AN

Almanack

For the Year of Our Lord

2001

ESTABLISHED 1868

BY

JOSEPH WHITAKER, FSA

CONTAINING AN ACCOUNT OF THE

ASTRONOMICAL AND OTHER PHENOMENA

AND

A vast Amount of INFORMATION respecting the
GOVERNMENT, FINANCES, POPULATION,
COMMERCE, and GENERAL STATISTICS of
the various Nations of the WORLD
with an INDEX containing
nearly 10,000
References

LONDON

OFFICE: 51 NINE ELMS LANE
LONDON SW8 5DR

The traditional design of the title page for Whitaker's Almanack which has appeared in each edition since 1868

Whitaker's Almanack

2001

LONDON
THE STATIONERY OFFICE

THE STATIONERY OFFICE LTD

51 Nine Elms Lane, London SW8 5DR

Whitaker's Almanack published annually since 1868

© 133rd edition The Stationery Office Ltd 2000

Standard edition

Cloth covers
0 11 7022 616

Leather binding
0 11 7022 608
Designed by Douglas Martin
Jacket designed by Compendium
Jacket photographs: PA Photos, Super Stock Ltd, Telegraph Colour Library
Typeset in Great Britain by Tradespools Ltd, Frome, Somerset
Printed and bound by LegoPrint S.P.A., Trento, Italy

Whitaker's Almanack Countries of the World Section was compiled with the assistance of: Military Balance (OUP); Keesings Worldwide; The Flag Institute; World Mineral Statistics (British Geological Survey); General Budget of the European Union 2001; Eurostat Yearbook; People in Power.

The Stationery Office's Accredited Agents
(*see* Yellow Pages)
and through good booksellers

EDITORIAL CONSULTANTS
Sally Whitaker
Gyles Brandreth
Rupert Pennant-Rea

EDITORIAL STAFF
Publisher: Tim Probart
Editor: Lauren Hill
Deputy Editor: Vanessa Taylor
Assistant Editors: Chris Sadowski, Tara West
Database Co-ordinator and Editorial Assistant: Arlene Zuccolo

EDITORIAL CONTACT DETAILS
Tel: 020-7873 8442
Fax: 020-7873 8723
Email: whitakers.almanack@theso.co.uk
Web: http://www.whitakers-almanack.co.uk

Published by The Stationery Office and available from:

The Publications Centre
(mail, telephone and fax orders only)
PO Box 276, London SW8 5DT
General enquiries/Telephone orders 0870-600 5522

The Stationery Office Bookshops
123 Kingsway, London WC2B 6PQ
020-7242 6393   Fax 020-7242 6394
16 Arthur Street, Belfast BTI 4GD
028-9023 8451   Fax 020-9023 5401
68-69 Bull Street, Birmingham B4 6AD
0121-236 9696   Fax 0121-236-9699
33 Wine Street, Cardiff CF1 2BZ
0117-926 4306   Fax 0117-929 4515
The Stationery Office Oriel Bookshop
18-19 High Street, Cardiff CF1 2BZ
029-2039 5548   Fax 029-2038 4347
71 Lothian Road, Edinburgh EH3 9AZ
0870-606 5566   Fax 0870-606 5588
9-21 Princess Street, Manchester M60 8AS
0161-834 7201   Fax 0161-833 0634

Contents

6

Preface

TO THE 133RD ANNUAL VOLUME

Welcome to the 133rd edition of *Whitaker's Almanack*. The last year has been a busy and eventful one, not just for the editorial and production team but for current affairs generally – London saw the return of a central governing authority in the form of a Mayor and Greater London Assembly; the Assembly was reinstated in Northern Ireland; Cherie Blair gave birth to baby Leo and sporting fever gripped the nation during the Euro 2000 football tournament and, of course, the Olympic Games.

This edition of *Whitaker's Almanack* brings a number of changes. Firstly, following developments in Scotland, Wales, Northern Ireland and London we have included a new section on regional/devolved government which includes election results and constituency and member information. Secondly, a new section, Information Technology and Computer Science, has been added to provide you with information on the growth of the IT industry from its humble beginnings to the multi-million pound Internet and e-commerce revolution that is taking place today. The Communications section has been overhauled to take account of technological advances within mobile telephony and the Environment section has been rewritten by an environmental journalist. We have also included results for a more diverse range of sports. While these additions and amendments have meant that in a small number of other sections we have had to reduce the amount of detail hitherto provided, I hope you will agree that the new material adds diversity to the Almanack, ensuring its appeal to a wider readership.

As ever, the research and compilation of this edition involved a lot of hard work and I would like to thank the editorial and production staff and the number of freelancers and contributors who applied a great deal of time and effort into assimilating *Whitaker's Almanack* to an extremely demanding schedule.

THE STATIONERY OFFICE LTD
51 Nine Elms Lane, London SW8 5DR
TEL: 020-7873 8442
FAX: 020-7873 8723
E-MAIL: whitakers.almanack@theso.co.uk

LAUREN HILL
Editor

The Year 2001

CHRONOLOGICAL CYCLES AND ERAS

Dominical Letter	G
Golden Number (Lunar Cycle)	VII
Julian Period	6714
Roman Indiction	9
Solar Cycle	22

	Beginning
Japanese year Heisei 13	1 January
Chinese year of the Dragon	24 January
Regnal year 50	6 February
Hindu new year	26 March
Indian (Saka) year 1923	26 March
Muslim year AH 1422	27 March
Sikh new year	13 April
Jewish year AM 5762	18 September
Roman year 2754 AUC	

RELIGIOUS CALENDARS

CHRISTIAN

Epiphany	6 January
Presentation of Christ in the Temple	2 February
Ash Wednesday	28 February
The Annunciation	25 March
Maundy Thursday	12 April
Good Friday	13 April
Easter Day (western churches)	15 April
Easter Day (Eastern Orthodox)	15 April
Rogation Sunday	20 May
Ascension Day	24 May
Pentecost (Whit Sunday)	3 June
Trinity Sunday	10 June
Corpus Christi	14 June
All Saints' Day	1 November
Advent Sunday	2 December
Christmas Day	25 December

HINDU

Makara Sankranti	14 January
Vasant Panchami (Sarasvati-puja)	29 January
Mahashivaratri	21 February
Holi	9 March
Chaitra (Hindu new year)	26 March
Ramanavami	2 April
Raksha-bandhan	4 August
Janmashtami	12 August
Ganesh Chaturthi, first day	22 August
Ganesh festival, last day	1 September
Durga-puja	17 October
Navaratri festival, first day	17 October
Sarasvati-puja	22 October
Dasara	26 October
Diwali, first day	12 November
Diwali, last day	16 November

JEWISH

Purim	9 March
Passover, first day	8 April
Feast of Weeks, first day	28 May
Jewish new year, first day	18 September
Yom Kippur (Day of Atonement)	27 September
Feast of Tabernacles, first day	2 October
Chanucah, first day	10 December

MUSLIM

Muslim new year	26 March
Ramadan, first day	17 November

SIKH

Birthday of Guru Gobind Singh Ji	5 January
Baisakhi Mela (Sikh new year)	13 April
Martyrdom of Guru Arjan Dev Ji	16 June
Birthday of Guru Nanak Dev Ji	11 November
Martyrdom of Guru Tegh Bahadur Ji	24 November

CIVIL CALENDAR

Accession of Queen Elizabeth II	6 February
Duke of York's birthday	19 February
St David's Day	1 March
Earl of Wessex's birthday	10 March
Commonwealth Day	12 March
St Patrick's Day	17 March
Birthday of Queen Elizabeth II	21 April
St George's Day	23 April
Europe Day	9 May
Coronation of Queen Elizabeth II	2 June
Duke of Edinburgh's birthday	10 June
The Queen's Official Birthday	16 June
Queen Elizabeth the Queen Mother's birthday	4 August
Princess Royal's birthday	15 August
Princess Margaret's birthday	21 August
Lord Mayor's Day	10 November
Remembrance Sunday	11 November
Prince of Wales's birthday	14 November
Wedding Day of Queen Elizabeth II	20 November
St Andrew's Day	30 November

LEGAL CALENDAR

LAW TERMS

Hilary Term	11 January to 11 April
Easter Term	24 April to 25 May
Trinity Term	5 June to 31 July
Michaelmas Term	1 October to 21 December

QUARTER DAYS

England, Wales and Northern Ireland

Lady	25 March
Midsummer	24 June
Michaelmas	29 September
Christmas	25 December

TERM DAYS

Scotland

Candlemas	28 February
Whitsunday	28 May
Lammas	28 August
Martinmas	28 November
Removal Terms	28 May, 28 November

2001

JANUARY

Sunday		7	14	21	28
Monday	1	8	15	22	29
Tuesday	2	9	16	23	30
Wednesday	3	10	17	24	31
Thursday	4	11	18	25	
Friday	5	12	19	26	
Saturday	6	13	20	27	

FEBRUARY

Sunday		4	11	18	25
Monday		5	12	19	26
Tuesday		6	13	20	27
Wednesday		7	14	21	28
Thursday	1	8	15	22	
Friday	2	9	16	23	
Saturday	3	10	17	24	

MARCH

Sunday		4	11	18	25
Monday		5	12	19	26
Tuesday		6	13	20	27
Wednesday		7	14	21	28
Thursday	1	8	15	22	29
Friday	2	9	16	23	30
Saturday	3	10	17	24	31

APRIL

Sunday	1	8	15	22	29
Monday	2	9	16	23	30
Tuesday	3	10	17	24	
Wednesday	4	11	18	25	
Thursday	5	12	19	26	
Friday	6	13	20	27	
Saturday	7	14	21	28	

MAY

Sunday		6	13	20	27
Monday		7	14	21	28
Tuesday	1	8	15	22	29
Wednesday	2	9	16	23	30
Thursday	3	10	17	24	31
Friday	4	11	18	25	
Saturday	5	12	19	26	

JUNE

Sunday		3	10	17	24
Monday		4	11	18	25
Tuesday		5	12	19	26
Wednesday		6	13	20	27
Thursday		7	14	21	28
Friday	1	8	15	22	29
Saturday	2	9	16	23	30

JULY

Sunday	1	8	15	22	29
Monday	2	9	16	23	30
Tuesday	3	10	17	24	31
Wednesday	4	11	18	25	
Thursday	5	12	19	26	
Friday	6	13	20	27	
Saturday	7	14	21	28	

AUGUST

Sunday		5	12	19	26
Monday		6	13	20	27
Tuesday		7	14	21	28
Wednesday	1	8	15	22	29
Thursday	2	9	16	23	30
Friday	3	10	17	24	31
Saturday	4	11	18	25	

SEPTEMBER

Sunday		2	9	16	23	30
Monday		3	10	17	24	
Tuesday		4	11	18	25	
Wednesday		5	12	19	26	
Thursday		6	13	20	27	
Friday		7	14	21	28	
Saturday	1	8	15	22	29	

OCTOBER

Sunday		7	14	21	28
Monday	1	8	15	22	29
Tuesday	2	9	16	23	30
Wednesday	3	10	17	24	31
Thursday	4	11	18	25	
Friday	5	12	19	26	
Saturday	6	13	20	27	

NOVEMBER

Sunday		4	11	18	25
Monday		5	12	19	26
Tuesday		6	13	20	27
Wednesday		7	14	21	28
Thursday	1	8	15	22	29
Friday	2	9	16	23	30
Saturday	3	10	17	24	

DECEMBER

Sunday		2	9	16	23	30
Monday		3	10	17	24	31
Tuesday		4	11	18	25	
Wednesday		5	12	19	26	
Thursday		6	13	20	27	
Friday		7	14	21	28	
Saturday	1	8	15	22	29	

PUBLIC HOLIDAYS	*England and Wales*	*Scotland*	*Northern Ireland*
New Year	†1 January	1, 2 January	†1 January
St Patrick s Day	—	—	‡19 March
*Good Friday	13 April	13 April	13 April
Easter Monday	16 April	—	16 April
Early May	†7 May	7 May	7 May
Spring	28 May	28 May	28 May
Battle of the Boyne	—	—	‡12 July
Summer	27 August	6 August	27 August
*Christmas	25, 26 December	25, †26 December	25, 26 December

*In England, Wales and Northern Ireland, Christmas Day and Good Friday are common law holidays
In the Channel Islands, Liberations Day is a bank and public holiday
† Subject to royal proclamation
‡Subject to proclamation by the Secretary of State for Northern Ireland.

2002

JANUARY

Sunday		6	13	20	27
Monday		7	14	21	28
Tuesday	1	8	15	22	29
Wednesday	2	9	16	23	30
Thursday	3	10	17	24	31
Friday	4	11	18	25	
Saturday	5	12	19	26	

FEBRUARY

Sunday		3	10	17	24
Monday		4	11	18	25
Tuesday		5	12	19	26
Wednesday		6	13	20	27
Thursday		7	14	21	28
Friday	1	8	15	22	
Saturday	2	9	16	23	

MARCH

Sunday		3	10	17	24	31
Monday		4	11	18	25	
Tuesday		5	12	19	26	
Wednesday		6	13	20	27	
Thursday		7	14	21	28	
Friday	1	8	15	22	29	
Saturday	2	9	16	23	30	

APRIL

Sunday		7	14	21	28
Monday	1	8	15	22	29
Tuesday	2	9	16	23	30
Wednesday	3	10	17	24	
Thursday	4	11	18	25	
Friday	5	12	19	26	
Saturday	6	13	20	27	

MAY

Sunday		5	12	19	26
Monday		6	13	20	27
Tuesday		7	14	21	28
Wednesday	1	8	15	22	29
Thursday	2	9	16	23	30
Friday	3	10	17	24	31
Saturday	4	11	18	25	

JUNE

Sunday		2	9	16	23	30
Monday		3	10	17	24	
Tuesday		4	11	18	25	
Wednesday		5	12	19	26	
Thursday		6	13	20	27	
Friday		7	14	21	28	
Saturday	1	8	15	22	29	

JULY

Sunday		7	14	21	28
Monday	1	8	15	22	29
Tuesday	2	9	16	23	30
Wednesday	3	10	17	24	31
Thursday	4	11	18	25	
Friday	5	12	19	26	
Saturday	6	13	20	27	

AUGUST

Sunday		4	11	18	25
Monday		5	12	19	26
Tuesday		6	13	20	27
Wednesday		7	14	21	28
Thursday	1	8	15	22	29
Friday	2	9	16	23	30
Saturday	3	10	17	24	31

SEPTEMBER

Sunday	1	8	15	22	29
Monday	2	9	16	23	30
Tuesday	3	10	17	24	
Wednesday	4	11	18	25	
Thursday	5	12	19	26	
Friday	6	13	20	27	
Saturday	7	14	21	28	

OCTOBER

Sunday		6	13	20	27
Monday		7	14	21	28
Tuesday	1	8	15	22	29
Wednesday	2	9	16	23	30
Thursday	3	10	17	24	31
Friday	4	11	18	25	
Saturday	5	12	19	26	

NOVEMBER

Sunday		3	10	17	24
Monday		4	11	18	25
Tuesday		5	12	19	26
Wednesday		6	13	20	27
Thursday		7	14	21	28
Friday	1	8	15	22	29
Saturday	2	9	16	23	30

DECEMBER

Sunday	1	8	15	22	29
Monday	2	9	16	23	30
Tuesday	3	10	17	24	31
Wednesday	4	11	18	25	
Thursday	5	12	19	26	
Friday	6	13	20	27	
Saturday	7	14	21	28	

PUBLIC HOLIDAYS	*England and Wales*	*Scotland*	*Northern Ireland*
New Year	†1 January	1, †2 January	†1 January
St Patrick's Day	—	—	‡18 March
*Good Friday	29 March	29 March	29 March
Easter Monday	1 April	—	1 April
Early May	†6 May	6 May	†6 May
Spring	27 May	†27 May	27 May
Battle of the Boyne	—	—	‡12 July
Summer	26 August	5 August	26 August
*Christmas	25, 26 December	25, †26 December	25, 26 December

FORTHCOMING EVENTS 2001

*Provisional dates

JANUARY
4–14	London International Boat Show, Earls Court, London
11–14 January	The Autosport Show, NEC, Birmingham

MARCH
8–11 March	Crufts Dog Show, NEC, Birmingham
17–10 June	Botticelli: The Drawings for Dante's Divine Comedy, Royal Academy of Arts

MAY
to October	Chichester Festival Theatre season
4 to 13 October	Pitlochry Festival Theatre season
17 to 26 August	Glyndebourne Festival Opera season
18 to 3 June	Bath International Music Festival
24–25	Chelsea Flower Show, Royal Hospital, Chelsea
25 to 3 June	The Hay Festival, Hay-on-Wye, Hereford

JUNE
8–24	Aldeburgh Festival of Music and the Arts, Saxmundham
30 to 15 July	Cheltenham International Festival of Music

JULY
2–5	The Royal Show, National Agriculture Centre, Stoneleigh Park
6–15	York Early Music Festival
12–22	Buxton Festival, Buxton Derbyshire
19–28	Welsh Proms, St David's Hall, Cardiff
20 to 15 September	BBC Broms, Royal Albert Hall, London

AUGUST
3–25	Edinburgh Military Tattoo, Edinburgh Castle
12 to 1 September	Edinburgh International Festival
18–25	Three Choirs Festival, Gloucester Cathedral
26–27	Notting Hill Carnival, London
31 to 4 November	Blackpool Illuminations

SEPTEMBER
10–13	TUC Annual Congress, Brighton
*14–23	Southampton International Boat Show, West Esplanade, Southampton
23–27	Liberal Democrat Party Conference, Bournemouth
30–4 October	Labour Party Conference, Brighton

OCTOBER
8–11	Conservative Party Conference, Blackpool
11 to 6 January2002	Painted Ladies: Portraits of Women at the Court of Charles II, National Portrait Gallery, London

NOVEMBER
21 to 2 December	Huddersfield Contemporary Music Festival
26–29 November	Smithfield Show, Earls Court, London
7–17 June	England v. Pakistan
8–20 July	England v. Zimbabwe

SPORTS EVENTS

AMERICAN SPORTS
10 July	Baseball – The All-star Game, Seattle, Washington
28 July	Football – Superbowl XXXV, Tampa, Florida

ATHLETICS
22 April	London Marathon
*27 July	British Grand Prix, Crystal Palace, London

CRICKET
Test Matches
22 February–19 March	Sri Lanka v. England (on tour in Sri Lanka)
17 May–4 June	England v. Pakistan
29 June–4 September	England v. West Indies
5 July–27 August	England v. Australia

One-Day Internationals
23–27 March	Sri Lanka v. England (on tour in Sri Lanka)
8 July	England v. Zimbabwe
9 July	England v. West Indies
13 July	England v. Zimbabwe
15 July	England v. West Indies
18 July	England v. Zimbabwe
20 July	England v. West Indies

Natwest Series
7 June	England v. Pakistan, Edgbaston
9 June	Pakistan v. Australia, Cardiff
10 June	England v. Australia, Bristol
12 June	England v. Pakistan, Lord's
14 June	England v. Australia, Old Trafford
16 June	Pakistan v. Australia, Durham
17 June	England v. Pakistan, Headingley
19 June	Pakistan v. Australia, Trent Bridge
21 June	England v. Australia, The Foster's Oval
23 June	Series Final, Lord's

CURLING
31 March–8 April	World Championships, Lausanne, Switzerland

EQUESTRIAN EVENTS
3–6 May	The Mitsubishi Motors Badminton Horse Trials, Badminton
9–13 May	Royal Windsor Horse Show, Home Park, Windsor
30 August–2 September	Burghley Horse Trials, Stamford
26–30 September	Horse of the Year Show, Wembley Arena, London

FOOTBALL
6 May	Welsh FA Cup Final, Millennium Stadium, Cardiff
12 May	FA Cup Final, *Millennium Stadium, Cardiff
26 May	Scottish FA Cup Final, Hampden Park, Glasgow

GOLF
4–9 June	The Amateur Championship, Prestwick/Kilmarnock
19–22 July	The Open, Royal Lytham & St Annes
11–22 August	The Walker Cup, Sea Island, Georgia USA
28–30 September	The Ryder Cup, Belfry

HORSERACING
15 March	Cheltenham Gold Cup
24 March	Dubai World Cup
24 March	Lincoln Handicap, Doncaster
7 April	Grand National, Aintree
5 May	2000 Guineas, Newmarket
6 May	1000 Guineas, Newmarket
8 June	The Oaks, Epsom Downs
8 June	Coronation Cup, Epsom Downs
9 June	The Derby, Epsom Downs
19–22 June	Royal Ascot
28 July	King George VI and Queen Elizabeth Diamond Stakes, Ascot
12 September	St Leger, Doncaster
6 October	Cambridgeshire Handicap, Newmarket
18 October	Cesarwitch Handicap, Newmarket

MOTOR SPORTS
*13 May	Formula 1: The British Grand Prix, Silverstone
27 May	Indy Cars: Indianapolis 500, Indianapolis, Indiana, USA
2–8 June	Motorcycles: TT Races, Isle of Man
16–17 June	Le Mans 24-Hour Race, Le Mans, France
*5 August	Motorcycles: World Superbikes, Brands Hatch
*23–25 November	Rallying: Rally of Great Britain, Cardiff

ROWING
24 March	The Oxford and Cambridge Boat Race
18–26 August	World Rowing Championships, Lucerne, Switzerland

RUGBY LEAGUE
28 April	Silk Cup Challenge Cup Final, Twickenham

RUGBY UNION   SIX NATIONS
3 February	Wales v. England, Cardiff
	France v. Scotland, Paris
4 February	Italy v. Ireland, Rome
17 February	Scotland v. Wales, Murrayfield
	Ireland v. France, Dublin
	England v. Italy, Twickenham
24 February	Tetley Bitter Cup Final, Twickenham
3 March	Wales v. Ireland, Cardiff
	England v. Scotland, Twickenham
	Italy v. France, Rome
17 March	France v. Wales, Paris
18 March	Scotland v. Italy, Murrayfield
24 March	Ireland v. England, Dublin
7 April	Italy v. Wales, Rome
	England v. France, Twickenham
	Scotland v. Ireland, Murrayfield

SHOOTING
11–21 July	Imperial Meeting, Bisley

SNOOKER
4–11 February	Benson & Hedges Masters, Wembley Conference Centre, London
21 April–7 May	Embassy World Championship, Crucible Theatre, Sheffield

TENNIS
15–28 January	Australian Open, Melbourne
28 May–12 June	French Open, Paris
25 June–8 July	The All-England Championships, Wimbledon, London
27 August–9 September	US Open Flushing Meadows, New York

YACHTING
16–28 July	Admiral Cup, Cowes, Isle of Wight
12 August	Fastnet Race, Cowes to Plymouth
4–11 August	Skandia Life Cowes Week, Isle of Wight

CENTENARIES OF 2001

1501	
17 January	Leonhard Fuchs, German botanist after whom the fuchsia was named, born
1701	
6 September	James II and VII, King 1685–9, died
27 November	Anders Celsius, Swedish astronomer, born
1801	
11 January	Domenico Cimarosa, Italian composer, died
21 February	Cardinal John Henry Newman, churchman and man of letters, born
2 April	Battle of Copenhagen
28 April	Anthony Ashley Cooper, 7th Earl of Shaftesbury, politician, reformer and philanthropist, born
14 June	Benedict Arnold, American general and turncoat, died
3 August	Sir Joseph Paxton, architect and landscape gardener, born
3 November	Karl Baedeker, German publisher and founder of Baedeker guidebooks, born
3 November	Vincenzo Bellini, Italian composer, born
1901	
16 January	Laura Riding, American poet and critic, born
22 January	Victoria, Queen 1837–1901, died

27 January	Giuseppe Verdi, Italian composer, died
1 February	Clark Gable, American actor, born
22 February	Stefan Lorant, Hungarian-born British photojournalist, first editor of Picture Post, born
28 February	Linus Pauling, American chemist, born
24 March	Charlotte Yonge, novelist, died
30 March	Sir John Stainer, composer, died
3 April	Richard D'Oyly Carte, producer of Gilbert and Sullivan operas and founder of the Savoy Theatre, died
15 April	Joe Davis, snooker player, born
7 May	Gary Cooper, American actor, born
12 June	Sir Norman Hartnell, couturier, born
13 July	Sir Reginald Goodall, conductor, born
20 July	Dilys Powell, film critic and reviewer, born
9 September	Henri de Toulouse-Lautrec, French painter, died
17 September	Sir Francis Chichester, yachtsman who made a solo circumnavigation of the world in 1966–7, born
10 October	Alberto Giacometti, Swiss sculptor and painter, born
6 November	Kate Greenaway, artist and illustrator, died
5 December	Walt Disney, American artist and animated film producer, born
10 December	Nobel Prizes awarded for the first time

CENTENARIES OF 2002

1602	
14 February	Francesco Cavalli, Italian composer, born
1702	
8 March	William III Orange, Dutch King 1689–1702, died
1802	
26 February	Victor Hugo, French novelist and poet, born
6 March	Sir Edwin Landseer, painter and sculptor, born
18 April	Erasmus Darwin, physician, free-thinker, poet and grandfather of Charles Darwin, died
12 June	Harriet Martineau, essayist and novelist, born
24 July	Alexandre Dumas, French novelist and playwright, born
15 November	George Romney, painter, died
1902	
5 January	Stella Gibbons, novelist, journalist and poet, born
31 January	Tallulah Bankhead, American actress, born
4 February	Charles Lindbergh, American aviator, born
27 February	John Steinbeck, American novelist, born
16 March	Dame Lucie Rie, Austrian-British potter, born

17 March	Bobby Jones, American golfer, born
26 March	Cecil Rhodes, colonialist, founder of Rhodesia, died
28 March	Dame Flora Robson, actress, born
29 March	Sir William Walton, composer, born
23 April	Halldor Laxness, Icelandic writer and Nobel literature laureate 1995, born
6 June	Lord Kings Norton Cox, aeronautical engineer, industrialist, chancellor of Cranfield University 1969–97, born
18 June	Samuel Butler, novelist, essayist and critic, died
28 June	Richard Rodgers, American composer, born
28 July	Sir Karl Popper, Austrian-British philosopher of natural and social science, born
31 July	Sir George Allen, cricketer, born
16 August	Georgette Heyer, novelist, born
19 August	Ogden Nash, American humorous poet, born
20 September	Florence Smith, poet, born
21 September	Sir Allen Lane, pioneer of paperback publishing, born
29 September	Emile Zola, French novelist, died
29 October	Susie Cooper, potter, born
9 December	R. A. Butler, Conservative politician, born
19 December	Sir Ralph Richardson, actor, born

Astronomy

The following pages give astronomical data for each month of the year 2001. There are four pages of data for each month. All data are given for 0h Greenwich Mean Time (GMT), i.e. at the midnight at the beginning of the day named. This applies also to data for the months when British Summer Time is in operation (for dates, *see* below).

The astronomical data are given in a form suitable for observation with the naked eye or with a small telescope. These data do not attempt to replace the *Astronomical Almanac* for professional astronomers.

A fuller explanation of how to use the astronomical data is given on pages 71–3.

CALENDAR FOR EACH MONTH

The calendar for each month shows dates of religious, civil and legal significance for the year 2001.

The days in bold type are the principal holy days and the festivals and greater holy days of the Church of England as set out in the calendar authorised for use from 1997. Observance of certain festivals and greater holy days is transferred if the day falls on a principal holy day. The calendar shows the date on which holy days and festivals are to be observed in 2001.

The days in small capitals are dates of significance in the calendars of non-Anglican denominations and non-Christian religions.

The days in italic type are dates of civil and legal significance. The royal anniversaries shown in italic type are the days on which the Union flag is to be flown.

The rest of the calendar comprises days of general interest and the dates of birth or death of well-known people.

Fuller explanations of the various calendars can be found under Time Measurement and Calendars (pages 81–9).

The zodiacal signs through which the Sun is passing during each month are illustrated. The date of transition from one sign to the next, to the nearest hour, is given under Astronomical Phenomena.

JULIAN DATE

The Julian date on 2001 January 0.0 is 2451909.5. To find the Julian date for any other date in 2001 (at 0h GMT), add the day-of-the-year number on the extreme right of the calendar for each month to the Julian date for January 0.0.

SEASONS

The seasons are defined astronomically as follows:

Spring from the vernal equinox to the summer solstice
Summer from the summer solstice to the autumnal equinox
Autumn from the autumnal equinox to the winter solstice
Winter from the winter solstice to the vernal equinox

The seasons in 2001 are:

Northern hemisphere

Vernal equinox	March 20d 14h GMT
Summer solstice	June 21d 08h GMT
Autumnal equinox	September 22d 23h GMT
Winter solstice	December 21d 19h GMT

Southern hemisphere

Autumnal equinox	March 20d 14h GMT
Winter solstice	June 21d 08h GMT
Vernal equinox	September 22d 23h GMT
Summer solstice	December 21d 19h GMT

The longest day of the year, measured from sunrise to sunset, is at the summer solstice. The longest day in the United Kingdom will fall on 21 June in 2001. *See also* page 81.

The shortest day of the year is at the winter solstice. The shortest day in the United Kingdom will fall on 21 December in 2001. *See also* page 81.

The equinox is the point at which day and night are of equal length all over the world. *See also* page 81.

In popular parlance, the seasons in the northern hemisphere comprise the following months:

Spring March, April, May
Summer June, July, August
Autumn September, October, November
Winter December, January, February

BRITISH SUMMER TIME

British Summer Time is the legal time for general purposes during the period in which it is in operation (*see also* page 75). During this period, clocks are kept one hour ahead of Greenwich Mean Time. The hour of changeover is 01h Greenwich Mean Time. The duration of Summer Time in 2001 is from March 25 01h GMT to October 28 01h GMT.

January 2001

FIRST MONTH, 31 DAYS, *Janus*, god of the portal, facing two ways, past and future

1	*Monday*	**Naming and Circumcision of Jesus**. J. Edgar Hoover b. 1895	*week 1 day* 1
2	*Tuesday*	General James Wolfe b. 1727. Frank Muir d. 1998	2
3	*Wednesday*	Josiah Wedgwood d. 1795. Norman Hepple d. 1994	3
4	*Thursday*	Giovanni Pergolesi b. 1710. T. S. Eliot d. 1965	4
5	*Friday*	Konrad Adenauer b. 1876. Calvin Coolidge d. 1933	5
6	*Saturday*	**The Epiphany**. Joan of Arc b. 1412	6
7	*Sunday*	**Baptism of Christ. 1st S. of Epiphany**	7
8	*Monday*	Robert Baden-Powell d. 1941. David Bowie b. 1947	*week 2 day* 8
9	*Tuesday*	Napoleon Bonaparte d. 1873. Dame Gracie Fields b. 1898	9
10	*Wednesday*	Archbishop William Laud d. 1645. Alexander Scriabin b. 1872	10
11	*Thursday*	Alan Paton b. 1903. Thomas Hardy d. 1928	11
12	*Friday*	Edmund Burke b. 1729. Nevil Shute d. 1960	12
13	*Saturday*	George Fox d. 1691. Stephen Collins Foster d. 1864	13
14	*Sunday*	**2nd S. of Epiphany**. Benedict Arnold b. 1741	14
15	*Monday*	Lloyd Bridges b. 1913. Martin Luther King b. 1929	*week 3 day* 15
16	*Tuesday*	André Michelin b. 1853. Gulf War began 1991	16
17	*Wednesday*	Benjamin Franklin b. 1706. Shari Lewis b. 1934	17
18	*Thursday*	A. A. Milne b. 1882. Hugh Gaitskell d. 1963	18
19	*Friday*	Edgar Allen Poe b. 1809. Patricia Highsmith b. 1921	19
20	*Saturday*	Federico Fellini b. 1920. King George V d. 1936	20
21	*Sunday*	**3rd S. of Epiphany**. Jack Nicklaus b. 1940	21
22	*Monday*	Battle of Rourke's Drift 1879. Sir Isaac Pitman d. 1897	*week 4 day* 22
23	*Tuesday*	Anna Pavlova d. 1931. Salvador Dalí d. 1989	23
24	*Wednesday*	Sir Edwin Chadwick b. 1800. Caligula d. AD 41	24
25	*Thursday*	**Conversion of St Paul**. Robert Burns b. 1759	25
26	*Friday*	Benjamin Haydon b. 1786. Al Capone d. 1947	26
27	*Saturday*	Wolfgang Amadeus Mozart b. 1756. Giuseppe Verdi d. 1901	27
28	*Sunday*	**4th S. of Epiphany**. Ronnie Scott b. 1927	28
29	*Monday*	Frederick Delius b. 1862. H. E. Bates d. 1974	*week 5 day* 29
30	*Tuesday*	Franklin D. Roosevelt b. 1882. Ferdinand Porsche d. 1951	30
31	*Wednesday*	Guy Fawkes d. 1606. Franz Schubert b. 1797	31

ASTRONOMICAL PHENOMENA

d	h	
4	09	Earth at perihelion (147 million km.)
6	02	Saturn in conjunction with Moon. Saturn 2° N.
6	15	Jupiter in conjunction with Moon. Jupiter 3° N.
9	20	Total eclipse of Moon (see page 71)
17	07	Venus at greatest elongation E.47°
17	22	Mars in conjunction with Moon. Mars 3° S.
20	00	Sun's longitude 300°≈
25	00	Saturn at stationary point
25	09	Jupiter at stationary point
26	04	Neptune in conjunction
26	05	Mercury in conjunction with Moon. Mercury 3° N.
28	14	Mercury at greatest elongation E.18°
28	20	Venus in conjunction with Moon. Venus 6° N.

MINIMA OF ALGOL

d	h	d	h	d	h
2	20.1	14	07.4	25	18.6
5	16.9	17	04.2	28	15.5
8	13.7	20	01.0	31	12.3
11	10.5	22	21.8		

CONSTELLATIONS

The following constellations are near the meridian at

	d	h		d	h
December	1	24	January	16	21
December	16	23	February	1	20
January	1	22	February	15	19

Draco (below the Pole), Ursa Minor (below the Pole), Camelopardus, Perseus, Auriga, Taurus, Orion, Eridanus and Lepus

THE MOON

Phases, Apsides and Node	d	h	m
☽ First Quarter	2	22	31
○ Full Moon	9	20	24
☾ Last Quarter	16	12	35
● New Moon	24	13	07
Perigee (357,130 km)	10	09	00
Apogee (406,562 km)	24	19	04

Mean longitude of ascending node on January 1, 106°

THE SUN   s.d. 16′.1

Day	Right Ascension h m s	Dec. ° ′	Equation of time m s	Rise 52° h m	Rise 56° h m	Transit h m	Set 52° h m	Set 56° h m	Sidereal time h m s	Transit of First Point of Aries h m s
1	18 46 15	23 01	− 3 25	8 08	8 31	12 04	15 59	15 36	6 42 50	17 14 20
2	18 50 40	22 56	− 3 53	8 08	8 31	12 04	16 00	15 38	6 46 47	17 10 24
3	18 55 05	22 50	− 4 21	8 08	8 31	12 05	16 02	15 39	6 50 44	17 06 28
4	18 59 29	22 44	− 4 48	8 08	8 30	12 05	16 03	15 40	6 54 40	17 02 32
5	19 03 52	22 38	− 5 16	8 07	8 30	12 05	16 04	15 42	6 58 37	16 58 36
6	19 08 15	22 31	− 5 42	8 07	8 29	12 06	16 05	15 43	7 02 33	16 54 40
7	19 12 38	22 23	− 6 08	8 06	8 28	12 06	16 07	15 45	7 06 30	16 50 44
8	19 17 00	22 16	− 6 34	8 06	8 28	12 07	16 08	15 46	7 10 26	16 46 48
9	19 21 22	22 07	− 6 59	8 05	8 27	12 07	16 09	15 48	7 14 23	16 42 52
10	19 25 43	21 59	− 7 24	8 05	8 26	12 08	16 11	15 49	7 18 20	16 38 56
11	19 30 04	21 50	− 7 48	8 04	8 25	12 08	16 12	15 51	7 22 16	16 35 00
12	19 34 24	21 40	− 8 11	8 03	8 24	12 08	16 14	15 53	7 26 13	16 31 05
13	19 38 43	21 30	− 8 34	8 03	8 23	12 09	16 15	15 55	7 30 09	16 27 09
14	19 43 02	21 20	− 8 56	8 02	8 22	12 09	16 17	15 56	7 34 06	16 23 13
15	19 47 20	21 09	− 9 18	8 01	8 21	12 09	16 18	15 58	7 38 02	16 19 17
16	19 51 37	20 58	− 9 38	8 00	8 20	12 10	16 20	16 00	7 41 59	16 15 21
17	19 55 54	20 46	− 9 59	7 59	8 19	12 10	16 21	16 02	7 45 55	16 11 25
18	20 00 10	20 34	−10 18	7 58	8 17	12 10	16 23	16 04	7 49 52	16 07 29
19	20 04 26	20 22	−10 37	7 57	8 16	12 11	16 25	16 06	7 53 49	16 03 33
20	20 08 40	20 09	−10 55	7 56	8 15	12 11	16 27	16 08	7 57 45	15 59 37
21	20 12 54	19 56	−11 13	7 55	8 13	12 11	16 28	16 10	8 01 42	15 55 41
22	20 17 08	19 43	−11 29	7 54	8 12	12 12	16 30	16 12	8 05 38	15 51 45
23	20 21 20	19 29	−11 45	7 53	8 10	12 12	16 32	16 14	8 09 35	15 47 50
24	20 25 32	19 14	−12 01	7 51	8 09	12 12	16 33	16 16	8 13 31	15 43 54
25	20 29 43	19 00	−12 15	7 50	8 07	12 12	16 35	16 18	8 17 28	15 39 58
26	20 33 53	18 45	−12 28	7 49	8 06	12 13	16 37	16 20	8 21 24	15 36 02
27	20 38 02	18 30	−12 41	7 47	8 04	12 13	16 39	16 22	8 25 21	15 32 06
28	20 42 11	18 14	−12 53	7 46	8 02	12 13	16 41	16 25	8 29 18	15 28 10
29	20 46 18	17 58	−13 04	7 44	8 00	12 13	16 42	16 27	8 33 14	15 24 14
30	20 50 25	17 42	−13 15	7 43	7 59	12 13	16 44	16 29	8 37 11	15 20 18
31	20 54 31	17 25	−13 24	7 41	7 57	12 13	16 46	16 31	8 41 07	15 16 22

DURATION OF TWILIGHT (in minutes)

Latitude	52°	56°	52°	56°	52°	56°	52°	56°
	1 January		11 January		21 January		31 January	
Civil	41	47	40	45	38	43	37	41
Nautical	84	96	82	93	80	90	78	87
Astronomical	125	141	123	138	120	134	117	130

THE NIGHT SKY

Mercury reaches its greatest eastern elongation (18°) on the 28th. Thus for the last ten days of the month it is an evening object and may be seen at the end of evening civil twilight low in the south-western sky. During this period its magnitude fades from −0.9 to 0.0. The thin crescent Moon will be seen near the planet on the evenings of the 25th and 26th, though on the first of these dates the Moon is only about one day old and is only likely to be seen under very good conditions.

Venus is at greatest eastern elongation on the 17th, and therefore is a brilliant evening object, magnitude −4.4, dominating the south-western sky for several hours after sunset. The crescent Moon will be seen in the proximity of the planet on the evenings of the 27–29th.

Mars, magnitude +1.2, is visible in the south-eastern quadrant of the sky in the early mornings, after about 03h. It crosses the meridian at about the time of beginning of morning civil twilight. At the beginning of the month Mars, in its eastward motion, moves from Virgo into Libra. The Moon, just after Last Quarter, passes north of Mars on the night of the 17–18th.

Jupiter, magnitude −2.6, is a brilliant evening object, visible high in the southern skies in the evening, and not setting in the west until the early hours of the morning. Jupiter and Saturn are only about 8° apart. The gibbous Moon passes 3–4° south of these planets on the 6th. Jupiter is retrograding slowly in Taurus, between the Pleiades and the Hyades, reaching its second stationary point on the 25th.

Saturn, magnitude 0.0, crosses the meridian in the early evening and remains visible in the western sky until the early hours of the morning. Saturn is retrograding slowly in Taurus, reaching its second stationary point on the 25th.

THE MOON

Day	RA	Dec.	Hor. par.	Semi-diam.	Sun's co-long.	PA of Bright Limb	Phase	Age	Rise 52°	Rise 56°	Transit	Set 52°	Set 56°
	h m	°	'	'	°	°	%	d	h m	h m	h m	h m	h m
1	23 26	− 8.8	54.7	14.9	344	249	32	6.3	11 38	11 44	17 13	22 59	22 55
2	0 11	− 4.4	55.3	15.1	356	247	41	7.3	11 56	11 58	17 56	—	—
3	0 57	+ 0.4	56.0	15.2	8	247	51	8.3	12 15	12 12	18 40	0 08	0 09
4	1 45	+ 5.3	56.8	15.5	20	248	61	9.3	12 34	12 28	19 27	1 20	1 25
5	2 34	+10.0	57.7	15.7	32	250	71	10.3	12 57	12 46	20 17	2 35	2 44
6	3 27	+14.5	58.7	16.0	45	253	80	11.3	13 25	13 09	21 11	3 53	4 07
7	4 24	+18.3	59.7	16.3	57	257	89	12.3	14 00	13 40	22 10	5 13	5 32
8	5 25	+21.1	60.5	16.5	69	262	95	13.3	14 48	14 24	23 13	6 31	6 54
9	6 29	+22.5	61.1	16.6	81	269	99	14.3	15 49	15 25	—	7 42	8 06
10	7 35	+22.2	61.4	16.7	93	84	100	15.3	17 04	16 42	0 18	8 41	9 03
11	8 40	+20.4	61.3	16.7	105	98	98	16.3	18 27	18 09	1 21	9 26	9 45
12	9 43	+17.1	61.0	16.6	117	104	93	17.3	19 52	19 39	2 22	10 01	10 15
13	10 42	+12.7	60.3	16.4	129	108	86	18.3	21 15	21 08	3 19	10 29	10 38
14	11 37	+ 7.8	59.5	16.2	142	110	77	19.3	22 35	22 33	4 12	10 52	10 56
15	12 29	+ 2.5	58.6	16.0	154	112	66	20.3	23 52	23 55	5 01	11 13	11 12
16	13 20	− 2.7	57.7	15.7	166	111	56	21.3	—	—	5 49	11 32	11 28
17	14 09	− 7.7	56.9	15.5	178	110	45	22.3	1 07	1 14	6 35	11 53	11 44
18	14 58	−12.1	56.1	15.3	190	108	35	23.3	2 19	2 31	7 22	12 15	12 02
19	15 47	−15.9	55.5	15.1	202	105	26	24.3	3 30	3 45	8 09	12 41	12 24
20	16 37	−19.0	55.0	15.0	215	101	18	25.3	4 37	4 57	8 57	13 11	12 51
21	17 28	−21.2	54.6	14.9	227	96	11	26.3	5 40	6 03	9 46	13 49	13 25
22	18 19	−22.3	54.3	14.8	239	90	6	27.3	6 36	7 00	10 35	14 33	14 09
23	19 11	−22.5	54.1	14.7	251	83	2	28.3	7 24	7 48	11 24	15 26	15 02
24	20 02	−21.7	54.0	14.7	263	67	0	29.3	8 04	8 25	12 12	16 25	16 04
25	20 52	−19.9	53.9	14.7	275	278	0	0.5	8 36	8 55	12 59	17 28	17 11
26	21 41	−17.2	54.0	14.7	288	262	2	1.5	9 03	9 17	13 44	18 34	18 21
27	22 28	−13.8	54.1	14.8	300	256	5	2.5	9 25	9 36	14 28	19 41	19 32
28	23 14	− 9.9	54.4	14.8	312	253	10	3.5	9 44	9 51	15 11	20 49	20 43
29	23 59	− 5.5	54.8	14.9	324	251	17	4.5	10 02	10 05	15 53	21 57	21 56
30	0 45	− 0.9	55.2	15.1	336	250	25	5.5	10 20	10 19	16 36	23 06	23 09
31	1 31	+ 3.9	55.8	15.2	349	250	34	6.5	10 38	10 33	17 21	—	—

MERCURY

Day	RA	Dec.	Diam.	Phase	Transit	5° high 52°	5° high 56°
	h m	°	"	%	h m	h m	h m
1	19 03	−24.6	5	99	12 22	15 11	14 30
3	19 17	−24.3	5	99	12 28	15 21	14 41
5	19 31	−23.9	5	98	12 34	15 31	14 53
7	19 46	−23.4	5	98	12 41	15 43	15 07
9	20 00	−22.8	5	97	12 47	15 55	15 21
11	20 14	−22.0	5	95	12 53	16 07	15 36
13	20 28	−21.2	5	93	12 59	16 20	15 51
15	20 41	−20.3	5	91	13 05	16 33	16 06
17	20 55	−19.3	5	88	13 10	16 47	16 21
19	21 07	−18.1	6	85	13 15	17 00	16 37
21	21 20	−17.0	6	81	13 19	17 12	16 51
23	21 31	−15.7	6	75	13 22	17 24	17 04
25	21 42	−14.5	6	69	13 25	17 34	17 16
27	21 51	−13.3	7	61	13 26	17 42	17 26
29	21 59	−12.1	7	53	13 25	17 48	17 34
31	22 04	−11.0	8	43	13 22	17 51	17 38

VENUS

Day	RA	Dec.	Diam.	Phase	Transit	5° high 52°	5° high 56°
	h m	°	"	%	h m	h m	h m
1	21 59	−13.9	21	59	15 16	19 28	19 11
6	22 19	−11.7	22	57	15 17	19 42	19 28
11	22 39	− 9.4	23	54	15 17	19 56	19 44
16	22 58	− 7.0	24	52	15 16	20 08	19 59
21	23 16	− 4.6	25	49	15 14	20 19	20 12
26	23 33	− 2.2	27	46	15 11	20 29	20 24
31	23 49	+ 0.2	29	43	15 07	20 38	20 35

MARS

Day	RA	Dec.	Diam.	Phase	Transit	5° high 52°	5° high 56°
1	14 12	−12.0	5	92	7 29	3 08	3 23
6	14 24	−12.9	5	92	7 21	3 05	3 21
11	14 35	−13.9	6	91	7 12	3 03	3 20
16	14 46	−14.8	6	91	7 04	3 00	3 18
21	14 57	−15.6	6	91	6 55	2 57	3 16
26	15 08	−16.4	6	91	6 47	2 54	3 14
31	15 20	−17.2	6	90	6 38	2 50	3 12

SUNRISE AND SUNSET

	London		Bristol		Birmingham		Manchester		Newcastle		Glasgow		Belfast	
	0°05′	51°30′	2°35′	51°28′	1°55′	52°28′	2°15′	53°28′	1°37′	54°59′	4°14′	55°52′	5°56′	54°35′
	h m	h m	h m	h m	h m	h m	h m	h m	h m	h m	h m	h m	h m	h m
1	8 06	16 02	8 16	16 12	8 18	16 05	8 25	16 01	8 31	15 49	8 47	15 54	8 46	16 09
2	8 06	16 03	8 16	16 13	8 18	16 06	8 25	16 02	8 31	15 50	8 47	15 55	8 46	16 10
3	8 06	16 04	8 16	16 15	8 18	16 07	8 24	16 03	8 31	15 52	8 47	15 57	8 46	16 11
4	8 05	16 06	8 15	16 16	8 18	16 08	8 24	16 04	8 30	15 53	8 46	15 58	8 45	16 13
5	8 05	16 07	8 15	16 17	8 17	16 09	8 24	16 05	8 30	15 54	8 46	15 59	8 45	16 14
6	8 05	16 08	8 15	16 18	8 17	16 11	8 23	16 07	8 29	15 56	8 45	16 01	8 44	16 15
7	8 04	16 09	8 14	16 19	8 16	16 12	8 23	16 08	8 29	15 57	8 45	16 02	8 44	16 17
8	8 04	16 11	8 14	16 21	8 16	16 13	8 22	16 10	8 28	15 59	8 44	16 04	8 43	16 18
9	8 03	16 12	8 13	16 22	8 15	16 15	8 22	16 11	8 27	16 00	8 43	16 06	8 42	16 20
10	8 03	16 13	8 13	16 24	8 15	16 16	8 21	16 13	8 27	16 02	8 42	16 07	8 42	16 21
11	8 02	16 15	8 12	16 25	8 14	16 18	8 20	16 14	8 26	16 03	8 41	16 09	8 41	16 23
12	8 02	16 16	8 11	16 26	8 13	16 19	8 20	16 16	8 25	16 05	8 40	16 11	8 40	16 25
13	8 01	16 18	8 11	16 28	8 13	16 21	8 19	16 17	8 24	16 07	8 39	16 12	8 39	16 26
14	8 00	16 19	8 10	16 29	8 12	16 22	8 18	16 19	8 23	16 09	8 38	16 14	8 38	16 28
15	7 59	16 21	8 09	16 31	8 11	16 24	8 17	16 20	8 22	16 10	8 37	16 16	8 37	16 30
16	7 58	16 22	8 08	16 33	8 10	16 25	8 16	16 22	8 21	16 12	8 36	16 18	8 36	16 31
17	7 57	16 24	8 07	16 34	8 09	16 27	8 15	16 24	8 20	16 14	8 35	16 20	8 35	16 33
18	7 56	16 26	8 06	16 36	8 08	16 29	8 14	16 26	8 19	16 16	8 34	16 22	8 34	16 35
19	7 55	16 27	8 05	16 37	8 07	16 31	8 13	16 27	8 17	16 18	8 32	16 24	8 33	16 37
20	7 54	16 29	8 04	16 39	8 06	16 32	8 11	16 29	8 16	16 20	8 31	16 26	8 31	16 39
21	7 53	16 31	8 03	16 41	8 05	16 34	8 10	16 31	8 15	16 21	8 30	16 28	8 30	16 41
22	7 52	16 32	8 02	16 42	8 03	16 36	8 09	16 33	8 13	16 23	8 28	16 30	8 29	16 43
23	7 51	16 34	8 01	16 44	8 02	16 38	8 08	16 35	8 12	16 25	8 27	16 32	8 27	16 45
24	7 50	16 36	8 00	16 46	8 01	16 39	8 06	16 37	8 10	16 27	8 25	16 34	8 26	16 46
25	7 49	16 37	7 58	16 48	8 00	16 41	8 05	16 38	8 09	16 29	8 23	16 36	8 24	16 48
26	7 47	16 39	7 57	16 49	7 58	16 43	8 03	16 40	8 07	16 31	8 22	16 38	8 23	16 50
27	7 46	16 41	7 56	16 51	7 57	16 45	8 02	16 42	8 06	16 33	8 20	16 40	8 21	16 52
28	7 44	16 43	7 54	16 53	7 55	16 47	8 00	16 44	8 04	16 35	8 18	16 42	8 20	16 54
29	7 43	16 45	7 53	16 55	7 54	16 48	7 59	16 46	8 02	16 38	8 17	16 44	8 18	16 56
30	7 42	16 46	7 51	16 56	7 52	16 50	7 57	16 48	8 01	16 40	8 15	16 46	8 16	16 58
31	7 40	16 48	7 50	16 58	7 51	16 52	7 56	16 50	7 59	16 42	8 13	16 49	8 15	17 00

JUPITER

Day	RA	Dec.	Transit	5° high 52°	5° high 56°
	h m	° ′	h m	h m	h m
1	4 01.1	+19 48	21 14	4 30	4 44
11	3 58.4	+19 43	20 33	3 47	4 01
21	3 57.0	+19 42	19 52	3 06	3 20
31	3 57.1	+19 44	19 13	2 27	2 41

Diameters – equatorial 45″ polar 42″

SATURN

Day	RA	Dec.	Transit	5° high 52°	5° high 56°
	h m	° ′	h m	h m	h m
1	3 31.2	+16 47	20 45	3 43	3 54
11	3 29.7	+16 45	20 04	3 02	3 13
21	3 29.0	+16 45	19 24	2 22	2 33
31	3 29.0	+16 48	18 45	1 43	1 54

Diameters – equatorial 19″ polar 17″
Rings – major axis 44″ minor axis 17″

URANUS

Day	RA	Dec.	Transit	10° high 52°	10° high 56°
	h m	° ′	h m	h m	h m
1	21 25.2	−15 53	14 40	17 55	17 27
11	21 27.2	−15 43	14 03	17 19	16 51
21	21 29.3	−15 33	13 26	16 43	16 16
31	21 31.6	−15 22	12 48	16 08	15 41

Diameter 4″

NEPTUNE

Day	RA	Dec.	Transit	10° high 52°	10° high 56°
	h m	° ′	h m	h m	h m
1	20 30.6	−18 46	13 46	16 37	16 00
11	20 32.1	−18 41	13 08	16 00	15 23
21	20 33.6	−18 36	12 30	15 23	14 47
31	20 35.1	−18 30	11 52	14 46	14 10

Diameter 2″

 # February 2001

SECOND MONTH, 28 or 29 DAYS. *Februa*, Roman festival of Purification

1	*Thursday*	Mary Wollstonecraft Shelley d. 1851. Clark Gable b. 1901	32
2	*Friday*	**Presentation of Christ in the Temple (Candlemas)**	33
3	*Saturday*	Walter Bagehot b. 1826. Woodrow Wilson d. 1924	34
4	*Sunday*	**4th S. before Lent.** Antonio Vivaldi b. 1678	35
5	*Monday*	Sir Robert Peel b. 1788. George Arliss d. 1946	*week 6 day* 36
6	*Tuesday*	*Queen's Accession 1952.* Joseph Priestley d. 1804	37
7	*Wednesday*	Sir Thomas More b. 1478. Adolphe Sax d. 1894	38
8	*Thursday*	Lana Turner b. 1920. Halldor Laxness d. 1998	39
9	*Friday*	John Hooper d. 1553. Brendan Behan b. 1923	40
10	*Saturday*	Samuel Plimsoll b. 1824. Maurice Schumann d. 1998	41
11	*Sunday*	**3rd S. before Lent.** William Henry Fox Talbot b. 1800	42
12	*Monday*	Charles Darwin b. 1809. Charles Schulz d. 2000	*week 7 day* 43
13	*Tuesday*	Massacre of Glencoe 1692. Léon Jean Goossens d. 1988	44
14	*Wednesday*	St Valentine's Day. Benvenuto Cellini d. 1571	45
15	*Thursday*	Herbert Asquith d. 1928. Graham Hill b. 1929	46
16	*Friday*	Lionel Lukin d. 1834. Sir Anthony Dowell b. 1943	47
17	*Saturday*	Johann Pestalozzi d. 1827. Sir Edward German b. 1862	48
18	*Sunday*	**2nd S. before Lent.** Michelangelo Buonarroti d. 1564	49
19	*Monday*	*Duke of York b. 1960.* Knut Hamsun d. 1952	*week 8 day* 50
20	*Tuesday*	Henry James Pye b. 1745. Ferruccio Lamborghini d. 1993	51
21	*Wednesday*	Jethro Tull d. 1741. Battle of Verdun 1915	52
22	*Thursday*	Frédéric Chopin d. 1810. Andy Warhol d. 1987	53
23	*Friday*	Constantine Karamanlis b. 1907. Sir Adrian Boult d. 1983	54
24	*Saturday*	Wilhelm Grimm b. 1786. Joseph Rowntree d. 1925	55
25	*Sunday*	**S. next before Lent.** Paul Julius von Reuter d. 1899	56
26	*Monday*	Frank Bridge b. 1879. Levi Eshkol d. 1969	*week 9 day* 57
27	*Tuesday*	Shrove Tuesday. Prof. Charles Best b. 1899	58
28	*Wednesday*	**Ash Wednesday.** King Edward IV b. 1442	59

ASTRONOMICAL PHENOMENA

d	h	
2	11	Saturn in conjunction with Moon. Saturn 2° N.
2	23	Jupiter in conjunction with Moon. Jupiter 3° N.
4	02	Mercury at stationary point
9	12	Uranus in conjunction
13	00	Mercury in inferior conjunction
15	11	Mars in conjunction with Moon. Mars 3° S.
18	14	Sun's longitude 330° $\mathcal{H}$
21	19	Mercury in conjunction with Moon. Mercury 6° N.
22	01	Venus at greatest brilliancy
25	16	Mercury at stationary point
26	17	Venus in conjunction with Moon. Venus 10° N.

MINIMA OF ALGOL

d	h	d	h	d	h
3	09.1	14	20.4	26	07.7
6	05.9	17	17.2		
9	02.8	20	14.0		
11	23.6	23	10.9		

CONSTELLATIONS

The following constellations are near the meridian at

	d	h		d	h
January	1	24	February	15	21
January	16	23	March	1	20
February	1	22	March	16	19

Draco (below the Pole), Camelopardus, Auriga, Taurus, Gemini, Orion, Canis Minor, Monoceros, Lepus, Canis Major and Puppis

THE MOON

Phases, Apsides and Node	d	h	m
☽ First Quarter	1	14	02
○ Full Moon	8	07	12
☾ Last Quarter	15	03	24
● New Moon	23	08	21
Perigee (356,852 km)	7	22	16
Apogee (406,331 km)	20	21	38

Mean longitude of ascending node on February 1, 104°

THE SUN s.d. 16′.1

Day	Right Ascension	Dec.	Equation of time	Rise 52°	Rise 56°	Transit	Set 52°	Set 56°	Sidereal time	Transit of First Point of Aries
	h m s	° ′	m s	h m	h m	h m	h m	h m	h m s	h m s
1	20 58 36	17 08	−13 33	7 40	7 55	12 14	16 48	16 33	8 45 04	15 12 26
2	21 02 41	16 51	−13 40	7 38	7 53	12 14	16 50	16 35	8 49 00	15 08 30
3	21 06 44	16 34	−13 47	7 37	7 51	12 14	16 52	16 38	8 52 57	15 04 35
4	21 10 47	16 16	−13 54	7 35	7 49	12 14	16 54	16 40	8 56 53	15 00 39
5	21 14 49	15 58	−13 59	7 33	7 47	12 14	16 55	16 42	9 00 50	14 56 43
6	21 18 50	15 40	−14 03	7 32	7 45	12 14	16 57	16 44	9 04 47	14 52 47
7	21 22 50	15 21	−14 07	7 30	7 43	12 14	16 59	16 46	9 08 43	14 48 51
8	21 26 49	15 02	−14 10	7 28	7 41	12 14	17 01	16 48	9 12 40	14 44 55
9	21 30 48	14 43	−14 12	7 26	7 39	12 14	17 03	16 51	9 16 36	14 40 59
10	21 34 46	14 24	−14 13	7 24	7 36	12 14	17 05	16 53	9 20 33	14 37 03
11	21 38 43	14 04	−14 14	7 23	7 34	12 14	17 07	16 55	9 24 29	14 33 07
12	21 42 39	13 44	−14 13	7 21	7 32	12 14	17 08	16 57	9 28 26	14 29 11
13	21 46 35	13 24	−14 12	7 19	7 30	12 14	17 10	16 59	9 32 22	14 25 15
14	21 50 30	13 04	−14 11	7 17	7 28	12 14	17 12	17 02	9 36 19	14 21 20
15	21 54 24	12 44	−14 08	7 15	7 25	12 14	17 14	17 04	9 40 16	14 17 24
16	21 58 17	12 23	−14 05	7 13	7 23	12 14	17 16	17 06	9 44 12	14 13 28
17	22 02 10	12 02	−14 01	7 11	7 21	12 14	17 18	17 08	9 48 09	14 09 32
18	22 06 02	11 41	−13 57	7 09	7 18	12 14	17 20	17 10	9 52 05	14 05 36
19	22 09 53	11 20	−13 51	7 07	7 16	12 14	17 21	17 13	9 56 02	14 01 40
20	22 13 44	10 58	−13 46	7 05	7 14	12 14	17 23	17 15	9 59 58	13 57 44
21	22 17 34	10 37	−13 39	7 03	7 11	12 14	17 25	17 17	10 03 55	13 53 48
22	22 21 23	10 15	−13 32	7 01	7 09	12 13	17 27	17 19	10 07 51	13 49 52
23	22 25 12	9 53	−13 24	6 59	7 06	12 13	17 29	17 21	10 11 48	13 45 56
24	22 29 00	9 31	−13 16	6 57	7 04	12 13	17 31	17 23	10 15 45	13 42 00
25	22 32 48	9 09	−13 07	6 54	7 01	12 13	17 32	17 26	10 19 41	13 38 05
26	22 36 35	8 46	−12 57	6 52	6 59	12 13	17 34	17 28	10 23 38	13 34 09
27	22 40 21	8 24	−12 47	6 50	6 56	12 13	17 36	17 30	10 27 34	13 30 13
28	22 44 07	8 01	−12 36	6 48	6 54	12 13	17 38	17 32	10 31 31	13 26 17

DURATION OF TWILIGHT (in minutes)

Latitude	52°	56°	52°	56°	52°	56°	52°	56°
	1 February		11 February		21 February		28 February	
Civil	37	41	35	39	34	38	34	38
Nautical	77	86	75	83	74	81	73	81
Astronomical	117	130	114	126	113	125	112	124

THE NIGHT SKY

Mercury is visible at the end of evening civil twilight, low above the south-western horizon for the first 3 or 4 days of the month, its magnitude fading rapidly from +0.1 to +0.9 during this time. Thereafter it is too close to the Sun for observation, as it passes through inferior conjunction on the 13th.

Venus, magnitude -4.6, continues to be visible as a magnificent object in the south-western sky in the evenings, attaining its greatest brilliancy on the 22nd. Keen-sighted observers may be able to detect the planet shortly before sunset, especially if they know exactly where to look and can shield their eyes from direct sunlight. At the end of the month the crescent Moon will be in the same area of the sky as Venus, though never closer than 11°.

Mars, magnitude +0.8, continues to be visible as a morning object in the south-eastern sky. Mars is in Libra at the beginning of the month, then moving eastwards into Scorpius before crossing into Ophiuchus at the very end of February. The Moon, at Last Quarter, passes north of Mars on the 15th.

Jupiter continues to be visible high in the south-western quadrant of the sky in the evenings, magnitude -2.4. By the end of the month the planet is setting over the west-north-western horizon shortly after midnight. Again the Moon, just after First Quarter, will be seen near both Jupiter and Saturn, passing south of them on the 2nd.

Saturn, magnitude +0.1, continues to be visible in the south-western quadrant of the sky in the evenings but by the end of the month is unlikely to be visible for long after 22h.

Zodiacal Light. The evening cone may be observed stretching up from the western horizon, along the ecliptic, after the end of twilight, from the 10th to the 24th. This faint phenomenon is only visible under good conditions and in the absence of both moonlight and artificial lighting.

THE MOON

Day	RA		Dec.	Hor. par.	Semi- diam.	Sun's co- long.	PA of Bright Limb	Phase	Age	Rise 52°	Rise 56°	Transit	Set 52°	Set 56°
	h	m	°	′	′	°	°	%	d	h m	h m	h m	h m	h m
1	2	18	+ 8.6	56.6	15.4	1	251	44	7.5	10 59	10 50	18 08	0 18	0 25
2	3	08	+13.0	57.4	15.6	13	254	55	8.5	11 23	11 09	18 58	1 32	1 44
3	4	02	+17.0	58.3	15.9	25	258	65	9.5	11 53	11 35	19 53	2 48	3 05
4	4	59	+20.1	59.3	16.1	37	262	75	10.5	12 33	12 11	20 51	4 05	4 26
5	6	00	+22.1	60.1	16.4	49	269	85	11.5	13 26	13 01	21 54	5 18	5 42
6	7	04	+22.6	60.8	16.6	61	276	92	12.5	14 32	14 09	22 58	6 22	6 46
7	8	09	+21.5	61.3	16.7	74	286	97	13.5	15 51	15 31	—	7 14	7 35
8	9	13	+18.8	61.4	16.7	86	318	100	14.5	17 17	17 02	0 00	7 54	8 11
9	10	15	+14.8	61.2	16.7	98	91	99	15.5	18 44	18 34	1 00	8 26	8 38
10	11	13	+ 9.9	60.7	16.5	110	103	96	16.5	20 09	20 04	1 57	8 52	8 59
11	12	08	+ 4.5	60.0	16.3	122	107	89	17.5	21 31	21 31	2 50	9 14	9 16
12	13	01	− 0.9	59.0	16.1	134	108	81	18.5	22 49	22 55	3 40	9 35	9 33
13	13	53	− 6.2	58.1	15.8	146	108	72	19.5	—	—	4 29	9 56	9 49
14	14	43	−11.0	57.1	15.6	159	106	62	20.5	0 05	0 15	5 17	10 18	10 07
15	15	33	−15.1	56.2	15.3	171	104	52	21.5	1 18	1 33	6 05	10 43	10 27
16	16	24	−18.4	55.5	15.1	183	100	42	22.5	2 28	2 47	6 53	11 12	10 53
17	17	15	−20.8	54.9	15.0	195	95	32	23.5	3 33	3 55	7 42	11 47	11 25
18	18	06	−22.2	54.5	14.8	207	90	24	24.5	4 31	4 56	8 31	12 30	12 05
19	18	58	−22.6	54.2	14.8	219	84	16	25.5	5 22	5 47	9 20	13 20	12 56
20	19	49	−22.0	54.0	14.7	232	78	10	26.5	6 04	6 27	10 09	14 17	13 55
21	20	39	−20.4	54.0	14.7	244	71	5	27.5	6 39	6 58	10 56	15 20	15 00
22	21	28	−17.9	54.0	14.7	256	61	2	28.5	7 07	7 23	11 42	16 25	16 10
23	22	16	−14.7	54.2	14.8	268	25	0	29.5	7 30	7 42	12 27	17 32	17 21
24	23	03	−10.8	54.4	14.8	280	278	1	0.7	7 50	7 59	13 10	18 40	18 33
25	23	48	− 6.5	54.7	14.9	293	261	3	1.7	8 09	8 13	13 53	19 48	19 46
26	0	34	− 1.9	55.1	15.0	305	256	7	2.7	8 26	8 27	14 35	20 58	21 00
27	1	19	+ 2.9	55.5	15.1	317	254	12	3.7	8 44	8 40	15 19	22 08	22 15
28	2	06	+ 7.6	56.0	15.3	329	254	20	4.7	9 03	8 55	16 05	23 21	23 32

MERCURY

Day	RA		Dec.	Diam.	Phase	Transit	5° high 52°	5° high 56°
	h	m	°	″	%	h m	h m	h m
1	22	06	-10.5	8	39	13 20	17 51	17 38
3	22	08	- 9.8	8	29	13 13	17 48	17 36
5	22	08	- 9.2	9	20	13 04	17 41	17 30
7	22	04	- 9.0	9	12	12 52	17 30	17 19
9	21	58	- 9.0	10	6	12 38	17 15	17 03
11	21	51	- 9.4	10	2	12 22	16 56	16 44
13	21	42	- 9.9	10	1	12 05	16 36	16 23
15	21	33	-10.6	10	2	11 48	7 21	7 35
17	21	25	-11.4	10	5	11 33	7 10	7 24
19	21	18	-12.2	10	9	11 19	7 00	7 16
21	21	13	-13.0	10	14	11 06	6 52	7 08
23	21	10	-13.6	10	20	10 56	6 46	7 03
25	21	09	-14.1	9	25	10 48	6 40	6 58
27	21	10	-14.5	9	31	10 41	6 36	6 54
29	21	12	-14.8	9	36	10 36	6 32	6 51
31	21	16	-15.0	8	40	10 32	6 30	6 48

VENUS

Day	RA		Dec.	Diam.	Phase	Transit	5° high 52°	5° high 56°
	h	m	°	″	%	h m	h m	h m
1	23	52	+ 0.7	29	43	15 06	20 39	20 37
6	0	07	+ 3.0	31	40	15 01	20 46	20 45
11	0	20	+ 5.3	33	36	14 54	20 50	20 52
16	0	31	+ 7.3	36	32	14 46	20 52	20 55
21	0	41	+ 9.3	38	28	14 36	20 52	20 56
26	0	49	+10.9	41	24	14 23	20 48	20 53
31	0	53	+12.3	45	19	14 08	20 39	20 46

MARS

Day	RA		Dec.	Diam.	Phase	Transit	5° high 52°	5° high 56°
1	15	22	-17.3	6	90	6 36	2 50	3 12
6	15	33	-18.0	7	90	6 28	2 46	3 09
11	15	44	-18.7	7	90	6 19	2 42	3 06
16	15	55	-19.3	7	90	6 10	2 37	3 03
21	16	05	-19.9	7	89	6 01	2 33	2 59
26	16	16	-20.4	8	89	5 52	2 27	2 55
31	16	26	-20.8	8	89	5 42	2 22	2 51

SUNRISE AND SUNSET

	London 0°05′ 51°30′		Bristol 2°35′ 51°28′		Birmingham 1°55′ 52°28′		Manchester 2°15′ 53°28′		Newcastle 1°37′ 54°59′		Glasgow 4°14′ 55°52′		Belfast 5°56′ 54°35′	
	h m	h m	h m	h m	h m	h m	h m	h m	h m	h m	h m	h m	h m	h m
1	7 39	16 50	7 48	17 00	7 49	16 54	7 54	16 52	7 57	16 44	8 11	16 51	8 13	17 03
2	7 37	16 52	7 47	17 02	7 48	16 56	7 52	16 54	7 55	16 46	8 09	16 53	8 11	17 05
3	7 35	16 54	7 45	17 04	7 46	16 58	7 51	16 56	7 53	16 48	8 07	16 55	8 09	17 07
4	7 34	16 55	7 44	17 05	7 44	17 00	7 49	16 58	7 52	16 50	8 05	16 57	8 07	17 09
5	7 32	16 57	7 42	17 07	7 42	17 02	7 47	17 00	7 50	16 52	8 03	16 59	8 05	17 11
6	7 30	16 59	7 40	17 09	7 41	17 04	7 45	17 02	7 48	16 54	8 01	17 02	8 04	17 13
7	7 29	17 01	7 39	17 11	7 39	17 05	7 43	17 04	7 46	16 56	7 59	17 04	8 02	17 15
8	7 27	17 03	7 37	17 13	7 37	17 07	7 41	17 06	7 44	16 58	7 57	17 06	8 00	17 17
9	7 25	17 05	7 35	17 15	7 35	17 09	7 39	17 08	7 42	17 01	7 55	17 08	7 58	17 19
10	7 23	17 06	7 33	17 16	7 33	17 11	7 38	17 10	7 40	17 03	7 53	17 10	7 56	17 21
11	7 22	17 08	7 32	17 18	7 32	17 13	7 36	17 12	7 37	17 05	7 51	17 12	7 54	17 23
12	7 20	17 10	7 30	17 20	7 30	17 15	7 34	17 14	7 35	17 07	7 48	17 15	7 51	17 25
13	7 18	17 12	7 28	17 22	7 28	17 17	7 32	17 16	7 33	17 09	7 46	17 17	7 49	17 27
14	7 16	17 14	7 26	17 24	7 26	17 19	7 30	17 18	7 31	17 11	7 44	17 19	7 47	17 29
15	7 14	17 15	7 24	17 26	7 24	17 21	7 27	17 20	7 29	17 13	7 42	17 21	7 45	17 31
16	7 12	17 17	7 22	17 27	7 22	17 23	7 25	17 22	7 27	17 15	7 39	17 23	7 43	17 34
17	7 10	17 19	7 20	17 29	7 20	17 24	7 23	17 23	7 24	17 17	7 37	17 26	7 41	17 36
18	7 08	17 21	7 18	17 31	7 18	17 26	7 21	17 25	7 22	17 19	7 35	17 28	7 38	17 38
19	7 06	17 23	7 16	17 33	7 16	17 28	7 19	17 27	7 20	17 22	7 33	17 30	7 36	17 40
20	7 04	17 25	7 14	17 35	7 14	17 30	7 17	17 29	7 18	17 24	7 30	17 32	7 34	17 42
21	7 02	17 26	7 12	17 36	7 11	17 32	7 15	17 31	7 15	17 26	7 28	17 34	7 32	17 44
22	7 00	17 28	7 10	17 38	7 09	17 34	7 13	17 33	7 13	17 28	7 25	17 36	7 29	17 46
23	6 58	17 30	7 08	17 40	7 07	17 36	7 10	17 35	7 11	17 30	7 23	17 39	7 27	17 48
24	6 56	17 32	7 06	17 42	7 05	17 38	7 08	17 37	7 08	17 32	7 21	17 41	7 25	17 50
25	6 54	17 34	7 04	17 44	7 03	17 39	7 06	17 39	7 06	17 34	7 18	17 43	7 23	17 52
26	6 52	17 35	7 02	17 45	7 01	17 41	7 04	17 41	7 04	17 36	7 16	17 45	7 20	17 54
27	6 50	17 37	7 00	17 47	6 59	17 43	7 01	17 43	7 01	17 38	7 13	17 47	7 18	17 56
28	6 48	17 39	6 58	17 49	6 56	17 45	6 59	17 45	6 59	17 40	7 11	17 49	7 15	17 58

JUPITER

Day	RA	Dec.	Transit	5° high 52°	56°
	h m	° ′	h m	h m	h m
1	3 57.1	+19 45	19 09	2 24	2 38
11	3 58.7	+19 52	18 31	1 47	2 01
21	4 01.7	+20 03	17 55	1 11	1 26
31	4 05.8	+20 16	17 20	0 37	0 52

Diameters – equatorial 40″ polar 38″

SATURN

Day	RA	Dec.	Transit	5° high 52°	56°
	h m	° ′	h m	h m	h m
1	3 29.0	+16 48	18 41	1 39	1 50
11	3 29.9	+16 54	18 03	1 01	1 12
21	3 31.5	+17 03	17 25	0 24	0 35
31	3 33.8	+17 14	16 48	23 45	23 56

Diameters – equatorial 18″ polar 17″
Rings – major axis 41″ minor axis 16″

URANUS

Day	RA	Dec.	Transit	10° high 52°	56°
	h m	° ′	h m	h m	h m
1	21 31.8	-15 21	12 45	9 26	9 52
11	21 34.1	-15 10	12 08	8 47	9 14
21	21 36.3	-14 59	11 31	8 09	8 35
31	21 38.5	-14 48	10 54	7 30	7 56

Diameter 4″

NEPTUNE

Day	RA	Dec.	Transit	10° high 52°	56°
	h m	° ′	h m	h m	h m
1	20 35.3	-18 30	11 48	8 55	9 30
11	20 36.8	-18 24	11 11	8 16	8 51
21	20 38.3	-18 19	10 33	7 38	8 12
31	20 39.7	-18 14	9 55	6 59	7 34

Diameter 2″

 # March 2001

THIRD MONTH, 31 DAYS. *Mars*, Roman god of battle

1	*Thursday*	**St David's Day.** David Niven b. 1910	60
2	*Friday*	Mikhail Gorbachev b. 1931. Howard Carter d. 1939	61
3	*Saturday*	Alexander Graham Bell b. 1847. Arthur Koestler d. 1983	62
4	*Sunday*	**1st S. of Lent.** RNLI founded 1824	63
5	*Monday*	King Henry II b. 1133. Josef Stalin d. 1953	*week 10 day* 64
6	*Tuesday*	Michelangelo Buonarroti b. 1475. Ivor Novello d. 1951	65
7	*Wednesday*	St Thomas Aquinas d. 1274. Sir Eduardo Paolozzi b. 1924	66
8	*Thursday*	Carl Philipp Emanuel Bach b. 1714. Sir William Walton d. 1983	67
9	*Friday*	Kaiser William I d. 1888. Yuri Gagarin b. 1934	68
10	*Saturday*	*Earl of Wessex b. 1964.* Michael O'Donovan d. 1966	69
11	*Sunday*	**2nd S. of Lent.** Luddite riots began 1811	70
12	*Monday*	Commonwealth Day. Ivar Kreuger d. 1932	*week 11 day* 71
13	*Tuesday*	Uranus discovered 1781. Sir Hugh Walpole b. 1884	72
14	*Wednesday*	Albert Einstein b. 1879.	73
15	*Thursday*	William Lamb b. 1779. Dr Benjamin Spock d. 1998	74
16	*Friday*	Camilo Castelo Branco b. 1825. William Beveridge d. 1963	75
17	*Saturday*	**St Patrick's Day.** Rudolf Nureyev b. 1938	76
18	*Sunday*	**3rd S. of Lent.** Neville Chamberlain b. 1869	77
19	*Monday*	**St Joseph of Nazareth.** Dr David Livingstone b. 1813	*week 12 day* 78
20	*Tuesday*	Spring begins. Ovid b. 43BC	79
21	*Wednesday*	Archbishop Thomas Cranmer d. 1556. Michael Heseltine b. 1933	80
22	*Thursday*	Sir Anthony van Dyck b. 1599. Jean-Baptiste Lully d. 1687.	81
23	*Friday*	*Princess Eugenie of York b. 1990.* Friedrich von Hayek d. 1992	82
24	*Saturday*	William Morris b. 1834. John Millington Synge d. 1909	83
25	*Sunday*	**4th S. of Lent. The Annunciation.** Mothering Sunday	84
26	*Monday*	Tennessee Williams b. 1911. David Lloyd George d. 1945	*week 13 day* 85
27	*Tuesday*	King James VI and I d. 1625. Sarah Vaughan b. 1924	86
28	*Wednesday*	Sir Dirk Bogarde b. 1921. Eugene Ionesco d. 1994	87
29	*Thursday*	Georges Seurat d. 1891. John Major b. 1943	88
30	*Friday*	Vincent van Gogh b. 1853. Sir John Stainer d. 1901	89
31	*Saturday*	Andrew Lang b. 1844. Eiffel Tower completed 1889	90

ASTRONOMICAL PHENOMENA

d	h	
1	19	Saturn in conjunction with Moon. Saturn 2° N.
2	10	Jupiter in conjunction with Moon. Jupiter 3° N.
9	01	Venus at stationary point
11	07	Mercury at greatest elongation W.27°
15	21	Mars in conjunction with Moon. Mars 2° S.
18	03	Pluto at stationary point
20	14	Sun's longitude 0° ♈
22	20	Mercury in conjunction with Moon. Mercury 2° N.
25	16	Venus in conjunction with Moon. Venus 13° N.
29	04	Saturn in conjunction with Moon. Saturn 2° N.
29	22	Jupiter in conjunction with Moon. Jupiter 2° N.
30	04	Venus in inferior conjunction

MINIMA OF ALGOL

d	h	d	h	d	h
1	04.5	12	15.8	24	03.1
4	01.3	15	12.6	26	23.9
6	22.1	18	09.4	29	20.7
9	19.0	21	06.3		

CONSTELLATIONS

The following constellations are near the meridian at

	d	h		d	h
February	1	24	March	16	21
February	15	23	April	1	20
March	1	22	April	15	19

Cepheus (below the Pole), Camelopardus, Lynx, Gemini, Cancer, Leo, Canis Minor, Hydra, Monoceros, Canis Major and Puppis

THE MOON

Phases, Apsides and Node		d	h	m
☽ First Quarter		3	02	03
○ Full Moon		9	17	23
☾ Last Quarter		16	20	45
● New Moon		25	01	21
Perigee (359,775 km)		8	08	54
Apogee (405,474 km)		20	11	24

Mean longitude of ascending node on March 1, 103°

THE SUN

s.d. 16′.1

Day	Right Ascension	Dec.	Equation of time	Rise 52°	Rise 56°	Transit	Set 52°	Set 56°	Sidereal time	Transit of First Point of Aries
	h m s	° ′	m s	h m	h m	h m	h m	h m	h m s	h m s
1	22 47 52	− 7 39	− 12 25	6 46	6 51	12 12	17 40	17 34	10 35 27	13 22 21
2	22 51 37	− 7 16	− 12 13	6 44	6 49	12 12	17 42	17 36	10 39 24	13 18 25
3	22 55 21	− 6 53	− 12 01	6 41	6 46	12 12	17 43	17 38	10 43 20	13 14 29
4	22 59 05	− 6 30	− 11 48	6 39	6 44	12 12	17 45	17 41	10 47 17	13 10 33
5	23 02 49	− 6 07	− 11 35	6 37	6 41	12 11	17 47	17 43	10 51 13	13 06 37
6	23 06 31	− 5 43	− 11 21	6 35	6 39	12 11	17 49	17 45	10 55 10	13 02 41
7	23 10 14	− 5 20	− 11 07	6 33	6 36	12 11	17 50	17 47	10 59 07	12 58 45
8	23 13 56	− 4 57	− 10 53	6 30	6 34	12 11	17 52	17 49	11 03 03	12 54 50
9	23 17 37	− 4 33	− 10 38	6 28	6 31	12 11	17 54	17 51	11 07 00	12 50 54
10	23 21 19	− 4 10	− 10 22	6 26	6 28	12 10	17 56	17 53	11 10 56	12 46 58
11	23 25 00	− 3 46	− 10 07	6 23	6 26	12 10	17 57	17 55	11 14 53	12 43 02
12	23 28 40	− 3 23	− 9 51	6 21	6 23	12 10	17 59	17 57	11 18 49	12 39 06
13	23 32 21	− 2 59	− 9 35	6 19	6 21	12 09	18 01	17 59	11 22 46	12 35 10
14	23 36 01	− 2 36	− 9 18	6 17	6 18	12 09	18 03	18 01	11 26 42	12 31 14
15	23 39 40	− 2 12	− 9 01	6 14	6 15	12 09	18 04	18 03	11 30 39	12 27 18
16	23 43 20	− 1 48	− 8 44	6 12	6 13	12 09	18 06	18 06	11 34 36	12 23 22
17	23 46 59	− 1 25	− 8 27	6 10	6 10	12 08	18 08	18 08	11 38 32	12 19 26
18	23 50 39	− 1 01	− 8 10	6 07	6 08	12 08	18 10	18 10	11 42 29	12 15 31
19	23 54 18	− 0 37	− 7 52	6 05	6 05	12 08	18 11	18 12	11 46 25	12 11 35
20	23 57 57	− 0 13	− 7 35	6 03	6 02	12 07	18 13	18 14	11 50 22	12 07 39
21	0 01 35	+ 0 10	− 7 17	6 00	6 00	12 07	18 15	18 16	11 54 18	12 03 43
22	0 05 14	+ 0 34	− 6 59	5 58	5 57	12 07	18 17	18 18	11 58 15	11 59 47
23	0 08 53	+ 0 58	− 6 41	5 56	5 54	12 07	18 18	18 20	12 02 11	11 55 51
24	0 12 31	+ 1 21	− 6 23	5 53	5 52	12 06	18 20	18 22	12 06 08	11 51 55
25	0 16 10	+ 1 45	− 6 05	5 51	5 49	12 06	18 22	18 24	12 10 05	11 47 59
26	0 19 48	+ 2 09	− 5 47	5 49	5 46	12 06	18 24	18 26	12 14 01	11 44 03
27	0 23 27	+ 2 32	− 5 29	5 46	5 44	12 05	18 25	18 28	12 17 58	11 40 07
28	0 27 05	+ 2 56	− 5 11	5 44	5 41	12 05	18 27	18 30	12 21 54	11 36 11
29	0 30 44	+ 3 19	− 4 53	5 42	5 39	12 05	18 29	18 32	12 25 51	11 32 16
30	0 34 22	+ 3 42	− 4 35	5 40	5 36	12 04	18 30	18 34	12 29 47	11 28 20
31	0 38 01	+ 4 06	− 4 17	5 37	5 33	12 04	18 32	18 36	12 33 44	11 24 24

DURATION OF TWILIGHT (in minutes)

Latitude	52°	56°	52°	56°	52°	56°	52°	56°
	1 March		11 March		21 March		31 March	
Civil	34	38	34	37	34	37	34	38
Nautical	73	81	73	80	74	82	76	84
Astronomical	112	124	113	125	116	129	120	136

THE NIGHT SKY

Mercury, despite the fact that it reaches greatest western elongation (27°) on the 11th, remains too close to the Sun for observation throughout March.

Venus is a brilliant object in the western sky in the early evenings, magnitude -4.3. The period available for observation is shortening very noticeably and by the end of the month the planet is setting before the Sun. However, Venus attains its greatest northern ecliptic latitude during the second part of the month, and also passes through inferior conjunction on the 30th. As a result it will be possible to see it as a morning object for the last ten days of March, low above the E.N.E. horizon shortly before sunrise. Thus there is about a week (between the 21st and the 28th, approximately) when it can be seen as both an evening and a morning object.

Mars continues to be visible in the south-eastern sky in the early mornings, its magnitude during the month brightening from +0.5 to -0.1. Mars is in the constellation of Ophiuchus, passing 5° north of Antares on the 4th. The Moon, near Last Quarter, is in the vicinity of Mars on the mornings of the 15th and 16th.

Jupiter, magnitude -2.2, continues to be visible in the south-western sky after sunset, though no longer visible after midnight. Jupiter is moving eastwards and slowly increasing the gap between itself and Saturn. The waxing crescent Moon passes south of both planets on the 1st-2nd and again on the 29th.

Saturn is still an evening object in the western sky but moving closer to the Sun and only visible for a short while after sunset. Its magnitude is +0.2.

Zodiacal Light. The evening cone may be observed, stretching up from the western horizon, along the ecliptic, after the end of twilight, from the 11th up to the 26th.

THE MOON

Day	RA (h m)	Dec. (°)	Hor. par. (')	Semi-diam. (')	Sun's co-long. (°)	PA of Bright Limb (°)	Phase (%)	Age (d)	Rise 52° (h m)	Rise 56° (h m)	Transit (h m)	Set 52° (h m)	Set 56° (h m)
1	2 55	+12.1	56.6	15.4	341	255	29	5.7	9 25	9 13	16 53	— -	
2	3 46	+16.2	57.3	15.6	354	258	39	6.7	9 52	9 36	17 44	0 35	0 50
3	4 41	+19.4	58.1	15.8	6	262	49	7.7	10 27	10 06	18 39	1 49	2 09
4	5 39	+21.7	58.8	16.0	18	268	60	8.7	11 12	10 48	19 38	3 02	3 25
5	6 40	+22.7	59.6	16.2	30	274	71	9.7	12 10	11 46	20 39	4 07	4 32
6	7 42	+22.3	60.2	16.4	42	281	81	10.7	13 22	12 59	21 41	5 03	5 26
7	8 45	+20.2	60.7	16.5	54	288	89	11.7	14 43	14 25	22 41	5 47	6 06
8	9 47	+16.8	60.9	16.6	67	297	96	12.7	16 09	15 56	23 38	6 22	6 36
9	10 46	+12.3	60.9	16.6	79	314	99	13.7	17 35	17 28	—	6 50	6 59
10	11 43	+ 7.0	60.6	16.5	91	62	100	14.7	19 00	18 58	0 33	7 14	7 18
11	12 38	+ 1.4	60.0	16.3	103	98	97	15.7	20 23	20 26	1 26	7 36	7 35
12	13 31	− 4.1	59.2	16.1	115	103	93	16.7	21 42	21 50	2 17	7 56	7 51
13	14 23	− 9.3	58.3	15.9	127	104	86	17.7	23 00	23 12	3 06	8 18	8 09
14	15 15	−13.9	57.3	15.6	139	103	78	18.7	—	—	3 56	8 42	8 28
15	16 07	−17.6	56.4	15.4	152	100	68	19.7	0 13	0 31	4 46	9 10	8 52
16	16 59	−20.4	55.7	15.2	164	96	59	20.7	1 22	1 44	5 36	9 44	9 22
17	17 51	−22.2	55.0	15.0	176	91	49	21.7	2 25	2 49	6 26	10 24	10 00
18	18 43	−22.8	54.5	14.9	188	86	39	22.7	3 19	3 44	7 15	11 12	10 47
19	19 35	−22.5	54.2	14.8	200	80	30	23.7	4 04	4 28	8 04	12 08	11 44
20	20 26	−21.1	54.1	14.7	212	75	22	24.7	4 41	5 02	8 52	13 09	12 48
21	21 15	−18.8	54.1	14.7	225	70	15	25.7	5 11	5 28	9 38	14 13	13 57
22	22 03	−15.8	54.2	14.8	237	64	9	26.7	5 35	5 49	10 23	15 20	15 08
23	22 50	−12.0	54.5	14.8	249	58	4	27.7	5 56	6 06	11 07	16 29	16 21
24	23 36	− 7.7	54.8	14.9	261	46	1	28.7	6 15	6 20	11 50	17 38	17 34
25	0 22	− 3.1	55.2	15.0	274	344	0	29.7	6 33	6 34	12 34	18 48	18 48
26	1 08	+ 1.8	55.6	15.2	286	272	1	0.9	6 50	6 47	13 17	19 59	20 04
27	1 55	+ 6.7	56.1	15.3	298	261	4	1.9	7 09	7 02	14 03	21 12	21 21
28	2 43	+11.3	56.6	15.4	310	259	9	2.9	7 30	7 19	14 50	22 26	22 41
29	3 34	+15.5	57.1	15.6	322	260	16	3.9	7 55	7 39	15 41	23 41	—
30	4 28	+19.0	57.6	15.7	335	263	24	4.9	8 26	8 06	16 34	—	0 00
31	5 25	+21.6	58.1	15.8	347	267	34	5.9	9 07	8 44	17 31	0 54	1 17

MERCURY

Day	RA (h m)	Dec. (°)	Diam. ('')	Phase (%)	Transit (h m)	5° high 52° (h m)	5° high 56° (h m)
1	21 12	-14.8	9	36	10 36	6 32	6 51
3	21 16	-15.0	8	40	10 32	6 30	6 48
5	21 21	-15.0	8	44	10 30	6 27	6 46
7	21 27	-14.9	8	48	10 28	6 25	6 43
9	21 34	-14.7	7	52	10 27	6 23	6 41
11	21 42	-14.5	7	55	10 27	6 21	6 39
13	21 51	-14.1	7	58	10 28	6 19	6 36
15	22 00	-13.6	7	61	10 29	6 17	6 33
17	22 09	-13.0	7	64	10 31	6 15	6 31
19	22 19	-12.3	6	66	10 33	6 13	6 28
21	22 29	-11.5	6	69	10 36	6 10	6 24
23	22 40	-10.6	6	71	10 38	6 08	6 21
25	22 51	- 9.7	6	73	10 42	6 05	6 17
27	23 02	- 8.7	6	75	10 45	6 03	6 14
29	23 14	- 7.5	6	77	10 48	6 00	6 10
31	23 25	- 6.4	6	79	10 52	5 57	6 06

VENUS

Day	RA (h m)	Dec. (°)	Diam. ('')	Phase (%)	Transit (h m)	5° high 52° (h m)	5° high 56° (h m)
1	0 52	+11.8	43	21	14 14	20 43	20 50
6	0 54	+13.0	47	17	13 57	20 31	20 39
11	0 54	+13.7	51	12	13 36	20 13	20 22
16	0 49	+13.9	54	8	13 12	19 49	19 58
21	0 41	+13.5	57	4	12 44	19 19	19 26
26	0 31	+12.4	59	2	12 14	18 43	18 50
31	0 20	+10.9	59	1	11 44	18 04	18 09

MARS

Day	RA (h m)	Dec. (°)	Diam. ('')	Phase (%)	Transit (h m)	5° high 52° (h m)	5° high 56° (h m)
1	16 22	-20.7	8	89	5 46	2 24	2 53
6	16 32	-21.1	8	89	5 37	2 18	2 48
11	16 42	-21.5	8	89	5 27	2 11	2 42
16	16 52	-21.9	9	89	5 17	2 04	2 36
21	17 01	-22.2	9	90	5 06	1 56	2 29
26	17 10	-22.5	10	90	4 55	1 48	2 21
31	17 18	-22.7	10	90	4 44	1 39	2 13

SUNRISE AND SUNSET

	London		Bristol		Birmingham		Manchester		Newcastle		Glasgow		Belfast	
	0° 05′	51° 30′	2° 35′	51° 28′	1° 55′	52° 28′	2° 15′	53° 28′	1° 37′	54° 59′	4° 14′	55° 52′	5° 56′	54° 35′
	h m	h m	h m	h m	h m	h m	h m	h m	h m	h m	h m	h m	h m	h m
1	6 46	17 41	6 55	17 51	6 54	17 47	6 57	17 47	6 56	17 42	7 08	17 51	7 13	18 00
2	6 43	17 42	6 53	17 52	6 52	17 49	6 54	17 49	6 54	17 44	7 06	17 53	7 11	18 02
3	6 41	17 44	6 51	17 54	6 50	17 50	6 52	17 51	6 52	17 46	7 03	17 56	7 08	18 04
4	6 39	17 46	6 49	17 56	6 47	17 52	6 50	17 53	6 49	17 48	7 01	17 58	7 06	18 06
5	6 37	17 48	6 47	17 58	6 45	17 54	6 47	17 54	6 47	17 50	6 58	18 00	7 03	18 08
6	6 35	17 49	6 45	17 59	6 43	17 56	6 45	17 56	6 44	17 52	6 56	18 02	7 01	18 10
7	6 32	17 51	6 42	18 01	6 41	17 58	6 43	17 58	6 42	17 54	6 53	18 04	6 59	18 12
8	6 30	17 53	6 40	18 03	6 38	18 00	6 40	18 00	6 39	17 56	6 50	18 06	6 56	18 14
9	6 28	17 55	6 38	18 05	6 36	18 01	6 38	18 02	6 37	17 58	6 48	18 08	6 54	18 16
10	6 26	17 56	6 36	18 06	6 34	18 03	6 36	18 04	6 34	18 00	6 45	18 10	6 51	18 18
11	6 23	17 58	6 33	18 08	6 31	18 05	6 33	18 06	6 32	18 02	6 43	18 12	6 49	18 20
12	6 21	18 00	6 31	18 10	6 29	18 07	6 31	18 08	6 29	18 04	6 40	18 14	6 46	18 22
13	6 19	18 02	6 29	18 12	6 27	18 08	6 28	18 09	6 27	18 06	6 37	18 16	6 44	18 24
14	6 17	18 03	6 27	18 13	6 24	18 10	6 26	18 11	6 24	18 08	6 35	18 18	6 41	18 26
15	6 14	18 05	6 24	18 15	6 22	18 12	6 24	18 13	6 22	18 10	6 32	18 20	6 39	18 28
16	6 12	18 07	6 22	18 17	6 20	18 14	6 21	18 15	6 19	18 12	6 30	18 23	6 36	18 30
17	6 10	18 08	6 20	18 18	6 17	18 16	6 19	18 17	6 16	18 14	6 27	18 25	6 34	18 32
18	6 08	18 10	6 18	18 20	6 15	18 17	6 16	18 19	6 14	18 16	6 24	18 27	6 31	18 33
19	6 05	18 12	6 15	18 22	6 13	18 19	6 14	18 21	6 11	18 18	6 22	18 29	6 29	18 35
20	6 03	18 13	6 13	18 23	6 10	18 21	6 12	18 22	6 09	18 20	6 19	18 31	6 26	18 37
21	6 01	18 15	6 11	18 25	6 08	18 23	6 09	18 24	6 06	18 22	6 17	18 33	6 24	18 39
22	5 59	18 17	6 09	18 27	6 06	18 24	6 07	18 26	6 04	18 24	6 14	18 35	6 21	18 41
23	5 56	18 19	6 06	18 29	6 03	18 26	6 04	18 28	6 01	18 26	6 11	18 37	6 19	18 43
24	5 54	18 20	6 04	18 30	6 01	18 28	6 02	18 30	5 59	18 28	6 09	18 39	6 16	18 45
25	5 52	18 22	6 02	18 32	5 59	18 30	5 59	18 32	5 56	18 30	6 06	18 41	6 14	18 47
26	5 49	18 24	5 59	18 34	5 56	18 31	5 57	18 33	5 54	18 32	6 03	18 43	6 11	18 49
27	5 47	18 25	5 57	18 35	5 54	18 33	5 55	18 35	5 51	18 34	6 01	18 45	6 09	18 51
28	5 45	18 27	5 55	18 37	5 52	18 35	5 52	18 37	5 48	18 36	5 58	18 47	6 06	18 53
29	5 43	18 29	5 53	18 39	5 49	18 37	5 50	18 39	5 46	18 38	5 56	18 49	6 03	18 55
30	5 40	18 30	5 50	18 40	5 47	18 38	5 47	18 41	5 43	18 40	5 53	18 51	6 01	18 57
31	5 38	18 32	5 48	18 42	5 44	18 40	5 45	18 43	5 41	18 42	5 50	18 53	5 58	18 58

JUPITER

Day	RA	Dec.		Transit	5° high	
					52°	56°
	h m	°	′	h m	h m	h m
1	4 04.9	+20	13	17 27	0 44	0 59
11	4 09.9	+20	29	16 53	0 11	0 26
21	4 16.0	+20	46	16 19	23 37	23 52
31	4 22.9	+21	05	15 47	23 06	23 22

Diameters – equatorial 37″ polar 35″

SATURN

Day	RA	Dec.		Transit	5° high	
					52°	56°
	h m	°	′	h m	h m	h m
1	3 33.3	+17	11	16 55	23 52	0 07
11	3 36.1	+17	24	16 19	23 16	23 28
21	3 39.5	+17	38	15 43	22 42	22 54
31	3 43.4	+17	53	15 07	22 08	22 20

Diameters – equatorial 17″ polar 16″
Rings – major axis 39″ minor axis 16″

URANUS

Day	RA	Dec.		Transit	10° high	
					52°	56°
	h m	°	′	h m	h m	h m
1	21 38.1	-14	50	11 01	7 38	8 04
11	21 40.2	-14	40	10 24	6 59	7 25
21	21 42.2	-14	30	9 46	6 21	6 46
31	21 44.0	-14	21	9 09	5 42	6 07

Diameter 4″

NEPTUNE

Day	RA	Dec.		Transit	10° high	
					52°	56°
	h m	°	′	h m	h m	h m
1	20 39.4	-18	15	10 02	7 07	7 41
11	20 40.7	-18	10	9 24	6 28	7 02
21	20 41.8	-18	06	8 46	5 49	6 23
31	20 42.8	-18	02	8 08	5 10	5 44

Diameter 2″

April 2001

FOURTH MONTH, 30 DAYS. *Aperire*, to open; Earth opens to receive seed

1	*Sunday*	**5th S. of Lent**. Prince Otto von Bismarck b. 1815		91
2	*Monday*	Hans Christian Andersen b. 1805. C. S. Forester d. 1966	*week 14 day*	92
3	*Tuesday*	Bartolomé Murillo d. 1682. Marlon Brando b. 1924		93
4	*Wednesday*	Sir William Siemens b. 1823. Karl Friedrich Benz d. 1941		94
5	*Thursday*	John Wisden d. 1884. Spencer Tracy b. 1900		95
6	*Friday*	Sir John Betjeman b. 1906. Igor Stravinsky d. 1971		96
7	*Saturday*	William Wordsworth b. 1770. Henry Ford d. 1947		97
8	*Sunday*	**Palm Sunday**. Sir Adrian Boult b. 1889		98
9	*Monday*	Lorenzo di Medici d. 1492. Jacques Villeneuve b. 1971	*week 15 day*	99
10	*Tuesday*	Civil Rights Bill passed by US Senate 1960		100
11	*Wednesday*	George Canning b. 1770. Sir Gerald du Maurier d. 1934		101
12	*Thursday*	**Maundy Thursday**. American Civil War started 1861		102
13	*Friday*	**Good Friday**. Seamus Heaney b. 1939		103
14	*Saturday*	Easter Eve. George Frederick Handel d. 1759		104
15	*Sunday*	**Easter Day**. Abraham Lincoln d. 1865		105
16	*Monday*	*Bank Holiday in England, Wales and Northern Ireland*	*week 16 day*	106
17	*Tuesday*	Sir Ian MacGregor d. 1998		107
18	*Wednesday*	Judge George Jeffreys d. 1689. Sir Roger de Grey b. 1918		108
19	*Thursday*	David Ricardo b. 1772. Anthony Tudor d. 1987		109
20	*Friday*	Pontiac d. 1769. Napoleon III b. 1808		110
21	*Saturday*	*Queen Elizabeth II b. 1926*. Mark Twain d. 1910		111
22	*Sunday*	**2nd S. of Easter**. Kathleen Ferrier b. 1912		112
23	*Monday*	**St George's Day**. Constantine Karamanlis d. 1998	*week 17 day*	113
24	*Tuesday*	Sir Stafford Cripps b. 1889. Wallis Simpson d. 1986		114
25	*Wednesday*	**St Mark**. Anders Celsius d. 1744		115
26	*Thursday*	David Hume b. 1711. Lucille Ball d. 1989		116
27	*Friday*	Bombing of Guernica 1937. Ulysses S. Grant b. 1822		117
28	*Saturday*	Anthony Ashley Cooper b. 1801. Benito Mussolini d. 1945		118
29	*Sunday*	**3rd S. of Easter**. Duke Ellington b. 1899		119
30	*Monday*	Queen Mary II b. 1662. A. E. Housman d. 1936	*week 18 day*	120

ASTRONOMICAL PHENOMENA

d	h	
8	15	Venus in conjunction with Mercury. Venus 9° N.
13	02	Mars in conjunction with Moon. Mars 1° S.
20	01	Sun's longitude 30° ♉
20	05	Venus at stationary point
21	03	Venus in conjunction with Moon. Venus 9° N.
23	09	Mercury in superior conjunction
23	16	Mercury in conjunction with Moon. Mercury 4° N.
25	16	Saturn in conjunction with Moon. Saturn 1° N.
26	13	Jupiter in conjunction with Moon. Jupiter 2° N.

MINIMA OF ALGOL

d	h	d	h	d	h
1	17.5	13	04.8	24	16.1
4	14.4	16	01.6	27	12.9
7	11.2	18	22.5	30	09.7
10	08.0	21	19.3		

CONSTELLATIONS

The following constellations are near the meridian at

	d	h		d	h
March	1	24	April	15	21
March	16	23	May	1	20
April	1	22	May	16	19

Cepheus (below the Pole), Cassiopeia (below the Pole), Ursa Major, Leo Minor, Leo, Sextans, Hydra and Crater

THE MOON

Phases, Apsides and Node	d	h	m
☽ First Quarter	1	10	49
○ Full Moon	8	03	22
☾ Last Quarter	15	15	31
● New Moon	23	15	26
☽ First Quarter	30	17	08
Perigee (364,809 km)	5	10	04
Apogee (404,505 km)	17	06	05

Mean longitude of ascending node on April 1, 101°

THE SUN

s.d. 16′.1

Day	Right Ascension	Dec. +	Equation of time	Rise 52°	Rise 56°	Transit	Set 52°	Set 56°	Sidereal time	Transit of First Point of Aries
	h m s	° ′	m s	h m	h m	h m	h m	h m	h m s	h m s
1	0 41 39	4 29	− 3 59	5 35	5 31	12 04	18 34	18 38	12 37 40	11 20 28
2	0 45 18	4 52	− 3 41	5 33	5 28	12 04	18 35	18 40	12 41 37	11 16 32
3	0 48 57	5 15	− 3 23	5 30	5 25	12 03	18 37	18 42	12 45 34	11 12 36
4	0 52 36	5 38	− 3 06	5 28	5 23	12 03	18 39	18 44	12 49 30	11 08 40
5	0 56 15	6 01	− 2 48	5 26	5 20	12 03	18 41	18 46	12 53 27	11 04 44
6	0 59 54	6 24	− 2 31	5 24	5 18	12 02	18 42	18 48	12 57 23	11 00 48
7	1 03 34	6 46	− 2 14	5 21	5 15	12 02	18 44	18 50	13 01 20	10 56 52
8	1 07 13	7 09	− 1 57	5 19	5 12	12 02	18 46	18 53	13 05 16	10 52 56
9	1 10 53	7 31	− 1 40	5 17	5 10	12 02	18 47	18 55	13 09 13	10 49 01
10	1 14 33	7 53	− 1 24	5 14	5 07	12 01	18 49	18 57	13 13 09	10 45 05
11	1 18 14	8 15	− 1 08	5 12	5 05	12 01	18 51	18 59	13 17 06	10 41 09
12	1 21 54	8 37	− 0 52	5 10	5 02	12 01	18 53	19 01	13 21 02	10 37 13
13	1 25 35	8 59	− 0 36	5 08	5 00	12 00	18 54	19 03	13 24 59	10 33 17
14	1 29 17	9 21	− 0 21	5 06	4 57	12 00	18 56	19 05	13 28 56	10 29 21
15	1 32 58	9 43	− 0 06	5 03	4 55	12 00	18 58	19 07	13 32 52	10 25 25
16	1 36 41	10 04	+ 0 08	5 01	4 52	12 00	18 59	19 09	13 36 49	10 21 29
17	1 40 23	10 25	+ 0 22	4 59	4 50	12 00	19 01	19 11	13 40 45	10 17 33
18	1 44 06	10 46	+ 0 36	4 57	4 47	11 59	19 03	19 13	13 44 42	10 13 37
19	1 47 49	11 07	+ 0 49	4 55	4 45	11 59	19 05	19 15	13 48 38	10 09 41
20	1 51 33	11 28	+ 1 02	4 53	4 42	11 59	19 06	19 17	13 52 35	10 05 46
21	1 55 17	11 48	+ 1 15	4 51	4 40	11 59	19 08	19 19	13 56 31	10 01 50
22	1 59 02	12 09	+ 1 27	4 48	4 37	11 58	19 10	19 21	14 00 28	9 57 54
23	2 02 47	12 29	+ 1 38	4 46	4 35	11 58	19 11	19 23	14 04 25	9 53 58
24	2 06 32	12 49	+ 1 49	4 44	4 32	11 58	19 13	19 25	14 08 21	9 50 02
25	2 10 18	13 08	+ 2 00	4 42	4 30	11 58	19 15	19 27	14 12 18	9 46 06
26	2 14 04	13 28	+ 2 10	4 40	4 28	11 58	19 16	19 29	14 16 14	9 42 10
27	2 17 51	13 47	+ 2 19	4 38	4 25	11 58	19 18	19 31	14 20 11	9 38 14
28	2 21 39	14 06	+ 2 29	4 36	4 23	11 57	19 20	19 33	14 24 07	9 34 18
29	2 25 27	14 25	+ 2 37	4 34	4 21	11 57	19 22	19 35	14 28 04	9 30 22
30	2 29 15	14 43	+ 2 45	4 32	4 18	11 57	19 23	19 37	14 32 00	9 26 26

DURATION OF TWILIGHT (in minutes)

Latitude	52°	56°	52°	56°	52°	56°	52°	56°
	1 April		11 April		21 April		30 April	
Civil	34	38	35	40	37	42	39	44
Nautical	76	85	79	90	84	96	89	105
Astronomical	121	137	128	148	138	167	152	200

THE NIGHT SKY

Mercury passes through superior conjunction on the 23rd and is therefore unsuitably placed for observation throughout the month.

Venus, magnitude -4.5, is a brilliant morning object, visible low above the E.N.E. horizon for a short while before sunrise. The old crescent Moon passes 9° south of the planet on the morning of the 21st.

Mars continues to be visible as a morning object, its magnitude brightening during the month from -0.2 to -1.0. By the end of the month it becomes visible shortly after midnight, low above the south-eastern horizon. On the morning of the 13th the gibbous Moon passes less than 1° north of the planet. At the beginning of April, Mars is in Ophiuchus but moves into Sagittarius at the very end of the month. Mars is still moving slowly southwards in declination, and by the end of April this has reached a value of -24°, so that from southern England it is still only about 15° above the horizon when it crosses the meridian, and only about 10° high from southern Scotland.

Jupiter is an evening object, magnitude -2.0, visible in the south-western sky for several hours after sunset. Jupiter is now about 10° further east than Saturn, passing 5° north of Aldebaran on the 16th. The crescent Moon passes 2° south of Jupiter on the 26th. The four Galilean satellites are readily observable with a small telescope or even a good pair of binoculars provided that they are held rigidly.

Saturn, magnitude +0.2, is still visible low in the western sky in the evenings but by the end of the month it has disappeared into the lengthening evening twilight. The crescent Moon passes 2° south of Saturn on the 25th.

THE MOON

Day	RA h m	Dec. °	Hor. par. '	Semi- diam. '	Sun's co- long. °	PA of Bright Limb °	Phase %	Age d	Rise 52° h m	Rise 56° h m	Transit h m	Set 52° h m	Set 56° h m
1	6 24	+22.9	58.7	16.0	359	272	45	6.9	9 59	9 34	18 30	2 01	2 26
2	7 25	+22.8	59.2	16.1	11	278	56	7.9	11 04	10 40	19 29	2 58	3 23
3	8 26	+21.3	59.6	16.2	23	284	67	8.9	12 20	11 59	20 28	3 45	4 06
4	9 26	+18.3	59.9	16.3	36	290	78	9.9	13 42	13 26	21 25	4 21	4 38
5	10 24	+14.3	60.1	16.4	48	296	87	10.9	15 06	14 56	22 19	4 51	5 02
6	11 20	+ 9.3	60.1	16.4	60	301	94	11.9	16 30	16 25	23 12	5 15	5 22
7	12 15	+ 3.8	59.8	16.3	72	311	98	12.9	17 53	17 54	—	5 37	5 39
8	13 08	− 1.8	59.4	16.2	84	2	100	13.9	19 15	19 20	0 03	5 57	5 54
9	14 00	− 7.3	58.8	16.0	96	88	99	14.9	20 34	20 45	0 53	6 18	6 11
10	14 53	− 12.2	58.0	15.8	109	98	95	15.9	21 52	22 07	1 43	6 41	6 29
11	15 46	− 16.4	57.2	15.6	121	98	90	16.9	23 05	23 26	2 34	7 07	6 50
12	16 39	− 19.7	56.4	15.4	133	96	83	17.9	—	—	3 25	7 38	7 17
13	17 32	− 21.9	55.7	15.2	145	92	75	18.9	0 13	0 37	4 16	8 16	7 52
14	18 26	− 23.0	55.1	15.0	157	87	66	19.9	1 12	1 38	5 07	9 02	8 36
15	19 18	− 23.0	54.6	14.9	169	82	56	20.9	2 02	2 27	5 58	9 55	9 31
16	20 10	− 21.9	54.3	14.8	182	78	47	21.9	2 42	3 05	6 46	10 55	10 33
17	21 00	− 19.9	54.2	14.8	194	73	37	22.9	3 14	3 33	7 33	11 59	11 41
18	21 48	− 17.0	54.3	14.8	206	69	29	23.9	3 40	3 55	8 19	13 06	12 51
19	22 35	− 13.4	54.4	14.8	218	65	20	24.9	4 02	4 13	9 03	14 14	14 04
20	23 22	− 9.2	54.8	14.9	230	62	13	25.9	4 21	4 28	9 46	15 22	15 17
21	0 07	− 4.6	55.2	15.0	243	58	7	26.9	4 39	4 42	10 29	16 32	16 31
22	0 53	+ 0.3	55.7	15.2	255	53	3	27.9	4 56	4 55	11 13	17 44	17 47
23	1 40	+ 5.2	56.3	15.3	267	37	1	28.9	5 14	5 09	11 58	18 58	19 06
24	2 29	+10.1	56.9	15.5	279	297	0	0.4	5 34	5 24	12 45	20 13	20 26
25	3 20	+14.6	57.4	15.6	292	267	2	1.4	5 57	5 43	13 36	21 30	21 48
26	4 14	+18.4	57.9	15.8	304	265	6	2.4	6 27	6 08	14 30	22 46	23 08
27	5 11	+21.3	58.3	15.9	316	267	13	3.4	7 04	6 42	15 26	23 56	—
28	6 10	+22.9	58.7	16.0	328	271	21	4.4	7 53	7 28	16 25	—	0 21
29	7 11	+23.2	58.9	16.1	340	277	31	5.4	8 55	8 30	17 24	0 57	1 22

MERCURY

Day	RA h m	Dec. °	Diam. "	Phase %	Transit h m	5° high 52° h m	5° high 56° h m
1	23 31	-5.7	6	81	10 54	5 56	6 04
3	23 43	-4.4	5	83	10 59	5 53	6 00
5	23 55	-3.0	5	85	11 03	5 50	5 56
7	0 08	-1.6	5	87	11 08	5 47	5 52
9	0 21	-0.1	5	89	11 13	5 44	5 48
11	0 34	+1.5	5	91	11 18	5 42	5 44
13	0 48	+3.1	5	93	11 24	5 39	5 40
15	1 02	+4.8	5	95	11 30	5 37	5 36
17	1 16	+6.5	5	97	11 37	5 34	5 32
19	1 31	+8.3	5	98	11 44	5 32	5 28
21	1 46	+10.1	5	99	11 51	5 30	5 25
23	2 02	+11.8	5	100	11 59	5 29	5 22
25	2 18	+13.6	5	100	12 08	18 50	18 59
27	2 34	+15.3	5	99	12 16	19 08	19 18
29	2 51	+16.9	5	96	12 25	19 26	19 37
31	3 07	+18.5	5	93	12 34	19 43	19 56

VENUS

Day	RA h m	Dec. °	Diam. "	Phase %	Transit h m	5° high 52° h m	5° high 56° h m
1	0 18	+10.5	59	1	11 38	5 18	5 13
6	0 09	+ 8.6	58	2	11 09	4 59	4 55
11	0 02	+ 6.8	55	5	10 43	4 42	4 40
16	23 59	+ 5.2	52	9	10 20	4 27	4 26
21	23 59	+ 4.0	48	14	10 01	4 14	4 14
26	0 03	+ 3.3	44	18	9 46	4 03	4 03
31	0 10	+ 3.0	41	23	9 34	3 52	3 52

MARS

Day	RA h m	Dec. °	Diam. "	Phase %	Transit h m	5° high 52° h m	5° high 56° h m
1	17 19	-22.8	10	90	4 41	1 37	2 11
6	17 27	-23.0	11	91	4 29	1 27	2 02
11	17 34	-23.3	12	91	4 16	1 16	1 52
16	17 40	-23.5	12	92	4 03	1 04	1 41
21	17 45	-23.7	13	92	3 48	0 52	1 29
26	17 50	-23.9	14	93	3 33	0 38	1 17
31	17 53	-24.1	14	94	3 16	0 24	1 03

SUNRISE AND SUNSET

	London 0°05' 51°30'		Bristol 2°35' 51°28'		Birmingham 1°55' 52°28'		Manchester 2°15' 53°28'		Newcastle 1°37' 54°59'		Glasgow 4°14' 55°52'		Belfast 5°56' 54°35'	
	h m	h m	h m	h m	h m	h m	h m	h m	h m	h m	h m	h m	h m	h m
1	5 36	18 34	5 46	18 44	5 42	18 42	5 42	18 44	5 38	18 44	5 48	18 55	5 56	19 00
2	5 34	18 35	5 44	18 45	5 40	18 44	5 40	18 46	5 36	18 45	5 45	18 57	5 53	19 02
3	5 31	18 37	5 41	18 47	5 37	18 45	5 38	18 48	5 33	18 47	5 43	18 59	5 51	19 04
4	5 29	18 39	5 39	18 49	5 35	18 47	5 35	18 50	5 31	18 49	5 40	19 01	5 48	19 06
5	5 27	18 40	5 37	18 50	5 33	18 49	5 33	18 52	5 28	18 51	5 37	19 03	5 46	19 08
6	5 25	18 42	5 35	18 52	5 31	18 51	5 30	18 53	5 26	18 53	5 35	19 05	5 44	19 10
7	5 22	18 44	5 32	18 54	5 28	18 52	5 28	18 55	5 23	18 55	5 32	19 07	5 41	19 12
8	5 20	18 45	5 30	18 55	5 26	18 54	5 26	18 57	5 21	18 57	5 30	19 09	5 39	19 14
9	5 18	18 47	5 28	18 57	5 24	18 56	5 23	18 59	5 18	18 59	5 27	19 11	5 36	19 16
10	5 16	18 49	5 26	18 59	5 21	18 58	5 21	19 01	5 16	19 01	5 24	19 13	5 34	19 18
11	5 13	18 50	5 23	19 00	5 19	18 59	5 19	19 03	5 13	19 03	5 22	19 15	5 31	19 19
12	5 11	18 52	5 21	19 02	5 17	19 01	5 16	19 04	5 11	19 05	5 19	19 17	5 29	19 21
13	5 09	18 54	5 19	19 04	5 15	19 03	5 14	19 06	5 08	19 07	5 17	19 19	5 26	19 23
14	5 07	18 55	5 17	19 05	5 12	19 05	5 12	19 08	5 06	19 09	5 14	19 21	5 24	19 25
15	5 05	18 57	5 15	19 07	5 10	19 06	5 09	19 10	5 03	19 11	5 12	19 23	5 22	19 27
16	5 03	18 59	5 13	19 09	5 08	19 08	5 07	19 12	5 01	19 13	5 09	19 25	5 19	19 29
17	5 00	19 00	5 11	19 10	5 06	19 10	5 05	19 13	4 59	19 15	5 07	19 27	5 17	19 31
18	4 58	19 02	5 08	19 12	5 03	19 12	5 02	19 15	4 56	19 17	5 04	19 29	5 14	19 33
19	4 56	19 04	5 06	19 14	5 01	19 13	5 00	19 17	4 54	19 19	5 02	19 32	5 12	19 35
20	4 54	19 05	5 04	19 15	4 59	19 15	4 58	19 19	4 51	19 21	4 59	19 34	5 10	19 37
21	4 52	19 07	5 02	19 17	4 57	19 17	4 56	19 21	4 49	19 22	4 57	19 36	5 07	19 39
22	4 50	19 09	5 00	19 19	4 55	19 19	4 54	19 23	4 47	19 24	4 55	19 38	5 05	19 41
23	4 48	19 10	4 58	19 20	4 53	19 20	4 51	19 24	4 44	19 26	4 52	19 40	5 03	19 42
24	4 46	19 12	4 56	19 22	4 51	19 22	4 49	19 26	4 42	19 28	4 50	19 42	5 01	19 44
25	4 44	19 14	4 54	19 24	4 49	19 24	4 47	19 28	4 40	19 30	4 47	19 44	4 58	19 46
26	4 42	19 15	4 52	19 25	4 47	19 25	4 45	19 30	4 38	19 32	4 45	19 46	4 56	19 48
27	4 40	19 17	4 50	19 27	4 44	19 27	4 43	19 32	4 35	19 34	4 43	19 48	4 54	19 50
28	4 38	19 19	4 48	19 29	4 42	19 29	4 41	19 33	4 33	19 36	4 40	19 50	4 52	19 52
29	4 36	19 20	4 46	19 30	4 40	19 31	4 39	19 35	4 31	19 38	4 38	19 52	4 50	19 54
30	4 34	19 22	4 44	19 32	4 38	19 32	4 37	19 37	4 29	19 40	4 36	19 54	4 47	19 56

JUPITER

Day	RA	Dec.	Transit	5° high 52°	56°
	h m	° '	h m	h m	h m
1	4 23.6	+21 07	15 44	23 03	23 19
11	4 31.4	+21 25	15 12	22 33	22 49
21	4 39.7	+21 44	14 41	22 04	22 21
31	4 48.6	+22 01	14 11	21 36	21 52

Diameters – equatorial 34" polar 32"

SATURN

Day	RA	Dec.	Transit	5° high 52°	56°
	h m	° '	h m	h m	h m
1	3 43.8	+17 54	15 04	22 04	22 16
11	3 48.2	+18 10	14 29	21 31	21 43
21	3 52.9	+18 26	13 54	20 58	21 11
31	3 57.9	+18 43	13 20	20 25	20 38

Diameters – equatorial 17" polar 15"
Rings – major axis 38" minor axis 16"

URANUS

Day	RA	Dec.	Transit	10° high 52°	56°
	h m	° '	h m	h m	h m
1	21 44.2	-14 20	9 05	5 38	6 03
11	21 45.8	-14 13	8 27	5 00	5 24
21	21 47.1	-14 06	7 49	4 21	4 45
31	21 48.2	-14 01	7 11	3 42	4 06

Diameter 4"

NEPTUNE

Day	RA	Dec.	Transit	10° high 52°	56°
	h m	° '	h m	h m	h m
1	20 42.9	-18 02	8 04	5 06	5 40
11	20 43.7	-17 59	7 25	4 27	5 01
21	20 44.2	-17 57	6 47	3 48	4 22
31	20 44.5	-17 55	6 08	3 09	3 43

Diameter 2"

May 2001

FIFTH MONTH, 31 DAYS. *Maia*, goddess of growth and increase

1	*Tuesday*	SS Philip and James. Dr David Livingstone d. 1873	121
2	*Wednesday*	Alessandro Scarlatti b. 1660. J. Edgar Hoover d. 1972	122
3	*Thursday*	Sugar Ray Robinson b. 1920.	123
4	*Friday*	Audrey Hepburn b. 1929. Diana Dors d. 1984	124
5	*Saturday*	Tammy Wynette b. 1942. Austin Reed d. 1954	125
6	*Sunday*	**4th S. of Easter**. Postage stamps first issued 1840	126
7	*Monday*	*Bank Holiday in UK*. Archibald Primrose b. 1847	*week 19 day* 127
8	*Tuesday*	Harry Selfridge d. 1947. Sir Dirk Bogarde d. 1999	128
9	*Wednesday*	George Fleming b. 1917. Aldo Moro d. 1978	129
10	*Thursday*	Fred Astaire b. 1899. Sir Henry Stanley d. 1904	130
11	*Friday*	Prime Minister Spencer Perceval assassinated 1812	131
12	*Saturday*	Sir Lennox Berkeley b. 1903. John Smith d. 1994	132
13	*Sunday*	**5th S. of Easter**. Fridtjof Nansen d. 1930	133
14	*Monday*	**St Matthias**. Eric Morecambe b. 1926	*week 20 day* 134
15	*Tuesday*	Pierre Curie b. 1859. Sir Robert Menzies d. 1978	135
16	*Wednesday*	First Academy Awards presented 1929	136
17	*Thursday*	Sandro Botticelli d. 1510. Dennis Potter b. 1935	137
18	*Friday*	Tsar Nicholas II b. 1868.	138
19	*Saturday*	Ho Chi-Minh b. 1890. Sir John Betjeman d. 1994	139
20	*Sunday*	**6th S. of Easter**. Linda McCartney d. 1998	140
21	*Monday*	King Henry VI d. 1471. Elizabeth Fry b. 1780	*week 21 day* 141
22	*Tuesday*	Blackwall Tunnel opened 1897	142
23	*Wednesday*	Carl Linnaeus b. 1707. Henrik Ibsen d. 1906	143
24	*Thursday*	**Ascension Day**. Harold Wilson d. 1995	144
25	*Friday*	Miles Davis b. 1926. Gustav Theodore Holst d. 1934	145
26	*Saturday*	American Civil War ended 1865	146
27	*Sunday*	**7th S. of Easter**. Jawaharlal Nehru d. 1964	147
28	*Monday*	*Bank Holiday in UK*. Ian Fleming b. 1908	*week 22 day* 148
29	*Tuesday*	Mount Everest conquered 1953	149
30	*Wednesday*	Alexander Pope d. 1744. Henry Addington b. 1757	150
31	*Thursday*	**Visit of Virgin Mary to Elizabeth**. Joseph Grimaldi d. 1837	151

ASTRONOMICAL PHENOMENA

d h
4 18	Venus at greatest brilliancy
7 06	Saturn in conjunction with Mercury. Saturn 4° S.
10 19	Mars in conjunction with Moon. Mars 2° S.
11 01	Neptune at stationary point
11 16	Mars at stationary point
16 11	Jupiter in conjunction with Mercury . Jupiter 3° S.
19 13	Venus in conjunction with Moon. Venus 4° N.
21 00	Sun's longitude 60° ♊
22 05	Mercury at greatest elongation E.22°
23 06	Saturn in conjunction with Moon. Saturn 1° N.
24 07	Jupiter in conjunction with Moon. Jupiter 1° N.
24 20	Mercury in conjunction with Moon. Mercury 3° N.
25 13	Saturn in conjunction
29 15	Uranus at stationary point

MINIMA OF ALGOL

Algol is inconveniently situated for observation during May

CONSTELLATIONS

The following constellations are near the meridian at

	d	h		d	h
April	1	24	May	16	21
April	15	23	June	1	20
May	1	22	June	15	19

Cepheus (below the Pole), Cassiopeia (below the Pole), Ursa Minor, Ursa Major, Canes Venatici, Coma Berenicies, Bootes, Leo, Virgo, Crater, Corvus and Hydra

THE MOON

Phases, Apsides and Node	d	h	m
○ Full Moon	7	13	53
☾ Last Quarter	15	10	11
● New Moon	23	02	46
☽ First Quarter	29	22	09
Perigee (369,419 km)	2	03	40
Apogee (404,144 km)	15	01	29
Perigee (368,033 km)	27	07	01

Mean longitude of ascending node on May 1, 99°

THE SUN   s.d. 16′.1

Day	Right Ascension	Dec. +	Equation of time	Rise 52°	Rise 56°	Transit	Set 52°	Set 56°	Sidereal time	Transit of First Point of Aries
	h m s	° ′	m s	h m	h m	h m	h m	h m	h m s	h m s
1	2 33 04	15 02	+2 53	4 30	4 16	11 57	19 25	19 39	14 35 57	9 22 31
2	2 36 53	15 20	+3 00	4 28	4 14	11 57	19 27	19 41	14 39 54	9 18 35
3	2 40 43	15 38	+3 07	4 27	4 12	11 57	19 28	19 43	14 43 50	9 14 39
4	2 44 34	15 55	+3 13	4 25	4 09	11 57	19 30	19 45	14 47 47	9 10 43
5	2 48 25	16 12	+3 18	4 23	4 07	11 57	19 32	19 47	14 51 43	9 06 47
6	2 52 16	16 29	+3 23	4 21	4 05	11 57	19 33	19 49	14 55 40	9 02 51
7	2 56 09	16 46	+3 28	4 19	4 03	11 57	19 35	19 51	14 59 36	8 58 55
8	3 00 01	17 03	+3 32	4 18	4 01	11 56	19 36	19 53	15 03 33	8 54 59
9	3 03 54	17 19	+3 35	4 16	3 59	11 56	19 38	19 55	15 07 29	8 51 03
10	3 07 48	17 35	+3 38	4 14	3 57	11 56	19 40	19 57	15 11 26	8 47 07
11	3 11 43	17 50	+3 40	4 12	3 55	11 56	19 41	19 59	15 15 23	8 43 11
12	3 15 38	18 06	+3 41	4 11	3 53	11 56	19 43	20 01	15 19 19	8 39 16
13	3 19 33	18 21	+3 42	4 09	3 51	11 56	19 44	20 03	15 23 16	8 35 20
14	3 23 30	18 35	+3 43	4 08	3 49	11 56	19 46	20 05	15 27 12	8 31 24
15	3 27 26	18 50	+3 42	4 06	3 47	11 56	19 47	20 07	15 31 09	8 27 28
16	3 31 24	19 04	+3 42	4 05	3 45	11 56	19 49	20 09	15 35 05	8 23 32
17	3 35 22	19 17	+3 40	4 03	3 44	11 56	19 50	20 10	15 39 02	8 19 36
18	3 39 20	19 31	+3 38	4 02	3 42	11 56	19 52	20 12	15 42 58	8 15 40
19	3 43 19	19 44	+3 36	4 00	3 40	11 56	19 53	20 14	15 46 55	8 11 44
20	3 47 19	19 57	+3 33	3 59	3 38	11 56	19 55	20 16	15 50 52	8 07 48
21	3 51 19	20 09	+3 29	3 58	3 37	11 57	19 56	20 17	15 54 48	8 03 52
22	3 55 20	20 21	+3 25	3 56	3 35	11 57	19 58	20 19	15 58 45	7 59 56
23	3 59 21	20 33	+3 20	3 55	3 34	11 57	19 59	20 21	16 02 41	7 56 01
24	4 03 23	20 44	+3 15	3 54	3 32	11 57	20 00	20 23	16 06 38	7 52 05
25	4 07 25	20 55	+3 09	3 53	3 31	11 57	20 02	20 24	16 10 34	7 48 09
26	4 11 28	21 06	+3 03	3 52	3 29	11 57	20 03	20 26	16 14 31	7 44 13
27	4 15 31	21 16	+2 56	3 51	3 28	11 57	20 04	20 27	16 18 27	7 40 17
28	4 19 35	21 26	+2 49	3 50	3 27	11 57	20 06	20 29	16 22 24	7 36 21
29	4 23 39	21 36	+2 42	3 49	3 25	11 57	20 07	20 30	16 26 21	7 32 25
30	4 27 44	21 45	+2 33	3 48	3 24	11 58	20 08	20 32	16 30 17	7 28 29
31	4 31 49	21 54	+2 25	3 47	3 23	11 58	20 09	20 33	16 34 14	7 24 33

DURATION OF TWILIGHT (in minutes)

Latitude	52°	56°	52°	56°	52°	56°	52°	56°
	1 May		11 May		21 May		31 May	
Civil	39	45	41	49	44	53	46	57
Nautical	90	106	97	121	106	143	116	TAN
Astronomical	154	209	179	TAN	TAN	TAN	TAN	TAN

THE NIGHT SKY

Mercury becomes visible as an evening object by about the 5th and remains so for the following three weeks, as it attains its greatest eastern elongation (22°) on the 22nd. This evening apparition of the planet is the most favourable one of the year for observers in the northern hemisphere. It may be seen low above the W.N.W. horizon at the end of civil twilight. During this period its magnitude fades from -1.1 to +1.0. A good opportunity of locating this elusive planet occurs on the evening of the 16th when it may be seen about 2.7° to the right and above Jupiter. On the evening of the 24th the thin crescent Moon, just under 2 days old, passes 3° south of Mercury.

Venus continues to be visible as a magnificent morning object, attaining its greatest brilliancy with a magnitude of −4.5, on the 4th. However, it is never visible for more than an hour before sunrise, low in the eastern sky. As seen through a telescope the apparent diameter shrinks from 41 to 26 arcseconds during May as its distance from the Earth increases. At the same time the phase increases from 23 to 45 per cent illuminated. The old crescent Moon will be seen near the planet on the mornings of the 19th and 20th.

Mars brightens considerably during the month, its magnitude changing from -1.1 to -2.0. The gibbous Moon will be seen near the planet on the 10th and 11th. Mars is in Sagittarius, reaching its first stationary point on the 11th, and then moving very slowly retrograde.

Jupiter, magnitude -1.9, is visible in the western sky in the early evening, for the first three weeks of the month. Thereafter it is lost in the lengthening twilight.

Saturn is unsuitably placed for observation throughout May, conjunction occurring on the 25th.

THE MOON

Day	RA h m	Dec. °	Hor. par. ′	Semi-diam. ′	Sun's co-long. °	PA of Bright Limb °	Phase %	Age d	Rise 52° h m	Rise 56° h m	Transit h m	Set 52° h m	Set 56° h m
1	9 11	+19.4	59.3	16.2	5	287	53	7.4	11 26	11 08	19 19	2 25	2 43
2	10 09	+15.6	59.4	16.2	17	292	65	8.4	12 47	12 35	20 12	2 55	3 09
3	11 04	+11.0	59.3	16.2	29	295	75	9.4	14 09	14 03	21 04	3 20	3 29
4	11 57	+ 5.7	59.2	16.1	41	298	84	10.4	15 31	15 29	21 54	3 41	3 45
5	12 50	+ 0.2	58.9	16.1	54	301	92	11.4	16 51	16 54	22 43	4 01	4 00
6	13 41	− 5.3	58.5	15.9	66	304	97	12.4	18 10	18 19	23 32	4 21	4 16
7	14 33	− 10.4	58.0	15.8	78	319	99	13.4	19 29	19 42	—	4 42	4 32
8	15 25	− 15.0	57.4	15.6	90	70	100	14.4	20 45	21 03	0 22	5 06	4 51
9	16 18	− 18.7	56.8	15.5	102	91	98	15.4	21 56	22 19	1 13	5 34	5 15
10	17 12	− 21.4	56.2	15.3	115	92	94	16.4	23 01	23 26	2 05	6 09	5 46
11	18 06	− 22.9	55.5	15.1	127	89	88	17.4	23 55	—	2 57	6 52	6 26
12	19 00	− 23.3	55.0	15.0	139	85	81	18.4	—	0 21	3 49	7 43	7 17
13	19 53	− 22.6	54.6	14.9	151	80	72	19.4	0 40	1 04	4 39	8 41	8 17
14	20 44	− 20.9	54.4	14.8	163	76	63	20.4	1 16	1 37	5 27	9 44	9 23
15	21 33	− 18.3	54.3	14.8	176	72	54	21.4	1 44	2 01	6 13	10 50	10 33
16	22 20	− 14.9	54.3	14.8	188	68	45	22.4	2 07	2 20	6 57	11 57	11 45
17	23 06	− 10.9	54.6	14.9	200	66	35	23.4	2 27	2 36	7 41	13 05	12 58
18	23 52	− 6.4	55.0	15.0	212	64	26	24.4	2 44	2 49	8 23	14 14	14 11
19	0 37	− 1.6	55.5	15.1	224	62	18	25.4	3 01	3 02	9 06	15 25	15 26
20	1 24	+ 3.4	56.2	15.3	237	62	11	26.4	3 18	3 15	9 51	16 37	16 43
21	2 12	+ 8.3	56.9	15.5	249	61	5	27.4	3 37	3 30	10 37	17 53	18 04
22	3 02	+ 13.1	57.6	15.7	261	58	2	28.4	3 59	3 47	11 27	19 11	19 27
23	3 56	+ 17.2	58.2	15.9	273	14	0	29.4	4 26	4 09	12 20	20 29	20 50
24	4 53	+ 20.6	58.8	16.0	286	273	1	0.9	5 01	4 39	13 17	21 44	22 09
25	5 53	+ 22.7	59.2	16.1	298	271	5	1.9	5 46	5 21	14 17	22 51	23 17
26	6 55	+ 23.4	59.5	16.2	310	275	11	2.9	6 44	6 19	15 18	23 46	—
27	7 57	+ 22.6	59.6	16.2	322	280	19	3.9	7 55	7 31	16 18	—	0 10
28	8 58	+ 20.3	59.5	16.2	335	285	29	4.9	9 13	8 54	17 15	0 28	0 48
29	9 56	+ 16.7	59.4	16.2	347	289	40	5.9	10 35	10 21	18 09	1 01	1 16
30	10 52	+ 12.3	59.2	16.1	359	293	51	6.9	11 57	11 48	19 01	1 27	1 37
31	11 45	+ 7.2	58.9	16.0	11	295	62	7.9	13 17	13 13	19 50	1 48	1 54

MERCURY

Day	RA h m	Dec. °	Diam. ″	Phase %	Transit h m	5° high 52° h m	5° high 56° h m
1	3 07	+18.5	5	93	12 34	19 43	19 56
3	3 24	+19.9	5	89	12 42	19 59	20 14
5	3 40	+21.1	6	84	12 51	20 15	20 31
7	3 56	+22.2	6	79	12 58	20 29	20 47
9	4 11	+23.2	6	73	13 06	20 42	21 00
11	4 26	+23.9	6	67	13 12	20 53	21 12
13	4 40	+24.5	7	61	13 18	21 02	21 22
15	4 53	+25.0	7	55	13 23	21 09	21 30
17	5 05	+25.3	7	50	13 27	21 14	21 35
19	5 16	+25.4	8	45	13 30	21 18	21 39
21	5 26	+25.5	8	40	13 31	21 19	21 40
23	5 35	+25.4	8	35	13 32	21 19	21 40
25	5 42	+25.2	9	30	13 31	21 16	21 37
27	5 48	+25.0	9	26	13 29	21 12	21 32
29	5 53	+24.6	10	22	13 26	21 06	21 26
31	5 57	+24.2	10	18	13 21	20 58	21 18

VENUS

Day	RA h m	Dec. °	Diam. ″	Phase %	Transit h m	5° high 52° h m	5° high 56° h m
1	0 10	+3.0	41	23	9 34	3 52	3 52
6	0 20	+3.0	38	27	9 24	3 41	3 42
11	0 32	+3.4	35	31	9 16	3 31	3 31
16	0 45	+4.1	32	35	9 09	3 21	3 21
21	1 00	+5.1	30	39	9 04	3 11	3 10
26	1 15	+6.2	28	42	9 01	3 02	3 00
31	1 32	+7.5	26	45	8 58	2 52	2 49

MARS

Day	RA h m	Dec. °	Diam. ″	Phase %	Transit h m	5° high 52° h m	5° high 56° h m
1	17 53	-24.1	14	94	3 16	0 24	1 03
6	17 55	-24.4	15	95	2 59	0 09	0 49
11	17 56	-24.7	16	95	2 40	23 49	0 34
16	17 55	-24.9	17	96	2 20	23 31	0 18
21	17 53	-25.2	18	97	1 58	23 13	0 01
26	17 50	-25.5	18	98	1 35	22 52	23 39
31	17 45	-25.8	19	99	1 11	22 31	23 19

SUNRISE AND SUNSET

	London		Bristol		Birmingham		Manchester		Newcastle		Glasgow		Belfast	
	0°05' 51°30'		2°35' 51°28'		1°55' 52°28'		2°15' 53°28'		1°37' 54°59'		4°14' 55°52'		5°56' 54°35'	
	h m	h m	h m	h m	h m	h m	h m	h m	h m	h m	h m	h m	h m	h m
1	4 32	19 24	4 42	19 34	4 37	19 34	4 34	19 39	4 26	19 42	4 34	19 56	4 45	19 58
2	4 30	19 25	4 40	19 35	4 35	19 36	4 32	19 41	4 24	19 44	4 31	19 58	4 43	20 00
3	4 29	19 27	4 39	19 37	4 33	19 37	4 30	19 42	4 22	19 46	4 29	20 00	4 41	20 01
4	4 27	19 28	4 37	19 38	4 31	19 39	4 28	19 44	4 20	19 48	4 27	20 02	4 39	20 03
5	4 25	19 30	4 35	19 40	4 29	19 41	4 27	19 46	4 18	19 49	4 25	20 04	4 37	20 05
6	4 23	19 32	4 33	19 42	4 27	19 43	4 25	19 48	4 16	19 51	4 23	20 06	4 35	20 07
7	4 21	19 33	4 32	19 43	4 25	19 44	4 23	19 49	4 14	19 53	4 21	20 08	4 33	20 09
8	4 20	19 35	4 30	19 45	4 23	19 46	4 21	19 51	4 12	19 55	4 18	20 10	4 31	20 11
9	4 18	19 36	4 28	19 46	4 22	19 48	4 19	19 53	4 10	19 57	4 16	20 12	4 29	20 12
10	4 16	19 38	4 26	19 48	4 20	19 49	4 17	19 55	4 08	19 59	4 14	20 13	4 27	20 14
11	4 15	19 40	4 25	19 49	4 18	19 51	4 15	19 56	4 06	20 01	4 12	20 15	4 25	20 16
12	4 13	19 41	4 23	19 51	4 17	19 52	4 14	19 58	4 04	20 02	4 10	20 17	4 23	20 18
13	4 12	19 43	4 22	19 53	4 15	19 54	4 12	20 00	4 02	20 04	4 09	20 19	4 22	20 20
14	4 10	19 44	4 20	19 54	4 13	19 56	4 10	20 01	4 01	20 06	4 07	20 21	4 20	20 21
15	4 09	19 46	4 19	19 56	4 12	19 57	4 09	20 03	3 59	20 08	4 05	20 23	4 18	20 23
16	4 07	19 47	4 17	19 57	4 10	19 59	4 07	20 05	3 57	20 10	4 03	20 25	4 16	20 25
17	4 06	19 49	4 16	19 59	4 09	20 00	4 06	20 06	3 55	20 11	4 01	20 27	4 15	20 27
18	4 04	19 50	4 14	20 00	4 07	20 02	4 04	20 08	3 54	20 13	3 59	20 28	4 13	20 28
19	4 03	19 52	4 13	20 01	4 06	20 03	4 02	20 09	3 52	20 15	3 58	20 30	4 12	20 30
20	4 02	19 53	4 12	20 03	4 04	20 05	4 01	20 11	3 51	20 16	3 56	20 32	4 10	20 32
21	4 00	19 54	4 10	20 04	4 03	20 06	4 00	20 12	3 49	20 18	3 54	20 34	4 08	20 33
22	3 59	19 56	4 09	20 06	4 02	20 08	3 58	20 14	3 48	20 20	3 53	20 35	4 07	20 35
23	3 58	19 57	4 08	20 07	4 01	20 09	3 57	20 15	3 46	20 21	3 51	20 37	4 06	20 36
24	3 57	19 58	4 07	20 08	3 59	20 10	3 56	20 17	3 45	20 23	3 50	20 39	4 04	20 38
25	3 56	20 00	4 06	20 10	3 58	20 12	3 54	20 18	3 43	20 24	3 48	20 40	4 03	20 39
26	3 54	20 01	4 05	20 11	3 57	20 13	3 53	20 20	3 42	20 26	3 47	20 42	4 02	20 41
27	3 53	20 02	4 04	20 12	3 56	20 14	3 52	20 21	3 41	20 27	3 46	20 43	4 00	20 42
28	3 52	20 03	4 03	20 13	3 55	20 16	3 51	20 22	3 40	20 29	3 44	20 45	3 59	20 44
29	3 51	20 05	4 02	20 15	3 54	20 17	3 50	20 24	3 38	20 30	3 43	20 46	3 58	20 45
30	3 51	20 06	4 01	20 16	3 53	20 18	3 49	20 25	3 37	20 32	3 42	20 48	3 57	20 46
31	3 50	20 07	4 00	20 17	3 52	20 19	3 48	20 26	3 36	20 33	3 41	20 49	3 56	20 48

JUPITER

Day	RA	Dec.	Transit	5° high	
				52°	56°
	h m	° '	h m	h m	h m
1	4 48.6	+22 01	14 11	21 36	21 52
11	4 57.9	+22 17	13 41	21 07	21 24
21	5 07.5	+22 32	13 11	20 39	20 56
31	5 17.3	+22 44	12 42	20 11	20 28

Diameters – equatorial 33″ polar 31″

SATURN

Day	RA	Dec.	Transit	5° high	
				52°	56°
	h m	° '	h m	h m	h m
1	3 57.9	+18 43	13 20	20 25	20 38
11	4 03.1	+18 59	12 46	19 53	20 06
21	4 08.4	+19 14	12 12	19 20	19 33
31	4 13.8	+19 29	11 38	18 47	19 01

Diameters – equatorial 16″ polar 15″
Rings – major axis 37″ minor axis 16″

URANUS

Day	RA	Dec.	Transit	10° high	
				52°	56°
	h m	° '	h m	h m	h m
1	21 48.2	-14 01	7 11	3 42	4 06
11	21 48.9	-13 58	6 32	3 03	3 27
21	21 49.4	-13 56	5 54	2 24	2 48
31	21 49.5	-13 56	5 14	1 45	2 09

Diameter 4″

NEPTUNE

Day	RA	Dec.	Transit	10° high	
				52°	56°
	h m	° '	h m	h m	h m
1	20 44.5	-17 55	6 08	3 09	3 43
11	20 44.7	-17 55	5 28	2 30	3 03
21	20 44.5	-17 56	4 49	1 51	2 24
31	20 44.2	-17 57	4 09	1 11	1 45

Diameter 2″

 **June 2001**

SIXTH MONTH, 30 DAYS. *Junius*, Roman *gens* (family)

1	*Friday*	Sir David Wilkie d. 1841. Marilyn Monroe b. 1926	152
2	*Saturday*	Thomas Hardy b. 1840. Sir Rex Harrison d. 1990	153
3	*Sunday*	**Pentecost (Whit Sunday).** Battle of Midway started 1942	154
4	*Monday*	Evacuation from Dunkirk completed 1942	*week 23 day* 155
5	*Tuesday*	Federico García Lorca b. 1898. Earl Kitchener d. 1916	156
6	*Wednesday*	Bjørn Borg b. 1956. John Paul Getty d. 1976	157
7	*Thursday*	Pietro Annigoni b. 1910. E. M. Forster d. 1970	158
8	*Friday*	Sir John Millais b. 1829. Sir Joseph Paxton d. 1865	159
9	*Saturday*	Ossie Clark b. 1942	160
10	*Sunday*	**Trinity Sunday.** *Duke of Edinburgh's Birthday b. 1921*	161
11	*Monday*	Jacques Cousteau b. 1910. John Wayne d. 1979	*week 24 day* 162
12	*Tuesday*	George Bush b. 1924. Sir Billy Butlin d. 1980	163
13	*Wednesday*	Dr Thomas Arnold b. 1795. Jesse Boot d. 1931	164
14	*Thursday*	**Corpus Christi.** Battle of Marengo 1800	165
15	*Friday*	Rt Revd Trevor Huddleston b. 1913. James Hunt d. 1993	166
16	*Saturday*	*Queen's Official Birthday.* John Churchill d. 1722. Tom Graveney b. 1927	167
17	*Sunday*	**1st S. after Trinity.** Father's Day. Cardinal Basil Hume d. 1999	168
18	*Monday*	Maxim Gorky d. 1936. Sir Paul McCartney b. 1942	*week 25 day* 169
19	*Tuesday*	Metropolitan Police founded 1829	170
20	*Wednesday*	Errol Flynn b. 1909. Sir William Golding d. 1993	171
21	*Thursday*	*Prince William of Wales b. 1982.* Summer begins	172
22	*Friday*	St John Fisher d. 1535. Sir Henry Rider Haggard b. 1856	173
23	*Saturday*	Lucrezia Borgia d. 1519. Anna Akhmatova b. 1889	174
24	*Sunday*	**2nd S. after Trinity. John the Baptist.** Midsummer's Day	175
25	*Monday*	Battle of Little Big Horn 1876	*week 26 day* 176
26	*Tuesday*	Samuel Crompton d. 1827. Laurie Lee b. 1914	177
27	*Wednesday*	Giorgio Vasari d. 1574. Charles Parnell b. 1846	178
28	*Thursday*	Henry VIII b. 1491. Archduke Ferdinand d. 1914	179
29	*Friday*	**SS Peter and Paul.** Trade Unions legalised 1871	180
30	*Saturday*	Tower Bridge opened 1894. Ruskin Spear b. 1911	181

ASTRONOMICAL PHENOMENA

d	h	
4	05	Mercury at stationary point
4	12	Pluto at opposition
6	20	Mars in conjunction with Moon. Mars 4° S.
8	06	Venus at greatest elongation W.46°
13	18	Mars at opposition
14	13	Jupiter in conjunction
16	13	Mercury in inferior conjunction
18	00	Venus in conjunction with Moon. Venus 2° N.
18	10	Jupiter in conjunction with Mercury. Jupiter 4° N.
19	22	Saturn in conjunction with Moon. Saturn 0.9° N.
21	00	Mercury in conjunction with Moon. Mercury 3° S.
21	03	Jupiter in conjunction with Moon. Jupiter 0.7° N.
21	08	Sun's longitude 90° ♋
21	12	Total eclipse of Sun (see page 66)
28	06	Mercury at stationary point

MINIMA OF ALGOL

Algol is inconveniently situated for observation during June

CONSTELLATIONS

The following constellations are near the meridian at

	d	h		d	h
May	1	24	June	15	21
May	16	23	July	1	20
June	1	22	July	16	19

Cassiopeia (below the Pole), Ursa Minor, Draco, Ursa Major, Canes Venatici, Bootes, Corona, Serpens, Virgo and Libra

THE MOON

Phases, Apsides and Node	d	h	m
○ Full Moon	6	01	39
☾ Last Quarter	14	03	28
● New Moon	21	11	58
☽ First Quarter	28	03	19
Apogee (404,629 km)	11	19	47
Perigee (363,132 km)	23	17	18

Mean longitude of ascending node on June 1, 98°

THE SUN   s.d. 16′.1

Day	Right Ascension h m s	Dec. + ° ′	Equation of time m s	Rise 52° h m	Rise 56° h m	Transit h m	Set 52° h m	Set 56° h m	Sidereal time h m s	Transit of First Point of Aries h m s
1	4 35 54	22 02	+2 16	3 46	3 22	11 58	20 10	20 34	16 38 10	7 20 37
2	4 40 00	22 10	+2 07	3 45	3 21	11 58	20 11	20 36	16 42 07	7 16 41
3	4 44 06	22 18	+1 57	3 44	3 20	11 58	20 12	20 37	16 46 03	7 12 46
4	4 48 12	22 25	+1 48	3 44	3 19	11 58	20 13	20 38	16 50 00	7 08 50
5	4 52 19	22 32	+1 37	3 43	3 18	11 58	20 14	20 39	16 53 56	7 04 54
6	4 56 26	22 38	+1 27	3 42	3 17	11 59	20 15	20 41	16 57 53	7 00 58
7	5 00 34	22 44	+1 16	3 42	3 17	11 59	20 16	20 42	17 01 50	6 57 02
8	5 04 42	22 50	+1 05	3 41	3 16	11 59	20 17	20 43	17 05 46	6 53 06
9	5 08 50	22 55	+0 53	3 41	3 15	11 59	20 18	20 44	17 09 43	6 49 10
10	5 12 58	23 00	+0 41	3 41	3 15	11 59	20 19	20 45	17 13 39	6 45 14
11	5 17 06	23 04	+0 29	3 40	3 14	12 00	20 19	20 45	17 17 36	6 41 18
12	5 21 15	23 08	+0 17	3 40	3 14	12 00	20 20	20 46	17 21 32	6 37 22
13	5 25 24	23 12	+0 05	3 40	3 14	12 00	20 21	20 47	17 25 29	6 33 26
14	5 29 33	23 15	−0 08	3 40	3 13	12 00	20 21	20 48	17 29 25	6 29 31
15	5 33 43	23 18	−0 21	3 39	3 13	12 00	20 22	20 48	17 33 22	6 25 35
16	5 37 52	23 20	−0 33	3 39	3 13	12 01	20 22	20 49	17 37 19	6 21 39
17	5 42 02	23 22	−0 46	3 39	3 13	12 01	20 23	20 49	17 41 15	6 17 43
18	5 46 11	23 24	−1 00	3 39	3 13	12 01	20 23	20 50	17 45 12	6 13 47
19	5 50 21	23 25	−1 13	3 39	3 13	12 01	20 23	20 50	17 49 08	6 09 51
20	5 54 31	23 26	−1 26	3 40	3 13	12 02	20 24	20 50	17 53 05	6 05 55
21	5 58 40	23 26	−1 39	3 40	3 13	12 02	20 24	20 50	17 57 01	6 01 59
22	6 02 50	23 26	−1 52	3 40	3 13	12 02	20 24	20 51	18 00 58	5 58 03
23	6 07 00	23 26	−2 05	3 40	3 14	12 02	20 24	20 51	18 04 55	5 54 07
24	6 11 09	23 25	−2 18	3 41	3 14	12 02	20 24	20 51	18 08 51	5 50 11
25	6 15 19	23 24	−2 31	3 41	3 14	12 03	20 24	20 51	18 12 48	5 46 15
26	6 19 28	23 22	−2 44	3 41	3 15	12 03	20 24	20 51	18 16 44	5 42 20
27	6 23 37	23 20	−2 57	3 42	3 15	12 03	20 24	20 50	18 20 41	5 38 24
28	6 27 46	23 17	−3 09	3 42	3 16	12 03	20 24	20 50	18 24 37	5 34 28
29	6 31 55	23 14	−3 21	3 43	3 17	12 03	20 24	20 50	18 28 34	5 30 32
30	6 36 04	23 11	−3 33	3 44	3 18	12 04	20 23	20 49	18 32 30	5 26 36

DURATION OF TWILIGHT (in minutes)

Latitude	52°	56°	52°	56°	52°	56°	52°	56°
	1 June		11 June		21 June		30 June	
Civil	47	58	48	61	49	63	49	62
Nautical	117	TAN	125	TAN	128	TAN	125	TAN
Astronomical	TAN	TAN	TAN	TAN	TAN	TAN	TAN	TAN

THE NIGHT SKY

Mercury passes through inferior conjunction on the 16th and is therefore too close to the Sun for observation throughout June.

Venus is a brilliant morning object in the eastern sky, magnitude −4.2. It reaches greatest western elongation (46°) on the 8th and by the end of June is visible for nearly two hours before sunrise. The old crescent Moon is in the vicinity of the planet on the mornings of the 17th to the 19th.

Mars, magnitude −2.4, reaches opposition on the 13th and therefore is available for observation throughout the hours of darkness. Because of the eccentricity of its orbit closest approach to the Earth occurs 8 days later than opposition. The Full Moon passes 3° north of Mars on the evening of the 6th. Mars is moving slowly retrograde, returning from Sagittarius into Ophiuchus at the very beginning of the month. Unfortunately this is a very disappointing opposition for observers in the British Isles. The declination of Mars is around −27° so that even from southern England its maximum altitude above the southern horizon (at transit) is only 12°, while from southern Scotland it is only 7°.

Jupiter, remains too close to the Sun for observation throughout the month, conjunction occurring on the 13th.

Saturn remains unsuitably placed for observation throughout the month.

Twilight. Reference to the section above shows that astronomical twilight last all night for a period around the summer solstice (i.e. in June and July), even in southern England. Under these conditions the sky never gets completely dark as the Sun is always less than 18° below the horizon.

THE MOON

Day	RA h m	Dec. °	Hor. par. ′	Semi-diam. ′	Sun's co-long. °	PA of Bright Limb °	Phase %	Age d	Rise 52° h m	Rise 56° h m	Transit h m	Set 52° h m	Set 56° h m
1	12 37	+ 1.7	58.5	15.9	23	296	73	8.9	14 36	14 37	20 38	2 08	2 09
2	13 27	− 3.7	58.1	15.8	36	296	82	9.9	15 54	16 00	21 26	2 27	2 23
3	14 17	− 8.9	57.7	15.7	48	295	90	10.9	17 11	17 22	22 15	2 47	2 39
4	15 09	−13.6	57.2	15.6	60	294	95	11.9	18 27	18 43	23 05	3 09	2 56
5	16 01	−17.6	56.7	15.4	72	294	99	12.9	19 40	20 01	23 56	3 34	3 17
6	16 54	−20.6	56.1	15.3	84	344	100	13.9	20 47	21 12	—	4 06	3 44
7	17 48	−22.6	55.6	15.2	97	87	99	14.9	21 47	22 13	0 48	4 45	4 20
8	18 42	−23.4	55.2	15.0	109	87	96	15.9	22 36	23 01	1 40	5 32	5 06
9	19 35	−23.1	54.7	14.9	121	83	92	16.9	23 15	23 38	2 31	6 28	6 02
10	20 27	−21.7	54.4	14.8	133	79	86	17.9	23 46	—	3 20	7 29	7 07
11	21 17	−19.3	54.2	14.8	145	75	78	18.9	—	0 05	4 07	8 35	8 16
12	22 05	−16.2	54.2	14.8	158	71	70	19.9	0 11	0 26	4 52	9 42	9 28
13	22 51	−12.4	54.3	14.8	170	69	61	20.9	0 32	0 43	5 36	10 49	10 40
14	23 36	− 8.1	54.6	14.9	182	67	52	21.9	0 50	0 57	6 18	11 57	11 52
15	0 21	− 3.4	55.0	15.0	194	66	42	22.9	1 07	1 10	7 00	13 06	13 05
16	1 07	+ 1.4	55.6	15.2	207	66	32	23.9	1 23	1 22	7 43	14 16	14 20
17	1 53	+ 6.4	56.4	15.4	219	66	23	24.9	1 41	1 35	8 27	15 29	15 38
18	2 42	+11.2	57.2	15.6	231	68	15	25.9	2 01	1 51	9 15	16 46	16 59
19	3 34	+15.6	58.0	15.8	243	71	8	26.9	2 25	2 10	10 06	18 04	18 23
20	4 30	+19.4	58.8	16.0	256	75	3	27.9	2 55	2 36	11 02	19 23	19 46
21	5 30	+22.0	59.5	16.2	268	77	0	28.9	3 36	3 12	12 02	20 35	21 01
22	6 32	+23.3	60.0	16.4	280	272	0	0.5	4 30	4 04	13 04	21 37	22 02
23	7 36	+23.0	60.3	16.4	292	276	3	1.5	5 37	5 12	14 07	22 26	22 48
24	8 40	+21.2	60.4	16.4	305	281	9	2.5	6 55	6 34	15 07	23 03	23 20
25	9 41	+17.9	60.2	16.4	317	286	17	3.5	8 19	8 03	16 04	23 32	23 44
26	10 38	+13.5	59.8	16.3	329	289	26	4.5	9 43	9 33	16 58	23 55	—
27	11 33	+ 8.5	59.4	16.2	341	292	37	5.5	11 05	11 00	17 48	—	0 02
28	12 25	+ 3.0	58.8	16.0	353	293	49	6.5	12 25	12 25	18 37	0 15	0 18
29	13 16	− 2.4	58.2	15.9	6	293	60	7.5	13 43	13 47	19 24	0 34	0 32
30	14 06	− 7.7	57.6	15.7	18	292	70	8.5	14 59	15 09	20 12	0 53	0 47

MERCURY

Day	RA h m	Dec. °	Diam. ″	Phase %	Transit h m	5° high 52° h m	5° high 56° h m
1	5 58	+24.0	10	17	13 18	20 54	21 13
3	6 00	+23.5	11	13	13 12	20 44	21 02
5	6 00	+23.0	11	10	13 03	20 32	20 50
7	5 59	+22.4	11	7	12 54	20 19	20 36
9	5 56	+21.8	12	5	12 44	20 05	20 21
11	5 53	+21.3	12	3	12 32	19 50	20 06
13	5 49	+20.7	12	1	12 20	19 35	19 50
15	5 44	+20.2	12	1	12 08	19 19	19 33
17	5 40	+19.7	12	1	11 55	4 46	4 32
19	5 35	+19.3	12	1	11 43	4 36	4 22
21	5 31	+19.0	12	2	11 31	4 26	4 12
23	5 27	+18.7	12	4	11 20	4 16	4 03
25	5 25	+18.6	11	7	11 10	4 06	3 53
27	5 23	+18.6	11	10	11 01	3 57	3 44
29	5 23	+18.7	10	13	10 53	3 48	3 35
31	5 24	+18.9	10	17	10 47	3 40	3 27

VENUS

Day	RA h m	Dec. °	Diam. ″	Phase %	Transit h m	5° high 52° h m	5° high 56° h m
1	1 36	+ 7.7	26	46	8 57	2 50	2 47
6	1 53	+ 9.1	24	48	8 55	2 41	2 37
11	2 12	+10.6	23	51	8 54	2 33	2 27
16	2 31	+12.0	22	54	8 54	2 24	2 18
21	2 51	+13.5	21	56	8 54	2 17	2 09
26	3 12	+15.0	20	58	8 55	2 10	2 01
31	3 33	+16.3	19	61	8 57	2 04	1 54

MARS

Day	RA h m	Dec. °	Diam. ″	Phase %	Transit h m	5° high 52° h m	5° high 56° h m
1	17 44	-25.9	19	99	1 06	3 41	2 53
6	17 38	-26.2	20	100	0 40	3 12	2 22
11	17 32	-26.4	20	100	0 14	2 43	1 52
16	17 24	-26.6	21	100	23 42	2 14	1 21
21	17 17	-26.7	21	100	23 15	1 46	0 52
26	17 10	-26.8	21	99	22 49	1 19	0 23
31	17 04	-26.8	21	98	22 23	0 52	23 52

SUNRISE AND SUNSET

	London		Bristol		Birmingham		Manchester		Newcastle		Glasgow		Belfast	
	0°05' 51°30'		2°35' 51°28'		1°55' 52°28'		2°15' 53°28'		1°37' 54°59'		4°14' 55°52'		5°56' 54°35'	
	h m	h m	h m	h m	h m	h m	h m	h m	h m	h m	h m	h m	h m	h m
1	3 49	20 08	3 59	20 18	3 51	20 21	3 47	20 27	3 35	20 34	3 40	20 51	3 55	20 49
2	3 48	20 09	3 58	20 19	3 50	20 22	3 46	20 29	3 34	20 35	3 39	20 52	3 54	20 50
3	3 47	20 10	3 58	20 20	3 50	20 23	3 45	20 30	3 33	20 37	3 38	20 53	3 53	20 51
4	3 47	20 11	3 57	20 21	3 49	20 24	3 44	20 31	3 32	20 38	3 37	20 54	3 52	20 52
5	3 46	20 12	3 56	20 22	3 48	20 25	3 44	20 32	3 32	20 39	3 36	20 55	3 51	20 54
6	3 45	20 13	3 56	20 23	3 47	20 26	3 43	20 33	3 31	20 40	3 35	20 57	3 51	20 55
7	3 45	20 14	3 55	20 24	3 47	20 27	3 42	20 34	3 30	20 41	3 35	20 58	3 50	20 56
8	3 44	20 15	3 55	20 24	3 46	20 27	3 42	20 35	3 30	20 42	3 34	20 59	3 50	20 57
9	3 44	20 15	3 54	20 25	3 46	20 28	3 41	20 36	3 29	20 43	3 33	21 00	3 49	20 57
10	3 44	20 16	3 54	20 26	3 46	20 29	3 41	20 36	3 29	20 44	3 33	21 00	3 48	20 58
11	3 43	20 17	3 53	20 27	3 45	20 30	3 41	20 37	3 28	20 44	3 32	21 01	3 48	20 59
12	3 43	20 18	3 53	20 27	3 45	20 30	3 40	20 38	3 28	20 45	3 32	21 02	3 48	21 00
13	3 43	20 18	3 53	20 28	3 45	20 31	3 40	20 38	3 27	20 46	3 31	21 03	3 47	21 00
14	3 43	20 19	3 53	20 29	3 44	20 32	3 40	20 39	3 27	20 47	3 31	21 03	3 47	21 01
15	3 43	20 19	3 53	20 29	3 44	20 32	3 40	20 40	3 27	20 47	3 31	21 04	3 47	21 02
16	3 42	20 20	3 53	20 30	3 44	20 33	3 39	20 40	3 27	20 48	3 31	21 05	3 47	21 02
17	3 42	20 20	3 53	20 30	3 44	20 33	3 39	20 40	3 27	20 48	3 31	21 05	3 47	21 03
18	3 42	20 20	3 53	20 30	3 44	20 33	3 39	20 41	3 27	20 49	3 31	21 05	3 47	21 03
19	3 43	20 21	3 53	20 31	3 44	20 34	3 39	20 41	3 27	20 49	3 31	21 06	3 47	21 03
20	3 43	20 21	3 53	20 31	3 44	20 34	3 40	20 41	3 27	20 49	3 31	21 06	3 47	21 04
21	3 43	20 21	3 53	20 31	3 45	20 34	3 40	20 42	3 27	20 49	3 31	21 06	3 47	21 04
22	3 43	20 21	3 53	20 31	3 45	20 34	3 40	20 42	3 27	20 50	3 31	21 06	3 47	21 04
23	3 43	20 22	3 54	20 31	3 45	20 34	3 40	20 42	3 28	20 50	3 32	21 07	3 48	21 04
24	3 44	20 22	3 54	20 31	3 45	20 35	3 41	20 42	3 28	20 50	3 32	21 07	3 48	21 04
25	3 44	20 22	3 54	20 31	3 46	20 35	3 41	20 42	3 28	20 50	3 32	21 07	3 48	21 04
26	3 45	20 22	3 55	20 31	3 46	20 34	3 42	20 42	3 29	20 50	3 33	21 06	3 49	21 04
27	3 45	20 22	3 55	20 31	3 47	20 34	3 42	20 42	3 29	20 49	3 33	21 06	3 49	21 04
28	3 46	20 21	3 56	20 31	3 47	20 34	3 43	20 42	3 30	20 49	3 34	21 06	3 50	21 04
29	3 46	20 21	3 56	20 31	3 48	20 34	3 43	20 41	3 31	20 49	3 35	21 06	3 51	21 03
30	3 47	20 21	3 57	20 31	3 49	20 34	3 44	20 41	3 31	20 48	3 35	21 05	3 51	21 03

JUPITER

Day	RA	Dec.		Transit	5° high	
					52°	56°
	h m	°	'	h m	h m	h m
1	5 18.3	+22	45	12 39	5 09	4 52
11	5 28.3	+22	55	12 09	4 39	4 21
21	5 38.3	+23	02	11 40	4 09	3 51
31	5 48.2	+23	07	11 10	3 39	3 21

Diameters – equatorial 32" polar 30"

SATURN

Day	RA	Dec.		Transit	5° high	
					52°	56°
	h m	°	'	h m	h m	h m
1	4 14.4	+19	30	11 35	4 25	4 11
11	4 19.7	+19	44	11 01	3 50	3 36
21	4 25.0	+19	56	10 26	3 14	3 00
31	4 30.1	+20	08	9 52	2 39	2 25

Diameters – equatorial 16" polar 15"
Rings – major axis 37" minor axis 16"

URANUS

Day	RA	Dec.		Transit	10° high	
					52°	56°
	h m	°	'	h m	h m	h m
1	21 49.5	-13	56	5 10	1 41	2 05
11	21 49.3	-13	57	4 31	1 01	1 25
21	21 48.8	-14	00	3 51	0 22	0 46
31	21 47.9	-14	05	3 11	23 38	0 07

Diameter 4"

NEPTUNE

Day	RA	Dec.		Transit	10° high	
					52°	56°
	h m	°	'	h m	h m	h m
1	20 44.2	-17	57	4 05	1 07	1 41
11	20 43.6	-17	59	3 25	0 28	1 01
21	20 42.9	-18	02	2 45	23 44	0 22
31	20 42.1	-18	05	2 05	23 04	23 38

Diameter 2"

July 2001

SEVENTH MONTH, 31 DAYS. *Julius* Caesar, formerly *Quintilis*, fifth month of Roman pre-Julian calendar

1	Sunday	**3rd S. after Trinity**. Harriet Beecher Stowe d. 1896		182
2	Monday	Sir Tyrone Guthrie b. 1900. Ernest Hemingway d. 1961	*week 27 day*	183
3	Tuesday	**St Thomas**. Theodor Herzl d. 1904		184
4	Wednesday	William Byrd d. 1623. Alec Bedser b. 1918		185
5	Thursday	Georges Pompidou b. 1911. Johnny Speight d. 1998		186
6	Friday	Sir Thomas More d. 1535. Tsar Nicholas I b. 1796		187
7	Saturday	Giancarlo Menotti b. 1911. Sir Allen Lane d. 1970		188
8	Sunday	**4th S. after Trinity**. Joseph Chamberlain b. 1836		189
9	Monday	Jan Van Eyck d. 1441. Ottorino Respighi b. 1879	*week 28 day*	190
10	Tuesday	Carl Orff b. 1895. Joe Davis d. 1978		191
11	Wednesday	Battle of Oudenarde 1708. George Gershwin d. 1937		192
12	Thursday	Pablo Neruda b. 1904. Charles Rolls d. 1910		193
13	Friday	Treaty of Berlin signed 1878. Baron Kenneth Clark b. 1903		194
14	Saturday	Alfred Krupp d. 1887. Woodrow Guthrie b. 1912		195
15	Sunday	**5th S. after Trinity**. Hammond Innes b. 1913		196
16	Monday	Anne of Cleves d. 1557. Ginger Rogers b. 1911	*week 29 day*	197
17	Tuesday	'Punch' first published 1841. Charles Grey d. 1845		198
18	Wednesday	W. G. Grace b. 1848. Sir Stanley Rous d. 1986		199
19	Thursday	Francesco Petrarch d. 1374. Vladimir Mayakovsky b. 1893		200
20	Friday	Sir Edmund Hillary b. 1919. Mark Boxer d. 1988		201
21	Saturday	Independence of Belgium 1831. Ernest Hemingway b. 1898		202
22	Sunday	**6th S. after Trinity. Mary Magdalene.**		203
23	Monday	Michael Foot b. 1913. Rosemary Sutcliff d. 1992	*week 30 day*	204
24	Tuesday	Simón Bolívar b. 1783. Peter Sellers d. 1980		205
25	Wednesday	**St James**. Elias Canetti b. 1905		206
26	Thursday	Carl Jung b. 1875. Terry Scott d. 1994		207
27	Friday	Alexandre Dumas b. 1824. Ferruccio Busoni d. 1924		208
28	Saturday	Antonio Vivaldi d. 1741.		209
29	Sunday	**7th S. after Trinity**. David Niven d. 1983		210
30	Monday	Henry Ford b. 1863. Prince Otto von Bismarck d. 1898	*week 31 day*	211
31	Tuesday	St Ignatius Loyola d. 1556. Franz Liszt d. 1886		212

ASTRONOMICAL PHENOMENA

d	h	
3	11	Mars in conjunction with Moon. Mars 6° S.
4	14	Earth at aphelion (152 million km.)
5	15	Partial eclipse of Moon (see page 66)
9	18	Mercury at greatest elongation W.21
12	22	Jupiter in conjunction with Mercury. Jupiter 2° N.
15	08	Saturn in conjunction with Venus. Saturn 0.7° N.
17	13	Saturn in conjunction with Moon. Saturn 0.6° N.
17	18	Venus in conjunction with Moon. Venus 0.3° S.
19	00	Jupiter in conjunction with Moon. Jupiter 0.2° N.
19	13	Mercury in conjunction with Moon. Mercury 1° S.
19	23	Mars at stationary point
22	18	Sun's longitude 120° ♌
30	12	Neptune at opposition
30	15	Mars in conjunction with Moon. Mars 6° S.

MINIMA OF ALGOL

d	h		d	h		d	h
2	11.6		13	22.9		25	10.1
5	08.4		16	19.7		28	06.9
8	05.3		19	16.5		31	03.7
11	02.1		22	13.3			

CONSTELLATIONS

The following constellations are near the meridian at

	d	h		d	h
June	1	24	July	16	21
June	15	23	August	1	20
July	1	22	August	16	19

Ursa Minor, Draco, Corona, Hercules, Lyra, Serpens, Ophiuchus, Libra, Scorpius and Sagittarius

THE MOON

Phases, Apsides and Node	d	h	m
○ Full Moon	5	15	04
☾ Last Quarter	13	18	45
● New Moon	20	19	44
☽ First Quarter	27	10	08
Apogee (405,567 km)	9	11	22
Perigee (359,027 km)	21	20	45

Mean longitude of ascending node on July 1, 96°

THE SUN

s.d. 16′.1

Day	Right Ascension	Dec. +	Equation of time	Rise 52°	Rise 56°	Transit	Set 52°	Set 56°	Sidereal time	Transit of First Point of Aries
	h m s	° ′	m s	h m	h m	h m	h m	h m	h m s	h m s
1	6 40 12	23 07	− 3 45	3 44	3 18	12 04	20 23	20 49	18 36 27	5 22 40
2	6 44 20	23 03	− 3 57	3 45	3 19	12 04	20 23	20 48	18 40 24	5 18 44
3	6 48 28	22 58	− 4 08	3 46	3 20	12 04	20 22	20 48	18 44 20	5 14 48
4	6 52 35	22 53	− 4 19	3 47	3 21	12 04	20 22	20 47	18 48 17	5 10 52
5	6 56 42	22 48	− 4 29	3 47	3 22	12 05	20 21	20 46	18 52 13	5 06 56
6	7 00 49	22 42	− 4 39	3 48	3 23	12 05	20 21	20 46	18 56 10	5 03 00
7	7 04 56	22 36	− 4 49	3 49	3 24	12 05	20 20	20 45	19 00 06	4 59 05
8	7 09 02	22 29	− 4 59	3 50	3 25	12 05	20 19	20 44	19 04 03	4 55 09
9	7 13 07	22 22	− 5 08	3 51	3 27	12 05	20 19	20 43	19 07 59	4 51 13
10	7 17 13	22 15	− 5 17	3 52	3 28	12 05	20 18	20 42	19 11 56	4 47 17
11	7 21 18	22 07	− 5 25	3 53	3 29	12 05	20 17	20 41	19 15 53	4 43 21
12	7 25 22	21 59	− 5 33	3 54	3 31	12 06	20 16	20 40	19 19 49	4 39 25
13	7 29 26	21 51	− 5 40	3 56	3 32	12 06	20 15	20 39	19 23 46	4 35 29
14	7 33 29	21 42	− 5 47	3 57	3 33	12 06	20 14	20 37	19 27 42	4 31 33
15	7 37 33	21 33	− 5 54	3 58	3 35	12 06	20 13	20 36	19 31 39	4 27 37
16	7 41 35	21 23	− 6 00	3 59	3 36	12 06	20 12	20 35	19 35 35	4 23 41
17	7 45 37	21 13	− 6 05	4 00	3 38	12 06	20 11	20 33	19 39 32	4 19 45
18	7 49 39	21 03	− 6 10	4 02	3 39	12 06	20 10	20 32	19 43 28	4 15 50
19	7 53 40	20 52	− 6 15	4 03	3 41	12 06	20 09	20 30	19 47 25	4 11 54
20	7 57 40	20 41	− 6 19	4 04	3 43	12 06	20 08	20 29	19 51 22	4 07 58
21	8 01 40	20 30	− 6 22	4 06	3 44	12 06	20 06	20 27	19 55 18	4 04 02
22	8 05 40	20 18	− 6 25	4 07	3 46	12 06	20 05	20 26	19 59 15	4 00 06
23	8 09 39	20 06	− 6 27	4 08	3 48	12 06	20 04	20 24	20 03 11	3 56 10
24	8 13 37	19 54	− 6 29	4 10	3 49	12 07	20 02	20 22	20 07 08	3 52 14
25	8 17 34	19 41	− 6 30	4 11	3 51	12 07	20 01	20 21	20 11 04	3 48 18
26	8 21 31	19 28	− 6 31	4 13	3 53	12 07	19 59	20 19	20 15 01	3 44 22
27	8 25 28	19 15	− 6 30	4 14	3 55	12 07	19 58	20 17	20 18 57	3 40 26
28	8 29 24	19 01	− 6 30	4 16	3 56	12 06	19 56	20 15	20 22 54	3 36 30
29	8 33 19	18 47	− 6 28	4 17	3 58	12 06	19 55	20 13	20 26 51	3 32 35
30	8 37 13	18 33	− 6 26	4 19	4 00	12 06	19 53	20 11	20 30 47	3 28 39
31	8 41 07	18 18	− 6 24	4 20	4 02	12 06	19 52	20 09	20 34 44	3 24 43

DURATION OF TWILIGHT (in minutes)

Latitude	52°	56°	52°	56°	52°	56°	52°	56°
	1 July		11 July		21 July		31 July	
Civil	48	61	46	58	44	53	41	49
Nautical	124	TAN	116	TAN	107	144	98	122
Astronomical	TAN	TAN	TAN	TAN	TAN	TAN	180	TAN

THE NIGHT SKY

Mercury remains too close to the Sun for observation throughout the month, despite the fact that it reaches its greatest western elongation (21°) on the 9th.

Venus continues to be visible as a magnificent morning object in the eastern sky before sunrise, magnitude -4.1. The old crescent Moon will be seen near Venus on the mornings of the 17th and 18th. Venus is moving eastwards amongst the stars, passing 3° north of Aldebaran on the 15th.

Mars is just past opposition so its magnitude fades during the month, from -2.2 to -1.5. At the beginning of the month it is still visible in the southern skies for the greater part of the night. Mars has now reached its most southerly declination (-27°) so that it will never be more than 12° above the horizon as seen from southern England, and only 7° from southern Scotland. The gibbous Moon passes north of the planet on the 3rd and again on the 30th. Mars reaches its second stationary point on the 19th, in Ophiuchus.

Jupiter is too close to the Sun for observation at the beginning of the month but by about the 12th it should be possible to glimpse it low above the east-north-eastern horizon around 03h. Its magnitude is -1.9. The old crescent Moon may be glimpsed just over 1° to the left and below the planet on the morning of the 19th.

Saturn, magnitude +0.2, gradually becomes a morning object, after the first week of the month. It will be difficult to observe at first, because of the long duration of twilight, but keen-sighted observers may be able to locate it low above the east-north-eastern horizon before the sky gets too bright. By the end of July it should be much easier to find, since it becomes visible by about 01h. On the 15th Venus passes within a degree south of Saturn. On the 17th the old crescent Moon, 3 days before New, may be seen about 6° to the right of the planet.

Neptune is at opposition on the 30th, in Capricornus. It is not visible to the naked eye since its magnitude is +7.8.

THE MOON

Day	RA h m	Dec. °	Hor. par. '	Semi-diam. '	Sun's co-long. °	PA of Bright Limb °	Phase %	Age d	Rise 52° h m	Rise 56° h m	Transit h m	Set 52° h m	Set 56° h m
1	14 56	− 12.5	57.0	15.5	30	290	79	9.5	16 14	16 29	21 01	1 14	1 03
2	15 47	− 16.6	56.5	15.4	42	286	87	10.5	17 27	17 47	21 51	1 38	1 22
3	16 39	− 19.9	56.0	15.2	55	282	93	11.5	18 36	19 00	22 41	2 07	1 46
4	17 32	− 22.1	55.5	15.1	67	276	97	12.5	19 38	20 04	23 33	2 42	2 18
5	18 26	− 23.3	55.1	15.0	79	268	100	13.5	20 31	20 57	—	3 26	3 00
6	19 19	− 23.3	54.7	14.9	91	97	100	14.5	21 14	21 38	0 24	4 18	3 53
7	20 12	− 22.2	54.4	14.8	103	85	98	15.5	21 48	22 08	1 14	5 18	4 54
8	21 02	− 20.1	54.2	14.8	115	80	95	16.5	22 15	22 31	2 02	6 22	6 02
9	21 51	− 17.2	54.1	14.7	128	75	90	17.5	22 37	22 49	2 48	7 29	7 13
10	22 38	− 13.6	54.1	14.7	140	72	83	18.5	22 56	23 04	3 32	8 36	8 25
11	23 23	− 9.4	54.2	14.8	152	70	76	19.5	23 13	23 17	4 14	9 43	9 36
12	0 07	− 4.9	54.5	14.9	164	68	67	20.5	23 29	23 29	4 56	10 51	10 48
13	0 52	− 0.2	55.0	15.0	177	68	58	21.5	23 45	23 42	5 37	11 59	12 01
14	1 37	+ 4.7	55.6	15.1	189	68	48	22.5	—	23 56	6 20	13 10	13 16
15	2 24	+ 9.5	56.3	15.3	201	70	38	23.5	0 03	—	7 05	14 23	14 34
16	3 13	+ 14.0	57.2	15.6	213	73	28	24.5	0 25	0 12	7 54	15 39	15 55
17	4 07	+ 18.0	58.1	15.8	225	77	19	25.5	0 51	0 34	8 46	16 56	17 17
18	5 04	+ 21.1	59.0	16.1	238	82	11	26.5	1 26	1 04	9 43	18 12	18 36
19	6 05	+ 23.0	59.9	16.3	250	90	5	27.5	2 13	1 48	10 45	19 20	19 45
20	7 09	+ 23.4	60.5	16.5	262	101	1	28.5	3 14	2 48	11 48	20 15	20 39
21	8 14	+ 22.1	61.0	16.6	274	241	0	0.2	4 29	4 06	12 51	20 59	21 18
22	9 18	+ 19.3	61.1	16.6	287	277	2	1.2	5 53	5 35	13 51	21 32	21 46
23	10 18	+ 15.1	60.9	16.6	299	284	7	2.2	7 20	7 08	14 48	21 58	22 07
24	11 16	+ 10.1	60.4	16.5	311	288	15	3.2	8 46	8 39	15 42	22 20	22 24
25	12 10	+ 4.6	59.8	16.3	323	290	24	4.2	10 10	10 08	16 33	22 40	22 39
26	13 03	− 1.1	59.0	16.1	336	291	34	5.2	11 30	11 33	17 22	22 59	22 54
27	13 54	− 6.5	58.2	15.9	348	290	45	6.2	12 48	12 57	18 10	23 20	23 10
28	14 44	− 11.5	57.4	15.6	0	288	56	7.2	14 05	14 18	18 58	23 42	23 28
29	15 35	− 15.8	56.7	15.4	12	285	67	8.2	15 18	15 36	19 48	—	23 50
30	16 27	− 19.2	56.0	15.3	25	281	76	9.2	16 28	16 51	20 38	0 09	—
31	17 20	− 21.7	55.5	15.1	37	275	84	10.2	17 32	17 57	21 29	0 42	0 20

MERCURY

Day	RA h m	Dec. °	Diam. "	Phase %	Transit h m	5° high 52° h m	5° high 56° h m
1	5 24	+18.9	10	17	10 47	3 40	3 27
3	5 27	+19.1	9	21	10 42	3 34	3 20
5	5 31	+19.5	9	25	10 38	3 28	3 14
7	5 36	+19.9	9	30	10 36	3 23	3 09
9	5 43	+20.3	8	35	10 35	3 19	3 04
11	5 51	+20.8	8	40	10 35	3 17	3 01
13	6 00	+21.2	7	46	10 37	3 16	3 00
15	6 11	+21.7	7	52	10 40	3 16	3 00
17	6 23	+22.0	7	58	10 45	3 18	3 01
19	6 36	+22.3	6	65	10 50	3 22	3 05
21	6 51	+22.5	6	71	10 57	3 27	3 10
23	7 06	+22.6	6	78	11 05	3 35	3 17
25	7 23	+22.5	6	84	11 14	3 44	3 27
27	7 40	+22.2	5	89	11 23	3 55	3 38
29	7 57	+21.8	5	93	11 33	4 07	3 51
31	8 15	+21.2	5	96	11 43	4 21	4 05

VENUS

Day	RA h m	Dec. °	Diam. "	Phase %	Transit h m	5° high 52° h m	5° high 56° h m
1	3 33	+16.3	19	61	8 57	2 04	1 54
6	3 55	+17.6	18	63	8 59	1 59	1 47
11	4 17	+18.8	17	65	9 02	1 55	1 42
16	4 41	+19.8	17	67	9 05	1 53	1 39
21	5 04	+20.6	16	69	9 09	1 52	1 37
26	5 28	+21.2	16	71	9 13	1 52	1 36
31	5 53	+21.7	15	73	9 18	1 54	1 38

MARS

Day	RA h m	Dec. °	Diam. "	Phase %	Transit h m	5° high 52° h m	5° high 56° h m
1	17 04	-26.8	21	98	22 23	0 52	23 52
6	16 59	-26.9	20	97	21 59	0 28	23 27
11	16 56	-26.9	20	96	21 36	0 05	23 05
16	16 54	-26.8	19	95	21 14	23 39	22 44
21	16 53	-26.8	18	94	20 55	23 19	22 24
26	16 54	-26.8	18	92	20 36	23 01	22 05
31	16 57	-26.9	17	91	20 20	22 44	21 48

SUNRISE AND SUNSET

	London		Bristol		Birmingham		Manchester		Newcastle		Glasgow		Belfast	
	0°05′	51°30′	2°35′	51°28′	1°55′	52°28′	2°15′	53°28′	1°37′	54°59′	4°14′	55°52′	5°56′	54°35′
	h m	h m	h m	h m	h m	h m	h m	h m	h m	h m	h m	h m	h m	h m
1	3 47	20 21	3 58	20 30	3 49	20 33	3 45	20 41	3 32	20 48	3 36	21 05	3 52	21 03
2	3 48	20 20	3 58	20 30	3 50	20 33	3 45	20 40	3 33	20 48	3 37	21 04	3 53	21 02
3	3 49	20 20	3 59	20 30	3 51	20 33	3 46	20 40	3 34	20 47	3 38	21 04	3 54	21 02
4	3 50	20 19	4 00	20 29	3 52	20 32	3 47	20 39	3 35	20 46	3 39	21 03	3 55	21 01
5	3 50	20 19	4 01	20 29	3 52	20 32	3 48	20 39	3 36	20 46	3 40	21 02	3 56	21 00
6	3 51	20 18	4 02	20 28	3 53	20 31	3 49	20 38	3 37	20 45	3 41	21 02	3 57	21 00
7	3 52	20 18	4 02	20 28	3 54	20 30	3 50	20 37	3 38	20 44	3 42	21 01	3 58	20 59
8	3 53	20 17	4 03	20 27	3 55	20 30	3 51	20 37	3 39	20 44	3 43	21 00	3 59	20 58
9	3 54	20 16	4 04	20 26	3 56	20 29	3 52	20 36	3 40	20 43	3 45	20 59	4 00	20 57
10	3 55	20 16	4 05	20 25	3 57	20 28	3 53	20 35	3 41	20 42	3 46	20 58	4 01	20 56
11	3 56	20 15	4 06	20 25	3 58	20 27	3 54	20 34	3 42	20 41	3 47	20 57	4 02	20 55
12	3 57	20 14	4 07	20 24	4 00	20 26	3 55	20 33	3 44	20 40	3 48	20 56	4 03	20 54
13	3 58	20 13	4 09	20 23	4 01	20 25	3 57	20 32	3 45	20 39	3 50	20 55	4 05	20 53
14	4 00	20 12	4 10	20 22	4 02	20 24	3 58	20 31	3 46	20 37	3 51	20 53	4 06	20 52
15	4 01	20 11	4 11	20 21	4 03	20 23	3 59	20 30	3 48	20 36	3 53	20 52	4 07	20 51
16	4 02	20 10	4 12	20 20	4 04	20 22	4 00	20 29	3 49	20 35	3 54	20 51	4 09	20 50
17	4 03	20 09	4 13	20 19	4 06	20 21	4 02	20 28	3 51	20 34	3 56	20 49	4 10	20 49
18	4 04	20 08	4 15	20 18	4 07	20 20	4 03	20 26	3 52	20 32	3 57	20 48	4 12	20 47
19	4 06	20 07	4 16	20 17	4 08	20 19	4 05	20 25	3 54	20 31	3 59	20 47	4 13	20 46
20	4 07	20 06	4 17	20 15	4 10	20 17	4 06	20 24	3 55	20 29	4 00	20 45	4 15	20 44
21	4 08	20 04	4 18	20 14	4 11	20 16	4 07	20 22	3 57	20 28	4 02	20 44	4 16	20 43
22	4 10	20 03	4 20	20 13	4 12	20 15	4 09	20 21	3 58	20 26	4 04	20 42	4 18	20 42
23	4 11	20 02	4 21	20 12	4 14	20 13	4 10	20 20	4 00	20 25	4 05	20 40	4 19	20 40
24	4 12	20 00	4 23	20 10	4 15	20 12	4 12	20 18	4 02	20 23	4 07	20 39	4 21	20 38
25	4 14	19 59	4 24	20 09	4 17	20 11	4 13	20 17	4 03	20 22	4 09	20 37	4 23	20 37
26	4 15	19 58	4 25	20 07	4 18	20 09	4 15	20 15	4 05	20 20	4 11	20 35	4 24	20 35
27	4 17	19 56	4 27	20 06	4 20	20 08	4 17	20 13	4 07	20 18	4 12	20 33	4 26	20 33
28	4 18	19 55	4 28	20 04	4 21	20 06	4 18	20 12	4 08	20 16	4 14	20 31	4 28	20 32
29	4 20	19 53	4 30	20 03	4 23	20 04	4 20	20 10	4 10	20 15	4 16	20 30	4 29	20 30
30	4 21	19 52	4 31	20 01	4 24	20 03	4 21	20 08	4 12	20 13	4 18	20 28	4 31	20 28
31	4 22	19 50	4 33	20 00	4 26	20 01	4 23	20 07	4 14	20 11	4 20	20 26	4 33	20 26

JUPITER

Day	RA	Dec.		Transit	5° high	
					52°	56°
	h m	°	′	h m	h m	h m
1	5 48.2	+23	07	11 10	3 39	3 21
11	5 58.1	+23	10	10 41	3 09	2 51
21	6 07.6	+23	10	10 11	2 39	2 21
31	6 16.9	+23	08	9 41	2 09	1 51

Diameters – equatorial 33″ polar 31″

SATURN

Day	RA	Dec.		Transit	5° high	
					52°	56°
	h m	°	′	h m	h m	h m
1	4 30.1	+20	08	9 52	2 39	2 25
11	4 34.9	+20	17	9 18	2 04	1 49
21	4 39.4	+20	26	8 43	1 28	1 13
31	4 43.5	+20	33	8 08	0 52	0 37

Diameters – equatorial 17″ polar 15″
Rings – major axis 38″ minor axis 17″

URANUS

Day	RA	Dec.		Transit	10° high	
					52°	56°
	h m	°	′	h m	h m	h m
1	21 47.9	-14	05	3 11	23 38	0 07
11	21 46.9	-14	11	2 31	22 59	23 23
21	21 45.6	-14	17	1 50	22 19	22 44
31	21 44.2	-14	25	1 09	21 39	22 04

Diameter 4″

NEPTUNE

Day	RA	Dec.		Transit	10° high	
					52°	56°
	h m	°	′	h m	h m	h m
1	20 42.1	-18 05		2 05	23 04	23 38
11	20 41.1	-18 09		1 25	22 25	22 59
21	20 40.0	-18 13		0 45	21 45	22 19
31	20 38.9	-18 18		0 04	21 05	21 40

Diameter 2″

August 2001

EIGHTH MONTH, 31 DAYS. *Augustus*, formerly *Sextilis*, sixth month of Roman pre-Julian calendar

1	*Wednesday*	Swiss Confederation founded 1291. Herman Melville b. 1819	213
2	*Thursday*	Thomas Gainsborough d. 1788. James Baldwin b. 1924	214
3	*Friday*	Sir Roger Casement d. 1916. P. D. James b. 1920	215
4	*Saturday*	*Queen Elizabeth the Queen Mother b. 1900*	216
5	*Sunday*	**8th S. after Trinity.** Neil Armstrong b. 1930	217
6	*Monday*	**The Transfiguration.** Daniel O'Connell b. 1775	*week 32 day* 218
7	*Tuesday*	Margaretha Macleod b. 1876. Sir Rabindranath Tagore d. 1941	219
8	*Wednesday*	*Princess Beatrice of York b. 1988.* Great Train Robbery 1963	220
9	*Thursday*	Henry V b. 1387. Dmitri Shostakovich d. 1975	221
10	*Friday*	Count Camillo Cavour b. 1810. Charles Keene b. 1823	222
11	*Saturday*	Sir Angus Wilson b. 1913. Andrew Carnegie d. 1919	223
12	*Sunday*	**9th S. after Trinity.** George Stephenson d. 1848	224
13	*Monday*	Battle of Blenheim 1704. John Logie Baird b. 1888	*week 33 day* 225
14	*Tuesday*	John Galsworthy b. 1867. William Hearst d. 1951	226
15	*Wednesday*	**Blessed Virgin Mary.** *Princess Royal b. 1950*	227
16	*Thursday*	Peterloo Massacre 1819. Ted Hughes b. 1930	228
17	*Friday*	Davy Crockett b. 1786. Ira Gershwin d. 1983	229
18	*Saturday*	Tara West b. 1977. Sir Frederick Ashton d. 1988	230
19	*Sunday*	**10th S. after Trinity.** Blaise Pascal d. 1662	231
20	*Monday*	Raymond Poincaré b. 1860. General William Booth d. 1912	*week 34 day* 232
21	*Tuesday*	*Princess Margaret b. 1930.* August Bournonville b. 1805	233
22	*Wednesday*	Deng Xiaoping b. 1904. Jomo Kenyatta d. 1978	234
23	*Thursday*	William Wallace d. 1305. Gene Kelly b. 1912	235
24	*Friday*	**St Bartholomew.** Mount Vesuvius erupted 7AD	236
25	*Saturday*	Michael Faraday d. 1867. Leonard Bernstein b. 1918	237
26	*Sunday*	**11th S. after Trinity.** Battle of Crecy 1346	238
27	*Monday*	*Bank Holiday in England, Wales and Northern Ireland*	*week 35 day* 239
28	*Tuesday*	St Augustine d. 430. Johann von Goethe b. 1749	240
29	*Wednesday*	Sir Charles Napier d. 1853. Ingrid Bergman b. 1915	241
30	*Thursday*	Raymond Massey b. 1896. Denis Healey b. 1917	242
31	*Friday*	Théophile Gautier b. 1811. Rocky Marciano d. 1969	243

ASTRONOMICAL PHENOMENA

d	h	
5	22	Mercury in superior conjunction
5	23	Jupiter in conjunction with Venus. Jupiter 1° N.
14	03	Saturn in conjunction with Moon. Saturn 0.2° N.
15	15	Uranus at opposition
15	20	Jupiter in conjunction with Moon. Jupiter 0.4° S.
16	13	Venus in conjunction with Moon. Venus 2° S.
20	02	Mercury in conjunction with Moon. Mercury 3° S.
23	01	Sun's longitude 150° ♍
23	16	Pluto at stationary point
27	13	Mars in conjunction with Moon. Mars 5° S.

MINIMA OF ALGOL

d	h	d	h	d	h
3	00.5	14	11.8	25	23.0
5	21.4	17	08.6	28	19.8
8	18.2	20	05.4	31	16.6
11	15.0	23	02.2		

CONSTELLATIONS

The following constellations are near the meridian at

	d	h		d	h
July	1	24	August	16	21
July	16	23	September	1	20
August	1	22	September	15	19

Draco, Hercules, Lyra, Cygnus, Sagitta, Ophiuchus, Serpens, Aquila and Sagittarius

THE MOON

Phases, Apsides and Node	d	h	m
○ Full Moon	4	05	56
☾ Last Quarter	12	07	53
● New Moon	19	02	55
☽ First Quarter	25	19	55
Apogee (406,269 km)	5	21	05
Perigee (357,157 km)	19	05	40

Mean longitude of ascending node on August 1, 94°

THE SUN
s.d. 16'.1

Day	Right Ascension	Dec. +	Equation of time	Rise 52°	Rise 56°	Transit	Set 52°	Set 56°	Sidereal time	Transit of First Point of Aries
	h m s	° ′	m s	h m	h m	h m	h m	h m	h m s	h m s
1	8 45 00	18 03	− 6 20	4 22	4 04	12 06	19 50	20 07	20 38 40	3 20 47
2	8 48 53	17 48	− 6 16	4 23	4 06	12 06	19 48	20 05	20 42 37	3 16 51
3	8 52 45	17 32	− 6 12	4 25	4 08	12 06	19 46	20 03	20 46 33	3 12 55
4	8 56 37	17 17	− 6 07	4 26	4 10	12 06	19 45	20 01	20 50 30	3 08 59
5	9 00 27	17 01	− 6 01	4 28	4 11	12 06	19 43	19 59	20 54 26	3 05 03
6	9 04 18	16 44	− 5 55	4 29	4 13	12 06	19 41	19 57	20 58 23	3 01 07
7	9 08 07	16 28	− 5 48	4 31	4 15	12 06	19 39	19 55	21 02 20	2 57 11
8	9 11 56	16 11	− 5 40	4 33	4 17	12 06	19 37	19 53	21 06 16	2 53 15
9	9 15 45	15 54	− 5 32	4 34	4 19	12 05	19 36	19 50	21 10 13	2 49 19
10	9 19 33	15 36	− 5 24	4 36	4 21	12 05	19 34	19 48	21 14 09	2 45 24
11	9 23 20	15 19	− 5 14	4 37	4 23	12 05	19 32	19 46	21 18 06	2 41 28
12	9 27 07	15 01	− 5 05	4 39	4 25	12 05	19 30	19 44	21 22 02	2 37 32
13	9 30 53	14 43	− 4 54	4 41	4 27	12 05	19 28	19 41	21 25 59	2 33 36
14	9 34 39	14 24	− 4 44	4 42	4 29	12 05	19 26	19 39	21 29 55	2 29 40
15	9 38 24	14 06	− 4 32	4 44	4 31	12 04	19 24	19 37	21 33 52	2 25 44
16	9 42 09	13 47	− 4 20	4 46	4 33	12 04	19 22	19 34	21 37 49	2 21 48
17	9 45 53	13 28	− 4 08	4 47	4 35	12 04	19 20	19 32	21 41 45	2 17 52
18	9 49 37	13 09	− 3 55	4 49	4 37	12 04	19 18	19 30	21 45 42	2 13 56
19	9 53 20	12 49	− 3 42	4 50	4 39	12 04	19 16	19 27	21 49 38	2 10 00
20	9 57 03	12 30	− 3 28	4 52	4 41	12 03	19 13	19 25	21 53 35	2 06 05
21	10 00 45	12 10	− 3 14	4 54	4 43	12 03	19 11	19 22	21 57 31	2 02 09
22	10 04 27	11 50	− 2 59	4 55	4 45	12 03	19 09	19 20	22 01 28	1 58 13
23	10 08 08	11 30	− 2 43	4 57	4 47	12 03	19 07	19 17	22 05 24	1 54 17
24	10 11 49	11 09	− 2 28	4 59	4 48	12 02	19 05	19 15	22 09 21	1 50 21
25	10 15 29	10 49	− 2 12	5 00	4 50	12 02	19 03	19 12	22 13 18	1 46 25
26	10 19 09	10 28	− 1 55	5 02	4 52	12 02	19 01	19 10	22 17 14	1 42 29
27	10 22 49	10 07	− 1 38	5 04	4 54	12 01	18 58	19 07	22 21 11	1 38 33
28	10 26 28	9 46	− 1 20	5 05	4 56	12 01	18 56	19 05	22 25 07	1 34 37
29	10 30 06	9 25	− 1 03	5 07	4 58	12 01	18 54	19 02	22 29 04	1 30 41
30	10 33 45	9 03	− 0 45	5 08	5 00	12 01	18 52	19 00	22 33 00	1 26 45
31	10 37 23	8 42	− 0 26	5 10	5 02	12 00	18 49	18 57	22 36 57	1 22 50

DURATION OF TWILIGHT (in minutes)

Latitude	52°	56°	52°	56°	52°	56°	52°	56°
	1 August		11 August		21 August		31 August	
Civil	41	48	39	45	37	42	35	40
Nautical	97	120	89	106	83	96	79	89
Astronomical	177	TAN	153	205	138	166	127	147

THE NIGHT SKY

Mercury passes through superior conjunction on the 5th and remains too close to the Sun for observation throughout August.

Venus, magnitude -4.0, is a magnificent morning object, visible in the eastern sky for several hours before dawn. The old crescent Moon is near the planet on the mornings of the 16th and 17th. Around the 22nd, Venus, continuing its eastward motion, passes south of the twins, Castor and Pollux.

Mars, its magnitude fading from -1.5 to -0.9 during the month, continues to be visible as an evening object, low in the south-western sky. The gibbous Moon will be seen near the planet on the evening of the 27th. Mars is in Ophiuchus.

Jupiter, magnitude -2.0, is a morning object, and by the end of the month becomes visible low above the east-north-eastern horizon shortly after midnight. Jupiter is in Gemini.

During the early part of the month Jupiter is near Venus, the two planets being only 1° apart on the night of the 5th–6th, Venus being obviously the brighter object. On the morning of the 16th, the old crescent Moon will be seen about 3° to the left of the planet.

Saturn continues to be visible as a morning object, magnitude +0.1. Saturn is in Taurus and by the end of the month the planet is visible low in the eastern sky by 23h.

Uranus is at opposition on the 15th, in Capricornus. Uranus is barely visible to the naked eye as its magnitude is +5.7, but it is readily located with only small optical aid.

Meteors. The maximum of the famous Perseid meteor shower occurs on the 12th. Unfortunately the Moon, at Last Quarter, rises shortly before 23h and will therefore provide some interference.

THE MOON

Day	RA h m	Dec. °	Hor. par. ′	Semi- diam. ′	Sun's co- long. °	PA of Bright Limb °	Phase %	Age d	Rise 52° h m	Rise 56° h m	Transit h m	Set 52° h m	Set 56° h m
1	18 13	− 23.1	55.0	15.0	49	269	91	11.2	18 27	18 54	22 20	1 23	0 58
2	19 06	− 23.4	54.6	14.9	61	262	95	12.2	19 13	19 38	23 10	2 13	1 46
3	19 58	− 22.6	54.3	14.8	73	251	99	13.2	19 50	20 11	23 58	3 10	2 45
4	20 49	− 20.7	54.1	14.7	86	208	100	14.2	20 19	20 36	—	4 13	3 51
5	21 38	− 18.0	54.0	14.7	98	95	99	15.2	20 42	20 56	0 45	5 19	5 02
6	22 25	− 14.5	54.0	14.7	110	81	97	16.2	21 02	21 11	1 29	6 26	6 13
7	23 11	− 10.5	54.0	14.7	122	75	93	17.2	21 19	21 24	2 12	7 33	7 25
8	23 55	− 6.1	54.2	14.8	134	72	88	18.2	21 35	21 37	2 54	8 40	8 36
9	0 39	− 1.4	54.5	14.9	146	71	81	19.2	21 51	21 49	3 35	9 48	9 48
10	1 24	+ 3.4	54.9	15.0	159	71	73	20.2	22 08	22 01	4 17	10 56	11 01
11	2 09	+ 8.2	55.5	15.1	171	72	63	21.2	22 27	22 16	5 00	12 07	12 16
12	2 57	+ 12.7	56.2	15.3	183	74	54	22.2	22 50	22 35	5 46	13 20	13 34
13	3 47	+ 16.8	57.0	15.5	195	77	43	23.2	23 20	23 00	6 35	14 35	14 53
14	4 42	+ 20.1	58.0	15.8	208	82	33	24.2	—	23 36	7 28	15 49	16 12
15	5 40	+ 22.5	58.9	16.1	220	87	23	25.2	0 00	—	8 26	16 59	17 25
16	6 42	+ 23.5	59.8	16.3	232	95	14	26.2	0 52	0 26	9 27	18 00	18 26
17	7 45	+ 22.9	60.6	16.5	244	103	7	27.2	2 00	1 35	10 30	18 50	19 11
18	8 49	+ 20.7	61.1	16.7	257	115	2	28.2	3 20	2 59	11 32	19 27	19 44
19	9 52	+ 17.1	61.4	16.7	269	175	0	29.2	4 48	4 32	12 32	19 57	20 08
20	10 52	+ 12.2	61.3	16.7	281	273	1	0.9	6 17	6 07	13 28	20 21	20 28
21	11 49	+ 6.7	60.9	16.6	293	284	6	1.9	7 44	7 40	14 22	20 43	20 44
22	12 44	+ 0.8	60.2	16.4	306	287	12	2.9	9 09	9 10	15 13	21 03	20 59
23	13 37	− 4.9	59.4	16.2	318	288	21	3.9	10 31	10 38	16 04	21 23	21 15
24	14 29	− 10.2	58.5	15.9	330	287	31	4.9	11 51	12 02	16 53	21 45	21 32
25	15 21	− 14.8	57.5	15.7	342	284	41	5.9	13 07	13 24	17 44	22 11	21 53
26	16 14	− 18.6	56.7	15.4	354	280	52	6.9	14 20	14 41	18 34	22 43	22 21
27	17 07	− 21.4	55.9	15.2	7	276	62	7.9	15 27	15 51	19 25	23 21	22 56
28	18 00	− 23.0	55.3	15.1	19	270	71	8.9	16 25	16 51	20 16	—	23 41
29	18 53	− 23.5	54.8	14.9	31	264	80	9.9	17 13	17 39	21 07	0 08	—
30	19 45	− 23.0	54.4	14.8	43	258	87	10.9	17 52	18 15	21 55	1 03	0 37
31	20 36	− 21.3	54.2	14.8	55	251	93	11.9	18 23	18 42	22 43	2 04	1 42

MERCURY

Day	RA h m	Dec. °	Diam. ″	Phase %	Transit h m	5° high 52° h m	5° high 56° h m
1	8 24	+20.8	5	97	11 47	4 28	4 13
3	8 41	+19.9	5	99	11 57	4 43	4 29
5	8 58	+18.9	5	100	12 06	19 12	19 25
7	9 15	+17.8	5	100	12 15	19 14	19 26
9	9 31	+16.5	5	99	12 23	19 15	19 25
11	9 47	+15.2	5	98	12 31	19 15	19 24
13	10 02	+13.8	5	97	12 38	19 15	19 22
15	10 16	+12.4	5	95	12 44	19 13	19 20
17	10 30	+10.9	5	94	12 50	19 11	19 16
19	10 44	+ 9.4	5	92	12 55	19 09	19 13
21	10 56	+ 7.9	5	90	13 00	19 06	19 08
23	11 09	+ 6.4	5	88	13 04	19 02	19 04
25	11 21	+ 4.9	5	86	13 08	18 59	18 59
27	11 32	+ 3.4	5	84	13 12	18 55	18 54
29	11 43	+ 2.0	5	83	13 15	18 50	18 48
31	11 54	+ 0.5	6	81	13 18	18 46	18 42

VENUS

Day	RA h m	Dec. °	Diam. ″	Phase %	Transit h m	5° high 52° h m	5° high 56° h m
1	5 57	+21.7	15	73	9 19	1 55	1 39
6	6 22	+21.9	15	75	9 24	1 59	1 43
11	6 47	+21.8	14	76	9 30	2 05	1 48
16	7 12	+21.5	14	78	9 35	2 12	1 56
21	7 38	+20.9	13	79	9 40	2 21	2 06
26	8 03	+20.1	13	81	9 46	2 31	2 17
31	8 27	+19.1	13	82	9 51	2 43	2 30

MARS

Day	RA h m	Dec. °	Diam. ″	Phase %	Transit h m	5° high 52° h m	5° high 56° h m
1	16 58	-26.9	17	91	20 16	22 41	21 45
6	17 02	-26.9	16	90	20 01	22 25	21 29
11	17 08	-26.9	16	89	19 47	22 11	21 14
16	17 15	-27.0	15	88	19 35	21 58	21 01
21	17 22	-27.0	15	88	19 23	21 46	20 49
26	17 31	-27.0	14	87	19 12	21 35	20 38
31	17 41	-27.0	13	86	19 03	21 26	20 29

SUNRISE AND SUNSET

	London		Bristol		Birmingham		Manchester		Newcastle		Glasgow		Belfast	
	0°05′	51°30′	2°35′	51°28′	1°55′	52°28′	2°15′	53°28′	1°37′	54°59′	4°14′	55°52′	5°56′	54°35′
	h m	h m	h m	h m	h m	h m	h m	h m	h m	h m	h m	h m	h m	h m
1	4 24	19 48	4 34	19 58	4 27	19 59	4 25	20 05	4 15	20 09	4 21	20 24	4 34	20 24
2	4 25	19 47	4 36	19 57	4 29	19 58	4 26	20 03	4 17	20 07	4 23	20 22	4 36	20 23
3	4 27	19 45	4 37	19 55	4 31	19 56	4 28	20 01	4 19	20 05	4 25	20 20	4 38	20 21
4	4 29	19 43	4 39	19 53	4 32	19 54	4 30	19 59	4 21	20 03	4 27	20 18	4 40	20 19
5	4 30	19 41	4 40	19 51	4 34	19 52	4 31	19 57	4 22	20 01	4 29	20 15	4 41	20 17
6	4 32	19 40	4 42	19 50	4 35	19 50	4 33	19 56	4 24	19 59	4 31	20 13	4 43	20 15
7	4 33	19 38	4 43	19 48	4 37	19 49	4 35	19 54	4 26	19 57	4 33	20 11	4 45	20 13
8	4 35	19 36	4 45	19 46	4 39	19 47	4 36	19 52	4 28	19 55	4 35	20 09	4 47	20 11
9	4 36	19 34	4 46	19 44	4 40	19 45	4 38	19 50	4 30	19 53	4 37	20 07	4 49	20 09
10	4 38	19 32	4 48	19 42	4 42	19 43	4 40	19 48	4 32	19 51	4 39	20 05	4 50	20 06
11	4 39	19 31	4 50	19 40	4 44	19 41	4 42	19 46	4 33	19 49	4 40	20 02	4 52	20 04
12	4 41	19 29	4 51	19 38	4 45	19 39	4 43	19 44	4 35	19 46	4 42	20 00	4 54	20 02
13	4 43	19 27	4 53	19 37	4 47	19 37	4 45	19 41	4 37	19 44	4 44	19 58	4 56	20 00
14	4 44	19 25	4 54	19 35	4 49	19 35	4 47	19 39	4 39	19 42	4 46	19 55	4 58	19 58
15	4 46	19 23	4 56	19 33	4 50	19 33	4 48	19 37	4 41	19 40	4 48	19 53	5 00	19 56
16	4 47	19 21	4 57	19 31	4 52	19 31	4 50	19 35	4 43	19 37	4 50	19 51	5 01	19 53
17	4 49	19 19	4 59	19 29	4 54	19 29	4 52	19 33	4 45	19 35	4 52	19 48	5 03	19 51
18	4 50	19 17	5 01	19 27	4 55	19 27	4 54	19 31	4 47	19 33	4 54	19 46	5 05	19 49
19	4 52	19 15	5 02	19 25	4 57	19 24	4 55	19 29	4 48	19 30	4 56	19 44	5 07	19 46
20	4 54	19 13	5 04	19 22	4 59	19 22	4 57	19 26	4 50	19 28	4 58	19 41	5 09	19 44
21	4 55	19 10	5 05	19 20	5 00	19 20	4 59	19 24	4 52	19 26	5 00	19 39	5 11	19 42
22	4 57	19 08	5 07	19 18	5 02	19 18	5 01	19 22	4 54	19 23	5 02	19 36	5 12	19 39
23	4 58	19 06	5 09	19 16	5 04	19 16	5 02	19 20	4 56	19 21	5 04	19 34	5 14	19 37
24	5 00	19 04	5 10	19 14	5 05	19 14	5 04	19 17	4 58	19 19	5 06	19 31	5 16	19 35
25	5 02	19 02	5 12	19 12	5 07	19 11	5 06	19 15	5 00	19 16	5 08	19 29	5 18	19 32
26	5 03	19 00	5 13	19 10	5 09	19 09	5 08	19 13	5 02	19 14	5 10	19 26	5 20	19 30
27	5 05	18 58	5 15	19 08	5 10	19 07	5 09	19 10	5 03	19 11	5 12	19 24	5 22	19 28
28	5 06	18 55	5 17	19 05	5 12	19 05	5 11	19 08	5 05	19 09	5 14	19 21	5 23	19 25
29	5 08	18 53	5 18	19 03	5 14	19 02	5 13	19 06	5 07	19 06	5 16	19 19	5 25	19 23
30	5 10	18 51	5 20	19 01	5 15	19 00	5 15	19 03	5 09	19 04	5 18	19 16	5 27	19 20
31	5 11	18 49	5 21	18 59	5 17	18 58	5 16	19 01	5 11	19 01	5 19	19 14	5 29	19 18

JUPITER

Day	RA	Dec.		Transit		5° high	
						52°	56°
	h m	°	′	h m		h m	h m
1	6 17.8	+23	07	9 38		2 06	1 48
11	6 26.6	+23	04	9 07		1 36	1 18
21	6 34.9	+22	58	8 36		1 06	0 48
31	6 42.5	+22	52	8 04		0 35	0 17

Diameters – equatorial 34″ polar 32″

SATURN

Day	RA	Dec.		Transit		5° high	
	h m	°	′	h m		h m	h m
1	4 43.9	+20	33	8 04		0 48	0 33
11	4 47.4	+20	39	7 28		0 12	23 53
21	4 50.4	+20	43	6 52		23 32	23 16
31	4 52.8	+20	46	6 15		22 54	22 39

Diameters – equatorial 18″ polar 16″
Rings – major axis 40″ minor axis 18″

URANUS

Day	RA	Dec.		Transit		10° high	
						52°	56°
	h m	°	′	h m		h m	h m
1	21 44.1	-14	25	1 05		4 31	4 06
11	21 42.6	-14	33	0 24		3 49	3 24
21	21 41.0	-14	41	23 39		3 08	2 42
31	21 39.5	-14	49	22 59		2 26	2 00

Diameter 4″

NEPTUNE

Day	RA	Dec.		Transit		10° high	
						52°	56°
	h m	°	′	h m		h m	h m
1	20 38.8	-18	18	0 00		2 55	2 20
11	20 37.7	-18	22	23 16		2 14	1 39
21	20 36.7	-18	26	22 35		1 33	0 58
31	20 35.7	-18	30	21 55		0 53	0 17

Diameter 2″

 # September 2001

NINTH MONTH, 30 DAYS. *Septem* (seven), seventh month of Roman pre-Julian calendar

1	*Saturday*	François Mauriac d. 1970	244
2	*Sunday*	**12th S. after Trinity.** Baron de Coubertin d. 1937	245
3	*Monday*	Sir John Rennie d. 1874. Frank Capra d. 1991	*week 36 day* 246
4	*Tuesday*	Anton Bruckner b. 1824. Forth Road Bridge opened 1964	247
5	*Wednesday*	Pieter Brueghel d. 1569. Arthur Koestler b. 1905	248
6	*Thursday*	Elie Halévy b. 1870. Hendrik Verwoerd d. 1966	249
7	*Friday*	Battle of Borodino 1812. Buddy Holly b. 1936	250
8	*Saturday*	Sir Peter Davies b. 1934. Richard Strauss d. 1949	251
9	*Sunday*	**13th S. after Trinity.** Mao Tse-Tung d. 1976	252
10	*Monday*	Treaty of St Germain signed 1919. Norman Morrice b. 1931	*week 37 day* 253
11	*Tuesday*	Jessica Mitford b. 1917. Salvador Allende d. 1973	254
12	*Wednesday*	Jean-Philippe Rameau d. 1764. Herbert Asquith b. 1852	255
13	*Thursday*	J. B. Priestley b. 1894. Leopold Stokowski d. 1977	256
14	*Friday*	**Holy Cross Day.** Dante Alighieri d. 1321	257
15	*Saturday*	*Prince Henry of Wales b. 1984.* Dame Agatha Christie b. 1890	258
16	*Sunday*	**14th S. after Trinity.** Count John McCormack d. 1945	259
17	*Monday*	US Constitution signed 1787. Stirling Moss b. 1929	*week 38 day* 260
18	*Tuesday*	Gerald Tyrwhitt-Wilson b. 1883. Agnes de Mille b. 1905	261
19	*Wednesday*	Battle of Poitiers 1356. Emil Zátopek b. 1922	262
20	*Thursday*	Florence Smith b. 1902. Jean Sibelius d. 1957	263
21	*Friday*	**St Matthew.** Sir Walter Scott d. 1832	264
22	*Saturday*	Irving Berlin d. 1989. Grandparent's Day	265
23	*Sunday*	**15th S. after Trinity.** Pablo Neruda d. 1973	266
24	*Monday*	Sir Ian MacGregor b. 1912. Dr Seuss d. 1991	*week 39 day* 267
25	*Tuesday*	Samuel Butler d. 1680. Mark Rothko b. 1903	268
26	*Wednesday*	George Gershwin b. 1898. Kier Hardie d. 1915	269
27	*Thursday*	Stockton-Darlington Railway opened 1825	270
28	*Friday*	Michael Somes b. 1917. Gamal Nasser d. 1970	271
29	*Saturday*	**St Michael and All Angels.** Sebastian Coe b. 1956	272
30	*Sunday*	**16th S. after Trinity.** Rudolph Diesel d. 1913	273

ASTRONOMICAL PHENOMENA

d	h	
10	13	Saturn in conjunction with Moon. Saturn 0.2° S.
12	13	Jupiter in conjunction with Moon. Jupiter 1° S.
15	09	Venus in conjunction with Moon. Venus 3° S.
18	23	Mercury at greatest elongation E.27°
19	08	Mercury in conjunction with Moon. Mercury 7° S.
22	23	Sun's longitude 180° ♎
25	00	Mars in conjunction with Moon. Mars 2° S.
27	00	Saturn at stationary point

MINIMA OF ALGOL

d	h	d	h	d	h
3	13.5	15	00.7	26	11.9
6	10.3	17	21.5	29	08.7
9	07.1	20	18.3		
12	03.9	23	15.1		

CONSTELLATIONS

The following constellations are near the meridian at

	d	h		d	h
August	1	24	September	15	21
August	16	23	October	1	20
September	1	22	October	16	19

Draco, Cepheus, Lyra, Cygnus, Vulpecula, Sagitta, Delphinus, Equuleus, Aquila, Aquarius and Capricornus

THE MOON

Phases, Apsides and Node	d	h	m
○ Full Moon	2	21	43
☾ Last Quarter	10	19	00
● New Moon	17	10	27
☽ First Quarter	24	09	31
Apogee (406,330 km)	1	23	25
Perigee (358,128 km)	16	15	47
Apogee (405,787 km)	29	05	33

Mean longitude of ascending node on September 1, 93°

THE SUN   s.d. 16′.1

Day	Right Ascension	Dec.		Equation of time	Rise 52°	Rise 56°	Transit	Set 52°	Set 56°	Sidereal time	Transit of First Point of Aries
	h m s	°	′	m s	h m	h m	h m	h m	h m	h m s	h m s
1	10 41 01	+8	20	− 0 07	5 12	5 04	12 00	18 47	18 54	22 40 53	1 18 54
2	10 44 38	+7	58	+0 12	5 13	5 06	12 00	18 45	18 52	22 44 50	1 14 58
3	10 48 15	+7	36	+0 31	5 15	5 08	11 59	18 43	18 49	22 48 47	1 11 02
4	10 51 52	+7	14	+0 51	5 17	5 10	11 59	18 40	18 47	22 52 43	1 07 06
5	10 55 29	+6	52	+1 11	5 18	5 12	11 59	18 38	18 44	22 56 40	1 03 10
6	10 59 05	+6	30	+1 31	5 20	5 14	11 58	18 36	18 41	23 00 36	0 59 14
7	11 02 41	+6	07	+1 52	5 21	5 16	11 58	18 33	18 39	23 04 33	0 55 18
8	11 06 17	+5	45	+2 12	5 23	5 18	11 58	18 31	18 36	23 08 29	0 51 22
9	11 09 53	+5	22	+2 33	5 25	5 20	11 57	18 29	18 34	23 12 26	0 47 26
10	11 13 29	+5	00	+2 54	5 26	5 22	11 57	18 26	18 31	23 16 22	0 43 30
11	11 17 04	+4	37	+3 15	5 28	5 24	11 57	18 24	18 28	23 20 19	0 39 35
12	11 20 40	+4	14	+3 36	5 30	5 26	11 56	18 22	18 26	23 24 16	0 35 39
13	11 24 15	+3	51	+3 57	5 31	5 28	11 56	18 19	18 23	23 28 12	0 31 43
14	11 27 50	+3	28	+4 18	5 33	5 30	11 56	18 17	18 20	23 32 09	0 27 47
15	11 31 26	+3	05	+4 39	5 34	5 31	11 55	18 15	18 18	23 36 05	0 23 51
16	11 35 01	+2	42	+5 01	5 36	5 33	11 55	18 12	18 15	23 40 02	0 19 55
17	11 38 36	+2	19	+5 22	5 38	5 35	11 54	18 10	18 12	23 43 58	0 15 59
18	11 42 11	+1	56	+5 43	5 39	5 37	11 54	18 08	18 10	23 47 55	0 12 03
19	11 45 47	+1	32	+6 05	5 41	5 39	11 54	18 05	18 07	23 51 51	0 08 07
20	11 49 22	+1	09	+6 26	5 43	5 41	11 53	18 03	18 04	23 55 48	0 04 11
21	11 52 57	+ 0	46	+ 6 47	5 44	5 43	11 53	18 01	18 02	23 59 44 { 0 00 15 / 23 56 20	
22	11 56 33	+0	22	+7 08	5 46	5 45	11 53	17 58	17 59	0 03 41	23 52 24
23	12 00 08	−0	01	+7 29	5 48	5 47	11 52	17 56	17 56	0 07 38	23 48 28
24	12 03 44	−0	24	+7 50	5 49	5 49	11 52	17 54	17 54	0 11 34	23 44 32
25	12 07 19	−0	48	+8 11	5 51	5 51	11 52	17 51	17 51	0 15 31	23 40 36
26	12 10 55	−1	11	+8 32	5 53	5 53	11 51	17 49	17 48	0 19 27	23 36 40
27	12 14 31	−1	34	+8 52	5 54	5 55	11 51	17 47	17 46	0 23 24	23 32 44
28	12 18 08	−1	58	+9 13	5 56	5 57	11 51	17 44	17 43	0 27 20	23 28 48
29	12 21 44	−2	21	+9 33	5 57	5 59	11 50	17 42	17 41	0 31 17	23 24 52
30	12 25 21	−2	44	+9 53	5 59	6 01	11 50	17 40	17 38	0 35 13	23 20 56

DURATION OF TWILIGHT (in minutes)

Latitude	52°	56°	52°	56°	52°	56°	52°	56°
	1 September		11 September		21 September		30 September	
Civil	35	39	34	38	34	37	34	37
Nautical	79	89	76	84	74	82	73	80
Astronomical	127	146	120	135	115	129	113	126

THE NIGHT SKY

Mercury is unfavourably placed for observation from these latitudes seven though it attains its greatest eastern elongation on the 18th.

Venus, magnitude -4.0, continues to be visible as a brilliant object in the eastern sky in the mornings. By the end of September it is still visible for about two hours before sunrise. On the mornings of the 14th-16th the old crescent Moon is in the vicinity of the planet. Venus passes within 1° of Regulus on the 20th.

Mars, magnitude -0.6, continues to be visible in the south-western quadrant of the evening sky though no longer visible after 21h by the end of the month. The Moon, near First Quarter, passes 2° north of Mars on the night of the 24th-25th.

Jupiter, magnitude -2.1, continues to be visible as a morning object in the eastern sky. By the end of the month it may be seen well before midnight. The old crescent Moon is near Jupiter on the mornings of the 12th and 13th.

Saturn, magnitude 0.0, is still a morning object, visible in the south-eastern quadrant of the sky: by the end of the month it crosses the meridian nearly 2 hours before sunrise. Saturn commences its retrograde motion after reaching its first stationary point on the 27th, in the constellation of Taurus. The Moon, at Last Quarter, is near Saturn on the 10th.

Zodiacal Light. The morning cone may be seen reaching up from the eastern horizon along the ecliptic, before the beginning of morning twilight, from the 17th to the end of the month.

THE MOON

Day	RA h m	Dec. °	Hor. par. '	Semi-diam. '	Sun's co-long. °	PA of Bright Limb °	Phase %	Age d	Rise 52° h m	Rise 56° h m	Transit h m	Set 52° h m	Set 56° h m
1	21 26	− 18.8	54.0	14.7	68	243	97	12.9	18 47	19 02	23 28	3 09	2 51
2	22 13	− 15.5	54.0	14.7	80	227	99	13.9	19 08	19 19	—	4 16	4 03
3	22 59	− 11.5	54.0	14.7	92	145	100	14.9	19 26	19 32	0 11	5 24	5 15
4	23 44	− 7.1	54.1	14.8	104	89	99	15.9	19 42	19 44	0 53	6 31	6 26
5	0 28	− 2.4	54.4	14.8	116	78	96	16.9	19 57	19 56	1 34	7 39	7 38
6	1 12	+ 2.4	54.7	14.9	128	75	91	17.9	20 14	20 08	2 16	8 47	8 51
7	1 57	+ 7.2	55.1	15.0	141	74	85	18.9	20 32	20 22	2 58	9 57	10 05
8	2 44	+11.8	55.6	15.1	153	75	77	19.9	20 53	20 39	3 42	11 08	11 21
9	3 33	+15.9	56.2	15.3	165	77	68	20.9	21 19	21 00	4 29	12 21	12 39
10	4 25	+19.5	56.9	15.5	177	81	59	21.9	21 53	21 30	5 20	13 35	13 57
11	5 21	+22.1	57.7	15.7	189	86	48	22.9	22 39	22 13	6 14	14 45	15 10
12	6 19	+23.5	58.6	16.0	202	92	37	23.9	23 38	23 12	7 12	15 48	16 14
13	7 21	+23.5	59.4	16.2	214	99	26	24.9	—	—	8 12	16 41	17 05
14	8 23	+22.0	60.2	16.4	226	106	17	25.9	0 51	0 27	9 13	17 22	17 42
15	9 25	+18.9	60.8	16.6	238	113	9	26.9	2 14	1 55	10 13	17 55	18 09
16	10 25	+14.5	61.2	16.7	251	123	3	27.9	3 42	3 29	11 11	18 21	18 30
17	11 23	+ 9.2	61.2	16.7	263	151	0	28.9	5 11	5 04	12 06	18 43	18 47
18	12 19	+ 3.3	60.9	16.6	275	262	1	0.6	6 38	6 37	12 59	19 04	19 02
19	13 14	− 2.6	60.4	16.5	287	280	4	1.6	8 04	8 08	13 51	19 24	19 18
20	14 08	− 8.4	59.6	16.2	299	284	10	2.6	9 28	9 37	14 43	19 46	19 34
21	15 02	− 13.5	58.7	16.0	312	283	17	3.6	10 49	11 03	15 34	20 10	19 54
22	15 56	− 17.7	57.7	15.7	324	280	26	4.6	12 06	12 26	16 27	20 40	20 19
23	16 50	− 20.9	56.8	15.5	336	276	36	5.6	13 17	13 41	17 19	21 17	20 52
24	17 45	− 22.9	56.0	15.3	348	271	46	6.6	14 20	14 46	18 11	22 01	21 34
25	18 39	− 23.8	55.3	15.1	1	266	56	7.6	15 12	15 39	19 02	22 54	22 28
26	19 32	− 23.4	54.7	14.9	13	261	66	8.6	15 54	16 18	19 52	23 54	23 30
27	20 23	− 22.0	54.4	14.8	25	255	74	9.6	16 27	16 48	20 40	—	—
28	21 13	− 19.7	54.1	14.7	37	250	82	10.6	16 53	17 10	21 25	0 59	0 39
29	22 01	− 16.5	54.0	14.7	49	245	89	11.6	17 14	17 27	22 09	2 06	1 50
30	22 47	− 12.7	54.1	14.7	61	239	94	12.6	17 33	17 41	22 51	3 13	3 03

MERCURY

Day	RA h m	Dec. °	Diam. "	Phase %	Transit h m	5° high 52° h m	5° high 56° h m
1	11 59	-0.2	6	80	13 19	18 43	18 39
3	12 10	-1.6	6	78	13 22	18 38	18 33
5	12 20	-3.0	6	76	13 24	18 33	18 27
7	12 29	-4.3	6	74	13 25	18 27	18 20
9	12 39	-5.6	6	71	13 27	18 22	18 13
11	12 48	-6.9	6	69	13 28	18 16	18 06
13	12 56	-8.1	6	67	13 28	18 10	17 59
15	13 04	-9.2	7	64	13 28	18 04	17 52
17	13 12	-10.3	7	61	13 28	17 57	17 44
19	13 19	-11.3	7	58	13 27	17 51	17 36
21	13 26	-12.2	7	54	13 26	17 44	17 29
23	13 32	-13.0	7	51	13 23	17 37	17 21
25	13 37	-13.7	8	46	13 20	17 30	17 13
27	13 41	-14.2	8	42	13 16	17 23	17 05
29	13 44	-14.6	8	37	13 11	17 15	16 57
31	13 45	-14.8	9	31	13 04	17 07	16 49

VENUS

Day	RA h m	Dec. °	Diam. "	Phase %	Transit h m	5° high 52° h m	5° high 56° h m
1	8 32	+18.8	13	83	9 52	2 45	2 32
6	8 57	+17.5	12	84	9 57	2 58	2 46
11	9 21	+16.0	12	85	10 01	3 11	3 01
16	9 45	+14.2	12	86	10 06	3 25	3 16
21	10 09	+12.4	12	88	10 10	3 39	3 32
26	10 33	+10.3	12	89	10 14	3 53	3 48
31	10 56	+ 8.2	11	90	10 17	4 08	4 05

MARS

Day	RA h m	Dec. °	Diam. "	Phase %	Transit h m	5° high 52° h m	5° high 56° h m
1	17 43	-27.0	13	86	19 01	21 24	20 27
6	17 54	-26.9	13	86	18 52	21 16	20 20
11	18 05	-26.8	12	85	18 44	21 09	20 14
16	18 17	-26.6	12	85	18 36	21 04	20 10
21	18 30	-26.4	11	85	18 29	20 59	20 08
26	18 43	-26.1	11	85	18 22	20 56	20 07
31	18 56	-25.7	11	85	18 16	20 54	20 07

SUNRISE AND SUNSET

	London 0°05' 51°30'		Bristol 2°35' 51°28'		Birmingham 1°55' 52°28'		Manchester 2°15' 53°28'		Newcastle 1°37' 54°59'		Glasgow 4°14' 55°52'		Belfast 5°56' 54°35'	
	h m	h m	h m	h m	h m	h m	h m	h m	h m	h m	h m	h m	h m	h m
1	5 13	18 47	5 23	18 57	5 19	18 56	5 18	18 59	5 13	18 59	5 21	19 11	5 31	19 15
2	5 14	18 44	5 24	18 54	5 20	18 53	5 20	18 56	5 15	18 56	5 23	19 09	5 33	19 13
3	5 16	18 42	5 26	18 52	5 22	18 51	5 22	18 54	5 16	18 54	5 25	19 06	5 34	19 10
4	5 18	18 40	5 28	18 50	5 24	18 49	5 23	18 51	5 18	18 51	5 27	19 03	5 36	19 08
5	5 19	18 38	5 29	18 48	5 25	18 46	5 25	18 49	5 20	18 49	5 29	19 01	5 38	19 05
6	5 21	18 35	5 31	18 45	5 27	18 44	5 27	18 47	5 22	18 46	5 31	18 58	5 40	19 03
7	5 22	18 33	5 32	18 43	5 29	18 42	5 29	18 44	5 24	18 44	5 33	18 56	5 42	19 00
8	5 24	18 31	5 34	18 41	5 30	18 39	5 30	18 42	5 26	18 41	5 35	18 53	5 44	18 58
9	5 26	18 29	5 36	18 39	5 32	18 37	5 32	18 39	5 28	18 39	5 37	18 50	5 45	18 55
10	5 27	18 26	5 37	18 36	5 33	18 35	5 34	18 37	5 29	18 36	5 39	18 48	5 47	18 53
11	5 29	18 24	5 39	18 34	5 35	18 32	5 35	18 35	5 31	18 34	5 41	18 45	5 49	18 50
12	5 30	18 22	5 40	18 32	5 37	18 30	5 37	18 32	5 33	18 31	5 43	18 42	5 51	18 48
13	5 32	18 19	5 42	18 29	5 38	18 28	5 39	18 30	5 35	18 28	5 45	18 40	5 53	18 45
14	5 34	18 17	5 44	18 27	5 40	18 25	5 41	18 27	5 37	18 26	5 47	18 37	5 55	18 43
15	5 35	18 15	5 45	18 25	5 42	18 23	5 42	18 25	5 39	18 23	5 49	18 34	5 56	18 40
16	5 37	18 13	5 47	18 23	5 43	18 20	5 44	18 22	5 41	18 21	5 50	18 32	5 58	18 38
17	5 38	18 10	5 48	18 20	5 45	18 18	5 46	18 20	5 42	18 18	5 52	18 29	6 00	18 35
18	5 40	18 08	5 50	18 18	5 47	18 16	5 48	18 17	5 44	18 16	5 54	18 27	6 02	18 33
19	5 42	18 06	5 52	18 16	5 49	18 13	5 49	18 15	5 46	18 13	5 56	18 24	6 04	18 30
20	5 43	18 03	5 53	18 13	5 50	18 11	5 51	18 13	5 48	18 10	5 58	18 21	6 06	18 28
21	5 45	18 01	5 55	18 11	5 52	18 09	5 53	18 10	5 50	18 08	6 00	18 19	6 07	18 25
22	5 46	17 59	5 56	18 09	5 54	18 06	5 55	18 08	5 52	18 05	6 02	18 16	6 09	18 23
23	5 48	17 56	5 58	18 06	5 55	18 04	5 56	18 05	5 54	18 03	6 04	18 13	6 11	18 20
24	5 50	17 54	6 00	18 04	5 57	18 01	5 58	18 03	5 56	18 00	6 06	18 11	6 13	18 17
25	5 51	17 52	6 01	18 02	5 59	17 59	6 00	18 00	5 57	17 58	6 08	18 08	6 15	18 15
26	5 53	17 49	6 03	17 59	6 00	17 57	6 02	17 58	5 59	17 55	6 10	18 05	6 17	18 12
27	5 54	17 47	6 04	17 57	6 02	17 54	6 03	17 55	6 01	17 53	6 12	18 03	6 18	18 10
28	5 56	17 45	6 06	17 55	6 04	17 52	6 05	17 53	6 03	17 50	6 14	18 00	6 20	18 07
29	5 58	17 43	6 08	17 53	6 05	17 50	6 07	17 51	6 05	17 47	6 16	17 57	6 22	18 05
30	5 59	17 40	6 09	17 50	6 07	17 47	6 09	17 48	6 07	17 45	6 18	17 55	6 24	18 02

JUPITER

Day	RA	Dec.		Transit	5° high 52°	56°
	h m	°	'	h m	h m	h m
1	6 43.2	+22	51	8 01	0 31	0 14
11	6 50.0	+22	44	7 29	0 00	23 39
21	6 55.9	+22	38	6 55	23 24	23 06
31	7 00.7	+22	32	6 21	22 50	22 32

Diameters – equatorial 37" polar 34"

SATURN

Day	RA	Dec.		Transit	5° high 52°	56°
	h m	°	'	h m	h m	h m
1	4 53.0	+20	46	6 11	22 50	22 35
11	4 54.6	+20	47	5 33	22 13	21 57
21	4 55.5	+20	47	4 55	21 34	21 19
31	4 55.6	+20	46	4 16	20 55	20 40

Diameters – equatorial 19" polar 17"
Rings – major axis 42" minor axis 19"

URANUS

Day	RA	Dec.		Transit	10° high 52°	56°
	h m	°	'	h m	h m	h m
1	21 39.3	-14	49	22 55	2 22	1 56
11	21 37.9	-14	56	22 14	1 40	1 14
21	21 36.7	-15	02	21 33	0 59	0 33
31	21 35.6	-15	07	20 53	0 18	23 47

Diameter 4"

NEPTUNE

Day	RA	Dec.	Diam	Phase	Transit	10° high 52°	56°
	h m	°	'			h m	h m	h m
1	20 35.6	-18	30		21 51	0 48	0 13
11	20 34.8	-18	33		21 11	0 08	23 28
21	20 34.1	-18	36		20 31	23 23	22 48
31	20 33.7	-18	38		19 51	22 43	22 07

Diameter 2"

 # October 2001

TENTH MONTH, 31 DAYS. *Octo* (eighth), eighth month of Roman pre-Julian Calendar

1	*Monday*	Annie Besant b. 1847. St Pancras Station opened 1868	*week 40 day* 274
2	*Tuesday*	Mahatma Gandhi b. 1869. Sir Peter Medawar d. 1987	275
3	*Wednesday*	St Francis of Assisi d. 1226. Thomas Wolfe b. 1900	276
4	*Thursday*	Rembrandt d. 1669. Buster Keaton b. 1895	277
5	*Friday*	Louis Lumière b. 1864. Jean Vigo d. 1934	278
6	*Saturday*	Charles Parnell d. 1891. Thor Heyerdahl b. 1914	279
7	*Sunday*	**17th S. of Trinity.** Edgar Allen Poe d. 1849	280
8	*Monday*	Henry Fielding d. 1754. Juan Perón b. 1895	*week 41 day* 281
9	*Tuesday*	Claude Perrault d. 1688. John Lennon b. 1940	282
10	*Wednesday*	Alberto Giacometti b. 1901. Yul Brynner d. 1985	283
11	*Thursday*	James Joule d. 1889. Jerome Robbins b. 1918	284
12	*Friday*	Columbus discovered the New World 1492	285
13	*Saturday*	Margaret Thatcher b. 1925. Sidney Webb d. 1947	286
14	*Sunday*	**18th S. of Trinity.** Bing Crosby d. 1977	287
15	*Monday*	Virgil b. 70 BC. Cole Porter d. 1964	*week 42 day* 288
16	*Tuesday*	Marie Antoinette d. 1793. Oscar Wilde b. 1854	289
17	*Wednesday*	Sir Philip Sidney d. 1586. Rita Hayworth b. 1918	290
18	*Thursday*	**St Luke.** Battle of Leipzig 1813	291
19	*Friday*	James Henry Hunt b. 1784. Harold French d. 1997	292
20	*Saturday*	Henry Temple b. 1784. Jack Buchanan d. 1957	293
21	*Sunday*	**19th S. of Trinity.** Sir Alan Cobham d. 1973	294
22	*Monday*	Ivan Bunin b. 1870. Pablo Casals d. 1973	*week 43 day* 295
23	*Tuesday*	Edward Smith-Stanley d. 1869. Pélé b. 1940	296
24	*Wednesday*	Dame Sybil Thorndike b. 1882. Christian Dior d. 1957	297
25	*Thursday*	Battle of Balaclava 1854. Sir Charles Hallé d. 1895	298
26	*Friday*	François Mitterrand b. 1916. William Temple d. 1944	299
27	*Saturday*	Dylan Thomas b. 1914. Sir Andrzej Panufnik d. 1991	300
28	*Sunday*	**SS Simon and Jude. 20th S. of Trinity**	301
29	*Monday*	Joseph Pulitzer d. 1911. Wall Street crashed 1929	*week 44 day* 302
30	*Tuesday*	R. B. Sheridan b. 1751. Sir Barnes Wallis d. 1979	303
31	*Wednesday*	John Keats b. 1795. Federico Fellini d. 1993	304

ASTRONOMICAL PHENOMENA

d	h	
1	19	Mercury at stationary point
7	19	Saturn in conjunction with Moon. Saturn 0.5° S.
10	01	Jupiter in conjunction with Moon. Jupiter 1° S.
14	02	Mercury in inferior conjunction
15	05	Venus in conjunction with Moon. Venus 4° S.
16	11	Mercury in conjunction with Moon. Mercury 6° S.
18	02	Neptune at stationary point
23	00	Mercury at stationary point
23	08	Sun's longitude 210° ♏
23	20	Mars in conjunction with Moon. Mars 0.1° N.
29	17	Mercury at greatest elongation W.19°
30	19	Venus in conjunction with Mercury . Venus 0.6° S.
30	23	Uranus at stationary point

MINIMA OF ALGOL

d	h	d	h	d	h
2	05.6	13	16.8	25	04.0
5	02.4	16	13.6	28	00.9
7	23.2	19	10.4	30	21.7
10	20.0	22	07.2		

CONSTELLATIONS

The following constellations are near the meridian at

	d	h		d	h
September	1	24	October	16	21
September	15	23	November	1	20
October	1	22	November	15	19

Ursa Major (below the Pole), Cepheus, Cassiopeia, Cygnus, Lacerta, Andromeda, Pegasus, Capricornus, Aquarius and Piscis Austrinus

THE MOON

Phases, Apsides and Node	d	h	m
○ Full Moon	2	13	49
☾ Last Quarter	10	04	20
● New Moon	16	19	23
☽ First Quarter	24	02	58
Perigee (361,860 km)	14	23	00
Apogee (404,935 km)	26	20	11

Mean longitude of ascending node on October 1, 91°

THE SUN
s.d. 16′.1

Day	Right Ascension	Dec.	Equation of time	Rise 52°	Rise 56°	Transit	Set 52°	Set 56°	Sidereal time	Transit of First Point of Aries
	h m s	° ′	m s	h m	h m	h m	h m	h m	h m s	h m s
1	12 28 58	3 08	+ 10 12	6 01	6 03	11 50	17 37	17 35	0 39 10	23 17 00
2	12 32 35	3 31	+ 10 32	6 02	6 05	11 49	17 35	17 33	0 43 07	23 13 05
3	12 36 12	3 54	+ 10 51	6 04	6 07	11 49	17 33	17 30	0 47 03	23 09 09
4	12 39 50	4 17	+ 11 10	6 06	6 09	11 49	17 31	17 27	0 51 00	23 05 13
5	12 43 28	4 40	+ 11 28	6 08	6 11	11 48	17 28	17 25	0 54 56	23 01 17
6	12 47 07	5 03	+ 11 46	6 09	6 13	11 48	17 26	17 22	0 58 53	22 57 21
7	12 50 46	5 26	+ 12 04	6 11	6 15	11 48	17 24	17 20	1 02 49	22 53 25
8	12 54 25	5 49	+ 12 21	6 13	6 17	11 48	17 22	17 17	1 06 46	22 49 29
9	12 58 05	6 12	+ 12 38	6 14	6 19	11 47	17 19	17 15	1 10 42	22 45 33
10	13 01 45	6 35	+ 12 54	6 16	6 21	11 47	17 17	17 12	1 14 39	22 41 37
11	13 05 26	6 58	+ 13 10	6 18	6 23	11 47	17 15	17 09	1 18 36	22 37 41
12	13 09 07	7 20	+ 13 25	6 19	6 25	11 46	17 13	17 07	1 22 32	22 33 46
13	13 12 49	7 43	+ 13 40	6 21	6 27	11 46	17 10	17 04	1 26 29	22 29 50
14	13 16 31	8 05	+ 13 54	6 23	6 29	11 46	17 08	17 02	1 30 25	22 25 54
15	13 20 14	8 27	+ 14 08	6 25	6 31	11 46	17 06	16 59	1 34 22	22 21 58
16	13 23 57	8 50	+ 14 21	6 26	6 33	11 46	17 04	16 57	1 38 18	22 18 02
17	13 27 41	9 12	+ 14 33	6 28	6 35	11 45	17 02	16 54	1 42 15	22 14 06
18	13 31 26	9 34	+ 14 45	6 30	6 37	11 45	17 00	16 52	1 46 11	22 10 10
19	13 35 11	9 55	+ 14 57	6 32	6 40	11 45	16 57	16 49	1 50 08	22 06 14
20	13 38 57	10 17	+ 15 08	6 33	6 42	11 45	16 55	16 47	1 54 05	22 02 18
21	13 42 43	10 38	+ 15 18	6 35	6 44	11 45	16 53	16 45	1 58 01	21 58 22
22	13 46 31	11 00	+ 15 27	6 37	6 46	11 44	16 51	16 42	2 01 58	21 54 26
23	13 50 18	11 21	+ 15 36	6 39	6 48	11 44	16 49	16 40	2 05 54	21 50 31
24	13 54 07	11 42	+ 15 44	6 41	6 50	11 44	16 47	16 38	2 09 51	21 46 35
25	13 57 56	12 03	+ 15 52	6 42	6 52	11 44	16 45	16 35	2 13 47	21 42 39
26	14 01 46	12 23	+ 15 58	6 44	6 54	11 44	16 43	16 33	2 17 44	21 38 43
27	14 05 36	12 44	+ 16 04	6 46	6 56	11 44	16 41	16 31	2 21 40	21 34 47
28	14 09 27	13 04	+ 16 10	6 48	6 58	11 44	16 39	16 28	2 25 37	21 30 51
29	14 13 19	13 24	+ 16 14	6 49	7 01	11 44	16 37	16 26	2 29 34	21 26 55
30	14 17 12	13 44	+ 16 18	6 51	7 03	11 44	16 35	16 24	2 33 30	21 22 59
31	14 21 05	14 03	+ 16 21	6 53	7 05	11 44	16 33	16 22	2 37 27	21 19 03

DURATION OF TWILIGHT (in minutes)

Latitude	52°	56°	52°	56°	52°	56°	52°	56°
	1 October		11 October		21 October		31 October	
Civil	34	37	34	37	34	38	36	40
Nautical	73	80	73	80	74	81	75	83
Astronomical	113	125	112	124	113	124	114	126

THE NIGHT SKY

Mercury passes through inferior conjunction on the 14th but then moves rapidly westwards from the Sun and for the last ten days of the month it is visible as a morning object, attaining its greatest western elongation (19°) on the 29th. It may be located low above the E.S.E. horizon at the beginning of morning twilight. This morning apparition is the most suitable one of the year for observers in the northern hemisphere. Its magnitude brightens from +0.9 to -0.7 during its period of visibility. Venus will be a useful guide to locating Mercury around the last two days of the month, when Mercury will be found about half-a-degree to the left of Venus.

Venus continues to be visible as a brilliant object in the eastern sky in the early mornings, magnitude -3.9, though it is gradually drawing closer to the Sun. The old crescent Moon is near Venus on the mornings of the 14th-16th.

Mars, magnitude -0.2, is still visible in the evenings, low above the south-western horizon. During the month Mars moves from Sagittarius into Capricornus. The Moon, only a few hours before First Quarter, passes extremely close to Mars on the evening of the 23rd, when Mars will appear to graze the upper limb of the Moon (which at that time will be unilluminated).

Jupiter, magnitude -2.3, continues to be visible as a brilliant morning object in the south-eastern sky. By the end of the month it may be seen low on the east-north-eastern horizon as early as 21h. The Moon, at Last Quarter, is near the planet on the night of the 9th-10th.

Saturn, although technically a morning object, is now visible in the eastern sky in the evenings and by the end of October is visible low above the E.N.E. horizon by about 19h. Its magnitude is -0.1. The gibbous Moon passes about a degree north of the planet on the evening of the 7th.

THE MOON

Day	RA h m	Dec. °	Hor. par. '	Semi-diam. '	Sun's co-long. °	PA of Bright Limb °	Phase %	Age d	Rise 52° h m	Rise 56° h m	Transit h m	Set 52° h m	Set 56° h m
1	23 33	− 8.3	54.2	14.8	74	231	98	13.6	17 49	17 53	23 33	4 21	4 15
2	0 17	− 3.6	54.4	14.8	86	209	100	14.6	18 04	18 04	—	5 30	5 27
3	1 01	+ 1.3	54.7	14.9	98	113	100	15.6	18 20	18 16	0 15	6 38	6 41
4	1 46	+ 6.2	55.1	15.0	110	84	98	16.6	18 37	18 29	0 57	7 48	7 55
5	2 33	+10.9	55.5	15.1	122	79	94	17.6	18 57	18 44	1 41	9 00	9 11
6	3 21	+15.2	56.0	15.3	134	79	89	18.6	19 21	19 04	2 27	10 13	10 29
7	4 13	+18.9	56.5	15.4	147	81	82	19.6	19 52	19 30	3 16	11 26	11 47
8	5 07	+21.8	57.1	15.6	159	85	73	20.6	20 33	20 07	4 09	12 37	13 02
9	6 04	+23.5	57.7	15.7	171	90	63	21.6	21 26	20 59	5 05	13 42	14 09
10	7 03	+23.9	58.4	15.9	183	96	52	22.6	22 32	22 06	6 03	14 37	15 02
11	8 04	+22.8	59.0	16.1	195	102	41	23.6	23 49	23 28	7 02	15 20	15 42
12	9 04	+20.3	59.6	16.2	208	108	30	24.6	—	—	8 00	15 54	16 11
13	10 03	+16.5	60.1	16.4	220	114	20	25.6	1 12	0 57	8 56	16 22	16 33
14	11 00	+11.6	60.5	16.5	232	119	11	26.6	2 39	2 29	9 51	16 45	16 51
15	11 56	+ 6.0	60.6	16.5	244	124	5	27.6	4 05	4 01	10 44	17 05	17 06
16	12 50	0.0	60.5	16.5	256	136	1	28.6	5 32	5 33	11 36	17 25	17 21
17	13 44	− 6.0	60.1	16.4	269	231	0	0.2	6 57	7 04	12 28	17 45	17 37
18	14 38	− 11.5	59.4	16.2	281	275	2	1.2	8 21	8 33	13 20	18 08	17 55
19	15 33	− 16.2	58.6	16.0	293	279	6	2.2	9 42	10 00	14 14	18 36	18 17
20	16 29	− 20.0	57.8	15.7	305	277	13	3.2	10 59	11 22	15 07	19 10	18 46
21	17 25	− 22.6	56.9	15.5	317	273	21	4.2	12 08	12 35	16 01	19 52	19 25
22	18 20	− 23.9	56.1	15.3	330	268	30	5.2	13 06	13 34	16 54	20 43	20 15
23	19 15	− 23.9	55.4	15.1	342	263	39	6.2	13 53	14 19	17 46	21 41	21 16
24	20 08	− 22.8	54.8	14.9	354	258	49	7.2	14 30	14 52	18 35	22 45	22 23
25	20 59	− 20.7	54.4	14.8	6	253	58	8.2	14 58	15 16	19 21	23 52	23 35
26	21 48	− 17.7	54.2	14.8	18	249	68	9.2	15 21	15 35	20 06	—	—
27	22 34	− 14.0	54.2	14.8	31	245	76	10.2	15 40	15 49	20 48	1 00	0 47
28	23 20	− 9.8	54.2	14.8	43	242	84	11.2	15 56	16 02	21 30	2 08	2 00
29	0 04	− 5.1	54.5	14.8	55	240	90	12.2	16 11	16 13	22 12	3 16	3 12
30	0 48	− 0.2	54.8	14.9	67	237	95	13.2	16 27	16 24	22 54	4 25	4 26

MERCURY

Day	RA h m	Dec. °	Diam. ''	Phase %	Transit h m	5° high 52° h m	5° high 56° h m
1	13 45	-14.8	9	31	13 04	17 07	16 49
3	13 45	-14.7	9	25	12 55	16 59	16 41
5	13 43	-14.4	9	19	12 45	16 52	16 34
7	13 39	-13.9	10	13	12 33	16 44	16 27
9	13 34	-13.0	10	8	12 19	16 36	16 20
11	13 27	-11.8	10	3	12 04	16 28	16 14
13	13 19	-10.4	10	1	11 48	7 18	7 30
15	13 11	-8.9	10	0	11 33	6 53	7 04
17	13 03	-7.4	10	3	11 18	6 30	6 40
19	12 58	-6.1	9	8	11 05	6 11	6 19
21	12 55	-5.2	9	16	10 55	5 55	6 02
23	12 54	-4.5	8	25	10 47	5 44	5 51
25	12 56	-4.3	8	35	10 41	5 37	5 44
27	13 00	-4.4	7	44	10 38	5 34	5 42
29	13 07	-4.9	7	54	10 37	5 36	5 43
31	13 14	-5.6	7	62	10 37	5 39	5 48

VENUS

Day	RA	Dec.	Diam.	Phase	Transit	5° high 52°	5° high 56°
1	10 56	+8.2	11	90	10 17	4 08	4 05
6	11 19	+5.9	11	91	10 20	4 23	4 22
11	11 42	+3.5	11	92	10 24	4 38	4 39
16	12 05	+1.1	11	93	10 27	4 54	4 56
21	12 28	-1.3	11	94	10 30	5 10	5 14
26	12 50	-3.7	11	94	10 33	5 26	5 32
31	13 14	-6.1	10	95	10 36	5 42	5 51

MARS

Day	RA	Dec.	Diam.	Phase	Transit	5° high 52°	5° high 56°
1	18 56	-25.7	11	85	18 16	20 54	20 07
6	19 10	-25.3	10	85	18 10	20 52	20 08
11	19 23	-24.7	10	85	18 04	20 52	20 11
16	19 37	-24.1	10	85	17 58	20 53	20 14
21	19 52	-23.4	9	85	17 53	20 54	20 17
26	20 06	-22.6	9	85	17 47	20 55	20 22
31	20 20	-21.7	9	85	17 42	20 57	20 26

SUNRISE AND SUNSET

	London		Bristol		Birmingham		Manchester		Newcastle		Glasgow		Belfast	
	0° 05′	51° 30′	2° 35′	51° 28′	1° 55′	52° 28′	2° 15′	53° 28′	1° 37′	54° 59′	4° 14′	55° 52′	5° 56′	54° 35′
	h m	h m	h m	h m	h m	h m	h m	h m	h m	h m	h m	h m	h m	h m
1	6 01	17 38	6 11	17 48	6 09	17 45	6 11	17 46	6 09	17 42	6 20	17 52	6 26	18 00
2	6 03	17 36	6 13	17 46	6 10	17 43	6 12	17 43	6 11	17 40	6 22	17 50	6 28	17 57
3	6 04	17 34	6 14	17 44	6 12	17 40	6 14	17 41	6 13	17 37	6 24	17 47	6 30	17 55
4	6 06	17 31	6 16	17 41	6 14	17 38	6 16	17 38	6 15	17 35	6 26	17 44	6 32	17 52
5	6 07	17 29	6 17	17 39	6 16	17 36	6 18	17 36	6 16	17 32	6 28	17 42	6 33	17 50
6	6 09	17 27	6 19	17 37	6 17	17 33	6 19	17 34	6 18	17 30	6 30	17 39	6 35	17 47
7	6 11	17 25	6 21	17 35	6 19	17 31	6 21	17 31	6 20	17 27	6 32	17 37	6 37	17 45
8	6 12	17 22	6 22	17 32	6 21	17 29	6 23	17 29	6 22	17 25	6 34	17 34	6 39	17 42
9	6 14	17 20	6 24	17 30	6 23	17 26	6 25	17 27	6 24	17 22	6 36	17 32	6 41	17 40
10	6 16	17 18	6 26	17 28	6 24	17 24	6 27	17 24	6 26	17 20	6 38	17 29	6 43	17 38
11	6 17	17 16	6 27	17 26	6 26	17 22	6 29	17 22	6 28	17 17	6 40	17 27	6 45	17 35
12	6 19	17 14	6 29	17 24	6 28	17 20	6 30	17 20	6 30	17 15	6 42	17 24	6 47	17 33
13	6 21	17 11	6 31	17 21	6 29	17 17	6 32	17 17	6 32	17 12	6 44	17 21	6 49	17 30
14	6 23	17 09	6 33	17 19	6 31	17 15	6 34	17 15	6 34	17 10	6 46	17 19	6 51	17 28
15	6 24	17 07	6 34	17 17	6 33	17 13	6 36	17 13	6 36	17 08	6 48	17 16	6 53	17 26
16	6 26	17 05	6 36	17 15	6 35	17 11	6 38	17 10	6 38	17 05	6 50	17 14	6 54	17 23
17	6 28	17 03	6 38	17 13	6 37	17 09	6 40	17 08	6 40	17 03	6 52	17 12	6 56	17 21
18	6 29	17 01	6 39	17 11	6 38	17 06	6 41	17 06	6 42	17 00	6 54	17 09	6 58	17 18
19	6 31	16 59	6 41	17 09	6 40	17 04	6 43	17 04	6 44	16 58	6 56	17 07	7 00	17 16
20	6 33	16 57	6 43	17 07	6 42	17 02	6 45	17 01	6 46	16 56	6 58	17 04	7 02	17 14
21	6 35	16 55	6 45	17 05	6 44	17 00	6 47	16 59	6 48	16 53	7 00	17 02	7 04	17 12
22	6 36	16 53	6 46	17 03	6 46	16 58	6 49	16 57	6 50	16 51	7 02	16 59	7 06	17 09
23	6 38	16 50	6 48	17 01	6 47	16 56	6 51	16 55	6 52	16 49	7 04	16 57	7 08	17 07
24	6 40	16 49	6 50	16 59	6 49	16 54	6 53	16 53	6 54	16 47	7 07	16 55	7 10	17 05
25	6 42	16 47	6 51	16 57	6 51	16 52	6 55	16 51	6 56	16 44	7 09	16 52	7 12	17 03
26	6 43	16 45	6 53	16 55	6 53	16 50	6 57	16 49	6 58	16 42	7 11	16 50	7 14	17 00
27	6 45	16 43	6 55	16 53	6 55	16 48	6 58	16 46	7 00	16 40	7 13	16 48	7 16	16 58
28	6 47	16 41	6 57	16 51	6 56	16 46	7 00	16 44	7 02	16 38	7 15	16 46	7 18	16 56
29	6 49	16 39	6 58	16 49	6 58	16 44	7 02	16 42	7 04	16 36	7 17	16 43	7 20	16 54
30	6 50	16 37	7 00	16 47	7 00	16 42	7 04	16 40	7 06	16 33	7 19	16 41	7 22	16 52
31	6 52	16 35	7 02	16 45	7 02	16 40	7 06	16 38	7 08	16 31	7 21	16 39	7 24	16 50

JUPITER

Day	RA	Dec.		Transit	5° high	
					52°	56°
	h m	°	′	h m	h m	h m
1	7 00.7	+22	32	6 21	22 50	22 32
11	7 04.4	+22	27	5 45	22 14	21 57
21	7 06.9	+22	24	5 08	21 38	21 20
31	7 08.0	+22	23	4 30	20 59	20 42

Diameters – equatorial 40″ polar 38″

SATURN

Day	RA	Dec.		Transit	5° high	
					52°	56°
	h m	°	′	h m	h m	h m
1	4 55.6	+20	46	4 16	20 55	20 40
11	4 54.9	+20	44	3 36	20 15	20 00
21	4 53.4	+20	41	2 55	19 35	19 20
31	4 51.3	+20	37	2 14	18 54	18 39

Diameters – equatorial 20″ polar 18″
Rings – major axis 45″ minor axis 20″

URANUS

Day	RA	Dec.		Transit	10° high	
					52°	56°
	h m	°	′	h m	h m	h m
1	21 35.6	-15	07	20 53	0 18	23 47
11	21 34.8	-15	11	20 13	23 33	23 07
21	21 34.3	-15	13	19 33	22 53	22 27
31	21 34.2	-15	13	18 54	22 14	21 47

Diameter 4″

NEPTUNE

Day	RA	Dec.		Transit	10° high	
					52°	56°
	h m	°	′	h m	h m	h m
1	20 33.7	-18	38	19 51	22 43	22 07
11	20 33.4	-18	39	19 12	22 04	21 28
21	20 33.4	-18	39	18 32	21 24	20 48
31	20 33.5	-18	39	17 53	20 45	20 09

Diameter 2″

 # November 2001

ELEVENTH MONTH, 30 DAYS. *Novem* (nine), ninth month of Roman pre-Julian calendar

1	*Thursday*	**All Saints Day**. Gary Player b. 1935	305
2	*Friday*	Daniel Boone b. 1734. Paavo Nurmi d. 1973	306
3	*Saturday*	Karl Baedeker b. 1801. Henri Matisse d. 1954	307
4	*Sunday*	**4th S. before Advent**. Yitzhak Rabin d. 1995	308
5	*Monday*	Gunpowder Plot 1605. Robert Maxwell d. 1991	*week 45 day* 309
6	*Tuesday*	Sir John Alcock b. 1892. Kate Greenaway d. 1901	310
7	*Wednesday*	Albert Camus b. 1913. Alexander Dubcek d. 1992	311
8	*Thursday*	Anton Rubinstein d. 1894. Lord Hunt d. 1999	312
9	*Friday*	Sir Giles Scott b. 1880. Charles de Gaulle d. 1970	313
10	*Saturday*	Richard Burton b. 1925. Leonid Brezhnev d. 1982	314
11	*Sunday*	**3rd S. before Advent**. Remembrance Sunday	315
12	*Monday*	Sinking of the Tirpitz 1944. Dolores Ibarruri d. 1989	*week 46 day* 316
13	*Tuesday*	St Augustine b. 354. Hon. George Grenville d. 1770	317
14	*Wednesday*	*Prince of Wales b. 1948*. Claude Monet b. 1840	318
15	*Thursday*	George Romney d. 1802. August Krogh b. 1874	319
16	*Friday*	Cardinal Pole d. 1558. Frank Bruno b. 1961	320
17	*Saturday*	Relief of Lucknow 1857. Martin Scorsese b. 1942	321
18	*Sunday*	**2nd S. before Advent**. Cab Calloway d. 1994	322
19	*Monday*	Charles I b. 1600. Thomas Shadwell d. 1692	*week 47 day* 323
20	*Tuesday*	*Queen's Wedding Day 1947*. Francisco Franco d. 1975	324
21	*Wednesday*	René Magritte b. 1898. Edward Bawden 1989	325
22	*Thursday*	Boris Becker b. 1967. Margaret Thatcher resigned 1990	326
23	*Friday*	Thomas Tallis d. 1585. Diana Quick b. 1946	327
24	*Saturday*	John Knox d. 1572. Baruch Spinoza b. 1632	328
25	*Sunday*	**Christ the King. S. next before Advent**	329
26	*Monday*	William Cowper b. 1731. Sojourner Truth d. 1883	*week 48 day* 330
27	*Tuesday*	Fanny Kemble b. 1809. Arthur Honegger d. 1955	331
28	*Wednesday*	Jean-Baptiste Lully b. 1632. Enid Blyton d. 1968	332
29	*Thursday*	Gaetano Donizetti b. 1798. Giacomo Puccini d. 1924	333
30	*Friday*	**St Andrew's Day**.	334

ASTRONOMICAL PHENOMENA

d	h	
2	16	Jupiter at stationary point
3	07	Venus in conjunction with Mercury. Venus 0.7 S.
3	22	Saturn in conjunction with Moon. Saturn 0.6° S.
6	08	Jupiter in conjunction with Moon. Jupiter 2° S.
14	03	Venus in conjunction with Venus 3° S.
14	09	Mercury in conjunction with Moon. Mercury 2° S.
21	21	Mars in conjunction with Moon. Mars 2° N.
22	06	Sun's longitude 240° ♐

MINIMA OF ALGOL

d	h	d	h	d	h
2	18.5	14	05.7	25	17.0
5	15.3	17	02.6	28	13.8
8	12.1	19	23.4		
11	08.9	22	20.2		

CONSTELLATIONS

The following constellations are near the meridian at

	d	h		d	h
October	1	24	November	15	21
October	16	23	December	1	20
November	1	22	December	16	19

Ursa Major (below the Pole), Cepheus, Cassiopeia, Andromeda, Pegasus, Pisces, Aquarius and Cetus

THE MOON

Phases, Apsides and Node	d	h	m
○ Full Moon	1	05	41
☽ Last Quarter	8	12	21
● New Moon	15	06	40
☾ First Quarter	22	23	21
○ Full Moon	30	20	49

Perigee (367,256 km)	11	17	24
Apogee (404,394 km)	23	15	45

Mean longitude of ascending node on November 1, 90°

THE SUN

s.d. 16′.1

Day	Right Ascension	Dec.	Equation of time	Rise		Transit	Set		Sidereal time	Transit of First Point of Aries
				52°	56°		52°	56°		
	h m s	° ′	m s	h m	h m	h m	h m	h m	h m s	h m s
1	14 25 00	14 23	+ 16 24	6 55	7 07	11 44	16 32	16 19	2 41 23	21 15 07
2	14 28 55	14 42	+ 16 25	6 57	7 09	11 44	16 30	16 17	2 45 20	21 11 11
3	14 32 51	15 01	+ 16 26	6 58	7 11	11 44	16 28	16 15	2 49 16	21 07 16
4	14 36 47	15 19	+ 16 26	7 00	7 13	11 44	16 26	16 13	2 53 13	21 03 20
5	14 40 45	15 38	+ 16 25	7 02	7 15	11 44	16 24	16 11	2 57 09	20 59 24
6	14 44 43	15 56	+ 16 23	7 04	7 18	11 44	16 23	16 09	3 01 06	20 55 28
7	14 48 42	16 14	+ 16 20	7 06	7 20	11 44	16 21	16 07	3 05 03	20 51 32
8	14 52 42	16 31	+ 16 17	7 07	7 22	11 44	16 19	16 05	3 08 59	20 47 36
9	14 56 43	16 49	+ 16 12	7 09	7 24	11 44	16 18	16 03	3 12 56	20 43 40
10	15 00 45	17 06	+ 16 07	7 11	7 26	11 44	16 16	16 01	3 16 52	20 39 44
11	15 04 48	17 23	+ 16 01	7 13	7 28	11 44	16 15	15 59	3 20 49	20 35 48
12	15 08 51	17 39	+ 15 54	7 15	7 30	11 44	16 13	15 57	3 24 45	20 31 52
13	15 12 56	17 55	+ 15 46	7 16	7 32	11 44	16 12	15 56	3 28 42	20 27 56
14	15 17 01	18 11	+ 15 37	7 18	7 34	11 44	16 10	15 54	3 32 38	20 24 01
15	15 21 07	18 27	+ 15 28	7 20	7 37	11 45	16 09	15 52	3 36 35	20 20 05
16	15 25 14	18 42	+ 15 17	7 22	7 39	11 45	16 07	15 50	3 40 32	20 16 09
17	15 29 22	18 57	+ 15 06	7 23	7 41	11 45	16 06	15 49	3 44 28	20 12 13
18	15 33 31	19 11	+ 14 54	7 25	7 43	11 45	16 05	15 47	3 48 25	20 08 17
19	15 37 40	19 25	+ 14 41	7 27	7 45	11 45	16 04	15 46	3 52 21	20 04 21
20	15 41 50	19 39	+ 14 27	7 28	7 47	11 46	16 02	15 44	3 56 18	20 00 25
21	15 46 01	19 53	+ 14 13	7 30	7 49	11 46	16 01	15 43	4 00 14	19 56 29
22	15 50 13	20 06	+ 13 58	7 32	7 51	11 46	16 00	15 41	4 04 11	19 52 33
23	15 54 26	20 19	+ 13 42	7 33	7 52	11 46	15 59	15 40	4 08 07	19 48 37
24	15 58 39	20 31	+ 13 25	7 35	7 54	11 47	15 58	15 39	4 12 04	19 44 41
25	16 02 53	20 43	+ 13 07	7 37	7 56	11 47	15 57	15 37	4 16 01	19 40 46
26	16 07 08	20 55	+ 12 49	7 38	7 58	11 47	15 56	15 36	4 19 57	19 36 50
27	16 11 24	21 06	+ 12 30	7 40	8 00	11 48	15 55	15 35	4 23 54	19 32 54
28	16 15 40	21 17	+ 12 10	7 41	8 02	11 48	15 54	15 34	4 27 50	19 28 58
29	16 19 57	21 27	+ 11 50	7 43	8 03	11 48	15 54	15 33	4 31 47	19 25 02
30	16 24 15	21 37	+ 11 29	7 44	8 05	11 49	15 53	15 32	4 35 43	19 21 06

DURATION OF TWILIGHT (in minutes)

Latitude	52°	56°	52°	56°	52°	56°	52°	56°
	1 November		11 November		21 November		30 November	
Civil	36	40	37	41	38	43	39	45
Nautical	75	84	78	87	80	90	82	93

THE NIGHT SKY

Mercury, magnitude -0.8, continues to be visible as a morning object for the first twelve days of the month, low above the E.S.E. horizon at the beginning of morning civil twilight. During this period Mercury and Venus are never more than 2° apart, and on the morning of the 3rd Venus passes only 0.7° south of Mercury. It is very unusual for Mercury and Venus to be so close to each other for such a long period (three weeks).

Venus, magnitude -3.9, continues to be visible as a brilliant object in the south-eastern sky in the early mornings before dawn. It is drawing towards the Sun, the period available for observation shortening noticeably during the month. Venus passes 4° north of Spica on the 2nd, while on the 14th the old crescent Moon passes 2° north of both Venus and Mercury.

Mars is still an evening object, magnitude +0.2, though by the end of the month it is no longer visible after 21h. The Moon, approaching First Quarter, passes 3° south of the planet on the evening of the 21st.

Jupiter, magnitude -2.5, is still a brilliant object in the night sky, visible from the late evening onwards. The gibbous Moon is in the vicinity of Jupiter on the 5th-6th.

Saturn, magnitude -0.3, is now visible for the greater part of the night. On the evening of the 3rd the gibbous Moon will be seen approaching the planet and then actually occulting it (see page 67).

Meteors. Although the Leonids do not usually produce a brilliant display there has been considerable activity during the last few years. Analysis of the observations thus obtained has led to predictions of considerable activity around November 17d 14h and again on November 18d 18h. From the British Isles the radiant will be below the horizon on both occasions but even so it might be worth while looking out after the radiant rises, say, after 22h 30m on the 17th and 18th. There will be no interference from moonlight.

THE MOON

Day	RA		Dec.	Hor. par.	Semi- diam.	Sun's co- long.	PA of Bright Limb	Phase	Age	Rise 52°	Rise 56°	Transit	Set 52°	Set 56°
	h	m	°	′	′	°	°	%	d	h m	h m	h m	h m	h m
1	2	20	+ 9.7	55.7	15.2	91	195	100	15.2	17 02	16 51	—	6 47	6 57
2	3	08	+14.2	56.2	15.3	103	94	99	16.2	17 24	17 08	0 24	8 02	8 16
3	3	59	+18.2	56.7	15.4	116	84	97	17.2	17 53	17 32	1 13	9 17	9 36
4	4	54	+21.4	57.2	15.6	128	85	92	18.2	18 30	18 05	2 05	10 30	10 54
5	5	51	+23.4	57.6	15.7	140	89	85	19.2	19 19	18 52	3 01	11 38	12 05
6	6	50	+24.2	58.1	15.8	152	94	77	20.2	20 21	19 55	3 58	12 36	13 03
7	7	50	+23.4	58.5	15.9	164	100	67	21.2	21 34	21 11	4 56	13 22	13 46
8	8	49	+21.3	58.9	16.0	176	105	56	22.2	22 54	22 37	5 54	13 58	14 17
9	9	47	+17.9	59.2	16.1	189	110	45	23.2	—	—	6 49	14 26	14 40
10	10	43	+13.3	59.5	16.2	201	114	33	24.2	0 18	0 05	7 43	14 49	14 58
11	11	37	+ 8.0	59.7	16.3	213	117	23	25.2	1 42	1 35	8 34	15 09	15 13
12	12	30	+ 2.3	59.7	16.3	225	119	14	26.2	3 05	3 04	9 25	15 28	15 27
13	13	23	− 3.6	59.6	16.2	237	120	7	27.2	4 29	4 33	10 15	15 47	15 41
14	14	16	− 9.3	59.3	16.1	249	123	2	28.2	5 52	6 02	11 06	16 08	15 57
15	15	10	−14.4	58.8	16.0	262	147	0	29.2	7 15	7 30	11 59	16 33	16 16
16	16	05	−18.6	58.2	15.9	274	268	1	0.7	8 35	8 56	12 53	17 03	16 42
17	17	02	−21.8	57.5	15.7	286	273	4	1.7	9 49	10 15	13 48	17 41	17 16
18	17	58	−23.6	56.7	15.5	298	270	9	2.7	10 54	11 22	14 42	18 29	18 01
19	18	55	−24.2	56.0	15.3	310	266	15	3.7	11 48	12 15	15 35	19 26	18 58
20	19	49	−23.5	55.4	15.1	323	261	23	4.7	12 29	12 54	16 26	20 29	20 05
21	20	42	−21.7	54.8	14.9	335	256	32	5.7	13 01	13 21	17 15	21 36	21 16
22	21	32	−19.0	54.5	14.8	347	252	41	6.7	13 26	13 42	18 00	22 44	22 29
23	22	19	−15.5	54.3	14.8	359	249	50	7.7	13 46	13 57	18 44	23 52	23 42
24	23	05	−11.4	54.2	14.8	11	246	60	8.7	14 03	14 10	19 26	—	—
25	23	49	− 6.9	54.4	14.8	24	244	69	9.7	14 18	14 22	20 07	1 00	0 54
26	0	33	− 2.0	54.7	14.9	36	243	77	10.7	14 33	14 33	20 48	2 08	2 07
27	1	18	+ 3.0	55.1	15.0	48	243	85	11.7	14 49	14 44	21 31	3 17	3 21
28	2	03	+ 7.9	55.7	15.2	60	244	91	12.7	15 06	14 57	22 16	4 29	4 37
29	2	51	+12.7	56.3	15.3	72	244	96	13.7	15 27	15 13	23 05	5 43	5 55
30	3	42	+17.0	56.9	15.5	84	243	99	14.7	15 53	15 34	23 57	6 59	7 17

MERCURY

Day	RA		Dec.	Diam.	Phase	Transit	5° high 52°	5° high 56°
	h	m	° ″	″	%	h m	h m	h m
1	13	19	- 6.0	6	66	10 38	5 42	5 51
3	13	28	- 6.9	6	72	10 40	5 50	5 59
5	13	39	- 8.0	6	78	10 42	5 58	6 09
7	13	50	- 9.2	6	83	10 45	6 08	6 20
9	14	01	-10.4	5	86	10 49	6 19	6 32
11	14	13	-11.6	5	89	10 53	6 30	6 44
13	14	25	-12.8	5	92	10 57	6 41	6 57
15	14	37	-14.0	5	94	11 01	6 53	7 10
17	14	49	-15.2	5	95	11 06	7 05	7 24
19	15	02	-16.3	5	97	11 10	7 17	7 38
21	15	14	-17.4	5	98	11 15	7 29	7 52
23	15	27	-18.4	5	98	11 20	7 41	8 06
25	15	40	-19.4	5	99	11 25	7 53	8 20
27	15	53	-20.3	5	99	11 30	8 06	8 34
29	16	06	-21.2	5	100	11 35	8 17	8 48
31	16	19	-21.9	5	100	11 41	8 29	9 02

VENUS

Day	RA		Dec.	Diam.	Phase	Transit	5° high 52°	5° high 56°
	h	m	° ′	″	%	h m	h m	h m
1	10	56	+8.2	11	90	10 17	4 08	4 05
6	11	19	+5.9	11	91	10 20	4 23	4 22
11	11	42	+3.5	11	92	10 24	4 38	4 39
16	12	05	+1.1	11	93	10 27	4 54	4 56
21	12	28	-1.3	11	94	10 30	5 10	5 14
26	12	50	-3.7	11	94	10 33	5 26	5 32
31	13	14	-6.1	10	95	10 36	5 42	5 51

MARS

Day	RA		Dec.	Diam.	Phase	Transit	5° high 52°	5° high 56°
1	20	23	-21.5	9	85	17 41	20 58	20 27
6	20	37	-20.6	9	85	17 35	21 00	20 32
11	20	52	-19.5	8	85	17 30	21 02	20 37
16	21	06	-18.4	8	86	17 25	21 05	20 41
21	21	20	-17.3	8	86	17 19	21 08	20 46
26	21	34	-16.0	8	86	17 13	21 11	20 51
31	21	48	-14.7	7	87	17 08	21 13	20 56

SUNRISE AND SUNSET

	London		Bristol		Birmingham		Manchester		Newcastle		Glasgow		Belfast	
	0°05′	51°30′	2°35′	51°28′	1°55′	52°28′	2°15′	53°28′	1°37′	54°59′	4°14′	55°52′	5°56′	54°35′
	h m	h m	h m	h m	h m	h m	h m	h m	h m	h m	h m	h m	h m	h m
1	6 54	16 33	7 04	16 43	7 04	16 38	7 08	16 36	7 10	16 29	7 23	16 37	7 26	16 48
2	6 56	16 31	7 06	16 42	7 06	16 36	7 10	16 34	7 12	16 27	7 26	16 35	7 28	16 46
3	6 57	16 30	7 07	16 40	7 07	16 34	7 12	16 33	7 14	16 25	7 28	16 32	7 30	16 44
4	6 59	16 28	7 09	16 38	7 09	16 32	7 14	16 31	7 16	16 23	7 30	16 30	7 32	16 42
5	7 01	16 26	7 11	16 36	7 11	16 31	7 16	16 29	7 18	16 21	7 32	16 28	7 34	16 40
6	7 03	16 25	7 13	16 35	7 13	16 29	7 18	16 27	7 20	16 19	7 34	16 26	7 36	16 38
7	7 04	16 23	7 14	16 33	7 15	16 27	7 19	16 25	7 22	16 17	7 36	16 24	7 38	16 36
8	7 06	16 21	7 16	16 31	7 17	16 26	7 21	16 23	7 24	16 15	7 38	16 22	7 40	16 34
9	7 08	16 20	7 18	16 30	7 18	16 24	7 23	16 22	7 26	16 13	7 40	16 20	7 42	16 32
10	7 10	16 18	7 20	16 28	7 20	16 22	7 25	16 20	7 28	16 12	7 42	16 19	7 44	16 30
11	7 11	16 17	7 21	16 27	7 22	16 21	7 27	16 18	7 30	16 10	7 45	16 17	7 46	16 29
12	7 13	16 15	7 23	16 25	7 24	16 19	7 29	16 17	7 32	16 08	7 47	16 15	7 48	16 27
13	7 15	16 14	7 25	16 24	7 26	16 18	7 31	16 15	7 34	16 06	7 49	16 13	7 50	16 25
14	7 17	16 12	7 27	16 22	7 27	16 16	7 33	16 14	7 36	16 05	7 51	16 11	7 52	16 24
15	7 18	16 11	7 28	16 21	7 29	16 15	7 35	16 12	7 38	16 03	7 53	16 10	7 54	16 22
16	7 20	16 10	7 30	16 20	7 31	16 13	7 36	16 11	7 40	16 02	7 55	16 08	7 56	16 21
17	7 22	16 08	7 32	16 18	7 33	16 12	7 38	16 09	7 42	16 00	7 57	16 06	7 58	16 19
18	7 23	16 07	7 33	16 17	7 35	16 11	7 40	16 08	7 44	15 58	7 59	16 05	8 00	16 18
19	7 25	16 06	7 35	16 16	7 36	16 09	7 42	16 06	7 46	15 57	8 01	16 03	8 02	16 16
20	7 27	16 05	7 37	16 15	7 38	16 08	7 44	16 05	7 48	15 56	8 03	16 02	8 03	16 15
21	7 28	16 04	7 38	16 14	7 40	16 07	7 45	16 04	7 50	15 54	8 05	16 00	8 05	16 13
22	7 30	16 02	7 40	16 13	7 41	16 06	7 47	16 03	7 52	15 53	8 07	15 59	8 07	16 12
23	7 32	16 01	7 41	16 12	7 43	16 05	7 49	16 01	7 54	15 52	8 09	15 57	8 09	16 11
24	7 33	16 00	7 43	16 11	7 45	16 04	7 51	16 00	7 55	15 50	8 11	15 56	8 11	16 10
25	7 35	16 00	7 45	16 10	7 46	16 03	7 52	15 59	7 57	15 49	8 13	15 55	8 13	16 09
26	7 36	15 59	7 46	16 09	7 48	16 02	7 54	15 58	7 59	15 48	8 14	15 54	8 14	16 07
27	7 38	15 58	7 48	16 08	7 49	16 01	7 56	15 57	8 01	15 47	8 16	15 53	8 16	16 06
28	7 39	15 57	7 49	16 07	7 51	16 00	7 57	15 56	8 02	15 46	8 18	15 52	8 18	16 05
29	7 41	15 56	7 51	16 06	7 53	15 59	7 59	15 56	8 04	15 45	8 20	15 51	8 19	16 04
30	7 42	15 55	7 52	16 06	7 54	15 58	8 00	15 55	8 06	15 44	8 21	15 50	8 21	16 04

JUPITER

Day	RA	Dec.		Transit	5° high	
					52°	56°
	h m	°	′	h m	h m	h m
1	7 08.0	+22	23	4 26	20 55	20 38
11	7 07.5	+22	25	3 46	20 15	19 58
21	7 05.6	+22	30	3 05	19 33	19 16
31	7 02.4	+22	36	2 22	18 50	18 33

Diameters – equatorial 44″ polar 41″

SATURN

Day	RA	Dec.		Transit	5° high	
					52°	56°
	h m	°	′	h m	h m	h m
1	4 51.1	+20	36	2 09	18 49	18 34
11	4 48.3	+20	31	1 27	18 08	17 53
21	4 45.2	+20	26	0 45	17 26	17 11
31	4 41.8	+20	20	0 02	16 44	16 29

Diameters – equatorial 20″ polar 19″
Rings – major axis 46″ minor axis 20″

URANUS

Day	RA	Dec.		Transit	10° high	
					52°	56°
	h m	°	′	h m	h m	h m
1	21 34.2	-15	13	18 50	22 10	21 43
11	21 34.4	-15	12	18 11	21 31	21 04
21	21 34.9	-15	09	17 32	20 53	20 26
31	21 35.7	-15	04	16 53	20 15	19 48

Diameter 4″

NEPTUNE

Day	RA	Dec.		Transit	10° high	
					52°	56°
	h m	°	′	h m	h m	h m
1	20 33.6	-18	39	17 49	20 41	20 05
11	20 34.0	-18	37	17 10	20 03	19 27
21	20 34.7	-18	35	16 32	19 24	18 49
31	20 35.5	-18	32	15 53	18 47	18 11

Diameter 2″

 # December 2001

TWELFTH MONTH, 31 DAYS. *Decem* (ten), tenth month of Roman pre-Julian calendar

1	*Saturday*	Woody Allen b. 1935. Stéphane Grappelli d. 1997	335
2	*Sunday*	**Advent Sunday.** St Paul's Cathedral opened 1697	336
3	*Monday*	Samuel Crompton b. 1753. John Flaxman d. 1826	*week 49 day* 337
4	*Tuesday*	John Cotton b. 1585. Benjamin Britten d. 1976	338
5	*Wednesday*	Gerardus Mercator d. 1594. Walt Disney b. 1901	339
6	*Thursday*	Finland declared independence 1917	340
7	*Friday*	St Ambrose d. 397. Lord Darnley b. 1545	341
8	*Saturday*	Jean Sibelius b. 1865. Bohuslav Martinu b. 1890	342
9	*Sunday*	**1st S. of Advent.** Dame Judi Dench b. 1934	343
10	*Monday*	Harold Alexander b. 1891. Luigi Pirandello d. 1936	*week 50 day* 344
11	*Tuesday*	James II fled from England 1688	345
12	*Wednesday*	Edvard Munch b. 1863. Robert Browning d. 1889	346
13	*Thursday*	Moses Maimonides d. 1204. Edward Blishen d. 1996	347
14	*Friday*	Alberto Morrocco b. 1917. Andrei Sakharov d. 1989	348
15	*Saturday*	Grigori Rasputin d. 1916. Edna O'Brien b. 1932	349
16	*Sunday*	**2nd S. of Advent.** Richard Bright d. 1858	350
17	*Monday*	Sir Humphrey Davy b. 1778. Suez Canal closes 1956	*week 51 day* 351
18	*Tuesday*	Joseph Grimaldi b. 1778. Paul Tortelier d. 1990	352
19	*Wednesday*	Sir Ralph Richardson b. 1902. Masaru Ibuka d. 1997	353
20	*Thursday*	John Croker b. 1780. John Steinbeck d. 1968	354
21	*Friday*	Winter begins. Josef Stalin b. 1879	355
22	*Saturday*	Jean Racine b. 1639. Beatrix Potter d. 1943	356
23	*Sunday*	**3rd S. of Advent.** Ronnie Scott d. 1996	357
24	*Monday*	Vasco da Gama d. 1524. George Crabbe b. 1754	*week 52 day* 358
25	*Tuesday*	**Christmas Day.** *Bank Holiday in the UK*	359
26	*Wednesday*	**St Stephen.** Boxing Day. *Bank Holiday in the UK*	360
27	*Thursday*	**St John.** Peter May d. 1994	361
28	*Friday*	**Holy Innocents.** Tay Bridge disaster 1879	362
29	*Saturday*	Harvey Smith b. 1938. Harold Macmillan d. 1986	363
30	*Sunday*	**1st S. of Christmas.** Sir Carol Reed b. 1906	364
31	*Monday*	John Wycliffe d. 1384. Henri Matisse b. 1869	*week 53 day* 365

ASTRONOMICAL PHENOMENA

d	h	
1	02	Saturn in conjunction with Moon. Saturn 0.5° S.
3	11	Jupiter in conjunction with Moon. Jupiter 2° S.
3	14	Saturn at opposition
4	22	Mercury in superior conjunction
7	04	Pluto in conjunction
14	06	Venus in conjunction with Moon. Venus 0.8° S.
14	21	Annular eclipse of Sun (see page 66)
15	08	Mercury in conjunction with Moon. Mercury 2° S.
21	00	Mars in conjunction with Moon. Mars 4° N.
21	19	Sun's longitude 270° ♋
28	08	Saturn in conjunction with Moon. Saturn 0.2° S.
30	14	Jupiter in conjunction with Moon. Jupiter 1° S.

MINIMA OF ALGOL

d	h	d	h	d	h
1	10.6	12	21.9	24	09.2
4	07.5	15	18.7	27	06.0
7	04.3	18	15.6	30	02.8
10	01.1	21	12.4		

CONSTELLATIONS

The following constellations are near the meridian at

	d	h		d	h
November	1	24	December	16	21
November	15	23	January	1	20
December	1	22	January	16	19

Ursa Major (below the Pole), Ursa Minor (below the Pole), Cassiopeia, Andromeda, Perseus, Triangulum, Aries, Taurus, Cetus and Eridanus

THE MOON

Phases, Apsides and Node	d	h	m
☾ Last Quarter	7	19	52
● New Moon	14	20	47
☽ First Quarter	22	20	56
○ Full Moon	30	10	40
Perigee (370,117 km)	6	22	42
Apogee (404,633 km)	21	13	01

Mean longitude of ascending node on December 1, 88°

THE SUN   s.d. 16′.1

Day	Right Ascension			Dec.		Equation of time		Rise		Transit		Set				Sidereal time			Transit of First Point of Aries		
								52°	56°			52°		56°							
	h	m	s	°	′	m	s	h m	h m	h	m	h	m	h	m	h	m	s	h	m	s
1	16	28	33	21	47	+11	07	7 46	8 07	11	49	15	52	15	31	4	39	40	19	17	10
2	16	32	52	21	56	+10	44	7 47	8 08	11	49	15	52	15	30	4	43	36	19	13	14
3	16	37	12	22	05	+10	21	7 48	8 10	11	50	15	51	15	29	4	47	33	19	09	18
4	16	41	32	22	13	+ 9	57	7 50	8 12	11	50	15	50	15	29	4	51	30	19	05	22
5	16	45	53	22	21	+ 9	33	7 51	8 13	11	51	15	50	15	28	4	55	26	19	01	26
6	16	50	14	22	28	+ 9	08	7 52	8 15	11	51	15	50	15	27	4	59	23	18	57	30
7	16	54	36	22	35	+ 8	43	7 54	8 16	11	52	15	49	15	27	5	03	19	18	53	35
8	16	58	59	22	42	+ 8	17	7 55	8 17	11	52	15	49	15	26	5	07	16	18	49	39
9	17	03	22	22	48	+ 7	50	7 56	8 19	11	52	15	49	15	26	5	11	12	18	45	43
10	17	07	45	22	54	+ 7	24	7 57	8 20	11	53	15	49	15	26	5	15	09	18	41	47
11	17	12	09	22	59	+ 6	56	7 58	8 21	11	53	15	48	15	25	5	19	05	18	37	51
12	17	16	34	23	04	+ 6	28	7 59	8 22	11	54	15	48	15	25	5	23	02	18	33	55
13	17	20	58	23	08	+ 6	00	8 00	8 23	11	54	15	48	15	25	5	26	59	18	29	59
14	17	25	23	23	12	+ 5	32	8 01	8 24	11	55	15	48	15	25	5	30	55	18	26	03
15	17	29	49	23	15	+ 5	03	8 02	8 25	11	55	15	49	15	25	5	34	52	18	22	07
16	17	34	14	23	18	+ 4	34	8 03	8 26	11	56	15	49	15	25	5	38	48	18	18	11
17	17	38	40	23	21	+ 4	05	8 03	8 27	11	56	15	49	15	25	5	42	45	18	14	15
18	17	43	06	23	23	+ 3	35	8 04	8 28	11	57	15	49	15	25	5	46	41	18	10	20
19	17	47	32	23	24	+ 3	06	8 05	8 28	11	57	15	50	15	26	5	50	38	18	06	24
20	17	51	59	23	26	+ 2	36	8 05	8 29	11	58	15	50	15	26	5	54	34	18	02	28
21	17	56	25	23	26	+ 2	06	8 06	8 30	11	58	15	50	15	27	5	58	31	17	58	32
22	18	00	51	23	26	+ 1	36	8 06	8 30	11	59	15	51	15	27	6	02	28	17	54	36
23	18	05	18	23	26	+ 1	06	8 07	8 31	11	59	15	52	15	28	6	06	24	17	50	40
24	18	09	44	23	25	+ 0	37	8 07	8 31	12	00	15	52	15	28	6	10	21	17	46	44
25	18	14	10	23	24	+ 0	07	8 08	8 31	12	00	15	53	15	29	6	14	17	17	42	48
26	18	18	37	23	22	− 0	23	8 08	8 31	12	01	15	54	15	30	6	18	14	17	38	52
27	18	23	03	23	20	− 0	52	8 08	8 32	12	01	15	54	15	31	6	22	10	17	34	56
28	18	27	29	23	17	− 1	22	8 08	8 32	12	02	15	55	15	32	6	26	07	17	31	00
29	18	31	55	23	14	− 1	51	8 08	8 32	12	02	15	56	15	33	6	30	03	17	27	05
30	18	36	20	23	11	− 2	20	8 08	8 32	12	03	15	57	15	34	6	34	00	17	23	09
31	18	40	45	23	06	− 2	49	8 08	8 31	12	03	15	58	15	35	6	37	57	17	19	13

DURATION OF TWILIGHT (in minutes)

Latitude	52°	56°	52°	56°	52°	56°	52°	56°
	1 December		11 December		21 December		31 December	
Civil	40	45	41	47	41	47	41	47
Nautical	82	93	84	96	85	97	84	96
Astronomical	123	138	125	141	126	142	125	141

THE NIGHT SKY

Mercury, not observable in December.

Venus, magnitude -3.9, is a morning object for the first two weeks of the month, visible for a short while before dawn, low above the south-eastern horizon.

Mars, magnitude +0.6, continues to be visible low in the south-western quadrant of the sky in the evenings. The Moon, just before First Quarter, passes 5° south of Mars on the night of the 20th.

Jupiter, magnitude -2.7, is moving towards opposition early next month and is therefore visible for the greater part of the night. By the end of the month it is visible low above the east-north-eastern horizon as soon as it gets dark. On the morning of the 3rd the gibbous Moon passes just south of the planet, while on the 30th, the Full Moon passes about 1° north of the planet.

Saturn, magnitude -0.4, reaches opposition on the 3rd and thus is visible throughout the hours of darkness. Saturn is moving slowly retrograde in Taurus, and passes 4° north of Aldebaran on the 12th, when it is nearly 2 magnitudes brighter than the star. Shortly after midnight on the 1st the Full Moon again occults the planet (see page 67). The Moon is again near Saturn on the morning of the 28th, though on this occasion no occultation is visible from the British Isles as the Moon will be seen to pass just below the planet.

Meteors. The maximum of the well-known Geminid meteor shower occurs on the night of the 13th-14th. Conditions are favourable since there will be no interference from moonlight.

THE MOON

Day	RA	Dec.	Hor. par.	Semi-diam.	Sun's co-long.	PA of Bright Limb	Phase	Age	Rise 52°	Rise 56°	Transit	Set 52°	Set 56°
	h m	°	′	′	°	° ′	%	d	h m	h m	h m	h m	h m
1	4 36	+20.5	57.5	15.7	96	125	100	15.7	16 27	16 04	—	8 15	8 38
2	5 34	+23.0	58.1	15.8	108	89	98	16.7	17 13	16 46	0 52	9 27	9 54
3	6 34	+24.2	58.5	15.9	121	91	95	17.7	18 12	17 44	1 51	10 31	10 58
4	7 35	+23.9	58.8	16.0	133	97	88	18.7	19 23	18 58	2 50	11 22	11 48
5	8 36	+22.0	59.1	16.1	145	102	80	19.7	20 42	20 22	3 49	12 02	12 23
6	9 35	+18.8	59.2	16.1	157	107	70	20.7	22 05	21 51	4 46	12 32	12 48
7	10 31	+14.5	59.2	16.1	169	111	60	21.7	23 28	23 19	5 40	12 56	13 06
8	11 25	+ 9.5	59.2	16.1	181	113	48	22.7	—	—	6 31	13 16	13 22
9	12 17	+ 3.9	59.1	16.1	194	115	37	23.7	0 50	0 47	7 20	13 35	13 35
10	13 08	− 1.9	58.9	16.0	206	115	26	24.7	2 11	2 13	8 09	13 53	13 49
11	14 00	− 7.5	58.6	16.0	218	114	17	25.7	3 32	3 39	8 59	14 12	14 03
12	14 52	−12.7	58.3	15.9	230	112	10	26.7	4 52	5 05	9 49	14 34	14 20
13	15 45	−17.2	57.9	15.8	242	109	4	27.7	6 12	6 31	10 41	15 01	14 42
14	16 41	−20.7	57.4	15.6	254	105	1	28.7	7 29	7 52	11 35	15 35	15 11
15	17 37	−23.1	56.8	15.5	267	264	0	0.1	8 38	9 05	12 29	16 18	15 51
16	18 33	−24.2	56.2	15.3	279	271	1	1.1	9 37	10 05	13 24	17 11	16 43
17	19 29	−24.0	55.7	15.2	291	266	5	2.1	10 24	10 51	14 16	18 12	17 46
18	20 23	−22.6	55.1	15.0	303	261	10	3.1	11 01	11 23	15 06	19 18	18 57
19	21 14	−20.1	54.7	14.9	315	256	17	4.1	11 28	11 46	15 54	20 27	20 10
20	22 03	−16.8	54.4	14.8	328	252	24	5.1	11 50	12 04	16 38	21 36	21 23
21	22 49	−12.9	54.2	14.8	340	249	33	6.1	12 08	12 18	17 21	22 43	22 36
22	23 34	− 8.5	54.2	14.8	352	247	42	7.1	12 24	12 29	18 02	23 51	23 48
23	0 18	− 3.8	54.4	14.8	4	246	51	8.1	12 39	12 40	18 42	—	—
24	1 02	+ 1.1	54.7	14.9	16	246	61	9.1	12 54	12 51	19 24	0 59	1 00
25	1 46	+ 6.0	55.2	15.0	28	247	70	10.1	13 10	13 03	20 07	2 08	2 14
26	2 33	+10.9	55.9	15.2	40	249	79	11.1	13 29	13 17	20 53	3 20	3 30
27	3 22	+15.3	56.6	15.4	53	252	86	12.1	13 52	13 35	21 43	4 34	4 50
28	4 14	+19.2	57.4	15.6	65	257	93	13.1	14 22	14 00	22 38	5 51	6 12
29	5 11	+22.2	58.2	15.9	77	263	97	14.1	15 02	14 37	23 36	7 06	7 32
30	6 11	+23.9	58.9	16.0	89	276	100	15.1	15 56	15 29	—	8 16	8 44
31	7 13	+24.1	59.5	16.5	101	84	100	16.1	17 05	16 39	0 37	9 14	9 41

MERCURY

Day	RA	Dec.	Diam.	Phase	Transit	5° high 52°	5° high 56°
	h m	°	″	%	h m	h m	h m
1	16 19	-21.9	5	100	11 41	8 29	9 02
3	16 32	-22.7	5	100	11 46	8 40	9 15
5	16 46	-23.3	5	100	11 52	8 52	9 28
7	16 59	-23.8	5	100	11 57	9 02	9 41
9	17 13	-24.3	5	100	12 03	14 53	14 13
11	17 26	-24.7	5	100	12 09	14 56	14 13
13	17 40	-25.0	5	99	12 15	14 59	14 15
15	17 54	-25.2	5	99	12 21	15 03	14 18
17	18 08	-25.3	5	98	12 27	15 08	14 23
19	18 22	-25.4	5	98	12 33	15 15	14 29
21	18 36	-25.3	5	97	12 39	15 22	14 37
23	18 50	-25.1	5	96	12 45	15 30	14 47
25	19 04	-24.8	5	94	12 52	15 39	14 57
27	19 18	-24.4	5	93	12 58	15 49	15 09
29	19 32	-24.0	5	91	13 03	16 00	15 22
31	19 45	-23.4	5	88	13 09	16 11	15 35

VENUS

Day	RA	Dec.	Diam.	Phase	Transit	5° high 52°	5° high 56°
	h m	°	″	%	h m	h m	h m
1	15 44	-19.0	10	98	11 05	7 30	7 56
6	16 10	-20.4	10	99	11 12	7 48	8 16
11	16 37	-21.6	10	99	11 18	8 04	8 35
16	17 04	-22.6	10	99	11 26	8 19	8 53
21	17 31	-23.2	10	100	11 33	8 32	9 08
26	17 58	-23.6	10	100	11 41	8 43	9 20
31	18 26	-23.7	10	100	11 49	8 51	9 29

MARS

Day	RA	Dec.	Diam.	Phase	Transit	5° high 52°	5° high 56°
1	21 48	-14.7	7	87	17 08	21 13	20 56
6	22 02	-13.4	7	87	17 02	21 16	21 00
11	22 16	-12.0	7	87	16 56	21 19	21 04
16	22 30	-10.6	7	88	16 50	21 21	21 08
21	22 43	-9.1	7	88	16 44	21 23	21 12
26	22 57	-7.6	6	88	16 38	21 26	21 16
31	23 10	-6.1	6	89	16 31	21 28	21 19

SUNRISE AND SUNSET

	London		Bristol		Birmingham		Manchester		Newcastle		Glasgow		Belfast	
	0°05′	51°30′	2°35′	51°28′	1°55′	52°28′	2°15′	53°28′	1°37′	54°59′	4°14′	55°52′	5°56′	54°35′
	h m	h m	h m	h m	h m	h m	h m	h m	h m	h m	h m	h m	h m	h m
1	7 44	15 55	7 53	16 05	7 55	15 58	8 02	15 54	8 07	15 43	8 23	15 49	8 22	16 03
2	7 45	15 54	7 55	16 04	7 57	15 57	8 03	15 53	8 09	15 43	8 25	15 48	8 24	16 02
3	7 46	15 54	7 56	16 04	7 58	15 56	8 05	15 53	8 11	15 42	8 26	15 47	8 26	16 01
4	7 48	15 53	7 58	16 03	8 00	15 56	8 06	15 52	8 12	15 41	8 28	15 46	8 27	16 01
5	7 49	15 53	7 59	16 03	8 01	15 55	8 07	15 52	8 13	15 40	8 29	15 46	8 28	16 00
6	7 50	15 52	8 00	16 03	8 02	15 55	8 09	15 51	8 15	15 40	8 31	15 45	8 30	16 00
7	7 51	15 52	8 01	16 02	8 04	15 55	8 10	15 51	8 16	15 39	8 32	15 45	8 31	15 59
8	7 53	15 52	8 02	16 02	8 05	15 54	8 11	15 50	8 17	15 39	8 33	15 44	8 32	15 59
9	7 54	15 52	8 04	16 02	8 06	15 54	8 13	15 50	8 19	15 39	8 35	15 44	8 34	15 58
10	7 55	15 51	8 05	16 02	8 07	15 54	8 14	15 50	8 20	15 38	8 36	15 43	8 35	15 58
11	7 56	15 51	8 06	16 01	8 08	15 54	8 15	15 50	8 21	15 38	8 37	15 43	8 36	15 58
12	7 57	15 51	8 07	16 01	8 09	15 54	8 16	15 50	8 22	15 38	8 38	15 43	8 37	15 58
13	7 58	15 51	8 08	16 01	8 10	15 54	8 17	15 49	8 23	15 38	8 39	15 43	8 38	15 58
14	7 59	15 51	8 09	16 01	8 11	15 54	8 18	15 50	8 24	15 38	8 40	15 43	8 39	15 58
15	8 00	15 51	8 09	16 02	8 12	15 54	8 19	15 50	8 25	15 38	8 41	15 43	8 40	15 58
16	8 00	15 52	8 10	16 02	8 13	15 54	8 20	15 50	8 26	15 38	8 42	15 43	8 41	15 58
17	8 01	15 52	8 11	16 02	8 13	15 54	8 20	15 50	8 27	15 38	8 43	15 43	8 42	15 58
18	8 02	15 52	8 12	16 02	8 14	15 54	8 21	15 50	8 28	15 39	8 44	15 43	8 42	15 58
19	8 02	15 52	8 12	16 03	8 15	15 55	8 22	15 51	8 28	15 39	8 45	15 44	8 43	15 59
20	8 03	15 53	8 13	16 03	8 15	15 55	8 22	15 51	8 29	15 39	8 45	15 44	8 44	15 59
21	8 04	15 53	8 13	16 04	8 16	15 56	8 23	15 51	8 29	15 40	8 46	15 44	8 44	16 00
22	8 04	15 54	8 14	16 04	8 16	15 56	8 23	15 52	8 30	15 40	8 46	15 45	8 45	16 00
23	8 05	15 54	8 14	16 05	8 17	15 57	8 24	15 52	8 30	15 41	8 47	15 46	8 45	16 01
24	8 05	15 55	8 15	16 05	8 17	15 57	8 24	15 53	8 31	15 42	8 47	15 46	8 46	16 01
25	8 05	15 56	8 15	16 06	8 18	15 58	8 24	15 54	8 31	15 42	8 47	15 47	8 46	16 02
26	8 06	15 56	8 15	16 07	8 18	15 59	8 25	15 55	8 31	15 43	8 47	15 48	8 46	16 03
27	8 06	15 57	8 16	16 07	8 18	16 00	8 25	15 55	8 31	15 44	8 48	15 49	8 46	16 04
28	8 06	15 58	8 16	16 08	8 18	16 00	8 25	15 56	8 32	15 45	8 48	15 50	8 46	16 04
29	8 06	15 59	8 16	16 09	8 18	16 01	8 25	15 57	8 32	15 46	8 48	15 51	8 46	16 05
30	8 06	16 00	8 16	16 10	8 18	16 02	8 25	15 58	8 32	15 47	8 48	15 52	8 46	16 06
31	8 06	16 01	8 16	16 11	8 18	16 03	8 25	15 59	8 31	15 48	8 47	15 53	8 46	16 07

JUPITER

Day	RA	Dec.		Transit	5° high	
					52°	56°
	h m	°	′	h m	h m	h m
1	7 02.4	+22	36	2 22	18 50	18 33
11	6 58.0	+22	43	1 39	18 06	17 48
21	6 52.7	+22	52	0 54	17 20	17 02
31	6 47.0	+23	00	0 09	16 34	16 16

Diameters – equatorial 47″ polar 44″

SATURN

Day	RA	Dec.		Transit	5° high	
					52°	56°
	h m	°	′	h m	h m	h m
1	4 41.8	+20	20	0 02	7 16	7 31
11	4 38.3	+20	14	23 15	6 33	6 47
21	4 35.0	+20	09	22 32	5 50	6 04
31	4 32.0	+20	04	21 50	5 07	5 21

Diameters – equatorial 20″ polar 19″
Rings – major axis 46″ minor axis 20″

URANUS

Day	RA	Dec.		Transit	10° high	
					52°	56°
	h m	°	′	h m	h m	h m
1	21 35.7	-15	04	16 53	20 15	19 48
11	21 36.9	-14	58	16 15	19 37	19 11
21	21 38.3	-14	51	15 37	19 00	18 35
31	21 40.0	-14	42	15 00	18 24	17 58

Diameter 4″

NEPTUNE

Day	RA	Dec.		Transit	10° high	
					52°	56°
	h m	°	′	h m	h m	h m
1	20 35.5	-18	32	15 53	18 47	18 11
11	20 36.6	-18	28	15 15	18 09	17 33
21	20 37.8	-18	24	14 37	17 31	16 56
31	20 39.1	-18	19	13 59	16 54	16 19

Diameter 2″

RISING AND SETTING TIMES

TABLE 1. SEMI-DIURNAL ARCS (HOUR ANGLES AT RISING/SETTING)

Dec. Latitude	0° h m	10° h m	20° h m	30° h m	40° h m	45° h m	50° h m	52° h m	54° h m	56° h m	58° h m	60° h m	Dec.
0°	6 00	6 00	6 00	6 00	6 00	6 00	6 00	6 00	6 00	6 00	6 00	6 00	0°
1°	6 00	6 01	6 01	6 02	6 03	6 04	6 05	6 05	6 06	6 06	6 06	6 07	1°
2°	6 00	6 01	6 03	6 05	6 07	6 08	6 10	6 10	6 11	6 12	6 13	6 14	2°
3°	6 00	6 02	6 04	6 07	6 10	6 12	6 14	6 15	6 17	6 18	6 19	6 21	3°
4°	6 00	6 03	6 06	6 09	6 13	6 16	6 19	6 21	6 22	6 24	6 26	6 28	4°
5°	6 00	6 04	6 07	6 12	6 17	6 20	6 24	6 26	6 28	6 30	6 32	6 35	5°
6°	6 00	6 04	6 09	6 14	6 20	6 24	6 29	6 31	6 33	6 36	6 39	6 42	6°
7°	6 00	6 05	6 10	6 16	6 24	6 28	6 34	6 36	6 39	6 42	6 45	6 49	7°
8°	6 00	6 06	6 12	6 19	6 27	6 32	6 39	6 41	6 45	6 48	6 52	6 56	8°
9°	6 00	6 06	6 13	6 21	6 31	6 36	6 44	6 47	6 50	6 54	6 59	7 04	9°
10°	6 00	6 07	6 15	6 23	6 34	6 41	6 49	6 52	6 56	7 01	7 06	7 11	10°
11°	6 00	6 08	6 16	6 26	6 38	6 45	6 54	6 58	7 02	7 07	7 12	7 19	11°
12°	6 00	6 09	6 18	6 28	6 41	6 49	6 59	7 03	7 08	7 13	7 20	7 26	12°
13°	6 00	6 09	6 19	6 31	6 45	6 53	7 04	7 09	7 14	7 20	7 27	7 34	13°
14°	6 00	6 10	6 21	6 33	6 48	6 58	7 09	7 14	7 20	7 27	7 34	7 42	14°
15°	6 00	6 11	6 22	6 36	6 52	7 02	7 14	7 20	7 27	7 34	7 42	7 51	15°
16°	6 00	6 12	6 24	6 38	6 56	7 07	7 20	7 26	7 33	7 41	7 49	7 59	16°
17°	6 00	6 12	6 26	6 41	6 59	7 11	7 25	7 32	7 40	7 48	7 57	8 08	17°
18°	6 00	6 13	6 27	6 43	7 03	7 16	7 31	7 38	7 46	7 55	8 05	8 17	18°
19°	6 00	6 14	6 29	6 46	7 07	7 21	7 37	7 45	7 53	8 03	8 14	8 26	19°
20°	6 00	6 15	6 30	6 49	7 11	7 25	7 43	7 51	8 00	8 11	8 22	8 36	20°
21°	6 00	6 16	6 32	6 51	7 15	7 30	7 49	7 58	8 08	8 19	8 32	8 47	21°
22°	6 00	6 16	6 34	6 54	7 19	7 35	7 55	8 05	8 15	8 27	8 41	8 58	22°
23°	6 00	6 17	6 36	6 57	7 23	7 40	8 02	8 12	8 23	8 36	8 51	9 09	23°
24°	6 00	6 18	6 37	7 00	7 28	7 46	8 08	8 19	8 31	8 45	9 02	9 22	24°
25°	6 00	6 19	6 39	7 02	7 32	7 51	8 15	8 27	8 40	8 55	9 13	9 35	25°
26°	6 00	6 20	6 41	7 05	7 37	7 57	8 22	8 35	8 49	9 05	9 25	9 51	26°
27°	6 00	6 21	6 43	7 08	7 41	8 03	8 30	8 43	8 58	9 16	9 39	10 08	27°
28°	6 00	6 22	6 45	7 12	7 46	8 08	8 37	8 52	9 08	9 28	9 53	10 28	28°
29°	6 00	6 22	6 47	7 15	7 51	8 15	8 45	9 01	9 19	9 41	10 10	10 55	29°
30°	6 00	6 23	6 49	7 18	7 56	8 21	8 54	9 11	9 30	9 55	10 30	12 00	30°
35°	6 00	6 28	6 59	7 35	8 24	8 58	9 46	10 15	10 58	12 00	12 00	12 00	35°
40°	6 00	6 34	7 11	7 56	8 59	9 48	12 00	12 00	12 00	12 00	12 00	12 00	40°
45°	6 00	6 41	7 25	8 21	9 48	12 00	12 00	12 00	12 00	12 00	12 00	12 00	45°
50°	6 00	6 49	7 43	8 54	12 00	12 00	12 00	12 00	12 00	12 00	12 00	12 00	50°
55°	6 00	6 58	8 05	9 42	12 00	12 00	12 00	12 00	12 00	12 00	12 00	12 00	55°
60°	6 00	7 11	8 36	12 00	12 00	12 00	12 00	12 00	12 00	12 00	12 00	12 00	60°
65°	6 00	7 29	9 25	12 00	12 00	12 00	12 00	12 00	12 00	12 00	12 00	12 00	65°
70°	6 00	7 56	12 00	12 00	12 00	12 00	12 00	12 00	12 00	12 00	12 00	12 00	70°
75°	6 00	8 45	12 00	12 00	12 00	12 00	12 00	12 00	12 00	12 00	12 00	12 00	75°
80°	6 00	12 00	12 00	12 00	12 00	12 00	12 00	12 00	12 00	12 00	12 00	12 00	80°

TABLE 2. CORRECTION FOR REFRACTION AND SEMI-DIAMETER

	m	m	m	m	m	m	m	m	m	m	m	m	
0°	3	3	4	4	4	5	5	5	6	6	6	7	0°
10°	3	3	4	4	4	5	5	6	6	6	7	7	10°
20°	4	4	4	4	5	5	6	7	7	8	8	9	20°
25°	4	4	4	4	5	6	7	8	8	9	11	13	25°
30°	4	4	4	5	6	7	8	9	11	14	21	—	30°

NB: Regarding Table 1. If latitude and declination are of the same sign, take out the respondent directly. If they are of opposite signs, subtract the respondent from 12h.
Example:

Lat.	Dec.	Semi-diurnal arc
+ 52°	+ 20°	7h 51m
+ 52°	− 20°	4h 09m

SUNRISE AND SUNSET

The local mean time of sunrise or sunset may be found by obtaining the hour angle from Table 1 and applying it to the time of transit. The hour angle is negative for sunrise and positive for sunset. A small correction to the hour angle, which always has the effect of increasing it numerically, is necessary to allow for the Sun's semi-diameter (16′) and for refraction (34′); it is obtained from Table 2. The resulting local mean time may be converted into the standard time of the country by taking the difference between the longitude of the standard meridian of the country and that of the place, adding it to the local mean time if the place is west of the standard meridian, and subtracting it if the place is east.

Example – Required the New Zealand Mean Time (12h fast on GMT) of sunset on May 23 at Auckland, latitude 36° 50′ S. (or minus), longitude 11h 39m E. Taking the declination as $+20°.6$ (page 33), we find:

	h m
Tabular entry for Lat. 30° and Dec. 20°, opposite signs	+ 5 11
Proportional part for 6° 50′ of Lat.	− 15
Proportional part for 0°.6 of Dec.	− 2
Correction (Table 2)	+ 4
Hour angle	4 58
Sun transits (page 33)	11 57
Longitudinal correction	+ 21
New Zealand Mean Time	17 16

MOONRISE AND MOONSET

It is possible to calculate the times of moonrise and moonset using Table 1, though the method is more complicated because the apparent motion of the Moon is much more rapid and also more variable than that of the Sun.

The parallax of the Moon, about 57′, is near to the sum of the semi-diameter and refraction but has the opposite effect on these times. It is thus convenient to neglect all three quantities in the method outlined below.

TABLE 3. LONGITUDE CORRECTION

X A	40m	45m	50m	55m	60m	65m	70m
h	m	m	m	m	m	m	m
1	2	2	2	2	3	3	3
2	3	4	4	5	5	5	6
3	5	6	6	7	8	8	9
4	7	8	8	9	10	11	12
5	8	9	10	11	13	14	15
6	10	11	13	14	15	16	18
7	12	13	15	16	18	19	20
8	13	15	17	18	20	22	23
9	15	17	19	21	23	24	26
10	17	19	21	23	25	27	29
11	18	21	23	25	28	30	32
12	20	23	25	28	30	33	35
13	22	24	27	30	33	35	38
14	23	26	29	32	35	38	41
15	25	28	31	34	38	41	44
16	27	30	33	37	40	43	47
17	28	32	35	39	43	46	50
18	30	34	38	41	45	49	53
19	32	36	40	44	48	51	55
20	33	38	42	46	50	54	58
21	35	39	44	48	53	57	61
22	37	41	46	50	55	60	64
23	38	43	48	53	58	62	67
24	40	45	50	55	60	65	70

Notation

φ	= latitude of observer
λ	= longitude of observer (measured positively towards the west)
T_{-1}	= time of transit of Moon on previous day
T_0	= time of transit of Moon on day in question
T_1	= time of transit of Moon on following day
δ_0	= approximate declination of Moon
δ_R	= declination of Moon at moonrise
δ_S	= declination of Moon at moonset
h_0	= approximate hour angle of Moon
h_R	= hour angle of Moon at moonrise
h_S	= hour angle of Moon at moonset
t_R	= time of moonrise
t_S	= time of moonset

Method

1. With arguments φ, δ_0 enter Table 1 on page 64 to determine h_0 where h_0 is negative for moonrise and positive for moonset.

2. Form approximate times from
$$t_R = T_0 + \lambda + h_0$$
$$t_S = T_0 + \lambda + h_0$$

3. Determine δ_R, δ_S for times t_R, t_S respectively.

4. Re-enter Table 1 on page 64 with
(a) arguments φ, δ_R to determine h_R
(b) arguments φ, δ_S to determine h_S

5. Form $t_R = T_0 + \lambda + h_R + AX$
$$t_S = T_0 + \lambda + h_S + AX$$

where $A = (\lambda + h)$

and $X = (T_0 - T_{-1})$ if $(\lambda + h)$ is negative
$X = (T_1 - T_0)$ if $(\lambda + h)$ is positive

AX is the respondent in Table 3.

Example – To find the times of moonrise and moonset at Vancouver ($\varphi = +49°$, $\lambda = +8h\ 12m$) on 2001 March 22. The starting data (page 26) are:

T_{-1} = 9h 38m
T_0 = 10h 23m
T_1 = 11h 07m
δ_0 = $-14°$

1. h_0 = 4h 53m
2. Approximate values
t_R = 22d 10h 25m + 8h 12m + ($-4h$ 53m)
   = 22d 13h 42m
t_S = 22d 10h 25m + 8h 12m + ($+4h$ 53m)
   = 22d 23h 28m
3. δ_R = $-13°.7$
δ_S = $-12°.2$
4. h_R = $-4h$ 56m
h_S = $+5h$ 02m
5. t_R = 22d 10h 23m + 8h 12m + ($-4h$ 56m) + 7m
   = 22d 13h 46m
t_S = 22d 10h 23m + 8h 12m + ($+5h$ 02m) + 24m
   = 23d 00h 01m

To get the LMT of the phenomenon the longitude is subtracted from the GMT thus:
Moonrise = 22d 13h 46m − 8h 12m = 22d 05h 34m
Moonset = 23d 00h 01m − 8h 12m = 22d 15h 49m

ECLIPSES AND OCCULTATIONS 2001

ECLIPSES

There will be four eclipses in 2001, two of the Sun and two of the Moon. (Penumbral lunar eclipses are not mentioned in this section as they are too difficult to observe.)

1. A total eclipse of the Moon on January 9 is visible from Australia, the western Pacific Ocean, Indonesia, the Philippines, Asia, the Indian Ocean, Africa, Europe (including the British Isles), the Atlantic Ocean, eastern South America, Greenland, Iceland, the Arctic Ocean, NE and North America, Bermuda and the extreme north of Canada. The partial eclipse begins at 18h 42m and ends at 21h 59m. Totality lasts from 19h 50m to 20h 52m.

2. A total eclipse of the Sun on June 21 is visible as a partial eclipse from most of South America, the Atlantic Ocean, Africa (except the north), the Southern Ocean, Madagascar and the western Indian Ocean. The eclipse begins at 09h 33m and ends at 14h 34m. The path of totality starts in the South Atlantic Ocean east of South America, crosses Angola, Zambia, northern Zimbabwe, Mozambique and southern Madagascar. Totality begins at 10h 36m and ends at 13h 32m. The maximum duration is 4m 57s.

3. A partial eclipse of the Moon on July 5 is visible from the Pacific Ocean, Australasia, the Indian Ocean, Asia (except the extreme north), eastern and southern Africa, Asia Minor and Antarctica. The eclipse begins at 13h 35m and ends at 16h 15m. At maximum eclipse 50 per cent of the Moon is obscured.

4. An annular eclipse of the Sun on December 14 is visible as a partial eclipse from the Pacific Ocean, Hawaii, the USA and part of Canada, the north-west of South America and the western Caribbean. The partial phase begins at 18h 03m and ends at 23h 41m. The track of annularity starts in the western North Pacific Ocean, and passes south of Hawaii before crossing southern Nicaragua and northern Costa Rica. The annular phase begins at 19h 08m and ends at 22h 36m. The maximum duration is 3m 54s.

LUNAR OCCULTATIONS

Observations of the times of occultations are made by both amateur and professional astronomers. Such observations are later analysed to yield accurate positions of the Moon; this is one method of determining the difference between ephemeris time and universal time.

Many of the observations made by amateurs are obtained with the use of a stop-watch which is compared with a time-signal immediately after the observation. Thus an accuracy of about one-fifth of a second is obtainable, though the observer's personal equation may amount to one-third or one-half of a second.

The list on page 67 includes most of the occultations visible under favourable conditions in the British Isles. No occultation is included unless the star is at least 10° above the horizon and the Sun sufficiently far below the horizon to permit the star to be seen with the naked eye or with a small telescope. The altitude limit is reduced from 10° to 2° for stars and planets brighter than magnitude 2.0 and such occultations are also predicted in daylight.

The column Phase shows (i) whether a disappearance (D) or reappearance (R) is to be observed; and (ii) whether it is at the dark limb (D) or bright limb (B). The column headed 'El. of Moon' gives the elongation of the Moon from the Sun, in degrees. The elongation increases from 0° at New Moon to 180° at Full Moon and on to 360° (or 0°) at New Moon again. Times and position angles (P), reckoned from the north point in the direction north, east, south, west, are given for Greenwich (lat. 51° 30′, long. 0°) and Edinburgh (lat. 56° 00′, long. 3° 12′ west).

The coefficients a and b are the variations in the GMT for each degree of longitude (positive to the west) and latitude (positive to the north) respectively; they enable approximate times (to within about 1m generally) to be found for any point in the British Isles. If the point of observation is $\Delta\lambda$ degrees west and $\Delta\varphi$ degrees north, the approximate time is found by adding $a.\Delta\lambda + b.\Delta\varphi$ to the given GMT.

Example: the disappearance of ZC648 on January 6 at Coventry, found from both Greenwich and Edinburgh.

	Greenwich	Edinburgh
	°	°
Longitude	0.0	+ 3.2
Long. of Coventry	+ 1.5	+ 1.5
$\Delta\lambda$	+ 1.5	-1.7
Latitude	+ 51.5	+ 56.0
Lat. of Coventry	+ 52.4	+ 52.4
$\Delta\phi$	+ 0.9	- 3.6
	h m	h m
GMT	23 43.2	23 32.1
$a.\Delta\lambda$	- 1.8	+ 1.9
$b.\Delta\phi$	- 1.9	+ 4.3
	23 39.5	23 38.3

If the occultation is given for one station but not the other, the reason for the suppression is given by the following code:

N = star not occulted
A = star's altitude less than 10° (2° for bright stars and planets)
S = Sun not sufficiently below the horizon
G = occultation is of very short duration

In some cases the coefficients a and b are not given; this is because the occultation is so short that prediction for other places by means of these coefficients would not be reliable.

LUNAR OCCULTATIONS 2001

		ZC No.	Mag.	Phase	El. of Moon	GREENWICH				EDINBURGH			
						UT	a	b	P	UT	a	b	P
						h m	m	m	°	h m	m	m	°
January	1	3536	4.7	D.D.	77	19 00.7	-1.4	-0.5	76	18 55.3	-1.1	-0.1	63
	1	5	4.7	D.D.	78	21 20.6	-1.1	-3.0	115	21 07.3	-0.8	-1.8	94
	6	648	3.9	D.D.	140	23 43.2	-1.2	-2.1	114	23 32.1	-1.1	-1.2	98
	7	653	4.8	D.D.	141	N				0 23.8	G		149
	7	658	4.2	D.D.	141	1 01.3	-0.8	-0.4	60	0 57.6	-0.8	0.0	46
	7	793	6.3	D.D.	152	21 04.9	-1.7	-0.6	118	21 00.0	-1.3	+0.3	100
	9	1125	6.5	D.D.	180	19 48.8	-1.1	-0.5	143	19 47.1	-0.6	+0.6	125
	9	1129	5.3	D.D.	180	N				20 21.6	G		157
	31	306	6.9	D.D.	80	17 59.5	-0.5	+2.7	9	N			
February	3	718	6.1	D.D.	117	17 56.9	-1.7	-0.1	116	17 54.2	-1.2	+0.8	100
	3	736	6.2	D.D.	120	22 41.9	-1.1	-0.4	67	22 37.8	-1.1	+0.1	53
	5	905	6.7	D.D.	134	0 15.7	-1.0	-0.6	68	0 10.7	-1.0	-0.2	55
	5	1047	5.2	D.D.	144	18 31.9	G		163	18 21.3	-1.0	+0.1	133
	28	401	6.3	D.D.	62	18 27.0	-0.8	+1.9	19	N			
March	3	847	3.0	D.D.	102	24 05.2	-0.3	-1.1	74	23 59.2	-0.5	-1.0	65
	4	847	3.0	R.B.	102	1 00.1	+0.1	-1.6	284	0 52.6	+0.1	-1.9	291
	5	1021	6.3	D.D.	115	0 15.2	-0.3	-1.8	107	0 06.2	-0.5	-1.6	99
	6	1295	6.5	D.D.	140	21 31.5	-1.5	+0.1	88	21 28.9	-1.3	+0.7	75
	6	1298	6.5	D.D.	141	22 05.4	-0.7	-3.6	162	21 50.7	-1.0	-1.9	145
April	1	1110	3.5	D.D.	97	22 55.8	+0.1	-2.9	149	22 43.3	-0.2	-2.6	139
	2	1128	6.9	D.D.	98	A				1 50.8	G		35
	2	1250	5.9	D.D.	109	22 09.2	-0.8	-1.8	118	21 59.1	-0.9	-1.5	110
	27	847	3.0	D.D.	47	N				9 34.5	-0.5	+0.6	137
	27	847	3.0	R.B.	47	N				10 02.6	+0.6	+2.8	198
	28	1078	5.9	D.D.	67	22 20.2	-0.3	-0.9	63	22 14.9	-0.5	-0.9	57
	29	1224	5.4	D.D	80	23 09.5	G		32	N			
May	25	1033	6.8	D.D.	36	20 49.4	-0.3	-0.5	47	S			
	30	1578	6.8	D.D.	91	A				0 11.1	-0.3	-1.2	58
June	23	1277	5.5	D.D.	33	A				21 48.9	+0.4	-1.5	117
	29	2008	6.7	D.D.	112	21 31.9	-1.0	-1.6	139	S			
July	26	1976	6.9	D.D.	83	21 38.2	-0.7	-1.4	79	21 29.3	-0.8	-1.5	76
	28	2213	5.9	D.D.	109	22 43.4	G		168	22 29.7	-0.9	-2.1	161
	29	2353	4.6	D.D.	121	23 05.6	-1.1	-1.7	115	22 55.2	-1.0	-1.5	110
August	30	2991	6.2	D.D.	146	19 41.0	-1.4	+1.5	55	A			
September	12	976	3.2	R.D.	285	0 28.6	G		197	0 42.1	+0.6	+2.2	213
	12	Jupiter	-2.2	D.B.	292	13 18.1	G		161	13 06.4	+0.5	-2.8	150
	12	Jupiter	-2.2	R.D.	293	13 41.0	G		209	13 38.5	-0.5	-0.5	220
	25	2834	5.0	D.D.	107	21 12.8	-1.7	-1.7	121	21 01.4	-1.5	-1.2	112
	27	3092	6.2	D.D.	129	22 17.3	-1.0	-0.1	49	22 14.4	-0.8	0.0	39
	28	3214	6.6	D.D.	139	21 22.0	G		133	21 11.0	-2.0	-0.2	119
October	22	2771	5.7	D.D.	75	18 22.6	-1.4	-0.6	79	18 15.9	-1.3	-0.5	74
	25	3164	4.7	D.D.	108	17 50.5	-1.7	+0.6	106	17 49.0	-1.4	+0.9	101
	25	3175	4.8	D.D.	109	21 44.9	-1.4	-1.3	94	21 35.8	-1.2	-0.9	82
	28	3536	4.7	D.D.	142	22 53.3	-1.3	-0.1	67	22 49.9	-1.0	+0.2	54
	29	5	4.7	D.D.	144	1 19.6	-1.3	-3.2	116	1 05.5	-1.0	-1.8	94
November	3	Saturn	-0.3	D.B.	212	21 04.5	0.0	+2.0	50	21 14.1	+0.1	+2.2	41
	3	Saturn	-0.3	R.D.	212	22 01.9	-0.7	+1.4	273	22 05.6	-0.7	+1.3	285
	19	2861	5.7	D.D.	55	18 22.2	-1.4	-1.6	111	A			
	28	401	6.3	D.D.	154	18 18.5	G		136	18 17.2	-1.0	+1.2	120
December	1	Saturn	-0.4	D.B.	183	2 23.5	-1.2	-0.8	83	2 17.4	-1.1	-0.3	69
	1	Saturn	-0.4	R.D.	184	3 33.7	-0.9	-0.9	255	3 26.2	-0.8	-1.3	267
	22	18	6.0	D.D.	90	19 56.7	-1.2	-0.2	63	19 53.4	-0.9	+0.2	49
	28	639	6.0	D.D.	151	N				3 24.8	G		150
	28	654	6.0	D.D.	151	A				5 09.3	+0.4	-1.8	111
	29	792	5.1	D.D.	164	4 10.0	-0.6	-0.2	44	4 07.8	-0.8	+0.3	31

MEAN PLACES OF STARS 2001.5

Name	Mag.	RA h	m	Dec °	'	Spectrum
a And *Alpheratz*	2.1	0	08.5	+29	06	A0p
β Cassiopeiae *Caph*	2.3	0	09.3	+59	09	F5
γ Pegasi *Algenib*	2.8	0	13.3	+15	12	B2
β Mensae	2.9	0	25.8	−77	15	G0
a Phoenicis	2.4	0	26.4	−42	18	K0
a Cassiopeiae *Schedar*	2.2	0	40.6	+56	33	K0
β Ceti *Diphda*	2.0	0	43.7	−17	59	K0
γ Cassiopeiae*	Var.	0	56.8	+60	43	B0p
β Andromedae *Mirach*	2.1	1	09.8	+35	38	M0
δ Cassiopeiae	2.7	1	25.9	+60	15	A5
a Eridani *Achernar*	0.5	1	37.8	−57	14	B5
β Arietis *Sheratan*	2.6	1	54.7	+20	49	A5
γ Andromedae *Almak*	2.3	2	04.0	+42	20	K0
a Arietis *Hamal*	2.0	2	07.3	+23	28	K2
a Ursae Minoris *Polaris*	2.0	2	33.5	+89	16	F8
β Persei *Algol**	Var.	3	08.3	+40	58	B8
a Persei *Mirfak*	1.8	3	24.4	+49	52	F5
η Tauri *Alcyone*	2.9	3	47.6	+24	07	B5p
a Tauri *Aldebaran*	0.9	4	36.0	+16	31	K5
β Orionis *Rigel*	0.1	5	14.6	−8	12	B8p
a Aurigae *Capella*	0.1	5	16.8	+46	00	G0
γ Orionis *Bellatrix*	1.6	5	25.2	+6	21	B2
β Tauri *Elnath*	1.7	5	26.4	+28	37	B8
δ Orionis	2.2	5	32.1	−0	18	B0
a Leporis	2.6	5	32.8	−17	49	F0
ε Orionis	1.7	5	36.3	−1	12	B0
ζ Orionis	1.8	5	40.8	−1	57	B0
κ Orionis	2.1	5	47.8	−9	40	B0
a Orionis *Betelgeuse*	Var.	5	55.3	+7	24	M0
β Aurigae *Menkalinan*	1.9	5	59.6	+44	57	A0p
β CMa *Mirzam*	2.0	6	22.8	−17	57	B1
a Carinae *Canopus*	− 0.7	6	24.0	−52	42	F0
γ Geminorum *Alhena*	1.9	6	37.8	+16	24	A0
a Canis Majoris *Sirius*	− 1.5	6	45.2	−16	43	A0
ε Canis Majoris	1.5	6	58.7	−28	58	B1
δ Canis Majoris	1.9	7	08.5	−26	24	F8p
a Geminorum *Castor*	1.6	7	34.7	+31	53	A0
a CMi *Procyon*	0.4	7	39.4	+5	13	F5
β Geminorum *Pollux*	1.1	7	45.4	+28	01	K0
ζ Puppis	2.3	8	03.6	−40	00	Od
γ Velorum	1.8	8	09.6	−47	20	Oap
ε Carinae	1.9	8	22.5	−59	31	K0
δ Velorum	2.0	8	44.7	−54	43	A0
λ Velorum *Suhail*	2.2	9	08.1	−43	26	K5
β Carinae	1.7	9	13.2	−69	43	A0
ι Carinae	2.2	9	17.1	−59	17	F0
κ Velorum	2.6	9	22.2	−55	01	B3
a Hydrae *Alphard*	2.0	9	27.7	−8	40	K2
a Leonis *Regulus*	1.3	10	08.5	+11	58	B8
γ Leonis *Algeiba*	1.9	10	20.1	+19	50	K0
β Ursae Majoris *Merak*	2.4	11	01.9	+56	22	A0
a Ursae Majoris *Dubhe*	1.8	11	03.8	+61	45	K0
δ Leonis	2.6	11	14.2	+20	31	A3
β Leonis *Denebola*	2.1	11	49.1	+14	34	A2
γ Ursae Majoris *Phecda*	2.4	11	53.9	+53	41	A0
γ Corvi	2.6	12	15.9	−17	33	B8
a Crucis	1.0	12	26.7	−63	06	B1
γ Crucis	1.6	12	31.2	−57	07	M3
γ Centauri	2.2	12	41.6	−48	58	A0
γ Virginis	2.7	12	41.7	−1	27	F0
β Crucis	1.3	12	47.8	−59	42	B1
ε Ursae Majoris *Alioth*	1.8	12	54.1	+55	57	A0p
a Canum Venaticorum	2.9	12	56.1	+38	19	A0p
ζ Ursae Majoris *Mizar*	2.1	13	24.0	+54	55	A2p
a Virginis *Spica*	1.0	13	25.3	−11	10	B2
ε Centauri	2.6	13	40.0	−53	28	B1
η Ursae Majoris *Alkaid*	1.9	13	47.6	+49	18	B3
β Centauri *Hadar*	0.6	14	03.9	−60	23	B1
θ Centauri	2.1	14	06.8	−36	23	K0
a Bootis *Arcturus*	0.0	14	15.7	+19	10	K0
a Centauri *Rigil Kent*	0.1	14	39.7	−60	50	G0
ε Bootis	2.4	14	45.1	+27	04	K0
β UMi *Kochab*	2.1	14	50.7	+74	09	K5
γ Ursae Minoris	3.1	15	20.7	+71	50	A2
a CrB *Alpecca*	2.2	15	34.8	+26	43	A0
β Trianguli Australis	3.0	15	55.3	−63	26	F0
δ Scorpii	2.3	16	00.4	−22	38	B0
β Scorpii	2.6	16	05.5	−19	49	B1
a Scorpii *Antares*	1.0	16	29.5	−26	26	M0
a Trianguli Australis	1.9	16	48.8	−69	02	K2
ε Scorpii	2.3	16	50.3	−34	18	K0
a Herculis†	Var	17	14.7	+14	23	M3
λ Scorpii	1.6	17	33.7	−37	06	B2
a Ophiuchi *Rasalhague*	2.1	17	35.0	+12	34	A5
θ Scorpii	1.9	17	37.4	−43	00	F0
κ Scorpii	2.4	17	42.6	−39	02	B2
γ Draconis	2.2	17	56.6	+51	29	K5
ε Sgr *Kaus Australis*	1.9	18	24.3	−34	23	A0
a Lyrae *Vega*	0.0	18	37.0	+38	47	A0
σ Sagittarii	2.0	18	55.4	−26	18	B3
β Cygni *Albireo*	3.1	19	30.8	+27	58	K0
a Aquilae *Altair*	0.8	19	50.9	+8	52	A5
a Capricorni	3.8	20	18.1	−12	32	G5
γ Cygni	2.2	20	22.3	+40	16	F8p
a Pavonis	1.9	20	25.8	−56	44	B3
a Cygni *Deneb*	1.3	20	41.5	+45	17	A2p
a Cephei *Alderamin*	2.4	21	18.6	+62	36	A5
ε Pegasi	2.4	21	44.3	+9	53	K0
δ Capricorni	2.9	21	47.1	−16	07	A5
a Gruis	1.7	22	08.3	−46	57	B5
δ Cephei†	3.7	22	29.2	+58	25	†
β Gruis	2.1	22	42.8	−46	53	M3
a PsA *Fomalhaut*	1.2	22	57.7	−29	37	A3
β Pegasi *Scheat*	2.4	23	03.8	+28	05	M0
a Pegasi *Markab*	2.5	23	04.8	+15	13	A0

*γ Cassiopeiae, 2000 mag. 2.2. β Persei, mag. 2.1 to 3.4. a Orionis, mag. 0.1 to 1.2.

†a Herculis, mag. 3.1 to 3.9. δ Cephei, mag. 3.7 to 4.4, spectrum F5 to G0.

The positions of heavenly bodies on the celestial sphere are defined by two co-ordinates, right ascension and declination, which are analogous to longitude and latitude on the surface of the Earth. If we imagine the plane of the terrestrial equator extended indefinitely, it will cut the celestial sphere in a great circle known as the celestial equator. Similarly the plane of the Earth's orbit, when extended, cuts in the great circle called the ecliptic. The two intersections of these circles are known as the First Point of Aries and the First Point of Libra. If from any star a perpendicular be drawn to the celestial equator, the length of this perpendicular is the star's declination. The arc, measured eastwards along the equator from the First Point of Aries to the foot of this perpendicular, is the right ascension. An alternative definition of right ascension is that it is the angle at the celestial pole (where the Earth's axis, if prolonged, would meet the sphere) between the great circles to the First Point of Aries and to the star.

The plane of the Earth's equator has a slow movement, so that our reference system for right ascension and declination is not fixed. The consequent alteration in these quantities from year to year is called precession. In right ascension it is an increase of about 3 seconds a year for equatorial stars, and larger or smaller changes in either direction for stars near the poles, depending on the right ascension of the star. In declination it varies between $+20''$ and $-20''$ according to the right ascension of the star.

A star or other body crosses the meridian when the sidereal time is equal to its right ascension. The altitude is then a maximum, and may be deduced by remembering that the altitude of the elevated pole is numerically equal to the latitude, while that of the equator at its intersection with the meridian is equal to the co-latitude, or complement of the latitude.

Thus in London (lat. 51° 30′) the meridian altitude of Sirius is found as follows:

	°	′
Altitude of equator	38	30
Declination south	16	43
Difference	21	47

The altitude of Capella (Dec. $+46°\ 00'$) at lower transit is:

	°	′
Altitude of pole	51	30
Polar distance of star	44	00
Difference	7	30

The brightness of a heavenly body is denoted by its magnitude. Omitting the exceptionally bright stars Sirius and Canopus, the twenty brightest stars are of the first magnitude, while the faintest stars visible to the naked eye are of the sixth magnitude. The magnitude scale is a precise one, as a difference of five magnitudes represents a ratio of 100 to 1 in brightness. Typical second magnitude stars are Polaris and the stars in the belt of Orion. The scale is most easily fixed in memory by comparing the stars with Norton's *Star Atlas* (*see* page 71). The stars Sirius and Canopus and the planets Venus and Jupiter are so bright that their magnitudes are expressed by negative numbers. A small telescope will show stars down to the ninth or tenth magnitude, while stars fainter than the twentieth magnitude may be photographed by long exposures with the largest telescopes.

MEAN AND SIDEREAL TIME

Acceleration						Retardation					
h	m	s	m	s	s	h	m	s	m	s	s
1	0	10	0	00	0	1	0	10	0	00	0
2	0	20	3	02	1	2	0	20	3	03	1
3	0	30	9	07	2	3	0	30	9	09	2
4	0	39	15	13	3	4	0	39	15	15	3
5	0	49	21	18	4	5	0	49	21	21	4
6	0	59	27	23	5	6	0	59	27	28	5
7	1	09	33	28	6	7	1	09	33	34	6
8	1	19	39	34	7	8	1	19	39	40	7
9	1	29	45	39	8	9	1	28	45	46	8
10	1	39	51	44	9	10	1	38	51	53	9
11	1	48	57	49	10	11	1	48	57	59	10
12	1	58	60	00		12	1	58	60	00	
13	2	08				13	2	08			
14	2	18				14	2	18			
15	2	28				15	2	27			
16	2	38				16	2	37			
17	2	48				17	2	47			
18	2	57				18	2	57			
19	3	07				19	3	07			
20	3	17				20	3	17			
21	3	27				21	3	26			
22	3	37				22	3	36			
23	3	47				23	3	46			
24	3	57				24	3	56			

The length of a sidereal day in mean time is 23h 56m 04s.09. Hence 1h MT = 1h + 9s.86 ST and 1h ST = 1h − 9s.83 MT.

To convert an interval of mean time to the corresponding interval of sidereal time, enter the acceleration table with the given mean time (taking the hours and the minutes and seconds separately) and add the acceleration obtained to the given mean time. To convert an interval of sidereal time to the corresponding interval of mean time, take out the retardation for the given sidereal time and subtract.

The columns for the minutes and seconds of the argument are in the form known as critical tables. To use these tables, find in the appropriate left-hand column the two entries between which the given number of minutes and seconds lies; the quantity in the right-hand column between these two entries is the required acceleration or retardation. Thus the acceleration for 11m 26s (which lies between the entries 9m 07s and 15m 13s) is 2s. If the given number of minutes and seconds is a tabular entry, the required acceleration or retardation is the entry in the right-hand column above the given tabular entry, e.g. the retardation for 45m 46s is 7s.

Example – Convert 14h 27m 35s from ST to MT

	h	m	s
Given ST	14	27	35
Retardation for 14h		2	18
Retardation for 27m 35s			5
Corresponding MT	14	25	12

For further explanation, *see* pages 73–4.

ECLIPSES AND SHADOW TRANSITS OF JUPITER'S SATELLITES 2001

GMT — *Sat.* — *Phen.*

JANUARY

d	h	m	Sat.	Phen.
2	19	46	I	Sh.I
2	21	57	I	Sh.E
3	19	18	I	Ec.R
8	19	51	II	Sh.E
9	21	42	I	Sh.I
10	21	13	I	Ec.R
11	18	21	I	Sh.E
11	18	45	III	Ec.R
15	19	52	II	Sh.I
18	18	06	I	Sh.I
18	20	17	I	Sh.E
18	20	34	III	Ec.D
24	19	22	II	Ec.R
25	20	02	I	Sh.I
26	19	32	I	Ec.R

FEBRUARY

d	h	m	Sat.	Phen.
3	18	37	I	Sh.E
5	18	40	III	Sh.I
9	19	33	II	Sh.E

JUNE

d	h	m	Sat.	Phen.
22	01	26	III	Sh.E
27	01	23	I	Sh.I

JULY

d	h	m	Sat.	Phen.
9	02	05	II	Sh.E
12	02	19	I	Ec.D
13	01	54	I	Sh.E
16	01	58	II	Sh.I
17	00	43	III	Ec.D
20	01	35	I	Sh.I
24	23	42	II	Ec.D
28	00	36	I	Ec.D
29	00	11	I	Sh.E

AUGUST

d	h	m	Sat.	Phen.
1	02	17	II	Ec.D
2	23	11	II	Sh.E
3	22	48	III	Sh.I
4	01	28	III	Sh.E
4	02	30	I	Ec.D
4	23	52	I	Sh.I
5	02	04	I	Sh.E
9	23	04	II	Sh.I
10	01	47	II	Sh.E
11	02	48	III	Sh.I
12	01	46	I	Sh.I
12	22	53	I	Ec.D
13	22	27	I	Sh.E
17	01	40	II	Sh.I
19	03	39	I	Sh.I
20	00	47	I	Ec.D
20	22	08	I	Sh.I
21	00	20	I	Sh.E
21	23	22	III	Ec.R
25	23	18	II	Ec.D
27	02	41	I	Ec.D
28	00	02	I	Sh.I
28	02	14	I	Sh.E
28	21	09	I	Ec.D
29	00	37	III	Ec.D
29	03	22	III	Ec.R

SEPTEMBER

d	h	m	Sat.	Phen.
2	01	53	II	Ec.D
3	22	54	II	Sh.E
4	01	55	I	Sh.I
4	04	08	I	Sh.E
4	23	03	I	Ec.D
5	20	24	I	Sh.I
5	22	36	I	Sh.E
8	21	26	III	Sh.I
9	04	27	II	Ec.D
10	22	47	II	Sh.I
11	01	31	II	Sh.E
11	03	49	I	Sh.I
12	00	57	I	Ec.D
12	22	17	I	Sh.I
13	00	30	I	Sh.E
15	22	41	III	Sh.I
16	01	26	III	Sh.E
18	01	23	II	Sh.I
18	04	07	II	Sh.E
19	02	51	I	Ec.D
19	20	17	II	Ec.D
20	00	11	I	Sh.I
20	02	23	I	Sh.E
20	21	20	I	Ec.D
21	20	51	I	Sh.E
23	02	39	III	Sh.I
25	03	59	II	Sh.I
26	04	45	I	Ec.D
26	19	22	III	Ec.R
26	22	51	II	Ec.D
27	02	04	I	Sh.I
27	04	16	I	Sh.E
27	23	13	I	Ec.D
28	20	02	I	Sh.E
28	20	32	I	Sh.I
28	22	45	I	Sh.E

OCTOBER

d	h	m	Sat.	Phen.
3	20	31	III	Ec.D
3	23	22	III	Ec.R
4	01	25	II	Ec.D
4	03	57	I	Sh.I
5	01	07	I	Ec.D
5	19	54	II	Sh.I
5	22	26	I	Sh.I
5	22	39	II	Sh.E
6	00	38	I	Sh.E
6	19	36	I	Ec.D
7	19	06	I	Sh.E
11	00	30	I	Ec.D
11	03	22	III	Ec.R
12	03	01	I	Ec.D
12	22	30	II	Sh.I
13	00	19	I	Sh.I
13	01	16	II	Sh.E
13	02	31	I	Sh.E
13	21	30	I	Ec.D
14	00	25	IV	Ec.D
14	01	46	IV	Ec.R
14	18	47	I	Sh.I
14	21	00	I	Sh.E
20	01	07	II	Sh.I
20	02	12	I	Sh.I
20	23	24	I	Ec.D
21	18	33	III	Sh.I
21	19	48	II	Ec.D
21	20	40	I	Sh.I
21	21	24	III	Sh.E
21	22	53	I	Sh.E
28	01	18	I	Ec.D
28	22	22	II	Ec.D
28	22	31	III	Sh.I
28	22	33	I	Sh.I
29	00	46	I	Sh.E
29	01	23	III	Sh.E
29	19	46	I	Ec.D
30	18	19	IV	Ec.D
30	19	15	I	Sh.E
30	19	47	II	Sh.E
30	20	03	IV	Ec.R

NOVEMBER

d	h	m	Sat.	Phen.
5	00	27	I	Sh.I
5	00	55	II	Ec.D
5	21	40	I	Ec.D
6	18	55	I	Sh.I
6	19	37	II	Sh.I
6	21	08	I	Sh.E
6	22	24	II	Sh.E
8	19	22	III	Ec.R
12	23	34	I	Ec.D
13	20	48	I	Sh.I
13	22	14	II	Sh.I
13	23	01	I	Sh.E
14	01	00	II	Sh.E
14	18	03	I	Ec.D
15	20	24	III	Ec.D
15	23	21	III	Ec.R
20	22	41	I	Sh.I
21	00	50	II	Sh.I
21	00	55	I	Sh.E
21	19	57	I	Ec.D
22	19	19	II	Ec.D
22	19	23	I	Sh.E
23	00	23	III	Sh.I
24	23	04	IV	Sh.I
28	00	35	I	Sh.I
28	21	51	I	Ec.D
29	19	03	I	Sh.I
29	21	17	I	Sh.E
29	21	53	II	Ec.D

DECEMBER

d	h	m	Sat.	Phen.
1	19	33	II	Sh.E
3	18	23	III	Sh.I
3	21	21	III	Sh.E
5	23	45	I	Ec.D
6	20	56	I	Sh.I
6	23	11	I	Sh.E
7	18	14	I	Ec.D
8	17	39	I	Sh.E
8	19	22	II	Sh.I
8	22	10	II	Sh.E
10	22	21	III	Sh.I
11	19	26	IV	Sh.E
13	22	50	I	Sh.I
14	20	08	I	Ec.D
15	19	33	I	Sh.E
15	21	58	II	Sh.I
21	22	02	I	Ec.D
22	19	12	I	Sh.I
22	21	27	I	Sh.E
24	18	52	II	Ec.D
28	20	20	III	Ec.D
29	21	06	I	Sh.I
30	18	26	I	Ec.D
31	17	50	I	Sh.E
31	21	27	II	Ec.D

Jupiter's satellites transit across the disk from east to west, and pass behind the disk from west to east. The shadows that they cast also transit across the disk. With the exception at times of Satellite IV, the satellites also pass through the shadow of the planet, i.e. they are eclipsed. Just before opposition the satellite disappears in the shadow to the west of the planet and reappears from occultation on the east limb. Immediately after opposition the satellite is occulted at the west limb and reappears from eclipse to the east of the planet. At times approximately two to four months before and after opposition, both phases of eclipses of Satellite III may be seen. When Satellite IV is eclipsed, both phases may be seen.

The times given refer to the centre of the satellite. As the satellite is of considerable size, the immersion and emersion phases are not instantaneous. Even when the satellite enters or leaves the shadow along a radius of the shadow, the phase can last for several minutes. With Satellite IV, grazing phenomena can occur so that the light from the satellite may fade and brighten again without a complete eclipse taking place.

The list of phenomena gives most of the eclipses and shadow transits visible in the British Isles under favourable conditions.

Ec. = Eclipse   R. = Reappearance
Sh. = Shadow transit   I. = Ingress
D. = Disappearance   E. = Egress

EXPLANATION OF ASTRONOMICAL DATA

Positions of the heavenly bodies are given only to the degree of accuracy required by amateur astronomers for setting telescopes, or for plotting on celestial globes or star atlases. Where intermediate positions are required, linear interpolation may be employed.

Definitions of the terms used cannot be given here. They must be sought in astronomical literature and textbooks. Probably the best source for the amateur is Norton's *Star Atlas and Reference Handbook* (Longman, 18th edition, 1989; £26.99), which contains an introduction to observational astronomy, and a series of star maps showing stars visible to the naked eye. Certain more extended ephemerides are available in the British Astronomical Association Handbook, an annual popular among amateur astronomers (Secretary: Burlington House, Piccadilly, London w1v 9AG).

A special feature has been made of the times when the various heavenly bodies are visible in the British Isles. Since two columns, calculated for latitudes 52° and 56°, are devoted to risings and settings, the range 50° to 58° can be covered by interpolation and extrapolation. The times given in these columns are Greenwich Mean Times for the meridian of Greenwich. An observer west of this meridian must add his/her longitude (in time) and vice versa.

In accordance with the usual convention in astronomy, + and − indicate respectively north and south latitudes or declinations.

All data are, unless otherwise stated, for 0h Greenwich Mean Time (GMT), i.e. at the midnight at the beginning of the day named. Allowance must be made for British Summer Time during the period that this is in operation (*see* pages 15 and 75).

PAGE ONE OF EACH MONTH

The calendar for each month is explained on page 15.

Under the heading Astronomical Phenomena will be found particulars of the more important conjunctions of the Sun, Moon and planets with each other, and also the dates of other astronomical phenomena of special interest.

Times of Minima of Algol are approximate times of the middle of the period of diminished light.

The Constellations listed each month are those that are near the meridian at the beginning of the month at 22h local mean time. Allowance must be made for British Summer Time if necessary. The fact that any star crosses the meridian 4m earlier each night or 2h earlier each month may be used, in conjunction with the lists given each month, to find what constellations are favourably placed at any moment. The table preceding the list of constellations may be extended indefinitely at the rate just quoted.

The principal phases of the Moon are the GMTs when the difference between the longitude of the Moon and that of the Sun is 0°, 90°, 180° or 270°. The times of perigee and apogee are those when the Moon is nearest to, and farthest from, the Earth, respectively. The nodes or points of intersection of the Moon's orbit and the ecliptic make a complete retrograde circuit of the ecliptic in about 19 years. From a knowledge of the longitude of the ascending node and the inclination, whose value does not vary much from 5°, the path of the Moon among the stars may be plotted on a celestial globe or star atlas.

PAGE TWO OF EACH MONTH

The Sun's semi-diameter, in arc, is given once a month.

The right ascension and declination (Dec.) is that of the true Sun. The right ascension of the mean Sun is obtained by applying the equation of time, with the sign given, to the right ascension of the true Sun, or, more easily, by applying 12h to the Sidereal Time. The direction in which the equation of time has to be applied in different problems is a frequent source of confusion and error. Apparent Solar Time is equal to the Mean Solar Time plus the Equation of Time. For example, at noon on August 8 the Equation of Time is − 5m 36s and thus at 12h Mean Time on that day the Apparent Time is 12h − 5m 36s = 11h 54m 24s.

The Greenwich Sidereal Time at 0h and the Transit of the First Point of Aries (which is really the mean time when the sidereal time is 0h) are used for converting mean time to sidereal time and vice versa.

The GMT of transit of the Sun at Greenwich may also be taken as the local mean time (LMT) of transit in any longitude. It is independent of latitude. The GMT of transit in any longitude is obtained by adding the longitude to the time given if west, and vice versa.

LIGHTING-UP TIME

The legal importance of sunrise and sunset is that the Road Vehicles Lighting Regulations 1989 (SI 1989 No. 1796) make the use of front and rear position lamps on vehicles compulsory during the period between sunset and sunrise. Headlamps on vehicles are required to be used during the hours of darkness on unlit roads or whenever visibility is seriously reduced. The hours of darkness are defined in these regulations as the period between half an hour after sunset and half an hour before sunrise.

In all laws and regulations 'sunset' refers to the local sunset, i.e. the time at which the Sun sets at the place in question. This common-sense interpretation has been upheld by legal tribunals. Thus the necessity for providing for different latitudes and longitudes, as already described, is evident.

SUNRISE AND SUNSET

The times of sunrise and sunset are those when the Sun's upper limb, as affected by refraction, is on the true horizon of an observer at sea-level. Assuming the mean refraction to be 34′, and the Sun's semi-diameter to be 16′, the time given is that when the true zenith distance of the Sun's centre is 90° + 34′ + 16′ or 90° 50′, or, in other words, when the depression of the Sun's centre below the true horizon is 50′. The upper limb is then 34′ below the true horizon, but is brought there by refraction. An observer on a ship might see the Sun for a minute or so longer, because of the dip of the horizon, while another viewing the sunset over hills or mountains would record an earlier time. Nevertheless, the moment when the true zenith distance of the Sun's centre is 90° 50′ is a precise time dependent only on the latitude and longitude of the place, and independent of its altitude above sea-level, the contour of its horizon, the vagaries of refraction or the small seasonal change in the Sun's semi-diameter; this moment is suitable in every way as a definition of sunset (or sunrise) for all statutory purposes. (For further information, *see* footnote on page 72.)

TWILIGHT

Light reaches us before sunrise and continues to reach us for some time after sunset. The interval between darkness and sunrise or sunset and darkness is called twilight. Astronomically speaking, twilight is considered to begin or end when the Sun's centre is 18° below the horizon, as no light from the Sun can then reach the observer. As thus defined twilight may last several hours; in high latitudes at the summer solstice the depression of 18° is not reached, and twilight lasts from sunset to sunrise.

The need for some sub-division of twilight is met by dividing the gathering darkness into four stages.

(1) *Sunrise or Sunset*, defined as above
(2) *Civil twilight*, which begins or ends when the Sun's centre is 6° below the horizon. This marks the time when operations requiring daylight may commence or must cease. In England it varies from about 30 to 60 minutes after sunset and the same interval before sunrise
(3) *Nautical twilight*, which begins or ends when the Sun's centre is 12° below the horizon. This marks the time when it is, to all intents and purposes, completely dark
(4) *Astronomical twilight*, which begins or ends when the Sun's centre is 18° below the horizon. This marks theoretical perfect darkness. It is of little practical importance, especially if nautical twilight is tabulated

To assist observers the durations of civil, nautical and astronomical twilights are given at intervals of ten days. The beginning of a particular twilight is found by subtracting the duration from the time of sunrise, while the end is found by adding the duration to the time of sunset. Thus the beginning of astronomical twilight in latitude 52°, on the Greenwich meridian, on March 11 is found as 06h 23m − 113m = 04h 30m and similarly the end of civil twilight as 17h 57m + 34m = 18h 31m. The letters TAN (twilight all night) are printed when twilight lasts all night.

Under the heading The Night Sky will be found notes describing the position and visibility of the planets and other phenomena.

PAGE THREE OF EACH MONTH

The Moon moves so rapidly among the stars that its position is given only to the degree of accuracy that permits linear interpolation. The right ascension (RA) and declination (Dec.) are geocentric, i.e. for an imaginary observer at the centre of the Earth. To an observer on the surface of the Earth the position is always different, as the altitude is always less on account of parallax, which may reach 1°.

The lunar terminator is the line separating the bright from the dark part of the Moon's disk. Apart from irregularities of the lunar surface, the terminator is elliptical, because it is a circle seen in projection. It becomes the full circle forming the limb, or edge, of the Moon at New and Full Moon. The selenographic longitude of the terminator is measured from the mean centre of the visible disk, which may differ from the visible centre by as much as 8°, because of libration.

Instead of the longitude of the terminator the Sun's selenographic co-longitude (Sun's co-long.) is tabulated. It is numerically equal to the selenographic longitude of the morning terminator, measured eastwards from the mean centre of the disk. Thus its value is approximately 270° at New Moon, 360° at First Quarter, 90° at Full Moon and 180° at Last Quarter.

The Position Angle (PA) of the Bright Limb is the position angle of the midpoint of the illuminated limb, measured eastwards from the north point on the disk. The Phase column shows the percentage of the area of the Moon's disk illuminated; this is also the illuminated percentage of the diameter at right angles to the line of cusps. The terminator is a semi-ellipse whose major axis is the line of cusps, and whose semi-minor axis is determined by the tabulated percentage; from New Moon to Full Moon the east limb is dark, and vice versa.

The times given as moonrise and moonset are those when the upper limb of the Moon is on the horizon of an observer at sea-level. The Sun's horizontal parallax (Hor. par.) is about

9″, and is negligible when considering sunrise and sunset, but that of the Moon averages about 57′. Hence the computed time represents the moment when the true zenith distance of the Moon is 90° 50′ (as for the Sun) minus the horizontal parallax. The time required for the Sun or Moon to rise or set is about four minutes (except in high latitudes). *See also* page 65 and footnote below.

The GMT of transit of the Moon over the meridian of Greenwich is given; these times are independent of latitude but must be corrected for longitude. For places in the British Isles it suffices to add the longitude if west, and vice versa. For other places a further correction is necessary because of the rapid movement of the Moon relative to the stars. The entire correction is conveniently determined by first finding the west longitude λ of the place. If the place is in west longitude, λ is the ordinary west longitude; if the place is in east longitude λ is the complement to 24h (or 360°) of the longitude and will be greater than 12h (or 180°). The correction then consists of two positive portions, namely λ and the fraction $\lambda/24$ (or $\lambda°/360$) multiplied by the difference between consecutive transits. Thus for Christchurch, New Zealand, the longitude is 11h 31m east, so $\lambda = 12$h 29m and the fraction $\lambda/24$ is 0.52. The transit on the local date 2001 March 21 is found as follows:

		d	h	m
GMT of transit at Greenwich	March	20	08	52
λ			12	29
0.52 × (8h 52m − 8h 04m)				25
GMT of transit at Christchurch		20	21	46
Corr. to NZ Standard Time			12	00
Local standard time of transit			21	09	46

As is evident, for any given place the quantities λ and the correction to local standard time may be combined permanently, being here 24h 29m.

Positions of Mercury are given for every second day, and those of Venus and Mars for every fifth day; they may be interpolated linearly. The diameter (Diam.) is given in seconds of arc. The phase is the illuminated percentage of the disk. In the case of the inner planets this approaches 100 at superior conjunction and 0 at inferior conjunction. When the phase is less than 50 the planet is crescent-shaped or horned; for greater phases it is gibbous. In the case of the exterior planet Mars, the phase approaches 100 at conjunction and opposition, and is a minimum at the quadratures.

Since the planets cannot be seen when on the horizon, the actual times of rising and setting are not given; instead, the time when the planet has an apparent altitude of 5° has been tabulated. If the time of transit is between 00h and 12h the time refers to an altitude of 5° above the eastern horizon; if between 12h and 24h, to the western horizon. The phenomenon tabulated is the one that occurs between sunset and sunrise. The times given may be interpolated for latitude and corrected for longitude, as in the case of the Sun and Moon.

SUNRISE, SUNSET AND MOONRISE, MOONSET

The tables have been constructed for the meridian of Greenwich and for latitudes 52° and 56°. They give Greenwich Mean Time (GMT) throughout the year. To obtain the GMT of the phenomenon as seen from any other latitude and longitude in the British Isles, first interpolate or extrapolate for latitude by the usual rules of proportion. To the time thus found, the longitude (expressed in time) is to be added if west (as it usually is in Great Britain) or subtracted if east. If the longitude is expressed in degrees and minutes of arc, it must be converted to time at the rate of 1° = 4m and 15′ = 1m.

A method of calculating rise and set times for other places in the world is given on pages 64 and 65

The GMT at which the planet transits the Greenwich meridian is also given. The times of transit are to be corrected to local meridians in the usual way, as already described.

PAGE FOUR OF EACH MONTH

The GMTs of sunrise and sunset for seven cities, whose adopted positions in longitude (W.) and latitude (N.) are given immediately below the name, may be used not only for these phenomena, but also for lighting-up times (*see* page 71 for a fuller explanation).

The particulars for the four outer planets resemble those for the planets on Page Three of each month, except that, under Uranus and Neptune, times when the planet is 10° high instead of 5° high are given; this is because of the inferior brightness of these planets. The diameters given for the rings of Saturn are those of the major axis (in the plane of the planet's equator) and the minor axis respectively. The former has a small seasonal change due to the slightly varying distance of the Earth from Saturn, but the latter varies from zero when the Earth passes through the ring plane every 15 years to its maximum opening half-way between these periods. The rings were last open at their widest extent (and Saturn at its brightest) in 1988; this will occur again in 2002. The Earth passed through the ring plane in 1995–6 and will do so again in 2009.

TIME

From the earliest ages, the natural division of time into recurring periods of day and night has provided the practical time-scale for the everyday activities of the human race. Indeed, if any alternative means of time measurement is adopted, it must be capable of adjustment so as to remain in general agreement with the natural time-scale defined by the diurnal rotation of the Earth on its axis. Ideally the rotation should be measured against a fixed frame of reference; in practice it must be measured against the background provided by the celestial bodies. If the Sun is chosen as the reference point, we obtain Apparent Solar Time, which is the time indicated by a sundial. It is not a uniform time but is subject to variations which amount to as much as a quarter of an hour in each direction. Such wide variations cannot be tolerated in a practical time-scale, and this has led to the concept of Mean Solar Time in which all the days are exactly the same length and equal to the average length of the Apparent Solar Day.

The positions of the stars in the sky are specified in relation to a fictitious reference point in the sky known as the First Point of Aries (or the Vernal Equinox). It is therefore convenient to adopt this same reference point when considering the rotation of the Earth against the background of the stars. The time-scale so obtained is known as Apparent Sidereal Time.

GREENWICH MEAN TIME

The daily rotation of the Earth on its axis causes the Sun and the other heavenly bodies to appear to cross the sky from east to west. It is convenient to represent this relative motion as if the Sun really performed a daily circuit around a fixed Earth. Noon in Apparent Solar Time may then be defined as the time at which the Sun transits across the observer's meridian. In Mean Solar Time, noon is similarly defined by the meridian transit of a fictitious Mean Sun moving uniformly in the sky with the same average speed as the true Sun. Mean Solar Time observed on the meridian of the transit circle telescope of the Old Royal Observatory at Greenwich is called Greenwich Mean Time (GMT). The mean solar day is divided into 24 hours and, for astronomical and other scientific purposes, these are numbered 0 to 23, commencing at midnight. Civil time is usually reckoned in two periods of 12 hours, designated a.m. (*ante meridiem*, i.e. before noon) and p.m. (*post meridiem*, i.e. after noon).

UNIVERSAL TIME

Before 1925 January 1, GMT was reckoned in 24 hours commencing at noon; since that date it has been reckoned from midnight. To avoid confusion in the use of the designation GMT before and after 1925, since 1928 astronomers have tended to use the term Universal Time (UT) or Weltzeit (WZ) to denote GMT measured from Greenwich Mean Midnight.

In precision work it is necessary to take account of small variations in Universal Time. These arise from small irregularities in the rotation of the Earth. Observed astronomical time is designated UT0. Observed time corrected for the effects of the motion of the poles (giving rise to a 'wandering' in longitude) is designated UT1. There is also a seasonal fluctuation in the rate of rotation of the Earth arising from meteorological causes, often called the annual fluctuation. UT1 corrected for this effect is designated UT2 and provides a time-scale free from short-period fluctuations. It is still subject to small secular and irregular changes.

APPARENT SOLAR TIME

As mentioned above, the time shown by a sundial is called Apparent Solar Time. It differs from Mean Solar Time by an amount known as the Equation of Time, which is the total effect of two causes which make the length of the apparent solar day non-uniform. One cause of variation is that the orbit of the Earth is not a circle but an ellipse, having the Sun at one focus. As a consequence, the angular speed of the Earth in its orbit is not constant; it is greatest at the beginning of January when the Earth is nearest the Sun.

The other cause is due to the obliquity of the ecliptic; the plane of the equator (which is at right angles to the axis of rotation of the Earth) does not coincide with the ecliptic (the plane defined by the apparent annual motion of the Sun around the celestial sphere) but is inclined to it at an angle of 23° 26′. As a result, the apparent solar day is shorter than average at the equinoxes and longer at the solstices. From the combined effects of the components due to obliquity and eccentricity, the equation of time reaches its maximum values in February (-14 minutes) and early November ($+16$ minutes). It has a zero value on four dates during the year, and it is only on these dates (approximately April 15, June 14, September 1 and December 25) that a sundial shows Mean Solar Time.

SIDEREAL TIME

A sidereal day is the duration of a complete rotation of the Earth with reference to the First Point of Aries. The term sidereal (or 'star') time is a little misleading since the time-scale so defined is not exactly the same as that which would be defined by successive transits of a selected star, as there is a small progressive motion between the stars and the First Point of Aries due to the precession of the Earth's axis. This makes the length of the sidereal day shorter than the true period of rotation by 0.008 seconds. Superimposed on this steady precessional motion are small oscillations (nutation), giving rise to fluctuations in apparent sidereal time amounting to as much as 1.2 seconds. It is therefore customary to employ Mean Sidereal Time, from which these fluctuations have been removed. The conversion of GMT to Greenwich sidereal time (GST) may be performed by adding the value of the GST at 0h on the day in question (Page Two of each month) to the GMT converted to sidereal time using the table on page 69.

Example – To find the GST at August 8d 02h 41m 11s GMT

	h	m	s
GST at 0h	21	06	16
GMT	2	41	11
Acceleration for 2h			20
Acceleration for 41m 11s			7
Sum = GST =	23	47	54

If the observer is not on the Greenwich meridian then his/her longitude, measured positively westwards from Greenwich, must be subtracted from the GST to obtain Local Sidereal Time (LST). Thus, in the above example, an observer 5h east of Greenwich, or 19h west, would find the LST as 4h 47m 54s.

EPHEMERIS TIME

An analysis of observations of the positions of the Sun, Moon and planets taken over an extended period is used in preparing ephemerides. (An ephemeris is a table giving the apparent position of a heavenly body at regular intervals of time, e.g. one day or ten days, and may be used to compare current observations with tabulated positions.) Discrepancies between the positions of heavenly bodies observed over a 300-year period and their predicted positions arose because the time-scale to which the observations were related was based on the assumption that the rate of rotation of the Earth is uniform. It is now known that this rate of rotation is variable. A revised time-scale, Ephemeris Time (ET), was devised to bring the ephemerides into agreement with the observations.

The second of ET is defined in terms of the annual motion of the Earth in its orbit around the Sun (1/31556925.9747 of the tropical year for 1900 January 0d 12h ET). The precise determination of ET from astronomical observations is a lengthy process as the requisite standard of accuracy can only be achieved by averaging over a number of years.

In 1976 the International Astronomical Union adopted a new dynamical time-scale for general use whose scale unit is the SI second (*see* Atomic Time). ET is now of little more than historical interest.

TERRESTRIAL DYNAMICAL TIME

The uniform time system used in computing the ephemerides of the solar system is Terrestrial Dynamical Time (TDT), which has replaced ET for this purpose. Except for the most rigorous astronomical calculations, it may be assumed to be the same as ET. During 2001 the estimated difference TDT – UT is about 66 seconds.

ATOMIC TIME

The fundamental standards of time and frequency must be defined in terms of a periodic motion adequately uniform, enduring and measurable. Progress has made it possible to use natural standards, such as atomic or molecular oscillations. Continuous oscillations are generated in an electrical circuit, the frequency of which is then compared or brought into coincidence with the frequency characteristic of the absorption or emission by the atoms or molecules when they change between two selected energy levels. The National Physical Laboratory (NPL) routinely uses clocks of high stability produced by locking a quartz oscillator to the frequencies defined by caesium or hydrogen atoms.

International Atomic Time (TAI), established through international collaboration, is formed by combining the readings of many caesium clocks and was set close to the astronomically based Universal Time (UT) near the beginning of 1958. It was formally recognized in 1971 and since 1988 January 1 has been maintained by the International Bureau of Weights and Measures (BIPM). The second markers are generated according to the International System (SI) definition adopted in 1967 at the 13th General Conference of Weights and Measures: 'The second is the duration of 9 192 631 770 periods of the radiation corresponding to the transition between the two hyperfine levels of the ground state of the caesium-133 atom.'

Civil time in almost all countries is now based on Co-ordinated Universal Time (UTC), which was adopted for scientific purposes on 1972 January 1. UTC differs from TAI by an integer number of seconds (determined from studies of the rate of rotation of the Earth) and was designed to make both atomic time and UT accessible with accuracies appropriate for most users. The UTC time-scale is adjusted by the insertion (or, in principle, omission) of leap seconds in order to keep it within ± 0.9 s of UT. These leap seconds are introduced, when necessary, at the same instant throughout the world, either at the end of December or at the end of June. So, for example, the 22nd leap second occurred at 0h UTC on 1999 January 1. All leap seconds so far have been positive, with 61 seconds in the final minute of the UTC month. The time 23h 59m 60s UTC is followed one second later by 0h 0m 00s of the first day of the following month. Notices concerning the insertion of leap seconds are issued by the International Earth Rotation Service (IERS) at the Observatoire de Paris.

RADIO TIME-SIGNALS

UTC is made generally available through time-signals and standard frequency broadcasts such as MSF in the UK, CHU in Canada and WWV and WWVH in the USA. These are based on national time-scales that are maintained in close agreement with UTC and provide traceability to the national time-scale and to UTC. The markers of seconds in the UTC scale coincide with those of TAI.

To disseminate the national time-scale in the UK, special signals are broadcast on behalf of the National Physical Laboratory from the BT (British Telecom) radio station at Rugby (call-sign MSF). The signals are controlled from a caesium beam atomic frequency standard and consist of a precise frequency carrier of 60 kHz which is switched off, after being on for at least half a second, to mark every second. The first second of the minute begins with a period of 500 ms with the carrier switched off, to serve as a minute marker. In the other seconds the carrier is always off for at least one tenth of a second at the start and then it carries an on-off code giving the British clock time and date, together with information identifying the start of the next minute. Changes to and from summer time are made following government announcements. Leap seconds are inserted as announced by the IERS and information provided by them on the difference between UTC and UT is also signalled. Other broadcast signals in the UK include the BBC six pips signal, the BT Timeline ('speaking clock'), the NPL Truetime service for computers, and a coded time-signal on the BBC 198 kHz transmitters which is used for timing in the electricity supply industry. From 1972 January 1 the six pips on the BBC have consisted of five short pips from second 55 to second 59 (six pips in the case of a leap second) followed by one lengthened pip, the start of which indicates the exact minute. From 1990 February 5 these signals have been controlled by the BBC with seconds markers referenced to the satellite-based US navigation system GPS

(Global Positioning System) and time and day referenced to the MSF transmitter. Formerly they were generated by the Royal Greenwich Observatory. The BT Timeline is compared daily with the National Physical Laboratory caesium beam atomic frequency standard at the Rugby radio station. The NPL Truetime service is directly connected to the national time-scale.

Accurate timing may also be obtained from the signals of international navigation systems such as the ground-based Omega, or the satellite-based American GPS or Russian GLONASS systems.

STANDARD TIME

Since 1880 the standard time in Britain has been Greenwich Mean Time (GMT); a statute that year enacted that the word 'time' when used in any legal document relating to Britain meant, unless otherwise specifically stated, the mean time of the Greenwich meridian. Greenwich was adopted as the universal meridian on 13 October 1884. A system of standard time by zones is used world-wide, standard time in each zone differing from that of the Greenwich meridian by an integral number of hours, either fast or slow. The large territories of the USA and Canada are divided into zones approximately 7.5° on either side of central meridians. (For time zones of countries of the world, *see* Index.)

Variations from the standard time of some countries occur during part of the year; they are decided annually and are usually referred to as Summer Time or Daylight Saving Time.

At the 180th meridian the time can be either 12 hours fast on Greenwich Mean Time or 12 hours slow, and a change of date occurs. The internationally recognised date or calendar line is a modification of the 180th meridian, drawn so as to include islands of any one group on the same side of the line, or for political reasons. The line is indicated by joining up the following co-ordinates:

Lat.	Long.	Lat.	Long.
60° S.	180°	48° N.	180°
51° S.	180°	53° N.	170° E.
45° S.	172.5° W.	65.5° N.	169° W.
15° S.	172.5° W.	75° N.	180°
5° S.	180°		

Changes to the date line would require an international conference.

BRITISH SUMMER TIME

In 1916 an Act ordained that during a defined period of that year the legal time for general purposes in Great Britain should be one hour in advance of Greenwich Mean Time. The Summer Time Acts 1922 and 1925 defined the period during which Summer Time was to be in force, stabilising practice until the Second World War.

During the war the duration of Summer Time was extended and in the years 1941 to 1945 and in 1947 Double Summer Time (two hours in advance of Greenwich Mean Time) was in force. After the war, Summer Time was extended each year in 1948–52 and 1961–4 by Order in Council.

Between 1968 October 27 and 1971 October 31 clocks were kept one hour ahead of Greenwich Mean Time throughout the year. This was known as British Standard Time.

The most recent legislation is the Summer Time Act 1972, which enacted that 'the period of summer time for the purposes of this Act is the period beginning at two o'clock, Greenwich mean time, in the morning of the day after the third Saturday in March or, if that day is Easter Day, the day after the second Saturday in March, and ending at two o'clock, Greenwich mean time, in the morning of the day after the fourth Saturday in October.'

The duration of Summer Time can be varied by Order in Council and in recent years alterations have been made to bring the operation of Summer Time in Britain closer to similar provisions in other countries of the European Union; for instance, since 1981 the hour of changeover has been 01h Greenwich Mean Time.

The duration of Summer Time in 2001 is:

March 25 01h GMT to October 28 01h GMT

MEAN REFRACTION

Alt.	Ref.		Alt.	Ref.		Alt.	Ref.	
°	′	′	°	′	′	°	′	′
1	20		3	12		7	54	
1	30	21	3	34	13	9	27	6
1	41	20	4	00	12	11	39	5
1	52	19	4	30	11	15	00	4
2	05	18	5	06	10	20	42	3
2	19	17	5	50	9	32	20	2
2	35	16	6	44	8	62	17	1
2	52	15	7	54	7	90	00	0
3	12	14						

The refraction table is in the form of a critical table (*see* page 69)

ASTRONOMICAL CONSTANTS

Solar parallax	8″.794
Astronomical unit	149597870 km
Precession for the year 2001	50″.291
Precession in right ascension	3s.075
Precession in declination	20″.043
Constant of nutation	9″.202
Constant of aberration	20″.496
Mean obliquity of ecliptic (2001)	23° 26′ 22″
Moon's equatorial hor. parallax	57′ 02″.70
Velocity of light in vacuo per second	299792.5 km
Solar motion per second	20.0 km
Equatorial radius of the Earth	6378.140 km
Polar radius of the Earth	6356.755 km
North galactic pole (IAU standard)	
	RA 12h 49m (1950.0). Dec. 27°.4 N.
Solar apex	RA 18h 06m Dec. + 30°

Length of year (in mean solar days)				
Tropical				365.24219
Sidereal				365.25636
Anomalistic (perihelion to perihelion)				365.25964
Eclipse				346.62000

Length of month (mean values)	d	h	m	s
New Moon to New	29	12	44	02.9
Sidereal	27	07	43	11.5
Anomalistic (perigee to perigee)	27	13	18	33.2

ELEMENTS OF THE SOLAR SYSTEM

Orb	Mean distance from Sun (Earth = 1)	km 10⁶	Sidereal period days	Synodic period days	Incl. of orbit to ecliptic ° ′	Diameter km	Mass (Earth = 1)	Period of rotation on axis days
Sun	—	—	—	—	—	1,392,530	332,946	25–35*
Mercury	0.39	58	88.0	116	7 00	4,879	0.0553	58.646
Venus	0.72	108	224.7	584	3 24	12,104	0.8150	243.019r
Earth	1.00	150	365.3	—	—	12,756e	1.0000	0.997
Mars	1.52	228	687.0	780	1 51	6,794e	0.1074	1.026
Jupiter	5.20	778	4,332.6	399	1 18	142,984e 133,708p	317.89	0.410e
Saturn	9.54	1427	10,759.2	378	2 29	120,536e 108,728p	95.18	0.426e
Uranus	19.18	2870	30,684.6	370	0 46	51,118e	14.54	0.718r
Neptune	30.06	4497	60,191.0	367	1 46	49,528e	17.15	0.671
Pluto	39.80	5954	91,708.2	367	17 09	2,302	0.002	6.387

e equatorial, p polar, r retrograde, * depending on latitude

THE SATELLITES

Name		Star mag.	Mean distance from primary	Sidereal period of revolution
EARTH			km	d
I	Moon	—	384,400	27.322
MARS				
I	Phobos	12	9,378	0.319
II	Deimos	13	23,459	1.262
JUPITER				
XVI	Metis	17	127,960	0.295
XV	Adrastea	19	128,980	0.298
V	Amalthea	14	181,300	0.498
XIV	Thebe	16	221,900	0.675
I	Io	5	421,600	1.769
II	Europa	5	670,900	3.552
III	Ganymede	5	1,070,000	7.155
IV	Callisto	6	1,883,000	16.689
XIII	Leda	20	11,094,000	239
VI	Himalia	15	11,480,000	251
X	Lysithea	18	11,720,000	259
VII	Elara	17	11,737,000	260
XII	Ananke	19	21,200,000	631r
XI	Carme	18	22,600,000	692r
VIII	Pasiphae	17	23,500,000	735r
IX	Sinope	18	23,700,000	758r
SATURN				
XVIII	Pan	—	133,583	0.575
XV	Atlas	18	137,640	0.602
XVI	Prometheus	16	139,353	0.613
XVII	Pandora	16	141,700	0.629
XI	Epimetheus	15	151,422	0.695
X	Janus	14	151,472	0.695
I	Mimas	13	185,520	0.942
II	Enceladus	12	238,020	1.370
III	Tethys	10	294,660	1.888
XIII	Telesto	19	294,660	1.888
XIV	Calypso	19	294,660	1.888
IV	Dione	10	377,400	2.737
XII	Helene	18	377,400	2.737

Name		Star mag.	Mean distance from primary	Sidereal period of revolution
SATURN			km	d
V	Rhea	10	527,040	4.518
VI	Titan	8	1,221,850	15.945
VII	Hyperion	14	1,481,100	21.277
VIII	Iapetus	11	3,561,300	79.330
IX	Pheobe	16	12,952,000	550.48r
URANUS				
VI	Cordelia	—	49,750	0.335
VII	Orphelia	—	53,760	0.376
VIII	Bianca	—	59,170	0.435
IX	Cressida	—	61,780	0.464
X	Desdemona	—	62,660	0.474
XI	Juliet	—	64,360	0.493
XII	Portia	—	66,100	0.513
XIII	Rosalind	—	69,930	0.558
XIV	Belinda	—	75,260	0.624
	S/1986U10	—	76,420	0.638
XV	Puck	—	86,000	0.762
V	Miranda	17	129,800	1.413
I	Ariel	14	191,200	2.520
II	Umbriel	15	266,000	4.144
III	Titania	14	435,800	8.706
IV	Oberon	14	583,600	13.463
	S/1997U1	—	7,164,600	579.4
	S/1997U2	—	12,174,700	1,283.7
NEPTUNE				
III	Naiad	25	48,230	0.294
IV	Thalassa	24	50,070	0.311
V	Despina	23	52,530	0.335
VI	Galatea	22	61,950	0.429
VII	Larissa	22	73,550	0.555
VIII	Proteus	20	117,650	1.122
I	Triton	13	354,760	5.877
II	Nereid	19	5,513,400	360.136
PLUTO				
I	Charon	17	19,600	6.387

THE EARTH

The shape of the Earth is that of an oblate spheroid or solid of revolution whose meridian sections are ellipses not differing much from circles, whilst the sections at right angles are circles. The length of the equatorial axis is about 12,756 km, and that of the polar axis is 12,714 km. The mean density of the Earth is 5.5 times that of water, although that of the surface layer is less. The Earth and Moon revolve about their common centre of gravity in a lunar month; this centre in turn revolves round the Sun in a plane known as the ecliptic, that passes through the Sun's centre. The Earth's equator is inclined to this plane at an angle of 23.4°. This tilt is the cause of the seasons. In mid-latitudes, and when the Sun is high above the Equator, not only does the high noon altitude make the days longer, but the Sun's rays fall more directly on the Earth's surface; these effects combine to produce summer. In equatorial regions the noon altitude is large throughout the year, and there is little variation in the length of the day. In higher latitudes the noon altitude is lower, and the days in summer are appreciably longer than those in winter.

The average velocity of the Earth in its orbit is 30 km a second. It makes a complete rotation on its axis in about 23h 56m of mean time, which is the sidereal day. Because of its annual revolution round the Sun, the rotation with respect to the Sun, or the solar day, is more than this by about four minutes (*see* page 73). The extremity of the axis of rotation, or the North Pole of the Earth, is not rigidly fixed, but wanders over an area roughly 20 metres in diameter.

TERRESTRIAL MAGNETISM

A magnetic compass points along the horizontal component of a magnetic line of force. These lines of force converge on the 'magnetic dip-poles', the places where a freely suspended magnetised needle would become vertical. Not only do these poles move with time, but their exact locations are ill-defined, particularly so in the case of the north dip-pole where the lines of force on the north side of it, instead of converging radially, tend to bunch into a channel. Although it is therefore unrealistic to attempt to specify the locations of the dip-poles exactly, the present approximate adopted positions are 81°.2 N., 110°.4 W., and 64°.6 S., 138°.2 E. The two magnetic dip-poles are thus not antipodal, the line joining them passing the centre of the Earth at a distance of about 1,250 km. The distances of the magnetic dip-poles from the north and south geographical poles are about 1,200 km and 2,800 km respectively.

There is also a 'magnetic equator', at all points of which the vertical component of the Earth's magnetic field is zero and a magnetised needle remains horizontal. This line runs between 2° and 10° north of the geographical equator in Asia and Africa, turns sharply south off the west African coast, and crosses South America through Brazil, Bolivia and Peru; it recrosses the geographical equator in mid-Pacific.

Reference has already been made to secular changes in the Earth's field. The following table indicates the changes in magnetic declination (or variation of the compass). Declination is the angle in the horizontal plane between the direction of true north and that in which a magnetic compass points. Similar, though much smaller, changes have occurred in 'dip' or magnetic inclination. Secular changes differ throughout the world. Although the London observations suggest a cycle with a period of several hundred years, an exact repetition is unlikely.

London		Greenwich	
1580	11° 15' E.	1900	16° 29' W.
1622	5° 56' E.	1925	13° 10' W.
1665	1° 22' W.	1950	9° 07' W.
1730	13° 00' W.	1975	6° 39' W.
1773	21° 09' W.	1998	3° 32' W.
1850	22° 24' W.		

In order that up-to-date information on declination may be available, many governments publish magnetic charts on which there are lines (isogonic lines) passing through all places at which specified values of declination will be found at the date of the chart.

In the British Isles, isogonic lines now run approximately north-east to south-west. Though there are considerable local deviations due to geological causes, a rough value of magnetic declination may be obtained by assuming that at 50° N. on the meridian of Greenwich, the value in 2001 is 2° 47' west and allowing an increase of 14' for each degree of latitude northwards and one of 27' for each degree of longitude westwards. For example, at 53° N., 5° W., declination will be about 2° 47' + 42' + 135', i.e. 5° 44' west. The average annual change at the present time is about 12' decrease.

The number of magnetic observatories is about 180, irregularly distributed over the globe. There are three in Great Britain, run by the British Geological Survey: at Hartland, north Devon; at Eskdalemuir, Dumfriesshire; and at Lerwick, Shetland Islands. The following are some recent annual mean values of the magnetic elements for Hartland.

Year	Declination West	Dip or inclination	Horizontal force	Vertical force
	° '	° '	gauss	gauss
1960	9 59	66 44	0.1871	0.4350
1965	9 30	66 34	0.1887	0.4354
1970	9 06	66 26	0.1903	0.4364
1975	8 32	66 17	0.1921	0.4373
1980	7 44	66 10	0.1933	0.4377
1985	6 56	66 08	0.1938	0.4380
1990	6 15	66 10	0.1939	0.4388
1995	5 33	66 07	0.1946	0.4395
1999	4 53	66 07	0.1950	0.4402

The normal worldwide terrestrial magnetic field corresponds approximately to that of a very strong small bar magnet near the centre of the Earth, but with appreciable smooth spatial departures. The origin and the slow secular change of the normal field are not fully understood but are generally ascribed to electric currents associated with fluid motions in the Earth's core. Superimposed on the normal field are local and regional anomalies whose magnitudes may in places approach that of the normal field; these are due to the influence of mineral deposits in the Earth's crust. A small proportion of the field is of external origin, mostly associated with electric currents in the ionosphere. The configuration of the external field and the ionisation of the atmosphere depend on the incident particle and radiation flux from the Sun. There are, therefore, short-term and non-periodic as well as diurnal, 27-day, seasonal and 11-year periodic changes in the magnetic field, dependent upon the position of the Sun and the degree of solar activity.

MAGNETIC STORMS

Occasionally, sometimes with great suddenness, the Earth's magnetic field is subject for several hours to marked disturbance. During a severe storm in 1989 the declination at Lerwick changed by almost 8° in less than an hour. In many instances such disturbances are accompanied by widespread displays of aurorae, marked changes in the incidence of cosmic rays, an increase in the reception of 'noise' from the Sun at radio frequencies, and rapid changes in the ionosphere and induced electric currents within the Earth which adversely affect radio and telegraphic communications. The disturbances are caused by changes in the stream of ionised particles which emanates from the Sun and through which the Earth is continuously passing. Some of these changes are associated with visible eruptions on the Sun, usually in the region of sun-spots. There is a marked tendency for disturbances to recur after intervals of about 27 days, the apparent period of rotation of the Sun on its axis, which is consistent with the sources being located on particular areas of the Sun.

ARTIFICIAL SATELLITES

To consider the orbit of an artificial satellite, it is best to imagine that one is looking at the Earth from a distant point in space. The Earth would be seen to be rotating about its axis inside the orbit described by the rapidly revolving satellite. The inclination of a satellite orbit to the Earth's equator (which generally remains almost constant throughout the satellite's lifetime) gives at once the maximum range of latitudes over which the satellite passes. Thus a satellite whose orbit has an inclination of 53° will pass overhead all latitudes between 53° S. and 53° N., but would never be seen in the zenith of any place nearer the poles than these latitudes. If we consider a particular place on the earth, whose latitude is less than the inclination of the satellite's orbit, then the Earth's rotation carries this place first under the northbound part of the orbit and then under the southbound portion of the orbit, these two occurrences being always less than 12 hours apart for satellites moving in direct orbits (i.e. to the east). (For satellites in retrograde orbits, the words 'northbound' and 'southbound' should be interchanged in the preceding statement.) As the value of the latitude of the observer increases and approaches the value of the inclination of the orbit, so this interval gets shorter until (when the latitude is equal to the inclination) only one overhead passage occurs each day.

OBSERVATION OF SATELLITES

The regression of the orbit around the Earth causes alternate periods of visibility and invisibility, though this is of little concern to the radio or radar observer. To the visual observer the following cycle of events normally occurs (though the cycle may start in any position): invisibility, morning observations before dawn, invisibility, evening observations after dusk, invisibility, morning observations before dawn, and so on. With reasonably high satellites and for observers in high latitudes around the summer solstice, the evening observations follow the morning observations without interruption as sunlight passing over the polar regions can still illuminate satellites which are passing over temperate latitudes at local midnight. At the moment all satellites rely on sunlight to make them visible, though a satellite with a flashing light has been suggested for a future launching. The observer must be in darkness or twilight in order to make any useful observations. (For durations of twilight; and sunrise and sunset times, *see* Page Two of each month.)

Some of the satellites are visible to the naked eye and much interest has been aroused by the spectacle of a bright satellite disappearing into the Earth's shadow. The event is even more interesting telescopically as the disappearance occurs gradually as the satellite traverses the Earth's penumbral shadow, and during the last few seconds before the eclipse is complete the satellite may change colour (in suitable atmospheric conditions) from yellow to red. This is because the last rays of sunlight are refracted through the denser layers of our atmosphere before striking the satellite.

Some satellites rotate about one or more axes so that a periodic variation in brightness is observed. This was particularly noticeable in several of the Soviet satellites.

Satellite research has provided some interesting results, including a revised value of the Earth's oblateness (1/298.2), and the discovery of the Van Allen radiation belts.

LAUNCHINGS

Apart from their names, e.g. Cosmos 6 Rocket, the satellites are also classified according to their date of launch. Thus 1961 a refers to the first satellite launching of 1961. A number following the Greek letter indicated the relative brightness of the satellites put in orbit. From the beginning of 1963 the Greek letters were replaced by numbers and the numbers by roman letters e.g. 1963–01A. For all satellites successfully injected into orbit the following table gives the designation and names of the main objects, the launch date and some initial orbital data. These are the inclination to the equator (i), the nodal period of revolution (P), and the apogee and perigee heights.

Although most of the satellites launched are injected into orbits less than 1,000 km high, there are an increasing number of satellites in geostationary orbits, i.e. where the orbital inclination is zero, the eccentricity close to zero, and the period of revolution is 1436.1 minutes. Thus the satellite is permanently situated over the equator at one selected longitude at a mean height of 35,786 km. This geostationary band is crowded. In one case there are four television satellites (Astra 1A, Astra 1B, Astra 1C and Astra 1D) orbiting within a few tens of kilometres of each other. In the sky they appear to be separated by only a few arc minutes.

In 1997 a number of *Iridium* satellites were launched into high inclination orbits. These are owned by the mobile telephone company Cellnet. For visual observers, these satellites have the interesting characteristic that the large aerials they carry can, when in exactly the right orientation with respect to the Sun and the observer, give off a 'flare' in brightness which can on occasion attain a magnitude of − 6, much brighter than Venus. The flare can be visible to the naked eye for nearly a minute.

The Russian Space Station, Mir, 1986–17A, which was launched in 1996, was scheduled to be decommissioned in 2000, but has since been granted a reprieve. When passing over Britain it can appear to be almost as bright as Jupiter on favourable transits, though only visable for four or five minutes on each pass.

The new International Space Station, ISS, 1998–67A, is currently being assembled in an orbit of similar size and inclination. It is already nearly as bright as Mir and will eventually become brighter as more parts are added to it.

ARTIFICIAL SATELLITE LAUNCHES 1999–2000

Designation	Satellite	Launch date	P	i	Apogee height	Perigee height
1999-			m	°	km	km
011	Wire, rocket	March 5	96.0	97.6	606	552
012	Globalstar M22, M41, M46, M37, rocket	March 15	103.6	52.0	967	907
013	Asiasat 3S, rocket, platform, rocket	March 21	827.7	13.2	35978	9692
014	Sealaunch Demo, rocket	March 28	645.1	1.3	36077	651
015	Progress M-41, rocket, Sputnik JR-3	April 2	91.5	51.7	367	351
016	Insat 2E, rocket	April 2	1430.0	0.2	35867	35488
017	USA 142, Titan 4, IUS1, IUS2	April 9	(unknown)			
018	Eutelsat W3, rocket	April 12	1436.0	0.0	35802	3577
019	Globalstar M45, M42, M44, M19, rocket	April 15	103.5	52.0	957	917
020	Landsat 7, rocket	April 15	98.7	98.3	710	702
021	Uosat 12, Snap 1, rocket	April 21	97.8	64.6	665	662
022	Abrixas, Megsat, rocket	April 28	96.3	48.5	615	567
023	USA 143, Milstar 2 F-1, rocket	April 30	147.3	28.0	5000	740
024	Orion 3, rocket	May 5	100.2	29.5	1387	172
025	Fengyun 1C, Shijian 5, rocket	May 10	102.2	98.8	868	849
026	Terriers, Mublcom, rocket, rocket	May 18	95.6	97.8	566	553
027	Nimiq 1, rocket, launcher, rocket	May 20	1143.5	3.2	35782	23929
028	USA 144, rocket	May 22	(No elements available)			
029	Kitsat 3, Tubsat, Oceansat, rocket	May 26	99.4	98.4	751	733
030	STS-96 Discovery F16, Starshine	May 27	92.3	51.6	424	370
031	Globalstar M52, M49, M25, M47, rocket	June 10	114.1	52.1	1426	1425
032	Iridiur SV14A, SV21A, rocket, Smart Dispenser	June.11	97.4	86.4	650	641
033	Astra 1H, rocket, platform, rocket	June 18	778.4	16.3	35842	7474
034	Quikscat, rocket	June 20	95.6	98.7	826	293
035	Fuse 1, rocket	June 24	100.1	25.0	783	767
036	Molniya 3-50, rocket, platform, rocket	July 8	737.1	62.9	40841	486
037	Globalstar MO-32, MO-30, MO-35, MO-31 rocket	July 10	113.1	52.1	1391	1363
038	Progress M-42, rocket	July 16	89.5	51.7	260	259
039	Okean-O, rocket	July 17	98.0	98.1	675	673
040	STS-93, CXO, rocket, rocket	July 23	90.1	28.5	303	280
041	Globalstar MO-26, MO-28, MO-43, MO-48 rocket	July 25	113.2	52.1	1393	1376
042	Telkom 1, rocket	August 12	1435.3	0.1	35888	35658
043	Globalstar MO-24, MO-27, MO-53, MO-54	August 17	113.2	52.1	1393	1375
044	Cosmos 2365, rocket	August 18	89.6	67.2	350	179
045	Cosmos 2366, rocket	August 26	104.9	83.0	1021	976
046	Koreasat 3, rocket	September 4	630.8	7.0	35770	224
047	Yamal 101-102, rocket, platform	September 6	641.1	49.3	36312	197
048	Foton 12, rocket	September 9	90.6	62.9	394	229
049	Globalstar MO-33, MO-50, MO-55, MO-58 rocket, rocket	September 22	103.7	52.0	972	912
050	Echostar 5, rocket, rocket	September 23	828.0	26.7	45538	144
051	Ikonos 2 (Athena Rocket)	September 24	98.4	98.2	695	691
052	Telstar 7, rocket	September 25	1562.6	1.9	59934	16544
053	LMI-1, rocket, platform, rocket	September 26	634.2	48.6	35926	241
054	Resurs F-1 M, rocket	September 28	89.1	82.4	243	232
055	Navstar SVN-46, rocket	October 7	357.9	39.0	20444	219
056	Directv 1-R, rocket	October10	1436.0	0.0	35792	35783
057	CBERS-1, SACI-1, rocket	October 14	100.0	98.6	763	747
058	Globalstar MO-31, MO-56, MO-57, MO-59, rocket, rocket	October 18	113.9	52.0	1412	1402

ARTIFICIAL SATELLITE LAUNCHES 1999–2000

Desig- nation	Satellite	Launch date	P	i	Apogee height	Perigee height
1999–			m	°	km	km
059	Orion 2, rocket	October 19	1436.0	0.1	35791	35782
060	GE 4, rocket	November 13	629.5	6.0	35715	211
061	Shenzhou 1, rocket	November 19	89.4	42.6	312	194
062	Globalstar MO-29, MO-34, MO-39, MO-61, rocket, rocket	November 22	103.5	52.0	955	909
063	UH F/O-10 USA-146, rocket	November 23	1227.5	7.2	36677	26539
064	Helios 1B, Clementine, rocket	December 3	98.2	98.1	688	682
065	Orbcomm FM-30, FM-31, FM-32, FM-33, FM-34, FM-35, FM-36, rocket	December 4	101.6	45.1	848	837
066	XMM, rocket	December 10	2625.0	40.1	65534	851
067	DMSP 5D-3/15	December 12	101.9	98.9	864	850
068	Terra, rocket	December 18	98.2	98.3	698	667
069	STS-103 Discovery	December 20	96.3	28.5	603	583
070	Kompsat, Acrimsat, Celestis-03, rocket	December 20	98.9	98.3	735	700
071	Galaxy 11, rocket	December 22	1029.7	0.5	38922	15886
072	Cosmos 2367, rocket	December 26	92.8	65.1	431	416
073	Cosmos 2368, rocket, platform, rocket	December 27	716.1	62.9	39716	558
2000-						
001	Mars Polar Lander, rocket	January 21		(Mars probe)		
002	Galaxy 10R, rocket	January 25	755.2	3.7	35815	6382
003	Zhongxing 22, rocket	January 25	755.7	24.4	41887	348
004	Ausasat 1, Opal, OCS, Falconsat, Jawsat	January 27	100.5	100.3	818	764
005	Progress M1-1, rocket	February 1	89.2	51.7	248	243
006	Cosmos 2369, rocket	February 3	102.0	71.1	866	861
007	Hispasat 1C, rocket	February 3	834.3	18.8	45742	236
008	Globalstar MO-60, MO-62, MO-63, MO-64, rocket	February 8	103.5	52.1	944	925
009	Dumsat, Fregat IRDT	February 8	96.6	64.9	619	594
010	STS-99 Endeavour F14	February 11	89.2	57.1	254	239

Time Measurement and Calendars

MEASUREMENTS OF TIME

Measurements of time are based on the time taken by the earth to rotate on its axis (day); by the moon to revolve round the earth (month); and by the earth to revolve round the sun (year). From these, which are not commensurable, certain average or mean intervals have been adopted for ordinary use.

THE DAY

The day begins at midnight and is divided into 24 hours of 60 minutes, each of 60 seconds. The hours are counted from midnight up to 12 noon (when the sun crosses the meridian), and these hours are designated a.m. (*ante meridiem*); and again from noon up to 12 midnight, which hours are designated p.m. (*post meridiem*), except when the 24-hour reckoning is employed. The 24-hour reckoning ignores a.m. and p.m., numbering the hours 0 to 23 from midnight.

Colloquially the 24 hours are divided into day and night, day being the time while the sun is above the horizon (including the four stages of twilight defined on page 72). Day is subdivided into morning, the early part of daytime, ending at noon; afternoon, from noon to about 6 p.m.; and evening, which may be said to extend from 6 p.m. until midnight. Night, the dark period between day and day, begins at the close of astronomical twilight (*see* page 72) and extends beyond midnight to sunrise the next day.

The names of the days are derived from Old English translations or adaptations of the Roman titles.

Sunday	Sun	Sol
Monday	Moon	Luna
Tuesday	Tiw/Tyr (god of war)	Mars
Wednesday	Woden/Odin	Mercury
Thursday	Thor	Jupiter
Friday	Frigga/Freyja (goddess of love)	Venus
Saturday	Saeternes	Saturn

THE MONTH

The month in the ordinary calendar is approximately the twelfth part of a year, but the lengths of the different months vary from 28 (or 29) days to 31.

THE YEAR

The equinoctial or tropical year is the time that the earth takes to revolve round the sun from equinox to equinox, i.e. 365.24219 mean solar days, or 365 days 5 hours 48 minutes and 45 seconds.

The calendar year usually consists of 365 days but a year containing 366 days is called bissextile (*see* Roman calendar, page 89) or leap year, one day being added to the month of February so that a date 'leaps over' a day of the week. In the Roman calendar the day that was repeated was the sixth day before the beginning of March, the equivalent of 24 February.

A year is a leap year if the date of the year is divisible by four without remainder, unless it is the last year of the century. The last year of a century is a leap year only if its number is divisible by 400 without remainder, e.g. the years 1800 and 1900 had only 365 days but the year 2000 has 366 days.

THE SOLSTICE

A solstice is the point in the tropical year at which the sun attains its greatest distance, north or south, from the Equator. In the northern hemisphere the furthest point north of the Equator marks the summer solstice and the furthest point south the winter solstice.

The date of the solstice varies according to locality. For example, if the summer solstice falls on 21 June late in the day by Greenwich time, that day will be the longest of the year at Greenwich though it may be by only a second, but it will fall on 22 June, local date, in Japan, and so 22 June will be the longest day there. The date of the solstice is also affected by the length of the tropical year, which is 365 days 6 hours less about 11 minutes 15 seconds. If a solstice happens late on 21 June in one year, it will be nearly six hours later in the next (unless the next year is a leap year), i.e. early on 22 June, and that will be the longest day.

This delay of the solstice does not continue because the extra day in leap year brings it back a day in the calendar. However, because of the 11 minutes 15 seconds mentioned above, the additional day in leap year brings the solstice back too far by 45 minutes, and the time of the solstice in the calendar is earlier, in a four-year pattern, as the century progresses. The last year of a century is in most cases not a leap year, and the omission of the extra day puts the date of the solstice later by about six hours too much. Compensation for this is made by the fourth centennial year being a leap year. The solstice has become earlier in date throughout this century and, because the year 2000 is a leap year, the solstice will get earlier still throughout the 21st century.

The date of the winter solstice, the shortest day of the year, is affected by the same factors as the longest day.

At Greenwich the sun sets at its earliest by the clock about ten days before the shortest day. The daily change in the time of sunset is due in the first place to the sun's movement southwards at this time of the year, which diminishes the interval between the sun's transit and its setting. However, the daily decrease of the Equation of Time causes the time of apparent noon to be continuously later day by day, which to some extent counteracts the first effect. The rates of the change of these two quantities are not equal or uniform; their combination causes the date of earliest sunset to be 12 or 13 December at Greenwich. In more southerly latitudes the effect of the movement of the sun is less, and the change in the time of sunset depends on that of the Equation of Time to a greater degree, and the date of earliest sunset is earlier than it is at Greenwich, e.g. on the Equator it is about 1 November.

THE EQUINOX

The equinox is the point at which the sun crosses the Equator and day and night are of equal length all over the world. This occurs in March and September.

DOG DAYS

The days about the heliacal rising of the Dog Star, noted from ancient times as the hottest period of the year in the northern hemisphere, are called the Dog Days. Their incidence has been variously calculated as depending on the Greater or Lesser Dog Star (Sirius or Procyon) and their duration has been reckoned as from 30 to 54 days. A generally accepted period is from 3 July to 15 August.

CHRISTIAN CALENDAR

In the Christian chronological system the years are distinguished by cardinal numbers before or after the birth of Christ, the period being denoted by the letters BC (Before Christ) or, more rarely, AC (*Ante Christum*), and AD (*Anno Domini* – In the Year of Our Lord). The correlative dates of the epoch are the fourth year of the 194th Olympiad, the 753rd year from the foundation of Rome, AM 3761 in Jewish chronology, and the 4714th year of the Julian period. The actual date of the birth of Christ is somewhat uncertain.

The system was introduced into Italy in the sixth century. Though first used in France in the seventh century, it was not universally established there until about the eighth century. It has been said that the system was introduced into England by St Augustine (AD 596), but it was probably not generally used until some centuries later. It was ordered to be used by the Bishops at the Council of Chelsea (AD 816).

THE JULIAN CALENDAR

In the Julian calendar (adopted by the Roman Empire in 45 BC, *see* page 89) all the centennial years were leap years, and for this reason towards the close of the 16th century there was a difference of ten days between the tropical and calendar years; the equinox fell on 11 March of the calendar, whereas at the time of the Council of Nicaea (AD 325), it had fallen on 21 March. In 1582 Pope Gregory ordained that 5 October should be called 15 October and that of the end-centennial years only the fourth should be a leap year (*see* page 81).

THE GREGORIAN CALENDAR

The Gregorian calendar was adopted by Italy, France, Spain and Portugal in 1582, by Prussia, the Roman Catholic German states, Switzerland, Holland and Flanders on 1 January 1583, by Poland in 1586, Hungary in 1587, the Protestant German and Netherland states and Denmark in 1700, and by Great Britain and Dominions (including the North American colonies) in 1752, by the omission of eleven days (3 September being reckoned as 14 September). Sweden omitted the leap day in 1700 but observed leap days in 1704 and 1708, and reverted to the Julian calendar by having two leap days in 1712; the Gregorian calendar was adopted in 1753 by the omission of eleven days (18 February being reckoned as 1 March). Japan adopted the calendar in 1872, China in 1912, Bulgaria in 1915, Turkey and Soviet Russia in 1918, Yugoslavia and Romania in 1919, and Greece in 1923.

In the same year that the change was made in England from the Julian to the Gregorian calendar, the beginning of the new year was also changed from 25 March to 1 January (*see* page 86).

THE ORTHODOX CHURCHES

Some Orthodox Churches still use the Julian reckoning but the majority of Greek Orthodox Churches and the Romanian Orthodox Church have adopted a modified 'New Calendar', observing the Gregorian calendar for fixed feasts and the Julian for movable feasts.

The Orthodox Church year begins on 1 September. There are four fast periods and, in addition to Pascha (Easter), twelve great feasts, as well as numerous commemorations of the saints of the Old and New Testaments throughout the year.

THE DOMINICAL LETTER

The dominical letter is one of the letters A–G which are used to denote the Sundays in successive years. If the first day of the year is a Sunday the letter is A; if the second, B; the third, C; and so on. A leap year requires two letters, the first for 1 January to 29 February, the second for 1 March to 31 December (*see* page 84).

EPIPHANY

The feast of the Epiphany, commemorating the manifestation of Christ, later became associated with the offering of gifts by the Magi. The day was of great importance from the time of the Council of Nicaea (AD 325), as the primate of Alexandria was charged at every Epiphany feast with the announcement in a letter to the churches of the date of the forthcoming Easter. The day was also of importance in Britain as it influenced dates, ecclesiastical and lay, e.g. Plough Monday, when work was resumed in the fields, fell on the Monday in the first full week after Epiphany.

LENT

The Teutonic word *Lent*, which denotes the fast preceding Easter, originally meant no more than the spring season; but from Anglo-Saxon times at least it has been used as the equivalent of the more significant Latin term Quadragesima, meaning the 'forty days' or, more literally, the fortieth day. Ash Wednesday is the first day of Lent, which ends at midnight before Easter Day.

PALM SUNDAY

Palm Sunday, the Sunday before Easter and the beginning of Holy Week, commemorates the triumphal entry of Christ into Jerusalem and is celebrated in Britain (when palm is not available) by branches of willow gathered for use in the decoration of churches on that day.

MAUNDY THURSDAY

Maundy Thursday is the day before Good Friday, the name itself being a corruption of *dies mandati* (day of the mandate) when Christ washed the feet of the disciples and gave them the mandate to love one another.

EASTER DAY

Easter Day is the first Sunday after the full moon which happens on, or next after, the 21st day of March; if the full moon happens on a Sunday, Easter Day is the Sunday after.

This definition is contained in an Act of Parliament (24 Geo. II c. 23) and explanation is given in the preamble to the Act that the day of full moon depends on certain tables that have been prepared. These tables are summarised in the early pages of the Book of Common Prayer. The moon referred to is not the real moon of the heavens, but a hypothetical moon on whose 'full' the date of Easter depends, and the lunations of this 'calendar' moon consist of twenty-nine and thirty days alternately, with certain necessary modifications to make the date of its full agree as nearly as possible with that of the real moon, which is known as the Paschal Full Moon.

A FIXED EASTER

In 1928 the House of Commons agreed to a motion for the third reading of a bill proposing that Easter Day shall, in the calendar year next but one after the commencement of the Act and in all subsequent years, be the first Sunday after the second Saturday in April. Easter would thus fall on the second or third Sunday in April, i.e. between 9 and 15 April (inclusive). A clause in the Bill provided that before it shall come into operation, regard shall be had to any opinion expressed officially by the various Christian churches. Efforts by the World Council of Churches to secure a unanimous choice of date for Easter by its member churches have so far been unsuccessful.

ROGATION DAYS

Rogation Days are the Monday, Tuesday and Wednesday preceding Ascension Day and from the fifth century were observed as public fasts with solemn processions and supplications. The processions were discontinued as religious observances at the Reformation, but survive in the ceremony known as 'beating the parish bounds'. Rogation Sunday is the Sunday before Ascension Day.

EMBER DAYS

The Ember Days at the four seasons are the Wednesday, Friday and Saturday (a) before the third Sunday in Advent,

(b) before the second Sunday in Lent, and (c) before the Sundays nearest to the festivals of St Peter and of St Michael and All Angels.

TRINITY SUNDAY

Trinity Sunday is eight weeks after Easter Day, on the Sunday following Pentecost (Whit Sunday). Subsequent Sundays are reckoned in the Book of Common Prayer calendar of the Church of England as 'after Trinity'.

Thomas Becket (1118–70) was consecrated Archbishop of Canterbury on the Sunday after Whit Sunday and his first act was to ordain that the day of his consecration should be held as a new festival in honour of the Holy Trinity. This observance spread from Canterbury throughout the whole of Christendom.

MOVABLE FEASTS TO THE YEAR 2035

Year	Ash Wednesday	Easter	Ascension	Pentecost (Whit Sunday)	Advent Sunday
2001	28 February	15 April	24 May	3 June	2 December
2002	13 February	31 March	9 May	19 May	1 December
2003	5 March	20 April	29 May	8 June	30 November
2004	25 February	11 April	20 May	30 May	28 November
2005	9 February	27 March	5 May	15 May	27 November
2006	1 March	16 April	25 May	4 June	3 December
2007	21 February	8 April	17 May	27 May	2 December
2008	6 February	23 March	1 May	11 May	30 November
2009	25 February	12 April	21 May	31 May	29 November
2010	17 February	4 April	13 May	23 May	28 November
2011	9 March	24 April	2 June	12 June	27 November
2012	22 February	8 April	17 May	27 May	2 December
2013	13 February	31 March	9 May	19 May	1 December
2014	5 March	20 April	29 May	8 June	30 November
2015	18 February	5 April	14 May	24 May	29 November
2016	10 February	27 March	5 May	15 May	27 November
2017	1 March	16 April	25 May	4 June	3 December
2018	14 February	1 April	10 May	20 May	2 December
2019	6 March	21 April	30 May	9 June	1 December
2020	26 February	12 April	21 May	31 May	29 November
2021	17 February	4 April	13 May	23 May	28 November
2022	2 March	17 April	26 May	5 June	27 November
2023	22 February	9 April	18 May	28 May	3 December
2024	14 February	31 March	9 May	19 May	1 December
2025	5 March	20 April	29 May	8 June	30 November
2026	18 February	5 April	14 May	24 May	29 November
2027	10 February	28 March	6 May	16 May	28 November
2028	1 March	16 April	25 May	4 June	3 December
2029	14 February	1 April	10 May	20 May	2 December
2030	6 March	21 April	30 May	9 June	1 December
2031	26 February	13 April	22 May	1 June	30 November
2032	11 February	28 March	6 May	16 May	28 November
2033	2 March	17 April	26 May	5 June	27 November
2034	22 February	9 April	18 May	28 May	3 December
2035	7 February	25 March	3 May	13 May	2 December

NOTES

Ash Wednesday (first day in Lent) can fall at earliest on 4 February and at latest on 10 March

Mothering Sunday (fourth Sunday in Lent) can fall at earliest on 1 March and at latest on 4 April

Easter Day can fall at earliest on 22 March and at latest on 25 April

Ascension Day is forty days after Easter Day and can fall at earliest on 30 April and at latest on 3 June

Pentecost (Whit Sunday) is seven weeks after Easter and can fall at earliest on 10 May and at latest on 13 June

Trinity Sunday is the Sunday after Whit Sunday

Corpus Christi falls on the Thursday after Trinity Sunday

Sundays after Pentecost – there are not less than 18 and not more than 23

Advent Sunday is the Sunday nearest to 30 November

EASTER DAYS AND DOMINICAL LETTERS 1500 TO 2035

Dates up to and including 1752 are according to the Julian calendar. For dominical letters in leap years, *see* page 82

		1500–1599	1600–1699	1700–1799	1800–1899	1900–1999	2000–2035
March							
d	22	1573	1668	1761	1818		
e	23	1505/16	1600	1788	1845/56	1913	2008
f	24		1611/95	1706/99		1940	
g	25	1543/54	1627/38/49	1722/33/44	1883/94	1951	2035
A	26	1559/70/81/92	1654/65/76	1749/58/69/80	1815/26/37	1967/78/89	
b	27	1502/13/24/97	1608/87/92	1785/96	1842/53/64	1910/21/32	2005/16
c	28	1529/35/40	1619/24/30	1703/14/25	1869/75/80	1937/48	2027/32
d	29	1551/62	1635/46/57	1719/30/41/52	1807/12/91	1959/64/70	
e	30	1567/78/89	1651/62/73/84	1746/55/66/77	1823/34	1902/75/86/97	
f	31	1510/21/32/83/94	1605/16/78/89	1700/71/82/93	1839/50/61/72	1907/18/29/91	2002/13/24
April							
g	1	1526/37/48	1621/32	1711/16	1804/66/77/88	1923/34/45/56	2018/29
A	2	1553/64	1643/48	1727/38	1809/20/93/99	1961/72	
b	3	1575/80/86	1659/70/81	1743/63/68/74	1825/31/36	1904/83/88/94	
c	4	1507/18/91	1602/13/75/86/97	1708/79/90	1847/58	1915/20/26/99	2010/21
d	5	1523/34/45/56	1607/18/29/40	1702/13/24/95	1801/63/74/85/96	1931/42/53	2015/26
e	6	1539/50/61/72	1634/45/56	1729/35/40/60	1806/17/28/90	1947/58/69/80	
f	7	1504/77/88	1667/72	1751/65/76	1822/33/44	1901/12/85/96	
g	8	1509/15/20/99	1604/10/83/94	1705/87/92/98	1849/55/60	1917/28	2007/12
A	9	1531/42	1615/26/37/99	1710/21/32	1871/82	1939/44/50	2023/34
b	10	1547/58/69	1631/42/53/64	1726/37/48/57	1803/14/87/98	1955/66/77	
c	11	1501/12/63/74/85/96	1658/69/80	1762/73/84	1819/30/41/52	1909/71/82/93	2004
d	12	1506/17/28	1601/12/91/96	1789	1846/57/68	1903/14/25/36/98	2009/20
e	13	1533/44	1623/28	1707/18	1800/73/79/84	1941/52	2031
f	14	1555/60/66	1639/50/61	1723/34/45/54	1805/11/16/95	1963/68/74	
g	15	1571/82/93	1655/66/77/88	1750/59/70/81	1827/38	1900/06/79/90	2001
A	16	1503/14/25/36/87/98	1609/20/82/93	1704/75/86/97	1843/54/65/76	1911/22/33/95	2006/17/28
b	17	1530/41/52	1625/36	1715/20	1808/70/81/92	1927/38/49/60	2022/33
c	18	1557/68	1647/52	1731/42/56	1802/13/24/97	1954/65/76	
d	19	1500/79/84/90	1663/74/85	1747/67/72/78	1829/35/40	1908/81/87/92	
e	20	1511/22/95	1606/17/79/90	1701/12/83/94	1851/62	1919/24/30	2003/14/25
f	21	1527/38/49	1622/33/44	1717/28	1867/78/89	1935/46/57	2019/30
g	22	1565/76	1660	1739/53/64	1810/21/32	1962/73/84	
A	23	1508	1671		1848	1905/16	2000
b	24	1519	1603/14/98	1709/91	1859		2011
c	25	1546	1641	1736	1886	1943	

HINDU CALENDAR

The Hindu calendar is a luni-solar calendar of twelve months, each containing 29 days, 12 hours. Each month is divided into a light fortnight (Shukla or Shuddha) and a dark fortnight (Krishna or Vadya) based on the waxing and waning of the moon. In most parts of India the month starts with the light fortnight, i.e. the day after the new moon, although in some regions it begins with the dark fortnight, i.e. the day after the full moon.

The new year begins in the month of Chaitra (March/April) and ends in the month of Phalgun (March). The twelve months, Chaitra, Vaishakh, Jyeshtha, Ashadh, Shravan, Bhadrapad, Ashvin, Kartik, Margashirsh, Paush, Magh and Phalgun, have Sanskrit names derived from twelve asterisms (constellations). There are regional variations to the names of the months but the Sanskrit names are understood throughout India.

Every lunar month must have a solar transit and is termed pure (shuddha). The lunar month without a solar transit is impure (mala) and called an intercalary month. An intercalary month occurs approximately every 32 lunar months, whenever the difference between the Hindu year of 360 lunar days (354 days 8 hours solar time) and the 365 days 6 hours of the solar year reaches the length of one Hindu lunar month (29 days 12 hours).

The leap month may be added at any point in the Hindu year. The name given to the month varies according to when it occurs but is taken from the month immediately following it. A leap month (Ashvin) occurs between September and October 2001.

The days of the week are called Raviwar (Sunday), Somawar (Monday), Mangalwar (Tuesday), Budhawar (Wednesday), Guruwar (Thursday), Shukrawar (Friday) and Shaniwar (Saturday). The names are derived from the Sanskrit names of the Sun, the Moon and five planets, Mars, Mercury, Jupiter, Venus and Saturn.

Most fasts and festivals are based on the lunar calendar but a few are determined by the apparent movement of the Sun, e.g. Sankranti and Pongal (in southern India), which are celebrated on 14/15 January to mark the start of the Sun's apparent journey northwards and a change of season.

Festivals celebrated throughout India are Chaitra (the New Year), Raksha-bandhan (the renewal of the kinship bond between brothers and sisters), Navaratri (a nine-night festival dedicated to the goddess Parvati), Dasara (the victory of Rama over the demon army), Diwali (a festival of lights), Makara Sankranti, Shivaratri (dedicated to Shiva), and Holi (a spring festival).

Regional festivals are Durga-puja (dedicated to the goddess Durga (Parvati)), Sarasvati-puja (dedicated to the goddess Sarasvati), Ganesh Chaturthi (worship of Ganesh on the fourth day (Chaturthi) of the light half of Bhadrapad), Ramanavami (the birth festival of the god Rama) and Janmashtami (the birth festival of the god Krishna).

The main festivals celebrated in Britain are Navaratri, Dasara, Durga-puja, Diwali, Holi, Sarasvati-puja, Ganesh Chaturthi, Raksha-bandhan, Ramanavami and Janmashtami.

For dates of the main festivals in 2001, *see* page 9.

JEWISH CALENDAR

The story of the Flood in the Book of Genesis indicates the use of a calendar of some kind and that the writers recognised thirty days as the length of a lunation. However, after the diaspora, Jewish communities were left in considerable doubt as to the times of fasts and festivals. This led to the formation of the Jewish calendar as used today. It is said that this was done in AD 358 by Rabbi Hillel II, though some assert that it did not happen until much later.

The calendar is luni-solar, and is based on the lengths of the lunation and of the tropical year as found by Hipparchus (*c*.120 BC), which differ little from those adopted at the present day. The year AM 5761 (2000–2001) is the 4th year of the 304th Metonic (Minor or Lunar) cycle of 19 years and the 21st year of the 206th Solar (or Major) cycle of 28 years since the Era of the Creation. Jews hold that the Creation occurred at the time of the autumnal equinox in the year known in the Christian calendar as 3760 BC (954 of the Julian period). The epoch or starting point of Jewish chronology corresponds to 7 October 3761 BC. At the beginning of each solar cycle, the Tekufah of Nisan (the vernal equinox) returns to the same day and to the same hour.

The hour is divided into 1080 minims, and the month between one new moon and the next is reckoned as 29 days, 12 hours, 793 minims. The normal calendar year, called a Regular Common year, consists of 12 months of 30 days and 29 days alternately. Since 12 months such as these comprise only 354 days, in order that each of them shall not diverge greatly from an average place in the solar year, a 13th month is occasionally added after the fifth month of the civil year (which commences on the first day of the month Tishri), or as the penultimate month of the ecclesiastical year (which commences on the first day of the month Nisan). The years when this happens are called Embolismic or leap years.

Of the 19 years that form a Metonic cycle, seven are leap years; they occur at places in the cycle indicated by the numbers 3, 6, 8, 11, 14, 17 and 19, these places being chosen so that the accumulated excesses of the solar years should be as small as possible.

A Jewish year is of one of the following six types:

Minimal Common	353 days
Regular Common	354 days
Full Common	355 days
Minimal Leap	383 days
Regular Leap	384 days
Full Leap	385 days

The Regular year has alternate months of 30 and 29 days. In a Full year, whether common or leap, Marcheshvan, the second month of the civil year, has 30 days instead of 29; in Minimal years Kislev, the third month, has 29 instead of 30. The additional month in leap years is called Adar I and precedes the month called Adar in Common years. Adar II is called Adar Sheni in leap years, and the usual Adar festivals are kept in Adar Sheni. Adar I and Adar II always have 30 days, but neither this, nor the other variations mentioned, is allowed to change the number of days in the other months, which still follow the alternation of the normal twelve.

These are the main features of the Jewish calendar, which must be considered permanent because as a Jewish law it cannot be altered except by a great Sanhedrin.

The Jewish day begins between sunset and nightfall. The time used is that of the meridian of Jerusalem, which is 2h 21m in advance of Greenwich Mean Time. Rules for the beginning of sabbaths and festivals were laid down for the latitude of London in the 18th century and hours for nightfall are now fixed annually by the Chief Rabbi.

JEWISH CALENDAR 5761–2

AM 5761 (761) is a Minimal Common year of 12 months, 50 sabbaths and 353 days. AM 5762 (762) is a year of 12 months, 49 sabbaths and 355 days.

Month (first day)	AM 5761	AM 5762
Tishri I	30 September 2000	18 September 2001
Marcheshvan I	30 October	18 October
Kislev I	28 November	16 November
Tebet I	27 December	16 December
Shebat I	25 January 2001	14 January 2002
*Adar I	24 February	13 February
†*Adar* II		
Nisan I	25 March	14 March
Iyar I	24 April	13 April
Sivan I	23 May	12 May
Tammuz I	22 June	11 June
Ab I	21 July	10 July
Elul I	20 August	9 August

*Known as Adar Rishon in leap years
†Known as Adar Sheni in leap years

JEWISH FASTS AND FESTIVALS

For dates of principal festivals in 2001, *see* page 9.

Tishri 1–2	Rosh Hashanah (New Year)
Tishri 3	*Fast of Gedaliah
Tishri 10	Yom Kippur (Day of Atonement)
Tishri 15–21	Succoth (Feast of Tabernacles)
Tishri 21	Hoshana Rabba
Tishri 22	Shemini Atseret (Solemn Assembly)
Tishri 23	Simchat Torah (Rejoicing of the Law)
Kislev 25	Chanucah (Dedication of the Temple) begins
Tebet 10	Fast of Tebet
†*Adar* 13	§Fast of Esther
†*Adar* 14	Purim
†*Adar* 15	Shushan Purim
Nisan 15–22	Pesach (Passover)
Sivan 6–7	Shavuot (Feast of Weeks)
Tammuz 17	*Fast of Tammuz
Ab 9	*Fast of Ab

*If these dates fall on the sabbath the fast is kept on the following day
†Adar Sheni in leap years
§This fast is observed on Adar 11 (or Adar Sheni 11 in leap years) if Adar 13 falls on a sabbath

THE MUSLIM CALENDAR

The Muslim era is dated from the *Hijrah*, or flight of the Prophet Muhammad from Mecca to Medina, the corresonding date of which in the Julian calendar is 16 July AD 622. The lunar *hijri* calendar is used principally in Iran, Egypt, Malaysia, Pakistan, Mauritania, various Arab states and certain parts of India. Iran uses the solar *hijri* calendar as well as the lunar *hijri* calendar. The dating system was adopted about AD 639, commencing with the first day of the month Muharram.

The lunar calendar consists of twelve months containing an alternate sequence of 30 and 29 days, with the intercalation of one day at the end of the twelfth month at stated intervals in each cycle of 30 years. The object of the intercalation is to reconcile the date of the first day of the month with the date of the actual new moon.

Some adherents still take the date of the evening of the first physical sighting of the crescent of the new moon as that of the first of the month. If cloud obscures the moon the present month may be extended to 30 days, after which the new month will begin automatically regardless of whether the moon has been seen. (Under religious law a month must have less than 31 days.) This means that the beginning of a new month and the date of religious festivals can vary from the published calendars.

In each cycle of 30 years, 19 years are common and contain 354 days, and 11 years are intercalary (leap years) of 355 days, the latter being called *kabisah*. The mean length of the Hijrah years is 354 days 8 hours 48 minutes and the period of mean lunation is 29 days 12 hours 44 minutes.

To ascertain if a year is common or kabisah, divide it by 30: the quotient gives the number of completed cycles and the remainder shows the place of the year in the current cycle. If the remainder is 2, 5, 7, 10, 13, 16, 18, 21, 24, 26 or 29, the year is kabisah and consists of 355 days.

MUSLIM CALENDAR 1421–22

Month (length)	1422 (1421) AH
Dhū'l-Qa'da (30)	(26 January)
Dhū'l-Hijjah (29 or 30)	(25 February)
Muharram (30)	26 March
Safar (29)	25 April
Rabi' I (30)	25 May
Rabi' II (29)	23 June
Jumada I (30)	22 July
Jumada II (29)	21 August
Rajab (30)	19 September
Sha'ban (29)	18 October
Ramadân (30)	17 November
Shawwâl (29)	16 December

MUSLIM FESTIVALS

Ramadan is a month of fasting for all Muslims because it is the month in which the revelation of the *Qur'an* (Koran) began. During Ramadan Muslims abstain from food, drink and sexual pleasure from dawn until after sunset throughout the month.

The two major festivals are *Id al-Fitr* and *Id al-Adha*. Id al-Fitr marks the end of the Ramadan fast and is celebrated on the day after the sighting of the new moon of the following month. Id al-Adha, the festival of sacrifice (also known as the great festival), celebrates the submission of the Prophet Ibrahim (Abraham) to God. Id al-Adha falls on the tenth day of Dhul-Hijjah, coinciding with the day when those on *hajj* (pilgrimage to Mecca) sacrifice animals.

Other days accorded special recognition are:

Muharram 1	New Year's Day
Muharram 10	Ashura (the day Prophet Noah left the Ark and Prophet Moses was saved from Pharaoh (Sunni), the death of the Prophet's grandson Husain (Shi'ite))
Rabi'u-l-Awwal (*Rabi' I*) 12	Mawlid al-Nabi (birthday of the Prophet Muhammad)
Rajab 27	Laylat al-Isra' wa'l-Mi'raj (The Night of Journey and Ascension)
Ramadân One of the odd-numbered nights in the last 10 of the month	Laylat al-Qadr (Night of Power)
Dhû'l-Hijjah 10	Id al-Adha (Festival of Sacrifice)

THE SIKH CALENDAR

The Sikh calendar is a lunar calendar of 365 days divided into 12 months. The length of the months varies between 29 and 32 days.

There are no prescribed feast days and no fasting periods. The main celebrations are Baisakhi Mela (the new year and the anniversary of the founding of the Khalsa), Diwali Mela (festival of light), Hola Mohalla Mela (a spring festival held in the Punjab), and the Gurpurbs (anniversaries associated with the ten Gurus).

For dates of the major celebrations in 2001, *see* page 9.

CIVIL AND LEGAL CALENDAR

THE HISTORICAL YEAR

Before 1752, two calendar systems were used in England. The civil or legal year began on 25 March and the historical year on 1 January. Thus the civil or legal date 24 March 1658 was the same day as the historical date 24 March 1659; a date in that portion of the year is written as 24 March 165$\frac{8}{9}$, the lower figure showing the historical year.

THE NEW YEAR

In England in the seventh century, and as late as the 13th, the year was reckoned from Christmas Day, but in the 12th century the Church in England began the year with the feast of the Annunciation of the Blessed Virgin ('Lady Day') on 25 March and this practice was adopted generally in the 14th century. The civil or legal year in the British Dominions (exclusive of Scotland) began with Lady Day until 1751. But in and since 1752 the civil year has begun with 1 January. New Year's Day in Scotland was changed from 25 March to 1 January in 1600.

Elsewhere in Europe, 1 January was adopted as the first day of the year by Venice in 1522, German states in 1544, Spain, Portugal and the Roman Catholic Netherlands in 1556, Prussia, Denmark and Sweden in 1559, France in 1564, Lorraine in 1579, the Protestant Netherlands in 1583, Russia in 1725, and Tuscany in 1751.

REGNAL YEARS

Regnal years are the years of a sovereign's reign and each begins on the anniversary of his or her accession, e.g. regnal year 50 of the present Queen begins on 6 February 2001.

The system was used for dating Acts of Parliament until 1962. The Summer Time Act 1925, for example, is quoted as 15 and 16 Geo. V c. 64, because it became law in the parliamentary session which extended over part of both of these regnal years. Acts of a parliamentary session during which a sovereign died were usually given two year numbers, the regnal year of the deceased sovereign and the regnal year of his or her successor, e.g. those passed in 1952 were dated 16 Geo. VI and 1 Elizabeth II. Since 1962 Acts of Parliament have been dated by the calendar year.

QUARTER AND TERM DAYS

Holy days and saints days were the usual means in early times for setting the dates of future and recurrent appointments. The quarter days in England and Wales are the feast of the Nativity (25 December), the feast of the Annunciation (25 March), the feast of St John the Baptist (24 June) and the feast of St Michael and All Angels (29 September).

The term days in Scotland are Candlemas (the feast of the Purification), Whitsunday, Lammas (Loaf Mass), and Martinmas (St Martin's Day). These fell on 2 February, 15 May, 1 August and 11 November respectively. However, by the Term and Quarter Days (Scotland) Act 1990, the dates of the term days were changed to 28 February (Candlemas), 28 May (Whitsunday), 28 August (Lammas) and 28 November (Martinmas).

RED-LETTER DAYS

Red-letter days were originally the holy days and saints days indicated in early ecclesiastical calendars by letters printed in red ink. The days to be distinguished in this way were approved at the Council of Nicaea in AD 325.

These days still have a legal significance, as judges of the Queen's Bench Division wear scarlet robes on red-letter days falling during the law sittings. The days designated as red-letter days for this purpose are:

Holy and saints days
The Conversion of St Paul, the Purification, Ash Wednesday, the Annunciation, the Ascension, the feasts of St Mark, SS Philip and James, St Matthias, St Barnabas, St John the Baptist, St Peter, St Thomas, St James, St Luke, SS Simon and Jude, All Saints, St Andrew

Civil calendar (for dates, *see* page 9)
The anniversaries of The Queen's accession, The Queen's birthday and The Queen's coronation, The Queen's official birthday, the birthday of the Duke of Edinburgh, the birthday of Queen Elizabeth the Queen Mother, the birthday of the Prince of Wales, St David's Day and Lord Mayor's Day

PUBLIC HOLIDAYS

Public holidays are divided into two categories, common law and statutory. Common law holidays are holidays 'by habit and custom'; in England, Wales and Northern Ireland these are Good Friday and Christmas Day.

Statutory public holidays, known as bank holidays, were first established by the Bank Holidays Act 1871. They were, literally, days on which the banks (and other public institutions) were closed and financial obligations due on that day were payable the following day. The legislation currently governing public holidays in the UK, which is the Banking and Financial Dealings Act 1971, stipulates the days that are to be public holidays in England, Wales, Scotland and Northern Ireland.

Certain holidays (indicated by * below) are granted annually by royal proclamation, either throughout the UK or in any place in the UK. The public holidays are:

England and Wales
*New Year's Day
Easter Monday
*The first Monday in May
The last Monday in May
The last Monday in August
26 December, if it is not a Sunday
27 December when 25 or 26 December is a Sunday

Scotland
New Year's Day, or if it is a Sunday, 2 January
2 January, or if it is a Sunday, 3 January
Good Friday
The first Monday in May
*The last Monday in May
The first Monday in August
Christmas Day, or if it is a Sunday, 26 December
*Boxing Day – if Christmas Day falls on a Sunday, 26 December is given in lieu and an alternative day is given for Boxing Day

Northern Ireland
*New Year's Day
17 March, or if it is a Sunday, 18 March
Easter Monday
*The first Monday in May
The last Monday in May
*12 July, or if it is a Sunday, 13 July
The last Monday in August
26 December, if it is not a Sunday
27 December if 25 or 26 December is a Sunday
For dates of public holidays in 2001 and 2002, *see* pages 10–11.

CHRONOLOGICAL CYCLES AND ERAS

SOLAR (OR MAJOR) CYCLE

The solar cycle is a period of twenty-eight years in any corresponding year of which the days of the week recur on the same day of the month.

METONIC (LUNAR, OR MINOR) CYCLE

In 432 BC, Meton, an Athenian astronomer, found that 235 lunations are very nearly, though not exactly, equal in duration to 19 solar years and so after 19 years the phases of the Moon recur on the same days of the month (nearly). The dates of full moon in a cycle of 19 years were inscribed in figures of gold on public monuments in Athens, and the number showing the position of a year in the cycle is called the golden number of that year.

JULIAN PERIOD

The Julian period was proposed by Joseph Scaliger in 1582. The period is 7980 Julian years, and its first year coincides with the year 4713 BC. The figure of 7980 is the product of the number of years in the solar cycle, the Metonic cycle and the cycle of the Roman indiction ($28 \times 19 \times 15$).

ROMAN INDICTION

The Roman indiction is a period of fifteen years, instituted for fiscal purposes about AD 300.

EPACT

The epact is the age of the calendar Moon, diminished by one day, on 1 January, in the ecclesiastical lunar calendar.

CHINESE CALENDAR

A lunar calendar was the sole calendar in use in China until 1911, when the government adopted the new (Gregorian) calendar for official and most business activities. The Chinese tend to follow both calendars, the lunar calendar playing an important part in personal life, e.g. birth celebrations, festivals, marriages; and in rural villages the lunar calendar dictates the cycle of activities, denoting the change of weather and farming activities.

The lunar calendar is used in Hong Kong, Singapore, Malaysia, Tibet and elsewhere in south-east Asia. The calendar has a cycle of 60 years. The new year begins at the first new moon after the sun enters the sign of Aquarius, i.e. the new year falls between 21 January and 19 February in the Gregorian calendar.

Each year in the Chinese calendar is associated with one of 12 animals: the rat, the ox, the tiger, the rabbit, the dragon, the snake, the horse, the goat or sheep, the monkey, the chicken or rooster, the dog, and the pig.

The date of the Chinese new year and the astrological sign for the years 2000–2005 are:

2000	5 February	Dragon
2001	24 January	Snake
2002	—	Horse
2003	—	Goat or Sheep
2004	—	Monkey
2005	—	Chicken/Rooster

COPTIC CALENDAR

In the Coptic calendar, which is used in parts of Egypt and Ethiopia, the year is made up of 12 months of 30 days each, followed, in general, by five complementary days. Every fourth year is an intercalary or leap year and in these years there are six complementary days. The intercalary year of the Coptic calendar immediately precedes the leap year of the Julian calendar. The era is that of Diocletian or the Martyrs, the origin of which is fixed at 29 August AD 284 (Julian date).

INDIAN ERAS

In addition to the Muslim reckoning, other eras are used in India. The Saka era of southern India, dating from 3 March AD 78, was declared the national calendar of the Republic of India with effect from 22 March 1957, to be used concurrently with the Gregorian calendar. As revised, the year of the new Saka era begins at the spring equinox, with five successive months of 31 days and seven of 30 days in ordinary years, and six months of each length in leap years. The year AD 2000 is 1922 of the revised Saka era.

The year AD 2001 corresponds to the following years in other eras:

Year 2058 of the Vikram Samvat era
Year 1408 of the Bengali San era
Year 1177 of the Kollam era
Vedanga Jyotisa year 2 of the five-yearly cycle (384th cycle of Paitamah Siddhanta)
Year 6002 of the Kaliyuga era
Year 2545 of the Buddha Nirvana era

JAPANESE CALENDAR

The Japanese calendar is essentially the same as the Gregorian calendar, the years, months and weeks being of the same length and beginning on the same days as those of the Gregorian calendar. The numeration of the years is different, based on a system of epochs or periods each of which begins at the accession of an Emperor or other important occurrence. The method is not unlike the British system of regnal years, except that each year of a period closes on 31 December. The Japanese chronology begins about AD 650 and the three latest epochs are defined by the reigns of Emperors, whose actual names are not necessarily used:

Epoch

Taishō 1 August 1912 to 25 December 1926
Shōwa 26 December 1926 to 7 January 1989
Heisei 8 January 1989

The year Heisei 13 begins on 1 January 2001.

The months are known as First Month, Second Month, etc., First Month being equivalent to January. The days of the week are Nichiyōbi (Sun-day), Getsuyōbi (Moon-day), Kayōbi (Fire-day), Suiyōbi (Water-day), Mokuyōbi (Wood-day), Kinyōbi (Metal-day), Doyōbi (Earth-day).

THE MASONIC YEAR

Two dates are quoted in warrants, dispensations, etc., issued by the United Grand Lodge of England, those for the current year being expressed as *Anno Domini* 2000 – *Anno Lucis* 6000. This *Anno Lucis* (year of light) is based on the Book of Genesis 1 : 3, the 4000-year difference being derived, in modified form, from *Ussher's Notation*, published in 1654, which places the Creation of the World in 4004 BC.

OLYMPIADS

Ancient Greek chronology was reckoned in Olympiads, cycles of four years corresponding with the periodic Olympic Games held on the plain of Olympia in Elis once every four years. The intervening years were the first, second, etc., of the Olympiad, which received the name of the victor at the Games. The first recorded Olympiad is that of Choroebus, 776 BC.

ZOROASTRIAN CALENDAR

Zoroastrians, followers of the Iranian prophet Zarathushtra (known to the Greeks as Zoroaster) are mostly to be found in Iran and in India, where they are known as Parsees.

The Zoroastrian era dates from the coronation of the last Zoroastrian Sasanian king in AD 631. The Zoroastrian calendar is divided into twelve months, each comprising 30 days, followed by five holy days of the Gathas at the end of each year to make the year consist of 365 days.

In order to synchronise the calendar with the solar year of 365 days, an extra month was intercalated once every 120 years. However, this intercalation ceased in the 12th century and the New Year, which had fallen in the spring, slipped back to August. Because intercalation ceased at different times in Iran and India, there was one month's difference between the calendar followed in Iran (Kadmi calendar) and that followed by the Parsees (Shenshai calendar). In 1906 a group of Zoroastrians decided to bring the calendar back in line with the seasons again and restore the New Year to 21 March each year (Fasli calendar).

The Shenshai calendar (New Year in August) is mainly used by Parsees. The Fasli calendar (New Year, 21 March) is mainly used by Zoroastrians living in Iran, in the Indian subcontinent, or away from Iran.

THE ROMAN CALENDAR

Roman historians adopted as an epoch the foundation of Rome, which is believed to have happened in the year 753 BC. The ordinal number of the years in Roman reckoning is followed by the letters AUC (*ab urbe condita*), so that the year 2001 is 2754 AUC (MMDCCLIV). The calendar that we know has developed from one said to have been established by Romulus using a year of 304 days divided into ten months, beginning with March. To this Numa added January and February, making the year consist of 12 months of 30 and 29 days alternately, with an additional day so that the total was 355. It is also said that Numa ordered an intercalary month of 22 or 23 days in alternate years, making 90 days in eight years, to be inserted after 23 February.

However, there is some doubt as to the origination and the details of the intercalation in the Roman calendar. It is certain that some scheme of this kind was inaugurated and not fully carried out, for in the year 46 BC Julius Caesar found that the calendar had been allowed to fall into some confusion. He sought the help of the Egyptian astronomer Sosigenes, which led to the construction and adoption (45 BC) of the Julian calendar, and, by a slight alteration, to the Gregorian calendar now in use. The year 46 BC was made to consist of 445 days and is called the Year of Confusion.

In the Roman (Julian) calendar the days of the month were counted backwards from three fixed points, or days, and an intervening day was said to be so many days before the next coming point, the first and last being counted. These three points were the Kalends, the Nones, and the Ides. Their positions in the months and the method of counting from them will be seen in the table below. The year containing 366 days was called *bissextilis annus*, as it had a doubled sixth day (*bissextus dies*) before the March Kalends on 24 February – *ante diem sextum Kalendas Martias*, or a.d. VI Kal. Mart.

Present days of the month	March, May, July, October have thirty-one days	January, August, December have thirty-one days	April, June, September, November have thirty days	February has twenty-eight days, and in leap year twenty-nine
1	Kalendis	Kalendis	Kalendis	Kalendis
2	VI ⎫	IV ⎫ ante Nonas	IV ⎫ ante Nonas	IV ⎫ ante Nonas
3	V ⎬ ante Nonas	III ⎭ Nonas	III ⎭ Nonas	III ⎭ Nonas
4	IV ⎪	pridie Nonas	pridie Nonas	pridie Nonas
5	III ⎭	Nonis	Nonis	Nonis
6	pridie Nonas	VIII ⎫	VIII ⎫	VIII ⎫
7	Nonis	VII	VII	VII
8	VIII ⎫	VI ⎬ ante Idus	VI ⎬ ante Indus	VI ⎬ ante Idus
9	VII	V ⎭	V ⎭	V ⎭
10	VI ⎬ ante Indus	IV	IV	IV
11	V ⎭	III ⎭	III ⎭	III ⎭
12	IV	pridie Idus	pridie Idus	pridie Idus
13	III	Idibus	Idibus	Idibus
14	pridie Idus	XIX ⎫	XVIII ⎫	XVI ⎫
15	Idibus	XVIII	XVII	XV
16	XVII ⎫	XVII	XVI	XIV
17	XVI	XVI	XV	XIII
18	XV	XV	XIV	XII
19	XIV	XIV	XIII	XI
20	XIII	XIII	XII ⎬ ante Kalendas (of the month following)	X ⎬ ante Kalendas Martias
21	XII	XII ⎬ ante Kalendas (of the month following)	XI	IX
22	XI ⎬ ante Kalendas (of the month following)	XI	X	VIII
23	X	X	IX	VII
24	IX	IX	VIII	*VI
25	VIII	VIII	VII	V
26	VII	VII	VI	IV
27	VI	VI	V	III ⎭
28	V	V	IV	pridie Kalendas
29	IV	IV	III ⎭	
30	III ⎭	III ⎭	pridie Kalendas (Maias, Quinctilis, Octobris, Decembris)	
31	pridie Kalendas (Aprilis, Iunias, Sextilis, Novembris)	pridie Kalendas (Februarias, Septembris Ianuarias)		*(repeated in leap year)

Calendar for Any Year 1780–2040

To select the correct calendar for any year between 1780 and 2040, consult the index below
*leap year

1780	N*	1813	K	1846	I	1879	G	1912	D*	1945	C	1978	A	2011	M
1781	C	1814	M	1847	K	1880	J*	1913	G	1946	E	1979	C	2012	B*
1782	E	1815	A	1848	N*	1881	M	1914	I	1947	G	1980	F*	2013	E
1783	G	1816	D*	1849	C	1882	A	1915	K	1948	J*	1981	I	2014	G
1784	J*	1817	G	1850	E	1883	C	1916	N*	1949	M	1982	K	2015	I
1785	M	1818	I	1851	G	1884	F*	1917	C	1950	A	1983	M	2016	L*
1786	A	1819	K	1852	J*	1885	I	1918	E	1951	C	1984	B*	2017	A
1787	C	1820	N*	1853	M	1886	K	1919	G	1952	F*	1985	E	2018	C
1788	F*	1821	C	1854	A	1887	M	1920	J*	1953	I	1986	G	2019	E
1789	I	1822	E	1855	C	1888	B*	1921	M	1954	K	1987	I	2020	H*
1790	K	1823	G	1856	F*	1889	E	1922	A	1955	M	1988	L*	2021	K
1791	M	1824	J*	1857	I	1890	G	1923	C	1956	B*	1989	A	2022	M
1792	B*	1825	M	1858	K	1891	I	1924	F*	1957	E	1990	C	2023	A
1793	E	1826	A	1859	M	1892	L*	1925	I	1958	G	1991	E	2024	D*
1794	G	1827	C	1860	B*	1893	A	1926	K	1959	I	1992	H*	2025	G
1795	I	1828	F*	1861	E	1894	C	1927	M	1960	L*	1993	K	2026	I
1796	L*	1829	I	1862	G	1895	E	1928	B*	1961	A	1994	M	2027	K
1797	A	1830	K	1863	I	1896	H*	1929	E	1962	C	1995	A	2028	N*
1798	C	1831	M	1864	L*	1897	K	1930	G	1963	E	1996	D*	2029	C
1799	E	1832	B*	1865	A	1898	M	1931	I	1964	H*	1997	G	2030	E
1800	G	1833	E	1866	C	1899	A	1932	L*	1965	K	1998	I	2031	G
1801	I	1834	G	1867	E	1900	G	1933	A	1966	M	1999	K	2032	J*
1802	K	1835	I	1868	H*	1901	E	1934	C	1967	A	2000	N*	2033	M
1803	M	1836	L*	1869	K	1902	G	1935	E	1968	D*	2001	C	2034	A
1804	B*	1837	A	1870	M	1903	I	1936	H*	1969	G	2002	E	2035	C
1805	E	1838	C	1871	A	1904	L*	1937	K	1970	I	2003	G	2036	F*
1806	G	1839	E	1872	D*	1905	A	1938	M	1971	K	2004	J*	2037	I
1807	I	1840	H*	1873	G	1906	C	1939	A	1972	N*	2005	M	2038	K
1808	L*	1841	K	1874	I	1907	E	1940	D*	1973	C	2006	A	2039	M
1809	A	1842	M	1875	K	1908	H*	1941	G	1974	E	2007	C	2040	B*
1810	C	1843	A	1876	N*	1909	K	1942	I	1975	G	2008	F*		
1811	E	1844	D*	1877	C	1910	M	1943	K	1976	J*	2009	I		
1812	H*	1845	G	1878	E	1911	A	1944	N*	1977	M	2010	K		

A

	January	February	March
Sun.	1 8 15 22 29	5 12 19 26	5 12 19 26
Mon.	2 9 16 23 30	6 13 20 27	6 13 20 27
Tue.	3 10 17 24 31	7 14 21 28	7 14 21 28
Wed.	4 11 18 25	1 8 15 22	1 8 15 22 29
Thur.	5 12 19 26	2 9 16 23	2 9 16 23 30
Fri.	6 13 20 27	3 10 17 24	3 10 17 24 31
Sat.	7 14 21 28	4 11 18 25	4 11 18 25

	April	May	June
Sun.	2 9 16 23 30	7 14 21 28	4 11 18 25
Mon.	3 10 17 24	1 8 15 22 29	5 12 19 26
Tue.	4 11 18 25	2 9 16 23 30	6 13 20 27
Wed.	5 12 19 26	3 10 17 24 31	7 14 21 28
Thur.	6 13 20 27	4 11 18 25	1 8 15 22 29
Fri.	7 14 21 28	5 12 19 26	2 9 16 23 30
Sat.	1 8 15 22 29	6 13 20 27	3 10 17 24

	July	August	September
Sun.	2 9 16 23 30	6 13 20 27	3 10 17 24
Mon.	3 10 17 24 31	7 14 21 28	4 11 18 25
Tue.	4 11 18 25	1 8 15 22 29	5 12 19 26
Wed.	5 12 19 26	2 9 16 23 30	6 13 20 27
Thur.	6 13 20 27	3 10 17 24 31	7 14 21 28
Fri.	7 14 21 28	4 11 18 25	1 8 15 22 29
Sat.	1 8 15 22 29	5 12 19 26	2 9 16 23 30

	October	November	December
Sun.	1 8 15 22 29	5 12 19 26	3 10 17 24 31
Mon.	2 9 16 23 30	6 13 20 27	4 11 18 25
Tue.	3 10 17 24 31	7 14 21 28	5 12 19 26
Wed.	4 11 18 25	1 8 15 22 29	6 13 20 27
Thur.	5 12 19 26	2 9 16 23 30	7 14 21 28
Fri.	6 13 20 27	3 10 17 24	1 8 15 22 29
Sat.	7 14 21 28	4 11 18 25	2 9 16 23 30

B (LEAP YEAR)

	January	February	March
Sun.	1 8 15 22 29	5 12 19 26	4 11 18 25
Mon.	2 9 16 23 30	6 13 20 27	5 12 19 26
Tue.	3 10 17 24 31	7 14 21 28	6 13 20 27
Wed.	4 11 18 25	1 8 15 22 29	7 14 21 28
Thur.	5 12 19 26	2 9 16 23	1 8 15 22 29
Fri.	6 13 20 27	3 10 17 24	2 9 16 23 30
Sat.	7 14 21 28	4 11 18 25	3 10 17 24 31

	April	May	June
Sun.	1 8 15 22 29	6 13 20 27	3 10 17 24
Mon.	2 9 16 23 30	7 14 21 28	4 11 18 25
Tue.	3 10 17 24	1 8 15 22 29	5 12 19 26
Wed.	4 11 18 25	2 9 16 23 30	6 13 20 27
Thur.	5 12 19 26	3 10 17 24 31	7 14 21 28
Fri.	6 13 20 27	4 11 18 25	1 8 15 22 29
Sat.	7 14 21 28	5 12 19 26	2 9 16 23 30

	July	August	September
Sun.	1 8 15 22 29	5 12 19 26	2 9 16 23 30
Mon.	2 9 16 23 30	6 13 20 27	3 10 17 24
Tue.	3 10 17 24 31	7 14 21 28	4 11 18 25
Wed.	4 11 18 25	1 8 15 22 29	5 12 19 26
Thur.	5 12 19 26	2 9 16 23 30	6 13 20 27
Fri.	6 13 20 27	3 10 17 24 31	7 14 21 28
Sat.	7 14 21 28	4 11 18 25	1 8 15 22 29

	October	November	December
Sun.	7 14 21 28	4 11 18 25	2 9 16 23 30
Mon.	1 8 15 22 29	5 12 19 26	3 10 17 24 31
Tue.	2 9 16 23 30	6 13 20 27	4 11 18 25
Wed.	3 10 17 24 31	7 14 21 28	5 12 19 26
Thur.	4 11 18 25	1 8 15 22 29	6 13 20 27
Fri.	5 12 19 26	2 9 16 23 30	7 14 21 28
Sat.	6 13 20 27	3 10 17 24	1 8 15 22 29

EASTER DAYS

March 26	1815, 1826, 1837, 1967, 1978, 1989
April 2	1809, 1893, 1899, 1961
April 9	1871, 1882, 1939, 1950, 2023, 2034
April 16	1786, 1797, 1843, 1854, 1865, 1911
	1922, 1933, 1995, 2006, 2017
April 23	1905

EASTER DAYS

April 1	1804, 1888, 1956, 2040
April 8	1792, 1860, 1928, 2012
April 22	1832, 1984

C

	January	February	March
Sun.	7 14 21 28	4 11 18 25	4 11 18 25
Mon.	1 8 15 22 29	5 12 19 26	5 12 19 26
Tue.	2 9 16 23 30	6 13 20 27	6 13 20 27
Wed.	3 10 17 24 31	7 14 21 28	7 14 21 28
Thur.	4 11 18 25	1 8 15 22	1 8 15 22 29
Fri.	5 12 19 26	2 9 16 23	2 9 16 23 30
Sat.	6 13 20 27	3 10 17 24	3 10 17 24 31

	April	May	June
Sun.	1 8 15 22 29	6 13 20 27	3 10 17 24
Mon.	2 9 16 23 30	7 14 21 28	4 11 18 25
Tue.	3 10 17 24	1 8 15 22 29	5 12 19 26
Wed.	4 11 18 25	2 9 16 23 30	6 13 20 27
Thur.	5 12 19 26	3 10 17 24 31	7 14 21 28
Fri.	6 13 20 27	4 11 18 25	1 8 15 22 29
Sat.	7 14 21 28	5 12 19 26	2 9 16 23 30

	July	August	September
Sun.	1 8 15 22 29	5 12 19 26	2 9 16 23 30
Mon.	2 9 16 23 30	6 13 20 27	3 10 17 24
Tue.	3 10 17 24 31	7 14 21 28	4 11 18 25
Wed.	4 11 18 25	1 8 15 22 29	5 12 19 26
Thur.	5 12 19 26	2 9 16 23 30	6 13 20 27
Fri.	6 13 20 27	3 10 17 24 31	7 14 21 28
Sat.	7 14 21 28	4 11 18 25	1 8 15 22 29

	October	November	December
Sun.	7 14 21 28	4 11 18 25	2 9 16 23 30
Mon.	1 8 15 22 29	5 12 19 26	3 10 17 24 31
Tue.	2 9 16 23 30	6 13 20 27	4 11 18 25
Wed.	3 10 17 24 31	7 14 21 28	5 12 19 26
Thur.	4 11 18 25	1 8 15 22 29	6 13 20 27
Fri.	5 12 19 26	2 9 16 23 30	7 14 21 28
Sat.	6 13 20 27	3 10 17 24	1 8 15 22 29

Easter Days

March 25	1883, 1894, 1951, 2035
April 1	1866, 1877, 1923, 1934, 1945, 2018, 2029
April 8	1787, 1798, 1849, 1855, 1917, 2007
April 15	1781, 1827, 1838, 1900, 1906, 1979, 1990, 2001
April 22	1810, 1821, 1962, 1973

D   (LEAP YEAR)

	January	February	March
Sun.	7 14 21 28	4 11 18 25	3 10 17 24 31
Mon.	1 8 15 22 29	5 12 19 26	4 11 18 25
Tue.	2 9 16 23 30	6 13 20 27	5 12 19 26
Wed.	3 10 17 24 31	7 14 21 28	6 13 20 27
Thur.	4 11 18 25	1 8 15 22 29	7 14 21 28
Fri.	5 12 19 26	2 9 16 23	1 8 15 22 29
Sat.	6 13 20 27	3 10 17 24	2 9 16 23 30

	April	May	June
Sun.	7 14 21 28	5 12 19 26	2 9 16 23 30
Mon.	1 8 15 22 29	6 13 20 27	3 10 17 24
Tue.	2 9 16 23 30	7 14 21 28	4 11 18 25
Wed.	3 10 17 24	1 8 15 22 29	5 12 19 26
Thur.	4 11 18 25	2 9 16 23 30	6 13 20 27
Fri.	5 12 19 26	3 10 17 24 31	7 14 21 28
Sat.	6 13 20 27	4 11 18 25	1 8 15 22 29

	July	August	September
Sun.	7 14 21 28	4 11 18 25	1 8 15 22 29
Mon.	1 8 15 22 29	5 12 19 26	2 9 16 23 30
Tue.	2 9 16 23 30	6 13 20 27	3 10 17 24
Wed.	3 10 17 24 31	7 14 21 28	4 11 18 25
Thur.	4 11 18 25	1 8 15 22 29	5 12 19 26
Fri.	5 12 19 26	2 9 16 23 30	6 13 20 27
Sat.	6 13 20 27	3 10 17 24 31	7 14 21 28

	October	November	December
Sun.	6 13 20 27	3 10 17 24	1 8 15 22 29
Mon.	7 14 21 28	4 11 18 25	2 9 16 23 30
Tue.	1 8 15 22 29	5 12 19 26	3 10 17 24 31
Wed.	2 9 16 23 30	6 13 20 27	4 11 18 25
Thur.	3 10 17 24 31	7 14 21 28	5 12 19 26
Fri.	4 11 18 25	1 8 15 22 29	6 13 20 27
Sat.	5 12 19 26	2 9 16 23 30	7 14 21 28

Easter Days

March 24	1940
March 31	1872, 2024
April 7	1844, 1912, 1996
April 14	1816, 1968

E

	January	February	March
Sun.	6 13 20 27	3 10 17 24	3 10 17 24 31
Mon.	7 14 21 28	4 11 18 25	4 11 18 25
Tue.	1 8 15 22 29	5 12 19 26	5 12 19 26
Wed.	2 9 16 23 30	6 13 20 27	6 13 20 27
Thur.	3 10 17 24 31	7 14 21 28	7 14 21 28
Fri.	4 11 18 25	1 8 15 22	1 8 15 22 29
Sat.	5 12 19 26	2 9 16 23	2 9 16 23 30

	April	May	June
Sun.	7 14 21 28	5 12 19 26	2 9 16 23 30
Mon.	1 8 15 22 29	6 13 20 27	3 10 17 24
Tue.	2 9 16 23 30	7 14 21 28	4 11 18 25
Wed.	3 10 17 24	1 8 15 22 29	5 12 19 26
Thur.	4 11 18 25	2 9 16 23 30	6 13 20 27
Fri.	5 12 19 26	3 10 17 24 31	7 14 21 28
Sat.	6 13 20 27	4 11 18 25	1 8 15 22 29

	July	August	September
Sun.	7 14 21 28	4 11 18 25	1 8 15 22 29
Mon.	1 8 15 22 29	5 12 19 26	2 9 16 23 30
Tue.	2 9 16 23 30	6 13 20 27	3 10 17 24
Wed.	3 10 17 24 31	7 14 21 28	4 11 18 25
Thur.	4 11 18 25	1 8 15 22 29	5 12 19 26
Fri.	5 12 19 26	2 9 16 23 30	6 13 20 27
Sat.	6 13 20 27	3 10 17 24 31	7 14 21 28

	October	November	December
Sun.	6 13 20 27	3 10 17 24	1 8 15 22 29
Mon.	7 14 21 28	4 11 18 25	2 9 16 23 30
Tue.	1 8 15 22 29	5 12 19 26	3 10 17 24 31
Wed.	2 9 16 23 30	6 13 20 27	4 11 18 25
Thur.	3 10 17 24 31	7 14 21 28	5 12 19 26
Fri.	4 11 18 25	1 8 15 22 29	6 13 20 27
Sat.	5 12 19 26	2 9 16 23 30	7 14 21 28

Easter Days

March 24	1799
March 31	1782, 1793, 1839, 1850, 1861, 1907
	1918, 1929, 1991, 2002, 2013
April 7	1822, 1833, 1901, 1985
April 14	1805, 1811, 1895, 1963, 1974
April 21	1867, 1878, 1889, 1935, 1946, 1957, 2019, 2030

F   (LEAP YEAR)

	January	February	March
Sun.	6 13 20 27	3 10 17 24	2 9 16 23 30
Mon.	7 14 21 28	4 11 18 25	3 10 17 24 31
Tue.	1 8 15 22 29	5 12 19 26	4 11 18 25
Wed.	2 9 16 23 30	6 13 20 27	5 12 19 26
Thur.	3 10 17 24 31	7 14 21 28	6 13 20 27
Fri.	4 11 18 25	1 8 15 22 29	7 14 21 28
Sat.	5 12 19 26	2 9 16 23	1 8 15 22 29

	April	May	June
Sun.	6 13 20 27	4 11 18 25	1 8 15 22 29
Mon.	7 14 21 28	5 12 19 26	2 9 16 23 30
Tue.	1 8 15 22 29	6 13 20 27	3 10 17 24
Wed.	2 9 16 23 30	7 14 21 28	4 11 18 25
Thur.	3 10 17 24	1 8 15 22 29	5 12 19 26
Fri.	4 11 18 25	2 9 16 23 30	6 13 20 27
Sat.	5 12 19 26	3 10 17 24 31	7 14 21 28

	July	August	September
Sun.	6 13 20 27	3 10 17 24 31	7 14 21 28
Mon.	7 14 21 28	4 11 18 25	1 8 15 22 29
Tue.	1 8 15 22 29	5 12 19 26	2 9 16 23 30
Wed.	2 9 16 23 30	6 13 20 27	3 10 17 24
Thur.	3 10 17 24 31	7 14 21 28	4 11 18 25
Fri.	4 11 18 25	1 8 15 22 29	5 12 19 26
Sat.	5 12 19 26	2 9 16 23 30	6 13 20 27

	October	November	December
Sun.	5 12 19 26	2 9 16 23 30	7 14 21 28
Mon.	6 13 20 27	3 10 17 24	1 8 15 22 29
Tue.	7 14 21 28	4 11 18 25	2 9 16 23 30
Wed.	1 8 15 22 29	5 12 19 26	3 10 17 24 31
Thur.	2 9 16 23 30	6 13 20 27	4 11 18 25
Fri.	3 10 17 24 31	7 14 21 28	5 12 19 26
Sat.	4 11 18 25	1 8 15 22 29	6 13 20 27

Easter Days

March 23	1788, 1856, 2008
April 6	1828, 1980
April 13	1884, 1952, 2036
April 20	1924

G

	January	February	March
Sun.	5 12 19 26	2 9 16 23	2 9 16 23 30
Mon.	6 13 20 27	3 10 17 24	3 10 17 24 31
Tue.	7 14 21 28	4 11 18 25	4 11 18 25
Wed.	1 8 15 22 29	5 12 19 26	5 12 19 26
Thur.	2 9 16 23 30	6 13 20 27	6 13 20 27
Fri.	3 10 17 24 31	7 14 21 28	7 14 21 28
Sat.	4 11 18 25	1 8 15 22	1 8 15 22 29

	April	May	June
Sun.	6 13 20 27	4 11 18 25	1 8 15 22 29
Mon.	7 14 21 28	5 12 19 26	2 9 16 23 30
Tue.	1 8 15 22 29	6 13 20 27	3 10 17 24
Wed.	2 9 16 23 30	7 14 21 28	4 11 18 25
Thur.	3 10 17 24	1 8 15 22 29	5 12 19 26
Fri.	4 11 18 25	2 9 16 23 30	6 13 20 27
Sat.	5 12 19 26	3 10 17 24 31	7 14 21 28

	July	August	September
Sun.	6 13 20 27	3 10 17 24 31	7 14 21 28
Mon.	7 14 21 28	4 11 18 25	1 8 15 22 29
Tue.	1 8 15 22 29	5 12 19 26	2 9 16 23 30
Wed.	2 9 16 23 30	6 13 20 27	3 10 17 24
Thur.	3 10 17 24 31	7 14 21 28	4 11 18 25
Fri.	4 11 18 25	1 8 15 22 29	5 12 19 26
Sat.	5 12 19 26	2 9 16 23 30	6 13 20 27

	October	November	December
Sun.	5 12 19 26	2 9 16 23 30	7 14 21 28
Mon.	6 13 20 27	3 10 17 24	1 8 15 22 29
Tue.	7 14 21 28	4 11 18 25	2 9 16 23 30
Wed.	1 8 15 22 29	5 12 19 26	3 10 17 24 31 ·
Thur.	2 9 16 23 30	6 13 20 27	4 11 18 25
Fri.	3 10 17 24 31	7 14 21 28	5 12 19 26
Sat.	4 11 18 25	1 8 15 22 29	6 13 20 27

EASTER DAYS

March 23	1845, 1913
March 30	1823, 1834, 1902, 1975, 1986, 1997
April 6	1806, 1817, 1890, 1947, 1958, 1969
April 13	1800, 1873, 1879, 1941, 2031
April 20	1783, 1794, 1851, 1862, 1919, 1930, 2003, 2014, 2025

I

	January	February	March
Sun.	4 11 18 25	1 8 15 22	1 8 15 22 29
Mon.	5 12 19 26	2 9 16 23	2 9 16 23 30
Tue.	6 13 20 27	3 10 17 24	3 10 17 24 31
Wed.	7 14 21 28	4 11 18 25	4 11 18 25
Thur.	1 8 15 22 29	5 12 19 26	5 12 19 26
Fri.	2 9 16 23 30	6 13 20 27	6 13 20 27
Sat.	3 10 17 24 31	7 14 21 28	7 14 21 28

	April	May	June
Sun.	5 12 19 26	3 10 17 24 31	7 14 21 28
Mon.	6 13 20 27	4 11 18 25	1 8 15 22 29
Tue.	7 14 21 28	5 12 19 26	2 9 16 23 30
Wed.	1 8 15 22 29	6 13 20 27	3 10 17 24
Thur.	2 9 16 23 30	7 14 21 28	4 11 18 25
Fri.	3 10 17 24	1 8 15 22 29	5 12 19 26
Sat.	4 11 18 25	2 9 16 23 30	6 13 20 27

	July	August	September
Sun.	5 12 19 26	2 9 16 23 30	6 13 20 27
Mon.	6 13 20 27	3 10 17 24 31	7 14 21 28
Tue.	7 14 21 28	4 11 18 25	1 8 15 22 29
Wed.	1 8 15 22 29	5 12 19 26	2 9 16 23 30
Thur.	2 9 16 23 30	6 13 20 27	3 10 17 24
Fri.	3 10 17 24 31	7 14 21 28	4 11 18 25
Sat.	4 11 18 25	1 8 15 22 29	5 12 19 26

	October	November	December
Sun.	4 11 18 25	1 8 15 22 29	6 13 20 27
Mon.	5 12 19 26	2 9 16 23 30	7 14 21 28
Tue.	6 13 20 27	3 10 17 24	1 8 15 22 29
Wed.	7 14 21 28	4 11 18 25	2 9 16 23 30
Thur.	1 8 15 22 29	5 12 19 26	3 10 17 24 31
Fri.	2 9 16 23 30	6 13 20 27	4 11 18 25
Sat.	3 10 17 24 31	7 14 21 28	5 12 19 26

EASTER DAYS

March 22	1818
March 29	1807, 1891, 1959, 1970
April 5	1795, 1801, 1863, 1874, 1885, 1931, 1942, 1953, 2015, 2026, 2037
April 12	1789, 1846, 1857, 1903, 1914, 1925, 1998, 2009
April 19	1829, 1835, 1981, 1987

H (LEAP YEAR)

	January	February	March
Sun.	5 12 19 26	2 9 16 23	1 8 15 22 29
Mon.	6 13 20 27	3 10 17 24	2 9 16 23 30
Tue.	7 14 21 28	4 11 18 25	3 10 17 24 31
Wed.	1 8 15 22 29	5 12 19 26	4 11 18 25
Thur.	2 9 16 23 30	6 13 20 27	5 12 19 26
Fri.	3 10 17 24 31	7 14 21 28	6 13 20 27
Sat.	4 11 18 25	1 8 15 22 29	7 14 21 28

	April	May	June
Sun.	5 12 19 26	3 10 17 24 31	7 14 21 28
Mon.	6 13 20 27	4 11 18 25	1 8 15 22 29
Tue.	7 14 21 28	5 12 19 26	2 9 16 23 30
Wed.	1 8 15 22 29	6 13 20 27	3 10 17 24
Thur.	2 9 16 23 30	7 14 21 28	4 11 18 25
Fri.	3 10 17 24	1 8 15 22 29	5 12 19 26
Sat.	4 11 18 25	2 9 16 23 30	6 13 20 27

	July	August	September
Sun.	5 12 19 26	2 9 16 23 30	6 13 20 27
Mon.	6 13 20 27	3 10 17 24 31	7 14 21 28
Tue.	7 14 21 28	4 11 18 25	1 8 15 22 29
Wed.	1 8 15 22 29	5 12 19 26	2 9 16 23 30
Thur.	2 9 16 23 30	6 13 20 27	3 10 17 24
Fri.	3 10 17 24 31	7 14 21 28	4 11 18 25
Sat.	4 11 18 25	1 8 15 22 29	5 12 19 26

	October	November	December
Sun.	4 11 18 25	1 8 15 22 29	6 13 20 27
Mon.	5 12 19 26	2 9 16 23 30	7 14 21 28
Tue.	6 13 20 27	3 10 17 24	1 8 15 22 29
Wed.	7 14 21 28	4 11 18 25	2 9 16 23 30
Thur.	1 8 15 22 29	5 12 19 26	3 10 17 24 31
Fri.	2 9 16 23 30	6 13 20 27	4 11 18 25
Sat.	3 10 17 24 31	7 14 21 28	5 12 19 26

EASTER DAYS

March 29	1812, 1964
April 5	1896
April 12	1868, 1936, 2020
April 19	1840, 1908, 1992

J (LEAP YEAR)

	January	February	March
Sun.	4 11 18 25	1 8 15 22 29	7 14 21 28
Mon.	5 12 19 26	2 9 16 23	1 8 15 22 29
Tue.	6 13 20 27	3 10 17 24	2 9 16 23 30
Wed.	7 14 21 28	4 11 18 25	3 10 17 24 31
Thur.	1 8 15 22 29	5 12 19 26	4 11 18 25
Fri.	2 9 16 23 30	6 13 20 27	5 12 19 26
Sat.	3 10 17 24 31	7 14 21 28	6 13 20 27

	April	May	June
Sun.	4 11 18 25	2 9 16 23 30	6 13 20 27
Mon.	5 12 19 26	3 10 17 24 31	7 14 21 28
Tue.	6 13 20 27	4 11 18 25	1 8 15 22 29
Wed.	7 14 21 28	5 12 19 26	2 9 16 23 30
Thur.	1 8 15 22 29	6 13 20 27	3 10 17 24
Fri.	2 9 16 23 30	7 14 21 28	4 11 18 25
Sat.	3 10 17 24	1 8 15 22 29	5 12 19 26

	July	August	September
Sun.	4 11 18 25	1 8 15 22 29	5 12 19 26
Mon.	5 12 19 26	2 9 16 23 30	6 13 20 27
Tue.	6 13 20 27	3 10 17 24 31	7 14 21 28
Wed.	7 14 21 28	4 11 18 25	1 8 15 22 29
Thur.	1 8 15 22 29	5 12 19 26	2 9 16 23 30
Fri.	2 9 16 23 30	6 13 20 27	3 10 17 24
Sat.	3 10 17 24 31	7 14 21 28	4 11 18 25

	October	November	December
Sun.	3 10 17 24 31	7 14 21 28	5 12 19 26
Mon.	4 11 18 25	1 8 15 22 29	6 13 20 27
Tue.	5 12 19 26	2 9 16 23 30	7 14 21 28
Wed.	6 13 20 27	3 10 17 24	1 8 15 22 29
Thur.	7 14 21 28	4 11 18 25	2 9 16 23 30
Fri.	1 8 15 22 29	5 12 19 26	3 10 17 24 31
Sat.	2 9 16 23 30	6 13 20 27	4 11 18 25

EASTER DAYS

March 28	1880, 1948, 2032
April 4	1920
April 11	1784, 1852, 2004
April 18	1824, 1976

K

	January	February	March
Sun.	3 10 17 24 31	7 14 21 28	7 14 21 28
Mon.	4 11 18 25	1 8 15 22	1 8 15 22 29
Tue.	5 12 19 26	2 9 16 23	2 9 16 23 30
Wed.	6 13 20 27	3 10 17 24	3 10 17 24 31
Thur.	7 14 21 28	4 11 18 25	4 11 18 25
Fri.	1 8 15 22 29	5 12 19 26	5 12 19 26
Sat.	2 9 16 23 30	6 13 20 27	6 13 20 27
	April	May	June
Sun.	4 11 18 25	2 9 16 23 30	6 13 20 27
Mon.	5 12 19 26	3 10 17 24 31	7 14 21 28
Tue.	6 13 20 27	4 11 18 25	1 8 15 22 29
Wed.	7 14 21 28	5 12 19 26	2 9 16 23 30
Thur.	1 8 15 22 29	6 13 20 27	3 10 17 24
Fri.	2 9 16 23 30	7 14 21 28	4 11 18 25
Sat.	3 10 17 24	1 8 15 22 29	5 12 19 26
	July	August	September
Sun.	4 11 18 25	1 8 15 22 29	5 12 19 26
Mon.	5 12 19 26	2 9 16 23 30	6 13 20 27
Tue.	6 13 20 27	3 10 17 24 31	7 14 21 28
Wed.	7 14 21 28	4 11 18 25	1 8 15 22 29
Thur.	1 8 15 22 29	5 12 19 26	2 9 16 23 30
Fri.	2 9 16 23 30	6 13 20 27	3 10 17 24
Sat.	3 10 17 24 31	7 14 21 28	4 11 18 25
	October	November	December
Sun.	3 10 17 24 31	7 14 21 28	5 12 19 26
Mon.	4 11 18 25	1 8 15 22 29	6 13 20 27
Tue.	5 12 19 26	2 9 16 23 30	7 14 21 28
Wed.	6 13 20 27	3 10 17 24	1 8 15 22 29
Thur.	7 14 21 28	4 11 18 25	2 9 16 23 30
Fri.	1 8 15 22 29	5 12 19 26	3 10 17 24 31
Sat.	2 9 16 23 30	6 13 20 27	4 11 18 25

EASTER DAYS

March 28	1869, 1875, 1937, 2027
April 4	1790, 1847, 1858, 1915, 1926, 1999, 2010, 2021
April 11	1819, 1830, 1841, 1909, 1971, 1982, 1993
April 18	1802, 1813, 1897, 1954, 1965
April 25	1886, 1943, 2038

M

	January	February	March
Sun.	2 9 16 23 30	6 13 20 27	6 13 20 27
Mon.	3 10 17 24 31	7 14 21 28	7 14 21 28
Tue.	4 11 18 25	1 8 15 22	1 8 15 22 29
Wed.	5 12 19 26	2 9 16 23	2 9 16 23 30
Thur.	6 13 20 27	3 10 17 24	3 10 17 24 31
Fri.	7 14 21 28	4 11 18 25	4 11 18 25
Sat.	1 8 15 22 29	5 12 19 26	5 12 19 26
	April	May	June
Sun.	3 10 17 24	1 8 15 22 29	5 12 19 26
Mon.	4 11 18 25	2 9 16 23 30	6 13 20 27
Tue.	5 12 19 26	3 10 17 24 31	7 14 21 28
Wed.	6 13 20 27	4 11 18 25	1 8 15 22 29
Thur.	7 14 21 28	5 12 19 26	2 9 16 23 30
Fri.	1 8 15 22 29	6 13 20 27	3 10 17 24
Sat.	2 9 16 23 30	7 14 21 28	4 11 18 25
	July	August	September
Sun.	3 10 17 24 31	7 14 21 28	4 11 18 25
Mon.	4 11 18 25	1 8 15 22 29	5 12 19 26
Tue.	5 12 19 26	2 9 16 23 30	6 13 20 27
Wed.	6 13 20 27	3 10 17 24 31	7 14 21 28
Thur.	7 14 21 28	4 11 18 25	1 8 15 22 29
Fri.	1 8 15 22 29	5 12 19 26	2 9 16 23 30
Sat.	2 9 16 23 30	6 13 20 27	3 10 17 24
	October	November	December
Sun.	2 9 16 23 30	6 13 20 27	4 11 18 25
Mon.	3 10 17 24 31	7 14 21 28	5 12 19 26
Tue.	4 11 18 25	1 8 15 22 29	6 13 20 27
Wed.	5 12 19 26	2 9 16 23 30	7 14 21 28
Thur.	6 13 20 27	3 10 17 24	1 8 15 22 29
Fri.	7 14 21 28	4 11 18 25	2 9 16 23 30
Sat.	1 8 15 22 29	5 12 19 26	3 10 17 24 31

EASTER DAYS

March 27	1785, 1842, 1853, 1910, 1921, 2005
April 3	1825, 1831, 1983, 1994
April 10	1803, 1814, 1887, 1898, 1955, 1966, 1977, 2039
April 17	1870, 1881, 1927, 1938, 1949, 2022, 2033
April 24	1791, 1859, 2011

L (LEAP YEAR)

	January	February	March
Sun.	3 10 17 24 31	7 14 21 28	6 13 20 27
Mon.	4 11 18 25	1 8 15 22 29	7 14 21 28
Tue.	5 12 19 26	2 9 16 23	1 8 15 22 29
Wed.	6 13 20 27	3 10 17 24	2 9 16 23 30
Thur.	7 14 21 28	4 11 18 25	3 10 17 24 31
Fri.	1 8 15 22 29	5 12 19 26	4 11 18 25
Sat.	2 9 16 23 30	6 13 20 27	5 12 19 26
	April	May	June
Sun.	3 10 17 24	1 8 15 22 29	5 12 19 26
Mon.	4 11 18 25	2 9 16 23 30	6 13 20 27
Tue.	5 12 19 26	3 10 17 24 31	7 14 21 28
Wed.	6 13 20 27	4 11 18 25	1 8 15 22 29
Thur.	7 14 21 28	5 12 19 26	2 9 16 23 30
Fri.	1 8 15 22 29	6 13 20 27	3 10 17 24
Sat.	2 9 16 23 30	7 14 21 28	4 11 18 25
	July	August	September
Sun.	3 10 17 24 31	7 14 21 28	4 11 18 25
Mon.	4 11 18 25	1 8 15 22 29	5 12 19 26
Tue.	5 12 19 26	2 9 16 23 30	6 13 20 27
Wed.	6 13 20 27	3 10 17 24 31	7 14 21 28
Thur.	7 14 21 28	4 11 18 25	1 8 15 22 29
Fri.	1 8 15 22 29	5 12 19 26	2 9 16 23 30
Sat.	2 9 16 23 30	6 13 20 27	3 10 17 24
	October	November	December
Sun.	2 9 16 23 30	6 13 20 27	4 11 18 25
Mon.	3 10 17 24 31	7 14 21 28	5 12 19 26
Tue.	4 11 18 25	1 8 15 22 29	6 13 20 27
Wed.	5 12 19 26	2 9 16 23 30	7 14 21 28
Thur.	6 13 20 27	3 10 17 24	1 8 15 22 29
Fri.	7 14 21 28	4 11 18 25	2 9 16 23 30
Sat.	1 8 15 22 29	5 12 19 26	3 10 17 24 31

EASTER DAYS

March 27	1796, 1864, 1932, 2016
April 3	1836, 1904, 1988
April 17	1808, 1892, 1960

N (LEAP YEAR)

	January	February	March
Sun.	2 9 16 23 30	6 13 20 27	5 12 19 26
Mon.	3 10 17 24 31	7 14 21 28	6 13 20 27
Tue.	4 11 18 25	1 8 15 22 29	7 14 21 28
Wed.	5 12 19 26	2 9 16 23	1 8 15 22 29
Thur.	6 13 20 27	3 10 17 24	2 9 16 23 30
Fri.	7 14 21 28	4 11 18 25	3 10 17 24 31
Sat.	1 8 15 22 29	5 12 19 26	4 11 18 25
	April	May	June
Sun.	2 9 16 23 30	7 14 21 28	4 11 18 25
Mon.	3 10 17 24	1 8 15 22 29	5 12 19 26
Tue.	4 11 18 25	2 9 16 23 30	6 13 20 27
Wed.	5 12 19 26	3 10 17 24 31	7 14 21 28
Thur.	6 13 20 27	4 11 18 25	1 8 15 22 29
Fri.	7 14 21 28	5 12 19 26	2 9 16 23 30
Sat.	1 8 15 22 29	6 13 20 27	3 10 17 24
	July	August	September
Sun.	2 9 16 23 30	6 13 20 27	3 10 17 24
Mon.	3 10 17 24 31	7 14 21 28	4 11 18 25
Tue.	4 11 18 25	1 8 15 22 29	5 12 19 26
Wed.	5 12 19 26	2 9 16 23 30	6 13 20 27
Thur.	6 13 20 27	3 10 17 24 31	7 14 21 28
Fri.	7 14 21 28	4 11 18 25	1 8 15 22 29
Sat.	1 8 15 22 29	5 12 19 26	2 9 16 23 30
	October	November	December
Sun.	1 8 15 22 29	5 12 19 26	3 10 17 24 31
Mon.	2 9 16 23 30	6 13 20 27	4 11 18 25
Tue.	3 10 17 24 31	7 14 21 28	5 12 19 26
Wed.	4 11 18 25	1 8 15 22 29	6 13 20 27
Thur.	5 12 19 26	2 9 16 23 30	7 14 21 28
Fri.	6 13 20 27	3 10 17 24	1 8 15 22 29
Sat.	7 14 21 28	4 11 18 25	2 9 16 23 30

EASTER DAYS

March 26	1780
April 2	1820, 1972
April 9	1944
April 16	2028
April 23	1848, 1916, 2000

GEOLOGICAL TIME

The earth is thought to have come into existence approximately 4,600 million years ago, but for nearly half this time, the Archean era, it was uninhabited. Life is generally believed to have emerged in the succeeding Proterozoic era. The Archean and the Proterozoic eras are often together referred to as the Precambrian.

Although primitive forms of life, e.g. algae and bacteria, existed during the Proterozoic era, it is not until the strata of Palaeozoic rocks is reached that abundant fossilised remains appear.

Since the Precambrian, there have been three great geological eras:

PALAEOZOIC ('ancient life')
c.570–c.245 million years ago

Cambrian – Mainly sandstones, slate and shales; limestones in Scotland. Shelled fossils and invertebrates, e.g. trilobites and brachiopods appear
Ordovician – Mainly shales and mudstones, e.g. in north Wales; limestones in Scotland. First fishes
Silurian – Shales, mudstones and some limestones, found mostly in Wales and southern Scotland
Devonian – Old red sandstone, shale, limestone and slate, e.g. in south Wales and the West Country
Carboniferous – Coal-bearing rocks, millstone grit, limestone and shale. First traces of land-living life
Permian – Marls, sandstones and clays. First reptile fossils

There were two great phases of mountain building in the Palaeozoic era: the Caledonian, characterised in Britain by NE–SW lines of hills and valleys; and the later Hercyian, widespread in west Germany and adjacent areas, and in Britain exemplified in E.–W. lines of hills and valleys.

The end of the Palaeozoic era was marked by the extensive glaciations of the Permian period in the southern continents and the decline of amphibians. It was succeeded by an era of warm conditions.

MESOZOIC ('middle forms of life')
c.245–c.65 million years ago

Triassic – Mostly sandstone, e.g. in the West Midlands
Jurassic – Mainly limestones and clays, typically displayed in the Jura mountains, and in England in a NE–SW belt from Lincolnshire and the Wash to the Severn and the Dorset coast
Cretaceous – Mainly chalk, clay and sands, e.g. in Kent and Sussex

Giant reptiles were dominant during the Mesozoic era, but it was at this time that marsupial mammals first appeared, as well as *Archaeopteryx lithographica*, the earliest known species of bird. Coniferous trees and flowering plants also developed during the era and, with the birds and the mammals, were the main species to survive into the Cenozoic era. The giant reptiles became extinct.

CENOZOIC ('recent life')
from c.65 million years ago

Palaeocene } The emergence of new forms of life,
Eocene } including existing species
Oligocene – Fossils of a few still existing species
Miocene – Fossil remains show a balance of existing and extinct species
Pliocene – Fossil remains show a majority of still existing species
Pleistocene – The majority of remains are those of still existing species

Holocene – The present, post-glacial period. Existing species only, except for a few exterminated by man

In the last 25 million years, from the Miocene through the Pliocene periods, the Alpine-Himalayan and the circum-Pacific phases of mountain building reached their climax. During the Pleistocene period ice-sheets repeatedly locked up masses of water as land ice; its weight depressed the land, but the locking-up of the water lowered the sea-level by 100–200 metres. The glaciations and interglacials of the Ice Age are difficult to date and classify, but recent scientific opinion considers the Pleistocene period to have begun approximately 1.64 million years ago. The last glacial retreat, merging into the Holocene period, was 10,000 years ago.

HUMAN DEVELOPMENT

Any consideration of the history of mankind must start with the fact that all members of the human race belong to one species of animal, i.e. *Homo sapiens*, the definition of a species being in biological terms that all its members can interbreed. As a species of mammal it is possible to group man with other similar types, known as the primates. Amongst these is found a sub-group, the apes, which includes, in addition to man, the chimpanzees, gorillas, orang-utans and gibbons. All lack a tail, have shoulder blades at the back, and a Y-shaped chewing pattern on the surface of their molars, as well as showing the more general primate characteristics of four incisors, a thumb which is able to touch the fingers of the same hand, and finger and toe nails instead of claws. The factors available to scientific study suggest that human beings have chimpanzees and gorillas as their nearest relatives in the animal world. However, there remains the possibility that there once lived creatures, now extinct, which were closer to modern man than the chimpanzees and gorillas, and which shared with modern man the characteristics of having flat faces (i.e. the absence of a pronounced muzzle), being bipedal, and possessing large brains.

There are two broad groups of extinct apes recognised by specialists. The ramapithecines, the remains of which, mainly jaw fragments, have been found in east Africa, Asia, and Turkey. They lived about 14 to 8 million years ago, and from the evidence of their teeth it seems they chewed more in the manner of modern man than the other presently living apes. The second group, the australopithecines, have left more numerous remains amongst which sub-groups may be detected, although the geographic spread is limited to south and east Africa. Living between 5 and 1.5 million years ago, they were closer relatives of modern man to the extent that they walked upright, did not have an extensive muzzle and had similar types of pre-molars. The first australopithecine remains were recognised at Taung in South Africa in 1924 and subsequent discoveries include those at the Olduvai Gorge in Tanzania. The most impressive discovery was made at Hadar, Ethiopia, in 1974 when about half a skeleton, known as 'Lucy', was found.

Also in east Africa, between 2 million and 1.5 million years ago, lived a hominid group which not only walked upright, had a flat face, and a large brain case, but also made simple pebble and flake stone tools. On present evidence these habilines seem to have been the first people to make tools, however crude. This facility is related to the larger brain size and human beings are the only animals to make implements to be used in other processes. These early pebble tool users, because of their distinctive

GEOLOGICAL TIME

Era	Period	Epoch	Date began*	Evolutionary stages
Cenozoic	Quaternary	Holocene	0.01	Man
		Pleistocene	1.64	
	Tertiary	Pliocene	5.2	
		Miocene	23.3	
		Oligocene	35.4	
		Eocene	56.5	
		Palaeocene	65.0	
Mesozoic	Cretaceous		145.6	
	Jurassic		208.0	First birds
	Triassic		245.0	First mammals
Palaeozoic	Permian		290.0	First reptiles
	Carboniferous		362.5	First amphibians and insects
	Devonian		408.5	
	Silurian		439.0	
	Ordovician		510.0	First fishes
	Cambrian		570.0	First invertebrates
Precambrian			4,600.0	First primitive life forms, e.g. algae and bacteria

* millions of years ago

characteristics, have been grouped as a separate sub-species, now extinct, of the genus *Homo* and are known as *Homo habilis*.

The use of fire, again a human characteristic, is associated with another group of extinct hominids whose remains, about a million years old, are found in south and east Africa, China, Indonesia, north Africa and Europe. Mastery of the techniques of making fire probably helped the colonization of the colder northern areas and in this respect the site of Vertesszollos in Hungary is of particular importance. *Homo erectus* is the name given to this group of fossils and it includes a number of famous individual discoveries, e.g. Solo Man, Heidelberg Man, and especially Peking Man who lived at the cave site at Choukoutien which has yielded evidence of fire and burnt bone.

The well-known group Neanderthal Man, or *Homo sapiens neandertalensis*, is an extinct form of modern man who lived between about 100,000 and 40,000 years ago, thus spanning the last Ice Age. Indeed, its ability to adapt to the cold climate on the edge of the ice-sheets is one of its characteristic features, the remains being found only in Europe, Asia and the Middle East. Complete neanderthal skeletons were found during excavations at Tabun in Israel, together with evidence of tool-making and the use of fire. Distinguished by very large brains, it seems that neanderthal man was the first to develop recognisable social customs, especially deliberate burial rites. Why the neanderthalers became extinct is not clear but it may be connected with the climatic changes at the end of the Ice Ages, which would have seriously affected their food supplies; possibly they became too specialised for their own good.

The Swanscombe skull is the only known human fossil remains found in England. Some specialists see Swanscombe Man (or, more probably, woman) as a neanderthaler. Others group these remains together with the Steinheim skull from Germany, seeing both as a separate sub-species. There is too little evidence as yet on which to form a final judgement.

Modern Man, *Homo sapiens sapiens*, the surviving sub-species of *Homo sapiens*, had evolved to our present physical condition and had colonised much of the world by about 30,000 years ago. There are many previously distinguished individual specimens, e.g. Cromagnon Man, which may now be grouped together as *Homo sapiens sapiens*. It was modern man who spread to the American continent by crossing the landbridge between Siberia and Alaska and thence moved south through North America and into South America. Equally it is modern man who over the last 30,000 years has been responsible for the major developments in technology, art and civilisation generally.

One of the problems for those studying fossil man is the lack in many cases of sufficient quantities of fossil bone for analysis. It is important that theories should be tested against evidence, rather than the evidence being made to fit the theory. The Piltdown hoax is a well-known example of 'fossils' being forged to fit what was seen in some quarters as the correct theory of man's evolution.

CULTURAL DEVELOPMENT

The Eurocentric bias of early archaeologists meant that the search for a starting point for the development and transmission of cultural ideas, especially by migration, trade and warfare, concentrated unduly on Europe and the Near East. The Three Age system, whereby pre-history was divided into a Stone Age, a Bronze Age and an Iron Age, was devised by Christian Thomsen, curator of the National Museum of Denmark in the early 19th century, to facilitate the classification of the museum's collections.

The descriptive adjectives referred to the materials from which the implements and weapons were made and came to be regarded as the dominant features of the societies to which they related. The refinement of the Three Age system once dominated archaeological thought and remains a generally accepted concept in the popular mind. However, it is now seen by archaeologists as an inadequate model for human development.

Common sense suggests that there were no complete breaks between one so-called Age and another, any more than contemporaries would have regarded 1485 as a complete break between medieval and modern English history. Nor can the Three Age system be applied universally. In some areas it is necessary to insert a Copper Age, while in Africa south of the Sahara there would seem to be no Bronze Age at all; in Australia, Old Stone Age societies survived, while in South America, New Stone Age communities existed into modern times. The civilisations in other parts of the world clearly invalidate a Eurocentric theory of human development.

The concept of the 'Neolithic revolution', associated with the domestication of plants and animals, was a development of particular importance in the human cultural pattern. It reflected change from the primitive hunter/gatherer economies to a more settled agricultural way of life and therefore, so the argument goes, made possible the development of urban civilisation. However, it can no longer be argued that this 'revolution' took place only in one area from which all development stemmed. Though it appears that the cultivation of wheat and barley was first undertaken, together with the domestication of cattle and goats/sheep, in the Fertile Crescent (the area bounded by the rivers Tigris and Euphrates), there is evidence that rice was first deliberately planted and pigs domesticated in south-east Asia, maize first cultivated in Central America and llamas first domesticated in South America. It has been recognised in recent years that cultural changes can take place independently of each other in different parts of the world at different rates and different times. There is no need for a general diffusionist theory.

Although scholars will continue to study the particular societies which interest them, it may be possible to obtain a reliable chronological framework, in absolute terms of years, against which the cultural development of any particular area may be set. The development and refinement of radio-carbon dating and other scientific methods of producing absolute chronologies is enabling the cross-referencing of societies to be undertaken. As the techniques of dating become more rigorous in application and the number of scientifically obtained dates increases, the attainment of an absolute chronology for prehistoric societies throughout the world comes closer to being achieved.

Tidal Tables

CONSTANTS

The constant tidal difference may be used in conjunction with the time of high water at a standard port shown in the predictions data (pages 98–103) to find the time of high water at any of the ports or places listed below.

These tidal differences are very approximate and should be used only as a guide to the time of high water at the places below. More precise local data should be obtained for navigational and other nautical purposes.

All data allow high water time to be found in Greenwich Mean Time; this applies also to data for the months when British Summer Time is in operation and the hour's time difference should be allowed for. Ports marked * are in a different time zone and the standard time zone difference also needs to be added/subtracted to give local time.

EXAMPLE

Required time of high water at Stranraer at 2 January 2001
Appropriate time of high water at Greenock

Afternoon tide 2 January	1720 hrs
Tidal difference	−0020 hrs
High water at Stranraer	1700 hrs

The columns headed 'Springs' and 'Neaps' show the height, in metres, of the tide above datum for mean high water springs and mean high water neaps respectively.

Port		Diff.		Springs	Neaps
		h	m	m	m
Aberdeen	Leith	−1	19	4.3	3.4
*Antwerp (Prosperpolder)	London	+0	50	5.8	4.8
Ardrossan	Greenock	−0	15	3.2	2.6
Avonmouth	London	−6	45	13.2	9.8
Ayr	Greenock	−0	25	3.0	2.5
Barrow (Docks)	Liverpool	0	00	9.3	7.1
Belfast	London	−2	47	3.5	3.0
Blackpool	Liverpool	−0	10	8.9	7.0
*Boulogne	London	−2	44	8.9	7.2
*Calais	London	−2	04	7.2	5.9
*Cherbourg	London	−6	00	6.4	5.0
Cobh	Liverpool	−5	55	4.2	3.2
Cowes	London	−2	38	4.2	3.5
Dartmouth	London	+4	25	4.9	3.8
*Dieppe	London	−3	03	9.3	7.3
Douglas, IOM	Liverpool	−0	04	6.9	5.4
Dover	London	−2	52	6.7	5.3
Dublin	London	−2	05	4.1	3.4
Dun Laoghaire	London	−2	10	4.1	3.4
*Dunkirk	London	−1	54	6.0	4.9
Fishguard	Liverpool	−4	01	4.8	3.4
Fleetwood	Liverpool	0	00	9.2	7.3
*Flushing	London	−0	15	4.7	3.9
Folkestone	London	−3	04	7.1	5.7
Galway	Liverpool	−6	08	5.1	3.9
Glasgow	Greenock	+0	26	4.7	4.0
Harwich	London	−2	06	4.0	3.4
*Le Havre	London	−3	55	7.9	6.6
Heysham	Liverpool	+0	05	9.4	7.4
Holyhead	Liverpool	−0	50	5.6	4.4
*Hook of Holland	London	−0	01	2.1	1.7
Hull (Albert Dock)	London	−7	40	7.5	5.8
Immingham	London	−8	00	7.3	5.8
Larne	London	−2	40	2.8	2.5
Lerwick	Leith	−3	48	2.2	1.6
Londonderry	London	−5	37	2.7	2.1
Lowestoft	London	−4	25	2.4	2.1
Margate	London	−1	53	4.8	3.9
Milford Haven	Liverpool	−5	08	7.0	5.2
Morecambe	Liverpool	+0	07	9.5	7.4
Newhaven	London	−2	46	6.7	5.1
Oban	Greenock	+5	43	4.0	2.9
*Ostend	London	−1	32	5.1	4.2
Plymouth (Devonport)	London	+4	05	5.5	4.4
Portland	London	+5	09	2.1	1.4
Portsmouth	London	−2	38	4.7	3.8
Ramsgate	London	−2	32	5.2	4.1
Richmond Lock	London	+1	00	4.9	3.7
Rosslare Harbour	Liverpool	−5	24	1.9	1.4
Rosyth	Leith	+0	09	5.8	4.7
*Rotterdam	London	+1	45	2.0	1.7
St Helier	London	+4	48	11.0	8.5
St Malo	London	+4	27	12.2	9.2
St Peter Port	London	+4	54	9.3	7.0
Scrabster	Leith	−6	06	5.0	4.0
Sheerness	London	−1	19	5.8	4.7
Shoreham	London	−2	44	6.3	4.9
Southampton (1st high water)	London	−2	54	4.5	3.7
Spurn Head	London	−8	25	6.9	5.5
Stornoway	Liverpool	−4	16	4.8	3.7
Stranraer	Greenock	−0	20	3.0	2.4
Stromness	Leith	−5	26	3.6	2.7
Swansea	London	−7	35	9.5	7.2
Tees (River Entrance)	Leith	+1	09	5.5	4.3
Tilbury	London	−0	49	6.4	5.4
Tobermory	Liverpool	−5	11	4.4	3.3
Tyne River (North Shields)	London	−10	30	5.0	3.9
Ullapool	Leith	−7	40	5.2	3.9
Walton-on-the-Naze	London	−2	10	4.2	3.4
Wick	Leith	−3	26	3.5	2.8
Zeebrugge	London	−0	55	4.8	3.9

PREDICTIONS

The data on pages 98–103 are daily predictions of the time and height of high water at London Bridge, Liverpool, Greenock and Leith. The time of the data is Greenwich Mean Time; this applies also to data for the months when British Summer Time is in operation and the hour's time difference should be allowed for. The datum of predictions for each port shows the difference of height, in metres from Ordnance data (Newlyn).

The tidal information for London Bridge, Liverpool, Greenock and Leith is reproduced with the permission of the UK Hydrographic Office and the Controller of HMSO. Crown copyright reserved.

JANUARY 2001   *High water*   GMT

		LONDON BRIDGE *Datum of predictions 3.20 m below				LIVERPOOL *Datum of predictions 4.93 m below				GREENOCK *Datum of predictions 1.62 m below				LEITH *Datum of predictions 2.90 m below			
		hr	ht m	hr	ht m	hr	ht m	hr	ht m	hr	ht m	hr	ht m	hr	ht m	hr	ht m
1	Monday	05 17	6.4	17 58	6.3	02 52	8.1	15 14	8.3	04 25	3.1	16 34	3.3	06 42	4.7	18 46	4.8
2	Tuesday	06 01	6.2	18 45	6.2	03 38	7.8	16 03	8.1	05 12	3.0	17 20	3.2	07 30	4.6	19 34	4.7
3	Wednesday	06 52	6.1	19 38	6.1	04 33	7.5	17 00	7.9	06 02	3.0	18 12	3.1	08 24	4.5	20 32	4.6
4	Thursday	07 50	6.0	20 38	6.0	05 37	7.5	18 05	7.9	06 56	2.9	19 12	3.0	09 24	4.5	21 37	4.6
5	Friday	08 56	6.0	21 45	6.1	06 45	7.6	19 11	8.1	07 59	2.9	20 25	3.0	10 28	4.6	22 44	4.7
6	Saturday	10 05	6.1	22 52	6.3	07 51	8.0	20 15	8.4	09 09	3.0	21 39	3.1	11 29	4.8	23 47	4.9
7	Sunday	11 13	6.4	23 54	6.5	08 49	8.5	21 13	8.9	10 14	3.2	22 41	3.2	—	—	12 26	5.1
8	Monday	—	—	12 14	6.7	09 42	9.0	22 07	9.3	11 08	3.3	23 36	3.3	00 45	5.2	13 18	5.3
9	Tuesday	00 49	6.8	13 12	7.0	10 32	9.5	22 59	9.6	11 56	3.5	—	—	01 38	5.5	14 05	5.6
10	Wednesday	01 41	7.0	14 05	7.2	11 22	9.8	23 49	9.8	00 28	3.4	12 42	3.7	02 27	5.7	14 50	5.7
11	Thursday	02 30	7.1	14 56	7.4	—	—	12 11	10.0	01 21	3.4	13 27	3.8	03 16	5.9	15 36	5.8
12	Friday	03 18	7.2	15 46	7.5	00 39	9.8	13 00	10.0	02 12	3.5	14 12	3.9	04 04	5.9	16 23	5.8
13	Saturday	04 04	7.2	16 34	7.5	01 29	9.7	13 49	9.9	03 01	3.4	14 57	3.9	04 53	5.8	17 12	5.7
14	Sunday	04 49	7.1	17 22	7.3	02 18	9.4	14 38	9.6	03 49	3.4	15 41	3.9	05 45	5.5	18 05	5.6
15	Monday	05 34	6.9	18 11	7.0	03 07	9.0	15 27	9.2	04 37	3.3	16 28	3.8	06 38	5.2	19 01	5.3
16	Tuesday	06 21	6.6	19 03	6.6	03 58	8.5	16 20	8.7	05 26	3.2	17 17	3.6	07 37	4.9	20 05	5.1
17	Wednesday	07 16	6.3	20 01	6.3	04 55	8.0	17 20	8.2	06 19	3.1	18 10	3.4	08 39	4.7	21 10	4.9
18	Thursday	08 22	6.1	21 06	6.0	06 01	7.7	18 30	7.8	07 18	3.0	19 09	3.2	09 42	4.5	22 14	4.7
19	Friday	09 32	6.0	22 10	6.0	07 13	7.6	19 43	7.8	08 38	3.0	20 32	3.0	10 47	4.5	23 21	4.7
20	Saturday	10 38	6.1	23 09	6.1	08 19	7.9	20 46	8.0	09 49	3.1	22 00	3.0	11 53	4.6	—	—
21	Sunday	11 38	6.3	—	—	09 13	8.2	21 39	8.2	10 44	3.2	22 59	3.1	00 24	4.8	12 51	4.8
22	Monday	00 03	6.4	12 32	6.5	09 59	8.6	22 23	8.5	11 29	3.3	23 47	3.1	01 19	4.9	13 38	4.9
23	Tuesday	00 52	6.5	13 20	6.6	10 39	8.8	23 02	8.6	—	—	12 10	3.4	02 04	5.0	14 17	5.1
24	Wednesday	01 36	6.6	14 04	6.7	11 16	9.0	23 37	8.7	00 28	3.1	12 49	3.5	02 43	5.1	14 52	5.2
25	Thursday	02 14	6.6	14 42	6.7	11 51	9.1	—	—	01 06	3.1	13 23	3.5	03 17	5.1	15 23	5.2
26	Friday	02 47	6.6	15 16	6.6	00 09	8.8	12 25	9.1	01 39	3.1	13 54	3.5	03 49	5.1	15 54	5.3
27	Saturday	03 18	6.5	15 47	6.6	00 43	8.8	12 59	9.1	02 11	3.1	14 24	3.5	04 22	5.1	16 26	5.3
28	Sunday	03 48	6.5	16 19	6.6	01 16	8.7	13 34	9.0	02 44	3.1	14 56	3.5	04 55	5.1	16 59	5.2
29	Monday	04 20	6.5	16 54	6.6	01 50	8.7	14 09	8.9	03 19	3.1	15 30	3.4	05 31	5.0	17 34	5.1
30	Tuesday	04 56	6.6	17 32	6.6	02 26	8.5	14 46	8.7	03 56	3.1	16 07	3.3	06 09	4.9	18 12	5.0
31	Wednesday	05 35	6.5	18 15	6.5	03 04	8.3	15 28	8.5	04 34	3.1	16 46	3.2	06 51	4.7	18 54	4.8

FEBRUARY 2001   *High water*   GMT

		LONDON BRIDGE				LIVERPOOL				GREENOCK				LEITH			
1	Thursday	06 20	6.4	19 03	6.3	03 50	8.0	16 18	8.2	05 16	3.0	17 29	3.1	07 38	4.6	19 42	4.7
2	Friday	07 13	6.2	19 58	6.1	04 47	7.7	17 20	7.9	06 03	2.9	18 22	3.0	08 34	4.5	20 43	4.6
3	Saturday	08 15	6.1	21 02	5.9	05 57	7.5	18 31	7.8	06 59	2.8	19 32	2.9	09 41	4.5	22 00	4.6
4	Sunday	09 25	6.0	22 15	6.0	07 12	7.7	19 45	8.1	08 16	2.8	21 06	2.9	10 52	4.6	23 18	4.7
5	Monday	10 42	6.1	23 28	6.2	08 24	8.2	20 54	8.5	09 43	3.0	22 25	3.0	12 00	4.8	—	—
6	Tuesday	11 55	6.5	—	—	09 25	8.8	21 54	9.1	10 48	3.2	23 26	3.2	00 27	5.0	12 59	5.2
7	Wednesday	00 30	6.5	12 57	6.9	10 20	9.4	22 48	9.5	11 40	3.4	—	—	01 25	5.4	13 50	5.5
8	Thursday	01 25	6.9	13 52	7.2	11 10	9.8	23 38	9.8	00 21	3.3	12 29	3.6	02 16	5.7	14 36	5.7
9	Friday	02 15	7.1	14 44	7.5	11 58	10.1	—	—	01 14	3.4	13 16	3.8	03 03	5.9	15 21	5.9
10	Saturday	03 03	7.3	15 32	7.6	00 26	9.9	12 45	10.2	02 03	3.4	14 01	3.9	03 49	5.9	16 07	6.0
11	Sunday	03 47	7.3	16 17	7.6	01 12	9.9	13 31	10.1	02 48	3.4	14 44	3.9	04 36	5.8	16 53	5.9
12	Monday	04 29	7.3	17 01	7.4	01 57	9.7	14 15	9.8	03 29	3.4	15 25	3.9	05 22	5.6	17 42	5.7
13	Tuesday	05 10	7.1	17 44	7.1	02 40	9.3	14 59	9.3	04 08	3.4	16 07	3.8	06 11	5.3	18 33	5.4
14	Wednesday	05 51	6.9	18 26	6.7	03 23	8.7	15 44	8.7	04 48	3.3	16 49	3.6	07 01	4.9	19 29	5.0
15	Thursday	06 34	6.5	19 11	6.2	04 10	8.1	16 35	8.0	05 29	3.1	17 33	3.4	07 56	4.6	20 31	4.7
16	Friday	07 26	6.1	20 06	5.8	05 07	7.6	17 41	7.4	06 17	3.0	18 23	3.1	08 57	4.4	21 37	4.5
17	Saturday	08 41	5.7	21 22	5.6	06 23	7.2	19 05	7.2	07 15	2.8	19 22	2.8	10 02	4.3	22 49	4.4
18	Sunday	10 06	5.7	22 34	5.6	07 45	7.4	20 22	7.4	09 06	2.8	21 37	2.7	11 17	4.3	—	—
19	Monday	11 13	5.9	23 34	5.9	08 49	7.8	21 20	7.8	10 20	3.0	22 47	2.8	00 04	4.4	12 28	4.5
20	Tuesday	—	—	12 10	6.2	09 39	8.3	22 06	8.2	11 09	3.2	23 35	2.9	01 04	4.6	13 21	4.8
21	Wednesday	00 27	6.2	13 00	6.5	10 21	8.7	22 45	8.5	11 52	3.3	—	—	01 50	4.8	14 01	5.0
22	Thursday	01 14	6.5	13 44	6.7	10 59	8.9	23 19	8.7	00 15	3.0	12 31	3.4	02 26	5.0	14 35	5.1
23	Friday	01 55	6.6	14 22	6.7	11 33	9.1	23 52	8.8	00 52	3.0	13 05	3.4	02 58	5.1	15 05	5.2
24	Saturday	02 31	6.6	14 56	6.7	—	—	12 06	9.2	01 23	3.0	13 34	3.3	03 26	5.2	15 34	5.3
25	Sunday	03 02	6.6	15 27	6.6	00 23	8.9	12 39	9.2	01 51	3.0	14 02	3.3	03 58	5.2	16 04	5.3
26	Monday	03 32	6.6	15 58	6.7	00 55	8.9	13 11	9.1	02 19	3.1	14 32	3.4	04 30	5.2	16 35	5.3
27	Tuesday	04 01	6.6	16 30	6.7	01 26	8.9	13 44	9.1	02 50	3.1	15 06	3.4	05 04	5.1	17 08	5.3
28	Wednesday	04 34	6.7	17 06	6.7	01 59	8.8	14 19	8.9	03 23	3.2	15 41	3.3	05 39	5.0	17 44	5.1

MARCH 2001 *High water* GMT

| | | LONDON BRIDGE |||| LIVERPOOL |||| GREENOCK |||| LEITH ||||
| | | *Datum of predictions 3.20 m below* |||| *Datum of predictions 4.93 m below* |||| *Datum of predictions 1.62 m below* |||| *Datum of predictions 2.90 m below* ||||
		hr	m	hr	m	hr	m	hr	m	hr	m	hr	m	hr	m	hr	m
1	Thursday	05 11	6.7	17 46	6.6	02 34	8.6	14 58	8.7	03 58	3.1	16 17	3.2	06 18	4.9	18 25	5.0
2	Friday	05 55	6.6	18 32	6.4	03 16	8.3	15 45	8.3	04 35	3.1	16 57	3.1	07 02	4.7	19 13	4.8
3	Saturday	06 46	6.3	19 24	6.0	04 09	7.8	16 47	7.8	05 17	2.9	17 46	2.9	07 54	4.5	20 13	4.6
4	Sunday	07 46	6.0	20 26	5.8	05 20	7.5	18 03	7.6	06 11	2.8	18 53	2.7	09 02	4.4	21 33	4.5
5	Monday	08 57	5.8	21 45	5.7	06 44	7.5	19 27	7.7	07 25	2.7	20 46	2.7	10 24	4.4	23 00	4.6
6	Tuesday	10 23	5.9	23 08	6.0	08 06	7.9	20 43	8.3	09 18	2.8	22 19	2.9	11 40	4.7	—	—
7	Wednesday	11 42	6.3	—	—	09 12	8.6	21 44	8.9	10 31	3.1	23 20	3.1	00 14	5.0	12 43	5.1
8	Thursday	00 13	6.4	12 45	6.8	10 07	9.3	22 36	9.5	11 25	3.4	—	—	01 13	5.3	13 34	5.4
9	Friday	01 09	6.8	13 38	7.2	10 55	9.8	23 23	9.8	00 12	3.2	12 13	3.6	02 02	5.6	14 19	5.7
10	Saturday	01 58	7.1	14 27	7.5	11 41	10.1	—	—	01 01	3.3	13 00	3.7	02 46	5.8	15 03	5.9
11	Sunday	02 43	7.3	15 13	7.6	00 07	10.0	12 26	10.2	01 45	3.4	13 44	3.8	03 30	5.9	15 47	6.0
12	Monday	03 26	7.4	15 55	7.5	00 50	9.9	13 08	10.1	02 25	3.4	14 25	3.9	04 13	5.7	16 31	5.9
13	Tuesday	04 06	7.4	16 35	7.3	01 30	9.7	13 49	9.7	03 01	3.4	15 04	3.8	04 57	5.5	17 17	5.7
14	Wednesday	04 44	7.2	17 12	7.1	02 09	9.3	14 29	9.2	03 35	3.4	15 43	3.7	05 41	5.2	18 05	5.3
15	Thursday	05 22	7.0	17 47	6.7	02 48	8.8	15 09	8.6	04 10	3.3	16 21	3.5	06 26	4.9	18 57	5.0
16	Friday	06 00	6.6	18 24	6.3	03 29	8.2	15 54	7.8	04 49	3.2	17 02	3.3	07 15	4.6	19 54	4.6
17	Saturday	06 44	6.1	19 06	5.9	04 18	7.5	16 54	7.2	05 32	3.0	17 49	3.0	08 12	4.3	20 59	4.3
18	Sunday	07 42	5.7	20 02	5.5	05 32	7.1	18 23	6.8	06 25	2.8	18 44	2.7	09 17	4.2	22 11	4.2
19	Monday	09 26	5.4	21 49	5.3	07 04	7.1	19 51	7.0	07 39	2.7	20 04	2.6	10 32	4.2	23 34	4.2
20	Tuesday	10 45	5.6	23 02	5.6	08 17	7.5	20 53	7.5	09 49	2.8	22 26	2.7	11 54	4.3	—	—
21	Wednesday	11 43	6.0	23 58	6.0	09 11	8.0	21 39	8.0	10 43	3.0	23 12	2.8	00 40	4.5	12 53	4.6
22	Thursday	—	—	12 33	6.4	09 55	8.5	22 19	8.4	11 26	3.2	23 51	2.9	01 25	4.8	13 35	4.9
23	Friday	00 46	6.4	13 17	6.6	10 33	8.8	22 54	8.7	—	—	12 04	3.2	02 00	5.0	14 09	5.1
24	Saturday	01 29	6.5	13 56	6.7	11 08	9.0	23 26	8.9	00 26	3.0	12 38	3.2	02 31	5.1	14 39	5.2
25	Sunday	02 06	6.6	14 30	6.7	11 41	9.1	23 57	9.0	00 56	3.0	13 06	3.2	03 00	5.2	15 08	5.3
26	Monday	02 39	6.6	15 02	6.7	—	—	12 13	9.2	01 22	3.1	13 35	3.2	03 30	5.3	15 38	5.4
27	Tuesday	03 10	6.6	15 33	6.8	00 28	9.0	12 46	9.2	01 50	3.1	14 07	3.3	04 02	5.3	16 10	5.4
28	Wednesday	03 40	6.7	16 06	6.8	01 00	9.0	13 19	9.2	02 20	3.2	14 42	3.3	04 36	5.3	16 45	5.4
29	Thursday	04 14	6.8	16 42	6.8	01 34	9.0	13 55	9.0	02 53	3.3	15 18	3.3	05 12	5.2	17 23	5.2
30	Friday	04 53	6.8	17 21	6.6	02 10	8.8	14 36	8.7	03 28	3.2	15 55	3.2	05 51	5.0	18 06	5.1
31	Saturday	05 37	6.6	18 06	6.3	02 52	8.4	15 24	8.2	04 04	3.2	16 36	3.0	06 36	4.8	18 57	4.8

APRIL 2001 *High water* GMT

| | | LONDON BRIDGE |||| LIVERPOOL |||| GREENOCK |||| LEITH ||||
		hr	m	hr	m	hr	m	hr	m	hr	m	hr	m	hr	m	hr	m
1	Sunday	06 27	6.3	18 57	5.9	03 46	7.9	16 27	7.7	04 46	3.0	17 27	2.8	07 28	4.6	19 59	4.6
2	Monday	07 28	6.0	20 01	5.6	04 59	7.5	17 49	7.4	05 41	2.8	18 41	2.6	08 39	4.4	21 22	4.5
3	Tuesday	08 44	5.8	21 27	5.6	06 28	7.5	19 17	7.6	06 58	2.8	20 46	2.6	10 05	4.4	22 48	4.7
4	Wednesday	10 16	5.9	22 51	5.9	07 51	7.9	20 30	8.2	08 58	2.8	22 12	2.9	11 22	4.7	—	—
5	Thursday	11 31	6.4	23 55	6.4	08 56	8.6	21 28	8.9	10 12	3.1	23 08	3.1	00 01	5.0	12 24	5.1
6	Friday	—	—	12 29	6.9	09 49	9.3	22 17	9.4	11 06	3.3	23 56	3.2	00 58	5.3	13 14	5.4
7	Saturday	00 48	6.9	13 20	7.3	10 36	9.7	23 02	9.7	11 53	3.5	—	—	01 44	5.6	13 59	5.7
8	Sunday	01 36	7.1	14 07	7.5	11 20	9.9	23 44	9.8	00 41	3.3	12 39	3.6	02 26	5.7	14 42	5.9
9	Monday	02 21	7.3	14 50	7.5	—	—	12 02	10.0	01 22	3.4	13 22	3.7	03 07	5.7	15 25	5.9
10	Tuesday	03 03	7.3	15 30	7.4	00 24	9.7	12 43	9.8	01 58	3.4	14 03	3.7	03 49	5.6	16 10	5.8
11	Wednesday	03 42	7.3	16 07	7.2	01 02	9.5	13 22	9.4	02 31	3.4	14 41	3.7	04 30	5.4	16 54	5.5
12	Thursday	04 19	7.2	16 40	6.9	01 39	9.1	14 00	8.9	03 04	3.4	15 18	3.6	05 11	5.2	17 40	5.2
13	Friday	04 56	6.9	17 12	6.7	02 16	8.7	14 38	8.4	03 38	3.4	15 57	3.4	05 53	4.9	18 29	4.8
14	Saturday	05 34	6.6	17 47	6.4	02 54	8.2	15 20	7.7	04 16	3.3	16 37	3.2	06 38	4.7	19 22	4.5
15	Sunday	06 16	6.2	18 27	6.0	03 39	7.6	16 13	7.1	04 58	3.1	17 24	2.9	07 30	4.4	20 21	4.2
16	Monday	07 08	5.7	19 18	5.6	04 43	7.1	17 36	6.7	05 49	2.9	18 20	2.7	08 34	4.2	21 27	4.1
17	Tuesday	08 26	5.4	20 36	5.3	06 17	7.0	19 07	6.8	06 54	2.7	19 30	2.6	09 44	4.1	22 42	4.2
18	Wednesday	10 05	5.5	22 19	5.5	07 35	7.3	20 13	7.3	08 43	2.7	21 37	2.6	11 01	4.2	23 56	4.4
19	Thursday	11 07	5.9	23 20	5.9	08 33	7.8	21 03	7.8	10 04	2.9	22 34	2.8	—	—	12 08	4.5
20	Friday	11 57	6.3	—	—	09 20	8.2	21 44	8.3	10 50	3.0	23 15	2.9	00 45	4.7	12 55	4.7
21	Saturday	00 10	6.2	12 42	6.6	10 00	8.6	22 20	8.6	11 27	3.1	23 50	3.0	01 23	4.9	13 32	5.0
22	Sunday	00 55	6.5	13 22	6.7	10 36	8.9	22 54	8.8	12 00	3.1	—	—	01 56	5.1	14 05	5.2
23	Monday	01 34	6.6	13 59	6.8	11 10	9.1	23 26	9.0	00 21	3.0	12 31	3.2	02 28	5.3	14 37	5.3
24	Tuesday	02 10	6.7	14 34	6.8	11 44	9.2	—	—	—	—	13 05	3.2	03 01	5.4	15 11	5.4
25	Wednesday	02 45	6.8	15 09	6.8	00 00	9.1	12 20	9.2	01 21	3.2	13 42	3.2	03 35	5.4	15 46	5.5
26	Thursday	03 21	6.8	15 45	6.8	00 35	9.1	12 58	9.2	01 54	3.3	14 20	3.3	04 11	5.4	16 25	5.4
27	Friday	03 59	6.9	16 23	6.8	01 13	9.1	13 38	9.0	02 28	3.4	15 00	3.2	04 49	5.3	17 07	5.3
28	Saturday	04 41	6.9	17 03	6.6	01 54	8.9	14 23	8.7	03 05	3.4	15 41	3.1	05 30	5.1	17 54	5.2
29	Sunday	05 27	6.7	17 48	6.3	02 40	8.5	15 15	8.3	03 44	3.3	16 28	3.0	06 17	4.9	18 48	4.9
30	Monday	06 20	6.4	18 41	5.9	03 37	8.1	16 20	7.8	04 28	3.1	17 28	2.8	07 13	4.7	19 54	4.7

MAY 2001 *High water* GMT

		LONDON BRIDGE *Datum of predictions 3.20 m below*				LIVERPOOL *Datum of predictions 4.93 m below*				GREENOCK *Datum of predictions 1.62 m below*				LEITH *Datum of predictions 2.90 m below*			
		hr	m (ht)	hr	m (ht)	hr	m (ht)	hr	m (ht)	hr	m (ht)	hr	m (ht)	hr	m (ht)	hr	m (ht)
1	Tuesday	07 23	6.0	19 48	5.7	04 50	7.7	17 40	7.5	05 26	2.9	18 55	2.6	08 27	4.5	21 14	4.6
2	Wednesday	08 43	5.9	21 16	5.7	06 14	7.7	19 01	7.7	06 49	2.8	20 39	2.7	09 50	4.6	22 34	4.8
3	Thursday	10 06	6.2	22 31	6.1	07 31	8.1	20 10	8.2	08 37	2.9	21 53	2.9	11 02	4.8	23 42	5.0
4	Friday	11 12	6.6	23 31	6.5	08 34	8.6	21 06	8.8	09 48	3.1	22 47	3.1	—	—	12 02	5.1
5	Saturday	—	—	12 07	7.0	09 27	9.1	21 55	9.2	10 43	3.3	23 33	3.2	00 37	5.2	12 53	5.4
6	Sunday	00 24	6.9	12 58	7.3	10 15	9.4	22 38	9.4	11 30	3.4	—	—	01 23	5.4	13 38	5.6
7	Monday	01 13	7.1	13 44	7.4	10 58	9.6	23 19	9.5	00 16	3.3	12 16	3.5	02 05	5.5	14 22	5.7
8	Tuesday	01 58	7.2	14 26	7.3	11 40	9.5	23 58	9.4	00 55	3.3	12 59	3.5	02 45	5.5	15 06	5.7
9	Wednesday	02 41	7.2	15 05	7.2	—	—	12 19	9.3	01 31	3.4	13 40	3.5	03 25	5.5	15 50	5.5
10	Thursday	03 21	7.1	15 40	7.0	00 35	9.2	12 57	9.0	02 04	3.4	14 18	3.4	04 05	5.4	16 34	5.3
11	Friday	03 58	7.0	16 11	6.8	01 11	9.0	13 34	8.7	02 38	3.4	14 56	3.3	04 45	5.2	17 18	5.1
12	Saturday	04 35	6.8	16 43	6.6	01 47	8.7	14 11	8.3	03 13	3.4	15 35	3.2	05 24	5.0	18 03	4.8
13	Sunday	05 12	6.5	17 18	6.4	02 26	8.3	14 51	7.8	03 49	3.3	16 17	3.1	06 06	4.7	18 51	4.5
14	Monday	05 54	6.2	17 59	6.1	03 09	7.9	15 39	7.3	04 30	3.1	17 05	2.9	06 54	4.5	19 44	4.3
15	Tuesday	06 42	5.8	18 48	5.8	04 03	7.4	16 43	6.9	05 18	2.9	18 00	2.7	07 51	4.3	20 41	4.2
16	Wednesday	07 42	5.6	19 51	5.5	05 18	7.2	18 09	6.9	06 18	2.8	19 01	2.6	08 56	4.2	21 43	4.2
17	Thursday	09 00	5.6	21 15	5.5	06 40	7.2	19 20	7.1	07 28	2.7	20 10	2.6	10 02	4.3	22 47	4.3
18	Friday	10 13	5.8	22 27	5.8	07 43	7.6	20 16	7.6	08 51	2.8	21 27	2.7	11 05	4.4	23 46	4.6
19	Saturday	11 10	6.1	23 23	6.1	08 34	8.0	21 01	8.1	09 55	2.9	22 24	2.9	12 00	4.6	—	—
20	Sunday	11 59	6.5	—	—	09 18	8.4	21 41	8.5	10 39	3.0	23 06	3.0	00 34	4.8	12 47	4.9
21	Monday	00 12	6.4	12 44	6.7	09 58	8.7	22 18	8.8	11 18	3.1	23 44	3.1	01 16	5.1	13 28	5.1
22	Tuesday	00 57	6.6	13 26	6.8	10 37	9.0	22 55	9.0	11 57	3.1	—	—	01 54	5.3	14 06	5.3
23	Wednesday	01 40	6.8	14 07	6.9	11 16	9.2	23 33	9.2	00 19	3.2	12 38	3.2	02 32	5.4	14 45	5.4
24	Thursday	02 22	6.9	14 47	6.9	11 58	9.3	—	—	00 56	3.3	13 21	3.2	03 09	5.5	15 26	5.5
25	Friday	03 04	7.0	15 28	6.9	00 14	9.3	12 41	9.2	01 34	3.4	14 05	3.2	03 49	5.5	16 09	5.5
26	Saturday	03 48	7.0	16 10	6.8	00 58	9.2	13 28	9.1	02 12	3.5	14 50	3.2	04 30	5.4	16 55	5.5
27	Sunday	04 34	7.0	16 53	6.7	01 45	9.0	14 17	8.8	02 51	3.5	15 38	3.1	05 15	5.3	17 45	5.3
28	Monday	05 23	6.8	17 40	6.4	02 36	8.8	15 11	8.5	03 34	3.4	16 33	3.0	06 05	5.1	18 41	5.1
29	Tuesday	06 17	6.5	18 34	6.2	03 34	8.5	16 14	8.1	04 22	3.3	17 39	2.8	07 04	4.9	19 46	4.9
30	Wednesday	07 21	6.3	19 41	6.0	04 41	8.2	17 25	7.9	05 22	3.1	18 55	2.8	08 15	4.8	21 00	4.8
31	Thursday	08 34	6.2	20 57	6.0	05 54	8.1	18 37	7.9	06 39	3.0	20 14	2.8	09 30	4.8	22 11	4.8

JUNE 2001 *High water* GMT

		LONDON BRIDGE				LIVERPOOL				GREENOCK				LEITH			
1	Friday	09 44	6.4	22 04	6.2	07 04	8.2	19 43	8.2	08 07	3.0	21 23	2.9	10 37	4.9	23 16	4.9
2	Saturday	10 46	6.6	23 04	6.5	08 07	8.5	20 40	8.6	09 20	3.1	22 19	3.0	11 37	5.1	—	—
3	Sunday	11 42	6.9	23 59	6.8	09 03	8.8	21 30	8.9	10 18	3.2	23 07	3.1	00 13	5.1	12 32	5.2
4	Monday	—	—	12 33	7.1	09 53	9.0	22 15	9.1	11 08	3.3	23 51	3.2	01 02	5.2	13 20	5.3
5	Tuesday	00 49	7.0	13 20	7.2	10 38	9.1	22 56	9.1	11 54	3.3	—	—	01 45	5.3	14 06	5.4
6	Wednesday	01 37	7.0	14 03	7.1	11 20	9.0	23 35	9.1	00 30	3.3	12 38	3.3	02 26	5.3	14 51	5.4
7	Thursday	02 22	7.0	14 42	7.0	11 59	8.9	—	—	01 08	3.3	13 19	3.2	03 06	5.3	15 34	5.3
8	Friday	03 03	6.9	15 17	6.8	00 11	9.0	12 36	8.7	01 43	3.4	13 59	3.2	03 44	5.3	16 16	5.2
9	Saturday	03 42	6.8	15 48	6.7	00 48	8.9	13 12	8.5	02 17	3.4	14 37	3.1	04 22	5.2	16 57	5.0
10	Sunday	04 18	6.6	16 20	6.6	01 25	8.7	13 49	8.3	02 52	3.4	15 17	3.1	04 59	5.0	17 37	4.8
11	Monday	04 54	6.4	16 55	6.4	02 03	8.5	14 28	8.0	03 28	3.3	15 59	3.0	05 38	4.9	18 20	4.7
12	Tuesday	05 33	6.2	17 35	6.3	02 44	8.2	15 10	7.7	04 06	3.2	16 45	2.9	06 22	4.7	19 06	4.5
13	Wednesday	06 17	6.1	18 22	6.0	03 30	7.9	16 00	7.4	04 49	3.0	17 34	2.8	07 11	4.5	19 56	4.4
14	Thursday	07 08	5.9	19 16	5.8	04 24	7.6	16 59	7.2	05 40	2.9	18 27	2.8	08 07	4.4	20 51	4.3
15	Friday	08 05	5.8	20 19	5.8	05 28	7.5	18 10	7.2	06 38	2.8	19 21	2.7	09 06	4.4	21 49	4.4
16	Saturday	09 09	5.9	21 26	5.8	06 36	7.5	19 15	7.5	07 42	2.8	20 20	2.7	10 07	4.4	22 48	4.5
17	Sunday	10 13	6.1	22 30	6.0	07 37	7.8	20 11	7.9	08 49	2.8	21 21	2.8	11 06	4.6	23 44	4.7
18	Monday	11 12	6.3	23 28	6.3	08 31	8.2	20 59	8.3	09 50	2.9	22 21	2.9	—	—	12 01	4.8
19	Tuesday	—	—	12 05	6.6	09 20	8.6	21 44	8.7	10 42	3.0	23 10	3.1	00 36	5.0	12 52	5.0
20	Wednesday	00 22	6.5	12 55	6.8	10 07	8.9	22 28	9.1	11 29	3.1	23 54	3.2	01 23	5.2	13 39	5.2
21	Thursday	01 13	6.8	13 43	6.9	10 53	9.2	23 13	9.3	—	—	12 17	3.2	02 06	5.4	14 25	5.4
22	Friday	02 02	7.0	14 29	7.0	11 41	9.3	23 59	9.4	00 36	3.3	13 06	3.2	02 48	5.5	15 10	5.6
23	Saturday	02 51	7.1	15 14	7.0	—	—	12 29	9.4	01 19	3.4	13 56	3.2	03 31	5.6	15 56	5.7
24	Sunday	03 39	7.2	16 00	7.0	00 47	9.3	13 20	9.3	02 01	3.5	14 47	3.2	04 16	5.6	16 44	5.6
25	Monday	04 28	7.2	16 45	6.9	01 37	9.4	14 11	9.1	02 44	3.6	15 39	3.1	05 03	5.5	17 35	5.5
26	Tuesday	05 17	7.1	17 32	6.7	02 29	9.2	15 03	8.9	03 29	3.6	16 34	3.1	05 54	5.4	18 30	5.3
27	Wednesday	06 09	6.9	18 23	6.5	03 23	9.0	15 58	8.5	04 18	3.5	17 32	3.0	06 51	5.2	19 30	5.1
28	Thursday	07 07	6.6	19 22	6.3	04 22	8.7	16 59	8.2	05 13	3.3	18 33	2.9	07 56	5.1	20 36	4.9
29	Friday	08 10	6.4	20 27	6.2	05 25	8.4	18 05	8.0	06 16	3.2	19 37	2.9	09 04	5.0	21 42	4.8
30	Saturday	09 15	6.4	21 33	6.2	06 32	8.2	19 11	8.0	07 28	3.1	20 45	2.9	10 10	4.9	22 46	4.7

JULY 2001   *High water*   GMT

		LONDON BRIDGE *Datum of predictions 3.20 m below*				LIVERPOOL *Datum of predictions 4.93 m below*				GREENOCK *Datum of predictions 1.62 m below*				LEITH *Datum of predictions 2.90 m below*			
		hr m	ht	hr m	ht	hr m	ht	hr m	ht	hr m	ht	hr m	ht	hr m	ht	hr m	ht
1	Sunday	10 16	6.4	22 36	6.4	07 39	8.2	20 13	8.2	08 46	3.1	21 48	2.9	11 12	4.9	23 47	4.8
2	Monday	11 14	6.6	23 34	6.5	08 40	8.3	21 08	8.4	09 54	3.1	22 41	3.0	—	—	12 12	5.0
3	Tuesday	—	—	12 08	6.7	09 34	8.5	21 55	8.7	10 50	3.1	23 28	3.1	00 41	4.9	13 07	5.1
4	Wednesday	00 29	6.7	12 57	6.9	10 21	8.6	22 38	8.9	11 39	3.1	—	—	01 30	5.0	13 56	5.1
5	Thursday	01 20	6.8	13 43	6.9	11 04	8.7	23 17	8.9	00 11	3.2	12 24	3.1	02 12	5.1	14 40	5.1
6	Friday	02 06	6.8	14 24	6.8	11 43	8.6	23 54	8.9	00 50	3.3	13 06	3.0	02 51	5.2	15 20	5.1
7	Saturday	02 49	6.8	15 00	6.7	—	—	12 19	8.6	01 26	3.3	13 45	3.0	03 28	5.2	15 58	5.1
8	Sunday	03 27	6.7	15 31	6.6	00 29	8.9	12 54	8.5	02 01	3.3	14 22	3.0	04 03	5.2	16 34	5.0
9	Monday	04 02	6.5	16 02	6.5	01 05	8.8	13 29	8.4	02 34	3.3	14 59	3.0	04 37	5.1	17 11	4.9
10	Tuesday	04 35	6.4	16 36	6.5	01 42	8.7	14 05	8.3	03 07	3.3	15 38	3.0	05 13	5.0	17 49	4.8
11	Wednesday	05 11	6.4	17 13	6.4	02 19	8.5	14 42	8.1	03 42	3.2	16 18	3.0	05 52	4.9	18 29	4.7
12	Thursday	05 50	6.3	17 54	6.3	02 59	8.3	15 23	7.9	04 20	3.1	17 01	2.9	06 34	4.8	19 14	4.6
13	Friday	06 33	6.2	18 40	6.1	03 43	8.0	16 10	7.6	05 02	3.0	17 46	2.9	07 19	4.6	20 03	4.5
14	Saturday	07 23	6.1	19 33	6.0	04 35	7.8	17 06	7.5	05 51	2.9	18 35	2.8	08 11	4.5	20 58	4.4
15	Sunday	08 19	6.0	20 33	5.9	05 35	7.7	18 12	7.5	06 48	2.8	19 28	2.8	09 11	4.5	21 58	4.5
16	Monday	09 22	6.0	21 39	6.0	06 40	7.7	19 19	7.7	07 56	2.8	20 31	2.8	10 16	4.5	23 00	4.6
17	Tuesday	10 28	6.1	22 47	6.1	07 45	8.0	20 21	8.1	09 09	2.8	21 41	2.9	11 21	4.7	—	—
18	Wednesday	11 32	6.4	23 51	6.4	08 47	8.4	21 16	8.6	10 15	2.9	22 42	3.0	00 01	4.8	12 23	4.9
19	Thursday	—	—	12 29	6.6	09 44	8.8	22 07	9.1	11 11	3.1	23 33	3.2	00 56	5.1	13 18	5.2
20	Friday	00 50	6.7	13 23	6.9	10 37	9.1	22 57	9.4	—	—	12 04	3.2	01 45	5.3	14 08	5.5
21	Saturday	01 46	7.0	14 13	7.0	11 28	9.4	23 46	9.7	00 20	3.4	12 58	3.2	02 30	5.5	14 56	5.7
22	Sunday	02 37	7.3	15 01	7.1	—	—	12 19	9.6	01 06	3.5	13 51	3.2	03 15	5.7	15 43	5.8
23	Monday	03 27	7.4	15 47	7.2	00 36	9.8	13 09	9.6	01 52	3.6	14 42	3.2	04 01	5.8	16 30	5.8
24	Tuesday	04 16	7.4	16 32	7.2	01 25	9.8	13 57	9.5	02 36	3.7	15 31	3.2	04 48	5.8	17 19	5.7
25	Wednesday	05 03	7.4	17 16	7.1	02 14	9.7	14 45	9.2	03 20	3.7	16 19	3.2	05 37	5.7	18 11	5.4
26	Thursday	05 51	7.1	18 01	6.9	03 03	9.3	15 34	8.8	04 05	3.6	17 06	3.2	06 30	5.5	19 05	5.1
27	Friday	06 41	6.8	18 51	6.6	03 54	8.9	16 26	8.4	04 52	3.5	17 54	3.1	07 29	5.2	20 05	4.9
28	Saturday	07 37	6.4	19 49	6.3	04 51	8.4	17 26	7.9	05 44	3.3	18 46	3.0	08 34	5.0	21 08	4.7
29	Sunday	08 39	6.2	20 57	6.1	05 56	7.9	18 36	7.7	06 41	3.1	19 50	2.9	09 40	4.8	22 12	4.6
30	Monday	09 43	6.0	22 07	6.0	07 10	7.7	19 46	7.8	07 56	2.9	21 13	2.9	10 48	4.7	23 19	4.6
31	Tuesday	10 45	6.1	23 12	6.2	08 19	7.8	20 47	8.0	09 34	2.9	22 18	3.0	11 56	4.7	—	—

AUGUST 2001   *High water*   GMT

		LONDON BRIDGE				LIVERPOOL				GREENOCK				LEITH			
1	Wednesday	11 43	6.3	—	—	09 18	8.0	21 39	8.4	10 40	2.9	23 09	3.1	00 23	4.7	12 57	4.8
2	Thursday	00 10	6.4	12 36	6.5	10 07	8.3	22 23	8.7	11 31	3.0	23 54	3.2	01 17	4.9	13 47	4.9
3	Friday	01 03	6.7	13 23	6.7	10 50	8.4	23 02	8.9	—	—	12 16	3.0	02 01	5.0	14 29	5.0
4	Saturday	01 51	6.8	14 06	6.8	11 28	8.6	23 38	9.0	00 34	3.3	12 56	3.0	02 38	5.2	15 05	5.1
5	Sunday	02 33	6.8	14 43	6.7	—	—	12 03	8.6	01 11	3.3	13 32	3.0	03 12	5.2	15 39	5.1
6	Monday	03 10	6.7	15 16	6.6	00 12	9.0	12 35	8.6	01 44	3.3	14 05	3.0	03 43	5.3	16 10	5.1
7	Tuesday	03 42	6.6	15 45	6.5	00 46	9.0	13 07	8.6	02 14	3.3	14 37	3.0	04 14	5.3	16 43	5.1
8	Wednesday	04 13	6.5	16 15	6.5	01 19	8.9	13 39	8.5	02 44	3.3	15 10	3.0	04 47	5.2	17 18	5.0
9	Thursday	04 44	6.5	16 47	6.5	01 52	8.8	14 13	8.4	03 16	3.3	15 45	3.1	05 22	5.1	17 55	4.9
10	Friday	05 19	6.5	17 23	6.5	02 27	8.6	14 48	8.2	03 51	3.2	16 22	3.0	05 59	5.0	18 35	4.8
11	Saturday	05 59	6.4	18 05	6.4	03 06	8.4	15 28	8.0	04 28	3.1	17 02	3.0	06 39	4.8	19 19	4.6
12	Sunday	06 43	6.2	18 53	6.2	03 52	8.1	16 19	7.7	05 10	3.0	17 46	2.9	07 25	4.7	20 10	4.5
13	Monday	07 35	6.0	19 50	6.0	04 50	7.8	17 22	7.5	06 01	2.8	18 38	2.8	08 21	4.5	21 12	4.4
14	Tuesday	08 36	5.9	20 56	5.9	05 57	7.6	18 36	7.5	07 09	2.7	19 42	2.8	09 32	4.5	22 22	4.5
15	Wednesday	09 47	5.8	22 11	6.0	07 12	7.7	19 51	7.9	08 36	2.7	21 05	2.8	10 49	4.6	23 32	4.7
16	Thursday	11 02	6.1	23 28	6.3	08 25	8.1	20 57	8.5	09 59	2.9	22 19	3.0	—	—	12 01	4.9
17	Friday	—	—	12 08	6.5	09 29	8.6	21 53	9.1	11 03	3.1	23 16	3.3	00 34	5.0	13 03	5.2
18	Saturday	00 33	6.7	13 04	6.8	10 24	9.1	22 43	9.6	11 57	3.2	—	—	01 27	5.4	13 54	5.6
19	Sunday	01 31	7.1	13 55	7.1	11 15	9.5	23 32	10.0	00 05	3.5	12 50	3.3	02 13	5.7	14 41	5.9
20	Monday	02 23	7.4	14 43	7.3	—	—	12 03	9.8	00 52	3.6	13 40	3.3	02 57	5.9	15 26	6.0
21	Tuesday	03 11	7.6	15 28	7.4	00 19	10.1	12 51	9.8	01 38	3.8	14 27	3.4	03 42	6.0	16 11	5.9
22	Wednesday	03 57	7.6	16 11	7.4	01 06	10.1	13 36	9.7	02 22	3.8	15 10	3.4	04 27	6.0	16 57	5.8
23	Thursday	04 42	7.5	16 52	7.3	01 51	9.9	14 19	9.4	03 03	3.9	15 50	3.4	05 15	5.9	17 45	5.5
24	Friday	05 25	7.2	17 33	7.1	02 36	9.4	15 03	8.9	03 44	3.8	16 29	3.3	06 05	5.6	18 35	5.2
25	Saturday	06 08	6.8	18 16	6.8	03 22	8.9	15 49	8.4	04 26	3.6	17 10	3.2	07 00	5.3	19 30	4.8
26	Sunday	06 54	6.4	19 05	6.3	04 13	8.2	16 43	7.8	05 10	3.4	17 54	3.1	08 03	4.9	20 31	4.6
27	Monday	07 49	5.9	20 13	5.9	05 17	7.5	17 56	7.4	06 00	3.1	18 48	2.9	09 11	4.6	21 37	4.4
28	Tuesday	09 03	5.6	21 39	5.7	06 41	7.2	19 19	7.4	07 01	2.8	20 17	2.8	10 22	4.5	22 49	4.4
29	Wednesday	10 15	5.7	22 51	5.9	08 01	7.3	20 27	7.7	09 25	2.7	21 56	3.0	11 39	4.5	—	—
30	Thursday	11 17	6.0	23 51	6.2	09 02	7.7	21 20	8.2	10 35	2.8	22 50	3.1	00 02	4.6	12 45	4.7
31	Friday	—	—	12 12	6.3	09 50	8.1	22 04	8.6	11 22	3.0	23 35	3.3	01 00	4.8	13 34	4.9

SEPTEMBER 2001　*High water*　GMT

		LONDON BRIDGE				LIVERPOOL				GREENOCK				LEITH			
		*Datum of predictions 3.20 m below				*Datum of predictions 4.93 m below				*Datum of predictions 1.62 m below				*Datum of predictions 2.90 m below			
		hr	ht m	hr	ht m	hr	ht m	hr	ht m	hr	ht m	hr	ht m	hr	ht m	hr	ht m
1	Saturday	00 43	6.6	13 01	6.6	10 31	8.4	22 43	8.9	—	—	12 02	3.0	01 44	5.0	14 12	5.1
2	Sunday	01 30	6.8	13 44	6.7	11 08	8.6	23 18	9.1	00 15	3.4	12 40	3.1	02 20	5.2	14 45	5.2
3	Monday	02 12	6.9	14 22	6.7	11 41	8.7	23 50	9.1	00 52	3.4	13 13	3.1	02 51	5.3	15 15	5.2
4	Tuesday	02 47	6.8	14 55	6.6	—	—	12 11	8.7	01 23	3.3	13 42	3.1	03 19	5.4	15 44	5.3
5	Wednesday	03 18	6.7	15 23	6.6	00 21	9.1	12 41	8.7	01 50	3.3	14 09	3.1	03 49	5.4	16 15	5.2
6	Thursday	03 46	6.6	15 50	6.5	00 52	9.0	13 11	8.7	02 18	3.3	14 38	3.2	04 20	5.4	16 48	5.2
7	Friday	04 15	6.6	16 20	6.6	01 23	8.9	13 42	8.6	02 49	3.3	15 10	3.2	04 53	5.3	17 23	5.1
8	Saturday	04 47	6.6	16 54	6.6	01 56	8.8	14 15	8.5	03 22	3.3	15 44	3.2	05 28	5.1	18 00	4.9
9	Sunday	05 24	6.5	17 34	6.5	02 33	8.5	14 53	8.2	03 58	3.2	16 20	3.1	06 08	5.0	18 42	4.8
10	Monday	06 06	6.3	18 21	6.3	03 18	8.1	15 41	7.8	04 36	3.1	17 01	3.0	06 54	4.8	19 32	4.6
11	Tuesday	06 56	6.0	19 17	6.0	04 15	7.7	16 46	7.5	05 22	2.9	17 50	2.9	07 50	4.6	20 34	4.5
12	Wednesday	07 55	5.7	20 24	5.8	05 29	7.4	18 07	7.4	06 31	2.7	18 57	2.8	09 03	4.5	21 52	4.5
13	Thursday	09 10	5.6	21 46	5.8	06 53	7.5	19 31	7.7	08 17	2.7	20 35	2.9	10 29	4.6	23 09	4.7
14	Friday	10 38	5.8	23 12	6.2	08 13	8.0	20 42	8.4	09 55	2.9	22 01	3.1	11 46	4.9	—	—
15	Saturday	11 48	6.3	—	—	09 17	8.6	21 38	9.2	10 57	3.1	22 58	3.4	00 14	5.1	12 48	5.3
16	Sunday	00 19	6.7	12 45	6.8	10 10	9.3	22 28	9.7	11 48	3.3	23 47	3.6	01 07	5.5	13 37	5.7
17	Monday	01 14	7.2	13 34	7.1	10 58	9.7	23 14	10.1	—	—	12 35	3.4	01 53	5.8	14 22	5.9
18	Tuesday	02 04	7.5	14 20	7.3	11 43	9.9	23 58	10.2	00 34	3.7	13 21	3.5	02 36	6.0	15 04	6.0
19	Wednesday	02 50	7.6	15 04	7.4	—	—	12 26	9.9	01 19	3.9	14 03	3.5	03 19	6.2	15 48	6.0
20	Thursday	03 34	7.6	15 45	7.4	00 42	10.1	13 09	9.7	02 02	3.9	14 41	3.5	04 04	6.1	16 32	5.8
21	Friday	04 15	7.4	16 25	7.4	01 25	9.8	13 49	9.4	02 42	3.9	15 16	3.5	04 51	5.9	17 17	5.5
22	Saturday	04 53	7.1	17 04	7.1	02 06	9.3	14 29	8.9	03 20	3.8	15 52	3.5	05 40	5.6	18 04	5.2
23	Sunday	05 30	6.8	17 43	6.8	02 49	8.7	15 11	8.3	03 59	3.6	16 30	3.4	06 33	5.2	18 55	4.8
24	Monday	06 07	6.3	18 27	6.3	03 35	7.9	16 00	7.7	04 41	3.4	17 13	3.2	07 34	4.8	19 54	4.6
25	Tuesday	06 47	5.9	19 24	5.8	04 36	7.2	17 11	7.2	05 28	3.1	18 04	3.0	08 41	4.5	21 01	4.4
26	Wednesday	07 48	5.4	21 08	5.5	06 10	6.9	18 46	7.1	06 26	2.8	19 13	2.9	09 53	4.3	22 14	4.4
27	Thursday	09 41	5.4	22 25	5.7	07 37	7.0	19 59	7.5	09 10	2.7	21 24	3.0	11 14	4.4	23 32	4.5
28	Friday	10 48	5.7	23 25	6.1	08 37	7.5	20 54	8.0	10 18	2.9	22 24	3.2	—	—	12 23	4.6
29	Saturday	11 44	6.1	—	—	09 24	8.0	21 38	8.5	11 00	3.0	23 09	3.3	00 33	4.8	13 10	4.9
30	Sunday	00 17	6.5	12 33	6.5	10 04	8.4	22 17	8.9	11 38	3.1	23 48	3.4	01 18	5.0	13 47	5.1

OCTOBER 2001　*High water*　GMT

		LONDON BRIDGE				LIVERPOOL				GREENOCK				LEITH			
1	Monday	01 03	6.8	13 16	6.7	10 40	8.7	22 52	9.1	—	—	12 12	3.2	01 53	5.2	14 17	5.2
2	Tuesday	01 43	6.9	13 54	6.7	11 12	8.8	23 23	9.1	00 24	3.4	12 44	3.2	02 23	5.3	14 46	5.3
3	Wednesday	02 17	6.8	14 27	6.7	11 42	8.9	23 53	9.1	00 55	3.4	13 11	3.2	02 51	5.4	15 14	5.4
4	Thursday	02 48	6.7	14 56	6.6	—	—	12 11	8.9	01 21	3.4	13 37	3.3	03 21	5.5	15 45	5.4
5	Friday	03 16	6.7	15 24	6.6	00 23	9.1	12 41	8.9	01 50	3.4	14 06	3.4	03 52	5.5	16 18	5.3
6	Saturday	03 45	6.7	15 54	6.7	00 56	9.0	13 13	8.8	02 23	3.4	14 38	3.4	04 26	5.4	16 53	5.2
7	Sunday	04 18	6.7	16 30	6.7	01 30	8.9	13 47	8.7	02 57	3.4	15 12	3.4	05 04	5.3	17 31	5.1
8	Monday	04 54	6.6	17 11	6.6	02 09	8.6	14 27	8.4	03 33	3.3	15 47	3.3	05 45	5.1	18 13	4.9
9	Tuesday	05 36	6.3	18 00	6.4	02 55	8.2	15 16	8.0	04 12	3.1	16 26	3.2	06 34	4.9	19 03	4.7
10	Wednesday	06 25	6.0	18 57	6.0	03 54	7.7	16 23	7.5	04 59	2.9	17 16	3.1	07 32	4.7	20 07	4.5
11	Thursday	07 24	5.6	20 06	5.8	05 12	7.3	17 47	7.4	06 13	2.7	18 26	2.9	08 48	4.6	21 30	4.5
12	Friday	08 44	5.5	21 34	5.8	06 42	7.5	19 15	7.8	08 13	2.7	20 13	3.0	10 14	4.7	22 49	4.8
13	Saturday	10 18	5.8	22 58	6.3	08 01	8.0	20 25	8.5	09 47	3.0	21 40	3.2	11 29	5.0	23 53	5.1
14	Sunday	11 26	6.3	—	—	09 01	8.7	21 20	9.2	10 44	3.2	22 37	3.5	—	—	12 28	5.4
15	Monday	00 00	6.8	12 21	6.8	09 51	9.3	22 08	9.8	11 31	3.4	23 26	3.7	00 45	5.5	13 17	5.7
16	Tuesday	00 53	7.3	13 10	7.1	10 36	9.7	22 53	10.1	—	—	12 15	3.5	01 31	5.9	14 00	5.9
17	Wednesday	01 41	7.5	13 55	7.3	11 19	9.9	23 36	10.1	00 12	3.8	12 57	3.6	02 14	6.1	14 41	5.9
18	Thursday	02 25	7.6	14 38	7.4	12 00	9.8	—	—	00 57	3.9	13 35	3.6	02 57	6.1	15 23	5.9
19	Friday	03 07	7.5	15 20	7.4	00 17	9.9	12 41	9.6	01 39	3.9	14 10	3.7	03 42	6.0	16 06	5.7
20	Saturday	03 46	7.3	16 00	7.3	00 58	9.6	13 19	9.3	02 19	3.8	14 45	3.7	04 29	5.8	16 49	5.5
21	Sunday	04 22	7.0	16 38	7.1	01 38	9.1	13 58	8.9	02 57	3.7	15 20	3.6	05 17	5.4	17 33	5.2
22	Monday	04 55	6.7	17 17	6.7	02 18	8.5	14 37	8.4	03 36	3.5	15 58	3.5	06 09	5.1	18 21	4.9
23	Tuesday	05 27	6.4	17 59	6.3	03 01	7.8	15 22	7.8	04 17	3.3	16 40	3.4	07 05	4.7	19 17	4.6
24	Wednesday	06 04	6.0	18 50	5.8	03 56	7.2	16 24	7.3	05 04	3.1	17 31	3.2	08 08	4.4	20 22	4.4
25	Thursday	06 52	5.6	20 14	5.4	05 24	6.8	18 00	7.1	06 02	2.8	18 34	3.0	09 15	4.3	21 33	4.3
26	Friday	08 33	5.3	21 49	5.5	06 56	6.9	19 19	7.4	07 22	2.7	20 14	3.0	10 29	4.3	22 46	4.5
27	Saturday	10 09	5.5	22 50	5.9	08 01	7.3	20 17	7.9	09 36	2.9	21 44	3.1	11 41	4.5	23 51	4.7
28	Sunday	11 07	5.9	23 42	6.3	08 49	7.9	21 04	8.3	10 23	3.0	22 33	3.3	—	—	12 32	4.8
29	Monday	11 56	6.3	—	—	09 30	8.3	21 44	8.7	11 02	3.2	23 14	3.4	00 39	4.9	13 10	5.0
30	Tuesday	00 27	6.6	12 40	6.5	10 06	8.7	22 19	9.0	11 38	3.3	23 49	3.4	01 16	5.1	13 42	5.2
31	Wednesday	01 07	6.8	13 19	6.6	10 39	8.9	22 52	9.1	—	—	12 10	3.3	01 49	5.3	14 13	5.4

NOVEMBER 2001   *High water*   GMT

		LONDON BRIDGE *Datum of predictions 3.20 m below						LIVERPOOL *Datum of predictions 4.93 m below						GREENOCK *Datum of predictions 1.62 m below						LEITH *Datum of predictions 2.90 m below					
		hr	m	ht	hr	m	ht	hr	m	ht	hr	m	ht	hr	m	ht	hr	m	ht	hr	m	ht	hr	m	ht
1	Thursday	01	42	6.8	13	54	6.7	11	10	9.0	23	24	9.2	00	20	3.4	12	38	3.4	02	20	5.4	14	44	5.4
2	Friday	02	15	6.8	14	27	6.7	11	41	9.1	23	57	9.2	00	51	3.4	13	06	3.4	02	53	5.5	15	17	5.5
3	Saturday	02	48	6.8	15	00	6.7	—			12	14	9.1	01	24	3.4	13	38	3.5	03	28	5.5	15	51	5.4
4	Sunday	03	21	6.8	15	36	6.8	00	32	9.1	12	50	9.0	02	00	3.4	14	12	3.6	04	05	5.5	16	28	5.4
5	Monday	03	55	6.7	16	15	6.8	01	11	9.0	13	29	8.9	02	38	3.4	14	47	3.6	04	45	5.4	17	07	5.2
6	Tuesday	04	34	6.6	16	59	6.7	01	54	8.7	14	13	8.6	03	17	3.3	15	25	3.5	05	30	5.2	17	51	5.0
7	Wednesday	05	16	6.3	17	49	6.4	02	44	8.3	15	06	8.2	04	01	3.1	16	06	3.4	06	21	5.0	18	43	4.8
8	Thursday	06	04	6.0	18	46	6.1	03	44	7.8	16	11	7.8	04	55	2.9	16	58	3.2	07	21	4.8	19	49	4.7
9	Friday	07	04	5.7	19	57	5.9	05	00	7.5	17	31	7.7	06	17	2.8	18	10	3.1	08	36	4.7	21	11	4.7
10	Saturday	08	28	5.6	21	23	6.0	06	25	7.6	18	52	8.0	08	02	2.8	19	48	3.1	09	56	4.8	22	27	4.9
11	Sunday	09	54	5.9	22	37	6.4	07	38	8.1	20	01	8.6	09	24	3.0	21	12	3.3	11	07	5.0	23	29	5.2
12	Monday	10	59	6.4	23	36	6.8	08	38	8.7	20	57	9.1	10	20	3.3	22	13	3.5	—			12	06	5.3
13	Tuesday	11	54	6.8	—			09	28	9.2	21	46	9.5	11	07	3.4	23	03	3.6	00	22	5.5	12	55	5.5
14	Wednesday	00	29	7.2	12	44	7.1	10	13	9.5	22	32	9.7	11	50	3.5	23	50	3.7	01	09	5.7	13	38	5.7
15	Thursday	01	17	7.4	13	31	7.3	10	56	9.7	23	14	9.8	—			12	30	3.6	01	54	5.9	14	20	5.7
16	Friday	02	01	7.4	14	16	7.3	11	36	9.7	23	55	9.6	00	34	3.7	13	08	3.7	02	39	5.9	15	01	5.7
17	Saturday	02	42	7.3	14	59	7.2	—			12	15	9.5	01	17	3.7	13	44	3.7	03	25	5.8	15	43	5.6
18	Sunday	03	20	7.1	15	39	7.1	00	35	9.3	12	54	9.2	01	58	3.7	14	20	3.7	04	11	5.6	16	25	5.4
19	Monday	03	54	6.9	16	18	6.9	01	14	8.9	13	31	8.9	02	37	3.6	14	56	3.7	04	58	5.3	17	06	5.2
20	Tuesday	04	25	6.6	16	57	6.6	01	53	8.4	14	11	8.5	03	16	3.5	15	34	3.6	05	45	5.0	17	50	5.0
21	Wednesday	04	58	6.4	17	37	6.3	02	34	7.9	14	54	8.1	03	58	3.3	16	15	3.5	06	35	4.7	18	40	4.7
22	Thursday	05	35	6.1	18	23	5.9	03	22	7.4	15	46	7.7	04	46	3.1	17	02	3.3	07	29	4.5	19	38	4.5
23	Friday	06	21	5.8	19	20	5.6	04	25	7.0	16	55	7.3	05	41	3.0	17	59	3.1	08	27	4.3	20	42	4.4
24	Saturday	07	22	5.5	20	38	5.5	05	51	6.9	18	19	7.3	06	45	2.9	19	06	3.0	09	29	4.3	21	47	4.4
25	Sunday	08	56	5.4	21	54	5.7	07	06	7.1	19	26	7.6	07	59	2.9	20	28	3.0	10	32	4.4	22	49	4.6
26	Monday	10	12	5.7	22	51	6.0	08	03	7.6	20	19	8.0	09	19	3.0	21	40	3.1	11	32	4.6	23	45	4.7
27	Tuesday	11	08	6.0	23	40	6.3	08	49	8.0	21	03	8.4	10	14	3.1	22	29	3.2	—			12	20	4.8
28	Wednesday	11	56	6.3	—			09	28	8.5	21	42	8.7	10	57	3.3	23	09	3.3	00	31	5.0	13	02	5.1
29	Thursday	00	24	6.6	12	40	6.5	10	04	8.8	22	19	9.0	11	33	3.4	23	45	3.3	01	12	5.1	13	39	5.3
30	Friday	01	06	6.7	13	21	6.7	10	39	9.0	22	56	9.2	—			12	06	3.4	01	51	5.3	14	16	5.4

DECEMBER 2001   *High water*   GMT

		LONDON BRIDGE						LIVERPOOL						GREENOCK						LEITH					
1	Saturday	01	45	6.8	14	01	6.8	11	15	9.2	23	35	9.2	00	23	3.3	12	41	3.5	02	29	5.4	14	52	5.5
2	Sunday	02	24	6.9	14	42	6.9	11	54	9.3	—			01	03	3.4	13	16	3.6	03	07	5.5	15	29	5.5
3	Monday	03	02	6.8	15	24	7.0	00	16	9.2	12	35	9.2	01	44	3.4	13	54	3.7	03	48	5.5	16	08	5.5
4	Tuesday	03	42	6.8	16	08	7.0	01	00	9.1	13	20	9.1	02	27	3.3	14	32	3.7	04	32	5.5	16	50	5.4
5	Wednesday	04	22	6.7	16	54	6.8	01	47	8.9	14	08	8.9	03	11	3.3	15	13	3.7	05	19	5.4	17	37	5.2
6	Thursday	05	06	6.5	17	44	6.6	02	36	8.6	15	01	8.7	04	00	3.2	15	58	3.6	06	11	5.2	18	30	5.1
7	Friday	05	54	6.2	18	41	6.4	03	36	8.2	16	01	8.4	04	59	3.0	16	51	3.4	07	09	5.0	19	33	4.9
8	Saturday	06	53	6.0	19	47	6.2	04	43	8.0	17	10	8.2	06	12	2.9	17	56	3.3	08	18	4.9	20	47	4.9
9	Sunday	08	08	5.9	21	00	6.2	05	57	7.9	18	22	8.2	07	32	3.0	19	15	3.3	09	31	4.8	21	59	5.0
10	Monday	09	24	6.1	22	09	6.4	07	08	8.1	19	31	8.5	08	49	3.1	20	37	3.3	10	39	4.9	23	02	5.1
11	Tuesday	10	30	6.3	23	09	6.6	08	11	8.5	20	32	8.8	09	50	3.2	21	45	3.4	11	40	5.1	23	59	5.3
12	Wednesday	11	28	6.6	—			09	05	8.8	21	26	9.1	10	41	3.3	22	41	3.5	—			12	32	5.2
13	Thursday	00	03	6.9	12	22	6.9	09	53	9.1	22	14	9.2	11	26	3.5	23	31	3.5	00	51	5.4	13	19	5.4
14	Friday	00	53	7.0	13	11	7.0	10	36	9.3	22	58	9.3	—			12	08	3.5	01	40	5.5	14	03	5.5
15	Saturday	01	39	7.1	13	58	7.1	11	17	9.4	23	39	9.2	00	15	3.5	12	47	3.6	02	27	5.5	14	44	5.5
16	Sunday	02	21	7.0	14	43	7.0	11	56	9.3	—			01	01	3.5	13	25	3.7	03	13	5.5	15	25	5.4
17	Monday	02	59	6.9	15	24	6.9	00	17	9.0	12	34	9.2	01	42	3.4	14	01	3.7	03	57	5.4	16	05	5.4
18	Tuesday	03	32	6.7	16	03	6.7	00	55	8.8	13	12	9.0	02	24	3.4	14	38	3.7	04	40	5.2	16	44	5.2
19	Wednesday	04	03	6.6	16	39	6.5	01	33	8.5	13	50	8.8	03	01	3.3	15	15	3.6	05	22	5.0	17	23	5.1
20	Thursday	04	36	6.4	17	17	6.3	02	12	8.2	14	31	8.5	03	42	3.2	15	54	3.5	06	04	4.8	18	06	4.9
21	Friday	05	13	6.3	17	57	6.1	02	54	7.9	15	14	8.2	04	25	3.1	16	35	3.4	06	49	4.6	18	53	4.7
22	Saturday	05	56	6.1	18	43	5.9	03	40	7.5	16	04	7.8	05	13	3.1	17	21	3.2	07	37	4.5	19	47	4.6
23	Sunday	06	46	5.9	19	35	5.8	04	36	7.2	17	03	7.6	06	05	3.0	18	14	3.1	08	31	4.4	20	45	4.5
24	Monday	07	47	5.7	20	35	5.7	05	45	7.1	18	10	7.5	06	59	2.9	19	12	3.0	09	28	4.4	21	46	4.5
25	Tuesday	08	55	5.7	21	41	5.8	06	55	7.3	19	16	7.7	07	59	2.9	20	19	3.0	10	26	4.4	22	45	4.5
26	Wednesday	10	03	5.8	22	44	6.0	07	55	7.7	20	13	8.0	09	06	3.0	21	29	3.0	11	25	4.6	23	43	4.7
27	Thursday	11	05	6.0	23	40	6.3	08	46	8.1	21	03	8.4	10	08	3.1	22	27	3.1	—			12	19	4.8
28	Friday	12	00	6.3	—			09	30	8.5	21	49	8.8	10	56	3.2	23	16	3.2	00	36	4.9	13	08	5.1
29	Saturday	00	31	6.6	12	51	6.6	10	13	8.9	22	34	9.1	11	39	3.4	—			01	24	5.1	13	51	5.2
30	Sunday	01	19	6.7	13	39	6.8	10	56	9.2	23	19	9.3	00	02	3.3	12	19	3.5	02	09	5.3	14	32	5.4
31	Monday	02	04	6.8	14	27	7.0	11	39	9.4	—			00	48	3.3	13	00	3.6	02	52	5.5	15	12	5.5

World Geographical Statistics

THE EARTH

The shape of the Earth is that of an oblate spheroid or solid of revolution whose meridian sections are ellipses, whilst the sections at right angles are circles.

DIMENSIONS

Equatorial diameter = 12,756.27 km (7,926.38 miles)
Polar diameter = 12,713.50 km (7,899.80 miles)
Equatorial circumference = 40,075.01 km (24,901.46 miles)
Polar circumference = 40,007.86 km (24,859.73 miles)

The equatorial circumference is divided into 360 degrees of longitude, which is measured in degrees, minutes and seconds east or west of the Greenwich meridian (0°) to 180°, the meridian 180° E. coinciding with 180° W. The dateline was internationally ratified on 13 October 1884.

Distance north and south of the Equator is measured in degrees, minutes and seconds of latitude. The Equator is 0°, the North Pole is 90° N. and the South Pole is 90° S. The Tropics lie at 23° 26′ N. (Tropic of Cancer) and 23° 26′ S. (Tropic of Capricorn). The Arctic Circle lies at 66° 34′ N. and the Antarctic Circle at 66° 34′ S. (NB The Tropics and the Arctic and Antarctic circles are affected by the slow decrease in obliquity of the ecliptic, of about 0.47 arcseconds per year. The effect of this is that the Arctic and Antarctic circles are currently moving towards their respective poles by about 14 metres per century, while the Tropics move towards the Equator by the same amount.

AREA, ETC.

The surface area of the Earth is 510,069,120 km² (196,938,800 miles²), of which the water area is 70.92 per cent and the land area is 29.08 per cent.

The velocity of a given point on the Earth's surface at the Equator is 1,669.79 km per hour (1,037.56 m.p.h.). The Earth's mean velocity in its orbit around the Sun is 107,229 km per hour (66,629 m.p.h.). The Earth's mean distance from the Sun is 149,597,870 km (92,955,807 miles).

OCEANS

AREA

	km²	miles²
Pacific	166,240,000	64,186,300
Atlantic	86,550,000	33,420,000
Indian	73,427,000	28,350,500
Arctic	9,485,000	3,662,000

The division by the Equator of the Pacific into the North and South Pacific and the Atlantic into the North and South Atlantic makes a total of six oceans.

GREATEST DEPTHS

Ocean	location	metres	feet
Pacific	Mariana Trench	10,920	35,827
Atlantic	Puerto Rico Trench	8,605	28,232
Indian	Java (Sunda) Trench	7,125	23,376
Arctic	Molloy Deep	5,680	18,399

SEAS

AREA

	km²	miles²
South China	2,974,600	1,148,500
Caribbean	2,515,900	971,400
Mediterranean	2,509,900	969,100
Bering	2,261,000	873,000
Gulf of Mexico	1,507,600	582,100
Okhotsk	1,392,000	537,500
Japan	1,012,900	391,100
Hudson Bay	730,100	281,900
East China	664,600	256,600
Andaman	564,880	218,100
Black Sea	507,900	196,100
Red Sea	453,000	174,900
North Sea	427,100	164,900
Baltic Sea	382,000	147,500
Yellow Sea	294,000	113,500
Persian/Arabian Gulf	230,000	88,800

GREATEST DEPTHS

	Maximum depth metres	feet
Caribbean	8,605	28,232
East China (Ryu Kyu Trench)	7,507	24,629
South China	7,258	23,812
Mediterranean (Ionian Basin)	5,150	16,896
Andaman	4,267	14,000
Bering	3,936	12,913
Gulf of Mexico	3,504	11,496
Okhotsk	3,365	11,040
Japan	3,053	10,016
Red Sea	2,266	7,434
Black Sea	2,212	7,257
North Sea	439	1,440
Hudson Bay	111	364
Baltic Sea	90	295
Yellow Sea	73	240
Persian Gulf	73	240

THE CONTINENTS

There are six geographic continents, although America is often divided politically into North and Central America, and South America.

AFRICA is surrounded by sea except for the narrow isthmus of Suez in the north-east, through which is cut the Suez Canal. Its extreme longitudes are 17° 20′ W. at Cape Verde, Senegal, and 51° 24′ E. at Ras Hafun, Somalia. Its extreme latitudes are 37° 20′ N. at Cape Blanc, Tunisia, and 34° 50′ S. at Cape Agulhas, South Africa, about 4,400 miles apart. The Equator passes through the middle of the continent.

NORTH AMERICA, including Mexico, is surrounded by ocean except in the south, where the isthmian states of CENTRAL AMERICA link North America with South America. Its extreme longitudes are 168° 5′ W. at Cape

Prince of Wales, Alaska, and 55° 40' W. at Cape Charles, Newfoundland. The extreme continental latitudes are the tip of the Boothia peninsula, NW Territories, Canada (71° 51' N.) and 14° 22' N. at Ocós in the south of Mexico.

SOUTH AMERICA lies mostly in the southern hemisphere; the Equator passes through the north of the continent. It is surrounded by ocean except where it is joined to Central America in the north by the narrow isthmus through which is cut the Panama Canal. Its extreme longitudes are 34° 47' W. at Cape Branco in Brazil and 81° 20' W. at Punta Pariña, Peru. The extreme continental latitudes are 12° 25' N. at Punta Gallinas, Colombia, and 53° 54' S. at the southernmost tip of the Brunswick peninsula, Chile. Cape Horn, on Cape Island, Chile, lies at 55° 59' S.

ANTARCTICA lies almost entirely within the Antarctic Circle (66° 34' S.) and is the largest of the world's glaciated areas. The continent has an area of 5.1 million square miles, 99 per cent of which is permanently ice-covered. The ice amounts to some 7.2 million cubic miles and represents more than 90 per cent of the world's fresh water. The environment is too hostile for unsupported human habitation.

ASIA is the largest continent and occupies 30 per cent of the world's land surface. The extreme longitudes are 26° 05' E. at Baba Buran, Turkey and 169° 40' W. at Mys Dežneva (East Cape), Russia, a distance of about 6,000 miles. Its extreme northern latitude is 77° 45' N. at Cape Čeljuskin, Russia, and it extends over 5,000 miles south to about 1° 15' N. of the Equator.

AUSTRALIA is the smallest of the continents and lies in the southern hemisphere. It is entirely surrounded by ocean. Its extreme longitudes are 113° 11' E. at Steep Point and 153° 11' E. at Cape Byron. The extreme latitudes are 10° 42' S. at Cape York and 39° S. at South East Point, Tasmania.

EUROPE, including European Russia, is the smallest continent in the northern hemisphere. Its extreme latitudes are 71° 11' N. at North Cape in Norway, and 36° 23' N. at Cape Matapan in southern Greece, a distance of about 2,400 miles. Its breadth from Cabo Carvoeiro in Portugal (9° 34' W.) in the west to the Kara River, north of the Urals (66° 30' E.) in the east is about 3,300 miles. The division between Europe and Asia is generally regarded as the watershed of the Ural Mountains; down the Ural river to Gur'yev, Kazakhstan; across the Caspian Sea to Apsheronskiy Poluostrov, near Baku; along the watershed of the Caucasus Mountains to Anapa and thence across the Black Sea to the Bosporus in Turkey; across the Sea of Marmara to Çanakkale Boğazi (Dardanelles).

	Area km²	miles²
Asia	43,998,000	16,988,000
*America	41,918,000	16,185,000
Africa	29,800,000	11,506,000
Antarctica	13,209,000	5,100,000
†Europe	9,699,000	3,745,000
Australia	7,618,493	2,941,526

*North and Central America has an area of 24,255,000 km² (9,365,000 miles²)

†Includes 5,571,000 km² (2,151,000 miles²) of former USSR territory, including the Baltic states, Belarus, Moldova, Ukraine, that part of Russia west of the Ural Mountains and Kazakhstan west of the Ural river. European Turkey (24,378 km²/9,412 miles²) comprises territory to the west and north of the Bosporus and the Dardanelles

GLACIATED AREAS

It is estimated that 15,915,000 km² (6,145,000 miles²) or 10.73 per cent of the world's land surface is permanently covered with ice.

	Area km²	miles²
South Polar regions	13,830,000	5,340,000
North Polar regions (incl. Greenland or Kalaallit Nunaat)	1,965,000	758,500
Alaska-Canada	58,800	22,700
Asia	37,800	14,600
South America	11,900	4,600
Europe	10,700	4,128
New Zealand	1,015	391
Africa	238	92

The largest glacier is the 515 km/320 mile-long Lambert-Fisher Ice Passage, Antarctica.

PENINSULAS

	Area km²	miles²
Arabian	3,250,000	1,250,000
Southern Indian	2,072,000	800,000
Alaskan	1,500,000	580,000
Labradorian	1,300,000	500,000
Scandinavian	800,300	309,000
Iberian	584,000	225,500

LARGEST ISLANDS

Island, and Ocean	Area km²	miles²
Greenland (Kalaallit Nunaat), Arctic	2,175,500	840,000
New Guinea, Pacific	821,030	317,000
Borneo, Pacific	725,450	280,100
Madagascar, Indian	587,040	226,658
Baffin Island, Arctic	507,451	195,928
Sumatra, Indian	427,350	165,000
Honshu, Pacific	227,413	87,805
*Great Britain, Atlantic	218,077	84,200
Victoria Island, Arctic	217,292	83,897
Ellesmere Island, Arctic	196,236	75,767
Sulawesi (Celebes), Indian	189,036	72,987
South Island, NZ, Pacific	151,213	58,384
Java, Indian	126,650	48,900
North Island, NZ, (Pacific)	114,487	44,204
Cuba, Atlantic	110,862	42,804
Newfoundland, Atlantic	108,855	42,030
Luzon, Pacific	105,360	40,680
Iceland, Atlantic	102,820	39,700
Mindanao, Pacific	95,247	36,775
Ireland, Atlantic	82,462	31,839

*Mainland only

LARGEST DESERTS

	Area (approx.) km²	miles²
The Sahara, N. Africa	8,400,000	3,250,000
Australian Desert	1,550,000	600,000
Arabian Desert	1,200,000	470,000
The Gobi, Mongolia/China	1,040,000	400,000
Kalahari Desert, Botswana/ Namibia/S. Africa	520,000	200,000
Takla Makan, Mongolia/China	320,000	125,000
*Kara Kum, Turkmenistan	310,000	120,000
Namib Desert, Namibia	285,000	110,000
Thar Desert, India/Pakistan	260,000	100,000
Somali Desert, Somalia	260,000	100,000
Atacama Desert, Chile	180,000	70,000
Sonoran Desert, USA/Mexico	180,000	70,000
Dasht-e Lut, Iran	52,000	20,000
Mojave Desert, USA	38,850	15,000

*Together with the Kyzyl Kum known as the Turkestan Desert

DEEPEST DEPRESSIONS

	Maximum depth below sea level metres	feet
Dead Sea, Jordan/Israel	408	1,338
Lake Assal, Djibouti	156	511
Turfan Depression, Sinkiang, China	153	505
Qattara Depression, Egypt	132	436
Mangyshlak peninsula, Kazakhstan	131	433
Danakil Depression, Ethiopia	116	383
Death Valley, California, USA	86	282
Salton Sink, California, USA	71	235
W. of Ustyurt plateau, Kazakhstan	70	230
Prikaspiyskaya Nizmennost', Russia/Kazakhstan	67	220
Lake Sarykamysh, Uzbekistan/ Turkmenistan	45	148
El Faiyûm, Egypt	44	147
Valdies peninsula, Lago Enriquillo, Dominican Republic	40	131
Lake Eyre, South Australia	16	52

The world's largest exposed depression is the Prikaspiyskaya Nizmennost' covering the hinterland of the northern third of the Caspian Sea, which is itself 28 m (92 ft) below sea level.

Western Antarctica and Central Greenland largely comprise crypto-depressions under ice burdens. The Antarctic Bentley subglacial trench has a bedrock 2,538 m (8,326 ft) below sea-level. In Greenland (lat. 73° N., long. 39° W.) the bedrock is 365 m (1,197 ft) below sea-level.

More than a quarter of the area of The Netherlands lies marginally below sea-level, an area of more than 10,000 km²/3,860 miles².

LONGEST MOUNTAIN RANGES

Range, and location	Length km	miles
Cordillera de Los Andes, W. South America	7,200	4,500
Rocky Mountains, W. North America	4,800	3,000
Himalaya-Karakoram-Hindu Kush, S. Central Asia	3,800	2,400
Great Dividing Range, E. Australia	3,600	2,250
Trans-Antarctic Mts, Antarctica	3,500	2,200
Atlantic Coast Range, E. Brazil	3,000	1,900
West Sumatran-Javan Range, Indonesia	2,900	1,800
Aleutian Range, Alaska and NW Pacific	2,650	1,650
Tien Shan, S. Central Asia	2,250	1,400
Central New Guinea Range, Irian Jaya/Papua New Guinea	2,000	1,250

HIGHEST MOUNTAINS

The world's 8,000-metre mountains (with six subsidiary peaks) are all in the Himalaya-Karakoram-Hindu Kush ranges.

Mountain	Height metres	feet
Mt Everest*	8,850	29,035
K2 (Chogori)†	8,607	28,238
Kangchenjunga	8,597	28,208
Lhotse	8,511	27,923
Makalu I	8,481	27,824
Lhotse Shar (II)	8,383	27,504
Dhaulagiri I	8,171	26,810
Manaslu I (Kutang I)	8,156	26,760
Cho Oyu	8,153	26,750
Nanga Parbat (Diamir)	8,125	26,660
Annapurna I	8,091	26,546
Gasherbrum I (Hidden Peak)	8,068	26,470
Broad Peak I	8,046	26,400
Shisham Pangma (Gosainthan)	8,046	26,400
Gasherbrum II	8,034	26,360
Makalu South-East	8,010	26,280
Broad Peak Central	8,000	26,246

*Named after Sir George Everest (1790–1866), Surveyor-General of India 1830–43, in 1863. He pronounced his name Eve-rest
†Formerly Godwin-Austin

The culminating summits in the other major mountain ranges are:

Mountain, by range or country	Height metres	feet
Pik Pobedy, Tien Shan	7,439	24,406
Cerro Aconcagua, Cordillera de Los Andes	6,960	22,834
Mt McKinley (S. Peak), Alaska Range	6,194	20,320
Kilimanjaro (Kibo), Tanzania	5,894	19,340
Hkakabo Razi, Myanmar	5,881	19,296
El'brus, (W. Peak), Caucasus	5,642	18,510
Citlaltépetl (Orizaba), Sierra Madre Oriental, Mexico	5,610	18,405
Vinson Massif, E. Antarctica	4,897	16,066
Puncak Jaya, Central New Guinea Range	4,884	16,023

Mountain, by range or country	*Height*	
	metres	feet
Mt Blanc, Alps	4,807	15,771
Klyuchevskaya Sopka, Kamchatka peninsula, Russia	4,750	15,584
Ras Dashan, Ethiopian Highlands	4,620	15,158
Zard Kūh, Zagros Mts, Iran	4,547	14,921
Mt Kirkpatrick, Trans Antarctic	4,529	14,860
Mt Belukha, Altai Mts, Russia/ Kazakhstan	4,505	14,783
Mt Elbert, Rocky Mountains	4,400	14,433
Mt Rainier, Cascade Range, N. America	4,392	14,410
Nevado de Colima, Sierra Madre Occidental, Mexico	4,268	14,003
Jebel Toubkal, Atlas Mts, N. Africa	4,165	13,665
Kinabalu, Crocker Range, Borneo	4,101	13,455
Kerinci, West Sumatran-Javan Range, Indonesia	3,800	12,467
Jabal an NabīShu'ayb, N. Tihāmat, Yemen	3,760	12,336
Mt Cook (Aorangi), Southern Alps, New Zealand	3,754	12,315
Teotepec, Sierra Madre del Sur, Mexico	3,703	12,149
Thaban Ntlenyana, Drakensberg, South Africa	3,482	11,425
Pico de Bandeira, Atlantic Coast Range	2,890	9,482
Shishaldin, Aleutian Range	2,861	9,387
Kosciusko, Great Dividing Range	2,228	7,310

HIGHEST VOLCANOES

Volcano (last major eruption), and location	*Height*	
	metres	feet
Ojos del Salado (1981), Andes, Argentina/Chile	6,880	22,572
Llullaillaco (1877), Andes, Argentina/Chile	6,723	22,057
San Pedro (1960), Andes, Chile	6,199	20,325
Guallatiri (1960, 1993), Andes, Chile	6,071	19,918
Cotopaxi (1940, 1975), Andes, Ecuador	5,897	19,347
Tupungatito (1986), Andes, Chile	5,640	18,504
Láscar (1995), Andes, Chile	5,591	18,346
Popocatépetl (1999), Mexico	5,465	17,930
Nevado del Ruiz (1985, 1991), Colombia	5,321	17,457
Sangay (1998), Andes, Ecuador	5,188	17,021
Irruputuncu (1995), Chile	5,163	16,939
Klyuchevskaya Sopka (1999), Kamchatka peninsula, Russia	4,835	15,863
Guagua Pichincha (1999), Andes, Ecuador	4,784	15,696
Purace (1977), Colombia	4,756	15,601
Wrongel (1907), Alaska, USA	4,316	14,163
Shasta (1786), California, USA	4,316	14,162
Galeras (1993), Colombia	4,275	14,028
Mauna Loa (1984, 1987), Hawaii Is.	4,170	13,680
Cameroon (1999), Cameroon	4,095	13,435

OTHER NOTABLE VOLCANOES

	Height	
	metres	feet
Erebus (1998), Ross Island, Antarctica	3,794	12,450
Fuji (1708), Honshu, Japan	3,775	12,388
Santa Maria (1902, 1998), Guatemala	3,772	12,375
Semeru (1998, 1999), Java, Indonesia	3,675	12,060
Mt Etna (1169, 1669, 1993, 1996-9), Sicily, Italy	3,368	11,053
Raung (1993, 1997), Java, Indonesia	3,322	10,932
Sheveluch (1997, 1999), Kamchatka, Russia	3,283	10,771
Llaima (1995), Chile	3,125	10,253
Mt St Helens (1980, 1986, 1991), Washington State, USA	2,549	8,363
Beerenberg (1985), Jan Mayen Island	2,277	7,470
Pinatubo (1991, 1995), Luzon, Philippines	1,598	5,249
Hekla (1981, 1991), Iceland	1,491	4,892
Mt Unzen (1792, 1991, 1996, 2000), Kyushu, Japan	1,360	4,462
Vesuvius (AD 79, 1631, 1944), Italy	1,281	4,203
Kilauea (1996, 1997-9), Hawaii, USA	1,249	4,009
Soufrière (1979, 1997), St Vincent	1,178	3,865
Stromboli (1996, 1997-9), Lipari Is., Italy	926	3,038
Soufrière Hills (1997-9), Montserrat	914	3,001
Krakatau (1883, 1995, 1999), Sunda Strait, Indonesia	813	2,667
Santoríni (Thíra) (1628 BC, 1950), Aegean Sea, Greece	564	1,850
Tristan da Cunha (1961), South Atlantic	243	800
Surtsey (1963-7), off Iceland	173	568

LARGEST LAKES

The areas of some of these lakes are subject to seasonal variation.

	Area		*Length*	
	km²	miles²	km	miles
Caspian Sea, Iran/ Azerbaijan/Russia/ Turkmenistan/ Kazakhstan	371,000	143,000	1,171	728
*Michigan–Huron, USA/Canada	117,610	45,300	1,010	627
Superior, Canada/ USA	82,100	31,700	563	350
Victoria, Uganda/ Tanzania/Kenya	69,500	26,828	362	225
Tanganyika, Dem. Rep. of Congo/ Tanzania/Zambia/ Burundi	32,900	12,665	725	450
Great Bear, Canada	31,328	12,096	309	192
‡Aral Sea, Kazakhstan/ Uzbekistan	30,700	11,850	320	200
†Baykal (*Baikal*), Russia	30,500	11,776	620	385
Malawi (Nyasa), Tanzania/Malawi/ Mozambique	28,900	11,150	580	360
Great Slave, Canada	28,570	11,031	480	298
Erie, Canada/USA	25,670	9,910	388	241

	Area km²	miles²	Length km	miles
Winnipeg, Canada	24,390	9,417	428	266
Ontario, Canada/USA	19,010	7,340	310	193
Balkhash, Kazakhstan	18,427	7,115	605	376
Ladozhskoye (Ladoga), Russia	17,700	6,835	193	120

*Lakes Michigan and Huron are regarded as lobes of the same lake. The Michigan lobe has an area of 57,750 km² (22,300 miles²) and the Huron lobe an area of 59,570 km² (23,000 miles²)
† World's deepest lake (1,940 m/6,365 ft)
‡ Northern part (Little Aral Sea) dammed off, 1997

UNITED KINGDOM, BY COUNTRY

	km²	miles²	km	miles
Lough Neagh, Northern Ireland	381.73	147.39	28.90	18.00
Loch Lomond, Scotland	71.12	27.46	36.44	22.64
Windermere, England	14.74	5.69	16.90	10.50
Lake Vyrnwy, Wales (artificial)	4.53	1.75	7.56	4.70
Llyn Tegid (Bala), Wales (natural)	4.38	1.69	5.80	3.65

River, source and outflow	Length km	miles
Tigris-Euphrates, R. Murat, E. Turkey – Persian Gulf	2,800	1,740
Zambezi, NW Zambia – S. Indian Ocean	2,735	1,700
Irrawaddy, R. Mali Hka, Myanmar – Andaman Sea	2,151	1,337
Don, SE of Novomoskovsk – Sea of Azov	1,969	1,224

BRITISH ISLES

	km	miles
Shannon, Co. Cavan, Rep. of Ireland – Atlantic Ocean	386	240
Severn, Powys, Wales – Bristol Channel	354	220
Thames, Gloucestershire, England – North Sea	346	215
Tay, Perthshire, Scotland – North Sea	188	117
Clyde, Lanarkshire, Scotland – Firth of Clyde	158	98¼
Tweed, Peeblesshire, Scotland – North Sea	155	96½
Bann (Upper and Lower), Co. Down, N. Ireland – Atlantic Ocean	122	76

LONGEST RIVERS

River, source and outflow	Length km	miles
Nile (Bahr-el-Nil), R. Luvironza, Burundi – E. Mediterranean Sea	6,825	4,240
Amazon (Amazonas), Lago Villafro, Peru – S. Atlantic Ocean	6,448	4,007
Yangtze-Kiang (Chang Jiang), Kunlun Mts, W. China – Yellow Sea	6,380	3,964
Mississippi-Missouri-Red Rock, Montana – Gulf of Mexico	5,970	3,710
Yenisey-Angara, W. Mongolia – Kara Sea	5,536	3,440
Huang He (Yellow River), Bayan Har Shan range, central China – Yellow Sea	5,463	3,395
Ob'-Irtysh, W. Mongolia – Kara Sea	5,410	3,362
Amur-Argun, R. Argun, Khingan Mts, N. China – Sea of Okhotsk	4,416	2,744
Lena-Kirenga, R. Kirenga, W. of Lake Baykal – Laptev Sea, Arctic Ocean	4,400	2,734
Zaïre (Congo), R. Lualaba, Dem. Rep. of Congo-Zambia – S. Atlantic Ocean	4,370	2,715
Mackenzie-Peace, Tatlatui Lake, British Columbia – Beaufort Sea	4,240	2,635
Mekong, Lants'ang, Tibet – South China Sea	4,184	2,600
Niger, Loma Mts, Guinea – Gulf of Guinea, E. Atlantic Ocean	4,170	2,590
Río de la Plata-Paraná, R. Paranáiba, central Brazil – S. Atlantic Ocean	4,000	2,485
Murray-Darling, SE Queensland – Lake Alexandrina, S. Australia	3,717	2,310
Volga, Valdai plateau – Caspian Sea	3,685	2,290

OTHER NOTABLE RIVERS

	km	miles
Rio Grande, USA–Mexican border	3,057	1,900
Ganges-Brahmaputra, R. Matsang, SW Tibet – Bay of Bengal	2,900	1,800
Indus, R. Sengge, SW Tibet – N. Arabian Sea	2,897	1,800
Danube (Donau), Black Forest, SW Germany – Black Sea	2,856	1,775

GREATEST WATERFALLS – BY HEIGHT

Waterfall, river and location	Total drop metres	feet	Greatest single leap metres	feet
Saltó Angel, Carrao Auyán Tepuí, Venezuela	979	3,212	807	2,648
Utigård, Jostedal Glacier, Norway	800	2,625	600	1,970
Mongefossen, Monge, Norway	774	2,540	—	—
Yosemite, Yosemite Creek, USA	739	2,425	435	1,430
Østre Mardøla Foss, Mardals, Norway	655	2,149	296	974
Tyssestrengane, Tysso, Norway	646	2,120	289	948
Cuquenán, Arabopó, Venezuela	610	2,000	—	—
Tugela, Tugela, Natal, S. Africa	580	1,904	410	1,350
Sutherland, Arthur, NZ	580	1,904	248	815
*Kjellfossen (Kile), Naeröfjord, Norway	561	1,841	149	490

*Volume often so low the fall atomizes into a 'bridal veil'

BRITISH ISLES, BY COUNTRY

	metres	feet		
Eas a' Chuàl Aluinn, Glas Bheinn, Sutherland, Scotland	200	658		
Powerscourt Falls, Dargle, Co. Wicklow, Rep. of Ireland	106	350		
Pistyll-y-Llyn, Powys/ Dyfed border, Wales	c.72	c.235	(cascades)	
Pistyll Rhyadr, Clwyd/ Powys border, Wales	71.5	235		(single leap)
Caldron Snout, R. Tees, Cumbria/Durham, England	61	200	(cascades)	

GREATEST WATERFALLS - BY VOLUME

Waterfall, river and location	Mean annual flow m³/sec	galls/sec
Inga (Congo dam site), Dem. Rep. of Congo	43,000	9,460,000
Khône, Mekong, Laos	42,500	9,350,000
Boyoma (Stanley), R. Lualaba, Dem. Rep. of Congo	c.17,000	c.3,750,000
Guayra (Sete Quedas), Brazil	13,000	2,860,000
Rio Paraná, Argentina/ Paraguay	11,900	2,619,000
Niagara (Horseshoe), R. Niagara/Lake Erie–Lake Ontario	6,000	1,320,000
Paulo Afonso, R. São Francisco, Brazil	2,830	622,500
Urubupunga, Alto Parañá, Brazil	2,745	604,000
Cataratas del Iguazú, R. Iguaçu, Brazil/Argentina	1,743	380,000
Patos-Maribando, Rio Grande, Brazil	1,500	330,000
Churchill, R. Churchill, Canada	1,132	215,000
Victoria (*Mosi-oa-tunya*), R. Zambezi, Zambia/ Zimbabwe	1,087	242,000

TALLEST DAMS

	metres	feet
*Rogun, R. Vakhsh, Tajikistan	335	1,098
Nurek, R. Vakhsh, Tajikistan	300	984
Grande Dixence, Switzerland	285	935
*Longtan, R. Hangshui, China	285	935
Inguri, Georgia	272	892
Vajont, Italy	262	859
Manuel M. Torres, Chicoasén, Mexico	261	856
Tehri, R. Bhagivathi, India	261	856

*Under construction

The world's most massive dam is the Syncrude Tailings dam in Alberta, Canada, which will have a volume of 540 million cubic metres/706 million cubic yards.

The Three Gorges Chang Jiang (Yangtze) Dam, China, with a crest length of 1,983 m/6,505 ft, is due for completion in 2009 (stage 3).

The Yacyretá-Apipe dam across the River Paraná, Argentina-Paraguay, is being completed to a length of 69,600 m/43.24 miles.

TALLEST INHABITED BUILDINGS

Building and city	Height metres	feet
*Shanghai World Financial Centre (2003)	460	1,509
Chongqing Tower, China	457	1,499
Petronas Towers I and II, Kuala Lumpur, Malaysia (1998)	451.9	1,482
Sears Tower, Chicago[1] (1974)	443	1,454
Jin Mao, Shanghai, China (1999)	420	1,378
One World Trade Center Tower, New York[2] (1972)	417	1,368
Xianmen Fairwell Int. Centre, China (2002)	397	1,302
CITIC Plaza, Guangzhou, China (1996)	391	1,283
Shun Hing Square, Shenzhen, China (1996)	384	1,260
Plaza Rakyat, Kuala Lumpur, Malaysia (1999)	382	1,254
Empire State Building, New York[3] (1931)	381	1,250
Central Plaza, Hong Kong (1992)	373	1,227
Bank of China Tower, Hong Kong (1998)	368	1,209
Emirates Tower One (2000)	350	1,148
T. & C. Tower, Kaohsiung, Taiwan (1998)	347	1,140
Amoco Building, Chicago (1973)	346	1,136
John Hancock Center, Chicago (1969)	343	1,127
Burjal Arab Hotal, Dubai (1999)	321	1,053
Baiyoke Tower II, Bangkok, Thailand (1998)	320	1,050

1. With TV antennae, 520 m/1,707 ft
2. With TV antennae, 521.2 m/1,710 ft; Two World Trade Center Tower (1973), 415 m/1,362 ft
3. With TV tower (added 1950–1), 430.9 m/1,414 ft

TALLEST STRUCTURES

*Collapsed during renovation, August 1991

Structure and location	Height metres	feet
*Warszawa Radio Mast, Konstantynow, Poland (1974)	646	2,120
KTHI-TV Mast, Blanchard, North Dakota (guyed) (1963)	629	2,063
CN Tower, Metro Centre, Toronto, Canada (1975)	555	1,822
Ostankino Tower, Moscow (1967)	537	1,762

LONGEST BRIDGES – BY SPAN

Bridge and location	Length metres	feet
SUSPENSION SPANS		
Akashi-Kaikyo, Shikoku, Japan (1998)	1,990	6,529
Storebaelt East Bridge, Denmark (1998)	1,624	5,328
Humber Estuary, Humberside, England (1981)	1,410	4,626
Jiangyin (Yangtze), China (1999)	1,385	4,544
Tsing Ma, Hong Kong, China (1997)	1,377	4,518
Verrazano Narrows, Brooklyn–Staten I, USA (1964)	1,298	4,260
Golden Gate, San Francisco Bay, USA (1937)	1,280	4,200
Hoga Kustan, Sweden (1997)	1,210	3,970
Mackinac Straits, Michigan, USA (1957)	1,158	3,800
Chesapeake Bay No.2, Virginia, USA (1999)	1,158	3,800
Minami Bisan-Seto, Japan (1988)	1,100	3,609
Bosporus II, Istanbul, Turkey (1988)	1,089	3,576
Bosporus I, Istanbul, Turkey (1973)	1,074	3,524
George Washington, Hudson River, New York City, USA (1931)	1,067	3,500
Kurushima III, Japan (1999)	1,030	3,379
Kurushima II, Japan (1999)	1,020	3,346
Ponte 25 de Abril (Tagus), Lisbon, Portugal (1966)	1,013	3,323
Firth of Forth (road), nr Edinburgh, Scotland (1964)	1,006	3,300
Kita Bisan-Seto, Japan (1988)	990	3,248
*Severn River, Severn Estuary, England (1966)	988	3,240

*The main span of the 5.15 km/3.2 mile long Second Severn bridging, opened in 1996, is 456 m/1,496 ft.

Bridge and location	Length	
	metres	feet
CANTILEVER SPANS		
Pont de Québec (rail-road), St Lawrence,		
Canada (1917)	548.6	1,800
Ravenswood, W. Virginia, USA	525.1	1,723
Firth of Forth (rail), nr Edinburgh,		
Scotland (1890)	521.2	1,710
Nanko, Osaka, Japan (1974)	510.0	1,673
Commodore Barry, Chester,		
Pennsylvania, USA	494.3	1,622
Greater New Orleans, Louisiana,		
USA (1988)	480.0	1,575
Howrah (rail-road), Calcutta, India	457.2	1,500
STEEL ARCH SPANS		
New River Gorge, Fayetteville,		
W. Virginia, USA (1977)	518.0	1,700
Bayonne (Kill van Kull), Bayonne, NJ –		
Staten I., USA (1931)	503.5	1,652
Sydney Harbour, Sydney, Australia (1932)	502.9	1,650

The 'floating' bridging at Evergreen Point, Seattle, Washington State, USA (1963), is 3,839 m/12,596 ft long, of which 2,310 m/7,578 ft floats.

The longest stretch of bridgings of any kind is that carrying the Interstate 55 and Interstate 10 highways at Manchac, Louisiana (1979), on twin concrete trestles over 55.21 km/34.31 miles.

LONGEST VEHICULAR TUNNELS

Tunnel and location	Length	
	km	miles
*Seikan (rail), Tsugaru Channel, Japan (1988)	53.90	33.49
*Channel Tunnel, Cheriton, Kent –		
Sangatte, Calais (1994)	49.94	31.03
Moscow metro, Belyaevo – Bittsevsky,		
Moscow, Russia (1979)	37.90	23.50
Northern line tube, East Finchley –		
Morden, London (1939)	27.84	17.30
†Laerdal-Aurland Road Link (2001)	24.50	15.22
*Oshimizu (rail), Honshū, Japan (1982)	22.17	13.78
Simplon II (rail), Brigue, Switzerland –		
Iselle, Italy (1922)	19.82	12.31
Simplon I (rail), Brigue, Switzerland –		
Iselle, Italy (1906)	19.80	12.30
*Shin-Kanmon (rail), Kanmon Strait, Japan		
(1975)	18.68	11.61
Great Appennine (rail), Vernio, Italy (1934)	18.49	11.49
St Gotthard (road), Göschenen –		
Airolo, Switzerland (1980)	16.32	10.14
Rokko (rail), Ōsaka – Kōbe, Japan (1972)	16.09	10.00

*Sub-aqueous; †Under construction.

The longest non-vehicular tunnelling in the world is the Delaware Aqueduct in New York State, USA, constructed in 1937–44 to a length of 168.9 km/105 miles.

BRITAIN – RAIL TUNNELS

	miles	yards
Severn, Bristol – Newport (1873–86)	4	484
Totley, Manchester – Sheffield	3	950
Standedge, Manchester – Huddersfield		
(1811)	3	66
Sodbury, Swindon – Bristol	2	924
Disley, Stockport – Sheffield	2	346
Ffestiniog, Llandudno – Blaenau Ffestiniog	2	338
Bramhope, Leeds – Harrogate	2	241
Cowburn, Manchester – Sheffield	2	182

The longest road tunnel in Britain is the Mersey Road Tunnel (1934), 3.42 km/2 miles 228 yards long. The longest canal tunnel, at Standedge, W. Yorks, is 5.13 km/3 miles 330 yards long; it was closed in 1944 but is currently being restored.

LONGEST SHIP CANALS

Canal (opening date)	Length		Min. depth	
	km	miles	metres	feet
White Sea-Baltic				
(formerly Stalin) (1933),				
of which Canalised river;				
51.5 km/32 miles	227	141.00	5.0	16.5
*Suez (1869)				
Links Red and	162	100.60	12.9	42.3
Mediterranean Seas				
V. I. Lenin Volga-Don				
(1952).				
Links Black and				
Caspian Seas	100	62.20	n/a	n/a
Kiel (or North Sea)				
(1895)				
Links North				
and Baltic Seas	98	60.90	13.7	45.0
*Houston (1940)				
Links inland city				
with sea	91	56.70	10.4	34.0
Alphonse XIII (1926)				
Gives Seville access				
to sea	85	53.00	7.6	25.0
Panama (1914)				
Links Pacific Ocean				
and Caribbean Sea;				
lake chain, 78.9 km/49	82	50.71	12.5	41.0
miles dug				
Manchester Ship (1894)				
Links city with				
Irish Channel	64	39.70	8.5	28.0
Welland (1932)				
Circumvents Niagara				
Falls and Rapids	43.5	27.00	8.8	29.0
Brussels (Rupel Sea)				
(1922)				

*Has no locks

The first section of China's Grand Canal, running 1,782 km/1,107 miles from Beijing to Hangzhou, was opened AD 610 and completed in 1283. Today it is limited to 2,000 tonne vessels.

The St Lawrence Seaway comprises the Beauharnois, Welland and Welland Bypass and Seaway 54–59 canals, and allows access to Duluth, Minnesota, USA via the Great Lakes from the Atlantic end of Canada's Gulf of St Lawrence, a distance of 3,769 km/2,342 miles. The St Lawrence Canal, completed in 1959, is 293 km/182 miles long.

Distances from London by Air

This list details the distances in miles from London, Heathrow, to various cities (airports) abroad.

To	Miles
Abidjan	3,197
Abu Dhabi (International)	3,425
Addis Ababa	3,675
Adelaide (International)	10,111
Aden	3,670
Algiers	1,035
Amman (Queen Alia)	2,287
Amsterdam	230
Ankara (Esenboga)	1,770
Athens	1,500
Atlanta	4,198
Auckland	11,404
Baghdad (Saddam)	2,551
Bahrain	3,163
Baku	2,485
Bangkok	5,928
Barbados	4,193
Barcelona (Muntadas)	712
Basle	447
Beijing (Capital)	5,063
Beirut	2,161
Belfast (Aldergrove)	325
Belgrade	1,056
Berlin (Tegel)	588
Bermuda	3,428
Berne	476
Bogotá	5,262
Bombay (Mumbai)	4,478
Boston	3,255
Brasilia	5,452
Bratislava	817
Brisbane (Eagle Farm)	10,273
Brussels	217
Bucharest (Otopeni)	1,307
Budapest	923
Buenos Aires	6,915
Cairo (International)	2,194
Calcutta	4,958
Calgary	4,357
Canberra	10,563
Cape Town	6,011
Caracas	4,639
Casablanca (Mohamed V)	1,300
Chicago (O'Hare)	3,941
Cologne	331
Colombo (Katunayake)	5,411
Copenhagen	608
Dakar	2,706
Dallas (Fort Worth)	4,736
Dallas (Lovefield)	4,732
Damascus (International)	2,223
Dar-es-Salaam	4,662
Darwin	8,613
Delhi	4,180
Denver	4,655
Detroit (Metropolitan)	3,754
Dhahran	3,143
Dhaka	4,976
Doha	3,253
Dubai	3,414
Dublin	279
Durban	5,937
Düsseldorf	310
Entebbe	4,033
Frankfurt (Main)	406
Freetown	3,046
Geneva	468
Gibraltar	1,084
Gothenburg (Landvetter)	664
Hamburg	463
Harare	5,156
Havana	4,647
Helsinki (Vantaa)	1,148
Hobart	10,826
Ho Chi Minh City	6,345
Hong Kong	5,990
Honolulu	7,220
Houston (Intercontinental)	4,821
Houston (William P. Hobby)	4,837
Islamabad	3,767
Istanbul	1,560
Jakarta (Halim Perdanakusuma)	7,295
Jeddah	2,947
Johannesburg	5,634
Kabul	3,558
Karachi	3,935
Kathmandu	4,570
Khartoum	3,071
Kiev (Borispol)	1,357
Kiev (Julyany)	1,337
Kingston, Jamaica	4,668
Kuala Lumpur (Subang)	6,557
Kuwait	2,903
Lagos	3,107
Larnaca	2,036
Lima	6,303
Lisbon	972
Lomé	3,129
Los Angeles (International)	5,439
Madras	5,113
Madrid	773
Malta	1,305
Manila	6,685
Marseille	614
Mauritius	6,075
Melbourne (Essendon)	10,504
Melbourne (Tullamarine)	10,499
Mexico City	5,529
Miami	4,414
Milan (Linate)	609
Minsk	1,176
Montego Bay	4,687
Montevideo	6,841
Montreal (Mirabel)	3,241
Moscow (Sheremetievo)	1,557
Munich (Franz Josef Strauss)	584
Muscat	3,621
Nairobi (Jomo Kenyatta)	4,248
Naples	1,011
Nassau	4,333
New York (J. F. Kennedy)	3,440
Nice	645
Oporto	806
Oslo (Fornebu)	722
Ottawa	3,321
Palma, Majorca (Son San Juan)	836
Paris (Charles de Gaulle)	215
Paris (Le Bourget)	215
Paris (Orly)	227
Perth, Australia	9,008
Port of Spain	4,404
Prague	649
Pretoria	5,602
Reykjavik (Domestic)	1,167
Reykjavik (Keflavik)	1,177
Rhodes	1,743
Rio de Janeiro	5,745
Riyadh (King Khaled) International	3,067
Rome (Fiumicino)	895
St John's, Newfoundland	2,308
St Petersburg	1,314
Salzburg	651
San Francisco	5,351
São Paulo	5,892
Sarajevo	1,017
Seoul (Kimpo)	5,507
Shanghai	5,725
Shannon	369
Singapore (Changi)	6,756
Sofia	1,266
Stockholm (Arlanda)	908
Suva	10,119
Sydney (Kingsford Smith)	10,568
Tangier	1,120
Tehran	2,741
Tel Aviv	2,227
Tokyo (Narita)	5,956
Toronto	3,544
Tripoli (International)	1,468
Tunis	1,137
Turin (Caselle)	570
Ulan Bator	4,340
Valencia	826
Vancouver	4,707
Venice (Tessera)	715
Vienna (Schwechat)	790
Vladivostok	5,298
Warsaw	912
Washington (Dulles)	3,665
Wellington	11,692
Yangon/Rangoon	5,582
Yokohama (Aomori)	5,647
Zagreb	848
Zürich	490

The United Kingdom

The United Kingdom comprises Great Britain (England, Wales and Scotland) and Northern Ireland. The Isle of Man and the Channel Islands are Crown dependencies with their own legislative systems, and not a part of the United Kingdom.

AREA AS AT 31 MARCH 1981

	Land miles²	km²	*Inland water miles²	km²	Total miles²	km²
United Kingdom	93,006	240,883	1,242	3,218	94,248	244,101
England	50,058	129,652	293	758	50,351	130,410
Wales	7,965	20,628	50	130	8,015	20,758
Scotland	29,767	77,097	653	1,692	30,420	78,789
†Northern Ireland	5,225	13,532	249	628	5,467	14,160
Isle of Man	221	572	—	—	221	572
Channel Islands	75	194	—	—	75	194

*Excluding tidal water
†Excluding certain tidal waters that are parts of statutory areas in Northern Ireland

POPULATION

The first official census of population in England, Wales and Scotland was taken in 1801 and a census has been taken every ten years since, except in 1941 when there was no census because of war. The last official census in the United Kingdom was taken on 21 April 1991 and the next is due in April 2001.

The first official census of population in Ireland was taken in 1841. However, all figures given below refer only to the area which is now Northern Ireland. Figures for Northern Ireland in 1921 and 1931 are estimates based on the censuses taken in 1926 and 1937 respectively.

Estimates of the population of England before 1801, calculated from the number of baptisms, burials and marriages, are:

1570	4,160,221	1670	5,773,646
1600	4,811,718	1700	6,045,008
1630	5,600,517	1750	6,517,035

Thousands	United Kingdom Total	Male	Female	England and Wales Total	Male	Female	Scotland Total	Male	Female	Northern Ireland Total	Male	Female
CENSUS RESULTS 1801–1991												
1801	—	—	—	8,893	4,255	4,638	1,608	739	869	—	—	—
1811	13,368	6,368	7,000	10,165	4,874	5,291	1,806	826	980	—	—	—
1821	15,472	7,498	7,974	12,000	5,850	6,150	2,092	983	1,109	—	—	—
1831	17,835	8,647	9,188	13,897	6,771	7,126	2,364	1,114	1,250	—	—	—
1841	20,183	9,819	10,364	15,914	7,778	8,137	2,620	1,242	1,378	1,649	800	849
1851	22,259	10,855	11,404	17,928	8,781	9,146	2,889	1,376	1,513	1,443	698	745
1861	24,525	11,894	12,631	20,066	9,776	10,290	3,062	1,450	1,612	1,396	668	728
1871	27,431	13,309	14,122	22,712	11,059	11,653	3,360	1,603	1,757	1,359	647	712
1881	31,015	15,060	15,955	25,974	12,640	13,335	3,736	1,799	1,936	1,305	621	684
1891	34,264	16,593	17,671	29,003	14,060	14,942	4,026	1,943	2,083	1,236	590	646
1901	38,237	18,492	19,745	32,528	15,729	16,799	4,472	2,174	2,298	1,237	590	647
1911	42,082	20,357	21,725	36,070	17,446	18,625	4,761	2,309	2,452	1,251	603	648
1921	44,027	21,033	22,994	37,887	18,075	19,811	4,882	2,348	2,535	1,258	610	648
1931	46,038	22,060	23,978	39,952	19,133	20,819	4,843	2,326	2,517	1,243	601	642
1951	50,225	24,118	26,107	43,758	21,016	22,742	5,096	2,434	2,662	1,371	668	703
1961	52,709	25,481	27,228	46,105	22,304	23,801	5,179	2,483	2,697	1,425	694	731
1971	55,515	26,952	28,562	48,750	23,683	25,067	5,229	2,515	2,714	1,536	755	781
1981	55,848	27,104	28,742	49,155	23,873	25,281	5,131	2,466	2,664	*1,533	750	783
1991	56,467	27,344	29,123	49,890	24,182	25,707	4,999	2,392	2,607	1,578	769	809
†RESIDENT POPULATION: PROJECTIONS (MID-YEAR)												
2001	59,618	29,377	30,241	52,818	26,062	26,756	5,106	2,484	2,622	1,694	830	864
2011	60,929	30,206	30,723	54,151	26,881	27,269	5,059	2,476	2,583	1,720	848	872
2021	62,244	30,916	31,328	55,526	27,614	27,913	4,993	2,449	2,544	1,724	853	871

*Figures include 44,500 non-enumerated persons
†Projections are 1996 based
Source: The Stationery Office – Annual Abstract 2000; ONS – Census reports (Crown copyright)

ISLANDS: Census Results 1901–91

	Isle of Man Total	Male	Female	Jersey Total	Male	Female	*Guernsey Total	Male	Female
1901	54,752	25,496	29,256	52,576	23,940	28,636	40,446	19,652	20,794
1911	52,016	23,937	28,079	51,898	24,014	27,884	41,858	20,661	21,197
1921	60,284	27,329	32,955	49,701	22,438	27,263	38,315	18,246	20,069
1931	49,308	22,443	26,865	50,462	23,424	27,038	40,643	19,659	20,984
1951	55,123	25,749	29,464	57,296	27,282	30,014	43,652	21,221	22,431
1961	48,151	22,060	26,091	57,200	27,200	30,000	45,068	21,671	23,397
1971	56,289	26,461	29,828	72,532	35,423	37,109	51,458	24,792	26,666
1981	64,679	30,901	33,778	77,000	37,000	40,000	53,313	25,701	27,612
1991	69,788	33,693	36,095	84,082	40,862	43,220	58,867	28,297	30,570

*Population of Guernsey, Herm, Jethou and Lithou. Figures for 1901–71 record all persons present on census night; census figures for 1981 and 1991 record all persons resident in the islands on census night
Source: 1991 Census

RESIDENT POPULATION

MID-YEAR ESTIMATE

	1988	1998
United Kingdom	57,158,000	59,237,000
England	47,633,000	49,495,000
Wales	2,854,000	2,933,000
Scotland	5,093,000	5,120,000
Northern Ireland	1,578,000	1,689,000

Source: The Stationery Office – *Annual Abstract of Statistics 2000* (Crown copyright)

BY AGE AND SEX 1998

Males	*Under 16*	*65 and over*
United Kingdom	6,210,000	3,824,000
England	5,172,000	3,212,000
Wales	307,000	210,000
Scotland	519,000	314,000
Northern Ireland	212,000	88,000

Females	*Under 16*	*60 and over*
United Kingdom	5,900,000	6,905,000
England	4,910,000	5,756,000
Wales	291,000	376,000
Scotland	494,000	605,000
Northern Ireland	202,000	168,000

Source: The Stationery Office – *Annual Abstract of Statistics 2000* (Crown copyright)

BY ETHNIC GROUP (1991 CENSUS (GREAT BRITAIN))

Ethnic group	*Estimated population*	*As % of ethnic minority population*
Caribbean	500,000	16.6
African	212,000	7
Other black	178,000	5.9
Indian	840,000	27.9
Pakistani	477,000	15.8
Bangladeshi	163,000	5.4
Chinese	157,000	5.2
Other Asian	198,000	6.6
Other	290,000	9.6
Total ethnic minority groups	3,015,000	100
White	51,874,000	—
All ethnic groups	54,889,000	—

Source: The Stationery Office – *Population Trends 72* (Crown copyright)

AVERAGE DENSITY *Persons per hectare*

	1981	1991
England	3.55	3.61
Wales	1.34	1.36
Scotland	0.66	0.65
Northern Ireland	1.12	1.11

Sources: ONS – Census reports (Crown copyright)

IMMIGRATION 1998
Acceptances for settlement in the UK by nationality

Region	*Number of persons*
Europe: total	7,570
European Economic Area	270
Remainder of Europe	7,300
Americas: total	10,780
USA	3,940
Canada	1,050
Africa: total	16,090
Asia: total	30,120
Indian sub-continent	16,420
Middle East	4,180
Oceania: total	3,690
British Overseas Citizens	960
Stateless	580
Total	69,790

Source: The Stationery Office – *Annual Abstract of Statistics 2000* (Crown copyright)

LIVE BIRTHS AND BIRTH RATES 1998

	Live births	*Birth rate**
United Kingdom	717,000	12.1
England and Wales	636,000	12.1
Scotland	57,000	11.2
Northern Ireland	24,000	14.1

*Live births per 1,000 population
Source: The Stationery Office – *Annual Abstract of Statistics 2000* (Crown copyright)

LEGAL ABORTIONS 1998p

Age group	England and Wales	Scotland
Under 16	3,759	285
16–19	33,236	2,694
20–34	116,581	7,943
35–44	23,750	1,481
45 and over	511	21
Total	190,261	

p provisional
Source: The Stationery Office – Annual Abstract of Statistics 2000
(Crown copyright)

BIRTHS OUTSIDE MARRIAGE (UK)

Age group	1988	1998
Under 20	51,000	49,000
20–24	76,000	77,000
25–29	42,000	70,000
Over 30	29,000	74,000
Total	198,000	270,000

Source: The Stationery Office – Annual Abstract of Statistics 2000
(Crown copyright)

MARRIAGE AND DIVORCE 1997p

	Marriages	Divorces
United Kingdom	310,218p	161,815
England and Wales	272,536p	146,689
Scotland	29,611	12,222
Northern Ireland	8,071	2,904

p provisional
Source: The Stationery Office – Annual Abstract of Statistics 2000
(Crown copyright)

DEATHS AND DEATH RATES 1998

Males	Deaths	Death rate*
United Kingdom	300,160	10.3
England and Wales	264,707	10.2
Scotland	28,132	11.3
Northern Ireland	7,321	8.9
Females		
United Kingdom	329,012	10.9
England and Wales	290,308	10.9
Scotland	31,032	11.8
Northern Ireland	7,672	8.9

*Deaths per 1,000 population
Sources: The Stationery Office – Annual Abstract of Statistics 2000
(Crown copyright); ONS; General Register Office for Scotland;
General Register Office (Northern Ireland)

INFANT MORTALITY 1998p
Deaths of infants under 1 year of age per 1,000 live births

	Number
United Kingdom	5.7
England and Wales	5.7
Scotland	5.6
Northern Ireland	5.6

p provisional
Sources: The Stationery Office – Annual Abstract of Statistics 2000
(Crown copyright)

LIFE EXPECTANCY LIFE TABLES 1996–98 (INTERIM FIGURES)

Age	England and Wales Male	Female	Scotland Male	Female	Northern Ireland Male	Female
0	74.8	79.8	72.4	77.9	74.2	79.5
5	70.4	75.3	67.9	73.4	69.7	75.0
10	65.5	70.4	63.0	68.4	64.7	70.0
15	60.5	65.4	58.1	63.5	59.8	65.1
20	55.7	60.5	53.3	58.6	55.0	60.2
25	50.9	55.6	48.6	53.7	50.2	55.3
30	46.1	50.7	43.9	48.8	45.5	50.3
35	41.4	45.8	38.2	43.9	40.7	45.5
40	36.6	41.0	34.5	39.1	35.9	40.6
45	31.9	36.2	29.9	34.4	31.3	35.9
50	27.4	31.6	25.5	29.9	26.8	31.2
55	23.0	27.0	21.3	25.5	22.4	26.7
60	18.9	22.7	17.5	21.3	18.3	22.4
65	15.2	18.6	14.0	17.3	14.7	18.3
70	11.8	14.8	11.0	13.8	11.5	14.5
75	9.1	11.5	8.5	10.7	8.8	11.3
80	6.8	8.6	6.3	7.9	6.6	8.4
85	5.0	6.3	4.7	5.6	4.9	6.1

Source: The Stationery Office – Annual Abstract of Statistics 2000 (Crown copyright)

DEATHS ANALYSED BY CAUSE 1998

	England and Wales	Scotland	N. Ireland
TOTAL DEATHS	555,015	59,164	14,933
Deaths from natural causes	536,396	56,579	14,271
Infectious and parasitic diseases	3,410	486	53
Neoplasms	138,306	14,907	3,769
Malignant neoplasm of stomach	6,442	680	215
Malignant neoplasm of trachea, bronchus and lung	30,199	3,984	775
Malignant neoplasm of breast	11,835	1,147	299
Malignant neoplasm of uterus	1,296	110	34
Malignant neoplasm of cervix	1,158	145	33
Benign and unspecified neoplasms	1,605	110	121
Leukaemia	3,551	329	93
Endocrine, nutritional and metabolic diseases and immunity disorders	7,542	797	85
Diabetes mellitus	5,938	574	55
Nutritional deficiencies	72	12	1
Other metabolic and immunity disorders	1,169	175	26
Diseases of blood and blood-forming organs	1,937	222	24
Anaemias	641	81	14
Mental disorders	10,430	1,725	145
Diseases of the nervous system and sense organs	10,035	894	240
Meningitis	216	6	4
Diseases of the circulatory system	226,677	25,253	6,367
Rheumatic heart disease	1,629	151	29
Hypertensive disease	3,122	277	72
Ischaemic heart disease	121,037	13,419	3,654
Diseases of pulmonary circulation and other forms of heart disease	26,377	2,784	680
Cerebrovascular disease	57,516	6,900	1,602
Diseases of the respiratory system	90,192	8,011	2,627
Influenza	129	12	2
Pneumonia	54,631	4,064	1,727
Bronchitis, emphysema	3,523	288	108
Asthma	1,366	120	44
Diseases of the digestive system	21,025	2,578	499
Ulcer of stomach and duodenum	3,935	314	80
Appendicitis	144	11	2
Hernia of the abdominal cavity and other intestinal obstruction	2,042	211	47
Chronic liver disease and cirrhosis	4,494	806	104
Diseases of the genitourinary system	6,946	890	265
Nephritis, nephrotic syndrome and nephrosis	2,946	570	164
Hyperplasia of prostate	207	7	5
Complications of pregnancy, childbirth and the puerperium	43	5	1
Abortion	7	–	–
Diseases of the skin and subcutaneous tissue	1,070	94	36
Diseases of the musculo-skeletal system	3,566	284	30
Congenital anomalies	1,247	176	70
Certain conditions originating in the perinatal period	124	165	64
Birth trauma, hypoxia, birth asphyxia and other respiratory conditions	94	82	21
Signs, symptoms and ill-defined conditions	13,846	398	149
Sudden infant death syndrome	236	79	4
Deaths from injury and poisoning	16,201	2,379	569
All accidents	10,351	1,388	381
Motor vehicle accidents	2,946	387	129
Suicide and self-inflicted injury	3,614	649	126
All other external causes	2,236	342	62

Source: The Stationery Office – *Annual Abstract of Statistics 2000* (Crown copyright)

The National Flag

The national flag of the United Kingdom is the Union Flag, generally known as the Union Jack.

The Union Flag is a combination of the cross of St George, patron saint of England, the cross of St Andrew, patron saint of Scotland, and a cross similar to that of St Patrick, patron saint of Ireland.

Cross of St George: cross Gules in a field Argent (red cross on a white ground)

Cross of St Andrew: saltire Argent in a field Azure (white diagonal cross on a blue ground)

Cross of St Patrick: saltire Gules in a field Argent (red diagonal cross on a white ground)

The Union Flag was first introduced in 1606 after the union of the kingdoms of England and Scotland under one sovereign. The cross of St Patrick was added in 1801 after the union of Great Britain and Ireland.

FLYING THE UNION FLAG

The correct orientation of the Union Flag when flying is with the broader diagonal band of white uppermost in the hoist (i.e. near the pole) and the narrower diagonal band of white uppermost in the fly (i.e. furthest from the pole).

It is the practice to fly the Union Flag daily on some customs houses. In all other cases, flags are flown on government buildings by command of The Queen. It is now customary for the Union Flag to be flown at Buckingham Palace when The Queen is not present.

Days for hoisting the Union Flag are notified to the Department for Culture, Media and Sport by The Queen's command and communicated by the department to the other government departments. On the days appointed, the Union Flag is flown on government buildings in the United Kingdom from 8 a.m. to sunset.

DAYS FOR FLYING FLAGS

The Queen's Accession	6 February
Birthday of The Duke of York	19 February
*St David's Day (in Wales only)	1 March
Birthday of The Prince Edward	10 March
Commonwealth Day** (2000)	12 March
Birthday of The Queen	21 April
*St George's Day (in England only)	23 April
†Europe Day	9 May
Coronation Day	2 June
Birthday of The Duke of Edinburgh	10 June
The Queen's Official Birthday 2001	16 June
Birthday of Queen Elizabeth the Queen Mother	4 August
Birthday of The Princess Royal	15 August
Birthday of The Princess Margaret	21 August
Remembrance Sunday 2001	10 November
Birthday of The Prince of Wales	14 November
The Queen's Wedding Day	20 November
*St Andrew's Day (in Scotland only)	30 November

‡The opening of Parliament by The Queen
‡The prorogation of Parliament by The Queen

*Where a building has two or more flagstaffs, the appropriate national flag may be flown in addition to the Union Flag, but not in a superior position
**Commonwealth Day is always the second Monday in March

†The Union Flag should fly alongside the European flag. On government buildings that have only one flagpole, the Union Flag should take precedence
‡Flags are flown whether or not The Queen performs the ceremony in person. Flags are flown only in the Greater London area

FLAGS AT HALF-MAST

Flags are flown at half-mast (i.e. two-thirds up between the top and bottom of the flagstaff) on the following occasions:

(a) From the announcement of the death up to the funeral of the Sovereign, except on Proclamation Day, when flags are hoisted right up from 11 a.m. to sunset

(b) The funerals of members of the royal family, subject to special commands from The Queen in each case

(c) The funerals of foreign rulers, subject to special commands from The Queen in each case

(d) The funerals of prime ministers and ex-prime ministers of the UK, subject to special commands from The Queen in each case

(e) Other occasions by special command of The Queen

On occasions when days for flying flags coincide with days for flying flags at half-mast, the following rules are observed. Flags are flown:

(a) although a member of the royal family, or a near relative of the royal family, may be lying dead, unless special commands be are received from The Queen to the contrary

(b) although it may be the day of the funeral of a foreign ruler

If the body of a very distinguished subject is lying at a government office, the flag may fly at half-mast on that office until the body has left (provided it is a day on which the flag would fly) and then the flag is to be hoisted right up. On all other government buildings the flag will fly as usual.

THE ROYAL STANDARD

The Royal Standard is hoisted only when The Queen is actually present in the building, and never when Her Majesty is passing in procession.

The Royal Family

THE SOVEREIGN

ELIZABETH II, by the Grace of God, of the United
Kingdom of Great Britain and Northern Ireland and of
her other Realms and Territories Queen, Head of the
Commonwealth, Defender of the Faith

Her Majesty Elizabeth Alexandra Mary of Windsor, elder
daughter of King George VI and of HM Queen Elizabeth
the Queen Mother
Born 21 April 1926, at 17 Bruton Street, London W1
Ascended the throne 6 February 1952
Crowned 2 June 1953, at Westminster Abbey
Married 20 November 1947, in Westminster Abbey, HRH
The Prince Philip, Duke of Edinburgh
Official residences: Buckingham Palace, London SW1A 1AA;
Windsor Castle, Berks; Palace of Holyroodhouse,
Edinburgh
Private residences: Sandringham, Norfolk; Balmoral
Castle, Aberdeenshire

HUSBAND OF THE QUEEN

HRH THE PRINCE PHILIP, DUKE OF EDINBURGH, KG, KT,
OM, GBE, AC, QSO, PC, Ranger of Windsor Park
Born 10 June 1921, son of Prince and Princess Andrew of
Greece and Denmark naturalised a British subject 1947,
created Duke of Edinburgh, Earl of Merioneth and Baron
Greenwich 1947

CHILDREN OF THE QUEEN

HRH THE PRINCE OF WALES (Prince Charles Philip
Arthur George), KG, KT, GCB and Great Master of the
Order of the Bath, AK, QSO, PC, ADC(P)
Born 14 November 1948, created Prince of Wales and
Earl of Chester 1958, succeeded as Duke of Cornwall, Duke
of Rothesay, Earl of Carrick and Baron Renfrew, Lord of
the Isles and Prince and Great Steward of Scotland 1952
Married 29 July 1981 Lady Diana Frances Spencer (Diana,
Princess of Wales (1961–97), youngest daughter of the 8th
Earl Spencer and the Hon. Mrs Shand Kydd), marriage
dissolved 1996
Issue:
(1) HRH Prince William of Wales (Prince William
Arthur Philip Louis), *born* 21 June 1982
(2) HRH Prince Henry of Wales (Prince Henry Charles
Albert David), *born* 15 September 1984
Residences of the Prince of Wales: St James's Palace, London
SW1A 1BS; Highgrove, Doughton, Tetbury, Glos GL8 8TN

HRH THE PRINCESS ROYAL (Princess Anne Elizabeth
Alice Louise), KG, GCVO
Born 15 August 1950, declared The Princess Royal 1987
Married (1) 14 November 1973 Captain Mark Anthony
Peter Phillips, CVO (*born* 22 September 1948); marriage
dissolved 1992; (2) 12 December 1992 Captain Timothy
James Hamilton Laurence, MVO, RN (*born* 1 March 1955)
Issue:
(1) Peter Mark Andrew Phillips, *born* 15 November 1977

(2) Zara Anne Elizabeth Phillips, *born* 15 May 1981
Residence: Gatcombe Park, Minchinhampton, Glos

HRH The Duke of York (Prince Andrew Albert Christian
Edward), CVO, ADC(P)
Born 19 February 1960, created Duke of York, Earl of
Inverness and Baron Killyleagh 1986
Married 23 July 1986 Sarah Margaret Ferguson, now
Sarah, Duchess of York (*born* 15 October 1959, younger
daughter of Major Ronald Ferguson and Mrs Hector
Barrantes), marriage dissolved 1996
Issue:
(1) HRH Princess Beatrice of York (Princess Beatrice
Elizabeth Mary), *born* 8 August 1988
(2) HRH Princess Eugenie of York (Princess Eugenie
Victoria Helena), *born* 23 March 1990
Residences: Buckingham Palace, London SW1A 1AA;
Sunninghill Park, Ascot, Berks

HRH THE EARL OF WESSEX (Prince Edward Antony
Richard Louis), CVO
Born 10 March 1964, created Earl of Wessex, Viscount
Severn 1999
Married 19 June 1999 Sophie Helen Rhys-Jones, now
HRH The Countess of Wessex (*born* 20 January 1965,
daughter of Mr and Mrs Christopher Rhys-Jones)
Residence: Bagshot Park, Bagshot, Surrey GU19 5HS

SISTER OF THE QUEEN

HRH THE PRINCESS MARGARET, COUNTESS OF
SNOWDON, CI, GCVO, Royal Victorian Chain, Dame Grand
Cross of the Order of St John of Jerusalem
Born 21 August 1930, younger daughter of King George
VI and HM Queen Elizabeth the Queen Mother
Married 6 May 1960 Antony Charles Robert Armstrong-
Jones, GCVO (*born* 7 March 1930, created Earl of Snowdon
1961); marriage dissolved 1978
Issue:
(1) David Albert Charles, Viscount Linley, *born* 3
November 1961, *married* 8 October 1993 the Hon.
Serena Stanhope, and has issue, Hon. Charles Patrick
Inigo Armstrong-Jones, *born* 1 July 1999
(2) Lady Sarah Chatto (Sarah Frances Elizabeth), *born* 1
May 1964, *married* 14 July 1994 Daniel Chatto, and
has issue, Samuel David Benedict Chatto, *born* 28
July 1996; Arthur Robert Nathaniel Chatto, *born* 5
February 1999
Residence: Kensington Palace, London W8 4PU

MOTHER OF THE QUEEN

HM QUEEN ELIZABETH THE QUEEN MOTHER (Elizabeth
Angela Marguerite), Lady of the Garter, Lady of the
Thistle, CI, GCVO, GBE, Dame Grand Cross of the Order of
St John of Jerusalem, Royal Victorian Chain, Lord Warden
and Admiral of the Cinque Ports and Constable of Dover
Castle
Born 4 August 1900, youngest daughter of the 14th Earl of
Strathmore and Kinghorne
Married 26 April 1923 (as Lady Elizabeth Bowes-Lyon)
Prince Albert, Duke of York, afterwards King George VI
(*see* page 126)

Residences: Clarence House, St James's Palace, London SW1A 1BA; Royal Lodge, Windsor Great Park, Berks; Castle of Mey, Caithness

---

AUNT OF THE QUEEN

HRH PRINCESS ALICE, DUCHESS OF GLOUCESTER (Alice Christabel), GCB, CI, GCVO, GBE, Grand Cordon of Al Kamal
Born 25 December 1901, third daughter of the 7th Duke of Buccleuch and Queensberry
Married 6 November 1935 (as Lady Alice Montagu-Douglas-Scott) Prince Henry, Duke of Gloucester, third son of King George V (*see* page 126)
Residence: Kensington Palace, London W8 4PU

COUSINS OF THE QUEEN

HRH THE DUKE OF GLOUCESTER (Prince Richard Alexander Walter George), KG, GCVO, Grand Prior of the Order of St John of Jerusalem
Born 26 August 1944
Married 8 July 1972 Birgitte Eva van Deurs, now HRH The Duchess of Gloucester, GCVO (*born* 20 June 1946, daughter of Asger Henriksen and Vivian van Deurs)
Issue:
(1)   Earl of Ulster (Alexander Patrick Gregers Richard), *born* 24 October 1974
(2)   Lady Davina Windsor (Davina Elizabeth Alice Benedikte), *born* 19 November 1977
(3)   Lady Rose Windsor (Rose Victoria Birgitte Louise), *born* 1 March 1980
Residence: Kensington Palace, London W8 4PU

HRH THE DUKE OF KENT (Prince Edward George Nicholas Paul Patrick), KG, GCMG, GCVO, ADC(P)
Born 9 October 1935
Married 8 June 1961 Katharine Lucy Mary Worsley, now HRH The Duchess of Kent, GCVO (*born* 22 February 1933, daughter of Sir William Worsley, Bt.)
Issue:
(1)   Earl of St Andrews (George Philip Nicholas), *born* 26 June 1962, *married* 9 January 1988 Sylvana Tomaselli, and has issue, Edward Edmund Maximilian George, Baron Downpatrick, *born* 2 December 1988; Lady Marina Charlotte Alexandra Katharine Windsor, *born* 30 September 1992; Lady Amelia Sophia Theodora Mary Margaret Windsor, *born* 24 August 1995
(2)   Lady Helen Taylor (Helen Marina Lucy), *born* 28 April 1964, *married* 18 July 1992 Timothy Taylor, and has issue, Columbus George Donald Taylor, *born* 6 August 1994; Cassius Edward Taylor, *born* 26 December 1996
(3)   Lord Nicholas Windsor (Nicholas Charles Edward Jonathan), *born* 25 July 1970
Residence: Wren House, Palace Green, London W8 4PY

HRH PRINCESS ALEXANDRA, THE HON. LADY OGILVY (Princess Alexandra Helen Elizabeth Olga Christabel), GCVO
Born 25 December 1936
Married 24 April 1963 The Rt. Hon. Sir Angus Ogilvy, KCVO (*born* 14 September 1928, second son of 12th Earl of Airlie)
Issue:
(1)   James Robert Bruce Ogilvy, *born* 29 February 1964, *married* 30 July 1988 Julia Rawlinson, and has issue,

Flora Alexandra Ogilvy, *born* 15 December 1994; Alexander Charles Ogilvy, *born* 12 November 1996
(2)   Marina Victoria Alexandra, Mrs Mowatt, *born* 31 July 1966, *married* 2 February 1990 Paul Mowatt (marriage dissolved 1997), and has issue, Zenouska May Mowatt, *born* 26 May 1990; Christian Alexander Mowatt, *born* 4 June 1993
Residence: Thatched House Lodge, Richmond Park, Surrey

HRH PRINCE MICHAEL OF KENT (Prince Michael George Charles Franklin), KCVO
Born 4 July 1942
Married 30 June 1978 Baroness Marie-Christine Agnes Hedwig Ida von Reibnitz, now HRH Princess Michael of Kent (*born* 15 January 1945, daughter of Baron Gunther von Reibnitz)
Issue:
(1)   Lord Frederick Windsor (Frederick Michael George David Louis), *born* 6 April 1979
(2)   Lady Gabriella Windsor (Gabriella Marina Alexandra Ophelia), *born* 23 April 1981
Residences: Kensington Palace, London W8 4PU; Nether Lypiatt Manor, Stroud, Glos GL6 7LS

ORDER OF SUCCESSION

1	HRH The Prince of Wales
2	HRH Prince William of Wales
3	HRH Prince Henry of Wales
4	HRH The Duke of York
5	HRH Princess Beatrice of York
6	HRH Princess Eugenie of York
7	HRH The Earl of Wessex
8	HRH The Princess Royal
9	Peter Phillips
10	Zara Phillips
11	HRH The Princess Margaret, Countess of Snowdon
12	Viscount Linley
13	Hon. Charles Armstrong-Jones
14	Lady Sarah Chatto
15	Samuel Chatto
16	Arthur Chatto
17	HRH The Duke of Gloucester
18	Earl of Ulster
19	Lady Davina Windsor
20	Lady Rose Windsor
21	HRH The Duke of Kent
22	Baron Downpatrick
23	Lady Marina Charlotte Windsor
24	Lady Amelia Windsor
25	Lord Nicholas Windsor
26	Lady Helen Taylor
27	Columbus Taylor
28	Cassius Taylor
29	Lord Frederick Windsor
30	Lady Gabriella Windsor
31	HRH Princess Alexandra, the Hon. Lady Ogilvy
32	James Ogilvy
33	Alexander Ogilvy
34	Flora Ogilvy
35	Marina, Mrs Paul Mowatt
36	Christian Mowatt
37	Zenouska Mowatt
38	The Earl of Harewood

The Earl of St Andrews and HRH Prince Michael of Kent both lost the right of succession to the throne through marriage to a Roman Catholic. Their children remain in succession provided that they are in communion with the Church of England

Royal Households

THE QUEEN'S HOUSEHOLD

Office: Buckingham Palace, London SW1A 1AA
Tel: 020-7930 4832
Web: http://www.royal.gov.uk

The Lord Chamberlain is the most senior member of The Queen's Household and under him come the heads of the six departments: the Private Secretary, the Keeper of the Privy Purse, the Comptroller of the Lord Chamberlain's Office, the Master of the Household, the Crown Equerry, and the Director of the Royal Collection. Positions in these departments are full-time salaried posts.

There are also a number of honorary or now largely ceremonial appointments which carry no remuneration or a small honorarium. In the following list, most honorary appointments have been placed at the end; however, where this is not the case, such appointments are indicated by an asterisk.

GREAT OFFICERS OF STATE
Lord Chamberlain, The Lord Camoys, GCVO, PC
Lord Steward, The Viscount Ridley, KG, GCVO, TD
Master of the Horse, The Lord Vestey

LADIES-IN-WAITING AND EQUERRIES
Mistress of the Robes, The Duchess of Grafton, GCVO
Ladies of the Bedchamber, The Countess of Airlie, DCVO;
The Lady Farnham, CVO
Women of the Bedchamber, Hon. Mary Morrison, DCVO
Lady Dugdale, DCVO; Mrs Robert de Pass;
Mrs Christian Adams (temp.)

THE PRIVATE SECRETARY'S OFFICE
Buckingham Palace, London SW1A 1AA

Private Secretary to The Queen, Sir Robin Janvrin,
KCVO, CB
Deputy Private Secretary, vacant
Communications Secretary, S. Lewis
Assistant Private Secretary, T. Hitchens
Special Assistant to the Private Secretary, A. Dent
Chief Clerk, Mrs G. Middleburgh, MVO
Secretary to the Private Secretary, Miss E. Ash

PRESS OFFICE
Press Secretary, G. Crawford, LVO
Deputy Press Secretary, Miss P. Russell-Smith
Assistant Press Secretaries, R. Arbiter, LVO; D. Tuck

THE QUEEN'S ARCHIVES
Round Tower, Windsor Castle, Berks

Keeper of The Queen's Archives, Sir Robin Janvrin,
KCVO, CB
Assistant Keeper, O. Everett, CVO
Registrar, Lady de Bellaigue, MVO

THE PRIVY PURSE AND TREASURER'S OFFICE
Buckingham Palace, London SW1A 1AA
Keeper of the Privy Purse and Treasurer to The Queen,
Sir Michael Peat, KCVO
Director of Property Services, J. Tiltman, LVO
Director of Royal Travel, Air Cdre the Hon. T. Elworthy

Director of Finance, Property Services and Royal Travel,
S. Cawley
Deputy Keeper of the Privy Purse and Deputy Treasurer,
J. Parsons, CVO
Chief Accountant and Paymaster, I. McGregor
Personnel Officer, Miss P. Lloyd
Land Agent, Sandringham, M. O'Lone, FRICS
Resident Factor, Balmoral, P. Ord, FRICS

THE LORD CHAMBERLAIN'S OFFICE
Buckingham Palace, London SW1A 1AA

Comptroller, Lt.-Col. W. H. M. Ross, CVO, OBE
Assistant Comptroller, Lt.-Col. R. Cartwright
Secretary, J. Spencer, MVO
Assistant Secretary, Miss A. Krysztofiak
State Invitations Assistant, J. O. Hope
Marshal of the Diplomatic Corps, Vice-Adm. Sir James
Weatherall, KBE
Vice-Marshal, Mrs K. Colvin

CENTRAL CHANCERY OF THE ORDERS OF KNIGHTHOOD
St James's Palace, London SW1A 1BS
Secretary, Lt.-Col. A. Mather, CVO, OBE
Assistant Secretary, Miss R. Wells, MVO

MASTER OF THE HOUSEHOLD'S DEPARTMENT
Buckingham Palace, London SW1A 1AA

Master of the Household, Maj.-Gen. Sir Simon Cooper,
KCVO
Deputy Master of the Household, Lt.-Col. C. Richards
Assistants to the Master of the Household, M. T. Parker,
MVO; A. Jarman; A. Smith
Chief Clerk, M. C. W. N. Jephson, LVO
Chief Housekeeper, Miss H. Colebrook, MVO
Palace Steward, P. S. Croasdale, RVM
Royal Chef, L. Mann, RVM
Superintendent, Windsor Castle, Maj. M. Davidson, MBE, BEM
Superintendent, The Palace of Holyroodhouse, Lt.-Col.
D. Anderson, OBE

ROYAL MEWS DEPARTMENT
Buckingham Palace, London SW1W 0QH

Crown Equerry, Lt.-Col. S. Gilbart-Denham, CVO
Superintendent, Royal Mews, Buckingham Palace,
Maj. I. Kelly

THE ROYAL COLLECTION
St James's Palace, London SW1A 1BS

*Director of Royal Collection and Surveyor of The Queen's
Works of Art,* H. Roberts, CVO, FSA
Surveyor of The Queen's Pictures, C. Lloyd, LVO
Trustee of Royal Collection, Dr E. Anderson
Librarian, The Royal Library, Windsor Castle, O. Everett,
CVO
Deputy Surveyor of The Queen's Works of Art, J. Marsden
Director of Media Affairs, R. Arbiter, LVO
Curator of the Print Room, The Hon. Mrs Roberts, LVO
Financial Director, M. Stevens
Financial Controller, Mrs G. Johnson, MVO
Administrator and Assistant to The Surveyors,
D. Rankin-Hunt, MVO, TD

Senior Picture Restorer, Miss V. Pemberton-Pigott, MVO
Chief Restorer, Old Master Drawings, A. Donnithorne
Senior Furniture Restorer, E. Fancourt, LVO, RVM
Armourer, J. Jackson, RVM
Chief Binder, R. Day, MVO, RVM

ROYAL COLLECTION ENTERPRISES LTD
Managing Director, M. E. K. Hewlett, LVO

ECCLESIASTICAL HOUSEHOLD
Clerk of the Closet, The Bishop of Derby
Deputy Clerk of the Closet, Revd W. Booth, LVO
Chaplains and Extra Chaplains to The Queen: approx. 30–40
Dean of the Chapels Royal, The Bishop of London
Sub-Dean of the Chapels Royal, Revd W. Booth, LVO
Organist, Choirmaster and Composer, R. J. Popplewell, MVO, FRCO, FRCM
Domestic Chaplain, Buckingham Palace, Revd W. Booth, LVO
Domestic Chaplain, Windsor Castle, The Dean of Windsor
Domestic Chaplain, Sandringham, Revd Canon G. R. Hall, LVO

MEDICAL HOUSEHOLD
Head of the Medical Household and Physician to The Queen, R. Thompson, DM, FRCP
Serjeant Surgeon, B. T. Jackson, FRCS
Apothecary to The Queen and to the Household, N. R. Southward, CVO
Apothecary to the Household at Windsor, J. Holliday
Apothecary to the Household at Sandringham, I. K. Campbell, D.Obst., FRCGP
Coroner of The Queen's Household, J. Burton, CBE

OTHER HONORARY/CEREMONIAL APPOINTMENTS
Lord High Almoner, The Bishop of Wakefield
Master of The Queen's Music, M. Williamson, CBE, AO
Poet Laureate (1999–2009), Prof. Andrew Motion
Keeper of the Royal Philatelic Collection, C. Goodwyn
Bargemaster, R. Crouch
Swan Warden, Prof. C. Perrins, LVO
Swan Marker, D. Barber

POLITICAL (GOVERNMENT WHIPS)
Captain, Honourable Corps of Gentlemen-at-Arms (Chief Whip in the Lords), The Lord Carter, PC
Captain, Queen's Bodyguard of the Yeomen of the Guard (Deputy Chief Whip in the Lords), The Lord McIntosh of Haringey
Lords-in-Waiting, The Lord Burlison of Rowlands; The Lord Hunt of King's Heath
Baronesses-in-Waiting, The Baroness Farrington of Ribbleton; The Baroness Ramsay of Cartvale; The Baroness Amos
Treasurer of the Household (Deputy Chief Whip in the Commons), K. Bradley, MP
Comptroller of the Household, T. McAvoy, MP
Vice-Chamberlain, G. Allen, MP

ARMED FORCES
Gold Sticks, HRH The Princess Royal, KG, GCVO; Gen. Sir Charles Guthrie, GCB, LVO, OBE
Vice-Admiral of the United Kingdom, Adm. Sir Nicholas Hunt, GCB, LVO
Rear-Admiral of the United Kingdom, Adm. Sir Jeremy Black, GBE, KCB, DSO
First and Principal Naval Aide-de-Camp, Adm. Sir Michael Boyce, GCB, OBE

Flag Aide-de-Camp, Rear-Adm. P. Spencer
Aides-de-Camp-General, Gen. Sir Charles Guthrie, GCB, LVO, OBE; Gen. Sir Roger Wheeler, GCB, CBE; Gen. Sir Michael Walker, KCB, CMG, CBE; Gen. Sir Alex Harley, KBE, CB
Air Aides-de-Camp, Air Chief Marshal Sir Richard Johns, GCB, CBE, LVO; Air Chief Marshal Sir Peter Squire, KCB, DFC, AFC
Gentleman Usher to the Sword of State, Adm. Sir Michael Layard, KCB, CBE
Constable and Governor of Windsor Castle, Gen. Sir Charles Palmer, KBE
Governor of Edinburgh Castle, Maj.-Gen. R.D.S. Gordon, CBE

BODYGUARDS

THE HONOURABLE CORPS OF GENTLEMEN-AT-ARMS
Captain, The Lord Carter, PC
Lieutenant, Lt.-Col. R. Mayfield, DSO
Clerk of the Cheque and Adjutant, Col. D. Fanshawe, OBE; *Gentlemen of the Corps*: 27

THE QUEEN'S BODY GUARD OF THE YEOMEN OF THE GUARD
Captain, The Lord McIntosh of Haringey
Lieutenant, Col. G. W. Tufnell
Clerk of the Cheque and Adjutant, Col. S. Longsdon
Yeomen of the Guard: 81

THE QUEEN'S HOUSEHOLD IN SCOTLAND
Hereditary Lord High Constable of Scotland, The Earl of Erroll
Hereditary Master of the Household in Scotland, The Duke of Argyll
Lord Lyon King of Arms, Sir Malcolm Innes of Edingight, KCVO, WS
Hereditary Banner-Bearer for Scotland, The Earl of Dundee
Hereditary Bearer of the National Flag of Scotland, The Earl of Lauderdale
Hereditary Keeper of the Palace of Holyroodhouse, The Duke of Hamilton and Brandon
Governor of Edinburgh Castle, Maj.-Gen. R. D. S. Gordon
Historiographer, Prof. T. C. Smout, CBE, FBA, FRSE, FSA Scot.
Botanist, Prof. D. Henderson, CBE, FRSE
Painter and Limner, vacant
Sculptor in Ordinary, Prof. Sir Eduardo Paolozzi, CBE, RA
Astronomer, Prof. J. Brown, Ph.D., FRSE
Heralds and Pursuivants, see page 282

ECCLESIASTICAL HOUSEHOLD
Dean of the Chapel Royal, Very Revd J. Harkness, CB, OBE, DD
Dean of the Order of the Thistle, Very Revd G. I. Macmillan, CVO
Chaplains in Ordinary: 10
Domestic Chaplain, Balmoral, Revd R. P. Sloan

MEDICAL HOUSEHOLD
Physicians in Scotland, P. Brunt, OBE, MD, FRCP; A. Toft, CBE, FRCPE
Surgeons in Scotland, J.Engeset, FRCS; I. Macintyre
Apothecary to the Household at Balmoral, D. J. A. Glass
Apothecary to the Household at the Palace of Holyroodhouse, Dr J. Cormack, MD, FRCPE, FRCGP

*ROYAL COMPANY OF ARCHERS (THE QUEEN'S BODYGUARD FOR SCOTLAND)

Captain-General and Gold Stick for Scotland, Maj. Sir Hew Hamilton-Dalrymple, Bt., KCVO
President of the Council and Silver Stick for Scotland, The Duke of Buccleuch and Queensberry, KT, VRD
Adjutant, Brig. The Hon. S. H. R. H Monro, CBE, ADC
Secretary, Capt. J. D. B. Younger
Treasurer, J. M. Haldane of Gleneagles
Members on the active list: *c.*400

HOUSEHOLD OF THE PRINCE PHILIP, DUKE OF EDINBURGH

Office: Buckingham Palace, London SW1A 1AA
Tel: 020-7930 4832
Treasurer, Sir Brian McGrath, KCVO
Private Secretary, Brig. M. G. Hunt-Davis, CVO, CBE
Equerry, Sqn Ldr L. Johnson
Temporary Equerries, Capt. J. Marot; Maj. P. Wise; Capt. B. Hancock
Chief Clerk and Accountant, P. Hughes

HOUSEHOLD OF QUEEN ELIZABETH THE QUEEN MOTHER

Office: Clarence House, St James's Palace, London SW1A 1BA
Tel: 020-7930 3141
Lord Chamberlain, The Earl of Crawford and Balcarres, KT, PC
Private Secretary, Comptroller and Equerry, Capt. Sir Alastair Aird, GCVO
Assistant Private Secretary and Equerry, Maj. R. Seymour, CVO
Treasurer and Extra Equerry, Hon. N. Assheton
Treasurer Emeritus and Equerry, Maj. Sir Ralph Anstruther, Bt., GCVO, MC
Equerry, Capt. T. Grayson (temp.)
Apothecary to the Household, Dr N. Southward, CVO
Surgeon-Apothecary to the Household (*Royal Lodge, Windsor*), J. Holliday
Ladies of the Bedchamber, The Lady Grimthorpe, DCVO; The Countess of Scarbrough
Clerk Comptroller, A. Kirkpatrick-Smith
Information Officer, Mrs R. Murphy, CVO
Clerks, Miss F. Fletcher, LVO; Mrs W. Stevens, LVO

HOUSEHOLD OF THE PRINCE OF WALES

Office: St James's Palace, London SW1A 1BS
Tel: 020-7930 4832
Private Secretary and Treasurer, S. M. J. Lamport, CVO
Deputy Private Secretary, M. Bolland
Assistant Private Secretaries, N. S. Archer; Miss E. Buchanan
Press Secretary, vacant
Deputy Press Secretary, Mrs C. Harris
Equerry, Lt. Cdr. W. N. Entwisle, RN
Secretary to the Duchy of Cornwall and Keeper of the Records, W. R. A. Ross

HOUSEHOLD OF THE DUKE OF YORK

Office: Buckingham Palace, London SW1A 1AA
Tel: 020-7930 4832
Private Secretary, Treasurer and Extra Equerry, Capt. R. N. Blair, LVO, RN
Comptroller and Deputy Private Secretary, Miss C. Manley, OBE
Equerry, Capt. R. J. Dilworth, RE

HOUSEHOLD OF THE EARL OF WESSEX

Office: Buckingham Palace, London SW1A 1AA
Tel: 020-7930 4832
Private Secretary, Lt.-Col. S. G. O'Dwyer, LVO
Clerk, Mrs L. Sharp, MVO

HOUSEHOLD OF THE PRINCESS ROYAL

Office: Buckingham Palace, London SW1A 1AA
Tel: 020-7930 4832
Private Secretary, Col. T. Earl, OBE
Assistant Private Secretary, Mrs S. Gee
Ladies-in-Waiting, Lady Carew Pole, LVO; Mrs Andrew Feilden, LVO; The Hon. Mrs Legge-Bourke, LVO; Mrs William Nunneley, LVO; Mrs Timothy Holderness-Roddam, LVO; Mrs Charles Ritchie, LVO; Mrs David Bowes Lyon; The Countess of Lichfield, LVO; Miss Victoria Legge-Bourke, LVO; Mrs Malcolm Innes, CVO; The Hon. Mrs Louloudis, LVO

HOUSEHOLD OF THE PRINCESS MARGARET, COUNTESS OF SNOWDON

Office: Kensington Palace, London W8 4PU
Tel: 020-7930 3141
Private Secretary, The Viscount Ullswater, PC
Treasurer, Maj. The Lord Napier and Ettrick, KCVO
Lady-in-Waiting, The Hon. Mrs Whitehead, LVO

HOUSEHOLD OF THE DUKE AND DUCHESS OF GLOUCESTER

Office: Kensington Palace, London W8 4PU
Tel: 020-7937 6374
Private Secretary, Comptroller and Equerry, Maj. N. M. L. Barne, LVO
Assistant Private Secretary to the Duchess of Gloucester, Miss S. Marland, LVO
Ladies-in-Waiting, Mrs Michael Wigley, CVO; Mrs Euan McCorquodale, LVO; Mrs Howard Page, LVO

HOUSEHOLD OF PRINCESS ALICE, DUCHESS OF GLOUCESTER

Office: Kensington Palace, London W8 4PU
Tel: 020-7937 6374
Private Secretary, Comptroller and Equerry, Maj. N. M. L. Barne, LVO
Ladies-in-Waiting, Dame Jean Maxwell-Scott, DCVO; Mrs Michael Harvey, LVO

HOUSEHOLD OF THE DUKE AND
DUCHESS OF KENT

Office: St James's Palace, London, SW1A 1BQ
Tel: 020-7930 4872

Private Secretary, N. C. Adamson, OBE
Temporary Equerry, Capt. C. MacRae
Ladies-in-Waiting, Mrs Colin Marsh, LVO; Mrs Julian
   Tomkins; Mrs Peter Troughton; Mrs Richard Beckett

HOUSEHOLD OF PRINCE AND PRINCESS
MICHAEL OF KENT

Office: Kensington Palace, London W8 4PU
Tel: 020-7938 3519

Private Secretary, N. Chance
Personal Secretaries, Miss C. Jenkins, Miss K. Garrod
Ladies-in-Waiting, The Hon. Mrs Sanders; Miss A. Frost;
   Mrs J. Kitchener-Fellowes; Miss J. MacLellan.

HOUSEHOLD OF PRINCESS ALEXANDRA,
THE HON. LADY OGILVY

Office: Buckingham Palace, London SW1A 1AA
Tel: 020-7930 1860

Private Secretary, Capt. R. N. Blair, LVO, RN
Lady-in-Waiting, The Lady Mary Mumford, DCVO

Royal Salutes

ENGLAND

A salute of 62 guns is fired on the wharf at the Tower of
London on the following occasions:
(a)   the anniversaries of the birth, accession and
      coronation of the Sovereign
(b)   the anniversary of the birth of HM Queen Elizabeth
      the Queen Mother
(c)   the anniversary of the birth of HRH Prince Philip,
      Duke of Edinburgh
A salute of 41 guns only is fired on extraordinary and
triumphal occasions, e.g. on the occasion of the Sovereign
opening, proroguing or dissolving Parliament in person,
or when passing through London in procession, except
when otherwise ordered.
   A salute of 41 guns is fired from the two saluting
stations
in London (the Tower of London and Hyde Park) on the
occasion of the birth of a royal infant.
Constable of the Royal Palace and Fortress of London,
   Field Marshal the Lord Inge, GCB
Lieutenant of the Tower of London, Lt.-Gen. Sir Anthony
   Denison-Smith, KBE
Resident Governor and Keeper of the Jewel House,
   Maj.-Gen. G. Field, CB, OBE

Master Gunner of St James's Park, Field Marshal the
Lord
   Vincent of Coleshill, GBE, KCB, DSO
Master Gunner within the Tower, Col. S. Lalor

SCOTLAND

Royal salutes are authorised at Edinburgh Castle and
Stirling Castle, although in practice Edinburgh Castle is
the only operating saluting station in Scotland.
   A salute of 21 guns is fired on the following occasions:
(a)   the anniversaries of the birth, accession and corona-
      tion of the Sovereign
(b)   the anniversary of the birth of HM Queen Elizabeth
      the Queen Mother
(c)   the anniversary of the birth of HRH Prince Philip,
      Duke of Edinburgh
   A salute of 21 guns is fired in Edinburgh on the
occasion of the opening of the General Assembly of the
Church of Scotland.
   A salute of 21 guns may also be fired in Edinburgh on
the arrival of HM The Queen, HM Queen Elizabeth the
Queen Mother, or a member of the royal family who is a
Royal Highness on an official visit.

Royal Finances

FUNDING

THE CIVIL LIST

The Civil List dates back to the late 17th century. It was
originally used by the sovereign to supplement hereditary
revenues for paying the salaries of judges, ambassadors and
other government officers as well as the expenses of the
royal household. In 1760 on the accession of George III it
was decided that the Civil List would be provided by
Parliament to cover all relevant expenditure in return for
the King surrendering the hereditary revenues of the
Crown. At that time Parliament undertook to pay the
salaries of judges, ambassadors, etc. In 1831 Parliament
agreed also to meet the costs of the royal palaces in return

for a reduction in the Civil List. Each sovereign has agreed
to continue this arrangement.
   The Civil List paid to The Queen is charged on the
Consolidated Fund. Until 1972, the amount of money
allocated annually under the Civil List was set for the
duration of a reign. The system was then altered to a fixed
annual payment for ten years but from 1975 high inflation
made an annual review necessary. The system of payments
reverted to the practice of a fixed annual payment for ten
years from 1 January 1991.
   The Civil List Acts provide for other members of the
royal family to receive parliamentary annuities from
government funds to meet the expenses of carrying out
their official duties. Since 1975 The Queen has reimbursed the Treasury for the annuities paid to the Duke of
Gloucester, the Duke of Kent and Princess Alexandra.
Since 1993 The Queen has reimbursed all the annuities

except those paid to herself, Queen Elizabeth the Queen Mother and the Duke of Edinburgh.

The Prince of Wales does not receive a parliamentary annuity. He derives his income from the revenues of the Duchy of Cornwall and these monies meet the official and private expenses of the Prince of Wales and his family.

The annual payments for the years 1991–2000:

The Queen	£7,900,000
Queen Elizabeth the Queen Mother	643,000
The Duke of Edinburgh	359,000
*The Duke of York	249,000
*†The Earl of Wessex	141,000
*The Princess Royal	228,000
*The Princess Margaret, Countess of Snowdon	219,000
*Princess Alice, Duchess of Gloucester	87,000
*The Duke of Gloucester	175,000
*The Duke of Kent	236,000
*Princess Alexandra	225,000
	10,462,000
*Refunded to the Treasury	1,560,000
Total	8,902,000

†The Earl of Wessex's annuity was increased from £96,000 upon his marriage in June 1999

GRANTS-IN-AID

The royal household receives grants-in-aid from two government departments to meet various official expenses. The Department for Culture, Media and Sport provides grant-in-aid to pay for the upkeep of English occupied royal palaces, which are used as offices, for official and ceremonial purposes and to which there is public access, and to meet the cost of media and information services. The Royal Travel grant-in-aid is provided by the Department of the Environment, Transport and the Regions to meet the cost of official royal travel by air and rail, using mainly aircraft from 32 (The Royal) Squadron, chartered commercial aircraft for major overseas state visits and the Royal Train.

Grants-in-aid for 1999–2000 were:

Property Services and Communications and Information	£15,000,000
Royal Travel	£9,300,000

THE PRIVY PURSE

The funds received by the Privy Purse pay for official expenses incurred by The Queen as head of state and for some of The Queen's private expenditure. The revenues of the Duchy of Lancaster are the principal source of income for the Privy Purse. The revenues of the Duchy were retained by George III in 1760 when the hereditary revenues were surrendered in exchange for the Civil List.

PERSONAL INCOME

The Queen's personal income derives mostly from investments, and is used to meet private expenditure.

DEPARTMENTAL VOTES

Items of expenditure connected with the official duties of the royal family which fall directly on votes of government departments include:

Ministry of Defence – equerries
Foreign and Commonwealth Office – Marshal of the Diplomatic Corps; costs (other than travel costs) associated with overseas visits at the request of government departments
HM Treasury – Central Chancery of the Orders of Knighthood
The Post Office – postal services

TAXATION

The sovereign is not legally liable to pay income tax, capital gains tax or inheritance tax. After income tax was reintroduced in 1842, some income tax was paid voluntarily by the sovereign but over a long period these payments were phased out. In 1992 The Queen offered to pay tax on a voluntary basis from 6 April 1993, and the Prince of Wales offered to pay tax on a voluntary basis on his income from the Duchy of Cornwall. (He was already taxed in all other respects.)

The main provisions for The Queen and the Prince of Wales to pay tax, set out in a Memorandum of Understanding on Royal Taxation presented to Parliament on 11 February 1993, are that The Queen will pay income tax and capital gains tax in respect of her private income and assets, and on the proportion of the income and capital gains of the Privy Purse used for private purposes. Inheritance tax will be paid on The Queen's assets, except for those which pass to the next sovereign, whether automatically or by gift or bequest. The Prince of Wales will pay income tax on income from the Duchy of Cornwall used for private purposes.

The Prince of Wales has confirmed that he intends to pay tax on the same basis following his accession to the throne.

Other members of the royal family are subject to tax as for any taxpayer.

Military Ranks and Titles

THE QUEEN

Lord High Admiral of the United Kingdom
Colonel-in-Chief
The Life Guards; The Blues and Royals (Royal Horse Guards and 1st Dragoons); The Royal Scots Dragoon Guards (Carabiniers and Greys); The Queen's Royal Lancers; Royal Tank Regiment; Corps of Royal Engineers; Grenadier Guards; Coldstream Guards; Scots Guards; Irish Guards; Welsh Guards; The Royal Welsh Fusiliers; The Queen's Lancashire Regiment; The Argyll and Sutherland Highlanders (Princess Louise's); The Royal Green Jackets; Adjutant General's Corps; The Royal Mercian and Lancastrian Yeomanry;

The Governor General's Horse Guards (of Canada); The King's Own Calgary Regiment; Canadian Forces Military Engineers Branch; Royal 22e Regiment (of Canada); Governor-General's Foot Guards (of Canada); The Canadian Grenadier Guards; Le Regiment de la Chaudiere (of Canada); 2nd Bn Royal New Brunswick Regiment (North Shore); The 48th Highlanders of Canada; The Argyll and Sutherland Highlanders of Canada (Princess Louise's); The Calgary Highlanders; Royal Australian Engineers; Royal Australian Infantry Corps; Royal Australian Army Ordnance Corps; Royal Australian Army Nursing Corps; The Corps of Royal New Zealand Engineers; Royal New Zealand Infantry Regiment; Royal Malta Artillery; The Malawi Rifles

Affiliated Colonel-in-Chief
The Queen's Gurkha Engineers

Captain-General
Royal Regiment of Artillery; The Honourable Artillery Company; Combined Cadet Force Association; Royal Regiment of Canadian Artillery; Royal Regiment of Australian Artillery; Royal Regiment of New Zealand Artillery; Royal New Zealand Armoured Corps

Patron
Royal Army Chaplains' Department

Air Commodore-in-Chief
Royal Auxiliary Air Force; Royal Air Force Regiment; Air Reserve (of Canada); Royal Australian Air Force Reserve; Territorial Air Force (of New Zealand)

Commandant-in-Chief
Royal Air Force College, Cranwell

Hon. Air Commodore
RAF Marham

HRH THE PRINCE PHILIP, DUKE OF EDINBURGH

Admiral of the Fleet
Field Marshal
Marshal of the Royal Air Force

Admiral of the Fleet, Royal Australian Navy
Field Marshal, Australian Military Forces
Marshal of the Royal Australian Air Force

Admiral of the Fleet, Royal New Zealand Navy
Field Marshal, New Zealand Army
Marshal of the Royal New Zealand Air Force
Captain-General, Royal Marines

Admiral
Royal Canadian Sea Cadets

Colonel-in-Chief
The Royal Gloucestershire, Berkshire and Wiltshire Regiment; The Highlanders (Seaforth, Gordons and Camerons); Corps of Royal Electrical and Mechanical Engineers; Intelligence Corps; Army Cadet Force Association; The Royal Canadian Regiment; The Royal Hamilton Light Infantry (Wentworth Regiment) (of Canada); The Cameron Highlanders of Ottawa; The Queen's Own Cameron Highlanders of Canada; The Seaforth Highlanders of Canada; The Royal Canadian Army Cadets; The Royal Corps of Australian Electrical and Mechanical Engineers; The Australian Cadet Corps

Deputy Colonel-in-Chief
The Queen's Royal Hussars (Queen's Own and Royal Irish)

Colonel
Grenadier Guards

Hon. Colonel
City of Edinburgh Universities Officers' Training Corps; The Trinidad and Tobago Regiment

Air Commodore-in-Chief
Air Training Corps; Royal Canadian Air Cadets

Hon. Air Commodore
RAF Kinloss

HM QUEEN ELIZABETH THE QUEEN MOTHER

Colonel-in-Chief
1st The Queen's Dragoon Guards; The Queen's Royal Hussars (Queen's Own and Royal Irish); 9th/12th Royal Lancers (Prince of Wales's); The King's Regiment; The Royal Anglian Regiment; The Light Infantry; The Black Watch (Royal Highland Regiment); Royal Army Medical Corps; The Black Watch (Royal Highland Regiment) of Canada; The Toronto Scottish Regiment; Canadian Forces Medical Services; Royal Australian Army Medical Corps; Royal New Zealand Army Medical Corps

Hon. Colonel
The Royal Yeomanry; The London Scottish; Inns of Court and City Yeomanry

Commandant-in-Chief
Women in the Royal Navy; Women, Royal Air Force; Royal Air Force Central Flying School

---

HRH THE PRINCE OF WALES

Rear Admiral, Royal Navy

Major-General, Army
Air Vice-Marshal, Royal Air Force

Colonel-in-Chief
The Royal Dragoon Guards; The 22nd (Cheshire) Regiment; The Royal Regiment of Wales (24th/41st Foot); The Parachute Regiment; The Royal Gurkha Rifles; Army Air Corps; The Royal Canadian Dragoons; Lord Strathcona's Horse (Royal Canadians); Royal Regiment of Canada; Royal Winnipeg Rifles; Air Reserve Group of Air Command (of Canada); Royal Australian Armoured Corps; The Royal Pacific Islands Regiment; Queen's Own Yeomanry

Deputy Colonel-in-Chief
The Highlanders (Seaforth, Gordons and Camerons)

Colonel
Welsh Guards

Air Commodore-in-Chief
Royal New Zealand Air Force

Hon. Air Commodore
RAF Valley

HRH THE DUKE OF YORK

Commander, Royal Navy

Admiral
Sea Cadet Corps

Colonel-in-Chief
The Staffordshire Regiment (The Prince of Wales's); The Royal Irish Regiment (27th (Inniskilling), 83rd, 87th and The Ulster Defence Regiment); Royal New Zealand Army Logistic Regiment; The Queen's York Rangers (First Americans)

Hon. Air Commodore
RAF Lossiemouth

HRH THE PRINCESS ROYAL

Rear Admiral
Chief Commandant for Women in the Royal Navy

Colonel-in-Chief
The King's Royal Hussars; Royal Corps of Signals; The Royal Scots (The Royal Regiment); The Worcestershire and Sherwood Foresters Regiment (29th/45th Foot); The Royal Logistic Corps; 8th Canadian Hussars (Princess Louise's); Canadian Forces Communications and Electronics Branch; The Grey and Simcoe Foresters; The Royal Regina Rifle Regiment; Royal Australian Corps of Signals; Royal New Zealand Corps of Signals; Royal New Zealand Nursing Corps

Colonel
Blues and Royals

Affiliated Colonel-in-Chief
The Queen's Gurkha Signals; The Queen's Own Gurkha Transport Regiment

Hon. Colonel
University of London Officers' Training Corps

Hon. Air Commodore
RAF Lyneham; University of London Air Squadron

HRH THE PRINCESS MARGARET, COUNTESS OF SNOWDON

Colonel-in-Chief
The Light Dragoons; The Royal Highland Fusiliers (Princess Margaret's Own Glasgow and Ayrshire Regiment); Queen Alexandra's Royal Army Nursing Corps; The Royal Highland Fusiliers of Canada; The Princess Louise Fusiliers (of Canada); The Bermuda Regiment

Deputy Colonel-in-Chief
The Royal Anglian Regiment

Hon. Air Commodore
RAF Coningsby

HRH PRINCESS ALICE, DUCHESS OF GLOUCESTER

Air Chief Marshal

Colonel-in-Chief
The King's Own Scottish Borderers; Royal Australian Corps of Transport

Deputy Colonel-in-Chief
The King's Royal Hussars; The Royal Anglian Regiment

Air Chief Commandant
Women, Royal Air Force

HRH THE DUKE OF GLOUCESTER

Hon. Air Marshal

Deputy Colonel-in-Chief
The Royal Gloucestershire, Berkshire and Wiltshire Regiment; The Royal Logistic Corps

Hon. Colonel
Royal Monmouthshire Royal Engineers (Militia)

Hon. Air Commodore
RAF Odiham

HRH THE DUCHESS OF GLOUCESTER

Colonel-in-Chief
Royal Australian Army Educational Corps; Royal New Zealand Army Educational Corps; Royal Army Dental Corps

Deputy Colonel-in-Chief
Adjutant-General's Corps

HRH THE DUKE OF KENT

Field Marshal
Hon. Air Chief Marshal

Colonel-in-Chief
The Royal Regiment of Fusiliers; The Devonshire and Dorset Regiment; The Lorne Scots (Peel, Dufferin and Hamilton Regiment)

Deputy Colonel-in-Chief
The Royal Scots Dragoon Guards (Carabiniers and Greys)

Colonel
Scots Guards

Hon. Air Commodore
RAF Leuchars

HRH THE DUCHESS OF KENT

Hon. Major-General

Colonel-in-Chief
The Prince of Wales's Own Regiment of Yorkshire

Deputy Colonel-in-Chief
The Royal Dragoon Guards; Adjutant-General's Corps; The Royal Logistic Corps

HRH PRINCE MICHAEL OF KENT

Major (retd), The Royal Hussars (Prince of Wales's Own)

Hon. Commodore
Royal Naval Reserve

HRH PRINCESS ALEXANDRA, THE HON. LADY OGILVY

Patron
Queen Alexandra's Royal Naval Nursing Service

Colonel-in-Chief
The King's Own Royal Border Regiment; The Queen's Own Rifles of Canada; The Canadian Scottish Regiment (Princess Mary's)

Deputy Colonel-in-Chief
The Queen's Royal Lancers; The Light Infantry

Deputy Hon. Colonel
The Royal Yeomanry

Patron and Air Chief Commandant
Princess Mary's Royal Air Force Nursing Service

The House of Windsor

King George V assumed by royal proclamation (17 July 1917) for his House and family, as well as for all descendants in the male line of Queen Victoria who are subjects of these realms, the name of Windsor.

KING GEORGE V (George Frederick Ernest Albert), second son of King Edward VII, *born* 3 June 1865; *married* 6 July 1893 HSH Princess Victoria Mary Augusta Louise Olga Pauline Claudine Agnes of Teck (Queen Mary, *born* 26 May 1867; *died* 24 March 1953); *succeeded* to the throne 6 May 1910; *died* 20 January 1936. *Issue:*

1. HRH PRINCE EDWARD Albert Christian George Andrew Patrick David, *born* 23 June 1894, *succeeded* to the throne as King Edward VIII, 20 January 1936; *abdicated* 11 December 1936; created *Duke of Windsor* 1937; *married* 3 June 1937, Mrs Wallis Simpson (Her Grace The Duchess of Windsor, *born* 19 June 1896; *died* 24 April 1986), *died* 28 May 1972

2. HRH PRINCE ALBERT Frederick Arthur George, *born* 14 December 1895, *created* Duke of York 1920; *married* 26 April 1923, Lady Elizabeth Bowes-Lyon, youngest daughter of the 14th Earl of Strathmore and Kinghorne (HM Queen Elizabeth the Queen Mother, *see* page 117), *succeeded* to the throne as King George VI, 11 December 1936; *died* 6 February 1952, having had issue (*see* page 117)

3. HRH PRINCESS (Victoria Alexandra Alice) MARY, *born* 25 April 1897, *created* Princess Royal 1932; *married* 28 February 1922, Viscount Lascelles, later the 6th Earl of Harewood (1882–1947), *died* 28 March 1965. *Issue:*
   (1) George Henry Hubert Lascelles, 7th Earl of Harewood, KBE, *born* 7 February 1923; *married* (1) 1949, Maria (Marion) Stein (marriage dissolved 1967); *issue*, (a) David Henry George,

Viscount Lascelles, *born* 1950; (b) James Edward, *born* 1953; (c) (Robert) Jeremy Hugh, *born* 1955; (2) 1967, Mrs Patricia Tuckwell; *issue*, (d) Mark Hubert, *born* 1964
   (2) Gerald David Lascelles (1924–98), *married* (1) 1952, Miss Angela Dowding (marriage dissolved 1978); *issue*, (a) Henry Ulick, *born* 1953; (2) 1978, Mrs Elizabeth Colvin; *issue*, (b) Martin David, *born* 1962

4. HRH PRINCE HENRY William Frederick Albert, *born* 31 March 1900, *created* Duke of Gloucester, Earl of Ulster and Baron Culloden 1928, *married* 6 November 1935, Lady Alice Christabel Montagu-Douglas-Scott, daughter of the 7th Duke of Buccleuch (HRH Princess Alice, Duchess of Gloucester, *see* page 118); *died* 10 June 1974. *Issue:*
   (1) HRH Prince William Henry Andrew Frederick, *born* 18 December 1941; *accidentally killed* 28 August 1972
   (2) HRH Prince Richard Alexander Walter George (HRH The Duke of Gloucester), *see* page 118

5. HRH PRINCE GEORGE Edward Alexander Edmund, *born* 20 December 1902, *created* Duke of Kent, Earl of St Andrews and Baron Downpatrick 1934, *married* 29 November 1934, HRH Princess Marina of Greece and Denmark (*born* 30 November os, 1906; *died* 27 August 1968); *killed on active service,* 25 August 1942. *Issue:*
   (1) HRH Prince Edward George Nicholas Paul Patrick (HRH The Duke of Kent), *see* page 118
   (2) HRH Princess Alexandra Helen Elizabeth Olga Christabel (HRH Princess Alexandra, the Hon. Lady Ogilvy), *see* page 118
   (3) HRH Prince Michael George Charles Franklin (HRH Prince Michael of Kent), *see* page 118

6. HRH PRINCE JOHN Charles Francis, *born* 12 July 1905; *died* 18 January 1919

Descendants of Queen Victoria

QUEEN VICTORIA (Alexandrina Victoria), *born* 24 May 1819; *succeeded* to the throne 20 June 1837; *married* 10 February 1840 (Francis) Albert Augustus Charles Emmanuel, Duke of Saxony, Prince of Saxe-Coburg and Gotha (HRH Albert, Prince Consort, *born* 26 August 1819, *died* 14 December 1861); *died* 22 January 1901. *Issue:*

1. HRH PRINCESS VICTORIA Adelaide Mary Louisa (Princess Royal) (1840–1901), *m.* 1858, Friedrich III (1831–88), German Emperor March–June 1888. *Issue:*
   (1) HIM Wilhelm II (1859–1941), German Emperor 1888–1918, *m.* (1) 1881 Princess Augusta Victoria of Schleswig-Holstein-Sonderburg-Augustenburg (1858–1921); (2) 1922 Princess Hermine of Reuss (1887–1947). *Issue:*
      (a) Prince Wilhelm (1882–1951), Crown Prince 1888–1918, *m.* 1905 Duchess Cecilie of Mecklenburg-Schwerin; *issue:* Prince Wilhelm (1906–40); Prince Louis Ferdinand (1907–94), *m.* 1938 Grand Duchess Kira (*see* page 128); Prince Hubertus (1909–50); Prince Friedrich Georg (1911–66); Princess Alexandrine Irene (1915–80); Princess Cecilie (1917–75)
      (b) Prince Eitel-Friedrich (1883–1942), *m.* 1906 Duchess Sophie of Oldenburg (marriage dissolved 1926)
      (c) Prince Adalbert (1884–1948), *m.* 1914 Duchess Adelheid of Saxe-Meiningen; *issue:* Princess Victoria Marina (1917–81); Prince Wilhelm Victor (1919–89)
      (d) Prince August Wilhelm (1887–1949), *m.* 1908 Princess Alexandra of Schleswig-Holstein-Sonderburg-Glücksburg (marriage dissolved 1920); *issue:* Prince Alexander (1912–85)
      (e) Prince Oskar (1888–1958), *m.* 1914 Countess von Ruppin; *issue:* Prince Oskar (1915–39); Prince Burchard (1917–88); Princess Herzeleide (1918–89); Prince Wilhelm-Karl (b. 1922)
      (f) Prince Joachim (1890–1920), *m.* 1916 Princess Marie of Anhalt; *issue:* Prince (Karl) Franz Joseph (1916–75), and has issue

      (g) Princess Viktoria Luise (1892–1980), *m.* 1913 Ernst, Duke of Brunswick 1913–18 (1887–1953); *issue:* Prince Ernst (1914–87); Prince Georg (b. 1915), *m.* 1946 Princess Sophie of Greece (*see* page 128) and has issue (two sons, one daughter); Princess Frederika (1917–81), *m.* 1938 Paul I, King of the Hellenes (*see* page 128); Prince Christian (1919–81); Prince Welf Heinrich (b. 1923)
   (2) Princess Charlotte (1860–1919), *m.* 1878 Bernhard, Duke of Saxe-Meiningen 1914 (1851–1914). *Issue:*
      Princess Feodora (1879–1945), *m.* 1898 Prince Heinrich XXX of Reuss
   (3) Prince Heinrich (1862–1929), *m.* 1888 Princess Irene of Hesse (*see* page 128). *Issue:*
      (a) Prince Waldemar (1889–1945), *m.* Princess Calixta Agnes of Lippe
      (b) Prince Sigismund (1896–1978), *m.*1919 Princess Charlotte of Saxe-Altenburg; *issue:* Princess Barbara (1920–94); Prince Alfred (b. 1924)
      (c) Prince Heinrich (1900–4)
   (4) Prince Sigismund (1864–6)
   (5) Princess Victoria (1866–1929), *m.* (1) 1890, Prince Adolf of Schaumburg-Lippe (1859–1916); (2) 1927 Alexander Zubkov
   (6) Prince Waldemar (1868–79)
   (7) Princess Sophie (1870–1932), *m.* 1889 Constantine I (1868–1923), King of the Hellenes 1913–17, 1920–3. *Issue:*
      (a) George II (1890–1947), King of the Hellenes 1923–4 and 1935–47, *m.* 1921 Princess Elisabeth of Roumania (marriage dissolved 1935) (*see* page 127)
      (b) Alexander I (1893–1920), King of the Hellenes 1917–20, *m.* 1919 Aspasia Manos; *issue:* Princess Alexandra (1921–93), *m.* 1944 King Petar II of Yugoslavia (*see* below)
      (c) Princess Helena (1896–1982), *m.* 1921 King Carol of Roumania (*see* below), (marriage dissolved 1928)

(d) Paul I (1901–64), King of the Hellenes 1947–64, *m.* 1938 Princess Frederika of Brunswick (*see* page 126); *issue:* King Constantine II (*b.* 1940), *m.* 1964 Princess Anne-Marie of Denmark (*see* page 128), and has issue (three sons, two daughters); Princess Sophie (*b.* 1938), *m.* 1962 Juan Carlos I of Spain (*see* page 128); Princess Irene (*b.* 1942)
(e) Princess Irene (1904–74), *m.* 1939 4th Duke of Aosta; *issue:* Prince Amedeo, 5th Duke of Aosta (*b.* 1943)
(f) Princess Katherine (Lady Katherine Brandram) (*b.* 1913), *m.* 1947 Major R. C. A. Brandram, MC, TD; *issue:* R. Paul G. A. Brandram (*b.* 1948)
(8) Princess Margarethe (1872–1954), *m.* 1893 Prince Friedrich Karl of Hesse (1868–1940). *Issue:*
(a) Prince Friedrich Wilhelm (1893–1916)
(b) Prince Maximilian (1894–1914)
(c) Prince Philipp (1896–1980), *m.* 1925 Princess Mafalda of Italy; *issue:* Prince Moritz (*b.* 1926); Prince Heinrich (*b.*1927); Prince Otto (*b.* 1937); Princess Elisabeth (*b.* 1940)
(d) Prince Wolfgang (1896–1989), *m.* (1) 1924 Princess Marie Alexandra of Baden; (2) 1948 Ottilie Möller
(e) Prince Richard (1901–69)
(f)Prince Christoph (1901–43), *m.* 1930 Princess Sophie of Greece (*see* below) and has issue (two sons, three daughters)

2. HRH PRINCE ALBERT EDWARD (HM King Edward VII), *b.* 9 November 1841, *m.* 1863 HRH Princess Alexandra of Denmark (1844–1925), *succeeded* to the throne 22 January 1901, *d.* 6 May 1910. *Issue:*
(1) Albert Victor, Duke of Clarence and Avondale (1864–92)
(2) George (HM KING GEORGE V) (*see* page 126)
(3) Louise (1867–1931) Princess Royal 1905–31, *m.* 1889 1st Duke of Fife (1849–1912). *Issue:*
(a) Princess Alexandra, Duchess of Fife (1891–1959), *m.* 1913 Prince Arthur of Connaught (*see* page 128)
(b) Princess Maud (1893–1945), *m.* 1923 11th Earl of Southesk (1893–1992); *issue:* The Duke of Fife (*b.* 1929)
(4) Victoria (1868–1935)
(5) Maud (1869–1938), *m.* 1896 Prince Carl of Denmark (1872–1957), later King Haakon VII of Norway 1905–57. *Issue:*
(a) Olav V (1903–91), King of Norway 1957–91, *m.* 1929 Princess Märtha of Sweden (1901–54); *issue:* Princess Ragnhild (*b.* 1930); Princess Astrid (*b.* 1932); Harald V, King of Norway (*b.* 1937)
(6) Alexander (6–7 April 1871)

3. HRH PRINCESS ALICE Maud Mary (1843–78), *m.* 1862 Prince Ludwig (1837–92), Grand Duke of Hesse 1877–92. *Issue:*
(1) Victoria (1863–1950), *m.* 1884 *Admiral of the Fleet* Prince Louis of Battenberg (1854–1921), *cr.* 1st Marquess of Milford Haven 1917. *Issue:*
(a) Alice (1885–1969), *m.* 1903 Prince Andrew of Greece (1882–1944); *issue:* Princess Margarita (1905–81), *m.* 1931 Prince Gottfried of Hohenlohe-Langenburg (*see* below); Princess Theodora (1906–69), *m.* Prince Berthold of Baden (1906–63) and has issue (two sons, one daughter); Princess Cecilie (1911–37), *m.* George, Grand Duke of Hesse (*see* below); Princess Sophie (*b.* 1914), *m.* (1) 1930 Prince Christoph of Hesse (*see* above); (2) 1946 Prince Georg of Hanover (*see* page 127); Prince Philip, Duke of Edinburgh (*b.* 1921) (*see* page 117)
(b) Louise (1889–1965), *m.* 1923 Gustaf VI Adolf (1882–1973), King of Sweden 1950–73
(c) George, 2nd Marquess of Milford Haven (1892–1938), *m.* 1916 Countess Nadejda, daughter of Grand Duke Michael of Russia; *issue:* Lady Tatiana (1917–88); David Michael, 3rd Marquess (1919–70)
(d) Louis, 1st Earl Mountbatten of Burma (1900–79), *m.* 1922 Edwina Ashley, daughter of Lord Mount Temple; *issue:* Patricia, Countess Mountbatten of Burma (*b.* 1924), Pamela (*b.* 1929)
(2) Elizabeth (1864–1918), *m.* 1884 Grand Duke Sergius of Russia (1857–1905)
(3) Irene (1866–1953), *m.* 1888 Prince Heinrich of Prussia (*see* page 126)
(4) Ernst Ludwig (1868–1937), Grand Duke of Hesse 1892–1918, *m.* (1) 1894 Princess Victoria Melita of Saxe-Coburg (*see* below) (marriage dissolved 1901) and (2) 1905 Princess Eleonore of Solms-Hohensolmslich. *Issue:*

(a) Princess Elizabeth (1895–1903)
(b) George, Hereditary Grand Duke of Hesse (1906–37), *m.* Princess Cecilie of Greece (*see* above), and had issue, two sons, accidentally killed with parents 1937
(c) Ludwig, Prince of Hesse (1908–68), *m.* 1937 Margaret, daughter of 1st Lord Geddes
(5) Frederick William (1870–3)
(6) Alix (Tsaritsa of Russia) (1872–1918), *m.* 1894 Nicholas II (1868–1918) Tsar of All the Russias 1894–1917, assassinated 16 July 1918. *Issue:*
(a) Grand Duchess Olga (1895–1918)
(b) Grand Duchess Tatiana (1897–1918)
(c) Grand Duchess Marie (1899–1918)
(d) Grand Duchess Anastasia (1901–18)
(e) Alexis, Tsarevich of Russia (1904–18)
(7) Marie (1874–8)

4. HRH PRINCE ALFRED Ernest Albert, Duke of Edinburgh, *Admiral of the Fleet* (1844–1900), *m.* 1874 Grand Duchess Marie Alexandrovna of Russia (1853–1920); succeeded as Duke of Saxe-Coburg and Gotha 22 August 1893. *Issue:*
(1) Alfred, Prince of Saxe-Coburg (1874–99)
(2) Marie (1875–1938), *m.* 1893 Ferdinand (1865–1927), King of Roumania 1914–27. *Issue:*
(a) Carol II (1893–1953), King of Roumania 1930–40, *m.* (2) 1921 Princess Helena of Greece (*see* above) (marriage dissolved 1928); *issue:* Michael (*b.* 1921), King of Roumania 1927–30, 1940–7, *m.* 1948 Princess Anne of Bourbon-Parma, and has issue (five daughters)
(b) Elisabeth (1894–1956), *m.* 1921 George II, King of the Hellenes (*see* page 126)
(c) Marie (1900–61), *m.* 1922 Alexander (1888–1934), King of Yugoslavia 1921–34; *issue:* Petar II (1923–70), King of Yugoslavia 1934–45, *m.* 1944 Princess Alexandra of Greece (*see* above) and has issue (Crown Prince Alexander, *b.* 1945); Prince Tomislav (*b.* 1928), *m.* (1) 1957 Princess Margarita of Baden (daughter of Princess Theodora of Greece and Prince Berthold of Baden, *see* above); (2) 1982 Linda Bonney; and has issue (three sons, one daughter); Prince Andrej (1929–90), *m.* (1) 1956 Princess Christina of Hesse (daughter of Prince Christoph of Hesse and Princess Sophie of Greece, *see* above); (2) 1963 Princess Kira-Melita of Leiningen (*see* below); and has issue (three sons, two daughters)
(d) Prince Nicolas (1903–78)
(e) Princess Ileana (1909–91), *m.* (1) 1931 Archduke Anton of Austria; (2) 1954 Dr Stefan Issarescu; *issue:* Archduke Stefan (*b.* 1932); Archduchess Maria Ileana (1933–59); Archduchess Alexandra (*b.* 1935); Archduke Dominic (*b.* 1937); Archduchess Maria Magdalena (*b.* 1939); Archduchess Elisabeth (*b.*1942)
(f) Prince Mircea (1913–16)
(3) Victoria Melita (1876–1936), *m.* (1) 1894 Grand Duke Ernst Ludwig of Hesse (*see* above) (marriage dissolved 1901); (2) 1905 the Grand Duke Kirill of Russia (1876–1938). *Issue:*
(a) Marie Kirillovna (1907–51), *m.* 1925 Prince Friedrich Karl of Leiningen; *issue:* Prince Emich (1926–91); Prince Karl (1928–90); Princess Kira-Melita (*b.* 1930), *m.* Prince Andrej of Yugoslavia (*see* above); Princess Margarita (*b.* 1932); Princess Mechtilde (*b.* 1936); Prince Friedrich (*b.* 1938)
(b) Kira Kirillovna (1909–67), *m.* 1938 Prince Louis Ferdinand of Prussia (*see* page 127); *issue:* Prince Friedrich Wilhelm (*b.* 1939); Prince Michael (*b.* 1940); Princess Marie (*b.* 1942); Princess Kira (*b.* 1943); Prince Louis Ferdinand (1944–77); Prince Christian (*b.* 1946); Princess Xenia (1949–92)
(c) Vladimir Kirillovich (1917–92), *m.* 1948 Princess Leonida Bagration-Mukhransky; *issue:* Grand Duchess Maria (*b.* 1953), and has issue
(4) Alexandra (1878–1942), *m.* 1896 Ernst, Prince of Hohenlohe Langenburg. *Issue:*
(a) Gottfried (1897–1960), *m.* 1931 Princess Margarita of Greece (*see* above); *issue:* Prince Kraft (*b.* 1935), Princess Beatrice (1936–97); Prince Georg Andreas (*b.* 1938), Prince Ruprecht (1944–76); Prince Albrecht (1944–92)
(b) Maria (1899–1967), *m.* 1916 Prince Friedrich of Schleswig-Holstein-Sonderburg-Glücksburg; *issue:* Prince Peter (1922–80); Princess Marie (*b.* 1927)
(c) Princess Alexandra (1901–63)
(d) Princess Irma (1902–86)

(5) Princess Beatrice (1884–1966), *m.* 1909 Alfonso of Orleans, Infante of Spain. *Issue:*
(*a*) Prince Alvaro (*b.* 1910), *m.* 1937 Carla Parodi-Delfino; *issue:* Doña Gerarda (*b.* 1939); Don Alonso (1941–75); Doña Beatriz (*b.* 1943); Don Alvaro (*b.* 1947)
(*b*) Prince Alonso (1912–36)
(*c*) Prince Ataulfo (1913–74)

5. HRH PRINCESS HELENA Augusta Victoria (1846–1923), *m.* 1866 Prince Christian of Schleswig-Holstein-Sonderburg-Augustenburg (1831–1917). *Issue:*
(1) Prince Christian Victor (1867–1900)
(2) Prince Albert (1869–1931), Duke of Schleswig-Holstein 1921–31
(3) Princess Helena (1870–1948)
(4) Princess Marie Louise (1872–1956), *m.* 1891 Prince Aribert of Anhalt (marriage dissolved 1900)
(5) Prince Harold (12–20 May 1876)

6. HRH PRINCESS LOUISE Caroline Alberta (1848–1939), *m.* 1871 the Marquess of Lorne, afterwards 9th Duke of Argyll (1845–1914); without issue

7. HRH PRINCE ARTHUR William Patrick Albert, Duke of Connaught, *Field Marshal* (1850–1942), *m.* 1879 Princess Louisa of Prussia (1860–1917). *Issue:*
(1) Margaret (1882–1920), *m.* 1905 Crown Prince Gustaf Adolf (1882–1973), afterwards King of Sweden 1950–73. *Issue:*
(*a*) Gustaf Adolf, Duke of Västerbotten (1906–47), *m.* 1932 Princess Sibylla of Saxe-Coburg-Gotha (*see below*); *issue:* Princess Margaretha (*b.* 1934); Princess Birgitta (*b.* 1937); Princess Désirée (*b.* 1938); Princess Christina (*b.* 1943); Carl XVI Gustaf, King of Sweden (*b.* 1946)
(*b*) Count Sigvard Bernadotte (*b.* 1907), *m.*; *issue:* Count Michael (*b.* 1944)
(*c*) Princess Ingrid (Queen Mother of Denmark) (*b.* 1910), *m.* 1935 Frederick IX (1899–1972), King of Denmark 1947–72; *issue:* Margrethe II, Queen of Denmark (*b.* 1940); Princess Benedikte (*b.* 1944); Princess Anne-Marie (*b.* 1946), *m.* 1964 Constantine II of Greece (*see page* 127)
(*d*) Prince Bertil, Duke of Halland (1912–97), *m.* 1976 Mrs Lilian Craig
(*e*) Count Carl Bernadotte (*b.* 1916), *m.* (1) 1946 Mrs Kerstin Johnson; (2) 1988 Countess Gunnila Bussler
(2) Arthur (1883–1938), *m.* 1913 HH the Duchess of Fife (*see* page 127). *Issue:*
Alastair Arthur, 2nd Duke of Connaught (1914–43)

(3) (Victoria) Patricia (1886–1974), *m.* 1919 Adm. Hon. Sir Alexander Ramsay. *Issue:*
Alexander Ramsay of Mar (*b.* 1919), *m.* 1956 Hon. Flora Fraser (Lady Saltoun)

8. HRH PRINCE LEOPOLD George Duncan Albert, Duke of Albany (1853–84), *m.* 1882 Princess Helena of Waldeck (1861–1922). *Issue:*
(1) Alice (1883–1981), *m.* 1904 Prince Alexander of Teck (1874–1957), *cr.* 1st Earl of Athlone 1917. *Issue:*
(*a*) Lady May (1906–94), *m.* 1931 Sir Henry Abel-Smith, KCMG, KCVO, DSO; *issue:* Anne (*b.* 1932); Richard (*b.* 1933); Elizabeth (*b.* 1936)
(*b*) Rupert, Viscount Trematon (1907–28)
(*c*) Prince Maurice (March–September 1910)
(2) Charles Edward (1884–1954), Duke of Albany 1884 until title suspended 1917, Duke of Saxe-Coburg-Gotha 1900–18, *m.* 1905 Princess Victoria Adelheid of Schleswig-Holstein-Sonderburg-Glücksburg. *Issue:*
(*a*) Prince Johann Leopold (1906–72), and has issue
(*b*) Princess Sibylla (1908–72), *m.* 1932 Prince Gustav Adolf of Sweden (*see above*)
(*c*) Prince Dietmar Hubertus (1909–43)
(*d*) Princess Caroline (1912–83), and has issue
(*e*) Prince Friedrich Josias (*b.* 1918), and has issue

9. HRH PRINCESS BEATRICE Mary Victoria Feodore (1857–1944), *m.* 1885 Prince Henry of Battenberg (1858–96). *Issue:*
(1) Alexander, 1st Marquess of Carisbrooke (1886–1960), *m.* 1917 Lady Irene Denison. *Issue:*
Lady Iris Mountbatten (1920–82), *m.*; *issue:* Robin A. Bryan (*b.* 1957)
(2) Victoria Eugénie (1887–1969), *m.* 1906 Alfonso XIII (1886–1941) King of Spain 1886–1931. *Issue:*
(*a*) Prince Alfonso (1907–38)
(*b*) Prince Jaime (1908–75), and has issue
(*c*) Princess Beatrice (*b.* 1909), and has issue
(*d*) Princess Maria (1911–96), and has issue
(*e*) Prince Juan (1913–93), Count of Barcelona; *issue:* Princess Maria (*b.* 1936); Juan Carlos I, King of Spain (*b.* 1938), *m.* 1962 Princess Sophie of Greece (*see* page 127) and has issue (one son, two daughters); Princess Margarita (*b.* 1939)
(*f*) Prince Gonzalo (1914–34)
(3) Major Lord Leopold Mountbatten (1889–1922)
(4) Maurice (1891–1914), died of wounds received in action

Kings and Queens

HOUSES OF CERDIC AND DENMARK

Reign

927–939 ÆTHELSTAN
Son of Edward the Elder, by Ecgwynn, and grandson of Alfred
Acceded to Wessex and Mercia *c.*924, established direct rule over Northumbria 927, effectively creating the Kingdom of England
Reigned 15 years

939–946 EDMUND I
Born 921, son of Edward the Elder, by Eadgifu
Married (1) Ælfgifu (2) Æthelflæd
Killed aged 25, *reigned* 6 years

946–955 EADRED
Son of Edward the Elder, by Eadgifu
Reigned 9 years

955–959 EADWIG
Born before 943, son of Edmund and Ælfgifu
Married Ælfgifu
Reigned 3 years

959–975 EDGAR I
Born 943, son of Edmund and Ælfgifu
Married (1) Æthelflæd (2) Wulfthryth (3) Ælfthryth
Died aged 32, *reigned* 15 years

975–978 EDWARD I (the Martyr)
*Born c.*962, son of Edgar and Æthelflæd
Assassinated aged *c.*16, *reigned* 2 years

978–1016 ÆTHELRED (the Unready)
*Born c.*968/969, son of Edgar and Ælfthryth
Married (1) Ælfgifu (2) Emma, daughter of Richard I, count of Normandy
1013–14 dispossessed of kingdom by Swegn Forkbeard (king of Denmark 987–1014)
Died aged *c.*47, *reigned* 38 years

1016 EDMUND II (Ironside)
Born before 993, son of Æthelred and Ælfgifu
Married Ealdgyth
Died aged over 23, *reigned* 7 months (April–November)

1016–1035 CNUT (Canute)
*Born c.*995, son of Swegn Forkbeard, king of Denmark, and Gunhild
Married (1) Ælfgifu (2) Emma, widow of Æthelred the Unready
Gained submission of West Saxons 1015, Northumbrians 1016, Mercia 1016, king of all

England after Edmund's death
King of Denmark 1019–35, king of Norway 1028–35
Died aged *c.*40, *reigned* 19 years

1035–1040 HAROLD I (Harefoot)
*Born c.*1016/17, son of Cnut and Ælfgifu
Married Ælfgifu
1035 recognized as regent for himself and his
brother Harthacnut; 1037 recognized as king
*Died aged c.*23, *reigned* 4 years

1040–1042 HARTHACNUT
*Born c.*1018, son of Cnut and Emma
Titular king of Denmark from 1028
Acknowledged king of England 1035–7 with
Harold I as regent; effective king after
Harold's death
Died aged c.24, *reigned* 2 years

1042–1066 EDWARD II (the Confessor)
Born between 1002 and 1005, son of Æthelred the
Unready and Emma
Married Eadgyth, daughter of Godwine, earl of
Wessex
Died aged over 60, *reigned* 23 years

1066 HAROLD II (Godwinesson)
*Born c.*1020, son of Godwine, earl of Wessex,
and Gytha
Married (1) Eadgyth (2) Ealdgyth
Killed in battle aged *c.*46, *reigned* 10 months
(January–October)

THE HOUSE OF NORMANDY

1066–1087 WILLIAM I (the Conqueror)
Born 1027/8, son of Robert I, duke of Normandy;
obtained the Crown by conquest
Married Matilda, daughter of Baldwin, count of
Flanders
Died aged *c.*60, *reigned* 20 years

1087–1100 WILLIAM II (Rufus)
Born between 1056 and 1060, third
son of William I;
succeeded his father in England only
Killed aged *c.*40, *reigned* 12 years

1100–1135 HENRY I (Beauclerk)
Born 1068, fourth son of William I
Married (1) Edith or Matilda, daughter of
Malcolm III of Scotland (2) Adela, daughter of
Godfrey, count of Louvain
Died aged 67, *reigned* 35 years

1135–1154 STEPHEN
Born not later than 1100, third son of Adela,
daughter of William I, and Stephen, count of Blois
Married Matilda, daughter of Eustace, count of
Boulogne
1141 (February–November) held captive by
adherents of Matilda, daughter of Henry I, who
contested the crown until 1153
Died aged over 53, *reigned* 18 years

THE HOUSE OF ANJOU (PLANTAGENETS)

1154–1189 HENRY II (Curtmantle)
Born 1133, son of Matilda, daughter of Henry
I, and Geoffrey, count of Anjou
Married Eleanor, daughter of William, duke of
Aquitaine, and divorced queen of Louis VII of
France
Died aged 56, *reigned* 34 years

1189–1199 RICHARD I (Coeur de Lion)
Born 1157, third son of Henry II
Married Berengaria, daughter of Sancho VI,
king of Navarre
Died aged 42, *reigned* 9 years

1199–1216 JOHN (Lackland)
Born 1167, fifth son of Henry II
Married (1) Isabella or Avisa, daughter of
William, earl of Gloucester (divorced) (2)
Isabella, daughter of Aymer, count of Angoulême
Died aged 48, *reigned* 17 years

1216–1272 HENRY III
Born 1207, son of John and Isabella of Angoulême
Married Eleanor, daughter of Raymond,

count of Provence
Died aged 65, *reigned* 56 years

1272–1307 EDWARD I (Longshanks)
Born 1239, eldest son of Henry III
Married (1) Eleanor, daughter of Ferdinand III,
king of Castile (2) Margaret, daughter of
Philip III of France
Died aged 68, *reigned* 34 years

1307–1327 EDWARD II
Born 1284, eldest surviving son of Edward I and
Eleanor
Married Isabella, daughter of Philip IV of France
Deposed January 1327, *killed* September 1327 aged
43, *reigned* 19 years

1327–1377 EDWARD III
Born 1312, eldest son of Edward II
Married Philippa, daughter of William, count of
Hainault
Died aged 64, *reigned* 50 years

1377–1399 RICHARD II
Born 1367, son of Edward (the Black Prince),
eldest son of Edward III
Married (1) Anne, daughter of Emperor Charles IV
(2) Isabelle, daughter of Charles VI of France
Deposed September 1399, *killed* February 1400 aged
33, *reigned* 22 years

THE HOUSE OF LANCASTER

1399–1413 HENRY IV
Born 1366, son of John of Gaunt, fourth son of
Edward III, and Blanche, daughter of Henry, duke
of Lancaster
Married (1) Mary, daughter of Humphrey, earl of
Hereford (2) Joan, daughter of Charles, king of
Navarre, and widow of John, duke of Brittany
Died aged *c.* 47, *reigned* 13 years

1413–1422 HENRY V
Born 1387, eldest surviving son of Henry IV and
Mary
Married Catherine, daughter of Charles VI of
France
Died aged 34, *reigned* 9 years

1422–1471 HENRY VI
Born 1421, son of Henry V
Married Margaret, daughter of René, duke of
Anjou and count of Provence
Deposed March 1461, *restored* October 1470
Deposed April 1471, *killed* May 1471 aged 49,
reigned 39 years

THE HOUSE OF YORK

1461–1483 EDWARD IV
Born 1442, eldest son of Richard of York
(grandson of Edmund, fifth son of
Edward III, and son of Anne, great-
granddaughter of Lionel, third son of
Edward III)
Married Elizabeth Woodville, daughter of
Richard, Lord Rivers, and widow of Sir
John Grey
Acceded March 1461, *deposed* October 1470,
restored April 1471
Died aged 40, *reigned* 21 years

1483 EDWARD V
Born 1470, eldest son of Edward IV
Deposed June 1483, *died* probably July–September
1483, aged 12, *reigned* 2 months (April–June)

1483–1485 RICHARD III
Born 1452, fourth son of Richard of York
Married Anne Neville, daughter of Richard,
earl of Warwick, and widow of Edward,
Prince of Wales, son of Henry VI
Killed in battle aged 32, *reigned* 2 years

THE HOUSE OF TUDOR

1485–1509 HENRY VII
Born 1457, son of Margaret Beaufort (great-
granddaughter of John of Gaunt, fourth son of

Edward III) and Edmund Tudor, earl of
Richmond
Married Elizabeth, daughter of Edward IV
Died aged 52, *reigned* 23 years

1509–1547 HENRY VIII
Born 1491, second son of Henry VII
Married (1) Catherine, daughter of
Ferdinand II, king of Aragon, and widow
of his elder brother Arthur (divorced) (2)
Anne, daughter of Sir Thomas Boleyn (executed)
(3) Jane, daughter of Sir John Seymour
(died in childbirth) (4) Anne, daughter of John,
duke of Cleves (divorced) (5) Catherine Howard,
niece of the Duke of Norfolk (executed) (6)
Catherine, daughter of Sir Thomas Parr and
widow of Lord Latimer
Died aged 55, *reigned* 37 years

1547–1553 EDWARD VI
Born 1537, son of Henry VIII and Jane Seymour
Died aged 15, *reigned* 6 years

1553 JANE
Born 1537, daughter of Frances (daughter of
Mary Tudor, the younger daughter of Henry VII)
and Henry Grey, duke of Suffolk
Married Lord Guildford Dudley, son of the
Duke of Northumberland
Deposed July 1553, *executed* February 1554
aged 16, *reigned* 14 days

1553–1558 MARY I
Born 1516, daughter of Henry VIII and
Catherine of Aragon
Married Philip II of Spain
Died aged 42, *reigned* 5 years

1558–1603 ELIZABETH I
Born 1533, daughter of Henry VIII and Anne
Boleyn
Died aged 69, *reigned* 44 years

BRITISH KINGS AND QUEENS SINCE 1603

THE HOUSE OF STUART

Reign

1603–1625 JAMES I (VI OF SCOTLAND)
Born 1566, son of Mary, queen of Scots
(granddaughter of Margaret Tudor, elder daughter
of Henry VII), and Henry Stewart, Lord Darnley
Married Anne, daughter of Frederick II of Denmark
Died aged 58, *reigned* 22 years
(*see also* page 133)

1625–1649 CHARLES I
Born 1600, second son of James I
Married Henrietta Maria, daughter of Henry IV of
France
Executed 1649 aged 48, *reigned* 23 years
COMMONWEALTH DECLARED 19 May 1649
1649–53 Government by a council of state
1653–8 Oliver Cromwell, Lord Protector
1658–9 Richard Cromwell, Lord Protector

1660–1685 CHARLES II
Born 1630, eldest son of Charles I
Married Catherine, daughter of John IV of Portugal
Died aged 54, *reigned* 24 years

1685–1688 JAMES II (VII of Scotland)
Born 1633, second son of Charles I
Married (1) Lady Anne Hyde, daughter of Edward,
earl of Clarendon (2) Mary, daughter of Alphonso,
duke of Modena
Reign ended with flight from kingdom December
1688
Died 1701 aged 67, *reigned* 3 years
INTERREGNUM 11 December 1688 to
12 February 1689

1689–1702 WILLIAM III
Born 1650, son of William II, prince of Orange, and
Mary Stuart, daughter of Charles I
Married Mary, elder daughter of James II
Died aged 51, *reigned* 13 years
and
1689–1694 MARY II
Born 1662, elder daughter of James II and Anne
Died aged 32, *reigned* 5 years

1702–1714 ANNE
Born 1665, younger daughter of James II and Anne
Married Prince George of Denmark, son of
Frederick III of Denmark
Died aged 49, *reigned* 12 years

THE HOUSE OF HANOVER

1714–1727 GEORGE I (Elector of Hanover)
Born 1660, son of Sophia (daughter of Frederick,
elector palatine, and Elizabeth Stuart, daughter of
James I) and Ernest Augustus, elector of Hanover
Married Sophia Dorothea, daughter of George
William, duke of Lüneburg-Celle
Died aged 67, *reigned* 12 years

1727–1760 GEORGE II
Born 1683, son of George I
Married Caroline, daughter of John Frederick,
margrave of Brandenburg-Anspach
Died aged 76, *reigned* 33 years

1760–1820 GEORGE III
Born 1738, son of Frederick, eldest son of George II
Married Charlotte, daughter of Charles Louis, duke
of Mecklenburg-Strelitz
Died aged 81, *reigned* 59 years
REGENCY 1811–20
Prince of Wales regent owing to the insanity of
George III

1820–1830 GEORGE IV
Born 1762, eldest son of George III
Married Caroline, daughter of Charles, duke of
Brunswick-Wolfenbüttel
Died aged 67, *reigned* 10 years

1830–1837 WILLIAM IV
Born 1765, third son of George III
Married Adelaide, daughter of George, duke of
Saxe-Meiningen
Died aged 71, *reigned* 7 years

1837–1901 VICTORIA
Born 1819, daughter of Edward, fourth son of
George III
Married Prince Albert of Saxe-Coburg and Gotha
Died aged 81, *reigned* 63 years

THE HOUSE OF SAXE-COBURG AND GOTHA

1901–1910 EDWARD VII
Born 1841, eldest son of Victoria and Albert
Married Alexandra, daughter of Christian IX of
Denmark
Died aged 68, *reigned* 9 years

THE HOUSE OF WINDSOR

1910–1936 GEORGE V
Born 1865, second son of Edward VII
Married Victoria Mary, daughter of Francis, duke of
Teck
Died aged 70, *reigned* 25 years

1936 EDWARD VIII
Born 1894, eldest son of George V
Married (1937) Mrs Wallis Simpson
Abdicated 1936, *died* 1972 aged 77, *reigned*
10 months (20 January to 11 December)

1936–1952 GEORGE VI
Born 1895, second son of George V
Married Lady Elizabeth Bowes-Lyon, daughter of
14th Earl of Strathmore and Kinghorne (*see also*
page 117)

1952–   ELIZABETH II
          Born 1926, elder daughter of George VI
          Married Philip, son of Prince Andrew of Greece
          (*see also* page 117)
          WHOM GOD PRESERVE

KINGS AND QUEENS OF SCOTS 1016 TO 1603

Reign
1016–1034   MALCOLM II
              Born c.954, son of Kenneth II
              Acceded to Alba 1005, secured Lothian c.1016,
              obtained Strathclyde for his grandson Duncan
              c.1016, thus reigning over an area approximately
              the same as that governed by later rulers of
              Scotland
              Died aged c.80, *reigned* 18 years

THE HOUSE OF ATHOLL

1034–1040   DUNCAN I
              Son of Bethoc, daughter of Malcolm II, and Crinan,
              mormaer of Atholl
              Married a cousin of Siward, earl of Northumbria
              Reigned 5 years
1040–1057   MACBETH
              Born c.1005, son of a daughter of Malcolm II and
              Finlaec, mormaer of Moray
              Married Gruoch, granddaughter of Kenneth III
              Killed aged c.52, *reigned* 17 years
1057–1058   LULACH
              Born c.1032, son of Gillacomgan, mormaer of
              Moray, and Gruoch (and stepson of Macbeth)
              Died aged c.26, *reigned* 7 months (August–March)
1058–1093   MALCOLM III (Canmore)
              Born c.1031, elder son of Duncan I
              Married (1) Ingibiorg (2) Margaret (St Margaret),
              granddaughter of Edmund II of England
              Killed in battle aged c.62, *reigned* 35 years
1093–1097   DONALD III BÁN
              Born c.1033, second son of Duncan I
              Deposed May 1094, *restored* November 1094,
              deposed October 1097, *reigned* 3 years
1094   DUNCAN II
              Born c.1060, elder son of Malcolm III and Ingibiorg
              Married Octreda of Dunbar
              Killed aged c.34, *reigned* 6 months (May–November)
1097–1107   EDGAR
              Born c.1074, second son of Malcolm III and
              Margaret
              Died aged c.32, *reigned* 9 years
1107–1124   ALEXANDER I (The Fierce)
              Born c.1077, fifth son of Malcolm III and Margaret
              Married Sybilla, illegitimate daughter of Henry I
              of England
              Died aged c.47, *reigned* 17 years
1124–1153   DAVID I (The Saint)
              Born c.1085, sixth son of Malcolm III and
              Margaret
              Married Matilda, daughter of Waltheof, earl of
              Huntingdon
              Died aged c.68, *reigned* 29 years
1153–1165   MALCOLM IV (The Maiden)
              Born c.1141, son of Henry, earl of Huntingdon,
              second son of David I
              Died aged c.24, *reigned* 12 years
1165–1214   WILLIAM I (The Lion)
              Born c.1142, brother of Malcolm IV
              Married Ermengarde, daughter of Richard, viscount
              of Beaumont
              Died aged c.72, *reigned* 49 years
1214–1249   ALEXANDER II
              Born 1198, son of William I
              Married (1) Joan, daughter of John, king of
              England (2) Marie, daughter of Ingelram de Coucy
              Died aged 50, *reigned* 34 years

1249–1286   ALEXANDER III
              Born 1241, son of Alexander II and Marie
              Married (1) Margaret, daughter of Henry III of
              England (2) Yolande, daughter of the Count of
              Dreux
              Killed accidentally aged 44, *reigned* 36 years
1286–1290   MARGARET (The Maid of Norway)
              Born 1283, daughter of Margaret (daughter of
              Alexander III) and Eric II of Norway
              Died aged 7, *reigned* 4 years

          FIRST INTERREGNUM 1290–2
          Throne disputed by 13 competitors. Crown
          awarded to John Balliol by adjudication of Edward I
          of England

THE HOUSE OF BALLIOL

1292–1296   JOHN (Balliol)
              Born c.1250, son of Dervorguilla, great-great-
              granddaughter of David I, and John de Balliol
              Married Isabella, daughter of John, earl of Surrey
              Abdicated 1296, *died* 1313 aged c.63, *reigned* 3 years

          SECOND INTERREGNUM 1296–1306
          Edward I of England declared John Balliol to have
          forfeited the throne for contumacy in 1296 and took
          the government of Scotland into his own hands

THE HOUSE OF BRUCE

1306–1329   ROBERT I (Bruce)
              Born 1274, son of Robert Bruce and Marjorie,
              countess of Carrick, and great-grandson of the
              second daughter of David, earl of Huntingdon,
              brother of William I
              Married (1) Isabella, daughter of Donald, earl of
              Mar (2) Elizabeth, daughter of Richard, earl of
              Ulster
              Died aged 54, *reigned* 23 years
1329–1371   DAVID II
              Born 1324, son of Robert I and Elizabeth
              Married (1) Joanna, daughter of Edward II of
              England (2) Margaret Drummond, widow of Sir
              John Logie (divorced)
              Died aged 46, *reigned* 41 years
              1332 Edward Balliol, son of John Balliol, crowned
              King of Scots September, expelled December
              1333–6 Edward Balliol restored as King of Scots

THE HOUSE OF STEWART

1371–1390   ROBERT II (Stewart)
              Born 1316, son of Marjorie (daughter of Robert I)
              and Walter, High Steward of Scotland
              Married (1) Elizabeth, daughter of Sir Robert Mure
              of Rowallan (2) Euphemia, daughter of Hugh, earl
              of Ross
              Died aged 74, *reigned* 19 years
1390–1406   ROBERT III
              Born c.1337, son of Robert II and Elizabeth
              Married Annabella, daughter of Sir John
              Drummond of Stobhall
              Died aged c.69, *reigned* 16 years
1406–1437   JAMES I
              Born 1394, son of Robert III
              Married Joan Beaufort, daughter of John, earl of
              Somerset
              Assassinated aged 42, *reigned* 30 years
1437–1460   JAMES II
              Born 1430, son of James I
              Married Mary, daughter of Arnold, duke of Gueldres
              Killed accidentally aged 29, *reigned* 23 years
1460–1488   JAMES III
              Born 1452, son of James II
              Married Margaret, daughter of Christian I of
              Denmark
              Assassinated aged 36, *reigned* 27 years
1488–1513   JAMES IV
              Born 1473, son of James III
              Married Margaret Tudor, daughter of Henry VII of
              England
              Killed in battle aged 40, *reigned* 25 years

1513–1542	**JAMES V** *Born* 1512, son of James IV *Married* (1) Madeleine, daughter of Francis I of France (2) Mary of Lorraine, daughter of the Duc de Guise *Died* aged 30, *reigned* 29 years
1542–1567	**MARY** *Born* 1542, daughter of James V and Mary *Married* (1) the Dauphin, afterwards Francis II of France (2) Henry Stewart, Lord Darnley (3) James Hepburn, earl of Bothwell *Abdicated* 1567, prisoner in England from 1568, *executed* 1587, *reigned* 24 years
1567–1625	**JAMES VI (and I of England)** *Born* 1566, son of Mary, queen of Scots, and Henry, Lord Darnley *Acceded* 1567 to the Scottish throne, *reigned* 58 years Succeeded 1603 to the English throne, so joining the English and Scottish crowns in one person. The two kingdoms remained distinct until 1707 when the parliaments of the kingdoms became conjoined For British Kings and Queens since 1603, *see* pages 130–1

WELSH SOVEREIGNS AND PRINCES

Wales was ruled by sovereign princes from the earliest times until
the death of Llywelyn in 1282. The first English Prince of Wales
was the son of Edward I, who was born in Caernarvon town on 25
April 1284. According to a discredited legend, he was presented to
the Welsh chieftains as their prince, in fulfilment of a promise that
they should have a prince who 'could not speak a word of English'
and should be native born. This son, who afterwards became
Edward II, was created 'Prince of Wales and Earl of Chester' at
the Lincoln Parliament on 7 February 1301.

The title Prince of Wales is borne after individual conferment
and is not inherited at birth, though some Princes have been
declared and styled Prince of Wales but never formally so created
(*s.*). The title was conferred on Prince Charles by The Queen on
26 July 1958. He was invested at Caernarvon on 1 July 1969.

INDEPENDENT PRINCES AD 844 TO 1282

844–878	Rhodri the Great
878–916	Anarawd, son of Rhodri
916–950	Hywel Dda, the Good
950–979	Iago ab Idwal (or Ieuaf)
979–985	Hywel ab Ieuaf, the Bad
985–986	Cadwallon, his brother
986–999	Maredudd ab Owain ap Hywel Dda
999–1008	Cynan ap Hywel ab Ieuaf
1018–1023	Llywelyn ap Seisyll
1023–1039	Iago ab Idwal ap Meurig
1039–1063	Gruffydd ap Llywelyn ap Seisyll
1063–1075	Bleddyn ap Cynfyn
1075–1081	Trahaern ap Caradog
1081–1137	Gruffydd ap Cynan ab Iago
1137–1170	Owain Gwynedd
1170–1194	Dafydd ab Owain Gwynedd
1194–1240	Llywelyn Fawr, the Great
1240–1246	Dafydd ap Llywelyn
1246–1282	Llywelyn ap Gruffydd ap Llywelyn

ENGLISH PRINCES SINCE 1301

1301	Edward (Edward II)
1343	Edward the Black Prince, son of Edward III
1376	Richard (Richard II), son of the Black Prince
1399	Henry of Monmouth (Henry V)
1454	Edward of Westminster, son of Henry VI
1471	Edward of Westminster (Edward V)
1483	Edward, son of Richard III (d. 1484)
1489	Arthur Tudor, son of Henry VII
1504	Henry Tudor (Henry VIII)
1610	Henry Stuart, son of James I (d. 1612)
1616	Charles Stuart (Charles I)

*c.*1638 (*s.*)	Charles Stuart (Charles II)
1688 (*s.*)	James Francis Edward Stuart (The Old Pretender), son of James II (d. 1766)
1714	George Augustus (George II)
1729	Frederick Lewis, son of George II (d. 1751)
1751	George William Frederick (George III)
1762	George Augustus Frederick (George IV)
1841	Albert Edward (Edward VII)
1901	George (George V)
1910	Edward (Edward VIII)
1958	Charles, son of Elizabeth II

PRINCESSES ROYAL

The style Princess Royal is conferred at the Sovereign's discretion
on his or her eldest daughter. It is an honorary title, held for life,
and cannot be inherited or passed on. It was first conferred on
Princess Mary, daughter of Charles I, in approximately 1642.

*c.*1642	Princess Mary (1631–60), daughter of Charles I
1727	Princess Anne (1709–59), daughter of George II
1766	Princess Charlotte (1766–1828), daughter of George III
1840	Princess Victoria (1840–1901), daughter of Victoria
1905	Princess Louise (1867–1931), daughter of Edward VII
1932	Princess Mary (1897–1965), daughter of George V
1987	Princess Anne (b. 1950), daughter of Elizabeth II

Precedence

ENGLAND AND WALES

The Sovereign
The Prince Philip, Duke of
 Edinburgh
The Prince of Wales
The Sovereign's younger sons
The Sovereign's grandsons
The Sovereign's cousins
Archbishop of Canterbury
Lord High Chancellor
Archbishop of York
The Prime Minister
Lord President of the Council
Speaker of the House of Commons
Lord Privy Seal
Ambassadors and High
 Commissioners
Lord Great Chamberlain
Earl Marshal
Lord Steward of the Household
Lord Chamberlain of the Household
Master of the Horse
Dukes, according to their patent of
 creation:
 (1) of England
 (2) of Scotland
 (3) of Great Britain
 (4) of Ireland
 (5) those created since the Union
Ministers and Envoys
Eldest sons of Dukes of Blood Royal
Marquesses, according to their
 patent of creation:
 (1) of England
 (2) of Scotland
 (3) of Great Britain
 (4) of Ireland
 (5) those created since the Union
Dukes' eldest sons
Earls, according to their patent of
 creation:
 (1) of England
 (2) of Scotland
 (3) of Great Britain
 (4) of Ireland
 (5) those created since the Union
Younger sons of Dukes of Blood
 Royal
Marquesses' eldest sons
Dukes' younger sons
Viscounts, according to their patent
 of creation:
 (1) of England
 (2) of Scotland
 (3) of Great Britain
 (4) of Ireland
 (5) those created since the Union
Earls' eldest sons
Marquesses' younger sons
Bishops of London, Durham and
 Winchester
Other English Diocesan Bishops,
 according to seniority of
 consecration

Suffragan Bishops, according to
 seniority of consecration
Secretaries of State, if of the degree
 of a Baron
Barons, according to their patent of
 creation:
 (1) of England
 (2) of Scotland
 (3) of Great Britain
 (4) of Ireland
 (5) those created since the Union
Treasurer of the Household
Comptroller of the Household
Vice-Chamberlain of the Household
Secretaries of State under the degree
 of Baron
Viscounts' eldest sons
Earls' younger sons
Barons' eldest sons
Knights of the Garter
Privy Counsellors
Chancellor of the Exchequer
Chancellor of the Duchy of
 Lancaster
Lord Chief Justice of England
Master of the Rolls
President of the Family Division
Vice-Chancellor
Lords Justices of Appeal
Judges of the High Court
Viscounts' younger sons
Barons' younger sons
Sons of Life Peers
Baronets, according to date of patent
Knights of the Thistle
Knights Grand Cross of the Bath
Members of the Order of Merit
Knights Grand Commanders of the
 Star of India
Knights Grand Cross of St Michael
 and St George
Knights Grand Commanders of the
 Indian Empire
Knights Grand Cross of the Royal
 Victorian Order
Knights Grand Cross of the British
 Empire
Companions of Honour
Knights Commanders of the Bath
Knights Commanders of the Star of
 India
Knights Commanders of St Michael
 and St George
Knights Commanders of the Indian
 Empire
Knights Commanders of the Royal
 Victorian Order
Knights Commanders of the British
 Empire
Knights Bachelor
Vice-Chancellor of the County
 Palatine of Lancaster
Judges of the Technology and
 Construction Court
Circuit judges and judges of the
 Mayor's and City of London Court
Companions of the Bath

Companions of the Star of India
Companions of St Michael and
 St George
Companions of the Indian Empire
Commanders of the Royal Victorian
 Order
Commanders of the British Empire
Companions of the Distinguished
 Service Order
Lieutenants of the Royal Victorian
 Order
Officers of the British Empire
Companions of the Imperial Service
 Order
Eldest sons of younger sons of Peers
Baronets' eldest sons
Eldest sons of Knights, in the same
 order as their fathers
Members of the Royal Victorian
 Order
Members of the British Empire
Younger sons of the younger sons
 of Peers
Baronets' younger sons
Younger sons of Knights, in the
 same order as their fathers
Naval, Military, Air, and other
 Esquires by office

SCOTLAND

The Sovereign
The Prince Philip, Duke of
 Edinburgh
The Lord High Commissioner to the
 General Assembly (while that
 Assembly is sitting)
The Duke of Rothesay (eldest son of
 the Sovereign)
The Sovereign's younger sons
The Sovereign's cousins
Lord-Lieutenant
Lord Provosts of those Cities
Sheriffs Principal, successively,
 within their own localities and
 during holding of office
Lord Chancellor of Great Britain
Moderator of the General Assembly
 of the Church of Scotland
Keepers of the Great Seal
The Presiding Officer
The Secretary of State for Scotland
Hereditary Lord High Constable of
 Scotland
Hereditary Master of the Household
Dukes, in same order as in England
Eldest sons of Dukes of the Blood
 Royal
Marquesses, as in England
Dukes' eldest sons
Earls, as in England
Younger sons of Dukes of Blood
 Royal
Marquesses' eldest sons
Dukes' younger sons
Lord Justice General
Lord Clerk Register
Lord Advocate

The Advocate-General
Lord Justice Clerk
Viscounts, as in England
Earls' eldest sons
Marquesses' younger sons
Lord-Barons, as in England
Viscounts' eldest sons
Earls' younger sons
Lord-Barons' eldest sons
Knights of the Garter
Knights of the Thistle
Privy Counsellors
Senators of College of Justice (Lords of Session)
Viscounts' younger sons
Lord-Barons' younger sons
Sons of Life Peers
Baronets
Knights Grand Cross, Grand Commander, and Knight Commanders, as in England
Solicitor-General for Scotland
Lord Lyon King of Arms
Sheriffs Principal, except as shown above
Knights Bachelor
Sheriffs
Commanders of the Royal Victorian Order
Companions of Orders, as in England
Commanders of the British Empire
Lieutenants of the Royal Victorian Order
Companions of the Distinguished Service Order
Eldest sons of younger sons of Peers
Baronets' eldest sons
Knights' eldest sons, as in England
Members of the Royal Victorian Order
Baronets' younger sons
Knights' younger sons
Queen's Counsel
Esquires
Gentlemen

WOMEN

Women take the same rank as their husbands or as their brothers; but the daughter of a peer marrying a commoner retains her title as Lady or Honourable. Daughters of peers rank next immediately after the wives of their elder brothers, and before their younger brothers' wives. Daughters of peers marrying peers of lower degree take the same order of precedence as that of their husbands; thus the daughter of a Duke marrying a Baron becomes of the rank of Baroness only, while her sisters married to commoners retain their rank and take precedence of the Baroness. Merely official rank on the husband's part does not give any similar precedence to the wife.

Peeresses in their own right take the same precedence as peers of the same rank, i.e. from their date of creation.

LOCAL PRECEDENCE

England and Wales
No written code of county or city order of precedence has been promulgated, but in counties the Lord Lieutenant stands first, and secondly (normally) the Sheriff, and therefore in cities and boroughs the Lord Lieutenant has social precedence over the Mayor; but at city or borough functions the Lord Mayor or Mayor will preside. At Oxford and Cambridge the High Sheriff takes precedence of the Vice-Chancellor.

Scotland
The Lord Provosts of the city districts of Aberdeen, Dundee, Edinburgh and Glasgow are Lord Lieutenants for those districts *ex officio* and take precedence as such.

Forms of address

It is only possible to cover here the forms of address for peers, baronets and knights, their wife and children, and Privy Counsellors. Greater detail should be sought in one of the publications devoted to the subject.

Both formal and social forms of address are given where usage differs; nowadays, the social form is generally preferred to the formal, which increasingly is used only for official documents and on very formal occasions.

F_ represents forename
S_ represents surname

BARON – *Envelope (formal)*, The Right Hon. Lord_; *(social)*, The Lord_. *Letter (formal)*, My Lord; *(social)*, Dear Lord_. *Spoken*, Lord_.

BARON'S WIFE – *Envelope (formal)*, The Right Hon. Lady_; *(social)*, The Lady_. *Letter (formal)*, My Lady; *(social)*, Dear Lady_. *Spoken*, Lady_.

BARON'S CHILDREN – *Envelope*, The Hon. F_ S_. *Letter*, Dear Mr/Miss/Mrs S_. *Spoken*, Mr/Miss/Mrs S_.

BARONESS IN OWN RIGHT – *Envelope*, may be addressed in same way as a Baron's wife or, if she prefers *(formal)*, The Right Hon. the Baroness_; *(social)*, The Baroness_. Otherwise as for a Baron's wife.

BARONET – *Envelope*, Sir F_ S_. Bt. *Letter (formal)*, Dear Sir; *(social)*, Dear Sir F_. *Spoken*, Sir F_.

BARONET'S WIFE – *Envelope*, Lady S_. *Letter (formal)*, Dear Madam; *(social)*, Dear Lady S_. *Spoken*, Lady S_.

COUNTESS IN OWN RIGHT – As for an Earl's wife.

COURTESY TITLES – The heir apparent to a Duke, Marquess or Earl uses the highest of his father's other titles as a courtesy title. The holder of a courtesy title is not styled The Most Hon. or The Right Hon., and in correspondence 'The' is omitted before the title. The heir apparent to a Scottish title may use the title 'Master' *(see below)*.

DAME – *Envelope*, Dame F_ S_, followed by appropriate post-nominal letters. *Letter (formal)*, Dear Madam; *(social)*, Dear Dame F_. *Spoken*, Dame F_.

DUKE – *Envelope (formal)*, His Grace the Duke of_; *(social)*, The Duke of_. *Letter (formal)*, My Lord Duke; *(social)*, Dear Duke. *Spoken (formal)*, Your Grace; *(social)*, Duke.

DUKE'S WIFE – *Envelope (formal)*, Her Grace the Duchess of_; *(social)*, The Duchess of_. *Letter (formal)*, Dear Madam; *(social)*, Dear Duchess. *Spoken*, Duchess.

DUKE'S ELDEST SON – *see* Courtesy titles.

Duke's YOUNGER SONS – *Envelope*, Lord F_ S_. *Letter (formal)*, My Lord; *(social)*, Dear Lord F_. *Spoken (formal)*, My Lord; *(social)*, Lord F_.

DUKE'S DAUGHTER – *Envelope*, Lady F_ S_. *Letter (formal)*, Dear Madam; *(social)*, Dear Lady F_. *Spoken*, Lady F_.

EARL – *Envelope (formal)*, The Right Hon. the Earl (of)_; *(social)*, The Earl (of)_. *Letter (formal)*, My Lord; *(social)*, Dear Lord_. *Spoken (formal)*, My Lord; *(social)*, Lord_.

EARL'S WIFE – *Envelope (formal)*, The Right Hon. the Countess (of)_; *(social)*, The Countess (of)_. *Letter (formal)*, Madam; *(social)*, Lady_. *Spoken (formal)*, Madam; *(social)*, Lady_.

EARL'S CHILDREN – *Eldest son, see* Courtesy titles. *Younger sons*, The Hon. F_ S_ (for forms of address, *see* Baron's children). *Daughters*, Lady F_ S_ (for forms of address, *see* Duke's daughter).

KNIGHT (Bachelor) – *Envelope*, Sir F_ S_. *Letter (formal)*, Dear Sir; *(social)*, Dear Sir F_. *Spoken*, Sir F_.

KNIGHT (ORDERS OF CHIVALRY) – *Envelope*, Sir F_ S_, followed by appropriate post-nominal letters. Otherwise as for Knight Bachelor.

KNIGHT'S WIFE – As for Baronet's wife.

LIFE PEER – As for Baron/Baroness in own right.

LIFE PEER'S WIFE – As for Baron's wife.

LIFE PEER'S CHILDREN – As for Baron's children.

MARQUESS – *Envelope (formal)*, The Most Hon. the Marquess of_; *(social)*, The Marquess of_. *Letter (formal)*, My Lord; *(social)*, Dear Lord_. *Spoken (formal)*, My Lord; *(social)*, Lord_.

MARQUESS'S WIFE – *Envelope (formal)*, The Most Hon. the Marchioness of_; *(social)*, The Marchioness of_. *Letter (formal)*, Madam; *(social)*, Dear Lady_. *Spoken*, Lady_.

MARQUESS'S CHILDREN – *Eldest son, see* Courtesy titles. *Younger sons*, Lord F_ S_ (for forms of address, *see* Duke's younger sons). *Daughters*, Lady F_ S_ (for forms of address, *see* Duke's daughter).

MASTER – The title is used by the heir apparent to a Scottish peerage, though usually the heir apparent to a Duke, Marquess or Earl uses his courtesy title rather than 'Master'. *Envelope*, The Master of_. *Letter (formal)*, Dear Sir; *(social)*, Dear Master of_. *Spoken (formal)*, Master, or Sir; *(social)*, Master, or Mr S_.

MASTER'S WIFE – Addressed as for the wife of the appropriate peerage style, otherwise as Mrs S_.

PRIVY COUNSELLOR – *Envelope*, The Right (or Rt.) Hon. F_ S_. *Letter*, Dear Mr/Miss/Mrs S_. *Spoken*, Mr/Miss/Mrs S_. It is incorrect to use the letters PC after the name in conjunction with the prefix The Right Hon., unless the Privy Counsellor is a peer below the rank of Marquess and so is styled The Right Hon. because of his rank. In this case only, the post-nominal letters may be used in conjunction with the prefix The Right Hon.

VISCOUNT – *Envelope (formal)*, The Right Hon. the Viscount_; *(social)*, The Viscount_. *Letter (formal)*, My Lord; *(social)*, Dear Lord_. *Spoken*, Lord_.

VISCOUNT'S WIFE – *Envelope (formal)*, The Right Hon. the Viscountess_; *(social)*, The Viscountess_. *Letter (formal)*, Madam; *(social)*, Dear Lady_. *Spoken*, Lady_.

VISCOUNT'S CHILDREN – As for Baron's children.

The Peerage

and Members of the House of Lords

The rules which govern the creation and succession of peerages are extremely complicated. There are, technically, five separate peerages, the Peerage of England, of Scotland, of Ireland, of Great Britain, and of the United Kingdom. The Peerage of Great Britain dates from 1707 when an Act of Union combined the two kingdoms of England and Scotland and separate peerages were discontinued. The Peerage of the United Kingdom dates from 1801 when Great Britain and Ireland were combined under an Act of Union. Some Scottish peers have received additional peerages of Great Britain or of the United Kingdom since 1707, and some Irish peers additional peerages of the United Kingdom since 1801.

The Peerage of Ireland was not entirely discontinued from 1801 but holders of Irish peerages, whether pre-dating or created subsequent to the Union of 1801, were not entitled to sit in the House of Lords if they had no additional English, Scottish, Great Britain or United Kingdom peerage. However, they are eligible for election to the House of Commons and to vote in parliamentary elections. An Irish peer holding a peerage of a lower grade which enabled him to sit in the House of Lords was introduced there by the title which enabled him to sit, though for all other purposes he was known by his higher title.

In the Peerage of Scotland there is no rank of Baron; the equivalent rank is Lord of Parliament, abbreviated to 'Lord' (the female equivalent is 'Lady'). All peers of England, Scotland, Great Britain or the United Kingdom who are 21 years or over, and of British, Irish or Commonwealth nationality were entitled to sit in the House of Lords until the House of Lords Act 1999, when hereditary peers lost the right to sit. Ninety-two hereditaries are to remain in the House of Lords for a transitional period. In the list below, these peers are indicated by the **. Ten hereditary peers received Life Peerages in 1999 enabling them to remain in the reformed chamber, and two further hereditary peers reverted to sitting by virtue of the Life Peerages they already held.

Hereditary Women Peers

Most hereditary peerages pass on death to the nearest male heir, but there are exceptions, and several are held by women.

A woman peer in her own right retains her title after marriage, and if her husband's rank is the superior she is designated by the two titles jointly, the inferior one second. Her hereditary claim still holds good in spite of any marriage whether higher or lower. No rank held by a woman can confer any title or even precedence upon her husband but the rank of a hereditary woman peer in her own right is inherited by her eldest son (or in some cases daughter).

After the Peerage Act 1963, hereditary women peers in their own right were entitled to sit in the House of Lords, subject to the same qualifications as men, until the House of Lords Act 1999.

Life Peers

Since 1876 non-hereditary or life peerages have been conferred on certain eminent judges to enable the judicial functions of the House of Lords to be carried out. These Lords are known as Lords of Appeal or law lords and, to date, such appointments have all been male.

Since 1958 life peerages have been conferred upon distinguished men and women from all walks of life, giving them seats in the House of Lords in the degree of Baron or Baroness. They are addressed in the same way as hereditary Lords and Barons, and their children have similar courtesy titles.

Peerages Extinct Since the Last Edition

BARONY: Wyfold (*cr.* 1919)

LIFE PEERAGES: Annan (*cr.* 1965); Braine of Wheatley (*cr.* 1992); Charteris of Amisfield (*cr.* 1978); Grey of Naunton (*cr.* 1968); Henderson of Brompton (*cr.* 1984); Hughes (*cr.* 1961); Jakobovits (*cr.* 1988); Mackenzie-Stuart (*cr.* 1988); Macleod of Borve (*cr.* 1971); Montague of Oxford (*cr.* 1997); Oram (*cr.* 1976); White (*cr.* 1970)

Disclaimer of Peerages

The Peerage Act 1963 enables peers to disclaim their peerages for life. Peers alive in 1963 could disclaim within twelve months after the passing of the Act (31 July 1963); a person subsequently succeeding to a peerage may disclaim within 12 months after the date of succession, or of reaching 21, if later. The disclaimer is irrevocable but does not affect the descent of the peerage after the disclaimant's death, and children of a disclaimed peer may, if they wish, retain their precedence and any courtesy titles and styles borne as children of a peer. The disclaimer permitted the disclaimant to sit in the House of Commons if elected as an MP. As the House of Lords Act 1999 removed hereditary peers from the House of Lords, they are now entitled to sit in the House of Commons without having to disclaim their titles.

The following peerages are currently disclaimed:

EARLDOMS: Durham (1970); Selkirk (1994)

VISCOUNTCIES: Camrose (1995); Hailsham (1963); Stansgate (1963)

BARONIES: Altrincham (1963); Merthyr (1977); Reith (1972); Sanderson of Ayot (1971); Silkin (1972)

PEERS WHO ARE MINORS (i.e. under 21 years of age)

MARQUESSES: Bristol (*b.* 1979)

EARLS: Craven (*b.* 1989)

BARONS: Elphinstone (*b.* 1980)

Contractions and Symbols

s.	Scottish title
I.	Irish title
*	The peer holds also an Imperial title, specified after the name by Engl., Brit. or UK
**	Hereditary peer remaining in the House of Lords for a transitional period
°	there is no 'of' in the title
b.	born
s.	succeeded
m.	married
w.	widower or widow
M.	minor
†	heir not ascertained at time of going to press

Hereditary Peers

PEERS OF THE BLOOD ROYAL

Style, His Royal Highness The Duke of _/His Royal Highness the Earl of_
Style of address (*formal*) May it please your Royal Highness; (*informal*) Sir

Created	Title, order of succession, name, etc.	Heir
	Dukes	
1337	*Cornwall*, Charles, Prince of Wales, s. 1952 (*see* page 117)	‡
1398	*Rothesay*, Charles, Prince of Wales, s. 1952 (*see* page 117)	‡
1986	*York* (1st), The Prince Andrew, Duke of York (*see* page 117)	None
1928	*Gloucester* (2nd), Prince Richard, Duke of Gloucester, s. 1974 (*see* page 118)	Earl of Ulster (*see* page 118)
1934	*Kent* (2nd), Prince Edward, Duke of Kent, s. 1942 (*see* page 118)	Earl of St Andrews (*see* page 118)
	Earl	
1999	*Wessex* (1st), The Prince Edward, Earl of Wessex (*see* page 117)	None

‡ The title is not hereditary but is held by the Sovereign's eldest son from the moment of his birth or the Sovereign's accession

DUKES

Coronet, Eight strawberry leaves
Style, His Grace the Duke of _
Wife's style, Her Grace the Duchess of _
Eldest son's style, Takes his father's second title as a courtesy title
Younger sons' style, 'Lord' before forename and family name
Daughters' style, 'Lady' before forename and family name
For forms of address, *see* page 135

Created	Title, order of succession, name, etc.	Heir
1868 I.	*Abercorn* (5th), James Hamilton, KG, b. 1934, s. 1979, m.	Marquess of Hamilton, b. 1969
1701 S.*	*Argyll* (12th) *and 5th UK Duke*, Argyll, 1892, Ian Campbell, b. 1937, s. 1973, m.	Marquess of Lorne, b. 1968
1703 S.	*Atholl* (11th), John Murray, b. 1929, s. 1996, m.	Marquess of Tullibardine, b. 1960
1682	*Beaufort* (11th), David Robert Somerset, b. 1928, s. 1984, w.	Marquess of Worcester, b. 1952
1694	*Bedford* (13th), John Robert Russell, b. 1917, s. 1953, m.	Marquess of Tavistock, b. 1940
1663 S.*	*Buccleuch and Queensberry* (11th) (S 1684) *and 8th Eng. Earl, Doncaster, 1662* (9th), Walter Francis John Montagu Douglas Scott, KT, VRD, b. 1923, s. 1973, m.	Earl of Dalkeith, KBE, b. 1954
1694	*Devonshire* (11th), Andrew Robert Buxton Cavendish, KG, MC, PC, b. 1920, s. 1950, m.	Marquess of Hartington, CBE, b. 1944
1947	*Edinburgh* (1st), HRH The Prince Philip, Duke of Edinburgh, (*see* page 117)	HRH The Earl of Wessex, (*see* page 117)
1900	*Fife* (3rd) *and 12th Scott. Earl, Southesk, 1633, S. 1992* (3rd), James George Alexander Bannerman Carnegie, b. 1929, s. 1959, (*see* page 128)	Earl of Southesk, b. 1961
1675	*Grafton* (11th), Hugh Denis Charles FitzRoy, KG, b. 1919, s. 1970, m.	Earl of Euston, b. 1947
1643 S.*	*Hamilton* (15th), *and Brandon* (12th) (*Brit.* 1711), Angus Alan Douglas Douglas-Hamilton, b. 1938, s. 1973.	Marquess of Douglas and Clydesdale, b. 1978
1766 I.*	*Leinster* (8th) *and 8th Brit. Visct.*, Leinster, 1747 *Premier Peer of Scotland* Gerald FitzGerald, b. 1914, s. 1976, m. *Premier Duke and Marquess of Ireland*	Marquess of Kildare, b. 1948
1719	*Manchester* (12th), Angus Charles Drogo Montagu, b. 1938, s. 1985, m.	Viscount Mandeville, b. 1962
1702	*Marlborough* (11th), John George Vanderbilt Henry Spencer-Churchill, b. 1926, s. 1972, m.	Marquess of Blandford, b. 1955
1707 S.*	** *Montrose* (8th) *and 6th Brit. Earl, Graham, 1722*, James Graham, b. 1935, s. 1992, m.	Marquess Graham, b. 1973
1483	** *Norfolk* (17th) *and 12th Eng. Baron, Beaumont* 1309, S. 1971 *and 4th UK Baron Howard of Glossop* 1869 S. 1972, Miles Francis Stapleton Fitzalan-Howard, KG, GCVO, CB, CBE, MC, b. 1915, s. 1975, m. *Premier Duke and Earl Marshal*	Earl of Arundel and Surrey b. 1956
1766	*Northumberland* (12th), Ralph George Algernon Percy, b. 1956, s. 1995, m.	Earl Percy, b. 1984

Created	Title, order of succession, name, etc.	Heir
1675	Richmond (10th) and Gordon (5th) (UK 1876) and Scott. Duke Lennox (10th), Charles Henry Gordon Lennox, b. 1929, s. 1989, m.	Earl of March and Kinrara, b. 1955
1707 S.*	Roxburghe (10th) and 5th UK Earl, Innes, 1837, Guy David Innes-Ker, b. 1954, s. 1974, m. Premier Baronet of Scotland	Marquess of Bowmont and Cessford b. 1981
1703	Rutland (11th), David Charles Robert Manners, b. 1959, s. 1999, m.	Hon. Edward J. F. M., b. 1965
1684	St Albans (14th), Murray de Vere Beauclerk, b. 1939, s. 1988, m.	Earl of Burford, b. 1965
1547	Somerset (19th), John Michael Edward Seymour, b. 1952, s. 1984, m.	Lord Seymour, b. 1982
1833	Sutherland and 5th UK Earl, Ellesmere, 1846, S. 1944 (6th), John Sutherland Egerton, TD, b. 1915, s. 1963, m.	Francis R. E., b. 1940
1814	Wellington (8th) and 9th Irish Earl, Mornington, 1760, Arthur Valerian Wellesley, KG, LVO, OBE, MC, b. 1915, s. 1972, m.	Marquess of Douro, b. 1945
1874	Westminster (6th), Gerald Cavendish Grosvenor, OBE, b. 1951, s. 1979, m.	Earl Grosvenor, b. 1991

MARQUESSES

Coronet, Four strawberry leaves alternating with four silver balls
Style, The Most Hon. the Marquess (of) _ . In Scotland the spelling 'Marquis' is preferred for pre-Union creations
Wife's style, The Most Hon. the Marchioness (of) _
Eldest son's style, Takes his father's second title as a courtesy title
Younger sons' style, 'Lord' before forename and family name
Daughters' style, 'Lady' before forename and family name
For forms of address, see page 135

Created	Title, order of succession, name, etc.	Heir
1916	Aberdeen (6th) and Temair and Scott. Earl, Aberdeen, 1682, Alastair Ninian John Gordon, b. 1920, s. 1984, m.	Earl Haddo, b. 1955
1876	Abergavenny (6th), Christopher George Charles Nevill, b. 1955, s. 2000, m.	David M. R., Nevill, b. 1941
1821	Ailesbury (8th), Michael Sidney Cedric Brudenell-Bruce, b. 1926, s. 1974	Earl of Cardigan, b. 1952
1831	Ailsa (8th) and 20th Scott. Earl, Cassillis, 1509, Archibald Angus Charles Kennedy, b. 1956, s. 1994	Lord David Kennedy, b. 1958
1815	Anglesey (7th), George Charles Henry Victor Paget, b. 1922, s. 1947, m.	Earl of Uxbridge, b. 1950
1789	Bath (7th), Alexander George Thynn, b. 1932, s. 1992, m.	Viscount Weymouth, b. 1974
1826	Bristol (8th), Frederick William Augustus Hervey, b. 1979, s. 1999, 1	Hon. Ronald F. W., H., b. 1919
1796	Bute (7th) and 12th Scott. Earl, Dumfries, 1633, John Colum Crichton-Stuart, b. 1958, s. 1993, m.	Earl of Dumfries, b. 1989
1812	°Camden (6th), David George Edward Henry Pratt, b. 1930, s. 1983	Earl of Brecknock, b. 1965
1815	** Cholmondeley (7th) and 11th Irish Visct., Cholmondeley, 1661, David George Philip Cholmondeley, b. 1960, s. 1990, 4, Lord Great Chamberlain	Charles G., C., b. 1959
1816	°Conyngham (7th) and 7th UK Baron, Minster, 1821, Frederick William Henry Francis Conyngham, b. 1924, s. 1974, m.	Earl of Mount Charles, b. 1951
1791 I.*	Donegall (7th) and 7th Brit. Baron, Fisherwick, 1970 and 6th Brit. Baron Templemore, 1831, s. 1953, Dermot Richard Claud Chichester, LVO, b. 1916, s. 1975, m.	Earl of Belfast, b. 1952
1789 I.*	Downshire (8th) and 8th Brit. Earl, Hillsborough, 1772, (Arthur) Robin Ian Hill, b. 1929, s. 1989, m.	Earl of Hillsborough, b. 1959
1801 I.*	Ely (8th) and 8th UK Baron, Loftus, 1801, Charles John Tottenham, b. 1913, s. 1969, m.	Viscount Loftus, b. 1943
1801	Exeter (8th), (William) Michael Anthony Cecil, b. 1935, s. 1988, m.	Lord Burghley, b. 1970
1800 I.*	Headfort (6th) and 4th UK Baron, Kenlis, 1831, Thomas Geoffrey Charles Michael Taylour, b. 1932, s. 1960, m.	Earl of Bective, b. 1959
1793	Hertford (9th) and 10th Irish Baron, Conway, 1712, Henry Jocelyn Seymour, b. 1958, s. 1997, m.	Earl of Yarmouth, b. 1993
1599 S.*	Huntly (13th) and 5th UK Baron, Meldrum, 1815, Granville Charles Gomer Gordon, b. 1944, s. 1987, m., Premier Marquess of Scotland	Earl of Aboyne, b. 1973
1784	Lansdowne (9th) and 9th Irish Earl, Kerry, 1723, Charles Maurice Mercer NairnePetty-Fitzmaurice, b. 1941, s. 1999, m.	Earl of Shelbourne, b. 1970
1902	Linlithgow (4th) and 10th Scott. Earl, Hopetoun, 1703, Adrian John Charles Hope, b. 1946, s. 1987, m.	Earl of Hopetown, b. 1971
1816 I.*	Londonderry (9th) and 6th UK Earl, Vane, 1823, Alexander Charles Robert Vane-Tempest-Stewart, b. 1937, s. 1955, m.	Viscount Castlereagh, b. 1972
1701 S.*	Lothian (12th) and 6th UK Baron, Kerr, 1821, Peter Francis Walter Kerr, KCVO, b. 1922, s. 1940, m.	Earl of Ancram, PC, MP, b. 1945
1917	Milford Haven (4th), George Ivar Louis Mountbatten, b. 1961, s. 1970, m.	Earl of Medina, b. 1991

Created	Title, order of succession, name, etc.	Heir
1838	*Normanby (5th) and 9th Irish Baron, Mulgrave,* 1767,	Earl of Mulgrave, *b.* 1994
	Constantine Edmund Walter Phipps, *b.* 1954, *s.* 1994, *m.*	
1812	*Northampton* (7th), Spencer Douglas David Compton, *b.* 1946, *s.* 1978, *m.*	Earl of Compton, *b.* 1973
1682 S.	*Queensberry* (12th), David Harrington Angus Douglas, *b.* 1929, *s.* 1954	Viscount Drumlanrig, *b.* 1967
1926	*Reading* (4th), Simon Charles Henry Rufus Isaacs, *b.* 1942, *s.* 1980, *m.*	Viscount Erleigh, *b.* 1986
1789	*Salisbury* (6th), Robert Edward Peter Cecil, *b.* 1916, *s.* 1972, *m.*,	Viscount Cranborne, PC,
	see also Baron Cecil, page 150	*b.* 1946 (*see also* Baron Cecil)
1800 I.*	*Sligo (11th) and 11th UK Baron, Monteagle,* 1806, Jeremy Ulick Browne,	Sebastian U., *B.*, *b.* 1964
	b. 1939, *s.* 1991, *m.*	
1787	°*Townshend* (7th), George John Patrick Dominic Townshend,	Viscount Raynham, *b.* 1945
	b. 1916, *s.* 1921, *w.*	
1694	°*Tweeddale (13th) and 4th UK Baron Tweddale,* 1881,	Lord, Charles D. M., *H.*,
	Edward Douglas John Hay, *b.* 1947, *s.* 1979	*b.* 1947
1789 I.*	*Waterford (8th) and 8th Brit. Baron Tyrone,* 1786, John Hubert de la Poer	Ear of Tyronel, *b.* 1958
	Beresford, *b.* 1933, *s.* 1934, *m.*	
1551	*Winchester* (18th), Nigel George Paulet, *b.* 1941, *s.* 1968, *m.*,	Earl of Wiltshire, *b.* 1969
	Premier Marquess of England	
1892	*Zetland (4th) and 6th UK Earl, Zetland,* 1838 *and 7th Brit.*	Earl of Ronaldshay, *b.* 1965
	Baron Dundas, 1794, Lawrence Mark Dundas, *b.* 1937, *s.* 1989, *m.*	

EARLS

Coronet, Eight silver balls on stalks alternating with eight gold strawberry leaves
Style, The Right Hon. the Earl (of) _
Wife's style, The Right Hon. the Countess (of) _
Eldest son's style, Takes his father's second title as a courtesy title
Younger sons' style, 'The Hon.' before forename and family name
Daughters' style, 'Lady' before forename and family name
For forms of address, *see* page 135

Created	Title, order of succession, name, etc.	Heir
1639 S.	*Airlie* (13th), David George Coke Patrick, OGILVY, KT, GCVO, PC,	Lord Ogilvy, *b.* 1958
	Royal Victorian, *b.* 1926, *s.* 1968, *m.*	
1696	*Albemarle* (10th), Rufus Arnold Alexis Keppel, *b.* 1965, *s.* 1979,	Crispian W. J., *K.*, *b.* 1948
1952	°*Alexander of Tunis* (2nd), Shane William Desmond Alexander,	Hon. Brian J., *A.*, *b.* 1939
	b. 1935, *s.* 1969, *m.*	
1662	*Annandale and Hartfell* (11th), Patrick Andrew Wentworth	Lord Johnstone, *b.* 1971
	Hope Johnstone, claim, *b.* 1941, *m.*	
1789	°*Annesley* (10th), Patrick Annesley, *b.* 1924, *s.* 1979, *m.*	Hon. Philip H., *A.*, *b.* 1927
1785	*Antrim* (9th), Alexander Randal Mark McDonnell, *b.* 1935, *s.* 1977, *m.*	Viscount Dunluce, *b.* 1967
1762	** *Arran and 5th UK Baron Sudley,* 1884 (9th), Arthur Desmond	Paul A., *G.*, CMG, CVO, *b.* 1921
	Colquhoun Gore, *b.* 1938, *s.* 1983, *m.*	
1955	°** *Attlee* (3rd), John Richard Attlee, *b.* 1956, *s.* 1991, *m.*	None
1714	*Aylesford* (11th), Charles Ian Finch-Knightley, *b.* 1918, *s.* 1958, *w.*	Lord Guernsey, *b.* 1947
1937	°** *Baldwin of Bewdley* (4th), Edward Alfred Alexander Baldwin, *b.* 1938,	Viscount Corvedale, *b.* 1973
	s. 1976, *m.*	
1922	*Balfour* (4th), Gerald Arthur James Balfour, *b.* 1925, *s.* 1968, *m.*	Eustace A. G., *B.*, *b.* 1921
1772	°*Bathurst* (8th), Henry Allen John Bathurst, *b.* 1927, *s.* 1943, *m.*	Lord Apsley, *b.* 1961
1919	°*Beatty* (3rd), David Beatty, *b.* 1946, *s.* 1972, *m.*	Viscount Borodale, *b.* 1973
1797	*Belmore* (8th), John Armar Lowry-Corry, *b.* 1951, *s.* 1960, *m.*	Viscount Corry, *b.* 1985
1739	*Bessborough (11th) and 8th UK Baron Duncannon,* 1834,	Viscount Duncannon, *b.* 1941
	Arthur Mountifort Longfield Ponsonby, *b.* 1912, *s.* 1993, *m.*	
1815	*Bradford* (7th), Richard Thomas Orlando Bridgeman, *b.* 1947, *s.* 1981, *m.*	Viscount Newport, *b.* 1980
1469	*Buchan (17th) and 8th UK Baron Erskine,* 1806, Malcolm Harry Erskine,	Lord Cardross, *b.* 1960
	b. 1930, *s.* 1984, *m.*	
1746	*Buckinghamshire* (10th), (George) Miles Hobart-Hampden,	Sir John Hobart, Bt., *b.* 1945
	b. 1944, *s.* 1983, *m.*	
1800	°*Cadogan* (8th), Charles Gerald John Cadogan, *b.* 1937, *s.* 1997, *m.*	Viscount Chelsea, *b.* 1966
1878	°*Cairns* (6th), Simon Dallas Cairns, CBE, *b.* 1939, *s.* 1989, *m.*	Viscount Garmoyle, *b.* 1965
1455	** *Caithness* (20th), Malcolm Ian Sinclair, PC, *b.* 1948, *s.* 1965, *w.*	Lord Berriedale, *b.* 1981
1800	*Caledon* (7th), Nicholas James Alexander, *b.* 1955, *s.* 1980, *m.*	Viscount Alexander, *b.* 1990
1661	*Carlisle (13th) and 13th Scott. Baron Ruthven of Freeland,* 1651,	Hon. Philip C. W., *H.*, *b.* 1963
	George William Beaumont Howard, *b.* 1949, *s.* 1994.	

Created	Title, order of succession, name, etc.	Heir
1793	** *Carnarvon* (7th), Henry George Reginald Molyneux Herbert, KCVO, KBE, *b.* 1924, *s.* 1987, *m.*	Lord Porchester, *b.* 1956
1748 I.*	*Carrick (10th) and 4th UK Baron Butler*, 1912, David James Theobald Somerset Butler, *b.* 1953, *s.* 1992, *m.*	Viscount Ikerrin, *b.* 1975
1800 I.	°*Castle Stewart* (8th), Arthur Patrick Avondale Stuart, *b.* 1928, *s.* 1961, *m.*	Viscount Stuart, *b.* 1953
1814	°*Cathcart (7th) and 16th Scott. Baron Cathcart*, 1447, Charles Alan Andrew Cathcart, *b.* 1952, *s.* 1999, *m.*	Lord Greenock, *b.* 1986
1647	*Cavan.* The 12th Earl died in 1988. Heir had not established his claim to the title at the time of going to press	Roger C. Lambart *b.* 1944
1827	°*Cawdor* (7th), Colin Robert Vaughan Campbell, *b.* 1962, *s.* 1993, *m.*	Hon. Frederick W., *C., b.* 1965
1801	*Chichester* (9th), John Nicholas Pelham, *b.* 1944, *s.* 1944, *m.*	Richard A. H., *P., b.* 1952
1803 I.	*Clancarty (9th) and 8th UK Visct. Clancarty*, 1823, Nicholas Power Richard Le Poer Trench, *b.* 1952, *s.* 1995.	None
1776 I.	*Clanwilliam (7th) and 5th UK Baron Clanwilliam*, 1828, John Herbert Meade, *b.* 1919, *s.* 1989, *m.*	Lord Gillford, *b.* 1960
1776	*Clarendon* (7th), George Frederick Laurence Hyde Villiers, *b.* 1933, *s.* 1955, *m.*	Lord Hyde, *b.* 1976
1620 I.	*Cork and Orrery* (14th) (I. 1660) *and 10th Brit. Baron Boyle of Marston*, 1711 (14th), John William Boyle, DSC, *b.* 1916, *s.* 1995, *m.*	Viscount Dungarvan, *b.* 1945
1850	*Cottenham* (8th), Kenelm Charles Everard Digby Pepys, *b.* 1948, *s.* 1968, *m.*	Viscount Crowhurst, *b.* 1983
1762 I.	** Courtown and 8th Brit. Baron Saltersford, 1796 (9th), James Patrick Montagu Burgoyne Winthrop, STOPFORD, *b.* 1954, *s.* 1975, *m.*	Viscount Stopford, *b.* 1988
1697	*Coventry* (11th), George William Coventry, *b.* 1934, *s.* 1940, *m.*	Francis H., *C., b.* 1912
1857	°*Cowley* (7th), Garret Graham Wellesley, *b.* 1934, *s.* 1975, *m.*	Viscount Dangan, *b.* 1965
1892	*Cranbrook* (5th), Gathorne Gathorne-Hardy, *b.* 1933, *s.* 1978, *m.*	Lord Medway, *b.* 1968
1801	*Craven* (9th), Benjamin Robert Joseph Craven, *b.* 1989, *s.* 1990, 1.	Rupert J. E., *C., b.* 1926
1398 S.*	*Crawford and Balcarres* (12th) (s. 1651) *and 5th UK Baron, Wigan*, 1826 *and Baron Balniel (life peerage)*, 1974 (29th), Robert Alexander Lindsay, KT, PC, *b.* 1927, *s.* 1975, *m., Premier Earl on Union Roll*	Lord Balniel, *b.* 1958
1861	*Cromartie* (5th), John Ruaridh Blunt Grant Mackenzie, *b.* 1948, *s.* 1989, *m.*	Viscount Tarbat, *b.* 1987
1901	*Cromer* (4th), Evelyn Rowland Esmond Baring, *b.* 1946, *s.* 1991, *m.*	Viscount Errington, *b.* 1994
1633 S.*	*Dalhousie (17th) and 5th UK Baron Ramsay*, 1875, James Hubert Ramsay, *b.* 1948, *s.* 1999, *m.*	Lord Ramsay, *b.* 1981
1725 I.	*Darnley and 20th Engl. Baron Clifton of Leighton Bromswold*, 1608 (11th), Adam Ivo Stuart Bligh, *b.* 1941, *s.* 1980, *m.*	Lord Clifton, *b.* 1968
1711	*Dartmouth* (10th), William Legge, *b.* 1949, *s.* 1997.	Hon. Rupert, *L., b.* 1951
1761	°*De La Warr* (11th), William Herbrand Sackville, *b.* 1948, *s.* 1988, *m.*	Lord Buckhurst, *b.* 1979
1622	*Denbigh and Desmond* (11th) (I. 1622) (12th), Alexander Stephen Rudolph Feilding, *b.* 1970, *s.* 1995, *m.*	William D., *F., b.* 1939
1485	*Derby* (19th), Edward Richard William Stanley, *b.* 1962, *s.* 1994, *m.*	Lord Stanley, *b.* 1998
1553	*Devon* (18th), Hugh Rupert Courtenay, *b.* 1942, *s.* 1998, *m.*	Lord Courtenay, *b.* 1975
1800 I.*	*Donoughmore (8th) and 8th UK Visct. Hutchinson*, 1821, Richard Michael John Hely-Hutchinson, *b.* 1927, *s.* 1981, *m.*	Viscount Suirdale, *b.* 1952
1661 I.*	*Drogheda (12th) and 3rd UK Baron Moore*, 1954, Henry Dermot Ponsonby Moore, *b.* 1937, *s.* 1989, *m.*	Viscount Moore, *b.* 1983
1837	*Ducie* (7th), David Leslie Moreton, *b.* 1951, *s.* 1991, *m.*	Lord Moreton, *b.* 1981
1860	*Dudley* (4th), William Humble David Ward, *b.* 1920, *s.* 1969, *m.*	Viscount Ednam, *b.* 1947
1660 S.*	** *Dundee (12th) and 2nd UK Baron Glassary*, 1954, Alexander Henry Scrymgeour, *b.* 1949, *s.* 1983, *m.*	Lord Scrymgeour, *b.* 1982
1669 S.	*Dundonald* (15th), Iain Alexander Douglas Blair Cochrane, *b.* 1961, *s.* 1986, *m.*	Lord Cochrane, *b.* 1991
1686 S.	*Dunmore* (12th), Malcolm Kenneth Murray, *b.* 1946, *s.* 1995, *m.*	Hon. Geoffrey C., *M., b.* 1949
1822 I.	*Dunraven and Mount-Earl* (7th), Thady Windham Thomas Wyndham-Quin, *b.* 1939, *s.* 1965, *m.*	None
1833	*Durham.* Antony Claud Frederick, Lambton, Disclaimed for life 1970. *b.* 1922, *s.* 1970, *m.*	Hon. Edward R., *L, b.* Hon. Edward R. *L.* (Baron Durham), *b.* 1961
1837	*Effingham (7th) and 17th Engl. Baron Howard of Effingham*, 1554, David Mowbray Algernon Howard, *b.* 1939, *s.* 1996, *m.*	Lord Howard of Effingham, *b.* 1971
1507 S.*	*Eglinton (18th) and Winton (9th) and 6th UK Earl Winton*, 1859, Archibald George Montgomerie, *b.* 1939, *s.* 1966, *m.*	Lord Montgomerie, *b.* 1966
1733 I.*	*Egmont (11th) and 9th Brit. Baron Lovel and Holland*, 1762, Frederick George Moore Perceval, *b.* 1914, *s.* 1932, *m.*	Viscount Perceval, *b.* 1934
1821	*Eldon* (5th), John Joseph Nicholas Scott, *b.* 1937, *s.* 1976, *m.*	Viscount Encombe, *b.* 1962
1633 S.*	*Elgin (11th) and Kincardine (15th)* (s. 1647) *and 4th UK Baron, Elgin*, 1849, Andrew Douglas Alexander Thomas Bruce, KT, *b.* 1924, *s.* 1968, *m.*	Lord Bruce, *b.* 1961
1789 I.*	*Enniskillen (7th) and 5th UK Baron, Grinstead*, 1815, Andrew John Galbraith Cole, *b.* 1942, *s.* 1989, *m.*	Arthur G., *C., b.* 1920

Created	Title, order of succession, name, etc.	Heir
1876 I.*	Erne (3rd) and 3rd UK Baron Fermanagh, 1876, Henry George Victor John Crichton, b. 1937, m.	Viscount Crichton, b. 1971
1452 S.	** Erroll (24th), Merlin Sereld Victor Gilbert, HAY, b. 1948, s. 1978, m. Hereditary Lord High Constable and Knight Marischal of Scotland	Lord Hay, b. 1984
1661	Essex (10th), Robert Edward de Vere Capell, b. 1920, s. 1981, m.	Viscount Essex, b. 1944
1711	°** Ferrers (13th), Robert Washington Shirley, PC, b. 1929, s. 1954, m.	Viscount Tamworth, b. 1952
1789	°Fortescue (8th), Charles Hugh Richard Fortescue, b. 1951, s. 1993, m.	Hon. Martin D., F., b. 1924
1841	Gainsborough (5th), Anthony Gerard Edward Noel, b. 1923, s. 1927, m.	Viscount Campden, b. 1950
1623 S.*	Galloway (13th) and 6th Brit. Baron of Garlies, 1796 (13th, Randolph Keith Reginald Stewart, b. 1928, s. 1978, w.	Andrew C., S., b. 1949
1703 S.*	Glasgow (10th) and 4th UK Baron, Farlie, 1897 (10th, Patrick Robin Archibald Boyle, b. 1939, s. 1984, m.	Viscount of Kelburn, b. 1978
1806 I.*	Gosford (7th) and 5th UK Baron, Worlingham, 1835, Charles David Nicholas Alexander John Sparrow, ACHESON, b. 1942, s. 1966, m.	Hon. Patrick B. V. M., A., b. 1915
1945	Gowrie (2nd) and 3rd UK Baron Ruthven of Gowrie, 1919, Alexander Patric Greysteil Hore-Ruthven, PC, b. 1939, s. 1955, m.	Viscount Ruthven of Canberra, b. 1964
1684 I.*	Granard (10th) and 5th UK Baron, Granard, 1806, Peter Arthur Edward Hastings Forbes, b. 1957, s. 1992, m.	Viscount Forbes, b. 1981
1833	°Granville (6th), Granville George Fergus Leveson-Gower, b. 1959, s. 1996, m.	Hon. Niall J., L.-G., b. 1963
1806	°Grey (6th), Richard Fleming George Charles Grey, b. 1939, s. 1963, m.	Philip K., G., b. 1940
1752	Guilford (10th), Piers Edward Brownlow North, b. 1971, s. 1999, m.	Hon. N., b. 1918
1619	Haddington (13th), John George Baillie-Hamilton, b. 1941, s. 1986, m.	Lord Binning, b. 1985
1919	°Haig (2nd), George Alexander Eugene Douglas Haig, OBE, b. 1918, s. 1928, m.	Viscount Dawick, b. 1961
1944	Halifax (3rd) and 5th UK Visct., Halifax, 1866, Charles Edward Peter Neil Wood, b. 1944, s. 1980, m.	Lord Irwin, b. 1977
1898	Halsbury (4th), Adam Edward Giffard, b. 1934, s. 2000, m.	
1754	Hardwicke (10th), Joseph Philip Sebastian Yorke, b. 1971, s. 1974,	Charles E., Y., b. 1951
1812	Harewood (7th), George Henry Hubert Lascelles, KBE, b. 1923, s. 1947, m., (see also page 127)	Viscount Lascelles, b. 1950
1742	Harrington (11th) and 8th Brit. Visct. Stanhope of Mahon, 1717, William Henry Leicester Stanhope, b. 1922, s. 1929, m.	Viscount (see also page 126), b. 1945
1809	Harrowby (7th), Dudley Danvers Granville Coutts Ryder, TD, b. 1922, s. 1987, m.	Viscount Petersham, b. 1951
1605	** Home (15th), David Alexander Cospatrick Douglas-Home, CVO, b. 1943, s. 1995, m.	Lord Dunglass, b. 1987
1821	°** Howe (7th), Frederick Richard Penn Curzon, b. 1951, s. 1984, m.	Viscount Curzon, b. 1994
1529	Huntingdon (16th), William Edward Robin Hood Hastings Bass, LVO, b. 1948, s. 1990, m.	Hon. Simon A. R. H., H. B., b. 1950
1885	Iddesleigh (4th), Stafford Henry Northcote, b. 1932, s. 1970, m.	Viscount St Cyres, b. 1957
1756	Ilchester (9th), Maurice Vivian de Touffreville Fox-Strangways, b. 1920, s. 1970, m.	Hon. Raymond G., F.-S., b. 1921
1929	Inchcape (4th), (Kenneth) Peter (Lyle) Mackay, b. 1943, s. 1994, m.	Viscount Glenapp, b. 1979
1919	Iveagh (4th), Arthur Edward Rory Guinness, b. 1969, s. 1992.	Hon. Rory M. B., G., b. 1974
1925	°Jellicoe (2nd), George Patrick John Rushworth Jellicoe, KBE, DSO, MC, PC, FRS, b. 1918, s. 1935, m.	Viscount Brocas, b. 1950
1697	Jersey (10th) and 13th Visct. Grandison, 1620, George Francis William Child Villiers, b. 1976, s. 1998.	Hon. Jamie C., V., b. 1994
1822 I.	Kilmorey (6th), Richard Francis Needham, KT, PC, b. 1942, s. 1977, m.	Viscount Newry and Morne, b. 1966
1866	Kimberley (4th), John Wodehouse, b. 1924, s. 1941, m.	Lord, b. 1951
1768 I.	Kingston (11th), Barclay Robert Edwin King-Tenison, b. 1943, s. 1948, m.	Viscount Kingsborough, b. 1969
1633 S.*	Kinnoull (15th) and 9th Brit. Baron Hay of Pedwardine, 1711, Arthur William George Patrick Hay, b. 1935, s. 1938, m.	Viscount Dupplin, b. 1962
1677 S.*	Kintore (13th) and 3rd UK Visct. Stonehaven, 1938, Michael Canning William John Keith, b. 1939, s. 1989, m.	Lord Inverurie, b. 1976
1914	°Kitchener of Khartoum (3rd), Henry Herbert Kitchener, TD, b. 1919, s. 1937,	None
1624	Lauderdale (17th), Patrick Francis Maitland, b. 1911, s. 1968, m.	Viscount Maitland, b. 1937
1837	Leicester (7th), Edward Douglas Coke, b. 1936, s. 1994, m.	Viscount Coke, b. 1965
1641 S.*	Leven (14th) and Melville (13th) (s. 1690), Alexander Robert Leslie Melville, b. 1924, s. 1947, m.	Lord Balgonie, b. 1954
1831	Lichfield (5th), Thomas Patrick John Anson, b. 1939, s. 1960.	Viscount Anson, b. 1978
1803 I.*	Limerick (6th) and 6th UK Baron Foxford, 1815, Patrick Edmund Pery, KBE, b. 1930, s. 1967, m.	Viscount Glentworth, b. 1963
1572	Lincoln (18th), Edward Horace Fiennes-Clinton, b. 1913, s. 1988, m.	Hon. Edward G., F.-C., b. 1943
1633 S.	** Lindsay (16th), James Randolph Lindesay-Bethune, b. 1955, s. 1989, m.	Viscount Garnock, b. 1990
1626	Lindsey (14th) and Abingdon (9th) (1682), Richard Henry Rupert Bertie, b. 1931, s. 1963, m.	Lord Norreys, b. 1958
1776 I.	Lisburne (8th), John David Malet Vaughan, b. 1918, s. 1965, m.	Viscount Vaughan, b. 1945

Created	Title, order of succession, name, etc.	Heir
1822 I.*	** Listowel (6th) and 4th UK Baron Hare, 1869, Francis Michael Hare, b. 1964, s. 1997, m.	Hon. Timothy P., H., b. 1966
1905	** Liverpool (5th), Edward Peter Bertram Savile Foljambe, b. 1944, s. 1969, m.	Viscount Hawkesbury, b. 1972
1945	°Lloyd George of Dwyfor (3rd), Owen Lloyd George, b. 1924, s. 1968, m.	Viscount Gwynedd, b. 1951
1785 I.*	Longford (7th) and 6th UK Baron, Silchester, 1821 and 1st UK Baron Pakenham, 1945, Francis Aungier Pakenham, KG, PC, b. 1905, s. 1961, m.	Thomas F. D., P., b. 1933
1807	Lonsdale (7th), James Hugh William Lowther, b. 1922, s. 1953, m.	Viscount Lowther, b. 1949
1838	Lovelace (5th) and 12th Brit. Baron King, 1725, Peter Axel William Locke King, b. 1951, s. 1964, m.	None
1795 I.*	Lucan (7th) and 3rd UK Baron Bingham, 1934, Richard John Bingham, b. 1934, s. 1964, m.	Lord Bingham, b. 1967
1880	Lytton (5th) and 18th Engl. Baron, Wentworth, 1529, John Peter Michael Scawen Lytton, b. 1950, s. 1985, m.	Viscount Bingham, b. 1989
1721	Macclesfield (9th), Richard Timothy George Mansfield Parker, b. 1943, s. 1992, m.	Hon. J. David G., P., b. 1945
1800	Malmesbury (6th), William James Harris, TD, b. 1907, s. 1950, w.	Viscount FitztHarris, b. 1946
1776 & 1792	Mansfield (8th) and Mansfield and 14th Scott. Visct. Stormont, 1621, William David Mungo James Murray, b. 1930, s. 1971, m.	Viscount Stormont, b. 1956
1565 S.*	**Mar and Kellie (16th) (s. 1616) (14th), James Thorne Erskine, b. 1949, s. 1994, m.	Hon. Alexander D., E., b. 1952
1785 I.	Mayo (10th), Terence Patrick Bourke, b. 1929, s. 1962,	Lord Naas, b. 1953
1627 I.*	Meath (15th) and 6th UK Baron, Chaworth, 1831, John Anthony Brabazon, b. 1941, s. 1998, m.	Lord Ardee, b. 1977
1766	Mexborough (8th), John Christopher George Savile, b. 1931, s. 1980, m.	Viscount Pollington, b. 1959
1813	Minto (6th), Gilbert Edward George Lariston Elliot-Murray-Kynynmound, OBE, b. 1928, s. 1975, m.	Viscount Melgund, b. 1953
1562 S.*	Moray (20th) and 12th Brit. Baron Stuart of Castle Stuart, 1796, Douglas John Moray Stuart, b. 1928, s. 1974, m.	Lord Downe, b. 1966
1815	Morley (6th), John St Aubyn Parker, KCVO, b. 1923, s. 1962, m.	Viscount Boringdon, b. 1956
1458	Morton (22nd), John Charles Sholto Douglas, b. 1927, s. 1976, m.	Lord Aberdour, b. 1952
1789	Mount Edgcumbe (8th), Robert Charles Edgcumbe, b. 1939, s. 1982,	Piers V., E., b. 1946
1831	Munster (7th), Anthony Charles FitzClarence, b. 1926, s. 1983, m.	None
1805	°Nelson (9th), Peter John Horatio Nelson, b. 1941, s. 1981, m.	Viscount Merton, b. 1971
1660 S.	Newburgh (12th), Don Filippo Giambattista Camillo Francesco Aldo Ma, Rospigliosi, b. 1942, s. 1986, m.	Princess Donna Benedetta F. M., R., b. 1974
1827 I.	Norbury (6th), Noel Terence Graham-Toler, b. 1939, s. 1955, m.	Viscount Glandine, b. 1967
1806 I.*	Normanton (6th) and 9th Brit. Baron, Mendip, 1794 and 4th UK Baron, Somerton, 1873, Shaun James Christian Welbore Ellis, AGAR, b. 1945, s. 1967, m.	Viscount Somerton b. 1982
1647 S.	** Northesk (14th), David John MacRae Carnegie, b. 1954, s. 1994, m.	Lord Rosehill, b. 1980
1801	** Onslow (7th), Michael William Coplestone Dillon Onslow, b. 1938, s. 1971, m.	Viscount Cranley, b. 1967
1696 S.	Orkney (9th), (Oliver) Peter St John, b. 1938, s. 1998, m.	Viscount Kirkwall, b. 1969
1328	Ormonde and Ossory. The 8th Marquess of Ormonde died in 1997, when the marquessate became extinct. The heir to his earldoms had not established his claim at the time of going to pressb. s. (see page 146)	Viscount Mountgarret, b. 1936 (see also page 146).
1925	Oxford and Asquith (2nd), Julian Edward George Asquith, KCMG, b. 1916, s. 1928, w.	Viscount Asquith, OBE, b. 1952
1929	°** Peel (3rd) and 4th UK Viscount Peel, 1895, William James Robert Peel, b. 1947, s. 1969, m.	Viscount Clanfield, b. 1976
1551	Pembroke (17th) and Montgomery (14th) (1605), Henry George Charles Alexander Herbert, b. 1939, s. 1969.	Lord Herbert, b. 1978
1605	Perth (17th), John David Drummond, PC, b. 1907, s. 1951, w.	Viscount Strathallan, b. 1935
1905	Plymouth (3rd) and 15th Engl. Baron, Windsor, 1529, Other Robert Ivor Windsor-Clive, b. 1923, s. 1943, m.	Viscount Windsor, b. 1951
1785	Portarlington (7th), George Lionel Yuill Seymour Dawson-Damer, b. 1938, s. 1959, m.	Viscount Carlow, b. 1965
1689	Portland (12th), Count Timothy Charles Robert Noel Bentinck, b. 1953, s. 1997, m.	Viscount Woodstock, b. 1984
1743	Portsmouth (10th), Quentin Gerard Carew Wallop, b. 1954, s. 1984, m.	Viscount Lymington, b. 1981
1804	Powis (8th) and 9th Irish Baron, Clive, 1762, John George Herbert, b. 1952, s. 1993, m.	Viscount Clive, b. 1979
1765	Radnor (8th), Jacob Pleydell-Bouverie, b. 1927, s. 1968, m.	Viscount Folkestone, b. 1955
1831 I.*	Ranfurly (7th) and 8th UK Baron, Ranfurly, 1826, Gerald Françoys Needham Knox, b. 1929, s. 1988, m.	Edward J., K., b. 1957
1771	Roden (10th), Robert John Jocelyn, b. 1938, s. 1993, m.	Viscount Jocelyn, b. 1989
1801	Romney (7th), Michael Henry Marsham, b. 1910, s. 1975, m.	Julian C., M., b. 1948

Created	Title, order of succession, name, etc.	Heir
1806 I.	*Rosse* (7th), William Brendan Parsons, *b.* 1936, *s.* 1979, *m.*	Lord Oxmanton, *b.* 1969
1703 S.*	*Rosebery (7th) and 3rd UK Earl Midlothian,* 1911, Neil Archibald Primrose, *b.* 1929, *s.* 1974, *m.*	Lord Dalmeny, *b.* 1967
1801	** *Rosslyn* (7th), Peter St Clair-Erskine, *b.* 1958, *s.* 1977, *m.*	Lord Loughborough, *b.* 1986
1457 S.	*Rothes* (21st), Ian Lionel Malcolm Leslie, *b.* 1932, *s.* 1975, *m.*	Lord Leslie, *b.* 1958
1861	°*Russell* (5th), Conrad Sebastian Robert Russell, FBA, *b.* 1937, *s.* 1987, *m.*	Viscount Amberley, *b.* 1968
1915	°*St Aldwyn* (3rd), Michael Henry Hicks Beach, *b.* 1950, *s.* 1992, *m.*	Hon. David S., *H. B.,* *b.* 1955
1815	*St Germans* (10th), Peregrine Nicholas Eliot, *b.* 1941, *s.* 1988,	Lord Eliot, *b.* 1966
1660	** *Sandwich* (11th), John Edward Hollister Montagu, *b.* 1943, *s.* 1995, *m.*	Viscount Hinchingbrooke, *b.* 1969
1690	*Scarbrough (12th) and 13th Irish Visct. Lumley,* 1628, Richard Aldred Lumley, *b.* 1932, *s.* 1969, *m.*	Viscount Lumley, *b.* 1973
1701 S.	*Seafield* (13th), Ian Derek Francis Ogilvie-Grant, *b.* 1939, *s.* 1969, *m.*	Viscount Reidhaven, *b.* 1963
1882	** *Selborne* (4th), John Roundell Palmer, KBE, FRS, *b.* 1940, *s.* 1971, *m.*	Viscount Wolmer, *b.* 1971
1646 S.	*Selkirk.* Disclaimed for life 1994. (*see* Lord Selkirk of Douglas, page 161)	Hon. John A., Douglas-Hamilton, *b.* 1978
1672	*Shaftesbury* (10th), Anthony Ashley-Cooper, *b.* 1938, *s.* 1961, *m.*	Lord Ashley, *b.* 1977
1756 I.*	*Shannon (9th) and 8th Brit. Baron Carleton,* 1786, Richard Bentinck Boyle, *b.* 1924, *s.* 1963,	Viscount Boyle, *b.* 1960
1442	** Shrewsbury (22nd) and Waterford and 7th Engl. Earl Talbot, 1784),, Charles Henry John Benedict Crofton Chetwynd, Chetwynd-Talbot, *b.* 1952, *s.* 1980, *m. Premier Earl of England and Ireland*	Viscount Ingestre, *b.* 1978
1961	*Snowdon (1st) and (life peer) Armstrong-Jones,* 1999, Antony Charles Robert Armstrong-Jones, GCVO, *b.* 1930, *s.m., (see also* page 117), Consta, e	Viscount Linley, *b.* 1961 (*see also* page 117)
1765	°*Spencer* (9th), Charles Edward Maurice Spencer, *b.* 1964, *s.* 1992,	Viscount Althorp, *b.* 1994
1703 S.*	*Stair (14th) and 7th UK Baron, Oxenfoord,* 1841, John David James Dalrymple, *b.* 1961, *s.* 1996.	Hon. David H., *D.,* *b.* 1963
1984	*Stockton* (2nd), Alexander Daniel Alan Macmillan, MEP, *b.* 1943, *s.* 1986, *m.*	Viscount Macmillan of Ovenden, *b.* 1974
1821	*Stradbroke* (6th), Robert Keith Rous, *b.* 1937, *s.* 1983, *m.*	Viscount Dunwich, *b.* 1961
1847	*Strafford* (8th), Thomas Edmund Byng, *b.* 1936, *s.* 1984, *m.*	Viscount Enfield, *b.* 1964
1606 S.*	*Strathmore (18th) and Kinghorne and 16th Scott. Earl, Strathmore, 1677 and 18th Scott. Earl, Kinghorne, 1606 and 5th UK Earl, Strathmore and Kinghorne,* 1937, Michael Fergus Bowes Lyon, *b.* 1957, *s.* 1987, *m.*	Lord Glamis, *b.* 1986
1603	*Suffolk (21st) and Berkshire* (14th) (1626), Michael John James George Robert Howard, *b.* 1935, *s.* 1941, *m.*	Viscount Andover, *b.* 1974
1955	*Swinton* (2nd), David Yarburgh Cunliffe-Lister, *b.* 1937, *s.* 1972, *m.*	Hon. Nicholas J., *C.-L.,* *b.* 1939
1714	*Tankerville* (10th), Peter Grey Bennet, *b.* 1956, *s.* 1980.	Revd the Hon. George A. G., *B.,* *b.* 1925
1822	°*Temple of Stowe* (8th), (Walter) Grenville Algernon Temple-Gore-Langton, *b.* 1924, *s.* 1988, *m.*	Lord Langton, *b.* 1955
1815	*Verulam (7th) and 11th Irish Visct. Grimston, 1719 and 16th Scott. Baron Forrester of Corstorphine,* 1633, John Duncan Grimston, *b.* 1951, *s.* 1973, *m.*	Viscount Grimston, *b.* 1978
1729	°*Waldegrave* (13th), James Sherbrooke Waldegrave, *b.* 1940, *s.* 1995, *m.*	Viscount Chewton, *b.* 1986
1759	*Warwick (9th) and Brooke* (9th) (Brit. 1746), Guy David Greville, *b.* 1957, *s.* 1996, *m.*	Lord Brooke, *b.* 1982
1633 S.*	*Wemyss (12th) and March* (8th) *and 5th UK Baron Wemyss,* 1821, Francis David Charteris, KT, *b.* 1912, *s.* 1937, *m.*	Lord Neidpath, *b.* 1948
1621 I.	*Westmeath* (13th), William Anthony Nugent, *b.* 1928, *s.* 1971, *m.*	Hon. Sean C. W., *N.,* *b.* 1965
1624	*Westmorland* (16th), Anthony David Francis Henry Fane, *b.* 1951, *s.* 1993, *m.*	Hon. Harry St C., *F.,* *b.* 1953
1876	*Wharncliffe* (5th), Richard Alan Montagu Stuart Wortley, *b.* 1953, *s.* 1987, *m.*	Viscount Carlton, *b.* 1980
1801	*Wilton (7th) and 8th UK Baron Ebury* (1857), Francis Egerton Grosvenor, *b.* 1934, *s.* 1999, *m.*	Hon. Julian Francis Martin, Grosvenor, *b.* 1959
1628	*Winchilsea and Nottingham* (12th) (1681) (17th), Daniel James Hatfield Finch Hatton, *b.* 1967, *s.* 1999, *m.*	Robin Heneage, *F.-H.,* *b.* 1939
1766	°*Winterton* (8th), (Donald) David Turnour, *b.* 1943, *s.* 1991, *m.*	Robert C., *T.,* *b.* 1950
1956	*Woolton* (3rd), Simon Frederick Marquis, *b.* 1958, *s.* 1969, *m.*	None
1837	*Yarborough* (8th), Charles John Pelham, *b.* 1963, *s.* 1991, *m.*	Lord Worsley, *b.* 1990

COUNTESSES IN THEIR OWN RIGHT

Style, The Right Hon. the Countess (of) _
Husband, Untitled
Children's style, As for children of an Earl
For forms of address, *see* page 135

Created	Title, order of succession, name, etc.	Heir
1643 S.	Dysart (11th in line), Rosamund Agnes, GREAVES, *b*. 1914, *s*. 1975.	Lady Katherine *Grant of Rothiemurchus, b*. 1918
1633 S.	*Loudoun* (13th in line), Barbara Huddleston Abney-Hastings, *b*. 1919, *s*. 1960, *m*.	Lord Mauchline, *b*. 1942
c.1115 S.	*Mar* (31st in line), Margaret of Mar, *b*. 1940, *s*. 1975, *m*., *Premier Earldom of Scotland*	Mistress of Mar, *b*. 1963
1947	°*Mountbatten of Burma* (2nd in line), Patricia Edwina Victoria Knatchbull, CBE, *b*. 1924, *s*. 1979, *m*.	Lord Romsey, *b*. 1947 *(see also* page 148)
c.1235 S.	*Sutherland* (24th in line), Elizabeth Millicent Sutherland, *b*. 1921, *s*. 1963, *m*.	Lord Strathnaver, *b*. 1947

VISCOUNTS

Coronet, Sixteen silver balls
Style, The Right Hon. the Viscount _
Wife's style, The Right Hon. the Viscountess _
Children's style, 'The Hon.' before forename and family name
In Scotland, the heir apparent to a Viscount may be styled 'The Master of _ (title of peer)'
For forms of address, *see* page 135

Created	Title, order of succession, name, etc.	Heir
1945	*Addison* (4th), William Matthew Wand Addison, *b*. 1945, *s*. 1992, *m*.	Hon. Paul W., *A., b*. 1973
1946	*Alanbrooke* (3rd), Alan Victor Harold Brooke, *b*. 1932, *s*. 1972.	None
1919	** *Allenby* (3rd), Lt.-Col. Michael Jaffray Hynman Allenby, *b*. 1931, *s*. 1984, *m*.	Hon. Henry J. H., *A., b*. 1968
1911	*Allendale* (3rd), Wentworth Hubert Charles Beaumont, *b*. 1922, *s*. 1956.	Hon. Wentworth P. I., *B., b*. 1948
1642 S.	*of Arbuthnott* (16th), John Campbell Arbuthnott, KT, CBE, DSC, FRSE, *b*. 1924, *s*. 1966, *m*.	Master of Arbuthnott, *b*. 1950
1751 I.	*Ashbrook* (11th), Michael Llowarch Warburton Flower, *b*. 1935, *s*. 1995, *m*.	Hon. Rowland F. W., *F., b*. 1975
1917	** *Astor* (4th) William Waldorf Astor, *b*. 1951, *s*. 1966, *m*.	Hon. William W., *A., b*. 1979
1781 I.	*Bangor* (8th), William Maxwell David Ward, *b*. 1948, *s*. 1993, *m*.	Hon. E. Nicholas, *W., b*. 1953
1925	*Bearsted* (5th), Nicholas Alan Samuel, *b*. 1950, *s*. 1996, *m*.	Hon. Harry R., *S., b*. 1988
1963	*Blakenham* (2nd), Michael John Hare, *b*. 1938, *s*. 1982, *m*.	Hon. Caspar J., *H., b*. 1972
1935	** *Bledisloe* (3rd), Christopher Hiley Ludlow Bathurst, QC, *b*. 1934, *s*. 1979.	Hon. Rupert E. L., *B., b*. 1964
1712	*Bolingbroke* (7th) *and St John* (8th) (1716), Kenneth Oliver Musgrave St John, *b*. 1927, *s*. 1974.	Hon. Henry F., *St J., b*. 1957
1960	*Boyd of Merton* (2nd), Simon Donald Rupert Neville Lennox-Boyd, *b*. 1939, *s*. 1983, *m*.	Hon. Benjamin A., *L.-B., b*. 1964
1717 I.*	*Boyne* (11th) *and 5th UK Baron Brancepeth*, 1866, Gustavus Michael Stucley Hamilton-Russell, *b*. 1965, *s*. 1995, *m*.	Hon. Brian G., *H.-R., b*. 1940
1929	*Brentford* (4th), Crispin William Joynson-Hicks, *b*. 1933, *s*. 1983, *m*.	Hon. Paul W., *J.-H., b*. 1971
1929	** *Bridgeman* (3rd), Robin John Orlando Bridgeman, *b*. 1930, *s*. 1982, *m*.	Hon. William O. C., *B., b*. 1968
1868	*Bridport* (4th) *and 7th Duke, Bronte in Sicily, 1799 and 6th Irish Baron Bridport*, 1794, Alexander Nelson Hood, *b*. 1948, *s*. 1969, *m*.	Hon. Peregrine A. N., *H., b*. 1974
1952	** *Brookeborough* (3rd), Alan Henry Brooke, *b*. 1952, *s*. 1987, *m*.	Hon. Christopher A., *B., b*. 1954
1933	*Buckmaster* (3rd), Martin Stanley Buckmaster, OBE, *b*. 1921, *s*. 1974.	Hon. Colin J., *B., b*. 1923
1939	*Caldecote* (3rd), Piers James Hampden Inskip, *b*. 1947, *s*. 1999, *m*.	Hon. Thomas J., *I., b*. 1985
1941	*Camrose*. Disclaimed for life 1995. (*see* Baron Hartwell, page 159)	Hon. Adrian M., Berry, *b*. 1937
1954	*Chandos* (3rd), Thomas Orlando Lyttelton, *b*. 1953, *s*. 1980, *m*.	Hon. Oliver A., *L., b*. 1986
1665 I.*	*Charlemont* (14th) *and 18th Irish Baron Caulfield of Charlemont*, 1620, John Day Caulfeild, *b*. 1934, *s*. 1985, *m*.	Hon. John D., *C., b*. 1966
1921	*Chelmsford* (4th), Frederic Corin Piers Thesiger, *b*. 1962, *s*. 1999.	
1717 I.	*Chetwynd* (10th), Adam Richard John Casson Chetwynd, *b*. 1935, *s*. 1965, *m*.	Hon. Adam D., *C., b*. 1969
1911	*Chilston* (4th), Alastair George Akers-Douglas, *b*. 1946, *s*. 1982, *m*.	Hon. Oliver I., *A.-D., b*. 1973

Created	Title, order of succession, name, etc.	Heir
1902	Churchill (3rd) and 5th UK Baron Churchill, 1815, w., Victor George Spencer, b. 1934, s. 1973.	None to Viscountcy. To Barony, Richard H. R. S., b. 1926
1718	Cobham (11th) and 8th Irish Baron Westcote, 1776, John William Leonard Lyttelton, b. 1943, s. 1977, m.	Hon. Christopher C., L., b. 1947
1902	** Colville (4th) of Culross and 13th Scott. Baron Colville of Culcross, 1604, John Mark Alexander Colville, QC, b. 1933, s. 1945, m.	Master of Colville, b. 1959
1826	Combermere (5th), Michael Wellington Stapleton-Cotton, b. 1929, s. 1969, m.	Hon. Thomas R. W., S.-C., b. 1969
1917	Cowdray (4th) and 4th UK Baron Cowdray, 1910, Michael Orlando Weetman Pearson, b. 1944, s. 1995, m.	Hon. Peregrine J. D., P., b. 1994
1927	** Craigavon (3rd), Janric Fraser Craig, b. 1944, s. 1974.	None
1886	Cross (3rd), Assheton Henry Cross, b. 1920, s. 1932.	None
1943	Daventry (4th), James Edward FitzRoy Newdegate, b. 1960, s. 2000, m.	
1937	Davidson (2nd), John Andrew Davidson, b. 1928, s. 1970, m.	Hon. Malcolm W. M., D., b. 1934
1956	De L'Isle (2nd) and 7th UK Baron de L'Isle and Dudley, 1835, Philip John Algernon Sidney, MBE, b. 1945, s. 1991, m.	Hon. Philip W. E., S., b. 1985
1776 I.*	De Vesci (7th) and 8th Irish Baron Knapton, 1750, Thomas Eustace Vesey, b. 1955, s. 1983, m.	Hon. Oliver I., V., b. 1991
1917	Devonport (3rd), Terence Kearley, b. 1944, s. 1973.	Chester D. H., K., b. 1932
1964	Dilhorne (2nd), John Mervyn Manningham-Buller, b. 1932, s. 1980, m.	Hon. James E., M.-B., b. 1956
1622 I.	Dillon (22nd), Henry Benedict Charles Dillon, b. 1973, s. 1982.	Hon. Richard A. L., D., b. 1948
1785 I.	Doneraile (10th), Richard Allen St Leger, b. 1946, s. 1983, m.	Hon. Nathaniel W. R. St J., St L., b. 1971
1680 I.*	Downe (11th) and 4th UK Baron Dawnay, 1897, John Christian George Dawnay, b. 1935, s. 1965, m.	Hon. Richard H., D., b. 1967
1959	Dunrossil (3rd), Andrew William Reginald Morrison, b. 1953, s. 2000, m.	
1964	Eccles (2nd), John Dawson Eccles, CBE, b. 1931, s. 1999, m.	Hon. William David, E., b. 1960
1897	Esher (4th), Lionel Gordon Baliol Brett, CBE, b. 1913, s. 1963, m.	Hon. Christopher L. B., B., b. 1936
1816	Exmouth (10th), Paul Edward Pellew, b. 1940, s. 1970, m.	Hon. Edward F., P., b. 1978
1620 S.	** Falkland (15th), Lucius Edward William Plantagenet Cary, b. 1935, s. 1984, m., Premier Scottish Viscount on the Roll	Master of Falkland, b. 1963
1720	Falmouth (9th) and 26th Engl. Baron Le Despencer, 1264, George Hugh Boscawen, b. 1919, s. 1962, m.	Hon. Evelyn A. H., B., b. 1955
1720 I.*	Gage (8th) and 7th Brit. Baron Gage, 1790, (Henry) Nicolas Gage, b. 1934, s. 1993, m.	Hon. Henry W., G., b. 1975
1727 I.	Galway (12th), George Rupert Monckton-Arundell, b. 1922, s. 1980, m.	Hon. J. Philip, M.-A., b. 1952
1478 I.*	Gormanston (17th) and 5th UK Baron Gormanston, 1868, Jenico Nicholas Dudley Preston, b. 1939, s. 1940, w., Premier Viscount of Ireland	Hon. Jenico F. T., P., b. 1974
1816 I.	Gort (9th), Foley Robert Standish Prendergast Vereker, b. 1951, s. 1995, m.	Hon. Robert F. P., V., b. 1993
1900	** Goschen (4th), Giles John Harry Goschen, b. 1965, s. 1977, m.	None
1849	Gough (5th), Shane Hugh Maryon Gough, b. 1941, s. 1951,	None
1937	Greenwood (3rd), Michael George Hamar Greenwood, b. 1923, s. 1998.	
1929	Hailsham. Disclaimed for life 1963. (see Lord Hailsham of St Marylebone, page 159)	†Rt. Hon. Douglas M., Hogg, QC, MP, b. 1945
1891	Hambleden (4th), William Herbert Smith, b. 1930, s. 1948, m.	Hon. William H. B., S., b. 1955
1884	Hampden (6th), Anthony David Brand, b. 1937, s. 1975, m.	Hon. Francis A., B., b. 1970
1936	Hanworth (3rd), David Stephen Geoffrey Pollock, b. 1946, s. 1996, m.	Hon. Richard C. S., P., b. 1951
1791 I.	Harberton (10th), Thomas de Vautort Pomeroy, b. 1910, s. 1980, w.	Henry Robert, P., b. 1958
1846	Hardinge (6th), Charles Henry Nicholas Hardinge, b. 1956, s. 1984, m.	Hon. Andrew H., H., b. 1960
1791 I.	Hawarden (9th), (Robert) Connan Wyndham Leslie Maude, b. 1961, s. 1991, m.	Hon. Varian J. C. E., M., b. 1997
1960	Head (2nd), Richard Antony Head, b. 1937, s. 1983, m.	Hon. Henry J., H., b. 1980
1550	Hereford (18th), Robert Milo Leicester Devereux, b. 1932, s. 1952, Premier Viscount of England	Hon. Charles R. de B., D., b. 1975
1842	Hill (8th), Antony Rowland Clegg-Hill, b. 1931, s. 1974, m.	Peter D. R. C., C.-H., b. 1945
1796	Hood (8th) and 7th Irish Baron, Hood, 1782, Henry Lyttleton Alexander, Hood, b. 1958, s. 1999, m.	Hon. Archibald Lyttleton Samuel, H., b. 1993
1956	Ingleby (2nd), Martin Raymond Peake, b. 1926, s. 1966, w.	None
1945	Kemsley (3rd), Richard Gomer Berry, b. 1951, s. 1999, m.	Hon. Edward, A. M., b. 1960
1911	Knollys (3rd), David Francis Dudley Knollys, b. 1931, s. 1966, m.	Hon. Patrick N. M., K., b. 1962
1895	Knutsford (6th), Michael Holland-Hibbert, b. 1926, s. 1986, m.	Hon. Henry T., H.-H., b. 1959
1945	Lambert (3rd), Michael John Lambert, b. 1912, s. 1989, m.	None
1954	Leathers (3rd), Christopher Graeme Leathers, b. 1941, s. 1996, m.	Hon. James F., L., b. 1969
1922	Leverhulme (3rd), Philip William Bryce Lever, KG, TD, b. 1915, s. 1949, w.	None
1781 I.	Lifford (9th), (Edward) James Wingfield Hewitt, b. 1949, s. 1987, m.	Hon. James T. W., H., b. 1979
1921	Long (4th), Richard Gerard Long, CBE, b. 1929, s. 1967, m.	Hon. James R., L., b. 1960

Created	Title, order of succession, name, etc.	Heir
1957	*Mackintosh of Halifax* (3rd), (John) Clive Mackintosh, *b.* 1958, *s.* 1980, *m.*	Hon. Thomas H. G., *M.*, *b.* 1985
1955	*Malvern* (3rd), Ashley Kevin Godfrey Huggins, *b.* 1949, *s.* 1978.	Hon. M. James, *H.*, *b.* 1928
1945	*Marchwood* (3rd), David George Staveley Penny, *b.* 1936, *s.* 1979, *w.*	Hon. Peter G. W., *P.*, *b.* 1965
1942	*Margesson* (2nd), Francis Vere Hampden Margesson, *b.* 1922, *s.* 1965, *m.*	Maj. Hon. Richard F. D., *M.*, *b.* 1960
1660 I.*	*Massereene (14th) and Ferrard* (7th) (1797) and 7th UK Baron, Oriel, 1821, , John David Clotworthy Whyte-Melville Foster, Skeffington, *b.* 1940, *s.* 1992, *m.*	Hon. Charles J. C. W.-M. F., *S.*, *b.* 1973
1802	*Melville* (9th), Robert David Ross Dundas, *b.* 1937, *s.* 1971, *m.*	Hon. Robert H. K., *D.*, *b.* 1984
1916	*Mersey (4th) and 13th Scott. Lord Nairne*, 1681 S. 1995, Richard Maurice Clive Bigham, *b.* 1934, *s.* 1979, *m.*	Hon. Edward J. H., Bigham, MASTER OF NAIRNE, *b.* 1966
1717 I.*	*Midleton (12th) and 9th Brit. Baron Brodrick of Peper Harow*, 1796, Alan Henry Brodrick, *b.* 1949, *s.* 1988, *m.*	Hon. Ashley R., *B.*, *b.* 1980
1962	*Mills* (3rd), Christopher Philip Roger Mills, *b.* 1956, *s.* 1988, *m.*	None
1716 I.	*Molesworth* (12th), Robert Bysse Kelham Molesworth, *b.* 1959, *s.* 1997.	Hon. William J. C., *M.*, *b.* 1960
1801 I.*	*Monck (7th) and 4th UK Baron, Monck*, 1866, Charles Stanley Monck, *b.* 1953, *s.* 1982.	Hon. George S., *M.*, *b.* 1957
1957	*Monckton of Brenchley* (2nd), Maj.-Gen. Gilbert Walter Riversdale Monckton, CB, OBE, MC, *b.* 1915, *s.* 1965, *m.*	Hon. Christopher W., *M.*, *b.* 1952
1946	*Montgomery of Alamein* (2nd), David Bernard Montgomery, CBE, *b.* 1928, *s.* 1976, *m.*	Hon. Henry D., *M.*, *b.* 1954
1550 I.*	*Mountgarret (17th) and 4th UK Baron Mountgarret*, 1911, Richard Henry Piers Butler, *b.* 1936, *s.* 1966, *m.*	Hon. Piers J. R., *B.*, *b.* 1961
1952	*Norwich* (2nd), John Julius Cooper, CVO, *b.* 1929, *s.* 1954, *m.*	Hon. Jason C. D. B., *C.*, *b.* 1959
1651 S.	** *of Oxfuird* (13th), George Hubbard Makgill, CBE, *b.* 1934, *s.* 1986, *m.*	Master, *b.* 1969
1873	*Portman* (10th), Christopher Edward Berkeley Portman, *b.* 1958, *s.* 1999, *m.*	Hon. Luke O. B., *P.*, *b.* 1984
1743 I.*	*Powerscourt (10th) and 4th UK Baron Powerscourt*, 1885, Mervyn Niall Wingfield, *b.* 1935, *s.* 1973, *m.*	Hon. Mervyn A., *W.*, *b.* 1963
1900	*Ridley* (4th), Matthew White Ridley, KG, GCVO, TD, *b.* 1925, *s.* 1964, *m.*, Lord Steward	Hon. Matthew W., *R.*, *b.* 1958
1960	*Rochdale* (2nd), St John Durival Kemp, *b.* 1938, *s.* 1993, *m.*	Hon. Jonathan H. D., *K.*, *b.* 1961
1919	*Rothermere* (4th), Harold Jonathan Esmond Vere Harmsworth, *b.* 1967, *s.* 1998, *m.*	Hon. Esmond Vyvyan, *H.*, *b.* 1967
1937	*Runciman* (3rd) *of Doxford and 4th UK Baron, Runciman*, 1933, Walter Garrison Runciman (Garry), CBE, FBA, *b.* 1934, *s.* 1989, *m.*	Hon. David W., *R.*, *b.* 1967
1918	** *St Davids (3rd) and 20th Engl. Baron Strange of Knokin*, 1299 *and 8th Engl. Baron, Hungerford*, 1426 *and Baron De Moleyns*, 1445, Colwyn Jestyn John Philipps, *b.* 1939, *s.* 1991, *m.*	Hon. Rhodri C., *P.*, *b.* 1966
1801	*St Vincent* (7th), Ronald George James Jervis, *b.* 1905, *s.* 1940, *m.*	Hon. Edward R. J., *J.*, *b.* 1951
1937	*Samuel* (3rd), David Herbert Samuel, OBE, PH.D., *b.* 1922, *s.* 1978, *m.*	Hon. Dan J., *S.*, *b.* 1925
1911	*Scarsdale (3rd) and 7th Brit. Baron Scarsdale*, 1761, Francis John Nathaniel Curzon, *b.* 1924, *s.* 1977, *m.*	Hon. Peter G. N., *C.*, *b.* 1949
1905	*Selby* (5th), Edward Thomas William Gully, *b.* 1967, *s.* 1997, *m.*	Hon. Christopher R. T., *G.*, *b.* 1993
1805	*Sidmouth* (7th), John Tonge Anthony Pellew Addington, *b.* 1914, *s.* 1976, *m.*	Hon. Jeremy F., *A.*, *b.* 1947
1940	** *Simon* (3rd), Jan David Simon, *b.* 1940, *s.* 1993, *m.*	None
1960	** *Slim* (2nd), John Douglas Slim, OBE, *b.* 1927, *s.* 1970, *m.*	Hon. Mark W. R., *S.*, *b.* 1960
1954	*Soulbury* (2nd), James Herwald Ramsbotham, *b.* 1915, *s.* 1971.	Hon. Sir Peter E., *R.*, GCMG, GCVO, *b.* 1919
1776 I.	*Southwell* (7th), Pyers Anthony Joseph Southwell, *b.* 1930, *s.* 1960, *m.*	Hon. Richard A. P., *S.*, *b.* 1956
1942	*Stansgate* Disclaimed for life 1963. (*Rt. Hon. Anthony Neil Wedgwood Benn*, MP, *b.* 1925, *s.* 1960, *m.*	Stephen M. W., *B.*, *b.* 1951
1959	*Stuart of Findhorn* (3rd), James Dominic Stuart, *b.* 1948, *s.* 1999, *m.*	Andrew M., *J.* Dominic, *S.*, *b.* 1957
1957	** *Tenby* (3rd), William Lloyd George, *b.* 1927, *s.* 1983, *m.*	Hon. Timothy H. G., *L. G.*, *b.* 1962
1952	*Thurso* (3rd), John Archibald Sinclair, *b.* 1953, *s.* 1995, *m.*	Hon. James A. R., *S.*, *b.* 1984
1721	*Torrington* (11th), Timothy Howard St George Byng, *b.* 1943, *s.* 1961, *m.*	John L., *B.*, MC, *b.* 1919
1936	*Trenchard* (3rd), Hugh Trenchard, *b.* 1951, *s.* 1987, *m.*	Hon. Alexander T., *T.*, *b.* 1978
1921	*Ullswater* (2nd), Nicholas James Christopher Lowther, PC, *b.* 1942, *s.* 1949, *m.*	Hon. Benjamin J., *L.*, *b.* 1975
1621 I.	*Valentia* (15th), Richard John Dighton Annesley, *b.* 1929, *s.* 1983, *m.*	Hon. Francis W. D., *A.*, *b.* 1959
1952	** *Waverley* (3rd), John Desmond Forbes Anderson, *b.* 1949, *s.* 1990.	None
1938	*Weir* (3rd), William Kenneth James Weir, *b.* 1933, *s.* 1975, *m.*	Hon. James W. H., *W.*, *b.* 1965
1918	*Wimborne (4th) and 5th UK Baron Wimborne*, 1880, Ivor Mervyn Vigors Guest, *b.* 1968, *s.* 1993.	Hon. Julian J., *G.*, *b.* 1945

BARONS/LORDS

Coronet, Six silver balls
Style, The Right Hon. the Lord _. In the Peerage of Scotland there is no rank of Baron; the equivalent rank is Lord of Parliament (*see* page 136) and Scottish peers should always be styled 'Lord', never 'Baron'
Wife's style, The Right Hon. the Lady _
Children's style, 'The Hon.' before forename and family name
In Scotland, the heir apparent to a Lord may be styled 'The Master of _ (title of peer)'
For forms of address, *see* page 135

Created	Title, order of succession, name, etc.	Heir
1911	*Aberconway* (3rd), Charles Melville McLaren, *b.* 1913, *s.* 1953, *m.*	Hon. H. Charles, *M.*, *b.* 1948
1873	** *Aberdare* (4th), Morys George Lyndhurst Bruce, KBE, PC, *b.* 1919, *s.* 1957, *m.*	Hon. Alastair J. L., *B.*, *b.* 1947
1835	*Abinger* (8th), James Richard Scarlett, *b.* 1914, *s.* 1943, *m.*	Hon. James H., *S.*, *b.* 1959
1869	*Acton* (4th), Richard Gerald Lyon-Dalberg-Acton, *b.* 1941, *s.* 1989, *m.*	Hon. John C. F. H., *L.-D.-A.*, *b.* 1966
1887	*Addington* (6th), Dominic Bryce Hubbard, *b.* 1963, *s.* 1982,	Hon. Michael W. L., *H.*, *b.* 1965
1896	*Aldenham (6th) and Hunsdon and Hunsdon* (4th) (1923), Vicary Tyser Gibbs, *b.* 1948, *s.* 1986, *m.*	Hon. Humphrey W. F., *G.*, *b.* 1989
1962	*Aldington* (1st) and 1st Baron Low (Life Peer 1999), Toby Austin, Richard William Low, KCMG, CBE, DSO, TD, PC, *b.* 1914.	Hon. Charles H. S., *L.*, *b.* 1948
1945	*Altrincham*. Disclaimed for life 1963. (*John Edward Poynder Grigg*, *b.* 1924, *s.* 1955, *m*).	Hon. Anthony U. D. D., *G.*, *b.* 1934
1929	*Alvingham* (2nd), Maj.-Gen. Robert Guy Eardley Yerburgh, CBE, *b.* 1926, *s.* 1955, *m.*	Capt. Hon. Robert R. G., *Y.*, *b.* 1956
1892	*Amherst of Hackney* (4th) William Hugh Amherst Cecil, *b.* 1940, *s.* 1980, *m.*	Hon. H. William A., *C.*, *b.* 1968
1881	*** *Ampthill* (4th), Geoffrey Denis Erskine Russell, CBE, PC, *b.* 1921, *s.* 1973,	Hon. David W. E., *R.*, *b.* 1947
1947	*Amwell* (3rd), Keith Norman Montague, *b.* 1943, *s.* 1990, *m.*	Hon. Ian K., *M.*, *b.* 1973
1863	*Annaly* (6th), Luke Richard White, *b.* 1954, *s.* 1990, *m.*	Hon. Luke H., *W.*, *b.* 1990
1885	*Ashbourne* (4th), Edward Barry Greynville Gibson, *b.* 1933, *s.* 1983, *m.*	Hon. Edward C. d'O., *G.*, *b.* 1967
1835	*Ashburton* (7th), John Francis Harcourt Baring, KG, KCVO, *b.* 1928, *s.* 1991, *m.*	Hon. Mark F. R., *B.*, *b.* 1958
1892	*Ashcombe* (4th), Henry Edward Cubitt, *b.* 1924, *s.* 1962, *m.*	Mark E., *C.*, *b.* 1964
1911	*Ashton of Hyde* (3rd), Thomas John Ashton, TD, *b.* 1926, *s.* 1983, *m.*	Hon. Thomas H., *A.*, *b.* 1958
1800 I.	*Ashtown* (7th), Nigel Clive Crosby Trench, KCMG, *b.* 1916, *s.* 1990, *m.*	Hon. Roderick N. G., *T.*, *b.* 1944
1956	*** *Astor of Hever* (3rd), John Jacob Astor, *b.* 1946, *s.* 1984, *m.*	Hon. Charles G. J., *A.*, *b.* 1990
1789 I.*	*Auckland* (10th) and 10th Brit. Baron Auckland, 1793, Robert Ian Burnard Eden, *b.* 1962, *s.* 1997, *m.*	Hon. Ronald J., *E.*, *b.* 1931
1313	*Audley.* The 25th Lord Audley died in July 1997, leaving three co-heiresses	
1900	*Avebury* (4th), Eric Reginald Lubbock, *b.* 1928, *s.* 1971, *m.*	Hon. Lyulph A. J., *L.*, *b.* 1954
1718 I.	*Aylmer* (13th), Michael Anthony Aylmer, *b.* 1923, *s.* 1982, *m.*	Hon. A. Julian, *A.*, *b.* 1951
1929	*Baden-Powell* (3rd), Robert Crause Baden-Powell, *b.* 1936, *s.* 1962, *m.*	Hon. David M., *B.-P.*, *b.* 1940
1780	*Bagot* (9th), Heneage Charles Bagot, *b.* 1914, *s.* 1979, *m.*	Hon. C. H. Shaun, *B.*, *b.* 1944
1953	*Baillieu* (3rd), James William Latham Baillieu, *b.* 1950, *s.* 1973, *m.*	Hon. Robert L., *B.*, *b.* 1979
1607 S.	*Balfour of Burleigh* (8th), Robert Bruce, FRSE, *b.* 1927, *s.* 1967, *m.*	Hon. Victoria B., *b.* 1973
1945	*Balfour of Inchrye* (2nd), Ian Balfour, *b.* 1924, *s.* 1988, *m.*	None
1924	*Banbury of Southam* (3rd), Charles William Banbury, *b.* 1953, *s.* 1981, *m.*	None
1698	*Barnard* (11th), Harry John Neville Vane, TD, *b.* 1923, *s.* 1964.	Hon. Henry F. C., *V.*, *b.* 1959
1887	*Basing* (5th), Neil Lutley Sclater-Booth, *b.* 1939, *s.* 1983, *m.*	Hon. Stuart W., *S.-B.*, *b.* 1969
1917	*Beaverbrook* (3rd), Maxwell William Humphrey Aitken, *b.* 1951, *s.* 1985, *m.*	Hon. Maxwell F., *A.*, *b.* 1977
1647 S.	*Belhaven and Stenton* (13th), Robert Anthony Carmichael Hamilton, *b.* 1927, *s.* 1961, *m.*	Master of Belhaven, *b.* 1953
1848 I.	*Bellew* (7th), James Bryan Bellew, *b.* 1920, *s.* 1981, *m.*	Hon. Bryan E., *B.*, *b.* 1943
1856	*Belper* (5th), Richard Henry Strutt, *b.* 1941, *s.* 1999, *m.*	Michael H., Richard H., *S.*, *b.* 1969
1938	*Belstead* (2nd), John Julian Ganzoni, PC, *b.* 1932, *s.* 1958.	None
1421	*Berkeley* (18th), Anthony Fitzhardinge Gueterbock, OBE, *b.* 1939, *s.* 1992, *m.*	Hon. Thomas F., *G.*, *b.* 1969
1922	*Bethell* (4th), Nicholas William Bethell, MEP, *b.* 1938, *s.* 1967, *m.*	Hon. James N., *B.*, *b.* 1967

Created	Title, order of succession, name, etc.	Heir
1938	*Bicester* (3rd), Angus Edward Vivian Smith, *b.* 1932, *s.* 1968,	Hugh C. V., *S.*, *b.* 1934
1903	*Biddulph* (5th), (Anthony) Nicholas Colin Maitland Biddulph, *b.* 1959, *s.* 1988, *m.*	Hon. Robert J., *M. B.*, *b.* 1994
1938	*Birdwood* (3rd), Mark William Ogilvie Birdwood, *b.* 1938, *s.* 1962, *m.*	None
1958	*Birkett* (2nd), Michael Birkett, *b.* 1929, *s.* 1962, *m.*	Hon. Thomas, *B.*, *b.* 1982
1907	*Blyth* (4th), Anthony Audley Rupert Blyth, *b.* 1931, *s.* 1977, *m.*	Hon. Riley A. J., *B.*, *b.* 1955
1797	*Bolton* (7th), Richard William Algar Orde-Powlett, *b.* 1929, *s.* 1963, *m.*	Hon. Harry A. N., *O.-P.*, *b.* 1954
1452 S.	*Borthwick* (24th), John Hugh Borthwick, *b.* 1940, *s.* 1997, *m.*	Hon. James H. A., *B. of Glengelt*, *b.* 1940
1922	*Borwick* (4th), James Hugh Myles Borwick, MC, *b.* 1917, *s.* 1961, *m.*	Hon. Robin S., *B.*, *b.* 1927
1761	*Boston* (10th), Timothy George Frank Boteler Irby, *b.* 1939, *s.* 1978, *m.*	Hon. George W. E. B., *I.*, *b.* 1971
1942	** *Brabazon of Tara* (3rd), Ivon Anthony Moore-Brabazon, *b.* 1946, *s.* 1974, *m.*	Hon. Benjamin R., *M.-B.*, *b.* 1983
1880	*Brabourne* (7th), John Ulick Knatchbull, CBE, *b.* 1924, *s.* 1943, *m.*	Lord, *b.* 1947 (*see* page 144)
1925	*Bradbury* (3rd), John Bradbury, *b.* 1940, *s.* 1994, *m.*	Hon. John, *B.*, *b.* 1973
1962	*Brain* (2nd), Christopher Langdon Brain, *b.* 1926, *s.* 1966, *m.*	Hon. Michael C., *B.*, DM, FRCP, *b.* 1928
1938	*Brassey of Apethorpe* (3rd), David Henry Brassey, OBE, *b.* 1932, *s.* 1967, *m.*	Hon. Edward, *B.*, *b.* 1964
1788	*Braybrooke* (10th), Robin Henry Charles Neville, *b.* 1932, *s.* 1990, *m.*	George, *N.*, *b.* 1943
1957	** *Bridges* (2nd), Thomas Edward Bridges, GCMG, *b.* 1927, *s.* 1969, *m.*	Hon. Mark T., *B.*, *b.* 1954
1945	*Broadbridge* (4th), Martin Hugh Broadbridge, *b.* 1929, *s.* 2000, *m.*	
1933	*Brocket* (3rd), Charles Ronald George Nall-Cain, *b.* 1952, *s.* 1967, *m.*	Hon. Alexander C. C., *N.-C.*, *b.* 1984
1860	** *Brougham and Vaux* (5th), Michael John Brougham, CBE, *b.* 1938, *s.* 1967	Hon. Charles W., *B.*, *b.* 1971
1945	*Broughshane* (3rd), (William) Kensington Davison, DSO, DFC, *b.* 1914, *s.* 1995.	None
1776	*Brownlow* (7th), Edward John Peregrine Cust, *b.* 1936, *s.* 1978, *m.*	Hon. Peregrine E. Q., *C.*, *b.* 1974
1942	*Bruntisfield* (2nd), John Robert Warrender, OBE, MC, TD, *b.* 1921, *s.* 1993, *m.*	Hon. Michael J. V., *W.*, *b.* 1949
1950	*Burden* (3rd), Andrew Philip Burden, *b.* 1959, *s.* 1995.	Hon. Fraser W. E., *B.*, *b.* 1964
1529	*Burgh* (7th), Alexander Peter Willoughby Leith, *b.* 1935, *s.* 1959, *m.*	Hon. A. Gregory D., *L.*, *b.* 1958
1903	** *Burnham* (6th), Hugh John Frederick Lawson, *b.* 1931, *s.* 1993, *m.*	Hon. Harry F. A., *L.*, *b.* 1968
1897	*Burton* (3rd), Michael Evan Victor Baillie, *b.* 1924, *s.* 1962, *m.*	Hon. Evan M. R., *B.*, *b.* 1949
1643	*Byron* (13th), Robert James Byron, *b.* 1950, *s.* 1989, *m.*	Hon. Charles R. G., *B.*, *b.* 1990
1937	*Cadman* (3rd), John Anthony Cadman, *b.* 1938, *s.* 1966, *m.*	Hon. Nicholas A. J., *C.*, *b.* 1977
1945	*Calverley* (3rd), Charles Rodney Muff, *b.* 1946, *s.* 1971, *m.*	Hon. Jonathan E., *M.*, *b.* 1975
1383	*Camoys* (7th), (Ralph) Thomas Campion George Sherman, STONOR, GCVO, PC, *b.* 1940, *s.* 1976, *m.*	Lord Chamberlain, Hon. R. William R. T., *S.*, *b.* 1974
1715 I.	*Carbery* (11th), Peter Ralfe Harrington Evans-Freke, *b.* 1920, *s.* 1970, *m.*	Hon. Michael P., *E.-F.*, *b.* 1942
1834 I.*	*Carew and 7th UK Baron, Carew*, 1838 (7th), Patrick Thomas Conolly-Carew, *b.* 1938, *s.* 1994, *m.*	Hon. William P., *C.-C.*, *b.* 1973
1916	*Carnock* (4th), David Henry Arthur Nicolson, *b.* 1920, *s.* 1982.	Nigel, *N.*, MBE, *b.* 1917
1796 I.*	*Carrington (6th) and 6th Brit. Baron Carrington*, 1797, Peter Alexander Rupert Carington, KG, GCMG, CH, MC, PC, *b.* 1919, *s.* 1938, *m.*	Hon. Rupert F. J., *C.*, *b.* 1948
1812	*Castlemaine* (8th), Roland Thomas John Handcock, MBE, *b.* 1943, *s.* 1973, *m.*	Hon. Ronan M. E., *H.*, *b.* 1989
1936	*Catto* (2nd), Stephen Gordon Catto, *b.* 1923, *s.* 1959, *m.*	Hon. Innes G., *C.*, *b.* 1950
1918	*Cawley* (3rd), Frederick Lee Cawley, *b.* 1913, *s.* 1954, *m.*	Hon. John F., *C.*, *b.* 1946
1603	*Cecil.* A subsidiary title of the Marquess of Salisbury. His heir Viscount Cranborne, PC, was given a Writ in Acceleration in this title to enable him to sit in the House of Lords whilst his father is still alive	
1937	*Chatfield* (2nd), Ernle David Lewis Chatfield, *b.* 1917, *s.* 1967, *m.*	
1858	*Chesham* (6th), Nicholas Charles Cavendish, *b.* 1941, *s.* 1989, *m.*	Hon. Charles G. C., *C.*, *b.* 1974
1945	*Chetwode* (2nd), Philip Chetwode, *b.* 1937, *s.* 1950, *m.*	Hon. Roger, *C.*, *b.* 1968
1945	*Chorley* (2nd), Roger Richard Edward Chorley, *b.* 1930, *s.* 1978, *m.*	Hon. Nicholas R. D., *C.*, *b.* 1966
1858	*Churston* (5th), John Francis Yarde-Buller, *b.* 1934, *s.* 1991, *m.*	Hon. Benjamin F. A., *Y.-B.*, *b.* 1974
1946	*Citrine* (3rd), Ronald Eric Citrine, *b.* 1919, *s.* 1997, *m.*	None
1800	*Clanmorris* (8th), Simon John Ward Bingham, *b.* 1937, *s.* 1988, *m.*	Robert D. de B., *B.*, *b.* 1942
1672	*Clifford of Chudleigh* (14th), Thomas Hugh Clifford, *b.* 1948, *s.* 1988, *m.*	Hon. Alexander T. H., *C.*, *b.* 1985
1299	*Clinton* (22nd), Gerard Nevile Mark Fane Trefusis, *b.* 1934, *m.*	Hon. Charles P. R. F., *T.*, *b.* 1962
1955	*Clitheroe* (2nd), Ralph John Assheton, *b.* 1929, *s.* 1984, *m.*	Hon. Ralph C., *A.*, *b.* 1962
1919	*Clwyd* (3rd), (John) Anthony Roberts, *b.* 1935, *s.* 1987, *m.*	Hon. J. Murray, *R.*, *b.* 1971
1948	*Clydesmuir* (3rd), David Ronald Colville, *b.* 1949, *s.* 1996, *m.*	Hon. Richard, *C.*, *b.* 1980

Created	Title, order of succession, name, etc.	Heir
1960	Cobbold (2nd), David Antony Fromanteel Lytton Cobbold, b. 1937, s. 1987, m.	Hon. Henry F., L. C., b. 1962
1919	Cochrane of Cults (4th), (Ralph Henry) Vere Cochrane, b. 1926, s. 1990, m.	Hon. Thomas H. V., C., b. 1957
1954	Coleraine (2nd), (James) Martin (Bonar) Law, b. 1931, s. 1980, m.	Hon. James P. B., L., b. 1975
1873	Coleridge (5th), William Duke Coleridge, b. 1937, s. 1984, m.	Hon. James D., C., b. 1967
1946	Colgrain (3rd), David Colin Campbell, b. 1920, s. 1973, m.	Hon. Alastair C. L., C., b. 1951
1917	** Colwyn (3rd), (Ian) Anthony Hamilton-Smith, CBE, b. 1942, s. 1966, m.	Hon. Craig P., H.-S., b. 1968
1956	Colyton (2nd), Alisdair John Munro Hopkinson, b. 1958, s. 1996, m.	Hon. James P. M., H., b. 1983
1841	Congleton (8th), Christopher Patrick Parnell, b. 1930, s. 1967, m.	Hon. John P. C., P., b. 1959
1927	Cornwallis (3rd), Fiennes Neil Wykeham Cornwallis, OBE, b. 1921, s. 1982, m.	Hon. F. W. Jeremy, C., b. 1946
1874	Cottesloe (5th), Cdr. John Tapling Fremantle, b. 1927, s. 1994, m.	Hon. Thomas F. H., F., b. 1966
1929	Craigmyle (4th), Thomas Columba Shaw, b. 1960, s. 1998, m.	Hon. Alexander F., S., b. 1988
1899	Cranworth (3rd), Philip Bertram Gurdon, b. 1940, s. 1964, m.	Hon. Sacha W. R., G., b. 1970
1959	** Crathorne (2nd), Charles James Dugdale, b. 1939, s. 1977, m.	Hon. Thomas A. J., D., b. 1977
1892	Crawshaw (5th), David Gerald Brooks, b. 1934, s. 1997, m.	Hon. John P., B., b. 1938
1940	Croft (3rd), Bernard William Henry Page Croft, b. 1949, s. 1997, m.	None
1797 I.	Crofton (7th), Guy Patrick Gilbert Crofton, b. 1951, s. 1989, m.	Hon. E. Harry P., C., b. 1988
1375	Cromwell (7th), Godfrey John Bewicke-Copley, b. 1960, s. 1982, m.	Hon. David G., B.-C., b. 1997
1947	Crook (2nd), Douglas Edwin Crook, b. 1926, s. 1989, m.	Hon. Robert D. E., C., b. 1955
1920	Cullen of Ashbourne (2nd), Charles Borlase Marsham Cokayne, MBE, b. 1912, s. 1932, w.	Hon. Edmund W. M., C., b. 1916
1914	Cunliffe (3rd), Roger Cunliffe, b. 1932, s. 1963, m.	Hon. Henry, C., b. 1962
1927	Daresbury (4th), Peter Gilbert Greenall, b. 1953, s. 1996, m.	Hon. Thomas E., G., b. 1984
1924	Darling (2nd), Robert Charles Henry Darling, b. 1919, s. 1936, m.	Hon. R. Julian H., D., b. 1944
1946	Darwen (3rd), Roger Michael Davies, b. 1938, s. 1988, m.	Hon. Paul, D., b. 1962
1932	Davies (3rd), David Davies, b. 1940, s. 1944, m.	Hon. David D., D., b. 1975
1812 I.	Decies (7th), Marcus Hugh Tristram de la Poer Beresford, b. 1948, s. 1992, m.	Hon. Robert M. D., de la P. B., b. 1988
1299	de Clifford (27th), John Edward Southwell Russell, b. 1928, s. 1982, m.	Hon. William S., R., b. 1930
1851	De Freyne (7th), Francis Arthur John French, b. 1927, s. 1935, m.	Hon. Fulke C. A. J., F., b. 1957
1821	Delamere (5th), Hugh George Cholmondeley, b. 1934, s. 1979, m.	Hon. Thomas P. G., C., b. 1968
1838	de Mauley (6th), Gerald John Ponsonby, b. 1921, s. 1962, m.	Hon. Col. Thomas M., P., TD, b. 1930
1937	** Denham (2nd), Bertram Stanley Mitford Bowyer, KBE, PC, b. 1927, s. 1948, m.	Hon. Richard G. G., B., b. 1959
1834	Denman (5th), Charles Spencer Denman, CBE, MC, TD, b. 1916, s. 1971, w.	Hon. Richard T. S., D., b. 1946
1885	Deramore (6th), Richard Arthur de Yarburgh-Bateson, b. 1911, s. 1964, m.	None
1887	De Ramsey (4th), John Ailwyn Fellowes, b. 1942, s. 1993, m.	Hon. Freddie J., F., b. 1978
1264	de Ros (28th), Peter Trevor Maxwell, b. 1958, s. 1983, m., Premier Baron of England	Hon. Finbar J., M., b. 1988
1881	Derwent (5th), Robin Evelyn Leo Vanden-Bempde-Johnstone, LVO, b. 1930, s. 1986, m.	Hon. Francis P. H., V.-B.-J., b. 1965
1831	de Saumarez (7th), Eric Douglas Saumarez, b. 1956, s. 1991, m.	Hon. Victor T., S., b. 1956
1910	de Villiers (3rd), Arthur Percy de Villiers, b. 1911, s. 1934.	Hon. Alexander C., de V., b. 1940
1930	Dickinson (2nd), Richard Clavering Hyett Dickinson, b. 1926, s. 1943, m.	Hon. Martin H., D., b. 1961
1620 I.*	Digby (12th), Edward Henry Kenelm Digby, KCVO, b. 1924, s. 1964, m.	Hon. Henry N. K., D., b. 1954
1765	Digby (6th), Edward Henry Kenelm Digby, KCVO, b. 1924, m.	Hon. Henry N. K., D., b. 1954
1615	Dormer (17th), Geoffrey Henry Dormer, b. 1920, s. 1995, m.	Hon. William R., D., b. 1960
1943	Dowding (3rd), Piers Hugh Tremenheere Dowding, b. 1948, s. 1992, m.	Hon. Mark D. J., D., b. 1949
1800 I.	Dufferin and Clandeboye. The 10th Baron died in 1991. Heir had not established his claim to the title at the time of going to press.	Sir John Blackwood, Bt., b. 1944
1929	Dulverton (3rd), (Gilbert) Michael Hamilton Wills, b. 1944, s. 1992, m.	Hon. Robert A. H., W., b. 1983
1800 I.	Dunalley (7th), Henry Francis Cornelius Prittie, b. 1948, s. 1992, m.	Hon. Joel H., P., b. 1981
1324 I.	Dunboyne (28th), Patrick Theobald Tower Butler, VRD, b. 1917, s. 1945, m.	Hon. John F., B., b. 1951
1892	Dunleath (6th), Brian Henry Mulholland, b. 1950, s. 1997, m.	Hon. Andrew H., M., b. 1981
1439 I.	Dunsany (20th), Edward John Carlos Plunkett, b. 1939, s. 1999, m.	Hon. Randal, P., b. 1983
1780	Dynevor (9th), Richard Charles Uryan Rhys, b. 1935, s. 1962.	Hon. Hugo G. U., R., b. 1966
1963	Egremont (2nd), John Max Henry Scawen Wyndham, b. 1948, s. 1972, m.	Hon. George R. V., W., b. 1983
1859	Leconfield (7th), John Max Henry Scawen Wyndham, b. 1948, m.	Hon. George R. V., W., b. 1983
1643	Elibank (14th), Alan D'Ardis Erskine-Murray, b. 1923, s. 1973, w.	Master, b. 1964
1802	Ellenborough (8th), Richard Edward Cecil Law, b. 1926, s. 1945, m.	Maj. Hon. Rupert E. H., L., b. 1955
1509 S.*	Elphinstone (19th), Alexander Mountstuart Elphinstone, b. 1980, s. 1994, I.	Hon. Angus J., E., b. 1982
1885	Elphinstone (5th), Alexander Mountstuart Elphinstone, b. 1980, I.	Hon. Angus J., E., b. 1982
1934	** Elton (2nd), Rodney Elton, TD, b. 1930, s. 1973, m.	Hon. Edward P., E., b. 1966

Created	Title, order of succession, name, etc.	Heir
1964	*Erroll of Hale* (1st) and 1st Baron Erroll of Kilmun (life peer 1999), Frederick James Erroll, TD, PC, *b.* 1914, *m.*	None
1627	*S. Fairfax of Cameron* (14th), Nicholas John Albert Fairfax, *b.* 1956, *s.* 1964, *m.*	Hon. Edward N. T., *F.*, *b.* 1984
1961	*Fairhaven* (3rd), Ailwyn Henry George Broughton, *b.* 1936, *s.* 1973, *m.*	Maj. Hon. James H. A., *B.*, *b.* 1963
1916	*Faringdon* (3rd), Charles Michael Henderson, *b.* 1937, *s.* 1977, *m.*	Hon. James H., *H.*, *b.* 1961
1756	*Farnham* (12th), Barry Owen Somerset Maxwell, *b.* 1931, *s.* 1957, *m.*	Hon. Simon K., *M.*, *b.* 1933
1856	*Fermoy* (6th), Patrick Maurice Burke Roche, *b.* 1967, *s.* 1984, *m.*	Hon. E. Hugh B., *R.*, *b.* 1972
1826	*Feversham* (6th), Charles Antony Peter Duncombe, *b.* 1945, *s.* 1963, *m.*	Hon. Jasper O. S., *D.*, *b.* 1968
1798 I.	*ffrench* (8th), Robuck John Peter Charles Mario ffrench, *b.* 1956, *s.* 1986, *m.*	Hon. John C. M. J. F., *ff.*, *b.* 1928
1909	*Fisher* (3rd), John Vavasseur Fisher, DSC, *b.* 1921, *s.* 1955, *m.*	Hon. Patrick V., *F.*, *b.* 1953
1295	*Fitzwalter* (21th), (Fitzwalter) Brook Plumptre, *b.* 1914, *m.*	Hon. Julian B., *P.*, *b.* 1952
1776	*Foley* (8th), Adrian Gerald Foley, *b.* 1923, *s.* 1927, *m.*	Hon. Thomas H., *F.*, *b.* 1961
1445	*Forbes* (22th), Nigel Ivan Forbes, KBE, *b.* 1918, *s.* 1953, *m.*, Premier Lord of Scotland	Master of Forbes, *b.* 1946
1821	*Forester* (8th), (George Cecil) Brooke Weld-Forester, *b.* 1938, *s.* 1977, *m.*	Hon. C. R. George, *W.-F.*, *b.* 1975
1922	*Forres* (4th), Alastair Stephen Grant Williamson, *b.* 1946, *s.* 1978, *m.*	Hon. George A. M., *W.*, *b.* 1972
1917	*Forteviot* (4th), John James Evelyn Dewar, *b.* 1938, *s.* 1993, *m.*	Hon. Alexander J. E., *D.*, *b.* 1971
1951	** *Freyberg* (3rd), Valerian Bernard Freyberg, *b.* 1970, *s.* 1993.	None
1917	*Gainford* (3rd), Joseph Edward Pease, *b.* 1921, *s.* 1971, *m.*	Hon. George, *P.*, *b.* 1926
1818	*Garvagh* (5th), (Alexander Leopold Ivor) George Canning, *b.* 1920, *s.* 1956, *m.*	Hon. Spencer G. S. de R., *C.*, *b.* 1953
1942	** *Geddes* (3rd), Euan Michael Ross Geddes, *b.* 1937, *s.* 1975, *m.*	Hon. James G. N., *G.*, *b.* 1969
1876	*Gerard* (5th), Anthony Robert Hugo Gerard, *b.* 1949, *s.* 1992, *m.*	Hon. Rupert B. C., *G.*, *b.* 1981
1824	*Gifford* (6th), Anthony Maurice Gifford, QC, *b.* 1940, *s.* 1961, *m.*	Hon. Thomas A., *G.*, *b.* 1967
1917	*Gisborough* (3rd), Thomas Richard John Long Chaloner, *b.* 1927, *s.* 1951, *m.*	Hon. T. Peregrine L., *C.*, *b.* 1961
1960	*Gladwyn* (2nd), Miles Alvery Gladwyn Jebb, *b.* 1930, *s.* 1996.	None
1899	*Glanusk* (5th), Christopher Russell Bailey, *b.* 1942, *s.* 1997, *m.*	Hon. Charles H., *B.*, *b.* 1976
1918	** *Glenarthur* (4th), Simon Mark Arthur, *b.* 1944, *s.* 1976, *m.*	Hon. Edward A., *A.*, *b.* 1973
1911	*Glenconner* (3rd), Colin Christopher Paget Tennant, *b.* 1926, *s.* 1983, *m.*	Hon. Cody, *T.*, *b.* 1994
1964	*Glendevon* (2nd), Julian John Somerset Hope, *b.* 1950, *s.* 1996.	Hon. Jonathan C., *H.*, *b.* 1952
1922	*Glendyne* (3rd), Robert Nivison, *b.* 1926, *s.* 1967, *m.*	Hon. John, *N.*, *b.* 1960
1939	** *Glentoran* (3rd), (Thomas) Robin (Valerian) Dixon, CBE, *b.* 1935, *s.* 1995, *m.*	Hon. Daniel G., *D.*, *b.* 1959
1909	*Gorell* (4th), Timothy John Radcliffe Barnes, *b.* 1927, *s.* 1963, *m.*	Hon. Ronald A. H., *B.*, *b.* 1931
1953	*Grantchester* (3rd), Christopher John Suenson-Taylor, *b.* 1951, *s.* 1995, *m.*	Hon. Jesse D., *S.-T.*, *b.* 1977
1782	*Grantley* (8th), Richard William Brinsley Norton, *b.* 1956, *s.* 1995,	Hon. Francis J. H., *N.*, *b.* 1960
1794 I.	*Graves* (9th), Evelyn Paget Graves, *b.* 1924, *s.* 1994, *m.*	Hon. Timothy E., *G.*, *b.* 1960
1445 S.	*Gray* (22nd), Angus Diarmid Ian Campbell-Gray, *b.* 1931, *s.* 1946, *m.*	Master of Gray, *b.* 1964
1950	*Greenhill* (3rd), Malcolm Greenhill, *b.* 1924, *s.* 1989.	None
1927	** *Greenway* (4th), Ambrose Charles Drexel Greenway, *b.* 1941, *s.* 1975, *m.*	Hon. Mervyn S. K., *G.*, *b.* 1942
1902	*Grenfell* (3rd), Julian Pascoe Francis St Leger Grenfell, *b.* 1935, *s.* 1976, *m.*	Francis P. J., *G.*, *b.* 1938
1944	*Gretton* (4th), John Lysander Gretton, *b.* 1975, *s.* 1989.	None
1397	*Grey of Codnor* (6th), Richard Henry Cornwall-Legh, *b.* 1936, *s.* 1996, *m.*	Hon. Richard S. C., *C.-L.*, *b.* 1976
1955	*Gridley* (3rd), Richard David Arnold Gridley, *b.* 1956, *s.* 1996, *m.*	Hon. Carl R., *G.*, *b.* 1981
1964	*Grimston of Westbury* (2nd), Robert Walter Sigismund Grimston, *b.* 1925, *s.* 1979, *m.*	Hon. Robert J. S., *G.*, *b.* 1951
1886	*Grimthorpe* (4th), Christopher John Beckett, OBE, *b.* 1915, *s.* 1963, *m.*	Hon. Edward J., *B.*, *b.* 1954
1945	*Hacking* (3rd), Douglas David Hacking, *b.* 1938, *s.* 1971, *m.*	Hon. Douglas F., *H.*, *b.* 1968
1950	*Haden-Guest* (5th), Christopher Haden-Guest, *b.* 1948, *s.* 1996, *m.*	Hon. Nicholas, *H.-G.*, *b.* 1951
1886	*Hamilton of Dalzell* (4th), James Leslie Hamilton, *b.* 1938, *s.* 1990, *m.*	Hon. Gavin G., *H.*, *b.* 1968
1874	*Hampton* (6th), Richard Humphrey Russell Pakington, *b.* 1925, *s.* 1974, *m.*	Hon. John H. A., *P.*, *b.* 1964
1939	*Hankey* (3rd), Donald Robin Alers Hankey, *b.* 1938, *s.* 1996, *m.*	Hon. Alexander M. A., *H.*, *b.* 1947
1958	*Harding of Petherton* (2nd), John Charles Harding, *b.* 1928, *s.* 1989, *m.*	Hon. William A. J., *H.*, *b.* 1969
1910	*Hardinge of Penshurst* (4th), Julian Alexander Hardinge, *b.* 1945, *s.* 1997.	Hon. Hugh F., *H.*, *b.* 1948
1876	*Harlech* (6th), Francis David Ormsby-Gore, *b.* 1954, *s.* 1985, *m.*	Hon. Jasset D. C., *O.-G.*, *b.* 1986
1939	*Harmsworth* (3rd), Thomas Harold Raymond Harmsworth, *b.* 1939, *s.* 1990, *m.*	Hon. Dominic M. E., *H.*, *b.* 1973
1815	*Harris* (8th), Anthony Harris, *b.* 1942, *s.* 1996, *m.*	Ronald G. T., *H.*, *b.* 1911
1954	*Harvey of Tasburgh* (2nd), Peter Charles Oliver Harvey, *b.* 1921, *s.* 1968, *w.*	Charles J. B., *H.*, *b.* 1951
1295	*Hastings* (22th), Edward Delaval Henry Astley, *b.* 1912, *s.* 1956, *m.*	Hon. Delaval T. H., *A.*, *b.* 1960
1835	*Hatherton* (8th), Edward Charles Littleton, *b.* 1950, *s.* 1985, *m.*	Hon. Thomas E., *L.*, *b.* 1977

Created	*Title, order of succession, name, etc.*	*Heir*
1776	*Hawke* (11th), Edward George Hawke, TD, *b.* 1950, *s.* 1992, *m.*	Hon. William M. T., *H.*, *b.* 1995
1927	*Hayter* (3rd), George Charles Hayter Chubb, KCVO, CBE, *b.* 1911, *s.* 1967, *m.*	Hon. G. William M., *C.*, *b.* 1943
1945	*Hazlerigg* (2nd), Arthur Grey Hazlerigg, MC, TD, *b.* 1910, *s.* 1949, *w.*	Hon. Arthur G., *H.*, *b.* 1951
1943	*Hemingford* (3rd), (Dennis) Nicholas Herbert, *b.* 1934, *s.* 1982, *m.*	Hon. Christopher D. C., *H.*, *b.* 1973
1906	*Hemphill* (5th), Peter Patrick Fitzroy Martyn Martyn-Hemphill, *b.* 1928, *s.* 1957, *m.*	Hon. Charles A. M., *M.-H.*, *b.* 1954
1799 I.*	** *Henley and 6th UK Baron Northington*, 1885 (8th), Oliver Michael Robert Eden, *b.* 1953, *s.* 1977, *m.*	Hon. John W. O., *E.*, *b.* 1988
1800 I.*	*Henniker* (8th), John Patrick Edward Chandos Henniker-Major, KCMG, CVO, MC, *b.* 1916, *s.* 1980, *m.*	Hon. Mark I. P. C., *H.-M.*, *b.* 1947
1866	*Hartismere* (4th), John Patrick Edward Chandos Henniker-Major, KCMG, CVO, MC, *b.* 1916, *m.*	Hon. Mark I. P. C., *H.-M.*, *b.* 1947
1886	*Herschell* (3rd), Rognvald Richard Farrer Herschell, *b.* 1923, *s.* 1929, *m.*	None
1935	*Hesketh* (3rd), Thomas Alexander Fermor-Hesketh, KBE, PC, *b.* 1950, *s.* 1955, *m.*	Hon. Frederick H., *F.-H.*, *b.* 1988
1828	*Heytesbury* (6th), Francis William Holmes Á Court, *b.* 1931, *s.* 1971, *m.*	Hon. James W., *H. Á. C.*, *b.* 1967
1886	*Hindlip* (6th), Charles Henry Allsopp, *b.* 1940, *s.* 1993, *m.*	Hon. Henry W., *A.*, *b.* 1973
1950	*Hives* (3rd), Matthew Peter Hives, *b.* 1971, *s.* 1997,	Hon. Michael B., *H.*, *b.* 1926
1912	*Hollenden* (4th), Ian Hampden Hope-Morley, *b.* 1946, *s.* 1999, *m.*	Hon. Edward, *H.-M.*, *b.* 1981
1897	*HolmPatrick* (4th), Hans James David Hamilton, *b.* 1955, *s.* 1991, *m.*	Hon. Ion H. J., *H.*, *b.* 1956
1797 I.	*Hotham* (8th), Henry Durand Hotham, *b.* 1940, *s.* 1967, *m.*	Hon. William B., *H.*, *b.* 1972
1881	*Hothfield* (6th), Anthony Charles Sackville Tufton, *b.* 1939, *s.* 1991, *m.*	Hon. William S., *T.*, *b.* 1977
1597	*Howard de Walden*, The 9th Baron Howard de Walden died in 1999, leaving four co-heiresses. *s.* 1946	
1930	*Howard of Penrith* (3rd), Philip Esme Howard, *b.* 1945, *s.* 1999, *m.*	Hon. Thomas Philip, *H.*, *b.* 1974
1960	*Howick of Glendale* (2nd), Charles Evelyn Baring, *b.* 1937, *s.* 1973, *m.*	Hon. David E. C., *B.*, *b.* 1975
1796 I.	*Huntingfield* (7th), Joshua Charles Vanneck, *b.* 1954, *s.* 1994, *m.*	Hon. Gerard C. A., *V.*, *b.* 1985
1866	** *Hylton* (5th), Raymond Hervey Jolliffe, *b.* 1932, *s.* 1967, *m.*	Hon. William H. M., *J.*, *b.* 1967
1933	*Iliffe* (3rd), Robert Peter Richard Iliffe, *b.* 1944, *s.* 1996, *m.*	Hon. Edward R., *I.*, *b.* 1968
1543 I.	*Inchiquin* (18th), Conor Myles John O'Brien, *b.* 1943, *s.* 1982, *m.*	Murrough R., *O.*, *b.* 1910
1962	*Inchyra* (2nd), Robert Charles Reneke Hoyer Millar, *b.* 1935, *s.* 1989, *m.*	Hon. C. James C. H., *M.*, *b.* 1962
1964	** *Inglewood* (2nd), (William) Richard Fletcher-Vane, MEP, *b.* 1951, *s.* 1989, *m.*	Hon. Henry W. F., *F.-V.*, *b.* 1990
1919	*Inverforth* (4th), Andrew Peter Weir, *b.* 1966, *s.* 1982,	Hon. John V., *W.*, *b.* 1935
1941	*Ironside* (2nd), Edmund Oslac Ironside, *b.* 1924, *s.* 1959, *m.*	Hon. Charles E. G., *I.*, *b.* 1956
1952	*Jeffreys* (3rd), Christopher Henry Mark Jeffreys, *b.* 1957, *s.* 1986, *m.*	Hon. Arthur M. H., *J.*, *b.* 1989
1906	*Joicey* (5th), James Michael Joicey, *b.* 1953, *s.* 1993, *m.*	Hon. William J., *J.*, *b.* 1990
1937	*Kenilworth* (4th), (John) Randle Siddeley, *b.* 1954, *s.* 1981, *m.*	Hon. William R. J., *S.*, *b.* 1992
1935	*Kennet* (2nd), Wayland Hilton Young, *b.* 1923, *s.* 1960, *m.*	Hon. W. A. Thoby, *Y.*, *b.* 1957
1776 I.*	*Kensington* (8th), Hugh Ivor Edwardes, *b.* 1933, *s.* 1981, *m.*	Hon. W. Owen A., *E.*, *b.* 1964
1886	*Kensington* (5th), Hugh Ivor Edwardes, *b.* 1933, *m.*	Hon. W. Owen A., *E.*, *b.* 1964
1951	*Kenswood* (2nd), John Michael Howard Whitfield, *b.* 1930, *s.* 1963, *m.*	Hon. Michael C., *W.*, *b.* 1955
1788	*Kenyon* (6th), Lloyd Tyrell-Kenyon, *b.* 1947, *s.* 1993, *m.*	Hon. Lloyd N., *T.-K.*, *b.* 1972
1947	*Kershaw* (4th), Edward John Kershaw, *b.* 1936, *s.* 1962, *m.*	Hon. John C. E., *K.*, *b.* 1971
1943	*Keyes* (2nd), Roger George Bowlby Keyes, *b.* 1919, *s.* 1945, *m.*	Hon. Charles W. P., *K.*, *b.* 1951
1909	*Kilbracken* (3rd), John Raymond Godley, DSC, *b.* 1920, *s.* 1950,	Hon. Christopher J., *G.*, *b.* 1945
1900	*Killanin* (4th), (George) Redmond Fitzpatrick Morris, *b.* 1947, *s.* 1999, *m.*	Luke M. G., *M.*, *b.* 1975
1943	*Killearn* (3rd), Victor Miles George Aldous Lampson, *b.* 1941, *s.* 1996, *m.*	Hon. Miles H. M., *L.*, *b.* 1977
1789 I.	*Kilmaine* (7th), John David Henry Browne, *b.* 1948, *s.* 1978, *m.*	Hon. John F. S., *B.*, *b.* 1983
1831	*Kilmarnock* (7th), Alastair Ivor Gilbert Boyd, *b.* 1927, *s.* 1975, *m.*	Hon. Robin J., *B.*, *b.* 1941
1941	*Kindersley* (3rd), Robert Hugh Molesworth Kindersley, *b.* 1929, *s.* 1976, *m.*	Hon. Rupert J. M., *K.*, *b.* 1955
1223 I.	*Kingsale* (35th), John de Courcy, *b.* 1941, *s.* 1969, *Premier Baron of Ireland*	Nevinson R., *de C.*, *b.* 1920
1902	*Kinross* (5th), Christopher Patrick Balfour, *b.* 1949, *s.* 1985, *m.*	Hon. Alan I., *B.*, *b.* 1978
1951	*Kirkwood* (3rd), David Harvie Kirkwood, PH.D., *b.* 1931, *s.* 1970, *m.*	Hon. James S., *K.*, *b.* 1937
1800 I.	*Langford* (9th), Col. Geoffrey Alexander Rowley-Conwy, OBE, *b.* 1912, *s.* 1953, *m.*	Hon. Owain G., *R.-C.*, *b.* 1958
1942	*Latham* (2nd), Dominic Charles Latham, *b.* 1954, *s.* 1970,	Anthony M., *L.*, *b.* 1954
1431	*Latymer* (8th), Hugo Nevill Money-Coutts, *b.* 1926, *s.* 1987, *m.*	Hon. Crispin J. A. N., *M.-C.*, *b.* 1955
1869	*Lawrence* (5th), David John Downer Lawrence, *b.* 1937, *s.* 1968,	None
1947	*Layton* (3rd), Geoffrey Michael Layton, *b.* 1947, *s.* 1989, *m.*	Hon. David, *L.*, MBE, *b.* 1914
1839	*Leigh* (5th), John Piers Leigh, *b.* 1935, *s.* 1979, *m.*	Hon. Christopher D. P., *L.*, *b.* 1960

Created	Title, order of succession, name, etc.	Heir
1962	*Leighton of St Mellons* (3rd), Robert William Henry Leighton Seager, *b.* 1955, *s.* 1998.	Hon. Simon J. L., *S.*, *b.* 1957
1797	*Lilford* (7th), George Vernon Powys, *b.* 1931, *s.* 1949, *m.*	Hon. Mark V., *P.*, *b.* 1975
1945	*Lindsay of Birker* (3rd), James Francis Lindsay, *b.* 1945, *s.* 1994, *m.*	Alexander S., *L.*, *b.* 1940
1758 I.	*Lisle* (8th), Patrick James Lysaght, *b.* 1931, *s.* 1998.	Hon. John N. G., *L.*, *b.* 1960
1850	*Londesborough* (9th), Richard John Denison, *b.* 1959, *s.* 1968, *m.*	Hon. James F., *D.*, *b.* 1990
1541 I.	*Louth* (16th), Otway Michael James Oliver Plunkett, *b.* 1929, *s.* 1950, *m.*	Hon. Jonathan O., *P.*, *b.* 1952
1458 S.*	*Lovat* (16th) *and 5th UK Baron, Lovat,* 1837, Simon Fraser, *b.* 1977, *s.* 1995.	Hon. Jack, *F.*, *b.* 1984
1946	*Lucas of Chilworth* (2nd), Michael William George Lucas, *b.* 1926, *s.* 1967, *m.*	Hon. Simon W., *L.*, *b.* 1957
1663	** *Lucas (11th) and Dingwall* (14th) (s. 1609), Ralph Matthew Palmer, *b.* 1951, *s.* 1991.	Hon. Lewis E., *P.*, *b.* 1987
1929	** *Luke* (3rd), Arthur Charles St John Lawson-Johnston, *b.* 1933, *s.* 1996, *m.*	Hon. Ian J. St J., *L.-J.*, *b.* 1963
1914	** *Lyell* (3rd), Charles Lyell, *b.* 1939, *s.* 1943.	None
1859	*Lyveden* (6th), Ronald Cecil Vernon, *b.* 1915, *s.* 1973, *m.*	Hon. Jack L., *V.*, *b.* 1938
1959	*MacAndrew* (3rd), Christopher Anthony Colin MacAndrew, *b.* 1945, *s.* 1989, *m.*	Hon. Oliver C. J., *M.*, *b.* 1983
1776 I.	*Macdonald* (8th), Godfrey James Macdonald of Macdonald, *b.* 1947, *s.* 1970, *m.*	Hon. Godfrey E. H. T., *M.*, *b.* 1982
1949	*Macdonald of Gwaenysgor* (2nd), Gordon Ramsay Macdonald, *b.* 1915, *s.* 1966, *m.*	None
1937	*McGowan* (3rd), Harry Duncan Cory McGowan, *b.* 1938, *s.* 1966, *m.*	Hon. Harry J. C., *M.*, *b.* 1971
1922	*Maclay* (3rd), Joseph Paton Maclay, *b.* 1942, *s.* 1969, *m.*	Hon. Joseph P., *M.*, *b.* 1977
1955	*McNair* (3rd), Duncan James McNair, *b.* 1947, *s.* 1989, *m.*	Hon. William S. A., *M.*, *b.* 1958
1951	*Macpherson of Drumochter* (2nd), (James) Gordon Macpherson, *b.* 1924, *s.* 1965, *m.*	Hon. James A., *M.*, *b.* 1979
1937	** *Mancroft* (3rd), Benjamin Lloyd Stormont Mancroft, *b.* 1957, *s.* 1987, *m.*	None
1807	*Manners* (5th), John Robert Cecil Manners, *b.* 1923, *s.* 1972, *m.*	Hon. John H. R., *M.*, *b.* 1956
1922	*Manton* (3rd), Joseph Rupert Eric Robert Watson, *b.* 1924, *s.* 1968, *m.*	Maj. Hon. Miles R. M., *W.*, *b.* 1958
1908	*Marchamley* (4th), William Francis Whiteley, *b.* 1968, *s.* 1994,	None
1964	*Margadale* (2nd), James Ian Morrison, TD, *b.* 1930, *s.* 1996, *m.*	Hon. Alastair J., *M.*, *b.* 1958
1961	*Marks of Broughton* (3rd), Simon Richard Marks, *b.* 1950, *s.* 1998, *m.*	Hon. Michael, *M.*, *b.* 1989
1964	*Martonmere* (2nd), John Stephen Robinson, *b.* 1963, *s.* 1989,	David A., *R.*, *b.* 1965
1776 I.	*Massy* (9th), Hugh Hamon John Somerset Massy, *b.* 1921, *s.* 1958, *m.*	Hon. David H. S., *M.*, *b.* 1947
1935	*May* (3rd), Michael St John May, *b.* 1931, *s.* 1950, *m.*	Hon. Jasper B. St J., *M.*, *b.* 1965
1928	*Melchett* (4th), Peter Robert Henry Mond, *b.* 1948, *s.* 1973,	None
1925	*Merrivale* (3rd), Jack Henry Edmond Duke, *b.* 1917, *s.* 1951, *m.*	Hon. Derek J. P., *D.*, *b.* 1948
1911	*Merthyr.* Disclaimed for life 1977. (*Trevor Oswin Lewis*, Bt, CBE, *b.* 1935, *s.* 1977, *m.*).	David T., *L.*, *b.* 1977
1919	*Meston* (3rd), James Meston, *b.* 1950, *s.* 1984, *m.*	Hon. Thomas J. D., *M.*, *b.* 1977
1838	** *Methuen* (7th), Robert Alexander Holt Methuen, *b.* 1931, *s.* 1994, *m.*	James P. A., Methuen-Campbell., *b.* 1952
1711	*Middleton* (12th), (Digby) Michael Godfrey John Willoughby, MC, *b.* 1921, *s.* 1970, *m.*	Hon. Michael C. J., *W.*, *b.* 1948
1939	*Milford* (4th), Guy Wogan Philipps, *b.* 1961, *s.* 1999, *m.*	Hon. Roland A., *P.*, *b.* 1962
1933	*Milne* (2nd), George Douglass Milne, TD, *b.* 1909, *s.* 1948, *m.*	Hon. George A., *M.*, *b.* 1941
1951	*Milner of Leeds* (2nd), Arthur James Michael Milner, AE, *b.* 1923, *s.* 1967, *m.*	Hon. Richard J., *M.*, *b.* 1959
1947	*Milverton* (2nd), Revd Fraser Arthur Richard Richards, *b.* 1930, *s.* 1978, *m.*	Hon. Michael H., *R.*, *b.* 1936
1873	*Moncreiff* (5th), Harry Robert Wellwood Moncreiff, *b.* 1915, *s.* 1942, *w.*	Hon. Rhoderick H. W., *M.*, *b.* 1954
1884	*Monk Bretton* (3rd), John Charles Dodson, *b.* 1924, *s.* 1933, *m.*	Hon. Christopher M., *D.*, *b.* 1958
1885	*Monkswell* (5th), Gerard Collier, *b.* 1947, *s.* 1984, *m.*	Hon. James A., *C.*, *b.* 1977
1728	** *Monson* (11th), John Monson, *b.* 1932, *s.* 1958, *m.*	Hon. Nicholas J., *M.*, *b.* 1955
1885	** *Montagu of Beaulieu* (3rd), Edward John Barrington Douglas-Scott-Montagu, *b.* 1926, *s.* 1929, *m.*	Hon. Ralph, *D.-S.-M.*, *b.* 1961
1839	*Monteagle of Brandon* (6th), Gerald Spring Rice, *b.* 1926, *s.* 1946, *m.*	Hon. Charles J. S., *R.*, *b.* 1953
1943	** *Moran* (2nd), (Richard) John (McMoran) Wilson, KCMG, *b.* 1924, *s.* 1977, *m.*	Hon. James M., *W.*, *b.* 1952
1918	*Morris* (3rd), Michael David Morris, *b.* 1937, *s.* 1975, *m.*	Hon. Thomas A. S., *M.*, *b.* 1982
1950	*Morris of Kenwood* (2nd), Philip Geoffrey Morris, *b.* 1928, *s.* 1954, *m.*	Hon. Jonathan D., *M.*, *b.* 1968
1831	*Mostyn* (5th), Roger Edward Lloyd Lloyd-Mostyn, MC, *b.* 1920, *s.* 1965, *m.*	Hon. Llewellyn R. L., *L.-M.*, *b.* 1948
1933	*Mottistone* (4th), David Peter Seely, CBE, *b.* 1920, *s.* 1966, *m.*	Hon. Peter J. P., *S.*, *b.* 1949
1945	*Mountevans* (3rd), Edward Patrick Broke Evans, *b.* 1943, *s.* 1974, *m.*	Hon. Jeffrey de C. R., *E.*, *b.* 1948
1283	** *Mowbray, Segrave* (27th) *and Stourton* (23rd) (1448) (26th), Charles Edward Stourton, CBE, *b.* 1923, *s.* 1965, *m.*	Hon. Edward W. S., *S.*, *b.* 1953

Created	Title, order of succession, name, etc.	Heir
1932	*Moyne* (3rd), Jonathan Bryan Guinness, *b.* 1930, *s.* 1992, *m.*	Hon. Jasper J. R., *G.*, *b.* 1954
1929	** *Moynihan* (4th), Colin Berkeley Moynihan, *b.* 1955, *s.* 1997, *m.*	Hon. Nicholas E. B., *M.*, *b.* 1994
1781 I.	*Muskerry* (9th), Robert Fitzmaurice Deane, *b.* 1948, *s.* 1988, *m.*	Hon. Jonathan F., *D.*, *b.* 1986
1627 S.*	*Napier and Ettrick* (5th) (UK 1872) (14th), Francis Nigel Napier, KCVO, *b.* 1930, *s.* 1954, *m.*	Master of Napier, *b.* 1962
1868	*Napier of Magdala* (6th), Robert Alan Napier, *b.* 1940, *s.* 1987, *m.*	Hon. James R., *N.*, *b.* 1966
1940	*Nathan* (2nd), Roger Carol Michael Nathan, *b.* 1922, *s.* 1963, *m.*	Hon. Rupert H. B., *N.*, *b.* 1957
1960	*Nelson of Stafford* (3rd), Henry Roy George Nelson, *b.* 1943, *s.* 1995, *m.*	Hon. Alistair W. H., *N.*, *b.* 1973
1959	*Netherthorpe* (3rd), James Frederick Turner, *b.* 1964, *s.* 1982, *m.*	Hon. Andrew J. E., *T.*, *b.* 1993
1946	*Newall* (2nd), Francis Storer Eaton Newall, *b.* 1930, *s.* 1963, *m.*	Hon. Richard H. E., *N.*, *b.* 1961
1776 I.	*Newborough* (8th), Robert Vaughan Wynn, *b.* 1949, *s.* 1998, *m.*	Hon. Charles H. R., *W.*, *b.* 1923
1892	*Newton* (5th), Richard Thomas Legh, *b.* 1950, *s.* 1992, *m.*	Hon. Piers R., *L.*, *b.* 1979
1930	*Noel-Buxton* (3rd), Martin Connal Noel-Buxton, *b.* 1940, *s.* 1980, *m.*	Hon. Charles C., *N.-B.*, *b.* 1975
1957	*Norrie* (2nd), (George) Willoughby Moke Norrie, *b.* 1936, *s.* 1977, *m.*	Hon. Mark W. J., *N.*, *b.* 1972
1884	** *Northbourne* (5th), Christopher George Walter James, *b.* 1926, *s.* 1982, *m.*	Hon. Charles W. H., *J.*, *b.* 1960
1866	** *Northbrook* (6th), Francis Thomas Baring, *b.* 1954, *s.* 1990, *m.*	None
1878	*Norton* (8th), James Nigel Arden Adderley, *b.* 1947, *s.* 1993, *m.*	Hon. Edward J. A., *A.*, *b.* 1982
1906	*Nunburnholme* (5th), Charles Thomas Wilson, *b.* 1935, *s.* 1998, *Oaksey* (see Trevethin and Oaksey, page 155).	Hon. Stephen C., *W.*, *b.* 1973
1950	*Ogmore* (2nd), Gwilym Rees Rees-Williams, *b.* 1931, *s.* 1976, *m.*	Hon. Morgan, *R.-W.*, *b.* 1937
1870	*O'Hagan* (4th), Charles Towneley Strachey, *b.* 1945, *s.* 1961.	Hon. Richard T., *S.*, *b.* 1950
1868	*O'Neill* (4th), Raymond Arthur Clanaboy O'Neill, TD, *b.* 1933, *s.* 1944, *m.*	Hon. Shane S. C., *O'N.*, *b.* 1965
1836 I.*	*Oranmore (4th) and Browne and 2nd UK Baron, Mereworth*, 1926, Dominick Geoffrey Edward Browne, *b.* 1901, *s.* 1927, *m.*	Hon. Dominick G. T., *B.*, *b.* 1929
1933	** *Palmer* (4th), Adrian Bailie Nottage Palmer, *b.* 1951, *s.* 1990, *m.*	Hon. Hugo B. R., *P.*, *b.* 1980
1914	*Parmoor* (4th), (Frederick Alfred) Milo Cripps, *b.* 1929, *s.* 1977.	Michael L. S., *C.*, *b.* 1942
1937	*Pender* (3rd), John Willoughby Denison-Pender, *b.* 1933, *s.* 1965, *m.*	Hon. Henry J. R., *D.-P.*, *b.* 1968
1866	*Penrhyn* (6th), Malcolm Frank Douglas-Pennant, DSO, MBE, *b.* 1908, *s.* 1967, *m.*	Hon. Nigel, *D.-P.*, *b.* 1909
1603	*Petre* (18th), John Patrick Lionel Petre, *b.* 1942, *s.* 1989, *m.*	Hon. Dominic W., *P.*, *b.* 1966
1918	*Phillimore* (5th), Francis Stephen Phillimore, *b.* 1944, *s.* 1994, *m.*	Hon. Tristan A. S., *P.*, *b.* 1977
1945	*Piercy* (3rd), James William Piercy, *b.* 1946, *s.* 1981.	Hon. Mark E. P., *P.*, *b.* 1953
1827	*Plunket* (8th), Robin Rathmore Plunket, *b.* 1925, *s.* 1975, *m.*	Hon. Shaun A. F. S., *P.*, *b.* 1931
1831	*Poltimore* (7th), Mark Coplestone Bampfylde, *b.* 1957, *s.* 1978, *m.*	Hon. Henry A. W., *B.*, *b.* 1985
1690 S.	*Polwarth* (10th), Henry Alexander Hepburne-Scott, TD, *b.* 1916, *s.* 1944, *m.*	Master of Polwarth, *b.* 1947
1930	*Ponsonby of Shulbrede* (4th), Frederick Matthew Thomas Ponsonby, *b.* 1958, *s.* 1990.	None
1958	*Poole* (2nd), David Charles Poole, *b.* 1945, *s.* 1993, *m.*	Hon. Oliver J., *P.*, *b.* 1972
1852	*Raglan* (5th), FitzRoy John Somerset, *b.* 1927, *s.* 1964.	Hon. Geoffrey, *S.*, *b.* 1932
1932	*Rankeillour* (4th), Peter St Thomas More Henry Hope, *b.* 1935, *s.* 1967.	Michael R., *H.*, *b.* 1940
1953	*Rathcavan* (3rd), Hugh Detmar Torrens O'Neill, *b.* 1939, *s.* 1994, *m.*	Hon. François H. N., *O'N.*, *b.* 1984
1916	*Rathcreedan* (3rd), Christopher John Norton, *b.* 1949, *s.* 1990, *m.*	Hon. Adam G., *N.*, *b.* 1952
1868	*Rathdonnell* (5th), Thomas Benjamin McClintock-Bunbury, *b.* 1938, *s.* 1959, *m.*	Hon. William L., *M.-B.*, *b.* 1966
1911	*Ravensdale* (3rd), Nicholas Mosley, MC, *b.* 1923, *s.* 1966, *m.*	Hon. Shaun N., *M.*, *b.* 1949
1821	*Ravensworth* (8th), Arthur Waller Liddell, *b.* 1924, *s.* 1950, *m.*	Hon. Thomas A. H., *L.*, *b.* 1954
1821	*Rayleigh* (6th), John Gerald Strutt, *b.* 1960, *s.* 1988, *m.*	Hon. John F., *S.*, *b.* 1993
1937	*Rea* (3rd), John Nicolas Rea, MD, *b.* 1928, *s.* 1981, *m.*	Hon. Matthew J., *R.*, *b.* 1956
1628 S.	** *Reay* (14th), Hugh William Mackay, *b.* 1937, *s.* 1963, *m.*	Master of Reay, *b.* 1965
1902	*Redesdale* (6th), Rupert Bertram Mitford, *b.* 1967, *s.* 1991, *m.*	None
1940	*Reith*. Disclaimed for life 1972. (*Christopher John Reith, b.* 1928, *s.* 1971, *m*).	Hon. James H. J., *R.*, *b.* 1971
1928	*Remnant* (3rd), James Wogan Remnant, CVO, *b.* 1930, *s.* 1967, *m.*	Hon. Philip J., *R.*, *b.* 1954
1806	*Rendlesham* (8th), Charles Anthony Hugh Thellusson, *b.* 1915, *s.* 1943, *w.*	Hon. Charles W. B., *T.*, *b.* 1954
1933	*Rennell* (3rd), (John Adrian) Tremayne Rodd, *b.* 1935, *s.* 1978, *m.*	Hon. James R. D. T., *R.*, *b.* 1978
1964	*Renwick* (2nd), Harry Andrew Renwick, *b.* 1935, *s.* 1973, *m.*	Hon. Robert J., *R.*, *b.* 1966
1885	*Revelstoke* (5th), John Baring, *b.* 1934, *s.* 1994.	Hon. James C., *B.*, *b.* 1938
1905	*Ritchie of Dundee* (5th), (Harold) Malcolm Ritchie, *b.* 1919, *s.* 1978, *m.*	Hon. C. Rupert R., *R.*, *b.* 1958
1935	*Riverdale* (3rd), Anthony Robert Balfour, *b.* 1960, *s.* 1998.	Hon. David R., *B.*, *b.* 1938
1961	*Robertson of Oakridge* (2nd), William Ronald Robertson, *b.* 1930, *s.* 1974, *m.*	Hon. William B. E., *R.*, *b.* 1975
1938	*Roborough* (3rd), Henry Massey Lopes, *b.* 1940, *s.* 1992, *m.*	Hon. Massey J. H., *L.*, *b.* 1969
1931	*Rochester* (2nd), Foster Charles Lowry Lamb, *b.* 1916, *s.* 1955, *w.*	Hon. David C., *L.*, *b.* 1944
1934	*Rockley* (3rd), James Hugh Cecil, *b.* 1934, *s.* 1976, *m.*	Hon. Anthony R., *C.*, *b.* 1961
1782	*Rodney* (10th), George Brydges Rodney, *b.* 1953, *s.* 1992, *m.*	Nicholas S. H., *R.*, *b.* 1947

Created	Title, order of succession, name, etc.	Heir
1651 S.*	Rollo and 5th UK Baron Dunning, 1869 (14th), David Eric Howard Rollo, b. 1943, s. 1997, m.	Master of Rollo, b. 1972
1959	Rootes (3rd), Nicholas Geoffrey Rootes, b. 1951, s. 1992, m.	William B., R., b. 1944
1796 I.*	Rossmore (7th) and 6th UK Baron, Rossmore, 1838, William Warner Westenra, b. 1931, s. 1958, m.	Hon. Benedict W., W., b. 1983
1939	** Rotherwick (3rd), (Herbert) Robin Cayzer, b. 1954, s. 1996, m.	Hon. H. Robin, C., b. 1989
1885	Rothschild (4th), (Nathaniel Charles) Jacob Rothschild, GBE, b. 1936, s. 1990, m.	Hon. Nathaniel P. V. J., R., b. 1971
1911	Rowallan (4th), John Polson Cameron Corbett, b. 1947, s. 1993.	Hon. Jason W. P. C., C., b. 1972
1947	Rugby (3rd), Robert Charles Maffey, b. 1951, s. 1990, m.	Hon. Timothy J. H., M., b. 1975
1919	Russell of Liverpool (3rd), Simon Gordon Jared Russell, b. 1952, s. 1981, m.	Hon. Edward C. S., R., b. 1985
1876	Sackville (6th), Lionel Bertrand Sackville-West, b. 1913, s. 1965, m.	Hugh R. I., S.-W., MC, b. 1919
1964	St Helens (2nd), Richard Francis Hughes-Young, b. 1945, s. 1980, m.	Hon. Henry T., H.-Y., b. 1986
1559	** St John of Bletso (21th), Anthony Tudor St John, b. 1957, s. 1978, m.	Hon. Oliver B., St J., b. 1995
1887	St Levan (4th), John Francis Arthur St Aubyn, DSC, b. 1919, s. 1978, m.	Hon. O. Piers, St. A., MC, b. 1920
1885	St Oswald (6th), Charles Rowland Andrew Winn, b. 1959, s. 1999, m.	Hon. Rowland C. S. H., W., b. 1986
1960	Sanderson of Ayot. Disclaimed for life 1971. (Alan Lindsay Sanderson, b. 1931, s. 1971, m).	Hon. Michael, S., b. 1959
1945	Sandford (2nd), Revd John Cyril Edmondson, DSC, b. 1920, s. 1959, m.	Hon. James J. M., E., b. 1949
1871	Sandhurst (5th), (John Edward) Terence Mansfield, DFC, b. 1920, s. 1964, m.	Hon. Guy R. J., M., b. 1949
1802	Sandys (7th), Richard Michael Oliver Hill, b. 1931, s. 1961, m.	The Marquess of Downshire (see page 138)
1888	Savile (3rd), George Halifax Lumley-Savile, b. 1919, s. 1931.	Hon. Henry L. T., L.-S., b. 1923
1447	Saye and Sele (21th), Nathaniel Thomas Allen Fiennes, b. 1920, s. 1968, m.	Hon. Richard I., F., b. 1959
1826	Seaford (6th), Colin Humphrey Felton Ellis, b. 1946, s. 1999, m.	Benjamin F. T., E., b. 1976
1932	** Selsdon (3rd), Malcolm McEacharn Mitchell-Thomson, b. 1937, s. 1963, m.	Hon. Callum M. M., M.-T., b. 1969
1489 S.	Sempill (21th), James William Stuart Whitemore Sempill, b. 1949, s. 1995, m.	Master of Sempill, b. 1979
1916	Shaughnessy (3rd), William Graham Shaughnessy, b. 1922, s. 1938, w.	Hon. Michael J., S., b. 1946
1946	Shepherd (2nd) and 1st Baron Shepherd of Spalding (life peer 1999), Malcolm Newton Shepherd, PC, b. 1918, s. 1954, w.	Hon. Graeme G., S., b. 1949
1964	Sherfield (2nd), Christopher James Makins, b. 1942, s. 1996, m.	Hon. Dwight W., M., b. 1951
1902	Shuttleworth (5th), Charles Geoffrey Nicholas Kay-Shuttleworth, b. 1948, s. 1975, m.	Hon. Thomas E., K.-S., b. 1976
1950	Silkin. Disclaimed for life 1972. (Arthur Silkin, b. 1916, s. 1972, m.	Hon. Christopher L., S., b. 1947
1963	Silsoe (2nd), David Malcolm Trustram Eve, QC, b. 1930, s. 1976, m.	Hon. Simon R. T., E., b. 1966
1947	Simon of Wythenshawe (2nd), Roger Simon, b. 1913, s. 1960, m.	Hon. Matthew, S., b. 1955
1449 S.	Sinclair (17th), Charles Murray Kennedy St Clair, CVO, b. 1914, s. 1957, m.	Master of Sinclair, b. 1968
1957	Sinclair of Cleeve (3rd), John Lawrence Robert Sinclair, b. 1953, s. 1985.	None
1919	Sinha (6th), Arup Kumar Sinha, b. 1966, s. 1999.	
1828	** Skelmersdale (7th), Roger Bootle-Wilbraham, b. 1945, s. 1973, m. .	Hon. Andrew, B.-W., b. 1977
1916	Somerleyton (3rd), Savile William Francis Crossley, GCVO, b. 1928, s. 1959, m.	Hon. Hugh F. S., C., b. 1971
1784	Somers (9th), Philip Sebastian Somers Cocks, b. 1948, s. 1995,	Alan B., C., b. 1930
1780	Southampton (6th), Charles James FitzRoy, b. 1928, s. 1989, m.	Hon. Edward C., F., b. 1955
1959	Spens (3rd), Patrick Michael Rex Spens, b. 1942, s. 1984, m.	Hon. Patrick N. G., S., b. 1968
1640	Stafford (15th), Francis Melfort William Fitzherbert, b. 1954, s. 1986, m.	Hon. Benjamin J. & B., F., b. 1983
1938	Stamp (4th), Trevor Charles Bosworth Stamp, MD, FRCP, b. 1935, s. 1987, m.	Hon. Nicholas C. T., S., b. 1978
1839	Stanley (8th) of Alderley and Sheffield (8th) (I. 1738) and 7th UK Baron, Eddisbury, 1848, Thomas Henry Oliver Stanley, b. 1927, s. 1971, m.	Hon. Richard O., S., b. 1956
1318	** Strabolgi (11th), David Montague de Burgh Kenworthy, b. 1914, s. 1953, m.	Andrew D. W., K., b. 1967
1954	Strang (2nd), Colin Strang, b. 1922, s. 1978, m.	None
1955	Strathalmond (3rd), William Roberton Fraser, b. 1947, s. 1976, m.	Hon. William G., F., b. 1976
1936	Strathcarron (2nd), David William Anthony Blyth Macpherson, b. 1924, s. 1937, m.	Hon. Ian D. P., M., b. 1949
1955	** Strathclyde (2nd), Thomas Galloway Dunlop du Roy de Blicquy, Galbraith, PC, b. 1960, s. 1985, m.	Hon. Charles W. du R. de B., G., b. 1962
1900	Strathcona and Mount Royal (4th), Donald Euan Palmer Howard, b. 1923, s. 1959, m.	Hon. D. Alexander S., H., b. 1961
1836	Stratheden and Campbell (6th) (1841) (6th), Donald Campbell, b. 1934, s. 1987, m.	Hon. David A., C., b. 1963
1884	Strathspey (6th), James Patrick Trevor Grant of Grant, b. 1943, s. 1992, m.	Hon. Michael P. F., G., b. 1953
1838	Sudeley (7th), Merlin Charles Sainthill Hanbury-Tracy, b. 1939, s. 1941.	D. Andrew J., H.-T., b. 1928

Created	Title, order of succession, name, etc.	Heir
1786	*Suffield* (11th), Anthony Philip Harbord-Hamond, MC, *b.* 1922, *s.* 1951, *w.*	Hon. Charles A. A., *H.-H.*, *b.* 1953
1893	*Swansea* (4th), John Hussey Hamilton Vivian, *b.* 1925, *s.* 1934, *m.*	Hon. Richard A. H., *V.*, *b.* 1957
1907	*Swaythling* (5th), Charles Edgar Samuel Montagu, *b.* 1954, *s.* 1998, *m.*	Hon. Anthony T. S., *M.*, *b.* 1931
1919	** *Swinfen* (3rd), Roger Mynors Swinfen Eady, *b.* 1938, *s.* 1977, *m.*	Hon. Charles R. P. S., *E.*, *b.* 1971
1935	*Sysonby* (3rd), John Frederick Ponsonby, *b.* 1945, *s.* 1956,	None
1831 I.	*Talbot of Malahide* (10th), Reginald John Richard Arundell, *b.* 1931, *s.* 1987, *m.*	Hon. Richard J. T., *A.*, *b.* 1957
1946	*Tedder* (3rd), Robin John Tedder, *b.* 1955, *s.* 1994, *m.*	Hon. Benjamin J., *T.*, *b.* 1985
1884	*Tennyson* (5th), Cdr. Mark Aubrey Tennyson, DSC, *b.* 1920, *s.* 1991, *m.*	Lt.-Cdr., James A., *T.*, DSC, *b.* 1913
1918	*Terrington* (5th), (Christopher) Montague Woodhouse, DSO, OBE, *b.* 1917, *s.* 1998, *w.*	Hon. Christopher R. J., *W.*, *b.* 1946
1940	*Teviot* (2nd), Charles John Kerr, *b.* 1934, *s.* 1968, *m.*	Hon. Charles R., *K.*, *b.* 1971
1616	*Teynham* (20th), John Christopher Ingham Roper-Curzon, *b.* 1928, *s.* 1972, *m.*	Hon. David J. H. I., *R.-C.*, *b.* 1965
1964	*Thomson of Fleet* (2nd), Kenneth Roy Thomson, *b.* 1923, *s.* 1976, *m.*	Hon. David K. R., *T.*, *b.* 1957
1792	*Thurlow* (8th), Francis Edward Hovell-Thurlow-Cumming-Bruce, KCMG, *b.* 1912, *s.* 1971, *w.*	Hon. Roualeyn R., *H.-T.-C.-B.*, *b.* 1952
1876	*Tollemache* (5th), Timothy John Edward Tollemache, *b.* 1939, *s.* 1975, *m.*	Hon. Edward J. H., *T.*, *b.* 1976
1564 S.	*Torphichen* (15th), James Andrew Douglas Sandilands, *b.* 1946, *s.* 1975, *m.*	Douglas R. A., *S.*, *b.* 1926
1947	** *Trefgarne* (2nd), David Garro Trefgarne, PC, *b.* 1941, *s.* 1960, *m.*	Hon. George G., *T.*, *b.* 1970
1921	*Trevethin and Oaksey* (2nd) (1947) John Geoffrey Tristram Lawrence, OBE, *b.* 1929, *s.* 1971, *m.*	Hon. Patrick J. T., *L.*, *b.* 1960
1880	*Trevor* (5th), Marke Charles Hill-Trevor, *b.* 1970, *s.* 1997, *m.*	Hon. Iain R., *H.-T.*, *b.* 1971
1461 I.	*Trimlestown* (21st), Raymond Charles Barnewall, *b.* 1930, *s.* 1997.	None
1940	*Tryon* (3rd), Anthony George Merrik Tryon, *b.* 1940, *s.* 1976.	Hon. Charles G. B., *T.*, *b.* 1976
1935	*Tweedsmuir* (3rd), William de l'Aigle Buchan, *b.* 1916, *s.* 1996, *m.*	Hon. John W. H. de l'A., *B.*, *b.* 1950
1523	*Vaux of Harrowden* (10th), John Hugh Philip Gilbey, *b.* 1915, *s.* 1977, *m.*	Hon. Anthony W., *G.*, *b.* 1940
1800 I.	*Ventry* (8th), Andrew Wesley Daubeny de Moleyns, *b.* 1943, *s.* 1987, *m.*	Hon. Francis W., *D. de M.*, *b.* 1965
1762	*Vernon* (10th), John Lawrance Vernon, *b.* 1923, *s.* 1963, *m.*	Anthony W., Vernon-Harcourt, *b.* 1939
1922	*Vestey* (3rd), Samuel George Armstrong Vestey, *b.* 1941, *s.* 1954, *m.*	Hon. William G., *V.*, *b.* 1983
1841	** *Vivian* (6th), Nicholas Crespigny Laurence Vivian, *b.* 1935, *s.* 1991, *m.*	Hon. Charles H. C., *V.*, *b.* 1966
1934	*Wakehurst* (3rd), (John) Christopher Loder, *b.* 1925, *s.* 1970, *m.*	Hon. Timothy W., *L.*, *b.* 1958
1723	** *Walpole and 8th Brit. Baron Walpole of Wolterton*, 1756 (10th), Robert Horatio Walpole, *b.* 1938, *s.* 1989, *m.*	Hon. Jonathan R. H., *W.*, *b.* 1967
1780	*Walsingham* (9th), John de Grey, MC, *b.* 1925, *s.* 1965, *m.*	Hon. Robert, *de. G.*, *b.* 1969
1936	*Wardington* (2nd), Christopher Henry Beaumont Pease, *b.* 1924, *s.* 1950, *m.*	Hon. William S., *P.*, *b.* 1925
1792 I.	*Waterpark* (7th), Frederick Caryll Philip Cavendish, *b.* 1926, *s.* 1948, *m.*	Hon. Roderick A., *C.*, *b.* 1959
1942	*Wedgwood* (4th), Piers Anthony Weymouth Wedgwood, *b.* 1954, *s.* 1970, *m.*	John, *W.*, CBE, MD, FRCP, *b.* 1919
1861	*Westbury* (5th), David Alan Bethell, CBE, MC, *b.* 1922, *s.* 1961, *m.*	Hon. Richard N., *B.*, MBE, *b.* 1950
1944	*Westwood* (3rd), (William) Gavin Westwood, *b.* 1944, *s.* 1991, *m.*	Hon. W. Fergus, *W.*, *b.* 1972
1935	*Wigram* (2nd), (George) Neville (Clive) Wigram, MC, *b.* 1915, *s.* 1960, *w.*	Maj. Hon. Andrew F. C., *W.*, MVO, *b.* 1949
1491	** *Willoughby de Broke* (21st), Leopold David Verney, *b.* 1938, *s.* 1986, *m.*	Hon. Rupert G., *V.*, *b.* 1966
1946	*Wilson* (2nd), Patrick Maitland Wilson, *b.* 1915, *s.* 1964, *w.*	None
1937	*Windlesham (3rd) and 1st UK Baron Hennessy (life peer 1999)* (5th) (1999), David James George Hennessy, CVO, PC, *b.* 1932, *s.* 1962, *w.*	Hon. James R., *H.*, *b.* 1968
1951	*Wise* (2nd), John Clayton Wise, *b.* 1923, *s.* 1968, *m.*	Hon. Christopher J. C., *W.*, Ph.D., *b.* 1949
1869	*Wolverton* (7th), Christopher Richard Glyn, *b.* 1938, *s.* 1988.	Hon. Andrew J., *G.*, *b.* 1943
1928	*Wraxall* (2nd), George Richard Lawley Gibbs, *b.* 1928, *s.* 1931.	Hon. Sir, Eustace H. B., *G.*, KCVO, CMG, *b.* 1929
1915	*Wrenbury* (3rd), Revd John Burton Buckley, *b.* 1927, *s.* 1940, *m.*	Hon. William E., *B.*, *b.* 1966
1838	*Wrottesley* (6th), Clifton Hugh Lancelot de Verdon Wrottesley, *b.* 1968, *s.* 1977.	Hon. Stephen J., *W.*, *b.* 1955
1919	*Wyfold* (3rd), Hermon Robert Fleming Hermon-Hodge, ERD, *b.* 1915, *s.* 1942.	None
1829	*Wynford* (8th), Robert Samuel Best, MBE, *b.* 1917, *s.* 1943, *m.*	Hon. John P. R., *B.*, *b.* 1950
1308	*Zouche* (18th), James Assheton Frankland, *b.* 1943, *s.* 1965, *m.*	Hon. William T. A., *F.*, *b.* 1984

BARONESSES/LADIES IN THEIR OWN RIGHT

Style, The Right Hon. the Lady _ , *or* The Right Hon. the Baroness _ , according to her preference. Either style may be used, except in the case of Scottish titles (indicated by S.), which are not baronies (*see* page 136) and whose holders are always addressed as Lady
Husband, Untitled
Children's style, As for children of a Baron
For forms of address, *see* page 135

Created	Title, order of succession, name, etc.	Heir
1664	*Arlington* (97th in line), Jennifer Jane Forwood, *b*. 1939, *m*.	Patrick John Dudley *Forwood*, *b*. 1967
1455	*Berners* (16th in line), Pamela Vivien Kirkham, *b*. 1929, *m*.	Hon. Rupert W. T. *K*., *b*. 1953
1529	*Braye* (8th in line), Mary Penelope Aubrey-Fletcher, *b*. 1941, *s*. 1985, *m*.	Two co-heiresses
1321	*Dacre* (27th in line), Rachel Leila Douglas-Home, *b*. 1929, *w*.	Hon. James T. A. *D.-H.*, *b*. 1952
1332	** *Darcy de Knayth* (18th in line), Davina Marcia Ingrams, DBE, *b*. 1938, *s*. 1943, *w*.	Hon. Caspar D. *I.*, *b*. 1962
1439	*Dudley* (14th in line), Barbara Amy Felicity Hamilton, *b*. 1907, *s*. 1972, *m*.	Hon. Jim A. H. *Wallace*, *b*. 1930
1490 S.	*Herries of Terregles* (14th in line), Anne Elizabeth Fitzalan-Howard, *b*. 1938, *s*. 1975, *m*.	Lady, Mary *Mumford*, CVO, *b*. 1940
1602 S.	*Kinloss* (12th in line), Beatrice Mary Grenville Freeman-Grenville, *b*. 1922, *s*. 1944, *m*.	Master of Kinloss, *b*. 1953
1445 S.	** *Saltoun* (20th in line), Flora Marjory Fraser, *b*. 1930, *s*. 1979, *m*.	Hon. Katharine I. M. I. *F.*, *b*. 1957
1628	*Strange* (16th in line), (Jean) Cherry Drummond of Megginch, *b*. 1928, *m*.	Hon. Adam H. *D. of M.*, *b*. 1953
1544/5	** *Wharton* (11th in line), Myrtle Olive Felix Robertson, *b*. 1934, *m*.	Hon. Myles C. D. *R.*, *b*. 1964
1313	*Willoughby de Eresby* (27th in line), (Nancy) Jane Marie Heathcote-Drummond-Willoughby, *b*. 1934, *s*. 1983,	Two co-heiresses

Life Peers

NEW LIFE PEERAGES *1 September 1999 to 31 August 2000*
NEW YEAR'S HONOURS (30 December 1999):
Sir John Birt; Rt. Hon. Sir Leon Brittan, QC;
Joel Joffe, CBE; Adam Patel; Sir Charles Powell,
KCMG; Sally, Lady Greengross, OBE
WORKING PEERS (30 March 2000): Baron Acton;
Kay Andrews, OBE; Michael Ashcroft; Baron Berkeley;
Alexander Bernstein; Angela Billingham; Daniel
Brennan, QC; Viscount Chandos; Sebastian Coe, OBE; Janet
Cohen; Matthew Evans, CBE; George Lennox Fyfe; Anne
Gibson, OBE; Lindsay Granshaw; Anthony Greaves; Baron
Grenfell; Robin Granville Hodgson, CBE; Julian Hunt, CB,
FRS; William Jordan, CBE;
Peter Layard; Earl of Mar and Kellie; Dame Sheila Masters,
DBE; Parry Mitchell; Kenneth Morgan;
Matthew Oakeshott; Bhikhu Parekh; Baron Ponsonby of
Shulbrede; Baron Redesdale; John Roper;
Rosalind Scott; David Shutt, OBE; Sir Leslie
Turnberg; Joan Walmsley

CREATED UNDER THE APPELLATE JURISDICTION ACT 1876 (AS AMENDED)

BARONS

Created
1986 *Ackner*, Desmond James Conrad Ackner, PC,
       b. 1920, *m.*
1980 *Bridge of Harwich*, Nigel Cyprian Bridge, PC,
       b. 1917, *m.*
1982 *Brightman*, John Anson Brightman, PC,
       b. 1911, *m.*
1991 *Browne-Wilkinson*, Nicolas Christopher Henry
       Browne-Wilkinson, PC, *b.* 1930, *m.*
       Lord of Appeal in Ordinary
1996 *Clyde*, James John Clyde, *b.* 1932, *m.*
       Lord of Appeal in Ordinary
1986 *Goff of Chieveley*, Robert Lionel Archibald
       Goff, PC, *b.* 1926, *m.*
1985 *Griffiths* (William) Hugh Griffiths, MC, PC,
       b. 1923, *m.*
1998 *Hobhouse of Woodborough*, John Stewart Hobhouse,
       PC, *b.* 1932, *m. Lord of Appeal in Ordinary*
1995 *Hoffmann*, Leonard Hubert Hoffmann, PC,
       b. 1934, *m. Lord of Appeal in Ordinary*
1997 *Hutton* (James) Brian (Edward) Hutton, PC,
       b. 1931, *m. Lord of Appeal in Ordinary*
1988 *Jauncey of Tullichettle*, Charles Eliot Jauncey,
       PC, *b.* 1925, *m.*
1977 *Keith of Kinkel*, Henry Shanks Keith, GBE, PC,
       b. 1922, *m.*
1979 *Lane*, Geoffrey Dawson Lane, AFC, PC,
       b. 1918, *m.*
1993 *Lloyd of Berwick*, Anthony John Leslie Lloyd, PC,
       b. 1929, *m. Lord of Appeal in Ordinary*
1998 *Millett*, Peter Julian Millett, PC, *b.* 1932, *m.*
       Lord of Appeal in Ordinary
1992 *Mustill*, Michael John Mustill, PC, *b.* 1931, *m.*
1994 *Nicholls of Birkenhead*, Donald James Nicholls, PC,
       b. 1933, *m. Lord of Appeal in Ordinary*
1994 *Nolan*, Michael Patrick Nolan, PC, *b.* 1928, *m.*
1986 *Oliver of Aylmerton*, Peter Raymond Oliver, PC,
       b. 1921, *m.*

1999 *Phillips of Worth Matravers*, Nicholas Addison
       Phillips, *b.* 1938, *m. Master of the Rolls*
1997 *Saville of Newdigate*, Mark Oliver Saville, PC,
       b. 1936, *m. Lord of Appeal in Ordinary*
1977 *Scarman*, Leslie George Scarman, OBE, PC,
       b. 1911, *m.*
1992 *Slynn of Hadley*, Gordon Slynn, PC, *b.* 1930,
       m. Lord of Appeal in Ordinary
1995 *Steyn*, Johan van Zyl Steyn, PC, *b.* 1932,
       m. Lord of Appeal in Ordinary
1982 *Templeman*, Sydney William Templeman,
       MBE, PC, *b.* 1920, *m.*
1964 *Wilberforce*, Richard Orme Wilberforce,
       CMG, OBE, PC, *b.* 1907, *m.*
1992 *Woolf*, Harry Kenneth Woolf, PC, *b.* 1933, *m.*
       Lord Chief Justice of England and Wales

CREATED UNDER THE LIFE PEERAGES ACT 1958

BARONS

Created
1998 *Ahmed*, Nazir Ahmed, *b.* 1957, *m.*
1996 *Alderdice*, John Thomas Alderdice, *b.* 1955, *m.*
1988 *Alexander of Weedon*, Robert Scott Alexander, QC,
       b. 1936, *m.*
1976 *Allen of Abbeydale*, Philip Allen, GCB, *b.* 1912, *m.*
1998 *Alli*, Waheed Alli.
1997 *Alton of Liverpool*, David Patrick Paul Alton,
       b. 1951, *m.*
1992 *Archer of Sandwell*, Peter Kingsley Archer, PC, QC,
       b. 1926, *m.*
1992 *Archer of Weston-super-Mare*, Jeffrey Howard
       Archer, *b.* 1940, *m.*
1988 *Armstrong of Ilminster*, Robert Temple Armstrong,
       GCB, CVO, *b.* 1927, *m.*
1992 *Ashley of Stoke*, Jack Ashley, CH, PC, *b.* 1922, *m.*
1993 *Attenborough*, Richard Samuel Attenborough, CBE,
       b. 1923, *m.*
1998 *Bach*, William Stephen Goulden Bach, *b.* 1946, *m.*
1997 *Bagri*, Raj Kumar Bagri, CBE, *b.* 1930, *m.*
1997 *Baker of Dorking*, Kenneth Wilfred Baker, CH, PC,
       b. 1934, *m.*
1974 *Balniel*, The Earl of Crawford and Balcarres.
1974 *Barber*, Anthony Perrinott Lysberg Barber, TD, PC,
       b. 1920, *m.*
1992 *Barber of Tewkesbury*, Derek Coates Barber,
       b. 1918, *m.*
1983 *Barnett*, Joel Barnett, PC, *b.* 1923, *m.*
1997 *Bassam of Brighton* (John) Steven Bassam,
       b. 1953.
1982 *Bauer*, Prof. Peter Thomas Bauer, D.Sc., FBA,
       b. 1915, *m.*
1967 *Beaumont of Whitley*, Revd Timothy Wentworth
       Beaumont, *b.* 1928, *m.*
1998 *Bell*, Timothy John Leigh Bell, *b.* 1941, *m.*
1979 *Bellwin*, Irwin Norman Bellow, *b.* 1923, *m.*
2000 *Bernstein of Craigweil*, Alexander Bernstein,
       b. 1936, *m.*
1997 *Biffen* (William) John Biffen, PC, *b.* 1930, *m.*
1996 *Bingham of Cornhill*, Thomas Henry Bingham, PC,
       b. 1933, *m.*
2000 *Birt*, John Francis Hodgess Birt, *b.* 1944, *m.*
1997 *Blackwell*, Norman Roy Blackwell, *b.* 1952, *m.*

1971   *Blake*, Robert Norman William Blake, FBA,
      b. 1916, w.

1994   *Blaker*, Peter Allan Renshaw Blaker, KCMG,
      PC, b. 1922, m.

1978   *Blease*, William John Blease, b. 1914, m.

1995   *Blyth of Rowington*, James Blyth, b. 1940, m.

1980   *Boardman*, Thomas Gray Boardman, MC, TD,
      b. 1919, m.

1996   *Borrie*, Gordon Johnson Borrie, QC, b. 1931, m.

1976   *Boston of Faversham*, Terence George Boston,
      QC, b. 1930, m.

1996   *Bowness*, Peter Spencer Bowness, CBE, b. 1943, m.

1999   *Bradshaw*, William Peter Bradshaw, b. 1936, m.

1998   *Bragg*, Melvyn Bragg, 1939, b. m.

1987   *Bramall*, Edwin Noel Westby Bramall, KG, GCB,
      OBE, MC, b. 1923, m. *Field Marshal*

2000   *Brennan*, Daniel Joseph Brennan, QC, b. 1942, m.

1999   *Brett*, William Henry Brett, b. 1942, m.

1976   *Briggs*, Asa Briggs, FBA, b. 1921, m.

2000   *Brittan of Spennithorne*, Leon Brittan,
      PC, QC, b. 1939, m.

1997   *Brooke of Alverthorpe*, Clive Brooke, b. 1942, m.

1975   *Brookes*, Raymond Percival Brookes, b. 1909, m.

1998   *Brookman*, David Keith Brookman, b. 1937, m.

1979   *Brooks of Tremorfa*, John Edward Brooks,
      b. 1927, m.

1974   *Bruce of Donington*, Donald William Trevor Bruce,
      b. 1912, m.

1976   *Bullock*, Alan Louis Charles Bullock, FBA,
      b. 1914, m.

1997   *Burlison*, Thomas Henry Burlison, b. 1936, m.

1998   *Burns*, Terence Burns, GCB, b. 1944, m.

1998   *Butler of Brockwell* (Frederick Edward) Robin
      Butler, GCB, CVO, b. 1938, m.

1985   *Butterworth*, John Blackstock Butterworth, CBE,
      b. 1918, m.

1978   *Buxton of Alsa*, Aubrey Leland Oakes Buxton,
      KCVO, MC, b. 1918, m.

1987   *Callaghan of Cardiff* (Leonard) James Callaghan,
      KG, PC, b. 1912, m.

1984   *Cameron of Lochbroom*, Kenneth John Cameron,
      PC, b. 1931, m.

1981   *Campbell of Alloway*, Alan Robertson Campbell, QC,
      b. 1917, m.

1974   *Campbell of Croy*, Gordon Thomas Calthrop
      Campbell, MC, PC, b. 1921, m.

1999   *Carlile of Berriew*, Alexander Charles Carlile,
      QC, b. 1948, m.

1987   *Carlisle of Bucklow*, Mark Carlisle, QC, PC,
      b. 1929, m.

1983   *Carmichael of Kelvingrove*, Neil George
      Carmichael, b. 1921, m.

1975   *Carr of Hadley* (Leonard) Robert Carr, PC,
      b. 1916, m.

1987   *Carter*, Denis Victor Carter, PC, b. 1932, m.

1977   *Carver* (Richard) Michael (Power) Carver,
      GCB, CBE, DSO, MC, b. 1915, m. *Field Marshal*

1990   *Cavendish of Furness* (Richard) Hugh Cavendish,
      b. 1941, m.

1996   *Chadlington*, Peter Selwyn Gummer, b. 1942, m.

1964   *Chalfont* (Alun) Arthur Gwynne Jones, OBE,
      MC, PC, b. 1919, m.

1985   *Chapple*, Francis (Frank) Joseph Chapple,
      b. 1921, w.

1987   *Chilver* (Amos) Henry Chilver, FRS, FEng.,
      b. 1926, m.

1977   *Chitnis*, Pratap Chidamber Chitnis, b. 1936, m.

1998   *Christopher*, Anthony Martin Grosvenor
      Christopher, CBE, b. 1925, m.

1992   *Clark of Kempston*, William Gibson Haig Clark,
      PC, b. 1917, m.

1998   *Clarke of Hampstead*, Anthony James Clarke,
      CBE, b. 1932, m.

1979   *Cledwyn of Penrhos*, Cledwyn Hughes, CH, PC,
      b. 1916, m.

1998   *Clement-Jones*, Timothy Francis Clement-Jones,
      CBE, b. 1949, m.

1990   *Clinton-Davis*, Stanley Clinton Clinton-Davis,
      PC, b. 1928, m.

1978   *Cockfield* (Francis) Arthur Cockfield,
      PC, b. 1916, w.

1987   *Cocks of Hartcliffe*, Michael Francis Lovell Cocks,
      PC, b. 1929, m.

2000   *Coe*, Sebastian Newbold Coe, OBE, b. 1956, m.

1981   *Constantine of Stanmore*, Theodore Constantine,
      CBE, AE, b. 1910, w.

1992   *Cooke of Islandreagh*, Victor Alexander Cooke,
      OBE, b. 1920, m.

1996   *Cooke of Thorndon*, Robin Brunskill Cooke,
      KBE, PC, Ph.D., b. 1926, m.

1997   *Cope of Berkeley*, John Ambrose Cope,
      PC, b. 1937, m.

1997   *Cowdrey of Tonbridge* (Michael) Colin Cowdrey,
      CBE, b. 1932, m.

1991   *Craig of Radley*, David Brownrigg Craig, GCB, OBE,
      b. 1929, m. *Marshal of the Royal Air Force*

1987   *Crickhowell* (Roger) Nicholas Edwards,
      PC, b. 1934, m.

1978   *Croham*, Douglas Albert Vivian Allen,
      GCB, b. 1917, w.

1995   *Cuckney*, John Graham Cuckney, b. 1925, m.

1996   *Currie of Marylebone*, David Anthony
      Currie, b. 1946, m.

1979   *Dacre of Glanton*, Hugh Redwald
      Trevor-Roper, b. 1914, w.

1993   *Dahrendorf*, Ralf Dahrendorf, KBE, Ph.D., D.Phil.,
      FBA, b. 1929, m.

1997   *Davies of Coity* (David) Garfield Davies,
      CBE, b. 1935, m.

1997   *Davies of Oldham*, Bryan Davies, b. 1939, m.

1993   *Dean of Harptree* (Arthur) Paul Dean,
      PC, b. 1924, m.

1998   *Dearing*, Ronald Ernest Dearing, CB, b. 1930, m.

1986   *Deedes*, William Francis Deedes, KBE, MC,
      PC, b. 1913, m.

1991   *Desai*, Prof. Meghnad Jagdishchandra Desai,
      Ph.D., b. 1940, m.

1997   *Dholakia*, Navnit Dholakia, OBE, b. 1937, m.

1970   *Diamond*, John Diamond, PC, b. 1907, m.

1997   *Dixon*, Donald Dixon, PC, b. 1929, m.

1993   *Dixon-Smith*, Robert William Dixon-Smith,
      b. 1934, m.

1988   *Donaldson of Lymington*, John Francis Donaldson,
      PC, b. 1920, m.

1985   *Donoughue*, Bernard Donoughue, D.Phil.,
      b. 1934, m.

1987   *Dormand of Easington*, John Donkin Dormand,
      b. 1919, m.

1994   *Dubs*, Alfred Dubs, b. 1932, m.

1995   *Eames*, Robert Henry Alexander Eames, Ph.D.,
      b. 1937, m.

1992   *Eatwell*, John Leonard Eatwell, Ph.D., b. 1945, m.

1983   *Eden of Winton*, John Benedict Eden, PC, b. 1925, m.

1999   *Elder*, Thomas Murray Elder.

1992   *Elis-Thomas*, Dafydd Elis Elis-Thomas, b. 1946, m.

1985   *Elliott of Morpeth*, Robert William Elliott, b. 1920, m.

1981   *Elystan-Morgan*, Dafydd Elystan
      Elystan-Morgan, b. 1932, m.

1980	*Emslie*, George Carlyle Emslie, MBE, PC, FRSE, *b.* 1919, *m.*	1970	*Hailsham of St Marylebone*, Quintin McGarel Hogg, KG, CH, PC, FRS, *b.* 1907, *w.*
1997	*Evans of Parkside*, John Evans, *b.* 1930, *m.*	1994	*Hambro*, Charles Eric Alexander Hambro, *b.* 1930, *m.*
2000	*Evans of Temple Guiting*, Matthew Evans, CBE, *b.* 1941, *m.*	1998	*Hamlyn*, Paul Bertrand Hamlyn, CBE, *b.* 1926, *m.*
1998	*Evans of Watford*, David Charles Evans, *b.* 1942, *m.*	1998	*Hanningfield*, Paul Edward Winston White, *b.* 1940, *m.*
1992	*Ewing of Kirkford*, Harry Ewing, *b.* 1931, *m.*	1983	*Hanson*, James Edward Hanson, *b.* 1922, *m.*
1983	*Ezra*, Derek Ezra, MBE, *b.* 1919, *m.*	1997	*Hardie*, Andrew Rutherford Hardie, QC, PC,
1997	*Falconer of Thoroton*, Charles Leslie Falconer, QC, *b.* 1951, *m.*		*b.* 1946, *m. Lord Advocate*
1983	*Fanshawe of Richmond*, Anthony Henry Fanshawe Royle, KCMG, *b.* 1927, *m.*	1997	*Hardy of Wath*, Peter Hardy, *b.* 1931, *m.*
1999	*Faulkner of Worcester*, Richard Oliver Faulkner, *b.* 1946, *m.*	1974	*Harmar-Nicholls*, Harmar Harmar-Nicholls, *b.* 1912, *m.*
1996	*Feldman*, Basil Feldman, *b.* 1926, *m.*	1974	*Harris of Greenwich*, John Henry Harris, PC, *b.* 1930, *m.*
1999	*Fellowes*, Robert Fellowes, PC, GCB, GCVO, *b.* 1941, *m.*	1998	*Harris of Haringey* (Jonathan) Toby Harris, *b.* 1953, *m.*
1999	*Filkin*, David Geoffrey Nigel Filkin, CBE, *b.* 1944, *m.*	1979	*Harris of High Cross*, Ralph Harris, *b.* 1924, *m.*
1983	*Fitt*, Gerard Fitt, *b.* 1926, *w.*	1996	*Harris of Peckham*, Philip Charles Harris, *b.* 1942, *m.*
1979	*Flowers*, Brian Hilton Flowers, FRS, *b.* 1924, *m.*	1999	*Harrison*, Lyndon Henry Arthur Harrison, *b.* 1947, *m.*
1967	*Foot*, John Mackintosh Foot, *b.* 1909, *m.*	1968	*Hartwell* (William) Michael Berry, MBE, TD,
1999	*Forsyth of Drumlean*, Michael Bruce Forsyth, *b.* 1954, *m.*		*b.* 1911, *w.*
1982	*Forte*, Charles Forte, *b.* 1908, *m.*	1993	*Haskel*, Simon Haskel, *b.* 1934, *m.*
1999	*Foster of Thames Bank*, Norman Robert Foster, OM, *b.* 1935, *m.*	1998	*Haskins*, Christopher Robin Haskins, *b.* 1937, *m.*
1989	*Fraser of Carmyllie*, Peter Lovat Fraser, PC, QC, *b.* 1945, *m.*	1990	*Haslam*, Robert Haslam, *b.* 1923, *m.*
1997	*Freeman*, Roger Norman Freeman, PC, *b.* 1942, *m.*	1997	*Hattersley*, Roy Sidney George Hattersley, PC, *b.* 1932, *m.*
2000	*Fyfe of Fairfield*, George Lennox Fyfe, *b.* 1941, *m.*	1992	*Hayhoe*, Bernard John (Barney) Hayhoe, PC, *b.* 1925, *m.*
1982	*Gallacher*, John Gallacher, *b.* 1920, *m.*	1992	*Healey*, Denis Winston Healey, CH, MBE, PC, *b.* 1917, *m.*
1997	*Garel-Jones* (William Armand) Thomas Tristan Garel-Jones, PC, *b.* 1941, *m.*	1997	*Higgins*, Terence Langley Higgins, KBE, PC, *b.* 1928, *m.*
1999	*Gavron*, Robert Gavron, CBE, *b.* 1930, *m.*	1979	*Hill-Norton*, Peter John Hill-Norton, GCB,
1992	*Geraint*, Geraint Wyn Howells, *b.* 1925, *m.*		*b.* 1915, *m. Admiral of the Fleet*
1975	*Gibson* (Richard) Patrick (Tallentyre) Gibson, *b.* 1916, *m.*	2000	*Hodgson of Astley Abbotts*, Robin Granville Hodgson, CBE, *b.* 1937, *m.*
1979	*Gibson-Watt* (James) David Gibson-Watt, MC, PC, *b.* 1918, *m.*	1997	*Hogg of Cumbernauld*, Norman Hogg, *b.* 1938, *m.*
1997	*Gilbert*, John William Gilbert, PC, Ph.D., *b.* 1927, *m.*	1979	*Holderness*, Richard Frederick Wood, PC, *b.* 1920, *m.*
1992	*Gilmour of Craigmillar*, Ian Hedworth John Little Gilmour, PC, *b.* 1926, *m.*	1991	*Hollick*, Clive Richard Hollick, *b.* 1945, *m.*
1994	*Gladwin of Clee*, Derek Oliver Gladwin, CBE, *b.* 1930, *m.*	1990	*Holme of Cheltenham*, Richard Gordon Holme, CBE, *b.* 1936, *m.*
1977	*Glenamara*, Edward Watson Short, CH, PC, *b.* 1912, *m.*	1979	*Hooson* (Hugh) Emlyn Hooson, QC, *b.* 1925, *m.*
1999	*Goldsmith*, Peter Henry Goldsmith, QC, *b.* 1950, *m.*	1995	*Hope of Craighead* (James Arthur) David Hope, PC, *b.* 1938, *m. Lord of Appeal in Ordinary*
1997	*Goodhart*, William Howard Goodhart, QC, *b.* 1933, *m.*	1992	*Howe of Aberavon* (Richard Edward) Geoffrey Howe, CH, PC, QC, *b.* 1926, *m.*
1997	*Gordon of Strathblane*, James Stuart Gordon, CBE, *b.* 1936, *m.*	1997	*Howell of Guildford*, David Arthur Russell Howell, PC, *b.* 1936, *m.*
1999	*Grabiner*, Anthony Stephen Grabiner, QC, *b.* 1945, *m.*	1978	*Howie of Troon*, William Howie, *b.* 1924, *m.*
1983	*Graham of Edmonton* (Thomas) Edward Graham, *b.* 1925, *m.*	1997	*Hoyle* (Eric) Douglas Harvey Hoyle, *b.* 1930, *w.*
1983	*Gray of Contin*, James (Hamish) Hector Northey Gray, PC, *b.* 1927, *m.*	1997	*Hughes of Woodside*, Robert Hughes, *b.* 1932, *m.*
1974	*Greene of Harrow Weald*, Sidney Francis Greene, CBE, *b.* 1910, *m.*	2000	*Hunt of Chesterton*, Julian Charles Roland Hunt, CBE, *b.* 1941, *m.*
1974	*Greenhill of Harrow*, Denis Arthur Greenhill, GCMG, OBE, *b.* 1913, *m.*	1997	*Hunt of Kings Heath*, Philip Alexander Hunt, OBE, *b.* 1949, *m.*
1975	*Gregson*, John Gregson, *b.* 1924.	1980	*Hunt of Tanworth*, John Joseph Benedict Hunt, GCB, *b.* 1919, *m.*
1991	*Griffiths of Fforestfach*, Brian Griffiths, *b.* 1941, *m.*	1997	*Hunt of Wirral*, David James Fletcher Hunt, MBE, PC, *b.* 1942, *m.*
2000	*Gueterbock*, Anthony Fitzhardinge, OBE, *b. m.*	1997	*Hurd of Westwell*, Douglas Richard Hurd, CH, CBE, PC, *b.* 1930, *m.*
1995	*Habgood*, Rt. Revd John Stapylton Habgood, PC, Ph.D., *b.* 1927, *w.*	1996	*Hussey of North Bradley*, Marmaduke James Hussey, *b.* 1923, *m.*
		1978	*Hutchinson of Lullington*, Jeremy Nicolas Hutchinson, QC, *b.* 1915, *m.*
		1999	*Imbert*, Peter Michael Imbert, QPM, *b.* 1933, *m.*

1997	*Inge*, Peter Anthony Inge, GCB, *b.* 1935, *m.* Field Marshal
1982	*Ingrow*, John Aked Taylor, OBE, TD, *b.* 1917, *m.*
1987	*Irvine of Lairg*, Alexander Andrew Mackay Irvine, PC, QC, *b.* 1940, *m.* Lord High Chancellor
1997	*Islwyn*, Royston John (Roy) Hughes, *b.* 1925, *m.*
1997	*Jacobs* (David) Anthony Jacobs, *b.* 1931, *m.*
1997	*Janner of Braunstone*, Greville Ewan Janner, QC, *b.* 1928, *w.*
1987	*Jenkin of Roding* (Charles) Patrick (Fleeming) Jenkin, PC, *b.* 1926, *m.*
1987	*Jenkins of Hillhead*, Roy Harris Jenkins, OM, PC, *b.* 1920, *m.*
1981	*Jenkins of Putney*, Hugh Gater Jenkins, *b.* 1908, *w.*
2000	*Joffe of Liddington*, Joel Goodman Joffe, CBE, *b.* 1932, *m.*
1987	*Johnston of Rockport*, Charles Collier Johnston, TD, *b.* 1915, *m.*
1997	*Jopling* (Thomas) Michael Jopling, PC, *b.* 1930, *m.*
2000	*Jordan*, William Brian Jordan, CBE, *b.* 1936, *m.*
1991	*Judd*, Frank Ashcroft Judd, *b.* 1935, *m.*
1980	*Keith of Castleacre*, Kenneth Alexander Keith, *b.* 1916, *m.*
1997	*Kelvedon* (Henry) Paul Guinness Channon, PC, *b.* 1935, *m.*
1996	*Kilpatrick of Kincraig*, Robert Kilpatrick, CBE, *b.* 1926, *m.*
1985	*Kimball*, Marcus Richard Kimball, *b.* 1928, *m.*
1983	*King of Wartnaby*, John Leonard King, *b.* 1918, *m.*
1999	*King of West Bromwich*, Tarsem King.
1993	*Kingsdown*, Robert (Robin) Leigh-Pemberton, KG, PC, *b.* 1927, *m.*
1994	*Kingsland*, Christopher James Prout, TD, PC, QC, *b.* 1942.
1999	*Kirkham*, Graham Kirkham, *b.* 1944, *m.*
1975	*Kirkhill*, John Farquharson Smith, *b.* 1930, *m.*
1987	*Knights*, Philip Douglas Knights, CBE, QPM, *b.* 1920, *m.*
1991	*Laing of Dunphail*, Hector Laing, *b.* 1923, *m.*
1999	*Laird*, John Dunn Laird, *b.* 1944, *m.*
1998	*Laming* (William) Herbert Laming, CBE, *b.* 1936, *m.*
1998	*Lamont of Lerwick*, Norman Stewart Hughson Lamont, PC, *b.* 1942.
1990	*Lane of Horsell*, Peter Stewart Lane, *b.* 1925, *w.*
1997	*Lang of Monkton*, Ian Bruce Lang, PC, *b.* 1940, *m.*
1992	*Lawson of Blaby*, Nigel Lawson, PC, *b.* 1932, *m.*
2000	*Layard*, Peter Richard Grenville Layard, *b.* 1934, *m.*
1999	*Lea of Crondall*, David Edward Lea, OBE, *b.* 1937, *m.*
1993	*Lester of Herne Hill*, Anthony Paul Lester, QC, *b.* 1936, *m.*
1997	*Levene of Portsoken*, Peter Keith Levene, KBE, *b.* 1941, *m.*
1997	*Levy*, Michael Abraham Levy, *b.* 1944, *m.*
1989	*Lewis of Newnham*, Jack Lewis, FRS, *b.* 1928, *m.*
1999	*Lipsey*, David Lawrence Lipsey, *b.* 1948, *m.*
1997	*Lloyd-Webber*, Andrew Lloyd Webber, *b.* 1948, *m.*
1997	*Lofthouse of Pontefract*, Geoffrey Lofthouse, *b.* 1925, *w.*
1974	*Lovell-Davis*, Peter Lovell Lovell-Davis, *b.* 1924, *m.*
1998	*Marshall of Knightsbridge*, Colin Marsh Marshall, *b.* 1933, *m.*
1988	*Macaulay of Bragar*, Donald Macaulay, QC, *b.* 1933, *m.*
1975	*McCarthy*, William Edward John McCarthy, D.Phil., *b.* 1925, *m.*
1976	*McCluskey*, John Herbert McCluskey, *b.* 1929, *m.*
1989	*McColl of Dulwich*, Ian McColl, CBE, FRCS, FRCSE, *b.* 1933, *m.*
1995	*McConnell*, Robert William Brian McConnell, PC (NI), *b.* 1922, *m.*
1998	*Macdonald of Tradeston*, Angus John Macdonald, CBE, *b.* 1940, *m.*
1991	*Macfarlane of Bearsden*, Norman Somerville Macfarlane, KT, FRSE, *b.* 1926, *m.*
1982	*McIntosh of Haringey*, Andrew Robert McIntosh, *b.* 1933, *m.*
1991	*Mackay of Ardbrecknish*, John Jackson Mackay, PC, *b.* 1938, *m.*
1979	*Mackay of Clashfern*, James Peter Hymers Mackay, KT, PC, FRSE, *b.* 1927, *m.*
1995	*Mackay of Drumadoon*, Donald Sage Mackay, PC, *b.* 1946, *m.*
1999	*MacKenzie of Culkein*, Hector Uisdean MacKenzie, *b.* 1940.
1998	*Mackenzie of Framwellgate*, Brian Mackenzie, OBE, *b.* 1943, *m.*
1974	*Mackie of Benshie*, George Yull Mackie, CBE, DSO, DFC, *b.* 1919, *m.*
1996	*MacLaurin*, Ian Charter MacLaurin, *b.* 1937, *w.*
1982	*MacLehose of Beoch* (Crawford) Murray MacLehose, KT, GBE, KCMG, KCVO, *b.* 1917, *m.*
1995	*McNally*, Tom McNally, *b.* 1943, *m.*
1991	*Marlesford*, Mark Shuldham Schreiber, *b.* 1931, *m.*
1981	*Marsh*, Richard William Marsh, PC, *b.* 1928, *m.*
1987	*Mason of Barnsley*, Roy Mason, PC, *b.* 1924, *m.*
1997	*Mayhew of Twysden*, Patrick Barnabas Burke Mayhew, QC, PC, *b.* 1929, *m.*
1984	*McAlpine of West Green* (Robert) Alistair McAlpine, *b.* 1942, *m.*
1992	*Merlyn-Rees*, Merlyn Merlyn-Rees, PC, *b.* 1920, *m.*
1978	*Mishcon*, Victor Mishcon, *b.* 1915, *m.*
2000	*Mitchell*, Parry Andrew Mitchell, *m.*
2000	*Mitford*, Rupert Bertram Redesdale, *b.* 1967, *m.*
1981	*Molloy*, William John Molloy, *b.* 1918.
1997	*Molyneaux of Killead*, James Henry Molyneaux, KBE, PC, *b.* 1920.
1997	*Monro of Langholm*, Hector Seymour Peter Monro, AE, PC, *b.* 1922, *m.*
1992	*Moore of Lower Marsh*, John Edward Michael Moore, PC, *b.* 1937, *m.*
1986	*Moore of Wolvercote*, Philip Brian Cecil Moore, GCB, GCVO, CMG, PC, *b.* 1921, *m.*
2000	*Morgan*, Kenneth Owen Morgan, *b.* 1934, *m.*
1990	*Morris of Castle Morris*, Brian Robert Morris, D.Phil., *b.* 1930, *m.*
1997	*Morris of Manchester*, Alfred Morris, PC, *b.* 1928, *m.*
1971	*Moyola*, James Dawson Chichester-Clark, PC (NI), *b.* 1923, *m.*
1985	*Murray of Epping Forest*, Lionel Murray, OBE, PC, *b.* 1922, *m.*
1979	*Murton of Lindisfarne* (Henry) Oscar Murton, OBE, TD, PC, *b.* 1914, *m.*
1997	*Naseby*, Michael Wolfgang Laurence Morris, PC, *b.* 1936, *m.*
1997	*Neill of Bladen* (Francis) Patrick Neill, QC, *b.* 1926, *m.*
1997	*Newby*, Richard Mark Newby, OBE, *b.* 1953, *m.*
1997	*Newton of Braintree*, Antony Harold Newton, OBE, PC, *b.* 1937, *m.*
1994	*Nickson*, David Wigley Nickson, KBE, FRSE, *b.* 1929, *m.*
1975	*Northfield* (William) Donald Chapman, *b.* 1923.
1998	*Norton of Louth*, Philip Norton, *b.* 1951.
1997	*Onslow of Woking*, Cranley Gordon Douglas Onslow, KCMG, PC, *b.* 1926, *m.*
1997	*Orme*, Stanley Orme, PC, *b.* 1923, *m.*

1992 Owen, David Anthony Llewellyn Owen,
CH, PC, b. 1938, m.
1999 Oxburgh, Ernest Ronald Oxburgh, KBE,
FRS, Ph.D., b. 1934, m.
1991 Palumbo, Peter Garth Palumbo, b. 1935, m.
2000 Parekh, Bhikhu Chhotalal Parekh, b. 1935, m.
1992 Parkinson, Cecil Edward Parkinson, PC, b. 1931, m.
1975 Parry, Gordon Samuel David Parry, b. 1925, m.
1999 Patel, Narendra Babubhai Patel, b. 1938, m.
2000 Patel of Blackburn, Adam Hafejee Patel, m.
1997 Patten, John Haggitt Charles Patten,
PC, b. 1945, m.
1996 Paul, Swraj Paul, b. 1931, m.
1990 Pearson of Rannoch, Malcolm Everard
MacLaren Pearson, b. 1942, m.
1979 Perry of Walton, Walter Laing Macdonald
Perry, OBE, FRS, FRSE, b. 1921, m.
1987 Peston, Maurice Harry Peston, b. 1931, m.
1983 Peyton of Yeovil, John Wynne William Peyton,
PC, b. 1919, m.
1998 Phillips of Sudbury, Andrew Wyndham Phillips,
OBE, b. 1939, m.
1996 Pilkington of Oxenford, Revd Canon Peter
Pilkington, b. 1933, w.
1992 Plant of Highfield, Prof. Raymond Plant, Ph.D.,
b. 1945, m.
1959 Plowden, Edwin Noel Plowden, GBE,
KCB, b. 1907, m.
1987 Plumb (Charles) Henry Plumb,
MEP, b. 1925, m.
1981 Plummer of St Marylebone (Arthur) Desmond
(Herne) Plummer, TD, b. 1914, w.
1990 Porter of Luddenham, George Porter, OM,
FRS, b. 1920, m.
2000 Powell of Bayswater, Charles David Powell,
KCMG, b. 1941, m.
1992 Prentice, Reginald Ernest Prentice, PC, b. 1923, m.
1987 Prior, James Michael Leathes Prior, PC,
b. 1927, m.
1982 Prys-Davies, Gwilym Prys Prys-Davies, b. 1923, m.
1997 Puttnam, David Terence Puttnam, CBE,
b. 1941, m.
1987 Pym, Francis Leslie Pym, MC, PC, b. 1922, m.
1982 Quinton, Anthony Meredith Quinton,
FBA, b. 1925, m.
1994 Quirk, Prof. (Charles) Randolph Quirk, CBE,
FBA, b. 1920, m.
1997 Randall of St Budeaux, Stuart Jeffrey
Randall, b. 1938, m.
1978 Rawlinson of Ewell, Peter Anthony Grayson
Rawlinson, PC, QC, b. 1919, m.
1976 Rayne, Max Rayne, b. 1918, m.
1997 Razzall (Edward) Timothy Razzall,
CBE, b. 1943, m.
1987 Rees, Peter Wynford Innes Rees,
PC, QC, b. 1926, m.
1988 Rees Mogg, William Rees-Mogg, b. 1928, m.
1991 Renfrew of Kaimsthorn (Andrew) Colin
Renfrew, FBA, b. 1937, m.
1999 Rennard, Christopher John Rennard,
MBE, b. 1960, m.
1979 Renton, David Lockhart-Mure Renton,
KBE, TD, DL, QC, b. 1908, w.
1997 Renton of Mount Harry (Ronald) Timothy
Renton, PC, b. 1932, m.
1997 Renwick of Clifton, Robin William Renwick,
KCMG, b. 1937, m.
1990 Richard, Ivor Seward Richard, PC, QC, b. 1932, m.
1979 Richardson, John Samuel Richardson, LVO,
MD, FRCP, b. 1910, m.

1983 Richardson of Duntisbourne, Gordon William
Humphreys Richardson, KG, MBE, TD,
PC, b. 1915, m.
1992 Rix, Brian Norman Roger Rix, CBE, b. 1924, m.
1997 Roberts of Conwy (Ieuan) Wyn (Pritchard)
Roberts, PC, b. 1930, m.
1999 Robertson of Port Ellen, George Islay MacNeill
Robertson, PC, b. 1946.
1992 Rodger of Earlsferry, Alan Ferguson Rodger,
PC, QC, FBA, b. 1944, m.
1992 Rodgers of Quarry Bank, William Thomas Rodgers,
PC, b. 1928, m.
1999 Rogan, Dennis Robert David Rogan, b. 1942, m.
1996 Rogers of Riverside, Richard George Rogers, RA,
RIBA, b. 1933, m.
1977 Roll of Ipsden, Eric Roll, KCMG, CB, b. 1907, w.
2000 Roper, John Francis Hodgess Roper, b. 1935, m.
1991 Runcie, Rt Revd Robert Alexander Kennedy
Runcie, MC, PC, Royal Victorian Chain,
b. 1921, m.
1997 Russell-Johnston (David) Russell Russell-Johnston,
b. 1932, m.
1975 Ryder of Eaton Hastings, Sydney Thomas Franklin
(Don) Ryder, b. 1916, m.
1997 Ryder of Wensum, Richard Andrew Ryder,
OBE, PC, b. 1949, m.
1996 Saatchi, Maurice Saatchi, b. 1946, m.
1989 Sainsbury of Preston Candover, John Davan
Sainsbury, KG, b. 1927, m.
1997 Sainsbury of Turville, David John Sainsbury,
b. 1940, m.
1997 Sandberg, Michael Graham Ruddock Sandberg,
CBE, b. 1927, m.
1985 Sanderson of Bowden, Charles Russell Sanderson,
b. 1933, m.
1998 Sawyer, Lawrence (Tom) Sawyer.
1979 Scanlon, Hugh Parr Scanlon, b. 1913, m.
1978 Sefton of Garston, William Henry Sefton, b. 1915, m.
1997 Selkirk of Douglas, James Alexander
Douglas-Hamilton, MSP, PC, QC, b. 1942, m.
1996 Sewel, John Buttifant Sewel, CBE, b. 1946.
1999 Sharman, Colin Morven Sharman,
OBE, b. 1943, m.
1994 Shaw of Northstead, Michael Norman Shaw,
b. 1920, m.
1959 Shawcross, Hartley William Shawcross, GBE,
PC, QC, b. 1902, m.
1994 Sheppard of Didgemere, Allan John George
Sheppard, KCVO, b. 1932, m.
1998 Sheppard of Liverpool, David Stuart
Sheppard, b. 1929, m.
1997 Shore of Stepney, Peter David Shore, PC,
b. 1924, m.
2000 Shutt of Greetland, David Trevor Shutt, OBE, b. m.
1980 Sieff of Brimpton, Marcus Joseph Sieff,
OBE, b. 1913, w.
1971 Simon of Glaisdale, Jocelyn Edward Salis Simon,
PC, b. 1911, m.
1997 Simon of Highbury, David Alec Gwyn Simon,
CBE, b. 1939, m.
1997 Simpson of Dunkeld, George Simpson, b. 1942, m.
1991 Skidelsky, Robert Jacob Alexander Skidelsky,
D.Phil., b. 1939, m.
1997 Smith of Clifton, Trevor Arthur Smith, b. 1937, m.
1999 Smith of Leigh, Peter Richard Charles Smith.
1990 Soulsby of Swaffham Prior, Ernest Jackson
Lawson Soulsby, Ph.D., b. 1926, m.
1987 St John of Fawsley, Norman Antony Francis
St John-Stevas, PC, b. 1929, m.
1983 Stallard, Albert William Stallard, b. 1921, m.

1997 *Steel of Aikwood*, David Martin Scott Steel,
PC, KBE, MSP, *b.* 1938, *m.*

1991 *Sterling of Plaistow*, Jeffrey Maurice Sterling,
CBE, *b.* 1934, *m.*

1987 *Stevens of Ludgate*, David Robert Stevens, *b.* 1936, *m.*

1999 *Stevenson of Coddenham*, Henry Dennistoun
Stevenson, CBE, *b.* 1945, *m.*

1992 *Stewartby* (Bernard Harold) Ian (Halley) Stewart,
RD, PC, FBA, FRSE, *b.* 1935, *m.*

1981 *Stodart of Leaston*, James Anthony Stodart,
PC, *b.* 1916, *m.*

1983 *Stoddart of Swindon*, David Leonard Stoddart,
b. 1926, *m.*

1969 *Stokes*, Donald Gresham Stokes, TD, FEng.,
b. 1914, *w.*

1997 *Stone of Blackheath*, Andrew Zelig Stone,
b. 1942, *m.*

1971 *Tanlaw*, Simon Brooke Mackay, *b.* 1934, *m.*

1996 *Taverne*, Dick Taverne, QC, *b.* 1928, *m.*

1978 *Taylor of Blackburn*, Thomas Taylor, CBE,
b. 1929, *m.*

1968 *Taylor of Gryfe*, Thomas Johnston Taylor,
FRSE, *b.* 1912, *m.*

1996 *Taylor of Warwick*, John David Beckett
Taylor, *b.* 1952, *m.*

1992 *Tebbit*, Norman Beresford Tebbit, CH, PC,
b. 1931, *m.*

1996 *Thomas of Gresford*, Donald Martin Thomas,
OBE, QC, *b.* 1937, *m.*

1987 *Thomas of Gwydir*, Peter John Mitchell
Thomas, PC, QC, *b.* 1920, *w.*

1997 *Thomas of Macclesfield*, Terence James Thomas,
CBE, *b.* 1937, *m.*

1981 *Thomas of Swynnerton*, Hugh Swynnerton Thomas,
b. 1931, *m.*

1977 *Thomson of Monifieth*, George Morgan Thomson,
KT, PC, *b.* 1921, *m.*

1990 *Tombs*, Francis Leonard Tombs,
FEng., *b.* 1924, *m.*

1998 *Tomlinson*, John Edward Tomlinson,
MEP, *b.* 1939.

1994 *Tope*, Graham Norman Tope, CBE, *b.* 1943, *m.*

1981 *Tordoff*, Geoffrey Johnson Tordoff, *b.* 1928, *m.*

1999 *Trotman*, Alexander Trotman, *b.* 1933.

1993 *Tugendhat*, Christopher Samuel Tugendhat,
b. 1937, *m.*

1990 *Varley*, Eric Graham Varley, PC, *b.* 1932, *m.*

1996 *Vincent of Coleshill*, Richard Frederick Vincent,
GBE, KCB, DSO, *b.* 1931, *m. (Field Marshal).*

1985 *Vinson*, Nigel Vinson, LVO, *b.* 1931, *m.*

1990 *Waddington*, David Charles Waddington,
GCVO, PC, QC, *b.* 1929, *m.*

1990 *Wade of Chorlton* (William) Oulton Wade,
b. 1932, *m.*

1992 *Wakeham*, John Wakeham, PC, *b.* 1932, *m.*

1999 *Waldegrave of North Hill*, William Arthur
Waldegrave, PC, *b.* 1946, *m.*

1997 *Walker of Doncaster*, Harold Walker,
PC, *b.* 1927, *m.*

1992 *Walker of Worcester*, Peter Edward Walker,
MBE, PC, *b.* 1932, *m.*

1974 *Wallace of Coslany*, George Douglas Wallace,
b. 1906, *m.*

1995 *Wallace of Saltaire*, William John Lawrence
Wallace, Ph.D., *b.* 1941, *m.*

1989 *Walton of Detchant*, John Nicholas Walton,
TD, FRCP, *b.* 1922, *m.*

1998 *Warner*, Norman Reginald Warner, *b.* 1940, *m.*

1997 *Watson of Invergowrie*, Michael Goodall Watson,
MSP, *b.* 1949, *m.*

1999 *Watson of Richmond*, Alan John Watson,
CBE, *b.* 1941, *m.*

1992 *Weatherill* (Bruce) Bernard Weatherill, PC,
b. 1920, *m.*

1977 *Wedderburn of Charlton* (Kenneth) William
Wedderburn, FBA, QC, *b.* 1927, *m.*

1976 *Weidenfeld* (Arthur) George Weidenfeld,
b. 1919, *m.*

1980 *Weinstock*, Arnold Weinstock, *b.* 1924, *m.*

1978 *Whaddon* (John) Derek Page, *b.* 1927, *m.*

1996 *Whitty*, John Lawrence (Larry) Whitty,
b. 1943, *m.*

1974 *Wigoder*, Basil Thomas Wigoder, QC,
b. 1921, *m.*

1985 *Williams of Elvel*, Charles Cuthbert Powell
Williams, CBE, *b.* 1933, *m.*

1992 *Williams of Mostyn*, Gareth Wyn Williams,
QC, *b.* 1941, *m.*

1999 *Williamson of Horton*, David Francis Williamson,
GCMG, CB, *b.* 1934, *m.*

1999 *Williamson of Horton*, David (Francis) Williamson,
GCMG, CB, *b.* 1934, *m.*

1992 *Wilson of Tillyorn*, David Clive Wilson, GCMG,
Ph.D., *b.* 1935, *m.*

1995 *Winston*, Robert Maurice Lipson Winston,
FRCOG, *b.* 1940, *m.*

1985 *Wolfson*, Leonard Gordon Wolfson, *b.* 1927, *m.*

1991 *Wolfson of Sunningdale*, David Wolfson, *b.* 1935, *m.*

1999 *Woolmer of Leeds*, Kenneth John Woolmer,
b. 1940, *m.*

1994 *Wright of Richmond*, Patrick Richard Henry
Wright, GCMG, *b.* 1931, *m.*

1978 *Young of Dartington*, Michael Young, Ph.D.,
b. 1915, *m.*

1984 *Young of Graffham*, David Ivor Young, PC,
b. 1932, *m.*

1992 *Younger of Prestwick*, The Viscount Younger of
Leckie.

BARONESSES

Created

1997 *Amos*, Valerie Ann Amos, *b.* 1954.

2000 *Andrews*, Elizabeth Kay Andrews, OBE.

1996 *Anelay of St Johns*, Joyce Anne Anelay, DBE,
b. 1947, *m.*

1999 *Ashton of Upholland*, Catherine Margaret
Ashton, *m.*

1999 *Barker*, Elizabeth Jean Barker, *b.* 1961.

1987 *Blackstone*, Tessa Ann Vosper Blackstone,
Ph.D., *b.* 1942, *m.*

1987 *Blatch*, Emily May Blatch, CBE, PC, *b.* 1937, *m.*

1999 *Blood*, May Blood, MBE, *b.* 1938.

1990 *Brigstocke*, Heather Renwick Brigstocke,
b. 1929, *w.*

1964 *Brooke of Ystradfellte*, Barbara Muriel Brooke,
DBE, *b.* 1908, *w.*

1998 *Buscombe*, Peta Jane Buscombe, *b.* 1954, *m.*

1996 *Byford*, Hazel Byford, DBE, *b.* 1941, *m.*

1982 *Carnegy of Lour*, Elizabeth Patricia Carnegy of
Lour, *b.* 1925.

1990 *Castle of Blackburn*, Barbara Anne Castle
PC, *b.* 1910, *w.*

1992 *Chalker of Wallasey*, Lynda Chalker, PC, *b.* 1942, *m.*

2000 *Cohen of Pimlico*, Janet Cohen, 1940, *m.*

1982 *Cox*, Caroline Anne Cox, *b.* 1937, *m.*

1998 *Crawley*, Christine Mary Crawley, MEP, *b.* 1950, *m.*

1990 *Cumberlege*, Julia Frances Cumberlege,
CBE, *b.* 1943, *m.*

1978 *David*, Nora Ratcliff David, *b.* 1913, *w.*

1993   *Dean of Thornton-le-Fylde*, Brenda Dean, PC, *b*. 1943, *m*.

1974   *Delacourt-Smith of Alteryn*, Margaret Rosalind Delacourt-Smith, *b*. 1916, *m*.

1991   *Denton of Wakefield*, Jean Denton, CBE, *b*. 1935, *w*.

1990   *Dunn*, Lydia Selina Dunn, DBE, *b*. 1940, *m*.

1990   *Eccles of Moulton*, Diana Catherine Eccles, *b*. 1933, *m*.

1972   *Elles*, Diana Louie Elles, *b*. 1921, *m*.

1997   *Emerton*, Audrey Caroline Emerton, DBE, *b*. 1935.

1974   *Falkender*, Marcia Matilda Falkender, CBE, *b*. 1932, *m*.

1994   *Farrington of Ribbleton*, Josephine Farrington, *b*. 1940, *m*.

1974   *Fisher of Rednal*, Doris Mary Gertrude Fisher, *b*. 1919, *w*.

1990   *Flather*, Shreela Flather, *m*.

1997   *Fookes*, Janet Evelyn Fookes, DBE, *b*. 1936.

1999   *Gale*, Anita Gale, *b*. 1940.

1981   *Gardner of Parkes* (Rachel) Trixie (Anne) Gardner, *b*. 1927, *m*.

2000   *Gibson of Market Rasen*, Anne Gibson, OBE, *b*. 1940, *m*.

1998   *Goudie*, Mary Teresa Goudie, *b*. 1946, *m*.

1993   *Gould of Potternewton*, Joyce Brenda Gould, *b*. 1932, *m*.

2000   *Greengross*, Sally Ralea Greengross, OBE, *b*. 1935, *m*.

1991   *Hamwee*, Sally Rachel Hamwee, *b*. 1947.

1999   *Hanham*, Joan Brownlow Hanham, CBE, *b*. 1939, *m*.

1999   *Harris of Richmond*, Angela Felicity Harris, *b*. 1944.

1996   *Hayman*, Helene Valerie Hayman, *b*. 1949, *m*.

1991   *Hilton of Eggardon*, Jennifer Hilton, QPM, *b*. 1936.

1995   *Hogg*, Sarah Elizabeth Mary Hogg, *b*. 1946, *m*.

1990   *Hollis of Heigham*, Patricia Lesley Hollis, D.Phil., *b*. 1941, *m*.

1985   *Hooper*, Gloria Dorothy Hooper, *b*. 1939.

1999   *Howells of St Davids*, Rosalind Particia-Anne Howells.

1965   *Hylton-Foster*, Audrey Pellew Hylton-Foster, DBE, *b*. 1908, *w*.

1991   *James of Holland Park*, Phyllis Dorothy White (P. D. James), OBE, *b*. 1920, *w*.

1992   *Jay of Paddington*, Margaret Ann Jay, PC, *b*. 1939, Lord Privy Seal, *w*.

1979   *Jeger*, Lena May Jeger, *b*. 1915, *w*.

1997   *Kennedy of the Shaws*, Helena Ann Kennedy, QC, *b*. 1950, *m*.

1997   *Knight of Collingtree* (Joan Christabel) Jill Knight, DBE, *b*. 1923, *w*.

1997   *Linklater of Butterstone*, Veronica Linklater, *b*. 1943, *m*.

1996   *Lloyd of Highbury*, Prof. June Kathleen Lloyd, DBE, FRCP, FRCPE, FRCGP, *b*. 1928.

1978   *Lockwood*, Betty Lockwood, *b*. 1924, *w*.

1997   *Ludford*, Sarah Ann Ludford, MEP, *b*. 1951, *m*.

1997   *Maddock*, Diana Margaret Maddock, *b*. 1945, *m*.

1991   *Mallalieu*, Ann Mallalieu, QC, *b*. 1945, *m*.

1970   *Masham of Ilton*, Susan Lilian Primrose Cunliffe-Lister, *b*. 1935, *m*. (*Countess of Swinton*).

1999   *Massey of Darwen*, Doreen Elizabeth Massey, *b*. 1938, *m*.

1979   *McFarlane of Llandaff*, Jean Kennedy McFarlane, *b*. 1926, *m*.

1999   *McIntosh of Hudnall*, Genista Mary McIntosh, *b*. 1946, *m*.

1998   *Miller of Chilthorne Domer*, Susan Elizabeth Miller, *b*. 1954.

1993   *Miller of Hendon*, Doreen Miller, MBE, *b*. 1933, *m*.

1997   *Nicholson of Winterbourne*, Emma Harriet Nicholson, MEP, *b*. 1941, *m*.

2000   *Northover*, Lindsay Patricia Granshaw, *m*.

1982   *Nicol*, Olive Mary Wendy Nicol, *b*. 1923, *m*.

2000   *Noakes*, Shiela Valerie Masters, DBE, *m*.

1991   *O'Cathain*, Detta O'Cathain, OBE, *b*. 1938, *m*.

1999   *O'Neill of Bengarve*, Onora Sylvia O'Neill, CBE, Ph.D., *b*. 1941.

1989   *Oppenheim-Barnes*, Sally Oppenheim-Barnes, PC, *b*. 1930, *m*.

1990   *Park of Monmouth*, Daphne Margaret Sybil Désirée Park, CMG, OBE, *b*. 1921.

1991   *Perry of Southwark*, Pauline Perry, *b*. 1931, *m*.

1974   *Pike* (Irene) Mervyn (Parnicott) Pike, DBE, *b*. 1918.

1997   *Pitkeathley*, Jill Elizabeth Pitkeathley, OBE, *b*. 1940.

1981   *Platt of Writtle*, Beryl Catherine Platt, CBE, FEng., *b*. 1923, *m*.

1999   *Prashar*, Usha Kumari Prashar, CBE, *b*. 1948, *m*.

1996   *Ramsay of Cartvale*, Margaret Mildred (Meta) Ramsay, *b*. 1936.

1994   *Rawlings*, Patricia Elizabeth Rawlings, *b*. 1939.

1997   *Rendell of Babergh*, Ruth Barbara Rendell, CBE, *b*. 1930, *m*.

1998   *Richardson of Calow*, Kathleen Margaret Richardson, OBE, *b*. 1938, *m*.

1979   *Ryder of Warsaw*, Margaret Susan Cheshire (Sue Ryder), CMG, OBE, *b*. 1923, *w*.

1997   *Scotland of Asthal*, Patricia Janet Scotland, QC, *m*.

2000   *Scott of Needham Market*, Rosalind Carol Scott, *m*.

1991   *Seccombe*, Joan Anna Dalziel Seccombe, DBE, *b*. 1930, *m*.

1967   *Serota*, Beatrice Serota, DBE, *b*. 1919, *m*.

1998   *Sharp of Guildford*, Margaret Lucy Sharp, *m*.

1973   *Sharples*, Pamela Sharples, *b*. 1923, *m*.

1995   *Smith of Gilmorehill*, Elizabeth Margaret Smith, *b*. 1940, *w*.

1999   *Stern*, Vivien Helen Stern, CBE, *b*. 1941.

1996   *Symons of Vernham Dean*, Elizabeth Conway Symons, *b*. 1951.

1992   *Thatcher*, Margaret Hilda Thatcher, KG, OM, PC, FRS, *b*. 1925, *m*.

1994   *Thomas of Walliswood*, Susan Petronella Thomas, OBE, *b*. 1935, *m*.

1998   *Thornton* (Dorothea) Glenys Thornton, *b*. 1952, *m*.

1980   *Trumpington*, Jean Alys Barker, PC, *b*. 1922, *w*.

1985   *Turner of Camden*, Muriel Winifred Turner, *b*. 1927, *m*.

1998   *Uddin*, Manzila Pola Uddin, *b*. 1959, *m*.

2000   *Walmsley*, Joan Margaret Walmsley, *m*.

1985   *Warnock*, Helen Mary Warnock, DBE, *b*. 1924, *w*.

1999   *Warwick of Undercliffe*, Diana Mary Warwick, *b*. 1945, *m*.

1999   *Whitaker*, Janet Alison Whitaker, *m*.

1996   *Wilcox*, Judith Ann Wilcox, *w*.

1999   *Wilkins*, Rosalie Catherine Wilkins, *b*. 1946.

1993   *Williams of Crosby*, Shirley Vivien Teresa Brittain Williams, PC, *b*. 1930, *m*.

1971   *Young*, Janet Mary Young, PC, *b*. 1926, *m*.

1997   *Young of Old Scone*, Barbara Scott Young, *b*. 1948.

Lords Spiritual

The Lords Spiritual are the Archbishops of Canterbury and York and 24 diocesan bishops of the Church of England. The Bishops of London, Durham and Winchester always have seats in the House of Lords; the other 21 seats are filled by the remaining diocesan bishops in order of seniority. The Bishop of Sodor and Man and the Bishop of Gibraltar are not eligible to sit in the House of Lords.

ARCHBISHOPS

Style, The Most Revd and Right Hon. the Lord
  Archbishop of _
Addressed as Archbishop, *or* Your Grace

Introduced to House of Lords
1991   *Canterbury* (103rd), George Leonard Carey, PC,
       Ph.D., *b*.1935, *m.*, *cons.* 1987, *trans.* 1991
1990   *York* (96th), David Michael Hope, KCVO, PC,
       D.Phil., *b.* 1940, *cons.* 1985, *elected* 1985, *trans.*
       1991, 1995

BISHOPS

Style, The Right Revd the Lord Bishop of _
Addressed as My Lord
elected date of election as diocesan bishop

Introduced to House of Lords (as at mid-2000)
1996   *London* (132nd), Richard John Carew Chartres,
       b. 1947, *m.*, *cons.* 1992
1994   *Durham* (93rd) (Anthony) Michael (Arnold)
       Turnbull, *b.* 1935, *m.*, *cons.* 1988, *elected* 1988,
       trans. 1994
1996   *Winchester* (96th), Michael Charles Scott-Joynt,
       b. 1943, *m.*, *cons.* 1987
1979   *Chichester* (102nd), Eric Waldram Kemp, DD,
       b. 1915, *m.*, *cons.* 1974, *elected* 1974
1989   *Lichfield* (97th), Keith Norman Sutton, *b.* 1934,
       m., *cons.* 1978, *elected* 1984
1990   *Bristol* (54th), Barry Rogerson, *b.* 1936, *m.*,
       cons. 1979, *elected* 1985
1993   *Lincoln* (70th), Robert Maynard Hardy,
       b. 1936, *m.*, *cons.* 1980, *elected* 1986
1993   *Oxford* (41st), Richard Douglas Harries,
       b. 1936, *m.*, *cons.* 1987, *elected* 1987
1994   *Birmingham* (7th), Mark Santer,
       b. 1936, *m.*, *cons.* 1981, *elected* 1987
1995   *Blackburn* (7th), Alan David Chesters,
       b. 1937, *m.*, *cons.* 1989, *elected* 1989
1996   *Carlisle* (65th), Ian Harland, *b.* 1932,
       m., *cons.* 1985, *elected* 1989
1997   *Hereford* (103rd), John Keith Oliver,
       b. 1935, *m.*, *cons.* 1990, *elected* 1990
1997   *Southwark* (9th), Thomas Frederick Butler,
       b. 1940, *m.*, *cons.* 1985, *elected* 1991
1997   *Bath and Wells* (77th), James Lawton Thompson,
       b. 1936, *m.*, *cons.* 1978, *elected* 1991
1997   *Wakefield* (11th), Nigel Simeon McCulloch,
       b. 1942, *m.*, *cons.* 1986, *elected* 1992
1997   *Bradford* (8th), David James Smith, *b.* 1935,
       m., *cons.* 1987, *elected* 1992
1997   *Manchester* (10th), Christopher John Mayfield,
       b. 1935, *m.*, *cons.* 1985, *elected* 1993

1998   *Salisbury* (77th), David Staffurth Stancliffe,
       b. 1942, *m.*, *cons.* 1993, *elected* 1993
1998   *Gloucester* (39th), David Edward Bentley,
       b. 1935, *m.*, *cons.* 1986, *elected* 1993
1999   *Rochester* (106th), Michael James Nazir-Ali, Ph.D.,
       b. 1949, *m.*, *cons.* 1984, *elected* 1995
1999   *Guildford* (8th), John Warren Gladwin,
       b. 1942, *m.*, *cons.* 1994, *elected* 1994
1999   *Portsmouth* (8th), Kenneth William Stevenson,
       b. 1949, *m.*, *cons.* 1995, *elected* 1995
1999   *Derby* (6th), Jonathan Sansbury Bailey,
       b. 1940, *m.*, *cons.* 1992, *elected* 1995
1999   *St Albans* (9th), Christopher William Herbert,
       b. 1944, *m.*, *cons.* 1995, *elected* 1995

Bishops awaiting seats, in order of seniority (as at mid-2000)
       Chelmsford (8th), John Freeman Perry, *b.* 1935,
       m., *cons.* 1989, *elected* 1996
       Peterborough (37th), Ian Cundy, *b.* 1945,
       m., *cons.* 1992, *elected* 1996
       Chester (40th), Peter Robert Forster, Ph.D., *b.*
       1950, *cons.* 1996, *elected* 1996
       St Edmundsbury and Ipswich (9th) (John Hubert)
       Richard Lewis, *b.* 1943, *m.*, *cons.* 1992,
       elected 1997
       Truro (14th), William Ind, *b.* 1942, *m.*, *cons.* 1987,
       elected 1997
       Worcester (112th), Peter Stephen Maurice Selby,
       b. 1941, *cons.* 1984, *elected* 1997
       Newcastle (11th) (John) Martin Wharton,
       b. 1944, *m.*, *cons.* 1992, *elected* 1997
       Sheffield (6th), John Nicholls, *b.* 1943, *m.*, *cons.* 1990,
       elected 1997
       Coventry (8th), Colin J. Bennetts, *b.* 1940, *m.*, *cons.*
       1994, *elected* 1997
       Liverpool (7th), James Jones, *b.* 1948, *m.*, *cons.* 1994,
       elected 1998
       Leicester (6th), Timothy John Stevens, *b.* 1946,
       m., *cons.* 1999, *elected* 1999
       Southwell (10th), George Henry Cassidy,
       b. 1942, *m.*, *cons.* 1999, *elected* 1999
       Norwich (71), Rt Revd Graham R. James,
       b. 1951, *m.*, *cons.* 1993, *elected* 1999
       Exeter (70), Rt. Revd Michael L. Langrish,
       b. 1946, *m.*, *cons.* 1993, *apptd* 2000

COURTESY TITLES

From this list it will be seen that, for example, the Marquess of Blandford is heir to the Dukedom of Marlborough, and Viscount Amberley to the Earldom of Russell. Titles of second heirs are also given, and the courtesy title of the father of a second heir is indicated by *; e.g. Earl of Burlington, eldest son of *Marquess of Hartington

For forms of address, *see* page 135

MARQUESSES

*Blandford –
  Marlborough, D.
Bowmont and Cessford –
  Roxburghe, D.
Douglas and Clydesdale –
  Hamilton, D.
*Douro – *Wellington, D.*
Graham – *Montrose, D.*
Hamilton – *Abercorn, D.*
*Hartington – *Devonshire,
  D.*
*Kildare – *Leinster, D.*
Lorne – *Argyll, D.*
*Tavistock – *Bedford, D.*
Tullibardine – *Atholl, D.*
*Worcester – *Beaufort, D.*

EARLS

Aboyne – *Huntly, M.*
Ancram – *Lothian, M.*
Arundel and Surrey –
  Norfolk, D.
*Bective – *Headfort, M.*
*Belfast – *Donegall, M.*
Brecknock – *Camden, M.*
Burford – *St Albans, D.*
Burlington – *Hartington,
  M.*
*Cardigan – *Ailesbury, M.*
Compton – *Northampton,
  M.*
*Dalkeith – *Buccleuch, D.*
Dumfries – *Bute, M.*
*Euston – *Grafton, D.*
Glamorgan – *Worcester,
  M.*
Grosvenor – *Westminster,
  D.*
*Haddo – *Aberdeen and
  Temair, M.*
Hillsborough – *Downshire,
  M.*
Hopetoun – *Linlithgow,
  M.*
March and Kinrara –
  Richmond, D.
Medina – *Milford Haven,
  M.*
*Mount Charles –
  Conyngham, M.
Mornington – *Douro, M.*
Mulgrave *Normanby, M.*
Percy – *Northumberland,
  D.*
Ronaldshay – *Zetland, M.*
*St Andrews – *Kent, D.*

*Shelburne – *Lansdowne,
  M.*
*Southesk – *Fife, D.*
Sunderland – *Blandford,
  M.*
*Tyrone – *Waterford, M.*
Ulster – *Gloucester, D.*
*Uxbridge – *Anglesey, M.*
Wiltshire – *Winchester,
  M.*
Yarmouth – *Hertford, M.*

VISCOUNTS

Althorp – *Spencer, E.*
Amberley – *Russell, E.*
Andover – *Suffolk and
  Berkshire, E.*
Anson – *Lichfield, E.*
Asquith – *Oxford and
  Asquith, E.*
Boringdon – *Morley, E.*
Borodale – *Beatty, E.*
Boyle – *Shannon, E.*
Brocas – *Jellicoe, E.*
Campden – *Gainsborough,
  E.*
Carlow – *Portarlington, E.*
Carlton – *Wharncliffe, E.*
Castlereagh – *Londonderry,
  M.*
Chelsea – *Cadogan, E.*
Chewton – *Waldegrave, E.*
Chichester – *Belfast, E.*
Clanfield – *Peel, E.*
Clive – *Powis, E.*
Coke – *Leicester, E.*
Corry – *Belmore, E.*
Corvedale – *Baldwin of
  Bewdley, E.*
Cranborne – *Salisbury, M.*
Cranley – *Onslow, E.*
Crichton – *Erne, E.*
Crowhurst – *Cottenham, E.*
Curzon – *Howe, E.*
Dangan – *Cowley, E.*
Dawick – *Haig, E.*
Drumlanrig – *Queensberry,
  M.*
Duncannon – *Bessborough,
  E.*
Dungarvan – *Cork and
  Orrery, E.*
Dunluce – *Antrim, E.*
Dunwich – *Stradbroke, E.*
Dupplin – *Kinnoull, E.*
Ebrington – *Fortescue, E.*
Ednam – *Dudley, E.*

Encombe – *Eldon, E.*
Enfield – *Strafford, E.*
Erleigh – *Reading, M.*
Errington – *Cromer, E.*
FitzHarris – *Malmesbury,
  E.*
Folkestone – *Radnor, E.*
Forbes – *Granard, E.*
Garmoyle – *Cairns, E.*
Garnock – *Lindsay, E.*
Glandine – *Norbury, E.*
Glenapp – *Inchcape, E.*
Glentworth – *Limerick, E.*
Grimstone – *Verulam, E.*
Gwynedd – *Lloyd George of
  Dwyfor, E.*
Hawkesbury – *Liverpool,
  E.*
Hinchingbrooke –
  Sandwich, E.
Ikerrin – *Carrick, E.*
Ingestre – *Shrewsbury, E.*
Ipswich – *Euston, E.*
Jocelyn – *Roden, E.*
Kelburn – *Glasgow, E.*
Kilwarlin – *Hillsborough,
  E.*
Kingsborough – *Kingston,
  E.*
Kirkwall – *Orkney, E.*
Knebworth – *Lytton, E.*
Lascelles – *Harewood, E.*
Linley – *Snowdon, E.*
Loftus – *Ely, M.*
Lowther – *Lonsdale, E.*
Lumley – *Scarbrough, E.*
Lymington – *Portsmouth,
  E.*
Macmillan of Ovenden –
  Stockton, E.
Maitland – *Lauderdale, E.*
Malden – *Essex, E.*
Mandeville – *Manchester,
  D.*
Melgund – *Minto, E.*
Merton – *Nelson, E.*
Moore – *Drogheda, E.*
Newport – *Bradford, E.*
Newry and Mourne –
  Kilmorey, E.
Parker – *Macclesfield, E.*
Perceval – *Egmont, E.*
Petersham – *Harrington,
  E.*
Pollington – *Mexborough,
  E.*
Raynham – *Townshend, M.*
Reidhaven – *Seafield, E.*
Ruthven of Canberra –
  Gowrie, E.
St Cyres – *Iddesleigh, E.*
Sandon – *Harrowby, E.*
Savernake – *Cardigan, E.*
Slane – *Mount Charles, E.*
Somerton – *Normanton, E.*
Stopford – *Courtown, E.*

Stormont – *Mansfield, E.*
Strathallan – *Perth, E.*
Stuart – *Castle Stewart, E.*
Suirdale – *Donoughmore,
  E.*
Tamworth – *Ferrers, E.*
Tarbat – *Cromartie, E.*
Vaughan – *Lisburne, E.*
Weymouth – *Bath, M.*
Windsor – *Plymouth, E.*
Wolmer – *Selborne, E.*
Woodstock – *Portland, E.*

BARONS (LORD)

Aberdour – *Morton, E.*
Apsley – *Bathurst, E.*
Ardee – *Meath, E.*
Ashley – *Shaftesbury, E.*
Balgonie – *Leven and
  Melville, E.*
Balniel – *Crawford and
  Balcarres, E.*
Berriedale – *Caithness, E.*
Bingham – *Lucan, E.*
Binning – *Haddington, E.*
Brooke – *Warwick, E.*
Bruce – *Elgin, E.*
Buckhurst – *De La Warr,
  E.*
Burghley – *Exeter, M.*
Cardross – *Buchan, E.*
Carnegie – *Southesk, E.*
Clifton – *Darnley, E.*
Cochrane – *Dundonald, E.*
Courtenay – *Devon, E.*
Dalmeny – *Rosebery, E.*
Doune – *Moray, E.*
Downpatrick –
  St Andrews, E.
Dunglass – *Home, E.*
Eliot – *St Germans, E.*
Eskdail – *Dalkeith, E.*
Formartine – *Haddo, E.*
Gillford – *Clanwilliam, E.*
Glamis – *Strathmore, E.*
Greenock – *Cathcart, E.*
Guernsey – *Aylesford, E.*
Hay – *Erroll, E.*
Herbert – *Pembroke, E.*
Howard of Effingham –
  Effingham, E.
Howland – *Tavistock, M*
Hyde – *Clarendon, E.*
Inverurie – *Kintore, E.*
Irwin – *Halifax, E.*
Johnstone – *Annandale and
  Hartfell, E.*
Kenlis – *Bective, E.*
Langton – *Temple of Stowe,
  E.*
La Poer – *Tyrone, E.*
Leslie – *Rothes, E.*
Loughborough – *Rosslyn,
  E.*
Maltravers – *Arundel and
  Surrey, E.*

Mauchline – *Loudoun, C.*
Medway – *Cranbrook, E.*
Montgomerie – *Eglinton and Winton, E.*
Moreton – *Ducie, E.*
Naas – *Mayo, E.*
Neidpath – *Wemyss and March, E.*

Norreys – *Lindsey and Abingdon, E.*
Ogilvy – *Airlie, E.*
Oxmantown – *Rosse, E.*
Paget de Beaudesert – **Uxbridge, E.*
Porchester – *Carnarvon, E.*
Ramsay – *Dalhousie, E.*

Romsey – *Mountbatten of Burma, C.*
Rosehill – *Northesk, E.*
Scrymgeour – *Dundee, E.*
Seymour – *Somerset, D.*
Stanley – *Derby, E.*
Strathnaver – *Sutherland, C.*

Wodehouse – *Kimberley, E.*
Worsley – *Yarborough, E.*

PEERS' SURNAMES WHICH DIFFER FROM THEIR TITLES

The following symbols indicate the rank of the peer holding each title:

C.	Countess
D.	Duke
E.	Earl
M.	Marquess
V.	Viscount
*	Life Peer

Where no designation is given, the title is that of an hereditary Baron or Baroness

Abney-Hastings – *Loudoun, C.*
Acheson – *Gosford, E.*
Adderley – *Norton*
Addington – *Sidmouth, V.*
Agar – *Normanton, E.*
Aitken – *Beaverbrook*
Akers-Douglas – *Chilston, V.*
Alexander – *A. of Tunis, E.*
Alexander – *A. of Weedon**
Alexander – *Caledon, E.*
Allen – *A. of Abbeydale**
Allen – *Croham**
Allsopp – *Hindlip*
Alton – *A. of Liverpool**
Anderson – *Waverley, V.*
Anelay – *A. of St Johns**
Annesley – *Valentia, V.*
Anson – *Lichfield, E.*
Archer – *A. of Sandwell**
Archer – *A. of Weston-super-Mare**
Armstrong – *A. of Ilminster**
Armstrong-Jones – *Snowdon, E.*
Arthur – *Glenarthur*
Arundell – *Talbot of Malahide*
Ashley – *A. of Stoke**
Ashley-Cooper – *Shaftesbury, E.*
Ashton – *A. of Hyde*
Asquith – *Oxford and Asquith, E.*
Assheton – *Clitheroe*
Astley – *Hastings*
Astor – *A. of Hever*
Aubrey-Fletcher – *Braye*
Bailey – *Glanusk*
Baillie – *Burton*
Baillie Hamilton – *Haddington, E.*

Baker – *B. of Dorking**
Baldwin – *B. of Bewdley, E.*
Balfour – *B. of Inchrye*
Balfour – *Kinross*
Balfour – *Riverdale*
Bampfylde – *Poltimore*
Banbury – *B. of Southam*
Barber – *B. of Tewkesbury**
Baring – *Ashburton*
Baring – *Cromer, E.*
Baring – *Howick of Glendale*
Baring – *Northbrook*
Baring – *Revelstoke*
Barker – *Trumpington**
Barnes – *Gorell*
Barnewall – *Trimlestown*
Bathurst – *Bledisloe, V.*
Beauclerk – *St Albans, D.*
Beaumont – *Allendale, V.*
Beaumont – *B. of Whitley**
Beckett – *Grimthorpe*
Bellow – *Bellwin**
Benn – *Stansgate, V.*
Bennet – *Tankerville, E.*
Bentinck – *Portland, E.*
Beresford – *Decies*
Beresford – *Waterford, M.*
Berry – *Camrose, V.*
Berry – *Hartwell**
Berry – *Kemsley, V.*
Bertie – *Lindsey, E.*
Best – *Wynford*
Bethell – *Westbury*
Bewicke-Copley – *Cromwell*
Bigham – *Mersey, V.*
Bingham – *B. of Cornhill**
Bingham – *Clanmorris*
Bingham – *Lucan, E.*
Blackwood – *Dufferin and Clandeboye*
Bligh – *Darnley, E.*
Blyth – *B. of Rowington**
Bootle-Wilbraham – *Skelmersdale*
Boscawen – *Falmouth, V.*
Boston – *B. of Faversham**
Bourke – *Mayo, E.*
Bowes Lyon – *Strathmore, E.*
Bowyer – *Denham*
Boyd – *Kilmarnock*
Boyle – *Cork and Orrery, E.*
Boyle – *Glasgow, E.*
Boyle – *Shannon, E.*
Brabazon – *Meath, E.*

Braine – *B. of Wheatley**
Brand – *Hampden, V.*
Brandon – *B. of Oakbrook**
Brassey – *B. of Apethorpe*
Brett – *Esher, V.*
Bridge – *B. of Harwich**
Bridgeman – *Bradford, E.*
Brodrick – *Midleton, V.*
Brooke – *Alanbrooke, V.*
Brooke – *Brookeborough, V.*
Brooke – *B. of Ystradfellte**
Brooks – *B. of Tremorfa**
Brooks – *Crawshaw*
Brougham – *Brougham and Vaux*
Broughton – *Fairhaven*
Browne – *Kilmaine*
Browne – *Oranmore and Browne*
Browne – *Sligo, M.*
Bruce – *Aberdare*
Bruce – *Balfour of Burleigh*
Bruce – *B. of Donington**
Bruce – *Elgin and Kincardine, E.*
Brudenell-Bruce – *Ailesbury, M.*
Buchan – *Tweedsmuir*
Buckley – *Wrenbury*
Butler – *Carrick, E.*
Butler – *Dunboyne*
Butler – *Lanesborough, E.*
Butler – *Mountgarret, V.*
Butler – *Ormonde, M.*
Buxton – *B. of Alsa**
Byng – *Strafford, E.*
Byng – *Torrington, V.*
Callaghan – *C. of Cardiff**
Cameron – *C. of Lochbroom**
Campbell – *Argyll, D.*
Campbell – *Breadalbane and Holland, E.*
Campbell – *C. of Alloway**
Campbell – *C. of Croy**
Campbell – *Cawdor, E.*
Campbell – *Colgrain*
Campbell – *Stratheden and Campbell*
Campbell-Gray – *Gray*
Canning – *Garvagh*
Capell – *Essex, E.*
Carington – *Carrington*
Carlisle – *C. of Bucklow**
Carmichael – *C. of Kelvingrove**

Carnegie – *Fife, D.*
Carnegie – *Northesk, E.*
Carr – *C. of Hadley**
Cary – *Falkland, V.*
Castle – *C. of Blackburn**
Caulfeild – *Charlemont, V.*
Cavendish – *C. of Furness**
Cavendish – *Chesham*
Cavendish – *Devonshire, D.*
Cavendish – *Waterpark*
Cayzer – *Rotherwick*
Cecil – *Amherst of Hackney*
Cecil – *Exeter, M.*
Cecil – *Rockley*
Cecil – *Salisbury, M.*
Chalker – *C. of Wallasey**
Chaloner – *Gisborough*
Channon – *Kelvedon**
Chapman – *Northfield**
Charteris – *C. of Amisfield**
Charteris – *Wemyss and March, E.*
Cheshire – *Ryder of Warsaw**
Chetwynd-Talbot – *Shrewsbury, E.*
Chichester – *Donegall, M.*
Chichester-Clark – *Moyola**
Child Villiers – *Jersey, E.*
Cholmondeley – *Delamere*
Chubb – *Hayter*
Clark – *C. of Kempston**
Clegg-Hill – *Hill, V.*
Clifford – *C. of Chudleigh*
Cochrane – *C. of Cults*
Cochrane – *Dundonald, E.*
Cocks – *C. of Hartcliffe**
Cocks – *Somers*
Cokayne – *Cullen of Ashbourne*
Coke – *Leicester, E.*
Cole – *Enniskillen, E.*
Collier – *Monkswell*
Colville – *Clydesmuir*
Colville – *C. of Culross, V.*
Compton – *Northampton, M.*
Conolly-Carew – *Carew*
Constantine – *C. of Stanmore**
Cooke – *C. of Islandreagh**
Cooke – *C. of Thorndon**
Cooper – *Norwich, V.*
Corbett – *Rowallan*
Courtenay – *Devon, E.*

Wilson – *W. of Tillyorn**
Windsor – *Gloucester, D.*
Windsor – *Kent, D.*
Windsor-Clive –
   Plymouth, E.
Wingfield – *Powerscourt,*
   V.
Winn – *St Oswald*
Wodehouse – *Kimberley,*
   E.
Wolfson – *W. of*
   *Sunningdale**
Wood – *Halifax, E.*
Wood – *Holderness**
Woodhouse – *Terrington*
Wright – *W. of Richmond**
Wyatt – *W. of Weeford**
Wyndham – *Egremont and*
   Leconfield
Wyndham-Quin –
   Dunraven, E.
Wynn – *Newborough*
Yarde-Buller – *Churston*
Yerburgh – *Alvingham*
Yorke – *Hardwicke, E.*
Young – *Kennet*
Young – *Y. of Dartington**
Young – *Y. of Graffham**
Younger – *Y. of Leckie, V.*
Younger – *Y. of Prestwick**

Orders of Chivalry

THE MOST NOBLE ORDER OF THE GARTER (1348)

KG

Ribbon, Blue
Motto, Honi soit qui mal y pense
(*Shame on him who thinks evil of it*)
The number of Knights Companions is limited to 24

SOVEREIGN OF THE ORDER
The Queen

LADIES OF THE ORDER
HM Queen Elizabeth the Queen Mother, 1936
HRH The Princess Royal, 1994

ROYAL KNIGHTS
HRH The Prince Philip, Duke of Edinburgh, 1947
HRH The Prince of Wales, 1958
HRH The Duke of Kent, 1985
HRH The Duke of Gloucester, 1997

EXTRA KNIGHTS COMPANIONS AND LADIES
HRH Princess Juliana of the Netherlands, 1958
HRH The Grand Duke of Luxembourg, 1972
HM The Queen of Denmark, 1979
HM The King of Sweden, 1983
HM The King of Spain, 1988
HM The Queen of the Netherlands, 1989
HIM The Emperor of Japan, 1998

KNIGHTS AND LADY COMPANIONS
The Earl of Longford, 1971
The Duke of Grafton, 1976
The Duke of Norfolk, 1983
The Lord Richardson of Duntisbourne, 1983
The Lord Carrington, 1985
The Lord Callaghan of Cardiff, 1987
The Viscount Leverhulme, 1988
The Lord Hailsham of St Marylebone, 1988
The Duke of Wellington, 1990
Field Marshal the Lord Bramall, 1990
Sir Edward Heath, 1992
The Viscount Ridley, 1992
The Lord Sainsbury of Preston Candover, 1992
The Lord Ashburton, 1994
The Lord Kingsdown, 1994
Sir Ninian Stephen, 1994
The Baroness Thatcher, 1995
Sir Edmund Hillary, 1995
The Duke of Devonshire, 1996
Sir Timothy Colman, 1996
The Duke of Abercorn, 1999
Sir William Gladstone, 1999

Prelate, The Bishop of Winchester
Chancellor, The Lord Carrington, KG, GCMG, CH, MC
Register, The Dean of Windsor
Garter King of Arms, P. Gwynn-Jones, CVO
Gentleman Usher of the Black Rod, Gen. Sir Edward Jones, KCB, CBE
Secretary, D. H. B. Chesshyre, LVO

THE MOST ANCIENT AND MOST NOBLE ORDER OF THE THISTLE (REVIVED 1687)

KT

Ribbon, Green
Motto, Nemo me impune lacessit (*No one provokes me with impunity*)
The number of Knights is limited to 16

SOVEREIGN OF THE ORDER
The Queen

LADY OF THE THISTLE
HM Queen Elizabeth the Queen Mother, 1937

ROYAL KNIGHTS
HRH The Prince Philip, Duke of Edinburgh, 1952
HRH The Prince of Wales, Duke of Rothesay, 1977

KNIGHTS AND LADIES
The Earl of Wemyss and March, 1966
Sir Donald Cameron of Lochiel, 1973
The Duke of Buccleuch and Queensberry, 1978
The Earl of Elgin and Kincardine, 1981
The Lord Thomson of Monifieth, 1981
The Lord MacLehose of Beoch, 1983
The Earl of Airlie, 1985
Capt. Sir Iain Tennant, 1986
The Viscount Younger of Leckie, 1995
The Viscount of Arbuthnott, 1996
The Earl of Crawford and Balcarres, 1996
Lady Marion Fraser, 1996
The Lord Macfarlane of Bearsden, 1996
The Lord Mackay of Clashfern, 1997

Chancellor, The Duke of Buccleuch and Queensberry, KT, VRD
Dean, The Very Revd G. I. Macmillan, CVO
Secretary and Lord Lyon King of Arms, Sir Malcolm Innes of Edingight, KCVO, WS
Usher of the Green Rod, Rear-Adm. C. H. Layman, CB, DSO, LVO

THE MOST HONOURABLE ORDER OF THE BATH (1725)

GCB *Military*   GCB *Civil*

GCB   Knight (or Dame) Grand Cross
KCB   Knight Commander
DCB   Dame Commander
CB   Companion

Ribbon, Crimson
Motto, Tria juncta in uno (*Three joined in one*)

Remodelled 1815, and enlarged many times since. The Order is divided into civil and military divisions. Women became eligible for the Order from 1 January 1971

THE SOVEREIGN
GREAT MASTER AND FIRST OR PRINCIPAL KNIGHT GRAND CROSS
HRH The Prince of Wales, KG, KT, GCB

Dean of the Order, The Dean of Westminster
Bath King of Arms, Gen. Sir Brian Kenny, GCB, CBE
Registrar and Secretary, Rear-Adm. D. E. Macey, CB
Genealogist, P. Gwynn-Jones, CVO
Gentleman Usher of the Scarlet Rod, Air Vice-Marshal Sir Richard Peirse, KCVO, CB
Deputy Secretary, The Secretary of the Central Chancery of the Orders of Knighthood

Chancery, Central Chancery of the
Orders of Knighthood, St James's
Palace, London SW1A 1BH

THE ORDER OF MERIT
(1902)

OM *Military*   OM *Civil*

OM

Ribbon, Blue and crimson

This Order is designed as a special
distinction for eminent men and
women without conferring a
knighthood upon them. The Order
is limited in numbers to 24, with
the addition of foreign honorary
members. Membership is of two
kinds, military and civil, the badge
of the former having crossed swords,
and the latter oak leaves

THE SOVEREIGN

HRH The Prince Philip, Duke of
Edinburgh, 1968
Sir George Edwards, 1971
Revd Prof. Owen Chadwick, KBE,
1983
Sir Andrew Huxley, 1983
Frederick Sanger, 1986
Prof. Sir Ernst Gombrich, 1988
Dr Max Perutz, 1988
Dame Cicely Saunders, 1989
The Lord Porter of Luddenham,
1989
The Baroness Thatcher, 1990
Dame Joan Sutherland, 1991
Prof. Francis Crick, 1991
Dame Ninette de Valois, 1992
Sir Michael Atiyah, 1992
Lucian Freud, 1993
The Lord Jenkins of Hillhead, 1993
Sir Aaron Klug, 1995
The Lord Foster of Thames Bank,
1997
Sir Denis Rooke, 1997
Sir James Black, 2000
Sir Anthony Caro, 2000
Sir Roger Penrose, 2000
Sir Tom Stoppard, 2000
Honorary Member, Nelson Mandela,
1995

Secretary and Registrar, Sir Edward
Ford, GCVO, KCB, ERD
Chancery, Central Chancery of the
Orders of Knighthood, St James's
Palace, London SW1A 1BH

THE MOST
DISTINGUISHED ORDER OF
ST MICHAEL AND
ST GEORGE (1818)

GCMG   KCMG

GCMG   Knight (or Dame)
              Grand Cross
KCMG   Knight Commander
DCMG   Dame Commander
CMG   Companion

Ribbon, Saxon blue, with scarlet
centre
Motto, Auspicium melioris aevi
(*Token of a better age*)

THE SOVEREIGN

GRAND MASTER
HRH The Duke of Kent, KG, GCMG,
GCVO, ADC

Prelate, The Rt. Revd Simon
Barrington-Ward
Chancellor, Sir Antony Acland,
GCMG, GCVO
Secretary, The Permanent Under-
Secretary of State at the Foreign
and Commonwealth Office and
Head of the Diplomatic Service
Registrar, Sir John Graham, Bt.,
GCMG
King of Arms, Sir Ewen Fergusson,
GCMG, GCVO
Gentleman Usher of the Blue Rod, Sir
John Margetson, KCMG
Dean, The Dean of St Paul's
Deputy Secretary, The Secretary of
the Central Chancery of the
Orders of Knighthood
Chancery, Central Chancery of the
Orders of Knighthood, St James's
Palace, London SW1A 1BH

THE MOST EMINENT
ORDER OF THE INDIAN
EMPIRE (1868)

GCIE   Knight Grand Commander
KCIE   Knight Commander
CIE   Companion

Ribbon, Imperial purple
Motto, Imperatricis auspiciis (*Under
the auspices of the Empress*)

THE SOVEREIGN

Registrar, The Secretary of the
Central Chancery of the Orders of
Knighthood
No conferments have been made
since 1947

THE IMPERIAL ORDER OF
THE CROWN OF INDIA
(1877) FOR LADIES

CI

Badge, the royal cipher in jewels
within an oval, surmounted by an
heraldic crown and attached to a
bow of light blue watered ribbon,
edged white
The honour does not confer any rank
or title upon the recipient
No conferments have been made
since 1947

HM The Queen, 1947
HM Queen Elizabeth the Queen
Mother, 1931
HRH The Princess Margaret,
Countess of Snowdon, 1947
HRH Princess Alice, Duchess of
Gloucester, 1937

THE ROYAL VICTORIAN
ORDER (1896)

GCVO   KCVO

GCVO   Knight or Dame
              Grand Cross
KCVO   Knight Commander
DCVO   Dame Commander
CVO   Commander
LVO   Lieutenant
MVO   Member

Ribbon, Blue, with red and white
edges
Motto, Victoria

THE SOVEREIGN

GRAND MASTER
HM Queen Elizabeth the Queen
Mother

Chancellor, The Lord Chamberlain
Secretary, The Keeper of the Privy
Purse
Registrar, The Secretary of the
Central Chancery of the Orders of
Knighthood
Chaplain, The Chaplain of the
Queen's Chapel of the Savoy
Hon. Genealogist, D. H. B. Chesshyre,
LVO

THE MOST EXCELLENT ORDER OF THE BRITISH EMPIRE (1917)

GBE   KBE

The Order was divided into military and civil divisions in December 1918

GBE   Knight or Dame Grand Cross
KBE   Knight Commander
DBE   Dame Commander
CBE   Commander
OBE   Officer
MBE   Member

Ribbon, Rose pink edged with pearl grey with vertical pearl stripe in centre (military division); without vertical pearl stripe (civil division)
Motto, For God and the Empire

THE SOVEREIGN

GRAND MASTER
HRH The Prince Philip, Duke of Edinburgh, KG, KT, OM, GBE, PC
Prelate, The Bishop of London
King of Arms, Air Chief Marshal Sir Patrick Hine, GCB, GBE
Registrar, The Secretary of the Central Chancery of the Orders of Knighthood
Secretary, The Secretary of the Cabinet and Head of the Home Civil Service
Dean, The Dean of St Paul's
Gentleman Usher of the Purple Rod, Sir Robin Gillett, Bt., GBE, RD
Chancery, Central Chancery of the Orders of Knighthood, St James's Palace, London SW1A 1BH

ORDER OF THE COMPANIONS OF HONOUR (1917)

CH

Ribbon, Carmine, with gold edges

This Order consists of one class only and carries with it no title. The number of awards is limited to 65 (excluding honorary members)

Anthony, Rt. Hon. John, 1981
Ashley of Stoke, The Lord, 1975
Astor, Hon. David, 1993
Attenborough, Sir David, 1995
Baker, Dame Janet, 1993
Baker of Dorking, The Lord, 1992

Brenner, Sydney, 1986
Brook, Peter, 1998
Brooke, Rt. Hon. Peter, 1992
Carrington, The Lord, 1983
Cledwyn of Penrhos, The Lord, 1976
de Valois, Dame Ninette, 1981
De Chastelain, Gen. John, 1999
Doll, Prof. Sir Richard, 1995
Fraser, Rt. Hon. Malcolm, 1977
Freud, Lucian, 1983
Glenamara, The Lord, 1976
Gorton, Rt. Hon. Sir John, 1971
Hailsham of St Marylebone, The Lord, 1974
Hamilton, Richard, 1999
Hawking, Prof. Stephen, 1989
Healey, The Lord, 1979
Heseltine, Rt. Hon. Michael, 1997
Hobsbawm, Prof. Eric, 1998
Hockney, David, 1997
Howe of Aberavon, The Lord, 1996
Hurd of Westwell, The Lord, 1995
Jones, James, 1977
King, Rt. Hon. Tom, 1992
Lange, Rt. Hon. David, 1989
Lasdun, Sir Denys, 1995
Lessing, Doris, 1999
Major, Rt. Hon. John, 1999
Milstein, César, 1994
Owen, The Lord, 1994
Patten, Rt. Hon. Christopher, 1998
Perutz, Dr Max, 1975
Powell, Sir Philip, 1984
Runciman, Hon. Sir Steven, 1984
Riley, Bridget, 1999
Sanger, Frederick, 1981
Sisson, Charles, 1993
Smith, Sir John, 1993
Somare, Rt. Hon. Sir Michael, 1978
Talboys, Rt. Hon. Sir Brian, 1981
Tebbit, The Lord, 1987
Trudeau, Rt. Hon. Pierre, 1984
Varah, Rev. Dr. Chad, 1999
Widdowson, Dr Elsie, 1993
Honorary Members, Lee Kuan Yew, 1970; Dr Joseph Luns, 1971

Secretary and Registrar, The Secretary of the Central Chancery of the Orders of Knighthood

THE DISTINGUISHED SERVICE ORDER (1886)

DSO

Ribbon, Red, with blue edges

Bestowed in recognition of especial services in action of commissioned officers in the Navy, Army and Royal Air Force and (since 1942) Mercantile Marine. The members are Companions only. A Bar may be awarded for any additional act of service

THE IMPERIAL SERVICE ORDER (1902)

ISO

Ribbon, Crimson, with blue centre

Appointment as Companion of this Order is open to members of the Civil Services whose eligibility is determined by the grade they hold. The Order consists of The Sovereign and Companions to a number not exceeding 1,900, of whom 1,300 may belong to the Home Civil Services and 600 to Overseas Civil Services. The then Prime Minister announced in March 1993 that he would make no further recommendations for appointments to the Order.

Secretary, The Secretary of the Cabinet and Head of the Home Civil Service
Registrar, The Secretary of the Central Chancery of the Orders of Knighthood, St James's Palace, London SW1A 1BH

THE ROYAL VICTORIAN CHAIN (1902)

It confers no precedence on its holders

HM THE QUEEN

HM Queen Elizabeth the Queen Mother, 1937

HRH Princess Juliana of the Netherlands, 1950
HM The King of Thailand, 1960
HM King Zahir Shah of Afghanistan, 1971
HM The Queen of Denmark, 1974
HM The King of Nepal, 1975
HM The King of Sweden, 1975
HM The Queen of the Netherlands, 1982
Gen. Antonio Eanes, 1985
HM The King of Spain, 1986
HM The King of Saudi Arabia, 1987
HRH The Princess Margaret, Countess of Snowdon, 1990
HE Richard von Weizsäcker, 1992
HM The King of Norway, 1994
The Earl of Airlie, 1997

Baronetage and Knightage

BARONETS

Style, 'Sir' before forename and surname, followed by 'Bt.'
Wife's style, 'Lady' followed by surname
For forms of address, *see* page 135

There are five different creations of baronetcies: Baronets of England (creations dating from 1611); Baronets of Ireland (creations dating from 1619); Baronets of Scotland or Nova Scotia (creations dating from 1625); Baronets of Great Britain (creations after the Act of Union 1707 which combined the kingdoms of England and Scotland); and Baronets of the United Kingdom (creations after the union of Great Britain and Ireland in 1801).

Badge of Baronets of the United Kingdom   *Badge of Baronets of Nova Scotia*

Badge of Ulster

The patent of creation limits the destination of a baronetcy, usually to male descendants of the first baronet, although special remainders allow the baronetcy to pass, if the male issue of sons fail, to the male issue of daughters of the first baronet. In the case of baronetcies of Scotland or Nova Scotia, a special remainder of 'heirs male and of tailzie' allows the baronetcy to descend to heirs general, including women. There are four existing Scottish baronets with such a remainder.

The Official Roll of Baronets is kept at the Home Office by the Registrar of the Baronetage. Anyone who considers that he is entitled to be entered on the Roll may petition the Crown through the Home Secretary. Every person succeeding to a baronetcy must exhibit proofs of succession to the Home Secretary. A person whose name is not entered on the Official Roll will not be addressed or mentioned by the title of baronet in any official document, nor will he be accorded precedence as a baronet.

BARONETCIES EXTINCT SINCE THE LAST EDITION
Kennard (*cr.* 1981); Makins (*cr.* 1903); Stewart (*cr.* 1937)

Registrar of the Baronetage, Miss C. E. C. Sinclair
Assistant Registrar, Mrs F. G. Bright
Office, Home Office, 50 Queen Anne's Gate, London SW1H 9AT. Tel: 020 7273 3498

KNIGHTS

Style, 'Sir' before forename and surname, followed by appropriate post-nominal initials if a Knight Grand Cross, Knight Grand Commander or Knight Commander

Wife's style, 'Lady' followed by surname
For forms of address, *see* page 135

The prefix 'Sir' is not used by knights who are clerics of the Church of England, who do not receive the accolade. Their wives are entitled to precedence as the wife of a knight but not to the style of 'Lady'.

Orders of Knighthood

Knight Grand Cross, Knight Grand Commander, and Knight Commander are the higher classes of the Orders of Chivalry (*see* pages 171–3). Honorary knighthoods of these Orders may be conferred on men who are citizens of countries of which The Queen is not head of state. As a rule, the prefix 'Sir' is not used by honorary knights.

Knights Bachelor

The Knights Bachelor do not constitute a Royal Order, but comprise the surviving representation of the ancient State Orders of Knighthood. The Register of Knights Bachelor, instituted by James I in the 17th century, lapsed, and in 1908 a voluntary association under the title of The Society of Knights (now The Imperial Society of Knights Bachelor by Royal Command) was formed with the primary objects of continuing the various registers dating from 1257 and obtaining the uniform registration of every created Knight Bachelor. In 1926 a design for a badge to be worn by Knights Bachelor was approved and adopted; in 1974 a neck badge and miniature were added.

Knight Principal, Sir Conrad Swan, KCVO
Chairman of Council, Sir Richard Gaskell.
Prelate, Rt. Revd and Rt. Hon. The Bishop of London
Registrar, Sir Robert Balchin
Hon. Treasurer, Sir Paul Judge.
Clerk to the Council, R. L. Jenkins, LVO, TD.
Office, 21 Old Buildings, Lincoln's Inn, London WC2A 3UJ

LIST OF BARONETS AND KNIGHTS

Revised to 31 August 2000
Peers are not included in this list

†	Not registered on the Official Roll of the Baronetage at the time of going to press
( )	The date of creation of the baronetcy is given in parenthesis
I	Baronet of Ireland
NS	Baronet of Nova Scotia
S	Baronet of Scotland

If a baronet or knight has a double-barrelled or hyphenated surname, he is listed under the final element of the name
A full entry in italic type indicates that the recipient of a knighthood died during the year in which the honour was conferred. The name is included for purposes of record

Abal, Sir Tei, Kt., CBE

Abbott, Sir Albert Francis, Kt., CBE

Abbott, *Adm.* Sir Peter Charles, GBE, KCB

Abdy, Sir Valentine Robert Duff, Bt. (1850)

Abel, Sir Seselo (Cecil) Charles Geoffrey, Kt., OBE

Abercromby, Sir Ian George, Bt. (s.1636)

Acheson, *Prof.* Sir (Ernest) Donald, KBE

Ackers, Sir James George, Kt.

Ackroyd, Sir Timothy Robert Whyte, Bt. (1956)

Acland, Sir Antony Arthur, GCMG, GCVO

Acland, *Lt.-Col.* Sir (Christopher) Guy (Dyke), Bt., MVO (1890)

Acland, Sir John Dyke, Bt. (1644)

Acland, *Maj.-Gen.* Sir John Hugh Bevil, KBE, CBE

Adam, Sir Christopher Eric Forbes, Bt. (1917)

Adams, Sir Philip George Doyne, KCMG

Adams, Sir William James, KCMG

Adrien, *Hon.* Sir Maurice Latour-, Kt.

Adsetts, Sir William Norman, Kt., OBE

Adye, Sir John Anthony, KCMG

Agnew, Sir Crispin Hamlyn, Bt. (s. 1629)

Agnew, Sir John Keith, Bt. (1895)

Aiken, *Air Chief Marshal* Sir John Alexander Carlisle, KCB

Aikens, Sir Richard John Pearson, Kt., QC

†Ainsworth, Sir Anthony Thomas Hugh, Bt. (1916)

Aird, *Capt.* Sir Alastair Sturgis, GCVO

Aird, Sir (George) John, Bt. (1901)

Airey, Sir Lawrence, KCB

Airy, *Maj.-Gen.* Sir Christopher John, KCVO, CBE

Aitchison, Sir Charles Walter de Lancey, Bt. (1938)

Akehurst, *Gen.* Sir John Bryan, KCB, CBE

Alberti, *Prof.* Kurt George Matthew Mayer, Kt.

Albu, Sir George, Bt. (1912)

Alcock, *Air Chief Marshal* Sir (Robert James) Michael, GCB, KBE

Aldous, *Rt. Hon.* Sir William, Kt.

Alexander, Sir Charles Gundry, Bt. (1945)

Alexander, Sir Claud Hagart-, Bt. (1886)

Alexander, Sir Douglas, Bt. (1921)

Alexander, *Prof.* Sir Kenneth John Wilson, Kt.

Alexander, Sir Michael O'Donal Bjarne, GCMG

†Alexander, Sir Patrick Desmond William Cable-, Bt. (1809)

Allan, Sir Anthony James Allan Havelock-, Bt. (1858)

Allen, *Prof.* Sir Geoffrey, Kt., Ph.D., FRS

Allen, Sir John Derek, Kt., CBE

Allen, *Hon.* Sir Peter Austin Philip Jermyn, Kt.

Allen, Sir Thomas Boaz, Kt., CBE

Allen, *Hon.* Sir William Clifford, KCMG, MP

Allen, Sir William Guilford, Kt.

Alleyne, Sir George Allanmoore Ogarren, Kt.

Alleyne, *Revd* Sir John Olpherts Campbell, Bt. (1769)

Alliance, Sir David, Kt., CBE

Allinson, Sir (Walter) Leonard, KCVO, CMG

Alliott, *Hon.* Sir John Downes, Kt.

Allison, *Air Chief Marshal* Sir John Shakespeare, KCB, CBE

Alment, Sir (Edward) Anthony John, Kt.

Althaus, Sir Nigel Frederick, Kt.

Ambo, *Rt. Revd* George, KBE

Amet, *Hon.* Sir Arnold Karibone, Kt.

Amies, Sir (Edwin) Hardy, KCVO

Amory, Sir Ian Heathcoat, Bt. (1874)

Anderson, Sir John Anthony, KBE

Anderson, *Maj.-Gen.* Sir John Evelyn, KBE

Anderson, Sir John Muir, Kt., CMG

Anderson, *Hon.* Sir Kevin Victor, Kt.

Anderson, Sir Leith Reinsford Steven, Kt., CBE

Anderson, *Vice-Adm.* Sir Neil Dudley, KBE, CB

Anderson, *Prof.* Sir (William) Ferguson, Kt., OBE

Anderton, Sir (Cyril) James, Kt., CBE, QPM

Andrew, Sir Robert John, KCB

Andrews, Sir Derek Henry, KCB, CBE

Andrews, *Hon.* Sir Dormer George, Kt.

Angus, Sir Michael Richardson, Kt.

Annesley, Sir Hugh Norman, Kt., QPM

Anson, *Vice-Adm.* Sir Edward Rosebery, KCB

Anson, Sir John, KCB

Anson, *Rear-Adm.* Sir Peter, Bt., CB (1831)

Anstey, *Brig.* Sir John, Kt., CBE, TD

Anstruther, *Maj.* Sir Ralph Hugo, Bt., GCVO, MC (s. 1694)

Antico, Sir Tristan Venus, Kt.

Antrobus, Sir Charles James, GCMG, OBE

Antrobus, Sir Edward Philip, Bt. (1815)

Appleyard, Sir Leonard Vincent, KCMG

Appleyard, Sir Raymond Kenelm, KBE

Arbuthnot, Sir Keith Robert Charles, Bt. (1823)

Arbuthnot, Sir William Reierson, Bt. (1964)

Arbuthnott, *Prof.* Sir John Peebles, Kt., Ph.D., FRSE

Archdale, *Capt.* Sir Edward Folmer, Bt., DSC, RN (1928)

Arculus, Sir Ronald, KCMG, KCVO

Armitage, *Air Chief Marshal* Sir Michael John, KCB, CBE

Armour, *Prof.* Sir James, Kt., CBE

†Armstrong, Sir Christopher John Edmund Stuart, Bt., MBE (1841)

Armytage, Sir John Martin, Bt. (1738)

Arnold, *Rt. Hon.* Sir John Lewis, Kt.

Arnold, Sir Malcolm Henry, Kt., CBE

Arnold, Sir Thomas Richard, Kt.

Arnott, Sir Alexander John Maxwell, Bt. (1896)

Arrindell, Sir Clement Athelston, GCMG, GCVO, QC

Arthur, *Lt.-Gen.* Sir (John) Norman Stewart, KCB

Arthur, Sir Stephen John, Bt. (1841)

Ash, *Prof.* Sir Eric Albert, Kt., CBE, FRS, FREng.

Ashburnham, Sir James Fleetwood, Bt. (1661)

Ashcroft, Sir Michael, KCMG

Ashdown, *Rt. Hon.* Sir Jeremy John Durham (Paddy), KBE

Ashley, Sir Bernard Albert, Kt.

Ashmore, *Admiral of the Fleet* Sir Edward Beckwith, GCB, DSC

Ashmore, *Vice-Adm.* Sir Peter William Beckwith, KCB, KCVO, DSC

Ashworth, Sir Herbert, Kt.

Aske, *Revd* Sir Conan, Bt. (1922)

Askew, Sir Bryan, Kt.

Asscher, Prof. Sir (Adolf) William, Kt., MD, FRCP

Astill, *Hon.* Sir Michael John, Kt.

Aston, Sir Harold George, Kt., CBE

Astor, *Hon.* Sir John Jacob, Kt., MBE

Astwood, *Hon.* Sir James Rufus, KBE

Atcherley, Sir Harold Winter, Kt.

Atiyah, Sir Michael Francis, Kt., OM, Ph.D., FRS

Atkins, *Rt. Hon.* Sir Anthony Robert James, Kt.

Atkinson, *Prof.* Sir Anthony Barnes, Kt.

Atkinson, *Air Marshal* Sir David William, KBE

Atkinson, Sir Frederick John, KCB

Atkinson, Sir John Alexander, KCB, DFC

Atkinson, Sir Robert, Kt., DSC, FREng.

Atopare, Sir Sailas, GCMG

Attenborough, Sir David Frederick, Kt., CH, CVO, CBE, FRS

Atwill, Sir (Milton) John (Napier), Kt.

Audland, Sir Christopher John, KCMG

Audley, Sir George Bernard, Kt.

Augier, *Prof.* Sir Fitz-Roy Richard, Kt.

Auld, *Rt. Hon.* Sir Robin Ernest, Kt.

Austin, Sir Anthony Leonard, Bt. (1894)

Austin, *Vice-Adm.* Sir Peter Murray, KCB

Austin, *Air Marshal* Sir Roger Mark, KCB, AFC

Axford, Sir William Ian, Kt.

Ayckbourn, Sir Alan, Kt., CBE

Aykroyd, Sir James Alexander Frederic, Bt. (1929)

Aykroyd, Sir William Miles, Bt., MC (1920)

Aylmer, Sir Richard John, Bt. (I. 1622)

Bacha, Sir Bhinod, Kt., CMG

Backhouse, Sir Jonathan Roger, Bt. (1901)

Bacon, Sir Nicholas Hickman Ponsonby, Bt. *Premier Baronet of England* (1611 and 1627)

Bacon, Sir Sidney Charles, Kt., CB, FREng.

Baddeley, Sir John Wolsey Beresford, Bt. (1922)

Baddiley, *Prof.* Sir James, Kt., Ph.D., D.Sc., FRS, FRSE

Badge, Sir Peter Gilmour Noto, Kt.

Badger, Sir Geoffrey Malcolm, Kt.

Baer, Sir Jack Mervyn Frank, Kt.

Bagge, Sir (John) Jeremy Picton, Bt. (1867)

Bagnall, *Air Marshal* Sir Anthony John Crowther, KCB, OBE

Bagnall, *Field Marshal* Sir Nigel Thomas, GCB, CVO, MC

Bailey, Sir Alan Marshall, KCB

Bailey, Sir Brian Harry, Kt., OBE

Bailey, Sir Derrick Thomas Louis, Bt., DFC (1919)

Bailey, Sir John Bilsland, KCB

Bailey, Sir Richard John, Kt., CBE

Bailey, Sir Stanley Ernest, Kt., CBE, QPM

Bailhache, Sir Philip Martin, Kt.

Baillie, Sir Gawaine George Hope, Bt. (1823)

Baines, *Prof.* Sir George Grenfell-, Kt., OBE

Baird, Sir David Charles, Bt. (1809)

†Baird, Sir James Andrew Gardiner, Bt. (S. 1695)

Baird, *Lt.-Gen.* Sir James Parlane, KBE, MD

Baird, *Air Marshal* Sir John Alexander, KBE

Baird, *Vice-Adm.* Sir Thomas Henry Eustace, KCB

Bairsto, *Air Marshal* Sir Peter Edward, KBE, CB

Baker, Sir Bryan William, Kt.

Baker, Sir Robert George Humphrey Sherston-, Bt. (1796)

Baker, *Hon.* Sir (Thomas) Scott (Gillespie), Kt.

Balchin, Sir Robert George Alexander, Kt.

Balderstone, Sir James Schofield, Kt.

Baldwin, *Prof.* Sir Jack Edward, Kt., FRS

Baldwin, Sir Peter Robert, KCB

Ball, *Air Marshal* Sir Alfred Henry Wynne, KCB, DSO, DFC

Ball, Sir Charles Irwin, Bt. (1911)

Ball, Sir Christopher John Elinger, Kt.

Ball, *Prof.* Sir Robert James, Kt., Ph.D.

Bamford, Sir Anthony Paul, Kt.

Banham, Sir John Michael Middlecott, Kt.

Bannerman, Sir David Gordon, Bt., OBE (S. 1682)

Bannister, Sir Roger Gilbert, Kt., · CBE, DM, FRCP

Barber, Sir (Thomas) David, Bt. (1960)

Barbour, *Very Revd* Sir Robert Alexander Stewart, KCVO, MC

Barclay, Sir Colville Herbert Sanford, Bt. (S. 1668)

Barclay, Sir David Rowat, Kt.

Barclay, Sir Frederick Hugh, Kt.

Barclay, Sir Peter Maurice, Kt., CBE

Barder, Sir Brian Leon, KCMG

Baring, Sir John Francis, Bt. (1911)

Barker, Sir Alwyn Bowman, Kt., CMG

Barker, Sir Colin, Kt.

Barker, *Hon.* Sir (Richard) Ian, Kt.

Barlow, Sir Christopher Hilaro, Bt. (1803)

Barlow, Sir Frank, Kt., CBE

Barlow, Sir (George) William, Kt., FREng.

Barlow, Sir John Kemp, Bt. (1907)

Barlow, Sir Thomas Erasmus, Bt., DSC (1902)

Barnard, Sir Joseph Brian, Kt.

Barnes, Sir (James) David (Francis), Kt., CBE

Barnes, Sir Kenneth, KCB

Barnewall, Sir Reginald Robert, Bt. (I. 1623)

Baron, Sir Thomas, Kt., CBE

Barraclough, *Air Chief Marshal* Sir John, KCB, CBE, DFC, AFC

Barraclough, Sir Kenneth James Priestley, Kt., CBE, TD

Barran, Sir David Haven, Kt.

Barran, Sir John Napoleon Ruthven, Bt. (1895)

Barratt, Sir Lawrence Arthur, Kt.

Barratt, Sir Richard Stanley, Kt., CBE, QPM

Barrett, *Lt.-Gen.* Sir David William Scott-, KBE, MC

Barrett, Sir Stephen Jeremy, KCMG

Barrington, Sir Alexander (Fitzwilliam Croker), Bt. (1831)

Barrington, Sir Nicholas John, KCMG, CVO

Barron, Sir Donald James, Kt.

Barrow, *Capt.* Sir Richard John Uniacke, Bt. (1835)

Barrowclough, Sir Anthony Richard, Kt., QC

Barry, Sir (Lawrence) Edward (Anthony Tress), Bt. (1899)

†Bartlett, Sir Andrew Alan, Bt. (1913)

Barttelot, *Col.* Sir Brian Walter de Stopham, Bt., OBE (1875)

Batchelor, Sir Ivor Ralph Campbell, Kt., CBE

Bate, Sir David Lindsay, KBE

Bate, Sir (Walter) Edwin, Kt., OBE

Bates, Sir Geoffrey Voltelin, Bt., MC (1880)

Bates, Sir Malcolm Rowland, Kt.

Bates, Sir Richard Dawson Hoult, Bt. (1937)

Batho, Sir Peter Ghislain, Bt. (1928)

Bathurst, *Admiral of the Fleet* Sir (David) Benjamin, GCB

Bathurst, Sir Frederick John Charles Gordon Hervey-, Bt. (1818)

Bathurst, Sir Maurice Edward, Kt., CMG, CBE, QC

Batten, Sir John Charles, KCVO

Battersby, *Prof.* Sir Alan Rushton, Kt., FRS

Battishill, Sir Anthony Michael William, GCB

Batty, Sir William Bradshaw, Kt., TD

Baxendell, Sir Peter Brian, Kt., CBE, FREng.

Bayliss, Sir Richard Ian Samuel, KCVO, MD, FRCP

Bayne, Sir Nicholas Peter, KCMG

Baynes, Sir John Christopher Malcolm, Bt. (1801)

Bazley, Sir Thomas John Sebastian, Bt. (1869)

Beach, *Gen.* Sir (William Gerald) Hugh, GBE, KCB, MC

Beale, *Lt.-Gen.* Sir Peter John, KBE, FRCP

Beament, Sir James William Longman, Kt., SC.D., FRS

Beamish, Sir Adrian John, KCMG

Beattie, *Hon.* Sir Alexander Craig, Kt.

Beattie, *Hon.* Sir David Stuart, GCMG, GCVO

Beauchamp, Sir Christopher Radstock Proctor-, Bt. (1745)

Beaumont, *Capt.* the Hon. Sir (Edward) Nicholas (Canning), KCVO

Beaumont, Sir George (Howland Francis), Bt. (1661)

Beaumont, Sir Richard Ashton, KCMG, OBE

Beavis, *Air Chief Marshal* Sir Michael Gordon, KCB, CBE, AFC

†Becher, Sir John William Michael Wrixon-, Bt. (1831)

Beck, Sir Edgar Philip, Kt.

Beckett, *Capt.* Sir (Martyn) Gervase, Bt., MC (1921)

Beckett, Sir Terence Norman, KBE, FREng.

Bedingfeld, *Capt.* Sir Edmund George Felix Paston-, Bt. (1661)

Beddoe, Sir David Sydney Rowe-, Kt.

Bedser, Sir Alec Victor, Kt., CBE

Beecham, Sir Jeremy Hugh, Kt.

Beecham, Sir John Stratford Roland, Bt. (1914)

Beeley, Sir Harold, KCMG, CBE

Beetham, *Marshal of the Royal Air Force* Sir Michael James, GCB, CBE, DFC, AFC

Beevor, Sir Thomas Agnew, Bt. (1784)

Beith, Sir John Greville Stanley, KCMG

Beldam, *Rt. Hon.* Sir (Alexander) Roy (Asplan), Kt.

Belich, Sir James, Kt.

Bell, Sir Brian Ernest, KBE

Bell, Sir (George) Raymond, KCMG, CB

Bell, Sir John Lowthian, Bt. (1885)

Bell, Hon. Sir Rodger, Kt.

Bell, Sir (William) Ewart, KCB

Bell, Sir William Hollin Dayrell Morrison-, Bt. (1905)

Bellamy, Hon. Sir Christopher William, Kt.

Bellew, Sir Henry Charles Gratton-, Bt. (1838)

Bellinger, Sir Robert Ian, GBE

†Bellingham, Sir Anthony Edward Norman, Bt. (1796)

Bengough, Col. Sir Piers, KCVO, OBE

Benn, Sir (James) Jonathan, Bt. (1914)

Bennett, Air Vice-Marshal Sir Erik Peter, KBE, CB

Bennett, Rt. Hon. Sir Frederic Mackarness, Kt.

Bennett, Sir Hubert, Kt.

Bennett, Hon. Sir Hugh Peter Derwyn, Kt.

Bennett, Sir John Mokonuiarangi, Kt.

Bennett, Gen. Sir Phillip Harvey, KBE, DSO

Bennett, Sir Reginald Frederick Brittain, Kt., VRD

Bennett, Sir Richard Rodney, Kt., CBE

Bennett, Sir Ronald Wilfrid Murdoch, Bt. (1929)

Benson, Sir Christopher John, Kt.

Benyon, Sir William Richard, Kt.

Beresford, Sir (Alexander) Paul, Kt., MP

Berger, Vice-Adm. Sir Peter Egerton Capel, KCB, LVO, DSC

Berghuser, Hon. Sir Eric, Kt., MBE

Beringer, Prof. Sir John Evelyn, Kt., CBE

Berman, Sir Franklin Delow, KCMG

Bernard, Sir Dallas Edmund, Bt. (1954)

Berney, Sir Julian Reedham Stuart, Bt. (1620)

Berridge, Prof. Sir Michael John, Kt., FRS

Berrill, Sir Kenneth Ernest, GBE, KCB

Berriman, Sir David, Kt.

Berry, Prof. Sir Colin Leonard, Kt., FRCPath.

Berry, Prof. Sir Michael Victor, Kt., FRS

Berthon, Vice-Adm. Sir Stephen Ferrier, KCB

Berthoud, Sir Martin Seymour, KCVO, CMG

Best, Sir Richard Radford, KCVO, CBE

Bethune, Hon. Sir (Walter) Angus, Kt.

Bett, Sir Michael, Kt., CBE

Bevan, Sir Martyn Evan Evans, Bt. (1958)

Bevan, Sir Timothy Hugh, Kt.

Beverley, Lt.-Gen. Sir Henry York La Roche, KCB, OBE, RM

Bibby, Sir Derek James, Bt., MC (1959)

Bichard, Sir Michael George, KCB

Bick, Hon. Sir Martin James Moore-, Kt.

Bickersteth, Rt. Revd Sir John Monier, KCVO

Biddulph, Sir Ian D'Olier, Bt. (1664)

Bide, Sir Austin Ernest, Kt.

Bidwell, Sir Hugh Charles Philip, GBE

Biggam, Sir Robin Adair, Kt.

Biggs, Vice-Adm. Sir Geoffrey William Roger, KCB

Biggs, Sir Norman Paris, Kt.

Bilas, Sir Angmai Simon, Kt., OBE

Billière, Gen. Sir Peter Edgar de la Cour de la, KCB, KBE, DSO, MC

Bingham, Hon. Sir Eardley Max, Kt., QC

Birch, Sir John Allan, KCVO, CMG

Birch, Sir Roger, Kt., CBE, QPM

Bird, Sir Richard Geoffrey Chapman, Bt. (1922)

Birkin, Sir John Christian William, Bt. (1905)

Birkin, Sir (John) Derek, Kt., TD

Birkmyre, Sir Archibald, Bt. (1921)

Birley, Sir Derek Sydney, Kt.

Birrell, Sir James Drake, Kt.

Birtwistle, Sir Harrison, Kt.

Bischoff, Winfried Franz Wilhelm, Kt.

Bishop, Sir Frederick Arthur, Kt., CB, CVO

Bishop, Sir Michael David, Kt., CBE

Bisson, Rt. Hon. Sir Gordon Ellis, Kt.

Black, Prof. Sir Douglas Andrew Kilgour, Kt., MD, FRCP

Black, Sir James Whyte, Kt., FRCP, FRS, OM

Black, Adm. Sir (John) Jeremy, GBE, KCB, DSO

Black, Sir Robert David, Bt. (1922)

Blackburne, Hon. Sir William Anthony, Kt.

Blacker, Gen. Sir (Anthony Stephen) Jeremy, KCB, CBE

Blacker, Gen. Sir Cecil Hugh, GCB, OBE, MC

Blackett, Sir Hugh Francis, Bt. (1673)

Blackham, Vice-Adm. Sir Jeremy Joe, KCB

Blacklock, Surgeon Capt. Prof. Sir Norman James, KCVO, OBE

Blackman, Sir Frank Milton, KCVO, OBE

Blackwell, Sir Basil Davenport, Kt., FREng.

Blackwood, Sir John Francis, Bt. (1814) (see also page 149)

Blair, Lt.-Gen. Sir Chandos, KCVO, OBE, MC

Blair, Sir Edward Thomas Hunter, Bt. (1786)

Blake, Sir Alfred Lapthorn, KCVO, MC

Blake, Sir Francis Michael, Bt. (1907)

Blake, Sir Peter James, KBE

Blake, Sir (Thomas) Richard (Valentine), Bt. (I. 1622)

Blaker, Sir John, Bt. (1919)

Blakiston, Sir Ferguson Arthur James, Bt. (1763)

Blanch, Sir Malcolm, KCVO

Bland, Sir (Francis) Christopher (Buchan), Kt.

Bland, Lt.-Col. Sir Simon Claud Michael, KCVO

Blank, Sir Maurice Victor, Kt.

Blatherwick, Sir David Elliott Spiby, KCMG, OBE

Blelloch, Sir John Nial Henderson, KCB

Blennerhassett, Sir (Marmaduke) Adrian Francis William, Bt. (1809)

Blewitt, Maj. Sir Shane Gabriel Basil, GCVO

Blofeld, Hon. Sir John Christopher Calthorpe, Kt.

Blois, Sir Charles Nicholas Gervase, Bt. (1686)

Blomefield, Sir Thomas Charles Peregrine, Bt. (1807)

Bloomfield, Sir Kenneth Percy, KCB

Blosse, Capt. Sir Richard Hely Lynch-, Bt. (1622)

Blount, Sir Walter Edward Alpin, Bt., DSC (1642)

Blundell, Sir Thomas Leon, Kt., FRS

Blunden, Sir George, Kt.

†Blunden, Sir Philip Overington, Bt. (I. 1766)

Blunt, Sir David Richard Reginald Harvey, Bt. (1720)

Blyth, Sir Charles (Chay), Kt., CBE, BEM

Boardman, Prof. Sir John, Kt., FSA, FBA

Bodey, Hon. Sir David Roderick Lessiter, Kt., QC

Bodmer, Sir Walter Fred, Kt., Ph.D., FRS

Body, Sir Richard Bernard Frank Stewart, Kt., MP

Boevey, Sir Thomas Michael Blake Crawley-, Bt. (1784)

Bogan, Sir Nagora, KBE

Boileau, Sir Guy (Francis), Bt. (1838)

Boles, Sir Jeremy John Fortescue, Bt. (1922)

Boles, Sir John Dennis, Kt., MBE

Bolland, Sir Edwin, KCMG

Bollers, Hon. Sir Harold Brodie Smith, Kt.

Bolt, Air Marshal Sir Richard Bruce, KBE, CB, DFC, AFC

Bolton, Sir Frederic Bernard, Kt., MC

Bona, Sir Kina, KBE

Bonallack, Sir Michael Francis, Kt., OBE

Bond, Sir John Reginald Hartnell, Kt.

Bond, Sir Kenneth Raymond Boyden, Kt.

Bond, Prof. Sir Michael Richard, Kt., FRCPsych., FRCPGlas., FRCSE

Bondi, Prof. Sir Hermann, KCB, FRS

Bonfield, Sir Peter Leahy, Kt., CBE, FREng.

Bonham, Maj. Sir Antony Lionel Thomas, Bt. (1852)

Bonington, Sir Christian John Storey, Kt., CBE

Bonsall, Sir Arthur Wilfred, KCMG, CBE

Bonsor, Sir Nicholas Cosmo, Bt. (1925)

Boolell, Sir Satcam, Kt.

Boord, Sir Nicolas John Charles, Bt. (1896)

Boorman, Lt.-Gen. Sir Derek, KCB

Booth, Sir Christopher Charles, Kt., MD, FRCP

Booth, Hon. Sir David Alwyn Gore-, KCMG, KCVO

Booth, Sir Douglas Allen, Bt. (1916)

Booth, Sir Gordon, KCMG, CVO

Booth, Sir Josslyn Henry Robert Gore-, Bt. (I. 1760)

Booth, Sir Michael Addison John Wheeler-, KCB

Boothby, Sir Brooke Charles, Bt. (1660)

Boreel, Sir Francis David, Bt. (1645)

Boreham, Hon. Sir Leslie Kenneth Edward, Kt.

Bornu, The Waziri of, KCMG, CBE

Borthwick, Sir John Thomas, Bt., MBE (1908)

Bossom, Hon. Sir Clive, Bt. (1953)

Boswall, Sir (Thomas) Alford Houstoun-, Bt. (1836)

Boswell, Lt.-Gen. Sir Alexander Crawford Simpson, KCB, CBE

Bosworth, Sir Neville Bruce Alfred, Kt., CBE

Bottomley, Sir James Reginald Alfred, KCMG

Boughey, Sir John George Fletcher, Bt. (1798)

Boulton, Sir Clifford John, GCB

Boulton, Sir (Harold Hugh) Christian, Bt. (1905)

Boulton, Sir William Whytehead, Bt., CBE, TD (1944)

Bourn, Sir John Bryant, KCB

Bovell, Hon. Sir (William) Stewart, Kt.

Bowater, Sir Euan David Vansittart, Bt. (1939)

Bowater, Sir (John) Vansittart, Bt. (1914)

Bowden, Sir Andrew, Kt., MBE

Bowden, Sir Frank, Bt. (1915)

Bowen, Sir Geoffrey Fraser, Kt.

Bowen, Sir Mark Edward Mortimer, Bt. (1921)

Bowett, Prof. Sir Derek William, Kt., CBE, QC, FBA

†Bowlby, Sir Richard Peregrine Longstaff, Bt. (1923)

Bowman, Sir Jeffery Haverstock, Kt.

Bowman, Sir Paul Humphrey Armytage, Bt. (1884)

Bowness, Sir Alan, Kt., CBE

Boyce, Adm. Sir Michael Cecil, GCB, OBE

Boyce, Sir Robert Charles Leslie, Bt. (1952)

Boyd, Sir Alexander Walter, Bt. (1916)

Boyd, Sir John Dixon Iklé, KCMG

Boyd, The Hon. Sir Mark Alexander Lennox-, Kt.

Boyd, Prof. Sir Robert Lewis Fullarton, Kt., CBE, D.SC., FRS

Boyes, Sir Brian Gerald Barratt-, KBE

Boyle, Sir Stephen Gurney, Bt. (1904)

Boynton, Sir John Keyworth, Kt., MC

Boys, Rt. Hon. Sir Michael Hardie, GCMG

Boyson, Rt. Hon. Sir Rhodes, Kt.

Brabham, Sir John Arthur, Kt., OBE

Bradbeer, Sir John Derek Richardson, Kt., OBE, TD

Bradbury, Surgeon Vice-Adm. Sir Eric Blackburn, KBE, CB

Bradbury, Prof. Sir Malcolm Stanley, Kt., CBE

Bradford, Sir Edward Alexander Slade, Bt. (1902)

Bradman, Sir Donald George, Kt.

Bradshaw, Sir Kenneth Anthony, KCB

Bradshaw, Lt.-Gen. Sir Richard Phillip, KBE

Brain, Sir (Henry) Norman, KBE, CMG

Braithwaite, Sir (Joseph) Franklin Madders, Kt.

Braithwaite, Rt. Hon. Sir Nicholas Alexander, Kt., OBE

Braithwaite, Sir Rodric Quentin, GCMG

Bramley, Prof. Sir Paul Anthony, Kt.

Branigan, Sir Patrick Francis, Kt., QC

Branson, Sir Richard Charles Nicholas, Kt.

Bratza, Sir Nicolas Duan, Kt., QC

Bray, Sir Theodor Charles, Kt., CBE

Brennan, Hon. Sir (Francis) Gerard, KBE

Brett, Sir Charles Edward Bainbridge, Kt., CBE

Brickwood, Sir Basil Greame, Bt. (1927)

Bridges, Hon. Sir Phillip Rodney, Kt., CMG

Brierley, Sir Ronald Alfred, Kt.

Bright, Sir Graham Frank James, Kt.

Bright, Sir Keith, Kt.

Brigstocke, Adm. Sir John Richard, KCB

Brinckman, Sir Theodore George Roderick, Bt. (1831)

†Brisco, Sir Campbell Howard, Bt. (1782)

Briscoe, Sir John Geoffrey James, Bt. (1910)

Brise, Sir John Archibald Ruggles-, Bt., CB, OBE, TD (1935)

Bristow, Hon. Sir Peter Henry Rowley, Kt.

Brittan, Sir Samuel, Kt.

Britton, Sir Edward Louis, Kt., CBE

†Broadbent, Sir Andrew George, Bt. (1893)

Brocklebank, Sir Aubrey Thomas, Bt. (1885)

Brodie, Sir Benjamin David Ross, Bt. (1834)

Broers, Prof. Sir Alec Nigel, Kt., Ph.D., FRS

Bromhead, Sir John Desmond Gonville, Bt. (1806)

Bromley, Sir Michael Roger, KBE

Bromley, Sir Rupert Charles, Bt. (1757)

†Brooke, Sir Alistair Weston, Bt. (1919)

Brooke, Sir Francis George Windham, Bt. (1903)

Brooke, Rt. Hon. Sir Henry, Kt.

Brooke, Sir (Richard) David Christopher, Bt. (1662)

Brooksbank, Sir (Edward) Nicholas, Bt. (1919)

Broom, Air Marshal Sir Ivor Gordon, KCB, CBE, DSO, DFC, AFC

Broomfield, Sir Nigel Hugh Robert Allen, KCMG

†Broughton, Sir David Delves, Bt. (1661)

Broun, Sir William Windsor, Bt. (S.1686)

Brown, Sir Allen Stanley, Kt., CBE

Brown, Sir (Austen) Patrick, KCB

Brown, Adm. Sir Brian Thomas, KCB, CBE

Brown, Sir (Cyril) Maxwell Palmer, KCB, CMG

Brown, Vice-Adm. Sir David Worthington, KCB

Brown, Sir Derrick Holden-, Kt.

Brown, Sir Douglas Denison, Kt.

Brown, Hon. Sir Douglas Dunlop, Kt.

Brown, Sir George Francis Richmond, Bt. (1863)

Brown, Sir George Noel, Kt.

Brown, Sir John, Kt.

Brown, Sir John Douglas Keith, Kt.

Brown, Sir John Gilbert Newton, Kt., CBE

Brown, Sir Mervyn, KCMG, OBE

Brown, Sir Peter Randolph, Kt.

Brown, Hon. Sir Ralph Kilner, Kt., OBE, TD

Brown, Sir Robert Crichton-, KCMG, CBE, TD

Brown, Rt. Hon. Sir Simon Denis, Kt.

Brown, Rt. Hon. Sir Stephen, GBE

Brown, Sir Stephen David Reid, KCVO

Brown, Sir Thomas, Kt.

Brown, Sir William Brian Piggott-, Bt. (1903)

Browne, Sir Anthony Arthur Duncan Montague-, KCMG, CBE, DFC

Browne, Sir (Edmund) John (Phillip), Kt., FREng.

Brownrigg, Sir Nicholas (Gawen), Bt. (1816)

Browse, Prof. Sir Norman Leslie, Kt., MD, FRCS

Bruce, Sir (Francis) Michael Ian, Bt. (S. 1628)

Bruce, Sir Hervey James Hugh, Bt. (1804)

Bruce, Rt. Hon. Sir (James) Roualeyn Hovell-Thurlow-Cumming-, Kt.

Brunner, Sir John Henry Kilian, Bt. (1895)

Brunton, Sir (Edward Francis) Lauder, Bt. (1908)

Brunton, Sir Gordon Charles, Kt.

Bryan, Sir Arthur, Kt.

Bryan, Sir Paul Elmore Oliver, Kt., DSO, MC

Bryce, Hon. Sir (William) Gordon, Kt., CBE

Bryson, Adm. Sir Lindsay Sutherland, KCB, FREng.

Buchan, Sir John, Kt., CMG

Buchanan, Sir Andrew George, Bt. (1878)

Buchanan, Sir Charles Alexander James Leith-, Bt. (1775)

Buchanan, Prof. Sir Colin Douglas, Kt., CBE

Buchanan, Vice-Adm. Sir Peter William, KBE

Buchanan, Sir (Ranald) Dennis, Kt., MBE

Buchanan, Sir Robert Wilson (Robin), Kt.

Buck, Sir (Philip) Antony (Fyson), Kt., QC

Buckland, Sir Ross, Kt.

Buckley, Sir John William, Kt.

Buckley, Lt.-Cdr. Sir (Peter) Richard, KCVO

Buckley, Hon. Sir Roger John, Kt.

Budd, Sir Alan Peter, Kt.

Bulkeley, Sir Richard Thomas Williams-, Bt. (1661)

Bull, Sir George Jeffrey, Kt.

Bull, Sir Simeon George, Bt. (1922)

Bullard, Sir Julian Leonard, GCMG

Bullus, Sir Eric Edward, Kt.

Bulmer, Sir William Peter, Kt.

Bultin, Sir Bato, Kt., MBE

Bunbury, Sir Michael William, Bt. (1681)

Bunbury, Sir (Richard David) Michael Richardson-, Bt. (I. 1787)

Bunch, Sir Austin Wyeth, Kt., CBE

Bunyard, Sir Robert Sidney, Kt., CBE, QPM

Burbidge, Sir Herbert Dudley, Bt. (1916)

Burdett, Sir Savile Aylmer, Bt. (1665)

Burgen, Sir Arnold Stanley Vincent, Kt., FRS

Burgess, Gen. Sir Edward Arthur, KCB, OBE

Burgess, Sir (Joseph) Stuart, Kt., CBE, Ph.D., FRSC

Burgh, Sir John Charles, KCMG, CB

Burke, Sir James Stanley Gilbert, Bt. (I. 1797)

Burke, Sir (Thomas) Kerry, Kt.

Burley, Sir Victor George, Kt., CBE

Burnet, Sir James William Alexander (Sir Alastair Burnet), Kt.

Burnett, Air Chief Marshal Sir Brian Kenyon, GCB, DFC, AFC

Burnett, Sir David Humphery, Bt., MBE, TD (1913)

Burnett, Sir John Harrison, Kt.

Burnett, Sir Walter John, Kt.

Burney, Sir Cecil Denniston, Bt. (1921)

Burns, Sir (Robert) Andrew, KCMG

Burrell, Sir John Raymond, Bt. (1774)

Burrows, Sir Bernard Alexander Brocas, GCMG

Burston, Sir Samuel Gerald Wood, Kt., OBE

Burt, Hon. Sir Francis Theodore Page, KCMG

Burton, Sir Carlisle Archibald, Kt., OBE

Burton, Sir George Vernon Kennedy, Kt., CBE

Burton, Lt.-Gen. Sir Edmund Fortescue Gerard, KBE

Burton, Sir Graham Stuart, KCMG

Burton, Sir Michael John, Kt., QC

Burton, Sir Michael St Edmund, KCVO, CMG

Bush, Adm. Sir John Fitzroy Duyland, GCB, DSC

Butler, Rt. Hon. Sir Adam Courtauld, Kt.

Butler, Hon. Sir Arlington Griffith, KCMG

Butler, Sir Michael Dacres, GCMG

Butler, Sir (Reginald) Michael (Thomas), Bt. (1922)

Butler, Hon. Sir Richard Clive, Kt.

†Butler, Sir Richard Pierce, Bt. (1628)

Butter, Maj. Sir David Henry, KCVO, MC

Butterfield, Hon. Sir Alexander Neil Logie, Kt.

Buxton, Sir Jocelyn Charles Roden, Bt. (1840)

Buxton, Rt. Hon. Sir Richard Joseph, Kt.

Buzzard, Sir Anthony Farquhar, Bt. (1929)

Byatt, Sir Hugh Campbell, KCVO, CMG

Byatt, Sir Ian Charles Rayner, Kt.

Byers, Sir Maurice Hearne, Kt., CBE, QC

Byford, Sir Lawrence, Kt., CBE, QPM

Byron, Sir Charles Michael Dennis, Kt.

Cable, Sir James Eric, KCVO, CMG

Cadbury, Sir (George) Adrian (Hayhurst), Kt.

Cadbury, Sir (Nicholas) Dominic, Kt.

Cadogan, Prof. Sir John Ivan George, Kt., CBE, FRS, FRSE

Cahn, Sir Albert Jonas, Bt. (1934)

Cain, Sir Henry Edney Conrad, Kt.

Caine, Sir Michael, Kt., CBE

Caines, Sir John, KCB

Calcutt, Sir David Charles, Kt., QC

Calderwood, Sir Robert, Kt.

Caldwell, Surgeon Vice-Adm. Sir (Eric) Dick, KBE, CB

Callan, Sir Ivan Roy, KCVO, CMG

Callaway, Prof. Sir Frank Adams, Kt., CMG, OBE

Calman, Prof. Sir Kenneth Charles, KCB, MD, FRCP, FRCS, FRSE

Calne, Prof. Sir Roy Yorke, Kt., FRS

Calthorpe, Sir Euan Hamilton Anstruther-Gough-, Bt. (1929)

Cameron of Lochiel, Sir Donald Hamish, KT, CVO, TD

Cameron, Sir Hugh Roy Graham, Kt., QPM

Campbell, Sir Alan Hugh, GCMG

Campbell, Prof. Sir Colin Murray, Kt.

Campbell, Prof. Sir Donald, Kt., CBE, FRCS, FRCPGlas.

Campbell, Sir Ian Tofts, Kt., CBE, VRD

Campbell, Sir Ilay Mark, Bt. (1808)

Campbell, Sir James Alexander Moffat Bain, Bt. (S. 1668)

Campbell, Sir Lachlan Philip Kemeys, Bt. (1815)

Campbell, Sir Niall Alexander Hamilton, Bt. (1831)

Campbell, Sir Robin Auchinbreck, Bt. (S. 1628)

Campbell, Sir Thomas Cockburn-, Bt. (1821)

Campbell, Hon. Sir Walter Benjamin, Kt.

Campbell, Rt. Hon. Sir William Anthony, Kt.

†Carden, Sir Christopher Robert, Bt. (1887)

Carden, Sir John Craven, Bt. (I. 1787)

Carew, Sir Rivers Verain, Bt. (1661)

Carey, Sir Peter Willoughby, GCB

Carlisle, Sir James Beethoven, GCMG

Carlisle, Sir John Michael, Kt.

Carlisle, Sir Kenneth Melville, Kt.

Carmichael, Sir David Peter William Gibson-Craig-, Bt. (S. 1702 and 1831)

Carnac, Revd Canon Sir (Thomas) Nicholas Rivett-, Bt. (1836)

Carnegie, Lt.-Gen. Sir Robin Macdonald, KCB, OBE

Carnegie, Sir Roderick Howard, Kt.

Carnwath, Sir Robert John Anderson, Kt., CVO

Caro, Sir Anthony Alfred, Kt., CBE, OM

Carpenter, Lt.-Gen. the Hon. Sir Thomas Patrick John Boyd-, KBE

Carr, Sir (Albert) Raymond (Maillard), Kt.

Carrick, Hon. Sir John Leslie, KCMG

Carrick, Sir Roger John, KCMG, LVO

Carsberg, Prof. Sir Bryan Victor, Kt.

Carswell, Rt. Hon. Sir Robert Douglas, Kt.

Carter, Sir Charles Frederick, Kt., FBA

Carter, Prof. Sir David Craig, Kt., FRCSE, FRCSGlas., FRCPE

Carter, Gen. Sir Evelyn John Webb-, KCVO, OBE

Carter, Sir John, Kt., QC

Carter, Sir John Alexander, Kt.

Carter, Sir John Gordon Thomas, Kt.

Carter, Sir Philip David, Kt., CBE

Carter, Sir Richard Henry Alwyn, Kt.

Carter, Sir William Oscar, Kt.

Cartland, Sir George Barrington, Kt., CMG

Cartledge, Sir Bryan George, KCMG

Cary, Sir Roger Hugh, Bt. (1955)

Casey, *Rt. Hon.* Sir Maurice Eugene, Kt.

Cash, Sir Gerald Christopher, GCMG, GCVO, OBE

Cass, Sir Geoffrey Arthur, Kt.

Cassel, Sir Harold Felix, Bt., TD, QC (1920)

Cassels, Sir John Seton, Kt., CB

Cassels, *Adm.* Sir Simon Alastair Cassillis, KCB, CBE

Cassidi, *Adm.* Sir (Arthur) Desmond, GCB

Castell, Sir William Martin, Kt.

Cater, Sir Jack, KBE

Catford, Sir (John) Robin, KCVO, CBE

Catherwood, Sir (Henry) Frederick (Ross), Kt.

Catling, Sir Richard Charles, Kt., CMG, OBE

Cave, Sir John Charles, Bt. (1896)

Cave, Sir Robert Cave-Browne-, Bt. (1641)

Cawley, Sir Charles Mills, Kt., CBE, Ph.D.

Cayley, Sir Digby William David, Bt. (1661)

Cayzer, Sir James Arthur, Bt. (1904)

Cazalet, *Hon.* Sir Edward Stephen, Kt.

Cazalet, Sir Peter Grenville, Kt.

Cecil, *Rear-Adm.* Sir (Oswald) Nigel Amherst, KBE, CB

Chadwick, *Revd Prof.* Sir Henry, KBE

Chadwick, *Rt. Hon.* Sir John Murray, Kt., ED

Chadwick, Sir Joshua Kenneth Burton, Bt. (1935)

Chadwick, *Revd Prof.* Sir (William) Owen, OM, KBE, FBA

Chalmers, Sir Iain Geoffrey, Kt.

Chalstrey, Sir (Leonard) John, Kt., MD, FRCS

Chan, *Rt. Hon.* Sir Julius, GCMG, KBE

Chance, Sir (George) Jeremy ffolliott, Bt. (1900)

Chandler, Sir Colin Michael, Kt.

Chandler, Sir Geoffrey, Kt., CBE

Chaney, *Hon.* Sir Frederick Charles, KBE, AFC

Chantler, *Prof.* Sir Cyril, Kt., MD, FRCP

Chaplin, Sir Malcolm Hilbery, Kt., CBE

Chapman, Sir David Robert Macgowan, Bt. (1958)

Chapman, Sir George Alan, Kt.

Chapman, Sir Sidney Brookes, Kt., MP

Chapple, *Field Marshal* Sir John Lyon, GCB, CBE

Charles, *Hon.* Sir Arthur William Hessin, Kt

Charles, Sir George Frederick Lawrence, KCMG, CBE

Charlton, Sir Robert (Bobby), Kt., CBE

Charnley, Sir (William) John, Kt., CB, FREng.

Chataway, *Rt. Hon.* Sir Christopher, Kt.

Chatfield, Sir John Freeman, Kt., CBE

Chaytor, Sir George Reginald, Bt. (1831)

Checketts, *Sqn. Ldr.* Sir David John, KCVO

Checkland, Sir Michael, Kt.

Cheetham, Sir Nicolas John Alexander, KCMG

Cheshire, *Air Chief Marshal* Sir John Anthony, KBE, CB

Chessells, Sir Arthur David (Tim), Kt.

Chesterton, Sir Oliver Sidney, Kt., MC

Chetwood, Sir Clifford Jack, Kt.

Chetwynd, Sir Arthur Ralph Talbot, Bt. (1795)

Cheung, Sir Oswald Victor, Kt., CBE

Cheyne, Sir Joseph Lister Watson, Bt., OBE (1908)

Chichester, Sir (Edward) John, Bt. (1641)

Chilcot, Sir John Anthony, GCB

Child, Sir (Coles John) Jeremy, Bt. (1919)

Chilton, *Brig.* Sir Frederick Oliver, Kt., CBE, DSO

Chilwell, *Hon.* Sir Muir Fitzherbert, Kt.

Chinn, Sir Trevor Edwin, Kt., CVO

Chipperfield, Sir Geoffrey Howes, KCB

Chisholm, Sir John Alexander Raymond, Kt., FREng.

Chitty, Sir Thomas Willes, Bt. (1924)

Cholmeley, Sir Hugh John Frederick Sebastian, Bt. (1806)

Chow, Sir Chung Kong, Kt.

Chow, Sir Henry Francis, Kt., OBE

Christie, Sir George William Langham, Kt.

Christie, Sir William, Kt., MBE

Christopherson, Sir Derman Guy, Kt., OBE, D.Phil., FRS, FREng.

Chung, Sir Sze-yuen, GBE, FREng.

Clapham, Sir Michael John Sinclair, KBE

Clark, Sir Francis Drake, Bt. (1886)

Clark, Sir John Allen, Kt.

Clark, Sir John Stewart-, Bt., MEP (1918)

Clark, Sir Jonathan George, Bt. (1917)

Clark, Sir Robert Anthony, Kt., DSC

Clark, Sir Robin Chichester-, Kt.

Clark, Sir Terence Joseph, KBE, CMG, CVO

Clark, Sir Thomas Edwin, Kt.

Clarke, *Hon.* Sir Anthony Petr, Kt.

Clarke, Sir Arthur Charles, Kt., CBE

Clarke, Sir (Charles Mansfield) Tobias, Bt. (1831)

Clarke, *Prof.* Sir Cyril Astley, KBE, MD, SC.D., FRS, FRCP

Clarke, Sir Ellis Emmanuel Innocent, GCMG

Clarke, Sir Jonathan Dennis, Kt.

Clarke, *Maj.* Sir Peter Cecil, KCVO

Clarke, Sir Robert Cyril, Kt.

Clarke, Sir Rupert William John, Bt., MBE (1882)

Clay, Sir Richard Henry, Bt. (1841)

Clayton, Sir David Robert, Bt. (1732)

Cleaver, Sir Anthony Brian, Kt.

Cleminson, Sir James Arnold Stacey, KBE, MC

Clerk, Sir John Dutton, Bt., CBE, VRD (S. 1679)

Clerke, Sir John Edward Longueville, Bt. (1660)

Clifford, Sir Roger Joseph, Bt. (1887)

Clothier, Sir Cecil Montacute, KCB, QC

Clucas, Sir Kenneth Henry, KCB

Clutterbuck, *Vice-Adm.* Sir David Granville, KBE, CB

Coates, Sir Anthony Robert Milnes, Bt. (1911)

Coates, Sir David Frederick Charlton, Bt. (1921)

Coats, Sir Alastair Francis Stuart, Bt. (1905)

Coats, Sir William David, Kt.

Cobham, Sir Michael John, Kt., CBE

Cochrane, Sir (Henry) Marc (Sursock), Bt. (1903)

Cockburn, Sir John Elliot, Bt. (S. 1671)

Cockshaw, Sir Alan, Kt., FREng.

Codrington, Sir Simon Francis Bethell, Bt. (1876)

Codrington, Sir William Alexander, Bt. (1721)

Coghill, Sir Egerton James Nevill Tobias, Bt. (1778)

Coghlin, *Hon.* Sir Patrick, Kt.

Cohen, Sir Edward, Kt.

Cohen, Sir Ivor Harold, Kt., CBE, TD

Cohen, *Prof.* Sir Philip, Kt., Ph.D, FRS

Cohen, Sir Stephen Harry Waley-, Bt. (1961)

Coldstream, Sir George Phillips, KCB, KCVO, QC

Cole, Sir (Alexander) Colin, KCB, KCVO, TD

Cole, Sir (Robert) William, Kt.

Coles, Sir (Arthur) John, GCMG

Colfox, Sir (William) John, Bt. (1939)

Collett, Sir Christopher, GBE

Collett, Sir Ian Seymour, Bt. (1934)

Collins, *Hon.* Sir Andrew David, Kt.

Collins, Sir Arthur James Robert, KCVO

Collins, Sir Bryan Thomas Alfred, Kt., OBE, QFSM

Collins, Sir John Alexander, Kt.

Collyear, Sir John Gowen, Kt., FREng.

Colman, *Hon.* Sir Anthony David, Kt.

Colman, Sir Michael Jeremiah, Bt. (1907)

Colman, Sir Timothy, KG

Colquhoun of Luss, Sir Ivar Iain, Bt. (1786)

Colt, Sir Edward William Dutton, Bt. (1694)

Colthurst, Sir Richard La Touche, Bt. (1744)

Coltman, Sir (Arthur) Leycester Scott, KBE, CMG

Colvin, Sir Howard Montagu, Kt., CVO, CBE, FBA

Compton, *Rt. Hon.* Sir John George Melvin, KCMG

Conant, Sir John Ernest Michael, Bt. (1954)

Condon, Sir Paul Leslie, Kt., QPM

Connell, *Hon.* Sir Michael Bryan, Kt.

Connery, Sir Sean, Kt.

Conran, Sir Terence Orby, Kt.

Cons, *Hon.* Sir Derek, Kt.

Constable, Sir Frederic Strickland-, Bt. (1641)

Constantinou, Sir Georkios, Kt., OBE

Cook, *Prof.* Sir Alan Hugh, Kt.

Cook, Sir Christopher Wymondham Rayner Herbert, Bt. (1886)

Cooke, Sir Charles Fletcher-, Kt., QC

Cooke, *Col.* Sir David William Perceval, Bt. (1661)

Cooke, Sir Howard Felix Hanlan, GCMG, GCVO

Cooksey, Sir David James Scott, Kt.

Cooper, *Rt. Hon.* Sir Frank, GCB, CMG

Cooper, Sir (Frederick Howard) Michael Craig-, Kt., CBE, TD

Cooper, *Gen.* Sir George Leslie Conroy, GCB, MC

Cooper, Sir Henry, Kt.

Cooper, Sir Louis Jacques Blom-, Kt., QC

Cooper, Sir Patrick Graham Astley, Bt. (1821)

Cooper, Sir Richard Powell, Bt. (1905)

Cooper, Sir Robert George, Kt., CBE

Cooper, *Maj.-Gen.* Sir Simon Christie, GCVO

Cooper, Sir William Daniel Charles, Bt. (1863)

Coote, Sir Christopher John, Bt., *Premier Baronet of Ireland* (I. 1621)

Copas, *Most Revd* Sir Virgil, KBE, DD

Copisarow, Sir Alcon Charles, Kt.

Corbett, *Maj.-Gen.* Sir Robert John Swan, KCVO, CB

Corby, Sir (Frederick) Brian, Kt.

Corfield, *Rt. Hon.* Sir Frederick Vernon, Kt., QC

Corfield, Sir Kenneth George, Kt., FREng.

Cork, Sir Roger William, Kt.

Corley, Sir Kenneth Sholl Ferrand, Kt.

Cormack, Sir Patrick Thomas, Kt., MP

Corness, Sir Colin Ross, Kt.

Cornforth, Sir John Warcup, Kt., CBE, D.Phil., FRS

Cortazzi, Sir (Henry Arthur) Hugh, GCMG

Cory, Sir (Clinton Charles) Donald, Bt. (1919)

Cossons, Sir Neil, Kt., OBE

Cotter, *Lt.-Col.* Sir Delaval James Alfred, Bt., DSO (I. 1763)

Cotterell, Sir John Henry Geers, Bt. (1805)

Cotton, Sir John Richard, KCMG, OBE

Cotton, *Hon.* Sir Robert Carrington, KCMG

Cottrell, Sir Alan Howard, Kt., Ph.D., FRS, FREng.

†Cotts, Sir Richard Crichton Mitchell, Bt. (1921)

Couper, Sir (Robert) Nicholas (Oliver), Bt. (1841)

Court, *Hon.* Sir Charles Walter Michael, KCMG, OBE

Cousins, *Air Chief Marshal* Sir David, KCB, AFC

Coutts, Sir David Burdett Money-, KCVO

Couzens, Sir Kenneth Edward, KCB

Covacevich, Sir (Anthony) Thomas, Kt., DFC

Coville, *Air Marshal* Sir Christopher Charles Cotton, KCB

Cowan, *Gen.* Sir Samuel, KCB, CBE

Coward, *Vice-Adm.* Sir John Francis, KCB, DSO

Cowen, *Rt. Hon. Prof.* Sir Zelman, GCMG, GCVO, QC

Cowie, Sir Thomas (Tom), Kt., OBE

Cowperthwaite, Sir John James, KBE, CMG

Cox, Sir Alan George, Kt., CBE

Cox, *Prof.* Sir David Roxbee, Kt., FRS

Cox, Sir Geoffrey Sandford, Kt., CBE

Cox, *Vice-Adm.* Sir John Michael Holland, KCB

Cradock, *Rt. Hon.* Sir Percy, GCMG

Craig, Sir (Albert) James (Macqueen), GCMG

Crane, *Hon.* Sir Peter Francis, Kt.

Craufurd, Sir Robert James, Bt. (1781)

Craven, Sir John Anthony, Kt.

Craven, *Air Marshal* Sir Robert Edward, KBE, CB, DFC

Crawford, *Prof.* Sir Frederick William, Kt., FREng.

Crawford, Sir (Robert) Stewart, GCMG, CVO

Crawford, *Vice-Adm.* Sir William Godfrey, KBE, CB, DSC

Creagh, *Maj.-Gen.* Sir (Kilner) Rupert Brazier-, KBE, CB, DSO

Cresswell, *Hon.* Sir Peter John, Kt.

Crill, Sir Peter Leslie, KBE

Cripps, Sir Cyril Humphrey, Kt.

Crisp, Sir (John) Peter, Bt. (1913)

Critchett, Sir Ian (George Lorraine), Bt. (1908)

Critchley, Sir Julian Michael Gordon, Kt.

Crocker, Sir Walter Russell, KBE

Croft, Sir Owen Glendower, Bt. (1671)

Croft, Sir Thomas Stephen Hutton, Bt. (1818)

†Crofton, Sir Hugh Denis, Bt. (1801)

Crofton, *Prof.* Sir John Wenman, Kt.

Crofton, Sir Malby Sturges, Bt. (1838)

Crookenden, *Lt.-Gen.* Sir Napier, KCB, DSO, OBE

Cross, *Air Chief Marshal* Sir Kenneth Brian Boyd, KCB, CBE, DSO, DFC

Crossland, *Prof.* Sir Bernard, Kt., CBE, FREng.

Cruthers, Sir James Winter, Kt.

Cubbon, Sir Brian Crossland, GCB

Cubitt, Sir Hugh Guy, Kt., CBE

Cullen, Sir (Edward) John, Kt., FREng.

Cumming, Sir William Gordon Gordon-, Bt. (1804)

Cuninghame, Sir John Christopher Foggo Montgomery-, Bt. (NS 1672)

Cuninghame, Sir Robert Henry Fairlie-, Bt. (S. 1630)

Cunliffe, Sir David Ellis, Bt. (1759)

Cunningham, *Lt.-Gen.* Sir Hugh Patrick, KBE

Cunynghame, Sir Andrew David Francis, Bt. (S. 1702)

†Currie, Sir Donald Scott, Bt. (1847)

Currie, Sir Neil Smith, Kt., CBE

Curtis, Sir Barry John, Kt.

Curtis, Sir (Edward) Leo, Kt.

Curtis, *Hon.* Sir Richard Herbert, Kt.

Curtis, Sir William Peter, Bt. (1802)

Curtiss, *Air Marshal* Sir John Bagot, KCB, KBE

Curwen, Sir Christopher Keith, KCMG

Cuschieri, *Prof.* Sir Alfred, Kt.

Cutler, Sir (Arthur) Roden, VC, KCMG, KCVO, CBE

Cutler, Sir Charles Benjamin, KBE, ED

Dacie, *Prof.* Sir John Vivian, Kt., MD, FRS

Dain, Sir David John Michael, KCVO

Dalrymple, *Maj.* Sir Hew Fleetwood Hamilton-, Bt., KCVO (S. 1697)

Dalton, Sir Alan Nugent Goring, Kt., CBE

Dalton, *Vice-Adm.* Sir Geoffrey Thomas James Oliver, KCB

Daly, *Lt.-Gen.* Sir Thomas Joseph, KBE, CB, DSO

Dalyell, Sir Tam (Thomas), Bt., MP (NS 1685)

Daniel, Sir Goronwy Hopkin, KCVO, CB, D.Phil.

Daniel, Sir John Sagar, Kt., D.Sc.

Daniell, Sir Peter Averell, Kt., TD

Darby, Sir Peter Howard, Kt., CBE, QFSM

Darell, Sir Jeffrey Lionel, Bt., MC (1795)

Dargie, Sir William Alexander, Kt., CBE

Dark, Sir Anthony Michael Beaumont-, Kt.

Darling, Sir Clifford, GCVO

Darvall, Sir (Charles) Roger, Kt., CBE

†Dashwood, Sir Edward John Francis, Bt., *Premier Baronet of Great Britain* (1707)

Dashwood, Sir Richard James, Bt. (1684)

Daunt, Sir Timothy Lewis Achilles, KCMG

Davey, *Hon.* Sir David Herbert Penry-, Kt.

David, Sir Jean Marc, Kt., CBE, QC

David, *His Hon.* Sir Robin (Robert) Daniel George, Kt., QC

Davidson, Sir Robert James, Kt., FREng.

†Davie, Sir Michael Ferguson-, Bt. (1847)

Davies, Sir Alan Seymour, Kt.

Davies, *Hon.* Sir (Alfred William) Michael, Kt.

Davies, Sir Alun Talfan, Kt., QC

Davies, Sir (Charles) Noel, Kt.

Davies, *Prof.* Sir David Evan Naughton, Kt., CBE, FRS, FREng.

Davies, *Hon.* Sir (David Herbert) Mervyn, Kt., MC, TD

Davies, Sir David John, Kt.

Davies, Sir Frank John, Kt., CBE

Davies, *Prof.* Sir Graeme John, Kt., FREng.

Davies, Sir John Howard, Kt.

Davies, *Vice-Adm.* Sir Lancelot Richard Bell, KBE

Davies, Sir Peter Maxwell, Kt., CBE

Davies, Sir Rhys Everson, Kt., QC

Davis, Sir Andrew Frank, Kt., CBE

Davis, Sir Colin Rex, Kt., CBE

Davis, Sir (Ernest) Howard, Kt., CMG, OBE

Davis, Sir John Gilbert, Bt. (1946)

Davis, Sir Peter John, Kt.

Davis, *Hon.* Sir Thomas Robert Alexander Harries, KBE

Davison, *Rt. Hon.* Sir Ronald Keith, GBE, CMG

Davson, Sir Christopher Michael Edward, Bt. (1927)

Dawanincura, Sir John Norbert, Kt., OBE

Dawbarn, Sir Simon Yelverton, KCVO, CMG

Dawson, *Hon.* Sir Daryl Michael, KBE, CB

Dawson, Sir Hugh Michael Trevor, Bt. (1920)

Dawtry, Sir Alan (Graham), Kt., CBE, TD

Day, Sir Derek Malcolm, KCMG

Day, *Air Marshal* Sir John Romney, KCB, OBE

Day, Sir (Judson) Graham, Kt.

Day, Sir Michael John, Kt., OBE

Day, Sir Simon James, Kt.

Deakin, Sir (Frederick) William (Dampier), Kt., DSO

Deane, *Hon.* Sir William Patrick, KBE

Dear, Sir Geoffrey James, Kt., QPM

de Bellaigue, Sir Geoffrey, GCVO

Debenham, Sir Gilbert Ridley, Bt. (1931)

de Deney, Sir Geoffrey Ivor, KCVO

de Hoghton, Sir (Richard) Bernard (Cuthbert), Bt. (1611)

De la Bère, Sir Cameron, Bt. (1953)

de la Rue, Sir Andrew George Ilay, Bt. (1898)

Dellow, Sir John Albert, Kt., CBE

de Montmorency, Sir Arnold Geoffroy, Bt. (I. 1631)

Denholm, Sir John Ferguson (Ian), Kt., CBE

Denman, Sir (George) Roy, KCB, CMG

Denny, Sir Anthony Coningham de Waltham, Bt. (I. 1782)

Denny, Sir Charles Alistair Maurice, Bt. (1913)

Dent, Sir John, Kt., CBE, FREng.

Denton, *Prof.* Sir Eric James, Kt., CBE, FRS

Derbyshire, Sir Andrew George, Kt.

Derham, Sir Peter John, Kt.

de Trafford, Sir Dermot Humphrey, Bt. (1841)

Deverell, *Lt.-Gen.* Sir John Freegard, KCB, OBE

Devesi, Sir Baddeley, GCMG, GCVO

De Ville, Sir Harold Godfrey Oscar, Kt., CBE

Devitt, Sir James Hugh Thomas, Bt. (1916)

de Waal, Sir (Constant Henrik) Henry, KCB, QC

Dewey, Sir Anthony Hugh, Bt. (1917)

Dewhurst, *Prof.* Sir (Christopher) John, Kt.

d'Eyncourt, Sir Mark Gervais Tennyson-, Bt. (1930)

Dhenin, *Air Marshal* Sir Geoffrey Howard, KBE, AFC, GM, MD

Dhrangadhra, HH the Maharaja Raj Saheb of, KCIE

Dibela, *Hon.* Sir Kingsford, GCMG

Dick, *Maj.-Gen.* Sir Iain Charles Mackay-, KCVO, MBE

Dickenson, Sir Aubrey Fiennes Trotman-, Kt.

Dickinson, Sir Harold Herbert, Kt.

Dickinson, Sir Samuel Benson, Kt.

Dilke, Sir Charles John Wentworth, Bt. (1862)

Dillon, *Rt. Hon.* Sir (George) Brian (Hugh), Kt.

Dixon, Sir Ian Leonard, Kt., CBE

Dixon, Sir Jeremy, Kt.

Dixon, Sir Jonathan Mark, Bt. (1919)

Djanogly, Sir Harry Ari Simon, Kt., CBE

Dobbs, *Capt.* Sir Richard Arthur Frederick, KCVO

Dobson, *Vice-Adm.* Sir David Stuart, KBE

Dobson, *Gen.* Sir Patrick John Howard-, GCB

Dodds, Sir Ralph Jordan, Bt. (1964)

Dodson, Sir Derek Sherborne Lindsell, KCMG, MC

Dodsworth, Sir John Christopher Smith-, Bt. (1784)

Doll, *Prof.* Sir (William) Richard (Shaboe), Kt., CH, OBE, FRS, DM, MD, D.Sc.

Dollery, Sir Colin Terence, Kt.

Donald, Sir Alan Ewen, KCMG

Donald, *Air Marshal* Sir John George, KBE

Donne, *Hon.* Sir Gaven John, KBE

Donne, Sir John Christopher, Kt.

Dookun, Sir Dewoonarain, Kt.

Dorey, Sir Graham Martyn, Kt.

Dorman, Sir Philip Henry Keppel, Bt.(1923)

Dougherty, *Maj.-Gen.* Sir Ivan Noel, Kt., CBE, DSO, ED

Doughty, Sir William Roland, Kt.

Douglas, Sir (Edward) Sholto, Kt.

Douglas, *Hon.* Sir Roger Owen, Kt.

Douglas, *Rt. Hon.* Sir William Randolph, KCMG

Dover, *Prof.* Sir Kenneth James, Kt., D.Litt., FBA, FRSE

Dowell, Sir Anthony James, Kt., CBE

Down, Sir Alastair Frederick, Kt., OBE, MC, TD

Downes, Sir Edward Thomas, Kt., CBE

Downey, Sir Gordon Stanley, KCB

Downs, Sir Diarmuid, Kt., CBE, FREng.

Downward, *Maj.-Gen.* Sir Peter Aldcroft, KCVO, CB, DSO, DFC

Downward, Sir William Atkinson, Kt.

Dowson, Sir Philip Manning, Kt., CBE, PRA

Doyle, Sir Reginald Derek Henry, Kt., CBE

D'Oyly, Sir Nigel Hadley Miller, Bt. (1663)

Drake, *Hon.* Sir (Frederick) Maurice, Kt., DFC

Drewry, *Lt-Gen.* Sir Christopher Francis, KCB, CBE

Dreyer, *Adm.* Sir Desmond Parry, GCB, CBE, DSC

Drinkwater, Sir John Muir, Kt., QC

Driver, Sir Antony Victor, Kt.

Driver, Sir Eric William, Kt.

Drummond, Sir John Richard Gray, Kt., CBE

Drury, Sir (Victor William) Michael, Kt., OBE

Dryden, Sir John Stephen Gyles, Bt. (1733 and 1795)

du Cann, *Rt. Hon.* Sir Edward Dillon Lott, KBE

†Duckworth, Sir Edward Richard Dyce, Bt. (1909)

du Cros, Sir Claude Philip Arthur Mallet, Bt. (1916)

Duffell, *Lt.-Gen.* Sir Peter Royson, KCB, CBE, MC

Duffus, *Hon.* Sir Herbert George Holwell, Kt.

Duffy, Sir (Albert) (Edward) Patrick, Kt., Ph.D.

Dugdale, Sir William Stratford, Bt., MC (1936)

Dummett, *Prof.* Sir Michael Anthony Eardley, Kt., FBA

Dunbar, Sir Archibald Ranulph, Bt. (S. 1700)

Dunbar, Sir David Hope-, Bt. (S. 1664)

Dunbar, Sir Drummond Cospatrick Ninian, Bt., MC (S. 1698)

Dunbar, Sir James Michael, Bt. (S. 1694)

†Dunbar of Hempriggs, Sir Richard Francis, Bt. (S. 1706)

Duncan, Sir James Blair, Kt.
Duncombe, Sir Philip Digby
Pauncefort-, Bt. (1859)
Dunham, Sir Kingsley Charles, Kt.,
PH.D., FRS, FRSE, FREng.
Dunlop, Sir Thomas, Bt. (1916)
Dunn, *Air Marshal* Sir Eric Clive,
KBE, CB, BEM
Dunn, *Air Marshal* Sir Patrick
Hunter, KBE, CB, DFC
Dunn, *Rt. Hon.* Sir Robin Horace
Walford, Kt., MC
Dunne, Sir Thomas Raymond, KCVO
Dunning, Sir Simon William Patrick,
Bt. (1930)
Dunstan, *Lt.-Gen.* Sir Donald
Beaumont, KBE, CB
Dunt, *Vice-Adm.* Sir John Hugh, KCB
†Duntze, Sir Daniel Evans, Bt. (1774)
Dupre, Sir Tumun, Kt., MBE
Dupree, Sir Peter, Bt. (1921)
Durand, Sir Edward Alan
Christopher David Percy, Bt.
(1892)
Durant, Sir (Robert) Anthony
(Bevis), Kt.
Durham, Sir Kenneth, Kt.
Durie, Sir Alexander Charles, Kt.,
CBE
Durkin, *Air Marshal* Sir Herbert,
KBE, CB
Durrant, Sir William Alexander
Estridge, Bt. (1784)
Duthie, *Prof.* Sir Herbert Livingston,
Kt.
Duthie, Sir Robert Grieve (Robin),
Kt., CBE
Dyer, *Prof.* Sir (Henry) Peter
(Francis) Swinnerton-, Bt., KBE,
FRS (1678)
Dyke, Sir David William Hart, Bt.
(1677)
Dyson, *Hon.* Sir John Anthony, Kt.
Eady, *Hon.* Sir David, Kt.
Earle, Sir (Hardman) George
(Algernon), Bt. (1869)
Easton, Sir Robert William Simpson,
Kt., CBE
Eaton, *Adm.* Sir Kenneth John, GBE,
KCB
Eberle, *Adm.* Sir James Henry Fuller,
GCB
Ebrahim, Sir (Mahomed)
Currimbhoy, Bt. (1910)
Echlin, Sir Norman David Fenton,
Bt. (I. 1721)
Eckersley, Sir Donald Payze, Kt.,
OBE
Edge, *Capt.* Sir (Philip) Malcolm,
KCVO
†Edge, Sir William, Bt. (1937)
Edmonstone, Sir Archibald Bruce
Charles, Bt. (1774)
Edwardes, Sir Michael Owen, Kt.
Edwards, Sir Christopher John
Churchill, Bt. (1866)
Edwards, Sir George Robert, Kt.,
OM, CBE, FRS, FREng.
Edwards, Sir Llewellyn Roy, Kt.
Edwards, *Prof.* Sir Samuel Frederick,
Kt., FRS

Egan, Sir John Leopold, Kt.
Egerton, Sir John Alfred Roy, Kt.
Egerton, Sir (Philip) John (Caledon)
Grey-, Bt. (1617)
Egerton, Sir Stephen Loftus, KCMG
Eichelbaum, *Rt. Hon.* Sir Thomas,
GBE
Elias, Sir Patrick, Kt., QC
Eliott of Stobs, Sir Charles Joseph
Alexander, Bt. (S. 1666)
Ellerton, Sir Geoffrey James, Kt.,
CMG, MBE
Elliot, Sir Gerald Henry, Kt.
Elliott, Sir Clive Christopher Hugh,
Bt. (1917)
Elliott, Sir David Murray, KCMG, CB
Elliott, *Prof.* Sir John Huxtable, Kt.,
FBA
Elliott, Sir Randal Forbes, KBE
Elliott, *Prof.* Sir Roger James, Kt., FRS
Elliott, Sir Ronald Stuart, Kt.
Ellis, Sir Ronald, Kt., FREng.
Ellison, *Col.* Sir Ralph Harry Carr-,
KCVO, TD
Elphinstone, Sir John, Bt. (S. 1701)
Elphinstone, Sir John Howard Main,
Bt. (1816)
Elton, Sir Arnold, Kt., CBE
Elton, Sir Charles Abraham
Grierson, Bt. (1717)
Elwes, Sir Jeremy Vernon, Kt., CBE
Elwood, Sir Brian George Conway,
Kt., CBE
Elworthy, Sir Peter Herbert, Kt.
Elyan, Sir (Isadore) Victor, Kt.
Emery, *Rt. Hon.* Sir Peter Frank
Hannibal, Kt., MP
Empey, Sir Reginald Norman
Morgan, Kt., OBE
Engle, Sir George Lawrence Jose,
KCB, QC
English, Sir Terence Alexander
Hawthorne, KBE, FRCS
Epstein, *Prof.* Sir (Michael) Anthony,
Kt., CBE, FRS
Errington, *Col.* Sir Geoffrey
Frederick, Bt., OBE (1963)
Errington, Sir Lancelot, KCB
Erskine, Sir (Thomas) David, Bt.
(1821)
Esmonde, Sir Thomas Francis
Grattan, Bt. (I. 1629)
Espie, Sir Frank Fletcher, Kt., OBE
Esplen, Sir John Graham, Bt. (1921)
Essenhigh, *Adm.* Sir Nigel Richard,
Kt.
Evans, Sir Anthony Adney, Bt. (1920)
Evans, *Rt. Hon.* Sir Anthony Howell
Meurig, Kt., RD
Evans, *Air Chief Marshal* Sir David
George, GCB, CBE
Evans, *Air Chief Marshal* Sir David
Parry-, GCB, CBE
Evans, *Hon.* Sir Haydn Tudor, Kt.
Evans, *Prof.* Sir John Grimley, Kt.,
FRCP
Evans, Sir John Stanley, Kt., QPM
Evans, Sir Richard Harry, Kt., CBE
Evans, Sir Richard Mark, KCMG,
KCVO
Evans, Sir Robert, Kt., CBE, FREng.

Evans, Sir (William) Vincent (John),
GCMG, MBE, QC
Eveleigh, *Rt. Hon.* Sir Edward
Walter, Kt., ERD
Everard, Sir Robin Charles, Bt.
(1911)
Everson, Sir Frederick Charles,
KCMG
Every, Sir Henry John Michael, Bt.
(1641)
Ewans, Sir Martin Kenneth, KCMG
†Ewart, Sir William Michael, Bt.
(1887)
Ewbank, *Hon.* Sir Anthony Bruce,
Kt.
Ewin, Sir (David) Ernest Thomas
Floyd, Kt., OBE, LVO
Ewing, Sir (Alistair) Simon Orr-, Bt.
(1963)
Ewing, Sir Ronald Archibald Orr-,
Bt. (1886)
Eyre, *Maj.-Gen.* Sir James Ainsworth
Campden Gabriel, KCVO, CBE
Eyre, Sir Reginald Edwin, Kt.
Eyre, Sir Richard Charles Hastings,
Kt., CBE
Faber, Sir Richard Stanley, KCVO,
CMG
Fagge, Sir John William Frederick,
Bt. (1660)
Fairbairn, Sir (James) Brooke, Bt.
(1869)
Fairclough, Sir John Whitaker, Kt.,
FREng.
Fairhall, *Hon.* Sir Allen, KBE
Fairweather, Sir Patrick Stanislaus,
KCMG
Falconer, *Hon.* Sir Douglas William,
Kt., MBE
†Falkiner, Sir Benjamin Simon
Patrick, Bt. (I. 1778)
Fall, Sir Brian James Proetel, GCVO,
KCMG
Falle, Sir Samuel, KCMG, KCVO, DSC
Fang, *Prof.* Sir Harry, Kt., CBE
Fareed, Sir Djamil Sheik, Kt.
Farmer, Sir Thomas, Kt., CBE
Farquhar, Sir Michael Fitzroy
Henry, Bt. (1796)
Farquharson, *Rt. Hon.* Sir Donald
Henry, Kt.
Farquharson, Sir James Robbie, KBE
Farrer, Sir (Charles) Matthew, GCVO
Farrington, Sir Henry Francis
Colden, Bt. (1818)
Tat, Sir (Maxime) Edouard (Lim
Man) Lim, Kt.
Faulkner, Sir (James) Dennis
(Compton), Kt., CBE, VRD
Fawcus, Sir (Robert) Peter, KBE, CMG
Fawkes, Sir Randol Francis, Kt.
Fay, Sir (Humphrey) Michael
Gerard, Kt.
Fayrer, Sir John Lang Macpherson,
Bt. (1896)
Fearn, Sir (Patrick) Robin, KCMG
Feilden, Sir Bernard Melchior, Kt.,
CBE
Feilden, Sir Henry Wemyss, Bt.,
(1846)
Fell, Sir David, KCB

Fender, Sir Brian Edward Frederick, Kt., CMG, Ph.D.

Fenn, Sir Nicholas Maxted, GCMG

Fennell, Hon. Sir (John) Desmond Augustine, Kt., OBE

Fennessy, Sir Edward, Kt., CBE

Ferguson, Sir Alexander Chapman, Kt., CBE

Ferguson, Sir Ian Edward Johnson-, Bt. (1906)

Fergusson of Kilkerran, Sir Charles, Bt. (S. 1703)

Fergusson, Sir Ewan Alastair John, GCMG, GCVO

Fergusson, Sir James Herbert Hamilton Colyer-, Bt. (1866)

Feroze, Sir Rustam Moolan, Kt., FRCS

Ferris, Hon. Sir Francis Mursell, Kt., TD

ffolkes, Sir Robert Francis Alexander, Bt, OBE (1774)

Field, Sir Malcolm David, Kt.

Fielding, Sir Colin Cunningham, Kt., CB

Fielding, Sir Leslie, KCMG

Fieldsend, Hon. Sir John Charles Rowell, KBE

Fiennes, Sir Ranulph Twisleton-Wykeham-, Bt., OBE (1916)

Figg, Sir Leonard Clifford William, KCMG

Figgis, Sir Anthony St John Howard, KCVO, CMG

Figures, Sir Colin Frederick, KCMG, OBE

Fingland, Sir Stanley James Gunn, KCMG

Finlay, Sir David Ronald James Bell, Bt. (1964)

Finney, Sir Thomas, Kt., OBE

Firth, Prof. Sir Raymond William, Kt., Ph.D., FBA

Fisher, Sir George Read, Kt., CMG

Fisher, Hon. Sir Henry Arthur Pears, Kt.

Fison, Sir (Richard) Guy, Bt., DSC (1905)

†Fitzgerald, Revd (Sir) Daniel Patrick, Bt. (1903)

FitzGerald, Sir George Peter Maurice, Bt., MC (The Knight of Kerry) (1880)

FitzHerbert, Sir Richard Ranulph, Bt. (1784)

Fitzpatrick, Gen. Sir (Geoffrey Richard) Desmond, GCB, GCVO, DSO, MBE, MC

Fitzpatrick, Air Marshal Sir John Bernard, KBE, CB

Flanagan, Sir Ronald, Kt., OBE

Fletcher, Sir Henry Egerton Aubrey-, Bt. (1782)

Fletcher, Sir James Muir Cameron, Kt.

Fletcher, Sir Leslie, Kt., DSC

Floissac, Hon. Sir Vincent Frederick, Kt., CMG, OBE, QC

Floyd, Sir Giles Henry Charles, Bt. (1816)

Foley, Lt.-Gen. Sir John Paul, KCB, OBE, MC

Foley, Sir (Thomas John) Noel, Kt., CBE

Follett, Prof. Sir Brian Keith, Kt., FRS

Foot, Sir Geoffrey James, Kt.

Foots, Sir James William, Kt.

Forbes, Hon. Sir Alastair Granville, Kt.

Forbes, Maj. Sir Hamish Stewart, Bt., MBE, MC (1823)

Forbes of Craigievar, Sir John Alexander Cumnock, Bt. (S. 1630)

Forbes, Vice-Adm. Sir John Morrison, KCB

Forbes, Hon. Sir Thayne John, Kt.

†Forbes of Pitsligo, Sir William Daniel Stuart-, Bt. (S. 1626)

Ford, Sir Andrew Russell, Bt. (1929)

Ford, Sir David Robert, KBE, LVO, OBE

Ford, Maj. Sir Edward William Spencer, GCVO, KCB, ERD

Ford, Air Marshal Sir Geoffrey Harold, KBE, CB, FREng.

Ford, Prof. Sir Hugh, Kt., FRS, FREng.

Ford, Sir James Anson St Clair-, Bt. (1793)

Ford, Sir John Archibald, KCMG, MC

Ford, Gen. Sir Robert Cyril, GCB, CBE

Foreman, Sir Philip Frank, Kt., CBE, FREng.

Forman, Sir John Denis, Kt., OBE

Forrest, Prof. Sir (Andrew) Patrick (McEwen), Kt.

Forrest, Rear-Adm. Sir Ronald Stephen, KCVO

Forster, Sir Archibald William, Kt., FREng.

Forte, Hon. Sir Rocco John Vincent, Kt.

Forwood, Sir Dudley Richard, Bt. (1895)

Foster, Prof. Sir Christopher David, Kt.

Foster, Sir John Gregory, Bt. (1930)

Foster, Sir Richard Anthony, Kt.

Foster, Sir Robert Sidney, GCMG, KCVO

Foulis, Sir Ian Primrose Liston-, Bt. (S. 1634)

Foulkes, Sir Nigel Gordon, Kt.

Fountain, Hon. Sir Cyril Stanley Smith, Kt.

Fowden, Sir Leslie, Kt., FRS

Fowke, Sir David Frederick Gustavus, Bt. (1814)

Fowler, Sir (Edward) Michael Coulson, Kt.

Fowler, Rt. Hon. Sir (Peter) Norman, Kt., MP

Fox, Rt. Hon. Sir (John) Marcus, Kt., MBE

Fox, Rt. Hon. Sir Michael John, Kt.

Fox, Sir Paul Leonard, Kt., CBE

France, Sir Christopher Walter, GCB

Francis, Sir Horace William Alexander, Kt., CBE, FREng.

Frank, Sir Douglas George Horace, Kt., QC

Frank, Sir Robert Andrew, Bt. (1920)

Franklin, Sir Michael David Milroy, KCB, CMG

Franks, Sir Arthur Temple, KCMG

Fraser, Sir Angus McKay, KCB, TD

Fraser, Sir Charles Annand, KCVO

Fraser, Gen. Sir David William, GCB, OBE

Fraser, Air Marshal Revd Sir (Henry) Paterson, KBE, CB, AFC

Fraser, Sir Iain Michael Duncan, Bt. (1943)

Fraser, Sir Ian James, Kt., CBE, MC

Fraser, Sir (James) Campbell, Kt.

Fraser, Sir William Kerr, GCB

Frederick, Sir Charles Boscawen, Bt. (1723)

Freeland, Sir John Redvers, KCMG

Freeman, Sir James Robin, Bt. (1945)

Freer, Air Chief Marshal Sir Robert William George, GBE, KCB

Freeth, Hon. Sir Gordon, KBE

French, Hon. Sir Christopher James Saunders, Kt.

Frere, Vice-Adm. Sir Richard Tobias, KCB

Fretwell, Sir (Major) John (Emsley), GCMG

Freud, Sir Clement Raphael, Kt.

Froggatt, Sir Leslie Trevor, Kt.

Froggatt, Sir Peter, Kt.

Frossard, Sir Charles Keith, KBE

Frost, Sir David Paradine, Kt., OBE

Frost, Sir Terence Ernest Manitou, Kt., RA

Fry, Sir Peter Derek, Kt.

Fry, Hon. Sir William Gordon, Kt.

Fuller, Sir James Henry Fleetwood, Bt. (1910)

Fuller, Hon. Sir John Bryan Munro, Kt.

Fung, Hon. Sir Kenneth Ping-Fan, Kt., CBE

Furness, Sir Stephen Roberts, Bt. (1913)

Gadsden, Sir Peter Drury Haggerston, GBE, FREng.

Gage, Hon. Sir William Marcus, Kt.

Gainsford, Sir Ian Derek, Kt., DDS

Gaius, Rt. Revd Saimon, KBE

Gallwey, Sir Philip Frankland Payne-, Bt. (1812)

Galsworthy, Sir Anthony Charles, KCMG

Gam, Rt. Revd Sir Getake, KBE

Gamble, Sir David Hugh Norman, Bt. (1897)

Gambon, Sir Michael John, Kt., CBE

Garden, Air Marshal Sir Timothy, KCB

Gardiner, Sir George Arthur, Kt.

Gardiner, Sir John Eliot, Kt., CBE

Gardner, Sir Edward Lucas, Kt., QC

Gardner, Sir Robert Henry Bruce-, Bt. (1945)

Garland, Hon. Sir Patrick Neville, Kt.

Garland, Hon. Sir Ransley Victor, KBE

Garlick, Sir John, KCB

Garner, Sir Anthony Stuart, Kt.

Garnett, *Vice-Adm.* Sir Ian David
Graham, KCB
Garnier, *Rear-Adm.* Sir John, KCVO,
CBE
Garrett, Sir Anthony Peter, Kt., CBE
Garrick, Sir Ronald, Kt., CBE, FREng.
Garrioch, Sir (William) Henry, Kt.
Garrod, *Lt.-Gen.* Sir (John) Martin
Carruthers, KCB, OBE
Garthwaite, Sir (William) Mark
(Charles), Bt. (1919)
Gaskell, Sir Richard Kennedy
Harvey, Kt.
Gatehouse, *Hon.* Sir Robert
Alexander, Kt.
Geno, Sir Makena Viora, KBE
George, Sir Arthur Thomas, Kt.
George, *Prof.* Sir Charles Frederick,
MD, FRCP
George, *Rt. Hon.* Sir Edward Alan
John, GBE
George, Sir Richard William, Kt.,
CVO
Gerken, *Vice-Adm.* Sir Robert
William Frank, KCB, CBE
Gery, Sir Robert Lucian Wade-,
KCMG, KCVO
Gethin, Sir Richard Joseph
St Lawrence, Bt. (I. 1665)
Getty, Sir (John) Paul, KBE
Ghurburrun, Sir Rabindrah, Kt.
Gibb, Sir Francis Ross (Frank), Kt.,
CBE, FREng.
Gibbings, Sir Peter Walter, Kt.
Gibbons, Sir (John) David, KBE
Gibbons, Sir William Edward
Doran, Bt. (1752)
Gibbs, *Hon.* Sir Eustace Hubert
Beilby, KCVO, CMG
Gibbs, *Rt. Hon.* Sir Harry Talbot,
GCMG, KBE
Gibbs, *Lt.-Col.* Sir Peter Evan
Wyldbore, KCVO
Gibbs, *Hon.* Sir Richard John
Hedley, Kt.
Gibbs, Sir Roger Geoffrey, Kt.
Gibbs, *Field Marshal* Sir Roland
Christopher, GCB, CBE, DSO, MC
†Gibson, *Revd* Sir Christopher
Herbert, Bt. (1931)
Gibson, *Vice-Adm.* Sir Donald
Cameron Ernest Forbes, KCB, DSC
Gibson, Sir Ian, Kt., CBE
Gibson, *Rt. Hon.* Sir Peter Leslie, Kt.
Gibson, *Rt. Hon.* Sir Ralph Brian, Kt.
Giddings, *Air Marshal* Sir (Kenneth
Charles) Michael, KCB, OBE, DFC,
AFC
Gielgud, Sir (Arthur) John, Kt., OM,
CH
Giffard, Sir (Charles) Sydney
(Rycroft), KCMG
Gilbert, Sir Arthur, Kt.
Gilbert, *Air Chief Marshal* Sir Joseph
Alfred, KCB, CBE
Gilbert, Sir Martin John, Kt., CBE
†Gilbey, Sir Walter Gavin, Bt. (1893)
Giles, *Rear-Adm.* Sir Morgan Charles
Morgan-, Kt., DSO, OBE, GM
Gill, Sir Anthony Keith, Kt., FREng.
Gillam, Sir Patrick John, Kt.

Gillen, *Hon.* Sir John de Winter, Kt.
Gillett, Sir Robin Danvers Penrose,
Bt., GBE, RD (1959)
Gilmour, *Col.* Sir Allan Macdonald,
KCVO, OBE, MC
Gilmour, Sir John Edward, Bt., DSO,
TD (1897)
Gina, Sir Lloyd Maepeza, KBE
Gingell, *Air Chief Marshal* Sir John,
GBE, KCB, KCVO
Girolami, Sir Paul, Kt.
Girvan, *Hon.* Sir (Frederick) Paul, Kt.
Gladstone, Sir (Erskine) William,
KG, Bt. (1846)
Glasspole, Sir Florizel Augustus,
GCMG, GCVO
Glen, Sir Alexander Richard, KBE,
DSC
Glenn, Sir (Joseph Robert)
Archibald, Kt., OBE
Glidewell, *Rt. Hon.* Sir Iain Derek
Laing, Kt.
Glover, *Gen.* Sir James Malcolm,
KCB, MBE
Glover, Sir Victor Joseph Patrick, Kt.
Glyn, Sir Richard Lindsay, Bt. (1759
and 1800)
Goavea, Sir Sinaka Vakai, KBE
Gobbo, Sir James Augustine, Kt., AC
Godber, Sir George Edward, GCB,
DM
Goff, Sir Robert (William) Davis-,
Bt. (1905)
Gold, Sir Arthur Abraham, Kt., CBE
Gold, Sir Joseph, Kt.
Goldberg, *Prof.* Sir Abraham, Kt.,
MD, D.Sc., FRCP
Goldberg, *Prof.* Sir David Paul
Brandes, Kt.
Goldman, Sir Samuel, KCB
Goldring, Sir John Bernard, Kt.
Gombrich, *Prof.* Sir Ernst Hans
Josef, Kt., OM, CBE, Ph.D., FBA, FSA
Gomersall, Sir Stephen John, KCMG
Gooch, Sir Timothy Robert, Bt., MBE
(1746)
Gooch, Sir Trevor Sherlock (Sir
Peter), Bt. (1866)
Good, Sir John Kennedy-, KBE
Goodall, Sir (Arthur) David Saunders,
GCMG
Goode, Prof. Sir Royston Miles, Kt.,
CBE, QC
Goodenough, Sir Anthony Michael,
KCMG
Goodenough, Sir William
McLernon, Bt. (1943)
Goodhart, Sir Philip Carter, Kt.
Goodhart, Sir Robert Anthony
Gordon, Bt. (1911)
Goodhew, Sir Victor Henry, Kt.
Goodison, Sir Alan Clowes, KCMG
Goodison, Sir Nicholas Proctor, Kt.
Goodlad, *Rt. Hon.* Sir Alastair
Robertson, KCMG
Goodman, Sir Patrick Ledger, Kt.,
CBE
Goodson, Sir Mark Weston Lassam,
Bt. (1922)
Goodwin, Sir Matthew Dean, Kt.,
CBE

†Goold, Sir George William, Bt.
(1801)
Gordon, Sir Andrew Cosmo Lewis
Duff-, Bt. (1813)
Gordon, Sir Charles Addison
Somerville Snowden, KCB
Gordon, Sir Gerald Henry, Kt., CBE,
QC
Gordon, Sir Keith Lyndell, Kt., CMG
Gordon, Sir (Lionel) Eldred (Peter)
Smith-, Bt. (1838)
Gordon, Sir Robert James, Bt.
(S. 1706)
Gordon, Sir Sidney Samuel, Kt., CBE
Gordon Lennox, Lord Nicholas
Charles, KCMG, KCVO
†Gore, Sir Nigel Hugh St George, Bt.
(I. 1622)
Gorham, Sir Richard Masters, Kt.,
CBE, DFC
Goring, Sir William Burton Nigel,
Bt. (1627)
Gorman, Sir John Reginald, Kt.,
CVO, CBE, MC
Gorst, Sir John Michael, Kt.
Gorton, *Rt. Hon.* Sir John Grey,
GCMG, CH
Goschen, Sir Edward Christian, Bt.,
DSO (1916)
Gosling, Sir (Frederick) Donald, Kt.
Goswell, Sir Brian Lawrence, Kt.
Goulden, Sir (Peter) John, KCMG
Goulding, Sir Marrack Irvine, KCMG
Goulding, Sir (William) Lingard
Walter, Bt. (1904)
Gourlay, *Gen.* Sir (Basil) Ian
(Spencer), KCB, OBE, MC, RM
Gourlay, Sir Simon Alexander, Kt.
Govan, Sir Lawrence Herbert, Kt.
Gow, *Gen.* Sir (James) Michael, GCB
Gowans, Sir James Learmonth, Kt.,
CBE, FRCP, FRS
†Graaff, Sir David de Villiers, Bt., MBE
(1911)
Grabham, Sir Anthony Henry, Kt.
Graham, Sir Alexander Michael, GBE
Graham, Sir James Bellingham, Bt.
(1662)
Graham, Sir James Fergus Surtees,
Bt. (1783)
Graham, Sir James Thompson, Kt.,
CMG
Graham, Sir John Alexander Noble,
Bt., GCMG (1906)
Graham, Sir John Alistair, Kt.
Graham, Sir John Moodie, Bt. (1964)
Graham, Sir Norman William, Kt.,
CB
Graham, Sir Peter, KCB, QC
Graham, Sir Peter Alfred, Kt., OBE
Graham, *Lt.-Gen.* Sir Peter Walter,
KCB, CBE
†Graham, Sir Ralph Stuart, Bt. (1629)
Graham, *Hon.* Sir Samuel Horatio,
Kt., CMG, OBE
Grandy, *Marshal of the Royal Air Force*
Sir John, GCB, GCVO, KBE, DSO
Grant, Sir Archibald, Bt. (S. 1705)
Grant, Sir Clifford, Kt.
Grant, Sir (John) Anthony, Kt.
Grant, Sir (Matthew) Alistair, Kt.

Grant, Sir Patrick Alexander Benedict, Bt. (S. 1688)
Grant, Lt.-Gen. Sir Scott Carnegie, KCB
Gray, Hon. Sir Charles Anthony St John, Kt., QC
Gray, Prof. Sir Denis John Pereira, Kt., OBE, FRCGP
Gray, Sir John Archibald Browne, Kt., SC.D., FRS
Gray, Sir John Walton David, KBE, CMG
Gray, Lt.-Gen. Sir Michael Stuart, KCB, OBE
Gray, Sir Robert McDowall (Robin), Kt.
Gray, Sir William Hume, Bt. (1917)
Graydon, Air Chief Marshal Sir Michael James, GCB, CBE
Grayson, Sir Jeremy Brian Vincent Harrington, Bt. (1922)
Green, Sir Allan David, KCB, QC
Green, Sir Andrew Fleming, KCMG
Green, Hon. Sir Guy Stephen Montague, KBE
Green, Sir Kenneth, Kt.
Green, Sir Owen Whitley, Kt.
†Green, Sir Simon Lycett, Bt., TD (1886)
Greenaway, Sir John Michael Burdick, Bt. (1933)
Greenbury, Sir Richard, Kt.
Greene, Sir (John) Brian Massy-, Kt.
Greener, Sir Anthony Armitage, Kt.
Greengross, Sir Alan David, Kt.
Greening, Rear-Adm. Sir Paul Woollven, GCVO
Greenstock, Sir Jeremy Quentin, KCMG
Greenwell, Sir Edward Bernard, Bt. (1906)
Gregson, Sir Peter Lewis, GCB
Greig, Sir (Henry Louis) Carron, KCVO, CBE
Grenside, Sir John Peter, Kt., CBE
Grey, Sir Anthony Dysart, Bt. (1814)
Grierson, Sir Michael John Bewes, Bt. (S.1685)
Grierson, Sir Ronald Hugh, Kt.
Griffin, Maj. Sir (Arthur) John (Stewart), KCVO
Griffin, Sir (Charles) David, Kt., CBE
Griffiths, Sir Eldon Wylie, Kt.
Griffiths, Sir John Norton-, Bt. (1922)
Grigson, Hon. Sir Geoffrey Douglas, Kt.
Grimwade, Sir Andrew Sheppard, Kt., CBE
Grindrod, Most Revd Sir John Basil Rowland, KBE
Grinstead, Sir Stanley Gordon, Kt.
Grose, Vice-Adm. Sir Alan, KBE
Grossart, Sir Angus McFarlane McLeod, Kt., CBE
Grotrian, Sir Philip Christian Brent, Bt. (1934)
Grove, Sir Charles Gerald, Bt. (1874)
Grove, Sir Edmund Frank, KCVO
Grugeon, Sir John Drury, Kt.

Grylls, Sir (William) Michael (John), Kt.
Guinness, Sir Howard Christian Sheldon, Kt., VRD
Guinness, Sir John Ralph Sidney, Kt., CB
Guinness, Sir Kenelm Ernest Lee, Bt. (1867)
Guise, Sir John Grant, Bt. (1783)
Gull, Sir Rupert William Cameron, Bt. (1872)
Gumbs, Sir Emile Rudolph, Kt.
Gunn, Prof. Sir John Currie, Kt., CBE
Gunn, Sir Robert Norman, Kt.
Gunn, Sir William Archer, KBE, CMG
†Gunning, Sir Charles Theodore, Bt. (1778)
Gunston, Sir John Wellesley, Bt. (1938)
Gurdon, Prof. Sir John Bertrand, Kt., D.Phil., FRS
Guthrie, Gen. Sir Charles Ronald Llewelyn, GCB, LVO, OBE
Guthrie, Sir Malcolm Connop, Bt. (1936)
Guy, Gen. Sir Roland Kelvin, GCB, CBE, DSO
Habakkuk, Sir John Hrothgar, Kt., FBA
Haddacks, Vice-Adm. Sir Paul Kenneth, KCB
Hadfield, Sir Ronald, Kt., QPM
Hadlee, Sir Richard John, Kt., MBE
Hague, Prof. Sir Douglas Chalmers, Kt., CBE
Halberg, Sir Murray Gordon, Kt., MBE
Hall, Sir Basil Brodribb, KCB, MC, TD
Hall, Sir Douglas Basil, Bt., KCMG (S. 1687)
Hall, Sir Ernest, Kt., OBE
Hall, Sir (Frederick) John (Frank), Bt. (1923)
Hall, Sir John, Kt.
Hall, Sir John Bernard, Bt. (1919)
Hall, Sir Laurence Charles Brodie-, Kt., AO, CMG
Hall, Sir Peter Edward, KBE, CMG
Hall, Prof. Sir Peter Geoffrey, Kt., FBA
Hall, Sir Peter Reginald Frederick, Kt., CBE
Hall, Sir Robert de Zouche, KCMG
Hall, Brig. Sir William Henry, KBE, DSO, ED
Halliday, Vice-Adm. Sir Roy William, KBE, DSC
Halpern, Sir Ralph Mark, Kt.
Halsey, Revd Sir John Walter Brooke, Bt. (1920)
Halstead, Sir Ronald, Kt., CBE
Ham, Sir David Kenneth Rowe-, GBE
Hambling, Sir (Herbert) Hugh, Bt. (1924)
Hamburger, Sir Sidney Cyril, Kt., CBE
Hamer, Hon. Sir Rupert James, KCMG, ED
Hamilton, Rt. Hon. Sir Archibald Gavin, Kt., MP

Hamilton, Sir Edward Sydney, Bt. (1776 and 1819)
Hamilton, Sir James Arnot, KCB, MBE, FREng.
Hamilton, Sir Malcolm William Bruce Stirling-, Bt. (S. 1673)
Hamilton, Sir (Robert Charles) Richard Caradoc, Bt. (S. 1646)
Hammick, Sir Stephen George, Bt. (1834)
Hammond, Sir Anthony Hilgrove, KCB, QC
Hampel, Sir Ronald Claus, Kt.
Hampshire, Sir Stuart Newton, Kt., FBA
Hampson, Sir Stuart, Kt.
Hampton, Sir (Leslie) Geoffrey, Kt.
Hancock, Sir David John Stowell, KCB
Hancock, Air Marshal Sir Valston Eldridge, KBE, CB, DFC
Hand, Most Revd Geoffrey David, KBE
Handley, Sir David John Davenport-, Kt., OBE
Hanham, Sir Michael William, Bt., DFC (1667)
Hanley, Rt. Hon. Sir Jeremy James, KCMG
Hanley, Sir Michael Bowen, KCB
Hanmer, Sir John Wyndham Edward, Bt. (1774)
Hann, Sir James, Kt., CBE
Hannam, Sir John Gordon, Kt.
Hannay, Sir David Hugh Alexander, GCMG
Hanson, Sir (Charles) Rupert (Patrick), Bt. (1918)
Hanson, Sir John Gilbert, KCMG, CBE
Hardcastle, Sir Alan John, Kt.
Hardie, Sir Douglas Fleming, Kt., CBE
Harding, Sir George William, KCMG, CVO
Harding, Marshal of the Royal Air Force Sir Peter Robin, GCB
Harding, Sir Roy Pollard, Kt., CBE
Hardman, Sir Henry, KCB
Hardy, Sir David William, Kt.
Hardy, Sir James Gilbert, Kt., OBE
Hardy, Sir Richard Charles Chandos, Bt. (1876)
Hare, Sir David, Kt., FRSL
Harford, Sir (John) Timothy, Bt. (1934)
Hargroves, Brig. Sir Robert Louis, Kt., CBE
Harington, Gen. Sir Charles Henry Pepys, GCB, CBE, DSO, MC
Harington, Sir Nicholas John, Bt. (1611)
Harland, Air Marshal Sir Reginald Edward Wynyard, KBE, CB
Harley, Gen. Sir Alexander George Hamilton, KBE, CB
Harman, Gen. Sir Jack Wentworth, GCB, OBE, MC
Harman, Hon. Sir Jeremiah LeRoy, Kt.
Harman, Sir John Andrew, Kt.

Harmsworth, Sir Hildebrand Harold, Bt. (1922)

Harris, *Prof.* Sir Alan James, Kt., CBE, FREng.

Harris, *Prof.* Sir Henry, Kt., FRCP, FRCPath., FRS

Harris, Sir Jack Wolfred Ashford, Bt. (1932)

Harris, *Air Marshal* Sir John Hulme, KCB, CBE

Harris, *Prof.* Sir Martin Best, Kt., CBE

Harris, Sir William Gordon, KBE, CB, FREng.

Harrison, Sir David, Kt., CBE, FREng.

Harrison, *Prof.* Sir Donald Frederick Norris, Kt., FRCS

Harrison, Sir Ernest Thomas, Kt., OBE

Harrison, Sir Francis Alexander Lyle, Kt., MBE, QC

Harrison, *Surgeon Vice-Adm.* Sir John Albert Bews, KBE

Harrison, *Hon.* Sir (John) Richard, Kt., ED

Harrison, *Hon.* Sir Michael Guy Vicat, Kt.

Harrison, Sir Michael James Harwood, Bt. (1961)

Harrison, *Prof.* Sir Richard John, Kt., FRS

Harrison, Sir (Robert) Colin, Bt. (1922)

Harrison, Sir Terence, Kt., FREng

Harrop, Sir Peter John, KCB

Hart, Sir Graham Allan, KCB

Hart, *Hon.* Sir Michael Christopher Campbell, Kt.

Hartwell, Sir (Francis) Anthony Charles Peter, Bt. (1805)

Harvey, Sir Charles Richard Musgrave, Bt. (1933)

Harvie, Sir John Smith, Kt., CBE

Haselhurst, *Rt. Hon.* Sir Alan Gordon Barraclough, Kt., MP

Haskard, Sir Cosmo Dugal Patrick Thomas, KCMG, MBE

Haslam, *Rear-Adm.* Sir David William, KBE, CB

Hassett, *Gen.* Sir Francis George, KBE, CB, DSO, LVO

Hastings, Sir Stephen Lewis Edmonstone, Kt., MC

Hatter, Sir Maurice, Kt.

Hatty, *Hon.* Sir Cyril James, Kt.

Havelock, Sir Wilfrid Bowen, Kt.

Hawkins, Sir Paul Lancelot, Kt., TD

†Hawkins, Sir Richard Caesar, Bt. (1778)

Hawley, Sir Donald Frederick, KCMG, MBE

†Hawley, Sir Henry Nicholas, Bt. (1795)

Haworth, Sir Philip, Bt. (1911)

Hawthorne, Sir Nigel Barnard, Kt., CBE

Hawthorne, *Prof.* Sir William Rede, Kt., CBE, Sc.D., FRS, FREng.

Hay, Sir David Osborne, Kt., CBE, DSO

Hay, Sir David Russell, Kt., CBE, FRCP, MD

Hay, Sir Hamish Grenfell, Kt.

Hay, Sir James Brian Dalrymple-, Bt. (1798)

Hay, Sir John Erroll Audley, Bt. (S. 1663)

†Hay, Sir Ronald Frederick Hamilton, Bt. (S. 1703)

Hayes, Sir Brian, Kt., CBE, QPM

Hayes, Sir Brian David, GCB

Hayr, *Air Marshal* Sir Kenneth William, KCB, KBE, AFC

Hayward, Sir Anthony William Byrd, Kt.

Hayward, Sir Jack Arnold, Kt., OBE

Haywood, Sir Harold, KCVO, OBE

Head, Sir Francis David Somerville, Bt. (1838)

Healey, Sir Charles Edward Chadwyck-, Bt. (1919)

Heap, Sir Peter William, KCMG

Hearne, Sir Graham James, Kt., CBE

Heath, *Rt. Hon.* Sir Edward Richard George, KG, MBE, MP

Heath, Sir Mark Evelyn, KCVO, CMG

Heathcote, *Brig.* Sir Gilbert Simon, Bt., CBE (1733)

Heathcote, Sir Michael Perryman, Bt. (1733)

Heatley, Sir Peter, Kt., CBE

Heaton, Sir Yvo Robert Henniker-, Bt. (1912)

Heiser, Sir Terence Michael, GCB

Hellaby, Sir (Frederick Reed) Alan, Kt.

Henao, Revd Sir Ravu, Kt., OBE

Henderson, Sir Denys Hartley, Kt.

Henderson, Sir (John) Nicholas, GCMG, KCVO

Henderson, Sir William MacGregor, Kt., D.Sc., FRS

Henley, Sir Douglas Owen, KCB

Hennessy, Sir James Patrick Ivan, KBE, CMG

†Henniker, Sir Adrian Chandos, Bt. (1813)

Henriques, *Hon.* Sir Richard Henry Quixano, Kt.

Henry, *Rt. Hon.* Sir Denis Robert Maurice, Kt.

Henry, *Hon.* Sir Geoffrey Arama, KBE

†Henry, Sir Patrick Denis, Bt. (1923)

Henry, *Hon.* Sir Trevor Ernest, Kt.

Hepburn, Sir John Alastair Trant Kidd Buchan-, Bt. (1815)

Herbecq, Sir John Edward, KCB

Herbert, *Adm.* Sir Peter Geoffrey Marshall, KCB, OBE

Herbert, Sir Walter William, Kt.

Hermon, Sir John Charles, Kt., OBE, QPM

Heron, Sir Conrad Frederick, KCB, OBE

Heron, Sir Michael Gilbert, Kt.

Hervey, Sir Roger Blaise Ramsay, KCVO, CMG

Heseltine, *Rt. Hon.* Sir William Frederick Payne, GCB, GCVO

Hetherington, Sir Arthur Ford, Kt., DSC, FREng.

Hetherington, Sir Thomas Chalmers, KCB, CBE, TD, QC

Hewetson, Sir Christopher Raynor, Kt., TD

Hewett, Sir Peter John Smithson, Bt., MM (1813)

Hewitt, Sir (Cyrus) Lenox (Simson), Kt., OBE

Hewitt, Sir Nicholas Charles Joseph, Bt. (1921)

Heygate, Sir Richard John Gage, Bt. (1831)

Heywood, Sir Peter, Bt. (1838)

Hezlet, *Vice-Adm.* Sir Arthur Richard, KBE, CB, DSO, DSC

Hibbert, Sir Jack, KCB

Hibbert, Sir Reginald Alfred, GCMG

Hickey, Sir Justin, Kt.

Hickman, Sir (Richard) Glenn, Bt. (1903)

Hicks, Sir Robert, Kt.

Hidden, *Hon.* Sir Anthony Brian, Kt.

Hielscher, Sir Leo Arthur, Kt.

Higgins, *Hon.* Sir Malachy Joseph, Kt.

Higginson, Sir Gordon Robert, Kt., Ph.D., FREng.

Hill, Sir Alexander Rodger Erskine-, Bt. (1945)

Hill, Sir Arthur Alfred, Kt., CBE

Hill, Sir Brian John, Kt.

Hill, Sir James Frederick, Bt. (1917)

Hill, Sir John McGregor, Kt., Ph.D., FREng.

Hill, Sir John Maxwell, Kt., CBE, DFC

†Hill, Sir John Rowley, Bt. (I. 1779)

Hill, *Vice-Adm.* Sir Robert Charles Finch, KBE, FREng.

Hillary, Sir Edmund, KG, KBE

Hillhouse, Sir (Robert) Russell, KCB

Hills, Sir Graham John, Kt.

Hine, *Air Chief Marshal* Sir Patrick Bardon, GCB, GBE

Hirsch, *Prof.* Sir Peter Bernhard, Kt., Ph.D., FRS

Hirst, *Rt. Hon.* Sir David Cozens-Hardy, Kt.

Hirst, Sir Michael William, Kt.

Hoare, *Prof.* Sir Charles Anthony Richard, Kt., FRS

Hoare, Sir Peter Richard David, Bt. (1786)

Hoare, Sir Timothy Edward Charles, Bt., OBE (I. 1784)

Hobart, Sir John Vere, Bt. (1914)

Hobbs, *Maj.-Gen.* Sir Michael Frederick, KCVO, CBE

Hobday, Sir Gordon Ivan, Kt.

Hobhouse, Sir Charles John Spinney, Bt. (1812)

Hockaday, Sir Arthur Patrick, KCB, CMG

Hockley, *Gen.* Sir Anthony Heritage Farrar-, GBE, KCB, DSO, MC

Hoddinott, Sir John Charles, Kt., CBE, QPM

†Hodge, Sir Andrew Rowland, Bt. (1921)

Hodge, Sir James William, KCVO, CMG

Hodge, Sir Julian Stephen Alfred, Kt.

Hodges, *Air Chief Marshal* Sir Lewis MacDonald, KCB, CBE, DSO, DFC

Hodgkin, Sir Gordon Howard Eliot, Kt., CBE

Hodgkinson, *Air Chief Marshal* Sir (William) Derek, KCB, CBE, DFC, AFC

Hodgson, Sir Maurice Arthur Eric, Kt., FREng.

Hodgson, *Hon.* Sir (Walter) Derek (Thornley), Kt.

Hodson, Sir Michael Robin Adderley, Bt. (I. 1789)

Hoffenberg, *Prof.* Sir Raymond, KBE

Hogg, Sir Christopher Anthony, Kt.

Hogg, *Vice-Adm.* Sir Ian Leslie Trower, KCB, DSC

Hogg, Sir Michael David, Bt. (1846)

†Hogg, Sir Michael Edward Lindsay-, Bt. (1905)

Holcroft, Sir Peter George Culcheth, Bt. (1921)

Holderness, Sir Martin William, Bt. (1920)

Holden, Sir Edward, Bt. (1893)

Holden, Sir John David, Bt. (1919)

Holder, Sir John Henry, Bt. (1898)

Holder, *Air Marshal* Sir Paul Davie, KBE, CB, DSO, DFC, ph.D.

Holdgate, Sir Martin Wyatt, Kt., CB, ph.D.

Holdsworth, Sir (George) Trevor, Kt., CVO

Holland, *Hon.* Sir Alan Douglas, Kt.

Holland, *Hon.* Sir Christopher John, Kt.

Holland, Sir Clifton Vaughan, Kt.

Holland, Sir Geoffrey, KCB

Holland, Sir Kenneth Lawrence, Kt., CBE, QFSM

Holland, Sir Philip Welsby, Kt.

Holliday, *Prof.* Sir Frederick George Thomas, Kt., CBE, FRSE

Hollings, *Hon.* Sir (Alfred) Kenneth, Kt., MC

Hollis, *Hon.* Sir Anthony Barnard, Kt.

Hollom, Sir Jasper Quintus, KBE

Holloway, *Hon.* Sir Barry Blyth, KBE

Holm, Sir Carl Henry, Kt., OBE

Holm, Sir Ian (Ian Holm Cuthbert), Kt., CBE

Holman, *Hon.* Sir (Edward) James, Kt.

Holmes, *Prof.* Sir Frank Wakefield, Kt.

Holmes, Sir John Eaton, KBE, CMG, CVO

Holmes, Sir Peter Fenwick, Kt., MC

Holroyd, *Air Marshal* Sir Frank Martyn, KBE, CB, FREng.

Holt, *Prof.* Sir James Clarke, Kt.

Holt, Sir Michael, Kt., CBE

Home, Sir William Dundas, Bt. (S. 1671)

Honeycombe, *Prof.* Sir Robert William Kerr, Kt., FRS, FREng.

Honywood, Sir Filmer Courtenay William, Bt. (1660)

Hood, Sir Harold Joseph, Bt., TD (1922)

Hookway, Sir Harry Thurston, Kt.

Hooper, *Hon.* Sir Anthony, Kt.

Hope, Sir Colin Frederick Newton, Kt.

Hope, *Rt. Revd and Rt. Hon.* Sir David Michael, KCVO

Hope, Sir John Carl Alexander, Bt. (S. 1628)

Hopkin, Sir (William Aylsham) Bryan, Kt., CBE

Hopkins, Sir Anthony Philip, Kt., CBE

Hopkins, Sir Michael John, Kt., CBE, RA, RIBA

Hopwood, *Prof.* Sir David Alan, Kt., FRS

Hordern, *Rt. Hon.* Sir Peter Maudslay, Kt.

Horlick, *Vice-Adm.* Sir Edwin John, KBE, FREng.

Horlick, Sir James Cunliffe William, Bt. (1914)

Horlock, *Prof.* Sir John Harold, Kt., FRS, FREng.

Hornby, Sir Derek Peter, Kt.

Hornby, Sir Simon Michael, Kt.

Horne, Sir Alan Gray Antony, Bt. (1929)

Horsfall, Sir John Musgrave, Bt., MC, TD (1909)

Horsley, *Air Marshal* Sir (Beresford) Peter (Torrington), KCB, CBE, LVO, AFC

†Hort, Sir Andrew Edwin Fenton, Bt. (1767)

Horton, Sir Robert Baynes, Kt.

Hosker, Sir Gerald Albery, KCB, QC

Hoskyns, Sir Benedict Leigh, Bt. (1676)

Hoskyns, Sir John Austin Hungerford Leigh, Kt.

Hotung, Sir Joseph Edward, Kt.

Houghton, Sir John Theodore, Kt., CBE, FRS

†Houldsworth, Sir Richard Thomas Reginald, Bt. (1887)

Hounsfield, Sir Godfrey Newbold, Kt., CBE

Hourston, Sir Gordon Minto, Kt.

House, *Lt.-Gen.* Sir David George, GCB, KCVO, CBE, MC

Houssemayne du Boulay, Sir Roger William, KCVO, CMG

Howard, Sir (Hamilton) Edward de Coucey, Bt., GBE (1955)

Howard, *Prof.* Sir Michael Eliot, Kt., CBE, MC

Howard, *Maj.-Gen.* Lord Michael Fitzalan-, GCVO, CB, CBE, MC

Howell, Sir Ralph Frederic, Kt.

Howells, Sir Eric Waldo Benjamin, Kt., CBE

Howes, Sir Christopher Kingston, KCVO, CB

Howlett, *Gen.* Sir Geoffrey Hugh Whitby, KBE, MC

Hoyle, *Prof.* Sir Fred, Kt., FRS

Hoyos, *Hon.* Sir Fabriciano Alexander, Kt.

Huggins, *Hon.* Sir Alan Armstrong, Kt.

Hughes, *Hon.* Sir Anthony Philip Gilson, Kt.

Hughes, Sir David Collingwood, Bt. (1773)

Hughes, Hon. Sir Davis, Kt.

Hughes, Sir Jack William, Kt.

Hughes, Sir Trevor Denby Lloyd-, Kt.

Hughes, Sir Trevor Poulton, KCB

Hull, *Prof.* Sir David, Kt.

Hulse, Sir Edward Jeremy Westrow, Bt. (1739)

Hume, Sir Alan Blyth, Kt., CB

Humphreys, Sir (Raymond Evelyn) Myles, Kt.

Hunt, Sir John Leonard, Kt.

Hunt, *Adm.* Sir Nicholas John Streynsham, GCB, LVO

Hunt, Sir Rex Masterman, Kt., CMG

Hunt, Sir Robert Frederick, Kt., CBE, FREng.

Hunt, Sir Julian Charles Roland, CB, Bt.

Hunter, Sir Alistair John, KCMG

Hunter, Sir Ian Bruce Hope, Kt., MBE

Hunter, *Prof.* Sir Laurence Colvin, Kt., CBE, FRSE

Hurn, Sir (Francis) Roger, Kt.

Hurrell, Sir Anthony Gerald, KCVO, CMG

Hurst, Sir Geoffrey Charles, Kt., MBE

Husbands, Sir Clifford Straugh, GCMG

Hutchinson, *Hon.* Sir Ross, Kt., DFC

Hutchison, *Lt.-Cdr.* Sir (George) Ian Clark, Kt., RN

Hutchison, Sir James Colville, Bt. (1956)

Hutchison, *Rt. Hon.* Sir Michael, Kt.

Hutchison, Sir Robert, Bt. (1939)

Huxley, *Prof.* Sir Andrew Fielding, Kt., OM, FRS

Huxtable, *Gen.* Sir Charles Richard, KCB, CBE

Hyatali, *Hon.* Sir Isaac Emanuel, Kt.

Hyslop, Sir Robert John (Robin) Maxwell-, Kt.

Ibbs, Sir (John) Robin, KBE

Imray, Sir Colin Henry, KBE, CMG

Ingham, Sir Bernard, Kt.

Ingilby, Sir Thomas Colvin William, Bt. (1866)

Inglis, Sir Brian Scott, Kt.

Inglis of Glencorse, Sir Roderick John, Bt. (S. 1703)

Ingram, Sir James Herbert Charles, Bt. (1893)

Ingram, Sir John Henderson, Kt., CBE

Inkin, Sir Geoffrey David, Kt., OBE

†Innes, Sir David Charles Kenneth Gordon, Bt. (NS 1686)

Innes of Edingight, Sir Malcolm Rognvald, KCVO

Innes, Sir Peter Alexander Berowald, Bt. (S. 1628)

Irvine, Sir Donald Hamilton, Kt., CBE, MD, FRCGP

Irving, *Prof.* Sir Miles Horsfall, Kt., MD, FRCS, FRCSE

Isaacs, Sir Jeremy Israel, Kt.

Isham, Sir Ian Vere Gyles, Bt. (1627)

Jack, *Hon.* Sir Alieu Sulayman, Kt.

Jack, Sir David, Kt., CBE, FRS, FRSE

Jack, Sir David Emmanuel, GCMG, MBE

Jackson, Sir (John) Edward, KCMG

Jackson, Sir Kenneth Joseph, Kt.

Jackson, *Lt.-Gen.* Sir Michael David, KCB, CBE

Jackson, Sir Michael Roland, Bt. (1902)

Jackson, Sir Nicholas Fane St George, Bt. (1913)

Jackson, Sir Robert, Bt. (1815)

Jackson, *Hon.* Sir Rupert Matthew, Kt., QC

Jackson, Sir William Thomas, Bt. (1869)

Jacob, Sir Isaac Hai, Kt., QC

Jacob, *Hon.* Sir Robert Raphael Hayim (Robin), Kt.

Jacobi, Sir Derek George, Kt., CBE

Jacobi, *Dr* Sir James Edward, Kt., OBE

Jacobs, *Hon.* Sir Kenneth Sydney, KBE

Jacobs, Sir Wilfred Ebenezer, GCMG, GCVO, OBE, QC

Jacomb, Sir Martin Wakefield, Kt.

Jaffray, Sir William Otho, Bt. (1892)

James, Sir Cynlais Morgan, KCMG

James, Sir John Nigel Courtenay, KCVO, CBE

James, Sir Stanislaus Anthony, GCMG, OBE

Jamieson, *Air Marshal* Sir David Ewan, KBE, CB

Jansen, Sir Ross Malcolm, KBE

Janvrin, Sir Robin Berry, KCVO, CB

Jardine of Applegirth, Sir Alexander Maule, Bt. (s. 1672)

Jardine, Sir Andrew Colin Douglas, Bt. (1916)

Jardine, *Maj.* Sir (Andrew) Rupert (John) Buchanan-, Bt., MC (1885)

Jarman, *Prof.* Sir Brian, Kt., OBE

Jarratt, Sir Alexander Anthony, Kt., CB

Jarvis, Sir Gordon Ronald, Kt.

Jawara, *Hon.* Sir Dawda Kairaba, Kt.

Jay, Sir Antony Rupert, Kt., CVO

Jay, Sir Michael Hastings, KCMG

Jeewoolall, Sir Ramesh, Kt.

Jefferson, Sir George Rowland, Kt., CBE, FREng.

Jefferson, Sir Mervyn Stewart Dunnington-, Bt. (1958)

Jeffreys, *Prof.* Sir Alec John, Kt., FRS

Jeffries, *Hon.* Sir John Francis, Kt.

Jehangir, Sir Hirji, Bt. (1908)

Jejeebhoy, Sir Jamsetjee, Bt. (1857)

Jenkins, Sir Brian Garton, GBE

Jenkins, Sir Elgar Spencer, Kt., OBE

Jenkins, Sir James Christopher, KCB, QC

Jenkins, Sir Michael Nicholas Howard, Kt., OBE

Jenkins, Sir Michael Romilly Heald, KCMG

Jenkinson, Sir John Banks, Bt. (1661)

†Jenks, Sir Maurice Arthur Brian, Bt. (1932)

Jenner, *Air Marshal* Sir Timothy Ivo, KCB

Jennings, Sir John Southwood, Kt., CBE, FRSE

Jennings, Sir Peter Neville Wake, Kt., CVO

Jennings, *Prof.* Sir Robert Yewdall, Kt., QC

Jephcott, Sir (John) Anthony, Bt. (1962)

Jessel, Sir Charles John, Bt. (1883)

Jewkes, Sir Gordon Wesley, KCMG

John, Sir David Glyndwr, KCMG

John, Sir Elton Hercules (Reginald Kenneth Dwight), Kt., CBE

Johns, *Air Chief Marshal* Sir Richard Edward, GCB, CBE, LVO

Johnson, *Rt. Hon.* Sir David Powell Croom-, Kt., DSC, VRD

Johnson, *Gen.* Sir Garry Dene, KCB, OBE, MC

Johnson, Sir John Rodney, KCMG

†Johnson, Sir Patrick Eliot, Bt. (1818)

Johnson, Sir Peter Colpoys Paley, Bt. (1755)

Johnson, *Hon.* Sir Robert Lionel, Kt.

Johnson, Sir Vassel Godfrey, Kt., CBE

Johnston, Sir John Baines, GCMG, KCVO

Johnston, *Lt.-Col.* Sir John Frederick Dame, GCVO, MC

Johnston, *Lt.-Gen.* Sir Maurice Robert, KCB, OBE

Johnston, Sir Thomas Alexander, Bt. (s. 1626)

Johnston, Sir William Robert Patrick Knox- (Sir Robin), Kt., CBE, RD

Johnstone, Sir (George) Richard Douglas, Bt. (s. 1700)

Johnstone, Sir (John) Raymond, Kt., CBE

Jolliffe, Sir Anthony Stuart, GBE

Jonas, Sir John Peter Jens, Kt., CBE

Jones, *Gen.* Sir (Charles) Edward Webb, KCB, CBE

Jones, Sir Christopher Lawrence-, Bt. (1831)

Jones, Sir David Akers-, KBE, CMG

Jones, *Air Marshal* Sir Edward Gordon, KCB, CBE, DSO, DFC

Jones, Sir Ewart Ray Herbert, Kt., D.Sc., Ph.D., FRS

Jones, Sir Harry George, Kt., CBE

Jones, Sir (John) Derek Alun-, Kt.

Jones, Sir John Henry Harvey-, Kt., MBE

Jones, Sir John Prichard-, Bt. (1910)

Jones, Sir Keith Stephen, Kt.

Jones, *Hon.* Sir Kenneth George Illtyd, Kt.

Jones, Sir Lyndon, Kt.

Jones, Sir (Owen) Trevor, Kt.

Jones, Sir (Peter) Hugh (Jefferd) Lloyd-, Kt.

Jones, Sir Richard Anthony Lloyd, KCB

Jones, Sir Robert Edward, Kt.

Jones, Sir Simon Warley Frederick Benton, Bt. (1919)

Jones, Sir Wynn Normington Hugh-, Kt., LVO

†Joseph, *Hon.* Sir James Samuel, Bt. (1943)

Jowitt, *Hon.* Sir Edwin Frank, Kt.

Joyce, *Lt.-Gen.* Sir Robert John Hayman-, KCB, CBE

Judge, *Rt. Hon.* Sir Igor, Kt.

Judge, Sir Paul Rupert, Kt.

Jugnauth, *Rt. Hon.* Sir Anerood, KCMG, QC

Jungius, *Vice-Adm.* Sir James George, KBE

Jupp, *Hon.* Sir Kenneth Graham, Kt., MC

Kaberry, *Hon.* Sir Christopher Donald, Bt. (1960)

Kalms, Sir (Harold) Stanley, Kt.

Kalo, Sir Kwamala, Kt., MBE

Kan Yuet-Keung, Sir, GBE

Kapi, *Hon.* Sir Mari, Kt., CBE

Kaputin, Sir John Rumet, KBE, CMG

Katz, Sir Bernard, Kt., FRS

Kausimae, Sir David Nanau, KBE

Kavali, Sir Thomas, Kt., OBE

Kawharu, *Prof.* Sir Ian Hugh, Kt.

Kay, *Prof.* Sir Andrew Watt, Kt.

Kay, *Hon.* Sir John William, Kt.

Kay, *Hon.* Sir Maurice Ralph, Kt.

Kaye, Sir John Phillip Lister Lister-, Bt. (1812)

Kaye, Sir Paul Henry Gordon, Bt. (1923)

Keane, Sir Richard Michael, Bt. (1801)

Kearney, *Hon.* Sir William John Francis, Kt., CBE

Keeble, Sir (Herbert Ben) Curtis, GCM

Keegan, Sir John Desmond Patrick, Kt., OBE

Keene, *Hon.* Sir David Wolfe, Kt.

Keith, *Prof.* Sir James, KBE

Kellett, Sir Stanley Charles, Bt. (1801)

Kelly, Sir David Robert Corbett, Kt., CBE

Kelly, *Rt. Hon.* Sir (John William) Basil, Kt.

Kemball, *Air Marshal* Sir (Richard) John, KCB, CBE

Kemp, Sir (Edward) Peter, KCB

Kenilorea, *Rt. Hon.* Sir Peter, KBE

Kennaway, Sir John Lawrence, Bt. (1791)

Kennedy, Sir Francis, KCMG, CBE

Kennedy, *Hon.* Sir Ian Alexander, Kt.

Kennedy, Sir Ludovic Henry Coverley, Kt.

†Kennedy, Sir Michael Edward, Bt. (1836)

Kennedy, *Rt. Hon.* Sir Paul Joseph Morrow, Kt.

Kennedy, *Air Chief Marshal* Sir Thomas Lawrie, GCB, AFC

Kenny, Sir Anthony John Patrick, Kt., D.Phil., D.Litt., FBA

Kenny, *Gen.* Sir Brian Leslie Graham,

GCB, CBE

Kentridge, Sir Sydney Woolf, KCMG, QC

Kenyon, Sir George Henry, Kt.

Kermode, Sir (John) Frank, Kt., FBA

Kermode, Sir Ronald Graham Quale, KBE

Kerr, *Hon.* Sir Brian Francis, Kt.

Kerr, *Adm.* Sir John Beverley, GCB

Kerr, Sir John Olav, KCMG

Kerr, *Rt. Hon.* Sir Michael Robert Emanuel, Kt.

Kerruish, Sir (Henry) Charles, Kt., OBE

Kerry, Sir Michael James, KCB, QC

Kershaw, Sir (John) Anthony, Kt., MC

Keswick, Sir John Chippendale Lindley, Kt.

Keys, Sir (Alexander George) William, Kt., OBE, MC

Kidd, Sir Robert Hill, KBE, CB

Kikau, *Ratu* Sir Jone Latianara, KBE

Killen, *Hon.* Sir Denis James, KCMG

Killick, Sir John Edward, GCMG

Kimber, Sir Charles Dixon, Bt. (1904)

King, Sir John Christopher, Bt. (1888)

King, *Vice-Adm.* Sir Norman Ross Dutton, KBE

King, Sir Wayne Alexander, Bt. (1815)

Kingman, *Prof.* Sir John Frank Charles, Kt., FRS

Kingsland, Sir Richard, Kt., CBE, DFC

Kinloch, Sir David, Bt. (S. 1686)

Kinloch, Sir David Oliphant, Bt. (1873)

Kipalan, Sir Albert, Kt.

Kirby, *Hon.* Sir Richard Clarence, Kt.

Kirkpatrick, Sir Ivone Elliott, Bt. (S. 1685)

Kirkwood, *Hon.* Sir Andrew Tristram Hammett, Kt.

Kitcatt, Sir Peter Julian, Kt., CB

Kitson, *Gen.* Sir Frank Edward, GBE, KCB, MC

Kitson, Sir Timothy Peter Geoffrey, Kt.

Kleinwort, Sir Richard Drake, Bt. (1909)

Klevan, *Hon.* Sir Rodney (Conrad), Kt., QC

Klug, Sir Aaron, Kt., OM

Kneller, Sir Alister Arthur, Kt.

Knight, Sir Arthur William, Kt.

Knight, Sir Harold Murray, KBE, DSC

Knight, *Air Chief Marshal* Sir Michael William Patrick, KCB, AFC

Knill, *Prof.* Sir John Lawrence, Kt., FREng.

†Knill, Sir Thomas John Pugin Bartholomew, Bt. (1893)

Knowles, Sir Charles Francis, Bt. (1765)

Knowles, Sir Durward Randolph, Kt., OBE

Knowles, Sir Leonard Joseph, Kt., CBE

Knowles, Sir Richard Marchant, Kt.

Knox, Sir Bryce Muir, KCVO, MC, TD

Knox, Sir David Laidlaw, Kt.

Knox, *Hon.* Sir John Leonard, Kt.

Knox, *Hon.* Sir William Edward, Kt.

Koraea, Sir Thomas, Kt.

Kornberg, *Prof.* Sir Hans Leo, Kt., D.Sc., Sc.D., Ph.D., FRS

Korowi, Sir Wiwa, GCMG

Krebs, *Prof.* Sir John Richard, Kt., D.Phil., FRS

Kroto, *Prof.* Sir Harold Walter, Kt., FRS

Kulukundis, Sir Elias George (Eddie), Kt., OBE

Kurongku, *Most Revd* Peter, KBE

Lacon, Sir Edmund Vere, Bt. (1818)

Lacy, Sir Hugh Maurice Pierce, Bt. (1921)

Lacy, Sir John Trend, Kt., CBE

Laddie, *Hon.* Sir Hugh Ian Lang, Kt.

Laidlaw, Sir Christophor Charles Fraser, Kt.

Laing, Sir (John) Martin (Kirby), Kt., CBE

Laing, Sir (John) Maurice, Kt.

Laing, Sir (William) Kirby, Kt., FREng.

Laird, Sir Gavin Harry, Kt., CBE

Lake, Sir (Atwell) Graham, Bt. (1711)

Laker, Sir Frederick Alfred, Kt.

Lakin, Sir Michael, Bt. (1909)

Laking, Sir George Robert, KCMG

Lamb, Sir Albert Thomas, KBE, CMG, DFC

Lambert, Sir Anthony Edward, KCMG

Lambert, Sir John Henry, KCVO, CMG

†Lambert, Sir Peter John Biddulph, Bt. (1711)

Lampl, Sir Frank William, Kt.

Landale, Sir David William Neil, KCVO

Landau, Sir Dennis Marcus, Kt.

Lander, Sir Stephen James, KCB

Lane, *Prof.* Sir David Philip, Kt., FRS, FRSE

Lang, *Lt.-Gen.* Sir Derek Boileau, KCB, DSO, MC

Langham, Sir James Michael, Bt. (1660)

Langlands, Sir Robert Alan, Kt.

Langley, *Hon.* Sir Gordon Julian Hugh, Kt.

Langley, *Maj.-Gen.* Sir Henry Desmond Allen, KCVO, MBE

Langrishe, Sir James Hercules, Bt. (I. 1777)

Lankester, Sir Timothy Patrick, KCB

Lapun, *Hon.* Sir Paul, Kt.

Larcom, Sir (Charles) Christopher Royde, Bt. (1868)

Large, Sir Andrew McLeod Brooks, Kt.

Large, Sir Peter, Kt., CBE

Lasdun, Sir Denys Louis, Kt., CH, CBE, FRIBA

Latham, *Hon.* Sir David Nicholas Ramsey, Kt.

Latham, Sir Michael Anthony, Kt.

Latham, Sir Richard Thomas Paul, Bt. (1919)

Latimer, Sir (Courtenay) Robert,

Kt., CBE

Latimer, Sir Graham Stanley, KBE

Lauder, Sir Piers Robert Dick-, Bt. (S. 1690)

Laughton, Sir Anthony Seymour, Kt.

Laurantus, Sir Nicholas, Kt., MBE

Laurence, Sir Peter Harold, KCMG, MC

Laurie, Sir Robert Bayley Emilius, Bt. (1834)

Lauterpacht, Sir Elihu, Kt., CBE, QC

Lauti, *Rt. Hon.* Sir Toaripi, GCMG

Lavan, *Hon.* Sir John Martin, Kt.

Law, *Adm.* Sir Horace Rochfort, GCB, OBE, DSC

Lawes, Sir (John) Michael Bennet, Bt. (1882)

Lawler, Sir Peter James, Kt., OBE

Lawrence, Sir David Roland Walter, Bt. (1906)

Lawrence, Sir George Alexander Waldemar, Bt. (1858)

Lawrence, Sir Guy Kempton, Kt., DSO, OBE, DFC

Lawrence, Sir Ivan John, Kt., QC

Lawrence, Sir John Patrick Grosvenor, Kt., CBE

Lawrence, Sir William Fettiplace, Bt. (1867)

Laws, *Rt. Hon.* Sir John Grant McKenzie, Kt.

Lawson, Sir Christopher Donald, Kt.

Lawson, *Col.* Sir John Charles Arthur Digby, Bt., DSO, MC (1900)

Lawson, Sir John Philip Howard-, Bt. (1841)

Lawson, *Gen.* Sir Richard George, KCB, DSO, OBE

Lawton, *Rt. Hon.* Sir Frederick Horace, Kt.

Layard, *Adm.* Sir Michael Henry Gordon, KCB, CBE

Lea, *Vice-Adm.* Sir John Stuart Crosbie, KBE

Lea, Sir Thomas William, Bt. (1892)

Leach, *Admiral of the Fleet* Sir Henry Conyers, GCB

Leahy, Sir Daniel Joseph, Kt.

Leahy, Sir John Henry Gladstone, KCMG

Learmont, *Gen.* Sir John Hartley, KCB, CBE

Leask, *Lt.-Gen.* Sir Henry Lowther Ewart Clark, KCB, DSO, OBE

Leather, Sir Edwin Hartley Cameron, KCMG, KCVO

Leaver, Sir Christopher, GBE

Le Bailly, *Vice-Adm.* Sir Louis Edward Stewart Holland, KBE, CB

Le Cheminant, *Air Chief Marshal* Sir Peter de Lacey, GBE, KCB, DFC

Lechmere, Sir Berwick Hungerford, Bt. (1818)

Ledger, Sir Philip Stevens, Kt., CBE, FRSE

Lee, Sir Arthur James, KBE, MC

Lee, *Air Chief Marshal* Sir David John Pryer, GBE, CB

Lee, *Brig.* Sir Leonard Henry, Kt., CBE

Lee, Sir Quo-wei, Kt., CBE

Leeds, Sir Christopher Anthony, Bt. (1812)
Lees, Sir David Bryan, Kt.
Lees, Sir Thomas Edward, Bt. (1897)
Lees, Sir Thomas Harcourt Ivor, Bt. (1804)
Lees, Sir (William) Antony Clare, Bt. (1937)
Leese, Sir John Henry Vernon, Bt. (1908)
Le Fanu, *Maj.* Sir (George) Victor (Sheridan), KCVO
le Fleming, Sir David Kelland, Bt. (1705)
Legard, Sir Charles Thomas, Bt. (1660)
Legg, Sir Thomas Stuart, KCB, QC
Leggatt, *Rt. Hon.* Sir Andrew Peter, Kt.
Leggatt, Sir Hugh Frank John, Kt.
Leggett, Sir Clarence Arthur Campbell, Kt., MBE
Leigh, Sir Geoffrey Norman, Kt.
Leigh, Sir Richard Henry, Bt. (1918)
Leighton, Sir Michael John Bryan, Bt. (1693)
Leitch, Sir George, KCB, OBE
Leith, Sir Andrew George Forbes-, Bt. (1923)
Le Marchant, Sir Francis Arthur, Bt. (1841)
Lemon, Sir (Richard) Dawnay, Kt., CBE
Leng, *Gen.* Sir Peter John Hall, KCB, MBE, MC
Lennard, *Revd* Sir Hugh Dacre Barrett-, Bt. (1801)
Leon, Sir John Ronald, Bt. (1911)
Leonard, *Rt. Revd and Rt. Hon.* Sir Graham Douglas, KCVO
Leonard, *Hon.* Sir (Hamilton) John, Kt.
Lepping, Sir George Geria Dennis, GCMG, MBE
Le Quesne, Sir (Charles) Martin, KCMG
Le Quesne, Sir (John) Godfray, Kt., QC
Leslie, Sir Colin Alan Bettridge, Kt.
Leslie, Sir John Norman Ide, Bt. (1876)
†Leslie, Sir (Percy) Theodore, Bt. (S. 1625)
Leslie, Sir Peter Evelyn, Kt.
Lester, Sir James Theodore, Kt.
Lethbridge, Sir Thomas Periam Hector Noel, Bt. (1804)
Lever, Sir Paul, KCMG
Lever, Sir (Tresham) Christopher Arthur Lindsay, Bt. (1911)
Levey, Sir Michael Vincent, Kt., LVO
Levine, Sir Montague Bernard, Kt.
Levinge, Sir Richard George Robin, Bt. (I. 1704)
Lewando, Sir Jan Alfred, Kt., CBE
Lewinton, Sir Christopher, Kt.
Lewis, Sir David Courtenay Mansel, KCVO
Lewis, Sir Terence Murray, Kt., OBE, GM, QPM
Lewthwaite, *Brig.* Sir Rainald

Gilfrid, Bt., CVO, OBE, MC (1927)
Ley, Sir Ian Francis, Bt. (1905)
Leyland, Sir Philip Vyvyan Naylor-, Bt. (1895)
Lickiss, Sir Michael Gillam, Kt.
Liddington, Sir Bruce, Kt.
Liggins, *Prof.* Sir Graham Collingwood, Kt., CBE, FRS
Lightman, *Hon.* Sir Gavin Anthony, Kt.
Lighton, Sir Thomas Hamilton, Bt. (I. 1791)
Limon, Sir Donald William, KCB
Linacre, Sir (John) Gordon (Seymour), Kt., CBE, AFC, DFM
Lindop, Sir Norman, Kt.
Lindsay, Sir James Harvey Kincaid Stewart, Kt.
Lindsay, *Hon.* Sir John Edmund Frederic, Kt.
Lindsay, Sir Ronald Alexander, Bt., (1962)
Lipton, Sir Stuart Anthony, Kt.
Lipworth, Sir (Maurice) Sydney, Kt.
Lithgow, Sir William James, Bt. (1925)
Little, *Most Revd* Sir Thomas Francis, KBE
Littler, Sir (James) Geoffrey, KCB
Livesay, *Adm.* Sir Michael Howard, KCB
Llewellyn, Sir David St Vincent, Bt. (1922)
Llewelyn, Sir John Michael Dillwyn-Venables-, Bt. (1890)
Lloyd, *Prof.* Sir Geoffrey Ernest Richard, Kt., FBA
Lloyd, Sir Ian Stewart, Kt.
Lloyd, Sir Nicholas Markley, Kt.
Lloyd, *Rt. Hon.* Sir Peter Robert Cable, Kt., MP
Lloyd, Sir Richard Ernest Butler, Bt. (1960)
Lloyd, *Hon.* Sir Timothy Andrew Wigram, Kt.
Loader, Sir Leslie Thomas, Kt., CBE
Loane, *Most Revd* Sir Marcus Lawrence, KBE
Lobo, Sir Rogerio Hyndman, Kt., CBE
Lockhart, Sir Simon John Edward Francis Sinclair-, Bt. (S. 1636)
†Loder, Sir Edmund Jeune, Bt. (1887)
Logan, Sir David Brian Carleton, KCMG
Logan, Sir Donald Arthur, KCMG
Logan, Sir Raymond Douglas, Kt.
Lokoloko, Sir Tore, GCMG, GCVO, OBE
Lombe, *Hon.* Sir Edward Christopher Evans-, Kt.
Longmore, *Hon.* Sir Andrew Centlivres, Kt.
Loram, *Vice-Adm.* Sir David Anning, KCB, CVO
Lorimer, Sir (Thomas) Desmond, Kt.
Los, *Hon.* Sir Kubulan, Kt., CBE
Lovell, Sir (Alfred Charles) Bernard, Kt., OBE, FRS

Lovelock, Sir Douglas Arthur, KCB
Loveridge, Sir John Warren, Kt.
Lovill, Sir John Roger, Kt., CBE
Low, Sir Alan Roberts, Kt.
Low, Sir James Richard Morrison-, Bt. (1908)
Lowe, *Air Chief Marshal* Sir Douglas Charles, GCB, DFC, AFC
Lowe, Sir Thomas William Gordon, Bt. (1918)
Lowry, Sir John Patrick, Kt., CBE
Lowson, Sir Ian Patrick, Bt. (1951)
Lowther, *Col.* Sir Charles Douglas, Bt. (1824)
Lowther, Sir John Luke, KCVO, CBE
Loyd, Sir Francis Alfred, KCMG, OBE
Loyd, Sir Julian St John, KCVO
Lu, Sir Tseng Chi, Kt.
Lucas, Sir Cyril Edward, Kt., CMG, FRS
Lucas, Sir Thomas Edward, Bt. (1887)
Luce, *Rt. Hon.* Sir Richard Napier, Kt.
Lucy, Sir Edmund John William Hugh Cameron-Ramsay-Fairfax, Bt. (1836)
Luddington, Sir Donald Collin Cumyn, KBE, CMG, CVO
Lumsden, Sir David James, Kt.
Lus, *Hon.* Sir Pita, Kt., OBE
Lush, *Hon.* Sir George Hermann, Kt.
Lushington, Sir John Richard Castleman, Bt. (1791)
Luttrell, *Col.* Sir Geoffrey Walter Fownes, KCVO, MC
Lyell, *Rt. Hon.* Sir Nicholas Walter, Kt., QC, MP
Lygo, *Adm.* Sir Raymond Derek, KCB
Lyle, Sir Gavin Archibald, Bt. (1929)
Lyne, Sir Roderic Michael John, KBE, CMG
Lyons, Sir Edward Houghton, Kt.
Lyons, Sir James Reginald, Kt.
Lyons, Sir John, Kt.
Lyons, Sir Michael Thomas, Kt.
McAlpine, Sir William Hepburn, Bt. (1918)
Macara, Sir Alexander Wiseman, Kt., FRCP, FRCGP
†Macara, Sir Hugh Kenneth, Bt. (1911)
Macartney, Sir John Barrington, Bt. (I. 1799)
Maclean, Sir Murdo, Kt.
MacSween, *Prof.* Sir Roderick Norman McIver, Kt.
McAvoy, Sir (Francis) Joseph, Kt., CBE
McCaffrey, Sir Thomas Daniel, Kt.
McCall, Sir (Charles) Patrick Home, Kt., MBE, TD
McCallum, Sir Donald Murdo, Kt., CBE, FREng.
McCamley, Sir Graham Edward, KBE
McCarthy, *Rt. Hon.* Sir Thaddeus Pearcey, KBE
McCartney, Sir (James) Paul, Kt., MBE
McClellan, *Col.* Sir Herbert Gerard Thomas, Kt., CBE, TD

McClintock, Sir Eric Paul, Kt.

McColl, Sir Colin Hugh Verel, KCMG

McCollum, *Rt. Hon.* Sir William, Kt.

McConnell, Sir Robert Shean, Bt. (1900)

McCorkell, *Col.* Sir Michael William, KCVO, OBE, TD

McCowan, *Rt. Hon.* Sir Anthony James Denys, Kt.

†McCowan, Sir David William, Bt. (1934)

McCullough, *Hon.* Sir (Iain) Charles (Robert), Kt.

MacDermott, *Rt. Hon.* Sir John Clarke, Kt.

McDermott, Sir (Lawrence) Emmet, KBE

Macdonald of Sleat, Sir Ian Godfrey Bosville, Bt. (s. 1625)

Macdonald, Sir Kenneth Carmichael, KCB

Macdonald, *Vice-Adm.* Sir Roderick Douglas, KBE

McDonald, Sir Tom, Kt., OBE

McDonald, Sir Trevor, Kt., OBE

MacDougall, Sir (George) Donald (Alastair), Kt., CBE, FBA

McDowell, Sir Eric Wallace, Kt., CBE

McDowell, Sir Henry McLorinan, KBE

Mace, *Lt.-Gen.* Sir John Airth, KBE, CB

McEwen, Sir John Roderick Hugh, Bt. (1953)

McFarland, Sir John Talbot, Bt. (1914)

Macfarlane, Sir (David) Neil, Kt.

Macfarlane, Sir George Gray, Kt., CB, FREng.

McFarlane, Sir Ian, Kt.

McGeoch, *Vice-Adm.* Sir Ian Lachlan Mackay, KCB, DSO, DSC

McGrath, Sir Brian Henry, KCVO

Macgregor, Sir Edwin Robert, Bt. (1828)

MacGregor of MacGregor, Sir Gregor, Bt. (1795)

McGregor, Sir Ian Alexander, Kt., CBE, FRS

McGrigor, *Capt.* Sir Charles Edward, Bt. (1831)

McIntosh, *Vice-Adm.* Sir Ian Stewart, KBE, CB, DSO, DSC

McIntosh, Sir Neil William David, Kt., CBE

McIntosh, Sir Ronald Robert Duncan, KCB

McIntyre, Sir Donald Conroy, Kt., CBE

McIntyre, Sir Meredith Alister, Kt.

MacKay, *Prof.* Sir Donald Iain, Kt., FRSE

McKay, Sir John Andrew, Kt., CBE

Mackechnie, Sir Alistair John, Kt.

McKee, *Maj.* Sir (William) Cecil, Kt., ERD

McKellen, Sir Ian Murray, Kt., CBE

Mackenzie, Sir Alexander Alwyne Henry Charles Brinton Muir-, Bt. (1805)

†Mackenzie, Sir (James William) Guy, Bt. (1890)

Mackenzie, *Gen.* Sir Jeremy John George, GCB, OBE

†Mackenzie, Sir Peter Douglas, Bt. (s. 1673)

†Mackenzie, Sir Roderick McQuhae, Bt. (s. 1703)

McKenzie, Sir Roy Allan, KBE

Mackerras, Sir (Alan) Charles (MacLaurin), Kt., CBE

Mackeson, Sir Rupert Henry, Bt. (1954)

MacKinlay, Sir Bruce, Kt., CBE

McKinnon, Sir James, Kt.

McKinnon, *Hon.* Sir Stuart Neil, Kt.

Mackintosh, Sir Cameron Anthony, Kt.

Macklin, Sir Bruce Roy, Kt., OBE

Mackworth, Sir Digby (John), Bt. (1776)

McLaren, Sir Robin John Taylor, KCMG

McLaughlin, Sir Justice, Kt.

Maclean of Dunconnell, Sir Charles Edward, Bt. (1957)

Maclean, Sir Donald Og Grant, Kt.

MacLean, *Vice-Adm.* Sir Hector Charles Donald, KBE, CB, DSC

Maclean, Sir Lachlan Hector Charles, Bt. (NS 1631)

McLeod, Sir Charles Henry, Bt. (1925)

McLeod, Sir Ian George, Kt.

MacLeod, Sir (John) Maxwell Norman, Bt. (1924)

Macleod, Sir (Nathaniel William) Hamish, KBE

McLintock, Sir (Charles) Alan, Kt.

McLintock, Sir Michael William, Bt. (1934)

Maclure, Sir John Robert Spencer, Bt. (1898)

McMahon, Sir Brian Patrick, Bt. (1817)

McMahon, Sir Christopher William, Kt.

Macmillan, Sir (Alexander McGregor) Graham, Kt.

MacMillan, *Lt.-Gen.* Sir John Richard Alexander, KCB, CBE

McMullin, *Rt. Hon.* Sir Duncan Wallace, Kt.

Macnaghten, Sir Patrick Alexander, Bt. (1836)

McNamara, *Air Chief Marshal* Sir Neville Patrick, KBE

Macnaughton, *Prof.* Sir Malcolm Campbell, Kt.

McNee, Sir David Blackstock, Kt., QPM

McNulty, Sir (Robert William) Roy, Kt., CBE

MacPhail, Sir Bruce Dugald, Kt.

Macpherson, Sir Ronald Thomas Steward (Tommy), CBE, MC, TD

Macpherson of Cluny, *Hon.* Sir William Alan, Kt., TD

McQuarrie, Sir Albert, Kt.

MacRae, Sir (Alastair) Christopher (Donald Summerhayes), KCMG

Macready, Sir Nevil John Wilfrid, Bt. (1923)

Mactaggart, Sir John Auld, Bt. (1938)

Macwhinnie, Sir Gordon Menzies, Kt., CBE

McWilliam, Sir Michael Douglas, KCMG

McWilliams, Sir Francis, GBE, FREng.

Madden, *Adm.* Sir Charles Edward, Bt., GCB (1919)

Maddocks, Sir Kenneth Phipson, KCMG, KCVO

Maddox, Sir John Royden, Kt.

Madel, Sir (William) David, Kt., MP

Madigan, Sir Russel Tullie, Kt., OBE

Magnus, Sir Laurence Henry Philip, Bt. (1917)

Maguire, *Air Marshal* Sir Harold John, KCB, DSO, OBE

Mahon, Sir (John) Denis, Kt., CBE

Mahon, Sir William Walter, Bt. (1819)

Maiden, Sir Colin James, Kt., D.Phil.

Main, Sir Peter Tester, Kt., ERD

Maingard de la Villeès Offrans, Sir Louis Pierre René, Kt., CBE

Maino, Sir Charles, KBE

†Maitland, Sir Charles Alexander, Bt. (1818)

Maitland, Sir Donald James Dundas, GCMG, OBE

Malcolm, Sir James William Thomas Alexander, Bt. (s. 1665)

Malet, Sir Harry Douglas St Lo, Bt. (1791)

Mallaby, Sir Christopher Leslie George, GCMG, GCVO

Mallick, *Prof.* Sir Netar Prakash, Kt., FRCP, FRCPEd.

Mallinson, Sir William James, Bt. (1935)

Malone, *Hon.* Sir Denis Eustace Gilbert, Kt.

Malpas, Sir Robert, Kt., CBE, FREng.

Mamo, Sir Anthony Joseph, Kt., OBE

Mance, *Hon.* Sir Jonathan Hugh, Kt.

Manchester, Sir William Maxwell, KBE

Mander, Sir Charles Marcus, Bt. (1911)

Manduell, Sir John, Kt., CBE

Mann, *Rt. Revd* Sir Michael Ashley, KCVO

Mann, Sir Rupert Edward, Bt. (1905)

Mansel, Sir Philip, Bt. (1622)

Mansfield, *Vice-Adm.* Sir (Edward) Gerard (Napier), KBE, CVO

Mansfield, *Prof.* Sir Peter, Kt., FRS

Mansfield, Sir Philip (Robert Aked), KCMG

Mantell, *Rt. Hon.* Sir Charles Barrie Knight, Kt.

Manton, Sir Edwin Alfred Grenville, Kt.

Manuella, Sir Tulaga, GCMG, MBE

Manzie, Sir (Andrew) Gordon, KCB

Mara, *Rt. Hon. Ratu* Sir Kamisese Kapaiwai Tuimacilai, GCMG, KBE

Margetson, Sir John William Denys, KCMG

Marjoribanks, Sir James Alexander Milne, KCMG

Mark, Sir Robert, GBE

Markham, Sir Charles John, Bt. (1911)

Marking, Sir Henry Ernest, KCVO, CBE, MC

Marling, Sir Charles William Somerset, Bt. (1882)

Marmot, Prof. Sir Michael Gideon, Kt.

Marr, Sir Leslie Lynn, Bt. (1919)

Marriner, Sir Neville, Kt., CBE

Marriott, Sir Hugh Cavendish Smith-, Bt. (1774)

Marriott, Sir John Brook, KCVO

†Marsden, Sir Simon Neville Llewelyn, Bt. (1924)

Marsh, *Prof.* Sir John Stanley, Kt., CBE

Marshall, Sir Arthur Gregory George, Kt., OBE

Marshall, Sir Denis Alfred, Kt.

Marshall, *Prof.* Sir (Oshley) Roy, Kt., CBE

Marshall, Sir Peter Harold Reginald, KCMG

Marshall, Sir Robert Braithwaite, KCB, MBE

Marshall, Sir (Robert) Michael, Kt.

Martin, Sir George Henry, Kt., CBE

Martin, *Vice-Adm.* Sir John Edward Ludgate, KCB, DSC

Martin, *Prof.* Sir Laurence Woodward, Kt.

Martin, Sir (Robert) Bruce, Kt., QC

Marychurch, Sir Peter Harvey, KCMG

Masefield, Sir Charles Beech Gordon, Kt.

Masefield, Sir Peter Gordon, Kt.

Masire, Sir Ketumile, GCMG

Mason, *Hon.* Sir Anthony Frank, KBE

Mason, Sir (Basil) John, Kt., CB, D.SC., FRS

Mason, *Prof.* Sir David Kean, Kt., CBE

Mason, Sir Frederick Cecil, KCVO, CMG

Mason, Sir Gordon Charles, Kt., OBE

Mason, Sir John Charles Moir, KCMG

Mason, Sir John Peter, Kt., CBE

Mason, *Prof.* Sir Ronald, KCB, FRS

Matane, Sir Paulias Nguna, Kt., CMG, OBE

Mather, Sir (David) Carol (Macdonell), Kt., MC

Mathers, Sir Robert William, Kt.

Matheson of Matheson, Sir Fergus John, Bt. (1882)

Matheson, Sir (James Adam) Louis, KBE, CMG, FREng.

Mathewson, Sir George Ross, Kt., CBE, Ph.D., FRSE

Matthews, Sir Peter Alec, Kt.

Matthews, Sir Peter Jack, Kt., CVO, OBE, QPM

Maud, The Hon. Sir Humphrey John Hamilton, KCMG

Mawhinney, *Rt. Hon.* Sir Brian Stanley, Kt., MP

Maxwell, Sir Michael Eustace George, Bt. (S. 1681)

Maxwell, Sir Nigel Mellor Heron-, Bt. (S. 1683)

May, *Rt. Hon.* Sir Anthony Tristram Kenneth, Kt.

May, Sir Kenneth Spencer, Kt., CBE

May, *Prof.* Sir Robert McCredie, Kt., FRS

Maynard, *Hon.* Sir Clement Travelyan, Kt.

Mayne, *Very Revd* Sir Michael Clement Otway, KCVO

Meadow, *Prof.* Sir (Samuel) Roy, Kt., FRCP, FRCPE

Medlycott, Sir Mervyn Tregonwell, Bt. (1808)

Megarry, *Rt. Hon.* Sir Robert Edgar, Kt., FBA

Melhuish, Sir Michael Ramsay, KBE, CMG

Mellon, Sir James, KCMG

Melville, Sir Leslie Galfreid, KBE

Melville, Sir Ronald Henry, KCB

Menter, Sir James Woodham, Kt., Ph.D., SC.D., FRS

Menteth, Sir James Wallace Stuart-, Bt. (1838)

Merifield, Sir Anthony James, KCVO, CB

Meyer, Sir Anthony John Charles, Bt. (1910)

Meyer, Sir Christopher John Rome, KCMG

Meyjes, Sir Richard Anthony, Kt.

Meyrick, Sir David John Charlton, Bt. (1880)

Meyrick, Sir George Christopher Cadafael Tapps-Gervis-, Bt. (1791)

Miakwe, *Hon.* Sir Akepa, KBE

Michael, Sir Peter Colin, Kt., CBE

Middleton, Sir Peter Edward, GCB

Miers, Sir (Henry) David Alastair Capel, KBE, CMG

Milbank, Sir Anthony Frederick, Bt. (1882)

Milburn, Sir Anthony Rupert, Bt. (1905)

Mildmay, Sir Walter John Hugh St John-, Bt. (1772)

Miles, Sir Peter Tremayne, KCVO

Miles, Sir William Napier Maurice, Bt. (1859)

Millais, Sir Geoffrey Richard Everett, Bt. (1885)

Millar, Sir Oliver Nicholas, GCVO, FBA

Millard, Sir Guy Elwin, KCMG, CVO

Miller, Sir Donald John, Kt., FRSE, FREng.

Miller, Sir Harry Holmes, Bt. (1705)

Miller, Sir Hilary Duppa (Hal), Kt.

Miller, *Lt.-Col.* Sir John Mansel, GCVO, DSO, MC

Miller, Sir (Oswald) Bernard, Kt.

Miller, Sir Peter North, Kt.

Miller, Sir Ronald Andrew Baird, Kt., CBE

Miller of Glenlee, Sir Stephen William Macdonald, Bt. (1788)

Millichip, Sir Frederick Albert (Bert), Kt.

Mills, *Vice-Adm.* Sir Charles Piercy, KCB, CBE, DSC

Mills, Sir Frank, KCVO, CMG

Mills, Sir John Lewis Ernest Watts, Kt., CBE

Mills, Sir Peter Frederick Leighton, Bt. (1921)

Milman, Sir David Patrick, Bt. (1800)

Milne, Sir John Drummond, Kt.

Milner, Sir Timothy William Lycett, Bt. (1717)

Mirrlees, *Prof.* Sir James Alexander, Kt., FBA

Mitchell, *Air Cdre* Sir (Arthur) Dennis, KBE, CVO, DFC, AFC

Mitchell, Sir David Bower, Kt.

Mitchell, Sir Derek Jack, KCB, CVO

Mitchell, *Prof.* Sir (Edgar) William John, Kt., CBE, FRS

Mitchell, *Rt. Hon.* Sir James Fitz Allen, KCMG

Mitchell, *Very Revd* Sir Patrick Reynolds, KCVO

Mitchell, *Hon.* Sir Stephen George, Kt.

Moate, Sir Roger Denis, Kt.

Mobbs, Sir (Gerald) Nigel, Kt.

Moberly, Sir John Campbell, KBE, CMG

Moberly, Sir Patrick Hamilton, KCMG

Moffat, Sir Brian Scott, Kt., OBE

Moffat, *Lt.-Gen.* Sir (William) Cameron, KBE

Mogg, *Gen.* Sir (Herbert) John, GCB, CBE, DSO

†Moir, Sir Christopher Ernest, Bt. (1916)

†Molony, Sir Thomas Desmond, Bt. (1925)

Monck, Sir Nicholas Jeremy, KCB

Montgomery, Sir (Basil Henry) David, Bt. (1801)

Montgomery, Sir (William) Fergus, Kt.

Mookerjee, Sir Birendra Nath, Kt.

Moollan, Sir Abdool Hamid Adam, Kt.

Moollan, *Hon.* Sir Cassam (Ismael), Kt.

Moon, Sir Peter Wilfred Giles Graham-, Bt. (1855)

†Moon, Sir Roger, Bt. (1887)

Moore, *Most Revd* Sir Desmond Charles, KBE

Moore, Sir Francis Thomas, Kt.

Moore, Sir Henry Roderick, Kt., CBE

Moore, *Maj.-Gen.* Sir (John) Jeremy, KCB, OBE, MC

Moore, Sir John Michael, KCVO, CB, DSC

Moore, Sir Lee Llewellyn, KCMG, QC

Moore, *Vice Adm.* Sir Michael Antony Claës, KBE, LVO

Moore, *Prof.* Sir Norman Winfrid, Bt. (1919)

Moore, Sir Patrick William Eisdell, Kt., OBE

Moore, Sir William Roger
Clotworthy, Bt., TD (1932)
Morauta, Sir Mekere, Kt.
Mordaunt, Sir Richard Nigel
Charles, Bt. (1611)
Moreton, Sir John Oscar, KCMG,
KCVO, MC
Morgan, *Vice-Adm.* Sir Charles
Christopher, KBE
Morgan, *His Hon. Maj.-Gen.* Sir
David John Hughes-, Bt., CB, CBE
(1925)
Morgan, Sir Graham, Kt.
Morgan, Sir John Albert Leigh,
KCMG
Morison, *Hon.* Sir Thomas Richard
Atkin, Kt.
Morland, *Hon.* Sir Michael, Kt.
Morland, Sir Robert Kenelm, Kt.
Morpeth, Sir Douglas Spottiswoode,
Kt., TD
†Morris, Sir Allan Lindsay, Bt. (1806)
Morris, *Air Marshal* Sir Arnold Alec,
KBE, CB, FREng.
Morris, Sir (James) Richard
(Samuel), Kt., CBE, FREng.
Morris, *Rt. Hon.* Sir John, Kt., QC
Morris, Sir Keith Elliot Hedley, KBE,
CMG
Morris, *Prof.* Sir Peter John, Kt., FRS
Morris, Sir Trefor Alfred, Kt., CBE,
QPM
Morris, *Very Revd* Sir William James,
KCVO, Ph.D.
Morrison, Sir (Alexander) Fraser,
Kt., CBE
Morrison, *Hon.* Sir Charles Andrew,
Kt.
Morrison, Sir Howard Leslie, Kt.,
OBE
Morrison, Sir Kenneth Duncan, Kt.,
CBE
Morritt, *Hon.* Sir (Robert) Andrew,
Kt., CVO
Morrow, Sir Ian Thomas, Kt.
Morse, Sir Christopher Jeremy,
KCMG
Mortimer, Sir John Clifford, Kt.,
CBE, QC
Morton, *Adm.* Sir Anthony Storrs,
GBE, KCB
Morton, Sir (Robert) Alastair
(Newton), Kt.
Moseley, Sir George Walker, KCB
Moser, *Prof.* Sir Claus Adolf, KCB,
CBE, FBA
Moses, *Hon.* Sir Alan George, Kt.
†Moss, Sir David John Edwards-,
Bt. (1868)
Moss, Sir David Joseph, KCVO, CMG
Moss, Sir Stirling Craufurd, Kt., OBE
Mostyn, *Gen.* Sir (Joseph) David
Frederick, KCB, CBE
†Mostyn, Sir William Basil John, Bt.
(1670)
Mott, Sir John Harmer, Bt. (1930)
Mottram, Sir Richard Clive, KCB
†Mount, Sir (William Robert)
Ferdinand, Bt. (1921)
Mountain, Sir Denis Mortimer, Bt.
(1922)

Mountfield, Sir Robin, KCB
Mowbray, Sir John, Kt.
Mowbray, Sir John Robert, Bt.
(1880)
Muir, Sir Laurence Macdonald, Kt.
†Muir, Sir Richard James Kay, Bt.
(1892)
Mulcahy, Sir Geoffrey John, Kt.
Mullens, *Lt.-Gen.* Sir Anthony
Richard Guy, KCB, OBE
Mummery, *Hon.* Sir John Frank, Kt.
Munby, *Hon.* Sir James Lawrence,
Kt.
Munn, Sir James, Kt., OBE
Munro, Sir Alan Gordon, KCMG
†Munro, Sir Kenneth Arnold
William, Bt. (S. 1634)
†Munro, Sir Keith Gordon, Bt. (1825)
Munro, Sir Sydney Douglas Gun-,
GCMG, MBE
Muria, *Hon.* Sir Gilbert John Baptist,
Kt.
Murphy, Sir Leslie Frederick, Kt.
Murray, *Rt. Hon.* Sir Donald Bruce,
Kt.
Murray, Sir James, KCMG
Murray, Sir John Antony
Jerningham, Kt., CBE
Murray, *Prof.* Sir Kenneth, Kt.,
FRCPath., FRS, FRSE
Murray, Sir Nigel Andrew Digby, Bt.
(S. 1628)
Murray, Sir Patrick Ian Keith, Bt.
(S. 1673)
†Murray, Sir Rowland William, Bt. (S.
1630)
Mursell, Sir Peter, Kt., MBE
Musgrave, Sir Christopher Patrick
Charles, Bt. (1611)
Musgrave, Sir Richard James, Bt.
(I. 1782)
Musson, *Gen.* Sir Geoffrey Randolph
Dixon, GCB, CBE, DSO
Myers, Sir Philip Alan, Kt., OBE, QPM
Myers, *Prof.* Sir Rupert Horace, KBE
Mynors, Sir Richard Baskerville, Bt.
(1964)
Naipaul, Sir Vidiadhar Surajprasad,
Kt.
Nairn, Sir Michael, Bt. (1904)
Nairn, Sir Robert Arnold Spencer-,
Bt. (1933)
Nairne, *Rt. Hon.* Sir Patrick
Dalmahoy, GCB, MC
Naish, Sir (Charles) David, Kt.
Nall, Sir Michael Joseph, Bt., RN
(1954)
Namaliu, *Rt. Hon.* Sir Rabbie
Langanai, KCMG
†Napier, Sir Charles Joseph, Bt.
(1867)
Napier, Sir John Archibald Lennox,
Bt. (S. 1627)
Napier, Sir Oliver John, Kt.
Nasmith, *Prof.* Sir James Duncan
Dunbar-, Kt., CBE, RIBA, FRSE
Neal, Sir Eric James, Kt., CVO
Neal, Sir Leonard Francis, Kt., CBE
Neale, Sir Gerrard Anthony, Kt.
Neave, Sir Paul Arundell, Bt. (1795)
Needham, *Rt. Hon.* Sir Richard (The

Earl of Kilmorey, *see* page 141)
Neill, *Rt. Hon.* Sir Brian Thomas, Kt.
Neill, *Rt. Hon.* Sir Ivan, Kt., PC (NI)
Neill, Sir (James) Hugh,KCVO, CBE,
TD
†Nelson, Sir Jamie Charles Vernon
Hope, Bt. (1912)
Nelson, *Hon.* Sir Robert Franklyn,
Kt.
Nelson, *Air Marshal* Sir (Sidney)
Richard (Carlyle), KCB, OBE, MD
Nepean, *Lt.-Col.* Sir Evan Yorke, Bt.
(1802)
Neuberger, *Hon.* Sir David Edmond,
Kt.
Neubert, Sir Michael John, Kt.
Neville, Sir Roger Albert Gartside,
Kt., VRD
New, *Maj.-Gen.* Sir Laurence
Anthony Wallis, Kt., CB, CBE
Newall, Sir Paul Henry, Kt., TD
Newby, *Prof.* Sir Howard Joseph, Kt.,
CBE
Newington, Sir Michael John, KCMG
Newman, Sir Francis Hugh Cecil,
Bt. (1912)
Newman, Sir Geoffrey Robert, Bt.
(1836)
Newman, *Hon.* Sir George Michael,
Kt.
Newman, Sir Kenneth Leslie, GBE,
QPM
Newman, *Vice-Adm.* Sir Roy
Thomas, KCB
Newman, *Col.* Sir Stuart Richard,
Kt., CBE, TD
Newsam, Sir Peter Anthony, Kt.
Newton, Sir (Charles) Wilfred, Kt.,
CBE
Newton, Sir (Harry) Michael (Rex),
Bt. (1900)
Newton, Sir Kenneth Garnar, Bt.,
OBE, TD (1924)
Ngata, Sir Henare Kohere, KBE
Nichol, Sir Duncan Kirkbride, Kt.,
CBE
Nicholas, Sir David, Kt., CBE
Nicholas, Sir John William, KCVO,
CMG
Nicholls, *Air Marshal* Sir John
Moreton, KCB, CBE, DFC, AFC
Nicholls, Sir Nigel Hamilton, KCVO,
CBE
Nichols, Sir Richard Everard, Kt.
Nicholson, Sir Bryan Hubert, Kt.
†Nicholson, Sir Charles Christian, Bt.
(1912)
Nicholson, *Rt. Hon.* Sir Michael, Kt.
Nicholson, Sir Paul Douglas, Kt.
Nicholson, Sir Robin Buchanan, Kt.,
Ph.D., FRS, FREng.
Nicoll, Sir William, KCMG
Nightingale, Sir Charles Manners
Gamaliel, Bt. (1628)
Nightingale, Sir John Cyprian, Kt.,
CBE, BEM, QPM
Nixon, Sir Simon Michael
Christopher, Bt. (1906)
Nixon, Sir Edwin Ronald, Kt., CBE
Noble, Sir David Brunel, Bt. (1902)
Noble, Sir Iain Andrew, Bt., OBE

(1923)

Noble, Sir (Thomas Alexander) Fraser, Kt., MBE

Nombri, Sir Joseph Karl, Kt., ISO, BEM

Norman, Sir Arthur Gordon, KBE, DFC

Norman, Sir Mark Annesley, Bt. (1915)

Norman, Sir Robert Henry, Kt., OBE

Norman, Sir Ronald, Kt., OBE

Norrington, Sir Roger Arthur Carver, Kt., CBE

Norris, *Air Chief Marshal* Sir Christopher Neil Foxley-, GCB, DSO, OBE

Norris, Sir Eric George, KCMG

Norriss, Air Marshal Sir Peter Coulson, KBE, CB, AFC

North, Sir Peter Machin, Kt., CBE, QC, DCL, FBA

North, Sir Thomas Lindsay, Kt.

North, Sir (William) Jonathan (Frederick), Bt. (1920)

Norton, *Vice-Adm. Hon.* Sir Nicholas John Hill-, KCB

Norwood, Sir Walter Neville, Kt.

Nossal, Sir Gustav Joseph Victor, Kt., CBE

Nott, *Rt. Hon.* Sir John William Frederic, KCB

Nourse, *Rt. Hon.* Sir Martin Charles, Kt.

Nugent, Sir John Edwin Lavallin, Bt. (I. 1795)

Nugent, *Maj.* Sir Peter Walter James, Bt. (1831)

Nugent, Sir Robin George Colborne, Bt. (1806)

Nursaw, Sir James, KCB, QC

Nurse, Sir Paul Maxime, Kt., ph.D.

Nuttall, Sir Nicholas Keith Lillington, Bt. (1922)

Nutting, Sir John Grenfell, Bt., QC (1903)

Oakeley, Sir John Digby Atholl, Bt. (1790)

Oakes, Sir Christopher, Bt. (1939)

Oakshott, Hon. Sir Anthony Hendrie, Bt. (1959)

Oates, Sir Thomas, Kt., CMG, OBE

Obolensky, *Prof.* Sir Dimitri, Kt.

O'Brien, Sir Frederick William Fitzgerald, Kt.

O'Brien, Sir Richard, Kt., DSO, MC

O'Brien, Sir Timothy John, Bt. (1849)

O'Brien, *Adm.* Sir William Donough, KCB, DSC

O'Connell, Sir Maurice James Donagh MacCarthy, Bt. (1869)

O'Connor, *Rt. Hon.* Sir Patrick McCarthy, Kt.

O'Dea, Sir Patrick Jerad, KCVO

Odell, Sir Stanley John, Kt.

Odgers, Sir Graeme David William, Kt.

O'Dowd, Sir David Joseph, Kt., CBE, QPM

Ogden, Sir (Edward) Michael, Kt.,

QC

Ogilvy, *Rt. Hon.* Sir Angus James Bruce, KCVO

Ogilvy, Sir Francis Gilbert Arthur, Bt. (s. 1626)

Ognall, *Hon.* Sir Harry Henry, Kt.

Ohlson, Sir Brian Eric Christopher, Bt. (1920)

Okeover, *Capt.* Sir Peter Ralph Leopold Walker-, Bt. (1886)

Olewale, *Hon.* Sir Niwia Ebia, Kt.

Oliphant, Sir Mark (Marcus Laurence Elwin), KBE, FRS

O'Loghlen, Sir Colman Michael, Bt. (1838)

Olver, Sir Stephen John Linley, KBE, CMG

Omand, Sir David Bruce, KCB

O'Neil, *Hon.* Sir Desmond Henry, Kt.

Ongley, *Hon.* Sir Joseph Augustine, Kt.

O'Nions, Prof. Sir Robert Keith, Kt., FRS, ph.D.

Onslow, Sir John Roger Wilmot, Bt. (1797)

Oppenheim, Sir Duncan Morris, Kt.

Oppenheimer, Sir Michael Bernard Grenville, Bt. (1921)

Orde, Sir John Alexander Campbell-, Bt. (1790)

O'Regan, *Dr* Sir Stephen Gerard (Tipene), Kt.

Orr, Sir David Alexander, Kt., MC

Osborn, Sir John Holbrook, Kt.

Osborn, Sir Richard Henry Danvers, Bt. (1662)

Osborne, Sir Peter George, Bt. (I.1629)

Osifelo, Sir Frederick Aubarua, Kt., MBE

Osmond, Sir Douglas, Kt., CBE

O'Sullevan, Sir Peter John, Kt., CBE

Oswald, *Admiral of the Fleet* Sir (John) Julian Robertson, GCB

Oswald, Sir (William Richard) Michael, KCVO

Otton, Sir Geoffrey John, KCB

Otton, *Rt. Hon.* Sir Philip Howard, Kt.

Oulton, Sir Antony Derek Maxwell, GCB, QC

Ouseley, Sir Herman George, Kt.

Outram, Sir Alan James, Bt. (1858)

Overall, Sir John Wallace, Kt., CBE, MC

Owen, Sir Geoffrey, Kt.

Owen, Sir Hugh Bernard Pilkington, Bt. (1813)

Owen, Sir Hugo Dudley Cunliffe-, Bt. (1920)

Owen, *Hon.* Sir John Arthur Dalziel, Kt.

Packer, Sir Richard John, KCB

Page, Sir (Arthur) John, Kt.

Page, Sir Frederick William, Kt., CBE, FREng.

Page, Sir John Joseph Joffre, Kt., OBE

Paget, Sir Julian Tolver, Bt., CVO

(1871)

Paget, Sir Richard Herbert, Bt. (1886)

Pain, *Lt.-Gen.* Sir (Horace) Rollo (Squarey), KCB, MC

Pain, *Hon.* Sir Peter Richard, Kt.

Paine, Sir Christopher Hammon, Kt., FRCP, FRCR

Palin, *Air Chief Marshal* Sir Roger Hewlett, KCB, OBE

Palliser, *Rt. Hon.* Sir (Arthur) Michael, GCMG

Palmer, Sir Derek James, Kt.

Palmer, Sir (Charles) Mark, Bt. (1886)

Palmer, Sir Geoffrey Christopher John, Bt. (1660)

Palmer, *Rt. Hon.* Sir Geoffrey Winston Russell, KCMG

Palmer, Sir John Chance, Kt.

Palmer, Sir John Edward Somerset, Bt. (1791)

Palmer, *Maj.-Gen.* Sir (Joseph) Michael, KCVO

Palmer, Sir Reginald Oswald, GCMG, MBE

Pantlin, Sir Dick Hurst, Kt., CBE

Paolozzi, Sir Eduardo Luigi, Kt., CBE, RA

Parbo, Sir Arvi Hillar, Kt.

Park, *Hon.* Sir Andrew Edward Wilson, Kt.

Park, *Hon.* Sir Hugh Eames, Kt.

Parker, Sir (Arthur) Douglas Dodds-, Kt.

Parker, Sir Eric Wilson, Kt.

Parker, *Hon.* Sir Jonathan Frederic, Kt.

Parker, *Maj.* Sir Michael John, KCVO, CBE

Parker, Sir Peter, KBE, LVO

Parker, Sir Richard (William) Hyde, Bt. (1681)

Parker, *Rt. Hon.* Sir Roger Jocelyn, Kt.

Parker, *Vice-Adm.* Sir (Wilfred) John, KBE, CB, DSC

Parker, Sir William Peter Brian, Bt. (1844)

Parkes, Sir Edward Walter, Kt., FREng.

Parkinson, Sir Nicholas Fancourt, Kt.

Parsons, Sir (John) Michael, Kt.

Parsons, Sir Richard Edmund (Clement Fownes), KCMG

Partridge, Sir Michael John Anthony, KCB

Pascoe, *Gen.* Sir Robert Alan, KCB, MBE

Pasley, Sir John Malcolm Sabine, Bt. (1794)

Paterson, Sir Dennis Craig, Kt.

Patnick, Sir (Cyril) Irvine, Kt., OBE

Pattie, *Rt. Hon.* Sir Geoffrey Edwin, Kt.

Pattinson, Sir (William) Derek, Kt.

Pattison, *Prof.* Sir John Ridley, Kt., DM, FRCPath.

Pattullo, Sir (David) Bruce, Kt., CBE

Paul, Sir John Warburton, GCMG,
OBE, MC
Paul, *Air Marshal* Sir Ronald Ian
Stuart-, KBE
Payne, Sir Norman John, Kt., CBE,
FREng.
Peach, Sir Leonard Harry, Kt.
Peacock, *Prof.* Sir Alan Turner, Kt.,
DSC
Pearce, Sir Austin William, Kt., CBE,
Ph.D., FREng.
Pearce, Sir (Daniel Norton) Idris,
Kt., CBE, TD
Pearse, Sir Brian Gerald, Kt.
Pearson, Sir Francis Nicholas Fraser,
Bt. (1964)
Pearson, *Gen.* Sir Thomas Cecil
Hook, KCB, CBE, DSO
Peart, *Prof.* Sir William Stanley, Kt.,
MD, FRS
Pease, Sir (Alfred) Vincent, Bt. (1882)
Pease, Sir Richard Thorn, Bt. (1920)
Peat, Sir Gerrard Charles, KCVO
Peat, Sir Michael Charles Gerrard,
KCVO
Peck, Sir Edward Heywood, GCMG
Peckham, *Prof.* Sir Michael John, Kt.,
FRCP, FRCPGlas., FRCR, FRCPath.
Pedder, *Air Marshal* Sir Ian Maurice,
KCB, OBE, DFC
Peek, *Vice-Adm.* Sir Richard Innes,
KBE, CB, DSC
Peek, Sir William Grenville, Bt.
(1874)
Peel, Sir John Harold, KCVO
Peel, Sir (William) John, Kt.
Peirse, Sir Henry Grant de la Poer
Beresford-, Bt. (1814)
Peirse, *Air Vice-Marshal* Sir Richard
Charles Fairfax, KCVO, CB
Pelgen, Sir Harry Friedrich, Kt., MBE
Peliza, Sir Robert John, KBE, ED
Pelly, Sir Richard John, Bt. (1840)
Pemberton, Sir Francis Wingate
William, Kt., CBE
Penrose, *Prof.* Sir Roger, Kt., FRS, OM
Pereira, Sir (Herbert) Charles, Kt.,
D.Sc., FRS
Perowne, *Vice-Adm.* Sir James
Francis, KBE, OBE
Perring, Sir John Raymond, Bt.
(1963)
Perris, Sir David (Arthur), Kt., MBE
Perry, Sir David Howard, KCB
Perry, Sir (David) Norman, Kt., MBE
Perry, Sir Michael Sydney, Kt., CBE
Pervez, Sir Mohammed Anwar, Kt.,
OBE
Pestell, Sir John Richard, KCVO
Peterkin, Sir Neville, Kt.
Peters, *Prof.* Sir David Keith, Kt.,
FRCP
Petersen, Sir Jeffrey Charles, KCMG
Petersen, Sir Johannes Bjelke-, KCMG
Peterson, Sir Christopher Matthew,
Kt., CBE, TD
†Petit, Sir Jehangir, Bt. (1890)
Peto, Sir Henry George Morton, Bt.
(1855)
Peto, Sir Michael Henry Basil, Bt.

(1927)
Peto, *Prof.* Sir Richard, Kt., FRS
Petrie, Sir Peter Charles, Bt., CMG
(1918)
Pettigrew, Sir Russell Hilton, Kt.
Pettit, Sir Daniel Eric Arthur, Kt.
Pettitt, Sir Dennis, Kt.
Philips, *Prof.* Sir Cyril Henry, Kt.
Phillips, Sir Fred Albert, Kt., CVO
Phillips, Sir (Gerald) Hayden, KCB
Phillips, Sir Henry Ellis Isidore, Kt.,
CMG, MBE
Phillips, Sir Horace, KCMG
Phillips, Sir John David, Kt., QPM
Phillips, Sir Peter John, Kt., OBE
Phillips, Sir Robin Francis, Bt. (1912)
Pickard, Sir (John) Michael, Kt.
Pickering, Sir Edward Davies, Kt.
Pickthorn, Sir James Francis Mann,
Bt. (1959)
Pidgeon, Sir John Allan Stewart, Kt.
†Piers, Sir James Desmond, Bt.
(I. 1661)
Pigot, Sir George Hugh, Bt. (1764)
Pigott, Sir Berkeley Henry Sebastian,
Bt. (1808)
Pike, *Lt.-Gen.* Sir Hew William
Royston, KCB, DSO, MBE
Pike, Sir Michael Edmund, KCVO,
CMG
Pike, Sir Philip Ernest Housden, Kt.,
QC
Pilditch, Sir Richard Edward, Bt.
(1929)
Pile, Sir Frederick Devereux, Bt., MC
(1900)
Pilkington, Sir Antony Richard, Kt.
Pilkington, Sir Thomas Henry
Milborne-Swinnerton-, Bt.
(S. 1635)
Pill, *Rt. Hon.* Sir Malcolm Thomas,
Kt.
Pinker, Sir George Douglas, KCVO
Pinsent, Sir Christopher Roy, Bt.
(1938)
Pippard, *Prof.* Sir (Alfred) Brian, Kt.,
FRS
Pirie, *Gp Capt* Sir Gordon Hamish,
Kt., CVO, CBE
Pitakaka, Sir Moses Puibangara,
GCMG
Pitcher, Sir Desmond Henry, Kt.
Pitman, Sir Brian Ivor, Kt.
Pitoi, Sir Sere, Kt., CBE
Pitt, Sir Harry Raymond, Kt., Ph.D.,
FRS
Pitts, Sir Cyril Alfred, Kt.
Plastow, Sir David Arnold Stuart, Kt.
Platt, Sir Harold Grant, Kt.
Plowman, *Hon.* Sir John Robin, Kt.,
CBE
Plumb, *Prof.* Sir John Harold, Kt.
Pohai, Sir Timothy, Kt., MBE
Pole, Sir (John) Richard (Walter
Reginald) Carew, Bt. (1628)
Pole, Sir Peter Van Notten, Bt.
(1791)
Polkinghorne, *Revd Canon* Sir John
Charlton, KBE, FRS
Pollen, Sir John Michael

Hungerford, Bt. (1795)
Pollock, Sir George Frederick, Bt.
(1866)
Pollock, Sir Giles Hampden
Montagu-, Bt. (1872)
Pollock, *Admiral of the Fleet* Sir
Michael Patrick, GCB, LVO, DSC
Ponsonby, Sir Ashley Charles Gibbs,
Bt., KCVO, MC (1956)
Pontin, Sir Frederick William, Kt.
Poole, *Hon.* Sir David Anthony, Kt.
Poore, Sir Herbert Edward, Bt.
(1795)
Pope, Sir Joseph Albert, Kt., D.Sc.,
Ph.D.
Popplewell, *Hon.* Sir Oliver Bury, Kt.
†Porritt, Sir Jonathon Espie, Bt.
(1963)
Portal, Sir Jonathan Francis, Bt.
(1901)
Porter, Sir John Simon Horsbrugh-,
Bt. (1902)
Porter, Sir Leslie, Kt.
Porter, *Air Marshal* Sir (Melvin)
Kenneth (Drowley), KCB, CBE
Porter, *Rt. Hon.* Sir Robert Wilson,
Kt., PC (NI), QC
Posnett, Sir Richard Neil, KBE, CMG
Potter, *Rt. Hon.* Sir Mark Howard,
Kt.
Potter, *Maj.-Gen.* Sir (Wilfrid) John,
KBE, CB
Potts, *Hon.* Sir Francis Humphrey,
Kt.
Pound, Sir John David, Bt. (1905)
Pountain, Sir Eric John, Kt.
Powell, Sir (Arnold Joseph) Philip,
Kt., CH, OBE, RA, FRIBA
Powell, Sir Nicholas Folliott
Douglas, Bt. (1897)
Powell, Sir Raymond, Kt., MP
Powell, Sir Richard Royle, GCB, KBE,
CMG
Power, Sir Alastair John Cecil, Bt.
(1924)
Power, *Hon.* Sir Noel Plunkett, Kt.
Prance, *Prof.* Sir Ghillean Tolmie,
Kt., FRS
Prendergast, Sir (Walter) Kieran,
KCVO, CMG
Prentice, *Hon.* Sir William Thomas,
Kt., MBE
Prescott, Sir Mark, Bt. (1938)
†Preston, Sir Philip Charles Henry
Hulton, Bt. (1815)
Prevost, Sir Christopher Gerald, Bt.
(1805)
Price, Sir Charles Keith Napier
Rugge-, Bt. (1804)
Price, Sir David Ernest Campbell,
Kt.
Price, Sir Francis Caradoc Rose, Bt.
(1815)
Price, Sir Frank Leslie, Kt.
Price, Sir Norman Charles, KCB
Price, Sir Robert John Green-, Bt.
(1874)
Prickett, *Air Chief Marshal* Sir
Thomas Other, KCB, DSO, DFC
Prideaux, Sir Humphrey Povah

Treverbian, Kt., OBE
†Primrose, Sir John Ure, Bt. (1903)
Pringle, *Air Marshal* Sir Charles
  Norman Seton, KBE, FREng.
Pringle, *Hon.* Sir John Kenneth, Kt.
Pringle, *Lt.-Gen.* Sir Steuart
  (Robert), Bt., KCB, RM (S. 1683)
Pritchard, Sir Neil, KCMG
Proby, Sir Peter, Bt. (1952)
Prosser, Sir Ian Maurice Gray, Kt.
Pryke, Sir Christopher Dudley, Bt.
  (1926)
Puapua, *Rt. Hon.* Sir Tomasi, KBE
Pugh, Sir Idwal Vaughan, KCB
Pullinger, Sir (Francis) Alan, Kt., CBE
Pumfrey, *Hon.* Sir Nicholas Richard,
  Kt.
Pumphrey, Sir (John) Laurence,
  KCMG
Purchas, *Rt. Hon.* Sir Francis Brooks,
  Kt.
Purves, Sir William, Kt., CBE, DSO
Purvis, *Vice-Adm.* Sir Neville, KCB
Quicke, Sir John Godolphin, Kt., CBE
Quigley, Sir (William) George
  (Henry), Kt., CB, Ph.D.
Quilliam, *Hon.* Sir (James) Peter, Kt.
Quilter, Sir Anthony Raymond
  Leopold Cuthbert, Bt. (1897)
Quinlan, Sir Michael Edward, GCB
Quinton, Sir James Grand, Kt.
Radcliffe, Sir Sebastian Everard, Bt.
  (1813)
Radda, *Prof.* Sir George Karoly, Kt.,
  CBE, FRS
Rae, *Hon.* Sir Wallace Alexander
  Ramsay, Kt.
Raeburn, Sir Michael Edward
  Norman, Bt. (1923)
Raeburn, *Maj.-Gen.* Sir (William)
  Digby (Manifold), KCVO, CB, DSO,
  MBE
Raikes, *Vice-Adm.* Sir Iwan Geoffrey,
  KCB, CBE, DSC
Raison, *Rt. Hon.* Sir Timothy Hugh
  Francis, Kt.
Ralli, Sir Godfrey Victor, Bt., TD
  (1912)
Ramdanee, Sir Mookteswar
  Baboolall Kailash, Kt.
Ramphal, Sir Shridath Surendranath,
  GCMG
Ramphul, Sir Baalkhristna, Kt.
Ramphul, Sir Indurduth, Kt.
Ramsay, Sir Alexander William
  Burnett, Bt. (1806)
Ramsay, Sir Allan John (Hepple),
  KBE, CMG
Ramsbotham, *Gen.* Sir David John,
  GCB, CBE
Ramsbotham, *Hon.* Sir Peter
  Edward, GCMG, GCVO
Ramsden, Sir John Charles Josslyn,
  Bt. (1689)
Randle, *Prof.* Sir Philip John, Kt.
Rank, Sir Benjamin Keith, Kt., CMG
Rankin, Sir Ian Niall, Bt. (1898)
Rasch, Sir Simon Anthony Carne, Bt.
  (1903)
Rashleigh, Sir Richard Harry, Bt.

(1831)
Ratford, Sir David John Edward,
  KCMG, CVO
Rattee, *Hon.* Sir Donald Keith, Kt.
Rattle, Sir Simon Dennis, Kt., CBE
Rault, Sir Louis Joseph Maurice,
  Kt.
Rawlins, *Surgeon Vice-Adm.* Sir John
  Stuart Pepys, KBE
Rawlins, *Prof.* Sir Michael David,
  Kt., FRCP, FRCPED
Rawlinson, Sir Anthony Henry John,
  Bt. (1891)
Read, *Air Marshal* Sir Charles
  Frederick, KBE, CB, DFC, AFC
Read, *Gen.* Sir (John) Antony
  (Jervis), GCB, CBE, DSO, MC
Read, Sir John Emms, Kt.
†Reade, Sir Kenneth Ray, Bt. (1661)
Reay, *Lt.-Gen.* Sir (Hubert) Alan
  John, KBE
Redgrave, *Maj.-Gen.* Sir Roy Michael
  Frederick, KBE, MC
Redmayne, Sir Nicholas, Bt. (1964)
Redwood, Sir Peter Boverton, Bt.
  (1911)
Reece, Sir Charles Hugh, Kt.
Reece, Sir James Gordon, Kt.
Rees, Sir (Charles William) Stanley,
  Kt., TD
Rees, Sir David Allan, Kt., Ph.D.,
  D.SC., FRS
Rees, *Prof.* Sir Martin John, Kt., FRS
Reeve, Sir Anthony, KCMG, KCVO
Reeves, *Most Revd* Paul Alfred, GCMG,
  GCVO
Reffell, *Adm.* Sir Derek Roy, KCB
Refshauge, *Maj.-Gen.* Sir William
  Dudley, Kt., CBE
Reid, Sir Alexander James, Bt. (1897)
Reid, Sir (Harold) Martin (Smith),
  KBE, CMG
Reid, Sir Hugh, Bt. (1922)
Reid, Sir Norman Robert, Kt.
Reid, Sir Robert Paul, Kt.
Reid, Sir William Kennedy, KCB
Reiher, Sir Frederick Bernard Carl,
  KBE, CMG
Reilly, *Lt.-Gen.* Sir Jeremy Calcott,
  KCB, DSO
Renals, Sir Stanley, Bt. (1895)
Rennie, Sir John Shaw, GCMG, OBE
Renouf, Sir Clement William Bailey,
  Kt.
Renshaw, Sir (Charles) Maurice
  Binc, Bt. (1903)
Renwick, Sir Richard Eustace, Bt.
  (1921)
Reporter, Sir Shapoor Ardeshirji,
  KBE
Reynolds, Sir David James, Bt. (1923)
Reynolds, Sir Peter William John,
  Kt., CBE
Rhodes, Sir Basil Edward, Kt., CBE,
  TD
Rhodes, Sir John Christopher
  Douglas, Bt. (1919)
Rhodes, Sir Peregrine Alexander,
  KCMG
Rice, *Maj.-Gen.* Sir Desmond Hind

Garrett, KCVO, CBE
Rice, Sir Timothy Miles Bindon, Kt.
Richard, Sir Cliff, Kt., OBE
Richards, Sir Brian Mansel, Kt., CBE,
  Ph.D.
Richards, Sir (Francis) Brooks,
  KCMG, DSC
Richards, *Lt.-Gen.* Sir John Charles
  Chisholm, KCB, KCVO, RM
Richards, Sir Rex Edward, Kt., D.SC.,
  FRS
Richards, *Hon.* Sir Stephen Price, Kt.
Richardson, Sir Anthony Lewis, Bt.
  (1924)
Richardson, *Rt. Hon.* Sir Ivor Lloyd
  Morgan, Kt.
Richardson, Sir (John) Eric, Kt., CBE
Richardson, Sir Michael John de
  Rougemont, Kt.
Richardson, *Lt.-Gen.* Sir Robert
  Francis, KCB, CVO, CBE
Richardson, Sir Simon Alaisdair
  Stewart-, Bt. (S. 1630)
Richardson, Sir Thomas Legh,
  KCMG
Richmond, Sir John Frederick, Bt.
  (1929)
Richmond, *Prof.* Sir Mark Henry,
  Kt., FRS
Ricketts, Sir Robert Cornwallis
  Gerald St Leger, Bt. (1828)
Riddell, Sir John Charles Buchanan,
  Bt., CVO (S. 1628)
Ridley, Sir Adam (Nicholas), Kt.
Ridley, Sir Michael Kershaw, KCVO
Ridley, Sir Nicholas Harold Lloyd,
  Kt.
Ridsdale, Sir Julian Errington, Kt.,
  CBE
Rifkind, *Rt. Hon.* Sir Malcolm Leslie,
  KCMG, QC
Rigby, Sir Anthony John, Bt. (1929)
Rimer, *Hon.* Sir Colin Percy
  Farquharson, Kt.
Ringadoo, *Hon.* Sir Veerasamy,
  GCMG
Ripley, Sir Hugh, Bt. (1880)
Risk, Sir Thomas Neilson, Kt.
Ritako, Sir Thomas Baha, Kt., MBE
Rix, *Hon.* Sir Bernard Anthony, Kt.
Rix, Sir John, Kt., MBE, FREng.
Robb, Sir John Weddell, Kt.
Roberts, *Hon.* Sir Denys Tudor Emil,
  KBE, QC
Roberts, Sir Derek Harry, Kt., CBE,
  FRS, FREng.
Roberts, Sir (Edward Fergus) Sidney,
  Kt., CBE
Roberts, *Prof.* Sir Gareth Gwyn, Kt.,
  FRS
Roberts, Sir Gilbert Howland
  Rookehurst, Bt. (1809)
Roberts, Sir Gordon James, Kt., CBE
Roberts, Sir Ivor Anthony, KCMG
Roberts, Sir Samuel, Bt. (1919)
Roberts, Sir Stephen James Leake,
  Kt.
Roberts, Sir William James Denby,
  Bt. (1909)
Robertson, Sir John Fraser, KCMG,

CBE
Robertson, Sir Lewis, Kt., CBE, FRSE
Robertson, *Prof.* Sir Rutherford
Ness, Kt., CMG
Robins, Sir Ralph Harry, Kt., FREng.
Robinson, Sir Albert Edward
Phineas, Kt.
†Robinson, Sir Christopher Philipse,
Bt. (1854)
Robinson, Sir Dominick Christopher
Lynch-, Bt. (1920)
Robinson, Sir Ian, Kt.
Robinson, Sir John James Michael
Laud, Bt. (1660)
Robinson, Sir Wilfred Henry
Frederick, Bt. (1908)
Robson, *Prof.* Sir James Gordon, Kt.,
CBE
Robson, Sir John Adam, KCMG
Robson, Sir Stephen Arthur, Kt., CB
Roch, *Rt. Hon.* Sir John Ormond, Kt.
Roche, Sir David O'Grady, Bt.
(1838)
Roche, Sir Henry John, Kt.
Rodgers, Sir (Andrew) Piers
(Wingate Aikin-Sneath), Bt. (1964)
Rodley, *Prof.* Sir Nigel, KBE
Rodrigues, Sir Alberto Maria, Kt.,
CBE, ED
Roe, *Air Chief Marshal* Sir Rex David,
GCB, AFC
Rogers, Sir Frank Jarvis, Kt.
Rogers, *Air Chief Marshal* Sir John
Robson, KCB, CBE
Rooke, Sir Denis Eric, Kt., OM, CBE,
FRS, FREng.
Ropner, Sir John Bruce Woollacott,
Bt. (1952)
Ropner, Sir Robert Douglas, Bt.
(1904)
Roscoe, Sir Robert Bell, KBE
Rose, *Rt. Hon.* Sir Christopher
Dudley Roger, Kt.
Rose, Sir Clive Martin,GCMG
Rose, Sir David Lancaster, Bt. (1874)
Rose, *Gen.* Sir (Hugh) Michael, KCB,
CBE, DSO, QGM
Rose, Sir Julian Day, Bt. (1872 and
1909)
Ross, Sir (James) Keith, Bt., RD, FRCS
(1960)
Ross, *Lt.-Gen.* Sir Robert Jeremy,
KCB, OBE
Ross, *Lt.-Col.* Sir Walter Hugh
Malcolm, KCVO, OBE
Rosser, Sir Melvyn Wynne, Kt.
Rossi, Sir Hugh Alexis Louis, Kt.
Rotblat, *Prof.* Sir Joseph, KCMG, CBE,
FRS
Roth, *Prof.* Sir Martin, Kt., MD, FRCP
Rothschild, Sir Evelyn Robert
Adrian de, Kt.
Rougier, *Hon.* Sir Richard George,
Kt.
Rowell, Sir John Joseph, Kt., CBE
Rowland, *Air Marshal* Sir James
Anthony, KBE, DFC, AFC
Rowland, Sir (John) David, Kt.
Rowlands, *Air Marshal* Sir John
Samuel, GC, KBE

Rowley, Sir Charles Robert, Bt.
(1836) †(1786)
Rowlinson, *Prof.* Sir John Shipley,
Kt., FRS
Roxburgh, *Vice-Adm.* Sir John
Charles Young, KCB, CBE, DSO, DSC
Royden, Sir Christopher John, Bt.
(1905)
Rudd, Sir (Anthony) Nigel (Russell),
Kt.
Rudge, Sir Alan Walter, Kt., CBE, FRS
Rumbold, Sir Henry John Sebastian,
Bt. (1779)
Rumbold, Sir Jack Seddon, Kt.
Runchorelal, Sir (Udayan) Chinubhai
Madhowlal, Bt. (1913)
Runciman, *Hon.* Sir James Cochran
Stevenson (Sir Steven), Kt., CH
Rusby, *Vice-Adm.* Sir Cameron, KCB,
LVO
†Russell, Sir (Arthur) Mervyn, Bt.
(1812)
Russell, Sir Charles Dominic, Bt.
(1916)
Russell, *Hon.* Sir David Sturrock
West-, Kt.
Russell, Sir George, Kt., CBE
Russell, *Prof.* Sir Peter Edward
Lionel, Kt., D.Litt., FBA
Russell, Sir (Robert) Mark, KCMG
Russell, *Rt. Hon.* Sir (Thomas)
Patrick, Kt.
Rutter, Sir Frank William Eden, KBE
Rutter, *Prof.* Sir Michael Llewellyn,
Kt., CBE, MD, FRS
Ryan, Sir Derek Gerald, Bt. (1919)
Rycroft, Sir Richard John, Bt. (1784)
Ryrie, Sir William Sinclair, KCB
Sabola, *Hon.* Sir Joaquim Claudino
Gonsalves-, Kt.
Sachs, *Hon.* Sir Michael Alexander
Geddes, Kt.
Sainsbury, *Rt. Hon.* Sir Timothy Alan
Davan, Kt.
†St Aubyn, Sir William
Molesworth-, Bt. (1689)
†St George, Sir John Avenel Bligh, Bt.
(I. 1766)
St Johnston, Sir Kerry, Kt.
Sainty, Sir John Christopher, KCB
Salisbury, Sir Robert William, Kt.
Salt, Sir Patrick MacDonnell, Bt.
(1869)
Salt, Sir (Thomas) Michael John, Bt.
(1899)
Sampson, Sir Colin, Kt., CBE, QPM
Samuel, Sir John Michael Glen, Bt.
(1898)
Samuelson, Sir (Bernard) Michael
(Francis), Bt. (1884)
Samuelson, Sir Sydney Wylie, Kt.,
CBE
Sanders, Sir John Reynolds
Mayhew-, Kt.
Sanders, Sir Robert Tait, KBE, CMG
Sanderson, Sir Frank Linton, Bt.
(1920)
Sarei, Sir Alexis Holyweek, Kt., CBE
Sarell, Sir Roderick Francis Gisbert,
KCMG, KCVO

Saunders, *Hon.* Sir John Anthony
Holt, Kt., CBE, DSO, MC
Saunders, Sir Peter, Kt.
Savage, Sir Ernest Walter, Kt.
Savile, Sir James Wilson Vincent,
Kt., OBE
Say, *Rt. Revd* Richard David, KCVO
Schiemann, *Rt. Hon.* Sir Konrad
Hermann Theodor, Kt.
Scholar, Sir Michael Charles, KCB
Scholey, Sir David Gerald, Kt., CBE
Scholey, Sir Robert, Kt., CBE, FREng.
Scholtens, Sir James Henry, KCVO
Schreier, Sir Bernard, Kt.
Schubert, Sir Sydney, Kt.
Scipio, Sir Hudson Rupert, Kt.
Scoon, Sir Paul, GCMG, GCVO, OBE
Scott, Sir Anthony Percy, Bt. (1913)
Scott, Sir (Charles) Peter, KBE, CMG
Scott, Sir David Aubrey, GCMG
Scott, Sir Dominic James Maxwell-,
Bt. (1642)
Scott, Sir Ian Dixon, KCMG, KCVO,
CIE
Scott, Sir James Jervoise, Bt. (1962)
Scott, Sir Kenneth Bertram Adam,
KCVO, CMG
Scott, Sir Michael, KCVO, CMG
Scott, *Rt. Hon.* Sir Nicholas Paul, KBE
Scott, Sir Oliver Christopher
Anderson, Bt. (1909)
Scott, *Prof.* Sir Philip John, KBE
Scott, *Rt. Hon.* Sir Richard Rashleigh
Folliott, Kt.
Scott, Sir Robert David Hillyer, Kt.
Scott, Sir Walter John, Bt. (1907)
Scott, *Rear-Adm.* Sir (William) David
(Stewart), KBE, CB
Scowen, Sir Eric Frank, Kt., MD,
D.Sc., LL D, FRCP, FRCS
Seale, Sir Clarence David, Kt.
Seale, Sir John Henry, Bt. (1838)
Seaman, Sir Keith Douglas, KCVO,
OBE
Sebastian, Sir Cuthbert Montraville,
GCMG, OBE
†Sebright, Sir Peter Giles Vivian,
Bt. (1626)
Seccombe, Sir (William) Vernon
Stephen, Kt.
Secombe, Sir Harry Donald, Kt., CBE
Seconde, Sir Reginald Louis, KCMG,
CVO
Sedley, *Rt. Hon.* Sir Stephen John, Kt.
Seely, Sir Nigel Edward, Bt. (1896)
Seeto, Sir Ling James, Kt., MBE
Seeyave, Sir Rene Sow Choung, Kt.,
CBE
Seligman, Sir Peter Wendel, Kt.,
CBE
Sellors, Sir Patrick John Holmes-,
KCVO, FRCS
Semple, Sir John Laughlin, KCB
Sergeant, Sir Patrick, Kt.
Series, Sir (Joseph Michel) Emile,
Kt., CBE
Serota, Sir Nicholas Andrew, Kt.
Serpell, Sir David Radford, KCB, CMG,
OBE
†Seton, Sir Charles Wallace, Bt.

(S. 1683)

Seton, Sir Iain Bruce, Bt. (S. 1663)

Severne, *Air Vice-Marshal* Sir John de Milt, KCVO, OBE, AFC

†Seymour, Sir Michael Patrick Culme-, Bt. (1809)

Shackleton, *Prof.* Sir Nicholas John, Kt., Ph.D., FRS

Shakerley, Sir Geoffrey Adam, Bt. (1838)

Shakespeare, Sir Thomas William, Bt. (1942)

Shand, Sir James, Kt., MBE

Sharp, Sir Adrian, Bt. (1922)

Sharp, Sir George, Kt., OBE

Sharp, Sir Kenneth Johnston, Kt., TD

Sharp, Sir Leslie, Kt., QPM

Sharp, Sir Richard Lyall, KCVO, CB

Sharp, Sir Sheridan Christopher Robin, Bt. (1920)

Sharpe, *Hon.* Sir John Henry, Kt., CBE

Sharples, Sir James, Kt., QPM

Shattock, Sir Gordon, Kt.

Shaw, Sir Brian Piers, Kt.

Shaw, Sir (Charles) Barry, Kt., CB, QC

Shaw, Sir (George) Neville Bowman-, Kt.

Shaw, *Prof.* Sir John Calman, Kt., CBE, FRSE

Shaw, Sir (John) Giles (Dunkerley), Kt.

Shaw, Sir John Michael Robert Best-, Bt. (1665)

Shaw, Sir Neil McGowan, Kt.

Shaw, Sir Robert, Bt. (1821)

Shaw, Sir Roy, Kt.

Shaw, Sir Run Run, Kt., CBE

Sheehy, Sir Patrick, Kt.

Sheen, *Hon.* Sir Barry Cross, Kt.

Sheffield, Sir Reginald Adrian Berkeley, Bt. (1755)

Shehadie, Sir Nicholas Michael, Kt., OBE

Sheil, *Hon.* Sir John, Kt.

Sheldon, *Hon.* Sir (John) Gervase (Kensington), Kt.

Shelley, Sir John Richard, Bt. (1611)

Shelton, Sir William Jeremy Masefield, Kt.

Shepheard, Sir Peter Faulkner, Kt., CBE

Shepherd, Sir Colin Ryley, Kt.

Shepperd, Sir Alfred Joseph, Kt.

Sher, Sir Antony, KBE

Sherlock, Sir Philip Manderson, KBE

Sherman, Sir Alfred, Kt.

Sherman, Sir Louis, Kt., OBE

Shields, Sir Neil Stanley, Kt., MC

Shields, *Prof.* Sir Robert, Kt., MD

Shiffner, Sir Henry David, Bt. (1818)

Silber, *Rt. Hon.* Sir Stephen Robert, Kt.

Shillington, Sir (Robert Edward) Graham, Kt., CBE

Shinwell, Sir (Maurice) Adrian, Kt.

Shock, Sir Maurice, Kt.

Short, Sir Apenera Pera, KBE

Short, *Brig.* Sir Noel Edward Vivian, Kt., MBE, MC

Shuckburgh, Sir Rupert Charles

Gerald, Bt. (1660)

Siaguru, Sir Anthony Michael, KBE

Siddall, Sir Norman, Kt., CBE, FREng.

Sidey, *Air Marshal* Sir Ernest Shaw, KBE, CB, MD

Sieff, *Hon.* Sir David, Kt.

Simeon, Sir John Edmund Barrington, Bt. (1815)

Simmons, *Air Marshal* Sir Michael George, KCB, AFC

Simmons, Sir Stanley Clifford, Kt., FRCS, FRCOG

Simms, Sir Neville Ian, Kt., FREng.

Simonet, Sir Louis Marcel Pierre, Kt., CBE

Simpson, *Hon.* Sir Alfred Henry, Kt.

Simpson, *Lt.-Gen.* Sir Roderick Alexander Cordy-, KBE, CB

Simpson, Sir William James, Kt.

Sims, Sir Roger Edward, Kt.

Sinclair, Sir Clive Marles, Kt.

Sinclair, Sir George Evelyn, Kt., CMG, OBE

Sinclair, Sir Ian McTaggart, KCMG, QC

Sinclair, *Air Vice-Marshal* Sir Laurence Frank, GC, KCB, CBE, DSO

Sinclair, Sir Patrick Robert Richard, Bt. (S. 1704)

Sinden, Sir Donald Alfred, Kt., CBE

Singer, *Prof.* Sir Hans Wolfgang, Kt.

Singer, *Hon.* Sir Jan Peter, Kt.

Singh, *Hon.* Sir Vijay Raghubir, Kt.

Sitwell, Sir (Sacheverell) Reresby, Bt. (1808)

Skeet, Sir Trevor Herbert Harry, Kt.

Skeggs, Sir Clifford George, Kt.

Skehel, Sir John James, Kt., FRS

Skempton, *Prof.* Sir Alec Wesley, Kt.

Skingsley, *Air Chief Marshal* Sir Anthony Gerald, GBE, KCB

Skinner, Sir (Thomas) Keith (Hewitt), Bt. (1912)

Skipwith, Sir Patrick Alexander d'Estoteville, Bt. (1622)

Skyrme, Sir (William) Thomas (Charles), KCVO, CB, CBE, TD

Slack, Sir William Willatt, KCVO, FRCS

Slade, Sir Benjamin Julian Alfred, Bt. (1831)

Slade, *Rt. Hon.* Sir Christopher John, Kt.

Slaney, *Prof.* Sir Geoffrey, KBE

Slater, *Adm.* Sir John (Jock) Cunningham Kirkwood, GCB, LVO

Sleight, Sir Richard, Bt. (1920)

Sloan, Sir Andrew Kirkpatrick, Kt., QPM

Sloman, Sir Albert Edward, Kt., CBE

Smart, *Prof.* Sir George Algernon, Kt., MD, FRCP

Smart, Sir Jack, Kt., CBE

Smedley, *Hon.* Sir (Frank) Brian, Kt.

Smedley, Sir Harold, KCMG, MBE

Smiley, *Lt.-Col.* Sir John Philip, Bt. (1903)

Smith, Sir Alan, Kt., CBE, DFC

Smith, Sir Alexander Mair, Kt., Ph.D.

Smith, Sir Andrew Colin Hugh-, Kt.

Smith, *Lt.-Gen.* Sir Anthony Arthur

Denison-, KBE

Smith, Sir Charles Bracewell-, Bt. (1947)

Smith, Sir Christopher Sydney Winwood, Bt. (1809)

Smith, *Prof.* Sir Colin Stansfield, Kt., CBE

Smith, Sir Cyril, Kt., MBE

Smith, *Prof.* Sir David Cecil, Kt., FRS

Smith, *Air Chief Marshal* Sir David Harcourt-, GBE, KCB, DFC

Smith, Sir David Iser, KCVO

Smith, Sir Douglas Boucher, KCB

Smith, Sir Dudley (Gordon), Kt.

Smith, *Prof.* Sir Eric Brian, Kt., Ph.D.

Smith, *Maj.-Gen.* Sir (Francis) Brian Wyldbore-, Kt., CB, DSO, OBE

Smith, *Prof.* Sir Francis Graham-, Kt., FRS

Smith, Sir Geoffrey Johnson, Kt., MP

Smith, Sir Graham William, Kt., CBE

Smith, Sir John Alfred, Kt., QPM

Smith, *Prof.* Sir John Cyril, Kt., CBE, QC, FBA

Smith, Sir John Hamilton-Spencer-, Bt. (1804)

Smith, Sir John Jonah Walker-, Bt. (1960)

Smith, Sir John Lindsay Eric, Kt., CH, CBE

Smith, Sir John Rathbone Vassar-, Bt. (1917)

Smith, Sir Joseph William Grenville, Kt., MD, FRCP

Smith, Sir Leslie Edward George, Kt.

Smith, *Maj.-Gen.* Sir Michael Edward Carleton-, Kt., CBE

Smith, Sir Michael John Llewellyn, KCVO, CMG

Smith, *Rt. Hon.* Sir Murray Stuart-, Kt.

Smith, Sir (Norman) Brian, Kt., CBE, Ph.D.

Smith, Sir Peter Brierley, Kt., CBE

†Smith, Sir Peter Frank Graham Newson-, Bt. (1944)

Smith, Sir Raymond Horace, KBE

Smith, Sir Robert Courtney, Kt., CBE

Smith, Sir Robert Haldane, Kt

Smith, Sir Robert Hill, Bt., MP (1945)

Smith, *Prof.* Sir Roland, Kt.

Smith, *Air Marshal* Sir Roy David Austen-, KBE, CB, CVO, DFC

Smith, *Gen.* Sir Rupert Anthony, KCB, DSO, OBE, QGM

Smith, Sir (Thomas) Gilbert, Bt. (1897)

Smith, Sir (William) Antony (John) Reardon-, Bt. (1920)

Smith, Sir (William) Richard Prince-, Bt. (1911)

Smithers, Sir Peter Henry Berry Otway, Kt., VRD, D.Phil.

Smyth, Sir Thomas Weyland Bowyer-, Bt. (1661)

Smyth, Sir Timothy John, Bt. (1955)

Soakimori, Sir Frederick Pa-Nukuanca, KBE, CPM

Soame, Sir Charles John Buckworth-Herne-, Bt. (1697)

Sobers, Sir Garfield St Auburn, Kt.

Solomon, Sir Harry, Kt.

Somare, *Rt. Hon.* Sir Michael Thomas, GCMG, CH

Somers, *Rt. Hon.* Sir Edward Jonathan, Kt.

Somerville, *Brig.* Sir John Nicholas, Kt., CBE

Somerville, Sir Quentin Charles Somerville Agnew-, Bt. (1957)

Sorrell, Sir Martin Stuart, Kt.

Soulsby, Sir Peter Alfred, Kt.

Soutar, *Air Marshal* Sir Charles John Williamson, KBE

South, Sir Arthur, Kt.

Southby, Sir John Richard Bilbe, Bt. (1937)

Southern, Sir Richard William, Kt., FBA

Southgate, Sir Colin Grieve, Kt.

Southgate, Sir William David, Kt.

Southward, Sir Leonard Bingley, Kt., OBE

Southwood, *Prof.* Sir (Thomas) Richard (Edmund), Kt., FRS

Souyave, *Hon.* Sir (Louis) Georges, Kt.

Sowrey, *Air Marshal* Sir Frederick Beresford, KCB, CBE, AFC

Sparkes, Sir Robert Lyndley, Kt.

Sparrow, Sir John, Kt.

Spearman, Sir Alexander Young Richard Mainwaring, Bt. (1840)

Spedding, *Prof.* Sir Colin Raymond William, Kt., CBE

Spedding, Sir David Rolland, KCMG, CVO, OBE

Speed, Sir (Herbert) Keith, Kt., RD

Speelman, Sir Cornelis Jacob, Bt. (1686)

Speight, *Hon.* Sir Graham Davies, Kt.

Spencer, Sir Derek Harold, Kt., QC

Spicer, Sir James Wilton, Kt.

Spicer, Sir Nicholas Adrian Albert, Bt., MB (1906)

Spicer, Sir (William) Michael Hardy, Kt., MP

Spiers, Sir Donald Maurice, Kt., CB, TD

Spooner, Sir James Douglas, Kt.

Spotswood, *Marshal of the Royal Air Force* Sir Denis Frank, GCB, CBE, DSO, DFC

Spratt, *Col.* Sir Greville Douglas, GBE, TD

Spring, Sir Dryden Thomas, Kt.

Squire, *Air Chief Marshal* Sir Peter Ted, KCB, DFC, AFC

Stabb, *Hon.* Sir William Walter, Kt., QC

Stainton, Sir (John) Ross, Kt., CBE

Stakis, Sir Reo Argiros, Kt.

Stamer, Sir (Lovelace) Anthony, Bt. (1809)

Stanbridge, *Air Vice-Marshal* Sir Brian Gerald Tivy,KCVO, CBE, AFC

Standard, Sir Kenneth Livingstone, Kt., MD

Stanier, Sir Beville Douglas, Bt. (1917)

Stanier, *Field Marshal* Sir John Wilfred, GCB, MBE

Stanley, *Rt. Hon.* Sir John Paul, Kt., MP

Staples, Sir James (Gerald James Arland), Bt. (I. 1628)

Stark, Sir Andrew Alexander Steel, KCMG, CVO

Starkey, Sir John Philip, Bt. (1935)

Starrit, Sir James, KCVO

Statham, Sir Norman, KCMG, CVO

Staughton, *Rt. Hon.* Sir Christopher Stephen Thomas Jonathan Thayer, Kt.

Staveley, Sir John Malfroy, KBE, MC

Stear, *Air Chief Marshal* Sir Michael James Douglas, KCB, CBE

Steel, Sir David Edward Charles, Kt., DSO, MC, TD

Steel, *Hon.* Sir David William, Kt.

Steele, Sir (Philip John) Rupert, Kt.

Steere, Sir Ernest Henry Lee-, KBE

Stephen, *Rt. Hon.* Sir Ninian Martin, KG, GCMG, GCVO, KBE

Stephens, Sir (Edwin) Barrie, Kt.

Stephenson, Sir Henry Upton, Bt. (1936)

Sternberg, Sir Sigmund, Kt.

Stevens, Sir Jocelyn Edward Greville, Kt., CVO

Stevens, Sir John, Kt.

Stevens, Sir Laurence Houghton, Kt., CBE

Stevenson, *Vice-Adm.* Sir (Hugh) David, KBE

Stevenson, Sir Simpson, Kt.

Stewart, Sir Alan, KBE

Stewart, Sir Alan d'Arcy, Bt. (I. 1623)

Stewart, Sir David James Henderson-, Bt. (1957)

Stewart, Sir David John Christopher, Bt. (1803)

Stewart, Sir Edward Jackson, Kt.

Stewart, *Prof.* Sir Frederick Henry, Kt., Ph.D., FRS, FRSE

Stewart, Sir Houston Mark Shaw-, Bt., MC, TD (S. 1667)

Stewart, Sir James Douglas, Kt.

Stewart, Sir James Moray, KCB

Stewart, Sir (John) Simon (Watson), Bt. (1920)

Stewart, Sir Robertson Huntly, Kt., CBE

Stewart, Sir Robin Alastair, Bt. (1960)

Stewart, *Prof.* Sir William Duncan Paterson, Kt., FRS, FRSE

Stibbon, *Gen.* Sir John James, KCB, OBE

Stirling, Sir Alexander John Dickson, KBE, CMG

Stirling, Sir Angus Duncan Aeneas, Kt.

Stockdale, Sir Arthur Noel, Kt.

Stockdale, Sir Thomas Minshull, Bt. (1960)

Stoddart, *Wg Cdr.* Sir Kenneth Maxwell, KCVO, AE

Stoker, *Prof.* Sir Michael George Parke, Kt., CBE, FRCP, FRS, FRSE

Stokes, Sir John Heydon Romaine, Kt.

Stones, Sir William Frederick, Kt., OBE

Stonhouse, *Revd* Sir Michael Philip, Bt. (1628)

Stonor, *Air Marshal* Sir Thomas Henry, KCB

Stoppard, Sir Thomas, Kt., CBE, OB

Storey, *Hon.* Sir Richard, Bt., CBE (1960)

Stott, Sir Adrian George Ellingham, Bt. (1920)

Stoute, Sir Michael Ronald, Kt.

Stow, Sir Christopher Philipson-, Bt., DFC (1907)

Stowe, Sir Kenneth Ronald, GCB, CVO

Stracey, Sir John Simon, Bt. (1818)

Strachan, Sir Curtis Victor, Kt., CVO

Strachey, Sir Charles, Bt. (1801)

Strang Steel, Sir (Fiennes) Michael, Bt. (1938)

Strawson, *Prof.* Sir Peter Frederick, Kt., FBA

Street, *Hon.* Sir Laurence Whistler, KCMG

Streeton, Sir Terence George, KBE, CMG

Stringer, Sir Donald Edgar, Kt., CBE

Stringer, Sir Howard, Kt.

Strong, Sir Roy Colin, Kt., Ph.D., FSA

Stronge, Sir James Anselan Maxwell, Bt. (1803)

Stroud, *Prof.* Sir (Charles) Eric, Kt., FRCP

Strutt, Sir Nigel Edward, Kt.,TD

Stuart, Sir James Keith, Kt.

Stuart, Sir Kenneth Lamonte, Kt.

Stuart, Sir Mark Moody-, KCMG

†Stuart, Sir Phillip Luttrell, Bt. (1660)

Stubbs, Sir William Hamilton, Kt., Ph.D.

Stucley, *Lt.* Sir Hugh George Coplestone Bampfylde, Bt. (1859)

Studd, Sir Edward Fairfax, Bt. (1929)

Studd, Sir Peter Malden, GBE, KCVO

Studholme, Sir Henry William, Bt. (1956)

†Style, Sir William Frederick, Bt. (1627)

Sugar, Sir Alan Michael, Kt.

Sugden, Sir Arthur, Kt.

Sullivan, *Hon.* Sir Jeremy Mirth, Kt.

Sullivan, Sir Richard Arthur, Bt. (1804)

Sumner, *Hon.* Sir Christopher John, Kt.

Sutherland, Sir John Brewer, Bt. (1921)

Sutherland, Sir Maurice, Kt.

Sutherland, *Prof.* Sir Stewart Ross, Kt., FBA

Sutherland, Sir William George MacKenzie, Kt.

Suttie, Sir James Edward Grant-, Bt. (S. 1702)

Sutton, Sir Frederick Walter, Kt., OBE

Sutton, *Air Marshal* Sir John Matthias Dobson, KCB

Sutton, Sir Richard Lexington, Bt. (1772)

Swaffield, Sir James Chesebrough, Kt., CBE, RD

Swaine, Sir John Joseph, Kt., CBE

Swan, Sir Conrad Marshall John

Fisher, KCVO, Ph.D.
Swan, Sir John William David, KBE
Swann, Sir Michael Christopher, Bt., TD (1906)
Swanwick, Sir Graham Russell, Kt., MBE
Swartz, Hon. Sir Reginald William Colin, KBE, ED
Sweeney, Sir George, Kt.
Sweetnam, Sir (David) Rodney, KCVO, CBE, FRCS
Swinburn, Lt.-Gen. Sir Richard Hull, KCB
Swinson, Sir John Henry Alan, Kt., OBE
Swinton, Maj.-Gen. Sir John, KCVO, OBE
Swire, Sir Adrian Christopher, Kt.
Swire, Sir John Anthony, Kt., CBE
Swynnerton, Sir Roger John Massy, Kt., CMG, OBE, MC
Sykes, Sir Francis John Badcock, Bt. (1781)
Sykes, Sir Hugh Ridley, Kt.
Sykes, Sir John Charles Anthony le Gallais, Bt. (1921)
Sykes, Prof. Sir (Malcolm) Keith, Kt.
Sykes, Sir Richard, Kt.
Sykes, Sir Tatton Christopher Mark, Bt. (1783)
Symington, Prof. Sir Thomas, Kt., MD, FRSE
Symons, Vice-Adm. Sir Patrick Jeremy, KBE
Synge, Sir Robert Carson, Bt. (1801)
Synnott, Adm. Sir Anthony Monckton, KBE
Tait, Adm. Sir (Allan) Gordon, KCB, DSC
Talbot, Hon. Sir Hilary Gwynne, Kt.
Talboys, Rt. Hon. Sir Brian Edward, CH, KCB
Tancred, Sir Henry Lawson-, Bt. (1662)
Tangaroa, Hon. Sir Tangoroa, Kt., MBE
Tange, Sir Arthur Harold, Kt., CBE
Tapsell, Sir Peter Hannay Bailey, Kt., MP
Tate, Sir (Henry) Saxon, Bt. (1898)
Tavaiqia, Ratu Sir Josaia, KBE
Tavare, Sir John, Kt., CBE
Tavener, Prof. Sir John Kenneth, Kt.
Taylor, Lt.-Gen. Sir Allan Macnab, KBE, MC
Taylor, Sir (Arthur) Godfrey, Kt.
Taylor, Sir Cyril Julian Hebden, Kt.
Taylor, Sir Edward Macmillan (Teddy), Kt., MP
Taylor, Rt. Revd John Bernard, KCVO
Taylor, Sir John Lang, KCMG
Taylor, Sir Nicholas Richard Stuart, Bt. (1917)
Taylor, Prof. Sir William, Kt., CBE
Teagle, Vice-Adm. Sir Somerford Francis, KBE
Tebbit, Sir Donald Claude, GCMG
Telford, Sir Robert, Kt., CBE, FREng.
Temple, Sir Rawden John Afamado, Kt., CBE, QC
Temple, Maj. Sir Richard Anthony

Purbeck, Bt., MC (1876)
Templeton, Sir John Marks, Kt.
Tenison, Sir Richard Hanbury-, KCVO
Tennant, Sir Anthony John, Kt.
Tennant, Capt. Sir Iain Mark, KT
Teo, Sir Fiatau Penitala, GCMG, GCVO, ISO, MBE
Terry, Air Marshal Sir Colin George, KBE, CB
Terry, Sir Michael Edward Stanley Imbert-, Bt. (1917)
Terry, Air Chief Marshal Sir Peter David George, GCB, AFC
Tett, Sir Hugh Charles, Kt.
Thatcher, Sir Denis, Bt., MBE, TD (1990)
Thesiger, Sir Wilfred Patrick, KBE, DSO
Thomas, Sir Derek Morison David, KCMG
Thomas, Sir (Godfrey) Michael (David), Bt. (1694)
Thomas, Sir Jeremy Cashel, KCMG
Thomas, Sir (John) Alan, Kt.
Thomas, Sir John Maldwyn, Kt.
Thomas, Prof. Sir John Meurig, Kt., FRS
Thomas, Sir Keith Vivian, Kt.
Thomas, Sir Quentin Jeremy, Kt., CB
Thomas, Sir Robert Evan, Kt.
Thomas, Hon. Sir Roger John Laugharne, Kt.
Thomas, Hon. Sir Swinton Barclay, Kt.
Thomas, Sir William James Cooper, Bt., TD (1919)
Thomas, Sir (William) Michael (Marsh), Bt. (1918)
Thompson, Sir Christopher Peile, Bt. (1890)
Thompson, Sir Clive Malcolm, Kt.
Thompson, Sir Donald, Kt.
Thompson, Sir Gilbert Williamson, Kt., OBE
Thompson, Surgeon Vice-Adm. Sir Godfrey James Milton-, KBE
Thompson, Sir (Humphrey) Simon Meysey-, Bt. (1874)
Thompson, Prof. Sir Michael Warwick, Kt., D.Sc
Thompson, Sir Nicholas Annesley, Bt. (1963)
Thompson, Sir Paul Anthony, Bt. (1963)
Thompson, Sir Peter Anthony, Kt.
Thompson, Sir Thomas d'Eyncourt John, Bt. (1806)
Thomson, Sir (Frederick Douglas) David, Bt. (1929)
Thomson, Sir John Adam, GCMG
Thomson, Sir John (Ian) Sutherland, KBE, CMG
Thomson, Sir Mark Wilfrid Home, Bt. (1925)
Thomson, Sir Thomas James, Kt., CBE, FRCP
Thorn, Sir John Samuel, Kt., OBE
Thorne, Sir Neil Gordon, Kt., OBE, TD
Thorne, Sir Peter Francis, KCVO, CBE

Thornton, Sir (George) Malcolm, Kt.
Thornton, Sir Peter Eustace, KCB
Thornton, Sir Richard Eustace, KCVO, OBE
Thorold, Sir (Anthony) Oliver, Bt. (1642)
Thorpe, Hon. Sir Mathew Alexander, Kt.
Thouron, Sir John Rupert Hunt, KBE
Thwaites, Sir Bryan, Kt., Ph.D.
Tibbits, Capt. Sir David Stanley, Kt., DSC
Tickell, Sir Crispin Charles Cervantes, GCMG, KCVO
Tidbury, Sir Charles Henderson, Kt.
Tikaram, Sir Moti, KBE
Tilt, Sir Robin Richard, Kt.
Tims, Sir Michael David, KCVO
Tindle, Sir Ray Stanley, Kt., CBE
Tippet, Vice-Adm. Sir Anthony Sanders, KCB
†Tipping, Sir David Gwynne Evans-, Bt. (1913)
Tirvengadum, Sir Harry Krishnan, Kt.
Titman, Sir John Edward Powis, KCVO
Tod, Air Marshal Sir John Hunter Hunter-, KBE, CB
Tod, Vice-Adm. Sir Jonathan James Richard, KCB, CBE
Todd, Prof. Sir David, Kt., CBE
Todd, Sir Ian Pelham, KBE, FRCS
Todd, Hon. Sir (Reginald Stephen) Garfield, Kt.
Tollemache, Sir Lyonel Humphry John, Bt. (1793)
Tololo, Sir Alkan, KBE
Tomkins, Sir Edward Emile, GCMG, CVO
Tomkys, Sir (William) Roger, KCMG
Tomlinson, Prof. Sir Bernard Evans, Kt., CBE
Tomlinson, Hon. Sir Stephen Miles, Kt.
Tooley, Sir John, Kt.
Tooth, Sir (Hugh) John Lucas-, Bt. (1920)
ToRobert, Sir Henry Thomas, KBE
Tory, Sir Geofroy William, KCMG
Touche, Sir Anthony George, Bt. (1920)
Touche, Sir Rodney Gordon, Bt. (1962)
Toulson, Hon. Sir Roger Grenfell, Kt.
Tovey, Sir Brian John Maynard, KCMG
ToVue, Sir Ronald, Kt., OBE
Towneley, Sir Simon Peter Edmund Cosmo William, KCVO
Townsend, Sir Cyril David, Kt.
Traill, Sir Alan Towers, GBE
Trant, Gen. Sir Richard Brooking, KCB
Treacher, Adm. Sir John Devereux, KCB
Trehane, Sir (Walter) Richard, Kt.
Treitel, Prof. Sir Guenter Heinz, Kt., FBA, QC
Trelawny, Sir John Barry Salusbury-, Bt. (1628)

Trench, Sir Peter Edward, Kt., CBE, TD

Trescowthick, Sir Donald Henry, KBE

†Trevelyan, Sir Edward (Norman), Bt. (1662)

Trevelyan, Sir Geoffrey Washington, Bt. (1874)

Trewby, *Vice-Adm.* Sir (George Francis) Allan, KCB, FREng.

Trezise, Sir Kenneth Bruce, Kt., OBE

Trippier, Sir David Austin, Kt., RD

Tritton, Sir Anthony John Ernest, Bt. (1905)

Trollope, Sir Anthony Simon, Bt. (1642)

Trotter, Sir Neville Guthrie, Kt.

Trotter, Sir Ronald Ramsay, Kt.

Troubridge, Sir Thomas Richard, Bt. (1799)

Troup, *Vice-Adm.* Sir (John) Anthony (Rose), KCB, DSC

Trowbridge, *Rear-Adm.* Sir Richard John, KCVO

Truscott, Sir George James Irving, Bt. (1909)

Tsang, Sir Donald Yam-keun, KBE

Tuck, Sir Bruce Adolph Reginald, Bt. (1910)

Tucker, *Hon.* Sir Richard Howard, Kt.

Tuckey, *Hon.* Sir Simon Lane, Kt.

Tuita, Sir Mariano Kelesimalefo, Kt., OBE

Tuite, Sir Christopher Hugh, Bt., ph.D. (1622)

Tuivaga, Sir Timoci Uluiburotu, Kt.

Tuke, Sir Anthony Favill, Kt.

Tumim, *His Hon.* Sir Stephen, Kt.

Tupper, Sir Charles Hibbert, Bt. (1888)

Turbott, Sir Ian Graham, Kt., CMG, CVO

Turing, Sir John Dermot, Bt. (s. 1638)

Turnbull, Sir Andrew, KCB, CVO

Turner, Sir Colin William Carstairs, Kt., CBE, DFC

Turner, *Hon.* Sir Michael John, Kt.

Turnquest, Sir Orville Alton, GCMG, QC

Tuti, *Revd* Dudley, KBE

Tweedie, *Prof.* Sir David Philip, Kt.

Tyree, Sir (Alfred) William, Kt., OBE

Tyrwhitt, Sir Reginald Thomas Newman, Bt. (1919)

Unsworth, *Hon.* Sir Edgar Ignatius Godfrey, Kt., CMG

Unwin, Sir (James) Brian, KCB

Ure, Sir John Burns, KCMG, LVO

Urquhart, Sir Brian Edward, KCMG, MBE

Urwick, Sir Alan Bedford, KCVO, CMG

Usher, Sir Andrew John, Bt. (1899)

Usher, Sir Leonard Gray, KBE

Ustinov, Sir Peter Alexander, Kt., CBE

Utting, Sir William Benjamin, Kt., CB

Vai, Sir Mea, Kt., CBE, ISO

Vallance, Sir Iain David Thomas, Kt.

Vallat, Sir Francis Aimé, GBE, KCMG, QC

Vallings, *Vice-Adm.* Sir George

Montague Francis, KCB

Vanderfelt, Sir Robin Victor, KBE

Vane, Sir John Robert, Kt., D.Phil., D.Sc., FRS

Vasquez, Sir Alfred Joseph, Kt., CBE, QC

Vaughan, Sir Gerard Folliott, Kt., FRCP

Vavasour, Sir Eric Michael Joseph Marmaduke, Bt. (1828)

Veale, Sir Alan John Ralph, Kt., FREng.

Verco, Sir Walter John George, KCVO

Vereker, Sir John Michael Medlicott, KCB

†Verney, Sir John Sebastian, Bt. (1946)

Verney, *Hon.* Sir Lawrence John, Kt., TD

Verney, Sir Ralph Bruce, Bt., KBE (1818)

Vernon, Sir James, Kt., CBE

Vernon, Sir Nigel John Douglas, Bt. (1914)

Vernon, Sir (William) Michael, Kt.

Vestey, Sir (John) Derek, Bt. (1921)

Vial, Sir Kenneth Harold, Kt., CBE

Vickers, *Lt.-Gen.* Sir Richard Maurice Hilton, KCB, CVO, OBE

Vincent, Sir William Percy Maxwell, Bt. (1936)

Vinelott, *Hon.* Sir John Evelyn, Kt.

Vines, Sir William Joshua, Kt., CMG

von Schramek, Sir Eric Emil, Kt.

†Vyvyan, Sir Ralph Ferrers Alexander, Bt. (1645)

Waddell, Sir James Henderson, Kt., CB

Wade, *Prof.* Sir Henry William Rawson, Kt., QC, FBA

Wade, *Air Chief Marshal* Sir Ruthven Lowry, KCB, DFC

Waine, *Rt. Revd* John, KCVO

Waite, *Rt. Hon.* Sir John Douglas, Kt.

Wake, Sir Hereward, Bt., MC (1621)

Wakefield, Sir (Edward) Humphry (Tyrell), Bt. (1962)

Wakefield, Sir Norman Edward, Kt.

Wakefield, Sir Peter George Arthur, KBE, CMG

Wakeford, *Air Marshal* Sir Richard Gordon, KCB, OBE, LVO, AFC

Wakeley, Sir John Cecil Nicholson, Bt., FRCS (1952)

†Wakeman, Sir Edward Offley Bertram, Bt. (1828)

Wales, Sir Robert Andrew, Kt.

Walford, Sir Christopher Rupert, Kt.

Walker, *Revd* Sir Alan Edgar, Kt., OBE

Walker, *Gen.* Sir Antony Kenneth Frederick, KCB

Walker, Sir Baldwin Patrick, Bt. (1856)

Walker, Sir (Charles) Michael, GCMG

Walker, Sir David Alan, Kt.

Walker, Sir Gervas George, Kt.

Walker, Sir Harold Berners, KCMG

Walker, *Maj.* Sir Hugh Ronald, Bt. (1906)

Walker, Sir James Graham, Kt., MBE

Walker, Sir James Heron, Bt. (1868)

Walker, Sir John Ernest, Kt., D.Phil., FRS

Walker, *Air Marshal* Sir John Robert, KCB, CBE, AFC

Walker, *Gen.* Sir Michael John Dawson, GCB, CMG, CBE

Walker, Sir Michael Leolin Forestier-, Bt. (1835)

Walker, Sir Miles Rawstron, Kt., CBE

Walker, Sir Patrick Jeremy, KCB

Walker, *Rt. Hon.* Sir Robert, Kt.

Walker, Sir Rodney Myerscough, Kt.

Walker, *Hon.* Sir Timothy Edward, Kt.

Walker, *Gen.* Sir Walter Colyear, KCB, CBE, DSO

Wall, Sir John Anthony, Kt., CBE

Wall, Sir (John) Stephen, KCMG, LVO

Wall, *Hon.* Sir Nicholas Peter Rathbone, Kt.

Wall, Sir Robert William, Kt., OBE

Wallace, *Lt.-Gen.* Sir Christopher Brooke Quentin, KBE

Wallace, Sir Ian James, Kt., CBE

Waller, *Hon.* Sir (George) Mark, Kt.

Waller, Sir Robert William, Bt. (I. 1780)

Walley, Sir John, KBE, CB

Wallis, Sir Peter Gordon, KCVO

Wallis, Sir Timothy William, Kt.

Walmsley, *Vice-Adm.* Sir Robert, KCB

Walsh, *Prof.* Sir John Patrick, KBE

†Walsham, Sir Timothy John, Bt. (1831)

Walters, *Prof.* Sir Alan Arthur, Kt.

Walters, Sir Dennis Murray, Kt., MBE

Walters, Sir Frederick Donald, Kt.

Walters, Sir Peter Ingram, Kt.

Walters, Sir Roger Talbot, KBE, FRIBA

Wamiri, Sir Akapite, KBE

Wan, Sir Wamp, Kt., MBE

Wanstall, *Hon.* Sir Charles Gray, Kt.

Ward, *Rt. Hon.* Sir Alan Hylton, Kt.

Ward, Sir John Devereux, Kt., CBE

Ward, Sir Joseph James Laffey, Bt. (1911)

Ward, *Maj.-Gen.* Sir Philip John Newling, KCVO, CBE

Ward, Sir Timothy James, Kt.

Wardale, Sir Geoffrey Charles, KCB

Wardlaw, Sir Henry (John), Bt. (s. 1631)

Waring, Sir (Alfred) Holburt, Bt. (1935)

Warmington, Sir David Marshall, Bt. (1908)

Warner, Sir (Edward Courtenay) Henry, Bt. (1910)

Warner, Sir Edward Redston, KCMG, OBE

Warner, *Prof.* Sir Frederick Edward, Kt., FRS, FREng.

Warner, Sir Gerald Chierici, KCMG

Warner, *Hon.* Sir Jean-Pierre Frank Eugene, Kt.

Warren, Sir (Frederick) Miles, KBE

Warren, Sir Kenneth Robin, Kt.

†Warren, Sir Michael Blackley, Bt. (1784)

Wass, Sir Douglas William Gretton,

GCB
Waterhouse, *Hon.* Sir Ronald
  Gough, Kt.
Waterlow, Sir Christopher Rupert,
  Bt. (1873)
Waterlow, Sir (James) Gerard, Bt.
  (1930)
Waters, *Gen.* Sir (Charles) John, GCB,
  CBE
Waters, Sir (Thomas) Neil (Morris),
  Kt.
Wates, Sir Christopher Stephen, Kt.
Watkins, *Rt. Hon.* Sir Tasker, VC, GBE
Watson, Sir Andrew Michael Milne-,
  Bt. (1937)
Watson, Sir Bruce Dunstan, Kt.
Watson, *Prof.* Sir David John, Kt.,
  PH.D.
Watson, Sir (James) Andrew, Bt.
  (1866)
Watson, Sir John Forbes Inglefield-,
  Bt. (1895)
Watson, *Vice-Adm.* Sir Philip
  Alexander, KBE, LVO
Watson, Sir Ronald Matthew, Kt.,
  CBE
Watt, *Surgeon Vice-Adm.* Sir James,
  KBE, FRCS
Watt, Sir James Harvie-, Bt. (1945)
Watts, Sir John Augustus Fitzroy,
  KCMG, CBE
Watts, Sir Arthur Desmond, KCMG
Watts, *Lt.-Gen.* Sir John Peter Barry
  Condliffe, KBE, CB, MC
Wauchope, Sir Roger (Hamilton)
  Don-, Bt. (S. 1667)
Weatherall, *Prof.* Sir David John, Kt.,
  FRS
Weatherall, *Vice-Adm.* Sir James
  Lamb, KBE
Weatherstone, Sir Dennis, KBE
Weaver, Sir Tobias Rushton, Kt., CB
Webb, *Prof.* Sir Adrian Leonard, Kt.
Webb, Sir Thomas Langley, Kt.
Webster, *Very Revd* Alan Brunskill,
  KCVO
Webster, *Vice-Adm.* Sir John
  Morrison, KCB
Webster, *Hon.* Sir Peter Edlin, Kt.
Wedderburn, Sir Andrew John
  Alexander Ogilvy-, Bt. (1803)
Wedgwood, Sir (Hugo) Martin, Bt.
  (1942)
Weekes, Sir Everton DeCourcey,
  KCMG, OBE
Weinberg, Sir Mark Aubrey, Kt.
Weir, Sir Michael Scott, KCMG
Weir, Sir Roderick Bignell, Kt.
Welby, Sir (Richard) Bruno
  Gregory, Bt. (1801)
Welch, Sir John Kemp-, Kt.
Welch, Sir John Reader, Bt. (1957)
Weldon, Sir Anthony William, Bt.
  (I. 1723)
Weller, Sir Arthur Burton, Kt., CBE
Wellings, Sir Jack Alfred, Kt., CBE
†Wells, Sir Christopher Charles, Bt.
  (1944)
Wells, Sir John Julius, Kt.
Wells, Sir William Henry Weston,
  Kt., FRICS
West, *Vice-Adm.* Sir Alan William

John, KCB
Westbrook, Sir Neil Gowanloch,
  Kt., CBE
Westerman, Sir (Wilfred) Alan, Kt.,
  CBE
Weston, Sir Michael Charles Swift,
  KCMG, CVO
Weston, Sir (Philip) John, KCMG
Whalen, Sir Geoffrey Henry, Kt., CBE
Wheeler, Sir Harry Anthony, Kt.,
  OBE
Wheeler, *Air Chief Marshal* Sir
  (Henry) Neil (George), GCB, CBE,
  DSO, DFC, AFC
Wheeler, *Rt. Hon.* Sir John Daniel, Kt.
Wheeler, Sir John Hieron, Bt. (1920)
Wheeler, *Gen.* Sir Roger Neil, GCB,
  CBE
Wheler, Sir Edward Woodford, Bt.
  (1660)
Whent, Sir Gerald Arthur, Kt., CBE
Whishaw, Sir Charles Percival Law,
  Kt.
Whistler, Sir Alan Charles Laurence,
  Kt., CBE
Whitaker, Sir John James Ingham
  (Jack), Bt. (1936)
White, Sir Christopher Robert
  Meadows, Bt. (1937)
White, *Hon.* Sir Christopher Stuart
  Stuart-, Kt.
White, Sir David Harry, Kt.
White, Sir Frank John, Kt.
White, Sir George Stanley James, Bt.
  (1904)
White, *Wg Cdr.* Sir Henry Arthur
  Dalrymple-, Bt., DFC (1926)
White, *Adm.* Sir Hugo Moresby,
  GCB, CBE
White, *Hon.* Sir John Charles, Kt.,
  MBE
White, Sir John Woolmer, Bt. (1922)
White, Sir Lynton Stuart, Kt., MBE,
  TD
White, Sir Nicholas Peter Archibald,
  Bt. (1802)
White, *Adm.* Sir Peter, GBE
Whitehead, Sir John Stainton, GCMG,
  CVO
Whitehead, Sir Rowland John
  Rathbone, Bt. (1889)
Whiteley, Sir Hugo Baldwin
  Huntington-, Bt. (1918)
Whiteley, *Gen.* Sir Peter John
  Frederick, GCB, OBE, RM
Whitfield, Sir William, Kt., CBE
Whitford, *Hon.* Sir John Norman
  Keates, Kt.
Whitmore, Sir Clive Anthony, GCB,
  CVO
Whitmore, Sir John Henry Douglas,
  Bt. (1954)
Whitney, Sir Raymond William, Kt.,
  OBE, MP
Whittome, Sir (Leslie) Alan, Kt.
Wickerson, Sir John Michael, Kt.
Wicks, Sir Nigel Leonard, GCB, CVO,
  CBE
†Wigan, Sir Michael Iain, Bt. (1898)
Wiggin, Sir Alfred William (Jerry),
  Kt., TD
†Wiggin, Sir Charles Rupert John, Bt.

(1892)
Wigram, *Revd Canon* Sir Clifford
  Woolmer, Bt. (1805)
Wilbraham, Sir Richard Baker, Bt.
  (1776)
Wilford, Sir (Kenneth) Michael,
  GCMG
Wilkes, *Prof.* Sir Maurice Vincent,
  Kt.
Wilkes, *Gen.* Sir Michael John, KCB,
  CBE
Wilkins, Sir Graham John, Kt.
Wilkinson, Sir (David) Graham
  (Brook) Bt. (1941)
Wilkinson, *Prof.* Sir Denys Haigh,
  Kt., FRS
Wilkinson, Sir Philip William, Kt.
Willcocks, Sir David Valentine, Kt.,
  CBE, MC
Willcocks, *Lt.-Gen.* Sir Michael
  Alan, Kt., CB
Williams, Sir Alastair Edgcumbe
  James Dudley-, Bt. (1964)
Williams, Sir Alwyn, Kt., PH.D., FRS,
  FRSE
Williams, Sir Arthur Dennis Pitt, Kt.
Williams, Sir (Arthur) Gareth
  Ludovic Emrys Rhys, Bt. (1918)
Williams, *Prof.* Sir Bernard Arthur
  Owen, Kt., FBA
Williams, *Prof.* Sir Bruce Rodda, KBE
Williams, Sir Charles Othniel, Kt.
Williams, Sir Daniel Charles, GCMG,
  QC
Williams, *Adm.* Sir David, GCB
Williams, *Prof.* Sir David Glyndwr
  Tudor, Kt.
Williams, Sir David Innes, Kt.
Williams, Sir David Reeve, Kt., CBE
Williams, *Hon.* Sir Denys Ambrose,
  KCMG
Williams, Sir Donald Mark, Bt.
  (1866)
Williams, *Prof.* Sir (Edward) Dillwyn,
  Kt., FRCP
Williams, *Hon.* Sir Edward Stratten,
  KCMG, KBE
Williams, Sir Francis Owen Garbett,
  Kt., CBE
Williams, *Prof.* Sir Glanmor, Kt.,
  CBE, FBA
Williams, Sir Henry Sydney, Kt., OBE
Williams, Sir (John) Kyffin, Kt., OBE,
  DL, RA
Williams, Sir (Lawrence) Hugh, Bt.
  (1798)
Williams, Sir Leonard, KBE, CB
Williams, Sir Osmond, Bt., MC
  (1909)
Williams, Sir Peter Michael, Kt.
Williams, *Prof.* Sir Robert Evan
  Owen, Kt., MD, FRCP
Williams, Sir (Robert) Philip
  Nathaniel, Bt. (1915)
Williams, Sir Robin Philip, Bt.
  (1953)
Williams, Sir (William) Maxwell
  (Harries), Kt.
Williamson, *Marshal of the Royal Air
  Force* Sir Keith Alec, GCB, AFC
Williamson, Sir (Nicholas Frederick)
  Hedworth, Bt. (1642)

Dames Grand Cross and Dames Commanders

Style, 'Dame' before forename and surname, followed by appropriate post-nominal initials. Where such an award is made to a lady already in enjoyment of a higher title, the appropriate initials follow her name
Husband, Untitled
For forms of address, *see* page 135

Dame Grand Cross and Dame Commander are the higher classes for women of the Order of the Bath, the Order of

St Michael and St George, the Royal Victorian Order, and the Order of the British Empire. Dames Grand Cross rank after the wives of Baronets and before the wives of Knights Grand Cross. Dames Commanders rank after the wives of Knights Grand Cross and before the wives of Knights Commanders.

Honorary Dames Commanders may be conferred on women who are citizens of countries of which The Queen is not head of state.

LIST OF DAMES
Revised to 31 August 2000

Women peers in their own right and life peers are not included in this list. Female members of the royal family are not included in this list; details of the orders they hold are given on pages 117–18

If a dame has a double barrelled or hyphenated surname, she is listed under the final element of the name.

A full entry in italic type indicates that the recipient of an honour died during the year in which the honour was conferred. The name is included for the purposes of record

Abaijah, Dame Josephine, DBE
Abel Smith, Lady, DCVO
Abergavenny, The Marchioness of, DCVO
Airlie, The Countess of, DCVO
Albemarle, The Countess of, DBE
Anderson, *Brig. Hon.* Dame Mary Mackenzie (Mrs Pihl), DBE
Andrews, Dame Julie, DBE
Anglesey, The Marchioness of, DBE
Anson, Lady (Elizabeth Audrey), DBE
Anstee, Dame Margaret Joan, DCMG
Arden, *Hon.* Dame Mary Howarth (Mrs Mance), DBE
Bainbridge, Dame Beryl, DBE
Baker, Dame Janet Abbott (Mrs Shelley), CH, DBE
Ballin, Dame Reubina Ann, DBE
Barrow, Dame Jocelyn Anita (Mrs Downer), DBE
Barstow, Dame Josephine Clare (Mrs Anderson), DBE
Basset, Lady Elizabeth, DCVO
Bassey, Dame Shirley, DBE
Bean, Dame Majorie Louise, DBE
Beaurepaire, Dame Beryl Edith, DBE
Beer, *Prof.* Dame Gillian Patricia Kempster, DBE, FBA
Bergquist, *Prof.* Dame Patricia Rose, DBE
Berry, Dame Alice Miriam, DBE
Bewley, Dame Beulah Rosemary, DBE
Black, *Hon.* Dame Jill Margaret, DBE
Blaize, Dame Venetia Ursula, DBE
Blaxland, Dame Helen Frances, DBE
Booth, *Hon.* Dame Margaret Myfanwy Wood, DBE
Bowman, Dame (Mary) Elaine Kellett, DBE

Bowtell, Dame Ann Elizabeth, DCB
Boyd, Dame Vivienne Myra, DBE
Bracewell, *Hon.* Dame Joyanne Winifred (Mrs Copeland), DBE
Brain, Dame Margaret Anne (Mrs Wheeler), DBE
Brazill, Dame Josephine (Sister Mary Philippa), DBE
Bridges, Dame Mary Patricia, DBE
Browne, Lady Moyra Blanche Madeleine, DBE
Bryans, Dame Anne Margaret, DBE
Buttfield, Dame Nancy Eileen, DBE
Byatt, Dame Antonia Susan, DBE, FRSL
Bynoe, Dame Hilda Louisa, DBE
Caldicott, Dame Fiona, DBE, FRCP, FRCPsych.
Cartwright, Dame Silvia Rose, DBE
Casey, Dame Stella Katherine, DBE
Charles, Dame (Mary) Eugenia, DBE
Chesterton, Dame Elizabeth Ursula, DBE
Clark, *Prof.* Dame Jill MacLeod, DBE
Clark, *Prof.* Dame (Margaret) June, DBE, Ph.D.
Collins, Dame Diana Clavering, DBE
Clay, Dame Marie Mildred, DBE
Clayton, Dame Barbara Evelyn (Mrs Klyne), DBE
Cleland, Dame Rachel, DBE
Coll, Dame Elizabeth Anne Loosemore Esteve-, DBE
Collarbone, Dame Patricia, DBE
Corsar, The Hon. Dame Mary Drummond, DBE
Daws, Dame Joyce Margaretta, DBE
Dell, Dame Miriam Patricia, DBE
Dench, Dame Judith Olivia (Mrs Williams), DBE
Descartes, Dame Marie Selipha Sesenne, BEM
de Valois, Dame Ninette, OM, CH, DBE
Devonshire, The Duchess of, DCVO
Digby, Lady, DBE
Donaldson, Dame (Dorothy) Mary (Lady Donaldson of Lymington), GBE
Duffield, Dame Vivien Louise, DBE, CBE
Dugdale, Kathryn, Lady, DCVO
Dumont, Dame Ivy Leona, DCMG
Dyche, Dame Rachael Mary, DBE
Ebsworth, *Hon.* Dame Ann Marian, DBE

Engel, Dame Pauline Frances (Sister Pauline Engel), DBE
Evans, Dame Anne Elizabeth Jane, DBE
Evans, Dame Lois Marie Browne-, DBE
Evison, Dame Helen June Patricia, DBE
Fenner, Dame Peggy Edith, DBE
Fielding, Dame Pauline, DBE
Fitton, Dame Doris Alice (Mrs Mason), DBE
Fort, Dame Maeve Geraldine, DCMG, DCVO
Fraser, Dame Dorothy Rita, DBE
Friend, Dame Phyllis Muriel, DBE
Fritchie, Dame Irene Tordoff (Dame Rennie Fritchie), DBE
Frost, Dame Phyllis Irene, DBE
Fry, Dame Margaret Louise, DBE
Gallagher, Dame Monica Josephine, DBE
Gardiner, Dame Helen Louisa, DBE, MVO
Giles, *Air Comdt.* Dame Pauline (Mrs Parsons), DBE, RRC
Goodman, Dame Barbara, DBE
Gordon, Dame Minita Elmira, GCMG, GCVO
Gow, Dame Jane Elizabeth (Mrs Whiteley), DBE
Grafton, The Duchess of, GCVO
Grant, Dame Mavis, DBE
Green, Dame Mary Georgina, DBE
Grey, Dame Beryl Elizabeth (Mrs Svenson), DBE
Grimthorpe, The Lady, DCVO
Guilfoyle, Dame Margaret Georgina Constance, DBE
Guthardt, *Revd Dr* Dame Phyllis Myra, DBE
Haig, Dame Mary Alison Glen-, DBE
Hale, *Hon.* Dame Brenda Marjorie (Mrs Farrand), DBE
Hallett, Dame Heather Carol, DBE, QC
Harper, Dame Elizabeth Margaret Way, DBE
Heilbron, *Hon.* Dame Rose, DBE
Herbison, Dame Jean Marjory, DBE, CMG
Hercus, *Hon.* Dame (Margaret) Ann, DCMG
Higgins, *Prof.* Dame Rosalyn, DBE, QC
Hill, *Air Cdre* Dame Felicity Barbara, DBE
Hiller, Dame Wendy (Mrs Gow), DBE
Hine, Dame Deirdre Joan, DBE, FRCP

Hird, Dame Thora (Mrs Scott), DBE
Hogg, *Hon.* Dame Mary Claire
(Mrs Koops), DBE
Hunter, Dame Pamela, DBE
Hurley, *Prof.* Dame Rosalinde
(Mrs Gortvai), DBE
Hussey, Lady Susan Katharine (Lady
Hussey of North Bradley), DCVO
Imison, Dame Tamsyn, DBE
Isaacs, Dame Albertha Madeline, DBE
James, Dame Naomi Christine
(Mrs Haythorne), DBE
Jenkins, Dame (Mary) Jennifer (Lady
Jenkins of Hillhead), DBE
Jones, Dame Gwyneth (Mrs Haberfeld-
Jones), DBE
Jones, Dame (Lilian) Pauline Neville-,
DCMG
Keegan, Dame Geraldine Mary
Marcella, DBE, OBE
Kekedo, Dame Rosalina Violet, DBE
Kelleher, Dame Joan, DBE
Kelly, Dame Lorna May Boreland, DBE
Kershaw, Dame Janet Elizabeth
Murray (Dame Betty), DBE
Kettlewell, *Comdt.* Dame Marion
Mildred, DBE
Kilpatrick, Dame Judith Ann Gladys,
DBE
Kirby, Dame Georgina Kamiria, DBE
Kirk, Dame (Lucy) Ruth, DBE
Kramer, *Prof.* Dame Leonie Judith, DBE
Laine, Dame Cleo (Clementine) Dinah
(Mrs Dankworth), DBE
Lamb, Dame Dawn Ruth, DBE
Lewis, Dame Edna Leofrida (Lady
Lewis), DBE
Litchfield, Dame Ruby Beatrice, DBE
Lott, Dame Felicity Ann Emwhyla
(Mrs Woolf), DBE
Lowrey, *Air Comdt.* Dame Alice, DBE,
RRC
Lympany, Dame Moura, DBE
Lynn, Dame Vera (Mrs Lewis), DBE
Mackinnon, Dame (Una) Patricia, DBE
McLaren, Dame Anne Laura, DBE,
FRCOG, FRS
Macmillan of Ovenden, Katharine,
Viscountess, DBE
Major, Dame Malvina Lorraine
(Mrs Fleming), DBE
Major, Dame Norma Christina
Elizabeth, DBE
Markova, Dame Alicia, DBE
Martin, Rosamund Mary Holland-,
Lady, DBE
Metcalf, Dame Helen, DBE
Metge, *Dr* Dame (Alice) Joan, DBE
Middleton, Dame Elaine Madoline,
DCMG, MBE
Miller, Dame Mary Elizabeth Hedley-,
DCVO, CB
Mills, Dame Barbara Jean Lyon, DBE,
QC
Mitchell, Dame Mona, DCVO
Moores, Dame Yvonne, DBE
Morrison, *Hon.* Dame Mary Anne,
DCVO
Mueller, Dame Anne Elisabeth, DCB

Muirhead, Dame Lorna Elizabeth Fox,
DBE
Muldoon, Thea Dale, Lady, DBE, QSO
Mumford, Lady Mary Katharine,
DCVO
Munro, Dame Alison, DBE
Murdoch, Dame Elisabeth Joy, DBE
Murray, Dame (Alice) Rosemary, DBE,
D.Phil.
Ogilvie, Dame Bridget Margaret, DBE,
Ph.D., D.Sc.
Oliver, Dame Gillian Frances, DBE
Ollerenshaw, Dame Kathleen Mary,
DBE, D.Phil.
Oxenbury, Dame Shirley Anne, DBE
Park, Dame Merle Florence
(Mrs Bloch), DBE
Paterson, Dame Betty Fraser Ross, DBE
Peake, *Air Cdre* Dame Felicity Hyde,
DBE, AE
Penhaligon, Dame Annette
(Mrs Egerton), DBE
Peters, Dame Mary Elizabeth, DBE,
CBE
Plowden, The Lady, DBE
Poole, Dame Avril Anne Barker, DBE
Porter, Dame Shirley (Lady Porter),
DBE
Prendergast, Dame Simone Ruth, DBE
Prentice, Dame Winifred Eva, DBE
Preston, Dame Frances Olivia
Campbell-, DCVO
Price, Dame Margaret Berenice, DBE
Purves, Dame Daphne Helen, DBE
Pyke, Lady, DBE
Quinn, Dame Sheila Margaret Imelda,
DBE
Rafferty, *Hon.* Anne Judith, DBE
Railton, Dame Ruth (Mrs King), DBE
Rankin, Lady Jean Margaret Florence,
DCVO
Reeves, Dame Helen May, DBE
Riddelsdell, Dame Mildred, DCB, CBE
Ridley, Dame (Mildred) Betty, DBE
Ridsdale, Dame Victoire Evelyn
Patricia (Lady Ridsdale), DBE
Rigg, Dame Diana, DBE
Rimington, Dame Stella, DCB
Robertson, *Comdt.* Dame Nancy
Margaret, DBE
Robottom, Dame Marlene, DBE
Roe, Dame Raigh Edith, DBE
Rothschild, Hon. Dame Miriam
Louisa, DBE, FRS
Rue, Dame (Elsie) Rosemary, DBE
Rumbold, *Rt. Hon.* Dame Angela Claire
Rosemary, DBE
Runciman of Doxford, The
Viscountess, DBE
Salas, Dame Margaret Laurence, DBE
Salmond, *Prof.* Dame Mary Anne, DBE
Saunders, Dame Cicely Mary Strode,
OM, DBE, FRCP
Sawyer, *Hon.* Dame Joan Augusta, DBE
Schwarzkopf, Dame Elisabeth
Friederike Marie Olga Legge-, DBE
Scott, Dame Jean Mary Monica
Maxwell-, DCVO

Seward, Dame Margaret Helen
Elizabeth, DBE
Shenfield, Dame Barbara Estelle, DBE
Sherlock, *Prof.* Dame Sheila Patricia
Violet, DBE, MD, FRCP
Shirley, Dame Stephanie, DBE
Shovelton, Dame Helena, DBE
Sibley, Dame Antoinette
(Mrs Corbett), DBE
Sloss, *Rt. Hon.* Dame (Ann) Elizabeth
(Oldfield) Butler-, DBE
Smieton, Dame Mary Guillan, DBE
Smith, *Hon.* Dame Janet Hilary
(Mrs Mathieson), DBE
Smith, Dame Margaret Natalie
(Maggie) (Mrs Cross), DBE
Smith, Dame Margot, DBE
Soames, Mary, Lady, DBE
Southgate, Prof. Dame Lesley Jill, DBE
Spark, Dame Muriel Sarah, DBE
Spencer, Dame Rosemary Jane, DCMG
Steel, *Hon.* Dame (Anne) Heather
(Mrs Beattie), DBE
Stephens, *Air Cmdt.* Dame Anne, DBE
Stewart, Dame Muriel Acadia, DBE
Strachan, Dame Valerie Patricia Marie,
DCB
Sutherland, Dame Joan (Mrs Bonynge),
OM, DBE
Sutherland, Dame Veronica Evelyn,
DBE, CMG
Szaszy, Dame Miraka Petricevich, DBE
Taylor, Dame Elizabeth, DBE
Taylor, Dame Jean Elizabeth, DCVO
Te Atairangikaahu, Te Arikinui, Dame,
DBE
Te Kanawa, Dame Kiri Janette, DBE
Thomas, Dame Maureen Elizabeth
(Lady Thomas), DBE
Thorneycroft, Carla, Lady, DBE
Tinson, Dame Sue, DBE
Tizard, Dame Catherine Anne, GCMG,
GCVO, DBE
Tokiel, Dame Rosa, DBE
Tutin, Dame Dorothy, DBE
Uprichard, Dame Mary Elizabeth, DBE
Uvarov, Dame Olga, DBE
Varley, Dame Joan Fleetwood, DBE
Wagner, Dame Gillian Mary Millicent
(Lady Wagner), DBE
Wall, (Alice) Anne, (Mrs Michael
Wall), DCVO
Warburton, Dame Anne Marion,
DCVO, CMG
Warwick, Dame Margaret Elizabeth
Harvey Turner-, DBE, FRCP,
FRCPEd.
Waterhouse, Dame Rachel Elizabeth,
DBE, Ph.D.
Webb, Prof. Dame Patricia, DBE
Weir, Dame Gillian Constance
(Mrs Phelps), DBE
Weston, Dame Margaret Kate, DBE
Williamson, Dame (Elsie) Marjorie,
DBE, Ph.D.
Winstone, Dame Dorothy Gertrude,
DBE, CMG
Wong Yick-ming, Dame Rosanna, DBE

Decorations and Medals

PRINCIPAL DECORATIONS AND MEDALS
In order of precedence

VICTORIA CROSS (VC), 1856 (*see* page 208)
GEORGE CROSS (GC), 1940 (*see* pages 208–9)
BRITISH ORDERS OF KNIGHTHOOD AND DISTINGUISHED
SERVICE ORDER.

Baronet's Badge
Knight Bachelor's Badge

DECORATIONS

Conspicuous Gallantry Cross (CGC), 1995
Royal Red Cross Class I (RRC), 1883
Distinguished Service Cross (DSC), 1914. For all ranks for
actions at sea
Military Cross (MC), December 1914. For all ranks for
actions on land
Distinguished Flying Cross (DFC), 1918. For all ranks for acts
of gallantry when flying in active operations against the
enemy
Air Force Cross (AFC), 1918. For all ranks for acts of courage
when flying, although not in active operations against the
enemy
Royal Red Cross Class II (ARRC)
Order of British India
Kaisar-i-Hind Medal
Order of St John

MEDALS FOR GALLANTRY AND DISTINGUISHED
CONDUCT

Union of South Africa Queen's Medal for Bravery, in Gold
Distinguished Conduct Medal (DCM), 1854
Conspicuous Gallantry Medal (CGM), 1874
Conspicuous Gallantry Medal (Flying)
George Medal (GM), 1940
Queen's Police Medal for Gallantry
Queen's Fire Service Medal for Gallantry
Royal West African Frontier Force Distinguished Conduct Medal
King's African Rifles Distinguished Conduct Medal
Indian Distinguished Service Medal
Union of South Africa Queen's Medal for Bravery, in Silver
Distinguished Service Medal (DSM), 1914
Military Medal (MM), 1916
Distinguished Flying Medal (DFM), 1918
Air Force Medal (AFM)
Constabulary Medal (Ireland)
Medal for Saving Life at Sea
Sea Gallantry Medal
Indian Order of Merit (Civil)
Indian Police Medal for Gallantry
Ceylon Police Medal for Gallantry
Sierra Leone Police Medal for Gallantry
Sierra Leone Fire Brigades Medal for Gallantry
Colonial Police Medal for Gallantry (CPM)
Queen's Gallantry Medal (QGM), 1974
Royal Victorian Medal (RVM), Gold, Silver and Bronze
British Empire Medal (BEM), (formerly the Medal of the Order
of the British Empire, for Meritorious Service; also includes
the Medal of the Order awarded before 29 December 1922)
Canada Medal
*Queen's Police (QPM) and Queen's Fire Service Medals (QFSM)
for Distinguished Service*
Queen's Volunteer Reserves Medal
Queen's Medal for Chiefs

WAR MEDALS AND STARS (in order of date)

Polar Medals (in order of date)

POLICE MEDALS FOR VALUABLE SERVICE

JUBILEE, CORONATION AND DURBAR MEDALS

*King George V, King George VI and Queen Elizabeth II Long and
Faithful Service Medals*

EFFICIENCY AND LONG SERVICE DECORATIONS AND
MEDALS

Medal for Meritorious Service
Accumulated Campaign Service Medal
The Medal for Long Service and Good Conduct (Military)
Naval Long Service and Good Conduct Medal
Royal Marines Meritorious Service Medal
Royal Air Force Meritorious Service Medal
Royal Air Force Long Service and Good Conduct Medal
*Medal for Long Service and Good Conduct (Ulster Defence
Regiment)*
Police Long Service and Good Conduct Medal
Fire Brigade Long Service and Good Conduct Medal
Colonial Police and Fire Brigades Long Service Medals
Colonial Prison Service Medal
Hong Kong Disciplined Services Medal
Army Emergency Reserve Decoration (ERD), 1952
Volunteer Officers' Decoration (VD)
Volunteer Long Service Medal
Volunteer Officers' Decoration for India and the Colonies
Volunteer Long Service Medal for India and the Colonies
Colonial Auxiliary Forces Officers' Decoration
Colonial Auxiliary Forces Long Service Medal
Medal for Good Shooting (Naval)
Militia Long Service Medal
Imperial Yeomanry Long Service Medal
Territorial Decoration (TD), 1908
Efficiency Decoration (ED)
Territorial Efficiency Medal
Efficiency Medal
Special Reserve Long Service and Good Conduct Medal
Decoration for Officers, Royal Navy Reserve (RD), 1910
Decoration for Officers, RNVR (VRD)
Royal Naval Reserve Long Service and Good Conduct Medal
RNVR Long Service and Good Conduct Medal
*Royal Naval Auxiliary Sick Berth Reserve Long Service and Good
Conduct Medal*
Royal Fleet Reserve Long Service and Good Conduct Medal
*Royal Naval Wireless Auxiliary Reserve Long Service and Good
Conduct Medal*
Air Efficiency Award (AE), 1942
Volunteer Reserves Service Medal
Ulster Defence Regiment Medal
Northern Ireland Home Service Medal
The Queen's Medal. For champion shots in the RN, RM,
RNZN, Army, RAF
Cadet Forces Medal, 1950
Coastguard Auxiliary Service Long Service Medal (formerly Coast
Life Saving Corps Service Medal)
Special Constabulary Long Service Medal
Royal Observer Corps Medal
Civil Defence Long Service Medal
*Ambulance Service (Emergency Duties) Long Service and Good
Conduct Medal*
Rhodesia Medal
Royal Ulster Constabulary Service Medal
Service Medal of the Order of St John
Badge of the Order of the League of Mercy
Voluntary Medical Service Medal, 1932
Women's Voluntary Service Medal
Colonial Special Constabulary Medal

FOREIGN ORDERS, DECORATIONS AND MEDALS
(IN ORDER OF DATE)

THE VICTORIA CROSS (1856)
FOR CONSPICUOUS BRAVERY

VC

Ribbon, Crimson, for all Services (until 1918 it was blue for the Royal Navy)

Instituted on 29 January 1856, the Victoria Cross was awarded retrospectively to 1854, the first being held by Lt. C. D. Lucas, RN, for bravery in the Baltic Sea on 21 June 1854 (gazetted 24 February 1857). The first 62 Crosses were presented by Queen Victoria in Hyde Park, London, on 26 June 1857.

The Victoria Cross is worn before all other decorations, on the left breast, and consists of a cross-pattée of bronze, one and a half inches in diameter, with the Royal Crown surmounted by a lion in the centre, and beneath there is the inscription *For Valour*. Holders of the VC receive a tax-free annuity of £1,300, irrespective of need or other conditions. In 1911, the right to receive the Cross was extended to Indian soldiers, and in 1920 to matrons, sisters and nurses, and the staff of the Nursing Services and other services pertaining to hospitals and nursing, and to civilians of either sex regularly or temporarily under the orders, direction or supervision of the naval, military, or air forces of the Crown.

SURVIVING RECIPIENTS OF THE VICTORIA CROSS
as at 31 August 2000

Agansing Rai, *Capt.*, MM (5th Royal Gurkha Rifles)
1944 *World War*
Annand, *Capt.* R. W. (Durham Light Infantry)
1940 *World War*
Bhan Bhagta Gurung, *Havildar* (2nd Gurkha Rifles)
1945 *World War*
Bhandari Ram, *Capt.* (10th Baluch Regiment)
1944 *World War*
Chapman, *Sgt.* E. T., BEM (Monmouthshire Regiment)
1945 *World War*
Cruickshank, *Flt. Lt.* J. A. (RAFVR)
1944 *World War*
Cutler, *Capt.* Sir Roden, AK, KCMG, KCVO, CBE (Australian Military Forces, 2/5th Field Artillery)
1941 *World War*
Fraser, *Lt.-Cdr.* I. E., DSC (RNR)
1945 *World War*
Ganju Lama, *Capt.*, MM (7th Gurkha Rifles)
1944 *World War*
Gardner, *Capt.* P. J., MC (Royal Tank Regiment)
1941 *World War*
Gould, *Lt.* T. W. (RN)
1942 *World War*
Jamieson, *Maj.* D. A., CVO (Royal Norfolk Regiment)
1944 *World War*
Kenna, *Pte.* E. (Australian Military Forces, 2/4th (NSW))
1945 *World War*
Kenneally, *Guardsman* J. P. (Irish Guards)
1943 *World War*
Lachhiman Gurung, *Havildar* (8th Gurkha Rifles)
1945 *World War*
Merritt, *Lt.-Col.* C. C. I., CD (South Saskatchewan Regiment)
1942 *World War*

Norton, *Capt.* G. R., MM (South African Forces, Kaffrarian Rifles)
1944 *World War*
Payne, *WO* K., DSC (USA) (Australian Army Training Team)
1969 *Vietnam*
Porteous, *Col.* P. A. (Royal Regiment of Artillery)
1942 *World War*
Rambahadur Limbu, *Capt.*, MVO (10th Princess Mary's Gurkha Rifles)
1965 *Sarawak*
Reid, *Flt. Lt.* W. (RAFVR)
1943 *World War*
Smith, *Sgt.* E. A., CD (Seaforth Highlanders of Canada)
1944 *World War*
Speakman-Pitts, *Sgt.* W. (Black Watch, attached KOSB)
1951 *Korea*
Tulbahadur Pun, *Lt.* (6th Gurkha Rifles)
1944 *World War*
Umrao Singh, *Sub Major* (Royal Indian Artillery)
1944 *World War*
Watkins, *Maj. Rt. Hon.* Sir Tasker, GBE (Welch Regiment)
1944 *World War*
Wilson, *Lt.-Col.* E. C. T. (East Surrey Regiment)
1940 *World War*

THE GEORGE CROSS (1940)
FOR GALLANTRY

GC

Ribbon, Dark blue, threaded through a bar adorned with laurel leaves

Instituted 24 September 1940 (with amendments, 3 November 1942)

The George Cross is worn before all other decorations (except the VC) on the left breast (when worn by a woman it may be worn on the left shoulder from a ribbon of the same width and colour fashioned into a bow). It consists of a plain silver cross with four equal limbs, the cross having in the centre a circular medallion bearing a design showing St George and the Dragon. The inscription *For Gallantry* appears round the medallion and in the angle of each limb of the cross is the Royal cypher 'G VI' forming a circle concentric with the medallion. The reverse is plain and bears the name of the recipient and the date of the award. The cross is suspended by a ring from a bar adorned with laurel leaves on dark blue ribbon one and a half inches wide.

The cross is intended primarily for civilians; awards to the fighting services are confined to actions for which purely military honours are not normally granted. It is awarded only for acts of the greatest heroism or of the most conspicuous courage in circumstances of extreme danger. From 1 April 1965, holders of the Cross have received a tax-free annuity, which is now £1,300. The cross has twice been awarded collectively rather than to an individual: to Malta (1942) and the Royal Ulster Constabulary (1999).

The royal warrant which ordained that the grant of the Empire Gallantry Medal should cease authorised holders of that medal to return it to the Central Chancery of the Orders of Knighthood and to receive in exchange the George Cross. A similar provision applied to posthumous awards of the Empire Gallantry Medal made after the outbreak of war in 1939. In October 1971 all surviving holders of the Albert Medal and the Edward Medal exchanged those decorations for the George Cross.

SURVIVING RECIPIENTS OF THE GEORGE CROSS
as at 31 August 2000

If the recipient originally received the Empire Gallantry Medal (EGM), the Albert Medal (AM) or the Edward Medal (EM), this is indicated by the initials in parenthesis.

Archer, *Col.* B. S. T., GC, OBE, ERD, 1941
Baker, J. T., GC (EM), 1929
Bamford, J., GC, 1952
Beaton, J., GC, CVO, 1974
Bridge, *Lt.-Cdr.* J., GC, GM and Bar, 1944
Butson, *Lt.-Col.* A. R. C., GC, CD, MD (AM), 1948
Bywater, R. A. S., GC, GM, 1944
Errington, H., GC, 1941
Farrow, K., GC (AM), 1948
Flintoff, H. H., GC (EM), 1944
Gledhill, A. J., GC, 1967
Gregson, J. S., GC (AM), 1943
Hawkins, E., GC (AM), 1943
Johnson, *WO1 (SSM)* B., GC, 1990
Kinne, D. G., GC, 1954
Lowe, A. R., GC (AM), 1949
Lynch, J., GC, BEM (AM), 1948
Moore, R. V., GC, CBE, 1940
Naughton, F., GC (EGM), 1937
Pearson, Miss J. D. M., GC (EGM), 1940
Pratt, M. K., GC, 1978
Purves, Mrs M., GC (AM), 1949
Raweng, Awang anak, GC, 1951
Riley, G., GC (AM), 1944
Rowlands, *Air Marshal* Sir John, GC, KBE, 1943
Sinclair, *Air Vice-Marshal* Sir Laurence, GC, KCB, CBE, DSO, 1941
Stevens, H. W., GC, 1958
Styles, *Lt.-Col.* S. G., GC, 1972
Walker, C., GC, 1972
Walker, C. H., GC (AM), 1942
Walton, E. W. K., GC (AM), DSO, 1948
Wilcox, C., GC (EM), 1949
Wiltshire, S. N., GC (EGM), 1930
Wooding, E. A., GC (AM), 1945

Chiefs of Clans and Names in Scotland

Only chiefs of whole Names or Clans are included, except certain special instances (marked *) who, though not chiefs of a whole name, were or are for some reason (e.g. the Macdonald forfeiture) independent. Under decision (*Campbell-Gray*, 1950) that a bearer of a 'double or triple-barrelled' surname cannot be held chief of a part of such, several others cannot be included in the list at present.

THE ROYAL HOUSE: HM The Queen

AGNEW: Sir Crispin Agnew of Lochnaw, Bt., QC, 6 Palmerston Road, Edinburgh EH9 1TN

ANSTRUTHER: Sir Ralph Anstruther of that Ilk, Bt., GCVO, MC, Balcaskie, Pittenweem, Fife KY10 2RD

ARBUTHNOTT: The Viscount of Arbuthnott, KT, CBE, DSC, Arbuthnott House, Laurencekirk, Kincardineshire AB30 1PA

BARCLAY: Peter C. Barclay of Towie Barclay and of that Ilk, 28A Gordon Place, London W8 4JE

BORTHWICK: The Lord Borthwick, Crookston, Heriot, Midlothian EH38 5YS

BOYD: The Lord Kilmarnock, 194 Regent's Park Road, London NW1 8XP

BOYLE: The Earl of Glasgow, Kelburn, Fairlie, Ayrshire KA29 0BE

BRODIE: Ninian Brodie of Brodie, Brodie Castle, Forres, Morayshire IV36 0TE

BRUCE: The Earl of Elgin and Kincardine, KT, Broomhall, Dunfermline, Fife KY11 3DU

BUCHAN: David S. Buchan of Auchmacoy, Auchmacoy House, Ellon, Aberdeenshire

BURNETT: J. C. A. Burnett of Leys, Crathes Castle, Banchory, Kincardineshire

CAMERON: Sir Donald Cameron of Lochiel, KT, CVO, TD, Achnacarry, Spean Bridge, Inverness-shire

CAMPBELL: The Duke of Argyll, Inveraray, Argyll PA32 8XF

CARMICHAEL: Richard J. Carmichael of Carmichael, Carmichael, Thankerton, Biggar, Lanarkshire

CARNEGIE: The Duke of Fife, Elsick House, Stonehaven, Kincardineshire AB3 2NT

CATHCART: vacant

CHARTERIS: The Earl of Wemyss and March, KT, Gosford House, Longniddry, East Lothian EH32 0PX

CLAN CHATTAN: M. K. Mackintosh of Clan Chattan, Maxwell Park, Gwelo, Zimbabwe

CHISHOLM: Hamish Chisholm of Chisholm (*The Chisholm*), Elmpine, Beck Row, Bury St Edmunds, Suffolk

COCHRANE: The Earl of Dundonald, Lochnell Castle, Ledaig, Argyllshire

COLQUHOUN: Sir Ivar Colquhoun of Luss, Bt., Camstraddan, Luss, Dunbartonshire G83 8NX

CRANSTOUN: David A. S. Cranstoun of that Ilk, Corehouse, Lanark

CRICHTON: vacant

CUMMING: Sir William Cumming of Altyre, Bt., Altyre, Forres, Moray

DARROCH: Capt. Duncan Darroch of Gourock, The Red House, Branksome Park Road, Camberley, Surrey

DAVIDSON: Alister G. Davidson of Davidson, 21 Winscombe Street, Takapuna, Auckland, New Zealand

DEWAR: Michael Dewar of that Ilk and Vogrie, Rectory Farm House, Charleton Musgrove, Wincanton, Somerset BA9 8ET

DRUMMOND: The Earl of Perth, PC, Stobhall, Perth PH2 6DR

DUNBAR: Sir James Dunbar of Mochrum, Bt., 211 Gardenville Drive, Yorktown, Va 23693, USA

DUNDAS: David D. Dundas of Dundas, 8 Derna Road, Kenwyn 7700, South Africa

DURIE: Andrew Durie of Durie, CBE, Finnich Malise, Croftamie, Stirlingshire G63 0HA

ELIOTT: Mrs Margaret Eliott of Redheugh, Redheugh, Newcastleton, Roxburghshire

ERSKINE: The Earl of Mar and Kellie, Erskine House, Kirk Wynd, Alloa, Clackmannan FK10 4JF

FARQUHARSON: Capt. A. Farquharson of Invercauld, MC, Invercauld, Braemar, Aberdeenshire AB35 5TT

FERGUSSON: Sir Charles Fergusson of Kilkerran, Bt., Kilkerran, Maybole, Ayrshire

FORBES: The Lord Forbes, KBE, Balforbes, Alford, Aberdeenshire AB33 8DR

FORSYTH: Alistair Forsyth of that Ilk, Ethie Castle, by Arbroath, Angus DD11 5SP

FRASER: The Lady Saltoun, Inverey House, Braemar, Aberdeenshire AB35 5YB

*FRASER (OF LOVAT): The Lord Lovat, Beaufort Lodge, Beauly, Inverness-shire IV4 7AZ

GAYRE: R. Gayre of Gayre and Nigg, Minard Castle, Minard, Inverary, Argyll PA32 8YB

GORDON: The Marquess of Huntly, Aboyne Castle, Aberdeenshire AB34 5JP

GRAHAM: The Duke of Montrose, Buchanan Auld House, Drymen, Stirlingshire

GRANT: The Lord Strathspey, The School House, Lochbuie, Mull, Argyllshire PA62 6AA

GRIERSON: Sir Michael Grierson of Lag, Bt., 40C Palace Road, London SW2 3NJ

HAIG: The Earl Haig, OBE, Bemersyde, Melrose, Roxburghshire TD6 9DP

HALDANE: Martin Haldane of Gleneagles, Gleneagles, Auchterarder, Perthshire

HANNAY: Ramsey Hannay of Kirkdale and of that Ilk, Cardoness House, Gatehouse-of-Fleet, Kirkcudbrightshire

HAY: The Earl of Erroll, Woodbury Hall, Sandy, Beds

HENDERSON: John Henderson of Fordell, 7 Owen Street, Toowoomba, Queensland, Australia

HUNTER: Pauline Hunter of Hunterston, Plovers Ridge, Lon Cecrist, Treaddur Bay, Holyhead, Gwynedd

IRVINE OF DRUM: David C. Irvine of Drum, Holly Leaf Cottage, Inchmarlo, Banchory, Aberdeenshire AB31 4BR

JARDINE: Sir Alexander Jardine of Applegirth, Bt., Ash House, Thwaites, Millom, Cumbria LA18 5HY

JOHNSTONE: The Earl of Annandale and Hartfell, Raehills, Lockerbie, Dumfriesshire

KEITH: The Earl of Kintore, The Stables, Keith Hall, Inverurie, Aberdeenshire AB51 0LD

KENNEDY: The Marquess of Ailsa, Cassillis House, Maybole, Ayrshire

KERR: The Marquess of Lothian, KCVO, Ferniehurst Castle, Jedburgh, Roxburghshire TN8 6NX

LAMONT: Peter N. Lamont of that Ilk, 209 Bungarribee Road, Blacktown, Australia

LEASK: Madam Leask of Leask, 1 Vincent Road, Sheringham, Norfolk

LENNOX: Edward J. H. Lennox of that Ilk, Tods Top Farm, Downton on the Rock, Ludlow, Shropshire

LESLIE: The Earl of Rothes, Tanglewood, West Tytherley, Salisbury, Wilts SP5 1LX

LINDSAY: The Earl of Crawford and Balcarres, KT, PC, Balcarres, Colinsburgh, Fife

LOCKHART: Angus H. Lockhart of the Lee, Newholme, Dunsyre, Lanark

LUMSDEN: Gillem Lumsden of that Ilk and Blanerne, Stapely Howe, Hoe Benham, Newbury, Berks

MACALESTER: William St J. S. McAlester of Loup and Kennox, Dun Skeig, 27 Durnham Road, Burton, Christchurch, Dorset BH23 7ND

McBAIN: J. H. McBain of McBain, 7025 North Finger Rock Place, Tucson, Arizona, USA

MACDONALD: The Lord Macdonald (*The Macdonald of Macdonald*), Kinloch Lodge, Sleat, Isle of Skye

*MACDONALD OF CLANRANALD: Ranald A. Macdonald of Clanranald, Mornish House, Killin, Perthshire FK21 8TX

*MACDONALD OF SLEAT (CLAN HUSTEAIN): Sir Ian Macdonald of Sleat, Bt., Thorpe Hall, Rudston, Driffield, N. Humberside YO25 0JE

*MACDONALD OF GLENGARRY: Ranald MacDonell of Glengarry, Elonbank, Castle Street, Fortrose, Ross-shire IV10 8TH

MACDOUGALL: vacant

MACDOWALL: Fergus D. H. Macdowall of Garthland, 16 Rowe Road, Ottawa, Ontario K29 2ZS

MACGREGOR: Brig. Sir Gregor MacGregor of MacGregor, Bt., Bannatyne, Newtyle, Blairgowrie, Perthshire PH12 8TR

MACINTYRE: James W. MacIntyre of Glenoe, 15301 Pine Orchard Drive, Apartment 3H, Silver Spring, Maryland, USA

MACKAY: The Lord Reay, 98 Oakley Street, London SW3

MACKENZIE: The Earl of Cromartie, Castle Leod, Strathpeffer, Ross-shire IV14 9AA

MACKINNON: Madam Anne Mackinnon of Mackinnon, 16 Purleigh Road, Bridgwater, Somerset

MACKINTOSH: *The Mackintosh of Mackintosh*, Moy Hall, Inverness IV13 7YQ

MACLACHLAN: vacant

MACLAREN: Donald MacLaren of MacLaren and Achleskine, Achleskine, Kirkton, Balquhidder, Lochearnhead

MACLEAN: The Hon. Sir Lachlan Maclean of Duart, Bt., CVO, Arngask House, Glenfarg, Perthshire PH2 9QA

MACLENNAN: vacant

MACLEOD: John MacLeod of MacLeod, Dunvegan Castle, Isle of Skye

MACMILLAN: George MacMillan of MacMillan, Finlaystone, Langbank, Renfrewshire

MACNAB: J. C. Macnab of Macnab (*The Macnab*), Leuchars Castle Farmhouse, Leuchars, Fife KY16 0EY

MACNAGHTEN: Sir Patrick Macnaghten of Macnaghten and Dundarave, Bt., Dundarave, Bushmills, Co. Antrim

MACNEACAIL: Iain Macneacail of Macneacail and Scorrybreac, 12 Fox Street, Ballina, NSW, Australia

MACNEIL OF BARRA: Ian R. Macneil of Barra (*The Macneil of Barra*), 95/6 Grange Loan, Edinburgh

MACPHERSON: The Hon. Sir William Macpherson of Cluny, TD, Newtown Castle, Blairgowrie, Perthshire

MACTAVISH: E. S. Dugald MacTavish of Dunardry, 2519 Vivaldi Lane, Four Seasons Estates, Gambrills, MD 21054, USA

MACTHOMAS: Andrew P. C. MacThomas of Finegand, c/o Roslin Cottage, Pitmedden, Aberdeenshire AB41 7NY

MAITLAND: The Earl of Lauderdale, 12 St Vincent Street, Edinburgh

MAKGILL: The Viscount of Oxfuird, Kenback, Stoke, Nr Andover, Hampshire SP11 0NP

MALCOLM (MACCALLUM): Robin N. L. Malcolm of Poltalloch, Duntrune Castle, Lochgilphead, Argyll

MAR: The Countess of Mar, St Michael's Farm, Great Witley, Worcs WR6 6JB

MARJORIBANKS: Andrew Marjoribanks of that Ilk, 10 Newark Street, Greenock

MATHESON: Maj. Sir Fergus Matheson of Matheson, Bt., Old Rectory, Hedenham, Bungay, Suffolk NR35 2LD

MENZIES: David R. Menzies of Menzies, Wester Auchnagallin Farmhouse, Braes of Castle Grant, Grantown on Spey PH26 3PL

MOFFAT: Madam Moffat of that Ilk, St Jasual, Bullocks Farm Lane, Wheeler End Common, High Wycombe

MONCREIFFE: vacant

MONTGOMERIE: The Earl of Eglinton and Winton, Balhomie, Cargill, Perth PH2 6DS

MORRISON: Dr Iain M. Morrison of Ruchdi, Magnolia Cottage, The Street, Walberton, Sussex

MUNRO: Hector W. Munro of Foulis, Foulis Castle, Evanton, Ross-shire IV16 9UX

MURRAY: The Duke of Atholl, Blair Castle, Blair Atholl, Perthshire

NESBITT (or NISBET): Robert Nesbitt of that Ilk, Upper Roundhurst Farm, Roundhurst, Haslemere, Surrey

NICOLSON: The Lord Carnock, 90 Whitehall Court, London SW1A 2EL

OGILVY: The Earl of Airlie, KT, GCVO, PC, Cortachy Castle, Kirriemuir, Angus

RAMSAY: The Earl of Dalhousie, Brechin Castle, Brechin, Angus DD7 6SH

RATTRAY: James S. Rattray of Rattray, Craighall, Rattray, Perthshire

RIDDELL: Sir John Riddell of Riddell, CB, CVO, Hepple, Morpeth, Northumberland

ROBERTSON: Alexander G. H. Robertson of Struan (*Struan-Robertson*), The Breach Farm, Goudhurst Road, Cranbrook, Kent

ROLLO: The Lord Rollo, Pitcairns, Dunning, Perthshire

ROSE: Miss Elizabeth Rose of Kilravock, Kilravock Castle, Croy, Inverness

ROSS: David C. Ross of that Ilk and Balnagowan, Shandwick, Perth Road, Stanley, Perthshire

RUTHVEN: The Earl of Gowrie, PC, 34 King Street, Covent Garden, London WC2

SCOTT: The Duke of Buccleuch and Queensberry, KT, VRD, Bowhill, Selkirk

SCRYMGEOUR: The Earl of Dundee, Birkhill, Cupar, Fife

SEMPILL: The Lord Sempill, 3 Vanburgh Place, Edinburgh, EH6 8AE

SHAW: John Shaw of Tordarroch, East Craig an Ron, 22 Academy Mead, Fortrose IV10 8TW

SINCLAIR: The Earl of Caithness, 137 Claxton Grove, London W6 8HB

SKENE: Danus Skene of Skene, Nether Pitlour, Strathmiglo, Fife

STIRLING: Fraser J. Stirling of Cader, 44A Oakley Street, London SW3 5HA

STRANGE: Maj. Timothy Strange of Balcaskie, Little Holme, Porton Road, Amesbury, Wilts

SUTHERLAND: The Countess of Sutherland, House of Tongue, Brora, Sutherland

SWINTON: John Swinton of that Ilk, 123 Superior Avenue SW, Calgary, Alberta, Canada

TROTTER: Alexander Trotter of Mortonhall, Charterhall, Duns, Berwickshire

URQUHART: Kenneth T. Urquhart of Urquhart, 507 Jefferson Park Avenue, Jefferson, New Orleans, La. 70121, USA

WALLACE: Ian F. Wallace of that Ilk, 5 Lennox Street, Edinburgh EH4 1QB

WEDDERBURN OF THAT ILK: The Master of Dundee, Birkhill, Cupar, Fife

WEMYSS: David Wemyss of that Ilk, Invermay, Forteviot, Perthshire

The Privy Council

The Sovereign in Council, or Privy Council, was the chief source of executive power until the system of Cabinet government developed in the 18th century. Now the Privy Council's main functions are to advise the Sovereign and to exercise its own statutory responsibilities independent of the Sovereign in Council (*see also* page 215).

Membership of the Privy Council is automatic upon appointment to certain government and judicial positions in the United Kingdom, e.g. Cabinet ministers must be Privy Counsellors and are sworn in on first assuming office. Membership is also accorded by The Queen to eminent people in the UK and independent countries of the Commonwealth of which Her Majesty is Queen, on the recommendation of the British Prime Minister. Membership of the Council is retained for life, except for very occasional removals.

The administrative functions of the Privy Council are carried out by the Privy Council Office (*see* page 353) under the direction of the President of the Council, who is always a member of the Cabinet.

President of the Council, The Rt. Hon. Margaret Beckett, MP
Clerk of the Council, A. Galloway

MEMBERS *as at 31 August 2000*

HRH The Duke of Edinburgh, 1951
HRH The Prince of Wales, 1977

Aberdare, Lord, 1974
Ackner, Lord, 1980
Airlie, Earl of, 1984
Aldington, Lord, 1954
Aldous, Sir William, 1995
Alebua, Ezekiel, 1988
Alison, Michael, 1981
Ampthill, Lord, 1995
Ancram, Michael, 1996
Anthony, Douglas, 1971
Arbuthnot, James, 1998
Archer of Sandwell, Lord, 1977
Armstrong, Hilary, 1999
Arnold, Sir John, 1979
Arthur, Hon. Owen, 1995
Ashdown, Paddy, 1989
Ashley of Stoke, Lord, 1979
Atkins, Sir Robert, 1995
Auld, Sir Robin, 1995
Baker of Dorking, Lord, 1984
Balcombe, Sir John, 1985
Barber, Lord, 1963
Barnett, Lord, 1975
Beckett, Margaret, 1993

Beith, Alan, 1992
Beldam, Sir Roy, 1989
Belstead, Lord, 1983
Benn, Anthony, 1964
Bennett, Sir Frederic, 1985
Biffen, Lord, 1979
Bingham of Cornhill, Lord, 1986
Birch, William, 1992
Bisson, Sir Gordon, 1987
Blair, Anthony, 1994
Blaker, Lord, 1983
Blanchard, Peter, 1998
Blatch, Baroness, 1993
Blunkett, David, 1997
Boateng, Paul, 1999
Bolger, James, 1991
Booth, Albert, 1976
Boothroyd, Betty, 1992
Boscawen, Hon. Robert, 1992
Bottomley, Virginia, 1992
Boyd, Colin, 2000
Boyson, Sir Rhodes, 1987
Braine of Wheatley, Lord, 1985
Brathwaite, Sir Nicholas, 1991
Bridge of Harwich, Lord, 1975
Brightman, Lord, 1979
Brittan of Spennithorne, Lord, 1981
Brook, Sir Henry, 1996
Brooke, Peter, 1988
Brown, Gordon, 1996
Brown, Nicholas, 1997
Brown, Sir Simon, 1992
Brown, Sir Stephen, 1983
Browne-Wilkinson, Lord, 1983
Butler, Sir Adam, 1984
Butler-Sloss, Dame Elizabeth, 1988
Buxton, Sir Richard, 1997
Byers, Stephen, 1998
Caborn, Richard, 1999
Caithness, Earl of, 1990
Callaghan of Cardiff, Lord, 1964
Cameron of Lochbroom, Lord, 1984
Camoys, Lord, 1997
Campbell of Croy, Lord, 1970
Campbell, Walter Menzies, 1998
Campbell, Sir William, 1999
Canterbury, The Archbishop of, 1991
Carlisle of Bucklow, Lord, 1979
Carr of Hadley, Lord, 1963
Carrington, Lord, 1959
Carswell, Sir Robert, 1993
Carter, Lord, 1997
Casey, Sir Maurice, 1986
Castle of Blackburn, Baroness, 1964
Chadwick, Sir John, 1997
Chalfont, Lord, 1964
Chalker of Wallasey, Baroness, 1987
Chan, Sir Julius, 1981
Chataway, Sir Christopher, 1970
Clark, David, 1997
Clark, Helen, 1990
Clark of Kempston, Lord, 1990
Clarke, Sir Anthony, 1998
Clarke, Kenneth, 1984
Clarke, Thomas, 1997
Cledwyn of Penrhos, Lord, 1966
Clinton-Davis, Lord, 1998
Clyde, Lord, 1996

Cockfield, Lord, 1982
Cocks of Hartcliffe, Lord, 1976
Colman, Fraser, 1986
Compton, Sir John, 1983
Concannon, John, 1978
Cook, Robin, 1996
Cooke of Thorndon, Lord, 1977
Cooper, Sir Frank, 1983
Cope of Berkeley, Lord, 1988
Corfield, Sir Frederick, 1970
Coulsfield, Lord, 2000
Cowen, Sir Zelman, 1981
Cradock, Sir Percy, 1993
Cranborne, Viscount, 1994
Crawford and Balcarres, Earl of, 1972
Creech, *Hon.* Wyatt, 1999
Crickhowell, Lord, 1979
Croom-Johnson, Sir David, 1984
Cullen, *Hon.* Lord, 1997
Cumming-Bruce, Sir Roualeyn, 1977
Cunningham, Jack, 1993
Curry, David, 1996
Darling, Alistair, 1997
Davies, Denzil, 1978
Davies, Ronald, 1997
Davis, David, 1997
Davis, Terry, 1999
Davison, Sir Ronald, 1978
Dean of Harptree, Lord, 1991
Dean of Thornton-le-Fylde, Baroness, 1998
Deedes, Lord, 1962
Dell, Edmund, 1970
Denham, John, 2000
Denham, Lord, 1981
Devonshire, Duke of, 1964
Dewar, Donald, 1996
Diamond, Lord, 1965
Dillon, Sir Brian, 1982
Dixon, Lord, 1996
Dobson, Frank, 1997
Donaldson of Lymington, Lord, 1979
Dorrell, Stephen, 1994
Douglas, Sir William, 1977
du Cann, Sir Edward, 1964
Dunn, Sir Robin, 1980
East, Paul, 1998
Eden of Winton, Lord, 1972
Eggar, Timothy, 1995
Eichelaum, Sir Thomas, 1989
Elias, *Hon.* Dame, Sian, 1999
Emery, Sir Peter, 1993
Emslie, Lord, 1972
Erroll of Hale, Lord, 1960
Esquivel, Manuel, 1986
Evans, Sir Anthony, 1992
Eveleigh, Sir Edward, 1977
Farquharson, Sir Donald, 1989
Fellowes, Lord, 1990
Ferrers, Earl, 1982
Field, Frank, 1997
Floissac, Sir Vincent, 1992
Foot, Michael, 1974
Forsyth of Drumlean, The Lord, 1995
Forth, Eric, 1997
Foster, Derek, 1993
Fowler, Sir Norman, 1979
Fox, Sir Marcus, 1995

Quin, Joyce, 1998
Radice, Giles, 1999
Raison, Sir Timothy, 1982
Ramsden, James, 1963
Rawlinson of Ewell, Lord, 1964
Redwood, John, 1993
Rees, Lord, 1983
Reid, John, 1998
Renton, Lord, 1962
Renton of Mount Harry, Lord, 1989
Richard, Lord, 1993
Richardson, Sir Ivor, 1978
Richardson of Duntisbourne, Lord, 1976
Rifkind, Sir Malcolm, 1986
Roberts of Conwy, Lord, 1991
Robertson of Port Ellen, Lord, 1997
Roch, Sir John, 1993
Rodger of Earlsferry, Lord, 1992
Rodgers of Quarry Bank, Lord, 1975
Rooker, Jeffrey, 1999
Rose, Sir Christopher, 1992
Ross, Hon. Lord, 1985
Rumbold, Dame Angela, 1991
Runcie, Lord, 1980
Russell, Sir Patrick, 1987
Ryder of Wensum, Lord, 1990
Sainsbury, Sir Timothy, 1992
St John of Fawsley, Lord, 1979
Sandiford, Erskine, 1989
Saville of Newdigate, Lord, 1994
Scarman, Lord, 1973
Schiemann, Sir Konrad, 1995
Scott, Sir Nicholas, 1989
Scott, Sir Richard, 1991
Seaga, Edward, 1981
Sedley, Sir Stephen, 1999
Selkirk of Douglas, Lord, 1996
Shawcross, Lord, 1946
Shearer, Hugh, 1969

Sheldon, Robert, 1977
Shephard, Gillian, 1992
Shepherd, Lord, 1965
Shipley, Jennifer, 1998
Shore of Stepney, Lord, 1967
Short, Clare, 1997
Simmonds, Kennedy, 1984
Simon of Glaisdale, Lord, 1961
Sinclair, Ian, 1977
Slade, Sir Christopher, 1982
Slynn of Hadley, Lord, 1992
Smith, Andrew, 1997
Smith, Christopher, 1997
Smith, Sir Geoffrey Johnson, 1996
Somare, Sir Michael, 1977
Somers, Sir Edward, 1981
Stanley, Sir John, 1984
Staughton, Sir Christopher, 1988
Steel of Aikwood, Lord, 1977
Stephen, Sir Ninian, 1979
Stephenson, Sir John, 1971
Stewartby, Lord, 1989
Steyn, Lord, 1992
Stodart of Leaston, Lord, 1974
Strang, Gavin, 1997
Strathclyde, Lord, 1995
Straw, Jack, 1997
Stuart-Smith, Sir Murray, 1988
Sutherland, Lord, 2000
Talboys, Sir Brian, 1977
Taylor, Ann, 1997
Tebbit, Lord, 1981
Templeman, Lord, 1978
Thatcher, Baroness, 1970
Thomas, Edmund, 1996
Thomas, Sir Swinton, 1994
Thomas of Gwydir, Lord, 1964
Thomson of Monifieth, Lord, 1966
Thorpe, Jeremy, 1967
Thorpe, Sir Matthew, 1995

Tipping, Andrew, 1998
Tizard, Robert, 1986
Trefgarne, Lord, 1989
Trimble, David, 1997
Trumpington, Baroness, 1992
Tuckey, Sir Simon, 1998
Ullswater, Viscount, 1994
Upton, Simon, 1999
Varley, Lord, 1974
Waddington, Lord, 1987
Waite, Sir John, 1993
Wakeham, Lord, 1983
Waldegrave, William, 1990
Walker of Doncaster, Lord, 1979
Walker of Worcester, Lord, 1970
Walker, Sir Robert, 1997
Waller, Sir Mark, 1996
Ward, Sir Alan, 1995
Watkins, Sir Tasker, 1980
Weatherill, Lord, 1980
Wheeler, Sir John, 1993
Widdecombe, Ann, 1997
Wigley, Dafydd, 1997
Wilberforce, Lord, 1964
Williams, Alan, 1977
Williams of Crosby, Baroness, 1974
Williams of Mostyn, Lord
Windlesham, Lord, 1973
Winti, Paias, 1987
Withers, Reginald, 1977
Woodhouse, Sir Owen, 1974
Woolf, Lord, 1986
Wylie, Hon. Lord, 1970
York, The Archbishop of, 1991
Young, Baroness, 1981
Young, Sir George, 1993
Young of Graffham, Lord, 1984
Younger of Leckie, Viscount, 1979
Zacca, Edward, 1992

The Privy Council of Northern Ireland

The Privy Council of Northern Ireland had responsibilities in Northern Ireland similar to those of the Privy Council in Great Britain until the Northern Ireland Act 1974 instituted direct rule and a UK Cabinet minister became responsible for the functions previously exercised by the Northern Ireland government.

Membership of the Privy Council of Northern Ireland is retained for life. Since the Northern Ireland Constitution Act 1973 no further appointments have been made. The postnominal initials PC (NI) are used to differentiate its members from those of the Privy Council.

MEMBERS *as at 31 August 2000*

Bailie, Robin, 1971
Bleakley, David, 1971
Craig, William, 1963
Dobson, John, 1969
Kelly, Sir Basil, 1969
Kirk, Herbert, 1962
Long, William, 1966
Lowry, The Lord, 1971
McConnell, The Lord, 1964
McIvor, Basil, 1971
Moyola, Lord, 1966

Neill, Sir Ivan, 1950
Porter, Sir Robert, 1969
Taylor, John, MP, 1970
West, Henry, 1960

Parliament

The United Kingdom constitution is not contained in any single document but has evolved in the course of time, formed partly by statute, partly by common law and partly by convention. A constitutional monarchy, the United Kingdom is governed by Ministers of the Crown in the name of the Sovereign, who is head both of the state and of the government.

The organs of government are the legislature (Parliament), the executive and the judiciary. The executive consists of HM Government (Cabinet and other Ministers), government departments and public corporations operating nationalised industries or social or cultural services (*see* Government Departments and Public Offices), and local authorities (*see* Local Government). The judiciary (*see* Law Courts and Offices) pronounces on the law, both written and unwritten, interprets statutes and is responsible for the enforcement of the law; the judiciary is independent of both the legislature and the executive.

THE MONARCHY

The Sovereign personifies the state and is, in law, an integral part of the legislature, head of the executive, head of the judiciary, commander-in-chief of all armed forces of the Crown and 'Supreme Governor' of the Church of England. The seat of the monarchy is in the United Kingdom. In the Channel Islands and the Isle of Man, which are Crown dependencies, the Sovereign is represented by a Lieutenant-Governor. In the member states of the Commonwealth of which the Sovereign is head of state, her representative is a Governor-General; in UK dependencies the Sovereign is usually represented by a Governor, who is responsible for the British Government.

Although in practice the powers of the monarchy are now very limited, restricted mainly to the advisory and ceremonial, there are important acts of government which require the participation of the Sovereign. These include summoning, proroguing and dissolving Parliament, giving royal assent to bills passed by Parliament, appointing important office-holders, e.g. government ministers, judges, bishops and governors, conferring peerages, knighthoods and other honours, and granting pardon to a person wrongly convicted of a crime. The Sovereign appoints the Prime Minister; by convention this office is held by the leader of the political party which enjoys, or can secure, a majority of votes in the House of Commons. In international affairs the Sovereign as head of state has the power to declare war and make peace, to recognise foreign states and governments, to conclude treaties and to annex or cede territory. However, as the Sovereign entrusts executive power to Ministers of the Crown and acts on the advice of her Ministers, which she cannot ignore, royal prerogative powers are in practice exercised by Ministers, who are responsible to Parliament.

Ministerial responsibility does not diminish the Sovereign's importance to the smooth working of government. She holds meetings of the Privy Council (*see* below), gives audiences to her Ministers and other officials at home and overseas, receives accounts of Cabinet decisions, reads dispatches and signs state papers; she must be informed and consulted on every aspect of national life; and she must show complete impartiality.

COUNSELLORS OF STATE

In the event of the Sovereign's absence abroad, it is necessary to appoint Counsellors of State under letters patent to carry out the chief functions of the Monarch, including the holding of Privy Councils and giving royal assent to acts passed by Parliament. The normal procedure is to appoint as Counsellors three or four members of the royal family among those remaining in the UK.

In the event of the Sovereign on accession being under the age of 18 years, or at any time unavailable or incapacitated by infirmity of mind or body for the performance of the royal functions, provision is made for a regency.

THE PRIVY COUNCIL

The Sovereign in Council, or Privy Council, was the chief source of executive power until the system of Cabinet government developed. Nowadays its main function is to advise the Sovereign to approve Orders in Council and to advise on the issue of royal proclamations. The Council's own statutory responsibilities (independent of the powers of the Sovereign in Council) include powers of supervision over the registering bodies for the medical and allied professions. A full Council is summoned only on the death of the Sovereign or when the Sovereign announces his or her intention to marry. (For full list of Counsellors, *see* The Privy Council section.)

There are a number of advisory Privy Council committees, whose meetings the Sovereign does not attend. Some are prerogative committees, such as those dealing with legislative matters submitted by the legislatures of the Channel Islands and the Isle of Man or with applications for charters of incorporation; and some are provided for by statute, e.g. those for the universities of Oxford and Cambridge and the Scottish universities.

The Judicial Committee of the Privy Council is the final court of appeal from courts of the UK dependencies, courts of independent Commonwealth countries which have retained the right of appeal, courts of the Channel Islands and the Isle of Man, some professional and disciplinary committees, and church sources. The Committee is composed of Privy Counsellors who hold, or have held, high judicial office, although usually only three or five hear each case.

Administrative work is carried out by the Privy Council Office under the direction of the President of the Council, a Cabinet Minister.

PARLIAMENT

Parliament is the supreme law-making authority and can legislate for the UK as a whole or for any parts of it separately (the Channel Islands and the Isle of Man are Crown dependencies and not part of the UK). The main functions of Parliament are to pass laws, to provide (by voting taxation) the means of carrying on the work of government and to scrutinise government policy and administration, particularly proposals for expenditure. International treaties and agreements are by custom presented to Parliament before ratification.

Parliament emerged during the late 13th and early 14th centuries. The officers of the King's household and the King's judges were the nucleus of early Parliaments, joined by such ecclesiastical and lay magnates as the King might summon to form a prototype 'House of Lords', and occasionally by the knights of the shires, burgesses and proctors of the lower clergy. By the end of Edward III's reign a 'House of Commons' was beginning to appear; the first known Speaker was elected in 1377.

Parliamentary procedure is based on custom and precedent, partly formulated in the Standing Orders of both Houses of Parliament, and each House has the right to control its own internal proceedings and to commit for contempt. The system of debate in the two Houses is similar; when a motion has been moved, the Speaker proposes the question as the subject of a debate. Members speak from wherever they have been sitting. Questions are decided by a vote on a simple majority. Draft legislation is introduced, in either House, as a bill. Bills can be introduced by a Government Minister or a private Member, but in practice the majority of bills which become law are introduced by the Government. To become law, a bill must be passed by each House (for parliamentary stages, see Bill, page 220) and then sent to the Sovereign for the royal assent, after which it becomes an Act of Parliament.

Proceedings of both Houses are public, except on extremely rare occasions. The minutes (called Votes and Proceedings in the Commons, and Minutes of Proceedings in the Lords) and the speeches (The Official Report of Parliamentary Debates, Hansard) are published daily. Proceedings are also recorded for transmission on radio and television and stored in the Parliamentary Recording Unit before transfer to the National Sound Archive. Television cameras have been allowed into the House of Lords since 1985 and into the House of Commons since 1989; committee meetings may also be televised.

By the Parliament Act of 1911, the maximum duration of a Parliament is five years (if not previously dissolved), the term being reckoned from the date given on the writs for the new Parliament. The maximum life has been prolonged by legislation in such rare circumstances as the two world wars (31 January 1911 to 25 November 1918; 26 November 1935 to 15 June 1945). Dissolution and writs for a general election are ordered by the Sovereign on the advice of the Prime Minister. The life of a Parliament is divided into sessions, usually of one year in length, beginning and ending most often in October or November.

DEVOLUTION

The Scottish Parliament elected in 1999 has legislative power over all devolved matters, i.e. matters not reserved to Westminster or otherwise outside its powers. The National Assembly for Wales elected in May 1999 has power to make secondary legislation in the areas where executive functions have been transferred to it. The New Northern Ireland Assembly elected in June 1998 was due to be formally established by legislation in 1999. The Assembly started sitting in July 1998. Following suspension in February 2000, it resumed sitting on 5 June 2000. It will have legislative authority in the fields currently administered by the Northern Ireland departments.

THE HOUSE OF LORDS
London SW1A 0PW
Tel: 020-7219 3000
Information Office: 020-7219 3107
E-mail: hlinfo@parliament.uk
Web: http://www.parliament.uk

The members of the House of Lords consist of the Lords Spiritual and Temporal. The Lords Spiritual are the Archbishops of Canterbury and York, the Bishops of London, Durham and Winchester, and the 21 senior diocesan bishops of the Church of England. The Lords Temporal currently consist of, life peers created under the Life Peerages Act 1958, 92 hereditary peers elected under the House of Lords Act 1999, and those Lords of Appeal in Ordinary created life peers under the Appellate Jurisdiction Act 1876, as amended (i.e. Law Lords). The House of Lords Act provides for 92 hereditary peers (42 Conservative, 28 cross-bench, three Liberal Democrat, two Labour, the Earl Marshal, the Lord Great Chamberlain and 15 others) to remain in the House of Lords until longer-term reform of the House has been carried out; elections to select those who remain were held in October and November 1999.

Peers are disqualified from sitting in the House if they are:

– aliens, i.e. any peer who is not a British citizen, a Commonwealth citizen (under the British Nationality Act 1981) or a citizen of the Republic of Ireland
– under the age of 21
– undischarged bankrupts or, in Scotland, those whose estate is sequestered
– convicted of treason

Bishops retire from their sees on reaching the age of 70 and cease to be members of the house at that time.

Peers who do not wish to attend sittings of the House of Lords may apply for leave of absence for the duration of a Parliament.

Until the beginning of this century the House of Lords had considerable power, being able to veto any bill submitted to it by the House of Commons, but those powers were greatly reduced by the Parliament Acts of 1911 and 1949 (see page 221).

Combined with its legislative role, the House of Lords has judicial powers as the ultimate Court of Appeal for courts in Great Britain and Northern Ireland, except for criminal cases in Scotland. These powers are exercised by the Lord Chancellor and the Lords of Appeal in Ordinary (the Law Lords) (see Law Courts and Offices).

Members of the House of Lords are unpaid. However, they are entitled to reimbursement of travelling expenses on parliamentary business within the UK and certain other expenses incurred for the purpose of attendance at sittings of the House, within a maximum for each day of £81.50 for overnight subsistence, £36.00 for day subsistence and incidental travel, and £35.00 for secretarial costs, postage and certain additional expenses.

COMPOSITION as at 5 June 2000

Archbishops and Bishops, 25
Life peers under the Appellate Jurisdiction Act 1876, 27
Life peers under the Life Peerages Act 1958, 552 (107 women)
Peers under the House of Lords Act 1999, 91 (4 women)
Total 695
Of whom:
    Peers on leave of absence from the House, 4

STATE OF PARTIES *as at 5 July 2000**
Conservative, 232
Labour, 199
Liberal Democrats, 63
Cross-bench, 164
Archbishops and Bishops, 25
Other, 8
Total: 691
* Excluding peers on leave of absence from the House

OFFICERS

The House is presided over by the Lord Chancellor, who is *ex officio* Speaker of the House. A panel of deputy Speakers is appointed by Royal Commission. The first deputy Speaker is the Chairman of Committees, appointed at the beginning of each session, a salaried officer of the House who takes the chair in committee of the whole House and in some select committees. He is assisted by a panel of deputy chairmen, headed by the salaried Principal Deputy Chairman of Committees, who is also chairman of the European Communities Committee of the House.

The permanent officers include the Clerk of the Parliaments, who is in charge of the administrative and procedural staff collectively known as the Parliament Office; the Gentleman Usher of the Black Rod, who is also Serjeant-at-Arms in attendance upon the Lord Chancellor and is responsible for security and for accommodation and services in the House of Lords; and the Yeoman Usher who is Deputy Serjeant-at-Arms and assists Black Rod in his duties.

Speaker (£167,760), The Lord Irvine of Lairg, PC, QC
  Private Secretary, Ms E. Hutchinson
Chairman of Committees (£66,294), The Lord Boston of
  Faversham, QC
Principal Deputy Chairman of Committees (£61,773),
  The Lord Tordoff

DEPARTMENT OF THE CLERK OF THE PARLIAMENTS

Clerk of the Parliaments (£127,872), J. M. Davies
Clerk Assistant and Clerk of Legislation (£75,374–£113,499),
  P. D. G. Hayter, LVO
Reading Clerk and Principal Finance Officer (£62,882–
  £101,254), M. G. Pownall
Counsel to Chairman of Committees (£62,882–£101,254), Sir
  James Nursaw, KCB, QC: Dr C. S. Kerse; D. W. Saunders
Principal Clerks (£57,367–£95,625), J. A. Vallance White,
  CB (*Judicial Office and Fourth Clerk at the Table*);
  B. P. Keith (*Journals*); D. R. Beamish (*Committees and
  Overseas Office*); E. C. Ollard, D.Phil. (*Establishment
  Officer*); Dr F. P. Tudor (*Private Bills*); R. H. Walters,
  D.Phil (*Public Bills*); A. Makower; T. V. Mohan (*Select
  Committees*)
Senior Clerks (£47,138–£75,601), S. P. Burton;
  Miss M. B. Robertson (*seconded as Secretary to the Leader
  of the House and Chief Whip*); T. E. Radice; D. J. Batt;
  E. R. Morgan; Dr E. A. Hopkins; Miss L. J. Mouland;
  J. A. Vaughan
Clerks (£16,714–£29,044), A. J. Mackersie; Miss K. S. Ball
Clerk of the Records (£47,138–£75,601), S. K. Ellison
Assistant Clerks of the Records (£32,065–£75,601),
  D. L. Prior; Dr C. Shenton
Librarian (£51,975–£85,047), D. L. Jones
Deputy Librarian (£36,313–£58,918), P. G. Davis, Ph.D.
Senior Library Clerks (£32,065–£48,584),
  Miss I. L. Victory, Ph.D.; S. Kennedy; H. C. Deadman
Library Clerk (£20,129–£26,366), I. S. Cruse
Examiners of Petitions for Private Bills (£47,138–£75,601),
  Dr F. P. Tudor; W. A. Proctor

Editor, Official Report (*Hansard*), (£47,138–£75,601),
  Mrs M. E. E. C. Villiers
Deputy Editor, Official Report (£36,313–£58,918),
  Mrs C. J. Boden

DEPARTMENT OF THE GENTLEMAN USHER OF THE BLACK ROD

Gentleman Usher of the Black Rod and Serjeant-at-Arms
  (£62,882–£101,254), Gen. Sir Edward Jones, KCB, CBE
Yeoman Usher of the Black Rod and Deputy Serjeant-at-Arms
  (£32,065–£48,584), Brig. H. D. C. Duncan, MBE

SELECT COMMITTEES

The main House of Lords select committees, as at April 2000, are as follows:
European Union – Sub-committees:
  A (*Economic and Financial Affairs, Trade and External
  Relations*) – *Chair*, The Lord Tomlinson; *Clerk*,
  Dr E. A. Hopkins
  B (*Energy, Industry and Transport*) – *Chair*, The Lord
  Geddes; *Clerk*, P. F. M. Wogan
  C (*Common Foreign and Security Policy*) – *Chair*, The Lord
  Havell of Guildford; *Clerk*, D. Batt
  D (*Environment, Agriculture, Public Health and Consumer
  Protection*) – *Chair*, The Earl of Selborne; *Clerk*,
  T. E. Radice
  E (*Law and Institutions*) – *Chair*, The Lord Hope of
  Craighead, PC; *Clerk*, S. P. Burton
  F (*Social Affairs, Education and Home Affairs*) – *Chair*, The
  Lord Wallace of Saltaire, PH.D.; *Clerk*, Dr C. S. Johnson
Science and Technology – *Chair*, The Lord Winston, FRCOG;
  Clerk, A. Makower
Delegated Powers and Deregulation – *Chair*, The Lord
  Alexander of Weedon, QC; *Clerk*, Dr F. P. Tudor
Monetary Policy Committee of the Bank of England – *Chair*,
  The Lord Peston; *Clerk*, S. P. Burton

THE HOUSE OF COMMONS

London SW1A 0AA
Tel: 020-7219 3000
Information Office: 020-7219 4272
Forthcoming business: 020-7219 5532
E-mail: hcinfo@parliament.uk
Web: http://www.parliament.uk

The members of the House of Commons are elected by universal adult suffrage. For electoral purposes, the United Kingdom is divided into constituencies, each of which returns one member to the House of Commons, the member being the candidate who obtains the largest number of votes cast in the constituency. To ensure equitable representation, the four Boundary Commissions keep constituency boundaries under review and recommend any redistribution of seats which may seem necessary because of population movements, etc. The number of seats was raised to 640 in 1945, reduced to 625 in 1948, and subsequently rose to 630 in 1955, 635 in 1970, 650 in 1983, 651 in 1992 and 659 in 1997. Of the present 659 seats, there are 529 for England, 40 for Wales, 72 for Scotland and 18 for Northern Ireland. The number of Scottish MPs at Westminster is likely to be cut by about 12 by 2007.

An electoral reform commission headed by Lord Jenkins of Hillhead proposed in October 1998 that the 'first-past-the-post' system of electing members of the House of Commons should be replaced by an alternative vote top-up system, under which 80–85 per cent of MPs would be elected by an alternative vote method and the remaining 15–20 per cent by an open-list system of proportional representation. A referendum will be held on the proposals at an unspecified future date.

ELECTIONS

Elections are by secret ballot, each elector casting one vote; voting is not compulsory. For entitlement to vote in parliamentary elections, *see* Legal Notes section. When a seat becomes vacant between general elections, a by-election is held.

British subjects and citizens of the Irish Republic can stand for election as Members of Parliament (MPs) provided they are 21 or over and not subject to disqualification. Those disqualified from sitting in the House include:

– undischarged bankrupts
– people sentenced to more than one year's imprisonment
– clergy of the Church of England, Church of Scotland, Church of Ireland and Roman Catholic Church
– members of the House of Lords
– holders of certain offices listed in the House of Commons Disqualification Act 1975, e.g. members of the judiciary, Civil Service, regular armed forces, police forces, some local government officers and some members of public corporations and government commissions

A candidate does not require any party backing but his or her nomination for election must be supported by the signatures of ten people registered in the constituency. A candidate must also deposit with the returning officer £500, which is forfeit if the candidate does not receive more than 5 per cent of the votes cast. All election expenses at a general election, except the candidate's personal expenses, are subject to a statutory limit of £4,965, plus 4.2 pence for each elector in a borough constituency or 5.6 pence for each elector in a county constituency.

See pages 226–33 for an alphabetical list of MPs, pages 236–68 for the results of the last general election, and page 233 for the results of by-elections since the general election.

STATE OF PARTIES *as at 4 July 2000*

Conservative, 160 (14 women)
Labour, 416 (101 women)
Liberal Democrats, 47 (4 women)
Plaid Cymru, 4
Scottish Labour, 1
Scottish Nationalist, 6 (2 women)
Sinn Fein, 2
Social Democratic Labour, 3
Ulster Democratic Unionist, 2
Ulster Unionist, 9
United Kingdom Unionist, 1
Independent (Martin Bell), 1
Member for Falkirk West (Dennis Canavan), 1
Member of Parliament for Brent East (Ken Livingstone), 1
*The Speaker and three Deputy Speakers, 4
Vacant seat (South Antrim), 1

Total, 659 (122 women)
Government majority, 178

* The Rt. Hon. Betty Boothroyd (*Lab*) resigned as Speaker and as MP for West Bromwich West on the 12 July 2000. For details of her successor *see* Stop Press.

BUSINESS

The week's business of the House is outlined each Thursday by the Leader of the House, after consultation between the Chief Government Whip and the Chief Opposition Whip. A quarter to a third of the time will be taken up by the Government's legislative programme and the rest by other business. As a rule, bills likely to raise political controversy are introduced in the Commons before going on to the Lords, and the Commons claims exclusive control in respect of national taxation and expenditure. Bills such as the Finance Bill, which imposes taxation, and the Consolidated Fund Bills, which author-ise expenditure, must begin in the Commons. A bill of which the financial provisions are subsidiary may begin in the Lords; and the Commons may waive its rights in regard to Lords' amendments affecting finance.

The Commons has a public register of MPs' financial and certain other interests; this is published annually as a House of Commons paper. Members must also disclose any relevant financial interest or benefit in a matter before the House when taking part in a debate, in certain other proceedings of the House, or in consultations with other MPs, with Ministers or with civil servants.

MEMBERS' PAY AND ALLOWANCES

Since 1911 members of the House of Commons have received salary payments; facilities for free travel were introduced in 1924. Salary rates since 1911 are as follows:

1911	£400 p.a.	1983 June	£15,308 p.a.
1931	360	1984 Jan	16,106
1934	380	1985 Jan	16,904
1935	400	1986 Jan	17,702
1937	600	1987 Jan	18,500
1946	1,000	1988 Jan	22,548
1954	1,250	1989 Jan	24,107
1957	1,750	1990 Jan	26,701
1964	3,250	1991 Jan	28,970
1972 Jan	4,500	1992 Jan	30,854
1975 June	5,750	1994 Jan	31,687
1976 June	6,062	1995 Jan	33,189
1977 July	6,270	1996 Jan	34,085
1978 June	6,897	1996 July	43,000
1979 June	9,450	1997 April	43,860
1980 June	11,750	1998 April	45,066
1981 June	13,950	1999 April	47,008
1982 June	14,510	2000 April	48,371

In 1969 MPs were granted an allowance for secretarial and research expenses, now known as the Office Costs Allowance. From April 2000 the allowance is £51,572 a year.

Since 1972 MPs have been able to claim reimbursement for the additional cost of staying overnight away from their main residence while on parliamentary business; this is known as the Additional Costs Allowance and from April 2000 is £13,322 a year.

Since 1980 each MP in receipt of the Office Costs Allowance has been able to contribute sums to an approved pension scheme for the provision of a pension, or other benefits, for or in respect of persons whose salary is met by him/her from the Office Costs Allowance.

MEMBERS' PENSIONS

Pension arrangements for MPs were first introduced in 1964. The arrangements currently provide a pension of one-fiftieth of salary for each year of pensionable service with a maximum of two-thirds of salary at age 65. Pension is payable normally at age 65, for men and women, or on later retirement. Pensions may be paid earlier, e.g. on retirement due to ill health or at age 60 after 20 years' service. The widow/widower of a former MP receives a pension of five-eighths of the late MP's pension. Pensions are index-linked. Members currently contribute six per cent of salary to the pension fund; there is an Exchequer contribution, currently slightly more than the amount contributed by MPs.

The House of Commons Members' Fund provides for annual or lump sum grants to ex-MPs, their widows or widowers, and children whose incomes are below certain limits or who are experiencing severe hardship. Members contribute £24 a year and the Exchequer £215,000 a year to the fund.

OFFICERS AND OFFICIALS

The House of Commons is presided over by the Speaker, who has considerable powers to maintain order in the House. A deputy Speaker, called the Chairman of Ways and Means, and two Deputy Chairmen may preside over sittings of the House of Commons; they are elected by the House, and, like the Speaker, neither speak nor vote other than in their official capacity.

The staff of the House are employed by a Commission chaired by the Speaker. The heads of the six House of Commons departments are permanent officers of the House, not MPs. The Clerk of the House is the principal adviser to the Speaker on the privileges and procedures of the House, the conduct of the business of the House, and committees. The Serjeant-at-Arms is responsible for security, ceremonial, and for accommodation in the Commons part of the Palace of Westminster.

*Speaker (£114,543), The Rt. Hon. Betty Boothroyd, MP (West Bromwich West)
Chairman of Ways and Means (£82,697), Sir Alan Haselhurst, MP (Saffron Walden)
First Deputy Chairman of Ways and Means (£78,539), Michael Martin, MP (Glasgow Springburn)
Second Deputy Chairman of Ways and Means (£78,539), Michael Lord, MP (Suffolk Central and Ipswich North)

* The Rt. Hon Betty Boothroyd resigned on the 12 July 2000. For details of her successor see Stop Press.

OFFICES OF THE SPEAKER AND CHAIRMAN OF WAYS AND MEANS

Speaker's Secretary (£45,810–£73,470), N. Bevan, CB
Chaplain to the Speaker, Revd Canon R. Wright
Secretary to the Chairman of Ways and Means (£30,967–£46,848 –£45,795), M. Hennessy

DEPARTMENT OF THE CLERK OF THE HOUSE

Clerk of the House of Commons (£127,872), W. R. McKay, CB
  Clerk Assistant (£68,840–£107,212), G. Cubie
Clerk of Committees (£68,840–£107,212), C. B. Winnifrith, CB
Clerk of Legislation (£68,640–£107,212), R. B. Sands
Principal Clerks (£62,882–£101,254)
  Journals, A. J. Hastings, CB
  Table Office, D. G. Millar
  Domestic Committees, M. R. Jack, Ph.D.
Principal Clerks (£51,975–£85,047)
  Overseas Office, R. W. G. Wilson
  Bills, Ms H. E. Irwin
  Select Committees, Mrs J. Sharpe; F. A. Cranmer; R. J. Rogers
  Delegated Legislation, W. A. Proctor
Deputy Principal Clerks (£47,138–£75,601), Ms A. Barry; C. R. M. Ward, Ph.D.; D. W. N. Doig; A. Sandall; D. L. Natzler; E.P. Silk; A. R. Kennon; L. C. Laurence Smyth; S. J. Patrick; D. J. Gerhold; C. J. Poyser; D. F. Harrison; S. J. Priestley; A. H. Doherty; P. A. Evans; R. I. S. Phillips; R. G. James, Ph.D.; Ms P. A. Helme; D. R. Lloyd; J. S. Benger, D.Phil.;

N. P. Walker; M. D. Hamlyn; Mrs E. J. Flood; P. C. Seaward, D.Phil.; A. Y. A. Azad; C. G. Lee
Senior Clerks (£30,967–£46,848), C. D. Stanton; C. A. Shaw; Ms L. M. Gardner; K. J. Brown, OBE; F. J. Reid; M. Hennessy; G. R. Devine; P. G. Moon; M. Clark; Mrs J. N. St J. Mulley; T. W. P. Healey; Mrs S. A. R. Davies; J. D. Whatley; K. C. Fox; J. D. W. Rhys; Mrs S. Craig; Miss E. S. Payne; Ms S. McGlashan; Mrs C. Oxborough; Ms J. Eldred (acting); S. T. Fiander (acting); D. H. Griffiths (acting); Ms R. Melling, CBE (acting); C. Wilson (acting)
Examiners of Petitions for Private Bills, Ms H. E. Irwin; Dr F. P. Tudor
Registrar of Members' Interests (£47,138–£75,601), D. W. N. Doig (seconded to Speaker's Office)
  Taxing Officer, Ms H. E. Irwin

VOTE OFFICE

Deliverer of the Vote (£47,138–£75,601), J. F. Collins
Deputy Deliverers of the Vote (£30,967–£46,848), O. B. T. Sweeney (Parliamentary); F. W. Hallett (Production); A. Powell (Development)

SPEAKER'S COUNSEL

Speaker's Counsel (£62,882–£101,254), J. Mason, CB
Speaker's Counsel (European legislation) (£62,882–£101,254), E. G. Vaux
Speaker's Assistant Counsel (£47,138–£75,601), A. Akbar; J. R. Mallinson

DEPARTMENT OF THE SERJEANT-AT-ARMS

Serjeant-at-Arms (£62,882–£101,254), P. N. W. Jennings, CVO
Deputy Serjeant-at-Arms (£47,138–£75,601), M. J. A. Cummins
Assistant Serjeants-at-Arms (£35,072–£56,801), P. A. J. Wright; J. M. Robertson; M. Harvey

DEPARTMENT OF THE LIBRARY

Librarian (£62,882–£101,254), Miss P. Baines
Directors (£47,138–£75,601), K. G. Cuninghame; Mrs J. Wainwright; R. Clements; R. Ware, D.Phil; Miss E. M. McInnes.
Heads of Sections (£35,072–£56,801), C. Pond, Ph.D.; Mrs C. Andrews; Mrs J. Lourie; C. Barclay; Mrs J. Fiddick; Mrs C. Gillie; R. Twigger; Mrs G. Allen; R. Cracknell
Senior Library Clerks (£30,967–£46,848), Ms F. Poole; T. Edmonds; Ms O. Gay; Dr D. Gore; B. Winetrobe; Miss M. Baber; Ms A. Walker; Mrs H. Holden; Mrs P. Carling; Mrs K. Greener; Ms P. Strickland; Miss V. Miller; M. P. Hillyard; Ms J. Roll; Ms W. Wilson; S. Wise; E. Wood; P. Bowers, Ph.D.; A. Seely; G. Danby, Ph.D.; B. C. Morgan; Miss L. Conway; C. Blair, Ph.D.; G. Vidler; C. Sear; Ms F. Whittle; M. Oakes (period); A. Presland (period); K. Parry (acting)

DEPARTMENT OF FINANCE AND ADMINISTRATION

Director of Finance and Administration (£62,882–£101,254), A. Walker
Head of the Establishments Office (£51,975–£85,047), B. Wilson
Head of the Fees Office (£47,138–£75,601), A. Cameron
Head of the Finance Office (£47,138–£75,601), M. Barram
Director of Internal Review Services (£35,072–£56,801), R. Russell

DEPARTMENT OF THE OFFICIAL REPORT

Editor (£51,975–£85,047), I. Church
Deputy Editors (£42,755–£67,163), W. G. Garland;
Miss L. Sutherland; Ms C. Fogarty

REFRESHMENT DEPARTMENT

Director of Catering Services (£51,975–£85,047),
Mrs S. Harrison
Food and Beverage Operations Manager (£30,967–£46,848),
R. Gibbs
Executive Chef (£30,967–£46,848), D. Dorricott
Financial Controller (£30,967–£46,848), Mrs J. Rissen

SELECT COMMITTEES

The more important committees, as at June 2000, are:

DEPARTMENTAL COMMITTEES

Agriculture B Chair, David Curry, MP; *Clerk*,
Ms L. M. Gardner
Culture, Media and Sport B Chair, Rt. Hon. Gerald
Kaufman, MP; *Clerks*, C. G. Lee; R. Cooke
Defence B Chair, Bruce George, MP; *Clerks*, P. A. Evans;
Mrs C. Oxborough
Education and Employment B Clerks, L. C. Laurence-Smyth;
T. P. W. Healey
  Sub-committees: Education B Chair, Barry Sheerman, MP;
  Clerk, L. C. Laurence-Smyth; *Employment B Chair*,
  Rt. Hon. Derek Foster, MP; *Clerk*, T. W. P. Healey
Environment, Transport and the Regions – Chair, Andrew
Bennett, MP; *Clerks*, Dr. D. F. Harrison; H. Yardley;
G. Devine
  Sub-committees: Environment B Chair, Andrew Bennett,
  MP; *Clerks*, Dr D. F. Harrison; H. A. Yardley; *Transport B
  Chair*, Gwyneth Dunwoody, MP; *Clerk*, G. R. Devine
Foreign Affairs B Chair, Donald Anderson, MP; *Clerks*,
E. P. Silk; Ms T. Brufal
Health B Chair, David Hinchliffe, MP; *Clerks*, J. S. Benger,
D.Phil.; T. Goldsmith
Home Affairs B Chair, Robin Corbett, MP; *Clerks*,
A. R. Kennon; M. P. Atkins
International Development B Chair, Bowen Wells, MP;
Clerks, A. Y. A. Azad; Ms J. Hughes
Northern Ireland – Chair, Rt. Hon. Peter Brooke, CH, MP;
Clerk, C. R. M. Ward
Science and Technology – Chair, Dr Michael Clark, MP;
Clerk, Mrs J. N. St J. Mulley
Scottish Affairs – Chair, David Marshall, MP; *Clerk*,
J. D. Whatley
Social Security – Chair, Archy Kirkwood, MP; *Clerks*,
P. G. Moon; T. Goldsmith
Trade and Industry – Chair, Martin O'Neill, MP; *Clerks*,
D. L. Natzler; Ms C. Littleboy
Treasury – Chair, Rt. Hon. Giles Radice, MP; *Clerks*,
S. J. Patrick; M. Egan
  Treasury sub-committee: Chair, Sir Michael Spicer, MP;
  Clerk, M. Egan
Welsh Affairs – Chair, Martyn Jones, MP; *Clerk*,
Ms P. A. Helme

NON-DEPARTMENTAL COMMITTEES

Deregulation – Chair, Peter Pike, MP; *Clerk*, Mrs S. Craig
Environmental Audit – Chair, John Horam, MP; *Clerk*,
F. J. Reid
European Scrutiny – Chair, James Hood, MP; *Clerks*,
Mrs E. J. Flood; Mrs S. Craig
Modernisation – Chair, Rt. Hon. Margaret Beckett, MP;
Clerks, C. B. Winnifrith, CB; A. Sandall
Procedure – Chair, Nicholas Winterton, MP; *Clerks*,
Dr. R. G. James; Ms S. McGlashan

Public Accounts – Chair, Rt. Hon. David Davis, MP; *Clerk*,
K. J. Brown, OBE
Public Administration – Chair, Tony Wright, MP; *Clerk*,
Ms A. Barry
Standards and Privileges – Chair, Rt. Hon. Robert Sheldon,
MP; *Clerks*, A. Sandall; S. Mark

PARLIAMENTARY INFORMATION

The following is a short glossary of aspects of the work of
Parliament. Unless otherwise stated, references are to
House of Commons procedures.

BILL – Proposed legislation is termed a bill. The stages
of a public bill (for private bills, *see* page 221) in the House
of Commons are as follows:
First Reading: This stage nowadays merely constitutes an
order to have the bill printed
Second Reading: The debate on the principles of the bill
Committee Stage: The detailed examination of a bill, clause
by clause. In most cases this takes place in a standing
committee, or the whole House may act as a committee.
A special standing committee may take evidence before
embarking on detailed scrutiny of the bill. Very rarely, a
bill may be examined by a select committee (*see* page 221)
Report Stage: Detailed review of a bill as amended in
committee
Third Reading: Final debate on a bill
Public bills go through the same stages in the House of
Lords, except that in almost all cases the committee stage
is taken in committee of the whole House.
A bill may start in either House, and has to pass through
both Houses to become law. Both Houses have to agree
the same text of a bill, so that the amendments made by the
second House are then considered in the originating
House, and if not agreed, sent back or themselves
amended, until agreement is reached.

CHILTERN HUNDREDS – A nominal office of profit
under the Crown, the acceptance of which requires an MP
to vacate his/her seat. The Manor of Northstead is similar.
These are the only means by which an MP may resign.

CONSOLIDATED FUND BILL – A bill to authorise issue of
money to maintain Government services. The bill is dealt
with without debate.

EARLY DAY MOTION – A motion put on the notice
paper by an MP without in general the real prospect of its
being debated. Such motions are expressions of backbench opinion.

FATHER OF THE HOUSE – The Member whose
continuous service in the House of Commons is the
longest. The present Father of the House is the Rt. Hon.
Sir Edward Heath, KG, MBE, MP, elected first in 1950.

HOURS OF MEETING – The House of Commons
normally meets Monday, Tuesday and Wednesday at
2.30 p.m., and on Thursdays at 11.30 a.m.; there are ten
Fridays without sittings in each session. From January
1999 until the end of the 1999–2000 session the Commons
is experimenting with sitting from 11.30 a.m. on Thursdays. (*See also* Westminster Hall Sittings, below). The
House of Lords normally meets at 2.30 p.m. Monday to
Wednesday and at 3 p.m. on Thursday. In the latter part of
the session, the House of Lords sometimes sits on Fridays
at 11 a.m.

LEADER OF THE OPPOSITION – In 1937 the office of Leader of the Opposition was recognised and a salary was assigned to the post. Since April 1999 the salary has been £105,957 (including parliamentary salary of £47,008). The present Leader of the Opposition is the Rt. Hon. William Hague, MP.

THE LORD CHANCELLOR – The Lord High Chancellor of Great Britain is (*ex officio*) the Speaker of the House of Lords. Unlike the Speaker of the House of Commons, he is a member of the Government, takes part in debates and votes in divisions. He has none of the powers to maintain order that the Speaker in the Commons has, these powers being exercised in the Lords by the House as a whole. The Lord Chancellor sits in the Lords on one of the Woolsacks, couches covered with red cloth and stuffed with wool. If he wishes to address the House in any way except formally as Speaker, he leaves the Woolsack.

NORTHERN IRELAND GRAND COMMITTEE – The Northern Ireland Grand Committee consists of all MPs representing constituencies in Northern Ireland, together with not more than 25 other MPs nominated by the Committee of Selection. The business of the committee includes questions, short debates, ministerial statements, bills, legislative proposals and other matters relating exclusively to Northern Ireland, and delegated legislation. In autumn 1999 the House will debate a proposal to suspend the work of the Committee during the experiment with sittings in Westminster Hall (*see* page 222).

The Northern Ireland Affairs Committee is one of the departmental select committees, empowered to examine the expenditure, administration and policy of the Northern Ireland Office and the administration and expenditure of the Crown Solicitor's Office.

OPPOSITION DAY – A day on which the topic for debate is chosen by the Opposition. There are 20 such days in a normal session. On 17 days, subjects are chosen by the Leader of the Opposition; on the remaining three days by the leader of the next largest opposition party.

PARLIAMENT ACTS 1911 AND 1949 – Under these Acts, bills may become law without the consent of the Lords, though the House of Lords has the power to delay a public bill for 13 months from its first second reading in the House of Commons.

PRIME MINISTER'S QUESTIONS – The Prime Minister answers questions from 3.00 to 3.30 p.m. on Wednesdays.

PRIVATE BILL – A bill promoted by a body or an individual to give powers additional to, or in conflict with, the general law, and to which a special procedure applies to enable people affected to object.

PRIVATE MEMBER'S BILL – A public bill promoted by a Member who is not a member of the Government.

PRIVATE NOTICE QUESTION – A question adjudged of urgent importance on submission to the Speaker (in the Lords, the Leader of the House), answered at the end of oral questions, usually at 3.30 p.m.

PRIVILEGE – The following are covered by the privilege of Parliament:

(i) freedom from interference in going to, attending at, and going from, Parliament
(ii) freedom of speech in parliamentary proceedings
(iii) the printing and publishing of anything relating to the proceedings of the two Houses is subject to privilege

(iv) each House is the guardian of its dignity and may punish any insult to the House as a whole

QUESTION TIME – Oral questions are answered by Ministers in the Commons from 2.30 to 3.30 p.m. every day except Friday. From January 1999 until the end of the 1999–2000 session the Commons experimented with taking questions on Thursdays from 11.30 a.m. to 12.30 p.m. Questions are also taken at the start of the Lords sittings, with a daily limit of four oral questions.

ROYAL ASSENT – The royal assent is signified by letters patent to such bills and measures as have passed both Houses of Parliament (or bills which have been passed under the Parliament Acts 1911 and 1949). The Sovereign has not given royal assent in person since 1854. On occasion, for instance in the prorogation of Parliament, royal assent may be pronounced to the two Houses by Lords Commissioners. More usually royal assent is notified to each House sitting separately in accordance with the Royal Assent Act 1967. The old French formulae for royal assent are then endorsed on the acts by the Clerk of the Parliaments.

The power to withhold assent resides with the Sovereign but has not been exercised in the UK since 1707.

SCOTTISH GRAND COMMITTEE – Established in its present form in 1957, the committee consists of all 72 MPs representing Scottish constituencies, with a quorum of ten. The functions of the committee are to consider the principle of all public bills relating exclusively to Scotland (constituting in effect the bill's second reading); to consider the Scottish estimates on not less than six days a session; and to consider matters relating exclusively to Scotland on not more than six days a session. From the beginning of the 1994–5 session, the committee's powers were enhanced to allow oral questions, short debates, ministerial statements, and consideration of appropriate statutory instruments. The committee can meet on appointed days at specified places in Scotland. In autumn 1999 the House will debate a proposal to suspend the work of the Committee during the experiment with sittings in Westminster Hall (*see* page 222).

The Scottish Affairs Committee, one of the departmental select committees, was empowered to examine the expenditure, administration and policy of the Scottish Office, and the expenditure and administration of the Lord Advocate's Office. Following devolution, the role of the select committee has been questioned. If it continues, it will be concerned with the role and responsibilities of the relevant Secretary of State and on occasion the policy of the UK departments as it affects Scotland.

SELECT COMMITTEES – Consisting usually of ten to 15 members of all parties, select committees are a means used by both Houses in order to investigate certain matters.

Most select committees in the House of Commons are tied to departments: each committee investigates subjects within a government department's remit. There are other select committees dealing with public accounts (i.e. the spending by the Government of money voted by Parliament) and European legislation, and also domestic committees dealing, for example, with privilege and procedure. Major select committees usually take evidence in public; their evidence and reports are published by The Stationery Office. House of Commons select committees are reconstituted after a general election. For main committees, *see* page 220.

The principal select committee in the House of Lords is that on the European Communities, which has, at present, six sub-committees dealing with all areas of Community policy. The House of Lords also has a select committee on science and technology, which appoints sub-committees to deal with specific subjects, and a select committee on delegated powers and deregulation. For committees, *see* page 217. In addition, *ad hoc* select committees have been set up from time to time to investigate specific subjects. There are also some joint committees of the two Houses, e.g. the committees on statutory instruments and on parliamentary privilege.

THE SPEAKER – The Speaker of the House of Commons is the spokesman and president of the Chamber. He or she is elected by the House at the beginning of each Parliament or when the previous Speaker retires or dies. The Speaker neither speaks in debates nor votes in divisions except when the voting is equal.

VACANT SEATS – When a vacancy occurs in the House of Commons during a session of Parliament, the writ for the by-election is moved by a Whip of the party to which the member whose seat has been vacated belonged. If the House is in recess, the Speaker can issue a warrant for a writ, should two members certify to him that a seat is vacant.

WELSH GRAND COMMITTEE – First appointed in the 1959–60 session, the committee consists of all 40 MPs representing Welsh constituencies plus not more than five other members nominated by the Committee of Selection. The functions of the committee are to consider the principle of all public bills referred to it (constituting in effect the second reading of such a bill); and to consider matters relating exclusively to Wales. Since 1996 the business of the committee may also include questions, ministerial statements and short debates. Since June 1996 members of the committee have been permitted to speak in Welsh. In autumn 1999 the House will debate a proposal to suspend the work of the Committee during the experiment with sittings in Westminster Hall.

The Welsh Affairs Committee, one of the departmental select committees, was empowered to examine the expenditure, administration and policy of the Welsh Office. Following devolution, the role of the select committee has been questioned. If it continues, it will be concerned with the role and responsibilities of the relevant Secretary of State and on occasion the policy of the UK departments as it affects Wales.

WESTMINSTER HALL SITTINGS – Following a report by the Modernisation of the House of Commons Select Committee, the Commons decided in May 1999 to set up a second debating forum for an experimental period from the start of the 1999–2000 session. It will be known as 'Westminster Hall' and sittings will be in the Grand Committee Room on Tuesdays from 10 a.m. to 1 p.m., Wednesdays from 9.30 a.m. to 2 p.m. and Thursdays from 2.30 p.m. for up to three hours. Sittings will be open to the public at the times indicated.

WHIPS – In order to secure the attendance of Members of a particular party in Parliament, particularly on the occasion of an important vote, Whips (originally known as 'Whippers-in') are appointed. The written appeal or circular letter issued by them is also known as a 'whip', its urgency being denoted by the number of times it is underlined. Failure to respond to a three-line whip is tantamount in the Commons to secession (at any rate temporarily) from the party. Whips are provided with office accommodation in both Houses, and Government and some Opposition Whips receive salaries from public funds.

PARLIAMENTARY EDUCATION UNIT – Norman Shaw Building (North), London SW1A 2TT.
Tel: 020-7219 2105
E-mail: edunit@parliament.uk
Web: http://www.explore-parliament.uk

GOVERNMENT OFFICE

The Government is the body of Ministers responsible for the administration of national affairs, determining policy and introducing into Parliament any legislation necessary to give effect to government policy. The majority of Ministers are members of the House of Commons but members of the House of Lords or of neither House may also hold ministerial responsibility. The Lord Chancellor is always a member of the House of Lords. The Prime Minister is, by current convention, always a member of the House of Commons.

THE PRIME MINISTER

The office of Prime Minister, which had been in existence for nearly 200 years, was officially recognised in 1905 and its holder was granted a place in the table of precedence. The Prime Minister, by tradition also First Lord of the Treasury and Minister for the Civil Service, is appointed by the Sovereign and is usually the leader of the party which enjoys, or can secure, a majority in the House of Commons. Other Ministers are appointed by the Sovereign on the recommendation of the Prime Minister, who also allocates functions amongst Ministers and has the power to obtain their resignation or dismissal individually.

The Prime Minister informs the Sovereign of state and political matters, advises on the dissolution of Parliament, and makes recommendations for important Crown appointments, the award of honours, etc.

As the chairman of Cabinet meetings and leader of a political party, the Prime Minister is responsible for translating party policy into government activity. As leader of the Government, the Prime Minister is responsible to Parliament and to the electorate for the policies and their implementation.

The Prime Minister also represents the nation in international affairs, e.g. summit conferences.

THE CABINET

The Cabinet developed during the 18th-century as an inner committee of the Privy Council, which was the chief source of executive power until that time. The Cabinet is composed of about 20 Ministers chosen by the Prime Minister, usually the heads of government departments (generally known as Secretaries of State unless they have a special title, e.g. Chancellor of the Exchequer), the leaders of the two Houses of Parliament, and the holders of various traditional offices.

The Cabinet's functions are the final determination of policy, control of government and co-ordination of government departments. The exercise of its functions is dependent upon enjoying majority support in the House of Commons. Cabinet meetings are held in private, taking place once or twice a week during parliamentary sittings and less often during a recess. Proceedings are confidential, the members being bound by their oath as Privy Counsellors not to disclose information about the proceedings.

The convention of collective responsibility means that the Cabinet acts unanimously even when Cabinet Ministers do not all agree on a subject. The policies of departmental Ministers must be consistent with the policies of the Government as a whole, and once the Government's policy has been decided, each Minister is expected to support it or resign.

The convention of ministerial responsibility holds a Minister, as the political head of his or her department, accountable to Parliament for the department's work. Departmental Ministers usually decide all matters within their responsibility, although on matters of political importance they normally consult their colleagues collectively. A decision by a departmental Minister is binding on the Government as a whole.

POLITICAL PARTIES

Before the reign of William and Mary the principal officers of state were chosen by and were responsible to the Sovereign alone and not to Parliament or the nation at large. Such officers acted sometimes in concert with one another but more often independently, and the fall of one did not, of necessity, involve that of others, although all were liable to be dismissed at any moment.

In 1693 the Earl of Sunderland recommended to William III the advisability of selecting a ministry from the political party which enjoyed a majority in the House of Commons and the first united ministry was drawn in 1696 from the Whigs, to which party the King owed his throne. This group became known as the Junto and was regarded with suspicion as a novelty in the political life of the nation, being a small section meeting in secret apart from the main body of Ministers. It may be regarded as the forerunner of the Cabinet and in course of time it led to the establishment of the principle of joint responsibility of Ministers, so that internal disagreement caused a change of personnel or resignation of the whole body of Ministers.

The accession of George I, who was unfamiliar with the English language, led to a disinclination on the part of the Sovereign to preside at meetings of his Ministers and caused the appearance of a Prime Minister, a position first acquired by Robert Walpole in 1721 and retained by him without interruption for 20 years and 326 days.

DEVELOPMENT OF PARTIES

In 1828 the Whigs became known as Liberals, a name originally given to it by its opponents to imply laxity of principles, but gradually accepted by the party to indicate its claim to be pioneers and champions of political reform and progressive legislation. In 1861 a Liberal Registration Association was founded and Liberal Associations became widespread. In 1877 a National Liberal Federation was formed, with headquarters in London. The Liberal Party was in power for long periods during the second half of the 19th-century and for several years during the first quarter of the 20th-century, but after a split in the party the numbers elected were small from 1931. In 1988, a majority of the Liberals agreed on a merger with the Social Democratic Party under the title Social and Liberal Democrats; since 1989 they have been known as the Liberal Democrats. A minority continue separately as the Liberal Party.

Soon after the change from Whig to Liberal the Tory Party became known as Conservative, a name believed to have been invented by John Wilson Croker in 1830 and to have been generally adopted about the time of the passing of the Reform Act of 1832 to indicate that the preservation of national institutions was the leading principle of the party. After the Home Rule crisis of 1886 the dissentient Liberals entered into a compact with the Conservatives,

under which the latter undertook not to contest their seats, but a separate Liberal Unionist organisation was maintained until 1912, when it was united with the Conservatives.

Labour candidates for Parliament made their first appearance at the general election of 1892, when there were 27 standing as Labour or Liberal-Labour. In 1900 the Labour Representation Committee was set up in order to establish a distinct Labour group in Parliament, with its own whips, its own policy, and a readiness to co-operate with any party which might be engaged in promoting legislation in the direct interest of labour. In 1906 the LRC became known as the Labour Party.

The Council for Social Democracy was announced by four former Labour Cabinet Ministers in January 1981 and in March 1981 the Social Democratic Party was launched. Later that year the SDP and the Liberal Party formed an electoral alliance. In 1988 a majority of the SDP agreed on a merger with the Liberal Party but a minority continued as a separate party under the SDP title. In 1990 it was decided to wind up the party organisation and its three sitting MPs were known as independent social democrats. None were returned at the 1992 general election.

Plaid Cymru was founded in 1926 to provide an independent political voice for Wales and to campaign for self-government in Wales.

The Scottish National Party was founded in 1934 to campaign for independence for Scotland.

The Social Democratic and Labour Party was founded in 1970, emerging from the civil rights movement of the 1960s, with the aim of promoting reform, reconciliation and partnership across the sectarian divide in Northern Ireland and of opposing violence from any quarter.

The Ulster Democratic Unionist Party was founded in 1971 to resist moves by the Ulster Unionist Party which were considered a threat to the Union. Its aim is to maintain Northern Ireland as an integral part of the UK.

The Ulster Unionist Council first met formally in 1905. Its objectives are to maintain Northern Ireland as an integral part of the UK and to promote the aims of the Ulster Unionist Party.

GOVERNMENT AND OPPOSITION

The government of the day is formed by the party which wins the largest number of seats in the House of Commons at a general election, or which has the support of a majority of members in the House of Commons. By tradition, the leader of the majority party is asked by the Sovereign to form a government, while the largest minority party becomes the official Opposition with its own leader and a 'Shadow Cabinet'. Leaders of the Government and Opposition sit on the front benches of the Commons with their supporters (the back-benchers) sitting behind them.

FINANCIAL SUPPORT

Financial support to Opposition parties in the House of Commons was introduced in 1975 and is commonly known as Short Money, after Edward Short, the Leader of the House at that time, who introduced the scheme. For 2000–1 financial support is:

Conservative	£3,485,131
Liberal Democrats	1,112.906
Plaid Cymru	63,454
SNP	138,106
SDLP	65,505
Democratic Unionists	34,744
Ulster Unionsts	142,333

A specific allocation for the Leader of the Opposition's office was introduced in April 1999 and has been set at £500,000 a year.

Financial support to the Opposition parties in the House of Lords was introduced in 1996 and is commonly known as Cranborne Money.

The parties included here are those with MPs sitting in the House of Commons in the present Parliament. Addresses of other political parties may be found in the Societies and Institutions section.

CONSERVATIVE AND UNIONIST PARTY

Central Office, 32 Smith Square,
London SW1P 3HH
Tel: 020-7222 9000; Fax: 020-7222 1135
E-mail: ccoffice@conservative-party.org.uk
Web: http://www.conservative-party.org.uk

Chairman, Rt. Hon. Michael Ancram, QC, MP
Deputy Chairman and Chief Executive, The Hon. David Prior, MP
Senior Vice-Chairman, Tim Collins, CBE, MP
Vice-Chairmen, N. Evans, MP (*Wales*); John Hayes, MP
Treasurer, M. Ashcroft
SHADOW CABINET *as at May 2000*
Leader of the Opposition, Rt. Hon. William Hague, MP
Agriculture, Fisheries and Food, Tim Yeo, MP
Cabinet Office, Duchy of Lancaster and Policy Renewal, Andrew Lansley, CBE, MP
Culture, Media and Sport, Peter Ainsworth, MP
Defence, Iain Duncan Smith, MP
Education and Employment, Theresa May, MP
Environment, Transport and the Regions, Archie Norman, MP
Foreign and Commonwealth Affairs, Rt. Hon. Francis Maude, MP
Health, Dr Liam Fox, MP
Home Affairs, Rt. Hon. Ann Widdecombe, MP
International Development, Gary Streeter, MP
Leader of the House of Commons and Constitutional Affairs, Rt. Hon. Sir George Young, Bt., MP
Leader of the House of Lords and Constitutional Affairs, The Lord Strathclyde, PC
Northern Ireland, Rt. Hon. Andrew Mackay, MP
Social Security, David Willetts, MP
Trade and Industry, Angela Browning, MP
Transport, Bernard Jenkin, MP
Treasury, Rt. Hon. Michael Portillo, MP
Chief Secretary to the Treasury, Rt. Hon. David Heathcoat-Amory, MP
Conservative Party Chairman, Rt. Hon. Michael Ancram, QC, MP
CHIEF WHIPS
House of Lords, The Lord Henley
House of Commons, Rt. Hon. James Arbuthnot, MP (*Chief Whip*); Patrick McLoughlin, MP (*Deputy Chief Whip*)

SCOTTISH CONSERVATIVE AND UNIONIST CENTRAL OFFICE

83 Princes Street, Edinburgh EH2 2ER
Tel: 0131-247 6890
Email: scuco@scottish.tory.org.uk

Chairman, R. Robertson
Deputy Chairman, B. Walker
Hon. Treasurer, D. Mitchell, CBE
Director, S. Turner

LABOUR PARTY

Millbank Tower, Millbank,
London SW1P 4GT
Tel: 020-7802 1000; Fax: 020-7802 1234
E-mail: information@new.labour.org.uk
Web: http://www.labour.org.uk

Parliamentary Party Leader, Rt. Hon. Anthony Blair, MP
Deputy Party Leader, Rt. Hon. John Prescott, MP
Leader in the Lords, The Baroness Jay of Paddington
Chair, Clive Soley, MP
Vice-Chair, Jean Corston, MP
Treasurer, Ms M. Prosser
General Secretary, Ms M. McDonagh
General Secretary, Scottish Labour Party, L. Quinn

LIBERAL DEMOCRATS

4 Cowley Street, London SW1P 3NB
Tel: 020-7222 7999; Fax: 020-7799 2170
E-mail: libdems@cix.co.uk
Web: http://www.libdems.org.uk

President, The Baroness Maddock
Hon. Treasurer, Reg Clark
Chief Executive, Hugh Rickard
Parliamentary Party Leader, Rt. Hon Charles Kennedy, MP
Leader in the Lords, The Lord Rodgers of Quarry Bank, PC
LIBERAL DEMOCRAT SPOKESMEN *as at May 2000*
Deputy Leader, Rt. Hon. Alan Beith, MP
Agriculture and Rural Affairs, Colin Breed, MP
Culture, Media and Sport, Constitution, Rt. Hon. Robert Maclennan, MP
Education and Employment, Phil Willis, MP
Environment, Don Foster, MP
Foreign Affairs, Defence and Europe, Rt. Hon. Menzies Campbell, MP
Home Affairs, Simon Hughes, MP
Health, Nick Harvey, MP
International Development, Dr, Jenny Tonge, MP
Social Security and Welfare, Prof. Steve Webb, MP
Trade and Industry, Dr Vincent Cable, MP
Treasury, Matthew Taylor, MP
Scotland, Rt. Hon. Jim Wallace, MP
Wales, Richard Livsey, MP
Chair of the Parliamentary Party, Malcolm Bruce, MP
LIBERAL DEMOCRAT WHIPS
House of Lords, The Lord Harris of Greenwich, PC
House of Commons, Paul Tyler, MP (*Chief Whip*); Andrew Stunell, MP (*Deputy Whip*)

LIBERAL DEMOCRATS WALES

Bay View House, 102 Bute Street, Cardiff CF1 6AD
Tel: 029-2031 3400; Fax: 029-2031 3401
E-mail: ldwales@cix.co.uk

Party President, Clive Lindley
Party Leader, Richard Livsey, CBE, MP
Chairman, P. Lloyd
Treasurer, G. Worley
Secretary, J. Bucree
Administrative Officer, Ms H. Northmore-Thomas
Chief Executive, C. Lines

SCOTTISH LIBERAL DEMOCRATS

4 Clifton Terrace, Edinburgh EH12 5DR
Tel: 0131-337 2314; Fax: 0131-337 3566
E-mail: scotlibdem@cix.co.uk
Web: http://www.scotlibdems.org.uk

Party President, Malcolm Bruce, MP
Party Leader, Jim Wallace, MP, MSP

Convener, Cllr I. Yuill
Treasurer, D. R. Sullivan
Chief Executive, K. Croft

PLAID CYMRU – THE PARTY OF WALES
18 Park Grove, Cardiff CF10 3BN
Tel: 029-2064 6000; Fax: 029-2064 6001
E-mail: post@plaidcymru.org
Web: http://www.plaidcymru.org

Party President, Dafydd Wigley, MP
Chairman, M. Phillips
Hon. Treasurer, vacant
Chief Executive/General Secretary, K. Davies

SCOTTISH NATIONAL PARTY
6 North Charlotte Street, Edinburgh EH2 4JH
Tel: 0131-226 3661; Fax: 0131-225 9597
Web: http://www.snp.org.uk

Parliamentary Party Leader, Alasdair Morgan, MP, MSP
Chief Whip, Alasdair Morgan, MP, MSP
National Convener, Alex Salmond, MP
Senior Vice-Convener, John Swinney, MP
National Treasurer, I. Blackford
National Secretary, S. Hosie

NORTHERN IRELAND

SOCIAL DEMOCRATIC AND LABOUR PARTY
121 Ormeau Road, Belfast BT7 1SH
Tel: 028-9024 7700; Fax: 028-9023 6699
E-mail: sdlp@indigo.ie
Web: http://www.sdlp.ie

Parliamentary Party Leader, John Hume, MP, MEP
Deputy Leader, Seamus Mallon, MP
Chief Whip, Eddie McGrady, MP
Chairman, J. Lennon
Hon. Treasurer, J. Stephenson
General Secretary, Mrs G. Cosgrove

ULSTER DEMOCRATIC UNIONIST PARTY
91 Dundela Avenue, Belfast BT4 3BU
Tel: 028-9047 1155; Fax: 028-9047 1797
E-mail: info@dup.org.uk
Web: http://www.dup.org.uk

Parliamentary Party Leader, Ian Paisley, MP, MEP, MLA
Deputy Leader, Peter Robinson, MP, MLA
Chairman, M. Morrow, MLA
Chief Executive, A. Ewart
Hon. Treasurer, G. Campbell, MLA
Party Secretary, N. Dodds, MLA

ULSTER UNIONIST PARTY
3 Glengall Street, Belfast BT12 5AE
Tel: 028-9032 4601; Fax: 028-9024 6738
E-mail: uup@uup.org
Web: http://www.uup.org

Party Leader, Rt. Hon. David Trimble, MP
Chief Whip, Revd Martin Smyth, MP
ULSTER UNIONIST COUNCIL
President, Sir Josias Cunningham
Chairman, The Lord Rogan
Hon. Treasurer, J. Allen, OBE
General Secretary, D. Boyd

For abbreviations, *see* page 235
*Member of last Parliament
†Elected at a by-election since the general election
For late amendments *see* Stop-press

*Abbott, Ms Diane J. (*b.* 1953) *Lab., Hackney North and Stoke Newington*, maj. 15,627
Adams, Gerard (Gerry) (*b.* 1948) *SF, Belfast West*, maj. 7,909
*Adams, Mrs K. Irene (*b.* 1948) *Lab., Paisley North*, maj. 12,814
*Ainger, Nicholas R. (*b.* 1949) *Lab., Carmarthen West and Pembrokeshire South*, maj. 9,621
*Ainsworth, Peter M. (*b.* 1956) *C., Surrey East*, maj. 15,093
*Ainsworth, Robert W. (*b.* 1952) *Lab., Coventry North East*, maj. 22,569
†Alexander, Douglas G. (*b.* 1967) *Lab., Paisley South*, maj. 2,731
Allan, Richard B. (*b.* 1966) *LD, Sheffield Hallam*, maj. 8,271
*Allen, Graham W. (*b.* 1953) *Lab., Nottingham North*, maj. 18,801
*Amess, David A.A. (*b.* 1952) *C., Southend West*, maj. 2,615
*Ancram, Rt. Hon. Michael A. F. J. K. (Earl of Ancram) (*b.* 1945) *C., Devizes*, maj. 9,782
*Anderson, Donald (*b.* 1939) *Lab., Swansea East*, maj. 25,569
*Anderson, Mrs Janet (*b.* 1949) *Lab., Rossendale and Darwen*, maj. 10,949
*Arbuthnot, Rt. Hon. James N. (*b.* 1952) *C., Hampshire North East*, maj. 14,398
*Armstrong, Miss Hilary J. (*b.* 1945) *Lab., Durham North West*, maj. 24,754
*Ashdown, Rt. Hon. J. J. D. (Paddy) (*b.* 1941) *LD, Yeovil*, maj. 11,403
*Ashton, Joseph W. (*b.* 1933) *Lab., Bassetlaw*, maj. 17,460
Atherton, Ms Candice K. (*b.* 1955) *Lab., Falmouth and Camborne*, maj. 2,688
Atkins, Ms Charlotte (*b.* 1950) *Lab., Staffordshire Moorlands*, maj. 10,049
*Atkinson, David A. (*b.* 1940) *C., Bournemouth East*, maj. 4,346
*Atkinson, Peter L. (*b.* 1943) *C., Hexham*, maj. 222
*Austin-Walker, John E. (*b.* 1944) *Lab., Erith and Thamesmead*, maj. 17,424
Baker, Norman J. (*b.* 1957) *LD, Lewes*, maj. 1,300
*Baldry, Antony B. (*b.* 1950) *C., Banbury*, maj. 4,737
Ballard, Mrs Jacqueline M. (*b.* 1953) *LD, Taunton*, maj. 2,443
*Banks, Anthony L. (*b.* 1943) *Lab., West Ham*, maj. 19,494
*Barnes, Harold (*b.* 1936) *Lab., Derbyshire North East*, maj. 18,321
*Barron, Kevin J. (*b.* 1946) *Lab., Rother Valley*, maj. 23,485
*Battle, John D. (*b.* 1951) *Lab., Leeds West*, maj. 19,771
*Bayley, Hugh (*b.* 1952) *Lab., City of York*, maj. 20,523
Beard, C. Nigel (*b.* 1936) *Lab., Bexleyheath and Crayford*, maj. 3,415
*Beckett, Rt. Hon. Margaret M. (*b.* 1943) *Lab., Derby South*, maj. 16,106
Begg, Ms Anne (*b.* 1955) *Lab., Aberdeen South*, maj. 3,365
*Beggs, Roy (*b.* 1936) *UUP, Antrim East*, maj. 6,389
*Beith, Rt. Hon. Alan J. (*b.* 1943) *LD, Berwick upon Tweed*, maj. 8,042
Bell, Martin, OBE (*b.* 1938) *Ind., Tatton*, maj. 11,077
*Bell, Stuart (*b.* 1938) *Lab., Middlesbrough*, maj. 25,018
*Benn, Rt. Hon. Anthony N. W. (*b.* 1925) *Lab., Chesterfield*, maj. 5,775
†Benn, Hilary J. (*b.* 1953) *Lab., Leeds Central*, maj. 2,293
*Bennett, Andrew F. (*b.* 1939) *Lab., Denton and Reddish*, maj. 20,311
*Benton, Joseph E. (*b.* 1933) *Lab., Bootle*, maj. 28,421
Bercow, John S. (*b.* 1963) *C., Buckingham*, maj. 12,386
*Beresford, Sir Paul (*b.* 1946) *C., Mole Valley*, maj. 10,221
*Bermingham, Gerald E. (*b.* 1940) *Lab., St Helens South*, maj. 23,739

*Berry, Roger L., D. Phil. (*b.* 1948) *Lab., Kingswood*, maj. 14,253
Best, Harold (*b.* 1939) *Lab., Leeds North West*, maj. 3,844
*Betts, Clive J.C. (*b.* 1950) *Lab., Sheffield Attercliffe*, maj. 21,818
Blackman, Ms Elizabeth M. (*b.* 1949) *Lab., Erewash*, maj. 9,135
*Blair, Rt. Hon. Anthony C. L. (*b.* 1953) *Lab., Sedgefield*, maj. 25,143
Blears, Hazel A. (*b.* 1956) *Lab., Salford*, maj. 17,069
Blizzard, Robert J. (*b.* 1950) *Lab., Waveney*, maj. 12,453
*Blunkett, Rt. Hon. David (*b.* 1947) *Lab., Sheffield Brightside*, maj. 19,954
Blunt, Crispin J. R. (*b.* 1960) *C., Reigate*, maj. 7,741
*Boateng, Paul Y. (*b.* 1951) *Lab., Brent South*, maj. 19,691
*Body, Sir Richard (*b.* 1927) *C., Boston and Skegness*, maj. 647
*Boothroyd, Rt. Hon. Betty (*b.* 1929) *The Speaker, West Bromwich West*, maj. 15,423
Borrow, David S. (*b.* 1952) *Lab., Ribble South*, maj. 5,084
*Boswell, Timothy E. (*b.* 1942) *C., Daventry*, maj. 7,378
*Bottomley, Peter J. (*b.* 1944) *C., Worthing West*, maj. 7,713
*Bottomley, Rt. Hon. Virginia H. B. M. (*b.* 1948) *C., Surrey South West*, maj. 2,694
*Bradley, Keith J. C. (*b.* 1950) *Lab., Manchester Withington*, maj. 18,581
Bradley, Peter C. S. (*b.* 1953) *Lab., Wrekin, The*, maj. 3,025
Bradshaw, Benjamin P. J. (*b.* 1960) *Lab., Exeter*, maj. 11,705
Brady, Graham (*b.* 1967) *C., Altrincham and Sale West*, maj. 1,505
Brake, Thomas A. (*b.* 1962) *LD, Carshalton and Wallington*, maj. 2,267
Brand, Dr Peter (*b.* 1947) *LD, Isle of Wight*, maj. 6,406
*Brazier, Julian W.H, TD (*b.* 1953) *C., Canterbury*, maj. 3,964
Breed, Colin E. (*b.* 1947) *LD, Cornwall South East*, maj. 6,480
Brinton, Ms Helen R. (*b.* 1954) *Lab., Peterborough*, maj. 7,323
*Brooke, Rt. Hon. Peter L., CH (*b.* 1934) *C., Cities of London and Westminster*, maj. 4,881
*Brown, Rt. Hon. J. Gordon, Ph.D. (*b.* 1951) *Lab., Dunfermline East*, maj. 18,751
*Brown, Nicholas H. (*b.* 1950) *Lab., Newcastle upon Tyne East and Wallsend*, maj. 23,811
Brown, Russell L. (*b.* 1951) *Lab., Dumfries*, maj. 9,643
Browne, Desmond (*b.* 1952) *Lab., Kilmarnock and Loudoun*, maj. 7,256
*Browning, Mrs Angela F. (*b.* 1946) *C., Tiverton and Honiton*, maj. 1,653
*Bruce, Ian C. (*b.* 1947) *C., Dorset South*, maj. 77
*Bruce, Malcolm G. (*b.* 1944) *LD, Gordon*, maj. 6,997
Buck, Ms Karen P. (*b.* 1958) *Lab., Regent's Park and Kensington North*, maj. 14,657
*Burden, Richard H. (*b.* 1954) *Lab., Birmingham Northfield*, maj. 11,443
Burgon, Colin (*b.* 1948) *Lab., Elmet*, maj. 8,779
Burnett, John P.A. (*b.* 1945) *LD, Devon West and Torridge*, maj. 1,957
*Burns, Simon H.M. (*b.* 1952) *C., Chelmsford West*, maj. 6,691
Burstow, Paul K. (*b.* 1962) *LD, Sutton and Cheam*, maj. 2,097
Butler, Ms Christine M. (*b.* 1943) *Lab., Castle Point*, maj. 1,116
*Butterfill, John V. (*b.* 1941) *C., Bournemouth West*, maj. 5,710
*Byers, Rt. Hon. Stephen J. (*b.* 1953) *Lab., Tyneside North*, maj. 26,643
Cable, Dr J. Vincent (*b.* 1943) *LD, Twickenham*, maj. 4,281
*Caborn, Richard G. (*b.* 1943) *Lab., Sheffield Central*, maj. 16,906
Campbell, Alan (*b.* 1957) *Lab., Tynemouth*, maj. 11,273
*Campbell, Mrs Anne (*b.* 1940) *Lab., Cambridge*, maj. 14,137
*Campbell, Ronald (*b.* 1943) *Lab., Blyth Valley*, maj. 17,736
*Campbell, Rt. Hon. W. Menzies, CBE, QC (*b.* 1941) *LD, Fife North East*, maj. 10,356

*Campbell-Savours, Dale N. (*b.* 1943) *Lab., Workington,* maj. 19,656

*Canavan, Dennis A. (*b.* 1942) *Lab., Falkirk West,* maj. 13,783

*Cann, James C. (*b.* 1946) *Lab., Ipswich,* maj. 10,439

Caplin, Ivor K. (*b.* 1958) *Lab., Hove,* maj. 3,959

Casale, Roger M. (*b.* 1960) *Lab., Wimbledon,* maj. 2,980

*Cash, William N. P. (*b.* 1940) *C., Stone,* maj. 3,818

Caton, Martin P. (*b.* 1951) *Lab., Gower,* maj. 13,007

Cawsey, Ian A. (*b.* 1960) *Lab., Brigg and Goole,* maj. 6,389

*Chapman, J. K. (Ben) (*b.* 1940) *Lab., Wirral South,* maj. 7,004

*Chapman, Sir Sydney (*b.* 1935) *C., Chipping Barnet,* maj. 1,035

Chaytor, David M. (*b.* 1949) *Lab., Bury North,* maj. 7,866

*Chidgey, David W. G. (*b.* 1942) *LD, Eastleigh,* maj. 754

*Chisholm, Malcolm G. R. (*b.* 1949) *Lab., Edinburgh North and Leith,* maj. 10,978

Chope, Christopher, R., OBE (*b.* 1947) *C., Christchurch,* maj. 2,165

*Church, Mrs Judith A. (*b.* 1953) *Lab., Dagenham,* maj. 17,054

*Clapham, Michael (*b.* 1943) *Lab., Barnsley West and Penistone,* maj. 17,267

*Clappison, W. James (*b.* 1956) *C., Hertsmere,* maj. 3,075

*Clark, Rt. Hon. David G., PH.D. (*b.* 1939) *Lab., South Shields,* maj. 22,153

Clark, Ms Lynda M. (*b.* 1949) *Lab., Edinburgh Pentlands,* maj. 4,862

*Clark, Dr Michael, PH.D. (*b.* 1935) *C., Rayleigh,* maj. 10,684

Clark, Paul G. (*b.* 1957) *Lab., Gillingham,* maj. 1,980

Clarke, Anthony R. (*b.* 1963) *Lab., Northampton South,* maj. 744

Clarke, Charles R. (*b.* 1950) *Lab., Norwich South,* maj. 14,239

*Clarke, Eric L. (*b.* 1933) *Lab., Midlothian,* maj. 9,870

*Clarke, Rt. Hon. Kenneth H., QC (*b.* 1940) *C., Rushcliffe,* maj. 5,055

*Clarke, Rt. Hon. Thomas, CBE (*b.* 1941) *Lab., Coatbridge and Chryston,* maj. 19,295

*Clelland, David G. (*b.* 1943) *Lab., Tyne Bridge,* maj. 22,906

*Clifton-Brown, Geoffrey R. (*b.* 1953) *C., Cotswold,* maj. 11,965

*Clwyd, Mrs Ann (*b.* 1937) *Lab., Cynon Valley,* maj. 19,755

Coaker, Vernon R. (*b.* 1953) *Lab., Gedling,* maj. 3,802

*Coffey, Ms M. Ann (*b.* 1946) *Lab., Stockport,* maj. 18,912

*Cohen, Harry M. (*b.* 1949) *Lab., Leyton and Wanstead,* maj. 15,186

Coleman, Iain (*b.* 1958) *Lab., Hammersmith and Fulham,* maj. 3,842

Collins, Timothy W. G. (*b.* 1964) *C., Westmorland and Lonsdale,* maj. 4,521

Colman, Anthony (*b.* 1943) *Lab., Putney,* maj. 2,976

*Connarty, Michael (*b.* 1947) *Lab., Falkirk East,* maj. 13,385

*Cook, Francis (*b.* 1935) *Lab., Stockton North,* maj. 21,357

*Cook, Rt. Hon. R. F. (Robin) (*b.* 1946) *Lab., Livingston,* maj. 11,747

Cooper, Ms Yvette (*b.* 1969) *Lab., Pontefract and Castleford,* maj. 25,725

*Corbett, Robin (*b.* 1933) *Lab., Birmingham Erdington,* maj. 12,657

*Corbyn, Jeremy B. (*b.* 1949) *Lab., Islington North,* maj. 19,955

*Cormack, Sir Patrick (*b.* 1939) *C., Staffordshire South,* maj. 7,821

*Corston, Ms Jean A. (*b.* 1942) *Lab., Bristol East,* maj. 16,159

Cotter, Brian J. (*b.* 1938) *LD, Weston-super-Mare,* maj. 1,274

*Cousins, James M. (*b.* 1944) *Lab., Newcastle upon Tyne Central,* maj. 16,480

*Cox, Thomas M. (*b.* 1930) *Lab., Tooting,* maj. 15,011

*Cran, James D. (*b.* 1944) *C., Beverley and Holderness,* maj. 811

Cranston, Ross F. (*b.* 1948) *Lab., Dudley North,* maj. 9,457

Crausby, David A. (*b.* 1946) *Lab., Bolton North East,* maj. 12,669

Cryer, Mrs C. Ann (*b.* 1939) *Lab., Keighley,* maj. 7,132

Cryer, John R. (*b.* 1964) *Lab., Hornchurch,* maj. 5,680

*Cummings, John S. (*b.* 1943) *Lab., Easington,* maj. 30,012

*Cunliffe, Lawrence F. (*b.* 1929) *Lab., Leigh,* maj. 24,496

*Cunningham, Rt. Hon. Dr. J. A. (Jack), PH.D. (*b.* 1939) *Lab., Copeland,* maj. 11,944

*Cunningham, James D. (*b.* 1941) *Lab., Coventry South,* maj. 10,953

*Cunningham, Ms Roseanna (*b.* 1951) *SNP, Perth,* maj. 3,141

*Curry, Rt. Hon. David M. (*b.* 1944) *C., Skipton and Ripon,* maj. 11,620

Curtis-Tansley, Ms Claire (*b.* 1958) *Lab., Crosby,* maj. 7,182

*Dalyell, Tam (*b.* 1932) *Lab., Linlithgow,* maj. 10,838

*Darling, Rt. Hon. Alistair M. (*b.* 1953) *Lab., Edinburgh Central,* maj. 11,070

Darvill, Keith E. (*b.* 1948) *Lab., Upminster,* maj. 2,770

Davey, Edward J. (*b.* 1965) *LD, Kingston and Surbiton,* maj. 56

Davey, Ms Valerie (*b.* 1940) *Lab., Bristol West,* maj. 1,493

*Davidson, Ian G. (*b.* 1950) *Lab. Co-op., Glasgow Pollok,* maj. 13,791

*Davies, Rt. Hon. D. J. Denzil (*b.* 1938) *Lab., Llanelli,* maj. 16,039

Davies, Geraint R. (*b.* 1960) *Lab., Croydon Central,* maj. 3,897

*Davies, J. Quentin (*b.* 1944) *C., Grantham and Stamford,* maj. 2,692

*Davies, Rt. Hon. Ronald (*b.* 1946) *Lab., Caerphilly,* maj. 25,839

*Davis, Rt. Hon. David M. (*b.* 1948) *C., Haltemprice and Howden,* maj. 7,514

*Davis, Terence A. G. (*b.* 1938) *Lab., Birmingham Hodge Hill,* maj. 14,200

Dawson, T. Hilton (*b.* 1953) *Lab., Lancaster and Wyre,* maj. 1,295

*Day, Stephen R. (*b.* 1948) *C., Cheadle,* maj. 3,189

Dean, Ms Janet E. A. (*b.* 1949) *Lab., Burton,* maj. 6,330

*Denham, John Y. (*b.* 1953) *Lab., Southampton Itchen,* maj. 14,209

*Dewar, Rt. Hon. Donald C. (*b.* 1937) *Lab., Glasgow Anniesland,* maj. 15,154

Dismore, Andrew H. (*b.* 1954) *Lab., Hendon,* maj. 6,155

Dobbin, James (*b.* 1941) *Lab. Co-op., Heywood and Middleton,* maj. 17,542

*Dobson, Rt. Hon. Frank G. (*b.* 1940) *Lab., Holborn and St Pancras,* maj. 17,903

Donaldson, Jeffrey M. (*b.* 1962) *UUP, Lagan Valley,* maj. 16,925

*Donohoe, Brian H. (*b.* 1948) *Lab., Cunninghame South,* maj. 14,869

Doran, Frank (*b.* 1949) *Lab., Aberdeen Central,* maj. 10,801

*Dorrell, Rt. Hon. Stephen J. (*b.* 1952) *C., Charnwood,* maj. 5,900

*Dowd, James P. (*b.* 1951) *Lab., Lewisham West,* maj. 14,337

Drew, David E. (*b.* 1952) *Lab. Co-op., Stroud,* maj. 2,910

Drown, Ms Julia K. (*b.* 1962) *Lab., Swindon South,* maj. 5,645

*Duncan, Alan J. C. (*b.* 1957) *C., Rutland and Melton,* maj. 8,836

*Duncan Smith, G. Iain (*b.* 1954) *C., Chingford and Woodford Green,* maj. 5,714

*Dunwoody, Hon. Mrs Gwyneth P. (*b.* 1930) *Lab., Crewe and Nantwich,* maj. 15,798

*Eagle, Ms Angela (*b.* 1961) *Lab., Wallasey,* maj. 19,074

Eagle, Ms Maria (*b.* 1961) *Lab., Liverpool Garston,* maj. 18,417

Edwards, Huw W. E. (*b.* 1953) *Lab., Monmouth,* maj. 4,178

Efford, Clive S. (*b.* 1958) *Lab., Eltham,* maj. 10,182

Ellman, Ms Louise J. (*b.* 1945) *Lab. Co-op., Liverpool Riverside,* maj. 21,799

*Emery, Rt. Hon. Sir Peter (*b.* 1926) *C., Devon East,* maj. 7,489

*Ennis, Jeffrey (*b.* 1952) *Lab., Barnsley East and Mexborough,* maj. 26,763

*Etherington, William (*b.* 1941) *Lab., Sunderland North,* maj. 19,697

*Evans, Nigel M. (*b.* 1957) *C., Ribble Valley,* maj. 6,640

*Ewing, Mrs Margaret A. (*b.* 1945) *SNP, Moray,* maj. 5,566

*Faber, David J. C. (*b.* 1961) *C., Westbury,* maj. 6,068

*Fabricant, Michael L. D. (*b.* 1950) *C., Lichfield,* maj. 238

Fallon, Michael C. (*b.* 1952) *C., Sevenoaks,* maj. 10,461

*Fearn, Ronald C., OBE (*b.* 1931) *LD, Southport,* maj. 6,160

*Field, Rt. Hon. Frank (b. 1942) Lab., Birkenhead, maj. 21,843
*Fisher, Mark (b. 1944) Lab., Stoke-on-Trent Central, maj. 19,924
Fitzpatrick, James (b. 1952) Lab., Poplar and Canning Town, maj. 18,915
Fitzsimons, Ms Lorna (b. 1967) Lab., Rochdale, maj. 4,545
Flight, Howard E. (b. 1948) C., Arundel and South Downs, maj. 14,035
Flint, Ms Caroline L. (b. 1961) Lab., Don Valley, maj. 14,659
*Flynn, Paul P. (b. 1935) Lab., Newport West, maj. 14,537
Follett, Ms D. Barbara (b. 1942) Lab., Stevenage, maj. 11,582
*Forth, Rt. Hon. Eric (b. 1944) C., Bromley and Chisleburst, maj. 11,118
*Foster, Rt. Hon. Derek (b. 1937) Lab., Bishop Auckland, maj. 21,064
*Foster, Donald M. E. (b. 1947) LD, Bath, maj. 9,319
Foster, Michael J. (b. 1946) Lab., Hastings and Rye, maj. 2,560
Foster, Michael J. (b. 1963) Lab., Worcester, maj. 7,425
*Foulkes, George (b. 1942) Lab. Co-op., Carrick, Cumnock and Doon Valley, maj. 21,062
*Fowler, Rt. Hon. Sir Norman (b. 1938) C., Sutton Coldfield, maj. 14,885
*Fox, Dr Liam (b. 1961) C., Woodspring, maj. 7,734
Fraser, Christopher J. (b. 1962) C., Dorset Mid and Poole North, maj. 681
*Fyfe, Ms Maria (b. 1938) Lab., Glasgow Maryhill, maj. 14,264
*Galbraith, Samuel L. (b. 1945) Lab., Strathkelvin and Bearsden, maj. 16,292
*Gale, Roger J. (b. 1943) C., Thanet North, maj. 2,766
*Galloway, George (b. 1954) Lab., Glasgow Kelvin, maj. 9,665
*Gapes, Michael J. (b. 1952) Lab. Co-op., Ilford South, maj. 14,200
Gardiner, Barry S. (b. 1957) Lab., Brent North, maj. 4,019
*Garnier, Edward H., QC (b. 1952) C., Harborough, maj. 6,524
George, Andrew H. (b. 1958) LD, St Ives, maj. 7,170
*George, Bruce T. (b. 1942) Lab., Walsall South, maj. 11,312
*Gerrard, Neil F. (b. 1942) Lab., Walthamstow, maj. 17,149
Gibb, Nicholas J. (b. 1960) C., Bognor Regis and Littlehampton, maj. 7,321
Gibson, Dr Ian (b. 1938) Lab., Norwich North, maj. 9,470
† Gidley, Sandra (b. 0) LD, Romsey, maj. 3,311
*Gillan, Mrs Cheryl E. K. (b. 1952) C., Chesham and Amersham, maj. 13,859
*Gill, Christopher J. RD (b. 1936) C., Ludlow, maj. 5,909
Gilroy, Mrs Linda (b. 1949) Lab. Co-op., Plymouth Sutton, maj. 9,440
*Godman, Norman A., PH.D. (b. 1938) Lab., Greenock and Inverclyde, maj. 13,040
*Godsiff, Roger D. (b. 1946) Lab., Birmingham Sparkbrook and Small Heath, maj. 19,526
Goggins, Paul G. (b. 1953) Lab., Wythenshawe and Sale East, maj. 15,019
*Golding, Mrs Llinos (b. 1933) Lab., Newcastle under Lyme, maj. 17,206
Gordon, Mrs Eileen (b. 1946) Lab., Romford, maj. 649
*Gorman, Mrs Teresa E. (b. 1931) C., Billericay, maj. 1,356
Gorrie, Donald C. E., OBE (b. 1933) LD, Edinburgh West, maj. 7,253
*Graham, Thomas (b. 1944) SLI, Renfrewshire West, maj. 7,979
Gray, James W. (b. 1954) C., Wiltshire North, maj. 3,475
Green, Damian H. (b. 1956) C., Ashford, maj. 5,355
*Greenway, John R. (b. 1946) C., Ryedale, maj. 5,058
Grieve, Dominic C. R. (b. 1956) C., Beaconsfield, maj. 13,987
Griffiths, Ms Jane P. (b. 1954) Lab., Reading East, maj. 3,795
*Griffiths, Nigel (b. 1955) Lab., Edinburgh South, maj. 11,452
*Griffiths, Winston J. (b. 1943) Lab., Bridgend, maj. 15,248
*Grocott, Bruce J. (b. 1940) Lab., Telford, maj. 11,290
Grogan, John T. (b. 1961) Lab., Selby, maj. 3,836
*Gummer, Rt. Hon. John S. (b. 1939) C., Suffolk Coastal, maj. 3,254

*Gunnell, W. John (b. 1933) Lab., Morley and Rothwell, maj. 14,750
*Hague, Rt. Hon. William J. (b. 1961) C., Richmond, maj. 10,051
*Hain, Peter G. (b. 1950) Lab., Neath, maj. 26,741
*Hall, Michael T. (b. 1952) Lab., Weaver Vale, maj. 13,448
Hall, Patrick (b. 1951) Lab., Bedford, maj. 8,300
*Hamilton, Rt. Hon. Sir Archibald (b. 1941) C., Epsom and Ewell, maj. 11,525
Hamilton, Fabian (b. 1955) Lab., Leeds North East, maj. 6,959
Hammond, Philip (b. 1955) C., Runnymede and Weybridge, maj. 9,875
Hancock, Michael T., CBE (b. 1946) LD, Portsmouth South, maj. 4,327
*Hanson, David G. (b. 1957) Lab., Delyn, maj. 11,693
*Harman, Rt. Hon. Harriet (b. 1950) Lab., Camberwell and Peckham, maj. 16,351
Harris, Dr Evan (b. 1965) LD, Oxford West and Abingdon, maj. 6,285
*Harvey, Nicholas B. (b. 1961) LD, Devon North, maj. 6,181
*Haselhurst, Rt. Hon. Sir Alan (b. 1937) C., Saffron Walden, maj. 10,573
*Hawkins, Nicholas J. (b. 1957) C., Surrey Heath, maj. 16,287
Hayes, John H. (b. 1958) C., South Holland and the Deepings, maj. 7,991
Heal, Mrs Sylvia L. (b. 1942) Lab. Co-op., Halesowen and Rowley Regis, maj. 10,337
*Heald, Oliver (b. 1954) C., Hertfordshire North East, maj. 3,088
Healey, John (b. 1960) Lab., Wentworth, maj. 23,959
*Heath, Rt. Hon. Sir Edward, KG, MBE (b. 1916) C., Old Bexley and Sidcup, maj. 3,569
Heath, David W. St J. (b. 1954) LD, Somerton and Frome, maj. 130
*Heathcoat-Amory, Rt. Hon. David P. (b. 1949) C., Wells, maj. 528
*Henderson, Douglas J. (b. 1949) Lab., Newcastle upon Tyne North, maj. 19,332
Henderson, Ivan J. (b. 1958) Lab., Harwich, maj. 1,216
Hepburn, Stephen (b. 1959) Lab., Jarrow, maj. 21,933
*Heppell, John B. (b. 1948) Lab., Nottingham East, maj. 15,419
*Heseltine, Rt. Hon. Michael R. D., CH (b. 1933) C., Henley, maj. 11,167
Hesford, Stephen (b. 1957) Lab., Wirral West, maj. 2,738
Hewitt, Ms Patricia H. (b. 1948) Lab., Leicester West, maj. 12,864
*Hill, T. Keith (b. 1943) Lab., Streatham, maj. 18,423
*Hinchliffe, David M. (b. 1948) Lab., Wakefield, maj. 14,604
*Hodge, Mrs Margaret E., MBE (b. 1944) Lab., Barking, maj. 15,896
*Hoey, Ms Catharine (Kate) L. (b. 1946) Lab., Vauxhall, maj. 18,660
*Hogg, Rt. Hon. Douglas M., QC (b. 1945) C., Sleaford and North Hykeham, maj. 5,123
*Home Robertson, John D. (b. 1948) Lab., East Lothian, maj. 14,221
*Hood, James (b. 1948) Lab., Clydesdale, maj. 13,809
*Hoon, Geoffrey W. (b. 1953) Lab., Ashfield, maj. 22,728
Hope, Philip I. (b. 1955) Lab. Co-op., Corby, maj. 11,860
Hopkins, Kelvin P. (b. 1941) Lab., Luton North, maj. 9,626
*Horam, John R. (b. 1939) C., Orpington, maj. 2,952
*Howard, Rt. Hon. Michael, QC (b. 1941) C., Folkestone and Hythe, maj. 6,332
*Howarth, Alan T., CBE (b. 1944) Lab., Newport East, maj. 13,523
*Howarth, George E. (b. 1949) Lab., Knowsley North and Sefton East, maj. 26,147
Howarth, J. Gerald D. (b. 1947) C., Aldershot, maj. 6,621
*Howells, Kim S., PH.D. (b. 1946) Lab., Pontypridd, maj. 23,129
Hoyle, Lindsay H. (b. 1957) Lab., Chorley, maj. 9,870

Hughes, Ms Beverley J. (*b.* 1950) *Lab., Stretford and Urmston,* maj. 13,640

*Hughes, Kevin M. (*b.* 1952) *Lab., Doncaster North,* maj. 21,937

*Hughes, Simon H. W. (*b.* 1951) *LD, Southwark North and Bermondsey,* maj. 3,387

Humble, Mrs Jovanka (Joan) (*b.* 1951) *Lab., Blackpool North and Fleetwood,* maj. 8,946

*Hume, John, MEP (*b.* 1937) *SDLP, Foyle,* maj. 13,664

*Hunter, Andrew R. F. (*b.* 1943) *C., Basingstoke,* maj. 2,397

Hurst, Alan A. (*b.* 1945) *Lab., Braintree,* maj. 1,451

*Hutton, John M. P. (*b.* 1955) *Lab., Barrow and Furness,* maj. 14,497

Iddon, Brian (*b.* 1940) *Lab., Bolton South East,* maj. 21,311

*Illsley, Eric E. (*b.* 1955) *Lab., Barnsley Central,* maj. 24,501

*Ingram, Rt. Hon. Adam P. (*b.* 1947) *Lab., East Kilbride,* maj. 17,384

*Jack, Rt. Hon. J. Michael (*b.* 1946) *C., Fylde,* maj. 8,963

*Jackson, Ms Glenda M., CBE (*b.* 1936) *Lab., Hampstead and Highgate,* maj. 13,284

*Jackson, Mrs Helen M. (*b.* 1939) *Lab., Sheffield Hillsborough,* maj. 16,451

*Jackson, Robert V. (*b.* 1946) *C., Wantage,* maj. 6,039

*Jamieson, David C. (*b.* 1947) *Lab., Plymouth Devonport,* maj. 19,067

*Jenkin, Hon. Bernard C. (*b.* 1959) *C., Essex North,* maj. 5,476

*Jenkins, Brian D. (*b.* 1942) *Lab., Tamworth,* maj. 7,496

Johnson, Alan A. (*b.* 1950) *Lab., Hull West and Hessle,* maj. 15,525

Johnson, Ms Melanie J. (*b.* 1955) *Lab., Welwyn Hatfield,* maj. 5,595

*Johnson Smith, Rt. Hon. Sir Geoffrey (*b.* 1924) *C., Wealden,* maj. 14,204

*Jones, Rt. Hon. S. Barry (*b.* 1938) *Lab., Alyn and Deeside,* maj. 16,403

Jones, Ms Fiona E. A. (*b.* 1957) *Lab., Newark,* maj. 3,016

Jones, Ms Helen M. (*b.* 1954) *Lab., Warrington North,* maj. 19,527

*Jones, Ieuan W. (*b.* 1949) *PC, Ynys Môn,* maj. 2,481

Jones, Ms Jennifer G. (*b.* 1948) *Lab., Wolverhampton South West,* maj. 5,118

*Jones, Jonathan O. (*b.* 1954) *Lab. Co-op., Cardiff Central,* maj. 7,923

*Jones, Ms Lynne M., PH.D. (*b.* 1951) *Lab., Birmingham Selly Oak,* maj. 14,088

*Jones, Martyn D. (*b.* 1947) *Lab., Clwyd South,* maj. 13,810

*Jones, Nigel D. (*b.* 1948) *LD, Cheltenham,* maj. 6,645

*Jowell, Rt. Hon. Tessa J. H. D. (*b.* 1947) *Lab., Dulwich and West Norwood,* maj. 16,769

*Kaufman, Rt. Hon. Gerald B. (*b.* 1930) *Lab., Manchester Gorton,* maj. 17,342

Keeble, Ms Sally C. (*b.* 1951) *Lab., Northampton North,* maj. 10,000

Keen, Mrs Ann L. (*b.* 1948) *Lab., Brentford and Isleworth,* maj. 14,424

*Keen, D. Alan (*b.* 1937) *Lab. Co-op., Feltham and Heston,* maj. 15,273

Keetch, Paul S. (*b.* 1961) *LD, Hereford,* maj. 6,648

Kelly, Ms Ruth M. (*b.* 1968) *Lab., Bolton West,* maj. 7,072

Kemp, Fraser (*b.* 1958) *Lab., Houghton and Washington East,* maj. 26,555

*Kennedy, Charles P. (*b.* 1959) *LD, Ross, Skye and Inverness West,* maj. 4,019

*Kennedy, Mrs Jane E. (*b.* 1958) *Lab., Liverpool Wavertree,* maj. 19,701

*Key, S. Robert (*b.* 1945) *C., Salisbury,* maj. 6,276

*Khabra, Piara S. (*b.* 1924) *Lab., Ealing Southall,* maj. 21,423

Kidney, David N. (*b.* 1955) *Lab., Stafford,* maj. 4,314

*Kilfoyle, Peter (*b.* 1946) *Lab., Liverpool Walton,* maj. 27,038

King, Andrew (*b.* 1948) *Lab., Rugby and Kenilworth,* maj. 495

King, Ms Oona T. (*b.* 1967) *Lab., Bethnal Green and Bow,* maj. 11,285

*King, Rt. Hon. Thomas J., CH (*b.* 1933) *C., Bridgwater,* maj. 1,796

Kingham, Ms Teresa J. (*b.* 1963) *Lab., Gloucester,* maj. 8,259

Kirkbride, Miss Julie (*b.* 1960) *C., Bromsgrove,* maj. 4,895

*Kirkwood, Archibald J. (*b.* 1946) *LD, Roxburgh and Berwickshire,* maj. 7,906

Kumar, Dr Ashok (*b.* 1956) *Lab., Middlesbrough South and Cleveland East,* maj. 10,607

Ladyman, Dr Stephen J. (*b.* 1952) *Lab., Thanet South,* maj. 2,878

Laing, Mrs Eleanor F. (*b.* 1958) *C., Epping Forest,* maj. 5,252

†Lait, Ms Jacqueline A. H. (*b.* 1947) *C., Beckenham,* maj. 1,227

†Lammy, David *Lab., Tottenham,* maj. 5,646

Lansley, Andrew D. (*b.* 1956) *C., Cambridgeshire South,* maj. 8,712

Lawrence, Mrs Jacqueline R. (*b.* 1948) *Lab., Preseli Pembrokeshire,* maj. 8,736

Laxton, Robert (*b.* 1944) *Lab., Derby North,* maj. 10,615

*Leigh, Edward J. E. (*b.* 1950) *C., Gainsborough,* maj. 6,826

Lepper, David (*b.* 1945) *Lab. Co-op., Brighton Pavilion,* maj. 13,181

Leslie, Christopher M. (*b.* 1972) *Lab., Shipley,* maj. 2,996

Letwin, Oliver (*b.* 1956) *C., Dorset West,* maj. 1,840

Levitt, Tom (*b.* 1954) *Lab., High Peak,* maj. 8,791

Lewis, Ivan (*b.* 1967) *Lab., Bury South,* maj. 12,433

Lewis, Dr Julian M. (*b.* 1951) *C., New Forest East,* maj. 5,215

*Lewis, Terence (*b.* 1935) *Lab., Worsley,* maj. 17,741

*Liddell, Rt. Hon. Helen (*b.* 1950) *Lab., Airdrie and Shotts,* maj. 15,412

*Lidington, David R., PH.D. (*b.* 1956) *C., Aylesbury,* maj. 8,419

*Lilley, Rt. Hon. Peter B. (*b.* 1943) *C., Hitchin and Harpenden,* maj. 6,671

Linton, J. Martin (*b.* 1944) *Lab., Battersea,* maj. 5,360

*Livingstone, Kenneth R. (*b.* 1945) *Lab., Brent East,* maj. 15,882

Livsey, Richard A. L., CBE (*b.* 1935) *LD, Brecon and Radnorshire,* maj. 5,097

*Lloyd, Anthony J. (*b.* 1950) *Lab., Manchester Central,* maj. 19,682

*Lloyd, Rt. Hon. Sir Peter (*b.* 1937) *C., Fareham,* maj. 10,358

*Llwyd, Elfyn (*b.* 1951) *PC, Meirionnydd nant Conwy,* maj. 6,805

Lock, David A. (*b.* 1960) *Lab., Wyre Forest,* maj. 6,946

*Lord, Michael N. (*b.* 1938) *C., Suffolk Central and Ipswich North,* maj. 3,538

Loughton, Timothy P. (*b.* 1962) *C., Worthing East and Shoreham,* maj. 5,098

Love, Andrew (*b.* 1949) *Lab. Co-op., Edmonton,* maj. 13,472

*Luff, Peter J. (*b.* 1955) *C., Worcestershire Mid,* maj. 9,412

*Lyell, Rt. Hon. Sir Nicholas, QC (*b.* 1938) *C., Bedfordshire North East,* maj. 5,883

*McAllion, John (*b.* 1948) *Lab., Dundee East,* maj. 9,961

*McAvoy, Thomas M. (*b.* 1943) *Lab. Co-op., Glasgow Rutherglen,* maj. 15,007

McCabe, Stephen J. (*b.* 1955) *Lab., Birmingham Hall Green,* maj. 8,420

McCafferty, Ms Christine (*b.* 1945) *Lab., Calder Valley,* maj. 6,255

*McCartney, Rt. Hon. Ian (*b.* 1951) *Lab., Makerfield,* maj. 26,177

*McCartney, Robert L., QC (NI) (*b.* 1936) *UKU, Down North,* maj. 1,449

McDonagh, Ms Siobhain A. (*b.* 1960) *Lab., Mitcham and Morden,* maj. 13,741

*Macdonald, Calum, A., PH.D. (*b.* 1956) *Lab., Western Isles,* maj. 3,576

McDonnell, John M. (*b.* 1951) *Lab., Hayes and Harlington,* maj. 14,291

*McFall, John (*b.* 1944) *Lab. Co-op., Dumbarton,* maj. 10,883

*McGrady, Edward K. (*b.* 1935) *SDLP, Down South,* maj. 9,933

*MacGregor, Rt. Hon. John R. R., OBE (*b.* 1937) *C., Norfolk South,* maj. 7,378

McGuinness, Martin (*b.* 1950) *SF, Ulster Mid,* maj. 1,883

McGuire, Mrs Anne (*b.* 1949) *Lab., Stirling,* maj. 6,411

McIntosh, Miss Anne C. B. (*b.* 1954) *C., Vale of York,* maj. 9,721

McIsaac, Ms Shona (*b.* 1960) *Lab., Cleethorpes,* maj. 9,176

*Mackay, Rt. Hon. Andrew J. (*b.* 1949) *C., Bracknell,* maj. 10,387

McKenna, Ms Rosemary (*b.* 1941) *Lab., Cumbernauld and Kilsyth,* maj. 11,128

*MacKinlay, Andrew S. (*b.* 1949) *Lab., Thurrock,* maj. 17,256

*Maclean, Rt. Hon. David J. (*b.* 1953) *C., Penrith and the Border,* maj. 10,233

*McLeish, Henry B. (*b.* 1948) *Lab., Fife Central,* maj. 13,713

*Maclennan, Rt. Hon. Robert A. R. (*b.* 1936) *LD, Caithness, Sutherland and Easter Ross,* maj. 2,259

*McLoughlin, Patrick A. (*b.* 1957) *C., Derbyshire West,* maj. 4,885

*McNamara, J. Kevin (*b.* 1934) *Lab., Hull North,* maj. 19,705

McNulty, Anthony J. (*b.* 1958) *Lab., Harrow East,* maj. 9,738

*MacShane, Denis, PH.D. (*b.* 1948) *Lab., Rotherham,* maj. 21,469

MacTaggart, Ms Fiona M. (*b.* 1953) *Lab., Slough,* maj. 13,071

McWalter, Tony (*b.* 1945) *Lab. Co-op., Hemel Hempstead,* maj. 3,636

*McWilliam, John D. (*b.* 1941) *Lab., Blaydon,* maj. 16,605

*Madel, Sir David (*b.* 1938) *C., Bedfordshire South West,* maj. 132

*Maginnis, Kenneth (*b.* 1938) *UUP, Fermanagh and South Tyrone,* maj. 13,688

*Mahon, Mrs Alice (*b.* 1937) *Lab., Halifax,* maj. 11,212

*Major, Rt. Hon. John, CH (*b.* 1943) *C., Huntingdon,* maj. 18,140

Malins, Humfrey J., CBE (*b.* 1945) *C., Woking,* maj. 5,678

Mallaber, Ms C. Judith (*b.* 1951) *Lab., Amber Valley,* maj. 11,613

*Mallon, Seamus (*b.* 1936) *SDLP, Newry and Armagh,* maj. 4,889

*Mandelson, Rt. Hon. Peter B. (*b.* 1953) *Lab., Hartlepool,* maj. 17,508

Maples, John C. (*b.* 1943) *C., Stratford-upon-Avon,* maj. 14,106

*Marek, John, PH.D. (*b.* 1940) *Lab., Wrexham,* maj. 11,762

*Marsden, Gordon (*b.* 1953) *Lab., Blackpool South,* maj. 11,616

Marsden, Paul W. B. (*b.* 1968) *Lab., Shrewsbury and Atcham,* maj. 1,670

*Marshall, David, PH.D (*b.* 1941) *Lab., Glasgow Shettleston,* maj. 15,868

*Marshall, James, PH.D. (*b.* 1941) *Lab., Leicester South,* maj. 16,493

Marshall-Andrews, Robert G., QC (*b.* 1944) *Lab., Medway,* maj. 5,354

*Martin, Michael J. (*b.* 1945) *Lab., Glasgow Springburn,* maj. 17,326

*Martlew, Eric A. (*b.* 1949) *Lab., Carlisle,* maj. 12,390

*Mates, Michael J. (*b.* 1934) *C., Hampshire East,* maj. 11,590

Maude, Rt. Hon. Francis A. A. (*b.* 1953) *C., Horsham,* maj. 14,862

*Mawhinney, Rt. Hon. Sir Brian, PH.D. (*b.* 1940) *C., Cambridgeshire North West,* maj. 7,754

*Maxton, John A. (*b.* 1936) *Lab., Glasgow Cathcart,* maj. 12,245

May, Mrs Theresa M. (*b.* 1956) *C., Maidenhead,* maj. 11,981

*Meacher, Rt. Hon. Michael H. (*b.* 1939) *Lab., Oldham West and Royton,* maj. 16,201

*Meale, J. Alan (*b.* 1949) *Lab., Mansfield,* maj. 20,518

Merron, Ms Gillian J. (*b.* 1959) *Lab., Lincoln,* maj. 11,130

*Michael, Rt. Hon. Alun E. (*b.* 1943) *Lab. Co-op., Cardiff South and Penarth,* maj. 13,881

*Michie, Mrs J. Ray (*b.* 1934) *LD, Argyll and Bute,* maj. 6,081

*Michie, William (*b.* 1935) *Lab., Sheffield Heeley,* maj. 17,078

*Milburn, Rt. Hon. Alan (*b.* 1958) *Lab., Darlington,* maj. 16,025

*Miller, Andrew P. (*b.* 1949) *Lab., Ellesmere Port and Neston,* maj. 16,036

*Mitchell, Austin V., D.Phil. (*b.* 1934) *Lab., Great Grimsby,* maj. 16,244

Moffatt, Mrs Laura J. (*b.* 1954) *Lab., Crawley,* maj. 11,707

*Moonie, Dr Lewis G. (*b.* 1947) *Lab. Co-op., Kirkcaldy,* maj. 10,710

Moore, Michael K. (*b.* 1965) *LD, Tweeddale, Ettrick and Lauderdale,* maj. 1,489

Moran, Ms Margaret (*b.* 1955) *Lab., Luton South,* maj. 11,319

Morgan, Alasdair N. (*b.* 1945) *SNP, Galloway and Upper Nithsdale,* maj. 5,624

*Morgan, H. Rhodri (*b.* 1939) *Lab., Cardiff West,* maj. 15,628

Morgan, Ms Julie (*b.* 1944) *Lab., Cardiff North,* maj. 8,126

*Morley, Elliot A. (*b.* 1952) *Lab., Scunthorpe,* maj. 14,173

*Morris, Ms Estelle (*b.* 1952) *Lab., Birmingham Yardley,* maj. 5,315

*Morris, Rt. Hon. John, QC (*b.* 1931) *Lab., Aberavon,* maj. 21,571

*Moss, Malcolm D. (*b.* 1943) *C., Cambridgeshire North East,* maj. 5,101

Mountford, Ms Kali C. J. (*b.* 1954) *Lab., Colne Valley,* maj. 4,840

*Mowlam, Rt. Hon. Marjorie, PH.D. (*b.* 1949) *Lab., Redcar,* maj. 21,664

*Mudie, George E. (*b.* 1945) *Lab., Leeds East,* maj. 17,466

*Mullin, Christopher J. (*b.* 1947) *Lab., Sunderland South,* maj. 19,638

Murphy, Denis (*b.* 1948) *Lab., Wansbeck,* maj. 22,367

Murphy, James (*b.* 1967) *Lab., Eastwood,* maj. 3,236

*Murphy, Paul P. (*b.* 1948) *Lab., Torfaen,* maj. 24,536

Naysmith, J. Douglas (*b.* 1941) *Lab. Co-op., Bristol North West,* maj. 11,382

*Nicholls, Patrick C. M. (*b.* 1948) *C., Teignbridge,* maj. 281

Norman, Archibald J. (*b.* 1954) *C., Tunbridge Wells,* maj. 7,506

Norris, Dan (*b.* 1960) *Lab., Wansdyke,* maj. 4,799

†Oaten, Mark (*b.* 1964) *LD, Winchester,* maj. 21,556

*O'Brien, Michael (*b.* 1954) *Lab., Warwickshire North,* maj. 14,767

†O'Brien, Stephen (*b.* 1957) *C., Eddisbury,* maj. 1,606

*O'Brien, William (*b.* 1929) *Lab., Normanton,* maj. 15,893

*O'Hara, Edward (*b.* 1937) *Lab., Knowsley South,* maj. 30,708

*Olner, William J. (*b.* 1942) *Lab., Nuneaton,* maj. 13,540

*O'Neill, Martin J. (*b.* 1945) *Lab., Ochil,* maj. 4,652

Opik, Lembit (*b.* 1965) *LD, Montgomeryshire,* maj. 6,303

Organ, Ms Diana M. (*b.* 1952) *Lab., Forest of Dean,* maj. 6,343

Osborne, Mrs Sandra C. (*b.* 1956) *Lab., Ayr,* maj. 6,543

*Ottaway, Richard G. J. (*b.* 1945) *C., Croydon South,* maj. 11,930

*Page, Richard L. (*b.* 1941) *C., Hertfordshire South West,* maj. 10,021

*Paice, James E. T. (*b.* 1949) *C., Cambridgeshire South East,* maj. 9,349

*Paisley, Revd Ian R. K., MEP (*b.* 1926) *DUP, Antrim North,* maj. 10,574

Palmer, Nicholas D. (*b.* 1950) *Lab., Broxtowe,* maj. 5,575

Paterson, Owen W. (*b.* 1956) *C., Shropshire North,* maj. 2,195

*Pearson, Ian P., PH.D. (*b.* 1959) *Lab., Dudley South,* maj. 13,027

*Pendry, Thomas (*b.* 1934) *Lab., Stalybridge and Hyde,* maj. 14,806

Perham, Ms Linda (*b.* 1947) *Lab., Ilford North,* maj. 3,224

*Pickles, Eric J. (*b.* 1952) *C., Brentwood and Ongar,* maj. 9,690

*Pickthall, Colin (*b.* 1944) *Lab., Lancashire West,* maj. 17,119

*Pike, Peter L. (*b.* 1937) *Lab., Burnley,* maj. 17,062

Plaskitt, James A. (*b.* 1954) *Lab., Warwick and Leamington,* maj. 3,398

Pollard, Kerry P. (*b.* 1944) *Lab., St Albans,* maj. 4,459

Pond, Christopher R. (*b.* 1952) *Lab., Gravesham,* maj. 5,779

*Pope, Gregory J. (*b.* 1960) *Lab., Hyndburn,* maj. 11,448

†Portillo, Rt. Hon. Michael (*b.* 1953) *C.*, *Kensington and Chelsea*, maj. 6,706

Pound, Stephen P. (*b.* 1948) *Lab.*, *Ealing North*, maj. 9,160

*Powell, Sir Raymond (*b.* 1928) *Lab.*, *Ogmore*, maj. 24,447

*Prentice, Ms Bridget T. (*b.* 1952) *Lab.*, *Lewisham East*, maj. 12,127

*Prentice, Gordon (*b.* 1951) *Lab.*, *Pendle*, maj. 10,824

*Prescott, Rt. Hon. John L. (*b.* 1938) *Lab.*, *Hull East*, maj. 23,318

*Primarolo, Ms Dawn (*b.* 1954) *Lab.*, *Bristol South*, maj. 19,328

Prior, Hon. David G. L. (*b.* 1954) *C.*, *Norfolk North*, maj. 1,293

Prosser, Gwynfor M. (*b.* 1943) *Lab.*, *Dover*, maj. 11,739

*Purchase, Kenneth (*b.* 1939) *Lab. Co-op.*, *Wolverhampton North East*, maj. 12,987

*Quin, Rt. Hon. Joyce G. (*b.* 1944) *Lab.*, *Gateshead East and Washington West*, maj. 24,950

Quinn, Lawrence W. (*b.* 1956) *Lab.*, *Scarborough and Whitby*, maj. 5,124

*Radice, Rt. Hon. Giles H. (*b.* 1936) *Lab.*, *Durham North*, maj. 26,299

Rammell, William E. (*b.* 1959) *Lab.*, *Harlow*, maj. 10,514

†Randall, A. John (*b.* 1955) *C.*, *Uxbridge*, maj. 3,766

Rapson, Sydney N. J. (*b.* 1942) *Lab.*, *Portsmouth North*, maj. 4,323

*Raynsford, W. R. N. (Nick) (*b.* 1945) *Lab.*, *Greenwich and Woolwich*, maj. 18,128

*Redwood, Rt. Hon. John A. D.Phil. (*b.* 1951) *C.*, *Wokingham*, maj. 9,365

Reed, Andrew J. (*b.* 1964) *Lab.*, *Loughborough*, maj. 5,712

*Reid, Rt. Hon. John, Ph.D. (*b.* 1947) *Lab.*, *Hamilton North and Bellshill*, maj. 17,067

*Rendel, David D. (*b.* 1949) *LD*, *Newbury*, maj. 8,517

*Robathan, Andrew R. G. (*b.* 1951) *C.*, *Blaby*, maj. 6,474

Robertson, Laurence A. (*b.* 1958) *C.*, *Tewkesbury*, maj. 9,234

*Robinson, Geoffrey (*b.* 1938) *Lab.*, *Coventry North West*, maj. 16,601

*Robinson, Peter D. (*b.* 1948) *DUP*, *Belfast East*, maj. 6,754

*Roche, Mrs Barbara M. R. (*b.* 1954) *Lab.*, *Hornsey and Wood Green*, maj. 20,499

*Roe, Mrs Marion A. (*b.* 1936) *C.*, *Broxbourne*, maj. 6,653

*Rogers, Allan R. (*b.* 1932) *Lab.*, *Rhondda*, maj. 24,931

*Rooker, Jeffrey W. (*b.* 1941) *Lab.*, *Birmingham Perry Barr*, maj. 18,957

*Rooney, Terence H. (*b.* 1950) *Lab.*, *Bradford North*, maj. 12,770

*Ross, Ernest (*b.* 1942) *Lab.*, *Dundee West*, maj. 11,859

*Ross, William (*b.* 1936) *UUP*, *Londonderry East*, maj. 3,794

*Rowe, Andrew J. B. (*b.* 1935) *C.*, *Faversham and Kent Mid*, maj. 4,173

*Rowlands, Edward (*b.* 1940) *Lab.*, *Merthyr Tydfil and Rhymney*, maj. 27,086

Roy, Frank (*b.* 1958) *Lab.*, *Motherwell and Wishaw*, maj. 12,791

Ruane, Christopher S. (*b.* 1958) *Lab.*, *Vale of Clwyd*, maj. 8,955

†Ruddock, Mrs Joan M. (*b.* 1943) *Lab.*, *Lewisham Deptford*, maj. 18,878

Ruffley, David L. (*b.* 1962) *C.*, *Bury St Edmunds*, maj. 368

Russell, Ms Christine M. (*b.* 1945) *Lab.*, *City of Chester*, maj. 10,553

Russell, Robert E. (*b.* 1946) *LD*, *Colchester*, maj. 1,581

Ryan, Ms Joan M. (*b.* 1955) *Lab.*, *Enfield North*, maj. 6,822

St Aubyn, Nicholas F. (*b.* 1955) *C.*, *Guildford*, maj. 4,791

*Salmond, Alexander E. A. (*b.* 1954) *SNP*, *Banff and Buchan*, maj. 12,845

Salter, Martin J. (*b.* 1954) *Lab.*, *Reading West*, maj. 2,997

Sanders, Adrian M. (*b.* 1959) *LD*, *Torbay*, maj. 12

Sarwar, Mohammad (*b.* 1952) *Lab.*, *Glasgow Govan*, maj. 2,914

Savidge, Malcolm K. (*b.* 1946) *Lab.*, *Aberdeen North*, maj. 10,010

Sawford, Philip A. (*b.* 1950) *Lab.*, *Kettering*, maj. 189

Sayeed, Jonathan (*b.* 1948) *C.*, *Bedfordshire Mid*, maj. 7,090

*Sedgemore, Brian C. J. (*b.* 1937) *Lab.*, *Hackney South and Shoreditch*, maj. 14,980

Shaw, Jonathan R. (*b.* 1966) *Lab.*, *Chatham and Aylesford*, maj. 2,790

*Sheerman, Barry J. (*b.* 1940) *Lab. Co-op.*, *Huddersfield*, maj. 15,848

*Sheldon, Rt. Hon. Robert E. (*b.* 1923) *Lab.*, *Ashton under Lyne*, maj. 22,965

*Shephard, Rt. Hon. Gillian P. (*b.* 1940) *C.*, *Norfolk South West*, maj. 2,464

*Shepherd, Richard C. S. (*b.* 1942) *C.*, *Aldridge-Brownhills*, maj. 2,526

Shipley, Ms Debra A. (*b.* 1957) *Lab.*, *Stourbridge*, maj. 5,645

*Short, Rt. Hon. Clare (*b.* 1946) *Lab.*, *Birmingham Ladywood*, maj. 23,082

*Simpson, Alan J. (*b.* 1948) *Lab.*, *Nottingham South*, maj. 13,364

Simpson, Keith (*b.* 1949) *C.*, *Norfolk Mid*, maj. 1,336

Singh, Marsha (*b.* 1954) *Lab.*, *Bradford West*, maj. 3,877

*Skinner, Dennis E. (*b.* 1932) *Lab.*, *Bolsover*, maj. 27,149

*Smith, Rt. Hon. Andrew D. (*b.* 1951) *Lab.*, *Oxford East*, maj. 16,665

Smith, Ms Angela E. (*b.* 1959) *Lab. Co-op.*, *Basildon*, maj. 13,280

*Smith, Rt. Hon. Christopher R., Ph.D. (*b.* 1951) *Lab.*, *Islington South and Finsbury*, maj. 14,563

Smith, Ms Geraldine (*b.* 1961) *Lab.*, *Morecambe and Lunesdale*, maj. 5,965

Smith, Ms Jacqueline J. (*b.* 1962) *Lab.*, *Redditch*, maj. 6,125

Smith, John W. P. (*b.* 1951) *Lab.*, *Vale of Glamorgan*, maj. 10,532

*Smith, Llewellyn T. (*b.* 1944) *Lab.*, *Blaenau Gwent*, maj. 28,035

Smith, Sir Robert, Bt. (*b.* 1958) *LD*, *Aberdeenshire West and Kincardine*, maj. 2,662

*Smyth, Revd W. Martin (*b.* 1931) *UUP*, *Belfast South*, maj. 4,600

*Snape, Peter C. (*b.* 1942) *Lab.*, *West Bromwich East*, maj. 13,584

*Soames, Hon. A. Nicholas W. (*b.* 1948) *C.*, *Sussex Mid*, maj. 6,854

*Soley, Clive S. (*b.* 1939) *Lab.*, *Ealing Acton and Shepherd's Bush*, maj. 15,647

Southworth, Ms Helen M. (*b.* 1956) *Lab.*, *Warrington South*, maj. 10,807

*Spellar, John F. (*b.* 1947) *Lab.*, *Warley*, maj. 15,451

Spelman, Mrs Caroline A. (*b.* 1958) *C.*, *Meriden*, maj. 582

*Spicer, Sir Michael (*b.* 1943) *C.*, *Worcestershire West*, maj. 3,846

*Spring, Richard J. G. (*b.* 1946) *C.*, *Suffolk West*, maj. 1,867

*Squire, Ms Rachel A. (*b.* 1954) *Lab.*, *Dunfermline West*, maj. 12,354

*Stanley, Rt. Hon. Sir John (*b.* 1942) *C.*, *Tonbridge and Malling*, maj. 10,230

Starkey, Mrs Phyllis M. (*b.* 1947) *Lab.*, *Milton Keynes South West*, maj. 10,292

*Steen, Sir Anthony (*b.* 1939) *C.*, *Totnes*, maj. 877

*Steinberg, Gerald N. (*b.* 1945) *Lab.*, *City of Durham*, maj. 22,504

*Stevenson, George W. (*b.* 1938) *Lab.*, *Stoke-on-Trent South*, maj. 18,303

Stewart, David J. (*b.* 1956) *Lab.*, *Inverness East, Nairn and Lochaber*, maj. 2,339

Stewart, Ian (*b.* 1950) *Lab.*, *Eccles*, maj. 21,916

Stinchcombe, Paul D. (*b.* 1962) *Lab.*, *Wellingborough*, maj. 187

Stoate, Howard G. A. (*b.* 1954) *Lab.*, *Dartford*, maj. 4,328

*Strang, Rt. Hon. Gavin S., Ph.D. (*b.* 1943) *Lab.*, *Edinburgh East and Musselburgh*, maj. 14,530

*Straw, Rt. Hon. J. W. (Jack) (*b.* 1946) *Lab.*, *Blackburn*, maj. 14,451

*Streeter, Gary N. (*b.* 1955) *C.*, *Devon South West*, maj. 7,433

Stringer, Graham E. (*b.* 1950) *Lab., Manchester Blackley,* maj. 19,588

Stuart, Mrs Gisela G. (*b.* 1955) *Lab., Birmingham Edgbaston,* maj. 4,842

Stunell, Andrew (*b.* 1942) *LD, Hazel Grove,* maj. 11,814

*Sutcliffe, Gerard (*b.* 1953) *Lab., Bradford South,* maj. 12,936

Swayne, Desmond A. (*b.* 1956) *C., New Forest West,* maj. 11,332

Swinney, John R. (*b.* 1964) *SNP, Tayside North,* maj. 4,160

Syms, Robert A. R. (*b.* 1956) *C., Poole,* maj. 5,298

*Tapsell, Sir Peter (*b.* 1930) *C., Louth and Horncastle,* maj. 6,900

Taylor, Ms Dari J. (*b.* 1944) *Lab., Stockton South,* maj. 11,585

Taylor, David L. (*b.* 1946) *Lab., Leicestershire North West,* maj. 13,219

*Taylor, Sir Edward (Teddy) (*b.* 1937) *C., Rochford and Southend East,* maj. 4,225

*Taylor, Ian C., MBE (*b.* 1945) *C., Esher and Walton,* maj. 14,528

*Taylor, Rt. Hon. John D. (*b.* 1937) *UUP, Strangford,* maj. 5,852

*Taylor, John M. (*b.* 1941) *C., Solihull,* maj. 11,397

*Taylor, Matthew O. J. (*b.* 1963) *LD, Truro and St Austell,* maj. 12,501

*Taylor, Rt. Hon. W. Ann (*b.* 1947) *Lab., Dewsbury,* maj. 8,323

*Temple-Morris, Peter (*b.* 1938) *Lab., Leominster,* maj. 8,835

Thomas, Gareth (*b.* 1954) *Lab., Clwyd West,* maj. 1,848

Thomas, Gareth R. (*b.* 1967) *Lab., Harrow West,* maj. 1,240

†Thomas, Simon (*b.* 0) *PC, Ceredigion,* maj. 4,948

Thompson, William J. (*b.* 1939) *UUP, Tyrone West,* maj. 1,161

*Timms, Stephen C. (*b.* 1955) *Lab., East Ham,* maj. 19,358

*Tipping, S. P. (Paddy) (*b.* 1949) *Lab., Sherwood,* maj. 16,812

Todd, Mark W. (*b.* 1954) *Lab., Derbyshire South,* maj. 13,967

Tonge, Dr Jennifer L. (*b.* 1941) *LD, Richmond Park,* maj. 2,951

*Touhig, J. Donnelly (Don) (*b.* 1947) *Lab. Co-op., Islwyn,* maj. 23,931

*Townend, John E. (*b.* 1934) *C., Yorkshire East,* maj. 3,337

*Tredinnick, David A. S. (*b.* 1950) *C., Bosworth,* maj. 1,027

*Trend, Hon. Michael St J. (*b.* 1952) *C., Windsor,* maj. 9,917

*Trickett, Jon H. (*b.* 1950) *Lab., Hemsworth,* maj. 23,992

*Trimble, Rt. Hon. W. David (*b.* 1944) *UUP, Upper Bann,* maj. 9,252

Truswell, Paul A. (*b.* 1955) *Lab., Pudsey,* maj. 6,207

*Turner, Dennis (*b.* 1942) *Lab. Co-op., Wolverhampton South East,* maj. 15,182

Turner, Desmond S. (*b.* 1939) *Lab., Brighton Kemptown,* maj. 3,534

Turner, Dr George (*b.* 1940) *Lab., Norfolk North West,* maj. 1,339

†Turner, Neil (*b.* 0) *Lab., Wigan,* maj. 6,729

Twigg, J. Derek (*b.* 1959) *Lab., Halton,* maj. 23,650

Twigg, Stephen (*b.* 1966) *Lab., Enfield Southgate,* maj. 1,433

*Tyler, Paul A., CBE (*b.* 1941) *LD, Cornwall North,* maj. 13,933

†Tynan, Bill (*b.* 0) *Lab., Hamilton South,* maj. 15,878

*Tyrie, Andrew G. (*b.* 1957) *C., Chichester,* maj. 9,734

*Vaz, N. Keith A. S. (*b.* 1956) *Lab., Leicester East,* maj. 18,422

*Viggers, Peter J. (*b.* 1938) *C., Gosport,* maj. 6,258

Vis, R. J. (Rudi) (*b.* 1941) *Lab., Finchley and Golders Green,* maj. 3,189

*Walker, A. Cecil (*b.* 1924) *UUP, Belfast North,* maj. 13,024

*Wallace, James R., QC (*b.* 1954) *LD, Orkney and Shetland,* maj. 6,968

*Walley, Ms Joan L. (*b.* 1949) *Lab., Stoke-on-Trent North,* maj. 17,392

Walter, Robert J. (*b.* 1948) *C., Dorset North,* maj. 2,746

Ward, Ms Claire M. (*b.* 1972) *Lab., Watford,* maj. 5,792

*Wardle, Charles F. (*b.* 1939) *C., Bexhill and Battle,* maj. 11,100

*Wareing, Robert N. (*b.* 1930) *Lab., Liverpool West Derby,* maj. 25,965

*Waterson, Nigel C. (*b.* 1950) *C., Eastbourne,* maj. 1,994

Watts, David L. (*b.* 1951) *Lab., St Helens North,* maj. 23,417

Webb, Prof. Steven J. (*b.* 1965) *LD, Northavon,* maj. 2,137

*Wells, Bowen (*b.* 1935) *C., Hertford and Stortford,* maj. 6,885

*Welsh, Andrew P. (*b.* 1944) *SNP, Angus,* maj. 10,189

White, Brian A. R. (*b.* 1957) *Lab., Milton Keynes North East,* maj. 240

Whitehead, Alan P. V. (*b.* 1950) *Lab., Southampton Test,* maj. 13,684

*Whitney, Sir Raymond, OBE (*b.* 1930) *C., Wycombe,* maj. 2,370

*Whittingdale, John F. L., OBE (*b.* 1959) *C., Maldon and Chelmsford East,* maj. 10,039

*Wicks, Malcolm H. (*b.* 1947) *Lab., Croydon North,* maj. 18,398

*Widdecombe, Rt. Hon. Ann N. (*b.* 1947) *C., Maidstone and the Weald,* maj. 9,603

*Wigley, Rt. Hon. Dafydd (*b.* 1943) *PC, Caernarfon,* maj. 7,949

*Wilkinson, John A. D. (*b.* 1940) *C., Ruislip-Northwood,* maj. 7,794

*Willetts, David L. (*b.* 1956) *C., Havant,* maj. 3,729

*Williams, Rt. Hon. Alan J. (*b.* 1930) *Lab., Swansea West,* maj. 14,459

*Williams, Dr Alan W. (*b.* 1945) *Lab., Carmarthen East and Dinefwr,* maj. 3,450

Williams, Mrs Betty H. (*b.* 1944) *Lab., Conwy,* maj. 1,596

Willis, G. Philip (*b.* 1941) *LD, Harrogate and Knaresborough,* maj. 6,236

Wills, Michael D. (*b.* 1952) *Lab., Swindon North,* maj. 7,688

*Wilshire, David (*b.* 1943) *C., Spelthorne,* maj. 3,473

*Wilson, Brian D. H. (*b.* 1948) *Lab., Cunninghame North,* maj. 11,039

*Winnick, David J. (*b.* 1933) *Lab., Walsall North,* maj. 12,588

*Winterton, Mrs J. Ann (*b.* 1941) *C., Congleton,* maj. 6,130

*Winterton, Nicholas R. (*b.* 1938) *C., Macclesfield,* maj. 8,654

Winterton, Ms Rosalie (*b.* 1958) *Lab., Doncaster Central,* maj. 17,856

*Wise, Mrs Audrey (*b.* 1935) *Lab., Preston,* maj. 18,680

Wood, Michael R. (*b.* 1946) *Lab., Batley and Spen,* maj. 6,141

Woodward, Shaun A. (*b.* 1958) *Lab., Witney,* maj. 7,028

Woolas, Philip J. (*b.* 1959) *Lab., Oldham East and Saddleworth,* maj. 3,389

*Worthington, Anthony (*b.* 1941) *Lab., Clydebank and Milngavie,* maj. 13,320

*Wray, James (*b.* 1938) *Lab., Glasgow Baillieston,* maj. 14,840

Wright, Anthony D. (*b.* 1954) *Lab., Great Yarmouth,* maj. 8,668

*Wright, Anthony W., D.Phil. (*b.* 1948) *Lab., Cannock Chase,* maj. 14,478

Wyatt, Derek M. (*b.* 1949) *Lab., Sittingbourne and Sheppey,* maj. 1,929

*Yeo, Timothy S. K. (*b.* 1945) *C., Suffolk South,* maj. 4,175

*Young, Rt. Hon. Sir George, BT. (*b.* 1941) *C., Hampshire North West,* maj. 11,551

BY-ELECTIONS SINCE THE GENERAL ELECTION

UXBRIDGE
(31 July 1997)
E.57,733 T.55.2%

J. Randall, *C.*	16,288
A. Slaughter, *Lab.*	12,522
K. Kerr, *LD*	1,792
Lord Sutch , *Loony*	396
Ms J. Leonard, *Soc.*	259
Ms F. Taylor, *BNP*	205
I. Anderson, *Nat. Dem.*	157
J. McCauley, *NF*	110
H. Middleton, *Original Lib. Party*	69
J. Feisenberger, *UK Ind.*	39
R. Carroll, *Emerald Rainbow Islands Dream Ticket*	30
C. majority	3,766

PAISLEY SOUTH
(6 November 1997)
E.54,040 T.42%

D. Alexander, *Lab.*	10,346
I. Blackford, *SNP*	7,615
Ms E. McCartin, *LD*	2,582
Ms S. Laidlaw, *C.*	1,643
J. Deighan, *ProLife*	578
F. Curran, *Soc. All. Fighting Corruption*	306
C. McLauchlan, *Scottish Ind. Lab.*	155
C. Herriot, *Soc. Lab.*	153
K. Blair, *NLP*	57
Lab. majority	2,731

BECKENHAM
(20 November 1997)
E.72,807 T.43.7%

Ms J. Lait, *C.*	13,162
R. Hughes, *Lab.*	11,935
Ms R. Vetterlein, *LD*	5,864
P. Rimmer, *Lib.*	330
J. McAuley, *NF*	267
L. Mead, *New Britain Ref.*	237
T. Campion, *Social Foundation*	69
J. Small, *NLP*	44
C. majority	1,227

WINCHESTER
(20 November 1997)
E.78,884 T.68.7%

M. Oaten, *LD*	37,006
G. Malone, *C.*	15,450
P. Davies, *Lab.*	944
R. Page, *Ref./UK Ind. Alliance*	521
'Lord' Sutch, *Loony*	316
R. Huggett, *Literal Dem.*	59
Ms R. Barry, *NLP*	48

R. Everest, *European C.*	40
LD majority	21,556

LEEDS CENTRAL
(10 June 1999)
E.66,983 T.19.6%

H. Benn, *Lab.*	6,361
P. Wild, *LD*	4,068
E. Wild, *C.*	1,618
Lab. majority	2,293

EDDISBURY
(22 July 1999)
E.67,086 T.51.4 %

S. O Brien, *C.*	15,465
Ms M. Hanson, *Lab.*	13,859
P. Roberts, *LD*	4,757
A. Hope, *Loony*	238
R. Everest, *Ind. Euro C.*	98
Ms D. Grice, *NLP*	80
C. majority	1,606

WIGAN
(23 September 1999)
E.64,775 T.25.0%

N. Turner, *Lab.*	9,641
T. Peet, *C.*	2,912
J. Rule, *LD*	2,148
J. Whittaker, *UK Ind.*	834
W. Kelly, *Soc. Lab.*	240
C. Maile, *Green*	190
S. Ebbs, *Nat. Dem. Res.*	100
P. Davis, *NLP*	64
D. Braid, *Rev.*	58
C. majority	6,729

HAMILTON SOUTH
(23 September 1999)
E.47,081 T.41.3%

B. Tynan, *Lab.*	7,172
A. Ewing, *SNP*	6,616
S. Blackall, *SSP*	1,847
C. Ferguson, *C.*	1,406
S. Mungall, *Watson*	1,075
M. MacLaren, *LD*	634
M. Burns, *ProLife.*	257
T. Dewar, *Soc. Lab.*	238
J. Reid, *SU*	113
A. McConnachie, *UK Ind.*	61
G. Stidolph, *NLP*	18
J. Moray, *SQ*	17
Lab. majority	556

KENSINGTON AND CHELSEA
(25 November 1999)
E.65,806 T.29.7%

Rt. Hon. M. Portillo, *C.*	11,004
R. Atkinson, *Lab.*	4,298

R. Woodthorpe Browne, *LD*	1,831
J. Stevens, *ProECP*	740
N. Hockney, *UK Ind.*	450
H. Charlton, *Green*	446
C. Burford, *Dem.*	182
C. Paisley, *LCA*	141
M. Irwin, *LWLC*	97
G. Oliver, *UKPP*	75
S. Scott-Fawcett, *Ref.*	57
L. Hodges, *DSSP*	48
G. Valente, *NLP*	35
L. Lovebucket, *PNDTP*	26
J. Davies, *Ind. ESCC*	24
P. May, *EPP*	24
A. Hope, *Loony*	20
T. Samuelson, *Stop*	15
C. majority	6,706

CEREDIGION
(3 February 2000)
E.55,025 T. 45.6%

S. Thomas, *PC*	10,716
M. Williams, *LD*	5,768
P. Davies, *C.*	4,138
M. Battle, *Lab.*	3,612
J. Bufton, *UK Ind.*	487
J. Berkeley Davies, *Ind. Green*	289
M. Shipton, *Match.*	55
PC majority	4,948

ROMSEY
(4 May 2000)
E.33,799 T. 55.64%

Sandra Gidley, *LD*	19,571
Timothy Palmer, *C*	16,260
Andrew Howard, *Lab*	1,451
Garry Rankin-Moore, *UK Ind.*	901
Derrick Large, *LCA*	417
Thomas Lamont, *Ind.*	109
LD Majority	3,311

TOTTENHAM
(22 June 2000)
E.64,554 T. 25.4%

David Lammy, *Lab*	8,785
Duncan Hames, *LD*	3,139
Jane Ellison, *C*	2,634
Weyman Bennett, *London, Soc. All.*	885
Peter Budge, *Green*	606
Erol Basarik, *Reform 2000*	177
Ashwin Tanna, *UK Ind.*	136
Derek Dorian de Braam, *Ind. Lab.*	55
Lab Majority	5,646

LEADERS OF THE OPPOSITION

The office of Leader of the Opposition was officially recognised in 1937 and a salary was assigned to the post.

Year	Name	Year	Name
1916	Herbert Asquith, *Liberal*	1951	Clement Attlee, *Labour*
1918	William Adamson, *Labour*	1955	Hugh Gaitskell, *Labour*
1921	John Clynes, *Labour*	1963	Harold Wilson, *Labour*
1922	Ramsay MacDonald, *Labour*	1965	Edward Heath, *Conservative*
	(leader of official Opposition)	1974	Edward Heath, *Conservative*
1924	Stanley Baldwin, *Conservative*	1970	Harold Wilson, *Labour*
1929	Stanley Baldwin, *Conservative*	1975	Margaret Thatcher, *Conservative*
1931	Arthur Henderson, *Labour*	1979	James Callaghan, *Labour*
	(leader of Labour Opposition)	1980	Michael Foot, *Labour*
1931	George Lansbury, *Labour*	1983	Neil Kinnock, *Labour*
1935	Clement Attlee, *Labour*	1992	John Smith, *Labour*
1945	Clement Attlee, *Labour*	1994	Anthony Blair, *Labour*
1945	Winston Churchill, *Conservative*	1997	William Hague, *Conservative*

GENERAL ELECTIONS since 1900

Year	Date	Party forming the Government	Year	Date	Party forming the Government
1900	28 Sept–24 Oct	Conservative	1970	18 June	Conservative
1906	12 Jan–7 Feb	Liberal	1974	28 Feb	Conservative
1910	14 Jan–9 Feb	Liberal	1974	10 Oct	Labour
1910	2–19 Dec	Liberal	1979	3 May	Conservative
1918	14 Dec	Coalition*	1983	9 June	Conservative
1922	15 Nov	Conservative	1987	11 June	Conservative
1923	6 Dec	Coalition†	1992	9 April	Conservative
1924	29 Oct	Conservative	1997	1 May	Labour
1929	30 May	Labour			
1931	27 Oct	National Government‡			
1935	14 Nov	Conservative			
1945	5 July	Labour			
1950	23 Feb	Labour			
1951	25 Oct	Conservative			
1955	26 May	Conservative			
1959	8 Oct	Conservative			
1964	15 Oct	Conservative			
1966	31 March	Labour			

*Coalition of Coalition Unionist (335 seats), Coalition Liberal (133) and Coalition Labour (10); opposition parties 229 seats, including 28 Liberal and 63 Labour

†Coalition of Labour (191 seats) and Liberal (159); opposition parties 265 seats, including Conservative 258

‡National Government of Conservative (473 seats), Liberal National (35), Liberal (33) and National Labour (13); opposition parties 61 seats, including Labour 52 and Independent Liberal 4

PARLIAMENTARY CONSTITUENCIES AS AT 1 MAY 1997

The results of voting in each parliamentary division at the general election of 1 May 1997 are given below. The majority in the 1992 general election, and any by-election between 1987 and 1992, is given below the 1992 result where the constituency covers the same area as in 1992. Where the boundaries of a constituency have changed since 1992, a notional result for 1992 is given.

Symbols

E. Total number of electors in the constituency at the 1997 general election

T. Turnout of electors at the 1997 general election

* Member of the last Parliament in unchanged constituency

† Member of the last Parliament in different constituency or one affected by boundary changes

Abbreviations

All.	Alliance Party (NI)
C.	Conservative
DUP	Democratic Unionist Party
Green	Green Party
Ind.	Independent
Lab.	Labour
Lab. Co-op.	Labour Co-operative
LD	Liberal Democrat
PC	Plaid Cymru
SDLP	Social Democratic and Labour Party
SF	Sinn Fein
SNP	Scottish National Party
UKU	United Kingdom Unionist
UUP	Ulster Unionist Party
ACA	Anti-Child Abuse
ACC	Anti-Corruption Candidate
Albion	Albion Party
Alt.	Alternative
ANP	All Night Party
Anti-maj.	Independent Anti-majority Democracy
AS	Anti-sleaze
Barts	Independent Save Barts Candidate
BDP	British Democratic Party
Beanus	Space Age Superhero from Planet Beanus
Beaut.	Independently Beautiful Party
Bert.	Berties Party
BFAIR	British Freedom and Individual Rights
BHMBCM	Black Haired Medium Build Caucasian Male
BHR	British Home Rule
B. Ind.	Beaconsfield Independent: Unity Through Electoral Reform
BIPF	British Isles People First Party
BNP	British National Party
Bypass	Newbury Bypass Stop Construction Now
Byro	Lord Byro versus the Scallywag Tories
Care	Care in the Community
CASC	Conservatives Against the Single Currency
CFSS	Country Field and Shooting Sports
Ch. D.	Christian Democrat
Ch. Nat.	Christian Nationalist
Choice	People's Choice
Ch. P.	Christian Party
Ch. U.	Christian Unity
Comm. L.	Communist League
Comm. P.	Communist Party of Britain
Constit.	Constitutionalist
Consult.	Independent Democracy Means Consulting the People

CRP	Community Representative Party
CSSPP	Common Sense Sick of Politicians Party
Cvty	Conservatory
D. Nat.	Democratic Nationalist
Dem	Democratic Party
Dream	Rainbow Dream Ticket Party
DSSP	Daily and Sunday Sport Party
Dynamic	First Dynamic Party
EDP	English Democratic Party
Embryo	Anti-Abortion Euthanasia Embryo Experiments
EPP	Equal Parenting Party
ESCC	Independent Environmentalist Stop Climatic Change
EUP	European Unity Party
Fair	Building a Fair Society
FDP	Fancy Dress Party
Fellowship	Fellowship Party for Peace and Justice
FEP	Full Employment Party
FP	Freedom Party
Glow	Glow Bowling Party
GRLNSP	Green Referendum Lawless Naturally Street Party
Heart	Heart 106.2 Alien Party
Hemp	Hemp Coalition
HR	Human Rights '97
Hum.	Humanist Party
IAC	Independent Anti-Corruption in Government/TGWU
Ind. AFE	Independent Against a Federal Europe
Ind. BB	Independent Back to Basics
Ind. CRP	Independent Conservative Referendum Party
Ind. Dean	Independent Royal Forest of Dean
Ind. Dem.	Independent Democrat
Ind. ECR	Independent English Conservative and Referendum
Ind. Euro C.	Independent Euro Conservative
Ind. F.	Independent Forester
Ind. Green	Independent Green: Your Children's Future
Ind. Hum.	English Independent Humanist Party
Ind. Is.	Island Independent
Ind. JRP	Justice and Renewal Independent Party
Ind. No	Independent No to Europe
IZB	Islam Zinda Baad Platform
JP	Justice Party
Juice	Juice Party
KBF	Keep Britain Free and Independent Party
Lab. Change	Labour Time for Change Candidate
LC	Loyal Conservative
LCA	Legalise Cannabis Alliance
LCP	Legalise Cannabis Party
LGR	Local Government Reform
Lib.	Liberal
Loc.	Local
Logic	Logic Party Truth Only Allowed
Loony	Monster Raving Loony Party
LWLC	Living Will Legalisation Campaign
Mal	Mal Voice of the People Party
Match	Wales on Sunday Match Funding Now
Miss M.	Miss Moneypenny's Glamorous One Party
MK	Mebyon Kernow
Mongolian	Mongolian Barbeque Great Place to Party
MRAC	Multi-racial Anti-Corruption Alliance
Nat. Dem.	National Democrat

Nat. Dem. Res.	National Democratic Resistance
New Way	New Millennium New Way Hemp Candidate
NF	National Front
NIFT	Former Captain NI Football Team
NIP	Northern Ireland Party
NI Women	Northern Ireland Women's Coalition
NLP	Natural Law Party
NLPC	New Labour Party Candidate
None	None of the Above Parties
NPC	Non-party Conservative
Pacifist	Pacifist for Peace, Justice, Co-operation, Environment
PAYR	Protecting All Your Rights Locally Effectively
PF	Pathfinders
PLP	People's Labour Party
Plymouth	Plymouth First Group
PNDTP	People's Net Dream Ticket Party
PP	People's Party
PPP	People's Party Party
ProECP	Pro Euro Conservative Party
ProLife	ProLife Alliance
PUP	Progressive Unionist Party
RA	Residents Association
Rain. Is.	Rainbow Connection Your Island Candidate
Rain. Ref.	Rainbow Referendum
R. Alt.	Radical Alternative
Ref.	Referendum Party
Ren. Dem.	Renaissance Democrat
Rep. GB	Republican Party of Great Britain
Rev.	Reverend
Rights	Charter for Basic Rights
Ronnie	Ronnie the Rhino Party
Route 66	Route 66 Party Posse Party
Scrapit	Scrapit Stop Avon Ring Road Now
SCU	Scottish Conservative Unofficial
SEP	Socialist Equality Party
SFDC	Stratford First Democratic Conservative
SG	Sub-genus Party
Shields	Pro Interests of South Shields People
SIP	Sheffield Independent Party
SLI	Scottish Labour Independent
Slough	People in Slough Shunning Useless Politicians
SLU	Scottish Labour Unofficial
Soc.	Socialist Party
Soc. Dem.	Social Democrat
Soc. Lab.	Socialist Labour Party
SPGB	Socialist Party of Great Britain
Spts All.	Sportsman's Alliance: Anything but Mellor
SSA	Scottish Socialist Alliance
SSP	Scottish Socialist Party
Stan	Happiness Stan's Freedom to Party Party
SQ	Status Quo
Stop	Stop Tobacco Companies Farming Our Children
SU	Scottish Unionist Party
Teddy	Teddy Bear Alliance Party
Top	Top Choice Liberal Democrat
21st Cent.	21st Century Independent Foresters
UA	Universal Alliance
UK Ind.	UK Independence Party
UKPP	UK Pensioners Party
Watson	Hamilton Accies Home Watson Away
WCCC	West Cheshire College in Crisis Party
Wessex	Wessex Regionalist
WP	Workers' Party
WRP	Workers' Revolutionary Party

ENGLAND

ALDERSHOT
E.76,189   T. 71.07%
G. Howarth, *C.*	23,119
A. Collett, *LD*	16,498
T. Bridgeman, *Lab.*	13,057
J. Howe, *UK Ind.*	794
A. Pendragon, *Ind.*	361
Dr D. Stevens, *BNP*	322

C. majority 6,621
(Boundary change: notional C.)

ALDRIDGE-BROWNHILLS
E.62,441   T. 74.26%
*R. Shepherd, *C.*	21,856
J. Toth, *Lab.*	19,330
Ms C. Downie, *LD*	5,184

C. majority 2,526
(April 1992, C. maj. 11,024)

ALTRINCHAM AND SALE WEST
E.70,625   T. 73.32%
G. Brady, *C.*	22,348
Ms J. Baugh, *Lab.*	20,843
M. Ramsbottom, *LD*	6,535
A. Landes, *Ref.*	1,348
J. Stephens, *ProLife*	313
Dr R. Mrozinski, *UK Ind.*	270
J. Renwick, *NLP*	125

C. majority 1,505
(Boundary change: notional C.)

AMBER VALLEY
E.72,005   T. 76.07%
Ms J. Mallaber, *Lab.*	29,943
†P. Oppenheim, *C.*	18,330
R. Shelley, *LD*	4,219
Mrs I. McGibbon, *Ref.*	2,283

Lab. majority 11,613
(Boundary change: notional C.)

ARUNDEL AND SOUTH DOWNS
E.67,641   T. 75.90%
H. Flight, *C.*	27,251
J. Goss, *LD*	13,216
R. Black, *Lab.*	9,376
†J. Herbert, *UK Ind.*	1,494

C. majority 14,035
(Boundary change: notional C.)

ASHFIELD
E.72,269   T. 70.02%
†G. Hoon, *Lab.*	32,979
M. Simmonds, *C.*	10,251
W. Smith, *LD*	4,882
M. Betts, *Ref.*	1,896
S. Belshaw, *BNP*	595

Lab. majority 22,728
(Boundary change: notional Lab.)

ASHFORD
E.74,149   T. 74.57%
D. Green, *C.*	22,899
J. Ennals, *Lab.*	17,544
J. Williams, *LD*	10,901
C. Cruden, *Ref.*	3,201
R. Boden, *Green*	660
S. Tyrell, *NLP*	89

C. majority 5,355
(April 1992, C. maj. 17,359)

ASHTON UNDER LYNE
E.72,206   T. 65.48%
†Rt. Hon. R. Sheldon, *Lab.*	31,919

R. Mayson, *C.*	8,954
T. Pickstone, *LD*	4,603
Mrs L. Clapham, *Ref.*	1,346
Prince Cymbal, *Loony*	458

Lab. majority 22,965
(Boundary change: notional Lab.)

AYLESBURY
E.79,047   T. 72.81%
†D. Lidington, *C.*	25,426
Ms S. Bowles, *LD*	17,007
R. Langridge, *Lab.*	12,759
M. John, *Ref.*	2,196
L. Sheaff, *NLP*	166

C. majority 8,419
(Boundary change: notional C.)

BANBURY
E.77,456   T. 75.46%
†A. Baldry, *C.*	25,076
Ms H. Peperell, *Lab.*	20,339
Mrs C. Bearder, *LD*	9,761
J. Ager, *Ref.*	2,245
Ms B. Cotton, *Green*	530
Mrs L. King, *UK Ind.*	364
I. Pearson, *NLP*	131

C. majority 4,737
(Boundary change: notional C.)

BARKING
E.53,682   T. 61.41%
†Mrs M. Hodge, *Lab.*	21,698
K. Langford, *C.*	5,802
M. Marsh, *LD*	3,128
C. Taylor, *Ref.*	1,283
M. Tolman, *BNP*	894
D. Mearns, *ProLife*	159

Lab. majority 15,896
(Boundary change: notional Lab.)

BARNSLEY CENTRAL
E.61,133   T. 59.68%
†E. Illsley, *Lab.*	28,090
S. Gutteridge, *C.*	3,589
D. Finlay, *LD*	3,481
J. Walsh, *Ref.*	1,325

Lab. majority 24,501
(Boundary change: notional Lab.)

BARNSLEY EAST AND
MEXBOROUGH
E.67,840   T. 63.88%
†J. Ennis, *Lab.*	31,699
Miss J. Ellison, *C.*	4,936
D. Willis, *LD*	4,489
K. Capstick, *Soc. Lab.*	1,213
A. Miles, *Ref.*	797
Ms J. Hyland, *SEP*	201

Lab. majority 26,763
(Boundary change: notional Lab.)

BARNSLEY WEST AND
PENISTONE
E.64,894   T. 65.04%
*M. Clapham, *Lab.*	25,017
P. Watkins, *C.*	7,750
Mrs W. Knight, *LD*	7,613
Mrs J. Miles, *Ref.*	1,828

Lab. majority 17,267
(April 1992, Lab. maj. 14,504)

BARROW AND FURNESS
E.66,960   T. 72.03%
*J. Hutton, *Lab.*	27,630
R. Hunt, *C.*	13,133
Mrs A. Metcalfe, *LD*	4,264
J. Hamzeian, *PLP*	1,995
D. Mitchell, *Ref.*	1,208

Lab. majority 14,497
(April 1992, Lab. maj. 3,578)

BASILDON
E.73,989   T. 71.74%
Ms A. Smith, *Lab. Co-op.*	29,646
J. Baron, *C.*	16,366
Ms L. Granshaw, *LD*	4,608
C. Robinson, *Ref.*	2,462

Lab. Co-op. majority 13,280
(Boundary change: notional C.)

BASINGSTOKE
E.77,035   T. 74.16%
†A. Hunter, *C.*	24,751
N. Lickley, *Lab.*	22,354
M. Rimmer, *LD*	9,714
E. Selim, *Ind.*	310

C. majority 2,397
(Boundary change: notional C.)

BASSETLAW
E.68,101   T. 70.37%
†J. Ashton, *Lab.*	29,298
M. Cleasby, *C.*	11,838
M. Kerrigan, *LD*	4,950
R. Graham, *Ref.*	1,838

Lab. majority 17,460
(Boundary change: notional Lab.)

BATH
E.70,815   T. 76.24%
†D. Foster, *LD*	26,169
Ms A. McNair, *C.*	16,850
T. Bush, *Lab.*	8,828
A. Cook, *Ref.*	1,192
R. Scrase, *Green*	580
P. Sandell, *UK Ind.*	315
N. Pullen, *NLP*	55

LD majority 9,319
(Boundary change: notional LD)

BATLEY AND SPEN
E.64,209   T. 73.14%
M. Wood, *Lab.*	23,213
†Mrs E. Peacock, *C.*	17,072
Mrs K. Pinnock, *LD*	4,133
E. Wood, *Ref.*	1,691
R. Smith, *BNP*	472
C. Lord, *Green*	384

Lab. majority 6,141
(Boundary change: notional C.)

BATTERSEA
E.66,928   T. 70.82%
M. Linton, *Lab.*	24,047
†J. Bowis, *C.*	18,687
Ms P. Keaveney, *LD*	3,482
M. Slater, *Ref.*	804
R. Banks, *UK Ind.*	250
J. Marshall, *Dream*	127

Lab. majority 5,360
(Boundary change: notional C.)

BEACONSFIELD
E.68,959 T. 72.80%

D. Grieve, C.	24,709
P. Mapp, LD	10,722
A. Hudson, Lab.	10,063
H. Lloyd, Ref.	2,197
C. Story, CASC	1,434
C. Cooke, UK Ind.	451
Ms G. Duval, ProLife	286
T. Dyball, NLP	193
R. Matthews, B. Ind.	146

C. majority 13,987
(Boundary change: notional C.)

BECKENHAM
E.72,807 T. 74.65%

†P. Merchant, C.	23,084
R. Hughes, Lab.	18,131
Ms R. Vetterlein, LD	9,858
L. Mead, Ref.	1,663
P. Rimmer, Lib.	720
C. Pratt, UK Ind.	506
J. Mcauley, NF	388

C. majority 4,953
(Boundary change: notional C.)
See also page 233

BEDFORD
E.66,560 T. 73.53%

P. Hall, Lab.	24,774
R. Blackman, C.	16,474
C. Noyce, LD	6,044
P. Conquest, Ref.	1,503
Ms P. Saunders, NLP	149

Lab. majority 8,300
(Boundary change: notional C.)

BEDFORDSHIRE MID
E.66,979 T. 78.41%

J. Sayeed, C.	24,176
N. Mallett, Lab.	17,086
T. Hill, LD	8,823
Mrs S. Marler, Ref.	2,257
M. Lorys, NLP	174

C. majority 7,090
(Boundary change: notional C.)

BEDFORDSHIRE NORTH EAST
E.64,743 T. 77.83%

†Rt. Hon. Sir N. Lyell, C.	22,311
J. Lehal, Lab.	16,428
P. Bristow, LD	7,179
J. Taylor, Ref.	2,490
L. Foley, Ind. C.	1,842
B. Bence, NLP	138

C. majority 5,883
(Boundary change: notional C.)

BEDFORDSHIRE SOUTH WEST
E.69,781 T. 75.76%

†Sir D. Madel, C.	21,534
A. Date, Lab.	21,402
S. Owen, LD	7,559
Ms R. Hill, Ref.	1,761
T. Wise, UK Ind.	446
A. Le Carpentier, NLP	162

C. majority 132
(Boundary change: notional C.)

BERWICK-UPON-TWEED
E.56,428 T. 74.08%

*A. Beith, LD	19,007
P. Brannen, Lab.	10,965

N. Herbert, C.	10,056
N. Lambton, Ref.	1,423
I. Dodds, UK Ind.	352

LD majority 8,042
(April 1992, LD maj. 5,043)

BETHNAL GREEN AND BOW
E.73,008 T. 61.20%

Ms O. King, Lab.	20,697
K. Choudhury, C.	9,412
S. N. Islam, LD	5,361
D. King, BNP	3,350
T. Milson, Lib.	2,963
S. Osman, Real Lab.	1,117
S. Petter, Green	812
M. Abdullah, Ref.	557
A. Hamid, Soc. Lab.	413

Lab. majority 11,285
(Boundary change: notional Lab.)

BEVERLEY AND HOLDERNESS
E.71,916 T. 73.62%

†J. Cran, C.	21,629
N. O'Neill, Lab.	20,818
J. Melling, LD	9,689
D. Barley, UK Ind.	695
S. Withers, NLP	111

C. majority 811
(Boundary change: notional C.)

BEXHILL AND BATTLE
E.65,584 T. 74.70%

†C. Wardle, C.	23,570
Mrs K. Field, LD	12,470
R. Beckwith, Lab.	8,866
Mrs V. Thompson, Ref.	3,302
J. Pankhurst, UK Ind.	786

C. majority 11,100
(Boundary change: notional C.)

BEXLEYHEATH AND CRAYFORD
E.63,334 T. 76.14%

N. Beard, Lab.	21,942
†D. Evennett, C.	18,527
Mrs F. Montford, LD	5,391
B. Thomas, Ref.	1,551
Ms P. Smith, BNP	429
W. Jenner, UK Ind.	383

Lab. majority 3,415
(Boundary change: notional C.)

BILLERICAY
E.76,550 T. 72.40%

†Mrs T. Gorman, C.	22,033
P. Richards, Lab.	20,677
G. Williams, LD	8,763
B. Hughes, LC	3,377
J. Buchanan, ProLife	570

C. majority 1,356
(Boundary change: notional C.)

BIRKENHEAD
E.59,782 T. 65.78%

*F. Field, Lab.	27,825
J. Crosby, C.	5,982
R. Wood, LD	3,548
M. Cullen, Soc. Lab.	1,168
R. Evans, Ref.	800

Lab. majority 21,843
(April 1992, Lab. maj. 17,613)

BIRMINGHAM EDGBASTON
E.70,204 T. 69.03%

Mrs G. Stuart, Lab.	23,554

A. Marshall, C.	18,712
J. Gallagher, LD	4,691
J. Oakton, Ref.	1,065
D. Campbell, BDP	443

Lab. majority 4,842
(Boundary change: notional C.)

BIRMINGHAM ERDINGTON
E.66,380 T. 60.87%

†R. Corbett, Lab.	23,764
A. Tompkins, C.	11,107
I. Garrett, LD	4,112
G. Cable, Ref.	1,424

Lab. majority 12,657
(Boundary change: notional Lab.)

BIRMINGHAM HALL GREEN
E.58,767 T. 71.16%

S. McCabe, Lab.	22,372
*A. Hargreaves, C.	13,952
A. Dow, LD	4,034
P. Bennett, Ref.	1,461

Lab. majority 8,420
(April 1992, C. maj. 3,665)

BIRMINGHAM HODGE HILL
E.56,066 T. 60.91%

*T. Davis, Lab.	22,398
E. Grant, C.	8,198
H. Thomas, LD	2,891
P. Johnson, UK Ind.	660

Lab. majority 14,200
(April 1992, Lab. maj. 7,068)

BIRMINGHAM LADYWOOD
E.70,013 T. 54.24%

†Ms C. Short, Lab.	28,134
S. Vara, C.	5,052
S. S. Marwa, LD	3,020
Mrs R. Gurney, Ref.	1,086
A. Carmichael, Nat. Dem.	685

Lab. majority 23,082
(Boundary change: notional Lab.)

BIRMINGHAM NORTHFIELD
E.56,842 T. 68.34%

†R. Burden, Lab.	22,316
A. Blumenthal, C.	10,873
M. Ashall, LD	4,078
D. Gent, Ref.	1,243
K. Axon, BNP	337

Lab. majority 11,443
(Boundary change: notional Lab.)

BIRMINGHAM PERRY BARR
E.71,031 T. 64.60%

†J. Rooker, Lab.	28,921
A. Dunnett, C.	9,964
R. Hassall, LD	4,523
S. Mahmood, Ref.	843
A. Baxter, Lib.	718
L. Windridge, BNP	544
A. S. Panesar, Fourth Party	374

Lab. majority 18,957
(Boundary change: notional Lab.)

BIRMINGHAM SELLY OAK
E.72,049 T. 70.16%

*Dr L. Jones, Lab.	28,121
G. Greene, C.	14,033
D. Osborne, LD	6,121
L. Marshall, Ref.	1,520
Dr G. Gardner, ProLife	417

P. Sherriff-Knowles, *Loony* 253
H. Meads, *NLP* 85
Lab. majority 14,088
(April 1992, Lab. maj. 2,060)

BIRMINGHAM SPARKBROOK AND
SMALL HEATH
E.73,130　T. 57.11%
†R. Godsiff, *Lab.* 26,841
K. Hardeman, *C.* 7,315
R. Harmer, *LD* 3,889
A. Clawley, *Green* 959
R. Dooley, *Ref.* 737
P. Patel, *Fourth Party* 538
R. M. Syed, *PAYR* 513
Ms S. Bi, *Ind.* 490
C. Wren, *Soc. Lab.* 483
Lab. majority 19,526
(Boundary change: notional Lab.)

BIRMINGHAM YARDLEY
E.53,058　T. 71.22%
*Ms E. Morris, *Lab.* 17,778
J. Hemming, *LD* 12,463
Mrs A. Jobson, *C.* 6,736
D. Livingston, *Ref.* 646
A. Ware, *UK Ind.* 164
Lab. majority 5,315
(April 1992, Lab. maj. 162)

BISHOP AUCKLAND
E.66,754　T. 68.88%
†Rt. Hon. D. Foster, *Lab.* 30,359
Mrs J. Fergus, *C.* 9,295
L. Ashworth, *LD* 4,223
D. Blacker, *Ref.* 2,104
Lab. majority 21,064
(Boundary change: notional Lab.)

BLABY
E.70,471　T. 76.05%
†A. Robathan, *C.* 24,564
R. Willmott, *Lab.* 18,090
G. Welsh, *LD* 8,001
R. Harrison, *Ref.* 2,018
J. Peacock, *BNP* 523
T. Stokes, *Ind.* 397
C. majority 6,474
(Boundary change: notional C.)

BLACKBURN
E.73,058　T. 65.01%
*J. Straw, *Lab.* 26,141
Ms S. Sidhu, *C.* 11,690
S. Fenn, *LD* 4,990
D. Bradshaw, *Ref.* 1,892
Mrs T. Wingfield, *Nat. Dem.* 671
Mrs H. Drummond, *Soc. Lab.* 637
R. Field, *Green* 608
Mrs M. Carmichael-Grimshaw,
　KBF 506
W. Batchelor, *CSSPP* 362
Lab. majority 14,451
(April 1992, Lab. maj. 6,027)

BLACKPOOL NORTH AND
FLEETWOOD
E.74,989　T. 71.67%
Mrs J. Humble, *Lab.* 28,051
†H. Elletson, *C.* 19,105
Mrs B. Hill, *LD* 4,600
Ms K. Stacey, *Ref.* 1,704
J. Ellis, *BNP* 288

Lab. majority 8,946
(Boundary change: notional C.)

BLACKPOOL SOUTH
E.75,720　T. 67.80%
G. Marsden, *Lab.* 29,282
R. Booth, *C.* 17,666
Mrs D. Holt, *LD* 4,392
Lab. majority 11,616
(Boundary change: notional C.)

BLAYDON
E.64,699　T. 70.98%
*J. McWilliam, *Lab.* 27,535
P. Maughan, *LD* 10,930
M. Watson, *C.* 6,048
R. Rook, *Ind. Lab.* 1,412
Lab. majority 16,605
(April 1992, Lab. maj. 13,343)

BLYTH VALLEY
E.61,761　T. 68.78%
*R. Campbell, *Lab.* 27,276
A. Lamb, *LD* 9,540
Mrs B. Musgrave, *C.* 5,666
Lab. majority 17,736
(April 1992, Lab. maj. 8,044)

BOGNOR REGIS AND
LITTLEHAMPTON
E.66,480　T. 69.86%
N. Gibb, *C.* 20,537
R. Nash, *Lab.* 13,216
Dr J. Walsh, *LD* 11,153
G. Stride, *UK Ind.* 1,537
C. majority 7,321
(Boundary change: notional C.)

BOLSOVER
E.66,476　T. 71.32%
†D. Skinner, *Lab.* 35,073
R. Harwood, *C.* 7,924
I. Cox, *LD* 4,417
Lab. majority 27,149
(Boundary change: notional Lab.)

BOLTON NORTH EAST
E.67,930　T. 72.44%
D. Crausby, *Lab.* 27,621
R. Wilson, *C.* 14,952
Dr E. Critchley, *LD* 4,862
D. Staniforth, *Ref.* 1,096
W. Kelly, *Soc. Lab.* 676
Lab. majority 12,669
(Boundary change: notional Lab.)

BOLTON SOUTH EAST
E.66,459　T. 65.23%
B. Iddon, *Lab.* 29,856
P. Carter, *C.* 8,545
F. Harasiwka, *LD* 3,805
W. Pickering, *Ref.* 973
L. Walch, *NLP* 170
Lab. majority 21,311
(Boundary change: notional Lab.)

BOLTON WEST
E.63,535　T. 77.37%
Ms R. Kelly, *Lab.* 24,342
†T. Sackville, *C.* 17,270
Mrs B. Ronson, *LD* 5,309
Mrs D. Kelly, *Soc. Lab.* 1,374
Mrs G. Frankl-Slater, *Ref.* 865

Lab. majority 7,072
(Boundary change: notional C.)

BOOTLE
E.57,284　T. 66.73%
†J. Benton, *Lab.* 31,668
R. Mathews, *C.* 3,247
K. Reid, *LD* 2,191
J. Elliott, *Ref.* 571
P. Glover, *Soc.* 420
S. Cohen, *NLP* 126
Lab. majority 28,421
(Boundary change: notional Lab.)

BOSTON AND SKEGNESS
E.67,623　T. 68.87%
†Sir R. Body, *C.* 19,750
P. McCauley, *Lab.* 19,103
J. Dodsworth, *LD* 7,721
C. majority 647
(Boundary change: notional C.)

BOSWORTH
E.68,113　T. 76.57%
†D. Tredinnick, *C.* 21,189
A. Furlong, *Lab.* 20,162
J. Ellis, *LD* 9,281
S. Halborg, *Ref.* 1,521
C. majority 1,027
(Boundary change: notional C.)

BOURNEMOUTH EAST
E.61,862　T. 70.20%
†D. Atkinson, *C.* 17,997
D. Eyre, *LD* 13,651
Mrs J. Stevens, *Lab.* 9,181
A. Musgrave-Scott, *Ref.* 1,808
K. Benney, *UK Ind.* 791
C. majority 4,346
(Boundary change: notional C.)

BOURNEMOUTH WEST
E.62,028　T. 66.22%
†J. Butterfill, *C.* 17,115
Ms J. Dover, *LD* 11,405
D. Gritt, *Lab.* 10,093
R. Mills, *Ref.* 1,910
Mrs L. Tooley, *UK Ind.* 281
J. Morse, *BNP* 165
A. Springham, *NLP* 103
C. majority 5,710
(Boundary change: notional C.)

BRACKNELL
E.79,292　T. 74.52%
†A. Mackay, *C.* 27,983
Ms A. Snelgrove, *Lab.* 17,596
A. Hilliar, *LD* 9,122
J. Tompkins, *New Lab.* 1,909
W. Cairns, *Ref.* 1,636
L. Boxall, *UK Ind.* 569
Ms D. Roberts, *ProLife* 276
C. majority 10,387
(Boundary change: notional C.)

BRADFORD NORTH
E.66,228　T. 63.26%
*T. Rooney, *Lab.* 23,493
R. Skinner, *C.* 10,723
T. Browne, *LD* 6,083
H. Wheatley, *Ref.* 1,227
W. Beckett, *Loony* 369
Lab. majority 12,770
(April 1992, Lab. maj. 7,664)

BRADFORD SOUTH
E.68,391   *T*. 65.88%
*G. Sutcliffe, *Lab.*   25,558
Mrs A. Hawkesworth, *C.*   12,622
A. Wilson-Fletcher, *LD*   5,093
Mrs M. Kershaw, *Ref.*   1,785
Lab. majority 12,936
(April 1992, Lab. maj. 4,902)
(June 1994, Lab. maj. 9,664)

BRADFORD WEST
E.71,961   *T*. 63.32%
M. Singh, *Lab.*   18,932
M. Riaz, *C.*   15,055
Mrs H. Wright, *LD*   6,737
A. Khan, *Soc. Lab.*   1,551
C. Royston, *Ref.*   1,348
J. Robinson, *Green*   861
G. Osborn, *BNP*   839
S. Shah, *Soc.*   245
Lab. majority 3,877
(April 1992, Lab. maj. 9,502)

BRAINTREE
E.72,772   *T*. 76.37%
A. Hurst, *Lab.*   23,729
†Rt. Hon. A. Newton, *C.*   22,278
T. Ellis, *LD*   6,418
N. Westcott, *Ref.*   2,165
J. Abbott, *Green*   712
M. Nolan, *New Way*   274
Lab. majority 1,451
(Boundary change: notional C.)

BRENT EAST
E.53,548   *T*. 65.87%
†K. Livingstone, *Lab.*   23,748
M. Francois, *C.*   7,866
I. Hunter, *LD*   2,751
S. Keable, *Soc. Lab.*   466
A. Shanks, *ProLife*   218
Ms C. Warrilo, *Dream*   120
D. Jenkins, *NLP*   103
Lab. majority 15,882
(Boundary change: notional Lab.)

BRENT NORTH
E.54,149   *T*. 70.50%
B. Gardiner, *Lab.*   19,343
†Rt. Hon. Sir R. Boyson, *C.*   15324
P. Lorber, *LD*   3,104
A. Davids, *NLP*   204
G. Clark, *Dream*   199
Lab. majority 4,019
(Boundary change: notional C.)

BRENT SOUTH
E.53,505   *T*. 64.48%
†P. Boateng, *Lab.*   25,180
S. Jackson, *C.*   5,489
J. Brazil, *LD*   2,670
Ms J. Phythian, *Ref.*   497
D. Edler, *Green*   389
C. Howard, *Dream*   175
Ms A. Mahaldar, *NLP*   98
Lab. majority 19,691
(Boundary change: notional Lab.)

BRENTFORD AND ISLEWORTH
E.79,058   *T*. 71.00%
Mrs A. Keen, *Lab.*   32,249
†N. Deva, *C.*   17,825
Dr G. Hartwell, *LD*   4,613

J. Bradley, *Green*   687
Mrs B. Simmerson, *UK Ind.*   614
M. Ahmed, *NLP*   147
Lab. majority 14,424
(Boundary change: notional C.)

BRENTWOOD AND ONGAR
E.66,005   *T*. 76.85%
†E. Pickles, *C.*   23,031
Mrs E. Bottomley, *LD*   13,341
M. Young, *Lab.*   11,231
Mrs A. Kilmartin, *Ref.*   2,658
Capt. D. Mills, *UK Ind.*   465
C. majority 9,690
(Boundary change: notional C.)

BRIDGWATER
E.73,038   *T*. 74.79%
*Rt. Hon. T. King, *C.*   20,174
M. Hoban, *LD*   18,378
R. Lavers, *Lab.*   13,519
Ms F. Evens, *Ref.*   2,551
C. majority 1,796
(April 1992, C. maj. 9,716)

BRIGG AND GOOLE
E.63,648   *T*. 73.53%
I. Cawsey, *Lab.*   23,493
D. Stewart, *C.*   17,104
Mrs M.-R. Hardy, *LD*   4,692
D. Rigby, *Ref.*   1,513
Lab. majority 6,389
(Boundary change: notional C.)

BRIGHTON KEMPTOWN
E.65,147   *T*. 70.81%
D. Turner, *Lab.*   21,479
†Sir A. Bowden, *C.*   17,945
C. Gray, *LD*   4,478
D. Inman, *Ref.*   1,526
Ms H. Williams, *Soc. Lab.*   316
J. Bowler, *NLP*   172
Ms L. Newman, *Loony*   123
R. Darlow, *Dream*   93
Lab. majority 3,534
(Boundary change: notional C.)

BRIGHTON PAVILION
E.66,431   *T*. 73.69%
D. Lepper, *Lab. Co-op.*   26,737
†Sir D. Spencer, *C.*   13,556
K. Blanshard, *LD*   4,644
P. Stocken, *Ref.*   1,304
P. West, *Green*   1,249
R. Huggett, *Ind. C.*   1,098
F. Stevens, *UK Ind.*   179
R. Dobbs, *SG*   125
A. Card, *Dream*   59
Lab. Co-op. majority 13,181
(Boundary change: notional C.)

BRISTOL EAST
E.68,990   *T*. 69.87%
†Ms J. Corston, *Lab.*   27,418
E. Vaizey, *C.*   11,259
P. Tyzack, *LD*   7,121
G. Philp, *Ref.*   1,479
P. Williams, *Soc. Lab.*   766
J. McLaggan, *NLP*   158
Lab. majority 16,159
(Boundary change: notional Lab.)

BRISTOL NORTH WEST
E.75,009   *T*. 73.65%
D. Naysmith, *Lab. Co-op.*   27,575
†M. Stern, *C.*   16,193
I. Parry, *LD*   7,263
C. Horton, *Ind. Lab.*   1,718
J. Quintanilla, *Ref.*   1,609
G. Shorter, *Soc. Lab.*   482
S. Parnell, *BNP*   265
T. Leighton, *NLP*   140
Lab. Co-op. majority 11,382
(Boundary change: notional Lab.
Co-op.)

BRISTOL SOUTH
E.72,393   *T*. 68.87%
†Ms D. Primarolo, *Lab.*   29,890
M. Roe, *C.*   10,562
S. Williams, *LD*   6,691
D. Guy, *Ref.*   1,486
J. Boxall, *Green*   722
I. Marshall, *Soc.*   355
Louis Taylor, *Glow*   153
Lab. majority 19,328
(Boundary change: notional Lab.)

BRISTOL WEST
E.84,870   *T*. 73.81%
Ms V. Davey, *Lab.*   22,068
†Rt. Hon. W. Waldegrave, *C.*   20,575
C. Boney, *LD*   17,551
Lady M. Beauchamp, *Ref.*   1,304
J. Quinnell, *Green*   852
R. Nurse, *Soc. Lab.*   244
J. Brierley, *NLP*   47
Lab. majority 1,493
(Boundary change: notional C.)

BROMLEY AND CHISLEHURST
E.71,104   *T*. 74.17%
†Rt. Hon. E. Forth, *C.*   24,428
R. Yeldham, *Lab.*   13,310
Dr P. Booth, *LD*   12,530
R. Bryant, *UK Ind.*   1,176
Ms F. Speed, *Green*   640
M. Stoneman, *NF*   369
G. Aitman, *Lib.*   285
C. majority 11,118
(Boundary change: notional C.)

BROMSGROVE
E.67,744   *T*. 77.07%
Miss J. Kirkbride, *C.*   24,620
P. McDonald, *Lab.*   19,725
Mrs J. Davy, *LD*   6,200
Mrs D. Winsor, *Ref.*   1,411
Mrs G. Wetton, *UK Ind.*   251
C. majority 4,895
(Boundary change: notional C.)

BROXBOURNE
E.66,720   *T*. 70.41%
†Mrs M. Roe, *C.*   22,952
B. Coleman, *Lab.*   16,299
Mrs J. Davies, *LD*   5,310
D. Millward, *Ref.*   1,633
D. Bruce, *BNP*   610
B. Cheetham, *Third Way*   172
C. majority 6,653
(Boundary change: notional C.)

BROXTOWE
E.74,144   *T*. 78.41%
N. Palmer, *Lab.*   27,343

†Sir J. Lester, *C.* 21,768
T. Miller, *LD* 6,934
R. Tucker, *Ref.* 2,092
Lab. majority 5,575
(Boundary change: notional C.)

BUCKINGHAM
*E.*62,945   *T.* 78.48%
J. Bercow, *C.* 24,594
R. Lehmann, *Lab.* 12,208
N. Stuart, *LD* 12,175
Dr G. Clements, *NLP* 421
C. majority 12,386
(Boundary change: notional C.)

BURNLEY
*E.*67,582   *T.* 66.95%
*P. Pike, *Lab.* 26,210
W. Wiggin, *C.* 9,148
G. Birtwistle, *LD* 7,877
R. Oakley, *Ref.* 2,010
Lab. majority 17,062
(April 1992, Lab. maj. 11,491)

BURTON
*E.*72,601   *T.* 75.08%
Ms J. Dean, *Lab.* 27,810
†Sir I. Lawrence, *C.* 21,480
D. Fletcher, *LD* 4,617
K. Sharp, *Nat. Dem.* 604
Lab. majority 6,330
(Boundary change: notional C.)

BURY NORTH
*E.*70,515   *T.* 78.07%
D. Chaytor, *Lab.* 28,523
*A. Burt, *C.* 20,657
N. Kenyon, *LD* 4,536
R. Hallewell, *Ref.* 1,337
Lab. majority 7,866
(April 1992, C. maj. 4,764)

BURY SOUTH
*E.*66,568   *T.* 75.60%
I. Lewis, *Lab.* 28,658
†D. Sumberg, *C.* 16,225
V. D'Albert, *LD* 4,227
B. Slater, *Ref.* 1,216
Lab. majority 12,433
(Boundary change: notional C.)

BURY ST EDMUNDS
*E.*74,017   *T.* 75.02%
D. Ruffley, *C.* 21,290
M. Ereira-Guyer, *Lab.* 20,922
D. Cooper, *LD* 10,102
I. McWhirter, *Ref.* 2,939
Mrs J. Lillis, *NLP* 272
C. majority 368
(Boundary change: notional C.)

CALDER VALLEY
*E.*74,901   *T.* 75.39%
Ms C. McCafferty, *Lab.* 26,050
*Sir D. Thompson, *C.* 19,795
S. Pearson, *LD* 8,322
A. Mellor, *Ref.* 1,380
Ms V. Smith, *Green* 488
C. Jackson, *BNP* 431
Lab. majority 6,255
(April 1992, C. maj. 4,878)

CAMBERWELL AND PECKHAM
*E.*50,214   *T.* 56.71%
†Ms H. Harman, *Lab.* 19,734

K. Humphreys, *C.* 3,383
N. Williams, *LD* 3,198
N. China, *Ref.* 692
Ms A. Ruddock, *Soc. Lab.* 685
G. Williams, *Lib.* 443
Ms J. Barker, *Soc.* 233
C. Eames, *WRP* 106
Lab. majority 16,351
(Boundary change: notional Lab.)

CAMBRIDGE
*E.*71,669   *T.* 71.63%
*Mrs A. Campbell, *Lab.* 27,436
D. Platt, *C.* 13,299
G. Heathcock, *LD* 8,287
W. Burrows, *Ref.* 1,262
Ms M. Wright, *Green* 654
Ms A. Johnstone, *ProLife* 191
R. Athow, *WRP* 107
Ms P. Gladwin, *NLP* 103
Lab. majority 14,137
(April 1992, Lab. maj. 580)

CAMBRIDGESHIRE NORTH EAST
*E.*76,056   *T.* 72.87%
†M. Moss, *C.* 23,855
Mrs V. Bucknor, *Lab.* 18,754
A. Nash, *LD* 9,070
M. Bacon, *Ref.* 2,636
C. Bennett, *Soc. Lab.* 851
L. Leighton, *NLP* 259
C. majority 5,101
(Boundary change: notional C.)

CAMBRIDGESHIRE NORTH WEST
*E.*65,791   *T.* 74.20%
†Rt. Hon. Dr B. Mawhinney, *C.* 23,488
L. Steptoe, *Lab.* 15,734
Mrs B. McCoy, *LD* 7,388
A.Watt, *Ref.* 1,939
W. Wyatt, *UK Ind.* 269
C. majority 7,754
(Boundary change: notional C.)

CAMBRIDGESHIRE SOUTH
*E.*69,850   *T.* 76.85%
A. Lansley, *C.* 22,572
J. Quinlan, *LD* 13,860
A. Gray, *Lab.* 13,485
R. Page, *Ref.* 3,300
D. Norman, *UK Ind.* 298
F. Chalmers, *NLP* 168
C. majority 8,712
(Boundary change: notional C.)

CAMBRIDGESHIRE SOUTH EAST
*E.*75,666   *T.* 75.08%
†J. Paice, *C.* 24,397
R. Collinson, *Lab.* 15,048
Ms S. Brinton, *LD* 14,246
J. Howlett, *Ref.* 2,838
K. Lam, *Fair* 167
P. While, *NLP* 111
C. majority 9,349
(Boundary change: notional C.)

CANNOCK CHASE
*E.*72,362   *T.* 72.37%
†Dr A. Wright, *Lab.* 28,705
J. Backhouse, *C.* 14,227
R. Kirby, *LD* 4,537
P. Froggatt, *Ref.* 1,663
W. Hurley, *New Lab.* 1,615

M. Conroy, *Soc. Lab.* 1,120
M. Hartshorn, *Loony* 499
Lab. majority 14,478
(Boundary change: notional Lab.)

CANTERBURY
*E.*74,548   *T.* 72.58%
†J. Brazier, *C.* 20,913
Ms C. Hall, *Lab.* 16,949
M. Vye, *LD* 12,854
J. Osborne, *Ref.* 2,460
G. Meaden, *Green* 588
J. Moore, *UK Ind.* 281
A. Pringle, *NLP* 64
C. majority 3,964
(Boundary change: notional C.)

CARLISLE
*E.*59,917   *T.* 72.78%
†E. Martlew, *Lab.* 25,031
R. Lawrence, *C.* 12,641
C. Mayho, *LD* 4,576
A. Fraser, *Ref.* 1,233
W. Stevens, *NLP* 126
Lab. majority 12,390
(Boundary change: notional Lab.)

CARSHALTON AND WALLINGTON
*E.*66,038   *T.* 73.33%
T. Brake, *LD* 18,490
*N. Forman, *C.* 16,223
A. Theobald, *Lab.* 11,565
J. Storey, *Ref.* 1,289
P. Hickson, *Green* 377
G. Ritchie, *BNP* 261
L. Povey, *UK Ind.* 218
LD majority 2,267
(April 1992, C. maj. 9,943)

CASTLE POINT
*E.*67,146   *T.* 72.34%
Ms C. Butler, *Lab.* 20,605
*Dr R. Spink, *C.* 19,489
D. Baker, *LD* 4,477
H. Maulkin, *Ref.* 2,700
Miss L. Kendall, *Consult.* 1,301
Lab. majority 1,116
(April 1992, C. maj. 16,830)

CHARNWOOD
*E.*72,692   *T.* 77.28%
†Rt. Hon. S. Dorrell, *C.* 26,110
D. Knaggs, *Lab.* 20,210
R. Wilson, *LD* 7,224
H. Meechan, *Ref.* 2,104
M. Palmer, *BNP* 525
C. majority 5,900
(Boundary change: notional C.)

CHATHAM AND AYLESFORD
*E.*69,172   *T.* 71.07%
J. Shaw, *Lab.* 21,191
R. Knox-Johnston, *C.* 18,401
R. Murray, *LD* 7,389
K. Riddle, *Ref.* 1,538
A. Harding, *UK Ind.* 493
T. Martel, *NLP* 149
Lab. majority 2,790
(Boundary change: notional C.)

CHEADLE
E.67,627   T. 77.58%
†S. Day, *C.* — 22,944
Mrs P. Calton, *LD* — 19,755
P. Diggett, *Lab.* — 8,253
P. Brook, *Ref.* — 1,511
C. majority 3,189
(Boundary change: notional C.)

CHELMSFORD WEST
E.76,086   T. 76.99%
†S. Burns, *C.* — 23,781
M. Bracken, *LD* — 17,090
Dr R. Chad, *Lab.* — 15,436
T. Smith, *Ref.* — 1,536
G. Rumens, *Green* — 411
M. Levin, *UK Ind.* — 323
C. majority 6,691
(Boundary change: notional C.)

CHELTENHAM
E.67,950   T. 74.03%
†N. Jones, *LD* — 24,877
J. Todman, *C.* — 18,232
B. Leach, *Lab.* — 5,100
Mrs A. Powell, *Ref.* — 1,065
K. Hanks, *Loony* — 375
G. Cook, *UK Ind.* — 302
Ms A. Harriss, *ProLife* — 245
Ms S. Brighouse, *NLP* — 107
LD majority 6,645
(Boundary change: notional LD)

CHESHAM AND AMERSHAM
E.69,244   T. 75.38%
†Mrs C. Gillan, *C.* — 26,298
M. Brand, *LD* — 12,439
P. Farrelly, *Lab.* — 10,240
P. Andrews, *Ref.* — 2,528
C. Shilson, *UK Ind.* — 618
H. Godfrey, *NLP* — 74
C. majority 13,859
(Boundary change: notional C.)

CHESTER, CITY OF
E.71,730   T. 78.43%
Ms C. Russell, *Lab.* — 29,806
†G. Brandreth, *C.* — 19,253
D. Simpson, *LD* — 5,353
R. Mullen, *Ref.* — 1,487
I. Sanderson, *Loony* — 204
J. Gerrard, *WCCC* — 154
Lab. majority 10,553
(Boundary change: notional C.)

CHESTERFIELD
E.72,472   T. 70.91%
*Rt. Hon. A. Benn, *Lab.* — 26,105
A. Rogers, *LD* — 20,330
M. Potter, *C.* — 4,752
N. Scarth, *Ind. OAP* — 202
Lab. majority 5,775
(April 1992, Lab. maj. 6,414)

CHICHESTER
E.74,489   T. 74.88%
A. Tyrie, *C.* — 25,895
Prof. P. Gardiner, *LD* — 16,161
C. Smith, *Lab.* — 9,605
D. Denny, *Ref.* — 3,318
J. Rix, *UK Ind.* — 800
C. majority 9,734

(Boundary change: notional C.)

CHINGFORD AND WOODFORD
GREEN
E.62,904   T. 70.66%
†I. Duncan Smith, *C.* — 21,109
T. Hutchinson, *Lab.* — 15,395
G. Seeff, *LD* — 6,885
A. Gould, *BNP* — 1,059
C. majority 5,714
(Boundary change: notional C.)

CHIPPING BARNET
E.69,049   T. 71.78%
†Sir S. Chapman, *C.* — 21,317
G. Cooke, *Lab.* — 20,282
S. Hooker, *LD* — 6,121
V. Ribekow, *Ref.* — 1,190
B. Miskin, *Loony* — 253
B. Scallan, *ProLife* — 243
Ms D. Dirksen, *NLP* — 159
C. majority 1,035
(Boundary change: notional C.)

CHORLEY
E.74,387   T. 77.58%
L. Hoyle, *Lab.* — 30,607
†D. Dover, *C.* — 20,737
S. Jones, *LD* — 4,900
A. Heaton, *Ref.* — 1,319
P. Leadbetter, *NLP* — 143
Lab. majority 9,870
(Boundary change: notional C.)

CHRISTCHURCH
E.71,488   T. 78.61%
C. Chope, *C.* — 26,095
†Mrs D. Maddock, *LD* — 23,930
C. Mannan, *Lab.* — 3,884
R. Spencer, *Ref.* — 1,684
R. Dickinson, *UK Ind.* — 606
C. majority 2,165
(Boundary change: notional C.)

CITIES OF LONDON AND
WESTMINSTER
E.69,047   T. 58.16%
†Rt. Hon. P. Brooke, *C.* — 18,981
Ms K. Green, *Lab.* — 14,100
M. Dumigan, *LD* — 4,933
Sir A. Walters, *Ref.* — 1,161
Ms P. Wharton, *Barts* — 266
C. Merton, *UK Ind.* — 215
R. Johnson, *NLP* — 176
N. Walsh, *Loony* — 138
G. Webster, *Hemp* — 112
J. Sadowitz, *Dream* — 73
C. majority 4,881
(Boundary change: notional C.)

CLEETHORPES
E.68,763   T. 73.40%
Ms S. McIsaac, *Lab.* — 26,058
†M. Brown, *C.* — 16,882
K. Melton, *LD* — 5,746
J. Berry, *Ref.* — 1,787
Lab. majority 9,176
(Boundary change: notional C.)

COLCHESTER
E.74,743   T. 69.58%
R. Russell, *LD* — 17,886
S. Shakespeare, *C.* — 16,305
R. Green, *Lab.* — 15,891

J. Hazell, *Ref.* — 1,776
Ms L. Basker, *NLP* — 148
LD majority 1,581
(Boundary change: notional C.)

COLNE VALLEY
E.73,338   T. 76.92%
Ms K. Mountford, *Lab.* — 23,285
*G. Riddick, *C.* — 18,445
N. Priestley, *LD* — 12,755
A. Brooke, *Soc. Lab.* — 759
A. Cooper, *Green* — 493
J. Nunn, *UK Ind.* — 478
Ms M. Staniforth, *Loony* — 196
Lab. majority 4,840
(April 1992, C. maj. 7,225)

CONGLETON
E.68,873   T. 77.56%
†Mrs A. Winterton, *C.* — 22,012
Mrs J. Walmsley, *LD* — 15,882
Ms H. Scholey, *Lab.* — 14,714
J. Lockett, *UK Ind.* — 811
C. majority 6,130
(Boundary change: notional C.)

COPELAND
E.54,263   T. 76.19%
*Rt. Hon. Dr J. Cunningham,
   Lab. — 24,025
A. Cumpsty, *C.* — 12,081
R. Putnam, *LD* — 3,814
C. Johnston, *Ref.* — 1,036
G. Hanratty, *ProLife* — 389
Lab. majority 11,944
(April 1992, Lab. maj. 2,439)

CORBY
E.69,252   T. 77.91%
P. Hope, *Lab. Co-op.* — 29,888
*W. Powell, *C.* — 18,028
I. Hankinson, *LD* — 4,045
S. Riley-Smith, *Ref.* — 1,356
I. Gillman, *UK Ind.* — 507
Ms J. Bence, *NLP* — 133
Lab. Co-op. majority 11,860
(April 1992, C. maj. 342)

CORNWALL NORTH
E.80,076   T. 73.16%
*P. Tyler, *LD* — 31,186
N. Linacre, *C.* — 17,253
Ms A. Lindo, *Lab.* — 5,523
Ms F. Odam, *Ref.* — 3,636
J. Bolitho, *MK* — 645
R. Winfield, *Lib.* — 186
N. Cresswell, *NLP* — 152
LD majority 13,933
(April 1992, LD maj. 1,921)

CORNWALL SOUTH EAST
E.75,825   T. 75.74%
C. Breed, *LD* — 27,044
W. Lightfoot, *C.* — 20,564
Mrs D. Kirk, *Lab.* — 7,358
J. Wonnacott, *UK Ind.* — 1,428
P. Dunbar, *MK* — 573
W. Weights, *Lib* — 268
Ms M. Hartley, *NLP* — 197
LD majority 6,480
(April 1992, C. maj. 7,704)

COTSWOLD
E.67,333　T. 75.92%
†G. Clifton-Brown, *C.*　23,698
D. Gayler, *LD*　11,733
D. Elwell, *Lab.*　11,608
R. Lowe, *Ref.*　3,393
Ms V. Michael, *Green*　560
H. Brighouse, *NLP*　129
C. majority 11,965
(Boundary change: notional C.)

COVENTRY NORTH EAST
E.74,274　T. 64.74%
†R. Ainsworth, *Lab.*　31,856
M. Burnett, *C.*　9,287
G. Sewards, *LD*　3,866
N. Brown, *Lib.*　1,181
R. Hurrell, *Ref.*　1,125
H. Khamis, *Soc. Lab.*　597
C. Sidwell, *Dream*　173
Lab. majority 22,569
(Boundary change: notional Lab.)

COVENTRY NORTH WEST
E.76,439　T. 71.07%
†G. Robinson, *Lab.*　30,901
P. Bartlett, *C.*　14,300
Dr N. Penlington, *LD*　5,690
D. Butler, *Ref.*　1,269
D. Spencer, *Soc. Lab.*　940
R. Wheway, *Lib.*　687
P. Mills, *ProLife*　359
L. Francis, *Dream*　176
Lab. majority 16,601
(Boundary change: notional Lab.)

COVENTRY SOUTH
E.71,826　T. 69.79%
†J. Cunningham, *Lab.*　25,511
P. Ivey, *C.*　14,558
G. MacDonald, *LD*　4,617
D. Nellist, *Soc.*　3,262
P. Garratt, *Ref.*　943
R. Jenking, *Lib.*　725
J. Astbury, *BNP*　328
Ms A.-M. Bradshaw, *Dream*　180
Lab. majority 10,953
(Boundary change: notional C.)

CRAWLEY
E.69,040　T. 73.03%
Mrs L. Moffatt, *Lab.*　27,750
Miss J. Crabb, *C.*　16,043
H. de Souza, *LD*　4,141
R. Walters, *Ref.*　1,931
E. Saunders, *UK Ind.*　322
A. Kahn, *JP*　230
Lab. majority 11,707
(Boundary change: notional C.)

CREWE AND NANTWICH
E.68,694　T. 73.67%
†Mrs G. Dunwoody, *Lab.*　29,460
M. Loveridge, *C.*　13,662
D. Cannon, *LD*　5,940
P. Astbury, *Ref.*　1,543
Lab. majority 15,798
(Boundary change: notional Lab.)

CROSBY
E.57,190　T. 77.18%
Ms C. Curtis-Tansley, *Lab.*　22,549
†Sir M. Thornton, *C.*　15,367
P. McVey, *LD*　5,080

J. Gauld, *Ref.*　813
J. Marks, *Lib.*　233
W. Hite, *NLP*　99
Lab. majority 7,182
(Boundary change: notional C.)

CROYDON CENTRAL
E.80,152　T. 69.62%
G. Davies, *Lab.*　25,432
†D. Congdon, *C.*　21,535
G. Schlich, *LD*　6,061
C. Cook, *Ref.*　1,886
M.-S. Barnsley, *Green*　595
J. Woollcott, *UK Ind.*　290
Lab. majority 3,897
(Boundary change: notional C.)

CROYDON NORTH
E.77,063　T. 68.21%
†M. Wicks, *Lab.*　32,672
I. Martin, *C.*　14,274
M. Morris, *LD*　4,066
R. Billis, *Ref.*　1,155
J. Feisenberger, *UK Ind.*　396
Lab. majority 18,398
(Boundary change: notional C.)

CROYDON SOUTH
E.73,787　T. 73.45%
†R. Ottaway, *C.*　25,649
C. Burling, *Lab.*　13,719
S. Gauge, *LD*　11,441
A. Barber, *Ref.*　2,631
P. Ferguson, *BNP*　354
A. Harker, *UK Ind.*　309
M. Samuel, *Choice*　96
C. majority 11,930
(Boundary change: notional C.)

DAGENHAM
E.58,573　T. 61.74%
†Mrs J. Church, *Lab.*　23,759
J. Fairrie, *C.*　6,705
T. Dobrashian, *LD*　2,704
S. Kraft, *Ref.*　1,411
W. Binding, *BNP*　900
R. Dawson, *Ind.*　349
M. Hipperson, *Nat. Dem.*　183
Ms K. Goble, *ProLife*　152
Lab. majority 17,054
(Boundary change: notional Lab.)

DARLINGTON
E.65,140　T. 73.95%
*A. Milburn, *Lab.*　29,658
P. Scrope, *C.*　13,633
L. Boxell, *LD*　3,483
M. Blakey, *Ref.*　1,399
Lab. majority 16,025
(April 1992, Lab. maj. 2,798)

DARTFORD
E.69,726　T. 74.57%
H. Stoate, *Lab.*　25,278
†R. Dunn, *C.*　20,950
Mrs D. Webb, *LD*　4,827
P. McHale, *BNP*　428
P. Homden, *FDP*　287
J. Pollitt, *Ch. D.*　228
Lab. majority 4,328
(Boundary change: notional C.)

DAVENTRY
E.80,151　T. 77.04%

†T. Boswell, *C.*　28,615
K. Ritchie, *Lab.*　21,237
J. Gordon, *LD*　9,233
Mrs B. Russocki, *Ref.*　2,018
B. Mahoney, *UK Ind.*　443
R. France, *NLP*　204
C. majority 7,378
(Boundary change: notional C.)

DENTON AND REDDISH
E.68,866　T. 66.92%
†A. Bennett, *Lab.*　30,137
Ms B. Nutt, *C.*　9,826
I. Donaldson, *LD*　6,121
Lab. majority 20,311
(Boundary change: notional Lab.)

DERBY NORTH
E.76,116　T. 73.76%
R. Laxton, *Lab.*　29,844
*Rt. Hon. G. Knight, *C.*　19,229
R. Charlesworth, *LD*　5,059
P. Reynolds, *Ref.*　1,816
J. Waters, *ProLife*　195
Lab. majority 10,615
(April 1992, C. maj. 4,453)

DERBY SOUTH
E.76,386　T. 67.84%
†Rt. Hon. Mrs M. Beckett, *Lab.*　29,154
J. Arain, *C.*　13,048
J. Beckett, *LD*　7,438
J. Browne, *Ref.*　1,862
R. Evans, *Nat. Dem.*　317
Lab. majority 16,106
(Boundary change: notional Lab.)

DERBYSHIRE NORTH EAST
E.71,653　T. 72.54%
*H. Barnes, *Lab.*　31,425
S. Elliott, *C.*　13,104
S. Hardy, *LD*　7,450
Lab. majority 18,321
(April 1992, Lab. maj. 6,270)

DERBYSHIRE SOUTH
E.76,672　T. 78.21%
M. Todd, *Lab.*　32,709
†Mrs E. Currie, *C.*　18,742
R. Renold, *LD*　5,408
R. North, *Ref.*　2,491
Dr I. Crompton, *UK Ind.*　617
Lab. majority 13,967
(Boundary change: notional C.)

DERBYSHIRE WEST
E.72,716　T. 78.23%
†P. McLoughlin, *C.*　23,945
S. Clamp, *Lab.*　19,060
C. Seeley, *LD*　9,940
J. Gouriet, *Ref.*　2,499
G. Meynell, *Ind. Green*　593
H. Price, *UK Ind.*　484
N. Delves, *Loony*　281
M. Kyslun, *Ind. BB*　81
C. majority 4,885
(Boundary change: notional C.)

DEVIZES
E.80,383　T. 74.69%
†Rt. Hon. M. Ancram, *C.*　25,710
A. Vickers, *LD*　15,928
F. Jeffrey, *Lab.*　14,551
J. Goldsmith, *Ref.*　3,021

S. Oram, *UK Ind.* 622
S. Haysom, *NLP* 204
C. majority 9,782
(Boundary change: notional C.)

DEVON EAST
*E.*69,094   *T.* 76.06%
†Rt. Hon. Sir P. Emery, *C.* 22,797
Miss R. Trethewey, *LD* 15,308
A. Siantonas, *Lab.* 9,292
W. Dixon, *Ref.* 3,200
G. Halliwell, *Lib.* 1,363
C. Giffard, *UK Ind.* 459
G. Needs, *Nat. Dem.* 131
C. majority 7,489
(Boundary change: notional C.)

DEVON NORTH
*E.*70,350   *T.* 77.94%
†N. Harvey, *LD* 27,824
R. Ashworth, *C.* 21,643
Mrs E. Brenton, *Lab.* 5,367
LD majority 6,181
(Boundary change: notional LD)

DEVON SOUTH WEST
*E.*69,293   *T.* 76.22%
†G. Streeter, *C.* 22,695
C. Mavin, *Lab.* 15,262
K. Baldry, *LD* 12,542
R. Sadler, *Ref.* 1,668
Mrs H. King, *UK Ind.* 491
J. Hyde, *NLP* 159
C. majority 7,433
(Boundary change: notional C.)

DEVON WEST AND TORRIDGE
*E.*75,919   *T.* 77.91%
J. Burnett, *LD* 24,744
I. Liddell-Grainger, *C.* 22,787
D. Brenton, *Lab.* 7,319
R. Lea, *Ref.* 1,946
M. Jackson, *UK Ind.* 1,841
M. Pithouse, *Lib.* 508
LD majority 1,957
(Boundary change: notional C.)

DEWSBURY
*E.*61,523   *T.* 70.01%
†Mrs A. Taylor, *Lab.* 21,286
Dr P. McCormick, *C.* 12,963
K. Hill, *LD* 4,422
Ms F. Taylor, *BNP* 2,232
Ms W. Goff, *Ref.* 1,019
D. Daniel, *Ind. Lab.* 770
I. McCourtie, *Green* 383
Lab. majority 8,323
(Boundary change: notional Lab.)

DONCASTER CENTRAL
*E.*67,965   *T.* 63.92%
Ms R. Winterton, *Lab.* 26,961
D. Turtle, *C.* 9,105
S. Tarry, *LD* 4,091
M. Cliff, *Ref.* 1,273
M. Kenny, *Soc. Lab.* 854
J. Redden, *ProLife* 697
P. Davies, *UK Ind.* 462
Lab. majority 17,856
(April 1992, Lab. maj. 10,682)

DONCASTER NORTH
*E.*63,019   *T.* 63.30%
†K. Hughes, *Lab.* 27,843

P. Kennerley, *C.* 5,906
M. Cook, *LD* 3,369
R. Thornton, *Ref.* 1,589
M. Swan, *AS Lab.* 1,181
Lab. majority 21,937
(Boundary change: notional Lab.)

DON VALLEY
*E.*65,643   *T.* 66.35%
Ms C. Flint, *Lab.* 25,376
Mrs C. Gledhill, *C.* 10,717
P. Johnston, *LD* 4,238
P. Davis, *Ref.* 1,379
N. Ball, *Soc. Lab.* 1,024
S. Platt, *Green* 493
Ms C. Johnson, *ProLife* 330
Lab. majority 14,659
(Boundary change: notional Lab.)

DORSET MID AND POOLE NORTH
*E.*67,049   *T.* 75.67%
C. Fraser, *C.* 20,632
A. Leaman, *LD* 19,951
D. Collis, *Lab.* 8,014
D. Nabarro, *Ref.* 2,136
C. majority 681
(Boundary change: notional C.)

DORSET NORTH
*E.*68,923   *T.* 76.30%
R. Walter, *C.* 23,294
Mrs P. Yates, *LD* 20,548
J. Fitzmaurice, *Lab.* 5,380
Mrs M. Evans, *Ref.* 2,564
Revd D. Wheeler, *UK Ind.* 801
C. majority 2,746
(Boundary change: notional C.)

DORSET SOUTH
*E.*66,318   *T.* 74.16%
†I. Bruce, *C.* 17,755
J. Knight, *Lab.* 17,678
M. Plummer, *LD* 9,936
P. McAndrew, *Ref.* 2,791
Capt. M. Shakesby, *UK Ind.* 861
G. Napper, *NLP* 161
C. majority 77
(Boundary change: notional C.)

DORSET WEST
*E.*70,369   *T.* 76.10%
O. Letwin, *C.* 22,036
R. Legg, *LD* 20,196
R. Bygraves, *Lab.* 9,491
P. Jenkins, *UK Ind.* 1,590
M. Griffiths, *NLP* 239
C. majority 1,840
(Boundary change: notional C.)

DOVER
*E.*68,669   *T.* 78.93%
G. Prosser, *Lab.* 29,535
†D. Shaw, *C.* 17,796
M. Corney, *LD* 4,302
Mrs S. Anderson, *Ref.* 2,124
C. Hyde, *UK Ind.* 443
Lab. majority 11,739
(Boundary change: notional C.)

DUDLEY NORTH
*E.*68,835   *T.* 69.45%
R. Cranston, *Lab.* 24,471
C. MacNamara, *C.* 15,014

G. Lewis, *LD* 3,939
M. Atherton, *Soc. Lab.* 2,155
S. Bavester, *Ref.* 1,201
G. Cartwright, *NF* 559
S. Darby, *Nat. Dem.* 469
Lab. majority 9,457
(Boundary change: notional Lab.)

DUDLEY SOUTH
*E.*66,731   *T.* 71.78%
†I. Pearson, *Lab.* 27,124
M. Simpson, *C.* 14,097
R. Burt, *LD* 5,214
C. Birch, *Ref.* 1,467
Lab. majority 13,027
(Boundary change: notional Lab.)

DULWICH AND WEST NORWOOD
*E.*69,655   *T.* 65.49%
†Ms T. Jowell, *Lab.* 27,807
R. Gough, *C.* 11,038
Mrs S. Kramer, *LD* 4,916
B. Coles, *Ref.* 897
Dr A. Goldie, *Lib.* 587
D. Goodman, *Dream* 173
E. Pike, *UK Ind.* 159
Capt. Rizz, *Rizz Party* 38
Lab. majority 16,769
(Boundary change: notional Lab.)

DURHAM NORTH
*E.*67,891   *T.* 69.48%
†G. Radice, *Lab.* 33,142
M. Hardy, *C.* 6,843
B. Moore, *LD* 5,225
I. Parkin, *Ref.* 1,958
Lab. majority 26,299
(Boundary change: notional Lab.)

DURHAM NORTH WEST
*E.*67,156   *T.* 68.97%
†Miss H. Armstrong, *Lab.* 31,855
Mrs L. St J. Howe, *C.* 7,101
A. Gillings, *LD* 4,991
R. Atkinson, *Ref.* 2,372
Lab. majority 24,754
(Boundary change: notional Lab.)

DURHAM, CITY OF
*E.*69,340   *T.* 70.86%
*G. Steinberg, *Lab.* 31,102
R. Chalk, *C.* 8,598
Dr N. Martin, *LD* 7,499
Ms M. Robson, *Ref.* 1,723
P. Kember, *NLP* 213
Lab. majority 22,504
(April 1992, Lab. maj. 15,058)

EALING ACTON AND SHEPHERD'S BUSH
*E.*72,078   *T.* 66.68%
†C. Soley, *Lab.* 28,052
Mrs B. Yerolemou, *C.* 12,405
A. Mitchell, *LD* 5,163
C. Winn, *Ref.* 637
J. Gilbert, *Soc. Lab.* 635
J. Gomm, *UK Ind.* 385
P. Danon, *ProLife* 265
C. Beasley, *Glow* 209
W. Edwards, *Ch. P.* 163
K. Turner, *NLP* 150
Lab. majority 15,647
(Boundary change: notional Lab.)

EALING NORTH
E.78,144   T. 71.31%
S. Pound, *Lab.*		29,904
†H. Greenway, *C.*		20,744
A. Gupta, *LD*		3,887
G. Slysz, *UK Ind.*		689
Ms A. Siebe, *Green*		502

Lab. majority 9,160
(Boundary change: notional C.)

EALING SOUTHALL
E.81,704   T. 66.88%
†P. Khabra, *Lab.*		32,791
J. Penrose, *C.*		11,368
Ms N. Thomson, *LD*		5,687
H. Brar, *Soc. Lab.*		2,107
N. Goodwin, *Green*		934
B. Cherry, *Ref.*		854
Ms K. Klepacka, *ProLife*		473
Dr R. Mead, *UK Ind.*		428

Lab. majority 21,423
(Boundary change: notional Lab.)

EASINGTON
E.62,518   T. 67.01%
*J. Cummings, *Lab.*		33,600
J. Hollands, *C.*		3,588
J. Heppell, *LD*		3,025
R. Pulfrey, *Ref.*		1,179
S. Colborn, *SPGB*		503

Lab. majority 30,012
(April 1992, Lab. maj. 26,390)

EASTBOURNE
E.72,347   T. 72.80%
†N. Waterson, *C.*		22,183
C. Berry, *LD*		20,189
D. Lines, *Lab.*		6,576
T. Lowe, *Ref.*		2,724
Mrs T. Williamson, *Lib.*		741
J. Dawkins, *UK Ind.*		254

C. majority 1,994
(Boundary change: notional C.)

EAST HAM
E.65,591   T. 60.81%
†S. Timms, *Lab.*		25,779
Miss A. Bray, *C.*		6,421
I. Khan, *Soc. Lab.*		2,697
M. Sole, *LD*		2,599
C. Smith, *BNP*		1,258
Mrs J. McCann, *Ref.*		845
G. Hardy, *Nat. Dem.*		290

Lab. majority 19,358
(Boundary change: notional Lab.)

EASTLEIGH
E.72,155   T. 76.91%
†D. Chidgey, *LD*		19,453
S. Reid, *C.*		18,699
A. Lloyd, *Lab.*		14,883
V. Eldridge, *Ref.*		2,013
P. Robinson, *UK Ind.*		446

LD majority 754
(Boundary change: notional C.)

ECCLES
E.69,645   T. 65.60%
I. Stewart, *Lab.*		30,468
G. Barker, *C.*		8,552
R. Boyd, *LD*		4,905
J. De Roeck, *Ref.*		1,765

Lab. majority 21,916
(Boundary change: notional Lab.)

EDDISBURY
E.65,256   T. 75.78%
†Rt.. Hon. A. Goodlad, *C.*		21,027
Ms M. Hanson, *Lab.*		19,842
D. Reaper, *LD*		6,540
Ms N. Napier, *Ref.*		2,041

C. majority 1,185
(Boundary change: notional C.)
See also page 233

EDMONTON
E.63,718   T. 70.37%
A. Love, *Lab. Co-op.*		27,029
*Dr I. Twinn, *C.*		13,557
A. Wiseman, *LD*		2,847
J. Wright, *Ref.*		708
B. Cowd, *BNP*		437
Mrs P. Weald, *UK Ind.*		260

Lab. Co-op. majority 13,472
(April 1992, C. maj. 593)

ELLESMERE PORT AND NESTON
E.67,573   T. 77.79%
†A. Miller, *Lab.*		31,310
Mrs L. Turnbull, *C.*		15,274
Ms J. Pemberton, *LD*		4,673
C. Rodden, *Ref.*		1,305

Lab. majority 16,036
(Boundary change: notional Lab.)

ELMET
E.70,423   T. 76.81%
C. Burgon, *Lab.*		28,348
*S. Batiste, *C.*		19,569
B. Jennings, *LD*		4,691
C. Zawadski, *Ref.*		1,487

Lab. majority 8,779
(April 1992, C. maj. 3,261)

ELTHAM
E.57,358   T. 75.71%
C. Efford, *Lab.*		23,710
C. Blackwood, *C.*		13,528
Ms A. Taylor, *LD*		3,701
M. Clark, *Ref.*		1,414
H. Middleton, *Lib.*		584
W. Hitches, *BNP*		491

Lab. majority 10,182
(Boundary change: notional C.)

ENFIELD NORTH
E.67,680   T. 70.43%
Ms J. Ryan, *Lab.*		24,148
M. Field, *C.*		17,326
M. Hopkins, *LD*		4,264
R. Ellingham, *Ref.*		857
Ms J. Griffin, *BNP*		590
Mrs J. O'Ware, *UK Ind.*		484

Lab. majority 6,822
(April 1992, C. maj. 9,430)

ENFIELD SOUTHGATE
E.65,796   T. 70.72%
S. Twigg, *Lab.*		20,570
†Rt. Hon. M. Portillo, *C.*		19,137
J. Browne, *LD*		4,966
N. Luard, *Ref.*		1,342
A. Storkey, *Ch. D.*		289
A. Malakouna, *Mal*		229

Lab. majority 1,433
(Boundary change: notional C.)

EPPING FOREST
E.72,795   T. 72.82%
Mrs E. Laing, *C.*		24,117
S. Murray, *Lab.*		18,865
S. Robinson, *LD*		7,074
J. Berry, *Ref.*		2,208
P. Henderson, *BNP*		743

C. majority 5,252
(Boundary change: notional C.)

EPSOM AND EWELL
E.73,222   T. 74.00%
†Rt. Hon. Sir A. Hamilton, *C.*		24,717
P. Woodford, *Lab.*		13,192
J. Vincent, *LD*		12,380
C. Macdonald, *Ref.*		2,355
H. Green, *UK Ind.*		544
H. Charlton, *Green*		527
Ms K. Weeks, *ProLife*		466

C. majority 11,525
(Boundary change: notional C.)

EREWASH
E.77,402   T. 77.95%
Ms E. Blackman, *Lab.*		31,196
†Mrs A. Knight, *C.*		22,061
Dr M. Garnett, *LD*		5,181
S. Stagg, *Ref.*		1,404
M. Simmons, *Soc. Lab.*		496

Lab. majority 9,135
(Boundary change: notional C.)

ERITH AND THAMESMEAD
E.62,887   T. 66.13%
†J. Austin-Walker, *Lab.*		25,812
N. Zahawi, *C.*		8,388
A. Grigg, *LD*		5,001
J. Flunder, *Ref.*		1,394
V. Dooley, *BNP*		718
M. Jackson, *UK Ind.*		274

Lab. majority 17,424
(Boundary change: notional Lab.)

ESHER AND WALTON
E.72,382   T. 74.14%
†I. Taylor, *C.*		26,747
Ms J. Reay, *Lab.*		12,219
G. Miles, *LD*		10,937
A. Cruickshank, *Ref.*		2,904
B. Collignon, *UK Ind.*		558
Ms S. Kay, *Dream*		302

C. majority 14,528
(Boundary change: notional C.)

ESSEX NORTH
E.68,008   T. 75.30%
†B. Jenkin, *C.*		22,480
T. Young, *Lab.*		17,004
A. Phillips, *LD*		10,028
R. Lord, *UK Ind.*		1,202
Ms S. Ransome, *Green*		495

C. majority 5,476
(Boundary change: notional C.)

EXETER
E.79,154   T. 78.16%
B. Bradshaw, *Lab.*		29,398
Dr A. Rogers, *C.*		17,693
D. Brewer, *LD*		11,148
D. Morrish, *Lib.*		2,062
P. Edwards, *Green*		643
Mrs C. Haynes, *UK Ind.*		638
J. Meakin, *UKPP*		282

Lab. majority 11,705
(Boundary change: notional C.)

FALMOUTH AND CAMBORNE
*E.*71,383   *T.* 75.13%

Ms C. Atherton, *Lab.*	18,151
*S. Coe, *C.*	15,463
Mrs T. Jones, *LD*	13,512
P. de Savary, *Ref.*	3,534
J. Geach, *Ind. Lab.*	1,691
P. Holmes, *Lib.*	527
R. Smith, *UK Ind.*	355
Ms R. Lewarne, *MK*	238
G. Glitter, *Loony*	161

Lab. majority 2,688
(April 1992, C. maj. 3,267)

FAREHAM
*E.*68,787   *T.* 75.85%

†Rt. Hon. Sir P. Lloyd, *C.*	24,436
M. Pryor, *Lab.*	14,078
Mrs G. Hill, *LD*	10,234
D. Markham, *Ref.*	2,914
W. O'Brien, *Ind. No*	515

C. majority 10,358
(Boundary change: notional C.)

FAVERSHAM AND KENT MID
*E.*67,490   *T.* 73.50%

†A. Rowe, *C.*	22,016
A. Stewart, *Lab.*	17,843
B. Parmenter, *LD*	6,138
R. Birley, *Ref.*	2,073
N. Davidson, *Loony*	511
M. Cunningham, *UK Ind.*	431
D. Currer, *Green*	380
Ms C. Morgan, *GRLNSP*	115
N. Pollard, *NLP*	99

C. majority 4,173
(Boundary change: notional C.)

FELTHAM AND HESTON
*E.*71,093   *T.* 65.58%

†A. Keen, *Lab. Co-op.*	27,836
P. Ground, *C.*	12,563
C. Penning, *LD*	4,264
R. Stubbs, *Ref.*	1,099
R. Church, *BNP*	682
D. Fawcett, *NLP*	177

Lab. Co-op. majority 15,273
(Boundary change: notional Lab.
Co-op.)

FINCHLEY AND GOLDERS GREEN
*E.*72,225   *T.* 69.65%

R. Vis, *Lab.*	23,180
†J. Marshall, *C.*	19,991
J. Davies, *LD*	5,670
G. Shaw, *Ref.*	684
A. Gunstock, *Green*	576
D. Barraclough, *UK Ind.*	205

Lab. majority 3,189
(Boundary change: notional C.)

FOLKESTONE AND HYTHE
*E.*71,153   *T.* 73.15%

†Rt. Hon. M. Howard, *C.*	20,313
D. Laws, *LD*	13,981
P. Doherty, *Lab.*	12,939
J. Aspinall, *Ref.*	4,188
J. Baker, *UK Ind.*	378
E. Segal, *Soc.*	182
R. Saint, *CFSS*	69

C. majority 6,332
(Boundary change: notional C.)

FOREST OF DEAN
*E.*63,465   *T.* 79.07%

Ms D. Organ, *Lab.*	24,203
†P. Marland, *C.*	17,860
Dr A. Lynch, *LD*	6,165
J. Hopkins, *Ref.*	1,624
G. Morgan, *Ind. Dean*	218
C. Palmer, *21st Cent.*	80
S. Porter, *Ind. F.*	34

Lab. majority 6,343
(Boundary change: notional Lab.)

FYLDE
*E.*71,385   *T.* 72.94%

†Rt. Hon. M. Jack, *C.*	25,443
J. Garrett, *Lab.*	16,480
W. Greene, *LD*	7,609
D. Britton, *Ref.*	2,372
T. Kerwin, *NLP*	163

C. majority 8,963
(Boundary change: notional C.)

GAINSBOROUGH
*E.*64,106   *T.* 74.56%

†E. Leigh, *C.*	20,593
P. Taylor, *Lab.*	13,767
N. Taylor, *LD*	13,436

C. majority 6,826
(Boundary change: notional C.)

GATESHEAD EAST AND WASHINGTON WEST
*E.*64,114   *T.* 67.19%

†Miss J. Quin, *Lab.*	31,047
Miss J. Burns, *C.*	6,097
A. Ord, *LD*	4,622
M. Daley, *Ref.*	1,315

Lab. majority 24,950
(Boundary change: notional Lab.)

GEDLING
*E.*68,820   *T.* 75.80%

V. Coaker, *Lab.*	24,390
*A. Mitchell, *C.*	20,588
R. Poynter, *LD*	5,180
J. Connor, *Ref.*	2,006

Lab. majority 3,802
(April 1992, C. maj. 10,637)

GILLINGHAM
*E.*70,389   *T.* 72.00%

P. Clark, *Lab.*	20,187
†J. Couchman, *C.*	18,207
R. Sayer, *LD*	9,649
G. Cann, *Ref.*	1,492
C. MacKinlay, *UK Ind.*	590
D. Robinson, *Loony*	305
C. Jury, *BNP*	195
Ms G. Duguay, *NLP*	58

Lab. majority 1,980
(Boundary change: notional C.)

GLOUCESTER
*E.*78,682   *T.* 73.61%

Ms T. Kingham, *Lab.*	28,943
†D. French, *C.*	20,684
P. Munisamy, *LD*	6,069
A. Reid, *Ref.*	1,482
A. Harris, *UK Ind.*	455
Ms M. Hamilton, *NLP*	281

Lab. majority 8,259
(Boundary change: notional C.)

GOSPORT
*E.*68,830   *T.* 70.25%

*P. Viggers, *C.*	21,085
I. Gray, *Lab.*	14,827
S. Hogg, *LD*	9,479
A. Blowers, *Ref.*	2,538
P. Ettie, *Ind.*	426

C. majority 6,258
(April 1992, C. maj. 16,318)

GRANTHAM AND STAMFORD
*E.*72,310   *T.* 73.25%

†Q. Davies, *C.*	22,672
P. Denning, *Lab.*	19,980
J. Sellick, *LD*	6,612
Ms M. Swain, *Ref.*	2,721
M. Charlesworth, *UK Ind.*	556
Ms R. Clark, *ProLife*	314
I. Harper, *NLP*	115

C. majority 2,692
(Boundary change: notional C.)

GRAVESHAM
*E.*69,234   *T.* 76.92%

C. Pond, *Lab.*	26,460
†J. Arnold, *C.*	20,681
Dr M. Canet, *LD*	4,128
Mrs P. Curtis, *Ref.*	1,441
A. Leyshon, *Ind.*	414
D. Palmer, *NLP*	129

Lab. majority 5,779
(Boundary change: notional C.)

GREAT GRIMSBY
*E.*65,043   *T.* 66.26%

*A. Mitchell, *Lab.*	25,765
D. Godson, *C.*	9,521
A. De Freitas, *LD*	7,810

Lab. majority 16,244
(April 1992, Lab. maj. 7,504)

GREAT YARMOUTH
*E.*68,625   *T.* 71.23%

A. Wright, *Lab.*	26,084
*M. Carttiss, *C.*	17,416
D. Wood, *LD*	5,381

Lab. majority 8,668
(April 1992, C. maj. 5,309)

GREENWICH AND WOOLWICH
*E.*61,352   *T.* 65.85%

†N. Raynsford, *Lab.*	25,630
M. Mitchell, *C.*	7,502
Mrs C. Luxton, *LD*	5,049
D. Ellison, *Ref.*	1,670
R. Mallone, *Fellowship*	428
D. Martin-Eagle, *Constit.*	124

Lab. majority 18,128
(Boundary change: notional Lab.)

GUILDFORD
*E.*75,541   *T.* 75.40%

N. St Aubyn, *C.*	24,230
Mrs M. Sharp, *LD*	19,439
J. Burns, *Lab.*	9,945
J. Gore, *Ref.*	2,650
R. McWhirter, *UK Ind.*	400
J. Morris, *Pacifist*	294

C. majority 4,791
(Boundary change: notional C.)

HACKNEY NORTH AND STOKE
NEWINGTON
E.62,045   T. 52.95%
*Ms D. Abbott, *Lab.* 21,110
M. Lavender, *C.* 5,483
D. Taylor, *LD* 3,806
Yen Chit Chong, *Green* 1,395
B. Maxwell, *Ref.* 544
D. Tolson, *None* 368
Miss L. Lovebucket, *Rain. Ref.* 146
Lab. majority 15,627
(April 1992, Lab. maj. 10,727)

HACKNEY SOUTH AND
SHOREDITCH
E.61,728   T. 54.67%
†B. Sedgemore, *Lab.* 20,048
M. Pantling, *LD* 5,068
C. O'Leary, *C.* 4,494
T. Betts, *New Lab.* 2,436
R. Franklin, *Ref.* 613
G. Callow, *BNP* 531
M. Goldman, *Comm. P.* 298
Ms M. Goldberg, *NLP* 145
W. Rogers, *WRP* 113
Lab. majority 14,980
(Boundary change: notional Lab.)

HALESOWEN AND ROWLEY
REGIS
E.66,245   T. 73.61%
Mrs S. Heal, *Lab.* 26,366
J. Kennedy, *C.* 16,029
Ms E. Todd, *LD* 4,169
P. White, *Ref.* 1,244
Ms K. Meeds, *Nat. Dem.* 592
T. Weller, *Green* 361
Lab. majority 10,337
(Boundary change: notional C.)

HALIFAX
E.71,701   T. 70.51%
*Mrs A. Mahon, *Lab.* 27,465
R. Light, *C.* 16,253
E. Waller, *LD* 6,059
Mrs C. Whitaker, *UK Ind.* 779
Lab. majority 11,212
(April 1992, Lab. maj. 478)

HALTEMPRICE AND HOWDEN
E.65,602   T. 75.53%
†Rt. Hon. D. Davis, *C.* 21,809
Ms D. Wallis, *LD* 14,295
G. McManus, *Lab.* 11,701
T. Pearson, *Ref.* 1,370
G. Bloom, *UK Ind.* 301
B. Stevens, *NLP* 74
C. majority 7,514
(Boundary change: notional C.)

HALTON
E.64,987   T. 68.38%
D. Twigg, *Lab.* 31,497
P. Balmer, *C.* 7,847
Ms J. Jones, *LD* 3,263
R. Atkins, *Ref.* 1,036
D. Proffitt, *Lib.* 600
J. Alley, *Rep. GB* 196
Lab. majority 23,650
(Boundary change: notional Lab.)

HAMMERSMITH AND FULHAM
E.78,637   T. 68.70%
I. Coleman, *Lab.* 25,262

†M. Carrington, *C.* 21,420
Ms A. Sugden, *LD* 4,728
Mrs M. Bremner, *Ref.* 1,023
W. Johnson-Smith, *New Lab.* 695
Ms E. Streeter, *Green* 562
G. Roberts, *UK Ind.* 183
A. Phillips, *NLP* 79
A. Elston, *Care* 74
Lab. majority 3,842
(Boundary change: notional C.)

HAMPSHIRE EAST
E.76,604   T. 75.88%
†M. Mates, *C.* 27,927
R. Booker, *LD* 16,337
R. Hoyle, *Lab.* 9,945
J. Hayter, *Ref.* 2,757
I. Foster, *Green* 649
S. Coles, *UK Ind.* 513
C. majority 11,590
(Boundary change: notional C.)

HAMPSHIRE NORTH EAST
E.69,111   T. 73.95%
†J. Arbuthnot, *C.* 26,017
I. Mann, *LD* 11,619
P. Dare, *Lab.* 8,203
D. Rees, *Ref.* 2,420
K. Jessavala, *Ind.* 2,400
C. Berry, *UK Ind.* 452
C. majority 14,398
(Boundary change: notional C.)

HAMPSHIRE NORTH WEST
E.73,222   T. 74.66%
†Rt. Hon. Sir G. 24,730
Young, Bt., *C.*
C. Fleming, *LD* 13,179
M. Mumford, *Lab.* 12,900
Mrs P. Callaghan, *Ref.* 1,533
T. Rolt, *UK Ind.* 1,383
W. Baxter, *Green* 486
H. Anscomb, *Bypass* 231
R. Dodd, *Ind.* 225
C. majority 11,551
(Boundary change: notional C.)

HAMPSTEAD AND HIGHGATE
E.64,889   T. 67.86%
†Ms G. Jackson, *Lab.* 25,275
Miss E. Gibson, *C.* 11,991
Mrs B. Fox, *LD* 5,481
Ms M. Siddique, *Ref.* 667
J. Leslie, *NLP* 147
R. Carroll, *Dream* 141
Miss P. Prince, *UK Ind.* 123
R. J. Harris, *Hum.* 105
Capt. Rizz, *Rizz Party* 101
Lab. majority 13,284
(Boundary change: notional Lab.)

HARBOROUGH
E.70,424   T. 75.27%
†E. Garnier, *C.* 22,170
M. Cox, *LD* 15,646
N. Holden, *Lab.* 13,332
N. Wright, *Ref.* 1,859
C. majority 6,524
(Boundary change: notional C.)

HARLOW
E.64,072   T. 74.62%
W. Rammell, *Lab.* 25,861

†J. Hayes, *C.* 15,347
Ms L. Spenceley, *LD* 4,523
M. Wells, *Ref.* 1,422
G. Batten, *UK Ind.* 340
J. Bowles, *BNP* 319
Lab. majority 10,514
(Boundary change: notional C.)

HARROGATE AND
KNARESBOROUGH
E.65,155   T. 73.14%
P. Willis, *LD* 24,558
†Rt. Hon. N. Lamont, *C.* 18,322
Ms B. Boyce, *Lab.* 4,159
J. Blackburn, *LC* 614
LD majority 6,236
(Boundary change: notional C.)

HARROW EAST
E.79,846   T. 71.37%
A. McNulty, *Lab.* 29,927
†H. Dykes, *C.* 20,189
B. Sharma, *LD* 4,697
B. Casey, *Ref.* 1,537
A. Scholefield, *UK Ind.* 464
A. Planton, *NLP* 171
Lab. majority 9,738
(Boundary change: notional C.)

HARROW WEST
E.72,005   T. 72.92%
G. Thomas, *Lab.* 21,811
*R. Hughes, *C.* 20,571
Mrs P. Nandhra, *LD* 8,127
H. Crossman, *Ref.* 1,997
Lab. majority 1,240
(Boundary change: notional C.)

HARTLEPOOL
E.67,712   T. 65.65%
*P. Mandelson, *Lab.* 26,997
M. Horsley, *C.* 9,489
R. Clark, *LD* 6,248
Miss M. Henderson, *Ref.* 1,718
Lab. majority 17,508
(April 1992, Lab. maj. 8,782)

HARWICH
E.75,775   T. 70.62%
I. Henderson, *Lab.* 20,740
†I. Sproat, *C.* 19,524
Mrs A. Elvin, *LD* 7,037
J. Titford, *Ref.* 4,923
R. Knight, *CRP* 1,290
Lab. majority 1,216
(Boundary change: notional C.)

HASTINGS AND RYE
E.70,388   T. 69.71%
M. Foster, *Lab.* 16,867
*Mrs J. Lait, *C.* 14,307
M. Palmer, *LD* 13,717
C. McGovern, *Ref.* 2,511
Ms J. Amstad, *Lib.* 1,046
W. Andrews, *UK Ind.* 472
D. Howell, *Loony* 149
Lab. majority 2,560
(April 1992, C. maj. 6,634)

HAVANT
E.68,420   T. 70.63%
†D. Willetts, *C.* 19,204
Ms L. Armstrong, *Lab.* 15,475

M. Kooner, *LD* — 10,806
A. Green, *Ref.* — 2,395
M. Atwal, *BIPF* — 442
C. majority 3,729
(Boundary change: notional C.)

HAYES AND HARLINGTON
*E.*56,829   *T.* 72.31%
J. McDonnell, *Lab.* — 25,458
A. Retter, *C.* — 11,167
A. Little, *LD* — 3,049
F. Page, *Ref.* — 778
J. Hutchins, *NF* — 504
D. Farrow, *ANP* — 135
Lab. majority 14,291
(Boundary change: notional C.)

HAZEL GROVE
*E.*63,694   *T.* 77.46%
A. Stunell, *LD* — 26,883
B. Murphy, *C.* — 15,069
J. Lewis, *Lab.* — 5,882
J. Stanyer, *Ref.* — 1,055
G. Black, *UK Ind.* — 268
D. Firkin-Flood, *Ind. Hum.* — 183
LD majority 11,814
(April 1992, C. maj. 929)

HEMEL HEMPSTEAD
*E.*71,468   *T.* 77.09%
A. McWalter, *Lab. Co-op.* — 25,175
†R. Jones, *C.* — 21,539
Mrs P. Lindsley, *LD* — 6,789
P. Such, *Ref.* — 1,327
Ms D. Harding, *NLP* — 262
Lab. Co-op. majority 3,636
(Boundary change: notional C.)

HEMSWORTH
*E.*66,964   *T.* 67.91%
†J. Trickett, *Lab.* — 32,088
N. Hazell, *C.* — 8,096
Ms J. Kirby, *LD* — 4,033
D. Irvine, *Ref.* — 1,260
Lab. majority 23,992
(Boundary change: notional Lab.)

HENDON
*E.*76,195   *T.* 65.67%
A. Dismore, *Lab.* — 24,683
†Sir J. Gorst, *C.* — 18,528
W. Casey, *LD* — 5,427
S. Rabbow, *Ref.* — 978
B. Wright, *UK Ind.* — 267
Ms S. Taylor, *WRP* — 153
Lab. majority 6,155
(Boundary change: notional C.)

HENLEY
*E.*66,424   *T.* 77.60%
†Rt. Hon. M. Heseltine, *C.* — 23,908
T. Horton, *LD* — 12,741
D. Enright, *Lab.* — 11,700
S. Sainsbury, *Ref.* — 2,299
Mrs S. Miles, *Green* — 514
N. Barlow, *NLP* — 221
T. Hibbert, *Whig Party* — 160
C. majority 11,167
(Boundary change: notional C.)

HEREFORD
*E.*69,864   *T.* 75.22%
P. Keetch, *LD* — 25,198

†Sir C. Shepherd, *C.* — 18,550
C. Chappell, *Lab.* — 6,596
C. Easton, *Ref.* — 2,209
LD majority 6,648
(Boundary change: notional C.)

HERTFORD AND STORTFORD
*E.*71,759   *T.* 76.03%
†B. Wells, *C.* — 24,027
S. Speller, *Lab.* — 17,142
M. Wood, *LD* — 9,679
H. Page Croft, *Ref.* — 2,105
B. Smalley, *UK Ind.* — 1,223
M. Franey, *ProLife* — 259
D. Molloy, *Logic* — 126
C. majority 6,885
(Boundary change: notional C.)

HERTFORDSHIRE NORTH EAST
*E.*67,161   *T.* 77.42%
†O. Heald, *C.* — 21,712
I. Gibbons, *Lab.* — 18,624
S. Jarvis, *LD* — 9,493
J. Grose, *Ref.* — 2,166
C. majority 3,088
(Boundary change: notional C.)

HERTFORDSHIRE SOUTH WEST
*E.*71,671   *T.* 77.31%
†R. Page, *C.* — 25,462
M. Wilson, *Lab.* — 15,441
Mrs A. Shaw, *LD* — 12,381
T. Millward, *Ref.* — 1,853
C. Adamson, *NLP* — 274
C. majority 10,021
(Boundary change: notional C.)

HERTSMERE
*E.*68,011   *T.* 74.03%
†J. Clappison, *C.* — 22,305
Ms E. Kelly, *Lab.* — 19,230
Mrs A. Gray, *LD* — 6,466
J. Marlow, *Ref.* — 1,703
R. Saunders, *UK Ind.* — 453
N. Kahn, *NLP* — 191
C. majority 3,075
(Boundary change: notional C.)

HEXHAM
*E.*58,914   *T.* 77.52%
*P. Atkinson, *C.* — 17,701
I. McMinn, *Lab.* — 17,479
Dr P. Carr, *LD* — 7,959
R. Waddell, *Ref.* — 1,362
D. Lott, *UK Ind.* — 1,170
C. majority 222
(April 1992, C. maj. 13,438)

HEYWOOD AND MIDDLETON
*E.*73,898   *T.* 68.41%
J. Dobbin, *Lab. Co-op.* — 29,179
S. Grigg, *C.* — 11,637
D. Clayton, *LD* — 7,908
Mrs C. West, *Ref.* — 1,076
P. Burke, *Lib.* — 750
Lab. Co-op. majority 17,542
(Boundary change: notional Lab. Co-op.)

HIGH PEAK
*E.*72,315   *T.* 79.03%
T. Levitt, *Lab.* — 29,052
†C. Hendry, *C.* — 20,261

Mrs S. Barber, *LD* — 6,420
C. Hanson-Orr, *Ref.* — 1,420
Lab. majority 8,791
(Boundary change: notional C.)

HITCHIN AND HARPENDEN
*E.*67,219   *T.* 77.99%
†Rt. Hon. P. Lilley, *C.* — 24,038
Ms R. Sanderson, *Lab.* — 17,367
C. White, *LD* — 10,515
D. Cooke, *NLP* — 290
J. Horton, *Soc.* — 217
C. majority 6,671
(Boundary change: notional C.)

HOLBORN AND ST PANCRAS
*E.*63,037   *T.* 60.28%
†F. Dobson, *Lab.* — 24,707
J. Smith, *C.* — 6,804
Ms J. McGuinness, *LD* — 4,750
Mrs J. Carr, *Ref.* — 790
T. Bedding, *NLP* — 191
S. Smith, *JP* — 173
Ms B. Conway, *WRP* — 171
M. Rosenthal, *Dream* — 157
P. Rice-Evans, *EUP* — 140
B. Quintavalle, *ProLife* — 114
Lab. majority 17,903
(Boundary change: notional Lab.)

HORNCHURCH
*E.*60,775   *T.* 72.30%
J. Cryer, *Lab.* — 22,066
*R. Squire, *C.* — 16,386
R. Martins, *LD* — 3,446
R. Khilkoff-Boulding, *Ref.* — 1,595
Miss J. Trueman, *Third Way* — 259
J. Sowerby, *ProLife* — 189
Lab. majority 5,680
(April 1992, C. maj. 9,165)

HORNSEY AND WOOD GREEN
*E.*74,537   *T.* 69.08%
*Mrs B. Roche, *Lab.* — 31,792
Mrs H. Hart, *C.* — 11,293
Ms L. Featherstone, *LD* — 5,794
Ms H. Jago, *Green* — 1,214
Ms R. Miller, *Ref.* — 808
P. Sikorski, *Soc. Lab.* — 586
Lab. majority 20,499
(April 1992, Lab. maj. 5,177)

HORSHAM
*E.*75,432   *T.* 75.78%
Rt. Hon. F. Maude, *C.* — 29,015
Mrs M. Millson, *LD* — 14,153
Ms M. Walsh, *Lab.* — 10,691
R. Grant, *Ref.* — 2,281
H. Miller, *UK Ind.* — 819
M. Corbould, *FEP* — 206
C. majority 14,862
(Boundary change: notional C.)

HOUGHTON AND WASHINGTON EAST
*E.*67,343   *T.* 62.10%
F. Kemp, *Lab.* — 31,946
P. Booth, *C.* — 5,391
K. Miller, *LD* — 3,209
J. Joseph, *Ref.* — 1,277
Lab. majority 26,555
(Boundary change: notional Lab.)

HOVE
*E.*69,016　*T.* 69.72%
I. Caplin, *Lab.*　21,458
R. Guy, *C.*　17,499
T. Pearce, *LD*　4,645
S. Field, *Ref.*　1,931
J. Furness, *Ind. C.*　1,735
P. Mulligan, *Green*　644
J. Vause, *UK Ind.*　209
Lab. majority 3,959
(April 1992, C. maj. 12,268)

HUDDERSFIELD
*E.*65,824　*T.* 67.69%
*B. Sheerman, *Lab. Co-op.*　25,171
W. Forrow, *C.*　9,323
G. Beever, *LD*　7,642
P. McNulty, *Ref.*　1,480
J. Phillips, *Green*　938
Lab. Co-op. majority 15,848
(April 1992, Lab. majority 7,258)

HULL EAST
*E.*68,733　*T.* 58.90%
*Rt. Hon. J. Prescott, *Lab.*　28,870
A. West, *C.*　5,552
J. Wastling, *LD*　3,965
G. Rogers, *Ref.*　1,788
Ms M. Nolan, *ProLife*　190
D. Whitley, *NLP*　121
Lab. majority 23,318
(April 1992, Lab. maj. 18,719)

HULL NORTH
*E.*68,106　*T.* 56.96%
*K. McNamara, *Lab.*　25,542
D. Lee, *C.*　5,837
D. Nolan, *LD*　5,667
A. Scott, *Ref.*　1,533
T. Brotheridge, *NLP*　215
Lab. majority 19,705
(April 1992, Lab. maj. 15,384)

HULL WEST AND HESSLE
*E.*65,840　*T.* 58.25%
A. Johnson, *Lab.*　22,520
R. Tress, *LD*　6,995
C. Moore, *C.*　6,933
R. Bate, *Ref.*　1,596
B. Franklin, *NLP*　310
Lab. majority 15,525
(Boundary change: notional Lab.)

HUNTINGDON
*E.*76,094　*T.* 74.86%
†Rt. Hon. J. Major, *C.*　31,501
J. Reece, *Lab.*　13,361
M. Owen, *LD*　8,390
D. Bellamy, *Ref.*　3,114
C. Coyne, *UK Ind.*　331
Ms V. Hufford, *Ch. D.*　177
D. Robertson, *Ind.*　89
C. majority 18,140
(Boundary change: notional C.)

HYNDBURN
*E.*66,806　*T.* 72.26%
†G. Pope, *Lab.*　26,831
P. Britcliffe, *C.*　15,383
L. Jones, *LD*　4,141
P. Congdon, *Ref.*　1,627
J. Brown, *IAC*　290

Lab. majority 11,448
(Boundary change: notional Lab.)

ILFORD NORTH
*E.*68,218　*T.* 71.60%
Ms L. Perham, *Lab.*　23,135
†V. Bendall, *C.*　19,911
A. Dean, *LD*　5,049
P. Wilson, *BNP*　750
Lab. majority 3,224
(Boundary change: notional C.)

ILFORD SOUTH
*E.*72,104　*T.* 69.37%
†M. Gapes, *Lab. Co-op.*　29,273
Sir N. Thorne, *C.*　15,073
Ms A. Khan, *LD*　3,152
D. Hodges, *Ref.*　1,073
B. Ramsey, *Soc. Lab.*　868
A. Owens, *BNP*　580
Lab. Co-op. majority 14,200
(Boundary change: notional C.)

IPSWICH
*E.*66,947　*T.* 72.24%
†J. Cann, *Lab.*　25,484
S. Castle, *C.*　15,045
N. Roberts, *LD*　5,881
T. Agnew, *Ref.*　1,637
W. Vinyard, *UK Ind.*　208
E. Kaplan, *NLP*　107
Lab. majority 10,439
(Boundary change: notional Lab.)

ISLE OF WIGHT
*E.*101,680　*T.* 71.95%
Dr P. Brand, *LD*　31,274
A. Turner, *C.*　24,868
Ms D. Gardiner, *Lab.*　9,646
T. Bristow, *Ref.*　4,734
M. Turner, *UK Ind.*　1,072
H. Rees, *Ind. Is.*　848
P. Scivier, *Green*　544
C. Daly, *NLP*　87
J. Eveleigh, *Rain. Is.*　86
LD majority 6,406
(April 1992, C. maj. 1,827)

ISLINGTON NORTH
*E.*57,385　*T.* 62.49%
*J. Corbyn, *Lab.*　24,834
J. Kempton, *LD*　4,879
S. Fawthrop, *C.*　4,631
C. Ashby, *Green*　1,516
Lab. majority 19,955
(April 1992, Lab. maj. 12,784)

ISLINGTON SOUTH AND FINSBURY
*E.*55,468　*T.* 63.67%
†C. Smith, *Lab.*　22,079
Ms S. Ludford, *LD*　7,516
D. Berens, *C.*　4,587
Miss J. Bryett, *Ref.*　741
A. Laws, *ACA*　171
M. Creese, *NLP*　121
E. Basarik, *Ind.*　101
Lab. majority 14,563
(Boundary change: notional Lab.)

JARROW
*E.*63,828　*T.* 68.84%
S. Hepburn, *Lab.*　28,497

M. Allatt, *C.*　6,564
T. Stone, *LD*　4,865
A. LeBlond, *Ind. Lab.*　2,538
P. Mailer, *Ref.*　1,034
J. Bissett, *SPGB*　444
Lab. majority 21,933
(Boundary change: notional Lab.)

KEIGHLEY
*E.*67,231　*T.* 76.57%
Mrs A. Cryer, *Lab.*　26,039
*G. Waller, *C.*　18,907
M. Doyle, *LD*　5,064
C. Carpenter, *Ref.*　1,470
Lab. majority 7,132
(April 1992, C. maj. 3,596)

KENSINGTON AND CHELSEA
*E.*67,786　*T.* 54.71%
Rt. Hon. A. Clark, *C.*　19,887
R. Atkinson, *Lab.*　10,368
R. Woodthorpe Browne, *LD*　5,668
Ms A. Ellis-Jones, *UK Ind.*　540
E. Bear, *Teddy*　218
G. Oliver, *UKPP*　176
Ms S. Hamza, *NLP*　122
P. Sullivan, *Dream*　65
P. Parliament, *Heart*　44
C. majority 9,519
(Boundary change: notional C.)
See also page 233

KETTERING
*E.*75,153　*T.* 75.79%
P. Sawford, *Lab.*　24,650
†Rt. Hon. R. Freeman, *C.*　24,461
R. Aron, *LD*　6,098
A. Smith, *Ref.*　1,551
Mrs R. le Carpentier, *NLP*　197
Lab. majority 189
(Boundary change: notional C.)

KINGSTON AND SURBITON
*E.*73,879　*T.* 75.35%
E. Davey, *LD*　20,411
†R. Tracey, *C.*　20,355
Ms S. Griffin, *Lab.*　12,811
Mrs G. Tchiprout, *Ref.*　1,470
Ms P. Burns, *UK Ind.*　418
C. Port, *Dream*　100
M. Leighton, *NLP*　100
LD majority 56
(Boundary change: notional C.)

KINGSWOOD
*E.*77,026　*T.* 77.75%
†Dr R. Berry, *Lab.*　32,181
J. Howard, *C.*　17,928
Mrs J. Pinkerton, *LD*　7,672
Ms A. Reather, *Ref.*　1,463
P. Hart, *BNP*　290
A. Harding, *NLP*　238
A. Nicolson, *Scrapit*　115
Lab. majority 14,253
(Boundary change: notional C.)

KNOWSLEY NORTH AND SEFTON EAST
*E.*70,918　*T.* 70.09%
†G. Howarth, *Lab.*　34,747
C. Doran, *C.*　8,600
D. Bamber, *LD*　5,499
C. Jones, *Soc. Lab.*　857

Lab. majority 26,147
(Boundary change: notional Lab.)

KNOWSLEY SOUTH
E.70,532   T. 67.47%
†E. O'Hara, Lab.   36,695
G. Robertson, C.   5,987
C. Mainey, LD   3,954
A. Wright, Ref.   954
Lab. majority 30,708
(Boundary change: notional Lab.)

LANCASHIRE WEST
E.73,175   T. 74.79%
†C. Pickthall, Lab.   33,022
C. Varley, C.   15,903
A. Wood, LD   3,938
M. Carter, Ref.   1,025
J. Collins, NLP   449
D. Hill, Home Rule   392
Lab. majority 17,119
(Boundary change: notional Lab.)

LANCASTER AND WYRE
E.78,168   T. 75.30%
H. Dawson, Lab.   25,173
†K. Mans, C.   23,878
J. Humberstone, LD   6,802
Mrs V. Ivell, Ref.   1,516
J. Barry, Green   795
Dr J. Whittaker, UK Ind.   698
Lab. majority 1,295
(Boundary change: notional C.)

LEEDS CENTRAL
E.67,664   T. 54.70%
†D. Fatchett, Lab.   25,766
E. Wild, C.   5,077
D. Freeman, LD   4,164
P. Myers, Ref.   1,042
D. Rix, Soc. Lab.   656
C. Hill, Soc.   304
Lab. majority 20,689
(Boundary change: notional Lab.)
See also page 233

LEEDS EAST
E.56,963   T. 62.83%
*G. Mudie, Lab.   24,151
J. Emsley, C.   6,685
Mrs M. Kirk, LD   3,689
L. Parish, Ref.   1,267
Lab. majority 17,466
(April 1992, Lab. maj. 12,697)

LEEDS NORTH EAST
E.63,185   T. 72.03%
F. Hamilton, Lab.   22,368
*T. Kirkhope, C.   15,409
Dr W. Winlow, LD   6,318
I. Rose, Ref.   946
Ms J. Egan, Soc. Lab.   468
Lab. majority 6,959
(April 1992, C. maj. 4,244)

LEEDS NORTH WEST
E.69,972   T. 70.57%
H. Best, Lab.   19,694
*Dr K. Hampson, C.   15,850
Mrs B. Pearce, LD   11,689
S. Emmett, Ref.   1,325
R. Lamb, Soc. Lab.   335
R. Toone, ProLife   251

D. Duffy, Ronnie   232
Lab. majority 3,844
(April 1992, C. maj. 7,671)

LEEDS WEST
E.63,965   T. 62.88%
*J. Battle, Lab.   26,819
J. Whelan, C.   7,048
N. Amor, LD   3,622
W. Finley, Ref.   1,210
D. Blackburn, Green   896
N. Nowosielski, Lib.   625
Lab. majority 19,771
(April 1992, Lab. maj. 13,828)

LEICESTER EAST
E.64,012   T. 69.37%
*K. Vaz, Lab.   29,083
S. Milton, C.   10,661
J. Matabudul, LD   3,105
P. Iwaniw, Ref.   1,015
S. Sidhu, Soc. Lab.   436
N. Slack, Glow   102
Lab. majority 18,422
(April 1992, Lab. maj. 11,316)

LEICESTER SOUTH
E.71,750   T. 67.06%
*J. Marshall, Lab.   27,914
C. Heaton-Harris, C.   11,421
B. Coles, LD   6,654
J. Hancock, Ref.   1,184
J. Dooher, Soc. Lab.   634
K. Sills, Nat. Dem.   307
Lab. majority 16,493
(April 1992, Lab. maj. 9,440)

LEICESTER WEST
E.64,570   T. 63.36%
Ms P. Hewitt, Lab.   22,580
R. Thomas, C.   9,716
M. Jones, LD   5,795
W. Shooter, Ref.   970
G. Forse, Green   586
D. Roberts, Soc. Lab.   452
Ms J. Nicholls, Soc.   327
A. Belshaw, BNP   302
C. Potter, Nat. Dem.   186
Lab. majority 12,864
(April 1992, Lab. maj. 3,978)

LEICESTERSHIRE NORTH WEST
E.65,069   T. 79.95%
D. Taylor, Lab.   29,332
R. Goodwill, C.   16,113
S. Heptinstall, LD   4,492
M. Abney-Hastings, Ref.   2,088
Lab. majority 13,219
(Boundary change: notional C.)

LEIGH
E.69,908   T. 65.69%
†L. Cunliffe, Lab.   31,652
E. Young, C.   7,156
P. Hough, LD   5,163
R. Constable, Ref.   1,949
Lab. majority 24,496
(Boundary change: notional Lab.)

LEOMINSTER
E.65,993   T. 76.60%
†P. Temple-Morris, C.   22,888
T. James, LD   14,053

R. Westwood, Lab.   8,831
A. Parkin, Ref.   2,815
Ms F. Norman, Green   1,086
R. Chamings, UK Ind.   588
J. Haycock, BNP   292
C. majority 8,835
(Boundary change: notional C.)

LEWES
E.64,340   T. 76.42%
N. Baker, LD   21,250
†T. Rathbone, C.   19,950
Dr M. Patton, Lab.   5,232
Mrs L. Butler, Ref.   2,481
J. Harvey, UK Ind.   256
LD majority 1,300
(Boundary change: notional C.)

LEWISHAM DEPTFORD
E.58,141   T. 57.87%
†Mrs J. Ruddock, Lab.   23,827
Mrs I. Kimm, C.   4,949
K. Appiah, LD   3,004
J. Mulrenan, Soc. Lab.   996
Ms S. Shepherd, Ref.   868
Lab. majority 18,878
(Boundary change: notional Lab.)

LEWISHAM EAST
E.56,333   T. 66.41%
†Ms B. Prentice, Lab.   21,821
P. Hollobone, C.   9,694
D. Buxton, LD   4,178
S. Drury, Ref.   910
R. Croucher, NF   431
P. White, Lib.   277
Capt. Rizz, Dream   97
Lab. majority 12,127
(Boundary change: notional Lab.)

LEWISHAM WEST
E.58,659   T. 64.00%
*J. Dowd, Lab.   23,273
Mrs C. Whelan, C.   8,936
Miss K. McGrath, LD   3,672
A. Leese, Ref.   1,098
N. Long, Soc. Lab.   398
Ms E. Oram, Lib.   167
Lab. majority 14,337
(April 1992, Lab. maj. 1,809)

LEYTON AND WANSTEAD
E.62,176   T. 63.24%
†H. Cohen, Lab.   23,922
R. Vaudry, C.   8,736
C. Anglin, LD   5,920
S. Duffy, ProLife   488
A. Mian, Ind.   256
Lab. majority 15,186
(Boundary change: notional Lab.)

LICHFIELD
E.62,720   T. 77.48%
†M. Fabricant, C.   20,853
Ms S. Woodward, Lab.   20,615
Dr P. Bennion, LD   5,473
G. Seward, Ref.   1,652
C. majority 238
(Boundary change: notional C.)

LINCOLN
E.65,485   T. 71.08%
Ms G. Merron, Lab.   25,563

A. Brown, *C.*   14,433
Ms L. Gabriel, *LD*   5,048
J. Ivory, *Ref.*   1,329
A. Myers, *NLP*   175
Lab. majority 11,130
(Boundary change: notional Lab.)

LIVERPOOL GARSTON
*E.*66,755   *T.* 65.14%
Ms M. Eagle, *Lab.*   26,667
Ms F. Clucas, *LD*   8,250
N. Gordon-Johnson, *C.*   6,819
F. Dunne, *Ref.*   833
G. Copeland, *Lib.*   666
J. Parsons, *NLP*   127
S. Nolan, *SEP*   120
Lab. majority 18,417
(Boundary change: notional Lab.)

LIVERPOOL RIVERSIDE
*E.*73,429   *T.* 51.93%
Ms L. Ellman, *Lab. Co-op.*   26,858
Ms B. Fraenkel, *LD*   5,059
D. Sparrow, *C.*   3,635
Ms C. Wilson, *Soc.*   776
D. Green, *Lib.*   594
G. Skelly, *Ref.*   586
Ms H. Neilson, *ProLife*   277
D. Braid, *MRAC*   179
G. Gay, *NLP*   171
Lab. Co-op. majority 21,799
(Boundary change: notional Lab.
Co-op.)

LIVERPOOL WALTON
*E.*67,527   *T.* 59.54%
*P. Kilfoyle, *Lab.*   31,516
R. Roberts, *LD*   4,478
M. Kotecha, *C.*   2,551
C. Grundy, *Ref.*   620
Ms L. Mahmood, *Soc.*   444
Ms H. Williams, *Lib.*   352
Ms V. Mearns, *ProLife*   246
Lab. majority 27,038
(April 1992, Lab. maj. 28,299)

LIVERPOOL WAVERTREE
*E.*73,063   *T.* 62.85%
†Ms J. Kennedy, *Lab.*   29,592
R. Kemp, *LD*   9,891
C. Malthouse, *C.*   4,944
P. Worthington, *Ref.*   576
K. McCullough, *Lib.*   391
Ms R. Kingsley, *ProLife*   346
Ms C. Corkhill, *WRP*   178
Lab. majority 19,701
(Boundary change: notional Lab.)

LIVERPOOL WEST DERBY
*E.*68,682   *T.* 61.38%
†R. Wareing, *Lab.*   30,002
S. Radford, *Lib.*   4,037
Ms A. Hines, *LD*   3,805
N. Morgan, *C.*   3,656
P. Forrest, *Ref.*   657
Lab. majority 25,965
(Boundary change: notional Lab.)

LOUGHBOROUGH
*E.*68,945   *T.* 75.95%
A. Reed, *Lab.*   25,448
K. Andrew, *C.*   19,736
Ms D. Brass, *LD*   6,190

R. Gupta, *Ref.*   991
Lab. majority 5,712
(Boundary change: notional C.)

LOUTH AND HORNCASTLE
*E.*68,824   *T.* 72.58%
†Sir P. Tapsell, *C.*   21,699
J. Hough, *Lab.*   14,799
Mrs F. Martin, *LD*   12,207
Ms R. Robinson, *Green*   1,248
C. majority 6,900
(Boundary change: notional C.)

LUDLOW
*E.*61,267   *T.* 75.55%
†C. Gill, *C.*   19,633
I. Huffer, *LD*   13,724
Ms N. O'Kane, *Lab.*   11,745
T. Andrewes, *Green*   798
E. Freeman-Keel, *UK Ind.*   385
C. majority 5,909
(Boundary change: notional C.)

LUTON NORTH
*E.*64,618   *T.* 73.25%
K. Hopkins, *Lab.*   25,860
D. Senior, *C.*   16,234
Mrs K. Newbound, *LD*   4,299
C. Brown, *UK Ind.*   689
A. Custance, *NLP*   250
Lab. majority 9,626
(Boundary change: notional C.)

LUTON SOUTH
*E.*68,395   *T.* 70.45%
Ms M. Moran, *Lab.*   26,428
†Sir G. Bright, *C.*   15,109
K. Fitchett, *LD*   4,610
C. Jacobs, *Ref.*   1,205
C. Lawman, *UK Ind.*   390
M. Scheimann, *Green*   356
Ms C. Perrin, *NLP*   86
Lab. majority 11,319
(Boundary change: notional C.)

MACCLESFIELD
*E.*72,049   *T.* 75.22%
†N. Winterton, *C.*   26,888
Ms J. Jackson, *Lab.*   18,234
M. Flynn, *LD*   9,075
C. majority 8,654
(Boundary change: notional C.)

MAIDENHEAD
*E.*67,302   *T.* 75.61%
Mrs T. May, *C.*   25,344
A. Ketteringham, *LD*   13,363
Ms D. Robson, *Lab.*   9,205
C. Taverner, *Ref.*   1,638
D. Munkley, *Lib.*   896
N. Spiers, *UK Ind.*   277
K. Ardley, *Glow*   166
C. majority 11,981
(Boundary change: notional C.)

MAIDSTONE AND THE WEALD
*E.*72,466   *T.* 73.98%
†Rt. Hon. Miss A.
   Widdecombe, *C.*   23,657
J. Morgan, *Lab.*   14,054
Mrs J. Nelson, *LD*   11,986
Ms S. Hopkins, *Ref.*   1,998
Ms M. Cleator, *Soc. Lab.*   979

Ms P. Kemp, *Green*   480
Mrs R. Owen, *UK Ind.*   339
J. Oldbury, *NLP*   115
C. majority 9,603
(Boundary change: notional C.)

MAKERFIELD
*E.*67,358   *T.* 66.83%
†I. McCartney, *Lab.*   33,119
M. Winstanley, *C.*   6,942
B. Hubbard, *LD*   3,743
A. Seed, *Ref.*   1,210
Lab. majority 26,177
(Boundary change: notional Lab.)

MALDON AND CHELMSFORD
EAST
*E.*66,184   *T.* 76.13%
†J. Whittingdale, *C.*   24,524
K. Freeman, *Lab.*   14,485
G. Pooley, *LD*   9,758
L. Overy-Owen, *UK Ind.*   935
Ms E. Burgess, *Green*   685
C. majority 10,039
(Boundary change: notional C.)

MANCHESTER BLACKLEY
*E.*62,227   *T.* 57.46%
G. Stringer, *Lab.*   25,042
S. Barclay, *C.*   5,454
S. Wheale, *LD*   3,937
P. Stanyer, *Ref.*   1,323
Lab. majority 19,588
(Boundary change: notional Lab.)

MANCHESTER CENTRAL
*E.*63,815   *T.* 52.55%
†A. Lloyd, *Lab.*   23,803
Ms A. Firth, *LD*   4,121
S. McIlwaine, *C.*   3,964
F. Rafferty, *Soc. Lab.*   810
J. Maxwell, *Ref.*   742
T. Rigby, *Comm L.*   97
Lab. majority 19,682
(Boundary change: notional Lab.)

MANCHESTER GORTON
*E.*64,349   *T.* 56.43%
†Rt. Hon. G. Kaufman, *Lab.*   23,704
Dr J. Pearcey, *LD*   6,362
G. Senior, *C.*   4,249
K. Hartley, *Ref.*   812
Dr S. Fitz-Gibbon, *Green*   683
T. Wongsam, *Soc. Lab.*   501
Lab. majority 17,342
(Boundary change: notional Lab.)

MANCHESTER WITHINGTON
*E.*66,116   *T.* 66.59%
†K. Bradley, *Lab.*   27,103
J. Smith, *C.*   8,522
Dr Y. Zalzala, *LD*   6,000
M. Sheppard, *Ref.*   1,079
S. Caldwell, *ProLife*   614
Ms J. White, *Soc.*   376
S. Kingston, *Dream*   181
M. Gaskell, *NLP*   152
Lab. majority 18,581
(Boundary change: notional Lab.)

MANSFIELD
*E.*67,057   *T.* 70.72%
*A. Meale, *Lab.*   30,556

T. Frost, *C.*	10,038		
P. Smith, *LD*	5,244		
W. Bogusz, *Ref.*	1,588		
Lab. majority 20,518			
(April 1992, Lab. maj. 11,724)			

MEDWAY
*E.*61,736   *T.* 72.47%

R. Marshall-Andrews, *Lab.*	21,858
*Dame P. Fenner, *C.*	16,504
R. Roberts, *LD*	4,555
J. Main, *Ref.*	1,420
Mrs S. Radlett, *UK Ind.*	405
Lab. majority 5,354	
(April 1992, C. maj. 8,786)	

MERIDEN
*E.*76,287   *T.* 71.73%

Mrs C. Spelman, *C.*	22,997
B. Seymour-Smith, *Lab.*	22,415
A. Dupont, *LD*	7,098
P. Gilbert, *Ref.*	2,208
C. majority 582	
(April 1992, C. maj. 14,699)	

MIDDLESBROUGH
*E.*70,931   *T.* 64.99%

†S. Bell, *Lab.*	32,925
L. Benham, *C.*	7,907
Miss A. Charlesworth, *LD*	3,934
R. Edwards, *Ref.*	1,331
Lab. majority 25,018	
(Boundary change: notional Lab.)	

MIDDLESBROUGH SOUTH AND
CLEVELAND EAST
*E.*70,481   *T.* 76.03%

Dr A. Kumar, *Lab.*	29,319
†M. Bates, *C.*	18,712
H. Garrett, *LD*	4,004
R. Batchelor, *Ref.*	1,552
Lab. majority 10,607	
(Boundary change: notional C.)	

MILTON KEYNES NORTH EAST
*E.*70,395   *T.* 72.78%

B. White, *Lab.*	20,201
†P. Butler, *C.*	19,961
G. Mabbutt, *LD*	8,907
M. Phillips, *Ref.*	1,492
A. Francis, *Green*	576
M. Simson, *NLP*	99
Lab. majority 240	
(Boundary change: notional C.)	

MILTON KEYNES SOUTH WEST
*E.*71,070   *T.* 71.42%

Mrs P. Starkey, *Lab.*	27,298
*B. Legg, *C.*	17,006
P. Jones, *LD*	6,065
H. Kelly, *NLP*	389
Lab. majority 10,292	
(April 1992, C. maj. 4,687)	

MITCHAM AND MORDEN
*E.*65,385   *T.* 73.33%

Ms S. McDonagh, *Lab.*	27,984
*Rt. Hon. Dame A. Rumbold, *C.*	14,243
N. Harris, *LD*	3,632
P. Isaacs, *Ref.*	810
Ms L. Miller, *BNP*	521
T. Walsh, *Green*	415
K. Vasan, *Ind.*	144

J. Barrett, *UK Ind.*	117
N. Dixon, *ACC*	80
Lab. majority 13,741	
(April 1992, C. maj. 1,734)	

MOLE VALLEY
*E.*69,140   *T.* 78.86%

†Sir P. Beresford, *C.*	26,178
S. Cooksey, *LD*	15,957
C. Payne, *Lab.*	8,057
N. Taber, *Ref.*	2,424
R. Burley, *Ind. CRP*	1,276
Capt. I. Cameron, *UK Ind.*	435
Ms J. Thomas, *NLP*	197
C. majority 10,221	
(Boundary change: notional C.)	

MORECAMBE AND LUNESDALE
*E.*68,013   *T.* 72.41%

Ms G. Smith, *Lab.*	24,061
†Sir M. Lennox-Boyd, *C.*	18,096
Mrs J. Greenwell, *LD*	5,614
I. Ogilvie, *Ref.*	1,313
D. Walne, *NLP*	165
Lab. majority 5,965	
(Boundary change: notional C.)	

MORLEY AND ROTHWELL
*E.*68,385   *T.* 67.12%

†J. Gunnell, *Lab.*	26,836
A. Barraclough, *C.*	12,086
M. Galdas, *LD*	5,087
D. Mitchell-Innes, *Ref.*	1,359
R. Wood, *BNP*	381
Ms P. Sammon, *ProLife*	148
Lab. majority 14,750	
(Boundary change: notional Lab.)	

NEW FOREST EAST
*E.*65,717   *T.* 74.64%

Dr J. Lewis, *C.*	21,053
G. Dawson, *LD*	15,838
A. Goodfellow, *Lab.*	12,161
C. majority 5,215	
(Boundary change: notional C.)	

NEW FOREST WEST
*E.*66,522   *T.* 74.79%

D. Swayne, *C.*	25,149
R. Hale, *LD*	13,817
D. Griffiths, *Lab.*	7,092
Mrs M. Elliott, *Ref.*	2,150
M. Holmes, *UK Ind.*	1,542
C. majority 11,332	
(Boundary change: notional C.)	

NEWARK
*E.*69,763   *T.* 74.50%

Ms F. Jones, *Lab.*	23,496
*R. Alexander, *C.*	20,480
P. Harris, *LD*	5,960
G. Creedy, *Ref.*	2,035
Lab. majority 3,016	
(April 1992, C. maj. 8,229)	

NEWBURY
*E.*73,680   *T.* 76.65%

†D. Rendel, *LD*	29,887
R. Benyon, *C.*	21,370
P. Hannon, *Lab.*	3,107
E. Snook, *Ref.*	992
Ms R. Stark, *Green*	644
R. Tubb, *UK Ind.*	302

Ms K. Howse, *Soc. Lab.*	174
LD majority 8,517	
(Boundary change: notional C.)	

NEWCASTLE-UNDER-LYME
*E.*66,686   *T.* 73.67%

*Mrs L. Golding, *Lab.*	27,743
M. Hayes, *C.*	10,537
Dr R. Studd, *LD*	6,858
Ms K. Suttle, *Ref.*	1,510
S. Mountford, *Lib.*	1,399
Ms B. Bell, *Soc. Lab.*	1,082
Lab. majority 17,206	
(April 1992, Lab. maj. 9,839)	

NEWCASTLE UPON TYNE
CENTRAL
*E.*69,781   *T.* 66.05%

†J. Cousins, *Lab.*	27,272
B. Newmark, *C.*	10,792
Ms R. Berry, *LD*	6,911
C. Coxon, *Ref.*	1,113
Lab. majority 16,480	
(Boundary change: notional Lab.)	

NEWCASTLE UPON TYNE EAST
AND WALLSEND
*E.*63,272   *T.* 65.73%

†N. Brown, *Lab.*	29,607
J. Middleton, *C.*	5,796
G. Morgan, *LD*	4,415
P. Cossins, *Ref.*	966
Ms B. Carpenter, *Soc. Lab.*	642
M. Levy, *Comm. P.*	163
Lab. majority 23,811	
(Boundary change: notional Lab.)	

NEWCASTLE UPON TYNE
NORTH
*E.*65,357   *T.* 69.20%

*D. Henderson, *Lab.*	28,125
G. White, *C.*	8,793
P. Allen, *LD*	6,578
Mrs D. Chipchase, *Ref.*	1,733
Lab. majority 19,332	
(April 1992, Lab. maj. 8,946)	

NORFOLK MID
*E.*75,311   *T.* 76.29%

K. Simpson, *C.*	22,739
D. Zeichner, *Lab.*	21,403
Mrs S. Frary, *LD*	8,617
N. Holder, *Ref.*	3,229
A. Park, *Green*	1,254
B. Parker, *NLP*	215
C. majority 1,336	
(Boundary change: notional C.)	

NORFOLK NORTH
*E.*77,113   *T.* 76.27%

D. Prior, *C.*	21,456
N. Lamb, *LD*	20,163
M. Cullingham, *Lab.*	14,736
J. Allen, *Ref.*	2,458
C. majority 1,293	
(April 1992, C. maj. 12,545)	

NORFOLK NORTH WEST
*E.*77,083   *T.* 74.72%

Dr G. Turner, *Lab.*	25,250
*H. Bellingham, *C.*	23,911
Ms E. Knowles, *LD*	5,513
R. Percival, *Ref.*	2,923

Lab. majority 1,339
(April 1992, C. maj. 11,564)

NORFOLK SOUTH
E.79,239   T. 78.37%
†Rt. Hon. J. MacGregor, *C.*   24935
Mrs B. Hacker, *LD*   17,557
Ms J. Ross, *Lab.*   16,188
Mrs P. Bateson, *Ref.*   2,533
Mrs S. Ross-Wagenknecht,
  Green   484
A. Boddy, *UK Ind.*   400
C. majority 7,378
(Boundary change: notional C.)

NORFOLK SOUTH WEST
E.80,236   T. 73.28%
†Rt. Hon. Mrs G. Shephard, *C.* 24694
A. Heffernan, *Lab.*   22,230
D. Buckton, *LD*   8,178
R. Hoare, *Ref.*   3,694
C. majority 2,464
(Boundary change: notional C.)

NORMANTON
E.62,980   T. 68.28%
†W. O'Brien, *Lab.*   26,046
Miss F. Bulmer, *C.*   10,153
D. Ridgway, *LD*   5,347
K. Shuttleworth, *Ref.*   1,458
Lab. majority 15,893
(Boundary change: notional Lab.)

NORTHAMPTON NORTH
E.73,664   T. 70.18%
Ms S. Keeble, *Lab.*   27,247
†A. Marlow, *C.*   17,247
Ms L. Dunbar, *LD*   6,579
D. Torbica, *UK Ind.*   464
B. Spivack, *NLP*   161
Lab. majority 10,000
(Boundary change: notional C.)

NORTHAMPTON SOUTH
E.79,384   T. 71.94%
A. Clarke, *Lab.*   24,214
†Rt. Hon. M. Morris, *C.*   23,470
A. Worgan, *LD*   6,316
C. Petrie, *Ref.*   1,405
D. Clark, *UK Ind.*   1,159
G. Woollcombe, *NLP*   541
Lab. majority 744
(Boundary change: notional C.)

NORTHAVON
E.78,943   T. 79.21%
Prof. S. Webb, *LD*   26,500
†Rt. Hon. Sir J. Cope, *C.*   24,363
R. Stone, *Lab.*   9,767
J. Parfitt, *Ref.*   1,900
LD majority 2,137
(Boundary change: notional C.)

NORWICH NORTH
E.72,521   T. 75.92%
Dr I. Gibson, *Lab.*   27,346
Dr R. Kinghorn, *C.*   17,876
P. Young, *LD*   6,951
A. Bailey-Smith, *Ref.*   1,777
H. Marks, *LCP*   512
J. Hood, *Soc. Lab.*   495
Mrs D. Mills, *NLP*   100
Lab. majority 9,470
(Boundary change: notional C.)

NORWICH SOUTH
E.70,009   T. 72.56%
C. Clarke, *Lab.*   26,267
B. Khanbhai, *C.*   12,028
A. Aalders-Dunthorne, *LD*   9,457
Dr D. Holdsworth, *Ref.*   1,464
H. Marks, *LCP*   765
A. Holmes, *Green*   736
B. Parsons, *NLP*   84
Lab. majority 14,239
(Boundary change: notional Lab.)

NOTTINGHAM EAST
E.65,581   T. 60.60%
*J. Heppell, *Lab.*   24,755
A. Raca, *C.*   9,336
K. Mulloy, *LD*   4,008
B. Brown, *Ref.*   1,645
Lab. majority 15,419
(April 1992, Lab. maj. 7,680)

NOTTINGHAM NORTH
E.65,698   T. 63.02%
*G. Allen, *Lab.*   27,203
Ms G. Shaw, *C.*   8,402
Ms R. Oliver, *LD*   3,301
J. Neal, *Ref.*   1,858
A. Belfield, *Soc.*   637
Lab. majority 18,801
(April 1992, Lab. maj. 10,743)

NOTTINGHAM SOUTH
E.72,418   T. 67.00%
*A. Simpson, *Lab.*   26,825
B. Kirsch, *C.*   13,461
G. Long, *LD*   6,265
K. Thompson, *Ref.*   1,523
Ms S. Edwards, *Nat. Dem.*   446
Lab. majority 13,364
(April 1992, Lab. maj. 3,181)

NUNEATON
E.72,032   T. 74.29%
*W. Olner, *Lab.*   30,080
R. Blunt, *C.*   16,540
R. Cockings, *LD*   4,732
R. English, *Ref.*   1,533
D. Bray, *Loc. Ind.*   390
P. Everitt, *UK Ind.*   238
Lab. majority 13,540
(April 1992, Lab. maj. 1,631)

OLD BEXLEY AND SIDCUP
E.68,044   T. 75.53%
†Rt. Hon. Sir E. Heath, *C.*   21,608
R. Justham, *Lab.*   18,039
I. King, *LD*   8,284
B. Reading, *Ref.*   2,457
C. Bullen, *UK Ind.*   489
Ms V. Tyndall, *BNP*   415
R. Stephens, *NLP*   99
C. majority 3,569
(Boundary change: notional C.)

OLDHAM EAST AND
SADDLEWORTH
E.73,189   T. 73.92%
P. Woolas, *Lab.*   22,546
†C. Davies, *LD*   19,157
J. Hudson, *C.*   10,666
D. Findlay, *Ref.*   1,116
J. Smith, *Soc. Lab.*   470
I. Dalling, *NLP*   146

Lab. majority 3,389
(Boundary change: notional C.)

OLDHAM WEST AND ROYTON
E.69,203   T. 66.09%
†M. Meacher, *Lab.*   26,894
J. Lord, *C.*   10,693
H. Cohen, *LD*   5,434
G. Choudhury, *Soc. Lab.*   1,311
P. Etherden, *Ref.*   1,157
Mrs S. Dalling, *NLP*   249
Lab. majority 16,201
(Boundary change: notional Lab.)

ORPINGTON
E.78,749   T. 76.40%
†J. Horam, *C.*   24,417
C. Maines, *LD*   21,465
Ms S. Polydorou, *Lab.*   10,753
D. Clark, *Ref.*   2,316
J. Carver, *UK Ind.*   526
R. Almond, *Lib.*   494
N. Wilton, *ProLife*   191
C. majority 2,952
(Boundary change: notional C.)

OXFORD EAST
E.69,339   T. 69.05%
†A. Smith, *Lab.*   27,205
J. Djanogly, *C.*   10,540
G. Kershaw, *LD*   7,038
M. Young, *Ref.*   1,391
C. Simmons, *Green*   975
W. Harper-Jones, *Embryo*   318
Dr P. Gardner, *UK Ind.*   234
J. Thompson, *NLP*   108
P. Mylvaganam, *Anti-maj.*   68
Lab. majority 16,665
(Boundary change: notional Lab.)

OXFORD WEST AND ABINGDON
E.79,329   T. 77.14%
Dr E. Harris, *LD*   26,268
L. Harris, *C.*   19,983
Ms S. Brown, *Lab.*   12,361
Mrs G. Eustace, *Ref.*   1,258
Dr M. Woodin, *Green*   691
R. Buckton, *UK Ind.*   258
Mrs L. Hodge, *ProLife*   238
Ms A.-M. Wilson, *NLP*   91
J. Rose, *LGR*   48
LD majority 6,285
(Boundary change: notional C.)

PENDLE
E.63,049   T. 74.60%
*G. Prentice, *Lab.*   25,059
J. Midgeley, *C.*   14,235
A. Greaves, *LD*   5,460
D. Hockney, *Ref.*   2,281
Lab. majority 10,824
(April 1992, Lab. maj. 2,113)

PENRITH AND THE BORDER
E.66,496   T. 73.63%
†Rt. Hon. D. Maclean, *C.*   23,300
G. Walker, *LD*   13,067
Mrs M. Meling, *Lab.*   10,576
C. Pope, *Ref.*   2,018
C. majority 10,233
(Boundary change: notional C.)

PETERBOROUGH
E.65,926   T. 73.46%
Ms H. Brinton, *Lab.*   24,365
Mrs J. Foster, *C.*   17,042
D. Howarth, *LD*   5,170
P. Slater, *Ref.*   924
C. Brettell, *NLP*   334
J. Linskey, *UK Ind.*   317
S. Goldspink, *ProLife*   275
Lab. majority 7,323
(Boundary change: notional C.)

PLYMOUTH DEVONPORT
E.74,483   T. 69.76%
†D. Jamieson, *Lab.*   31,629
A. Johnson, *C.*   12,562
R. Copus, *LD*   5,570
C. Norsworthy, *Ref.*   1,486
Mrs C. Farrand, *UK Ind.*   478
S. Ebbs, *Nat. Dem.*   238
Lab. majority 19,067
(Boundary change: notional Lab.)

PLYMOUTH SUTTON
E.70,666   T. 67.43%
Mrs L. Gilroy, *Lab. Co-op.*   23,881
A. Crisp, *C.*   14,441
S. Melia, *LD*   6,613
T. Hanbury, *Ref.*   1,654
R. Bullock, *UK Ind.*   499
K. Kelway, *Plymouth*   396
F. Lyons, *NLP*   168
Lab. Co-op. majority 9,440
(Boundary change: notional C.)

PONTEFRACT AND CASTLEFORD
E.62,350   T. 66.39%
Ms Y. Cooper, *Lab.*   31,339
A. Flook, *C.*   5,614
W. Paxton, *LD*   3,042
R. Wood, *Ref.*   1,401
Lab. majority 25,725
(April 1992, Lab. maj. 23,495)

POOLE
E.66,078   T. 70.84%
R. Syms, *C.*   19,726
A. Tetlow, *LD*   14,428
H. White, *Lab.*   10,100
J. Riddington, *Ref.*   1,932
P. Tyler, *UK Ind.*   487
Mrs J. Rosta, *NLP*   137
C. majority 5,298
(Boundary change: notional C.)

POPLAR AND CANNING TOWN
E.67,172   T. 58.46%
J. Fitzpatrick, *Lab.*   24,807
B. Steinberg, *C.*   5,892
Ms J. Ludlow, *LD*   4,072
J. Tyndall, *BNP*   2,849
I. Hare, *Ref.*   1,091
Ms J. Joseph, *Soc. Lab.*   557
Lab. majority 18,915
(Boundary change: notional Lab.)

PORTSMOUTH NORTH
E.64,539   T. 70.14%
S. Rapson, *Lab.*   21,339
†P. Griffiths, *C.*   17,016
S. Sollitt, *LD*   4,788
S. Evelegh, *Ref.*   1,757
P. Coe, *UK Ind.*   298

C. Bex, *Wessex*   72
Lab. majority 4,323
(Boundary change: notional C.)

PORTSMOUTH SOUTH
E.80,514   T. 64.21%
M. Hancock, *LD*   20,421
*D. Martin, *C.*   16,094
A. Burnett, *Lab.*   13,086
C. Trim, *Ref.*   1,629
J. Thompson, *Lib.*   184
Mrs J. Evans, *UK Ind.*   141
W. Treend, *NLP*   140
LD majority 4,327
(April 1992, C. maj. 242)

PRESTON
E.72,933   T. 65.92%
†Mrs A. Wise, *Lab.*   29,220
P. Gray, *C.*   10,540
W. Chadwick, *LD*   7,045
J. C. Porter, *Ref.*   924
J. Ashforth, *NLP*   345
Lab. majority 18,680
(Boundary change: notional Lab.)

PUDSEY
E.70,922   T. 74.35%
P. Truswell, *Lab.*   25,370
P. Bone, *C.*   19,163
Dr J. Brown, *LD*   7,375
D. Crabtree, *Ref.*   823
Lab. majority 6,207
(April 1992, C. maj. 8,972)

PUTNEY
E.60,176   T. 73.11%
A. Colman, *Lab.*   20,084
*Rt. Hon. D. Mellor, *C.*   17,108
R. Pyne, *LD*   4,739
Sir J. Goldsmith, *Ref.*   1,518
W. Jamieson, *UK Ind.*   233
L. Beige, *Stan*   101
M. Yardley, *Spts All.*   90
J. Small, *NLP*   66
Ms A. Poole, *Beaut.*   49
D. Vanbraam, *Ren. Dem.*   7
Lab. majority 2,976
(April 1992, C. maj. 7,526)

RAYLEIGH
E.68,737   T. 74.65%
†Dr M. Clark, *C.*   25,516
R. Ellis, *Lab.*   14,832
S. Cumberland, *LD*   10,137
A. Farmer, *Lib.*   829
C. majority 10,684
(Boundary change: notional C.)

READING EAST
E.71,586   T. 70.15%
Ms J. Griffiths, *Lab.*   21,461
†J. Watts, *C.*   17,666
R. Samuel, *LD*   9,307
D. Harmer, *Ref.*   1,042
J. Buckley, *NLP*   254
Miss A. Thornton, *UK Ind.*   252
Ms B. Packer, *BNP*   238
Lab. majority 3,795
(Boundary change: notional C.)

READING WEST
E.69,073   T. 70.05%
M. Salter, *Lab.*   21,841

N. Bennett, *C.*   18,844
Mrs D. Tomlin, *LD*   6,153
S. Brown, *Ref.*   976
I. Dell, *BNP*   320
D. Black, *UK Ind.*   255
Lab. majority 2,997
(Boundary change: notional C.)

REDCAR
E.68,965   T. 70.99%
†Dr M. Mowlam, *Lab.*   32,972
A. Isaacs, *C.*   11,308
Ms J. Benbow, *LD*   4,679
Lab. majority 21,664
(Boundary change: notional Lab.)

REDDITCH
E.60,841   T. 73.55%
Ms J. Smith, *Lab.*   22,280
Miss A. McIntyre, *C.*   16,155
M. Hall, *LD*   4,935
R. Cox, *Ref.*   1,151
P. Davis, *NLP*   227
Lab. majority 6,125
(Boundary change: notional C.)

REGENT'S PARK AND
KENSINGTON NORTH
E.73,752   T. 64.19%
Ms K. Buck, *Lab.*   28,367
P. McGuinness, *C.*   13,710
Miss E. Gasson, *LD*   4,041
Ms S. Dangoor, *Ref.*   867
J. Hinde, *NLP*   192
Ms D. Sadowitz, *Dream*   167
Lab. majority 14,657
(Boundary change: notional Lab.)

REIGATE
E.64,750   T. 74.40%
C. Blunt, *C.*   21,123
A. Howard, *Lab.*   13,382
P. Samuel, *LD*   9,615
†Sir G. Gardiner, *Ref.*   3,352
R. Higgs, *Ind.*   412
S. Smith, *UK Ind.*   290
C. majority 7,741
(Boundary change: notional C.)

RIBBLE SOUTH
E.71,670   T. 77.06%
D. Borrow, *Lab.*   25,856
†Rt. Hon. R. Atkins, *C.*   20,772
T. Farron, *LD*   5,879
G. Adams, *Ref.*   1,475
N. Ashton, *Lib.*   1,127
Ms B. Leadbetter, *NLP*   122
Lab. majority 5,084
(Boundary change: notional C.)

RIBBLE VALLEY
E.72,664   T. 78.75%
†N. Evans, *C.*   26,702
M. Carr, *LD*   20,062
M. Johnstone, *Lab.*   9,013
J. Parkinson, *Ref.*   1,297
Miss N. Holmes, *NLP*   147
C. majority 6,640
(Boundary change: notional C.)

RICHMOND (Yorks)
E.65,058   T. 73.38%
†Rt. Hon. W. Hague, *C.*   23,326

S. Merritt, *Lab.* 13,275
Mrs J. Harvey, *LD* 8,773
A. Bentley, *Ref.* 2,367
C. majority 10,051
(Boundary change: notional C.)

RICHMOND PARK
*E.*71,572 *T.* 79.43%
Dr J. Tonge, *LD* 25,393
†Rt. Hon. J. Hanley, *C.* 22,442
Ms S. Jenkins, *Lab.* 7,172
J. Pugh, *Ref.* 1,467
D. Beaupre, *Loony* 204
B. D'Arcy, *NLP* 102
P. Davies, *Dream* 73
LD majority 2,951
(Boundary change: notional C.)

ROCHDALE
*E.*68,529 *T.* 70.16%
Ms L. Fitzsimons, *Lab.* 23,758
†Miss E. Lynne, *LD* 19,213
M. Turnberg, *C.* 4,237
G. Bergin, *BNP* 653
S. Mohammed, *IZB* 221
Lab. majority 4,545
(Boundary change: notional LD)

ROCHFORD AND SOUTHEND
EAST
*E.*72,848 *T.* 63.97%
†Sir E. Taylor, *C.* 22,683
N. Smith, *Lab.* 18,458
Ms P. Smith, *LD* 4,387
B. Lynch, *Lib.* 1,070
C. majority 4,225
(Boundary change: notional C.)

ROMFORD
*E.*59,611 *T.* 70.66%
Mrs E. Gordon, *Lab.* 18,187
†Sir M. Neubert, *C.* 17,538
N. Meyer, *LD* 3,341
S. Ward, *Ref.* 1,431
T. Hurlstone, *Lib.* 1,100
M. Carey, *BNP* 522
Lab. majority 649
(Boundary change: notional C.)

ROMSEY
*E.*67,306 *T.* 76.99%
†M. Colvin, *C.* 23,834
M. Cooper, *LD* 15,249
Ms J. Ford, *Lab.* 9,623
Dr A. Sked, *UK Ind.* 1,824
M. Wigley, *Ref.* 1,291
C. majority 8,585
(Boundary change: notional C.)
see also page 233

ROSSENDALE AND DARWEN
*E.*69,749 *T.* 73.42%
†Mrs J. Anderson, *Lab.* 27,470
Mrs P. Buzzard, *C.* 16,521
B. Dunning, *LD* 5,435
R. Newstead, *Ref.* 1,108
A. Wearden, *BNP* 674
Lab. majority 10,949
(Boundary change: notional Lab.)

ROTHER VALLEY
*E.*68,622 *T.* 67.26%
*K. Barron, *Lab.* 31,184
S. Stanbury, *C.* 7,699

S. Burgess, *LD* 5,342
S. Cook, *Ref.* 1,932
Lab. majority 23,485
(April 1992, Lab. maj. 17,222)

ROTHERHAM
*E.*59,895 *T.* 62.86%
*D. MacShane, *Lab.* 26,852
S. Gordon, *C.* 5,383
D. Wildgoose, *LD* 3,919
R. Hollibone, *Ref.* 1,132
A. Neal, *ProLife* 364
Lab. majority 21,469
(April 1992, Lab. maj. 17,561)

RUGBY AND KENILWORTH
*E.*79,384 *T.* 77.10%
A. King, *Lab.* 26,356
†J. Pawsey, *C.* 25,861
J. Roodhouse, *LD* 8,737
M. Twite, *NLP* 251
Lab. majority 495
(Boundary change: notional C.)

RUISLIP-NORTHWOOD
*E.*60,393 *T.* 74.24%
†J. Wilkinson, *C.* 22,526
P. Barker, *Lab.* 14,732
C. Edwards, *LD* 7,279
Ms C. Griffin, *NLP* 296
C. majority 7,794
(Boundary change: notional C.)

RUNNYMEDE AND WEYBRIDGE
*E.*72,177 *T.* 71.44%
P. Hammond, *C.* 25,051
I. Peacock, *Lab.* 15,176
G. Taylor, *LD* 8,397
P. Rolt, *Ref.* 2,150
S. Slater, *UK Ind.* 625
J. Sleeman, *NLP* 162
C. majority 9,875
(Boundary change: notional C.)

RUSHCLIFFE
*E.*78,735 *T.* 78.89%
*Rt. Hon. K. Clarke, *C.* 27,558
Ms J. Pettit, *Lab.* 22,503
S. Boote, *LD* 8,851
Miss S. Chadd, *Ref.* 2,682
J. Moore, *UK Ind.* 403
Ms A. Maszwska, *NLP* 115
C. majority 5,055
(April 1992, C. maj. 19,766)

RUTLAND AND MELTON
*E.*70,150 *T.* 75.02%
†A. Duncan, *C.* 24,107
J. Meads, *Lab.* 15,271
K. Lee, *LD* 10,112
R. King, *Ref.* 2,317
J. Abbott, *UK Ind.* 823
C. majority 8,836
(Boundary change: notional C.)

RYEDALE
*E.*65,215 *T.* 74.80%
†J. Greenway, *C.* 21,351
J. Orrell, *LD* 16,293
Ms A. Hiles, *Lab.* 8,762
J. Mackfall, *Ref.* 1,460
S. Feaster, *UK Ind.* 917
C. majority 5,058
(Boundary change: notional C.)

SAFFRON WALDEN
*E.*74,097 *T.* 76.99%
†Sir A. Haselhurst, *C.* 25,871
M. Caton, *LD* 15,298
M. Fincken, *Lab.* 12,275
R. Glover, *Ref.* 2,308
I. Evans, *UK Ind.* 658
B. Tyler, *Ind.* 486
C. Edwards, *NLP* 154
C. majority 10,573
(Boundary change: notional C.)

ST ALBANS
*E.*65,560 *T.* 77.49%
K. Pollard, *Lab.* 21,338
D. Rutley, *C.* 16,879
A. Rowlands, *LD* 10,692
J. Warrilow, *Ref.* 1,619
Ms S. Craigen, *Dream* 166
I. Docker, *NLP* 111
Lab. majority 4,459
(Boundary change: notional C.)

ST HELENS NORTH
*E.*71,380 *T.* 68.97%
D. Watts, *Lab.* 31,953
P. Walker, *C.* 8,536
J. Beirne, *LD* 6,270
D. Johnson, *Ref.* 1,276
R. Waugh, *Soc. Lab.* 832
R. Rudin, *UK Ind.* 363
Lab. majority 23,417
(April 1992, Lab. maj. 16,244)

ST HELENS SOUTH
*E.*66,526 *T.* 66.53%
†G. Bermingham, *Lab.* 30,367
Ms M. Russell, *C.* 6,628
B. Spencer, *LD* 5,919
W. Holdaway, *Ref.* 1,165
Ms H. Jump, *NLP* 179
Lab. majority 23,739
(Boundary change: notional Lab.)

ST IVES
*E.*71,680 *T.* 75.20%
A. George, *LD* 23,966
W. Rogers, *C.* 16,796
C. Fegan, *Lab.* 8,184
M. Faulkner, *Ref.* 3,714
Mrs P. Garnier, *UK Ind.* 567
G. Stephens, *Lib.* 425
K. Lippiatt, *R. Alt.* 178
W. Hitchins, *BHMBCM* 71
LD majority 7,170
(April 1992, C. maj. 1,645)

SALFORD
*E.*58,610 *T.* 56.51%
Ms H. Blears, *Lab.* 22,848
E. Bishop, *C.* 5,779
N. Owen, *LD* 3,407
R. Cumpsty, *Ref.* 926
Ms S. Herman, *NLP* 162
Lab. majority 17,069
(Boundary change: notional Lab.)

SALISBURY
*E.*78,973 *T.* 73.75%
*R. Key, *C.* 25,012
Ms Y. Emmerson-Peirce, *LD* 18,736
R. Rogers, *Lab.* 10,242
N. Farage, *UK Ind.* 3,332

H. Soutar, *Green* 623
W. Holmes, *Ind.* 184
Mrs S. Haysom, *NLP* 110
C. majority 6,276
(April 1992, C. maj. 8,973)

SCARBOROUGH AND WHITBY
E.75,862 T. 71.61%
L. Quinn, *Lab.* 24,791
*J. Sykes, *C.* 19,667
M. Allinson, *LD* 7,672
Ms S. Murray, *Ref.* 2,191
Lab. majority 5,124
(April 1992, C. maj. 11,734)

SCUNTHORPE
E.60,393 T. 68.84%
†E. Morley, *Lab.* 25,107
M. Fisher, *C.* 10,934
G. Smith, *LD* 3,497
P. Smith, *Ref.* 1,637
B. Hopper, *Soc. Lab.* 399
Lab. majority 14,173
(Boundary change: notional Lab.)

SEDGEFIELD
E.64,923 T. 72.57%
†Rt. Hon. A. Blair, *Lab.* 33,526
Mrs E. Pitman, *C.* 8,383
R. Beadle, *LD* 3,050
Miss M. Hall, *Ref.* 1,683
B. Gibson, *Soc. Lab.* 474
Lab. majority 25,143
(Boundary change: notional Lab.)

SELBY
E.75,141 T. 74.95%
J. Grogan, *Lab.* 25,838
K. Hind, *C.* 22,002
E. Batty, *LD* 6,778
D. Walker, *Ref.* 1,162
P. Spence, *UK Ind.* 536
Lab. majority 3,836
(Boundary change: notional C.)

SEVENOAKS
E.66,474 T. 75.44%
M. Fallon, *C.* 22,776
J. Hayes, *Lab.* 12,315
R. Walshe, *LD* 12,086
N. Large, *Ref.* 2,138
Ms M. Lawrence, *Green* 443
M. Ellis, *PF* 244
A. Hankey, *NLP* 147
C. majority 10,461
(Boundary change: notional C.)

SHEFFIELD ATTERCLIFFE
E.68,548 T. 64.65%
*C. Betts, *Lab.* 28,937
B. Doyle, *C.* 7,119
Mrs G. Smith, *LD* 6,973
J. Brown, *Ref.* 1,289
Lab. majority 21,818
(April 1992, Lab. maj. 15,480)

SHEFFIELD BRIGHTSIDE
E.58,930 T. 57.47%
*D. Blunkett, *Lab.* 24,901
F. Butler, *LD* 4,947
C. Buckwell, *C.* 2,850
B. Farnsworth, *Ref.* 624
P. Davidson, *Soc. Lab.* 482

R. Scott, *NLP* 61
Lab. majority 19,954
(April 1992, Lab. maj. 22,681)

SHEFFIELD CENTRAL
E.68,667 T. 53.04%
†R. Caborn, *Lab.* 23,179
A. Qadar, *LD* 6,273
M. Hess, *C.* 4,341
A. D'Agorne, *Green* 954
A. Brownlow, *Ref.* 863
K. Douglas, *Soc.* 466
Ms M. Aitken, *ProLife* 280
M. Driver, *WRP* 63
Lab. majority 16,906
(Boundary change: notional Lab.)

SHEFFIELD HALLAM
E.62,834 T. 72.38%
R. Allan, *LD* 23,345
†Sir I. Patnick, *C.* 15,074
S. Conquest, *Lab.* 6,147
I. Davidson, *Ref.* 788
P. Booler, *SIP* 125
LD majority 8,271
(Boundary change: notional C.)

SHEFFIELD HEELEY
E.66,599 T. 64.96%
*W. Michie, *Lab.* 26,274
R. Davison, *LD* 9,196
J. Harthman, *C.* 6,767
D. Mawson, *Ref.* 1,029
Lab. majority 17,078
(April 1992, Lab. maj. 14,954)

SHEFFIELD HILLSBOROUGH
E.74,642 T. 71.04%
*Mrs H. Jackson, *Lab.* 30,150
A. Dunworth, *LD* 13,699
D. Nuttall, *C.* 7,707
J. Rusling, *Ref.* 1,468
Lab. majority 16,451
(April 1992, Lab. maj. 7,068)

SHERWOOD
E.74,788 T. 75.59%
*P. Tipping, *Lab.* 33,071
R. Spencer, *C.* 16,259
B. Moult, *LD* 4,889
L. Slack, *Ref.* 1,882
P. Ballard, *BNP* 432
Lab. majority 16,812
(April 1992, Lab. maj. 2,910)

SHIPLEY
E.69,281 T. 76.32%
C. Leslie, *Lab.* 22,962
*Rt. Hon. Sir M. Fox, *C.* 19,966
J. Cole, *LD* 7,984
Dr S. Ellams, *Ref.* 1,960
Lab. majority 2,996
(April 1992, C. maj. 12,382)

SHREWSBURY AND ATCHAM
E.73,542 T. 75.25%
P. Marsden, *Lab.* 20,484
*D. Conway, *C.* 18,814
Mrs A. Woolland, *LD* 13,838
D. Barker, *Ref.* 1,346
D. Rowlands, *UK Ind.* 477
A. Dignan, *CFSS* 257
A. Williams, *PPP* 128

Lab. majority 1,670
(April 1992, C. maj. 10,965)

SHROPSHIRE NORTH
E.70,852 T. 72.71%
O. Paterson, *C.* 20,730
I. Lucas, *Lab.* 18,535
J. Stevens, *LD* 10,489
D. Allen, *Ref.* 1,764
C. majority 2,195
(Boundary change: notional C.)

SITTINGBOURNE AND SHEPPEY
E.63,850 T. 72.30%
D. Wyatt, *Lab.* 18,723
†Sir R. Moate, *C.* 16,794
R. Truelove, *LD* 8,447
P. Moull, *Ref.* 1,082
C. Driver, *Loony* 644
N. Risi, *UK Ind.* 472
Lab. majority 1,929
(Boundary change: notional C.)

SKIPTON AND RIPON
E.72,042 T. 75.44%
†Rt. Hon. D. Curry, *C.* 25,294
T. Mould, *LD* 13,674
R. Marchant, *Lab.* 12,171
Mrs N. Holdsworth, *Ref.* 3,212
C. majority 11,620
(Boundary change: notional C.)

SLEAFORD AND NORTH HYKEHAM
E.71,486 T. 74.39%
†Rt. Hon. D. Hogg, *C.* 23,358
S. Harriss, *Lab.* 18,235
J. Marriott, *LD* 8,063
P. Clery, *Ref.* 2,942
R. Overton, *Ind.* 578
C. majority 5,123
(Boundary change: notional C.)

SLOUGH
E.70,283 T. 67.91%
Ms F. MacTaggart, *Lab.* 27,029
Mrs P. Buscombe, *C.* 13,958
C. Bushill, *LD* 3,509
Ms A. Bradshaw, *Lib.* 1,835
T. Sharkey, *Ref.* 1,124
P. Whitmore, *Slough* 277
Lab. majority 13,071
(Boundary change: notional Lab.)

SOLIHULL
E.78,898 T. 74.66%
†J. Taylor, *C.* 26,299
M. Southcombe, *LD* 14,902
Ms R. Harris, *Lab.* 14,334
M. Nattrass, *Ref.* 2,748
J. Caffery, *ProLife* 623
C. majority 11,397
(Boundary change: notional C.)

SOMERTON AND FROME
E.73,988 T. 77.58%
D. Heath, *LD* 22,684
†M. Robinson, *C.,* 22,554
R. Ashford, *Lab.* 9,385
R. Rodwell, *Ref.* 2,449
R. Gadd, *UK Ind.* 331
LD majority 130
(Boundary change: notional C.)

SOUTHAMPTON ITCHEN
E.76,869　T. 70.06%

†J. Denham, *Lab.*	29,498
P. Fleet, *C.*	15,289
D. Harrison, *LD*	6,289
J. Clegg, *Ref.*	1,660
K. Rose, *Soc. Lab.*	628
C. Hoar, *UK Ind.*	172
G. Marsh, *Soc.*	113
Ms R. Barry, *NLP*	110
F. McDermott, *ProLife*	99

Lab. majority 14,209
(Boundary change: notional Lab.)

SOUTHAMPTON TEST
E.72,983　T. 71.85%

A. Whitehead, *Lab.*	28,396
†Sir J. Hill, *C.*	14,712
A. Dowden, *LD*	7,171
P. Day, *Ref.*	1,397
H. Marks, *LCP*	388
A. McCabe, *UK Ind.*	219
P. Taylor, *Glow*	81
J. Sinel, *NLP*	77

Lab. majority 13,684
(Boundary change: notional Lab.)

SOUTHEND WEST
E.66,493　T. 69.95%

†D. Amess, *C.*	18,029
Mrs N. Stimson, *LD*	15,414
A. Harley, *Lab.*	10,600
C. Webster, *Ref.*	1,734
B. Lee, *UK Ind.*	636
P. Warburton, *NLP*	101

C. majority 2,615
(April 1992, C. maj. 11,902)

SOUTH HOLLAND AND THE
DEEPINGS
E.69,642　T. 71.98%

J. Hayes, *C.*	24,691
J. Lewis, *Lab.*	16,700
P. Millen, *LD*	7,836
G. Erwood, *NPC*	902

C. majority 7,991
(Boundary change: notional C.)

SOUTHPORT
E.70,194　T. 72.08%

R. Fearn, *LD*	24,346
*M. Banks, *C.*	18,186
Ms S. Norman, *Lab.*	6,125
F. Buckle, *Ref.*	1,368
Ms S. Ashton, *Lib.*	386
E. Lines, *NLP*	93
M. Middleton, *Nat. Dem.*	92

LD majority 6,160
(April 1992, C. maj. 3,063)

SOUTH SHIELDS
E.62,261　T. 62.60%

†Dr D. Clark, *Lab.*	27,834
M. Hoban, *C.*	5,681
D. Ord, *LD*	3,429
A. Loraine, *Ref.*	1,660
I. Wilburn, *Shields*	374

Lab. majority 22,153
(Boundary change: notional Lab.)

SOUTHWARK NORTH AND
BERMONDSEY
E.65,598　T. 62.19%

†S. Hughes, *LD*	19,831

J. Fraser, *Lab.*	16,444
G. Shapps, *C.*	2,835
M. Davidson, *BNP*	713
W. Newton, *Ref.*	545
I. Grant, *Comm L.*	175
J. Munday, *Lib.*	157
Ms I. Yngvison, *Nat. Dem.*	95

LD majority 3,387
(Boundary change: notional LD)

SPELTHORNE
E.70,562　T. 73.58%

*D. Wilshire, *C.*	23,306
K. Dibble, *Lab.*	19,833
E. Glynn, *LD*	6,821
B. Coleman, *Ref.*	1,495
J. Fowler, *UK Ind.*	462

C. majority 3,473
(April 1992, C. maj. 19,843)

STAFFORD
E.67,555　T. 76.64%

D. Kidney, *Lab.*	24,606
D. Cameron, *C.*	20,292
Mrs P. Hornby, *LD*	5,480
S. Culley, *Ref.*	1,146
A. May, *Loony*	248

Lab. majority 4,314
(Boundary change: notional C.)

STAFFORDSHIRE MOORLANDS
E.66,095　T. 77.34%

Ms C. Atkins, *Lab.*	26,686
Dr A. Ashworth, *C.*	16,637
Mrs C. Jebb, *LD*	6,191
D. Stanworth, *Ref.*	1,603

Lab. majority 10,049
(Boundary change: notional Lab.)

STAFFORDSHIRE SOUTH
E.68,896　T. 74.19%

†Sir P. Cormack, *C.*	25,568
Ms J. LeMaistre, *Lab.*	17,747
Mrs J. Calder, *LD*	5,797
P. Carnell, *Ref.*	2,002

C. majority 7,821
(Boundary change: notional C.)

STALYBRIDGE AND HYDE
E.65,468　T. 65.80%

†T. Pendry, *Lab.*	25,363
N. de Bois, *C.*	10,557
M. Cross, *LD*	5,169
R. Clapham, *Ref.*	1,992

Lab. majority 14,806
(Boundary change: notional Lab.)

STEVENAGE
E.66,889　T. 76.82%

Ms B. Follett, *Lab.*	28,440
†T. Wood, *C.*	16,858
A. Wilcock, *LD*	4,588
J. Coburn, *Ref.*	1,194
D. Bundy, *ProLife*	196
A. Calcraft, *NLP*	110

Lab. majority 11,582
(Boundary change: notional C.)

STOCKPORT
E.65,232　T. 71.54%

†Ms A. Coffey, *Lab.*	29,338
S. Fitzsimmons, *C.*	10,426
Mrs S. Roberts, *LD*	4,951

W. Morley-Scott, *Ref.*	1,280
G. Southern, *Soc. Lab.*	255
C. Newitt, *Loony*	213
C. Dronfield, *Ind.*	206

Lab. majority 18,912
(Boundary change: notional Lab.)

STOCKTON NORTH
E.64,380　T. 69.08%

†F. Cook, *Lab.*	29,726
B. Johnston, *C.*	8,369
Mrs S. Fletcher, *LD*	4,816
K. McConnell, *Ref.*	1,563

Lab. majority 21,357
(Boundary change: notional Lab.)

STOCKTON SOUTH
E.68,470　T. 76.12%

Ms D. Taylor, *Lab.*	28,790
†T. Devlin, *C.*	17,205
P. Monck, *LD*	4,721
J. Horner, *Ref.*	1,400

Lab. majority 11,585
(Boundary change: notional C.)

STOKE-ON-TRENT CENTRAL
E.64,113　T. 62.77%

*M. Fisher, *Lab.*	26,662
N. Jones, *C.*	6,738
E. Fordham, *LD*	4,809
P. Stanyer, *Ref.*	1,071
M. Coleman, *BNP*	606
Ms F. Oborski, *Lib.*	359

Lab. majority 19,924
(April 1992, Lab. maj. 13,420)

STOKE-ON-TRENT NORTH
E.59,030　T. 65.50%

†Ms J. Walley, *Lab.*	25,190
C. Day, *C.*	7,798
H. Jebb, *LD*	4,141
Ms J. Tobin, *Ref.*	1,537

Lab. majority 17,392
(Boundary change: notional Lab.)

STOKE-ON-TRENT SOUTH
E.69,968　T. 66.08%

*G. Stevenson, *Lab.*	28,645
Mrs S. Scott, *C.*	10,342
P. Barnett, *LD*	4,710
R. Adams, *Ref.*	1,103
Mrs A. Micklem, *Lib.*	580
S. Batkin, *BNP*	568
B. Lawrence, *Nat. Dem.*	288

Lab. majority 18,303
(April 1992, Lab. maj. 6,909)

STONE
E.68,242　T. 77.77%

†W. Cash, *C.*	24,859
J. Wakefield, *Lab.*	21,041
B. Stamp, *LD*	6,392
Ms A. Winfield, *Lib.*	545
Ms D. Grice, *NLP*	237

C. majority 3,818
(Boundary change: notional C.)

STOURBRIDGE
E.64,966　T. 76.50%

Ms D. Shipley, *Lab.*	23,452
†W. Hawksley, *C.*	17,807
C. Bramall, *LD*	7,123
P. Quick, *Ref.*	1,319

Lab. majority 5,645
(Boundary change: notional C.)

STRATFORD-ON-AVON
E.81,434   T. 76.26%
J. Maples, C.   29,967
Dr S. Juned, LD   15,861
S. Stacey, Lab.   12,754
A. Hilton, Ref.   2,064
J. Spilsbury, UK Ind.   556
J. Brewster, NLP   307
S. Marcus, SFDC   306
Ms S. Miller, ProLife   284
C. majority 14,106
(Boundary change: notional C.)

STREATHAM
E.74,509   T. 60.24%
†K. Hill, Lab.   28,181
E. Noad, C.   9,758
R. O'Brien, LD   6,082
J. Wall, Ref.   864
Lab. majority 18,423
(Boundary change: notional Lab.)

STRETFORD AND URMSTON
E.69,913   T. 69.65%
Ms B. Hughes, Lab.   28,480
J. Gregory, C.   14,840
J. Bridges, LD   3,978
Ms C. Dore, Ref.   1,397
Lab. majority 13,640
(Boundary change: notional Lab.)

STROUD
E.77,494   T. 80.45%
D. Drew, Lab. Co-op.   26,170
†R. Knapman, C.   23,260
P. Hodgkinson, LD   9,502
J. Marjoram, Green   3,415
Lab. Co-op. majority 2,910
(Boundary change: notional C.)

SUFFOLK CENTRAL AND
IPSWICH NORTH
E.70,222   T. 75.22%
†M. Lord, C.   22,493
Ms C. Jones, Lab.   18,955
Dr M. Goldspink, LD   10,886
Ms S. Bennell, Ind.   489
C. majority 3,538
(Boundary change: notional C.)

SUFFOLK COASTAL
E.74,219   T. 75.80%
†Rt. Hon. J. Gummer, C.   21,696
M. Campbell, Lab.   18,442
Ms A. Jones, LD   12,036
S. Caulfield, Ref.   3,416
A. Slade, Green   514
Ms F. Kaplan, NLP   152
C. majority 3,254
(Boundary change: notional C.)

SUFFOLK SOUTH
E.67,323   T. 77.20%
†T. Yeo, C.   19,402
P. Bishop, Lab.   15,227
Mrs K. Pollard, LD   14,395
C. de Chair, Ref.   2,740
Mrs A. Holland, NLP   211
C. majority 4,175
(Boundary change: notional C.)

SUFFOLK WEST
E.68,638   T. 71.51%
†R. Spring, C.   20,081
M. Jefferys, Lab.   18,214
A. Graves, LD   6,892
J. Carver, Ref.   3,724
A. Shearer, NLP   171
C. majority 1,867
(Boundary change: notional C.)

SUNDERLAND NORTH
E.64,711   T. 59.05%
†W. Etherington, Lab.   26,067
A. Selous, C.   6,370
G. Pryke, LD   3,973
M. Nicholson, Ref.   1,394
K. Newby, Loony   409
Lab. majority 19,697
(Boundary change: notional Lab.)

SUNDERLAND SOUTH
E.67,937   T. 58.77%
†C. Mullin, Lab.   27,174
T. Schofield, C.   7,536
J. Lennox, LD   4,606
M. Wilkinson, UK Ind.   609
Lab. majority 19,638
(Boundary change: notional Lab.)

SURREY EAST
E.72,852   T. 75.02%
†P. Ainsworth, C.   27,389
Ms B. Ford, LD   12,296
D. Ross, Lab.   11,573
M. Sydney, Ref.   2,656
A. Stone, UK Ind.   569
Ms S. Bartrum, NLP   173
C. majority 15,093
(Boundary change: notional C.)

SURREY HEATH
E.73,813   T. 74.14%
†N. Hawkins, C.   28,231
D. Newman, LD   11,944
Ms S. Jones, Lab.   11,511
J. Gale, Ref.   2,385
R. Squire, UK Ind.   653
C. majority 16,287
(Boundary change: notional C.)

SURREY SOUTH WEST
E.72,350   T. 78.03%
*Rt. Hon. Mrs V. Bottomley, C. 25,165
N. Sherlock, LD   22,471
Ms M. Leicester, Lab.   5,333
Mrs J. Clementson, Ref.   2,830
J. Kirby, UK Ind.   401
Ms J. Quintavalle, ProLife   258
C. majority 2,694
(April 1992, C. maj. 14,975)

SUSSEX MID
E.68,784   T. 77.73%
†N. Soames, C.   23,231
Mrs M. Collins, LD   16,377
M. Hamilton, Lab.   9,969
T. Large, Ref.   3,146
J. Barnett, UK Ind.   606
E. Tudway, Ind. JRP   134
C. majority 6,854
(Boundary change: notional C.)

SUTTON AND CHEAM
E.62,785   T. 75.01%
P. Burstow, LD   19,919
*Lady O. Maitland, C.   17,822
M. Allison, Lab.   7,280
P. Atkinson, Ref.   1,784
S. McKie, UK Ind.   191
Ms D. Wright, NLP   96
LD majority 2,097
(April 1992, C. maj. 10,756)

SUTTON COLDFIELD
E.71,864   T. 72.92%
*Rt. Hon. Sir N. Fowler, C.   27,373
A. York, Lab.   12,488
J. Whorwood, LD   10,139
D. Hope, Ref.   2,401
C. majority 14,885
(April 1992, C. maj. 26,036)

SWINDON NORTH
E.65,535   T. 73.66%
M. Wills, Lab.   24,029
G. Opperman, C.   16,341
M. Evemy, LD   6,237
Ms G. Goldsmith, Ref.   1,533
A. Fiskin, NLP   130
Lab. majority 7,688
(Boundary change: notional Lab.)

SWINDON SOUTH
E.70,207   T. 72.87%
Ms J. Drown, Lab.   23,943
†S. Coombs, C.   18,298
S. Pajak, LD   7,371
D. Mackintosh, Ref.   1,273
R. Charman, Route 66   181
K. Buscombe, NLP   96
Lab. majority 5,645
(Boundary change: notional C.)

TAMWORTH
E.67,205   T. 74.18%
†B. Jenkins, Lab.   25,808
Lady A. Lightbown, C.   18,312
Mrs J. Pinkett, LD   4,025
Mrs D. Livesey, Ref.   1,163
C. Lamb, UK Ind.   369
Ms C. Twelvetrees, Lib.   177
Lab. majority 7,496
(Boundary change: notional C.)

TATTON
E.63,822   T. 76.45%
M. Bell, Ind.   29,354
†N. Hamilton, C.   18,277
S. Hill, Ind.   295
S. Kinsey, Ind.   187
B. Penhaul, Miss M.   128
J. Muir, Albion   126
M. Kennedy, NLP   123
D. Bishop, Byro   116
R. Nicholas, Ind.   113
J. Price, Juice   73
Ind. majority 11,077
(Boundary change: notional C.)

TAUNTON
E.79,783   T. 76.47%
Mrs J. Ballard, LD   26,064
*D. Nicholson, C.   23,621
Ms E. Lisgo, Lab.   8,248
B. Ahern, Ref.   2,760

L. Andrews, *BNP*   318
LD majority 2,443
(April 1992, C. maj. 3,336)

TEIGNBRIDGE
*E.*81,667   *T.* 77.08%
†P. Nicholls, *C.*   24,679
R. Younger-Ross, *LD*   24,398
Ms S. Dann, *Lab.*   11,311
S. Stokes, *UK Ind.*   1,601
N. Banwell, *Green*   817
Mrs L. Golding, *Dream*   139
C. majority 281
(Boundary change: notional C.)

TELFORD
*E.*56,558   *T.* 65.62%
†B. Grocott, *Lab.*   21,456
B. Gentry, *C.*   10,166
N. Green, *LD*   4,371
C. Morris, *Ref.*   1,119
Lab. majority 11,290
(Boundary change: notional Lab.)

TEWKESBURY
*E.*68,208   *T.* 76.46%
L. Robertson, *C.*   23,859
J. Sewell, *LD*   14,625
K. Tustin, *Lab.*   13,665
C. majority 9,234
(Boundary change: notional C.)

THANET NORTH
*E.*71,112   *T.* 68.84%
*R. Gale, *C.*   21,586
Ms I. Johnston, *Lab.*   18,820
P. Kendrick, *LD*   5,576
M. Chambers, *Ref.*   2,535
Ms J. Haines, *UK Ind.*   438
C. majority 2,766
(April 1992, C. maj. 18,210)

THANET SOUTH
*E.*62,792   *T.* 71.65%
Dr S. Ladyman, *Lab.*   20,777
†Rt. Hon. J. Aitken, *C.*   17,899
Ms B. Hewett-Silk, *LD*   5,263
C. Crook, *UK Ind.*   631
D. Wheatley, *Green*   418
Lab. majority 2,878
(Boundary change: notional C.)

THURROCK
*E.*71,600   *T.* 65.94%
*A. MacKinlay, *Lab.*   29,896
A. Rosindell, *C.*   12,640
J. White, *LD*   3,843
P. Compobassi, *UK Ind.*   833
Lab. majority 17,256
(April 1992, Lab. maj. 1,172)

TIVERTON AND HONITON
*E.*75,744   *T.* 78.06%
†Mrs A. Browning, *C.*   24,438
Dr J. Barnard, *LD*   22,785
J. King, *Lab.*   7,598
S. Lowings, *Ref.*   2,952
Mrs J. Roach, *Lib.*   635
Ms E. McIvor, *Green*   485
D. Charles, *Nat. Dem.*   236
C. majority 1,653
(Boundary change: notional C.)

TONBRIDGE AND MALLING
*E.*64,798   *T.* 75.97%
†Rt. Hon. Sir J. Stanley, *C.*   23,640
Mrs B. Withstandley, *Lab.*   13,410
K. Brown, *LD*   9,467
J. Scrivenor, *Ref.*   2,005
Mrs B. Bullen, *UK Ind.*   502
G. Valente, *NLP*   205
C. majority 10,230
(Boundary change: notional C.)

TOOTING
*E.*66,653   *T.* 69.17%
*T. Cox, *Lab.*   27,516
J. Hutchings, *C.*   12,505
S. James, *LD*   4,320
Mrs A. Husband, *Ref.*   829
J. Rattray, *Green*   527
P. Boddington, *BFAIR*   161
J. Koene, *Rights*   94
D. Bailey-Bond, *Dream*   83
P. Miller, *NLP*   70
Lab. majority 15,011
(April 1992, Lab. maj. 4,107)

TORBAY
*E.*72,258   *T.* 73.79%
A. Sanders, *LD*   21,094
*R. Allason, *C.*   21,082
M. Morey, *Lab.*   7,923
G. Booth, *UK Ind.*   1,962
B. Cowling, *Lib.*   1,161
P. Wild, *Dream*   100
LD majority 12
(April 1992, C. maj. 5,787)

TOTNES
*E.*70,473   *T.* 76.30%
†Sir A. Steen, *C.*   19,637
R. Chave, *LD*   18,760
V. Ellery, *Lab.*   8,796
Ms P. Cook, *Ref.*   2,552
C. Venmore, *Loc. C.*   2,369
H. Thomas, *UK Ind.*   999
A. Pratt, *Green*   548
J. Golding, *Dream*   108
C. majority 877
(Boundary change: notional C.)

TOTTENHAM
*E.*66,173   *T.* 56.98%
*B. Grant, *Lab.*   26,121
A. Scantlebury, *C.*   5,921
N. Hughes, *LD*   4,064
P. Budge, *Green*   1,059
Ms E. Tay, *ProLife*   210
C. Anglin, *WRP*   181
Ms T. Kent, *SEP*   148
Lab. majority 20,200
(April 1992, Lab. maj. 11,968)
See also page 233

TRURO AND ST AUSTELL
*E.*76,824   *T.* 73.87%
*M. Taylor, *LD*   27,502
N. Badcock, *C.*   15,001
M. Dooley, *Lab.*   8,697
C. Hearn, *Ref.*   3,682
A. Haithwaite, *UK Ind.*   576
Mrs D. Robinson, *Green*   482
D. Hicks, *MK*   450
Mrs L. Yelland, *PP*   240

P. Boland, *NLP*   117
LD majority 12,501
(April 1992, LD maj. 7,570)

TUNBRIDGE WELLS
*E.*65,259   *T.* 74.10%
A. Norman, *C.*   21,853
A. Clayton, *LD*   14,347
P. Warner, *Lab.*   9,879
T. Macpherson, *Ref.*   1,858
M. Anderson Smart, *UK Ind.*   264
P. Levy, *NLP*   153
C. majority 7,506
(Boundary change: notional C.)

TWICKENHAM
*E.*73,281   *T.* 79.34%
Dr V. Cable, *LD*   26,237
†T. Jessel, *C.*   21,956
Ms E. Tutchell, *Lab.*   9,065
Miss J. Harrison, *Ind. ECR*   589
T. Haggar, *Dream*   155
A. Hardy, *NLP*   142
LD majority 4,281
(Boundary change: notional C.)

TYNE BRIDGE
*E.*61,058   *T.* 57.08%
†D. Clelland, *Lab.*   26,767
A. Lee, *C.*   3,861
Mrs M. Wallace, *LD*   2,785
G. Oswald, *Ref.*   919
Ms E. Brunskill, *Soc.*   518
Lab. majority 22,906
(Boundary change: notional Lab.)

TYNEMOUTH
*E.*66,341   *T.* 77.11%
A. Campbell, *Lab.*   28,318
M. Callanan, *C.*   17,045
A. Duffield, *LD*   4,509
C. Rook, *Ref.*   819
Dr F. Rogers, *UK Ind.*   462
Lab. majority 11,273
(Boundary change: notional C.)

TYNESIDE NORTH
*E.*66,449   *T.* 67.90%
†S. Byers, *Lab.*   32,810
M. McIntyre, *C.*   6,167
T. Mulvenna, *LD*   4,762
M. Rollings, *Ref.*   1,382
Lab. majority 26,643
(Boundary change: notional Lab.)

UPMINSTER
*E.*57,149   *T.* 72.30%
K. Darvill, *Lab.*   19,085
†Sir N. Bonsor, *C.*   16,315
Mrs P. Peskett, *LD*   3,919
T. Murray, *Ref.*   2,000
Lab. majority 2,770
(Boundary change: notional C.)

UXBRIDGE
*E.*57,497   *T.* 72.26%
†Sir M. Shersby, *C.*   18,095
D. Williams, *Lab.*   17,371
Dr A. Malyan, *LD*   4,528
G. Aird, *Ref.*   1,153
Ms J. Leonard, *Soc.*   398
C. majority 724
(Boundary change: notional C.)
See also page 233

VALE OF YORK
E.70,077   T. 76.01%
Miss A. McIntosh, *C.*   23,815
M. Carter, *Lab.*   14,094
C. Hall, *LD*   12,656
C. Fairclough, *Ref.*   2,503
A. Pelton, *Soc. Dem.*   197
C. majority 9,721
(Boundary change: notional C.)

VAUXHALL
E.70,402   T. 55.49%
†Ms K. Hoey, *Lab.*   24,920
K. Kerr, *LD*   6,260
R. Bacon, *C.*   5,942
I. Driver, *Soc. Lab.*   983
S. Collins, *Green*   864
R. Headicar, *SPGB*   97
Lab. majority 18,660
(Boundary change: notional Lab.)

WAKEFIELD
E.73,210   T. 68.96%
†D. Hinchliffe, *Lab.*   28,977
J. Peacock, *C.*   14,373
D. Dale, *LD*   5,656
S. Shires, *Ref.*   1,480
Lab. majority 14,604
(Boundary change: notional Lab.)

WALLASEY
E.63,714   T. 73.52%
*Ms A. Eagle, *Lab.*   30,264
Mrs P. Wilcock, *C.*   11,190
P. Reisdorf, *LD*   3,899
R. Hayes, *Ref.*   1,490
Lab. majority 19,074
(April 1992, Lab. maj. 3,809)

WALSALL NORTH
E.67,587   T. 64.07%
*D. Winnick, *Lab.*   24,517
M. Bird, *C.*   11,929
Ms T. O'Brien, *LD*   4,050
D. Bennett, *Ref.*   1,430
M. Pitt, *Ind.*   911
A. Humphries, *NF*   465
Lab. majority 12,588
(April 1992, Lab. maj. 3,824)

WALSALL SOUTH
E.64,221   T. 67.33%
*B. George, *Lab.*   25,024
L. Leek, *C.*   13,712
H. Harris, *LD*   2,698
Dr T. Dent, *Ref.*   1,662
Mrs L. Meads, *NLP*   144
Lab. majority 11,312
(April 1992, Lab. maj. 3,178)

WALTHAMSTOW
E.63,818   T. 62.76%
†N. Gerrard, *Lab.*   25,287
Mrs J. Andrew, *C.*   8,138
Dr J. Jackson, *LD*   5,491
Revd G. Hargreaves, *Ref.*   1,139
Lab. majority 17,149
(Boundary change: notional Lab.)

WANSBECK
E.62,998   T. 71.70%
D. Murphy, *Lab.*   29,569
A. Thompson, *LD*   7,202

P. Green, *C.*   6,299
P. Gompertz, *Ref.*   1,146
Dr N. Best, *Green*   956
Lab. majority 22,367
(April 1992, Lab. maj. 18,174)

WANSDYKE
E.69,032   T. 79.27%
D. Norris, *Lab.*   24,117
M. Prisk, *C.*   19,318
J. Manning, *LD*   9,205
K. Clinton, *Ref.*   1,327
T. Hunt, *UK Ind.*   438
P. House, *Loony*   225
Ms S. Lincoln, *NLP*   92
Lab. majority 4,799
(Boundary change: notional C.)

WANTAGE
E.71,657   T. 78.23%
*R. Jackson, *C.*   22,311
Ms C. Wilson, *Lab.*   16,272
Ms J. Riley, *LD*   14,822
S. Rising, *Ref.*   1,549
Ms M. Kennet, *Green*   640
Count N. Tolstoy-Miloslausky,
UK Ind.   465
C. majority 6,039
(April 1992, C. maj. 16,473)

WARLEY
E.59,758   T. 65.08%
†J. Spellar, *Lab.*   24,813
C. Pincher, *C.*   9,362
J. Pursehouse, *LD*   3,777
K. Gamre, *Ref.*   941
Lab. majority 15,451
(Boundary change: notional Lab.)

WARRINGTON NORTH
E.72,694   T. 70.50%
Ms H. Jones, *Lab.*   31,827
Ms R. Lacey, *C.*   12,300
I. Greenhalgh, *LD*   5,308
Dr A. Smith, *Ref.*   1,816
Lab. majority 19,527
(Boundary change: notional Lab.)

WARRINGTON SOUTH
E.72,262   T. 76.23%
Ms H. Southworth, *Lab.*   28,721
C. Grayling, *C.*   17,914
P. Walker, *LD*   7,199
G. Kelly, *Ref.*   1,082
S. Ross, *NLP*   166
Lab. majority 10,807
(Boundary change: notional C.)

WARWICK AND LEAMINGTON
E.79,374   T. 75.71%
J. Plaskitt, *Lab.*   26,747
†Sir D. Smith, *C.*   23,349
N. Hicks, *LD*   7,133
Mrs V. Davis, *Ref.*   1,484
P. Baptie, *Green*   764
G. Warwick, *UK Ind.*   306
M. Gibbs, *EDP*   183
R. McCarthy, *NLP*   125
Lab. majority 3,398
(Boundary change: notional C.)

WARWICKSHIRE NORTH
E.72,602   T. 74.71%
†M. O'Brien, *Lab.*   31,669

S. Hammond, *C.*   16,902
W. Powell, *LD*   4,040
R. Mole, *Ref.*   917
C. Cooke, *UK Ind.*   533
I. Moorecroft, *Bert.*   178
Lab. majority 14,767
(Boundary change: notional Lab.)

WATFORD
E.74,015   T. 74.63%
Ms C. Ward, *Lab.*   25,019
R. Gordon, *C.*   19,227
A. Canning, *LD*   9,272
Dr P. Roe, *Ref.*   1,484
L. Davis, *NLP*   234
Lab. majority 5,792
(Boundary change: notional C.)

WAVENEY
E.75,266   T. 75.21%
R. Blizzard, *Lab.*   31,846
†D. Porter, *C.*   19,393
C. Thomas, *LD*   5,054
N. Clark, *Ind.*   318
Lab. majority 12,453
(Boundary change: notional C.)

WEALDEN
E.79,519   T. 74.32%
†Rt. Hon. Sir G. Johnson Smith,
C.   29,417
M. Skinner, *LD*   15,213
N. Levine, *Lab.*   10,185
B. Taplin, *Ref.*   3,527
Mrs M. English, *UK Ind.*   569
P. Cragg, *NLP*   188
C. majority 14,204
(Boundary change: notional C.)

WEAVER VALE
E.66,011   T. 73.17%
†M. Hall, *Lab.*   27,244
J. Byrne, *C.*   13,796
T. Griffiths, *LD*   5,949
R. Cockfield, *Ref.*   1,312
Lab. majority 13,448
(Boundary change: notional Lab.)

WELLINGBOROUGH
E.74,955   T. 75.10%
P. Stinchcombe, *Lab.*   24,854
*Sir P. Fry, *C.*   24,667
P. Smith, *LD*   5,279
A. Ellwood, *UK Ind.*   1,192
Ms A. Lowrys, *NLP*   297
Lab. majority 187
(April 1992, C. maj. 11,816)

WELLS
E.72,178   T. 78.11%
*Rt. Hon. D. Heathcoat-Amory,
C.   22,208
Dr P. Gold, *LD*   21,680
M. Eavis, *Lab.*   10,204
Mrs P. Phelps, *Ref.*   2,196
Ms L. Royse, *NLP*   92
C. majority 528
(April 1992, C. maj. 6,649)

WELWYN HATFIELD
E.67,395   T. 78.59%
Ms M. Johnson, *Lab.*   24,936
†D. Evans, *C.*   19,341
R. Schwartz, *LD*   7,161

E. Cox, *RA* 1,263
Ms H. Harold, *ProLife* 267
Lab. majority 5,595
(Boundary change: notional C.)

WENTWORTH
*E.*63,951 *T.* 65.33%
J. Healey, *Lab.* 30,225
K. Hamer, *C.* 6,266
J. Charters, *LD* 3,867
A. Battley, *Ref.* 1,423
Lab. majority 23,959
(April 1992, Lab. maj. 22,449)

WEST BROMWICH EAST
*E.*63,401 *T.* 65.44%
†P. Snape, *Lab.* 23,710
B. Matsell, *C.* 10,126
M. Smith, *LD* 6,179
G. Mulley, *Ref.* 1,472
Lab. majority 13,584
(Boundary change: notional Lab.)

WEST BROMWICH WEST
*E.*67,496 *T.* 54.37%
†Rt. Hon. Miss B. Boothroyd,
    Speaker 23,969
R. Silvester, *Lab. Change* 8,546
S. Edwards, *Nat. Dem.* 4,181
Speaker majority 15,423
(Boundary change: notional Lab.)

WESTBURY
*E.*74,301 *T.* 76.38%
†D. Faber, *C.* 23,037
J. Miller, *LD* 16,969
K. Small, *Lab.* 11,969
G. Hawkins, *Lib.* 1,956
N. Hawkings-Byass, *Ref.* 1,909
R. Westbury, *UK Ind.* 771
C. Haysom, *NLP* 140
C. majority 6,068
(Boundary change: notional C.)

WEST HAM
*E.*57,058 *T.* 58.99%
†A. Banks, *Lab.* 24,531
M. MacGregor, *C.* 5,037
Ms S. McDonough, *LD* 2,479
K. Francis, *BNP* 1,198
T. Jug, *Loony* 300
J. Rainbow, *Dream* 116
Lab. majority 19,494
(Boundary change: notional Lab.)

WESTMORLAND AND LONSDALE
*E.*68,389 *T.* 74.29%
T. Collins, *C.* 21,470
S. Collins, *LD* 16,949
J. Harding, *Lab.* 10,459
M. Smith, *Ref.* 1,931
C. majority 4,521
(Boundary change: notional C.)

WESTON-SUPER-MARE
*E.*72,445 *T.* 73.68%
B. Cotter, *LD* 21,407
Mrs M. Daly, *C.* 20,133
D. Kraft, *Lab.* 9,557
T. Sewell, *Ref.* 2,280
LD majority 1,274
(Boundary change: notional C.)

WIGAN
*E.*64,689 *T.* 67.74%
†R. Stott, *Lab.* 30,043
M. Loveday, *C.* 7,400
T. Beswick, *LD* 4,390
A. Bradborne, *Ref.* 1,450
C. Maile, *Green* 442
W. Ayliffe, *NLP* 94
Lab. majority 22,643
(Boundary change: notional Lab.)
See also page 233

WILTSHIRE NORTH
*E.*77,237 *T.* 75.11%
J. Gray, *C.* 25,390
S. Cordon, *LD* 21,915
N. Knowles, *Lab.* 8,261
Ms M. Purves, *Ref.* 1,774
A. Wood, *UK Ind.* 410
Ms J. Forsyth, *NLP* 263
C. majority 3,475
(Boundary change: notional C.)

WIMBLEDON
*E.*64,070 *T.* 75.47%
R. Casale, *Lab.* 20,674
*Dr C. Goodson-Wickes, *C.* 17,694
Ms A. Willott, *LD* 8,014
H. Abid, *Ref.* 993
R. Thacker, *Green* 474
Ms S. Davies, *ProLife* 346
M. Kirby, *Mongolian* 112
G. Stacey, *Dream* 47
Lab. majority 2,980
(April 1992, C. maj. 14,761)

WINCHESTER
*E.*78,884 *T.* 78.66%
M. Oaten, *LD* 26,100
†G. Malone, *C.* 26,098
P. Davies, *Lab.* 6,528
P. Strand, *Ref.* 1,598
R. Huggett, *Top* 640
D. Rumsey, *UK Ind.* 476
J. Browne, *Ind. AFE* 307
P. Stockton, *Loony* 307
LD majority 2
(Boundary change: notional C.)
See also page 233

WINDSOR
*E.*69,132 *T.* 73.46%
†M. Trend, *C.* 24,476
C. Fox, *LD* 14,559
Mrs A. Williams, *Lab.* 9,287
J. McDermott, *Ref.* 1,676
P. Bradshaw, *Lib.* 388
Mrs E. Bigg, *UK Ind.* 302
Mr R. Parr, *Dynamic* 93
C. majority 9,917
(Boundary change: notional C.)

WIRRAL SOUTH
*E.*59,372 *T.* 81.01%
†B. Chapman, *Lab.* 24,499
L. Byrom, *C.* 17,495
P. Gilchrist, *LD* 5,018
D. Wilcox, *Ref.* 768
Ms J. Nielsen, *ProLife* 264
G. Mead, *NLP* 51
Lab. majority 7,004
(Boundary change: notional C.)

WIRRAL WEST
*E.*60,908 *T.* 76.98%
S. Hesford, *Lab.* 21,035
*Rt. Hon. D. Hunt, *C.* 18,297
J. Thornton, *LD* 5,945
D. Wharton, *Ref.* 1,613
Lab. majority 2,738
(April 1992, C. maj. 11,064)

WITNEY
*E.*73,520 *T.* 76.72%
S. Woodward, *C.* 24,282
A. Hollingsworth, *Lab.* 17,254
Mrs A. Lawrence, *LD* 11,202
G. Brown, *Ref.* 2,262
M. Montgomery, *UK Ind.* 765
Ms S. Chapple-Perrie, *Green* 636
C. majority 7,028
(Boundary change: notional C.)

WOKING
*E.*70,053 *T.* 72.68%
H. Malins, *C.* 19,553
P. Goldenberg, *LD* 13,875
Ms K. Hanson, *Lab.* 10,695
H. Bell, *Ind. C.* 3,933
C. Skeate, *Ref.* 2,209
M. Harvey, *UK Ind.* 512
Miss D. Sleeman, *NLP* 137
C. majority 5,678
(Boundary change: notional C.)

WOKINGHAM
*E.*66,161 *T.* 75.74%
†Rt. Hon. J. Redwood, *C.* 25,086
Dr R. Longton, *LD* 15,721
Ms P. Colling, *Lab.* 8,424
P. Owen, *Loony* 877
C. majority 9,365
(Boundary change: notional C.)

WOLVERHAMPTON NORTH EAST
*E.*61,642 *T.* 67.17%
K. Purchase, *Lab. Co-op.* 24,534
D. Harvey, *C.* 11,547
B. Niblett, *LD* 2,214
C. Hallmark, *Lib.* 1,560
A. Muchall, *Ref.* 1,192
M. Wingfield, *Nat. Dem.* 356
Lab. Co-op. majority 12,987
(Boundary change: notional Lab. Co-op.)

WOLVERHAMPTON SOUTH EAST
*E.*54,291 *T.* 64.15%
*D. Turner, *Lab. Co-op.* 22,202
W. Hanbury, *C.* 7,020
R. Whitehouse, *LD* 3,292
T. Stevenson-Platt, *Ref.* 980
N. Worth, *Soc. Lab.* 689
K. Bullman, *Lib.* 647
Lab. Co-op. majority 15,182
(April 1992, Lab. maj. 10,240)

WOLVERHAMPTON SOUTH WEST
*E.*67,482 *T.* 72.49%
Ms J. Jones, *Lab.* 24,657
*N. Budgen, *C.* 19,539
M. Green, *LD* 4,012
M. Hyde, *Lib.* 713
Lab. majority 5,118
(April 1992, C. maj. 4,966)

WOODSPRING
*E.*69,964   *T.* 78.51%
†Dr L. Fox, *C.*   24,425
Mrs N. Kirsen, *LD*   16,691
Ms D. Sander, *Lab.*   11,377
R. Hughes, *Ref.*   1,614
Dr R. Lawson, *Green*   667
A. Glover, *Ind.*   101
M. Mears, *NLP*   52
C. majority 7,734
(Boundary change: notional C.)

WORCESTER
*E.*69,234   *T.* 74.56%
M. Foster, *Lab.*   25,848
N. Bourne, *C.*   18,423
P. Chandler, *LD*   6,462
Mrs P. Wood, *UK Ind.*   886
Lab. majority 7,425
(Boundary change: notional C.)

WORCESTERSHIRE MID
*E.*68,381   *T.* 74.32%
†P. Luff, *C.*   24,092
Mrs D. Smith, *Lab.*   14,680
D. Barwick, *LD*   9,458
T. Watson, *Ref.*   1,780
D. Ingles, *UK Ind.*   646
A. Dyer, *NLP*   163
C. majority 9,412
(Boundary change: notional C.)

WORCESTERSHIRE WEST
*E.*64,712   *T.* 76.25%
†Sir M. Spicer, *C.*   22,223
M. Hadley, *LD*   18,377
N. Stone, *Lab.*   7,738
Ms S. Cameron, *Green*   1,006
C. majority 3,846
(Boundary change: notional C.)

WORKINGTON
*E.*65,766   *T.* 75.08%
†D. Campbell-Savours, *Lab.*   31,717
R. Blunden, *C.*   12,061
P. Roberts, *LD*   3,967
G. Donnan, *Ref.*   1,412
C. Austin, *UA*   217
Lab. majority 19,656
(Boundary change: notional Lab.)

WORSLEY
*E.*68,978   *T.* 67.82%
†T. Lewis, *Lab.*   29,083
D. Garrido, *C.*   11,342
R. Bleakley, *LD*   6,356
Lab. majority 17,741
(Boundary change: notional Lab.)

WORTHING EAST AND
SHOREHAM
*E.*70,771   *T.* 72.87%
T. Loughton, *C.*   20,864
M. King, *LD*   15,766
M. Williams, *Lab.*   12,335
J. McCulloch, *Ref.*   1,683
Mrs R. Jarvis, *UK Ind.*   921
C. majority 5,098
(Boundary change: notional C.)

WORTHING WEST
*E.*71,329   *T.* 72.12%
†P. Bottomley, *C.*   23,733
C. Hare, *LD*   16,020
J. Adams, *Lab.*   8,347
N. John, *Ref.*   2,313
T. Cross, *UK Ind.*   1,029
C. majority 7,713
(Boundary change: notional C.)

WREKIN, THE
*E.*59,126   *T.* 76.56%
P. Bradley, *Lab.*   21,243
P. Bruinvels, *C.*   18,218
I. Jenkins, *LD*   5,807
Lab. majority 3,025
(Boundary change: notional C.)

WYCOMBE
*E.*73,589   *T.* 71.10%
†Sir R. Whitney, *C.*   20,890
C. Bryant, *Lab.*   18,520
P. Bensilum, *LD*   9,678
A. Fulford, *Ref.*   2,394
J. Laker, *Green*   716
M. Heath, *NLP*   121
C. majority 2,370
(Boundary change: notional C.)

WYRE FOREST
*E.*73,063   *T.* 75.35%
D. Lock, *Lab.*   26,843

†A. Coombs, *C.*   19,897
D. Cropp, *LD*   4,377
W. Till, *Ref.*   1,956
C. Harvey, *Lib.*   1,670
J. Millington, *UK Ind.*   312
Lab. majority 6,946
(Boundary change: notional C.)

WYTHENSHAWE AND SALE EAST
*E.*71,986   *T.* 63.25%
P. Goggins, *Lab.*   26,448
P. Fleming, *C.*   11,429
Ms V. Tucker, *LD*   5,639
B. Stanyer, *Ref.*   1,060
J. Flannery, *Soc. Lab.*   957
Lab. majority 15,019
(Boundary change: notional Lab.)

YEOVIL
*E.*74,165   *T.* 72.88%
†Rt. Hon. J. D. D. Ashdown,
   LD   26,349
N. Cambrook, *C.*   14,946
P. Conway, *Lab.*   8,053
J. Beveridge, *Ref.*   3,574
D. Taylor, *Green*   728
J. Archer, *Musician*   306
C. Hudson, *Dream*   97
LD majority 11,403
(Boundary change: notional LD)

YORK, CITY OF
*E.*79,383   *T.* 73.50%
*H. Bayley, *Lab.*   34,956
S. Mallett, *C.*   14,433
A. Waller, *LD*   6,537
J. Sheppard, *Ref.*   1,083
M. Hill, *Green*   880
E. Wegener, *UK Ind.*   319
A. Lightfoot, *Ch. Nat.*   137
Lab. majority 20,523
(April 1992, Lab. maj. 6,342)

YORKSHIRE EAST
*E.*69,409   *T.* 70.55%
†J. Townend, *C.*   20,904
I. Male, *Lab.*   17,567
D. Leadley, *LD*   9,070
R. Allerston, *Soc. Dem.*   1,049
M. Cooper, *Nat. Dem.*   381
C. majority 3,337
(Boundary change: notional C.)

WALES

ABERAVON
*E.*50,025   *T.* 71.89%
*Rt. Hon. J. Morris, *Lab.*   25,650
R. McConville, *LD*   4,079
P. Harper, *C.*   2,835
P. Cockwell, *PC*   2,088
P. David, *Ref.*   970
Capt. Beany, *Beanus*   341
Lab. majority 21,571
(April 1992, Lab. maj. 21,310)

ALYN AND DEESIDE
*E.*58,091   *T.* 72.21%
†B. Jones, *Lab.*   25,955
T. Roberts, *C.*   9,552

Mrs E. Burnham, *LD*   4,076
M. Jones, *Ref.*   1,627
Mrs S. Hills, *PC*   738
Lab. majority 16,403
(Boundary change: notional Lab.)

BLAENAU GWENT
*E.*54,800   *T.* 72.32%
*L. Smith, *Lab.*   31,493
Mrs G. Layton, *LD*   3,458
Mrs M. Williams, *C.*   2,607
J. Criddle, *PC*   2,072
Lab. majority 28,035
(April 1992, Lab. maj. 30,067)

BRECON AND RADNORSHIRE
*E.*52,142   *T.* 82.24%
R. Livsey, *LD*   17,516
*J. Evans, *C.*   12,419
C. Mann, *Lab.*   11,424
Ms E. Phillips, *Ref.*   900
S. Cornelius, *PC*   622
LD majority 5,097
(April 1992, C. maj. 130)

BRIDGEND
*E.*59,721   *T.* 72.44%
*W. Griffiths, *Lab.*   25,115
D. Davies, *C.*   9,867

A. McKinlay, *LD* — 4,968
T. Greaves, *Ref.* — 1,662
D. Watkins, *PC* — 1,649
Lab. majority 15,248
(April 1992, Lab. maj. 7,326)

CAERNARFON
E.46,815   T. 72.65%
*D. Wigley, *PC* — 17,616
E. Williams, *Lab.* — 9,667
E. Williams, *C.* — 4,230
Ms M. McQueen, *LD* — 1,686
C. Collins, *Ref.* — 811
PC majority 7,949
(April 1992, PC maj. 14,476)

CAERPHILLY
E.64,621   T. 70.05%
*R. Davies, *Lab.* — 30,697
R. Harris, *C.* — 4,858
L. Whittle, *PC* — 4,383
A. Ferguson, *LD* — 3,724
M. Morgan, *Ref.* — 1,337
Mrs C. Williams, *ProLife* — 270
Lab. majority 25,839
(April 1992, Lab. maj. 22,672)

CARDIFF CENTRAL
E.60,354   T. 70.01%
*J. Owen Jones, *Lab. Co-op.* — 18,464
Mrs J. Randerson, *LD* — 10,541
D. Melding, *C.* — 8,470
T. Burns, *Soc. Lab.* — 2,230
W. Vernon, *PC* — 1,504
N. Lloyd, *Ref.* — 760
C. James, *Loony* — 204
A. Hobbs, *NLP* — 80
Lab. Co-op. majority 7,923
(April 1992, Lab. maj. 3,465)

CARDIFF NORTH
E.60,430   T. 80.24%
Ms J. Morgan, *Lab.* — 24,460
*G. Jones, *C.* — 16,334
R. Rowland, *LD* — 5,294
Dr C. Palfrey, *PC* — 1,201
E. Litchfield, *Ref.* — 1,199
Lab. majority 8,126
(April 1992, C. maj. 2,969)

CARDIFF SOUTH AND PENARTH
E.61,838   T. 68.57%
*A. Michael, *Lab. Co-op.* — 22,647
Mrs C. Roberts, *C.* — 8,766
Dr S. Wakefield, *LD* — 3,964
J. Foreman, *New Lab.* — 3,942
D. Haswell, *PC* — 1,356
P. Morgan, *Ref.* — 1,211
M. Shepherd, *Soc.* — 344
Ms B. Caves, *NLP* — 170
Lab. Co-op. majority 13,881
(April 1992, Lab. maj. 10,425)

CARDIFF WEST
E.58,198   T. 69.21%
†R. Morgan, *Lab.* — 24,297
S. Hoare, *C.* — 8,669
Ms J. Gasson, *LD* — 4,366
Ms G. Carr, *PC* — 1,949
T. Johns, *Ref.* — 996
Lab. majority 15,628
(Boundary change: notional Lab.)

CARMARTHEN EAST AND DINEFWR
E.53,079   T. 78.62%
†Dr A. Wynne Williams, *Lab.* — 17,907
R. Thomas, *PC* — 14,457
E. Hayward, *C.* — 5,022
Mrs J. Hughes, *LD* — 3,150
I. Humphreys-Evans, *Ref.* — 1,196
Lab. majority 3,450
(Boundary change: notional Lab.)

CARMARTHEN WEST AND PEMBROKESHIRE SOUTH
E.55,724   T. 76.52%
†N. Ainger, *Lab.* — 20,956
O. J. Williams, *C.* — 11,335
R. Llewellyn, *PC* — 5,402
K. Evans, *LD* — 3,516
Mrs J. Poirrier, *Ref.* — 1,432
Lab. majority 9,621
(Boundary change: notional Lab.)

CEREDIGION
E.54,378   T. 73.90%
†C. Dafis, *PC* — 16,728
R. Harris, *Lab.* — 9,767
D. Davies, *LD* — 6,616
Dr F. Aubel, *C.* — 5,983
J. Leaney, *Ref.* — 1,092
PC majority 6,961
(Boundary change: notional PC)

CLWYD SOUTH
E.53,495   T. 73.62%
†M. Jones, *Lab.* — 22,901
B. Johnson, *C.* — 9,091
A. Chadwick, *LD* — 3,684
G. Williams, *PC* — 2,500
A. Lewis, *Ref.* — 1,207
Lab. majority 13,810
(Boundary change: notional Lab.)

CLWYD WEST
E.53,467   T. 75.29%
G. Thomas, *Lab.* — 14,918
†R. Richards, *C.* — 13,070
E. Williams, *PC* — 5,421
G. Williams, *LD* — 5,151
Ms H. Collins, *Ref.* — 1,114
D. Neal, *Cvty* — 583
Lab. majority 1,848
(Boundary change: notional C.)

CONWY
E.55,092   T. 75.44%
Mrs B. Williams, *Lab.* — 14,561
R. Roberts, *LD* — 12,965
D. Jones, *C.* — 10,085
R. Davies, *PC* — 2,844
A. Barham, *Ref.* — 760
R. Bradley, *Alt. LD* — 250
D. Hughes, *NLP* — 95
Lab. majority 1,596
(April 1992, C. maj. 995)

CYNON VALLEY
E.48,286   T. 69.22%
*Mrs A. Clwyd, *Lab.* — 23,307
A. Davies, *PC* — 3,552
H. Price, *LD* — 3,459

A. Smith, *C.* — 2,262
G. John, *Ref.* — 844
Lab. majority 19,755
(April 1992, Lab. maj. 21,364)

DELYN
E.53,693   T. 74.02%
†D. Hanson, *Lab.* — 22,300
Mrs K. Lumley, *C.* — 10,607
P. Lloyd, *LD* — 4,160
A. Drake, *PC* — 1,558
Ms E. Soutter, *Ref.* — 1,117
Lab. majority 11,693
(Boundary change: notional Lab.)

GOWER
E.57,691   T. 75.12%
M. Caton, *Lab.* — 23,313
A. Cairns, *C.* — 10,306
H. Evans, *LD* — 5,624
E. Williams, *PC* — 2,226
R. Lewis, *Ref.* — 1,745
A. Popham, *FP* — 122
Lab. majority 13,007
(April 1992, Lab. maj. 7,018)

ISLWYN
E.50,540   T. 72.03%
*D. Touhig, *Lab. Co-op.* — 26,995
C. Worker, *LD* — 3,064
R. Walters, *C.* — 2,864
D. Jones, *PC* — 2,272
Mrs S. Monaghan, *Ref.* — 1,209
Lab. Co-op. majority 23,931
(April 1992, Lab. maj. 24,728)
(Feb. 1995, Lab. maj. 13,097)

LLANELLI
E.58,323   T. 70.66%
†Rt. Hon. D. Davies, *Lab.* — 23,851
M. Phillips, *PC* — 7,812
A. Hayes, *C.* — 5,003
N. Burree, *LD* — 3,788
J. Willock, *Soc. Lab.* — 757
Lab. majority 16,039
(Boundary change: notional Lab.)

MEIRIONNYDD NANT CONWY
E.32,345   T. 75.98%
*E. Llwyd, *PC* — 12,465
H. Rees, *Lab.* — 5,660
J. Quin, *C.* — 3,922
Mrs B. Feeley, *LD* — 1,719
P. Hodge, *Ref.* — 809
PC majority 6,805
(April 1992, PC maj. 4,613)

MERTHYR TYDFIL AND RHYMNEY
E.56,507   T. 69.27%
*T. Rowlands, *Lab.* — 30,012
D. Anstey, *LD* — 2,926
J. Morgan, *C.* — 2,508
A. Cox, *PC* — 2,344
A. Cowdell, *Old Lab.* — 691
R. Hutchings, *Ref.* — 660
Lab. majority 27,086
(April 1992, Lab. maj. 26,713)

MONMOUTH
E.60,703   T. 80.76%
H. Edwards, *Lab.* — 23,404
*R. Evans, *C.* — 19,226

M. Williams, *LD* — 4,689
N. Warry, *Ref.* — 1,190
A. Cotton, *PC* — 516
Lab. majority 4,178
(April 1992, C. maj. 3,204)

MONTGOMERYSHIRE
E.42,618   T. 74.91%
L. Opik, *LD* — 14,647
G. Davies, *C.* — 8,344
Ms A. Davies, *Lab.* — 6,109
Ms H. M. Jones, *PC* — 1,608
J. Bufton, *Ref.* — 879
Ms S. Walker, *Green* — 338
LD majority 6,303
(April 1992, LD maj. 5,209)

NEATH
E.55,525   T. 74.28%
*P. Hain, *Lab.* — 30,324
D. Evans, *C.* — 3,583
T. Jones, *PC* — 3,344
F. Little, *LD* — 2,597
P. Morris, *Ref.* — 975
H. Marks, *LCP* — 420
Lab. majority 26,741
(April 1992, Lab. maj. 23,975)

NEWPORT EAST
E.50,997   T. 73.06%
†A. Howarth, *Lab.* — 21,481
D. Evans, *C.* — 7,958
A. Cameron, *LD* — 3,880
A. Scargill, *Soc. Lab.* — 1,951
G. Davis, *Ref.* — 1,267
C. Holland, *PC* — 721
Lab. majority 13,523
(April 1992, Lab. maj. 9,899)

NEWPORT WEST
E.53,914   T. 74.57%
*P. Flynn, *Lab.* — 24,331
P. Clarke, *C.* — 9,794
S. Wilson, *LD* — 3,907
C. Thompsett, *Ref.* — 1,199
H. Jackson, *PC* — 648
H. Moelwyn Hughes, *UK Ind.* — 323
Lab. majority 14,537
(April 1992, Lab. maj. 7,779)

OGMORE
E.52,078   T. 73.10%
*Sir R. Powell, *Lab.* — 28,163
D. Unwin, *C.* — 3,716
Ms K. Williams, *LD* — 3,510
J. Rogers, *PC* — 2,679

Lab. majority 24,447
(April 1992, Lab. maj. 23,827)

PONTYPRIDD
E.64,185   T. 71.44%
*Dr K. Howells, *Lab.* — 29,290
N. Howells, *LD* — 6,161
J. Cowen, *C.* — 5,910
O. Llewelyn, *PC* — 2,977
J. Wood, *Ref.* — 874
P. Skelly, *Soc. Lab.* — 380
R. Griffiths, *Comm. P.* — 178
A. Moore, *NLP* — 85
Lab. majority 23,129
(April 1992, Lab. maj. 19,797)

PRESELI PEMBROKESHIRE
E.54,088   T. 78.40%
Mrs J. Lawrence, *Lab.* — 20,477
R. Buckland, *C.* — 11,741
J. Clarke, *LD* — 5,527
A. Lloyd Jones, *PC* — 2,683
D. Berry, *Ref.* — 1,574
Ms M. Scott Cato, *Green* — 401
Lab. majority 8,736
(Boundary change: notional C.)

RHONDDA
E.57,105   T. 71.46%
*A. Rogers, *Lab.* — 30,381
Ms L. Wood, *PC* — 5,450
Dr R. Berman, *LD* — 2,307
S. Whiting, *C.* — 1,551
S. Gardiner, *Ref.* — 658
K. Jakeway, *Green* — 460
Lab. majority 24,931
(April 1992, Lab. maj. 28,816)

SWANSEA EAST
E.57,373   T. 67.41%
*D. Anderson, *Lab.* — 29,151
Ms C. Dibble, *C.* — 3,582
E. Jones, *LD* — 3,440
Ms M. Pooley, *PC* — 1,308
Ms C. Maggs, *Ref.* — 904
R. Job, *Soc.* — 289
Lab. majority 25,569
(April 1992, Lab. maj. 23,482)

SWANSEA WEST
E.58,703   T. 68.94%
*Rt. Hon. A. Williams, *Lab.* — 22,748
A. Baker, *C.* — 8,289
J. Newbury, *LD* — 5,872
D. Lloyd, *PC* — 2,675
D. Proctor, *Soc. Lab.* — 885

Lab. majority 14,459
(April 1992, Lab. maj. 9,478)

TORFAEN
E.60,343   T. 71.67%
*P. Murphy, *Lab.* — 29,863
N. Parish, *C.* — 5,327
Ms J. Gray, *LD* — 5,249
Ms D. Holler, *Ref.* — 1,245
R. Gough, *PC* — 1,042
R. Coghill, *Green* — 519
Lab. majority 24,536
(April 1992, Lab. maj. 20,754)

VALE OF CLWYD
E.52,418   T. 74.65%
C. Ruane, *Lab.* — 20,617
D. Edwards, *C.* — 11,662
D. Munford, *LD* — 3,425
Ms G. Kensler, *PC* — 2,301
S. Vickers, *Ref.* — 834
S. Cooke, *UK Ind.* — 293
Lab. majority 8,955
(Boundary change: notional C.)

VALE OF GLAMORGAN
E.67,213   T. 80.21%
J. Smith, *Lab.* — 29,054
†W. Sweeney, *C.* — 18,522
Mrs S. Campbell, *LD* — 4,945
Ms M. Corp, *PC* — 1,393
Lab. majority 10,532
(Boundary change: notional C.)

WREXHAM
E.50,741   T. 71.78%
Dr J. Marek, *Lab.* — 20,450
S. Andrew, *C.* — 8,688
A. Thomas, *LD* — 4,833
J. Cronk, *Ref.* — 1,195
K. Plant, *PC* — 1,170
N. Low, *NLP* — 86
Lab. majority 11,762
(Boundary change: notional Lab.)

YNYS MÔN
E.52,952   T. 75.41%
*I. W. Jones, *PC* — 15,756
O. Edwards, *Lab.* — 13,275
G. Owen, *C.* — 8,569
D. Burnham, *LD* — 1,537
H. Gray Morris, *Ref.* — 793

SCOTLAND

ABERDEEN CENTRAL
PC majority 2,481
(April 1992, PC maj. 1,106)
E.54,257   T. 65.64%
F. Doran, *Lab.* — 17,745
Mrs J. Wisely, *C.* — 6,944
B. Topping, *SNP* — 5,767
J. Brown, *LD* — 4,714
J. Farquharson, *Ref.* — 446
Lab. majority 10,801
(Boundary change: notional Lab.)

ABERDEEN NORTH
E.54,302   T. 70.74%
M. Savidge, *Lab.* — 18,389
B. Adam, *SNP* — 8,379
J. Gifford, *C.* — 5,763
M. Rumbles, *LD* — 5,421
A. Mackenzie, *Ref.* — 463
Lab. majority 10,010
(Boundary change: notional Lab.)

ABERDEEN SOUTH
E.60,490   T. 72.84%
Ms A. Begg, *Lab.* — 15,541

N. Stephen, *LD* — 12,176
†R. Robertson, *C.* — 11,621
J. Towers, *SNP* — 4,299
R. Wharton, *Ref.* — 425
Lab. majority 3,365
(Boundary change: notional C.)

ABERDEENSHIRE WEST AND
KINCARDINE
E.59,123   T. 73.05%
Sir R. Smith, *LD* — 17,742
†G. Kynoch, *C.* — 15,080

Ms J. Mowatt, *SNP* 5,639
Ms Q. Khan, *Lab.* 3,923
S. Ball, *Ref.* 805
LD majority 2,662
(Boundary change: notional C.)

AIRDRIE AND SHOTTS
*E.*57,673　*T.* 71.40%
†Mrs H. Liddell, *Lab.* 25,460
K. Robertson, *SNP* 10,048
Dr N. Brook, *C.* 3,660
R. Wolseley, *LD* 1,719
C. Semple, *Ref.* 294
Lab. majority 15,412
(Boundary change: notional Lab.)

ANGUS
*E.*59,708　*T.* 72.14%
†A. Welsh, *SNP* 20,792
S. Leslie, *C.* 10,603
Ms C. Taylor, *Lab.* 6,733
Dr R. Speirs, *LD* 4,065
B. Taylor, *Ref.* 883
SNP majority 10,189
(Boundary change: notional SNP)

ARGYLL AND BUTE
*E.*49,451　*T.* 72.23%
*Mrs R. Michie, *LD* 14,359
Prof. N. MacCormick, *SNP* 8,278
R. Leishman, *C.* 6,774
A. Syed, *Lab.* 5,596
M. Stewart, *Ref.* 713
LD majority 6,081
(April 1992, LD maj. 2,622)

AYR
*E.*55,829　*T.* 80.17%
Mrs S. Osborne, *Lab.* 21,679
†P. Gallie, *C.* 15,136
I. Blackford, *SNP* 5,625
Miss C. Hamblen, *LD* 2,116
J. Enos, *Ref.* 200
Lab. majority 6,543
(Boundary change: notional Lab.)

BANFF AND BUCHAN
*E.*58,493　*T.* 68.69%
†A. Salmond, *SNP* 22,409
W. Frain-Bell, *C.* 9,564
Ms M. Harris, *Lab.* 4,747
N. Fletcher, *LD* 2,398
A. Buchan, *Ref.* 1,060
SNP majority 12,845
(Boundary change: notional SNP)

CAITHNESS, SUTHERLAND AND
EASTER ROSS
*E.*41,566　*T.* 70.18%
†R. Maclennan, *LD* 10,381
J. Hendry, *Lab.* 8,122
E. Harper, *SNP* 6,710
T. Miers, *C.* 3,148
Ms C. Ryder, *Ref.* 369
J. Martin, *Green* 230
M. Carr, *UK Ind.* 212
LD majority 2,259
(Boundary change: notional LD)

CARRICK, CUMNOCK AND DOON
VALLEY
*E.*65,593　*T.* 74.96%
†G. Foulkes, *Lab. Co-op.* 29,398

A. Marshall, *C.* 8,336
Mrs C. Hutchison, *SNP* 8,190
D. Young, *LD* 2,613
J. Higgins, *Ref.* 634
Lab. Co-op. majority 21,062
(Boundary change: notional Lab.
Co-op.)

CLYDEBANK AND MILNGAVIE
*E.*52,092　*T.* 75.03%
†A. Worthington, *Lab.* 21,583
J. Yuill, *SNP* 8,263
Ms N. Morgan, *C.* 4,885
K. Moody, *LD* 4,086
I. Sanderson, *Ref.* 269
Lab. majority 13,320
(Boundary change: notional Lab.)

CLYDESDALE
*E.*63,428　*T.* 71.60%
*J. Hood, *Lab.* 23,859
A. Doig, *SNP* 10,050
M. Izatt, *C.* 7,396
Mrs S. Grieve, *LD* 3,796
K. Smith, *BNP* 311
Lab. majority 13,809
(April 1992, Lab. maj. 10,187)

COATBRIDGE AND CHRYSTON
*E.*52,024　*T.* 72.30%
†T. Clarke, *Lab.* 25,697
B. Nugent, *SNP* 6,402
A. Wauchope, *C.* 3,216
Mrs M. Daly, *LD* 2,048
B. Bowsley, *Ref.* 249
Lab. majority 19,295
(Boundary change: notional Lab.)

CUMBERNAULD AND KILSYTH
*E.*48,032　*T.* 75.00%
Ms R. McKenna, *Lab.* 21,141
C. Barrie, *SNP* 10,013
I. Sewell, *C.* 2,441
J. Biggam, *LD* 1,368
Ms J Kara, *ProLife* 609
K. McEwan, *SSA* 345
Ms P. Cook, *Ref.* 107
Lab. majority 11,128
(April 1992, Lab. maj. 9,215)

CUNNINGHAME NORTH
*E.*55,526　*T.* 74.07%
*B. Wilson, *Lab.* 20,686
Mrs M. Mitchell, *C.* 9,647
Ms K. Nicoll, *SNP* 7,584
Ms K. Freel, *LD* 2,271
Ms L. McDaid, *Soc. Lab.* 501
I. Winton, *Ref.* 440
Lab. majority 11,039
(April 1992, Lab. maj. 2,939)

CUNNINGHAME SOUTH
*E.*49,543　*T.* 71.54%
*B. Donohoe, *Lab.* 22,233
Mrs M. Burgess, *SNP* 7,364
Mrs P. Paterson, *C.* 3,571
E. Watson, *LD* 1,604
K. Edwin, *Soc. Lab.* 494
A. Martlew, *Ref.* 178
Lab. majority 14,869
(April 1992, Lab. maj. 10,680)

DUMBARTON
*E.*56,229　*T.* 73.39%
*J. McFall, *Lab. Co-op.* 20,470
W. Mackechnie, *SNP* 9,587
P. Ramsay, *C.* 7,283
A. Reid, *LD* 3,144
L. Robertson, *SSA* 283
G. Dempster, *Ref.* 255
D. Lancaster, *UK Ind.* 242
Lab. Co-op. majority 10,883
(April 1992, Lab. maj. 6,129)

DUMFRIES
*E.*62,759　*T.* 78.92%
R. Brown, *Lab.* 23,528
S. Stevenson, *C.* 13,885
R. Higgins, *SNP* 5,977
N. Wallace, *LD* 5,487
D. Parker, *Ref.* 533
Ms E. Hunter, *NLP* 117
Lab. majority 9,643
(Boundary change: notional C.)

DUNDEE EAST
*E.*58,388　*T.* 69.41%
†J. McAllion, *Lab.* 20,718
Ms S. Robison, *SNP* 10,757
B. Mackie, *C.* 6,397
Dr G. Saluja, *LD* 1,677
E. Galloway, *Ref.* 601
H. Duke, *SSA* 232
Ms E. MacKenzie, *NLP* 146
Lab. majority 9,961
(Boundary change: notional Lab.)

DUNDEE WEST
*E.*57,346　*T.* 67.67%
†E. Ross, *Lab.* 20,875
J. Dorward, *SNP* 9,016
N. Powrie, *C.* 5,105
Dr E. Dick, *LD* 2,972
Ms M. Ward, *SSA* 428
J. MacMillan, *Ref.* 411
Lab. majority 11,859
(Boundary change: notional Lab.)

DUNFERMLINE EAST
*E.*52,072　*T.* 70.25%
†Rt. Hon. G. Brown, *Lab.* 24,441
J. Ramage, *SNP* 5,690
I. Mitchell, *C.* 3,656
J. Tolson, *LD* 2,164
T. Dunsmore, *Ref.* 632
Lab. majority 18,751
(Boundary change: notional Lab.)

DUNFERMLINE WEST
*E.*52,467　*T.* 69.44%
†Ms R. Squire, *Lab.* 19,338
J. Lloyd, *SNP* 6,984
Mrs E. Harris, *LD* 4,963
K. Newton, *C.* 4,606
J. Bain, *Ref.* 543
Lab. majority 12,354
(Boundary change: notional Lab.)

EAST KILBRIDE
*E.*65,229　*T.* 74.81%
†A. Ingram, *Lab.* 27,584
G. Gebbie, *SNP* 10,200
C. Herbertson, *C.* 5,863
Mrs K. Philbrick, *LD* 3,527
J. Deighan, *ProLife* 1,170

Ms J. Gray, *Ref.* 306
E. Gilmour, *NLP* 146
Lab. majority 17,384
(Boundary change: notional Lab.)

EAST LOTHIAN
*E.*57,441 *T.* 75.61%
†J. Home Robertson, *Lab.* 22,881
M. Fraser, *C.* 8,660
D. McCarthy, *SNP* 6,825
Ms A. MacAskill, *LD* 4,575
N. Nash, *Ref.* 491
Lab. majority 14,221
(Boundary change: notional Lab.)

EASTWOOD
*E.*66,697 *T.* 78.32%
J. Murphy, *Lab.* 20,766
P. Cullen, *C.* 17,530
D. Yates, *SNP* 6,826
Dr C. Mason, *LD* 6,110
D. Miller, *Ref.* 497
Dr M. Tayan, *ProLife* 393
D. McPherson, *UK Ind.* 113
Lab. majority 3,236
(Boundary change: notional C.)

EDINBURGH CENTRAL
*E.*63,695 *T.* 67.09%
†A. Darling, *Lab.* 20,125
M. Scott-Hayward, *C.* 9,055
Ms F. Hyslop, *SNP* 6,750
Ms K. Utting, *LD* 5,605
Ms L. Hendry, *Green* 607
A. Skinner, *Ref.* 495
M. Benson, *Ind. Dem.* 98
Lab. majority 11,070
(Boundary change: notional Lab.)

EDINBURGH EAST AND
MUSSELBURGH
*E.*59,648 *T.* 70.61%
†Dr G. Strang, *Lab.* 22,564
D. White, *SNP* 8,034
K. Ward, *C.* 6,483
Dr C. MacKellar, *LD* 4,511
J. Sibbet, *Ref.* 526
Lab. majority 14,530
(Boundary change: notional Lab.)

EDINBURGH NORTH AND LEITH
*E.*61,617 *T.* 66.45%
†M. Chisholm, *Lab.* 19,209
Ms A. Dana, *SNP* 8,231
E. Stewart, *C.* 7,312
Ms H. Campbell, *LD* 5,335
A. Graham, *Ref.* 441
G. Brown, *SSA* 320
P. Douglas-Reid, *NLP* 97
Lab. majority 10,978
(Boundary change: notional Lab.)

EDINBURGH PENTLANDS
*E.*59,635 *T.* 76.70%
Ms L. Clark, *Lab.* 19,675
†Rt. Hon. M. Rifkind, *C.* 14,813
S. Gibb, *SNP* 5,952
Dr J. Dawe, *LD* 4,575
M. McDonald, *Ref.* 422
R. Harper, *Green* 224
A. McConnachie, *UK Ind.* 81
Lab. majority 4,862
(Boundary change: notional C.)

EDINBURGH SOUTH
*E.*62,467 *T.* 71.78%
†N. Griffiths, *Lab.* 20,993
Miss E. Smith, *C.* 9,541
M. Pringle, *LD* 7,911
Dr J. Hargreaves, *SNP* 5,791
I. McLean, *Ref.* 504
B. Dunn, *NLP* 98
Lab. majority 11,452
(Boundary change: notional Lab.)

EDINBURGH WEST
*E.*61,133 *T.* 77.91%
D. Gorrie, *LD* 20,578
†Rt. Hon. Lord J. Douglas-
Hamilton, *C.* 13,325
Ms L. Hinds, *Lab.* 8,948
G. Sutherland, *SNP* 4,210
Dr S. Elphick, *Ref.* 277
P. Coombes, *Lib.* 263
A. Jack, *AS* 30
LD majority 7,253
(Boundary change: notional C.)

FALKIRK EAST
*E.*56,792 *T.* 73.24%
†M. Connarty, *Lab.* 23,344
K. Brown, *SNP* 9,959
M. Nicol, *C.* 5,813
R. Spillane, *LD* 2,153
S. Mowbray, *Ref.* 326
Lab. majority 13,385
(Boundary change: notional Lab.)

FALKIRK WEST
*E.*52,850 *T.* 72.60%
†D. Canavan, *Lab.* 22,772
D. Alexander, *SNP* 8,989
Mrs C. Buchanan, *C.* 4,639
D. Houston, *LD* 1,970
Lab. majority 13,783
(Boundary change: notional Lab.)

FIFE CENTRAL
*E.*58,315 *T.* 69.90%
†H. McLeish, *Lab.* 23,912
Mrs P. Marwick, *SNP* 10,199
J. Rees-Mogg, *C.* 3,669
R. Laird, *LD* 2,610
J. Scrymgeour-Wedderburn, *Ref.* 375
Lab. majority 13,713
(Boundary change: notional Lab.)

FIFE NORTH EAST
*E.*58,794 *T.* 71.16%
*M. Campbell, *LD* 21,432
A. Bruce, *C.* 11,076
C. Welsh, *SNP* 4,545
C. Milne, *Lab.* 4,301
W. Stewart, *Ref.* 485
LD majority 10,356
(Boundary change: notional LD)

GALLOWAY AND UPPER
NITHSDALE
*E.*52,751 *T.* 79.65%
A. Morgan, *SNP* 18,449
†Rt. Hon. I. Lang, *C.* 12,825
Ms K. Clark, *Lab.* 6,861
J. McKerchar, *LD* 2,700
R. Wood, *Ind.* 566

A. Kennedy, *Ref.* 428
J. Smith, *UK Ind.* 189
SNP majority 5,624
(Boundary change: notional C.)

GLASGOW ANNIESLAND
*E.*52,955 *T.* 63.98%
†Rt. Hon. D. Dewar, *Lab.* 20,951
Dr W. Wilson, *SNP* 5,797
A. Brocklehurst, *C.* 3,881
C. McGinty, *LD* 2,453
A. Majid, *ProLife* 374
W. Bonnar, *SSA* 229
A. Milligan, *UK Ind.* 86
Ms G. McKay, *Ref.* 84
T. Pringle, *NLP* 24
Lab. majority 15,154
(Boundary change: notional Lab.)

GLASGOW BAILLIESTON
*E.*51,152 *T.* 62.27%
†J. Wray, *Lab.* 20,925
Mrs P. Thomson, *SNP* 6,085
M. Kelly, *C.* 2,468
Ms S. Rainger, *LD* 1,217
J. McVicar, *SSA* 970
J. McClafferty, *Ref.* 188
Lab. majority 14,840
(Boundary change: notional Lab.)

GLASGOW CATHCART
*E.*49,312 *T.* 69.17%
†J. Maxton, *Lab.* 19,158
Ms M. Whitehead, *SNP* 6,913
A. Muir, *C.* 4,248
C. Dick, *LD* 2,302
Ms Z. Indyk, *ProLife* 687
R. Stevenson, *SSA* 458
S. Haldane, *Ref.* 344
Lab. majority 12,245
(Boundary change: notional Lab.)

GLASGOW GOVAN
*E.*49,836 *T.* 64.70%
M. Sarwar, *Lab.* 14,216
Ms N. Sturgeon, *SNP* 11,302
W. Thomas, *C.* 2,839
R. Stewart, *LD* 1,915
A. McCombes, *SSA* 755
P. Paton, *SLU* 325
I. Badar, *SLI* 319
Z. J. Abbasi, *SCU* 221
K. MacDonald, *Ref.* 201
J. White, *BNP* 149
Lab. majority 2,914
(Boundary change: notional Lab.)

GLASGOW KELVIN
*E.*57,438 *T.* 56.85%
†G. Galloway, *Lab.* 16,643
Ms S. White, *SNP* 6,978
Ms E. Buchanan, *LD* 4,629
D. McPhie, *C.* 3,539
A. Green, *SSA* 386
R. Grigor, *Ref.* 282
V. Vanni, *SPGB* 102
G. Stidolph, *NLP* 95
Lab. majority 9,665
(Boundary change: notional Lab.)

GLASGOW MARYHILL
*E.*52,523 *T.* 56.59%
†Ms M. Fyfe, *Lab.* 19,301

J. Wailes, *SNP* 5,037
Ms E. Attwooll, *LD* 2,119
S. Baldwin, *C.* 1,747
Ms L. Blair, *NLP* 651
Ms A. Baker, *SSA* 409
J. Hanif, *ProLife* 344
R. Paterson, *Ref.* 77
S. Johnstone, *SEP* 36
Lab. majority 14,264
(Boundary change: notional Lab.)

GLASGOW POLLOK
*E.*49,284   *T.* 66.56%
†I. Davidson, *Lab. Co-op.* 19,653
D. Logan, *SNP* 5,862
T. Sheridan, *SSA* 3,639
E. Hamilton, *C.* 1,979
D. Jago, *LD* 1,137
Ms M. Gott, *ProLife* 380
D. Haldane, *Ref.* 152
Lab. Co-op. majority 13,791
(Boundary change: notional Lab. Co-op.)

GLASGOW RUTHERGLEN
*E.*50,646   *T.* 70.14%
†T. McAvoy, *Lab. Co-op.* 20,430
I. Gray, *SNP* 5,423
R. Brown, *LD* 5,167
D. Campbell Bannerman, *C.* 3,288
G. Easton, *Ind. Lab.* 812
Ms R. Kane, *SSA* 251
Ms J. Kerr, *Ref.* 150
Lab. Co-op. majority 15,007
(Boundary change: notional Lab. Co-op.)

GLASGOW SHETTLESTON
*E.*47,990   *T.* 55.87%
†D. Marshall, *Lab.* 19,616
H. Hanif, *SNP* 3,748
C. Simpson, *C.* 1,484
Ms K. Hiles, *LD* 1,061
Ms C. McVicar, *SSA* 482
R. Currie, *BNP* 191
T. Montguire, *Ref.* 151
J. Graham, *WRP* 80
Lab. majority 15,868
(Boundary change: notional Lab.)

GLASGOW SPRINGBURN
*E.*53,473   *T.* 59.05%
†M. Martin, *Lab.* 22,534
J. Brady, *SNP* 5,208
M.Holdsworth, *C.* 1,893
J. Alexander, *LD* 1,349
J. Lawson, *SSA* 407
A. Keating, *Ref.* 186
Lab. majority 17,326
(Boundary change: notional Lab.)

GORDON
*E.*58,767   *T.* 71.89%
†M. Bruce, *LD* 17,999
J. Porter, *C.* 11,002
R. Lochhead, *SNP* 8,435
Ms L. Kirkhill, *Lab.* 4,350
F. Pidcock, *Ref.* 459
LD majority 6,997
(Boundary change: notional C.)

GREENOCK AND INVERCLYDE
*E.*48,818   *T.* 71.05%

†Dr N. Godman, *Lab.* 19,480
B. Goodall, *SNP* 6,440
R. Ackland, *LD* 4,791
H. Swire, *C.* 3,976
Lab. majority 13,040
(Boundary change: notional Lab.)

HAMILTON NORTH AND BELLSHILL
*E.*53,607   *T.* 70.88%
†Dr J. Reid, *Lab.* 24,322
M. Matheson, *SNP* 7,255
G. McIntosh, *C.* 3,944
K. Legg, *LD* 1,924
R. Conn, *Ref.* 554
Lab. majority 17,067
(Boundary change: notional Lab.)

HAMILTON SOUTH
*E.*46,562   *T.* 71.07%
†G. Robertson, *Lab.* 21,709
I. Black, *SNP* 5,831
R. Kilgour, *C.* 2,858
R. Pitts, *LD* 1,693
C. Gunn, *ProLife* 684
S. Brown, *Ref.* 316
Lab. majority 15,878
(Boundary change: notional Lab.)
See also page 233

INVERNESS EAST, NAIRN AND LOCHABER
*E.*65,701   *T.* 72.71%
D. Stewart, *Lab.* 16,187
F. Ewing, *SNP* 13,848
S. Gallagher, *LD* 8,364
Mrs M. Scanlon, *C.* 8,355
Ms W. Wall, *Ref.* 436
M. Falconer, *Green* 354
D. Hart, *Ch. U.* 224
Lab. majority 2,339
(Boundary change: notional LD)

KILMARNOCK AND LOUDOUN
*E.*61,376   *T.* 77.24%
D. Browne, *Lab.* 23,621
A. Neil, *SNP* 16,365
D. Taylor, *C.* 5,125
J. Stewart, *LD* 1,891
W. Sneddon, *Ref.* 284
W. Gilmour, *NLP* 123
Lab. majority 7,256
(April 1992, Lab. maj. 6,979)

KIRKCALDY
*E.*52,186   *T.* 67.02%
†L. Moonie, *Lab. Co-op.* 18,730
S. Hosie, *SNP* 8,020
Miss C. Black, *C.* 4,779
J. Mainland, *LD* 3,031
V. Baxter, *Ref.* 413
Lab. Co-op. majority 10,710
(Boundary change: notional Lab. Co-op.)

LINLITHGOW
*E.*53,706   *T.* 73.84%
†T. Dalyell, *Lab.* 21,469
K. MacAskill, *SNP* 10,631
T. Kerr, *C.* 4,964
A. Duncan, *LD* 2,331
K. Plomer, *Ref.* 259

Lab. majority 10,838
(Boundary change: notional Lab.)

LIVINGSTON
*E.*60,296   *T.* 71.04%
†Rt. Hon. R. Cook, *Lab.* 23,510
P. Johnston, *SNP* 11,763
H. Craigie Halkett, *C.* 4,028
E. Hawthorn, *LD* 2,876
Ms H. Campbell, *Ref.* 444
M. Culbert, *SPGB* 213
Lab. majority 11,747
(Boundary change: notional Lab.)

MIDLOTHIAN
*E.*47,552   *T.* 74.13%
†E. Clarke, *Lab.* 18,861
L. Millar, *SNP* 8,991
Miss A. Harper, *C.* 3,842
R. Pinnock, *LD* 3,235
K. Docking, *Ref.* 320
Lab. majority 9,870
(Boundary change: notional Lab.)

MORAY
*E.*58,302   *T.* 68.21%
†Mrs M. Ewing, *SNP* 16,529
A. Findlay, *C.* 10,963
L. Macdonald, *Lab.* 7,886
Ms D. Storr, *LD* 3,548
P. Mieklejohn, *Ref.* 840
SNP majority 5,566
(Boundary change: notional SNP)

MOTHERWELL AND WISHAW
*E.*52,252   *T.* 70.08%
F. Roy, *Lab.* 21,020
J. McGuigan, *SNP* 8,229
S. Dickson, *C.* 4,024
A. Mackie, *LD* 2,331
C. Herriot, *Soc. Lab.* 797
T. Russell, *Ref.* 218
Lab. majority 12,791
(Boundary change: notional Lab.)

OCHIL
*E.*56,572   *T.* 77.40%
†M. O'Neill, *Lab.* 19,707
G. Reid, *SNP* 15,055
A. Hogarth, *C.* 6,383
Mrs A. Watters, *LD* 2,262
D. White, *Ref.* 210
I. McDonald, *D. Nat.* 104
M. Sullivan, *NLP* 65
Lab. majority 4,652
(Boundary change: notional Lab.)

ORKNEY AND SHETLAND
*E.*32,291   *T.* 64.00%
*J. Wallace, *LD* 10,743
J. Paton, *Lab.* 3,775
W. Ross, *SNP* 2,624
H. Vere Anderson, *C.* 2,527
F. Adamson, *Ref.* 820
Ms C. Wharton, *NLP* 116
A. Robertson, *Ind.* 60
LD majority 6,968
(April 1992, LD maj. 5,033)

PAISLEY NORTH
*E.*49,725   *T.* 68.65%
†Mrs I. Adams, *Lab.* 20,295
I. Mackay, *SNP* 7,481
K. Brookes, *C.* 3,267

A. Jelfs, *LD* — 2,365
R. Graham, *ProLife* — 531
E. Mathew, *Ref.* — 196
Lab. majority 12,814
(Boundary change: notional Lab.)

PAISLEY SOUTH
E.54,040   T. 69.12%
†G. McMaster, *Lab. Co-op.* — 21,482
W. Martin, *SNP* — 8,732
Ms E. McCartin, *LD* — 3,500
R. Reid, *C.* — 3,237
J. Lardner, *Ref.* — 254
S. Clerkin, *SSA* — 146
Lab. Co-op. majority 12,750
(Boundary change: notional Lab. Co-op.)
See also page 233

PERTH
E.60,313   T. 73.87%
†Ms R. Cunningham, *SNP* — 16,209
J. Godfrey, *C.* — 13,068
D. Alexander, *Lab.* — 11,036
C. Brodie, *LD* — 3,583
R. MacAuley, *Ref.* — 366
M. Henderson, *UK Ind.* — 289
SNP majority 3,141
(Boundary change: notional C.)

RENFREWSHIRE WEST
E.52,348   T. 76.00%
†T. Graham, *Lab.* — 18,525
C. Campbell, *SNP* — 10,546
C. Cormack, *C.* — 7,387
B. MacPherson, *LD* — 3,045
S. Lindsay, *Ref.* — 283
Lab. majority 7,979
(Boundary change: notional Lab.)

ROSS, SKYE AND INVERNESS WEST
E.55,639   T. 71.81%
†C. Kennedy, *LD* — 15,472
D. Munro, *Lab.* — 11,453
Mrs M. Paterson, *SNP* — 7,821
Miss M. Macleod, *C.* — 4,368
L. Durance, *Ref.* — 535
A. Hopkins, *Green* — 306
LD majority 4,019
(Boundary change: notional LD)

ROXBURGH AND BERWICKSHIRE
E.47,259   T. 73.91%
†A. Kirkwood, *LD* — 16,243
D. Younger, *C.* — 8,337
Ms H. Eadie, *Lab.* — 5,226
M. Balfour, *SNP* — 3,959
J. Curtis, *Ref.* — 922
P. Neilson, *UK Ind.* — 202
D. Lucas, *NLP* — 42
LD majority 7,906
(Boundary change: notional LD)

STIRLING
E.52,491   T. 81.84%
Mrs A. McGuire, *Lab.* — 20,382
†Rt. Hon. M. Forsyth, *C.* — 13,971
E. Dow, *SNP* — 5,752
A. Tough, *LD* — 2,675
W. McMurdo, *UK Ind.* — 154
Ms E. Olsen, *Value Party* — 24
Lab. majority 6,411
(Boundary change: notional C.)

STRATHKELVIN AND BEARSDEN
E.62,974   T. 78.94%
†S. Galbraith, *Lab.* — 26,278

D. Sharpe, *C.* — 9,986
G. McCormick, *SNP* — 8,111
J. Morrison, *LD* — 4,843
D. Wilson, *Ref.* — 339
Ms J. Fisher, *NLP* — 155
Lab. majority 16,292
(Boundary change: notional Lab.)

TAYSIDE NORTH
E.61,398   T. 74.25%
J. Swinney, *SNP* — 20,447
†W. Walker, *C.* — 16,287
I. McFatridge, *Lab.* — 5,141
P. Regent, *LD* — 3,716
SNP majority 4,160
(Boundary change: notional C.)

TWEEDDALE, ETTRICK AND LAUDERDALE
E.50,891   T. 76.64%
M. Moore, *LD* — 12,178
K. Geddes, *Lab.* — 10,689
A. Jack, *C.* — 8,623
I. Goldie, *SNP* — 6,671
C. Mowbray, *Ref.* — 406
J. Hein, *Lib.* — 387
D. Paterson, *NLP* — 47
LD majority 1,489
(Boundary change: notional LD)

WESTERN ISLES
E.22,983   T. 70.08%
*C. Macdonald, *Lab.* — 8,955
Dr A. Lorne Gillies, *SNP* — 5,379
J. McGrigor, *C.* — 1,071
N. Mitchison, *LD* — 495
R. Lionel, *Ref.* — 206

NORTHERN IRELAND

ANTRIM EAST
Lab. majority 3,576
(April 1992, Lab. maj. 1,703)
E.58,963   T. 58.26%
†R. Beggs, *UUP* — 13,318
S. Neeson, *All.* — 6,929
J. McKee, *DUP* — 6,682
T. Dick, *C.* — 2,334
W. Donaldson, *PUP* — 1,757
D. O'Connor, *SDLP* — 1,576
R. Mason, *Ind.* — 1,145
Ms C. McAuley, *SF* — 543
Ms M. McCann, *NLP* — 69
UUP majority 6,389
(Boundary change: notional UUP)

ANTRIM NORTH
E.72,411   T. 63.78%
*Revd I. Paisley, *DUP* — 21,495
J. Leslie, *UUP* — 10,921
S. Farren, *SDLP* — 7,333
J. McCarry, *SF* — 2,896
Dr D. Alderdice, *All.* — 2,845
Ms B. Hinds, *NI Women* — 580
J. Wright, *NLP* — 116
DUP majority 10,574
(April 1992, DUP maj. 14,936)

ANTRIM SOUTH
E.69,414   T. 57.91%
†C. Forsythe, *UUP* — 23,108

D. McClelland, *SDLP* — 6,497
D. Ford, *All.* — 4,668
H. Smyth, *PUP* — 3,490
H. Cushinan, *SF* — 2,229
Ms B. Briggs, *NLP* — 203
UUP majority 16,611
(Boundary change: notional UUP)
See also page 233

BELFAST EAST
E.61,744   T. 63.21%
†P. Robinson, *DUP* — 16,640
R. Empey, *UUP* — 9,886
J. Hendron, *All.* — 9,288
Miss S. Dines, *C.* — 928
D. Corr, *SF* — 810
Mrs P. Lewsley, *SDLP* — 629
D. Dougan, *NIFT* — 541
J. Bell, *WP* — 237
D. Collins, *NLP* — 70
DUP majority 6,754
(Boundary change: notional DUP)

BELFAST NORTH
E.64,577   T. 64.19%
†C. Walker, *UUP* — 21,478
A. Maginness, *SDLP* — 8,454
G. Kelly, *SF* — 8,375
T. Campbell, *All.* — 2,221
P. Emerson, *Green* — 539

P. Treanor, *WP* — 297
Ms A. Gribben, *NLP* — 88
UUP majority 13,024
(Boundary change: notional UUP)

BELFAST SOUTH
E.63,439   T. 62.24%
†Revd M. Smyth, *UUP* — 14,201
Dr A. McDonnell, *SDLP* — 9,601
D. Ervine, *PUP* — 5,687
S. McBride, *All.* — 5,112
S. Hayes, *SF* — 2,019
Ms A. Campbell, *NI Women* — 1,204
Miss M. Boal, *C.* — 962
N. Cusack, *Ind. Lab.* — 292
P. Lynn, *WP* — 286
J. Anderson, *NLP* — 120
UUP majority 4,600
(Boundary change: notional UUP)

BELFAST WEST
E.61,785   T. 74.27%
G. Adams, *SF* — 25,662
†Dr J. Hendron, *SDLP* — 17,753
F. Parkinson, *UUP* — 1,556
J. Lowry, *WP* — 721
L. Kennedy, *HR* — 102
Ms M. Daly, *NLP* — 91
SF majority 7,909
(Boundary change: notional SDLP)

DOWN NORTH
E.63,010   T. 58.03%
†R. McCartney, UKU   12,817
A. McFarland, UUP   11,368
Sir O. Napier, All.   7,554
L. Fee, C.   1,810
Miss M. Farrell, SDLP   1,602
Ms J. Morrice, NI Women   1,240
T. Mullins, NLP   108
R. Mooney, NIP   67
UKU majority 1,449
(Boundary change: notional Popular
Unionist)

DOWN SOUTH
E.69,855   T. 70.84%
†E. McGrady, SDLP   26,181
D. Nesbitt, UUP   16,248
M. Murphy, SF   5,127
J. Crozier, All.   1,711
Ms R. McKeon, NLP   219
SDLP majority 9,933
(Boundary change: notional SDLP)

FERMANAGH AND SOUTH
TYRONE
E.64,600   T. 74.75%
†K. Maginnis, UUP   24,862
G. McHugh, SF   11,174
T. Gallagher, SDLP   11,060
S. Farry, All.   977
S. Gillan, NLP   217
UUP majority 13,688
(Boundary change: notional UUP)

FOYLE
E.67,620   T. 70.71%
†J. Hume, SDLP   25,109
M. McLaughlin, SF   11,445
W. Hay, DUP   10,290
Mrs H.-M. Bell, All.   817

D. Brennan, NLP   154
SDLP majority 13,664
(Boundary change: notional SDLP)

LAGAN VALLEY
E.71,225   T. 62.21%
J. Donaldson, UUP   24,560
S. Close, All.   7,635
E. Poots, DUP   6,005
Ms D. Kelly, SDLP   3,436
S. Sexton, C.   1,212
Ms S. Ramsey, SF   1,110
Ms F. McCarthy, WP   203
H. Finlay, NLP   149
UUP majority 16,925
(Boundary change: notional UUP)

LONDONDERRY EAST
E.58,831   T. 64.77%
†W. Ross, UUP   13,558
G. Campbell, DUP   9,764
A. Doherty, SDLP   8,273
M. O'Kane, SF   3,463
Ms Y. Boyle, All.   2,427
J. Holmes, C.   436
Ms C. Gallen, NLP   100
I. Anderson, Nat. Dem.   81
UUP majority 3,794
(Boundary change: notional UUP)

NEWRY AND ARMAGH
E.70,652   T. 75.40%
†S. Mallon, SDLP   22,904
D. Kennedy, UUP   18,015
P. McNamee, SF   11,218
P. Whitcroft, All.   1,015
D. Evans, NLP   123
SDLP majority 4,889
(Boundary change: notional SDLP)

STRANGFORD
E.69,980   T. 59.47%
†Rt. Hon. J. Taylor, UUP   18,431

Mrs I. Robinson, DUP   12,579
K. McCarthy, All.   5,467
P. O'Reilly, SDLP   2,775
G. Chalk, C.   1,743
G. O Fachtna, SF   503
Mrs S. Mullins, NLP   121
UUP majority 5,852
(Boundary change: notional UUP)

TYRONE WEST
E.58,168   T. 79.55%
W. Thompson, UUP   16,003
J. Byrne, SDLP   14,842
P. Doherty, SF   14,280
Ms A. Gormley, All.   829
T. Owens, WP   230
R. Johnstone, NLP   91
UUP majority 1,161
(Boundary change: notional DUP)

ULSTER MID
E.58,836   T. 86.12%
M. McGuinness, SF   20,294
†Revd W. McCrea, DUP   18,411
D. Haughey, SDLP   11,205
E. Bogues, All.   460
Mrs M. Donnelly, WP   238
Ms M. Murray, NLP   61
SF majority 1,883
(Boundary change: notional DUP)

UPPER BANN
E.70,398   T. 67.88%
*D. Trimble, UUP   20,836
Ms B. Rodgers, SDLP   11,584
Ms B. O'Hagan, SF   5,773
M. Carrick, DUP   5,482
Dr W. Ramsay, All.   3,017
T. French, WP   554
B. Price, C.   433
J. Lyons, NLP   108
UUP majority 9,252
(Boundary change: notional UUP)

Regional Government

GREATER LONDON AUTHORITY (GLA)

Romney House, 43 Marsham Street, London SW1P 3PY
Tel: 020-7983 4000; Press Office: 020-7983 4071/4072/
4090/4067/4228; Email: mayor@london.gov.uk;
Web: http://www.london.gov.uk

On the 7 May 1998, London voted in favour of the formation of the Greater London Authority. The first elections to the GLA were on Thursday, 4 May 2000 and the new Authority took over its responsibilities on 3 July 2000.

The GLA consists of a directly elected mayor, The Mayor of London and a separately elected assembly, The London Assembly. The Mayor has the key role of decision making with the Assembly performing the tasks of regulating and scrutinising these decisions. In addition, the GLA has around 400 permanent staff to support the activities of the Mayor and the Assembly, which are overseen by a Head of Paid Service. The Mayor may appoint two political advisors but he/she may not appoint the Head of Paid Service, the Monitoring Officer or the Chief Finance Officer. These must be appointed by the Assembly. The Mayor is also responsible for appointing a Cabinet.

ELECTIONS

The Assembly will be elected every four years at the same time as the Mayor and consists of 25 members. There is one member from each of the 14 GLA Constituencies topped up with 11 London members who are representatives of political parties or individuals standing as independent candidates.

The GLA constituencies are: Barnet and Camden; Bexley and Bromley; Brent and Harrow; City and London East, covering Barking and Dagenham and the City of London; Newham and Tower Hamlets; Croydon and Sutton; Ealing and Hillingdon; Enfield and Haringey; Greenwich and Lewisham; Havering and Redbridge; North East, covering Hackney, Islington and Waltham Forest; Lambeth and Southwark; West Central, covering Hammersmith and Fulham, Kensington and Chelsea and Westminster; South West, covering Hounslow, Kingston upon Thames and Richmond upon Thames; Merton and Wandsworth.

FUNDING

The GLA is responsible for funding Transport for London, the London Development Agency, the Metropolitan Police Authority and the London Fire and Emergency Planning Authority. Budgets are set by the Mayor, and scrutinised by the Assembly. Funds are allocated subject to safeguards on service standards. The GLA has inherited its funding from the various bodies that it is replacing. This is thought to amount to around £3 billion. The GLA also receives a government grant to cover the cost of the Mayor, Assembly and additional staff. The contribution of the London taxpayer to the cost of the GLA is around £1.70 per person per year, (3p per day).

TRANSPORT FOR LONDON (TfL)

The TfL is run by a board of 8–15 members appointed by the mayor. Its role will be:

- to manage the buses, Croydon Tramlink and the Docklands Light Railway (DLR)
- to manage the underground once Public Private partnership contracts are in place
- to manage an important network of roads to be known as the GLA Road Network
- to regulate taxis and minicabs
- to run the London River services and promote the river for passenger and freight movement
- to help to co-ordinate the Dial-a-Ride and Taxicard schemes for door-to-door services for transport users with mobility problems
- to take responsibility for traffic lights

London Borough Councils will maintain the role of highway and traffic authorities for 95 per cent of London's roads. Bodies such as London Transport and London Underground will be wound up and their powers transferred to TfL.

Transitional Chief Executive, Anthony Mayer.

SPATIAL DEVELOPMENT STRATEGY (SDS)

The Mayor of London is responsible for strategic planning in London in the form of a Spatial Planning Strategy. This sets priorities and provides direction for the future development of London. It replaces regional planning guidance provided by the Secretary of State.

London Borough Councils continue to deal with all planning applications and produce development plans.

LONDON DEVELOPMENT AGENCY (LDA)

The LDA promotes economic development and regeneration. It is one of the eight regional development agencies. The key aspects of the LDA's role are:

- to promote business efficiency, investment and competitiveness
- to promote employment
- to enhance the skills of local people
- to create sustainable development

The London Boroughs retain powers to promote economic development in their local areas.

THE ENVIRONMENT

The Mayor will be required to formulate strategies to tackle London's environmental issues including the quality of water, air and land; the use of energy and London's contribution to climate change targets; ground water levels and traffic emissions; municipal waste management.

METROPOLITAN POLICE AUTHORITY (MPA)

This body, which oversees the policing of London consists of 12 members of the assembly, including the deputy mayor, four magistrates and seven independents. The role of the MPA is:

- to maintain an efficient and effective police force
- to publish an annual policing plan
- to set police targets and monitor performance
- to be part of the appointment, discipline and removal of senior officers
- to be responsible for the performance budget

The boundaries of the metropolitan police districts have been changed to be in line with the 32 London boroughs. Areas beyond the GLA remit have been incorporated into the Surrey, Hertfordshire and Essex police areas. The City of London has its own police force.

LONDON FIRE AND EMERGENCY PLANNING AUTHORITY (LFEPA)

On 3 July 2000, the existing London Fire and Civil Defence Authority became the London Fire and Emergency Planning Authority. It consists of 17 members, 9 will be drawn from the new assembly and eight will be nominated by the London Boroughs. The role of LFEPA will be:

- to set the strategy for the provision of fire services
- to ensure that the fire brigade can meet all the normal requirements efficiently
- to ensure that effective arrangements are made for the fire brigade to receive emergency calls and deal with them promptly
- to ensure that information useful to the development of the fire brigades is gathered
- to assist the boroughs with their emergency planning training and exercises

HEALTH

Healthcare in London continues to be the remit of the NHS and the London Ambulance Service. The NHS London Regional Office are fully supported by the GLA in its development of strategies to improve the health of Londoners.

THE CULTURAL STRATEGY GROUP FOR LONDON (CSGL)

The GLA aims to provide a wide ranging culture strategy, encompassing the arts, sport and tourism. The CSGL provides advice and guidance to the GLA on this matter. It is envisaged that the GLA will:

- produce a strategy for the cultural development of London
- to endorse and bid for major sporting events which London may host
- to develop the creative industries' contribution to the London economy
- to take over management of Trafalgar Square and Parliament Square
- to develop a policy for the development of tourism in London

The GLA will be housed at the temporary address shown above until its new premises are complete. The new GLA building will be built on a brown field site on the south bank of the river Thames, adjacent to Tower Bridge. The building is a distinctive glass globe with a purpose built assembly chamber and offices for 400 people. It will stand fifty metres high, with 21,700 square metres of floor space.

SALARIES *as at July 2000*

Mayor, £86,832*

Assembly Member, £34,438

*Reduced by a third if the Mayor is an MP

MAYOR'S ADVISORY CABINET

Deputy Mayor and Spatial development and strategic planning, Nicky Gavron

Police, Toby Harris

Human rights and equalities, Graham Tope

Chair, London Fire and Emergency Planning Authority, Val Shawcross

Environment, Darren Johnson

City and business, Judith Mayhew

Homelessness, Glenda Jackson

Consultation and local government, John McDonnell

Chair of the London Development Agency, George Barlow

Regeneration, Kumar Murshid

Race relations, Lee Jasper

Women and equality, Diane Abbott

Community relations, Richard Stone

London Voluntary Services Council, Sean Baine

Disability rights, Caroline Gooding

GREATER LONDON ASSEMBLY MEMBERS
as at 31 July 2000

The Mayor, Ken Livingstone, *(Ind.)*

Anderson, Victor *(Green), London List*

Arbour, Anthony *(C.), South West,* maj. 7,059

Barnes, Richard *(C.), Ealing and Hillingdon,* maj. 6,812

Briggs, John *(Lab.), City and East,* maj. 26,121

Bloom, Louise *(LD), London List*

OVERALL RESULTS IN MAYORAL ELECTION *as at May 2000*

First Pref	Party	Votes	%
Ken Livingstone	Ind.	667,877	39.0
Steven Norris	C.	464,434	27.1
Frank Dobson	Lab.	223,884	13.1
Susan Kramer	LD	203,452	11.9
Ram Gidoomal	CPA	42,060	2.4
Darren Johnson	Green	38,121	2.2
Michael Newland	BNP	33,569	2.0
Damian Hockney	UK Ind.	16,234	1.0
Geoffrey Ben-Nathan	PMSS	9,956	0.6
Ashwin Kumar Tanna	Ind.	9,015	0.5
Geoffrey Clements	Natural Law Party	5,470	0.3

Second Pref	Party	Votes	%
Susan Kramer	LD	404,815	28.5
Frank Dobson	Lab.	228,095	16.0
Darren Johnson	Green	192,764	13.6
Steven Norris	C.	188,041	13.2
Ken Livingstone	Ind.	178,809	12.6
Ram Gidoomal	CPA	56,489	4.0
Michael Newland	BNP	45,337	3.2
Damian Hockney	UK Ind.	43,672	3.1
Ashwin Kumar Tanna	Ind.	41,766	2.9
Geoffrey Ben-Nathan	PMSS	23,021	1.6
Geoffrey Clements	Natural Law Party	18,185	1.3

Bray, Angie (C.), *West Central*, maj. 18,279
Coleman, Brian (C.), *Barnet and Camden*, maj. 551
Duvall, Len (*Lab.*), *Greenwich and Lewisham*, maj. 17,985
Evans, Jeremy Roger (C.), *Havering and Redbridge*, maj. 8,269
Featherstone, Lynne (*LD*), *London List*
Gavron, Nicky (*Lab.*), *Enfield and Haringey*, maj. 3,302
Hamwee, Baroness Sally (*LD*), *London List*
Harris, Lord Toby (*Lab.*) *Brent and Harrow*, maj. 4,380
Heath, Samantha (*Lab.*), *London List*
Hillier, Meg (*Lab.*), *North East*, maj. 17,603
Howlett, Elizabeth (C.), *Merton and Wandsworth*, maj. 12,870
Johnson, Darren (*Green*), *London List*
Jones, Jennifer (*Green*), *London List*
*Lammy, David (*Lab.*), *London List*
Neill, Bob (C.), *Bexley and Bromley*, maj. 34,559
Ollerenshaw, Eric (C.), *London List*
Pelling, Andrew John (C.), *Croydon and Sutton*, maj. 17,087
Phillips, Trevor (*Lab.*), *London List*
Shawcross, Valerie (*Lab.*), *Lambeth and Southwark*, maj. 15,493
Tope, Graham (*LD*), *London List*
* David Lammy was elected Member of Parliament for Tottenham following a by-election in June 2000. His status as a member of the Greater London Assembly is unconfirmed at the time of going to press.

THE NATIONAL ASSEMBLY FOR WALES

Cathays Park, Cardiff CF1 3NQ
Tel: 029-2082 5111
National Assembly Information Line: 029-2089 8200
E-mail: webmaster@wales.gov.uk
Web: http://www.wales.gov.uk

In July 1997, the Government announced plans to establish a National Assembly for Wales. In a referendum on 18 September 1997 about 50 per cent of the electorate voted, of whom 50.3 per cent voted in favour of the Assembly. Elections are to be held every four years. The first elections were held on 6 May 1999 when about 46 per cent of the electorate voted.

The first session was held on 10 May 1999 and the Assembly was officially opened on 26 May at Crickhowell House, Cardiff; a new building to house the Assembly is under construction in Cardiff.

The Assembly has 60 members (including the Presiding Officer), comprising 40 constituency members and 20 additional regional members from party lists. It can introduce only secondary legislation and has no power to raise or lower income tax.

The National Assembly for Wales has responsibility in Wales for ministerial functions relating to health and personal social services; education, except for terms and conditions of service and student awards; training; the Welsh language, arts and culture; the implementation of the Citizen's Charter in Wales; local government; housing; water and sewerage; environmental protection; sport; agriculture and fisheries; forestry; land use, including town and country planning and countryside and nature conservation; new towns; non-departmental public bodies and appointments in Wales; ancient monuments and historic buildings and the Welsh Arts Council; roads; tourism; financial assistance to industry; the Strategic Development Scheme in Wales and the Programme for the Valleys; and the operation of the European Regional Development Fund in Wales and other European Union matters.

SALARIES FROM 1 APRIL 2000:

First Secretary	£66,173
Assembly Secretary/Presiding Officer	£34,327
Assembly Members	£35,437*

*Reduced by two-thirds if the member is already an MP or an MEP
First Secretary, Assembly Member and Presiding Officer also receive the Assembly Member salary

THE WELSH CABINET
First Secretary of the Assembly, Rhodri Morgan, MP, AM
Private Secretary, Ms A. Coleman
Special Advisers, P. Griffiths; M. Drakeford; Ms R. Jones; G. Vidler
Secretary for Economic Development, Rhodri Morgan, MP, AM
Secretary for Education Up to Age 16, Rosemary Butler, AM
Secretary for Health and Social Services, Jane Hutt, AM
Secretary for Post-16 Education and Training, Tom Middlehurst, AM
Secretary for Local Government and Housing, Peter Law, AM
Secretary for Agriculture and the Rural Economy, Christine Gwyther, AM
Secretary for the Environment, Planning and Transport, Sue Essex, AM
Trefnydd Manager, Andrew Davies, AM
Finance Secretary, Edwina Hart, AM
Permanent Secretary (G1), J. D. Shortridge
Clerk to the Assembly, J. W. Lloyd, CB

OFFICE OF THE PRESIDING OFFICER
Deputy Clerk (G3), Mrs B. Wilson

COMMITTEE SECRETARIAT
Grade 5, Ms M. Knox

CABINET EXECUTIVE
Head, B. Mitchell

CABINET SECRETARIAT
Grade 5, L. Conway

OFFICE OF THE COUNSEL GENERAL
Counsel General, W. Roddick, QC

COMMUNICATIONS DIRECTORATE
Head, M. Brooke

ESTABLISHMENT GROUP
Director of Personnel (G3), P. Gregory

FINANCE GROUP
Principal Finance Officer (G3), D. T. Richards

ECONOMIC AFFAIRS, TRANSPORT, PLANNING AND ENVIRONMENT
Senior Director (G2), D. W. Jones

AGRICULTURE DEPARTMENT
Head of Department (G3), H. D. Brodie

ECONOMIC DEVELOPMENT DEPARTMENT
Head of Department (G3), D. Pritchard

EUROPEAN AFFAIRS DIVISION
Head, M. Cochlin

SOCIAL POLICY AND LOCAL GOVERNMENT
Senior Director (G2), G. C. G. Craig

TRAINING AND EDUCATION DEPARTMENT
Head of Department (G3), R. J. Davies

OFFICE OF HM CHIEF INSPECTOR FOR SCHOOLS IN WALES – ESTYN
Chief Inspector (G4), Miss S. Lewis

SOCIAL SERVICES AND COMMUNITIES GROUP
Director, Ms H. Thomas

LOCAL GOVERNMENT GROUP
Head of Group (G3), A. Peat

NHS DIRECTORATE
Director (G3), vacant

HEALTH PROTECTION AND IMPROVEMENT DIRECTORATE
Chief Medical Officer (G3), Dr R. Hall

NURSING DIVISION
Chief Nursing Officer, Miss R. Kennedy

TRANSPORT, PLANNING AND ENVIRONMENT GROUP
Head of Group (G3), M. L. Evans

EXECUTIVE AGENCIES

CADW: WELSH HISTORIC MONUMENTS
Crown Building, Cathays Park, Cardiff CF1 3NQ
Tel: 029-2050 0200; Fax: 029-2082 6375

Cadw supports the preservation, conservation, appreciation and enjoyment of the built heritage in Wales.
Chief Executive, T. Cassidy

PLANNING INSPECTORATE
Crown Buildings, Cathays Park, Cardiff CF1 3NQ
Tel: 029-2082 3892; Fax: 029-208 25150

The Inspectorate is a joint executive agency of the Department of the Environment, Transport and the Regions and the National Assembly for Wales.
Chief Executive and Chief Planning Inspector (G3),
C. Shepley

MEMBERS OF THE WELSH ASSEMBLY

Barrett, Ms Lorraine, *Lab. Co-op.*, *Cardiff South and Penarth*, maj. 6,803
Bates, Mick, *LD*, *Montgomeryshire*, maj. 5,504
Black, Peter, *LD*, *South Wales West region*
Bourne, Prof. Nicholas, *C.*, *Wales Mid and West region*
Butler, Ms Rosemary, *Lab.*, *Newport West*, maj. 4,710
Cairns, Alun, *C.*, *South Wales West region*
Chapman, Ms Christine, *Lab. Co-op.*, *Cynon Valley*, maj. 677
Dafis, Cynog G., *MP*, *PC*, *Wales Mid and West region*
Davidson, Ms Jane, *Lab.*, *Pontypridd*, maj. 1,575
Davies, Andrew, *Lab.*, *Swansea West*, maj. 1,926
Davies, David, *C.*, *Monmouth*, maj. 2,712
Davies, Geraint, *PC*, *Rhondda*, maj. 2,285
Davies, Glyn, *C.*, *Wales Mid and West region*
Davies, Ms Janet, *PC*, *South Wales West region*
Davies, Ms Jocelyn, *PC*, *South Wales East region*
Davies, Rt. Hon. Ronald, *MP*, *Lab.*, *Caerphilly*, maj. 2,861
Edwards, Richard, *Lab.*, *Preseli Pembrokeshire*, maj. 2,738
Elis Thomas, Dafydd, *PC*, *Meirionnydd Nant Conwy*, maj. 8,742
Essex, Ms Sue, *Lab.*, *Cardiff North*, maj. 2,304
Evans, Delyth, *Lab.*, *Wales Mid and West region*
Feld, Ms Val, *Lab.*, *Swansea East*, maj. 3,781
German, Michael, *LD*, *South Wales East region*
Gibbons, Brian, *Lab.*, *Aberavon*, maj. 6,743
Graham, William, *C.*, *South Wales East region*
Gregory, Ms Janice, *Lab.*, *Ogmore*, maj. 4,565
Griffiths, John, *Lab. Co-op.*, *Newport East*, maj. 5,111
Gwyther, Ms Christine, *Lab.*, *Carmarthen West and Pembrokeshire South*, maj. 1,492
Halford, Ms Alison, *Lab.*, *Delyn*, maj. 5,417
Hancock, Brian, *PC*, *Islwyn*, maj. 604
Hart, Ms Edwina, *Lab.*, *Gower*, maj. 3,160
Humphreys, Ms Christine, *LD*, *Wales North region*

Hutt, Ms Jane, *Lab.*, *Vale of Glamorgan*, maj. 926
Jarman, Ms Pauline, *PC*, *South Wales Central region*
Jones, Ms Ann, *Lab.*, *Vale of Clwyd*, maj. 3,341
Jones, Carwyn, *Lab.*, *Bridgend*, maj. 4,258
Jones, Elin, *PC*, *Ceredigion*, maj. 10,249
Jones, Gareth, *PC*, *Conwy*, maj. 114
Jones, Ms Helen Mary, *PC*, *Llanelli*, maj. 688
Jones, Ieuan W., *MP*, *PC*, *Ynys Môn*, maj. 9,288
Law, Peter, *Lab. Co-op.*, *Blaenau Gwent*, maj. 10,568
Lewis, Huw, *Lab. Co-op.*, *Merthyr Tydfil and Rhymney*, maj. 4,214
Lloyd, Dr David, *PC*, *South Wales West region*
Marek, John, *MP*, *PH.D.*, *Lab.*, *Wrexham*, maj. 6,472
Melding, David, *C.*, *South Wales Central region*
Middlehurst, Tom, *Lab.*, *Alyn and Deeside*, maj. 6,359
Morgan, H. Rhodri, *MP*, *Lab.*, *Cardiff West*, maj. 10,859
Morgan, Jonathan, *C.*, *South Wales Central region*
Neagle, Ms Lynne, *Lab.*, *Torfaen*, maj. 5,285
Pugh, Alun, *Lab.*, *Clwyd West*, maj. 760
Randerson, Ms Jenny, *LD*, *Cardiff Central*, maj. 3,168
Richards, Rod, *C.*, *Wales North region*
Rogers, Peter, *C.*, *Wales North region*
Ryder, Ms Janet, *PC*, *Wales North region*
Sinclair, Ms Karen, *Lab.*, *Clwyd South*, maj. 3,685
Thomas, Ms Gwenda, *Lab.*, *Neath*, maj. 2,618
Thomas, Owen John, *PC*, *South Wales Central region*
Thomas, Rhodri, *PC*, *Carmarthen East and Dinefwr*, maj. 6,980
Wigley, Rt. Hon. Dafydd, *MP*, *PC*, *Caernarfon*, maj. 12,273
Williams, Ms Kirsty, *LD*, *Brecon and Radnorshire*, maj. 5,852
Williams, Dr Phil, *PC*, *South Wales East region*

STATE OF THE PARTIES *as at May 2000*

	Constituency AMs	Regional AMs	Total
Labour	27	1	28
Plaid Cymru	8†	8	16†
Conservative	1	8	9
Liberal Democrats	3	3	6
The Presiding Officer	1	0	1
(The Lord Elis-Thomas)			

†Excludes the Presiding Officer, who has no party allegiance while in post

Welsh Assembly AS AT MAY 2000

CONSTITUENCIES

ABERAVON (S. WALES WEST)
E. 49,786   *T.* 46.79%

B. Gibbons, *Lab.*	11,941
Ms J. Davies, *PC*	5,198
K. Davies, *LD*	3,165
Ms M. E. Davies, *C.*	1,624
Beany, *Bean*	849
D. Pudner, *United Soc.*	517

Lab. majority 6,743

ALYN AND DEESIDE (WALES N.)
E. 59,386   *T.* 32.04%

T. Middlehurst, *Lab.*	9,772
N. Formstone, *C.*	3,413
Ms A. Owen, *PC*	2,304
J. Clarke, *LD*	1,879
J. Cooksey, *Ind.*	1,333
G. Davies, *Comm.*	329

Lab. majority 6,359

BLAENAU GWENT (S. WALES EAST)
E. 53,919   *T.* 48.21%

P. Law, *Lab. Co-op.*	16,069
P. Williams, *PC*	5,501
K. Rogers, *LD*	2,980
D. Thomas, *C.*	1,444

Lab. Co-op. majority 10,568

BRECON AND RADNORSHIRE (WALES MID AND W.)
E. 51,166   *T.* 57.10%

Ms K. Williams, *LD*	13,022
N. Bourne, *C.*	7,170
I. Janes, *Lab. Co-op.*	5,165
D. Patterson, *PC*	2,356
M. Shaw, *Ind.*	1,502

LD majority 5,852

BRIDGEND (S. WALES WEST)
E. 60,234   *T.* 41.56%

C. Jones, *Lab.*	9,321
A. Cairns, *C.*	5,063
J. Canning, *PC*	4,919
R. Humphreys, *LD*	3,910
A. Jones, *Ind.*	1,819

Lab. majority 4,258

CAERNARFON (WALES N.)
E. 47,213   *T.* 60.32%

D. Wigley, *PC*	18,748
T. Jones, *Lab.*	6,475
Ms B. Naish, *C.*	2,464
D. Shankland, *LD*	791

PC majority 12,273

CAERPHILLY (S. WALES EAST)
E. 65,997   *T.* 43.20%

R. Davies, *Lab.*	12,602
R. Gough, *PC*	9,741
M. German, *LD*	3,543
Ms M. Taylor, *C.*	2,213
T. Richards, *United Soc.*	412

Lab. majority 2,861

CARDIFF CENTRAL (S. WALES CENTRAL)
E. 57,815   *T.* 44.75%

Ms J. Randerson, *LD*	10,937
M. Drakeford, *Lab.*	7,769
O. J. Thomas, *PC*	3,795
S. Jones, *C.*	3,034
J. Goss, *United Soc.*	338

LD majority 3,168

CARDIFF NORTH (S. WALES CENTRAL)
E. 61,398   *T.* 51.33%

Ms S. Essex, *Lab.*	12,198
J. Morgan, *C.*	9,894
A. Meikle, *LD*	5,088
C. Mann, *PC*	4,337

Lab. majority 2,304

CARDIFF SOUTH AND PENARTH (S. WALES CENTRAL)
E. 61,149   *T.* 37.67%

Ms L. Barrett, *Lab. Co-op.*	11,057
Ms M. Davies, *C.*	4,254
J. Rowlands, *PC*	3,931
Ms J. Maw-Cornish, *LD*	2,890
D. Bartlett, *United Soc.*	355
J. Foreman, *Ind. Lab.*	339
T. Davies, *Celtic All.*	210

Lab. Co-op. majority 6,803

CARDIFF WEST (S. WALES CENTRAL)
E. 57,717   *T.* 40.22%

R. Morgan, *Lab.*	14,305
Ms M. Boult, *C.*	3,446
Ms E. Bush, *PC*	3,402
D. Garrow-Smith, *LD*	2,063

Lab. majority 10,859

CARMARTHEN EAST AND DINEFWR (WALES MID AND W.)
E. 53,634   *T.* 60.88%

R. Thomas, *PC*	17,328
C. Llewellyn, *Lab.*	10,348
Ms H. Stoddart, *C.*	2,776
Ms J. Hughes, *LD*	2,202

PC majority 6,980

CARMARTHEN WEST AND PEMBROKESHIRE SOUTH (WALES MID AND W.)
E. 55,655   *T.* 50.58%

Ms C. Gwyther, *Lab.*	9,891
R. Llewellyn, *PC*	8,399
D. Edwards, *C.*	5,079
E. Davies, *Ind.*	2,090
R. Williams, *LD*	1,875
G. Fry, *TFPW*	815

Lab. majority 1,492

CEREDIGION (WALES MID AND W.)
E. 55,311   *T.* 57.67%

E. Jones, *PC*	15,258
Ms M. Battle, *Lab.*	5,009
D. Lloyd Evans, *Ind.*	4,114
D. Evans, *LD*	3,571
H. Lloyd Davies, *C.*	2,944
D. Bradney, *Green*	1,002

PC majority 10,249

CLWYD SOUTH (WALES N.)
E. 53,843   *T.* 40.51%

Ms K. Sinclair, *Lab.*	9,196
H. Williams, *PC*	5,511
D. R. Jones, *C.*	4,167
D. Burnham, *LD*	2,432
M. Jones, *United Soc.*	508

Lab. majority 3,685

CLWYD WEST (WALES N.)
E. 53,952   *T.* 46.77%

A. Pugh, *Lab.*	7,824
R. Richards, *C.*	7,064
Ms E. Williams, *PC*	6,886
Ms R. Feeley, *LD*	3,462

Lab. majority 760

CONWY (WALES N.)
E. 55,189   *T.* 49.11%

G. Jones, *PC*	8,285
Ms C. Sherrington, *Lab.*	8,171
D. I. Jones, *C.*	5,006
Ms C. Humphreys, *LD*	4,480
G. Edwards, *Ind.*	1,160

PC majority 114

CYNON VALLEY (S. WALES CENTRAL)
E. 47,619   *T.* 45.50%

Ms C. Chapman, *Lab. Co-op.*	9,883
P. Richards, *PC*	9,206
Ms A. Willott, *LD*	1,531
E. Hayward, *C.*	1,046

Lab. Co-op. majority 677

DELYN (WALES N.)
E. 54,047   T. 44.13%
Ms A. Halford, *Lab.*	10,672
Ms K. Lumley, *C.*	5,255
Ms M. Ellis, *PC*	4,837
Ms E. Burnham, *LD*	3,089

Lab. majority 5,417

GOWER (S. WALES WEST)
E. 58,523   T. 47.33%
Ms E. Hart, *Lab.*	9,813
D. Jones, *PC*	6,653
A. Jones, *C.*	3,912
H. Evans, *LD*	3,260
R. Lewis, *Ind.*	2,307
I. Richard, *PRP*	1,755

Lab. majority 3,160

ISLWYN (S. WALES EAST)
E. 50,600   T. 47.29%
B. Hancock, *PC*	10,042
S. Williams, *Lab.*	9,438
Ms C. Bennett, *LD*	2,351
C. Stevens, *C.*	1,621
I. Thomas, *United Soc.*	475

PC majority 604

LLANELLI (WALES MID AND W.)
E. 58,371   T. 48.63%
Ms H. M. Jones, *PC*	11,973
Ms A. Garrard, *Lab. Co-op.*	11,285
T. Dumper, *LD*	2,920
B. Harding, *C.*	1,864
A. Popham, *Ind.*	345

PC majority 688

MEIRIONNYDD NANT CONWY (WALES MID AND W.)
E. 32,922   T. 57.33%
D. Elis Thomas, *PC*	12,034
Ms D. Jones, *Lab.*	3,292
O. J. Williams, *C.*	2,170
G. Worley, *LD*	1,378

PC majority 8,742

MERTHYR TYDFIL AND RHYMNEY (S. WALES EAST)
E. 55,858   T. 44.91%
H. Lewis, *Lab. Co-op.*	11,024
A. Cox, *PC*	6,810
A. Rogers, *Ind.*	3,746
E. Jones, *LD*	1,682
Ms C. Hyde, *C.*	1,246
M. Jenkins, *United Soc.*	580

Lab. Co-op. majority 4,214

MONMOUTH (S. WALES EAST)
E. 61,999   T. 51.13%
D. Davies, *C.*	12,950
Ms C. Short, *Lab.*	10,238
C. Lines, *LD*	4,639
M. Hubbard, *PC*	1,964
A. Carrington, *TFPW*	1,911

C. majority 2,712

MONTGOMERYSHIRE (WALES MID AND W.)
E. 43,386   T. 49.41%
M. Bates, *LD*	10,374
G. Davies, *C.*	4,870
D. Senior, *PC*	3,554
C. Hewitt, *Lab.*	2,638

LD majority 5,504

NEATH (S. WALES WEST)
E. 56,085   T. 47.95%
Ms G. Thomas, *Lab.*	12,234
T. Jones, *PC*	9,616
D. Davies, *LD*	2,631
Ms J. Chambers, *C.*	1,895
N. Duncan, *United Soc.*	519

Lab. majority 2,618

NEWPORT EAST (S. WALES EAST)
E. 54,196   T. 35.45%
J. Griffiths, *Lab. Co-op.*	9,497
M. Major, *C.*	4,386
A. Cameron, *LD*	2,684
C. Holland, *PC*	2,647

Lab. Co-op. majority 5,111

NEWPORT WEST (S. WALES EAST)
E. 57,243   T. 42.34%
Ms R. Butler, *Lab.*	11,538
W. Graham, *C.*	6,828
R. Vickery, *PC*	3,053
Ms V. Watkins, *LD*	2,820

Lab. majority 4,710

OGMORE (S. WALES WEST)
E. 51,998   T. 41.54%
Ms J. Gregory, *Lab.*	10,407
J. Rogers, *PC*	5,842
R. Hughes, *Ind.*	2,439
Ms S. Waye, *LD*	1,496
C. Smart, *C.*	1,415

Lab. majority 4,565

PONTYPRIDD (S. WALES CENTRAL)
E. 64,597   T. 45.71%
Ms J. Davidson, *Lab.*	11,330
B. Hancock, *PC*	9,755
G. Orsi, *LD*	5,240
Ms S. Ingerfield, *C.*	2,485
P. Phillips, *Ind.*	436
R. Griffiths, *Comm.*	280

Lab. majority 1,575

PRESELI PEMBROKESHIRE (WALES MID AND W.)
E. 54,225   T. 53.63%
R. Edwards, *Lab.*	9,977
C. Bryant, *PC*	7,239
F. Aubel, *C.*	6,585
D. Lloyd, *LD*	3,338
A. Luke, *Ind.*	1,944

Lab. majority 2,738

RHONDDA (S. WALES CENTRAL)
E. 55,398   T. 50.22%
G. Davies, *PC*	13,558
W. David, *Lab.*	11,273
M. Williams, *LD*	1,303
G. Summers, *Ind.*	913
P. Hobbins, *C.*	774

PC majority 2,285

SWANSEA EAST (S. WALES WEST)
E. 57,766   T. 36.07%
Ms V. Feld, *Lab.*	9,495
J. Ball, *PC*	5,714
P. Black, *LD*	3,963
W. Hughes, *C.*	1,663

Lab. majority 3,781

SWANSEA WEST (S. WALES WEST)
E. 59,369   T. 39.97%

A. Davies, *Lab.*	8,217
D. Lloyd, *PC*	6,291
P. Valerio, *C.*	3,643
J. Newbury, *LD*	3,543
D. Evans, *Ind.*	996
J. Harris, *PRP*	774
A. Thraves, *United Soc.*	263

Lab. majority 1,926

TORFAEN (S. WALES EAST)
E. 61,037   T. 39.19%

Ms L. Neagle, *Lab.*	9,080
M. Gough, *Ind. Lab.*	3,795
Ms I. Nutt, *Ind.*	2,828
N. Turner, *PC*	2,614
Ms J. Gray, *LD*	2,614
Ms K. Thomas, *C.*	2,152
S. Smith, *Local Soc.*	839

Lab. majority 5,285

VALE OF CLWYD (WALES N.)
E. 51,124   T. 43.43%

Ms A. Jones, *Lab.*	8,359
R. Salisbury, *C.*	5,018
Ms S. Brynach, *PC*	4,295
G. Clague, *Dem. All.*	1,908
P. Lloyd, *LD*	1,376
D. Roberts, *Ind.*	661
D. Pennant, *Ind.*	586

Lab. majority 3,341

VALE OF GLAMORGAN (S. WALES CENTRAL)
E. 67,804   T. 48.31%

Ms J. Hutt, *Lab.*	11,448
D. Melding, *C.*	10,522
C. Franks, *PC*	7,848
F. Little, *LD*	2,938

Lab. majority 926

WREXHAM (WALES N.)
E. 50,932   T. 34.19%

J. Marek, *Lab.*	9,239
Ms C. O'Toole, *LD*	2,767
Ms F. Elphick, *C.*	2,747
Ms J. Ryder, *PC*	2,659

Lab. majority 6,472

YNYS MON (WALES N.)
E. 52,571   T. 59.56%

I. W. Jones, *PC*	16,469
A. Owen, *Lab.*	7,181
P. Rogers, *C.*	6,031
J. Clarke, *LD*	1,630

PC majority 9,288

REGIONS

SOUTH WALES CENTRAL
E. 473,494   T. 45.51%

Lab.	79,564 (36.92%)
PC	58,080 (26.95%)
C.	34,944 (16.22%)
LD	30,911 (14.35%)
Green	5,336 (2.48%)
Soc.Lab.	2,822 (1.31%)
Ind. Matt.	1,524 (0.71%)
NLP	665 (0.31%)
Comm.	652 (0.30%)
United Soc.	602 (0.28%)
Ind. Phill.	378 (0.18%)

Lab. majority 21,484
(May 1997, Lab. maj. 131,398)

Additional Members elected: J. Morgan, *C.*;
  D. Melding, *C.*; Ms P. Jarman, *PC*; O. J. Thomas, *PC*

SOUTH WALES EAST
E. 460,846   T. 43.95%

Lab.	83,953 (41.45%)
PC	49,139 (24.26%)
C.	33,947 (16.76%)
LD	24,757 (12.22%)
Soc. Lab.	4,879 (2.41%)
Green	4,055 (2.00%)
United Soc.	903 (0.45%)
NLP	898 (0.44%)

Lab. majority 34,814
(May 1997, Lab. maj. 163,134)
Additional Members elected: W. Graham, *C.*;
  M. German, *LD*; Ms J. Davies, *PC*; Dr P. Williams, *PC*

SOUTH WALES WEST
E. 393,758   T. 42.44%

Lab.	70,625 (42.26%)
PC	50,757 (30.37%)
C.	20,993 (12.56%)
LD	18,527 (11.09%)
Green	4,082 (2.44%)
United Soc.	1,257 (0.75%)
NLP	676 (0.40%)
PRP	204 (0.12%)

Lab. majority 19,868
(May 1997, Lab. maj. 142,286)
Additional Members elected: A. Cairns, *C.*; P. Black, *LD*;
  Dr D. Lloyd, *PC*; Ms J. Davies, *PC*

WALES MID AND WEST
E. 404,667   T. 54.21%

PC	84,554 (38.55%)
Lab.	53,842 (24.55%)
C.	36,622 (16.70%)
LD	31,683 (14.44%)
Green	7,718 (3.52%)
Soc. Lab.	3,019 (1.38%)
Ind. Turner	1,214 (0.55%)
NLP	705 (0.32%)

PC majority 30,712
(May 1997, Lab. maj. 52,382)
Additional Members elected: G. Davies, *C.*;
  Prof. N. Bourne, *C.*; *A. Michael, *Lab.*; C. Dafis, *PC*
*A. Michael resigned in March 2000. Replaced by D. Evans,
  see members list, page 272

WALES NORTH
E. 478,252   T. 45.06%

Lab.	73,673 (34.19%)
PC	69,518 (32.26%)
C.	41,700 (19.35%)
LD	22,130 (10.27%)
Green	4,667 (2.17%)
Rhuddlan	1,353 (0.63%)
NLP	917 (0.43%)
United Soc.	828 (0.38%)
Comm.	714 (0.33%)

Lab. majority 4,155
(May 1997, Lab. maj. 80,590)
Additional Members elected: P. Rogers, *C.*; R. Richards,
  C.; Ms C. Humphreys, *LD*; Ms J. Ryder, *PC*

THE SCOTTISH PARLIAMENT
Edinburgh EH99 1SP. Tel: 0131-348 5000;
Web http://www.scotland.gov.uk

In July 1997, the Government announced plans to establish a Scottish Parliament. In a referendum on 11 September 1997 about 62 per cent of the electorate voted, of whom 74.3 per cent voted in favour of the Parliament and 63.5 in favour of its having tax-raising powers. Elections are to be held every four years. The first elections were held on 6 May 1999 when about 59 per cent of the electorate voted. The first session was held on 12 May 1999 and the Scottish Parliament was officially opened on 1 July 1999 at the Edinburgh Assembly Hall; a new building to house the Parliament is under construction in Edinburgh.

The Scottish Parliament has 129 members (including the Presiding Officer), comprising 73 constituency members and 56 additional regional members from party lists. It can introduce primary legislation and has the power to raise or lower the basic rate of income tax by up to three pence in the pound.

The Scottish Parliament is responsible for: education; health; law; environment; economic development; local government; housing; police; fire services; planning; financial assistance to industry; tourism; some transport; heritage and the arts; agriculture; forestry; food standards.

SALARIES FROM 1 APRIL 2000:

First Minister	£66,173*
Ministers	£34,326*
Lord Advocate	£86,103
Solicitor-General for Scotland	£73,684
Junior Ministers	£17,807*
MSPs	£41,255†
Presiding Officer	£34,326*
Deputy Presiding Officers	£17,807*

*In addition to the MSP salary
†Reduced by two-thirds (to £13,364) if the member is already an MP or an MEP

THE SCOTTISH EXECUTIVE
St Andrew's House, Regent Road,
Edinburgh EH1 3DG. Tel: 0131-556 8400; E-mail: ceu
@scotland.gov.uk; Web: http://www.scotland.gov.uk

The Scottish Executive is responsible in Scotland for all matters not reserved to Westminster under devolution, including education, health, social work, law and order, agriculture and the environment.

In addition there are a number of Scottish departments for which the Executive has some degree of responsibility; these include the Scottish Courts Administration, the General Register Office, the National Archives of Scotland (formerly the Scottish Record Office) and the Department of the Registers of Scotland.

First Minister, The Rt. Hon. Donald Dewar, MP, MSP (Lab.)
Deputy First Minister and Minister for Justice, Jim Wallace, QC, MP, MSP (LD)
Finance Minister, Jack McConnell, MSP (Lab.)
Minister for Health and Community Care, Susan Deacon, MSP (Lab.)
Minister for Communities, Wendy Alexander, MSP (Lab.)
Minister for Transport and the Environment, Sarah Boyack, MSP (Lab.)
Minister for Enterprise and Lifelong Learning, Henry McLeish, MP, MSP (Lab.)
Minister for Rural Affairs, Ross Finnie, MSP (LD)

Minister for Education and Children, Sam Galbraith, MP, MSP (Lab.)
Minister for Parliament and Chief Whip, Tom McCabe, MSP (Lab.)
Lord Advocate, Colin Boyd, QC
Solicitor-General, Neil Davidson, QC

JUNIOR MINISTERS (NOT MEMBERS OF THE SCOTTISH EXECUTIVE)

Deputy Minister for Justice, Angus Mackay, MSP
Deputy Minister for Community Care, Iain Gray, MSP
Deputy Minister for Local Government, Frank McAveety, MSP
Deputy Minister for Social Inclusion, Equality and the Voluntary Sector, Jackie Baillie, MSP
Deputy Minister for Enterprise and Lifelong Learning, Nicol Stephen, MSP
Deputy Minister for Highlands and Islands and Gaelic, Alasdair Morrison, MSP
Deputy Minister for Fisheries, John Home Robertson, MSP
Deputy Minister for Culture and Sport, Rhona Brankin, MSP
Deputy Minister for Children and Education, Peter Peacock, MSP
Deputy Minister for Parliament and Whip, Iain Smith, MSP

SCOTTISH EXECUTIVE CORPORATE SERVICES
16 Waterloo Place, Edinburgh EH1 3DN
Tel: 0131-556 8400
Principal Establishment Officer (SCS), Mrs A. Robson

DIRECTORATE OF ADMINISTRATIVE SERVICES
Saughton House, Broomhouse Drive,
Edinburgh EH11 3DX
Tel: 0131-556 8400

SCOTTISH EXECUTIVE FINANCE
Victoria Quay, Edinburgh EH6 6QQ
Tel: 0131-556 8400
Principal Finance Officer (SCS), Dr P. S. Collings

SCOTTISH EXECUTIVE SECRETARIAT
St Andrew's House, Regent Road, Edinburgh EH1 3DG
Tel: 0131-5568400
Head of Secretariat, R. S. B. Gordon

SCOTTISH EXECUTIVE POLICY UNIT
Head of Unit (SCS), P. J. Rycroft

SCOTTISH EXECUTIVE INFORMATION DIRECTORATE
Head of Information Directorate (SCS), R. Williams

SOLICITOR'S OFFICE
For the Scottish Executive
Solicitor (SCS), R. M. Henderson

SCOTTISH EXECUTIVE RURAL AFFAIRS DEPARTMENT
Pentland House, 47 Robb's Loan, Edinburgh EH14 1TY
Tel: 0131-5568400
Head of Department (SCS), J. S. Graham

EXECUTIVE AGENCIES

FISHERIES RESEARCH SERVICES
Marine Laboratory, PO Box 101, Victoria Road,
Aberdeen AB11 9DB
Tel: 01224-876544; Fax: 01224-295511

SCOTTISH AGRICULTURAL SCIENCE AGENCY
82 Craigs Road, East Craig, Edinburgh EH12 8NJ
Tel: 0131-244 8890; Fax: 0131-244 8988

SCOTTISH FISHERIES PROTECTION AGENCY
Pentland House, 47 Robb's Loan, Edinburgh EH14 1TY
Tel: 0131-556 8400; Fax: 0131-244 6086
Chief Executive, Capt. P. Du Vivier, RN

SCOTTISH EXECUTIVE DEVELOPMENT
DEPARTMENT
Victoria Quay, Edinburgh EH6 6QQ
Tel: 0131-556 8400
Head of Department (SCS), K. MacKenzie, CB

INQUIRY REPORTERS
2 Greenside Lane, Edinburgh EH1 3AG
Tel: 0131-2445649
Chief Reporter (SCS), R. M. Hickman

TRUNK ROADS DESIGN AND CONSTRUCTION DIVISION
Victoria Quay, Edinburgh EH6 6QQ
Tel: 0131-556 8400
Chief Engineers (SCS), J. A. Howison (*Roads*);
  N. B. MacKenzie (*Bridges*)

SCOTTISH EXECUTIVE EDUCATION
DEPARTMENT
Victoria Quay, Edinburgh EH6 6QQTel: 0131-556 8400
Secretary (SCS), J. Elvidge

HM INSPECTORS OF SCHOOLS
Senior Chief Inspector (SCS), D. A. Osler

EXECUTIVE AGENCIES

HISTORIC SCOTLAND
Longmore House, Salisbury Place, Edinburgh EH9 1SH
Tel: 0131-668 8600; Fax: 0131-668 8699

SCOTTISH PUBLIC PENSIONS AGENCY
St Margaret's House, 151 London Road,
Edinburgh EH8 7TG
Tel: 0131-556 8400; Fax: 0131-244 3334

SCOTTISH EXECUTIVE ENTERPRISE AND
LIFELONG LEARNING DEPARTMENT
Meridian Court, 5 Cadogan Street, Glasgow G2 6AT
Tel: 0141-248 2855
Secretary (SCS), E. Frizzell

ECONOMIC DEVELOPMENT, ADVICE AND EMPLOYMENT
ISSUES
Under-Secretary (SCS), M. B. Foulis

ENTERPRISE AND INDUSTRIAL EXPANSION
Meridian Court, 5 Cadogan Street, Glasgow G2 6AT
Tel: 0141-248 2855
Under-Secretary (SCS), S. Hampson

LIFELONG LEARNING GROUP
Europa House, 450 Argyle Street, Glasgow G2 8LG
Tel: 0141-248 2855
Under Secretary (SCS), E. J. Weeple

LOCATE IN SCOTLAND
120 Bothwell Street, Glasgow G2 7JP
Tel: 0141-248 2700
Director (SCS), M. Togneri

SCOTTISH TRADE INTERNATIONAL
120 Bothwell Street, Glasgow G2 7JP
Tel: 0141-248 2700
Director, D. Taylor

EXECUTIVE AGENCY

STUDENT AWARDS AGENCY FOR SCOTLAND
Gyleview House, 3 Redheughs Rigg,
Edinburgh EH12 9HH
Tel: 0131-476 8212; Fax: 0131-244 5887
Chief Executive, K. MacRae

SCOTTISH EXECUTIVE HEALTH
DEPARTMENT
St Andrew's House, Edinburgh EH1 3DG
Tel: 0131-5568400

NATIONAL HEALTH SERVICE IN SCOTLAND
MANAGEMENT EXECUTIVE
Acting Chief Executive (SCS), Prof. Sir David Carter,
FRCSE, FRCS Glas, FRCPE

HEALTH POLICY UNIT
Head of Unit (SCS), G. Robson

STATE HOSPITAL
Carstairs Junction, Lanark ML11 8RP
Tel: 01555-840293
Chairman, D. N. James

COMMON SERVICES AGENCY
Trinity Park House, South Trinity Road,
Edinburgh EH5 3SE
Tel: 0131-552 6255
Chairman, G. R. Scaife, CB
General Manager, Dr F. Gibb

SCOTTISH EXECUTIVE JUSTICE
DEPARTMENT
Saughton House, Broomhouse Drive,
Edinburgh EH11 3XD
Tel: 0131-556 8400
Secretary (SCS), J. Gallagher

SOCIAL WORK AND SERVICES GROUP AND
INSPECTORATE
James Craig Walk, Edinburgh EH1 3BA
Tel: 0131-556 8400
Under Secretary (SCS), Mrs G. M. Stewart

OFFICE OF THE SCOTTISH
PARLIAMENTARY COUNSEL
Victoria Quay, Edinburgh EH6 6QQ
Tel: 0131-556 8400
First Scottish Parliamentary Counsel, J. C. McCluskie,
  CB, QC

PRIVATE LEGISLATION OFFICE UNDER
THE PRIVATE LEGISLATION PROCEDURE
(SCOTLAND) ACT 1936
50 Frederick Street, Edinburgh EH2 1EN
Tel: 0131-226 6499
Senior Counsel, G. S. Douglas, QC

EXECUTIVE AGENCIES

NATIONAL ARCHIVES OF SCOTLAND

REGISTERS OF SCOTLAND

SCOTTISH PRISON SERVICE

GENERAL REGISTER OFFICE FOR SCOTLAND
New Register House, Edinburgh EH1 3YT
Tel: 0131-334 0380; Fax: 0131-314 4400;
Web http://www.gro-scotland.gov.uk
Registrar-General (SCS), J. N. Randall

MENTAL WELFARE COMMISSION FOR
SCOTLAND
K Floor, Argyle House, 3 Lady Lawson Street,
Edinburgh EH3 9SH
Tel: 0131-222 6111
Chairman, I. J. Reid, OBE
Director, Dr J. A. T. Dyer

MEMBERS OF THE SCOTTISH PARLIAMENT

Adam, Brian, SNP, Scotland North East region
Aitken, William, C., Glasgow region
Alexander, Ms Wendy, Lab., Paisley North, maj. 4,616
Baillie, Ms Jackie, Lab., Dumbarton, maj. 4,758
Barrie, Scott, Lab., Dunfermline West, maj. 5,021
Boyack, Ms Sarah, Lab., Edinburgh Central, maj. 4,626
Brankin, Ms Rhona, Lab. Co-op., Midlothian, maj. 5,525
Brown, Robert, LD, Glasgow region
Campbell, Colin, SNP, Scotland West region
Canavan, Dennis A., MP, Lab., Falkirk West, maj. 12,192
Chisholm, Malcolm G. R., MP, Lab., Edinburgh North and
  Leith, maj. 7,736
Craigie, Ms Cathy, Lab., Cumbernauld and Kilsyth,
  maj. 4,259
Crawford, Bruce, SNP, Scotland Mid and Fife region
Cunningham, Ms Roseanna, MP, SNP, Perth, maj. 2,027
Curran, Ms Margaret, Lab., Glasgow Baillieston, maj. 3,072
Davidson, David, C., Scotland North East region
Deacon, Ms Susan, Lab., Edinburgh East and Musselburgh,
  maj. 6,714
Dewar, Rt. Hon. Donald C., MP, Lab., Glasgow Anniesland,
  maj. 10,993
Selkirk of Douglas, The Lord, PC, QC, C., Lothians region
Eadie, Ms Helen, Lab. Co-op., Dunfermline East, maj. 8,699
Elder, Ms Dorothy, SNP, Glasgow region
Ewing, Fergus, SNP, Inverness East, Nairn and Lochaber,
  maj. 441
Ewing, Mrs Margaret A., MP, SNP, Moray, maj. 4,129
Ewing, Dr Winnifred, SNP, Highlands and Islands region
Fabiani, Ms Linda, SNP, Scotland Central region
Farquhar-Munro, John, LD, Ross, Skye and Inverness West,
  maj. 1,539
Ferguson, Ms Patricia, Lab., Glasgow Maryhill, maj. 4,326
Fergusson, Alex, C., Scotland South region
Finnie, Ross, LD, Scotland West region
Galbraith, Samuel L., MP, Lab., Strathkelvin and Bearsden,
  maj. 12,121
Gallie, Phil, C., Scotland South region
Gibson, Kenneth, SNP, Glasgow region
Gillon, Ms Karen, Lab., Clydesdale, maj. 3,880 (elected as
  Karen Turnbull)
Godman, Ms Patricia, Lab., Renfrewshire West, maj. 2,893
Goldie, Miss Annabel, C., Scotland West region
Gorrie, Donald C. E., MP, OBE, LD, Scotland Central region
Grahame, Ms Christine, SNP, Scotland South region (elected
  as Christine Creech)
Grant, Ms Rhoda, Lab., Highlands and Islands region
Gray, Iain, Lab., Edinburgh Pentlands, maj. 2,885
Hamilton, Duncan, SNP, Highlands and Islands region
Harding, Keith, C., Scotland Mid and Fife region
Harper, Robin, Green, Lothians region
Henry, Hugh, Lab., Paisley South, maj. 4,495
Home Robertson, John D., MP, Lab., East Lothian,
  maj. 10,946
Hughes, Ms Janice, Lab., Glasgow Rutherglen, maj. 7,287
Hyslop, Ms Fiona, SNP, Lothians region
Ingram, Adam, SNP, Scotland South region
Jackson, Gordon, QC, Lab., Glasgow Govan, maj. 1,756
Jackson, Dr Sylvia, Lab., Stirling, maj. 3,981
Jamieson, Ms Cathy, Lab. Co-op., Carrick, Cumnock and
  Doon Valley, maj. 8,803
Jamieson, Ms Margaret, Lab., Kilmarnock and Loudoun,
  maj. 2,760
Jenkins, Ian, LD, Tweeddale, Ettrick and Lauderdale,
  maj. 4,478
Johnston, Nicholas, C., Scotland Mid and Fife region

Johnstone, Alex, C., Scotland North East region
Kerr, Andy, Lab., East Kilbride, maj. 6,499
Lamont, Johann, Lab. Co-op., Glasgow Pollock, maj. 4,642
Livingstone, Ms Marilyn, Lab. Co-op., Kirkcaldy, maj. 4,475
Lochhead, Richard, SNP, Scotland North East region
Lyon, George, LD, Argyll and Bute, maj. 2,057
McAllion, John, MP, Lab., Dundee East, maj. 2,854
MacAskill, Kenny, SNP, Lothians region
McAveety, Frank, Lab. Co-op., Glasgow Shettleston,
  maj. 5,467
McCabe, Tom, Lab., Hamilton South, maj. 7,176
McConnell, Jack, Lab., Motherwell and Wishaw, maj. 5,076
Macdonald, Lewis, Lab., Aberdeen Central, maj. 2,696
MacDonald, Ms Margo, SNP, Lothians region
MacGrigor, Jamie, C., Highlands and Islands region
McGugan, Ms Irene, SNP, Scotland North East region
Macintosh, Ken, Lab., Eastwood, maj. 2,125
McIntosh, Mrs Lindsay, C., Scotland Central region
MacKay, Angus, Lab., Edinburgh South, maj. 5,424
MacLean, Ms Kate, Lab., Dundee West, maj. 121
McLeish, Henry B., MP, Lab., Fife Central, maj. 8,675
McLeod, Ms Fiona, SNP, Scotland West region
McLetchie, David, C., Lothians region
McMahon, Michael, Lab., Hamilton North and Bellshill,
  maj. 5,606
Macmillan, Ms Maureen, Lab., Highlands and Islands region
McNeil, Duncan, Lab., Greenock and Inverclyde, maj. 4,313
McNeill, Ms Pauline, Lab., Glasgow Kelvin, maj. 4,408
McNulty, Des, Lab., Clydebank and Milngavie, maj. 4,710
Martin, Paul, Lab., Glasgow Springburn, maj. 7,893
Marwick, Ms Tricia, SNP, Scotland Mid and Fife region
Matheson, Michael, SNP, Scotland Central region
Monteith, Brian, C., Scotland Mid and Fife region
Morgan, Alasdair N., MP, SNP, Galloway and Upper
  Nithsdale, maj. 3,201
Morrison, Alasdair, Lab., Western Isles, maj. 2,093
Muldoon, Bristow, Lab., Livingston, maj. 3,904
Mulligan, Ms Mary, Lab., Linlithgow, maj. 2,928
Mundell, David, C., Scotland South region
Murray, Dr Elaine, Lab., Dumfries, maj. 3,654
Neil, Alex, SNP, Scotland Central region
Oldfather, Ms Irene, Lab., Cunninghame South, maj. 6,541
Paterson, Gil, SNP, Scotland Central region
Peacock, Peter, Lab., Highlands and Islands region
Peattie, Ms Cathy, Lab., Falkirk East, maj. 4,139
Quinan, Lloyd, SNP, Scotland West region
Radcliffe, Ms Nora, LD, Gordon, maj. 4,195
Raffan, Keith, LD, Scotland Mid and Fife region
Reid, George, SNP, Scotland Mid and Fife region
Robison, Ms Shona, SNP, Scotland North East region
Robson, Euan, LD, Roxburgh and Berwickshire, maj. 3,585
Rumbles, Mike, LD, Aberdeenshire West and Kincardine,
  maj. 2,289
Russell, Michael, SNP, Scotland South region
Salmond, Alex E.A., MP, SNP, Banff and Buchan, maj. 11,292
Scanlon, Mrs Mary, C., Highlands and Islands region
Scott, John, C., Ayr, maj. 3,344 (by-election in June 2000 due
  to resignation of Ian Welsh)
Scott, Tavish, LD, Shetland, maj. 3,194
Sheridan, Tommy, SSP, Glasgow region
Simpson, Richard, Lab., Ochil, maj. 1,303
Smith, Ms Elaine, Lab., Coatbridge and Chryston,
  maj. 10,404
Smith, Iain, LD, Fife North East, maj. 5,064
Smith, Ms Margaret, LD, Edinburgh West, maj. 4,583
Steel, Rt. Hon. Sir David (The Lord Steel of Aikwood),
  KBE, PC, LD, Lothians region
Stephen, Nicol, LD, Aberdeen South, maj. 1,760
Stone, Jamie, LD, Caithness, Sutherland and Easter Ross,
  maj. 4,391

Sturgeon, Ms Nicola, *SNP, Glasgow region*
Swinney, John R., MP, *SNP, Tayside North*, maj. 4,192
Thomson, Ms Elaine, *Lab., Aberdeen North*, maj. 398
Tosh, Murray, *C., Scotland South region*
Ullrich, Ms Kay, *SNP, Scotland West region*
Wallace, Ben, *C., Scotland North East region*
Wallace, James R., MP, QC, *LD, Orkney*, maj. 4,619
Watson, Mike (The Lord Watson of Invergowrie),
  Lab., Glasgow Cathcart, maj. 5,374
Welsh, Andrew P., MP, *SNP, Angus*, maj. 8,901
White, Ms Sandra, *SNP, Glasgow region*
Whitefield, Ms Karen, *Lab., Airdrie and Shotts*, maj. 8,985
Wilson, Allan, *Lab., Cunninghame North*, maj. 4,796
Wilson, Andrew, *SNP, Scotland Central region*
Young, John, OBE, *C., Scotland West region*

STATE OF THE PARTIES *as at May 2000*

	Constituency MSPs	Regional MSPs	Total
Scottish Labour Party	52	3	55
Scottish National Party	7	28	35
Scottish Conservative and Unionist Party	1	18	19
Scottish Liberal Democrats	12	4†	16†
Scottish Green Party	0	1	1
Scottish Socialist Party	0	1	1
Independent (Dennis Canavan)	1	0	1
The Presiding Officer (Rt. Hon. Sir David Steel, KBE, MSP)	0	1	1

†Excludes the Presiding Officer, who has no party allegiance while in post
Deputy Presiding Officers, George Reid, MSP (*SNP*); Patricia Ferguson, MSP (*Lab.*)

Scottish Parliament AS AT JULY 2000

CONSTITUENCIES

ABERDEEN CENTRAL
(Scotland North East region)
E. 52,715 *T.* 50.26%

L. Macdonald, *Lab.*	10,305
R. Lochhead, *SNP*	7,609
Ms E. Anderson, *LD*	4,403
T. Mason, *C.*	3,655
A. Cumbers, *SSP*	523

Lab. majority 2,696

ABERDEEN NORTH
(Scotland North East region)
E. 54,553 *T.* 51.00%

Ms E. Thomson, *Lab.*	10,340
B. Adam, *SNP*	9,942
J. Donaldson, *LD*	4,767
I. Haughie, *C.*	2,772

Lab. majority 398

ABERDEEN SOUTH
(Scotland North East region)
E. 60,579 *T.* 57.26%

N. Stephen, *LD*	11,300
M. Elrick, *Lab.*	9,540
Ms N. Milne, *C.*	6,993
Ms I. McGugan, *SNP*	6,651
S. Sutherland, *SWP*	206

LD majority 1,760

ABERDEENSHIRE WEST AND
KINCARDINE
(Scotland North East region)
E. 60,702 *T.* 58.87%

M. Rumbles, *LD*	12,838
B. Wallace, *C.*	10,549
Ms M. Watt, *SNP*	7,699
G. Guthrie, *Lab.*	4,650

LD majority 2,289

AIRDRIE AND SHOTTS
(Scotland Central region)
E. 58,481 *T.* 56.79%

Ms K. Whitefield, *Lab.*	18,338
G. Paterson, *SNP*	9,353
P. Ross-Taylor, *C.*	3,177
D. Miller, *LD*	2,345

Lab. majority 8,985

ANGUS
(Scotland North East region)
E. 59,891 *T.* 57.66%

A. Welsh, *SNP*	16,055
R. Harris, *C.*	7,154
I. McFatridge, *Lab.*	6,914
R. Speirs, *LD*	4,413

SNP majority 8,901

ARGYLL AND BUTE
(Highlands and Islands region)
E. 49,609 *T.* 64.86%

G. Lyon, *LD*	11,226
D. Hamilton, *SNP*	9,169
H. Raven, *Lab.*	6,470
D. Petrie, *C.*	5,312

LD majority 2,057

AYR
(Scotland South region)
E. 56,338 *T.* 66.48%

I. Welsh, *Lab.*	14,263
P. Gallie, *C.*	14,238
R. Mullin, *SNP*	7,291
Ms E. Morris, *LD*	1,662

Lab. majority 25

By-election held on 16 March 2000 *see* p 284

BANFF AND BUCHAN
(Scotland North East region)
E. 57,639 *T.* 55.06%

A. Salmond, *SNP*	16,695
D. Davidson, *C.*	5,403
M. Mackie, *LD*	5,315
Ms M. Harris, *Lab.*	4,321

SNP majority 11,292

CAITHNESS, SUTHERLAND AND
EASTER ROSS
(Highlands and Islands region)
E. 41,581 *T.* 62.60%

J. Stone, *LD*	10,691
J. Hendry, *Lab.*	6,300
Ms J. Urquhart, *SNP*	6,035
R. Jenkins, *C.*	2,167
J. Campbell, *Ind.*	554
E. Stewart, *Ind.*	282

LD majority 4,391

CARRICK, CUMNOCK AND
DOON VALLEY
(Scotland South region)
E. 65,580   *T.* 62.66%

Ms C. Jamieson, *Lab. Co-op.*	19,667
A. Ingram, *SNP*	10,864
J. Scott, *C.*	8,123
D. Hannay, *LD*	2,441

Lab. Co-op. majority 8,803

CLYDEBANK AND MILNGAVIE
(Scotland West region)
E. 52,461   *T.* 63.55%

D. McNulty, *Lab.*	15,105
J. Yuill, *SNP*	10,395
R. Ackland, *LD*	4,149
Ms D. Luckhurst, *C.*	3,688

Lab. majority 4,710

CLYDESDALE
(Scotland South region)
E. 64,262   *T.* 60.61%

Ms K. Turnbull, *Lab.*	16,755
Ms A. Winning, *SNP*	12,875
C. Cormack, *C.*	5,814
Ms S. Grieve, *LD*	3,503

Lab. majority 3,880

COATBRIDGE AND CHRYSTON
(Scotland Central region)
E. 52,178   *T.* 57.87%

Ms E. Smith, *Lab.*	17,923
P. Kearney, *SNP*	7,519
G. Lind, *C.*	2,867
Ms J. Hook, *LD*	1,889

Lab. majority 10,404

CUMBERNAULD AND KILSYTH
(Scotland Central region)
E. 49,395   *T.* 61.97%

Ms C. Craigie, *Lab.*	15,182
A. Wilson, *SNP*	10,923
H. O'Donnell, *LD*	2,029
R. Slack, *C.*	1,362
K. McEwan, *SSP*	1,116

Lab. majority 4,259

CUNNINGHAME NORTH
(Scotland West region)
E. 55,867   *T.* 59.95%

A. Wilson, *Lab.*	14,369
Ms K. Ullrich, *SNP*	9,573
M. Johnston, *C.*	6,649
C. Irving, *LD*	2,900

Lab. majority 4,796

CUNNINGHAME SOUTH
(Scotland South region)
E. 50,443   *T.* 56.06%

Ms I. Oldfather, *Lab.*	14,936
M. Russell, *SNP*	8,395
M. Tosh, *C.*	3,229
S. Ritchie, *LD*	1,717

Lab. majority 6,541

DUMBARTON
(Scotland West region)
E. 56,090   *T.* 61.86%

Ms J. Baillie, *Lab.*	15,181
L. Quinan, *SNP*	10,423
D. Reece, *C.*	5,060
P. Coleshill, *LD*	4,035

Lab. majority 4,758

DUMFRIES
(Scotland South region)
E. 63,162   *T.* 60.93%

Ms E. Murray, *Lab.*	14,101
D. Mundell, *C.*	10,447
S. Norris, *SNP*	7,625
N. Wallace, *LD*	6,309

Lab. majority 3,654

DUNDEE EAST
(Scotland North East region)
E. 57,222   *T.* 55.33%

J. McAllion, *Lab.*	13,703
Ms S. Robison, *SNP*	10,849
I. Mitchell, *C.*	4,428
R. Lawrie, *LD*	2,153
H. Duke, *SSP*	530

Lab. majority 2,854

DUNDEE WEST
(Scotland North East region)
E. 55,725   *T.* 52.19%

Ms K. MacLean, *Lab.*	10,925
C. Cashley, *SNP*	10,804
G. Buchan, *C.*	3,345
Ms E. Dick, *LD*	2,998
J. McFarlane, *SSP*	1,010

Lab. majority 121

DUNFERMLINE EAST
(Scotland Mid and Fife region)
E. 52,087   *T.* 56.94%

Ms H. Eadie, *Lab. Co-op.*	16,576
D. McCarthy, *SNP*	7,877
Ms C. Ruxton, *C.*	2,931
F. Lawson, *LD*	2,275

Lab. Co-op. majority 8,699

DUNFERMLINE WEST
(Scotland Mid and Fife region)
E. 53,112   *T.* 57.75%

S. Barrie, *Lab.*	13,560
D. Chapman, *SNP*	8,539
Ms E. Harris, *LD*	5,591
J. Mackie, *C.*	2,981

Lab. majority 5,021

EAST KILBRIDE
(Scotland Central region)
E. 66,111   *T.* 62.49%

A. Kerr, *Lab.*	19,987
Ms L. Fabiani, *SNP*	13,488
C. Stevenson, *C.*	4,465
E. Hawthorn, *LD*	3,373

Lab. majority 6,499

EAST LOTHIAN
(Scotland South region)
E. 58,579   *T.* 64.16%

J. Home Robertson, *Lab.*	19,220
C. Miller, *SNP*	8,274
Ms C. Richard, *C.*	5,941
Ms J. Hayman, *LD*	4,147

Lab. majority 10,946

EASTWOOD
(Scotland West region)
E. 67,248   *T.* 67.51%

K. Macintosh, *Lab.*	16,970
J. Young, *C.*	14,845
Ms R. Findlay, *SNP*	8,760
Ms A. McCurley, *LD*	4,472
M. Tayan, *Ind.*	349

Lab. majority 2,125

EDINBURGH CENTRAL
(Lothians region)
E. 65,945   *T.* 56.73%

Ms S. Boyack, *Lab.*	14,224
I. McKee, *SNP*	9,598
A. Myles, *LD*	6,187
Ms J. Low, *C.*	6,018
K. Williamson, *SSP*	830
B. Allingham, *Ind. Dem.*	364
W. Wallace, *Braveheart*	191

Lab. majority 4,626

EDINBURGH EAST AND MUSSELBURGH
(Lothians region)
E. 60,167   *T.* 61.48%

Ms S. Deacon, *Lab.*	17,086
K. MacAskill, *SNP*	10,372
J. Balfour, *C.*	4,600
Ms M. Thomas, *LD*	4,100
D. White, *SSP*	697
M. Heavey, *Ind. You*	134

Lab. majority 6,714

EDINBURGH NORTH AND LEITH
(Lothians region)
E. 62,976   *T.* 58.19%

M. Chisholm, *Lab.*	17,203
Ms A. Dana, *SNP*	9,467
J. Sempill, *C.*	5,030
S. Tombs, *LD*	4,039
R. Brown, *SSP*	907

Lab. majority 7,736

EDINBURGH PENTLANDS
(Lothians region)
E. 60,029   *T.* 65.97%

I. Gray, *Lab.*	14,343
D. McLetchie, *C.*	11,458
S. Gibb, *SNP*	8,770
I. Gibson, *LD*	5,029

Lab. majority 2,885

EDINBURGH SOUTH
(Lothians region)
E. 64,100   *T.* 62.61%

A. MacKay, *Lab.*	14,869
Ms M. MacDonald, *SNP*	9,445
M. Pringle, *LD*	8,961
I. Whyte, *C.*	6,378
W. Black, *SWP*	482

Lab. majority 5,424

EDINBURGH WEST
(Lothians region)
E. 61,747   *T.* 67.34%

Ms M. Smith, *LD*	15,161
Lord J. Douglas-Hamilton, *C.*	10,578
Ms C. Fox, *Lab.*	8,860
G. Sutherland, *SNP*	6,984

LD majority 4,583

FALKIRK EAST
(Scotland Central region)
E. 57,345   *T.* 61.40%

Ms C. Peattie, *Lab.*	15,721
K. Brown, *SNP*	11,582
A. Orr, *C.*	3,399
G. McDonald, *LD*	2,509
R. Stead, *Soc. Lab.* 1,643	
V. MacGrain, *SFPP* 358	

Lab. majority 4,139

FALKIRK WEST
(Scotland Central region)
E. 53,404   *T.* 63.04%

D. Canavan, *Falkirk W.*	18,511
R. Martin, *Lab.*	6,319
M. Matheson, *SNP*	5,986
G. Miller, *C.*	1,897
A. Smith, *LD*	954

Falkirk W. majority 12,192

FIFE CENTRAL
(Scotland Mid and Fife region)
E. 58,850   *T.* 55.82%

H. McLeish, *Lab.*	18,828
Ms P. Marwick, *SNP*	10,153
Ms J. A. Liston, *LD*	1,953
K. Harding, *C.*	1,918

Lab. majority 8,675

FIFE NORTH EAST
(Scotland Mid and Fife region)
E. 60,886   *T.* 59.03%

I. Smith, *LD*	13,590
E. Brocklebank, *C.*	8,526
C. Welsh, *SNP*	6,373
C. Milne, *Lab.*	5,175
D. Macgregor, *Ind.*	1,540
R. Beveridge, *Ind.*	737

LD majority 5,064

GALLOWAY AND UPPER NITHSDALE
(Scotland South region)
E. 53,057   *T.* 66.56%

A. Morgan, *SNP*	13,873
A. Fergusson, *C.*	10,672
J. Stevens, *Lab.*	7,209
Ms J. Mitchell, *LD*	3,562

SNP majority 3,201

GLASGOW ANNIESLAND
(Glasgow region)
E. 54,378   *T.* 52.37%

D. Dewar, *Lab.*	16,749
K. Stewart, *SNP*	5,756
W. Aitken, *C.*	3,032
I. Brown, *LD*	1,804
Ms A. Lynch, *SSP*	1,000
E. Boyd, *Soc. Lab.*	139

Lab. majority 10,993

GLASGOW BAILLIESTON
(Glasgow region)
E. 49,068   *T.* 48.32%

Ms M. Curran, *Lab.*	11,289
Ms D. Elder, *SNP*	8,217
J. McVicar, *SSP*	1,864
Ms K. Pickering, *C.*	1,526
Ms J. Fryer, *LD*	813

Lab. majority 3,072

GLASGOW CATHCART
(Glasgow region)
E. 51,338   *T.* 52.55%

M. Watson, *Lab.*	12,966
Ms M. Whitehead, *SNP*	7,592
Ms M. Leishman, *C.*	3,311
C. Dick, *LD*	2,187
R. Slorach, *SWP*	920

Lab. majority 5,374

GLASGOW GOVAN
(Glasgow region)
E. 53,257　T. 49.52%

G. Jackson, *Lab.*	11,421
Ms N. Sturgeon, *SNP*	9,665
Ms T. Ahmed-Sheikh, *C.*	2,343
M. Aslam Khan, *LD*	1,479
C. McCarthy, *SSP*	1,275
J. Foster, *Comm. Brit.* 190	
Lab. majority 1,756	

GLASGOW KELVIN
(Glasgow region)
E. 61,207　T. 46.34%

Ms P. McNeill, *Lab.*	12,711
Ms S. White, *SNP*	8,303
Ms M. Craig, *LD*	3,720
A. Rasul, *C.*	2,253
Ms H. Ritchie, *SSP*	1,375
Lab. majority 4,408	

GLASGOW MARYHILL
(Glasgow region)
E. 56,469　T. 40.75%

Ms P. Ferguson, *Lab.*	11,455
W. Wilson, *SNP*	7,129
Ms C. Hamblen, *LD*	1,793
G. Scott, *SSP*	1,439
M. Fry, *C.*	1,194
Lab. majority 4,326	

GLASGOW POLLOCK
(Glasgow region)
E. 47,970　T. 54.37%

J. Lamont, *Lab. Co-op.*	11,405
K. Gibson, *SNP*	6,763
T. Sheridan, *SSP*	5,611
R. O'Brien, *C.*	1,370
J. King, *LD*	931
Lab. Co-op. majority 4,642	

GLASGOW RUTHERGLEN
(Glasgow region)
E. 51,012　T. 56.89%

Ms J. Hughes, *Lab.*	13,442
T. Chalmers, *SNP*	6,155
R. Brown, *LD*	5,798
I. Stewart, *C.*	2,315
W. Bonnar, *SSP*	832
J. Nisbet, *Soc. Lab.* 481	
Lab. majority 7,287	

GLASGOW SHETTLESTON
(Glasgow region)
E. 50,592　T. 40.58%

F. McAveety, *Lab. Co-op.*	11,078
J. Byrne, *SNP*	5,611
Ms R. Kane, *SSP*	1,640
C. Bain, *C.*	1,260
L. Clarke, *LD*	943
Lab. Co-op. majority 5,467	

GLASGOW SPRINGBURN
(Glasgow region)
E. 55,670　T. 43.77%

P. Martin, *Lab.*	14,268
J. Brady, *SNP*	6,375
M. Roxburgh, *C.*	1,293
M. Dunnigan, *LD*	1,288
J. Friel, *SSP*	1,141
Lab. majority 7,893	

GORDON
(Scotland North East region)
E. 59,497　T. 56.51%

Ms N. Radcliffe, *LD*	12,353
A. Stronach, *SNP*	8,158
A. Johnstone, *C.*	6,602
Ms G. Carlin-Kulwicki, *Lab.*	3,950
H. Watt, *Ind.*	2,559
LD majority 4,195	

GREENOCK AND INVERCLYDE
(Scotland West region)
E. 48,584　T. 58.95%

D. McNeil, *Lab.*	11,817
R. Finnie, *LD*	7,504
I. Hamilton, *SNP*	6,762
R. Wilkinson, *C.*	1,699
D. Landels, *SSP*	857
Lab. majority 4,313	

HAMILTON NORTH AND BELLSHILL
(Scotland Central region)
E. 53,992　T. 57.82%

M. McMahon, *Lab.*	15,227
Ms K. McAlorum, *SNP*	9,621
S. Thomson, *C.*	3,199
Ms J. Struthers, *LD*	2,105
Ms K. McGavigan, *Soc. Lab.*	1,064
Lab. majority 5,606	

HAMILTON SOUTH
(Scotland Central region)
E. 46,765　T. 55.43%

T. McCabe, *Lab.*	14,098
A. Ardrey, *SNP*	6,922
Ms M. Mitchell, *C.*	2,918
J. Oswald, *LD*	1,982
Lab. majority 7,176	

INVERNESS EAST, NAIRN AND
LOCHABER
(Highlands and Islands region)
E. 66,285　T. 63.10%

F. Ewing, *SNP*	13,825
Ms J. Aitken, *Lab.*	13,384
D. Fraser, *LD*	8,508
Ms M. Scanlon, *C.*	6,107
SNP majority 441	

KILMARNOCK AND LOUDOUN
(Scotland Central region)
E. 61,454　T. 64.03%

Ms M. Jamieson, *Lab.*	17,345
A. Neil, *SNP*	14,585
L. McIntosh, *C.*	4,589
J. Stewart, *LD*	2,830
Lab. majority 2,760	

KIRKCALDY
(Scotland Mid and Fife region)
E. 51,640　T. 54.88%

Ms M. Livingstone, *Lab.Co-op.*	13,645
S. Hosie, *SNP*	9,170
M. Scott-Hayward, *C.*	2,907
J. Mainland, *LD*	2,620
Lab. Co-op. majority 4,475	

LINLITHGOW
(Lothians region)
E. 54,262   T. 62.26%

Ms M. Mulligan, *Lab.*	15,247
S. Stevenson, *SNP*	12,319
G. Lindhurst, *C.*	3,158
J. Barrett, *LD*	2,643
Ms I. Ovenstone, *Ind.*	415

Lab. majority 2,928

LIVINGSTON
(Lothians region)
E. 62,060   T. 58.93%

B. Muldoon, *Lab.*	17,313
G. McCarra, *SNP*	13,409
D. Younger, *C.*	3,014
M. Oliver, *LD*	2,834

Lab. majority 3,904

MIDLOTHIAN
(Lothians region)
E. 48,374   T. 61.51%

Ms R. Brankin, *Lab. Co-op.*	14,467
A. Robertson, *SNP*	8,942
J. Elder, *LD*	3,184
G. Turnbull, *C.*	2,544
D. Pryde, *Ind.*	618

Lab. Co-op. majority 5,525

MORAY
(Highlands and Islands region)
E. 58,388   T. 57.50%

Mrs M. Ewing, *SNP*	13,027
A. Farquharson, *Lab.*	8,898
A. Findlay, *C.*	8,595
Ms P. Kenton, *LD*	3,056

SNP majority 4,129

MOTHERWELL AND WISHAW
(Scotland Central region)
E. 52,613   T. 57.71%

J. McConnell, *Lab.*	13,955
J. McGuigan, *SNP*	8,879
W. Gibson, *C.*	3,694
J. Milligan, *Soc. Lab.*	1,941
R. Spillane, *LD*	1,895

Lab. majority 5,076

OCHIL
(Scotland Mid and Fife region)
E. 57,083   T. 64.58%

R. Simpson, *Lab.*	15,385
G. Reid, *SNP*	14,082
N. Johnston, *C.*	4,151
Earl of Mar and Kellie, *LD*	3,249

Lab. majority 1,303

ORKNEY
(Highlands and Islands region)
E. 15,658   T. 56.95%

J. Wallace, *LD*	6,010
C. Zawadzki, *C.*	1,391
J. Mowat, *SNP*	917
A. Macleod, *Lab.*	600

LD majority 4,619

PAISLEY NORTH
(Scotland West region)
E. 49,020   T. 56.61%

Ms W. Alexander, *Lab.*	13,492
I. Mackay, *SNP*	8,876
P. Ramsay, *C.*	2,242
Ms T. Mayberry, *LD*	2,133
Ms F. Macdonald, *SSP*	1,007

Lab. majority 4,616

PAISLEY SOUTH
(Scotland West region)
E. 53,637   T. 57.15%

H. Henry, *Lab.*	13,899
W. Martin, *SNP*	9,404
S. Callison, *LD*	2,974
Ms S. Laidlaw, *C.*	2,433
P. Mack, *Ind.*	1,273
Ms J. Forrest, *SWP*	673

Lab. majority 4,495

PERTH
(Scotland Mid and Fife region)
E. 61,034   T. 61.27%

Ms R. Cunningham, *SNP*	13,570
I. Stevenson, *C.*	11,543
Ms J. Richards, *Lab.*	8,725
C. Brodie, *LD*	3,558

SNP majority 2,027

RENFREWSHIRE WEST
(Scotland West region)
E. 52,452   T. 64.89%

Ms P. Godman, *Lab.*	12,708
C. Campbell, *SNP*	9,815
Ms A. Goldie, *C.*	7,243
N. Ascherson, *LD*	2,659
A. McGraw, *Ind.*	1,136
P. Clark, *SWP*	476

Lab. majority 2,893

ROSS, SKYE AND INVERNESS
WEST
(Highlands and Islands Region)
E. 55,845   T. 63.42%

J. Farquhar-Munro, *LD*	11,652
D. Munro, *Lab.*	10,113
J. Mather, *SNP*	7,997
J. Scott, *C.*	3,351
D. Briggs, *Ind.*	2,302

LD majority 1,539

ROXBURGH AND BERWICKSHIRE
(Scotland South region)
E. 47,639   T. 58.52%

E. Robson, *LD*	11,320
A. Hutton, *C.*	7,735
S. Crawford, *SNP*	4,719
Ms S. McLeod, *Lab.*	4,102

LD majority 3,585

SHETLAND
(Highlands and Islands region)
E. 16,978   T. 58.77%

T. Scott, *LD*	5,435
J. Wills, *Lab.*	2,241
W. Ross, *SNP*	1,430
G. Robinson, *C.*	872

LD majority 3,194

STIRLING
(Scotland Mid and Fife region)
E. 52,904   T. 67.68%

Ms S. Jackson, *Lab.*	13,533
Ms A. Ewing, *SNP*	9,552
B. Monteith, *C.*	9,158
I. Macfarlane, *LD*	3,407
S. Kilgour, *Ind.*	155
Lab. majority 3,981	

STRATHKELVIN AND BEARSDEN
(Scotland West region)
E. 63,111   T. 67.17%

S. Galbraith, *Lab.*	21,505
Ms F. McLeod, *SNP*	9,384
C. Ferguson, *C.*	6,934
Ms A. Howarth, *LD*	4,144
Ms M. Richards, *Anti-Drug*	423
Lab. majority 12,121	

TAYSIDE NORTH
(Scotland Mid and Fife region)
E. 61,795   T. 61.58%

J. Swinney, *SNP*	16,786
M. Fraser, *C.*	12,594
Ms M. Dingwall, *Lab.*	5,727
P. Regent, *LD*	2,948
SNP majority 4,192	

TWEEDDALE, ETTRICK AND
LAUDERDALE
(Scotland South region)
E. 51,577   T. 65.37%

I. Jenkins, *LD*	12,078
Ms C. Creech, *SNP*	7,600
G. McGregor, *Lab.*	7,546
J. Campbell, *C.*	6,491
LD majority 4,478	

WESTERN ISLES
(Highlands and Islands region)
E. 22,412   T. 62.26%

A. Morrison, *Lab.*	7,248
A. Nicholson, *SNP*	5,155
J. MacGrigor, *C.*	1,095
J. Horne, *LD*	456
Lab. majority 2,093	

BY-ELECTIONS
AYR (16 MARCH 2000)
T. 57%

J. Scott, *C.*	12,580
J. Mather, *SNP*	9,236
R. Millar, *Lab.*	7,054
J. Stewart, *SSP*	1,345
S. Ritchie, *LD*	800
G. Corbett, *Green*	460
W. Botcherby, *Ind*	186
A. McConnachie, *UK Ind*	113
R. Graham, *ProLife*	111
K. Dhillon, *Ind*	15
C. majority 3,344	

REGIONS

GLASGOW
E. 531,956   T. 48.19%

Lab.	112,588 (43.92%)
SNP	65,360 (25.50%)
C.	20,239 (7.90%)
SSP	18,581 (7.25%)
LD	18,473 (7.21%)
Green	10,159 (3.96%)
Soc. Lab.	4,391 (1.71%)
ProLife	2,357 (0.92%)
SUP	2,283 (0.89%)
Comm. Brit.	521 (0.20%)
Humanist	447 (0.17%)
NLP	419 (0.16%)
SPGB	309 (0.12%)
Choice	221 (0.09%)
Lab.majority 47,228	

(May 1997, Lab. maj. 166,061)

Additional Members
W. Aitken, *C.*; R. Brown, *LD*; Ms D. Elder, *SNP*;
Ms S. White, *SNP*; Ms N. Sturgeon, *SNP*; K. Gibson,
SNP; T. Sheridan, *SSP*

HIGHLANDS AND ISLANDS
E. 326,553   T. 61.76%

SNP	55,933 (27.73%)
Lab.	51,371 (25.47%)
LD	43,226 (21.43%)
C.	30,122 (14.94%)
Green	7,560 (3.75%)
Ind. Noble	3,522 (1.75%)
Soc. Lab.	2,808 (1.39%)
Highlands	2,607 (1.29%)
SSP	1,770 (0.88%)
Mission	1,151 (0.57%)
Int. Ind.	712 (0.35%)
NLP	536 (0.27%)
Ind. R.	354 (0.18%)
SNP majority 4,562	

(May 1997, LD maj. 1,388)

Additional Members
J. MacGrigor, *C.*; Mrs M. Scanlon, *C.*; Ms M. MacMillan,
Lab.; P. Peacock, *Lab.*; Ms R. Grant, *Lab.*; Mrs W. Ewing,
SNP; D. Hamilton, *SNP*

LOTHIANS
E. 539,656   T. 61.25%

Lab.	99,908 (30.23%)
SNP	85,085 (25.74%)
C.	52,067 (15.75%)
LD	47,565 (14.39%)
Green	22,848 (6.91%)
Soc. Lab.	10,895 (3.30%)
SSP	5,237 (1.58%)
Lib.	2,056 (0.62%)
Witchery	1,184 (0.36%)
ProLife	898 (0.27%)
Rights	806 (0.24%)
NLP	564 (0.17%)
Braveheart	557 (0.17%)
SPGB	388 (0.12%)
Ind. Voice	256 (0.08%)
Ind. Ind.	145 (0.04%)
Anti-Corr.	54 (0.02%)
Lab. majority	14,823

(May 1997, Lab. maj. 101,991)

Additional Members
Lord James Douglas Hamilton, *C.*; D. McLetchie, *C.*;
Rt. Hon. Sir David Steel, *LD*; K. MacAskill, *SNP*;
Ms M. MacDonald, *SNP*; Ms F. Hyslop, *SNP*;
R. Harper, *Green*

SCOTLAND CENTRAL
E. 551,733   *T.* 59.90%

Lab.	129,822 (39.28%)
SNP	91,802 (27.78%)
C.	30,243 (9.15%)
Falkirk W.	27,700 (8.38%)
LD	20,505 (6.20%)
Soc. Lab.	10,956 (3.32%)
Green	5,926 (1.79%)
SSP	5,739 (1.74%)
SUP	2,886 (0.87%)
ProLife	2,567 (0.78%)
SFPP	1,373 (0.42%)
NLP	719 (0.22%)
Ind. Prog.	248 (0.08%)

Lab. majority 38,020
(May 1997, Lab. maj. 143,376)

Additional Members
Mrs L. McIntosh, *C.*; D. Gorrie, *LD*; A. Neil, *SNP*;
M. Matheson, *SNP*; Ms L. Fabiani, *SNP*; A. Wilson, *SNP*;
G. Paterson, *SNP*

SCOTLAND MID AND FIFE
E. 509,387   *T.* 60.01%

Lab.	101,964 (33.36%)
SNP	87,659 (28.68%)
C.	56,719 (18.56%)
LD	38,896 (12.73%)
Green	11,821 (3.87%)
Soc. Lab.	4,266 (1.40%)
SSP	3,044 (1.00%)
ProLife	735 (0.24%)
NLP	558 (0.18%)

Lab. majority 14,305
(May 1997, Lab. maj. 54,087)

Additional Members
N. Johnston, *C.*; B. Monteith, *C.*; K. Harding, *C.*;
K. Raffan, *LD*; B. Crawford, *SNP*; G. Reid, *SNP*;
Ms P. Marwick, *SNP*

SCOTLAND NORTH EAST
E. 518,521   *T.* 55.05%

SNP	92,329 (32.35%)
Lab.	72,666 (25.46%)
C.	52,149 (18.27%)
LD	49,843 (17.46%)
Green	8,067 (2.83%)
Soc.Lab.	3,557 (1.25%)
SSP	3,016 (1.06%)
Ind. Watt.	2,303 (0.81%)
Ind. SB	770 (0.27%)
NLP	746 (0.26%)

SNP majority 19,663
(May 1997, Lab. maj. 17,518)

ADDITIONAL MEMBERS
D. Davidson, *C.*; A. Johnstone, *C.*; B. Wallace, *C.*;
R. Lochhead, *SNP*; Ms S. Robison, *SNP*; B. Adam, *SNP*;
Ms I. McGugan, *SNP*

SCOTLAND SOUTH
E. 510,634   *T.* 62.35%

Lab.	98,836 (31.04%)
SNP	80,059 (25.15%)
C.	68,904 (21.64%)
LD	38,157 (11.99%)
Soc. Lab.	13,887 (4.36%)
Green	9,468 (2.97%)
Lib.	3,478 (1.09%)
SSP	3,304 (1.04%)
UK Ind.	1,502 (0.47%)
NLP	775 (0.24%)

Lab. majority 18,777
(May 1997, Lab. maj. 79,585)

Additional Members
P. Gallie, *C.*; D. Mundell, *C.*; M. Tosh, *C.*; A. Fergusson,
C.; M. Russell, *SNP*; A. Ingram, *SNP*; Ms C. Creech, *SNP*

SCOTLAND WEST
E. 498,466   *T.* 62.27%

Lab.	119,663 (38.55%)
SNP	80,417 (25.91%)
C.	48,666 (15.68%)
LD	34,095 (10.98%)
Green	8,175 (2.63%)
SSP	5,944 (1.91%)
Soc. Lab.	4,472 (1.44%)
ProLife	3,227 (1.04%)
Individual	2,761 (0.89%)
SUP	1,840 (0.59%)
NLP	589 (0.19%)
Ind. Water	565 (0.18%)

Lab. majority 39,246
(May 1997, Lab. maj. 115,995)

Additional Members
Miss A. Goldie, *C.*; J. Young, *C.*; R. Finnie, *LD*; L. Quinan,
SNP; Ms F. McLeod, *SNP*; Ms K. Ullrich, *SNP*;
C. Campbell, *SNP*

NORTHERN IRELAND ASSEMBLY
Parliament Buildings, Stormont, Belfast BT4 3SW
Tel: 028-9052 1137; Fax: 028-9052 1961
Web: http://www.ni-assembly.gov.uk

The Assembly has 108 members elected by single transferable vote (six from each of the 18 Westminster constituencies). The first elections took place on 25 June 1998 and members met for the first time on 1 July. Safeguards ensure that key decisions have cross-community support. The executive powers of the Assembly will be discharged by an executive committee comprising a First Minister and Deputy First Minister (jointly elected by the Assembly on a cross-community basis) and up to ten ministers with departmental responsibilities. Ministerial posts will be allocated on the basis of the number of seats each party holds.

The Assembly met in shadow form several times, pending the establishment of an Executive and the transfer of powers from Parliament. After devolution it will have executive and legislative authority over those areas formerly the responsibility of the Northern Ireland government departments (*see* Government Departments and Public Offices section). Its powers might be extended further in future.

Power was initially due to be transferred to the new Executive on 10 March 1999, but disagreements emerged over whether Sinn Féin should be allowed to enter the

Executive before IRA weapons had been decommissioned. Further deadlines of 2 April and 30 June were also missed. On 15 July the Assembly met to nominate ministers, with the transfer of power to follow on 18 July. However, as the decommissioning issue had still not been resolved, Unionists failed to nominate ministers (the UUP boycotting the meeting itself) and the process collapsed. On 20 July the two Prime Ministers announced a review of the implementation of the Agreement to be facilitated by former Senator George Mitchell. The scope of the review was tightly drawn, focusing only on the practical implementation of the three principles set out above, effectively decommissioning the Executive. The timing of the review dove-tailed with the inevitably sensitive publication of the Patten Commission's report on policing.

Following a series of meetings involving the parties in London, Mitchell's interim report of 15 November stated that he was increasingly more confident that the parties could find a way through the impasse.

On 18 November, following statements from the UUP, Sinn Féin and one from the IRA, George Mitchell concluded the review indicating that he now believed there was a basis for devolution to occur, for the institutions to be established and for decommissioning to take place as soon as possible. He concluded that devolution should take effect, the Executive Committee should meet and paramilitary organisations should appoint their authorised representatives to the IICD in that order and all in the same day. On 20 November the Secretary of State announced support for the Mitchell proposals and stated that the Assembly should meet on 29 November for the purpose of running d'Hondt procedure for appointing shadow ministers and devolution should take effect after the necessary Parliamentary procedures had been completed on 2 December.

Powers were devolved to Assembly and other institutions established on 2 December on a basis agreed by the parties during the Mitchell review. The Mitchell review created the expectation that the establishment of the institutions and the appointment of authorised representatives produced conditions in which Sinn Féin could influence bringing about the start of decommissioning. But it was a matter of political reality that if decommissioning did not occur by the end of January it would be very difficult for David Trimble to continue as leader of the Ulster Unionist Party (UUP) beyond this. In late November the Council of the UUP had endorsed the Mitchell outcome but, reflecting the political reality, also recommend that progress on the timing and modalities of decommissioning be reviewed at the end of January 2000 through reports presented to the two governments by the IICD.

Devolution and the institutions were able to flourish on the basis of sufficient cross community support. Unfortunately that support began to ebb when the anticipated progress on decommissioning failed to materialise at the end of January. The two Governments took receipt of General de Chastelain's 31 January report but held back publication in order to explore any hope of credible progress on decommissioning. Both governments tried further efforts to gain clarity on the decommissioning issue.

The Secretary of State announced the suspension legislation on 3 February and warned publicly that it would come into effect on Friday 11 February. On the morning of 11 February, there was some sign that a new IRA proposal was emerging. The Irish Government presented a new position from its leadership. There were still only words and no timescale, but it did include clearer and less equivocal words than before. Unfortunately this was not enough to avert the collapse of the institutions.

Suspension meant that the Assembly could not meet or conduct any business. Parliament Buildings remained open for use by Assembly Members for the purpose of carrying out constituency work and they continued to be paid salaries and allowances – set at the lower pre-devolution shadow rate to reflect the supension of Assembly business.

Following a period of intensive discussions with pro-Agreement parties during 4 and 5 May at Hillsborough, the Prime Minister and Taoiseach issued a joint statement committing both Government's proposals. On May 6, the IRA responded with a significant and forthcoming statement in which they recognised that:

– the implementation of what the Governments had agreed would provide a new context in which Republicans could pursue their political objectives peacefully;
– in that new context the IRA leadership would initiate a process that would completely and verifiably put arms beyond use;
– the IRA would renew contact with the Decommissioning Commission;
– agreed, as a confidence building measure, to open a number of arms dumps to independent inspectors reporting to the Decommissioning Commission on a regular basis to verify that arms remain secure.

The pro-Agreement parties welcomed these developments. The UUP leader, David Trimble said that the IRA statement appeared to break new ground. The Prime Minister and the Taoiseach on 8 May that they were asking former Finnish President Martti Ahtisaari and Cyril Ramaphosa, the ANC negotiator, to become the independent inspectors. On 9 May, the Chief Constable of the RUC recognised that the IRA statement marked a significant reduction in the overall threat and announced a number of measures, spread across Northern Ireland, designed as a return to more normal policing.

The Government published the Police Bill on 16 May and gave assurances to Unionists that the legal description of the new police service would incorporate the RUC, while the operational and working name would change to Police Service of Northern Ireland. The Government also took an enabling power to resolve the flying of flags over Government buildings if the devolved Executive could not.

A week later than originally envisaged the Ulster Unionist Council endorsed the Government's proposals on 27 May and devolved government was restored to Northern Ireland with effect from midnight on 29 May.

SALARIES *as at April 2000*

First Minister	£66,173*
Deputy First Minister	£66,173*
Minister/Presiding Officer	£34,327*
Assembly Member	£39,139

*Also receive the Assembly Member salary

NORTHERN IRELAND EXECUTIVE

Castle Buildings Stormont, Belfast BT4 3SG
Tel: 028-9052 0700; Fax: 028-9052 8195
Web: http://www.northernireland.gov.uk

First Minster, David Trimble, MLA
Deputy First Minister, Seamus Mallon, MLA
Minister of Agriculture and Rural Development, Brid Rogers, MLA
Minster of Culture and Arts and Leisure, Michael McGimpsey, MLA
Minister of Education, Martin McGuiness, MLA
Minister for Enterprise, Trade and Investment, Sir Reg

Empey, MLA
Minister for Environment, Sam Foster, MLA
Minister for Finance and Personnel, Mark Durkan, MLA
Minister of Health, Social Services and Public Safety,
   Bairbre de Brún, MLA
*Minister of Higher and Further Education, Training and
   Employment*, Sean Farren, MLA
Minister for Regional Development, Peter Robinson, MLA
Minister for Social Development, Nigel Dodds, MLA

OFFICE OF THE FIRST MINISTER AND DEPUTY MINISTER
Castle Buildings, Stormont Estate, Belfast BT4 3SR
Tel: 028-9052 8400

DEPARTMENT OF AGRICULTURE AND RURAL DEVELOPMENT
Dundonald House, Upper Newtownards Road,
Belfast BT4 3SB
Tel: 028-9052 0100; Fax: 028-9052 5015

EXECUTIVE AGENCIES
INTERVENTION BOARD

RIVERS AGENCY, 4 Hospital Road, Belfast BT8 8JP.
   Tel: 028-9025 3355
FOREST SERVICE, Dundonald House, Upper
   Newtownards Road, Belfast BT4 3SB.
   Tel: 028-9052 4480

DEPARTMENT OF CULTURE, ARTS AND LEISURE
20–24 York Street, Belfast BT15 1AQ
Tel: 028-9025 8825

DEPARTMENT OF EDUCATION
Rathgael House, 43 Balloo Road, Bangor,
Co. Down BT19 7PR
Tel: 028-9127 9279; Fax: 028-9127 9100

DEPARTMENT OF ENTERPRISE, TRADE AND INVESTMENT
Netherleigh, Massey Avenue, Belfast BT4 2JP
Tel: 028-9052 9900; Fax: 028-9052 9550

INDUSTRIAL DEVELOPMENT BOARD, IDB House,
   64 Chichester Street, Belfast BT14JX.
   Tel: 028-9023 3233

EXECUTIVE AGENCIES
INDUSTRIAL RESEARCH AND TECHNOLOGY UNIT, 17
   Antrim Road, Lisburn BT28 3AL. Tel: 028-9262 3000

DEPARTMENT OF THE ENVIRONMENT
Clarence Court, 10–18 Adelaide Street, Belfast BT2 8GB
Tel: 028-9054 0540

EXECUTIVE AGENCIES
DRIVER AND VEHICLE LICENSING AGENCY (NORTHERN
   IRELAND), County Hall, Castlerock Road, Coleraine,
   Co. Londonderry BT51 3HS. Tel: 01265-41200
DRIVER AND VEHICLE TESTING AGENCY (NORTHERN
   IRELAND), Balmoral Road, Belfast BT12 6QL.
   Tel: 028-9068 1831
ENVIRONMENT AND HERITAGE SERVICE, Commonwealth
   House, Castle Street, Belfast BT1 1GU.
   Tel: 028-9025 1477
PLANNING SERVICE, Clarence Court, 10–18 Adelaide
   Street, Belfast BT2 8GB. Tel: 028-9054 0540

DEPARTMENT OF FINANCE AND PERSONNEL
Rathgael House, Balloo Road, Bangor BT19 7NA
Tel: 028-9127 9279

EXECUTIVE AGENCIES
BUSINESS DEVELOPMENT SERVICE, Craigantlet Buildings,
   Stoney Road, Belfast BT4 3SX. Tel: 028-9052 0400
CONSTRUCTION SERVICE, Churchill House, Victoria
   Square, Belfast BT1 4QW. Tel: 028-9052 0250
GOVERNMENT PURCHASING AGENCY, Rosepark House,
   Upper Newtownards Road, Belfast BT4 3NR.
   Tel: 028-9052 0400
LAND REGISTERS OF NORTHERN IRELAND, Lincoln
   Building, 27–45 Great Victoria Street, Belfast BT2 7SL.
   Tel: 028-9025 1555
NORTHERN IRELAND STATISTICS AND RESEARCH
   AGENCY, McAuley House, 2–14 Castle Street, Belfast
   BT1 1SA. Tel: 028-9034 8100
RATE COLLECTION AGENCY, Oxford House, 49–55
   Chichester Street, Belfast BT1 4HH Tel: 028-9025 2252
VALUATION AND LANDS AGENCY, Queen's Court, 56–66
   Upper Queen Street, Belfast BT1 6FD.
   Tel: 028-9025 0700

DEPARTMENT OF HEALTH AND SOCIAL SERVICES NORTHERN IRELAND
Castle Buildings, Stormont, Belfast BT4 3SJ
Tel: 028-9052 0000; Fax: 028-9052 0572

HEALTH AND SOCIAL SERVICES BOARDS
— *see* Social Welfare section

EXECUTIVE AGENCIES
NORTHERN IRELAND HEALTH AND SOCIAL SERVICES
   ESTATES AGENCY, Stoney Road, Dundonald,
   Belfast BT16 1US. Tel: 028-9052 0025

DEPARTMENT OF HIGHER AND FURTHER EDUCATION, TRAINING AND EMPLOYMENT
Adelaide House, Adelaide Street, Belfast BT2 8FD
Tel: 028-9025 7777; Fax 028-9025 7783

DEPARTMENT FOR REGIONAL DEVELOPMENT
Clarence Court, 10–18 Adelaide Street, Belfast BT2 8GB
Tel: 028-9054 0540; Fax: 028-9054 0064

DEPARTMENT FOR SOCIAL DEVELOPMENT
Churchill House, Victoria Square, Belfast BT2 4BA
Tel: 028-9056 9100

THE FOLLOWING BODIES WILL ALSO BECOME
OPERATIONAL:

BRITISH-IRISH COUNCIL
NORTH/SOUTH MINISTERIAL COUNCIL
CIVIC FORUM
BRITISH-IRISH INTERGOVERNMENTAL CONFERENCE

NORTHERN IRELAND ASSEMBLY MEMBERS

Adams, Gerry, (*SF*), *West Belfast*
Adamson, Dr Ian, (*UUP*), *East Belfast*
*Agnew, Fraser, (*UUAP*), *North Belfast*
Alderdice, Lord, (*Speaker*), *East Belfast*
Armitage, Ms Pauline, (*UUP*), *East Londonderry*
Armstrong, Billy, (*UUP*), *Mid Ulster*
Attwood, Alex, (*SDLP*), *West Belfast*
Beggs, Roy, (*UUP*), *East Antrim*
Bell, Eileen, (*All.*), *North Down*

Benson, Tom, (*UUP*), *Strangford*
Berry, Paul, (*DUP*), *Newry and Armagh*
Birnie, Esmond, (*UUP*), *South Belfast*
†Boyd, Norman, (*NIUP*), *South Antrim*
Bradley, P. J. (*SDLP*), *South Down*
Byrne, Joe, (*SDLP*), *West Tyrone*
Campbell, Gregory, (*DUP*), *East Londonderry*
Carrick, Mervyn, (*DUP*), *Upper Bann*
Carson, Ms Joan, (*UUP*), *Ferm and South Tyrone*
Close, Seamus, (*All.*), *Lagan Valley*
Clyde, Wilson, (*DUP*), *South Antrim*
Cobain, Fred, (*UUP*), *North Belfast*
Coulter, Robert, (*UUP*), *North Antrim*
Dallat, John, (*SDLP*), *East Londonderry*
Davis, Ivan, (*UUP*), *Lagan Valley*
Brun, Ms Bairbre de, (*SF*), *West Belfast*
Dodds, Nigel, (*DUP*), *North Belfast*
Doherty, Srthur, (*SDLP*), *East Londonderry*
Doherty, Pat, (*SF*), *West Tyrone*
*Douglas, Boyd, (*UUAP*), *East Londonderry*
Durkan, Mark, (*SDLP*), *Foyle*
Empey, Reg, (*UUP*), *East Belfast*
Ervine, David, (*PUP*), *East Belfast*
Farren, Sean, (*SDLP*), *North Antrim*
Fee, John, (*SDLP*), *Newry and Armagh*
Ford, David, (*All.*), *South Antrim*
Foster, Sam, (*UUP*), *Ferm and South Tyrone*
Gallagher, Tommy, (*SDLP*), *Ferm and South Tyrone*
Gibson, Oliver, (*DUP*), *West Tyrone*
Gildernew, Michelle, (*SF*), *Ferm and South Tyrone*
‡Gorman, John, (*UUP*), *North Down*
Hanna, Carmel. (*SDLP*), *South Belfast*
Haughey, Denis, (*SDLP*), *Mid Ulster*
Hay, William, (*DUP*), *Foyle*
Hendron, Joe, (*SDLP*), *West Belfast*
Hilditch, David, (*DUP*), *East Antrim*
Hume, John, (*SDLP*), *Foyle*
Hussey, Derek, (*UUP*), *West Tyrone*
§Hutchinson, Bill, (*PUP*), *North Belfast*
Hutchinson, Roger, (*Ind Unionist*), *East Antrim*
Kane, (*DUP*), *North Antrim*
Kelly, Gerrym (*SF*), *North Belfast*
Kelly, Jon, (*SF*), *Mid Ulster*
Kennedy, Danny, (*UUP*), *Newry and Armagh*
Leslie, James, (*UUP*), *North Antrim*
Lewsley, Patricia, (*SDLP*), *Lagan Valley*
Maginness, Alban, (*SDLP*), *North Belfast*
Mallon, Seamus, (*SDLP*), *Newry and Armagh*
McCarthy, Keiran, (*All.*), *Strangford*
McCartney, Robert, (*UKUP*), *North Down*
McClarty, David, (*UUP*), *East Londonderry*
McCrea, William, (*DUP*), *Mid Ulster*
‡McClelland, Donovan, (*SDLP*), *South Antrim*
McDonnell, Alasdair, (*SDLP*), *South Belfast*
McElduff, Barry, (*SF*), *West Tyrone*
McFarland, Alan, (*UUP*), *North Down*
McGimpsey, Michael, (*UUP*), *South Belfast*
McGrady, Eddie, (*SDLP*), *South Down*
McGuiness, Martin, (*SF*), *Mid Ulster*
McHugh, Gerry, (*SF*), *Ferm and South Tyrone*
McLaughlin, Mitchel, (*SF*), *Foyle*
McMenamin, Eugene, (*SDLP*), *West Tyrone*
McNamee, Pat, (*SF*), *Newry and Armagh*
McWilliams, Prof. Monica, (*NIWC*), *South Belfast*
Molloy, Francie, (*SF*), *Mid Ulster*
Murphy, Connor, (*SF*), *Newry and Armagh*
Murphy, Mick, (*SF*), *South Down*
‡Morrice, Ms Jane, (*NIWC*), *North Down*
Morrow, Maurice, (*DUP*), *Ferm and South Tyrone*
Neeson, Sean, (*All.*), *East Antrim*

Nelis, Ms Mary, (*SF*), *Foyle*
Nesbitt, Dermot, (*UUP*), *South Down*
O'Connor, Danny, (*SDLP*), *East Antrim*
O'Hagan, Dara, (*SF*), *Upper Bann*
O'Neill, Eamon, (*SDLP*), *South Down*
Paisley, Rev Dr Ian, (*DUP*), *North Antrim*
Poots, Edwin, (*DUP*), *Lagan Valley*
Ramsey, Sue, (*SF*), *West Belfast*
Robinson, Isis, (*DUP*), *Strangford*
Robinson, Ken, (*UUP*), *East Anrtim*
Robinson, Mark, (*DUP*), *South Belfast*
Robinson, Peter, (*DUP*), *East Belfast*
†Roche, Patrick, (*NIUP*), *Lagan Valley*
Rodgers, Brid, (*SDLP*), *Upper Bann*
Savage, George, (*UUP*), *Upper Bann*
Shannon, Jim, (*DUP*), *Strangford*
Shipley-Dalton, Duncan, (*UUP*), *South Antrim*
Taylor, The Rt. Hon. John, (*UUP*), *Strangford*
Tierney, John, (*SDLP*), *Foyle*
Trimble, The Rt. Hon. David, (*UUP*), *Upper Bann*
Watson, Denis, (*UUAP*), *Upper Bann*
Weir, Peter, (*UUP*), *North Down*
Wells, Jim, (*DUP*), *South Down*
†Wilson, Cedric, (*NIUP*), *Strangford*
Wilson, Jim, (*UUP*) *South Antrim*
Wilson, Sammy, (*DUP*), *East Belfast*

* Elected as independent candidates, formed the United
Unionist Assembly Party (UUAP) with effect from 21
September 1998
† Elected as UK Unionist Candidates, formed Northern
Ireland Unionist Party (NIUP) with effect from 15 January
1999
‡ Elected as Deputy Speakers of the Northern Ireland
Assembly 31 January 2000
§ Mr Hutchinson was expelled from the Northern Ireland
Unionist Party (NIUP) with effect from 2 December 1999

STATE OF THE PARTIES *as at July 2000*

UUP	Ulster Unionist Party	28
SDLP	Social Democratic and Labour Party	24
DUP	Democratic Unionist Party	20
SF	Sinn Fein	18
All.	All.	6
†NIUP	Northern Ireland Unionist Party	3
*UUAP	United Unionist Assembly Party	3
NIWC	Northern Ireland Women's Coalition	2
PUP	Progressive Unionist Party	2
UKUP	UK Unionist Party	1
§Ind Unionist	Independent Unionist	1

The Government

Prime Minister, First Lord of the Treasury and Minister for the Civil Service
The Rt. Hon. Anthony (Tony) Blair, MP, since May 1997
Deputy Prime Minister and Secretary of State for the Environment, Transport and the Regions
The Rt. Hon. John Prescott, MP, since May 1997
Chancellor of the Exchequer
The Rt. Hon. Gordon Brown, MP, since May 1997
Secretary of State for Foreign and Commonwealth Affairs
The Rt. Hon. Robin Cook, MP, since May 1997
Lord Chancellor
The Lord Irvine of Lairg, PC, QC, since May 1997
Secretary of State for the Home Department
The Rt. Hon. Jack Straw, MP, since May 1997
Secretary of State for Education and Employment
The Rt. Hon. David Blunkett, MP, since May 1997
President of the Council and Leader of the House of Commons
The Rt. Hon. Margaret Beckett, MP, since July 1998
Minister for the Cabinet Office and Chancellor of the Duchy of Lancaster
The Rt. Hon. Dr Marjorie (Mo) Mowlam, MP, since October 1999
Secretary of State for Scotland
The Rt. Hon. Dr John Reid, MP, since May 1999
Secretary of State for Defence
The Rt. Hon. Geoff Hoon, MP, since October 1999
Secretary of State for Health
The Rt. Hon. Alan Milburn, MP, since October 1999
Parliamentary Secretary to the Treasury (Chief Whip)
The Rt. Hon. Ann Taylor, MP
Secretary of State for Culture, Media and Sport
The Rt. Hon. Chris Smith, MP, since May 1997
Secretary of State for Northern Ireland
The Rt. Hon. Peter Mandelson, MP, since October 1999
Secretary of State for Wales
The Rt. Hon. Paul Murphy, MP, since July 1999
Secretary of State for International Development
The Rt. Hon. Clare Short, MP, since May 1997
Secretary of State for Social Security
The Rt. Hon. Alistair Darling, MP, since July 1998
Minister of Agriculture, Fisheries and Food
The Rt. Hon. Nick Brown, MP, since July 1998
Leader of the House of Lords and Minister for Women
The Baroness Jay of Paddington*, since July 1998
Secretary of State for Trade and Industry
The Rt. Hon. Stephen Byers, MP, since January 1999
Chief Secretary to the Treasury
The Rt. Hon. Andrew Smith, MP, since October 1999

The Minister of State at the Department of the Environment, Transport and the Regions with responsibility for Transport, and the Government Chief Whip in the House of Lords will attend Cabinet meetings although they are not members of the Cabinet.

* Appointed as Lord Privy Seal

LAW OFFICERS

Attorney-General
The Lord Williams of Mostyn, QC, since July 1999
Lord Advocate
Colin Boyd, QC, since February 2000
Solicitor-General
Ross Cranston, MP, since July 1998
Solicitor-General for Scotland
Neil Davidson, QC
Advocate-General for Scotland
Dr Lynda Clark, QC, MP

MINISTERS OF STATE

Agriculture, Fisheries and Food
The Rt. Hon. Joyce Quin, MP
The Baroness Hayman
Cabinet Office
The Lord Falconer of Thoroton, QC
The Rt. Hon. Ian McCartney, MP
Defence
John Spellar, MP (*Armed Forces*)
The Baroness Symons of Vernham Dean (*Defence Procurement*)
Education and Employment
The Rt. Hon. Tessa Jowell, MP (*Employment, Welfare to Work and Equal Opportunities*)
Estelle Morris, MP (*School Standards*)
The Baroness Blackstone, Ph.D. (*Education and Employment in the Lords*)
Environment, Transport and the Regions
The Lord Macdonald of Tradeston (*Transport*)
The Rt. Hon. Michael Meacher, MP (*Environment*)
The Rt. Hon. Hilary Armstrong, MP (*Local Government, Regions*)
The Rt. Hon. Nick Raynsford, MP (*Housing, Planning*)
Foreign and Commonwealth Office
Keith Vaz, MP (Minister for Europe)
Peter Hain, MP
John Battle, MP
Health
John Denham, MP (*NHS Structure and Resources*)
John Hutton, MP (*Social Care and Mental Health*)
Home Office
The Rt. Hon. Paul Boateng, MP
Charles Clarke, MP
Barbara Roche, MP
Northern Ireland Office
The Rt. Hon. Adam Ingram, MP
Scotland Office
Brian Wilson, MP
Social Security
Jeff Rooker, MP
Trade and Industry
The Rt. Hon. Helen Liddell, MP (*Energy, Competitiveness in Europe*)
The Rt. Hon. Richard Caborn, MP (*Trade*)
Patricia Hewitt, MP (Small Business and E-Commerce)

Treasury
Dawn Primarolo, MP (*Paymaster-General*)
Stephen Timms, MP (*Financial Secretary*)
Melanie Johnson, MP (*Economic Secretary*)

UNDER-SECRETARIES OF STATE

Agriculture, Fisheries and Food
Elliot Morley, MP
Culture, Media and Sport
Alan Howarth, MP (*Arts*)
Kate Hoey, MP (*Sport*)
Janet Anderson, MP (*Tourism, Film, Broadcasting*)
Defence
Dr Lewis Moonie, MP
Education and Employment
Margaret Hodge, MP (*Employment, Equal Opportunities*)
Malcolm Wicks, MP (*Lifelong Learning*)
Jacqui Smith, MP (*School Standards*)
Michael Wills, MP (*Learning and Technology*)
Environment, Transport and the Regions
The Lord Whitty
Keith Hill, MP
Chris Mullin, MP
Beverley Hughes, MP
Foreign and Commonwealth Office
The Baroness Scotland of Asthal
Health
Yvette Cooper, MP
The Lord Hunt of King's Heath, OBE
Gisela Stuart, MP
Home Office
Michael O'Brien, MP
The Lord Bassam of Brighton
International Development
George Foulkes, MP
Lord Chancellor's Department
Jane Kennedy, MP
David Lock, MP
Northern Ireland Office
George Howarth, MP
Social Security
The Baroness Hollis of Heigham, D.Phil. (*Child Benefit, Child Support, War Pensions*)
Angela Eagle, MP (*Income-related Benefits, International and Green Issues*)
Hugh Bayley, MP (*Disability and Sickness Benefits, Deregulation, Independent Living Fund*)
Trade and Industry
Dr Kim Howells, MP (*Consumers and Corporate Affairs*)
Alan Johnson, MP (*Competitiveness*)
The Lord Sainsbury of Turville§ (*Science and Innovation*)
Welsh Office
David Hanson, MP

§ Unpaid

GOVERNMENT WHIPS

HOUSE OF LORDS

Captain of the Honourable Corps of Gentlemen-at-Arms (Chief Whip)
The Lord Carter, PC
Captain of The Queen's Bodyguard of the Yeoman of the Guard (Deputy Chief Whip)
The Lord McIntosh of Haringey
Lords-in-Waiting
The Lord Burlison; The Lord Bach
Baronesses-in-Waiting
The Baroness Farrington of Ribbleton; The Baroness Ramsay of Cartvale; The Baroness Amos

HOUSE OF COMMONS

Parliamentary Secretary to the Treasury (Chief Whip)
The Rt. Hon. Ann Taylor, MP
Treasurer of HM Household (Deputy Chief Whip)
Keith Bradley, MP
Comptroller of HM Household
Thomas McAvoy, MP
Vice-Chamberlain of HM Household
Graham Allen, MP
Lords Commissioners
Robert Ainsworth, MP; James Dowd, MP; Clive Betts, MP; David Jamieson, MP; Gregory Pope, MP
Assistant Whips
David Clelland, MP; Kevin Hughes, MP; Anne McGuire, MP; Michael Hall, MP; Anthony McNulty, MP; Gerry Sutcliffe, MP; Donnelly Touhig, MP

Government Departments and Public Offices

This section covers central Government departments, executive agencies, regulatory bodies, other statutory independent organisations, and bodies which are government-financed or whose head is appointed by a Government Minister.

THE CIVIL SERVICE

Under the Next Steps programme, launched in 1988, many semi-autonomous executive agencies have been established to carry out much of the work of the Civil Service. Executive agencies operate within a framework set by the responsible minister which specifies policies, objectives and available resources. All executive agencies are set annual performance targets by their Minister. Each agency has a chief executive, who is responsible for the day-to-day operations of the agency and who is accountable to the minister for the use of resources and for meeting the agency's targets. The minister accounts to Parliament for the work of the agency. Nearly 80 per cent of civil servants now work in executive agencies. In October 1999 there were about 466,500 permanent civil servants.

The Senior Civil Service was created in 1996 and on 1 April 2000 comprised 3,180 staff from Permanent Secretary to the former Grade 5 level, including all agency chief executives. All Government departments and executive agencies are now responsible for their own pay and grading systems for civil servants outside the Senior Civil Service. In practice the grades of the former Open structure are still in use in some organisations. The Open structure represented the following:

Grade	Title
1	Permanent Secretary
1A	Second Permanent Secretary
2	Deputy Secretary
3	Under-Secretary
4	Chief Scientific Officer B, Professional and Technology Directing A
5	Assistant Secretary, Deputy Chief Scientific Officer, Professional and Technology Directing B
6	Senior Principal, Senior Principal Scientific Officer, Professional and Technology Superintending Grade
7	Principal, Principal Scientific Officer, Principal Professional and Technology Officer

SALARIES 2000–1

MINISTERIAL SALARIES *from 1 April 2000*

Ministers who are Members of the House of Commons receive a parliamentary salary (£48,371) in addition to their ministerial salary.

*Prime Minister	£110,287
*Cabinet minister (Commons)	£66,172
*†Cabinet minister (Lords)	£85,983
Minister of State (Commons)	£34,326
Minister of State (Lords)	£66,294
Parliamentary Under-Secretary (Commons)	£26,053
Parliamentary Under-Secretary (Lords)	£57,244

*These Ministers have yet to decide whether to take the full salaries provided for them for the financial year 2000–1. For the time being they will draw the following ministerial salaries: Prime Minister, £64,580; Cabinet minister (Commons), £48,516; Cabinet minister (Lords), £72,729
†Except the Lord Chancellor, who receives a salary of £167,760

SPECIAL ADVISERS' SALARIES *from 1 April 1999*

Special advisers to government ministers are paid out of public funds; their salaries are negotiated individually, but are usually in the range £26,728 to £78,186. At March 1999 there were 66 special advisers.

CIVIL SERVICE SALARIES *from 1 April 2000*

Senior Civil Service (SCS)

Secretary of the Cabinet and Head of the Home Civil Service	£98,400–£168,910
Permanent Secretary	£101,254–£173,808
Band 9	£89,996–£127,452
Band 8	£82,341–£120,249
Band 7	£75,374–£113,499
Band 6	£68,840–£107,212
Band 5	£62,882–£101,254
Band 4	£57,367–£95,625
Band 3	£51,975–£85,047
Band 2	£47,138–£75,601
Band 1	£42,755–£67,163

Staff are placed in pay bands according to their level of responsibility and taking account of other factors such as experience and marketability. Movement within and between bands is based on performance. A recruitment and retention allowance of up to £3,000 may be paid in certain circumstances in addition to the salary ranges shown for bands 1 to 9.

Other Civil Servants

Following the delegation of responsibility for pay and grading to Government departments and agencies from 1 April 1996, it is no longer possible to show service-wide pay rates for staff outside the Senior Civil Service. The following table will however give an indication of the percentage of civil servants at a given salary level.

Non-Industrial Staff by Gross Salary Band as at 1 April 1999

Salary Band	Per Cent
£5,001–£10,000	8.3
£10,001–£15,000	37.0
£15,001–£20,000	23.4
£20,001–£25,000	16.4
£25,001–£30,000	6.5
£30,001–£35,000	3.1
£35,001–£40,000	1.9
£40,001–£45,000	1.3
£45,001–£50,000	0.7
£50,001–£55,000	0.0
£55,001–£60,000	0.3
£60,001–£65,000	0.1
£65,001–£70,000	0.1
£70,001–£75,000	0.0
£75,001 +	0.1

Source: Government Statistical Service – *Civil Service Statistics 1999*

GOVERNMENT DEPARTMENTS

MINISTRY OF AGRICULTURE, FISHERIES AND FOOD
Nobel House, 17 Smith Square, London SW1P 3JR
Tel: 020-7238 3000; Fax: 020-7238 6591
Email: helpline@inf.maff.gov.uk
Web: http://www.maff.gov.uk/maffhome.htm

The Ministry of Agriculture, Fisheries and Food is responsible for Government policies on agriculture, horticulture and fisheries in England and for policies relating to the safety and quality of food in the UK as a whole, including composition, labelling, additives, contaminants and new production processes. In association with the agriculture departments of the Scottish Executive, the National Assembly for Wales and the Northern Ireland Office and with the Intervention Board (*see* page 337), the Ministry is responsible for negotiations in the EU on the common agricultural and fisheries policies, and for single European market questions relating to its responsibilities. Its remit also includes international agricultural and food trade policy.

The Ministry exercises responsibilities for the protection and enhancement of the countryside and the marine environment, for flood defence and for other rural issues. It is the licensing authority for veterinary medicines and the registration authority for pesticides. It administers policies relating to the control of animal, plant and fish diseases. It provides scientific, technical and professional services and advice to farmers, growers and ancillary industries, and it commissions research to assist in the formulation and assessment of policy and to underpin applied research and development work done by industry. Responsibility for food safety and standards was transferred to the new Food Standards Agency in April 2000.

Minister of Agriculture, Fisheries and Food, The Rt. Hon. Nick Brown, MP
 Principal Private Secretary (G7), A. Slade
 Private Secretary, Ms F. James
 Parliamentary Private Secretary, Ruth Kelly, MP
Minister of State, The Rt. Hon. Joyce Quin, MP
 Private Secretary, Ms T. Hart
Minister of State, The Baroness Hayman
 Private Secretary, V. Platten
Parliamentary Secretary, Elliot Morley, MP
 Private Secretary, M. Livesey
Parliamentary Clerk, Ms C. Dix
Permanent Secretary (SCS), B. Bender, CB
 Private Secretary, L. Burdett

ESTABLISHMENTS GROUP
Director of Establishments (SCS), R. A. Saunderson

DIVISION
Head of Division (SCS), B. Jones

PERSONNEL DIVISION
Head of Division (SCS), Ms T. Newell

BUILDING AND ESTATE MANAGEMENT
Eastbury House, 30–34 Albert Embankment, London SE1 7TL
Tel: 020-7238 6000
Head of Division (SCS), J. A. S. Nickson

INFORMATION TECHNOLOGY DIRECTORATE
Government Buildings, Epsom Road, Guildford, Surrey GU1 2LD
Tel: 01483-403757
Acting Director (SCS), S. Soper
Acting Head of Strategies (G6), A. Hill
Head of Applications (G6), P. Barber
Head of Infrastructure (G6), D. Brown

COMMUNICATIONS DIRECTORATE
Nobel House, 17 Smith Square, London SW1P 3JR
Tel: 020-7238 6000; helpline 0645-335577
Director of Communications (SCS), R. Lowson
Chief Press Officer (G7), M. Smith
Chief Publicity Officer (G7), N. Wagstaffe
Principal Librarian (G7), P. McShane

AGENCY OWNERSHIP UNIT
3–8 Whitehall House (West Block), London SW1A 2HH
Head of Unit (SCS), Dr M. Tas

FINANCE DEPARTMENT
3–8 Whitehall Place (West Block), London SW1A 2HH
Tel: 020-7238 6000
Principal Finance Officer (SCS), P. Elliott

FINANCIAL POLICY DIVISION
Head of Division (SCS), B. J. Harding

PROCUREMENT AND CONTRACTS DIVISION
19–29 Woburn Place, London WC1H 0LU
Tel: 020-7273 3000
Head of Division (SCS), D. Rabey

AUDIT, CONSULTANCY AND MANAGEMENT SERVICES
19–29 Woburn Place, London WC1H 0LU
Tel: 020-7273 3000
Director of Audit (SCS), D. V. Fisher

RESOURCE MANAGEMENT STRATEGY UNIT
19–29 Woburn Place, London WC1H 0LU
Tel: 020-7273 3000
Head of Unit (SCS), D. V. Fisher

RESOURCE MANAGEMENT DIVISION
Foss House, Kings Pool, 1–2 Peasholme Green, York YO1 7PX
Tel: 01904-455328
Head of Division (G6), Mrs J. Flint

BUSINESS PLANNING UNIT
Head of Unit (G7), V. Bodnar

LEGAL DEPARTMENT
55 Whitehall, London SW1A 2EY
Tel: 020-7238 6000
Legal Adviser and Solicitor (SCS), Miss K. M. S. Morton
Principal Assistant Solicitors (SCS), D. J. Pearson; Ms C. A. Crisham

LEGAL DIVISIONS
Assistant Solicitor, Division A1 (SCS), P. Davis
Assistant Solicitor, Division A2 (SCS), Ms A. Werbicki
Assistant Solicitor, Division A3 (SCS), C. Gregory
Assistant Solicitor, Division A4 (SCS), C. Allen
Assistant Solicitor, Division A5 (SCS), N. Lambert

Assistant Solicitor, Division B1 (*SCS*), Ms S. Spence
Assistant Solicitor, Division B2 (*SCS*), M. Patel
Assistant Solicitor, Division B3 (*SCS*), I. Corbett

INVESTIGATION UNIT
Chief Investigation Officer (*G7*), Miss J. Panting

ECONOMICS AND STATISTICS
3–8 Whitehall Place (West Block), London SW1A 2HH
Tel: 020-7238 6000

Head of Economics and Statistics Group (*SCS*), D. Thompson

DIVISIONS

Senior Economic Adviser, Economics and Statistics (*Farm Business*) (*G6*), J. Watson
Senior Economic Adviser, Economics (*International*) (*SCS*), N. Atkinson
Senior Economic Adviser, Economics (*Resource Use*) (*SCS*), J. P. Muriel

TRANSMISSABLE SPONGIFORM ENCEPHALOPATHIES RESEARCH AND SURVEILLANCE UNIT
Eastbury House, 30–34 Albert Embankment, London SE17 7TL *Head of Unit* (*SCS*), Dr Mandy Bailey

CHANGE MANAGEMENT UNIT
3–8 Whitehall Place (West Block), London SW1P 2HH
Head of Unit, David Rossington

STATISTICS DIVISION
Foss House, Kings Pool, 1–2 Peasholme Green,
York YO1 7PX
Tel: 01904-455332

Chief Statistician (*Commodities and Food*) (*SCS*), S. Platt
Chief Statistician (*Census and Surveys*) (*SCS*), P. F. Helm

CHIEF SCIENTIST'S GROUP
1A Page Street, London SW1P 4PQ
Tel: 020-7904 6000

Chief Scientist (*SCS*), Dr D. W. F. Shannon

DIVISIONS

Head, Agriculture, Environment and Food Technology (*SCS*), Dr J. C. Sherlock
Head, Veterinary, Food and Aquatic Science (*SCS*), Dr K. J. MacOwan
Head, Research Policy and International (*SCS*), A. R. Burne

FISHERIES DEPARTMENT
Nobel House, 17 Smith Square,
London SW1P 3JR
Fisheries Secretary (*SCS*), S.Wentworth

DIVISIONS

Head, Fisheries I (*SCS*), P. M. Boyling
Head, Fisheries II (*SCS*), C. I. Llewellyn
Head, Fisheries III (*SCS*), Miss S. Brown
Head, Fisheries IV (*SCS*), B. S. Edwards
Chief Inspector, Sea Fisheries Inspectorate (*G6*), S. G. Ellson

AGRICULTURAL CROPS AND COMMODITIES DIRECTORATE
3–8 Whitehall Place (West Block), London SW1A 2HH
Tel: 020-7238 6000

Deputy Secretary (*SCS*), Ms V. K. Timms, CB

EUROPEAN UNION AND INTERNATIONAL POLICY
Head of Group (*SCS*), A. J. Lebrecht

DIVISIONS
Head, European Union and Agriculture Strategy (*SCS*), T. Eddy
Head, European Union and International Division (*SCS*), D. Dawson

AGRICULTURE GROUP
Head of Group (*SCS*), D. Hunter

DIVISIONS

Head, Horticulture, Potatoes and HMI (*SCS*), G. W. Noble
Head, New Crops and Sugar (*SCS*), H. B. Brown
Head, Arable Crops (*SCS*), A. Kuyk
Head, Beef and Sheep (*SCS*), R. Cowan
Head, Livestock Schemes (*SCS*), A. Taylor
Head, Milk, Pigs, Eggs and Poultry (*SCS*), G. Ross
Head Plant Health and PHSI (*SCS*), A. Perrins

FOOD INDUSTRY, COMPETITIVENESS AND CONSUMERS
Head (*SCS*), J. Robbs

DIVISIONS

Head, Food and Drinks Industry (*SCS*), Miss C. J. Rabagliati
Head, International Relations and Export Promotion (*SCS*), D. V. Orchard
Head, Agricultural Resources and Better Regulation (*SCS*), Mrs A. Blackburn
Head, Marketing, Competition and Consumers (*SCS*), Ms J. Allfrey
Head, Genetic Modification and Agricultural Group Co-ordination Division, Ms S. Hendry (*G6*)
Head, Flood and Coastal Defence (*SCS*), J. Park
Head, BSE Enquiry Liaison Unit, Ms A. Waters (*G6*)

PLANT VARIETY RIGHTS OFFICE AND SEED DIVISION
White House Lane, Huntingdon road, Cambridge CB3 0LF
Head of Office (*SCS*), D. Boreham

REGIONAL SERVICES AND DEFENCE GROUP
3–8 Whitehall Place (West Block), London SW1A 2HH
Tel: 020-7238 6000

Head of Group (*SCS*), Mrs K. J. A. Brown

DIVISIONS
Head of CAP Schemes Management Division (*SCS*), Mrs J. Purnell

REGIONAL ORGANISATION
Head, Regional Support Unit (*G7*), D. Putley
Regional Service Centres
ANGLIA REGION, Block B, Government Buildings, Brooklands Avenue, Cambridge CB2 2DR.
Tel: 01223-462727. *Regional Director*, M. Edwards
EAST MIDLANDS REGION, Block 7, Government Buildings, Chalfont Drive, Nottingham NG8 3SN.
Tel: 0115-929 0634. *Regional Director*, G. Norbury
NORTH-EAST REGION, Government Buildings, Crosby Road, Northallerton, N. Yorks DL6 1AD.
Tel: 01609-773751. *Regional Director*, P. Watson
NORTHERN REGION, Eden Bridge House, Lowther Street, Carlisle, Cumbria CA3 8DX. Tel: 01228-523400.
Regional Director, I. G. Pearson
NORTH MERCIA REGION, Electra Way, Crewe Business Park, Crewe, Cheshire CW1 6GL.
Tel: 01270-754000. *Regional Director (Acting)*, A. Percival

SOUTH-EAST REGION, Block A, Government Buildings, Coley Park, Reading, Berks RG1 6DT. Tel: 01889-581222. *Regional Director (Acting)*, W. Duncan

SOUTH MERCIA REGION, Block C, Government Buildings, Whittington Road, Worcester WR5 2LQ. Tel: 01905-763355. *Regional Director*, B. Davies

SOUTH-WEST REGION, Clyst House, Winslade Park, Clyst St Mary, Exeter EX5 1DY. Tel: 01392-447400. *Regional Director*, M. R. W. Highman

WESSEX REGION, Block 3, Government Buildings, Burghill Road, Westbury-on-Trym, Bristol BS10 6NJ.Tel: 0117-959 1000. *Regional Director (Acting)*, Ms C. Deakins

ANIMAL HEALTH AND ENVIRONMENT GROUP
Deputy Secretary (SCS), Ms J. Bacon

ENVIRONMENT GROUP
Head of Group (SCS), D. J. Coates
Head, Rural Division (SCS), Ms L. Cornish
Head, Conservation Management Division (SCS), T. J. Osmond
Head, Rural and Marine Environment (SCS), P. Cleasby

ANIMAL HEALTH GROUP
1A Page Street, London SW1P 4PQ
Tel: 020-7904 6000
Head of Group (SCS), N. Thornton

DIVISIONS

Head, Animal Health (BSE and International Trade) (SCS), P. Nash
Head, Animal Health (Disease Control) (SCS), Ms V. Smith
Head, Services (G6), Ms C. Harrold
Head, Animal Welfare (SCS), C. J. Ryder
Head, Bovine Tuberculosis (SCS), R. Hathaway

CHIEF VETERINARY OFFICER'S GROUP
1A Page Street, London SW1P 4PQ
Tel: 020-7904 6000
Chief Veterinary Officer (SCS), J. M. Scudamore
Deputy Chief Veterinary Officer (Services) (SCS), M. Atkinson

DIVISIONS

Head of Veterinary Services East (SCS), G. Jones
Head of Veterinary Services West (SCS), J. Cross
Head of Veterinary Services North (SCS), R. Drummond
Head of Veterinary Services Resources (SCS), Ms B. Phillip
Assistant Chief Veterinary Officer (Scotland), L. Gardner
Head of Veterinary Services (Scotland) (SCS), D. McIntosh
Assistant Chief Veterinary Officer (Wales), A. Edwards
Deputy Chief Veterinary Officer (Policy)(SCS), R. Cawthorne
Head, Veterinary International Trade Team (SCS), R. A. Bell
Head, Veterinary Notifiable Disease Team (Exotic Diseases) (SCS), Dr D. Matthews
Head, Veterinary Notifiable Disease Team (Endemic Animal Diseases and Zoonoses) (SCS), Dr Debbie Reynolds
Head, Welfare Team (SCS), D. Pritchard

EXECUTIVE AGENCIES

CENTRAL SCIENCE LABORATORY
Sand Hutton, York YO41 1LZ
Tel: 01904-462000; Fax: 01904-462111

The agency provides MAFF with technical support and policy advice on the protection and quality of the food supply and on related environmental issues.
Chief Executive (G3), Prof. P. I. Stanley
Research Directors (G5), Prof. A. R. Hardy *(Agriculture and Environment)*; Prof. J. Gilbert *(Food)*

CENTRE FOR ENVIRONMENT, FISHERIES AND AQUACULTURE SCIENCE
Pakefield Road, Lowestoft, Suffolk NR33 0HT
Tel: 01502-562244; Fax: 01502-513865

The Agency, established in April 1997, provides research and consultancy services in fisheries science and management, aquaculture, fish health and hygiene, environmental impact assessment, and environmental quality assessment.
Chief Executive, Dr P. Greig-Smith

FARMING AND RURAL CONSERVATION AGENCY
Nobel House, 17 Smith Square, London SW1P 3JR
Tel: 020-7238 5432; Fax: 020-7238 5588

The Agency, established in April 1997, is responsible jointly to MAFF and the National Assembly for Wales. It assists the Government in the design, development and implementation of policies on the integration of farming and conservation, environmental protection, rural land use and the diversification of the rural economy. This includes agri-environment schemes such as Environmentally Sensitive Areas, Countryside Stewardship and access, rural development, milk hygiene inspections and wildlife management.
Chief Executive (SCS), Miss S. Nason

INTERVENTION BOARD
—see pages 337

PESTICIDES SAFETY DIRECTORATE
Mallard House, Kings Pool, 3 Peasholme Green, York YO1 7PX
Tel: 01904-640500; Fax: 01904-455733

The Pesticides Safety Directorate is responsible for the evaluation and approval of pesticides and the development of policies relating to them, in order to protect consumers, users and the environment.
Chief Executive (G4), Dr H. K. Wilson
Director (Policy) (G5), J. A. Bainton
Director (Approvals) (G5), Dr A. D. Martin

VETERINARY LABORATORIES AGENCY
Woodham Lane, New Haw, Addlestone, Surrey KT15 3NB
Tel: 01932-341111; Fax: 01932-347046

The Veterinary Laboratories Agency provides scientific and technical expertise in animal and public health.
Chief Executive, Dr S. Edwards
Director of Research, Dr J. A. Morris
Acting Director of Surveillance and Laboratory Services, R. Hancock
Director of Finance, C. Morrey
Laboratory Secretary, C. Edwards

VETERINARY MEDICINES DIRECTORATE
Woodham Lane, New Haw, Addlestone, Surrey KT1 3LS
Tel: 01932-336911; Fax: 01932-336618

The Veterinary Medicines Directorate is responsible for all aspects of the authorisation and control of veterinary medicines, including post-authorisation surveillance of residues in meat and animal products, and the provision of policy advice to Ministers.
Chief Executive and Director of Veterinary Medicines (G4), Dr J. M. Rutter

Director (Policy) (G5), R. Anderson
Director (Licensing) (G5), S. Dean
Secretary and Head of Business Unit (G6), J. FitzGerald
Licensing Manager, Pharmaceuticals and Feed Additives (G6),
J. P. O'Brien
Licensing Manager, Immunologicals (G6),
Dr D. J. K. Mackay

THE CABINET OFFICE
70 Whitehall, London SW1A 2AS
Tel: 020-7270 3000
Web: http://www.cabinet-office.gov.uk

The Cabinet Office comprises the Secretariat, who support Ministers collectively in the conduct of Cabinet business; and units responsible for modernising Government and helping to improve the quality, coherence and responsiveness of public services. By 2008, the Government hopes to be able to deliver all its services electronically. It is also responsible for Senior Civil Service and public appointments, market testing and efficiency in the Civil Service, and Civil Service recruitment. The Cabinet Office supports the Prime Minister in his capacity as Minister for the Civil Service, with responsibility for day-to-day supervision delegated to the Minister for the Cabinet Office, who is also responsible for the Central Office of Information (see page 296).

Prime Minister and Minister for the Civil Service,
 The Rt. Hon. Tony Blair, MP
Minister for the Cabinet Office and Chancellor
 of the Duchy of Lancaster,
 The Rt. Hon. Dr Marjorie (Mo) Mowlam, MP
 Principal Private Secretary (SCS), Dr J. Fuller
 Parliamentary Private Secretary, Margaret Moran, MP
 Private Secretary, S. Poole
 Special Advisers, N. Warner; A. Lappin
Minister of State, The Lord Falconer of Thoroton, QC
 Private Secretary, M. Langdale
 Parliamentary Private Secretary, C. Leslie, MP
Minister of State, The Rt. Hon. Ian McCartney, MP
 Private Secretary, Ms N. Pitts
 Parliamentary Private Secretary, Frank Doran, MP
 Parliamentary Secretary, Graham Stringer, MP
Secretary of the Cabinet and Head of the Home Civil Service,
 Sir Richard Wilson, KCB
 Private Secretary (SCS), R. Abel
 Permanent Secretary, Ms M. MacDonald
Private Secretary, P. White
 Chief Scientific Adviser, vacant

PRIME MINISTER'S OFFICE
10 Downing Street, London SW1A 2AA
Tel: 020-7270 3000; Fax: 020-7925 0918
Web: http://www.number-10.gov.uk
Principal Private Secretary, J. J. Heywood
Chief of Staff (£91,014), J. Powell
Deputy Chief of Staff, P. McFadden
Private Secretaries, J. Sawers (Foreign Affairs); C. Sumner
 (Parliamentary Affairs); D. North (Home Affairs);
 S. Virley (Economic Affairs); A. Wechsberg,
 M. Tatham (Assistant on Foreign Affairs);
 M. Cleaver (Foreign Affairs/Assistant Private Secretary)
Diary Secretary, Ms K. Garvey
Special Assistant for Presentation and Planning,
 Ms A. Hunter
Assistant to Mrs Blair, Ms F. Millar
Political Secretary, Ms S. Morgan
Head of Policy Unit, D. Miliband

Policy Unit, G. Mulgan; R. Liddle; D. Scott;
 Ms E. Lloyd; P. Hyman; J. Purnell; R. Hill;
 G. Norris; A. Adonis; C. Oppenheim; E. Richards,
 J. Gallagher, B. Hackland
Parliamentary Private Secretary, B. Grocott, MP
Chief Press Secretary (£91,014), A. Campbell
Deputy Press Secretary, G. Smith
Special Advisers, Press Office, Ms H. Coffman; L. Price
Press Officers, T. Joseph; D. Peel; J. Braithwaite
Strategic Communications Unit, P. Bassett; D. Bradshaw;
 J. Humphreys; L. McNeil; P. Brown
Secretary for Appointments, and Ecclesiastical Secretary
 to the Lord Chancellor, W. Chapman
Parliamentary Clerk, C. Barbour

SECRETARIATS

ECONOMIC AND DOMESTIC SECRETARIAT
Head (SCS), S. Chakrabarti
Deputy Heads (SCS), Ms. L. Bell; P. Britton

DEFENCE AND OVERSEAS AFFAIRS SECRETARIAT
Head of Secretariat and Chairman of the Joint Intelligence
 Committee (SCS), P. Rikketts
Deputy Head (SCS), D. Fisher
Head of Division, N. Sanderson
Chief of Assessments Staff, J. Day

INTELLIGENCE CO-ORDINATION GROUP
Head (SCS), The Hon M. Pakenham, CMG
Head of Security Division (SCS), Ms E. Chivers

EUROPEAN AFFAIRS SECRETARIAT
Head (SCS), S. Wall
Deputy Heads (SCS), M. Donnelly

CONSTITUTION SECRETARIAT
Director (SCS), J. Tross
Head of Other Constitutional Reform Team (SCS),
 Ms J. Simpson
Head of Legal Advisers, Ms R. Jeffreys

CENTRAL SECRETARIAT
Director (SCS), Ms S. Phippard
Deputy Director (SCS), P. Calcutt, OBE

CEREMONIAL BRANCH
Ashley House, 2 Monck Street, London SW1P 2BQ
 Tel: 020-7270 1234
Honours Nomination Unit: Tel: 020-7276 2775
Ceremonial Officer (SCS), Mrs G. Catto

PUBLIC SERVICE DELIVERY

MODERNISING PUBLIC SERVICES GROUP
Director (SCS), J. Stephens
Deputy Directors (SCS), S. O'Leary, OBE;
 M. Sweetman; A. Whysall; J. Cowper

CENTRAL IT UNIT
Tel: 020-7270 1234
Director (SCS), D. Cooke
Deputy Directors (SCS), J. Crump; M. Gladwyn;
 Mrs A. Steward; I. White; P. Waller

REGULATORY IMPACT UNIT
Director (SCS), P. Wynn Owen
Deputy Directors (SCS), D. Hayler; C. Hayes;
 Ms A. French
Legal Adviser, P. Bovey

MODERNISING GOVERNMENT
Director, A. Wells
Deputy Director (SCS), J. Cowper

CIVIL SERVICE MANAGEMENT

CENTRAL GOVERNMENT NATIONAL TRAINING
ORGANISATION (CGNTO)
Room 69/1 GOOGS, Horse Guards Road, London
SW1P 3AL
Tel: 020-7270 1597; Fax: 020-7270 6640;
Email: secretariat@cgnto.org.uk
Council Members, B. Fox; J. Barker; R. Green;
Ms A. Perkins; R. Dudding; C. MacDonald; B. Mitchell;
B. Richardson;
M. Grannatt; P. Joyce; J. Sheldon; Cllr J. Stocks;
N. Starritt; D. Laughrin; I. Magee
Head of Secretariat, John Barker

CENTRE FOR MANAGEMENT AND POLICY STUDIES
(CMPS)
Director-General, Prof. R. Amman
Directors (SCS), R. Green; S. Duncan

CIVIL SERVICE COLLEGE DIRECTORATE
Sunningdale Park, Ascot, Berks SL5 0QE
Tel: 01344-634000; Fax: 01344-634233
11 Belgrave Road, London SW1 4RB
Tel: 020-7834 6644; Fax: 01344-634451
199 Cathedral Street, Glasgow G4 0QU
Tel: 0141-553 6021; Fax: 0141-553 6171
Suite 19, 1 St Colme Street, Edinburgh EH3 6AA
Tel: 0131-220 8267; Fax: 0131-220 8367
The College provides training in management and
professional skills for the public and private sectors. From
1 April 2000 it ceased to be an executive agency of the
Cabinet Office, but was integrated into the Governments
Centre for Management and Policy Studies.
Director, E. Wooldridge
Business Executives, Prof. R. Amann; Ms S. Duncan;
R. Green; Ms L. Chapman; Mrs N. Oppenheimer;
B. Sutcliffe; C. Parry

CIVIL SERVICE CORPORATE
MANAGEMENT COMMAND
Senior Director (SCS), B. M. Fox, CB
Directors (SCS), J. Barker; Ms S. Hinkley, CBE
Deputy Directors (SCS), Ms A. Schofield; Ms J. Lemprière;
C. J. Parry; Ms E. Goodison; D. G. Pain; S. Mitha

GOVERNMENT INFORMATION AND
COMMUNICATION SERVICES
*Head of Government Information and Communication Services
(SCS)*, M. Granatt
Director, Development Centre (SCS), C. Skinner
Deputy Director, Ms S. Jenkins

OFFICE OF THE COMMISSIONER FOR
PUBLIC APPOINTMENTS (OCPA)
Tel: 020-7270 6472
The role of the Commissioner for Public Appointments is
to monitor, regulate, report and advise on 12,500
ministerial public appointments to executive non-depart-
mental public bodies, public corporations, nationalised
industries, utility regulators and NHS bodies. The
Commissioner is appointed by an Order-in-Council.
Commissioner, Dame Rennie Fritchie
Head of Office (SCS), J. Barron

OFFICE OF THE CIVIL SERVICE
COMMISSIONERS (OCSC)
Tel: 020-7270 5081; Fax: 020-7270 5967
First Commissioner, The Baroness Usha Prashar, CBE
Commissioners (part-time), D. J. Burr; Ms S. Forbes;
H. J. F. McLean, CBE; Sir Leonard Peach; J. Shrigley;
K. Singh, CBE; C. Stevens, CB; Dame Rennie Fritchie
Secretary to the Commissioners and Head of the Office (SCS),
J. K. Barron

CROSS-CUTTING ISSUES

SOCIAL EXCLUSION UNIT
Tel: 020-7270 5211
Director of Unit (SCS), Ms M. Wallace, OBE
Deputy Directors, Ms Z. Peatfield; A. Patel

UK ANTI DRUGS CO-ORDINATION UNIT
Tel: 020-7270 5399
UK Anti-Drugs Co-ordinator (£106,057), K. Hellawell
Deputy Co-ordinator, M. Trace
Private Secretary, V. Baggarley
Director, J. Critchley

WOMEN'S UNIT
10 Great George Street, London SW1P 3AE
Tel: 020-7273 8808
Head of Unit (SCS), Ms F. Reynolds, CBE
Deputy Director, G. Kidd

PERFORMANCE AND INNOVATION UNIT
Tel: 020-7270 1512
Director (SCS), vacant
Deputy Director (SCS), J. Rentoul

INFORMATION, ESTABLISHMENT
AND ORGANISATION

Queen Anne's Chambers, 28 Broadway, London SW1H 9JS
Director of Information (SCS), P. Martin
Principal Establishment and Finance Officer (SCS), P. Wardle
Deputy Directors (SCS), Miss E. Chennells; D. Brennan;
R. Harris; K. Tolladay
Ministers' Adviser on Agencies, C. Brendish, CBE

HER MAJESTY'S STATIONERY OFFICE
St Clements House, 2–16 Colegate, Norwich NR3 1BQ
Tel: 01603-621000
Controller (SCS), Mrs C. Tullo

EXECUTIVE AGENCY

GOVERNMENT CAR AND DESPATCH AGENCY
46 Ponton Road, London SW8 5AX
Tel: 020-7217 3839; Fax: 020-7217 3840;
Email: gcda@compuserve.com
The Agency provides secure transport and document
transfers between Government departments.
Chief Executive, N. Matheson

CENTRAL OFFICE OF INFORMATION
Hercules Road, London SE1 7DU
Tel: 020-7928 2345; Fax: 020-7928 5037

The Central Office of Information (COI) is a Government department which offers consultancy, procurement
and project management services to central Government
for publicity. Though the majority of the COI's work is for
Government departments in the UK, it also procures a

range of publicity materials for overseas consumption. Administrative responsibility for the COI rests with the Minister for the Cabinet Office.
Chief Executive (G3), Miss C. Fisher
Senior Personal Secretary, Mrs I. MacMull

MANAGEMENT BOARD
Members, K. Williamson; P. Buchanan; I. Hamilton; R. Haslam; Mrs S. Whetton; M. Reid
Secretary, Mrs I. MacMull

DIRECTORS
Director, Client Services, I. Hamilton
Director, Marketing Communications, P. Buchanan
Director, Films, Radio and Events, S. Whetton
Director, Publications, M. Reid
Director, Central Services, K. Williamson
Director, Regional Network, R. Haslam

NETWORK OFFICES
EASTERN, 2nd Floor, Block A1, Westbrook Centre, Milton Road, Cambridge CB4 1YG. *Network Director*, R. Humphries
MIDLANDS EAST, Belgrave Centre, Talbot Street, Nottingham NG1 5GG, P. Smith
MIDLANDS WEST, Five Ways House, Islington Row, Middleway, Edgbaston, Birmingham B15 1SH. *Network Director*, B. Garner
NORTH-EAST, Wellbar House, Gallowgate, Newcastle upon Tyne NE1 4TB. *Network Director*, Ms L. Taylor
NORTH-WEST, Sunley Tower, Piccadilly Plaza, Manchester M1 4BD. *Network Director*, Mrs E. Jones
SOUTH-EAST, Hercules Road, London SE1 7DU. *Network Director*, Ms V. Burdon
SOUTH-WEST, The Pithay, Bristol BS1 2NF. *Network Director*, P. Whitbread
YORKSHIRE AND HUMBERSIDE, City House, New Station Street, Leeds LS1 4JG. *Network Director*, Ms W. Miller

DEPARTMENT FOR CULTURE, MEDIA AND SPORT
2–4 Cockspur Street, London SW1Y 5DH
Tel: 020-7211 6200; Fax: 020-7211 6032
Email: enquiries@culture.gov.uk
Web: http://www.culture.gov.uk

The Department for Culture, Media and Sport was established in July 1997 and is responsible for Government policy relating to the arts, broadcasting, the press, museums and galleries, libraries, sport and recreation, historic buildings and ancient monuments, tourism, and the music industry. It is responsible for policy on the National Lottery and the Millennium, and sponsors the Millennium Commission.
Secretary of State for Culture, Media and Sport, The Rt. Hon. Chris Smith, MP
Private Secretary, F. Muir
Special Advisers, A. Burnham; Ms R. Mackenzie, OBE
Parliamentary Private Secretary, Ms F. Mactaggart, MP
Parliamentary Under-Secretaries, Alan Howarth, MP (*Arts*); Kate Hoey, MP (*Sport*); Janet Anderson, MP (*Tourism, Film and Broadcasting*)
Private Secretaries, S. Cooper; S. Harding; T. Edmunds
Permanent Secretary (SCS), R. Young
Private Secretary, Ms C. Page

MUSEUMS, GALLERIES, LIBRARIES AND HERITAGE GROUP
Head of Group (SCS), Ms A. Stewart
Head, Libraries and Information Division (SCS), J. Evans

Head, Buildings, Monuments and Sites (SCS), N. Pittman
Head, Museums, Galleries and Cultural Property (SCS), H. Corner
Director, Government Art Collection (SCS), Ms P. Johnson

STRATEGY AND COMMUNICATION GROUP
Head of Group (SCS), P. Bolt
Head of News, I. Hepplewhite
Head of Promotions and Publicity Unit, G. Newsom
Head of Strategy, S. Cove

FINANCE AND CENTRAL GROUP
Head of Group (SCS), A. Ramsay
Head, Finance Division (SCS), vacant
Head, National Lottery Division (SCS), A. McLellan
Head, Personnel and Central Services Division (SCS), Ms R. Siemaszko
Head, Central Appointments Unit, Ms R. Griggs
Head, Internal Audit, D. Rix

CREATIVE INDUSTRIES, MEDIA AND BROADCASTING GROUP
Head of Group (SCS), N. J. Kroll
Head, Broadcasting Division (SCS), D. Kahn
Head, Media Division (SCS), M. Seeney
Head, Creative Industries, A. Ferries

REGIONS, TOURISM, MILLENNIUM AND INTERNATIONAL GROUP
Head of Group, B. Leonard
Head, Tourism Division (SCS), S. Broadley
Head, Millennium Unit, Miss C. Pillman
Head, Local, Regional and International Division (SCS), P. Douglas

EDUCATION, TRAINING, ARTS AND SPORT
Head of Group, Ms P. Drew
Head, Arts Division (SCS), W. Nye
Head, Sports Division (SCS), H. Reeves
Head, Education (SCS), A. Dyer

EXECUTIVE AGENCY

ROYAL PARKS AGENCY
The Old Police House, Hyde Park, London W2 2UH
Tel: 020-7298 2000; Fax: 020-7298 2005

The Agency is responsible for maintaining and developing the royal parks.
Chief Executive (G5), W. Weston

DEPARTMENT FOR EDUCATION AND EMPLOYMENT
Sanctuary Buildings, Great Smith Street, London SW1P 3BT Tel: 0870-001 2345;
Fax: 020-7925 6000 Email: info@dfee.gov.uk
Web: http://www.dfee.gov.uk
Caxton House, Tothill Street, London SW1H 9NF
Tel: 020-7273 3000; Fax: 020-7273 5124
Moorfoot, Sheffield S1 4PQ
Tel: 0114-275 5275; Fax: 0114-259 4724
Mowden Hall, Staindrop Road, Darlington DL3 9BG
Tel: 01325-460155

The Department for Education and Employment was formed in July 1995, bringing together the functions of the former Department for Education with the training and labour market functions of the former Employment Department Group. It includes an executive agency, the Employment Service. The Department aims to support economic growth and improve the nation's competitiveness and quality of life by raising standards of education and training and by promoting an efficient and flexible labour market.

Secretary of State for Education and Employment,
  The Rt. Hon. David Blunkett, MP
  Principal Private Secretary, M. Wardle
  Special Advisers, C. Ryan; Ms S. Linden;
  N. Pearce; T. Engel
  Parliamentary Private Secretary, Ms J. Corston, MP
Minister of State, The Rt. Hon. Tessa Jowell, MP
  (Employment, Welfare to Work and Equal Opportunities)
  Private Secretary, D. Nickerson
Parliamentary Private Secretary, Ms J. Ryan, MP
  Minister of State, Estelle Morris, MP *(School Standards)*
  Private Secretary, J. Whitfield
Minister in the Lords, The Baroness Blackstone, PH.D.
  (Education and Employment)
  Private Secretary, E. Wilkinson
  Parliamentary Private Secretary, T. McNulty, MP
Parliamentary Under-Secretaries of State, Margaret Hodge,
  MP *(Employment and Equal Opportunities)*; Malcolm
  Wicks, MP *(Lifelong Learning)*; Jacqui Smith, MP
  (School Standards); Michael Wills, MP
  (Learning and Technology)
  Private Secretaries, L. Carter; K. Lumley;
S. Bartlett; S. Kennett
  Permanent Secretary, Sir Michael Bichard, KCB
  Private Secretary, M. Doherty

EMPLOYMENT, EQUALITY AND INTERNATIONAL RELATIONS DIRECTORATE
Director-General, C. Tucker

INTERNATIONAL
Director, C. Tucker, CB
Heads of Divisions, Ms W. Harris *(European Union)*;
  Ms E. Trewartha *(European Social Fund)*;
  M. Niven *(International Relations)*

EMPLOYMENT POLICY
Director, M. J. Richardson
Heads of Divisions, T. Moore *(Structural Unemployment
  Policy)*; E. Galvin *(Adults Disadvantage Policy Division)*;
  C. Barnham *(Welfare to Work)*; B. Wells *(Economy and
  Labour Market)*;
  N. Atkinson *(Learning and Workbank Project)*; M. Daly
  (DfEE/ES New Agency Division)

OPPORTUNITY AND DIVERSITY GROUP
Director, Ms S. Trundle, OBE
Heads of Divisions, Ms C. Slocock *(Childcare Unit)*;
  Ms J. Eastabrook *(Sex and Race Equality)*; Ms E. Tillett
  (Disability Policy); M. Craske *(Overseas Labour Service)*

FINANCE AND ANALYTICAL SERVICES DIRECTORATE
Director-General, P. Shaw

FINANCE
Heads of Divisions, Mrs S. Todd *(Planning and Expenditure)*;
  S. Burt *(Capital Investment)*; Mrs C. Hunter *(Programmes)*;
  R. Wye *(Efficiency)*; P. Connor *(Financial Accounting)*;
  N. Thirtle *(Internal Audit)*

ANALYTICAL SERVICES
Director, D. Allnutt
Heads of Divisions, M. Britton *(Qualifications, Pupil Assessment and IT)*; J. Elliott *(Youth and Further Education)*;

S. Field *(Higher Education, Evaluation Strategy and
  International)*;
  B. Butcher *(Employability and Adult Learning)*;
  R. Bartholomew *(Equal Opportunities and Research
  Programmes)*; Ms A. Brown *(Schools, Teachers and
  Resources)*

LIFELONG LEARNING DIRECTORATE
Director-General, N. Stuart *Director,* J. Hedger
Heads of Divisions, P. Holme *(Resources and Contract
  Management Divison)*; S. Orr *(Quality and Financial
  Assurance Division)*; A. Weinstock *(Millennium
  Volunteers Unit)*

LEARNING QUALITY AND DELIVERY DIRECTORATE
Director, P. Lauener
Heads of Divisions, J. Reid *(LSC Implementation)*; P. Houten
  (Post 16 Implementation); P. Mucklow *(LSC Policy,
  Structure and Appointments)*; A. McCully *(Post 16
  Legislation Division)*; M. Stock *(LSC/ALI Information and
  Business Systems)*

QUALIFICATIONS
Director, R. Hull
Heads of Division, J. West *(Qualifications at Work)*; C.
  Johnson *(School and College Qualifications)*; M. Stark
  (Review of Support for Adult Learning)

FURTHER EDUCATION AND TRAINING
Director, D. Forrester
Heads of Division, C. Tyler *(Connexions Unit)*; S. Hillier
  (FE Funding and Organisation); A. Clarke *(Standards
  Quality and Access)*; A. Davis *(Partnership Skills and Young
  People)*; S. Geary *(Youth Support Service Implementation)*;
  T. Fellowes *(Further Education and 16–19 Student
  Support)*

HIGHER EDUCATION
Director, N. Sanders
Heads of Divisions, M. Hipkins *(HE Funding and Organisation)*; N. Flint *(Student Support 1)*; B. Evans *(Student
  Support 2)*;
  P. Cohen *(Higher Education: Quality and Employability)*

ADULT LEARNING GROUP
Director, D. Grover
Heads of Divisions, vacant *(Basic Skills Unit)*; J. Temple
  (Skills Unit); T. Down *(Individual Learning)*; L. Ammon
  (Workspace Learning); J. Pugh *(Lifelong Learning and
  Technologies Division)*; J. Fuller *(National Training
  Organisation)*

LEGAL ADVISER'S OFFICE
Legal Adviser, D. Macrae
Heads of Divisions, F. Clarke; S. Harker; Miss D. Collins;
  A. Preston; P. Kilgarriff

CORPORATE SERVICES AND DEVELOPMENT DIRECTORATE
Director, Mrs H. Douglas
Heads of Divisions, R. Hinchcliffe *(Information Systems)*;
  M. Shipp *(Personnel)*; P. Neill *(Procurement and
  Contracting)*;
  J. Gordon *(Training and Development)*; L. Webb *(Facilities Management)*; G. Archer (Leadership and Change
  Division); N. Parker *(Senior Equal Opportunities Adviser)*

SCHOOLS DIRECTORATE
Director-General, D. Normington

SCHOOLS ORGANISATION AND FUNDING GROUP

Director, Ms H. Williams
Heads of Divisions, Ms E. Wylie (*LEA Support*); K. Beeton (*School Capital and Buildings*); A. Wye (*Schools and LEA Funding*); Ms C. Macready (*School Admissions and Governance*)

TEACHERS

Director, P. Makeham
Heads of Divisions, Ms A. Jackson (*Teachers' Pay and Policy*); G. Holley (*Teacher Supply and Training*); Ms P. Jones (*Teachers' Standards and Pensions*); Ms C. Bienkowska (*School Leadership*); R. Harrison (*Teacher Development*)

PUPIL SUPPORT AND INCLUSION

Director, R. Smith
Heads of Divisions, B. Shaw (*School Inclusion*); M. Phipps (*Pupil Support and Independent Schools*); C. Wells (*Special Educational Needs*); A. Cranston (*Early Years*)
Head of Sure Start Unit, Ms N. Eisenstadt
Deputy Head of Sure Start Unit, Ms S. Thomson
Schools Plus, Susan Johnson and Anne-Marie Lawlor

CURRICULUM, COMMUNICATIONS GROUP

Director, Ms I. Wilde
Heads of Divisions, I. Berry (*Curriculum*); S. Edwards (*School Communications*); N. Baxter (*Parents and Performance Tables*), Dick Palmer (*ICT Strategy Unit*); D. Brown (*National Grid for Learning*)

STANDARDS AND EFFECTIVENESS UNIT

Head of Unit, Prof. M. Barber
Heads of Divisions, S. Adamson (*Pupil Standards*); Ms S. Scales (*LEA Improvement*); D. Sandeman (*School Effectiveness*); S. Crowne (School Improvement); J. Benham (Diversity and Best Practice); C. Wormald (Excellent in cities Unit)

STRATEGY AND COMMUNICATIONS DIRECTORATE

Director, P. Wanless
Heads of Divisions, Ms J. Simpson (*Head of News*); T. Cook (*Media Relations*); J. Ross (*Publicity*); vacant (*Strategy*); G. McKenzie (*Regional Policy Division*); N. Houston (Speeches and General Briefing); R. Bicknell (Communications and Knowledge Management Division)

EXECUTIVE AGENCY

THE EMPLOYMENT SERVICE

Caxton House, Tothill Street, London SW1H 9NA
Tel: 020-7273 6060; Fax: 020-7273 6099

The aims of the Employment Service are to contribute to high levels of employment and growth by helping all people without a job to find work and by helping employers to fill their vacancies, and to help individuals lead rewarding working lives.

Chief Executive, L. Lewis
Director of Jobcentre Services, Ms C. Dodgson, CB
Director of Human Resources, K. White
Director of Welfare to Work Delivery, R. Foster
Director for Finance and Commercial and Corporate Services, M. Neale
Non-Executive Directors, R. Dykes; Ms L. de Groot; C. Cox
Regional Directors, Ms D. Ross (*East Midlands and Eastern*); S. Holt, OBE (*London and South-East*); V. Robinson (*Northern*); Ms M. John (*North-West*); K.Pascoe (*South-West*); Ms R. Thew (*West Midlands*); R. Lasko (*Yorkshire and Humberside*)
Director for Scotland, A. R. Brown
Director for Wales, Mrs S. Keyse

DEPARTMENT OF THE ENVIRONMENT, TRANSPORT AND THE REGIONS
Eland House, Bressenden Place, London SW1E 5DU
Great Minster House, 76 Marsham Street, London SW1P 4DR
Ashdown House, 123 Victoria Street, London SW1E 6DE
Tel: 020-7944 3000 Web: http://www.detr.gov.uk

The Department of the Environment, Transport and the Regions (DETR) was formed in June 1997 by the merger of the Department of the Environment and the Department of Transport. It is responsible for policies relating to the environment, housing, transport services, rural affairs, planning, local government, regional development, regeneration, the construction industry and health and safety. The Department's Ministers are based at Eland House.

Deputy Prime Minister and Secretary of State for the Environment, Transport and the Regions, The Rt. Hon. John Prescott, MP
Private Secretary, P. Unwin
Special Advisers, J. Irvin; Ms J. Hammell
Parliamentary Private Secretary, J. Heppell, MP
Minister for Transport, The Lord Macdonald of Tradeston
Private Secretary, S. Davies
Special Adviser, A. Long
Parliamentary Private Secretary, P. Woolas, MP
Minister of State, The Rt. Hon. Michael Meacher, MP (*Environment*)
Private Secretary, C. Bird
Parliamentary Private Secretary, T. Rooney, MP
Minister of State, The Rt. Hon. Hilary Armstrong, MP (*Local Government, Regions*)
Private Secretary, T. Wechsler
Special Adviser, D. Wilson
Parliamentary Private Secretary, Ms S. Keeble, MP
Minister of State, Nick Raynsford, MP (*Housing, Planning*)
Private Secretary, M. Leach
Special Adviser, P. Hackett
Parliamentary Private Secretary, P. Hope, MP
Parliamentary Under-Secretaries of State, The Lord Whitty; Keith Hill, MP; Chris Mullin, MP; Beverley Hughes, MP
Private Secretaries, Ms J. Borg; Ms K. Braddick; C. Brain; R. O'Donnell
Parliamentary Clerk, Ms M. Cameron
Permanent Secretary (*SCS*), Sir Richard Mottram, KCB
Private Secretary, M. Capstick

*DIRECTORATE OF COMMUNICATION
Director (*SCS*), A. Evans
Deputy Directors (*SCS*), C. Skinner (*Marketing and Corporate Communications*); D. Plews (*Deputy Prime Minister's Press Secretary*)

†ENVIRONMENT PROTECTION GROUP
Director-General (*SCS*), Miss D. A. Nichols

ENERGY, ENVIRONMENT AND WASTE DIRECTORATE
Director (*SCS*), P. Ward
Heads of Divisions (*SCS*), L. Packer (*Sustainable Energy Policy*); D. Vincent (*Energy and Environment; Best Practice*); T. Ilott (*Environment, Business and Consumers*); B. Ryder (*Environment and Business 6–7*); Ms S. Ellis (*Waste Policy*); D. Prior (*Joint Environmental Markets Unit*); S. Hewitt (*Waste Strategy*)

---

* Based at Eland House
† Based at Ashdown House

ENVIRONMENT: RISK AND ATMOSPHERE
DIRECTORATE

Director (SCS), H. Derwent
Heads of Divisions (SCS), Dr P. Hinchcliffe (*Chemicals and Biotechnology*); R. Wood (*Radioactive Substances*); P. Betts (*Global Atmosphere*); M. Hurst (*Air and Environment Quality 1–5*); M. Williams (*Air and Environment, Scientific Branches*)

†ENVIRONMENT PROTECTION STRATEGY
DIRECTORATE

Director (SCS), A. Burchell
Heads of Divisions (SCS), Mrs H. C. Hillier (*EP Statistics and Information Management*); J. Bradley (*Environment Agency Sponsorship and Navigation*); Ms S. McCabe (*Environment Protection International*); R. Wilson (*Environment Protection Economics*); J. Adams (*Sustainable Development Unit*);
Mrs J. Bailey (*Environment Agency Review Team*);
Mrs D. Hayes (*Sustainable Development Secretariat*)

WATER AND LAND DIRECTORATE

Director (SCS), A. H. Davis
Heads of Divisions (SCS), M. Rouse (*Drinking Water Inspectorate*); A. Simcock (*Marine, Land and Liabilities*); S. Hoggan (*Water Quality*); B. Dinwiddy (*Water Supply and Regulation*)

†FINANCE GROUP

Director and Principal Finance Officer (SCS), J. Ballard
Heads of Divisions (SCS), D. McCarthy (*Finance Programmes*);
K. Arnold (*Finance Sponsorship and Programme*); R. Anderson (*Finance Departmental Administration*); A. Beard (*Finance Accounting Services*); C. Arnott (*Internal Audit*);
Ms A. Rutherford (*Finance Business Co-ordination*)

*HOUSING, CONSTRUCTION,
REGENERATION AND COUNTRYSIDE
GROUP

Director-General (SCS), Mrs M. McDonald, CB

HOUSING

Director (SCS), M. Gahagan
Heads of Divisons (SCS), Mrs J. Littlewood (*Research, Analysis and Evaluation*); B. Oelman (*Housing Data and Statistics*); P. Cox (*Housing and Urban Economics*); M. Jones (*Housing Policy, Renewal and Ownership*); M. Faulkner (*Housing Private Rented Sector*); Mrs H. Chipping (*Local Authority Housing Finance*); R. Horsman (*Housing Associations and Private Finance*); N. Murphy (*Homelessness and Housing Management*)

CONSTRUCTION DIRECTORATE

Director (SCS), J. Hobson
Heads of Divisions (SCS), N. Dorling (*Construction Industry Sponsorship*); J. Stambollouian (*Construction Innovation and Research Management*); vacant (*Export Promotion and Construction Materials*); P. Everall (*Building Regulations*); B. Davies (*Construction Market Intelligence*)

WILDLIFE AND COUNTRYSIDE DIRECTORATE

Director (SCS), Ms S. Lambert
Heads of Divisions (SCS), R. M. Pritchard (*European Wildlife*); R. Hepworth (*Global Wildlife*); H. Cleary

---

* Based at Eland House
†Based at Ashdown House

(*Rural Development*); Ms S. Carter (*Countryside*); C. Braun (*Countryside Legislation*)

REGENERATION DIRECTORATE

Director (SCS), P. Evans
Heads of Divisions (SCS), J. Roberts; Ms L. Simcock, P. Houston; J. Bright

ROUGH SLEEPERS UNIT

Director (SCS), Ms L. Casey
Head of Division (SCS), vacant

INTEGRATED TRANSPORT TASKFORCE TEAM

Director-General (SCS), W. Rickett
Deputy Director (SCS), Ms M. Phillips, CB
Heads of Divisons (SCS), Ms L. Robinson (*Transport, Delivery and Presentation*); I. Todd (*Transport, Environment and Taxation*); D. Hulls (*Transport Finance*); Ms B. Hills (*Transport Strategy*)

*LEGAL GROUP
Director-General (SCS), D. Hogg

COUNTRYSIDE, PLANNING AND TRANSPORT

Director (SCS), Ms S. Unerman
Heads of Divisions (SCS), N. Lefton (*Countryside and Environmental Liability*); Ms G. Hedley-Dent (*Planning*); R. Lines (*Highways*); D. Ingham (*Road Traffic*); A. Jones (*Aviation*); H. Kayan (*Marine*); Ms J.-A. McKenzie (*Railways*)

COMMERCIAL, ENVIRONMENT, HOUSING AND
LOCAL GOVERNMENT

Director (SCS), C. Muttukamaru
Heads of Divisions (SCS), J. Comber (*Environment (National)*);
D. Jordan (*Local Government (Finance)*); Ms P. Conlon (*Local Government (General)*); J. Wright (*Housing and Land*); N. Thomas (*Greater London Authority Implementation*);
D. Aries (*Commercial and Establishments*); Ms D. Phillips (*Devolution and Regional Government*)

ENVIRONMENT (INTERNATIONAL AND EC)

Director (SCS), P. Szell
Head of Division (SCS), A. McGlone

LEGISLATIVE UNIT

Director (SCS), A. Roberts

REGIONAL CO-ORDINATION UNIT

Director-General (SCS), R. Smith
Director (SCS), A. Wells
Heads of Divisions (SCS), Mrs J. Scones (*Government Offices Central Unit*); M. Ross (*RCU1*)

*LOCAL AND REGIONAL GOVERNMENT
GROUP

Director-General (SCS), P. Wood

LOCAL GOVERNMENT DIRECTORATE

Director (SCS), A. Whetnall
Heads of Divisions (SCS), P. Rowsell (*Local Government Sponsorship*); J. R. Footitt (*Local Government Competition and Quality*); T. Redpath (*Local Government Legislation*); T. Crossley (*Local Government Pensions*)

LOCAL GOVERNMENT FINANCE POLICY
DIRECTORATE

Director (SCS), M. Lambirth

Heads of Divisions (SCS), R. J. Gibson (*Local Government Grant Distribution*); Mrs M. Green (*Local Government Finance Statistics*); Ms P. Williams (*Local Government Capital Finance*); S. Claughton (*Local Government Taxation*); I. Scotter (*Local Government Revenue Expenditure*)

REGIONAL POLICY UNIT
Director (SCS), D. Wilkinson
Heads of Divisions (SCS), W. Arnold (*RPU1*);
A. Murray (*RPU2*)

REGIONAL OFFICES
— see page 333

‡PLANNING, ROADS AND LOCAL TRANSPORT
Director-General (SCS), vacant

MOBILITY AND INCLUSION UNIT
Head of Unit (SCS), Miss E. A. Frye, OBE

PLANNING DIRECTORATE
Director (SCS), J. Jacobs
Heads of Divisions (SCS), J. Channing (*Planning and Policies*); C. Bowden (*Development Control Policy*); M. R. Ash (*Plans and Compensation*); vacant (*Environmental Assessment, International Planning and Research*); A. M. Oliver (*Planning and Land Use Statistics*); L. Hicks (*Minerals and Waste Planning*); J. M. Leigh-Pollitt (*Land and Property*)

ROADS AND TRAFFIC
Director (SCS), D. Roberts
Heads of Divisions (SCS), T. Worsley (*Highways, Economics and Traffic Appraisal*); N. McDonald (*Roads Policy*); M. Talbot (*Traffic Management and Tolls*); R. Donachie (*Transport Statistics: Roads*)

INTEGRATED AND LOCAL TRANSPORT
Director (SCS), R. Bird
Heads of Divisions (SCS), E. C. Neve (*Buses and Taxis*); K. Lloyd (*Local Transport Policy*); A. S. D. Whybrow (*Charging and Local Transport*); M. Walsh (*Economics, Local Transport and General*); P. Capell (*Transport Statistics: Personal Travel*)

ROAD AND ENVIRONMENT SAFETY
Director (SCS), J. Plowman
Heads of Divisions (SCS), M. Fendick (*Vehicle Standards and Engineering*); R. Peal (*Road Safety*); R. Jones (*Licensing, Road Worthiness and Insurance*); Dr T. Carter (*Chief Medical Adviser*); M. Brasher (*Driver, Vehicle Operator Task Force*)

‡RAILWAYS, AVIATION LOGISTICS AND MARITIME
Director-General (SCS), D. Rowlands

RAILWAYS
Director (SCS), R. Linnard
Heads of Divisions (SCS), Ms A. Munro (*Railways Major Project*); S. Connolly (*Railways Economics and Finance*); P. Thomas (*Railways International and General*); M. Coulshed (*Railways Sponsorship*)

LONDON UNDERGROUND TASK GROUP
Director (SCS), M. Fuhr
Heads of Division (SCS), Mrs B. Bostock (*London Transport*);

R. Bennett and I. Jordan (*London Underground Task Group*)

AVIATION
Director (SCS), R. Griffins
Heads of Divisions (SCS), M. Fawcett (*Airports Policy*); M. C. Mann (*Economics, Aviation, Maritime and International*); Ms E. Duthie (*Aviation Environmental*); M. Smethers (*Multilateral*); A. T. Baker (*International Aviation Negotiation*); D. McMillan (*Air Traffic*); I. McBrayne (*Civil Aviation*)

AIR ACCIDENTS INVESTIGATION BRANCH
Berkshire Copse Road, Aldershot, Hants GU112HH
Tel: 01252-510300
Chief Inspector of Air Accidents, K. P. R. Smart, CBE
Deputy Chief Inspector, R. McKinlay

LOGISTICS AND MARITIME TRANSPORT
Director (SCS), B. Wadsworth
Heads of Divisions (SCS), Ms A. Moss (*Road Haulage*); M. Hughes (*Transport Statistics Freight*); D. Liston-Jones (*Traffic Area Network Unit*); D. Cooke (*Shipping Policy 1*); G. D. Rowe (*Shipping Policy 2*); J. F. Wall, CMG (*Shipping Policy 3*); T. Allan (*DETR Rep IMO*)

MARINE ACCIDENTS INVESTIGATION BRANCH
Carlton House, Carlton Place, Southampton SO15 2DZ
Tel: 023-8039 5500
Chief Inspector of Marine Accidents, Rear-Adm. J. Lang
Deputy Chief Inspector, S. Harwood

TRANSPORT SECURITY
Director (SCS), D. Lord
Head of Division and Deputy Director (SCS), W. Gillan

*STRATEGY AND CORPORATE SERVICES GROUP
Director-General (SCS), R. S. Dudding
Heads of Divisions (SCS), I. Harris (*Working Environment*); G. Jones (*Procurement, Policy and Advice*); R. Long (*IT Services*)

HUMAN RESOURCES
Director (SCS), Mrs H. Parker-Brown
Heads of Divisions (SCS), M. Dutta (*Business Services*); M. Bailey (*Customer Services*); Mrs V. Penney (*Information Services*); Mrs S. Bishop (*Performance and Development Services*)

CHIEF ECONOMIST
Director and Chief Economist (SCS), C. Riley
Head of Division (SCS), N. Campbell (*Central Economics and Policy*)

CENTRAL STRATEGY (AND CHIEF SCIENTIST)
Director (and Chief Scientist) (SCS), D. Fisk
Heads of Divisions (SCS), J. Stevens (*Europe, Transport and General*); J. Grubb (*Health and Safety Sponsorship*); A. Apling (*Science and Technology Policy*); I. Heawood (*Information Management*); G. Pendlebury (*Policy Strategy and Integration*); P. Walton (*Corporate, Business and Agencies*)

---

* Based at Eland House
†Based at Ashdown House
‡Based at Great Minster House

EXECUTIVE AGENCIES

DRIVER AND VEHICLE LICENSING AGENCY

Longview Road, Morriston, Swansea SA6 7JL
Tel: 0870 240 0010 (*Vehicles Customer Services*);
0870 240 0009 (*Drivers Customer Services*)

The Agency's responsibilities are the issuing of driving licences, the registration and licensing of vehicles in Great Britain, and the collection and enforcement of vehicle excise duty in the UK.
Chief Executive, Dr S. J. Ford, CBE

DRIVING STANDARDS AGENCY

Stanley House, Talbot Street, Nottingham NG1 5GU
Tel: 0115-947 4222; Fax: 0115-955 7334

The Agency's role is to carry out driving tests and approve driving instructors.
Chief Executive, G. Austin

HIGHWAYS AGENCY

St Christopher House, Southwark Street,
London SE1 0TE
Tel: 0645-556575; Fax: 020-7921 4899
Email: ha_info@highways.gov.uk
Web: http://www.highways.gov.uk

The Agency is responsible for the operation, management and maintenance of the motorway and trunk road network and for road construction and improvement.
Chief Executive, L. J. Haynes

MARITIME AND COASTGUARD AGENCY

Spring Place, 105 Commercial Road, Southampton
SO15 1EG
Tel: 023-8032 9100; Email: infoline@swan.mcagency.
org.uk; Web: http://www.mcagency .org.uk

The Agency was formed in April 1998 by the merger of the Coastguard Agency and the Marine Safety Agency. Its role is to develop, promote and enforce high standards of marine safety; to minimise loss of life amongst seafarers and coastal users; and to minimise pollution from ships of the sea and coastline.
Chief Executive, M. Storey
Chief Coastguard, J. Astbury

PLANNING INSPECTORATE

Tollgate House, Houlton Street, Bristol BS2 9DJ
Tel: 0117-987 8000; Fax: 0117 987 8408;
Email: enquiries.pins@gtnet.gov.uk
Web: http://www.open.gov.uk/pi/pihome.htm

The Inspectorate is responsible for casework involving planning, housing, roads, environmental and related legislation. It is a joint executive agency of the Department of the Environment, Transport and the Regions and the National Assembly for Wales.
Chief Executive and Chief Planning Inspector, C. Shepley

QUEEN ELIZABETH II CONFERENCE CENTRE

Broad Sanctuary, London SW1 P3EE
Tel: 020-7222 5000; Fax: 020-7798 4200

The Centre provides conference and banqueting facilities for both private sector and government use.
Chief Executive, M. C. Buck

THE RENT SERVICE

Clifton House, 1st Floor, 87-113 Euston Road, London
NW1 2RA
Tel: 020-7554 2450; Fax: 020-7554 2490

Established in October 1999, the Agency took over responsibility of the former Rent Officer Service which operated through 77 separate units based in local authorities.
Chief Executive, S. Williams

VEHICLE CERTIFICATION AGENCY

1 Eastgate Office Centre, Eastgate Road, Bristol BS5 6XX
Tel: 0117-951 5151; Fax: 0117-952 4103

The Agency tests and certificates vehicles to UK and international standards.
Chief Executive, D. W. Harvey

VEHICLE INSPECTORATE

Berkeley House, Croydon Street, Bristol BS5 0DA
Tel: 0117-954 3200; Fax: 0117-954 3212

The Agency carries out annual testing and inspection of heavy goods and other vehicles and administers the MOT testing scheme.
Chief Executive, M. Newey

TRAFFIC AREA OFFICES AND COMMISSIONERS

Senior Traffic Commissioner, M. W. Betts, CBE
Eastern, G. Simms
North-Eastern and North-Western, T. Macartney
Scottish, M. W. Betts, CBE
South-Eastern and Metropolitan, C. Heaps
Western, P. Brown
Wales and West Midlands, D. Dixon

FOREIGN AND COMMONWEALTH OFFICE

King Charles Street, London SW1A 2AH
Tel: 020-7270 3000
Web: http://www.fco.gov.uk

The Foreign and Commonwealth Office provides, mainly through diplomatic missions, the means of communication between the British Government and other governments and international governmental organisations for the discussion and negotiation of all matters falling within the field of international relations. It is responsible for alerting the Government to the implications of developments overseas; for protecting British interests overseas; for protecting British citizens abroad; for explaining British policies to, and cultivating friendly relations with, governments overseas; and for the discharge of British responsibilities to the UK overseas territories.
Secretary of State for Foreign and Commonwealth Affairs,
The Rt. Hon. Robin Cook, MP
  Principal Private Secretary, S. L. Cowper-Coles, CMG, LVO
  Special Advisers, M. Williams D. Clark
  Parliamentary Private Secretary, K. Purchase, MP
Minister for Europe, Keith Vaz, MP
  Private Secretary, J. Morrison
Minister of State, Peter Hain, MP
Minister of State, John Battle, MP
  Private Secretaries to the Ministers of State, F. Baker; H. Shorter
Parliamentary Under-Secretary of State, The Baroness Scotland of Asthal
  Private Secretary, C. Newns
Permanent Under-Secretary of State and Head of HM Diplomatic Service, Sir John Kerr, KCMG
  Private Secretary, Dr V. Rangarajan
Chief Executive, †*British Trade International*,
  Sir David Wright, KCMG, LVO
Deputy Under-Secretaries, C. Hum, CMG (*Chief Clerk*);

C. Budd, CMG (*EU/Economic Director*); E. Jones Parry,
CMG (*Political Director*); D. Manning, CMG

HEADS OF DEPARTMENTS

African Department (Equatorial), J. Bevan
African Department (Southern), N. R. Chrimes
Aviation and Maritime Department, N. A. Ling
Central and North-West European Department,
  Sir John Ramsden, Bt.
Change Management Unit, Ms S. Matthews
China/Hong Kong Department, D. A. Warren
Common Foreign and Security Policy Department, C. Roberts
Commonwealth Co-ordination Department, C. C. Bright
Consular Division, D. J. R. Taylor
Counter-Terrorism Policy Department, V. Fean
Cultural Relations Department, Ms A. W. Lewis
Devolved Administration Department, Dr J. Milligan
Drugs and International Crime Department, M. Ryder
Eastern Department, A. F. Pringle
Eastern Adriatic Department, T. R. V. Phillips
Economic Relations Department, C. Butler
Environment, Science and Energy Department, J. Ashton
European Union Department (Bi-lateral), J. Cresswell, CVO
European Union Department (External), S. Featherstone
European Union Department (Internal), M. J. Lyall-Grant
FCO Services, N. Hook (*Head, Conference and Visits Group*);
  Ms V. Life (*Head, Consultancy Group*); J. Elgie (*Head,
  Estates Group*); J. Thompson, MBE (*Head, Information
  Management Group*); Ms J. Link (*Head, Resource
  Management Group*); M. Carr (*Head, Support Group*);
  N. Stickells (*Head, Technical Group*)
Financial Compliance Unit, M. Purves
Financial Policy Department, M. J. Brown
Honours Department, R. M. Sands
Human Rights Policy Department, Dr Carolyn Browne
Information Department, P. J. Dun
*Internal Audit Department, R. A. Elias
†Invest in Britain Bureau, A. Fraser (*Chief Executive*)
†Joint Export Promotion Directorate, D. Hall, CMG
Latin America and Caribbean Department, H. G. Hogger
Middle East Department, E. G. M. Chaplin
Migration and Visa Department, R. M. White, MBE
Near East and North Africa Department, C. N. R. Prentice
News Department, N. K. Darroch, CMG
Non-Proliferation Department, P. W. Hare, LVO
North America Department, P. J. Priestley, CBE
North-East Asia and Pacific Department, P. Carter
OSCE and Council of Europe Department, A. E. Huckle
Overseas Territories Department, C. J. B. White
Parliamentary Relations Department, A. Henderson(*Head*);
  P. R. O. Bromley (*Deputy Head and Parliamentary Clerk*)
Personnel Command, P. Jones (*Asst. Director, Personnel
  Management*); T. Simmons (*Asst. Director, Performance
  Issues*); Ms E. Kennedy (*Asst. Director, *Medical and
  Welfare*); S. Wightman (*Asst. Director, Personnel Policy*);
  R. T. Fell, CVO (*Asst. Director, Personnel Services*);
  C. Edgerton, OBE, T. Malcomson (*Asst. Directors,
  Prosper*); Ms A. Cookson-Hall (*Head, Recruitment*);
  Dr Vanessa Davies (*Head, Diplomatic Service Language
  Centre*); Ms J. Bennet, Ms A. Kirk (*Heads,
  Grading Review Team*)
Policy Planning Staff, R. Clarke
Policy, Resources and Personnel Directorate, D. J. Hall (*Trade*);
  C. Stilt; I. Fletcher
Protocol Department, Mrs K. F. Colvin (*Head of Department
  and First Vice-Marshal of the Diplomatic Corps*)
Purchasing Directorate, M. J. H. Gower
Republic of Ireland Department, G. Fergusson
Research Analysis, R. D. Lavers
Resources, P. Collecott

Resource Management, Ms J. Link
Resources Planning, R. Kinchen
Royal Matters Department, B. England
Security Strategy Unit, T. J. Duggin
Security Policy Department, A. M. Thompson
South Asian Department, S. N. Evans, OBE
South-East Asian Department, R. Gordon
Support Group, M. Carr
Technical Support, N. Stickells
United Nations Department, S. Pattison
Whitehall Liaison Department, L. Parker

EXECUTIVE AGENCY

WILTON PARK CONFERENCE CENTRE
Wiston House, Steyning, W. Sussex BN4 43DZ
Tel: 01903-815020; Fax: 01903-879647

Wilton Park organises international affairs conferences
and is hired out to Government departments and
commercial users.
Chief Executive and Director, C. B. Jennings

CORPS OF QUEEN'S MESSENGERS
Support Group, Foreign and Commonwealth Office,
London SW1 A2AH
Tel: 020-7270 2779

Superintendent of the Corps of Queen's Messengers,
  A. C. Brown
Queen's Messengers, P. Allen; R. Allen; Maj. A. N. D. Bols;
  Maj. P. C. H. Dening-Smitherman; Sqn. Ldr.
  J. S. Frizzell; Capt. N. C. E. Gardner; Maj. D. A.
  Griffiths; A. Hill; R. Long; Maj. K. J. Rowbottom; Maj.
  M. R. Senior; Cdr. K. M. C. Simmons, AFC; Maj. J. S.
  Steele; Maj. J. E. A. Andre; W. Lisle; Maj. J. H. Steele;
  J. A. Hatfield

DEPARTMENT OF HEALTH
Richmond House, 79 Whitehall, London SW1A 2NL
Tel: 020-7210 3000
Web: http://www.open.gov.uk/doh/dhhome.htm

The Department of Health is responsible for the provision
of the National Health Service in England and for social
care, including oversight of personal social services run by
local authorities in England for children (except day care,
which is now the responsibility of the DfEE), the elderly,
the infirm, the handicapped and other persons in need. It is
responsible for health promotion and has functions
relating to public and environmental health, food safety
and nutrition. The Department is also responsible for the
ambulance and emergency first aid services, under the
Civil Defence Act 1948. The Department represents the
UK at the European Union and other international
organisations including the World Health Organisation.
It also supports UK-based healthcare and pharmaceutical
industries. Responsibility for food safety was transferred
to the Food Standards Agency, in April 2000.

The Department of Health has announced preparations
to form the General Social Care Council (GSCC) in
April 2001. This body will be responsible for increasing
standards in the Social Care workforce in England
(Scotland, Wales and Northern Ireland will have their
own regulatory bodies).

---

*Joint Foreign and Commonwealth Office / Department for
  International Development department
†Joint Foreign and Commonwealth Office / Department of
  Trade and Industry directorate

Secretary of State for Health, The Rt. Hon. Alan Milburn, MP
Principal Private Secretary, J. Grauberg
Private Secretaries, H. Rogers; S. Waring
Special Advisers, S. Stevens; D. Murphy
Parliamentary Private Secretary, J. Fitzpatrick, MP
Minister of State, John Denham, MP (*NHS Structure and Resources*)
Private Secretary, T. Fretten
Parliamentary Private Secretary, P. Goggins, MP
Minister of State, John Hutton, MP (*Social Care and Mental Health*)
Private Secretary, J. Adedeji
Parliamentary Private Secretary, M. Eagle, MP
Parliamentary Under-Secretaries of State,
Yvette Cooper, MP; The Lord Hunt of Kings Heath, OBE; Gisela Stuart, MP
Private Secretaries, P. Mcnaught; Ms H. McLain; K. Holton
Parliamentary Clerk, J. Mean
Permanent Secretary (*SCS*), C. Kelly
Private Secretary, H. Causley
Chief Medical Officer (*SCS*), Prof. L. Donaldson, FRCSEd., FRCP
Acting Chief Executive, NHS Executive (*SCS*), Neil McKay
Deputy Chief Medical Officers (*SCS*), Dr Patricia Troop; Dr Sheila Adam

REGIONAL CHAIRMEN'S MEETING
Chairman, The Secretary of State for Health
Members, John Denham, MP (*Minister of State*); John Hutton, MP (*Minister of State*); Yvette Cooper, MP (*Parliamentary Under-Secretary*); The Lord Hunt of Kings Heath (*Parliamentary Under-Secretary*); Gisela Stuart, MP (*Parliamentary Under-Secretary*); Prof. L. Donaldson, FRCSEd., FRCP (*Chief Medical Officer*); Neil McKay (*Acting Chief Executive, NHS Executive*); C. Kelly (*Permanent Secretary*); Ms S. Mullally (*Chief Nursing Officer*); C. Wilkinson; Mrs Z. Manzoor, CBE; D. Nicholson; Mrs R. Varley; Miss J. Trotter, OBE; I. Mills; W. Wells; Prof. J. Higgins

CORPORATE MANAGEMENT DIRECTORATE GROUP
Head of Group (*SCS*), Ms A. Perkins

STATISTICS DIVISION
Director of Statistics (*SCS*), J. Fox
Chief Statisticians (*SCS*), R. K. Willmer; A. Roberts; J. Stokoe; A. Sutherland

INTERNATIONAL AND CONSTITUTIONAL BRANCH (ICB)
Branch Head (*SCS*), N. Boyd

PERSONNEL SERVICES
Director of Personnel (*SCS*), F. Goldhill
Heads of Branches (*SCS*), C. Muir; I. Forsyth; A. Davey

INFORMATION SERVICES DIVISION
Head of Division (*SCS*), Dr A. A. Holt
Heads of Branches, Mrs L. Wishart; C. Horsey; M. Rainsford; Mrs J. Dainty; R. Long; P. G. Cobb; P. Charman; Mrs D. McDonagh

RESOURCE MANAGEMENT AND FINANCE
Head of Division (*SCS*), D. Clark
Heads of Branches, P. Kendall; B. Burleigh; S. Mitchell, P. Lemmey

MEDICINES, PHARMACY AND INDUSTRY DIVISION (MPI)
Head of Division, A. McKeon
Heads of Branches, M. Brownlee; K. Guiness; J. Middeton

ECONOMICS AND OPERATIONAL RESEARCH DIVISION (HEALTH)
Chief Economic Adviser (*SCS*), C. H. Smee, CB
Heads of Branches, Dr S. Harding; Dr G. Royston; A. Hare; N. York; M. Minford

COMMUNICATIONS DIRECTORATE
Director of Communications (*SCS*), Mrs H. McCallum
Deputy Directors, S. Jarvis (*Media*); W. Roberts (*Campaigns*); P. Addison-Child (*Corporate Communications*)

SOLICITOR'S OFFICE
Solicitor (*SCS*), M. Morgan
Director of Legal Services (*SCS*), Mrs G. S. Kerrigan

PUBLIC HEALTH POLICY GROUP

PUBLIC HEALTH DIVISION
Head of Division, Prof. D. Nutbeam
Heads of Branches, M. Fry; Ms I. Sharp; M. Haroon; C. Kenny (*Acting*); N. Dean; Ms J. Walden; Ms C. Hamlyn; Dr M. O'Mahony; A. Smith

WINTER AND EMERGENCY SERVICES CAPACITY PLANNING TEAM (WEST)
Head of Branch, Ms A. Sergeant

SOCIAL CARE GROUP
Chief Social Services Inspector, Ms D. Platt
Head of Social Care Policy, D. Walden
Deputy Chief Inspectors, D. Gilroy; Ms A. Nottage
Heads of Branches (*SCS*), Miss A. Stephenson; R. Wilson (*Section Head*); Ms. C. Brock; B. Clark; G. Denham; Ms A. Gross
Assistant Chief Inspector (*HQ*), J. Cleary
Assistant Chief Inspectors (*Regions*), J. Cypher; B. Riddell; A. Jones; C. P. Brearley; J. Fraser; Mrs L. Hoare; Ms J. Owen; Miss F. McCabe; R. Balte

NURSING GROUP
Chief Nursing Officer/Director of Nursing (*SCS*), Ms S. Mullally
Assistant Chief Nursing Officers (*SCS*), Mrs G. Stephens; D. Moore; D. Innes (*Acting*)

QUALITY MANAGEMENT BRANCH
Acting Branch Head, Julian Brookes

RESEARCH AND DEVELOPMENT DIVISION
Director of Research and Development, Prof. Sir John Pattison
Deputy Director of Research and Development (*SCS*), Dr C. Henshall
Heads of Branches (*SCS*), Dr P. Greenaway; Mrs J. Griffin; Ms A. Kauder; M. Taylor

NHS EXECUTIVE
Quarry House, Quarry Hill, Leeds LS2 7UE
Tel: 0113-254 5000
Chief Executive (*Acting*), Neil McKay
Director of Human Resources, H. Taylor, CB
Director of Finance and Performance, C. Reeves, CBE
Medical Director, Dr Sheila Adam
Director of Research and Development, Prof. Sir John Pattison
Director of Planning and Performance Management, vacant

Director of National Cancer Services, Prof. M. Richards
Director of Counter Fraud Services, J. Gee
Director of Operation, R. Kerr, CBE

HUMAN RESOURCES

Director of Human Resources, H Taylor, CB
Deputy Director of Human Resources (SCS), S. Barnett
Heads of Branches, H. Tolland; Ms K. Barnard;
Ms R. Roughton; Ms E. Al-Khatifa; R. Cairncross;
T. Sands; H. Fields; D. Amos; Dr R. J. Moore

INFORMATION POLICY UNIT
Head of Unit (SCS), Dr P. Drury

PLANNING DIRECTORATE
Director (SCS), vacant
Chief Economic Adviser, C. Smee, CB
Head of Planning, Ms P. Dash
Head of Information Policy Unit, P. Drury
Director of Statistics, J. Fox

HEALTH SERVICES DIRECTORATE
Director (SCS), Dr Sheila Adam
Heads of Branches, M. Brown; Ms J. McKessack;
L. Percival; D. Hewlett; Ms K. Tyson; Dr V. Day;
H. Shirely-Quirk; P. Hampshire; C. Robinson;
A. Sheehan; J. Mahoney; A. Humphrey; A. Mithani;
M. Davies; Dr G. Chapman; M. McGovern (*Acting*);
Dr J. Carpenter; J. Boyington; Dr F. Harvey

PRIMARY CARE DIVISION
Head of Division, M. Farrar
Chief Dental Officer, J. R. Wild
Chief Pharmaceutical Officer (Acting), Mrs J. Howe
Heads of Branches, Miss H. Robinson (*Dental and Optical
Services*); K. Guinness (*Pharmacy and Prescribing*); vacant
(*White Paper Implementation Team*); M. Farrar
(*General Medical Services*); H. Gwynn (*Cardiac Services*)

FINANCE AND PERFORMANCE DIRECTORATE
Director (SCS), C. L. Reeves, CBE
Deputy Directors, B. McCarthy; Ms C. Daws; M. Harris,
CBE (*Acting*)
Heads of Branches, Dr S. Peck; M. Sturges; A. Angilley;
J. Thomlinson; P. Coates; J. Copeland; P. Taylor;
A. MacLellan; I. Ellul; J. Stopes-Roe; S. Emslie;
L. Eccles

DIRECTORATE OF COUNTER FRAUD SERVICES
Director, J. GEE

REGIONAL OFFICES
— *see* Social Welfare section

ADVISORY COMMITTEES

ADVISORY COMMITTEE ON THE MICROBIOLOGICAL
SAFETY OF FOOD, Room 502A, Skipton House, 80
London Road, London SE1 6LH. Tel: 020-7972 5050.
Chairman, Prof. D. Georgarla, CBE, Ph.D.
COMMITTEE ON THE SAFETY OF MEDICINES, Market
Towers, 1 Nine Elms Lane, London SW8 5NQ.
Tel: 020-7273 0451. *Chairman*,
Prof. A. M. Breckenridge, CBE, FRCP, FRCPEd., FRSE
MEDICINES COMMISSION, Market Towers, 1 Nine Elms
Lane, London SW8 5NQ. Tel: 020-7273 0652.
Chairman, Prof. D. H. Lawson, CBE, FRCPEd., FRCP
(Glas.)

SPECIAL HEALTH AUTHORITIES

DENTAL VOCATIONAL TRAINING AUTHORITY, Master's
House, Temple Grove, Compton Place Road,
Eastbourne, E. Sussex BN20 8AD. Tel: 01323-431189.
Chairman, R. Davies; *Secretary*, Ms J. Verity
FAMILY HEALTH SERVICES APPEAL AUTHORITY, 30
Victoria Avenue, Harrogate HG1 5PR.
Tel: 01423-535415. *Chief Executive*, D. J. Laverick
HEALTH DEVELOPMENT AGENCY, Trevelyan House,
30 Great Peter Street, London SW1P 2HW.
Tel: 0171-222 5300. *Chair*, Ms Y. Buckland;
Chief Executive, Prof R. Parish
MENTAL HEALTH ACT COMMISSION – *see* page 320
MICROBIOLOGICAL RESEARCH AUTHORITY, Porton
Down, Salisbury, Wilts SP4 0JG. Tel: 01980-612100.
Chairman, Sir William Stewart, FRS;
Director, Dr R. H. Gilmour
NATIONAL BLOOD AUTHORITY, Oak House, Reeds
Crescent, Watford, Herts WD1 1QH.
Tel: 01923-486800. *Chairman*, M. Fogden, CB;
Chief Executive, M. Gorham
NATIONAL INSTITUTE OF CLINICAL EXCELLENCE, 90
Long Acre, London WC2E 9RZ. Tel: 020-7849 3444.
Chairman, Sir Michael Rawlins;
Chief Executive, A. Dillon
NHS INFORMATION AUTHORITY, 15 Frederick Road,
Edgbaston, Birmingham B15 1JD.Tel: 0121-625 1992.
Chairman, Prof. A. Bellingham, CBE;
Chief Executive, N. Bell
NHS LITIGATION AUTHORITY, Mapier Health, 24-28
High Holburn, London WC13 6AZ. Tel: 020-7430 8700.
Chairman, Ron Bradshaw; *Chief Executive*, S. Walker
NHS PURCHASING AND SUPPLY AGENCY, Premier House,
60 Caversham Road, Reading, Berks RG1 7EB.
Tel: 0118-980 8600. *Chairman*, D. Hall, CBE, TD;
Chief Executive, D. Eaton
PRESCRIPTION PRICING AUTHORITY, Bridge House,
152 Pilgrim Street, Newcastle upon Tyne NE1 6SN.
Tel: 0191-232 5371. *Chairman*, Prof. D. J. Johns;
Chief Executive, N. Scholte
UK TRANSPLANT SUPPORT SERVICE AUTHORITY,
Fox Den Road, Stoke Gifford, Bristol BS34 8RR.
Tel: 0117-975 7575. *Chairman*, J. F. Shaw;
Chief Executive, Mrs R. Balderson

SPECIAL HOSPITALS

ASHWORTH HOSPITAL, Parkbourn, Maghull, Merseyside
L31 1HW. Tel: 0151-473 0303. *Chief Executive (Acting)*,
L. Boswell
BROADMOOR HOSPITAL, Crowthorne, Berks RG45 7EG.
Tel: 01344-773111. *Chief Executive*, Dr J. Hollyman
RAMPTON HOSPITAL, Retford, Notts DN22 0PD.
Tel: 01777-248321. *Chief Executive*, Mrs S. Foley

EXECUTIVE AGENCIES

MEDICINES CONTROL AGENCY (MCA)
Market Towers, 1 Nine Elms Lane, London SW8 5NQ
Tel: 020-7273 0000; Fax: 020-7273 0353

The MCA is responsible for safeguarding public health by
ensuring all medicines on the UK market meet appropriate standards of safety, quality and efficacy. This is
achieved by a system of licensing, inspection, enforcement
and monitoring of medicines after they have been licensed.
Chief Executive, Dr K. H. Jones, CB

MEDICAL DEVICES AGENCY
Hannibal House, Elephant and Castle, London SE1 6TQ
Tel: 020-7972 8000; Fax: 020-7972 8108;
Email: mail@medicaldevices.gov.uk;
Web: http://www.medical-devices.gov.uk

The Agency safeguards the performance, quality and safety of medical devices and ensures that they comply with relevant EU directives.
Chief Executive, Dr D. Jefferys

NHS ESTATES

1 Trevelyan Square, Boar Lane, Leeds LS1 6AE
Tel: 0113-254 7000; Fax: 0113-254 7299;
Email: nhs.estates@doh.gov.uk

NHS Estates provides advice and guidance in the area of healthcare estate and facilities management to the NHS and the healthcare industry.
Chief Executive, Mrs K. Priestley

NHS PENSIONS

Hesketh House, 200–220 Broadway, Fleetwood, Lancs FY7 8LG
Tel: 01253-774774; Fax: 01253-774860

NHS Pensions administers the NHS occupational pension scheme.
Chief Executive, A. F. Cowan

HOME OFFICE

50 Queen Anne's Gate, London SW1H9AT
Tel: 020-7273 4000; Fax: 020-7273 2190
Email: gen.ho@gtnet.gov.uk
Web: http://www.homeoffice.gov.uk

The Home Office deals with those internal affairs in England and Wales which have not been assigned to other Government departments. The Home Office statement of purpose is to build a safe, just and tolerant society, in which the rights and responsibilities of individuals, families and communities are properly balanced, and the protection and security of the public are maintained. The Home Secretary is particularly concerned with the administration of justice; criminal law; the treatment of offenders, including probation and the prison service; the police; immigration and nationality; passport policy matters; community relations; certain public safety matters; and fire and civil emergencies services. The Home Secretary personally is the link between The Queen and the public, and exercises certain powers on her behalf, including that of the royal pardon.

Other subjects dealt with include electoral arrangements; ceremonial and formal business connected with honours; scrutiny of local authority by-laws; granting of licences for scientific procedures involving animals; cremations, burials and exhumations; firearms; dangerous drugs and poisons; general policy on laws relating to shops, liquor licensing, gaming and marriage; theatre and cinema licensing; and race relations policy.

The Home Secretary is also the link between the UK Government and the governments of the Channel Islands and the Isle of Man.

Secretary of State for the Home Department, The Rt. Hon. Jack Straw, MP
Principal Private Secretary (SCS), Ms H. Jackson
Private Secretaries, Ms A. Pearce; S. Harrison; Ms M. Goldstein
Assistant Private Secretary, Ms J. Fowler
Special Advisers, E. Owen; J. Russell
Minister of State, The Rt. Hon. Paul Boateng, MP
Private Secretary, S. Hayes
Minister of State, Charles Clarke, MP
Private Secretary, Ms J. Russell
Minister of State, Barbara Roche, MP
Private Secretary, Ms C. Hume

Parliamentary Under-Secretaries of State, Michael O'Brien, MP; The Lord Bassam of Brighton
Private Secretaries, L. Bailey; P. Morrison
Parliamentary Clerk, Ms D. Caddle
Permanent Under-Secretary of State (SCS), D. B. Omand
Private Secretary, Ms G. Kirton
Chief Medical Officer (at Department of Health), Prof. L. Donaldson, QHP, FRCSEd., FRCP

COMMUNICATION DIRECTORATE

Director (SCS), B. Butler
Deputy Head of Communication (Head of News) (SCS), Ms P. Teare
Head of Publicity and Corporate Services (SCS), Miss A. Nash
Head of Internal Communications (SCS), P. Samuels
Assistant Director and Head of Information Services Group (G6), P. Griffiths

CONSTITUTIONAL AND COMMUNITY POLICY DIRECTORATE

Director (SCS), Miss C. Sinclair
Heads of Units (SCS), Mrs G. Catto; T. Cobley; M. de Pulford; E. Grant; L. Hughes; Ms S. Marshall; N. Varney

ANIMALS (SCIENTIFIC PROCEDURES) INSPECTORATE

Chief Inspector (SCS), Dr J. Richmond
Superintendent Inspector (SCS), Dr J. Anderson
Inspectors (G6), Dr R. Curtis; Dr V. Navaratnam; Dr C. Wilkins

GAMING BOARD FOR GREAT BRITAIN

—see page 333

CORPORATE DEVELOPMENT DIRECTORATE

Director (SCS), Dr D. Pepper
Heads of Units (SCS), T. Edwards; Ms S. Rae
Senior Principal (G6), T. Williams

CORPORATE RESOURCES DIRECTORATE

Grenadier House, 99–105 Horseferry Road, London SW1P 2DD
Tel: 020-7273 4000
Queen Anne's Gate, London SW1H 9AT
Tel: 020-7273 4000

Director (SCS), Ms L. Lockyer
Heads of Units (SCS), Ms D. Loudon; Ms E. Moody; S. Wharton, N. Benger
Senior Principals (G6), A. Ford; D. McDonough; D. G. Jones

CRIMINAL POLICY GROUP

Directors (SCS), J. Halliday, CB; Mrs S. Street
Heads of Units (SCS), S. Atkins; M. Boyle; Ms F. Clarkson; Ms G. Fletcher-Cooke; M. Lewer; J. Powls; Dr D. Jones; Ms C. Byrne; I. Chisholm; S. Hickson; H. Marriage; A. Norbury; J. Powls; Miss C. Stewart; J. Thompson; H. Webber
Senior Principals (G6), J. Furniss; Mrs A. Johnstone; A. Macfarlane; J. Nicholson; Ms L. Rogerson; S. Thornton; Mrs J. Burhams; S. Trimmins; T. Woolfenden; D. Perry

HOME OFFICE CRIME PREVENTION COLLEGE

The Hawkhills, Easingwold, York YO6 3EG
Tel: 01347-825060
Director, S. Trimmins

HM INSPECTORATE OF PROBATION
Chief Inspector (SCS), Sir Graham Smith, CBE
Assistant Chief Inspector (G6), J. Kuipers

FIRE AND EMERGENCY PLANNING
DIRECTORATE
Horseferry House, Dean Ryle Street, London SW1P 2AW
Tel: 020-7273 4000
50 Queen Anne's Gate, London SW1H 9AT
Tel: 020-7273 4000
Director (SCS), C. Everett
Heads of Units (SCS), P. Davies; E. Guy; Mrs V. Harris;
   Miss S. Hart; Dr D. Peace

HM FIRE SERVICE INSPECTORATE
HM Chief Inspector, G. Meldrum, CBE, QFSM
HM Territorial Inspectors, A. R. Currie, OBE, QFSM;
   P. Morphew, QFSM; A. Rule, QFSM; J. G. Russel, QFSM
Lay Inspector, vacant
HM Inspectors, R. A. M. Baillie, QFSM; D. Berry;
   G. P. Bowles; S. D. Christian; D. Kent; C. Moseley;
   R. Pearce; E. G. Pearn, OBE, QFSM; K. Phillips;
   M. Robinson; B. J. Unger; A. C. Wells, QFSM
Principal (G7), Miss K. Kirton

EMERGENCY PLANNING COLLEGE
The Hawkhills, Easingwold, Yorks YO6 3EG
Tel: 01347-821406

IMMIGRATION AND NATIONALITY
DIRECTORATE, AND EUROPEAN AND
INTERNATIONAL UNIT
Whitgift Centre, Block A, 15 Wellesley Road,
Croydon, Surrey CR9 3LY
Tel: 0870 606 7766
Apollo House, 36 Wellesley Road, Croydon,
Surrey CR9 3RR
Tel: 020-8686 0333
50 Queen Anne's Gate, London SW1H 9AT
Tel: 020-7273 4000
India Buildings, 3rd Floor, Water Street, Liverpool L2 0QN
Tel: 0151-237 5200
Director-General (SCS), S. Boys Smith
Deputy Directors-General (SCS), M. J. Eland (*Policy*);
   Miss K. Collins (*Operations*); Dr C. Mace (*Projects*)
Heads of Directorates (SCS), J. Acton; Miss V. M. Dews;
   B. Eagle; Mrs E. C. L. Pallett; J. Potts; R. M. Whalley;
   R. G. Yates
Senior Principals (G6), P. Dawson; B. Downie;
   P. Wheelhouse

IMMIGRATION SERVICE
Director (Ports) (SCS), T. Farrage, CBE
Deputy Director (G6), V. Hogg
Director (Enforcement) (SCS), I. Boon
Deputy Director (G6), C. Harbin

EUROPEAN INTERNATIONAL UNIT
Head of Unit (SCS), P. Edwards

LEGAL ADVISERS' BRANCH
Legal Adviser (SCS), D. Seymour
Deputy Legal Advisers (SCS), Mrs S. A. Evans; T.
   Middleton
Assistant Legal Advisers (SCS), R. J. Clayton; J. R. O'Meara;
   R. Green; S. A. Parker

ORGANISED AND INTERNATIONAL
CRIME DIRECTORATE
Director (SCS), J. Warne

PLANNING, FINANCE AND
PERFOMANCE GROUP
50 Queen Anne's Gate, London SW1H 9AT
Tel: 020-7273 4000
Horseferry House, Dean Ryle Street,
London SW1P 2AW
Tel: 020-7273 4000
Directors (SCS), R. Fulton; L. Haugh
Heads of Units (SCS), C. Harnett; A. Mortimer
Senior Principal (G6), P. Dare

POLICING AND CRIME
REDUCTION GROUP
Director (SCS), J. Lyon
Head of Unit (SCS), N. Benger
Senior Principal (G6), R. Ginman

NATIONAL POLICE TRAINING
National Director of Police Training, I. McDonald
Corporate Services, Senior Principal (G6), S. Wells

NATIONAL POLICE TRAINING
Bramshill House, Bramshill, Hook, Hants RG27 0JW
Tel: 01256-602100
Head of Higher Training, I. McDonald

HENDON DATA CENTRE
Aerodrome Road, Colindale, London NW9 5LN
Tel: 020-8200 2424
Head of Unit (G6), J. Ladley

POLICE SCIENTIFIC DEVELOPMENT BRANCH
Sandridge, St Albans, Herts AL4 9HQ
Tel: 01727-865051
Director (SCS), B. R. Coleman, OBE
Chief Scientist/Deputy Director (G6), Dr P. Young
Langhurst House, Langhurstwood Road,
Nr Horsham, W. Sussex RH12 4WX
Tel: 01403-255451
Head of Langhurst Facility (G6), Dr G. Thomas

HM INSPECTORATE OF CONSTABULARY
HM Chief Inspector of Constabulary (SCS),
   Sir David O'Dowd, CBE, QPM
HM Inspectors (SCS), D. Crompton, CBE, QPM;
   K. Povey, QPM; C. Smith, CBE, CVO, QPM;
   P. J. Winship, CBE, QPM; D. Blakey, CBE, QPM
Senior Principal (G6), L. Davidoff

METROPOLITAN POLICE COMMITTEE
AND SECRETARIAT
Clive House, Petty France, London SW1H 9HD
Tel: 020-7273 4000
Head of Secretariat (SCS), P. Honour

RESEARCH, DEVELOPMENT AND
STATISTICS DIRECTORATE
Director (SCS), Dr P. Wiles
Heads of Units (SCS), Dr G. Laycock; C. Lewis;
   D. Moxon; R. Price; P. Ward; Dr J. Youell
Senior Principals (G6), G. Barclay; Ms M. Colledge;
   P. Collier; Mrs P. Dowdeswell; Ms M. FitzGerald;
   P. Goldblatt; Mrs C. Lehman; Mrs P. Mayhew, OBE;
   R. Walmsley; B. Webb

PERFORMANCE AND STRATEGY UNIT
Head of Unit (SCS), C. Allars

HM INSPECTORATE OF PRISONS
HM Chief Inspector, Gen. Sir David Ramsbotham, GCB, CBE
HM Deputy Chief Inspector, C. Allen
HM Inspectors (Governor 1), R. Jacques; G. Hughes;
J. Podmore

PRISONS OMBUDSMAN
— *see* page 353

PAROLE BOARD FOR ENGLAND AND WALES
— *see* page 351

HM PRISON SERVICE
— *see* Prison Service section, 391–395

FIRE SERVICE COLLEGE
Moreton-in-Marsh, Glos GL56 0RH
Tel: 01608-650831
An executive agency of the Home Office.
Chief Executive and Commandant, T. Glossop, QFSM
College Secretary, P. Taylor

UK PASSPORT AGENCY
Clive House, Petty France, London SW1H 9HD
Tel: 020-7799 2728
An executive agency of the Home Office.
Chief Executive (SCS), B. L. Herdan
Deputy Chief Executive and Director of Operations (G6),
K. J. Sheehan
Director of Systems (G6), J. Davies
CRIMINAL RECORDS BUREAU, Room 466/68, India
Buildings, Water Street, Liverpool L2 0UZ.
Tel: 0151-224 8068. *Programme Manager (G6)*,
G. Ryan

DEPARTMENT FOR INTERNATIONAL DEVELOPMENT
94 Victoria Street, London SW1E 5JL
Tel: 020-7917 7000; Fax: 020-7917 0019
Web: http://www.dfid.gov.uk
Abercrombie House,
Eaglesham Road, East Kilbride, Glasgow G758EA
Tel: 01355-844000; Fax: 01355-844099

The Department for International Development (DFID)
was established in May 1997 from the former Overseas
Development Administration of the Foreign and Commonwealth Office. It takes the lead on British policy
towards developing countries. It also manages the development assistance budget, including financial aid and
technical assistance (specialist staff abroad and training
facilities in the UK), whether provided directly to devel-
oping countries or through the various multilateral aid
organisations, including the EU, the World Bank and the
UN agencies.
Secretary of State for International Development,
The Rt. Hon. Clare Short, MP
  Private Secretary, C. Austin
  Special Advisers, D. Sullivan; D. Mepham
  Parliamentary Private Secretary, D. Turner, MP
Parliamentary Under-Secretary, George Foulkes, MP
Permanent Secretary (SCS), Sir John Vereker, KCB
  Private Secretary, A. Mungar

PROGRAMMES
Director-General (SCS), B. R. Ireton
Head, Conflict and Humanitarian Affairs Department (SCS),
Dr M. Kapila

AFRICA
Head (SCS), G. Stegmann
Heads of Departments (SCS), Mrs B. M. Kelly, CBE
  (Africa, Greater Horn and Co-ordination); B. Thomson
  (West and North Africa); M. Lowcock *(Eastern Africa)*;
  Ms C. Sergeant *(Eastern Africa, Tanzania)*; G. Teskey
  (Eastern Africa, Uganda); J. R. Drummond
  (Central Africa); J. H. S. Chard *(Southern Africa)*

ASIA AND PACIFIC
Head (SCS), M. Dinham
Heads of Departments (SCS), Ms. S. Smith *(East Asia and
  Pacific)*; R. Graham-Harrison *(India)*; Ms M. H. Vowles
  (Western Asia); M. Mallalieu *(South-East Asia)*;
  K. L. Sparkhall *(Bangladesh)*

EASTERN EUROPE AND WESTERN HEMISPHERE
Head (SCS), J. Kerby
Heads of Departments (SCS), C. Curran *(Caribbean)*
  Ms A. Archbald *(Latin America, Caribbean and Atlantic)*

ECONOMICS, STATISTICS AND ENTERPRISE
Director, and Chief Economic Adviser (SCS), A. Coverdale
Chief Statistician (SCS), A. B. Williams
Head, Asia Regional and Economic Policy, P. J. Ackroyd
Head, Africa Policy and Economics, P. J. Landymore
Head, Development Economic Policy Research (SCS),
  P. D. Grant
Head, Enterprise Development, D. Stanton
Head, Asia Regional Economic Policy, P. Ackroyd
Head, Western Hemisphere and Eastern Europe, Ms C. Laing

EDUCATION DIVISION
Chief Education Adviser (SCS), Ms M. A. Harrison

HEALTH AND POPULATION DIVISION
Chief Health and Population Adviser, J. Lobb-Levitt

INTERNATIONAL DEVELOPMENT AFFAIRS
Director (SCS), J. A. L. Faint
Heads of Departments (SCS), A. Smith *(European Union)*;
  E. Hawthorne *(International Economic Policy)*;
  M. Mosselmans *(United Nations and Commonwealth)*;
  M. E. Cund *(International Financial Institutions)*

RURAL LIVELIHOODS AND ENVIRONMENT
Chief Natural Resources Adviser (SCS), A. J. Bennett, CMG
Head, Environment Policy Department (SCS), A. Davis
Head, Rural Livelihoods, J. M. Scott
Head, Social Development, Dr M. Schultz

RESOURCES
Director-General (SCS), R. G. Manning
Heads of Departments (SCS) R. Wilson *(Governance)*;
  R. Stevenson *(Business Partnership)*; D. Sands-Smith
  (Aid Policy); C. Raynor *(Finance)*; M. Smithson *(Accounts)*;
  R. A. Elias *(Internal Audit Unit)*; C. Kirk *(Evaluation)*;
  D. Richards *(Human Resources Policy)*; J. Anning *(Human
  Resources Operations)*; vacant *(Civil Society)*; P. Brough
  (Overseas Pensions); D. Gillett *(Information Systems and
  Services)*; R. Calvert *(Information)*

OTHER RELATED ORGANISATIONS

CDC CAPITAL PARTNERS
One Bessborough Gardens, London SW1V 2JQ
Tel: 020-7828 4488; Fax: 020-7282 6505
The Commonwealth Development Corporation has now
become CDC Capital Partners, a public limited company
with the Department of International Development as its

100% shareholder. At a later date CDC plans to become a public private partnership with the Government maintaining the majority of the shareholding.
Chairman, The Lord Cairns, CBE
Deputy Chairman, Ms J. Almond
Chief Executive, Dr A. Gillespie

LORD CHANCELLOR'S DEPARTMENT
Selborne House, 54–60 Victoria Street,
London SW1E 6QW Tel: 020-7210 8500
Email: enquiries.lcdhq@gtnet.gov.uk
Web: http://www.open.gov.uk/lcd

The Lord Chancellor appoints Justices of the Peace (except in the Duchy of Lancaster) and advises the Crown on the appointment of most members of the higher judiciary. He is responsible for promoting general reforms in the civil law, for the procedure of the civil courts and for the Community Legal Service. He is a member of the Cabinet. He also has ministerial responsibility for magistrates' courts, which are administered locally. Administration of the Supreme Court and county courts in England and Wales was taken over by the Court Service, an executive agency of the department, in 1995.

The Lord Chancellor is also responsible for ensuring that letters patent and other formal documents are passed in the proper form under the Great Seal of the Realm, of which he is the custodian. The work in connection with this is carried out under his direction in the Office of the Clerk of the Crown in Chancery.

The Lord Chancellor is also the senior Lord of Appeal in Ordinary and speaker of the House of Lords.
Lord Chancellor (£167,760), The Lord Irvine of Lairg, PC, QC
　Principal Private Secretary, Ms D. Matthews
　Special Adviser, G. Hart
Parliamentary Secretaries, Jane Kennedy, MP;
　David Lock, MP
　Private Secretaries, R. Moore; M. Charles
Permanent Secretary (*SCS*), Sir Hayden Phillips, KCB
　Private Secretary, B. Lee

CROWN OFFICE
House of Lords, London SW1A 0PW
Tel: 020-7219 4713

Clerk of the Crown in Chancery (*SCS*),
　Sir Hayden Phillips, KCB
Deputy Clerk of the Crown in Chancery (*SCS*),
　M. Huebner, CB
Clerk of the Chamber, C. I. P. Denyer

JUDICIAL GROUP
Tel: 020-7210 8500

Director (*SCS*), Mrs E. J. Grimsey
Heads of Divisions (*SCS*), D. E. Staff (*Policy and Conditions of Service*); D. Gladwell (*Senior Appointment and Silk*);
　Mrs C. Pulford (*District Bench and Tribunals*);
　S. Humphries (*Magistrates' Appointments*);
　P. L. Jacob (*Judicial Policy*)
Judicial Studies Board
9th Floor, Millbank Tower, London SW1P 4QW
Tel: 020-7925 4762

Secretary (SCS), E. S. Adams

POLICY GROUP
Tel: 020-7210 8719

Director-General (*SCS*), Ms J. MacNaughton
Heads of Divisions (*SCS*), A. Cogbill (*Civil Justice and Legal*

Services Directorate); J. Tanner (*Civil Justice*); H. Burns (*Civil Law Development*); D. A. Hill (*Legal Aid Division*); C. Myerscough (*Community Legal Services*); P. Harris (*Legal Services*); Ms A. Finlay (*Public and Private Rights Directorate*); Ms M. Pigott, Ms J. Killick (*Family Policy*); B. Wells (*Administrative Justice*); D. Lye (Children and Advisory Service); Ms C. Colins, Ms K. Di Lorenzo (*Human Rights and Constitution Division*); Mrs K. Allen (Policy Group Secretariat); M. Ormerod (*Criminal Justice Group*); M. Kron (*Criminal Courts Review*); P. Stockton (*Criminal Justice*); Ms. S. Field (*Magistrates' Court*); P. White (*Magistrates' Courts IT*);

LEGAL ADVISER'S GROUP
Tel: 020-7210 0711

Legal Adviser (*SCS*), P. Jenkins
Heads of Divisions (*SCS*), P. Fish (*Legal Advice and Litigation*); A. Wallace (*International and Common Law Services*); M. Collon (*Drafting Services*)

COMMUNICATIONS GROUP
Tel: 020-7210 8672

Director of Communications (*SCS*), A. Percival, LVO

CORPORATE SERVICES GROUP
Tel: 020-7210 8503

Director of Corporate Services (*SCS*), Ms. J. Rowe
Heads of Divisions (*SCS*), R. Sams, (*Personnel*); S. Smith (*Finance*) A. Pay (*Accountancy*); A. Rummins (*Internal Assurance*); A. Maultby (*Information Management Unit*); R. Atkinson (*Facilities and Support Services*); K. Garrett (*Statutory Publications*); D. Houtley (*Information Technology*); B. Eadie (*Corporate Services Secretariat*)

ECCLESIASTICAL PATRONAGE
10 Downing Street, London SW1A 2AA
Tel: 020-7930 4433

Secretary for Ecclesiastical Patronage, J. H. Holroyd, CB
Assistant Secretary for Ecclesiastical Patronage,
　N. C. Wheeler

HM MAGISTRATES' COURTS' SERVICE INSPECTORATE
Southside, 105 Victoria Street, London SW1E 6QJ
Tel: 020-7210 1655

Chief Inspector (*SCS*), C. J. A. Chivers
Senior Inspectors (*SCS*), D. Gear; C. Monson; Ms S. Steel

LORD CHANCELLOR'S ADVISORY COMMITTEE ON STATUTE LAW
Room 6.06, Selborne House, 54-60 Victoria Street,
London SW1E 6QW
Tel: 020-7210 2615; Fax: 020-7210 2678

The Advisory Committee advises the Lord Chancellor on all matters relating to the revision, modernisation and publication of the statute book.
Chairman, The Lord Chancellor,
　The Rt. Hon. the Lord Irvine of Lairg
Deputy Chairman, Sir Hayden Phillips, KCB
Members, The Hon. Mr Justice Carnwath, CVO;
　The Hon. Lord Gill; J. M. Davies; J. C. McCluskie, CB, QC; R. Henderson; P. Jenkins; Mrs C. Tullo; W. R. McKay, CB; K. Garrett; E. G. Cauldwell, CB; P. J. Layden, TD; G. Gray; Miss J. Wheldon, CB, QC; Ms J. Rowe; A. Pawsey
Secretary, N. Hodgett

EXECUTIVE AGENCY

THE COURT SERVICE

Southside, 105 Victoria Street, London SW1E 6QT
Tel: 020-7210 1646; Fax: 020-7210 2059
E mail cust.ser.cs@gtnet.gov.uk
Web: http://www.courtservice.gov.uk

The Court Service provides administrative support to the Supreme Court, the Crown Court, county courts and a number of tribunals in England and Wales.
Chief Executive (SCS), I. Magee
Director of Operational Policy (SCS), Miss B. Kenny
Director of Finance (SCS), vacant
Change Director (SCS), K. Pogson
Director of Purchasing and Contract Management (SCS), vacant
Head of Information Services Division (SCS), Ms A. Vernon
Head of Personnel and Training (SCS), Ms H. Dudley
Director of Civil and Family Operations (SCS), S. Smith
Director of Criminal Operations (SCS), N. J. Smedley
Director of Tribunals (SCS), P. Stockton

Supreme Court Group
Strand, London WC2A 2LL
Tel: 020-7936 6000
Director (SCS), I. Hyams

For Supreme Court departments and offices and circuit administrators, *see* Law Courts and Offices section

NORTHERN IRELAND OFFICE

11 Millbank, London SW1P 4PN
Tel: 020-72103000
Castle Buildings, Stormont, Belfast BT43SG
Tel: 01232-520700; Fax: 01232-528195
Web: http://www.nics.gov.uk/centgov/nio/nio.htm

The Northern Ireland Office was established in 1972, when the Northern Ireland (Temporary Provisions) Act transferred the legislative and executive powers of the Northern Ireland Parliament and Government to the UK Parliament and a Secretary of State.

The Northern Ireland Office is responsible primarily for security issues, law and order and prisons, and for matters relating to the political and constitutional future of the province. It also deals with international issues as they affect Northern Ireland. Following an earlier suspension of the Assembly, devolution took place on the 29 May 2000.

Under the terms of the 1998 Belfast Agreement, power was due to be devolved to the New Northern Ireland Assembly in 1999; the Assembly would then take on responsibility for the relevant areas of work currently undertaken by the departments of the Northern Ireland Office. In December 1998 the creation of ten new departments was agreed: agriculture and rural development; the environment; regional development; social development; education; higher education, training and employment; enterprise, trade and investment; culture, arts and leisure; health, social services and public safety; and finance and personnel. Each department is headed by a member of the power-sharing executive (*see* Regional Government Section) which is headed by the First Minister and Deputy First Minister. Six cross-border implementation bodies have also been established, dealing with inland waterways, food safety, trade and business development, EU programmes, language, and aquaculture.
Secretary of State for Northern Ireland,
The Rt. Hon. Peter Mandelson,MP
Parliamentary Private Secretary, H. Jackson, MP

Minister of State, The Rt. Hon. Adam Ingram, MP
Parliamentary Private Secretary, D. Browne, MP
Parliamentary Under-Secretaries of State,
George Howarth, MP
Permanent Under-Secretary of State (SCS), J. Pilling, CB
Second Permanent Under-Secretary of State, Head of the Northern Ireland Civil Service, G. Loughran

LONDON
SCS, (Political Director)
SCS, (Associate Political Director); (International and Planning); (Constitutional and Political); (Rights and European); (Personnel and Office Services)
SCS, (Director of Information Services)

BELFAST
SCS, (Political Director)
SCS, (Associate Political Director); (Security); (Criminal Justice); (Political); (Personnel and Finance)

NORTHERN IRELAND INFORMATION SERVICE
Castle Buildings, Stormont, Belfast BT4 3SG
Tel: 01232-520700

EXECUTIVE AGENCIES
COMPENSATION AGENCY, Royston House, Upper Queen Street, Belfast BT1 6FD. Tel: 01232-2499444
FORENSIC SCIENCE AGENCY, Seapark, 151 Belfast Road, Carrickfergus, Co. Antrim BT38 8PL.
Tel: 01232-365744
NORTHERN IRELAND PRISON SERVICE, *see* Prison Service section

SCOTLAND OFFICE
Dover House, Whitehall, London SW1A 2AU
Tel: 0171-270 3000; Fax: 0171-270 6730

The Scotland Office is the department of the Secretary of State for Scotland, who represents Scottish interests in the Cabinet on matters reserved to the UK Parliament, i.e. constitutional matters, financial and economic matters, defence and international relations, immigration, social security, various matters relating to the single market with the UK (energy, transport, consumer protection) and employment. It also supports the Advocate General, the legal adviser to the UK Government on Scottish law.
See also Scottish Executive, Regional Government Section.
Secretary of State for Scotland,
The Rt. Hon. Dr John Reid, MP
Private Secretary (SCS), Ms J. Colquhoun
Minister of State, Brian Wilson, MP
Private Secretary, D. Ferguson
Advocate-General for Scotland, Lynda Clark, MP
Private Secretary, Ms C. Keggie
Head of Department (SCS), I. Gordon

DEPARTMENT OF SOCIAL SECURITY
Richmond House, 79 Whitehall, London SW1A 2NS
Tel: 020-7238 0800

The Department of Social Security (DSS) is responsible for the payment of benefits including child benefit, one-parent benefit, income support and family credit. It administers the Social Fund, and is responsible for assessing the means of applicants for legal aid. It is also responsible for the payment of war pensions and the operation of the child maintenance system. Responsibility for the operation of the national insurance contributions scheme was transferred from the DSS to the Inland Revenue in April 1999.

Secretary of State for Social Security, The Rt. Hon. Alistair Darling, MP
  Principal Private Secretary, N. Couling
  Special Advisers, E. Johnson; A. Maugham
  Parliamentary Private Secretary, Ms A. Coffey, MP
Minister of State, Jeff Rooker, MP
  Private Secretary, Ms D. Whitehead
Parliamentary Under-Secretaries of State, The Baroness Hollis of Heigham, D.Phil. (*Family Policy, Child Benefit, Child Support, War Pensions*); Angela Eagle, MP (*Income-related Benefits, International and Green Issues*); Hugh Bayley, MP (*Disability and Sickness Benefits, Deregulation, Independent Living Fund*)
  Private Secretaries, Ms H. Bees; Ms T. Griffiths; Ms M. Curran
Permanent Secretary (SCS), Ms R. Lomax
  Private Secretary, C. Jackson

CORPORATE MANAGEMENT GROUP
Director (SCS), J. Tross

PERSONNEL AND HQ SUPPORT SERVICES DIRECTORATE
Director, M. Cayley

ANALYTICAL SERVICES DIVISION
The Adelphi, 1–11 John Adam Street, London WC2N 6HT
Tel: 020-7962 8000

Director (SCS), D. Stanton
Chief Statistician (SCS), N. Dyson
Senior Economic Advisers (SCS), J. Ball; G. Harris; R. D'Souza
Operational Research Service (SCS), D. Barnbrook
Chief Research Officers (SCS), Ms S. Duncan; S. Rice

PLANNING AND FINANCE DIVISION
Director, P. Mosley

INFORMATION DIRECTORATE
Director of Information (SCS), S. MacDowall
Deputy Head of Information (G6), J. Bretherton
Chief Press Officer (G7), Ms S. Lewis
Chief Publicity Officer (G7), Mrs A. Hall

SOCIAL SECURITY POLICY GROUP
Head of Policy Group (SCS), P. R. C. Gray, CB
Policy Directors (SCS), Miss M. Peirson, CB (*Pensions and NI*); D. Brereton (*Income Support*); U. Brennan (*Disability, Sickness and Career Benefit*); Ms J. Collinson (*Welfare Reform*)
Chief Medical Adviser and Medical Policy Director, Dr M. Aylward

SOLICITOR'S OFFICE
Solicitor and Head of Law and Special Policy Group (SCS), Mrs M. A. Morgan, CB

SOLICITOR'S DIVISION A
New Court, 48 Carey Street, London WC2A 2LS
Tel: 020-7412 1466

Legal Director (SCS), J. A. Catlin
Assistant Legal Director (SCS), Ms F. A. Logan; S. Cooper; Ms C. Cooper; P. Milledge; Ms A. McGaughrin

SOLICITOR'S DIVISION B
New Court, 48 Carey Street, London WC2A 2LS
Tel: 020-7412 1528

Solicitor and Head of Law and Special Policy Group (SCS), Mrs M. A. Morgan, CB
Assistant Solicitors (SCS), Ms S. Edwards; R. S. Powell; Mrs A. James

SOLICITOR'S DIVISION C
New Court, 48 Carey Street, London WC2A 2LS
Tel: 020-7412 1342

Legal Director (SCS), Mrs G. S. Kerrigan
Assistant Solicitors (SCS), Miss M. E. Trefgarne; Mrs S. Walker; K. Baulblys; D. Dunleavy; Ms R. Sandby-Thomas

BENEFITS FRAUD INSPECTORATE
Berkeley House, 12A North Park Road, Harrogate HG1 5QA
Tel: 01423-832922

Director-General (SCS), C. Bull

EXECUTIVE AGENCIES

APPEALS SERVICE AGENCY
— *see* Tribunals section

BENEFITS AGENCY
Quarry House, Quarry Hill, Leeds LS2 7UA
Tel: 0113-232 4000

The Agency administers claims for and payments of social security benefits.
Chief Executive, P. Mathison
  Private Secretary, R. Baldwin
Directors, J. Codling (*Finance*); M. Fisher (*Personnel and Communications*); S. Heminsley (*Strategic and Planning*); A. Cleveland (*Operations Support*); N. Haighton (*Projects*)

Medical Policy
Principal Medical Officers, Dr M. Aylward; Dr P. Dewis; Dr P. Sawney; Dr A. Braidwood; Dr P. Stidolph

CHILD SUPPORT AGENCY
DSS Long Benton, Benton Park Road, Newcastle upon Tyne NE98 1YX
Tel: 0191-213 5000

The Agency was set up in April 1993. It is responsible for the administration of the Child Support Act and for the assessment, collection and enforcement of maintenance payments for all new cases.
Chief Executive, Ms F. Boardman
Directors, M. Davison; C. Peters; M. Isaacs; T. Read

INFORMATION TECHNOLOGY SERVICES AGENCY
4th Floor, Verulam Point, Station Way, St Albans, Herts AL1 5HE
Tel: 01727-815835; Fax: 01727-833740

The Agency maintains and oversees policies on information technology strategy, procurement, technical standards and security.
Chief Executive, G. McCorkell
Directors, J. Thomas; J. Brewood; G. Brown; B. Barnes; B. Gormley; J. Delamere; C. Nicholls
Non-Executive Directors, K. Pfotzer; K. Bogg

WAR PENSIONS AGENCY
Norcross, Blackpool, Lancs FY5 3WP
Tel: 01253-338816
Email: warpensions@gtnet.gov.uk

The Agency administers the payment of war disablement and war widows' pensions and provides welfare services and support to war disablement pensioners, war widows and their dependants and carers.
Chief Executive, G. Hextall
Central Advisory Committee on War Pensions
Rm 6303, War Pensions Agency, Norcross,
Blackpool, FY5 3WP
Tel: 01253 338816
Email: warpensions@gtnet.gov.uk
Secretary, C. Pike

ADVISORY BODIES
SOCIAL SECURITY ADVISORY COMMITTEE, New Court,
48 Carey Street, London WC2A 2LS.
Tel: 020-7412 1508; Fax: 020-7412 1570;
Email: ssac@ms42.dss.gov.uk;
Web: http://www.ssac.org.uk
Chairman, Lt.-Gen. Sir Thomas Boyd-Carpenter, KBE;
Secretary, Ms G. Saunders

DEPARTMENT OF TRADE AND INDUSTRY
1 Victoria Street, London SW1H 0ET
Tel: 020-7215 5000; Fax: 020-7222 2629
Web: http://www.dti.gov.uk

The Department is responsible for international trade policy, including the development of UK trade interests in the European Union, GATT, OECD, UNCTAD and other international organisations; policy in relation to industry and commerce, including industrial relations policy; policy towards small firms; regional industrial assistance; legislation and policy in relation to the Post Office; competition policy and consumer protection; the development of national policies in relation to all forms of energy and the development of new sources of energy, including international aspects of energy policy; policy on science and technology research and development; space policy; standards, quality and design; and company legislation.
Secretary of State for Trade and Industry,
  The Rt. Hon. Stephen Byers, MP
Principal Private Secretary, Ms. B. Kelly
Private Secretaries, B. Hoskins; E. Barker
Minister of State, The Rt. Hon. Helen Liddell, MP
  (*Energy and Competitiveness in Europe*)
Minister of State, The Rt. Hon. Richard Caborn, MP (*Trade*)
Minister of State, Patricia Hewitt, MP (*Small Business and E-commerce*)
Parliamentary Under-Secretaries of State,
  Dr Kim Howells, MP (*Consumers and Corporate Affairs*); Alan Johnson, MP (*Competitiveness*);
  The Lord Sainsbury of Turville (*Science and Innovation*)
  Private Secretaries, G. Maybury; Ms G. Jeffrey;
  Ms B. Eggleton
Parliamentary Clerk, T.Williams
Permanent Secretary, Sir Michael Scholar, KCB
  Private Secretary, Ms J. Davis
Chief Scientific Adviser and Head of Office of Science and Technology, Sir Robert May, FRS
  Private Secretary, Dr N. Moisewitsch
British Trade International Chief Executive,
  Sir David Wright, KCMG, LVO

Directors-General, Dr J. Taylor, OBE, FEng., FRS
  (*Director-General of the Research Councils*);
  A. Hutton, CB (*Trade Policy*); M. Gibson (*Enterprise and Innovation*); Dr C. Bell (*Competition and Markets Group*); D. Nissen, CB
  (*The Solicitor*); Ms A. Walker (*Energy*); J. Phillips
  (*Resources and Services*); J. Spencer (*Business Competitiveness*) vacant (*Fair Trading*)

DIVISIONAL ORGANISATION

†BRITISH NATIONAL SPACE CENTRE
Director-General (SCS), Dr C. Hicks
Deputy Director-General (SCS), D.Leadbeater
Directors (SCS), A. Cooper; Dr P. Murdin;
  Miss P. Freedman

BPT DIRECTORATE – BNFL PUBLIC PRIVATE PARTNERSHIP
Directors, J. Rhodes; Dr D. Walker
Deputy Directors, Ms R. Loebl; Ms P. Ciniewicz;
  N. Woodage

CENTRAL DIRECTORATE
Director of Competitiveness Unit (SCS), D. Evans
Directors (SCS), Ms S. Chambers; M. Higson; P. Bunn

†CHEMICALS AND BIOTECHNOLOGY DIRECTORATE
Director of Chemicals and Biotechnology (SCS), D. Davis
Directors (SCS), Ms M. Darnbrough; one vacancy

PUBLICITY AND INTERNAL COMMUNICATIONS DIRECTORATE/NEWSROOM
Deputy Director of News (SCS), C. Seabrook
Director of Public Information (SCS), P. Burke

†COMMUNICATIONS AND INFORMATION INDUSTRIES DIRECTORATE
Director of Communications and Information Industries (SCS), W. MacIntyre
Directors (SCS), N.Worman; D. Lumley; D. Love;
  C. Holmes; Mrs G. Alliston

COMPANY LAW AND INVESTIGATIONS DIRECTORATE
Director of Company Law and Investigations (SCS),
  R. Rogers
Directors (SCS), J. Grewe; G. Harp; J. Gardner;
  J. Sibley; R. Burns; Ms B. Chase; A. Robertshaw

COMPETITION POLICY AND UTILITIES REVIEW DIRECTORATE
Director of Team (SCS), Ms R. Anderson
Directors (SCS), Dr A. Eggington; D. Miner;
  J. May; R. Bent

CONSUMER AFFAIRS DIRECTORATE
Director of Consumer Affairs (SCS), J. Rees
Directors (SCS), P. Mason; Ms J. Munday; H. Ewing;
  A. Willcocks

CONSUMER GOODS, BUSINESS AND POSTAL SERVICES DIRECTORATE
Director of Consumer Goods, Business and Postal Services (SCS), D. Davis
Directors (SCS), B. Hopson; Ms J. Britton

ECONOMICS AND STATISTICS DIRECTORATE
Chief Economic Adviser (SCS), D. R. Coates
Directors (SCS), K. Warwick; Ms J. Dougharty; A. Rees

EMPLOYMENT RELATIONS DIRECTORATE
Director of Industrial Relations (SCS), S. Haddrill
Directors (SCS), Dr E. Baker; R.Niblett;
  Ms N. Carter; K. Masson; M. Beatson

ENERGY POLICY, ANALYSIS, TECHNOLOGY AND
COAL DIRECTORATE
*Director of Energy Policy, Analysis, Technology and Coal
(SCS)*, N. Hirst
Directors (SCS), G. C. White; N. Peace; J. Doddrell;
  P. Mason; A. Wright

ENU – ENERGY UTILITIES DIRECTORATE
Deputy Director General, N. Hirst
Director, I. Fletcher
Deputy Director, Dr G. Bryce

†ENGINEERING INDUSTRIES DIRECTORATE
Director of Engineering Industries (SCS), M. O'Shea
Directors (SCS), J. Hunt; D. Way; R. Kingcombe;
  H. Brown; I. Cameron; J. Dennis; Ms E. Zimmer

ENGINEERING INSPECTORATE
Director of Engineering Inspectorate (SCS), Dr P. Fenwick

ENVIRONMENT DIRECTORATE
Director of Environment (SCS), Dr J. Dennis
Director (SCS), D. Prior

ESTATES AND FACILITIES MANAGEMENT
DIRECTORATE
Director (SCS), M. Coolican

EUROPEAN POLICY DIRECTORATE
Kingsgate House, 66–74 Victoria Street,
  London SW1E 6SW
Director (SCS), N. McMillan, CMG

EXPORT CONTROL AND NON-PROLIFERATION
DIRECTORATE
Kingsgate House, 66–74 Victoria Street,
  London SW1E 6SW
Director of Export Control and Non-Proliferation (SCS),
  Ms S. Haird
Director (SCS), J. Neve

EXPORT SERVICES DIRECTORATE
Kingsgate House, 66–74 Victoria Street,
  London SW1E 6SW
Director (SCS), A. Reynolds

FINANCE AND RESOURCE MANAGEMENT
DIRECTORATE
Director of Finance and Resource Management (SCS),
  E. Hosker
Directors (SCS), E. Hosker; K. Hills;
  N. Nandra; H. Savill; D. Windle

‡INDUSTRY ECONOMICS AND STATISTICS
DIRECTORATE
Director (SCS), Dr N. Owen

†INFORMATION MANAGEMENT AND PROCESS
ENGINEERING DIRECTORATE
Director (SCS), R. Wheeler

BUSINESS GROUP 4 AND BUSINESS GROUP 5
BG4 Director, B. Gallaher
BG5 Director, K. Forrest

INNOVATION SERVICES
Director of Innovation Policy and Standards (SCS), R. Foster
Directors (SCS), J. Barber; D. Reed; S. I. Chanik

INNOVATION UNIT
Directors (SCS), Dr A. Keddie; J. Reynolds

†INTERNAL AUDIT DIRECTORATE
Director of Internal Audit (SCS), R. Louth

INTERNATIONAL ECONOMICS DIRECTORATE
Kingsgate House, 66–74 Victoria Street,
London SW1E 6SW
Director (SCS), C. Moir

INVEST UK
Chief Executive (SCS), A. Fraser
Director, Operations, A. Morgan
Director, International, D. Cockerham

LEGAL RESOURCE MANAGEMENT AND
BUSINESS LAW UNIT
10 Victoria Street, London SW1H 0NN
The Solicitor and Director-General (SCS), D. Nissen, CB
Director (SCS), C. Warren

LEGAL SERVICES DIRECTORATE A
10 Victoria Street, London SW1H 0NN
Director of Legal A (SCS), J. Stanley
Legal Directors (SCS), J. Roberts; Miss N. O'Flynn;
  S.Hyett; Miss G. Richmond

LEGAL SERVICES DIRECTORATE B
10 Victoria Street, London SW1H 0NN
Director of Legal B (SCS), P. Bovey
Legal Directors (SCS), R. Baker; B.Welch; R. Perkins;
  Ms S. Hardy; C. Raikes; Ms N. Arora

LEGAL SERVICES DIRECTORATE C
10 Victoria Street, London SW1H 0NN
Director of Legal C (SCS), Ms A. Brett-Holt
Legal Directors (SCS), M.Bucknill; A. Woods;
  M. Smith; T. Susman

LEGAL SERVICES DIRECTORATE D
10 Victoria Street, London SW1H 0NN
Director of Legal D (SCS), Mrs T. Dunstan
Directors (SCS), S. Milligan; L. Nawbatt

NEW ISSUES AND DEVELOPING COUNTRIES
Kingsgate House, 66–74 Victoria Street,
London SW1E 6SW
Director (SCS), C. Bridge

NUCLEAR INDUSTRIES DIRECTORATE
Director of Nuclear Industries (SCS), H. Leiser
Directors (SCS), Dr M. Draper; Dr E. Drage;
  I. Downing; S. Bowen; D. Walker

OFFICE OF SCIENCE AND TECHNOLOGY: SCIENCE
AND ENGINEERING BASE DIRECTORATE
Albany House, 84–86 Petty France, London SW1H 9ST
Director, Science and Engineering Base (SCS),
  Dr M. Earwicker
Directors (SCS), Dr F. Saunders; R. King; Dr K. Root

---

†At 151 Buckingham Palace Road, London SW1W 9SS

OFFICE OF SCIENCE AND TECHNOLOGY:
TRANSDEPARTMENTAL SCIENCE AND
TECHNOLOGY DIRECTORATE
Albany House, 84–86 Petty France, London SW1H 9ST
Director, Transdepartmental Science and Technology (SCS),
Ms J. Durning
Directors (SCS), S. Spivey; Mrs P. Sellers; M. Parker;
Ms J. Darrell
OIL AND GAS DIRECTORATE
1 Victoria Street, London SW1H 0ET
Director of Oil and Gas (SCS), G. Dart
Directors (SCS), J. R. V. Brooks, CBE; G. Riggs;
S. Toole; M. Graham

Atholl House, 86–88 Guild Street, Aberdeen AB11 6AR
Tel: 01224-254059
Director of Reform and Energy Regulation, K. Long
Directors of Oil and Gas (SCS), S. Toole; J. Campbell

REGIONAL ASSISTANCE DIRECTORATE
Director of Regional Assistance (SCS), A. Steele
Director (SCS), S. Robins

REGIONAL EUROPEAN FUNDS DIRECTORATE
Director (SCS), K. Masson

REGIONAL POLICY DIRECTORATE
Director (SCS), D. Smith

SENIOR STAFF MANAGEMENT DIRECTORATE
Director (SCS), Ms K. Elliott

SMALL BUSINESS SERVICE
Chief Executive, D. Irwin
Deputy Chief Executive, P. Waller
Directors, H. Merrifield; P. Jackson; J. Hobday;
M. Cocks; R. Allpress

STAFF PERSONNEL OPERATIONS DIRECTORATE
Director (SCS), R. Wright

STAFF POLICY AND PAY DIRECTORATE
Director (SCS), Ms B. Habberjam

TRADE FACILITATION AND IMPORT POLICY
DIRECTORATE
Kingsgate House, 66–74 Victoria Street,
London SW1E 6SW
Director (SCS), A. Berry

TRADE POLICY DIRECTORATE
Kingsgate House, 66–74 Victoria Street,
London SW1E 6SW
Director (SCS), C. Bridge

BRITISH TRADE INTERNATIONAL
Kingsgate House, 66–74 Victoria Street,
London SW1E 6SW Tel: 020-7215 5000

British Trade International brings together the Department of Trade and Industry and the Foreign and
Commonwealth Office export and investment operations.
Chairmen, The Rt. Hon. Richard Caborn, MP *(Minister
for Trade, DTI);* J. Battle, MP *(Minister of State, FCO)*
Vice-Chairmen, HRH The Duke of Kent, KG, GCMG,
GCVO; Sir David John, KCMG
Chief Executive, Sir David Wright, KCMG, LVO
Group Members, R. Turner, OBE; V. Brown;
A. Summers; Ms G. Goucher, MBE; R. Orgill;
K. Pathak; P. Westmacott; W. Thomson; G. Robson;
D. Jones; J. Spencer; P. Mason; A. Hingston

TRADE PARTNERS UK
The Trade Partners UK network provides services to
British exporters and investors at home and overseas.

*Deputy Chief Executive and Group Director, Central Services
Group (SCS),* D. Hall
Group Director, Regional Group, I. Jones
Group Director, International Group (SCS), Q. Quayle
Group Director, Business Group (SCS), D. Warren
Group Director, Strategy and Communications Group (SCS),
S. Lyle-Smythe

EXECUTIVE AGENCIES

COMPANIES HOUSE
Companies House, Crown Way, Cardiff CF14 3UZ
Tel: 029-2038 0801; Fax: 029-2038 0900
London Information Centre, 21 Bloomsbury Street,
London WC1B 3XD
37 Castle Terrace, Edinburgh EH1 2EB
Tel: 0131-535 5800; Fax: 0131-535 5820

Companies House incorporates companies, registers
company documents and provides company information.
Registrar of Companies for England and Wales, J. Holden
Registrar for Scotland, J. Henderson

EMPLOYMENT TRIBUNALS SERVICE
19–29 Woburn Place, London WC1H 0LU
Tel: 020-7273 8666; Fax: 020-7273 8670
The Service became an executive agency in 1997 and
brought together the administrative support for the
employment tribunals and the Employment Appeal
Tribunal.
Chief Executive, R. Heathcote

THE INSOLVENCY SERVICE
PO Box 203, 21 Bloomsbury Street, London WC1B 3QW
Tel: 020-7637 1110; Fax: 020-7636 4709
The Service administers and investigates the affairs of
bankrupts and companies in compulsory liquidation; deals
with the disqualification of directors in all corporate
failures; regulates insolvency practitioners and their
professional bodies; provides banking and investment
services for bankruptcy and liquidation estates; and advises
Ministers on insolvency policy issues.
Inspector-General and Chief Executive, P. R. Joyce, CB
Deputy Inspectors-Generals, D. J. Flynn; L. T. Cramp

NATIONAL WEIGHTS AND MEASURES
LABORATORY (NWML)
Stanton Avenue, Teddington, Middx TW11 0JZ
Tel: 020-8943 7272; Fax: 020-8943 7270;
Web: http://www.nwml.gov.uk

The Laboratory administers weights and measures
legislation, carries out type examination, calibration and
testing, and runs courses on meteorological topics. The
status of the NWML is currently under review.
Chief Executive, Dr S. Bennett

PATENT OFFICE
—see page 351

RADIOCOMMUNICATIONS AGENCY
Wyndham House, 189 Marsh Wall, London E14 9SX
Tel: 020-7211 0211; Fax: 020-7211 0507;
library.ra@gtnet.gov.uk;
Web: http://www.radio.gov.uk

The Agency is responsible for the management of the
radio spectrum used for civilian purposes within the UK. It
also represents UK radio interests internationally.
Chief Executive, D. Hendon

HM TREASURY
Parliament Street, London SW1P 3AG
Tel: 020-7270 5000
Web: http://www.hm-treasury.gov.uk

The Office of the Lord High Treasurer has been continuously in commission for well over 200 years. The Lord High Commissioners of HM Treasury are the First Lord of the Treasury (who is also the Prime Minister), the Chancellor of the Exchequer and five junior Lords (who are Government whips in the House of Commons). This Board of Commissioners is assisted at present by the Chief Secretary, the Parliamentary Secretary who is also the Government Chief Whip, the Paymaster-General, the Financial Secretary, the Economic Secretary, the Minister of State and the Permanent Secretary.

The Prime Minister is not primarily concerned in the day-to-day aspects of Treasury business; the management of the Treasury devolves upon the Chancellor of the Exchequer and the other Treasury Ministers.

The Chief Secretary is responsible for public expenditure planning and control; public sector pay; value for money in the public services; public/private partnerships and procurement policy; strategic oversight of banking, financial services and insurance; departmental investment strategies; welfare reform; devolution; and resource accounting and budgeting. From April 2000 he is responsible for a new Office of Government Commerce which centralises Government procurement activities.

The Paymaster-General is responsible for the Inland Revenue, Customs and Excise and the Treasury, with overall responsibility for the Finance Bill. She leads on personal and business taxation, VAT and European/international tax issues. The Paymaster-General's Office is part of the National Investment and Loans Office.

The Financial Secretary is responsible for growth and productivity; small firms and venture capital; science, research and development; competition and deregulation policy; environmental issues; export credit; most Customs and Excise taxes; vehicle excise duty; and parliamentary financial business.

The Economic Secretary is responsible for National Savings, the Debt Management Office, the National Investment and Loans Office, the Office for National Statistics, the Royal Mint, and the Government Actuary's Department; banking, financial services and insurance; foreign exchange reserves; debt management policy; women's issues; and charity taxation.

Prime Minister and First Lord of the Treasury,
  The Rt. Hon. Tony Blair, MP
Chancellor of the Exchequer,
  The Rt. Hon.Gordon Brown, MP
  Principal Private Secretary, T. Scholar
Private Secretaries, N. Jokey; M. Bowman
  Special Advisers, E. Balls; E. Miliband; I. Austin;
  P. Andrew
Council of Economic Advisers, C. Wales; P. Gregg;
  Ms S. Vadera
  Parliamentary Private Secretary, vacant
Chief Secretary to the Treasury, The Rt. Hon. Andrew
  Smith, MP
  Private Secretary, Ms D. Nickerson
Paymaster-General, Dawn Primarolo, MP
  Private Secretary, Ms S. Knight
  Parliamentary Private Secretary, John Healy, MP
Financial Secretary to the Treasury, Stephen Timms, MP
  Private Secretary, C. Martin

Economic Secretary, Melanie Johnson, MP
  Private Secretary, Ms J. Daniels
*Parliamentary Secretary to the Treasury and Government
  Chief Whip,* The Rt. Hon. Ann Taylor, MP
  Private Secretary, M. Maclean
Treasurer of HM Household and Deputy Chief Whip,
  Keith Bradley, MP
Comptroller of HM Household, Thomas McAvoy, MP
Vice-Chamberlain of HM Household, Graham Allen, MP
Lord Commissioners of the Treasury, Robert Ainsworth, MP;
  James Dowd, MP; Clive Betts, MP; David Jamieson, MP;
  Jane Kennedy, MP
Assistant Whips, David Clelland, MP; Kevin Hughes, MP;
  Greg Pope, MP; Anne McGuire, MP; Michael Hall, MP;
  Gerry Sutcliffe, MP
Parliamentary Clerk, D. S. Martin
Permanent Secretary to the Treasury, Sir AndrewTurnbull,
  KCB, CVO
  Private Secretary, J. Pavel
Head of Government Accountancy Service and Chief Accountancy Adviser to the Treasury, A.Likierman

DIRECTORATES

Head of Ministerial Support Team (SCS), T. Scholar
Head of Communications Team (SCS), M. Elham
Head of Strategy Team (SCS), R. Brightwell

MACROECONOMIC POLICY AND INTERNATIONAL
FINANCE
*Director, and Head of the Government Economic Service
  (SCS),* A. O'Donnell
Deputy Directors (SCS), J. Cunliffe; J. Taylor; I. Rogers
Heads of Teams (SCS), C. M. Kelly; A. Kilpatrick;
  D. Ramsden; M. Glycopantis; A. Lewis; S. Brooks;
  D. Lawton; M. Richardson; R. Todd

BUDGET AND PUBLIC FINANCES
Director (SCS), R. Culpin
Deputy Directors (SCS), N. Macpherson; C. J. Mowl
Heads of Teams (SCS), P. Curwen; Ms M. Dawes;
  I. Taylor; M. Williams; G. Parker; A. Gibbs;
  D. Deaton; C. Maxwell
Heads of Teams, I. Walker, M. Swan

PUBLIC SERVICES
Director (SCS), E. J. W. Gieve, CB
Deputy Directors (SCS), Miss G. M. Noble, CB;
  †A. Sharples; Ms L. de Groot †J. Grice
Heads of Teams (SCS), Ms A. Charlesworth; T. Dowse;
  E. Evans; D. Franklin; N. Holgate A. Ritchie;
  Ms H. Tuffs; P. Williams; R. Brown; A. Bridges;
  Mrs H. John; J. Richardson; P. Kane; S. Meek;
  Mrs R. Dunn; P. Brook; Miss T. Finkelstein;
  D. Franklin

FINANCIAL MANAGEMENT, REPORTING AND AUDIT
Director (Chief Accountancy Adviser) (SCS), A. Likierman
Deputy Director (SCS), †B. Glicksman
Heads of Teams (SCS), D. Loweth; K. Ross;
  I. Carruthers; R. Brightwell
Heads of Teams, K. Ross; C. Butler; Miss A. M. Jones

FINANCE, REGULATION AND INDUSTRY
Director (SCS), Dr S. Robson, CB
Deputy Directors (SCS), H. J. Bush, CB; R. Fellgett

---

* In addition to a parliamentary salary of £48,371; the Chief Whip is entitled to the ministerial salary shown but in common with other Cabinet Ministers takes only £48,516

Heads of Teams (SCS), Mrs P. C. Diggle; C. Ford;
D. Griffiths; J. Halligan; D. Roe; P. Rutman;
P. Schofield; Ms S. Mullen; J. Kingman

PERSONNEL, ACCOMMODATION AND INFORMATION
SERVICES
Director (SCS), Miss M. O'Mara
Head of Team (SCS), J. Dodds; J. Hibberd
Heads of Teams, P. Pegler
† Combined deputy director and head of team

EXECUTIVE AGENCIES

NATIONAL SAVINGS
—*see* page 347

OFFICE FOR NATIONAL STATISTICS
— *see* page 348

ROYAL MINT
— *see* page 358

UNITED KINGDOM DEBT MANAGEMENT OFFICE
Cheapside House, 138 Cheapside, London EC2V 6BB
Tel: 020-7862 6500; Fax: 0171 862 6509

The UK Debt Management Office was launched as an
executive agency of the Treasury in April 1998 after the
transfer from the Bank of England to the Treasury of
responsibility for debt management, the sale of gilts and
oversight of the gilts market. It took over responsibility for
the management of the Exchequer's daily cash flows in
April 2000.
Chief Executive, M. L. Williams

OTHER BODIES

OFFICE OF GOVERNMENT COMMERCE (OGC)
Fleetbank House, 2-6 Salisbury Square,
London EC4Y 8JX Tel: 020-7211 1300;
Web: http://www.ogc.gov.uk

The Office of Government Commerce was set up on the
1 April 2000. It is a unique body within government,
overseen by a supervisory board of Ministers and officials
from across the departments of government. Its aim is to
achieve the best value for money for the Government's
commercial relationships and coherence of purchasing
activity across 200 Government departments, non-governmental bodies and agencies. The OGC is an office of
HM Treasury.
Chief Executive, P. Gershon
Deputy Chief Executive, B. Rigby

THE BUYING AGENCY
Royal Liver Building, Pier Head, Liverpool L3 1PE
Tel: 0151-227 4262; Fax: 0151-227 3315

The Agency provides a professional purchasing service to
Government departments and other public bodies. From
April 2000 it became part of the Office of Government
Commerce reporting to the Chief Secretary to the
Treasury.
Chief Executive (SCS), S. P. Sage

CCTA (CENTRAL COMPUTER AND
TELECOMMUNICATIONS AGENCY)
Rosebery Court, St Andrew's Business Park,
Norwich NR7 0HS
Tel: 01603-704567; Fax: 01603-704817
Steel House, 11 Tothill Street, London SW1H 9NF
Tel: 020-7273 6565; Fax: 020-7273 6555

CCTA is and executive agency of the Office of Government Commerce, part of HM Treasury. CCTA is the
centre of expertise on IT within government, and at the

heart of the UK government's modernisation initiative. Its
aim is to help the public sector to improve the delivery of
their services through the best use of IT.
Chief Executive, R. Assirati

THE TREASURY SOLICITOR
DEPARTMENT OF HM PROCURATOR-GENERAL AND
TREASURY SOLICITOR
Queen Anne's Chambers, 28 Broadway, London SW1H 9JS
Tel: 020-7210 3000; Fax: 020-7210 3004

The Treasury Solicitor's Department provides legal
services for many Government departments. Those without their own lawyers are provided with legal advice, and
both they and other departments are provided with
litigation services. The Treasury Solicitor is also the
Queen's Proctor, and is responsible for collecting Bona
Vacantia on behalf of the Crown. The Department
became an executive agency in 1996.
HM Procurator-General and Treasury Solicitor (SCS), Sir A.
H. Hammond, KCB
Deputy Treasury Solicitor (SCS), A. M. Inglese

LITIGATION DIVISION
SCS, R. Aitken; Mrs D. Babar; P. Bennett; D. Brummell;
L. John-Charles; A. D. Lawton; A. Leithead;
B. McHenry; B. McKay; P. R. Messer; Ms L. Nicoll;
Mrs J. B. C. Oliver; D. Palmer; S. Parkinson;
R. J. Phillips; A. J. Sandal

QUEEN'S PROCTOR DIVISION
Queen's Proctor (SCS), Sir A. H. Hammond, KCB
Assistant Queen's Proctor (SCS), Mrs D. Babar

RESOURCES AND SERVICES DIVISION
*Principal Establishment and Finance Officer and Security
Officer (SCS)*, J. P. Burnett
Assistant Director Establishments (G7), Ms H.Donnelly
Assistant Director Finance (G7), C. A. Woolley
Assistant Director Information Systems (G7), M. Gabbidon
Business Support Manager (SEO), E. Blishen
Assistant Director Personnel and Training, Ms M Esplin

BONA VACANTIA DIVISION
SCS, Ms L. Addison

EUROPEAN DIVISION
SCS, J. E. Collins; A. Ridout; M. C. P. Thomas

CULTURE, MEDIA AND SPORT DIVISION
SCS, Ms I. Letwin

CABINET OFFICE AND CENTRAL ADVISORY DIVISION
SCS, M. C. L. Carpenter; C. House

MINISTRY OF DEFENCE ADVISORY DIVISION
Metropole Building, Northumberland Avenue,
London WC2N 5BL
Tel: 020-7218 4691

SCS, N. Beach; Mrs V. Collett; M. Hemming; Ms F. Nash

DEPARTMENT FOR EDUCATION AND EMPLOYMENT
ADVISORY DIVISION
Caxton House, Tothill Street, London SW1H 9NF
Tel: 020-72733000

SCS, F. D. W. Clarke; Ms D. Collins; S. T. Harker;
P. Kilgarriff; N. A. D. Lambert; D. Macrae; A. Preston

HM TREASURY ADVISORY DIVISION
Allington Towers, 19 Allington Street, London SW1E 5EB
Tel: 020-7270 3000

SCS, M. A. Blythe; J. R. J. Braggins; Ms R. Ford;
J. Jones; R. Ricks; Miss J. V. Stokes

CONSTITUTIONAL REFORM DIVISION
70 Whitehall, London SW1A 2AS
Tel: 020-7270 6093
SCS, Miss R. A. Jeffreys

WALES OFFICE
Gwydyr House, Whitehall, London SW1A 2ER
Tel: 0171-270 3000

The Wales Office is the Office of the Secretary of State for Wales, who represents Welsh interests in the Cabinet.
Secretary of State for Wales, The Rt. Hon. Paul Murphy, MP
Parliamentary Under-Secretary, David Hanson, MP
Head of Department, Ms A. Jackson

PUBLIC OFFICES

ADJUDICATOR'S OFFICE
Haymarket House, 28 Haymarket, London SW1Y 4SP
Tel: 020-7930 2292; Fax: 020-7930 2298

The Adjudicator's Office opened in 1993 and investigates complaints about the way the Inland Revenue (including the Valuation Office Agency) and Customs and Excise have handled a person's affairs.
The Adjudicator, Dame Barbara Mills, DBE, QC
Head of Office, C. Gordon

ADVISORY, CONCILIATION AND ARBITRATION SERVICE
Brandon House, 180 Borough High Street,
London SE1 1LW
Tel: 020-7210 3613; Fax: 020-7210 3708

The Advisory, Conciliation and Arbitration Service (ACAS) was set up under the Employment Protection Act 1975 (the provisions now being found in the Trade Union and Labour Relations (Consolidation) Act 1992). ACAS is directed by a Council consisting of a full-time chairman and part-time employer, trade union and independent members, all appointed by the Secretary of State for Trade and Industry. The functions of the Service are to promote the improvement of industrial relations in general, to provide facilities for conciliation, mediation and arbitration as means of avoiding and resolving industrial disputes, and to provide advisory and information services on industrial relations matters to employers, employees and their representatives.
ACAS has regional offices in Birmingham, Bristol, Cardiff, Fleet, Glasgow, Leeds, Liverpool, London, Manchester, Newcastle upon Tyne and Nottingham.
Chairman, vacant
Chief Conciliator (G4), D. Evans

ANCIENT MONUMENTS BOARD FOR SCOTLAND
Longmore House, Salisbury Place,
Edinburgh EH9 1SH
Tel: 0131-668 8764; Fax: 0131-668 8765;
Email: ancient.monuments@scotland.gov.uk

The Ancient Monuments Board for Scotland advises the Scottish Ministers on the exercise of their functions, under the Ancient Monuments and Archaeological Areas Act 1979, of providing protection for monuments of national importance.

Chairman, Prof. Michael Lynch, Ph.D., FRSE, FSA Scot.
Members, A. Wright, FSA Scot.; Dr A. Ritchie, OBE, Ph.D., FRSE, FSA, FSA Scot.; Prof. C. D. Morris, FRSE, FSA, FSA Scot.; R. J. Mercer, FRSE, FSA, FSAScot.; Miss L. M. Thoms, FSA Scot.; J. Higgitt, FSA, FSA Scot.; Dr C. Swanson, Ph.D., FSA Scot.; M. Baughan; Dr J. Cannizzo, Ph.D., FSA Scot.; Dr S. Peake, Ph.D.; M. J. Taylor; Ms J. Harden, FSA Scot.; Cllr J. A. McFadden, CBE; Cllr E. F. Scott, FSA Scot.;
Secretary, R. A. J. Dalziel
Assessor, Dr D. J. Breeze, Ph.D., FRSE, FSA, FSAScot.

ANCIENT MONUMENTS BOARD FOR WALES
Crown Buildings, Cathays Park, Cardiff CF10 3NQ
Tel: 029-2050 0200; Fax: 029-2082 6375;
Email: cadw@wales.gsi.gov.uk;
Web: http://www.cadw.wales.gov.uk

The Ancient Monuments Board for Wales advises the National Assembly for Wales on its statutory functions in respect of ancient monuments.
Chairman, Prof. R. R. Davies, CBE, D.Phil., FBA
Members, R. G. Keen; Prof. Wendy Davies, Ph.D., FBA; M. J. Garner; Prof. R. A. Griffiths, Ph.D., D.Litt.; R. Brewer, FSA
Secretary, Mrs J. Booker

ARTS COUNCILS

The Arts Council of Great Britain was established as an independent body in 1946 to be the principal channel for the Government's support of the arts. In 1994 the Scottish and Welsh Arts Councils became autonomous and the Arts Council of Great Britain became the Arts Council of England.
The Arts Councils are responsible for the distribution of the proceeds of the National Lottery allocated to the arts (*see* Lotteries and Gaming section).

ARTS COUNCIL OF ENGLAND
14 Great Peter Street, London SW1P 3NQ
Tel: 020-7333 0100; Fax: 020-7973 6590
The Arts Council is the national body for the arts in England.Its objectives are to develop and improve the understanding and practice of the arts and to increase their accessibility to the public. The Council funds the major arts organisations in England and the ten Regional Arts Boards. It is funded by a grant from the Department for Culture, Media and Sport and the lottery but operates at 'arm's length' from Government as regards artistic decision-making, although it is expected to account for such decisions to the Government and the public. The Council also provides advice, information and help to artists and arts organisations. Its members are unpaid.
The Government grant for 2000–1 is £237.3 million.
Chairman, G. Robinson
Members, D. Anderson; D. Brierley, CBE; Ms D. Bull, CBE; Prof. C. Frayling; A. Gormley; A. Kapoor; Prof. J. MacGregor; Prof. A. Motion; Ms P. Skene; Ms H. Strong
Chief Executive, P. Hewitt

REGIONAL ARTS BOARDS
EASTERN ARTS BOARD, Cherry Hinton Hall, Cherry Hinton Road, Cambridge CB1 8DW.
Tel: 01223-215355. *Chair,* Prof. S. Timperley

EAST MIDLANDS ARTS BOARD, Mountfields House, Epinal Way, Loughborough, Leics LE11 0QE. Tel: 01509-218292. *Chair,* Prof. R. Cowell

LONDON ARTS BOARD, Elme House, 133 Long Acre, London WC2E 9AF. Tel: 020-7240 1313. *Chair,* vacant

NORTHERN ARTS BOARD, Central Square, Forth Street, Newcastle upon Tyne NE7 3PJ. Tel: 0191-255 8500. *Chair,* G. Loggie

NORTH-WEST ARTS BOARD, Manchester House, 22 Bridge Street, Manchester M3 3AB. Tel: 0161-834 6644. *Chair,* T. Bloxham, MBE

SOUTH-EAST ARTS BOARD, Union House, Eridge Road, Tunbridge Wells, Kent TN4 8HF. Tel: 01892-507200. *Chair,* R. Reed

SOUTHERN ARTS BOARD, 13 St Clement Street, Winchester SO23 9DQ. Tel: 01962-855099. *Chair,* D. Astor

SOUTH WEST ARTS , Bradninch Place, Gandy Street, Exeter EX4 3LS. Tel: 01392-218188. *Chair,* Prof. A. Livingston

WEST MIDLANDS ARTS BOARD, 82 Granville Street, Birmingham B1 2LH. Tel: 0121-631 3121. *Chair,* R. Natkiel

YORKSHIRE ARTS BOARD, 21 Bond Street, Dewsbury, W. Yorks WF13 1AX. Tel: 01924-455555. *Chair,* C. Price

SCOTTISH ARTS COUNCIL

12 Manor Place, Edinburgh EH3 7DD
Tel: 0131-226 6051; Fax: 0131-225 9833;
Email: administrator@ scottisharts.org.uk
Web: http://www.sca.org.uk

The Scottish Arts Council funds arts organisations in Scotland with the concept of providing leadership and developing new ideas and initiatives. It has two main sources of funding: the Scottish Executive (2000-1 £29.7m) and Lottery funding through the Department of Culture, Media and Sport (2000-1 £19.7m).
Chairman, M. Linklater
Members, Ms S. Ainsley; Cllr Elizabeth Cameron; R. Chester; W. English; J. Faulds; Ms D. Idiens; Ms M. Marshall; Dr Ann Matheson, OBE; J. Scott Moncrieff; R. Presswood; W. Speirs
Director, Ms T. Jackson

ARTS COUNCIL OF WALES

9 Museum Place, Cardiff CF10 3NX
Tel: 029-2037 6500; Fax: 029-2022 1447

The Arts Council of Wales funds arts organisations in Wales and is funded by the National Assembly for Wales. The grant for 2000–2001 is about £15.4 million.
Chairman, Ms S. Crouch
Members, D. Davies; Dr H. Walford Davies; E. Fivet; S. Garrett; E. ap Gwyn; H. James; D. Jones; P. Ryan, OBE; R. Davies; G. Lewis; A. Lloyd; C. Thomas
Chief Executive, Ms J. Weston

ARTS COUNCIL OF NORTHERN IRELAND

MacNeice House, 77 Malone Road, Belfast BT9 6AQ
Tel: 028-90-38 5210; Fax: 028-9066 1715;
Email: publicaffairs@artscouncil-ni.org
Web: http://www.artscouncil-ni.org

The Arts Council of Northern Ireland is the prime distributor of Government funds in support of the arts in Northern Ireland. It is funded by the Department of Education for Northern Ireland, and the grant for 1999–2000 is £6.89 million.
Chairman, Prof. B. Walker
Vice-Chairman, Ms E. O'Baoill

Members, Ms M. Armstrong; D. Boyd; Cllr M. Bradley; Dr M. Crozier; R. Dunn; Dr Tess Hurson; D. Hyndman; Ms J. Jordan; J. Kerr; Prof. B. McClelland; Ms G. Moriarty; A. Shortt; Mrs. M. Yeomans
Chief Executive, B. Ferran

ART GALLERIES AND ASSOCIATED BODIES

NATIONAL GALLERIES OF SCOTLAND

The Mound, Edinburgh EH2 2EL
Tel: 0131-624 6200; Fax: 0131-343 3250
The National Galleries of Scotland comprise the National Gallery of Scotland, the Scottish National Portrait Gallery, the Scottish National Gallery of Modern Art and the Dean Gallery. There are also outstations at Paxton House, Berwickshire, and Duff House, Banffshire. Total Government grant-in-aid for 1999–2000 is £10.197 million.

TRUSTEES
Chairman of the Trustees, The Countess of Airlie, CVO
Trustees, Ms V. Atkinson; J. H. Blair; G. J. N. Gemmell, CBE; Lord Gordon of Strathblane, CBE; A. P. Leitch; Prof. Christina Lodder; Dr I. McKenzie Smith, OBE; Dr M. Shea; G. Weaver; Prof. I. Whyte

OFFICERS
Director (G4), T. Clifford
Keeper of Conservation (G6), M. Gallagher
Head of Press and Information (G7), Mrs A. M. Wagener
Keeper of Education (G7), M. Cassin
Registrar (G7), Miss A. Buddle
Secretary (G6), Ms S. Edwards
Buildings (G7), R. Galbraith
Keeper, National Gallery of Scotland (G6), M. Clarke
Keeper, Scottish National Portrait Gallery (G6), J. Holloway
   Curator of Photography, Miss S. F. Stevenson
Keeper, Scottish National Gallery of Modern Art and Dean Gallery (G6), R. Calvocoressi

NATIONAL GALLERY

Trafalgar Square, London WC2N 5DN
Tel: 020-7839 3321; Fax: 020-7747 2403
The National Gallery, which houses a permanent collection of western painting from the 13th to the 20th century, was founded in 1824, following a parliamentary grant of £60,000 for the purchase and exhibition of the Angerstein collection of pictures. The present site was first occupied in 1838; an extension to the north of the building with a public entrance in Orange Street was opened in 1975, and the Sainsbury wing was opened in 1991. Total Government grant-in-aid for 1999–2000 was £19.478 million.

BOARD OF TRUSTEES
Chairman, P. Hughes, CBE
Trustees, Lady Bingham; Sir Mark Richmond, SC.D., FRS; Lady Monck; Sir Ewen Fergusson, GCMG, GCVO; R. Gavron, CBE; C. Le Brun; The Hon. R. G. H. Seitz; Dr D. Landau; Sir Colin Southgate; J. Snow; Prof. Dawn Ades; Lady Hopkins

OFFICERS
Director, R. N. MacGregor
Keeper, Dr N. Penny
Senior Curator, D. Jaffé
Chief Restorer, M. H. Wyld, CBE
Head of Exhibitions, M. J. Wilson
Scientific Adviser, Dr A. Roy
Director of Administration, J. MacAuslan

Head of Press and Public Relations, Miss J. Liddiard
Director of Communications, D. Savelkoul

NATIONAL PORTRAIT GALLERY
St Martin's Place, London WC2H 0HE
Tel: 020-7306 0055; Fax: 020-7306 0058

A grant was made in 1856 to form a gallery of the portraits of the most eminent persons in British history. The present building was opened in 1896 and an extension in 1933. There are four regional partnerships displaying portraits in appropriate settings: Montacute House, Gawthorpe Hall, Beningbrough Hall and Bodelwyddan Castle. Total Government grant-in-aid for 2000–1 is £5.138 million.

BOARD OF TRUSTEES
Chairman, H. Keswick
Trustees, The Rt. Hon. Margaret Beckett, MP;
  Prof. Phillip King; Ms. F. Fraser; Ms T. Green;
  M. Hastings; H. Keswick; The Lord Morris of Castle
  Morris; T. Phillips, RA; Prof. The Earl Russell, FBA;
  Ms. C. Tomalin; J. Tusa; D. Scholey, CBE;
  Ms A. Shulman; Sir John Weston; Baroness
  Willoughby de Eresby
Director (G3), C. Saumarez Smith, PH.D.

ROYAL FINE ART COMMISSION FOR SCOTLAND
Bakehouse Close, 146 Canongate, Edinburgh EH8 8DD
Tel: 0131-556 6699; Fax: 0131-556 6633;
Web: http://www.rfacs.com

The Commission was established in 1927 and advises Ministers and local authorities on the visual impact and quality of design of construction projects. It is an independent body and gives its opinions impartially.
Chairman, The Rt. Hon. The Lord Cameron of
  Lochbroom, PC, FRSE
Commissioners, Prof. G. Benson; W. A. Cadell;
  Mrs K. Dalyell; Ms J. Malvenan; R. G. Maund;
  M. Murray; D. Page; B. Rae; Prof. R. Russell;
  M. Turnbull; A. Wright
Secretary, C. Prosser

TATE BRITAIN
Millbank, London SW1P 4RG
Tel: 020-7887 8000; Fax: 020-7887 8007

Tate Britain displays the national collection of British art. The gallery opened in 1897, the cost of erection (£80,000) being defrayed by Sir Henry Tate, who also contributed the nucleus of the present collection. The Turner wing was opened in 1910, and further galleries and a new sculpture hall followed in 1937. In 1979 a further extension was built, and the Clore Gallery, for the Turner collection, was opened in 1987. Tate consists of four galleries: Tate Britain and Tate Modern in London, Tate Liverpool and Tate St Ives.

BOARD OF TRUSTEES
Chairman, D. Verey
Trustees, Prof. Dawn Ades; Ms V. Barnsley;
  The Hon. Mrs J. de Botton; Sir Richard Carew Pole;
  P. Doig; Prof. J. Latto; Sir Christopher Mallaby,
  GCMG, GCVO; J. Snow; J. Studzinski; Ms G. Wearing;
  W. Woodrow

OFFICERS
Director, Sir Nicholas Serota
Director of National Programmes, S. Nairne
Director of Collections, J. Lewison
Director, Tate Modern, L. Nittve
Director, Tate Britain, S. Deuchar

Curator, Tate Liverpool, L. Biggs
Curator, Tate St Ives, S. Daniel-McElvoy

TATE MODERN
Bankside, London SE1 9TG
Tel: 020-7887 8000

Opened on 11 May 2000, Tate Modern displays the Tate collection of international modern art dating from 1900 to the present day. It includes works by Dalí, Picasso, Matisse, and Warhol as well as many contemporary works. It is housed in the former Bankside Power Station in London, redesigned by the Swiss architects Herzog & de Meuron.

WALLACE COLLECTION
Hertford House, Manchester Square, London W1M 6BN
Tel: 020-7935 0687; Fax: 020-7224 2155

The Wallace Collection was bequeathed to the nation by the widow of Sir Richard Wallace, Bt. in 1897, and Hertford House was subsequently acquired by the Government. Total Government grant-in-aid for 1999–2000 is £2.453 million.
Director, Miss R. J. Savill
Head of Administration, N. Paladina

ASSEMBLY OMBUDSMAN FOR NORTHERN IRELAND AND NORTHERN IRELAND COMMISSIONER FOR COMPLAINTS
Progressive House, 33 Wellington Place, Belfast BT1 6HN
Tel: 028-9023 3821; Fax: 028-9023 4912;
Email: ombudsman@ni-ombudsman.org.uk;
Web: http://www.ni-ombudsman.org.uk

The Ombudsman is appointed under legislation with powers to investigate complaints by people claiming to have sustained injustice in consequence of maladministration arising from action taken by a Northern Ireland Government department, or any other public body within his remit. Staff are presently seconded from the Northern Ireland Civil Service.
Ombudsman, T. Frawley
Deputy Ombudsman, J. MacQuarrie
Directors, C. O'Hare; R. Doherty; H. Mallon

AUDIT COMMISSIONS

ACCOUNTS COMMISSION FOR SCOTLAND
see Audit Scotland

AUDIT COMMISSION FOR LOCAL AUTHORITIES AND THE NATIONAL HEALTH SERVICE IN ENGLAND AND WALES
1 Vincent Square, London SW1P 2PN
Tel: 020-7828 1212; Fax: 020-7976 6187

The Audit Commission was set up in 1983 and is responsible for appointing external auditors to local authorities, including the Greater London Authority, and local National Health Service bodies in England and Wales. It is also responsible for promoting the proper stewardship of public finances and value for money in the services provided by local authorities and health bodies.

The Commission has a chairman, a deputy chairman and up to 18 members who, though appointed by the Secretary of State for the Environment, Transport and the Regions in consultation with the Secretary of State for Wales and the Health Secretaries in England and Wales, are responsible to Parliament.
Chair, Dame Helena Shovelton, DBE

Deputy Chairman, J. Orme
Members, Sir Peter Soulsby; Mrs I. Tarry, CBE;
  J. R. Foster; Sir Ronald Watson, CBE; Ms. R. Lowe;
  Mrs A. Fresko; Cllr R. Arthur; Sir. David Williams;
  Prof Sue Richards; Dr Judy Curson;
  Sir Graham Hart; Ms E. Filkin; B. Wolfe;
  Ms J. Baddeley
Controller of Audit, A. Foster
Commission Secretary, Ms C. Baldwinson
Chief Executive of District Audit Service, D. Prince

AUDIT SCOTLAND
110 George Street, Edinburgh EH2 4LH
Tel: 0131-477 1234; Fax: 0131-477 4567;
Web: http://www.audit-scotland.gov.uk

Audit Scotland was set up on 1 April 2000 to provide services to the Accounts Commission and the Auditor General for Scotland. Together they help to ensure that the Scottish Executive and public sector bodies in Scotland are held accountable for the proper, efficient and effective use of around £17 billion of public funds. Audit Scotland's work covers around 250 bodies including local authorities, police and fire boards; NHS boards and trusts; further education colleges; water authorities; departments of the Scottish Executive; executive agencies such as the Prison Service and non-departmental public bodies such as Scottish Enterprise. Audit Scotland carries out financial and regularity audits to ensure that the public sector bodies adhere to the highest standards of financial management and governance. It also performs audits to ensure that these bodies achieve the best value for money. All of Audit Scotland's work in connection with local authorities, fire and police boards is carried out for the Accounts Commission while its other work is undertaken for the Auditor General.
Auditor General, R. W. Black
Controller of Audit, R. Hinds
Secretary, W. F. Magee

BANK OF ENGLAND
Threadneedle Street, London EC2R 8AH
Tel: 020-7601 4444; Fax: 020-7601 4771;
Email: enquiries@bankofengland.co.uk
Web: http://www.bankofengland

The Bank of England was incorporated in 1694 under royal charter. It is the banker of the Government and manages the note issue. Since May 1997 it has been operationally independent and its Monetary Policy Committee has had responsibility for setting short-term interest rates to meet the Government's inflation target. As the central reserve bank of the country, the Bank keeps the accounts of British banks, who maintain with it a proportion of their cash resources, and of most overseas central banks. The Bank has three main areas of activity: Monetary Stability, Market Operations and Financial Stability. Its responsibility for banking supervision has been transferred to the Financial Services Authority. (*See also* Manual Services Regulation Section).
Governor, The Rt. Hon. E. A. J. George
Deputy Governors, D. Clementi; M. A. King
Non-Executive Directors, R. Bailie, OBE; A. R. F. Buxton;
  Sir David Cooksey; H. J. Davies; Sir Ian Gibson;
  G. Hawker; Mrs F. A. Heaton; Sir John Keswick;
  Dame Sheila Masters, DBE; Ms S. McKechnie, OBE;
  W. Morris; J. Neill, CBE, Ph.D.; N. I. Simms;
  J. Stretton; Ms K. A. O'Donovan

Monetary Policy Committee, The Governor; the Deputy
  Governors; I. Plenderleith; Dr D. Julius; J. Vickers;
  Dr S. Wadhwani; Prof. S. Nickell, C. J. Allsopp
Advisers to the Governor, Sir Peter Petrie;
  L. Berkowitz; R. Brealey
*Chief Cashier and Deputy Director, Banking and
  Market Services*, Ms M. V. Lowther
Chief Registrar, G. P. Sparkes
General Manager, Printing Works, A. W. Jarvis
Secretary, P. D. Rodgers
The Auditor, K. Butler

BOARD OF CUSTOMS AND EXCISE
*New King's Beam House, 22 Upper Ground,
London SE1 9PJ
Tel: 020-76201313
Web: http://www.open.gov.uk/customs/c.htm

Commissioners of Customs were first appointed in 1671 and housed by the King in London. The Excise Department was formerly under the Inland Revenue Department and was amalgamated with the Customs Department in 1909.

HM Customs and Excise is responsible for collecting and administering customs and excise duties and VAT, and advises the Chancellor of the Exchequer on any matters connected with them. The Department is also responsible for preventing and detecting the evasion of revenue laws and for enforcing a range of prohibitions and restrictions on the importation of certain classes of goods. In addition, the Department undertakes certain agency work on behalf of other departments, including the compilation of UK overseas trade statistics from customs import and export documents.

THE BOARD
Chairman (G1), R. Broadbent
  Private Secretaries, Ms D. Morris, Ms A. Lakemen
Commissioners (G3), P. R. H. Allen; M. R. Brown;
  R. N. McAfee; M. W. Norgrove; T. Byrne; M. Eland;
  M. Hansons (*Non Executive*) Ms R. Pickauence;
  D. Spencer
Solicitor, D. Pickup

COMMUNICATIONS DIVISION
Tel: 020-7865 5335

HEAD OF COMMUNICATIONS DIVISION, P. Rose

LOGISTICS GROUP, Alexander House, 21 Victoria Avenue,
  Southend-on-Sea SS99 1AA, Tel: 01702-348944
Director, A. Paynter

POLICY GROUP
Director, M. Eland

HUMAN RESOURCE GROUP
Director, P. R. H. Allen

OUTPUTS (MANAGEMENT) GROUP
Director, R. N. McAfee

Tariff and Statistical Office
Portcullis House, 27 Victoria Avenue, Southend-on-Sea
SS2 6AL
Tel: 01702-348944

Controller, M. McDowall

---

* Unless otherwise stated, this is the address and telephone number of directorates of the Board

Accounting Services Division
Alexander House, 21 Victoria Avenue, Southend-on-Sea
SS99 1AA
Tel: 01702-348944
Accountant and Comptroller-General, D. Robinson

OUTPUTS (DELIVERY) GROUP
Director, M. W. Norgrove

OUTPUTS (FRAUD) GROUP
Director, T. Byrne

National Investigation Service
Custom House, Lower Thames Street, London EC3R 6EE
Tel: 020-7283 5353
Chief Investigation Officer, P. Evans

SOLICITOR'S OFFICE
Solicitor, D. Pickup
Deputy Solicitor, G. Fotherby

COLLECTORS OF HM CUSTOMS AND EXCISE (*G5*)
Eastern England, J. Hendry
East, A. Durrant
London, J. Maclean *London International*, M. Hill
Northern Ireland, B. Logan
North-west, A. Allen
Scotland, I. Mackay
South-east, J. Tullberg
South-east (Central), M. Peach
South-west, H. Burnard
Wales, B. Flavill
West Midlands, D. Garlick
Yorkshire, Humber and the North East, H. Peden

BOARD OF INLAND REVENUE
Somerset House, Strand, London WC2R 1LB
Tel: 020-7438 6622

The Board of Inland Revenue was constituted under the Inland Revenue Board Act 1849. The Board administers and collects direct taxes – income tax, corporation tax, capital gains tax, inheritance tax, stamp duty, and petroleum revenue tax – and advises the Chancellor of the Exchequer on policy questions involving them. The Department's Valuation Office is an executive agency responsible for valuing property for tax purposes. The Contributions Agency of the Department of Social Security, which is responsible for the collection of contributions under the National Insurance scheme, became part of the Inland Revenue in April 1999 and is now an executive office called the National Insurance Contributions Office. The Contributions Unit of the Social Security Agency in Northern Ireland also transferred to the Inland Revenue in April 1999.

THE BOARD
Chairman (G1), N. Montagu, CB
  Private Secretary, Ms C. Lunney
Deputy Chairmen (G2), vacant
Director-General (G2), T. J. Flesher
Director-General, Strategic Service Delivery (G2),
  Miss A. Chant

DIVISIONS
Director, Human Resources Division (G3), J. Gant
Director, Business and Management Services Division (G3), J. Yard
Head, Strategy and Planning Division, P. Wardle
Principal Finance Officer (G3), R. R. Martin
Director, Business Operations Division (G3), D. A. Smith
Director, Analytical Services Division (G3), R. G. Ward

Director, Business Tax Division (G3), Ms J. Williams
Director, Management Support Unit (G3), K. Hodgson
Director, International Division (G3), G. Makhlouf
Director, Compliance Division (G3), E. J. Gribbon
Director, Personal Tax Division (G3), B. A. Mace
Director, Capital and Savings Division (G3), D. Hartnett

EXECUTIVE OFFICES
ACCOUNTS OFFICE (CUMBERNAULD), St Mungo's Road,
  Cumbernauld, Glasgow G70 5TR.
  Director, A. Geddes, OBE
ACCOUNTS OFFICE (SHIPLEY), Shipley, Bradford,
  W. Yorks BD98 8AA. *Director*, R. J. Warner
CAPITAL TAXES OFFICE, Ferrers House, PO Box 38,
  Castle Meadow Road, Nottingham NG2 1BB.
  Director, E. McKeegan
CAPITAL TAXES OFFICE (SCOTLAND), Mulberry House,
  16 Picardy Place, Edinburgh EH1 3NB.
  Registrar, Mrs J. Templeton
COMMUNICATIONS UNITS, Ground Floor, New Wing
  Somerset House, Strand, London WC2R 1LB.
  Director of Communications, Ms N. Walters
ENFORCEMENT OFFICE, Durrington Bridge House,
  Barrington Road, Worthing, W. Sussex BN12 4SE.
  Director, Mrs C. A. Mellor
FINANCIAL ACCOUNTING OFFICE, South Block,
  Barrington Road, Worthing, W. Sussex BN12 4XH.
  Director, Ms M. McLeish
FINANCIAL INTERMEDIARIES AND CLAIMS OFFICE,
  St John's House, Merton Road, Bootle L26 9BB;
  Fitz Roy House, PO Box 46, Castle Meadow,
  Nottingham NG2 1BD. *Director*, J. Johnson
INTERNAL AUDIT OFFICE, 2nd Floor (North), 22
  Kingsway, London WC2B 6NR. *Director*, N. R. Buckley
NATIONAL INSURANCE CONTRIBUTIONS OFFICE, DSS
  Longbenton, Benton Park Road, Newcastle upon
  Tyne NE98 1ZZ. *Chief Executive (G3)*, G. Bertram, CB
OIL TAXATION OFFICE, Melbourne House, Aldwych,
  London WC2B 4LL. *Director*, B. Mountain
PENSION SCHEME OFFICE, Yorke House, PO Box 62,
  Castle Meadow Road, Nottingham NG2 1BG.
  Director, G. Neild
SOLICITOR'S OFFICE, East Wing, Somerset House,
  London WC2R 1LB. *Solicitor (G2)*, P. Ridd
SOLICITOR'S OFFICE (SCOTLAND), Clarendon House,
  114–116 George Street, Edinburgh EH2 4LH.
  Solicitor, I. K. Laing
SPECIAL COMPLIANCE OFFICE, Angel Court, 199 Borough
  High Street, London SE1 1HZ. *Director*, J. Middleton
STAMP OFFICE, Ground Floor, PO Box 38, Ferrers House,
  Castle Meadow, Nottingham NG2 1BB.
  Director, Ms. L. Martin
TRAINING OFFICE, Lawress Hall, Riseholme Park,
  Lincoln LN2 2BJ. *Director*, Ms L. Hinnigan

REGIONAL EXECUTIVE OFFICES

INLAND REVENUE EAST, Churchgate, New Road,
  Peterborough PE1 1TD. *Director*, S. Banyard
INLAND REVENUE LARGE BUSINESS OFFICE, 1st Floor
  North, 22 Kingsway, London WC2B 6NR.
  Director, Mrs M. E. Williams
INLAND REVENUE LONDON, New Court, Carey Street,
  London WC2A 2JE. *Director*, C. R. Massingale
INLAND REVENUE NORTH, 3rd Floor, Dunedin House,
  Columbia Drive, Stockton on Tees TS17 6QZ.
  Director, R. Cooke
INLAND REVENUE NORTH-WEST, The Triad, Stanley
  Road, Bootle, Merseyside L75 2DD.
  Director, G. W. Lunn

INLAND REVENUE SOUTH-EAST, 4th Floor, Dukes Court, Dukes Street, Woking GU21 5XR. *Director*, T. Sleeman
INLAND REVENUE SOUTH-WEST, 3rd Floor, Longbrook House, New North Road, Exeter EX4 4UA. *Director*, T. Sleeman
INLAND REVENUE SOUTH YORKSHIRE, Concept House, 5 Young Street, Sheffield S1 4LF. *Director*, Ms M. Hay
INLAND REVENUE WALES AND MIDLANDS, 1st Floor, Phase II Building, Ty Glas Avenue, Llanishen, Cardiff CF14 5TS; 550 Streetsbrook Road, Solihull, West Midlands B91 1QU. *Director*, M. W. Kirk
INLAND REVENUE SCOTLAND, Clarendon House, 114–116 George Street, Edinburgh EH2 4LH. *Director*, I. S. Gerrie
INLAND REVENUE NORTHERN IRELAND, Dorchester House, 52–58 Great Victoria Street, Belfast BT2 7QE. *Director*, D. Hinstridge

VALUATION OFFICE AGENCY
New Court, 48 Carey Street, London WC2A 2JE
Tel: 020-7506 0701; Fax: 020-7506 1998;
Web: http://www.voa.gov.uk
50 Frederick Street, Edinburgh EH2 1NG
Tel: 0131-465 0700; Fax: 0131-465 0799

Chief Executive, M. A. Johns
Chief Valuer, Scotland, A. Ainslie
Chief Valuer, Wales, P. Clement

ADJUDICATOR'S OFFICE
— *see* page 317

BOUNDARY COMMISSIONS

The Commissions are constituted under the Parliamentary Constituencies Act 1986. The Speaker of the House of Commons is *ex officio* chairman of all four commissions in the UK. Each of the four commissions is required by law to keep the parliamentary constituencies in their part of the UK under review. The latest report was completed in April 1995 and its proposals took effect at the 1997 general election. The next report must be submitted before April 2007.

ENGLAND
1 Drummond Gate, London SW1V 2QQ
Tel: 020-7533 5177; Fax: 020-7533 5176

Deputy Chairman, The Hon. Mr Justice Harrison
Joint Secretaries, R. Farrance; M. Rawlings

WALES
1 Drummond Gate, London SW1V 2QQ
Tel: 020-7533 5172; Fax: 020-7533 5176

Deputy Chairman, The Hon. Mr Justice Kay
Joint Secretaries, R. Farrance; M. Rawlings

SCOTLAND
3 Drumsheugh Gardens, Edinburgh EH3 7QJ
Tel: 0131-538 7200; Fax: 0131-538 7240

Deputy Chairman, The Hon. Lady Cosgrove
Secretary, R. Smith

NORTHERN IRELAND
REL Division, 11 Millbank, London SW1P 4PN
Tel: 020-7210 6569

Deputy Chairman, The Hon. Mr Justice Coghlin
Secretary, Mrs L. Rogers

BRITISH BROADCASTING CORPORATION
Broadcasting House, Portland Place, London W1A 1AA
Tel: 020-7580 4468; BBC Information Line 0870 010 0222
Web: http://www.bbc.co.uk
Television Centre, Wood Lane, London W12 7RJ
Tel: 020-8743 8000

The BBC was incorporated under royal charter in 1926 as successor to the British Broadcasting Company Ltd. The BBC's current charter came into force on 1 May 1996 and extends to 31 December 2006. The chairman, vice-chairman and other governors are appointed by The Queen-in-Council. The BBC is financed by revenue from receiving licences for the home services and by grant-in-aid from Parliament for the World Service (radio).
For services, *see* Broadcasting section.

BOARD OF GOVERNORS
Chairman, Sir Christopher Bland
Vice-Chairman, The Baroness Young of Old Scone
National Governors, Prof. F. Monds (*N. Ireland*);
    R. S. Jones, OBE (*Wales*); Sir Robert Smith (*Scotland*)
Governors, Sir Richard Eyre, CBE; A. White, CBE; Dame
    Pauline Neville-Jones, DCMG; A. Young;
    Ms H. Rabbatts; Baroness Hogg; R. Sondhi

BOARD OF MANAGEMENT
EXECUTIVE COMMITTEE
Director-General and Editor-in-Chief, G. Dyke
    (from April 2000)
Directors, M. Thompson (*Television*); Ms J. Barmsky
    (*Radio*); M. Byford (*BBC World Service*); T. Hall (*News*);
    A. Yentob (*Drama, Entertainment and Children*);
    P. Loughrey (*National and Regions*); J. Smith (*Finance,
    Property and Business Affairs*); G. Jones (*Human Resources
    and Internal Communications*); P. Langsdale (*Distribution
    and Technology*); M. Bannister (*Marketing and
    Communications*); Ms L. Heggessey (*Factual*);
    M. Stevenson (*Learning*); R. Sambrook (*Sport*);
    Ms C. Thomson (*Public Policy*); Ms C. Fairbairn
    (*Strategy*); A. Highfield (*New Media*)
Chief Executives, Ms M. Salmon (*BBC Resources Ltd.*);
    R. Gavin (*BBC Worldwide*)

OTHER SENIOR STAFF
Controller, BBC1, P. Salmon
Controller, BBC2, Ms J. Root
Controller, Radio 1, A. Parfitt
Controller, Radio 2, J. Moir
Controller, Radio 3, R. Wright
Controller, Radio 4, J. Boyle
Controller, Radio 5 Live, B. Shennan
Controller, BBC Scotland, J. McCormick
Controller, BBC Wales, G. Talfan Davies
Controller, BBC N. Ireland, Ms A. Carragher
Controller, English Regions, A. Griffee

THE BRITISH COUNCIL

10 Spring Gardens, London SW1A 2BN
Tel: 020-7930 8466; Fax: 020-7839 6347
Bridgewater House, 58 Whitworth Street,
Manchester M15 4AA
Tel: 0161-957 7755; Fax: 0161-957 7762
Arts Division: 11 Portland Place, London W1N 4EJ
Tel: 020-7389 3001; Fax: 020-7389 3199

The British Council was established in 1934, incorporated by Royal Charter in 1940 and granted a supplemental charter in 1993. It is an independent, non-political organisation which promotes Britain abroad. It is the UK's international organisation for educational and cultural relations. The British Council is represented in 243 towns and cities in 110 countries and runs 222 libraries and information centres and 136 teaching centres around the world.

Total income in 1999–2000, including Foreign and Commonwealth Office grants and contracted money, was £429.560 million.

Chairman, The Baroness Kennedy of The Shaws, QC
Deputy Chairman, Sir Tim Lankester, KCB
Director-General, D. Green, CMG

BRITISH FILM COMMISSION

10 Little Portland Street, London W1N 5DF
Tel: 020-7224 5000; Fax: 020-7224 1013

The British Film Commission was set up in 1991 and is funded by the Department for Culture, Media and Sport. The Commission promotes the UK as an international production centre, encourages the use of locations, facilities, services and personnel, and provides, at no charge to the film makers, comprehensive advice and information relating to the practical aspects of filming in the UK.

In April 2000, the Government launched the Film Council to take a leading role in the development of the British film industry.

Commissioner and Chief Executive, S. Norris

BRITISH FILM INSTITUTE

21 Stephen Street, London W1P 2LN
Tel: 020-7255 1444; Fax: 020-7436 0439;
Web: http://www.bfi.org.uk

The British Film Institute was established in in 1933. It consists of three main departments: bfi Education, which comprises the bfi National Library, bfi publishing and bfi education projects, which encourages life-long learning about the moving image; bfi Exhibition, which runs the National Film Theatre, the London Film Festival and supports local cinemas and festivals UK wide; and bfi Collections, which preserves and promotes the UK's moving image heritage. The bfi also runs the London Imax Cinema, featuring the UK's largest screen. Grant-in-aid from the British Film Commission for 2000–1 is £16 million.

In April 2000, the Government launched the Film Council to take a leading role in the development of the British film industry.

Chairman, Ms J. Bakewell, CBE
Deputy Chairman, E. Senat
Director, J. Teckman
Deputy Director, R. Collins

BRITISH PHARMACOPOEIA COMMISSION

Market Towers, 1 Nine Elms Lane, London SW8 5NQ
Tel: 020-7273 0561; Fax: 020-7273 0566

The British Pharmacopoeia Commission sets standards for medicinal products used in human and veterinary medicines and is responsible for publication of the British Pharmacopoeia (a publicly available statement of the standard that a product must meet throughout its shelf-life), the British Pharmacopoeia (Veterinary) and the selection of British Approved Names. It has 13 members who are appointed by the Secretary of State for Health, the Minister for Agriculture, Fisheries and Food, the Scottish Ministers, the National Assembly for Wales, and the relevant Northern Ireland departments.

Chairman, Prof. D. Calam, OBE, D.Phil.
Vice-Chairman, Prof. J. A. Goldsmith
Secretary and Scientific Director, Dr R. C. Hutton

BRITISH RAILWAYS BOARD AND SHADOW STRATEGIC RAIL AUTHORITY

55 Victoria Street, London SW1H 0EU
Tel: 020-7654 6000; Fax: 020-7654 6010

The British Railways Board came into being in 1963 under the terms of the Transport Act 1962. Under the Railways Act 1993, the activities of the Board were restructured and largely transferred to the private sector. Its residual responsibilities include disposing of surplus land and advising the Government on rail policy issues.

The Government announced in July 1998 that British Rail's residual functions would be taken over by a Strategic Rail Authority, which has been operating in shadow form since 1 April 1999 and will do so until the required legislation in enacted, probably in 2000. When the authority is set up it will also incorporate the functions of the Passenger Franchising Director and some functions currently exercised by the Rail Regulator and the Department of the Environment, Transport and the Regions. Its main responsibilities will be strategic planning, co-ordinating and supervising the activities of the rail industry, and the disbursement of public funds.

Chairman, British Railways Board and Shadow Strategic Rail Authority, Sir Alastair Morton
Vice-Chairman, J. J. Jerram, CBE
Non-executive Members (part-time), L. D. Adams, OBE;
  D. A. Begg; Lord Bradshaw; W. Gallagher;
  D. Grayson, CBE; Mrs. A. Hemmingway;
  D. G. Jeffries, CBE; P .H. Kent, CBE; J. Mayhew;
  A. Montague; D. A. Quarmby; Ms J. Rubin; K. Small
Secretary, P. Trewin

BRITISH STANDARDS INSTITUTION (BSI)

389 Chiswick High Road, London W4 4AL
Tel: 020-8996 9000; Fax: 020-8996 7344

The British Standards Institution is the recognised authority in the UK for the preparation and publication of national standards for industrial and consumer products. About 90 per cent of its standards work is now internationally linked. British Standards are issued for voluntary adoption, though in a number of cases compliance with a British Standard is required by legislation. Industrial and consumer products certified as complying with the relevant British Standard may carry

the Institution's certification trade mark, known as the 'Kitemark'.
Chairman, V. E. Thomas, CBE

BRITISH TOURIST AUTHORITY
Thames Tower, Black's Road, London W6 9EL
Tel: 020-8846 9000; Fax: 020-8563 0302

Established under the Development of Tourism Act 1969, the British Tourist Authority is responsible for promoting tourism to Great Britain from overseas. It also has a general responsibility for the promotion and development of tourism and tourist facilities within Great Britain as a whole, and for advising the Secretary of State for Culture, Media and Sport on tourism matters.
Chairman (part-time), D. Quarmby
Chief Executive, J. Hamblin

BRITISH WATERWAYS
Willow Grange, Church Road, Watford, Herts WD1 3QA
Tel: 01923-226422; Fax: 01923-201400;
Email: enquiries@bwmedia.demon.co.uk;
Web: http://www.british waterways.co.uk

British Waterways conserves and manages over 2,000 miles of canals and rivers in England, Scotland and Wales. It is responsible to the Secretary of State for the Environment, Transport and the Regions. Its responsibilities include maintaining the waterways and structures on and around them; looking after wildlife and the waterway environment; and ensuring that canals and rivers are safe and enjoyable places to visit.
Chairman (part-time), Dr G. Greener
Members (part-time), D. H. R. Yorke; Sir Neil Cossons; Ms J. Elvey; Ms J. Lewis-Jones; Ms C. Dobson; P. King; P. Soulsby; C. Christie
Chief Executive, D. Fletcher
Director of Corporate Services, R. J. Duffy

BROADCASTING STANDARDS COMMISSION
7 The Sanctuary, London SW1P 3JS
Tel: 020-7808 1000; Fax: 020-7233 0397

The Commission was established in April 1997 under the Broadcasting Act 1996. It is an independent organisation representing the interests of the consumer, and its remit covers all television and radio broadcasting. The Commission considers the portrayal of violence and sexual conduct and matters of taste and decency. It also provides redress for people who believe they have been unfairly treated or subjected to unwarranted infringement of privacy. The Commission conducts research into standards and fairness in broadcasting and produces codes of practice, and it considers and adjudicates on complaints. Members of the Commission are appointed by the Secretary of State for Culture, Media and Sport. The appointments are part-time.
Chair (£45,210), Lord Holme
Deputy Chairmen (£34,000–£36,000), Ms J. Leighton; Mrs S. Warner
Commissioners (each £14,960), D. Boulton; Dame Fiona Caldicott, DBE; U. Dholakia; S. Heppel, CB; Revd Rose Hudson Wilkin; J. Mitchell; Ms S. O'Sullivan; Ms S. Wyn Thomas
Director, S. Whittle

THE BROADS AUTHORITY
Thomas Harvey House, 18 Colegate, Norwich NR3 1BQ
Tel: 01603-610734; Fax: 01603-765710;
Web: http://www.broads-authority.gov.uk

The Broads Authority is a special statutory authority set up under the Norfolk and Suffolk Broads Act 1988. The functions of the Authority are to conserve and enhance the natural beauty of the Broads; to provide integrated management of the land and water space of the area; to promote the enjoyment of the Broads by the public; and to protect the interests of navigation. The Authority comprises 35 members, appointed by the local authorities in the area covered, environmental conservation bodies, the Environment Agency, and the Great Yarmouth Port Authority.
Chairman, The Viscountess Knollys
Chief Executive, Prof. M. A. Clark, OBE

BUILDING SOCIETIES COMMISSION
25 The North Colonnade, Canary Wharf,
London E14 5HS
Tel: 020-7676 1000

The Building Societies Commission was established by the Building Societies Act 1986. The Commission is responsible for the supervision of building societies and administers the system of prudential regulation. It also advises the Treasury and other Government departments on matters relating to building societies.
  The functions of the Commission should will to the Financial Services Authority on implementation of the Financial Services and Markets Act.

BUILDING SOCIETIES COMMISSION
Chairman, G. E. Fitchew
Deputy Chairman, Ms C. Sergeant
Commissioners, S. Mundy; J. M. Palmer; *F. G. Sunderland; *Sir James Birrell; *N. Fox Bassett; *F. E. Worsley
Secretary, G. Johnson

CENTRAL ARBITRATION COMMITTEE
Third Floor, Discovery House, 28–42 Banner Street,
London EC1Y 8QE Tel: 020-7251 9747

The Central Arbitration Committee arbitrates on trade disputes; adjudicates on disclosure of information and complaints; also determines claims for statutory recognition under the employment Relations Act 1999 and certain issues relating to the implementation of the European Works Council Directive.
Chairman, Sir Michael Burton
Secretary, C. Johnston

CERTIFICATION OFFICE FOR TRADE UNIONS AND EMPLOYERS' ASSOCIATIONS
180 Borough High Street, London SE1 1LW
Tel: 020-7210 3734/5; Fax: 020-7210 3612

The Certification Office is an independent statutory authority. The Certification Officer is appointed by the Secretary of State for Trade and Industry and is responsible for receiving and scrutinising annual returns from trade unions and employers' associations; for determining complaints concerning trade union elections, certain ballots and certain breaches of trade union rules; for ensuring observance of statutory requirements governing mergers between trade unions and employers' associations; for overseeing the political funds and finances of trade unions and employers' associations; and for certifying the independence of trade unions.

Certification Officer, E. G. Whybrew
Assistant Certification Officer, G. S. Osborne

SCOTLAND
58 Frederick Street, Edinburgh EH21 LN
Tel: 0131-226 3224; Fax: 0131-200 1300

Assistant Certification Officer for Scotland, J. L. J. Craig

CHARITY COMMISSION

Harmsworth House, 13–15 Bouverie Street,
London EC4Y 8DP
Tel: 0870 333 0123; Fax: 020-7674 2310
Web: http://www.charity-commission.gov.uk
2nd Floor, 20 King's Parade, Queen's Dock,
Liverpool L3 4DQ
Tel: 0870 333 0123; Fax: 0151-703 1557
Woodfield House, Tangier, Taunton, Somerset TA1 4BL
Tel: 0870 333 0123; Fax: 01823-345008

The Charity Commission for England and Wales is the Government Department whose aim is to give the public confidence in the integrity of charity. It also carries out the functions of the registration, monitoring and support of charities and the investigation of alleged wrong-doing. The Commission maintains a computerised register of some 187,000 charities. It is accountable to the courts and for its efficiency to the Home Secretary. There are five Commissioners appointed by the Home Office for a fixed term and the Commission has Offices in London, Liverpool and Taunton.

Chief Commissioner (G3), J. Stoker
Legal Commissioner (G3), M. Carpenter
Commissioners (part-time) (G4), J. Bonds; Ms J. Warburton; Ms J. Unwin
Heads of Legal Sections (G5), J. A. Dutton; G. S. Goodchild; K. M. Dibble; S. Slack
Executive Director (G4), Ms L. Berry
Head of Policy Division (G5), R. Carter
Establishment Officer (G5), Ms C. Stewart
Information Systems Controller (G5), Ms G.Cruickshank

The offices responsible for charities in Scotland and Northern Ireland are:
SCOTLAND – Scottish Charities Office, Crown Office, 25 Chambers Street, Edinburgh EH1 1LA.
Tel: 0131-226 2626
NORTHERN IRELAND – Department of Health and Social Services, Charities Branch, Annexe 3, Castle Buildings, Stormont Estate, Belfast BT4 3RA.

CHURCH COMMISSIONERS

1 Millbank, London SW1P 3JZ
Tel: 020-7898 1000; Fax: 020-7898 1131
Email: commissioners.enquiry@c-of-e.org.uk
Web: http://www.cofe.anglican.org

The Church Commissioners were established in 1948 by the amalgamation of Queen Anne's Bounty (established 1704) and the Ecclesiastical Commissioners (established 1836). They are responsible for the management of most of the Church of England's assets, the income from which is predominantly used to pay, house and pension the clergy. The Commissioners own 128,000 acres of agricultural land, a number of residential estates in central London, and commercial property in Great Britain. They also carry out administrative duties in connection with pastoral reorganisation and redundant churches.

The Commissioners are: the Archbishops of Canterbury and of York; four bishops, three clergy and four lay persons elected by the respective houses of the General Synod; two deans or provosts elected by all the deans and provosts; three persons nominated by The Queen; three persons nominated by the Archbishops of Canterbury and York; three persons nominated by the Archbishops after consultation with others including the lord mayors of London and York and the vice-chancellors of the universities of Oxford and Cambridge; the First Lord of the Treasury; the Lord President of the Council; the Home Secretary; the Lord Chancellor; the Secretary of State for Culture, Media and Sport; and the Speaker of the House of Commons.

INCOME AND EXPENDITURE
for year ended 31 December 1999

	£ million
Net income	140.7
Investments	92.6
Property	42.7
Interest from loans, etc.	16.3
Total expenditure	156.1
Parish ministry support	20.6
Bishop and cathedral clergy stipends	6.6
Bishops' housing	3.3
Grants to cathedrals	2.6
Financial provision for resigning clergy	1.8
Clergy pensions and CHARM subsidy	86.9
Transitional support for pension contributions	17.3
Church buildings	1.0
Bishops' working cost	8.5
Commissioners' administration of national church functions	5.5
Administration costs of other church bodies	2.0

CHURCH ESTATES COMMISSIONERS
First, J. Sclater, CVO
Second, S. Bell, MP
Third, The Viscountess Brentford

OFFICERS
Secretary, H. H. Hughes
Deputy Secretary (Finance and Investment), C. W. Daws
Official Solicitor, S. Jones
Assistant Secretaries:
   The Accountant, M. Adams
   Management Accountant, B. J. Hardy
   Chief Surveyor, A. C. Brown
   Computer Manager, J. W. Ferguson
   Bishoprics Secretary, E. G. Peacock
   Investments Manager, A. S. Hardy
   Pastoral, Houses and Redundant Churches, M. D. Elengorn
   Senior Architect, J. A. Taylor

CIVIL AVIATION AUTHORITY

CAA House, 45–59 Kingsway, London WC2B 6TE
Tel: 020-7379 7311; Fax: 020-7240 1153

The CAA is responsible for the economic regulation of UK airlines and for the safety regulation of UK civil aviation by the certification of airlines and aircraft and by licensing aerodromes, flight crew and aircraft engineers. Through its subsidiary company, National Air Traffic

Services Ltd (NATS), it is also responsible for the provision of air traffic control and telecommunications services. The Government announced in July 1999 that it planned to separate regulation from service provision and sell 51 per cent of NATS to the private sector.

The CAA advises the Government on aviation issues, represents consumer interests, conducts economic and scientific research, produces statistical data, and provides specialist services and other training and consultancy services to clients world-wide.

Chairman, Sir Malcolm Field
Secretary, R. J. Britton

THE COAL AUTHORITY

200 Lichfield Lane, Mansfield, Notts NG18 4RG
Tel: 01623-427162; Fax: 01623-622072
Email: coalauthority@coal.gov.uk
Web: http://www.coal.gov.uk

The Coal Authority was established under the Coal Industry Act 1994 to manage certain functions previously undertaken by British Coal, including ownership of unworked coal. It is responsible for licensing coal mining operations and for providing information on coal reserves and past and future coal mining. It settles subsidence claims not falling on coal mining operators. It deals with the management and disposal of property, and with surface hazards such as abandoned coal mine shafts.

Chairman, J. Harris
Chief Executive, K. J. Fergusson

COLLEGE OF ARMS (OR HERALDS COLLEGE)

Queen Victoria Street, London EC4V 4BT
Tel: 020-7248 2762; Fax: 020-7248 6448

The Sovereign's Officers of Arms (Kings, Heralds and Pursuivants of Arms) were first incorporated by Richard III. The powers vested by the Crown in the Earl Marshal (the Duke of Norfolk) with regard to state ceremonial are largely exercised through the College. The College is also the official repository of the arms and pedigrees of English, Welsh, Northern Irish and Commonwealth (except Canadian) families and their descendants, and its records include official copies of the records of Ulster King of Arms, the originals of which remain in Dublin. The 13 officers of the College specialise in genealogical and heraldic work for their respective clients.

Arms have been and still are granted by letters patent from the Kings of Arms. A right to arms can only be established by the registration in the official records of the College of Arms of a pedigree showing direct male line descent from an ancestor already appearing therein as being entitled to arms, or by making application through the College of Arms for a grant of arms. Grants are made to corporations as well as to individuals.

The College of Arms is open Monday–Friday 10–4.

Earl Marshal, The Duke of Norfolk, KG, GCVO, CB, CBE, MC

KINGS OF ARMS
Garter, P. L. Gwynn-Jones, CVO, FSA
Clarenceux, D. H. B. Chesshyre, LVO, FSA
Norroy and Ulster, T. Woodcock, LVO, FSA

HERALDS
Richmond (and Earl Marshal's Secretary), P. L. Dickinson
York, H. E. Paston-Bedingfeld

Chester (and Registrar), T. H. S. Duke
Lancaster, R. J. B. Noel
Windsor, W. G. Hunt, TD

PURSUIVANTS
Rouge Croix, D. V. White
Rouge Dragon, C. E. A. Cheesman, PH.D.

COMMISSION FOR ARCHITECTURE AND THE BUILT ENVIRONMENT

7 St James's Square, London SW1Y 4JU
Tel: 020-7839 6537; Fax: 020-7839 8475
Email: enquiries@cabe.org.uk
Web: http://www.cabe.org.uk

The Commission for Architecture and the Built Environment (CABE) replaced the Royal Fine Art Commission (RFAC) in August 1999. It has taken over the RFAC's design review function, and is also responsible for promoting the importance of high quality architecture and urban design and encouraging the understanding of architecture through educational and regional initiatives.

Chairman, S. A. Lipton
Chief Executive, J. Rouse

COMMISSION FOR INTEGRATED TRANSPORT

Romney House, 5th Floor, Tufton Street,
London SW1P 3RA
Tel: 020-7944 4101/4813; Fax: 020-7944 2919;
Email: cfit@detr.gsi.gov.uk

The Commission for Integrated Transport was proposed in the 1998 Transport White Paper and was set up in June 1999. Its role is to provide independent expert advice to the Government in order to achieve a transport system that supports sustainable development. Members of the Commission are appointed by the Secretary of State for the Environment, Transport and the Regions.

Chairman (£25,000), Prof. D. Begg
Vice-Chairman (£17,500), Sir Trevor Chinn
Members (£5,000 each), Lord Bradshaw; L. Christensen, CBE; N. Gavron; S. Joseph; D. Leeder; Ms L. Matson; W. Morris; J. O'Brien; Ms V. Palmer; M. Parker; N. Reilly
Ex-Officio Members, Sir Malcolm Field (*Chairman, Civil Aviation Authority*); P. Nutt (*Chief Executive, Highways Agency*); Sir Alastair Morton (*Chairman, British Railways Board and Head, Shadow Strategic Rail Authority*); Ms J. Wilmot (*Chair, Disabled Persons Transport Advisory Committee*)
Secretary (G7), P. Carey

COMMISSION FOR RACIAL EQUALITY

Elliot House, 10–12 Allington Street, London SW1E 5EH
Tel: 020-7828 7022; Fax: 020-7630 7605

The Commission was established in 1977 under the Race Relations Act 1976. Its duties are to work towards the elimination of discrimination and promote equality of opportunity, to encourage good relations between different racial groups and to monitor the working of the Race Relations Act. It is funded by the Home Office.

Chairman, Gurbux Singh (£81,000)
Deputy Chairmen, Ms B. Bernard; Dr M. Jogee
Commissioners, M. Amran; Dr R. Chandran;

M. Hastings; S. Malik; Ms J. Mellor; P. Passley;
Ms S. Patel; B. Purkiss; Ms C. Short; Dr J. Singh;
R. Singh; Ms G. Sootarsing; K. Jandu
Chief Executive, Ms S. Parsons

COMMITTEE ON STANDARDS IN PUBLIC LIFE

35 Great Smith Street, London SW1P 3BQ
Tel: 020-7276 2595; Fax: 020-7276 2585
Email: neil@gtnet.gov.uk
Web: http://www.public-standards.gov.uk

The Committee on Standards in Public Life was set up
in October 1994. It is a standing body whose chairman
and members are appointed by the Prime Minister;
three members are nominated by the leaders of the three
main political parties. The committee's remit is to examine concerns about standards of conduct of all holders
of public office, including arrangements relating to
financial and commercial activities, and to make recommendations as to any changes in present arrangements
which might be required to ensure the highest standards
of propriety in public life. It is also charged with reviewing issues in relation to the funding of political parties.
The committee does not investigate individual allegations of misconduct.
Chairman, The Lord Neill of Bladen, QC
Members, Ms A. Abraham, Sir Clifford Boulton, GCB;
    Prof. Alice Brown; Sir Anthony Cleaver;
    The Lord Goodhart, QC; F. Heaton
    The Rt. Hon. J. MacGregor, OBE, MP;
    The Lord Shore of Stepney, PC;
    Sir William Utting, CB
Secretary (SCS), Mrs S. Tyerman

COMMONWEALTH INSTITUTE

230 Kensington High Street, London W8 6NQ
Tel: 020-7603 4535; Fax: 020-7602 7374
Email: info@commonwealth.org.uk
Web: http://www.commonwealth.org.uk

The Commonwealth Institute is responsible for promoting the contemporary Commonwealth in the UK and
other member countries through exhibitions, educational
programmes, publications, resources and information.
The Institute houses the Commonwealth Resource
Centre (CRC) and Literature Library and a Conference
and Events Centre.
    The Institute was established in 1958 and is an
independent statutory body funded by the British
government with contributions from other Commonwealth governments. On 1 January 2000 it became a
company limited by guarantee and a registered charity. It
is controlled by a Board of Trustees elected by the Board of
Govenors. All the Commonwealth High Commissioners
to London are *ex-officio* governors of the Institute in
addition to other governors appointed by the Board of
Trustees.
Chairman, D. A. Thompson
Chief Executive, D. French
Commercial Director, P. Kennedy
Director of Education, S. Brace
Director of Finance, Ms. J. Curry
Director of Public Affairs, G. Carter

COMMONWEALTH WAR GRAVES COMMISSION

2 Marlow Road, Maidenhead, Berks SL6 7DX
Tel: 01628-634221; Fax: 01628-771208
Email: general.enq@cwgc.org
Web: http://www.cwgc.org

The Commonwealth War Graves Commission (formerly
Imperial War Graves Commission) was founded by royal
charter in 1917. It is responsible for the commemoration
of 1,695,098 members of the forces of the Commonwealth
who fell in the two world wars. More than one million
graves are maintained in 23,216 burial grounds throughout the world. Over three-quarters of a million men and
women who have no known grave or who were cremated
are commemorated by name on memorials built by the
Commission.
    The funds of the Commission are derived from the six
participating governments, i.e. the UK, Canada, Australia,
India, New Zealand and South Africa.
President, HRH The Duke of Kent, KG, GCMG, GCVO, ADC
Chairman, The Secretary of State for Defence in the UK
Vice-Chairman, Adm. Sir John Kerr, GCB
Members, The High Commissioners in London for
    Canada, New Zealand, South Africa, Australia and
    India; Prof. R. J. O'Neill, AO; Mrs L. Golding, MP;
    J. Wilkinson, MP; Sir John Gray, KBE, CMG;
    P. D. Orchard-Lisle, CBE, TD; Air Chief Marshal
    Sir Michael Stear, KCB, CBE; Dame Susan Tinson,
    DBE; Gen. Sir John Wilsey, GCB, CBE
Director-General and Secretary to the Commission,
    R. E. Kellaway
Deputy Director-General, R. J. Dalley
Legal Adviser and Solicitor, G. C. Reddie
Directors, D. R. Parker (*Information and Secretariat*);
    A. Coombe (*Works*); R. D. Wilson (*Administration*);
    D. C. Parker (*Horticulture*); D. G. Storey (*Personnel*)
IMPERIAL WAR GRAVES ENDOWMENT FUND
Trustees, A. C. Barker (*Chairman*); Adm. Sir John Kerr,
    GCB; C. G. Clarke
Secretary to the Trustees, R. D. Wilson

COMPETITION COMMISSION

New Court, 48 Carey Street, London WC2A 2JT
Tel: 020-7271 0100; Fax: 020-7271 0367

The Commission was established in 1948 as the
Monopolies and Restrictive Practices Commission (later
the Monopolies and Mergers Commission); it became the
Competition Commission in April 1999 under the
Competition Act 1998. Its role is to investigate and report
on matters which are referred to it by the Secretary of State
for Trade and Industry or the Director-General of Fair
Trading or, in the case of regulated utilities, by the
appropriate regulator. It has no power to initiate its own
investigations.
    The Appeals Tribunal of the Competition Commission
hears appeals against decisions by the Director-General of
Fair Trading and the utility regulators in respect of the
prohibitions on anti-competitive agreements and abuse of
a dominant position.
    The Commission has a full-time chairman, two part-
time deputy chairmen and about 36 reporting panel
members and 25 specialist panel members to carry out
investigations. All are appointed by the Secretary of State
for Trade and Industry.
Chairman, Dr D. Morris, PH.D.

Deputy Chairmen, P. G. Corbett, CBE;
Mrs D. P. B. Kingsmill, CBE
President, Appeal Tribunals, His Hon. Sir Christopher
Bellamy, QC
Members, H. G. C. Aldous; Prof. J. Beatson, QC;
R. Bertram; Mrs S. Brown; Prof. M. Cave;
A. T. Clothier; R. H. F. Croft, CB; C. Darke;
N. Garthwaite; Prof. P. Geroski; Prof. C. Graham;
G. H. Hadley; D. B. Hammond; Ms J. C. Hanratty;
C. Henderson, CB; D. J. Jenkins, MBE; R. Lyons;
P. MacKay, CB; Dr E. M. Monck; Ms K. M. H.
Mortimer; R. J. Munson; Prof. D. M. G. Newbery, FBA;
Dr Gill Owen; Prof. D. Parker; A. Pryor, CB;
R. A. Rawlinson; Prof. Judith Rees; T. S. Richmond,
MBE; J. Rickford; E. J. Seddon; Dame Helena Shovelton,
DBE; G. H. Stacy, CBE; J. D. Stark; Prof. A. Steele;
M. R. Webster; A. M. Young
Appeal Panel Members, Sir Christopher Bellamy, QC;
B. D. Colgate; P. Grant-Hutchinson; Mrs S. Hewitt;
Ms A. M. Kelly; M. R. Prosser, OBE; Dr A. J. Pryor,
CB; A. Scott, TD; D. L. Summers
Appeal Panel Registrar, C. Dhanowa
Secretary, Miss P. Boys

COUNCIL ON TRIBUNALS
7th Floor, 22 Kingsway, London WC2B 6LE
Tel: 020-7947 7045; Fax: 020-7947 7044

The Council on Tribunals is an independent body that
operates under the Tribunals and Inquiries Act 1992.
It consists of 16 members appointed by the Lord
Chancellor and the Scottish Ministers; one member is
appointed to represent the interests of people in Wales.
The Scottish Committee of the Council generally considers Scottish tribunals and matters relating only to
Scotland.
    The Council advises on and keeps under review the
constitution and working of administrative tribunals, and
considers and reports on administrative procedures relating to statutory inquiries. Some 70 tribunals are currently
under the Council's supervision. It is consulted by and
advises Government departments on a wide range of
subjects relating to adjudicative procedures.
Chairman, The Rt. Hon. The Lord Newton of Braintree
Members, The Parliamentary Commissioner for
Administration (*ex officio*); R. J. Elliot, WS (*Chairman
of the Scottish Committee*); Mrs C. Berkeley;
S. M. D. Brown; S. R. Davie, CB; J. H. Eames;
Mrs A. Galbraith; Mrs S. R. Howdle; I. J. Irvine; S. Jones,
CBE; Prof. T. M. Partington; I. D. Penman, CB;
D. G. Readings; E. P. Roberts; P. A. A. Waring
Secretary, Mrs P. J. Fairbairn

SCOTTISH COMMITTEE OF THE COUNCIL ON TRIBUNALS
44 Palmerston Place, Edinburgh EH12 5BJ
Tel: 0131-220 1236; Fax: 0131-225 4271;
Email: sccot@gtnet.gov.uk
Chairman, R. J. Elliot
Members, The Parliamentary Commissioner for
Administration (*ex officio*); Mrs P. Y. Berry, MBE;
Mrs B. Bruce; D. Graham; I. J. Irvine; I. D. Penman, CB;
Mrs. M. Wood
Secretary, Mrs E. M. MacRae

COUNTRYSIDE AGENCY
John Dower House, Crescent Place, Cheltenham,
Glos GL50 3RA
Tel: 01242-521381; Fax: 01242-584270

The Countryside Agency was set up in April 1999 by the
merger of the Countryside Commission with parts of the
Rural Development Commission. It is a Government
agency which promotes the conservation and enhancement of the countryside in England and undertakes
activities aimed at stimulating job creation and the
provision of essential services in the countryside. The
Agency is funded by an annual grant from the Department
of the Environment, Transport and the Regions, and
board members are appointed by the Secretary of State.
Chairman, E. Cameron
Deputy Chair, Ms P. Warhurst
Members, Ms K. Ashbrook; Ms J. Bradbury;
the Rt. Revd Bishop of Blackburn; M. Doughty;
Dr Victoria Edwards, FRICS; P. Fane; A. Hams, OBE;
Prof. P. Lowe; Ms C. Mack; FCA; L. Frank-Riley;
Ms F. Rowe; Ms. S. Stapley; D. Woodhall, CBE
Chief Executive, R. G. Wakeford
Directors, Miss M. A. Clark, OBE; D. Coleman;
J. Tomlinson

COUNTRYSIDE COUNCIL FOR
WALES/CYNGOR CEFN GWLAD CYMRU
Plas Penrhos, Ffordd Penrhos, Bangor LL57 2LQ
Tel: 01248-385500; Fax: 01248-385505

The Countryside Council for Wales is the Government's
statutory adviser on sustaining natural beauty, wildlife and
the opportunity for outdoor enjoyment in Wales and its
inshore waters. It is funded by the National Assembly for
Wales and accountable to the First Secretary, who
appoints its members.
Chairman, J. Lloyd Jones, OBE
Chief Executive, P. E. Loveluck, CBE
Senior Director and Chief Scientist, Dr M. E. Smith
Director, Countryside Policy, Dr J. Taylor
Director, Conservation, Dr D. Parker

COURT OF THE LORD LYON
HM New Register House, Edinburgh EH1 3YT
Tel: 0131-556 7255; Fax: 0131-557 2148

The Court of the Lord Lyon is the Scottish Court of
Chivalry (including the genealogical jurisdiction of the
Ri-Sennachie of Scotland's Celtic Kings). The Lord Lyon
King of Arms has jurisdiction, subject to appeal to the
Court of Session and the House of Lords, in questions of
heraldry and the right to bear arms. The Court also
administers the Scottish Public Register of All Arms and
Bearings and the Public Register of All Genealogies.
Pedigrees are established by decrees of Lyon Court and
by letters patent. As Royal Commissioner in Armory, the
Lord Lyon grants patents of arms (which constitute the
grantee and heirs noble in the Noblesse of Scotland) to
'virtuous and well-deserving' Scotsmen and to petitioners
(personal or corporate) in The Queen's overseas realms
of Scottish connection, and issues birthbrieves.
Lord Lyon King of Arms, Sir Malcolm Innes of Edingight,
KCVO, WS

HERALDS
Albany, J. A. Spens, MVO, RD, WS
Rothesay, Sir Crispin Agnew of Lochnaw, Bt., QC
Ross, C. J. Burnett, FSA Scot.

PURSUIVANTS
Kintyre, J. C. G. George
Unicorn, Alastair Campbell of Airds, FSA Scot.
Carrick, Mrs C. G. W. Roads, MVO, FSA Scot.

Lyon Clerk and Keeper of Records, Mrs C. G. W. Roads, MVO, FSA Scot.
Procurator-Fiscal, D. I. K. MacLeod, WS
Herald Painter, Mrs J. Phillips
Macer, A. M. Clark

COVENT GARDEN MARKET AUTHORITY
Covent House, New Covent Garden Market,
London SW8 5NX
Tel: 020-7720 2211; Fax: 020-7622 5307
Email: info@cgma.gov.uk
Web: http://www.cgma.gov.uk

The Covent Garden Market Authority is constituted under the Covent Garden Market Acts 1961 to 1977, the members being appointed by the Minister of Agriculture, Fisheries and Food. The Authority owns and operates the 56-acre New Covent Garden Markets (fruit, vegetables, flowers) which have been trading since 1974.
Chairman (part-time), L. Mills, CBE
General Manager, Dr P. M. Liggins
Secretary, C. Farey

CRIMINAL CASES REVIEW COMMISSION
Alpha Tower, Suffolk Street Queensway,
Birmingham B1 1TT
Tel: 0121-633 1800; Fax: 0121-633 1823/1804

The Criminal Cases Review Commission is an independent body set up under the Criminal Appeal Act 1995. It is a non-departmental public body reporting to Parliament via the Home Secretary. It is responsible for investigating suspected miscarriages of justice in England, Wales and Northern Ireland, and deciding whether or not to refer cases back to an appeal court. Membership of the Commission is by royal appointment; the senior executive staff are appointed by the Commission.
Chairman, Sir Frederick Crawford, FREng.
Members, B. Capon; L. Elks; A. Foster; Ms J. Gort; Ms F. King; J. Knox; D. Kyle; J. Leckey; Prof. L. Leigh; J. MacKeith; K. Singh; B. Skitt; E. Weiss
Chief Executive, Ms G. Stacey
Director of Finance and Personnel, D. Robson
Legal Advisers, J. Wagstaff; M. Aspinall
Police Adviser, R. Barrington

CRIMINAL INJURIES COMPENSATION AUTHORITY (CICA)
Morley House, Holborn Viaduct, London EC1A 2JQ
Tel: 020-7842 6800; Fax: 020-7436 0804
Web: http://www.cica.gov.uk
Tay House, 300 Bath Street, Glasgow G2 4JR
Tel: 0141-331 2726; Fax: 0141-331 2287

All applications for compensation for personal injury arising from crimes of violence in England, Scotland and Wales are dealt with at the above locations. (Separate arrangements apply in Northern Ireland.) Applications received up to 31 March 1996 are assessed on the basis of common law damages under the 1990 compensation scheme. Applications received later than 1 April 1996 are assessed under a tariff-based scheme, made under the Criminal Injuries Compensation Act 1995, by the Criminal Injuries Compensation Authority (CICA). There is a separate avenue of appeal to the Criminal Injuries Compensation Appeals Panel (CICAP). In 1999–2000 total compensation paid was £194.34 million.
Chief Executive, Howard Webber
Deputy Chief Executive, E. McKeown
Head of Legal Services, Ms A. M. Johnstone
Press enquiries, Ms J Hay

CRIMINAL INJURIES COMPENSATION APPEALS PANEL (CICAP)
11th Floor, Cardinal Tower, 12 Farringdon Road,
London EC1M 3HS
Tel: 020-7549 4600; Fax: 020-7549 4643
Email: info@cicap.gov.uk
Web: http://www.cicap.gov.uk
Chairman, Michael Lewer, QC
Secretary, Ms. V. Jenson

CROFTERS COMMISSION
4–6 Castle Wynd, Inverness IV2 3EQ
Tel: 01463-663450; Fax: 01463-711820

The Crofters Commission was established in 1955 under the Crofters (Scotland) Act. It advises the Scottish Ministers on all matters relating to crofting. It seeks to develop and promote thriving crofting communities and to simplify relevant legislation. It administers the Crofting Counties Agricultural Grants Scheme, Livestock Improvement Schemes and the Croft Entrant Scheme. It also provides a free enquiry service.
Chairman, I. MacAskill
Secretary (G6), M.Grantham

CROWN ESTATE
16 Carlton House Terrace, London SW1Y 5AH
Tel: 020-7210 4377; Fax: 020-7930 8187

The Crown Estate includes substantial blocks of urban property, primarily in London, almost 120,000 hectares of agricultural land and extensive marine holdings throughout the United Kingdom. Its origins go back to the reign of King Edward the Confessor and, until the accession of King George III, the Sovereign received its rents and profits. However, since 1760 the annual surplus, after deducting management expenses, has been surrendered by the Sovereign to Parliament to help meet the cost of civil government. In return, the Sovereign receives the Civil List and the Government meets other official expenditure incurred in support of the Sovereign.
  In the year ended 31 March 1999, the gross revenue from the Crown Estate totalled £173.6 million and £125.8 million was paid to the Exchequer as surplus revenue.
First Commissioner and Chairman (part-time), Sir Denys Henderson
Second Commissioner and Chief Executive, Sir Christopher Howes, KCVO, CB
Commissioners (part-time), The Lord De Ramsey; I. D. Grant, CBE; Mrs H. M. R. Chapman, CBE, FRICS; R. R. Spinney, FRICS; D. T. Y. Curry, CBE
Commissioner and Director of Finance and Administration, R. Bright

Director of Urban Estates, D. A. Bickmore
Rural Estate, C. Bourchier
Urban, Central London Estate, Ms E. Miller
Urban, Regent Street Estate, M. W. Dillon
Urban, Regional Estate, A. Meakin
Urban, Residential Estate, R. Wyatt
Urban, Special Projects, L. Colgan
Marine Estate, F. G. Parrish
Finance and Information Systems, J. G. Lelliott
Internal Audit, J. Ford
Corporate Policy and Personnel, M. J. Gravestock
Communications Manager, Miss I. Belcher

SCOTLAND
10 Charlotte Square, Edinburgh EH2 4BR
Tel: 0131-226 7241; Fax: 0131-220 1366
Head of Scottish Estate, M. Cunliffe

WINDSOR ESTATE
The Great Park, Windsor, Berks SL4 2HT
Tel: 01753-860222; Fax: 01753-859617
Deputy Ranger, P. Everrett

DEER COMMISSION FOR SCOTLAND
Knowsley, 82 Fairfield Road, Inverness IV3 5LH
Tel: 01463-231751; Fax: 01463-712931
Email: deercom@aol.com
Web: http://www.dcs.gov.uk

The Deer Commission for Scotland has the general functions of furthering the conservation and control of deer in Scotland. It has the statutory duty, with powers, to prevent damage to agriculture, forestry and the habitat by deer. It is funded by the Scottish Executive.
Chairman (part-time), A. Raven
Director, N. Reiter
Technical Director, R. W. Youngson

DESIGN COUNCIL
34 Bow Street, London WC2E 7DL
Tel: 020-7420 5200; Fax: 020-7420 5300

The Design Council is a campaigning and lobbying organisation which works with partners in business, education and Government to promote the effective use of good design. It is a registered charity with a Royal Charter and is funded by grant in aid from the Department of Trade and Industry.
Chairman, C. Frayling
Chief Executive, A. Summers

DISABILITY RIGHTS COMMISSION (DRC)
DRC Contact Centre, Stratford upon Avon CV37 9BR
Tel: DRC Helpline, 08457 622633
Web: http://www.drc-gb.org

The Commission is an executive non-departmental public body established in April 2000. Its role is to advise Government on issues of discrimination against disabled people and the operation of the Disability Discrimination Act 1995. It will promote good practice to employers and service providers and provide advice and information.
Chair, B. Massie
Chief Executive, R. Niven

Commissioners, Saghir Alam; Ms K. Allen;
Ms. J. Campbell; M. Devenney; R. Exell;
Dr K. Fitzpatrick; J. Hougham; P. Humphrey;
C. Low; Mrs E. Noad; Ms E. Rank-Petruzzietto;
Ms P. Russell; J. Strachan; Ms J. White

THE DUCHY OF CORNWALL
10 Buckingham Gate, London SW1E 6LA
Tel: 020-7834 7346; Fax: 020-7931 9541

The Duchy of Cornwall was created by Edward III in 1337 for the support of his eldest son Edward, later known as the Black Prince. It is the oldest of the English duchies. The duchy is acquired by inheritance by the sovereign's eldest son either at birth or on the accession of his parent to the throne, whichever is the later. The primary purpose of the estate remains to provide an income for the Prince of Wales. The estate is mainly agricultural and based in the south-west of England. A recent purchase has increased the landholding to approximately 150,000 acres in 26 counties. The duchy also has some residential property, a number of shops and offices, and a Stock Exchange portfolio. Prince Charles is the 24th Duke of Cornwall.

THE PRINCE'S COUNCIL
Chairman, HRH The Prince of Wales, KG, KT, GCB
Lord Warden of the Stannaries, The Earl Peel
Receiver-General, The Rt. Hon. J. H. Leigh-Pemberton
Attorney-General to the Prince of Wales, N. Underhill, QC
Secretary and Keeper of the Records, W. R. A. Ross
Other members, R. Broadhurst; The Earl of Cairns;
A. M. J. Galsworthy; W. N. Hood, CBE;
Sir Christopher Howes, CB; S. Lamport;
The Marquess of Lansdowne; J. E. Pugsley

OTHER OFFICERS
Auditors, I. Brindle; R. Hughes
Sheriff (2000–1), Lady Banham

THE DUCHY OF LANCASTER
Lancaster Place, Strand, London WC2E 7ED
Tel: 020-7836 8277; Fax: 020-7836 3098

The estates and jurisdiction known as the Duchy of Lancaster have belonged to the reigning monarch since 1399 when John of Gaunt's son came to the throne as Henry IV. As the Lancaster Inheritance it goes back as far as 1265 when Henry III granted his youngest son Edmund lands and possessions following the Baron's war. In 1267 Henry gave Edmund the County, Honor and Castle of Lancaster and created him the first Earl of Lancaster. In 1351 Edward III created Lancaster a County Palatine.

The Chancellor of the Duchy of Lancaster is responsible for the administration of the Duchy, the appointment of justices of the peace in Lancashire, Greater Manchester and Merseyside and ecclesiastical patronage in the Duchy gift.
Chancellor of the Duchy of Lancaster (and Minister for the Cabinet Office), The Rt. Hon. Dr Marjorie Mowlam, MP
Chairman of the Duchy Council, Sir Michael Bunbury, BT
Attorney-General, R. G. B. McCombe, QC
Receiver-General, Sir Michael Peat, KCVO
Clerk of the Council and Chief Executive, P. R. Clarke
Chief Clerk and Secretary for Appointments,
Col. F. N. J. Davies

ECGD (EXPORT CREDITS GUARANTEE DEPARTMENT)
PO Box 2200, 2 Exchange Tower, Harbour Exchange Square, London E14 9GS
Tel: 020-7512 7000; Fax: 020-7512 7649

ECGD (Export Credits Guarantee Department), the UK's official export credit insurer, is a Government department responsible to the Secretary of State for Trade and Industry and functions under the Export and Investment Guarantees Act 1991. This enables ECGD to facilitate UK exports by making available export credit insurance to firms engaged in selling overseas and to guarantee repayment to banks providing finance for capital goods. The Act also empowers ECGD to insure UK companies investing overseas against political risks such as war, expropriation and restrictions on remittances.
Chief Executive, H. V. B. Brown
Group Directors (G3), V. P. Lunn-Rockliffe
  (*Asset Management*); J. R. Weiss (*Underwriting*);
  T. M. Jaffray (*Resource Management*)

DIVISIONS
Director, Finance (G5), R. J. Healey
Director, Central Services (G5), P. J. Callaghan
Directors, Underwriting Divisions (G5), G. G. W. Welsh
  (*Division 1*); J. C. W. Croall (*Division 2*); M. D. Pentecost
  (*Division 3*); R. Gotts (*Division 4*); S. R. Dodgson
  (*Division 5*); C. J. Leeds (*Division 6*)
Director, Office of the General Counsel (G5), N. Ridley
Director, International Debt (G5), Ms L. Woods
Director, Claims (G5), R. F. Lethbridge
Director, Treasury and Export Finance (G5), J. S. Snowdon
Director, Risk Management (G5), P. J. Radford
Director, External Relations (G5), Mrs M. E. Maddox
Director, IT Services (G6), E. J. Walsby
Director, Internal Audit (G6), G. Cassell
Director, Operational Research (G6), Ms R. Kaufman

EXPORT GUARANTEES ADVISORY COUNCIL
Chairman, D. H. A. Harrison
Other Members, Ms E. Airey; Dr A. K. Banerji;
  R. F. T. Binyon; A. Brown; S. J. Doughty;
  D. McLachlan; P. J. Mason;
  Sir David Wright, KCMG, LVO

ENGLISH HERITAGE (HISTORIC BUILDINGS AND MONUMENTS COMMISSION FOR ENGLAND)
23 Savile Row, London W1X 1AB
Tel: 020-7973 3000; Fax: 020-7973 3001

English Heritage was established under the National Heritage Act 1983. On 1 April 1999 it merged with the Royal Commission on the Historical Monuments of England to become the new lead body for England's historic environment. Its duties are to carry out and sponsor archaeological, architectural and scientific survey and research designed to increase the understanding of England's past and its changing condition; to offer expert advice and skills and give grants to secure the preservation of listed buildings, cathedrals, churches, archaeological sites, ancient monuments and historic houses of England; to encourage the imaginative re-use of historic buildings to aid regeneration of the centres of cities, towns and villages; to manage the historic monuments and historic buildings in England; and to curate and make publicly accessible the National Monuments Record, whose records of over one million historic sites and buildings, and collections of more that 12 million photographs, maps, drawings and reports constitute the central database and archive to England's historic environment
Chairman, Sir Neil Cossons
Commissioners, Miss A. Arrowsmith; Ms B. Cherry;
  Cllr P. Davis; A. Fane; The Lord Faringdon;
  Prof. E. Fernie, CBE; Lady Gass; HRH The Duke of
  Gloucester, KG, GCVO; P. Gough, CBE; L. Grossman;
  Mrs C. Lycett-Green; Ms K. McLeod;
  Prof. R. Morris, FSA; Miss S. Underwood
Chief Executive, Ms P. Alexander

NATIONAL MONUMENTS RECORD, National Monuments Record Centre, Kemble Drive, Swindon SN2 2GZ.
  Tel: 01793-414600; Fax: 01793-414606. *London Search Room:* 55 Blandford Street, London SW1H 3AF. Tel: 020-7208 8200; Fax: 020-7224 5333

ENGLISH NATURE
Northminster House, Peterborough PE1 1UA
Tel: 01733-455000; Fax: 01733-568834

English Nature (the Nature Conservancy Council for England) was established in 1991 and is responsible for advising the Secretary of State for the Environment, Transport and the Regions on nature conservation in England. It promotes, directly and through others, the conservation of England's wildlife and natural features. It selects, establishes and manages National Nature Reserves and identifies and notifies Sites of Special Scientific Interest. It provides advice and information about nature conservation, and supports and conducts research relevant to these functions. Through the Joint Nature Conservation Committee (*see* page xxx), it works with its sister organisations in Scotland and Wales on UK and international nature conservation issues.
Chairman, The Baroness Young of Old Scone
Chief Executive, D. Arnold-Forster
Directors, Dr K. L. Duff; Miss C. E. M. Wood;
  Ms S. Collins; A. E. Brown

THE ENVIRONMENT AGENCY
Rio House, Waterside Drive, Aztec West, Almondsbury, Bristol BS32 4UD
Tel: 01454-624400; Fax: 01454-624409
Email: enquiries@environment-agency.gov.uk

The Environment Agency was established in 1996 under the Environment Act 1995 and is a non-departmental public body sponsored by the Department of the Environment, Transport and the Regions, MAFF and the National Assembly for Wales. The Agency is responsible for pollution prevention and control in England and Wales, and for the management and use of water resources, including flood defences, fisheries and navigation. It has head offices in London and Bristol and eight regional offices.

THE BOARD
Chairman, Sir John Harman
Members, C. Beardwood; A. J. P. Dalton; A. Dare, CBE;
  E. Gallagher; N. Haigh, OBE; C.Hampson, CBE;
  Prof. R. Macrory; Prof. Jacqueline McGlade;
  G. Manning, OBE; Dr A. Powell; Prof. D. Ritchie;
  A. Rogers; G. Wardell

THE EXECUTIVE
Chief Executive, E. Gallagher
Director of Finance, N. Reader
Director of Personnel, G. Duncan
Director of Environmental Protection, Dr P. Leinster
Director of Water Management, G. Mance
Director of Operations, A. Robertson
Director of Corporate Affairs, vacant
Director of Legal Services, R. Navarro
Chief Scientist, Dr John Murlis

EQUAL OPPORTUNITIES COMMISSION
Arndale House, Arndale Centre, Manchester M4 3EQ
Tel: 0161-833 9244; Fax: 0161-838 8312

Press Office, 36 Broadway, London SW1H 0XH.
Tel: 020-7222 1110
Other Offices, St Stephens House, 279 Bath Street,
Glasgow G2 4JL Tel: 0141-248 5833; Windsor House,
Windsor Place, Cardiff CF10 3GE Tel: 029-2034 3552

The Commission was set up in 1975 as a result of the
passing of the Sex Discrimination Act. It works towards
the elimination of discrimination on the grounds of sex or
marital status and to promote equality of opportunity
between men and women generally. It is responsible to the
Department for Education and Employment.
Chair, Ms J. Mellor
Deputy Chair, Ms J. Watson
Members, Mrs M. Berg; Ms K. Carberry; Ms F. Cannon;
Ms J. Drake; R. Grayson; Ms E. Hodder; R. Penn;
Prof. T. Rees; Mr S. Sharma; P. Smith;
Dr J. Stringer; Ms T. Woodcraft
Chief Executive, Ms L. Berry

EQUAL OPPORTUNITIES COMMISSION FOR NORTHERN
IRELAND
Andras House, 60 Great Victoria Street, Belfast BT2 7BB
Tel: 028-9050 0600; Fax: 028-9033 1544
Chief Commissioner, Ms J.Harbison
Chief Executive, Ms E. Collins

FILM COUNCIL
10 Little Portland Street, London W1W 7JG
Tel: 020-7861 7861; Fax: 020-7861 7862

The Council was created in April 2000 by the Department
for Culture, Media and Sport to develop a coherent
strategy for the development and leadership of film culture
and the film industry. It will be responsible for the majority
of the Department for Culture, Media and Sport funding
for film as well as lottery and grant-in-aid (with the
exception of the National Film and Television School).
Chairman, A. Parker
Deputy Chairman, S. Till
Chief Executive, J. Woodward

FOOD STANDARDS AGENCY (UK)
Hannibal House, London SE1 6YA
Tel: 020-7972 2416; Fax: 020-7972 5140
Web: http://www.foodstandards.gov.uk

The Food Standards Agency was established by Act of
Parliament (the Food Standards Act 1999) in April 2000 to
protect public health from risks arising in connection with
the consumption of food, and otherwise to protect the
interests of consumers in relation to food. The Agency has
the general function of developing policy in these areas

and provides information and advice to the Government,
other public bodies and consumers. It also sets standards
for and monitors food law enforcement by local authorities. The Agency is a UK body and has executive offices
in Scotland, Wales and Northern Ireland. It is advised by
advisory committees on food safety matters of special
interest to each of these areas.
Chairman, Prof. Sir John Krebs
Deputy Chairman, Ms S. Leather
Chief Executive, G. Podger

EXECUTIVE AGENCY

MEAT HYGIENE SERVICE
Foss House, Kings Pool, 1–2 Peasholme Green,
York YO1 7PX
Tel: 01904-455655; Fax: 01904-455502

The Agency was launched in April 1995 and from the
1 April became an executive agency of the Food Standards
Agency. It protects public health and promotes animal
welfare through veterinary supervision and meat inspection in licensed fresh meat establishments.
Chief Executive (G4), J. McNeill

FOOD STANDARDS AGENCY SCOTLAND
St Magnus House, 25 Guild Street, Aberdeen, AB11 6NG
Tel: 01224 285100;
Email: scotland@foodstandards.gsi.gov.uk
Web: http://www foodstandards.gov.uk/scotland
Scottish Food Advisory Committee
Chairman, Sir John Arbuthnott

FOOD STANDARDS AGENCY WALES
1st Floor, Southgate House, Wood Street,
Cardiff CF10 1EW
Tel: 029-2067 8999;
Email: hilary.neathy@foodstandards.gsi.gov.uk
Web: http://www.foodstandards.gov.uk/wales
Advisory Committee for Wales
Chair, Ms A. Hemingway

FOOD STANDARDS AGENCY
NORTHERN IRELAND
Tel: 028-9052 2675
Email: gerry.rickard@dhsspsni.gov.uk
Web: http://www.foodstandards.gov.uk/n_ireland
Advisory Committee for Northern Ireland
Chairman, M. Walker

FOREIGN COMPENSATION COMMISSION
Room 3.G.9, 1 Palace Street, London SW1E 5HE
Tel: 020-7238 4419; Fax: 020-7238 4594

The Commission was set up by the Foreign Compensation Act 1950 primarily to distribute, under Orders in
Council, funds received from other governments in
accordance with agreements to pay compensation for
expropriated British property and other losses sustained
by British nationals.
Chairman, A. W. E. Wheeler, CBE
Secretary, A. N. Grant

FORESTRY COMMISSION
231 Corstorphine Road, Edinburgh EH12 7AT
Tel: 0131-334 0303; Fax: 0131-334 3047

The Forestry Commission is the Government department
responsible for forestry policy in Great Britain. It reports
directly to forestry Ministers (i.e. the Minister of

Agriculture, Fisheries and Food, the Scottish Ministers and the National Assembly for Wales), to whom it is responsible for advice on forestry policy and for the implementation of that policy.

The Commission's principal objectives are to protect Britain's forests and woodlands; expand Britain's forest area; enhance the economic value of the forest resources; conserve and improve the biodiversity, landscape and cultural heritage of forests and woodlands; develop opportunities for woodland recreation; and increase public understanding of and community participation in forestry. Forest Enterprise, a trading body operating as an executive agency of the Commission, manages its forestry estate on a multi-use basis.

Chairman (part-time), Sir Peter Hutchison, Bt., CBE
Director-General and Deputy Chairman (G2), D. J. Bills
Secretary to the Commissioners (G5), F. Strang

FOREST ENTERPRISE HEADQUARTERS, 231 Corstorphine Road, Edinburgh EH12 7AT. Tel: 0131-334 0303. *Chief Executive*, Dr B. McIntosh

FOREST RESEARCH, Alice Holt Lodge, Wrecclesham, Farnham, Surrey GU10 4LU. Tel: 01420-222555; Northern Research Station, Roslin, Midlothian EH25 9SY. Tel: 0131-445 2176. *Chief Executive*, J. Dewar

FRIENDLY SOCIETIES COMMISSION
15th Floor, 25 The North Colonnade, Canary Wharf, London E14 5HS
Tel: 020-7676 1000; Fax: 020-7676 9700

The Friendly Societies Commission was established by the Friendly Societies Act 1992. It is responsible for the supervision of friendly societies and administers the system of prudential regulation. It also advises the Treasury and other Government departments on matters relating to friendly societies.

The Government has proposed to Parliament that the functions of the Commission should pass to the Financial Services Authority (*see* page 640) on implementation of the Financial Services and Markets Bill.

FRIENDLY SOCIETIES COMMISSION
Chairman, M. Roberts
Commissioners, F. da Rocha; *B. Richardson; *J. A. Geddes; *Ms S. Brown; *Ms P. Triggs
*non executive

SECRETARIAT
Miss J. Erskine; Miss L. Gammans

GAMING BOARD FOR GREAT BRITAIN
Berkshire House, 168–173 High Holborn, London WC1V 7AA
Tel: 020-7306 6200; Fax: 020-7306 6266
Web: http://www.gbgb.org.uk

The Board was established in 1968 and is responsible to the Home Secretary. It is the regulatory body for casinos, bingo clubs, gaming machines and the larger society and all local authority lotteries in Great Britain. Its functions are to ensure that those involved in organising gaming and lotteries are fit and proper to do so and to keep gaming free from criminal infiltration; to ensure that gaming and lotteries are run fairly and in accordance with the law; and to advise the Home Secretary on developments in gaming and lotteries.
Chairman (part-time) (£38,704), P. Dean, CBE
Secretary, T. Kavanagh

GOVERNMENT ACTUARY'S DEPARTMENT
New King's Beam House, 22 Upper Ground, London SE1 9RJ
Tel: 020-7211 2601; Fax: 020-7211 2640/2650
Email: enquiries@gad.gov.uk
Web: http://www.gad.gov.uk

The Government Actuary provides a consulting service to Government departments, the public sector, and overseas governments. The actuaries advise on social security schemes and superannuation arrangements in the public sector at home and abroad, on population and other statistical studies, and on Government supervision of insurance companies, friendly societies and pension funds.
Government Actuary, C. D. Daykin, CB
Directing Actuaries, D. G. Ballantine; T. W. Hewitson; A. G. Young
Chief Actuaries, E. I. Battersby; Ms C. Cresswell; Mrs B. J. Hall; A. I. Johnston; D. Lewis; J. C. A. Rathbone; G. T. Russell; P. J. Tuley

GOVERNMENT HOSPITALITY FUND
8 Cleveland Row, London SW1A 1DH
Tel: 020-7210 4282; Fax: 020-7930 1148

The Government Hospitality Fund was instituted in 1908 for the purpose of organising official hospitality on a regular basis with a view to the promotion of international goodwill. It is responsible to the Foreign and Commonwealth Office.
Minister in Charge, The Baroness Symons of Vernham Dean
Secretary, Col. T. Earl

GOVERNMENT OFFICES FOR THE REGIONS

The Government Offices for the Regions were established in 1994. The regional directors are accountable to the Secretary of State for the Environment, Transport and the Regions, the Secretary of State for Trade and Industry, and the Secretary of State for Education and Employment. The offices' role is to promote a coherent approach to competitiveness, sustainable economic development and regeneration using public and private resources.

CENTRAL UNIT, 1st Floor, Eland House, Bressenden Place, London SW1E 5DU
Tel: 020-7944 5157; Fax: 020-7944 5019

Director (G3), A. Wells
Head of Unit (G5), Mrs J. Scoones

EAST MIDLANDS
Secretariat: The Belgrave Centre, Stanley Place, Talbot Street, Nottingham NG1 5GG
Tel: 0115-971 9971; Fax: 0115-971 2404;
Email: enquiries.goem@go-regions.gov.uk;
Web: http://www.go-em.gov.uk
Regional Director (G3), D. Morrison
Directors (G5), Dr S. Kennett (*Environment and Community Development*); R. Poole (*Competitiveness and European Policy*); S. McIntyre (*Skills and Enterprise*); (*G6*), R. Smith (*Corporate Affairs*)

EAST OF ENGLAND
Secretariat: Building A, Westbrook Centre, Milton Road, Cambridge CB4 1YG
Tel: 01223 346719; Fax: 01223-346705

Regional Director (G3), A. Riddell
Directors (G5), C. Dunabin (*Housing, Environment and Regeneration*); Ms C. Bowdler (*Planning and Transport*); M. Oldham (*Economic Development*); J. Street (*Skills and Enterprise*); (*G6*), Chris Beesley (*Strategy and Resources*)

LONDON
Secretariat: Riverwalk House, 157–161 Millbank, London SW1P 4RR
Tel: 020-7217 3456; Fax: 020-7217 3450

Director of Office (G2), Miss E. C. Turton, CB
Directors (G3), J. A. Owen (*Skills, Education and Regeneration*); R. Allan (*New London Governance*); (*G5*), A. Sargent (*Skills and Education*); Mrs J. Bridges (*Planning*); K. Timmins (*Enterprise and North-West*); Ms M. Winckler (*London East and European Programmes*); P. Sanders (*Transport for London Bill Division*); A. Melville (*Greater London Authority Implementation*); A. Weedon (*Transport Task Force*); Ms C. Lyons (*Corporate*); J. Sienkiewicz (*London Development Unit*); R. Wragg (*Operations and Business Management*); N. Robinson (*Exports and Trade, and Business Development*); P. Fiddeman (*Regeneration London South*); B. Mann (*Home Office Liaison*); Z. Kowalczyk (*London Readiness 2000/Millennium Access*); G. Williams (*Transport for London Project Division*)

NORTH-EAST
Secretariat: Wellbar House, Gallowgate, Newcastle upon Tyne NE1 4TD
Tel: 0191-201 3300; Fax: 0191-202 3998;
Web: http://www.go-ne.gov.uk

Regional Director (G3), Dr R. Dobbie, CB
Directors (G5), J. Darlington (*Planning, Environment and Transport*); Miss D. Caudle (*Education, Skills, Enterprise and Regeneration*); A. Dell (*Europe, Industry, Trade and Technology*); (*G6*), Mrs D. Pearce (*Strategy and Resources*)

NORTH-WEST
Secretariat: 12th Floor, Sunley Tower, Piccadilly Plaza, Manchester M1 4BE
Tel: 0161-952 4000; Fax: 0161-952 4099

Regional Director (G3), K. Barnes
Directors, (G5), P. Styche (*Communities*); D. Duff (*Skills and Enterprise*); Dr D. Highham (*Business and Europe*); (*G6*), I. Jamieson (*Europe, Manchester*); Ms S. Yates (*Europe, Liverpool*); Ms E. Hughes (*Planning and Environment/Regional Policy and Co-ordination*); D. Hopewell (*Corporate Services*); N. Burke (*Skills and Enterprise, New Business*) (*acting*); M. Hill (*Skills and Enterprise, Operations*) (*acting*)

SOUTH-EAST
Secretariat: 2nd Floor, Bridge House, 1 Walnut Tree Close, Guildford, Surrey GU1 4GA
Tel: 01483-882481; Fax: 01483-882269

Regional Director (G3), D. Saunders
Directors (G5), Mr C. Byrne (*Hants/IOW*); N. Wilson (*Berks/Oxon/Bucks*); A. Campbell (*Kent*); D. Andrews (*Surrey/E. and W. Sussex*); Mrs C. Dixon (*Regional Strategy Team*)

SOUTH-WEST
Secretariat: 5th Floor, The Pithay, Bristol BS1 2PB
Tel: 0117-900 1700; Fax: 0117-900 1900

Regional Director (G3), Ms J. Henderson
Directors (G5), R. Bayly (*Devon and Cornwall*); Ms C. Carrington (*Environment and Regeneration*); T. Shearer (*Competitiveness and Skills*); (*G6*) M. Davey (*Corporate Services*)

WEST MIDLANDS
Secretariat: 6th Floor, 77 Paradise Circus, Queensway, Birmingham B1 2DT
Tel: 0121-212 5000; Fax: 0121-212 5456

Regional Director (G3), D. Ritchie
Directors (G5), C. Marsh (*Corporate Affairs and Europe Division*); Mrs P. Holland (*Local Government Division*); (*G6*) D. Way (*Business and Learning Division*)

YORKSHIRE AND THE HUMBER
Secretariat: PO Box 213, City House, New Station Street, Leeds LS1 4US
Tel: 0113-280 0600; Fax: 0113-283 6394

Regional Director (G3), Ms F. Everiss
Directors (G5), G. Dyche (*Strategy and Europe*); S. Perryman (*Business, Enterprise and Skills*); (*G6*), J. Jarvis (*Planning and Transport*); M. Doxey (*Personnel and Resources*); Ms M. Jackson (*Regeneration*) (*acting*)

HEALTH AND SAFETY COMMISSION
Rose Court, 2 Southwark Bridge, London SE1 9HS
Tel: 020-7717 6000; Fax: 020-7717 6717

The Health and Safety Commission was created under the Health and Safety at Work etc. Act 1974, with duties to reform health and safety law, to propose new regulations, and generally to promote the protection of people at work and of the public from hazards arising from industrial and commercial activity, including major industrial accidents and the transportation of hazardous materials. The members of the Commission are appointed by the Secretary of State for the Environment, Transport and the Regions. The Commission is made up of representatives of employers, trades unions and local authorities, and has a full-time chairman.
Chairman, W. Callaghan
Members, Ms A. Gibson; Dr M. McKiernan;
  Ms J. Edmond-Smith; G. Brumwell; Ms M. Burns;
  S. Hamid; A. Chowdry; O. Tudor; R. Symons, CBE
Secretary, T. A. Gates

HEALTH AND SAFETY EXECUTIVE
Rose Court, 2 Southwark Bridge, London SE1 9HS
Tel: 020-7717 6000; Fax: 020-7717 6717

The Health and Safety Executive is the Health and Safety Commission's major instrument. Through its inspectorates it enforces health and safety law in the majority of industrial premises. The Executive advises the Commission in its major task of laying down safety standards through regulations and practical guidance for many industrial processes. The Executive is also the licensing authority for nuclear installations and the reporting officer on the severity of nuclear incidents in Britain, and it is responsible for the Channel Tunnel Safety Authority.
Director-General, Miss J. H. Bacon, CB
Deputy Director-General, D. C. T. Eves, CB
  (*HM Chief Inspector of Factories*)
Director, Field Operations Directorate, Dr A. Ellis
Director, Science and Technology, Dr J. McQuaid, CB
Director, Safety Policy, C. Norris
Director, Health Directorate, Dr P. J. Graham
Director, Resources and Planning, R. Hillier
HM Chief Inspector of Nuclear Installations,
  Dr L. G. Williams
HM Chief Inspector of Mines, B. Langdon, CBE
HM Chief Inspecting Officer of Railways, V. Coleman

HIGHLANDS AND ISLANDS ENTERPRISE
Bridge House, 20 Bridge Street, Inverness IV1 1QR
Tel: 01463-234171; Fax: 01463-244469
Email: hie.general@hient.co.uk
Web: http://www.hie.co.uk

Highlands and Islands Enterprise (HIE) was set up under the Enterprise and New Towns (Scotland) Act 1991. Its role is to design, direct and deliver enterprise development, training, environmental and social projects and services. HIE is made up of a strategic core body and ten Local Enterprise Companies (LECs) to which many of its individual functions are delegated.
Chairman, Dr J. Hunter
Chief Executive, I. A. Robertson, CBE

HISTORIC BUILDINGS COUNCIL FOR SCOTLAND
Longmore House, Salisbury Place, Edinburgh EH9 1SH
Tel: 0131-668 8600; Fax: 0131-668 8788

The Historic Buildings Council for Scotland is the advisory body to the Scottish Ministers on matters related to buildings of special architectural or historical interest and in particular to proposals for awards by them of grants for the repair of buildings of outstanding architectural or historical interest or lying within outstanding conservation areas.
Chairman, Sir Raymond Johnstone, CBE
Members, R. Cairns; Mrs P. Chalmers; Bishop M. Conti; Ms L. Davidson; Mrs A. Dundas-Bekker; Revd G. Forbes; Dr J. Frew; D. Gauci; M. Hopton; E. Jamieson; Mrs P. Robertson; Ms F. Sinclair
Secretary, Mrs S. Williamson

HISTORIC BUILDINGS COUNCIL FOR WALES
Cathays Park, Cardiff CF1 3NQ
Tel: 029-2050 0200; Fax: 029-20-82 6375

The Council's function is to advise the National Assembly for Wales on the built heritage through Cadw: Welsh Historic Monuments, which is an executive agency of the Assembly.
Chairman, T. Lloyd, FSA
Members, Dr P. Morgan; Mrs S. Furse; Dr S. Unwin; Dr E. Wiliam; Miss E. Evans; Dr R. Wools
Secretary, Mrs J. Booker

HISTORIC ROYAL PALACES
Hampton Court Palace, East Molesey, Surrey KT8 9AU
Tel: 020-8781 9500; Fax: 020-8781 9754

Historic Royal Palaces was formerly an executive agency of the Department for Culture, Media and Sport; it is now a non-departmental public body with charitable trust status. The Secretary of State for Culture, Media and Sport is still accountable to Parliament for the care, conservation and presentation of the palaces, which are owned by the Sovereign in right of the Crown. The chairman of the trustees is appointed by The Queen on the advice of the Secretary of State.

Historic Royal Palaces is responsible for the Tower of London, Hampton Court Palace, Kensington Palace State Apartments and the Royal Ceremonial Dress Collection, Kew Palace with Queen Charlotte's Cottage, and the Banqueting House, Whitehall.
TRUSTEES
Chairman, The Earl of Airlie, KT, GCVO, PC
Appointed by The Queen, The Lord Camoys, GCVO, PC; Sir Michael Peat, KCVO; H. Roberts, CVO, FSA
Appointed by the Secretary of State, M. Herbert, CBE; Ms A. Heylin, OBE; S. Jones, LVO; Ms J. Sharman, CBE
Ex officio, Field Marshal the Lord Inge, GCB (*Constable of the Tower of London*)
OFFICERS
Chief Executive, A. Coppin
Director of Finance, Ms A. McLeish
Director of Human Resources, G. Josephs
Surveyor of the Fabric, R. Davidson
Curator, Dr E. Impey
Director, Palaces Group, D. McGuinnes
Resident Governor, HM Tower of London, Maj.-Gen. G. Field, CB, OBE

HOME-GROWN CEREALS AUTHORITY
Caledonia House, 223 Pentonville Road, London N1 9HY
Tel: 020-7520 3926; Fax: 020-7520 3954

Set up under the Cereals Marketing Act 1965, the HGCA Board consists of seven members representing UK cereal growers, seven representing dealers in, or processors of, grain and two independent members. HGCA's functions are to improve the production and marketing of UK-grown cereals and oilseeds through a research and development programme, to provide a market information service, and to promote UK cereals in export markets.
Chairman (part-time) (£22,243), A. Pike
Chief Executive, P. V. Biscoe

HORSERACE TOTALISATOR BOARD
Tote House, 74 Upper Richmond Road, London SW15 2SU
Tel: 020-8874 6411; Fax: 020-8874 6107
Web: http://www.tote.co.uk

The Horserace Totalisator Board (the Tote) was established by the Betting, Gaming and Lotteries Act 1963. Its function is to operate totalisators on approved racecourses in Great Britain, and it also provides on- and off-course cash and credit offices. Under the Horserace Totalisator and Betting Levy Board Act 1972, it is further empowered to offer bets at starting price (or other bets at fixed odds) on any sporting event, and under the Horserace Totalisator Board Act 1997 to take bets on any event, except the National Lottery. The chairman and members of the Board are appointed by the Home Secretary.

The Government announced in March 2000 that the Tote would be sold to a racing trust, subject to the necessary legislation going through Parliament.
Chairman, P. I. Jones
Chief Executive, W. J. Heaton

HOUSING CORPORATION
149 Tottenham Court Road, London W1P 0BN
Tel: 020-7393 2000; Fax: 020-7393 2111
Email: enquiries@housingcorp.gov.uk
Web: http://www.housingcorp.gov.uk

Established by Parliament in 1964, the Housing Corporation regulates, funds and promotes the proper performance of registered social landlords, which are non-profit
making bodies run by voluntary committees. There are
over 2,200 registered social landlords, most of which are
housing associations, and they now provide homes for
more than 1.5 million people. Under the Housing Act
1996, the Corporation's regulatory role was widened to
embrace new types of landlords, in particular local housing
companies. The Corporation is funded by the Department of the Environment, Transport and the Regions.
Chairman, The Rt. Hon. Baroness Dean of
 Thornton-le-Fylde, PC
Deputy Chairman, E. Armitage
Acting Chief Executive, S. Dow

HUMAN FERTILISATION AND EMBRYOLOGY AUTHORITY
Paxton House, 30 Artillery Lane, London E1 7LS
Tel: 020-7377 5077; Fax: 020-7377 1871

The Human Fertilization and Embryology Authority
(HFEA) was established under the Human Fertilisation
and Embryology Act 1990. Its function is to license the
following activities: the creation or use of embryos outside
the body in the provision of infertility treatment services;
the use of donated gametes in infertility treatment; the
storage of gametes or embryos; and research on human
embryos. It maintains a confidential database of all such
treatments and of egg and sperm donors, and provides
information to patients, clinics and the public. The HFEA
also keeps under review information about embryos and,
when requested to do so, gives advice to the Secretary of
State for Health.
Chairman, Mrs R. Deech
Deputy Chairman, Mrs J. Denton
Members, Prof. Brenda Almond; Dr S. Avery;
 Prof. D. Barlow; Mrs M. E. Coath; Prof. Christine
 Gosden; Prof. A. Grubb; Prof. H. Leese; Prof. S. Lewis;
 Prof. P. Brando; Dr Anne McLaren; Dr S. Muhammed;
 Ms S. Nathan; Ms S. Nebhrajani; The Rt. Revd Bishop
 of Rochester; Dr F. Shenfield; Prof. A. Templeton;
 Julia, Lady Tugendhat; Mrs L. Woods
Chief Executive, Mrs S. McCarthy

HUMAN GENETICS COMMISSION
Room 401, Wellington House, 133–155 Waterloo Road,
London SE1 8UG Tel: 020-7972 4017;
Fax: 020-7972 4196, Email: hgc@doh.gov.uk
Web: http://www.hgc.gov.uk

The Human Genetics Commission was established in
1999, subsuming three previous advisory committees.
Its remit is to give Ministers strategic advice on how
developments in human genetics will impact on people
and on health care, focusing in particular on the special
and ethical implications.
Chairman, Baroness H. Kennedy of the Shaws, QC
Vice Chair, Prof. A. McCall Smith

Members; Dr W. Albert, Prof. E. Anionwu; Prof. J. Burn;
 Prof. J. Durant; Ms R. Evans; Prof. P. Goodfellow;
 Dr H. Harris; Prof. J. Harris; Ms H. Newiss;
 Prof. J. Polkinghorne; Prof. B. Ponder;
 Prof. M. Richards; Dr G. Samuels; Mr G. Watts;
 Mr P. Webb; Prof. V. von Heyningen; Ms R. Deech;
 Mrs J. Axelby; Prof. N. Nevin; Dr R. Skinner
Head of Secretariat, Dr D. Coles

INDEPENDENT HOUSING OMBUDSMAN
Norman House, 105–109 Strand, London WC2R 0AA
Tel: 020-7836 3630; 0345-125973; Fax: 020-7836 3900
Email: ombudsman@ihos.org.uk
Web: http://www.ihos.org.uk

The Independent Housing Ombudsman (IHO) was
established in 1997 under the Housing Act 1996. The
Ombudsman deals with complaints against registered
social landlords (not including local authorities) and some
private landlords. IHO is also managing the pilot Tenancy
Deposit Scheme aimed at protecting the deposits of
private tenants and resolving any disputes over their return
quickly, cheaply and fairly.
Ombudsman, R. Jefferies
Chair of Board, Ms P. Brown
General Manager, L. Greenberg

INDEPENDENT INTERNATIONAL COMMISSION ON DECOMMISSIONING
Dublin Castle, Block M, Ship Street, Dublin 2
Tel: 00 353 1-478 0111; Fax: 00 353 1-478 0600
Rosepark House, Upper Newtownards Road,
Belfast BT4 3NX
Tel: 028-90-48 8600; Fax: 028-9048 8601

The Commission was established by agreement between
the British and Irish Governments in August 1997. Its
objective is to facilitate the decommissioning of illegally-
held firearms and explosives in accordance with the relevant legislation in both jurisdictions. Its members are
appointed jointly by the two Governments; staff are
appointed by the Commission. All are drawn from
countries other than the UK and the Republic of Ireland.
Chairman, Gen. J. de Chastelain (Canada)
Commissioners, Brig. T. Nieminen (Finland);
 A. Sens (USA)
Chief of Staff, C. E. Garrard (Canada)

INDEPENDENT REVIEW SERVICE FOR THE SOCIAL FUND
4th Floor, Centre City Podium, 5 Hill Street,
Birmingham B5 4UB
Tel: 0121-606 2100; Fax: 0121-606 2180

The Social Fund Commissioner is appointed by the
Secretary of State for Social Security. The Commissioner
appoints Social Fund Inspectors, who provide an independent review of decisions made by Social Fund Officers in
the Benefits Agency of the Department of Social Security.
Social Fund Commissioner, J. Scampion

INDEPENDENT TELEVISION COMMISSION
33 Foley Street, London W1P 7LB
Tel: 020-7255 3000; Fax: 020-7306 7800

The Independent Television Commission replaced the Independent Broadcasting Authority in 1991. The Commission is responsible for licensing and regulating all commercially funded television services broadcast from the UK. Members are appointed by the Secretary of State for Culture, Media and Sport.
Chairman, Sir Robin Biggam
Members, A. Balls, CB; C. Brendish; Ms. B. Donoghue;
    Sir Michael Checkland; Ms J. Goffe; J. Kelly;
    Dr Maria Moloney (*Member for Northern Ireland*);
    Prof. D. L. Morgan, D.Phil. (*Member for Wales*);
    Dr M. Shea, CVO (*Member for Scotland*)
Chief Executive, P. Rogers
Secretary and Director of Administration, M. Redley

INDUSTRIAL INJURIES ADVISORY COUNCIL
6th Floor, The Adelphi, 1–11 John Adam Street,
London WC2N 6HT
Tel: 020-7962 8066; Fax: 020-7712 2255
Email: iiac@dial.pipex.com; Web: http://www.iiac.org.uk

The Industrial Injuries Advisory Council is a statutory body under the Social Security Administration Act 1992 which considers and advises the Secretary of State for Social Security on regulations and other questions relating to industrial injuries benefits or their administration.
Chairman, Prof. A. J. Newman Taylor, OBE, FRCP
Secretary, A. Packer

INTELLIGENCE SERVICES TRIBUNAL
PO Box 4823, London SW1A 9XD
Tel: 020-7273 4383

The Intelligence Services Act 1994 established a tribunal of three senior members of the legal profession, independent of the Government and appointed by The Queen, to investigate complaints from any person about anything which they believe the Secret Intelligence Service or the Government Communications Headquarters has done to them or to their property.
President, The Rt. Hon. Lord Justice Simon Brown
Vice-President, Sheriff J. McInnes, QC
Member, Sir Richard Gaskell
Secretary, N. Brooks

INTERCEPTION COMMISSIONER
c/o PO Box 12376, London SW1P 1XU
Tel: 020-7273 4096

The Commissioner is appointed by the Prime Minister. He keeps under review the issue by Secretaries of State of warrants under the Interception of Communications Act 1985 and safeguards made in respect of intercepted material obtained through the use of such warrants. He is also required to give all such assistance as the Interception of Communications Tribunal may require to enable it to carry out its functions, and to submit an annual report to the Prime Minister with respect to the carrying out of his functions.
Commissioner, The Lord Nolan, PC
    Private Secretary, N. Brooks

INTERCEPTION OF COMMUNICATIONS TRIBUNAL
PO Box 12376, London SW1P 1XU
Tel: 020-7273 4096

Under the Interception of Communications Act 1985, the Tribunal is required to investigate complaints from any person who believes that communications sent to or by them have been intercepted in the course of their transmission by post or by means of a public telecommunications system. The Tribunal comprises senior members of the legal profession, who are appointed by The Queen.
President, Sir William Macpherson of Cluny
Vice-President, Sir David Calcutt, QC
Members, P. Scott, QC; R. Seabrook, QC; W. Carmichael
Secretary, N. Brooks

INTERVENTION BOARD
PO Box 69, Reading RG1 3YD
Tel: 0118-958 3626; Fax: 0118-953 1370

The Intervention Board was established as a Government department in 1972 and became an executive agency in 1990. The Board is responsible for the implementation of European Union regulations covering the market support arrangements of the Common Agricultural Policy. Members are appointed by and are responsible to the four agriculture Ministers in the UK.
Chairman, I. Kent
Chief Executive (*G3*), G. Trevelyan
Directors (*G5*), H. MacKinnon (*Operations*);
    J. P. Bradbury (*Operations*, Newcastle);
    Mrs A. Parker (*Corporate Services*); P. Kent (*Legal*);
    G. Trantham (*Finance*)

JOINT NATURE CONSERVATION COMMITTEE
Monkstone House, City Road, Peterborough PE1 1JY
Tel: 01733-562626; Fax: 01733-555948

The Committee was established under the Environmental Protection Act 1990. It advises the Government and others on UK and international nature conservation issues and disseminates knowledge on these subjects. It establishes common standards for the monitoring of nature conservation and research, and provides guidance to English Nature, Scottish Natural Heritage, the Countryside Council for Wales and the Department of the Environment for Northern Ireland.
Chairman, Sir Angus Stirling
Managing Director, D. Steer
Director, Dr M. A. Vincent

LAND REGISTRIES

HM LAND REGISTRY
Lincoln's Inn Fields, London WC2A 3PH
Tel: 020-7917 8888; Fax: 020-7955 0110

The registration of title to land was first introduced in England and Wales by the Land Registry Act 1862; HM Land Registry operates today under the Land Registration Acts 1925 to 1997. The object of registering title to land is to create and maintain a register of landowners whose title is guaranteed by the state and so to simplify the transfer, mortgage and other dealings with real property. Registration on sale is now compulsory throughout England and Wales. The register has been open to inspection by the public since 1990.

HM Land Registry is an executive agency and Trading Fund administered under the Lord Chancellor by the Chief Land Registrar.

HEADQUARTERS OFFICE
Chief Land Registrar and Chief Executive, P. Collis
Solicitor to Land Registry, C. J. West
Director of Corporate Services, E. G. Beardsall
Director of Operations, A. Howarth
Director of Practice and Legal Services, J. V. Timothy
Director of Information Systems, P. J. Smith, OBE
Director of Facilities, P. R. Laker
Director of Personnel, J. Hodder
Director of Finance, Ms H. Jackson
Director of Communication, A. Pemberton
Director of Service Development, P. Norman

COMPUTER SERVICES DIVISION
Burrington Way, Plymouth PL5 3LP
Tel: 01752-635600
Head of IT Services Division, P. A. Maycock
Head of IT Development Division, J. Formby
Head of IT Management Services, K. Deards

LAND CHARGES AND AGRICULTURAL
CREDITS DEPARTMENT
Burrington Way, Plymouth PL5 3LP
Tel: 01752-635600
Superintendent of Land Charges, J. Hughes

DISTRICT LAND REGISTRIES
BIRKENHEAD (OLD MARKET HOUSE) – Old Market House, Hamilton Street, Birkenhead CH41 5FL. Tel: 0151-473 1110. *District Land Registrar*, P. J. Brough
BIRKENHEAD (ROSEBRAE COURT), Woodside Ferry Approach, Birkenhead L41 6DU. Tel: 0151-472 6666. *District Land Registrar*, M. G. Garwood
COVENTRY – Leigh Court, Torrington Avenue, Coventry CV4 9XZ. Tel: 024-7686 0860. *District Land Registrar*, T. H. O. Lewis
CROYDON – Sunley House, Bedford Park, Croydon CR9 3LE. Tel: 020-8781 9100. *District Land Registrar*, F. M. Twambley
DURHAM (BOLDON HOUSE) – Boldon House, Wheatlands Way, Pity Me, Durham DH1 5GJ. Tel: 0191-301 2345. *District Land Registrar*, R. B. Fearnley
DURHAM (SOUTHFIELD HOUSE) – Southfield House, Southfield Way, Durham DH1 5TR. Tel: 0191-301 3500. *District Land Registrar*, P. J. Timothy
GLOUCESTER – Twyver House, Bruton Way, Gloucester GL1 1DQ. Tel: 01452-511111. *District Land Registrar*, W. W. Budden
HARROW – Lyon House, Lyon Road, Harrow, Middx HA1 2EU. Tel: 020-8235 1181. *District Land Registrar*, C. Tate
KINGSTON UPON HULL – Earle House, Portland Street, Hull HU2 8JN. Tel: 01482-223244. *District Land Registrar*, S. R. Coveney
LANCASHIRE – Birkenhead House, East Beach, Lytham, Lancs FY8 5AB. Tel: 01253-849849. *District Land Registrar*, Mrs L. Wallwork
LEICESTER – Westbridge Place, Leicester LE3 5DR. Tel: 0116-265 4000. *District Land Registrar*, Mrs J. A. Goodfellow
LYTHAM – Birkenhead House, East Beach, Lytham, Lancs FY8 5AB. Tel: 01253-849849. *District Land Registrar*, J. G. Cooper

NOTTINGHAM (EAST) – Robins Wood Road, Nottingham NG8 3RQ. Tel: 0115-906 5353. *District Land Registrar*, P. A. Brown
NOTTINGHAM (WEST) – Chalfont Drive, Nottingham NG8 3RN. Tel: 0115-935 1166. *District Land Registrar*, Ms A. M. Goss
PETERBOROUGH – Touthill Close, City Road, Peterborough PE1 1XN. Tel: 01733-288288. *District Land Registrar*, C. W. Martin
PLYMOUTH – Plumer House, Tailyour Road, Crownhill, Plymouth PL6 5HY. Tel: 01752-636000. *District Land Registrar*, A. J. Pain
PORTSMOUTH – St Andrews Court, St Michael's Road, Portsmouth PO1 2JH. Tel: 023-9276 8888. *District Land Registrar*, S. R. Sehrawat
STEVENAGE – Brickdale House, Swingate, Stevenage, Herts SG1 1XG. Tel: 01438-788888. *District Land Registrar*, M. Croker
SWANSEA – Ty Bryn Glas, High Street, Swansea SA1 1PW. Tel: 01792-458877. *District Land Registrar*, G. A. Hughes
TELFORD – Parkside Court, Hall Park Way, Telford TF3 4LR. Tel: 01952-290355. *District Land Registrar*, A. M. Lewis
TUNBRIDGE WELLS – Forest Court, Forest Road, Tunbridge Wells, Kent TN2 5AQ. Tel: 01892-510015. *District Land Registrar*, G. R. Tooke
WALES – Ty Cwm Tave, Phoenix Way, Llansamlet, Swansea SA7 9FQ. Tel: 01792-355000. *District Land Registrar*, T. M. Lewis
WEYMOUTH – Melcombe Court, 1 Cumberland Drive, Weymouth, Dorset DT4 9TT. Tel: 01305-363636. *District Land Registrar*, Mrs P. M. Reeson
YORK – James House, James Street, York YO1 3YZ. Tel: 01904-450000. *District Land Registrar*, Mrs R. F. Lovel

REGISTERS OF SCOTLAND
Meadowbank House, 153 London Road, Edinburgh EH8 7AU
Tel: 0131-659 6111; Fax: 0131-479 3688
Customer Service Centre: 0845-6070161

Registers of Scotland is the executive agency responsible for framing and maintaining records relating to property and other legal documents in Scotland. The agency holds 15 registers: two property registers (General Register of Sasines and Land Register of Scotland) and 13 chancery and judicial registers (Register of Deeds in the Books of Council and Session; Register of Protests; Register of Judgments; Register of Service of Heirs; Register of the Great Seal; Register of the Quarter Seal; Register of the Prince's Seal; Register of Crown Grants; Register of Sheriffs' Commissions; Register of the Cachet Seal; Register of Inhibitions and Adjudications; Register of Entails; and Register of Hornings).
Chief Executive and Keeper of the Registers of Scotland, A. W. Ramage
Deputy Keeper, A. G. Rennie
Managing Director, F. Manson

LAW COMMISSION
Conquest House, 37–38 John Street, London WC1N 2BQ
Tel: 020-7453 1220; Fax: 020-7453 1297
Web: http://www.lawcom.gov.uk

The Law Commission was set up in 1965, under the Law Commissions Act 1965, to make proposals to the Government for the examination of the law in England

and Wales and for its revision where it is unsuited for modern requirements, obscure, or otherwise unsatisfactory. It recommends to the Lord Chancellor programmes for the examination of different branches of the law and suggests whether the examination should be carried out by the Commission itself or by some other body. The Commission is also responsible for the preparation of Consolidation and Statute Law (Repeals) Bills.
Chairman, The Hon. Mr Justice Carnwath, CVO
Commissioners, C. Harpum; Miss D. Faber;
Judge A. Wilkie, QC; Prof H. Beale
Secretary, M. W. Sayers

LAW OFFICERS' DEPARTMENTS
Legal Secretariat to the Law Officers, Attorney-General's Chambers, 9 Buckingham Gate, London SW1E 6JP
Tel: 020-7271 2400; Fax: 020-7271 2430;
Email: lslo@gtnet.gov.uk; Web: http://www.lslo.gov.uk
Attorney-General's Chambers, Royal Courts of Justice, Belfast BT1 3JY
Tel: 01232-235111; Fax: 01232-546049

The Law Officers of the Crown for England and Wales are the Attorney-General and the Solicitor-General. The Attorney-General, assisted by the Solicitor-General, is the chief legal adviser to the Government and is also ultimately responsible for all Crown litigation. He has overall responsibility for the work of the Law Officers' Departments (the Treasury Solicitor's Department, the Crown Prosecution Service, the Serious Fraud Office and the Legal Secretariat to the Law Officers). He has a specific statutory duty to superintend the discharge of their duties by the Director of Public Prosecutions (who heads the Crown Prosecution Service) and the Director of the Serious Fraud Office. The Director of Public Prosecutions for Northern Ireland is also responsible to the Attorney-General for the performance of his functions. The Attorney-General has additional responsibilities in relation to aspects of the civil and criminal law.
Attorney-General (*£90,125), The Lord Williams of
Mostyn, QC
Private Secretary, R. Cazalet
Parliamentary Private Secretary, M. Foster, MP
Solicitor-General, Ross Cranston, MP
Private Secretary, R. Cazalet
Legal Secretary (*G2*), D. Seymour
Deputy Legal Secretary (*G3*), S. Parkinson
In addition to a parliamentary salary of £48,371

LEARNING AND SKILLS COUNCIL
DfEE, Room W3B, Moorfoot, Sheffield S1 4PQ

The Learning and Skills Council will be established in April 2001 to replace the Further Education Funding Council and the Training and Enterprise Councils. It will be a non-departmental public body that will advise the government on future National Learning Targets and be responsible for the allocation of £6 billion of public money. Its objective is to ensure that high quality post-16 provision is available to meet the needs of employers, individuals and communities. The LSC will operate through 47 local departments, which will work to promote the equality of opportunity in the workplace, aiming to ensure that the needs of the most disadvantaged in the labour market are met. These local departments will in most cases have coterminous boundaries with Small business service franchises.

Chairman, B. Sanderson
Chief Executive, J. Harwood

LEGAL SERVICES COMMISSION
85 Gray's Inn Road, London WC1X 8TX
Tel: 020-7759 0000; Fax: 020-7759 0546
Web: http://www.legalservices.gov.uk

On 1 April 2000, the Legal Aid Board was replaced by the Legal Services Commission (LSC), which runs two schemes the civil scheme for funding civil cases as part of the Community Legal Service, and a scheme for funding criminal cases. Under the Community Legal Service the LSC has an important role in co-ordinating and working in a partnership with other funders of legal services, such as local authorities. The LSC also directly funds legal services for eligible clients.
The criminal scheme will continue largely as it was run by the Legal Aid Board until the creation of the Criminal Defence Service, when further changes will be made to the ways in which criminal cases are funded. The new scheme will ensure that people suspected or accused of a crime are properly represented, while securing better value for money than is possible under the legal aid scheme.
Chairman, P. G. Birch, CBE
Members, S. Orchard, CBE (*Chief Executive*); M. Barnes, CBE; R. Buxton (*Director of Operations*); A. Edwards; P. Ely; B. Harvey (*Director of Resources and Supplier Development*); Ms J. Herzog; Mrs S. Hewitt; Ms Y. Mosquito; R. Penn; J. Shearer

LIBRARIES

THE BRITISH LIBRARY
96 Euston Road, London NW1 2DB
Tel: 020-7412 7000

The British Library was established in 1973. It is the UK's national library and occupies a key position in the library and information network. The Library aims to serve scholarship, research, industry, commerce and all other major users of information. Its services are based on collections which include over 18 million volumes, 1 million discs, and 55,000 hours of tape recordings. The Library is now based at two sites: London (St Pancras and Colindale) and Boston Spa, W. Yorks. Government grant-in-aid to the British Library in 2000–1 is £84.48 million. The Library's sponsoring department is the Department for Culture, Media and Sport.
Access to the reading rooms at St Pancras is limited to holders of a British Library Reader's Pass; information about eligibility is available from the Reader Admissions Office. The exhibition galleries and public areas are open to all, free of charge.
Opening hours of services vary; some services may close for one week each year. Specific information should be checked by telephone.

BRITISH LIBRARY BOARD
Chairman, Dr J. M. Ashworth
Chief Executive and Deputy Chairman, Ms L. Brindley
Deputy Chief Executive, D. Russon
Director-General, Collections and Services, D. Bradbury
Part-time Members, H. Boyd-Carpenter, CVO;
Prof. M.Anderson, OBE, FBA, FRSE; Sir Matthew Farrer, GCVO; C. G. R. Leach, Ph.D.; B. Naylor; Dr Jessica Rawson, CBE, FBA; J. Ritblat; The Viscount Runciman of Doxford, CBE, FBA; P. Scherer; Prof. L. Colley

BRITISH LIBRARY, BOSTON SPA
Boston Spa, Wetherby, W. Yorks LS23 7BQ
Tel: 01937-546000

PUBLIC SERVICES, *Director*, M. Smith
Deputy Director, R. Smith
COLLECTION MANAGEMENT, *Director*, S. Ede
INFORMATION SYSTEMS. Tel: 01937-546879.

BRITISH LIBRARY, ST PANCRAS
96 Euston Road, London NW1 2DB
Tel: 020-7412 7000

PRESS AND PUBLIC RELATIONS. Tel: 020-7412 7111
EXHIBITIONS SERVICE AND VISITOR SERVICES.
Tel: 020-7412 7332
EDUCATION SERVICE, Tel: 020-7412 7797

READER SERVICES AND COLLECTION DEVELOPMENT.
Director, M. J. Crump
Reader Admissions. Tel: 020-7412 7677
Reader Services. Tel: 020-7412 7676
*West European Collections, Slavonic and East European
Collections, English Language Collections.*
Tel: 020-7412 7676
Newspaper Library, Colindale Avenue, London NW9 5HE.
Tel: 020-7412 7353

NATIONAL PRESERVATION OFFICE. Tel: 020-7412 7612

SPECIAL COLLECTIONS. Tel: 020-7412 7513.
Director, Dr A.Prochaska
Oriental and India Office Collections. Tel: 020-7412 7873
Western Manuscripts. Tel: 020-7412 7513
Map Library. Tel: 020-7412 7700
Music Library. Tel: 020-7412 7772
Philatelic Collections. Tel: 020-7412 7635
National Sound Archive. Tel: 020-7412 7440

SCIENCE, TECHNOLOGY AND BUSINESS
Science and Technology. Tel: 020-7412 7494/7496
British and EPO Patents. Tel: 020-7412 7919
Foreign Patents. Tel: 020-7412 7902
Business. Tel: 020-7412 7454
Social Policy Information Service. Tel: 020-7412 7536

NATIONAL LIBRARY OF SCOTLAND
George IV Bridge, Edinburgh EH1 1EW
Tel: 0131-226 4531; Fax: 0131-622 4803

The Library, which was founded as the Advocates' Library in 1682, became the National Library of Scotland in 1925. It is funded by the Scottish Executive. It contains about seven million books and pamphlets, 20,000 current periodicals, 350 newspaper titles and 120,000 manuscripts. It has an unrivalled Scottish collection.

The Reading Room is for reference and research which cannot conveniently be pursued elsewhere. Admission is by ticket issued to an approved applicant. Opening hours: Reading Room, weekdays, 9.30–8.30 (Wednesday, 10–8.30); Saturday 9.30–1. Map Library, weekdays, 9.30–5 (Wednesday, 10–5); Saturday 9.30–1. Exhibition, weekdays, 10–5; Saturday 10–5; Sunday 2–5. Scottish Science Library, weekdays, 9.30–5 (Wednesday, 10–8.30).
Chairman of the Trustees, Prof. Michael Anderson, OBE, PH.D., FBA, FRSE
Librarian and Secretary to the Trustees (G4), I. D. McGowan
Secretary of the Library (G6), M. C. Graham
Director of General Collections, vacant
Director of Special Collections, M. C. T. Simpson
Director of Public Services, A. M. Marchbank

NATIONAL LIBRARY OF WALES/LLYFRGELL GENEDLAETHOL CYMRU
Aberystwyth SY23 3BU
Tel: 01970-632800; Fax: 01970-615709

The National Library of Wales was founded by royal charter in 1907, and is funded by the National Assembly for Wales. It contains about four million printed books, 40,000 manuscripts, four million deeds and documents, numerous maps, prints and drawings, and a sound and moving image collection. It specialises in manuscripts and books relating to Wales and the Celtic peoples. It is the repository for pre-1858 Welsh probate records, manorial records and tithe documents, and certain legal records. Readers' room open weekdays, 9.30–6 (Saturday 9.30–5); closed first week of October. Admission by reader's ticket to the Reading Rooms but fee entry to the exhibition programme.
President, Dr R. Brinley Jones
Librarian (G4), A. M. W. Green
Heads of Departments (G6), M. W. Mainwaring
(*Administration and Technical Services*); G. Jenkins
(*Manuscripts and Records*); Dr W. R. M. Griffiths
(*Printed Books*); Dr D. H. Owen (*Pictures and Maps*)

LIGHTHOUSE AUTHORITIES

CORPORATION OF TRINITY HOUSE
Trinity House, Tower Hill, London EC3N 4DH
Tel: 020-7481 6900; Fax: 020-7480 7662

Trinity House, the first general lighthouse and pilotage authority in the kingdom, was granted its first charter by Henry VIII in 1514. The Corporation is the general lighthouse authority for England, Wales and the Channel Islands and maintains 72 lighthouses, 13 major floating aids to navigation (e.g. light vessels) and more than 420 buoys. The Corporation also has certain statutory jurisdiction over aids to navigation maintained by local harbour authorities and is responsible for dealing with wrecks dangerous to navigation, except those occurring within port limits or wrecks of HM ships.

The Trinity House Lighthouse Service is maintained out of the General Lighthouse Fund which is provided from light dues levied on ships calling at ports of the UK and the Republic of Ireland. The Corporation is also a deep-sea pilotage authority and a charitable organisation.

The affairs of the Corporation are controlled by a board of Elder Brethren and the Secretary. A separate board, which comprises Elder Brethren, senior staff and outside representatives, currently controls the Lighthouse Service. The Elder Brethren also act as nautical assessors in marine cases in the Admiralty Division of the High Court of Justice.

ELDER BRETHREN
Master, HRH The Prince Philip, Duke of Edinburgh, KG, KT
Deputy Master, Rear-Adm. P. B. Rowe, CBE, LVO
Wardens, Capt. C. M. C. Stewart; Sir Brian Shaw
Elder Brethren, HRH The Prince of Wales, KG, KT; HRH The Duke of York, CVO, ADC; Capt. Sir David Tibbits, DSC, RN; Capt. D. A. G. Dickens; Capt. J. E. Bury; Capt. J. A. N. Bezant, DSC, RD, RNR (retd.); Capt. D. J. Cloke; Capt. Sir Miles Wingate, KCVO; The Rt. Hon. Sir Edward Heath, KG, MBE, MP; Capt. I. R. C. Saunders; Capt. P. F. Mason, CBE; Capt. T. Woodfield, OBE; The Lord Simon of Glaisdale, PC; Capt. D. T. Smith, RN; Cdr. Sir Robin Gillett, Bt.,

GBE, RD, RNR; Capt. Sir Malcolm Edge, KCVO; The Lord Cuckney; Capt. D. J. Orr; The Lord Carrington, KG, GCMG, CH, MC, PC; The Lord Mackay of Clashfern, KT, PC; Sir Adrian Swire; The Lord Sterling of Plaistow, CBE, RNR; Cdr. M. J. Rivett-Carnac, RN; Adm. Sir Jock Slater, GCB, LVO, ADC; Capt. J. R. Burton-Hall, RD; Capt. I. Gibb, FRSA; Cdre P. J. Melson, CBE, RN; Capt. D. C. Glass

OFFICERS
Secretary, R. F. Dobb
Director of Finance, K. W. Clark
Director of Engineering, M. G. B. Wannell
Director of Administration, D. I. Brewer
Head of Human Resources, vacant
Legal and Insurance Manager, J. D. Price
Navigation Manager, Mrs K. Hossain
Head of Management Services, S. J. W. Dunning
Deputy Director of Engineering, P. N. Hyde
Senior Inspector of Shipping, J. R. Dunnett
Media and Communication Officer, H. L. Cooper

NORTHERN LIGHTHOUSE BOARD
84 George Street, Edinburgh EH2 3DA
Tel: 0131-473 3100; Fax: 0131-220 2093
Email: enquiries@nlb.org.uk
Web: http://www.nlb.org.uk
The Lighthouse Board is the general lighthouse authority for Scotland and the Isle of Man. The board owes its origin to an Act of Parliament passed in 1786. At present the Commissioners operate under the Merchant Shipping Act 1995 and are 19 in number.
The Commissioners control 84 major automatic lighthouses, 116 minor lights and many lighted and unlighted buoys. They have a fleet of two motor vessels.

COMMISSIONERS
The Lord Advocate; the Solicitor-General for Scotland; the Lord Provosts of Edinburgh, Glasgow and Aberdeen; the Provost of Inverness; the Convener of Argyll and Bute Council; the Sheriffs-Principal of North Strathclyde, Tayside, Central and Fife, Grampian, Highlands and Islands, South Strathclyde, Dumfries and Galloway, Lothians and Borders, and Glasgow and Strathkelvin; Capt. D. M. Cowell; Adm. Sir Michael Livesay, KCB; The Lord Maclay; P. MacKay, CB; Capt. K. MacLeod.

OFFICERS
Chief Executive, Capt. J. B. Taylor, RN
Director of Finance, D. Gorman
Director of Engineering, W. Paterson
Director of Operations and Navigational Requirements, P. J. Christmas

---

LOCAL COMMISSIONERS

COMMISSION FOR LOCAL ADMINISTRATION IN ENGLAND
21 Queen Anne's Gate, London SW1H 9BU
Tel: 020-7915 3210; Fax: 020-7233 0396
Local Commissioners (local government ombudsmen) are responsible for investigating complaints from members of the public against local authorities (but not town and parish councils); English Partnerships (planning matters only); Housing Action Trusts; education appeal committees; police aunthorities and certain other authorities. The Commissioners are appointed by the Crown on the recommendation of the Secretary of State for the Environment, Transport and the Regions.

Certain types of action are excluded from investigation, including personnel matters and commercial transactions unless they relate to the purchase or sale of land. Complaints can be sent direct to the Local Government Ombudsman or through a councillor, although the Local Government Ombudsman will not consider a complaint unless the council has had an opportunity to investigate and reply to a complainant.
A free leaflet *Complaint about the council? How to complain to the Local Government Ombudsman* is available from the Commission's office.
Chairman and Chief Executive of the Commission and Local Commissioner (£127,872), E. B. C. Osmotherly, CB
Vice-Chairman and Local Commissioner (£96,873), Mrs P. A. Thomas
Local Commissioner (£95,873), J. R. White
Member (*ex officio*), The Parliamentary Commissioner for Administration
Deputy Chief Executive and Secretary (£60,831), N. J. Karney

COMMISSION FOR LOCAL ADMINISTRATION IN WALES
Derwen House, Court Road, Bridgend CF31 1BN
Tel: 01656-661325; Fax: 01656-658317
Email: enquiries@ombudsman-wales.org
Web: http://www.ombudsman-wales.org
The Local Commissioner for Wales has similar powers to the Local Commissioners in England. The Commissioner is appointed by the Crown on the recommendation of the Secretary of State for Wales. A free leaflet *Your Local Ombudsman in Wales* is available from the Commission's office.
Local Commissioner, E. R. Moseley
Secretary, D. Bowen
Member (*ex officio*), The Parliamentary Commissioner for Administration

COMMISSIONER FOR LOCAL ADMINISTRATION IN SCOTLAND
23 Walker Street, Edinburgh EH3 7HX
Tel: 0131-225 5300; Fax: 0131-225 9495
Email: commissioner@ombudslgscot.org.uk
Web: http://www.ombudslgscot.org.uk

The Local Commissioner for Scotland has similar powers to the Local Commissioners in England, and is appointed by the Crown on the recommendation of the First Minister.
Local Commissioner, vacant
Deputy Commissioner and Secretary, Ms J. H. Renton

LONDON REGIONAL TRANSPORT
55 Broadway, London SW1H 0BD
Tel: 020-7222 5600

Subject to the financial objectives and principles approved by the Secretary of State for the Environment, Transport and the Regions, London Regional Transport has a general duty to provide or secure the provision of public transport services for Greater London.
Chairman (*non-executive*), Sir Malcolm Bates
Chief Executive, D. Tunnicliffe, CBE
Member, and Managing Director of London Transport Buses, C. Hodson, CBE
Member, and Managing Director of London Underground Ltd, D. Smith

LORD GREAT CHAMBERLAIN'S OFFICE
House of Lords, London SW1A 0PW
Tel: 020-7219 3100; Fax: 020-7219 2500

The Lord Great Chamberlain is a Great Officer of State, the office being hereditary since the grant of Henry I to the family of De Vere, Earls of Oxford. It is now a joint hereditary office between the Cholmondeley and Carington families. The Lord Great Chamberlain is responsible for the royal apartments of the Palace of Westminster, i.e. The Queen's Robing Room, the Royal Gallery and, in conjunction with the Lord Chancellor and the Speaker, Westminster Hall. The Lord Great Chamberlain has particular responsibility for the internal administrative arrangements within the House of Lords for State Openings of Parliament.
Lord Great Chamberlain, The Marquess of Cholmondeley
Secretary to the Lord Great Chamberlain,
  Gen. Sir Edward Jones, KCB, CBE
Clerks to the Lord Great Chamberlain, Ms J. Perodeau;
  Ms R. English

LORD PRIVY SEAL'S OFFICE
Privy Council Office, 68 Whitehall, London SW1A 2AT
Tel: 020-7270 3000

The Lord Privy Seal is a member of the Cabinet and Leader of the House of Lords. She has no departmental portfolio, but is a member of a number of domestic and economic Cabinet committees. She is responsible to the Prime Minister for the organisation of Government business in the House and has a responsibility to the House itself to advise it on procedural matters and other difficulties which arise.
Lord Privy Seal, Leader of the House of Lords and Minister
  for Women, The Baroness Jay of Paddington, PC
Principal Private Secretary, W. Connon
Private Secretary (House of Lords), Miss M. Robertson
Special Advisers, Ms J. Gibbons; Ms C. Cozens

MENTAL HEALTH ACT COMMISSION
Maid Marian House, 56 Hounds Gate,
Nottingham NG1 6BG
Tel: 0115-943 7100; Fax: 0115-943 7101

The Mental Health Act Commission was established in 1983. Its functions are to keep under review the operation of the Mental Health Act 1983; to visit and meet patients detained under the Act; to investigate complaints falling within the Commission's remit; to operate the consent to treatment safeguards in the Mental Health Act; to publish a biennial report on its activities; to monitor the implementation of the Code of Practice; and to advise Ministers. Commissioners are appointed by the Secretary of State for Health.
Chairman, Miss M. Clayton
Vice-Chairman, Prof. R. Williams
Acting Chief Executives, Ms C. Robinson; P. Hampshire

MILLENNIUM COMMISSION
Portland House, Stag Place, London SW1E 5EZ
Tel: 020-7880 2001; Fax: 020-7880 2000;
Email: info@millennium.gov.uk

The Millennium Commission was established in February 1994 and is accountable to the Department for Culture, Media and Sport. It is an independent body which distributes money from National Lottery proceeds to projects to mark the millennium.
Chairman, The Rt. Hon. Chris Smith, MP
Members, Prof. Heather Couper, FRAS; The Earl of
  Dalkeith; The Lord Glentoran, CBE; S. Jenkins;
  Ms F. Benjamin; The Rt. Hon. M. Heseltine, MP; The
  Rt. Hon. Dr Marjorie Mowlam, MP; Ms J. Donovan, CBE
Director, M. O'Connor

MUSEUMS

THE BRITISH MUSEUM
Great Russell Street, London WC1B 3DG
Tel: 020-7636 1555; Fax: 020-7323 8614

The British Museum houses the national collection of antiquities, ethnography, coins and paper money, medals, and prints and drawings. The British Museum may be said to date from 1753, when Parliament approved the holding of a public lottery to raise funds for the purchase of the collections of Sir Hans Sloane and the Harleian manuscripts, and for their proper housing and maintenance. The building (Montagu House) was opened in 1759. The present buildings were erected between 1823 and the present day, and the original collection has increased to its present dimensions by gifts and purchases. Total government grant-in-aid for 1999–2000 is £34.7 million.

BOARD OF TRUSTEES
Appointed by the Sovereign, HRH The Duke of
  Gloucester, KG, GCVO
Appointed by the Prime Minister, C. Allen-Jones;
  H. Askari; N. Barber; Prof. Gillian Beer, FBA;
  Sir John Boyd, KCMG; Sir John Browne, FREng.;
  The Rt. Hon Countess of Dalkeith; Sir Michael
  Hopkins, CBE, RA, RIBA; Sir Joseph Hotung;
  Prof. M. Kemp, FBA; D. Lindsell; C. McCall, QC;
  Sir Martin Rees, FRS, Dr Anna Ritchie; E. Salama
Nominated by the Learned Societies, Prof. Jean Thomas,
  CBE (*Royal Society*); T. Phillips, RA (*Royal Academy*);
  Sir Keith Thomas, FBA (*British Academy*); The Lord
  Renfrew of Kaimsthorn, FBA, FSA (*Society of Antiquaries*)
Appointed by the Trustees of the British Museum,
  G. C. Greene, CBE (*Chairman*); Sir David Attenborough,
  CH, CVO, CBE, FRS; Dr Jennifer Montagu, FBA;
  Sir Claus Moser, KCB, CBE, FBA; J. Tusa

OFFICERS
Director, Dr R. G. W. Anderson, FRSC, FSA
Managing Director, Ms S. Taverne
Director of Marketing and Public Affairs, Dr C. Homden
Director of Finance and Resources, C. Herring
Secretary, Mrs C. Nihoul Parker
Head of Exhibitions, G. A. L. House
Head of Media and Public Relations, A. E. Hamilton
Head of Design, Miss M. Hall, OBE
Head of Education, J. F. Reeve
Head of Administration, C. E. I. Jones
Head of Building Development and Planning, K. T. Stannard
Head of Building Management, T. R. A. Giles
Head of Finance, Miss S. E. Davies
Head of Personnel and Office Services, Miss B. A. Hughes
Head of Visitor Services, Ms L. Lee
Head of Membership Development, Ms S. Carthew
Head of Marketing Communications, M. Ladds
Director of Human Resources, I. Black

KEEPERS
Keeper of Prints and Drawings, A. V. Griffiths
Keeper of Coins and Medals, Dr A. M. Burnett

Keeper of Egyptian Antiquities, W. V. Davies
Keeper of Western Asiatic Antiquities, Dr J. E. Curtis
Keeper of Greek and Roman Antiquities, Dr D. J. R. Williams
Keeper of Medieval and Later Antiquities, J. Cherry
Keeper of Prehistory and Early Europe, vacant
Keeper of Japanese Antiquities, V. T. Harris
Keeper of Oriental Antiquities, R. J. Knox
Keeper of Ethnography, B. J. Mack
Keeper of Scientific Research, Dr S. G. E. Bowman
Keeper of Conservation, W. A. Oddy

IMPERIAL WAR MUSEUM
Lambeth Road, London SE1 6HZ
Tel: 020-7416 5000; Fax: 020-7416 5374

The Museum, founded in 1917, illustrates and records all aspects of the two world wars and other military operations involving Britain and the Commonwealth since 1914. It was opened in its present home, formerly Bethlem Hospital or Bedlam, in 1936. The Museum also administers HMS Belfast in the Pool of London, Duxford Airfield near Cambridge and the Cabinet War Rooms in Westminster.
   Total Government grant-in-aid for 1999–2000 is £11.662 million.

OFFICERS
Director-General, R. W. K. Crawford
Secretary and Director of Finance, J. Card
Assistant Directors, D. A. Needham (Administration);
   Miss K. J. Carmichael (Collections); G. Marsh
   (Planning and Development)
Director of Duxford Airfield, E. O. Inman, OBE
Director of HMS Belfast, E. J. Wenzel

KEEPERS
Public Services Division, C. Dowling, D.Phil.
Department of Documents, R. W. A. Suddaby
Department of Exhibits and Firearms, D. J. Penn
Department of Printed Books, R. Golland
Department of Art, Miss A. H. Weight
Department of Film, R. B. N. Smither
Department of Photographs, Ms B. Kinally
Department of Sound Records, Mrs M. A. Brooks
Department of Marketing and Trading, Miss A. Godwin
Curator of the Cabinet War Rooms, P. Reed

MUSEUM OF LONDON
London Wall, London EC2Y 5HN
Tel: 020-7600 3699; Fax: 020-7600 1058
Email: info@museumoflondon.org.uk
Web: http://www.museumoflondon.org.uk

The Museum of London illustrates the history of London from prehistoric times to the present day. It opened in 1976 and is based on the amalgamation of the former Guildhall Museum and London Museum. The Museum is controlled by a Board of Governors, appointed (nine each) by the Government and the Corporation of London. The Museum is currently funded jointly by the Department for Culture, Media and Sport and the Corporation of London, each contributing £4.360 million in 1999–2000.
Chairman of Board of Governors, R. Hambro
Director, Dr S. Thurley

NATIONAL ARMY MUSEUM
Royal Hospital Road, London SW3 4HT
Tel: 020-77300717; Fax: 020-7823 6573

The National Army Museum covers the history of five centuries of the British Army. It was established by royal charter in 1960. Total Government grant-in-aid for 1999–2000 is £3.2 million.

Director, I. G. Robertson
Assistant Directors, D. K. Smurthwaite; A. J. Guy;
   P. B. Boyden

NATURAL HISTORY MUSEUM
Cromwell Road, London SW7 5BD
Tel: 020-7942 5000

The Natural History Museum originates from the natural history departments of the British Museum, which grew extensively during the 19th century; in 1860 the natural history collection was moved from Bloomsbury to a new location. Part of the site of the 1862 International Exhibition in South Kensington was acquired for the new museum, and the Museum opened to the public in 1881. In 1963 the Natural History Museum became completely independent with its own board of trustees. The Walter Rothschild Zoological Museum, Tring, bequeathed by the second Lord Rothschild, has formed part of the Museum since 1938. The Geological Museum merged with the Natural History Museum in 1985. Total Government grant-in-aid for 2000–1 is £30.408 million.

BOARD OF TRUSTEES
Appointed by the Prime Minister, The Lord Oxburgh,
   KBE, Ph.D., FRS(Chairman); Sir Crispin Tickell, GCMG,
   KCVO; Dame Anne McLaren, DBE, FRS, FRCOG;
   Sir Richard Sykes, FRS; Miss J. Mayhew;
   Ms J. Bennett; Prof. M. Hassell, FRS; O. Stocken
Appointed by the Secretary of State for Culture, Media and
   Sport, Prof. C. Leaver, CBE, FRS, FRSE
Appointed by the Trustees of the Natural History Museum,
   The Lord Palumbo; Prof. Sir K. O'Nions, FRS;
   Prof. Linda Partridge, FRS, FRSE

SENIOR STAFF
Director, Dr N. R. Chalmers.
Director of Science, Prof. P. Henderson, D.Phil.
Head of Audit and Review, D. Thorpe
Keeper of Botany, Dr R. Bateman
Director of Development and Marketing, Ms S. Amert
Keeper of Entomology, Dr R. Vane-Wright
Director of Estates, G. Pellow
Head of Education and Exhibitions, Dr G. Clarke
Director of Finance, N. Greenwood
Head of Library and Information Services, Dr R. G. Lester
Keeper of Mineralogy, Prof. A. Fleet
Keeper of Palaeontology, Prof. S. K. Donovan
Director of Human Resources, D. Hill
Head of Visitor Services, Ms D. Carndlin
Keeper of Zoology, Prof. P. Rainbow
Policy and Planning Co-ordinator, P. Kirkman
Director, Tring Zoological Museum, Mrs T. Wild

NATIONAL MARITIME MUSEUM
Greenwich, London SE10 9NF
Tel: 020-8858 4422; Fax: 020-8312 6632

Established by Act of Parliament in 1934, the National Maritime Museum illustrates the maritime history of Great Britain in the widest sense, underlining the importance of the sea and its influence on the nation's power, wealth, culture, technology and institutions. The Museum is in three groups of buildings in Greenwich Park – the main building, the Queen's House (built by Inigo Jones, 1616–35) and the Royal Observatory (including Wren's Flamsteed House). In May 1999, a £20 million Heritage Lottery supported project opened 16 new galleries in a glazed courtyard in the Museum's west wing. Total Government grant-in-aid for 1999–2000 was £10.425 million.
Director, R. L. Ormond

NATIONAL MUSEUMS AND GALLERIES ON MERSEYSIDE
PO Box 33, 127 Dale Street, Liverpool L69 3LA
Tel: 0151-207 0001; Fax: 0151-478 4790

The Board of Trustees of the National Museums and Galleries on Merseyside is responsible for the Liverpool Museum, the Merseyside Maritime Museum (incorporating HM Customs and Excise National Museum), the Museum of Liverpool Life, the Lady Lever Art Gallery, the Walker Art Gallery and Sudley House, and the Conservation Centre. Total Government grant-in-aid for 2001–2 is £13.6 million.
Chairman of the Board of Trustees, D. McDonnell
Director, Sir Richard Foster
Keeper of Art Galleries, J. Treuherz
Keeper of Conservation, A. Durham
Keeper, Liverpool Museum, Ms L. Knowles
Keeper, Merseyside Maritime Museum and Museum of Liverpool Life, M. Stammers

NATIONAL MUSEUMS AND GALLERIES OF WALES/AMGUEDDFEYDD AC ORIELAU CENEDLAETHOL CYMRU
Cathays Park, Cardiff CF10 3NP
Tel: 029-2039 7951; Fax: 029-2037 3219
Email: post@nmgw.co.uk; Web: http://www/nmgw.ac.uk

The National Museums and Galleries of Wales comprise the National Museum and Gallery Cardiff, the Museum of Welsh Life St Fagans, the Roman Legionary Museum Caerleon, Turner House Gallery Penarth, the Welsh Slate Museum Llanberis, the Segontium Roman Museum Caernarfon and the Museum of the Welsh Woollen Industry Dre-fach, Felindre. Total funding from the National Assembly for Wales for 1999–2000 is £13.9 million.
President, M. C. T. Prichard, CBE
Vice-President, A. Thomas

OFFICERS
Director, A. Southall
Directors, C. Thomas (*Public Affairs*); ; Dr E. Wiliam (*Collections and Education and Deputy Director*); J. Williams-Davies, (*Museum of Welsh Life*); M. Tooby (*National Museum and Gallery*)
Keeper of Geology, M. G. Bassett, PH.D.
Keeper of Bio-diversity and Systematic Biology, Dr P. G. Oliver
Keeper of Art, O. Fairclough
Keeper of Archaeology, R. Brewer
Manager, Roman Legionary Museum, B. Lewis
Keeper in Charge, Turner House Gallery, O. Fairclough
Keeper, Welsh Slate Museum and Segontium Roman Museum, D.Roberts, PH.D.
Manager, Museum of the Welsh Woollen Industry, S. Moss

NATIONAL MUSEUMS OF SCOTLAND
Chambers Street, Edinburgh EH1 1JF
Tel: 0131-225 7534; Fax: 0131-220 4819

The National Museums of Scotland comprise the Royal Museum of Scotland, the Scottish United Services Museum, the Scottish Agricultural Museum, the Museum of Flight, Shambellie House Museum of Costume and the Museum of Scotland. Total funding from the Scottish Executive for 2000–1 is £14.2 million.

BOARD OF TRUSTEES
Chairman, Sir Robert Smith, FSA Scot.
Members, Prof T. Devine; Dr L. Glasser, MBE, FRSE; S. G. Gordon, CBE; G. Johnston, OBE, TD;
Ms C. Macaulay; N. McIntosh, CBE; Prof. A. Manning, OBE; Prof. J. Murray; Sir William Purves, CBE, DSO; Dr A. Ritchie, OBE; The Countess of Rosebery; I. Smith; The Lord Wilson of Tillyorn, GCMG

OFFICERS
Director, M. Jones, FSA, FSAScot., FRSA
Depute Director (Collections) and Keeper of History and Applied Art, Miss D. Idiens, FRSA, FSA Scot.
Development Director, C. McCallum
Keeper of Archaeology, D. V. Clarke, PH.D., FSA, FSA Scot.
Keeper of Geology and Zoology, M. Shaw, D.Phil.
Keeper of Social and Technological History, G. Sprott
Head of Public Affairs, Ms M. Bryden
Head of Museum Services, S. R. Elson, FSA Scot.

RESOURCE: THE COUNCIL FOR MUSEUMS, ARCHIVES AND LIBRARIES
16 Queen Anne's Gate, London SW1H 9AA
Tel: 020-7233 4200; Fax: 020-7233 3686
Web: http://www.resource.gov.uk

On 1 April 2000, the Museums and Galleries Commission and the Library and Information Commission merged to form Resource: The Council for Museums, Archives and Libraries. This new strategic agency will work with museums, libraries and archives across the UK.
Chairman, Lord Evans
Chief Executive, N. Mackay
Board Members, L. Grossman; Ms K. Knight; V. Gray; M. Wood; A. Chowdhury; Dr M. Crozier; V. Griffiths; N. Hodgson; M. Jones; N. MacGregor; E. J. Ryder; M. Stevenson; Prof L. Young

ROYAL AIR FORCE MUSEUM
Grahame Park Way, London NW9 5LL
Tel: 0870 870 4868; Fax: 020-7942 4447

Situated on the former airfield at RAF Hendon, the Museum illustrates the development of aviation from before the Wright brothers to the present-day RAF. Total Government grant-in-aid for 1999–2000, including funding for the aerospace museum at Cosford, is £3.7 million.
Director, Dr M. A. Fopp
Assistant Directors, H. Hall; A. Wright
Senior Keeper, P. Elliott

THE SCIENCE MUSEUM
Exhibition Road, London SW7 2DD
Tel: 0870 870 4868; Fax: 020-7942 4447

The Science Museum, part of the National Museum of Science and Industry, houses the national collections of science, technology, industry and medicine. The Museum began as the science collection of the South Kensington Museum and first opened in 1857. In 1883 it acquired the collections of the Patent Museum and in 1909 the science collections were transferred to the new Science Museum, leaving the art collections with the Victoria and Albert Museum. The Wellcome wing was recently opened in July 2000.

Some of the Museum's commercial aircraft, agricultural machinery, and road and rail transport collections are at Wroughton, Wilts. The National Museum of Science and Industry also incorporates the National Railway Museum, York and the National Museum of Photography, Film and Television, Bradford.

Total Government grant-in-aid for 2000–1 is £24,329 million.

OFFICERS
Director, Dr L. Sharp
Head of Personnel and Legal Services, A. Mather
Head of Finance, Ms A. Caine
Head of Information Systems, S. Gordon
Head of Estates, J. Bevin
Assistant Director and Head of Collections Division, D. Swade
Head of Physical Sciences and Engineering Group (acting),
 Dr A. Q. Morton
Head of Life and Communications Technologies Group,
 Dr R. F. Bud
Head of Collections Management Group, Dr S. Keene
Assistant Director and Head of Public Affairs Division,
 C. M. Pemberton
Head of Corporate Relations, F. Kirk
Head of Commercial Development, M. Sullivan
Head of Marketing and Communications, R. Hopson
Head of Wellcome Wing Commercial and Access, B. Jones
*Assistant Director, Wellcome Wing Project Director and Head
 of Science Communication Division*, Prof J. R. Durant
Head of Education and Programmes, Dr R. Jackson
Head of Exhibition and Wellcome Wing Content,
 Dr G. Farmelo
Head of Design, T. Molloy
Head of National Railway Museum, A. Scott
*Head of National Museum of Photography, Film
 and Television*, Ms A. Nevill

VICTORIA AND ALBERT MUSEUM
Cromwell Road, London SW7 2RL
Tel: 020-7942 2000

The Victoria and Albert Museum is the national museum of fine and applied art and design. It descends directly from the Museum of Manufactures, which opened in Marlborough House in 1852 after the Great Exhibition of 1851. The Museum was moved in 1857 to become part of the South Kensington Museum. It was renamed the Victoria and Albert Museum in 1899. It also houses the National Art Library and Print Room.

The Museum administers three branch museums: the National Museum of Childhood in Bethnal Green, the Theatre Museum in Covent Garden, and the Wellington Museum at Apsley House. The museum in Bethnal Green was opened in 1872 and the building is the most important surviving example of the type of glass and iron construction used by Paxton for the Great Exhibition. Total Government grant-in-aid for 2000–1 is £30.458 million.

OFFICERS
Director, Dr A. C. N. Borg, CBE, FSA
Assistant Director, J. W. Close
Senior Chief Curator, Dr D. Swallow
Chief Curator, Ceramics and Glass, Dr O. Watson
Director of Collections, vacant
Director of Collections Services, vacant
Head of Conservation, Dr J. Ashley-Smith
Director of Corporate Communications, vacant
Director of Development, Mrs L. Morrison
Director of Facilities Management, R. P. Whitehouse
Chief Curator, Far Eastern, Miss R. Kerr
Director of Finance and Central Services, Miss R. M. Sykes
Chief Curator, Furniture and Woodwork, C. Wilk
Chief Curator, Indian and South-East Asian, vacant
Acting Head of Information Systems Services, A. Mabogunje
Director of Learning and Visitor Services, D. Anderson, OBE
Director of Major Projects, Mrs G. F. Miles
Chief Curator, Metalwork, Silver and Jewellery, vacant
Chief Librarian, National Art Library, vacant
Director of Personnel, Mrs G. Henchley
Chief Curator, Prints, Drawings and Paintings,
 Miss S. B. Lambert
Head of Records and Collections Services, A. Seal
Head of Research, P. Greenhalgh
Head of Safety and Security, R. Bland
Chief Curator, Sculpture, Dr P. E. D. Williamson
Chief Curator, Textiles and Dress, Mrs V. D. Mendes
Managing Director, V. and A. Enterprises Ltd, M. Cass
Director of the National Museum of Childhood, Ms D. Lees
Director of the Theatre Museum, Miss M. Benton
Head of the Wellington Museum, Miss A. Robinson

NATIONAL AUDIT OFFICE
157–197 Buckingham Palace Road, London SW1W 9SP
Tel: 020-7798 7000; Fax: 020-7828 3774
Email: nao@gtnet.gov.uk; Web: http://www.noa.gov.uk
Audit House, 23–24 Park Place, Cardiff CF1 3BA
Tel: 01222-378661; Fax: 01222-388415

The National Audit Office came into existence under the National Audit Act 1983 to replace and continue the work of the former Exchequer and Audit Department. The Act reinforced the Office's total financial and operational independence from the Government and brought its head, the Comptroller and Auditor-General, into a closer relationship with Parliament as an officer of the House of Commons.

The National Audit Office provides independent information, advice and assurance to Parliament and the public about all aspects of the financial operations of Government departments and many other bodies receiving public funds. It does this by examining and certifying the accounts of these organisations and by regularly publishing reports to Parliament on the results of its value for money investigations of the economy, efficiency and effectiveness with which public resources have been used. The National Audit Office is also the auditor by agreement of the accounts of certain international and other organisations. In addition, the Office authorises the issue of public funds to Government departments.

Comptroller and Auditor-General, Sir John Bourn, KCB
 Private Secretary, M. Davies
Deputy Comptroller and Auditor-General, T. Burr
Deputy Auditor-General, M. C. Pfleger
Assistant Auditors-General, J. Colman; J. Marshall;
 Miss C. Mawhood; M. Sinclair; Ms W. Kenway-Smith

NATIONAL CONSUMER COUNCIL
20 Grosvenor Gardens, London SW1W 0DH
Tel: 020-7730 3469; Fax: 020-7730 0191
Web: http://www.ncc.org.uk

The National Consumer Council (NCC) was set up by the Government in 1975 to give an independent voice to consumers in the UK. Its role is to advocate the consumer interest to decision-makers in national and local government, industry and regulatory bodies, business and the professions. It does this through a combination of research and campaigning. NCC is a non-profit making company limited by guarantee and is largely funded by grant-in-aid from the Department of Trade and Industry.
Chairman, D. Hatch, CBE
Vice-Chairman, Mrs D. Hutton, CBE
Director, Ms A. Bradley

NATIONAL ENDOWMENT FOR SCIENCE, TECHNOLOGY AND THE ARTS (NESTA)
Fishmongers' Chambers, 110 Upper Thames Street, London EC4R 3JT
Tel: 020-7645 9500; Fax: 020-7645 9501

The National Endowment for Science, Technology and the Arts (NESTA) was established under the National Lottery Act 1998 with a £200 million endowment from the proceeds of the National Lottery. Its aims are to help talented individuals; to enable innovative ideas to be successfully commercially exploited; and to promote public knowledge of science, technology and the arts.
Chairman, The Lord Puttnam, CBE
Trustees, Dame Bridget Ogilvie, DBE; Prof. Sir Martin Rees, FRS; Dr C. Evans, OBE; Ms C. Vorderman; D. Wardell; F. Matarasso; The Baroness McIntosh of Hudnall; Ms C. McKeever; Ms J. Kirkpatrick; Ms S. Hunter; D. Alexander; D. Wanless
Chief Executive, J. Newton

NATIONAL HERITAGE MEMORIAL FUND
7 Holbein Place, London SW1W 8NR
Tel: 020-7591 6000; Fax: 020-7591 6001

The National Heritage Memorial Fund is an independent body established in 1980 as a memorial to those who have died for the UK. The Fund is empowered by the National Heritage Act 1980 to give financial assistance towards the cost of acquiring, maintaining or preserving land, buildings, works of art and other objects of outstanding interest which are also of importance to the national heritage. The Fund is administered by 15 trustees who are appointed by the Prime Minister.
The National Lottery Act 1993 designated the Fund as distributor of the heritage share of proceeds from the National Lottery. As a result, the Fund now operates two funds: the Heritage Memorial Fund and the Heritage Lottery Fund. The Heritage Memorial Fund receives an annual grant from the Department for Culture, Media and Sport; the grant for 1999–2000 is £2.5 million.
Chairman, Dr E. Anderson
Trustees, Prof. C. Baines; R. Boas; Sir Richard Carew Pole, Bt.; Sir Angus Grossart; Mrs C. Hubbard; J. Keegan; Mrs P. Lankester; Prof. P. Miss S. Palmer; Earl of Dalkeith; Prof. T. Pritchard; Ms M. A. Sieghart; Dame Sue Tinson, DBE
Director, Ms A. Case

NATIONAL INVESTMENT AND LOANS OFFICE
1 King Charles Street, London SW1A 2AP
Tel: 020-7270 3861; Fax: 020-7270 6075

The National Investment and Loans Office is a non-ministerial Government department which was set up in 1980 by the merger of the National Debt Office and the Public Works Loan Board. The Office provides the staff and administrative support for the National Debt Commissioners, the Public Works Loan Commissioners and the Office of HM Paymaster-General. The National Debt Office is responsible for managing the investment portfolios of certain public funds and the management of some residual operations relating to the national debt. The function of the Public Works Loan Board is to make loans from the National Loans Fund to local authorities and certain other statutory bodies, primarily for capital purposes.
The Office of HM Paymaster-General has continuously existed in its present form since 1836; the Paymaster-General has responsibilities assigned from time to time by the Prime Minister and is currently a Treasury minister. The Assistant Paymaster-General is responsible for the banking and financial information services provided to the Government and public sector bodies by the Office of HM Paymaster-General.
Director, Ian Peattie
Establishment Officer, D. Hockey

NATIONAL DEBT OFFICE
020-7270 3868
Comptroller-General, Ian Peattie

PUBLIC WORKS LOAN BOARD
020-7270 3874
Chairman, A. D. Loehnis, CMG
Deputy Chairman, Miss V. J. DiPalma, OBE
Other Commissioners, Dame Sheila Masters, DBE; Mrs R. V. Hale; J. A. Parkes, CBE; J. Andrews; B. Tanner, CBE; T. Fellowes; Mrs R. Terry; D. W. Midgley; L. M. Nippers; Mrs S. Wood
Secretary, Ian Peattie
Assistant Secretary, M. Frankel

OFFICE OF HM PAYMASTER-GENERAL
020-7270 6074
Paymaster-General, Dawn Primarolo, MP
Assistant Paymaster-General, Ian Peattie
Head of Banking, Lee Palmer
BANKING OPERATIONS, National Investment and Loans Office, Sutherland House, Russell Way, Crawley, W. Sussex RH10 1UH. Tel: 01293-604410.
Banking Manager, Peter Harris

NATIONAL LOTTERY CHARITIES BOARD
St Vincent House, 16 Suffolk Street, London SW1Y 4NL
Tel: 020-7747 5299; Fax: 020-7747 5220
Web: http://www.nlcb.org.uk

The Board was set up under the National Lottery Act 1993 to distribute funds from the Lottery to support charitable, benevolent and philanthropic organisations. The chair and members are appointed by the Secretary of State for Culture, Media and Sport. The Board's main aim is to help meet the needs of those at greatest disadvantage in society and to improve the quality of life in the community through grants programmes in the UK

and an international grants programme for UK-based agencies working abroad.
Chair, Lady Brittan, CBE
Deputy Chairman, Sir Adam Ridley
Members, Mrs T.Baring, CBE; A.Bhatia, OBE; S. Burkeman; J. Carroll; Mrs A. Clark; Ms K. Hampton; T. Jones, OBE; Ms A. Jordan; Mrs B. Lowndes, MBE; R. Martineau; W. Osborne; R. Partington; J. Simpson, OBE; N. Stewart, OBE; Mrs E. Watkins
Chief Executive, T. Hornsby

NATIONAL LOTTERY COMMISSION
2 Monck Street, London SW1P 2BQ
Tel: 020-7227 2000; Fax: 020-7227 2005;
Web: http://www.natlotcomm.gov.uk

The National Lottery Commission replaced the Office of the National Lottery (OFLOT) in April 1999 under the National Lottery Act 1998. The Commission is responsible for the granting, varying and enforcing of licences to run the National Lottery. Its duties are to ensure that the National Lottery is run with all due propriety, that the interests of players are protected, and, subject to these two objectives, that returns to the 'good causes' are maximised.
Chairman, Dame Helena Shovelton, DBE
Commissioners, Ms H. Blume; Ms H. Spicer; R. Squire; B. Pomeroy
Chief Executive, M. Harris
Director of Licensing, K. Jones
Director of Compliance and Resources, Ms M. Phillips
For details of National Lottery operations, *see* Lotteries and Gaming section

NATIONAL PHYSICAL LABORATORY
Queens Road, Teddington, Middx TW11 0LW
Tel: 020-8977 3222; Fax: 020-8943 6458

The Laboratory is the UK's national standards laboratory. It develops, maintains and disseminates national measurement standards for physical quantities such as mass, length, time, temperature, voltage, force and pressure. It also conducts underpinning research on engineering materials and information technology and disseminates good measurement practice. It is Government-owned but contractor-operated.
Managing Director, Dr R. McGuiness
Director of Marketing and Knowledge Transfer, D. C. Richardson

NATIONAL RADIOLOGICAL PROTECTION BOARD
Chilton, Didcot, Oxon OX11 0RQ
Tel: 01235-831600; Fax: 01235-833891
Web: http://www.nrpb.org.uk

The National Radiological Protection Board is an independent statutory body created by the Radiological Protection Act 1970. It is the national point of authoritative reference on radiological protection for both ionising and non-ionising radiations, and has issued recommendations on limiting human exposure to electromagnetic fields and radiation from a range of sources, including X-rays, the Sun, base stations and mobile phones. Its sponsoring department is the Department of Health.
Chairman, Sir Walter Bodmer, Ph.D., FRCPath., FRS
Director, Prof. R. H. Clarke

NATIONAL SAVINGS
375 Kensington High Street, London W14 8SD
Tel: 020-7605 9300;
Web: http://www.nationalsavings.co.uk

National Savings was established as a Government department in 1969. It became an executive agency of the Treasury in 1996 and is responsible for the design, marketing and administration of savings and investment products for personal savers and investors. In April 1999 Siemens Business Services took over all the back office functions at National Savings.
Chief Executive, P. Bareau
Personnel Director, D. S. Speedie
Finance Director, R. Douglas
Commercial Director, C. Moxey
Sourcing Director, Ms J. Bevan
For details of schemes, *see* National Savings section

NEW OPPORTUNITIES FUND
Heron House, 322 High Holborn, London WC1V 7PW
Tel: 020-7211 1800; Fax: 020-7211 1750;
Email: enquiries@nof.org.uk
Web: http://www.nof.org.uk

The New Opportunities Fund is a Lottery Distributor created to distribute grants to health, education and environment projects across the UK. The New Opportunities Fund intends to fund projects that will improve people's quality of life, address the needs of those people who are most disadvantaged in society, encourage community participation and complement relevant local and national strategies and programmes.
Chair of the Board, The Baroness Pitkeathley
Members of the Board, Ms J. Barrow; Prof. E. Bolton, CB; Ms N. Clarke; Prof. A. Patmore, CBE; D. Mackie; D. Campbell; Prof. S. Griffiths; Ms M. Letts; Ms R. McDonough
Chief Executive, S. Dunmore

NORTHERN IRELAND AUDIT OFFICE
106 University Street, Belfast BT7 1EU
Tel: 02890-251000; Fax: 02890-251106

The primary aim of the Northern Ireland Audit Office is to provide independent assurance, information and advice to Parliament on the proper accounting for Northern Ireland departmental and certain other public expenditure, revenue, assets and liabilities; on regularity and propriety; and on the economy, efficiency and effectiveness of the use of resources.
Comptroller and Auditor-General for Northern Ireland, J. M. Dowdall

NORTHERN IRELAND HUMAN RIGHTS COMMISSION
Temple Court, 39–41 North Street, Belfast BT1 1NA
Tel: 028-9024 3987; Fax: 028-9024 7844
Email: nihrc@belfast.org.uk; Web: http://www.nihrc.org

The Northern Ireland Human Rights Commission was set up in March 1999. Its main functions are to keep under the review the law and practice relating to human rights in Northern Ireland, to advise the Government and to promote an awareness of human rights in Northern Ireland. The Commission consists of one full-time

commissioner and nine part-time commissioners, all appointed by the Secretary of State for Northern Ireland.
Chief Commissioner (£55,000), Prof. B. Dickson
Commissioners (£8,000 each), Prof. C. Bell;
Ms M-A. Dinsmore, QC; T. Donnelly, MBE;
The Revd H. Good, OBE; Prof. T. Hadden;
Ms A. Hegarty; Ms P. Kelly;
Ms I. McCormack; F. McGuinness

OCCUPATIONAL PENSIONS REGULATORY AUTHORITY

Invicta House, Trafalgar Place, Brighton BN1 4DW
Tel: 01273-627600; Fax: 01273-627760
Email: helpdesk@opra.gov.uk

The Occupational Pensions Regulatory Authority (OPRA) was set up under the Pensions Act 1995 and became fully operational on 6 April 1997. It is the independent, statutory regulator of occupational pension schemes in the UK.
Chairman, J. Hayes, CBE
Chief Executive, Mrs C. Instance

OFFICE FOR NATIONAL STATISTICS

1 Drummond Gate, London SW1V 2QQ
Tel: 020-7533 5888; Email: info@statistic.gov.uk
Web: http://www.statistics.gov.uk

The Office for National Statistics was created in 1996 by the merger of the Central Statistical Office and the Office of Population, Censuses and Surveys. It is an executive agency of the Treasury and is responsible for preparing and interpreting key economic statistics for Government policy; collecting and publishing business statistics; publishing annual and monthly statistical digests; providing researchers, analysts and other customers with a statistical service; administration of the marriage laws and local registration of births, marriages and deaths in England and Wales; provision of population estimates and projections and statistics on health and other demographic matters in England and Wales; population censuses in England and Wales; surveys for Government departments and public bodies; and promoting these functions within the UK, the European Union and internationally to provide a statistical service to meet European Union and international requirements.

Following the publication of the White Paper, 'Building Trust in Statistics', National Statistics was launched in June 2000. Headed by the National Statistician, and overseen by an independent Statistics Commission, the National Statistics 'brand' encompasses the output of the ONS, plus many of the key public interest statistics produced by other Government departments.
National Statistician, Registrar General for England and Wales and the Head of the Government Statistical Service, Len Cook
Directors, Ms S. Linacre (*Methods and Quality*);
A. Goldsmith (*Finance and Corporate Affairs, also Principal Finance Officer*); J. Kidgell (*Economic Statistics*); J. Pullinger (*Social Statistics*)
Principal Establishment Officer, E. Williams
Head of Communication, Ms H. Rafalowska
Parliamentary Clerk, J. Bailey

FAMILY RECORDS CENTRE, 1 Myddelton Street, London EC1R 1UW. Tel: 020-8392 5300. Open Mon., Wed., Fri. 9 a.m.–5 p.m.; Tues. 10 a.m.–7 p.m.; Thurs. 9 a.m.–7 p.m.; Sat. 9.30 a.m.–5 p.m.

OFFICE FOR STANDARDS IN EDUCATION (OFSTED)

Alexandra House, 33 Kingsway, London WC2B 6SE
Tel: 020-7421 6800; Fax: 020-7421 6707

OFSTED is a non-ministerial Government department established in 1992 to keep the Secretary of State and the public informed about the standards and management of schools in England, and to establish and monitor an independent inspection system for maintained schools in England. *See also* Education section.
HM Chief Inspector, C. Woodhead
Directors of Inspection, M. J. Tomlinson, CBE; D. Taylor
Director of Policy, Planning and Resources,
  Miss J. M. Phillips, CBE

DIVISION MANAGERS
Personnel Management, A. White
Contracts, C. Bramley
Communications, Media and Public Relations, J. Lawson
Information Systems, M. Worthy
Administrative Support and Estate Management, K. Francis
Inspection Quality, P. Matthews
LEA Inspections, D. Singleton
School Improvement, Ms E. Passmore, OBE
Nursery and Primary, K. Lloyd
Secondary and Independent, M. Raleigh
Post-Compulsory, S. Grix
Special Educational Needs, C. Marshall
Research, Analysis and International, Ms C. Agambar
Teacher Education and Training, C. Gould
Nursery Education Scheme, D. Bradley
Subject Specialist Advisers, N. Bufton; B. Ponchaud;
  A.Dobson; M. Ive; P. Smith; Ms J. Mills; C. Stretch;
  P. Jones; J. Hertrich; Ms B. Wintersgill; G. Goldstein
There are about 200 HM Inspectors

OFFICE FOR THE REGULATION OF ELECTRICITY AND GAS

Brookmount Buildings, 42 Fountain Street,
Belfast BT1 5EE
Tel: 028-90-31 1575 (*Electricity*); 028-90-31 4212 (*Gas*);
Fax: 028-9031 1740; Email: ofreg@nics.gov.uk;
Web: http://www.ofreg.nics.gov.uk

The Office for the Regulation of Electricity and Gas (OFREG) is the combined regulatory body for the electricity and gas supply industries in Northern Ireland.
Director-General of Electricity Supply and Director-General of Gas for Northern Ireland, D. B. McIldoon

OFFICE OF GAS AND ELECTRICITY MARKETS

9 Millbank, London
Tel: 020-7828 0898; Fax: 020-7932 1600
SCOTLAND: Regent Court, 70 West Regent Street,
Glasgow G2 2QZ
Tel: 0141-331 2678; Fax: 0141-331 2777

The Office of Gas and Electricity Markets (Ofgem) was formed in 1999 by the merger of the separate regulators for electricity and gas set up under the Electricity Act 1989 and the Gas Act 1986 respectively. It is the independent regulatory body for the electricity and gas supply industries in England, Scotland and Wales. Its functions are to promote competition and to protect customers' interests in relation to prices, security of supply and quality of services.

Director-General, C. McCarthy
Deputy Directors-General, J. Neilson (*Customers and Supply*); Dr Eileen Marshall, CBE (*Competition and Trading Arrangements*); R. Morse (*Regulation and Financial Affairs*)
Chief Operating Officer, Ms G. Whittington
Director, Public Affairs, Ms S. Harrison

OFFICE OF FAIR TRADING

Fleetbank House, 2–6 Salisbury Square,
London EC4Y 8JX
Tel: 020-7211 8000; Fax: 020-7211 8800

The Office of Fair Trading is a non-ministerial Government department headed by the Director-General of Fair Trading. It keeps commercial activities in the UK under review and seeks to protect consumers against unfair trading practices. The Director-General's consumer protection duties under the Fair Trading Act 1973, together with his responsibilities under the Consumer Credit Act 1974, the Estate Agents Act 1979, the Control of Misleading Advertisements Regulations 1988, and the Unfair Terms in Consumer Contracts Regulations 1999, are administered by the Office's Consumer Affairs Division. The Competition Policy Division is concerned with monopolies and mergers (under the Fair Trading Act 1973) and the Director-General's other responsibilities for competition matters, including those under the Competition Act 1998, the Financial Services Act 1986 and the Broadcasting Act 1990. The Office is the UK competent authority on the application of the European Commission's competition rules, and also liaises with the Commission on consumer protection initiatives.
Director-General, J. Bridgeman

CONSUMER AFFAIRS DIVISION
Director (G3), Miss C. Banks
Assistant Directors (G5), R. Watson; M. Graham; D. Wray

COMPETITION POLICY DIVISION
Divisional Director (G3), Mrs M. J. Bloom
Branch Directors (G5), A. J. White; A. Walker-Smith; E. L. Whitehorn; S. Wood; Dr D. Mason; Dr G. Davis; A. Williams
Chief Economist, P. G. A. Banford

LEGAL DIVISION
Divisional Director (G3), Miss P. Edwards
Branch Directors (G5), M. A. Khan; S. Brindley
Establishment and Finance Officer (G5), Mrs R. Heyhoe
Chief Information Officer (G6), D. Hill

OFFICE OF MANPOWER ECONOMICS

Oxford House, 76 Oxford Street, London W1N 9FD
Tel: 020-7467 7244; Fax: 020-7467 7248

The Office of Manpower Economics was set up in 1971. It is an independent non-statutory organisation which is responsible for servicing independent review bodies which advise on the pay of various public service groups the Pharmacists Review Panel and the Police Negotiating Board. The Office is also responsible for servicing *ad hoc* bodies of inquiry and for undertaking research into pay and associated matters as requested by the Government.
OME Director, M. J. Horsman
Director, Health Secretariat, and OME Deputy Director, G. S. Charles

Director, Armed Forces' Secretariat, Mrs C. Haworth
Director, Senior Salaries Secretariat,
Ms. R. McCarthy-Ward *Director, School Teachers' Secretariat*, Mrs E. M. Melling
Press Liaison Officer, M. C. Cahill

OFFICE OF TELECOMMUNICATIONS (OFTEL)

50 Ludgate Hill, London EC4M 7JJ
Tel: 020-7634 8700; Fax: 020-7 634 8943

The Office of Telecommunications (Oftel) is the regulator, or 'watchdog', for the UK telecommunications industry. Oftel is a Government department but is independent of ministerial control. Oftel's aim is for customers to get the best deal in terms of quality, choice and value for money. Its strategy to achieve this goal is through four objectives: effective competition benefiting consumers; well informed consumers; adequately protected consumers; and prevention of significant anti-competitive practice. Oftel is responsible for ensuring that holders of telecommunications licences comply with their licence conditions, and has powers under the Competition Act 1999 to deal with anti-competitive practices and cartels. The Director-General has a duty to consider all reasonable complaints about telecommunications services.
Director-General, D. Edmonds
Director of Operations, Miss A. Lambert
Director of Regulatory Policy, C. Kenny
Director of Compliance, vacant
Director of Technology, P. Walker
Director of Strategy and Forecasting, A. Bell
Director of Business Support, D. Smith
Director of Communications, D. Stroud

OFFICE OF THE DATA PROTECTION COMMISSIONER

Wycliffe House, Water Lane, Wilmslow,
Cheshire SK9 5AF
Tel: 01625-545745; Fax: 01625-524510
Email: mail@dataprotection.gov.uk
Web: http://www.dataprotection.gov.uk

The Office of the Data Protection Registrar was created by the Data Protection Act 1984; the Registrar was renamed the Data Protection Commissioner on 1 March 2000 under the Data Protection Act 1998. It is the Commissioner's duty to compile and maintain the register of data controllers and to provide facilities for members of the public to examine the register; to promote observance of data protection principles; to disseminate information about the Data Protection Act; to encourage the production of codes of practice by trade associations and other bodies; to guide data users in complying with data protection principles; and to co-operate with other parties to the Council of Europe Convention and act as UK authority for the purposes of Article 13 of the Convention.
Commissioner, Mrs E. France

OFFICE OF THE LEGAL SERVICES OMBUDSMAN

22 Oxford Court, Oxford Street, Manchester M2 3WQ
Tel: 0845 601 0794; Fax: 0161-236 2651
Email: enquiries.olso@gtnet.gov.uk

The Legal Services Ombudsman is appointed by the Lord Chancellor under the Courts and Legal Services Act 1990 to oversee the handling of complaints against solicitors, barristers, licensed conveyancers and legal executives by their professional bodies. A complainant must first complain to the relevant professional body before raising the matter with the Ombudsman. The Ombudsman is independent of the legal profession and her services are free of charge.

Legal Services Ombudsman, Ms A. Abraham
Secretary, S. D. Entwisle

OFFICE OF THE SCOTTISH LEGAL SERVICES OMBUDSMAN
Mulberry House, 16–22 Picardy Place,
Edinburgh EH1 3JT
Tel: 0131-556 5574; Fax: 0131-556 1519;
Email: complaints@legal-ombud.org.uk
Web: http://www.scot-legal.ombud.org.uk

Scottish Legal Services Ombudsman, G. S. Watson

OFFICE OF THE LORD ADVOCATE
Crown Office, 25 Chambers Street, Edinburgh EH1 1LA
Tel: 0131-226 2626; Fax: 0131-226 6910

The Law Officers for Scotland are the Lord Advocate and the Solicitor-General for Scotland.
Lord Advocate, The Rt. Hon. Colin Boyd, QC
Solicitor-General for Scotland, Neil F. Davidson, QC
    Private Secretary to the Law Officers, J. Gibbons

OFFICE OF THE PARLIAMENTARY
COMMISSIONER FOR ADMINISTRATION
AND HEALTH SERVICE COMMISSIONER
Millbank Tower, Millbank, London SW1P 4QP
Tel: 0845-015 4033; Fax: 020-7217 4000
Web: http://www.ombudsman.org.uk

The Parliamentary Commissioner for Administration (the Parliamentary Ombudsman) is independent of Government and is an officer of Parliament. He is responsible for investigating complaints referred to him by MPs from members of the public who claim to have sustained injustice in consequence of maladministration by or on behalf of Government departments and certain non-departmental public bodies. In March 1999 an additional 158 public bodies were brought within the jurisdiction of the Parliamentary Commissioner. Certain types of action by Government departments or bodies are excluded from investigation. The Parliamentary Commissioner is also responsible for investigating complaints, referred by MPs, alleging that access to official information has been wrongly refused under the Code of Practice on Access to Government Information 1994.

The Health Service Commissioners (the Health Service Ombudsmen) for England, for Scotland and for Wales are responsible for investigating complaints against National Health Service authorities and trusts that are not dealt with by those authorities to the satisfaction of the complainant. Complaints can be referred direct by the member of the public who claims to have sustained injustice or hardship in consequence of the failure in a service provided by a relevant body, failure of that body to provide a service or in consequence of any other action by that body. The Ombudsmens' jurisdiction now covers complaints about family doctors, dentists, pharmacists and opticians, and complaints about actions resulting from clinical judgment. The Health Service Ombudsmen are also responsible for investigating complaints that information has been wrongly refused under the Code of Practice on Openness in the National Health Service 1995. The three offices are presently held by the Parliamentary Commissioner.

Parliamentary Commissioner and Health Service
    Commissioner (G1), M. S. Buckley
Deputy Parliamentary Commissioner (G3), J. E. Avery, CB

Deputy Health Service Commissioner (G3), Ms H. Scott
Directors, Parliamentary Commissioner (G5),
    Ms J. Binstead; N. Cleary; Mrs S. P. Maunsell;
    G. Monk; A. Watson
Directors, Health Service Commissioners (G5),
    Ms H. Bainbridge; N. J. Jordan; D. R. G. Pinchin;
    R. Tyrrell
Finance and Establishment Officer (G5), J. Stevens

For Scotland, *see* Scottish Parliamentary Commissioner for Administration

For Wales, *see* Welsh Administration Ombudsman

OFFICE OF THE PENSIONS OMBUDSMAN
6th Floor, 11 Belgrave Road, London SW1V 1RB
Tel: 020-7834 9144; Fax: 020-7821 0065

The Pensions Ombudsman is appointed under the Pension Schemes Act 1993 as amended by the Pensions Act 1995. He investigates and decides complaints and disputes concerning occupational pension schemes. Complaints concerning personal pensions would normally be dealt with only if outside the jurisdiction of the Personal Investment Authority. The Ombudsman is completely independent and there is no charge for bringing a complaint or dispute to him.

Pensions Ombudsman, Dr J. T. Farrand, QC

OFFICE OF THE RAIL REGULATOR
1 Waterhouse Square, 138–142 Holborn,
London EC1N 2TQ
Tel: 020-7282 2000; Fax: 020-7282 2047
Email: orr@dial.pipex.com
Web: http://www.rail-reg.gov.uk

The Office of the Rail Regulator was set up under the Railways Act 1993. The Regulator's main functions are the licensing of operators of railway assets; the approval of agreements for access by those operators to track, stations and light maintenance depots; the enforcement of domestic competition law; and consumer protection. The Regulator also sponsors a network of Rail Users' Consultative Committees, which represent the interests of passengers.

Subject to parliamentary approval of the necessary legislation, the consumer protection function of the Rail Regulator will be taken over by the new Strategic Rail Authority when it is set up, and the Rail Regulator will become subject to strategic guidance from the Secretary of State.

Rail Regulator, T. Winsor
Director of Strategy Planning and Communications, K. Webb
Director of Network Regulation, M. Beswick
Director of Operator Regulation, Ms M. Leech
Chief Economist and Director of Economics and Finance,
    P. Plummer
Chief Legal Adviser and Director of Legal Services,
    M. Brocklehurst

OFFICE OF WATER SERVICES
Centre City Tower, 7 Hill Street, Birmingham B5 4UA
Tel: 0121-625 1300; Fax: 0121-625 1400
Email: enquiries@ofwat.gtnet.gov.uk
Web: http://www.open.gov.uk/ofwat/

The Office of Water Services (Ofwat) was set up under the Water Act 1989 and is a non-ministerial Government

department headed by the Director-General of Water Services. It is the independent economic regulator of the water and sewerage companies in England and Wales. Ofwat's main duties are to ensure that the companies can finance and carry out the functions specified in the Water Industry Act 1991 and to protect the interests of water customers. There are ten regional customer service committees which are concerned solely with the interests of water customers. Representation of customer interests at national level is the responsibility of the Ofwat National Customer Council (ONCC).
Director-General of Water Services, vacant
Chairman, Ofwat National Customer Council, Ms S. Reiter

OMBUDSMEN
— *see* Local Commissioners *and* Parliamentary Commissioner. For non-statutory Ombudsmen, *see* Index

ORDNANCE SURVEY
Romsey Road, Maybush, Southampton SO1 64GU
Tel: 023-8079 2000; Fax: 023-8079 2452

Ordnance Survey is the national mapping agency for Britain. It is a Government department and executive agency operating as a Trading Fund and reporting to the Secretary of State for the Environment, Transport and the Regions.
Director-General and Chief Executive, Ms V. Lawrence

PARADES COMMISSION
12th Floor, Windsor House, 6–12 Bedford Street, Belfast BT2 7EL
Tel: 029-9054 8900; Fax: 029-9032 2988

The Parades Commission was set up under the Public Processions (Northern Ireland) Act 1998. Its function is to encourage and facilitate local accommodation on contentious parades; where this is not possible, the Commission is empowered to make legal determinations about such parades, which may include imposing conditions on aspects of the notified parade.
The chairman and members are appointed by the Secretary of State for Northern Ireland; the membership must, as far as is practicable, be representative of the community in Northern Ireland.
Chairman, A. J. Holland
Members, J. Cousins; Revd R. Magee; W. Martin; P. Osborne; Sir J. Pringle; P. Quinn
Secretary (G5), D. J. R. Hill

PARLIAMENTARY COMMISSIONER FOR STANDARDS
House of Commons, London SW1A 0AA
Tel: 020-7219 0320

Following recommendations of the Committee on Standards in Public Life, the House of Commons agreed to the appointment of an independent Parliamentary Commissioner for Standards with effect from November 1995. The Commissioner has responsibility for maintaining and monitoring the operation of the Register of Members' Interests; advising Members of Parliament and the select committee on standards and privileges, on the interpretation of the rules on disclosure and advocacy, and on other questions of propriety; and receiving and, if she thinks fit, investigating complaints about the conduct of MPs.
Parliamentary Commissioner for Standards, Ms E. Filkin

PARLIAMENTARY COUNSEL
36 Whitehall, London SW1A 2AY
Tel: 020-7210 6637; Fax: 020-7210 6632

Parliamentary Counsel draft all Government bills (i.e. primary legislation) except those relating exclusively to Scotland. They also advise on all aspects of parliamentary procedure in connection with such bills and draft Government amendments to them as well as any motions (including financial resolutions) necessary to secure their introduction into, and passage through, Parliament.
First Counsel (SCS), E. G. Caldwell, CB
Counsel (SCS), E. G. Bowman, CB; G. B. Sellers, CB; E. R. Sutherland, CB; P. F. A. Knowles, CB; S. C. Laws, CB; R. S. Parker, CB; Miss C. E. Johnston, CB; P. J. Davies; J. M. Sellers

PAROLE BOARD FOR ENGLAND AND WALES
Abell House, John Islip Street, London SW1P 4LH
Tel: 020-7217 5314; Fax: 020-7217 5793
Email: info@paroleboard.gov.uk
Web: http://www.paroleboard.gov.uk

The Board was constituted under the Criminal Justice Act 1967 and continued under the Criminal Justice Act 1991. It is an executive non-departmental public body and its duty is to advise the Home Secretary with respect to matters referred to it by him which are connected with the early release or recall of prisoners. Its functions include giving directions concerning the release on licence of prisoners serving discretionary life sentences and of certain prisoners serving long-term determinate sentences.
Chairman, The Baroness Prashar, CBE
Vice-Chairman, The Hon. Mr Justice Scott Baker
Chief Executive, J. Casey

PAROLE BOARD FOR SCOTLAND
Saughton House, Broomhouse Drive, Edinburgh EH11 3XD
Tel: 0131-244 8755; Fax: 0131-244 6974

The Board directs and advises the Scottish Minister on the release of prisoners on licence, and related matters.
Chairman, Dr J. J. McManus
Vice-Chairman, H. Hyslop
Secretary, H. P. Boyle

PATENT OFFICE
Concept House, Cardiff Road, Newport NP10 8QQ
Tel: 0845-9500505; Fax: 01633-814444
Email: enquiries@patent.gov.uk
Web: http://www.patent.gov.uk

The Patent Office is an executive agency of the Department of Trade and Industry. The duties of the Patent Office are to administer the Patent Acts, the Registered Designs Act and the Trade Marks Act, and to deal with questions relating to the Copyright, Designs and Patents Act 1988. The Search and Advisory Service carries out commercial searches through patent information. In 1997 the Office granted 2,792 patents and registered 9,592 designs and 27,897 trade marks.
Comptroller-General, Ms A. Brimelow
Director, Intellectual Property Policy Directorate, G. Jenkins
Director, Patents and Designs, R. J. Marchant

Director and Assistant Registrar of Trade Marks, P. Lawrence
*Director, Administration and Resources and Secretary to the
Patent Office*, C. Octon
Director, Copyright, J. Startup
Director, Finance, J. Thompson

HM PAYMASTER-GENERAL, OFFICE OF
— *see* National Investment and Loans Office

PENSIONS COMPENSATION BOARD
11 Belgrave Road, London SW1V 1RB
Tel: 020-7828 9794; Fax: 020-7931 7239

The Pensions Compensation Board was established under
the Pensions Act 1995 and is funded by a levy paid by all
eligible occupational pension schemes. Its function is to
compensate occupational pension schemes for losses due
to dishonesty where the employer is insolvent.
Chairman, Dr J. T. Farrand, QC
Secretary, M. Lydon

POLICE COMPLAINTS AUTHORITY
10 Great George Street, London SW1P 3AE
Tel: 020-7273 6450; Fax: 020-7273 6401;
Web: http://www.pca.gov.uk

The Police Complaints Authority was established under
the Police and Criminal Evidence Act 1984 to provide
an independent system for dealing with complaints by
members of the public against police officers in England
and Wales. It is funded by the Home Office. The authority
has powers to supervise the investigation of certain
categories of serious complaints and examines all completed investigations to decide whether officers should
face misconduct proceedings. It does not deal with police
operational matters; these are usually dealt with by the
Chief Constable of the relevant force.
Chairman, Sir Alistair Graham
Deputy Chair, Ms M. Meacher
Members, Mrs A. Boustred; I. Bynoe; Ms J. Dobry;
J. Elliott; D. Gear; Miss M. Mian; Mrs C. Mitchell;
A. Potts; Mrs W. Towers; A. Williams, MBE

**INDEPENDENT COMMISSION FOR POLICE
COMPLAINTS FOR NORTHERN IRELAND**
— *see* Police Ombudsman for Northern Ireland in Stop
press

**POLITICAL HONOURS SCRUTINY
COMMITTEE**
Ashley House, 2 Monck Street, London SW1P 2BQ
Tel: 020-7276 2770; Fax: 020-7276 2766

The function of the Political Honours Scrutiny Committee (a committee of Privy Councillors) was last set out
in full in an Order in Council in May 1997. Subsequent
Orders in Council have been made announcing changes
in the committee's membership. The Prime Minister
submits certain particulars to the Committee about
persons proposed to be recommended for honour for
their political services. From mid 2000 these exclude
Peerage candidates who will be referred for scrutiny to
the Appointments Commission. The Committee, after
such enquiry as it thinks fit, reports to the Prime Minister
whether, so far as it believes, the persons whose names
are submitted are fit and proper persons to be
recommended.

Chairman, The Lord Thomson of Monifieth, KT, PC
Members, The Baroness Dean of Thornton-le-Fylde,
PC; The Lord Hurd of Westwell, CH, CBE
Secretary, Mrs P. G. W. Catto

PORT OF LONDON AUTHORITY
Devon House, 58–60 St Katharine's Way, London E1 9LB
Tel: 020-7265 2656; Fax: 020-7265 2699;
Web: http://www.portoflondon.co.uk

The Port of London Authority is a public trust constituted
under the Port of London Act 1908 and subsequent
legislation. It is the governing body for the Port of
London, covering the tidal portion of the River Thames
from Teddington to the seaward limit. The Board comprises a chairman and up to seven but not less than four
non-executive members appointed by the Secretary of
State for the Environment, Transport and the Regions,
and up to four but not less than one executive members
appointed by the Board.
Chairman, Sir Brian Shaw
Vice-Chairman, The Baroness Wilcox
Chief Executive, S. Cuthbert
Secretary, G. E. Ennals

THE POST OFFICE
148 Old Street, London EC1V 9HQ
Tel: 020-72502888

Crown services for the carriage of Government dispatches
were set up in about 1516. The conveyance of public
correspondence began in 1635 and the mail service was
made a parliamentary responsibility with the setting up of
a Post Office in 1657. Telegraphs came under Post Office
control in 1870 and the Post Office Telephone Service
began in 1880. The National Girobank service of the
Post Office began in 1968. The Post Office ceased to be
a Government department in 1969 when responsibility
for the running of the postal, telecommunications,
giro and remittance services was transferred to a public
authority called The Post Office. The 1981 British
Telecommunications Act separated the functions of
the Post Office, making it solely responsible for postal
services and Girobank. Girobank was privatised in
1990. In July 1999 the Government announced plans to
turn the Post Office into a public limited company, give
it greater commercial freedom and set up an independent
regulator to protect consumer interests. The Postal
Services Bill of January 2000 outlined a universal service
and universal tariff system to be introduced at the time
of privatisation.
   The chairman, chief executive and members of the Post
Office Board are appointed by the Secretary of State for
Trade and Industry but responsibility for the running of
the Post Office as a whole rests with the Board in its
corporate capacity.

POST OFFICE BOARD
Chairman, Dr N. Bain
Chief Executive, J. Roberts, CBE
Members, M. Kitchener (*Managing Director, Finance*);
J. Cope (*Managing Director, Strategy and Personnel*)
Secretary, J. Evans

PRIME MINISTER'S OFFICE
—*see* page 295

PRISONS OMBUDSMAN FOR ENGLAND AND WALES
Ashley House, 2 Monck Street, London SW1P 2BQ
Tel: 020-7276 2876; Fax: 020-7276 2860
Email: prisonsombudsman@homeoffice.gsi.gov.uk

The post of Prisons Ombudsman was instituted in 1994. The Ombudsman is appointed by the Home Secretary and is an independent point of appeal for prisoners' grievances about their lives in prison, including disciplinary issues. The Ombudsman can investigate complaints about almost any aspect of prison life, assuming prisoners have completed the Prison Service's internal complaints procedure.
Prisons Ombudsman, Stephen Shaw

For Scotland, *see* Scottish Prisons Complaints Commission

PRIVY COUNCIL OFFICE
2 Carlton Gardens, London SW1Y 5AA
Tel: 020-7210 1033; Fax: 020-7210 1071

The Office is responsible for the arrangements leading to the making of all royal proclamations and Orders in Council; for certain formalities connected with ministerial changes; for considering applications for the granting (or amendment) of royal charters; for the scrutiny and approval of by-laws and statutes of chartered bodies; and for the appointment of high sheriffs and many Crown and Privy Council appointments to governing bodies.
President of the Council (and Leader of the House of Commons), The Rt. Hon. Margaret Beckett, MP
  Private Secretary, J. Capstick
Parliamentary Secretary, Paddy Tipping, MP
Clerk of the Council, A. K. Galloway
Deputy Clerk of the Council, G. C. Donald
Senior Clerk, Miss M. A. McCullagh
Registrar, J. A. C. Watherston

PUBLIC HEALTH LABORATORY SERVICE
61 Colindale Avenue, London NW9 5DF
Tel: 020-8200 1295; Fax: 020-8358 3130/3131;
Email: phls@phls.nhs.uk

The Public Health Laboratory Service comprises eight groups of laboratories, the Central Public Health Laboratory, the Communicable Disease Surveillance Centre and the Headquarters. The PHLS seeks to protect the population from infection through detection, diagnosis, surveillance, prevention and control of infections and communicable diseases. It keeps track of what infections are appearing where, advises on remedial or preventive action and provides clinical diagnostic services.
Chairman (£15,500), Prof. Sir Leslie Turnberg, MD
Deputy Chairman, R. Tabor
Director, Dr Diana Walford, FRCP,FRCPath.
Deputy Directors, Prof. B. I. Duerden, MD, FRCPath.
  (*Medical Director*); K. M. Saunders (*Corporate Planning and Resources*)
Board Secretary, K. M. Saunders

CENTRAL PUBLIC HEALTH LABORATORY
Colindale Avenue, London NW9 5HT
Director, Prof. S. P. Borriello

COMMUNICABLE DISEASES SURVEILLANCE CENTRE
Colindale Avenue, NW9 5EQ
Director, vacant

PHLS GROUPS OF LABORATORIES AND GROUP DIRECTORS
East, Dr P. M. B.White
Midlands, Dr R. E.Warren
North, Dr N. F. Lightfoot
North-West, Dr I. Farrell
South-West, Prof. K. A. V.Cartwright
London and South-East, Dr R. Gross
Trent, Dr P. J. Wilkinson
Wales, Dr A. J. Howard
OTHER SPECIAL LABORATORIES AND UNITS
ANAEROBE REFERENCE UNIT, Public Health Laboratory, Cardiff. *Head*, Prof. B. I. Duerden
ANTIVIRAL SUSCEPTIBILITY REFERENCE UNIT, Public Health Laboratory, Birmingham. *Head*, Dr D. P. Pillay
CRYPTOSPRORIDIUM REFERENCE UNIT, Public Health Laboratory, Rhyl. *Head*, Dr Rachel Chalmers
FOOD MICROBIOLOGY RESEARCH UNIT, Public Health Laboratory, Exeter. *Head*, Prof. T. J. Humphrey
GENITO-URINARY INFECTIONS REFERENCE LABORATORY, Public Health Laboratory, Bristol. *Head*, Dr A. J. Herring
LEPTOSPIRA REFERENCE LABORATORY, Public Health Laboratory, Hereford. *Director*, Dr T. J. Coleman
LYME DISEASE REFERENCE UNIT, Public Health Laboratory, Southampton. *Head*, Dr S. O'Connell
MALARIA REFERENCE LABORATORY, London School of Hygiene and Tropical Medicine, London WC1E 7HT. *Directors*, Prof. D. J. Bradley; Dr D. C. Warhurst
MENINGOCOCCAL REFERENCE LABORATORY, Public Health Laboratory, Manchester. *Director*, Dr E. Kaczmarski
MYCOBACTERIUM REFERENCE UNIT, Public Health Laboratory, Dulwich, London. *Director*, Dr F. Drobniewski
MYCOLOGY REFERENCE LABORATORY, Public Health Laboratory, Bristol. *Head*, Dr D. Warnock; University of Leeds. *Head*, Prof. E. G. V. Evans
PARASITOLOGY REFERENCE LABORATORY, Hospital for Tropical Diseases, London. *Director*, Dr P. L. Chiodini
TOXOPLASMA REFERENCE LABORATORY, Public Health Laboratory, Swansea. *Head*, D. H. M. Joynson
WATER AND ENVIRONMENTAL MICROBIOLOGY RESEARCH UNIT, Public Health Laboratory, Nottingham. *Head*, Dr J. V. Lee

PUBLIC TRUST OFFICE
Stewart House, 24 Kingsway, London WC2B 6JX
Tel: 020-7664 7000; Fax: 020-7664 7702
COURT FUNDS OFFICE, 22 Kingsway, London WC2B 6LE
Tel: 020-7936 6000; Fax: 020-7936 6882
email enquiries@publictrust.gov.uk
Web: http://www.publictrust.gov.uk

The Public Trust Office became an executive agency of the Lord Chancellor's Department in 1994. The chief executive of the agency holds the statutory title of Accountant-General of the Supreme Court.
  The Public Trustee, through the Public Trust Office, is a trust corporation created to undertake the business of executorships and trusteeship; acting as executor or administrator of the estate of a deceased person, or as trustee of a will or settlement. The Public Trustee is also responsible for the performance of all the administrative, but not the judicial, tasks required of the Court of

Protection under Part VII of the Mental Health Act 1983, relating to the management and administration of the property and affairs of persons suffering from mental disorder. The Public Trustee also acts as Receiver when so directed by the Court, usually where there is no other person willing or able so to act. The Office also deals with the registration of Enduring Powers of Attorney.

The Accountant-General of the Supreme Court, through the Court Funds Office, is responsible for the investment and accounting of funds in court for persons under a disability, monies in court subject to litigation and statutory deposits.

The Office is currently undergoing a process of restructuring and some functions will be reallocated to other organisations during 2000–1.

Acting Chief Executive (Accountant-General), N. J. Snedley
Acting Public Trustee, Ms. J. Martin
Assistant Public Trustee, vacant
Investment Manager, H. Stevenson
Chief Property Adviser, A. Nightingale

MENTAL HEALTH SECTOR
Head of Mental Health Services, P. L. Hales

TRUSTS AND FUNDS SECTOR
Director of Mental Health and Trusts Services, F. J. Eddy
Principal of Court Funds Office, Ms. P. MacDermott
Director of Finance, R. Yates
Divisional Manager, Trust Division, M. Munt
Finance Officer, M. Guntrip

PLANNING AND PAY POLICY
Head of Human Resources and Planning, D. Adams
Head of Client Services, A. McDonald

PUBLIC WORKS LOAN BOARD
—*see* National Investment and Loans Office

QUEST (THE QUALITY, EFFICIENCY AND STANDARDS TEAM)
c/o Department for Culture, Media and Sport,
2–4 Cockspur Street, London SW1Y 5DH
Tel: 020-7211 6200; Fax: 020-7211 6032

Quest was established in 1999. Its role is to monitor the quality of performance in organisations sponsored by the Department for Culture, Media and Sport and to provide independent advice to the Secretary of State.
Chief Executive, T. Suter

THE RADIO AUTHORITY
Holbrook House, 14 Great Queen Street,
London WC2B 5DG
Tel: 020-74302724; Fax: 020-7405 7062

The Radio Authority was established in 1991 under the Broadcasting Act 1990. It is the regulator and licensing authority for all independent radio services. Members of the Authority are appointed by the Secretary of State for Culture, Media and Sport; senior executive staff are appointed by the Authority.
Chairman, Richard Hooper
Deputy Chairman, David Witherow
Members, Mrs H. Tennant; F. Sharkey; Ms S. Hewitt; Ms S. Nathan; Ms K. O'Rourke
Chief Executive, A. Stoller
Deputy Chief Executive, D.Vick
Secretary to the Authority and Director of Legal Affairs, Ms E. Salomon

RECORD OFFICES

ADVISORY COUNCIL ON PUBLIC RECORDS
Secretariat: Public Record Office, Kew, Richmond, Surrey TW9 4DU
Tel: 020-8876 3444 ext. 2351; Fax: 020-8392 5295

Council members are appointed by the Lord Chancellor, under the Public Records Act 1958, to advise him on matters concerning public records in general and, in particular, on those aspects of the work of the Public Record Office which affect members of the public who make use of it.
Chairman, The Master of the Rolls
Secretary, T. R. Padfield

CORPORATION OF LONDON RECORDS OFFICE
Guildhall, London EC2 P2EJ
Tel: 020-73321251; Fax: 020-7710 8682
Email: clro@corpoflondon.gov.uk
Web: http://www.cityof london.gov.uk/archives/clro

The Corporation of London Records Office contains the municipal archives of the City of London which are regarded as the most complete collection of ancient municipal records in existence. The collection includes charters of William the Conqueror, Henry II, and later kings and queens to 1957; ancient custumals: Liber Horn, Dunthorne, Custumarum, Ordinacionum, Memorandorum and Albus, Liber de Antiquis Legibus, and collections of statutes; continuous series of judicial rolls and books from 1252 and Council minutes from 1275; records of the Old Bailey and Guildhall sessions from 1603; financial records from the 16th century; the records of London Bridge from the 12th century; and numerous subsidiary series and miscellanea of historical interest. The Readers' Room is open Monday–Friday, 9.30–4.45.
Keeper of the City Records, The Town Clerk
City Archivist, J. R. Sewell
Deputy City Archivist, Mrs J. M. Bankes

HOUSE OF LORDS RECORD OFFICE (THE PARLIAMENTARY ARCHIVES)
House of Lords, London SW1A 0PW
Tel: 020-7219 3074; Fax: 020-7219 2570
Web: hlro@parliament.uk

Since 1497, the records of Parliament have been kept within the Palace of Westminster. They are in the custody of the Clerk of the Parliaments. In 1946 a record department was established to supervise their preservation and their availability to the public. The search room of the office is open to the public Monday–Friday, 9.30–5 (Tuesday to 8, by appointment).

Some three million documents are preserved, including Acts of Parliament from 1497, journals of the House of Lords from 1510, minutes and committee proceedings from 1610, and papers laid before Parliament from 1531. Amongst the records are the Petition of Right, the Death Warrant of Charles I, the Declaration of Breda, and the Bill of Rights. The House of Lords Record Office also has charge of the journals of the House of Commons (from 1547), and other surviving records of the Commons (from 1572), including documents relating to private bill legislation from 1818. Among other documents are the records of the Lord Great Chamberlain, the political papers of certain members of the two Houses, and documents relating to Parliament acquired on behalf of the nation. A permanent exhibition was established in the Royal Gallery in 1979.
Clerk of the Records, S. K. Ellison
Assistant Clerks of the Records, D. L. Prior; Dr C. Shenton

NATIONAL ARCHIVES OF SCOTLAND

HM General Register House, Edinburgh EH1 3YY
Tel: 0131-535 1314; Fax: 0131-535 1360

The history of the national archives of Scotland can be traced back to the 13th century. The National Archives of Scotland (formerly the Scottish Record Office) is an executive agency of the Scottish Executive and keeps the administrative records of pre-Union Scotland, the registers of central and local courts of law, the public registers of property rights and legal documents, and many collections of local and church records and private archives. Certain groups of records, mainly the modern records of Government departments in Scotland, the Scottish railway records, the plans collection, and private archives of an industrial or commercial nature, are preserved in the branch repository at the West Register House in Charlotte Square. The search rooms in both buildings are open Monday–Friday, 9–4.45. A permanent exhibition at the West Register House and changing exhibitions at the General Register House are open to the public on weekdays, 10–4. The National Register of Archives (Scotland) is based in the West Register House.
Keeper of the Records of Scotland, P. M. Cadell
Deputy Keeper, Dr P. D. Anderson

THE PUBLIC RECORD OFFICE

Kew, Richmond, Surrey TW9 4DU
Tel: 020-8876 3444; Fax: 020-8878 8905

The Public Record Office, originally established in 1838 under the Master of the Rolls, was placed under the direction of the Lord Chancellor in 1958; it became an executive agency in 1992. The Lord Chancellor appoints a Keeper of Public Records, whose duties are to co-ordinate and supervise the selection of records of Government departments and the law courts for permanent preservation, to safeguard the records and to make them available to the public. There is a separate record office for Scotland, now called the National Archives of Scotland (*see* page 337).

The Office holds records of central Government dating from the Domesday Book (1086) to the present. Under the Public Records Act 1967 they are normally open to inspection when 30 years old, and are then available, without charge, in the reading rooms (Monday, Wednesday, Friday, Saturday, 9.30–5; Tuesday 10–7; Thursday 9.30–7).
Keeper of Public Records (G3), Mrs S. Tyacke, CB
Director, Public Services Division (G5), Dr E. Hallam Smith
Director, Government, Corporate and Information Services Division (G5), Dr D. Simpson

PUBLIC RECORD OFFICE (NORTHERN IRELAND)

66 Balmoral Avenue, Belfast BT9 6NY
Tel: 01232-251318; Fax: 01232-255999

The Public Record Office (Northern Ireland) is responsible for identifying and preserving Northern Ireland's archival heritage and making it available to the public. It is an executive agency of the Department of Culture, Arts and Leisure. The search room is open on weekdays, 9.15–4.15 (Thursday, 9.15–8.45).
Chief Executive, vacant

ROYAL COMMISSION ON HISTORICAL MANUSCRIPTS

Quality House, Quality Court, Chancery Lane, London WC2A 1HP
Tel: 020-72421198; Fax: 020-7831 3550
Email: nra@hmc.gov.uk
Web: http://www.hmc.gov.uk

The Commission was set up by royal warrant in 1869 to enquire and report on collections of papers of value for the study of history which were in private hands. In 1959 a new warrant enlarged these terms of reference to include all historical records, wherever situated, outside the Public Records and gave it added responsibilities as a central co-ordinating body to promote, assist and advise on their proper preservation and storage. The Commission is sponsored by the Department for Culture, Media and Sport.

The Commission also maintains the National Register of Archives (NRA), which contains over 42,000 unpublished lists and catalogues of manuscript collections describing the holdings of local record offices, national and university libraries, specialist repositories and others in the UK and overseas. The NRA can be searched using computerised indices which are available in the Commission's search room.

The Commission also administers the Manorial and Tithe Documents Rules on behalf of the Master of the Rolls.
Chairman, The Lord Bingham of Cornhill, PC
Commissioners, Sir Patrick Cormack, FSA,MP; The Lord Egremont and Leconfield; Sir Matthew Farrer, GCVO; Sir John Sainty, KCB, FSA; Very Revd H. E. C. Stapleton, FSA; Sir Keith Thomas, FBA; The Earl of Scarbrough; Mrs A. Dundas-Bekker; G. E. Aylmer, D.Phil, FBA; Mrs S. J. Davies, Ph.D.; Mrs A. Prochaska, Ph.D.; Miss R. Dunhill, FSA; Dr Caroline Barron, FSA; Prof. T. C. Smout, CBE, Ph.D., FBA, FRSE, FSA Scot.
Secretary, C. J. Kitching, Ph.D., FSA

SCOTTISH RECORDS ADVISORY COUNCIL

HM General Register House, Edinburgh EH1 3YY
Tel: 0131-535 1314; Fax: 0131-535 1360;
Web: http://www.nas.gov.uk

The Council was established under the Public Records (Scotland) Act 1937. Its members are appointed by the First Minister and it may submit proposals or make representations to the First Minister, the Lord Justice General or the Lord President of the Court of Session on questions relating to the public records of Scotland.
Chairman, Prof. Anne Crowther
Secretary, Dr A. Rosie

REGISTRAR OF PUBLIC LENDING RIGHT

Richard House, Sorbonne Close, Stockton on Tees TS17 6DA
Tel: 01642-604699; Fax: 01642-615641

Under the Public Lending Right system, in operation since 1983, payment is made from public funds to authors whose books are lent out from public libraries. Payment is made once a year and the amount each author receives is proportionate to the number of times (established from a sample) that each registered book has been lent out during the previous year. The Registrar of PLR, who is appointed by the Secretary of State for Culture, Media and Sport, compiles the register of authors and books. From 1 July 2000 authors resident in all EC countries are eligible to apply. (The term 'author' covers writers, illustrators, translators, and some editors/compilers.)

A payment of 2.18 pence was made in 1999–2000 for each estimated loan of a registered book, up to a top limit of £6,000 for the books of any one registered author; the money for loans above this level is used to augment the

remaining PLR payments. In February 2000, the sum of £4,206 million was made available for distribution to 30,674 registered authors and assignees as the annual payment of PLR.
Registrar, Dr J. G. Parker
Chairman of Advisory Committee, C. Francis

REGISTRY OF FRIENDLY SOCIETIES
Victory House, 30–34 Kingsway, London WC2B 6ES
Tel: 020-7663 5282/5124/5269/5299

The Registry of Friendly Societies is a non-ministerial Government department comprising the Registry and the Assistant Registrar of Friendly Societies for Scotland.

The Central Office of the Registry of Friendly Societies provides a public registry for mutual organisations registered under the Building Societies Act 1986, the Friendly Societies Acts 1974 and 1992, and the Industrial and Provident Societies Act 1965. The Chief Registrar is responsible for the supervision of credit unions, and advises the Government on issues affecting them.

The Registry of Friendly Societies will be subsumed into the Financial Services Authority (*see* page 640) at a date to be fixed.

CENTRAL OFFICE OF THE REGISTRY
Chief Registrar, G. E. Fitchew
Assistant Registrars, Ms S. Eden; S. Mundy; E. Engstrom; N. Fawcett
Establishment and Finance Officer, R. E. Merrick

REGISTRY OF FRIENDLY SOCIETIES, SCOTLAND
58 Frederick Street, Edinburgh EH2 1NB
Tel: 0131-226 3224
Assistant Registrar, J. L. J. Craig, WS

REVIEW BODIES

The secretariat for these bodies is provided by the Office of Manpower Economics (*see* page 349)

ARMED FORCES PAY
The Review Body on Armed Forces Pay was appointed in 1971 to advise the Prime Minister on the pay and allowances of members of naval, military and air forces of the Crown and of any women's service administered by the Defence Council.
Chairman, The Baroness Dean of Thornton-le-Fylde, PC
Members, Mrs K. Coleman, OBE; J. Davies; Vice-Adm.
Sir Toby Frere, KCB; The Lord Gladwin of Clee, CBE;
Prof. D. Greenaway; Ms G. Haskins; M. Ward

DOCTORS' AND DENTISTS' REMUNERATION
The Review Body on Doctors' and Dentists' Remuneration was set up in 1971 to advise the Government on the remuneration of doctors and dentists taking any part in the National Health Service.
Chairman, C. B. Gough
Members, Mrs M. Alderson; A. Hawksworth;
Miss C. Hui; Dr G. Jones; C. King, CBE;
Prof. S. McLean

NURSING STAFF, MIDWIVES, HEALTH VISITORS AND PROFESSIONS ALLIED TO MEDICINE
The Review Body for nursing staff, midwives, health visitors and professions allied to medicine was set up in 1983 to advise the Government on the remuneration of nursing staff, midwives and health visitors employed in the National Health Service; and also of physiotherapists, radiographers, occupational therapists, orthoptists, chiropodists, dietitians and related grades employed in the National Health Service.
Chairman, Prof. C. Booth
Members, Ms U. Banerjee; J. Bartlett; Mrs M. Davies;
M. Malone-Lee, CB; C. Monks, OBE;
Prof P Weetman

SCHOOL TEACHERS
The School Teachers' Review Body (STRB) was set up under the School Teachers' Pay and Conditions Act 1991. It is required to examine and report on such matters relating to the statutory conditions of employment of school teachers in England and Wales as may be referred to it by the Secretary of State for Education and Employment.
Chairman, A. Vineall
Members, P. Gedling; Miss J. Langdon; R. Pearson;
J. Singh; Mrs P. Sloane

SENIOR SALARIES
The Senior Salaries Review Body (formerly the Top Salaries Review Body) was set up in 1971 to advise the Prime Minister on the remuneration of the judiciary, senior civil servants and senior officers of the armed forces. In 1993 its remit was extended to cover the pay, pensions and allowances of MPs, Ministers and others whose pay is determined by a Ministerial and Other Salaries Order, and the allowances of peers. The Terms of Reference were again revised in 1998.
Chairman, Sir Michael Perry, CBE
Members, The Hon. M. Beloff, QC; D. Clayman;
Prof. S. Dawson; The Baroness Dean of
Thornton-le-Fylde, PC; Sir Terry Heiser, GCB;
Sir Sydney Lipworth, QC; Prof. Sir David Williams, QC;
George Staple, CB, QC

ROYAL BOTANIC GARDEN EDINBURGH
20A Inverleith Row, Edinburgh EH3 5LR
Tel: 0131-552 7171; Fax: 0131-248 2901
Email: press@rbge.org.uk; Web: http://www.rbge.org.uk

The Royal Botanic Garden Edinburgh (RBGE) originated as the Physic Garden, established in 1670 beside the Palace of Holyroodhouse. The Garden moved to its present 28-hectare site at Inverleith, Edinburgh, in 1821. There are also three specialist gardens: Benmore Botanic Garden, near Dunoon, Argyllshire; Logan Botanic Garden, near Stranraer, Wigtownshire; and Dawyck Botanic Garden, near Stobo, Peeblesshire. Since 1986 RBGE has been administered by a board of trustees established under the National Heritage (Scotland) Act 1985. It receives an annual grant from the Rural Affairs Department of the Scottish Executive.

RBGE is an international centre for scientific research on plant diversity and for horticulture education and conservation. It has an extensive library, a herbarium with over two million preserved plant specimens, and over 20,000 species in the living collections. Public opening hours: Edinburgh site, daily (except Christmas Day and New Year's Day) November–January 9.30–4; February and October 9.30–5; March and September 9.30–6; April–August 9.30–7; Specialist Gardens, 1 March–31 October 9.30–6. Admission free to Edinburgh site; admission charge to Specialist Gardens.
Chairman of the Board of Trustees, Dr P. Nicholson
Regius Keeper, Prof. S. Blackmore

ROYAL BOTANIC GARDENS KEW
Richmond, Surrey TW9 3AB
Tel: 020-8332 5000; Fax: 020-8332 5197
Wakehurst Place, Ardingly, nr Haywards Heath,
W. Sussex RH17 6TN
Tel: 01444-894066; Fax: 01444-894069

The Royal Botanic Gardens (RBG) Kew were originally laid out as a private garden for Kew House for George III's mother, Princess Augusta, in 1759. They were much enlarged in the 19th century, notably by the inclusion of the grounds of the former Richmond Lodge. In 1965 the garden at Wakehurst Place was acquired; it is owned by the National Trust and managed by RBG Kew. Under the National Heritage Act 1983 a board of trustees was set up to administer the gardens, which in 1984 became an independent body supported by grant-in-aid from the Ministry of Agriculture, Fisheries and Food.

The functions of RBG Kew are to carry out research into plant sciences, to disseminate knowledge about plants and to provide the public with the opportunity to gain knowledge and enjoyment from the gardens' collections. There are extensive national reference collections of living and preserved plants and a comprehensive library and archive. The main emphasis is on plant conservation and bio-diversity.

The gardens are open daily (except Christmas Day and New Year's Day) from 9.30 a.m. (Wakehurst, 10 a.m.). The closing hour varies from 4 p.m. in mid-winter to 6 p.m. on weekdays and 7.30 p.m. on Sundays and Bank Holidays in mid-summer. Admission, 2000, £5.00; concessionary schemes available. Glasshouses (Kew only), 9.30–4.30 (winter); 9.30–5.30 (summer). No dogs except guide-dogs for the blind.

BOARD OF TRUSTEES
Chairman, The Viscount Blakenham
Members, Sir Jeffery Bowman (*Queen's Trustee*);
   Miss M. Black, CBE; Prof. M. Crawley;
   Prof. H. Dickinson; Miss A. Ford; Mrs R. Franklin;
   S. de Grey, CBE; R. Lapthorne, CBE; I. Oag;
   Prof. J. S. Parker; Prof. C. Payne, OBE
Director, Prof. P. Crane

ROYAL COMMISSION FOR THE EXHIBITION OF 1851
Sherfield Building, Imperial College of Science, Technology and Medicine, London SW7 2AZ
Tel: 020-7594 8790; Fax: 020-7594 8794;
Email: royalcom1851@ic.ac.uk
Web: http://www.royalcommission1851.org.uk

The Royal Commission was incorporated by supplemental charter as a permanent commission after winding up the affairs of the Great Exhibition of 1851. Its object is to promote scientific and artistic education by means of funds derived from its Kensington estate, purchased with the surplus left over from the Great Exhibition. Annual charitable expenditure on educational grants is about £1 million.
President, HRH The Prince Philip,
   Duke of Edinburgh,KG, KT, PC
Chairman, Board of Management, Sir Denis Rooke, OM,
   CBE, FRS, FREng.
Secretary to Commissioners, J. P. W. Middleton,CB

ROYAL COMMISSION ON ENVIRONMENTAL POLLUTION
1st Floor, Steel House, 11 Tothill Street,
London SW1H 9RE
Tel: 020-7273 6635; Email: enquiries@rcep.org.uk

The Commission was set up in 1970 to advise on national and international matters concerning the pollution of the environment.
Chairman, Prof. Sir Thomas Blundell
Members, Revd Prof. M. C. Banner; Dr I. Graham-Bryce;
   Prof. R. Clift, OBE, FREng.; J. Flemming;
   Sir Martin Holdgate, CB; Prof. B. Hoskins, CBE, FRS;
   Prof. R. Macrory; Sir Michael Marmot, PH.D.;
   Mrs C. Miller, FRSA; Dr Susan Owens, OBE;
   Prof. Jane Plant, CBE, FRSA; J. Roberts
Secretary, D. R. Lewis

ROYAL COMMISSION ON THE ANCIENT AND HISTORICAL MONUMENTS OF SCOTLAND
John Sinclair House, 16 Bernard Terrace,
Edinburgh EH8 9NX
Tel: 0131-662 1456; Fax: 0131-662 1477

The Royal Commission was established in 1908 and is appointed to provide for the survey and recording of ancient and historical monuments connected with the culture, civilisation and conditions of life of the people in Scotland from the earliest times. It is funded by the Scottish Executive. The Commission compiles and maintains the National Monuments Record of Scotland as the national record of the archaeological and historical environment. The National Monuments Record is open for reference Monday–Thursday 9.30–4.30, Friday 9.30–4.
Chairman, Mrs Kathleen Dalyell
Commissioners, Prof. J. M. Coles, PH.D., FBA;
   Prof. T. C. Smout, CBE, PH.D., FRSE, FBA;
   Prof. R. A. Paxton, MBE, FRSE; Dr Barbara Crawford,
   FSA, FSA Scot.; Miss A. C. Riches, OBE, FSA;
   J. W. T. Simpson, FSA Scot.; Dr M. A. Mackay, PH.D.;
   Dr A. Macdonald, PH.D.; Prof. C. D. Morris,
   FSA, FRSE; Dr J. Murray, PH.D.
Secretary, R. J. Mercer, FSA, FRSE

ROYAL COMMISSION ON THE ANCIENT AND HISTORICAL MONUMENTS OF WALES
Crown Building, Plas Crug, Aberystwyth SY23 1NJ
Tel: 01970-621200; Fax: 01970-627701

The Royal Commission was established in 1908 and is currently empowered by a royal warrant of 1992 to survey, record, publish and maintain a database of ancient and historical and maritime sites and structures, and landscapes in Wales. The Commission is funded by the National Assembly for Wales and is also responsible for the National Monuments Record of Wales, which is open daily for public reference, for the supply of archaeological information to the Ordnance Survey, for the co-ordination of archaeological aerial photography in Wales, and for sponsorship of the regional Sites and Monuments Records.
Chairman, Prof. R. A. Griffiths, PH.D., D.Litt.
Commissioners, D. W. Crossley, FSA; J. Newman, FSA;
   U. B. Smith, PH.D.; Mrs A. Nicol; Prof. P. Sims-
   Williams, FBA; Prof. G. J. Wainwright, MBE, PH.D., FSA;
   E. Wiliam, PH.D., FSA
Secretary, P.R.White, FSA

THE ROYAL MINT
Llantrisant, Pontyclun CF72 8YT
Tel: 01443-623060; Fax: 01443-623185;
Web: http://www.royalmint.com

The prime responsibility of the Royal Mint is the provision of United Kingdom coinage, but it actively competes in world markets for a share of the available circulating coin business and about half of the 25,000 tonnes of coins and blanks it produces annually are exported. The Mint also manufactures special proof and uncirculated quality coins in gold, silver and other metals; military and civil decorations and medals; commemorative and prize medals; and royal and official seals.

The Royal Mint became an executive agency of the Treasury in 1990. The Government announced in July 1999 that the Royal Mint would be given greater commercial freedom to expand its business into new areas and develop partnerships with the private sector.
Master of the Mint, The Chancellor of the Exchequer
 (*ex officio*)
Deputy Master and Comptroller, R. de L. Holmes

ROYAL NATIONAL THEATRE BOARD
South Bank, London, SE1 9PX
Tel: 020-7452 3333; Fax: 020-7452 3344

The chairman and members of the Board of the Royal National Theatre are appointed by the Secretary of State for Culture, Media and Sport.
Chairman, Sir Christopher Hogg
Members, Ms J. Bakewell, CBE; The Hon. P. Benson;
 Sir David Hancock, KCB; G. Hutchings; Ms K. Jones;
 Ms S. MacGregor, OBE; B. Okri; M.Oliver;
 Sir Tom Stoppard, OM, CBE; P. Wiegand;
 Prof. Lola Young
Company Secretary, Mrs M. McGregor
Director, T. Nunn, CBE
Executive Director, The Baroness McIntosh of Hudnall

SCOTTISH CRIMINAL CASES REVIEW COMMISSION
5th Floor, Portland House, 17 Renfield Street,
Glasgow G2 5AH
Tel: 0141-270 7030; Fax: 0141-270 7040

The Commission is a non-departmental public body which started operating on 1 April 1999. It took over from the Secretary of State for Scotland powers to consider alleged miscarriages of justice in Scotland and refer cases meeting the relevant criteria to the Appeal Court for review. Members are appointed by Her Majesty The Queen on the recommendation of the First Minister; senior executive staff are appointed by the Commission.
Chairperson (£360 per day), Prof. Sheila McLean
Members (£210 per day), A. Bonnington; Prof. P. Duff;
 The Very Revd G. Forbes; A. Gallen; Sir G. Gordon,
 CBE, QC; W. Taylor, QC
Chief Executive, Ms C. A. Kelly

SCOTTISH ENTERPRISE
120 Bothwell Street, Glasgow G2 7JP
Tel: 0141-248 2700; Fax: 0141-221 3217

Scottish Enterprise was established in 1991 and its purpose is to create jobs and prosperity for the people of Scotland. It is funded largely by the Scottish Executive and is responsible to the Scottish Ministers. Working in partnership with the private and public sectors, Scottish Enterprise aims to further the development of Scotland's economy, to enhance the skills of the Scottish workforce and to promote Scotland's international competitiveness. Through Locate in Scotland, Scottish Enterprise is concerned with attracting firms to Scotland, and through Scottish Trade International it helps Scottish companies to compete in world export markets. Scottish Enterprise has a network of 13 Local Enterprise Companies that deliver economic development services at local level.
Chairman (£31,567), Sir Ian Wood, CBE
Chief Executive, Dr R. Crawford

SCOTTISH ENVIRONMENT PROTECTION AGENCY
Erskine Court, The Castle Business Park, Stirling FK9 4TR
Tel: 01786-457700; Fax: 01786-446885

The Scottish Environment Protection Agency came into being on 1 April 1996 under the Environment Act 1995. It is responsible for controlling pollution to land, air and water in Scotland. It receives funding from the Scottish Executive.
Chairman, K. Collins
Chief Executive, A. Paton
Director of Finance, J. Ford
Director of Environmental Strategy, Ms P. Henton
Director, North Region, Prof. D. Mackay
Director, East Region, W. Halcrow
Director, West Region, J. Beveridge

SCOTTISH EXECUTIVE
— *see Regional Government section*

SCOTTISH HOMES
Thistle House, 91 Haymarket Terrace,
Edinburgh EH12 5HE
Tel: 0131-313 0044; Fax: 0131-313 2680

Scottish Homes, the national housing agency for Scotland, aims to improve the quality and variety of housing available in Scotland by working in partnership with the public and private sectors. The agency is a major funder of new and improved housing provided by housing associations and private developers. It is currently transferring its own rented houses to alternative landlords. It is also involved in housing research. Board members are appointed by the First Minister.
Chairman, J. Ward, CBE
Chief Executive, vacant

SCOTTISH LAW COMMISSION
140 Causewayside, Edinburgh EH9 1PR
Tel: 0131-668 2131; Fax: 0131-662 4900

The Commission keeps the law in Scotland under review and makes proposals for its development and reform. It is responsible to the Scottish Ministers through the Scottish Executive Justice Department (*see* pages xxx).
Chairman (*part-time*), The Hon. Lord Gill
Commissioners (*full-time*), Prof. G. Maher;
 Prof. K. G. C. Reid; Prof. J. M. Thomson;
 (*part-time*) P. S. Hodge, QC
Secretary, N. Raven

SCOTTISH LEGAL AID BOARD
44 Drumsheugh Gardens, Edinburgh EH3 7SW
Tel: 0131-226 7061; Fax: 0131-220 4878

The Scottish Legal Aid Board was set up under the Legal Aid (Scotland) Act 1986. It is responsible for ensuring that advice, assistance and representation are available in accordance with the Act. Members are appointed by the First Minister.
Chairman, Mrs J. Couper
Members, B. C. Adair; Mrs K. Blair; W. Gallagher;
    Sheriff A. Jessop; N. Kuenssberg; Prof. J. P. Percy;
    D. O'Carroll; Mrs Y. Osman; Mrs M. Scanlan;
    M. C. Thomson, QC; A. F. Wylie, QC
Chief Executive, L. Montgomery

SCOTTISH NATURAL HERITAGE
12 Hope Terrace, Edinburgh EH9 2AS
Tel: 0131-447 4784; Fax: 0131-446 2277

Scottish Natural Heritage was established in 1992 under the Natural Heritage (Scotland) Act 1991. It provides advice on nature conservation to all those whose activities affect wildlife, landforms and features of geological interest in Scotland, and seeks to develop and improve facilities for the enjoyment and understanding of the Scottish countryside. It is funded by the Scottish Executive.
Chairman, Dr J. Markland, CBE
Chief Executive, R. Crofts, CBE
Chief Scientific Adviser, M. B.Usher
Directors of Operations, J. Thomson (*West*);
    I. Jardine (*East*); J. Watson (*North*)
Director of Corporate Services, I. Edgeler

SCOTTISH PARLIAMENTARY COMMISSIONER FOR ADMINISTRATION
28 Thistle Street, Edinburgh EH2 1EN
Tel: 0845-601 0456; Fax: 0131-226 4447

The Scottish Parliamentary Commissioner for Administration was appointed in July 1999 to investigate complaints made to him by Members of the Scottish Parliament on behalf of members of the public who have suffered an injustice through maladministration by the Scottish Executive and a wide range of public bodies involved in devolved Scottish affairs.
Scottish Parliamentary Commissioner for Administration,
    M. S. Buckley

SCOTTISH PRISONS COMPLAINTS COMMISSION
Government Buildings, Broomhouse Drive,
Edinburgh EH11 3XD
Tel: 0131-244 8423; Fax: 0131-244 8430

The Commission was established in 1994. It is an independent body to which prisoners in Scottish prisons can make application in relation to any matter where they have failed to obtain satisfaction from the Prison Service's internal grievance procedures. Clinical judgments made by medical officers, matters which are the subject of legal proceedings and matters relating to sentence, conviction and parole decision-making are excluded from the Commission's jurisdiction. The Commissioner is appointed by the First Minister.
Commissioner, Miss J. N. Aitken

SEA FISH INDUSTRY AUTHORITY
18 Logie Mill, Logie Green Road, Edinburgh EH7 4HG
Tel: 0131-5583331; Fax: 0131-558 1442

Established under the Fisheries Act 1981, the Authority is required to promote the efficiency of the sea fish industry. It carries out research relating to the industry and gives advice on related matters. It provides training, promotes the marketing, consumption and export of sea fish and sea fish products, and may provide financial assistance for the improvement of fishing vessels in respect of essential safety equipment. It is responsible to the Ministry of Agriculture, Fisheries and Food.
Chairman, E. Davey
Chief Executive, A. C. Fairbairn

THE SECURITY AND INTELLIGENCE SERVICES

Under the Intelligence Services Act 1994, the Intelligence and Security Committee of Parliamentarians was established to oversee the work of GCHQ, MI5 and MI6; in 1999 an Investigator was appointed to the committee in order to reinforce the authority of its findings and establish public confidence in the oversight system. The Act also established the Intelligence Services Tribunal (*see* pages 312–3), which hears complaints made against GCHQ and MI6. The Security Service Tribunal and Commissioner (*see* below) investigate complaints about MI5.

DEFENCE INTELLIGENCE STAFF
— *see* Defence section

GOVERNMENT COMMUNICATIONS HEADQUARTERS (GCHQ)
Priors Road, Cheltenham, Glos GL52 5AJ
Tel: 01242-221491; Fax: 01242-574349

GCHQ produces signals intelligence in support of national security and the UK's economic wellbeing, and in the prevention or detection of serious crime. It also provides advice and assistance to Government departments, the armed forces and other national infrastructure bodies on the security of their communications and information systems. It was placed on a statutory footing by the Intelligence Services Act 1994 and is headed by a director who is directly accountable to the Foreign Secretary. A new building to house GCHQ is to be constructed in Cheltenham, with the anticipated completion date of early 2003.
Director, F. N. Richards, CVO, CMG

NATIONAL CRIMINAL INTELLIGENCE SERVICE
PO Box 8000, London SE11 5EN
Tel: 020-7238 8000;
Web: http://www.ncis.gov.uk

The National Criminal Intelligence Service (NCIS) provides intelligence about serious and organised crime to law enforcement, government and other relevant national and international agencies. On 1 April 1998 NCIS was placed on a statutory footing. It is accountable to the NCIS Service Authority.
Director-General, J.Abbott, QPM, CBE
Deputy Director-General (Director (Intelligence)),
    R. Gaspar, QPM
Director, International Division, N. Bailey
Director, UK Division, V. Harvey
Director, Resources Division, N. Beard

SERVICE AUTHORITY
PO Box 2600, London SW1V 2WG
Tel: 020-7238 2600

The Service Authority for NCIS is responsible for ensuring its effective operation. It operates with the Service Authority for the National Crime Squad (*see* page 374). There are 26 members of the authorities, of whom the chairman and nine others serve as 'core members' on both authorities.

Chairman, Rt. Hon. Sir John Wheeler
Clerk, T. Simmons
Treasurer, P. Derrick

THE SECRET INTELLIGENCE SERVICE (MI6)
PO Box 1300, London SE1 1BD

The Secret Intelligence Service produces secret intelligence in support of the Government's security, defence, foreign and economic policies. It was placed on a statutory footing by the Intelligence Services Act 1994 and is headed by a chief, known as 'C', who is directly accountable to the Foreign Secretary.

Chief, R. B. Dearlove, OBE

THE SECURITY SERVICE (MI5)
PO Box 3255, London SW1P 1AE
Tel: 020-7930 9000

The function of the Security Service is the protection of national security, in particular against threats from espionage, terrorism, sabotage and the proliferation of weapons of mass destruction, from the activities of agents of foreign powers, and from actions intended to overthrow or undermine parliamentary democracy by political, industrial or violent means. It is also the Service's function to safeguard the economic well-being of the UK against threats posed by the actions or intentions of persons outside the British Islands. Under the Security Service Act 1996, the Service's role was extended to support the police and customs in the prevention and detection of serious crime.

The Security Service was placed on a statutory footing by the Security Service Act 1989 and is headed by a director-general who is directly accountable to the Home Secretary for the operations and efficiency of the Service.

Director-General, Sir Stephen Lander, KCB

SECURITY SERVICE COMMISSIONER
c/o PO Box 18, London SE1 0TZ
Tel: 020-7273 4095

The Commissioner is appointed by the Prime Minister. He keeps under review the issue of warrants by the Home Secretary under the Intelligence Services Act 1994, and is required to help the Security Service Tribunal by investigating complaints which allege interference with property and by offering all such assistance in discharging its functions as it may require. He is also required to submit an annual report on the discharge of his functions to the Prime Minister.

Commissioner, The Rt.Hon.Lord Justice Simon Brown
 Private Secretary, Miss R. E. Morrison

SECURITY SERVICE TRIBUNAL
PO Box 18, London SE1 0TZ
Tel: 020-7273 4095

The Security Service Act 1989 established a tribunal of three to five senior members of the legal profession, independent of the Government and appointed by The Queen, to investigate complaints from any person about anything which they believe the Security Service has done to them or to their property.

President, The Rt. Hon. Lord Justice Simon Brown
Vice-President, Sheriff J. McInnes, QC
Member, Sir Richard Gaskell
Secretary, N. R. Brooks

SENTENCE REVIEW COMMISSIONERS
PO Box 1011, Belfast BT2 7SR
Tel: 01232-549412; Fax: 01232-549427
Email: sentrev@belfast.org.uk
Web: http://www.sentencereview.org.uk

The Sentence Review Commissioners are appointed by the Secretary of State for Northern Ireland to consider applications from prisoners serving sentences in Northern Ireland for declarations that they are entitled to early release in accordance with the provisions of the Northern Ireland (Sentences) Act 1998. The commissioners have been appointed until 31 July 2000 and are served by staff seconded from the Northern Ireland Office.

Joint Chairmen, Sir John Belloch, KCB; B. Currin
Commissioners, Dr Silvia Casale; Dr P. Curran;
 I. Dunbar, CB; Mrs M. Gilpin; Dr A. Grounds;
 Ms C. McGrory; Dr D. Morrow; D. Wall
Secretary (SCS)

SERIOUS FRAUD OFFICE
Elm House, 10–16 Elm Street, London WC1X 0BJ
Tel: 020-7239 7272; Fax: 020-7837 1689
Email: public.enquiries@sfo.gov.uk

The Serious Fraud Office works under the superintendence of the Attorney-General. Its remit is to investigate and prosecute serious and complex fraud. (Other fraud cases are handled by the fraud divisions of the Crown Prosecution Service.) The scope of its powers covers England, Wales and Northern Ireland. The staff includes lawyers, accountants and other support staff; investigating teams work closely with the police.

Director, Mrs R. Wright

SMALL BUSINESS COUNCIL
Victoria Street, London SW1H 0ET
Tel: 020-7215 5365;
Email: enquiries@sbs.gsi.gov.uk
Web: http://www.businessadviceonline.org

The Small Business Council was set up in March 2000. It is a Non-Departmental Public Body independent of Government acting in an advisory capacity to the Small Business Service. The Council also reports to the Secretary for Trade and Industry on the needs of small businesses.

Chairman, W. Sargent
Members, Ms S. Anderson; J. Braithwaite; Dr Marion
 Carter; Ms S. Gemmell; W. Herriot; W. Jeffrey;
 P. Morgan; Dr R. Parkinson; K. Patel; Mrs. M. Pathak;
 C. Perry; I. Rees; R. Singh; M. Snyder; Prof. D. Storey;
 Mrs. M. Tarn; Ms Y. Thompson; J. Torrance;
 Ms B. Webster

SMALL BUSINESS SERVICE
1 Victoria Street, London SW1 0ET
Tel: 020-7215 5365;
Email: enquiries@sbs.gsi.gov.uk
Web: http://www.businessadviceonline.org

The Small Business Service was set up by the government in April 2000. The role of the Service will be to provide a voice for small businesses in Government, to improve the coherence and quality of Government support for the small business, and to help small businesses on issues of regulation. There will be (from April 2001) 45 local Business Link franchises throughout England largely coterminous in their boundaries with the new Learning and Skills Councils.
Chief Executive, D. Irwin
Deputy Chief Executive, P.Waller

SOCIAL SECURITY, CHILD SUPPORT AND PENSIONS JOINT AUTHORITY
The Adelphi, 1–11 John Adam Street, London WC2N 6HT
Tel: 020-7962 8426; Fax: 020-7962 8110

Previously the National Insurance Joint Authority, the Authority's function is to co-ordinate the operation of social security legislation in Great Britain and Northern Ireland, including the necessary financial adjustments between the two National Insurance Funds.
Members, The Secretary of State for Social Security; the Northern Ireland Minister for Social Development and the Chancellor of the Exchequer
Secretary, Ms B. West

STATISTICS COMMISSION
10 Great George Street, London SW1P 3AE
Tel: 020-7273 8343;
E-mail statscom@btinternet.com
Web: http://www.statscom.org.uk

The objectives and structure of the Statistics Commission were laid out in the white paper 'Building Trust in Statistics' in October 1999. It will be an independent, non-executive body which will check the integrity and independence of National Statistics. It will also aim to ensure that National Statistics are responsive to public needs.
Chairman, Sir John Kingman, FRS
Members, Miss C. Bowe; Sir Kenneth Calman; Miss P. Hodgson; Prof. D. Rind; Mrs J. Trewdale; D. Wanless; M. Weale

TOURISM BODIES

The English Tourism Council, the Scottish Tourist Board, the Wales Tourist Board and the Northern Ireland Tourist Board are responsible for developing and marketing the tourist industry in their respective countries.
ENGLISH TOURISM COUNCIL, Thames Tower, Black's Road, London W6 9EL. Tel: 020-8563 3000; Web: http://www.englishtourism.org.uk.
Chief Executive, Ms M. Lynch
SCOTTISH TOURIST BOARD, 23 Ravelston Terrace, Edinburgh EH4 3TP. Tel: 0131-332 2433; Thistle House, Beechwood Park North, Inverness IV2 3ED. Tel: 01463-716996. *Chief Executive*, T. Buncle

WALES TOURIST BOARD, Brunel House, 2 Fitzalan Road, Cardiff CF2 1UY. Tel: 01222-475272.
Chief Executive, J. Jones
NORTHERN IRELAND TOURIST BOARD, St Anne's Court, 59 North Street, Belfast BT1 1NB. Tel: 01232-231221.
Chief Executive, I. Henderson

UNITED KINGDOM SPORTS COUNCIL (UK SPORT)
40 Bernard Street, London WC1N 1ST
Tel: 020-7841 9500; Fax: 020-7841 8850

The UK Sports Council (UK Sport) was established by Royal Charter in January 1997. Its role is to focus on high performance sport at UK level, with the aim of achieving sporting excellence in world competition. It promotes the development of sport and fosters the provision of sporting facilities. It works to combat drug misuse, deals with international relations and organises major events. It also distributes the funds allocated to sport from the proceeds of the National Lottery.
Chairman, Sir Rodney Walker
Chief Executive, R. Callicott

UNRELATED LIVE TRANSPLANT REGULATORY AUTHORITY
Department of Health, c/o Room 311, Wellington House, 133–155 Waterloo Road, London SE1 8UG
Tel: 020-7972 4812; Fax: 020-7972 4852

The Unrelated Live Transplant Regulatory Authority (ULTRA) is a statutory body established in 1990. In every case where the transplant of an organ within the definition of the Human Organ Transplants Act 1989 is proposed between a living donor and a recipient who are not genetically related, the proposal must be referred to ULTRA. Applications must be made by registered medical practitioners.
The Authority comprises a chairman and ten members appointed by the Secretary of State for Health. The secretariat is provided by Department of Health officials.
Chairman, Prof. Sir Rodrick MacSween
Members, Mrs J. H. Callman; Dr J. F. Douglas; Dr H. Draper; Miss P. M. Franklin; Dr S. Fuggle; A. J. Hooker; Prof. A. Rees; Mrs S. J. Sullivan
Administrative Secretary, E. Scarlett
Medical Secretary, Dr P. Doyle

UK ATOMIC ENERGY AUTHORITY
Harwell, Didcot, Oxon OX11 0RA
Tel: 01235-820220; Fax: 01235-436401

The UKAEA was established by the Atomic Energy Authority Act 1954 and took over responsibility for the research and development of the civil nuclear power programme. The Authority's commercial arm, AEA Technology PLC, was privatised in 1996. UKAEA is responsible for the safe management and decommissioning of its radioactive plant and for maximising the income from the buildings and land on its sites. UKAEA also undertakes special nuclear tasks for the Government, including the UK's contribution to the international fusion programme.
Chairman, Adm. Sir Kenneth Eaton
Chief Executive, Dr J. McKeown

WALES YOUTH AGENCY
Leslie Court, Lon-y-Llyn, Caerphilly CF83 1BQ
Tel: 029-2085 5700; Fax: 029-2085 5701
Email: way@wya.org.uk
Web: http://www.way.org.uk

The Wales Youth Agency is an independent organisation funded by the National Assembly for Wales. Its functions include the encouragement and development of the partnership between statutory and voluntary agencies relating to young people; the promotion of staff development and training; and the extension of marketing and information services in the relevant fields. The board of directors do not receive a salary.
Chairman of the Board of Directors, R. Noble
Vice-Chairman of the Board of Directors, Dr H. Williamson
Chief Executive, B. Williams

WELSH ADMINISTRATION OMBUDSMAN
5th Floor, Capital Tower, Greyfriars Road,
Cardiff CF10 3AG
Tel: 0845-601 0987; Fax: 029-2022 6909
Web: http://www.ombudsman.org.uk

The Welsh Administration Ombudsman was appointed in July 1999 to investigate complaints by members of the public who have suffered an injustice through maladministration by the National Assembly for Wales and certain public bodies involved in devolved Welsh affairs.
Welsh Administration Ombudsman, M. S. Buckley

WELSH DEVELOPMENT AGENCY
Principality House, The Friary, Cardiff CF10 3FE
Tel: 01443-845500; Fax: 01443-845589

The Agency was established under the Welsh Development Agency Act 1975. Its remit is to help further the regeneration of the economy and improve the environment in Wales. Under the Government of Wales Act 1998, the Land Authority for Wales and the Development Board for Rural Wales merged with the Welsh Development Agency. The Agency is sponsored by the National Assembly for Wales.

The Agency's priorities are to create new businesses and to encourage existing small firms to grow. Its main activities include promoting Wales as a location for inward investment, helping to boost the growth, profitability and competitiveness of indigenous Welsh companies, providing investment capital for industry, encouraging investment by the private sector in property development, grant-aiding land reclamation, and stimulating quality urban and rural development.
Chairman, D. Rowe-Beddoe
Deputy Chairman, G. Hawker
Chief Executive, W. B. Willott, CB

WOMEN'S NATIONAL COMMISSION
Room 56/4, Cabinet Office, Horse Guards Road,
London SW1P 3AL
Tel: 020-7238 0386; Fax: 020-7238 0387

The Women's National Commission is an independent advisory committee to the Government. Its remit is to ensure that the informed opinions of women are given their due weight in the deliberations of the Government and in public debate on matters of public interest including those of special interest to women. The Commission's sponsoring department is the Cabinet Office.
Chair, Baroness Christine Crawley of Edgbaston
Director, Ms J. Veitch

European Parliament

European Parliament elections take place at five-yearly intervals; the first direct elections to the Parliament were held in 1979. In mainland Britain MEPs were elected in all constituencies on a first-past-the-post basis until the elections of June 1999; in Northern Ireland three MEPs have been elected by the single transferable vote system of proportional representation since 1979. From 1979 to 1994 the number of seats held by the UK in the European Parliament was 81. At the June 1994 election the number of seats increased to 87 (England 71, Wales 5, Scotland 8, Northern Ireland 3).

At the European Parliament elections held on 10 June 1999, all British MEPs were elected under a 'closed-list' regional system of proportional representation, with England being divided into nine regions and Scotland and Wales each constituting a region. Parties submitted a list of candidates for each region in their own order of preference. Voters voted for a party or an independent candidate, and the first seat in each region was allocated to the party or candidate with the highest number of votes. The rest of the seats in each region were then allocated broadly in proportion to each party's share of the vote. Each region returned the following number of members: East Midlands, 6; Eastern, 8; London, 10; North East, 4; North West, 10; South East, 11; South West, 7; West Midlands, 8; Yorkshire and the Humber, 7; Wales, 5; Scotland, 8.

If a vacancy occurs due to the resignation or death of an MEP, the vacancy is filled by the next available person on that party's list. If an independent MEP resigns or dies, a by-election is held. Where an MEP leaves the party on whose list he/she was elected, there is no requirement to resign and he/she can remain in office until the next election.

British subjects and citizens of the Irish Republic are eligible for election to the European Parliament provided they are 21 or over and not subject to disqualification. Since 1994, nationals of member states of the European Union have had the right to vote in elections to the European Parliament in the UK as long as they are entered on the electoral register.

MEPs currently receive a salary from the parliaments or governments of their respective member states, set at the level of the national parliamentary salary and subject to national taxation rules (for salary of British MPs, *see* Parliament section). A proposal that all MEPs should be paid the same rate of salary out of the EU budget, and subject to the EC tax rate, was under negotiation between the European Parliament and the Council of Ministers at the time of going to press.

UK MEMBERS AS AT 28 JULY 2000

* Denotes membership of the last European Parliament
† see Replacements since the last election
‡ Subsequently left UK Independence Party and now sits as an independent

Atkins, Rt. Hon. Sir Robert (*b.* 1946), *C., North West*
Attwooll, Ms Elspeth M.-A. (*b.* 1943), *LD, Scotland*
*Balfe, Richard A. (*b.* 1944), *Lab., London*
Beazley, Christopher J. P. (*b.* 1952), *C., Eastern*
Bethell, The Lord (*b.* 1938), *C., London*
*Bowe, David R. (*b.* 1955), *Lab., Yorkshire and the Humber*
Bowis, John C., OBE (*b.* 1945), *C., London*
Bradbourn, Philip, OBE (*b.* 1951), *C., West Midlands*
Bushill-Matthews, Philip (*b.* 1943), *C., West Midlands*

Callanan, Martin (*b.* 1961), *C., North East*
Cashman, Michael (*b.* 1950), *Lab., West Midlands*
*Chichester, Giles B. (*b.* 1946), *C., South West*
Clegg, Nicholas W. P. (*b.* 1967), *LD, East Midlands*
*Corbett, Richard (*b.* 1955), *Lab., Yorkshire and the Humber*
*Corrie, John A. (*b.* 1935), *C., West Midlands*
Davies, Christopher G. (*b.* 1954), *LD, North West*
Deva, Niranjan J. A. (Nirj), FRSA (*b.* 1948), *C., South East*
†*Donnelly, Alan J. (*b.* 1957), *Lab., North East*
Dover, Den (*b.* 1938), *C., North West*
Duff, Andrew N. (*b.* 1950), *LD, Eastern*
*Elles, James E. M. (*b.* 1949), *C., South East*
Evans, Ms Jillian R. (*b.* 1959), *PC, Wales*
Evans, Jonathan P., FRSA (*b.* 1950), *C., Wales*
*Evans, Robert J. E. (*b.* 1956), *Lab., London*
Farage, Nigel (*b.* 1964), *UK Ind., South East*
*Ford, J. Glyn (*b.* 1950), *Lab., South West*
Foster, Mrs Jacqui (*b.* 1947), *C., North West*
Gill, Ms Neena (*b.* 1956), *Lab., West Midlands*
Goodwill, Robert (*b.* 1956), *C., Yorkshire and the Humber*
†*Green, Mrs Pauline (*b.* 1948), *Lab., London*
Hannan, Daniel (*b.* 1971), *C., South East*
Harbour, Malcolm (*b.* 1947), *C., West Midlands*
Heaton-Harris, Christopher (*b.* 1967), *C., East Midlands*
Helmer, Roger (*b.* 1944), *C., East Midlands*
‡Holmes, Michael (*b.* 1938), *UK Ind., South West*
*Howitt, Richard (*b.* 1961), *Lab., Eastern*
Hudghton, Ian (*b.* 1951), *SNP, Scotland*
*Hughes, Stephen S. (*b.* 1952), *Lab., North East*
Huhne, Christopher M. P., OBE (*b.* 1954), *LD, South East*
*Hume, John, MP (*b.* 1937), *SDLP, Northern Ireland*
Inglewood, The Lord (*b.* 1951), *C., North West*
*Jackson, Mrs Caroline F., D.Phil. (*b.* 1946), *C., South West*
Khanbhai, Bashir (*b.* 1945), *C., Eastern*
*Kinnock, Mrs Glenys E. (*b.* 1944), *Lab., Wales*
Kirkhope, Timothy J. R. (*b.* 1945), *C., Yorkshire and the Humber*
Lambert, Ms Jean D. (*b.* 1950), *Green, London*
Lucas, Ms Caroline, Ph.D. (*b.* 1960), *Green, South East*
Ludford, The Baroness (*b.* 1951), *LD, London*
Lynne, Ms Elizabeth (*b.* 1948), *LD, West Midlands*
*McAvan, Ms Linda (*b.* 1962), *Lab., Yorkshire and the Humber*
*McCarthy, Ms Arlene (*b.* 1960), *Lab., North West*
MacCormick, Prof. D. Neil, FBA (*b.* 1941), *SNP, Scotland*
*McMillan-Scott, Edward H. C. (*b.* 1949), *C., Yorkshire and the Humber*
*McNally, Mrs Eryl M. (*b.* 1942), *Lab., Eastern*
*Martin, David W. (*b.* 1954), *Lab., Scotland*
*Miller, William (*b.* 1954), *Lab., Scotland*
Moraes, Claude (*b.* 1965), *Lab., London*
*Morgan, Ms Eluned (*b.* 1967), *Lab., Wales*
*Murphy, Simon F., D.Ph. (*b.* 1962), *Lab., West Midlands*
Newton Dunn, William F. (Bill) (*b.* 1941), *C., East Midlands*
Nicholson of Winterbourne, The Baroness (*b.* 1941), *LD, South East*
*Nicholson, James F. (*b.* 1945), *UUP, Northern Ireland*
O'Toole, Ms Barbara M. (Mo) (*b.* 1960), *Lab., North East*
*Paisley, Revd Ian R. K., MP (*b.* 1926), *DUP, Northern Ireland*
Parish, Neil (*b.* 1956), *C., South West*

*Perry, Roy J. (*b.* 1943), *C., South East*
*Provan, James L. C. (*b.* 1936), *C., South East*
Purvis, John R., CBE (*b.* 1938), *C., Scotland*
*Read, Ms I. M. (Mel) (*b.* 1939), *Lab., East Midlands*
*Simpson, Brian (*b.* 1953), *Lab., North West*
*Skinner, Peter W. (*b.* 1959), *Lab., South East*
Stevenson, Struan (*b.* 1948), *C., Scotland*
Stihler, Catherine D. (*elected Catherine Taylor*) (*b.* 1973), *Lab., Scotland*
Stockton, The Earl of (*b.* 1943), *C., South West*
*Sturdy, Robert W. (*b.* 1944), *C., Eastern*
Sumberg, David A. G. (*b.* 1941), *C., North West*

Tannock, Dr Charles (*b.* 1957), *C., London*
Titford, Jeffrey (*b. 1933*), *UK Ind., Eastern*
*Titley, Gary (*b.* 1950), *Lab., North West*
Van Orden, Geoffrey (*b.* 1945), *C., Eastern*
Villiers, Ms Theresa (*b.* 1968), *C., London*
Wallis, Ms Diana P. (*b.* 1954), *LD, Yorkshire and the Humber*
*Watson, Graham R. (*b.* 1956), *LD, South West*
*Watts, Mark F. (*b.* 1964), *Lab., South East*
*Whitehead, Philip (*b.* 1937), *Lab., East Midlands*
Wyn, Eurig (*b.* 1944), *PC, Wales*
*Wynn, Terence (*b.* 1946), *Lab., North West*

UK REGIONS AS AT 10 JUNE 2000

Abbreviations

ACPFCA	Anti-Corruption Pro Family Christian Alliance
AHRPE	Architect Human Rights Peace in Europe
Anti VAT	Independent Anti Value Added Tax
EFP	English Freedom Party
Ind. Profit	Independent Making a Profit in Europe
Ind. Stable	Independent Open Democracy for Stability
Lower Tax	Account for Lower Scottish Taxes
MEP Ind.	MEP Independent Labour
Soc. All.	Socialist Alliance
SSP	Scottish Socialist Party
WW	Weekly Worker

For other abbreviations, *see* page 235

EASTERN
(Bedfordshire; Cambridgeshire; Essex; Hertfordshire; Luton; Norfolk; Peterborough; Southend-on-Sea; Suffolk; Thurrock)

E.4,019,916	T.24.74%
C.	425,091 (42.75%)
Lab.	250,132 (25.15%)
LD	118,822 (11.95%)
UK Ind.	88,452 (8.89%)
Green	61,334 (6.17%)
Lib.	16,861 (1.70%)
Pro Euro C.	16,340 (1.64%)
BNP	9,356 (0.94%)
Soc. Lab.	6,143 (0.62%)
NLP	1,907 (0.19%)
C. majority	174,959
(June 1994, Lab. maj. 90,087)	

MEMBERS ELECTED
*R. Sturdy, *C.*
C. Beazley, *C.*
B. Khanbhai, *C.*
G. Van Orden, *C.*
*Ms E. McNally, *Lab.*
*R. Howitt, *Lab.*
A. Duff, *LD*
J. Titford, *UK Ind.*

EAST MIDLANDS
(Derby; Derbyshire; Leicester; Leicestershire; Lincolnshire; Northamptonshire; Nottingham; Nottinghamshire; Rutland)

E.3,170,517	T.22.83%
C.	285,662 (39.47%)
Lab.	206,756 (28.57%)
LD	92,398 (12.77%)
UK Ind.	54,800 (7.57%)
Green	38,954 (5.38%)
Alt. Lab.	17,409 (2.41%)
Pro Euro C.	11,359 (1.57%)
BNP	9,342 (1.29%)
Soc. Lab.	5,528 (0.76%)
NLP	1,525 (0.21%)
C. majority	78,906
(June 1994, Lab. maj. 229,680)	

MEMBERS ELECTED
R. Helmer, *C.*
W. Newton Dunn, *C.*
C. Heaton-Harris, *C.*
*Ms M. Read, *Lab.*
*P. Whitehead, *Lab.*
N. Clegg, *LD*

LONDON

E.4,940,493	T.23.10%
Lab.	399,466 (35.00%)
C.	372,989 (32.68%)
LD	133,058 (11.66%)
Green	87,545 (7.67%)
UK Ind.	61,741 (5.41%)
Soc. Lab.	19,632 (1.72%)
BNP	17,960 (1.57%)
Lib.	16,951 (1.49%)
Pro Euro C.	16,383 (1.44%)
AHRPE	4,851 (0.43%)
Anti VAT	2,596 (0.23%)
Hum.	2,586 (0.23%)
Hemp	2,358 (0.21%)
NLP	2,263 (0.20%)
WW	846 (0.07%)
Lab. majority	26,477
(June 1994, Lab. maj. 346,850)	

MEMBERS ELECTED
Miss T. Villiers, *C.*
Dr C. Tannock, *C.*
The Lord Bethell, *C.*
J. Bowis, *C.*
*Ms P. Green, *Lab.*
C. Moraes, *Lab.*
*R. Evans, *Lab.*
*R. Balfe, *Lab.*
Ms S. Ludford, *LD*
Ms J. Lambert, *Green*

NORTH EAST
(Co. Durham; Darlington; Hartlepool; Middlesbrough; Northumberland; Redcar and Cleveland; Stockton-on-Tees; Tyne and Wear)

E.1,954,076	T.19.74%
Lab.	162,573 (42.15%)
C.	105,573 (27.37%)
LD	52,070 (13.50%)
UK Ind.	34,063 (8.83%)
Green	18,184 (4.71%)
Soc. Lab.	4,511 (1.17%)
BNP	3,505 (0.91%)
Pro Euro C.	2,926 (0.76%)
SPGB	1,510 (0.39%)
NLP	826 (0.21%)
Lab. majority	57,000
(June 1994, Lab. maj. 330,689)	

MEMBERS ELECTED
M. Callanan, *C.*
*A. Donnelly, *Lab.*
*S. Hughes, *Lab.*
Ms M. O'Toole, *Lab.*

NORTHERN IRELAND
Northern Ireland forms a three-member seat with a single transferable vote system

E.1,190,160	T.57.77%
First Count	
*Revd I. Paisley, *DUP*	192,762
*J. Hume, *SDLP*	190,731
*J. Nicholson, *UUP*	119,507
M. McLaughlin, *SF*	117,643
D. Ervine, *PUP*	22,494
R. McCartney, *UKU*	20,283
S. Neeson, *All.*	14,391
J. Anderson, *NLP*	998

MEMBERS ELECTED
*Revd I. Paisley, *DUP*
*J. Hume, *SDLP*
*J. Nicholson, *UUP* (elected on third count)

NORTH WEST
(Blackburn-with-Darwen; Blackpool; Cheshire; Cumbria; Greater Manchester; Halton; Lancashire; Merseyside; Warrington)

E.5,170,524	T.19.67%
C.	360,027 (35.39%)
Lab.	350,511 (34.46%)
LD	119,376 (11.74%)
UK Ind.	66,779 (6.57%)
Green	56,828 (5.59%)
Lib.	22,640 (2.23%)

BNP	13,587 (1.34%)
Soc. Lab.	11,338 (1.11%)
Pro Euro C.	9,816 (0.97%)
ACPFCA	2,251 (0.22%)
NLP	2,114 (0.21%)
Ind. Hum.	1,049 (0.10%)
WW	878 (0.09%)
C. majority	9,516

(June 1994, Lab. maj. 444,569)

MEMBERS ELECTED

The Lord Inglewood, C.
Sir Robert Atkins, C.
D. Sumberg, C.
D. Dover, C.
Mrs J. Foster, C.
*Ms A. McCarthy, Lab.
*G. Titley, Lab.
*T. Wynn, Lab.
*B. Simpson, Lab.
C. Davies, LD

SCOTLAND

E.3,979,845	T.24.83%
Lab.	283,490 (28.68%)
SNP	268,528 (27.17%)
C.	195,296 (19.76%)
LD	96,971 (9.81%)
Green	57,142 (5.78%)
SSP	39,720 (4.02%)
Pro Euro C.	17,781 (1.80%)
UK Ind.	12,549 (1.27%)
Soc. Lab.	9,385 (0.95%)
BNP	3,729 (0.38%)
NLP	2,087 (0.21%)
Lower Tax	1,632 (0.17%)
Lab. majority	14,962

(June 1994, Lab. maj. 148,718)

MEMBERS ELECTED

S. Stevenson, C.
J. Purvis, C.
*D. Martin, Lab.
*W. Miller, Lab.
Ms C. Taylor, Lab.
Ms E. Attwooll, LD
*I. Hudghton, SNP
Prof. N. MacCormick, SNP

SOUTH EAST

(Bracknell Forest; Brighton and Hove; Buckinghamshire; East Sussex; Hampshire; Isle of Wight; Kent; Medway; Milton Keynes; Oxfordshire; Portsmouth; Reading; Slough; Southampton; Surrey; West Berkshire; West Sussex; Windsor and Maidenhead; Wokingham)

E.5,972,945	T.24.95%
C.	661,931 (44.42%)
Lab.	292,146 (19.61%)
LD	228,136 (15.31%)
UK Ind.	144,514 (9.70%)
Green	110,571 (7.42%)
Pro Euro C.	27,305 (1.83%)
BNP	12,161 (0.82%)
Soc. Lab.	7,281 (0.49%)
NLP	2,767 (0.19%)
Ind. Stable	1,857 (0.12%)
Ind. Profit	1,400 (0.09%)
C. majority	369,785

(June 1994, C. maj. 230,122)

MEMBERS ELECTED

*J. Provan, C.
*R. Perry, C.
D. Hannan, C.
*J. Elles, C.
N. Deva, C.
*P. Skinner, Lab.
*M. Watts, Lab.
The Baroness Nicholson of Winterbourne, LD
C. Huhne, LD
Dr Caroline Lucas, Green
N. Farage, UK Ind.

SOUTH WEST

(Bath and North-East Somerset; Bournemouth; Bristol; Cornwall; Devon; Dorset; Gloucestershire; North Somerset; Plymouth; Poole; Scilly Isles; Somerset; South Gloucestershire; Swindon; Torbay; Wiltshire)

E.3,747,620	T.27.81%
C.	434,645 (41.70%)
Lab.	188,362 (18.07%)
LD	171,498 (16.45%)
UK Ind.	111,012 (10.65%)
Green	86,630 (8.31%)
Lib.	21,645 (2.08%)
Pro Euro C.	11,134 (1.07%)
BNP	9,752 (0.94%)
Soc. Lab.	5,741 (0.55%)
NLP	1,968 (0.19%)
C. majority	246,283

(June 1994, LD maj. 3,796)

MEMBERS ELECTED

*Dr Caroline Jackson, C.
*G. Chichester, C.
The Earl of Stockton, C.
N. Parish, C.
*G. Ford, Lab.
*G. Watson, LD
M. Holmes, UK Ind.

WALES

E.2,211,162	T.28.33%
Lab.	199,690 (31.88%)
PC	185,235 (29.57%)
C.	142,631 (22.77%)
LD	51,283 (8.19%)
UK Ind.	19,702 (3.15%)
Green	16,146 (2.58%)
Pro Euro C.	5,834 (0.93%)
Soc. Lab.	4,283 (0.68%)
NLP	1,621 (0.26%)
Lab. majority	14,455

(June 1994, Lab. maj. 368,271)

MEMBERS ELECTED

J. Evans, C.
*Ms G. Kinnock, Lab.
*Ms E. Morgan, Lab.
Ms J. Evans, PC
E. Wyn, PC

WEST MIDLANDS

(Herefordshire; Shropshire; Staffordshire; Stoke-on-Trent; Telford and Wrekin; Warwickshire; West Midlands Metropolitan County; Worcestershire)

E.4,001,942	T.21.21%
C.	321,719 (37.91%)
Lab.	237,671 (28.00%)
LD	95,769 (11.28%)
UK Ind.	49,621 (5.85%)
Green	49,440 (5.83%)
MEP Ind.	36,849 (4.34%)
Lib.	14,954 (1.76%)
BNP	14,344 (1.69%)
Pro Euro C.	11,144 (1.31%)
Soc. All.	7,203 (0.85%)
Soc. Lab.	5,257 (0.62%)
EFP	3,066 (0.36%)
NLP	1,647 (0.19%)
C. majority	84,048

(June 1994, Lab. maj. 268,888)

MEMBERS ELECTED

*J. Corrie, C.
P. Bushill-Matthews, C.
M. Harbour, C.
P. Bradbourn, C.
*S. Murphy, Lab.
M. Cashman, Lab.
Ms N. Gill, Lab.
Ms E. Lynne, LD

YORKSHIRE AND THE HUMBER

(East Riding of Yorkshire; Kingston-upon-Hull; North East Lincolnshire; North Lincolnshire; North Yorkshire; South Yorkshire; West Yorkshire; York)

E.3,767,227	T.19.75%
C.	272,653 (36.64%)
Lab.	233,024 (31.32%)
LD	107,168 (14.40%)
UK Ind.	52,824 (7.10%)
Green	42,604 (5.73%)
Alt. Lab.	9,554 (1.28%)
BNP	8,911 (1.20%)
Pro Euro C.	8,075 (1.09%)
Soc. Lab.	7,650 (1.03%)
NLP	1,604 (0.22%)
C. majority	39,629

(June 1994, Lab. maj. 344,310)

MEMBERS ELECTED

*E. McMillan-Scott, C.
T. Kirkhope, C.
R. Goodwill, C.
*Ms L. McAvan, Lab.
*D. Bowe, Lab.
*R. Corbett, Lab.
Ms D. Wallis, LD

REPLACEMENTS SINCE THE LAST ELECTION

LONDON
2000; Pauline Green replaced by Mary Honeyball, Lab

NORTH EAST
2000; Alan Donnelly replaced by Gordon Adam, Lab

Prime Ministers since 1782

Over the centuries there has been some variation in the determination of the dates of appointment of Prime Ministers. Where possible, the date given is that on which a new Prime Minister kissed the Sovereign's hands and accepted the commission to form a ministry. However, until the middle of the 19th century the dating of a commission or transfer of seals could be the date of taking office. Where the composition of the Government changed, e.g. became a coalition, but the Prime Minister remained the same, the date of the change of government is given.

The Marquess of Rockingham, *Whig*, 27 March 1782
The Earl of Shelburne, *Whig*, 4 July 1782
The Duke of Portland, *Coalition*, 2 April 1783
William Pitt, *Tory*, 19 December 1783
Henry Addington, *Tory*, 17 March 1801
William Pitt, *Tory*, 10 May 1804
The Lord Grenville, *Whig*, 11 February 1806
The Duke of Portland, *Tory*, 31 March 1807
Spencer Perceval, *Tory*, 4 October 1809
The Earl of Liverpool, *Tory*, 8 June 1812
George Canning, *Tory*, 10 April 1827
Viscount Goderich, *Tory*, 31 August 1827
The Duke of Wellington, *Tory*, 22 January 1828
The Earl Grey, *Whig*, 22 November 1830
The Viscount Melbourne, *Whig*, 16 July 1834
The Duke of Wellington, *Tory*, 17 November 1834
Sir Robert Peel, *Tory*, 10 December 1834
The Viscount Melbourne, *Whig*, 18 April 1835
Sir Robert Peel, *Tory*, 30 August 1841
Lord John Russell (subsequently the Earl Russell), *Whig*, 30 June 1846
The Earl of Derby, *Tory*, 23 February 1852
The Earl of Aberdeen, *Peelite*, 19 December 1852
The Viscount Palmerston, *Liberal*, 6 February 1855
The Earl of Derby, *Conservative*, 20 February 1858
The Viscount Palmerston, *Liberal*, 12 June 1859
The Earl Russell, *Liberal*, 29 October 1865
The Earl of Derby, *Conservative*, 28 June 1866

Benjamin Disraeli, *Conservative*, 27 February 1868
William Gladstone, *Liberal*, 3 December 1868
Benjamin Disraeli, *Conservative*, 20 February 1874
William Gladstone, *Liberal*, 23 April 1880
The Marquess of Salisbury, *Conservative*, 23 June 1885
William Gladstone, *Liberal*, 1 February 1886
The Marquess of Salisbury, *Conservative*, 25 July 1886
William Gladstone, *Liberal*, 15 August 1892
The Earl of Rosebery, *Liberal*, 5 March 1894
The Marquess of Salisbury, *Conservative*, 25 June 1895
Arthur Balfour, *Conservative*, 12 July 1902
Sir Henry Campbell-Bannerman, *Liberal*, 5 December 1905
Herbert Asquith, *Liberal*, 7 April 1908
Herbert Asquith, *Coalition*, 25 May 1915
David Lloyd-George, *Coalition*, 7 December 1916
Andrew Bonar Law, *Conservative*, 23 October 1922
Stanley Baldwin, *Conservative*, 22 May 1923
Ramsay MacDonald, *Labour*, 22 January 1924
Stanley Baldwin, *Conservative*, 4 November 1924
Ramsay MacDonald, *Labour*, 5 June 1929
Ramsay MacDonald, *Coalition*, 24 August 1931
Stanley Baldwin, *Coalition*, 7 June 1935
Neville Chamberlain, *Coalition*, 28 May 1937
Winston Churchill, *Coalition*, 10 May 1940
Winston Churchill, *Conservative*, 23 May 1945
Clement Attlee, *Labour*, 26 July 1945
Sir Winston Churchill, *Conservative*, 26 October 1951
Sir Anthony Eden, *Conservative*, 6 April 1955
Harold Macmillan, *Conservative*, 10 January 1957
Sir Alec Douglas-Home, *Conservative*, 19 October 1963
Harold Wilson, *Labour*, 16 October 1964
Edward Heath, *Conservative*, 19 June 1970
Harold Wilson, *Labour*, 4 March 1974
James Callaghan, *Labour*, 5 April 1976
Margaret Thatcher, *Conservative*, 4 May 1979
John Major, *Conservative*, 28 November 1990
Anthony Blair, *Labour*, 2 May 1997

Speakers of the Commons since 1708

The date of appointment given is the day on which the Speaker was first elected by the House of Commons. The appointment requires royal approbation before it is confirmed and this is usually given within a few days. The present Speaker is the 155th, however, she announced her retirement in July 2000.

PARLIAMENT OF GREAT BRITAIN
Sir Richard Onslow (*Lord Onslow*), 16 November 1708
William Bromley, 25 November 1710
Sir Thomas Hanmer, 16 February 1714
Spencer Compton (*Earl of Wilmington*), 17 March 1715
Arthur Onslow, 23 January 1728
Sir John Cust, 3 November 1761
Sir Fletcher Norton (*Lord Grantley*), 22 January 1770
Charles Cornwall, 31 October 1780
Hon. William Grenville (*Lord Grenville*), 5 January 1789
Henry Addington (*Viscount Sidmouth*), 8 June 1789

PARLIAMENT OF THE UNITED KINGDOM
Sir John Mitford (*Lord Redesdale*), 11 February 1801

Charles Abbot (*Lord Colchester*), 10 February 1802
Charles Manners-Sutton (*Viscount Canterbury*), 2 June 1817
James Abercromby (*Lord Dunfermline*), 19 February 1835
Charles Shaw-Lefevre (*Viscount Eversley*), 27 May 1839
J. Evelyn Denison (*Viscount Ossington*), 30 April 1857
Sir Henry Brand (*Viscount Hampden*), 9 February 1872
Arthur Wellesley Peel (*Viscount Peel*), 26 February 1884
William Gully (*Viscount Selby*), 10 April 1895
James Lowther (*Viscount Ullswater*), 8 June 1905
John Whitley, 27 April 1921
Hon. Edward Fitzroy, 20 June 1928
Douglas Clifton-Brown (*Viscount Ruffside*), 9 March 1943
William Morrison (*Viscount Dunrossil*), 31 October 1951
Sir Harry Hylton-Foster, 20 October 1959
Horace King (*Lord Maybray-King*), 26 October 1965
Selwyn Lloyd (*Lord Selwyn-Lloyd*), 12 January 1971
George Thomas (*Viscount Tonypandy*), 2 February 1976
Bernard Weatherill (*Lord Weatherill*), 15 June 1983
Betty Boothroyd, 27 April 1992

Law Courts and Offices

THE JUDICIAL COMMITTEE OF THE PRIVY COUNCIL

The Judicial Committee of the Privy Council is primarily the final court of appeal for the United Kingdom overseas and those independent Commonwealth countries which have retained the avenue of appeal upon achieving independence (Antigua and Barbuda, The Bahamas, Barbados, Belize, Brunei, Dominica, Grenada, Jamaica, Kiribati, Mauritius, New Zealand, St Christopher and Nevis, St Lucia, St Vincent and the Grenadines, Trinidad and Tobago, and Tuvalu). The Committee also hears appeals from the Channel Islands and the Isle of Man and the disciplinary and health committees of the medical and allied professions. It has a limited jurisdiction to hear appeals under the Pastoral Measure 1983. In 1999 the Judicial Committee heard 64 appeals and 82 petitions for special leave to appeal.

Under the devolution legislation enacted in 1998, the Judicial Committee of the Privy Council is the final arbiter in disputes as to the legal competence of things done or proposed by the devolved legislative and Executive authorities in Scotland, Wales and Northern Ireland.

The members of the Judicial Committee include the Lord Chancellor, the Lords of Appeal in Ordinary (*see* page 368), other Privy Counsellors who hold or have held high judicial office and certain judges from the Commonwealth.

PRIVY COUNCIL OFFICE (JUDICIAL COMMITTEE),
Downing Street, London SW1A 2AJ. Tel: 020-7270 0483.
Registrar of the Privy Council, J. A. C. Watherston; *Chief Clerk*, F. G. Hart

The Judicature of England and Wales

The legal system of England and Wales is separate from those of Scotland and Northern Ireland and differs from them in law, judicial procedure and court structure, although there is a common distinction between civil law (disputes between individuals) and criminal law (acts harmful to the community).

The supreme judicial authority for England and Wales is the House of Lords, which is the ultimate Court of Appeal from all courts in Great Britain and Northern Ireland (except criminal courts in Scotland) for all cases except those concerning the interpretation and application of European Community law, including preliminary rulings requested by British courts and tribunals, which are decided by the European Court of Justice (*see* European Union section). Under the Human Rights Act 1998, which came into force in October 2000, the European Convention on Human Rights will be incorporated into British law; unresolved cases will still be referred to the European Court of Human Rights. As a Court of Appeal the House of Lords consists of the Lord Chancellor and the Lords of Appeal in Ordinary (law lords).

SUPREME COURT OF JUDICATURE

The Supreme Court of Judicature comprises the Court of Appeal, the High Court of Justice and the Crown Court. The High Court of Justice is the superior civil court and is divided into three divisions. The Chancery Division is concerned mainly with equity, bankruptcy and contentious probate business. The Queen's Bench Division deals with commercial and maritime law, serious personal injury and medical negligence cases, cases involving a breach of contract and professional negligence actions. The Family Division deals with matters relating to family law. Sittings are held at the Royal Courts of Justice in London or at 126 District Registries outside the capital. High Court judges sit alone to hear cases at first instance. The Restrictive Practices Court, set up under the Restrictive Trade Practices Act 1956, and the Technology and Construction Court, which deals with cases which require expert evidence on technical and other issues concerning mainly the construction industry, defective products, property valuations, and landlord and tenant disputes, are also currently part of the High Court, although the Restrictive Practices Court is due to be abolished following the establishment of the Competition Commission (*see* Government Department and Public Offices section). Appeals from the High Court are heard in the Court of Appeal (Civil Division), presided over by the Master of the Rolls, and may go on to the House of Lords.

In December 1999 the Lord Chancellor announced that a wide ranging, independent review of the criminal courts in England and Wales would take place. Lord Justice Auld is to lead the review into how the criminal courts work at every level.

CRIMINAL CASES

In criminal matters the decision to prosecute in the majority of cases rests with the Crown Prosecution Service, the independent prosecuting body in England and Wales (*see* pages 376–7). The Service is headed by the Director of Public Prosecutions, who works under the superintendence of the Attorney-General. Certain categories of offence continue to require the Attorney-General's consent for prosecution.

The Crown Court sits in about 90 centres, divided into six circuits, and is presided over by High Court judges, full-time circuit judges, and part-time recorders and assistant recorders, sitting with a jury in all trials which are contested. There were 266 assistant recorders at 30 June 1999. The Crown Court deals with trials of the more serious criminal offences, the sentencing of offenders committed for sentence by magistrates' courts (when the magistrates consider their own power of sentence inadequate), and appeals from magistrates' courts. Magistrates usually sit with a circuit judge or recorder to deal with appeals and committals for sentence. Appeals from the Crown Court, either against sentence or conviction, are made to the Court of Appeal (Criminal Division), presided over by the Lord Chief Justice. A further appeal from the Court of Appeal to the House of Lords can be brought if a point of law of general public importance is considered to be involved.

Minor criminal offences (summary offences) are dealt with in magistrates' courts, which usually consist of three unpaid lay magistrates (justices of the peace) sitting without a jury, who are advised on points of law and procedure by a legally-qualified clerk to the justices. There were 30,260 justices of the peace at 1 January 1999. In busier courts a full-time, salaried and legally-qualified stipendiary magistrate presides alone. Cases involving people under 18 are heard in youth courts, specially constituted magistrates' courts which sit apart from other courts. Preliminary proceedings in a serious case to decide whether there is evidence to justify committal for trial in the Crown Court are also dealt with in the magistrates' courts. Appeals from magistrates' courts against sentence or conviction are made to the Crown Court. Appeals upon a point of law are made to the High Court, and may go on to the House of Lords.

CIVIL CASES

Most minor civil cases are dealt with by the county courts, of which there are about 222 (details may be found in the local telephone directory). Cases are heard by circuit judges or district judges. There were 403 district judges at 31 May 2000. For cases involving small claims there are special simplified procedures. Where there are financial limits on county court jurisdiction, claims which exceed those limits may be tried in the county courts with the consent of the parties, subject to the Court's agreement, or in certain circumstances on transfer from the High Court. Outside London, bankruptcy proceedings can be heard in designated county courts. Magistrates' courts can deal with certain classes of civil case and committees of magistrates license public houses, clubs and betting shops. For the implementation of the Children Act 1989, a new structure of hearing centres was set up in 1991 for family proceedings cases, involving magistrates' courts (family proceedings courts), divorce county courts, family hearing centres and care centres. Appeals in family matters heard in the family proceedings courts go to the Family Division of the High Court; affiliation appeals and appeals from decisions of the licensing committees of magistrates go to the Crown Court. Appeals from county courts may be heard in the High Court of Appeal (civil division) and may go on to the House of Lords.

CORONERS' COURTS

Coroners' courts investigate violent and unnatural deaths or sudden deaths where the cause is unknown. Cases may be brought before a local coroner (a senior lawyer or doctor) by doctors, the police, various public authorities or members of the public. Where a death is sudden and the cause is unknown, the coroner may order a post-mortem examination to determine the cause of death rather than hold an inquest in court.

Judicial appointments are made by The Queen; the most senior appointments are made on the advice of the Prime Minister and other appointments on the advice of the Lord Chancellor.

Under the provisions of the Criminal Appeal Act 1995, a Commission was set up to direct and supervise investigations into possible miscarriages of justice and to refer cases to the courts on the grounds of conviction and sentence (*see* Parliament section); these functions were formerly the responsibility of the Home Secretary.

THE HOUSE OF LORDS
AS FINAL COURT OF APPEAL

The Lord High Chancellor (£167,760)
The Rt. Hon. the Lord Irvine of Lairg, *born* 1940, *apptd* 1997

LORDS OF APPEAL IN ORDINARY (each £152,072)
Style, The Rt. Hon. Lord —

Rt. Hon. Lord Slynn of Hadley, *born* 1930, *apptd* 1992
Rt. Hon. Lord Nicholls of Birkenhead, *born* 1933, *apptd* 1994
Rt. Hon. Lord Steyn, *born* 1932, *apptd* 1995
Rt. Hon. Lord Hoffman, *born* 1934, *apptd* 1995
Rt. Hon. Lord Hope of Craighead, *born* 1938, *apptd* 1996
Rt. Hon. Lord Clyde, *born* 1932, *apptd* 1996
Rt. Hon. Lord Hutton, *born* 1931, *apptd* 1997
Rt. Hon. Lord Saville of Newdigate, *born* 1936, *apptd* 1997
Rt. Hon. Lord Hobhouse of Woodborough, *born* 1932, *apptd* 1998
Rt. Hon. Lord Millett, *born* 1932, *apptd* 1998
Rt. Hon. Lord Bingham of Cornhill, *born* 1933, *apptd* 2000

Judicial Office of the House of Lords, House of Lords, London SW1A 0PW. Tel: 020-7219 3111
Registrar, The Clerk of the Parliaments

SUPREME COURT OF JUDICATURE

COURT OF APPEAL

The Master of the Rolls (£157,390), The Rt. Hon. Lord Phillips of Worth Matravers, *born* 1938, *apptd* 2000,
Secretary, Mrs L. Grace
Clerk, Ms J. Jones

LORDS JUSTICES OF APPEAL (each £144,549)
Style, The Rt. Hon. Lord/Lady Justice [surname]

Rt. Hon. Sir Martin Nourse, *born* 1932, *apptd* 1985
Rt. Hon. Sir Paul Kennedy, *born* 1935, *apptd* 1992
Rt. Hon. Sir Simon Brown, *born* 1937, *apptd* 1992
Rt. Hon. Sir Christopher Rose, *born* 1937, *apptd* 1992
Rt. Hon. Sir John Roch, *born* 1934, *apptd* 1993
Rt. Hon. Sir Peter Gibson, *born* 1934, *apptd* 1993
Rt. Hon. Sir Denis Henry, *born* 1931, *apptd* 1993
Rt. Hon. Sir Swinton Thomas, *born* 1931, *apptd* 1994
Rt. Hon. Sir Andrew Morritt, CVO, *born* 1938, *apptd* 1994
Rt. Hon. Sir Philip Otton, *born* 1933, *apptd* 1995
Rt. Hon. Sir Robin Auld, *born* 1937, *apptd* 1995
Rt. Hon. Sir Malcolm Pill, *born* 1938, *apptd* 1995
Rt. Hon. Sir William Aldous, *born* 1936, *apptd* 1995
Rt. Hon. Sir Alan Ward, *born* 1938, *apptd* 1995
Rt. Hon. Sir Konrad Schiemann, *born* 1937, *apptd* 1995
Rt. Hon. Sir Mathew Thorpe, *born* 1938, *apptd* 1995
Rt. Hon. Sir Mark Potter, *born* 1937, *apptd* 1996
Rt. Hon. Sir Henry Brooke, *born* 1936, *apptd* 1996
Rt. Hon. Sir Igor Judge, *born* 1941, *apptd* 1996
Rt. Hon. Sir Mark Waller, *born* 1940, *apptd* 1996
Rt. Hon. Sir John Mummery, *born* 1938, *apptd* 1996
Rt. Hon. Sir Charles Mantell, *born* 1937, *apptd* 1997
Rt. Hon. Sir John Chadwick, ED, *born* 1941, *apptd* 1997
Rt. Hon. Sir Robert Walker, *born* 1938, *apptd* 1997
Rt. Hon. Sir Richard Buxton, *born* 1938, *apptd* 1997
Rt. Hon. Sir Anthony May, *born* 1940, *apptd* 1997
Rt. Hon. Sir Simon Tuckey, *born* 1941, *apptd* 1998
Rt. Hon. Sir Anthony Clarke, *born* 1943, *apptd* 1998
Rt. Hon. Sir John Laws, *born* 1945, *apptd* 1999
Rt. Hon. Sir Stephen Sedley, *born* 1939, *apptd* 1999
Rt. Hon. Sir Jonathan Mance, *born* 1943, *apptd* 1999
Rt. Hon. Dame Brenda Hale, *born* 1945, *apptd* 1999
Rt. Hon. Sir David Latham, *born* 1942, *apptd* 2000
Rt. Hon Sir John William Kay, *born* 1943, *apptd.* 2000
Rt. Hon. Sir Bernard Anthony Rix, *born* 1944, *apptd* 2000

Ex officio Judges, The Lord High Chancellor; the Lord Chief Justice of England; the Master of the Rolls; the President of the Family Division; and the Vice-Chancellor

COURT OF APPEAL (CIVIL DIVISION)
Vice-President, The Rt Hon. Lord Justice Nourse

COURT OF APPEAL (CRIMINAL DIVISION)
Vice-President, The Rt. Hon. Lord Justice Rose
Judges, The Lord Chief Justice of England; the Master of the Rolls; Lords Justices of Appeal; and Judges of the High Court of Justice

COURT-MARTIAL APPEAL COURT
Judges, The Lord Chief Justice of England; the Master of the Rolls; Lords Justices of Appeal; and Judges of the High Court of Justice

HIGH COURT OF JUSTICE

CHANCERY DIVISION

President, The Lord High Chancellor
The Vice-Chancellor (£152,072), The Rt. Hon. Sir Richard Scott, *born* 1934, *apptd* 1994
  Clerk, W. Northfield, BEM

JUDGES (each £127,872)
Style, The Hon. Mr/Mrs Justice [surname]

Hon. Sir Donald Rattee, *born* 1937, *apptd* 1989
Hon. Sir Francis Ferris, TD, *born* 1932, *apptd* 1990
Hon. Sir Jonathan Parker, *born* 1937, *apptd* 1991
Hon. Sir John Lindsay, *born* 1935, *apptd* 1992
Hon. Dame Mary Arden, DBE, *born* 1947, *apptd* 1993
Hon. Sir Edward Evans-Lombe, *born* 1937, *apptd* 1993
Hon. Sir Robin Jacob, *born* 1941, *apptd* 1993
Hon. Sir William Blackburne, *born* 1944, *apptd* 1993
Hon. Sir Gavin Lightman, *born* 1939, *apptd* 1994
Hon. Sir Robert Carnwath, *born* 1945, *apptd* 1994
Hon. Sir Colin Rimer, *born* 1944, *apptd* 1994
Hon. Sir Hugh Laddie, *born* 1946, *apptd* 1995
Hon. Sir Timothy Lloyd, *born* 1946, *apptd* 1996
Hon. Sir David Neuberger, *born* 1948, *apptd* 1996
Hon. Sir Andrew Park, *born* 1939, *apptd* 1997
Hon. Sir Nicholas Pumfrey, *born* 1951, *apptd* 1997
Hon. Sir Michael Hart, *born* 1948, *apptd* 1998
Hon. Sir Lawrence Collins, *born* 1941, *apptd* 2000
Hon. Sir Nicholas Patten, *born* 1950, *apptd* 2000

HIGH COURT OF JUSTICE IN BANKRUPTCY
Judges, The Vice-Chancellor and judges of the Chancery Division of the High Court

COMPANIES COURT
Judges, The Vice Chancellor and judges of the Chancery Division of the High Court

PATENT COURT (APPELLATE SECTION)
Judge, The Hon. Mr Justice Jacob

QUEEN'S BENCH DIVISION

The Lord Chief Justice of England and Wales (£165,260)
  The Rt. Hon. the Lord Woolf, *born* 1933, *apptd* 2000
  Private Secretary, E. Adams
  Clerk, J. Bond
Vice-President, The Rt. Hon. Lord Justice Kennedy

JUDGES (each £127,872)
Style, The Hon. Mr/Mrs Justice [surname]

Hon. Sir Patrick Garland, *born* 1929, *apptd* 1985
Hon. Sir Michael Turner, *born* 1931, *apptd* 1985
Hon. Sir John Alliott, *born* 1932, *apptd* 1986
Hon. Sir Humphrey Potts, *born* 1931, *apptd* 1986
Hon. Sir Richard Rougier, *born* 1932, *apptd* 1986
Hon. Sir Stuart McKinnon, *born* 1938, *apptd* 1988
Hon. Sir Scott Baker, *born* 1937, *apptd* 1988
Hon. Sir Douglas Brown, *born* 1931, *apptd* 1996
Hon. Sir Michael Morland, *born* 1929, *apptd* 1989
Hon. Sir Roger Buckley, *born* 1939, *apptd* 1989
Hon. Sir Anthony Hidden, *born* 1936, *apptd* 1989
Hon. Sir Michael Wright, *born* 1932, *apptd* 1990
Hon. Sir John Blofeld, *born* 1932, *apptd* 1990
Hon. Sir Peter Cresswell, *born* 1944, *apptd* 1991
Hon. Dame Ann Ebsworth, DBE, *born* 1937, *apptd* 1992
Hon. Sir Christopher Holland, *born* 1937, *apptd* 1992
Hon. Sir Richard Curtis, *born* 1933, *apptd* 1992
Hon. Dame Janet Smith, DBE, *born* 1940, *apptd* 1992
Hon. Sir Anthony Colman, *born* 1938, *apptd* 1992
Hon. Sir John Dyson, *born* 1943, *apptd* 1993
Hon. Sir Thayne Forbes, *born* 1938, *apptd* 1993
Hon. Sir Michael Sachs, *born* 1932, *apptd* 1993
Hon. Sir Stephen Mitchell, *born* 1941, *apptd* 1993
Hon. Sir Rodger Bell, *born* 1939, *apptd* 1993
Hon. Sir Michael Harrison, *born* 1939, *apptd* 1993
Hon. Dame Heather Steel, DBE, *born* 1940, *apptd* 1993
Hon. Sir William Gage, *born* 1938, *apptd* 1993
Hon. Sir Andrew Longmore, *born* 1944, *apptd* 1993
Hon. Sir Thomas Morison, *born* 1939, *apptd* 1993
Hon. Sir David Keene, *born* 1941, *apptd* 1994
Hon. Sir Andrew Collins, *born* 1942, *apptd* 1994
Hon. Sir Maurice Kay, *born* 1942, *apptd* 1995
Hon. Sir Anthony Hooper, *born* 1937, *apptd* 1995
Hon. Sir Alexander Butterfield, *born* 1942, *apptd* 1995
Hon. Sir George Newman, *born* 1941, *apptd* 1995
Hon. Sir David Poole, *born* 1938, *apptd* 1995
Hon. Sir Martin Moore-Bick, *born* 1946, *apptd* 1995
Hon. Sir Gordon Langley, *born* 1943, *apptd* 1995
Hon. Sir Roger Thomas, *born* 1947, *apptd* 1996
Hon. Sir Robert Nelson, *born* 1942, *apptd* 1996
Hon. Sir Roger Toulson, *born* 1946, *apptd* 1996
Hon. Sir Michael Astill, *born* 1938, *apptd* 1996
Hon. Sir Alan Moses, *born* 1945, *apptd* 1996
Hon. Sir Timothy Walker, *born* 1946, *apptd* 1996
Hon. Sir David Eady, *born* 1943, *apptd* 1997
Hon. Sir Jeremy Sullivan, *born* 1945, *apptd* 1997
Hon. Sir David Penry-Davey, *born* 1942, *apptd* 1997
Hon. Sir Stephen Richards, *born* 1950, *apptd* 1997
Hon. Sir David Steel, *born* 1943, *apptd* 1998
Hon. Sir Rodney Klevan, *born* 1940, *apptd* 1998
Hon. Sir Charles Gray, *born* 1942, *apptd* 1998
Hon. Sir Nicolas Bratza, *born* 1945, *apptd* 1998
Hon. Sir Michael Burton, *born* 1946, *apptd* 1998
Hon. Sir Rupert Jackson, *born* 1948, *apptd* 1998
Hon. Dame Heather Hallett, *born* 1949, *apptd* 1999
Hon. Sir Patrick Elias, *born* 1947, *apptd* 1999
Hon. Sir Richard Aikens, *born* 1948, *apptd* 1999
Hon. Sir Stephen Silber, *born* 1944, *apptd* 1999
Hon. Sir John Goldring, *born* 1944, *apptd* 1999
Hon. Sir Peter Crane, *born* 1940, *apptd* 2000
Hon. Dame Anne Rafferty, *born* 1951, *apptd* 2000
Hon. Sir Geoffrey Grigson, *born* 1944, *apptd* 2000
Hon. Sir Richard Gibbs, *born* 1941, *apptd* 2000
Hon. Sir Richard Henriques, *born* 1943, *apptd* 2000
Hon. Sir Stephen Tomlinson, *born* 1952, *apptd* 2000
Hon. Sir Andrew Smith, *born* 1947, *apptd* 2000
Hon. Sir Stanley Burnton, *born* 1942, *apptd* 2000

Hon. Sir Patrick Hunt, *born* 1943, *apptd* 2000
Hon. Sir Christopher Pitchford, *born* 1942,
apptd 2000

FAMILY DIVISION

President (£152,072), The Rt. Hon. Dame Elizabeth
Butler-Sloss, DBE, *born* 1933, *apptd* 1999
Secretary, Mrs S. Leung
Clerk, Mrs S. Bell

JUDGES (each £127,872)
Style, The Hon. Mr/Mrs Justice [surname]

Hon. Sir Robert Johnson, *born* 1933, *apptd* 1989
Hon. Dame Joyanne Bracewell, DBE, *born* 1934, *apptd* 1990
Hon. Sir Michael Connell, *born* 1939, *apptd* 1991
Hon. Sir Peter Singer, *born* 1944, *apptd* 1993
Hon. Sir Nicholas Wilson, *born* 1945, *apptd* 1993
Hon. Sir Nicholas Wall, *born* 1945, *apptd* 1993
Hon. Sir Andrew Kirkwood, *born* 1944, *apptd* 1993
Hon. Sir Hugh Bennett, *born* 1943, *apptd* 1995
Hon. Sir Edward Holman, *born* 1947, *apptd* 1995
Hon. Dame Mary Hogg, DBE, *born* 1947, *apptd* 1995
Hon. Sir Christopher Sumner, *born* 1939, *apptd* 1996
Hon. Sir Anthony Hughes, *born* 1948, *apptd* 1997
Hon. Sir Arthur Charles, *born* 1948, *apptd* 1998
Hon. Sir David Bodey, *born* 1947, *apptd* 1998
Hon. Dame Jill Black, *born* 1954, *apptd* 1999
Hon. Sir James Munby, *born* 1949, *apptd* 2000

RESTRICTIVE PRACTICES COURT

Room 410, Thomas More Building, Royal Courts of
Justice, Strand, London WC2A 2LL
Tel: 020-7947 6727

President, The Hon. Mr Justice Buckley
Judges, The Hon. Mr Justice Ferris; The Hon. Mr Justice
Lightman
Lay Members, B. M. Currie; Sir Lewis Robertson, CBE;
R. Garrick, CBE; S. J. Ahearne; J. A. Graham;
Mrs D. H. Hatfield; J. A. Scott; B. D. Colgate;
J. A. C. King
Clerk of the Court, M. Buckley

TECHNOLOGY AND CONSTRUCTION COURT

St Dunstan's House, 133–137 Fetter Lane,
London EC4A 1HD
Tel: 020-7947 7427

JUDGES (each £103,516)
The Hon. Mr Justice Dyson (*Presiding Judge*)
His Hon. Judge Bowsher, QC
His Hon. Judge Havery, QC
His Hon. Judge Lloyd, QC
His Hon. Judge Seymour, QC
His Hon. Judge Thornton, QC
His Hon. Judge Wilcox
His Hon. Judge Toulmin, CMG, QC
Court Manager, Miss B. Joy

LORD CHANCELLOR'S DEPARTMENT

— *see* Government Departments and Public Offices

SUPREME COURT DEPARTMENTS AND OFFICES

Royal Courts of Justice, London WC2A 2LL
Tel: 020-7947 6000

DIRECTOR'S OFFICE
Director, I. Hyams
Group Manager and Deputy Director, J. Selch
Group Manager, Family Proceedings and Probate Service,
R. P. Knight
Finance and Performance Officer, K. T. Fairweather

ADMIRALTY AND COMMERCIAL REGISTRY AND
MARSHAL'S OFFICE
Registrar (£76,921), P. Miller
Admiralty Marshal and Court Manager, K. Houghton

BANKRUPTCY DEPARTMENT
Chief Registrar (£95,873), M. C. B. Buckley
Bankruptcy Registrars (£76,921), W. S. James;
J. A. Simmonds; P. J. S. Rawson; S. Baister;
G. W. Jaques
Court Manager, Miss B. Flaxman

CENTRAL OFFICE OF THE SUPREME COURT
*Senior Master of the Supreme Court (QBD), and Queen's
Remembrancer* (£95,873), R. L. Turner
Masters of the Supreme Court (QBD) (£76,921),
D. L. Prebble; G. H. Hodgson; J. Trench; M. Tennant;
P. Miller; N. O. G. Murray; I. H. Foster; G. H. Rose;
P. G. A. Eyre; H. J. Leslie; J. G. G. Ungley
Court Manager, M. A. Brown

CHANCERY DIVISION
Senior Court Manager, P. Emery

CHANCERY CHAMBERS
Chief Master of the Supreme Court (£95,873),
J. I. Winegarten
Masters of the Supreme Court (£76,921), J. A. Moncaster;
R. A. Bowman; N. W. Bragge; T. J. Bowles
Court Manager, G. Robinson
Conveyancing Counsel of the Supreme Court, W. D. Ainger;
H. M. Harrod; A. C. Taussig

COMPANIES COURT
Registrar (£76,921), M. Buckley
Court Manager, M. A. Brown

COURT OF APPEAL CIVIL DIVISION
Head of the Civil Appeals Office (£95,873), R. A. Venne
Court Manager, Miss H. M. Goddard

COURT OF APPEAL CRIMINAL DIVISION
Registrar (£95,873), M. McKenzie, CB, QC
Deputy Registrar, Mrs L. G. Knapman
Chief Clerk, M. Bishop

COURTS-MARTIAL APPEALS OFFICE
Registrar (£95,873), M. McKenzie, CB, QC
Chief Clerk, M. Bishop

CROWN OFFICE OF THE SUPREME COURT
Master of the Crown Office, and Queen's Coroner and Attorney
(£95,873), M. McKenzie, CB, QC
Head of Crown Office, Mrs L. G. Knapman
Chief Clerk, M. Bishop

EXAMINERS OF THE COURT

Empowered to take examination of witnesses in all Divisions of the High Court

A. G. Dyer; A. W. Hughes; Mrs G. M. Kenne; R. M. Planterose; Miss V. E. I. Selvaratnam

RESTRICTIVE PRACTICES COURT

Clerk of the Court, M. Buckley
Court Manager, Miss B. Flaxman

SUPREME COURT COSTS OFFICE

Senior Cost Judge (£95,873), P. T. Hurst
Masters of the Supreme Court (£76,921), M. Ellis;
    T. H. Seager Berry; C. C. Wright; P. R. Rogers;
    G. N. Pollard; J. E. O'Hare; C. D. N. Campbell
Court Manager, D. O'Riordan

COURT OF PROTECTION

Stewart House, 24 Kingsway, London WC2B 6HD
Tel: 020-7664 7000

Master (£95,873), D. A. Lush

ELECTION PETITIONS OFFICE

Room E113, Royal Courts of Justice, Strand, London
WC2A 2LL
Tel: 020-7947 6131

The office accepts petitions and deals with all matters relating to the questioning of parliamentary, European Parliament and local government elections, and with applications for relief under the Representation of the People legislation.

Prescribed Officer, R. L. Turner
Chief Clerk, Miss J. L. Waine

OFFICE OF THE LORD CHANCELLOR'S VISITORS

Stewart House, 24 Kingsway, London WC2B 6HD
Tel: 020-7664 7317

Legal Visitor, A. R. Tyrrell
Medical Visitors, K. Khan; W. B. Sprey; E. Mateu;
    S. E. Mahapatra; A. Bailey; A. Kaeser

OFFICIAL RECEIVERS' DEPARTMENT

21 Bloomsbury Street, London WC1B 3SS
Tel: 020-7323 3090

Senior Official Receiver, M. C. A. Osborne
Official Receivers, M. J. Pugh; L. T. Cramp; J. Norris

OFFICIAL SOLICITOR'S DEPARTMENT

81 Chancery Lane, London WC2B 6HD
Tel: 020-7911 7105

Official Solicitor to the Supreme Court, P. M. Harris
Deputy Official Solicitor, H. J. Baker
Chief Clerk, R. Lancaster

PRINCIPAL REGISTRY (FAMILY DIVISION)

First Avenue House, 42–49 High Holborn, London
WC1V 6NP
Tel: 020-7947 6000

Senior District Judge (£95,873), G. B. N. A. Angel
District Judges (£80,921), B. P. F. Kenworthy-Browne;
    Mrs K. T. Moorhouse; M. J. Segal; R. Conn;
    Miss I. M. Plumstead; G. J. Maple; Miss H. C. Bradley;
    K. J. White; A. R. S. Bassett-Cross; N. A. Grove;
    M. C. Berry; Miss S. M. Bowman; C. Million; P. Waller;
    Miss P. Cushing; R. Harper; G. C. Brasse;
    Miss D. C. Redgrave
Family and Probate Service Group Manager, R. P. Knight

District Probate Registrars

Birmingham and Stoke-on-Trent, C. Marsh
Brighton and Maidstone, P. Ellwood
Bristol, Exeter and Bodmin, R. H. P. Joyce

Cardiff, Bangor and Carmarthen, R. F. Yeldam
Ipswich, Norwich and Peterborough, D. N. Mee
Leeds, Lincoln and Sheffield, A. P. Dawson
Liverpool, Lancaster and Chester, C. Fox
Manchester and Nottingham, M. A. Moran
Newcastle, Carlisle, York and Middlesbrough, P. Sanderson
Oxford, Gloucester and Leicester, R. R. Da Costa
Winchester, A. K. Biggs

JUDGE ADVOCATES

OFFICE OF THE JUDGE ADVOCATE OF THE FLEET

c/o The Crown Court at Chichester, Southgate,
Chichester PO19 1SX. Tel: 01243 520750
Judge Advocate of the Fleet (£95,873), His Hon. Judge
    Sessions

OFFICE OF THE JUDGE ADVOCATE-GENERAL OF THE FORCES

(*Joint Service for the Army and the Royal Air Force*)
22 Kingsway, London WC2B 6LE
Tel: 020-7218 8079
Judge Advocate-General (£95,873), His Hon. Judge
    J. W. Rant, CB, QC
Vice-Judge Advocate-General (£92,253), E. G. Moelwyn-Hughes
Judge Advocates (£76,921), M. A. Hunter; J. P. Camp;
    Miss S. E. Woollam; R. C. C. Seymour; I. H. Pearson;
    R. G. Chapple; J. F. T. Bayliss
Style for Judge Advocates, Judge Advocate [surname]

HIGH COURT AND CROWN COURT CENTRES

First-tier centres deal with both civil and criminal cases and are served by High Court and circuit judges. Second-tier centres deal with criminal cases only and are served by High Court and circuit judges. Third-tier centres deal with criminal cases only and are served only by circuit judges.

MIDLAND AND OXFORD CIRCUIT

First-tier – Birmingham, Lincoln, Nottingham, Oxford,
    Stafford, Warwick
Second-tier – Leicester, Northampton, Shrewsbury,
    Worcester
Third-tier – Coventry, Derby, Grimsby, Hereford,
    Peterborough, Stoke-on-Trent, Wolverhampton
Circuit Administrator, P. Handcock, The Priory Courts,
    6th Floor, 33 Bull Street, Birmingham B4 6DS.
    Tel: 0121-681 3201
Group Managers: Birmingham Group, Mrs K. Hoyte;
    Coventry Group, Mrs D. Ponsonby; *Lincoln Group*,
    A. Phillips; *Northampton Group*, K. Dickerson; *Nottingham Group*, Mrs E. A. Folman; *Stafford Group*, D. Bennett

NORTH-EASTERN CIRCUIT

First-tier – Leeds, Newcastle upon Tyne, Sheffield,
    Teesside
Second-tier – Bradford, York
Third-tier – Doncaster, Durham, Kingston-upon-Hull
Circuit Administrator, P. J. Farmer, 18th Floor, West
    Riding House, Albion Street, Leeds LS1 5AA.
    Tel: 0113-251 1200
Group Managers: Bradford Group, F. Taylor; *Leeds Group*,
    P. M. Norris; *Newcastle upon Tyne Group*,
    Miss S. Proudlock; *Sheffield Group*, G. Bingham, OBE;
    Teesside Group, Miss E. Yates

NORTHERN CIRCUIT

First-tier – Carlisle, Liverpool, Manchester (Crown Square), Preston

Third-tier – Barrow-in-Furness, Bolton, Burnley, Lancaster; Manchester (Minshull Street)

Circuit Administrator, R. A. Vincent, 15 Quay Street, Manchester M60 9FD. Tel: 0161-833 1005

Group Managers: Liverpool Group, Mrs J. Roche; *Manchester Central Group*, Mrs C. A. Mayer; *Outer Manchester Group*, S. Townley; *Preston Group*, B. Wilson

SOUTH-EASTERN CIRCUIT

First-tier – Chelmsford, Lewes, Norwich

Second-tier – Ipswich, London (Central Criminal Court), Luton, Maidstone, Reading, St Albans

Third-tier – Aylesbury, Basildon, Bury St Edmunds, Cambridge, Canterbury, Chichester, Croydon, Guildford, King's Lynn, London (Blackfriars, Harrow, Inner London Sessions House, Isleworth, Kingston, Middlesex Guildhall, Snaresbrook, Southwark, Wood Green, Woolwich) Southend

Circuit Administrator, R. J. Clark, CBE, New Cavendish House, 18 Maltravers Street, London WC2R 3EU. Tel: 020-7947 7235

Provincial Administrator, J. Powell, 1st Floor, Steeple House, Church Lane, Chelmsford CM1 1NH. Tel: 01245-257425

Group Managers: Chelmsford Group, M. Littlewood; *Kingston Group*, D. Thompson; *Lewes Group*, B. Macbeth; *London Group (Civil)*, vacant; *London Group (Crime)*, K. Budgen; *Luton Group*, M. McIver; *Maidstone Group*, Mrs L. Lennon

The High Court in Greater London sits at the Royal Courts of Justice.

WALES AND CHESTER CIRCUIT

First-tier – Caernarfon, Cardiff, Chester, Mold, Swansea

Second-tier – Carmarthen, Merthyr Tydfil, Newport, Welshpool

Third-tier – Dolgellau, Haverfordwest, Knutsford, Warrington

Circuit Administrator, P. Risk, Churchill House, Churchill Way, Cardiff CF10 4HH. Tel: 029-2041 5501

Group Managers: Cardiff Group, G. Pickett; *Chester Group*, G. Kenney; *Swansea Group*, Mrs D. Thomas

WESTERN CIRCUIT

First-tier – Bristol, Exeter, Truro, Winchester

Second-tier – Dorchester, Gloucester, Plymouth, Weymouth

Third-tier – Barnstaple, Bournemouth, Newport (IOW), Portsmouth, Salisbury, Southampton, Swindon, Taunton

Circuit Administrator, D. Ryan, Bridge House, Sion Place, Clifton, Bristol BS8 4BN. Tel: 0117-974 3763

Group Managers: Bristol Group, N. Jeffery; *Exeter Group*, D. Gentry; *Winchester Group*, A. Bean

CIRCUIT JUDGES

Senior Circuit Judges, each £103,516

Circuit Judges at the Central Criminal Court, London (Old Bailey Judges), each £103,516

Circuit Judges, each £95,873

Style, His/Her Hon. Judge [surname]

Senior Presiding Judge, The Rt. Hon. Lord Justice Judge

MIDLAND AND OXFORD CIRCUIT

Presiding Judges, The Hon. Mr Justice Astill

F. A. Allan; Miss C. Alton; B. J. Appleby, QC; D. P. Bennett; R. S. A. Benson; J. G. Boggis, QC; R. W. A. Bray; D. W. Brunning; N. B. Cameron Coles, QC; J. J. Cavell; F. A. Chapman; P. N. R. Clark; M. F. Coates; R. R. B. Cole; I. Collis; T. G. E. Corrie; *P. J. Crawford, QC (*Recorder of Birmingham*)*; Mrs P. A. Deeley; P. N. de Mille; C. H. Durman; H. W. P. Eccles, QC; B. A. Farrer, QC; Miss E. N. Fisher; J. E. Fletcher; A. C. Geddes; J. Hall; V. E. Hall; D. R. D. Hamilton; S. T. Hammond; G. C. W. Harris, QC; M. J. Heath; Miss E. J. Hindley, QC; C. R. Hodson; J. R. Hopkin; Mrs H. M. Hughes; R. H. Hutchinson; R. A. G. Inglis; A. A. Jenkins; R. P. V. Jenkins; A. W. P. King; D. L. McCarthy; A. W. McCreath; M. N. McKenna; A. G. MacDuff, QC; D. D. McEvoy, QC; J. V. Machin; M. H. Mander; L. Marshall; K. Matthewman, QC; W. D. Matthews; H. R. Mayor, QC; A. P. Mitchell; N. J. Mitchell; P. R. Morrell; J. I. Morris; M. D. Mott; A. J. D. Nicholl; S. Oliver-Jones, QC; R. T. N. Orme; R. C. C. O'Rorke; J. F. F. Orrell; D. S. Perrett, QC; C. J. Pitchers; R. F. D. Pollard; D. P. Pugsley; J. R. Pyke; R. J. Rubery; J. A. O. Shand; D. P. Stanley; P. J. Stretton; G. C. Styler; A. B. Taylor; J. J. Teare; R. S. W. F. Tonking; J. J. Wait; J. C. Warner; H. Wilson; J. W. Wilson

NORTH-EASTERN CIRCUIT

Presiding Judges, The Hon. Mr Justice Henriques; The Hon. Mr Justice Bennett

J. R. S. Adams; J. Altman; P. J. B. Armstrong; P. M. Baker, QC; T. W. Barber; J. E. Barry; G. N. Barr Young; R. Bartfield; C. O. J. Behrens; D. R. Bentley, QC; P. H. Bowers; A. N. J. Briggs; D. A. Bryant; J. W. M. Bullimore; B. Bush; M. C. Carr; M. L. Cartlidge; P. J. Charlesworth; G. Cliffe; P. J. Cockroft; G. J. K. Coles, QC; J. Crabtree; M. T. Cracknell; W. H. R. Crawford, QC; Mrs J. Davies; I. J. Dobkin; E. J. Faulks; Miss A. C. Finnerty; P. J. Fox, QC; A. N. Fricker, QC; M. S. Garner; A. R. Goldsack, QC; R. A. Grant; S. P. Grenfell; S. J. Gullick; G. F. R. Harkins; T. S. A. Hawkesworth, QC; P. J. M. Heppel, QC; T. Hewitt; *T. D. T. Hodson (*Recorder of Newcastle upon Tyne*)*; P. M. L. Hoffman; D. P. Hunt; N. H. Jones, QC; R. A. Jordan; G. H. Kamil; T. D. Kent-Jones, TD; G. M. Lightfoot; R. P. Lowden; A. G. McCallum; C. I. McGonigal; K. M. P. Macgill; M. K. Mettyear; Mrs J. P. Moir; R. J. Moore; M. J. A. Murphy, QC; A. L. Myerson, QC; D. A. Orde; J. Prophet; P. E. Robertshaw; R. M. Scott; L. Spittle; Mrs L. Sutcliffe; J. A. Swanson; M. J. Taylor; R. C. Taylor; J. D. G. Walford; M. Walker; P. H. C. Walker; *B. Walsh, QC; C. T. Walton; G. Whitburn, QC; J. S. Wolstenholme; D. R. Wood

NORTHERN CIRCUIT

Presiding Judge, The Hon. Mr Justice Forbes; The Hon. Mr Justice Douglas Brown

M. P. Allweis; J. F. Appleton; R. K. Atherton; S. W. Baker; A. W. Bell; R. C. W. Bennett; Miss I. Bernstein; A. N. H. Blake; C. Bloom, QC; R. Brown; J. K. Burke, QC; I. B. Campbell; F. B. Carter, QC; B. I. Caulfield; D. Clark; *D. C. Clarke, QC (*Recorder of Liverpool*)*; G. M. Clifton; I. W. Crompton; *R. E. Davies, QC (*Recorder of Manchester*)*; Miss A. E. Downey; B. R. Duckworth; S. B. Duncan; Miss D. B. Eaglestone; T. K. Earnshaw; G. A. Ensor; D. M. Evans, QC; S. J. D. Fawcus; P. S. Fish; J. R. B. Geake; D. S. Gee; W. George; J. A. D. Gilliland, QC; I. M. Hamilton; J. A. Hammond; M. Hedley; T. B. Hegarty, QC; M. J. Henshell; F. R. B. Holloway; R. C. Holman; N. J. G. Howarth; G. W. Humphries; C. E. F. James; P. M. Kershaw, QC *(Commercial Circuit Judge)*; Miss L. J. Kushner, QC; H. L. Lachs; P. M. Lakin; B. W. Lewis; R. J. D. Livesey, QC; A. P. Lyon; D. Lynch; D. I. Mackay; J. B. Macmillan;

D. G. Maddison; B. C. Maddocks; C. J. Mahon; J. A. Morgan; W. P. Morris; T. J. Mort; *C. P. L. Openshaw, QC; F. D. Owen, TD; J. A. Phillips; J. C. Phipps; D. A. Pirie; A. J. Proctor; J. H. Roberts; Miss G. D. Ruaux; H. S. Singer; E. Slinger; A. C. Smith; W. P. Smith; Miss E. M. Steel; D. R. Swift; C. B. Tetlow; J. P. Townend; I. J. C. Trigger; P. W. G. Urquhart; K. H. P. Wilkinson; B. Woodward

SOUTH-EASTERN CIRCUIT

Presiding Judges, The Hon. Mr Justice Aikens; The Hon. Mr Justice Moses

J. D. R. Adams; M. F. Addison; P. C. Ader; Mrs S. C. Andrew; A. R. L. Ansell; M. G. Anthony; S. A. Anwyl, QC; E. H. Bailey; M. F. Baker, QC; A. F. Balston; G. S. Barham; C. J. A. Barnett, QC; W. E. Barnett, QC; R. A. Barratt, QC; K. Bassingthwaighte; *G. A. Bathurst Norman; P. J. L. Beaumont, QC; N. E. Beddard; R. V. M. E. Behar; Mrs C. V. Bevington; M. G. Binning; J. E. Bishop; B. M. B. Black; H. O. Blacksell, QC; J. G. Boal, QC; A. V. Bradbury; P. N. Brandt; R. G. Brown; J. M. Bull, QC; *N. M. Butter, QC; The Hon. C. W. Byers; H. J. Byrt, QC; J. Q. Campbell; M. J. Carroll; B. E. F. Catlin; *B. L. Charles, QC; P. C. L. Clark; P. C. Clegg; Miss S. Coates; N. J. Coleman; S. H. Colgan; P. H. Collins; C. C. Colston, QC; S. S. Coltart; Viscount Colville of Culross, QC; J. S. Colyer, QC; C. D. Compston; T. A. C. Coningsby, QC; J. G. Connor; R. D. Connor; M. J. Cook; R. A. Cooke; M. R. Coombe; P. E. Copley; Dr E. Cotran; P. R. Cowell; R. C. Cox; M. L. S. Cripps; C. A. Critchlow; J. F. Crocker; D. L. Croft, QC; H. M. Crush; D. M. Cryan; P. Curl; Mrs P. M. T. Dangor; G. L. Davies; W. L. M. Davies, QC; M. Dean, QC; P. G. Dedman; W. N. Denison, QC (*Common Serjeant*); J. E. Devaux; M. N. Devonshire, TD; P. H. Downes; W. H. Dunn, QC; C. M. Edwards; D. F. Elfer; QC; D. R. Ellis; R. C. Elly; C. Elwen; F. P. L. Evans; Miss D. Faber; J. D. Farnworth; P. Fingret; P. E. J. Focke, QC; P. Ford; G. C. F. Forrester; Ms D. A. Freedman; R. Gee; L. Gerber; C. A. H. Gibson; Miss A. F. Goddard, QC; S. A. Goldstein; C. G. M. Gordon; J. B. Gosschalk; A. A. Goymer; M. Graham, QC; B. S. Green, QC; A. E. Greenwood; R. B. Groves, TD, VRD; D. F. Hallett; A. B. R. Hallgarten, QC; Miss G. Hallon; J. Hamilton; Miss S. Hamilton, QC; C. R. H. Hardy; B. Hargrove, OBE, QC; M. F. Harris; A. M. Harvey; W. G. Hawkesworth; R. G. Hawkins, QC; J. M. Haworth; R. J. Haworth; R. M. Hayward; A. N. Hitching; H. E. G. Hodge, OBE; D. Holden; K. M. J. Hollis; J. F. Holt; A. C. W. Horderm, QC; K. A. D. Hornby; M. Hucker; Sir David Hughes-Morgan, BT., CB, CBE; J. G. Hull, QC; M. J. Hyam (*Recorder of London*); D. A. Inman; A. B. Issard-Davies; Dr P. J. E. Jackson; T. J. C. Joseph; I. G. F. Karsten, QC; S. S. Katkhuda; C. J. B. Kemp; M. Kennedy, QC; A. M. Kenny; T. R. King; B. J. Knight, QC; L. G. Krikler; L. H. C. Lait; P. St J. H. Langan, QC; Capt. J. B. R. Langdon, RN; P. H. Latham; R. Laurie; T. Lawrence; D. M. Levy, QC; C. C. D. Lindsay, QC; S. H. Lloyd; F. R. Lockhart; J. A. M. Lowen; Mrs C. M. Ludlow; Capt. S. Lyons; A. G. McDowall; R. J. McGregor-Johnson; B. M. McIntyre; K. A. Machin, QC; R. G. McKinnon; W. N. McKinnon; K. C. Macrae; T. Maher; F. J. M. Marr-Johnson; D. N. N. Martineau; N. A. Medawar, QC; D. B. Meier; D. J. Mellor; G. D. Mercer; D. Q. Miller; Miss A. E. Mitchell; F. I. Mitchell; H. M. Morgan; D. Morton Jack; R. T. Moss; Miss M. J. S. Mowat; T. M. E. Nash; M. H. D. Neligan; Mrs M. F. Norrie; Brig. A. P. Norris, OBE; P. W. O'Brien; M. A. Oppenheimer; D. C. J. Paget, QC; Ms M. J. Parker; D. J. Parry; A. Patience, QC; Mrs N. Pearce; Prof. D. S. Pearl; Miss V. A. Pearlman; B. P. Pearson; N. A. J. Philpot; T. D. Pillay; D. C. Pitman; J. R. Platt; J. R. Playford, QC;

P. B. Pollock; T. G. Pontius; W. D. C. Poulton; S. Pratt; R. J. C. V. Prendergast; J. E. Previté, QC; B. H. Pryor, QC; J. E. Pullinger; D. W. Radford; J. W. Rant, CB, QC; E. V. P. Reece; J. R. Reid, QC; M. P. Reynolds; M. S. Rich, QC; D. J. Richardson; N. P. Riddell; G. Rivlin, QC; S. D. Robbins; J. M. Roberts; D. A. H. Rodwell, QC; G. H. Rooke, TD, QC; W. M. Rose; P. C. R. Rountree; J. H. Rucker; T. R. G. Ryland; J. E. A. Samuels, QC; R. B. Sanders; A. R. G. Scott-Gall; J. S. Sennitt; D. Serota, QC; J. L. Sessions; D. R. A. Sich; A. G. Simmons; K. T. Simpson; P. R. Simpson; M. Singh, QC; S. P. Sleeman; C. M. Smith, QC; S. A. R. Smith; Miss Z. P. Smith; R. J. Southan; S. B. Spence; S. M. Stephens, QC; N. A. Stewart; D. M. A. Stokes, QC; W. F. C. Thomas; P. J. Thompson; A. G. Y. Thorpe; C. H. Tilling; C. J. M. Tyrer; Mrs A. P. Uziell-Hamilton; J. E. van der Werff; A. O. R. Vick, QC; T. L. Viljoen; J. P. Wadsworth, QC; Miss A. P. Wakefield; R. Wakefield; R. Walker; S. P. Waller; D. B. Watling, QC; A. R. Webb; C. S. Welchman; A. F. Wilkie, QC; S. R. Wilkinson; R. J. Winstanley; D. Worsley; E. G. Wrintmore; M. P. Yelton; K. H. Zucker, QC

WALES AND CHESTER CIRCUIT

Presiding Judges, The Hon. Mr Justice Maurice Kay; The Hon. Mr Justice Connell; The Hon. Mr Justice Thomas

K. E. Barnett; M. R. Burr; G. H. F. Carson; N. M. Chambers, QC; S. P. Clarke; T. R. Crowther, QC; J. T. Curran; Miss J. M. P. Daley; G. H. M. Daniel; D. T. A. Davies; J. B. S. Diehl, QC; R. T. Dutton; D. E. H. Edwards; G. O. Edwards, QC; The Lord Elystan-Morgan; *D. R. Evans, QC; M. R. Furness; J. W. Gaskell; D. R. Halbert; D. J. Hale; Miss J. E. Hayward; G. R. Hickinbottom; R. P. Hughes; P. J. Jacobs; G. J. Jones; H. D. H. Jones; G. E. Kilfoil; C. G. Masterman; D. G. Morgan; D. G. Morris; D. C. Morton; T. H. Moseley; G. A. L. Price, QC; P. J. Price, QC; E. J. Prosser, QC; D. W. Richards; J. M. T. Rogers, QC; A. A. Wallace; J. G. Williams, QC

WESTERN CIRCUIT

Presiding Judges, The Hon. Mrs Justice Hallett, DBE; The Hon. Mr Justice Toulson

P. R. Barclay; J. F. Beashel; R. H. Bond; Miss J. A. M. Bonvin; C. L. Boothman; M. J. L. Brodrick; J. M. J. Burford; QC; R. D. H. Bursell, QC; A. V. Chubb; M. G. Cotterill; G. W. A. Cottle; K. C. Cutler; P. M. Darlow; S. C. Darwall Smith; Mrs S. P. Darwall Smith; Mrs L. H. Davies; *M. Dyer; Ms J. A. Exton; J. D. Foley; R. H. Griffith-Jones; D. L. Griffiths; J. D. Griggs; Mrs C. M. A. Hagen; P. J. C. R. Hooton; M. K. Harington; G. B. Hutton; R. E. Jack, QC; J. R. Jarvis; A. G. H. Jones; T. Longbotham; T. N. Mackean; Miss S. M. D. McKinney; I. S. McKintosh; J. G. McNaught; The Lord Meston, QC; T. J. Milligan; D. W. Morgan; J. Neligan; S. K. O'Malley; S. K. Overend; R. Price; R. C. Pryor, QC; M. W. Roach; J. N. P. Rudd; A. Rutherford; Miss A. O. H. Sander; D. H. D. Selwood; R. M. Shawcross; D. A. Smith, QC; W. E. M. Taylor; P. M. Thomas; A. A. R. Thompson, QC; D. K. Ticehurst, QC; D. I. H. Tyzack, QC; R. C. B. Wade; D. M. Webster, QC; J. H. Weeks, QC; J. S. Wiggs; J. A. J. Wigmore; J. C. Willis

RECORDERS (each £422 per day)

F. A. Abbott; R. D. I. Adam; J. F. Akast; D. J. Ake; R. Akenhead, QC; I. D. G. Alexander, QC; C. D. Allan, QC; C. J. Alldis; J. H. Allen, QC; D. M. Altaras; A. J. Anderson, QC; W. P. Andreae-Jones, QC; Mrs E. H. Andrew; P. J. Andrews, QC; R. A. Anelay, QC; J. M. Appleby; Miss L. E. Appleby, QC; B. J. Argyle; E. K. Armitage, QC; G. K. Arran; S. J. Ashurst; E. G. Aspley; P. Atherton; N. J. Atkinson, QC;

D. J. M. Aubrey, QC; D. S. Aubrey; M. G. Austin-Smith, QC; M. J. S. Axtell; W. S. Aylen, QC; P. D. Babb; J. F. Badenoch, QC; P. G. N. Badge; Miss P. H. Badley; A. B. Baillie; N. R. J. Baker, QC; Miss A. Ball, QC; C. G. Ball, QC; A. Barker, QC; B. J. Barker, QC; G. E. Barling, QC; D. N. Barnard;H. J. Barnes; T. P. Barnes, QC; A. J. Barnett; Miss F. J. Baron, QC; D. A. Bartlett; G. R. Bartlett, QC; J. C. T. Barton, QC; D. C. Bate, QC; S. D. Batten, QC; P. D. Batty, QC; J. J. Baughan, QC; J. F. T. Bayliss; R. A. Bayliss; D. M. Bean; C. M. Beale; J. Beatson; S. J. Bedford; R. W. Belben; J. K. Benson; P. C. Benson; R. A. Benson, QC; H. L. Bentham, QC; D. M. Berkson; C. R. Berry; M. Bethel, QC; J. P. V. Bevan; Mrs M. O. Bickford-Smith; N. Bidder; I. G. Bing; P. V. Birkett, QC; M. I. Birnbaum; W. J. Birtles; P. W. Birts, QC; M. J. Black, QC; B. G. D. Blair, QC; W. J. L. Blair, QC; P. E. Bleasdale; R. H. L. Blomfield, TD; D. J. Blunt, QC; O. S. P. Blunt, QC; Miss B. M. Bolton; G. T. K. Boney, QC; Ms C. Booth, QC; J. J. Boothby; D. J. Boulton; S. N. Bourne-Arton, QC; M. J. Bowerman; Ms M. R. Bowron; W. Boyce; S. C. Boyd, QC; J. J. Boyle; D. L. Bradshaw; W. T. S. Braithwaite, QC; G. B. Breen; D. J. Brennan, QC; M. L. Brent, QC; G. J. B. G. Brice, QC; A. J. Brigden; D. R. Bright; R. P. Brittain; R. A. Britton; J. Bromley-Davenport; L. F. M. Brown; S. C. Brown, QC; D. J. M. Browne, QC; J. N. Browne; A. J. N. Brunner, QC; R. V. Bryan; Miss B. M. Bucknall, QC; J. E. Bullen; J. P. Burke, QC; L. S. Burn; H. W. Burnett, QC; R. H. Burns; F. G. Burrell, QC; K. Bush; A. J. Butcher, QC; C. M. Butler; Miss J. Butler; M. D. Byrne; D. W. Caddick; D. Calvert-Smith, QC; R. Camden Pratt, QC; Miss S. M. C. Cameron; A. N. Campbell, QC; Ms A. R. Campbell; J. M. Caplan, QC; G. M. C. Carey, QC; A. C. Carlile, QC, MP; H. B. H. Carlisle, QC; J. J. Carter-Manning, QC; R. Carus, QC; Mrs J. R. Case; P. D. Cattan; Miss M. T. Catterson; R. M. Challinor; Miss D. C. Champion; C. B. Chandler; V. R. Chapman; J. M. Cherry, QC; A. C. Chippindall; C. F. Chruszcz, QC; C. H. Clark, QC; C. S. C. S. Clarke, QC; T. N. Clark; P. W. Clarke; P. R. J. Clarkson, QC; T. Clayson; A. S. L. Cleary; W. Clegg, QC; P. Clements; T. A. Clover; W. P. Coates; D. J. Cocks, QC; J. J. Coffey, QC; T. A. Coghlan, QC; J. L. Cohen; L. F. R. Cohen, QC; W. J. Coker, QC; A. J. S. Coleman; A. R. Collender; P. N. Collier, QC; M. G. Collins, QC; Mrs J. R. Comyns; D. G. Conlin; A. D. Conrad; C. S. Cook; J. L. Cooke, QC; N. O. Cooke; K. B. Coonan, QC; A. E. M. Cooper; P. J. Cooper, QC; C. J. Cornwall; P. J. Cosgrove, QC; Miss D. R. Cotton, QC; J. S. Coward, QC; T. G. Cowling; Mrs L. M. Cox, QC; P. Crampin, QC; L. S. Crawford; N. Crichton; D. I. Crigman, QC; D. R. Crome; S. R. Crookenden, QC; Mrs J. E. Crowley; J. D. Crowley, QC; T. S. Culver; Miss E. A. M. Curnow, QC; P. D. Curran; J. W. O. Curtis, QC; M. J. Curwen; A. J. G. Dalziel; A. M. Darroch; C. P. M. Davidson; A. M. Davies; A. R. M. Davies; H. Davies; J. T. L. Davies; Miss N. V. Davies, QC; R. L. Davies, QC; N. A. L. Davis, QC; E. E. Davis; A. W. Dawson; D. H. Day, QC; Ms M. R. de Haas, QC; P. A. de la Piquerie; M. A. de Navarro, QC; R. L. Denyer, QC; H. A. D. de Silva; P. N. Digney; C. E. Dines; A. D. Dinkin, QC; D. R. Dobbin; R. S. Dodds; P. Dodgson; R. A. M. Doggett; Ms B. Dohmann, QC; D. T. Donaldson, QC; A. M. Donne, QC; A. F. S. Donovan; A. K. Dooley; Ms J. M. R. Dowell; J. Dowse; M. J. Dudley; J. R. Duggan; P. R. Dunkels, QC; J. D. Durham Hall, QC; R. M. Eades; C. N. Edelman, QC; A. J. C. Edis, QC; A. H. Edwards; Miss S. M. Edwards, QC; A. J. C. Edwards-Stuart, QC; A. J. Elleray, QC; G. Elias, QC; E. A. Elliott; J. A. Elvidge; R. M. Englehart, QC; D. A. Evans, QC; D. H. Evans, QC; F. W. H. Evans, QC; G. J. Evans; G. W. R. Evans, QC; I. Evans; M. Evans; M. J. Evans; M. A. Everall, QC; T. M. Faber; R. B. Farley, QC; P. M. Farmer, QC; D. J. Farrer, QC; P. E. Feinberg, QC; J. F.

Q. Fenwick, QC; R. Fernyhough, QC; M. C. Field; R. A. Field, QC; J. E. Finestein; D. T. Fish; D. P. Fisher, QC; G. D. Flather, CBE, QC; R. A. Flowerdew; N. M. Ford, QC; R. A. Fordham, QC; B. C. Forster; M. D. P. Fortune; D. R. Foskett, QC; I. H. Foster; J. R. Foster, QC; D. P. Friedman, QC; S. A. Furst, QC; C. J. E. Gardner, QC; P. R. Garlick, QC; C. R. Garside, QC; R. C. Gaskell; J. B. Gateshill; S. A. G. L. Gault; A. H. Gee, QC; I. W. Geering, QC; D. S. Geey; C. R. George, QC; S. M. Gerlis; D. C. Gerrey; S. J. Gibbons, QC; A. J. Gilbart, QC; F. H. S. Gilbert, QC; N. J. Gilchrist; K. Gillance; N. B. D. Gilmour, QC; L. Giovenne; R. P. Glancy, QC; A. T. Glass, QC; M. G. J. Gledhill; H. B. Globe, QC; Miss E. Gloster, QC; H. K. Goddard, QC; H. A. Godfrey, QC; Ms L. S. Godfrey, QC; J. J. Goldberg, QC; I. S. Goldrein, QC; P. H. Goldsmith, QC; A. J. Goldstaub, QC; L. C. Goldstone, QC; A. J. J. Gompertz, QC; Miss R. M. Goode; J. R. W. Goss; T. J. C. Goudie, QC; G. Gozem; The Lord Grabiner, QC; H. Green, QC; Miss J. E. G. Greenberg, QC; J. C. Greenwood; J. G. Grenfell, QC; D. E. Griffith-Jones; J. P. G. Griffiths, QC; M. G. Grills; M. S. E. Grime, QC; P. Grobel; P. H. Gross, QC; B. P. Gulbenkian; J. D. Guthrie, QC; A. S. Hacking, QC; J. W. Haines; N. J. Hall; S. J. Hall; J. P. N. Hallam; A. N. R. Hamilton; G. M. Hamilton, TD, QC; P. L. Hamlin; J. L. Hand, QC; G. T. Harrap; P. J. Harrington, QC; D. M. Harris, QC; R. D. Harrison; R. M. Harrison, QC; H. M. Harrod; J. M. Harrow; C. A. Hart-Leverton, QC; B. Harvey; J. G. Harvey; M. L. T. Harvey, QC; D. W. Hatton, QC; A. M. D. Havelock-Allan, QC; The Hon. P. N. Havers, QC; R. W. P. H. Hay; Prof. D. J. Hayton; R. Hayward-Smith, QC; R. Hedgeland; A. T. Hedworth, QC; R. A. Henderson, QC; R. C. Herman; M. S. Heslop QC; J. W. Hillyer; A. J. H. Hilton, QC; J. W. Hirst, QC; W. T. J. Hirst; J. D. Hitchen; S. A. Hockman, QC; A. J. C. Hoggett, QC; T. V. Holroyde, QC; R. M. Hone; G. A. J. Hooper; A. D. Hope; S. J. Hopkins; M. A. P. Hopmeier; M. Horowitz, QC; Miss R. Horwood-Smart; C. P. Hotten, QC; B. F. Houlder, QC; M. N. Howard; C. I. Howells; M. J. Hubbard, QC; D. L. Hughes; Miss J. C. A. Hughes, QC; Miss K. L. Hughes; P. T. Hughes, QC; T. M. Hughes, QC; L. D. Hull; Capt. D. R. Humphrey, RN; W. G. B. Hungerford; D. R. N. Hunt, QC; I. G. A. Hunter, QC; M. A. Hunter; G. N. N. Huskinson; M. Hussain, QC; J. G. K. Hyland; R. Ibbotson; M. D. Inman, QC; P. R. Isaacs; S. L. Isaacs; S. M. Jack; D. G. A. Jackson; M. R. Jackson; I. E. Jacob; N. F. B. Jarman, QC; J. M. Jarvis, QC; A. H. Jeffreys; D. A. Jeffreys, QC; J. Jenkins, QC; J. J. Jenkins; Miss A. M. Jolles; D. A. F. Jones; D. L. Jones; N. G. Jones; P. H. F. Jones; S. E. Jones, QC; W. J. Jones; R. C. Jose; Ms W. R. Joseph, QC; H. M. Joy; P. S. L. Joyce, QC; R. W. S. Juckes; M. L. Kallipetis, QC; Miss L. N. R. Kamill; R. G. Kaye, QC; D. B. Kealy; K. R. Keen, QC; Mrs S. M. Keen; B. R. Keith, QC; W. A. Kennedy; D. Kennett Brown; D. M. Kerr; L. D. Kershen, QC; M. I. Khan; G. M. P. F. Khayat, QC; C. A. Kinch; T. R. A. King, QC; Mrs F. M. Kirkham; M. S. Knott; Miss P. E. Knowles; C. J. Knox; Miss J. C. M. Korner, QC; S. E. Kramer, QC; P. E. Kyte, QC; N. R. W. Lambert; D. C. Lamdin; A. T. Lancaster; D. A. Landau; D. G. Lane, QC; B. F. J. Langstaff, QC; R. B. Latham, QC; S. W. Lawler, QC; Sir Ivan Lawrence, QC; Miss E. A. Lawson, QC; M. H. Lawson, QC; G. S. Lawson-Rogers, QC; P. L. O. Leaver, QC; D. Lederman, QC; B. W. T. Leech; I. Leeming, QC; C. H. de V. Leigh, QC; H. B. G. Lett; B. L. Lever; B. H. Leveson, QC; A. E. Levy, QC; M. E. Lewer, QC; J. A. Lewis; K. M. J. Lewison, QC; S. J. Linehan, QC; R. A. Lissack, QC; G. W. Little; B. J. E. Livesey, QC; C. G. Llewellyn-Jones, QC; L. J. R. Lobo; QC; J. Lockhart-Mummery, QC; A. J. C. Lodge, QC; D. C. Lovell-Pank, QC; A. C. Lowcock; G. W. Lowe; Rt. Hon. Sir Nicholas Lyell, QC, MP; P. G. McCahill, QC; R. G. B. McCombe, QC;

G. F. McDermott; A. E. McFarlane, QC; R. D. Machell, QC; C. C. Mackay, QC; D. L. Mackie; N. A. McKittrick; I. A. B. McLaren, QC; I. McLeod; N. R. B. Macleod, QC; Ms J. Macur, QC; A. G. Mainds; A. H. R. Maitland; A. R. Malcolm; H. J. Malins; M. E. Mann, QC; The Hon. G. R. J. Mansfield; R. L. Marks; J. W. Marrin, QC; A. L. Marriott, QC; G. M. Marriott; A. S. Marron, QC; P. Marsh; R. G. Marshall-Andrews, QC; G. C. Marson; H. R. A. Martineau; S. A. Maskrey, QC; C. P. Mather; D. Matheson, QC; P. R. Matthews; Mrs S. P. Matthews, QC; P. B. Mauleverer, QC; R. B. Mawrey, QC; J. F. M. Maxwell; R. Maxwell, QC; Mrs P. R. May; R. M. J. Meeke; G. M. Mercer; N. F. Merriman, QC; C. S. J. Metcalf; J. T. Milford, QC; K. S. H. Miller; P. W. Miller; R. A. Miller; S. M. Miller, QC; C. J. Millington; C. E. Million; J. B. M. Milmo, QC; D. C. Milne, QC; C. J. M. Miskin, QC; Miss C. M. Miskin; A. R. Mitchell, QC; C. R. Mitchell; D. C. Mitchell; J. R. Mitchell; J. E. Mitting, QC; F. R. Moat; E. G. Moelwyn-Hughes; C. R. D. Moger, QC; D. R. P. Mole, QC; M. G. C. Moorhouse; A. G. Moran, QC; P. B. Morgan; A. P. Morris, QC; C. Morris-Coole; H. A. C. Morrison, OBE; R. F. Morrison; G. E. Morrow, QC; M. G. M. Morse; C. J. Moss, QC; P. C. Mott, QC; R. W. Moxon-Brown, QC; J. H. Muir; F. J. Muller, QC; A. H. Munday, QC; G. S. Murdoch, QC; I. P. Murphy, QC; A. C. Murray; C. M. Murray; N. O. G. Murray; N. J. Mylne, QC; H. G. Narayan; A. R. H. Newman, QC; Miss L. A. Newton; A. I. Niblett; G. Nice, QC; A. E. R. Noble; B. Nolan, QC; M. C. Norman; J. M. Norris; P. H. Norris; G. Nuttall; J. G. Nutting, QC; D. P. O'Brien, QC; Mrs F. M. T. Oldham; M. D. Oldham; R. W. Onions; M. N. O'Sullivan; D. B. W. Ouseley, QC; N. D. Padfield, QC; Miss A. M. Page, QC; S. R. Page; A. O. Palmer, QC; A. W. Palmer, QC; D. P. Pannick, QC; A. D. W. Pardoe, QC; S. A. B. Parish; P. L. Parker; G. C. Parkins, QC; G. E. Parkinson; M. P. Parroy, QC; D. J. T. Parry; E. O. Parry; N. S. K. Pascoe, QC; Miss A. E. H. Pauffley, QC; J. G. Paulusz; W. E. Pawlak; F. M. Pearce; D. J. Pearce-Higgins, QC; R. J. Pearse Wheatley; The Hon. I. J. C. Peddie, QC; J. V. Pegden; J. Perry, QC; M. Pert, QC; N. M. Peters, QC; J. R. D. Philips; D. J. Phillips, QC; W. B. Phillips; M. A. Pickering, QC; J. K. Pickup; The Hon. B. M. D. Pitt; Miss E. F. Platt, QC; R. Platts; R. O. Plender, QC; Miss J. C. Plumptre; Miss I. M. Plumstead; S. D. Popat; A. R. Porten, QC; L. R. Portnoy; J. R. L. Posnansky, QC; Mrs R. M. Poulet, QC; S. R. Powles, QC; D. Price; J. A. Price, QC; J. C. Price; N. P. L. Price, QC; R. Price Lewis; R. B. L. Prior; F. S. K. Privett; H. W. Prosser; A. C. Pugh, QC; G. V. Pugh, QC; G. F. Pulman, QC; C. P. B. Purchas, QC; R. M. Purchas, QC; N. R. Purnell, QC; P. O. Purnell, QC; Q. C. W. Querelle; N. P. Quinn; D. A. Radcliffe; Mrs N. P. Radford; T. W. H. Raggatt, QC; Miss E. A. Ralphs; J. Y. Randall, QC; A. D. Rawley, QC; J. E. Rayner James, QC; P. R. Raynor, QC; J. H. Reddihough; M. H. Redfern, QC; A. R. F. Redgrave, QC; D. W. Rees; G. W. Rees; P. Rees; C. E. Reese, QC; P. C. Reid; D. J. Rennie; R. E. Rhodes, QC; T. Rigby; S. V. Riordan, QC; G. Risius; Miss J. H. Ritchie, QC; J. M. G. Roberts, QC; T. D. Roberts; A. J. Robertson; G. R. Robertson, QC; V. Robinson, QC; D. E. H. Robson, QC; G. W. Roddick, QC; Miss M. B. Roddy; Miss D. J. Rodgers; P. F. G. Rook, QC; J. G. Ross; J. G. Ross Martyn; P. C. Rouch; J. J. Rowe, QC; R. J. Royce, QC; M. W. Rudland; P. E. B. M. Rueff; A. A. Rumbelow, QC; N. J. Rumfitt, QC; R. J. Rundell; J. R. T. Rylance; C. R. A. Sallon, QC; C. N. Salmon; D. A. Salter; G. R. Sankey, QC; N. L. Sarony; J. H. B. Saunders, QC; M. P. Sayers, QC; R. J. Scholes, QC; T. J. W. Scott; Miss P. Scriven, QC; R. J. Seabrook, QC; C. Seagroatt, QC; W. P. L. Sellick; O. M. Sells, QC; A. J. Seys-Llewellyn; A. R. F. Sharp; P. P. Shears; S. J. Sher, QC; Miss D. A. Sherwin; Miss J. Shipley; P. C. H. Simon, QC; Miss E. A. Slade, QC; A. T. Smith, QC;

D. Smith; P. W. Smith, QC; R. D. H. Smith, QC; C. J. Smyth; R. C. Southwell, QC, R. C. E. Southwell; M. H. Spence, QC; Sir Derek Spencer, QC; J. Spencer, QC; M. G. Spencer, QC; R. G. Spencer; S. M. Spencer, QC; R. V. Spencer Bernard; D. P. Spens, QC; R. W. Spon-Smith; D. Steer, QC; M. T. Steiger, QC; Mrs L. J. Stern, QC; A. W. Stevenson, TD; J. S. H. Stewart, QC; S. P. Stewart, QC; W. R. Stewart Smith; A. C. Steynor; G. J. C. Still; D. A. Stockdale, QC; Mrs D. M. Stocken; M. G. T. Stokes, QC; J. B. Storey, QC; T. M. F. Stow, QC; D. M. A. Strachan, QC; M. Stuart-Moore; J. H. Stuart-Smith, QC; F. R. C. Such; A. B. Suckling, QC; Ms L. E. Sullivan, QC; D. M. Sumner; J. P. C. Sumption, QC; M. A. Supperstone, QC; P. J. Susman; R. P. Sutton, QC; N. H. Sweeney; Miss C. J. Swift, QC; M. R. Swift, QC; Miss H. H. Swindells, QC; P. Sycamore; C. J. M. Symons, QC; J. P. Tabor, QC; J. A. Tackaberry, QC; P. J. Talbot, QC; R. K. K. Talbot; R. B. Tansey, QC; J. B. C. Tanzer; Miss S. A. M. Tapping; G. F. Tattersall, QC; E. T. H. Teague; N. J. M. Teare, QC; R. H. Tedd, QC; A. D. Temple, QC; V. B. A. Temple, QC; M. H. Tennant; The Lord Thomas of Gresford, OBE, QC; P. A. Thomas; R. L. Thomas, QC; R. M. Thomas; R. U. Thomas, QC; Miss S. M. Thomas; C. F. J. Thompson; R. E. T. Thorn, QC; A. R. Thornhill, QC; P. R. Thornton, QC; A. C. Tickle; M. B. Tillett, QC; J. W. Tinnion; R. N. Titheridge, QC; P. J. H. Towler; J. B. S. Townend, QC; C. M. Treacy, QC; H. B. Trethowan; A. D. H. Trollope, QC; D. W. Tucker; M. G. Tugendhat, QC; H. W. Turcan; D. A. Turner, QC; J. Turner; P. A. Twigg, QC; J. F. Uff, QC; R. P. A. Ullstein, QC; N. E. Underhill, QC; J. G. G. Ungley; P. C. Upward, QC; H. V. C. Vagg; N. P. Valios, QC; N. C. van der Bijl; D. A. J. Vaughan, QC; M. J. D. Vere-Hodge, QC; C. J. Vosper; S. P. Waine; R. M. Wakerley, QC; Mrs E. A. Walker; R. A. Walker, QC; R. J. Walker, QC; Sir Jonah Walker-Smith, Bt.; T. M. Walsh; J. J. Wardlow; B. B. Warner; J. Warren, QC; N. J. Warren; N. R. Warren, QC; D. E. B. Waters; Miss B. J. Watson; Sir James Watson, Bt.; B. J. Waylen; A. S. Webster; M. R. West; L. J. West-Knights; G. B. N. White; W. J. M. White; D. R. B. Whitehouse, QC; R. P. Whitehurst; P. G. Whiteman, QC; P. J. M. Whiteman, TD; A. Whitfield, QC; S. J. P. Widdup; C. T. Wide, QC; R. Wigglesworth; Mrs M. Wilby; N. V. M. Wilkinson, QC; Miss E. Willers; G. H. G. Williams, QC; Miss J. A. Williams; J. L. Williams, QC; M. J. Williams; W. L. Williams, QC; Miss H. E. Williamson, QC; S. W. Williamson, QC; A. J. D. Wilson, QC; A. M. Wilson, QC; I. K. R. Wilson; C. Wilson-Smith, QC; G. W. Wingate-Saul, QC; Miss S. E. Wollam; H. Wolton, QC; M. M. Wood, QC; N. A. Wood; R. L. J. Wood, QC; W. R. Wood; Miss S. Woodley, QC; J. T. Woods; W. C. Woodward, QC; Miss S. E. Woollam; A. P. L. Woolman; T. H. Workman; Miss A. M. Worrall, QC; P. F. Worsley, QC; J. J. Wright; N. A. Wright; D. E. M. Young, QC; M. K. Zeidman, QC

STIPENDIARY MAGISTRATES

PROVINCIAL
(each £76,921)

Avon, D. L. Thomas, *apptd* 1999
Cheshire, P. K. Dodd, OBE, *apptd* 1991
Chesterfield, M. G. Friel, *apptd* 1997
Derbyshire, M. J. Friel, *apptd* 1997; Mrs J. H. Alderson, *apptd* 1997
Devon, P. H. Wassall, *apptd* 1994
Dorset, P. R. Farmer, *apptd* 1998
East and West Sussex, P. C. Tain, *apptd* 1992; Mrs A. M. Arnold, *apptd* 1999
Essex, K. A. Gray, *apptd* 1995

Greater Manchester, A. Berg, *apptd* 1994; C. R. Darnton, *apptd* 1994; M. A. Abelson, *apptd* 1998
Hampshire, T. G. Cowling, *apptd* 1989; J. I. Woollard, *apptd* 1998; Mrs M. Shelvey, *apptd* 1999
Humberside, N. H. White, *apptd* 1985
Lancashire/Merseyside, J. Finestein, *apptd* 1992
Leeds, N. R. Cadbury, *apptd* 1997
Leicestershire, D. M. Meredith, *apptd* 1995; R. Holland, *apptd* 1999
Merseyside, D. R. G. Tapp, *apptd* 1992; P. S. Ward, *apptd* 1994; P. J. Firth, *apptd* 1994
Middlesex, N. A. McKittrick, *apptd* 1989; S. N. Day, *apptd* 1991; C. S. Wiles, *apptd* 1996
Mid Glamorgan, Miss P. J. Watkins, *apptd* 1995
Norfolk, N. P. Heley, *apptd* 1994
North-East London, G. E. Cawdron, *apptd* 1993
Nottinghamshire, P. F. Nuttall, *apptd* 1991; M. L. R. Harris, *apptd* 1991
Shropshire, P. H. R. Browning, *apptd* 1994
South Glamorgan, G. R. Watkins, *apptd* 1993
South Wales and Gwent, D. V. Manning-Davies, *apptd* 1996; Miss P. J. Watkins, *apptd* 1995
South Yorkshire, J. A. Browne, *apptd* 1992; W. D. Thomas, *apptd* 1989; M. A. Rosenberg, *apptd* 1993; P. H. F. Jones, *apptd* 1995; Mrs S. E. Driver, *apptd* 1995
Staffordshire, P. G. G. Richards, *apptd* 1991
West Midlands, W. M. Probert, *apptd* 1983; B. Morgan, *apptd* 1989; I. Gillespie, *apptd* 1991; M. F. James, *apptd* 1991; C. M. McColl, *apptd* 1994; J. A. Jellema, *apptd* 1998; D. J. Chinery, *apptd* 1998
West Yorkshire, Mrs P. A. Hewitt, *apptd* 1990; G. A. K. Hodgson, *apptd* 1993; N. R. Cadbury, *apptd* 1997, R. W. Anderson, *apptd* 1999

METROPOLITAN

Chief Metropolitan Stipendiary Magistrate and Chairman of Magistrates' Courts Committee for Inner London Area (£95,873), G. E. Parkinson, *apptd* 1997 (*Bow Street*)
Magistrates (each £80,921)

Bow Street, The Chief Magistrate; T. Workman, *apptd* 1986; C. L. Pratt, *apptd* 1990; H. N. Evans, *apptd* 1994
Camberwell Green, C. P. M. Davidson, *apptd* 1984; R. House, *apptd* 1995; Mrs L. Morgan, *apptd* 1995; Miss C. S. R. Tubbs, *apptd* 1996; K. Grant, *apptd* 1999
Greenwich, D. A. Cooper, *apptd* 1991; M. Kelly, *apptd* 1992; P. S. Wallis, *apptd* 1993; H. C. F. Riddle, *apptd* 1995
Highbury Corner, M. A. Johnstone, *apptd* 1980; Miss D. Quick, *apptd* 1986; I. M. Baker, *apptd* 1990; A. T. Evans, *apptd* 1990; Mrs L. Morgan, *apptd* 1995; P. A. M. Clark, *apptd* 1996; J. Perkins, *apptd* 1999
Horseferry Road, A. R. Davies, *apptd* 1985; G. Breen, *apptd* 1986; G. Wicks, *apptd* 1987; Mrs K. R. Keating, *apptd* 1987; Mrs E. Rees, *apptd* 1994
Inner London and City Family Proceedings Court, N. Crichton, *apptd* 1987
Marylebone, D. Kennett Brown, *apptd* 1982; Ms G. Babington-Browne, *apptd* 1991; Miss E. Roscoe, *apptd* 1994
South-Western, C. D. Voelcker, *apptd* 1982; A. W. Ormerod, *apptd* 1988; Miss D. Wickham, *apptd* 1989
Thames, Mrs J. Comyns, *apptd* 1982; S. E. Dawson, *apptd* 1984; I. G. Bing, *apptd* 1989; A. Baldwin, *apptd* 1990; W. A. Kennedy, *apptd* 1991
Tower Bridge, C. S. F. Black, *apptd* 1993; M. Read, *apptd* 1993; S. Somjee, *apptd* 1995
West London Magistrates' Court, K. L. Maitland-Davies, *apptd* 1984; T. English, *apptd* 1986; B. Loosley, *apptd* 1989; J. Philips, *apptd* 1989; D. L. Thomas, *apptd* 1990; D. Simpson, *apptd* 1993; J. Coleman, *apptd* 1995; Miss D. Lachhar, *apptd* 1996

MAGISTRATES' COURTS COMMITTEE FOR THE INNER LONDON AREA
65 Romney Street, London SW1P 3RD
Tel: 0845 600 8889
Justices' Chief Executive and Clerk to the Committee (£93,203), Miss C. Glenn
Training and Development Manager (£27,600–£37,500), Miss J. Whitby

---

CROWN PROSECUTION SERVICE
50 Ludgate Hill, London EC4M 7EX
Tel: 020-7796 8000
E-mail: enquiries@cps.gov.uk
Web: http://www.cps.gov.uk

The Crown Prosecution Service (CPS) is responsible for the independent review and conduct of criminal proceedings instituted by police forces in England and Wales, with the exception of cases conducted by the Serious Fraud Office (*see* Government Departments and Public Offices section) and certain minor offences.

The Service is headed by the Director of Public Prosecutions (DPP), who works under the superintendence of the Attorney-General, and a chief executive. The Service comprises a headquarters and 42 Areas, each Area corresponding to a police area in England and Wales. Each Area is headed by a Chief Crown Prosecutor, supported by an Area Business Manager.

Director of Public Prosecutions (SCS), D. Calvert-Smith, QC
Chief Executive (SCS), M. E. Addison
Directors (SCS), C. Newell (*Casework*); G. Patten (*Policy*); J. Graham (*Finance*); L. Carey (*Business Information Systems*); I. Seehra (*Human Resources*)
Head of Communications (SCS), Mrs L. Salisbury
Head of Management Audit Services (SCS), Ms. R. Read

CPS AREAS

ENGLAND

CPS AVON AND SOMERSET, 2nd Floor, Froomsgate House, Rupert Street, Bristol BS1 2QJ. Tel: 0117-930 2800. *Chief Crown Prosecutor (SCS)*, D. Archer; *Area Business Manager*, Ms L. Burton
CPS BEDFORDSHIRE, Sceptre House, 7–9 Castle Street, Luton LU1 3AJ. Tel: 01582-816600. *Chief Crown Prosecutor (SCS)*, Ms M. Townsend; *Area Business Manager*, Ms J. Altham
CPS CAMBRIDGESHIRE, Justinian House, Spitfire Close, Ermine Business Park, Huntingdon, Cambs PE18 6XY. Tel: 01480-825200. *Chief Crown Prosecutor (SCS)*, R. Crowley; *Area Business Manager*, I. Farrell
CPS CHESHIRE, 2nd Floor, Windsor House, Pepper Street, Chester CH1 1TD. Tel: 01244-408600. *Chief Crown Prosecutor (SCS)*, B. Hughes; *Area Business Manager*, Mrs E. Sherwood
CPS CLEVELAND, 5 Linthorpe Road, Middlesbrough, Cleveland TS1 1TX. Tel: 01642-204500. *Chief Crown Prosecutor (SCS)*, D. Magson; *Area Business Manager*, Mrs M. Phillips
CPS CUMBRIA, 1st Floor, Stocklund House, Castle Street, Carlisle CA3 8SY. Tel: 01228-882900. *Chief Crown Prosecutor (SCS)*, D. Farmer; *Area Business Manager*, J. Pears
CPS DERBYSHIRE, 7th Floor, St Peter's House, Gower Street, Derby DE1 1SB. Tel: 01332-614000. *Chief Crown Prosecutor (SCS)*, D. Adams; *Area Business Manager*, Mrs A. Clarke

CPS DEVON AND CORNWALL, Hawkins House, Pynes Hill, Rydon Lane, Exeter EX2 5SS. Tel: 01392-288000. *Chief Crown Prosecutor (SCS)*, A. Cresswell; *Area Business Manager*, J. Nettleton

CPS DORSET, 1st Floor, Oxford House, Oxford Road, Bournemouth BH8 8HA. Tel: 01202-498700. *Chief Crown Prosecutor (SCS)*, J. Revell; *Area Business Manager*, J. Putman

CPS DURHAM, Elvet House, Hallgarth Street, Durham DH1 3AT. Tel: 0191-383 5800. *Chief Crown Prosecutor (SCS)*, J. Corringhan; *Area Business Manager*, B. Feetham

CPS ESSEX, County House, 100 New London Road, Chelmsford CM2 0RG. Tel: 01245-455800. *Chief Crown Prosecutor (SCS)*, J. Bell; *Area Business Manager*, P. Overett

CPS GLOUCESTERSHIRE, 2 Kimbrose Way, Gloucester GL1 2DB. Tel: 01452-872400. *Chief Crown Prosecutor (SCS)*, W. Cole; *Area Business Manager*, W. Hollins

CPS GREATER MANCHESTER, PO Box 237, 8th Floor, Sunlight House, Quay Street, Manchester M60 3PS. Tel: 0161-827 4700. *Chief Crown Prosecutor (SCS)*, T. Taylor; *Area Business Manager*, K. Fox

CPS HAMPSHIRE, 3rd Floor, Black Horse House, 8–10 Leigh Road, Eastleigh, Hants SO50 9FH. Tel: 01703 673800. *Chief Crown Prosecutor (SCS)*, R. Daw; *Area Business Manager*, M. Sunderland

CPS HERTFORDSHIRE, Queen's House, 58 Victoria Street, St Albans, Herts AL1 3HZ. Tel: 01727-798700. *Chief Crown Prosecutor (SCS)*, C. Ingham; *Area Business Manager*, L. Carroll

CPS HUMBERSIDE, 2nd Floor, King William House, Lowgate, Hull HU1 1RS. Tel: 01482-621000. *Chief Crown Prosecutor (SCS)*, B. Marshall; *Area Business Manager*, Ms C. Skidmore

CPS KENT, Priory Gate, 29 Union Street, Maidstone, Kent ME14 1PT. Tel: 01622-356300. *Chief Crown Prosecutor (SCS)*, Ms E. Howe; *Area Business Manager*, K. Mitchell

CPS LANCASHIRE, 3rd Floor, Unicentre, Lord's Walk, Preston PR1 1DH. Tel: 01772-208100. *Chief Crown Prosecutor (SCS)*, D. Dickenson; *Area Business Manager*, G. Rankin

CPS LEICESTERSHIRE, Princes Court, 34 York Road, Leicester LE1 5TU. Tel: 0116-204 6700. *Chief Crown Prosecutor (SCS)*, M. Howard; *Area Business Manager*, Ms L. Jones

CPS LINCOLNSHIRE, Crosstrend House, 10A Newport, Lincoln LN1 3DF. Tel: 01522-585900. *Chief Crown Prosecutor (SCS)*, Ms A. Kerr; *Area Business Manager*, Ms A. Garbett

CPS LONDON (METROPOLITAN), 4th Floor, 50 Ludgate Hill, London EC4M 7EX. Tel: 020-7796 8000. *Chief Crown Prosecutor (SCS)*, P. Boeuf; *Assistant Chief Crown Prosecutors (SCS)*, Mrs A. Saunders; Ms M. Werrett; H. Cohen; *Area Business Manager*, A. Machray

CPS MERSEYSIDE, 7th Floor (South), Royal Liver Building, Pier Head, Liverpool L3 1HN. Tel: 0151-239 6400. *Chief Crown Prosecutor (SCS)*, J. Holt; *Area Business Manager*, Ms D. King

CPS NORFOLK, Haldin House, Old Bank of England Court, Queen Street, Norwich NR2 4SX. Tel: 01603-693000. *Chief Crown Prosecutor (SCS)*, P. Tidey; *Area Business Manager*, A. Mardell

CPS NORTH YORKSHIRE, 6th Floor, Ryedale Building, 60 Piccadilly, York YO1 1NS. Tel: 01904-731700. *Chief Crown Prosecutor (SCS)*, R. Turnbull; *Area Business Manager*, R. Cragg

CPS NORTHAMPTONSHIRE, Beaumont House, Cliftonville, Northampton NN1 5BE. Tel: 01604-823600.

Chief Crown Prosecutor (SCS), C. Chapman; *Area Business Manager*, J. Stephenson

CPS NORTHUMBRIA, 1st Floor, Benton House, 136 Sandyford Road, Newcastle upon Tyne NE2 1QE. Tel: 0191-260 4200. *Chief Crown Prosecutor (SCS)*, Ms N. Reasbeck; *Area Business Manager*, S. Guy

CPS NOTTINGHAMSHIRE, 2 King Edward Court, King Edward Street, Nottingham NG1 1EL. Tel: 0115-852 3300. *Chief Crown Prosecutor (SCS)*, P. Lewis; *Area Business Manager*, Mrs G. Pessol

CPS SOUTH YORKSHIRE, Greenfield House, 32 Scotland Street, Sheffield S3 7DQ. Tel: 0114-229 8600. *Chief Crown Prosecutor (SCS)*, Mrs J. Walker; *Area Business Manager*, C. Day

CPS STAFFORDSHIRE, 11A Princes Street, Stafford ST16 2EU. Tel: 01785-272200. *Chief Crown Prosecutor (SCS)*, H. Ireland; *Area Business Manager*, B. Laybourne

CPS SUFFOLK, Saxon House, 1 Cromwell Square, Ipswich IP1 1TS. Tel: 01473-282100. *Chief Crown Prosecutor (SCS)*, C. Yule; *Area Business Manager*, Mrs D. Waddington

CPS SURREY, One Onslow Street, Guildford, Surrey GU1 4YA. Tel: 01483-468200. *Chief Crown Prosecutor (SCS)*, Ms S. Hebblethwaite; *Area Business Manager*, M. Wray

CPS SUSSEX, Unit 3, Clifton Mews, Clifton Hill, Brighton BN1 3HR. Tel: 01273-765600. *Chief Crown Prosecutor (SCS)*, M. Kennedy; *Area Business Manager*, B. Shepherd

CPS THAMES VALLEY, The Courtyard, Lombard Street, Abingdon, Oxon OX14 5SE. Tel: 01235-551900. *Chief Crown Prosecutor (SCS)*, S. Clements; *Area Business Manager*, G. Choldcroft

CPS WARWICKSHIRE, Rossmore House, 10 Newbold Terrace, Leamington Spa, Warks CV32 4EA. Tel: 01926-455000. *Chief Crown Prosecutor (SCS)*, M. Lynn; *Area Business Manager*, Mrs S. Petyt

CPS WEST MERCIA, Artillery House, Heritage Way, Droitwich, Worcester WR9 8YB. Tel: 01905-825000. *Chief Crown Prosecutor (SCS)*, J. England; *Area Business Manager*, L. Sutton

CPS WEST MIDLANDS, 14th Floor, Colmore Gate, 2 Colmore Row, Birmingham B3 2QA. Tel: 0121-262 1300. *Chief Crown Prosecutor (SCS)*, D. Blundell; *Area Business Manager*, M. Grist

CPS WEST YORKSHIRE, Oxford House, Oxford Row, Leeds LS1 3BE Tel: 0113-290 2700. *Chief Crown Prosecutor (SCS)*, N. Franklin; *Area Business Manager*, R. Stevenson

CPS WILTSHIRE, 2nd Floor, Fox Talbot House, Bellinger Close, Malmesbury Road, Chippenham, Wilts SN15 1BN. Tel: 01249-766100. *Chief Crown Prosecutor (SCS)*, N. Hawkins; *Area Business Manager*, N. Nabi

WALES

CPS DYFED-POWYS, Heol Penlanffos, Tanerdy, Carmarthen, Dyfed SA31 2EZ. Tel: 01267-242100. *Chief Crown Prosecutor (SCS)*, S. Rowlands; *Area Business Manager*, Mrs C. Jones

CPS GWENT, 6th Floor, Chartist Tower, Upper Dock Street, Newport, Gwent NP9 1DW. Tel: 01633-261100. *Chief Crown Prosecutor (SCS)*, C. Woolley; *Area Business Manager*, B. Fullerton

CPS NORTH WALES, Llys Eirias, Heritage Gate, Bromfield House, Ellice Way, Wrexham LL13 7YW. Tel: 01978 346000. *Chief Crown Prosecutor (SCS)*, P. Whittaker; *Area Business Manager*, Mrs A. Walsh

CPS SOUTH WALES, 20st Floor, Capital Tower, Greyfriars Road, Cardiff CF1 3PL. Tel: 029-2080 3900. *Chief Crown Prosecutor (SCS)*, H. Heycock; *Area Business Manager*, I. Edmondson

The Scottish Judicature

Scotland has a legal system separate from and differing greatly from the English legal system in enacted law, judicial procedure and the structure of courts.

In Scotland the system of public prosecution is headed by the Lord Advocate and is independent of the police, who have no say in the decision to prosecute. The Lord Advocate, discharging his functions through the Crown Office in Edinburgh, is responsible for prosecutions in the High Court, sheriff courts and district courts. Prosecutions in the High Court are prepared by the Crown Office and conducted in court by one of the law officers, by an advocate-depute, or by a solicitor advocate. In the inferior courts the decision to prosecute is made and prosecution is preferred by procurators fiscal, who are lawyers and full-time civil servants subject to the directions of the Crown Office. A permanent legally-qualified civil servant known as the Crown Agent is responsible for the running of the Crown Office and the organisation of the Procurator Fiscal Service, of which he is the head.

Scotland is divided into six sheriffdoms, each with a full-time sheriff principal. The sheriffdoms are further divided into sheriff court districts, each of which has a legally-qualified resident sheriff or sheriffs, who are the judges of the court.

In criminal cases sheriffs principal and sheriffs have the same powers; sitting with a jury of 15 members, they may try more serious cases on indictment, or, sitting alone, may try lesser cases under summary procedure. Minor summary offences are dealt with in district courts which are administered by the district and the islands local government authorities and presided over by lay justices of the peace (of whom there are about 4,000) and, in Glasgow only, by stipendiary magistrates. Juvenile offenders (children under 16) may be brought before an informal children's hearing comprising three local lay people. The superior criminal court is the High Court of Justiciary which is both a trial and an appeal court. Cases on indictment are tried by a High Court judge, sitting with a jury of 15, in Edinburgh and on circuit in other towns. Appeals from the lower courts against conviction or sentence are heard also by the High Court, which sits as an appeal court only in Edinburgh. There is no further appeal to the House of Lords in criminal cases.

In civil cases the jurisdiction of the sheriff court extends to most kinds of action. Appeal against decisions of the sheriff may be made to the sheriff principal and thence to the Court of Session, or direct to the Court of Session, which sits only in Edinburgh. The Court of Session is divided into the Inner and the Outer House. The Outer House is a court of first instance in which cases are heard by judges sitting singly, sometimes with a jury of 12. The Inner House, itself subdivided into two divisions of equal status, is mainly an appeal court. Appeals may be made to the Inner House from the Outer House as well as from the sheriff court. An appeal may be made from the Inner House to the House of Lords.

The judges of the Court of Session are the same as those of the High Court of Justiciary, the Lord President of the Court of Session also holding the office of Lord Justice General in the High Court. Senators of the College of Justice are Lords Commissioners of Justiciary as well as judges of the Court of Session. On appointment, a Senator takes a judicial title, which is retained for life. Although styled 'The Hon./Rt. Hon. Lord —', the Senator is not a peer.

The office of coroner does not exist in Scotland. The local procurator fiscal inquires privately into sudden or suspicious deaths and may report findings to the Crown Agent. In some cases a fatal accident inquiry may be held before the sheriff.

COURT OF SESSION AND HIGH COURT OF JUSTICIARY

The Lord President and Lord Justice General (£157,390)
The Rt. Hon. the Lord Rodger of Earlsferry, *born* 1944, *apptd* 1996
  Secretary, A. Maxwell

INNER HOUSE

Lords of Session (each £144,549)

FIRST DIVISION
The Lord President
Rt. Hon. Lord Sutherland (Ranald Sutherland), *born* 1932, *apptd* 1985
Rt. Hon. Lord Prosser (William Prosser), *born* 1934, *apptd* 1986
Rt. Hon. Lord Cameron of Lochbroom, *born* 1931, *apptd* 1989

SECOND DIVISION
Lord Justice Clerk (£152,072), The Rt. Hon. Lord Cullen (William Cullen), *born* 1935, *apptd* 1997
Rt. Hon. Lord Kirkwood (Ian Kirkwood), *born* 1932, *apptd* 1987
Rt. Hon. Lord Coulsfield (John Cameron), *born* 1934, *apptd* 1987
Rt. Hon. Lord Milligan (James Milligan) *born* 1934, *apptd* 1988

OUTER HOUSE

Lords of Session (each £127,872)

Hon. Lord Marnoch (Michael Bruce), *born* 1938, *apptd* 1990
Hon. Lord MacLean (Ranald MacLean), *born* 1938, *apptd* 1990
Hon. Lord Penrose (George Penrose), *born* 1938, *apptd* 1990
Hon. Lord Osborne (Kenneth Osborne), *born* 1937, *apptd* 1990
Hon. Lord Abernethy (Alistair Cameron), *born* 1938, *apptd* 1992
Hon. Lord Johnston (Alan Johnston), *born* 1942, *apptd* 1994
Hon. Lord Gill (Brian Gill), *born* 1942, *apptd* 1994
Hon. Lord Hamilton (Arthur Hamilton), *born* 1942, *apptd* 1995
Hon. Lord Dawson (Thomas Dawson), *born* 1948, *apptd* 1995
Hon. Lord Macfadyen (Donald Macfadyen), *born* 1945, *apptd* 1995
Hon. Lady Cosgrove (Hazel Aronson), *born* 1946, *apptd* 1996
Hon. Lord Nimmo Smith (William Nimmo Smith), *born* 1942, *apptd* 1996
Hon. Lord Philip (Alexander Philip), *born* 1942, *apptd* 1996
Hon. Lord Kingarth (Derek Emslie), *born* 1949, *apptd* 1997
Hon. Lord Bonomy (Iain Bonomy), *born* 1946, *apptd* 1997
Hon. Lord Eassie (Ronald Mackay), *born* 1945, *apptd* 1997
Hon. Lord Reed (Robert Reed), *born* 1956, *apptd* 1998
Hon. Lord Wheatley (John Wheatley), *born* 1941, *apptd* 2000
Hon. Lady Paton (Ann Paton), *born* 1952, *apptd* 2000

Hon. Lord Carloway (Colin Sutherland), *born* 1954, *apptd* 2000
Hon. Lord Clarke (Matthew Clarke), *born* 1947, *apptd* 2000
Rt. Hon. Lord Hardie (Andrew Hardie), *born* 1946, *apptd* 2000
Rt. Hon. Lord Mackay of Drumadoon (Donald Mackay), *born* 1946, *apptd* 2000
Hon. Lord McEwan (Robin McEwan), *born* 1943, *apptd* 2000

COURT OF SESSION AND HIGH COURT OF JUSTICIARY

Parliament House, Parliament Square, Edinburgh EH1 1HQ
Tel: 0131-225 2595

Principal Clerk of Session and Justiciary (£33,391–£55,711), J. L. Anderson
Deputy Principal Clerk of Justiciary and Administration (£29,277–£45,365), T. Higgins
Deputy Principal Clerk of Session and Principal Extractor (£29,277–£45,365), A. Finlayson
Deputy Principal Clerk (Keeper of the Rolls) (£29,277–£45,365), D. Shand
Depute Clerks of Session and Justiciary (£22,348–£29,381), N. J. Dowie; I. F. Smith; T. Higgins; T. B. Cruickshank; Q. A. Oliver; F. Shannly; A. S. Moffat; G. G. Ellis; W. Dunn; A. M. Finlayson; C. C. Armstrong; R. Jenkins; J. O. McLean; M. Weir; R. M. Sinclair; E. G. Appelbe; B. Watson; D. W. Cullen; I. D. Martin; N. McGinley; J. Lynn; E. Dickson; K. D. Carter; F. Petrie; D. Fraser; S. M. Fowler; W. G. Combe; R. T. MacPherson; P. McFarlane; D. Bruton

SCOTTISH EXECUTIVE COURTS GROUP

Hayweight House, 23 Lauriston Street, Edinburgh EH3 9DQ
Tel: 0131-229 9200

Courts Group is responsible for the provision of sufficient Judges and Sheriffs for the needs of the programme of the supreme and Sheriffs Court in Scotland. It is also responsible for the promotion, through the reform of law of Scotland, of the independence, integrity and quality of the judicial process in civil proceedings (and in relation to evidence, in criminal proceedings). It also has a role in the development of the private international law of Scotland and the relationship between the Scottish Legal System and other legal systems including those in Europe and the United Kingdom; and provides resources for the efficient administration of a number of tribunals and small departments.
Head of Judicial Appointments and Finance Division (SCS), D. Stewart
Head of Civil Law and International Division (SCS), P. M. Beaton

SCOTTISH COURT SERVICE

Hayweight House, 23 Lauriston Street, Edinburgh EH3 9DQ
Tel: 0131-229 9200

The Scottish Court Service is an executive agency within the Scottish Executive Justice Department. It is responsible to the Scottish Ministers for the provision of staff, court houses and associated services for the Supreme and Sheriff Courts.
Chief Executive, J. Ewing

SHERIFF COURT OF CHANCERY

27 Chambers Street, Edinburgh EH1 1LB
Tel: 0131-225 2525

The Court deals with service of heirs and completion of title in relation to heritable property.
Sheriff of Chancery, C. G. B. Nicholson, QC

HM COMMISSARY OFFICE

27 Chambers Street, Edinburgh EH1 1LB
Tel: 0131-225 2525

The Office is responsible for issuing confirmation, a legal document entitling a person to execute a deceased person's will, and other related matters.
Commissary Clerk, J. M. Ross

SCOTTISH LAND COURT

1 Grosvenor Crescent, Edinburgh EH12 5ER
Tel: 0131-225 3595

The court deals with disputes relating to agricultural and crofting land in Scotland.
Chairman (£103,516), The Hon. Lord McGhie (James McGhie), QC
Members, D. J. Houston; D. M. Macdonald; J. Kinloch (*part-time*)
Principal Clerk, K. H. R. Graham, WS

SHERIFFDOMS

SALARIES

Sheriff Principal	£103,516
Sheriff	£95,873
Area Director	£32,293–£63,490
Sheriff Clerk	£12,719–£43,873

*Floating Sheriff

GRAMPIAN, HIGHLANDS AND ISLANDS

Sheriff Principal, D. J. Risk, QC
Area Director North, J. Robertson

SHERIFFS AND SHERIFF CLERKS

Aberdeen and Stonehaven, D. Kelbie; L. A. S. Jessop; A. Pollock; Mrs A. M. Cowan; C. J. Harris, QC; I. H. L. Miller; *G. K. Buchanan; *Sheriff Clerks*, Mrs E. Laing (*Aberdeen*); B. McBride (*Stonehaven*)
Peterhead and Banff, K. A. McLernan; *D. J. Cusine; *Sheriff Clerk*, A. Hempseed (*Peterhead*); *Sheriff Clerk Depute*, Mrs F. L. MacPherson (*Banff*)
Elgin, N. McPartlin; *Sheriff Clerk*, M. McBey
Inverness, Lochmaddy, Portree, Stornoway, Dingwall, Tain, Wick and Dornoch, W. J. Fulton; D. Booker-Milburn; J. O. A. Fraser; I. A. Cameron; *Sheriff Clerks*, J. Robertson (*Inverness*); W. Cochrane (*Dingwall*); *Sheriff Clerks Depute*, Miss M. Campbell (*Lochmaddy and Portree*); Miss A. B. Armstrong (*Stornoway*); L. MacLachlan (*Tain*); Mrs J. McEwan (*Wick*); K. Kerr (*Dornoch*)
Kirkwall and Lerwick, C. S. Mackenzie; *Sheriff Clerks Depute*, vacant (*Kirkwall*); M. Flanagan (*Lerwick*)
Fort William, C. G. McKay (also *Oban*); *Sheriff Clerk Depute*, D. Hood

TAYSIDE, CENTRAL AND FIFE

Sheriff Principal, R. A. Dunlop, QC
Area Director East, M. Bonar

SHERIFFS AND SHERIFF CLERKS

Arbroath and Forfar, K. A. Veal; *C. N. R. Stein; *Sheriff Clerks*, M. Herbertson (*Arbroath*); S. Munro (*Forfar*)
Dundee, R. A. Davidson; A. L. Stewart, QC; *J. P. Scott; G. J. Evans (also *Cupar*); *P. P. Davies; *J. K. Tierney; *Sheriff Clerk*, D. Nicoll

Perth, M. J. Fletcher; Mrs F. L. Reith, QC; *D. Pyle; *L. D. R. Foulis *Sheriff Clerk*, J. Murphy
Falkirk, A. V. Sheehan; A. J. Murphy; *C. Caldwell *Sheriff Clerk*, R. McMillan
Stirling, The Hon. R. E. G. Younger; *A. W. Robertson *Sheriff Clerk*, J. Clark
Alloa, W. M. Reid; *Sheriff Clerk*, R. G. McKeand
Cupar, G. J. Evans (also *Dundee*); *Sheriff Clerk*, R. Hughes
Dunfermline, J. S. Forbes; *G. W. M. Liddle; Mrs I. G. McColl; N. C. Stewart; *Sheriff Clerk*, W. McCulloch
Kirkcaldy, F. J. Keane; Mrs L. G. Patrick; *I. D. Dunbar; *B. G. Donald; *Sheriff Clerk*, W. Jones

LOTHIAN AND BORDERS

Sheriff Principal, C. G. B. Nicholson, QC
Area Director East, M. Bonar

SHERIFFS AND SHERIFF CLERKS

Edinburgh, R. G. Craik, QC (also *Peebles*); R. J. D. Scott (also *Peebles*); Miss I. A. Poole; A. M. Bell; J. M. S. Horsburgh, QC; G. W. S. Presslie (also *Haddington*); J. A. Farrell; *A. Lothian; I. D. Macphail, QC; C. N. Stoddart; A. B. Wilkinson, QC; N. M. P. Morrison, QC; *Miss M. M. Stephen; Mrs M. L. E. Jarvie, QC; *Mrs K. E. C. Mackie; *N. J. MacKinnon; *Sheriff Clerk*, J. Ross
Peebles, R. G. Craik, QC (also *Edinburgh*); R. J. D. Scott (also *Edinburgh*); *Sheriff Clerk Depute*, M. L. Kubeczka
Linlithgow, H. R. MacLean; G. R. Fleming; *P. Gillam; *Sheriff Clerk*, R. D. Sinclair
Haddington, G. W. S. Presslie (also *Edinburgh*); *Sheriff Clerk*, J. O'Donnell
Jedburgh and Duns, T. A. K. Drummond, QC; *Sheriff Clerk*, I. W. Williamson
Selkirk, T. A. K. Drummond, QC; *Sheriff Clerk Depute*, L. McFarlane

NORTH STRATHCLYDE

Sheriff Principal, B. A. Kerr, QC
Area Director West, I. Scott

SHERIFFS AND SHERIFF CLERKS

Oban, C. G. McKay (also *Fort William*); *Sheriff Clerk Depute*, J. G. Whitelaw
Dumbarton, J. T. Fitzsimons; T. Scott; S. W. H. Fraser; *Sheriff Clerk*, P. Corcoran
Paisley, J. Spy; C. K. Higgins; N. Douglas; D. J. Pender; *W. Dunlop; G. C. Kavanagh (also *Campbeltown*); *Sheriff Clerk*, Miss S. Hindes
Greenock, J. Herald (also *Rothesay*); Sir Stephen Young; *Mrs R. Swanney; *Sheriff Clerk*, J. Tannahill
Kilmarnock, T. M. Croan; D. B. Smith; T. F. Russell; *Mrs I. S. Donald; *Sheriff Clerk*, G. Waddell
Dunoon, Mrs C. M. A. F. Gimblett; *Sheriff Clerk Depute*, Mrs C. Carson
Campbeltown, *W. Dunlop (also *Paisley*); *Sheriff Clerk Depute*, P. G. Hay
Rothesay, J. Herald (also *Greenock*); *Sheriff Clerk Depute*, Mrs C. K. McCormick

GLASGOW AND STRATHKELVIN

Sheriff Principal, E. F. Bowen, QC
Area Director West, I. Scott

SHERIFFS AND SHERIFF CLERKS

Glasgow, B. Kearney; B. A. Lockhart; Mrs A. L. A. Duncan; A. C. Henry; J. K. Mitchell; A. G. Johnston; J. P. Murphy; Miss S. A. O. Raeburn, QC; D. Convery; J. McGowan; I. A. S. Peebles, QC; C. W. McFarlane, QC; K. M. Maciver; H. Matthews, QC; J. A. Baird; Miss R. E. A. Rae, QC; Mrs P. M. M. Bowman; A. W. Noble; J. D. Friel; Mrs D. M. MacNeill, QC; J. A. Taylor;

C. A. L. Scott; * S. Cathcart; *Ms L. M. Ruxton; *Sheriff Clerk*, R. Cockburn

SOUTH STRATHCLYDE, DUMFRIES AND GALLOWAY

Sheriff Principal, J. C. McInnes, QC
Area Director West, I. Scott

SHERIFFS AND SHERIFF CLERKS

Hamilton, L. Cameron; D. C. Russell; V. J. Canavan (also *Airdrie*); W. E. Gibson; J. H. Stewart; H. S. Neilson; S. C. Pender; *Sheriff Clerk*, P. Feeney
Lanark, J. D. Allan; *Miss J. Powrie; *A. D. Vannett; *T. Welsh, QC; *Sheriff Clerk*, A. Whyte
Ayr, N. Gow, QC; *D. W. McIntyre; C. B. Miller; *Sheriff Clerk*, Miss C. D. Cockburn
Stranraer and Kirkcudbright, J. R. Smith (also *Dumfries*); *Sheriff Clerks*, W. McIntosh (*Stranraer*); B. Lindsay (*Kirkcudbright*)
Dumfries, K. G. Barr; ; J. R. Smith (also *Stranraer and Kirkcudbright*); K. A. Ross; *Sheriff Clerk*, P. McGonigle
Airdrie, V. J. Canavan (also *Hamilton*); R. H. Dickson; I. C. Simpson; J. C. Morris, QC; *Sheriff Clerk*, D. Forrester

STIPENDIARY MAGISTRATES

GLASGOW

R. Hamilton, *apptd* 1984; J. B. C. Nisbet, *apptd* 1984; R. B. Christie, *apptd* 1985; Mrs J. A. M. MacLean, *apptd* 1990

CROWN OFFICE AND PROCURATOR FISCAL SERVICE

CROWN OFFICE
25 Chambers Street, Edinburgh EH1 1LA
Tel: 0131-226 2626;
Web: http://www.crownoffice.gov.uk
Crown Agent (£80,020–£116,860), A. C. Normand
Deputy Crown Agent (£55,750–£92,930), F. R. Crowe

PROCURATORS FISCAL

SALARIES

Regional Procurator Fiscal (SCS Band 5)	£62,882–£101,254
Regional Procurator Fiscal (SCS Band 4)	£57,367–£95,6256
	£55,750–£92,930
Procurator Fiscal – upper level	£42,755–£67,163
Procurator Fiscal – lower level	£36,900–£44,786

GRAMPIAN, HIGHLAND AND ISLANDS REGION

Regional Procurator Fiscal, Mrs E. Angiolini (*Aberdeen*)
Procurators Fiscal, E. K. Barbour (*Stonehaven*); A. J. M. Colley (*Banff*); A. B. Hutchinson (*Peterhead*); D. J. Dickson (*Elgin*); G. Aitken (*Wick*); J. F. Bamber (*Portree, Lochmaddy*); D. S. Teale (*Stornoway*); Mrs B. Bott (*Inverness*); R. W. Urquhart (*Kirkwall, Lerwick*); D. J. Buchanan (*Fort William*); A. N. MacDonald (*Dingwall, Dornoch, Tain*)

TAYSIDE, CENTRAL AND FIFE REGION

Regional Procurator Fiscal, B. K. Heywood (*Dundee*)
Procurators Fiscal, J. I. Craigen (*Forfar*); I. A. McLeod (*Perth*); W. J. Gallacher (*Falkirk*); C. Ritchie (*Stirling and Alloa*); E. B. Russell (*Cupar*); R. G. Stott (*Dunfermline*); Miss H. M. Clark (*Kirkcaldy*); A. J. Wheelan (*Arbroath*)

LOTHIAN AND BORDERS REGION

Regional Procurator Fiscal, N. McFadyen (*Edinburgh*)

Procurators Fiscal, Mrs C. P. Dyer (*Linlithgow*); A. J. P. Reith (*Haddington*); A. R. G. Fraser (*Duns, Jedburgh*); Mrs L. E. Thomson (*Selkirk, Peebles*)

NORTH STRATHCLYDE REGION
Regional Procurator Fiscal, W. A. Gilchrist (*Paisley*)
Procurators Fiscal, F. Redman (*Campbeltown*); C. C. Donnelly (*Dumbarton*); W. S. Carnegie (*Greenock, Rothesay*); D. L. Webster (*Dunoon*); J. Watt (*Kilmarnock*); B. R. Maguire (*Oban*)

GLASGOW AND STRATHKELVIN REGION
Regional Procurator Fiscal, L. A. Higson (*Glasgow*)

SOUTH STRATHCLYDE, DUMFRIES AND GALLOWAY REGION
Regional Procurator Fiscal, D. A. Brown (*Hamilton*)
Procurators Fiscal, S. R. Houston (*Lanark*); J. T. O'Donnell (*Ayr*); A. S. Kennedy (*Stranraer*); D. J. Howdle (*Dumfries, Kirkudbright*); D. Spiers (*Airdrie*)

Northern Ireland Judicature

In Northern Ireland the legal system and the structure of courts closely resemble those of England and Wales; there are, however, often differences in enacted law.

The Supreme Court of Judicature of Northern Ireland comprises the Court of Appeal, the High Court of Justice and the Crown Court. The practice and procedure of these courts is similar to that in England. The superior civil court is the High Court of Justice, from which an appeal lies to the Northern Ireland Court of Appeal; the House of Lords is the final civil appeal court.

The Crown Court, served by High Court and county court judges, deals with criminal trials on indictment. Cases are heard before a judge and, except those involving offences specified under emergency legislation, a jury. Appeals from the Crown Court against conviction or sentence are heard by the Northern Ireland Court of Appeal; the House of Lords is the final court of appeal.

The decision to prosecute in cases tried on indictment and in summary cases of a serious nature rests in Northern Ireland with the Director of Public Prosecutions, who is responsible to the Attorney-General. Minor summary offences are prosecuted by the police.

Minor criminal offences are dealt with in magistrates' courts by a legally qualified resident magistrate and, where an offender is under 17, by juvenile courts each consisting of a resident magistrate and two lay members specially qualified to deal with juveniles (at least one of whom must be a woman). On 6 August 1999 there were 937 justices of the peace in Northern Ireland. Appeals from magistrates' courts are heard by the county court, or by the Court of Appeal on a point of law or an issue as to jurisdiction.

Magistrates' courts in Northern Ireland can deal with certain classes of civil case but most minor civil cases are dealt with in county courts. Judgments of all civil courts are enforceable through a centralised procedure administered by the Enforcement of Judgments Office.

SUPREME COURT OF JUDICATURE

The Royal Courts of Justice, Belfast BT1 3JF
Tel: 028-9023 5111
Lord Chief Justice of Northern Ireland (£157,390)

The Rt. Hon. Sir Robert Carswell, *born* 1934, *apptd* 1997
Principal Secretary, G. W. Johnston

LORDS JUSTICES OF APPEAL (each £144,549)
Style, The Rt. Hon. Lord Justice [surname]

Rt. Hon. Sir Michael Nicholson, *born* 1933, *apptd* 1995
Rt. Hon. Sir William McCollum, *born* 1933, *apptd* 1997
Rt. Hon. Sir Anthony Campbell, *born* 1936, *apptd* 1998

PUISNE JUDGES (each £3127,872)
Style, The Hon. Mr Justice [surname]

Hon. Sir John Sheil, *born* 1938, *apptd* 1989
Hon. Sir Brian Kerr, *born* 1948, *apptd* 1993
Hon. Sir Malachy Higgins, *born* 1944, *apptd* 1993
Hon. Sir Paul Girvan, *born* 1948, *apptd* 1995
Hon. Sir Patrick Coghlin, *born* 1945, *apptd* 1997
Hon. Sir John Gillen, *born* 1947, *apptd* 1998
Hon. Sir Richard McLaughlin, *born* 1947, *apptd* 1999

MASTERS OF THE SUPREME COURT (each £76,921)
Master, Queen's Bench and Appeals and Clerk of the Crown, J. W. Wilson, QC
Master, High Court, Mrs D. M. Kennedy
Master, Office of Care and Protection, F. B. Hall
Master, Chancery Office, R. A. Ellison
Master, Bankruptcy and Companies Office, C. W. G. Redpath
Master, Probate and Matrimonial Office, Miss M. McReynolds
Master, Taxing Office, J. C. Napier

OFFICIAL SOLICITOR
Official Solicitor to the Supreme Court of Northern Ireland, Miss B. M. Donnelly

COUNTY COURTS

JUDGES (each £103,516)

Style, His/Her Hon. Judge [surname]

Judge Curran, QC; Judge Gibson, QC; Judge Petrie, QC; Judge Smyth, QC; Judge Markey, QC; Judge McKay, QC; Judge Smyth, QC (*Chief Social Security and Child Support Commissioner*); Judge Brady, QC; Judge Foote, QC; Her Hon. Judge Philpott, QC; Judge McFarland; Judge Lockie

RECORDERS (each £103,516)
Belfast, Judge Hart, QC
Londonderry, Judge Burgess

MAGISTRATES' COURTS

RESIDENT MAGISTRATES (each £76,921)
There are 17 resident magistrates in Northern Ireland.

CROWN SOLICITOR'S OFFICE
PO Box 410, Royal Courts of Justice, Belfast BT1 3JY
Tel: 028-9054 2555
Crown Solicitor, N. P. Roberts

DEPARTMENT OF THE DIRECTOR OF PUBLIC PROSECUTIONS
Royal Courts of Justice, Belfast BT1 3NX
Tel: 028-9054 2444

Director of Public Prosecutions, A. Fraser, CB, QC
Deputy Director of Public Prosecutions, W. R. Junkin

NORTHERN IRELAND COURT SERVICE
Windsor House, Bedford Street, Belfast BT2 7LT
Tel: 028-9032 8594
Director (*G3*)

Tribunals

AGRICULTURAL LAND TRIBUNALS
c/o Rural and Marine Environment Division,
Ministry of Agriculture, Fisheries and Food,
Nobel House, 17 Smith Square, London SW1P 3JR
Tel: 020-7238 6991

Agricultural Land Tribunals settle disputes and other issues between agricultural landlords and tenants, and drainage disputes between neighbours.

There are seven tribunals covering England and one covering Wales. For each tribunal the Lord Chancellor appoints a chairman and one or more deputies (barristers or solicitors of at least seven years standing). The Lord Chancellor also appoints lay members to three statutory panels: the 'landowners' panel, the 'farmers' panel and the 'drainage' panel.

Each tribunal is an independent statutory body with jurisdiction only within its own area. A separate tribunal is constituted for each case, and consists of a chairman (who may be the chairman or one of the deputy chairmen) and two lay members nominated by the chairman.
Chairmen (England) (£271 a day), W. D. Greenwood;
K. J. Fisher; P. A. de la Piquerie; A. G. Donn; His
Hon. Judge Lee; G. L. Newsom; His
Hon. Judge Robert Taylor
Chairman (Wales) (£271 a day), W. J. Owen

APPEALS SERVICE
Whittington House, 19–30 Alfred Place,
London WC1E 7LW
Tel: 020-7712 2600

The Service is responsible for the functioning of tribunals hearing appeals concerning child support assessments, social security benefits and vaccine damage payments. Judicial authority for the Service rests with the President, while administrative responsibility is exercised by the Appeals Service Agency, which is an executive agency of the Department of Social Security.
President, His Hon. Judge Michael Harris
Chief Executive, Appeals Service Agency, N. Ward

COMMONS COMMISSIONERS
Room 818, Tollgate House, Houlton Street,
Bristol BS2 9DJ
Tel: 0117-987 8928

The Commons Commissioners are responsible for deciding disputes arising under the Commons Registration Act 1965. They also enquire into the ownership of unclaimed common land and village greens. Commissioners are appointed by the Lord Chancellor.
Chief Commons Commissioner (part-time), D. M. Burton
Commissioner, I. L. R. Romer (part-time)
Clerk, H. Thomas

COPYRIGHT TRIBUNAL
Harmsworth House, 13–15 Bouverie Street,
London EC4Y 8DP
Tel: 020-7596 6510; Fax 020-7596-6526;
Email: copyright.tribunal@patent.gov.uk;
Web: http://www.patent.gov.uk

The Copyright Tribunal resolves disputes over copyright licences, principally where there is collective licensing.

The chairman and two deputy chairmen are appointed by the Lord Chancellor. Up to eight ordinary members are appointed by the Secretary of State for Trade and Industry.
Chairman (£316 a day), C. P. Tootal
Secretary, Miss J. E. M. Durdin

GENERAL COMMISSIONERS OF INCOME TAX
Lord Chancellor's Department, Selborne House,
54–60 Victoria Street, London SW1E 6QW
Tel: 020-7210 8728

General Commissioners of Income Tax operate under the Taxes Management Act 1970. They are unpaid judicial officers who sit in some 460 Divisions throughout the United Kingdom to hear appeals against decisions by the Inland Revenue on a variety of taxation matters. The Commissioners' jurisdiction was extended in 1999 to hear National Insurance appeals. The Lord Chancellor appoints General Commissioners (except in Scotland, where they are appointed by the Scottish Executive). There are approximately 3,000 General Commissioners sitting throughout the United Kingdom. In each Division, Commissioners appoint a Clerk, who is normally legally qualified, who makes the administrative arrangements for appeal hearings and advises the Commissioners on points of law and procedure. The Lord Chancellor's Department pays the Clerks' remuneration.

Appeals from the General Commissioners are by way of case stated, on a point of law, to the High Court (the Court of Session in Scotland or the Court of Appeal in Northern Ireland).

In 1999, approximately 85,000 cases were listed before the General Commissioners.

PROTECTION TRIBUNAL
c/o The Home Office, Queen Anne's Gate,
London SW1H 9AT
Tel: 020-7273 3755

The Data Protection Tribunal determines appeals against decisions of the Data Protection Commissioner. The chairman and deputy chairman are appointed by the Lord Chancellor and must be legally qualified. Lay members are appointed by the Home Secretary to represent the interests of data users or data subjects. A tribunal consists of a legally-qualified chairman sitting with equal numbers of the lay members appointed to represent the interests of data users and data subjects.
Chairman (£394 a day), J. A. C. Spokes, QC
Secretary, R. Hartley

EMPLOYMENT TRIBUNALS

CENTRAL OFFICE (ENGLAND AND WALES)
19–29 Woburn Place, London WC1H 0LU
Tel: 020-7273 8666

Employment Tribunals for England and Wales sit in 12 regions. The tribunals deal with matters of employment law, redundancy, dismissal, contract disputes, sexual, racial and disability discrimination, and related areas of dispute which may arise in the workplace. A central registration unit records all applications and maintains a public register at Southgate Street, Bury St Edmunds, Suffolk IP33 2AQ. The tribunals are funded by the Department of Trade and Industry; administrative support is provided by the Employment Tribunals Service.

Chairmen, who may be full-time or part-time, are legally qualified. They are appointed by the Lord Chancellor. Tribunal members are appointed by the Secretary of State for Trade and Industry.
President (£103,516), His Hon. Judge Prophet

CENTRAL OFFICE (SCOTLAND)
Eagle Building, 215 Bothwell Street, Glasgow G2 7TS
Tel: 0141-204 0730

Tribunals in Scotland have the same remit as those in England and Wales. Chairmen are appointed by the Lord President of the Court of Session and lay members by the Secretary of State for Trade and Industry.
President (£95,873), C. M. Milne

EMPLOYMENT APPEAL TRIBUNAL

Central Office: Audit House, 58 Victoria Embankment,
London EC4Y 0DS
Tel: 020-7273 1041
Divisional Office: 52 Melville Street, Edinburgh EH3 7HF
Tel: 0131-225 3963;
Web: http://www.employmentappeals.gov.uk

The Employment Appeal Tribunal hears appeals on a question of law arising from any decision of an employment tribunal. A tribunal consists of a high court judge and two lay members, one from each side of industry. They are appointed by The Queen on the recommendation of the Lord Chancellor and the Secretary of State for Trade and Industry. Administrative support is provided by the Employment Tribunals Service.
President, The Hon. Mr Justice Lindsay
Scottish Chairman, The Hon. Lord Johnston
Registrar, Miss V. J. Selio
Deputy Registrar, Ms J. Johnson

IMMIGRATION APPELLATE AUTHORITIES

Taylor House, 88 Rosebery Avenue, London EC1R 4QU
Tel: 020-7862 4200

The Immigration Appeal Adjudicators hear appeals from immigration decisions concerning the need for, and refusal of, leave to enter or remain in the UK, refusals to grant asylum, decisions to make deportation orders and directions to remove persons subject to immigration control from the UK. The Immigration Appeal Tribunal hears appeals direct from decisions to make deportation orders in matters concerning conduct contrary to the public good, and from refusals to grant asylum. Its principal jurisdiction is, however, the hearing of appeals from adjudicators by the party (Home Office or individual) who is aggrieved by the decision. Appeals are subject to leave being granted by the tribunal.

An adjudicator sits alone. The tribunal sits in divisions of three, normally a legally qualified member and two lay members. Members of the tribunal and adjudicators are appointed by the Lord Chancellor.

IMMIGRATION APPEAL TRIBUNAL
President, The Hon. Mr Justice Collins
Vice-Presidents, A. F. Hatt; M. Rapinet; A. O'Brien-Quinn; Mrs D. J. Drew; Dr H. H. W. Storey; J. G. Freeman; D. Allen; J. Barnes; K. Drabu; J. Fox; P. Moulden; C. Ockelton

IMMIGRATION APPEAL ADJUDICATORS
Chief Adjudicator, His Hon. Judge Dunn, QC
Deputy Chief Adjudicator, J. Latter

INDUSTRIAL TRIBUNALS AND THE FAIR EMPLOYMENT TRIBUNAL (NORTHERN IRELAND)

Long Bridge House, 20–24 Waring Street, Belfast BT1 2EB
Tel: 028-9032 7666

The industrial tribunal system in Northern Ireland was set up in 1965 and has a similar remit to the employment tribunals in the rest of the UK. There is also in Northern Ireland a Fair Employment Tribunal, which hears and determines individual cases of alleged religious or political discrimination in employment. Employers can appeal to the Fair Employment Tribunal if they consider the directions of the Equality Commission to be unreasonable, inappropriate or unnecessary, and the Equality Commission can make application to the Tribunal for the enforcement of undertakings or directions with which an employer has not complied.

The president, vice-president and part-time chairmen of the Fair Employment Tribunal are appointed by the Lord Chancellor. The full-time chairman and the part-time chairmen of the industrial tribunals and the panel members to both the industrial tribunals and the Fair Employment Tribunal are appointed by the Department of Higher and Further Education Training and Employment.
President of the Industrial Tribunals and the Fair Employment Tribunal (£103,516), J. Maguire, CBE
Vice-President of the Industrial Tribunals and the Fair Employment Tribunal, Mrs M. P. Price
Secretary, Mrs P. McVeigh

LANDS TRIBUNAL

48–49 Chancery Lane, London WC2A 1JR
Tel: 020-7947 7200

The Lands Tribunal is an independent judicial body which determines questions relating to the valuation of land, rating appeals from valuation tribunals, the discharge or modification of restrictive covenants, and compulsory purchase compensation. The tribunal may also arbitrate under references by consent. The president and members are appointed by the Lord Chancellor.
President (£103,516), G. R. Bartlett, QC
Members (£95,873), P. H. Clarke, FRICS; N. J. Rose, FRICS; P. R. Francis
Member (part-time), His Hon. Judge Rich, QC
Registrar, D. Scannell

LANDS TRIBUNAL FOR SCOTLAND
1 Grosvenor Crescent, Edinburgh EH12 5ER
Tel: 0131-225 7996

The Lands Tribunal for Scotland has the same remit as the tribunal for England and Wales but also covers questions relating to tenants' rights to buy their homes under the Housing (Scotland) Act 1987. The president is appointed by the Lord President of the Court of Session.
President (£103,516), The Hon. Lord McGhie, QC
Members (£95,873), J. Devine, FRICS; A. R. MacLeary, FRICS
Member (part-time) (£33,409), R. A. Edwards, CBE, WS
Clerk, N. M. Tainsh

MENTAL HEALTH REVIEW TRIBUNALS
Secretariat: Health Service Directorate,
Room 326 Wellington House, 133–155 Waterloo Road,
London SE1 8UG
Tel: 020-7972 4503/4577

The Mental Health Review Tribunals are independent judicial bodies which review the cases of patients compulsorily detained under the provisions of the Mental Health Act 1983. They have the power to discharge the patient, to recommend leave of absence, delayed discharge, transfer to another hospital or that a guardianship order be made, to reclassify both restricted and unrestricted patients, and to recommend consideration of a supervision application. There are four tribunals in England, each headed by a regional chairman who is appointed by the Lord Chancellor on a part-time basis. Each tribunal is made up of at least three members, and must include a lawyer, who acts as president (£239 a day), a medical member (£226 a day) and a lay member (£97 a day).

There are five regional offices:

LIVERPOOL, 3rd Floor, Cressington House, 249 St Mary's Road, Garston, Liverpool L19 0NF. Tel: 0151-728 5400
LONDON (NORTH), Spur 3, Block 1, Government Buildings, Honeypot Lane, Stanmore, Middx HA7 1AY. Tel: 020-7972 3754
LONDON (SOUTH), Block 3, Crown Offices, Kingston Bypass Road, Surbiton, Surrey KT6 5QN. Tel: 020-8268 4549
NOTTINGHAM, Spur A, Block 5, Government Buildings, Chalfont Drive, Western Boulevard, Nottingham NG8 3RZ. Tel: 0115-942 8308
WALES, 4th Floor, Crown Buildings, Cathays Park, Cardiff CF1 3NQ. Tel: 029-2082 5328

NATIONAL HEALTH SERVICE TRIBUNAL

The NHS Tribunal considers representations that the continued inclusion of a doctor, dentist, optician or pharmacist on a health authority's list would be prejudicial to the efficiency of the service concerned. The tribunal sits when required, usually in London. The chairman is appointed by the Lord Chancellor and members by the Secretary of State for Health.
Chairman, A. Whitfield, QC
Deputy Chairmen, Miss E. Platt, QC; Dr R. N. Ough
Clerk, T. L. Rayson, OBE, 38D Rayleigh Road, Thundersley SS7 3TA. Tel: 01268-774481

NATIONAL HEALTH SERVICE TRIBUNAL (SCOTLAND)
Clerk: 66 Queen Street, Edinburgh EH2 4NE
Tel: 0131-226 4771

The tribunal considers representations that the continued inclusion of a doctor, dentist, optometrist or pharmacist on a health board's list would be prejudicial to the efficiency of the service concerned. The tribunal sits when required and is composed of a chairman, one lay member, and one practitioner member drawn from a representative professional panel. The chairman is appointed by the Lord President of the Court of Session, and the lay member and the members of the professional panel are appointed by the First Minister.
Chairman, M. G. Thomson, QC
Lay member, J. D. M. Robertson
Clerk to the Tribunal, D. G. Brash, WS

PENSIONS APPEAL TRIBUNALS

CENTRAL OFFICE (ENGLAND AND WALES)
48–49 Chancery Lane, London WC2A 1JFR
Tel: 020-7947 7032/3; Fax: 020-7947 7054

The Pensions Appeal Tribunals are responsible for hearing appeals from ex-servicemen or women and widows who have had their claims for a war pension rejected by the Secretary of State for Social Security. The Entitlement Appeal Tribunals hear appeals in cases where the Secretary of State has refused to grant a war pension. The Assessment Appeal Tribunals hear appeals against the Secretary of State's assessment of the degree of disablement caused by an accepted condition. The tribunal members are appointed by the Lord Chancellor.
President (£76,921), Dr H. M. G. Concannon
Tribunal Manager, Miss N. Collins

PENSIONS APPEAL TRIBUNALS FOR SCOTLAND
20 Walker Street, Edinburgh EH3 7HS
Tel: 0131-220 1404
President (£298 a day), C. N. McEachran, QC

OFFICE OF THE SOCIAL SECURITY AND CHILD SUPPORT COMMISSIONERS
5th Floor, Newspaper House, 8–16 Great New Street,
London EC4A 3BN
Tel: 020-7353 5145
23 Melville Street, Edinburgh EH3 7PW
Tel: 0131-225 2201

The Social Security Commissioners are the final statutory authority to decide appeals relating to entitlement to social security benefits. The Child Support Commissioners are the final statutory authority to decide appeals relating to child support. Appeals may be made in relation to both matters only on a point of law. The Commissioners' jurisdiction covers England, Wales and Scotland. There are 17 commissioners; they are all qualified lawyers.
Chief Social Security Commissioner and Chief Child Support Commissioner (£103,516), His Hon. Judge Machin, QC
Secretary, L. Pereira (*London*); Mrs M. Watts (*Edinburgh*)

OFFICE OF THE SOCIAL SECURITY COMMISSIONERS AND CHILD SUPPORT COMMISSIONERS FOR NORTHERN IRELAND
Lancashire House, 5 Linenhall Street, Belfast BT2 8AA
Tel: 028-9033 2344

The role of Northern Ireland Social Security Commissioners and Child Support Commissioners is similar to that of the Commissioners in Great Britain. There are two commissioners for Northern Ireland.
Chief Commissioner (£103,516), His Hon. Judge Martin, QC
Registrar of Appeals, W. R. Brown

SOLICITORS' DISCIPLINARY TRIBUNAL
3rd Floor, Gate House, 1 Farringdon Street, London EC4M 7NS
Tel: 020-7329 4808

The Solicitors' Disciplinary Tribunal is an independent statutory body whose members are appointed by the Master of the Rolls. The tribunal considers applications made to it alleging either professional misconduct and/or a breach of the statutory rules by which solicitors are bound against an individually named solicitor, former solicitor, registered foreign lawyer, or solicitor's clerk. The president and solicitor members do not receive remuneration.
President, G. B. Marsh
Clerk, Mrs S. C. Elson

SCOTTISH SOLICITORS' DISCIPLINE TRIBUNAL
22 Rutland Square, Edinburgh EH1 2BB
Tel: 0131-229 5860

The Scottish Solicitors' Discipline Tribunal is an independent statutory body with a panel of 18 members, ten of whom are solicitors; members are appointed by the Lord President of the Court of Session. Its principal function is to consider complaints of misconduct against solicitors in Scotland.
Chairman, J. W. Laughland
Clerk, J. M. Barton, WS

SPECIAL COMMISSIONERS OF INCOME TAX
15–19 Bedford Avenue, London WC1B 3AS
Tel: 020-7631 4242

The Special Commissioners are an independent body appointed by the Lord Chancellor to hear complex appeals against decisions of the Board of Inland Revenue and its officials. In addition to the Presiding Special Commissioner there is one full-time and 11 deputy special commissioners; all are legally qualified.
Presiding Special Commissioner, His Hon. Stephen Oliver, QC
Special Commissioner, T. H. K. Everett
Clerk, R. P. Lester

SPECIAL IMMIGRATION APPEALS COMMISSION
Taylor House, 88 Rosebery Avenue, London EC1R 4QU
Tel: 020-7862 4200

The Commission was set up under the Special Immigration Appeals Commission Act 1998. Its main function is to consider appeals against orders for deportations in cases which involve, in the main, considerations of national security. Members are appointed by the Lord Chancellor.
Chairman, The Hon. Mr Justice Potts
Secretary, S. Hill

TRAFFIC COMMISSIONERS
c/o Scottish Traffic Area, Argyle House, 3 Lady Lawson Street, Edinburgh EH3 9SE
Tel: 0131-529 8500

The Traffic Commissioners are responsible for licensing operators of heavy goods and public service vehicles. They also have responsibility for appeals relating to the licensing of operators and for disciplinary cases involving the conduct of drivers of these vehicles. There are six Commissioners in the seven traffic areas covering Britain. Each Traffic Commissioner constitutes a tribunal for the purposes of the Tribunals and Inquiries Act 1971.
Senior Traffic Commissioner (£59,431), M. W. Betts, CBE

TRANSPORT TRIBUNAL
48–49 Chancery Lane, London WC2A 1JR
Tel: 020-7947 7493

The Transport Tribunal hears appeals against decisions made by Traffic Commissioners at public inquiries. The tribunal consists of a legally-qualified president, two legal members who may sit as chairmen, and five lay members. The president and legal members are appointed by the Lord Chancellor and the lay members by the Secretary of State for the Environment, Transport and the Regions.
President (part-time), H. B. H. Carlisle, QC
Legal member (part-time) (£290 a day), His Hon. Judge Brodrick
Lay members (£232 a day), D. Yeomans; J. W. Whitworth; P. Steel; P. Rogers; L. Milliken
Secretary, P. J. Fisher

VALUATION TRIBUNALS
Valuation Tribunal Management Board 2nd Floor, Walton House, 11 Parade, Leamington Spa, Warks CV32 4DG
Tel: 01926-421875

The Valuation Tribunals hear appeals concerning the council tax, non-domestic rating and land drainage rates in England and Wales. There are 56 tribunals in England and four in Wales; those in England are funded by the Department of the Environment, Transport and the Regions and those in Wales by the National Assembly for Wales. A separate tribunal is constituted for each hearing, and normally consists of a chairman and two other members. Members are appointed by the local authorities and serve on a voluntary basis. The Valuation Tribunal Management Board considers all matters affecting valuation tribunals in England, and the Council

of Wales Valuation Tribunals performs the same func-
tion in Wales.
Chairman, Valuation Tribunal Management Board,
P.Wood, OBE
Valuation Tribunals National Officer, B. P. Massen, MBE
President, Council of Wales Valuation Tribunals,
    J. H. Owens.

VAT AND DUTIES TRIBUNALS
15–19 Bedford Avenue, London WC1B 3AS
Tel: 020-7631 4242

VAT and Duties Tribunals are administered by the Lord
Chancellor in England and Wales, and by the First
Minister in Scotland. They are independent, and decide
disputes between taxpayers and Customs and Excise. In
England and Wales, the president and chairmen are
appointed by the Lord Chancellor and members by the
Treasury. Chairmen in Scotland are appointed by the
Lord President of the Court of Session.
President, His Hon. Stephen Oliver, QC
Vice-President, England and Wales, A. W. Simpson
Vice-President, Scotland, T. G. Coutts, QC
Vice-President, Northern Ireland, His Hon. J. McKee, QC
Registrar, R. P. Lester

TRIBUNAL CENTRES
EDINBURGH, 44 Palmerston Place, Edinburgh EH12 5BJ.
Tel: 0131-226 3551
LONDON (including Belfast), 15–19 Bedford Avenue,
London WC1B 3AS. Tel: 020-7631 4242
MANCHESTER, Warwickgate House, Warwick Road, Old
Trafford, Manchester M16 0GP. Tel: 0161-872 6471

The Police Service

There are 52 police forces in the United Kingdom, each responsible for policing in its area. Most police force areas are coterminous with one or more local authority areas. Policing in London is carried out by the Metropolitan Police and the City of London Police; in Northern Ireland by the Royal Ulster Constabulary; and by the Isle of Man, States of Jersey, and Guernsey forces in their respective islands and bailiwicks. National services include the National Missing Persons Bureau and the National Crime Squad.

The police authorities of English and Welsh forces comprise local councillors, magistrates and independent members. In Scotland, there are six joint police boards made up of local councillors; the other two police authorities are councils. In London the authority for the Metropolitan Police is the Home Secretary, advised by the Metropolitan Police Committee; for the City of London Police the authority is a committee of the Corporation of London and includes councillors and magistrates. In Northern Ireland the Secretary of State appoints the police authority.

Police authorities are financed by central and local government grants and a precept on the council tax. Subject to the approval of the Home Secretary (in England and Wales) and to regulations, they appoint the chief constable. In England and Wales they are responsible for publishing annual policing plans and annual reports, setting local objectives and a budget, and levying the precept. The police authorities in Scotland are responsible for setting a budget, providing the resources necessary to police the area adequately, appointing officers of the rank of Assistant Chief Constable and above, and determining the number of officers and civilian staff in the force. The structure and responsibilities of the police authority in Northern Ireland are under review.

The Home Secretary, the Secretary of State for Northern Ireland and the Scottish Executive are responsible for the organisation, administration and operation of the police service. They make regulations covering matters such as police ranks, discipline, hours of duty, and pay and allowances. All police forces are subject to inspection by HM Inspectors of Constabulary, who report to the Home Secretary, Scottish Executive or Secretary of State for Northern Ireland. In Scotland, a review of the structure of police forces began in April 1998. In Northern Ireland a commission on policing was established by the Belfast Agreement in April 1998. It made recommendations to the Secretary of State in September 1999.

In April 1999 the Home Secretary set targets for recruitment of officers from ethnic minorities for each force in England and Wales to achieve within ten years. From autumn 2000 targets for promotion and retention of these officers will also be set.

COMPLAINTS

The investigation and resolution of a serious complaint against a police officer in England and Wales is subject to the scrutiny of the Police Complaints Authority. An officer who is dismissed, required to resign or reduced in rank, whether as a result of a complaint or not, may appeal to a police appeals tribunal established by the relevant police authority. In Scotland, chief constables are obliged to investigate a complaint against one of their officers; if there is a suggestion of criminal activity, the complaint is investigated by an independent public prosecutor. In Northern Ireland complaints are investigated by the Independent Commission for Police Complaints, which was replaced by the Police Ombudsman in April 2000.

BASIC RATES OF PAY
since 1 September 1999

Chief Constable	
No fixed term	£73,616–£105,270
Fixed term appointment	£77,301–£110,406
Assistant Chief Constable – designated Deputy	
No fixed term	80% of their Chief Constable's pay or £70,151, whichever is higher
Fixed term appointment	80% of their Chief Constable's pay or £74,040, whichever is higher
Assistant Chief Constable	
No fixed term	£61,428–£70,515
Fixed term appointment	£64,500–£74,040
Superintendent	£43,143–£53,556
Chief Inspector	£36,729–£41,190
Inspector	£32,862–£37,266
Sergeant	£25,407–£29,634
Constable	£16,635–£26,325
Metropolitan Police	
Metropolitan Commissioner	£121,300–£137,000
Deputy Commissioner	£103,155–£116,559
Assistant Commissioner	£93,276–£102,699
Commander	£61,428–£74,040

The rank of Chief Superintendent was abolished in April 1995. Existing appointments continue and receive the higher ranges of the pay scale for Superintendents

THE SPECIAL CONSTABULARY

Each police force has its own special constabulary, made up of volunteers who work in their spare time. Special Constables have full police powers.

NATIONAL CRIME SQUAD

Headquarters: PO Box 2500, London SW1V 2WF.
Tel: 020-7238 2500
Director General, Roy Penrose, OBE, QPM
(Retires 31 December 2000)

NCS SERVICE AUTHORITY

Headquarters: PO Box 2600, London SW1V 2WG.
Tel: 020-7238 2600
Chairman, Rt. Hon. Sir John Wheeler
Clerk, T. Simmons
Treasurer, P. Derrick

NATIONAL MISSING PERSONS BUREAU

Headquarters: New Scotland Yard, Broadway, London SW1H 0BG. Tel: 020-7230 1212
Director, C. J. Coombes

POLICE INFORMATION TECHNOLOGY ORGANISATION

Headquarters: Horseferry House, Dean Ryle Street, London SW1P 2AW. Tel: 020-8358 5497

Chairman, Sir Trefor Morris
Chief Executive, vacant

FORENSIC SCIENCE SERVICE
Headquarters: Priory House, Gooch Street North,
Birmingham B5 6QQ. Tel: 0121-607 6800
Chief Executive, Dr J. Thompson

POLICE FORCES AND AUTHORITIES

Strength: actual strength of force as at mid 2000
Chair: chairman/convener of the police authority/police
committee/joint police board

ENGLAND

AVON AND SOMERSET CONSTABULARY, PO Box 37,
Valley Road, Portishead, North Somerset BS20 8QJ.
Tel: 01275-818181. *Strength,* 2,999; *Chief Constable,*
S. Pilkington, QPM; *Chairman of Police Authority,*
J. Christensen
BEDFORDSHIRE POLICE, Woburn Road, Kempston,
Beds MR43 3AX. Tel: 01234-841212; Fax: 01234-842006.
Strength, 1,054; *Chief Constable,* M. O' Byrne, QPM;
Chairman, A. Hefferman
CAMBRIDGESHIRE CONSTABULARY, Hinchingbrooke
Park, Huntingdon, Cambs PE29 6NP.
Tel: 01480-456111. *Strength,* 1,320; *Chief Constable,*
D. G. Gunn; *Chairman,* J. Reynolds
CHESHIRE CONSTABULARY, Nuns Road, Chester CH1 2PP.
Tel: 01244-350000; Fax: 01244-612269. *Strength,*
2,053; *Chief Constable,* N. K. Burgess, QPM;
Chairman, Mrs. M. Chapman
CLEVELAND POLICE, PO Box 70, Ladgate Lane,
Middlesbrough TS8 9EH. Tel: 01642-326326. *Strength,*
1,449; *Chief Constable,* B. Shaw; *Chairman,* K. Walker
CUMBRIA CONSTABULARY, Carleton Hall, Penrith,
Cumbria CA10 2AU. Tel: 01768-891999. *Strength,* 1,090;
Chief Constable, C. Phillips; *Chairman,* R. Watson
DERBYSHIRE CONSTABULARY, Butterley Hall, Ripley,
Derbys DE5 3RS. Tel: 01773-570100. *Strength,* 1,844;
Chief Constable, J. F. Newing, CBE, QPM;
Chairman, K. Wilkinson
DEVON AND CORNWALL CONSTABULARY Middlemoor,
Exeter EX2 7HQ. Tel: 0990-777444. *Strength,* 2,841;
Chief Constable, Sir John Evans, QPM; *Chairman of
Police Authority,* G. Greenslade
DORSET POLICE HEADQUARTERS Winfrith, Dorchester,
Dorset DT2 8DZ. Tel: 01929-462727. *Strength,* 1,310;
Chief Constable, Mrs J. Stichbury; *Chairman of Police
Authority,* P. I. Jones
DURHAM CONSTABULARY HEADQUARTERS Aykley Heads,
Durham City DH1 5TT. Tel: 0191-386 4929. *Strength,*
1,570; *Chief Constable,* G. Hedges, QPM; *Chairman of
Police Authority,* J. Knox
ESSEX POLICE, PO Box 2, Springfield, Chelmsford,
Essex CM2 6DA. Tel: 01245-491491. *Strength,* 2,928;
Chief Constable, D. F. Stevens, QPM; *Chairman,* E. A. Peel
GLOUCESTERSHIRE CONSTABULARY, Holland House,
Lansdown Road, Cheltenham GL51 6QH.
Tel: 01242-521321; Fax: 01242-221362. *Strength,*
1,122; *Chief Constable,* A. J. P. Butler, QPM;
Chairman, Brig. M. Browne, CBE
GREATER MANCHESTER POLICE, PO Box 22,
Chester House, Boyer Street, Manchester M16 0RE.
Tel: 0161-872 5050; Fax: 0161-856 2666. *Strength,*
6,840; *Chief Constable,* D. Wilmat; *Chairman,*
S. Murphy

HAMPSHIRE CONSTABULARY HEADQUARTERS, West Hill,
Winchester, Hants SO22 5DB. Tel: 0845-045 4545.
Strength, 3,456; *Chief Constable,* P. R. Kernaghan,
QPM; *Chairman,* R. A. Culver
HERTFORDSHIRE CONSTABULARY, Stanborough Road,
Welwyn Garden City, Herts AL8 6XF.
Tel: 01707-354200. *Strength,* 1,923; *Chief Constable,*
P. Acres; *Chairman of Police Authority,* P. Holland
HUMBERSIDE POLICE, Queens Gardens, Kingston upon
Hull HU1 3DJ. Tel: 01482-326111. *Strength,* 2,850;
Chief Constable, D. Westwood; *Chairman,* vacant
KENT CONSTABULARY, Sutton Road, Maidstone, Kent
ME15 9BZ. Tel: 01622-690690; Fax: 01622-690511.
Strength, 3,300; *Chief Constable,* J. D. Phillips, QPM;
Chairperson, Mrs. P. Stubbs
LANCASHIRE CONSTABULARY, PO Box 77, Hutton,
Preston PR4 5SB. Tel: 01772-614444. *Strength,* 3,298;
Chief Contstable, Ms P. Clare; *Chairman of Police
Authority,* Dr R. B. Henig
LEICESTERSHIRE CONSTABULARY, St John's, Narborough,
Leicester LE9 5BX. Tel: 0116-222 2222. *Strength,* 1,993;
Chief Constable, D. J. Wyrko, QPM; *Chairman,*
D. J. Saville
LINCOLNSHIRE POLICE, PO Box 999, Lincoln LN5 7PH.
Tel: 01522-532222. *Strength,* 1,145; *Chief Constable,*
R. J. N. Childs; *Chairman of Police Authority
Committee,* M. D. Kennedy
MERSEYSIDE POLICE, PO Box 59, Canning Place,
Liverpool L69 1JD. Tel: 0151-709 6010;
Fax: 0151-777 8999. *Strength,* 4,210;
Chief Constable, N. Bettison; *Chair,*
Ms C. Gustafson
NORFOLK CONSTABULARY, Police Headquarters,
Martineau Lane, Norwich NR1 2DJ. Tel: 01603-768769.
Strength, 1,394; *Chief Constable,* K. Williams;
Chairman of Police Authority Committee, J. Wilson
NORTH YORKSHIRE POLICE, Newby Wiske Hall, Newby
Wiske, Northallerton, N. Yorks DL7 9HA.
Tel: 01609-783131. *Strength,* 1,321; *Chief Constable,*
D. R. Kenworthy; *Chairman,* Mrs A. F. Harris
NORTHAMPTONSHIRE POLICE, Wootton Hall
Northampton NN4 0JQ. Tel: 01604-700700. *Strength,*
1,150; *Chief Executive,* C. Fox; *Chair of Police
Authority Committee,* Dr M. Dickie
NORTHUMBRIA POLICE, Force Headquarters, North
Road, Ponteland, Newcastle upon Tyne NE20 0BL.
Tel: 01661-872555. *Strength,* 3,800; *Chief Constable,*
C. Strachan; *Chairman,* G. Gill
NOTTINGHAMSHIRE POLICE, Sherwood Lodge,
Arnold, Nottingham NG5 8PP. Tel: 0115-967 0999; Fax:
0115-976 1900. *Strength,* 2,233; *Chief Constable,* C.
Bailey; *Chairman,* R. A. Hassett
SOUTH YORKSHIRE POLICE, Snig Hill, Sheffield S3 8LY.
Tel: 0114-220 2020. *Strength,* 3,157; *Chief Constable,*
M. Hedges; *Chairman,* C. Swindell
STAFFORDSHIRE POLICE, Cannock Road, Stafford
ST17 0QG. Tel: 01785-257717; Fax: 01785-232313.
Strength, 2,255; *Chief Constable,* J. Giffard;
Chairman, T. Meir
SUFFOLK CONSTABULARY HEADQUARTERS, Force
Headquarters, Portal Avenue, Martlesham Heath,
Ipswich IP5 3QS. Tel: 01473-613500. *Strength,* 1,182;
Chief Constable, P. J. Scott-Lee, QPM; *Chairman,*
M. N. Smith
SURREY POLICE, Mount Browne, Sandy Lane, Guildford,
Surrey GU3 1HG. Tel: 01483-571212. *Strength,* 2,084;
Chief Constable, D. O'Connor; *Chairman,* A. Peirce

SUSSEX POLICE, Malling House, Church Lane, Lewes, E. Sussex BN7 2DZ. Tel: 0845-607 0999. *Strength*, 2,938; *Chief Constable*, P. C. Whitehouse, QPM; *Chairman of Police Authority*, Mrs M. A. Johnson

THAMES VALLEY POLICE, Oxford Road, Kidlington, Oxon OX5 2NX. Tel: 01865-846000. *Strength*, 3,800; *Chief Constable*, C. Pollard, QPM; *Chairman of Police Authority*, G. Maybury

WARWICKSHIRE CONSTABULARY, Police HQ, PO Box 4, Leek Wootton, Warwick CV35 7QB. Tel: 01926-415000; Fax: 01926-850362. *Strength*, 923; *Acting Chief Constable*, M. Brewer; *Chairman*, J. Rennie

WEST MERCIA CONSTABULARY, Hindlip Hall, PO Box 55, Worcester WR3 8SP. Tel: 01905-723000. *Strength*, 2,007; *Chief Constable*, P. Hampson, QPM; *Chairman*, B. Watkins

WEST MIDLANDS POLICE, PO Box 52, Lloyd House, Colmore Circus, Queensway, Birmingham B4 6NQ. Tel: 0121-626 5000; Fax: 0121-626 5695. *Strength*, 7,435; *Chief Constable*, E. Crew, QPM; *Chairman*, B. Jones

WEST YORKSHIRE POLICE, PO Box 9, Laburnum Road, Wakefield, W. Yorks WF1 3QP. Tel: 01924-375222. *Strength*, 4,982; *Chief Constable*, G. Moore; *Chairman*, N. Taggart

WILTSHIRE CONSTABULARY, Police Headquarters, London Road, Devizes, Wilts SN10 2DN. Tel: 01380-722341. *Strength*, 1,075; *Chief Constable*, Miss E. Neville; *Chairman*, H. A. Woolnough

WALES

DYFED-POWYS POLICE, PO Box 99, Llangunnor, Carmarthen, Carmarthenshire SA31 2PF. Tel: 01267-222020. *Strength*, 1,045; *Chief Constable*, T. Grange; *Chairman*, M. Waterworth

GWENT POLICE, Police Headquarters, Turnpike Road, Croesyceiliog, Cwmbran, Gwent NP44 2XJ. Tel: 01633-838111. *Strength*, 1,262; *Chief Constable*, K. Turner; *Chairman*, D. Turnbull

NORTH WALES POLICE, Glan-y-don, Colwyn Bay, Conwy LL29 8AW. Tel: 01492-517171. *Strength*, 1,409; *Chief Constable*, M. J. Argent, QPM; *Chairman of Police Authority*, M. C. King

SOUTH WALES POLICE, Police Headquarters, Cowbridge Road, Bridgend CF31 3SU. Tel: 01656-655555. *Strength*, 2,999; *Chief Constable*, A. T. Burden; *Chairman*, R. Thomas

SCOTLAND

CENTRAL SCOTLAND POLICE, Randolphfield, Stirling FK8 2HD. Tel: 01786-456000. *Strength*, 725; *Chief Constable*, A. Cameron; *Convenor, Joint Police Board*, I. Miller

DUMFRIES AND GALLOWAY CONSTABULARY, Police Headquarters, Cornwall Mount, Dumfries DG1 1PZ. Tel: 01387-252112. *Strength*, 448; *Chief Constable*, W. Rae, QPM; *Chairman*, B. Conchie

FIFE CONSTABULARY, Police Headquarters, Detroit Road, Glenrothes, Fife KY6 2RJ. Tel: 01592-418888. *Strength*, 854; *Chief Constable*, J. P. Hamilton; *Chairman*, A. Keddie

GRAMPIAN POLICE, Force Headquarters, Queen Street, Aberdeen AB10 1ZA. Tel: 01224-386000. *Strength*, 1,220; *Chief Constable*, A. G. Brown; *Convenor of Police Authority Committee*, Ms M. Stewart

LOTHIAN AND BORDERS POLICE, Fettes Avenue, Edinburgh EH4 1RB. Tel: 0131-311 3131. *Strength*, 2,615; *Chief Constable*, Sir Roy Cameron, Kt, QPM; *Convenor of Police Authority*, Ms L. Hinds

NORTHERN CONSTABULARY, Old Perth Road, Inverness IV2 3SY. Tel: 01463-715555; Fax: 01463-720373.

Strength, 659; *Chief Constable*, W. Robertson; *Chairman*, J. Home

STRATHCLYDE POLICE, HQ, 173 Pitt Street, Glasgow G2 4JS. Tel: 0141-532 2000. *Strength*, 7,352; *Chief Constable*, J. Orr, OBE, QPM; *Convenor of Strathclyde Joint Police Board*, B. A. Maan

TAYSIDE POLICE, PO Box 59, West Bell Street, Dundee DD1 9JU. Tel: 01382-223200. *Strength*, 1,150; *Chief Constable*, (until December) W. A. Spence, QPM; (from January 2001) vacant; *Chairman*, J. Corrigan

NORTHERN IRELAND

ROYAL ULSTER CONSTABULARY, G. C., RUC Headquarters, Brooklyn, 65 Knock Road, Belfast BT5 6LD. Tel: 028-9065 0222. *Strength*, 8,415; *Chief Constable*, Sir Ronnie Flanagan, Kt, OBE; *Chairman of Police Authority*, P. Armstrong, CBE

CHANNEL ISLANDS

ISLAND POLICE FORCE, Hospital Lane, St. Peter Port, Guernsey GY1 2QN. Tel: 01481-725111; Fax: 01481-45136. *Strength*, 147; *Chief Constable*, M. H. Wyeth; *President*, M. Torode

ISLE OF MAN CONSTABULARY, Police Headquarters, Glencrutchery Road, Douglas, Isle of Man IM2 4RG. Tel: 01624-631212. *Strength*, 241; *Chief Constable*, M. Culverhouse; *Chairman, Minister for Home Affairs*, A. Bell

STATES OF JERSEY POLICE, Rouge Bouillon, PO Box 789, St Helier, Jersey JE2 3ZA. Tel: 01534-612612. *Strength*, 241; *Chief Officer*, R. H. Le Breton; *Chairman*, A. Laizell

---

METROPOLITAN POLICE SERVICE
New Scotland Yard, Broadway, London SW1H 0BG
Tel 020-7230 1212

Establishment, 26,500

Commissioner, Sir John Stevens, QPM,
Deputy Commissioner, Ian Blair, QPM,
Receiver, P. Fletcher

OPERATIONAL AREAS

Assistant Commissioners, A. Dunn, QPM *(Strategic Development)*; W. I. R. Johnston, QPM (*Territorial Policing*)

Deputy Assistant Commissioner, S. E. Becks, R. Clark, QPM; T. Ghaffur; J. G. D. Grieve, CBE, QPM; A. S. Trotter; B. Wilding, QPM; M. Todd

Commanders, M. Craik; D. N. Croll, QPM; R. Cullen; R. Currie, QPM; M. J. Gerrard; D. E. Gilbertson; T. J. Godwin; P. C. Hagon; G. P. James; B. J. Luckhurst; M. Messinger; S. Roberts; A. G. Shave; D. L. Smith; P. L. Tomkins

SPECIALIST OPERATIONS DEPARTMENT

Assistant Commissioner, D. C. Veness, QPM

Deputy Assistant Commissioner, W. I. Griffiths, QPM

Commanders, A. J. Brown; P. J. Clarke; M. A. Fuller; C. A. Howlett; N. G. Mulvihill, QPM; R. C. Pearce

COMPLAINTS INVESTIGATION BUREAU

Commander, A. C. Hayman

INSPECTORATE

Chief Superintendent, I. Nettleship

CITY OF LONDON POLICE
26 Old Jewry, London EC2R 8DJ
Tel 020-7601 2222

Strength, 730

Commissioner (£99,129), P. Nove, QPM
Assistant Commissioner (£79,302), J. Hart, QPM
Commander (£71,466), J. Davison
Chairman of Police Committee, S. A. Sellon OBE, TD, DL

BRITISH TRANSPORT POLICE
15 Tavistock Place, London WC1H 9SJ
Tel 020-7388 7541

Strength (March 2000), 2,073

British Transport Police is the national police force for the railways in England, Wales and Scotland, including the London Underground system, the Docklands Light Railway, the Midland Metro Tram system and Croydon Tramlink. The Chief Constable reports to the British Transport Police Committee. The members of the Committee are appointed by the British Railways Board and include representatives of Railtrack and London Underground Ltd as well as independent members. Officers are paid the same as other police forces.
Chief Constable, D. J. Williams, QPM
Deputy Chief Constable, J. A. Lake

MINISTRY OF DEFENCE POLICE
MDP Wethersfield, Braintree, Essex CM7 4AZ
Tel 01371-854000

Strength (March 2000), 3,526 operational staff and 266 civilian support staff

The Ministry of Defence Police is a civilian police force geared to meeting the requirements of the MOD and other customers including visiting forces, the Royal Mint and the Royal Ordnance. The Policing Team initiative has recently been expanded to meet policing demands across a wider area than previously. Other specialist services include marine policing, dogs, firearms and Police Search Teams. The Force also has its own Criminal Investigation Department with specialist officers working in the field of fraud investigation and can also offer crime prevention advice, including the services of Crime Prevention Officers, Community Liaison Officers, trained Architectural Liaison Officers and a growing network of Wildlife Liaison Officers. MDP officers are also serving as a part of the British contingent of police officers supporting the United Nations peace keeping initiative in Kosovo.
Chief Constable, W. E. E. Boreham, OBE
Deputy Chief Constable, A. V. Comben
Head of Secretariat, P. A. Crowther

ROYAL PARKS CONSTABULARY
The Old Police House, Hyde Park,
London W2 2UH
Tel 020-7298 2000

Strength (July 2000), 155

The Royal Parks Constabulary is maintained by the Royal Parks Agency, an executive agency of the Department for Culture, Media and Sport, and is responsible for the policing of eight royal parks in and around London. These comprise an area in excess of 5,000 acres. Officers of the force are appointed under the Parks Regulations Act 1872 as amended and are paid around 85 per cent of the Metropolitan Police rate.
Chief Officer, W. Ross, OBE
Deputy Chief Officer, A. McLean

UK ATOMIC ENERGY AUTHORITY
CONSTABULARY
Building E6, Culham Science Centre, Abingdon,
Oxon OX14 3DB
Tel 01235-463760

Strength (June 2000), 498

The Constabulary is responsible for policing UK Atomic Energy Authority and British Nuclear Fuels PLC establishments and for escorting nuclear material between establishments. The Chief Constable is responsible, through the Atomic Energy Authority Police Authority, to the President of the Board of Trade. Officers are paid around 95 per cent of the rate paid to other police forces.
Chief Constable, W. F. Pryke
Assistant Chief Constable, P. P. Crossan

STAFF ASSOCIATIONS

Police officers are not permitted to join a trade union or to take strike action. All ranks have their own staff associations.

ASSOCIATION OF CHIEF POLICE OFFICERS OF ENGLAND, WALES AND NORTHERN IRELAND, 7th Floor, 25 Victoria Street, London SW1H 0EX. Tel: 020-7227 3434. *General Secretary*, Miss M. C. E. Barton, OBE

THE POLICE SUPERINTENDENTS' ASSOCIATION OF ENGLAND AND WALES, 67A Reading Road, Pangbourne, Reading RG8 7JD. Tel: 0118-984 4005. *Secretary*, Supt. P. Williams

THE POLICE FEDERATION OF ENGLAND AND WALES, 15–17 Langley Road, Surbiton, Surrey KT6 6LP. Tel: 020-8399 2224. *General Secretary*, J. Moseley

ASSOCIATION OF CHIEF POLICE OFFICERS IN SCOTLAND, Police Headquarters, Fettes Avenue, Edinburgh EH4 1RB. Tel: 0131-311 3051. *Hon. Secretary*, H. R. Cameron, QPM

THE ASSOCIATION OF SCOTTISH POLICE SUPERINTENDENTS, Secretariat, 173 Pitt Street, Glasgow G2 4JS. Tel: 0141-221 5796. *President*, Chief Supt. S. Davidson

THE SCOTTISH POLICE FEDERATION, 5 Woodside Place. Glasgow G3 7QF. Tel: 0141-332 5234. *General Secretary*, D. J. Keil, QPM

THE SUPERINTENDENTS' ASSOCIATION OF NORTHERN IRELAND, RUC Training Centre, Garnerville Road, Belfast BT4 2NX. Tel: 028-9070 0660. *Hon. Secretary*, Supt. M. Dyer

THE POLICE FEDERATION FOR NORTHERN IRELAND, Royal Ulster Constabulary, Garnerville, Garnerville Road, Belfast BT4 2NX. Tel: 028-9076 0831. *Secretary*, D. A. McClurg

The Prison Service

The prison services in the United Kingdom are the responsibility of the Home Secretary, the Scottish Executive Justice Department and the Secretary of State for Northern Ireland. The chief executive officers of the Prison Service, the Scottish Prison Service and the Northern Ireland Prison Service are responsible for the day-to-day running of the system.

There are 136 prison establishments in England and Wales, 20 in Scotland and four in Northern Ireland. Convicted prisoners are classified according to their assessed security risk and are housed in establishments appropriate to that level of security. There are no open prisons in Northern Ireland. Female prisoners are housed in women's establishments or in separate wings of mixed prisons. Remand prisoners are, where possible, housed separately from convicted prisoners. Offenders under the age of 21 are usually detained in a young offenders' institution, which may be a separate establishment or part of a prison.

Eight prisons are now run by the private sector, and in England and Wales all escort services have been contracted out to private companies. Two prisons are being built and financed under the Private Finance Initiative and will also be run by private contractors. In Scotland, one prison (Kilmarnock) was built and financed by the private sector and is being operated by private contractors.

There are independent prison inspectorates in England and Wales and Scotland which report annually on conditions and the treatment of prisoners. HM Chief Inspector of Prisons for England and Wales also performs an inspectorate role for prisons in Northern Ireland. Every prison establishment also has an independent board of visitors or visiting committee made up of local volunteers. Any prisoner whose complaint is not satisfied by the internal complaints procedures may complain to the Prisons Ombudsman for England and Wales or the Scottish Prisons Complaints Commission. There is no Prisons Ombudsman for Northern Ireland, but complaints by prisoners regarding maladministration may be made to the Parliamentary Commissioner for Administration.

AVERAGE PRISON POPULATION 1999–2000 (UK)

	Remand	Sentenced	Other
ENGLAND AND WALES			
Male	11,581	49,418	536
Female	741	2,514	22
Total	12,323	51,933	559
SCOTLAND			
Male	n/a	n/a	—
Female	n/a	n/a	—
Total	975	4,999	—
N. IRELAND			
Male	346	811	4
Female	10	8	0
Total	356	819	4
UK TOTAL	13,654	58,726	563

The projected prison population for 2006 in England and Wales is 66,700 if custody rates and sentence lengths remain at 1998 levels

Sources: Home Office – *Research Development Statistics*; Scottish Prison Service – *Annual Report and Accounts 1999–2000*; Northern Ireland Prison Service – *Annual Report 1999–2000*

SENTENCED PRISON POPULATION BY SEX AND OFFENCE (ENGLAND AND WALES)
as at June 1999

	Male	Female
Violence against the person	10,429	429
Sexual offences	4,929	17
Burglary	8,622	158
Robbery	6,174	157
Theft, handling	4,021	390
Fraud and forgery	993	111
Drugs offences	7,294	875
Other offences	5,178	220
Offence not known	1,222	74
In default of payment of a fine	94	5
Total	48,956	2,436

Source: Home Office – *Research Development Statistics*

AVERAGE SENTENCED POPULATION BY LENGTH OF SENTENCE 1999 (ENGLAND AND WALES)

	Adults	Young Offenders
Less than 12 months	5,721	2,006
12 months to less than 4 years	15,048	4,674
4 years to less than 10 years	15,090	1,466
10 years less than life	3,410	60
Life	4,078	139
Total	43,347	8,345

Source: Home Office – *Research Development Statistics*

AVERAGE DAILY SENTENCED POPULATION BY LENGTH OF SENTENCE 1998–9 (SCOTLAND)

	Adults	Young Offenders
Less than 4 years	1,987	502
4 years or over (including life)	2,333	176
Total	4,320	678

Source: Scottish Prison Service – *Annual Report and Accounts 1999–2000*

PRISON SUICIDES 1999 (ENGLAND AND WALES)

Males	86
Females	5
Total	91
Rate per 1,000 prisoners in custody	1.40

Source: Home Office – *Research Development Statistics*

AVERAGE NUMBER OF PRISON SERVICE STAFF 1998–9 (GREAT BRITAIN)

	England and Wales	Scotland
No. of prison service staff	43,088	4,870

Sources: HM Prison Service – *Annual Report and Accounts 1999–2000*; Scottish Prison Service – *Annual Report and Accounts 1999–2000*

OPERATING COSTS OF PRISON SERVICE IN ENGLAND AND WALES 1999–2000

	£ million
Staff costs	1,044.7
Other operating costs	849.3
Operating income	(20.0)
Net operating costs before notional charge on capital employed	1,874
Charge on capital employed	254.9
Net operating costs	2,128.9
Average cost per prisoner place (reflecting establishment costs only)	£21,751

Source: HM Prison Service – *Annual Report and Accounts 1999–2000*

OPERATING COSTS OF SCOTTISH PRISON SERVICE
1999–2000

	£
Total income	1,734,000
Total expenditure	219,975,000
Staff costs	127,724,000
Running costs	73,489,000
Other current expenditure	18,762,000
Operating deficit	(218,241,000)
Cost of capital charges	(23,349,000)
Interest payable and similar charges	(154,000)
Interest receivable	93,000
Lockerbie Trial Costs	3,387
Deficit for financial year	(244,899,000)
Average annual cost per prisoner per place	£28,375

Source: Scottish Prison Service – Annual Report and Accounts 1999–2000

OPERATING COSTS OF NORTHERN IRELAND
PRISON SERVICE 1999–2000

	£'000
Income	463
Expenditure	
Staff Costs	99,397
Depreciation and other charges	5,598
Other Operating Costs	25, 827
Total	130,822
Net cost of Operations	260,507
Average annual cost per prisoner place	77,749

Source: Northern Ireland Prison Service – Annual Report and Accounts 1999–2000

THE PRISON SERVICES

HM PRISON SERVICE

Cleland House, Page Street, London SW1P 4LN
Tel: 020-7217 6000; Fax: 020-7217 6403
SALARIES 1999–2000

Governor 1	£53,658–£55,510
Governor 2	£48,452–£49,939
Governor 3	£41,844–£43,026
Governor 4	£35,089–£36,956
Governor 5	£30,336–£33,102

THE PRISON SERVICE MANAGEMENT BOARD

Director-General (SCS), M. Narey
  Private Secretary, Ms R. Goodwin
  Staff Officer, vacant
Prisons and Probation Minister, Chairman of the
  Strategy Board for Correctional Services,
  The Rt. Hon. Paul Boateng, MP
Director, Criminal Policy Group, Home Office, Ms S. Street
Deputy Director-General (SCS), P. Wheatley
Director of High Security Prisons (SCS), P. Atherton
Director of Security (SCS), B. Clark
Director of Personnel (SCS), G. Hadley
Director of Finance (SCS), J. Le Vay
Director of Corporate Affairs (SCS), Ms C. Pelham
Director of Regimes (SCS), K. D. Sutton
Head of the Prison Health Policy Unit (SCS),
  Dr F. Harvey
Non-Executive Members, Sir Duncan Nichol, CBE;
  Mrs R. Thomson, CBE; P. Carter
Board Secretary and Head of Secretariat,
  Ms C. Checksfield
Chaplain-General and Archdeacon of the Prison Service,
  Ven. D. Fleming

Muslim Advisor, M. Ahmed
Race Equality Advisor, Ms J. Clements
Legal Adviser, T. Middleton

AREA MANAGERS (SCS)
Eastern, M. Spurr; East Midlands (North),
D. Waplington; East Midlands (South), M. Egan; London, A.
Smith; North East, R. Mitchell; North West (Lancashire and
Cumbria), T. Fitzpatrick; North West (Manchester, Mersey
and Cheshire), I. Lockwood; South East (Thames Valley and
Hampshire), Mrs S. Payne; South East (Kent Surrey and
Sussex), T. Murtagh; South West, J. Petherick; Wales, J.
May; West Midlands, B. Payling; Yorkshire and Humberside,
P. Earnshaw
Operational Manager for Women's Prisons, N. Clifford

PRISON ESTABLISHMENTS

CNA Average number of in use certified normal accom-
modation places without overcrowding
1999–2000
Prisoners/Young Offenders Average number of
prisoners/young offenders 1999–2000
ACKLINGTON, Morpeth, Northumberland NE65 9XH.
  CNA, 782. Prisoners, 726. Governor, P. Atkinson
ALBANY, Newport, Isle of Wight PO30 5RS. CNA, 436.
  Prisoners, 429. Governor, K. Munns
ALTCOURSE (private prison), Higher Lane, Fazakerley,
  Liverpool L9 7AG. CNA, 600. Prisoners, 669.
  Director, W. MacGowan
†‡ASHFIELD (from December 1999), Shortwood Road,
  Pucklechurch, Bristol BS16 9QT. CNA, 400.
  Director, N. Pascoe
ASHWELL, Oakham, Leics LE15 7LF. CNA, 484. Prisoners,
  483. Governor, D. Walmsley
*‡ASKHAM GRANGE, Askham Richard, York YO2 3PT.
  CNA, 130. Prisoners and Young Offenders, 121. Governor,
  I. Simmonds
‡AYLESBURY, Bierton Road, Aylesbury, Bucks HP20 1EH.
  CNA, 351. Young Offenders, 443. Governor, S. Bryans
BEDFORD, St Loyes Street, Bedford MK40 1HG. CNA, 352.
  Prisoners, 400. Governor, T. Ireson
†BELMARSH, Western Way, Thamesmead, London
  SE28 0EB. CNA, 843. Prisoners, 788.
  Governor, W. S. Duff
BIRMINGHAM, Winson Green Road, Birmingham B18 4AS.
  CNA, 724. Prisoners, 1,100. Governor, C. Scott, OBE
BLAKENHURST (private prison), Hewell Lane, Redditch,
  Worcs B97 6QS. CNA, 647. Prisoners, 850. Director,
  P. Siddons
BLANTYRE HOUSE, Goudhurst, Cranbrook, Kent
  TN17 2NH. CNA, 120. Prisoners, 120.
  Governor, C. Bartlett
BLUNDESTON, Lowestoft, Suffolk NR32 5BG. CNA, 424.
  Prisoners, 424. Governor, vacant
†‡BRINSFORD, New Road, Featherstone, Wolverhampton
  WV10 7PY. CNA, 477. Young Offenders, 509.
  Governor, C. Davidson
BRISTOL, Cambridge Road, Bristol BS7 8PS. CNA, 386.
  Prisoners, 602. Governor, N. Wall
BRIXTON, PO Box 369, Jebb Avenue, London SW2 5XF.
  CNA, 693. Prisoners, 659. Governor, R. Chapman
*†‡BROCKHILL, Redditch, Worcs B97 6RD. CNA, 159.
  Prisoners and Young Offenders, 159. Governor, V. Bird
BUCKLEY HALL (private prison), Buckley Farm Lane,
  Rochdale, Lancs OL12 9DP. CNA, 350. Prisoners, 382.
  Director, S. Mitson
BULLINGDON, PO Box 50, Bicester, Oxon OX6 0PR. CNA,
  773. Prisoners, 897. Acting Governor, L. Serjeant
*‡BULLWOOD HALL, High Road, Hockley, Essex SS5 4TE.
  CNA, 1840. Prisoners and Young Offenders, 140. Governor,
  Mrs V. Hart

CAMP HILL, Newport, Isle of Wight PO30 5PB. *CNA,* 474. *Prisoners,* 472. *Governor,* R. Oliver

CANTERBURY, 46 Longport, Canterbury CT1 1PJ. *CNA,* 196. *Prisoners,* 283. *Governor,* Ms J. Galbally

††CARDIFF, Knox Road, Cardiff CF2 1UG. *CNA,* 525. *Prisoners and Young Offenders,* 722. *Governor,* J. Thomas-Ferrand

‡CASTINGTON, Morpeth, Northumberland NE65 9XG. *CNA,* 420. *Young Offenders,* 210. *Governor,* M. Lees

CHANNINGS WOOD, Denbury, Newton Abbott, Devon TQ12 6DW. *CNA,* 482. *Prisoners,* 615. *Governor,* N. Evans

††CHELMSFORD, 200 Springfield Road, Chelmsford, Essex CM2 6LQ. *CNA,* 448. *Prisoners and Young Offenders,* 501. *Governor,* Ms A. Gomme

COLDINGLEY, Bisley, Woking, Surrey GU24 9EX. *CNA,* 286. *Prisoners,* 290. *Governor,* E. R. Butt

*COOKHAM WOOD, Rochester, Kent ME1 3LU. *CNA,* 120. *Prisoners,* 149. *Governor,* S. West

DARTMOOR, Princetown, Yelverton, Devon PL20 6RR. *CNA,* 691. *Prisoners,* 692. *Governor,* J. Lawrence

‡DEERBOLT, Bowes Road, Barnard Castle, Co. Durham DL12 9BG. *CNA,* 486. *Young Offenders,* 457. *Governor,* P. Copple

††DONCASTER (private prison), Off North Bridge, Marshgate, Doncaster DN5 8UX. *CNA,* 771. *Prisoners and Young Offenders,* 1,052. *Director,* K. Rogers

††DORCHESTER, North Square, Dorchester DT1 1JD. *CNA,* 172. *Prisoners and Young Offenders,* 230. *Governor,* R. Bateman

‡DOVER, The Citadel, Western Heights, Dover CT17 9DR. *CNA,* 264. *Young Offenders,* 247. *Governor,* C. Kershaw

DOWNVIEW, Sutton Lane, Sutton, Surrey SM2 5PD. *CNA,* 327. *Prisoners,* 340. *Governor,* C. Lambert

*‡DRAKE HALL, Eccleshall, Staffs ST21 6LQ. *CNA,* 295. *Prisoners and Young Offenders,* 295. *Governor,* P. Tidball

*†DURHAM, Old Elvet, Durham DH1 3HU. *CNA,* 686. *Prisoners,* 902. *Governor,* M. Newell

*‡EAST SUTTON PARK, Sutton Valence, Maidstone, Kent ME17 3DF. *CNA,* 94. *Prisoners and Young Offenders,* 79. *Governor,* Revd R. Carter

*††EASTWOOD PARK, Falfield, Wotton-under-Edge, Glos GL12 8DB. *CNA,* 255. *Prisoners and Young Offenders,* 288. *Governor,* P. Winkley.

ELMLEY, Church Road, Eastchurch, Sheerness, Kent ME12 4AY. *CNA,* 763. *Prisoners,* 950. *Governor,* B. Pollett

ERLESTOKE HOUSE, Devizes, Wilts SN10 5TU. *CNA,* 310. *Prisoners,* 300. *Governor,* Mrs J. Blake

EVERTHORPE, Brough, E. Yorks HU15 1RB. *CNA,* 438. *Prisoners,* 464. *Governor,* P. Midgley

††EXETER, New North Road, Exeter EX4 4EX. *CNA,* 321. *Prisoners and Young Offenders,* 527. *Governor,* G. Deighton

FEATHERSTONE, New Road, Wolverhampton WV10 7PU. *CNA,* 599. *Prisoners,* 599. *Governor,* M. Pascoe

††FELTHAM, Bedfont Road, Feltham, Middx TW13 4ND. *CNA,* 848. *Prisoners and Young Offenders,* 878. *Governor,* W. Payne

FORD, Arundel, W. Sussex BN18 0BX. *CNA,* 501. *Prisoners,* 355. *Governor,* K. Kan

FOREST BANK (from December 1999), Agecroft Road, Pendlebury, Manchester M27 8UE. *CNA,* 800. *Director,* M. Goodwin

*‡FOSTON HALL, Foston, Derbys DE65 5DN. *CNA,* 174. *Prisoners and Young Offenders,* 174. *Governor,* Ms P. Scriven

FRANKLAND, Brasside, Durham DH1 5YD. *CNA,* 655. *Prisoners,* 530. *Governor,* I. Woods

FULL SUTTON, Full Sutton, York YO41 1PS. *CNA,* 602. *Prisoners,* 530. *Governor,* D. Roberts

GARTH, Ulnes Walton Lane, Leyland, Preston PR5 3NE. *CNA,* 633. *Prisoners,* 646. *Governor,* W. Rose-Quirie, OBE

GARTREE, Gallow Field Road, Market Harborough, Leics LE16 7RP. *CNA,* 366. *Prisoners,* 356. *Governor,* S. McAllister

††GLEN PARVA, Tigers Road, Wigston, Leicester LE8 4TN. *CNA,* 720. *Young Offenders,* 828. *Governor,* C. Bushell

††GLOUCESTER, Barrack Square, Gloucester GL1 2JN. *CNA,* 235. *Prisoners and Young Offenders,* 327. *Governor,* R. Booty

GRENDON/SPRING HILL, HMP Grendon, Grendon Underwood, Aylesbury, Bucks HP18 0TL. *CNA,* 497. *Prisoners,* 499. *Governor,* T. C. Newell

‡GUYS MARSH, Shaftesbury, Dorset SP7 0AH. *CNA,* 504. *Prisoners and Young Offenders,* 507. *Governor,* Mrs D. Calvert

§HASLAR, 2 Dolphin Way, Gosport, Hants PO12 2AW. *CNA,* 160. *Prisoners,* 142. *Governor,* B. McAlley

‡HATFIELD, Thorne Road, Hatfield, Doncaster DN7 6EL. *CNA,* 180. *Young Offenders,* 155. *Governor,* M. Read

HAVERIGG, Millom, Cumbria LA18 4NA. *CNA,* 402. *Prisoners,* 530. *Governor,* G. Brunskill

HEWELL GRANGE, Redditch, Worcs B97 6QQ. *CNA,* 203. *Prisoners,* 203. *Governor,* N. Croft

HIGH DOWN, Sutton Lane, Sutton, Surrey SM2 5PJ. *CNA,* 649. *Prisoners,* 714. *Governor,* D. Wilson

*HIGHPOINT, Stradishall, Newmarket, Suffolk CB8 9YG. *CNA,* 810. *Prisoners,* 812. *Governor,* R. Woolford

††HINDLEY, Gibson Street, Bickershaw, Wigan, Lancs WN2 5TH. *CNA,* 547. *Prisoners and Young Offenders,* 493. *Governor,* J. Heavens

‡HOLLESLEY BAY COLONY, Woodbridge, Suffolk IP12 3JW. *CNA,* 464. *Prisoners and Young Offenders,* 361. *Governor,* S. Robinson

*††HOLLOWAY, Parkhurst Road, London N7 0NU. *CNA,* 477. *Prisoners and Young Offenders,* 492. *Governor,* D. Lancaster

HOLME HOUSE, Holme House Road, Stockton-on-Tees TS18 2QU. *CNA,* 971. *Prisoners,* 963. *Governor,* D. Crouch

††HULL, Hedon Road, Hull HU9 5LS. *CNA,* 675. *Prisoners and Young Offenders,* 494. *Governor,* S. Wagstaffe

‡HUNTERCOMBE, Huntercombe Place, Nuffield, Henley-on-Thames RG9 5SB. *CNA,* 360. *Young Offenders,* 376. *Governor,* P. Manwaring

KINGSTON, 122 Milton Road, Portsmouth PO3 6AS. *CNA,* 193. *Prisoners,* 175. *Governor,* S. McLean

KIRKHAM, Freckleton Road, Preston PR4 2RN. *CNA,* 606. *Prisoners,* 658. *Governor,* A. F. Jennings, OBE

KIRKLEVINGTON GRANGE, Yarm, Cleveland TS15 9PA. *CNA,* 183. *Prisoners,* 166. *Governor,* Ms S. Anthony

LANCASTER, The Castle, Lancaster LA1 1YL. *CNA,* 150. *Prisoners,* 216. *Governor,* J. Illingsworth

††LANCASTER FARMS, Far Moor Lane, Stone Row Head, off Quernmore Road, Lancaster LA1 3QZ. *CNA,* 496. *Prisoners and Young Offenders,* 456. *Governor,* D. Thomas

---

* Women's establishment or establishment with units for women
†Remand Centre or establishment with units for remand prisoners
‡Young Offender Institution or establishment with units for young offenders
§Immigration Holding Centre

LATCHMERE HOUSE, Church Road, Ham Common, Richmond, Surrey TW10 5HH. *CNA*, 193. *Prisoners*, 171. *Governor*, T. Hinchliffe

LEEDS, Armley, Leeds LS12 2TJ. *CNA*, 797. *Prisoners*, 1,233. *Governor*, R. Daly

LEICESTER, Welford Road, Leicester LE2 7AJ. *CNA*, 219. *Prisoners*, 346. *Governor*, D. Bamber

†‡LEWES, Brighton Road, Lewes, E. Sussex BN7 1EA. *CNA*, 485. *Prisoners and Young Offenders*, 483. *Governor*, J. F. Dixon

LEYHILL, Wotton-under-Edge, Glos GL12 8BT. *CNA*, 410. *Prisoners*, 422. *Governor*, D. T. Williams

LINCOLN, Greetwell Road, Lincoln LN2 4BD. *CNA*, 360. *Prisoners*, 474. *Governor*, vacant

§LINDHOLME, Bawtry Road, Hatfield Woodhouse, Doncaster DN7 6EE. *CNA*, 530. *Prisoners*, 666. *Governor*, vacant

LITTLEHEY, Perry, Huntingdon, Cambs PE18 0SR. *CNA*, 624. *Prisoners*, 648. *Governor*, C. Morris

LIVERPOOL, 68 Hornby Road, Liverpool L9 3DF. *CNA*, 1,260. *Prisoners*, 1,510. *Governor*, C. Sheffield

LONG LARTIN, South Littleton, Evesham, Worcs WR11 5TZ. *CNA*, 456. *Prisoners*, 344. *Governor*, J. Mullen

LOWDHAM GRANGE (private prison), Lowdham, Notts NG14 7TA. *CNA*, 504. *Prisoners*, 506. *Director*, R. Tasker

*†‡LOW NEWTON, Brasside, Durham DH1 5SD. *CNA*, 215. *Prisoners and Young Offenders*, 295. *Governor*, M. Kirby

MAIDSTONE, 36 County Road, Maidstone ME14 1UZ. *CNA*, 549. *Prisoners*, 576. *Governor*, M. Conway

MANCHESTER, Southall Street, Manchester M60 9AH. *CNA*, 953. *Prisoners*, 1,074. *Acting Governor*, M. Shann

‡MOORLAND, Bawtry Road, Hatfield Woodhouse, Doncaster DN7 6BW. *CNA*, 740. *Prisoners and Young Offenders*, 760. *Governor*, B. McCourt

MORTON HALL, Swinderby, Lincoln LN6 9PS. *CNA*, 208. *Prisoners*, 185. *Governor*, M. Murphy

THE MOUNT, Molyneaux Avenue, Bovingdon, Hemel Hempstead HP3 0NZ. *CNA*, 705. *Prisoners*, 745. *Governor*, P. Wailen

*†‡NEW HALL, Dial Wood, Flockton, Wakefield WF4 4AX. *CNA*, 327. *Prisoners and Young Offenders*, 366. *Governor*, M. Shepherd

†‡NORTHALLERTON, 15A East Road, Northallerton, N. Yorks DL6 1NW. *CNA*, 152. *Prisoners and Young Offenders*, 271. *Governor*, D. P. G. Appleton

NORTH SEA CAMP, Freiston, Boston, Lincs PE22 0QX. *CNA*, 208. *Prisoners*, 192. *Governor*, M. A. Lewis

†‡NORWICH, Mousehold, Norwich NR1 4LU. *CNA*, 564. *Prisoners and Young Offenders*, 744. *Governor*, M. Knight

NOTTINGHAM, Perry Road, Sherwood, Nottingham NG5 3AG. *CNA*, 466. *Prisoners*, 440. *Governor*, K. Beaumont

‡ONLEY, Willoughby, Rugby, Warks CV23 8AP. *CNA*, 400. *Young Offenders*, 580. *Governor*, D. Watson

†‡PARC (private prison), Heol Hopcyn John, Bridgend CF35 6AR. *CNA*, 800. *Prisoners and Young Offenders*, 411. *Director*, R. Woolford

PARKHURST, Newport, Isle of Wight PO30 5NX. *CNA*, 482. *Prisoners*, 443. *Governor*, D. M. Morrison

PENTONVILLE, Caledonian Road, London N7 8TT. *CNA*, 897. *Prisoners*, 1,175. *Governor*, R. Duncan

‡PORTLAND, Easton, Portland, Dorset DT5 1DL. *CNA*, 512. *Young Offenders*, 534. *Governor*, K. Lockyer

‡PRESCOED, 47 Maryport Street, Usk, Gwent NP5 1XP. *CNA*, see Usk. *Prisoners and Young Offenders*, see Usk. *Governor*, R. J. Comber

PRESTON, 2 Ribbleton Lane, Preston PR1 5AB. *CNA*, 343. *Prisoners*, 679. *Governor*, A. Scott

RANBY, Ranby, Retford, Notts DN22 8EV. *CNA*, 725. *Prisoners*, 740. *Governor*, J. Slater

†‡READING, Forbury Road, Reading RG1 3HY. *CNA*, 204. *Prisoners and Young Offenders*, 245. *Governor*, C. Norman

*RISLEY, Risley, Warrington WA3 6BP. *CNA*, 851. *Prisoners*, 868. *Governor*, C. McConnell

†‡ROCHESTER, 1 Fort Road, Rochester, Kent ME1 3QS. *CNA*, 433. *Prisoners and Young Offenders*, 366. *Governor*, T. Robson

*SEND, Ripley Road, Send, Woking, Surrey GU23 7LJ. *CNA*, 220. *Prisoners*, 200. *Governor*, T. Beeston

SHEPTON MALLET, Cornhill, Shepton Mallet, Somerset BA4 5LU. *CNA*, 184. *Prisoners*, 224. *Governor*, R. Bennett

SHREWSBURY, The Dana, Shrewsbury SY1 2HR. *CNA*, 323. *Prisoners*, 323. *Governor*, A. Bramley

STAFFORD, 54 Gaol Road, Stafford ST16 3AW. *CNA*, 627. *Prisoners*, 627. *Governor*, P. Wright

STANDFORD HILL, Church Road, Eastchurch, Isle of Sheppey, Kent ME12 4AA. *CNA*, 384. *Prisoners*, 217. *Governor*, J. Robinson

STOCKEN, Stocken Hall Road, Stretton, nr Oakham, Leics LE15 7RD. *CNA*, 556. *Prisoners*, 572. *Governor*, R. Curtis

‡STOKE HEATH, Stoke Heath, Market Drayton, Shropshire TF9 2JL. *CNA*, 644. *Young Offenders*, 633. *Governor*, J. Alldridge

*‡STYAL, Wilmslow, Cheshire SK9 4HR. *CNA*, 412. *Prisoners and Young Offenders*, 438. *Governor*, Ms M. Moulden

SUDBURY, Ashbourne, Derbys DE6 5HW. *CNA*, 519. *Prisoners*, 494. *Governor*, vacant

SWALESIDE, Brabazon Road, Eastchurch, Isle of Sheppey, Kent ME12 4AX. *CNA*, 632. *Prisoners*, 616. *Governor*, E. Willett

†SWANSEA, 200 Oystermouth Road, Swansea SA1 3SR. *CNA*, 251. *Prisoners*, 336. *Governor*, Miss V. O'Dea

‡SWINFEN HALL, Lichfield, Staffs WS14 9QS. *CNA*, 320. *Young Offenders*, 295. *Governor*, Ms J. P. Francis

‡THORN CROSS, Arley Road, Appleton Thorn, Warrington WA4 4RL. *CNA*, 316. *Young Offenders*, 224. *Governor*, Mrs C. James

USK, 47 Maryport Street, Usk, Gwent NP5 1XP. *CNA* (*Usk and Prescoed*), 206. *Prisoners* (*Usk and Prescoed*), 281. *Governor*, R. J. Comber

THE VERNE, Portland, Dorset DT5 1EQ. *CNA*, 552. *Prisoners*, 570. *Governor*, M. Cook

WAKEFIELD, 5 Love Lane, Wakefield WF2 9AG. *CNA*, 747. *Prisoners*, 555. *Governor*, D. Shaw

WANDSWORTH, Heathfield Road, London SW18 3HS. *CNA*, 1,102. *Prisoners*, 1,094. *Governor*, S. Rimmer

WAYLAND, Griston, Thetford, Norfolk IP25 6RL. *CNA*, 620. *Prisoners*, 648. *Governor*, Mrs K. Crawley

WEALSTUN, Wetherby, W. Yorks LS23 7AZ. *CNA*, 632. *Prisoners*, 603. *Governor*, S. Tasker

WEARE, Portland Dock, Castletown, Portland, Dorset DT5 1PZ. *CNA*, 400. *Prisoners*, 312. *Governor*, Ms S. F. McCormick

WELLINGBOROUGH, Millers Park, Doddington Road, Wellingborough, Northants NN8 2NH. *CNA*, 511. *Prisoners*, 430. *Governor*, E. Willetts

‡WERRINGTON, Werrington, Stoke-on-Trent ST9 0DX. *CNA*, 188. *Young Offenders*, 106. *Governor*, S. Habgood

‡WETHERBY, York Road, Wetherby, W. Yorks LS22 5ED. *CNA*, 360. *Young Offenders*, 347. *Governor*, vacant

WHATTON, 14 Cromwell Road, Nottingham NG13 9FQ. *CNA*, 275. *Prisoners*, 267. *Governor*, vacant

WHITEMOOR, Longhill Road, March, Cambs PE15 0PR. *CNA*, 522. *Prisoners*, 454. *Governor*, T. Williams

*WINCHESTER, Romsey Road, Winchester SO22 5DF. *CNA*, 463. *Prisoners*, 576. *Governor*, R. J. Gaines

THE WOLDS (private prison), Everthorpe, Brough,
E. Yorks HU15 2JZ. *CNA*, 360. *Prisoners*, 399.
Director, D. McDonnell
†‡§WOODHILL, Tattenhoe Street, Milton Keynes MK44DA.
CNA, 672. *Prisoners and Young Offenders*, 693. *Governor*,
Mrs M. Boon
WORMWOOD SCRUBS, PO Box 757, Du Cane Road,
London W12 0AE. *CNA*, 938. *Prisoners*, 1,122. *Governor*,
S. Moore
WYMOTT, Ulnes Walton Lane, Leyland, Preston PR5 3LW.
CNA, 809. *Prisoners*, 797. *Governor*, R. Doughty

SCOTTISH PRISON SERVICE

Calton House, 5 Redheughs Rigg, Edinburgh EH12 9HW
Tel: 0131-556 8400

SALARIES 1999–2000

Senior managers in the Scottish Prison Service, including
governors and deputy governors of prisons, are paid across
three pay bands:

Band I	£36,725–£55,700
Band H	£30,600–£47,275
Band G	£25,600–£38,925

Chief Executive of Scottish Prison Service (SCS),
A. Cameron
Director of Custody, J. Durno, OBE
Director, Human Resources, P. Russell
Director, Finance and Information Systems, W.Pretswell
Director, Strategy and Corporate Affairs, Ms J. Hutchison
Deputy Director, Regime Services and Supplies, J. McNeill
Deputy Director, Estates and Buildings, D. Bentley
Area Director, South and West, M. Duffy
Area Director, North and East, P. Withers
Head of Training, Scottish Prison Service College,
J. Matthews
Head of Communications, T. Fox

PRISON ESTABLISHMENTS

Prisoners/Young Offenders Average number of prisoners/
young offenders 1999–2000
*ABERDEEN, Craiginches, Aberdeen AB9 2HN. *Prisoners*,
181. *Governor*, I. Gunn
BARLINNIE, Barlinnie, Glasgow G33 2QX. *Prisoners*, 1,124.
Governor, R. L. Houchin
CASTLE HUNTLY, Castle Huntly, Longforgan, nr Dundee
DD2 5HL. *Prisoners*, 106. *Governor*, M. McAlpine
*‡CORNTON VALE, Cornton Road, Stirling FK9 5NY.
Prisoners and Young Offenders, 180. *Governor*,
Mrs K. Donegan
*‡DUMFRIES, Terregles Street, Dumfries DG2 9AX. *Young
Offenders*, 137. *Governor*, C. McGeever
EDINBURGH, 33 Stenhouse Road, Edinburgh EH1 3LN.
Prisoners, 731. *Governor*, R. MacCowan
‡GLENOCHIL, King O'Muir Road, Tullibody,
Clackmannanshire FK10 3AD. *Prisoners and Young Offen-
ders*, 573. *Governor*, A. Spencer
GREENOCK, Gateside, Greenock PA16 9AH. *Prisoners*, 236.
Governor, A. Park
*INVERNESS, Porterfield, Inverness IV2 3HH. *Prisoners*, 122.
Governor, A. MacDonald
KILMARNOCK (private prison), Bowhouse, Mauchline
Road, Kilmarnock KA1 5JH. *Prisoners*, 500. *Director*,
J. Bywalec
LOW MOSS, Low Moss, Bishopbriggs, Glasgow G64 2QB.
Prisoners, 362. *Governor*, E. Murch
NORANSIDE, Noranside, Fern, by Forfar, Angus DD8 3QY.
Prisoners, 102. *Governor*, K. Rennie
PERTH, 3 Edinburgh Road, Perth PH2 8AT. *Prisoners*, 477.
Governor, W. Millar
PETERHEAD, Salthouse Head, Peterhead, Aberdeenshire

AB4 6YY. *Prisoners*, 297. *Governor*, W. Rattray; *Governor*,
Peterhead Unit, B. McConnell
‡POLMONT, Brightons, Falkirk, Stirlingshire FK2 0AB.
Young Offenders, 443. *Governor*, D. Gunn
SHOTTS, Shotts ML7 4LF. *Prisoners*, 467. *Governor*,
W. McKinlay; *Governor, Shotts Unit*, G. Storer

NORTHERN IRELAND PRISON SERVICE

Dundonald House, Upper Newtownards Road, Belfast
BT4 3SU
Tel: 028-90 52 0700; Fax: 028-90 52 5160;
Web http://www.niprisonservice.gov.uk

Salaries 1999–2000

Governor 1	£53,658–£55,510
Governor 2	£48,452–£49,939
Governor 3	£41,844–£43,026
Governor 4	£35,089–£36,956
Governor 5	£24,600–£33,102

A Northern Ireland allowance is also payable

PRISON ESTABLISHMENTS

Prisoners/Young Offenders Average number of prisoners/
young offenders 1998–9
‡HYDEBANK WOOD, Hospital Road, Belfast BT8 8NA.
Young Offenders, 173
*‡MAGHABERRY, Old Road, Ballinderry Upper, Lisburn,
Co. Antrim BT28 2PT. *Prisoners and Young Offenders*, 502
§Magilligan, Point Road, Magilligan, Co. Londonderry
BT49 0LR. *Prisoners*, 340

* Women's establishment or establishment with units for
women
†Remand Centre or establishment with units for remand
prisoners
‡Young Offender Institution or establishment with units for
young offenders
§Immigration Holding Centre

Defence

The armed forces of the United Kingdom comprise the Royal Navy, the Army and the Royal Air Force. The Queen is commander-in-chief of all the armed forces. The Ministry of Defence, headed by a Secretary of State, provides the support structure for the armed forces. Within the Ministry of Defence, the Defence Council has overall responsibility for running the armed forces. The Chief of Staff of each service reports through the Chief of the Defence Staff to the Secretary of State on matters relating to the running of his service. The Chief of Staff also chairs the executive committee of the appropriate service board, which manages the service in accordance with centrally determined objectives and budgets. The military-civilian Central Staffs, headed by the Vice-Chief of the Defence Staff and the Second Permanent Under-Secretary of State, are responsible for policy, operational requirements, commitments, financial management, re-source planning and civilian personnel management. The Defence Procurement Agency is responsible for purchasing equipment. The Defence Scientific Staff and the Defence Intelligence Staff also form part of the Ministry of Defence.

A permanent Joint Headquarters for the conduct of joint operations was set up at Northwood in 1996. The Joint Headquarters connects the policy and strategic functions of the MoD Head Office with the conduct of operations and is intended to strengthen the policy/executive division. A Joint Rapid Deployment Force was established in August 1996 and a Joint Rapid Reaction Force was set up in April 1999 and will be fully in place by October 2001.

Britain pursues its defence and security policies through its membership of NATO (to which most of its armed forces are committed), the Western European Union, the European Union, the Organisation for Security and Co-operation in Europe and the UN (see International Organisations section).

ARMED FORCES STRENGTHS as at 1 October 1999

All Services	212,400
Men	196,540
Women	15,860
Royal Naval Services	43,700
Army	113,500
Royal Air Force	55,200

Source: Ministry of Defence: The Military Balance 1999–2000 (OUP)

SERVICE PERSONNEL

1 October 1999

	Royal Navy	Army	RAF	All Services
1975 strength	76,200	167,100	95,000	338,300
1990 strength	63,200	152,800	89,700	305,700
1999 strength	43,700	113,500	55,200	212,400

Source: Ministry of Defence: The Military Balance 1999–2000 (OUP)

CIVILIAN PERSONNEL

1 June

1975 level	316,700
1990 level	172,300
1999 level	117,700
2000 level	99,142

Source: The Ministry of Defence The Military Balance 1999–2000 (OUP)

DEPLOYMENT OF UK PERSONNEL

SERVICE PERSONNEL IN UK as at July 1999

	England	Wales	Scotland	N. Ireland[3]	Total
All Services	144,350	3,272	14,937	8,994	171,553
Officers	24,647	419	1,742	927	27,735
Other Ranks	119,703	2,853	13,195	8,067	143,818
Army[2]	69,040	897	3,814	7,717	81,468
Officers	9,489	112	373	767	10,741
Soldiers	59,551	785	3,441	6,950	70,727
Navy[1,2]	35,726	28	5,086	173	41,013
Officers	6,533	11	584	13	7,141
Ratings	29,193	17	4,502	160	33,872
RAF[2]	39,584	2,347	6,037	1,104	49,072
Officers	8,625	296	785	147	9,853
Aircrew	30,959	2,051	5,252	957	39,219

1. Naval Service personnel on sea service in home waters are included against the local authority containing the home port of their ship.
2. The titles Naval Service, Army and Royal Air Force include Nursing services.
3. The Home battalions of the Royal Irish Regiment are excluded from the UK Northern Ireland figures.

Source: Ministry of Defence: Defence Analytical Service Agency

SERVICE PERSONNEL OVERSEAS as at 1 July 2000

All Services	42,920
Officers	5,879
Other Ranks	37,041
Army	30,775
Officers	3,679
Soldiers	27,096
Navy	5,171
Officers	899
Ratings	4,272
RAF	6,974
Officers	1,301
Aircrew	5,673

Source: Ministry of Defence: Defence Analytical Service Agency

NUCLEAR FORCES

Britain's nuclear forces comprise four ballistic missile submarines carrying Trident missiles and equipped with nuclear warheads. All nuclear free-fall bombs have been taken out of service.

ARMS CONTROL

The 1990 Conventional Armed Forces in Europe Treaty (the CFE Treaty), which is currently being revised, commits all NATO and former Warsaw Pact members to limiting five major classes of conventional weapons. In 1968 Britain signed the Nuclear Non-Proliferation Treaty, which was indefinitely and unconditionally extended in 1995 and in 1996 signed a Comprehensive Nuclear Test Ban Treaty. Britain was a party to the 1972 Biological and Toxin Weapons Convention, which provides for a world-wide ban on biological weapons, and the 1993 Chemical Weapons Convention, which came into force in 1997 and provides for a world-wide ban on chemical weapons. In 1997 Britain signed the Ottawa Convention, which provides for an immediate ban on the use, production and transfer of anti-personnel land-mines;

Britain ratified the Convention on 31 July 1998 and it came into force on 1 March 1999.

DEFENCE BUDGET

Estimated Outturn	£ billion
2000–2001	22.820
2001–2002	23.408
2002–2003	24.036
2003–2004	24.816

Sources: Ministry of Defence: Defence Analytical Service Agency

The defence settlement under the 2000 Comprehensive Spending Review estimates that defence expenditure will rise from approximately £23 billion this year to almost £25 billion by 2004–2005.

Over the period of the Spending Review, defence as a percentage of GDP will fall from 2.4 per cent this year to 2.3 per cent by 2003–2004, reflecting the fact that GDP is forecast to grow strongly. As a share of total Government expenditure, defence spending will remain at a round 6 per cent.

MINISTRY OF DEFENCE
Main Building, Whitehall, London SW1A 2HB
Tel 0171-218 9000
Public Enquiry Office: Tel 0171-218 6645
Web http://www.mod.uk

For ministerial and civil service salaries, *see* page 291
For Services salaries, *see* pages 406–8
Officers promoted in an acting capacity to a more senior rank are listed under the more senior rank. Promotion to five-star rank is no longer usual in peacetime.

For changes after 31 August 2000, *see* Stop-press

Secretary of State for Defence, Rt. Hon. Geoff Hoon, MP
  Private Secretary (SCS), J. Miller
  Special Advisers, A. McGowan, A. Hood
  Parliamentary Private Secretary, Ms S. Heal, MP
Minister of State for the Armed Forces, John Spellar, MP
  Private Secretary (SCS), D. Applegate
Minister of State for Defence Procurement, The Baroness Symons of Vernham Dean
  Private Secretary (SCS), D. E. A. Hatcher
  Parliamentary Private Secretary, Gillian Merron, MP
Parliamentary Under-Secretary of State, Dr Lewis Moonie, MP
  Private Secretary (SCS), A. Dwyer
Permanent Under-Secretary of State (SCS), K. R. Tebbit, CMG
Chief of the Defence Staff, Gen. Sir Charles Guthrie, GCB, LVO, OBE, ADC *(Gen.)*

THE DEFENCE COUNCIL

The Defence Council is responsible for running the Armed Forces. The Crown Office announced that as of the 5th November 1999, the constitution of the defence council would be arranged in the following way. It is chaired by the Principal Secretary of State for Defence and consists of: the Ministers of State for the Armed Forces; the Minister of State for Defence Procurement; the Parliamentary Under-Secretary of State for Defence; the Chief of the Defence Staff; the Permanent Under-Secretary of State of the Ministry of Defence; the Chief of the Naval Staff and First Sea Lord; the Chief of the General Staff; the Chief of the Air Staff; the Vice-Chief of the Defence Staff; the Chief of Defence Procurement for the Ministry of Defence; the Chief Scientific Adviser of the Ministry of Defence; the Chief of Defence Logistics and the Second Permanent Under-Secretary of State of the Ministry of Defence.

CHIEFS OF STAFF

CHIEF OF THE NAVAL STAFF
Chief of the Naval Staff and First Sea Lord, Adm. Sir Michael Boyce, GCB, OBE, ADC
Asst Chief of the Naval Staff, Rear-Adm. J. M. Burnell-Nugent
Secretariat (Naval Staff) (SCS), C. Verey

CHIEF OF THE GENERAL STAFF
Chief of the General Staff, Gen. Sir Michael Walker, GCB, CMG, CBE, ADC *(Gen.)*
Asst Chief of the General Staff, Maj.-Gen. K. O'Donoghue, CBE
Director-General, Development and Doctrine, Maj.-Gen. C. L. Elliott, CB, MBE

CHIEF OF THE AIR STAFF
Chief of the Air Staff, Air Chief Marshal Sir Peter Squire, AFC, ADC, KCB, DFC
Asst Chief of the Air Staff, Air Vice-Marshal P. O. Sturley
Secretariat (Air Staff) (SCS), M. J. D. Fuller
British-American Community Relations Co-ordinator, Air Marshal Sir John Kemball, KCB, CBE, RAF (retd)
Chief Executive, National Air Traffic Services (SCS), D. J. McLauchlan
Director, Airspace Policy, Air Vice-Marshal J. R. D. Arscott

CENTRAL STAFFS

Vice-Chief of the Defence Staff, Adm. Sir Peter Abbott, GBE, KCB
Second Permanent Under-Secretary of State (SCS), R. T. Jackling, CB, CBE
Deputy CDS (Equipment Capability), Vice-Adm. Sir Jeremy Blackham, KCB
Asst CDS, Operational Requirements (Sea Systems), Rear-Adm. R. J. G. Ward
Asst CDS, Operational Requirements (Land Systems), Maj.-Gen. P. J. Russell-Jones, OBE
Asst CDS, Operational Requirements (Air Systems), Air Vice-Marshal S. M. Nicholl, CBE, AFC
Deputy CDS (Personnel), Air Marshal M. D. Pledger, OBE, AFC
Asst CDS (Programmes), Maj.-Gen. J. P. Kiszely, MC
Asst Under-Secretary of State (Service Personnel Policy) (SCS), D. Bowen
Defence Housing Executive (SCS), C. J. I. James
Surgeon-General, Lt.-Gen. R. C. Menzies, OBE, QHS
Chief of Staff to the Surgeon-General, Rear-Adm. C. D. Stanford
Chief Executive, Defence Medical Training Organisation, Brig. J. R. Brown
Chief Executive, Defence Secondary Care Organisation, J. F. Tuckett
Deputy Under-Secretary of State (Resources, Programmes and Finance) (SCS), C. V. Balmer
Asst Under-Secretary of State (Programmes) (SCS), T. A. Woolley
Asst Under-Secretary of State (Systems) (SCS), N. K. J. Witney
Asst Under-Secretary of State (Financial Management) (SCS), D. G. Jones
Asst Under-Secretary of State (General Finance) (SCS), C. Sanders
Defence Services Secretary, Rear-Adm. R. B. Lees
Deputy CDS (Commitments), Lt.-Gen. A. D. Pigott, CBE

Asst CDS (Operations), Air Vice-Marshall. G. L. Torpy, CBE, DSO
Asst Under-Secretary of State (Home and Overseas) (SCS), E. V. Buckley, CB
Chief of Defence Logistics, Gen. Sir Samuel Cowan, KCB, CBE
Chief of Staff to the Chief of Defence Logistics, (Operations and Business Development), Rear-Admiral M. G. Wood, CBE
Deputy to the Chief of Defence Logistics, J. R. C. Oughton
Asst CDS (Logistics), Air Vice-Marshal D. C. Couzens
Director of Policy (SCS), R. P. Hatfield, CBE
Asst CDS (Policy), Maj. Gen. J. G. Reith, CBE
Deputy Under-Secretary of State (Civilian Management) (SCS), J. Howe
Asst Under-Secretary of State, Civilian Management (Personnel) (SCS), B. A. E. Taylor
Chief Constable, MOD Police,W. E. E. Boreham, OBE
Asst Under-Secretary of State (Security and Support) (SCS), A. G. Rucker
Legal Adviser (SCS), M. J. Hemming
Director-General, Information and Communications Services (SCS), A. C. Sleigh
Defence Estate Organisation (SCS), B. L. Hirst
Commandant, Joint Services Command and Staff College, Air Vice-Marshal B. K. Burridge, CBE

DEFENCE INFORMATION STAFF

Director-General of Corporate Communications (SCS), J. Pitt-Brooke
Director, Information Strategy and News (SCS), Ms O. Muirhead
Director, Internal Communications and Media Training (SCS), A. Boardman
Director, Public Relations (Navy), Cdre H. Edelston
Director, Public Relations (Army), Brig. S. Roberts
Director, Public Relations (RAF), Air Cdre D. Walker

DEFENCE INTELLIGENCE STAFF

Old War Office Building, Whitehall, London SW1A 2EU
Tel 0171-218 6645; fax 0171-218 1562

Chief of Defence Intelligence,Vice-Adm. Sir Alan West, KCB, DSC
Deputy Chief of Defence Intelligence and Head of Defence Intelligence Analysis Staff (SCS), J. N. L. Morrison
Director, Intelligence Programmes and Resources (SCS), P. I. Bailey
Director, Defence Intelligence Secretariat and Communications Information Systems (SCS), R. C. Hack
Director, Regional Assessments, Brig. N. J. Cottam, OBE
Director, Intelligence Global Issues (SCS), J. M. Cunningham
Director-General, Intelligence and Geographic Resources, Air Vice-Marshal J. C. French, CBE

DEFENCE SCIENTIFIC STAFF

Chief Scientific Adviser (SCS), Prof. Sir David Davies, KBE (until Jan. 2000); Prof. Sir Keith O'Nions, FRS (from Jan. 2000)
Chief Scientist (SCS), G. H. B. Jordan
Deputy Chief Scientists (Scrutiny and Analysis) (SCS), M. J. Earwicker; P. M. Sutcliffe
Asst Chief Scientific Adviser (Nuclear) (SCS), P. W. Roper
Nuclear Weapon Safety Adviser (SCS), Dr A. Ferguson

SECOND SEA LORD/COMMANDER-IN-CHIEF NAVAL HOME COMMAND

Second Sea Lord and C.-in-C. Naval Home Command, Vice-Adm. P. Spencer, ADC

Director-General, Naval Personnel (Strategy and Plans) and Chief of Staff to Second Sea Lord and C.-in-C. Naval Home Command, Rear-Adm. R. G. Lockwood
Asst Under-Secretary of State (Naval Personnel) (SCS), B. Miller
Flag Officer Training and Recruiting and Chief Executive, Naval Recruiting and Training Agency, Rear-Adm. J. Chadwick
Naval Secretary and Chief Executive, Naval Manning Agency, Rear-Adm. J. M. de Halpert
Director-General, Naval Medical Services, vacant
Director-General, Naval Chaplaincy Services, Revd Dr C. Stewart

NAVAL SUPPORT COMMAND

Chief of Fleet Support, Rear-Adm. B. B. Perowne
Asst Under-Secretary of State (Fleet Support) (SCS), D. J. Gould
Chief Executive, Ships Support Agency (SCS), J. Coles
Chief Executive, Naval Bases and Supply Agency, Rear-Adm. B. B. Perowne
Chief Naval Engineer Officer, Rear-Adm. J. Chadwick
Director-General, Aircraft (Navy), vacant
Flag Officer Scotland, N. England and N. Ireland, and Naval Base Commander Clyde, Rear-Adm. D. J. Anthony, CBE

COMMANDER-IN-CHIEF FLEET

C.-in-C. Fleet, Adm. Sir Nigel Essenhigh, KCB
Deputy Commander Fleet, Vice-Adm. F. M. Malbon
Chief of Staff (Operations) and Flag Officer Submarines, Rear-Adm. R. P. Stevens, OBE
Chief of Staff (Corporate Development), Rear- Adm. J. Reeve
Flag Officer Surface Flotilla, Rear-Adm. I. A. Forbes, CBE
Flag Officer Sea Training, Rear-Adm. A. K. Backus, OBE
Commander, UK Task Group/Commander, Anti-Submarine Warfare Strike Force, Rear-Adm. S. R. Meyer
Flag Officer Naval Aviation, Rear-Adm. I. R. Henderson, CBE
Commandant-General, Royal Marines, Maj.-Gen. R. H. G. Fulton

ADJUTANT-GENERAL'S DEPARTMENT

Adjutant-General, Lt.-Gen. T. J. Granville-Chapman, CBE
Chief of Staff, Maj-Gen. A. P. N. Currie
Head, Command Secretariat (SCS), M. E. McLoughlin
Director-General, Army Training and Recruiting and Chief Executive, Army Training and Recruiting Agency, Maj.-Gen. A. M. D. Palmer, CBE
Chaplain-General, Revd Ven J Blackburn
Director-General, Army Medical Services, Maj.-Gen. D. S. Jolliffe, QHP
Director, Army Legal Services, Maj.-Gen. G. Risius
Military Secretary and Chief Executive, Army Personnel Centre, Maj.-Gen. A. S. H. Irwin, CBE
Commandant, Royal Military Academy, Sandhurst, Maj.-Gen. A. G. Denaro, CBE
Commandant, Royal Military College of Science, Maj.-Gen. J. C. B. Sutherell

COMMANDER-IN-CHIEF LAND COMMAND

C.-in-C., Land Command, Gen. Sir Michael Jackson, KCB, CBE, DSO (Commander-in-Chief Headquarters Land Command)
Deputy C.-in-C., Land Command, and Inspector-General, Territorial Army, Lt.-Gen. Sir John Deverell, KCB, OBE
Chief of Staff, HQ Land Command, Maj.-Gen. F. R. Viggers, MBE

Deputy Chief of Staff, HQ Land Command, Maj.-Gen.
P. A. Chambers, MBE

HQ STRIKE COMMAND

Air Officer Commanding-in-Chief, Air Chief Marshal
Sir Peter Squire, KCB, DFC, AFC, ADC
Chief of Staff and Deputy C.-in-C., Air Marshal
T. I. Jenner, CB
Senior Air Staff Officer, Air Vice-Marshal
N. J. Sudborough OBE
*Air Officer Logistics and Communications Information
Systems*, Air Vice-Marshal P. J. Scott
Air Officer Administration, Air Vice-Marshal A. J. Burton
Head, Command Secretariat (SCS), C. J. Wright
Air Officer Commanding, No. 1 Group, Air Vice-Marshal
Air Office Commanding, No. 38 Group, Air Vice-Marshal
K. D. Filbey, CBE

HQ LOGISTICS COMMAND

Air Officer Commanding-in-Chief, Air Vice-Marshal
G. Skinner, CBE
*Chief of Staff (Air Officer Commanding Directly Administered
Units)*, vacant
Command Secretary (SCS), H. Griffiths
*Air Officer Communications Information Systems and Support
Services*, Air Vice-Marshal P. Liddell
Director-General, Support Management (RAF), Air
Vice-Marshal P. W. Henderson, CB, MBE

HQ PERSONNEL AND TRAINING
COMMAND

*Air Member for Personnel and Commander-in-Chief
Personnel and Training Command*, Air Marshal
Sir John Day
Chief of Staff, Air Vice-Marshal R. A. Wright, AFC
Chief Executive, Training Group Defence Agency, Air Vice-
Marshal I. S. Corbitt
*Air Officer Administration and Air Officer Commanding
Directly Administered Units*, Air Vice-Marshal
C. Davison, MBE
Commandant, RAF College, Cranwell, Air Vice-Marshall
H. G. Mackay, OBE, AFC
*Air Secretary and Chief Executive, RAF Personnel
Management Agency*, Air Vice-Marshal I. M. Stewart,
AFC
Director-General, Medical Services (RAF), Air
Vice-Marshal C. J. Sharples, QHP
Director, Legal Services (RAF), Air Vice-Marshal
J. Weeden
Chaplain-in-Chief (RAF), Revd A. P. Bishop, QHC
Command Secretary (SCS), L. D. Kyle

DEFENCE PROCUREMENT AGENCY
MOD Abbey Wood, Bristol BS34 8JH
Tel 0117-913 0000

*Chief of Defence Procurement and Chief Executive,
Defence Procurement Agency*, Vice-Adm. Sir Robert
Walmsley, KCB
*Deputy Chief of Defence Procurement (Operations) and
Controller Aircraft*, Air Marshal Sir Peter Norriss, KBE,
CB, AFC
Deputy Chief Executive (SCS), Miss S. Scholefield, CMG
Executive Director 1 (SCS), I. Fauset
Executive Director 2, Maj.-Gen P. Gilchrist
Executive Director 3 (SCS), G. N. Beaven
Executive Director 4, and Controller of the Navy, Rear-Adm.
N. C. F. Guild

Executive Director 5 (SCS), S. Porter
Executive Director 6 (SCS), S. Webb
Engineering Adviser and President of the Ordnance Board,
Maj.-Gen. L. D. Curran

OTHER DEFENCE AGENCIES

ARMED FORCES PERSONNEL ADMINISTRATION AGENCY,
Building 182, RAF Innsworth, Gloucester GL3 1HW.
Tel: 01452-712612 ext. 7347. *Chief Executive*, T. S. Lord
ARMY BASE REPAIR ORGANISATION, Building 200,
Monxton Road, Andover, Hants SP11 8HT. Tel: 01264-
383295. *Chief Executive*, J. R. Drew, CBE
ARMY PERSONNEL CENTRE, Kentigern House, 65 Brown
Street, Glasgow G2 8EX. Tel: 0141-224 3010. *Chief
Executive*, Maj.-Gen. A. S. H. Irwin, CBE
ARMY TRAINING AND RECRUITING AGENCY, Trenchard
Lines, Upavon, Pewsey, Wilts SN9 6BE. Tel: 01980-
615024. *Chief Executive*, Maj.-Gen. A. M. D. Palmer,
CBE
BRITISH FORCES POST OFFICE, Inglis Barracks, Mill Hill,
London NW7 1PX. Tel: 0181-818 6313. E-mail:
bfpo@compuserve.com *Director and Chief Executive*,
Brig. B. J. Cash
DEFENCE ANALYTICAL SERVICES AGENCY,
Northumberland House, Northumberland Avenue,
London WC2N 5BP. Tel: 0171-218 0729. *Chief Executive*,
C. Youngson
DEFENCE AVIATION REPAIR AGENCY, DARA Head Office,
Building 145, St Athan, Barry, Vale of Glamorgan CF62
4WA. Tel: 01446-798893. *Chief Executive*, S. R. Hill, OBE
DEFENCE BILLS AGENCY, Room 410, Mersey House,
Drury Lane, Liverpool L2 7PX. Tel: 0151-242 2234.
Chief Executive, I. S. Elrick
DEFENCE CLOTHING AND TEXTILES AGENCY,
Skimmingdish Lane, Caversfield, Oxon OX6 9TS. Tel:
01869-875501. *Chief Executive*, Brig. M. J. Roycroft
DEFENCE COMMUNICATION SERVICES AGENCY, Basil Hill
Site, Park Lane, Wilts SN13 9NR. Tel:01225-814829
Building 111, Basil Hill Barracks, Park Lane, Corsham,
Wilts SN13 9NR. Tel: 01225-814886. *Chief Executive*,
Maj.-Gen. A. Raper, CBE
DEFENCE DENTAL AGENCY, RAF Halton, Aylesbury,
Bucks HP22 5PG. Tel: 01296-623535, ext. 6762. E-mail
hqdda.demon.co.uk *Chief Executive*, Air Vice-Marshal
I. G. McIntyre, QHDS
DEFENCE ESTATES, St George's House, Blakemore Drive,
Sutton Coldfield, W. Midlands B75 7RL. Tel: 0121-311
3850. *Chief Executive*, I. Andrews, CBE
DEFENCE EVALUATION AND RESEARCH AGENCY, Ively
Road, Farnborough, Hants GU14 0LX. Tel: 01252-
394500. *Chief Executive*, Sir John Chisholm
DEFENCE GEOGRAPHIC AND IMAGERY INTELLIGENCE
AGENCY, Watson Building, Elmwood Avenue, Feltham,
Middx TW13 7AH. Tel: 020-8818 2422. *Chief Executive*,
Brig. A. P. Walker, OBE
DEFENCE HOUSING EXECUTIVE, 8th Floor,
St Christopher House, Southwark Street, London
SE1 0TE. Tel: 0171-921 1033. *Chief Executive*, J. Wilson
DEFENCE INTELLIGENCE AND SECURITY CENTRE,
Chicksands, Shefford, Beds SG17 5PR. Tel: 01462-
752125. *Chief Executive*, Brig. C. G. Holtom
DEFENCE MEDICAL TRAINING ORGANISATION, Building
87, Fort Blockhouse, Gosport, Hants PO12 2AB. Tel:
01705-765284/765438. *Chief Executive*,
Brig. J. R. Brown
DEFENCE SECONDARY CARE AGENCY, Room 4/152,
St Christopher House, Southwark Street, London
SE1 0TD. Tel: 020-7305 6190. *Chief Executive*,
Mr J. Tuckett

DEFENCE STORAGE AND DISTRIBUTION AGENCY,
Ploughley Road, Lower Arncott, Bicester, Oxon
OX6 0LD. Tel: 01869-256840. *Chief Executive*, Brig.
P. D. Foxton

DEFENCE TRANSPORT AND MOVEMENTS AGENCY,
Monxton Road, Andover, Hants SP11 8HT. Tel: 01264-
382537. *Chief Executive*, Air Cdre Whalley

DEFENCE VETTING AGENCY, Room Building 107,
Imphal Barracks, Fulford Road, York YO10 4AS . Tel:
01904 662444. *Chief Executive*, M. P. B. G. Wilson

DISPOSAL SALES AGENCY, 7th Floor, 6 Hercules Road,
London SE1 7DJ. Tel: 020-761 8853. *Chief Executive*,
S. Taylor

JOINT AIR RECONNAISSANCE INTELLIGENCE CENTRE,
RAF Brampton, Huntingdon, Cambs PE28 4YG. Tel:
01480-52151, ext. 7837. *Officer Commanding*,
Gp Capt S. J. Lloyd

LOGISTIC INFORMATION SYSTEMS AGENCY, Monxton
Road, Andover, Hants SP11 8HT. Tel: 01264-382025.
Chief Executive, Brig. P. A. Flanagan

MEDICAL SUPPLIES AGENCY, Drummond Barracks,
Ludgershall, Andover, Hants SP11 9RU. Tel: 01264
798622. *Chief Executive*, B. E. Nimick

METEOROLOGICAL OFFICE, London Road, Bracknell,
Berks RG12 2SZ. Tel: 01344-420242. *Chief Executive*,
P. D. Ewins

MINISTRY OF DEFENCE POLICE, Wethersfield, Braintree,
Essex CM7 4AZ. Tel: 01371-854000. *Chief Executive*,
Chief Constable W. E. E. Boreham, OBE

NAVAL BASES AND SUPPLY AGENCY, Room 8, C Block,
Ensleigh, Bath BA1 5AB. Tel: 01225-467400. *Chief
Executive*, Rear-Adm. B. B. Perowne

NAVAL MANNING AGENCY, Victory Building, HM Naval
Base, Portsmouth PO1 3LS. Tel: 023-9272 7402. *Chief
Executive*, Rear-Adm. J. M. de Halpert

NAVAL RECRUITING AND TRAINING AGENCY, Victory
Building, HM Naval Base, Portsmouth PO1 3LS.
Tel: 023-9272 7602. *Chief Executive*, Rear-Adm.
J. Chadwick

PAY AND PERSONNEL AGENCY, Warminster Road, Bath
BA1 5AA. Tel: 01225-828533. *Chief Executive*,
M. A. Rowe

RAF PERSONNEL MANAGEMENT AGENCY, RAF
Innsworth, Gloucester GL3 1EZ. Tel: 01452-712612,
ext. 7849. *Chief Executive*, Air Vice-Marshal
I. M. Stewart, AFC

RAF SIGNALS ENGINEERING ESTABLISHMENT, RAF
Henlow, Beds SG16 6DN. Tel: 01462-851515, ext. 7625.
Director, Air Vice-Marshal C. M. Davison

SERVICE CHILDREN'S EDUCATION, HQ SCE, Building 5,
Wegberg Military Complex, BFPO 40. Tel: 00-49 2161-
908 2372. *Chief Executive*, D. G. Wadsworth

SHIPS SUPPORT AGENCY, B Block, Room 102, Foxhill,
Bath BA1 5AB. Tel: 01225-882348. *Chief Executive*,
J. D. Coles

TRAINING GROUP DEFENCE AGENCY, RAF Innsworth,
Gloucester GL3 1EZ. Tel: 01452-712612, ext. 5344. *Chief
Executive*, Air Vice-Marshal I. S. Corbitt

UNITED KINGDOM HYDROGRAPHIC OFFICE, Admiralty
Way, Taunton, Somerset TA1 2DN. Tel: 01823-337900.
E-mail: name@ukho.gov.uk Web: www.ukho.gov.uk
Chief Executive, and Hydrographer of the Royal Navy,
Rear-Adm. J. P. Clarke, CB, LVO, MBE

The Royal Navy

LORD HIGH ADMIRAL OF THE UNITED KINGDOM
HM The Queen

ADMIRALS OF THE FLEET
HRH The Prince Philip, Duke of Edinburgh, KG, KT, OM,
GBE, AC, QSO, PC, *apptd* 1953
The Lord Hill-Norton, GCB, *apptd* 1971
Sir Michael Pollock, GCB, LVO, DSC, *apptd* 1974
Sir Edward Ashmore, GCB, DSC, *apptd* 1977
Sir Henry Leach, GCB, *apptd* 1982
Sir Julian Oswald, GCB, *apptd* 1993
Sir Benjamin Bathurst, GCB, *apptd* 1995

ADMIRALS
Boyce, Sir Michael, GCB, OBE, ADC (*Chief of the Naval Staff
and First Sea Lord*)
Abbott, Sir Peter, GBE, KCB (*Vice-Chief of the Defence Staff*)
Essenhigh, Sir Nigel, KCB (*C.-in-C. Fleet, C.-in-C.
Eastern Atlantic Area and Commander Allied Forces
North-Western Europe*)
Perowne, J. F., OBE (Deputy Supreme Allied Commander
Atlantic)

VICE-ADMIRALS
Garnett, Sir Ian, KCB (*Chief of Joint Operations*)
Haddacks, Sir Paul, KCB (*Director of NATO Military Staff*)
Blackham, Sir Jeremy, KCB (*Deputy CDS (Equipment
Capability)*)
West, Sir Alan, KCB, DSC (*Chief of Defence Intelligence*)
McAnally, J. H. S., LVO (*Commandant, Royal College of
Defence Studies*)
Malbon, F. M. (*Deputy Commander Fleet*)
Band, J. (*Team Leader, Defence Training and Education
Study*) (from 11 Jan. 2000)
Spencer, P., ADC (*C.-in-C. Naval Home Command and
Second Sea Lord*)

REAR-ADMIRALS
Clarke, J. P., CB, LVO, MBE (*Hydrographer of the Navy and
Chief Executive, UK Hydrographic Office*)
Franklyn, P. M., CB, MVO (*Flag Officer Scotland, N. England
and N. Ireland*)
Lees, R. B. (*Defence Services Secretary*)
Ross, A. B., CB, CBE (*Asst Director Operations Divn
International Military Staff*)
Perowne, B. B. (*Chief Executive, Naval Bases and Supply
Agency and Chief of Fleet Support*)
Forbes, I. A., CBE (*Flag Officer Surface Flotilla*)
Gough, A. B., CB (CDS *Policy and Requirements*)
Lipplett, R. J., MBE (*Chief of Staff to Commander, Allied
Naval Forces Southern Europe, and Senior British Officer
Southern Region*)
Gregory, A. M., OBE (*Naval Base Commander Clyde*)
Moore, S., CB (CDS *Operations*)
Dunt, P. A. (*Director General Personnel Strategy and Plans*)
Burch, J. A., CBE (*Director General Aircraft (Navy)*)
Stevens, R. P., OBE (*Chief of Staff (Operations), Flag
Officer Submarines, COMSUBEASTLANT and
COMSUBNORTHWEST*)
Henderson, I. R., CBE (*Flag Officer Naval Aviation*)
Chadwick, J. (*Flag Officer Training and Recruiting and Chief
Executive, Naval Recruiting and Training Agency and Chief
Naval Engineer Officer*)

de Halpert, J. M. (*Naval Secretary/Chief Executive, Naval Manning Agency*)

HRH The Prince of Wales, KG, KT, GCB and Great Master of the Order of the Bath, AK, QSO, PC, ADC (P)

Wood, M. G., CBE (*Chief of Staff to Chief of Defence Logistics (Operations and Business Development)*)

Stanford, C. D. (*Chief of Staff to the Surgeon-General*)

Burnell-Nugent, J. M. (*Asst Chief of the Naval Staff*)

Meyer, S. R. (*Commander, UK Task Group/Commander, Anti-Submarine Warfare Strike Force*)

Backus, A. K., OBE (*Flag Officer Sea Training*)

Clare, R. A. G. (*Director of Operational Management NATO Regional Command North*)

Guild, N. C. F. (*Executive Director 4, Defence Procurement Agency*)

Ward, R. J. G. (*Asst CDS Operational Requirements (Sea Systems)*)

Anthony, D. J., MBE (*Flag Officer Scotland, N. England and N. Ireland, and Naval Base Commander Clyde*)

Reeve, J. (*Chief of Staff (Corporate Development)*) to C.-in-C. Fleet)

Lockwood, R. G. (*Director-General, Naval Personnel (Strategy and Plans) and Chief of Staff to Second Sea Lord and C.-in-C. Naval Home Command*)

Stanhope, M. (*Director of Operational Management, NATO Regional Command North*)

Enquiries regarding records of serving officers should be directed to The Naval Secretary, Room 161, Victory Building, HM Naval Base, Portsmouth, Hants PO1 3LS. Tel: 023-9272 7402.

Enquiries regarding records of retired officers should be directed to the Officers Mobilisation Section, Room 171, Victory Building, HM Naval Base, Portsmouth, Hants PO1 3LS. Tel: 023-9272 7431

HM FLEET *as at autumn 2000*

SUBMARINES

Trident	Vanguard, Vengeance, Victorious, Vigilant
Fleet	Sceptre, Sovereign, Spartan, Splendid, Superb, Talent, Tireless, Torbay, Trafalgar, Trenchant, Triumph, Turbulent
ANTI-SUBMARINE WARFARE CARRIERS	Ark Royal, Illustrious, Invincible
ASSAULT SHIPS	Fearless, Intrepid
LANDING PLATFORM HELICOPTER	Ocean
DESTROYERS	
Type 42	Cardiff, Edinburgh, Exeter, Glasgow, Gloucester, Liverpool, Manchester, Newcastle, Nottingham, Southampton, St Albans, York
FRIGATES	
Type 23	Argyll, Grafton, Iron Duke, Lancaster, Marlborough, Monmouth, Montrose, Norfolk, Northumberland, Richmond, Somerset, Sutherland, Westminster
Type 22	Campbeltown, Chatham, Cornwall, Coventry, Cumberland, Sheffield
OFFSHORE PATROL	
Castle Class	Dumbarton Castle, Leeds Castle
Island Class	Alderney, Anglesey, Guernsey, Lindisfarne, Shetland
MINEHUNTERS	
Hunt Class	Atherstone, Brecon, Brocklesby, Cattistock, Chiddingfold, Cottesmore, Dulverton, Hurworth, Ledbury, Middleton, Quorn
Sandown Class	Bridport, Cromer, Grimsby, Inverness, Pembroke, Penzance, Sandown, Walney, Blyth
PATROL CRAFT	
River Class	Orwell
Coastal Training Craft*	Archer, Biter, Blazer, Charger, Dasher, Example, Exploit, Explorer, Express, Puncher, Pursuer, Raider, Smiter, Tracker
Gibraltar Search and Rescue Craft	Ranger, Trumpeter
ICE PATROL SHIP	Endurance
SURVEY SHIPS	Beagle, Bulldog, Gleaner, Herald, Roebuck, Scott
SOLD/DECOMMISSIONED 1998	Arun, Beaver, Blackwater, Boxer, London, Orkney, Spey, Brave, Birmingham, Bicester, Berkeley

*Operated by the University Royal Naval Units

OTHER PARTS OF THE NAVAL SERVICE

ROYAL MARINES

The Royal Marines were formed in 1664 and are part of the Naval Service. Their primary purpose is to conduct amphibious and land warfare. The principal operational units are 3 Commando Brigade Royal Marines, an amphibious all-arms brigade trained to operate in arduous environments, which is a core element of the UK's Joint Rapid Reaction Force; Comacchio Group Royal Marines, which is responsible for the security of nuclear weapon facilities; and Special Boat Service Royal Marines, the maritime special forces. The Royal Marines also provide detachments for warships and land-based naval parties as required. The Royal Marines Band Service provides military musical support for the Naval Service. The headquarters of the Royal Marines is at Portsmouth, along with the Royal Marines School of Music, and principal bases are at Plymouth, Arbroath, Poole, Taunton and Chivenor. The Corps of Royal Marines is about 6,500 strong.

Commandant-General, Royal Marines, Maj.-Gen. R. H. G. Fulton

Chief of Staff, NATO Joint Headquarters North, Maj.-Gen. D. Wilson, OBE

Director-General, Joint Doctrine and Concepts Centre, Maj.-Gen. A. A. Milton, OBE, ADC

ROYAL MARINES RESERVE (RMR)

The Royal Marines Reserve is a commando-trained volunteer force with the principal role, when mobilised, of supporting the Royal Marines. There are RMR centres in London, Glasgow, Bristol, Liverpool and Newcastle. The current strength of the RMR is about 1,000.

Director, RMR, Col. A. W. MacCormick

ROYAL FLEET AUXILIARY SERVICE (RFA)

The Royal Fleet Auxiliary Service is a civilian-manned flotilla of 22 ships. Its primary role is to supply the Royal Navy at sea with food, fuel, ammunition and spares, enabling it to maintain operations away from its home ports. In addition the RFA provides the Royal Navy with sea-borne aviation training facilities as well as secure logistic support and amphibious operations capability for the Army and Royal Marines.

FLEET AIR ARM

The Fleet Air Arm was founded in 1914 as the Royal Naval Air Service and operates some 240 fixed wing aircraft and helicopters for the Royal Navy. Sea Harrier fighters provide air defence/strike capability for the fleet, and Sea King and Lynx helicopters provide commando support, anti-submarine, anti-surface, airborne early warning and search and rescue capability. In 1999 the strength of the FAA was 5,600.

ROYAL NAVAL RESERVE (RNR)

The Royal Naval Reserve is an integral part of the Naval Service. It comprises up to 3,850 men and women nationwide who volunteer to train in their spare time to enable the Royal Navy to meet its operational commitments, at sea and ashore, in crisis or war.

The standard annual training commitment is 24 days, including 12 days' continuous training. Daily pay scales range from £46 to £148 for officers and from £26 to £64 for ratings. A tax-free bounty is also payable, the amount depending on the length of service.

Director, Naval Reserves, Capt J. A. Rimington, RN

QUEEN ALEXANDRA'S ROYAL NAVAL NURSING SERVICE

The first nursing sisters were appointed to naval hospitals in 1884 and the Queen Alexandra's Royal Naval Nursing Service (QARNNS) gained its current title in 1902. Nursing ratings were introduced in 1960 and men were integrated into the Service in 1982; QARNNS recruits qualified nurses as both officers and ratings and student nurse training can be undertaken in the Service. Female medical assistants were introduced between 1987–1998, although no longer recruited some continue to serve in QARNNS.

Patron, HRH Princess Alexandra, the Hon. Lady Ogilvy, GCVO

Matron-in-Chief and Director of Naval Nursing Services, Capt. J. C. Brown

---

The Army

THE QUEEN

FIELD MARSHALS

HRH The Prince Philip, Duke of Edinburgh, KG, KT, OM, GBE, AC, QSO, PC, *apptd* 1953
The Lord Carver, GCB, CBE, DSO, MC, *apptd* 1973
Sir Roland Gibbs, GCB, CBE, DSO, MC, *apptd* 1979
The Lord Bramall, KG, GCB, OBE, MC, *apptd* 1982
Sir John Stanier, GCB, MBE, *apptd* 1985
Sir Nigel Bagnall, GCB, CVO, MC, *apptd* 1988
The Lord Vincent of Coleshill, GBE, KCB, DSO (Col. Cmdt. RA), *apptd* 1991

Sir John Chapple, GCB, CBE, *apptd* 1992
HRH The Duke of Kent, KG, GCMG, GCVO, ADC, *apptd* 1993
The Lord Inge, GCB (Col. Green Howards, Col. Cmdt. APTC), *apptd* 1994

GENERALS

Guthrie, Sir Charles, GCB, LVO, OBE, ADC *(Gen.),* Col. LG *(Chief of the Defence Staff)*
Wheeler, Sir Roger, GCB, CBE, ADC *(Gen.),* Col. Cmdt. Int. Corps, Col. R. Irish, Hon. Col. Oxford University Officers' Training Corps
Walker, Sir Michael, GCB, CMG, CBE, ADC (Chief Of The General Staff) *(Gen.), (Chief of the General Staff)*
Harley, Sir Alexander, KBE, CB, ADC *(Gen.),* Col. Cmdt. RHA
Cowan, Sir Samuel, KCB, CBE, Col. Cmdt. Bde of Gurkhas *(Chief of Defence Logistics)*
Smith, Sir Rupert, KCB, DSO, OBE, QGM, Col. Cmdt. REME *(d.saceur)*
Jackson, Sir Michael, KCB, CBE, DSO, Col. Cmdt. Parachute Regiment, Col. Cmdt. AG Corps, Hon. Col. The Rifle Volunteers *(C.-in-C., Land)*

LIEUTENANT-GENERALS

Pike, Sir Hew, KCB, DSO, MBE *(GOC Northern Ireland)*
Deverell, Sir John, KCB, OBE, Col. Cmdt. Lt. Col. Cmdt. SASC *(Deputy C.-in-C., Land Command, and Inspector-General, Territorial Army)*
Willcocks, Sir Michael, KCB, Col. Cmdt. RA *(UK Military Rep. at NATO HQ)*
Foley, Sir John, *(Lieutenant-Governor and Commander-in-Chief of Guernsey)*
Drewry, C. F., CBE *(Commander, ACE Rapid Reaction Corps)*
Pigott, A. D., CBE, Col. The Queen's Gurkha Engineers, Col. Cmdt. RE *(Deputy CDS (Commitments))* Menzies, R. C., OBE, QHS *(Surgeon-General)*
Cordy-Simpson, R., KBE, CB, Col. The Light Dragoons *(President Royal British Legion)*
Granville-Chapman, T. J., CBE

MAJOR-GENERALS

Cordingley, P. A. J., DSO, Col. RDG
McAfee, R. W. M., CB, Col. Cmdt. RTR *(Commander Multinational Divn Central (Airmobile))*
Drewienkiewicz, K. J., CB, Col. Cmdt. RE *(Head of British Contingent to Kosovo Monitoring Mission)*
Sulivan, T. J., CBE *(GOC HQ 4 Divn)*
Delves, C. N. G. *(Chief of Joint Forces Operational Readiness and Training)*
Elliott, C. L., CB, MBE *(Director-General, Development and Doctrine)*
Kiszely, J. P., MC *(Asst CDS (Programmes))*
O'Donoghue, K., CBE *(Asst Chief of the General Staff)*
Webb-Carter, E. J., OBE, Col. DWR *(GOC London District)*
Irwin, A. S. H., CBE, Col. Cmdt. The Scottish Division *(Military Secretary and Chief Executive, Army Personnel Centre)*
Trousdell, P. C. C., Col. The Queen's Own Gurkha Transport Regiment *(Deputy Commander (Operations) Stabilisation Force Bosnia Herzogovina)*
Chambers, P. A., MBE *(Deputy Chief of Staff, HQ Land Command)*
Besgrove, P. V. R., CBE, Col. Cmdt. REME *(Asst. Chief of Staff (Resources) HQ Allied Forces Southern Europe)*
Searby, R. V. *(Senior British Loan Service Officer, Oman)*
Russell-Jones, P. J., OBE, Col. Cmdt. Corps of Royal Engineers *(Asst CDS, Operational Requirements (Land Systems))*

Risius, G. (*Director, Army Legal Services*)

Reith, J. G., CB, CBE (*Asst CDS (Policy)*)

Milne, J. (*Director Support, HQ Allied Land Forces Central Europe*)

Pringle, A. R. D., CB, CBE, Col. Cmdt. RGJ (*Chief of Staff to Chief of Joint Operations*)

Raper, A. J., CBE (*Chief Executive, Defence Communications Services Agency*)

Ridgway, A. P., CBE (*Chief of Staff HQ ACE Rapid Reaction Corps*)

Truluck, A. E. G., CBE (*Executive Assistant to the Chief of Staff Supreme HQ Allied Powers Europe*)

Currie, A. P. N. (*Chief of Staff to Adjutant-General*)

Lyons, A. W., CBE (*Director-General, Logistic Support (Army)*)

Watt, C. R., CBE (*GOC 1 (UK) Armd Divn*)

Ramsay, A. I., CBE, DSO, Col. Cmdt. RHF (*Commander British Forces Cyprus*)

HRH The Prince of Wales, KG, KT, GCB and Great Master of the Order of the Bath, AK, QSO, PC, ADC(P) Dannatt, F. R., CBE, MC (*GOC 3 (UK) Divn*)

Curran, L. D., Col. Cmdt. REME (*Engineering Adviser, Defence Procurement Agency and President of the Ordnance Board*)

Grant Peterkin, A. P., OBE (*General Officer, Commanding 5th Division*)

Palmer, A. M. D., CBE (*Director-General, Army Training and Recruiting and Chief Executive, Army Training and Recruiting Agency*)

Sutherell, J. C. B., CBE, Col. Cmdt. The Queens Division (*Commandant, RMCS*)

Viggers, F. R., MBE (*Chief of Staff, HQ Land Command*)

Gordon, R. D. S., CBE (*GOC HQ 2 Divn*)

Moore-Bick, J. D., CBE (*Military Assistant to the High Representative in Bosnia-Herzogovina*)

Judd, D. L. (Quartermaster General)

Gilchrist, P., Master General of the Ordnance, Col. Cmdt. RAC (*Executive Director 2, Defence Procurement Agency*)

Brims, R. V., CBE, (*Commander Multinational Divn. (South West) Bosnia-Herzogovina*)

Jolliffe, D. S. QHP, (*Director General, Army Medical Services*)

Messervy-Whiting, G. G., (*Head Interim Military Staff EU Brussels*)

Viggars, F. R. MBE, (*Deputy Colonel Commandant Adjutant General's Corps*)

CONSTITUTION OF THE ARMY

The regular forces include the following arms, branches and corps. They are listed in accordance with the order of precedence within the British Army. All enquiries with regard to records of serving personnel (Regular and Territorial Army) should be directed to Relations with the Public, Army Personnel Office, Kentigern House, 65 Brown Street, Glasgow G2 8EX. Tel: 0141-224 8883/8880/8881/8884.

THE ARMS

HOUSEHOLD CAVALRY – The Household Cavalry Regiment (The Life Guards and The Blues and Royals)

ROYAL ARMOURED CORPS – Cavalry Regiments: 1st The Queen's Dragoon Guards; The Royal Scots Dragoon Guards (Carabiniers and Greys); The Royal Dragoon Guards; The Queen's Royal Hussars (The Queen's Own and Royal Irish); 9th/12th Royal Lancers (Prince of Wales's); The King's Royal Hussars; The Light Dragoons; The Queen's Royal Lancers; Royal Tank Regiment, comprising two regular regiments

ARTILLERY – Royal Regiment of Artillery

ENGINEERS – Corps of Royal Engineers

SIGNALS – Royal Corps of Signals

THE INFANTRY

The Foot Guards and regiments of Infantry of the Line are grouped in divisions as follows:

GUARDS DIVISION – Grenadier, Coldstream, Scots, Irish and Welsh Guards. *Divisional Office*, HQ Infantry, Warminster Training Centre, Warminster, Wilts. *Training Centre*, Infantry Training Centre, Vimy Barracks, Catterick, N. Yorks

SCOTTISH DIVISION – The Royal Scots (The Royal Regiment); The Royal Highland Fusiliers (Princess Margaret's Own Glasgow and Ayrshire Regiment); The King's Own Scottish Borderers; The Black Watch (Royal Highland Regiment); The Highlanders (Seaforth, Gordons and Camerons); The Argyll and Sutherland Highlanders (Princess Louise's). *Divisional Office*, HQ Infantry, Warminster Training Centre, Warminster, Wilts. *Training Centre*, Infantry Training Centre, Vimy Barracks, Catterick, N. Yorks

QUEEN'S DIVISION – The Princess of Wales's Royal Regiment (Queen's and Royal Hampshire's); The Royal Regiment of Fusiliers; The Royal Anglian Regiment. *Divisional Office*, HQ Infantry, Warminster Training Centre, Warminster, Wilts. *Training Centre*, Infantry Training Centre, Vimy Barracks, Catterick, N. Yorks

KING'S DIVISION – The King's Own Royal Border Regiment; The King's Regiment; The Prince of Wales's Own Regiment of Yorkshire; The Green Howards (Alexandra, Princess of Wales's Own Yorkshire Regiment); The Queen's Lancashire Regiment; The Duke of Wellington's Regiment (West Riding). *Divisional Office*, HQ Infantry, Warminster Training Centre, Warminster, Wilts. *Training Centre*, Infantry Training Centre, Vimy Barracks, Catterick, N. Yorks

PRINCE OF WALES'S DIVISION – The Devonshire and Dorset Regiment; The Cheshire Regiment; The Royal Welch Fusiliers; The Royal Regiment of Wales (24th/41st Foot); The Royal Gloucestershire, Berkshire and Wiltshire Regiment; The Worcestershire and Sherwood Foresters Regiment (29th/45th Foot); The Staffordshire Regiment (The Prince of Wales's). *Divisional Office*, HQ Infantry, Warminster Training Centre, Warminster, Wilts. *Training Centre*, Infantry Training Centre, Vimy Barracks, Catterick, N. Yorks

LIGHT DIVISION – The Light Infantry; The Royal Green Jackets. *Divisional Office*, HQ Infantry, Warminster Training Centre, Warminster, Wilts. *Training Centre*, Infantry Training Centre, Vimy Barracks, Catterick, N. Yorks

THE ROYAL IRISH REGIMENT (one general service and six home service battalions) – 27th (Inniskilling), 83rd, 87th and the Ulster Defence Regiment. *Regimental HQ and Training Centre*, St Patrick's Barracks, BFPO 808

BRIGADE OF GURKHAS – The Royal Gurkha Rifles; The Queen's Gurkha Engineers; Queen's Gurkha Signals; The Queen's Own Gurkha Transport Regiment. *Regimental HQ*, Airfield Camp, Netheravon, Wilts. *Gurkha Company*, Infantry Training Centre, Vimy Barracks, Catterick, N. Yorks

THE PARACHUTE REGIMENT (three regular battalions) – *Regimental HQ*, Browning Barracks, Aldershot, Hants. *Training Centre*, Infantry Training Centre, Vimy Barracks, Catterick, N. Yorks

SPECIAL AIR SERVICE REGIMENT – *Regimental HQ and Training Centre*, Stirling Lines, Hereford

ARMY AIR CORPS – *Regimental HQ* and *Training Centre*, Middle Wallop, Stockbridge, Hants

SERVICES/ARMS*

Royal Army Chaplains Department – *Regimental HQ*, HQ AG, Upavon, Pewsey, Wilts. *Training Centre*, Armed Forces Chaplaincy Centre, Amport House, Amport, Andover, Hants

The Royal Logistic Corps – *Regimental HQ*, Blackdown Barracks, Deepcut, Camberley, Surrey. *Training Centre*, Princess Royal Barracks, Deepcut, Camberley, Surrey

Royal Army Medical Corps – *Regimental HQ*, Keogh Barracks, Ash Vale, Aldershot, Hants. *Training Centre*, Defence Medical Services Training Centre, Keogh Barracks, Ash Vale, Aldershot, Hants

Corps of Royal Electrical and Mechanical Engineers – *Regimental HQ* and *Training Centre*, Hazebrouck Barracks, Isaac Newton Road, Arborfield, Reading, Berks

Adjutant-General's Corps – *Corps HQ* and *Training Centre*, Worthy Down, Winchester, Hants

Royal Army Veterinary Corps – *Regimental HQ*, Defence Animal Centre, Welby Lane Camp, Melton Mowbray, Leicestershire

Small Arms School Corps – *Regimental HQ*, Warminster Training Centre, Warminster, Wilts

Royal Army Dental Corps – *Regimental HQ*, Keogh Barracks, Ash Vale, Aldershot, Hants. *Training Centre*, Defence Dental Agency Training Establishment, Evelyn Woods Road, Aldershot, Hants

*Intelligence Corps – *Corps HQ* and *Training Centre*, Chicksands, Shefford, Beds

Army Physical Training Corps – *Regimental HQ*, Army School of Physical Training, Fox Lines, Queen's Avenue, Aldershot, Hants General Service Corps

Queen Alexandra's Royal Army Nursing Corps – *Regimental HQ*, Keogh Barracks, Ash Vale, Aldershot, Hants. *Training Centre*, Health Studies Division, Royal Defence Medical College, Vulcan Block, Fort Blockhouse, Gosport, Hants

Corps of Army Music – *Corps HQ* and *Training Centre*, Army School of Music, Kneller Hall, Kneller Road, Twickenham, Middx

ARMY EQUIPMENT HOLDINGS *as at August 1999*

Tanks	373
Armoured combat vehicles	2,920
Artillery pieces	406
Large landing craft	2
Helicopters	232

THE TERRITORIAL ARMY (TA)

The Territorial Army provides formed units and individuals as an essential part of the Army's order of battle for operations across all military tasks in order to ensure that the Army is capable of mounting and sustaining operations at nominated states of readiness. It also provides a basis for regeneration, while at the same time maintaining links with the local community and society at large. From 1 July 1999 its established strength is 41,204.

Members of the TA receive pay at the rate appropriate to their rank. From 1 April 2000, the minimum daily pay for an officer is £46.14 and for a soldier is £26.31. Pay rises with rank and length of service. Members who complete their annual training requirements (27 and 19 days respectively for members of the Independent and Specialist TA) and are certified as efficient receive a single bounty ranging from £100 to £1,050.

Inspector-General, Lt.-Gen. Sir John Deverell, KCB, OBE

QUEEN ALEXANDRA'S ROYAL ARMY
NURSING CORPS

The Queen Alexandra's Royal Army Nursing Corps (QARANC) was founded in 1902 as Queen Alexandra's Imperial Military Nursing Service (QAIMNS) and gained its present title in 1949. The QARANC has trained nurses for the register since 1950 and also trains and employs Health Care Assistants to Level 3 NVQ. The Corps also recruits qualified nurses as Officers and other ranks and in 1992 male nurses already serving in the Army were transferred to the QARANC. QARANC personnel serve in all four corners of the world in both peacetime and operational environments.

Colonel-in-Chief, HRH The Princess Margaret, Countess of Snowdon, CI, GCVO

Director of Army Nursing Services (DANS) and Matron in Chief Army, Col. B. C. McEvilly

The Royal Air Force

THE QUEEN

MARSHALS OF THE ROYAL AIR FORCE

HRH The Prince Philip, Duke of Edinburgh, KG, KT, OM, GBE, AC, QSO, PC, *apptd* 1953

Sir John Grandy, GCB, GCVO, KBE, DSO, *apptd* 1971

Sir Denis Spotswood, GCB, CBE, DSO, DFC, *apptd* 1974

Sir Michael Beetham, GCB, CBE, DFC, AFC, *apptd* 1982

Sir Keith Williamson, GCB, AFC, *apptd* 1985

The Lord Craig of Radley, GCB, OBE, *apptd* 1988

AIR CHIEF MARSHALS

Johns, Sir Richard, GCB, CBE, LVO, ADC (*Chief of Air Staff*)

Squire, Sir Peter, KCB, DFC, AFC, ADC (*Chief of the Air Staff*) (*Air Officer Commanding-in-Chief, HQ Strike Command, and Commander Allied Air Forces NW Europe*)

Bagnall, Sir Anthony, KCB, OBE (*Commander-in-Chief Strike Command*)

AIR MARSHALS

Day, Sir John, KCB, OBE (*Air Member for Personnel/ C.-in-C., Personnel and Training Command*)

Coville, Sir Christopher, KCB (*Deputy C.-in-C., Allied Forces Central Europe*)

Jenner, T. I., CB (*Chief of Staff and Deputy C.-in-C., HQ Strike Command*)

Norriss, Sir Peter, KBE, CB, AFC (*Deputy Chief of Defence Procurement (Operations) and Controller of the Navy*)

Pledger, M. D., OBE, AFC (*Deputy CDS (Personnel)*)

Goodall, R. H., CB, CBE, AFC (*Chief of Staff, Component Command Air North*)

Spink, C. R., CBE (*Director General, Saudi Arabia Armed Forces Project*)

AIR VICE-MARSHALS

Stables, A. J., CBE (*due to retire Nov 2000*)

French, J. C., CBE (*Director-General, Intelligence and Geographic Resources*)

Thompson, J. H., CB (*Defence Attache and Head of British Defence Staff Washington*)

Stewart, I. M., AFC (*Air Secretary and Chief Executive, RAF Personnel Management Agency*)

Weeden, J. (*Director, Legal Services (RAF)*)

Wright, R. A., AFC (*Chief of Staff, HQ Personnel and Training Command and Asst Chief of Staff Policy and Requirements SHAPE*)

McIntyre, I. G., QHDS (*Chief Executive, Defence Dental Agency*)

Sharples, C. J., QHP (*Director-General, Medical Services (RAF)*)

Burridge, B. K., CBE (*Commandant, Joint Services Command and Staff College*)

Filbey, K. D., CBE (*AOC No. 38 Group*)

Sturley, P.O., CB, MBE (*Asst Chief of the Air Staff*)

Henderson, P. W., CB, MBE (*Director-General, Support Management, HQ Logistics Command*)

Nicholl, S. M., CBE, AFC (*Asst CDS Operational Requirements (Air Systems)*)

Niven, D. M., CBE (*Commander, Joint Helicopter Command*)

Scott, P. J. (*Air Officer Logistics and Communications Information Systems, HQ Strike Command*)

Burton, A. J., OBE (*Air Officer Administration, HQ Strike Command*)

Rimmer, T. W., OBE (*Commander British Forces Cyprus and Administrator of the Sovereign Base Areas of Akrotiri and Dhekelia*)

Nicholson, A. A., CBE, LVO (*Integration and Aerospace Adviser, Defence Procurement Agency*)

HRH The Prince of Wales, KG, KT, GCB and Great Master of the Order of the Bath, AK, QSO, PC, ADC(P)

Gardiner, M. J., OBE (*Deputy Commander, Interim Combined Air Operations Centre No. 4*)

Couzens, D. C. (*Asst CDS (Logistics)*)

Liddell, P. (*Air Officer Communications Information Systems and Support Services*)

Harris, P. V., AFC

Arscott, J. R. D. (*Director, Airspace Policy*)

Skinner, G., CBE (*Air Officer C.-in-C., HQ Logistics Command*)

Corbitt, I. S., (*Air Officer Training and Chief Executive, Training Group Defence Agency*)

Roser, P. W., MBE (*Senior Directing Staff (Air)*, Royal College of Defence Studies)

Davison, C., MBE (*Air Officer Administration and Air Officer Commanding Directly Administered Units, HQ Personnel and Training Command*)

Sudborough, N.J., OBE (*Deputy Chief of Staff Operations Strike Command*)

Torpy, G. L. CBE, DSO (*Asst CDS (Operations)*)

Mackay, H. G., OBE, AFC (*Commandant, RAF College, Cranwell*)

Davidson, C. M., (*Air Officer Administration and Air Officer Commanding Directly Administered Units Headquarters Personnel and Training Command*)

CONSTITUTION OF THE ROYAL AIR FORCE

The RAF consists of three commands: Strike Command, Personnel and Training Command and Logistics Command. Strike Command is responsible for all the RAF's front-line forces. The restructured Strike Command, implemented on 1 April 2000, was split into three organisational groups, each responsible for specific operational duties. No 1 Group now contains the tactical fast jet forces, with No 2 Group providing the overarching enabling forces – Air Transport, Air Refuelling and Strategic Reconnaissance. No 3 Group is comprised of the Nimrod MPA force, Search and Rescue helicopters and the newly created Joint Force 2000 – a combination of the RAF Harrier GR7 and RN Harrier FA2 squadrons. Personnel and Training Command is responsible for personnel administration and training in the RAF. Logistics Command is responsible for all logistics, engineering and material support.

Enquiries regarding records of serving officers should be directed to the RAF Personnel Management Agency (*see* Defence Agencies, above).

RAF EQUIPMENT *as at 1 July 2000*

AIRCRAFT

Tornado ADV	93
Tornado IDS	127
Harrier	64
Jaguar	53
Canberra	7
Nimrod	27
VC10	24
Tristar	9
Hercules	55
BAe 125	6
BAe 146	3
Sentry	7
Hawk	107
Bulldog	105
Domenie	10
Islander	2
Jetstream	11
Tucano	86

HELICOPTERS

Chinook	38
Puma	41
Sea King	25
Wessex	15
Gazelle	1

ROYAL AUXILIARY AIR FORCE (RAuxAF)

Formed in 1924, the Auxiliary Air Force received the prefix 'Royal' in 1947 in recognition of its war record. The RAuxAF amalgamated with the Royal Air Force Volunteer Reserve in 1997. The RAuxAF supports the RAF in many roles, including maritime air operations, air and ground defence of airfields, air movements, aero-medical evacuation, intelligence and public relations.

The minimum annual commitment for reservists is 27 days, including 15 days' continuous training. Pay scales are equivalent to regular rates less a percentage, made on a pro-rata daily basis. An annual bounty is also payable, the amount depending on the length of service.

Air Commodore-in-Chief, HM The Queen

PRINCESS MARY'S ROYAL AIR FORCE NURSING SERVICE

The Princess Mary's Royal Air Force Nursing Service (PMRAFNS) was formed on 1st June 1918 as the Royal Air Force Nursing Service. In June 1923, His Majesty King George V gave his Royal Assent for the Royal Air Force Nursing Service to be known as the Princess Mary's Royal Air Force Nursing Service. Men were integrated into the PMRAFNS in 1980 and now serve as officers and other ranks. Student nurse training is undertaken and qualified RN's, RM's and RMN's are recruited to the commissioned branches of the PMRAFNS.

Patron and Air Chief Commandant, HRH Princess Alexandra, the Hon. Lady Ogilvy, GCVO

Matron-in-Chief and Director RAF Nursing Service, Air Cdre R.H. Williams

SERVICE SALARIES

The following rates of pay apply from 1 April 2000.

OFFICERS' SALARIES

MAIN SCALE

The pay rates shown are for Army personnel. The rates apply also to personnel of equivalent rank and pay band in the other services (*see* page 407 for table of relative ranks).

Rank	Daily	Annual
Second Lieutenant	£49.66	£18,125.90
Lieutenant		
On appointment	£59.70	£21,790.50
After 1 year in rank	£61.27	£22,363.55
After 2 years in rank	£62.84	£22,936.60
After 3 years in rank	£64.41	£23,509.65
After 4 years in rank	£65.98	£24,082.70
Captain		
On appointment	£76.12	£27,783.80
After 1 year in rank	£78.18	£28,535.70
After 2 years in rank	£80.24	£29,287.60
After 3 years in rank	£82.30	£30,039.50
After 4 years in rank	£84.36	£30,791.40
After 5 years in rank	£86.42	£31,543.30
After 6 years in rank	£88.48	£32,295.20
Major		
On appointment	£95.89	£34,999.85
After 1 year in rank	£98.26	£35,864.90
After 2 years in rank	£100.63	£36,729.95
After 3 years in rank	£103.00	£37,595.00
After 4 years in rank	£105.37	£38,460.05
After 5 years in rank	£107.74	£39,325.10
After 6 years in rank	£110.11	£40,190.15
After 7 years in rank	£112.48	£41,055.20
After 8 years in rank	£114.85	£41,920.25
Special List Lieutenant-Colonel	£132.64	£48,413.60
Lieutenant-Colonel		
On appointment with less than 19 years' service	£135.26	£49,369.90
After 2 years in the rank or with 19 years' service	£138.82	£50,669.30

Rank	Daily	Annual
Lieutenant-Colonel *contd*		
After 4 years in the rank or with 21 years' service	£142.38	£51,968.70
After 6 years in the rank or with 23 years' service	£145.94	£53,268.10
After 8 years in the rank or with 25 years' service	£149.50	£54,567.50
Colonel		
On appointment	£156.63	£57,169.95
After 2 years in the rank	£160.75	£58,673.75
After 4 years in the rank	£164.87	£60,177.55
After 6 years in the rank	£168.99	£61,681.35
After 8 years in the rank	£173.11	£63,185.15
Brigadier	£191.31	£69.828.15
Major-General		
Range 1	£201.32	£73,481
Range 2	£207.84	£75,861
Range 3	£216.06	£78,862
Lieutenant-General		
Range 4	£229.42	£83,740
Range 5	£250.13	£91,296
General		
Range 6	£307.43	£112,211
Range 7	£325.05	£118,642
Range 8	£401.77	£146,645

Field Marshal – appointments to this rank will not usually be made in peacetime. The salary for existing holders of the rank is equivalent to the salary of a range 8 General

---

SALARIES OF OFFICERS COMMISSIONED FROM THE RANKS (LIEUTENANTS AND CAPTAINS ONLY)

YEARS OF COMMISSIONED SERVICE	YEARS OF NON-COMMISSIONED SERVICE FROM AGE 18					
	Less than 12 years		12 years but less than 15 years		15 years or more	
	Daily	Annual	Daily	Annual	Daily	Annual
On commissioning	£83.86	£30,609	£87.89	£32,080	£91.92	£33,551
After 1 year's service	£85.88	£31,346	£89.91	£32,817	£93.96	£34,295
After 2 years' service	£87.89	£32,080	£91.92	£33,551	£95.26	£34,770
After 3 years' service	£89.91	£32,817	£93.96	£34,295	£96.56	£35,244
After 4 years' service	£91.92	£33,551	£95.26	£34,770	£97.86	£35,719
After 5 years' service	£93.96	£34,295	£96.56	£35,244	£99.16	£36,193
After 6 years' service	£95.26	£34,770	£97.86	£35,719	£100.46	£36,668
After 8 years' service	£96.56	£35,244	£99.16	£36,193	£101.76	£37,142
After 10 years' service	£97.86	£35,719	£100.46	£36,668	£101.76	£37,142
After 12 years' service	£99.16	£36,193	£101.76	£37,142	£101.76	£37,142
After 14 years' service	£100.46	£36,668	£101.76	£37,142	£101.76	£37,142
After 16 years' service	£101.76	£37,142	£101.76	£37,142	£101.76	£37,142

SOLDIERS' SALARIES

The pay structure below officer level is divided into pay bands. Jobs at each rank are allocated to bands according to their score in the job evaluation system. Length of service is from age 18.

Scale A: committed to serve for less than 6 years, or those with less than 9 years' service who are serving on Open Engagement

Scale B: committed to serve for 6 years but less than 9 years

Scale C: committed to serve for 9 years or more, or those with more than 9 years' service who are serving on Open Engagement

Daily rates of pay effective from 1 April 2000 are:

RANK   SCALE A

	Band 1	Band 2	Band 3	
Private				
Class 4	£28.34	—	—	
Class 3	£31.89	£37.01	£42.70	
Class 2	£35.64	£40.81	£46.49	
Class 1	£38.76	£43.92	£49.59	
Lance Corporal				
Class 3	£38.76	£43.92	£49.59	
Class 2	£41.26	£46.41	£52.53	
Class 1	£44.38	£49.53	£55.66	
Corporal				
Class 2	£47.18	£52.29	£58.38	
Class 1	£50.65	£55.74	£61.83	
	Band 4	Band 5	Band 6	Band 7
Sergeant	£55.71	£61.24	£67.28	—
Staff Sergeant	£58.90	£64.42	£70.50	£77.79
Warrant Officer				
Class 2	£62.97	£68.52	£75.97	£83.44
Class 1	£67.15	£72.69	£80.24	£87.68

SCALE B

	Band 1	Band 2	Band 3	
Private				
Class 4	£28.64	—	—	
Class 3	£32.19	£37.31	£43.00	
Class 2	£35.94	£41.11	£46.79	
Class 1	£39.06	£44.22	£49.89	

SCALE B

	Band 1	Band 2	Band 3	
Lance Corporal				
Class 3	£39.06	£44.22	£49.89	
Class 2	£41.56	£46.71	£52.83	
Class 1	£44.68	£49.83	£55.96	
Corporal				
Class 2	£47.48	£52.59	£58.68	
Class 1	£50.95	£56.04	£62.13	
	Band 4	Band 5	Band 6	Band 7
Sergeant	£56.01	£61.54	£67.58	—
Staff Sergeant	£59.20	£64.72	£70.80	£78.09
Warrant Officer				
Class 2	£63.27	£68.82	£76.27	£83.74
Class 1	£67.45	£72.99	£80.54	£87.98

SCALE C

	Band 1	Band 2	Band 3	
Private				
Class 4	£29.09	—	—	
Class 3	£32.64	£37.76	£43.45	
Class 2	£36.39	£41.56	£47.24	
Class 1	£39.51	£44.67	£50.34	
Lance Corporal				
Class 3	£39.51	£44.67	£50.34	
Class 2	£42.01	£47.16	£53.28	
Class 1	£45.13	£50.28	£56.41	
Corporal				
Class 2	£47.93	£53.04	£59.13	
Class 1	£51.40	£56.49	£62.58	
	Band 4	Band 5	Band 6	Band 7
Sergeant	£56.46	£61.99	£68.03	—
Staff Sergeant	£59.65	£65.17	£71.25	£78.54
Warrant Officer				
Class 2	£63.72	£69.27	£76.72	£84.19
Class 1	£67.90	£73.44	£80.99	£88.43

RELATIVE RANK – ARMED FORCES

Royal Navy	Army	Royal Air Force
1 Admiral of the Fleet	1 Field Marshal	1 Marshal of the RAF
2 Admiral (Adm.)	2 General (Gen.)	2 Air Chief Marshal
3 Vice-Admiral (Vice-Adm.)	3 Lieutenant-General (Lt.-Gen.)	3 Air Marshal
4 Rear-Admiral (Rear-Adm.)	4 Major-General (Maj.-Gen.)	4 Air Vice-Marshal
5 Commodore (Cdre)	5 Brigadier (Brig.)	5 Air Commodore (Air Cdre)
6 Captain (Capt.)	6 Colonel (Col.)	6 Group Captain (Gp Capt.)
7 Commander (Cdr.)	7 Lieutenant-Colonel (Lt.-Col.)	7 Wing Commander (Wg Cdr.)
8 Lieutenant-Commander (Lt.-Cdr.)	8 Major (Maj.)	8 Squadron Leader (Sqn Ldr)
9 Lieutenant (Lt.)	9 Captain (Capt.)	9 Flight Lieutenant (Flt. Lt.)
10 Sub-Lieutenant (Sub-Lt.)	10 Lieutenant (Lt.)	10 Flying Officer (FO)
11 Acting Sub-Lieutenant (Acting Sub-Lt.)	11 Second Lieutenant (2nd Lt.)	11 Pilot Officer (PO)

SERVICE RETIRED PAY ON COMPULSORY RETIREMENT

Those who leave the services having served at least five years, but not long enough to qualify for the appropriate immediate pension, now qualify for a preserved pension and terminal grant, both of which are payable at age 60. The tax-free resettlement grants shown below are payable on release to those who qualify for a preserved pension and who have completed nine years service from age 21 (officers) or 12 years from age 18 (other ranks).

The annual rates for army personnel are given. The rates apply also to personnel of equivalent rank in the other services, including the nursing services.

OFFICERS

Applicable to officers who give full pay service on the active list on or after 31 March 2000. Senior officers (*) can elect to receive a pension calculated as a percentage of their pensionable earnings.

No. of years reckonable service over age 21	Capt. and below	Major	Lt.-Col.	Colonel	Brigadier	Major-General*	Lieutenant-General*	General*
16	£9,204	£10,961	£14,441	—	—	—	—	—
17	£9,628	£11,482	£15,109	—	—	—	—	—
18	£10,052	£12,002	£15,777	£18,269	—	—	—	—
19	£10,477	£12,523	£16,445	£19,043	—	—	—	—
20	£10,901	£13,043	£17,113	£19,816	—	—	—	—
21	£11,325	£13,564	£17,781	£20,590	—	—	—	—
22	£11,749	£14,084	£18,449	£21,363	£24,556	—	—	—
23	£12,173	£14,605	£19,117	£22,137	£25,332	—	—	—
24	£12,597	£15,125	£19,785	£22,910	£26,108	£28,443	—	—
25	£13,022	£15,646	£20,453	£23,684	£26,884	£29,289	—	—
26	£13,446	£16,167	£21,121	£24,457	£27,660	£30,134	—	—
27	£13,870	£16,687	£21,789	£25,231	£28,436	£30,979	£35,643	—
28	£14,294	£17,208	£22,457	£26,004	£29,212	£31,824	£36,616	—
29	£14,718	£17,728	£23,125	£26,778	£29,988	£32,670	£37,588	—
30	£15,142	£18,249	£23,793	£27,551	£30,763	£33,515	£38,561	£50,925
31	£15,567	£18,769	£24,461	£28,325	£31,539	£34,360	£39,533	£52,209
32	£15,991	£19,290	£25,124	£29,098	£32,315	£35,206	£40,506	£53,493
33	£16,415	£19,810	£25,797	£29,872	£33,091	£36,051	£41,478	£54,777
34	£16,839	£20,331	£26,465	£30,645	£33,867	£36,896	£42,451	£56,062

WARRANT OFFICERS, NCOs AND PRIVATES

Applicable to soldiers who give full pay service on or after 31 March 2000.

No. of years reckonable service	Below Corporal	Corporal	Sergeant	Staff Sergeant	Warrant Officer Class II	Warrant Officer Class I
22	£5,344	£6,751	£7,477	£8,512	£8,799	£9,727
23	£5,530	£6,987	£7,738	£8,809	£9,111	£10,076
24	£5,717	£7,222	£7,999	£9,106	£9,422	£10,426
25	£5,903	£7,458	£8,260	£9,403	£9,734	£10,775
26	£6,090	£7,693	£8,521	£9,701	£10,045	£11,125
27	£6,276	£7,929	£8,782	£9,998	£10,357	£11,474
28	£6,463	£8,165	£9,043	£10,295	£10,669	£11,824
29	£6,649	£8,400	£9,304	£10,592	£10,980	£12,173
30	£6,836	£8,636	£9,565	£10,889	£11,292	£12,523
31	£7,022	£8,871	£9,826	£11,186	£11,603	£12,872
32	£7,209	£9,107	£10,087	£11,483	£11,915	£13,222
33	£7,395	£9,343	£10,348	£11,780	£12,227	£13,571
34	£7,582	£9,578	£10,609	£12,078	£12,538	£13,921
35	£7,768	£9,814	£10,870	£12,375	£12,850	£14,270
36	£7,955	£10,049	£11,131	£12,672	£13,161	£14,620
37	£8,141	£10,285	£11,392	£12,969	£13,473	£14,969

RESETTLEMENT GRANTS

Terminal grants are in each case three times the rate of retired pay or pension. There are special rates of retired pay for certain other ranks not shown above. Lower rates are payable in cases of voluntary retirement.

A gratuity of £3,130 is payable for officers with short service commissions for each year completed. Resettlement grants are: officers £10,765; non-commissioned ranks £7,034.

Religion in the UK

There are two established, i.e. state, churches in the United Kingdom: the Church of England and the Church of Scotland. There are no established churches in Wales or Northern Ireland, though the Church in Wales, the Scottish Episcopal Church and the Church of Ireland are members of the Anglican Communion.

About 65 per cent of the population of the UK (38.1 million people) would call itself broadly Christian (in the Trinitarian sense), with 45 per cent (26.1 million) identifying with Anglican churches, 10 per cent (5.7 million) with the Roman Catholic Church, 4 per cent (2.6 million) with Presbyterian Churches, 2 per cent (1.3 million) with the Methodist Churches and 4 per cent (2.6 million) with other Christian churches; but only about 8.7 per cent of the population of Great Britain (3.98 million people) regularly attends a Christian church. Church attendance in Northern Ireland is estimated at 30–35 per cent of the population.

About 2 per cent of the population (1.3 million people) is affiliated to non-Trinitarian churches, e.g. Jehovah s Witnesses, the Church of Jesus Christ of Latter-Day Saints (Mormons), the Church of Christ, Scientist and the Unitarian churches.

A further 5 per cent of the population (3.25 million people) are adherents of other faiths, including Hinduism, Islam, Judaism and Sikhism.

About 28 per cent of the population is non-religious.

ADHERENTS TO RELIGIONS IN UK *(millions)*

	1975	1985	1995
Christian (Trinitarian)	40.2	39.1	38.1
Non-Trinitarian	0.7	1.0	1.3
Hindu	0.3	0.4	0.4
Jew	0.4	0.3	0.3
Muslim	0.4	0.9	1.2
Sikh	0.2	0.3	0.6
Other	0.1	0.3	0.3
Total	42.3	42.3	42.2

PERCENTAGE OF UK POPULATION ADHERING TO RELIGIONS

	1975	1985	1995
Christian (Trinitarian)	72	69	65
Non-Trinitarian	1	2	2
Non-Christian religions	3	3	5
All religions	76	74	72

Source: Christian Research/Paternoster Publishing – *UK Christian Handbook Religious Trends No. 1 1998–9;* figures in text are for 1995

INTER-CHURCH AND INTER-FAITH CO-OPERATION

The main umbrella body for the Christian churches in the UK is the Churches Together in Britain and Ireland. There are also ecumenical bodies in each of the constituent countries of the UK: Churches Together in England, Action of Churches Together in Scotland, CYTUN (Churches Together in Wales), and the Irish Council of Churches. The Free Churches' Council comprises most of the Free Churches in England and Wales, and the Evangelical Alliance represents evangelical Christians.

The Inter Faith Network for the United Kingdom promotes co-operation between faiths, and the Council of Christians and Jews works to improve relations between the two religions. Churches Together in Britain and Ireland also has a Commission on Inter Faith Relations.

ACTION OF CHURCHES TOGETHER IN SCOTLAND, Scottish Churches House, Kirk Street, Dunblane, Perthshire FK15 0AJ. Tel: 01786-823588. *General Secretary,* Revd Dr K. Franz
CHURCHES TOGETHER IN BRITAIN AND IRELAND, Inter-Church House, 35–41 Lower Marsh, London SE1 7SA. Tel: 020-7523 2121. *General Secretary,* Dr D. Goodbourn
CHURCHES TOGETHER IN ENGLAND, 101 Queen Victoria Street, London EC4V 4EN. Tel: 020-7332 8230/1/2. *Executive Officer,* Ms J. Lampard
COUNCIL OF CHRISTIANS AND JEWS, Drayton House, 30 Gordon Street, London WC1H 0AN. Tel: 020-7388 3322. *Director,* Sr M. Shepherd, NDS
CYTUN (CHURCHES TOGETHER IN WALES), Ty John Penri, 11 St Helen's Road, Swansea SA1 4AL. Tel: 01792-460876. *General Secretary,* Revd G. Abraham-Williams
EVANGELICAL ALLIANCE, Whitefield House, 186 Kennington Park Road, London SE11 4BT. Tel: 020-7207 2100. *General Director,* Revd J. Edwards
FREE CHURCHES' COUNCIL, 27 Tavistock Square, London WC1H 9HH. Tel: 020-7387 8413. *General Secretary,* Revd G. H. Roper
INTER FAITH NETWORK FOR THE UNITED KINGDOM, 5–7 Tavistock Place, London WC1H 9SN. Tel: 020-7388 0008. *Director,* B. Pearce
IRISH COUNCIL OF CHURCHES, Inter-Church Centre, 48 Elmwood Avenue, Belfast BT9 6AZ. Tel: 028-9066 3145. *General Secretary,* Dr R. D. Stevens

Christianity

Christianity is a monotheistic faith based on the person and teachings of Jesus Christ and all Christian denominations claim his authority. Central to its teaching is the concept of God and his son Jesus Christ, who was crucified and resurrected in order to enable mankind to attain salvation.

The Jewish scriptures predicted the coming of a *Messiah,* an 'anointed one', who would bring salvation. To Christians, Jesus of Nazareth, a Jewish rabbi (teacher), who was born in Palestine, was the promised Messiah. Jesus' birth, teachings, crucifixion and subsequent resurrection are recorded in the *Gospels,* which, together with other scriptures that summarise Christian belief, form the *New Testament.* This, together with the Hebrew scriptures, entitled the *Old Testament* by Christians, makes up the *Bible,* the sacred texts of Christianity.

BELIEFS

Christians believe that sin distanced mankind from God, and that Jesus was the Son of God, sent to redeem mankind from that sin by his death. In addition, many believe that Jesus will return again at some future date, triumph over evil and establish a kingdom on earth, thus inaugurating a new age. The Gospel assures Christians that those who believe in Jesus and obey his teachings will be forgiven their sins and will be resurrected from the dead.

PRACTICES

Christian practices vary widely between different Christian churches, but prayer is universal to all, as is charity, giving for the maintenance of the church buildings, for the work of the church, and to the poor and needy. In addition, certain days of observance, i.e. the *Sabbath*, *Easter*, and *Christmas* are celebrated by most Christians. The Orthodox, Roman Catholic and Anglican churches celebrate many more days of observance, based on saints and significant events in the life of Jesus. The belief in sacraments, physical signs believed to have been ordained by Jesus Christ to symbolise and convey spiritual gifts, varies greatly between Christian denominations; *Baptism* and the *Eucharist* are practised by most Christians. Baptism, symbolising repentance and faith in Jesus is an act marking entry into the Christian community; the Eucharist, the ritual re-enactment of the Last Supper, Jesus' final meal with his disciples, is also practised by most denominations. Other sacraments, such as anointing the sick, the laying on of hands to symbolise the passing on of the office of priesthood or to heal the sick and speaking in tongues, where it is believed that the person is possessed by the Holy Spirit, the Spirit of God, are less common. In denominations where infant baptism is practised, confirmation is common, where the person now repeats the commitments made for him or her at infancy. Matrimony and the ordination of priests are also widely believed to be sacraments. Many Protestants only view baptism and the Eucharist as sacraments; the Quakers and the Salvation Army reject the use of sacraments.

Most Christians believe that God actively guides the Church.

THE EARLY CHURCH

The apostles were Jesus' first converts and are recognised by Christians as the founders of the Christian community. The new faith spread rapidly throughout the eastern provinces of the Roman Empire. Early Christianity was subject to great persecution until AD 313, when Emperor Constantine's Edict of Toleration confirmed its right to exist and it became established as the religion of the Roman Empire in AD 381.

The Christian faith was slowly formulated in the first millennium of the Christian era. Between AD 325 and 787 there were seven Oecumenical Councils at which bishops from the entire Christian world assembled to resolve various doctrinal disputes. The estrangement between East and West began after Constantine moved the centre of the Roman Empire from Rome to Constantinople, and it grew after the division of the Roman Empire into eastern and western halves. Linguistic and cultural differences between Greek East and Latin West served to encourage separate ecclesiastical developments which became pronounced in the tenth and early 11th centuries.

Administration of the church was divided between five ancient patriarchates: Rome and all the West, Constantinople (the imperial city – the 'New Rome'), Jerusalem and all Palestine, Antioch and all the East, and Alexandria and all Africa. Of these, only Rome was in the Latin West and after the schism in 1054, Rome developed a structure of authority centralised on the Papacy, while the Orthodox East maintained the style of localised administration.

Papal authority over the doctrine and jurisdiction of the Church in western Europe was unrivalled after the split with the Eastern Orthodox Church until the Protestant Reformation in the 16th century.

CHRISTIANITY IN BRITAIN

An English Church already existed when Pope Gregory sent Augustine to evangelise the English in AD 596. Conflicts between Church and State during the Middle Ages culminated in the Act of Supremacy in 1534, which repudiated papal supremacy and declared King Henry VIII to be the supreme head of the Church in England. Since 1559 the English monarch has been termed the Supreme Governor of the Church of England.

In 1560 the jurisdiction of the Roman Catholic Church in Scotland was abolished and the first assembly of the Church of Scotland ratified the Confession of Faith, drawn up by a committee including John Knox. In 1592 Parliament passed an Act guaranteeing the liberties of the Church and its presbyterian government. King James VI (James I of England) and later Stuart monarchs attempted to reintroduce episcopacy, but a presbyterian church was finally restored in 1690 and secured by the Act of Settlement (1690) and the Act of Union (1707).

PORVOO DECLARATION

The Porvoo Declaration was drawn up by representatives of the British and Irish Anglican churches and the Nordic and Baltic Lutheran churches and was approved by the General Synod of the Church of England in July 1995. Churches that approve the Declaration regard baptised members of each other's churches as members of their own, and allow free interchange of episcopally ordained ministers within the rules of each church.

Non-Christian Religions

BAHÁ'Í FAITH

Mirza Husayn-'Ali, known as *Baha'u'lláh* (Glory of God) was born in Iran in 1817 and became a follower of the *Bab*, a religious reformer and prophet who was imprisoned for his beliefs and executed on the grounds of heresy in 1850. *Baha'u'lláh* was himself imprisoned in 1852, and in 1853 he had a vision that he was the Promised One foretold by the *Bab*.

The Bahá'í faith recognises the unity and relativity of religious truth and teaches that there is only one God, whose will has been revealed to mankind by a series of messengers, such as Zoroaster, Abraham, Moses, Buddha, Krishna, Christ, Muhammad, the Báb and Bahá'u'lláh.

THE BAHÁ'Í INFORMATION OFFICE, 27 Rutland Gate, London SW7 1PD. Tel: 020-7584 2566

BUDDHISM

Buddhism originated in northern India, in the teachings of Siddharta Gautama, who was born near Kapilavastu about 560 BC.

Fundamental to Buddhism is the concept that there is no such thing as a permanent soul or self; when someone dies, consciousness is the only one of the elements of which they were composed which is lost. All the other elements regroup in a new body and carry with them the consequences of the conduct of the earlier life (known as the law of *karma*). This cycle of death and rebirth is broken only when the state of *nirvana* has been reached. Buddhism steers a middle path between belief in personal immortality and belief in death as the final end.

The Four Noble Truths of Buddhism (*dukkha*, suffering; *tanha*, a thirst or desire for continued existence which causes dukkha; *nirvana*, the final liberation from desire and ignorance; and *ariya*, the path to nirvana) are all held to be universal and to sum up the *dhamma* or true nature of life. Necessary qualities to promote spiritual development are *sila* (morality), *samadhi* (meditation) and *panna* (wisdom).

There are two main schools of Buddhism: *Theravada* Buddhism, the earliest extant school, which is more traditional, and *Mahayana* Buddhism, which began to develop about 100 years after the Buddha's death and is more liberal; it teaches that all people may attain Buddhahood. Important schools which have developed within Mahayana Buddhism are *Zen* Buddhism, *Nichiren* Buddhism and *Pure Land* Buddhism or *Amidism*. There are also distinctive Tibetan forms of Buddhism. Buddhism began to establish itself in the West in the early 20th century.

The scripture of Theravada Buddhism is the *Pali Canon*, which dates from the first century BC. Mahayana Buddhism uses a Sanskrit version of the Pali Canon but also has many other works of scripture.

There are estimated to be at least 300 million Buddhists world-wide, and more than 500 groups and centres, an estimated 25,000 adherents and up to 20 temples or monasteries in the UK.

BRITISH BUDDHIST ASSOCIATION, 11 Biddulph Road, London W9. Tel: 020-7286 5575
FRIENDS OF THE WESTERN BUDDHIST ORDER, Padmaloka , Lesingham House, Surlingham, Norwich NR14 7AL. Tel: 01508- 88310
SOKA GAKKAI UK, Taplow Court, Taplow, Maidenhead, Berkshire SL6 0ER. Tel: 01628-773163
THE BUDDHIST SOCIETY, 58 Eccleston Square, London SW1V1PH. Tel: 020-7834 5858. *General Secretary*, R. C. Maddox
TIBET FOUNDATION, 2 Bloomsbury Way, London WC1A 2SH. Tel: 020-7404 2889

HINDUISM

Hinduism has no historical founder but had become highly developed in India by about 1200 BC. Its adherents originally called themselves Aryans; Muslim invaders first called the Aryans 'Hindus' (derived from 'Sindhu', the name of the river Indus) in the eighth century.

Most Hindus hold that *satya* (truthfulness), *ahimsa* (non-violence), honesty, physical labour and tolerance of other faiths are essential for good living. They believe in one supreme spirit (*Brahman*), and in the transmigration of *atman* (the soul). Most Hindus accept the doctrine of *karma* (consequences of actions), the concept of *samsara* (successive lives) and the possibility of all atmans achieving *moksha* (liberation from samsara) through *jnana* (knowledge), *yoga* (meditation), *karma* (work or action) and *bhakti* (devotion).

Most Hindus offer worship to *murtis* (images or statues) representing different aspects of Brahman, and follow their *dharma* (religious and social duty) according to the traditions of their *varna* (social class), *ashrama* (stage in life), *jati* (caste) and *kula* (family).

Hinduism's sacred texts are divided into *shruti* ('heard' or divinely inspired), including the *Vedas*; or *smriti* ('remembered' tradition), including the *Ramayana*, the *Mahabharata*, the *Puranas* (ancient myths), and the sacred law books. Most Hindus recognise the authority of the *Vedas*, the oldest holy books, and accept the philosophical teachings of the *Upanishads*, the *Vedanta Sutras* and the *Bhagavad-Gita*.

Brahman is formless, limitless and all-pervading, and is represented in worship by murtis which may be male or female and in the form of a human, animal or bird. Brahma, Vishnu and Shiva are the most important gods worshipped by Hindus; their respective consorts are Saraswati, Lakshmi and Durga or Parvati, also known as Shakti. There are believed to have been ten *avatars* (incarnations) of Vishnu, of whom the most important are Rama and Krishna. Other popular gods are Ganesha, Hanuman and Subrahmanyam. All gods are seen as aspects of the supreme God, not as competing deities.

There are an estimated 800 million Hindus world-wide; there are about 380,000 adherents and over 150 temples in the UK.

ARYA PRATINIDHI SABHA (UK) AND ARYA SAMAJ LONDON, 69A Argyle Road, London W13 0LY. Tel: 020-8991 1732. *President*, Prof. S. N. Bharadwaj
BHARATIYA VIDYA BHAVAN, Institute of Indian Art and Culture, 4A Castletown Road, London W14 9HQ. Tel: 020-7381 4608. *Executive Director*, Dr M. N. Nandakumara
INTERNATIONAL SOCIETY FOR KRISHNA CONSCIOUSNESS (ISKCON), Bhaktivedanta Manor, Dharam Marg, Hilfield Lane, Aldenham, Watford, Herts WD2 8EZ. Tel: 01923-857244. *Governing Body Commissioner*, P. Latai
NATIONAL COUNCIL OF HINDU TEMPLES (UK), Bhaktivedanta Manor, Dharam Marg, Hilfield Lane, Aldenham, Watford WD2 8EZ. Tel: 01923-856269/ 857244. *Secretary*, V. P. Aery
SWAMINARAYAN HINDU MISSION (SHREE SWAMINARAYAN MANDIR), 105–119 Brentfield Road, London NW10 8JP. Tel: 020-8965 2651. *Sadhu*, Atmaswarup Das
VISHWA HINDU PARISHAD (UK), 48 Wharfedale Gardens, Thornton Heath, Surrey CR76LB. Tel: 020-8684 9716. *General Secretary*, K. Ruparelia

ISLAM

Islam (which means 'peace arising from submission to the will of Allah' in Arabic) is a monotheistic religion which was taught in Arabia by the Prophet Muhammad, who was born in (Makkah) in AD 570. Islam spread to Egypt, North Africa, Spain and the borders of China in the century following the Prophet's death, and is now the predominant religion in Indonesia, the Near and Middle East, northern and parts of western Africa, Pakistan, Bangladesh, Malaysia and some of the former Soviet republics. There are also large Muslim communities in other countries.

For Muslims (adherents of Islam), there is one God (*Allah*), who holds absolute power. His commands were revealed to mankind through the prophets, who include Abraham, Moses and Jesus, but his message was gradually corrupted until revealed finally and in perfect form to Muhammad through the angel *Jibril* (Gabriel) over a period of 23 years. This last, incorruptible message has been recorded in the *Qur'an* (Koran), which contains 114 divisions called *surahs*, each made up of *ayahs*, and is held to be the essence of all previous scriptures. The *Ahadith* are the records of the Prophet Muhammad's deeds and sayings (the *Sunnah*) as recounted by his immediate followers. A culture and a system of law and theology gradually developed to form a distinctive Islamic civilisation. Islam makes no distinction between sacred and worldly affairs and provides rules for every aspect of human life. The *Shari'ah* is the sacred law of Islam based upon prescriptions derived from the Qur'an and the *Sunnah* of the Prophet.

The 'five pillars of Islam' are *shahadah* (a declaration of faith in the oneness and supremacy of Allah and the messengership of Muhammad); *salat* (formal prayer, to be performed five times a day facing the *Ka'bah* (sacred house) in the holy city of Makkah); *zakat* (welfare due); *sawm* (fasting during the month of Ramadan); and *hajj* (pilgrimage to Makkah); some Muslims would add *jihad* (striving for the cause of good and resistance to evil).

Two main groups developed among Muslims. *Sunni* Muslims accept the legitimacy of Muhammad's first four *caliphs* (successors as head of the Muslim community) and of the authority of the Muslim community as a whole. About 90 per cent of Muslims are Sunni Muslims. *Shi'ites* recognise only Muhammad's son-in-law Ali as his rightful successor and the *Imams* (descendants of Ali, not to be confused with *imams* (prayer leaders or religious teachers)) as the principal legitimate religious authority. The largest group within Shi'ism is *Twelver Shi'ism*, which has been the official school of law and theology in Iran since the 16th century; other subsects include the *Ismailis* and the *Druze*, the latter being an offshoot of the Ismailis and differing considerably from the main body of Muslims.

Islam was first known in western Europe in the eighth century when 800 years of Muslim rule began in Spain. Later, Islam spread to eastern Europe. More recently, Muslims came to Europe from Africa, the Middle East and Asia in the late 19th century. Both the Sunni and Shi'ah traditions are represented in Britain, but the majority of Muslims in Britain adhere to Sunni Islam.

There are about 1,000 million Muslims world-wide, with more than nearly two million adherents and about 1,200 mosques in Britain.

IMAMS AND MOSQUES COUNCIL, 20–22 Creffield Road, London W5 3RP. Tel: 020-8992 6636. *Director of the Council and Principal of the Muslim College*, Dr M. A. Z. Badawi

ISLAMIC CULTURAL CENTRE, 146 Park Road, London NW87RG. Tel: 020-7724 3363. *Director*, H. Al-Majed

MUSLIM COUNCIL OF BRITAIN, P.O. Box 52, Wembley, Middx HA9 7AL. Tel: 020-8903 9024. *Secretary-General*, Yousuf Bhailok

MUSLIM WORLD LEAGUE, 46 Goodge Street, London W1P 1FJ. Tel: 020-7636 7568. *Deputy Director*, G. Rahman

UNION OF MUSLIM ORGANISATIONS OF THE UK AND EIRE, 109 Campden Hill Road, London W8 7TL. Tel: 020-7229 0538/7221 6608. *General Secretary*, Dr S. A. Pasha

JAINISM

Jainism traces its history to Vardhamana Jnatiputra, known as *Mahavira* (The Great Hero) whose traditional dates were 599–527 BC. He was the last of a series of 24 *Jinas* (those who overcome) or *Tirthankaras* (Those who show a way across the ocean of life) stretching back to remote antiquity. Born to a noble family in north-eastern India, he renounced the world for the life of a wandering ascetic and after 12 years of austerity and meditation he attained enlightenment. He then preached his message until, at the age of 72, he passed away and reached *moksha*, total liberation from the cycle of death and rebirth.

Jains believe that the universe is eternal and self-subsisting: there is no omnipotent creator God ruling it and the destiny of the individual is in his or her own hands.

There are about 25,000 Jains in Britain, sizeable communities in North America and East Africa and smaller groups in many other countries.

JAIN CENTRE, Oxford Street, Leicester LE1 5XU Tel: 0116-254 3091

JUDAISM

Judaism is the oldest monotheistic faith. The primary authority of Judaism is the Hebrew Bible or *Tanakh*, which records how the descendants of Abraham were led by Moses out of their slavery in Egypt to Mount Sinai where God's law (*Torah*) was revealed to them as the chosen people. The *Talmud*, which consists of commentaries on the *Mishnah* (the first text of rabbinical Judaism), is also held to be authoritative, and may be divided into two main categories: the *halakah* (dealing with legal and ritual matters) and the *Aggadah* (dealing with theological and ethical matters not directly concerned with the regulation of conduct). The *Midrash* comprises rabbinic writings containing biblical interpretations in the spirit of the Aggadah. The *halakah* has become a source of division; Orthodox Jews regard Jewish law as derived from God and therefore unalterable; Reform and Liberal Jews seek to interpret it in the light of contemporary considerations; and Conservative Jews aim to maintain most of the traditional rituals but to allow changes in accordance with tradition. Reconstructionist Judaism, a 20th-century movement, regards Judaism as a culture rather than a theological system and accepts all forms of Jewish practice.

The family is the basic unit of Jewish ritual, with the synagogue playing an important role as the centre for public worship and religious study. A synagogue is led by a group of laymen who are elected to office. The Rabbi is primarily a teacher and spiritual guide. The Sabbath is the central religious observance. For details of the Jewish calendar, fasts and festivals, *see* page 85. Most British Jews are descendants of either the *Ashkenazim* of central and eastern Europe or the *Sephardim* of Spain, Portugal and the Middle East..

The Chief Rabbi of the United Hebrew Congregations of the Commonwealth is appointed by a Chief Rabbinate Conference, and is the rabbinical authority of the mainstream Orthodox sector of the Ashkenazi Jewish community. His authority is not recognised by the Reform Synagogues of Great Britain (the largest progressive group), the Union of Liberal and Progressive Synagogues, the Union of Orthodox Hebrew Congregations, the Federation of Synagogues, the Sephardi community, or the Assembly of Masorti Synagogues. He is, however, generally recognised both outside the Jewish community and within it as the public religious representative of the totality of British Jewry. The Chief Rabbi is President of the Beth Din of the United Synagogue.

A *Beth Din* (Court of Judgement) is a rabbinic court. The *Dayanim* (Assessors) adjudicate in disputes or on matters of Jewish law and tradition; they also oversee dietary law administration.

The Board of Deputies of British Jews, established in 1760, is the representative body of British Jewry.

There are over 12.5 million Jews world-wide; in Great Britain and Ireland there are an estimated 285,000 adherents and about 365 synagogues. Of these, 191 congregations and about 150 rabbis and ministers are under the jurisdiction of the Chief Rabbi; 99 orthodox congregations have a more independent status; and 79 congregations are outside the jurisdiction of the Chief Rabbi.

CHIEF RABBINATE, Adler House, 735 High Road, London N12 0US. Tel: 020-8343 6301. *Chief Rabbi*, Prof. Jonathan Sacks; *Executive Director*, Mrs S. Weinberg

BETH DIN (COURT OF THE CHIEF RABBI), 735 High Road, London N12 0US. Tel: 020-8343 6280. *Registrar*, D. Frei; *Dayanim*, Dayan C.Ehrentreu; Rabbi Dayan I. Binstock; Rabbi C. D. Kaplin; Dayan M. Gelley

BOARD OF DEPUTIES OF BRITISH JEWS, Commonwealth House, 1–19 New Oxford Street, London WC1A 1NU. Tel: 020-7543 5400. *President*, E. Tabachnik, QC; *Director-General*, N. A. Nagler

ASSEMBLY OF MASORTI SYNAGOGUES, 1097 Finchley Road, London NW11 0PU. Tel: 020-8201 8772. *Director*, Dr. H. Freedman

FEDERATION OF SYNAGOGUES, 65 Watford Way, London NW4 3AQ. Tel: 020-8202 2263. *Head of Administration*, G. D. Coleman

BETH DIN OF THE FEDERATION OF SYNAGOGUES, 65 Watford Way, London NW43AQ. Tel: 020-8202 2263. *Registrar*, Rabbi S. Zaiden; *Dayanim*, Dayan Y. Y. Lichtenstein, Dayan B. Berkovits, Dayan M. D. Elzas

REFORM SYNAGOGUES OF GREAT BRITAIN, The Sternberg Centre for Judaism, 80 East End Road, London N3 2SY. Tel: 020-8349 5640. *Chief Executive*, Rabbi T. Bayfield

SPANISH AND PORTUGUESE JEWS' CONGREGATION, 2 Ashworth Road, London W9 1JY. Tel: 020-7289 2573. *Chief Administrator and Secretary*, H. Miller

UNION OF LIBERAL AND PROGRESSIVE SYNAGOGUES, The Montagu Centre, 21 Maple Street, London W1P 6DS. Tel: 020-7580 1663. *Executive Director*, Rabbi Dr C. H. Middleburgh

UNION OF ORTHODOX HEBREW CONGREGATIONS, 140 Stamford Hill, London N16 6QT. Tel: 020-8802 6226.

UNITED SYNAGOGUE HEAD OFFICE, Adler House, 735 High Road, London N12 0US. Tel: 020-8343 8989. *Chief Executive*, George Willman

---

SIKHISM

The Sikh religion dates from the birth of Guru Nanak in the Punjab in 1469. 'Guru' means teacher but in Sikh tradition has come to represent the divine presence of God giving inner spiritual guidance. Nanak's role as the human vessel of the divine guru was passed on to nine successors, the last of whom (Guru Gobind Singh) died in 1708. The immortal guru is now held to reside in the sacred scripture, *Guru Granth Sahib*, and so to be present in all Sikh gatherings.

Guru Nanak taught that there is one God and that different religions are like different roads leading to the same destination. He condemned religious conflict, ritualism and caste prejudices. The fifth Guru, Guru Arjan Dev, largely compiled the Sikh Holy Book, a collection of hymns (*gurbani*) known as the *Adi Granth*. It includes the writings of the first five Gurus and the ninth Guru, and selected writings of Hindu and Muslim saints whose views are in accord with the Gurus' teachings. Guru Arjan Dev also built the Golden Temple at Amritsar, the centre of Sikhism. The tenth Guru, Guru Gobind Singh, passed on the guruship to the sacred scripture, Guru Granth Sahib. He also founded the *Khalsa*, an order intended to fight against tyranny and injustice. Male initiates to the order added 'Singh' to their given names and women added 'Kaur'. Guru Gobind Singh also made five symbols obligatory: *kaccha* (a special undergarment), *kara* (a steel bangle), *kirpan* (a small sword), *kesh* (long unshorn hair, and consequently the wearing of a turban), and *kangha* (a comb). These practices are still compulsory for those Sikhs who are initiated into the Khalsa (the *Amritdharis*). Those who do not seek initiation are known as *Sehajdharis*.

There are about 20 million Sikhs world-wide and about 400,000 adherents and 250 gurdwaras in Great Britain. Every gurdwara manages its own affairs and there is no central body in the UK. The Sikh Missionary Society provides an information service.

SIKH MISSIONARY SOCIETY UK, 10 Featherstone Road, Southall, Middx UB2 5AA. Tel: 020-8574 1902. *Hon. General Secretary*, K. S. Rai

WORLD SIKH FOUNDATION (THE SIKH COURIER INTERNATIONAL), 33 Wargrave Road, South Harrow, Middx HA2 8LL. Tel: 020-8864 9228. *Secretary*, Mrs H. B. Bharara

---

ZOROASTRIANISM

Zoroastrianism was founded by Zarathushtra (or Zoroaster in its hellenised form) in Persia. Linguistic analysis of the earliest extant Zoroastrian texts suggests that he lived around 1500 BC. Zarathushtra's words are recorded in five poems called the *Gathas*, which, together with other scriptures, forms the *Avestan*.

Zoroastrianism teaches that there is one God, *Ahura Mazda* (the Wise Lord), and that all creation stems ultimately from God; the Gathas teach that human beings have free will, are responsible for their own actions and can choose between good and evil: Choosing *Asha* (truth or righteousness) leads to happiness for the individual and society, whereas choosing evil leads to unhappiness and conflict.

WORLD ZOROASTRIAN ORGANISATION, 135 Tennison Road, London SE25 5NF.

The Churches

For changes notified after 31 August, *see* Stop-press

The Church of England

The Church of England is the established church in England and seeks to serve the nation through its dioceses and parishes. It traces its life back to the first coming of Christianity to England. Its position is defined by the ancient creeds of the Church and by the Thirty-nine articles of Religion (1571), the Book of Common Prayer (1662) and the Ordinal. The Church of England is thus both catholic and reformed. It is the mother church of the Anglican Communion.

THE ANGLICAN COMMUNION

The Anglican Communion consists of 40 independent provincial or national Christian churches throughout the world, many of which are in Commonwealth countries and originated from missionary activity by the Church of England. Every ten years all the bishops in the Communion meet at the Lambeth Conference, convened by the Archbishop of Canterbury. The Conference has no policy-making authority but is an important forum for discussing and forming consensus around issues of common concern. The Anglican Consultative Council was set up in 1968 to liaise between the member churches and provinces of the Anglican Communion. It meets every three years. Meetings of the Anglican primates have taken place every two years since 1979.

There are about 70 million Anglicans and 800 archbishops and bishops world-wide.

STRUCTURE

The Church of England is divided into the two provinces of Canterbury and York, each under an archbishop. The two provinces are subdivided into 44 dioceses.

Decisions on matters concerning the Church of England are made by the General Synod, established in 1970. It also discusses and expresses opinion on any other matter of religious or public interest. The General Synod has 580 members in total, divided between three houses: the House of Bishops, the House of Clergy and the House of Laity. It is presided over jointly by the Archbishops of Canterbury and York and normally meets twice a year. The Synod has the power, delegated by Parliament, to frame statute law (known as a Measure) on any matter concerning the Church of England. A Measure must be laid before both Houses of Parliament, who may accept or reject it but cannot amend it. Once accepted the Measure is submitted for royal assent and then has the full force of law. In addition to the General Synod, there are Synods at diocesan level

The Archbishops' Council was established in January 1999. Its creation was the result of changes to the Church of England's national structure proposed in 1995 and subsequently approved by the Synod and Parliament. The Council's purpose, set out in the National Institutions Measure 1998, is to co-ordinate, promote and further the work and mission of the Church of England. It reports frequently to the General Synod. The Archbishops' Council comprises three *ex-officio* members: the Archbishops of Canterbury and York (joint presidents) and a Church Estates Commissioners, ten elected members: the two persons elected by the Convocations of Prolocutors; the Chairman and Vice-Chairman of the House of Laity,

elected by that House; two bishops, two clergy and two lay members each elected by their respective Houses of the General Synod; and up to six members appointed by the two archbishops with the approval of the General Synod.

There are also a number of national boards, councils and other bodies working on matters such as social responsibility, mission, Christian unity and education which report to the General Synod through the Archbishops' Council.

GENERAL SYNOD OF THE CHURCH OF ENGLAND, Church House, Great Smith Street, London SW1P 3NZ. Tel: 020-7222 9011. *Joint* Presidents, The Archbishops of Canterbury and York. *Secretary-General*, P. Mawer
HOUSE OF BISHOPS: *Chairman*, The Archbishop of Canterbury; *Vice-Chairman*, The Archbishop of York
HOUSE OF CLERGY: *Chairman (alternating)*, Canon J. Stanley; Canon H. Wilcox
HOUSE OF LAITY: *Chairman*, Dr C. Baxter; *Vice-Chairman*, Dr P. Giddings
ARCHBISHOPS' COUNCIL, Church House, Great Smith Street, London SW1P 3NZ. Tel: 020-7898 1000. *Joint Presidents*, The Archbishops of Canterbury and York. *Secretary-General*, P. Mawer.

THE ORDINATION OF WOMEN

The canon making it possible for women to be ordained to the priesthood was promulgated in the General Synod in February 1994 and the first 32 women priests were ordained on 12 March 1994.

MEMBERSHIP

In 1998, 177,000 people were baptised. Also 1998 the Church of England had an electoral roll membership of 1.3 million, and each week about 1 million people attended Sunday services. At December 1999 there were two archbishops and 102 diocesan, suffragan and (stipendiary) assistant bishops. In 1999 there were 8,356 other male and 1,061 female full-time stipendiary clergy, and over 16,000 churches and places of worship. (The Diocese in Europe is not included in these figures.)

FULL-TIME DIOCESAN CLERGY 1998 AND CHURCH ELECTORAL ROLLS 1997

	Clergy		Membership
	Male	*Female*	
Bath and Wells	216	28	42,500
Birmingham	173	30	19,500
Blackburn	230	12	38,300
Bradford	106	9	13,300
Bristol	127	23	20,200
Canterbury	156	16	21,800
Carlisle	145	14	25,200
Chelmsford	377	46	53,200
Chester	262	21	50,900
Chichester	330	8	61,400
Coventry	134	17	17,700
Derby	169	17	21,900
Durham	200	30	28,900

	Clergy		Membership
	Male	*Female*	
Ely	137	20	21,200
Europe	120	7	8,800

Exeter	244	14	35,000
Gloucester	142	16	26,900
Guildford	177	30	31,500
Hereford	399	16	19,400
Leicester	143	22	16,600
Lichfield	314	46	54,300
Lincoln	187	40	31,500
Liverpool	221	36	33,300
London	501	52	57,800
Manchester	259	32	39,500
Newcastle	133	15	17,800
Norwich	184	17	26,700
Oxford	386	69	64,600
Peterborough	146	17	19,800
Portsmouth	105	11	19,200
Ripon and Leeds	131	22	20,100
Rochester	202	24	12,200
St Albans	243	45	45,500
St Edmundsbury and Ipswich	146	14	26,100
Salisbury	203	27	47,100
Sheffield	166	25	21,500
Sodor and Man	22	0	3,000
Southwark	318	67	46,400
Southwell	145	27	18,900
Truro	126	34	17,700
Wakefield	157	19	34,100
Winchester	221	14	43,500
Worcester	134	20	23,200
York	242	29	39,500
Total	8,579	1,068	1,347,500

STIPENDS 1999–2000

Archbishop of Canterbury	£55,660
Archbishop of York	£48,770
Bishop of London	£45,480
Other diocesan bishops	£30,210
Suffragan bishops	£24,790
Deans and provosts	£24,790
Residentiary canons	£20,200
Incumbents and clergy of similar status	£16,420*

*National Stipends Benchmark

CANTERBURY

103RD ARCHBISHOP AND PRIMATE OF ALL ENGLAND
Most Revd and Rt. Hon. George L.Carey, Ph.D., *cons.* 1987, *trans.* 1991, *apptd* 1991; Lambeth Palace, London SE1 7JU. *Signs* George Cantuar
BISHOPS SUFFRAGAN
Dover, Rt. Revd Stephen S. Venner, *cons* 1994, *apptd* 1999; Upway, St Martin's Hill, Canterbury, Kent CT1 1PR
Maidstone, vacant; Bishop's House, Pett Lane, Charing, Ashford, Kent TN27 0DL
Ebbsfleet, *cons. apptd* (provincial episcopal visitor);
Richborough, Rt. Revd Edwin Barnes, *cons.* 1995, *apptd* 1995 (provincial episcopal visitor); 14 Hall Place Gardens, St Albans, Herts AL1 3SP
DEAN
Very Revd John Arthur Simpson, *apptd* 1986

CANONS RESIDENTIARY
P. Brett, *apptd* 1983; R. H. C. Symon, *apptd* 1994; Dr M. Chandler, *apptd* 1995; Ven. J. Pritchard, *apptd* 1996

Organist, D. Flood, FRCO, *apptd* 1988

ARCHDEACONS
Canterbury, Ven. J. Pritchard, *apptd* 1996
Maidstone, Ven. P. Evans, *apptd* 1989

Vicar-General of Province and Diocese, Chancellor S. Cameron, QC
Commissary-General, His Hon. Judge Richard Walker
Joint Registrars of the Province, F. E. Robson, OBE; B. J. T. Hanson, CBE
Diocesan Registrar and Legal Adviser, R. H. B. Sturt
Diocesan Secretary, D. Kemp, Diocesan House, Lady Wootton's Green, Canterbury CT1 1NQ.
Tel: 01227-459401

YORK

96TH ARCHBISHOP AND PRIMATE OF ENGLAND
Most Revd and Rt. Hon. David M. Hope, KCVO, D.Phil., LL D, *cons.* 1985, *trans.* 1995, *apptd* 1995; Bishopthorpe, York YO23 2GE. *Signs* David Ebor:
BISHOPS SUFFRAGAN
Hull, Rt. Revd Richard M. C. Frith, *cons.* 1998, *apptd* 1998; Hullen House, Woodfield Lane, Hessle, Hull HU13 0ES
Selby, Rt. Revd Humphrey V. Taylor, *cons.* 1991, *apptd* 1991; 10 Precentor's Court, York YO1 2EJ
Whitby, Rt. Revd Robert S. Ladds, *cons.* 1999, *apptd* 1999; 60 West Green, Stokesley, Middlesbrough TS9 5BD
Beverley, Rt. Revd M. Jarrett, *apptd* 2000 (provincial episcopal visitor); 3 North Lane, Roundhay, Leeds LS8 2QJ
DEAN
Very Revd Raymond Furnell, *apptd* 1994

CANONS RESIDENTIARY
G. Webster, *apptd* 1999;
P. J. Ferguson, *apptd* 1995; E. R. Norman, Ph.D., DD, *apptd* 1999; J. L. Draper, *apptd* 2000

CANONS LAY
J. L. Mackinlay, *apptd* 2000; Mrs E. C. Rymer, *apptd* 2000; Dr A. J. Warren, *apptd* 2000; Brig. P. J. Lyddon (as Chapter Steward), *apptd* 2000

Organist, P. Moore, FRCO, *apptd* 1983

ARCHDEACONS
Cleveland, Ven. C. J. Hawthorn, *apptd* 1991
East Riding, Ven. P. R. W. Harrison, *apptd* 1998
York, Ven. R. Seed, *apptd* 1999

Official Principal and Auditor of the Chancery Court, Sir John Owen, QC
Chancellor of the Diocese, His Hon. Judge Coningsby, QC, *apptd* 1977
Vicar-General of the Province and Official Principal of the Consistory Court, His Hon. Judge Coningsby, QC
Registrar and Legal Secretary, L. P. M. Lennox
Diocesan Secretary, C. Sheppard, Diocesan House, Aviator Court, Clifton Moor, York YO30 4WJ.
Tel: 01904-699500

LONDON (Province of Canterbury)

132ND BISHOP
Rt. Revd and Rt. Hon Richard J. C. Chartres, *cons.* 1992, *apptd* 1995; The Old Deanery, Dean's Court, London EC4V 5AA. *Signs* Richard Londin

AREA BISHOPS
Edmonton, Rt. Revd Peter W. Wheatley, *cons.* 1999, *apptd* 1999; 27 Thurlow Road, London NW3 5PP
Kensington, Rt. Revd Michael Colclough, *cons.* 1996, *apptd* 1996; 19 Campden Hill Square, London W8 7JY
Stepney, Rt. Revd Dr John M. Sentamu, *cons.* 1996, *apptd* 1996; 63 Coborn Road, London E3 2DB
Willesden, Rt. Revd Graham G. Dow, *cons.* 1992, *apptd* 1992; 173 Willesden Lane, London NW6 7YN

BISHOP SUFFRAGAN
Fulham, Rt. Revd John Broadhurst, *cons.* 1996, *apptd* 1996; 26 Canonbury Park South, London N1 2FN

DEAN OF ST PAUL'S
Very Revd John H. Moses, PH.D., *apptd* 1996

CANONS RESIDENTIARY
R. J. Halliburton, *apptd* 1990; M. J. Saward, *apptd* 1991; S. J. Oliver, *apptd* 1997; P. Buekrer, *apptd* 1999

Registrar and Receiver of St Paul's, Brig. R. W. Acworth, CBE

Organist, J. Scott, FRCO, *apptd* 1990

ARCHDEACONS
Charing Cross, Ven. Dr W. Jacob, *apptd* 1996
Hackney, Ven. L. Dennen, *apptd* 1999
Hampstead, Ven. M. Lawson, *apptd* 1999
London, Ven. P. Delaney, *apptd* 1999
Middlesex, Ven. M. Colmer, *apptd* 1996
Northolt, Ven. P. Broadbent, *apptd* 1995

Chancellor, Miss S. Cameron, QC, *apptd* 1992
Registrar and Legal Secretary, P. C. E. Morris
Diocesan Secretary, K. Robinson

DURHAM (Province of York)

70TH BISHOP
Rt. Revd A. Michael A.Turnbull, *cons.* 1988, *apptd* 1994; Auckland Castle, Bishop Auckland DL14 7NR. *Signs* Michael Dunelm

BISHOP SUFFRAGAN
Jarrow, Rt. Revd Alan Smithson, *cons.* 1990, *apptd* 1990; The Old Vicarage, Hallgarth, Pittington, Durham DH6 1AB

DEAN
Very Revd John R. Arnold, *apptd* 1989

CANONS RESIDENTIARY
D. W. Brown, *apptd* 1990; T. Willmott, *apptd* 1997; M. Kitchen, *apptd* 1997; D. J. Whittington, *apptd* 1998; N. Stock, *apptd* 1998

Organist, J. B. Lancelot, FRCO, *apptd* 1985

ARCHDEACONS
Auckland, Ven. G. G. Gibson, *apptd* 1993
Durham, Ven. T. Willmott, *apptd* 1997
Sunderland, Ven. F. White, *apptd* 1997

Chancellor, His Hon. Judge Bursell, QC, *apptd* 1989
Registrar and Legal Secretary, A. N. Fairclough
Diocesan Secretary, J. P. Cryer, Auckland Castle, Bishop Auckland, Co. Durham DL14 7QJ.
Tel: 01388-604515

WINCHESTER (Canterbury)

96TH BISHOP
Rt. Revd Michael C. Scott-Joynt, *cons.* 1987, *trans.* 1995, *apptd* 1995; Wolvesey, Winchester SO23 9ND.
Signs Michael Winton

BISHOPS SUFFRAGAN
Basingstoke, Rt. Revd Dr. Geoffrey Rowell, *cons.* 1994, *apptd* 1994; Bishopswood End, Kingswood Rise, Four Marks, Alton, Hants GU34 5BD
Southampton, Rt. Revd Jonathan M. Gledhill, *cons.* 1996, *apptd* 1996; Ham House, The Crescent, Romsey SO51 7NG

DEAN
Very Revd Michael Till, *apptd* 1996

Dean of Jersey (A Peculiar), Very Revd John Seaford, *apptd* 1993
Dean of Guernsey (A Peculiar), Very Revd Marc Trickey, *apptd* 1995

CANONS RESIDENTIARY
A. K. Walker, *apptd* 1987; P. B. Morgan, *apptd* 1994; C. Stewart, *apptd* 1997; Ven. J. A. Guille, *apptd* 1998

Organist, D. Hill, FRCO, *apptd* 1988

ARCHDEACONS
Bournemouth, Ven. A. G. Harbidge, *apptd* 1998
Winchester, Ven. J. A. Guille, *apptd* 1998

Chancellor, C. Clark, *apptd* 1993
Registrar and Legal Secretary, P. M. White
Diocesan Secretary, R. Anderton, Church House, 9 The Close, Winchester, Hants SO23 9LS.
Tel: 01962-844644

BATH AND WELLS (Canterbury)

76TH BISHOP
Rt. Revd James L. Thompson, *cons.* 1978, *apptd* 1991; The Palace, Wells BA5 2PD. *Signs* James Bath & Wells

BISHOP SUFFRAGAN
Taunton, Rt. Revd Andrew John Radford, *cons.* Dec. 1998, *apptd* 1998; The Bishop's Lodge, Monkton Heights, West Monkton, Taunton, Somerset TA2 8LU

DEAN
Very Revd Richard Lewis, *apptd* 1990

CANONS RESIDENTIARY
R. Acworth, *apptd* 1993; P. G. Walker, *apptd* 1994; M. W. Matthews, *apptd* 1997; P. H. F. Woodhouse, *apptd* 2000

Organist, M. Archer, *apptd* 1996

ARCHDEACONS
Bath, Ven. R. J. S. Evens, *apptd* 1996
Taunton, Ven. J. P. C. Reed, *apptd* 1999
Wells, Ven. R. Acworth, *apptd* 1993

Chancellor, T. Briden, *apptd* 1993
Registrar and Legal Secretary, T. Berry
Diocesan Secretary, N. Denison, The Old Deanery, Wells, Somerset BA5 2UG. Tel: 01749-670777

BIRMINGHAM (Canterbury)

7TH BISHOP
Rt. Revd Mark Santer, *cons.* 1981, *apptd* 1987; Bishop's Croft, Harborne, Birmingham B17 0BG. *Signs* Mark Birmingham

BISHOP SUFFRAGAN
Aston, Rt. Revd John Austin, *cons.* 1992, *apptd* 1992; Strensham House, 8 Strensham Hill, Moseley, Birmingham B13 8AG

PROVOST
The Very Revd Gordon Hursell, *apptd* 2000

CANONS RESIDENTIARY
Ven. C. J. G. Barton, *apptd* 1990; Revd D. Lee, *apptd* 1996; Revd G. O'Neill, *apptd* 1997

Organist, M. Huxley, FRCO, *apptd* 1986

ARCHDEACONS
Aston, Ven. C. J. G. Barton, *apptd* 1990
Birmingham, Ven. J. F. Duncan, *apptd* 1985

Chancellor, His Hon. Judge Aglionby, *apptd* 1970
Registrar and Legal Secretary, H. Carslake
Diocesan Secretary, J. Drennan, 175 Harborne Park Road, Harborne, Birmingham B17 0BH. Tel: 0121-427 5141

BLACKBURN (York)

7TH BISHOP
Rt. Revd Alan D. Chesters, *cons.* 1989, *apptd* 1989; Bishop's House, Ribchester Road, Blackburn BB1 9EF. *Signs* Alan Blackburn

BISHOPS SUFFRAGAN
Burnley, Rt. Revd Martyn W. Jarrett, *cons.* 1994, *apptd* 1994; Dean House, 449 Padiham Road, Burnley BB12 6TE
Lancaster, Rt. Revd Stephen Pedley, *cons.* 1998, *apptd* 1997; The Vicarage, Shireshead, Forton, Preston PR3 0AE

PROVOST
Very Revd David Frayne, *apptd* 1992

CANONS RESIDENTIARY
D. M. Galilee, *apptd* 1995; A. D. Hindley, *apptd* 1996; P. J. Ballard, *apptd* 1998; A. Clitherow, *apptd* 2000

Organist, R. Tanner, *apptd* 1998

ARCHDEACONS
Blackburn, Ven. F. J. Marsh, *apptd* 1996
Lancaster, Ven. C. H. Williams, *apptd* 1999

Chancellor, J. W. M. Bullimore, *apptd* 1990
Registrar and Legal Secretary, T. A. Hoyle
Diocesan Secretary, Revd M. J. Wedgeworth, Diocesan Office, Cathedral Close, Blackburn BB1 5AA. Tel: 01254-54421

BRADFORD (York)

8TH BISHOP
Rt. Revd David J. Smith, *cons.* 1987, *apptd* 1992; Bishopscroft, Ashwell Road, Heaton, Bradford BD9 4AU. *Signs* David Bradford

DEAN
Very Revd John S. Richardson, *apptd* 1990

CANONS RESIDENTIARY
C. G. Lewis, *apptd* 1993; vacant

Organist, A. Horsey, FRCO, *apptd* 1986

ARCHDEACONS
Bradford, Ven. G. A. Wilkinson, *apptd* 1999
Craven, Ven. M. L. Grundy, *apptd* 1994

Chancellor, J. de G. Walford, *apptd* 1999
Registrar and Legal Secretary, J. G. H. Mackrell
Diocesan Secretary, M. Halliday, Cathedral Hall, Stott Hill, Bradford BD1 4ET. Tel: 01274-725958

BRISTOL (Canterbury)

54TH BISHOP
Rt. Revd Barry Rogerson, *cons.* 1979, *apptd* 1985; Bishop's House, Clifton Hill, Bristol BS8 1BW. *Signs* Barry Bristol

BISHOP SUFFRAGAN
Swindon, Rt. Revd Michael Doe, *cons.* 1994, *apptd* 1994; Mark House, Field Rise, Old Town, Swindon SN1 4HP

DEAN
Very Revd Robert W. Grimley, *apptd* 1997

CANONS RESIDENTIARY
P. F. Johnson, *apptd* 1990; D. R. Holt, *apptd* 1998; B. D. Clover, *apptd* 1999

Organist, M. Lee, *apptd* 1998

ARCHDEACONS
Bristol, Ven. T. E. McClure, apptd 1999
Swindon, Ven. A. F. Hawker, *apptd* 1998

Chancellor, Sir David Calcutt, QC, *apptd* 1971
Registrar and Legal Secretary, T. Berry
Diocesan Secretary, Mrs L. Farrall, Diocesan Church House, 23 Great George Street, Bristol, Avon BS1 5QZ. Tel: 0117-921 4411

CARLISLE (York)

65TH BISHOP
Rt. Revd Graham Dow, *cons.* 1985, *apptd* 2000; Rose Castle, Dalston, Carlisle CA5 7BZ. *Signs* Graham Carliol

BISHOP SUFFRAGAN
Penrith, Rt. Revd Richard Garrard, *cons.* 1994, *apptd* 1994; Holm Croft, Castle Road, Kendal, Cumbria LA9 7AU

DEAN
Very Revd Graeme P. Knowles, *apptd* 1998

CANONS RESIDENTIARY
R. A. Chapman, *apptd* 1978; Ven. D. C. Turnbull, *apptd* 1993; D. W. V. Weston, *apptd* 1994; C. Hill, *apptd* 1996

Organist, J. Suter, FRCO, *apptd* 1991

ARCHDEACONS
Carlisle, Ven. D. C. Turnbull, *apptd* 1993
West Cumberland, Ven. A. N. Davis, *apptd* 1996
Westmorland and Furness, Ven. G. A. Howe, *apptd* 2000

Chancellor, His Hon. Judge Aglionby, *apptd* 1991
Registrar and Legal Secretary, Mrs S. Holmes
Diocesan Secretary, Canon C. Hill, Church House, West Walls, Carlisle CA3 8UE. Tel: 01228-522573

CHELMSFORD (Canterbury)

8TH BISHOP
Rt. Revd John F. Perry, *cons.* 1989, *apptd* 1996;
Bishopscourt, Margaretting, Ingatestone CM4 0HD.
Signs John Chelmsford

BISHOPS SUFFRAGAN
Barking, Rt. Revd Roger F. Sainsbury, *cons.* 1991, *apptd*
1991; 110 Capel Road, Forest Gate, London E7 0JS
Bradwell, Rt. Revd Laurence Green, *cons.* 1993, *apptd* 1993;
The Vicarage, Orsett Road, Horndon-on-the-Hill,
Stanford-le-Hope, Essex SS17 8NS
Colchester, Rt. Revd Edward Holland, *cons.* 1986, *apptd*
1995; 1 Fitzwalter Road, Lexden, Colchester CO3 3SS

PROVOST
Very Revd Peter S. M. Judd, *apptd* 1997

CANONS RESIDENTIARY
T. Thompson, *apptd* 1988; B. P. Thompson, *apptd* 1988;
D. Knight, *apptd* 1991; A. Knowles, *apptd* 1998

Master of Music, P. Nardone, *apptd* 2000

ARCHDEACONS
Colchester, Ven. M. W. Wallace, *apptd* 1997
Harlow, Ven. P. F. Taylor, *apptd* 1996
Southend, Ven. D. Jennings, *apptd* 1992
West Ham, Ven. M. J. Fox, *apptd* 1996

Chancellor, Miss S. M. Cameron, QC, *apptd* 1970
Registrar and Legal Secretary, B. Hood
Diocesan Secretary, D. Phillips, 53 New Street, Chelmsford, Essex CM1 1AT. Tel: 01245-294400

CHESTER (York)

40TH BISHOP
Rt. Revd Peter R. Forster, Ph.D., *cons.* 1996, *apptd* 1996;
Bishop's House, Chester CH1 2JD. *Signs* Peter Cestr

BISHOPS SUFFRAGAN
Birkenhead, Rt. Revd David A. Urquhart, *cons.* 2000,
apptd 2000; Bishop's Lodge, 67 Bidston Road,
Oxton, Birkenhead CH43 6TR
Stockport, Rt. Revd Geoffrey M.Turner, *cons.* 1994, *apptd*
1994; Bishop's Lodge, Back Lane, Dunham Town,
Altrincham, Cheshire WA14 4SG

DEAN
Very Revd Dr Stephen S.Smalley, *apptd* 1986

CANONS RESIDENTIARY
R. M. Rees, *apptd* 1990; J. M. Roff, *apptd* 2000;
Dr T. J. Dennis, *apptd* 1994; J. W. S. Newcome, *apptd*
1994

Organist and Director of Music, D. G. Poulter, FRCO,
apptd 1997

ARCHDEACONS
Chester, Ven. C. Hewetson, *apptd* 1994
Macclesfield, Ven. R. J. Gillings, *apptd* 1994

Chancellor, D. G. P. Turner, QC, *apptd* 1998
Registrar and Legal Secretary, A. K. McAllester
Diocesan Secretary, S. P. A. Marriott, Church House,
Lower Lane, Aldford, Chester CH3 6HP.
Tel: 01244-620444

CHICHESTER (Canterbury)

102ND BISHOP
Rt. Revd Eric W. Kemp, DD, *cons.* 1974, *apptd* 1974;
The Palace, Chichester PO19 1PY. *Signs* Eric Cicestr

BISHOPS SUFFRAGAN
Horsham, Rt. Revd Lindsay G. Urwin, *cons.* 1993, *apptd*
1993; Bishop's House, 21 Guildford Road, Horsham,
W. Sussex RH12 1LU
Lewes, Rt. Revd Wallace P. Benn, *cons.* 1997, *apptd* 1997;
16A Prideaux Road, Eastbourne, E. Sussex BN21 2NB

DEAN
Very Revd John D.Treadgold, LVO, *apptd* 1989

CANONS RESIDENTIARY
R. T. Greenacre, *apptd* 1975; F. J. Hawkins, *apptd* 1981;
P. G. Atkinson, *apptd* 1997; C. Lansdale, *apptd.* 1999;
D. McKittrick, *apptd.* 1999

Organist, A. J. Thurlow, FRCO, *apptd* 1980

ARCHDEACONS
Chichester, Ven. M. Brotherton, *apptd* 1991
Horsham, Ven. W. C. L. Filby, *apptd* 1983
Lewes and Hastings, Ven. N. S. Reade, *apptd* 1997

Chancellor, M. Hill
Registrar and Legal Secretary, C. Butcher
Diocesan Secretary, J. Prichard, Diocesan Church House,
211 New Church Road, Hove, E. Sussex BN3 4ED.
Tel: 01273-421021

COVENTRY (Canterbury)

8TH BISHOP
Rt. Revd Colin J. Bennetts; *cons.* 1994, *apptd* 1997; The
Bishop's House, 23 Davenport Road, Coventry CV5 6PW.
Signs Colin Coventry

BISHOP SUFFRAGAN
Warwick, Rt. Revd Anthony M. Priddis, *cons.* 1996, *apptd*
1996; 139 Kenilworth Road, Coventry CV4 7AF

DEAN
vacant
CANONS RESIDENTIARY
J. C. Burch, *apptd* 1995; A. White, *apptd* 1998; S. A. Beake,
apptd 2000

Director of Music, R. Jeffcoat, *apptd* 1997

ARCHDEACONS
Coventry, 1989 vacant
Warwick, Ven. M. J. J. Paget-Wilkes, *apptd* 1990

Chancellor, Sir William Gage, *apptd* 1980
Registrar and Legal Secretary, D. J. Dumbleton
Diocesan Secretary, Mrs I. Chapman, Church House,
Palmerston Road, Coventry CV5 6FJ. Tel: 024-
7667 4328

DERBY (Canterbury)

6TH BISHOP
Rt. Revd Jonathan S. Bailey, *cons.* 1992, *apptd* 1995; Derby
Church House, Full Street, Derby DE1 3DR. *Signs*
Jonathan Derby

BISHOP SUFFRAGAN
Repton, Rt. Revd David C. Hawtin, *cons.*1999, *apptd* 1999; Repton House, Lea, Matlock, Derbys DE4 5JP

PROVOST
Very Revd Michael F. Perham, *apptd* 1998

CANONS RESIDENTIARY
G. A. Chesterman, *apptd* 1989; B. V. Gauge, *apptd* 1999; G. O. Marshall, *apptd* 1992; D. C. Truby, *apptd* 1998

Organist, P.Gould, *apptd* 1982

ARCHDEACONS
Chesterfield, Ven. D. C. Garnett, *apptd* 1996
Derby, Ven. I. Gatford, *apptd* 1992

Chancellor, J. W. M. Bullimore, *apptd* 1981
Registrar and Legal Secretary, J. S. Battie
Diocesan Secretary, R. J. Carey, Derby Church House, Full Street, Derby DE1 3DR. Tel: 01332-382233

ELY (Canterbury)

BISHOP
Rt. Revd Dr Anthony Russell, *cons.* 1988, *apptd* 2000; The Bishop's House, Ely, Cambs CB7 4DW

BISHOP SUFFRAGAN
Huntingdon, Rt. Revd John R. Flack, *cons.* 1997, *apptd* 1996; 14 Lynn Road, Ely, Cambs CB6 1DA

DEAN
Very Revd Michael Higgins, *apptd* 1991

CANONS RESIDENTIARY
J. Inge, *apptd* 1996; P. M. Stills, *apptd* 2000

Organist, P. Trepte, FRCO, *apptd* 1991

ARCHDEACONS
Ely, Ven. J. Watson, *apptd* 1993
Huntingdon, Ven. J. Beer, *apptd* 1997
Wisbech, Ven. J. Rone, *apptd* 1995

Chancellor, W. Gage, QC
Joint Registrars, W. H. Godfrey; P. F. B. Beesley (*Legal Secretary*)
Diocesan Secretary, Dr M. Lavis, Bishop Woodford House, Barton Road, Ely, Cambs CB7 4DX. Tel: 01353-652701

EXETER (Canterbury)

70TH BISHOP
Rt. Revd Michael L. Langrish, *cons.* 1993, *apptd* 2000; The Palace, Exeter, EX1 1HY. *Signs* Michael Exon

BISHOPS SUFFRAGAN
Crediton, Rt. Revd Richard S. Hawkins, *cons.* 1988, *apptd* 1996; 10 The Close, Exeter EX1 1EZ
Plymouth, Rt. Revd John H. Garton, *cons.* 1996, *apptd* 1996; 31 Riverside Walk, Tamerton Foliot, Plymouth PL5 4AQ

DEAN
Very Revd Keith B. Jones, *apptd* 1996

CANONS RESIDENTIARY
N. Collings, *apptd* 1999;
D. J. Ison, *apptd* 1997

Director of Music, A. T. S. Millington, *apptd* 1999

ARCHDEACONS
Barnstaple, Ven. T. Lloyd, *apptd* 1989
Exeter, Ven. A. F. Tremlett, *apptd* 1994
Plymouth, vacant
Totnes, Preb. R. T. Gilpin, *apptd* 1996

Chancellor, Sir David Calcutt, QC, *apptd* 1971
Registrar and Legal Secretary, R. K. Wheeler
Diocesan Secretary, M. Beedell, Diocesan House, Palace Gate, Exeter, Devon EX1 1HX. Tel: 01392-72686

GIBRALTAR IN EUROPE (Canterbury)

BISHOP
Rt. Revd John Hind, *cons.* 1991, *apptd* 1993; 14 Tufton Street, London SW1P 3QZ

BISHOP SUFFRAGAN
In Europe Rt. Revd Henry Scriven, *cons.* 1995, *apptd* 1994; 14 Tufton Street, London SW1P 3QZ

Dean, Cathedral Church of the Holy Trinity, Gibraltar, Very Revd J. K. Robinson
Chancellor, Pro-Cathedral of St Paul, Valletta, Malta, Canon A.Woods
Chancellor, Pro-Cathedral of the Holy Trinity, Brussels, Belgium, Canon N.Walker

ARCHDEACONS
Eastern, Rt. Revd H. Scriven (*acting*)
North-West Europe, Ven. G. G. Allen
France, Ven. M. Draper, OBE
Gibraltar, Very Revd. K.Robinson
Italy, Ven. W. G. Reid
Scandinavia and Germany, Ven. D. Ratcliff
Switzerland, Ven. P. J. Hawker, OBE

Chancellor, Sir David Calcutt, QC
Registrar and Legal Secretary, J. G. Underwood
Diocesan Secretary, A. C. Mumford, 14 Tufton Street, London SW1P 3QZ. Tel: 020-7898 1155

GLOUCESTER (Canterbury)

39TH BISHOP
Rt. Revd David Bentley, *cons.* 1986, *apptd* 1993; Bishopscourt, Gloucester GL1 2BQ. *Signs* David Gloucestr

BISHOP SUFFRAGAN
Tewkesbury, Rt. Revd John S. Went, *cons.* 1995, *apptd* 1995; Green Acre, Hempsted, Gloucester GL2 6LG

DEAN
Very Revd Nicholas A. S. Bury, *apptd* 1997

CANONS RESIDENTIARY
R. D. M. Grey, *apptd* 1982; N. Chatfield, *apptd* 1992; N. Heavisides, *apptd* 1993; C. H. Morgan, *apptd* 1996

Organist, D.Briggs, FRCO, *apptd* 1994

ARCHDEACONS
Cheltenham, Ven. H. S. Ringrose, *apptd* 1998
Gloucester, vacant

Chancellor and Vicar-General, Ms D. J. Rodgers, *apptd* 1990
Registrar and Legal Secretary, C. G. Peak
Diocesan Secretary, M. Williams, Church House, College Green, Gloucester GL1 2LY. Tel: 01452-410022

GUILDFORD (Canterbury)

8TH BISHOP
Rt. Revd John W. Gladwin, *cons.* 1994, *apptd* 1994; Willow Grange, Woking Road, Guildford GU4 7QS. *Signs* John Guildford

BISHOP SUFFRAGAN
Dorking, Rt. Revd Ian Brackley, *cons.* 1996, *apptd* 1995; Dayspring, 13 Pilgrims Way, Guildford GU4 8AD

DEAN
Very Revd Alexander G. Wedderspoon, *apptd* 1987

CANONS RESIDENTIARY
Dr Maureen Palmer, *apptd* 1996

Organist, S. Farr, FRCO, *apptd* 1999

ARCHDEACONS
Dorking, Ven. M. Wilson, *apptd* 1996
Surrey, Ven. R. Reiss, *apptd* 1996

Chancellor, His Hon. Judge Goodman
Registrar and Legal Secretary, P. Beesley
Diocesan Secretary, S. Marriott

HEREFORD (Canterbury)

103RD BISHOP
Rt. Revd John Oliver, *cons.* 1990, *apptd* 1990; The Palace, Hereford HR4 9BN. *Signs* John Hereford

BISHOP SUFFRAGAN
Ludlow, Rt. Revd Dr John Saxbee, *cons.* 1994, *apptd* 1994; Bishop's House, Halford, Craven Arms, Shropshire SY7 9BT

DEAN
Very Revd Robert A. Willis, *apptd* 1992

CANONS RESIDENTIARY
P. Iles, *apptd* 1983; J. Tiller, *apptd* 1984; M. W. Hooper, *apptd* 1997

Organist, Dr R. Massey, FRCO, *apptd* 1974

ARCHDEACONS
Hereford, Ven. M. W. Hooper, *apptd* 1997
Ludlow, Rt. Revd J. C. Saxbee, *apptd* 1992

Chancellor, J. M. Henty
Joint Registrars and Legal Secretaries, V. T. Jordan; P. F. B. Beesley
Diocesan Secretary, Miss S. Green, The Palace, Hereford HR4 9BL. Tel: 01432-353863

LEICESTER (Canterbury)

6TH BISHOP
Rt. Revd Timothy J. Stevens, *cons.* 1995, *apptd* 1999; Bishop's Lodge, 10 Springfield Road, Leicester LE2 3BD. *Signs* Timothy Leicester

STIPENDIARY ASSISTANT BISHOP
Rt. Revd William Down, *cons.* 1990, *apptd* 1995

PROVOST
Very Revd Vivienne F. Faull, *apptd* 2000

CANONS RESIDENTIARY
M. T. H. Banks, *apptd* 1988; M. Wilson, *apptd* 1988

Organist, J. T. Gregory, *apptd* 1994

ARCHDEACONS
Leicester, Ven. M.Edson, *apptd* 1994
Loughborough, Ven. I. Stanes, *apptd* 1992

Chancellor, N. Seed, *apptd* 1989
Registrars and Legal Secretaries, P. C. E. Morris; R. H. Bloor
Diocesan Secretary, A. Howard; Church House, 3–5 St Martin's East, Leicester LE1 5FX. Tel: 0116-262 7445

LICHFIELD (Canterbury)

97TH BISHOP
Rt. Revd Keith N. Sutton, *cons.* 1978, *apptd* 1984; Bishop's House, The Close, Lichfield WS13 7LG. *Signs* Keith Lichfield

BISHOPS SUFFRAGAN
Shrewsbury, Rt. Revd David M. Hallatt, *cons.* 1994, *apptd* 1994; 68 London Road, Shrewsbury SY2 6PG
Stafford, Rt. Revd Christopher J. Hill, *cons.* 1996, *apptd* 1996; Ash Garth, Broughton Crescent, Barlaston, Staffs ST12 9DD
Wolverhampton, Rt. Revd Michael G. Bourke, *cons.* 1993, *apptd* 1993; 61 Richmond Road, Wolverhampton WV3 9JH

DEAN
Very Revd Michael Yorke, *apptd* 1999

CANONS RESIDENTIARY
A. N. Barnard, *apptd* 1977; C. W. Taylor, *apptd* 1995; Ven. G. Frost, *apptd* 1998

Organist, A. Lumsden, *apptd* 1992

ARCHDEACONS
Lichfield, Ven. G. Frost, *apptd* 1998
Salop, Ven . J. B. Hall, *apptd* 1998
Stoke-on-Trent, Ven. A. G. C. Smith, *apptd* 1997
Walsall, Ven. A. G. Sadler, *apptd* 1997

Chancellor, His Hon. Judge Shand
Registrar and Legal Secretary, J. P. Thorneycroft
Diocesan Secretary, D. R. Taylor, St Mary's House, The Close, Lichfield, Staffs WS13 7LD. Tel: 01543-306030

LINCOLN (Canterbury)

70TH BISHOP
Rt. Revd Robert M. Hardy, *cons.* 1980, *apptd* 1987; Bishop's House, Eastgate, Lincoln LN2 1QQ. *Signs* Robert Lincoln

BISHOPS SUFFRAGAN
Grantham, Rt. Revd Alastair L. J. Redfern, *cons.* 1997, *apptd* 1997; Fairacre, 234 Barrowby Road, Grantham, Lincs NG31 8NP

Grimsby, Rt. Revd David D. J. Rossdale, *cons.* 2000, *apptd* 2000; Bishop's House, Church Lane, Irby-upon-Humber, Grimsby DN37 7JR

DEAN
Very Revd Alexander F. Knight, *apptd* 1998

CANONS RESIDENTIARY
B. R. Davis, *apptd* 1977; A. J. Stokes, *apptd* 1992; V. White, *apptd* 1994

Organist, C. S. Walsh, FRCO, *apptd* 1988

ARCHDEACONS
Lincoln, Ven. A. Hawes, *apptd* 1995
Lindsey, vacant
Stow, Ven. R. J. Wells, *apptd* 1989

Chancellor, Peter N. Collier, QC, *apptd* 1999
Registrar and Legal Secretary, D. M. Wellman
Diocesan Secretary, P. Hamlyn Williams, The Old Palace,
Lincoln LN2 1PU. Tel: 01522-529241

LIVERPOOL (York)

7TH BISHOP
Rt. Revd James Jones, *cons.* 1994, *apptd* 1998; Bishop's
Lodge, Woolton Park, Liverpool L25 6DT. *Signs* James
Liverpool

BISHOP SUFFRAGAN
Warrington, vacant; 34 Central Avenue, Eccleston Park,
Prescot, Merseyside L34 2QP

DEAN
Rt. Revd Dean Dr Rupert W. N. Hoare

CANONS RESIDENTIARY
D. J. Hutton, *apptd* 1983; M. C. Boyling, *apptd* 1994;
N. T. Vincent, *apptd* 1995;

Organist, Prof. I. Tracey, *apptd* 1980

ARCHDEACONS
Liverpool, Ven. R. L. Metcalf, *apptd* 1994
Warrington, Ven. C. D. S. Woodhouse, *apptd* 1981

Chancellor, R. G. Hamilton
Registrar and Legal Secretary, R. H. Arden
Diocesan Secretary, K. Cawdron, Church House, 1 Hanover Street, Liverpool L1 3DW. Tel: 0151-709 9722

MANCHESTER (York)

10TH BISHOP
Rt. Revd Christopher J. Mayfield, *cons.* 1985, *apptd* 1993;
Bishopscourt, Bury New Road, Manchester M7 4LE.
Signs Christopher Manchester

BISHOPS SUFFRAGAN
Bolton, Rt. Revd David K. Gillett, *cons.* 1999, *apptd* 1999;
4 Bishop's Lodge, Bolton Road, Hawkshaw, Bury BL8 4JN
Hulme, Rt. Revd Stephen R. Lowe, *cons.* 1999, *apptd.* 1999;
14 Moorgate Avenue, Withington, Manchester M20 1HE
Middleton, Rt. Revd Michael A. O. Lewis, *cons.* 1999, apptd
1999; The Hollies, Manchester Road, Rochdale
OL11 3QY

DEAN
Very Revd Kenneth Riley, *apptd* 1993

CANONS RESIDENTIARY
J. R. Atherton, Ph.D., *apptd* 1984; A. E. Radcliffe, *apptd*
1991; P. Denby, *apptd* 1995

Organist, C. Stokes, *apptd* 1992

ARCHDEACONS
Bolton, Ven. L. M. Davies, *apptd* 1992
Manchester, Ven. A. Wolstencroft, *apptd* 1998
Rochdale, Ven. A. Ballard, *apptd* 2000

NEWCASTLE (York)

11TH BISHOP
Rt. Revd J. Martin Wharton, *cons.* 1992, *apptd* 1997;
Bishop's House, 29 Moor Road South, Gosforth,
Newcastle upon Tyne NE3 1PA. *Signs*
Martin Newcastle

STIPENDIARY ASSISTANT BISHOP
Rt. Revd Paul Richardson, *cons.* 1987, *apptd* 1999

PROVOST
Very Revd Nicholas G. Coulton, *apptd* 1990

CANONS RESIDENTIARY
R. Langley, *apptd* 1985; P. R. Strange, *apptd* 1986;
Ven. P. Elliott, *apptd* 1993; G. V. Miller, *apptd* 1999

Organist, T. G. Hone, FRCO, *apptd* 1987

ARCHDEACONS
Lindisfarne, Ven. M. E. Bowering, *apptd* 1987
Northumberland, Ven. P. Elliott, *apptd* 1993

Chancellor, Prof. D. McClean, *apptd* 1998
Registrar and Legal Secretary, Mrs B. J. Lowdon
Diocesan Secretary, P. Davies, Church House, Grainger
Park Road, Newcastle upon Tyne NE4 8SX.
Tel: 0191-273 0120

NORWICH (Canterbury)

71ST BISHOP
Rt Revd Graham R. James, *cons.* 1993, *apptd* 2000; Bishop's
House, Norwich NR3 1SB. *Signs* Graham Norvic

BISHOPS SUFFRAGAN
Lynn, Rt. Revd A. C. Foottit, *cons.* 1999, *apptd* 1999
Thetford, Rt. Revd Hugo F. de Waal, *cons.* 1992, *apptd*
1992; Rectory Meadow, Bramerton,
Norwich NR14 7DW

DEAN
Very Revd Stephen Platten, *apptd* 1995

CANONS RESIDENTIARY
J. M. Haselock, *apptd* 1998; Ven. C. J. Offer, *apptd* 1994;
R. J. Hanmer, *apptd* 1994; M. Kitchener, *apptd* 1999

Organist, D. Dunnett, *apptd* 1996

ARCHDEACONS
Lynn, Ven. M. C. Gray, *apptd* 1999
Norfolk, Ven. A. M. Handley, *apptd* 1993
Norwich, Ven. C. J. Offer, *apptd* 1994

Chancellor, The Hon. Mr Justice Blofeld, *apptd* 1998
Registrar and Legal Secretary, J. W. F. Herring
Diocesan Secretary, D. Adeney, Diocesan House, 109
Dereham Road, Easton, Norwich, Norfolk NR9 5ES.
Tel: 01603-880853

OXFORD (Canterbury)

41ST BISHOP
Rt. Revd Richard D. Harries, *cons.* 1987, *apptd* 1987;
Diocesan Church House, North Hinksey, Oxford
OX2 0NB. *Signs* Richard Oxon

AREA BISHOPS
Buckingham, Rt. Revd Michael A. Hill, *cons.* 1998, *apptd* 1998; 28 Church Street, Great Missenden, Bucks HP16 0AZ
Dorchester, Rt. Revd Colin Fletcher, *cons.* 2000, *apptd* 2000; 12 Sandy Lane, Yarnton, Oxon OX5 1PB
Reading, Rt. Revd Dominic Walker, *cons.* 1997, *apptd* 1997; Bishop's House, Tidmarsh Lane, Tidmarsh, Reading RG8 8HA

DEAN OF CHRIST CHURCH
Very Revd John H. Drury, *apptd* 1991

CANONS RESIDENTIARY
O. M. T. O'Donovan, D.Phil., *apptd* 1982; J. M. Pierce, *apptd* 1987; J. S. K. Ward, *apptd* 1991; R. Jeffery, *apptd* 1996; Prof. J. Webster, *apptd* 1996; Prof. H. M. R. E. Mayr-Harting, *apptd* 1997; Ven. J. A. Morrison, *apptd* 1998

Organist, S. Darlington, FRCO, *apptd* 1985

ARCHDEACONS
Berkshire, Ven. N. A. Russell, *apptd* 1998
Buckingham, Ven. D. Goldie, *apptd* 1998
Oxford, Ven. J. A. Morrison, *apptd* 1998

Chancellor, P. T. S. Boydell, QC, *apptd* 1958
Joint Registrars and Legal Secretariesy, Dr F. E. Robson and Revd. J. Rees
Diocesan Secretary, R. Pearce, Diocesan Church House, North Hinksey, Oxford OX2 0NB. Tel: 01865-208202

PETERBOROUGH (Canterbury)

37TH BISHOP
Rt. Revd Ian P. M. Cundy, *cons.* 1992, *apptd* 1996; The Palace, Peterborough PE1 1YA. *Signs* Ian Petriburg

BISHOP SUFFRAGAN
Brixworth, Rt. Revd Paul E. Barber, *cons.* 1989, *apptd* 1989; 4 The Avenue, Dallington, Northampton NN1 4RZ

DEAN
Very Revd Michael Bunker, *apptd* 1992

CANONS RESIDENTIARY
T. R. Christie, *apptd* 1980; J. Higham, *apptd* 1983; P. A. Spence, *apptd* 1998; D. Painter, *apptd* 2000

Organist, C. S. Gower, FRCO, *apptd* 1977

ARCHDEACONS
Northampton, Ven. M. R. Chapman, *apptd* 1991
Oakham, Ven. D. Painter, *apptd* 2000

Chancellor, T. A. C. Coningsby, QC, *apptd* 1989
Registrar and Legal Secretary, R. Hemingray
Diocesan Secretary, Revd Canon R. J. Cattle, The Palace, Peterborough, Cambs PE1 1YB. Tel: 01733-887000

PORTSMOUTH (Canterbury)

8TH BISHOP
Rt. Revd Dr Kenneth W. Stevenson, *cons.* 1995, *apptd* 1995; Bishopsgrove, 26 Osborn Road, Fareham, Hants PO16 7DQ. *Signs* Kenneth Portsmouth

PROVOST
The Very Revd Dr William H. Taylor, *apptd* 2000; Provost's House, 13 Pembroke Road, Portsmouth PO1 2NS.

CANONS RESIDENTIARY
D. T. Isaac, *apptd* 1990; Jane B. Hedges, *apptd* 1993; G. Kirk, *apptd* 1998; I. Jagger, *apptd* 1998

Organist, D. J. C. Price, *apptd* 1996

ARCHDEACONS
Isle of Wight, Ven. K. M. L. H. Banting, *apptd* 1996
Portsdown, Ven. C. Lowson, *apptd* 1999
The Meon, Ven. N. P. Hancock, *apptd* 1999

Chancellor, His Hon. Judge Aglionby, *apptd* 1978
Registrar and Legal Secretary, Miss H. A. G. Tyler
Diocesan Secretary, M. F. Jordan, Cathedral House, St Thomas's Street, Portsmouth, Hants PO1 2HA. Tel: 023-9282 5731

RIPON AND LEEDS (York)

BISHOP
Rt. Revd John R. Packer, *apptd* 2000; Bishop Mount, Ripon HG4 5DP

BISHOP SUFFRAGAN
Knaresborough, Rt. Revd Frank V. Weston, *cons.* 1997, *apptd* 1997; 16 Shaftesbury Avenue, Roundhay, Leeds LS8 1DT

DEAN
Very Revd John Methuen, *apptd* 1995

CANONS RESIDENTIARY
M. R. Glanville-Smith, *apptd* 1990
K. Punshon, *apptd* 1996

Organist, K. Beaumont, FRCO, *apptd* 1994

ARCHDEACONS
Leeds, Ven. J. M. Oliver, *apptd* 1992
Richmond, Ven. K. Good, *apptd* 1993

Chancellor, His Hon. Judge Grenfell, *apptd* 1992
Registrars and Legal Secretaries, C. T. Tunnard, Mrs N. Harding
Diocesan Secretary, P. M. Arundel, Diocesan Office, St Mary's Street, Leeds LS9 7DP. Tel: 0113-248 7487

ROCHESTER (Canterbury)

106TH BISHOP
Rt. Revd Dr Michael Nazir-Ali, *cons.* 1984, *apptd* 1994; Bishopscourt, Rochester ME1 1TS. *Signs* Michael Roffen

BISHOP SUFFRAGAN
Tonbridge, Rt. Revd Brian A. Smith, *cons.* 1993, *apptd* 1993; Bishop's Lodge, 48 St Botolph's Road, Sevenoaks TN13 3AG

DEAN
Very Revd Edward F. Shotter, *apptd* 1990

CANONS RESIDENTIARY
E. R. Turner, *apptd* 1981; J. M. Armson, *apptd* 1989; C. J. Meyrick, *apptd* 1998

Organist, R. Sayer, FRCO, *apptd* 1995

ARCHDEACONS
Bromley, Ven. G. Norman, *apptd* 1994
Rochester, vacant
Tonbridge, Ven. Judith Rose, *apptd* 1996

Chancellor, His Hon. Judge Goodman, *apptd* 1971
Registrar and Legal Secretary, M. Thatcher

Diocesan Secretary, Mrs L. Gilbert, St Nicholas Church, Boley Hill, Rochester ME1 1SL. Tel: 01634-830333

ST ALBANS (Canterbury)

9TH BISHOP
Rt. Revd Christopher W. Herbert, *cons.* 1995, *apptd* 1995; Abbey Gate House, St Albans AL3 4HD. *Signs* Christopher St Albans

BISHOPS SUFFRAGAN
Bedford, Rt. Revd John H. Richardson, *cons.* 1994, *apptd* 1994; 168 Kimbolton Road, Bedford MK41 8DN
Hertford, Rt. Revd Robin J. N. Smith, *cons.* 1990, *apptd* 1990; Hertford House, Abbey Mill Lane, St Albans AL3 4HE

DEAN
Very Revd Christopher Lewis, *apptd* 1993

CANONS RESIDENTIARY
M. Sansom, *apptd* 1988; C. R. J. Foster, *apptd* 1994; I. R. Lane, *apptd* 2000

Organist, A. Lucas, *apptd* 1998

ARCHDEACONS
Bedford, Ven. M. L. Lesiter, *apptd* 1993
Hertford, Ven. T. P. Jones, *apptd* 1997
St Albans, Ven. R. I. Cheetham, *apptd* 1999

Chancellor, His Hon. Judge Bursell, QC, *apptd* 1992
Registrar and Legal Secretary, D. N. Cheetham
Diocesan Secretary, L. Nicholls, Holywell Lodge, 41 Holywell Hill, St Albans AL1 1HE. Tel: 01727-854532

ST EDMUNDSBURY AND IPSWICH (Canterbury)

9th Bishop
Rt. Revd J. H. Richard Lewis, *cons.* 1992, *apptd* 1997; Bishop's House, 4 Park Road, Ipswich IP1 3ST. *Signs* Richard St Edmundsbury and Ipswich

BISHOP SUFFRAGAN
Dunwich, Rt. Revd Clive Young, *cons.* 1999, *apptd* 1999; 28 Westerfield Road, Ipswich IP4 2UJ

PROVOST
Very Revd J. Atwell, *apptd* 1995

CANONS RESIDENTIARY
A. M. Shaw, *apptd* 1989; M. E. Mingins, *apptd* 1993; J. Parr, *apptd* 1999

Organist, J. Thomas, *apptd* 1997

ARCHDEACONS
Ipswich, Ven. T. A. Gibson, *apptd* 1987
Sudbury, Ven. J. Cox, *apptd* 1995
Suffolk, Ven. G. Arrand, *apptd* 1994

Chancellor, The Hon. Mr Justice Blofeld, *apptd* 1974
Registrar and Legal Secretary, J. Hall
Diocesan Secretary, N. Edgell, Churchgates House, Cutler Street, Ipswich IP1 1QU. Tel: 01473-298500

SALISBURY (Canterbury)

77TH BISHOP
Rt. Revd David S. Stancliffe, *cons.* 1993, *apptd* 1993; South Canonry, The Close, Salisbury SP1 2ER. *Signs* David Sarum

BISHOPS SUFFRAGAN
Ramsbury, Rt. Revd Peter F. Hullah, *cons.* 1999, *apptd* 1999
Sherborne, Rt. Revd John D. G. Kirkham, *cons.* 1976, *apptd* 1976; Little Bailie, Sturminster Marshall, Wimborne BH21 4AD

DEAN
Very Revd Derek Watson, *apptd* 1996

CANONS RESIDENTIARY
D. J. C. Davies, *apptd* 1985; D. M. K. Durston, *apptd* 1992; June Osborne, *apptd* 1995

Organist, S. R. A. Lole, *apptd* 1997

ARCHDEACONS
Dorset, Ven. A. J. Magowan, *apptd* 2000
Sherborne, Ven. P. C. Wheatley, *apptd* 1991
Wilts, Ven. B. J. Hopkinson, *apptd* 1986 (Sarum), 1998 (Wilts)

Chancellor, His Hon. Judge Wiggs, *apptd* 1997
Registrar and Legal Secretary, A. Johnson
Diocesan Secretary, Revd Karen Curnock, Church House, Crane Street, Salisbury SP1 2QB. Tel: 01722-411922

SHEFFIELD (York)

6TH BISHOP
Rt. Revd John (Jack) Nicholls, *cons.* 1990, *apptd* 1997; Bishopscroft, Snaithing Lane, Sheffield S10 3LG. *Signs* Jack Sheffield

BISHOP SUFFRAGAN
Doncaster, Rt. Revd Cyril Guy Ashton, *cons.* 2000, *apptd* 2000; Bishop's House, 3 Farrington Court, Wickersley, Rotherham SL6 1JQ

PROVOST
Very Revd Michael Sadgrove, *apptd* 1995

CANONS RESIDENTIARY
T. M. Page, *apptd* 1982; C. M. Smith, *apptd* 1991; Ms J. E. M. Sinclair, *apptd* 1993; Ven. R. F. Blackburn, *apptd* 1999

Organist, N.Taylor, *apptd* 1997

ARCHDEACONS
Doncaster, Ven. B. L. Holdridge, *apptd* 1994
Sheffield, Ven. R. F. Blackburn, *apptd* 1999

Chancellor, Prof. J. D. McClean, *apptd* 1992
Registrar and Legal Secretary, Mrs M. Myers
Diocesan Secretary, C. A. Beck, FCIS, Diocesan Church House, 95–99 Effingham Street, Rotherham S65 1BL. Tel: 01709-511116

SODOR AND MAN (York)

79TH BISHOP
Rt. Revd Noel D. Jones, CB, *cons.* 1989, *apptd* 1989; The Bishop's House, Quarterbridge Road, Douglas, Isle of Man IM2 3RF. *Signs* Noel Sodor and Man

CANONS
B. H. Kelly, *apptd* 1980; F. H. Bird, *apptd* 1993; D. Whitworth, *apptd* 1996; M. Convery, *apptd* 1999

ARCHDEACON
Isle of Man, Ven. B. H. Partington, *apptd* 1996

Vicar-General and Chancellor, Ms C. Faulds
Registrar and Legal Secretary, C. J. Callow
Diocesan Secretary, Mrs C. Roberts, Holly Cottage,

Ballaughton Meadows, Douglas, Isle of Man IM2 1JG.
Tel: 01624-626994

SOUTHWARK (Canterbury)

9TH BISHOP
Rt. Revd Thomas F. Butler, PH.D, LL D, *cons.* 1985, *apptd*
1998; Bishop's House, 38 Tooting Bec Gardens,
London SW16 1QZ. *Signs* Thomas Southwark

AREA BISHOPS
Croydon, Rt. Revd Dr Wilfred D. Wood, DD, *cons.* 1985,
apptd 1985; St Matthew's House, George Street,
Croydon CR0 1PE
Kingston upon Thames, Rt Revd Peter B. Price, *cons.* 1997,
apptd 1998; *Kingston Episcopal Area Office*, Whitelands
College, West Hill, London SW15 3SN
Woolwich, Rt. Revd Colin O. Buchanan, *cons.* 1985, *apptd*
1996; 37 South Road, Forest Hill, London SE23 2UJ

DEAN
Very Revd Colin B. Slee, *apptd* 1994

CANONS RESIDENTIARY
Helen Cunliffe, *apptd* 1995; J. John, *apptd* 1997;
B. Saunders, *apptd* 1997; A. P. Nunn, *apptd* 1999;
S. Roberts, *apptd* 2000

Organist, P. Wright, FRCO, *apptd* 1989

ARCHDEACONS
Croydon, Ven. V. A. Davies, *apptd* 1994
Lambeth, Ven. N. Barnes, *apptd* 2000
Lewisham, Ven. D. J. Atkinson, *apptd* 1996
Reigate, vacant
Southwark, Ven. D. L. Bartles-Smith, *apptd* 1985
Wandsworth, Ven. D. Gerrard, *apptd* 1989

Chancellor, C. George, QC
Registrar and Legal Secretary, P. Morris
Diocesan Secretary, S. Parton, Trinity House, 4 Chapel
Court, Borough High Street, London SE1 1HW.
Tel: 020-7403 8686

SOUTHWELL (York)

10TH BISHOP
Rt. Revd George H. Cassidy, *cons.* 1999, *apptd* 1999;
Bishop's Manor, Southwell NG25 0JR. *Signs* George
Southwell

BISHOP SUFFRAGAN
Sherwood, Rt. Revd Alan W. Morgan, *cons.* 1989, *apptd*
1989; Dunham House, Westgate, Southwell, Notts
NG25 0JL

DEAN
Very Revd David Leaning, *apptd* 1991

CANONS RESIDENTIARY
I. G. Collins, *apptd* 1985; G. A. Hendy *apptd* 1997;
R. H. Davey, *apptd* 1999

Organist, P. Hale, *apptd* 1989

ARCHDEACONS
Newark, Ven. N. Peyton, *apptd* 1999
Nottingham, Ven. G. Ogilvie, *apptd* 1996

Chancellor, J. Shand, *apptd* 1981
Registrar and Legal Secretary, C. C. Hodson
Diocesan Secretary, P. Prentis, Dunham House, Westgate,
Southwell, Notts NG25 0JL. Tel: 01636-814331

TRURO (Canterbury)

14TH BISHOP
Rt. Revd William Ind, *cons.* 1987, *apptd* 1997; Lis Escop,
Truro TR3 6QQ. *Signs* William Truro

BISHOP SUFFRAGAN
St Germans, Revd Royden Screech, *cons.* 2000, *apptd* 2000

DEAN
Very Revd Michael A. Moxon, LVO, *apptd* 1998

CANONS RESIDENTIARY
P. R. Gay, *apptd* 1994; K. P. Mellor, *apptd* 1994;
P. D. Goodridge, *apptd* 1996; P. Robson, *apptd* 1999

Organist, A. Nethsingha, FRCO, *apptd* 1994

ARCHDEACONS
Cornwall, Ven. R. D. C. Whiteman, *apptd* 2000
Bodmin, Ven. C. Coehn, *apptd* 2000

Chancellor, T. Briden, *apptd* 1998
Registrar and Legal Secretary, M. J. Follett
Diocesan Secretary, B. C. Laite, Diocesan House, Kenwyn,
Truro TR1 3DU. Tel: 01872-274351

WAKEFIELD (York)

11TH BISHOP
Rt. Revd Nigel S. McCulloch, *cons.* 1986, *apptd* 1992;
Bishop's Lodge, Woodthorpe Lane, Wakefield WF2 6JL.
Signs Nigel Wakefield

BISHOP SUFFRAGAN
Pontefract, Rt. Revd David C. James, *cons.* 1998, *apptd*
1998; Pontefract House, 181A Manygates Lane,
Wakefield WF2 7DR

PROVOST
Very Revd George P. Nairn-Briggs, *apptd* 1997

CANONS RESIDENTIARY
R. Capper, *apptd* 1997; R. Gage, *apptd* 1997; I. Gaskell,
apptd 1998; J. Holmes, *apptd* 1998

Organist, J. Bielby, FRCO, *apptd* 1972

ARCHDEACONS
Halifax, Ven. R. Inwood, *apptd* 1995
Pontefract, Ven. A. Robinson, *apptd* 1997

Chancellor, P. Collier, QC, *apptd* 1992
Registrar and Legal Secretary, L. Box
Diocesan Secretary, A. W. Ellis, Church House, 1 South
Parade, Wakefield WF1 1LP. Tel: 01924-371802

WORCESTER (Canterbury)

112TH BISHOP
Rt. Revd Dr Peter S. M. Selby, *cons.* 1984, *apptd* 1997; The
Bishop's House, Hartlebury Castle, Kidderminster
DY11 7XX. *Signs* Peter Wigorn:

AREA BISHOP
Dudley Rt. Revd David S. Walker, *cons.* 2000,
apptd 2000; The Bishop's House,
Bishop's Walk, Cradley Heath B64 7RH

DEAN
Very Revd Peter J. Marshall, *apptd* 1997

CANONS RESIDENTIARY
I. M. MacKenzie, *apptd* 1989; B. B. Ruddock, *apptd.* 1999;
J. D. Tetley, *apptd* 1999

Organist, A. Lucas, *apptd* 1996

ARCHDEACONS
Dudley, Ven. J. R. Gathercole, *apptd* 1987
Worcester, Ven. Dr J. D. Tetley

Chancellor, C. Mynors, *apptd* 1999
Registrar and Legal Secretary, M. Huskinson
Diocesan Secretary, R. Higham, The Old Palace,
Deansway, Worcester WR1 2JE. Tel: 01905-20537

ROYAL PECULIARS

WESTMINSTER
The Collegiate Church of St Peter
Dean, Very Revd Dr A. W. Carr, *apptd* 1997
Sub Dean and Archdeacon, D. H. Hutt, *apptd* 1995
Canons of Westminster, D. H. Hutt, *apptd* 1995;
M. J. Middleton, *apptd* 1997; R. Wright, *apptd* 1998;
Dr N. T. Wright, *apptd* 1999
Chapter Clerk and Receiver-General, Maj.-Gen. D. Burden,
CB, CBE, *apptd* 199, Chapter Office, 20 Dean's Yard,
London SW1P 3PA
Organist, J. O'Donnell, *apptd* 1999
Registrar, S. J. Holmes, MVO,
Legal Secretary, C. Vyse, *apptd* 2000

WINDSOR
The Queen's Free Chapel of St George within Her Castle of Windsor
Dean, Rt. Revd D. J. Conner, *apptd* 1998
Canons Residentiary, J. A. White, *apptd* 1982;
L. F. P. Gunner, *apptd* 1996; B. P. Thompson, Ph.D.,
apptd 1998; J. A. Ovenden, *apptd* 1998
Chapter Clerk, Lt.-Col. N. J. Newman, *apptd* 1990,
Chapter Office, The Cloisters, Windsor Castle,
Windsor, Berks SL4 1NJ
Organist, J. Rees-Williams, FRCO, *apptd* 1991

Other Anglican Churches

THE CHURCH IN WALES

The Anglican Church was the established church in Wales
from the 16th century until 1920, when the estrangement
of the majority of Welsh people from Anglicanism
resulted in disestablishment. Since then the Church in
Wales has been an autonomous province consisting of six
sees. The bishops are elected by an electoral college
comprising elected lay and clerical members, who also
elect one of the diocesan bishops as Archbishop of Wales.

The legislative body of the Church in Wales is the
Governing Body, which has 365 members divided
between the three orders of bishops, clergy and laity. Its
President is the Archbishop of Wales and it meets twice
annually. Its decisions are binding upon all members of the
Church. The Church's property and finances are the
responsibility of the Representative Body. There are about
96,000 members of the Church in Wales, with about 700
stipendiary clergy and 1,142 parishes.

THE GOVERNING BODY OF THE CHURCH IN WALES,
39 Cathedral Road, Cardiff CF1 9XF. Tel: 029-2023
1638. *Secretary-General*, J. W. D. McIntyre

10TH ARCHBISHOP OF WALES, Most Revd
Dr Rowan D. Wilkins, *elected* 1999, installed 2000

BISHOPS
Bangor (*79th*), Rt. Revd F. J. Saunders Davies, *b.* 1937, *cons.*
2000, *elected* 1999; Ty'r Esgob, Bangor, Gwynedd LL57
2SS. Signs Saunders Bangor, *Stipendiary clergy*, 60
Llandaff (*102nd*), Rt. Revd Dr Barry C. Morgan, *b.* 1947,
cons. 1993, *elected* 1999; Llys Esgob, The Cathedral
Green, Llandaff, Cardiff CF5 2YE. Signs Barry Landav.
Stipendiary clergy, 164
Monmouth (*8th*), Rt. Most-Revd Dr Rowan D. Williams,
b. 1950, *cons.* 1992, *elected* 1992; Bishopstow, Stow Hill,
Newport NP2 4EA. Signs Rowan Cambrensis. *Stipendiary
clergy*, 106
St Asaph (*74th*), Rt. Revd John S. Davies, *b.* 1943, *cons.*
1999, *elected* 1999; Esgobty, St Asaph, Denbighshire
LL17 0TW. Signs John St Asaph. *Stipendiary clergy*, 112
St David's (*126th*), Rt. Revd D. Huw Jones, *b.* 1934, *cons.*
1993, *elected* 1995; Llys Esgob, Abergwili, Carmarthen
SA31 2JG. Signs Huw St Davids. *Stipendiary clergy*, 135
Swansea and Brecon (*8th*), Rt. Revd Anthony E. Pierce,
b. 1941, *cons.* 1999, *elected* 1999; Ely Tower, Brecon,
Powys LD3 9DE. Signs Anthony Swansea & Brecon.
Stipendiary clergy, 86

The stipend of a diocesan bishop of the Church in Wales is
£26,674 a year from 1998

THE SCOTTISH EPISCOPAL CHURCH

The Scottish Episcopal Church was founded after the Act
of Settlement (1690) established the presbyterian nature of
the Church of Scotland. The Scottish Episcopal Church is
in full communion with the Church of England but is
autonomous. The governing authority is the General
Synod, an elected body of approximately 170 members
which meets once a year. The diocesan bishop who
convenes and presides at meetings of the General Synod is
called the Primus and is elected by his fellow bishops.

There are 49,995 members of the Scottish Episcopal
Church, of whom 31,247 are communicants. There are
seven bishops, 315 serving clergy, and 310 churches and
places of worship.

THE GENERAL SYNOD OF THE SCOTTISH EPISCOPAL
CHURCH, 21 Grosvenor Crescent, Edinburgh EH12 5EE.
Tel: 0131-225 6357. *Secretary-General*, J. F. Stuart

PRIMUS OF THE SCOTTISH EPISCOPAL CHURCH, Most
Revd Richard F. Holloway (Bishop of Edinburgh),
elected 1992

BISHOPS
Aberdeen and Orkney, A. Bruce Cameron, *b.* 1941, *cons.*
1992, *elected* 1992. *Clergy*, 40
Argyll and the Isles, Douglas M. Cameron, *b.* 1935, *cons.*
1993, *elected* 1992. *Clergy*, 16
Brechin, Neville Chamberlain, *b.* 1939, *cons.* 1997, *elected*
1997. *Clergy*, 24
Edinburgh, Richard F. Holloway, *b.* 1933, *cons.* 1986,
elected 1986. *Clergy*, 90
Glasgow and Galloway, Idris Jones, *b.* 1943, *cons.* 1998,
elected 1998. *Clergy*, 68
Moray, Ross and Caithness, John Crook, *b.* 1940,
cons. 1999, *elected* 1999. *Clergy*, 25

St Andrews, Dunkeld and Dunblane, Michael H. G. Henley, *b.* 1938, *cons.* 1995, *elected* 1995. *Clergy*, 52

The minimum stipend of a diocesan bishop of the Scottish Episcopal Church was £23,355 in 2000 (e.g. 1.5× the minimum clergy stipend of £15,570)

THE CHURCH OF IRELAND

The Anglican Church was the established church in Ireland from the 16th century but never secured the allegiance of a majority of the Irish and was disestablished in 1871. The Church in Ireland is divided into the provinces of Armagh and Dublin, each under an archbishop. The provinces are subdivided into 12 dioceses.

The legislative body is the General Synod, which has 660 members in total, divided between the House of Bishops and the House of Representatives. The Archbishop of Armagh is elected by the House of Bishops; other episcopal elections are made by an electoral college.

There are about 375,000 members of the Church of Ireland, with two archbishops, ten bishops, about 600 clergy and about 1,000 churches and places of worship.

CENTRAL OFFICE, Church of Ireland House, Church Avenue, Rathmines, Dublin 6. Tel: 00-353-1-497 8422. *Chief Officer and Secretary of the Representative Church Body*, R. H. Sherwood; *Assistant Secretary of the General Synod*, V. F. Beatty

PROVINCE OF ARMAGH

ARCHBISHOP OF ARMAGH AND PRIMATE OF ALL IRELAND, Most Revd Robert H. A. Eames, PH.D., *b.* 1937, *cons.* 1975, *trans.* 1986. *Clergy*, 51

BISHOPS
Clogher, Brian D. A. Hannon, *b.* 1936, *cons.* 1986, *apptd* 1986. *Clergy*, 32
Connor, James E. Moore, *b.* 1933, *cons.* 1995, *apptd* 1995. *Clergy*, 106
Derry and Raphoe, James Mehaffey, PH.D., *b.* 1931, *cons.* 1980, *apptd* 1980. *Clergy*, 50
Down and Dromore, Harold C. Miller, *b.* 1950, *cons.* 1997, *apptd* 1997. *Clergy*, 109
Kilmore, Elphin and Ardagh, Michael H. G. Mayes, *b.* 1941, *cons.* 1993, *apptd* 1993. *Clergy*, 24
Tuam, Killala and Achonry, Richard C. A. Henderson, *b.* 1957, *cons.* 1998, *apptd* 1998. *Clergy*, 12

PROVINCE OF DUBLIN

ARCHBISHOP OF DUBLIN, BISHOP OF GLENDALOUGH, AND PRIMATE OF IRELAND, Most Revd Walton N. F. Empey, *b.* 1934, *cons.* 1981, *trans.* 1985, 1996. *Clergy*, 90

BISHOPS
Cashel and Ossory, John R. W. Neill, *b.* 1945, *cons.* 1986, *trans.* 1997. *Clergy*, 37
Cork, Cloyne and Ross, W. Paul Colton, *b.* 1960, *cons.* 1999, *apptd* 1999. *Clergy*, 28
Limerick and Killaloe, vacant
Meath and Kildare (Most Revd) Robert L. Clarke, PH.D., *b.* 1949, *cons.* 1996, *apptd* 1996. *Clergy*, 23

OVERSEAS

PRIMATES

PRIMATE AND PRESIDING BISHOP OF AOTEAROA, NEW ZEALAND AND POLYNESIA, Rt. Revd John Paterson (Bishop of Auckland), *cons.* 1995, *apptd* 1998

PRIMATE OF AUSTRALIA Most Revd Peter Carnley (Archbishop of Perth), *cons.* 1981, *apptd* 2000
PRIMATE OF BRAZIL, Most Revd Glauco Soares de Lima (Bishop of São Paulo), *cons.* 1989, *apptd* 1994
ARCHBISHOP OF THE PROVINCE OF BURUNDI, Most Revd Samuel Ndayisenga (Bishop of Buye), *apptd* 1998
ARCHBISHOP AND PRIMATE OF CANADA, Most Revd Michael G. Peers, *cons.* 1977, *elected* 1986
ARCHBISHOP OF THE PROVINCE OF CENTRAL AFRICA, vacant
PRIMATE OF THE CENTRAL REGION OF AMERICA, Most Revd Cornelius J. Wilson (Bishop of Costa Rica), *cons.* 1978, *apptd* 1998
ARCHBISHOP OF THE PROVINCE OF CONGO, Most Revd Patrice Byankya Njojo (Bishop of Boga), *cons.* 1980, *apptd* 1992
PRIMATE OF THE PROVINCE OF HONG KONG SHENG KUNG HUI, Most Revd Peter Kwong (Bishop of Hong Kong Island), *cons.* 1981, *apptd* 1998
ARCHBISHOP OF THE PROVINCE OF THE INDIAN OCEAN, Most Revd Remi Rabenirina (Bishop of Antananarivo), *cons.* 1984, *apptd* 1995
PRESIDENT-BISHOP OF JERUSALEM AND THE MIDDLE EAST, Most Revd Iraj Mottahedeh, *apptd* 2000
ARCHBISHOP OF THE PROVINCE OF KENYA, Most Revd Dr David M. Gitari (Bishop of Nairobi), *cons.* 1975, *apptd* 1996
ARCHBISHOP OF THE PROVINCE OF KOREA, Most Revd Paul Hwan Yoon (Bishop of Taejon), *cons.* 1987, *apptd* 2000
ARCHBISHOP OF THE PROVINCE OF MELANESIA, Most Revd Ellison L. Pogo (Bishop of Central Melanesia), *cons.* 1981, *apptd* 1994
ARCHBISHOP OF MEXICO, Most Revd Samuel Espinoza (Bishop of Western Mexico), *cons.* 1981, *elected* 1995
ARCHBISHOP OF THE PROVINCE OF MYANMAR (until February 2001) Most Revd Andrew Mya Han (Bishop of Yangon), *cons.* 1988, *apptd* 1988
ARCHBISHOP OF THE PROVINCE OF NIGERIA, Most Revd Peter Akinola (Bishop of Abuja), *cons.* 1989, *apptd* 2000
PRIMATE OF NIPPON SEI KO KAI, Rt. Revd John Jun'Ichiro Furumoto (Bishop of Kobe), *elected* 2000
ARCHBISHOP OF PAPUA NEW GUINEA, Most Revd James Ayong (Bishop of Aipo Rongo), *cons.* 1995, *elected* 1996
PRIME BISHOP OF THE PHILIPPINES, Most Revd Ignacio C. Soliba, *cons.* 1991, *apptd* 1997
ARCHBISHOP OF THE PROVINCE OF RWANDA, Most Revd Emmanuel Kolini Mboni (Bishop of Kigali), *cons.* 1980, *apptd* 1997
PRIMATE OF THE PROVINCE OF SOUTH EAST ASIA, Most Revd Ping Chung Yong (Bishop of Sabah), *cons.* 1990 *apptd* 1999
METROPOLITAN OF THE PROVINCE OF SOUTHERN AFRICA, Most Revd Winston H. N. Ndungane (Archbishop of Cape Town), *cons.* 1991, *trans.* 1996
PRESIDING BISHOP OF THE SOUTHERN CONE OF AMERICA, Rt. Revd Maurice Sinclair (Bishop of Northern Argentina), *cons.* 1990
ARCHBISHOP OF THE PROVINCE OF THE SUDAN, Most Revd Joseph Marona (Bishop of Juba) *cons.* 1984, *apptd* 2000
ARCHBISHOP OF THE PROVINCE OF TANZANIA, Most Revd Donald L. Mtetemela (Bishop of Ruaha), *cons.* 1982, *apptd* 1998
ARCHBISHOP OF THE PROVINCE OF UGANDA, Most Revd Livingstone Mpalanyi-Nkoyoyo. *cons.* 1980
PRESIDING BISHOP AND PRIMATE OF THE USA, Most Revd Frank T. Griswold III, *cons.* 1985, *apptd* 1997
ARCHBISHOP OF THE PROVINCE OF WEST AFRICA, Most Revd Robert Okine (Bishop of Koforidua), *cons.* 1981, *apptd* 1993

ARCHBISHOP OF THE PROVINCE OF THE WEST INDIES, Most Revd Drexel Gomez (Bishop of Nassau and the Bahamas), *cons.* 1972, *apptd* 1998

OTHER CHURCHES AND
EXTRA-PROVINCIAL DIOCESES

ANGLICAN CHURCH OF BERMUDA, Rt. Revd Ewen Ratteray, *apptd* 1996
CHURCH OF CEYLON: This Church comes under the Metropolitical authority of the Archbishop of Canterbury.
Bishop of Colombo, Rt. Revd Kenneth Michael James Fernando, *cons.* 1992
Bishop of Kurunagala, Rt. Revd Andrew O. Kumarage, *cons.* 1984
EPISCOPAL CHURCH OF CUBA, Rt. Revd Jorge Perera Hurtado, *apptd* 1995
LUSITANIAN CHURCH (*Portuguese Episcopal Church*), Rt. Revd Fernando da Luz Soares, *apptd* 1971
SPANISH REFORMED EPISCOPAL CHURCH, Rt. Revd Carlos Lozano Lopez, *apptd* 1995
EXTRA-PROVINCIAL TO PROVINCE IX OF THE EPISCOPAL CHURCH IN THE USA:
PUERTO RICO, Rt. Revd David Andres Alvarez-Velazquez, *cons.* 1987
VENEZUELA, Rt. Revd Orlando Guerrero, *cons.* 1995

MODERATORS OF CHURCHES IN FULL
COMMUNION WITH THE ANGLICAN
COMMUNION

CHURCH OF NORTH INDIA, Rt. Revd Vinod Peter (Bishop of Nagpur), *apptd* 1998
CHURCH OF SOUTH INDIA, Most Revd Joseph Samuel (Bishop of East Kerala), *cons.* 1990, *apptd* 2000
CHURCH OF PAKISTAN, Rt. Revd Samuel Azariah, Bishop of Raiwind
CHURCH OF BANGLADESH, Rt. Revd Barnabas Mondal, *cons.* 1975, *apptd* 1975

The Church of Scotland

The Church of Scotland is the established (i.e. national) church of Scotland. The Church is Reformed and evangelical in doctrine, and presbyterian in constitution, i.e. based on a hierarchy of councils of ministers and elders and, since 1990, of members of a diaconate. At local level the kirk session consists of the parish minister and ruling elders. At district level the presbyteries, of which there are 47, consist of all the ministers in the district, one ruling elder from each congregation, and those members of the diaconate who qualify for membership. The General Assembly is the supreme authority, and is presided over by a Moderator chosen annually by the Assembly. The Sovereign, if not present in person, is represented by a Lord High Commissioner who is appointed each year by the Crown.

The Church of Scotland has about 700,000 members, 1,200 ministers and 1,600 churches. There are about 100 ministers and other personnel working overseas.

Lord High Commissioner (1999), The Lord Hogg of Cumbernauld
Moderator of the General Assembly (1999), The Rt. Revd John B. Cairns
Principal Clerk, Revd F. A. J. Macdonald
Depute Clerk, Revd M. A. MacLean

Procurator, R. A. Dunlop, QC
Law Agent and Solicitor of the Church, Mrs J. S. Wilson
Parliamentary Agent, I. McCulloch (*London*)
General Treasurer, D. F. Ross
Secretary, Church and Nation Committee, Revd Dr D. Sinclair
CHURCH OFFICE, 121 George Street, Edinburgh EH2 4YN.
Tel: 0131-225 5722

PRESBYTERIES AND CLERKS

Edinburgh, Revd W. P. Graham
West Lothian, Revd D. Shaw
Lothian, J. D. McCulloch
Melrose and Peebles, Revd J. H. Brown
Duns, Revd A. C. D. Cartwright
Jedburgh, Revd A. D. Reid
Annandale and Eskdale, Revd C. B. Haston
Dumfries and Kirkcudbright, Revd G. M. A. Savage
Wigtown and Stranraer, Revd D. Dutton
Ayr, Revd J. Crichton
Irvine and Kilmarnock, Revd C. G. F. Brockie
Ardrossan, Revd D. Broster
Lanark, Revd I. D. Cunningham
Paisley, Revd D. Kay
Greenock, Revd D. Mill
Glasgow, Revd A. Cunningham
Hamilton, Revd J. H. Wilson
Dumbarton, Revd D. P. Munro
South Argyll, M. A. J. Gossip
Dunoon, Revd R. Samuel
Lorn and Mull, Revd W. Hogg
Falkirk, Revd D. E. McClements
Stirling, Revd B. W. Dunsmore
Dunfermline, Revd W. E. Farquhar
Kirkcaldy, Revd B. L. Tomlinson
St Andrews, Revd P. Meager
Dunkeld and Meigle, Revd A. B. Reid
Perth, Revd A. M. Millar
Dundee, Revd J. A. Roy
Angus, Revd M. I. G. Rooney
Aberdeen, Revd A. Douglas
Kincardine and Deeside, Revd J. W. S. Brown
Gordon, Revd I. U. Thomson
Buchan, Revd R. Neilson
Moray, Revd D. J. Ferguson
Abernethy, Revd J. A. I. MacEwan
Inverness, Revd A. S. Younger
Lochaber, Revd A. Ramsay
Ross, Revd R. M. MacKinnon
Sutherland, Revd J. L. Goskirk
Caithness, Revd M. G. Mappin
Lochcarron/Skye, Revd A. I. Macarthur
Uist, Revd M. Smith
Lewis, Revd T. S. Sinclair
Orkney (Finstown), Revd T. Hunt
Shetland (Lerwick), Revd N. R. Whyte
England (London), Revd W. A. Cairns
Europe (Geneva), Revd J. W. McLeod
The minimum stipend of a minister in the Church of Scotland in 1998 was £16,737

The Roman Catholic Church

The Roman Catholic Church is one world-wide Christian Church acknowledging as its head the Bishop of Rome, known as the Pope (Father). The Pope is held to be the successor of St Peter and thus invested with the power which was entrusted to St Peter by Jesus Christ. A direct line of succession is therefore claimed from the earliest Christian communities. With the fall of the Roman Empire the Pope also became an important political leader. His temporal power is now limited to the 107 acres of the Vatican City State.

The Pope exercises spiritual authority over the Church with the advice and assistance of the Sacred College of Cardinals, the supreme council of the Church. He is also advised about the concerns of the Church locally by his ambassadors, who liaise with the Bishops' Conference in each country.

In addition to advising the Pope, those members of the Sacred College of Cardinals who are under the age of 80 also elect a successor following the death of a Pope. The assembly of the Cardinals at the Vatican for the election of a new Pope is known as the Conclave in which, in complete seclusion, the Cardinals elect by a secret ballot; a two-thirds majority is necessary before the vote can be accepted as final. When a Cardinal receives the necessary votes, the Dean of the Sacred College formally asks him if he will accept election and the name by which he wishes to be known. On his acceptance of the office the Conclave is dissolved and the First Cardinal Deacon announces the election to the assembled crowd in St Peter's Square. On the first Sunday or Holyday following the election, the new Pope assumes the pontificate at High Mass in St Peter's Square. A new pontificate is dated from the assumption of the pontificate.

The number of cardinals was fixed at 70 by Pope Sixtus V in 1586, but has been steadily increased since the pontificate of John XXIII and at the end of December 1999 stood at 154, plus two cardinals created 'in pectore' (their names being kept secret by the Pope for fear of persecution; they are thought to be Chinese).

The Roman Catholic Church universally and the Vatican City State are run by the Curia, which is made up of the Secretariat of State, the Sacred Council for the Public Affairs of the Church, and various congregations, secretariats and tribunals assisted by commissions and offices. The congregations are permanent commissions for conducting the affairs of the Church and are made up of cardinals, one of whom occupies the office of prefect. Below the Secretariat of State and the congregations are the secretariats and tribunals, all of which are headed by cardinals. (The Curial cardinals are analagous to ministers in charge of government departments.)

The Vatican State has its own diplomatic service, with representatives known as nuncios. Papal nuncios with full diplomatic recognition are given precedence over all other ambassadors to the country to which they are appointed; where precedence is not recognised the Papal representative is known as a pro-nuncio. Where the representation is only to the local churches and not to the government of a country, the Papal representative is known as an apostolic delegate. The Roman Catholic Church has an estimated 890.9 million adherents world-wide.

SOVEREIGN PONTIFF

His Holiness Pope John Paul II (Karol Wojtyla), *born* Wadowice, Poland, 18 May 1920; *ordained priest* 1946; *appointed Archbishop of Kraków* 1964; *created Cardinal* 1967; *assumed pontificate* 16 October 1978

SECRETARIAT OF STATE

Secretary of State, HE Cardinal Angelo Sodano
First Section (General Affairs), Mgr G. Re (Archbishop of Vescovio)

Second Section (Relations with other states), Mgr J. L. Tauran (Archbishop of Telepte)

BISHOPS' CONFERENCE

The Roman Catholic Church in England and Wales is governed by the Bishops' Conference, membership of which includes the Diocesan Bishops, the Apostolic Exarch of the Ukrainians, the Bishop of the Forces and the Auxiliary Bishops. The Conference is headed by the President and Vice-President. There are five departments, each with an episcopal chairman: the Department for Christian Life and Worship (the Archbishop of Southwark), the Department for Mission and Unity (the Archbishop of Westminster), the Department for Catholic Education and Formation (the Bishop of Leeds), the Department for Christian Responsibility and Citizenship (the Bishop of East Anglia), and the Department for International Affairs (the Bishop of Leeds).

The Bishops' Standing Committee, made up of all the Archbishops and the chairman of each of the above departments, has general responsibility for continuity and policy between the plenary sessions of the Conference. It prepares the Conference agenda and implements its decisions. It is serviced by a General Secretariat. There are also agencies and consultative bodies affiliated to the Conference.

The Bishops' Conference of Scotland has as its president Archbishop Winning of Glasgow and is the permanently constituted assembly of the Bishops of Scotland. To promote its work, the Conference establishes various agencies which have an advisory function in relation to the Conference. The more important of these agencies are called Commissions and each one has a Bishop President who, with the other members of the Commissions, are appointed by the Conference.

The Irish Episcopal Conference has as its acting president Archbishop Connell of Dublin. Its membership comprises all the Archbishops and Bishops of Ireland and it appoints various Commissions to assist it in its work. There are three types of Commissions: (a) those made up of lay and clerical members chosen for their skills and experience, and staffed by full-time expert secretariats; (b) Commissions whose members are selected from existing institutions and whose services are supplied on a part-time basis; and (c) Commissions of Bishops only.

The Roman Catholic Church in Britain and Ireland has an estimated 8,992,000 members, 11 archbishops, 67 bishops, 11,260 priests, and 8,588 churches and chapels open to the public.

Bishops' Conferences secretariats:

ENGLAND AND WALES, 39 Eccleston Square, London SW1V 1PD. Tel: 020-7630 8220. *General Secretary*, The Rt. Revd Arthur Roche

SCOTLAND, Candida Casa, 8 Corsehill Road, Ayr KA7 2ST. Tel: 01292-256750. *General Secretary*, The Rt. Revd Maurice Taylor (Bishop of Galloway)

IRELAND, Iona, 65 Newry Road, Dundalk, Co. Louth. *Executive Secretary*, Revd Hugh G. Connelly

GREAT BRITAIN

APOSTOLIC NUNCIO TO GREAT BRITAIN
The Most Revd Pablo Puente, 54 Parkside, London SW19 5NE. Tel: 020-8946 1410

ENGLAND AND WALES

THE MOST REVD ARCHBISHOPS

Westminster, Cormac Murphy-O'Connor, *cons.* 1977, *apptd* 2000
  Auxiliaries, Vincent Nichols, *cons.* 1992; James J. O'Brien, *cons.* 1977; Patrick O'Donoghue, *cons.* 1993
  Clergy, 762
  Archbishop's Residence, Archbishop's House, Ambrosden Avenue, London SW1P 1QJ. Tel: 020-7798 9033
Birmingham, Vincent Nichols, *cons.* 1992, *apptd* 2000
  Auxiliaries, Philip Pargeter, *cons.* 1990
  Clergy, 511
  Diocesan Curia, Cathedral House, St Chad's Queensway, Birmingham B4 6EX. Tel: 0121-236 5535
Cardiff, John A. Ward, *cons.* 1980, *apptd* 1983
  Clergy, 126
  Diocesan Curia, Archbishop's House, 41–43 Cathedral Road, Cardiff CF11 9HD. Tel: 029-2022 0411
Liverpool, Patrick Kelly, *cons.* 1984, *apptd* 1996
  Auxiliary, Vincent Malone, *cons.* 1989
  Clergy, 522
  Diocesan Curia, 152 Brownlow Hill, Liverpool L3 5RQ. Tel: 0151-709 4801
Southwark, Michael Bowen, *cons.* 1970, *apptd* 1977
  Auxiliaries, Charles Henderson, *cons.* 1972; Howard Tripp, *cons.* 1980; John Jukes, *cons.* 1980
  Clergy, 518
  Diocesan Curia, Archbishop's House, 150 St George's Road, London SE1 6HX. Tel: 020-7928 5592

THE RT. REVD BISHOPS

Arundel and Brighton, vacant
  Clergy, 27. *Diocesan Curia*, Bishop's House, The Upper Drive, Hove, E. Sussex BN3 6NE. Tel: 01273-506387
Brentwood, Thomas McMahon, *cons.* 1980, *apptd* 1980.
  Clergy, 175. *Bishop's Office*, Cathedral House, Ingrave Road, Brentwood, Essex CM15 8AT. Tel: 01277-232266
Clifton, Mervyn Alexander, *cons.* 1972, *apptd* 1974.
  Clergy, 254. *Diocesan Curia*, Egerton Road, Bishopston, Bristol BS7 8HU. Tel: 0117-983 3907
East Anglia, Peter Smith, *cons.* 1995, *apptd* 1995. *Clergy*, 164. *Diocesan Curia*, The White House, 21 Upgate, Poringland, Norwich NR1 47SH. Tel: 01508-492202
Hallam, John Rawsthorne, *cons.* 1981, *apptd* 1997. *Clergy*, 91. *Bishop's Residence*, 'Quarters', Carsick Hill Way, Sheffield S10 3LY. Tel: 0114-230 9101
Hexham and Newcastle, Michael Ambrose Griffiths, *cons.* 1992. *Clergy*, 261. *Diocesan Curia*, Bishop's House, East Denton Hall, 800 West Road, Newcastle upon Tyne NE5 2BJ. Tel: 0191-228 0003
Lancaster, vacant
  Clergy, 248. *Bishop's Residence*, Bishop's House, Cannon Hill, Lancaster LA1 5NG. Tel: 01524-32231
Leeds, David Konstant, *cons.* 1977, *apptd* 1985. *Clergy*, 254. *Diocesan Curia*, Hinsley Hall, 62 Headingley Lane, Leeds LS6 2BX. Tel: 0113-261 8000
Menevia (*Wales*), Daniel Mullins, *cons.* 1970, *apptd* 1987. *Clergy*, 60. *Diocesan Curia*, 27 Convent Street, Swansea SA1 2BX. Tel: 01792-644017
Middlesbrough, John Crowley, *cons.* 1986, *apptd* 1992. *Clergy*, 182. *Diocesan Curia*, 50A The Avenue, Linthorpe, Middlesbrough, Cleveland TS5 6QT. Tel: 01642-850505
Northampton, Patrick Leo McCartie, *cons.* 1977, *apptd* 1990. *Clergy*, 159. *Diocesan Curia*, Bishop's House, Marriott Street, Northampton NN2 6AW. Tel: 01604-715635
Nottingham, James McGuinness, *cons.* 1972, *apptd* 1974. *Clergy*, 214. *Diocesan Curia*, Willson House, Derby Road, Nottingham NG1 5AW. Tel: 0115-953 9800

Plymouth, Christopher Budd, *cons.* 1986. *Clergy*, 170. *Diocesan Curia*, Bishop's House, 31 Wyndham Street West, Plymouth PL1 5RZ. Tel: 01752-224414
Portsmouth, F. Crispian Hollis, *cons.* 1987, *apptd* 1989. *Clergy*, 282. *Bishop's Residence*, Bishop's House, Edinburgh Road, Portsmouth, Hants PO1 3HG. Tel: 023-9282 0894
Salford, Terence J. Brain, *cons.* 1991, *apptd* 1997. *Clergy*, 380. *Diocesan Curia*, Cathedral House, 250 Chapel Street, Salford M3 5LL. Tel: 0161-834 9052
Shrewsbury, Brian Noble, *cons.* 1995, *apptd* 1995. *Clergy* 202. *Diocesan Curia*, 2 Park Road South, Birkenhead, Wirral L43 4UX. Tel: 0151-652 9855
Wrexham (*Wales*), Edwin Regan, *apptd* 1994. *Clergy*, 83. *Diocesan Curia*, Bishop's House, Sontley Road, Wrexham, Clwyd LL13 7EW. Tel: 01978-262726

SCOTLAND

THE MOST REVD ARCHBISHOPS

St Andrews and Edinburgh, Keith Patrick O'Brien, *cons.* 1985
  Clergy, 188
  Diocesan Curia, 113 Whitehouse Loan, Edinburgh EH9 1BD. Tel: 0131-452 8244
Glasgow, HE Cardinal Thomas Winning, *cons.* 1971, *apptd* 1974
  Clergy, 257
  Diocesan Curia, 196 Clyde Street, Glasgow G1 4JY. Tel: 0141-226 5898

THE RT. REVD BISHOPS

Aberdeen, Mario Conti, *cons.* 1977. *Clergy*, 54. *Bishop's Residence*, 3 Queen's Cross, Aberdeen AB2 6BR. Tel: 01224-319154
Argyll and the Isles, Ian Murray, *cons.* 1999. *Clergy*, 33. *Diocesan Curia*, St Columba's Cathedral, Esplanade, Oban, Argyll PA34 5AB. Tel: 01631-571003
Dunkeld, Vincent Logan, *cons.* 1981. *Clergy*, 52. *Diocesan Curia*, 29 Roseangle, Dundee DD1 4LR. Tel: 01382-25453
Galloway, Maurice Taylor, *cons.* 1981. *Clergy*, 59. *Diocesan Curia*, 8 Corsehill Road, Ayr KA7 2ST. Tel: 01292-266750
Motherwell, Joseph Devine, *cons.* 1977, *apptd* 1983. *Clergy*, 163. *Diocesan Curia*, Coursington Road, Motherwell ML1 1PW. Tel: 01698-269114
Paisley, John A. Mone, *cons.* 1984, *apptd* 1988. *Clergy*, 87. *Diocesan Curia*, Cathedral House, 8 East Buchanan Street, Paisley, Renfrewshire PA1 1HS. Tel: 0141-889 3601

BISHOPRIC OF THE FORCES

Francis Walmsley, *cons.* 1979. Administration: AGPDO, Middle Hill, Aldershot, Hants GU11 1PP. Tel: 01252-349004

IRELAND

There is one hierarchy for the whole of Ireland. Several of the dioceses have territory partly in the Republic of Ireland and partly in Northern Ireland.

APOSTOLIC NUNCIO TO IRELAND
  Most Revd Giovanni Ceirano (titular Archbishop of Tigimma), 183 Navan Road, Dublin 7. Tel: (00353)(1)-380577
THE MOST REVD ARCHBISHOPS
Armagh, Sean Brady, *cons.* 1995, *apptd* 1996
  Auxiliary, Gerard Clifford, *cons.* 1991

Clergy, 183
Diocesan Curia, Ara Coeli, Armagh BT61 7QY. Tel: 028-3752 2045
Cashel, Dermot Clifford, *cons*. 1986, *apptd* 1988
Clergy, 136
Archbishop's Residence, Archbishop's House, Thurles, Co. Tipperary. Tel: (00 353)(504)-21512
Dublin, Desmond Connell, *cons*. 1988, *apptd* 1988
Auxiliaries, James Moriarty, *cons*. 1991; Eamonn Walsh, *cons*. 1990; Fiachra O'Ceallaigh, *cons* 1994; Martin Drennan, *cons*. 1997; Raymond Field, *cons*. 1997
Clergy, 994
Archbishop's Residence, Archbishop's House, Drumcondra, Dublin 9. Tel: (00 353)(1)-837 3732
Tuam, Michael Neary, *cons*. 1992, *apptd* 1995
Clergy, 180
Archbishop's Residence, Archbishop's House, Tuam, Co. Galway. Tel: (00 353)(93)-24166

THE MOST REVD BISHOPS

Achonry, Thomas Flynn, *cons*. 1975. *Clergy*, 62. *Bishop's Residence*, Bishop's House, Ballaghadaderreen, Co. Roscommon. Tel: (00 353)(907)-60021
Ardagh and Clonmacnois, Colm O'Reilly, *cons*. 1983. *Clergy*, 100. *Diocesan Office*, Bishop's House, St Michael's, Longford, Co. Longford. Tel: (00 353)(43)-46432
Clogher, Joseph Duffy, *cons*. 1979. *Clergy*, 108. *Bishop's Residence*, Bishop's House, Monaghan. Tel: (00 353)(47)-81019
Clonfert, Joseph Kirby, *cons*. 1988. *Clergy*, 71. *Bishop's Residence*, St Brendan's, Coorheen, Loughrea, Co. Galway. Tel: (00 353)(91)-41560
Cloyne, John Magee, *cons*. 1987. *Clergy*, 158. *Diocesan Centre*, Cobh, Co. Cork. Tel: (00 353)(21)-811430
Cork and Ross, John Buckley, *cons*. 1984, *apptd* 1998. *Clergy*, 338. *Diocesan Office*, Bishop's House, Redemption Road, Cork. Tel: (00 353)(21)-301717
Derry, Seamus Hegarty, *cons*. 1984, *apptd* 1994. *Clergy*, 157. *Bishop's Residence*, Bishop's House, St Eugene's Cathedral, Derry BT48 9AP. Tel: 028-7126 2302
Auxiliary, Francis Lagan, *cons*. 1988
Down and Connor, Patrick J. Walsh, *cons*. 1983, *apptd* 1991. *Clergy*, 248. *Bishop's Residence*, Lisbreen, 73 Somerton Road, Belfast, Co. Antrim BT15 4DE. Tel: 028-9077 6185
Auxiliaries, Anthony Farquhar, *cons*. 1983; Michael Dallat, *cons*. 1994
Dromore, John McAreavey, *cons*. 1999. *Clergy*, 78. *Bishop's Residence*, Bishop's House, Violet Hill, Newry, Co. Down BT35 6PN. Tel: 028-3026 2444
Elphin, Christopher Jones, *cons*. 1994. *Clergy*, 101. *Bishop's Residence*, St Mary's, Sligo. Tel: (00 353)(71)-62670
Ferns, Brendon Comiskey, *cons*. 1980. *Clergy*, 161. *Bishop's Office*, Bishop's House, Summerhill, Wexford. Tel: (00 353)(53)-22177
Galway and Kilmacduagh, James McLoughlin, *cons*. 1993. *Clergy*, 90. *Diocesan Office*, The Cathedral, Galway. Tel: (00 353)(91)-63566
Kerry, William Murphy, *cons*. 1995. *Clergy*, 149. *Bishop's Residence*, Bishop's House, Killarney, Co. Kerry. Tel: (00 353)(64)-31168
Kildare and Leighlin, Laurence Ryan, *cons*. 1984. *Clergy*, 136. *Bishop's Residence*, Bishop's House, Carlow. Tel: (00 353)(503)-31102
Killala, Thomas Finnegan, *cons*. 1970. *Clergy*, 62. *Bishop's Residence*, Bishop's House, Ballina, Co. Mayo. Tel: (00 353)(96)-21518
Killaloe, William Walsh, *cons*. 1994. *Clergy*, 149. *Bishop's Residence*, Westbourne, Ennis, Co. Clare. Tel: (00 353)(65)-28638

Kilmore, Francis McKiernan, *cons*. 1972. *Coadjutor*, Leo O'Reilly. *Clergy*, 115. *Bishop's Residence*, Bishop's House, Cullies, Co. Cavan. Tel: (00 353)(49)-31496
Limerick, Donal Murray, *cons*. 1996. *Clergy*, 152. *Diocesan Offices*, 66 O'Connell Street, Limerick. Tel: (00 353)(61)-315856
Meath, Michael Smith, *cons*. 1984, *apptd* 1990. *Clergy*, 141. *Bishop's Residence*, Bishop's House, Dublin Road, Mullingar, Co. Westmeath. Tel: (00 353)(44)-48841
Ossory, Laurence Forristal, *cons*. 1980. *Clergy*, 111. *Bishop's Residence*, Sion House, Kilkenny. Tel: (00 353)(56)-62448
Raphoe, Philip Boyce, *cons*. 1994. *Clergy*, 96. *Bishop's Residence*, Ard Adhamhnáin, Letterkenny, Co. Donegal. Tel: (00 353)(74)-21208
Waterford and Lismore, William Lee, *cons*. 1993. *Clergy*, 130. *Bishop's Residence*, Woodleigh, Summerville Avenue, Waterford. Tel: (00 353)(51)-71432

PATRIARCHS IN COMMUNION WITH THE ROMAN CATHOLIC CHURCH

Alexandria, HB Stephanos II Ghattas (Patriarch for Catholic Copts)
Antioch, HB Ignace Antoine II Hayek (Patriarch for Syrian rite Catholics); HB Maximos V. Hakim (Patriarch for Greek Melekite rite Catholics); HE Cardinal Nasrallah Pierre Sfeir (Patriarch for Maronite rite Catholics)
Jerusalem, HB Michel Sabbah (Patriarch for Latin rite Catholics); HB Maximos V. Hakim (Patriarch for Greek Melekite rite Catholics)
Babilonia of the Chaldeans, HB Raphael I Bidawid
Cilicia of the Armenians, HB Jean Pierre XVIII Kasparian (Patriarch for Armenian rite Catholics)
Oriental India, Archbishop Raul Nicolau Gonsalves
Lisbon, vacant
Venice, HE Cardinal Marco Ce

Other Churches in the UK

AFRICAN AND AFRO-CARIBBEAN CHURCHES

There are more than 160 Christian churches or groups of African or Afro-Caribbean origin in the UK. These include the Apostolic Faith Church, the Cherubim and Seraphim Church, the New Testament Church Assembly, the New Testament Church of God, the Wesleyan Holiness Church and the Aladura Churches.

The Afro-West Indian United Council of Churches and the Council of African and Afro-Caribbean Churches UK (which was initiated as the Council of African and Allied Churches in 1979 to give one voice to the various Christian churches of African origin in the UK) are the media through which the member churches can work jointly to provide services they cannot easily provide individually.

There are about 70,000 adherents of African and Afro-Caribbean churches in the UK, and about 1,000 congregations. The Afro-West Indian United Council of Churches has about 30,000 individual members, 135 ministers and own 65 places of worship. The Council of African and Afro-Caribbean Churches UK has about 17,000 members, 250 ministers and 125 congregations.

AFRO-WEST INDIAN UNITED COUNCIL OF CHURCHES, c/o New Testament Church of God, Arcadian Gardens, High Road, London N22 5AA. Tel: 020-8888 9427. *Secretary*, Bishop E. Brown

COUNCIL OF AFRICAN AND AFRO-CARIBBEAN CHURCHES UK, 31 Norton House, Sidney Road, London SW9 0UJ. Tel: 020-7274 5589. *Chairman*, His Grace The Most Revd Father Olu A. Abiola

ASSOCIATED PRESBYTERIAN CHURCHES OF SCOTLAND

The Associated Presbyterian Churches came into being in 1989 as a result of a division within the Free Presbyterian Church of Scotland. Following two controversial disciplinary cases, the culmination of deepening differences within the Church, a presbytery was formed calling itself the Associated Presbyterian Churches (APC). The Associated Presbyterian Churches has about 1,000 members, 15 ministers and 20 churches.

Clerk of the Scottish Presbytery, Revd A. N. McPhail, Fernhill, Polvinster Road, Oban PA34 5TN. Tel: 01631-567076

THE BAPTIST CHURCH

Baptists trace their origins to John Smyth, who in 1609 in Amsterdam reinstituted the baptism of conscious believers as the basis of the fellowship of a gathered church. Members of Smyth's church established the first Baptist church in England in 1612. They came to be known as 'General' Baptists and their theology was Arminian, whereas a later group of Calvinists who adopted the baptism of believers came to be known as 'Particular' Baptists. The two sections of the Baptists were united into one body, the Baptist Union of Great Britain and Ireland, in 1891. In 1988 the title was changed to the Baptist Union of Great Britain.

Baptists emphasise the complete autonomy of the local church, although individual churches are linked in various kinds of associations. There are international bodies (such as the Baptist World Alliance) and national bodies, but some Baptist churches belong to neither. However, in Great Britain the majority of churches and associations belong to the Baptist Union of Great Britain. There are also Baptist Unions in Wales, Scotland and Ireland which are much smaller than the Baptist Union of Great Britain, and there is some overlap of membership.

There are over 40 million Baptist church members world-wide; in the Baptist Union of Great Britain there are 144,932 members, 1,780 pastors and 2,110 churches. In the Baptist Union of Scotland there are 14,881 members, 132 pastors and 173 churches. In the Baptist Union of Wales there are 21,800 members, 110 pastors and 527 churches. In the Association of Baptist Churches there are 8,378 members, 90 pastors and 110 churches.

President of the Baptist Union of Great Britain (2000–1), Prof. G. Ashworth

General Secretary, Revd D. R. Coffey, Baptist House, PO Box 44, 129 Broadway, Didcot, Oxon OX11 8RT. Tel: 01235-517700

THE CONGREGATIONAL FEDERATION

The Congregational Federation was founded by members of Congregational churches in England and Wales who did not join the United Reformed Church in 1972. There are also churches in Scotland and Australia affiliated to the Federation. The Federation exists to encourage congregations of believers to worship in free assembly, but it has no authority over them and emphasises their right to independence and self-government.

The Federation has 11,923 members, 71 recognised ministers and 313 churches in England, Wales and Scotland.

President of the Federation (2000–1), Revd. J. Smith

General Secretary, Revd. M. Heaney, The Congregational Centre, 48 Castle Gate, Nottingham NG1 7AS. Tel: 0115-911 1460

THE FREE CHURCH OF ENGLAND

The Free Church of England is a union of two bodies in the Anglican tradition, the Free Church of England, founded in 1844 as a protest against the Oxford Movement in the established Church, and the Reformed Episcopal Church, founded in America in 1873 but which also had congregations in England. As both Churches sought to maintain the historic faith, tradition and practice of the Anglican Church since the Reformation, they decided to unite as one body in England in 1927. The historic episcopate was conferred on the English Church in 1876 through the line of the American bishops, who had pioneered an open table Communion policy towards members of other denominations.

The Free Church of England has 1,500 members, 42 ministers and 25 churches in England. It also has three house churches and three ministers in New Zealand, and one church and one minister in St Petersburg, Russia.

General Secretary, Revd R. E. Talbot, 32 Bonnywood Road, Hassocks, W. Sussex BN6 8HR. Tel: 01273-845092

THE FREE CHURCH OF SCOTLAND

The Free Church of Scotland was formed in 1843 when over 400 ministers withdrew from the Church of Scotland as a result of interference in the internal affairs of the church by the civil authorities. In 1900, all but 26 ministers joined with others to form the United Free Church (most of which rejoined the Church of Scotland in 1929). In 1904 the remaining 26 ministers were recognised by the House of Lords as continuing the Free Church of Scotland.

The Church maintains strict adherence to the Westminster Confession of Faith (1648) and accepts the Bible as the sole rule of faith and conduct. Its General Assembly meets annually. It also has links with Reformed Churches overseas. The Free Church of Scotland has 5,000 communicating members, 90 ministers and 110 churches.

General Treasurer, I. D. Gill, The Mound, Edinburgh EH1 2LS. Tel: 0131-226 5286

THE FREE PRESBYTERIAN CHURCH OF SCOTLAND

The Free Presbyterian Church of Scotland was formed in 1893 by two ministers of the Free Church of Scotland who refused to accept a Declaratory Act passed by the Free Church General Assembly in 1892. The Free Presbyterian Church of Scotland is Calvinistic in doctrine and emphasises observance of the Sabbath. It adheres strictly to the Westminster Confession of Faith of 1648.

The Church has about 3,000 members in Scotland and about 4,000 in overseas congregations. It has 20 ministers and 50 churches.
Moderator, Revd K. D. Macleod, BSc., Free Presbyterian Manse, Leverburgh, Harris, Western Isles HS5 3UA
Clerk of Synod, Revd J. MacLeod, 16 Matheson Road, Stornoway, Isle of Lewis HS1 2LA. Tel: 01851-702755

THE INDEPENDENT METHODIST CHURCHES

The Independent Methodist Churches seceded from the Wesleyan Methodist Church in 1805 and remained independent when the Methodist Church in Great Britain was formed in 1932. They are mainly concentrated in the industrial areas of the north of England.

The churches are Methodist in doctrine but their organisation is congregational. All the churches are members of the Independent Methodist Connexion of Churches. The controlling body of the Connexion is the Annual Meeting, to which churches send delegates. The Connexional President is elected annually. Between annual meetings the affairs of the Connexion are handled by departmental committees. Ministers are appointed by the churches and trained through the Connexion. The ministry is open to both men and women and is unpaid.

There are 2,552 members, 108 ministers and 98 churches in Great Britain.
Connexional President (2000–1), A. G. Mort
General Secretary, W. C. Gabb, 66 Kirkstone Drive, Loughborough LE11 3RW

THE LUTHERAN CHURCH

Lutheranism is based on the teachings of Martin Luther, the German leader of the Protestant Reformation. The authority of the scriptures is held to be supreme over Church tradition and creeds, and the key doctrine is that of justification by faith alone.

Lutheranism is one of the largest Protestant denominations and it is particularly strong in northern Europe and the USA. Some Lutheran churches are episcopal, while others have a synodal form of organisation; unity is based on doctrine rather than structure. Most Lutheran churches are members of the Lutheran World Federation, based in Geneva.

Lutheran services in Great Britain are held in 17 languages to serve members of different nationalities. English-language congregations are members either of the Lutheran Church in Great Britain, or of the Evangelical Lutheran Church of England. The Lutheran Church in Great Britain and other Lutheran churches in Britain are members of the Lutheran Council of Great Britainn most, which represents them and co-ordinates their common work.

There are over 70 million Lutherans world-wide; in Great Britain there are about 100,000 members, 50 clergy and 100 congregations.
General Secretary of the Lutheran Council of Great Britain, Revd T. Bruch, 30 Thanet Street, London WC1H 9QH. Tel: 020-7554 2900

THE METHODIST CHURCH

The Methodist movement started in England in 1729 when the Revd John Wesley, an Anglican priest, and his brother Charles met with others in Oxford and resolved to conduct their lives and study by 'rule and method'. In 1739 the Wesleys began evangelistic preaching and the first Methodist chapel was founded in Bristol in the same year. In 1744 the first annual conference was held, at which the Articles of Religion were drawn up. Doctrinal emphases included repentance, faith, the assurance of salvation, social concern and the priesthood of all believers. After John Wesley's death in 1791 the Methodists withdrew from the established Church to form the Methodist Church. Methodists gradually drifted into many groups, but in 1932 the Wesleyan Methodist Church, the United Methodist Church and the Primitive Methodist Church united to form the Methodist Church in Great Britain as it now exists.

The governing body and supreme authority of the Methodist Church is the Conference, but there are also 33 district synods, consisting of all the ministers and selected lay people in each district, and circuit meetings of the ministers and lay people of each circuit.

There are over 60 million Methodists world-wide; in Great Britain (1998 figures) there are 353,330 members, 3,727 ministers, 10,746 lay preachers and 6,452 churches.
President of the Conference in Great Britain (2000–1), Revd I. J. Bhogal
Vice-President of the Conference (2000–1), Sr E. Williams
Secretary of the Conference, Revd Dr N. T. Collinson, Methodist Church, Conference Office, 25 Marylebone Road, London NW1 5JR. Tel: 020-7486 5502

THE METHODIST CHURCH IN IRELAND

The Methodist Church in Ireland is closely linked to British Methodism but is autonomous. It has 16,599 members, 199 ministers, 297 lay preachers and 223 churches.
President of the Methodist Church in Ireland (2000–1), Revd Dr S. K. Todd, Woolhara Park, Cork, Republic of Ireland. Tel: 00-353-21 292503
Secretary of the Methodist Church in Ireland, Revd E. T. I. Mawhinney, 1 Fountainville Avenue, Belfast BT9 6AN. Tel: 028-9032 4554

THE (EASTERN) ORTHODOX CHURCH

The Eastern (or Byzantine) Orthodox Church is a communion of self-governing Christian churches recognising the honorary primacy of the Oecumenical Patriarch of Constantinople.

The position of Orthodox Christians is that the faith was fully defined during the period of the Oecumenical Councils. In doctrine it is strongly trinitarian, and stresses the mystery and importance of the sacraments. It is episcopal in government. The structure of the Orthodox Christian year differs from that of western Churches.

Orthodox Christians throughout the world are estimated to number about 300 million.

PATRIARCHS OF THE EASTERN ORTHODOX CHURCH
Archbishop of Constantinople, New Rome and Oecumenical Patriarch, Vartholomaeos, *elected* 1991
Pope and Patriarch of Alexandria and All Africa, Petros VII, *elected* 1997
Patriarch of Antioch and All the East, Ignatios IV, *elected* 1979
Patriarch of Jerusalem and All Palestine, Diodoros, *elected* 1981
Patriarch of Moscow and All Russia, Alexei II, *elected* 1990

Archbishop of Pec, Metropolitan of Belgrade and Karlovci, Patriarch of Serbia, Pavle, *elected* 1990
Archbishop of Bucharest and Patriarch of Romania, Teoctist, *elected* 1986
Metropolitan of Sofia and Patriarch of Bulgaria, Maxim, *elected* 1971
Archbishop of Tbilisi and Mtskheta, Catholicos-Patriarch of All Georgia, Ilia II, *elected* 1977

HEADS OF AUTOCEPHALOUS ORTHODOX CHURCHES

Archbishop of Cyprus, Chrysostomos, *elected* 1977
Archbishop of Athens and All Greece, Christodoulos, *elected* 1998
Metropolitan of Warsaw and All Poland, Sawa, *elected* 1998
Archbishop of Tirana and All Albania, Anastas, *elected* 1992
Archbishop of Prague and All the Czech Lands and Slovakia, Nikolaji, *elected* 2000

EASTERN ORTHODOX CHURCHES IN THE UK

THE PATRIARCHATE OF ANTIOCH

There are ten parishes served by 14 clergy. In Great Britain the Patriarchate is represented by the Revd Fr Samir Gholam, 1A Redhill Street, London NW1 4BG. Tel: 020-7383 0403.

THE GREEK ORTHODOX CHURCH (PATRIARCHATE OF CONSTANTINOPLE)

The presence of Greek Orthodox Christians in Britain dates back at least to 1677 when Archbishop Joseph Geogirenes of Samos fled from Turkish persecution and came to London. The present Greek cathedral in Moscow Road, Bayswater, was opened for public worship in 1879 and the Diocese of Thyateira and Great Britain was established in 1922. There are now 117 parishes and other communities (including monasteries) in Great Britain, served by seven bishops, 107 clergy and about 100 churches.

In Great Britain the Patriarchate of Constantinople is represented by Archbishop Gregorios of Thyateira and Great Britain, 5 Craven Hill, London W2 3EN. Tel: 020-7723 4787.

THE RUSSIAN ORTHODOX CHURCH (PATRIARCHATE OF MOSCOW) AND THE RUSSIAN ORTHODOX CHURCH OUTSIDE RUSSIA)

The records of Russian Orthodox Church activities in Britain date from the visit to England of Tsar Peter I in the early 18th century. Clergy were sent from Russia to serve the chapel established to minister to the staff of the Imperial Russian Embassy in London.

In Great Britain the Patriarchate of Moscow is represented by Metropolitan Anthony of Sourozh, 67 Ennismore Gardens, London SW7 1NH. Fax only: 020-7584 9864. He is assisted by one archbishop, one vicar bishop and 26 clergy. There are 27 parishes and smaller communities.

The Russian Orthodox Church Outside Russia is represented by Archbishop Mark of Berlin, Germany and Great Britain, c/o 57 Harvard Road, London W4 4ED. Tel: 020-8742 3493. There are eight communities, including two monasteries, served by seven clergy.

THE SERBIAN ORTHODOX CHURCH (PATRIARCHATE OF SERBIA)

There are 33 parishes and smaller communities in Great Britain served by 12 clergy. The Patriarchate of Serbia is represented by the Episcopal Vicar, the Very Revd Milenko Zebic, 131 Cob Lane, Bournville, Birmingham B30 1QE. Tel: 0121-458 5273.

OTHER NATIONALITIES

Most of the Ukrainian parishes in Britain have joined the Patriarchate of Constantinople, leaving a small number of Ukrainian parishes in Britain under the care of other patriarchates (not all of which are recognised by the other Orthodox Churches). The Latvian, Polish and some Belorussian parishes are also under the care of the Patriarchate of Constantinople. The Patriarchate of Romania has one parish served by two clergy. The Patriarchate of Bulgaria has one parish served by one priest. The Belorussian Autocephalous Orthodox Church has five parishes served by two priests.

THE ORIENTAL ORTHODOX CHURCHES

The term 'Oriental Orthodox Churches' is now generally used to describe a group of six ancient eastern churches which reject the Christological definition of the Council of Chalcedon (AD 451) and use Christological terms in different ways from the Eastern Orthodox Church. There are about 34 million members of the Oriental Orthodox Churches.

PATRIARCHS OF THE ORIENTAL ORTHODOX CHURCHES

ARMENIAN ORTHODOX CHURCH – *Supreme Patriarch Catholicos of All Armenians (Etchmiadzin)*, Karekin II, *elected* 1999; *Catholicos of Cilicia*, Aram I, *elected* 1995; *Patriarch of Jerusalem*, Torkom II, *elected* 1994; *Patriarch of Constantinople*, Mesrob II, *elected* 1998
COPTIC ORTHODOX CHURCH – *Pope of Alexandria and Patriarch of the See of St Mark*, Shenouda III, *elected* 1971
ERITREAN ORTHODOX CHURCH – *Patriarch of Eritrea*, Philipos I, *elected* 1998
ETHIOPIAN ORTHODOX CHURCH – *Patriarch of Ethiopia*, Paulos, *elected* 1992
MALANKARA ORTHODOX SYRIAN CHURCH – *Catholicos of the East*, Basilios Mar Thoma Mathews II, *elected* 1991
SYRIAN ORTHODOX CHURCH – *Patriarch of Antioch and All the East*, Ignatius Zakka I, *elected* 1980

ORIENTAL ORTHODOX CHURCHES IN THE UK

THE ARMENIAN ORTHODOX CHURCH (PATRIARCHATE OF ETCHMIADZIN)

The Armenian Orthodox Church is the longest-established Oriental Orthodox community in Great Britain. It is represented by Archbishop Yeghishe Gizirian, Armenian Primate of Great Britain, Armenian Vicarage, Iverna Gardens, London W8 6TP. Tel: 020-7937 0152.

THE COPTIC ORTHODOX CHURCH

The Coptic Orthodox Church is the largest Oriental Orthodox community in Great Britain. It has four dioceses (Birmingham; Scotland, Ireland and north-east England; the British Orthodox Church; and churches directly under Pope Shenouda III). The senior bishop in Great Britain is Metropolitan Seraphim, 10 Heathwood Gardens, London SE7 8EP. Tel: 020-8854 3090.

THE ERITREAN ORTHODOX CHURCH

In Great Britain the Eritrean Orthodox Church is represented by Bishop Markos, 11 Anfield Close, Weir Road, London SW12 0NT. Tel: 020-8675 5115.

THE ETHIOPIAN ORTHODOX CHURCH
The head of the Ethiopian Orthodox Tewahedo Church is His Grace Abuna Esaias, Archbishop of Western Europe, 9 Philip House, Mortimer Place, London NW6 5PB. Tel: 020-7624 3744.

THE MALANKARA ORTHODOX SYRIAN CHURCH
The Malankara Orthodox Syrian Church is part of the Diocese of Europe under Metropolitan Thomas Mar Makarios. His representative in Great Britain is Fr M. S. Skariah, Paramula House, 44 Newbury Road, Newbury Park, Ilford, Essex IG2 7HD. Tel: 020-8599 3836.

THE SYRIAN ORTHODOX CHURCH
The Syrian Orthodox Church in Great Britain comes under the Patriarchal Vicar, whose representative is Fr Touma Hazim Dakkama, Antiochian, 5 Canning Road, Croydon CR0 6QA. Tel: 020-8654 7531. The Indian congregation under the Syrian Patriarch of Antioch is represented by Fr Eldhose Koungampillil, 1 Roslyn Court, Roslyn Avenue, East Barnet, Herts EN4 8DJ. Tel: 020-8368 2794.

THE COUNCIL OF ORIENTAL ORTHODOX CHURCHES, 34 Chertsey Road, Church Square, Shepperton, Middx TW17 9LF. Tel: 020-8368 8447. *Secretary*, Deacon Aziz M. A. Nour

PENTECOSTAL CHURCHES

Pentecostalism is inspired by the descent of the Holy Spirit upon the apostles at Pentecost. The movement began in Los Angeles, USA, in 1906 and is characterised by baptism with the Holy Spirit, divine healing, speaking in tongues (glossolalia), and a literal interpretation of the scriptures. The Pentecostal movement in Britain dates from 1907. Initially, groups of Pentecostalists were led by laymen and did not organise formally. However, in 1915 the Elim Foursquare Gospel Alliance (more usually called the Elim Pentecostal Church) was founded in Ireland by George Jeffreys and in 1924 about 70 independent assemblies formed a fellowship, the Assemblies of God in Great Britain and Ireland. The Apostolic Church grew out of the 1904–5 revivals in South Wales and was established in 1916, and the New Testament Church of God was established in England in 1953. In recent years many aspects of Pentecostalism have been adopted by the growing charismatic movement within the Roman Catholic, Protestant and Eastern Orthodox churches.

There are about 105 million Pentecostalists worldwide, with about 200,000 adult adherents in Great Britain and Ireland.

THE APOSTOLIC CHURCH, International Administration Offices, PO Box 389, 24–27 St Helens Road, Swansea SA1 1ZH. Tel: 01792-473992. *President*, Pastor R. W. Jones; *Administrator*, Pastor A. Saunders. The Apostolic Church has about 130 churches, 5,500 adherents and 83 ministers

THE ASSEMBLIES OF GOD IN GREAT BRITAIN AND IRELAND, General Offices, 16 Bridgford Road, West Bridgford, Nottingham NG2 6AF. Tel: 0115-981 1188. *General Superintendent*, P.C. Weaver; *General Administrator*, D. H. Gill. The Assemblies of God has 640 churches, about 75,000 adherents (including children) and 860 accredited ministers

THE ELIM PENTECOSTAL CHURCH, PO Box 38, Cheltenham, Glos GL50 3HN. Tel: 01242-519904. *General Superintendent*, Revd J. J. Glass; *Administrator*, Pastor B. Hunter. The Elim Pentecostal Church has

600 churches, 68,500 adherents and 650 accredited ministers

THE NEW TESTAMENT CHURCH OF GOD, Main House, Overstone Park, Overstone, Northampton NN6 0AD. Tel: 01604-643311. *National Overseer*, Revd Dr R. O. Brown. The New Testament Church of God has 105 organised congregations, 7,971 baptised members, about 20,000 adherents and 252 accredited ministers

THE PRESBYTERIAN CHURCH IN IRELAND

The Presbyterian Church in Ireland is Calvinistic in doctrine and presbyterian in constitution. Presbyterianism was established in Ireland as a result of the Ulster plantation in the early 17th century, when English and Scottish Protestants settled in the north of Ireland.

There are 21 presbyteries and five regional synods under the chief court known as the General Assembly. The General Assembly meets annually and is presided over by a Moderator who is elected for one year. The ongoing work of the Church is undertaken by 18 boards under which there are a number of specialist committees.

There are about 285,000 Presbyterians in Ireland, mainly in the north, in 557 congregations and with 400 ministers.

Moderator (2000–1), Rt. Revd Dr T. Morrow
Clerk of Assembly and General Secretary, Very Revd Dr S. Hutchinson, Church House, Belfast BT1 6DW. Tel: 028-9032 2284

THE PRESBYTERIAN CHURCH OF WALES

The Presbyterian Church of Wales or Calvinistic Methodist Church of Wales is Calvinistic in doctrine and presbyterian in constitution. It was formed in 1811 when Welsh Calvinists severed the relationship with the established church by ordaining their own ministers. It secured its own confession of faith in 1823 and a Constitutional Deed in 1826, and since 1864 the General Assembly has met annually, presided over by a Moderator elected for a year. The doctrine and constitutional structure of the Presbyterian Church of Wales was confirmed by Act of Parliament in 1931–2.

The Church has 45,700 members, 124 ministers and 881 churches.

Moderator (2000–1), Revd J. E.-Wynne Davies
General Secretary, Revd W. G. Edwards, 53 Richmond Road, Cardiff CF24 3WJ. Tel: 029-2049 4913

THE RELIGIOUS SOCIETY OF FRIENDS (QUAKERS)

Quakerism is a movement, not a church, which was founded in the 17th century by George Fox and others in an attempt to revive what they saw as 'primitive Christianity'. The movement was based originally in the Midlands, Yorkshire and north-west England, but there are now Quakers in 36 countries around the world. The colony of Pennsylvania, founded by William Penn, was originally Quaker.

Emphasis is placed on the experience of God in daily life rather than on sacraments or religious occasions. There is no church calendar. Worship is largely silent and there are no appointed ministers; the responsibility for conducting a meeting is shared equally among those present. Social reform and religious tolerance have always been important to Quakers, together with a commitment to non-violence in resolving disputes.

There are 213,800 Quakers world-wide, with over 19,000 in Great Britain and Ireland. There are about 490 meeting houses in Great Britain.

CENTRAL OFFICES: (GREAT BRITAIN) Friends House, 173 Euston Road, London NW1 2BJ. Tel: 020-7663 1000; (IRELAND) Swanbrook House, Morehampton Road, Dublin 4. Tel: (00 353)(1)-683684

THE SALVATION ARMY

The Salvation Army was founded by a Methodist minister, William Booth, in the east end of London in 1865, and has since become established in 107 countries world-wide. It was first known as the Christian Mission, and took its present name in 1878 when it adopted a quasi-military command structure intended to inspire and regulate its endeavours and to reflect its view that the Church was engaged in spiritual warfare. Salvationists emphasise evangelism, social work and the relief of poverty.

The world leader, known as the General, is elected by a High Council composed of the Chief of the Staff and senior ranking officers known as commissioners.

There are about 1.5 million members, 17,201 active officers (full-time ordained ministers) and 15,670 worship centres and outposts world-wide. In Great Britain and Ireland there are 62,836 members, 1,638 active officers and 810 worship centres.

General, J. Gowans
UK Territorial Commander, A. Hughes
TERRITORIAL HEADQUARTERS, 101 Newington Causeway, London SE1 6BN. Tel: 020-7367 4500

THE SEVENTH-DAY ADVENTIST CHURCH

The Seventh-day Adventist Church was founded in 1863 in the USA. Its members look forward to the second coming of Christ and observe the Sabbath (the seventh day) as a day of rest, worship and ministry. The Church bases its faith and practice wholly on the Bible and has developed 27 fundamental beliefs.

The World Church is divided into 12 divisions, each made up of unions of churches. The Seventh-day Adventist Church in the British Isles is known as the British Union of Seventh-day Adventists and is a member of the Trans-European Division. In the British Isles the administrative organisation of the church is arranged in three tiers: the local churches; the regional conferences for south England, north England, Wales, Scotland and Ireland; and the national 'union' conference.

There are about 9 million Adventists and 43,848 churches in 205 countries world-wide. In the UK and Ireland there are 20,110 members, 152 ministers and 240 churches.

President of the British Union Conference, Pastor C. R. Perry
BRITISH ISLES HEADQUARTERS, Stanborough Park, Watford WD2 6JP. Tel: 01923-672251

UNDEB YR ANNIBYNWYR CYMRAEG
The Union of Welsh Independents

The Union of Welsh Independents was formed in 1872 and is a voluntary association of Welsh Congregational Churches and personal members. It is mainly Welsh-speaking. Congregationalism in Wales dates back to 1639 when the first Welsh Congregational Church was opened in Gwent. Member churches are Calvinistic in doctrine, although a wide range of interpretations is permitted, and congregationalist in organisation. Each church has complete independence in the government and administration of its affairs.

The Union has around 37,000 members, 204 ministers and 514 member churches.

President of the Union (2000–1), Revd. D. M. Jones
General Secretary, Revd D. Myrddin Hughes, Tŷ John Penry, 11 Heol Sant Helen, Swansea SA1 4AL. Tel: 01792-652542

THE UNITED REFORMED CHURCH

The United Reformed Church was first formed by the union of most of the Congregational churches in England and Wales with the Presbyterian Church of England in 1972.

Congregationalism dates from the mid 16th century. It is Calvinistic in doctrine, and its followers form independent self-governing congregations bound under God by covenant, a principle laid down in the writings of Robert Browne (1550–1633). From the late 16th century the movement was driven underground by persecution, but the cause was defended at the Westminster Assembly in 1643 and the Savoy Declaration of 1658 laid down its principles. Congregational churches formed county associations for mutual support and in 1832 these associations merged to form the Congregational Union of England and Wales.

Presbyterianism in England also dates from the mid 16th century, and was Calvinistic and evangelical in its doctrine. It was governed by a hierarchy of courts.

In the 1960s there was close co-operation locally and nationally between Congregational and Presbyterian Churches. This led to union negotiations and a Scheme of Union, supported by Act of Parliament in 1972. In 1981 a further unification took place, with the Reformed Association of Churches of Christ becoming part of the URC. In 2000 a third union took place, with the Congregational Union of Scotland. In its basis the United Reformed Church reflects local church initiative and responsibility with a conciliar pattern of oversight. The General Assembly is the central body, and is made up of equal numbers of ministers and lay members.

The United Reformed Church is divided into 13 synods, each with a Synod Moderator, and 78 districts. There are 96,500 members, 657 full-time stipendiary ministers, 77 part-time stipendiary ministers, 190 non-stipendiary ministers, 10 active CRCUS, and 1,765 local churches.

General Secretary, Revd A. G. Burnham, 86 Tavistock Place, London WC1H 9RT. Tel: 020-7916 2020

THE WESLEYAN REFORM UNION

The Wesleyan Reform Union was founded by Methodists who left or were expelled from Wesleyan Methodism in 1849 following a period of internal conflict. Its doctrine is conservative evangelical and its organisation is congregational, each church having complete independence in the government and administration of its affairs. The main concentration of churches is in Yorkshire.

The Union has 2,147 members, 22 ministers, 122 lay preachers and 112 churches.

President (2000–1), M. J. Mumford
General Secretary, Revd A. J. Williams, Wesleyan Reform Church House, 123 Queen Street, Sheffield S1 2DU. Tel: 0114-272 1938

Non-Trinitarian Churches

THE CHURCH OF CHRIST, SCIENTIST

The Church of Christ, Scientist was founded by Mary Baker Eddy in the USA in 1879 to 'reinstate primitive Christianity and its lost element of healing'. Christian Science teaches the need for spiritual regeneration and salvation from sin, but is best known for its reliance on prayer alone in the healing of sickness. Adherents believe that such healing is a law, or Science, and is in direct line with that practised by Jesus Christ (revered, not as God, but as the Son of God) and by the early Christian Church.

The denomination consists of The First Church of Christ, Scientist, in Boston, Massachusetts (the Mother Church) and its branch churches in over 60 countries world-wide. Branch churches are democratically governed by their members, while a five-member Board of Directors, based in Boston, is authorised to transact the business of the Mother Church. The Bible and Mary Baker Eddy's book, *Science and Health with Key to the Scriptures*, are used at services; there are no clergy. Those engaged in full-time healing are called practitioners, of whom there are 3,500 world-wide.

No membership figures are available, since Mary Baker Eddy felt that numbers are no measure of spiritual vitality and ruled that such statistics should not be published. There are over 2,400 branch churches world-wide, including nearly 200 in the UK.

CHRISTIAN SCIENCE COMMITTEE ON PUBLICATION, 2 Elysium Gate, 126 New Kings Road, London SW6 4LZ. Tel: 020-7371 0600. *District Manager for Great Britain and Ireland*, H. Joynes

THE CHURCH OF JESUS CHRIST OF LATTER-DAY SAINTS

The Church (often referred to as 'the Mormons') was founded in New York state, USA, in 1830, and came to Britain in 1837. The oldest continuous branch in the world is to be found in Preston, Lancs. Mormons are Christians who claim to belong to the 'Restored Church' of Jesus Christ. They believe that true Christianity died when the last original apostle died, but that it was given back to the world by God and Christ through Joseph Smith, the Church's founder and first president. They accept and use the Bible as scripture, but believe in continuing revelation from God and use additional scriptures, including *The Book of Mormon: Another Testament of Jesus Christ*. The importance of the family is central to the Church's beliefs and practices. Church members set aside Monday evenings as Family Home Evenings when Christian family values are taught. Polygamy was formally discontinued in 1890.

The Church has no paid ministry; local congregations are headed by a leader chosen from amongst their number. The world governing body, based in Utah, USA, is the three-man First Presidency, assisted by the Quorum of the Twelve Apostles.

There are more than 10 million members world-wide, with about 180,000 adherents in Britain in over 350 congregations.

President of the Europe North Area (including Britain), Elder W. Rolfe Kerr

BRITISH HEADQUARTERS, Church Offices, 751 Warwick Road, Solihull, W. Midlands B91 3DQ. Tel: 0121-712 1202

JEHOVAH'S WITNESSES

The movement now known as Jehovah's Witnesses grew from a Bible study group formed by Charles Taze Russell in 1872 in Pennsylvania, USA. In 1896 it adopted the name of the Watch Tower Bible and Tract Society, and in 1931 its members became known as Jehovah's Witnesses. Jehovah's (God's) Witnesses believe in the Bible as the word of God, and consider it to be inspired and historically accurate. They take the scriptures literally, except where there are obvious indications that they are figurative or symbolic, and reject the doctrine of the Trinity. Witnesses also believe that the earth will remain for ever and that all those approved of by Jehovah will have eternal life on a cleansed and beautified earth; only 144,000 will go to heaven to rule with Christ. They believe that the second coming of Christ began in 1914 and his thousand-year reign on earth is imminent, and that Armageddon (a final battle in which evil will be defeated) will precede Christ's rule of peace. They refuse to take part in military service, and do not accept blood transfusions. They publish two magazines, *The Watchtower* and *Awake!*

The 13-member world governing body is based in New York, USA. Witnesses world-wide are divided into branches, countries or areas, districts, circuits and congregations. There are overseers at each level, and two assemblies are held annually for each circuit. There is no paid ministry, but each congregation has elders assigned to look after various duties and every Witness is assigned homes to visit in their congregation.

There are over 5 million Jehovah's Witnesses world-wide, with 130,000 Witnesses in the UK organised into over 1,400 congregations.

BRITISH ISLES HEADQUARTERS, Watch Tower House, The Ridgeway, London NW7 1RN. Tel: 020-8906 2211

UNITARIAN AND FREE CHRISTIAN CHURCHES

Unitarianism has its historical roots in the Judaeo-Christian tradition but rejects the deity of Christ and the doctrine of the trinity. It allows the individual to embrace insights from all the world's faiths and philosophies, as there is no fixed creed. It is accepted that beliefs may evolve in the light of personal experience.

Unitarian communities first became established in Poland and Transylvania in the 16th century. The first avowedly Unitarian place of worship in the British Isles opened in London in 1774. The General Assembly of Unitarian and Free Christian Churches came into existence in 1928 as the result of the amalgamation of two earlier organisations.

There are about 7,000 Unitarians in Great Britain and Ireland, and 150 Unitarian ministers. About 200 self-governing congregations and fellowship groups, including a small number overseas, are members of the General Assembly.

GENERAL ASSEMBLY OF UNITARIAN AND FREE CHRISTIAN CHURCHES, Essex Hall, 1–6 Essex Street, Strand, London WC2R3HY. Tel: 020-7240 2384. *General Secretary*, J. J. Teagle

Education

For addresses of national education departments, *see* Government Departments and Public Offices. For other addresses, *see* Education Directory

Responsibility for education in England lies with the Secretary of State for Education and Employment; in Wales, with the First Secretary of the National Assembly for Wales; in Scotland, with Scottish Ministers; and with Education Ministers in Northern Ireland.

The main concerns of the education departments (the Department for Education and Employment (DfEE) in England; the National Assembly for Wales Education Department; the Scottish Executive Department of Education and the Department of Enterprise and Lifelong Learning; the Departments of Education (DE) and Higher and Further Education, Training and Employment (DHFETE) in Northern Ireland are the formulation of national policies for education and the maintenance of consistency in educational standards. They are responsible for the broad allocation of resources for education, for the rate and distribution of educational building and for the supply, training and superannuation of teachers (in England through the Teacher Training Agency).

EXPENDITURE

In the UK in 1997–8, expenditure on education was (£ million):

Schools	22,574.0
Further and higher education	9,499.4
Other education and related expenditure	3,344.6

Most of this expenditure is incurred by local authorities, which make their own expenditure decisions according to their local situations and needs. Expenditure on education by central government departments, in real terms, was (£ million):

	1999–2000 estimated outturn	2000–1 planned
DfEE	15,779	18,251
National Assembly for Wales	509.2	726.1
Scottish Executive	1,860.8	1,994.6
Northern Ireland Assembly	1,555	1,660

The bulk of direct expenditure by the DfEE, the National Assembly for Wales and the Scottish Executive is directed towards supporting higher education in universities and colleges through the Higher Education Funding Councils (HEFCs) and further education and sixth form colleges through the Further Education Funding Councils (FEFCs). In addition, the DfEE funds student support in England and Wales, the City Technology Colleges (CTCs), the City College for the Technology of the Arts, and pays grants under the specialist schools programme.

In Wales the National Assembly also funds curriculum development, educational services and research and supports bilingual education. In Scotland the main elements of central government expenditure, in addition to those outlined above, are grant-aided special schools, student awards and bursaries (through the Student Awards Agency for Scotland), teachers, curriculum development, special educational needs, community education and further and higher education through the Funding Councils. In Northern Ireland central government directly funds higher education, teacher education,

teacher salaries and superannuation, student awards, further education, grant-maintained integrated schools, and voluntary grammar schools.

Current net expenditure on education by local education authorities in England, Wales, and Scotland, and education and library boards in Northern Ireland is (£ million):

	1999–2000 estimated outturn	2000–1 planned
England	22.942	21.500
Wales	1,427	1,476
Scotland	2,637.7	2,717.1
Northern Ireland	938*	905

LOCAL EDUCATION ADMINISTRATION

In England and Wales the education service is administered by local education authorities (LEAs), which carry the day-to-day responsibility for providing most state primary and secondary education in their areas. They share with the FEFCs the duty to provide adult education to meet local needs.

The LEAs own and maintain most schools and some colleges, build new ones and provide equipment. LEAs are financed largely from the council tax and aggregate external finance (AEF) from the Department for the Environment, Transport and the Regions in England and the National Assembly for Wales.

All LEA-maintained schools manage their own budgets. The LEA allocates funds to the school, largely on the basis of pupil numbers, and the school governing body is responsible for overseeing spending and for most aspects of staffing, including appointments and dismissals. LEAs have powers to monitor, maintain and improve standards. An Education Association can be set up to take over the management of failing schools where both the LEA and the governing body have not brought about improvements identified as necessary by inspection.

The duty of providing education locally in Scotland rests with the education authorities. They are responsible for the construction of buildings, the employment of teachers and other staff and the provision of equipment and materials. Devolved School Management is in place for all primary, secondary and special schools.

Education authorities are required to establish school boards consisting of parents and teachers as well as co-opted members, responsible among other things for the appointment of staff.

Education is administered locally in Northern Ireland by five education and library boards, whose costs are met in full by central government. All grant-aided schools include elected parents and teachers on their boards of governors. Provision has been made for schools wishing to provide integrated education to have grant-maintained integrated status from the outset. All schools and colleges of further education have full responsibility for their own budgets, including staffing costs. The Council for Catholic Maintained Schools forms an upper tier of management for Catholic schools and provides advice on matters relating to management and administration.

THE INSPECTORATE

The Office for Standards in Education (OFSTED) is a non-ministerial government department in England headed by HM Chief Inspector of Schools (HMCI). OFSTED's remit is regularly to inspect and report on all maintained schools in England; local education authorities (supported by the Audit Commission); initial teacher training; adult and youth education; and nursery education providers. Subject to the will of Parliament, from September 2001, OFSTED will have responsibility for the regulation, registration and inspection of all childcare provision in England and educational provision for all 16- to 19-year-olds, including sixth form and further education colleges as well as schools. A new Adult Learning Inspectorate (ADI) is also planned.

Teams of OFSTED-trained accredited inspectors, including educationalists and lay people, carry out inspections in schools according to the Framework for Inspection of Schools to ensure consistency in the process of inspection and the criteria used. HM Inspectors (HMI) within OFSTED report on good practice in schools and on other educational issues based on inspection evidence. From 1997 for secondary and from 1998 for primary, schools are inspected once every six years or more frequently if there is cause. A summary of the inspection report must be sent to the parents of each pupil by the school, followed by a copy of the governors' action plan thereon.

There are about 200 HMIs on OFSTED's permanent staff, about 2,000 registered inspectors and about 7,500 team inspectors, who work on contract to OFSTED.

Estyn: Arolygiaeth Ei Mawrhydi Dros Addysg A Hyfforddiant yng Nghymru (Her Majesty's Inspectorate for Education and Training in Wales) has a remit which includes that carried out in England by OFSTED and other bodies. Estyn inspects funded nursery provision, maintained schools, local education authorities, teacher education and training and adult and youth education, among others. Estyn also inspects establishments of further education at the request of the Further Education Funding Council for Wales. Its remit also includes advice to the National Assembly for Wales on a wide range of education and training matters.

There are 43 HMIs, about 177 registered inspectors and 512 team members in Wales.

HM Inspectors of Schools in Scotland inspect and publish reports on a wide range of educational provision including pre-school, nursery, primary and special schools, further education institutions, teacher education and community education. HMIs work in teams alongside lay members and associate assessors, who are practising teachers seconded for the inspection. HMI monitor how well schools, colleges and other providers of education are performing and help to raise standards and improve quality in education in Scotland by leading and supporting the development of educational initiatives. The inspection of higher education is the responsibility of inspectors appointed to the Higher Education Funding Council for Scotland.

There are 84 HMIs and eight Chief Inspectors in Scotland.

Inspection is carried out in Northern Ireland by the Department of Education's Education and Training Inspectorate, using teams which, on occasion, include lay people. The Inspectorate also advises government. From September 1999 a seven-year cycle of inspection was introduced.

There are one Chief Inspector and 61 members of the Inspectorate in Northern Ireland.

SCHOOLS AND PUPILS

Schooling is compulsory in Great Britain for all children between five and 16 years and between four and 16 years in Northern Ireland. Provision is being increased for pre-school children and many pupils remain at school after the minimum leaving age. No fees are charged in any publicly maintained school in England, Wales and Scotland. In Northern Ireland, fees may be charged in voluntary schools and are paid by pupils in preparatory departments of grammar schools, but pupils admitted to the secondary departments of grammar schools, unless they come from outside the province, do not pay fees.

The 'Parents' Charter', available free from education departments, is a booklet telling parents about the education system. Schools are now required to make available information about themselves, their truancy rates, destinations of leavers, their public examination and (in England, Wales and Northern Ireland) national test results. Parents in England and Wales must receive a written yearly progress report on all aspects of their child's achievements. There is a similar commitment for Northern Ireland. In Scotland the school report card gives parents information on their child's progress.

FALL AND RISE IN NUMBERS

In nursery and primary education, and increasingly in secondary education, pupil numbers in the UK declined through the 1980s. In maintained nursery and primary schools they had dropped to 4.9 million in 1991, had risen to 5.4 million by 1999 and are expected to decline to 4.9 million by 2005. In secondary schools pupil numbers peaked at 4.5 million in 1981, had fallen to 3.4 million by 1991, had risen to 3.8 million by 1999 and are projected to remain at around that figure until 2010.

ENGLAND AND WALES

There are two main types of school in England and Wales: publicly maintained schools, which charge no fees; and independent schools, which charge fees. Publicly maintained schools, with the exception of City Technology Colleges, are maintained by local education authorities.

Publicly funded schools are in the process of being classified as community, voluntary or foundation schools; those in the last two classes may express a preference as to category. Community (formerly county) schools are owned by LEAs and wholly funded by them. They are non-denominational and provide primary and secondary education. The voluntary category includes those schools which have a particular religious ethos and comprises two subdivisions, voluntary controlled and voluntary aided. The latter includes schools formerly classed as special agreement and former grant-maintained schools, which had originally been voluntary aided or special agreement schools or were founded by promoters. Voluntary schools provide primary and secondary education. Although the buildings are in many cases provided by the voluntary bodies (mainly religious denominations), they are financially maintained by an LEA. In the case of voluntary controlled schools the LEA bears all costs. In voluntary aided schools, although the managers or governors are responsible for repairs, improvements and alterations to the building, central government may reimburse up to 85 per cent of approved capital expenditure, while the LEA pays for internal maintenance and other running costs. In the case of former special agreement schools, the LEA may, by special agreement, pay between one-half and three-quarters of the cost of building a new or extending an existing school, usually a secondary school. Foundation schools are former grant-maintained (GM) schools which were originally county and voluntary controlled schools or were established by the Funding Agency for Schools. Under the previous administration all secondary and primary schools, whether maintained or independent, were eligible to apply for grant-maintained status subject to a ballot of parents. GM schools were maintained directly by the Secretary of State (through the Funding Agency for Schools) and the former Welsh Office, not the LEA; those arrangements no longer apply and they are now included in LEA funding arrangements. They are wholly run by their own governing body. About 60 per cent of the GM schools established were secondary schools.

The number of schools by category in 1999 was:

Under the Local Management of Schools (LMS)

	England	Wales
Maintained schools	28,783	2,186
Community	13,790	1,612
Voluntary	7,067	277
controlled	2,795	116
aided	4,272	161
Foundation	859	20
CTCs and CCTAs*	15	–
Independent schools	2,067	54
TOTAL	33,865	2,240

* In England only

initiative, LEAs are required to delegate the entire school budget, including staffing costs, directly to those schools that wish it. LEAs continue to retain responsibility for various common services, including transport and special educational needs units. The LEA acts as admission authority for most community and some voluntary schools.

Governing bodies – All publicly maintained schools have a governing body, usually made up of a number of parent and local community representatives, governors appointed by the LEA if the school is LEA maintained, the headteacher (unless he or she chooses otherwise), and serving teachers. Schools can appoint up to four sponsor governors from business who will be expected to provide financial and managerial assistance. Governing bodies are responsible for the overall policies of schools and their academic aims and objectives. They also control matters of school discipline, the appointment and dismissal of staff and act as the admission authority for voluntary aided and all foundation schools.

The Specialist Schools Programme – The programme is open to all state secondary schools in England which teach the national curriculum and wish to specialise in the teaching of technology, mathematics and science, modern foreign languages, sports and the arts. In addition to the normal funding arrangements, the schools receive business sponsorship (up to four sponsor governors may sit on governing bodies) and complementary capital grants up to £100,000 from central government, together with extra annual funding of £120 a pupil (for four years initially) to assist the delivery of an enhanced curriculum. By September 2000, there were 288 technology colleges, 85 language colleges, 60 sports colleges and 49 arts colleges.

City Technology Colleges (CTCs) and *City Colleges for the Technology of the Arts (CCTAs)* are state-aided but independent of LEAs. Their aim is to widen the choice of secondary education in disadvantaged urban areas and to teach a broad curriculum with an emphasis on science,

technology, business understanding and arts technologies. Capital costs are shared by government and business sponsors, and running costs are covered by a per capita grant from the DfEE in line with comparable costs in an LEA maintained school. The first city technology college opened in 1988 in Solihull. The first CCTA, known as Britschool, opened in Croydon in 1991.

SCOTLAND

Education authority schools (known as public schools) are financed by local government, partly through revenue support grants from central government, and partly from local taxation. Devolved management from the local authority to the school is in place for more than 88 per cent of all school level expenditure. A small number of grant-aided schools, mainly in the special sector, are conducted by boards of managers and receive grants direct from the Scottish Executive Education Department. Under the previous administration a category of self-governing schools was created. Such schools opted to be managed entirely by a board of management but remained in the public sector and were funded by direct government grant. Two were established but one has since been returned to the education authority framework.

Independent schools charge fees and receive no direct grant, but are subject to inspection and registration.

The number of schools by category in 1999 was:

Publicly maintained schools:	
Education authority	4,054
Self-governing	1
Independent schools	207
TOTAL	4,262

NORTHERN IRELAND

Controlled schools are maintained by the education and library boards with all costs paid from public funds. Voluntary maintained schools, mainly under Roman Catholic management, receive grants towards capital costs and running costs in whole or in part. Voluntary grammar schools may be under denominational or non-denominational management and receive grants from DENI. Voluntary maintained and voluntary grammar schools can apply for designation as a new category of voluntary school, which is eligible for a 100 per cent as opposed to 85 per cent grant. Such schools are managed by a board of governors on which no single interest group has a majority of nominees. All grant-aided schools include elected parents and teachers on their boards of governors, whose responsibilities also include financial management under the Local Management of Schools (LMS) initiative. All schools now have fully delegated budgets. The majority of children in Northern Ireland are educated in schools which in practice are segregated on religious lines. Integrated schools exist to educate Protestant and Roman Catholic children together. There are two types: grant-maintained integrated schools which are funded by DENI; and controlled integrated schools funded by the education and library boards. Procedures are in place for balloting parents in existing segregated schools to determine whether they want instead to have integrated schools, subject to the satisfaction of certain criteria. By September 2000, 45 integrated schools had been established, 17 of them secondary.

The number of schools by category in 1999–2000 was:

Grant-aided schools:

Controlled	654
Maintained	552
Voluntary grammar	54
Integrated schools	43
Independent schools	22
TOTAL	1,325

THE STATE SYSTEM

PRE-SCHOOL EDUCATION – Pre-school education is for children from two to five years and is not compulsory, although a free place is available for each four-year-old who requires it and free provision for three-year-olds is being increased. Northern Ireland has a compulsory school starting age of four as of September each year but there too pre-school provision is being increased. Pre-school education takes place in nursery schools (1,668 in the public sector in 1999) or, in England, nursery classes in primary schools. The number of children receiving pre-school education in the UK in 1998–9 was (thousands):

In maintained nursery schools	79.1
In primary schools	997.7
In non-maintained nursery schools	70.8
In special schools	7.8
TOTAL	1,155.4

Education authorities are responsible for planning, co-ordinating and delivering nursery education in their areas using a range of providers on the basis of an Early Years Development Plan, in partnership with parents and the private and voluntary sectors. All providers of pre-school education are subject to inspection.

PRIMARY EDUCATION – Primary education begins at five years in Great Britain and four years in Northern Ireland. In England, Wales and Northern Ireland the transfer to secondary school is generally made at 11 years. In Scotland, the primary school course lasts for seven years and pupils' transfer to secondary courses at about the age of 12.

Primary schools (UK) 1998–9

No. of primary schools	23,114
No. of pupils (thousands)	5,029.0
Pupils aged 2–4 years	996.7

Primary schools consist mainly of infant schools for children aged five to seven, junior schools for those aged seven to 11, and combined junior and infant schools for both age groups. First schools in some parts of England cater for ages five to ten as the first stage of a three-tier system: first, middle and secondary.

	1997–8	1998–9
England	23.7	23.5
Wales	n/a	23.0
Scotland	19.9	19.4
Northern Ireland	19.9	19.9
UK	21.2	23.0

Pupil-teacher ratios in maintained primary schools were:
The average size of classes as taught was 25.5 in 1998.

MIDDLE SCHOOLS – Middle schools (which take children from first schools), mostly in England, cover varying age ranges between eight and 14 and usually lead on to comprehensive upper schools.

SECONDARY EDUCATION – Secondary schools are for children aged 11 to 16 and for those who choose to stay on

to 18. At 16, many students prefer to move on to tertiary or sixth form colleges. Most secondary schools in England, Wales and Scotland are co-educational. The largest secondary schools have over 1,500 pupils but only 33 per cent of schools take over 1,000 pupils.

Secondary schools 1999

	England	Wales*	Scotland	Northern Ireland
No. of pupils (000s)	3,121.9	201.9	313.2	153.9
% 16 to 18 age group	21.4%*	37.0%*	36.6%*	41.6%
Average class size	21.9	20.6	19.2	n/a
Pupil-teacher ratio	17.0	16.5	13.0	14.6

*1998 data

In England and Wales the main types of maintained secondary schools are: comprehensive schools (86.2 per cent of pupils in England, 100 per cent in Wales), whose admission arrangements are without reference to ability or aptitude; deemed middle schools for children aged variously between eight and 14 years who then move on to senior comprehensive schools at 12, 13 or 14 (5.0 per cent of pupils in England); secondary modern schools (2.9 per cent of pupils in England) providing a general education with a practical bias; secondary grammar schools (4.5 per cent of pupils in England) with selective intake providing an academic course from 11 to 16–18 years; and technical schools (0.2 per cent of pupils in England), providing an integrated academic and technical education.

In Scotland all pupils in education authority secondary schools attend schools with a comprehensive intake. Most of these schools provide a full range of courses appropriate to all levels of ability from first to sixth year.

In most areas of Northern Ireland there is a selective system of secondary education with pupils transferring either to grammar schools (34.1 per cent of pupils in 1999) or secondary schools (65.9 per cent of pupils in 1999) at 11–12 years of age. Parents can choose the school they would like their children to attend and all those who apply must be admitted if they meet the criteria. If a school is over-subscribed beyond its statutory admissions number, selection is on the basis of published criteria, which, for most grammar schools, place emphasis on performance in the transfer procedure tests which are set and administered by the Northern Ireland Council for the Curriculum, Examinations and Assessment. When parents consider that a school has not applied its criteria fairly they have access to independent appeals tribunals. Grammar schools provide an academic type of secondary education with A-levels at the end of the seventh year, while secondary non-grammar schools follow a curriculum suited to a wider range of aptitudes and abilities.

SPECIAL EDUCATION – Wherever possible, children with special needs are educated in ordinary schools, taking the parents' wishes into account, and schools are required to publish their policy for pupils with special educational needs. LEAs in England and Wales and Education and Library Boards in Northern Ireland are required to identify and secure provision for the needs of children with learning difficulties, to involve the parents in any decision and draw up a formal statement of the child's special educational needs and how they intend to meet them, all within statutory time limits.

In Scotland, school placing is a matter of agreement between education authorities and parents. Parents have the right to say which school they want their child to attend, and a right of appeal where their wishes are not being met. Whenever possible, children with special needs are integrated into ordinary schools.

Maintained special schools are run by education authorities which pay all the costs of maintenance, but under the terms of Local Management of Schools (LMS), those able and wishing to manage their own budgets may choose to do so. Non-maintained special schools are run by voluntary bodies; they may receive some grant from central government for capital expenditure and for equipment but their current expenditure is met primarily from the fees charged to education authorities for pupils placed in the schools. Some independent schools provide education wholly or mainly for children with special educational needs and are required to meet similar standards to those for maintained and non-maintained special schools.

The number of pupils with statements of special needs in January 1999 was (thousands):

In special schools: total	101.2
England	87.3
Wales	3.6
Scotland	6.5
N. Ireland	3.8
In public sector primary and secondary schools: total	172.8
England	147.1
Wales	12.9
Scotland	8.5
N. Ireland	4.3

ALTERNATIVE PROVISION

There is no legal obligation on parents in the UK to educate their children at school provided that the local education authority is satisfied that the child is receiving full-time education suited to its age, abilities and aptitudes.

INDEPENDENT SCHOOLS

Independent schools charge fees and are owned and managed under special trusts, with profits being used for the benefit of the schools concerned. There is a wide variety of provision, from kindergartens to large day and boarding schools, and from experimental schools to traditional institutions. A number of independent schools have been instituted by religious and ethnic minorities.

The term public school is often applied to those independent schools in membership of the Headmasters' and Headmistresses' Conference, the Governing Bodies Association or the Governing Bodies of Girls' Schools Association.

Preparatory schools are so-called because they prepare pupils for the common entrance examination to senior independent schools. Most cater for pupils from about seven to 13 years. The common entrance examination is set by the Common Entrance Examination Board, but marked by the independent school to which the pupil intends to go. It is taken at 13 by boys, and between 11 and 13 by girls.

Most independent schools in Scotland follow the same examination system as England, Wales and Northern Ireland, i.e. GCSE followed by A-levels.

The number of schools and pupils in 1998–9 was:

	No. of schools	No. of pupils (000s)	% of school population	Pupil-teacher ratio
England	2,231	575.0	7.4	10.0
Wales	57	9.8	1.9	9.9
Scotland	175	31.3	3.8	10.4
N. Ireland	22	1.3	0.4	10.0

ASSISTED PLACES SCHEME

The Assisted Places Scheme ceased to operate after the September 1997 and is being phased out. Pupils in secondary education holding their places at the beginning of the 1997–8 school year will keep them until they have completed their education at their current school. Those at the primary stage will hold them until they have completed that phase of their education, although some may exceptionally be allowed to do so for a further period to complete their secondary education. The scheme enables children to attend independent secondary schools which their parents could not otherwise afford. The proportion of pupils receiving full fee remission is about 47 per cent. In the 1999–2000 academic year, about 23,930 places were offered at the 455 participating schools in England and Wales. In Scotland 2,054 pupils participated in the scheme in 49 schools.

The scheme is administered and funded in England by the DfEE and in Wales and Scotland by the respective education departments. The scheme does not operate in Northern Ireland as the independent sector admits non-fee-paying pupils. There is, however, a similar scheme known as the Talented Children's Scheme to help pupils gifted in music and dance.

THE CURRICULUM

ENGLAND

The national curriculum was introduced in primary and secondary schools between autumn 1989 and autumn 1996, for the period of compulsory schooling from five to 16. It is mandatory in all maintained schools. As originally proposed, it was widely criticised for being too prescriptive and time-consuming. Following revision in 1994 its requirements were substantially reduced; the revisions were implemented from September 1995 for key stages one to three and from September 1996 for key stage four. A second review was completed in August 1999 and a revised curriculum was introduced in schools from September 2000.

The statutory subjects at key stages one and two (five–11-year olds) are:

Core subjects	Foundation subjects
English	Design and technology
Information and communication technology	Mathematics
History	Science
Geography	Art and design
Music	Physical education

At key stage three (11- to 14-year-olds) a modern foreign language is introduced. At key stage four (14- to 16-year-olds) pupils are required to continue to study the core subjects, physical education, design and technology and information and communication technology. Citizenship will become a compulsory subject for secondary pupils from 2002. Other foundation subjects are optional and others, such as drama, dance and classical languages are taught when the resources of individual schools permit. Religious education must be taught across all key stages, following a locally agreed syllabus; parents have the right to remove their children if they wish.

Statutory assessment takes place on entry to primary school and national tests and tasks in English and mathematics at key stage one, with the addition of science at key stages two and three, are in place. Teachers make their own assessments of their pupils' progress to set alongside the test results. At key stage four the GCSE and vocational equivalents are the main form of assessment.

The DfEE publishes tables showing pupils' performance in A-level, AS-level, GCSE and GNVQ examinations school by school. Local education authorities are required to publish similar information in November each year showing the results of national curriculum tests and teacher assessments for seven-, 11- and 14-year-olds. Approximately 600,000 pupils in each of the age groups take the tests each year.

NATIONAL TESTING AND TEACHERS'
ASSESSMENT RESULTS IN CORE SUBJECTS 1999

Percentage of pupils reaching the expected level of performance at that age:

	Key stage 1 7-year olds (level 2)	Key stage 2 11-year olds (level 4)	Key stage 3 14-year olds (level 5)
English	79.5	68.5	63.5
Mathematics	86.0	69.0	63.0
Science	87.0	76.0	57.5

National targets have been set for 11-year-olds: 80 per cent to reach level four in the English test and 75 per cent to reach level four in the mathematics test by 2002.

The Qualifications and Curriculum Authority (QCA) is an independent government agency funded by the DfEE. It is responsible for ensuring that the curriculum and qualifications available to young people and adults are of high quality, coherent and flexible and its remit ranges from the under-fives to higher level vocational qualifications.

WALES

The national curriculum was introduced simultaneously in Wales and, although it is broadly similar, has separate and distinctive characteristics which are reflected, where appropriate, in the programmes of study. A review of the curriculum in Wales has been completed and changes were introduced from September 2000. Welsh is compulsory for pupils at all key stages, either as a teaching medium or as a second language. In 1999 some 27 per cent of primary schools used Welsh as the sole or main medium of instruction and a further five per cent used it for part of the curriculum. Over 22 per cent of secondary schools taught Welsh both as a first and second language, while 69 per cent taught it as a second language only. Schools perform tests and tasks in Welsh in addition to those in the other subjects of the national curriculum.

The National Assembly for Wales and local education authorities publish tables showing pupils' performance in examinations and national curriculum tests. Approximately 38,000 pupils in each of the age groups take the tests each year.

NATIONAL TESTING AND TEACHERS'
ASSESSMENT RESULTS IN CORE SUBJECTS 1999

Percentage of pupils reaching the expected level of performance at that age:

	Key stage 1 7-year olds (level 2)	Key stage 2 11-year olds (level 4)	Key stage 3 14-year olds (level 5)
WALES			
English	80.0	65.0	62.0
Welsh (first language)	86.0	63.0	71.0
Mathematics	84.0	65.0	64.0
Science	85.0	71.0	60.0

National targets have been set as follows: 70–80 per cent to reach the expected level of performance for that age at key stages two and three in English, Welsh, mathematics and science by 2002 and 80–85 per cent by 2004.

Awdurdod Cymwysterau, Cwricwlwm ac Asesu Cymru (ACCAC)/the Qualifications, Curriculum and Assessment Authority for Wales advises government on matters within its remit. ACCAC is funded by the National Assembly for Wales.

SCOTLAND

The content and management of the curriculum in Scotland are not prescribed by statute but are the responsibility of education authorities and individual headteachers. Advice and guidance are provided by the Scottish Executive Education Department and the Scottish Consultative Council on the Curriculum, which also has a developmental role. Guidance for the pre-school sector describes the nature of the pre-school experience, sets out features of learning in key aspects of the child's early development and identifies appropriate learning experiences for children and opportunities for collaboration with other agencies. For the five–14 age group there are guidelines on the structure and balance of the curriculum as well as for each of the curriculum areas, although they are currently under review. There are also guidelines on assessment across the whole curriculum, on reporting to parents, and on standardised national tests for English language and mathematics at five levels. The curriculum for 14- to 16-year-olds includes study within each of eight modes: language and communication, mathematical studies, science, technology, social studies, creative activities, physical education, and religious and moral education. There are recommendations for the percentage of time to be devoted to each area over the two years. Provision is made for teaching in Gaelic in Gaelic-speaking areas. Testing is carried out on a voluntary basis when the teacher deems it appropriate; most pupils are expected to move from one level to the next at roughly two-year intervals. National testing is largely in place in most primary schools but secondary school participation rates are lower.

For 16- to 18-year-olds, a new unified framework of courses and awards, known as 'Higher Still', which will bring together both academic and vocational courses, was introduced in 1999. The SQA awards the new certificates.

NORTHERN IRELAND

A curriculum common to all grant-aided schools exists. Pupils are required to study religious education and, depending on which key stage they have reached, certain subjects from six broad areas of study: English, mathematics, science and technology; the environment and society; creative and expressive studies and, in key stages three and four, language studies. The statutory curriculum requirements at key stages one to three have been revised and new programmes of study were introduced in September 1996. Six cross-curricular educational themes, which include information technology and education for mutual understanding, are woven through the main subjects of the curriculum. Irish is a foundation subject in schools that use it as a medium of instruction.

The assessment of pupils is broadly in line with practice in England and Wales and takes place at the ages of eight, 11 and 14. The GCSE is used to assess 16-year-olds.

NATIONAL TESTING AND TEACHERS' ASSESSMENT
RESULTS IN CORE SUBJECTS 2000
(1999 KEY STAGE 3)

Percentage of pupils reaching the expected level of performance at that age (at key stage 3, teacher assessed level (test level in brackets)):

	Key stage 1 8-year olds (level 2)	Key stage 2 11-year olds (level 4)	Key stage 3 14-year olds (level 5)
English	94	71	72 (67)
Mathematics	94	75	71 (69)
Science	—	—	70 (64)

National targets have been set for 11-year-olds: 80 per cent to reach level four in English and mathematics by 2002.

The Northern Ireland Council for the Curriculum, Examinations and Assessment (NICCEA) monitors and advises the Department of Education and teachers on all matters relating to the curriculum, assessment arrangements and examinations in grant-aided schools. It conducts GCSE, A- and AS-level examinations, pupil assessment at key stages one, two and three and administers the transfer procedure tests.

THE PUBLIC EXAMINATION SYSTEM

ENGLAND, WALES AND NORTHERN IRELAND

Until the end of 1987, secondary school pupils at the end of compulsory schooling around the age of 16, and others, took the General Certificate of Education (GCE) Ordinary-level or the Certificate of Secondary Education (CSE). From 1988 these were replaced by a single system of examinations, the General Certificate of Secondary Education (GCSE), which is usually taken after five years of secondary education. The GCSE is the main method of assessing the performance of pupils at age 16 in all national curriculum subjects required to be assessed at the end of compulsory schooling. The structure of the examination is being adapted in accordance with national curriculum requirements; new subject criteria published in 1995 to govern GCSE syllabuses introduced in 1996 for first examination in 1998. GCSE short-course qualifications are available in some subjects. As a rule the syllabus takes half the time of a full GCSE course.

The GCSE differs from its predecessors in that there are syllabuses based on national criteria covering course objectives, content and assessment methods; differentiated assessment (i.e. different papers or questions for different ranges of ability) and grade-related criteria (i.e. grades awarded on absolute rather than relative performance). The GCSE certificates are awarded on a seven-point scale, A to G. From 1994 there has been an additional 'starred' A grade (A*), to recognise the achievement of the highest attainers at GCSE. Grades A to C are the equivalent of the corresponding O-level grades A to C or CSE grade 1. Grades D, E, F and G record achievement at least as high as that represented by CSE

grades 2 to 5. All GCSE syllabuses, assessments and grading procedures are monitored by the Qualifications and Curriculum Authority to ensure that they conform to the national criteria

In the UK in 1997–8, 96.6 per cent of all 15- to 16-year-old entrants achieved one or more graded GCSE, SCE Standard Grade, or equivalent result, while 48.6 per cent achieved five or more results at grade C or better.

Many maintained schools offer BTEC Firsts and an increasing number offer BTEC Nationals. National Vocational Qualifications (NVQs) in the form of General NVQs (GNVQs) are also available to students in schools. The Part 1 GNVQ is a shortened version of the full GNVQ. Designed for 14- to 16-year-olds, it is a two-year course at Foundation and Intermediate levels, the former broadly equivalent to two GCSEs at grades D to G, the latter at grades A* to C. It has been available in schools since September 1999. The Vocational A-level, formerly the Advanced GNVQ equivalent to two A-levels, has been revised and expanded and is available in three, six and 12 units, equivalent to AS-level (three units), A-level (six units) and two A levels (12 units).

Those who choose to continue their education after GCSE may also take General Certificate of Education (GCE) Advanced (A-level) examinations. A-level courses usually last two years and have traditionally provided the foundation for entry to higher education. A separate Advanced Supplementary level examination was introduced in 1987 as an alternative to, and to complement, A-levels. The course was designed to last two years and required not less than half the teaching time of the corresponding A-level course. The syllabus covered not less than half the content of the corresponding A-level syllabus and, where possible, was related to it. From summer 2000 revised A-level syllabuses have been introduced for examination in summer 2002 and Advanced Subsidiary level examinations have replaced Advanced Supplementary level examinations for examination in summer 2001. The new A-level qualification is normally composed of six units (three A2 units and three AS units), the latter being less demanding and constituting the new AS-level qualification, which represents the first half of a full A-level. Students who go on to complete the full A-level will be assessed on their attainment in all six units, which may be taken either in stages or all at the end of the course. Candidates have the choice between end-of-course or staged assessment, with limits on coursework. A-levels and AS-levels are marked on a six-point scale: from A to E (pass) and U (unclassified), which is not certificated.

In the UK in 1997–8, 331.0 thousand students achieved one or more passes at A-level or SCE H-grade (an increase of ten per cent on the previous year). Of those in Great Britain who entered for A-level or SCE H-grade examinations, 32.9 per cent studied sciences (58.6 per cent boys, 41.4 per cent girls) and 67.1 per cent studied arts/social studies (40.5 per cent of boys, 59.5 per cent of girls).

Most examining boards allow the option of an additional paper of greater difficulty to be taken by A-level candidates. From September 2000 such will be known as Advanced Extension Awards (formerly Special-level or Scholarship-level). Papers are available in most of the traditional academic subjects and are marked on a three-point scale.

The City & Guilds Diploma of Vocational Education is intended for a wide ability range. Within guidelines and to meet specified criteria, schools and colleges design their own courses, which stress activity-based learning, core skills which include application of number, communication and information technology, and work experience.

The Diploma is of value to those who want to find out what aptitudes they may have and to prepare themselves for work, but who may not yet be committed to a particular occupation. It can be taken alongside GCSEs and can provide a context for the introduction of GNVQ units into the key stage four curriculum.

The various examining boards in England have combined into three unitary awarding bodies, which offer both academic and vocational qualifications: GNVQs, GCSEs, AS and A-levels. The new bodies are the Assessment and Qualifications Alliance (AQA), Edexcel and Oxford, Cambridge and RSA Examinations (OCR). At present the existing examination boards are still separate bodies, although they work together in many ways to meet the needs of schools and colleges.

Scotland

Scotland has its own system of public examinations. At the end of the fourth year of secondary education, at about the age of 16, or earlier if appropriate, pupils take the Standard Grade of the Scottish Certificate of Education. Standard Grade courses and examinations have been designed to suit every level of ability, with assessment against nationally determined standards of performance.

For most courses there are three separate examination papers at the end of the two-year Standard Grade course. They are set at Credit (leading to awards at grade 1 or 2), General (leading to awards at grade 3 or 4) and Foundation (leading to awards at grade 5 or 6) levels. Grade 7 is available to those who, although they have completed the course, have not attained any of these levels. Normally pupils will take examinations covering two pairs of grades, either grades 1–4 or grades 3–6. Most candidates take seven or eight Standard Grade examinations.

Above Standard Grade, Higher Grade will be available after a one-year course in the fifth or sixth year of secondary school until 2000–1.

The one-year Certificate of Sixth Year Studies (CSYS) will be available until 2001–2.

A new system of courses and qualifications is being phased in under the 'Higher Still' reforms, bringing together academic and vocational qualifications. National Qualifications will replace Highers, CSYS and National Certificate modules, for everyone studying beyond Standard Grade in Scottish schools, and for non-advanced students in further education colleges. National Qualifications will be available at five levels: Access, Intermediate 1, Intermediate 2, Higher, and Advanced Higher, the latter available from 2000–1. Courses will be made up of internally assessed units with external assessment of the full course determining the grade (A to C). Students possessing a number of units and courses may be able to build them into a Scottish Group Award. The core skills of communication, numeracy, problem-solving, information technology and working with others are embedded in the Higher Still qualifications, although the skills and levels covered vary between subjects; there will also be separate core skills units.

All of these qualifications are awarded by the Scottish Qualifications Authority (SQA).

The International Baccalaureate is an internationally recognised two-year pre-university course and examination designed to facilitate the mobility of students and to promote international understanding. There are 33 schools and colleges in the UK which offer the International Baccalaureate diploma.

RECORDS OF ACHIEVEMENT

The National Record of Achievement (NRA) is under review. Subject to evaluation, it will be replaced in England, Wales and Northern Ireland by the Progress file after a three year trial period starting in July 1999. In Scotland the Scottish Qualifications Authority issues a Scottish Qualifications Certificate recording all qualifications achieved at all levels which it has either awarded or accredited.

TEACHERS

ENGLAND AND WALES

Teachers at state primary and secondary schools are required to have successfully completed a course of initial teacher training, traditionally either a Bachelor of Education (BEd) degree or the Postgraduate Certificate of Education (PGCE) at an accredited institution. New entrants to the profession are statutorily required to serve a one-year induction period during which they will have a structured programme of support. In recent years various employment-based routes to teaching have been developed. The Graduate Teacher Programme allows mature graduates with teaching experience to undergo between one term's and one year's school-based training. The schools involved receive up to £13,000 to cover the trainee's salary on top of the existing grant of up to £4,000 for undertaking training. The Registered Teacher Scheme is designed to attract into the teaching profession entrants over 24 years of age without formal teaching qualifications but with relevant training and experience; entrants are paid a salary and undertake one to two years higher education depending on whether they possess relevant teaching experience. Teachers in further education are not required to have Qualified Teacher Status, though roughly half have a teaching qualification and most have industrial, commercial or professional experience. A qualification for aspiring head-teachers, the National Professional Qualification for Headship (NPQH), was introduced in September 1997 and will be mandatory by 2002.

Teacher training is now largely school-based, with student teachers on secondary PGCE courses spending two-thirds of their training in the classroom. Changes have also been made to primary phase teacher training to make it more school-based and to give schools a role in course design and delivery. Individual schools or consortia of schools and CTCs can bid for funds from the DfEE to carry out their own teacher training, including recruitment of students, subject to approval of their proposed training programme by the Teacher Training Agency (TTA) and monitoring and evaluation by OFSTED and Estyn. Funds are given to schools to meet the costs of designing and delivering the courses.

The TTA funds all types of teacher training in England, whether run by universities, colleges or schools, and some educational research. In Wales funding is undertaken by the Higher Education Funding Council for Wales. On an integrated England and Wales basis the TTA also acts as a central source of information and advice about entry to teaching, and has responsibilities relating to the continuing professional development of teachers. An independent professional council, the General Teaching Council, has been established to advise the Secretary of State and the TTA, with a separate council for Wales.

The Specialist Teacher Assistant (STA) scheme provides trained support to qualified teachers in the teaching of reading, writing and arithmetic to young pupils.

SHORTAGE SUBJECTS

Because of a shortage of teachers in England and Wales in certain secondary subjects, from September 2000 graduates training for a PGCE who then take up a post as teachers of mathematics, modern foreign languages (including Welsh in Wales), science or technology, received a training salary of £6,000 (£150 per week) and a further £4,000 lump sum after completing induction and obtaining a permanent appointment. A training salary for postgraduates training as primary teachers is being trialled during 2000–1. Furthermore, providers of initial teacher training in England and Wales may receive funds from the TTA to help promote courses in certain subjects and to offer students on courses in those subjects financial support. The subjects are: science; mathematics; modern languages (including Welsh in Wales); design and technology; information technology; religious education; music, and geography.

SCOTLAND

The General Teaching Council (GTC) for Scotland advises central government on matters relating to teachers and teacher education. All teachers in maintained schools must be registered with the GTC, initially for a two-year probationary period which can be extended if necessary. Only graduates are accepted as entrants to the profession; primary school teachers undertake either a four-year vocational degree course or a one-year postgraduate course, while teachers of academic subjects in secondary schools undertake the latter. Most initial teacher training is classroom-based. The Scottish Qualification for Headship has been introduced for aspiring head teachers. The colleges of education provide both in-service and pre-service training for teachers which is subject to inspection by HM Inspectors. All pre-service courses must be approved by the Scottish Executive Education Department and, if appropriate, validated by a higher education institution and accredited by the GTC. The colleges are funded by the Scottish Higher Education Funding Council.

NORTHERN IRELAND

All new entrants to teaching in grant-aided schools are graduates and hold an approved teaching qualification. Teacher training is provided by the two universities and two colleges of education. The colleges are concerned with teacher education mainly for the primary school sector. They also provide BEd courses for intending secondary school teachers of religious education, commercial studies, and craft, design and technology. With these exceptions, the professional training of teachers for secondary schools is provided in the education departments of the universities. A review of primary and secondary teacher training has taken place as a result of which all student teachers spend more time in the classroom. All newly qualified teachers undertake a two-year induction period. The General Teaching Council for Northern Ireland is to be established in 2001 to advise government on professional issues, to maintain a register of teachers and to act as a disciplinary body.

ACCREDITATION OF TRAINING INSTITUTIONS

Advice to central government on the accreditation, content and quality of initial teacher training courses is given in England by the TTA, in Wales by the HEFCW and in Northern Ireland by validating bodies (by the General Teaching Council for Northern Ireland when established). These bodies also monitor and disseminate good practice, assisted in Northern Ireland by the Teacher Education Committee. In Scotland the General Teaching Council advises the Scottish Executive Education Department on the professional suitability of all training courses in colleges of education.

SERVING TEACHERS 1997–8 (*full-time and part-time*) (thousands)

Public sector schools	447.4
Nursery and primary	210.7
Secondary	220.1
Special	16.6
TOTAL	464.0

SALARIES

Qualified teachers in England, Wales and Northern Ireland, other than heads and deputy heads, are paid on an 18-point scale. Entry points and placement depend on qualifications and experience. There are additional cash allowances for management responsibilities, special needs work and recruitment and retention factors as calculated by the relevant body, i.e. the governing body or the LEA. A new career grade of 'Advanced Skills Teacher' has been introduced to enhance prospects in the classroom for the most able teachers. The introduction of the government's proposal, that high-performing teachers as assessed against national standards should receive a performance-related pay increase of an extra £2,000 a year, has been delayed following a legal challenge. There is a statutory superannuation scheme in maintained schools.

Teachers in Scotland are paid on a ten-point scale. The entry point depends on type of qualification, and additional allowances are payable' under' certain circumstances.

Salaries from 1 April 2000

	England, Wales and N. Ireland	Scotland
Head	£32,184–£72,312*	£34,407–£54,774
Deputy head	£28,158–£46,320	£33,708–£40,986
Advanced skills teacher	£26,943–£42,981	
Teacher	£15,141–£38,262	£14,022–£28,881

* Until 31 August 2000

FURTHER EDUCATION

Further education is defined as all provision outside schools to people aged over 16 of education up to and including A-level and its equivalent.

ENGLAND AND WALES

Further education and sixth form colleges are funded directly by central government through the Further Education Funding Council for England (FEFCE) and the Further Education Funding Council for Wales (FEFCW). The Councils have a duty to secure provision of adequate facilities in their areas and are also responsible for the assessment of quality, in which their inspectorates play a key role. The colleges are controlled by autonomous further education corporations, which include substantial representation from industry and commerce, and which own their own assets and employ their own staff. Their funding is determined in part by the number of students enrolled and their level of achievement. From April 2001 a new Learning and Skills Council operating through

47 regional councils will take over the role of the FEFCE and the training functions of Training and Enterprise Councils. Its counterpart in Wales will be the National Council for Education and Training in Wales.

Teaching staff in further education establishments are not necessarily required to have teaching qualifications although many do so, but they are subject to regular appraisal of teaching performance. It is planned to introduce a mandatory professional qualification for college principals.

Further education tends to be broadly vocational in purpose and employers are often involved in designing courses. It ranges from lower-level technical and commercial courses and government-sponsored training, through courses for those aiming at higher-level posts in industry, commerce and administration, to professional courses. Facilities exist for GCE A- and AS-levels, GCSEs, GNVQs and a full range of vocational qualifications (*see* below). These courses can form the foundation for progress to higher education qualifications. Many students attend part-time, either through day or block release from employment, or in the evenings.

The main courses and examinations in the vocational field, all of which link in with the National Vocational Qualification (NVQ) framework (*see* below), are offered by the following bodies, but there are also many others.

The Edexcel Foundation was formed by the merger of the Business and Technology Education Council (BTEC) and London Examinations. It provides programmes of study across a wide range of subject areas. The main qualifications offered are GCSEs, AS and A-levels, GNVQs, NVQs, BTEC First, National and Higher National diplomas and certificates, key skills and entry certificates.

City & Guilds specialise in developing qualifications and assessments for work-related and leisure qualifications. They offer nationally and internationally recognised certificates in over 500 vocational qualifications. The progressive structure of awards spans seven levels, from foundation to the highest level of professional competence.

RSA Examinations Board schemes cover a wide range of vocational qualifications, including accounting, business administration, customer service, management, language schemes, information technology and teaching qualifications. A wide range of NVQs and GNVQs are offered and a policy operates of credit accumulation, so that candidates can take a single unit or complete qualifications.

There are 435 further education establishments (of which 107 are sixth form colleges) in England and 26 in Wales. In England (1998–9) there were 900.2 thousand full-time and sandwich-course students and 2,149.9 thousand part-time students. In Wales (1997–8) there were 44.2 thousand full-time and sandwich students and 162.1 thousand part-time students.

SCOTLAND

Further education comprises all provision outside schools to those aged over 16. It includes National Qualifications, SVQ work-based awards, SCE Higher Grade and occasionally GCE A-level.

Responsibility for further education lies with the Scottish Executive under the Minister for Enterprise and Lifelong Learning through the Scottish Further Education Funding Council. There are 47 further education colleges of which 43 are self-governing incorporated colleges run by their own boards of management. The boards include the principal, staff and student representatives among their ten to 16 members; at least half the members

must have experience of commerce, industry or the practice of a profession. Two colleges, on Orkney and Shetland, are under Islands Council control and two others, Sàbhal Mor Ostaig (the Gaelic college on Skye) and Newbattle Abbey are run by trustees.

The Scottish Qualifications Authority (SQA) is the statutory awarding body for qualifications in the national education system in schools and colleges; the national accrediting body for work-based SVQs; and the main awarding body for work-related and work-based qualifications. It awards at non-advanced level the National Certificate, which is available in over 4,000 individual modules embracing a wide range of subjects and covers the whole range of non-advanced further education provision. Students may study for the National Certificate on a full-time, part-time, open learning or work-based learning basis. National Certificate modules can be taken in further education colleges, secondary schools and other centres, normally from the age of 16 onwards. New unified National Qualifications for non-advanced post-16 education began to be phased in from August 1999 under the Higher Still reforms, which bring together academic and vocational qualifications. National Qualification courses will be available at five levels, (Access, Intermediate 1, Intermediate 2, Higher and Advanced Higher) and will replace Higher Grades, CSYS, General Scottish Vocational Qualifications (GSVQ) and National Certificate modules, but not Standard Grade or Scottish Vocational Qualifications (SVQ).

SQA also offers modular advanced-level HNC/HND qualifications, which are available in further education colleges and higher education institutions. SQA accredits and awards SVQs which have mutual recognition with the NVQs available in the rest of the UK. SVQs are workplace assessed, but can also be taken in further education colleges and other centres where work-place conditions can be simulated.

In the academic year 1998–9 there were 36,874 full-time and sandwich-course students and 253,411 part-time students on non-advanced vocational courses of further education in further education colleges (excluding Newbattle Abbey College).

NORTHERN IRELAND

All further education colleges are free-standing corporate bodies like their counterparts in the rest of the UK. Planning is the responsibility of the Department of Education for Northern Ireland, which funds the colleges directly. The colleges own their own property, are responsible for their own services and employ their own staff.

The governing bodies of the colleges must include at least 50 per cent membership from the professions, local business or industry, or other fields of employment relevant to the activities of the college.

In 1999–2000 Northern Ireland had 17 institutions of further education, and there were 20,558 full-time students and 57,277 part-time students on vocational further education courses.

STUDENT SUPPORT

At present 16- to 19-year-olds may receive means-tested discretionary payments from LEAs, while adults may apply for access funds allocated by central government through the FEFCs. The means-tested Education Maintenance Allowance (EMA) for 16- to 18-year-old students in both schools and colleges is a weekly allowance worth up to £30 a week which is being piloted in certain areas where there are problems of poverty and low staying-on rates. EMAs are payable subject to conditions laid out under a learning agreement. The access fund scheme is also being extended.

NATIONAL VOCATIONAL QUALIFICATIONS

National Vocational Qualifications (NVQs) are workplace based occupational qualifications. In September 1992 General National Vocational Qualifications (GNVQs) were introduced into colleges and schools as a vocational alternative to academic qualifications. GNVQs cover six broad categories in the NVQ framework and are aimed at those wishing to familiarise themselves with a range of opportunities. In September 2000 the Vocational A level has been introduced. It operates at three levels: the three unit vocational A level (known as Vocational AS), equivalent to one GCE AS-level; the six unit Vocational A level, equivalent to one GCE A-level; and the 12 unit Vocational A level (double award) equivalent to two A-levels (formerly Advanced GNVQ). Part one GNVQ comprises Intermediate GNVQ, equivalent to two GCSEs at A* to C grade and Foundation GNVQ, equivalent to two GCSEs at D to G grade. The full GNVQ , also at Intermediate and Foundation level, is similarly equivalent to four GCSEs.

HIGHER EDUCATION

The term higher education is used to describe education above A-level, Higher and Advanced Higher Grade and their equivalent, which is provided in universities, colleges of higher education and in some further education colleges.

FURTHER EDUCATION, HIGHER EDUCATION

The Further and Higher Education Act 1992 and parallel legislation in Scotland removed the distinction between higher education provided by the universities and that provided in England and Wales by the former polytechnics and colleges of higher education and in Scotland by the former central institutions and others. It allowed all polytechnics, and other higher education institutions which satisfy the necessary criteria, to award their own taught course and research degrees and to adopt the title of university. All the polytechnics, art colleges and some colleges of higher education have since done so. The change of name does not affect the legal constitution of the institutions. Funding is by the Higher Education Funding Councils for England, Wales and Scotland and directly by the Department of Education in Northern Ireland.

The number of students in higher education in the UK in 1998–9 was (thousands):
The proportion of the 18- to 21-year-old population

Full-time, sandwich	1,294.1
% female	52.5
Part-time	786.9
% female	54.3
TOTAL	2,081.0
of which overseas	9.1

undertaking full-time and part-time courses in higher education in the UK was 31 per cent in 1998–9. In the same year, 30 per cent of undergraduates in the first year of a first degree course were aged 21 years or over, while 72.6 per cent of first year postgraduate students were aged 25 years or over. The number of full-time and part-time undergraduate students on science courses (excluding medicine and related courses) in 1998–9 was 284 thousand, of whom 33.7 per cent were female.

UNIVERSITIES AND COLLEGES

Responsibility for universities rests in England with the Secretary of State for Education and Employment and with Education Ministers in Scotland, Northern Ireland and Wales. Advice to government on matters relating to the universities is provided by the Higher Education Funding Councils for England, Wales and Scotland, and by the Higher Education Council in Northern Ireland. The HEFCs receive a block grant from central government which they allocate to the universities and colleges. The grant is allocated directly to institutions by central government in Northern Ireland on the advice of the Northern Ireland Higher Education Council.

There are now 88 universities in the UK, where only 47 existed prior to the Further and Higher Education Acts 1992. Of the 88, 71 are in England (including one federal university), two (one a federal institution) in Wales, 13 in Scotland and two in Northern Ireland.

The pre-1992 universities each have their own system of internal government but broad similarities exist. Most are run by two main bodies: the senate, which deals primarily with academic issues and consists of members elected from within the university; and the council, which is the supreme body and is responsible for all appointments and promotions, and bidding for and allocation of financial resources. At least half the members of the council are drawn from outside the university. Joint committees of senate and council are becoming increasingly common.

Those universities which were formerly polytechnics (38) or other higher education institutions (three) and the colleges of higher education (60) are run by higher education corporations (HECs), which are controlled by boards of governors. At least half the members of each board must be drawn from industry, business, commerce and the professions.

The non-residential Open University provides courses nationally leading to degrees. Teaching is through a combination of television and radio programmes, correspondence, tutorials, short residential courses and local audio-visual centres. No qualifications are needed for entry. The Open University offers a modular programme of undergraduate courses by credit accumulation and post-experience and postgraduate courses, including a programme of higher degrees which comprises BPhil, MPhil and PhD through research, and MA, MBA and MSc through taught courses. The Open University in England, Wales and Northern Ireland is funded by the Higher Education Funding Council for England. Scottish students are funded by the Scottish Higher Education Funding Council. The Open University's recurrent grant for 1998–9 was £125.1 million from the Higher Education Funding Council for England and £4.3 million from the Teacher Training Agency. In 2000 about 130,000 undergraduates were registered of whom about 54 per cent were women. Estimated cost (2000) of a six-credit degree was around £4,400 including course fees of about £3,200.

The independent University of Buckingham provides a two-year course leading to a bachelor's degree and its tuition fees were £9,996 for 2000.

The University for Industry (UfI) was launched in autumn 2000 in England, Wales and Northern Ireland to promote learning ranging from basic skills to specialised technological and management skills. UfI will operate through learning centres; 11,000 are planned by March 2001. The Scottish UfI operates within the distinctive Scottish system.

ENGLAND AND WALES

In 1998–9 full-time and part-time student enrolments were (thousands):

England

Undergraduates	1,087.7
% overseas	9.9
Postgraduates	264.3
% overseas	27.8

Wales

Undergraduates	72.2
% overseas	8.9
Postgraduates	13.6
% overseas	31.6

Higher education courses funded by the HEFCs are also taught in some further education colleges. In England in 1998–9 there were about 45 thousand full-time and part-time students (2.3 per cent of total higher education student numbers) on such courses and about 4,600 (4.6 per cent of higher education student numbers) in Wales.

SCOTLAND

The Scottish Higher Education Funding Council (SHEFC) funds 21 institutions of higher education, including 13 universities. The universities are broadly managed as described above and the remaining colleges are managed by independent governing bodies which include representatives of industrial, commercial, professional and educational interests. Most of the courses outside the universities have a vocational orientation and a substantial number are sandwich courses.

Student enrolments in 1998–9 in universities and other higher education institutions were (thousands):

Undergraduates	144.5
% overseas	6.5
Postgraduates	17.8
% overseas	33.4

There were 272 thousand students on higher education courses in further education colleges, amounting to 0.15 per cent of the total.

NORTHERN IRELAND

In Northern Ireland higher education is provided in the 17 colleges of further education, the two universities and the two colleges of education. As well as offering first and postgraduate degrees, the University of Ulster offers courses leading to the BTEC Higher National Diploma and professional qualifications. Applications to undertake courses of higher education other than degree courses are made to the institutions direct. Higher education student enrolments in 1998–9 were (thousands):

Undergraduates	29.7
% overseas	14.1
Postgraduates	7.4
% overseas	19.3

In 1999–2000 there were 11,544 students enrolled on higher education courses in the institutions of further education, 27.2 per cent of Further and Higher Education higher education student numbers.

ACADEMIC STAFF

Each university and college appoints its own academic staff on its own conditions. However, there is a common salary structure and, except for Oxford and Cambridge, a common career structure in the pre-1992 universities and a common salary structure for the post-1992 universities. The Universities and Colleges Employers Association (UCEA) acts as a pay agency for universities and colleges.

Teaching staff in higher education require no formal teaching qualification, but the Institute of Teaching and Learning in Higher Education, funded by the Higher Education Funding Councils, has been established to set up an accreditation scheme for higher education teachers and to encourage innovation in teaching and learning. Teacher trainers are required to spend a certain amount of time in schools to ensure that they have sufficient recent practical experience.

In 1998–9, there were 103,995 full-time and part-time teaching and research staff (UK nationals) in institutions of higher education in the UK.

Salary scales for staff in the pre-1992 universities differ from those in the former polytechnics and colleges; it is planned eventually to amalgamate them. The salary scales for non-clinical academic staff in the pre-1992 universities are (1 April 1999):

Professor	from £36,401
Senior lecturer	£31,563–£38,561
Lecturer grade B	£23,521–£30,065
Lecturer grade A	£16,286–£21,579

The salaries of clinical academic staff are kept broadly comparable to those of doctors and dentists in the National Health Service.

Salary scales for lecturers in the former polytechnics, now universities, and colleges of higher education in England, Wales and Northern Ireland (from September 1999) (Scotland as of 1 April 1998 in parenthesis) are:

Head of Department	from £27,225 min (£34,861–£46,508)
Principal lecturer	£28,717–£36,436
Senior lecturer	£23,184–£30,636 (£26,140–£38,037)
Lecturer	£14,902–£24,842 (£15,885–£31,658)

FINANCE

Although universities and colleges are expected to look to a wider range of funding sources than before, and to generate additional revenue in collaboration with industry, they are still largely financed, directly or indirectly, from government resources.

In 1998–9 the total income of institutions of higher education in the UK was £12,112.7 million (£11,632.0 million in 1997–8). Grants from the funding councils amounted to £4,918.5 million (£4,514.3 million in 1997–8), forming 40.6 per cent of total income (38.8 per cent in 1997–8). Income from research grants and contracts was £1,834.7 million, 15.1 per cent of total income (14.9 per cent in 1997–8).

In the academic year 1998–9 the HEFCE's and HEFCW's recurrent grant to institutions outside their sector for the provision of higher education courses was £144.1 million.

COURSES

In the UK all universities and some colleges award their own degrees and other qualifications and may act as awarding and validating bodies for neighbouring colleges which are not yet accredited. The Quality Assurance Agency for Higher Education, funded by institutional contributions, advises government on applications for degree-awarding powers.

Higher education courses last full-time for at least four weeks or, if part-time, involve more than 60 hours of instruction. Facilities exist for full-time and part-time study, day release, sandwich or block release. Credit accumulation and transfer (CATS) is a system of study which allows a student to achieve a final qualification by accumulating credits for courses of study successfully achieved, or even professional experience, over a period. Credit transfer information and values are carried on an electronic database called ECCTIS 2000, which is available in most careers offices and many schools and colleges.

Higher education courses comprise: first degree and postgraduate (including research); Diploma in Higher Education (DipHE); Higher National Diploma (HND) and Higher National Certificate (HNC); and preparation for professional examinations. The in-service training of teachers is also included, but is funded in England by the TTA, not the HEFCE.

The Diploma of Higher Education (DipHE) is a two-year diploma usually intended to serve as a stepping-stone to a degree course or other further study. The DipHE is awarded by the institution itself if it is accredited; by an accredited institution of its choice if not. The BTEC Higher National Certificate (HNC) is awarded after two years part-time study. The BTEC Higher National Diploma (HND) is awarded after two years full-time, or three years sandwich-course or part-time study.

With the exception of certain Scottish universities where master is sometimes used for a first degree in arts subjects, undergraduate courses lead to the title of Bachelor, Bachelor of Arts (BA) and Bachelor of Science (BSc) being the most common. For a higher degree the titles are: Master of Arts (MA), Master of Science (MSc) and the research degrees of Master of Philosophy (MPhil) and Doctor of Philosophy (PhD or, at a few universities, DPhil).

Most undergraduate courses at universities and colleges of higher education run for three years, but some take up to four years. They include modern language courses and honours courses at Scottish universities and the University of Keele. Professional courses in subjects such as medicine, veterinary science and architecture take longer.

Postgraduate studies vary in length. Certificates, diplomas or masters degrees usually take one year full-time or two years part-time. Research degrees take from two to three years full-time.

Post-experience short courses are forming an increasing part of higher education provision, reflecting the need to update professional and technical training. Most of these courses fund themselves.

ADMISSIONS

The target proportion of the 18- to 19-year-old age group entering full-time higher education for 2000–1 was set at 32 to 34 per cent. Institutions suffer financial penalties if the number of students laid down for them by the Funding Councils is exceeded, but the individual university or college decides which students to accept. The formal entry requirements to most degree courses are two A-levels at grade E or above (or equivalent), and to HND courses one A-level (or equivalent). In practice, most offers of places require qualifications in excess of this, higher requirements usually reflecting the popularity of a course. These requirements do not, however, exclude applications from students with a variety of non-GCSE qualifications or unquantified experience and skills.

For admission to a degree, DipHE or HND, potential students apply through a central clearing house, (UCAS). Applicants are supplied with an application form and a UCAS Handbook, available from schools, colleges and careers offices or direct from UCAS, and may apply to a maximum of six institutions/courses. The only exception among universities is the Open University, which conducts its own admissions.

Applications for undergraduate teacher training courses are made through UCAS. Details of initial teacher training courses in Scotland can be obtained from colleges of education and those universities offering such courses, and from the Committee of Scottish Higher Education Principals (COSHEP).

For admission as a postgraduate student, universities and colleges normally require a good first degree in a subject related to the proposed course of study or research, but other experience and qualifications will be considered on merit. Most applications are made to individual institutions but there are two clearing houses of relevance. Postgraduate teacher training courses in England and Wales utilise the Graduate Teacher Training Registry. Applications to postgraduate teacher training courses in Scotland are made through the Teacher Education Admissions Clearing House (TEACH). Applications for PGCE courses at institutions in Northern Ireland are made to the Department of Education. For social work the Social Work Admissions System operates.

FEES

From September 1998 new entrants to undergraduate courses have paid, directly to the institution, an annual contribution to their fees (up to £1,050 in 2000-1) depending on their own level of income and that of their spouse or parents. Students from EU member countries pay fees at home student rates and those at institutions in England, Wales and Northern Ireland will also be liable to make an annual contribution to fees assessed against family income. Among the classes of students exempt from payment are: Scottish domiciled and EU students at Scottish institutions; students from England, Wales and Northern Ireland in the fourth year of a four-year degree course at a Scottish institution; existing students with mandatory awards (*see* below), for whom the grant-awarding body pays; post-graduate certificate of education students (not in Scotland); and medical students in the fifth year of their course.

Universities and colleges are free to set their own charges for students from non-EU countries, whose fees are meant to cover the cost of their education. Financial help is available under a number of schemes.

For postgraduate students, the maximum tuition fee that will be reimbursed through the awards system is £2,740 in 2000–1.

STUDENT SUPPORT

STUDENT GRANTS

Students in the UK who started a full-time or sandwich undergraduate course of higher education since the academic year commencing in September 1998 are no longer eligible for a grant. Grants for such students have been replaced by loans which are partly means-tested, although some students, such as single parents and those with dependants are entitled to apply for an additional means-tested supplementary grant for help in meeting certain living costs and for each child at school. Disabled students are eligible for non means-tested disabled students allowances. Students who started their courses before September 1998 and certain others continue for the duration of their course to be eligible for means-tested maintenance grants, from which a parental contribution is deductible on a sliding scale dependent on income or, for married students, from their spouse's income. However, a parental contribution is not deducted from the grant to students over 25 years of age who have been self-supporting for any three years before the beginning of their course.

Grants are paid by the local education authority for the area in which the student lives in England, Wales and Northern Ireland. The cost is reimbursed by central government. For students resident in Scotland grants are made by central government through the Students Awards Agency.

The means-tested maintenance grant, usually paid once a term, covers periods of attendance during term as well as the Christmas and Easter vacations, but not the summer vacation. The basic grant rates for 2000-1 (rates for Scottish students in parenthesis) are:

Living in

College/lodgings in London area	£2,335 (£2,255)
College/lodgings outside London area	£1,900 (£1,825)
Parental home	£1,555 (£1,345)

Additional allowances are available if, for example, the course requires a period of study abroad.

Expenditure on mandatory awards in 1998–9 was £1,831.4 million; about one million mandatory awards were made.

STUDENT LOANS

In the academic year 2000–1 students are eligible to apply for interest-free loans of up to £4,590 through LEAs in England and Wales, education and library boards in Northern Ireland and the Students Awards Agency in Scotland.

Loans are available to students on designated courses, which are those full-time or sandwich courses leading to: a degree; the Diploma of Higher Education; the Higher National Diploma; initial teacher-training courses (not in Scotland), including those for the postgraduate certificate of education and the art teachers' certificate or diploma; a university certificate or diploma course lasting at least three years and other qualifications which are specifically designated as being comparable to first degree courses. Certain residency conditions also apply. Loans of up to £500 are available to part-time students on low incomes. In 1998–9, 659.5 thousand loans were taken up, to the value of £1,233.5 million. Repayment arrangements differ for students who embarked upon higher education courses before the 1998–9 academic year and those starting thereafter. The former normally repay on a mortgage-style basis over five to seven years, although repayment can be deferred if annual income is at or below 85 per cent of national average earnings (£18,192 at 31 August 2000). The latter will not be required to make repayments if their annual income is below £10,000; otherwise nine per cent of the income above that amount is taken to repay the loan.

ACCESS AND HARDSHIP FUNDS

Access funds are allocated by central government to the appropriate Funding Councils in England and Wales and to the Students Award Agency in Scotland and administered by further and higher education institutions. In Northern Ireland they are allocated by central government directly to the institution. They provide non-repayable bursaries of up to £1,000 mainly to mature students, but also to students with dependants, whose access to education might otherwise be inhibited by financial considerations or where real financial difficulties are faced. Hardship loans provide sums of up to £500 for students who are eligible for means-tested loans.

POSTGRADUATE AWARDS

Grants for postgraduate study are discretionary. They comprise studentship awards, which cover students undertaking research degrees or taught masters degrees, are dependent on the class of first degree (especially for research degrees) and are not means-tested; 30-week bursaries, which are means-tested and are available for certain vocational and diploma courses; and flat-rate maintenance grants which have replaced the latter for new entrants from the academic year 2000–1. Postgraduate students, with the exception of students in England, Wales and Northern Ireland on loan-bearing diploma courses such as teacher training, are not eligible to apply for student loans.

For students resident in England and Wales funding is provided by the DfEE through the Arts and Humanities Research Board, research councils and the Ministry of Agriculture, Fisheries and Food.

In Scotland postgraduate funding is provided by central government through the Students Awards Agency for Scotland, the Scottish Executive Rural Affairs Department and the research councils as in England and Wales.

Awards in Northern Ireland are made by DFHETE, the Department of Agriculture and the research councils.

The rates for 30-week bursaries for non loan-bearing courses of professional and vocational training in 2000–1 (Scottish rates in parenthesis) are:

Living in

College/lodgings in London area	£4,215 (£3,853)
College/lodgings outside London area	£3,160 (£3,032)
Parental home	£2,650 (£2,291)

Flat-rate maintenance grants (2000–1) were: £4,100 (London); £3,300 (elsewhere).

Studentship awards for 2000–1 are payable at between £8,500 (London) and £6,810 (elsewhere).

ADULT AND CONTINUING EDUCATION

In the UK, the responsibility for securing adult and continuing education leading to academic or vocational qualifications is statutory. In England, Wales and Scotland it is shared between various bodies: the Further Education Funding Councils (FEFCs) (from April 2001 the Learning and Skills councils in England and the National Council for Education and Training in Wales) are responsible for and fund those courses which take place in their sector and lead to academic and vocational qualifications, prepare students to undertake further or higher education courses, or confer basic skills; the Higher Education Funding Councils fund advanced courses of continuing education. The LEAs have the power, although not the duty, to provide those courses which do not fall within the remit of the Funding Councils. Funding in Northern Ireland is through the education and library boards.

GRANTS, ADULT EDUCATION

Adult education takes place in 'area' adult education centres (England and Wales), vocational further education colleges and evening centres (Scotland), community schools (Northern Ireland), the adult studies departments of colleges of further and higher education and universities.

The involvement of universities in adult education and continuing education has diversified considerably. Birkbeck College in the University of London caters solely for part-time students. Those institutions and colleges formerly in the PCFC sector in England and Wales, because of their range of courses and flexible patterns of student attendance, provide opportunities in the field of adult and continuing education. The Forum for the Advancement of Continuing Education (FACE) promotes collaboration between institutions of higher education active in this area. The Open University, in partnership with the BBC, provides distance teaching leading to first degrees, and also offers post-experience and higher degree courses.

Of the voluntary bodies, the biggest is the Workers' Educational Association (WEA) which operates throughout the UK, reaching about 150,000 adult students annually. The FEFCs (from April 2001 the Learning and Skills Council and the National Council for Education and Training in Wales) and LEAs make grants towards provision.

NIACE, the national organisation for adult learning has a broad remit to promote lifelong learning opportunities for adults. NIACE works to develop increased participation in education and training. It does this through research and project work, conferences, publications and the provision of an information service to educational providers. NIACE Cymru, the Welsh committee, receives financial support from the National Assembly for Wales, support in kind from local authorities, and advises government, voluntary bodies and education providers on adult continuing education and training matters in Wales. In Scotland advice on adult and community education, and promotion thereof, is provided by Community Learning Scotland. Following the demise of the Northern Ireland Council for Adult Education, its functions have been taken over by the Department of Education until a successor body can be set up.

The Universities' Association for Continuing Education (UACE) represents the continuing education and lifelong learning community within higher education and is open to universities and higher education institutions.

GRANTS

Adult education bursaries for students at the long-term residential colleges of adult education are the responsibility of the colleges themselves. The awards are administered for the colleges by the Awards Officer of the Residential Colleges Committee for students resident in England and are funded by the FEFCE (from April 2001 the Learning and Skills Council) in English colleges; for colleges in Wales they are funded and administered by the FEFCW (from April 2001 the National Council for Education and Training in Wales); for colleges in Scotland they are funded by central government and administered by the Scottish FEFC; and for colleges in Northern Ireland they are funded by central government and administered by the education and library boards.

Education Directory

ENGLAND

COUNTY COUNCILS

BEDFORDSHIRE, County Hall, Cauldwell Street, Bedford MK42 9AP. Tel: 01234-363222. *Director*, P. Brett

BUCKINGHAMSHIRE, County Hall, Walton Street, Aylesbury HP20 1UA. Tel: 01296-382602. *Director*, D. McGahey

CAMBRIDGESHIRE, Education Information Office, Box ELH 1500, Shire Hall, Cambridge CB3 0AP. Tel: 01223-717667. *Director*, A. Baxter

CHESHIRE, County Hall, Chester CH1 1SQ. Tel: 01244-602424. *Director of Education*, D. Cracknell

CORNWALL, County Hall, Truro TR1 3AY. Tel: 01872-322000. *Secretary for Education*, J. Harris

CUMBRIA, 5 Portland Square, Carlisle CA1 1PU. Tel: 01228-606868. *Director*, J. Nellist

DERBYSHIRE, County Hall, Matlock DE4 3AG. Tel: 01629-585641. *Chief Education Officer*, R. V. Taylor

DEVON, County Hall, Topsham Road, Exeter EX2 4QD. Tel: 01392-382059. *Director of Education, Arts and Libraries*, A. Smith

DORSET, County Hall, Colliton Park, Dorchester DT1 1XJ. Tel: 01305-224171. *Director*, D. Goddard

DURHAM, County Hall, Durham DH1 5UL. Tel: 0191-383 3319. *Director*, K. Mitchell

EAST SUSSEX, County Hall, St Anne's Crescent, Lewes BN7 1SG. Tel: 01273-481316. *Director of Education*, Ms D. Stokoe

ESSEX, PO Box 47, Chelmsford CM2 6WN. Tel: 01245-492211. *Director of Learning Services*, P. A. Lincoln

GLOUCESTERSHIRE, Shire Hall, Westgate Street, Gloucester GL1 2TG. Tel: 01452-425300. *Director*, R. Crouch

HAMPSHIRE, The Castle, Winchester SO23 8UG. Tel: 01962-841841. *County Education Officer*, A. J. Seber

HERTFORDSHIRE, County Hall, Pegs Lane, Hertford SG13 8DE. Tel: 01992-555555. *Director*, R. Shostak

ISLE OF WIGHT, County Hall, High Street, Newport PO30 1UD. Tel: 01983-823400. *Director*, A. Kaye

KENT, Sessions House, County Hall, Maidstone ME14 1XQ. Tel: 01622-671411. *Strategic Director Education and Libraries*, N. Henwood

LANCASHIRE, PO Box 61, County Hall, Preston PR1 8RJ. Tel: 01772-254868. *Director of Education and Cultural Services*, C. J. Trinick

LEICESTERSHIRE, County Hall, Glenfield, Leicester LE38RF. Tel: 0116-265 6301. *Director*, Mrs J. A. M. Strong

LINCOLNSHIRE, County Offices, Newland, Lincoln LN1 1YQ. Tel: 01522-552222. *Director of Education and Cultural Services*, Dr C. Berry

NORFOLK, County Hall, Martineau Lane, Norwich NR1 2DH. Tel: 01603-222146. *Director*, Dr B. C. Slater

NORTH YORKSHIRE, County Hall, Northallerton N. Yorks DL7 8AE. Tel: 01609-780780. *Director*, Miss C. Welbourn

NORTHAMPTONSHIRE, Education and Community Learning, PO Box 233, County Hall, Northampton NN1 1AZ. Tel: 01604-236252. *Strategic Director*, Mrs B. Bignold

NORTHUMBERLAND, County Hall, Morpeth NE61 2EF. Tel: 01670-533601. *Director*, Dr L. Davis

NOTTINGHAMSHIRE, County Hall, West Bridgford, Nottingham NG2 7QP. Tel: 0115-982 3823. *Director*, R. Valentine

OXFORDSHIRE, Education Department, Macclesfield House, New Road, Oxford OX1 1NA. Tel: 01865-815449. *Chief Education Officer*, G. Badman

SHROPSHIRE, The Shirehall, Abbey Foregate, Shrewsbury SY2 6ND. Tel: 01743-254302. *Corporate Director – Education Services*, Ms E. Nicholson

SOMERSET, County Hall, Taunton TA1 4DY. Tel: 01823-355790. *Corporate Director – Education*, M. Jennings

STAFFORDSHIRE, Education Offices, Tipping Street, Stafford ST16 2DH. Tel: 01785-223121. *Director*, Dr P. J. Hunter

SUFFOLK, St Andrew House, County Hall, Ipswich IP4 1LJ. Tel: 01473-584631. *Director*, D. J. Peachey

SURREY, County Hall, Penrhyn Road, Kingston upon Thames KT1 2DN. Tel: 0845-600 9009. *Director*, Dr P. Gray

WARWICKSHIRE, PO Box 24, 22 Northgate Street, Warwick CV34 4SR. Tel: 01926-410410. *County Education Officer*, E. Wood

WEST SUSSEX, County Hall, Chichester PO19 1RF. Tel: 01243-777129. *Director of Education and the Arts*, R. D. C. Bunker

WILTSHIRE, County Hall, Bythesea Road, Trowbridge BA14 8JB. Tel: 01225-713000. *Chief Education Officer*, R. W. Wolfson

WORCESTERSHIRE, County Hall, Spetchley Road, Worcester WR5 2NP. Tel: 01905-763763. *Director of Educational Services*, J. Kramer

UNITARY COUNCILS

BARNSLEY, Berneslai Close, Barnsley S70 2HS. Tel: 01226-773500. *Executive Director-Education*, Ms J. Potter

BATH AND NORTH-EAST SOMERSET, PO Box 25, Riverside, Temple Street, Keynsham, Bristol BS31 1DN. Tel: 01225-394200. *Education Director*, D. Williams

BIRMINGHAM, Education Offices, Margaret Street, Birmingham B3 3BU. Tel: 0121-303 2590/2872. *Chief Education Officer*, Prof. T. Brighouse

BLACKBURN WITH DARWEN, Town Hall, Blackburn BB1 7DY. Tel: 01254-585541. *Director of Education and Training*, M. Pattison

BLACKPOOL, Progress House, Clifton Road, Blackpool FY4 4US. Tel: 01253-476555. *Director of Education and Cultural Services*, Dr D. Sanders

BOLTON, Paderborn House, Civic Centre, Bolton BL1 1JW. Tel: 01204-333333. *Director*, Mrs M. Blenkinsop

BOURNEMOUTH, Dorset House, 20–22 Christchurch Road, Bournemouth BH1 3NL. Tel: 01202-456219. *Director*, K. Shaikh

BRACKNELL FOREST, Edward Elgar House, Skimped Hill Lane, Bracknell Berks RG12 1LY. Tel: 01344-424642. *Director of Education*, T. Eccleston

BRADFORD, Flockton House, Flockton Road, Bradford BD4 7RY. Tel: 01274-751840. *Director*, Mrs D. Cavanagh

BRIGHTON AND HOVE, PO Box 2503, Kings House, Grand Avenue, Hove BN3 2SU. Tel: 01273-290000. *Strategic Director of Education and Lifelong Learning*, D. Hawker

BRISTOL, The Council House, College Green, Bristol BS99 7EW. Tel: 0117-903 7961. *Director of Education and Lifelong Learning*, R. Riddell

BURY, Athenaeum House, Market Street, Bury BL9 0SW. Tel: 0161-253 5652. *Chief Education Officer*, H. Williams

CALDERDALE, Northgate House, Northgate, Halifax HX1 1UN. Tel: 01422-357257. *Group Director, Schools and Children's Services*, Ms C. White

COVENTRY, Council Offices, Earl Street, Coventry CV1 5RS. Tel: 024-7683 1505. *Strategic Director for Lifelong Learning*, Ms C. Goodwin

DARLINGTON, Town Hall, Darlington DL1 5QT. Tel: 01325-380651. *Director*, G. Pennington

DERBY, Middleton House, 27 St Mary's Gate, Derby DE1 3NN. Tel: 01332-716924. *Director*, A. Flack

DONCASTER, Directorate of Education and Culture, The Council House, College Road, Doncaster DN1 3AD. Tel: 01302-737103. *Executive Director*, M. Simpson

DUDLEY, Westox House, 1 Trinity Road, Dudley DY1 1JQ. Tel: 01384-814225. *Chief Education Officer*, R. P. Colligan

EAST RIDING OF YORKSHIRE, County Hall, Beverley HU17 9BA. Tel: 01482-887700. *Director*, J. Ginnever

GATESHEAD, Civic Centre, Regent Street, Gateshead NE8 1HH. Tel: 0191-477 1011. *Director*, B. H. Edwards

HALTON, Grosvenor House, Halton Lea, Runcorn WA7 2WD. Tel: 0151-424 2061. *Director*, G. Talbot

HARTLEPOOL, Civic Centre, Victoria Road, Hartlepool TS24 8AY. Tel: 01429-266522. *Director*, J. J. Fitt

HEREFORDSHIRE, Brockington, 35 Hafod Road, Hereford HR1 1SH. Tel: 01432-260000. *Director*, Dr E. Oram

KINGSTON UPON HULL, Essex House, Manor Street, Kingston upon Hull HU1 1YD. Tel: 01482-613161. *Group Director Learning Services*, Miss J. E. Taylor

KIRKLEES, Oldgate House, 2 Oldgate, Huddersfield HD1 6QW . Tel: 01484-225242. *Chief Education Officer*, G. Tonkin

KNOWSLEY, Education Offices, Huyton Hey Road, Huyton, Knowsley L36 9YH. Tel: 0151-443 3220. *Director*, S. Munby

LEEDS, Merrion House, Merrion Way, 110 Merrion Centre, Leeds LS2 8DT. Tel: 0113-247 5590. *Director*, K. Burton

LEICESTER, Marlborough House, 38 Welford Road, Leicester LE2 7AA. Tel: 0116-252 7807. *Director*, S. Andrews

LIVERPOOL, 4th Floor, 4 Renshaw Street, Liverpool L1 4NX. Tel: 0151-233 3000. *Executive Director*, C. Hilton

LUTON, Unity House, 111 Stuart Street, Luton LU1 5NP. Tel: 01582-546000. *Director*, T. Dessent

MANCHESTER, Cumberland House, Crown Square, Manchester M60 3BB. Tel: 0161-234 7125. *Director*, D. Johnston

MEDWAY, Compass Centre, Chatham Maritime, Chatham Kent ME7 4OD. Tel: 01634-881638. *Director of Education*, R. Bolsin

MIDDLESBROUGH, PO Box 69, Vancouver House, Gurney Street, Middlesbrough TS1 1QP. Tel: 01642-262001. *Corporate Director of Education*, Dr B. Comiskey

MILTON KEYNES, Saxon Court, 502 Avebury Boulevard, Milton Keynes MK9 3HS. Tel: 01908-253325. *Director*, A. Flack

NEWCASTLE UPON TYNE, Civic Centre, Newcastle upon Tyne NE1 8PU. Tel: 0191-232 8520 ext. 5301. *Director of Education and Libraries*, P. Turner

NORTH EAST LINCOLNSHIRE, Education Department, 7 Eleanor Street, Grimsby DN32 9DU. Tel: 01472-323021. *Director of Education*, G. Hill

NORTH LINCOLNSHIRE, PO Box 35, Hewson House, Station Road, Brigg DN20 8XJ. Tel: 01724-297240 *Director of Education and Personal Development*, Dr T. W. Thomas

NORTH SOMERSET, Town Hall, Weston-super-Mare BS23 1AE. Tel: 01934-888888. *Director*, J. Simpson

NORTH TYNESIDE, Town Hall, High Street East, Wallsend, Tyne & Wear NE28 7RR. Tel: 0191-200 6565. *Acting Chief Education Officer*, P. Parish

NOTTINGHAM CITY, Sandfield Centre, Sandfield Road, Nottingham NG7 1QH. Tel: 0115-915 0706. *Director*, P. Roberts

OLDHAM, PO Box 40, Civic Centre, West Street, Oldham OL1 1XJ. Tel: 0161-911 4200. *Executive Director, Education and Leisure Services*, Ms C. Berry

PETERBOROUGH, Bayard Place, Broadway, Peterborough PE1 1FB. Tel: 01733-748000. *Director*, R. Clayton

PLYMOUTH, Civic Centre, Armada Way, Plymouth PL1 2EW. Tel: 01752-668000. *Director for Lifelong Learning*, S. Faruqi

POOLE, Civic Centre, Poole Dorset BH15 2RU. Tel: 01202-633202. *Policy Director – Education*, Dr S. Goodwin

PORTSMOUTH, Civic Offices, Guildhall Square, Portsmouth PO1 2AL. Tel: 023-9282 2251. *City Education Officer*, J. Gaskin

READING, Civic Centre, Reading RG1 7TD. Tel: 0118-939 0900. *Director of Education and Community Services*, A. Daykin

REDCAR AND CLEVELAND, Council Offices, Kirkleatham Street, Redcar TS10 1YA. Tel: 01642-444342. *Director*, P. Scott

ROCHDALE, PO Box 70, Municipal Offices, Smith Street, Rochdale OL16 1YD. Tel: 01706-647474. *Director of Education*, B. Atkinson

ROTHERHAM, Education Office, Norfolk House, Walker Place, Rotherham S65 1AS. Tel: 01709-822500. *Acting Executive Director for Education, Culture and Leisure Services*, Ms D. Billups

RUTLAND, Catmose, Oakham Rutland LE15 6HP. Tel: 01572-722577. *Director of Education and Youth*, Ms C. Chambers

SALFORD, Chapel Street, Salford M3 5TL. Tel: 0161-832 9751. *Director of Education and Leisure*, M. Carriline

SANDWELL, PO Box 41, Shaftesbury House, 402 High Street, West Bromwich B70 9LT. Tel: 0121-525 7366. *Executive Director, Education and Lifelong Learning*, S. Gallacher

SEFTON, Town Hall, Trinity Road, Bootle Merseyside L20 7AE. Tel: 0151-922 4040. *Director*, Ms E. Simpson

SHEFFIELD, Education Department, Leopold Street, Sheffield S1 1RJ. Tel: 0114-273 5722. *Executive Director of Education*, J. Crossley-Holland

SLOUGH, Town Hall, Bath Road, Slough SL1 3UQ. Tel: 01753-875712. *Chief Officer*, J. Christie

SOLIHULL, PO Box 20, Council House, Solihull B91 3QU. Tel: 0121-704 6656. *Director*, D. Nixon

SOUTH GLOUCESTERSHIRE, Bowling Hill, Chipping Sodbury S. Glos BS37 6JX. Tel: 01454-868686. *Director of Education*, Ms T. Gillespie

SOUTH TYNESIDE, Town Hall and Civic Offices, Westoe Road, South Shields NE33 2RL. Tel: 0191-427 1717. *Director*, I. Reid

SOUTHAMPTON, Civic Centre, Southampton SO14 7LP. Tel: 023-8083 2771. *Director*, R. Hogg

SOUTHEND, Civic Centre, Victoria Avenue, Southend-on-Sea SS2 6ER. Tel: 01702-215890. *Education and Library Services Director*, S. Hay

ST HELENS, Rivington Centre, Rivington Road, St Helens WA10 4ND. Tel: 01744-455321. *Director of Community Education and Leisure Services*, Ms S. Richardson

STOCKPORT, Town Hall, Stockport SK1 3XE. Tel: 0161-474 3808. *Chief Education Officer*, M. K. J. Hunt

STOCKTON-ON-TEES, Municipal Buildings, PO Box 228, Church Road, Stockton-on-Tees TS18 1XE. Tel: 01642-393441. *Director of Education, Leisure and Cultural Services*, S. T. Bradford

STOKE-ON-TRENT, PO Box 758, Civic Centre, Glebe Street, Stoke-on-Trent ST4 4SY. Tel: 01782-232014. *Director*, N. Rigby PH.D.

SUNDERLAND, PO Box 101, Civic Centre, Sunderland SR2 7DN. Tel: 0191-553 1000. *Director of Education and Community Services*, Dr J. W. Williams

SWINDON, Civic Offices, Euclid Street, Swindon SN1 2JH. Tel: 01793-463069. *Director*, M. Lusty

TAMESIDE, Council Offices, Wellington Road, Ashton under Lyne Lancs OL6 6DL. Tel: 0161-342 2201. *Director of Education and Cultural Services*, P. Lawday

TELFORD AND WREKIN, Civic Offices,. Telford Shropshire TF3 4WF. Tel: 01952-202402. *Corporate Director*, Mrs C. Davies

THURROCK, PO Box 118, Grays Essex RM17 6GF. Tel: 01375-652652. *Director of Education*, R. Wilkins

TORBAY, Oldway Mansion, Paignton Devon TQ3 2TE. Tel: 01803-208208. *Director*, G. Cane

TRAFFORD, PO Box 40, Trafford Town Hall, Talbot Road, Stretford, Trafford Greater Manchester M32 0EL. Tel: 0161-912 1212. *Director Education, Arts and Leisure*, C. Pratt

WAKEFIELD, County Hall, Bond Street, Wakefield WF1 2QW. Tel: 01924-305500. *Chief Education Officer*, J. McLeod

WALSALL, Civic Centre, Darwall Street, Walsall WS1 1TP. Tel: 01922-652301. *Chief Education Officer*, H. Smith

WARRINGTON, New Town House, Buttermarket Street, Warrington Cheshire WA1 2NJ. Tel: 01925-442901. *Director*, M. L. Roxburgh

WEST BERKSHIRE, Avonbank House, West Street, Newbury Berks RG14 1BZ. Tel: 01635-519722. *Corporate Director*, J. Mercer

WIGAN, Gateway House, Standishgate, Wigan Lancs WN1 1AE. Tel: 01942-828891. *Director*, R. J. Clark

WINDSOR AND MAIDENHEAD, Town Hall, St Ives Road, Maidenhead Berks SL6 1RF. Tel: 01628-796367. *Director*, M. Peckham

WIRRAL, Hamilton Building, Conway Street, Birkenhead CH41 4FD. Tel: 0151-666 2121. *Director*, C. Rice

WOKINGHAM, PO Box 156, Shute End, Wokingham Berks RG40 1WN. Tel: 0118-974 6100. *Director*, A. Roberts

WOLVERHAMPTON, Civic Centre, St Peter's Square, Wolverhampton WV1 1RR. Tel: 01902-554177 *Co-ordinating Director for Lifelong Learning*, R. Lockwood

YORK, 10–12 George Hudson Street, York YO1 6ZG. Tel: 01904-613161. *Director of Educational Services*, M. Peters

LONDON

*Inner London borough

BARKING AND DAGENHAM, Town Hall, Barking Essex IG11 7LU. Tel: 020-8592 4500. *Director of Education, Arts and Libraries*, A. Larbalestier

BARNET, The Old Town Hall, Friern Barnet Lane, London N11 3DL. Tel: 020-8359 3048. *Head of Education*, Ms L. Stone

BEXLEY, Hill View, Hill View Drive, Welling, Kent DA16 3RY. Tel: 020-8303 7777. *Director*, P. McGee

BRENT, Chesterfield House, 9 Park Lane, Wembley, Middx HA9 7RW. Tel: 020-8937 3190. *Director*, Ms J. Griffin

BROMLEY, Civic Centre, Stockwell Close, Bromley BR1 3UH. Tel: 020-8313 4066. *Director*, K. Davis

*CAMDEN, Crowndale Centre, 218–220 Eversholt Street, London NW1 1BD. Tel: 020-7974 1505. *Director*, R. Litchfield

*CITY OF LONDON, Education Department, Corporation of London, PO Box 270, Guildhall, London EC2P 2EJ. Tel: 020-7332 1750. *City Education Officer*, D. Smith

*CITY OF WESTMINSTER, City Hall, 64 Victoria Street, London SW1E 6QP. Tel: 020-7641 1947. *Director*, J. Harris

CROYDON, Taberner House, Park Lane, Croydon CR9 3JS. Tel: 020-8760 5555. *Director*, D. Sands

EALING, Perceval House, 14–16 Uxbridge Road, London W5 2HL. Tel: 020-8758 5410. *Director*, A. Parker

ENFIELD, PO Box 56, Civic Centre, Silver Street, Enfield, Middx EN1 3XQ. Tel: 020-8379 3201. *Director*, Ms E. Graham

*GREENWICH, Riverside House, Woolwich High Street, London SE18 6DN. Tel: 020-8921 8230. *Director*, G. Gyte

*HACKNEY, Edith Cavell Building, Enfield Road, London N1 5BA. Tel: 020-8356 5000. *Director*, Ms E. Reid

*HAMMERSMITH, Cambridge House, Cambridge Grove, London W6 0LE. Tel: 020-8748 3020. *Director*, Ms C. Whatford

HARINGEY, 48 Station Road, Wood Green, London N22 7TY. Tel: 020-8489 0000. *Interim Director*, S. Jenkin

HARROW, PO Box 22, Civic Centre, Station Road, Harrow HA1 2UW. Tel: 020-8424 1307. *Director*, P. A. Osburn

HAVERING, The Broxhill Centre, Broxhill Road, Harold Hill, Romford RM4 1XN. Tel: 01708-434343. *Executive Director Children and Lifelong Learning*, S. Evans

HILLINGDON, Civic Centre, High Street, Uxbridge UB8 1UW. Tel: 01895-250528. *Corporate Director - Education, Youth and Leisure Services*, P. O'Hear

HOUNSLOW, Civic Centre, Lampton Road, Hounslow, Middx TW3 4DN. Tel: 020-8583 2000. *Director*, J. D. Tricket

*ISLINGTON, Laycock Street, Islington, London N1 1TH. Tel: 020-7527 5753. *Director of Education Services*, J. Suter

*KENSINGTON AND CHELSEA, Town Hall, Hornton Street, London W8 7NX. Tel: 020-7361 3033. *Director*, R. Wood

KINGSTON UPON THAMES, Guildhall 2, Kingston upon Thames KT1 1EU. Tel: 020-8547 5220. *Director*, J. Braithwaite

*LAMBETH, International House, Canterbury Crescent, London SW9 7QE. Tel: 020-7926 1000. *Acting Director*, A. Wood

*LEWISHAM, 3rd Floor, Laurence House, 1 Catford Road, London SE6 4RU. Tel: 020-8314 8527. *Executive Director – Education and Culture*, Ms A. Efunshile

MERTON, Civic Centre, London Road, Morden, Surrey SM4 5DX. Tel: 020-8545 3251. *Director of Education, Leisure and Libraries*, Ms J. Cairns

NEWHAM, Broadway House, 322 High Street, Stratford, London E15 1AJ. Tel: 020-8555 5552. *Director*, I. Harrison

REDBRIDGE, Lynton House, 255–259 High Road, Ilford, Essex IG1 1NN. Tel: 020-8478 3020. *Chief Education Officer*, J. Pallett

RICHMOND UPON THAMES, 1st Floor, Regal House, London Road, Twickenham TW1 3QS. Tel: 020-8891 7500. *Acting Chief Education Officer*, P. Lomax

*SOUTHWARK, John Smith House, 144–152 Walworth Road, London SE17 1JL. Tel: 020-7525 5050. *Strategic Director of Education and Lifelong Learning*, Dr R. Smith

SUTTON, The Grove, Carshalton Surrey SM5 3AL. Tel: 020-8770 6568. *Strategic Director*, Dr I. Birnbaum

*TOWER HAMLETS, Town Hall, Mulberry Place, 5 Clove Crescent, London E14 2BG. Tel: 020-7364 5000. *Corporate Director – Education*, Ms C. Gilbert

WALTHAM FOREST, Leyton Municipal Offices, High Road, Leyton, London E10 5QJ. Tel: 020-8527 5544 ext. 5015. *Chief Education Officer*, vacant

*WANDSWORTH, Town Hall, Wandsworth High Street, London SW18 2PU. Tel: 020-8871 8013. *Director*, P. Robinson

WALES

ANGLESEY, Swyddfa'r Sir, Llangefni Anglesey LL77 7EY. Tel: 01248-752921. *Director*, R. P. Jones

BLAENAU GWENT, Victoria House, Victoria Business Park, Ebbw Vale NP23 6ER. Tel: 01495-355434. *Director*, B. Mawby

BRIDGEND, Sunnyside, Bridgend CF31 4AR. Tel: 01656-642600. *Director of Education, Leisure and Community Services*, D. Matthews

CAERPHILLY, Council Offices, Caerphilly Road, Ystrad Mynach, Hengoed CF82 7EP. Tel: 01443-815588. *Director*, D. Hopkins

CARDIFF, County Hall, Atlantic Wharf, Cardiff CF10 4UW. Tel: 029-2087 2700. *Head of Service – Schools Services*, H. Knight

CARMARTHENSHIRE, Pibwrlwyd, Carmarthen SA31 2NH. Tel: 01267-224501. *Director of Education and Community Services*, vacant

CEREDIGION, Swyddfa'r Sir, Marine Terrace, Aberystwyth SY23 2DE. Tel: 01970-633600. *Director*, R. J. Williams

CONWY, Government Buildings, Dinerth Road, Colwyn Bay LL28 4UL. Tel: 01492-575031. *Director*, R. E. Williams

DENBIGHSHIRE, Phase 4, County Hall, Mold Flintshire CH7 6GR. Tel: 01824-706777. *Director*, vacant

FLINTSHIRE, County Hall, Mold CH7 6NW. Tel: 01352-704010. *Director of Education and Recreation*, K. McDonogh

GWYNEDD, Shirehall Street, Caernarfon LL55 1SH. Tel: 01286-677162. *Director*, D. Whittall

MERTHYR TYDFIL, Ty Keir Hardie, Riverside Court, Avenue De Clichy, Merthyr Tydfil CF47 8XD. Tel: 01685-724614. *Director*, D. Jones

MONMOUTHSHIRE, County Hall, Cwmbran NP44 2XH. Tel: 01633-644487. *Director of Lifelong Learning and Leisure*, P. Cooke

NEATH PORT TALBOT, Civic Centre, Port Talbot SA13 1PJ. Tel: 01639-763298. *Director*, V. Thomas

NEWPORT, Civic Centre, Newport NP20 4UR. Tel: 01633-232204. *Director*, G. Bingham

PEMBROKESHIRE, County Hall, Haverfordwest SA61 1TP. Tel: 01437-764551. *Director*, G. Davies

POWYS, County Hall, Llandrindod Wells LD1 5LG. Tel: 01597-826000. *Director*, M. Barker M.Sc.

RHONDDA, CYNON, TAFF, Education Centre, Grawen Street, Porth CF39 0BU. Tel: 01443-687666. *Group Director, Education and Children's Services*, D. Jones

SWANSEA, County Hall, Oystermouth Road, Swansea SA1 3SN. Tel: 01792-636351. *Director*, R. Parry

TORFAEN, County Hall, Croesyceiliog, Cwmbran Torfaen NP44 2WN. Tel: 01633-648610. *Director*, M. de Val

VALE OF GLAMORGAN, Civic Offices, Holton Road, Barry CF63 4RU. Tel: 01446-709360. *Director*, B. Jeffreys

WREXHAM, Ty Henblas, Queen's Square, Wrexham LL13 8AZ. Tel: 01978-297420. *Director*, T. Garner

SCOTLAND

ABERDEEN CITY, Summerhill Education Centre, Stronsay Drive, Aberdeen AB15 6JA. Tel: 01224-346060. *Director*, J. Stodter

ABERDEENSHIRE, Woodhill House, Westburn Road, Aberdeen AB16 5GB. Tel: 01224-665420. *Director*, H. Vernal

ANGUS, County Buildings, Market Street, Forfar DD8 3WE. Tel: 01307-461460. *Director*, J. Anderson

ARGYLL AND BUTE, Argyll House, Alexandra Parade, Dunoon PA23 8AJ. Tel: 01369-704000. *Director*, A. C. Morton

CITY OF EDINBURGH, Wellington Court, 10 Waterloo Place, Edinburgh EH1 3EG. Tel: 0131-469 3000. *Director*, R. Jobson

CLACKMANNANSHIRE, Lime Tree House, Alloa FK10 1EX. Tel: 01259-452431. *Executive Director Education and Community Services*, K. Bloomer

DUMFRIES AND GALLOWAY, Education Department, 30 Edinburgh Road, Dumfries DG1 1JG. Tel: 01387-260419. *Director for Education*, F. Sanderson

DUNDEE CITY, Floor 8, Tayside House, Crichton Street, Dundee DD1 3RJ. Tel: 01382-433088. *Director of Education*, Mrs A. Wilson

EAST AYRSHIRE, Council Headquarters, London Road, Kilmarnock KA3 7BU. Tel: 01563-576017. *Director*, J. Mulgrew

EAST DUNBARTONSHIRE, Boclair House, 100 Milngavie Road, Bearsden, Glasgow G61 2TQ. Tel: 0141-578 8000. *Director*, Ms S. Bruce

EAST LOTHIAN, John Muir House, Haddington EH41 3HA. Tel: 01620-827562. *Director*, A. Blackie

EAST RENFREWSHIRE, Council Offices, Eastwood Park, Rouken Glen Road, Giffnock G46 6UG. Tel: 0141-577 3431. *Director*, Mrs E. J. Currie

EILEAN SIAR/WESTERN ISLES, Council Offices, Sandwick Road, Stornoway, Isle of Lewis HS1 2BW. Tel: 01851-703773. *Acting Director*, M. Macleod

FALKIRK, McLaren House, Marchmont Avenue, Polmont, Falkirk FK2 0NZ. Tel: 01324-506600. *Director*, Dr G. Young

FIFE, Rothesay House, North Street, Glenrothes KY7 5PN. Tel: 01592-413656. *Director*, A. McKay

GLASGOW CITY, Nye Bevan House, 20 India Street, Glasgow G2 4PF. Tel: 0141-287 6898. *Director*, K. Corsar

HIGHLAND, Council Buildings, Glenurquhart Road, Inverness IV3 5NX. Tel: 01463-702802. *Director*, B. Robertson

INVERCLYDE, 105 Dalrymple Street, Greenock PA15 1HT. Tel: 01475-712824. *Director*, B. McLeary

MIDLOTHIAN, Fairfield House, 8 Lothian Road, Dalkeith EH22 3ZJ. Tel: 0131-270 7500. *Director*, D. MacKay

MORAY, Council Offices, High Street, Elgin IV30 1BX. Tel: 01343-563171. *Director of Educational Services*, D. M. Duncan

NORTH AYRSHIRE, Cunninghame House, Irvine KA12 8EE. Tel: 01294-324400. *Corporate Director – Educational Services*, J. Travers

NORTH LANARKSHIRE, Municipal Buildings, Kildonan Street, Coatbridge ML5 3BT. Tel: 01236-812222. *Director*, M. O'Neill

ORKNEY ISLANDS, Council Offices, School Place, Kirkwall Orkney KW15 1NY. Tel: 01856-873535. *Director*, L. Manson

PERTH AND KINROSS, Blackfriars, Perth PH1 5LU. Tel: 01738-476200. *Education Director and Children's Services*, W. Frew

RENFREWSHIRE, Council Headquarters, South Building, Cotton Street, Paisley PA1 1LE. Tel: 0141-842 5601. *Director*, Ms S. Rae

SCOTTISH BORDERS, Council Headquarters, Newtown St Boswells, Melrose, Roxburghshire TD6 0SA. Tel: 01835-824000. *Director*, J. Christie

SHETLAND ISLANDS, Hayfield House, Hayfield Lane, Lerwick, Shetland ZE1 0QD. Tel: 01595-744000. *Head of Education Service*, M. Payton

SOUTH AYRSHIRE, County Buildings, Wellington Square, Ayr KA7 1DR. Tel: 01292-612201. *Director of Educational Services*, M. McCabe

SOUTH LANARKSHIRE, Council Headquarters, Almada Street, Hamilton ML3 0AE. Tel: 01698-454545. *Executive Director*, Ms M. Allan

STIRLING, Viewforth, Stirling FK8 2ET. Tel: 01786-442678. *Director of Children's Services*, G. Jeyes

WEST DUNBARTONSHIRE, Garshake Road, Dumbarton G82 3PU. Tel: 01389-737301. *Director of Education and Cultural Services*, I. McMurdo

WEST LOTHIAN, Lindsay House, South Bridge Street, Bathgate EH48 1TS. Tel: 01506-776000. *Corporate Manager*, R. Stewart

NORTHERN IRELAND

BELFAST EDUCATION AND LIBRARY BOARD, 40 Academy Street, Belfast BT1 2NQ. Tel: 028-9056 4122. *Chief Executive*, D. Cargo

NORTH EASTERN EDUCATION AND LIBRARY BOARD, County Hall, 182 Galgorm Road, Ballymena, Co. Antrim BT42 1HN. Tel: 028-2565 3333. *Chief Executive*, G. Topping

SOUTH EASTERN, Grahamsbridge Road, Dundonald BT16 2HS. Tel: 028-9056 6200. *Chief Executive*, J. B. Fitzsimons

SOUTHERN EDUCATION AND LIBRARY BOARD, 3 Charlemont Place, The Mall, Armagh BT61 9AX Tel: 028-3751 2200. *Chief Executive*, Mrs H. McClenagahan

WESTERN, 1 Hospital Road, Omagh, Co. Tyrone BT79 0AW. Tel: 028-8241 1411. *Chief Executive*, P. J. Martin

ISLANDS

GUERNSEY, Grange Road, St Peter Port, Guernsey GY1 1RQ. Tel: 01481-710821. *Director*, D. T. Neale

ISLE OF MAN, Murray House, 5–11 Mount Havelock, Douglas, Isle of Man IM1 2SG. Tel: 01624-685820. *Director*, R. B. Cowin

ISLES OF SCILLY, Town Hall, St Mary's, Isles of Scilly TR21 0LW. Tel: 01720-422537 ext. 145. *Secretary for Education*, P. S. Hygate

JERSEY, PO Box 142, Jersey JE4 8QJ. Tel: 01534-509500. *Director*, T. W. McKeon

---

ADVISORY BODIES

SCHOOLS

BRITISH EDUCATIONAL COMMUNICATIONS AND TECHNOLOGY AGENCY, Milburn Hill Road, Science Park, Coventry CV4 7JJ. Tel: 024-7641 6994. *Chief Executive*, O. Lynch

EDUCATION OTHERWISE, PO Box 7420, London N9 9SG. Helpline: 0870-730 0074

INTERNATIONAL BACCALAUREATE ORGANISATION, Peterson House, Fortran Road, St Mellons, Cardiff CF3 0WB. Tel: 029-2077 4000. *Director of Academic Affairs*, Dr H. Drennen

NATIONAL ADVISORY COUNCIL FOR EDUCATION AND TRAINING TARGETS, Dunford Lodge, Storth Lane, Ranmoor, Sheffield S10 3HN. Tel: 0114-259 7887. *Director*, J. Dewsbury

SPECIAL EDUCATIONAL NEEDS TRIBUNAL, 7th Floor, Windsor House, 50 Victoria Street, London SW1H 0NW. Tel: 020-7925 6925. *President*, T. Aldridge

INDEPENDENT SCHOOLS

GOVERNING BODIES ASSOCIATION, The Ancient Foresters, Bush End, Takeley, Bishop's Stortford, Herts CM22 6NN. Tel: 01279-871865. *Secretary*, F. V. Morgan

GOVERNING BODIES OF GIRLS' SCHOOLS ASSOCIATION, The Ancient Foresters, Bush End, Takeley, Bishop's Stortford, Herts CM22 6NN. Tel: 01279-871865. *Secretary*, F. V. Morgan

INDEPENDENT SCHOOLS COUNCIL, Grosvenor Gardens House, 35–37 Grosvenor Gardens, London SW1W 0BS. Tel: 020-7798 1590. *General Secretary*, Dr A. B. Cooke

INDEPENDENT SCHOOLS EXAMINATIONS BOARD, Jordan House, Christchurch Road, New Milton, Hants BH25 6QU. Tel: 01425-621111. *Administrator*, Mrs J. Williams

FURTHER EDUCATION

FURTHER EDUCATION DEVELOPMENT AGENCY (FEDA), Citadel Place, Tinworth Street, London SE11 5EH. Tel: 020-7840 5400. *Chief Executive*, C. Hughes

Regional Advisory Councils

ASSOCIATION OF COLLEGES IN THE EASTERN REGION, Suite 1, Lancaster House, Meadow Lane, St Ives, Huntingdon, Cambs PE27 4LG. Tel: 01223-424022. *Chief Executive*, N. Brenton

ASSOCIATION OF SOUTH EAST COLLEGES, Building 33, The University of Reading, London Road, Reading RG1 5AQ. Tel: 0118-931 6320. *Secretary*, B. Fryatt

CENTRA (EDUCATION AND TRAINING SERVICES) LTD, Duxbury Park, Duxbury Hall Road, Chorley, Lancs PR7 4AT. Tel: 01257-241428. *Chief Executive*, P. Wren

EMFEC (EAST MIDLAND FURTHER EDUCATION COUNCIL), Robins Wood House, Robins Wood Road, Aspley, Nottingham NG8 3NH. Tel: 0115-854 1616. *Chief Executive*, Ms J. Gardiner

NCFE, Portland House, New Bridge Street, Newcastle upon Tyne NE1 8AN. Tel: 0191-201 3100. *Chief Executive*, J. F. Pearce

SOUTH WEST ASSOCIATION FOR EDUCATION AND TRAINING, Bishops Hull House, Bishops Hull, Taunton, Somerset TA1 5RA. Tel: 01823-335491. *Chief Executive*, Ms L. McGrath

SOUTHERN REGIONAL COUNCIL FOR EDUCATION AND TRAINING, Building 33, The University of Reading, London Road, Reading RG1 5AQ. Tel: 0118-931 6320. *Chief Executive*, B. J. Knowles

WELSH JOINT EDUCATION COMMITTEE, 245 Western Avenue, Cardiff CF5 2YX. Tel: 029-2026 5000. *Examinations Secretary*, B. Evans

HIGHER EDUCATION

ASSOCIATION OF COMMONWEALTH UNIVERSITIES, John Foster House, 36 Gordon Square, London WC1H 0PF. Tel: 020-7380 6700. *Secretary-General*, Prof. M. G. Gibbons

COMMITTEE OF SCOTTISH HIGHER EDUCATION PRINCIPALS (COSHEP), 53 Hanover Street, Edinburgh EH2 2PJ. Tel: 0131-226 1111. *Director*, D. Caldwell

COMMITTEE OF VICE-CHANCELLORS AND PRINCIPALS OF THE UNIVERSITIES OF THE UNITED KINGDOM, Woburn House, 20 Tavistock Square, London WC1H 9HQ. Tel: 020-7419 4111. *Chairman*, H. Newby

NORTHERN IRELAND HIGHER EDUCATION COUNCIL, 4th Floor, Room 407, Adelaide House, 39–49 Adelaide Street, Belfast BT2 8FD. Tel: 028-9025 7722. *Chairman*, Sir Kenneth Bloomfield KCB

QUALITY ASSURANCE AGENCY FOR HIGHER EDUCATION, Southgate House, Southgate Street, Gloucester GL1 1UB. Tel: 01452-557000. *Chief Executive*, J. Randall

CURRICULUM COUNCILS

AWDURDOD CYMWYSTERAU, CWRICWLWM AC ASESU CYMRU/QUALIFICATIONS, CURRICULUM AND ASSESSMENT AUTHORITY FOR WALES, Castle Buildings, Womanby Street, Cardiff CF10 9SX. Tel: 029-2037 5400. *Chief Executive*, J. V. Williams

NORTHERN IRELAND COUNCIL FOR THE CURRICULUM, EXAMINATIONS AND ASSESSMENT, Clarendon Dock, 29 Clarendon Road, Belfast BT1 3BG. Tel: 028-9026 1200. *Chief Executive*, G. Boyd

QUALIFICATIONS AND CURRICULUM AUTHORITY, 29 Bolton Street, London . Tel: 020-7509 5555. *Chairman*, Sir William Stubbs Ph.D.

SCOTTISH CONSULTATIVE COUNCIL ON THE CURRICULUM, Gardyne Road, Broughty Ferry, Dundee DD5 1NY. Tel: 01382-455053. *Chief Executive*, M. Baughan

EXAMINING BODIES

ASSESSMENT AND QUALIFICATIONS ALLIANCE (AQA), Staghill House, Guildford Surrey GU2 7XJ. Tel: 01483-506506. *Director-General*, Ms K. Tattersall

ASSESSMENT AND QUALIFICATIONS ALLIANCE (AQA), Devas Street, Manchester M15 6EX. Tel: 0161-953 1180. *Director-General* Ms K. Tattersall

THE EDEXCEL FOUNDATION, Stewart House, 32 Russell Square, London WC1B 5DN. Tel: 020-7393 4444. *Chief Executive*, Dr C. Townsend

OXFORD, CAMBRIDGE AND RSA EXAMINATIONS (OCR), 1 Regent Street, Cambridge CB2 1GG. Tel: 01223-552552. *Chief Executive*, B. Swift

GCSE

THE EDEXCEL FOUNDATION, *see above*

NORTHERN IRELAND COUNCIL FOR THE CURRICULUM, EXAMINATIONS AND ASSESSMENT. Tel: 01232-261200. *Chief Executive*, G. Boyd

OXFORD, CAMBRIDGE AND RSA EXAMINATIONS, *see above*

WELSH JOINT EDUCATION COMMITTEE, 245 Western Avenue, Cardiff CF5 2YX. Tel: 029-2026 5000. *Chief Executive*, I. Hume

A-LEVEL

NORTHERN IRELAND COUNCIL FOR THE CURRICULUM, EXAMINATIONS AND ASSESSMENT EXAMINATIONS AND ASSESSMENT, Clarendon Dock, 29 Clarendon Road, Belfast BT1 3BG. Tel: 028-9026 1200. *Chief Executive*, Mrs C. Coxhead

WELSH JOINT EDUCATION COMMITTEE, 245 Western Avenue, Cardiff CF5 2YX. Tel: 029-2026 5000. *Chief Executive* I. Hume

SCOTLAND

SCOTTISH QUALIFICATIONS AUTHORITY, Hanover House, 24 Douglas Street, Glasgow G2 7NQ. Tel: 0141-248 7900. *Chief Executive*, R. Tuck

FURTHER EDUCATION

CITY & GUILDS, 1 Giltspur Street, London EC1A 9DD. Tel: 020-7294 2468. *Director-General*, N. Carey

THE EDEXCEL FOUNDATION, *see above*

OXFORD, CAMBRIDGE AND RSA EXAMINATIONS, *see above*

FUNDING COUNCILS

FURTHER EDUCATION

FURTHER EDUCATION FUNDING COUNCIL FOR ENGLAND, Cheylesmore House, Quinton Road, Coventry CV1 2WT. Tel: 024-7686 3000. *Chief Executive*, Prof. D. Melville

FURTHER EDUCATION FUNDING COUNCIL FOR WALES, Linden Court, The Orchards, Ilex Close, Cardiff CF14 5DZ. Tel: 029-2076 1861. *Chief Executive*, S. Martin

SCOTTISH FURTHER EDUCATION FUNDING COUNCIL, Donaldson House, 97 Haymarket Terrace, Edinburgh EH12 5HD. Tel: 0131-313 6500. *Chief Executive*, Prof. J. Sizer, CBE

HIGHER EDUCATION

HIGHER EDUCATION FUNDING COUNCIL FOR ENGLAND, Northavon House, Coldharbour Lane, Bristol BS16 1QD. Tel: 0117-931 7317. *Chief Executive*, Sir Brian Fender, Kt.

HIGHER EDUCATION FUNDING COUNCIL FOR WALES, Linden Court, The Orchards, Ilex Close, Cardiff CF14 5DZ. Tel: 029-2076 1861. *Chief Executive*, S. Martin

SCOTTISH HIGHER EDUCATION FUNDING COUNCIL, Donaldson House, 97 Haymarket Terrace, Edinburgh EH12 5HD. Tel: 0131-313 6500. *Chief Executive*, Prof. J. Sizer, CBE

STUDENT AWARDS AGENCY FOR SCOTLAND, Gyleview House, 3 Redheughs Rigg, Edinburgh EH12 9HH. Tel: 0131-244 5890. *Chief Executive*, D. Stephen

STUDENT LOANS COMPANY LTD, 100 Bothwell Street, Glasgow G2 7JD. Tel: 0141-306 2000. *Chief Executive*, C. Ward

TEACHER TRAINING AGENCY, Portland House, Stag Place, London SW1E 5TT. Tel: 020-7925 3700. *Chairman*, Prof. C. Booth

ADMISSIONS AND COURSE INFORMATION

CAREERS RESEARCH AND ADVISORY CENTRE, Sheraton House, Castle Park, Cambridge CB3 0AX. Tel: 01223-460277. *Chief Executive*, D. Thomas

COMMITTEE OF SCOTTISH HIGHER EDUCATION PRINCIPALS (COSHEP), St Andrew House, 141 West Nile Street, Glasgow G1 2RN. Tel: 0141-353 1880. *Secretary*, Dr R. L. Crawford

GRADUATE TEACHER TRAINING REGISTRY, Rosehill, New Barn Lane, Cheltenham, Glos GL52 3LZ. Tel: 01242-544600. *Small Systems Unit Manager*, Mrs J. Pearce

SOCIAL WORK ADMISSIONS SYSTEM, Rosehill, New Barn Lane, Cheltenham, Glos GL52 3LZ. Tel: 01242-544600. *Small Systems Unit Manager*, Mrs J. Pearce

UNIVERSITIES AND COLLEGES ADMISSIONS SERVICE, Rosehill, New Barn Lane, Cheltenham, Glos GL52 3LZ. Tel: 01242-222444. *Chief Executive*, M. A. Higgins

UNIVERSITIES

THE UNIVERSITY OF ABERDEEN (1495)
Aberdeen AB24 3FX
Tel: 01224-272000
Chancellor, The Lord Wilson of Tillyorn, GCMG (1997)
Vice-Chancellor and Principal, Prof. C. D. Rice
Secretary, S. Cannon
Rector, Miss C. Dickson Wright

THE UNIVERSITY OF ABERTAY DUNDEE (1994)
Bell Street, Dundee DD1 1HG
Tel: 01382-308080
Chancellor, The Rt. Hon. Earl of Airlie, KT, GCVO, PC (1994)
Vice-Chancellor, Prof. B. King
Registrar, Dr D. Button
Secretary and Director of Operations, Ms C. Lamb

ANGLIA POLYTECHNIC UNIVERSITY (1992)
Bishop Hall Lane, Chelmsford CM1 1SQ
Tel: 01245-493131
Chancellor, vacant
Vice-Chancellor, M. Malone-Lee, CB
Secretary and Clerk, S. G. Bennett

ASTON UNIVERSITY (1895)
Aston Triangle, Birmingham B4 7ET
Tel: 0121-359 3611
Chancellor, Sir Adrian Cadbury (1979)
Vice-Chancellor, Prof. M. Wright
Registrar and Secretary, R. D. A. Packham

THE UNIVERSITY OF BATH (1966)
Bath BA2 7AY
Tel: 01225-826826
Chancellor, The Lord Tugendhat (1998)
Vice-Chancellor, Prof. V. D. VandeLinde
Registrar, J. A. Bursey

THE UNIVERSITY OF BIRMINGHAM (1900)
Edgbaston, Birmingham B45 2TT
Tel: 0121-414 3344
Chancellor, Sir Alexander Jarratt, CB (1983)
Vice-Chancellor, Prof. M. Irvine, ph.D., FRSE
Registrar and Secretary, D. J. Allen

BOURNEMOUTH UNIVERSITY (1992)
Fern Barrow, Poole BH12 5BB
Tel: 01202-524111
Chancellor, The Baroness Cox (1992)
Vice-Chancellor, Prof. G. Slater
Registrar, N. O. G. Richardson

THE UNIVERSITY OF BRADFORD (1966)
Richmond Road, Bradford BD7 1DP
Tel: 01274-232323
Chancellor, The Baroness Lockwood (1997)
Vice-Chancellor, Prof. C. Bell
Registrar and Secretary, N. J. Andrew

THE UNIVERSITY OF BRIGHTON (1992)
Lewes Road, Brighton BN2 4AT
Tel: 01273-600900
Chairman of the Board, C. Hume
Director, Prof. Sir David Watson
Deputy Director, D. E. House
Secretary, Ms C. E. Moon

THE UNIVERSITY OF BRISTOL (1909)
Tyndall Avenue, Bristol BS8 1TH
Tel: 0117-928 9000
Chancellor, Sir Jeremy Morse, KCMG (1989)
Vice-Chancellor, Sir John Kingman, FRS
Registrar, D. Pretty,
Secretary, Dr K. McKenzie, D.Phil.

BRUNEL UNIVERSITY (1966)
Uxbridge UB8 3PH
Tel: 01895-274000
Chancellor, The Lord Wakeham, PC, DL (1998)
Vice-Chancellor and Principal, Prof. M. J. H. Sterling
   ph.D, FREng.
Academic Registrar, J. B. Alexander

THE UNIVERSITY OF BUCKINGHAM (1983)
Buckingham MK18 1EG
Tel: 01280-814080
Chancellor, Sir Martin Jacomb (1998)
Vice-Chancellor, Prof. R. H. Taylor
Registrar and Secretary, S. Cooksey

THE UNIVERSITY OF CAMBRIDGE
Trinity Lane, Cambridge CB2 1TN
Tel: 01223-337733

UNIVERSITY OFFICERS, ETC.

Chancellor, HRH The Prince Philip, Duke of
   Edinburgh KG, KT, OM, GBE, PC (1977)
Vice-Chancellor, Prof. Sir Alec Broers, FRS (1996)
Deputy High Steward, The Lord Richardson of
   Duntisbourne, MBE, TD, PC (1983)
Commissary, The Lord Oliver of Aylmerton
   (*Trinity Hall*) PC (1989)
Orator, A. J. Bowen (*Jesus*), (1993)
Registrary, T. J. Mead (*Wolfson*), ph.D (1997)
Librarian, P. K. Fox (*Selwyn*) (1994)
Treasurer, Mrs J. Womack (*Trinity Hall*) (1993)
Secretary-General of the Faculties, D. A. Livesey
   (*Emmanuel*), ph.D (1992)
Director of the Fitzwilliam Museum, D. D. Robinson
   (*Clare*) (1995)
High Steward, The Lord Runcie, PC, DD (1991)
Proctors, Dr F. H. King (*Magdalene*); R. J. Stibbs
   (*Downing*) (2000)

COLLEGES AND HALLS, ETC.
with dates of foundation

CHRIST'S (1505), *Master*, A. J. Munro, ph.D. (1995)
CHURCHILL (1960), *Master*, Sir John Boyd, KCMG (1996)
CLARE (1326), *Master*, Prof. B. A. Hepple, LLD (1993)
CLARE HALL (1966), *President*, Prof. Dame Gillian Beer,
   DBE, Litt.D., FBA (1994)
CORPUS CHRISTI (1352), *Master*, Prof. Sir Tony Wrigley,
   ph.D. (1994)
DARWIN (1964), *Master*, Prof. Sir Geoffrey Lloyd, ph.D.,
   FBA (1989)
DOWNING (1800), *Master*, Prof. D. A. King, FRS (1995)
EMMANUEL (1584), *Master*, Prof. J. E. Ffowcs-Williams,
   Sc.D. (1996)
FITZWILLIAM (1966), *Master*, Prof. B. F. G. Johnston
GIRTON (1869), *Mistress*, Prof. A. M. Strathern, ph.D.
   (1998)
GONVILLE AND CAIUS (1348), *Master*, N. McKendrick
   (1996)
HOMERTON (1824) (for B.Ed. Students), *Principal*,
   Mrs K. B. Pretty, ph.D. (1991)
HUGHES HALL (1885) (for post-graduate students),
   President, Prof. P. Richards (1998)
JESUS (1496), *Master*, vacant
KING'S (1441), *Provost*, Prof. P. P. G. B. Bateson, Sc.D., FRS
   (1987)
*LUCY CAVENDISH COLLEGE (1965) (for women research
   students and mature and affiliated undergraduates),
   President, The Baroness Perry of Southwark (1994)
MAGDALENE (1542), *Master*, Prof. Sir John Gurdon,
   D.Phil, FRS (1995)
*NEW HALL (1954), *President*, Mrs A. Lonsdale (1996)
*NEWNHAM (1871), *Principal*, Baroness O'Neill, CBE
   (1992)
PEMBROKE (1347), *Master*, Sir Roger Tomkys, KCMG
   (1992)
PETERHOUSE (1284), *Master*, Prof. Sir John Meurig
   Thomas, FRS (1993)
QUEENS' (1448), *President*, The Lord Eatwell

ROBINSON (1977), *Warden*, Prof. the Lord Lewis of
Newnham, SC.D., FRS (1977)
ST CATHARINE'S (1473), *Master*, D. S. Ingram, SC.D. (2000)
ST EDMUND'S (1896), *Master*, Prof. R. B. Heap, SC.D. (1996)
ST JOHN'S (1511), *Master*, Prof. P. Goddard, Ph.D., FRS
(1994)
SELWYN (1882), *Master*, Prof. R. J. Bowring, Litt.D. (2000)
SIDNEY SUSSEX (1596), *Master*, Prof. S. N. Dawson (1999)
TRINITY (1546), *Master*, Prof. A. K. Sen (1998)
TRINITY HALL (1350), *Master*, Sir John Lyons, Ph.D. (1984)
WOLFSON (1965), *President*, G. Johnson, Ph.D. (1994)
* College for women only

THE UNIVERSITY OF CENTRAL ENGLAND
IN BIRMINGHAM (1992)
Perry Barr, Birmingham B42 2SU
Tel: 0121-331 5000
Chancellor, I. McArdle
Vice-Chancellor, Dr P. C. Knight, CBE
Registrar and Secretary, Ms M. Penlington

THE UNIVERSITY OF CENTRAL
LANCASHIRE (1992)
Preston PR1 2HE
Tel: 01772-201201
Chancellor, Sir Francis Kennedy, KCMG, CBE (1995)
Vice-Chancellor, Dr M. McVicar
Registrar, Ms L. Munro
Secretary, Mrs P. M. Ackroyd

CITY UNIVERSITY (1966)
Northampton Square, London EC1V 0HB
Tel: 020-7477 8000
Chancellor, The Rt. Hon. the Lord Mayor of London,
Vice-Chancellor, Prof. D. W. Rhind
Academic Registrar, A. H. Seville, Ph.D.
Secretary, M. M. O'Hara

COVENTRY UNIVERSITY (1992)
Priory Street, Coventry CV1 5FB
Tel: 024-7688 7688
Chancellor, The Lord Plumb (1995)
Vice-Chancellor, Dr M. Goldstein, CBE, Ph.D.
Academic Registrar, Dr J. Gledhill, Ph.D.
Secretary, Mrs L. Arlidge

CRANFIELD UNIVERSITY (1969)
MK43 0AL
Tel: 01234-750111
Chancellor, The Lord Vincent of Coleshill,
GBE, KCB, DSO (1998)
Vice-Chancellor, Prof. F. R. Hartley, D.Sc
Academic Registrar and Secretary, D. J. Buck

DE MONTFORT UNIVERSITY (1992)
The Gateway, Leicester LE1 9BH
Tel: 0116-255 1551
Chancellor, Baroness Prashar of Runnymede,
CBE (1998)
Vice-Chancellor, Prof. P. Tasker
Academic Registrar, V. E. Critchlow
Secretary, Mrs A. Hayter

THE UNIVERSITY OF DERBY (1993)
Kedleston Road, Derby DE22 1GB
Tel: 01332-890600
Chancellor, Sir Christopher Ball, FRSA
Vice-Chancellor, Prof. R. Waterhouse
Registrar, Mrs J. M. Fry, B.Sc

THE UNIVERSITY OF DUNDEE (1967)
Dundee DD1 4HN
Tel: 01382-344000

Chancellor, Sir James Black, FRCP, FRS (1992)
Vice-Chancellor, Sir Alan Langlands
Secretary, R. Seaton
Rector, T. Slattery, 1998–2001.

THE UNIVERSITY OF DURHAM
Durham DH1 3HP
Tel: 0191-374 2000
Chancellor, Sir Peter Ustinov, CBE, FRSL
Vice-Chancellor, Prof. Sir Kenneth Calman, KCB, MD
Registrar and Secretary, J. V. Hogan, Ph.D

COLLEGES

COLLINGWOOD, *Principal*, Prof. G. H. Blake, Ph.D.
GRADUATE SOCIETY, *Principal*, vacant
GREY, *Master*, V. E. Watts
HATFIELD, *Master*, Prof. T. P. Burt, Ph.D.
ST AIDAN'S, *Principal*, J. S. Ashworth
ST CHAD'S, *Principal*, Revd J. P. M. Cassidy, Ph.D.
ST CUTHBERT'S SOCIETY, *Principal*, B. Robertson
ST HILD AND ST BEDE, *Acting Principal*,
J. A. Pearson, Ph.D.
ST JOHN'S, *Principal*, Rt. Revd S. W. Sykes
ST MARY'S, *Principal*, Miss J. L. Hobbs
TREVELYAN, *Principal*, vacant
UNIVERSITY, *Master*, Prof. M. E. Tucker, Ph.D.
USHAW, *President*, Revd J. O'Keefe
VAN MILDERT, *Acting Principal*, G. Patterson

THE UNIVERSITY OF EAST ANGLIA (1963)
Norwich NR4 7TJ
Tel: 01603-456161
Chancellor, Sir Geoffrey Allen, FRS, FREng. (1994)
Vice-Chancellor, V. Watts
Registrar and Secretary, B. Summers

THE UNIVERSITY OF EAST LONDON (1898)
Longbridge Road, Dagenham RM8 2AS
Tel: 020-8223 3000
Chancellor, The Lord Rix, CBE, DL, Kt. (1997)
Vice-Chancellor, Prof. F. W. Gould
Registrar and Secretary, A. Ingle

THE UNIVERSITY OF EDINBURGH (1583)
South Bridge, Edinburgh EH8 9YL
Tel: 0131-650 1000
Chancellor, HRH The Prince Philip, Duke of Edinburgh,
KG, KT, OM, GBE, PC, FRS (1952)
Vice-Chancellor, Prof. Sir Stewart Sutherland, FBA, FRSE
Secretary, Dr M. Lowe, Ph.D.
Rector, R. Harper

THE UNIVERSITY OF ESSEX (1964)
Wivenhoe Park, Colchester CO4 3SQ
Tel: 01206-873333
Chancellor, The Lord Nolan, PC (1997)
Vice-Chancellor, Prof. I. Crewe
Registrar and Secretary, T. Rich, Ph.D.

THE UNIVERSITY OF EXETER (1955)
The Queen's Drive, Exeter EX4 4QJ
Tel: 01392-263263
Chancellor, The Lord Alexander of Weedon
(1998), QC
Vice-Chancellor, Sir Geoffrey Holland, KCB
Registrar and Secretary, I. H. C. Powell

THE UNIVERSITY OF GLAMORGAN (1992)
Pontypridd CF37 1DL
Tel: 01443-480480; Freephone: 0800-716925
Chancellor, The Rt. Hon. Lord Merlyn-Rees, PC, QC (1994)
Vice-Chancellor, Prof. Sir Adrian Webb
Registrar, J. O'Shea
Secretary, J. L. Bracegirdle

THE UNIVERSITY OF GLASGOW (1451)
The University Avenue, Glasgow G12 8QQ
Tel: 0141-339 8855
Chancellor, Sir William Kerr Fraser, GCB, FRSE
Vice-Chancellor, Prof. Sir Graeme Davies, FREng, FRSE
Secretary, D. Mackie, FRSA
Rector, R. Kemp 1999–2002

GLASGOW CALEDONIAN UNIVERSITY (1993)
Cowcaddens Road, Glasgow G4 0BA
Tel: 0141-331 3000
Chancellor, The Lord Nickson KBE (1993)
Vice-Chancellor, Dr I. A. Johnston, Ph.D., CB
Secretary, B. M. Murphy

THE UNIVERSITY OF GREENWICH (1992)
Bexley Road, London SE9 2PQ
Tel: 020-8331 8000
Chancellor, Lord Holme of Cheltenham, CBE
Vice-Chancellor, Prof. R. Trainor
Academic Registrar, Miss C. Rose
Secretary, J. M. Charles

HERIOT-WATT UNIVERSITY (1966)
Edinburgh EH14 4AS
Tel: 0131-449 5111
Chancellor, The Lord Mackay of Clashfern, Kt, PC (1979)
Vice-Chancellor, Prof. J. S. Archer, FREng.
Secretary, P. L. Wilson

THE UNIVERSITY OF HERTFORDSHIRE (1992)
College Lane, Hatfield AL10 9AB
Tel: 01707-284000
Chancellor, The Lord MacLaurin of Knebworth (1996)
Vice-Chancellor, Prof. N. K. Buxton
Registrar and Secretary, P. G. Jeffreys

THE UNIVERSITY OF HUDDERSFIELD (1992)
Queensgate, Huddersfield HD1 3DH
Tel: 01484-422288
Chancellor, Sir Ernest Hall, OBE (1996)
Vice-Chancellor, Prof. J. R. Tarrant
Secretary, T. Menes

THE UNIVERSITY OF HULL (1954)
Cottingham Road, Hull HU6 7RX
Tel: 01482-346311
Chancellor, The Lord Armstrong of Ilminster,
    GCB, CVO (1994)
Vice-Chancellor, Dr D. J. Drewry
Registrar, D. J. Lock

KEELE UNIVERSITY (1962)
Newcastle under Lyme ST5 5BG
Tel: 01782-621111
Chancellor, Sir Claus Moser, KCB, CBE, FBA (1986)
Vice-Chancellor, Prof. J. V. Finch, CBE, DL, Ph.D.
Registrar and Secretary, S. J. Morris

THE UNIVERSITY OF KENT AT
CANTERBURY (1965)
Canterbury CT2 7NZ
Tel: 01227-764000
Chancellor, Sir Crispin Tickell, GCMG, KCVO
Vice-Chancellor, Prof. R. Sibson, Ph.D.
Registrar and Secretary, N. A. McHard

KINGSTON UNIVERSITY (1992)
53–57 High Street, Kingston upon Thames KT1 1LQ
Tel: 020-8547 2000
Chancellor, Sir Peter Hall
Vice-Chancellor, Prof. P. Scott
Registrar, Mrs A. Stokes
Secretary, R. S. Abdula, MBE

THE UNIVERSITY OF LANCASTER (1964)
Bailrigg, Lancaster LA1 4YW
Tel: 01524-65201
Chancellor, HRH Princess Alexandra, the
    Hon. Lady Ogilvy, GCVO (1964)
Vice-Chancellor, Prof. W. Ritchie, OBE
Secretary, Miss F. Aiken

THE UNIVERSITY OF LEEDS (1904)
Leeds LS2 9JT
Tel: 0113-243 1751
Chancellor, Lord Bragg of Wigton
Vice-Chancellor, Prof. A. G. Wilson,
Registrar and Secretary, D. S. Robinson, Ph.D.

LEEDS METROPOLITAN UNIVERSITY (1992)
Calverley Street, Leeds LS1 3HE
Tel: 0113-283 2600
Chancellor, L. Silver, OBE (1989)
Vice-Chancellor, Prof. L. Wagner, CBE
Secretary, M. Wilkinson

THE UNIVERSITY OF LEICESTER (1957)
The University Road, Leicester LE1 7RH
Tel: 0116-252 2522
Chancellor, Sir Michael Atiyah, OM, FRS,
    Ph.D., D.Sc. (1995)
Vice-Chancellor, Prof. R. Burgess Ph.D.
Registrar and Secretary, K. J. Julian

THE UNIVERSITY OF LINCOLNSHIRE AND
HUMBERSIDE (1992)
Cottingham Road, Hull HU6 7RT
Tel: 01522-882000
Chancellor, Dr J. H. Hooper, CBE
Vice-Chancellor, Prof. R. P. King
Registrar, F. Marks

THE UNIVERSITY OF LIVERPOOL (1903)
Abercromby Square, Liverpool L69 3BX
Tel: 0151-794 2000
Chancellor, The Lord Owen, CH, PC (1996)
Vice-Chancellor, Prof. P. N. Love, CBE
Registrar and Secretary, M. D. Carr

LIVERPOOL JOHN MOORES UNIVERSITY (1992)
70 Mount Pleasant, Liverpool L3 5UX
Tel: 0151-231 2121
Chancellor, Ms C. Booth, QC
Vice-Chancellor, Prof. M. Brown
Registrar and Secretary, Ms A. Wild

THE UNIVERSITY OF LONDON (1836)
Malet Street, London WC1E 7HU
Tel: 020-7862 8000
Visitor, HM The Queen in Council
Chancellor, HRH The Princess Royal, KG, GCVO, FRS
    (1981)
Vice-Chancellor, Prof. G. J. Zellick, Ph.D.
Chairman of the Council, The Lord Woolf, PC
Chairman of Convocation, D. D. A. Leslie
Academic Registrar, Mrs G. F. Roberts
Director of Administration, J. R. Davidson

COLLEGES
BIRKBECK COLLEGE, Malet Street, London WC1E 7HX.
    Master, Prof. T. O'Shea
GOLDSMITHS COLLEGE, Lewisham Way, New Cross,
    London SE4 6NW. *Warden*, Prof. B. Pimlott, FBA
HEYTHROP COLLEGE, Kensington Square, London W8
    5HQ. *Principal*, Revd Dr J. McDade, SJ

IMPERIAL COLLEGE OF SCIENCE, TECHNOLOGY AND MEDICINE (includes Imperial College Schools of Medicine at Charing Cross, Hammersmith and St Mary's hospitals and at the National Heart and Lung Institute), South Kensington, London SW7 2AZ. *Rector*, Lord Oxburgh, KBE, FRS

INSTITUTE OF EDUCATION, 20 Bedford Way, London WC1H 0AL. *Director*, Prof. P. Mortimore, OBE

KING'S COLLEGE LONDON, (includes King's College School of Medicine and Dentistry, United Medical and Dental Schools of Guy's and St Thomas' Hospitals), Strand, London WC2R 2LS. *Principal*, Prof. A. Lucas, Ph.D.

LONDON BUSINESS SCHOOL, Sussex Place, Regent's Park, London NW1 4SA. *Principal*, Prof. J. Quelch

LONDON SCHOOL OF ECONOMICS AND POLITICAL SCIENCE, Houghton Street, London WC2A 2AE. *Director*, Prof. A. Giddens

LONDON SCHOOL OF HYGIENE AND TROPICAL MEDICINE, Keppel Street, London WC1E 7HT. *Dean*, Prof. H. Spencer

QUEEN MARY AND WESTFIELD COLLEGE, (incorporating St Bartholomew's and the Royal London School of Medicine and Dentistry and the London Hospital Medical College), Mile End Road, London E1 4NS. *Principal*, Prof. A. Smith

ROYAL ACADEMY OF MUSIC, Marylebone Road, London NW1 2BS. *Director*, Dr C. Price

ROYAL HOLLOWAY, Egham Hill, Egham, Surrey TW20 0EX. *Principal*, Prof. D. Bone

ROYAL VETERINARY COLLEGE, Royal College Street, London NW1 0TU. *Principal and Dean*, Prof. L. E. Lanyon, Ph.D.

ST GEORGE'S HOSPITAL MEDICAL SCHOOL, Cranmer Terrace, London SW17 0RE. *Dean*, Prof. R. Boyd, FRCP

SCHOOL OF ORIENTAL AND AFRICAN STUDIES, Thornhaugh Street, Russell Square, London WC1H 0XG. *Director*, Sir Tim Lankester, KCB

SCHOOL OF PHARMACY, 29–39 Brunswick Square, London WC1N 1AX. *Dean*, Prof. A. T. Florence, CBE, Ph.D., FRSE

UNIVERSITY COLLEGE LONDON, (including UCL Medical School), Gower Street, London WC1E 6BT. *Provost*, Prof. C. Llewellyn-Smith, FRS

WYE COLLEGE, Wye, near Ashford, Kent TN25 5AH. *Principal*, Prof. J. H. D. Prescott, Ph.D.

INSTITUTES

BRITISH INSTITUTE IN PARIS, 9–11 rue de Constantine, 75340 Paris, Cedex 07, France. *Director*, Prof. C. L. Campos, *London office:* Senate House, Malet Street, London WC1E 7HU, CBE, Ph.D.

CENTRE FOR DEFENCE STUDIES, King's College London, Strand, London WC2R 2LS. *Director*, Prof. L. Freedman, CBE, FBA

COURTAULD INSTITUTE OF ART, North Block, Somerset House, Strand, London WC2R 0RN. *Director*, Prof. E. C. Fernie, CBE, FSA, FRSE

INSTITUTE OF ADVANCED LEGAL STUDIES, Charles Clore House, 17 Russell Square, London WC1B 5DR. *Director*, Prof. B. A. K. Rider

INSTITUTE OF CANCER RESEARCH, Royal Cancer Hospital, Chester Beatty Laboratories, 17A Onslow Gardens, London SW7 3AL. *Chief Executive*, Dr P. Rigby

INSTITUTE OF CLASSICAL STUDIES, Senate House, Malet Street, London WC1E 7HU. *Director*, Prof. G. B. Waywell, FSA

INSTITUTE OF COMMONWEALTH STUDIES, 27–28 Russell Square, London WC1B 5DS. *Director*, Prof. P. Caplan

INSTITUTE OF ENGLISH STUDIES, Senate House, Malet Street, London WC1E 7HU. *Director*, Prof. W. Gould

INSTITUTE OF GERMANIC STUDIES, 29 Russell Square, London WC1B 5DP. *Director*, Prof. R. Görner

INSTITUTE OF HISTORICAL RESEARCH, Senate House, Malet Street, London WC1E 7HU. *Director*, Prof. D. Cannadine

INSTITUTE OF LATIN AMERICAN STUDIES, 31 Tavistock Square, London WC1H 9HA. *Director*, Prof. J. Dunkerley

INSTITUTE OF PSYCHIATRY, De Crespigny Park, Denmark Hill, London SE5 8AF. *Dean*, Prof. S. Checkley

INSTITUTE OF ROMANCE STUDIES, Senate House, Malet Street, London WC1E 7HU. *Director*, Prof. J. Labanyi

INSTITUTE OF UNITED STATES STUDIES, Senate House, Malet Street, London WC1E 7HU. *Director*, Prof. G. L. McDowell, Ph.D.

SCHOOL OF ADVANCED STUDY, Senate House, Malet Street, London WC1E 7HU. *Dean*, Prof. T. C. Daintith

UNIVERSITY MARINE BIOLOGICAL STATION MILLPORT, Isle of Cumbrae, Scotland KA28 0EG. *Director*, Dr R. Ormond

WARBURG INSTITUTE, Woburn Square, London WC1H 0AB. *Director*, Prof. C. N. J. Mann, Ph.D., CBE

ASSOCIATE INSTITUTES

INSTITUTE OF ZOOLOGY, Royal Zoological Society, Regent's Park, London NW1 4RY. *Director*, Prof. M. Gosling

LONDON SCHOOL OF JEWISH STUDIES, 44A Albert Road, London NW4 2SJ. *Principal*, Prof. D. H. Ruben

ROYAL COLLEGE OF MUSIC, Prince Consort Road, London SW7 2BS. *Director*, Dr J. Ritterman

LONDON GUILDHALL UNIVERSITY (1992)
31 Jewry Street, London EC3N 2EY
Tel: 020-7320 1000
Patron, HRH The Prince Philip, Duke of Edinburgh, KG, KT, OM, GBE, PC (1952)
Chancellor, Lord Limerick
Provost, Prof. R. Floud, D.Phil.
Registrar, Ms J. Grinstead
Secretary, M. Weaver

LOUGHBOROUGH UNIVERSITY (1966)
Loughborough LE11 3TU
Tel: 01509-263171
Chancellor, Sir Denis Rooke, CBE, FRS, FREng. (1989)
Vice-Chancellor, Prof. D.Wallace, FRS, FRSE
Registrar and Secretary, J. Town

THE UNIVERSITY OF LUTON (1993)
Park Square, Luton LU1 3JU
Tel: 01582-734111
Chancellor, Sir David Plastow
Vice-Chancellor, Dr D. John

THE UNIVERSITY OF MANCHESTER (1851)
Oxford Road, Manchester M13 9PL
Tel: 0161-275 2000
Chancellor, The Lord Flowers, FRS (1994)
Vice-Chancellor, Prof. M. B. Harris, CBE, DL, Ph.D.
Registrar and Secretary, E. Newcomb, FRSA

THE UNIVERSITY OF MANCHESTER INSTITUTE OF SCIENCE AND TECHNOLOGY (UMIST) (1824)
Manchester M60 1QD
Tel: 0161-236 3311
Chancellor, Prof. Sir Roland Smith, Ph.D. (1995)
Vice-Chancellor, Prof. R. F. Boucher, CBE, Ph.D., Ceng, FRSA, FREng.
Registrar and Secretary, J. Baldwin

MANCHESTER METROPOLITAN
UNIVERSITY (1992)
All Saints, Manchester M15 6BH
Tel: 0161-247 2000
Chancellor, The Duke of Westminster, OBE, TD (1993)
Vice-Chancellor, Mrs A. V. Burslem, OBE
Academic Registrar, J. D. M. Karczewski-Slowikowski
Secretary, T. A. Hendley, FCIS

MIDDLESEX UNIVERSITY (1992)
White Hart Lane, London N17 8HR
Tel: 020-8 411 5000
Chancellor, The Rt. Hon. Lord Sheppard
of Didgemere, KT., KGVC
Vice-Chancellor, Prof. M. Driscoll
Registrar, G. Jones

NAPIER UNIVERSITY (1992)
219 Colinton Road, Edinburgh EH14 1DJ
Tel: 0131-444 2266
Chancellor, The Viscount Younger of Leckie,
KT, KCVO, TD, PC, FRSE (1993)
Vice-Chancellor, Prof. J. Mavor
Academic Registrar, Mrs L. Fraser
Secretary, Dr G. Webber

THE UNIVERSITY OF NEWCASTLE
UPON TYNE (1834)
6 Kensington Terrace, Newcastle upon Tyne NE1 7RU
Tel: 0191-222 6000
Chancellor, Rt. Hon. C. Patten, CH
Vice-Chancellor, J. R. G. Wright
Registrar, D. E. T. Nicholson

THE UNIVERSITY OF NORTH LONDON (1992)
166–220 Holloway Road, London N7 8DB
Tel: 020-7607 2789
Vice-Chancellor, B. A. Roper
Secretary, J. McParland

THE UNIVERSITY OF NORTHUMBRIA AT
NEWCASTLE (1992)
Ellison Place, Newcastle upon Tyne NE1 8ST
Tel: 0191-232 6002
Chancellor, The Lord Glenamara, CH, PC (1984)
Vice-Chancellor, Prof. G. Smith
Registrar, Mrs C. Penna
Secretary, R. A. Bott

THE UNIVERSITY OF NOTTINGHAM (1948)
University Park, Nottingham NG7 2RD
Tel: 0115-951 5151
Chancellor, The Lord Dearing, CB (1993)
Vice-Chancellor, Prof. Sir Colin Campbell, DL
Registrar, K. H. Jones

NOTTINGHAM TRENT UNIVERSITY (1992)
Burton Street, Nottingham NG1 4BU
Tel: 0115-941 8418
Vice-Chancellor, Prof. R. Cowell, Ph.D.
Registrar, D. W. Samson
Secretary, S. Smith

THE UNIVERSITY OF OXFORD
Wellington Square, Oxford OX1 2JD
Tel: 01865-270000
Chancellor, The Lord Jenkins of Hillhead (*Balliol*),
elected 1987, OM, PC
Vice-Chancellor, Dr C. R. Lucas (*Balliol*), elected 1997
Proctors, Dr R. H. A. Jenkyns (*Lady Margaret Hall*);
Dr A. M. Hart (*Exeter*), elected 1999
Assessor, Prof. R. A. Mayou (*Nufield*), elected 1999
Public Orator, Prof. J. Griffin (*Balliol*), elected 1992

Bodley's Librarian, R. P. Carr (*Balliol*), elected 1997
Keeper of Archives, D. G. Vaisey (*Exeter*), elected 1995
Director of the Ashmolean Museum, Dr C. Brown
(*Worcester*), elected 1998
Registrar of the University, D. R. Holmes (*St John's*),
elected 1998
Surveyor to the University, P. M. R. Hill (*St Cross*),
elected 1993,
Secretary of Faculties, A. P. Weale (*Worcester*),
elected 1984
Secretary of the Chest, J. R. Clements (*Merton*), elected 1995
High Steward, The Lord Goff of Chieveley, PC (*Lincoln* and
New College), elected, 1990
Assessor, P. W. Smith (*Pembroke*), elected 1999

OXFORD COLLEGES AND HALLS
with dates of foundation
ALL SOULS (1438), *Warden*, Prof. J. Davis, FBA, Ph.D. (1995)
BALLIOL (1263), *Acting Master*, A. Graham (1998)
BLACKFRIARS (1221), *Regent*, Revd F. G. Kerr (1998)
BRASENOSE (1509), *Principal*, The Lord Windlesham, BT,
CVO, PC, D.Litt (1989)
CAMPION HALL (1896), *Master*, Revd Dr G. J. Hughes,
D.Phil. (1998)
CHRIST CHURCH (1546), *Dean*, Very Revd J. H. Drury
(1991)
CORPUS CHRISTI (1517), *President*, Prof. Sir Keith
Thomas, FBA (1986)
EXETER (1314), *Rector*, Dr M. Butler (1993)
GREEN (1979), *Warden*, Sir John Hanson, KCMG, CBE
(1997)
GREYFRIARS (1910), *Warden*, Revd T. G. Weinandy, Ph.D.
(1996)
HARRIS MANCHESTER (1786), *Principal*, Revd R. Waller,
Ph.D. (1990)
HERTFORD (1874), *Principal*, Sir Walter Bodmer, FRS,
FRCPath. (1996)
JESUS (1571), *Principal*, Sir Peter North, CBE, QC, FBA
(1984)
KEBLE (1868), *Warden*, Dr A. Cameron, FBA, FSA (1994)
KELLOGG (1990), *President*, Dr G. P. Thomas, (1990)
LADY MARGARET HALL (1878), *Principal*, Sir Brian Fall,
GVCO, KCMG (1995)
LINACRE (1962), *Principal*, Dr P. A. Slack, FBA (1996)
LINCOLN (1427), *Rector*, Prof. P. Langford, (2000)
MAGDALEN (1458), *President*, A. D. Smith, CBE (1988)
MANSFIELD (1886), *Principal*, Prof. D. I. Marquand, (1996)
MERTON (1264), *Warden*, Dr J. Rawson, CBE, FBA (1994)
NEW COLLEGE (1379), *Warden*, Dr. A. J. Ryan, FBA (1996)
NUFFIELD (1958), *Warden*, A. Atkinson, FBA (1994)
ORIEL (1326), *Provost*, Dr E. W. Nicholson,
DD, FBA (1990)
PEMBROKE (1624), *Master*, Dr R. Stevens, DCL (1993)
QUEEN'S (1340), *Provost*, Sir Alan Budd (1999)
REGENT'S PARK (1810), *Principal*, Revd P. S. Fiddes,
D.Phil. (1989)
ST ANNE'S (1952 (Society of Oxford Home-Students
(1879)), *Principal*, Mrs R. L. Deech (1991)
ST ANTONY'S (1953), *Warden*, Sir Marrack Goulding,
KCMG (1997)
ST BENET'S HALL (1897), *Master*, Revd H. Wansbrough,
OSB (1991)
ST CATHERINE'S (1963), *Master*, Sir Peter Williams, CBE,
FREng., FRS (2000)
ST CROSS (1965), *Master*, Dr R. C. Repp (1987)
ST EDMUND HALL (c.1278), *Principal*,
Prof. D. M. P. Mingos, (1999)
*ST HILDA'S (1893), *Principal*, Miss E. Llewellyn-Smith,
CB (1990)
ST HUGH'S (1886), *Principal*, D. Wood, CBE, QC (1991)

St John's (1555), *President*, Dr W. Hayes (1987)
St Peter's (1929), *Master*, Dr J. P. Barron, FSA (1991)
Somerville (1879), *Principal*, Dame Fiona Caldicott, DBE, FRCP, FRCPsych., FRCPI (1996)
Templeton (1965), *President*, Sir David Rowland (1998)
Trinity (1554), *President*, The Hon. Michael J. Beloff, QC (1996)
University (1249), *Master*, Baron Butler of Brockwell, GCB, CVO (1998)
Wadham (1610), *Warden*, J. S. Flemming, FBA (1993)
Wolfson (1966), *President*, Prof. Sir Gareth Roberts, FRS (2000)
Worcester (1714), *Provost*, R. G. Smethurst (1991)
Wycliffe Hall (1877), *Principal*, Revd A. E. McGrath, D.Phil. (1995)
*College for women only

OXFORD BROOKES UNIVERSITY (1993)
Gipsy Lane, Oxford OX3 0BP
Tel: 01865-484848
Chancellor, vacant
Vice-Chancellor, Prof. G. Upton
Registrar, Ms E. Winders

THE UNIVERSITY OF PAISLEY (1992)
Paisley PA1 2BE
Tel: 0141-848 3000
Chancellor, Sir Robert Easton, CBE (1993)
Vice-Chancellor and Principal, Prof. R. W. Shaw, CBE
Registrar, D. Rigg
Secretary, J. Fraser

THE UNIVERSITY OF PLYMOUTH (1992)
Drake Circus, Plymouth PL4 8AA
Tel: 01752-600600
Vice-Chancellor, Prof. J. Bull
Academic Registrar and Secretary, Miss J. Hopkinson

THE UNIVERSITY OF PORTSMOUTH (1992)
Winston Churchill Avenue, Portsmouth PO1 2UP
Tel: 023-9284 8484
Chancellor, The Lord Palumbo (1992)
Vice-Chancellor, Prof. J. Craven
Academic Registrar, A. Rees
Secretary, Dr M. Bateman

QUEEN'S UNIVERSITY OF BELFAST (1908)
Belfast BT7 1NN
Tel: 028-9024 5133
Chancellor, Sen. G. Mitchell
Vice-Chancellor, Prof. G. Bain
Registrar, J. O'Kane

THE UNIVERSITY OF READING (1926)
PO Box 217, Reading RG6 6AH
Tel: 0118-987 5123
Chancellor, The Lord Carrington, KG, GCMG (1992)
Vice-Chancellor, Prof. R. Williams
Registrar, D. C. R. Frampton

ROBERT GORDON UNIVERSITY (1992)
Schoolhill, Aberdeen AB10 1FR
Tel: 01224-262000
Chancellor, Sir Bob Reid, (1993)
Vice-Chancellor, Prof. W. Stevely, B.Sc., D.Phil.
Secretary, Dr A. Graves, D.Phil.

THE UNIVERSITY OF ST ANDREWS (1411)
College Gate, St Andrews KY16 9AJ
Tel: 01334-476161
Chancellor, Sir Kenneth Dover, DLitt., FRSE, FBA (1981)
Master and Acting Principal, Prof. C. A. Vincent
Secretary and Registrar, D. J. Corner
Rector, A. Neil (2000–2003)

THE UNIVERSITY OF SALFORD (1967)
Salford M5 4WT
Tel: 0161-295 5000
Chancellor, Sir Walter Bodmer, Ph.D., FRS
Vice-Chancellor, Prof. M. Harloe
Registrar, Dr M. D. Winton Ph.D.

THE UNIVERSITY OF SHEFFIELD (1905)
Western Bank, Sheffield S10 2TN
Tel: 0114-222 2000
Chancellor, Sir Peter Middleton, GCB
Vice-Chancellor, Prof. Sir Gareth Roberts, Kt., FRS, Ph.D.
Registrar and Secretary, Dr D. E. Fletcher, Ph.D.

SHEFFIELD HALLAM UNIVERSITY (1992)
Howard Street, Sheffield S1 1WB
Tel: 0114-225 5555
Chancellor, Sir Bryan Nicholson (1992)
Vice-Chancellor, Prof. D. Green
Registrar, Ms J. Tory
Secretary, Ms S. Neocosmos

THE UNIVERSITY OF SOUTHAMPTON (1952)
Highfield, Southampton SO17 1BJ
Tel: 023-8059 5000
Chancellor, The Earl of Selbourne, KBE, FRS (1996)
Vice-Chancellor, Prof. H. Newby, CBE, Ph.D.
Registrar and Secretary, J. F. D. Lauwerys

SOUTH BANK UNIVERSITY (1992)
103 Borough Road, London SE1 0AA
Tel: 020-7928 8989
Chancellor, Sir Trevor McDonald
Vice-Chancellor, Prof. G. Bernbaum
Registrar, R. Phillips
Secretary, Ms K. Stephenson

STAFFORDSHIRE UNIVERSITY (1992)
College Road, Stoke-on-Trent ST4 2DE
Tel: 01782-294000
Chancellor, The Lord Ashley of Stoke, CH, PC (1993)
Vice-Chancellor, Prof. C. E. King, Ph.D., DL, D.Litt, FRSA
Dean of Students and Academic Registrar, Ms F. Francis
Secretary, K. Sproston

THE UNIVERSITY OF STIRLING (1967)
Stirling FK9 4LA
Tel: 01786-473171
Chancellor, Dame Diana Rigg, DBE
Vice-Chancellor, Prof. A. Miller, CBE, FRSE
Academic Registrar, D. G. Wood
Secretary, K. J. Clarke

THE UNIVERSITY OF STRATHCLYDE (1796)
John Anderson Campus, Glasgow G1 1XQ
Tel: 0141-552 4400
Chancellor, The Rt. Hon. Lord Hope of Craighead PC (1998)
Vice-Chancellor, (until December) Prof. Sir John Arbuthnott, FRSE, FRC; (from January 2001) Prof. A. Hamnett
Academic Registrar, Dr S. M. Mellows
Secretary, Dr P. W. A. West
Chairman of Court, Dr R. A. Johnson

THE UNIVERSITY OF SUNDERLAND (1992)
Ryhope Road, Sunderland SR2 7EE
Tel: 0191-515 2000
Chancellor, The Lord Puttnam, CBE (1998)
Vice-Chancellor, Prof. P. Fidler, MBE
Registrar, S. Porteous
Secretary, J. D. Pacey
Rector, Revd P. Hutchinson

THE UNIVERSITY OF SURREY (1966)
Guildford GU2 5XH
Tel: 01483-300800
Chancellor, HRH The Duke of Kent,
    KG, GCMG, GCVO (1977)
Vice-Chancellor, Prof. P. J. Dowling, FRS, FREng.
Registrar, P. J. Beardsley
Secretary, U. Davies

THE UNIVERSITY OF SURREY ROEHAMPTON
Roehampton Lane, London SW15 5PU
Tel: 020-8392 3000/3232
Secretary, A. Skinner

THE UNIVERSITY OF SUSSEX (1961)
Brighton BN1 9RH
Tel: 01273-606755
Chancellor, The Lord Attenborough, KT, CBE (1998)
Vice-Chancellor, Prof. M. A. M. Smith
Registrar, N. Gershon

THE UNIVERSITY OF TEESSIDE (1992)
Middlesbrough TS1 3BA
Tel: 01642-218121
Chancellor, The Rt. Hon. Sir Leon Brittan, QC (1993)
Vice-Chancellor, Prof. D. Fraser
Registrar, Ms J. Walters
Secretary, J. M. McClintock

THAMES VALLEY UNIVERSITY (1992)
St Mary's Road, London W5 5RF
Tel: 020-8579 5000
Pro-Chancellor, The Lord Paul, CBE
Vice-Chancellor, Prof. K. Barker, CBE
Secretary, S. Denton

THE UNIVERSITY OF ULSTER (1984)
Cromore Road, Coleraine, Co. Londonderry BT52 1SA
Tel: 028-7034 4141
Chancellor, Rabbi J. Neuberger (1993)
Vice-Chancellor, Prof. P. G. McKenna, Ph.D

THE UNIVERSITY OF WALES (1893)
King Edward VII Avenue, Cardiff CF10 3NS
Tel: 029-2038 2656
Chancellor, HRH The Prince of Wales,
    KG, KT, GCB, PC (1976)
Senior Vice-Chancellor, Prof. K. G. Robbins,
    D.Phil., DLitt., FRSE
Secretary-General, vacant
Secretary to the Council, L. E. Williams, Ph.D.

MEMBER INSTITUTIONS

UNIVERSITY OF WALES, ABERYSTWYTH, Old College,
    King Street, Aberystwyth SY23 2AX. Tel: 01970-623111.
    Vice-Chancellor, Prof. D. Llwyd Morgan, D.Phil, D.Litt
    (1995)
UNIVERSITY OF WALES, BANGOR, Bangor LL57 2DG. Tel:
    01248-351151. *Vice-Chancellor*, Prof. H. R. Evans, Ph.D.,
    FREng. (1995)
UNIVERSITY OF WALES, CARDIFF, PO Box 920,
    Cardiff CF10 3XP. Tel: 029-2087 4000. *Vice-Chancellor*,
    Prof. Sir Brian Smith, Ph.D., D.SC. (1993)
UNIVERSITY OF WALES, LAMPETER, Lampeter
    SA48 7ED. Tel: 01570-422351. *Vice-Chancellor*,
    Prof. K. G. Robbins, D.Litt., D.Phil., FRSE (1992)
UNIVERSITY OF WALES, SWANSEA, Singleton Park,
    Swansea SA2 8PP. Tel: 01792-205678. *Vice-Chancellor*,
    Prof. R. H. Williams, Ph.D., D.SC., FRS (1994)
UNIVERSITY OF WALES COLLEGE OF MEDICINE,
    Heath Park, Cardiff CF14 4XN. Tel: 029-2074 7747.
    Vice-Chancellor, Prof. I. R. Cameron, DM, FRCP (1994)

UNIVERSITY OF WALES COLLEGE, NEWPORT,
    Caerleon Campus, PO Box 179, Newport NP6 1YG.
    Tel: 01633-430088. *Principal*, Prof. K. J. Overshott,
    Ph.D. (1990)
UNIVERSITY OF WALES INSTITUTE, CARDIFF,
    Llandaff Centre, Western Avenue, Cardiff CF5 2SG.
    Tel: 029-2050 6070. *Principal*, A. J. Chapman, Ph.D.
    (1998)

THE UNIVERSITY OF WARWICK (1965)
Coventry CV4 7AL
Tel: 024-7652 3523
Chancellor, Sir Shridath Surendranath Ramphal,
    GCMG, QC (1989)
Vice-Chancellor, Prof. Sir Brian Follett, FRS
Registrar, Dr J. W. Nicholls
Administravie Secretary, Ms C. Charlton

THE UNIVERSITY OF WESTMINSTER (1992)
309 Regent Street, London W1B 2UW
Tel: 020-7911 5000
Vice-Chancellor and Rector, Dr G. M. Copland (1996)
Academic Registrar, Ms E. Green

THE UNIVERSITY OF THE WEST OF
ENGLAND (1992)
Coldharbour Lane, Bristol BS16 1QY
Tel: 0117-965 6261
Chancellor, The Rt. Hon. Dame Elizabeth Butler-Sloss,
    DBE (1993)
Vice-Chancellor, A. C. Morris
Academic Secretary, Ms C. Webb

THE UNIVERSITY OF WOLVERHAMPTON
(1992)
Wulfruna Street, Wolverhampton WV1 1SB
Tel: 01902-321000
Chancellor, Lord Paul of Marylebone
Vice-Chancellor, Prof. J. S. Brooks, Ph.D.
Secretary, A. W. Lee

THE UNIVERSITY OF YORK (1963)
York YO10 5DD
Tel: 01904-430000
Chancellor, Dame Janet Baker, CH, DBE (1991)
Vice-Chancellor, Prof. R. U. Cooke, Ph.D.
Registrar and Secretary, D. J. Foster

OPEN UNIVERSITY (1969)
Milton Keynes MK7 6AA
Tel: 01908-274066
Head of Student Services Registry, Ms H. Niven
Chancellor, The Rt. Hon. Betty Boothroyd, MP
Vice-Chancellor, Sir John Daniel
Secretary, F. Woodburn

ROYAL COLLEGE OF ART (1837)
Kensington Gore, London SW7 2EU
Tel: 020-7590 4444
Provost, The Earl of Snowdon, GCVO (1995)
Rector, Prof. C. Frayling, Ph.D.
Registrar, A. Selby, B.SC.

COLLEGES

It is not possible to name here all the colleges offering courses of higher or further education. The list does not include colleges forming part of a polytechnic or a university. The English colleges that follow are confined to those in the Higher Education Funding Council for England sector; there are many more colleges in England providing higher education courses, some with HEFCFE funding.

The list of colleges in Wales, Scotland and Northern Ireland include institutions providing at least one full-time course leading to a first degree granted by an accredited validating body.

ENGLAND

BATH SPA UNIVERSITY COLLEGE, Newton Park, Newton St Loe, Bath BA2 9BN. Tel: 01225-875875. *Director,* F. Morgan

BISHOP GROSSETESTE COLLEGE, Lincoln LN1 3DY. Tel: 01522-527347. *Principal,* Prof. E. Baker

BOLTON INSTITUTE OF HIGHER EDUCATION, Deane Road, Bolton BL3 5AB. Tel: 01204-528851. *Principal,* Ms M. Temple

BRETTON HALL, West Bretton, Wakefield, W. Yorks WF4 4LG. Tel: 01924-830261. *Principal,* Prof. G. H. Bell

BUCKINGHAMSHIRE CHILTERNS UNIVERSITY COLLEGE, Queen Alexandra Road, High Wycombe, Bucks HP11 2JZ. Tel: 01494-522141. *Director,* Prof. P. B. Mogford

CANTERBURY CHRIST CHURCH UNIVERSITY COLLEGE, North Holmes Road, Canterbury, Kent CT1 1QU. Tel: 01227-767700. *Principal,* Prof. M. Wright

CHELTENHAM AND GLOUCESTER COLLEGE OF HIGHER EDUCATION COLLEGE OF HIGHER EDUCATION, PO Box 220, The Park, Cheltenham, Glos GL50 2QF. Tel: 01242-532700. *Director,* Miss J. O. Trotter, OBE

CO-OPERATIVE COLLEGE, Stanford Hall, Loughborough, Leics LE12 5QP. Tel: 01509-857212. *Chief Executive and Principal,* M. Wilson

DARTINGTON COLLEGE OF ARTS, Totnes, Devon TQ9 6EJ. Tel: 01803-862224. *Principal,* Prof. K. Thompson

EDGE HILL COLLEGE OF HIGHER EDUCATION, St Helens Road, Ormskirk, Lancs L39 4QP. Tel: 01695-575171. *Chief Executive,* Dr J. Cater

FALMOUTH COLLEGE OF ARTS, Woodlane, Falmouth, Cornwall TR11 4RH. Tel: 01326-211077. *Principal,* Prof. A. G. Livingston

FIRCROFT COLLEGE, 1018 Bristol Road, Selly Oak, Birmingham B29 6LH. Tel: 0121-472 0116. *Principal,* Ms F. Larden

FORUM FOR THE ADVANCEMENT OF CONTINUING EDUCATION (FACE), Regional Office, Widening Participation Unit, University of East London, Romford Road, London E15 4LZ. Tel: 020-8223 4936

HARPER ADAMS UNIVERSITY COLLEGE, Newport, Shropshire TF10 8NB. Tel: 01952-820280. *Principal,* Prof. E. W. Jones

HILLCROFT COLLEGE, South Bank, Surbitons, Surrey KT6 6DF. Tel: 020-8399 2688. *Principal,* Ms J. Ireton

HOMERTON COLLEGE, Cambridge CB2 2PH. Tel: 01223-507111. *Principal,* Dr K. Pretty, PH.D.

KENT INSTITUTE OF ART AND DESIGN, Oakwood Park, Maidstone, Kent ME16 8AG. Tel: 01622-757286. *Director,* Prof. V. Grylls

KING ALFRED'S COLLEGE, Sparkford Road, Winchester, Hants SO22 4NR. Tel: 01962-841515. *Acting Principal,* Prof. C. Turner

LIVERPOOL HOPE UNIVERSITY COLLEGE, Hope Park, Liverpool L16 9JD. Tel: 0151-291 3000. *Rector and Chief Executive,* Prof. S. Lee

LLANDRILLO COLLEGE, Llandudno Road, Rhos-on-Sea, Colwyn Bay, Conwy LL28 4HZ. Tel: 01492-546666. *Principal,* W. S. H. Evans

NATIONAL INSTITUTE OF ADULT CONTINUING EDUCATION, 21 De Montfort Street, Leicester LE1 7GE. Tel: 0116-204 4200. *Director,* A. Tuckett

NEWMAN COLLEGE OF HIGHER EDUCATION, Genners Lane, Bartley Green, Birmingham B32 3NT. Tel: 0121-476 1181. *Principal,* Mrs P. Taylor

NORTHERN COLLEGE, Wentworth Castle, Stainborough, Barnsley, S. Yorks S75 3ET. Tel: 01226-776000. *Principal and Chief Executive,* Dr J. A. Jowitt

PLATER COLLEGE, Pullens Lane, Oxford OX3 0DT. Tel: 01865-740500. *Principal,* M. Blades

QUEEN MARGARET UNIVERSITY COLLEGE, Clerwood Terrace, Edinburgh EH12 8TS. Tel: 0131-317 3000. *Principal,* Prof. J. Stringer

RCN INSTITUTE, The Royal College of Nursing, 20 Cavendish Square, London W1M 0AB. Tel: 020-7647 3700. *Director,* Prof. A. L. Kitson

ROSE BRUFORD COLLEGE, Lamorbey Park, Sidcup, Kent DA15 9DF. Tel: 020-8300 3024. *Principal,* Prof. R. Ely

ROYAL AGRICULTURAL COLLEGE, Cirencester, Glos GL7 6JS. Tel: 01285-652531. *Principal,* Prof. J. B. Dent

ROYAL NORTHERN COLLEGE OF MUSIC, 124 Oxford Road, Manchester M13 9RD. Tel: 0161-907 5200. *Principal,* Prof. E. Gregson

RUSKIN COLLEGE, Walton Street, Oxford OX1 2HE. Tel: 01865-554331. *Principal,* J. Durcan

SOUTHAMPTON INSTITUTE, East Park Terrace, Southampton SO14 0YN. Tel: 023-8031 9000. *Principal,* Dr R. Brown

ST MARTIN'S COLLEGE, Lancaster LA1 3JD. Tel: 01524-384384. *Principal,* Prof. C. J. Carr

SURREY INSTITUTE OF ART AND DESIGN, UNIVERSITY COLLEGE, Falkner Road, Farnham, Surrey GU9 7DS. Tel: 01252-722441. *Director,* Prof. E. Thomas

THE CENTRAL SCHOOL OF SPEECH AND DRAMA SPEECH AND DRAMA, Embassy Theatre, 64 Eton Avenue, London NW3 3HY. Tel: 020-7722 8183. *Principal,* Prof. G. Crossley

THE COLLEGE OF RIPON AND YORK ST JOHN, Lord Mayor's Walk, York YO31 7EX. Tel: 01904-656771. *Principal,* Prof. D. Willcocks

THE LONDON INSTITUTE, 65 Davies Street, London W1Y 2AA. Tel: 020-7514 6000. *Rector,* Sir William Stubbs

THE RESIDENTIAL COLLEGES COMMITTEE, c/o Ruskin College, Oxford OX1 2HE. Tel: 01865-556360. *Awards Officer,* Mrs F. A. Bagchi

THE UNIVERSITIES ASSOCIATION FOR CONTINUING EDUCATION, University of Cambridge Board of Continuing Education, Madingley Hall, Madingley, Cambridge CB3 8AQ. Tel: 01954-280279. *Administrator,* Ms S. Irwin

THE UNIVERSITY OF BIRMINGHAM, WESTHILL, Weoley Park Road, Selly Oak, Birmingham B29 6LL Tel: 0121-472 7245. *Principal and Vice-Chancellor,* Prof. J. H. Y. Briggs

TRINITY AND ALL SAINTS' COLLEGE, Brownberrie Lane, Horsforth, Leeds LS18 5HD. Tel: 0113-283 7100. *Principal,* Dr M. J. Coughlan

UNIVERSITY COLLEGE CHESTER, Parkgate Road, Chester CH1 4BJ. Tel: 01244-375444. *Principal,* Prof. T. J. Wheeler

UNIVERSITY COLLEGE CHICHESTER, College Lane, Chichester, W. Sussex PO19 4PE. Tel: 01243-816000. *Director,* P. E. D. Robinson

UNIVERSITY COLLEGE NORTHAMPTON, Park Campus, Boughton Green Road, Northampton NN2 7AL. Tel: 01604-735500. *Rector*, Dr S. M. Gaskell

UNIVERSITY COLLEGE OF ST MARK AND ST JOHN, Derriford Road, Plymouth PL6 8BH. Tel: 01752-636700. *Principal*, Dr W. J. Rea

UNIVERSITY COLLEGE WORCESTER, Henwick Grove, Worcester WR2 6AJ. Tel: 01905-855000. *Principal*, Ms D. Urwin

UNIVERSITY OF WALES INSTITUTE CARDIFF, Llandaff Campus, Western Avenue, Cardiff CF5 2YB. Tel: 029-2041 6070. *Principal*, Prof A. J. Chapman

WINCHESTER SCHOOL OF ART, Park Avenue, Winchester, Hants SO23 8DL. Tel: 023-8059 6900. *Principal*, P. Pilgrim

WORKERS' EDUCATIONAL ASSOCIATION, Temple House, 17 Victoria Park Square, London E2 9PB. Tel: 020-8983 1515. *General Secretary*, R. Lochrie

WALES

CARMARTHENSHIRE COLLEGE, Graig Campus, Sandy Road, Llanelli SA15 4DN. Tel: 01554-748000. *Principal*, B. Robinson

COLEG HARLECH, Harlech Gwynedd LL46 2PU. Tel 01766-780363. *Acting Warden*, Dr D. R. Wiltshire

NIACE DYSGU CYMRU, 245 Western Avenue, Cardiff CF5 2YX. Tel: 029-2026 5002. *Director for Wales*, Ms A. Poole

NORTH EAST WALES INSTITUTE OF HIGHER EDUCATION, Plas Coch, Mold Road, Wrexham LL11 2AW. Tel: 01978-290666. *Acting Principal*, Prof. R. D. Jones

SWANSEA INSTITUTE OF HIGHER EDUCATION, Mount Pleasant, Swansea SA1 6ED. Tel: 01792-481000. *Principal*, Prof. D. Warner

TRINITY COLLEGE, Carmarthen SA31 3EP. Tel: 01267-676767. *Principal*, Dr M. Hughes

WELSH COLLEGE OF MUSIC AND DRAMA, Castle Grounds, Cathays Park, Cardiff CF10 3ER. Tel: 029-2034 2854. *Principal*, E. Fivet

SCOTLAND

BELL COLLEGE OF TECHNOLOGY, Almada Street, Hamilton Lanarkshire ML3 0JB. Tel: 01698-283100. *Principal*, Dr K. J. MacCallum

COMMUNITY LEARNING SCOTLAND, Rosebery House, 9 Haymarket Terrace, Edinburgh EH12 5EZ. Tel: 0131-313 2488. *Chief Executive*, C. McConnell

DUMFRIES AND GALLOWAY COLLEGE, Heathhall, Dumfries DG1 3QZ. Tel: 01387-261261. *Principal*, T. Jakimciw

FIFE COLLEGE OF FURTHER AND HIGHER EDUCATION, St Brycedale Avenue, Kirkcaldy Fife KY1 1EX. Tel: 01592-268591. *Principal*, Mrs J. S. R. Johnston

GLASGOW SCHOOL OF ART, 167 Renfrew Street, Glasgow G3 6RQ. Tel: 0141-353 4500. *Director*, Ms S. Reid

INVERNESS COLLEGE, Longman Road, Inverness IV1 1SA. Tel: 01463-273000. *Principal*, Dr G. Clark

LEWS CASTLE COLLEGE, Stornoway, Isle of Lewis HS2 0XR. Tel: 01851-770000. *Principal*, D. Green

MORAY COLLEGE, Moray Street, Elgin, Moray IV30 1JJ. Tel: 01343-576000. *Acting Principal*, B. G. Cooper

NEWBATTLE ABBEY COLLEGE, Dalkeith, Midlothian EH22 3LL. Tel: 0131-663 1921. *Principal*, Ms A. Southwood

NORTHERN COLLEGE, Hilton Place, Aberdeen AB24 4FA. Tel: 01224-283500. *Principal*, D. Adams

ORKNEY COLLEGE, Kirkwall, Orkney KW15 1LX. Tel: 01856-872839. *Principal*, P. Scott

ROYAL SCOTTISH ACADEMY OF MUSIC AND DRAMA MUSIC AND DRAMA, 100 Renfrew Street, Glasgow G2 3DB. Tel: 0141-332 4101. *Principal*, Sir Philip Ledger, KT., CBE, FRSE

SÀBHAL MÒR OSTAIG, Sleat, Isle of Skye IV44 8RQ. Tel: 01471-888000. *Director*, N. N. Gillies

SAC (SCOTTISH AGRICULTURAL COLLEGE), Central Office, West Mains Road, Edinburgh EH9 3JG. Tel: 0131-535 4000. *Principal*, K. A. Linklater

THURSO COLLEGE, Ormlie Road, Thurso, Caithness KW14 7EE. Tel: 01847-896161. *Principal*, H. Logan

NORTHERN IRELAND

ST MARY'S UNIVERSITY COLLEGE, 191 Falls Road, Belfast BT12 6FE. Tel: 028-9032 7678. *Principal*, Very Revd Prof. M. O'Callaghan

---

ADULT CONTINUING EDUCATION

NATIONAL INSTITUTE OF ADULT CONTINUING EDUCATION, 21 De Montfort Street, Leicester LE1 7GE. Tel: 0116-204 4200. *Director*, A. Tuckett

NIACE DYSGU CYMRU, 245 Western Avenue, Cardiff CF5 2YX. Tel: 029-2026 5002. *Director for Wales*, Ms A. Poole

THE RESIDENTIAL COLLEGES COMMITTEE, c/o Ruskin College, Oxford OX1 2HE. Tel: 01865-556360. *Awards Officer*, Mrs F. A. Bagchi

COMMUNITY LEARNING SCOTLAND, Rosebery House, 9 Haymarket Terrace, Edinburgh EH12 5EZ. Tel: 0131-313 2488. *Chief Executive*, C. McConnell

THE UNIVERSITIES ASSOCIATION FOR CONTINUING EDUCATION, University of Cambridge Board of Continuing Education, Madingley Hall, Madingley, Cambridge CB3 8AQ. Tel: 01954-280279. *Administrator*, Ms S. Irwin

WORKERS' EDUCATIONAL ASSOCIATION, Temple House, 17 Victoria Park Square, London E2 9PB. Tel: 020-8983 1515. *General Secretary*, R. Lochrie

LONG-TERM RESIDENTIAL COLLEGES FOR ADULT EDUCATION

COLEG HARLECH, Harlech, Gwynedd LL46 2PU. Tel: 01766-780363. *Acting Warden*, Dr D. R. Wiltshire

CO-OPERATIVE COLLEGE, Stanford Hall, Loughborough, Leics LE12 5QP. Tel: 01509-857212. *Chief Executive and Principal*, M. Wilson

FIRCROFT COLLEGE, 1018 Bristol Road, Selly Oak, Birmingham B29 6LH. Tel: 0121-472 0116. *Principal*, Ms F. Larden

FORUM FOR THE ADVANCEMENT OF CONTINUING EDUCATION (FACE), Regional Office, Widening Participation Unit, University of East London, Romford Road, London E15 4LZ. Tel: 020-8223 4936

HILLCROFT COLLEGE, South Bank, Surbiton, Surrey KT6 6DF. Tel: 020-8399 2688. *Principal*, Ms J. Ireton

NEWBATTLE ABBEY COLLEGE, Dalkeith, Midlothian EH22 3LL. Tel: 0131-663 1921. *Principal*, Ms A. Southwood

NORTHERN COLLEGE, Wentworth Castle, Stainborough, Barnsley, S. Yorks S75 3ET. Tel: 01226-776000. *Principal and Chief Executive*, Dr J. A. Jowitt

PLATER COLLEGE, Pullens Lane, Oxford OX3 0DT. Tel: 01865-740500. *Principal*, M. Blades

RUSKIN COLLEGE, Walton Street, Oxford OX1 2HE. Tel: 01865-554331. *Principal*, J. Durcan

PROFESSIONAL EDUCATION
Excluding postgraduate study

The organisations listed below are those which, by providing specialist training or conducting examinations, control entry into a profession, or are responsible for maintaining a register of those with professional qualifications in their sector.

Many professions now have a largely graduate entry, and possession of a first degree can exempt entrants from certain of the professional examinations. Enquiries about obtaining professional qualifications should be made to the relevant professional organisation(s). Details of higher education providers of first degrees may be found in *University and College Entrance: Official Guide* (available from UCAS).

EU RECOGNITION

It is now possible for those with professional qualifications obtained in the UK to have these recognised in other European Union countries. A booklet, *Europe Open for Professions*, and further information can be obtained from: DEPARTMENT OF TRADE AND INDUSTRY, Bay 212, Kingsgate House, 66–74 Victoria Street, London SW1E 6SW. Tel: 020-7215 4648. *Contact*, Ms A. Wilson

ACCOUNTANCY

The main bodies granting membership on examination after a period of practical work are:
ASSOCIATION OF CHARTERED CERTIFIED ACCOUNTANTS (ACCA), 29 Lincoln's Inn Fields, London WC2A 3EE. Tel: 020-7242 6855. *Chief Executive*, Ms A. Rose
CIMA (THE CHARTERED INSTITUTE OF MANAGEMENT ACCOUNTANTS), 63 Portland Place, London W1B 1AB. Tel: 020-7637 2311. *Chief Executive*, J. Chester
INSTITUTE OF CHARTERED ACCOUNTANTS IN ENGLAND AND WALES, Chartered Accountants' Hall, PO Box 433, Moorgate Place, London EC2P 2BJ. Tel: 020-7920 8100. *Secretary General*, J. Collier
INSTITUTE OF CHARTERED ACCOUNTANTS OF SCOTLAND, CA House, 21 Haymarket Yards, Edinburgh EH12 5BG. Tel: 0131-347 0100. *Chief Executive*, D. A. Brew

ACTUARIAL SCIENCE

Two professional organisations grant qualifications after examination:
INSTITUTE OF ACTUARIES, Staple Inn Hall, High Holborn, London WC1V 7QJ. Tel: 020-7632 2100. *Secretary General*, G. B. L. Campbell
THE FACULTY OF ACTUARIES IN SCOTLAND, Maclaurin House, 18 Dublin Street, Edinburgh EH2 3PP. Tel: 0131-240 1300. *Secretary*, W. Mair

ARCHITECTURE

The Education Committee of the Royal Institute of British Architects sets standards and guides the whole system of architectural education throughout the UK. RIBA recognises courses at 35 schools of architecture in the UK for exemption from their own examinations as well as 65 courses overseas.
ARCHITECTS REGISTRATION BOARD, 8 Weymouth Street, London W1W 5BU. Tel: 020-7580 5861. *Chief Officer and Registrar*, R. Vaughan
ROYAL INSTITUTE OF BRITISH ARCHITECTS, 66 Portland Place, London W1N 4AD. Tel: 020-7580 5533

Schools of architecture outside the universities include:
THE ARCHITECTURAL ASSOCIATION (INC.), 34–36 Bedford Square, London WC1B 3ES. Tel: 020-7887 4018. *Secretary*, E. Le Maistre
THE PRINCE'S FOUNDATION, 19–22 Charlotte Road, London EC2A 3SG. Tel: 020-7916 7380. *Head of School*, D. Luwts

BANKING

Professional organisations granting qualifications after examination are:
THE CHARTERED INSTITUTE OF BANKERS, 90 Bishopsgate, London EC2N 4AS. Tel: 020-7444 7111. *Chief Executive Officer*, G. Shreeve
THE CHARTERED INSTITUTE OF BANKERS IN SCOTLAND, Drumsheugh House, 38B Drumsheugh Gardens, Edinburgh EH3 7SW. Tel: 0131-473 7777. *Chief Executive*, C. W. Munn

BUILDING

Examinations are conducted by:
THE CHARTERED INSTITUTE OF BUILDING, Englemere, King's Ride, Ascot, Berks SL5 7TB. Tel: 01344-630700. *Chief Executive*, C. Blythe
THE INSTITUTE OF BUILDING CONTROL, 92–104 East Street, Epsom, Surrey KT17 1EB. Tel: 01372-745577. *Chief Executive*, J. Parrott
THE INSTITUTE OF CLERKS OF WORKS OF GREAT BRITAIN, 41 The Mall, London W5 3TJ. Tel: 020-8579 2917/8. *General Secretary*, D. McGeorge

BUSINESS, MANAGEMENT AND ADMINISTRATION

Professional bodies conducting training and/or examinations in business, administration, management or commerce include:
AMETS (ASSOCIATION FOR MANAGEMENT EDUCATION AND TRAINING IN SCOTLAND), c/o Cottrell Building, University of Stirling, Stirling FK9 4LA. Tel: 01786-460906. *Chairman*, Prof. F. Pignatelli
CHARTERED INSTITUTE OF PERSONNEL AND DEVELOPMENT, IPD House, Camp Road, London SW19 4UX. Tel: 020-8971 9000. *Director-General*, G. Armstrong
HENLEY MANAGEMENT COLLEGE, Greenlands, Henley on Thames, Oxon RG9 3AU. Tel: 01491-571454. *Principal*, R. Wild
INSTITUTE OF CHARTERED SECRETARIES AND ADMINISTRATORS, 16 Park Crescent, London W1N 4AH. Tel: 020-7580 4741. *Chief Executive*, M. J. Ainsworth
INSTITUTE OF CHARTERED SHIPBROKERS, 3 St Helen's Place, London EC3A 6EJ. Tel: 020-7628 5559. *Director*, Mrs B. Fletcher
INSTITUTE OF MANAGEMENT, Management House, Cottingham Road, Corby, Northants NN17 1TT. Tel: 01536-204222. *Director-General*, Ms M. Chapman
INSTITUTE OF QUALITY ASSURANCE, 12 Grosvenor Crescent, London SW1X 7EE. Tel: 020-7245 6722. *Chief Executive*, Frank Steer, MBE
THE ASSOCIATION OF MBAs, 15 Duncan Terrace, London N1 8BZ. Tel: 020-7837 3375. *Director*, M. Jones
THE CAM FOUNDATION, Abford House, 15 Wilton Road, London SW1V 1NJ. Tel: 020-7828 7506. *Chief Executive*, D. Royston-Lee
THE CHARTERED INSTITUTE OF HOUSING, Octavia House, Westwood Business Park, Westwood Way, Coventry CV4 8JP. Tel: 024-7685 1700. *Chief Executive*, D. Butler

THE CHARTERED INSTITUTE OF PURCHASING AND SUPPLY, Easton House, Easton on the Hill, Stamford, Lincs PE9 3NZ. Tel: 01780-756777. *Chief Executive*, C. Holden

THE INSTITUTE OF ADMINISTRATIVE MANAGEMENT, 40 Chatsworth Parade, Petts Wood, Orpington, Kent BR5 1RW. Tel: 01689-875555. *Chief Executive*, Prof. G. Robinson

THE INSTITUTE OF EXPORT, Export House, 64 Clifton Street, London EC2A 4HB. Tel: 020-7247 9812. *Director-General*, I. J. Campbell

THE INSTITUTE OF HEALTHCARE MANAGEMENT, 7-10 Chandos Street, London W1M 9DE. Tel: 020-7460 7654. *Chief Executive*, S. Marples

CHIROPRACTIC

Chiropractic obtained statutory regulation by the Chiropractic Act 1994. There are four professional associations, which operate voluntary registers. The General Chiropractic Council opened its register in June 1999 and when this closes in June 2001, it will be an offence to use the title chiropractor unless registered with the General Chiropractic Council.

The General Chiropractic Council has accredited four training centres for chiropractic in the UK.

BRITISH CHIROPRACTIC ASSOCIATION, Blagrave House, Blagrave Street, Reading, Berks RG1 1QB. Tel: 0118-950 5950

GENERAL CHIROPRACTIC COUNCIL, PO Box 23050, London W11 3WH. Tel: 020-7713 5155

SCOTTISH CHIROPRACTIC ASSOCIATION, St Boswells Chiropractic Clinic, 16 Jenny Moores Road, St Boswells, Melrose TD6 0AL. Tel: 01835-824026

DANCE

The Council for Dance Education and Training (CDET) has accredited courses at the following: Arts Education Schools, Tring Park and London; Central School of Ballet; Doreen Bird College of Performing Arts; Elmhurst–The School for Dance and Performing Arts; English National Ballet School; The Hammond School; The Italia Conti Academy of Theatre Arts Ltd; Laban Centre, London; Laine Theatre Arts Ltd; London Contemporary Dance School; London Studio Centre; Midlands Academy of Dance and Drama; Merseyside Dance and Drama Centre; Northern Ballet School; Performers College; Stella Mann College; Studios La Pointe; Royal Academy of Dancing; The Urdang Academy.

The accreditation of a course in a school does not necessarily imply that other courses of a different type or duration in the same school are also accredited.

CDET has approved the teacher registration systems of the following: Association of American Dancing; British Ballet Organisation; British Theatre Dance Association; Cecchetti Society; Imperial Society of Teachers of Dancing; Royal Academy of Dancing.

IMPERIAL SOCIETY OF TEACHERS OF DANCING, Imperial House, 22-26 Paul Street, London EC2A 4QE. Tel: 020-7377 1577. *Chief Executive*, M. J. Browne

INTERNATIONAL DANCE TEACHERS' ASSOCIATION, International House, 76 Bennett Road, Brighton BN2 5JL. Tel: 01273-685652

ROYAL ACADEMY OF DANCING, 36 Battersea Square, London SW11 3RA. Tel: 020-7326 8000. *Chief Executive*, L. Rittner

ROYAL BALLET SCHOOL, 155 Talgarth Road, London W14 9DE. Tel: 020-8748 6335. *Director*, Ms G. Stock, AM

DEFENCE

ROYAL COLLEGE OF DEFENCE STUDIES, Seaford House, 37 Belgrave Square, London SW1X 8NS. Tel: 020-7915 4800. *Commandant*, Vice-Adm. J. H. S. McAnally, LVO

JOINT SERVICES COMMAND AND STAFF COLLEGE, Faringdon Road, Watchfield, Swindon, Wilts SN6 8TS. Tel: 01793-788555. *Commandant*, Air Vice-Marshal B. K. Burridge, CBE

ROYAL NAVAL COLLEGE

BRITANNIA ROYAL NAVAL COLLEGE, Dartmouth, Devon TQ6 0HJ. Tel: 01803-677108. *Commodore*, Cdre M. W. G. Kerr, RN

MILITARY COLLEGES

DIRECTORATE OF EDUCATIONAL AND TRAINING SERVICES (ARMY), Trenchard Lines, Upavon, Pewsey, Wilts SN9 6BE. Tel: 01980-618719/618710. *Director*, Brig. P. S. Purves

ROYAL MILITARY ACADEMY SANDHURST, Camberley, Surrey GU15 4PQ. Tel: 01276-63344. *Commandant*, Maj Gen A. G. Denaro, CBE

ROYAL MILITARY COLLEGE OF SCIENCE, Cranfield University, RMCS Shrivenham, Swindon SN6 8LA. Tel: 01793-785435

ROYAL AIR FORCE COLLEGES

ROYAL AIR FORCE COLLEGE, Cranwell, Sleaford, Lincs NG3 48HB. Provides initial training for all officer entrants to the RAF. Also provides initial specialist and postgraduate training for engineering and supply officers. The RAF College is the site of the Joint Elementary Flying School for pilots of all three services, Number 3 Flying Training School and the RAF Central Flying School. It is also the headquarters for the RAF University Air Squadrons, and is responsible for supervision of the Air Cadet Organisation. *Air Officer Commanding and Commandant*, Air Vice-Marshal H. G. Mackay, OBE, AFC, BSC, FRAES, RAF

ROYAL AIR FORCE TRAINING, DEVELOPMENT AND SUPPORT UNIT, RAF Halton, Aylesbury, Bucks HP22 5PG. Tel: 01296-623535 ext. 6210. *Commanding Officer*, Gp Capt A. Harris, RAF

DENTISTRY

In order to practise in the UK, a dentist must be entered with the General Dental Council. To be registered a person must be qualified in one of the following ways: hold the degree or diploma in dental surgery of a university in the UK or hold the licentiate in dental surgery awarded by one of the Royal Surgical Colleges in the UK; completed the Council's statutory examination (soon to be replaced by the International Qualifying Examination (IQE)); be an European Community or European Economic Area national holding an appropriate European diploma; hold a registered overseas diploma or be an EEA national holding a primary dental qualification from outside the EEA but has acquired a right to practise in the EEA. The holder of a dental degree or diploma other than those referred to above may be eligible for temporary registration to enable him or her to practise dentistry in the United Kingdom for a limited period and in specified posts without the need to take further examinations. The Dentists Register is maintained by:

GENREAL DENTAL COUNCIL, 37 Wimpole Street, London W1M 8DQ. Tel: 020-7887 3800

SCOTTISH COUNCIL FOR POSTGRADUATE MEDICAL AND
DENTAL EDUCATION, 4th Floor, Hobart House, 80
Hanover Street, Edinburgh EH2 1EL. Tel: 0131-225
4365

DIETETICS

The professional association is the British Dietetic
Association. Full membership is open to dietitians holding
a recognised qualification, who may also become State
Registered Dietitians through the Council for Professions
Supplementary to Medicine (*see* Medicine).
THE BRITISH DIETETIC ASSOCIATION, 7th Floor,
Elizabeth House, 22 Suffolk Street Queensway,
Queensway, Birmingham B1 1LS. Tel: 0121-643 5483

DRAMA

The national validating body for courses providing
training in drama for the professional theatre is the
National Council for Drama Training. It currently has
accredited courses at the following: Academy of Live and
Recorded Arts; Arts Educational Schools; Birmingham
School of Speech Training and Dramatic Art; Bristol Old
Vic Theatre School; Central School of Speech and
Drama; Drama Centre, London; Drama Studio, London;
Guildford School of Acting; Guildhall School of Music
and Drama, London; London Academy of Music and
Dramatic Art; Manchester Metropolitan University
School of Theatre; Mountview Theatre School; Oxford
School of Drama, Woodstock; Queen Margaret Uni-
versity College, Edinburgh; Rose Bruford College, Sid-
cup; Royal Academy of Dramatic Art, London; Royal
Scottish Academy of Music and Drama; Webber Douglas
Academy of Dramatic Art, London; Welsh College of
Music and Drama.
The accreditation of a course in a school does not
necessarily imply that other courses of different type or
duration in the same school are also accredited.
NATIONAL COUNCIL FOR DRAMA TRAINING, 5 Tavistock
Place, London WC1H 9SS. Tel: 020-7387 3650

ENGINEERING

The Engineering Council promotes and leads the
engineering profession through the 38 nominated engineering institutions who are represented on its Board for
Engineers' Regulation. Working with and through the
institutions, the Council sets the standards for the
registration of individuals, and also the accreditation for
academic courses in universities and colleges and the
practical training in industry.
The principal qualifying bodies are:
BRITISH COMPUTER SOCIETY, 1 Sanford Street, Swindon
SN1 1HJ. Tel: 01793-417417. *Chief Executive*, Ms J. Scott
CHARTERED INSTITUTE OF BUILDING SERVICES
ENGINEERS, 222 Balham High Road, London SW12 9BS.
Tel: 020-8675 5211. *Chief Executive*, R. John
INSTITUTION OF CHEMICAL ENGINEERS, Davis Building,
165-189 Railway Terrace, Rugby, Warks CV21 3HQ. Tel:
01788-578214. *Chief Executive*, Dr T. J. Evans
INSTITUTION OF ELECTRICAL ENGINEERS, Savoy Place,
London WC2R 0BL. Tel: 020-7344 5445. *Chief Executive*,
Dr A. Roberts
INSTITUTION OF GAS ENGINEERS, 21 Portland Place,
London W1N 3AF. Tel: 020-7636 6603. *Chief Executive
Officer*, C. Bleach
INSTITUTION OF MECHANICAL ENGINEERS, 1 Birdcage
Walk, London SW1H 9JJ. Tel: 020-7222 7899. *Director-
General*, Sir Michael Moore, KBE, LVO

INSTITUTION OF MINING AND METALLURGY, Danum
House, South Parade, Doncaster, S. Yorks DN1 2DY.
Tel: 01302-320486. *Secretary*, Dr G. J. M. Woodrow
INSTITUTION OF STRUCTURAL ENGINEERS, 11 Upper
Belgrave Street, London SW1X 8BH. Tel: 020-7235 4535.
Chief Executive and Secretary, Dr K. J. Eaton
INSTITUTION OF STRUCTURAL ENGINEERS, (Scottish
Branch), 15 Beresford Place, East Trinity Road,
Edinburgh EH5 3SL. Tel: 0131-552 8852. *Chief Executive
and Secretary*, Dr K. J. Eaton
ROYAL AERONAUTICAL SOCIETY, 4 Hamilton Place,
London W1V 0BQ. Tel: 020-7499 3515. *Director*, K. Mans
ROYAL INSTITUTION OF NAVAL ARCHITECTS, 10 Upper
Belgrave Street, London SW1X 8BQ.
Tel: 020-7235 4622. *Chief Executive*, T. Blakeley
THE ENGINEERING COUNCIL, 10 Maltravers Street,
London WC2R 3ER. Tel: 020-7557 6418
THE INSTITUTE OF MARINE ENGINEERS, 80 Coleman
Street, London EC2R 5BJ. Tel: 020-7382 2600.
Director-General, K. F. Read
THE INSTITUTE OF MATERIALS, 1 Carlton House Terrace,
London SW1Y 5DB. Tel: 020-7451 7300. *Chief Executive*,
Dr B. Rickinson
THE INSTITUTE OF MEASUREMENT AND CONTROL, 87
Gower Street, London WC1E 6AF. Tel: 020-7387 4949.
Secretary, M. Yates
THE INSTITUTION OF CIVIL ENGINEERS, 1 Great George
Street, London SW1P 3AA. Tel: 020-7222 7722. *Chief
Executive and Secretary*, M. Casebourne

FILM AND TELEVISION

Postgraduate training for those intending to make a career
in film, television and media production is provided by the
National Film and Television School, which provides
courses in animation direction, documentary direction,
fiction direction, producing, screenwriting, screen design,
editing, cinematography, screen sound, screen music and
television producing/direction. Short courses, enabling
professionals to update or expand their skills are run by the
National Short Course Training Programme. There is
also the Finishing School, a new industry-accredited,
Digital Post-Production training workshop and creative
laboratory.
NATIONAL FILM AND TELEVISION SCHOOL, Station Road,
Beaconsfield. Bucks HP9 1LJ. Tel: 01494-671234 ext.
205. *Director* S. Bayly

FORESTRY AND TIMBER STUDIES

Professional organisations include:
COMMONWEALTH FORESTRY ASSOCIATION, c/o Oxford
Forestry Institute, South Parks Road, Oxford OX1 3RB.
Tel: 01865-271037. *Chairman*, Dr J. S. Maini
INSTITUTE OF CHARTERED FORESTERS, 7A St Colme
Street, Edinburgh EH3 6AA. Tel: 0131-225 2705.
Executive Director, Mrs M. W. Dick, FRSA
ROYAL FORESTRY SOCIETY OF ENGLAND, WALES AND
NORTHERN IRELAND, 102 High Street, Tring, Herts
HP23 4AF. Tel: 01442-822028. *Director*, Dr J. E. Jackson
ROYAL SCOTTISH FORESTRY SOCIETY, Hagg-on-Esk,
Canonbie, Dumfriesshire DG14 0BE. Tel: 01387-371518.
President, P. J. Fothergill

FUEL AND ENERGY SCIENCE

The principal professional bodies are:
THE INSTITUTE OF PETROLEUM, 61 New Cavendish
Street, London W1M 8AR. Tel: 020-7467 7100.
Director-General, J. Pym

HOTELKEEPING, CATERING AND INSTITUTIONAL MANAGEMENT

The qualifying professional body in these areas is:
HOTEL AND CATERING INTERNATIONAL MANAGEMENT ASSOCIATION, 191 Trinity Road, London SW17 7HN. Tel: 020-8672 4251. *Chief Executive*, D. Wood

INDUSTRIAL AND VOCATIONAL TRAINING

The NTO National Council represents the network of employer-led national training organisations (NTOs). NTOs represent the education and training interests of their respective sectors to government and ensure the development and adoption of occupational standards, particularly through National and Scottish Vocational Qualifications and learning initiatives including Modern Apprenticeship and National Traineeship.
NTO NATIONAL COUNCIL, 10 Meadowcourt, Amos Road, Sheffield S9 1BX. Tel: 0114-261 9926

INSURANCE

Organisations conducting examinations and awarding diplomas are:
ASSOCIATION OF AVERAGE ADJUSTERS, The Baltic Exchange, St Mary Axe, London EC3A 8BH. Tel: 020-7623 5501. *Chairman*, M. Duncan
THE CHARTERED INSTITUTE OF LOSS ADJUSTERS, Peninsular House, 36 Monument Street, London EC3R 8LJ. Tel: 020-7337 9960. *Executive Director*, G. L. Cave
THE CHARTERED INSURANCE INSTITUTE, 20 Aldermanbury, London EC2V 7HY. Tel: 020-8989 8464. *Director-General*, D. Bland

JOURNALISM

Courses for trainee newspaper journalists are available at 30 centres. One-year full-time courses are available for selected students and 18-week courses for graduates. Particulars of all these courses are available from the National Council for the Training of Journalists (NCTJ). Short courses for mid-career development can be arranged, as can various distance learning courses. The NCTJ also offers Assessor, Internal Verifier (IV) and Accreditation of Prior Achievement (APA) training, and NVQs.

For periodical journalists, there are nine centres running courses approved by the Periodicals Training Council (PTC). The PTC also offers NVQs and information on best practice training.
NATIONAL COUNCIL FOR THE TRAINING OF JOURNALISTS, Latton Bush Centre, Southern Way, Harlow, Essex CM18 7BL. Tel: 01279-430009
THE PERIODICALS TRAINING COUNCIL, Queens House, 55–56 Lincoln Inn Field, London WC2A 3LJ. Tel: 020-7404 4168

LAW

THE BAR

Admission to the Bar of England and Wales is controlled by the Inns of Court, admission to the Bar of Northern Ireland by the Honorable Society of the Inn of Court of Northern Ireland and admission as an Advocate of the Scottish Bar is controlled by the Faculty of Advocates. The governing body of the barristers' branch of the legal profession in England and Wales is the General Council of the Bar (the Bar Council). The governing body in Northern Ireland is the Honorable Society of the Inn of Court of Northern Ireland, and the Faculty of Advocates is the governing body of the Scottish Bar. The education and examination of students training for the Bar of England and Wales is regulated by the General Council of the Bar. Those who intend to practise at the Bar of England and Wales must pass the Bar's vocational course. The Inns of Court School of Law is the largest provider of initial training for those wishing to practise at the Bar, but seven other institutions have been validated to provide the course. Applications are handled by the Bar Council's Centralised Applications Clearing House (CACH).

CACH, THE EDUCATION AND TRAINING DEPARTMENT, The General Council of the Bar, 2–3 Curistor Street, London EC4A 1NE. Tel: 020-7440 4000. *Chief Executive*, N. Morison
FACULTY OF ADVOCATES, Advocates Library, Parliament House, Edinburgh EH1 1RF. Tel: 0131-226 5071. *Dean*, G. N. H. Emslie, QC
THE GENERAL COUNCIL OF THE BAR, 3 Bedford Row, London WC1R 4DB. Tel: 020-7242 0082
THE HONORABLE SOCIETY OF THE INN OF COURT OF NORTHERN IRELAND, Royal Courts of Justice, Belfast BT1 3JF. Tel: 028-9023 5111
INNS OF COURT SCHOOL OF LAW, 4 Gray's Inn Place, Gray's Inn, London WC1R 5DX. Tel: 020-7404 5787

The Inns of Court

GRAY'S INN, 8 South Square, London WC1R 5ET. Tel: 020-7458 7800. *Treasurer*, L. Read, QC
INNER TEMPLE, London EC4Y 7HL. Tel: 020-7797 8250. *Treasurer*, S. Brodie, QC
LINCOLN'S INN, London WC2A 3TL. Tel: 020-7405 1393. *Under-Treasurer*, Col. D. Hills, MBE
MIDDLE TEMPLE, London EC4Y 9AT. Tel: 020-7427 4800. *Treasurer*, The Hon. Sir Charles McCullogh

SOLICITORS

Qualifications for solicitors are obtainable only from one of the Law Societies, which control the education and examination of trainee solicitors and the admission of solicitors.
THE COLLEGE OF LAW, Braboeuf Manor, St Catherine's, Guildford, Surrey GU3 1HA. Tel: 01483-460200
THE LAW SOCIETY OF ENGLAND AND WALES, 113 Chancery Lane, London WC2A 1PL. Tel: 020-7320 5902
LAW SOCIETY OF NORTHERN IRELAND, Law Society House, 98 Victoria Street, Belfast BT1 3JZ. Tel: 028-9023 1614. *Chief Executive and Secretary*, J. W. Bailie
LAW SOCIETY OF SCOTLAND, 26 Drumsheugh Gardens, Edinburgh EH3 7YR. Tel: 0131-226 7411
OFFICE FOR THE SUPERVISION OF SOLICITORS, Victoria Court, 8 Dormer Place, Leamington Spa, Warks CV32 5AE. Tel: 01926-820082. *Director*, J. Wagstaffe

LIBRARIANSHIP AND INFORMATION SCIENCE/MANAGEMENT

The Library Association accredits degree and postgraduate courses in library and information science which are offered by 17 universities in the UK. A full list of accredited degree and postgraduate courses is available from its Information Services and on its web site (http://www.la-hq.org.uk) The Association also maintains a professional register of Chartered Members.
THE LIBRARY ASSOCIATION, 7 Ridgmount Street, London WC1E 7AE. Tel: 020-7636 7543

MEDICINE

All doctors must be registered with the General Medical Council. In order to register, medical students must complete an undergraduate medical degree at one of the

19 universities with medical schools, followed by a year of general clinical training. Once registered, doctors undertake general professional and basic specialist training as senior house officers. Further specialist training is provided by the royal colleges, faculties and societies listed below. The General Medical Council keeps a register of those doctors who have been awarded Certificates of Completion of Specialist Training.

The United Examining Board holds qualifying examinations for candidates who have trained overseas. These candidates must also have spent a period at a UK medical school.

GENERAL MEDICAL COUNCIL, 178 Great Portland Street, London W1N 6JE. Tel: 020-7580 7642

UNITED EXAMINING BOARD, Apothecaries Hall, Black Friars Lane, London EC4V 6EJ. Tel: 020-7236 1180. *Chairman*, Prof J. S. P. Lumley

COLLEGES/SOCIETIES HOLDING POSTGRADUATE MEMBERSHIP AND DIPLOMA EXAMINATIONS

FACULTY OF ACCIDENT AND EMERGENCY MEDICINE, Royal College of Surgeons of England, 35–43 Lincoln's Inn Fields, London WC2A 3PN. Tel: 020-7405 7071. *President*, I. W. R. Anderson

FACULTY OF PUBLIC HEALTH MEDICINE, 4 St Andrews Place, London NW1 4LB. Tel: 020-7935 0243. *Faculty Secretary*, P. Scourfield

ROYAL COLLEGE OF ANAESTHETISTS, 48–49 Russell Square, London WC1B 4JY. Tel: 020-7813 1900. *President*, Prof. P. Hatton

ROYAL COLLEGE OF OBSTETRICIANS AND GYNAECOLOGISTS, 27 Sussex Place, Regent's Park, London NW1 4RG. Tel: 020-7772 6200. *President*, Prof. R. Shaw

ROYAL COLLEGE OF PAEDIATRICS AND CHILD HEALTH, 50 Hallam Street, London W1W 6DE. Tel: 020-7307 5600. *Secretary*, L. Tyler

ROYAL COLLEGE OF PATHOLOGISTS, 2 Carlton House Terrace, London SW1Y 5AF. Tel: 020-7451 6700. *College Secretary*, D. Ross

ROYAL COLLEGE OF PHYSICIANS, 11 St Andrews Place, Regent's Park, London NW1 4LE. Tel: 020-7935 1174. *President*, Prof. Sir George Alberti

ROYAL COLLEGE OF PHYSICIANS AND SURGEONS OF GLASGOW, 232–242 St Vincent Street, Glasgow G2 5RJ. Tel: 0141-221 6072. *President*, Prof. A. R. Lorimer, FRCPGlasg.

ROYAL COLLEGE OF PHYSICIANS OF EDINBURGH, 9 Queen Street, Edinburgh EH2 1JQ. Tel: 0131-225 7324. *President*, Prof. J. C. Petrie

ROYAL COLLEGE OF PSYCHIATRISTS, 17 Belgrave Square, London SW1X 8PG. Tel: 020-7235 2351. *President*, Prof. J. L. Cox

ROYAL COLLEGE OF RADIOLOGISTS, 38 Portland Place, London W1N 4JQ. Tel: 020-7636 4432. *President*, Prof. P. Armstrong

ROYAL COLLEGE OF SURGEONS OF EDINBURGH, Nicolson Street, Edinburgh EH8 9DW. Tel: 0131-527 1600. *President*, Prof. J. G. Temple

THE ROYAL COLLEGE OF SURGEONS OF ENGLAND, 35–43 Lincoln's Inn Fields, London WC2A 3PN. Tel: 020-7405 3474. *President*, B. Jackson

SOCIETY OF APOTHECARIES OF LONDON, 14 Black Friars Lane, London EC4V 6EJ. Tel: 020-7236 1189. *Clerk*, R. J. Stringer

PROFESSIONS SUPPLEMENTARY TO MEDICINE

The standard of professional education in art, drama and music therapies, biomedical sciences, chiropody, dietetics,

occupational therapy, orthoptics, prosthetics and orthotics, physiotherapy and radiography is the responsibility of nine professional boards, which also publish an annual register of qualified practitioners. The work of the boards is co-ordinated by the Council for Professions Supplementary to Medicine.

In January 2000 three new boards were established, covering speech and language therapists, clinical scientists and paramedics.

COUNCIL FOR PROFESSIONS SUPPLEMENTARY TO MEDICINE, Park House, 184 Kennington Park Road, London SE11 4BU. Tel: 020-7582 0866

ART, DRAMA AND MUSIC THERAPIES

A postgraduate qualification in the relevant therapy is required. There are five institutions in the UK offering courses in art therapy and six offering courses in music therapy.

ASSOCIATION OF PROFESSIONAL MUSIC THERAPISTS, 26 Hamlyn Road, Glastonbury, Somerset BA6 8HT. Tel: 01458-834919. *Administrator*, Mrs D. Asbridge

BRITISH ASSOCIATION OF ART THERAPISTS, Mary Ward House, 5 Tavistock Place, London WC1H 9SN. Tel: 020-7383 3774. *Administrator*, Ms D. Haworth

BRITISH ASSOCIATION OF DRAMATHERAPISTS, 41 Broomhouse Lane, London SW6 3DP. Tel: 020-7731 0160. *Administrator*, Ms J. Eckley

BIOMEDICAL SCIENCES

Qualifications from higher education establishments and training in medical laboratories are required for membership of the Institute of Biomedical Science.

INSTITUTE OF BIOMEDICAL SCIENCES, 12 Coldbath Square, London EC1R 5HL. Tel: 020-7713 0214

CHIROPODY

Professional recognition is granted by the Society of Chiropodists and Podiatrists to students who are awarded B.Sc. degrees in Podiatry or Podiatric Medicine after attending a course of full-time training for three or four years at one of the 13 recognised schools in the UK (ten in England and Wales, two in Scotland and one in Northern Ireland). Qualifications granted and degrees recognised by the Society are approved by the Chiropodists Board for the purpose of State Registration, which is a condition of employment within the National Health Service.

SOCIETY OF CHIROPODISTS AND PODIATRISTS, 53 Welbeck Street, London W1M 7HE. Tel: 020-7486 3381

OCCUPATIONAL THERAPY

The professional qualification may be obtained upon successful completion of a validated course in any of the 28 institutions approved by the College of Occupational Therapists. The courses are normally degree-level courses based in higher education institutions.

COLLEGE OF OCCUPATIONAL THERAPISTS, 106–114 Borough High Street, London SE1 1LB. Tel: 020-7357 6480

FACULTY OF OCCUPATIONAL MEDICINE, 6 St Andrew's Place, London NW1 4LB. Tel: 020-7317 5890. *Secretary*, Ms F. Quinn

ORTHOPTICS

Orthoptists undertake the diagnosis and treatment of all types of squint and other anomalies of binocular vision, working in close collaboration with ophthalmologists. The training and maintenance of professional standards are the responsibility of the Orthoptists Board of the Council for the Professions Supplementary to Medicine.

The professional body is the British Orthoptic Society. Training is at degree level.

THE BRITISH ORTHOPTIC SOCIETY, Tavistock House North, Tavistock Square, London WC1H 9HX. Tel: 020-7387 7992

PHYSIOTHERAPY

Full-time three- or four-year degree courses are available at 30 higher education institutions in the UK. Information about courses leading to eligibility for Membership of the Chartered Society of Physiotherapy and to State Registration is available from the Chartered Society of Physiotherapy.

THE CHARTERED SOCIETY OF PHYSIOTHERAPY, 14 Bedford Row, London WC1R 4ED. Tel: 020-7306 6666

PROSTHETICS AND ORTHOTICS

Prosthetists provide artificial limbs, while orthotists provide devices to support or control a part of the body. It is necessary to obtain an honours degree to become a prosthetist/orthotist. Courses are available at two institutions in the UK.

BRITISH ASSOCIATION OF PROSTHETISTS AND ORTHOTISTS, Sir James Clark Building, Abbey Mill Business Centre, Paisley PA1 1TJ. Tel: 0141-561 7217

RADIOGRAPHY AND RADIOTHERAPY

In order to practise both diagnostic and therapeutic radiography in the UK, it is necessary to have successfully completed a course of education and training recognised by the Privy Council. Such courses are offered by universities throughout the UK and lead to the award of a degree in radiography. Further information is available from the college.

COLLEGE OF RADIOGRAPHERS, 2 Carriage Row, 183 Eversholt Street, London NW1 1BU. Tel: 020-7740 7200

COMPLEMENTARY MEDICINE

Professional courses are validated by:

INSTITUTE FOR COMPLEMENTARY MEDICINE, PO Box 194, London SE16 7QZ. Tel: 020-7237 5165. *Director*, A. Baird

MERCHANT NAVY TRAINING SCHOOLS

OFFICERS

WARSASH MARITIME CENTRE, Southampton Institute, Newtown Road, Warsash, Southampton SO31 9ZL. Tel: 01489-576161. *Dean*, Capt G. B. Angas

SEAFARERS

NATIONAL SEA TRAINING CENTRE, North West Kent College, Dering Way, Gravesend, Kent DA12 2JJ. Tel: 01322-629600. *Director of Faculty - NSTC*, R. Macdonald

MUSIC

The Associated Board of the Royal Schools of Music conducts graded music examinations in over 80 countries and provides other services to music education through its professional development department and publishing company.

ASSOCIATED BOARD OF THE ROYAL SCHOOLS OF MUSIC, 14 Bedford Square, London WC1B 3JG. Tel: 020-7636 5400. *Chief Executive*, R. Morris

GUILDHALL SCHOOL OF MUSIC AND DRAMA, Silk Street, Barbican, London EC2Y 8DT. Tel: 020-7628 2571. *Principal*, Dr I. Horsbrugh

LONDON COLLEGE OF MUSIC AND MEDIA, Thames Valley University, St Mary's Road, London W5 5RF. Tel: 020-8231 2304. *Director and Dean*, Mrs P. Thompson

ROYAL ACADEMY OF MUSIC, Marylebone Road, London NW1 5HT. Tel: 020-7873 7373. *Principal*, C. Price

ROYAL COLLEGE OF ORGANISTS, 7 St Andrew Street, London EC4A 3LQ. Tel: 020-7936 3606. *Senior Executive*, A. Dear

ROYAL NORTHERN COLLEGE OF MUSIC, 124 Oxford Road, Manchester M13 9RD. Tel: 0161-907 5200. *Principal*, Prof. E. Gregson

ROYAL SCOTTISH ACADEMY OF MUSIC AND DRAMA, 100 Renfrew Street, Glasgow G2 3DB. Tel: 0141-332 4101. *Principal*, Sir Philip Ledger, CBE

TRINITY COLLEGE OF MUSIC, 11–13 Mandeville Place, London W1M 6AQ. Tel: 020-7487 9647. *Principal*, G. Henderson

NURSING

All nurses must be registered with the UK Central Council for Nursing, Midwifery and Health Visiting. Courses leading to registration as a nurse are at least three years in length. There are also some programmes which are combined with degrees. Students study in colleges of nursing or in institutions of higher education. Courses offer a combination of theoretical and practical experience in a variety of settings. Different courses lead to different types of registration, including: Registered Nurse (RN), Registered Mental Nurse (RMN), Registered Mental Handicap Nurse (RMHN), Registered Sick Children's Nurse (RSCN), Registered Midwife (RM) and Registered Health Visitor (RHV). The various national boards, listed below, are responsible for validating courses in nursing. In February 1999 the Government announced plans to replace these boards and the UK Central Council with a single UK-wide body. Health visitors will continue to have separate registration and representation on the new body.

The Royal College of Nursing is the largest professional union representing nurses and provides higher education through its Institute.

ENGLISH NATIONAL BOARD FOR NURSING, MIDWIFERY AND HEALTH VISITING, Victory House, 170 Tottenham Court Road, London W1P 0HA. Tel: 020-7391 6229. *Chief Executive*, A. P. Smith, CBE

NATIONAL BOARD FOR NURSING, MIDWIFERY AND HEALTH VISITING FOR NORTHERN IRELAND, Centre House, 79 Chichester Street, Belfast BT1 4JE. Tel: 028-9023 8152. *Chief Executive*, Prof. O. D'A Slevin

NATIONAL BOARD FOR NURSING, MIDWIFERY AND HEALTH VISITING FOR SCOTLAND, 22 Queen Street, Edinburgh EH2 1NT. Tel: 0131-226 7371. *Chief Executive*, D. C. Benton

UK CENTRAL COUNCIL FOR NURSING, MIDWIFERY AND HEALTH VISITING, 23 Portland Place, London W1N 4JT. Tel: 020-7637 7181

WELSH NATIONAL BOARD FOR NURSING, MIDWIFERY AND HEALTH VISITING, 2nd Floor, Golate House, 101 St Mary Street, Cardiff CF10 1DX. Tel: 029-2026 1400. *Chief Executive*, D. A. Ravey

OPHTHALMIC AND DISPENSING OPTICS

Professional bodies are:

THE ASSOCIATION OF BRITISH DISPENSING OPTICIANS, 6 Hurlingham Business Park, Sulivan Road, London SW6 3DU. Tel: 020-7736 0088. *General-Secretary*, Sir Anthony Garrett, CBE

THE COLLEGE OF OPTOMETRISTS, 42 Craven Street, London WC2N 5NG. Tel: 020-7839 6000. *Secretary*, P. D. Leigh

OSTEOPATHY

Osteopathy is the first of the professions previously outside conventional medical sevrvices to achieve statutory recognition under a new body the General Osteopathic Council. Since May 2000 all pracitising osteopaths have had to be registered with the Gencral Osteopathic Council and the title 'osteopath' is protected by law. To gain entry to the register all newly qualified osteopaths have to be in possession of a recognised qualification from a course of training accredited by the General Osteopathic Council. The General Osteopathic Council is responsible for regulating, developing, and promoting the profession.
GENERAL OSTEOPATHIC COUNCIL, Osteopathy House, 176 Tower Bridge Road, London SE1 3LU.
Tel: 020-7357 6655

PHARMACY

Information may be obtained from the Secretary and Registrar of the Royal Pharmaceutical Society of Great Britain.
FACULTY OF PHARMACEUTICAL MEDICINE, 1 St Andrew's Place, London NW1 4LB. Tel: 020-7224 0343. *Faculty Administrator*, Mrs K. Swanston

PHOTOGRAPHY

The professional body is:
BRITISH INSTITUTE OF PROFESSIONAL PHOTOGRAPHY, Fox Talbot House, Amwell End, Ware, Herts SG12 9HN.
Tel: 01920-464011. *Chief Executive*, A. Mair

PRINTING

Details of training courses in printing can be obtained from the Institute of Printing and the British Printing Industries Federation. In addition to these examining and organising bodies, examinations are held by various independent regional examining boards in further education.
BRITISH PRINTING INDUSTRIES FEDERATION, 11 Bedford Row, London WC1R 4DX. Tel: 020-7915 8300
INSTITUTE OF PRINTING, The Mews, Hill House, Clanricarde Road, Tunbridge Wells, Kent TN1 1PJ.
Tel: 01892-538118

SCIENCE

Professional qualifications are awarded by:
THE INSTITUTE OF BIOLOGY, 20–22 Queensberry Place, London SW7 2DZ. Tel: 020-7581 8333. *Chief Executive*, Prof. A. D. B. Malcolm
THE ROYAL SOCIETY OF CHEMISTRY, Burlington House, Piccadilly, London W1V 0BN. Tel: 020-7437 8656. *Secretary-General and Chief Executive*, Dr D. Giachardi
THE INSTITUTE OF PHYSICS, 76 Portland Place, London W1N 3DH. Tel: 020-7470 4800. *Chief Executive*, Dr A. Jones

SPEECH AND LANGUAGE THERAPY

The Royal College of Speech and Language Therapists provides details of courses leading to qualification as a speech and language therapist. Other professionals may become Affiliates of the College. A directory of registered members is published annually.
ROYAL COLLEGE OF SPEECH AND LANGUAGE THERAPISTS, 2 White Hart Yard, London SE1 1NX. Tel: 020-7378 1200

SURVEYING

The qualifying professional bodies include:
ARCHITECTURE AND SURVEYING INSTITUTE, St Mary House, 15 St Mary Street, Chippenham, Wilts SN15 3WD. Tel: 01249-444505. *Chief Executive*, I. N. Norris
ASSOCIATION OF BUILDING ENGINEERS, Lutyens House, Billing Brook Road, Weston Favell, Northampton NN3 8NW. Tel: 01604-404121. *Chief Executive*, D. R. Gibson
INSTITUTE OF REVENUES, RATING AND VALUATION, 41 Doughty Street, London WC1N 2LF. Tel: 020-7831 3505. *Director*, Ms K. Aldred
THE ROYAL INSTITUTION OF CHARTERED SURVEYORS, 12 Great George Street, London SW1P 3AD. Tel: 020-7222 7000. *Chief Executive*, J. H. A. J. Armstrong

TEACHING

Teachers in maintained schools must acquire Qualified Teacher Status (QTS) by completing a programme of Initial Teacher Training. Those without a first degree may take a Bachelor of Education (B.Ed) or a Bachelor of Arts/Science (BA/B.Sc) with QTS, full-time for three or four years, depending on the programme followed. These degrees combine subject and professional studies with teaching practice. Shortened courses of these degrees are available for those who have successfully completed one or two years of higher education. Flexible routes into teaching are increasing, including part-time, distance learning and modular courses. Alternatively, teachers can gain QTS through employment-based training, following individual training plans while in post.

For those who already have a first degree, the most common route is through a one-year Postgraduate Certificate of Education (PGCE). This may be taken full-time or part-time, or as a distance-learning programme. Postgraduates may also gain QTS through training in a school (School-Centred Initial Teacher Training). Since January 1998, graduates have been able to join the Graduate Teacher Programme which provides teaching and training for one year.

Details of courses in England and Wales are contained in the *NATFHE Handbook of Initial Teacher Training in England and Wales 2000*, in *University and College Entrance: 2000 (The Big Book)* published by UCAS and on the UCAS website (http://www.ucas.ac.uk). Further information about teaching in England and Wales is available from the Teaching Information Line, 01245-454454. Details of courses in Scotland can be obtained from universities and the Graduate Teacher Training Registry (GTTR). Each university chooses whether to receive applications direct or through the GTTR. Details of courses in Northern Ireland can be obtained from the Department of Education for Northern Ireland. Applications for teacher training courses in Northern Ireland are made to the institutions direct.
TEACHER TRAINING AGENCY, Portland House, Stag Place, London SW1E 5TT. Tel: 020-7925 3755

TEXTILES

THE TEXTILE INSTITUTE, 4th Floor, St James's Buildings, Oxford Street, Manchester M1 6FQ. Tel: 0161-237 1188. *Director-General*, T. D. Hennessey

THEOLOGICAL COLLEGES

The current approximate number of students training for the ministry is shown in parenthesis.

ANGLICAN

COLLEGE OF THE RESURRECTION, Mirfield, W. Yorks WF14 0BW. Tel: 01924-490441. (40). *Principal*, Revd C. Irvine

CRANMER HALL, St John's College, Durham DH1 3RJ. Tel: 0191-374 3579. (60). *Principal*, The Rt. Revd S. W. Sykes

OAK HILL COLLEGE, Chase Side, Southgate, London N14 4PS. Tel: 0208-449 0467. (90). *Principal*, Revd Dr D. Peterson

RIDLEY HALL, Cambridge CB3 9HG. Tel: 01223-741080. (109). *Principal*, Revd G. Cray

RIPON COLLEGE, Cuddesdon, Oxford OX44 9EX. Tel: 01865-874427. (75). *Principal*, Revd J. Clarke

ST JOHN'S COLLEGE, Chilwell Lane, Bramcote, Nottingham NG9 3DS. Tel: 0115-925 1114. (110). *Principal*, Canon Dr C. Baxter

ST MICHAEL'S THEOLOGICAL COLLEGE, Llandaff, Cardiff CF5 2YJ. Tel: 029-2056 3379. (30). *Principal*, Revd Dr J. Holdsworth

ST STEPHEN'S HOUSE, 16 Marston Street, Oxford OX4 1JX. Tel: 01865-247874. (60). *Principal*, Revd Dr J. P. Sheehy

THEOLOGICAL INSTITUTE OF THE SCOTTISH EPISCOPAL CHURCH, Old Coates House, 32 Manor Place, Edinburgh EH3 7EB. Tel: 0131-220 2272. (28). *Principal*, Revd Canon Dr M. Fuller

TRINITY COLLEGE, Stoke Hill, Bristol BS9 1JP. Tel: 0117-968 2803. (200). *Principal*, Revd Dr F. Bridger

WESTCOTT HOUSE, Jesus Lane, Cambridge CB5 8BP. Tel: 01223-741000. (65). *Principal*, Revd M. Roberts

WYCLIFFE HALL THEOLOGICAL COLLEGE, 54 Banbury Road, Oxford OX2 6PW. Tel: 01865-274200. (70). *Principal*, Revd Prof. A. E. McGrath

BAPTIST

BRISTOL BAPTIST COLLEGE, The Promenade, Clifton, Bristol BS8 3NF. Tel: 0117-946 7050. (26). *Principal*, Revd C. Ellis

NORTHERN BAPTIST COLLEGE, Luther King House, Brighton Grove, Rusholme, Manchester M14 5JP. Tel: 0161-224 6404. (30). *Principal*, Revd Dr R. Kidd

NORTH WALES BAPTIST COLLEGE, Ffordd Ffriddoedd, Bangor LL57 2EH. Tel: 01248-362608. (6). *Warden*, Revd Dr D. D. Morgan

REGENT'S PARK COLLEGE, Oxford OX1 2LB. Tel: 01865-288120. (25). *Principal*, Revd Dr P. S. Fiddes

THE SCOTTISH BAPTIST COLLEGE, 12 Aytoun Road, Glasgow G41 5RN. Tel: 0141-424 0747. (14). *Principal*, Dr K. B. E. Roxburgh

SOUTH WALES BAPTIST COLLEGE, 54 Richmond Road, Cardiff CF24 3UR. Tel: 029-2025 6066. (26). *Principal*, Revd D. H. Matthews

CHURCH OF SCOTLAND

NEW COLLEGE, Mound Place, Edinburgh EH1 2LX. Tel: 0131-650 8916. (20). *Principal*, Revd Dr D. Lyall

TRINITY COLLEGE, Faculty of Divinity, University of Glasgow, Glasgow G12 8QQ. Tel: 0141-330 6840. (20). *Principal*, Revd Dr D. M. Murray

CONGREGATIONAL

SCOTTISH CONGREGATIONAL COLLEGE, 340 Cathedral Street, Glasgow G1 2BQ. Tel: 0141-332 7667. (4). *Principal*, Revd J. W. Dyce

ECUMERICAL

THE QUEEN'S FOUNDATION FOR ECUMERICAL THEOLOGICAL INFORMATION, Somerset Road, Edgbaston, Birmingham B15 2QH, Tel: 0121-454 1527. (120). *Principal*, Revd P. Fisher

METHODIST

EDGHILL THEOLOGICAL COLLEGE, 9 Lennoxvale, Belfast BT9 5BY. Tel: 028-9066 5870. (25). *Principal*, Dr D. Cooke

HARTLEY VICTORIA COLLEGE, Luther King House, Brighton Grove, Rusholme, Manchester M14 5JP. Tel: 0161-249 2516. (40). *Principal*, Revd Dr J. A. Harrod

WESLEY COLLEGE, College Park Drive, Henbury Road, Bristol BS10 7QD. Tel: 0117-959 1200. *Principal*, Revd Dr N. Richardson

WESLEY THEOLOGICAL COLLEGE, Wesley House, Jesus Lane, Cambridge CB5 8BJ. Tel: 01223-741033. (30). *Principal*, Revd Dr P. Luscombe

WESLEY STUDY CENTRE, 55 The Avenue, Durham DH1 4EB. Tel: 0191-374 3580. (25). *Director*, Revd R. Walton

NON-DENOMINATIONAL

CHRIST'S COLLEGE, 25 High Street, Old Aberdeen, Aberdeen AB24 3EE. Tel: 01224-272138. (30). *Master*, Very Revd Prof. A. Main

ST MARY'S COLLEGE, The University, St Andrews, Fife KY16 9JU. Tel: 01334-462850. (175). *Principal*, Prof. R. A. Piper

SPURGEON'S COLLEGE, South Norwood Hill, London SE25 6DJ. Tel: 020-8653 0850. (100). *Principal*, Revd Dr N. Wright

PRESBYTERIAN

UNION THEOLOGICAL COLLEGE, 108 Botanic Avenue, Belfast BT7 1JT. Tel: 028-9062 4574 ext 24. (186). *Principal*, Revd J. C. McCullough

PRESBYTERIAN CHURCH OF WALES

UNITED THEOLOGICAL COLLEGE, Aberystwyth, Ceredigion SY23 2LT. Tel: 01970-624574. (3). *Principal*, Revd Dr J. Tudno Williams

ROMAN CATHOLIC

ALLEN HALL, 28 Beaufort Street, London SW3 5AA. Tel: 020-7351 1296. (40). *Rector*, Revd J. Overton

CAMPION HOUSE COLLEGE, 112 Thornbury Road, Isleworth, Middx TW7 4NN. Tel: 020-8560 1924. (12). *Principal*, Revd M. Barrow SJ

OSCOTT COLLEGE, Chester Road, Sutton Coldfield, West Midlands B73 5AA. Tel: 0121-354 2490. (40). *Rector*, Monsignor K. McDonald

ST JOHN'S SEMINARY, Wonersh, Guildford, Surrey GU5 0QX. (45). Tel: 01483-892217. *Rector*, Revd K. Haggerty

SCOTUS COLLEGE, 2 Chesters Road, Bearsden, Glasgow G61 4AG. Tel: 0141-942 8384. (21). *Rector*, Revd N. Donnachie

USHAW COLLEGE, Durham DH7 9RH. Tel: 0191-373 1366. (40). *President*, Revd J. O'Keefe

UNITARIAN

UNITARIAN COLLEGE, Luther King House, Brighton Grove, Rusholme, Manchester M14 5JP. Tel: 0161-224 2849. (5). *Principal*, Revd Dr L. Smith

UNITED REFORMED

NORTHERN COLLEGE, Luther King House, Brighton Grove, Rusholme, Manchester M14 5JP. (49). Tel: 0161-224 4381. *Principal*, Revd Dr D. R. Peel

WESTMINSTER COLLEGE, Madingley Road, Cambridge CB3 0AA. Tel: 01223-741084. (45). *Principal*, Revd Dr D. Cornick

JEWISH

LONDON SCHOOL OF JEWISH STUDIES, Schaller House,
44a Albert Road, London NW4 2SJ. Tel: 020-8203 6427.
(10). *Principal*, Dr A. Weiss

LEO BAECK COLLEGE, Sternberg Centre for Judaism, 80
East End Road, London N3 2SY. Tel: 020-8349 5600.
(27). *Principal*, Rabbi Prof. J. Magonet

VETERINARY MEDICINE

The regulatory body for veterinary medicine is the Royal
College of Veterinary Surgeons, which keeps the register
of those entitled to practise veterinary medicine. In
order to be registered, a person must complete a five-year
undergraduate degree (BVetMed, BVSc., BVMS, BVM
and S) at one of the six authorised institutions in the UK.

The British Veterinary Association is the professional
body representing veterinary surgeons. The British
Veterinary Nursing Association is the professional body
representing veterinary nurses who are also registered
with the Royal College of Veterinary Surgeons.

BRITISH VETERINARY NURSING ASSOCIATION, Terminus
House, Terminus Street, Harlow, Essex CM20 1XA.
Tel: 01279-450567

ROYAL COLLEGE OF VETERINARY SURGEONS, Belgravia
House, 62-64 Horseferry Road, London SW1P 2AF.
Tel: 020-7222 2001

Independent Schools

The following pages list those independent schools whose Head is a member of the Headmasters' and Headmistresses' Conference, the Society of Headmasters and Headmistresses of Independent Schools or the Girls' Schools Association.

THE HEADMASTERS' AND HEADMISTRESSES' CONFERENCE

Chairman (2000), T. D. Wheare (Bryanston); (from Jan. 2001) C. D. Brown (Norwich)
Secretary, G. H. Lucas, 130 Regent Road, Leicester LE1 7PG

Membership Secretary, D. E. Prince
† Girls in VI form
‡ Co-educational

Name of School	Founded	No. of pupils	Annual fees £ Boarding	Day	Head (with date of appointment)
ENGLAND AND WALES					
Abbotsholme School, Rocester	1889	220‡	14,519	7,008	Dr S. Tommis (1999)
Abingdon School, Oxon	1256	790	13,155	7,170	M. St J. Parker (1975)
Ackworth School, W. Yorks	1779	340‡	12,033	6,843	M. J. Dickinson (1995)
Aldenham School, Elstree, Herts	1597	405†	14,490	10,215	R. S. Harman (2000)
Alleyn's School, London SE22	1619	920‡	—	7,425	Dr C. H. R. Niven (1992)
Ampleforth College (*RC*), N. Yorks	1802	505†	14,805	7,644	Revd G. F. L. Chamberlain, OSB (1993)
Ardingly College, Haywards Heath	1858	410‡	14,205	10,650	J. Franklin (1998)
Arnold School, Blackpool	1896	800‡	—	4,900	W. T. Gillen (1993)
Ashville College, Harrogate	1877	586‡	11,800	6,350	M. H. Crosby (1987)
Bablake School, Coventry	1560	850‡	—	4,497	Dr S. Nuttall (1991)
Bancroft's School, Woodford Green, Essex	1727	791‡	—	7,398	Dr P. R. Scott (1996)
Barnard Castle School, Co. Durham	1883	495‡	11,181	6,618	M. D. Featherstone (1997)
Batley Grammar School, W. Yorks	1612	450‡	—	5,205	B. Battye (1998)
Bedales School, Petersfield	1893	400‡	16,587	12,681	Mrs A. A. Willcocks (1995)
Bedford Modern School	1566	1100	—	6,114	S. Smith (1997)
Bedford School	1552	662	13,440	8,460	Dr I. P. Evans (1990)
Berkhamsted Collegiate School, Herts	1541	1000‡	13,668	8,592	Dr P. Chadwick (*Principal*) (1996)
Birkdale School, Sheffield	1904	500‡	—	5,766	R. J. Court (1998)
Birkenhead School, Merseyside	1860	581	—	4,776	S. J. Haggett (1988)
Bishop's Stortford College, Herts	1868	367‡	12,498	9,012	J. G. Trotman (1997)
Bloxham School, Banbury	1860	362‡	15,150	11,850	D. K. Exham (1991)
Blundell's School, Tiverton	1604	370‡	14,070	8,580	J. Leigh (1992)
Bolton School	1641	850	—	5,664	A. W. Wright (1983)
Bootham School, York	1823	396‡	12,825	8,385	I. M. Small (1988)
Bradfield College, Reading	1850	580‡	16,125	12,094	P. B. Smith (1985)
Bradford Grammar School	1548	1035‡	—	5,700	S. R. Davidson (1996)
Brentwood School, Essex	1557	1080‡	13,489	7,760	J. A. B. Kelsall (1993)
Brighton College, E. Sussex	1845	545‡	15,423	9,948	Dr A. F. Seldon (1997)
Bristol Cathedral School	1140	450‡	—	5,088	K. J. Riley (1993)
Bristol Grammar School	1532	1030‡	—	5,160	Dr D. J. Mascord (1999)
Bromsgrove School, Worcs	1553	675‡	12,975	7,920	T. M. Taylor (1996)
Bryanston School, Blandford Forum	1928	640‡	16,755	12,507	T. D. Wheare (1983)
Bury Grammar School, Lancs	1573	650	—	4,770	K. Richards (1990)
Canford School, Wimbourne	1923	567	16,170	12,135	J. D. Lever (1992)
Caterham School, Surrey	1811	709	14,817	7,944	R. A. E. Davey (1995)
Charterhouse, Godalming	1611	675	15,588	12,882	Revd J. S. Witheridge (1996)
Cheadle Hulme School, Cheshire	1855	1138	—	5,415	D. J. Wilkinson (1990)
Cheltenham College, Glos	1841	520	15,900	11,955	P. A. Chamberlain (1997)
Chetham's School of Music, Manchester	1653	270	17,595	13,620	Mrs C. J. Moreland (1999)
Chigwell School, Essex	1629	400	12,264	8,067	D. F. Gibbs (1996)
Christ College, Brecon	1541	320	12,102	9,378	D. P. Jones (1996)
Christ's Hospital, Horsham	1552	800‡	varies		— Dr P. C. D. Southern (1996)
Churcher's College, Petersfield	1722	570‡	—	6,555	G. W. Buttle (1988)
City of London Freemen's School, Ashtead	1854	400‡	11,997	7,497	D. C. Haywood (1986)
City of London, London EC4	1442	875	—	7,671	D. Levin (1999)
Clifton College, Bristol	1862	667‡	15,000	10,500	M. S. Spurr (2000)
Colfe's School, London SE12	1652	693‡	—	6,822	Dr D. J. Richardson (1990)

Name of School	Founded	No. of pupils	Annual fees £		Head (with date of appointment)
			Boarding	Day	
Colston's Collegiate School, Bristol	1710	500‡	10,800		4,700 D. G. Crawford (1995)
Cranleigh School, Surrey	1865	480†	15,450		11,553 G. Waller (1997)
Culford School, Bury St Edmunds	1881	365‡	14,211		9,249 J. S. Richardson (1992)
Dame Allan's Boys' School, Newcastle upon Tyne	1705	490†	—		5,022 D. W. Welsh (*Principal*) (1996)
Dauntsey's School, Devizes	1542	660‡	14,025		8,490 S. B. Roberts (1997)
Dean Close School, Cheltenham	1886	433‡	15,930		11,130 Revd T. M. Hastie-Smith (1998)
Denstone College, Uttoxeter	1868	370‡	11,085		7,353 D. M. Derbyshire (1997)
Downside School (*RC*), Somerset	1606	280	14,172		7,260 Revd Dom. A. Sutch (1995)
Dulwich College, London SE21	1619	1400	15,975		8,175 G. G. Able (*Master*) (1997)
Durham School	1414	325‡	12,966		8,487 N. G. Kern (1997)
Eastbourne College	1867	500‡	14,460		9,690 C. M. P. Bush (1993)
Ellesmere College, Shropshire	1884	450‡	13,800		9,141 B. J. Wignall (1996)
Eltham College, London SE9	1842	590†	15,282		7,398 P. J. Henderson (2000)
Emanuel School, London SW11	1594	760‡	—		7,341 Mrs A-M. Sutcliffe (1998)
Epsom College, Surrey	1853	660‡	15,423		9,141 S. B. Borthwick (2000)
Eton College, Windsor	1440	1284	15,660		— J. E. Lewis (1994)
Exeter School	1633	685‡	—		5,535 N. W. Gamble (1992)
Felsted School, Dunmow, Essex	1564	390‡	15,720		11,490 S. C. Roberts (1993)
Forest School, London E17	1834	1000‡	11,826		7,545 A. G. Boggis (*Warden*) (1992)
Framlingham College, Woodbridge, Suffolk	1864	420‡	12,111		7,773 Mrs. G. M. Randall (1994)
Frensham Heights, Farnham	1925	320‡	14,985		10,080 P. M. de Voil (1993)
Giggleswick School, Settle	1499	325‡	15,402		7,830 A. P. Millard (1993)
The Grange School, Northwich, Cheshire	1933	650‡	—		5,080 Mrs J. E. Stephen (1997)
Gresham's School, Holt, Norfolk	1555	525‡	15,555		11,940 J. H. Arkell (1991)
Haberdashers' Aske's School, Elstree, Herts	1690	1100	—		7,650 J. W. R. Goulding (1996)
Haileybury, Hertford	1862	640‡	15,510		11,220 S. A. Westley (*Master*) (1996)
Hampton School, Middx	1556	992	—		7,065 B. R. Martin (1997)
Harrow School, Middx	1572	790	16,860		— B. J. Lenon (1999)
Hereford Cathedral School	1384	600‡	—		6,027 Dr H. C. Tomlinson (1987)
Highgate School, London N6	1565	575	—		8,970 R. P. Kennedy (1989)
Hulme Grammar School, Oldham	1611	604	—		4,455 K. E. Jones (2000)
Hurstpierpoint College, Hassocks, W. Sussex	1849	350‡	13,950		11,295 S. D. A. Meek (1995)
Hymers College, Hull	1889	740	—		4,851 J. C. Morris (1990)
Ipswich School	1390	585	11,274		6,507 I. G. Galbraith (1993)
John Lyon School, Harrow	1876	525	—		7,335 Revd T. J. Wright (1986)
Kelly College, Tavistock	1877	350‡	14,580		9,165 M. Turner (1995)
Kent College, Canterbury	1885	470‡	13,005		7,242 E. B. Halse (1995)
Kimbolton School, Huntingdon	1600	570‡	11,205		6,615 R. V. Peel (1987)
King Edward VI School, Southampton	1553	978‡	—		6,399 P. B. Hamilton (1996)
King Edward VII and Queen Mary School, Lytham St Annes	1908	760‡	—		4,770 P. J. Wilde, (*Principal*) (1999)
King Edward's School, Bath	1552	700‡	—		5,997 P. J. Winter (1993)
King Edward's School, Birmingham	1552	883	—		5,835 R. M. Dancey (*Chief Master*) (1998)
King Edward's School, Witley, Surrey	1553	465‡	12,465		8,225 K. Fulton-Peebles (2000)
King Henry VIII School, Coventry	1545	809‡	—		5,184 G. D. Fisher (2000)
King's College School, London SW19	1829	700	—		9,150 A. C. V. Evans (1997)
King's College, Taunton	1879	430‡	13,950		9,180 R. S. Funnell (1988)
King's School, Bruton, Somerset	1519	360‡	13,860		10,050 R. I. Smyth (1993)
King's School, Canterbury	600	754‡	15,780		11,010 Revd Canon K. H. Wilkinson (1996)
King's School, Chester	1541	550‡	—		6,075 T. J. Turvey (2000)
King's School, Ely	973	395‡	14,706		10,099 R. H. Youdale (1992)
King's School, Gloucester	1541	300‡	12,000		7,500 P. Lacey (1992)
King's School, Macclesfield	1502	1050‡	—		5,010 Dr S. Coyne (2000)
King's School, Rochester, Kent	604	313‡	15,765		9,165 Dr I. R. Walker (1986)
King's School, Worcester	1541	788‡	—		6,681 T. H. Keyes (1998)
Kingston Grammar School, Surrey	1561	605‡	—		7,380 C. D. Baxter (1991)
Kingswood School, Bath	1748	486‡	13,999		7,954 G. M. Best (1987)
Lancing College, W. Sussex	1848	430†	15,750		11,775 P. M. Tinniswood (1998)
Latymer Upper School, London W6	1624	950‡	—		7,560 C. Diggory (1991)
Leeds Grammar School	1552	1010	—		6,567 Dr M. Bailey (1999)
Leicester Grammar School	1981	670‡	—		5,520 J. B. Sugden (1989)
Leighton Park School, Reading	1890	360‡	13,455		9,414 J. Dunston (1996)

Name of School	Founded	No. of pupils	Annual fees £		Head (with date of appointment)
			Boarding	Day	
The Leys School, Cambridge	1875	500‡	14,505	6,495	Revd Dr J. C. A. Barrett (1990)
Liverpool College	1840	700‡	—	6,081	J. P. Siviter (Principal) (1997)
Llandovery College, Carmarthenshire	1848	185‡	12,468	8,280	P. A. Hogan (2000)
Lord Wandsworth College, Long Sutton, Hants	1912	485‡	12,555	9,675	I. G. Power (1997)
Loughborough Grammar School	1495	970	9,837	5,481	P. B. Fisher (1998)
Magdalen College School, Oxford	1480	550	—	6,033	A. D. Halls (Master) (1998)
Malvern College, Worcs	1862	537‡	15,930	10,095	H. C. K. Carson (1997)
Manchester Grammar School	1515	1425	—	5,400	Dr G. M. Stephen (High Master) (1994)
Marlborough College, Wilts	1843	830‡	16,410	12,300	E. J. H. Gould (Master) (1993)
Merchant Taylors' School, Liverpool	1620	711	—	4,599	S. J. R. Dawkins (1986)
Merchant Taylors' School, Northwood, Middx	1561	775	13,500	8,000	J. R. Gabitass (1991)
Millfield, Street, Somerset	1935	1215‡	16,770	10,980	P. M. Johnson (1998)
Mill Hill School, London NW7	1807	565‡	14,085	9,225	W. R. Winfield (1995)
Monkton Combe School, Bath	1868	330‡	15,405	10,512	M. J. Cuthbertson (1990)
Monmouth School	1614	570	11,199	6,720	T. H. P. Haynes (1995)
Mount St Mary's College (RC), Sheffield	1842	250‡	11,580	6,585	P. MacDonald (1998)
Newcastle-under-Lyme School	1602	1100‡	—	4,782	Dr R. M. Reynolds (Principal) (1990)
Norwich School	1156	615†	—	5,919	C. D. Brown, MA (1984)
Nottingham High School	1513	832	—	5,994	C. S. Parker, CBE (1995)
Oakham School, Rutland	1584	778‡	14,910	8,910	A. R. M. Little (1996)
The Oratory School (RC), Woodcote, Berks	1859	400	15,510	10,875	C. I. Dytor (2000)
Oundle School, Northants	1556	830‡	16,206	—	Dr R. Townsend (1999)
Pangbourne College, Berks	1917	320‡	14,745	10,710	Dr. K. Greig (2000)
Perse School, Cambridge	1615	590‡	—	6,687	N. P. V. Richardson (1994)
Plymouth College	1877	580‡	11,718	6,147	A. J. Morsley (1992)
Pocklington School, York	1514	585‡	10,197	6,255	N. Clements (2000)
Portsmouth Grammar School	1732	800‡	—	6,000	Dr T. R. Hands, D.Phil. (1997)
Prior Park College (RC), Bath	1830	500‡	13,485	7,485	Dr R. G. G. Mercer, MA, D.Phil. (1996)
Queen Elizabeth GS, Wakefield	1591	680†	—	5,307	R. P. Mardling (1985)
Queen Elizabeth's GS, Blackburn	1567	860†	—	5,400	Dr D. S. Hempsall (1995)
Queen Elizabeth's Hospital, Bristol	1590	540			S. W. Holliday (2000)
Queen's College, Taunton	1843	520‡	11,340	7,434	C. T. Bradnock (1991)
Radley College, Abingdon	1847	620	16,410	—	A. W. McPhail (Warden) (2000)
Ratcliffe College (RC), Leicester	1844	495‡	11,514	7,647	P. Farrar (1999)
Reading Blue Coat School	1646	600‡	12,720	6,960	S. J. W. McArthur (1997)
Reed's School, Cobham, Surrey	1813	330‡	13,578	10,263	D. W. Jarrett (1997)
Reigate Grammer School, Surrey	1675	805‡	—	6,708	Dr P. V. Dixon (1996)
Rendcomb College, Cirencester	1920	250‡	10,260	7,800	G. Holden (1999)
Repton School, Derby	1557	542‡	15,075	11,175	G. E. Jones (1987)
Rossall School, Fleetwood, Lancs	1844	390‡	14,175	5,325	G. S. M. Pengelley (2000)
Royal Grammar School, Guildford	1509	840	—	7,431	T. M. S. Young (1992)
Royal Grammar School, Newcastle upon Tyne	1545	925	—	5,139	J. F. X. Miller (1994)
Royal Grammar School, Worcester	1291	726	—	5,796	W. A. Jones (1993)
Royal Hospital School, Ipswich	1712	690‡	11,079	7,182	N. K. D. Ward (1995)
Rugby School	1567	743‡	16,380	9,840	M. B. Mavor, CVO (1990)
Rydal Penrhos School, Colwyn Bay	1885	447‡	12,686	8,121	M. S. James, (Principal) (1998)
Ryde School with Upper Chine, Isle of Wight	1921	420‡	10,500	5,400	Dr N. J. England (1997)
St Albans School	948	700†	—	7,305	A. R. Grant (1993)
St Bede's College (RC), Manchester	1876	995‡	—	4,845	J. Byrne (1983)
St Bees School, Cumbria	1583	300‡	14,499	9,528	P. J. Capes (2000)
St Benedict's School (RC), London W5	1902	548†	—	6,510	Dr A. J. Dachs (1986)
St Dunstan's College, London SE6	1888	960‡	—	6,933	D. I. Davies (1998)
St Edmund's College (RC), Ware, Herts	1568	373‡	12,825	8,025	D. J. J. McEwen (1984)
St Edmund's School, Canterbury	1749	270‡	15,642	10,095	A. N. Ridley (1994)
St Edward's School, Oxford	1863	600‡	16,230	11,985	D. Christie (Warden) (1988)
St George's College (RC), Addlestone, Surrey	1869	986‡	—	7,650	J. A. Peake (1994)
St John's School, Leatherhead, Surrey	1851	420†	14,250	10,050	C. H. Tongue (1993)
St Lawrence College in Thanet, Ramsgate	1879	350‡	15,540	9,975	M. Slater (1996)
St Mary's College (RC), Liverpool	1919	620‡	—	4,740	W. Hammond (1991)

Name of School	Founded	No. of pupils	Annual fees £ Boarding	Annual fees £ Day	Head (with date of appointment)
St Paul's School, London SW13	1509	787	14,910	9,870	R. S. Baldock (*High Master*) (1992)
St Peter's School, York	627	500‡	13,056	7,776	A. F. Trotman (1995)
Sedbergh School, Cumbria	1525	282	15,495	11,190	C. H. Hirst (1995)
Sevenoaks School, Kent	1432	960‡	15,219	9,270	T. R. Cookson (1996)
Sherborne School, Dorset	1550	520	16,290	12,210	S. F. Eliot (2000)
Shiplake College, Henley-on-Thames	1959	290	14,400	9,714	N. V. Bevan (1988)
Shrewsbury School	1552	700	15,975	11,250	F. E. Maidment (1988)
Silcoates School, Wakefield	1820	450‡	—	6,354	A. P. Spillane (1992)
Solihull School	1560	787†	—	5,277	P. S. J. Derham (1996)
Stamford School, Lincs	1532	684	11,352	5,832	Dr P. R. Mason (*Principal*) (1997)
Stockport Grammar School	1487	1005‡	—	5,175	I. Mellor (1996)
Stonyhurst College (*RC*), Clitheroe	1593	400‡	14,940	9,018	A. J. F. Aylward (1996)
Stowe School, Bucks	1923	575‡	16,545	12,405	J. G. L. Nichols (1989)
Sutton Valence School, Kent	1576	420‡	14,820	9,480	N. A. Sampson (1994)
Taunton School	1846	465‡	13,995	8,985	J. P. Whiteley (1997)
Tettenhall College, Wolverhampton	1863	300‡	10,800	6,594	Dr P. C. Bodkin (1994)
Tonbridge School, Kent	1553	710	16,767	11,847	J. M. Hammond (1990)
Trent College, Nottingham	1868	640‡	12,382	7,628	J. S. Lee (1988)
Trinity School, Croydon	1596	860	—	7,238	C. J. Tarrant (1999)
Truro School	1880	756‡	11,520	5,961	G. A. G. Dodd (1993)
University College School, London NW3	1830	700	—	8,475	K. J. Durham (1996)
Uppingham School, Oakham, Rutland	1584	660†	16,275	11,400	Dr S. C. Winkley, D.Phil. (1991)
Warwick School	914	800	13,407	6,315	Dr P. J. Cheshire (1988)
Wellingborough School, Northants	1595	348‡	—	6,870	F. R. Ullmann (1993)
Wellington College, Crowthorne, Berks	1859	805	16,380	12,285	A. H. Monro (*Master*) (2000)
Wellington School, Somerset	1837	560‡	10,515	5,763	A. J. Rogers (1990)
Wells Cathedral School, Somerset	909	550‡	13,353	7,929	Ms E. Cairncross (2000)
West Buckland School, Barnstaple, Devon	1858	489‡	11,745	6,630	J. F. Vick (1997)
Westminster School, London SW1	1560	652†	16,068	12,069	T. Jones-Parry (1998)
Whitgift School, South Croydon	1596	1100	—	7,812	C. A. Barnett, MA, D.Phil. (1991)
William Hulme's GS, Manchester	1887	625‡	—	5,121	S. R. Patriarca (2000)
Winchester College	1382	680	17,319	16,455	E. N. Tate, MA, Ph.D. (2000)
Wisbech Grammar School, Cambs	1379	762‡	—	5,985	R. S. Repper (1988)
Wolverhampton Grammar School	1512	760‡	—	6,420	Dr B. Trafford (1990)
Woodbridge School, Suffolk	1662	547‡	12,672	7,290	S. H. Cole (1994)
Woodhouse Grove School, Bradford	1812	608‡	11,700	6,795	D. C. Humphreys (1996)
Worksop College, Notts	1895	380‡	13,575	9,300	R. A. Collard (1994)
Worth School (*RC*), Crawley	1959	410	14,808	10,767	Fr C. Jamison (1994)
Wrekin College, Telford	1880	340‡	14,340	8,670	S. G. Drew (1998)
Wycliffe College, Stonehouse, Glos	1882	406‡	15,585	10,530	Dr R. A. Collins (1998)
Yarm School, Stockton-on-Tees	1978	550†	—	6,480	D. M. Dunn (1999)

SCOTLAND

Name of School	Founded	No. of pupils	Annual fees £ Boarding	Annual fees £ Day	Head (with date of appointment)
Daniel Stewart's and Melville College, Edinburgh	1855	760†	11,424	5,775	J. N. D. Gray (*Principal*) (2000)
Dollar Academy, Clackmannanshire	1818	749‡	11,988	5,400	J. S. Robertson (*Rector*) (1994)
The High School of Dundee	1239	720‡	—	5,325	A. M. Duncan (1997)
The Edinburgh Academy	1824	458†	13,464	6,315	J. V. Light (*Rector*) (1995)
Fettes College, Edinburgh	1870	401‡	15,927	10,746	M. C. B. Spens (1998)
George Heriot's School, Edinburgh	1628	885‡	—	5,106	A. G. Hector (1998)
George Watson's College, Edinburgh	1741	1273‡	11,274	5,430	F. E. Gerstenberg (*Principal*) (1985)
Glasgow Academy	1845	600‡	—	5,424	D. Comins (*Rector*) (1994)
Glenalmond College, Perth	1841	400‡	15,300	10,200	I. G. Templeton (*Warden*) (1992)
Gordonstoun School, Elgin	1934	430‡	15,765	11,571	M. C. Pyper (1990)
High School of Glasgow	1124	668‡	—	5,463	R. G. Easton (*Rector*) (1983)
Hutcheson's Grammar School, Glasgow	1641	1250‡	—	5,024	J. G. Knowles (*Rector*) (1999)
Kelvinside Academy, Glasgow	1878	330‡	—	5,460	J. L. Broadfoot (*Rector*) (1998)
Loretto School, Musselburgh	1827	275‡	14,795	9,600	K. J. Budge (1995)
Merchiston Castle School, Edinburgh	1833	365‡	15,300	10,350	A. R. Hunter (1998)
Morrison's Academy, Crieff	1860	362‡	13,200	5,340	G. H. Edwards (*Rector*) (1996)
Robert Gordon's College, Aberdeen	1729	962‡	—	5,330	B. R. W. Lockhart (1996)
St Aloysius' College, Glasgow	1859	837‡	—	4,300	Fr. A. Porter, SJ (1995)
St Columba's School, Kilmacolm	1897	360‡	—	4,713	A. H. Livingstone (1987)
Strathallan School, Perth	1912	400‡	15,024	10,350	B. K. Thompson (2000)

Name of School	Founded	No. of pupils	Annual fees £ Boarding	Day	Head (with date of appointment)
NORTHERN IRELAND					
Bangor Grammar School	1856	494	—	250	N. D. Argent (1998)
Belfast Royal Academy	1785	1397‡	—	80	W. S. F. Young (2000)
Campbell College, Belfast	1894	690	6,759	1,389	Dr R. J. I. Pollock (1987)
Coleraine Academical Institution	1860	406	—	75	R. S. Forsythe (1984)
Methodist College, Belfast	1865	570‡	3,905	—	T. W. Mulryne (*Principal*) (1988)
Portora Royal School, Enniskillen	1608	110	—	42	R. L. Bennett (1983)
Royal Belfast Academical Institution	1810	1050	—	540	R. M. Ridley (*Principal*) (1990)
CHANNEL ISLANDS AND ISLE OF MAN					
Elizabeth College, Guernsey	1563	470†	—	3,090	D. E. Toze (1998)
King William's College, Isle of Man	1668	280‡	13,545	9,630	P. K. Fulton-Peebles (*Principal*) (1996)
Victoria College, Jersey	1852	622†	—	2,268	R. Cook (2000)
EUROPE					
Aiglon College, Switzerland	1949	250‡	Fr. 60,160	Fr. 39,560	Acting: S. R. Braidwood (2000)
British School in The Netherlands	1935	606‡	—	Gld. 21,950	J. Hollis (1997)
British School of Brussels	1969	560‡	—	Euro 18,330	Ms J. M. Bray (*Principal*) (1990)
British School of Paris	1954	360	Fr. 119,000	Fr. 90,000	M. W. Honour (*Principal*) (1992)
The International School of Geneva	1924	1210	—	Fr. 19,915	D. Billingsley, (*Director-General*) (2000)
King's College, Madrid	1969	600	Pesetas 2.2m	Pesetas 1.2m	C. T. Gill Leech (1996)
St Columba's College, Dublin	1843	305	Ir. £8,250	Ir £4,600	T. E. Macey (1988)
St Edward's College, Malta	1929	330	—	LM. 858	W. Dimech (1997)
St George's British International School, Rome	1958	280	—	L. 3.08m	Mrs B. Gardner (*Principal*) (1994)

THE SOCIETY OF HEADMASTERS AND HEADMISTRESSES OF INDEPENDENT SCHOOLS

The Society was founded in 1961 and, in general, represents smaller boarding schools.

General Secretary, I. D. Cleland, Celedston, Rhosesmor Road, Halkyn, Holywell CH8 8 DL. Tel: 01352-781102

Headmasters/mistresses of the following schools are members of both HMC and SHMIS; details of these schools appear in the HMC list: Abbotsholme School, Ackworth School, Bedales School, Churcher's College, Colston's Collegiate School, King's School, Tynemouth, Leighton Park School, Lord Wandsworth College, Pangbourne College, Reading Blue Coat, Reed's School, Rendcomb College, Royal Hospital Schools, Rydal Penrhos School, Ryde School, St Columba's, St George's College, Shiplake College, Silcoates School, Tettenhall College, Wisbech Grammar School, Yarm School.

The Headmistresses of King Edward VI High School for Girls and Moira House are members of both SHMIS and GSA; details of the schools are given in the GSA list.
† Girls in VI form
‡ Co-educational

Name of School	Founded	No. of pupils	Annual fees £ Boarding	Day	Head (with date of appointment)
ENGLAND AND WALES					
Abbey Gate College, Saighton, Chester	1977	270‡	—	5,439	E. W. Mitchell (1991)
Austin Friars School (RC), Carlisle	1951	295‡	—	5,565	Revd D. Middleton (1996)
Battle Abbey School, E. Sussex	1912	140‡	11,910	7,380	R. Clark (1998)
Bearwood College, Wokingham	1827	250‡	12,825	7,650	S. G. G. Aiano (1998)
Bedstone College, Bucknell, Shropshire	1948	165‡	12,834	6,774	M. S. Symonds (1990)
Bentham Grammar School, N. Yorks	1726	173‡	11,490	5,820	Miss R. E. Colman (1999)
Bethany School, Cranbrook, Kent	1866	290‡	12,513	8,043	N. Dorey (1998)
Box Hill School, Dorking	1959	320‡	12,894	7,527	Dr R. A. S. Atwood (1987)
Claremont Fan Court School, Esher	1978	307‡	12,420	7,710	Mrs. P. B. Farrar (*Principal*) (1994)
Clayesmore School, Blandford Forum	1896	287‡	14,280	10,131	D. J. Beeby (1986)
Cokethorpe School, Witney, Oxon	1957	300‡	13,900	4,800	P. J. S. Cantwell (1995)
Duke of York's Royal Military School, Dover	1803	500‡	975	—	J. Cummings (1999)
Elmhurst – The School for Dance and Performing Arts, Camberley	1922	55‡	12,123	8,892	J. McNamara (*Principal*) (1995)
Embley Park School, Romsey, Hants	1946	285‡	11,970	7,317	D. F. Chapman (1987)
Ewell Castle School, Epsom	1926	300	—	6,015	R. A. Fewtrell (*Principal*) (1983)
Friends' School, Saffron Walden	1702	200‡	12,900	7,740	Ms J. E. Laing (1996)

Name of School	Founded	No. of pupils	Annual fees £		Head (with date of appointment)
			Boarding	Day	
Fulneck School, Pudsey, W. Yorks	1753	240‡	10,995	5,985	Mrs H. Gordon, (Principal) (1996)
Grenville College, Bideford	1954	260‡	12,330	6,105	Dr M. C. V. Cane
Halliford School, Shepperton, Middx	1921	320†	—	5,985	J. R. Crook (1984)
Hipperholme Grammar School, Halifax	1648	300‡	—	4,950	C. C. Robinson (1988)
Kingham Hill School, Chipping Norton	1886	230‡	12,723	7,788	M. Morris (2000)
Kirkham Grammar School, Preston	1549	626‡	9,375	4,875	B. Stacey (1991)
Langley School, Norwich	1910	285‡	12,630	6,555	J. G. Malcolm (1997)
La Retraite Swan, Salisbury	1953	90‡	—	6,150	Mrs R. A. Simmons (1994)
Lincoln Minster School (CSC)	1996	315‡	11,355	6,000	C. Rickart (1999)
Lomond School, Helensburgh, Argyll and Bute	1977	306‡	12,458	5,811	A. D. Macdonald (1986)
Milton Abbey School, Blandford Forum	1954	80	14,175	10,275	W. J. Hughes-D'Aeth (1995)
Oswestry School, Shropshire	1407	320‡	12,726	7,590	P. K. Smith (1995)
The Purcell School (music), Harrow	1962	155‡	17,511	10,494	J. Tolputt (1999)
Rannoch School, Rannoch, By Pitlochry	1959	190‡	14,000	7,500	Dr J. D. Halliday (1997)
Rishworth School, W. Yorks	1724	348‡	12,045	6,225	R. A. Baker (1999)
Rougemont School, Newport	1974	330‡	—	5,163	I. Brown (1995)
Royal Russell School, Croydon	1853	497‡	13,440	7,050	Dr J. R. Jennings (1996)
Royal School, Dungannon, N. Ireland	1608	630‡	4,200	110	P. D. Hewitt (1984)
Royal Wolverhampton School, Wolverhampton	1850	302‡	13,560	6,615	T. Brooker (2000)
Ruthin School, Denbighshire	1574	170‡	12,390	7,935	J. S. Rowlands (1993)
St Bede's School, Hailsham	1978	550‡	14,475	8,820	R. A. Perrin (1978)
St Christopher School, Letchworth	1915	380‡	13,317	7,548	C. Reid (1980)
St David's College, Llandudno	1965	220‡	12,066	7,845	W. Seymour (1991)
St Edward's School, Cheltenham	1987	450‡	—	6,810	A. J. Martin (1991)
Scarborough College, N. Yorks	1898	330‡	8,631	6,240	T. L. Kirkup (1996)
Seaford College, Petworth, W. Sussex	1884	217‡	14,100	9,390	T. J. Mullins (1997)
Shebbear College, North Devon	1841	200‡	11,985	6,420	L. D. Clark (1997)
Sibford School, Banbury	1842	242†	12,675	6,285	Ms S. Freestone (1997)
Sidcot School, North Somerset	1699	342‡	13,350	7,200	A. Slesser (1997)
Stafford Grammar School	1982	320‡	—	4,941	M. Darley (1998)
Stanbridge Earls School, Romsey, Hants	1952	200‡	15,000	11,100	H. Moxon (1984)
Sunderland High School (CSC)	1884	300‡	—	4,797	Dr A. Slater (1998)
Thetford Grammar School, Norfolk	1119	200‡	—	5,520	J. R. Weeks (1990)
Warminster School, Wilts	1707	300‡	11,925	6,705	D. Dowdles (1998)
Yehudi Menuhin School (music), Surrey	1963	51‡	varies	—	P. N. Chisholm (1988)

THE GIRL'S SCHOOLS ASSOCIATION

13 Regent Road, Leicester LE1 7PG. Tel: 0116-254 1619
President, Mrs L. Warrington
Secretary, Ms S. Cooper

Headmasters/mistresses of the following schools are members of both HMC and GSA; details of these schools appear in the HMC list; Berkamsted Collegiate School, Rydal Penrhos School, Stamford Endowed Schools

§ Girls Day School Trust, 100 Rochester Row, London SW1P 1JP. Tel: 020-7393 6666
† Boys in VI
‡ Co-educational

Name of School	Founded	No. of pupils	Annual fees £		Head (with date of appointment)
ENGLAND AND WALES			Boarding	Day	
Abbey School, Reading	1887	665	—	5,760	Miss B. C. L. Sheldon (1991)
Abbot's Hill, Hemel Hempstead	1912	164	13,500	8,160	Mrs K. Lewis (1997)
Adcote School for Girls, Shrewsbury	1907	80	12,150	6,975	Mrs A. E. Read (1997)
Alderley Edge School for Girls	1880	100	—	4,635	Ms P. A. Bristow (1997)
Alice Ottley School, Worcester	1883	500	—	6,381	Mrs M. Chapman (1999)
Amberfield School, Ipswich	1927	151	—	5,130	M. L. Amphlett Lewis (1992)
Ashford School, Kent	1898	340	13,671	7,869	Mrs P. Holloway (2000)
§Atherley School, Southampton	1926	250	11,649	4,992	Mrs M. Bradley (1999)
Badminton School, Bristol	1858	380	14,400	8,100	Mrs J. A. Scarrow (1997)
Bedford High School	1882	666	11,649	6,261	Mrs B. E. Stanley (1995)
Bedgebury School, Goudhurst, Kent	1920	259	14,010	8,700	Mrs H. Moriarty (2000)
Beechwood Sacred Heart (RC), Tunbridge Wells	1915	130	13,185	8,085	N. R. Beesley (1999)

Name of School	Founded	No. of pupils	Annual fees £ Boarding	Day	Head (with date of appointment)
Benenden School, Cranbrook, Kent	1923	450	16,050	—	Mrs C. M. Oulton (2000)
Bolton School	1877	802	—	5,664	Miss E. J. Panton (1994)
Bradford Girls' Grammar School	1875	620	—	5,541	Mrs L. J. Warrington (1987)
Brigidine School, Windsor	1948	160	—	6,405	Mrs M. B. Cairns (1986)
Bruton School, Somerset	1900	457	11,610	6,750	Mrs B. Bates (1999)
Burgess Hill School, W. Sussex	1906	370	11,865	7,020	Mrs R. F. Lewis (1992)
Bury Grammar School, Lancs	1884	761	—	4,800	Miss C. H. Thompson (1998)
Casterton School, Carnforth, Lancs	1823	354	11,403	7,254	A. F. Thomas (1990)
Channing School, London N6	1885	350	—	6,735	Mrs E. Radice (1999)
Cheltenham Ladies' College, Glos	1853	840	15,135	9,780	Mrs A. V. Tuck (*Principal*) (1996)
City of London School for Girls, London EC2	1894	546	—	7,137	Mrs Y. A. Burne, Ph.D. (1995)
Clifton High School, Bristol	1877	345	9,615	5,565	Mrs M. C. Culligan (1998)
Cobham Hall, Kent	1962	200	14,985	10,005	Mrs R. J. McCarthy (1989)
Colston's Girls' School, Bristol	1891	440	—	4,830	Mrs J. P. Franklin (1989)
Combe Bank School, Sevenoaks	1868	221	—	7,845	Mrs R. Martin (2000)
Cranford House School, Moulsford, Oxon	1931	87	—	5,850	Mrs A. B. Gray (1992)
Croham Hurst School, South Croydon	1899	350	—	5,850	Miss S. C. Budgen (1994)
Dame Alice Harpur School, Bedford	1882	723	—	6,216	Mrs J. Berry (2000)
Dame Allan's Girls' School, Newcastle upon Tyne	1705	430†	—	5,022	D. W. Welsh (*Principal*) (1996)
Downe House, Thatcham	1907	530	15,900	11,526	Mrs E. McKendrick (1997)
Dunottar School, Reigate	1926	255	—	6,495	Miss M. J. Skinner (1997)
Durham High School for Girls	1884	261	—	5,790	Mrs A. J. Templeman (1998)
Edgbaston High School for Girls, Birmingham	1876	500	—	5,085	Miss E. M. Mullenger (1998)
Farlington School, Horsham	1896	260	12,315	7,635	Mrs P. M. Mawer (1992)
Farnborough Hill, Hants	1889	500	—	6,093	Miss J. Thomas (1997)
Farringtons and Stratford House, Chislehurst	1911	250	13,470	6,840	Mrs C. E. James (1999)
Francis Holland School, London NW1	1878	375	—	2,440	Mrs G. Low (1998)
Francis Holland School, London SW1	1881	250	—	8,130	Miss S. J. Pattenden (1997)
Gateways School, Harewood, W. Yorks	1941	220	—	5,550	Mrs D. Davidson (1997)
Godolphin and Latymer School, London W6	1905	700	—	7,380	Miss M. Rudland (1986)
Godolphin School, Salisbury	1726	410	14,025	8,400	Miss M. J. Horsburgh (1996)
Greenacre School, Banstead	1933	225	—	6,450	Mrs P. M. Wood (1990)
§Guildford High School	1888	580	—	7,002	Mrs S. H. Singer (1991)
Haberdashers' Aske's School for Girls, Elstree, Herts	1690	812	—	5,805	Mrs P. Penney (1991)
Haberdashers' Monmouth School	1892	575	11,256	6,021	Dr B. Despontin, Ph.D. (1997)
Harrogate Ladies' College	1893	370	12,465	7,635	Dr M. J. Hustler (1996)
Headington School, Oxford	1915	570	12,705	6,960	Mrs H. A. Fender (1996)
Heathfield School, Ascot, Berks	1899	235	16,275	—	Mrs J. M. Benammar (1992)
Hethersett Old Hall School, Norwich	1928	174	12,255	6,150	Mrs J. Mark (2000)
Highclare School, Birmingham	1932	214†	—	5,445	Mrs C. A. Hanson (1974)
Hollygirt School, Nottingham	1877	231	—	4,584	Mrs M. I. Connolly (1997)
Holy Child School, Birmingham	1936	152	—	5,367	Mrs J. M. C. Hill (1993)
Holy Trinity College, Bromley	1886	222	—	5,595	Mrs D. A. Bradshaw (1994)
Holy Trinity School, Kidderminster	1903	163	—	4,950	Mrs E. L. Thomas (1998)
Howell's School, Denbigh	1859	220	11,085	7,485	Mrs S. Gordon (1998)
§Hull High School	1890	164	—	5,112	Mrs M. A. Benson (1994)
Hulme Grammar School, Oldham	1895	511	—	4,743	Miss M. S. Smolenski (1992)
James Allen's Girls' School, London SE22	1741	740	—	7,413	Mrs M. O. Gibbs (1994)
Kent College, Tunbridge Wells	1886	264	14,220	8,790	Miss B. J. Crompton (1990)
King Edward VI High School for Girls, Birmingham	1883	543	—	5,688	Ms S. H. Evans (1996)
King's High School for Girls, Warwick	1879	547	—	5,784	Mrs J. M. Anderson (1987)
Kingsley School, Leamington Spa	1884	460	—	4,725	Mrs Mannion Watson (1997)
Lady Eleanor Holles School, Hampton, Middx	1710	719	—	7,380	Miss E. M. Candy (1981)
La Sagesse High School, Newcastle upon Tyne	1906	300	—	5,058	Miss L. Clark (1994)
Lavant House and Rosemead, Chichester	1952	95	12,405	7,125	Mrs S. E. Watkins (1996)
Leeds Girls' High School	1876	589	—	5,871	Ms S. Fishburn (1997)
Leicester High School	1906	302	—	5,550	Mrs P. A. Watson (1992)
Lodge School, Purley, Surrey	1916	120	—	5,730	Miss P. Maynard (1998)
Loughborough High School	1850	558	—	5,337	Miss J. E. L. Harvatt (1978)

Name of School	Founded	No. of pupils	Annual fees £		Head (with date of appointment)
			Boarding	Day	
Luckley-Oakfield School, Wokingham	1895	285	12,102	7,092	R. C. Blake (1984)
Malvern Girls' College, Worcs	1893	430	14,700	9,810	Mrs P. M. C. Leggate (1997)
Manchester High School	1874	731	—	5,130	Mrs C. Lee-Jones (1998)
Manor House School, Little Bookham, Surrey	1927	163	—	6,990	Mrs A. Morris (2000)
Marymount International School, Kingston upon Thames	1955	245	17,165	10,000	Sr R. Sheridan (1990)
Maynard School, Exeter	1658	429	—	5,610	Dr D. M. West (2000)
Merchant Taylors' School, Liverpool	1888	660	—	4,599	Mrs J. I. Mills (1994)
Moira Girls School, Eastbourne	1875	210	13,500	8,400	Mrs A. Harris (Principal) (1997)
More House School, London SW1	1953	220	—	7,095	Mrs L. Falconer (1999)
Moreton Hall, Oswestry	1913	260	14,850	10,200	J. Forster (1992)
Mount School, York	1785	264	12,795	8,025	Miss B. J. Windle (1986)
Newcastle upon Tyne Church High School	1885	363	—	5,190	Mrs L. G. Smith (1995)
New Hall School, Chelmsford	1642	370	13,680	8,910	Sr Anne-Marie (1996)
Northampton High School	1878	570	—	5,340	Mrs L. A. Mayne (1988)
North Foreland Lodge, Hook	1909	180	15,600	9,600	Miss S. Cameron (1996)
North London Collegiate School, Edgware	1850	760	—	6,990	Mrs B. McCabe (1997)
Northwood College, Middx	1878	460	—	6,567	Mrs A. Mayou (1991)
Notre Dame Senior School, Cobham, Surrey	1937	330	—	6,585	Mrs M. McSwiggan (1999)
Ockbrook School, Derby	1799	490	9,099	4,959	Miss D. P. Bolland (1995)
Old Palace School, Croydon	1889	547	—	5,748	Mrs J. Hancock (2000)
Palmers Green High School, London N21	1905	140	—	6,045	Mrs S. Grant (1989)
Parsons Mead, Ashtead, Surrey	1897	160	12,084	6,996	Mrs P. Taylor (2000)
Perse School for Girls, Cambridge	1881	530	—	6,372	Miss H. S. Smith (1989)
Peterborough High School	1895	160	10,623	5,289	Mrs S. A. Dixon (1999)
Pipers Corner School, High Wycombe	1930	300	12,225	7,332	Mrs V. M. Stattersfield (1996)
Polam Hall School, Darlington	1848	289	12,285	5,715	Mrs H. C. Hamilton (1987)
Princess Helena College, Hitchin, Herts	1820	150	13,260	8,955	Mrs A. M. Hodgkiss (1997)
Prior's Field, Godalming	1902	235	13,188	8,820	Mrs J. Dwyer (1999)
Queen Anne's School, Reading	1894	325	14,910	10,808	Mrs D. Forbes (1993)
Queen Ethelburga's College, York	1912	200	15,087	9,237	Mrs E. I. E. Taylor (1997)
Queen Margaret's School, York	1901	365	13,224	8,379	Dr G. A. H. Chapman (1993)
Queen's College, London W1	1848	380	—	7,815	Miss M. M. Connell (1999)
Queen's Gate School, London SW7	1891	260	—	7,350	Mrs A. M. Holyoak (Principal) (1989)
Queen's School, Chester	1878	468	—	5,550	Miss D. M. Skilbeck (1989)
Queenswood, Hatfield, Herts	1894	390	15,510	11,940	Ms C. Farr (Principal) (1996)
Redland High School for Girls, Bristol	1882	483	—	5,340	Mrs C. Lear (1971)
Red Maids' School, Bristol	1634	465	9,600	4,800	Miss S. Hampton (1987)
Roedean School, Brighton	1885	425	15,750	9,750	Mrs P. Metham (1997)
Royal Masonic School, Herts	1788	520	10,566	6,429	Mrs I. M. Andrews (1992)
Rye St Antony School (RC), Oxford	1930	330	11,085	6,345	Miss A. M. Jones (1990)
St Albans High School	1889	564	—	6,360	Mrs C. Y. Daly (1994)
St Andrew's School, Bedford	1897	147	—	5,415	Mrs J. E. Marsland (2000)
St Anne's School, Windermere	1863	160‡	11,400	6,300	Miss W. A. Ellis (1999)
St Antony's-Leweston School (RC), Sherborne	1891	240	13,539	8,919	H. J. MacDonald (1999)
St Catherine's School, Guildford	1885	515	11,865	7,230	Mrs A. M. Phillips (1999)
St David's School, Ashford, Middx	1716	238†	11,850	6,750	Ms P. A. Bristow (1999)
St Dunstan's Abbey School, Plymouth	1850	166†	10,884	5,860	Mrs B. K. Brown (1998)
St Elphin's School, Matlock	1844	160	11,670	6,798	Mrs V. E. Fisher (1995)
St Felix School, Southwold, Suffolk	1897	150	12,615	8,340	R. Williams (1998)
St Francis' College (RC), Letchworth	1933	182	13,020	6,690	Miss M. Hegarty (1993)
St Gabriel's School, Newbury	1929	187	—	6,687	D. J. Cobb (1990)
St George's School, Ascot, Berks	1924	270	14,970	9,585	Mrs J. Grant Peterkin (1999)
St George's School, Edgbaston	1999	290	—	5,325	Miss H. J. Phillips (1999)
School of St Helen and St Katharine, Abingdon	1903	550	—	5,937	Mrs C. L. Hall (1993)
St Helen's School, Northwood, Middx	1899	632	12,432	6,600	Mrs M. Morris (Acting) (2000)
St James' School, West Malvern	1896	150	14,865	9,150	Mrs S. Kershaw (1998)
St Joseph's Convent School (RC), Reading	1894	300	—	5,595	Mrs V. M. Brookes (1990)
St Leonards-Mayfield School, Mayfield	1872	400	12,900	8,600	Mrs J. Dalton (2000)
St Margaret's School, Exeter	1904	356	—	5,085	Mrs D. D'Albertanson (1993)
St Margaret's School, Bushey, Herts	1749	320	12,825	7,590	Miss M. de Villiers (1992)
St Martin's School, Solihull	1941	240	—	5,490	Mrs S. J. Williams (1988)
St Mary's Convent School, Worcester	1934	200	—	4,935	C. Garner (1997)

Name of School	Founded	No. of pupils	Annual fees £		Head (with date of appointment)
			Boarding	Day	
St Mary's Hall, Brighton	1836	254	11,709	7,428	Mrs S. M. Meek (1997)
St Mary's School (RC), Ascot, Berks	1885	353	15,300	10,185	Mrs M. Breen (1999)
St Mary's School, Calne, Wilts	1873	300	14,490	9,150	Mrs C. J. Shaw (1996)
St Mary's School, Cambridge	1898	460	13,650	6,180	Mrs G. Piotrowska (1998)
St Mary's School, Colchester	1908	240	—	5,025	Mrs G. M. G. Mouser (1981)
St Mary's School, Gerrards Cross	1872	148	—	6,695	Mrs F. Balcombe (1995)
St Mary's School (RC), Shaftesbury	1945	325	13,125	8,520	Mrs S. Pennington (1998)
St Mary's School, Wantage, Oxon	1873	200	15,075	10,050	Mrs S. Bodinham (1994)
St Nicholas' School, Fleet, Hants	1935	156	—	5,955	Mrs A. V. Whatmough (1995)
St Paul's Girls' School, London W6	1904	670	—	8,208	Miss E. Diggory (High Mistress) (1998)
St Swithun's School, Winchester	1884	471	14,505	8,790	Dr H. L. Harvey (1995)
St Teresa's School, Dorking	1928	340	13,050	7,380	Mrs M. E. Prescott (1997)
School of S. Mary and S. Anne, Abbots Bromley, Staffs	1874	186	12,675	8,136	Mrs M. Steel (1998)
Sherborne School for Girls, Dorset	1899	370	14,970	11,250	Mrs G. Kerton-Johnson (1999)
Sir William Perkins's School, Chertsey, Surrey	1725	583	—	6,120	Miss S. Ross (1994)
Stonar School, Melksham, Wilts	1895	325	11,880	6,600	Mrs C. Homan (1997)
Stover School, Newton Abbot	1932	216	11,385	5,685	P. E. Bujak (1994)
§Surbiton High School, Kingston-upon-Thames	1884	648	—	3,660	Miss M. G. Perry (1993)
Talbot Heath, Bournemouth	1886	390	11,190	6,450	Mrs C. Dipple (1991)
Teesside High School, Stockton-on-Tees	1970	350	—	5,000	Mrs H. J. French (2000)
§Tormead School, Guildford	1905	504	—	6,330	Mrs H. E. M. Alleyne (1992)
Tudor Hall School, Banbury	1850	262	12,780	7,980	Miss N. Godfrey (1984)
Wakefield Girls' High School	1878	692†	—	5,307	Mrs P. A. Langham (1988)
Walthamstow Hall, Sevenoaks	1838	250	15,240	8,580	Mrs J. S. Lang (1984)
Wentworth College, Bournemouth	1871	225	10,950	6,885	Miss S. D. Coe (1991)
Westfield School, Newcastle upon Tyne	1960	235	—	5,085	Mrs M. Farndale (1991)
Westholme School, Blackburn	1923	713	—	4,305	Mrs L. Croston (Principal) (1988)
Westonbirt School, Tetbury, Glos	1928	200	14,760	10,287	Mrs M. Henderson (1999)
Wispers School, Haslemere, Surrey	1947	120	12,255	7,890	L. H. Beltran (1980)
Withington Girls' School, Manchester	1890	530	—	5,040	Mrs J. D. Pickering (2000)
Woldingham School, Surrey	1842	550	15,285	9,033	Mrs M. M. Ribbins (1997)
Wychwood School, Oxford	1897	140	9,540	5,985	Mrs S. Wingfield Digby (1997)
Wycombe Abbey School, High Wycombe	1896	513	16,200	12,150	Mrs P. E. Davies (1998)
Wykeham House School, Fareham, Hants	1913	147	—	5,184	Mrs R. M. Kamaryc (1995)
SCOTLAND					
Kilgraston School for Girls, Bridge of Earn, Perth	1920	200	13,560	7,995	Mrs J. L. Austin (1993)
Laurel Park School, Glasgow	1996	286	—	4,986	Mrs E. Surber (1995)
Mary Erskine School, Edinburgh	1694	685‡	11,424	5,454	D. Gray (Principal) (2000)
St George's School, Edinburgh	1888	550	10,905	5,580	Dr J. McClure (1994)
St Margaret's School, Aberdeen	1846	200	—	4,878	Miss A. C. Ritchie (1998)
St Margaret's School, Edinburgh	1890	370	10,260	5,010	Miss A. Mitchell (1994)
CHANNEL ISLANDS					
The Ladies' College, Guernsey	1872	350	—	2,760	Miss M. E. Macdonald (Principal) (1992)

Health

SELECTED CAUSES OF DEATH, BY GENDER AND
AGE 1998 (UNITED KINGDOM)

	Under 1*	1–14	15–24	25–34	35–54	55–64	65–74	75 and over	All ages
Males									
Circulatory diseases	43	45	108	392	7,272	13,777	33,000	68,452	123,089
Cancer	15	234	224	437	6,339	12,712	26,051	35,502	81,514
Respiratory diseases	97	79	73	142	1,161	2,676	9,095	32,143	45,466
Injury and poisoning	40	291	1,576	2,549	3,530	1,194	1,044	1,979	12,203
Infectious diseases	68	71	49	92	333	252	407	773	2,045
Other causes*	2,064	369	567	1,072	4,092	3,167	6,121	18,391	35,843
All males (number)	2,327	1,089	2,597	4,684	22,727	33,778	75,718	157,240	300,160
Females									
Circulatory diseases	30	50	66	251	2,576	5,681	20,344	106,110	135,108
Cancer	8	131	142	507	7,597	10,255	19,729	37,099	75,468
Respiratory diseases	63	68	58	100	825	1,847	7,214	45,189	55,364
Injury and poisoning	31	166	456	545	1,101	476	740	3,431	6,946
Infectious diseases	65	55	49	69	167	159	340	1,000	1,904
Other causes*	1,555	305	283	499	2,453	2,456	5,833	40,838	54,222
All females (number)	1,752	775	1,054	1,971	14,719	20,874	54,200	233,667	329,012

* Deaths at under 28 days are not assigned a specific cause and are entered under 'other'.
Source: Office for National Statistics, Mortality Statistics Section

NOTIFICATIONS OF INFECTIOUS DISEASES (UK) 1998

Measles	4,540
Mumps	1,917
Rubella	4,064
Whooping cough	1,902
Scarlet fever	4,708
Dysentery	1,934
Food poisoning	105,060
Typhoid and paratyphoid fevers	252
Hepatitis	3,781
Tuberculosis	6,605
Malaria	1,163

Source: The Stationery Office – *Annual Abstract of Statistics 2000* (Crown copyright)

HIV/AIDS AND SEXUALLY TRANSMITTED DISEASES (ENGLAND)

	1987	1998
HIV cases diagnosed	1,917	2,275
Exposure category		
Homosexual intercourse	73%	48%
Heterosexual intercourse	9%	39%
Injecting drug use	12%	4%
Blood products	2%	0.3%
Aids cases diagnosed	640	581
Sexually transmitted diseases (new cases) (1997)		
All, except HIV/AIDS	—	455,500
Syphilis	2,400	1,300
Gonorrhoea	46,300	15,400
Chlamydia	—	54,400
Herpes	18,900	27,400
Wart virus	52,200	106,000

Source: The Stationery Office – *Health and Personal Social Services Statistics for England 1999* (Crown copyright)

CURRENT SMOKERS (UNITED KINGDOM)
By gender and socio-economic group Percentage

	1982	1998–99
Males		
Professional	20	15
Employers and managers	29	21
Intermediate and junior non-manual	30	23
Skilled manual	42	33
Semi-skilled manual	47	38
Unskilled manual	49	45
Females		
Professional	21	14
Employers and managers	29	20
Intermediate and junior non-manual	30	24
Skilled manual	39	30
Semi-skilled manual	36	33
Unskilled manual	41	43

Source: The Stationery Office – *Social Trends 30* (Crown copyright)

ADULTS CONSUMING OVER SELECTED WEEKLY LIMITS OF ALCOHOL, *by Gender and Age*
Percentage

	1998–99
Men	
16–24	36
25–44	27
45–64	30
65 and over	16
All aged 16 and over	27
Women	
16–24	25
25–44	16
45–64	16
65 and over	6
All aged 16 and over	15

Source: The Stationery Office – *Social Trends 30* (Crown copyright)

Social Welfare

National Health Service

The National Health Service (NHS) came into being on 5 July 1948 under the National Health Service Act 1946, covering England and Wales, and under separate legislation for Scotland and Northern Ireland. The NHS is now administered by the Secretary of State for Health (in England), the National Assembly for Wales, the Scottish Executive and the Secretary of State for Northern Ireland.

The function of the NHS is to provide a comprehensive health service designed to secure improvement in the physical and mental health of the people and to prevent, diagnose and treat illness. It was founded on the principle that treatment should be provided according to clinical need rather than ability to pay, and should be free at the point of delivery. However, prescription charges were provided for by legislation in 1949 and implemented in 1952, and charges for some dental and ophthalmic treatment have also been introduced.

The NHS covers a comprehensive range of hospital, specialist, family practitioner (medical, dental, ophthalmic and pharmaceutical), artificial limb and appliance, ambulance, and community health services. Everyone normally resident in the UK is entitled to use any of these services.

STRUCTURE

The structure of the NHS remained relatively stable for the first 30 years of its existence. In 1974, a three-tier management structure comprising Regional Health Authorities, Area Health Authorities and District Management Teams was introduced in England, and the NHS became responsible for community health services. In 1979 Area Health Authorities were abolished and District Management Teams were replaced by District Health Authorities.

The National Health Service and Community Care Act 1990 provided for more streamlined Regional Health Authorities and District Health Authorities, and for the establishment of Family Health Services Authorities (FHSAs) and NHS Trusts. The concept of the 'internal market' was introduced into health care, whereby care was provided through NHS contracts where health authorities or boards and GP fundholders (the purchasers) were responsible for buying health care from hospitals, non-fundholding GPs, community services and ambulance services (the providers).

NHS Trusts operate as self-governing health care providers independent of health authority control and responsible to the Secretary of State. Until 1999 they derived their income principally from contracts to provide services to health authorities and fund-holding GPs. In Northern Ireland, 20 health and social services trusts are responsible for providing health and social services in an organisational model unique to Northern Ireland.

The Act also paved the way for the Community Care reforms, which were introduced in April 1993 and changed the way care is administered for elderly people, the mentally ill, the physically handicapped and people with learning disabilities.

The eight Regional Health Authorities in England were abolished in April 1996 and replaced by eight regional offices which, together with the headquarters in Leeds, form the NHS Executive. The regional offices are part of the Department of Health, and their functions include financial and performance monitoring of local purchasers and providers, public health, regional research and development, and education programmes.

In April 1996 the District Health Authorities and Family Health Service Authorities were merged to form 100 unified Health Authorities (HAs) in England. The HAs are responsible for health and health services in their areas. They are also responsible for assessing the health care needs of the local population and developing integrated strategies for meeting these needs in partnership with GPs and in consultation with the public, hospitals and others. HAs' resources are allocated by the NHS Executive headquarters, to which they are also accountable for their performance. HA chairmen are appointed by the Health Secretary and non-executive members by the regional offices of the NHS Executive.

In Wales the chairman and non-executive members of the five HAs which replaced the former 17 HAs and FHSAs in April 1996 are appointed by the First Secretary. Health Solutions Wales provides a range of specialist services to the NHS in Wales. In Scotland there are 15 Health Boards with similar responsibilities to those of HAs. In Northern Ireland there are four Health and Social Services Boards.

There are also Community Health Councils (called Local Health Councils in Scotland and Health and Social Services Councils in Northern Ireland) throughout the UK; their role is to represent the interests of the public to health authorities and boards. The Government announced in March 1998 that public consultation and patient representation in the NHS would be increased.

Under the Health Act 1999 the NHS internal market in England was replaced by teams of GPs and community nurses working together in primary care groups (see page 489) from 1 April 1999. Long-term service agreements are beginning to replace annual contracts between primary care groups, health authorities, and NHS Trusts. A National Institute for Clinical Excellence has been established to produce new national guidelines and National Service Frameworks are being prepared to guarantee consistency in access to services. The first of these, published in late 1999, addressed mental health and coronary heart disease services. A Commission for Health Improvement was established in autumn 1999 to promote best practice. In Scotland, the Act replaced the internal market with Local Health Care Co-operatives (see page 489) from 1 April 1999. The NHS Trusts were reorganised into 13 primary care trusts and 15 acute care trusts, responsible to the Health Boards. In Wales the internal market was replaced by a system of Local Health Groups (see page 489). In Scotland the Scottish Health Technology Assessment Centre provide guidelines to promote best practice.

FINANCE

UNITED KINGDOM

The NHS is still funded mainly through general taxation, although in recent years more reliance has been placed on the NHS element of National Insurance contributions, patient charges and other sources of income. In 1999–2000 just over 93 per cent of NHS expenditure was financed from general taxation and National Insurance Contributions. Forecast UK Gross Expenditure on the NHS in 1999–2000 is 5.9 per cent of GDP and is set to rise to 6.0 per cent for the first time in 2000–1. The Government announced in July 1998 that an additional £21,000 million would be spent on the NHS between 1999 and 2002. In the March 2000 Budget the Government unveiled its plans to put extra funding into the NHS in order for it to grow by one half in cash terms and by one third in real terms by 2005. Their objectives include 7,000 extra beds in hospitals and intermediate care; over 100 new hospitals by 2010 and 500 new one-stop primary care centres; over 3,000 GP premises modernised and 250 new scanners; cleaner wards and better hospital food; more IT systems in every hospital and GP surgery; 7,500 more consultants and 2,000 more GPs; 20,000 extra nurses and 6,500 extra therapists; 1,000 more medical school places and childcare support for NHS staff with 100 on-site nurseries.

NATIONAL HEALTH CURRENT EXPENDITURE 1998–9

	£ million
National Health Service:	
Hospitals, Community Health Services and Family Health Services	43,600
Departmental administration	227
Other central services	3,357
Less payments by patients	−944
TOTAL	45,346

PERSONAL SOCIAL SERVICES CURRENT EXPENDITURE 1998–9

	£ million
Central government	53
Local authorities running expenses	11,439
Capital expenditure	191
TOTAL	11,683

Source: The Stationery Office – *Annual Abstract of Statistics 2000* (Crown copyright)

WALES

CENTRAL GOVERNMENT HEALTH FUNDING 1997–8

	£ thousand
Central administration	6,904
Hospital, community and cash limited family health services	1,851,757
NHS Trusts	159,266
Demand-led (non-cash limited) family health services	425,705
Other health services	61,951
Welfare foods	12,773
TOTAL	2,518,356

Source: Welsh Office

SCOTLAND

NET COSTS OF THE NATIONAL HEALTH SERVICE 1996–7

	£ thousand
Central administration	8,378
Total NHS cost	4,377,923
NHS contributions	468,770
Net costs to Exchequer	3,909,153
Health Board administration	89,282
Hospital and community health services	3,108,575
Family practitioner services	986,616
Central health services	120,586

State hospital	22,400
Training	3,326
Research	10,517
Disabled services	2,331
Welfare foods	13,835
Miscellaneous health services	20,455
TOTAL	4,386,301

Source: Scottish Office – *Annual Abstract of Statistics 1998* (Crown copyright)

TOTAL NHS EXPENDITURE PER HEAD OF POPULATION 2000–1

	NET £	GROSS £
UK	967	906
England	949	885
Scotland	1,094	1,026
Wales	976	958
Northern Ireland	912	898

Source: Department of Health

ORGANISATIONS

HEALTH AUTHORITIES (ENGLAND)

There are 100 health authorities in England. For details, contact the relevant NHS Executive regional office (*see* below).

NHS EXECUTIVE REGIONAL OFFICES

EASTERN, 6–12 Capital Drive, Linford Wood, Milton Keynes MK14 6QP. Tel: 01908-844400. *Chairman*, Mrs R. Varley; *Regional Director*, P. Houghton Relocating in Dec 2000: Victoria House 2, Capital Park, Fulbourn, Cambridge CB1 5XB.

LONDON, 40 Eastbourne Terrace, London W2 3QR. Tel: 020-7725 5300. *Chairman*, I. Mills; *Regional Director*, N. Crisp

NORTHERN AND YORKSHIRE, John Snow House, Durham University Science Park, Durham DH1 3YG. Tel: 0191-301 1325. *Chairman*, Mrs Z. Manzoor; *Regional Director*, P. Garland

NORTH WEST, 930–932 Birchwood Boulevard, Millennium Park, Birchwood, Warrington WA3 7QN. Tel: 01925-704000. *Chairman*, Prof. Jean Higgins; *Regional Director*, Prof. R. Tinston

SOUTH EAST, 40 Eastbourne Terrace, London W2 3QR. Tel: 020-7725 2500. *Chairman*, Sir William Wells; *Regional Director*, B. Stocking

SOUTH WEST, Westward House, Lime Kiln Close, Stoke Gifford, Bristol BS34 8SR. Tel: 0117-984 1750. *Chairman*, Miss J. Trotter, OBE; *Regional Director*, A. Laurance

TRENT, Fulwood House, Old Fulwood Road, Sheffield S10 3TH. Tel: 0114-263 0300. *Chairman*, Dr P. Barrett; *Acting Regional Director*, D. Nicholson

WEST MIDLANDS, Bartholomew House, 142 Hagley Road, Birmingham B16 9PA. Tel: 0121-224 4600. *Chairman*, C. Wilkinson; *Regional Director*, S. Day

HEALTH BOARDS (SCOTLAND)

ARGYLL AND CLYDE, Ross House, Hawkhead Road, Paisley PA2 7BN. Tel: 0141-842 7200. *Chairman*, M. D. Jones; *General Manager*, N. McConachie

AYRSHIRE AND ARRAN, PO Box 13, Boswell House, 10 Arthur Street, Ayr KA7 1QJ. Tel: 01292-611040. *Chairman*, Dr J. Morrow; *Chief Executive*, Mrs W. Hatton

BORDERS, Newstead, Melrose, Roxburghshire TD9 0SE. Tel: 01896-825500. *Chairman*, D. A. C. Kilshaw, OBE; *General Manager*, Dr L. Burley

DUMFRIES AND GALLOWAY, Grierson House, The Crichton Royal, Bankend Road, Dumfries DG1 4ZG. Tel: 01387-272700. *Chairman*, J. Ross, CBE; *General Manager*, N. Campbell
FIFE, Springfield House, Cupar KY15 9UP. Tel: 01334-656200. *Chairman*, Mrs C. Stenhouse; *General Manager*, M. Murray
FORTH VALLEY, 33 Spittal Street, Stirling FK8 1DX. Tel: 01786-463031. *Chairman*, E. Bell-Scott; *General Manager*, D. Hird
GRAMPIAN, Summerfield House, 2 Eday Road, Aberdeen AB15 6RE. Tel: 01224-663456. *Chairman*, Dr C. E. MacLeod,CBE; *General Manager*, F. E. L. Hartnett, OBE
GREATER GLASGOW, Dalian House, PO Box 15329, 350 St Vincent Street, Glasgow G3 8YZ. Tel: 0141-201 4444. *Chairman*, Prof. D. Hamblen; *Chief Executive*, C. J. Spry
HIGHLAND, Beechwood Park, Inverness IV2 3HG. Tel: 01463-717123. *Chairman*, Mrs C. Thomson; *Acting General Manager*, E. Baigal
LANARKSHIRE, 14 Beckford Street, Hamilton, Lanarkshire ML3 0TA. Tel: 01698-281313. *Chairman*, I. Livingstone, CBE; *General Manager*, Prof. T. A. Divers
LOTHIAN, Deaconess House, 148 Pleasance, Edinburgh EH8 9RS. Tel: 0131-536 9000. *Chairman*, Mrs M. Ford; *General Manager*, T. Jones
ORKNEY, Garden House, New Scapa Road, Kirkwall, Orkney KW15 1BQ. Tel: 01856-885400. *Chairman*, I. Leslie; *General Manager*, J. Wellden
SHETLAND, Brevik House, South Road, Lerwick ZE1 0TG. Tel: 01595-696767. *Chairman*, J. Telford; *Chief Executive*, B. J. Atherton
TAYSIDE, Gateway House, Luna Place, Dundee Technology Park, Dundee DD2 1TP. Tel: 01382-561818. *Chairman*, Mrs F. Havenga; *General Manager*, T. Brett
WESTERN ISLES, 37 South Beach Street, Stornoway, Isle of Lewis HS1 2BN. Tel: 01851-702997. *Chairman*, A. Matheson; *General Manager*, M. Maclennan

HEALTH AUTHORITIES (WALES)

BRO TAF, 17 Churchill House, Churchill Way, Cardiff CF10 4TW. Tel: 029-2040 2402. *Chairman*, S. Jones; *Chief Executive*, Mrs J. Williams
DYFED POWYS, PO Box 13, St David's Hospital, Carmarthen SA31 3YH. Tel: 01267-225225. *Chairman*, Ms M. Price; *Chief Executive*, S. Gray
GWENT, Mamhilad House, Mamhilad Park Estate, Pontypool NP4 0YP. Tel: 01495-765065. *Chairman*, Mrs F. Peel; *Chief Executive*, G. Coomber
IECHYD MORGANNWG, 41 High Street, Swansea SA1 1LT. Tel: 01792-458066. *Chairman*, D. H. Thomas; *Chief Executive*, Ms J. Perrin
NORTH WALES, Preswylfa, Hendy Road, Mold CH7 1PZ. Tel: 01352-700227. *Chairman*, Mrs E. Rowlands; *Chief Executive*, D. Hands
HEALTH SOLUTIONS WALES, Brunnell House, 2 Fitzellen Road, Cardiff CF24 0HA. Tel: 029-2050 0500.

NORTHERN IRELAND HEALTH AND SOCIAL SERVICES BOARDS

EASTERN, Champion House, 12–22 Linenhall Street, Belfast BT2 8BS. Tel: 028-9032 1313. *Chairman*, D. McGuiness; *Chief Executive*, Dr M. P. J. Kilbane, FRCP
NORTHERN, County Hall, 182 Galgorm Road, Ballymena BT42 1QB. Tel: 028-2565 3333. *Chairman*, M. A. Wood; *Chief Executive*, J. S. MacDonell

SOUTHERN, Tower Hill, Armagh BT61 7DR. Tel: 028-3741 0041. *Chairman*, W. Gillespie; *Chief Executive*, B. P. Cunningham
WESTERN, 15 Gransha Park, Clooney Road, Londonderry BT47 6FN. Tel: 028-7186 0086. *Chairman*, J. Bradley; *Chief Executive*, T. J. Frawley

HEALTH PROMOTION AUTHORITIES

HEALTH PROMOTION ENGLAND, 50 Eastbourne Terrace, London W2 3QR. Tel: 020-7413 2627. *General Manager*, Geof Webb
HEALTH EDUCATION BOARD FOR SCOTLAND, Woodburn House, Canaan Lane, Edinburgh EH10 4SG. Tel: 0131-536 5500. *Chairman*, D. R. Campbell; *Chief Executive*, Prof. A. Tannahill
HEALTH PROMOTION AGENCY FOR NORTHERN IRELAND, 18 Ormeau Avenue, Belfast BT2 8HS. Tel: 028-9031 1611; *Chief Executive*, Dr B. Gaffney

---

EMPLOYEES AND SALARIES

EMPLOYEES

NHS HOSPITAL AND COMMUNITY HEALTH SERVICES – ALL NON-MEDICAL STAFF (*England*) *as at September 1999**

Ambulance service	15,910
Administration and estates	204,617
Healthcare assistants and other support staff	115,024
Nursing, midwifery and health visiting	431,103
Nursing, midwifery and health visiting learners	1,945
Scientific, therapeutic and technical	128,293
Other non-medical staff	675
All non-medical staff	897,567

* Figures exclude agency staff
Source: The Department of Health – *1999 Non-medical Workforce Census*

SALARIES *as at 1 April 2000*

General Practitioners (GPs), dentists, optometrists and pharmacists are self-employed, and are employed by the NHS under contract. GPs are paid for their NHS work in accordance with a scheme of remuneration which includes a basic practice allowance, capitation fees, reimbursement of certain practice expenses and payments for out-of-hours work. Dentists receive payment for items of treatment for individual adult patients and, in addition, a continuing care payment for those registered with them. Optometrists receive approved fees for each sight test they carry out. Pharmacists receive professional fees from the NHS and are refunded the cost of prescriptions supplied.

Consultant	£47,345–£61,605†
Specialist Registrar	£23,300–£33,965†
Registrar	£23,300–£28,625†
Senior House Officer	£20,845–£27,845†
House Officer	£16,710–£18,860†
GP	*£54,220
Nursing Grades G–I (Senior Ward Sister)	£20,830–£29,205
Nursing Grade F (Ward Sister)	£17,655–£22,860
Nursing Grade E (Senior Staff Nurse)	£15,920–£19,220
Nursing Grade D (Staff Nurse)	£14,890–£16,445
Nursing Grade C (Enrolled Nurse)	£12,135–£14,890
Nursing Grades A–B (Nursing Auxiliary)	£9,000–£12,135

* average intended net remuneration
† 1999 figure – wage increases to be announced in October 2000

HEALTH SERVICES

PRIMARY AND COMMUNITY HEALTH CARE

Primary and community health care services comprise the family health services (i.e. the general medical, personal medical, pharmaceutical, dental, and ophthalmic services) and community services (including preventive activities such as vaccination, immunisation and fluoridation) commissioned by HAs and provided by NHS Trusts, health centres and clinics. Nursing services including practice nurses, district nurses and health visitors, community psychiatric nurses, school nurse and ante- and post-natal care are also an integral part of primary and community health care.

FAMILY DOCTOR SERVICE

In England and Wales the Family Doctor Service (or General Medical Service) is now the responsibility of the HAs. In late 1999 a pilot scheme of 19 walk-in centres, where people may consult a doctor without an appointment between the hours of 7 a.m. and 10 p.m., was introduced. They are responsible to HAs and work closely with primary care groups.

Any doctor may take part in the Family Doctor Service (provided the area in which he/she wishes to practise has not already an adequate number of doctors) and about 29,000 GPs in England and Wales do so. The distribution of GPs is controlled by the Medical Practices Committee, a statutory body. The average number of patients on a doctor's list in the UK as at October 1999 was 1,791. GPs may also have private fee-paying patients.

The Government has replaced the fundholding system by allowing the new primary care groups and trusts to assume one of four levels of responsibility. In April 1999 481 primary care groups became operational in England, covering populations of between 46,000 and 257,000. They operate as a committee of a Health Authority and are responsible for health improvement, primary and community health service development and commissioning secondary care services where appropriate. Primary care groups operate at one of two levels of responsibility. At level one, the group advises the Health Authority and is responsible for less than 40 per cent of the group's unified budget. Level two primary care groups are responsible for 40 per cent of the group's unified budget, rising to 60 per cent in their second year of operation. A board consisting of GPs, nurses, a social services officer, a health authority representative and a local member of the public administers each group.

From 1 April 2000, Primary Care Trusts became operational in England. They are free-standing statutory bodies undertaking many of the functions previously exercised by Health Authorities. They operate at one of two levels. Level three Trusts are able to commission services with greater scope than a level two primary care group, but not directly provide them. Those at level four are able to commission and directly provide services and run community hospitals and health services.

In Scotland, fundholding was replaced by over 70 Local Health Care Co-operatives on 1 April 1999. These, consisting of GPs and others involved in primary care, are responsible for developing health care in their area.

In Wales 22 Local Health Groups were set up by the Health Authorities and began work in April 1999. They are coterminous with local authority areas. At present, they advise Health Authorities but in the future they will assume responsibility for commissioning services and devising strategies for improved health. They will also integrate the delivery of primary and community care. A governing body including GPs and other health professionals, social services and community representatives administers each group.

Everyone aged 16 or over can choose their doctor (parents or guardians choose for children under 16); the doctor is free to accept a person or not. Should a patient have difficulty in registering with a doctor, HAs have powers to assign the patient to a GP. A person may change their doctor if they wish, by going to the surgery of a GP of their choice who is willing to accept them, and either handing in their medical card to register or filling in a form. When people are away from home they can still use the Family Doctor Service if they ask to be treated as temporary residents, and in an emergency, any doctor in the service will give treatment and advice. A number of drop-in medical centres are being set up where anyone can consult a doctor.

PHARMACEUTICAL SERVICE

Patients may obtain medicines, appliances and oral contraceptives prescribed under the NHS from any pharmacy whose owner has entered into arrangements with the HA to provide this service; the number of these pharmacies in England and Wales in March 1998 was about 10,500. There are also some appliance suppliers who only provide special appliances. In rural areas, where access to a pharmacy may be difficult, patients may be able to obtain medicines, etc., from their doctor.

Except for contraceptives (for which there is no charge), a charge of £6.00 is payable for each item supplied unless the patient is exempt and the declaration on the back of the prescription form is completed. Prepayment certificates (£31.40 valid for four months, £86.20 valid for a year) may be purchased by those patients not entitled to exemption who require frequent prescriptions.

The following people are exempt from prescription charges:

- children under 16
- full-time students under 19
- men and women aged 60 and over
- pregnant women who hold an exemption certificate
- women who have had a baby in the last 12 months and who hold an exemption certificate
- people suffering from certain medical conditions who hold an exemption certificate
- people who receive income support, full working families' tax credit or credit reduced by up to £70, full disabled person's tax credit or credit reduced by up to £70 or income-based jobseeker's allowance, and their partners
- people who are named on an HC2 certificate issued by the Health Benefits Division
- war pensioners (for their accepted disablements)

Booklet HC11, available from main post offices and local social security offices, gives further details.

The number of prescriptions dispensed in the community in 1999 was:

England and Wales	511,600,000
Scotland	60,362,413
Northern Ireland	22,171,000*

* 1998 figure

DENTAL SERVICE

Dentists, like doctors, may take part in the NHS and also have private patients. About 17,000 dentists in England provide NHS general dental services. They are responsible to the HAs in whose areas they provide services.

Patients may go to any dentist who is taking part in the NHS and is willing to accept them. Patients are required to pay 80 per cent of the cost of NHS dental treatment. Since 1 April 1999 the maximum charge for a course of treatment has been £348. There is no charge for arrest of bleeding or repairs to dentures; home visits by the dentist or re-opening a surgery in an emergency are charged for as treatment given in the normal way. The following people are exempt from dental charges or have charges remitted:

- people under 18
- full-time students under 19
- women who were pregnant when accepted for treatment
- women who have had a child in the previous 12 months
- people who receive income support, full working families' tax credit or credit reduced by up to £70, full disabled person's tax credit or credit reduced by up to £70, or income-based jobseeker's allowance, and their partners
- people who are named on an HC2 certificate issued by the Health Benefits Division

Booklet HC11, available from main post offices and local social security offices, gives further details.

GENERAL DENTAL SERVICE 1999–2000 (ENGLAND)

Number of dentists	17,821
Number of patients registered	
Adults	16,800,000
Children	6,900,000
Number of courses of treatment	
Adults	25,900,000
Expenditure (£ million)	
Gross expenditure	1,480
Paid by patients	430
Paid out of public funds	1,050

Source: Department of Health

GENERAL OPHTHALMIC SERVICES

General Ophthalmic Services are administered by HAs. Testing of sight may be carried out by any ophthalmic medical practitioner or ophthalmic optician (optometrist). The optician must give the prescription to the patient, who can take this to any supplier of glasses to have them dispensed. Only registered opticians can supply glasses to children and to people registered as blind or partially sighted.

The NHS sight test costs £15.01. Those on a low income may qualify for help with the cost. The test is available free to:

- people aged 60 or over
- children under 16*
- full-time students under 19*
- people who receive income support, income-based jobseeker's allowance, full working families' tax credit or credit reduced by up to £70, full disabled person's tax credit or credit reduced by up to £70, and their partners*
- people who are named on an HC2 certificate issued by the Health Benefits Division*
- people prescribed complex lenses*
- people registered as blind or partially sighted
- diagnosed diabetic and glaucoma patients
- people advised by an ophthalmologist that they are at risk of glaucoma

The categories indicated by * above are automatically entitled to help with the purchase of glasses under an NHS voucher scheme, as are people whose spectacles are lost or damaged as a result of illness. Booklet HC11, available from main post offices and local social security offices, gives further details.

Diagnosis and specialist treatment of eye conditions, and the provision of special glasses, are available through the Hospital Eye Service.

COMMUNITY CHILD HEALTH SERVICES

Pre-school services at GP surgeries or child health clinics provide regular monitoring of children's physical, mental and emotional health and development, and advice to parents on their children's health and welfare.

The School Health Service provides for the medical and dental examination of schoolchildren, and advises the local education authority, the school, the parents and the pupil of any health factors which may require special consideration during the pupil's school life. GPs are increasingly undertaking child health monitoring in order to improve the preventive health care of children.

HEALTH ACTION ZONES

Health Action Zones aim to improve health services and tackle health inequalities in certain areas, working with the primary care groups in their area. The first 11 zones were set up in April 1998 and by April 1999 a total of 26 were in existence. Each zone receives funding for seven years.

HOSPITALS AND OTHER SERVICES

Hospital, medical, dental, nursing, ophthalmic and ambulance services are provided by the NHS to meet all reasonable requirements. Facilities for the care of expectant and nursing mothers and young children, and other services required for the diagnosis and treatment of illness, are also provided. Rehabilitation services (occupational therapy, physiotherapy and speech therapy) may also be provided, and surgical and medical appliances are supplied where appropriate. Specialists and consultants who work in NHS hospitals can also engage in private practice, including the treatment of their private patients in NHS hospitals.

PRIVATE FINANCE INITIATIVE

The Private Finance Initiative (PFI) was launched in 1992, and involves the private sector in designing, building, financing and operating new hospitals, which are then leased to the NHS. In July 1997 a new programme of hospital building under the PFI was announced by the Government.

CHARGES

Certain hospitals have accommodation in single rooms or small wards which, if not required for patients who need privacy for medical reasons, may be made available to patients who desire it as an amenity for a small charge. These patients are still NHS patients and are treated as such.

In a number of hospitals, accommodation is available for the treatment of private in-patients who undertake to pay the full costs of hospital accommodation and services and (usually) separate medical fees to a specialist as well. The amount of the medical fees is a matter for agreement between doctor and patient. Hospital charges for private in-patients are set locally at a commercial rate.

There is no charge for drugs supplied to NHS hospital in-patients, but out-patients pay £6.00 an item unless they are exempt. With certain exceptions, hospital out-patients have to pay fixed charges for dentures, contact lenses and certain appliances. Glasses may be obtained either from the hospital or an optician, and the charge will be related to the type of lens prescribed and the choice of frame.

AMBULANCE SERVICE

The NHS provides emergency ambulance services free of charge via the 999 emergency telephone service. There are 35 ambulance services in the UK. Helicopter ambulances are used in some areas where access may be difficult or heavy traffic could hinder road progress, and an air ambulance service is available throughout Scotland. Non-emergency ambulance services are provided free of charge to patients who are deemed to require them on medical grounds.

In 1999–2000 in England about 4,100,000 emergency calls were made to the ambulance service, an increase of 7.9 per cent on the previous year. There were about 2,900,000 emergency patient journeys. The Patients' Charter requires emergency ambulances to respond to 95 per cent of calls within 14 minutes in urban areas and 19 minutes in rural areas, and to reach 50 per cent of cases within eight minutes. In 1999–2000, of the 20 ambulance services that had introduced call prioritisation by 31 March 2000, 16 ambulance services met the Charter standard for responding to life-threatening emergencies and 14 met the standard for non-life threatening emergencies. Of the 12 ambulance services whose calls are not prioritised, one achieved the Charter Standard.

NHS DIRECT

NHS Direct is a telephone service staffed by nurses which gives patients advice on how to look after themselves as well as directing them to the appropriate part of the NHS for treatment if necessary. Tel: 0845-4647

BLOOD SERVICES

There are four national bodies which co-ordinate the blood donor programme in each constituent country of the UK. About two million donations of blood are given each year; donors give blood at local centres on a voluntary basis.

NATIONAL BLOOD AUTHORITY, Oak House, Reeds Crescent, Watford, Herts WD1 1QH. Tel: 01923-486800. *Chairman*, M. Fogden, CB; *Chief Executive*, M. Gorham
SCOTTISH NATIONAL BLOOD TRANSFUSION SERVICE, 21 Ellens Glen Road, Edinburgh EH17 7QT. Tel: 0131-536 5701. *National Director*, A. McMillan-Douglas
WELSH BLOOD SERVICE, Ely Valley Road, Talbot Green, Pontyclun CF72 9WB. Tel: 01443-622000. *Director*, Dr F. G. Williams
NORTHERN IRELAND BLOOD TRANSFUSION SERVICE, Belfast City Hospital Complex, Lisburn Road, Belfast BT9 7TS. Tel: 028-9032 1414

HOSPICES

Hospice or palliative care may be available for patients with life-threatening illnesses. It may be provided at the patient's home or in a voluntary or NHS hospice or in hospital, and is intended to ensure the best possible quality of life for the patient during their illness, and to provide help and support to both the patient and the patient's family. The National Council for Hospices and Specialist Palliative Care Services co-ordinates NHS and voluntary services in England, Wales and Northern Ireland; the Scottish Partnership Agency for Palliative and Cancer Care performs the same function in Scotland.

NATIONAL COUNCIL FOR HOSPICE AND SPECIALIST PALLIATIVE CARE SERVICES, 1st Floor, 34–44 Britannia Street, London WC1X 9JG. Tel: 020-7520 8299. *Executive Director*, Ms E. S. Richardson
SCOTTISH PARTNERSHIP AGENCY FOR PALLIATIVE AND CANCER CARE, 1A Cambridge Street, Edinburgh EH1 2DY. Tel: 0131-229 0538. *Director*, Mrs M. Stevenson

NUMBER OF BEDS AND PATIENT ACTIVITY 1998

	England*	Wales
In-patients:		
Average daily available beds	194,000	14,200
Average daily occupation of beds	157,000	–
Persons waiting for admission at 31 March	1,158,000	61,800
Day-case admissions	3,071,000	328,000
Ordinary admissions	8,459,000	522,700
Out-patient attendances:		
New patients	11,529,000	691,300
Total attendances	41,635,000	2,667,400
Accident and emergency:		
New patients	12,794,000	831,000
Total attendances	14,364,000	982,000
Ward attendances	1,034,000	n/a

* 1997 figures
n/a not available

SCOTLAND

In-patients:	
Average available staffed beds	36,800
Average occupied beds	29,500
Out-patient attendances:	
New patients	2,715,000
Total attendances	6,331,000

Source: The Stationery Office – *Annual Abstract of Statistics 2000* (Crown copyright)

WAITING LISTS

At the end of May 2000 the total number of patients waiting to be admitted to NHS hospitals in England was 1,052,900, a decrease of 3.9 per cent on the previous year. The number of patients who had been waiting more than one year was 50,900, an increase of 5.3 per cent on the previous year. Under the Patient's Charter, patients are guaranteed admission within 18 months of being placed on a waiting list however, 15 patients had been waiting longer than 18 months at the end of May 2000.

NHS CHARTERS

The original Patient's Charter was published in 1991 and came into force in 1992; an expanded version was published in 1995. The Charter sets out the rights of patients in relation to the NHS (i.e. the standards of service which all patients will receive at all times); and patients' reasonable expectations (i.e. the standards of service that the NHS aims to provide, even if they cannot in exceptional circumstances be met). The Charter covers areas such as access to services, personal treatment of patients, the provision of information, registering with a doctor, hospital waiting times, care in hospitals, community services, ambulance waiting times, dental, optical and pharmaceutical services, and maternity services. In England there are separate Patient's Charter leaflets setting out standards in relation to services for children and young people, maternity services, mental health services and blood donation.

Further information is available free of charge from the National Health Information Service (Tel: 0800-665544).

Health authorities and boards, NHS Trusts and GP practices may also have their own local charters setting out the standard of service they aim to provide.

COMPLAINTS

The Patient's Charter includes the right to have any complaint about the service provided by the NHS dealt with quickly, with a full written reply being provided by a relevant chief executive. There are two levels to the NHS complaints procedure: the first level involves resolution of a complaint locally, following a direct approach to the relevant service provider; the second level involves an independent review procedure if the complaint is not resolved locally. As a final resort, patients may approach the Health Service Commissioner or Ombudsman (*see* page 350) (in Northern Ireland, the Commissioner for Complaints if they are dissatisfied with the response of the NHS to a complaint.

In 1998–9 there were 86,013 written complaints about hospital and community health services, of which 63 per cent were resolved locally within the target period of four weeks; two per cent of complainants requested an independent review. Hospital and Community Trusts received 93 per cent of the total number of complaints with Ambulance Trusts receiving just under five per cent and Health Authorities just over three per cent.

NHS TRIBUNALS

The National Health Service Tribunal and the National Health Service Tribunal (Scotland) (*see* Tribunals) consider representations that the continued inclusion of a doctor, dentist, optician or pharmacist on the list of a health authority or health board would be prejudicial to the efficiency of the service concerned. The Mental Health Review Tribunals (*see* Tribunals) are responsible for reviewing the cases of patients compulsorily detained under the Mental Health Act 1983.

RECIPROCAL ARRANGEMENTS

Citizens of countries in the European Economic Area (EEA – *see* European Union) are entitled to receive emergency health care either free of charge or for a reduced charge when they are temporarily visiting other member states of the EEA. Form E111, available at post offices, should be obtained before travelling. Non-EEA nationals, or visitors receiving routine, non-emergency care, are normally required to pay for treatment in Britain. There are bilateral agreements with several other countries, including Australia and New Zealand, for the provision of urgent medical treatment either free of charge or for a reduced charge.

Personal Social Services

The Secretary of State for Health is responsible, under the Local Authority Social Services Act 1970, for the provision of social services for elderly people, disabled people, families and children, and those with mental disorders. Personal Social Services are administered by local authorities according to policies and standards set by central government. Each authority has a Director of Social Services and a Social Services Committee responsible for the social services functions placed upon them. Local authorities provide, enable and commission care after assessing the needs of their population. The private and voluntary sectors also play an important role in the delivery of social services, and an estimated six million people in Great Britain provide substantial regular care for a member of their family.

The Community Care reforms introduced in 1993 were intended to enable vulnerable groups to live in the community rather than in residential homes wherever possible, and to offer them as independent a lifestyle as possible.

At 31 March 1999, there were 345,000 residential places in 24,800 residential and nursing care homes in England. About 261,000 residents were supported by local authorities (compared to 186,000 in 1995).

FINANCE

The Personal Social Services programme is financed partly by central government, with decisions on expenditure allocations being made at local authority level.

STAFF

STAFF OF LOCAL AUTHORITY SOCIAL SERVICES DEPARTMENTS 1999 (ENGLAND)

Full-time equivalents

Area office/field work staff	110,900
Residential care staff	59,200
Day care staff	30,800
Central/strategic HQ staff	16,500
Other staff	2,300
Total staff	221,700

Source: Department of Health

ELDERLY PEOPLE

Services for elderly people are designed to enable them to remain living in their own homes for as long as possible. Local authority services include advice, domestic help, meals in the home, alterations to the home to aid mobility, emergency alarm systems, day and/or night attendants, laundry services and the provision of day centres and recreational facilities. Charges may be made for these services. Respite care may also be provided in order to allow carers temporary relief from their responsibilities.

Local authorities and the private sector also provide 'sheltered housing' for elderly people, sometimes with resident wardens.

If an elderly person is admitted to a residential home, charges are made according to a means test; if the person cannot afford to pay, the costs are met by the local authority.

The Royal Commission on Long-Term Care reported in March 1999. Its proposals are being considered by the Government.

DISABLED PEOPLE

Services for disabled people are designed to enable them to remain living in their own homes wherever possible. Local authority services include advice, adaptations to the home, meals in the home, help with personal care, occupational therapy, educational facilities and recreational facilities. Respite care may also be provided in order to allow carers temporary relief from their responsibilities.

Special housing may be available for disabled people who can live independently, and residential accommodation for those who cannot.

FAMILIES AND CHILDREN

Local authorities are required to provide services aimed at safeguarding the welfare of children in need and, wherever possible, allowing them to be brought up by their families. Services include advice, counselling, help in the home and the provision of family centres. Many authorities also provide short-term refuge accommodation for women and children.

DAY CARE

In allocating day-care places to children, local authorities give priority to children with special needs, whether in terms of their health, learning abilities or social needs. They also provide a registration and inspection service in relation to childminders, play groups and private day nurseries in the local authority area. In England in August 2000 there were approximately 7,000 day nurseries providing 170,000 places, 98,500 registered child-minders providing 365,000 places, and 14,500 play groups providing 362,000 places.

A national child care strategy is being developed by the Government, under which day care and out-of-school child care facilities will be extended to match more closely the needs of working parents.

CHILD PROTECTION

Children considered to be at risk of physical injury, neglect or sexual abuse are placed on the local authority's child protection register. Local authority social services staff, school nurses, health visitors and other agencies work together to prevent and detect cases of abuse. In England at 31 March 1998 there were 31,600 children on child protection registers, a two per cent decrease from March 1997. This figure represents 28 children per 10,000 of population aged under 18. Of these, 39 per cent were at risk of neglect, 33 per cent of physical abuse, 20 per cent of sexual abuse and 16 per cent of emotional abuse.

LOCAL AUTHORITY CARE

Local authorities are required to provide accommodation for children who have no parent or guardian or whose parents or guardians are unable or unwilling to care for them. A family proceedings court may also issue a care order in cases where a child is being neglected or abused, or is not attending school; the court must be satisfied that this would positively contribute to the well-being of the child.

The welfare of children in local authority care must be properly safeguarded. Children may be placed with foster families, who receive payments to cover the expenses of caring for the child or children, or in residential care. Children's homes may be run by the local authority or by the private or voluntary sectors; all homes are subject to inspection procedures. In England at 31 June 2000, 55,300 children were in the care of local authorities. Of these, 65 per cent were placed with foster parents and four per cent were placed for adoption.

ADOPTION

Local authorities are required to provide an adoption service, either directly or via approved voluntary societies. In England and Wales in 1998, 4,387 children (2,214 boys and 2,173 girls) were adopted.

PEOPLE WITH LEARNING DISABILITIES

Services for people with learning disabilities (i.e. mental handicap) are designed to enable them to remain living in the community wherever possible. Local authority services include short-term care, support in the home, the provision of day care centres, and help with other activities outside the home. Residential care is provided for the severely or profoundly disabled.

MENTALLY ILL PEOPLE

Under the Care Programme Approach, mentally ill people should be assessed by specialist services and receive a care plan, and a key worker should be appointed for each patient. Regular reviews of the patient's progress should be conducted. Local authorities provide help and advice to mentally ill people and their families, and places in day centres and social centres. Social workers can apply for a mentally disturbed person to be compulsorily detained in hospital. Where appropriate, mentally ill people are provided with accommodation in special hospitals, local authority accommodation, or homes run by private or voluntary organisations. Patients who have been discharged from hospitals may be placed on a supervision register. In July 1998 the Government announced that the system of care for mentally ill people would be replaced. A Mental Health National Service Framework was published in September 1999 setting the first ever national standards on how to prevent and treat mental illness. The government has pledged £700 million in the next two years in a drive to build modern and dependable mental health services. In Scotland a committee has been established to review mental health legislation and will report to the Scottish Parliament in late 2000.

LOCAL AUTHORITY-SUPPORTED RESIDENTS IN STAFFED RESIDENTIAL AND NURSING CARE (ENGLAND)
as at 31 March 1998

All staffed homes	249,438
Local authority staffed	54,611
Independent residential care	121,923
Independent nursing care	72,904
People aged 65 and over	202,722
People aged under 65	
Physically/sensorily disabled adults	8,734
People with mental health problems	9,277
People with learning disabilities	26,029
Other people	2,676

Source: The Stationery Office – Health and Personal Social Services Statistics for England 1999 (Crown copyright)

LOCAL AUTHORITY PERSONAL SOCIAL SERVICES GROSS EXPENDITURE BY CLIENT GROUP 1997–8 (ENGLAND)

£ million	Elderly	Children	Learning disability	Adults	Mental health	HQ costs	Total
HQ costs	—	—	—	—	—	128	128
Area officers/senior managers	104	155	26	27	24	—	336
Care management/care assessment	279	354	58	78	95	—	863
Residential care	2,942	690	737	200	208	—	4,776
Non-residential care	1,541	952	487	382	169	—	3,531
Field social work	464	105	17	17	18	—	203
Other	—	—	—	147	—	—	147
TOTAL	4,912	2,256	1,324	850	515	128	9,984

Source: The Stationery Office – Health and Personal Social Services Statistics for England 1999 (Crown copyright)

National Insurance and Related Cash Benefits

NB All leaflets referred to in this section can be obtained from local social security offices unless an alternative source is given

The state insurance and assistance schemes, comprising schemes of national insurance and industrial injuries insurance, national assistance, and non-contributory old age pensions, came into force from 5 July 1948. The Ministry of Social Security Act 1966 replaced national assistance and non-contributory old age pensions with a scheme of non-contributory benefits. These and subsequent measures relating to social security provision in Great Britain were consolidated by the Social Security Act 1975, the Social Security (Consequential Provisions) Act 1975, and the Industrial Injuries and Diseases (Old Cases) Act 1975. Corresponding measures were passed for Northern Ireland. The Social Security Pensions Act 1975 introduced a new state pensions scheme in 1978, and the graduated pension scheme 1961 to 1975 has been wound up, existing rights being preserved. Under the Pensions Act 1995 the age of retirement is to be 65 for both men and women, this being phased in between 2010 and 6 April 2020. The Pensioners' Payments and Social Security Act 1979 provided for a Christmas bonus for pensioners in 1979 and in succeeding years. The Child Benefit Act 1975 replaced family allowances (introduced 1946) with child benefit and one-parent benefit. Some of this legislation has been superseded by the provisions of the Social Security Acts 1969 to 1992. The Government is reforming the social security system. The Welfare Reform and Pensions Bill became law on 11 November 1999. Changes in benefits will come into effect from April 2001. Details of changes, where known, are included.

NATIONAL INSURANCE SCHEME

The National Insurance (NI) scheme operates under the Social Security Contributions and Benefits Act 1992 and the Social Security Administration Act 1992, and orders and regulations made thereunder. The scheme is financed by contributions payable by earners, employers and others (see below) and by a Treasury grant. Money collected under the scheme is used to finance the National Insurance Fund (from which contributory benefits are paid) and to contribute to the cost of the National Health Service.

NATIONAL INSURANCE FUND

Approximate receipts and payments of the National Insurance Fund for the year ended 31 March 2000 were:

Receipts	£'000
Balance, 1 April 1999 (provisional)	9,608,000
Contributions under the Social Security Acts (net of SSP and SMP)	49,402,000
Treasury grant	0
Compensation from Consolidated Fund for SSP and SMP recoveries	590,000
Compensation from Consolidated Fund for contribution holidays for employers taking on formerly long-term unemployed	2,000
Income from investments	780,000
State scheme premiums	49,000
	50,823,000

Payments	£'000
Benefits	464,266,000
Personal pensions contracted-out rebates and age-related rebates for contracted out money purchase schemes	2,127,000
Transfers to Northern Ireland	230,000
Administration	783,000
Redundancy payments (net)	126,000
Balance, 31 March 2000	12,193,000
	61,716,000

CONTRIBUTIONS

There are six classes of NI contributions:

Class 1	paid by employees and their employers
Class 1A	paid by employers who provide employees with cars/fuel for private use
Class 1B	paid by employers in value of any items included on a PAYE settlement with the Inland Revenue
Class 2	paid by self-employed people
Class 3	voluntary contributions paid to protect entitlement to certain benefits
Class 4	paid by the self-employed on their taxable profits over a set limit

The lower and upper earnings limits and the percentage rates referred to below apply from 3 April 2000 to 2 April 2001.

CLASS 1

Class 1 contributions are paid where a person:

– is an employed earner (employee) or office holder (e.g. company director)
– is 16 or over and under state pension age
– earns at or above £76.00 per week (including overtime pay, bonus, commission, etc., without deduction of superannuation contributions)

Class 1 contributions are made up of primary and secondary contributions. Primary contributions are those paid by the employee and these are deducted from earnings by the employer. Primary contributions are not paid on earnings below the lower earnings limit. They are payable at the rate of ten per cent on earnings between £76.00 and the upper earnings limit of £535.00 per week (8.4 per cent for contracted-out employment, see page 496).

Some married women or widows pay a reduced rate of 3.85 per cent on earnings between the lower and upper earnings limits. It is no longer possible to elect to pay the reduced rate but those who had reduced liability before 12 May 1977 may retain it so long as certain conditions are met. See leaflet CA09 (widows) or leaflet CA13 (married women).

Secondary contributions are paid by employers of employed earners at the rate of 12.2 per cent on all earnings at or above the secondary earnings threshold of £84.00 per week. Employers operating contracted-out salary related schemes (see page 496) pay reduced contributions of 9.2 per cent; those with contracted-out money-purchase schemes (see page 496) also pay 9.2 per cent. There is no upper earnings limit for employers' contributions. The contracted-out rate applies only to that portion of earnings between the lower and upper earnings limits. Employers' contributions below and above those respective limits are assessed at the appropriate not contracted-out rate.

CLASS 2

Class 2 contributions are paid where a person is self-employed and is 16 or over and under state pension age.

Contributions are paid at a flat rate of £2.00 per week regardless of the amount earned. However, those with earnings of less than £3,825 a year can apply for Small Earnings Exception, e.g. exemption from liability to pay Class 2 contributions. Those granted exemption from Class 2 contributions may pay Class 2 or Class 3 contributions voluntarily. Self-employed earners (whether or not they pay Class 2 contributions) may also be liable to pay Class 4 contributions based on profits. There are special rules for those who are concurrently employed and self-employed.

Married women and widows can no longer choose not to pay Class 2 contributions but those who elected not to pay Class 2 contributions before 12 May 1977 may retain the right so long as certain conditions are met.

Class 2 contributions are collected by the National Insurance Contributions Office (NICO), an executive agency of the Inland Revenue, by direct debit or quarterly bills. See leaflets CA03 and CA02.

CLASS 3

Class 3 contributions are voluntary flat-rate contributions of £6.55 per week payable by persons over the age of 16 who would otherwise be unable to qualify for retirement pension and certain other benefits because they have an insufficient record of Class 1 or Class 2 contributions. This may include those who are not working, those not liable for Class 1 or Class 2 contributions or those excepted from Class 2 contributions. Married women and widows who on or before 11 May 1977 elected not to pay Class 1 (full rate) or Class 2 contributions cannot pay Class 3 contributions while they retain this right.

Class 3 contributions are collected by the NICO by quarterly bills or direct debit. See leaflet CA08.

CLASS 4

Self-employed people whose profits and gains are over £4,385 a year pay Class 4 contributions in addition to Class 2 contributions. This applies to self-employed earners over 16 and under the state pension age. Class 4 contributions are calculated at seven per cent of annual profits or gains between £4,385 and £27,820. The maximum Class 4 contribution payable on £27,820 or more is £1,640.45.

Class 4 contributions are assessed and collected by the Inland Revenue together with Schedule D tax. It is possible, in some circumstances, to apply for exceptions from liability to pay Class 4 contributions or to have the amount of contribution reduced (where Class 1 contributions are payable on earnings assessed for Class 4 contributions). See leaflet CA03.

PENSIONS

The Social Security Pensions Act came into force in 1978. It aimed to:
- reduce reliance on means-tested benefit in old age, widowhood and chronic ill-health
- ensure that occupational pension schemes which are contracted out of the state scheme fulfil the conditions of a good scheme
- ensure that pensions are adequately protected against inflation
- ensure that men and women are treated equally in state and occupational schemes
Legislation and regulations introduced since 1978 go further towards fulfilling these aims and more changes came into effect in April 1997 (see below). One of the changes is to equalise the state pension age for men (currently 65 years) and women (currently 60 years) from 6 April 2020.

The change will be phased in over the ten years leading up to 6 April 2020. As a result the state pension age is as follows:
- the pension age for men remains at 65
- the pension age for women born on or before 5 April 1950 remains at 60
- the pension age for women born on or after 6 April 1955 is now 65
- for women born after 5 April 1950 and before 6 April 1955, the pension age is 60 plus one month for every month, or part of a month, that their date of birth fell after 5 April 1950.
The Welfare Reform and Pensions Bill provides for the sharing of pensions between divorcing couples.

STATE PENSION SCHEME

The state pension scheme consists of the basic flat-rate pension and the state earnings-related pension scheme (SERPS), also known as additional pension.

The amount of basic pension paid is dependent on the number of 'qualifying years' a person has in their 'working life'. A 'qualifying year' is a tax year in which a person pays Class 1 (at the standard rate), 2 or 3 NI contributions for the whole year (see above). Those in receipt of invalid care allowance, disabled person's tax credit, jobseeker's allowance, incapacity benefit, severe disablement allowance or approved training have contributions credited to them for each week they receive benefit or fulfil certain other conditions. For those reaching pensionable age on or after 6 April 1999, a Class 3 credit of earnings will be awarded for each week from 6 April 1995 that family credit or, subsequently, working families tax credit, has been received. 'Working life' is counted from the start of the tax year in which a person reaches 16 to the end of the tax year before the one in which they reach pensionable age: for men this is normally 49 years and for women this varies between 44 and 49 years because the state pension ages vary (see above). To get the full rate (100 per cent) basic pension a person must have qualifying years for about 90 per cent of their working life. To get the minimum basic pension (25 per cent) a person will need ten or eleven qualifying years. Married women who are not entitled to a pension on their own contributions may get a pension on their husband's contributions. It is possible for people who are unable to work because they care for children or a sick or disabled person at home to reduce the number of qualifying years required. This is called home responsibilities protection (HRP) and can be given for any tax year since April 1978; the number of years for which HRP is given is deducted from the number of qualifying years needed.

The amount of SERPS or additional pension paid depends on the amount of earnings a person has between the lower and upper earnings limits (see page 494) for each complete tax year between 6 April 1978 (when the scheme started) and the tax year before they reach state pension age. The right to additional pension does not depend on the person's right to basic pension. The amount of additional pension paid also depends on when a person reaches retirement; changes phased in from 6 April 1999 mean that pensions are calculated differently from that date. Women widowed before 6 April 2000 inherit all their late husband's additional pension and women widowed on or after this date will inherit half of the husband's additional pension.

There are four categories of state pension provided under the Social Security Contributions and Benefits Act 1992:
- Category A, a contributory pension made up of basic and additional elements, payable to those of pensionable age who satisfy the entitlement conditions described above (see pages 499–500)

– Category B, a contributory pension made up of basic and additional elements, payable to married women and widows and based on their husband's contributions. This category of pension is to be extended to men whose wives were born after 5 April 1950 from 6 April 2010 (*see* page 498)

– Category C, a non-contributory pension payable to those who reached pensionable age before 5 July 1948 (*see* page 499)

– Category D, a non-contributory pension for those over 80 (*see* page 499)

Graduated retirement benefit is also available to those who paid graduated NI contributions into the scheme when it existed between April 1961 and April 1975.

It is possible to find out how much basic and additional pension a person might receive by filling in form BR19, available from local social security offices or by telephoning 0191-225 5240.

The Welfare Reform and Pensions Bill will make changes to pensions. SERPS will be replaced by a second state pension from 2002. This will initially be earnings-related, but will subsequently be paid at a flat rate, targeted towards low earners. It will provide a guaranteed minimum income. Under certain circumstances, people not working (such as disabled people and those caring for children or sick relatives) will receive credits into the scheme as though they had earned £9,000 per year. As with SERPS, a person will be entitled to contract out into an occupational, personal or new stakeholder pension scheme. Stakeholder pensions will be available from 2001. They will be targeted at those earning between £9,000 and £18,500 who have no occupational or appropriate personal scheme to join. Higher earners will also be able to join a stakeholder scheme if they wish.

CONTRACTED-OUT OCCUPATIONAL AND PERSONAL PENSION SCHEMES

Under the Pensions Schemes Act 1993, an employer can contract out of SERPS those employees who are members of an occupational scheme, so long as the occupational scheme satisfies certain conditions. The occupational pension took the place of the additional pension from April 1997 (previously it took the place of part of the additional pension); the state remains responsible for the flat rate state basic pension. Until April 1997 members of contracted-out occupational and personal pension schemes accrued additional pension in the same way as someone who is not contracted-out but the rate payable was reduced by contracted-out deductions. Since 5 April 1997, it has not been possible to accrue any SERPS while being a member of a contracted-out occupational or personal pension scheme. Members are still entitled to those rights earned before April 1997. Since April 1997 there have been age-related NI contribution rebates for people who leave SERPS and become members of either a COMP (*see* below) or an appropriate personal pension scheme; these will be lower for younger people and higher for older people.

There are three types of contracted-out occupational schemes.

Contracted-Out Salary-Related Scheme (COSR)

– this scheme must provide a pension related to earnings

– the pension provided must not be less than a person's guaranteed minimum pension (GMP), i.e. worth about the same as the additional pension provided by the state scheme had the member remained in the State scheme

– any notional additional pension earned from 6 April 1978 to 5 April 1997 will be reduced by the amount of GMP earned during that period (the contracted-out deduction)

– from 6 April 1997 these schemes no longer provide a GMP but do have to satisfy a new scheme-based test, certified by an actuary, before a contracting-out certificate can be issued

Contracted-Out Money Purchase Scheme (COMP)

– this scheme must provide a pension based on the value of the fund built up, i.e. the money paid in, along with returns from investment

– part of the pension, known as protected rights, takes the place of the additional pension. A contracted-out deduction, which may be more or less than the pension provided by the scheme, will be made from any additional pension earned from 6 April 1987 to 5 April 1997

In contracted-out occupational pension schemes, both the employee and employer pay lower NI contribution rates in recognition that SERPS will not be paid.

Contracted-Out Mixed Benefit Scheme (COMBS)

A mixed benefit scheme has two active sections, one salary-related and the other money purchase. Scheme rules set out which section individual employees may join and the circumstances (if any) in which members may move between sections. Each section must satisfy the respective contracting-out conditions for COSRs and COMPs.

Appropriate Personal Pension Schemes

The option of a personal pension scheme is open to all employees, even if their employer has an occupational pension scheme. A personal pension scheme must provide a pension based on the value of the fund built up, i.e. the money paid in, along with returns from investment. Part of the pension, known as protected rights, takes the place of the additional pension. A contracted-out deduction, which may be more or less than the pension provided by the scheme, will be made from any additional pension earned from 6 April 1987 to 5 April 1997.

Employees who are members of a personal pension plan and their employers pay NI contributions at the full rate and the Inland Revenue pays the difference between the full rate and the contracted-out rate into the personal pension scheme.

A Pensions Ombudsman deals with complaints about maladministration of pensions schemes. The Occupational Pensions Board, which supervised contracting-out and approved personal pension schemes, was abolished in April 1997 and replaced by the Occupational Pensions Regulatory Authority. *See* leaflet NP46.

BENEFITS

Leaflets relating to the various benefits and contribution conditions for different benefits are available from local social security offices; leaflets NI196 *Social Security Benefit Rates*, FB2 *Which Benefit?* and MG1 *A Guide to Benefits* are general guides to benefits, benefit rates and contributions.

The benefits payable under the Social Security Acts are:

CONTRIBUTORY BENEFITS

Jobseeker's allowance (contribution-based)
Incapacity benefit
Maternity allowance
Widow's benefit (comprising widow's payment,
    widowed mother's allowance and widow's pension)
Retirement pensions, categories A and B

NON-CONTRIBUTORY BENEFITS AND TAX CREDITS

Child benefit
Guardian's allowance
Jobseeker's allowance (income-based)

Invalid care allowance
Severe disablement allowance
Attendance allowance
Disability living allowance
Disabled person's tax credit
Retirement pensions, categories C and D
Income support
Working families tax credit
Housing benefit
Council tax benefit
Social fund

BENEFITS FOR INDUSTRIAL INJURIES AND
DISABLEMENT

Other
Statutory sick pay
Statutory maternity pay

TAX CREDITS

Under the Tax Credits Act 1999, Family Credit and Disability Working Allowance (both non-contributory benefits) were replaced by Working Families Tax Credit and Disabled Person's Tax Credit from 5 October 1999. Both of these are administered by the Inland Revenue. The first payments were made from April 2000. People receiving Family Credit or Disability Working Allowance on 5 October 1999 continue to receive their benefits until the award expires, when they will be able to change to the new tax credits. From April 2000 employees will receive the credits from their employer along with their wages or salary. Self-employed applicants will be paid direct by the Inland Revenue. Further information and application forms are available from Inland Revenue Tax Enquiry Centres, Benefits Agency offices, Jobcentres, post offices and Citizens' Advice Bureaux.

WORKING FAMILIES TAX CREDIT

Working Families Tax Credit is a system of tax credits paid to couples (married or unmarried) or lone parents who have at least one child living with them and where at least one partner works at least 16 hours per week. The credit is not payable if any savings exceed £8,000.

Working Families Tax Credit will usually be paid at the same rate for 26 weeks. There are four elements:
– a basic credit of £52.30 per family per week
– a credit of £11.05 per week where one earner works at least 30 hours per week
– a credit for each child at the rate of £20.95 per week from birth , £20.90 from the September following their 11th birthday and £25.95 from the September following their 16th birthday up to the day before their 19th birthday
– a childcare credit (in certain circumstances) of up to 70 per cent of eligible childcare costs up to a maximum of £100 per week for one child and £150 per week for two or more children

If net income is below £90 per week, the maximum tax credit is payable. If net income exceeds £90 per week, the total tax credit is reduced by 55p for each £1.00 above £90.

DISABLED PERSON'S TAX CREDIT

Disabled Person's Tax Credit is a system of tax credits for people who are working at least 16 hours per week but have an illness or disability which puts them at a disadvantage in getting a job. To qualify, a person must have one of the 'qualifying benefits' or have had them up to 182 days before applying. The credit is not payable if any savings exceed £16,000.

Disabled Person's Tax Credit will usually be paid at the same rate for 26 weeks. There are five elements:

– a basic credit of £54.30 per week for a single person or £83.55 for a couple
– a credit of £11.05 per week where one applicant works at least 30 hours per week
– a credit for each child at the rate of £19.85 from birth (rising by £1.10 plus inflation from April 2000), £20.90 from the September following their 11th birthday and £25.95 from the September following their 16th birthday up to the day before their 19th birthday
– a disabled child's tax credit of £21.90 per week
– a childcare credit (in certain circumstances) of up to 70 per cent of eligible childcare costs up to a maximum of £100 per week for one child and £150 per week for two or more children

If net income is below £70 per week for a single person or £90 per week for a couple or lone parent, the maximum tax credit is payable. If net income exceeds these thresholds, the total tax credit is reduced by 55p for each £1.00 above the threshold.

CONTRIBUTORY BENEFITS

Entitlement to contributory benefits depends on contribution conditions being satisfied either by the claimant or by some other person (depending on the kind of benefit). The class or classes of contribution which for this purpose are relevant to each benefit are:

Jobseeker's allowance (contribution-based)	Class 1
Incapacity benefit	Class 1 or 2
Maternity allowance	Class 1 or 2
Widow's benefits	Class 1, 2 or 3
Retirement pensions, categories A and B	Class 1, 2 or 3

The system of contribution conditions relates to yearly levels of earnings on which contributions have been paid.

JOBSEEKER'S ALLOWANCE

Jobseeker's allowance (JSA) replaced unemployment benefit and income support for unemployed people under pension age from 7 October 1996. There are two routes of entitlement. Contribution-based JSA is paid as a personal rate (i.e. additional benefit for dependants is not paid) to those who have made sufficient NI contributions in two particular tax years. Savings and partner's earnings are not taken into account and payment can be made for up to six months. Those who do not qualify for contribution-based JSA, those who have exhausted their entitlement to contribution-based JSA or those for whom contribution-based JSA provides insufficient income may qualify for income-based JSA. The amount paid depends on age and number of dependants and income and savings are taken into account. Income-based JSA may comprise three parts: a personal allowance for the jobseeker and his/her partner and one for each child or young person for whom they are responsible; premiums for groups of people with special needs; and housing costs. This is payable for the claimant and their dependants for as long as they satisfy the rules. Rates of jobseeker's allowance correspond to income support rates.

Claims for this benefit are made through Employment Service Job centres. A person wishing to claim jobseeker's allowance must be unemployed, capable of work and available for any work which they can reasonably be expected to do, usually for at least 40 hours per week. They must agree and sign a 'jobseeker's agreement', which will set out each claimant's plans to find work, and must actively seek work. If they refuse work or training their benefit may be suspended for between two and six weeks.

A person will be disqualified from jobseeker's allowance if they have left a job voluntarily or through misconduct, if they refuse to take up an offer of employment or if they fail to attend a training scheme or employment programme. In these circumstances, it may be possible to receive hardship payments, particularly where the claimant or their family is vulnerable, e.g. if sick or pregnant, or for those with children or caring responsibilities. *See* leaflet JSAL5.

INCAPACITY BENEFIT

Incapacity benefit is available to those who are incapable of work but cannot get statutory sick pay from their employer. It is not payable to those over state pension age. However, people who are already in receipt of short-term incapacity benefit when they reach state pension age may continue to receive this benefit for up to 52 weeks. The Welfare Reform and Pensions Bill will restrict eligibility for incapacity benefit to people who have paid National Insurance contributions in the previous two years. The Bill also provides for the reduction of the amount of incapacity benefit payable where a claimant receives more than a specified amount of occupational or personal pension. Severely disabled people aged between 16 and 19 should receive incapacity benefit without meeting the national insurance contribution conditions under the Government's proposals. There are three rates of incapacity benefit:

– short-term lower rate for the first 28 weeks of sickness
– short-term higher rate from weeks 29 to 52
– long-term rate after week 52

The terminally ill and those entitled to the highest rate care component of disability living allowance are paid the long-term rate after 28 weeks. Incapacity benefit is taxable after 28 weeks.

Two rates of age addition are paid with long-term benefit based on the claimant's age when incapacity started. The higher rate is payable where incapacity for work commenced before the age of 35; and the lower rate where incapacity commenced before the age of 45. Increases for dependants are also payable with short and long-term incapacity benefit.

There are two medical tests of incapacity: the 'own occupation' test and the 'all work' test. Those who worked before becoming incapable of working will be assessed, for the first 28 weeks of incapacity, on their ability to do their own job. After 28 weeks (or from the start of incapacity for those who were not working) claimants are assessed on their ability to carry out a range of work-related activities. The 'all work' test applies to most former sickness and invalidity benefit claimants. The Government plans to replace the 'all work' test with a new 'personal capability assessment.' *See* leaflets IB202 and SD1.

MATERNITY ALLOWANCE

The maternity allowance (MA) scheme covers women who are self-employed or otherwise do not qualify for statutory maternity pay (*see* page 503). In order to qualify, the woman must have been working and paying standard rate NI contributions for at least 26 weeks in the 66-week period which ends with the week before the week in which the baby is due. A woman can choose to start receiving MA between the beginning of the 11th week before the week in which the baby is due and the Sunday after the baby is born, depending on when she stops working. MA is paid for a period of up to 18 weeks. MA is only paid while the woman is not working. *See* leaflet NI17A.

WIDOW'S BENEFITS

Only the late husband's contributions of any class count for widow's benefit in any of its three forms:
Widow's payment – may be received by a woman who at her husband's death is under 60, or whose husband was not

entitled to a Category A retirement pension when he died. It is a single tax-free lump sum payable immediately the woman becomes a widow
Widowed mother's allowance – a taxable benefit payable to a widow if she is entitled or treated as entitled to child benefit, or if she is expecting her husband's baby
Widow's pension – a widow may receive this pension if aged 45 or over at the time of her husband's death (40 or over if widowed before 11 April 1988) or when her widowed mother's allowance ends. If aged 55 or over (50 or over if widowed before 11 April 1988) she will receive the full widow's pension rate

It is not possible to receive widowed mother's allowance and widow's pension at the same time, and widow's benefit in any form ceases upon remarriage or during a period in which a widow lives with a man as his wife. Different rules and conditions (other than those mentioned) apply to women widowed before 11 April 1988. The Welfare Reform and Pensions Bill will replace the widow's payment with a £2,000 bereavement payment and the introduction of widowed parent's allowance and bereavement allowance. All of the new benefits will be payable to both widowers and widows who are eligible. *See* leaflet NP45.

RETIREMENT PENSION: CATEGORIES A AND B

A Category A pension is payable for life to men and women who reach state pension age and who satisfy the contributions conditions (*see* page 494). A Category B pension is payable for life to a spouse and is based on their wife or husband's contributions. It becomes payable only when the wife or husband has claimed their pension and the spouse has reached state pension age. It is also payable on widowhood after the state retirement age regardless of whether the wife or husband had qualified for their pension. There are special rules for those who are widowed before reaching pensionable age.

A person may defer claiming their pension for five years after state pension age. In doing so they may earn increments which will increase the weekly amount paid when they claim their pension. If a married man defers his Category A pension, his wife cannot claim a Category B pension on his contributions but she may earn increments on her pension during this time. A woman can defer her Category B pension, and earn increments, even if her husband is claiming his Category A pension.

The basic state pension is £67.50 per week plus any additional (earnings-related) pension the person may be entitled to (*see* page 494). An increase of £40.40 is paid for an adult dependant, providing the dependant's earnings do not exceed the rate of jobseeker's allowance for a single person (*see* below). It is also possible to get an increase of Category A and B pensions for a child or children. An age addition of 25p per week is payable if a retirement pensioner is aged 80 or over.

Since 1989 pensioners have been allowed to have unlimited earnings without affecting their retirement pension. Income support is payable on top of a pension where a pension does not give the person enough to live on and to those who are entitled to retirement pension but who have not claimed it. Pensioners may also be entitled to housing and council tax benefits.

GRADUATED RETIREMENT BENEFIT

Graduated NI contributions were first payable from 1961 and were calculated as a percentage of earnings between certain bands. They were discontinued in 1975. Any graduated pension which an employed person over 18 and under 70 (65 for a woman) had earned by paying graduated contributions will be paid when the contributor claims retirement pension or at 70 (65 for a woman), in addition to any retirement pension for which he or she qualifies. A wife can get a graduated pension in return for her own graduated contributions, but not for her husband's.

Graduated retirement benefit is at a weekly rate for each 'unit' of graduated contributions paid by the employee (half a unit or more counts as a whole unit); the rate varies from person to person. A unit of graduated pension can be calculated by adding together all graduated contributions and dividing by 7.5 (men) or 9.0 (women). If a person defers making a claim beyond 65 (60 for a woman), entitlement may be increased by one seventh of a penny per £1 of its weekly rate for each complete week of deferred retirement, as long as the retirement is deferred for a minimum of seven weeks.

WEEKLY RATES OF BENEFIT

from April 2000

Jobseeker's allowance (contribution-based)

Person under 18	£31.45
Person aged 18–24	41.35
Person over 25	52.20

Short-term incapacity benefit

Person under pension age – lower rate	50.90
*Person under pension age – higher rate	60.20
Increase for adult dependant	31.50
*Person over pension age	64.75
Increase for adult dependant	31.50

Long-term incapacity benefit

Person (under or over pension age)	67.50
Increase for adult dependant	40.40
Age addition – lower rate	7.10
Age addition – higher rate	14.20

Invalidity allowance: maximum amount payable

Higher rate	14.20
Middle rate	9.00
Lower rate	4.50

Maternity allowance

Employed	60.20
Self-employed or unemployed	52.25

Widow's benefits

Widow's payment (lump sum)	1,000.00
†Widowed mother's allowance	67.50
†Widow's pension	67.50

* *Retirement pension: categories A and B*

Single person	67.50
Increase for wife/other adult dependant	40.40

* These benefits attract an increase for each dependent child (in addition to child benefit) of £9.85 for the first or only child and £11.35 for each subsequent child
† To rise to £2,000 under Welfare Reform and Pensions Bill

NON-CONTRIBUTORY BENEFITS

These benefits are paid from general taxation and are not dependent on NI contributions. Unless otherwise stated, a benefit is tax-free and is not means tested.

CHILD BENEFIT

Child benefit is payable for virtually all children aged under 16, and for those aged 16 to 18 who are studying full-time up to and including A-level or equivalent standard. It is also payable for a short period if the child has left school recently and is registered for work or work-based training for young people at a careers office.

A higher rate of benefit (child benefit (lone parent)) may be paid to a person who is responsible for bringing up one or more children on his/her own. It is a flat rate benefit payable for the eldest child only. Since 6 July 1998 child benefit (lone parent) has not been available to new lone

parents but it may still be payable in certain circumstances. *See* leaflets CH1 and CH11.

GUARDIAN'S ALLOWANCE

Where the parents of a child are dead, the person who has the child in his/her family may claim a guardian's allowance in addition to child benefit. In exceptional circumstances the allowance is payable on the death of only one parent. *See* leaflet NI14.

INVALID CARE ALLOWANCE

Invalid care allowance (ICA) is a taxable benefit payable to people of working age who give up the opportunity of full-time paid employment because they are regularly and substantially engaged (spending at least 35 hours per week as a carer) in caring for a severely disabled person. To qualify for ICA a person must be caring for someone in receipt of one of the following benefits:
– the middle or highest rate of disability living allowance care component
– either rate of attendance allowance
– constant attendance allowance, paid at not less than the normal maximum rate, under the industrial injuries or war pension schemes
See leaflets FB31 and SD1.

SEVERE DISABLEMENT ALLOWANCE

Persons who have been incapable of work for a continuous period of at least 28 weeks but who do not qualify for contributory incapacity benefit may be entitled to severe disablement allowance (SDA). This benefit is available to people over 16 and under 65. Those who are over 65 can only get SDA if they were entitled to it on the day before their 65th birthday. People who became incapable of work on or before their 20th birthday do not have to have their disability assessed but those who became incapable after their 20th birthday must be assessed as at least 80 per cent disabled. When the Welfare Reform and Pensions Bill is enacted, Severe Disablement Allowance will not be available to new claimants from April 2001. *See* leaflet NI252.

ATTENDANCE ALLOWANCE

This is payable to disabled people who claim after the age of 65 and who need a lot of care or supervision because of physical or mental disability for a period of at least six months. People not expected to live for six months because of an illness do not have to wait six months. The allowance has two rates: the lower rate is for day or night care, and the higher rate is for day and night care. *See* leaflets DS702 and SD1.

DISABILITY LIVING ALLOWANCE

This is payable to disabled people who claim before the age of 65 who have personal care and mobility needs because of an illness or disability for a period of at least three months and are likely to have those needs for a further six months or more. People not expected to live for six months because of an illness do not have to wait three months. The allowance has two components: the care component, which has three rates, and the mobility component, which has two rates. The rates depend on the care and mobility needs of the claimant. The mobility component is currently payable only to those aged five or over, but the Government plans to extend it to those aged over three. A Disability Income Guarantee will also be introduced. *See* leaflets DS704 and SD1.

RETIREMENT PENSION: CATEGORIES C AND D

A Category C pension is provided, subject to a residence test, for persons who were over pensionable age on 5 July

500   Social Welfare

1948, and for the wives and widows of men who qualified if they are over pension age. A Category D pension is provided for people aged 80 and over if they are not entitled to another category of pension or are entitled to less than the Category D rate.

WEEKLY RATES OF BENEFIT
from April 2000
Child benefit

Eldest child	£15.00
Eldest child of certain lone parents	17.10
Each subsequent child	10.00
Guardian's allowance	
Eldest child	9.85
Each subsequent child	11.35
*Invalid care allowance	39.95
Increase for wife/other adult dependant	23.90
Severe disablement allowance	
†Basic rate	40.80
Under 40	14.20
40–49	9.00
50–59	4.50
Increase for wife/other adult dependant	23.95
Attendance allowance	
Higher rate	53.55
Lower rate	35.80
Disability living allowance	
Care component	
Higher rate	53.55
Middle rate	35.80
Lowest rate	14.20
Mobility component	
Higher rate	37.40
Lower rate	14.20
*Retirement pension: categories *C and D*	
Single person	40.40
Increase for wife/other adult dependant	24.15
(not payable with Category D pension)	

* These benefits attract an increase for each dependent child (in addition to child benefit) of £9.85 for the first or only child and £11.35 for each subsequent child
† The age addition applies to the age when incapacity began

INCOME SUPPORT

Income support is a benefit for those aged 16 and over whose income is below a certain level. It can be paid to people who are not expected to sign on as unemployed (income support for unemployed people was replaced by jobseeker's allowance in October 1996) and who are:
– incapable of work due to sickness or disability
– bringing up children alone
– 60 or over
– looking after a person who has a disability
– registered blind
Some people who are not in these categories may also be able to claim income support.

Income support is also payable to people who work for less than 16 hours a week on average (or 24 hours for a partner). Some people can claim income support if they work longer hours.

Income support is not payable if the claimant, or claimant and partner, have capital or savings in excess of £8,000. For capital and savings in excess of £3,000, a deduction of £1 is made for every £250 or part of £250 held. Different limits apply to people permanently in residential care and nursing homes: the upper limit is £16,000 and deductions apply for capital in excess of £10,000.

Sums payable depend on fixed allowances laid down by law for people in different circumstances. If both partners are entitled to income support, either may claim it for the couple. People receiving income support may be able to receive housing benefit, help with mortgage or home loan interest and help with health care. They may also be eligible for help with exceptional expenses from the Social Fund. Special rates may apply to some people living in residential care or nursing homes. Leaflet IS20 gives a detailed explanation of income support.

In October 1998 the Government's voluntary New Deal for Lone Parents programme became available throughout the UK. All lone parents receiving income support are assigned a personal adviser at a jobcentre who will provide guidance and support with a view to enabling the claimant to find work.

INCOME SUPPORT PREMIUMS

Income support premiums are additional weekly payments for those with special needs. People qualifying for more than one premium will normally only receive the highest single premium for which they qualify. However, family premium, disabled child premium, severe disability premium and carer premium are payable in addition to other premiums.
People with children may qualify for:
– the family premium if they have at least one child (a higher rate is paid to lone parents, although from 6 April 1998 it has not generally been available to new claimants)
– the disabled child premium if they have a child who receives disability living allowance or is registered blind
Carers may qualify for:
– the carer premium if they or their partner are in receipt of invalid care allowance
Long-term sick or disabled people may qualify for:
– the disability premium if they or their partner are receiving certain benefits because they are disabled or cannot work; are registered blind; or if the claimant has been incapable of work or receiving statutory sick pay for at least 364 days (196 days if the person is terminally ill), including periods of incapacity separated by eight weeks or less
– the severe disability premium if the person lives alone and receives attendance allowance or the middle or higher rate of disability living allowance care component and no one receives invalid care allowance for caring for that person. This premium is also available to couples where both partners meet the above conditions
People aged 60 and over may qualify for:
– the pensioner premium if they or their partner are aged 60 to 74
– the enhanced pensioner premium if they or their partner are aged 75 to 79
– the higher pensioner premium if they or their partner are aged 80 or over. This is also available to people over 60 who receive attendance allowance, disability living allowance, long-term incapacity benefit or severe disablement allowance, or who are registered blind

WEEKLY RATES OF BENEFIT
from April 2000
Income support
Single person

under 18	£31.45
under 18 (higher)	41.35
aged 18–24	41.35
aged 25 and over	52.50
aged under 18 and a single parent (lower)	31.45
aged under 18 and a single parent (higher)	41.35

aged 18 and over and a single parent	52.20
Couples*	
both under 18	62.35
one or both aged 18 or over	81.95
For each child in a family from birth	
until September following 16th birthday	26.60
†from September following 16th birthday	31.75
to day before 19th birthday	
Premiums	
Family premium	14.25
Family (lone parent) premium	15.90
Disabled child premium	22.25
Carer premium	14.15
Disability premium	
Single	22.25
Couple	31.75
Severe disability premium	
Single	40.20
Couple (one person qualified)	40.20
Couple (both qualified)	80.40
Pensioner premium	
Single	26.25
Couple	40.00
Higher pensioner premium	
Single	33.85
Couple	43.40
Enhanced pensioner premium	
Single	28.65
Couple	43.40

* Where one or both partners are aged under 18, their personal allowance will depend on their situation
† If in full-time education up to A-level or equivalent standard

HOUSING BENEFIT

Housing benefit is designed to help people with rent (including rent for accommodation in guest houses, lodgings or hostels). It does not cover mortgage payments. The amount of benefit paid depends on:
– the income of the claimant, and partner if there is one, including earned income, unearned income (any other income including some other benefits) and savings
– number of dependants
– certain extra needs of the claimant, partner or any dependants
– number and gross income of people sharing the home who are not dependent on the claimant
– how much rent is paid
Housing benefit is not payable if the claimant, or claimant and partner, have savings of over £16,000. The amount of benefit is affected if savings held exceed £3,000. Housing benefit is not paid for meals, fuel or certain service charges that may be included in the rent. Deductions are also made for most non-dependants who live in the same accommodation as the claimant (and their partner).

The maximum amount of benefit (which is not necessarily the same as the amount of rent paid) may be paid where the claimant is in receipt of income support or income-based jobseeker's allowance or where the claimant's income is less than the amount allowed for their needs. Any income over that allowed for their needs will mean that their benefit is reduced.

Claims for housing benefit are made to the local council. Those who are also claiming income support or income-based jobseeker's allowance may claim housing benefit at the local benefits or employment services office. *See* leaflets RR1 and RR2.

COUNCIL TAX BENEFIT

Nearly all the rules which apply to housing benefit apply to council tax benefit, which helps people on low incomes to pay council tax bills. The amount payable depends on how much council tax is paid and who lives with the claimant. The benefit may be available to those receiving income support or income-based jobseeker's allowance or to those whose income is less than that allowed for their needs. Any income over that allowed for their needs will mean that their council tax benefit is reduced. Deductions are made for non-dependants.

The maximum amount that is payable for those living in properties in council tax bands A to E is 100 per cent of the claimant's council tax liability. This also applies to those living in properties in bands F to H who were in receipt of the benefit at 31 March 1998 if they have remained in the same property. From 1 April 1998 council tax benefit for new claimants living in property bands F to H (or existing claimants moving into these bands) was restricted to the level payable for band E.

If a person shares a home with one or more adults (not their partner) who are on a low income, it may be possible to claim a second adult rebate. Those who are entitled to both council tax benefit and second adult rebate will be awarded whichever is the greater. Second adult rebate may be claimed by those not in receipt of council tax benefit.

THE SOCIAL FUND

The Social Fund helps people with expenses which are difficult to meet from regular income. Regulated maternity and funeral payments are decided by Decision Makers; cold weather payments and winter fuel payments are made automatically. These payments are not limited by the district's Social Fund budget. Discretionary community care grants, and budgeting and crisis loans are decided by Social Fund Officers and come out of a yearly budget which is allocated to each district (1999–2000, grants £98 million; loans £436.7 million; £0.5 million set aside as a contingency reserve). *See* leaflet SB16.

REGULATED PAYMENTS

Maternity Payments

From April 2000 the Maternity Payment Scheme was replaced by the State Maternity Grant Scheme. A payment of up to £200 for each baby expected, born, adopted or the subject of a parental order (in the case of surrogacy), will be linked to the claimant seeking advice on the welfare of the baby. It is payable to people on income support, income-based jobseeker's allowance, disabled person's tax credit and working families tax credit and does not have to be repaid.

Funeral Payments

Payable for the necessary cost of burial or cremation, plus other funeral expenses reasonably incurred up to £600, to people receiving income support, income-based jobseeker's allowance, disabled person's tax credit, working families' tax credit, council tax benefit or housing benefit who have good reason for taking responsibility for the funeral expenses. These payments are recoverable from any estate of the deceased.

Cold Weather Payments

A payment of £8.50 when the average temperature over seven consecutive days is recorded as or forecast to be 0°C or below in their area. Payments are made to people on income support or income-based jobseeker's allowance and who have a child under five or whose benefit includes a pensioner or disability premium. They do not have to be repaid.

Winter Fuel Payments

An annual payment of £100 per household paid automatically to eligible pensioners. Payments are made before Christmas and do not have to be repaid.

DISCRETIONARY PAYMENTS

Community Care Grants

These are intended to help people on income support or income-based jobseeker's allowance (or those likely to receive these benefits on leaving residential or institutional accommodation) to live as independently as possible in the community; ease exceptional pressures on families; care for a prisoner or young offender released on temporary licence; help people set up home as part of a resettlement programme and/or assist with certain travelling expenses. They do not have to be repaid.

Budgeting Loans

These are interest-free loans to people who have been receiving income support or income-based jobseeker's allowance for at least 26 weeks, for intermittent expenses that may be difficult to budget for.

Crisis Loans

These are interest-free loans to anyone, whether receiving benefit or not, who is without resources in an emergency, where there is no other means of preventing serious damage or serious risk to their health or safety.

SAVINGS

Savings over £500 (£1,000 for people aged 60 or over) are taken into account for maternity and funeral payments, community care grants and budgeting loans. All savings are taken into account for crisis loans. Savings are not taken into account for cold weather or winter fuel payments.

INDUSTRIAL INJURIES AND DISABLEMENT BENEFITS

The industrial injuries scheme, administered under the Social Security Contributions and Benefits Act 1992, provides a range of benefits designed to compensate for disablement resulting from an industrial accident (i.e. an accident arising out of and in the course of an employed earner's employment) or from a prescribed disease due to the nature of a person's employment. Those who are self-employed are not covered by this scheme.

INDUSTRIAL INJURIES DISABLEMENT BENEFIT

A person must be at least 14 per cent disabled (except for certain respiratory diseases) in order to qualify for this benefit. The amount paid depends on the degree of disablement:

- those assessed as 14–19 per cent disabled are paid at the 20 per cent rate
- those with disablement of over 20 per cent will have the percentage rounded up or down to the nearest ten per cent, e.g. a disablement of 44 per cent will be paid at the 40 per cent rate while a disablement of 45 per cent will be paid at the 50 per cent rate

Benefit is payable 15 weeks (90 days) after the date of the accident or onset of the disease and may be payable for a limited period or for life. The benefit is payable whether the person works or not and those who are incapable of work are entitled to draw statutory sick pay or incapacity benefit in addition to industrial injuries disablement benefit. It may also be possible to claim the following allowances:

- reduced earnings allowance for those who are unable to return to their regular work or work of the same standard and who had their accident (or whose disease started) before 1 October 1990
- retirement allowance for those who were entitled to reduced earnings allowance who have reached state pension age

- constant attendance allowance for those with a disablement of 100 per cent who need constant care. There are four rates of allowance depending on how much care the person needs
- exceptionally severe disablement allowance for those who are entitled to constant care attendance allowance at one of the higher rates and who need constant care permanently

See leaflets NI6 and N12.

OTHER BENEFITS

People who are disabled because of an accident or disease that was the result of work that they did before 5 July 1948 are not entitled to industrial injuries disablement benefit. They may, however, be entitled to payment under the workmen's compensation scheme or the pneumoconiosis, byssinosis and miscellaneous diseases benefit scheme. See leaflets WS1 and PN1.

WEEKLY RATES OF BENEFIT

from April 2000
*Disablement benefit/pension
Degree of disablement

100 per cent	£109.30
90	98.37
80	87.44
70	76.51
60	65.58
50	54.65
40	43.72
30	32.79
20	21.86
†Unemployability supplement	67.50
Addition for adult dependant (subject to earnings rule)	40.40
Reduced earnings allowance (maximum)	43.72
Retirement allowance (maximum)	10.93
Constant attendance allowance (normal maximum rate)	43.80
Exceptionally severe disablement allowance	43.80

* There is a weekly benefit for those under 18 with no dependants which is set at a lower rate
† This benefit attracts an increase for each dependent child (in addition to child benefit) of £9.85 for the first child and £11.35 for each subsequent child

CLAIMS AND QUESTIONS

With a few exceptions, claims and questions relating to social security benefits are decided in agencies. The decision makers act impartially. See leaflets GL24 and NI260(DMA).

Entitlement to benefit (including disablement questions) and regulated Social Fund payments is determined by decision makers. A claimant who is dissatisfied with that decision can ask for an explanation and review of the decision. If they are still dissatisfied they can go to the Appeals Service, an independent tribunal. There is a further right of appeal to a Social Security Commissioner against the tribunal's decision but leave to appeal must first be obtained. Appeals to the Commissioner must be on a point of law. Provision is also made for the determination of certain questions by the Secretary of State for Social Security.

Decisions on applications to the discretionary Social Fund are made by Social Fund Officers. Applicants can ask for a review within 28 days of the date on the decision letter. The Social Fund Review Officer will review the case and there is a further right of review to an independent Social Fund Inspector.

Reviews of housing and council tax benefit decisions are dealt with initially by the council. The claimant must ask for a review within six weeks of being told how much benefit they will receive. Further reviews are dealt with by an independent review board.

OTHER BENEFITS

STATUTORY SICK PAY

Employers usually pay statutory sick pay (SSP) to their employees for up to 28 weeks of sickness in any period of incapacity for work that lasts longer than four days. SSP is paid at £59.55 per week and is subject to PAYE tax and NI deductions. Employees who cannot obtain SSP may be able to claim incapacity benefit. Employers may be able to recover some SSP costs. *See* leaflets NI244 and NI245.

STATUTORY MATERNITY PAY

In general, employers pay statutory maternity pay (SMP) to pregnant women who have been employed by them full or part-time for at least 26 weeks before the end of the 'qualifying week', which is 15 weeks before the week the baby is due, and whose earnings on average at least equal the lower earnings limit applied to NI contributions. All women who meet these conditions receive payment of 90 per cent of their average earnings for six weeks, followed by a maximum of 12 weeks at £59.55. SMP can be paid from the beginning of the 11th week before the week in which the baby is due but women can decide to begin maternity leave later than this. SMP is not payable for any week in which the woman works. Employers are reimbursed for 92 per cent of the SMP they pay (105 per cent for those whose annual NI liability (excluding Class 1A) is £20,000 or less). *See* Leaflet NI17A.

War Pensions

The War Pensions Agency, an executive agency of the Department of Social Security (DSS), awards war pensions under The Naval, Military and Air Forces, Etc. (Disablement and Death) Service Pensions Order 1983 to members of the armed forces in respect of service after 4 August 1914. There is also a scheme for civilians and civil defence workers in respect of the 1939–45 war, and other schemes for groups such as merchant seamen and Polish armed forces who served under British command.

PENSIONS

War disablement pension is awarded for the disabling effects of any injury, wound or disease which is the result of, or has been aggravated by, conditions of service in the armed forces. It can only be paid once the person has left the armed forces. The amount of pension paid depends on the severity of disablement, which is assessed by comparing the health of the claimant with that of a healthy person of the same age and sex. The person's earning capacity or occupation are not taken into account in this assessment. A pension is awarded if the person has a disablement of 20 per cent or more and a lump sum is usually payable to those with a disablement of less than 20 per cent. No award is made for noise-induced sensorineural hearing loss where the assessment of disablement is less than 20 per cent.

War widow's pension is payable where the husband's death was due to, or hastened by, his service in the armed forces or where the husband was in receipt of a war disablement pension constant attendance allowance (or would have been had he not been in hospital). A war widow's pension is also payable if the husband was getting unemployability supplement at the time of his death and his pensionable disablement was at least 80 per cent. Most war widows receive a standard rank-related rate but a lower weekly rate is payable to war widows of men below the rank of Lieutenant-Colonel who are under the age of 40, without children and capable of maintaining themselves. This is increased to the standard rate at age 40. Allowances are paid for children (in addition to child benefit) and adult dependents. An age allowance may also be given when the woman reaches 65 and increased at age 70 and age 80.

A war widower's pension may be payable to a man whose wife died because of service in the armed forces, if he was dependent on his wife before her death and cannot support himself.

All war pensions and war widow's pensions are tax-free and pensioners living overseas receive the same amount as those resident in the UK.

SUPPLEMENTARY ALLOWANCES

A number of supplementary allowances may be awarded to a war pensioner which are intended to meet various needs which may result from disablement or death and take account of its particular effect on the pensioner or spouse. The principal supplementary allowances are unemployability supplement, allowance for lowered standard of occupation and constant attendance allowance. Others include exceptionally severe disablement allowance, severe disablement occupational allowance, treatment allowance, mobility supplement, comforts allowance, clothing allowance, age allowance and widow's age allowance. There is a rent allowance available on a war widow's pension.

SOCIAL SECURITY BENEFITS

Most social security benefits are paid in addition to the basic war disablement pension or war widow's pension. Any retirement pension for which a war widow qualifies on her own NI contribution record can be paid in addition to her war widow's pension.

A war pensioner or war widow who claims income support, working families tax credit or disabled person's tax credit has the first £10 a week of pension disregarded. A similar provision operates for housing benefit and council tax benefit; but the local authority may, at its discretion, disregard any or all of the balance.

CLAIMS AND QUESTIONS

To claim a war pension it is necessary to contact the nearest war pensioners' welfare service office, the address of which is available from local social security offices, or to write to the War Pensions Agency, Norcross, Blackpool FY5 3WP. Claims can also be made through authorised agents, usually ex-service organisations such as the RBL, BLESMA etc.

The war pensioners' welfare service advises and assists war pensioners and widows on any matters affecting their welfare. General advice on any war pensions matter can be obtained by ringing the War Pensions Freeline (UK only) on 0800-169 2277. If living overseas ring 00 44 1253 866043; E-mail: warpensions@gtnet.gov.uk; Web: http://www.dss.gov.uk/wpa/index.htm

The Water Industry

ENGLAND AND WALES

The water industry supplies 58 million people 18,000 million litres of water every day. Around 3 million tests are carried out to check water quality every year and 99.78 per cent of samples meet all British/European standards.

In England and Wales the Secretary of State for the Environment, Transport and the Regions and the National Assembly for Wales have overall responsibility for water policy and set the environmental and health and safety standards for the water industry. The Drinking Water Inspectorate acts on their behalf as the regulator of drinking water quality.

The Director-General of Water Services, as the independent economic regulator, is responsible for ensuring that the private water companies are able to fulfil their statutory obligation to provide water supply and sewerage services, and for protecting the interests of consumers.

The Minister of Agriculture, Fisheries and Food and the National Assembly for Wales are responsible for policy relating to land drainage, flood protection, sea defences and the protection and development of fisheries.

The Environment Agency is responsible for water quality and the control of pollution, the management of water resources and nature conservation.

THE WATER COMPANIES

Until 1989 nine regional water authorities in England and the Welsh Water Authority in Wales were responsible for water supply and the development of water resources, sewerage and sewage disposal, pollution control, freshwater fisheries, flood protection, water recreation, and environmental conservation. The Water Act 1989 provided for the creation of a privatised water industry under public regulation, and the functions of the regional water authorities were taken over by ten holding companies and

the regulatory bodies and has since been consolidated into the Water Industry Act 1991.

Of the 99 per cent of the population of England and Wales who are connected to a public water supply, 78 per cent are supplied by the water companies (through their principal operating subsidiaries, the water service companies). The remaining 22 per cent are supplied by statutory water companies which were already in the private sector. Most of these have public limited company (PLC) status and many are now in foreign ownership or are part of larger multi-utility companies. They are represented by Water UK, which also represents the ten water service companies responsible for sewerage and sewage disposal in England and Wales, and the state-owned water authorities of Scotland and Northern Ireland. Water UK is the trade association for all the water service companies except Mid Kent Water.

Limited competition exists in the water industry, with large industrial customers being able to negotiate separate supply arrangements. Discussions are underway to determine the feasibility and future extent of competition.

WATER UK, 1 Queen Anne's Gate, London, SW1H 9BT. Tel: 020-7344 1844. *Chief Executive*, Ms P. Taylor

Water Service Companies

ANGLIAN WATER SERVICES LTD, Anglian House, Ambury Road, Huntingdon, Cambs PE18 6NZ
DWR CYMRU (WELSH WATER), Cambrian Way, Brecon, Powys LD3 7HP
NORTHUMBRIAN WATER LTD, Abbey Road, Pity Me, Durham DH1 5FJ
NORTH WEST WATER LTD, Dawson House, Liverpool Road, Great Sankey, Warrington WA5 3LW
SEVERN TRENT WATER LTD, 2297 Coventry Road, Sheldon, Birmingham B26 3PU
SOUTHERN WATER SERVICES LTD, Southern House, Yeoman Road, Worthing, W. Sussex BN13 3NX

WATER SUPPLY AND CONSUMPTION 1998–9

| | Supply | | Consumption | | | |
	Supply from treatment works (*Ml/day*)	Total leakage (*Ml/day*)	Household (*l/head/day*) Unmetered	Metered	Non-household (*l/prop/day*) Unmetered	Metered
WATER SERVICE COMPANIES						
Anglian	1,112.1	201.0	166.8	148.4	528.0	3,268.4
Dwr Cymru (Welsh)	948.8	306.0	162.5	160.3	801.8	2,687.8
North West	1,977.3	510.3	152.0	138.7	701.8	2,715.9
Northumbrian	776.8	170.7	165.8	141.7	926.7	5,046.3
Severn Trent	1,869.0	344.2	154.0	141.0	600.0	2,484.7
South West	433.7	91.6	174.5	133.4	1,243.2	1,651.5
Southern	588.4	94.8	170.2	148.4	829.7	2,704.7
Thames	2,481.0	770.4	181.0	163.0	831.6	3,376.8
Wessex	387.1	100.3	160.0	132.2	2,042.3	2,656.8
Yorkshire	1,238.5	332.8	151.3	131.6	123.2	2,677.1
Total	11,812.7	2,922.2	—	—	—	—
Average	—	—	162.7	145.3	772.3	2,846.0
WATER COMPANIES						
Total	3,331.0	664.3	—	—	—	—
Average	—	—	177.6	153.8	952.9	3,258.0

Source: Office of Water Services

SOUTH WEST WATER SERVICES LTD, Peninsula House, Rydon Lane, Exeter EX2 7HR
THAMES WATER UTILITIES LTD, Gainsborough House, Manor Farm Road, Reading RG2 0JN
WESSEX WATER SERVICES LTD, Wessex House, Passage Street, Bristol BS2 0JQ
YORKSHIRE WATER SERVICES LTD, Western House, Western Way, Halifax Road, Bradford BD6 2LZ

REGULATORY BODIES

The Office of Water Services (Ofwat) (*see* page 350) was set up under the Water Act 1989 and is the independent economic regulator of the water and sewerage companies in England and Wales. Ofwat's main duty is to ensure that the companies can finance and carry out their statutory functions and to protect the interests of water customers. Ofwat is a non-ministerial government department headed by the Director-General of Water Services, who is appointed by the Secretary of State for the Environment, Transport and the Regions and the Secretary of State for Wales. Under the Competition Act 1998, from 1 March 2000 the Competition Commission (*see* page 327) will hear appeals against the regulator's decisions regarding anti-competitive agreements and abuse of a dominant position in the marketplace. The Environment Agency (*see* page 331) has statutory duties and powers in relation to water resources, pollution control, flood defence, fisheries, recreation, conservation and navigation in England and Wales.

The Drinking Water Inspectorate is responsible for assessing the quality of the drinking water supplied by the water companies, inspecting the companies themselves and investigating any accidents affecting drinking water quality. The Chief Inspector presents an annual report to the Secretary of State for the Environment, Transport and the Regions and to the National Assembly for Wales.

METHODS OF CHARGING

In England and Wales, most domestic customers still pay for domestic water supply and sewerage services through charges based on the old rateable value of their property, although about 20 per cent of householders are now charged according to consumption, which is recorded by meter. Industrial and most commercial customers are charged according to consumption.

Under the Water Industry Act 1999, water companies can continue basing their charges on the old rateable value of property. Domestic customers can continue paying on an unmeasured basis unless they choose to pay according to consumption. After having a meter installed (which is free of charge), a customer can revert to unmeasured charging within 12 months. Domestic, school and hospital customers cannot be disconnected for non-payment.

In November 1999 Ofwat set new price limits for the period 2000–5. The average reduction in prices for the first year, 2000–1, is 12.3 per cent.

SCOTLAND

Overall responsibility for national water policy in Scotland rested with the Secretary of State for Scotland until July 1999 when it was devolved to the Scottish Ministers.

Until The Local Government etc. (Scotland) Act 1994, water supply and sewerage services were local authority responsibilities. The Central Scotland Water Development Board had the function of developing new sources of water supply for the purpose of providing water in bulk to water authorities whose limits of supply were within the board's area. Under the Act, three new public water authorities, covering the north, east and west of Scotland

respectively, took over the provision of water and sewerage services from April 1996. The Central Scotland Water Development Board was then abolished. The new authorities were responsible to the Secretary of State for Scotland, and since July 1999 have been responsible to the Scottish Ministers. The Act also established the Scottish Water and Sewerage Customers Council representing consumer interests. It monitored the performance of the authorities; approved charges schemes; investigated complaints; and advised the Secretary of State. The Water Industry Act 1999, whose Scottish provisions were accepted by the Scottish Executive, abolished the Scottish Water and Sewerage Customers Council and replaced it in November 1999 by a Water Industry Commissioner who promotes the interests of customers. The Commissioner makes long-term recommendations about charging and efficiency to the Scottish Ministers and is advised by three water industry consultative committees (one for each water authority).

The Scottish Environment Protection Agency (SEPA) (*see* page 358) is responsible for promoting the cleanliness of Scotland's rivers, lochs and coastal waters. SEPA is also responsible for controlling pollution.

WATER RESOURCES 1998

	No.	Yield (Ml/day)
Reservoirs and lochs	321	3,099
Feeder intakes	23	—
River intakes	247	452
Bore-holes	41	81
Underground springs	85	27
Total	*717	3,659

* Including compensation reservoirs

WATER CONSUMPTION 1998

TOTAL (*Ml/day*)	2,328.6
Potable	2,316.6
Unmetered	1,917.4
Metered	399.3
Non-potable[†]	11.9
TOTAL (*l/head/day*)	465.2
Unmetered	358
Metered and non-potable[†]	81.7

[†]'Non-potable' supplied for industrial purposes. Metered supplies in general relate to commercial and industrial use and unmetered to domestic use
Source: The Scottish Office

EAST OF SCOTLAND WATER AUTHORITY, Pentland Gait, 597 Calder Road, Edinburgh EH11 4HJ. Tel: 0131-453 7500. *Chief Executive*, R. Rennet
NORTH OF SCOTLAND WATER AUTHORITY, Cairngorm House, Beechwood Business Park, Inverness IV2 3ED. Tel: 01463-245400. *Chief Executive*, A. Findlay
WATER INDUSTRY COMMISSIONER FOR SCOTLAND, Ochil House, Springkerse Business Park, Stirling FK7 7XE. Tel: 01786-430200. *Commissioner:* A. D. Sutherland.
WEST OF SCOTLAND WATER AUTHORITY, 419 Balmore Road, Glasgow G22 6NU. Tel: 0141-355 5333. *Chief Executive*, E. Chambers

METHODS OF CHARGING

The water authorities set charges for domestic and non-domestic water and sewerage provision through charges schemes which have to be approved by the Scottish Water and Sewerage Customers Council. The authorities must publish a summary of their charges schemes.

NORTHERN IRELAND

In Northern Ireland ministerial responsibility for water services lies with the Minister of the Department for Regional Development. The Water Service, which is an executive agency of the Department for Regional Development, is responsible for policy and co-ordination with regard to supply, distribution and cleanliness of water, and the provision and maintenance of sewerage services.

The Water Service is divided into four regions, the Eastern, Northern, Western and Southern Divisions. These are based in Belfast, Ballymena, Londonderry and Craigavon respectively.

METHODS OF CHARGING

Until last year Water Service was funded mainly through the regional rate (part or which was appropriated in-aid of the Department) and direct charges principally for metered water. However, the regional rate is no longer appropriated-in-aid and following Devolution the Water Service is now funded by Parliamentary Vote and direct charges.

All properties, which are not exclusively domestic, are metered. They are, however, granted an allowance of 200 cubic meters per annum to reflect domestic usage – this is known as the domestic usage allowance. Customers are charged only for water used in excess of the domestic usage allowance together with a standing charge, which is intended to cover the costs of meter provision, maintenance, reading and billing. This allowance is not granted if rates are not paid on the property. Traders operating from industrial derated premises are required to pay for the treatment and disposal of the trade effluent which they discharge into the public sewer.

Energy

The main primary sources of energy in Britain are oil, natural gas, coal, nuclear power and water power. The main secondary sources (e.g. sources derived from the primary sources) are electricity, coke and smokeless fuels, and petroleum products. The Department of the Environment, Transport and the Regions is responsible for promoting energy efficiency.

INDIGENOUS PRODUCTION OF PRIMARY FUELS
Million tonnes of oil equivalent

	1998	1999p
Coal	27.0	25.2
Petroleum	145.2	150.0
Natural gas	90.3	99.6
Primary electricity		
Nuclear	23.28	22.38
Natural flow hydro	0.50	0.54
Total	286.2	297.7

p provisional

INLAND ENERGY CONSUMPTION BY PRIMARY FUEL
Million tonnes of oil equivalent, seasonally adjusted

	1998	1999p
Coal	43.1	38.2
Petroleum	76.7	73.4
Natural gas	92.2	91.0
Primary electricity	25.19	22.38
Nuclear	23.28	22.38
Natural flow hydro	0.50	0.53
Net imports	1.41	1.07
Total	237.2	235.9

p provisional

TRADE IN FUELS AND RELATED MATERIALS 1999

	Quantity*	Value†
IMPORTS		
Coal and other solid fuel	14.6	599
Crude petroleum	32.7	2,273
Petroleum products	20.0	1,961
Natural gas	0.3	27
Electricity	1.2	396
Total	68.8	5,256
Total (fob)‡	—	4,704
EXPORTS		
Coal and other solid fuel	0.8	61
Crude petroleum	80.4	5,993
Petroleum products	30.4	2,854
Natural gas	4.1	227
Electricity	—	9
Total	115.7	9,145
Total (fob)‡	—	9,145

*Million tonnes of oil equivalent
†£ million
‡Adjusted to exclude estimated costs of insurance, freight, etc.
Source: Department of Trade and Industry – *Energy Trends June 2000* (Crown Copyright)

OIL

Until the 1960s Britain imported almost all its oil supplies. In 1969 oil was discovered in the Arbroath field of the UK Continental Shelf (UKCS). The first oilfield to be brought into production was the Argyll field in 1975, and since the mid-1970s Britain has been a major producer of crude oil.

Licences for exploration and production are granted to companies by the Department of Trade and Industry; the leading British oil companies are British Petroleum (BP) and Shell Transport and Trading. At the end of 1998, 1,021 offshore licences and 150 onshore licences had been awarded, and there were 121 offshore oilfields in production. In 1998 there were 10 oil refineries and four smaller refining units processing crude and process oils. There are estimated to be reserves of 1,800 million tonnes of oil in the UKCS. Royalties are payable on fields approved before April 1982 and petroleum revenue tax is levied on fields approved between 1975 and March 1993.

DRILLING ACTIVITY 1999

Number of wells started	Offshore	Onshore
Exploration and appraisal	36	8
Exploration	16	—
Appraisal	20	—
Development	234	11

VALUE OF UKCS OIL AND GAS PRODUCTION AND INVESTMENT
£ million

	1998	1999p
Total income	16,950	19,364
Operating costs	4,190	4,239
Exploration expenditure	762	457
Gross trading profits*	11,289	13,464
Percentage contribution to GVA	1.5	1.8
Capital investment	5,086	3,166
Percentage contribution to industrial investment	18	13

*Net of stock appreciation
p provisional

INDIGENOUS PRODUCTION AND REFINERY RECEIPTS

	1998	1999p
Indigenous production (thousand tonnes)	132,633	137,099
Crude oil	124,222	128,262
NGLs*	8,411	8,837
Refinery receipts (thousand tonnes)		
Indigenous	46,382	50,886
Other†	1,255	2,113
Net foreign imports	46,434	36,346

p provisional
*Natural gas liquids: condensates and petroleum gases derived at onshore treatment plants
†Mainly recycled products

DELIVERIES OF PETROLEUM PRODUCTS FOR INLAND
CONSUMPTION BY ENERGY USE
Thousand tonnes

	1998	1999
Electricity generators	924	773
Gas works	47	51
Iron and steel industry	499	500
Other industries	5,678	5,385
Transport	47,831	47,860
Domestic	3,190	2,875
Other	3,042	2,648
Total	61,210	60,092

Source: Department of Trade and Industry – *Energy Trends*
June 2000 (Crown Copyright)

GAS

From the late 18th-century gas in Britain was produced
from coal. In the 1960s town gas began to be produced
from oil-based feedstocks using imported oil. In 1965 gas
was discovered in the North Sea in the West Sole field,
which became the first gasfield in production in 1967, and
from the late 1960s natural gas began to replace town gas.
Britain is now the world's fourth largest producer of
gas and in 1998 only 1.5 per cent of gas available for
consumption in the UK was imported. From October
1998 Britain was connected to the continental European
gas system via a pipeline from Bacton, Norfolk to
Zeebrugge, Belgium.

By the end of 1998 there were 80 offshore gasfields producing natural gas and associated gas (mainly methane).
There is estimated to be 1,795,000 million cubic metres of
recoverable gas reserves. There are about 9,419km of
major submarine pipelines for transporting hydrocarbons,
and onshore pipelines for carrying refined products and
chemicals. Natural gas is transported around Britain by
about 273,000km of pipelines supplied by seven coastal
terminals. This pipeline system is owned by Transco and
licensed gas shippers are allowed access under a network
code. New arrangements for trading within the pipeline
system were introduced on 1 October 1999. Greater efficiency in balancing supply and demand is expected to
achieve savings which will be reflected in lower prices.

The Office of Gas and Electricity Markets is the
regulator for the gas industry. It was formed in 1999 by
the merger of the Office of Gas Supply and the Office of
Electricity Regulation. Under the Competition Act 1998,
from 1 March 2000 the Competition Commission has
heard appeals against the regulator's decisions regarding
anti-competitive agreements and abuse of a dominant
position in the marketplace.

The gas industry in Britain was nationalised in 1949
and operated as the Gas Council. The Gas Council was
replaced by the British Gas Corporation in 1972 and the
industry became more centralised. The British Gas
Corporation was privatised in 1986 as British Gas PLC.

In 1993 the Monopolies and Mergers Commission
found that British Gas's integrated business in Great
Britain as a gas trader and the owner of the gas transportation system could be expected to operate against the
public interest. In February 1997 British Gas demerged its
trading arm and now operates as two separate companies:
BG PLC, which runs the Transco pipeline business in
Britain and oil and gas exploration and production in the
UK and abroad; and, Centrica PLC, which runs the trading
and, services operations under the British Gas brand name
in Great Britain.

Competition was gradually introduced into the industrial gas market from 1986. Supply of gas to the domestic
market was opened to companies other than British Gas,
starting in April 1996 with a pilot project in the West
Country and Wales. From spring 1997 competition was
progressively introduced throughout the rest of Britain
in stages which were completed in May 1998. With the
electricity market also open, many suppliers now offer
their customers both gas and electricity. Some gas
companies have become part of larger multi-utility
companies, often operating internationally.

BG PLC, 100 Thames Valley Park Drive, Reading RG6 1PT.
Tel: 0118-935 3222. *Chairman,* R. V. Giordano;
Chief Executive, D. Varney

CENTRICA PLC, Charter Court, 50 Windsor Road, Slough,
Berks SL1 2HA. Tel: 01753-758000. *Chief Executive,*
R. Gardner

NATURAL GAS PRODUCTION AND SUPPLY
GWh

	1998	1999p
Gross gas production	1,048,353	1,51,689
Exports	31,604	85,188
Imports	10,582	12,862
Gas available	956,076	1,010,068
Gas transmitted‡	948,401	1,011,215

p provisional
‡ Figures differ from gas available mainly because of stock changes

NATURAL GAS CONSUMPTION
GWh

	1998	1999p
Electricity generators	253,348	307,247
Iron and steel industry	22,754	22,425
Other industries	175,747	181,771
Domestic	360,266	355,346
Public administration, commerce	118,860	124,165
and agriculture		
Total	928,176	990,954

p provisional
Source: Department of Trade and Industry – *Energy Trends*
June 2000 (Crown Copyright)

COAL

Coal has been mined in Britain for centuries and the
availability of coal was crucial to the industrial revolution
of the 18th- and 19th-centuries. Mines were in private
ownership until 1947 when they were nationalised and
came under the management of the National Coal Board,
later the British Coal Corporation. In addition to
producing coal at its own deep-mine and opencast sites,
of which there were 850 in 1955, British Coal was
responsible for licensing private operators.

Under the Coal Industry Act 1994, the Coal Authority
was established to take over ownership of coal reserves and
to issue licences to private mining companies as part of the
privatisation of British Coal. The Coal Authority also
deals with the physical legacy of mining, e.g. subsidence
damage claims, and is responsible for holding and making
available all existing records. The mines were sold as five
separate businesses in 1994 and coal production in the UK
is now undertaken entirely in the private sector. At the end
of 1997 there were 20 large deep mines in operation.

The main UK customer for coal is the electricity supply industry, but the latter's demand for coal declined and National Power announced that it expected to close ten of its 18 coal-fired power stations by 2000. However, following a review of energy policy, the Government announced measures in its October 1998 Energy White Paper which included a freeze on new applications to build gas-fired power stations in order to increase opportunities for coal-fired power stations. The Government also hopes that reform of the electricity wholesale market (the Pool, see below) will allow coal to compete better with other fuels.

Following the implementation of the Pool Reform, the moratorium on new gas-fired power stations will be lifted. This is expected in the autumn 2000. The government has also announced that it is in discussions with the European Commission on the potential of making available temporary state aid for the coal industry; such aid to end with the termination of the European Coal and Steel Community Treaty in 2002.

COAL PRODUCTION AND FOREIGN TRADE
Thousand tonnes

	1998	1999p
Total production	41,428	37,478
Deep-mined	25,014	20,889
Opencast	15,033	15,275
Imports	21,233	20,758
Exports	944	762

p provisional

INLAND COAL USE
Thousand tonnes

	1998	1999p
Fuel producers		
Collieries	5	10
Electricity generators	48,521	41,087
Coke ovens	8,695	8,558
Other conversion industries	643	646
Total	66,039	56,837
Final users		
Industry	2,714	3,008
Domestic	2,182	2,837
Public administration, commerce and agriculture	279	691

p provisional
Source: Department of Trade and Industry – *Energy Trends June 2000* (Crown Copyright)

ELECTRICITY

The first power station in Britain generating electricity for public supply began operating in 1882. In the 1930s a national transmission grid was developed, and it was reconstructed and extended in the 1950s and 1960s. Power stations were operated by the Central Electricity Generating Board.

Under the Electricity Act 1989, 12 regional electricity companies (RECs), which are responsible for the distribution of electricity from the national grid to consumers, were formed from the former area electricity boards in England and Wales. Four companies were formed from the Central Electricity Generating Board: three generating companies (National Power PLC, Nuclear Electric PLC and PowerGen PLC) and the National Grid Company PLC, which owns and operates the transmission

system. National Power and PowerGen were floated on the stock market in 1991. Nuclear Electric was split into two parts in 1995; the part comprising the more modern nuclear stations was incorporated into a new company, British Energy, which was floated on the stock market in 1996. Magnox Electric, which owns the magnox nuclear reactors, remained in the public sector and was integrated into British Nuclear Fuels (BNFL) in 1999. Ownership of the National Grid Company was transferred to the RECs and it was subsequently floated in 1995.

Generators sell the electricity they produce into an open commodity market (the Pool) from which buyers purchase. The Regulator and Government have announced their intention to replace the Pool with a new system of bilateral trading from November 2000. The introduction of competition into the domestic electricity market was completed in May 1999. With the gas market also open, many suppliers now offer their customers both gas and electricity.

Electricity companies can now also sell gas to their customers. Similarly, gas companies can also offer electricity. Some electricity companies have bought others, and there is a trend towards larger multi-utility companies, often operating internationally.

In Scotland, three new companies were formed under the Electricity Act 1989: Scottish Power PLC and Scottish Hydro-Electric PLC, which are responsible for generation, transmission, distribution and supply; and Scottish Nuclear Ltd. Scottish Power and Scottish Hydro-Electric were floated on the stock market in 1991 (the latter merged with Southern Electric in 1998 to become Scottish and Southern Energy PLC); Scottish Nuclear was incorporated into British Energy in 1995.

In Northern Ireland, Northern Ireland Electricity PLC was set up in 1993 under a 1991 Order in Council. It is responsible for transmission, distribution and supply and has been floated on the stock market. There is no Pool in Northern Ireland; three private companies are responsible for electricity generation and the electricity is sold to Northern Ireland Electricity under a series of power purchase agreements.

The Office of Gas and Electricity Markets is the regulator for the electricity industry. It was formed in 1999 by the merger of the Office of Electricity Regulation and the Office of Gas Supply. Under the Competition Act 1998, the Competition Commission now hears appeals against the regulator's decisions regarding anti-competitive agreements and abuse of a dominant position in the marketplace.

The Electricity Association is the electricity industry's main trade association, providing representational and professional services for the electricity companies. EA Technology Ltd provides distribution and utilisation research, development and technology transfer.

NUCLEAR POWER

Nuclear reactors began to supply electricity to the national grid in 1956. It is generated at six magnox reactors, seven advanced gas-cooled reactors (AGRs) and one pressurised water reactor (PWR), Sizewell 'B' in Suffolk. Nuclear stations now generate about 29 per cent of the UK's electricity.

In preparation for privatisation, the nuclear industry was restructured in December 1995. A holding company, British Energy PLC, was formed with two operational subsidiaries, Nuclear Electric Ltd and Scottish Nuclear Ltd. Nuclear Electric operates the five AGRs and the PWR in England and Wales; Scottish Nuclear operates the two AGRs in Scotland. British Energy was floated on the stock market in 1996. The Magnox reactors were transferred to Magnox Electric PLC, and later to British Nuclear Fuels Ltd (BNFL). BNFL is in public ownership, providing reprocessing, waste management and effluent treatment services. The UK Atomic Energy Authority is responsible for the decommissioning of nuclear reactors and other nuclear facilities used in research and development. UK Nirex, which is owned by the nuclear generating companies and the Government, is responsible for the disposal of intermediate and some low-level nuclear waste. The Nuclear Installations Inspectorate of the Health and Safety Executive is the nuclear industry's regulator.

ELECTRICITY UTILITIES

BRITISH ENERGY PLC, 10 Lochside Place, Edinburgh EH12 9DF. Tel: 0131-527 2000
BNFL MAGNOX GENERATION PLC, Berkeley Centre, Berkeley, Glos GL13 9PB. Tel: 01453-810451
EAST MIDLANDS ELECTRICITY PLC, PO Box 44, Wollaton, Nottingham NG8 1EZ. Tel: 0115-929 1151
EASTERN ELECTRICITY PLC, PO Box 40, Wherstead Park, Wherstead, Ipswich IP9 2AQ. Tel: 01473-688688
FIRST HYDRO COMPANY, Bala House, Lakeside Business Village, St David's Park, Ewloe CH5 3XJ. Tel: 01244-520234
GENERAL PUBLIC UTILITIES, Whittington Hall, Whittington WR5 2RB. Tel: 0845-735 3637.
GUERNSEY ELECTRICITY, PO Box 4, Electricity House, North Side, Vale, Guernsey GY1 3AD. Tel: 01481-46931
HYDER PLC, Newport Road, St Mellons, Cardiff CF3 9XW. Tel: 029-2079 2111
JERSEY ELECTRICITY, PO Box 45, Queens Road, St Helier, Jersey JE4 8NY. Tel: 01534-505000
LONDON ELECTRICITY PLC, Templar House, 81–87 High Holborn, London WC1V 6NU. Tel: 020-7242 9050
MANWEB PLC, Manweb House, Kingsfield Court, Chester Business Park, Chester CH4 9RF. Tel: 0845-272 3636
MANX ELECTRICITY AUTHORITY, PO Box 177, Douglas, Isle of Man IM99 1PS. Tel: 01624-687687
NATIONAL GRID COMPANY PLC, National Grid House, Kirby Corner Road, Coventry CV4 8JY. Tel: 024-7642 3000
NATIONAL POWER PLC, Windmill Hill Business Park, Whitehill Way, Swindon, Wilts SN5 9FH. Tel: 01793-877777
NIGEN LTD., AES Kilroot Power Station, Larne Road, Carrickfergus, Co. Antrim BT38 7LX. Tel: 028-9335 1644
NORTHERN ELECTRIC PLC, Carliol House, Market Street, Newcastle upon Tyne NE1 6NE. Tel: 0191-210 2000
NORTHERN IRELAND ELECTRICITY PLC, 120 Malone Road, Belfast BT9 5HT. Tel: 028-9066 1100
NORWEB PLC, Oakland House, Talbot Road, Old Trafford, Manchester M16 0HQ. Tel: 0161-873 8000
POWERGEN PLC, Westwood Way, Westwood Business Park, Coventry CV4 8LG. Tel: 024-7642 4000
PREMIER POWER LTD, Ballylumford, Islandmagee, Larne, Co. Antrim BT40 3RS. Tel: 028-9335 1644
SCOTTISH AND SOUTHERN ENERGY PLC, 10 Dunkeld Road, Perth PH1 5WA. Tel: 01738-452100
SCOTTISH POWER PLC, 1 Atlantic Quay, Glasgow G2 8SP. Tel: 0141-248 8200
SEEBOARD PLC, Forest Gate, Brighton Road, Crawley, W. Sussex RH11 9BH. Tel: 01293-565888
SWEB PLC, 300 Park Avenue, Aztec West, Almondsbury, Bristol BS32 4SE. Tel: 01454-201101
YORKSHIRE ELECTRICITY GROUP PLC, Wetherby Road, Scarcroft, Leeds LS15 3HS. Tel: 0113-289 2123

ELECTRICITY ASSOCIATION LTD, 30 Millbank, London SW1P 4RD. Tel: 020-7963 5700
EA TECHNOLOGY LTD, Capenhurst, Chester CH1 6ES. Tel: 0151-339 4181

ELECTRICITY GENERATION, SUPPLY AND CONSUMPTION
GWh

	1997	1998
Electricity generated: total	345,342	358,248
Major power producers: total	324,143	334,972
Conventional steam stations	133,132	134,317
Nuclear stations	98,146	100,140
Gas turbines and oil engines	459	221
Combined cycle gas turbine stations	86,974	93,832
Hydro-electric stations:		
Natural flow	3,337	4,240
Pumped storage	1,486	1,624
Renewables other than hydro	609	590
Other generators	21,199	23,276
Electricity used on works: total	16,369	17,777
Major generating companies	15,404	16,471
Other generators	956	1,306
Electricity supplied (gross): total	328,973	340,471
Major power producers: total	308,739	318,501
Conventional steam stations	127,075	127,581
Nuclear stations	89,341	91,186
Gas turbines and oil engines	436	211
Combined cycle gas turbine stations	86,609	93,005
Hydro-electric stations:		
Natural flow	3,299	4,228
Pumped storage	1,439	1,569
Renewables other than hydro	540	722
Other generators	20,234	21,970
Electricity used in pumping		
Major power producers	2,477	2,594
Electricity supplied (net): total	326,496	337,877
Major power producers	306,262	315,907
Other generators	20,234	21,970
Net imports	16,575	12,468
Electricity available	343,071	350,345
Losses in transmission, etc.	25,585	26,076
Electricity consumption: total	317,486	324,269
Fuel industries	8,235	7,575
Final users: total	309,251	316,694
Industrial sector	104,743	107,226
Domestic sector	104,455	109,610
Other sectors	100,053	99,858

Source: The Stationery Office – Annual Abstract of Statistics 2000

RENEWABLE SOURCES

Renewable sources of energy principally include biofuels, hydro, wind and solar. Renewable sources accounted for 2.9 million tonnes of oil equivalent of primary energy use in 1998; of this, about 2.0 million tonnes was used to generate electricity and about 0.9 million tonnes to generate heat.

The Non-Fossil Fuel Obligation (NFFO) Renewables Orders have, to date been, the Government's principal mechanism for developing renewable energy sources. NFFO Renewables Orders require the regional electricity companies to buy specified amounts of electricity from specified non-fossil fuel sources. The technologies covered by NFFO Orders have included landfill gas, municipal and industrial waste, small-scale hydro, on-shore wind and energy crops. The fifth NFFO Renewables Order was made in September 1998. In Scotland a similar system of Scottish Renewables Orders exists. The third Order was made in February 1999 and covers wave energy, the first time that this technology has been supported by a Renewables Order. Energy policy was devolved to the Scottish Parliament in July 1999.

The Government intends to achieve 10 per cent of the UK's electricity needs from renewables by 2010. Plans are also being made to determine how renewables can contribute to meeting commitments to future reductions in greenhouse gases.

RENEWABLE ENERGY SOURCES 1999

	Percentages
Biofuels	81.1
Landfill gas	19.7
Sewage gas	6.3
Wood combustion	24.4
Straw combustion	2.5
Refuse combustion	19.9
Other biofuels	8.3
Hydro	15.9
Large-scale	15.2
Small-scale	0.7
Wind	2.6
Active solar heating	0.4
Total	100

Source: Department of Trade and Industry

Transport

CIVIL AVIATION

Since the privatisation of British Airways in 1987, UK airlines have been operated entirely by the private sector. In 1998, total capacity on British airlines amounted to 42,002,000,000 tonne-km, of which 31,815,000,000 tonne-km was on scheduled services. British airlines carried 97.9 million passengers, 65.4 million on scheduled services and 165,212 on charter flights.

Leading British airlines include British Airways, Britannia Airways, British Midland, Monarch Airlines and Virgin Atlantic.

There are 142 licensed civil aerodromes in Britain, with Heathrow and Gatwick handling the highest volume of passengers. BAA PLC owns and operates the seven major airports: Heathrow, Gatwick, Stansted, Southampton, Glasgow, Edinburgh and Aberdeen, which between them handle about 70 per cent of air passengers and 81 per cent of air cargo traffic in Britain. Many other airports, including Manchester, are controlled by local authorities or private companies. In the 1999 Budget, the Government announced it was setting up a review of competition in the airports sector.

The Civil Aviation Authority (CAA), an independent statutory body, is responsible for the economic regulation of UK airlines and for the safety regulation of the UK civil aviation industry. Through its wholly-owned subsidiary, National Air Traffic Services (NATS), the CAA plans and provides air traffic control services throughout the United Kingdom and over the North Atlantic – more than a million square miles – and at most of Britain's major airports. In 1999 the Government announced plans to establish a public private partnership for NATS. This would enable NATS to obtain the investment it needs to handle increasing traffic and exploit new business opportunities. The Government's proposals continue to make progress through Parliament.

The CAA is responsible for ensuring that UK airlines provide services at the lowest charges possible, given the requirement to meet stringent safety standards. It is also responsible for the economic regulation of the larger airports.

All commercial airline companies must be granted an Air Operator's Certificate, which is issued by the CAA to operators meeting the required safety standards. The CAA also issues airport safety licences, which must be obtained by any airport used for public transport and training flights. All British-registered aircraft must be granted an airworthiness certificate, and the CAA also issues professional licences to pilots, flight crew, ground engineers and air traffic controllers.

AIR PASSENGERS 1999*

ALL UK AIRPORTS: TOTAL	169,649,921
LONDON AREA AIRPORTS: TOTAL	108,953,719
Battersea Heliport	5,255
Gatwick (BAA)	30,563,621
Heathrow (BAA)	62,268,292
London City	1,385,968
Luton	5,284,810
Southend	3,770
Stansted (BAA)	9,447,258

OTHER UK AIRPORTS: TOTAL	60,690,947
Aberdeen (BAA)	2,467,514
Barra	7,291
Barrow-in-Furness	125
Belfast City	1,284,148
Belfast International	3,035,907
Benbecula (HIAL)	34,703
Biggin Hill	6,263
Birmingham	7,013,867
Blackpool	117,581
Bournemouth	279,029
Bristol	1,993,331
Cambridge	14,430
Campbeltown (HIAL)	8,446
Cardiff	1,330,277
Carlisle	333
Coventry	2,862
Dundee	30,410
East Midlands	2,229,536
Edinburgh (BAA)	5,119,258
Exeter	297,040
Glasgow (BAA)	6,813,955
Gloucestershire	2,192
Hawarden	4,612
Humberside	427,870
Inverness (HIAL)	348,679
Islay (HIAL)	20,704
Isle of Man	700,592
Kent International	1,511
Kirkwall (HIAL)	87,956
Leeds/Bradford	1,462,497
Lerwick (Tingwall)	4,239
Liverpool	1,304,959
Londonderry	103,504
Lydd	3,430
Manchester	17,577,765
Newcastle upon Tyne	2,994,051
Norwich	342,681
Penzance Heliport	126,609
Plymouth	148,940
Prestwick	710,623
St Mary's, Isles of Scilly	133,806
Scatsta	93,171
Sheffield City	75,157
Shoreham	1,820
Southampton (BAA)	755,432
Stornoway (HIAL)	89,946
Sumburgh (HIAL)	265,645
Teesside	736,822
Tiree (HIAL)	5,249
Tresco, Isles of Scilly (H)	38,258
Unst	1,771
Wick (HIAL)	34,150

CHANNEL IS. AIRPORTS: TOTAL	2,719,336
Alderney	73,099
Guernsey	926,076
Jersey	1,720,161

*Total terminal, transit, scheduled and charter passengers

Source: Civil Aviation Authority

RAILWAYS

Britain pioneered railways and a railway network was developed across Britain by private companies in the course of the 19th century. In 1948 the main railway companies were nationalised and were run by a public authority, the British Transport Commission. The Commission was replaced by the British Railways Board in 1963, operating as British Rail. On 1 April 1994, responsibility for managing the railway infrastructure passed to a newly-formed company, Railtrack; the British Railways Board continued as operator of all train services until they were sold or franchised to the private sector. All passenger activities have now been franchised and all British Rail's freight, technical support and specialist function businesses have been sold. The Board still has certain functions, including overall responsibility for the British Transport Police.

PRIVATISATION

Since 1 April 1994, ownership of operational track and land has been vested in Railtrack, which was floated on the Stock Exchange in 1996. Railtrack manages the track and charges for access to it and is responsible for signalling and timetabling. It does not operate train services. It owns the stations, and leases most of them out to the train operating companies. Infrastructure support functions are now provided by private sector companies. Railtrack invests in infrastructure principally using finance raised by track charges, and takes investment decisions in consultation with rail operators. Railtrack is also responsible for overall safety on the railways.

Proposals to privatise part of London Underground were announced in July 1997 with more details being given in June 1999. The Government intends the infrastructure to be run by private companies, with the operating company remaining in public ownership. In June 1999 the Government announced that the lines would be leased in three groups. The first group, lines close to the surface, would be leased to Railtrack with a view to integrating them into the national railway network. The remaining lines will be leased in two groups. In September 1999 London Underground created three infrastructure divisions and reorganised the operation sides of the management, to replicate the structure that will apply under the Public Private Partnership. The arrangements will be tested and modified during this 'shadow running' period until transfer to the private sector. London Transport is now running a new competition for the sub-surface lines in parallel with those for the deep tubes; an invitation to Tender has been issued and bids are due on 15 September 2000. In 1997–8 there were 832 million passenger journeys, including 384 million using season tickets.

RAIL REGULATOR

The independent Rail Regulator is responsible for the licensing of new railway operators, approving access agreements, promoting the use and development of the network, preventing anti-competitive practices (in conjunction with the Director-General of Fair Trading) and protecting the interests of rail users. The Regulator will publish the conclusions of his review of Railtrack's funding arrangements in September 2000, for implementation in April 2001. He has indicated that he will seek to tighten the regime to promote improvements in the infrastructure. The White Paper *New Deal for Transport* contains proposals to strengthen the Regulator's power to impose sanctions and broaden the scope of his duties.

Separate regulations, which took effect on 28 June 1998, established licensing and access arrangements for certain international train services in Great Britain. These are overseen by the International Rail Regulator, a position held by the Rail Regulator.

The White Paper *New Deal for Transport*, published in July 1998, announced plans to establish a Strategic Rail Authority (SRA) to manage passenger railway franchising, take responsibility for increasing the use of the railways for freight transport, and lead strategic planning of passenger and freight rail services. In December 1999 the Government published its Transport Bill which will give the SRA its full powers. The SRA began work in shadow form in April 1999, using the existing powers of the Franchising Director and British Rail.

SERVICES

For privatisation, domestic passenger services were divided into 25 train-operating units, which have been franchised to private sector operators via a competitive tendering process overseen by the Director of the Office of Passenger Rail Franchising (OPRAF). The franchise agreements were for between five and 15 years. The Government continues to subsidise loss-making but socially necessary rail services. The Franchising Director is responsible for monitoring the performance of the franchisees, allocating and administering government subsidy payments, proposing closures to the Rail Regulator and designating experimental services.

There are currently 25 train operating companies: Anglia Railways; Cardiff Railway; Central Trains; Chiltern Railways; Connex South Central; Connex South Eastern; Eurostar (which is not subject to a franchise agreement); Gatwick Express; Great Eastern Railway; Great North Eastern Railway; Great Western Trains; Island Line (Isle of Wight); LTS Rail (London to Southend and Shoeburyness); Merseyrail Electrics; Midland Mainline; North Western Trains; Northern Spirit; Scotrail Railways; Silverlink Train Services (North London); South West Trains; Thameslink Rail; Thames Trains; Virgin Trains (which operates two franchises); Wales and West Passenger Trains; and West Anglia Great Northern Railway.

Railtrack publishes a national timetable which contains details of rail services operated over the Railtrack network, coastal shipping information and connections with Ireland, the Isle of Man, the Isle of Wight, the Channel Islands and some European destinations.

The national rail enquiries service offers information about train times and fares for any part of the country:

National Rail Enquiries	0345-484950
London Transport	020-7222 1234
Eurostar	0345-303030

Rail Users' Consultative Committees monitor the policies and performance of train and station operators in their area (there are nine, covering Great Britain). They are statutory bodies and have a legal right to make recommendations for changes. The London Regional Passengers Committee represents users of buses, the underground and the Docklands Light Railway as well as users of rail services in the London area.

British Rail's passenger rolling stock was divided between three subsidiary companies, which were privatised in 1996. The companies lease rolling stock to passenger service operators. On privatisation, British Rail's bulk freight haulage companies and Rail Express Systems, which carries Royal Mail traffic, were sold to English, Welsh and Scottish Railways, which also purchased Railfreight Distribution (international freight) in 1997. In 1997–8 an average 1,159,000 tonnes of freight was transported by an average of 1,900 trains a day.

RAILTRACK, Railtrack House, Euston Square, London NW1 2EE. Tel: 020-7557 8000. *Chairman*, Sir Robert Horton. *Chief Executive*, G. Corbett

ASSOCIATION OF TRAIN OPERATING COMPANIES, 40 Bernard Street, London WC1N 1BY. Tel: 020-7904 3010. *Chairman*, I. W. Warburton

OFFICE OF PASSENGER RAIL FRANCHISING (OPRAF), 55 Victoria Street, London SW1H 0EU. Tel: 020-7654 6000. *Franchising Director*, M. Grant

OFFICE OF THE RAIL REGULATOR (ORR) 1 Waterhouse Square, 138–142 Holborn, London EC1N 2TQ. Tel: 020-7282 2000. *Rail Regulator*, T. Winsor

SHADOW STRATEGIC RAIL AUTHORITY, 55 Victoria Street, London, SW1H 0EU. Tel: 020-7654 6000 Web: http://www.sra.gov.uk *Chairman*, Sir Alastair Morton

RAILTRACK

At 31 March 1999, Railtrack had about 20,000 miles of standard gauge lines and sidings in use, representing 10,343 miles of route of which 3,208 miles were electrified. Standard rail on main line has a weight of 110 lb per yard. Railtrack owns 2,495 stations, 90 light maintenance depots, about 40,000 bridges, viaducts and tunnels, and over 9,000 level crossings.

Passenger journeys made in 1998–9 totalled 892.3 million, including 390 million made by holders of season tickets. The average distance of each passenger journey on ordinary fare was 28.97 miles; and on season ticket, 16 miles. Passenger stations in use numbered 2,500. The number of ticket transactions in the year was 329.3 million, earning a total ticket revenue of £3,100 million.

In 1999–2000 Railtrack showed an operating profit of £471 million and a pre-tax profit of £428 million. On 31 March 1999 Railtrack employed 10,838 staff.

	£ million
Income	
Passenger	2,169
Freight	169
Property rental	131
Commercial and development property sales	41
Other	63
Total	2,573
Costs	
Production and management	547
Infrastructure maintenance	694
Joint industry costs	227
Depreciation	634
Total	2,102

RAIL SAFETY

The Railways (Safety Case) Regulations 1994 require infrastructure controllers (e.g. Railtrack, London Underground) to have systems in place to manage safety on the railway networks for which they are responsible.

Each infrastructure controller is required to present a Railway Safety Case (RSC) to the Railway Inspectorate (part of the Health and Safety Executive). The RSC must be accepted by the Inspectorate, and is subject to regular compliance audits.

The infrastructure controllers require companies wishing to operate services to present an RSC. The RSC must be accepted by the infrastructure controller before a train or station operator can receive a licence and begin to provide services. If any revision is required, the RSC must be re-presented. RSCs must be thoroughly reviewed at least every three years. The Inspectorate may examine the RSC of train and service operators as part of its general inspection activities.

Proposed amendments to the Railways (Safety Case) Regulations were being consulted upon in June and July 2000. If made, the amendments will, inter alia, transfer the responsibility for acceptance of RSCs of train and station operators from the infrastructure controllers to the Health and Safety Executive.

ACCIDENTS ON RAILWAYS

	1997–8	1998–9
Train accidents: total	1,863	1,728
Persons killed: total	10	3
Passengers	7	0
Railway staff	0	0
Others	3	3
Persons injured: total	244	88
Passengers	190	40
Railway staff	39	31
Others	15	13
Other accidents through movement of		
railway vehicles		
Persons killed	32	27
Persons injured	883	982
Other accidents on railway premises		
Persons killed	64	7
Passengers	4	3
Railway staff	0	3
Others	2	1
Persons injured	4,186	4,172
Trespassers and suicides		
Persons killed	265	249
Persons injured	136	153

THE CHANNEL TUNNEL

The earliest recorded scheme for a submarine transport connection between Britain and France was in 1802. Tunnelling has begun simultaneously on both sides of the Channel three times: in 1881, in the early 1970s, and on 1 December 1987, when construction workers began to bore the first of the three tunnels which form the Channel Tunnel. They 'holed through' the first tunnel (the service tunnel) on 1 December 1990 and tunnelling was completed in June 1991. The tunnel was officially inaugurated by The Queen and President Mitterrand of France on 6 May 1994.

The submarine link comprises three tunnels. There are two rail tunnels, each carrying trains in one direction, which measure 24.93ft (7.6m) in diameter. Between them lies a smaller service tunnel, measuring 15.75ft (4.8m) in diameter. The service tunnel is linked to the rail tunnels by 130 cross-passages for maintenance and safety purposes. The tunnels are 31 miles (50km) long, 24 miles (38km) of which is under the sea-bed at an average depth of 132ft (40m). The rail terminals are situated at Folkestone and Calais, and the tunnels go underground at Shakespeare Cliff, Dover, and Sangatte, west of Calais.

Eurostar is the high speed passenger train connecting London with Paris in three hours and Brussels in two hours 40 minutes, via the Channel Tunnel. There are up to 24 trains each way per day on the Paris route and ten each way per day on the Brussels route. Some trains stop en route at Ashford (Kent), Calais and Lille. Connecting services from Edinburgh and Manchester via London began in 1997. The introduction of through services from these cities, not stopping in London, is the subject of a government review, due to report in late 1999. Vehicle shuttle services operate between Folkestone and Calais.

RAIL LINKS

The route for the British Channel Tunnel Rail Link will run from Folkestone to a new terminal at St Pancras station, London, with new intermediate stations at Ebbsfleet, Kent, and Stratford, east London; at present services run into a terminal at Waterloo station, London.

Construction of the rail link is financed by the private sector with a substantial government contribution. A private sector consortium, London and Continental Railways Ltd (LCR), is responsible for the design, construction and ownership of the rail link, and comprises Union Railways and the UK operator of Eurostar. Construction was expected to be completed in 2003, but on 28 January 1998 LCR informed the Government that it was unable to fulfil its obligations. On 3 June 1998 the Government announced a new funding agreement with LCR. The rail link will be constructed in two phases: phase one, from the Channel Tunnel to Fawkham Junction (where an existing connection allows trains to continue to Waterloo), began in October 1998 and will be completed in 2003; phase two, from Fawkham Junction to St Pancras, will be built between 2001 and 2007. Railtrack will buy phase one when it is completed and has an option to buy phase two by 2003.

Infrastructure developments in France have been completed and high-speed trains run from Calais to Paris, linking the Channel Tunnel with the high-speed European network.

ROADS

HIGHWAY AUTHORITIES

The powers and responsibilities of highway authorities in England and Wales are set out in the Highways Acts 1980; for Scotland there is separate legislation.

Responsibility for trunk road motorways and other trunk roads in Great Britain rests in England with the Secretary of State for the Environment, Transport and the Regions, in Scotland with the Scottish Executive, and in Wales with the National Assembly for Wales. The costs of construction, improvement and maintenance are paid for by central government. The White Paper *New Deal for Transport*, published in July 1998, restated and revised the Highways Agency's responsibility for operating, maintaining and improving the trunk road network.

The highway authority for non-trunk roads in England, Wales and Scotland is, in general, the unitary authority, county council or London borough council in whose area the roads lie.

In Northern Ireland the Department of the Environment for Northern Ireland is the statutory road authority responsible for public roads and their maintenance and construction; the Roads Service executive agency carries out these functions on behalf of the Department.

FINANCE

The Government contributes towards capital expenditure through grants and credit approvals in England and Transport Grant (TG) in Wales. Grant rates are determined by the Secretary of State for the Environment, Transport and the Regions in England, the Scottish Executive and the National Assembly for Wales in each country respectively. Grant is paid at 50 per cent of expenditure accepted for grant in England and Wales.

In England Transport Supplementary Grant (TSG) is paid towards capital spending on highways and the regulation of traffic; other capital spending is financed by credit approvals and specific grants. Current expenditure is funded by revenue support grant (i.e. central government grants to local authorities for non-specific services). From 2000–1 all bridge assessment and strengthening, and structural maintenance of principal road carriage ways will be funded entirely through credit approvals. In Wales TG is paid towards capital expenditure only; current expenditure is funded by revenue support grant.

For the financial year 2000–1 local authorities in England will receive £22 million in TSG and £720 million in credit approvals. Total estimated expenditure on building and maintaining motorways and trunk roads in England in 1999–2000 was £1,389 million; estimated outturn for 2000–1 is £1,430 million.

For the financial year 2000–1 local authorities in Wales will receive up to £18.2 million in TG. Total expenditure on motorways and trunk roads in Wales in 1999–2000 was £112.44 million and estimated expenditure in 2000–1 is £117.3 million.

Until 1999, the Scottish Office received a block vote from Parliament, and the Secretary of State for Scotland determined how much was spent on roads. Since 1 July 1999 all decisions on transport expenditure have been devolved to the Scottish Executive. Total expenditure on building and maintaining trunk roads in Scotland was estimated at £17 million in 1998–9.

In Northern Ireland estimated expenditure on roads for 1998–9 was £147.7 million and £155.6 million has been allocated for expenditure in 1999–2000.

The Government is considering the possibility of introducing tolls on certain roads. The Transport Bill currently before Parliament contains proposals to enable local authorities to levy charges for driving cars in congested areas or for workplace charging. In 2000–1, £18 million has been allocated to a number of pilot authorities to develop charging schemes.

PRIVATE FINANCE

Private finance is being increasingly used to help finance road schemes. The current targeted programme of road improvements contains two design, build, finance and operate road contracts with a capital value of £360 million which will deliver five of the road schemes in the Government s targeted programme of improvements.

TARGETED PROGRAMME OF IMPROVEMENTS (TPI)

The 1998 Roads Review increased the emphasis given to making better use of the existing road network and improving road maintenance. It resulted in a carefully targeted £1,400 million programme of 37 trunk road improvements to be started by 2005. In February 2000, the Government announced the acceleration of the TPI with the result that 13 rather than seven schemes will now start in 2000–1. A series of studies is also underway looking at traffic problems not addressed by the TPI. Road schemes that emerge from these studies will be progressed through the regional planning guidance (RPG) system. This is now the method by which truck road schemes will enter the TPI. Four additional schemes with a value of £100 million were added to the TPI in March 2000.

ROAD LENGTHS

(in miles) *as at April 1999*

	Total roads	Trunk roads (including motorways)	Motorways*
England	177,124	6,554	1,781
Wales	20,877	1,062	82
Scotland	33,115	2,154	229
N. Ireland	15,211	153[†]	82

*There were in addition 26.1 miles of local authority motorway in England
[†] 1997 figure

MOTORWAYS

England and Wales:

M1	London to Yorkshire
M2	London to Faversham
M3	London to Southampton
M4	London to South Wales
M5	Birmingham to Exeter
M6	Catthorpe to Carlisle
M10	St Albans spur
M11	London to Cambridge
M18	Rotherham to Goole
M20	London to Folkestone
M23	London to Gatwick
M25	London orbital
M26	M20 to M25 spur
M27	Southampton bypass
M32	M4 to Bristol spur
M40	London to Birmingham
M41	London to West Cross
M42	South-west of Birmingham to Measham
M45	Dunchurch spur
M50	Ross spur
M53	Chester to Birkenhead
M54	M6 to Telford
M55	Preston to Blackpool
M56	Manchester to Chester
M57	Liverpool outer ring
M58	Liverpool to Wigan
M60	Manchester ring road
M61	Manchester to Preston
M62	Liverpool to Hull
M65	Calder Valley
M67	Manchester Hyde to Denton
M69	Coventry to Leicester
M180	South Humberside

Scotland:

M8	Edinburgh-Newhouse, Baillieston-West Ferry Interchange
M9	Edinburgh to Dunblane
M73	Maryville to Mollinsburn
M74	Glasgow-Gretna,
M77	Ayr Road Route
M80	Stirling to Haggs/Glasgow (M8) to Stepps
M90	Inverkeithing to Perth
M876	Dennyloanhead (M80) to Kincardine Bridge

Northern Ireland:

M1	Belfast to Dungannon
M2	Belfast to Antrim
M2	Ballymena bypass
M3	Belfast Cross Harbour Bridge
M5	M2 to Greencastle
M12	M1 to Craigavon
M22	Antrim to Randalstown

ROAD USE

ESTIMATED TRAFFIC ON ALL ROADS (GREAT BRITAIN) 1999

Million vehicle kilometres

All motor vehicles	467,100
Cars and taxis	380,300
Two-wheeled motor vehicles	4,000
Buses and coaches	5,000
Light vans	44,400
Other goods vehicles	32,800
Total goods vehicles	77,200
Pedal cycles	4,200

ROAD GOODS TRANSPORT (GREAT BRITAIN) 1999
Analysis by mode of working and by gross weight of vehicle

Estimated tonne kilometres (thousand million)	149.2
Own account	38.3
Public haulage	110.9
By gross weight of vehicle (billion tonne kilometres)	
Estimated tonnes carried (millions)	1,567.0
Own account	576.0
Public haulage	991.0
By gross weight of vehicle (million tonnes)	
Not over 25 tonnes	346.0
Over 25 tonnes	1,221.0

ROAD PASSENGER SERVICES

Until 1988 most road passenger transport services in Great Britain were provided by the public sector; the National Bus Company was the largest bus and coach operator in England and Wales and the Scottish Bus Group the largest operator in Scotland. The privatisation of the National Bus Company was completed in 1988 and that of the Scottish Bus Group in 1991. London Transport's bus operating subsidiaries were privatised by the end of 1994. Almost all bus and coach services in Great Britain are now provided by private sector companies.

Bus services outside London were deregulated in 1986, although local authorities can subsidise the provision of socially necessary services after competitive tendering. In London, London Transport retains overall responsibility for the provision of services.

The largest bus operators in Great Britain are Stagecoach Holdings, FirstGroup (formerly FirstBus) and Arriva (formerly Cowie British Bus), which between them account for over 50 per cent of all bus services (by turnover). There are also 17 municipal bus companies in England and Wales, and thousands of smaller private sector operators. National Express runs a national network of coach routes, mainly operating through franchises.

In Northern Ireland, almost all passenger transport services are provided by subsidiaries of Translink (formerly the Northern Ireland Transport Holding Company), which is publicly owned. The two main operators are Citybus Ltd (in Belfast) and Ulsterbus Ltd (outside Belfast). There are also about 75 small private sector operators.

The transport White Paper announced plans to promote bus use, primarily through agreements between local authorities and bus operators to improve the standard and efficiency of services in an area.

There are about 64,000 licensed taxis in Great Britain, of which about 19,000 are in London. There are also about 74,000 licensed private hire vehicles in Great Britain outside London, and an estimated 60,000 in London; an exact figure is not known because a new licensing system is being introduced in 2000.

BUSES AND COACHES (GREAT BRITAIN) 1998–9

Number of vehicles (31 March 1999)	79,300
Vehicle kilometres (millions)	4,300
Local bus passenger journeys (millions)	4,248
Passenger receipts (£ million)	3,942

ROAD SAFETY

The Government in 1987 set a target of reducing road traffic casualties by a third by the year 2000 compared to the average for 1981–5. Measures to achieve this were successful in reducing the number of deaths on the road by 39 per cent by 1998, and the number of serious casualties by 45 per cent. Over the same period the number of slight casualties increased by 16 per cent, but as road traffic increased by 55 per cent, the number of casualties per 100 km travelled has increased by only 1 per cent. In 1998, fatalities were reduced by 5 per cent from 1997, and all casualties decreased by 1 per cent.

In March 2000, the Government published a new road safety strategy, 'Tomorrow's Roads' – Safer for Everyone' which set new casualty reduction targets for 2010. The new targets include a 40 per cent reduction in the overall number of people killed or seriously injured in road accidents, a 50 per cent reduction in the number of children killed or seriously injured and a 10 per cent reduction in the slight casualty rate, all compared with the average for 1994–8.

The previous target was to reduce casualties by a third by 2000 compared to the average for 1981–5. Measures to achieve this were successful in reducing the number of deaths on the road by 39 per cent by 1998 and the number of seriously injured by 45 per cent. Both figures represent a 5 per cent reduction compared to 1997. The total number of casualties rose by 1 per cent taking into account a 16 per cent rise in slight casualties although this is considerably less than the 55 per cent rise in traffic between the average for 1981–9 and 1998.

ROAD ACCIDENT CASUALTIES

	Fatal	Serious	Slight	All Severities
England	2,922	33,710	248,494	285,126
Wales	191	1,678	12,478	14,347
Scotland	310	3,734	16,793	20,837
Great Britain	3,423	39,122	277,765	320,310

	Killed	Injured
1965	7,952	389,985
1970	7,499	355,869
1975	6,366	318,584
1980	6,010	323,000
1985	5,165	312,359
1990	5,217	335,924
1995	3,621	306,885
1996	3,598	316,704
1997	3,599	323,945
1998	3,421	321,791

Source: Department of the Environment, Transport and the Regions

DRIVING LICENCES

It is necessary to hold a valid full licence in order to drive on public roads in the UK. Learner drivers must obtain a provisional driving licence before starting to learn to drive and must then pass theory and practical tests to obtain a full driving licence. Application forms for a driving licence (form D1) are available from post offices. A phased introduction of driving licences including the driver's photograph began in July 1998; all licences for newly qualified drivers will include a photograph, and qualified drivers will be issued with the new licence when their licence details need updating.

There are separate tests for driving motor cycles, cars, passenger-carrying vehicles (PCVs) and large goods vehicles (LGVs). Drivers must hold full car entitlement before they can apply for PCV or LGV entitlements. At 3 April 1999, 38 million people in the UK (20.9 male, 17.1 female) held a valid driving licence (full or provisional). The minimum age for driving motor cars, light goods vehicles up to 3.5 tonnes and motor cycles is 17 (moped, 16). Since June 1997, drivers who collect six or more penalty points within two years of qualifying lose their licence and are required to take another test. A leaflet, *What You Need to Know About Driving Licences* (form D100), is available from post offices.

The Driver and Vehicle Licensing Agency is responsible for issuing driving licences, registering and licensing vehicles, and collecting excise duty in Great Britain. In Northern Ireland the Driver and Vehicle Licensing Agency (Northern Ireland) has similar responsibilities.

DRIVING LICENCE FEES *as at 1 April 2000*

First provisional licence	£23.50
Changing a provisional to a full licence after passing a driving test	£8.50
Renewal of licence	£8.50
Renewal of licence including PCV or LGV entitlements	£28.50
Renewal after disqualification	£24.50
Renewal after drinking and driving disqualification	£33.50
Medical renewal	free
Medical renewal (over 70)	free
Duplicate Licence	£13.50
Exchange licence	£13.50
Removing endorsements	£13.50
Replacement (change of name or address)	free

DRIVING TESTS

The Driving Standards Agency is responsible for carrying out driving tests and approving driving instructors in Great Britain. In Northern Ireland the Driver and Vehicle Testing Agency (Northern Ireland) is responsible for testing drivers and vehicles.

In 1999–2000, almost 1.2 million driving tests, nearly 55,500 vocational tests (lorries and buses) and over 96,500 motorcycle tests were conducted in Great Britain. In the same period, 1.1 million theory tests were conducted. In 1998–9, almost 1.2 million car driving tests were conducted in Great Britain of which 45.9 per cent resulted in a pass. In addition over 49,000 lorry tests were undertaken, of which 51.9 per cent were successful. Over 83,000 motorcycle tests were undertaken, of which 67.9 per cent were successful. There were more than 7,600 bus tests, with a pass rate of 47.8 per cent. In the same period, 1.2 million theory tests were conducted. A new, longer driving test was introduced on 4 May 1999.

Since 1 March 1997 driving test candidates have been required to produce photographic confirmation of their identity.

*DRIVING TEST FEES (weekday rate/evening and Saturday rate) *as at 1 April 2000*

For cars	£36.75/£46
†For motor cycles	£45/£55
For lorries, buses	£73.50/£92

*Since 1 July 1996 most candidates for car and motor cycle tests have also been required to take a written driving theory test, for which there is a separate fee of £15.50. Theory tests for lorry and bus drivers were introduced on 1 January 1997
†Before riding on public roads, learner motor cyclists and learner moped riders are required to have completed Compulsory Basic Training, provided by DSA-approved training bodies. The Compulsory Basic Training certificate costs £8.00. All exemptions from CBT were removed on 1 January 1997

An extended driving test was introduced in 1992 for those convicted of dangerous driving. The fee is £73.50/£92 (car) or £90/£110 (motorcycle).

MOTOR VEHICLES

Vehicles must be licensed by the DVLA or the DVLNI before they can be driven on public roads. They must also be approved as roadworthy by the Vehicle Certification Agency. The Vehicle Inspectorate carries out annual testing and inspection of goods vehicles, buses and coaches.

There were 27.9 million vehicles registered at the DVLA at December 1998:

Private and light goods	24,840,942
Motor cycles, scooters, mopeds	701,692
Coaches and buses	80,862
Large goods vehicles	419,526
Electric vehicles	11,020
Others	1,926,884
Total	27,980,926

VEHICLE LICENCES

Registration and first licensing of vehicles is through local offices (known as Vehicle Registration Offices) of the Driver and Vehicle Licensing Agency in Swansea. Local facilities for relicensing are available at any post office which deals with vehicle licensing. Applicants will need to take their vehicle registration document; if this is not available the applicant must complete form V62 which is held at post offices. Postal applications can be made to the post offices shown on form V100, available at any post office. This form also provides guidance on registering and licensing vehicles.

Details of the present duties chargeable on motor vehicles are available at post offices and Vehicle Registration Offices. The Vehicle Excise and Registration Act 1994 provides *inter alia* that any vehicle kept on a public road but not used on roads is chargeable to excise duty as if it were in use. All non-commercial vehicles constructed before 1 January 1973 are exempt from vehicle excise duty.

VEHICLE EXCISE DUTY RATES *from 22 March 2000*

	Twelve months £	Six months £
Motor Cars		
Light vans, cars, taxis, etc.	155.00	85.25
Under 1100 cc[†]	100.00	55.00
Over 1100 cc[†]	155.00	85.25
Motor Cycles		
With or without sidecar, not over 150 cc	15.00	—
With or without sidecar, 150–250 cc	40.00	—
Others	60.00	33.00
Electric motorcycles (including tricycles)	15.00	—
Tricycles (not over 450 kg)		
Not over 150 cc	15.00	—
Others	60.00	33.00
*Buses**		
Seating 9–16 persons	165.00	90.75
	(155.00)	(85.25)
Seating 17–35 persons	220.00	121.00
	(155.00)	(85.25)
Seating 36–60 persons	330.00	181.00
	(155.00)	(85.25)
Seating over 60 persons	500.00	275.00
	(155.00)	(85.25)

*Figures in parentheses refer to reduced pollution vehicles.
[†]Rate from 1 June 1999

MoT TESTING

Cars, motor cycles, motor caravans, light goods and dual-purpose vehicles more than three years old must be covered by a current MoT test certificate. However, some vehicles i.e. minibuses may require a certificate at one year old. All certificates must be renewed annually. The MoT testing scheme is administered by the Vehicle Inspectorate on behalf of the Secretary of State for Transport.

A fee is payable to MoT testing stations, which must be authorised to carry out tests. The maximum fees, which are prescribed by regulations, are:

For cars and light vans	£32.11
For solo motor cycles	£13.04
For motor cycle combinations	£21.80
For three-wheeled vehicles	£25.63
Private passenger vehicles and ambulances	
With 9–12 passenger seats	£33.91
13–16 passenger seats	£39.18
Over 16 passenger seats	£53.36
For light goods vehicles between 3,000 and 3,500 kg	£33.80

METHOD OF TRAVEL TO WORK, *Great Britain* (*percentage**)

	1993	1997
Car, van, minibus, works van	68	71
Bus, coach, private bus	9	8
Train (incl. Underground and light rail)	5	6
Walk	12	11
Other	5	5
All	100	100

*All figures are rounded
Source: DETR/The Stationery Office – *Focus on Personal Travel 1998* (Crown copyright)

SHIPPING AND PORTS

Since earliest times sea trade has played a central role in Britain's economy. By the 17th century Britain had built up a substantial merchant fleet and by the early 20th century it dominated the world shipping industry. In recent years the size and tonnage of the UK-registered trading fleet have declined; the UK-flagged merchant fleet now constitutes about 1 per cent of the world fleet. In December 1998 the Government published a document, *British Shipping: Charting a New Course*, which outlined strategies to promote the long-term interests of British shipping.

Freight is carried by liner and bulk services, almost all scheduled liner services being containerised. About 95 per cent by weight of Britain's overseas trade is carried by sea; this amounts to 75 per cent of its total value. Passengers and vehicles are carried on roll-on, roll-off ferries, hovercraft, hydrofoils and high-speed catamarans. There are about 53 million ferry passengers a year, of whom 33 million travel internationally. The leading British operators of passenger services are P&O Stena, Stena Line (which has a Swedish parent company) and P&O European Ferries.

Lloyd's of London provides the most comprehensive shipping intelligence service in the world. *Lloyd's Shipping Index*, published daily, lists some 25,000 ocean-going vessels and gives the latest known report of each.

PORTS

There are about 70 commercially significant ports in Great Britain, including such ports as London, Dover,

Forth, Tees and Hartlepool, Grimsby and Immingham, Sullom Voe, Milford Haven, Southampton, Felixstowe and Liverpool. Belfast is the principal freight port in Northern Ireland.

Broadly speaking, ports are owned and operated by private companies, local authorities or trusts. The largest operator is Associated British Ports (formerly the British Transport Docks Board, privatised in 1981), which owns 23 ports. Total traffic through British ports in 1999 amounted to 566 million tonnes, a slight decrease on the previous year's figure of 568 million tonnes.

MARINE SAFETY

By 1 October 2002 all roll-on, roll-off ferries operating to and from the UK will be required to meet the new international safety standards on stability established by the Stockholm Agreement.

The Maritime and Coastguard Agency (MCA) was established on 1 April 1998 by the merger of the Coastguard Agency and the Marine Safety Agency. It is an executive agency of the Department of the Environment, Transport and the Regions. The Agency's aims are to minimise loss of life amongst seafarers and coastal users, respond to maritime emergencies 24 hours a day, develop, promote and enforce high standards of marine safety and to minimise the risk of pollution of the marine environment from ships and where pollution occurs, minimise the impact on UK interests. Each year HM Coastguard co-ordinate Search and Rescue for around 11,000 incidents saving around 250 lives.

Locations hazardous to shipping in coastal waters are marked by lighthouses and other lights and buoys. The lighthouse authorities are the Corporation of Trinity House (for England, Wales and the Channel Islands), the Northern Lighthouse Board (for Scotland and the Isle of Man), and the Commissioners of Irish Lights (for Northern Ireland and the Republic of Ireland). Trinity House maintains 72 lighthouses, 13 major floating aids to navigation and more than 429 buoys; and the Northern Lighthouse Board 84 lighthouses, 116 minor lights and many buoys.

Harbour authorities are responsible for pilotage within their harbour areas; and the Ports Act 1991 provides for the transfer of lights and buoys to harbour authorities where these are used for mainly local navigation.

UK-REGISTERED TRADING VESSELS OF 500 GROSS TONS AND OVER as at end 1998

Type of vessel	No.	Gross tonnage
Tankers[1]	145	2,977,000
Bulk carriers[2]	26	854,000
Specialised carriers[3]	11	49,000
Container (fully cellular)[4]	45	1,379,000
Ro-Ro[5]	92	1,123,000
Other general cargo[6]	86	307,000
Passenger[7]	11	358,000
TOTAL	416	7,048,000

[1] Includes oil, gas, chemical and other specialised tankers
[2] Includes combination bulk carriers: ore/oil and ore/bulk/oil carriers
[3] Includes livestock, car and chemical carriers
[4] Fully cellular container ships only.
[5] Ro-Ro passenger and cargo vessels.
[6] Reefer vessels, general cargo/passenger vessels, and single and multi-deck general cargo vessels.
[7] Cruise liner and other passenger

Source: The Stationery Office – *Annual Abstract of Statistics 2000*

SEABORNE TRADE OF THE UK 1996

EXPORTS (INCLUDING RE-EXPORTS) PLUS IMPORTS BY SEA

	Million tonnes
By weight	
All cargo	354.3
Dry cargo	203.4
Tanker cargo	150.9
	£ million
By value	
All cargo	260,900
Dry cargo	244,700
Tanker cargo	16,300

Source: The Stationery Office – *Annual Abstract of Statistics 1999*

PASSENGER MOVEMENT BY SEA 1998p

*Arrivals plus departures at UK seaports by place of embarkation or landing**

All passenger movements	33,275,000
Irish Republic	4,610,000
Belgium	1,747,000
France[†]	23,908,000
Netherlands	1,767,000
Other EU countries	1,024,000
Other European and Mediterranean countries[‡]	192,000

p provisional
* Passengers are included at both departure and arrival if their journeys begin and end at a UK seaport
† Includes hovercraft passengers
‡ Includes North Africa and Middle East Mediterranean countries

Source: The Stationery Office – *Annual Abstract of Statistics 2000*

Communications

Postal Services

Responsibility for running postal services rests in the UK with the Post Office, which the Government plans to change from a public authority into a public limited company. All shares will be owned by the Government. An independent postal services regulator will be appointed. The Secretary of State for Trade and Industry has powers to suspend the letter monopoly of the Post Office in certain areas and to issue licences to other bodies to provide an alternative service.

As the range of postal services increases it is not possible for us to include full details and costings for each one. Below are details of a number of popular services along with costings where available at the time of going to press.

For further details, please contact the relevant service provider, i.e. Royal Mail or Parcelforce. For a quick reference guide to the price of postal services consult the Royal Mail's postal calculator at http://www.royalmail.com

INLAND POSTAL SERVICES AND REGULATIONS

INLAND LETTER POST RATES*

Not over	1st class[†]	2nd class[†]
60 g	27p	19p
100 g	41p	33p
150 g	57p	44p
200 g	72p	54p
250 g	84p	66p
300 g	96p	76p
350 g	£1.09	87p
400 g	£1.24	£1.00
450 g	£1.41	£1.14
500 g	£1.58	£1.30
600 g	£1.90	£1.52
700 g	£2.39	£1.74
750 g	£2.56	£1.85 (not
800 g	£2.77	Admissible
900 g	£3.05	over 750 g)
1,000 g	£3.32	
Each extra 250 g or part thereof	81p	

UK PARCEL RATES

Not over	
1 kg	£3.00
2 kg	£4.15
4 kg	£6.30
6 kg	£6.80
8 kg	£7.80
10 kg	£8.40

*Postcards travel at the same rates as letter post
[†]First class letters are normally delivered the following day and second class post within three days

AIRMAIL LETTER RATES

Europe: Letters

Not over		Not over	
20 g	36p	280 g	£2.30
40 g	50p	300 g	£2.45
60 g	65p	320 g	£2.60
80 g	80p	340 g	£2.75
100 g	95p	360 g	£2.90
120 g	£1.10	380 g	£3.05
140 g	£1.25	400 g	£3.20
160 g	£1.40	420 g	£3.35
180 g	£1.55	440 g	£3.50
200 g	£1.70	460 g	£3.65
220 g	£1.85	480 g	£3.80
240 g	£2.00	500 g	£3.95
260 g	£2.15	1,000 g	£7.70
		*2,000 g	£15.20

*Max. 2 kg
Postcards to Europe travel at 20 g letter rate

Outside Europe: Letters

	Not over 10 g	Not over 20 g	Over 20 g
Zone 1	45p	65p	Varies
Zone 2	45p	65p	Varies

For airmail letter zones outside Europe, *see* pages 521–3

SPECIAL DELIVERY SERVICES

DATAPOST

A guaranteed service for the delivery of documents and packages.

ROYAL MAIL SPECIAL DELIVERY

A guaranteed next working day delivery service by 12.00 p.m. to most UK destinations for first class letters and packets. The fee is £3.50. Compensation of up to £250 can be awarded for an item if next working day delivery is not achieved, provided that items are posted before latest recommended posting times.

RECORDED MAIL

Provides a record of posting and delivery of letters and ensures a signature on delivery. This service is recommended for items of little or no monetary value. All packets must be handed to the post office and a certificate of posting issued. Charges: 63p plus postage (inland); £2.60 plus postage (international).

REDIRECTION

By agent of addressee: mail other than parcels, business reply and freepost items may be reposted free not later than the day after delivery (not counting Sundays and public holidays) if unopened and if original addressee's name is unobscured. Parcels may be redirected free within the same time limits only if the original and substituted address are in the same local parcel delivery area (or the London postal area). Registered packets must be taken to a post office and are re-registered free up to the day after delivery.

By the Post Office: a printed form obtainable from the Post Office must be signed by the person to whom the letters are to be addressed. A fee is payable for each different surname on the application form. Charges: up to 1 calendar month, £12.60 (abroad, £12.60); up to 3 calendar months, £21.00 (£27.30); up to 12 calendar months, £63.00 (£63.00).

REGISTERED MAIL (INTERNATIONAL)

All packets must be handed to the post office and a certificate of posting obtained. Charges (plus postage)

Compensation up to	Registered fee plus postage
£500	£3.15

Airmail and IDD Codes

AIRMAIL ZONES (AZ)

The table includes airmail letter zones for countries outside Europe, and destinations to which European and European Union airmail letter rates apply (*see also* page 520).

(*Source: Post Office*)
1 airmail zone 1
2 airmail zone 2
e Europe

INTERNATIONAL DIRECT DIALLING (IDD)

International dialling codes are composed of four elements which are dialled in sequence:

(i)   the international code
(ii)   the country code (*see* below)
(iii) the area code
(iv)   the customer's telephone number

Calls to some countries must be made via the international operator. (*Source:BT*)

† Connection is currently unavailable
‡ Calls must be made via the international operator
p A pause in dialling is necessary whilst waiting for a second tone
* Varies in some areas
** Varies depending on carrier

Country	AZ	IDD from UK	IDD to UK
Afghanistan	1	†	†
Albania	e	00 355	00 44
American Samoa	2	00 684	00 44
Algeria	1	00 213	00p44
Andorra	e	00 376	00 44
Angola	1	00 244	00 44
Anguilla	1	00 1 264	011 44
Antigua and Barbuda	1	00 1 268	011 44
Argentina	1	00 54	00 44
Armenia	e	00 374	810 44
Aruba	1	00 297	00 44
Ascension Island	1	00 247	00 44
Australia	2	00 61	00 11 44
Austria	e	00 43	00 44
Azerbaijan	e	00 994	810 44
Azores	e	00 351	00 44
Bahamas	1	00 1 242	011 44
Bahrain	1	00 973	0 44
Bangladesh	1	00 880	00 44
Barbados	1	00 1 246	011 44
Belarus	e	00 375	810 44
Belgium	e	00 32	00 44
Belize	1	00 501	00 44
Benin	1	00 229	00p44
Bermuda	1	00 1 441	011 44
Bhutan	1	00 975	00 44

Country	AZ	IDD from UK	IDD to UK
Bosnia-Hercegovina	e	00 387	00 44
Botswana	1	00 267	00 44
Brazil	1	00 55	00 44
British Virgin Islands	1	00 1 284	011 44
Brunei	1	00 673	00 44
Bulgaria	e	00 359	00 44
Burkina Faso	1	00 226	00 44
Burundi	1	00 257	90 44
Cambodia	1	00 855	00 44
Cameroon	1	00 237	00 44
Canada	1	00 1	011 44
Canary Islands	e	00 34	00 44
Cape Verde	1	00 238	0 44
Cayman Islands	1	00 1 345	011 44
Central African Republic	1	00 236	19 44
Chad	1	00 235	15 44
Chile	1	00 56	00 44
China	2	00 86	00 44
Hong Kong	1	00 852	001 44
Colombia	1	00 57	009 44
Comoros	1	00 269	00 44
Congo, Dem. Rep. of	1	00 243	00 44
Congo, Republic of	1	00 242	00 44
Cook Islands	2	00 682	00 44
Costa Rica	1	00 506	00 44
Cote d'Ivoire	1	00 225	00 44
Croatia	e	00 385	00 44
Cuba	1	00 53	119 44
Cyprus	e	00 357	00 44
Czech Republic	e	00 420	00 44
Denmark	e	00 45	00 44
Djibouti	1	00 253	00 44
Dominica	1	00 1 767	011 44
Dominican Republic	1	00 1 809	011 44
Ecuador	1	00 593	00 44
El Salvador	1	00 503	0 44
Egypt	1	00 20	00 44
Equatorial Guinea	1	00 240	00 44
Eritrea	1	00 291	00 44
Estonia	e	00 372	800 44
Ethiopia	1	00 251	00 44
Falkland Islands	1	00 500	0 44
Faroe Islands	1	00 298	009 44
Fiji	2	00 679	05 44
Finland	e	00 358	00 44**
France	e	00 33	00 44
French Guiana	1	00 594	00 44
French Polynesia	2	00 689	00 44
Gabon	1	00 241	00 44
The Gambia	1	00 220	00 44
Georgia	e	00 995	810 44
Germany	e	00 49	00 44
Ghana	1	00 233	00 44
Gibraltar	e	00 350	00 44
Greece	e	00 30	00 44

Country	AZ	IDD from UK	IDD to UK
Grenada	1	00 1 473	011 44
Guadeloupe	1	00 590	00 44
Guam	2	00 1 671	001 44
Guatemala	1	00 502	00 44
Guinea	1	00 224	00 44
Guinea-Bissau	1	00 245	099 44
Guyana	1	00 592	001 44
Haiti	1	00 509	00 44
Honduras	1	00 504	00 44
Hungary	e	00 36	00 44
Iceland	e	00 354	00 44
India	1	00 91	00 44
Indonesia	1	00 62	001 44**
			00844**
Iran	1	00 98	00 44
Iraq	1	00 964	00 44
Ireland, Republic of	e	00 353	00 44
Israel	1	00 972	00 44**
Italy	e	00 39	00 44
Jamaica	1	00 1 876	011 44
Japan	2	00 81	001 44**
			004144**
			006144**
Jordan	1	00 962	00 44*
Kazakhstan	e	00 7	810 44
Kenya	1	00 254	00 44
Kiribati	2	00 686	00 44
Korea, North	2	00 850	00 44
Korea, South	2	00 82	001 44**
			00244**
Kuwait	1	00 965	00 44
Kyrgystan	e	00 996	00 44
Laos	1	00 856	00 44
Latvia	e	00 371	00 44
Lebanon	1	00 961	00 44
Lesotho	1	00 266	00 44
Liberia	1	00 231	00 44
Libya	1	00 218	00 44
Liechtenstein	e	00 423	00 44
Lithuania	e	00 370	810 44
Luxembourg	e	00 352	00 44
Macao	1	00 853	00 44
Macedonia	e	00 389	99 44
Madagascar	1	00 261	00 44
Madeira	e	00 351 91	00 44*
Malawi	1	00 265	101 44
Malaysia	1	00 60	00 44
Maldives	1	00 960	00 44
Mali	1	00 223	00 44
Malta	e	00 356	00 44
Mariana Islands, Northern	2	00 1 670	011 44
Marshall Islands	2	00 692	011 44
Martinique	1	00 596	00 44
Mauritania	1	00 222	00 44
Mauritius	1	00 230	00 44
Mayotte	1	00 269	10 44
Mexico	1	00 52	98 44
Micronesia, Federated States of	2	00 691	011 44
Moldova	e	00 373	810 44
Monaco	e	00 377	00 44
Mongolia	2	00 976	00 44
Montenegro	e	00 381	99 44
Montserrat	1	00 1 664	011 44
Morocco	1	00 212	00p44
Mozambique	1	00 258	00 44
Myanmar	1	00 95	00 44

Country	AZ	IDD from UK	IDD to UK
Namibia	1	00 264	00 44
Nauru	2	00 674	00 44
Nepal	1	00 977	00 44
Netherlands	e	00 31	00 44
Netherlands Antilles	1	00 599	00 44
New Caledonia	2	00 687	00 44
New Zealand	2	00 64	00 44
Nicaragua	1	00 505	00 44
Niger	1	00 227	00 44
Nigeria	1	00 234	009 44
Niue	2	00 683	00 44
Norfolk Island	2	00 672	0101 44
Norway	e	00 47	00 44
Oman	1	00 968	00 44
Pakistan	1	00 92	00 44
Palau	2	00 680	011 44
Panama	1	00 507	00 44
Papua New Guinea	2	00 675	05 44
Paraguay	1	00 595	00 44**
			00 344**
Peru	1	00 51	00 44
Philippines	2	00 63	00 44
Poland	e	00 48	00 44
Portugal	e	00 351	00 44
Puerto Rico	1	00 1 787	011 44
Qatar	1	00 974	00 44
Réunion	1	00 262	00 44
Romania	1	00 40	00 44
Russia	e	00 7	810 44
Rwanda	1	00 250	00 44
St Christopher and Nevis	1	00 1 869	011 44
St Helena	1	00 290	0 44
St Lucia	1	00 1 758	011 44
St Pierre and Miquelon	1	00 508	00 44
St Vincent and the Grenadines	1	00 1 784	001 44
Samoa	2	00 685	0 44
San Marino	e	00 378	00 44
Saõ Tomé and Princípe	1	00 239	00 44
Saudi Arabia	1	00 966	00 44
Senegal	1	00 221	00p44
Serbia	e	00 381	99 44
Seychelles	1	00 248	00 44
Sierra Leone	1	00 232	00 44
Singapore	1	00 65	001 44
Slovak Republic	e	00 421	00 44
Slovenia	e	00 386	00 44
Solomon Islands	2	00 677	00 44
Somalia	1	00 252	16 44
South Africa	1	00 27	09 44
Spain	e	00 34	00 44
Sri Lanka	1	00 94	00 44
Sudan	1	00 249	00 44
Suriname	1	00 597	00 44
Swaziland	1	00 268	00 44
Sweden	e	00 46	007 44**
			00944**
			008744**
Switzerland	e	00 41	00 44
Syria	1	00 963	00 44
Taiwan	2	00 886	002 44
Tajikistan	e	00 7	810 44
Tanzania	1	00 255	00 44
Thailand	1	00 66	001 44

Country	AZ	IDD from UK	IDD to UK
Tibet	1	00 86	00 44
Togo	1	00 228	00 44
Tonga	2	00 676	00 44
Trinidad and Tobago	1	00 1 868	011 44
Tristan da Cunha	1	00 2 897	‡
Tunisia	1	00 216	00 44
Turkey	e	00 90	00 44
Turkmenistan	e	00 993	810 44
Turks and Caicos Islands	1	00 1 649	0 44
Tuvalu	2	00 688	00 44
Uganda	1	00 256	00 44
Ukraine	e	00 380	810 44
United Arab Emirates	1	00 971	00 44
Uruguay	1	00 598	00 44
USA	1	00 1	011 44
Uzbekistan	e	00 998	810 44
Vanuatu	2	00 678	00 44
Vatican City State	e	00 390 66982	00 44
Venezuela	1	00 58	00 44
Vietnam	1	00 84	00 44
Virgin Islands (US)	1	00 1 340	011 44
Yemen	1	00 967	00 44
Yugoslav Fed. Rep.	e	00 381	99 44
Zambia	1	00 260	00 44
Zimbabwe	1	00 263	00 44

The UK Communications Industry

Regular readers will notice that the structure of this section has changed. In the past, information online rental and call charges was included, however, due to the increasing number of suppliers in this sector inclusion of such tariffs is no longer possible. Instead we have provided an insight into the structure and current technological advances of the UK communications industry. For specific details of services and tariffs, please contact suppliers direct. A list of contacts can be found on page 526.

The UK has historically been an attractive market for many industries due to its strategic location and importance as a global player. The communications industry is no exception. Compared with other world markets the UK's communications industry is relatively mature; liberalisation of service provision was introduced early and as a result an advanced range of services is available through a choice of competitive suppliers. The appeal of the industry is also reflected in the amount of inward investment attracted to each of the communications sectors.

The communications industry now encompasses fixed line telephony services, mobile telephony services, multi-channel TV, Digital TV and the internet and where these previously operated as separate sectors; the definition between them is becoming increasingly blurred.

There are two ways in which this convergence can be tracked:

- convergence between telecommunications services – e.g. fixed mobile offerings
- convergence between telecommunications and other communications industries – the convergence between telecommunications and the internet is the most notable

REGULATION

The regulation of the telecommunications industry in the UK falls under the jurisdiction of Oftel. The Radiocommunications Agency, which is part of the Department of Trade and Industry (DTI), is responsible for radio frequency allocation.

Oftel was created by the 1984 Telecommunications Act and was empowered ensure that the UK communications industry became as competitive as possible. In order to achieve this Oftel has authority over licensing procedures, tariffing, interconnection as well as acting as an arbitrator between operators.

The policies adopted and enforced by Oftel have been largely driven by the European Commission (with the support of the Parliament and Council of Ministers) since the European Court of Justice allowed the European Commission to apply the competition rules of the Treaty of Rome to telecommunications (in 1985) and the formation of DGXIII (Telecommunications, Information Industries and Innovation) in 1986.

In general policy has been aimed at providing access to networks and public services and guarantee harmonised, objective, transparent and non-discriminatory conditions based on the so called 'Open Network Provision' (ONP) principles which aim to ensure fair competition and access for new entrants. To date the Commission has addressed:

- *Interconnection*
  New operators often construct their own long distance networks but it does not make economic sense to run a second line to every home so this last part of the network (referred to either as the 'last mile' or the 'Local Loop') is owned by the incumbent and accessed by the new entrant for a fee. Calls to fixed telephones from mobile telephone must also be routed over the Local Loop.
- *Universal Service*
  This is the stipulation by which services must be provided to all customers irrespective of their location. New entrants often have to contribute to the cost of universal service provision. In the UK in 1996, the government and the EU agreed to offer grants to Vodafone and Cellnet to extend their mobile telephony coverage to sparsely populated areas of Scotland
- *Number Portability*
  This allows the customer to keep his or her telephone number even if they change service provider so the telephone number is seen to belong to the customer not the service provider. Number portability was introduced to the UK's fixed line communications industry in June 1997 and to the mobile industry in January 1999.
- *Licensing*
  The provision of and requirements of the licensing process.
- *Incumbent's Tariffs*
  This provision is to stop incumbent operators abusing their positions as providers of both local, national and long distance services by cross-subsiding one with another.
- *Cable Television Networks*
  Many incumbents also own Cable TV networks but EU legislation requires that cable TV networks be operated as separate legal entities.

524   Communications

In the UK the two major pieces of legislation that have shaped the communications industry are the 1981 and the 1984 Telecommunications Acts. The former divided the General Post Office (which prior to this had provided telecommunications services) into British Telecommunications (BT) and the Post Office and made provision for the introduction of competition. The latter established BT as a public limited company and created Oftel as the industry watchdog.

Since its creation, Oftel has licensed hundreds of companies to compete in the various sectors of the UK communications industry. These licenses are divided into the following four categories:

- PTO or Public Telecommunications Operator (a total of 39 licensed to date)
- IFS or International Facilities Based Service Provider (110 licensed to date)
- ISVR or International Simple Voice Reseller (179 licensed to date)
- Satellite Services Provider (36 licensed to date)

It must be noted that not all these license are current, some operators may have ceased to exist or may never have begun operations.

PTOs can provide either fixed or mobile services and will own their network (the physical infrastructure over which the call is routed). IFS providers also own infrastructure although this is limited by the nature of the services they offer e.g. international calls only. ISVR providers do not own any infrastructure but buy capacity from other operators. Finally, as the name suggests, Satellite Services Providers offer satellite-based services.

Since much of the early regulation of the UK telecommunications industry was concerned with the promotion of competition and since this has by and large been achieved in most of the sectors covered by Oftel the regulator has announced that it intends to take a much 'softer' approach to regulation in the future. In light of this Oftel's activities can broadly be divided into:

- Continuing to review its current customer protection policies
- Policing the regulation of licenses
- Conducting separate twice yearly reviews of each sector – fixed, mobile, internet access and interactive broadcasting – to monitor for anti-competitive behaviour, excessive profits and market share

One aspect of the industry the regulator will continue to monitor closely is the development of mobile internet access. Oftel is currently allowing operators to develop mobile internet access services unhindered but may look again at mobile internet access if or when it becomes a vital way of accessing information and services.

FIXED COMMUNICATIONS

The fixed line communications sector is still dominated by the ex-incumbent BT despite facing competition since 1984, when Cable & Wireless subsidiary Mercury was licensed as the UK's second fixed line operator. This duopoly existed until 1991 when further entrants were allowed.

BT now competes with new entrants in all of its core telephony areas; local, national and international calls. Since no operator can hope to take on BT in all its markets at once, competitors have tended to focus on one area in particular. The UK has witnessed the entrance of cable television operators (e.g. TeleWest, NTL and Cable & - Wireless Communications), utilities companies who previously operated their own private networks (e.g. Energis) and broadcasting companies (e.g. BskyB) to the fixed telephony provision sector.

The emergence of strong competition in all areas of operation has meant that fixed line operators are no longer content and indeed can no longer make a strong business case in providing basic telephony connection and services. The trend is now towards the development of value added services and in the convergence with other communications related industries – in particular the internet. Fixed line operators are positioning themselves to capitalise on the growth of the internet not just in the increase of usage through connection charges but in becoming internet service providers themselves. Customers are looking for higher speed services at a reasonable cost and in the short to medium term operators are achieving this through the deployment of digital ISDN lines.

MARKET SIZE – GROWTH OF FIXED LINE CONNECTIONS IN THE UK

In total there are estimated to be 32.1 million lines in the UK, 73 per cent of which are residential.

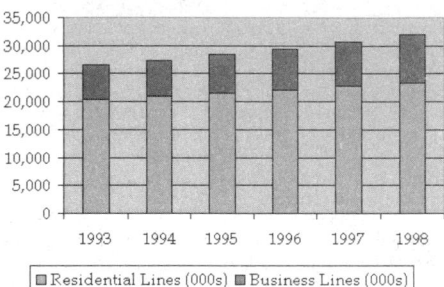

☐ Residential Lines (000s)   ■ Business Lines (000s)

1998 Fixed Line Call Breakdown (millions)

Total Calls	Local	National	International	To Mobiles
142,897	90,070	43,577	5,462	3,788
100%	63%	30.6%	3.8%	2.6

Oftel figures show that in 1998 there were a total of 142,897 million calls made over the UK's fixed line networks. Overall BT still retains a 74.5 per cent market share although in some sectors – most notably international business calls its share is much weaker (39 per cent).

The strongest competitor is Cable & Wireless Communications (C&WC) who began operations in 1984, in the form of Mercury Communications. C&WC as the company stands today is the result of the merger of Cable & Wireless' UK fixed line subsidiary, Mercury, and its three cable operators Videotron, Bell Cablemedia and NYNEX. C&WC now operates in local, national and international telephony provision as well as in the cable television sector. Despite this the operator only has an estimated 11.8 per cent share of the entire fixed line telephony market.

The various cable television operators, who offer fixed line services account for 5 per cent and the remaining 8.7 per cent is distributed among other, mainly niche operators.

The largest market segment is the residential user group but the most profitable is the business user group whose calling pattern is during peak times e.g. during working hours, and involves more international calls.

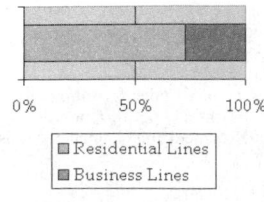

0%   50%   100%

☐ Residential Lines
■ Business Lines

BT still retains 82 per cent of all residential calls made but in recent years this grip in the market is weakening due to the attractive packages offered by the cable operators and other alternative operators and BT in continuing to lose ground. Residential calling patterns increasingly include Internet access calls and all of the major operators are addressing this burgeoning market either by launching Internet Service Provider (ISP) activities themselves or by partnering with existing ISPs. BT itself is taking a two-pronged approach to tackling this area by promoting its BT Highway transmission service and in offering BT Click Internet access.

The business segment is also fiercely contended. Operators here have a much larger scope for offering innovative value added services such as high speed transmission facilities, Virtual Private Networks, internet access and so on. In this area BT is facing competition from highly specialised niche operators such as ACC Telecom, Telstra UK and COLT – even the traditionally residential focused cable operators are attracting an increasing proportion of business customers. These operators are focusing on a specific market (ACC is now the UK's leading supplier to universities), a region (COLT's business is built around its London network and offers services to the multinational corporates sited there) or simply in offering cheaper international calls to lucrative business customers (Telstra).

The result is that the provision of international calls (particularly for business users but also for residential customers) has become the most competitive segment. The barrier to entry this market is much lower as no infrastructure is required. Here BT is estimated to have an overall 64.8 per cent market share, but its share for international business calls has dropped to 39.5 per cent from 57 per cent the previous year. BT hopes that its alliance with the US based AT&T which specialises in developing solutions for corporate customers will help address this area.

CABLE TV OPERATORS

Both the Telecommunications Act of 1984 and the Broadcasting Act of 1990 cover cable television operators. The former covers cable infrastructure while the latter covers the content of the services. The 1984 Cable and Broadcasting Act established the Cable Communications Association and empowered it to grant franchises for the installation and operation cable networks. These franchises could further be licensed to provide telephony services by applying for a license from the DTI. However, the cable operators' licenses stipulate that they may provide local calls only within their franchised areas and that all national and international calls must be routed through BT or C&WC. Of the 132 franchises in the UK 129 of them offer telephony. In 1998 the cable operators passed 11 million households.

The cable industry is coming out of a period of con-solidation which has left just three cable operators; C&WC, Telewest and NTL. All three have reported that the ability to offer a bundled telephony and cable television package has improved the take up of cable services in the UK. Indeed the cable operators now have more cable telephony customers than multi-channel customers. In 1998 figures released showed that there were 2.7 million multi-channel subscribers and 3.5 million cable telephony customers. They are an increasing threat to BT's dominance over the local telephony sector.

PAGING

Paging in the UK, as in many European countries, has been declining in popularity since mobile telephony has decreased in price and particularly since the uptake of pre-paid mobile services and the development of Short Message Service (SMS) based applications where mobile subscribers can send text messages to one another. Many industry observers view SMS as the death knell for paging.

Currently paging services in the UK are provided by four operators; BT Mobile, Vodapage, Page One Com-munications and Hutchison. BT Mobile is by far the largest operator and still has over one million customers. It operates two brands, BT Advanced Messaging for business users and Easy Reach for private users. Vodapage is part of the Vodafone AirTouch group of operations and is the next largest with around half the number of subscribers of BT Mobile. It operates the Business Paging service and Vodazap for residential customers. Neither Page One nor Hutchison make their subscriber figures available.

SATELLITE MARKET

The satellite services sector offers another method of transmission of communications content, whether it is voice, television or data. Satellite telephony itself, as promoted by the failed Iridium venture, has no future in the UK. Everything about the UK communications market is against the introduction of satellite based telephony; existing telephony services, both fixed and mobile, offer near total coverage of the UK and the pricing of satellite telephony would not be competitive in terms of airtime charges or handset cost.

Once again BT is the dominant player in the market sector. BT has two main satellite services:

- The Global Satellite Services Division which provides satellite solutions to large corporate customers and Very Small Aperture Terminal (VSAT) capability supply to BT joint ventures in Europe
- Broadcast Services which is responsible for television uplinks for satellite news gathering services

Satellite Information Services (SIS) is the largest business services player in the UK. SIS core activity is in news gathering, but the company has also acquired a license to interconnect with the telephone infrastructure (PSTN) which gives the possibility of simultaneous voice and broadcast signal transmission.

Other players in the UK satellite services sector are Kingston Satellite Services, a subsidiary of Kingston Communications and joint venture with British Aerospace and Alphameric.

Satellite broadcasting is also beginning to play its part in the communications industry. BskyB, which operates the Sky and Sky Digital brands, has a subscriber base of around 6.8 million although some of the subscribers take the service as part of a cable offering. In keeping with the general trend to convergence of communications services in the UK, BskyB announced that it would be offering international telecommunications services in November 1997 in partnership with another international reseller. While they are not expected to become a major player in the telecommunications industry as such it was a slight blow to the cable television operators whose competitive advantage over BskyB had been the ability to offer telecommunications services in a bundled packed with multi-channel television.

MOBILE COMMUNICATIONS

Mobile telephony services in the UK are currently provided by four operators. However a further operator is due to enter the scene in 2001 following the licensing for so called third Generation or Universal Mobile Tele-communications System (UMTS) services.

CURRENT MOBILE MARKET

Operator	Ownership	Technology	Launch Date
BT Cellnet	100% BT	Tacs-900	January 1985
		GSM	January 1994
Vodafone	100% Vodafone	Tacs-900	January 1985
	AirTouch	GSM	July 1992
One2One	100% Deutsche	GSM 1800	September 1993
	Telekom		
Orange	100% France	GSM 1800	April 1994
	Telecom		
TIW	100% TIW	UMTS	To begin
			operations 2001

MARKET SHARE

	BT Cellnet	Vodafone	One2One	Orange
Current Subscriber Base	8,404,000	8,670,668	5,018,000	5,970,000
Total Market Share	27.6%	32%	18.4%	22%

SUBSCRIBER GROWTH

Jan 1996	5,410,000	9.4%
Jan 1997	6,810,000	11.7%
Jan 1998	8,344,000	14.3%
Jan 1999	13,001,000	22.3%
Jan 2000	23,944,000	41%
April 2000	27,062,668	46.3%

UNIVERSAL MOBILE TELECOMMUNICATIONS SYSTEM (UMTS)

The UK was the third European country to license 3G operators after Finland and Spain but was the first to auction its licenses. Auctions are not new to the European communications industry, many of the second and third entrants had to bid for their license, what is spectacular about the UK's 3G auction is the height of the bids. While industry observers has speculated that the auction might reach £4 billion, in the event a total of £22 billion was raised.

As in the fixed line communications, mobile operators are no longer content to offer connection, voice telephony and standard applications e.g. voicemail, SMS, bundled airtime and so on. Competition has driven down prices and therefore revenue from the basic services and operators are now seeking to differentiate themselves by offering innovative value added services. The most important of these to date is the development of Wireless Application Protocol applications.

WAP is a language that allows data from the internet to be viewed from the mobile phone. To date applications have been uninspiring, news and weather reports, sports information, horoscopes, etc, but it important for the development of 3G services that subscribers accept the idea of internet based services.

UMTS will offer subscribers much faster transfer rates (up to 2 mbps is commonly quoted) which will expand the facility of the network to include full internet browsing and streamed video content.

PUBLIC MOBILE RADIO (PMR)

There is a fifth operational national mobile network which must be mentioned in a discussion of the communications industry in the UK. Dolphin Telecom operates a national mobile network based on the TETRA standard. Public Mobile Radio (PMR) or Public Access Mobile Radio (PAMR) as it is also referred to differs from other mobile networks in its ability to allow group communication, a single user has the ability to push a button which allows them to broadcast to members of a pre-selected group. Most often PMRs are used by the emergency services but the Dolphin network interconnects with the fixed network and is offered primarily to business users as the UK's fifth mobile network. However the take up of services has been much slower than anticipated.

British Telecom
81 Newgate Street, London EC1A 7AJ
Tel: 020-7356 5000; Fax: 020-7356 5520
Web: http://www.bt.com

CABLE & WIRELESS COMMUNICATIONS
26 Red Lion Square, London WC1R 4HQ
Tel: 020-7528 2000; Fax: 020-7528 2181
Web: http://www.cwc.com

BT CELLNET
260 Bath Road, Slough, Berk SL1 4DX
Tel: 01753-565 000; Fax: 01753-565 010
Web: http://www.cellnet.co.uk

COLT TELECOMMUNICATIONS
Bishopsgate Court, 4 Norton Folgate, London, E1 6DQ
Tel: 020 7390 3900; fax: 020 7390 3901
Web: http://www.colt.co.uk

DOLPHIN TELECOM
The Crescent, Jays Close, Basingstoke,
Hampshire RG22 4BS
Tel: 01256-811822; Fax: 01256-474537
Web: http://www.dolphin-telecom.co.uk

ENERGIS
Carmelite, 50 Victoria Embankment,
London EC4Y 0DE
Tel: 020-7206 5555; Fax: 020-7206 5500
Web: http://www.energis.co.uk

KINGSTON COMMUNICATIONS
Telephone House, Carr Lane, Kingston upon Hull
HU1 3RE
Tel: 01482-602 100; Fax: 01482-320 652

NTL GROUP
Bristol House, Farnborough Aerospace Centre,
Farnborough, Hampshire, GU14 6XP
Tel: 01962-822 817; Fax: 01962-822 820
Web: http://www.ntl.co.uk

ORANGE PLC
The Economist Building, 25 St James Street,
London SW1A 1HA
Tel: 020-7766 1766; Fax: 020-7766 1767
Web: http://www.orange.co.uk

ONE2ONE
Imperial Place, Maxwell Road, Borehamwood
WD6 1EA
Tel: 020-8214 2121; Fax: 020-8214 3601
Web: http://www.one2one.co.uk

TELEWEST PLC
Genesis Business Park, Albert Drive, Woking,
Surrey GU21 5RW
Tel: 01483-750900; Fax: 01483-750901
Web: http://www.telewest.co.uk

VODAFONE GROUP
The Courtyard, 2–4 London Road, Newbury,
Berkshire RG14 1JX
Tel: 01635-33251; Fax: 01635-45713
Web: http://www.vodafone.co.uk

Information Technology and Computer Science

It can be asserted that there have been three marvels of the twentieth century: modern medicine, nuclear fusion and the computer. It can be further asserted that modern medicine and nuclear fusion might not have so advanced were it not for the invention of the computer.

So rapid has the pace of the computer's development been and so broad the field of computer science that no article of such brevity can be wholly accurate or complete.

ANCESTRY

The ancestors to the modern century computer are the *Difference Engine* and *Analytical Engine* devised by mathematician Charles Babbage. Designed in 1820 to automatically compute mathematical tables, construction of his mechanical, clockwork-like *Difference Engine* was abandoned by Babbage in the 1840s due to financial problems, personal tragedy and a disagreement with head engineer Joseph Clement.

In 1834 Babbage began work on his *Analytical Engine*. Unlike the *Difference Engine*, the *Analytical Engine* was designed as a general purpose tool with a store to hold information and a mill to take information input on punched cards and translate it into results, or output, on similar punched cards.

Following the financial problems with the incomplete *Difference Engine* project, Babbage was unable to secure further government funding for his *Analytical Engine* and it was not until 1991 that an actual engine was built by a group of historical enthusiasts.

FIRST GENERATION

Babbage's work relied heavily on mechanics and physical machinery. It was not until the twentieth century invention of the electrical vacuum tube and then the transistor that computers became a feasible means to solving problems.

War has been a significant factor in the development of the computer. In 1943, during World War II, the British and Americans developed electronic computers. *Colossus*, a British effort, was specifically developed to crack the German coding cipher *Lorenz* whilst an American effort, *Harvard Mark I*, was developed as a more general purpose electromechanical programmable computer.

Regarded as early 'first generation' computers, these machines primarily comprised wired circuits and vacuum valves. Punched cards were employed as the input, output and main storage systems.

Following on from initial developments, *ENIAC* (*Electronic Numerical Integrator and Computer*) was completed in 1946 by the Americans. Capable of carrying out 100,000 calculations a second, it was remarkable for its day. Like all first generation machines, *ENIAC* was huge and power hungry (weighing 30 tonnes and consuming 25 kilowatts of electricity).

SECOND GENERATION

Similar to light bulbs, valves were prone to failure, requiring tedious checks to resolve problems (*ENIAC* alone contained 18,000 vacuum valves). In 1947 the transistor was invented. Performing the same role as a vacuum valve but less prone to failure, smaller and more efficient, the transistor allowed smaller 'second generation' computers to be developed throughout the 1950s and early 1960s.

Computers remained the province of government and universities due to their scale of cost and size. Their use was significant in nuclear weapon and power generation research and development - one field drove the other.

THIRD GENERATION

In 1958 Jack St Claire Kilby produced the first integrated circuit, a 'micro-chip'. A micro-chip is comprised of a large number of transistors and other components bonded to a single substrate – typically a wafer of silicon, interconnected by a surface film of conductive material rather than by wires. By reducing distance between components, savings are made in both size and electricity. In 1963 the first 'third generation' computers based on 'micro-chip' technology appeared.

FOURTH GENERATION

In 1971 Intel produced the first 'microprocessor' heralding a 'fourth generation' of computers. The Intel 4004 (capable of 60,000 instructions per second) grouped much of the processing functions onto a single micro-chip. Around the same time Intel invented the RAM (random access memory) chip which grouped significant amounts of memory onto a single chip. Intel remain today as a leading chip manufacturer. Successive microprocessors had ever-increasing calculating ability while the capacity of RAM increased also. Super computers and mainframes utilising scores of microprocessors had terrific power in the order of 150 million instructions per second.

The power of the computer has exponentially increased as science has scaled down the size and electrical consumption of the core component (the transistor) from thumb size to far smaller than the thickness of a human hair, allowing a greater density and thus increasing the total power of the computer. Developments such as multiple-layer circuits and the use of copper instead of gold continue to yield gains in size and performance through miniaturisation.

The microprocessor facilitated the advent of immensely powerful supercomputers and also allowed small and affordable micro or personal computers. Early micro computers included the Altair 8800 in 1974, the Apple I & II, Commodore PET through to the IBM PC based on Intel's 8086 in 1981. The 8086 chip began a dynasty of hugely successful microprocessors for Intel that continues today with the Pentium III range.

IBM's original PC set a standard which was effectively wrestled from IBM by companies making clones or copies of the IBM design. IBM designed the initial PC only to see other companies take the lion's share of the market. The operating system supplier Microsoft made thousands of times more money out of the IBM PC than IBM ever did.

In the mid 1980s Apple Computer abandoned its highly successful Apple II computer range to produce the Apple Lisa and Apple Macintosh computers utilising the Motorola 68000 processor. Being the first widely available commercial computers with a graphical mouse/pointer driven interface they were relatively expensive compared to the command line (text only) operated IBM PC clones. The Lisa was abandoned but the Apple Macintosh today ranks as the second largest personal computer system.

In the early 1990s RISC (reduced instruction set computing) became common. Compared with conventional CISC (complex instruction set computing) chips, a RISC processor uses a small set of highly efficient instruction types in combinations to achieve the same result as one CISC instruction. Because of performance optimisation the RISC chip can often perform some tasks more quickly than a CISC chip.

The first RISC chips were installed in UNIX servers and workstations. In the mid-1990s Apple Computer teamed up with IBM and Motorola to produce the PowerPC chip. Apple stopped shipping personal computers with the ageing 68040 CISC chip and instead utilised the PowerPC chip. Around that time Intel began shipping the Pentium CISC chip. Successive releases have produced ever faster versions of the PowerPC and Intel chip sets. For example: from an initial speed of 66 MHz in the mid-1990s, the PowerPC chip was released at 1,000 MHz in 2000.

Next Generation

Most modern computers are still regarded as 'fourth generation' as they use essentially the same technology, albeit highly miniaturised. The future of computer technology is widely thought to be dependent on the physics of light. Already used extensively in the computer industry for high speed communications, laser light offers possibilities for both calculation and storage.

As has been seen, there is huge diversity in the field of computer science and processor types are no exception – there have been literally hundreds of design families and thousands of processor models, and constraints of space preclude discussion of them all here.

Programming Languages

A multitude of programming languages have been devised with the common purpose of devising a program of instructions for computers to follow to achieve a task. Programming languages are categorised by generation:

1GL or first-generation language is the machine language that the processor chips execute. Instructions and arguments are in binary form (strings of zeros and ones). For the very early computers machine language was the only choice as there was often insufficient resources to support assembly language or even an operating system. Machine language tends to be highly specific to a particular processor or processor family.

2GL or second-generation language. Assembly language is a human-understandable language insofar as uses names instead of numbers. An assembler program takes assembly language and turns it into a machine code program. Very common on early systems where resources (speed, storage) were at a premium, it is typically only used today as an output from 3GL and higher systems. It is rare for the assembly language of two different processor families to be identical but they all share similar syntax. Assembly language programs do not lend themselves to being used on different hardware platforms.

3GL or third-generation language is a 'high-level' programming language. Typically more readable and concise than assembly language, 3GL programs are converted by a compiler program into either machine or assembly language for later execution. 3GL languages allow programs to be converted or ported from one operating system or hardware platform to another (with varying degrees of effort) and allow more complex data structures and program flows than 2GLs. 4GL or fourth-generation language is designed to be closer to natural language than a 3GL language. Languages for accessing databases are often described as 4GLs.

5GL or fifth-generation language programming uses graphical development environments to create source language to be compiled with a 3GL or 4GL language compiler. Often 5GLs are used to develop prototype applications which have the look and feel of a final application but often without the underlying power provided by a 3GL or 4GL. Often a mix of generations is used, with a high level language (4 or 5GL) used to produce interface elements and a lower level language used to provide the processing power.

Operating Systems

An operating system (OS) is a set of utility programs that acts as the liaison between the computer user, the computer hardware (processor unit, memory) and its peripherals (hard disk, mouse, display, printer, network etc) and the program that a user is running (e.g. a spreadsheet).

The first computers had no operating system, and each program had to directly control the hardware on its own adding greatly to the burden of programming a computer. Initial input was by setting dials and switches (or even plugging cables), with calculation results shown on dials. The input was in the form of elementary machine language encoded in binary.

The early code-breaking systems utilised teletype paper tape. Then came punched cards – where instructions were laboriously encoded onto cardboard cards that were fed through the machine telling it both what to do and giving it the information or data to compute. The result was either produced onto further punched cards or output on to rudimentary display panels.

The use of punched cards allowed some routine components or programs to be re-used (by re-using routines on sets of cards). Later development of memory chips, magnetic tape and hard disks have allowed more extensive programs and information to be stored, executed and re-executed.

Early OS were hardware- and vendor-specific with assembly language or machine code the programming language. Each computer model or series tended to have its own specific operating system.

In 1969 a major mainstream operating systems, UNIX, was first released. Originated at Bell Labs in the USA, it was based on 'Multics', an earlier time-sharing system. UNIX was one of the first operating systems that could be ported (converted) to a variety of system hardware. This ability was made largely through the use of the 'C' programming language which was first defined and developed around the same time.

UNIX has evolved into many different versions or 'strains' due in part to the fact that the source code is largely free and written in C. UNIX systems were keystones in the development of the Internet and a large proportion of Internet servers today are UNIX-driven. UNIX is available on more hardware platforms than any other OS, although there is no dominant version of UNIX with a dozen or so major versions.

In 1979 Digital Equipment Corporation (DEC) released VMS (Virtual Memory System) as the operating system for the DEC VAX mini-computer. The main features of VMS was the adoption of a 32-bit virtual memory system that allowed use of hard disk as virtual memory in place of actual RAM chips. There have been many operating systems devised and abandoned over the years.

Personal Computer Operating Systems

Throughout the 1990s the personal computer world has been dominated by two main players – Microsoft and Apple Computer. Although not a significant manufacturer of computer equipment itself, Microsoft Corporation has built on its market share secured in the 1980s with MS-DOS to become the market leading operating system provider. Microsoft's MS Windows range of personal computer operating systems are installed on more computers than any other commercial operating system. Concern over the market dominance of Microsoft has led to legislatures in the US and European Union bringing anti-trust (anti-monopoly) lawsuits against the company. Success or failure for Microsoft in such litigation is likely to significantly shape the future of computing over the first decade of the new millennium.

Microsoft's main rival is Apple Computer. Established in the 1970s, Apple became highly successful with its Apple I, II and III range of personal computers and is one of the few of a flock of personal computer companies from that time who have continued to manufacture both their own operating system and hardware to run upon it.

Unlike Microsoft, Apple's strategy has been to control both the hardware and software of their systems. The Apple Macintosh operating system (MacOS) can only be run on Apple Macintosh hardware. This has resulted in a benefit that is also a curse – the Macintosh is a quality product but quality tends to cost. Microsoft benefited from the production of a huge volume of less expensive PCs, while Apple sells on quality and features. Both have significant benefits and downfalls. Many other operating systems exist but tend to be brand- or hardware-specific.

'THE NET'

Prior to the Internet or 'the Net' as it is known colloquially, computers tended to be connected together by hardware and protocols that were peculiar to each particular connection. Typically, links were point-to-point (a link had to be directly and physically established between the two computers).

As in other areas of computing, the military had an important influence on the development of what was to become 'the Net'. In 1969 ARPANET was formed by the US Department of Defence. A main concern was to establish a way for the computer capability of the military to be dispersed so that no one centre was critical to the operation of the network as a whole. This was achieved by interconnecting computers both directly and by way of other intermediary computers; thus if one link or 'node' computer was hit by a nuclear bomb, other pathways of communication could be established. The interconnections, when drawn, appeared as a mesh or net or web.

ARPANET was extended to non-military users such as universities early in the 1970s, with initial international links appearing in 1972. Early network research lead to the protocol of request for comments (RFC) whereby ideas in development can be adopted and studied by other computer users, who will comment on it, expand it and improve on it allowing a de facto standard to quickly evolve. The collaboration ethos instilled in the RFC protocol has fuelled development of the Internet and related computer fields. RFC number 1 was written in 1969 and there are well over 2,000 today.

Early Internet was merely a means for computers rather than people to communicate and was a side-effect of research into networking. It was not 'the Web' and web pages and e-mail as we know it did not exist – these were the days of command line, text-only green screens (if not Teletype printer/keyboards).

The introduction of domain names (e.g. ditdit.co.uk) in 1984 offered an easier means of using the Web. Prior to domain names one had to remember IP numbers (e.g. 192.168.1.100) for accessing destination computers. The use of e-mail increased and implementations improved as various RFCs were adopted as standards; however, the Internet was primarily limited to government agencies, the military, academic and research organisations and some big businesses.

In 1989 what most people perceive as 'the Net' was born. It was effectively invented at CERN (the European Particle Physics Laboratory) by Tim Berners-Lee as a way for scientists to share information by placing it in a prescribed format (defined in an RFC) on a server. Initially text only, development of computer capability allowed inclusion of images through use of a program called NCSA Mosaic – the first graphical 'browser' (see glossary).

By 1993 a whole new industry of ISPs (Internet Service Providers) had begun, allowing computer users to dial up via a modem and access the Internet and to view the Web through their browser of choice. The leading two browsers today, Netscape and Microsoft Explorer, were both based on the open source code of NCSA Mosaic.

In the mid 1990s the term 'information superhighway' was coined to refer to the Internet. Sadly, the Internet is not a superhighway – it suffers from rush hours, traffic jams and link closures despite the fact that new connections are added at a frantic pace.

Developments of the late 1990s have allowed music, video, games, text, graphics and even telephone conversations to co-exist on the same Internet. The core technologies underpinning the Internet are TCP/IP, routers and domain names (see glossary).

The future of the Internet is likely to see the majority of telephone calls and probably video being transmitted over the Internet for at least part of its journey. Expansion of fibre-optic cable networks to homes and business will underpin this. The advent of high-capacity mobile phones will also facilitate and demand expansion of the Internet.

Simple but successful virus attacks like the 'love bug' computer virus of early 2000 show how much the world depends on and is affected by Internet technology. With no central governing body or legal jurisdiction the legal implications of the Internet will continue to puzzle for years to come.

GLOSSARY OF IT TERMS

The following is a selected list of modern computing terms. It is by no means exhaustive but is intended to cover those that the average computer user might encounter. Some obvious, well known definitions have been omitted e.g. mouse, keyboard, display.

Kbps: kilo bits per second – measure of transmission speed, denoting 1,000 bits transmitted per second.

Mbps: mega bits per second – denoting 1 million bits transmitted per second.

Gbps: giga bits per second – denoting 1,000 million bits transmitted per second.

10-BaseT: 10 Mbps Ethernet. *See also* Ethernet.

100-BaseT: 100 Mbps Ethernet. *See also* Ethernet.

1000-BaseT: 1000 Mbps or 1 Gbps Ethernet also known as Gigabit Ethernet. *See also* Ethernet.

10-Base2: 2 Mbps Ethernet over co-axial cable. (*See* Ethernet)

ADB: a defunct proprietary standard formerly built into Apple Macintosh computers to connect keyboard and mice and other input peripherals, ADB has now been supplanted by USB. *See also* USB.

ADSL: Asymmetric Digital Subscriber Line – a high speed digital protocol that allows continuous connection over standard copper wire to the Internet at over 265 kbps for sending and at least twice as fast for receiving. Common in North America and parts of Europe it has various sub types and speeds with several Mbps possible in some forms. Expected to be available in the United Kingdom in 2000. ADSL is ideal for receiving streamed video and audio and is seen as the replacement for modems (which presently have a maximum download throughput of 56 kbps).

Animated Gif: a multi-layered Gif file that allows simple animations to be created by transitions between the layers. Banner advertising on the Internet tends to utilise animated Gifs.

Applet: a very small application that is run in a special environment to provide a specialised function. For example Java applets provide special functions to web pages and are run in the Java virtual machine environment from which they derive their functionality.

ATA: Advanced Technology Attachment – ANSI name for IDE. *See* IDE.

Browser: typically referring to a 'web browser' that allows a computer user to view web page content on their computer. Browsers can be designed for different specialist functions such as presenting image libraries, databases or computer code to users in a friendly format.

BASIC: Beginners All Purpose Symbolic Instruction Code – was designed for mainframe computers in 1963. Included on many personal computers in the 1970s (due to its minimal memory requirements) it became popular for beginners and non-professional programmers. Available on most operating systems, BASIC has been further popularised by Microsoft Visual Basic (an object-oriented graphical language).

Bytecode: file format which is the product of a compiler. Bytecode allows programs written in Java or PERL to be executed on virtual machines on any supporting platform.

Cat-5: an electrical performance and cable quality standard prescribed to support high-speed Ethernet networks.

C: A 3GL programming language developed in the late 1960s in parallel with the UNIX operating system. Primarily limited to UNIX until the mid 1980s when standards emerged (the POSIX standard among others) allowing C to be widely adopted on many operating systems. UNIX used C as its core programming language.

C++: 3GL programming language invented by Bell Labs in 1985 with a final standard ratified in the late 1990s. Hugely popular, it has overthrown C as the language of choice for professional operating system and application developers. Based on C it uses the object-oriented programming model.

CD: Compact Disc – a digital disk format capable of storing 650 megabytes of information on each of its two sides. Information is read by a laser head that detects pits etched into the substrate of the spinning disk and interprets them as information. Widely used in an audio format for storing recorded music. The computer format CD-ROM is likely to be superseded by the higher capacity DVD in the next few years. CD-RAM/ CD-RW is a modifiable version and CD-R is a write once, read many format – both use lasers to alter the disk substrate to make the pits interpreted later as information. (CD-ROM is pressed by machine and die).

CGI: Common Gateway Interface – specification for how a web server and web page interact with applications on the server to accept process and return web content dynamically. Typically CGI handles form submission and searches.

COBOL: Common Business Oriented Language – was released in 1960. Its authors aimed to produce a programming language that was easy to understand and use, more like English and less like code. COBOL in all its versions has been widely adopted for the development of business and financial systems. Many such systems have been evolving since the early days of COBOL when system resources were limited and much of the work required to fix the so called Millennium bug

was work to correct flaws in major COBOL-based systems. Millennium preparation for many organisations involved replacing legacy COBOL systems with more modern solutions using standard relational database and internet tools. COBOL is still commercially available today.

DNS: Domain Name Server – a server that translates domain names into the IP numbers used by programs to directly access computers on the Internet. Each server has a telephone number and a name and DNS is analogous to the directory enquiries service, providing a means of locating my computer connected to the Internet.

Domain: a set of words, numbers and letters separated by dots used to identify an Internet server or group of servers, e.g. www.southpac.co.uk, where 'www' denotes a web server, 'SouthPac' denotes the organisation name, 'co' denotes that the organisation is a company and 'uk' denotes United Kingdom (there are alternates for every country but 'us' is seldom used for United States). Alternative include: org – organisation; net – network; gov – government; co/com – company.

DVD: Digital Versatile Disc – DVD-ROM is a high-capacity disk format that has the same front factor as CD-ROM. Unlike the CD-ROM, however, DVD-ROM can store several Gigabytes of information on each surface and can have 4 readable surfaces (through laser focusing technology) compared with CD-ROM's two surfaces of 650 Megabytes. DVD-RAM is a modifiable version of DVD. Various formats of DVD are available, the most common being that used to store high-quality digital video, an alternative to the laser disk or video tape. *See also* CD-ROM.

E-mail: An e-mail message is a document that is addressed to one or more persons from an individual. Usually containing a message, it can also include other documents and e-mail is the modern version of the telex, telegram, postcard and letter for exchanging information electronically. The advent of the Internet has seen an explosion in the use of e-mail in modern life.

Ethernet: a local area network type that typically utilises twisted pair cables directly between a central switch or hub. Utilising simple, standard and relatively cheap cable and connectors (RJ-45) Ethernet has become the standard for local area networks. Spreads of 10 Mbps (10-BaseT) and 100 Mbps (100-BaseT) are common with 1000 Mbps (1000-BaseT) also available. Ethernet employs a system whereby each computer listens for information addressed to its own unique address. Before transmitting, each computer waits for silence on the line; if multiple computers start transmitting simultaneously, they each detect the 'collision' and wait a random period of time before listening for silence and re-transmitting, thus allowing communications to resume much like polite society. Ethernet reliability depends on the hub or switch rather than on one individual computer. Ethernet is also available over co-axial (television style) cable typically at 2 Mbps (10-Base2); although higher speeds are available, they are less common as co-axial cable is less resilient than twisted pair. 10-Base2 does not employ hubs or switches and comprises an open ended 'daisy-chain' of computers connected to the network. A break in the chain will divide the network into two or ever cause it to fail.

File Server: a computer on a network that stores computer files that users can access from other computers on the network. Popular modern systems include Windows NT, UNIX, Novell NetWare and AppleShare IP.

Fire Wall: computer or device to protect a network from security risks posed by the Internet, just as a firewall or fire-door protects parts of a building from a fire raging on the other side.

Firewire: developed primarily by Apple Computer and Sony, Firewire is being used as a high-performance hot-plugable replacement for SCSI for connection of hard disks, scanners and digital video and still cameras. *See also* SCSI.

Flash: a de facto standard for providing online animated web content from something as simple as an animated logo or button to an online video game. Flash is primarily produced by Macromedia Director and can be programmed with the logo language.

FORTRAN: FORmula TRANslation is a 3GL programming language designed for users and creators of scientific algorithms rather than business solutions. Today it has been succeeded by C for most applications but many legacy FORTRAN applications still exist and many developers still use it.

FTP: File Transfer Protocol – an Internet protocol whereby an FTP client program can request listings of files on a remote server and exchange files with that server. Publicly accessible FTP servers allow Anonymous FTP which does not require a password or user name, whereas while private ones do.

GIF: Graphics Interchange Format – compressed graphic format most suitable for logos and non-photographic images. Invented by Unisys to allow images to be electronically sent in an efficient manner. Royalties due to Unisys for any implementation of GIF have lead to the development of a replacement format, PNG.

Hot-plugable: adjective to describe the ability of a protocol or device to be connected and disconnected as required without restarting the computer or device.

HTTP: Hypertext Transfer Protocol – an Internet protocol whereby a web server sends web pages, images and files to a web browser. HTTP is a perpetually evolving application protocol.

IMAP: Internet Mail Access Protocol – an Internet protocol offered as a replacement for POP3. IMAP allows a user to review manipulate and store e-mail on a central server from one or more workstations without necessitating message removal from the server. Advanced versions such as IMAP4 allow multiple users to have shared mailboxes or folders on the e-mail server.

Internet: An abstract concept applied to describe the global network of INTER-connected computer NET-works of computers. *See* body of article.

Intranet: Subset of the Internet, using Internet protocols but on a local srea network. Common today for publishing information and services within a company or office.

Extranet: Secure subset of the internet, using Internet protocols. Common today for exchanging information and services between a specific group or organisation. Security prevents outsiders from accessing the Extranet.

IP Address/IP Number: typically of the form *number1.number2.number3.number4* e.g. 192.168.1.100, an IP Address is unique to the computer that possesses it. Its purpose is similar to that of a telephone number, each digit allowing an internet or network connection to be made between computers. When transmitting, a computer quotes the destination address and its own address and the information is routed accordingly using those numbers. *See also* router. The widely used IP Address scheme is running out of unique numbers and an extended scheme is being phased in to replace it, although this is likely to take many years.

IRC: Internet Relay Chat – protocol that allows users to 'chat' online with other users using their keyboards. Under IRC a user can log into various chat rooms under their own name or an alias and have a text 'conversation' in real time with other users. IRC spans the globe and allows a person to build a persona based entirely on what they type.

ISDN: Integrated Services Digital Network – widely adopted in the United Kingdom and Europe but not North America, ISDN allows both digital computer data and voice telephony to coexist simultaneously on the same cable circuits. Data can be digital exchanged at 64 kbps on one pair of copper wires, and up to 128 kbps for a typical installation of two pairs. Typically used for point-to-point file transfer of large documents when first introduced, more recently it has been used for 'dial-up' Internet for small- to medium-sized business. In the UK, widespread adoption has been hampered by pricing structures (a 128 kbps connection incurs a call charges for two lines per minute). Introduction of ADSL is likely to limit or reduce market penetration of ISDN.

IDE: Integrated Drive Electronics – a standard electronic interface used between computer disk storage devices. The IDE interface is based on the IBM PC ISA 16-bit bus standard. *See also* ATA.

Java: a development environment that allows development of cross-platform applications or applets typically utilised by web sites or Intranets. Java applications are compiled into Java Virtual Machine code in the same way as normal programs and thus cannot be modified by end users and is relatively efficient when compared to Java Script. Java is related to C++, an object-oriented development language used to develop many modern operating systems and as such can be used to develop sophisticated web-based programs.

Java Script: Netscape version of Java code that is executed or interpreted on the web user's machine each time it is run and is thus less efficient than compiled Java applets. Unlike compiled Java, Java Script is typically provided in source form and is modifiable by the end user.

Java Virtual Machine (JVM): Java applets and Java scripts are required by Java standard to be run on any operating system that has a Java Virtual Machine which must provide a standard suite of facilities to the Java program. Microsoft among others have produced their own extensions to Java that are outside the standard, causing problems to MacOS users and others who do not have access to the Microsoft extensions.

JPEG: Joint Photographic Experts Group – compressed graphic format most suitable for compression of photographic images. Image data is compressed in manner that simplifies the image, losing definition in the process. As the level of compression increases so too does the image degradation.

MacOS: operating system developed by Apple Computer for use on their own Macintosh personal and server computers. Presently a co-operative multitasking system with version 9, it will become a more powerful operating system with MacOS X (10) which is a pre-emptive multitasking operating system based on UNIX.

Novell NetWare – introduced in the late 1980s, NetWare was one of the first network server operating systems and until MS Windows NT4 overtook it in the mid- to late-1990s it was the market leader.

Modem: modulator/demodulator – a device that modulates digital signals from a computer into analogue signals for transmission over a standard telephone line and demodulates an incoming analogue signal and converts it to a digital signal for the computer.

MP3: motion picture group 1 layer 3 – popular format for compressing audio information for transmission over the Internet for later playback on personal computers and hand-held music players and other devices.

MPEG: Motion Picture Encoding Group – popular format standards for compressing video and audio information for transmission over the Internet for later playback on personal computers and on some hand-held devices.

MS-DOS: Microsoft Corporation's Disk Operating System – an early OS developed but not invented by Microsoft for use on early Intel-based personal computers. MS-DOS is believed by many to still be a core for Microsoft's more modern operating systems. *See also*: PC-DOS; Operating System.

Name Server: See DNS

Network Server: both Print Servers and File Servers are types of network server. Other types of network service include provision of configuration or security controls etc.

News: see NNTP.

News Group: See NNTP.

NNTP: Network News Transfer Protocol – an Internet protocol that implements a bulletin board, but on a global scale. Using a NNTP browser one can subscribe to one or more news groups of a huge diversity of topics from Archaeology to Zebras. Messages are posted to a virtual notice board by users through their news browser software to a news group on their local server which in turn passes it to other servers higher up in the hierarchy. To simplify, the hierarchy ends at a server for each country which passes the messages back down the chain in its own country and to its peers abroad (in actuality countries are irrelevant and network boundaries are important). Network News generates huge volumes each day and messages are discarded off servers after an amount of time specified by the individual server manager for each specific group. This period could be minutes, hours or days. Moderated news requires a news group administrator to approve each message before it is posted to a moderated news group. News groups can be specific to a particular organisation, country or network. There is no central store for news and no central control of content.

Operating System (OS): computer software developed to provide computer programs with standard facilities to interact with users and with computer hardware (via drivers). *See also* MS-DOS, PC-DOS, UNIX, MacOS, Windows 3.1.1, 95/98, NT 3/4, 2000.

PERL: Practical Extraction and Reporting Language – language used to develop CGIs. Compiled into Byte-code, a PERL program can be run on any computer supporting the PERL virtual machine.

Parallel: adjective to describe a communications type to denote that bits of information are sent in groups simultaneously side by side over multiple pairs within a single cable. Commonly used to connect PCs and printers.

PC-DOS: very closely related to MS-DOS and providing the same functionality. Initially adopted by IBM as the operating system for their personal computers but was finally abandoned as MS-DOS became ubiquitous. *See also*: PC-DOS; Operating System.

POP3: Post Office Protocol 3 – an Internet protocol whereby a workstation can collect e-mail from a personal mailbox on an e-mail server and move it to a mailbox typically on a user's own machine. Mail collection typically copies the messages from the server to the local machine before deleting them from the server.

PNG: an improved royalty-free graphics file replacement for GIF.

Print Server: a computer or device on a network that manages the sharing of one or more printers between multiple computers over a network. Many modern printers have a print server built in, although early printers almost always needed a print server to be actively shared.

RJ-45: a standard for cable connectors in Ethernet networks.

Router: where multiple networks are joined together, a router acts like a very fast sorting office, examining the destination address of each information packet and passing or routing it to the appropriate network. Routers select the most efficient general route for packets of information based on current system demands.

SCSI: Small Computer System Interface – available in a variety of performance specifications. Typically used for connection of high speed hard disks, scanners, specialist printers and removable drives, SCSI was until recently shipped as standard on all Apple Macintosh computers and is common on UNIX servers and workstations. SCSI has been replaced by Firewire on Apple Macintosh and is becoming more common on other platforms. It is less common than ATA/IDE on Intel-based PCs partly due to expense. *See also* ATA, IDE, Firewire.

Serial: adjective to describe a communication type to denote that bits of information are sent one after another down a single wire pair as opposed to being sent in parallel. Commonly for mice and keyboards, and on Macintosh computers for printers. (*See* Parallel).

SMTP: Simple Mail Transfer Protocol – an Internet protocol whereby a workstation can send e-mail to a server or whereby two servers can exchange e-mail.

Stuffit: popular Apple Macintosh mechanism to compress information for transmission and later expansion without loss of information. Stuffit is a proprietary brand name of Aladdin Systems. *See also* Zip.

TCP/IP: Transmission Control Protocol/Internet Protocol – a protocol which is the life blood of the Internet, TCP/IP defines how information and requests generated by all other protocols are transmitted and received over the Internet. The majority of information on the Internet is chopped up into small chunks or packets of information which are addressed with a destination and origination address. It sometimes happens that a packet gets lost and TCP/IP dictates how such a loss is handled.

Token ring: Historically popular but less so today, a token ring is a form of network that takes the form of a ring connecting each computer. An electronic token (or tokens) is passed around the ring to each computer in turn. Possession of the token allows a computer to transmit for a limited period of time. Token ring is less resilient than Ethernet as any break or flaw in the ring can seriously degrade performance or cause it to fail completely.

USB: Universal Serial Bus – new standard for connecting serial devices such as scanners, mice, keyboards, modems and printers to computers. With USB, speeds of 10 Mbps and higher are possible. Has replaced standard serial ports and ADB connections on Apple Macintosh computers. USB devices can be hot-plugged as required. *See also* ADB.

URL: Uniform Resource Locator – address of an Internet file accessible on the Internet. Typically the server and path to an image, HTML page, CGI, Java applet or other Internet content available to web browsers.

Virus: a computer program or script written for the express purpose of replicating itself onto as many machines as possible (much like its biological namesake) often with negative side effects to the host computer and computer network. Such effects vary from harmless screen messages to deletion or corruption of document integrity, network overload or compromising of security or

privacy. The typical motive is notoriety for the author.
Most viruses are not particularly sophisticated and tend
to capitalise on specific flaws or features of a particular
operating system or program. Very few viruses are truly
self-modifying and simply robotically clone themselves.
Historically transmitted by floppy disk between offices
and over networks within offices, the prevalence of
e-mail means viruses can spread globally within hours.

Windows 3.1.1: Microsoft's initial credible implementation of an graphical user interface operating system
(GUI OS) implementation. Still used by many companies but superseded by successive MS Windows releases.

Windows 95: Microsoft's highly successful upgrade to 3.1.1
providing more features but consuming more resources.

Windows 98: essentially a bug-fix, correcting problems
with Windows 95.

Windows NT 3: appearing to the user as a 32 bit
implementation of Windows 3.1.1, Windows NT was
marketed as a stable and powerful business operating
system. NT was mainly adopted by organisations as
a server operating system and thus competing with
Novell NetWare. Subsequently has been superseded
by Windows NT 4.

Windows NT 4: This evolution of Windows NT 3 is
marketed as Windows NT 4 Workstation for business
machines and as NT 4 Workstation for network servers.
Significant in-built network administration and work
group features coupled with the highly successful
graphical interface of Windows 95 have led to Windows
NT being a leading operating system market.

XML: Extensible Mark-up Language; similar to HTML
but more powerful, XML allows pages of information to
be encoded for publishing on the web and for traditional
paper publishing. It is extensible in so much as XML
primaries can be combined to extend the language
providing greater functionality.

Zip: compression – a popular mechanism on PCs to
compress information for transmission and later expansion without loss of information. *See also* Stuffit.

Zip DRIVE: – a popular 3.5" inexpensive removable disk
format capable of storing either 100 or 250 Megabytes of
information depending on format. Zip is a proprietary
brand name of Iomega.

Local Government

Major changes in local government were introduced in England and Wales in 1974 and in Scotland in 1975 by the Local Government Act 1972 and the Local Government (Scotland) Act 1973. Further significant alterations were made in England by the Local Government Acts of 1985 and 1992.

The structure in England was based on two tiers of local authorities (county councils and district councils) in the non-metropolitan areas; and a single tier of metropolitan councils in the six metropolitan areas of England and London borough councils in London.

Following reviews of the structure of local government in England by the Local Government Commission, 46 unitary (all-purpose) authorities were created between April 1995 and April 1998 to cover certain areas in the non-metropolitan counties. The remaining county areas continue to have two tiers of local authorities. The county and district councils in the Isle of Wight were replaced by a single unitary authority on 1 April 1995; the former counties of Avon, Cleveland, Humberside and Berkshire have been replaced by unitary authorities; and Hereford and Worcester was replaced by a new county council for Worcestershire (with district councils) and a unitary authority for Herefordshire.

The Local Government (Wales) Act 1994 and the Local Government etc. (Scotland) Act 1994 abolished the two-tier structure in Wales and Scotland with effect from 1 April 1996, replacing it with a single tier of unitary authorities.

Local authorities are empowered or required by various Acts of Parliament to carry out functions in their areas. The legislation concerned comprises public general Acts and 'local' Acts which local authorities have promoted as private bills.

ELECTIONS

Local elections are normally held on the first Thursday in May. Generally, all British subjects, citizens of the Republic of Ireland, Commonwealth and other European Union citizens who are 18 years or over and resident on the qualifying date in the area for which the election is being held, are entitled to vote at local government elections. A register of electors is prepared and published annually by local electoral registration officers.

A returning officer has the overall responsibility for an election. Voting takes place at polling stations, arranged by the local authority and under the supervision of a presiding officer specially appointed for the purpose. Candidates, who are subject to various statutory qualifications and disqualifications designed to ensure that they are suitable persons to hold office, must be nominated by electors for the electoral area concerned.

In England, the Local Government Commission is responsible for carrying out periodic reviews of electoral arrangements and making recommendations to the Secretary of State for changes found necessary. In Wales and Scotland these matters are the responsibility of the Local Government Boundary Commission for Wales and the Local Boundary Commission for Scotland respectively.

LOCAL GOVERNMENT COMMISSION FOR ENGLAND, Dolphyn Court, 10–11 Great Turnstile, Lincoln's Inn Fields, London WC1V 7JU. Tel: 020-7430 8400
LOCAL GOVERNMENT BOUNDARY COMMISSION FOR WALES, Caradog House, 1–6 St Andrew's Place, Cardiff CF1 3BE. Tel: 029-2039 5031
LOCAL GOVERNMENT BOUNDARY COMMISSION FOR SCOTLAND, 3 Drumsheugh Gardens, Edinburgh EH3 7QJ. Tel: 0131-538 7510

INTERNAL ORGANISATION

The council as a whole is the final decision-making body within any authority. Councils are free to a great extent to make their own internal organisational arrangements. A local Government Bill is currently progressing through Parliament which proposes new management arrangements with a separate executive arm of the council. The current plan envisages that these arrangements will be implemented in June 2002.

Normally, questions of policy are settled by the full council, while the administration of the various services is the responsibility of committees of councillors. Day-to-day decisions are delegated to the council's officers, who act within the policies laid down by the councillors.

FINANCE

Local government in England, Wales and Scotland is financed from four sources: the council tax, non-domestic rates, government grants, and income from fees and charges for services.

COUNCIL TAX

Under the Local Government Finance Act 1992, from 1 April 1993 the council tax replaced the community charge (which had been introduced in April 1989 in Scotland and April 1990 in England and Wales in place of domestic rates).

The council tax is a local tax levied by each local council. Liability for the council tax bill usually falls on the owner-occupier or tenant of a dwelling which is their sole or main residence. Council tax bills may be reduced because of the personal circumstances of people resident in a property, and there are discounts in the case of dwellings occupied by fewer than two adults.

In England, each county council, each district council and each police authority sets its own council tax rate. The district councils collect the combined council tax, and the county councils and police authorities claim their share from the district councils' collection funds. In Wales, each unitary authority and each police authority sets its own council tax rate. The unitary authorities collect the combined council tax and the police authorities claim their share from the funds. In Scotland, each island council and unitary authority sets its own rate of council tax.

The tax relates to the value of the dwelling. Each dwelling is placed in one of eight valuation bands, ranging from A to H, based on the property's estimated market value as at 1 April 1991.

The valuation bands and ranges of values in England, Wales and Scotland are:

England

A	Up to £40,000	E	£88,001–£120,000
B	£40,001–£52,000	F	£120,001–£160,000
C	£52,001–£68,000	G	£160,001–£320,000
D	£68,001–£88,000	H	Over £320,000

Wales

A	Up to £30,000	E	£66,001–£90,000
B	£30,001–£39,000	F	£90,001–£120,000
C	£39,001–£51,000	G	£120,001–£240,000
D	£51,001–£66,000	H	Over £240,000

Scotland

A	Up to £27,000	E	£58,001–£80,000
B	£27,001–£35,000	F	£80,001–£106,000
C	£35,001–£45,000	G	£106,001–£212,000
D	£45,001–£58,000	H	Over £212,000

The Council tax within a local area varies between the different bands according to proportions laid down by law. The charge attributable to each band as a proportion of the Band D charge set by the council is approximately:

A	67%	E	122%
B	78%	F	144%
C	89%	G	167%
D	100%	H	200%

The Band D rate is given in the tables on the following pages. There may be variations from the given figure within each district council area because of different parish or community precepts being levied.

NON-DOMESTIC RATES

Non-domestic (business) rates are collected by billing authorities; these are the district councils in those areas of England with two tiers of local government and unitary authorities in other parts of England, in Wales and in Scotland. In respect of England and Wales, the Local Government Finance Act 1988 provides for liability for rates to be assessed on the basis of a poundage (multiplier) tax on the rateable value of property (hereditaments). Separate multipliers are set by the Secretary of State for the Environment, Transport and the Regions in England, the National Assembly for Wales and the Scottish Executive, and rates are collected by the billing authority for the area where a property is located. Rate income collected by billing authorities is paid into a national non-domestic rating (NNDR) pool and redistributed to individual authorities on the basis of the adult population figure as prescribed by the Secretary of State for the Environment, Transport and the Regions, the National Assembly for Wales or the Scottish Executive. The rates pools are maintained separately in England, Wales and Scotland. A actual payment of rates in certain cases is subject to transitional arrangements, to phase in the larger increases and reductions in rates resulting from the effects of the 2000 revaluation.

Rates are levied in Scotland in accordance with the Local Government (Scotland) Act 1975. For 1995–6, the Secretary of State for Scotland prescribed a single non-domestic rates poundage to apply throughout the country at the same level as the uniform business rate (UBR) in England. Rate income is pooled and redistributed to local authorities on a per capita basis. For the year 1995–6 payment of rates was subject to transitional arrangements to phase in the effect of the 1995 revaluation.

Rateable values for the 2000 rating lists came into force on 1 April 2000. They are derived from the rental value of property as at 1 April 1993 and determined on certain statutory assumptions by the Valuation Office Agency in England and Wales, and by Regional Assessors in Scotland. New property which is added to the list, and significant changes to existing property, necessitate amendments to the rateable value on the same basis. Rating lists (valuation rolls in Scotland) remain in force until the next general revaluation. Such revaluations take place every five years, the next being in 2005.

Certain types of property are exempt from rates, e.g. agricultural land and buildings, certain businesses and places of public religious worship. Charities and other non-profit-making organisations may receive full or partial relief. Empty property is liable to pay rates at 50 per cent, except for certain specified classes which are exempt entirely.

GOVERNMENT GRANTS

In addition to specific grants in support of revenue expenditure on particular services, central government pays revenue support grant to local authorities. This grant is paid to each local authority so that if each authority spends at the level of its standard spending assessment, all authorities in the same class can set broadly the same council tax.

COMPLAINTS

Commissioners for Local Administration in England, Wales and Scotland are responsible for investigating complaints from members of the public who claim to have suffered injustice as a consequence of maladministration in local government or in certain local bodies.

The Northern Ireland Commissioner for Complaints fulfils a similar function in Northern Ireland, investigating complaints about local authorities and certain public bodies.

Complaints are made to the relevant local authority in the first instance and complainants may approach the Commissioners if not satisfied. Complaints may also be made directly to the Commissioners.

The Local Government Bill includes a provision for the setting up of a Standards Board and Adjudication Panel in England. The Standards Board will investigate allegations that councillors have breached the council's Code of Conduct and if there is evidence of wrongdoing the Adjudication Panel will consider the report of investigations and if it is upheld, impose a penalty.

In Wales the Commission for Local Administration in Wales will undertake the role of the Standards Board.

THE QUEEN'S REPRESENTATIVES

The Lord-Lieutenant of a county is the permanent local representative of the Crown in that county. The appointment of Lord-Lieutenants is now regulated by the Lieutenancies Act 1997. They are appointed by the Sovereign on the recommendation of the Prime Minister. The retirement age is 75. The office of Lord-Lieutenant dates from 1557, and its holder was originally responsible for the maintenance of order and for local defence in the county. The duties of the post include attending on royalty during official visits to the county, performing certain duties in connection with armed forces of the Crown (and in particular the reserve forces), and making presentations of honours and awards on behalf of the Crown. In England, Wales and Northern Ireland, the Lord-Lieutenant usually also holds the office of *Custos Rotulorum*. As such, he or she acts as head of the county's commission of the peace (which recommends the appointment of magistrates).

The office of Sheriff (from the Old English shire-reeve) of a county was created in the tenth century. The Sheriff was the special nominee of the Sovereign, and the office reached the peak of its influence under the Norman kings. The Provisions of Oxford (1258) laid down a yearly tenure of office. Since the mid-16th century the office has been purely civil, with military duties taken over by the Lord-Lieutenant of the county. The Sheriff (commonly known as 'High Sheriff') attends on royalty during official visits to the county, acts as the returning officer during parliamentary elections in county constituencies, attends the opening ceremony when a High Court judge goes on circuit, executes High Court writs, and appoints under-sheriffs to act as deputies. The appointments and duties of the High Sheriffs in England and Wales are laid down by the Sheriffs Act 1887.

The serving High Sheriff submits a list of names of possible future sheriffs to a tribunal which chooses three names to put to the Sovereign. The tribunal nominates the High Sheriff annually on 12 November and the Sovereign picks the name of the Sheriff to succeed in the following year. The term of office runs from 25 March to the following 24 March (the civil and legal year before 1752). No person may be chosen twice in three years if there is any other suitable person in the county.

CIVIC DIGNITIES

District councils in England may petition for a royal charter granting borough or 'city' status to the district. Local councils in Wales may petition for a royal charter granting county borough or 'city' status to the council.

In England and Wales the chairman of a borough or county borough council may be called a mayor, and the chairman of a city council a Lord Mayor. Parish councils in England and community councils in Wales may call themselves 'town councils', in which case their chairman is the town mayor.

In Scotland the chairman of a local council may be known as a convenor; a provost is the equivalent of a mayor. The chairmen of the councils for the cities of Aberdeen, Dundee, Edinburgh and Glasgow are Lord Provosts.

ENGLAND

There are currently 34 non-metropolitan counties; all are divided into non-metropolitan districts. In addition, there are 45 unitary authorities (13 created in April 1996, 13 in April 1997 and 19 in April 1998). At present there are 238 non-metropolitan districts. The populations of most of the new unitary authorities are in the range of 100,000 to 300,000. The non-metropolitan districts have populations broadly in the range of 60,000 to 100,000; some, however, have larger populations, because of the need to avoid dividing large towns, and some in mainly rural areas have smaller populations.

The main conurbations outside Greater London – Tyne and Wear, West Midlands, Merseyside, Greater Manchester, West Yorkshire and South Yorkshire – are divided into 36 metropolitan districts, most of which have a population of over 200,000.

There are also about 10,000 parishes, in 219 of the non-metropolitan and 18 of the metropolitan districts.

ELECTIONS

For districts, non-metropolitan counties and for about 8,000 parishes, there are elected councils, consisting of directly elected councillors. The councillors elect annually one of their number as chairman.

Generally, councillors serve four years and there are no elections of district and parish councillors in county election years. In metropolitan districts, one-third of the councillors for each ward are elected each year except in the year when county elections take place elsewhere. Non-metropolitan districts can choose whether to have elections by thirds or whole council elections. In the former case, one-third of the council, as nearly as may be, is elected in each year of metropolitan district elections. If whole council elections are chosen, these are held in the year midway between county elections.

FUNCTIONS

In non-metropolitan areas, functions are divided between the districts and counties, those requiring the larger area or population for their efficient performance going to the county. The metropolitan district councils, with the larger population in their areas, already had wider functions than non-metropolitan councils, and following abolition of the metropolitan county councils were given most of their functions also. A few functions continue to be exercised over the larger area by joint bodies, made up of councillors from each district.

The allocation of functions is as follows:

County councils: education; strategic planning; traffic, transport and highways; fire service; consumer protection; refuse disposal; smallholdings; social services; libraries

Non-metropolitan district councils: local planning; housing; highways (maintenance of certain urban roads and off-street car parks); building regulations; environmental health; refuse collection; cemeteries and crematoria

Unitary councils: their functions are all those listed above, except that the fire service is exercised by a joint body

Concurrently by county and district councils: recreation (parks, playing fields, swimming pools); museums; encouragement of the arts, tourism and industry

The Police and Magistrates Court Act 1994 set up police authorities in England and Wales separate from the local authorities.

PARISH COUNCILS

Parishes with 200 or more electors must generally have parish councils, which means that over three-quarters of the parishes have councils. A parish council comprises at least five members, the number being fixed by the district council. Elections are held every four years, at the time of the election of the district councillor for the ward including the parish. All parishes have parish meetings, comprising the electors of the parish. Where there is no council, the meeting must be held at least twice a year.

Parish council functions include: allotments; encouragement of arts and crafts; community halls, recreational facilities (e.g. open spaces, swimming pools), cemeteries and crematoria; and many minor functions. They must also be given an opportunity to comment on planning applications. They may, like county and district councils, spend limited sums for the general benefit of the parish. They levy a precept on the district councils for their funds.

The Local Government and Rating Act 1997 gave additional powers to parish councils to spend money on community transport initiatives and crime prevention equipment.

FINANCE

Aggregate external finance for 2000–1 was originally determined at £41,856 million. Of this, specific and special grants were estimated at £6,927 million; £19,470 million was in respect of revenue support grant and £15,400 million was support from the national non-domestic rate pool. Total standard spending by local authorities considered for grant purposes was £53,761 million.

In England, the average council tax per dwelling in 2000–1 is £697, an increase of 6.2 per cent from the 1999–2000 level. The average council tax is £710 in shire areas, £713 in London and £650 in metropolitan areas. In England, the average council tax bill for a Band D dwelling (occupied by two adults) for 2000–1 is £847, an increase of 6.1 per cent from the 1999–2000 level. The average Band D council tax is £843 in shire areas, £778 in London and £919 in metropolitan areas.

The provisional amount estimated to be raised from national non-domestic rates from central and, local lists is £13,196 million. Total rateable value held on draft local authority lists at 31 December 1999 was £37,770 million. The amount of national non-domestic rates to be redistributed to authorities from the pool in 2000–1 was £15,400 million. The national non-domestic rate multiplier, or poundage, for 2000–1 is 41.6p.

Under the Local Government and Housing Act 1989, local authorities have four main ways of paying for capital expenditure: borrowing and other forms of extended credit; capital grants from central government towards some types of capital expenditure; 'usable' capital receipts from the sale of land, houses and other assets; and revenue.

The amount of capital expenditure which a local authority can finance by borrowing (or other forms of credit) is effectively limited by the credit approvals issued to it by central government. Most credit approvals can be used for any local authority service; these are known as basic credit approvals. Others (supplementary credit approvals) are for particular projects or services.

Generally, the 'usable' part of a local authority's capital receipts consists of 25 per cent of receipts from the sale of council houses. The balance has to be set aside as provision for repaying debt and meeting other credit liabilities. Since 1 September 1998, local authorities have been free to use all receipts from the sale of other property and assets.

EXPENDITURE

Local authority budgeted net revenue expenditure for 2000–1 was (2000–1 cash prices):

Service	£m
Education	23,470
Personal social services	10,272
Police	7,331
Highway maintenance	2,036
Fire	1,517
Civil defence and other Home Office services	610
Magistrates courts	322
Public transport and parking	850
Housing benefit administration	5,830
Non-housing revenue account housing	442
Libraries, culture and heritage	1,020
Sport	543
Local environmental services	6,557
Other services	426
Net current expenditure	61,227
Capital charges	2,083
Capital charged to revenue	620
Other non-current expenditure	2,377
Interest receipts	−797
Gross revenue expenditure	65,509

Specific and special grants outside AEF	−8,475
Revenue expenditure	57,034
Specific and special grants inside AEF	−3,603
Net revenue expenditure	53,431

AEF = aggregate external finance

LONDON

Since the abolition of the Greater London Council in 1986, the Greater London area has not had a single local government body. The area is divided into 32 borough councils, which have a status similar to the metropolitan district councils in the rest of England, and the Corporation of the City of London.

In March 1998 the Government announced proposals for a Greater London Authority (GLA) covering the area of the 32 London boroughs and the City of London, which would comprise a directly elected mayor and a 25-member assembly. A referendum was held in London on 7 May 1998; the turnout was approximately 34 per cent, of whom 72 per cent voted in favour of the GLA. The independent candidate for London Mayor, Ken Livingstone, was elected on 4 May 2000 and the Authority assumed its responsibilities on 3 July 2000. The GLA is responsible for transport, economic development, strategic planning, culture, health, the environment, the police and fire and emergency planning. The separately elected assembly will scrutinise the mayor's activities and approve plans and budgets. There are 14 Constituency Assembly members, each representing a separate area of London (each constituency is made up of two or three complete London boroughs). Eleven additional members, making up the total Assembly complement of 25 members, are elected on a Londonwide basis, either as independents or from party political lists on the basis of proportional representation. Parties or independent candidates must secure at least five per cent of the vote to be entitled to additional seats.

LONDON BOROUGH COUNCILS

The London boroughs have whole council elections every four years, in the year immediately following the county council election year. The next elections will be in 2002.

The borough councils have responsibility for the following functions: building regulations; cemeteries and crematoria; consumer protection; education; youth employment; environmental health; electoral registration; food; drugs; housing; leisure services; libraries; local planning; local roads; museums; parking; recreation (parks, playing fields, swimming pools); refuse collection and street cleansing; social services; town planning; and traffic management.

THE CORPORATION OF LONDON

The Corporation of London is the local authority for the City of London. Its legal definition is 'The Mayor and Commonalty and Citizens of the City of London'. It is governed by the Court of Common Council, which consists of the Lord Mayor, 24 other aldermen, and 130 common councilmen. The Lord Mayor and two sheriffs are nominated annually by the City Guilds (the livery companies) and elected by the Court of Aldermen. Aldermen and councilmen are elected from the 25 wards into which the City is divided; councilmen must stand for re-election annually. The Council is a legislative assembly, and there are no political parties.

The Corporation has the same functions as the London borough councils. In addition, it runs the City of London Police; is the health authority for the Port of London; has health control of animal imports throughout Greater London, including at Heathrow airport; owns and manages public open spaces throughout Greater London; runs the Central Criminal Court; and runs Billingsgate, Smithfield and Spitalfields markets.

THE CITY GUILDS (LIVERY COMPANIES)

The livery companies of the City of London grew out of early medieval religious fraternities and began to emerge as trade and craft guilds, retaining their religious aspect, in the 12th century. From the early 14th century, only members of the trade and craft guilds could call themselves citizens of the City of London. The guilds began to be called livery companies, because of the distinctive livery worn by the most prosperous guild members on ceremonial occasions, in the late 15th century.

By the early 19th century the power of the companies within their trades had begun to wane, but those wearing the livery of a company continued to play an important role in the government of the City of London. Liverymen still have the right to nominate the Lord Mayor and sheriffs, and most members of the Court of Common Council are liverymen.

GREATER LONDON SERVICES

After the abolition of the Greater London Council (GLC) in 1986, the London boroughs took over most of its functions. Successor bodies have also been set up for certain functions. The London Residuary Body (LRB) was set up in 1986 to deal with residual matters of the GLC. It completed its work and was wound up in 1995.

WALES

The Local Government (Wales) Act 1994 abolished the two-tier structure of eight county and 37 district councils which had existed since 1974, and replaced it, from 1 April 1996, with 22 unitary authorities. The new authorities were elected in May 1995. Each unitary authority has inherited all the functions of the previous county and district councils, except fire services (which are provided by three combined fire authorities, composed of representatives of the unitary authorities) and National Parks (which are the responsibility of three independent National Park authorities).

The Police and Magistrates Courts Act 1994 set up four police authorities with effect from 1 April 1995: Dyfed-Powys, Gwent, North Wales, and South Wales.

COMMUNITY COUNCILS

In Wales community councils are the equivalent of parishes in England. Unlike England, where many areas are not in any parish, communities have been established for the whole of Wales, approximately 865 communities in all. Community meetings may be convened as and when desired.

Community councils exist in 735 communities and further councils may be established at the request of a community meeting. Community councils have broadly the same range of powers as English parish councils. Community councillors are elected for a term of four years.

FINANCE

Aggregate external finance for 2000–1 (excluding specific grants) is £2,688 million. This comprises revenue support grant of £2,033 million, support from the national non-domestic rate pool of £638 million, and £17 million in council tax reduction grants. Total standard spending by local authorities considered for grant purposes is £3,307 million.

The average Band D council tax levied in Wales for 2000–1 is £669, comprising unitary authorities £573, police authorities £80, community councils £16 and an average grant reduction of £17.

EXPENDITURE

Local authority budgeted net revenue expenditure for 1999–2000 was (1999–2000 cash prices):

Service	£m
Education	1,427
Personal social services	616
Police	372
Highway maintenance	145
Fire	95
Probation and other Home Office services	35
Magistrates courts	19
Public transport and parking	18
Housing and council tax benefit	360
Non-housing revenue account housing	17
Libraries, museums and art galleries	50
Swimming pools and recreation	55
Local environmental services	314
Other services	97
Net current expenditure	3,620
Capital charges	259
Capital charged to revenue	19
Other non-current expenditure	11
Interest receipts	−20
Gross revenue expenditure	3,890
Specific grants outside AEF	−459
Revenue expenditure	3,431
Specific grants inside AEF	−68
Net revenue expenditure	3,362

AEF = aggregate external finance

SCOTLAND

The Local Government etc. (Scotland) Act 1994 abolished the two-tier structure of nine regional and 53 district councils which had existed since 1975 and replaced it, from 1 April 1996, with 29 unitary authorities on the mainland; the three islands councils remained. The new authorities were elected in April 1995. Each unitary authority has inherited all the functions of the regional and district councils, except water and sewerage (now provided by three public bodies whose members were appointed by the Secretary of State for Scotland; this power has now been devolved to the Scottish Executive) and reporters panels (now a national agency).

In July 1999 the Scottish Parliament assumed responsibility for legislation on local government. The Government had established a Commission on Local Government and the Scottish Parliament (the McIntosh Commission) to make recommendations on the relationship between local authorities and the new Parliament and on increasing local authorities accountability. The Commission reported to the First Minister of the Scottish Parliament in June 1999.

Following this, the Scottish Executive established the 'Renewing Local Democracy' working group to consider ways in which council membership could be made more attractive and councils could become more representative of the make-up of the community and advise on the appropriate numbers of members for each council, taking account of new management arrangements and characteristics. They also investigated which method of election would be most appropriate, taking account of the following criteria; proportionality and the councillor-ward link, fair provision for independents, allowance for geographical diversity and a close fit between council wards and natural communities, and advise on an appropriate system of remuneration for councillors, taking account of available resources.

The Scottish Executive also set up the Leadership Advisory Panel in October 1999 following the recommendations of the McIntosh Report. The panel is working closely with all Scottish local authorities conducting reviews of their policy development and decision-making structures.

ELECTIONS

The unitary authorities consist of directly elected councillors. Elections take place every three years; the next elections are in 2002. In 2000 the register showed 4,009,424 electors in Scotland.

FUNCTIONS

The functions of the councils and islands councils are: education; social work; strategic planning; the provision of infrastructure such as roads; consumer protection; flood prevention; coast protection; valuation and rating; the police and fire services; civil defence; electoral registration; public transport; registration of births, deaths and marriages; housing; leisure and recreation; development control and building control; environmental health; licensing; allotments; public conveniences; and the administration of district courts.

COMMUNITY COUNCILS

Unlike the parish councils and community councils in England and Wales, Scottish community councils are not local authorities. Their purpose as defined in statute is to ascertain and express the views of the communities they represent, and to take in the interests of their communities such actions as appears to be expedient or practicable. Over 1,000 community councils have been established under schemes drawn up by district and islands councils in Scotland.

Since April 1996 community councils have had an enhanced role, becoming statutory consultees on local planning issues and on the decentralisation schemes which the new councils have to draw up for delivery of services.

FINANCE

Figures for 1999–2000 show total receipts from non-domestic rates of £1,326,000,000 and £1,070 million from the council tax. The unified business rate for 1998–9 was 48p for property with a rateable value of less than £10,000 and 48.9p otherwise. The average Band D council tax payable was £827.

EXPENDITURE

Local authority current expenditure supported by aggregate external finance for 2000–1 was (2000–1 cash prices):

Service	£m
Tourism	9
Roads and transport	352
Housing	4
Other environmental services	720
Law, order and protective services	950
Education	2,997
Arts and libraries	121
Social work services	1,223
Housing benefit administration	35
Sheltered employment	10
Consumer protection	17
Total	6,441
Total excluding housing benefits, sheltered employment and consumer protection	6,379

NORTHERN IRELAND

For the purpose of local government Northern Ireland has a system of 26 single-tier district councils.

ELECTIONS

There are 582 members of the councils, elected for periods of four years at a time on the principle of proportional representation.

FUNCTIONS

The district councils have three main roles. These are:

Executive: responsibility for a wide range of local services including building regulations; community services; consumer protection; cultural facilities; environmental health; miscellaneous licensing and registration provisions, including dog control; litter prevention; recreational and social facilities; refuse collection and disposal; street cleansing; and tourist development

Representative: nominating representatives to sit as members of the various statutory bodies responsible for the administration of regional services such as drainage, education, fire, health and personal social services, housing, and libraries

Consultative: acting as the medium through which the views of local people are expressed on the operation in their area of other regional services, notably conservation (including water supply and sewerage services), planning and roads, provided by those departments of central government which have an obligation, statutory or otherwise, to consult the district councils about proposals affecting their areas

FINANCE

Local government in Northern Ireland is funded by a system of rates (a local property tax calculated by using the rateable value of a property multiplied by an amount per pound of rateable value). Rates are collected by the Rate Collection Agency, an executive agency within the Department of the Environment for Northern Ireland. A general revaluation of non-domestic properties became effective on 1 April 1997. As a result of this, separate regional rates are now made at standard uniform amounts by the Department of Finance and Personnel for both domestic and non-domestic sectors. District councils now make their individual district rates on the same basis.

In 1997–8 approximately £495 million was raised in rates. The average domestic poundage levied was 189.59p and the average non-domestic rate poundage was 41.37p.

Political Composition of Local Councils

AS AT END MAY 2000

Abbreviations:

C.	Conservative
Com.	Communist
Dem.	Democrat
Green	Green
Ind.	Independent
Lab.	Labour
Lib.	Liberal
LD	Liberal Democrat
MK	Mebyon Kernow
NP	Non-political/Non-party
PC	Plaid Cymru
RA	Ratepayers'/Resident's Associations
SD	Social Democrat
SNP	Scottish National Party

ENGLAND

COUNTY COUNCILS

Bedfordshire	C. 25, Lab. 14, LD 10
Buckinghamshire	C. 38, LD 10, Lab. 4, vacant 1
Cambridgeshire	C. 33, LD 16, Lab. 10
Cheshire	Lab. 19, C. 18, LD 10, vacant 1
Cornwall	Ind. 31, LD 30, Lab. 8, vacant 1
Cumbria	Lab. 43, C. 24, LD 12, Ind. 4
Derbyshire	Lab. 44, C. 12, LD 6, Ind. 2
Devon	LD 29, C. 15, Lab. 4, Lib. 2
Dorset	LD 21, C. 15, Lab. 5, Ind. 1
Durham	Lab. 52, Ind. 4, LD 3, C. 2
East Sussex	C. 20, LD 17, Lab. 7
Essex	C. 38, Lab. 24, LD 14, Ind. 3
Gloucestershire	C. 23, LD 20, Lab. 15, Ind. 3, vacant 1
Hampshire	C. 42, LD 22, Lab. 8, Ind. 2
Hertfordshire	C. 40, Lab. 28, LD 8, Ind. 1
Kent	C. 45, Lab. 23, LD 16
Lancashire	Lab. 46, C. 23, LD 7, Other 2
Leicestershire	C. 25, Lab. 17, LD 11, Others 1
Lincolnshire	C. 43, Lab. 19, LD 11, Ind. 3
Norfolk	C. 37, Lab. 33, LD 13, Ind. 1
Northamptonshire	Lab. 38, C. 27, LD 3
Northumberland	Lab. 42, C. 15, LD 8, Ind. 1
North Yorkshire	C. 38, LD 19, Lab. 11, Ind. 6
Nottinghamshire	Lab. 41, C. 17, LD 4 vacant 1
Oxfordshire	C. 27, LD 21, Lab. 20, Green 2
Shropshire	C. 20, LD 12, Others 6
Somerset	LD 36, C. 18, Lab. 3
Staffordshire	Lab. 40, C. 20, LD 2
Suffolk	Lab. 32, C. 31, LD 14, Ind. 3
Surrey	C. 48, LD 16, Lab. 6, RA 4, Ind. 2
Warwickshire	Lab. 31, C. 21, LD 7, Other 1
West Sussex	C. 38, LD 23, Lab. 9, Ind. 1
Wiltshire	C. 25, LD 16, Lab. 4, Ind. 2
Worcestershire	C. 25, Lab 21, LD 8, Lib.1

UNITARY COUNCIL

Barnsley	Lab. 52, Ind. 7, C. 3, LD 3 Others 1

Bath and North-East Somerset	LD 30, Lab. 17, C. 15, Ind. Lab. 2
Birmingham	Lab. 66, C. 28, LD 18, Others 5
Blackburn with Darwen	Lab. 36, C. 20, LD 6
Blackpool	Lab. 24, C. 16, LD 4
Bolton	Lab. 34, C. 15, LD 11
Bournemouth	C. 27, LD 18, Lab. 6
Bracknell Forest	C. 30, Lab. 10
Bradford	Lab. 41, C. 37, LD 11, Green 1
Brighton and Hove	Lab. 45, C. 27, LD 3
Bristol	Lab. 36, LD 24, C. 10
Bury	C. 32, Lab. 13, LD 2, vacant 1
Calderdale	C. 28, LD 15, Lab. 10, Ind. 1
Coventry	Lab. 35, C. 15, Others 3, SD 1
Darlington	Lab. 35, C. 15, LD 2
Derby	Lab. 29, C. 9, LD 6
Doncaster	Lab. 41, LD 9, C. 6, Others 4, Ind. 2, Ind. Lab. 1
Dudley	Lab. 43, C. 18, LD 11
East Riding of Yorkshire	C. 27, LD 22, Lab. 12, Ind. 6
Gateshead	Lab. 47, LD 18, Lib. 1
Halton	Lab. 43, LD 7, Others 4, C. 1
Hartlepool	Lab. 21, LD 14, C. 9, Ind. 2, Ind. C. 1
Herefordshire	LD 21, Ind. 14, Lab. 4
Isle of Wight	LD 18, C. 13, Ind. 7, Others 5, Lab. 4, Lib. 1
Kingston upon Hull	Lab. 44, LD 10, Ind. 2, Ind. Lab. 2
Kirklees	LD 29, Lab. 25, C. 15, Green 3
Knowsley	Lab. 61, LD 4, vacant 1
Leeds	Lab. 61, LD 19, C. 16, Green 2, Ind. 1
Leicester	Lab. 30, LD 16, C. 10
Liverpool	LD 69, Lab. 20, Others 5, Lib. 4, Ind. 1
Luton	Lab. 36, LD 9, C. 3
Manchester	Lab. 77, LD 21
Medway	C. 38, Lab. 25, LD 15, Others 2
Middlesbrough	Lab. 41, LD 7, C. 4, Ind. 1
Milton Keynes	Lab. 22, LD 20, C. 8, Ind. 1
Newcastle upon Tyne	Lab. 63, LD 13, vacant 2
North-East Lincolnshire	Lab. 22, C. 11, LD 5, Ind. 4
North Lincolnshire	Lab. 23, C. 19
North Somerset	C. 32, Lab. 13, LD 11, Ind. 3, Others 1
North Tyneside	Lab. 34, C. 17, LD 9
Nottingham	Lab. 40, C. 11, LD 4
Oldham	LD 31, Lab. 25, Green 2
Peterborough	C. 27, Lab. 22, Lib. 3, Other 2, Ind. 1
Plymouth	C. 39, Lab. 21
Poole	LD 19, C. 17, Lab. 3
Portsmouth	C. 16, Lab. 15, LD 8
Reading	Lab. 36, LD 6, C. 3
Redcar and Cleveland	Lab. 32, C. 14, LD 11, Ind. 2
Rochdale	Lab. 31, LD 21, C. 8
Rotherham	Lab. 57, Ind. 4, LD 1
Rutland	Ind. 10, LD 4, Others 2, Green 1
St Helens	Lab. 35, LD 15, C. 4
Salford	Lab. 52, LD 5, C. 3
Sandwell	Lab. 55, Lib. 10, C. 6, Ind. 1
Sefton	LD 25, Lab. 22, C. 19
Sheffield	LD 48, Lab. 36, Ind. 2, C. 1
Slough	Lab. 26, C. 8, Lib. 4, Ind. 2, LD 1
Solihull	C. 28, Lab. 14, Lib. 9
Southampton	Lab. 22, LD 16, C. 7
South Gloucestershire	LD 37, Lab. 23, C. 10
Southend	C. 25, LD 9, Lab. 5

Due to a typesetting error a number of political compositions within the Local Government section were output incorrectly. The correct political compositions for these councils (at the time of going to press) are given below. We apologise for any inconvenience this may cause.

C.	Conservative
Lab	Labour
LD	Liberal Democrat
Lib	Liberal
Ind	Independent
NP	Non political
PC	Plaid Cymru
RA	Ratepayer/Residents' Association
SNP	Scottish National Party
SSP	Scottish Socialist Party

ENGLISH COUNTY, DISTRICT & UNITARY COUNCILS

Buckinghamshire	C. 38, Ind. 1, Lab. 4, LD 10, vacant 1
Cornwall	C. 8, Ind. 31, Lab. 8, LD 30, Lib. 1, vacant 1
Devon	C. 15, Ind. 4, Lab. 4, LD 29, Lib. 2
Gloucestershire	C. 23, Ind. 3, Lab. 15, LD 20, Others 1, vacant 1
Shropshire	C. 20, Lab. 6, LD 12, Others 6
Worcestershire	C. 25, Ind. 1, Ind. Lab. 1, Lab 21, LD 8, Lib.1
Alnwick	C.2, Ind.12, Lab.2, LD.13, Others 1
Ashfield	C. 1, Ind. 2, Lab. 29, LD 1
Ashford	C.24, Ind.2, Ind.Con.1, Lab.12, LD.9, Others 1
Aylesbury Vale	C.25, Ind.7, Lab.1, LD.25
Babergh	C.10, Ind.13, Lab.5, LD.13, Others 1
Barnsley	C. 3, Ind. 7, Lab. 52, LD 3 Others 1
Basingstoke and Deane	C.24, Ind.2, Lab.15, LD 15, Others 1
Bassetlaw	C. 14 Ind. 2, Lab. 31 LD 2
Bournemouth	C. 27, Ind. 6, Lab. 6, LD 18
Braintree	Lab. 30, C. 16, Ind. 7, LD. 3, Green 2
Brentwood	C.10, Ind Con 1, Lab.2, LD.25, Lib.1
Bridgnorth	C. 3, Ind. 9, Ind. C. 4, Lab. 4, LD 4, Others 9
Brighton and Hove	C. 27, Green 3, Lab. 45, LD 3
Canterbury	C.18, Lab.13, LD 18,
Caradon	C.1, Ind.19, Lab.2, LD 19
Cheltenham	C. 24, LD 11, Lab. 2, Others 2
Chester-le-Street	C. 1, Ind. 1, Lab. 30, LD 1
Corby	C. 1, Ind. 1, Lab. 26, LD 1
Cotswold	C. 14, Ind. 18, Ind. C. 2, Lab. 2, LD 7, RA 2
Crewe and Nantwich	Lab. 29, C. 21, LD 4, Ind. 1, vacant 1
Derwentside	Ind. 6, Lab. 47, Others 1, vacant 1
Dover	C. 26, Ind. 1, Lab. 28, LD 1
Easington	Ind. 4, Ind. Lab. 1, Lab. 45, LD 1

Eastbourne	C. 15, LD 15
East Devon	C. 38, Ind. 5, Lab. 1, LD 15, Lib. 1
Eden	C. 3, Ind. 30, Lab. 2, LD 3
Forest Heath	C. 21, Ind. 1, Lab. 1, LD 2
Harlow	C. 8, Lab. 26, LD 8
Herefordshire	C. 21, Ind. 14, Lab. 4, LD 21
Kerrier	C. 4, Ind. 18, Lab. 10, LD 10 Lib. 1, Others 1
Kingston upon Hull	C. 2, Ind. 2, Ind. Lab. 2 Lab. 44, LD 10
Lewes	C. 16, Ind. 1, LD 30, RA 1
Maldon	C. 18, Ind. 6, Lab. 6
Mid Devon	C. 2, Ind. 18, Lab. 1, LD 18, Lib. 1
Mid Suffolk	C. 14, Ind. 4, Ind. Lab. 2, Lab. 6, LD 14
Mid Sussex	C. 29, Ind. 2, Lab. 2, LD 21
Malvern Hills	C. 18, Green 1, Ind. 8, Ind.C. 3, LD 11, Others 1
North Kesteven	C. 15, Ind. 4, Lab. 6, LD 6
North Shropshire	C. 9, Ind.24, Lab. 5, LD 1, vacant 1
North Somerset	C. 32, Green 1, Ind. 3, Lab. 13, LD 11, Others 1
North Warwickshire	C. 9, Ind. 1, Lab. 22, Lib. 9
Oldham	C. 2, Green 2, Lab. 25, LD 31
Peterborough	C. 27, Ind. 1, Lab. 22, LD 2, Lib. 3, Other 2
Restormel	C. 13, Ind. 12, Lab. 1, LD 16, Others 1, vacant 1
Rochford	C. 19, Lab. 9, LD 9, Others 3
Rotherham	C. 4, Ind. 4, Lab. 57, LD 1
Rother	C. 29, Ind. 4, Lab. 4, LD 8
Rushcliffe	C. 31, Ind. 1, Lab. 11, LD 11
Rushmoor	C. 24, Ind. 1, Lab. 10, LD 10
Rutland	C. 1, Green 1, Ind. 10, Lab. 2, LD 4, Others 2
St Edmundsbury	C. 24, Ind. 2, Lab. 16, LD 2
Sevenoaks	C. 33, Ind. 2, Lab. 9, LD 9
Shepway	C. 30, Lab. 13, LD 13
South Hams	C. 29, Ind. 4, Lab. 3, LD 4
South Kesteven	C. 29, Ind. 12, Lab. 12, LD 3, Others 1, vacant 1
South Norfolk	C. 16, Ind. 2, Lab. 2, LD 27
South Oxfordshire	C. 20, Ind. 3, Lab. 7, LD 20
Stevenage	C. 3, Lab. 33, LD 3
Stroud	C. 23, Green 4, Ind. 4, Lab. 18, LD 6
Surrey Heath	C. 22 Lab. 7, LD 7
Tameside	C. 6, Lab. 47, LD 2, Others 2
Taunton Deane	C. 21, Ind. 5, Lab. 5, LD 23
Teignbridge	C. 19, Ind. 19, Lab. 1, LD 17, Others 2
Telford and Wrekin	C. 15, Ind. 4, Lab. 30, LD 4, RA 1
Wakefield	C. 6, Ind. Lab. 1, Lab. 54, LD. 1, Others 1
Wear Valley	Ind. 5, Lab. 30, LD 5
West Berkshire	C. 14, Ind. 1, LD 38, vacant 1

West Lindsey	C. 9, *Ind.* 9, *Lab.* 3, *LD* 16
West Wiltshire	C. 10, *Ind.* 2, *Lab.* 2, *LD* 26, *Others* 3
Weymouth and Portland	C. 5, *Lab.* 13, *LD* 12, *Others* 5
Wokingham	C. 27, *LD* 27

LONDON, WALES, SCOTLAND

Lewisham	C. 2, *Ind.* 1, *Ind.* Lab 1, *Lab.* 59, *LD* 4
Merton	C. 10, *Ind.* 3, *Ind. Lab.* 3, *Lab.* 38, *LD* 3
Sutton	C. 5, *Lab.* 5, *LD* 46
Blaenau Gwent	*Ind.* 2, *Ind.Lab.* 1, *Lab.* 34, *LD* 1, *Others* 4
Bridgend	C. 1, *Ind.* 4, *Ind. Lab.* 1, *Lab.* 40, *LD* 6, *PC* 2
Cardiff	C. 5, *Ind. Lab.* 1, *Lab.* 50, *LD* 18, *PC* 1
Carmarthenshire	*Ind.* 25, *Ind.* Lab 3, *Lab.* 28, *LD* 1, *PC* 14, *RA* 2, *vacant* 1
Denbighshire	C. 2, *Ind.* 17, *Lab.* 14, *LD* 1, *NP* 1, *PC* 8, *Others* 4

Monmouthshire	C.19, *Ind.*3, *Lab.*18, *LD* 1, *Others* 1
Neath Port Talbot	*Ind.* 3, *Ind.Lab.* 1, *Lab.* 40, *LD* *PC* 10, *RA* 5, *Others* 3
Torfaen	C. 1, *Ind.* 3, *Lab.* 39, *LD* 1
Angus	C. 2, *Ind.* 3, *Lab.* 1, *LD* 2, *SNI* 21
Argyll and Bute	C.4, *Ind.* 4, *Lab.* 1, *LD.* 6, *NP.* 16, *SNP.*5
Dumfries and Galloway	C.8, *Ind.*13, *Ind. Lab.*1, *Lab.*13, *LD* 6, *SNP* 5, *Others* 1
City of Edinburgh	C. 13, *Lab.* 31, *LD* 13, *SNP* 1
East Ayrshire	C. 1, *Lab.* 17, *SNP* 13, *vacant*
Fife	C. 1, *Comm.* 1, *Ind.* 1, *Lab.* 43 *LD* 21, *SNP* 9, *Others* 1
Glasgow City	C. 1, *Lab.* 74, *LD* 1, *SNP* 2, *SS* 1
Moray	C. 1, *Ind.* 13, *Lab.* 6, *LD* 2, *SN* 2, *Others* 2
North Ayrshire	C. 2, *Ind.* 1, *Lab.* 25, *SNP* 2
Perth and Kinross	C. 11, *Ind.* 2, *Lab.* 6, *LD* 6, *SN* 16
Scottish Borders	C. 1, *Ind.* 14, *Lab.* 1, *LD* 14, *SNP* 4

South Tyneside	*Lab.* 50, *LD* 6, *Others* 4
Stockport	*LD* 32, *Lab.* 22, *C.* 6, *Ind.* 3
Stockton-on-Tees	*Lab.* 38, *C.* 12, *LD* 5
Stoke-on-Trent	*Lab.* 32, *Ind.* 15, *LD* 7, *C.* 6
Sunderland	*Lab.* 62, *C.* 10, *LD* 3
Swindon	*Lab.* 28, *C.* 23, *LD* 8
Tameside	*Lab.* 47, *C.* 6, *Others* 2
Telford and Wrekin	*Lab.* 30, *C.* 15, *LD* 4, *RA* 1
Thurrock	*Lab.* 37, *C.* 11, *Ind.* 1
Torbay	*C.* 32, *LD* 4
Trafford	*Lab.* 33, *C.* 26, *LD* 3, *Ind. C.* 1
Wakefield	*Lab.* 54, *C.* 6, *Others* 1
Walsall	*Lab.* 27, *C.* 26, *Lib.* 7
Warrington	*Lab.* 43, *LD* 13, *C.* 4
West Berkshire	*LD* 38, *C.* 14, *vacant* 1
Wigan	*Lab.* 69, *LD* 2, *C.* 1
Windsor and Maidenhead	*C.* 29, *LD* 21, *Others* 7, *Lab.* 1
Wirral	*Lab.* 33, *C.* 20, *LD* 12, *vacant* 1
Wokingham	*C.* 27, *LD* 27
Wolverhampton	*Lab.* 33, *C.* 24, *LD* 3
York	*Lab.* 25, *LD* 24, *C.* 3, *Ind.* 1

DISTRICT COUNCILS

* Denotes councils where one-third of Councillors retire
each year except in the year of county council elections

*Adur	*C.* 15, *Lab.* 13, *LD* 9, *Ind.* 2
Allerdale	*Lab.* 36, *C.* 10, *LD* 7, *Ind.* 3
Alnwick	*LD* 13, *Ind.* 12, *Lab.* 2, *Others* 1
Amber Valley	*C.* 32, *Lab.* 12, *Ind.* 1
Arun	*C.* 35, *LD* 10, *Lab.* 8, *Ind.* 2, *vacant* 1
Ashfield	*Lab.* 29, *Ind.* 2, *LD* 1
Ashford	*C.* 24, *Lab.* 12, *LD* 9, *Ind.* 2, *Others* 1
Aylesbury Vale	*LD* 25, *Ind.* 7, *Lab.* 1
Babergh	*LD* 13, *C.* 11, *Lab.* 5, *Others* 1
*Barrow-in-Furness	*Lab.* 18, *C.* 17, *Others* 3
*Basildon	*Lab.* 20, *C.* 18, *LD* 4
*Basingstoke and Deane	*C.* 24, *LD* 15, *Ind.* 2, *Others* 1
*Bassetlaw	*Lab.* 31, *C.* 14, *LD* 2, *Ind.* 2
*Bedford	*Lab.* 18, *LD* 16, *C.* 13, *Ind.* 6
Berwick-upon-Tweed	*LD* 18, *Ind.* 5, *Others* 4, *C.* 3, *Lab.* 1
Blaby	*C.* 25, *LD* 8, *Lab.* 6
Blyth Valley	*Lab.* 36, *LD* 8, *Ind.* 3, *C.* 2
Bolsover	*Lab.* 32, *Ind.* 4, *RA* 1
Boston	*C.* 13, *Lab.* 11, *Ind.* 5, *LD* 3
Braintree	*C.* 16, *Ind.* 7, *LD* 3, *Green* 2
Breckland	*C.* 34, *Lab.* 14, *Ind.* 3, *LD* 2
*Brentwood	*LD* 25, *C.* 10, *Lab.* 2, *Lib.* 1
Bridgnorth	*Others* 9, *LD* 4, *C.* 3
Broadland	*C.* 25, *Others* 14, *LD* 8, *Ind.* 2
Bromsgrove	*C.* 30, *Lab.* 7, *RA* 2
*Broxbourne	*C.* 35, *Lab.* 3
Broxtowe	*Lab.* 25, *C.* 12, *LD* 11, *Ind.* 1
*Burnley	*Lab.* 24, *Ind.* 11, *LD* 9, *C.* 3, *Others* 1
*Cambridge	*LD* 23, *Lab.* 16, *C.* 3
*Cannock Chase	*Lab.* 27, *C.* 8, *LD* 7
Canterbury	*LD* 18, *Lab.* 13
Caradon	*LD* 19, *Lab.* 2, *C.* 1
*Carlisle	*C.* 30, *Lab.* 14, *LD* 6, *Ind.* 2
Carrick	*LD* 26, *C.* 9, *Ind.* 7, *Lab.* 2, *vacant* 1
Castle Morpeth	*Ind.* 11, *Lab.* 10, *LD* 7, *C.* 4, *Green* 1

Castle Point	*Lab.* 24, *C.* 15
Charnwood	*Lab.* 24, *C.* 21, *LD* 6, *Ind.* 1
Chelmsford	*LD* 27, *C.* 22, *Lab.* 5, *Ind.* 2
*Cheltenham	*C.* 24, *LD* 11, *Others* 2
*Cherwell	*C.* 33, *Lab.* 13, *LD* 4, *Ind.* 2
Chesterfield	*Lab.* 28, *LD* 19
Chester-le-Street	*Lab.* 30, *LD* 1
*Chester	*Lab.* 21, *LD* 19, *C.* 18, *Ind.* 2
Chichester	*C.* 29, *LD* 19, *Ind.* 2
Chiltern	*C.* 29, *LD* 19, *RA* 2
*Chorley	*Lab.* 31, *C.* 9, *LD* 6, *Ind.* 2
Christchurch	*C.* 17, *LD* 5, *Ind.* 3
*Colchester	*LD* 23, *C.* 22, *Lab.* 14, *RA* 1
*Congleton	*LD* 34, *C.* 13, *Lab.* 1
Copeland	*Lab.* 30, *C.* 17, *Ind.* 3, *LD* 1
Corby	*Lab.* 26, *LD* 1
Cotswold	*Ind.* 18, *C.* 14, *LD* 7, *RA* 2
*Craven	*C.* 18, *Ind.* 12, *LD* 4
*Crawley	*Lab.* 23, *C.* 6, *LD* 2, *vacant* 1
*Crewe and Nantwich	*Lab.* 29, *C.* 21, *LD* 4, *vacant* 1
Dacorum	*C.* 25, *Lab.* 20, *LD* 6, *Ind.* 1
Dartford	*Lab.* 28, *C.* 14, *Others* 4, *Ind. Lab.* 1
*Daventry	*C.* 20, *Lab.* 13, *LD* 3, *Ind.* 2
Derbyshire Dales	*C.* 20, *LD* 9, *Lab.* 6, *Ind.* 3, *vacant* 1
Derwentside	*Lab.* 47, *Ind.* 6, *vacant* 1
Dover	*Lab.* 28, *C.* 26, *LD* 1
Durham	*Lab.* 33, *LD* 13, *Ind.* 3
Easington	*Lab.* 45, *Ind.* 4, *LD* 1
*Eastbourne	*LD* 15
East Cambridgeshire	*LD* 20, *Ind.* 12, *Lab.* 4, *C.* 1
East Devon	*C.* 38, *LD* 15, *Ind.* 5, *Lib.* 1
East Dorset	*C.* 26, *LD* 9, *Ind.* 1
East Hampshire	*C.* 22, *LD* 17, *Ind.* 3
East Hertfordshire	*C.* 31, *LD* 9, *Lab.* 8, *Ind.* 2
*Eastleigh	*LD* 28, *C.* 9, *Lab.* 7
East Lindsey	*Ind.* 35, *Lab.* 9, *LD* 8, *C.* 7, *Green* 1
East Northamptonshire	*C.* 21, *Lab.* 15
East Staffordshire	*Lab.* 28, *C.* 15, *LD* 3
Eden	*Ind.* 30, *LD* 3, *Lab.* 2
*Ellesmere Port and Neston	*Lab.* 36, *C.* 6, *LD* 1
*Elmbridge	*RA* 25, *C.* 22, *LD* 9, *Ind.* 3, *Lab.* 1
*Epping Forest	*C.* 20, *LD* 15, *Lab.* 12, *Others* 8, *Ind. C.* 3, *vacant* 1
Epsom and Ewell	*RA* 27, *LD* 9, *Lab.* 3
Erewash	*Lab.* 28, *C.* 16, *LD* 4
*Exeter	*Lab.* 22, *LD* 8, *C.* 6, *Lib.* 4
*Fareham	*C.* 29, *LD* 11, *Lab.* 2
Fenland	*C.* 29, *Lab.* 7, *Ind.* 3, *LD* 1
Forest Heath	*C.* 21, *LD* 2, *Lab.* 1, *Ind.* 1
Forest of Dean	*Lab.* 30, *Ind.* 13, *LD* 6, *Others* 2
Fylde	*C.* 21, *Ind.* 12, *Others* 11, *LD* 3, *Lab.* 2
Gedling	*C.* 29, *Lab.* 18, *LD* 7, *Ind.* 3
*Gloucester	*Lab.* 20, *C.* 10, *LD* 8, *Ind.* 1
*Gosport	*C.* 13, *Lab.* 12, *LD* 5
Gravesham	*Lab.* 29, *C.* 15
*Great Yarmouth	*C.* 26, *Lab.* 22
Guildford	*LD* 19, *C.* 17, *Lab.* 6, *Ind.* 3
Hambleton	*C.* 35, *Ind.* 6, *LD* 4, *Lab.* 2
Harborough	*C.* 16, *LD* 14, *Ind.* 4, *Lab.* 3
*Harlow	*Lab.* 26, *LD* 8
*Harrogate	*LD* 40, *C.* 18, *Lab.* 1
*Hart	*C.* 19, *LD* 12, *Ind.* 4
*Hastings	*Lab.* 19, *LD* 11, *C.* 2
*Havant	*C.* 20, *Lab.* 11, *LD* 8, *Ind.* 3
*Hertsmere	*C.* 22, *Lab.* 12, *LD* 5

High Peak	*Lab.* 27, *C.* 10, *LD* 5, *Ind.* 2
Hinckley and Bosworth	*LD* 14, *C.* 11, *Lab.* 9
Horsham	*C.* 24, *LD* 16, *Ind.* 3
*Huntingdonshire	*C.* 37, *LD* 13, *Ind.* 3
*Hyndburn	*C.* 31, *Lab.* 15, *vacant* 1
*Ipswich	*Lab.* 30, *C.* 15, *LD* 2, *vacant* 1
Kennet	*C.* 23, *Ind.* 11, *Lab.* 4, *LD* 2
Kerrier	*Ind.* 18, *Lab.* 10, *LD* 10, *C.* 4, *Lib.* 1, *Others* 1
Kettering	*Lab.* 22, *C.* 18, *Ind.* 4, *LD* 1
King's Lynn and West Norfolk	*Lab.* 27, *LD* 5, *Others* 1
Lancaster	*Ind.* 23, *Lab.* 17, *C.* 9, *LD* 6, *Green* 5
Lewes	*LD* 30, *C.* 16, *RA* 1
Lichfield	*C.* 29, *Lab.* 24, *LD* 2, *Ind.* 1
*Lincoln	*Lab.* 29, *C.* 4
*Macclesfield	*C.* 37, *LD* 14, *Lab.* 6, *Others* 3
*Maidstone	*LD* 22, *C.* 16, *Lab.* 12, *Ind.* 5
Maldon	*C.* 18, *Lab.* 6
Malvern Hills	*C.* 18, *LD* 11, *Ind.* 8, *Ind. C.* 3, *Others* 1
Mansfield	*Lab.* 39, *C.* 5, *LD* 2
Melton	*Lab.* 11, *C.* 9, *Ind.* 6
Mendip	*C.* 18, *LD* 16, *Lab.* 10, *Ind.* 2
Mid Bedfordshire	*C.* 35, *Lab.* 7, *LD* 6, *Ind.* 5
Mid Devon	*LD* 18, *C.* 2, *Lib.* 1
Mid Suffolk	*LD* 14, *Lab.* 6, *Ind.* 4, *Ind. Lab.* 2
*Mid Sussex	*C.* 29, *LD* 21, *Lab.* 2
*Mole Valley	*C.* 19, *LD* 14, *Ind.* 7, *Lab.* 1
Newark and Sherwood	*Lab.* 26, *C.* 20, *LD* 5, *Ind.* 3
*Newcastle under Lyme	*Lab.* 30, *Lib.* 16, *C.* 9, *Ind.* 1
New Forest	*C.* 31, *LD* 24, *Ind.* 3
Northampton	*Lab.* 28, *LD* 11, *C.* 8
North Cornwall	*Ind.* 25, *LD* 10, *C.* 3
North Devon	*LD* 26, *Ind.* 11, *C.* 5, *Others* 2
North Dorset	*C.* 17, *LD* 10, *Ind.* 6
North East Derbyshire	*Lab.* 38, *C.* 10, *LD* 3, *Ind.* 2
*North Hertfordshire	*C.* 29, *Lab.* 18, *LD* 2
North Kesteven	*C.* 15, *LD* 6, *Ind.* 4
North Norfolk	*Others* 17, *LD* 12, *Lab.* 10, *Ind.* 7
North Shropshire	*Ind.* 24, *C.* 9, *Lab.* 5, *vacant* 1
North Warwickshire	*Lab.* 22, *Lib.* 9, *Ind.* 1
North West Leicestershire	*Lab.* 31, *C.* 8, *Ind. C.* 1
North Wiltshire	*LD* 26, *C.* 20, *Lab.* 4, *Ind.* 2
*Norwich	*Lab.* 26, *LD* 21, *C.* 1
*Nuneaton and Bedworth	*Lab.* 35, *C.* 10
*Oadby and Wigston	*LD* 22, *C.* 4
Oswestry	*Ind.* 14, *Lab.* 6, *LD* 5, *C.* 4
*Oxford	*Lab.* 22, *LD* 20, *Green* 8, *C.* 1
*Pendle	*Lab.* 24, *LD* 18, *C.* 9
*Penwith	*C.* 10, *Ind.* 9, *LD* 7, *Others* 5, *Lab.* 3
*Preston	*Lab.* 24, *C.* 17, *LD* 12, *Ind. Lab.* 3, *Ind.* 1
*Purbeck	*C.* 17, *Ind. C.* 4, *Ind.* 3
*Redditch	*Lab.* 17, *C.* 10, *LD* 2
*Reigate and Banstead	*C.* 32, *Lab.* 8, *RA* 6, *LD* 4, *vacant* 1
Restormel	*LD* 16, *C.* 13, *Ind.* 12, *vacant* 1
Ribble Valley	*C.* 19, *LD* 17, *Ind.* 2, *Lab.* 1
Richmondshire	*Ind.* 18, *LD* 9, *C.* 6, *SDP* 1
*Rochford	*C.* 19, *LD* 9, *Others* 3
*Rossendale	*C.* 24, *Lab.* 12
Rother	*C.* 29, *LD* 8, *Lab.* 4
*Rugby	*Lab.* 18, *C.* 14, *LD* 9, *Ind.* 7
*Runnymede	*C.* 33, *Ind.* 6, *Lab.* 3
Rushcliffe	*C.* 31, *LD* 11, *Ind.* 1
*Rushmoor	*C.* 24, *LD* 10, *Ind.* 1
Ryedale	*C.* 11, *Ind.* 6, *LD* 5, *Lab.* 1
*St Albans	*LD* 23, *C.* 19, *Lab.* 15, *Ind.* 1
St Edmundsbury	*C.* 24, *Lab.* 16, *LD* 2
Salisbury	*C.* 27, *LD* 15, *Lab.* 11, *Ind.* 3, *Others* 2
Scarborough	*C.* 17, *Ind.* 16, *Lab.* 11, *LD* 5
Sedgefield	*Lab.* 43, *Ind.* 4, *LD* 2
Sedgemoor	*C.* 31, *Lab.* 16, *LD* 3
Selby	*Lab.* 20, *C.* 15, *Ind.* 5, *LD* 1
Sevenoaks	*C.* 33, *LD* 9, *Ind.* 2
Shepway	*C.* 30, *LD* 13
*Shrewsbury and Atcham	*Lab.* 18, *C.* 16, *LD* 11, *Ind.* 3
*South Bedfordshire	*C.* 26, *LD* 17, *Lab.* 7, *Ind.* 3
South Bucks	*C.* 27, *Ind.* 10, *LD* 3
*South Cambridgeshire	*C.* 20, *LD* 15, *Ind.* 14, *Lab.* 5, *vacant* 1
South Derbyshire	*Lab.* 24, *C.* 10
South Hams	*C.* 29, *LD* 4, *Lab.* 3
South Holland	*C.* 20, *Ind.* 10, *Others* 4, *Lab.* 3, *LD* 1
South Kesteven	*C.* 29, *Lab.* 12, *LD* 3, *vacant* 1
*South Lakeland	*LD* 21, *C.* 17, *Lab.* 9, *Ind.* 5
South Norfolk	*LD* 27, *C.* 16, *Lab.* 2
South Northamptonshire	*C.* 28, *Lab.* 7, *Ind.* 4, *LD* 3
South Oxfordshire	*LD* 20, *Lab.* 7, *Ind.* 3
South Ribble	*Lab.* 21, *C.* 18, *LD* 12, *Others* 3
South Shropshire	*Ind.* 24, *LD* 14, *Green* 2
South Somerset	*LD* 41, *C.* 13, *Ind.* 6
South Staffordshire	*C.* 37, *Lab.* 10, *Ind.* 2, *LD* 1
Spelthorne	*C.* 27, *Lab.* 9, *LD* 4
*Staffordshire Moorlands	*C.* 17, *Lab.* 15, *Others* 12, *LD* 9, *Ind.* 3
Stafford	*Lab.* 28, *C.* 23, *LD* 8, *Ind.* 1
*Stevenage	*Lab.* 33, *LD* 3
*Stratford	*C.* 28, *LD* 18, *Ind.* 7, *Lab.* 2
*Stroud	*C.* 23, *Lab.* 18, *LD* 6, *Ind.* 4
Suffolk Coastal	*C.* 36, *LD* 10, *Lab.* 8, *Ind.* 1
Surrey Heath	*C.* 22 *Lab.* 7, *LD* 7
*Swale	*LD* 22, *C.* 15, *Lab.* 10
*Tamworth	*Lab.* 16, *C.* 13, *Ind.* 1
*Tandridge	*C.* 29, *LD* 10, *Lab.* 3
Taunton Deane	*LD* 23, *C.* 21, *Lab.* 5
Teesdale	*Ind.* 12, *Lab.* 9, *Others* 8, *vacant* 1
Teignbridge	*Ind.* 19, *LD* 17, *Others* 2, *Lab.* 1
Tendring	*Lab.* 23, *C.* 17, *Ind.* 11, *LD* 9
Test Valley	*C.* 28, *LD* 14, *Ind.* 2
Tewkesbury	*C.* 13, *Ind.* 11, *Lab.* 8, *LD* 4
Thanet	*Lab.* 33, *C.* 17, *Ind.* 3, *vacant* 1
*Three Rivers	*LD* 26, *C.* 15, *Lab.* 7
*Tonbridge and Malling	*C.* 27, *LD* 21, *Lab.* 7
Torridge	*Ind.* 13, *LD* 12, *Others* 4, *Lab.* 2
*Tunbridge Wells	*C.* 28, *LD* 12, *Lab.* 7, *Ind.* 1
Tynedale	*C.* 23, *Lab.* 13, *LD* 10, *Ind.* 6
Uttlesford	*LD* 18, *C.* 16, *Ind.* 6, *Lab.* 2
Vale of White Horse	*LD* 33, *C.* 15, *Lab.* 2, *Ind.* 1
Vale Royal	*Lab.* 33, *C.* 16, *LD* 8
Wansbeck	*Lab.* 25, *LD* 20
Warwick	*Lab.* 16, *LD* 13, *C.* 10, *Ind.* 6
*Watford	*Lab.* 18, *LD* 10, *C.* 8
*Waveney	*Lab.* 28, *C.* 13, *LD* 4, *Ind.* 2, *Others* 1
Waverley	*C.* 31, *LD* 24, *Lab.* 2
Wealden	*C.* 34, *LD* 22, *Ind.* 2
Wear Valley	*Lab.* 30, *LD* 5

Wellingborough	Lab. 20, C. 15, Ind. C. 1
*Welwyn Hatfield	Lab. 25, C. 23
West Devon	Ind. 12, C. 10, LD 8
West Dorset	C. 22, LD 15, Others 14, Lab. 4
*West Lancashire	Lab. 31, C. 22, Ind. 2
*West Lindsey	LD 16, Ind. 9, Lab. 3
*West Oxfordshire	C. 26, LD 13, Ind. 8, Lab. 2
West Somerset	C. 18, Ind. 8, Lab. 4, LD 1
West Wiltshire	LD 26, C. 10, Others 3, Lab. 2
*Weymouth and Portland	Lab. 13, LD 12, Others 5
*Winchester	LD 36, C. 10, Ind. 5, Lab. 4
*Woking	LD 16, C. 14, Lab. 5, Ind. 1
*Worcester	Lab. 15, C. 11, Ind. 4, LD 1
*Worthing	C. 20, LD 16
Wychavon	C. 31, LD 11, Lab. 5, Ind. 2
Wycombe	C. 42, Lab. 9, LD 7, Ind. 2
Wyre	C. 35, Lab. 19, LD 2
*Wyre Forest	Others 22, Lab. 11, C. 5, LD 4

Conwy	Lab. 19, LD 15, Ind. 13, PC 7, C. 5
Denbighshire	Ind. 17, Lab. 14, PC 8, Others 4, C. 2, NP 1
Flintshire	Lab. 42, Others 19, LD 7, PC 2
Gwynedd	PC 43, Ind. 20, Lab. 12, LD 6, Others 2
Merthyr Tydfil	Lab. 16, Ind. 12, PC 4, vacant 1
Monmouthshire	C. 19, Lab. 18, Ind. 3, Others 1
Neath Port Talbot	Lab. 40, PC 10, RA 5, Others 3, LD 2, Ind. Lab. 1
Newport	Lab. 39, C. 5, Ind. 2, LD 1
Pembrokeshire	Ind. 38, Lab. 13, C. 4, LD 3, PC 2
Powys	Others 73
Rhondda, Cynon, Taff	PC 42, Lab. 26, Ind. 5, LD 2
Swansea	Lab. 47, LD 11, Ind. 7, C. 4, PC 2, Others 1
Torfaen	Lab. 39, Ind. 3, LD 1
Vale of Glamorgan	C. 22, Lab. 18, PC 6, LD 1
Wrexham	Lab. 26, Ind. 8, LD 7, Ind. Lab. 5, C. 4, Others 1

GREATER LONDON COUNCILS

Barking and Dagenham	Lab. 46, RA 3, LD 2
Barnet	C. 28, Lab. 26, LD 6
Bexley	C. 32, Lab. 24, LD 6
Brent	Lab. 43, C. 19, LD 6
Bromley	C. 29, LD 24, Lab. 7
Camden	Lab. 42, C. 11, LD 6
City of Westminster	C. 47, Lab. 13
Croydon	Lab. 38, C. 31, LD 1
Ealing	Lab. 55, C. 13, LD 3
Enfield	Lab. 42, C. 23, Ind. 1
Greenwich	Lab. 52, C. 8, LD 2
Hackney	Lab. 29, LD 17, C. 11, Green 2, Ind. 1
Hammersmith and Fulham	Lab. 35, C. 14, Ind. 1
Haringey	Lab. 54, LD 3, C. 2
Harrow	Lab. 32, C. 20, Lib. 9, Ind. 2
Havering	Lab. 31, RA 16, C. 13, LD 3
Hillingdon	C. 33, Lab. 32, LD 4
Hounslow	Lab. 44, C. 11, LD 4, Others 1
Islington	LD 27, Lab. 25
Kensington and Chelsea	C. 39, Lab. 15
Kingston upon Thames	C. 20, LD 19, Lab. 10, Ind. C. 1
Lambeth	Lab. 41, LD 18, C. 5
Lewisham	Lab. 59, LD 4, C. 2, Ind. Lab 1
Merton	Lab. 38, C. 10, LD 3
Newham	Lab. 59, Others 1
Redbridge	Lab. 29, C. 24, LD 9
Richmond upon Thames	LD 34, C. 14, Lab. 4
Southwark	Lab. 32, LD 27, C. 4, Ind. 1
Sutton	LD 46, Lab. 5
Tower Hamlets	Lab. 41, C. 8, Ind. 1
Waltham Forest	Lab. 30, C. 14, LD 12, Ind. 1
Wandsworth	C. 50, Lab. 11

WALES

Anglesey	Ind. 27, PC 8, Lab. 4, C. 1
Blaenau Gwent	Lab. 34, Others 4, Ind. 2, LD 1
Bridgend	Lab. 40, LD 6, Ind. 4, PC 2, Ind. Lab. 1
Caerphilly	PC 38, Lab. 28, Ind. 4, LD 3
Cardiff	Lab. 50, LD 18, C. 5, PC 1
Carmarthenshire	Lab. 28, Ind. 25, PC 14, Ind. Lab 3, RA 2, vacant 1
Ceredigion	Ind. 21, PC 13, LD 7, Others 2, Lab. 1

SCOTLAND

Aberdeen City	Lab. 22, LD 12, C. 6, SNP 3
Aberdeenshire	LD 28, SNP 23, Ind. 10, Com. 7
Angus	SNP 21, Ind. 3, LD 2, Lab.1
Argyll and Bute	NP 16, LD 6, SNP 5, Ind. 4, Lab. 1
City of Edinburgh	Lab. 31, LD 13, SNP 1
Clackmannanshire	SNP 10, Lab. 7, C. 1
Dumfries and Galloway	Lab. 13, C. 8, LD 6, SNP 5, Others 1
Dundee City	Lab. 14, SNP 10, C. 4, Ind. 1
East Ayrshire	Lab. 17, SNP 13, vacant 1
East Dunbartonshire	Lab. 11, LD 10, C. 3
East Lothian	Lab. 16, C. 5, SNP 2
East Renfrewshire	Lab. 9, C. 8, LD 2, RA 1
Eilean Siar/Western Isles	Ind. 23, Lab. 5, SNP 3
Falkirk	Lab. 15, SNP 9, Others 4, Ind. 2, vacant 1
Fife	Lab. 43, LD 21, SNP 9, Others 1
Glasgow City	Lab. 74, SNP 2, Others 1
Highland	Ind. 49, Lab. 11, LD 10, SNP 9, vacant 1
Inverclyde	Lab. 11, LD 8, C. 1
Midlothian	Lab. 17, LD 1
Moray	Ind. 13, Lab. 6, Others 2, C. 1
North Ayrshire	Lab. 25, SNP 2, Ind. 1
North Lanarkshire	Lab. 56, SNP 12, Ind. 2
Orkney Islands	Ind. 21
Perth and Kinross	SNP 16, C. 11, LD 6, Ind. 2
Renfrewshire	Lab. 21, SNP 15, LD 3, C. 1
Scottish Borders	LD 14, SNP 4, Lab. 1
Shetland Islands	Ind. 13, LD 8, Others 1
South Ayrshire	Lab. 17, C. 13
South Lanarkshire	Lab. 54, SNP 10, C. 2, LD 1
Stirling	Lab. 11, C. 10, SNP 1
West Dunbartonshire	Lab. 12, SNP 7, Others 3
West Lothian	Lab. 20, SNP 11, C. 1

England

The Kingdom of England lies between 55°46′ and 49°57′ 30″ N. latitude (from a few miles north of the mouth of the Tweed to the Lizard), and between 1°46′ E. and 5°43′ W. (from Lowestoft to Land's End). England is bounded on the north by the Cheviot Hills; on the south by the English Channel; on the east by the Straits of Dover (Pas de Calais) and the North Sea; and on the west by the Atlantic Ocean, Wales and the Irish Sea. It has a total area of 130,410 sq. km (50,351 sq. miles): land 129,652 sq. km (50,058 sq. miles); inland water 758 sq. km (293 sq. miles).

POPULATION

The population at the 1991 census was 47,055,204. The average density of the population in 1991 was 3.6 persons per hectare.

FLAG

The flag of England is the cross of St George, a red cross on a white field (cross gules in a field argent). The cross of St George, the patron saint of England, has been used since the 13th century.

RELIEF

There is a marked division between the upland and lowland areas of England. In the extreme north the Cheviot Hills (highest point, The Cheviot, 2,674 ft) form a natural boundary with Scotland. Running south from the Cheviots, though divided from them by the Tyne Gap, is the Pennine range (highest point, Cross Fell, 2,930 ft), the main orological feature of the country. The Pennines culminate in the Peak District of Derbyshire (Kinder Scout, 2,088 ft). West of the Pennines are the Cumbrian mountains, which include Scafell Pike (3,210 ft), the highest peak in England, and to the east are the Yorkshire Moors, their highest point being Urra Moor (1,490 ft).

In the west, the foothills of the Welsh mountains extend into the bordering English counties of Shropshire (the Wrekin, 1,334 ft; Long Mynd, 1,694 ft) and Hereford and Worcester (the Malvern Hills – Worcestershire Beacon, 1,394 ft). Extensive areas of highland and moorland are also to be found in the south-western peninsula formed by Somerset, Devon and Cornwall: principally Exmoor (Dunkery Beacon, 1,704 ft), Dartmoor (High Willhays, 2,038 ft) and Bodmin Moor (Brown Willy, 1,377 ft). Ranges of low, undulating hills run across the south of the country, including the Cotswolds in the Midlands and south-west, the Chilterns to the north of London, and the North (Kent) and South (Sussex) Downs of the south-east coastal areas.

The lowlands of England lie in the Vale of York, East Anglia and the area around the Wash. The lowest-lying are the Cambridgeshire Fens in the valleys of the Great Ouse and the River Nene, which are below sea-level in places. Since the 17th century extensive drainage has brought much of the Fens under cultivation. The North Sea coast between the Thames and the Humber, low-lying and formed of sand and shingle for the most part, is subject to erosion and defences against further incursion have been built along many stretches.

HYDROGRAPHY

The Severn is the longest river in Great Britain, rising in the north-eastern slopes of Plynlimon (Wales) and entering England in Shropshire with a total length of 354 km (220 miles) from its source to its outflow into the Bristol Channel, where it receives on the east the Bristol Avon, and on the west the Wye, its other tributaries being the Vyrnwy, Tern, Stour, Teme and Upper (or Warwickshire) Avon. The Severn is tidal below Gloucester, and a high bore or tidal wave sometimes reverses the flow as high as Tewkesbury (13½ miles above Gloucester). The scenery of the greater part of the river is very picturesque and beautiful, and the Severn is a noted salmon river, some of its tributaries being famous for trout. Navigation is assisted by the Gloucester and Berkeley Ship Canal (16¾ miles), which admits vessels of 350 tons to Gloucester. The Severn Tunnel was begun in 1873 and completed in 1886 at a cost of £2 million and after many difficulties from flooding. It is 4 miles 628 yards in length (of which 2¼ miles are under the river). The Severn road bridge between Haysgate, Gwent, and Almondsbury, Glos, with a centre span of 3,240 ft, was opened in 1966.

The longest river wholly in England is the Thames, with a total length of 346 km (215 miles) from its source in the Cotswold hills to the Nore, and is navigable by ocean-going ships to London Bridge. The Thames is tidal to Teddington (69 miles from its mouth) and forms county boundaries almost throughout its course; on its banks are situated London, Windsor Castle, the oldest royal residence still in regular use, Eton College and Oxford, the oldest university in the kingdom.

Of the remaining English rivers, those flowing into the North Sea are the Tyne, Wear, Tees, Ouse and Trent from the Pennine Range, the Great Ouse (160 miles), which rises in Northamptonshire, and the Orwell and Stour from the hills of East Anglia. Flowing into the English Channel are the Sussex Ouse from the Weald, the Itchen from the Hampshire Hills, and the Axe, Teign, Dart, Tamar and Exe from the Devonian hills. Flowing into the Irish Sea are the Mersey, Ribble and Eden from the western slopes of the Pennines and the Derwent from the Cumbrian mountains.

The English Lakes, noteworthy for their picturesque scenery and poetic associations, lie in Cumbria, the largest being Windermere (10 miles long), Ullswater and Derwent Water.

ISLANDS

The Isle of Wight is separated from Hampshire by the Solent. The capital, Newport, stands at the head of the estuary of the Medina, Cowes (at the mouth) being the chief port. Other centres are Ryde, Sandown, Shanklin, Ventnor, Freshwater, Yarmouth, Totland Bay, Seaview and Bembridge.

Lundy (the name means Puffin Island), 11 miles northwest of Hartland Point, Devon, is about two miles long and about half a mile wide on average, with a total area of about 1,116 acres, and a population of about 20. It became the property of the National Trust in 1969 and is now principally a bird sanctuary.

The Isles of Scilly consist of about 140 islands and skerries (total area, 10 sq. km/6 sq. miles) situated 28 miles south-west of Land's End. Only five are inhabited: St Mary's, St Agnes, Bryher, Tresco and St Martin's. The population is 1,978. The entire group has been designated a Conservation Area, a Heritage Coast, and an Area of Outstanding Natural Beauty, and has been given National Nature Reserve status by the Nature Conservancy Council because of its unique flora and fauna. Tourism and the winter/spring flower trade for the home market form the basis of the economy of the Isles. The island group is a recognised rural development area.

EARLY HISTORY

Archaeological evidence suggests that England has been inhabited since at least the Palaeolithic period, though the extent of the various Palaeolithic cultures was dependent upon the degree of glaciation. The succeeding Neolithic and Bronze Age cultures have left abundant remains throughout the country, the best-known of these being the henges and stone circles of Stonehenge (ten miles north of Salisbury, Wilts) and Avebury (Wilts), both of which are believed to have been of religious significance. In the latter part of the Bronze Age the Goidels, a people of Celtic race, and in the Iron Age other Celtic races of Brythons and Belgae, invaded the country and brought with them Celtic civilisation and dialects, place names in England bearing witness to the spread of the invasion over the whole kingdom.

THE ROMAN CONQUEST

The Roman conquest of Gaul (57–50 BC) brought Britain into close contact with Roman civilisation, but although Julius Caesar raided the south of Britain in 55 BC and 54 BC, conquest was not undertaken until nearly 100 years later. In AD 43 the Emperor Claudius dispatched Aulus Plautius, with a well-equipped force of 40,000, and himself followed with reinforcements in the same year. Success was delayed by the resistance of Caratacus (Caractacus), the British leader from AD 48–51, who was finally captured and sent to Rome, and by a great revolt in AD 61 led by Boudicca (Boadicea), Queen of the Iceni; but the south of Britain was secured by AD 70, and Wales and the area north to the Tyne by about AD 80.

In AD 122, the Emperor Hadrian visited Britain and built a continuous rampart, since known as Hadrian's Wall, from Wallsend to Bowness (Tyne to Solway). The work was entrusted by the Emperor Hadrian to Aulus Platorius Nepos, legate of Britain from AD 122 to 126, and it was intended to form the northern frontier of the Roman Empire.

The Romans administered Britain as a province under a Governor, with a well-defined system of local government, each Roman municipality ruling itself and its surrounding territory, while London was the centre of the road system and the seat of the financial officials of the Province of Britain. Colchester, Lincoln, York, Gloucester and St Albans stand on the sites of five Roman municipalities, and Wroxeter, Caerleon, Chester, Lincoln and York were at various times the sites of legionary fortresses. Well-preserved Roman towns have been uncovered at or near Silchester (*Calleva Atrebatum*), ten miles south of Reading, Wroxeter (*Viroconium Cornoviorum*), near Shrewsbury, and St Albans (*Verulamium*) in Hertfordshire.

Four main groups of roads radiated from London, and a fifth (the Fosse) ran obliquely from Lincoln through Leicester, Cirencester and Bath to Exeter. Of the four groups radiating from London, one ran south-east to Canterbury and the coast of Kent, a second to Silchester and thence to parts of western Britain and south Wales, a third (later known as Watling Street) ran through St Albans to Chester, with various branches, and the fourth reached Colchester, Lincoln, York and the eastern counties.

In the fourth century Britain was subject to raids along the east coast by Saxon pirates, which led to the establishment of a system of coastal defences from the Wash to Southampton Water, with forts at Brancaster, Burgh Castle (Yarmouth), Walton (Felixstowe), Bradwell, Reculver, Richborough, Dover, Lympne, Pevensey and Porchester (Portsmouth). The Irish (Scoti) and Picts in the north were also becoming more aggressive; from about AD 350 incursions became more frequent and more formidable. As the Roman Empire came under attack increasingly towards the end of the fourth century, many troops were removed from Britain for service in other parts of the empire. The island was eventually cut off from Rome by the Teutonic conquest of Gaul, and with the withdrawal of the last Roman garrison early in the fifth century, the Romano-British were left to themselves.

SAXON SETTLEMENT

According to legend, the British King Vortigern called in the Saxons to defend him against the Picts, the Saxon chieftains being Hengist and Horsa, who landed at Ebbsfleet, Kent, and established themselves in the Isle of Thanet; but the events during the one and a half centuries between the final break with Rome and the re-establishment of Christianity are unclear. However, it would appear that in the course of this period the raids turned into large-scale settlement by invaders traditionally known as Angles (England north of the Wash and East Anglia), Saxons (Essex and southern England) and Jutes (Kent and the Weald), which pushed the Romano-British into the mountainous areas of the north and west, Celtic culture outside Wales and Cornwall surviving only in topographical names. Various kingdoms were established at this time which attempted to claim overlordship of the whole country, hegemony finally being achieved by Wessex (capital, Winchester) in the ninth century. This century also saw the beginning of raids by the Vikings (Danes), which were resisted by Alfred the Great (871–99), who fixed a limit to the advance of Danish settlement by the Treaty of Wedmore (878), giving them the area north and east of Watling Street, on condition that they adopt Christianity.

In the tenth century the kings of Wessex recovered the whole of England from the Danes, but subsequent rulers were unable to resist a second wave of invaders. England paid tribute (*Danegeld*) for many years, and was invaded in 1013 by the Danes and ruled by Danish kings from 1016 until 1042, when Edward the Confessor was recalled from exile in Normandy. On Edward's death in 1066 Harold Godwinson (brother-in-law of Edward and son of Earl Godwin of Wessex) was chosen King of England. After defeating (at Stamford Bridge, Yorkshire, 25 September) an invading army under Harald Hadraada, King of Norway (aided by the outlawed Earl Tostig of Northumbria, Harold's brother), Harold was himself defeated at the Battle of Hastings on 14 October 1066, and the Norman conquest secured the throne of England for Duke William of Normandy, a cousin of Edward the Confessor.

CHRISTIANITY

Christianity reached the Roman province of Britain from Gaul in the third century (or possibly earlier); Alban, traditionally Britain's first martyr, was put to death as a Christian during the persecution of Diocletian (22 June 303), at his native town Verulamium; and the Bishops of Londinium, Eboracum (York), and Lindum (Lincoln) attended the Council of Arles in 314. However, the Anglo-Saxon invasions submerged the Christian religion in England until the sixth century when conversion was undertaken in the north from 563 by Celtic missionaries from Ireland led by St Columba, and in the south by a mission sent from Rome in 597 which was led by St Augustine, who became the first archbishop of Canterbury. England appears to have been converted again by the end of the seventh century and followed, after the Council of Whitby in 663, the practices of the Roman Church, which brought the kingdom into the mainstream of European thought and culture.

PRINCIPAL CITIES

BIRMINGHAM

Birmingham is Britain's second city. It is a focal point in national communications networks with a rapidly expanding international airport. The generally accepted derivation of 'Birmingham' is the *ham* (dwelling-place) of the *ing* (family) of *Beorma*, presumed to have been Saxon. During the Industrial Revolution the town grew into a major manufacturing centre and in 1889 was granted city status.

Despite the decline in manufacturing, Birmingham is still a major hardware trade and motor component industry centre. As well as the National Exhibition Centre and the Aston Science Park, recent developments include the International Convention Centre, the National Indoor Arena and Brindleyplace.

The principal buildings are the Town Hall (1834–50); the Council House (1879); Victoria Law Courts (1891); Birmingham University (1906–9); the 13th century Church of St Martin-in-the-Bull-Ring (rebuilt 1873); Our Lady, Help of Christians Church; the Cathedral (formerly St Philip's Church) (1711) and the Roman Catholic Cathedral of St Chad (1839–41).

BRADFORD

Bradford lies on the southern edge of the Yorkshire Dales National Park, including within its boundaries the village of Haworth, home of the Brontë sisters, and Ilkley Moor.

Originally a Saxon township, Bradford received a market charter in 1251 but developed only slowly until the industrialisation of the textile industry brought rapid growth during the 19th century; it was granted its city charter in 1897. The prosperity of that period is reflected in much of the city's architecture, particularly the public buildings: City Hall (1873), Wool Exchange (1867), St George's Hall (concert hall, 1853), Cartwright Hall (art gallery, 1904) and the Technical College (1882). Other chief buildings are the Cathedral (15th century) and Bolling Hall (14th century).

Textiles still play an important part in the city's economy but industry is now more broadly based, including engineering, micro-electronics, printing and chemicals. The city has a strong financial services sector, and a growing tourism industry.

BRISTOL

Bristol was a Royal Borough before the Norman Conquest. The earliest form of the name is *Bricgstow*. In 1373 Edward III granted Bristol county status.

The chief buildings include the 12th century Cathedral (with later additions), with Norman chapter house and gateway, the 14th century Church of St Mary Redcliffe, Wesley's Chapel, Broadmead, the Merchant Venturers' Almshouses, the Council House (1956), Guildhall, Exchange (erected from the designs of John Wood in 1743), Cabot Tower, the University and Clifton College. The Roman Catholic Cathedral at Clifton was opened in 1973.

The Clifton Suspension Bridge, with a span of 702 feet over the Avon, was projected by Brunel in 1836 but was not completed until 1864. Brunel's *SS Great Britain*, the first ocean-going propeller-driven ship, is now being restored in the City Docks from where she was launched in 1843. The docks themselves have been extensively restored and redeveloped and are becoming a focus for the arts and recreation.

CAMBRIDGE

Cambridge, a settlement far older than its ancient university, lies on the River Cam or Granta. The city is a county town and regional headquarters. Its industries include electronics, high technology research and development, and biotechnology. Among its open spaces are Jesus Green, Sheep's Green, Coe Fen, Parker's Piece, Christ's Pieces, the University Botanic Garden, and the Backs, or lawns and gardens through which the Cam winds behind the principal line of college buildings. East of the Cam, King's Parade, upon which stand Great St Mary's Church, Gibbs' Senate House and King's College Chapel with Wilkins' screen, joins Trumpington Street to form one of the most beautiful throughfares in Europe.

University and college buildings provide the outstanding features of Cambridge architecture but several churches (especially St Benet's, the oldest building in the city, and St Sepulchre's, the Round Church) are also notable. The Guildhall (1939) stands on a site of which at least part has held municipal buildings since 1224.

CANTERBURY

Canterbury, the Metropolitan City of the Anglican Communion, dates back to prehistoric times. It was the Roman *Durovernum Cantiacorum* and the Saxon *Cant-wara-byrig* (stronghold of the men of Kent). Here in 597 St Augustine began the conversion of the English to Christianity, when Ethelbert, King of Kent, was baptised.

Of the Benedictine St Augustine's Abbey, burial place of the Jutish Kings of Kent (whose capital Canterbury was), only ruins remain. St Martin's Church, on the eastern outskirts of the city, is stated by Bede to have been the place of worship of Queen Bertha, the Christian wife of King Ethelbert, before the advent of St Augustine.

In 1170 the rivalry of Church and State culminated in the murder in Canterbury Cathedral, by Henry II's knights, of Archbishop Thomas Becket. His shrine became a great centre of pilgrimage, as described in Chaucer's *Canterbury Tales*. After the Reformation pilgrimages ceased, but the prosperity of the city was strengthened by an influx of Huguenot refugees, who introduced weaving. The poet and playwright Christopher Marlowe was born and reared in Canterbury, and there are also literary associations with Defoe, Dickens, Joseph Conrad and Somerset Maugham.

The Cathedral, with architecture ranging from the 11th to the 15th centuries, is world famous. Modern pilgrims are attracted particularly to the Martyrdom, the Black Prince's Tomb, the Warriors' Chapel and the many examples of medieval stained glass.

The medieval city walls are built on Roman foundations and the 14th century West Gate is one of the finest buildings of its kind in the country.

The 1,000-seat Marlowe Theatre is a centre for the Canterbury Arts Festival each autumn.

CARLISLE

Carlisle is situated at the confluence of the River Eden and River Caldew, 309 miles north-west of London and about ten miles from the Scottish border. It was granted a charter in 1158.

The city stands at the western end of Hadrian's Wall and dates from the original Roman settlement of *Luguvalium*. Granted to Scotland in the tenth century, Carlisle is not included in the Domesday Book. William Rufus reclaimed the area in 1092 and the castle and city walls were built to guard Carlisle and the western border; the citadel is a Tudor addition to protect the south of the city. Border disputes were common until the problem of the Debateable Lands was settled in 1552. During the Civil War the city remained Royalist; in 1745 Carlisle was besieged for the last time by the Young Pretender.

The Cathedral, originally a 12th century Augustinian priory, was enlarged in the 13th and 14th centuries after the diocese was created in 1133. To the south is a restored Tithe Barn and nearby the 18th century church of St Cuthbert, the third to stand on a site dating from the seventh century.

Carlisle is the major shopping, commercial and agricultural centre for the area, and industries include the manufacture of metal goods, biscuits and textiles. However, the largest employer is the services sector, notably in central and local government, retailing and transport. The city has an important communications position at the centre of a network of major roads, as a stage on the main west coast rail services, and with its own airport at Crosby-on-Eden.

CHESTER

Chester is situated on the River Dee, and was granted borough and city status in 1974. Its recorded history dates from the first century when the Romans founded the fortress of *Deva*. The city's name is derived from the Latin *castra* (a camp or encampment). During the Middle Ages, Chester was the principal port of north-west England but declined with the silting of the Dee estuary and competition from Liverpool. The city was also an important military centre, notably during Edward I's Welsh campaigns and the Elizabethan Irish campaigns. During the Civil War, Chester supported the King and was besieged from 1643 to 1646. Chester's first charter was granted *c.* 1175 and the city was incorporated in 1506. The office of Sheriff is the earliest created in the country (*c.* 1120s), and in 1992 the Mayor was granted the title of Lord Mayor. He/she also enjoys the title 'Admiral of the Dee'.

The city's architectural features include the city walls (an almost complete two-mile circuit), the unique 13th century Rows (covered galleries above the street-level shops), the Victorian Gothic Town Hall (1869), the Castle (rebuilt 1788 and 1822) and numerous half-timbered buildings. The Cathedral was a Benedictine abbey until the Dissolution. Remaining monastic buildings include the chapter house, refectory and cloisters and there is a modern free-standing bell tower. The Norman church of St John the Baptist was a cathedral church in the early Middle Ages.

Chester is a thriving retail, business and tourist centre.

COVENTRY

Coventry is an important industrial centre, producing vehicles, machine tools, agricultural machinery, man-made fibres, aerospace components and telecommunications equipment. New investment has come from financial services, power transmission, professional services, leisure and education.

The city owes its beginning to Leofric, Earl of Mercia, and his wife Godiva who, in 1043, founded a Benedictine monastery. The guildhall of St Mary dates from the 14th century, three of the city's churches date from the 14th and 15th centuries, and 16th century almshouses may still be seen. Coventry's first cathedral was destroyed at the Reformation, its second in the 1940 blitz (the walls and spire remain) and the new cathedral designed by Sir Basil Spence, consecrated in 1962, now draws numerous visitors.

Coventry is the home of the University of Warwick and its Science Park, Coventry University, the Westwood Business Park, the Cable and Wireless College, the Museum of British Road Transport and the Coventry Arena.

DERBY

Derby stands on the banks of the River Derwent, and its name dates back to 880 when the Danes settled in the locality and changed the original Saxon name of *Northworthy* to *Deoraby*.

Derby has a wide range of industries including aero engines, cars, pipework, specialised mechanical engineering equipment, textiles, chemicals, plastics and the Royal Crown Derby porcelain. The city is an established railway centre with rail research, engineering, safety testing, infrastructure and train-operating companies.

Buildings of interest include St Peter's Church and the Old Abbey Building (14th century), the Cathedral (1525), St Mary's Roman Catholic Church (1839) and the Industrial Museum, formerly the Old Silk Mill (1721). The traditional city centre is complemented by the Eagle Centre and 'out-of-centre' retail developments. In addition to the Derby Playhouse, the Assembly Rooms are a multi-purpose venue.

The first charter granting a Mayor and Aldermen was that of Charles I in 1637. Previous charters date back to 1154. It was granted city status in 1977.

DURHAM

The city of Durham is a district in the county of Durham and a major tourist attraction because of its prominent Norman Cathedral and Castle set high on a wooded peninsula overlooking the River Wear. The Cathedral was founded as a shrine for the body of St Cuthbert in 995. The present building dates from 1093 and among its many treasures is the tomb of the Venerable Bede (673–735). Durham's Prince Bishops had unique powers up to 1836, being lay rulers as well as religious leaders. As a palatinate Durham could have its own army, nobility, coinage and courts. The Castle was the main seat of the Prince Bishops for nearly 800 years; it is now used as a college by the University. The University, founded on the initiative of Bishop William Van Mildert, is England's third oldest.

Among other buildings of interest is the Guildhall in the Market Place which dates originally from the 14th century. Work has been carried out to conserve this area as part of the city's contribution to the Council of Europe's Urban Renaissance Campaign. Annual events include Durham's Regatta in June (claimed to be the oldest rowing event in Britain) and the Annual Gala (formerly Durham Miners' Gala) in July.

The economy has undergone a significant change with the replacement of mining as the dominant industry by 'white collar' employment. Although still a predominantly rural area, the industrial and commercial sector is growing and a wide range of manufacturing and service industries are based on industrial estates in and around the city. A research and development centre, linked to the University, also plays an important role in the local economy.

EXETER

Exeter lies on the River Exe ten miles from the sea. It was granted a charter by Henry II. The Romans founded

Isca Dumnoniorum in the first century AD, and in the third century a stone wall (much of which remains) was built, providing protection against Saxon, and then Danish invasions. After the Conquest, the city led resistance to William in the west until reduced by siege. The Normans built the ringwork castle of Rougemont, the gatehouse and one tower of which remain, although the rest was pulled down in 1784. The first bridge across the Exe was built in the early 13th century. The city's main port was situated downstream at Topsham until the construction in the 1560s of the first true canal in England, the redevelopment of which in 1700 brought seaborne trade direct to the city. Exeter was the Royalist headquarters in the west during the Civil War.

The diocese of Exeter was established by Edward the Confessor in 1050, although a minster existed near the Cathedral site from the late seventh century. A new cathedral was built in the 12th century but the present building, which incorporates the Norman Towers, was begun *c*. 1275 and completed about a century later. The Guildhall dates from the 12th century and there are many other medieval buildings in the city, as well as architecture in the Georgian and Regency styles, and the Custom House (1680). Damage suffered by bombing in 1942 led to the redevelopment of the city centre.

Exeter's prosperity from medieval times was based on trade in wool and woollen cloth (commemorated by Tuckers Hall), which flourished until the late 18th century when export trade was hit by the French wars. Subsequently Exeter has developed as an administrative and commercial centre, notably in the distributive trades, light manufacturing industries and tourism.

KINGSTON UPON HULL

Hull (officially Kingston upon Hull) lies at the junction of the River Hull with the Humber, 22 miles from the North Sea. It is one of the major seaports of the United Kingdom, comprising 2,000 acres in four main dock installations. The port provides a wide range of cargo services, including ro-ro and container traffic, and handles a million passengers annually on daily sailings to Rotterdam and Zeebrugge. There is a variety of manufacturing and service industries, as well as increasing tourism and conference business.

The city, restored after heavy air raid damage during the Second World War, has good office and administrative buildings, its municipal centre being the Guildhall, its educational centres the University of Hull and the University of Lincolnshire and Humberside and its religious centre the Parish Church of the Holy Trinity. The old town area has been renovated and includes a marina and shopping complex. Just west of the city is the Humber Bridge, the world's longest single-span suspension bridge.

Kingston upon Hull was so named by Edward I. City status was accorded in 1897 and the office of Mayor raised to the dignity of Lord Mayor in 1914.

LEEDS

Leeds, situated in the lower Aire Valley, is a junction for road, rail, canal and air services and an important manufacturing and commercial centre. Seventy-three per cent of employment is in services, notably the distributive trades, public administration, medical services and business services. The main manufacturing industries are mechanical engineering, printing and publishing, metal goods and furniture.

The principal buildings are the Civic Hall (1933), the Town Hall (1858), the Municipal Buildings and Art Gallery (1884) with the Henry Moore Gallery (1982), the Corn Exchange (1863) and the University. The Parish Church (St Peter's) was rebuilt in 1841; the 17th century St John's Church has a fine interior with a famous English Renaissance screen; the last remaining 18th century church in the city is Holy Trinity in Boar Lane (1727). Kirkstall Abbey (about three miles from the centre of the city), founded by Henry de Lacy in 1152, is one of the most complete examples of Cistercian houses now remaining. Temple Newsam, birthplace of Lord Darnley, was acquired by the Council in 1922. The present house was largely rebuilt by Sir Arthur Ingram in about 1620. Adel Church, about five miles from the centre of the city, is a fine Norman structure. The new Royal Armouries Museum houses the collection of antique arms and armour formerly held at the Tower of London.

Leeds was first incorporated by Charles I in 1626. The earliest forms of the name are *Loidis* or *Ledes*, the origins of which are obscure.

LEICESTER

Leicester is situated geographically in the centre of England. It dates back to pre-Roman times and was one of the Five Danish Boroughs of the Danelaw. In 1589 Queen Elizabeth I granted a charter to the city and the ancient title was confirmed by letters patent in 1919.

The principal industries are hosiery, knitwear, footwear manufacturing and engineering. The growth of Leicester as a hosiery centre increased rapidly from the introduction there of the first stocking frame in 1670 and today it has some of the largest hosiery factories in the world.

The principal buildings are the Town Hall, the New Walk Centre, the University of Leicester, De Montfort University, De Montfort Hall, one of the finest concert halls in the provinces seating over 2,750 people, and the Granby Halls, an indoor sports facility. The ancient churches of St Martin (now Leicester Cathedral), St Nicholas, St Margaret, All Saints, St Mary de Castro, and buildings such as the Guildhall, the 14th century Newarke Gate, the Castle and the Jewry Wall Roman site still exist. The Haymarket Theatre was opened in 1973 and The Shires shopping centre in 1992.

LINCOLN

Situated 40 miles inland on the River Witham, Lincoln derives its name from a contraction of *Lindum Colonia*, the settlement founded in AD 48 by the Romans to command the crossing of Ermine Street and Fosse Way. Sections of the third-century Roman city wall can be seen, including an extant gateway (Newport Arch), and excavations have discovered traces of a sewerage system unique in Britain. The Romans also drained the surrounding fenland and created a canal system, laying the foundations of Lincoln's agricultural prosperity and also of the city's importance in the medieval wool trade as a port and Staple town.

As one of the Five Boroughs of the Danelaw, Lincoln was an important trading centre in the ninth and tenth centuries and medieval prosperity from the wool trade lasted until the 14th century, enabling local merchants to build parish churches (of which three survive), and attracting in the 12th century a Jewish community (Jew's House and Court, Aaron's House). However, the removal of the Staple to Boston in 1369 heralded a decline from which the city only recovered fully in the 19th century when improved fen drainage made Lincoln agriculturally important and improved canal and rail links led to industrial development, mainly in the manufacture of machinery, components and engineering products.

The castle was built shortly after the Conquest and is unusual in having two mounds; on one motte stands a Keep (Lucy's Tower) added in the 12th century. It currently houses one of the four surviving copies of the Magna Carta. The Cathedral was begun c. 1073 when the first Norman bishop moved the see of Lindsey to Lincoln, but was mostly destroyed by fire and earthquake in the 12th century. Rebuilding was begun by St Hugh and completed over a century later. Other notable architectural features are the 12th century High Bridge, the oldest in Britain still to carry buildings, and the Guildhall situated above the 15th–16th century Stonebow gateway.

LIVERPOOL

Liverpool, on the right bank of the River Mersey, three miles from the Irish Sea, is the United Kingdom's foremost port for the Atlantic trade. Tunnels link Liverpool with Birkenhead and Wallasey.

There are 2,100 acres of dockland on both sides of the river and the Gladstone and Royal Seaforth Docks can accommodate Panamax-sized vessels. Approximately 31 million tonnes of cargo is handled annually. The main cargoes are crude oil, grain, fossil fuels, edible oils, timber, scrap metal, containers and break-bulk cargo. Liverpool Free Port, Britain's largest, was opened in 1984.

Liverpool was created a free borough in 1207 and a city in 1880. From the early 18th century it expanded rapidly with the growth of industrialisation and the Atlantic trade. Surviving buildings from this period include the Bluecoat Chambers (1717, formerly the Bluecoat School), the Town Hall (1754, rebuilt to the original design 1795), and buildings in Rodney Street, Canning Street and the suburbs. Notable from the 19th and 20th centuries are the Anglican Cathedral, built from the designs of Sir Giles Gilbert Scott (the foundation stone was laid in 1904, and the building was completed only in 1980), the Catholic Metropolitan Cathedral (designed by Sir Frederick Gibberd, consecrated 1967) and St George's Hall (1838–54), regarded as one of the finest modern examples of classical architecture. The refurbished Albert Dock (designed by Jesse Hartley) contains the Merseyside Maritime Museum and Tate Gallery, Liverpool.

In 1852 an Act was obtained for establishing a public library, museum and art gallery; as a result Liverpool had one of the first public libraries in the country. The Brown, Picton and Hornby libraries now form one of the country's major libraries. The Victoria Building of Liverpool University, the Royal Liver, Cunard and Mersey Docks and Harbour Company buildings at the Pier Head, the Municipal Buildings and the Philharmonic Hall are other examples of the city's fine buildings.

MANCHESTER

Manchester (the *Mamucium* of the Romans, who occupied it in AD 79) is a commercial and industrial centre with a population engaged in the engineering, chemical, clothing, food processing and textile industries and in education. Banking, insurance and a growing leisure industry are among the prime commercial activities. The city is connected with the sea by the Manchester Ship Canal, opened in 1894, 35½ miles long, and accommodating ships up to 15,000 tons. Manchester Airport handles 15 million passengers yearly.

The principal buildings are the Town Hall, erected in 1877 from the designs of Alfred Waterhouse, with a large extension of 1938; the Royal Exchange (1869, enlarged 1921); the Central Library (1934); Heaton Hall; the 17th century Chetham Library; the Rylands Library (1900), which includes the Althorp collection; the University

precinct; the 15th century Cathedral (formerly the parish church) and G-MEX exhibition centre. Recent developments include the Manchester Arena, the largest indoor arena in Europe, and the Bridgewater Hall. Manchester is the home of the Hallé Orchestra, the Royal Northern College of Music, the Royal Exchange Theatre and seven public art galleries. Metrolink, the light rail system, opened in 1992.

The Commonwealth Games are to be held in Manchester in 2002 and new sports facilities include a stadium, a swimming pool complex and the National Cycling Centre.

The town received its first charter of incorporation in 1838 and was created a city in 1853.

NEWCASTLE UPON TYNE

Newcastle upon Tyne, on the north bank of the River Tyne, is eight miles from the North Sea. A cathedral and university city, it is the administrative, commercial and cultural centre for north-east England and the principal port. It is an important manufacturing centre with a wide variety of industries.

The principal buildings include the Castle Keep (12th century), Black Gate (13th century), Blackfriars (13th century), West Walls (13th century), St Nicholas's Cathedral (15th century, fine lantern tower), St Andrew's Church (12th–14th century), St John's (14th–15th century), All Saints (1786 by Stephenson), St Mary's Roman Catholic Cathedral (1844), Trinity House (17th century), Sandhill (16th century houses), Guildhall (Georgian), Grey Street (1834–9), Central Station (1846–50), Laing Art Gallery (1904), University of Newcastle Physics Building (1962) and Medical Building (1985), Civic Centre (1963), Central Library (1969) and Eldon Square Shopping Development (1976). Open spaces include the Town Moor (927 acres) and Jesmond Dene. Nine bridges span the Tyne at Newcastle.

The city s name is derived from the 'new castle' (1080) erected as a defence against the Scots. In 1400 it was made a county, and in 1882 a city.

NORWICH

Norwich grew from an early Anglo-Saxon settlement near the confluence of the Rivers Yare and Wensum, and now serves as provincial capital for the predominantly agricultural region of East Anglia. The name is thought to relate to the most northerly of a group of Anglo-Saxon villages or *wics*. The city's first known charter was granted in 1158 by Henry II.

Norwich serves its surrounding area as a market town and commercial centre, banking and insurance being prominent among the city's businesses. From the 14th century until the Industrial Revolution, Norwich was the regional centre of the woollen industry, but now the biggest single industry is financial services and principal trades are engineering, printing, shoemaking, double glazing, the production of chemicals and clothing, food processing and technology. Norwich is accessible to seagoing vessels by means of the River Yare, entered at Great Yarmouth, 20 miles to the east.

Among many historic buildings are the Cathedral (completed in the 12th century and surmounted by a 15th century spire 315 feet in height), the keep of the Norman castle (now a museum and art gallery), the 15th century flint-walled Guildhall (now a tourist information centre), some 30 medieval parish churches, St Andrew's and Blackfriars' Halls, the Tudor houses preserved in Elm Hill and the Georgian Assembly House.

The University of East Anglia is on the city's western boundary.

NOTTINGHAM

Nottingham stands on the River Trent and is connected by canal with the Atlantic Ocean and the North Sea. *Snotingaham* or *Notingeham*, literally the homestead of the people of Snot, is the Anglo-Saxon name for the Celtic settlement of *Tigguocobauc*, or the house of caves. In 878, Nottingham became one of the Five Boroughs of the Danelaw. William the Conqueror ordered the construction of Nottingham Castle, while the town itself developed rapidly under Norman rule. Its laws and rights were later formally recognised by Henry II's charter in 1155. The Castle became a favoured residence of King John. In 1642 King Charles I raised his personal standard at Nottingham Castle at the start of the Civil War.

Nottingham is home to Notts County FC (the world's oldest football league side), Nottingham Racecourse and the National Watersports Centre. The principal industries include textiles, pharmaceuticals, food manufacturing, engineering and telecommunications. There are two universities within the city boundaries.

Architecturally, Nottingham has a wealth of notable buildings, particularly those designed in the Victorian era by T. C. Hine and Watson Fothergill. The City Council owns the Castle, of Norman origin but restored in 1878, Wollaton Hall (1580–8), Newstead Abbey (home of Lord Byron), the Guildhall (1888) and Council House (1929). St Mary's, St Peter's and St Nicholas's Churches are of interest, as is the Roman Catholic Cathedral (Pugin, 1842–4).

Nottingham was granted city status in 1897.

OXFORD

Oxford is a university city, an important industrial centre, and a market town. Industry played a minor part in Oxford until the motor industry was established in 1912.

It is for its architecture that Oxford is of most interest to the visitor, its oldest specimens being the reputedly Saxon tower of St Michael's church, the remains of the Norman castle and city walls, and the Norman church at Iffley. It is chiefly famous, however, for its Gothic buildings, such as the Divinity Schools, the Old Library at Merton College, William of Wykeham's New College, Magdalen College and Christ Church and many other college buildings. Later centuries are represented by the Laudian quadrangle at St John's College, the Renaissance Sheldonian Theatre by Wren, Trinity College Chapel, and All Saints Church; Hawksmoor's mock-Gothic at All Souls College, and the 18th century Queen's College. In addition to individual buildings, High Street and Radcliffe Square, just off it, both form architectural compositions of great beauty. Most of the Colleges have gardens, those of Magdalen, New College, St John's and Worcester being the largest.

PLYMOUTH

Plymouth is situated on the borders of Devon and Cornwall at the confluence of the Rivers Tamar and Plym. The city has a long maritime history; it was the home port of Sir Francis Drake and the starting point for his circumnavigation of the world, as well as the last port of call for the *Mayflower* when the Pilgrim Fathers sailed for the New World in 1620. Today Plymouth is host to many international yacht races. The Barbican harbour area has many Elizabethan buildings and on Plymouth Hoe stands Smeaton's lighthouse, the third to be built on the Eddystone Rocks 13 miles offshore.

The city centre was rebuilt following extensive war damage, and comprises a large shopping centre, municipal offices, law courts and public buildings. The main employment is provided at the naval base, though many industrial firms and service industries have become established in the post-war period and the city is a growing tourism centre. In 1982 the Theatre Royal was opened. In conjunction with the Cornwall County Council, the Tamar Bridge was constructed linking the city by road with Cornwall.

PORTSMOUTH

Portsmouth occupies Portsea Island, Hampshire, with boundaries extending to the mainland. It is a centre of industry and commerce, including many high technology and manufacturing industries. It is the British headquarters of several major international companies. The Royal Navy base still has a substantial work-force, although this has decreased in recent years. The commercial port and continental ferry port is owned and run by the City Council, and carries passengers and vehicles to France and northern Spain.

A major port since the 16th century, Portsmouth is also a thriving seaside resort catering for thousands of visitors annually. Among many historic attractions are Lord Nelson's flagship, *HMS Victory*, the Tudor warship *Mary Rose*, Britain's first 'ironclad' warship, *HMS Warrior*, the D-Day Museum, Charles Dickens' birthplace at 393 Old Commercial Road, the Royal Naval and Royal Marine museums, Southsea Castle (built by Henry VIII), Fort Nelson on Portsdown Hill, the Sealife Centre and the Round Tower and Point Battery, which for hundreds of years have guarded the entrance to Portsmouth Harbour.

ST ALBANS

The origins of St Albans, situated on the River Ver, stem from the Roman town of *Verulamium*. Named after the first Christian martyr in Britain, who was executed here, St Albans has developed around the Norman Abbey and Cathedral Church (consecrated 1115), built partly of materials from the old Roman city. The museums house Iron Age and Roman artefacts and the Roman Theatre, unique in Britain, has a stage as opposed to an amphitheatre. Archaeological excavations in the city centre have revealed evidence of pre-Roman, Saxon and medieval occupation.

The town's significance grew to the extent that it was a signatory and venue for the drafting of the Magna Carta. It was also the scene of riots during the Peasants' Revolt, the French King John was imprisoned here after the Battle of Poitiers, and heavy fighting took place during the Wars of the Roses.

Previously controlled by the Abbot, the town achieved a charter in 1553 and city status in 1877. The street market, first established in 1553, is still an important feature of the city, as are many hotels and inns which survive from the days when St Albans was an important coach stop. Tourist attractions include historic churches and houses, and a 15th century clock tower.

The city now contains a wide range of firms, with special emphasis on information and legal services. In addition, it is the home of the Royal National Rose Society, and of Rothamsted Park, the agricultural research centre.

SHEFFIELD

Sheffield, the centre of the special steel and cutlery trades, is situated at the junction of the Sheaf, Porter, Rivelin and Loxley valleys with the River Don. Though its cutlery, silverware and plate have long been famous, Sheffield has other and now more important industries: special and alloy steels, engineering, tool-making, medical equipment and media-related industries (in its new Cultural Industries Quarter). Sheffield has two universities and is an important research centre.

The parish church of St Peter and St Paul, founded in the 12th century, became the Cathedral Church of the Diocese of Sheffield in 1914. The Roman Catholic Cathedral Church of St Marie (founded 1847) was created Cathedral for the new diocese of Hallam in 1980. Parts of the present building date from c.1435. The principal buildings are the Town Hall (1897), the Cutlers' Hall (1832), City Hall (1932), Graves Art Gallery (1934), Mappin Art Gallery, the Crucible Theatre and the restored 19th century Lyceum theatre, which dates from 1897 and was reopened in 1990. Three major sports venues were opened in 1990 to 1991. The National Centre for Popular Music was opened in 1999.

Sheffield was created a city in 1893.

SOUTHAMPTON

Southampton is the leading British deep-sea port on the Channel and is situated on one of the finest natural harbours in the world. The first charter was granted by Henry II and Southampton was created a county of itself in 1447. In 1964 it was granted city status.

There were Roman and Saxon settlements on the site of the city, which has been an important port since Anglo-Saxon times due to its natural deep-water harbour. The oldest church is St Michael's (1070) which has an unusually tall spire built in the 18th century as a landmark for navigators of Southampton Water. Other buildings and monuments within the city walls are the Bargate, the Tudor House Museum, God's House Tower, the Tudor Merchants Hall, the Weigh-house, West Gate, King John's House, Long House, Wool House, the ruins of Holy Rood Church, St Julien's Church and the Mayflower Memorial. The medieval town walls, built for artillery, are among the most complete in the UK. Public open spaces total over 1,000 acres and comprise nine per cent of the city's area. The Common covers an area of 328 acres in the central district of the city and is mostly natural parkland. A recent addition to work in marine technology in Southampton is Europe's leading oceanography research centre, which is part of the University.

STOKE-ON-TRENT

Stoke-on-Trent, standing on the River Trent and familiarly known as The Potteries, is the main centre of employment for the population of North Staffordshire. The city is the largest clayware producer in the world (china, earthenware, sanitary goods, refractories, bricks and tiles) and also has a wide range of other manufacturing industry, including steel, chemicals, engineering and tyres. Extensive reconstruction has been carried out in recent years.

The city was formed by the federation of the separate municipal authorities of Tunstall, Burslem, Hanley, Stoke, Fenton, and Longton in 1910 and received its city status in 1925.

WINCHESTER

Winchester, the ancient capital of England, is situated on the River Itchen. The city is rich in architecture of all types but the Cathedral takes pride of place. The longest Gothic cathedral in the world, it was built in 1079–93 and exhibits examples of Norman, early English and Perpendicular styles. The author Jane Austen is buried in the Cathedral. Winchester College, founded in 1382, is one of the most famous public schools, the original building (1393) remaining largely unaltered. St Cross Hospital, another great medieval foundation, lies one mile south of the city. The almshouses were founded in 1136 by Bishop Henry de Blois, and Cardinal Henry Beaufort added a new almshouse of 'Noble Poverty' in 1446. The chapel and dwellings are of great architectural interest, and visitors may still receive the 'Wayfarer's Dole' of bread and ale.

Excavations have done much to clarify the origins and development of Winchester. Part of the forum and several of the streets of the Roman town have been discovered; excavations in the Cathedral Close have uncovered the entire site of the Anglo-Saxon cathedral (known as the Old Minster) and parts of the New Minster which was built by Alfred's son Edward the Elder and is the burial place of the Alfredian dynasty. The original burial place of St Swithun, before his remains were translated to a site in the present cathedral, was also uncovered.

Excavations in other parts of the city have thrown much light on Norman Winchester, notably on the site of the Royal Castle (adjacent to which the new Law Courts have been built) and in the grounds of Wolvesey Castle, where the great house built by Bishops Giffard and Henry de Blois in the 12th century has been uncovered. The Great Hall, built by Henry III between 1222 and 1236 survives and houses the Arthurian Round Table.

YORK

The city of York is an archiepiscopal seat. Its recorded history dates from AD 71, when the Roman Ninth Legion established a base under Petilius Cerealis which later became the fortress of *Eburacum*. In Anglo-Saxon times the city was the royal and ecclesiastical centre of Northumbria, and after capture by a Viking army in AD 866 it became the capital of the Viking kingdom of Jorvik. By the 14th century the city had become a great mercantile centre, mainly because of its control of the wool trade, and was used as the chief base against the Scots. Under the Tudors its fortunes declined, though Henry VIII made it the headquarters of the Council of the North. Excavations on many sites, including Coppergate, have greatly expanded knowledge of Roman, Viking and medieval urban life.

With its development as a railway centre in the 19th century the commercial life of York expanded. The principal industries are the manufacture of chocolate, scientific instruments and sugar. It is the location of several government departments.

The city is rich in examples of architecture of all periods. The earliest church was built in AD 627 and, in the 12th to 15th centuries, the present Minster was built in a succession of styles. Other examples within the city are the medieval city walls and gateways, churches and guildhalls. Domestic architecture includes the Georgian mansions of The Mount, Micklegate and Bootham.

English Counties and Shires

LORD-LIEUTENANTS AND HIGH SHERIFFS

County/Shire	Lord-Lieutenant	High Sheriff, 2000–1
Bedfordshire	S. C. Whitbread	T. F. Wells
Berkshire	P. L. Wroughton	J. H. L. Puxley
Bristol	J. Tidmarsh, MBE	Dr C. St John Hartnell
Buckinghamshire	Sir Nigel Mobbs	M. H. T. Jourdan
Cambridgeshire	J. G. P. Crowden	A. F. Pemberton
Cheshire	W. A. Bromley-Davenport	S. Chantler
Cornwall	Lady Holborow	Lady Frances Banham
Cumbria	J. A. Cropper	The Lady Hothfield
Derbyshire	J. K. Bather	Mrs M. Boissier
Devon	E. Dancer, CBE	Maj. R. Rayner
Dorset	Capt. M. Fulford-Dobson, RN	M. J. A. Bond
Durham	Sir Paul Nicholson	Mrs E. Smyth
East Riding of Yorkshire	R. Marriott, TD	C. M. Oughtred
East Sussex	Mrs. P. Stewart-Roberts, OBE	W. Fane de Salis
Essex	The Lord Braybrooke	J. G. S. Coode-Adams
Gloucestershire	H. W. G. Elwes	Maj. J. V. Eyre
Greater London	The Lord Imbert, QPM	M. P. S. Barton
Greater Manchester	Col. J. B. Timmins, OBE, TD	Maj. J. N. Abbott, TD, DL
Hampshire	Mrs F. M. Fagan	Maj. J. Groves
Herefordshire	Sir Thomas Dunne, KCVO	Mrs T. Hone
Hertfordshire	S. A. Bowes Lyon	E. Faure-Walker
Isle of Wight	C. D. J. Bland	Dr C. N. A. Mobbs
Kent	The Lord Kingsdown, KG, PC	R. F. Loder-Symonds
Lancashire	The Lord Shuttleworth	R. N. Swarbrick, CBE, DL
Leicestershire	T. G. M. Brooks	R. A. Wessel
Lincolnshire	Mrs B. K. Cracroft-Eley	R. W. Parker
Merseyside	A. W. Waterworth	W. D. Fulton, DL
Norfolk	Sir Timothy Colman, KG	R. W. Jewson
Northamptonshire	Lady Juliet Townsend, LVO	A. G. Stoughton-Harris, CBE
Northumberland	Sir John Riddell	S. C. Enderby
North Yorkshire	The Lord Crathorne	The Hon. G. Turton
Nottinghamshire	Sir Andrew Buchanan, Bt.	Mrs B. A. Vere-Laurie
Oxfordshire	H. L. J. Brunner	R. H. Lethbridge
Rutland	Air Chief Marshal Sir Thomas Kennedy, GCB, AFC	Lt.-Col. Bingley
Shropshire	A. E. H. Heber-Percy	R. P. Corbett
Somerset	Lady Gass	Mrs A. B. Yeoman, OBE
South Yorkshire	The Earl of Scarbrough	Col. G. Norton, TD
Staffordshire	J. A. Hawley, TD	D. Elliot
Suffolk	The Lord Belstead, PC	J. Clement
Surrey	Mrs S. J. F. Goad	M. G. More-Molyneux
Tyne and Wear	Sir Ralph Carr-Ellison, KCVO, TD	J. T. Ward
Warwickshire	M. Dunne	J. S. Hammon
West Midlands	R. R. Taylor, OBE	J. F. Woolridge, CBE
West Sussex	H. Wyatt	R. R. Loder
West Yorkshire	J. Lyles, CBE	F. R. Fenton
Wiltshire	Lt.-Gen. Sir Maurice Johnston, KCB, OBE	R. N. Lawton, CBE
Worcestershire	Sir Thomas Dunne, KCVO	Mrs T. Hone

COUNTY COUNCILS: Area, Population, Finance

Council	Administrative headquarters	Area (hectares)	Population	Total demand upon collection fund 2000–1
Bedfordshire	County Hall, Bedford	119,220	524,105	£98,100,000.00
Buckinghamshire	County Hall, Aylesbury	156,538	632,487	£128,000,000.00
Cambridgeshire	Shire Hall, Cambridge	305,399	645,125	£118,028,000.00
Cheshire	County Hall, Chester	208,344	956,616	£183,646,553.00
Cornwall	County Hall, Truro	354,810	468,425	£105,974,048.00
Cumbria	The Courts, Carlisle	681,000	483,163	£114,678,000.00
Derbyshire	County Hall, Matlock	262,858	928,636	£173,339,000.00
Devon	County Hall, Exeter	670,343	1,009,950	£651,340,000.00
Dorset	County Hall, Dorchester	254,375	645,166	£107,500,000.00
Durham	County Hall, Durham	223,180	593,430	£99,035,000.00
East Sussex	Pelham House, St Andrew's Lane, Lewes	172,500	690,447	£128,532,000.00
Essex	County Hall, Chelmsford	344,781	1,528,577	£315,481,000.00
Gloucestershire	Shire Hall, Gloucester	265,535	528,370	£120,000,000.00
Hampshire	The Castle, Winchester	367,915	1,541,547	£299,586,000.00
Hertfordshire	County Hall, Hertford	164,306	975,829	£255,690,628.00
Kent	County Hall, Maidstone	354,296	1,508,873	£321,100,000.00
Lancashire	County Hall, Preston	289,780	1,383,998	£275,900,000.00
Leicestershire	County Hall, Glenfield, Leicester	208,380	867,521	£136,867,050.00
Lincolnshire	County Offices, Newland, Lincoln	588,000	584,534	£433,412,000.00
Norfolk	County Hall, Norwich	537,234	745,613	£174,100,000.00
Northamptonshire	County Hall, Northampton	236,737	578,807	£127,600,000.00
Northumberland	County Hall, Morpeth	502,594	307,709	£76,380,000.00
North Yorkshire	County Hall, Northallerton	830,399	556,200	£130,100,000.00
Nottinghamshire	County Hall, Nottingham	208,510	993,872	£186,322,000.00
Oxfordshire	County Hall, Oxford	260,595	547,584	£145,000,000.00
Shropshire	The Shirehall, Shrewsbury	319,736	406,387	£63,326,388.00
Somerset	County Hall, Taunton	345,233	460,368	£111,895,240.23
Staffordshire	County Buildings, Stafford	262,355	1,031,135	£160,923,909.00
Suffolk	County Hall, Ipswich	380,207	636,266	£142,700,000.00
Surrey	County Hall, Kingston upon Thames	167,011	1,018,003	£288,100,000.00
Warwickshire	Shire Hall, Warwick	198,054	484,247	£122,687,564.00
West Sussex	County Hall, Chichester	199,025	702,290	£187,757,000.00
Wiltshire	County Hall, Trowbridge	348,070	564,471	£103,534,400.00
Worcestershire	County Hall, Worcester	173,529	531,909	£118,532,000.00

COUNTY COUNCILS: OFFICERS AND CHAIRMEN

Council	Chief Executive	County Treasurer	Chairman of County Council
Bedfordshire	D. Bell	*vacant*	J. Saunders
Buckinghamshire	I. Crookall	S. Nolan	K. I. Ross
Cambridgeshire	A. Barnish	M. Parsons	J. Eddy
Cheshire	C. Cheesman	A. Cope	D. Newton
Cornwall	P. Davies	F. P. Twyning	J. M. Philp
Cumbria	*vacant*	R. F. Mather	W. Minto, CBE, DL, FRSA
Derbyshire	A. R. N. Hodgson	P. Swaby	G. Bratt
Devon	P. Jenkinson	Mrs J. Stanhope	F. Symons
Dorset	D. H. Jenkins	A. P. Peel	Mrs A. P. Hymers
Durham	K. W. Smith	J. Kirkby	J. Richardson
East Sussex	Mrs C. Miller	J. Howes	R. Stevens
Essex	K. W. S. Ashurst	K. D. Neale	J. Pike
Gloucestershire	R. Cockcroft	R. Potter	Dr J. Cardwell
Hampshire	P. C. B. Robertson	J. C. Pittam	F. A. J. Emery-Wallis, CBE, DL
Hertfordshire	W. D. Ogley	A. Laycock	Ms H. Burningham
Kent	M. Pitt	D. Lewis	Mrs B. Trench
Lancashire	M. B. Winterbottom	B. Aldred	R. Clark
Leicestershire	J. B. Sinnott	A. Youd	J. F. Howard
Lincolnshire	D. Bowles	P. Moore *(acting)*	W. R. Wyrill, OBE
Norfolk	T. J. Byles	R. D. Summers	J. Sheppard
Northamptonshire	A. Elliston *(acting)*	S. Wood	H. T. K. Graham
Northumberland	A. Clarke	C. Burns	Dr G. H. Fisher
North Yorkshire	J. Walker	J. S. Moore	R. Wilson
Nottinghamshire	P. J. Housden	R. Latham	J. T. Napier
Oxfordshire	J. Harwood	C. Gray	D. Green
Shropshire	N. T. Pursey	K. Dixon	Mrs P. Larney
Somerset	Dr D. Radford	C. N. Bilsland	H. P. N. Temperley
Staffordshire	B. A. Price, CBE	R. G. Tettenborn, OBE	T. R. Wright
Suffolk	Mrs L. Homer	M. More	Dr A. D. Lower
Surrey	P. Coen	M. Taylor	Dr B. J. Coffin
Warwickshire	I. G. Caulfield	D. Clarke	M. Singh
West Sussex	D. P. Rigg	Mrs H. Kilpatrick	I. R. W. Elliott
Wiltshire	Dr K. Robinson	D. Chalker	Lt.-Col. D. B. W. Jarvis
Worcestershire	R. Sykes	M. Weaver	P. Carter

Unitary Councils

SMALL CAPITALS denote CITY status
§ Denotes Borough status
Source of population figures: ONS Monitor PP1 97/1, 28 August 1997

Council	Population	Band D charge 2000	Chief Executive	Mayor (a) Lord Mayor (b) Chairman 2000–1
§Barnsley	220,937	£844.88	P. J. Coppard	A. Whittaker
Bath and North-East Somerset	164,700	£870.53	J. Everitt	J. Bailey
BIRMINGHAM	961,041	£937.53	Sir Michael Lyons	(a) Ms T. Stewart
§Blackburn with Darwen	136,612	£964.61	P. S. Watson	J. Bury
§Blackpool	1,51200	£564.08	G. E. Essex-Crosby	G. Heap
§Bolton	258,584	£924.53	B. Knight	A. Wilkinson
§Bournemouth	160,700	£764.33	D. Newell	B. Grower
§Bracknell Forest	110,000	£743.68	G. S. Mitchell	J. M. B. Egan
BRADFORD	457,344	£834.24	I. Stewart	(a) J. S. King
§Brighton and Hove	245,000	£780.62	G. Jones	A. Durr
BRISTOL	399,600	£999.12	C. Reynell	(a) G. Robertson
§Bury	176,760	£851.30	D. Taylor	W. Johnson, MBE
§Calderdale	191,585	£911.33	P. Sheehan	G. T. Hall
COVENTRY	294,387	£1,019.82	I. Roxburgh	(a) Ms S. Collins
§Darlington	101,000	£687.49	B. Keel	Ms D. Long
DERBY	235,238	£827.30	R. H. Cowlishaw	A. Kalia
§Doncaster	288,854	£800.00	A. M. Taylor	M. Edgar
§Dudley	304,615	£836.06	A. Sparke	G. Davies
East Riding of Yorkshire	310,800	£833.83	D. Stephenson	(b) N. Hall
§Gateshead	199,588	£1,006.65	L. N. Elton	P. Wilson
§Halton	123,038	£736.73	M. Cuff	Ms J. Devaney
Hartlepool	92,000	£1,021.18	B. J. Dinsdale	F. Rogers
Herefordshire	167,000	£774.67	N. Pringle	(b) R. Thomas
Isle of Wight	125,466	£828.65	B. Quoroll	(b) V. J. Morey
KINGSTON UPON HULL	266,900	£794.14	I. Crookham	(a) Mrs B. Ware
§Kirklees	373,510	£908.10	A. Elson	Ms A. Denham
§Knowsley	152,091	£986.65	S. Gallagher	R. Maguire
LEEDS	680,722	£802.03	P. Rogerson	(a) B. P. Atha
LEICESTER	270,493	£873.48	R. Green	(a) Mrs B. Chambers
LIVERPOOL	452,450	£1,171.54	D. Henshaw	(a) E. M. Clein
§Luton	181,500	£760.81	Mrs K. Jones	W. Akbar
§MANCHESTER	404,861	£1,006.04	H. Bernstein	(a) H. Barrett
Medway	239,978	£700.98	Ms J. Armitt	R. Andrews
Middlesbrough	144,500	£842.32	J. E. Foster	Ms K. Bevington
§Milton Keynes	204,415	£786.22	H. Miller	A. Woodcock
NEWCASTLE UPON TYNE	259,541	£1,005.79	K. G. Lavery	(a) P. Thomson
North-East Lincolnshire	168,000	£917.14	J. Leivers	Ms J. Hyldon-King
North Lincolnshire	152,423	£947.00	M. Garnett	M. Todd
North Somerset	177,000	£779.95	P. May	I. Parker
§North Tyneside	192,286	£967.21	Executive Directorate	D. Charlton
NOTTINGHAM	284,000	£921.86	E. F. Cantle	(a) I. W. Malcolm
§Oldham	216,531	£962.10	A. W. Kilburn	R. Knowles
PETERBOROUGH	159,900	£821.35	P. Martin	R. Pobgee, MBE
PLYMOUTH	255,800	£764.47	Mrs A. Stone	(a) D. Camp
§Poole	139,200	£790.20	J. Brooks	Mrs J. Jones
PORTSMOUTH	190,400	£702.27	N. Gurney	(a) B. Maine
§Reading	142,851	£799.00	Ms J. Markham	R. Green
Redcar and Cleveland	140,200	£1,080.99	C. Moore	A. Dobson
§Rochdale	2,02164	£909.42	R. Ellis	B. Leather
§Rotherham	251,637	£781.58	A. G. Carruthers, B.SC.	I. G. Logan
Rutland	34,600	£992.64	Dr J. R. Morphet	(b) Wg Cdr R. D. Toy
§St Helens	178,764	£962.88	Mrs C. Hudson	Mrs P. Robinson
SALFORD	220,463	£1,033.26	J. C. Willis	B. Warner
§Sandwell	290,091	£898.04	F. N. Summers	Ms J. Marson
§Sefton	289,542	£950.15	G. J. Haywood	Ms W. Jones

Council	Population	Band D charge 2000	Chief Executive	Mayor (a) Lord Mayor (b) Chairman 2000–1
SHEFFIELD	501,202	£935.84	R. W. Kerslake	(a) Ms P. Midgley
§Slough	108,000	£713.51	Ms C. Coppell	R. Webb
§Solihull	199,859	£775.00	vacant	H. Cox
SOUTHAMPTON	2,14859	£751.72	J. Cairns	P. Wakeford
South Gloucestershire	239,000	£859.25	M. Robinson	(b) A. Adams
§Southend	172,300	£733.70	J. K. M. Krawiec	G. Longley
§South Tyneside	154,697	£929.52	P. J. Haigh	Mrs M. Brady
§Stockport	284,395	£952.78	J. R. Schultz	Ms M. Rowles
§Stockton-on-Tees	179,000	£899.50	G. Garlick	P. Andrew
STOKE-ON-TRENT	254,300	£787.27	B. Smith	(a) Ms B. Dunn
§SUNDERLAND	28,9040	£856.03	C. W. Sinclair, Ph. D.	B. Dodds
§Swindon	177,118	£741.91	P. Doherty	A. Archer
§Tameside	216,431	£938.16	M. J. Greenwood	B. Wild
Telford and Wrekin	151,500	£783.00	M. Frater	(b) C. Mason
§Thurrock	132,283	£716.40	K. Barnes	J. M. Norris
§Torbay	119,674	£791.54	A. J. Hodgkiss	C. Charlwood
§Trafford	212,731	£722.97	Ms C. Hassan	J. Ackerley
WAKEFIELD	310,915	£1,621.82	M. Pullan	N. J. Hazell, MBE
§Walsall	259,488	£857.84	H. Bhogal	B. Douglas-Maul
§Warrington	187,000	£761.94	S. Broomhead	Ms S. E. Woodyatt, MBE
West Berkshire	144,000	£881.36	Ms S. Manzie	(b) P. Barnett
§Wigan	306,521	£886.76	S. M. Jones	Mrs J. Hurst
§Windsor and Maidenhead	132,465	£777.54	D. C. Lunn	J. Webb
§Wirral	330,795	£1,030.72	S. Maddox	Mrs K. Wood
Wokingham	142,767	£888.54	Ms J. Earl	(b) Mrs D. Tomlin
§Wolverhampton	242,190	£997.56	D. B. Anderson	T. Singh
YORK	175,925	£687.00	D. Clark	(a) S. Braund

District Councils

SMALL CAPITALS denote CITY status
§ Denotes Borough status
Source of population figures: ONS Monitor PP1 97/1, 28 August 1997

Council	Population	Band D charge 2000	Chief Executive	Chairman (a) Mayor (b) Lord Mayor 2000–1
Adur, W. Sussex	58,019	£837.11	I. Lowrie	(b) J. Phillips
§Allerdale, Cumbria	95,702	£908.89	M. Phillips	A. Shith
Alnwick, Northumberland	30,081	£956.25	L. A. B. St Ruth	(b) G. R. Arckless
Amber Valley, Derbys	111,897	£929.54	P. M. Carney	J. Nelson
Arun, W. Sussex	129,357	£775.94	I. Sumnall	(b) Mrs R. Cooper
Ashfield, Notts	108,364	£982.73	E. N. Bernasconi	(b) D. Hague
§Ashford, Kent	92,331	£792.26	A. Baker	A. J. Hoad
Aylesbury Vale, Bucks	145,931	£815.48	B. Hurles	(b) C. R. James
Babergh, Suffolk	79,632	£751.00	P. Barnes	(b) P. Jones
§Barrow-in-Furness, Cumbria	73,125	£943.28	T. O. Campbell	J. R. Richardson
Basildon, Essex	161,124	£867.60	J. Robb	(b) Mrs L. Gordon
§Basingstoke and Deane, Hants	144,790	£796.35	Mrs K. E. P. Sporle	Mrs M. J. Tucker
Bassetlaw, Notts	103,979	£970.04	J. Molloy	(b) D. Walsh
§Bedford, Beds	133,692	£909.07	S. Field	Ms H. Mitchell

Council	Population	Band D charge 2000	Chief Executive	Chairman (a) Mayor (b) Lord Mayor 2000–1
§Berwick-upon-Tweed, Northumberland	26,731	£943.89	P. Rutherford (*acting*)	G. Exley
Blaby, Leics	82,700	£870.80	E. Hemsley	(*b*) Mrs J. L. Weatherstone
§Blyth Valley, Northumberland	79,584	£939.57	G. Paul	R. Sanderson
Bolsover, Derbys	70,437	£965.44	J. R. Fotherby	(*b*) D. E. Reynolds
§Boston, Lincs	53,226	£834.33	M. James	G. Danby
Braintree, Essex	118,883	£820.17	Ms A. F. Ralph	(*b*) K. Boylan
Breckland, Norfolk	107,167	£784.37	R. N. Garnett	(*b*) Mrs S. Matthews
§Brentwood, Essex	70,597	£818.28	B. McLintock; D. Marchant	D. Minns
Bridgnorth, Salop	50,511	£824.65	Mrs T. M. Elliott	(*b*) Ms M. Winckler
Broadland, Norfolk	106,292	£822.84	C. Bland (*acting*)	(*b*) D. Thompson
Bromsgrove, Worcs	91,544	£781.37	D. A. H. Bryant	(*b*) Mrs A. Doyle
§Broxbourne, Herts	81,449	£759.42	M. J. Walker	Mrs E. M. White
§Broxtowe, Notts	107,137	£975.45	M. Brown	R. Collins
§Burnley, Lancs	91,130	£998.05	Dr G. Taylor	R. Malik
CAMBRIDGE	91,933	£796.26	R. Hammond	Ms E. Knowles
Cannock Chase, Staffs	88,833	£818.79	M. G. Kemp	(*b*) R. J. Todd
CANTERBURY, Kent	123,947	£811.88	C. Carmichael	(*a*) Miss J. Samper
Caradon, Cornwall	76,516	£789.12	Dr J. Neal	(*b*) T. G. Smale
CARLISLE, Cumbria	100,562	£927.81	P. Stybelski	R. Knapton
Carrick, Cornwall	82,725	£828.79	J. P. Winskill	(*b*) Mrs S. C. Shaw
§Castle Morpeth, Northumberland	50,299	£963.44	P. Wilson	F. Harrington
§Castle Point, Essex	86,560	£863.91	B. Rollinson	A. Goldsworthy
§Charnwood, Leics	141,806	£858.89	S. M. Peatfield	N. C. N. Bird
§Chelmsford, Essex	152,418	£808.30	M. Easteal	C. Stephenson
§Cheltenham, Glos	103,115	£830.93	L. Davison	Ms D. Pennell
Cherwell, Oxon	117,832	£772.98	G. J. Handley	(*b*) Mrs C. A. Fulljames
§Chesterfield, Derbys	99,403	£907.23	D. R. Shaw	M. Leverton
Chester-le-Street, Co. Durham	52,641	£867.69	J. A. Greensmith	(*b*) I. Wilson
CHESTER, Cheshire	115,971	£930.00	P. F. Durham	(*a*) R. Jones
Chichester, W. Sussex	101,358	£806.76	J. S. Marsland	(*b*) C. W. Spawton
Chiltern, Bucks	89,838	£822.23	A. Goodrum	(*b*) D. W. Phillips
§Chorley, Lancs	96,504	£946.32	J. W. Davies	T. McGowan
§Christchurch, Dorset	40,865	£858.86	M. A. Turvey	E. N. Speadbury
§Colchester, Essex	142,515	£820.80	J. Cobley	C. Garnett
§Congleton, Cheshire	84,525	£907.81	P. Cooper	R. Lowe
§Copeland, Cumbria	71,296	£906.90	Dr J. Stanforth	R. Simpson
§Corby, Northants	53,044	£814.27	N. Rudd	Ms J. Field
Cotswold, Glos	73,965	£832.27	N. C. Abbott	(*b*) B. I. Evans
Craven, N. Yorks	49,891	£777.96	Miss R. Mann	(*b*) P. Walbank
§Crawley, W. Sussex	87,644	£796.59	M. D. Sander	M. Qamaruddin
§Crewe and Nantwich, Cheshire	103,164	£922.19	A. Wenham	Ms B. Bickerton
§Dacorum, Herts	134,733	£784.86	P. Walker	H. Chapman
§Dartford, Kent	79,439	£824.67	G. Harris	M. Dando
Daventry, Northants	62,886	£765.18	S. Atkinson	(*b*) G. Morrott
Derbyshire Dales, Derbys	67,562	£943.96	D. Wheatcroft	(*b*) Mrs C. Crowther
Derwentside, Co. Durham	86,046	£937.80	*vacant*	(*b*) O. Johnson
Dover, Kent	103,216	£803.06	J. P. Moir, TD	(*b*) F. E. Woodbridge, MBE
DURHAM	80,669	£873.99	C. Shearsmith	G. Wharton
Easington, Co. Durham	97,824	£996.77	P. Wilding	(*b*) W. R. Peardon
§Eastbourne, E. Sussex	81,395	£851.52	*vacant*	M. Tunwell
East Cambridgeshire	60,416	£767.46	R. C. Carr	(*b*) Ms S. Friend-Smith
East Devon	115,873	£805.00	F. J. Vallender	(*b*) B. C. J. Hughes
East Dorset	78,698	£888.14	A. Breakwell	(*b*) P. G. Gutteridge
East Hampshire	103,460	£839.68	P. Burton	(*b*) Sqn. Ldr. G. Whittle
East Hertfordshire	115,818	£769.53	R. J. Bailey	R. Gilbert
§Eastleigh, Hants	105,999	£831.44	C. Tapp	P. Humphreys
East Lindsey, Lincs	116,957	£763.93	P. Haigh	(*b*) M. Clark
East Northamptonshire	67,686	£782.88	R. K. Heath	(*b*) R. Underwood
§East Staffordshire	97,105	£829.07	F. W. Saunders	P. Haynes
Eden, Cumbria	45,581	£930.94	I. W. Bruce	(*b*) Mrs N. Walker
§Ellesmere Port and Neston, Cheshire	80,873	£927.65	S. Ewbank	P. Shephard
§Elmbridge, Surrey	114,479	£817.37	M. Lockwood	A. Hopkins
Epping Forest, Essex	116,027	£835.08	J. Burgess	(*b*) R. Heath

Council	Population	Band D charge 2000	Chief Executive	Chairman (a) Mayor (b) Lord Mayor 2000–1
§Epsom and Ewell, Surrey	67,007	£801.64	D. J. Smith	N. Petrie
§Erewash, Derbys	106,101	£916.12	vacant	Ms P. Phillips
EXETER, Devon	98,125	£792.72	P. Bostock	Mrs M. Evans
Fareham, Hants	99,262	£802.35	A. A. Davies	Capt. K. B. Estlin, RN
Fenland, Cambs	74,426	£792.65	N. R. Topliss	(b) J. L. Barker
Forest Heath, Suffolk	54,843	£719.21	D. W. Burnip	(b) W. J. Bishop
Forest of Dean, Glos	75,351	£854.16	Ms M. Holborow	(b) B. W. Hobman
§Fylde, Lancs	70,999	£928.98	J. R. Wilkinson	P. J. Hayhurst
§Gedling, Notts	110,133	£953.20	D. Kennedy	D. Walker
GLOUCESTER	101,608	£827.21	G. Garbutt	T. L. Haines
§Gosport, Hants	75,061	£827.93	M. C. Crocker	A. H. G. Hayward
§Gravesham, Kent	92,454	£791.60	E. C. Anderson	Ms P. Mersh
§Great Yarmouth, Norfolk	87,724	£827.98	R. W. Packham	(b) B. J. E. Collins
§Guildford, Surrey	127,500	£813.80	D. T. Watts, FRSA	Ms S. Thornberry
Hambleton, N. Yorks	79,425	£736.68	P. Simpson	(b) D. A. Howey
Harborough, Leics	67,607	£628.71	M. C. Wilson	(b) R. Vickers
Harlow, Essex	74,629	£924.87	D. Patterson	(b) T. Abel
§Harrogate, N. Yorks	143,526	£805.67	P. M. Walsh	Mrs P. Marsh
Hart, Hants	80,921	£823.20	G. R. Jelbart	(b) C. Lynch
§Hastings, E. Sussex	80,820	£874.96	R. Mawford	J. Dowling
§Havant, Hants	11,9697	£816.47	R. D. Smith	P. G. Quick
§Hertsmere, Herts	87,590	£800.17	P. H. Copland	Ms A. Attwood
§High Peak, Derbys	87,900	£935.19	R. P. H. Brady	Ms J. McGrother
§Hinckley and Bosworth, Leics	96,201	£826.93	J. Corry	D. S. Cope
Horsham, W. Sussex	108,562	£770.73	M. J. Pearson	(b) Mrs E. G. Kitchen
Huntingdonshire, Cambs	144,075	£750.00	D. Monks	(b) K. Reynolds
§Hyndburn, Lancs	78,390	£982.46	M. J. Chambers	D. Hayes
§Ipswich, Suffolk	116,956	£885.42	J. D. Hehir	D. Edwards
Kennet, Wilts	68,526	£826.18	M. J. Boden	(b) Mrs S. M. Findlay
Kerrier, Cornwall	87,566	£820.98	G. G. Cox	(b) Mrs W. Lawrence
§Kettering, Northants	78,200	£773.94	D. Cook	J. Coleman
§King's Lynn and West Norfolk	131,000	£827.11	Dr G. Taylor	C. Walters
LANCASTER, Lancs	123,856	£940.14	M. Cullinan	Mrs E. Jones
Lewes, E. Sussex	87,389	£878.66	J. N. Crawford	(b) Ms M. E. Messer
Lichfield, Staffs	92,679	£808.43	J. T. Thompson	(b) T. V. Finn
LINCOLN	81,987	£851.85	A. Taylor	R. Coupland
§Macclesfield, Cheshire	151,590	£852.40	B. W. Longden	G. W. Wright
§Maidstone, Kent	137,000	£848.86	D. Petford	D. Daley
Maldon, Essex	52,843	£796.95	E. A. P. Plumridge	(b) R. Pipe
Malvern Hills, Worcs	86,902	£801.53	C. J. Bocock	(b) P. Raven
Mansfield, Notts	100,386	£989.91	R. P. Goad	(b) R. Spate
§Melton, Leics	45,112	£851.41	P. M. Murphy	N. Angrave
Mendip, Somerset	95,603	£832.25	G. Jeffs	(b) C. Lockey
Mid Bedfordshire, Beds	109,801	£919.14	C. A. Tucker	(b) Mrs F. Chapman
Mid Devon, Devon	64,258	£823.87	M. I. R. Bull	(b) Mrs J. Campbell
Mid Suffolk, Suffolk	78,383	£780.45	G. R. Chilton	(b) Ms C. E. Jones
Mid Sussex, W. Sussex	126,000	£797.13	W. J. H. Hatton	(b) Mrs C. Field
Mole Valley, Surrey	79,220	£787.08	Mrs H. Kerswell	(b) P. Seabrook
Newark and Sherwood, Notts	102,784	£1,023.85	R. G. Dix	(b) F. S. Jackson
§Newcastle under Lyme, Staffs	119,091	£812.04	F. Harley	Mrs S. T. Butler
New Forest, Hants	160,456	£836.98	D. Yates	(b) A. Rice, TD
§Northampton	180,567	£850.36	R. J. B. Morris	Dr V. Dams
North Cornwall	73,800	£832.93	D. Brown	(b) R. W. Flower
North Devon	84,800	£838.35	D. T. Cunliffe	(b) H. Hopkins
North Dorset	52,110	£854.90	A. Greaves	(b) Mrs D. L. Jones, MBE
North East Derbyshire	97,570	£968.02	Ms C. A. Gilby	(b) K. Savidge
North Hertfordshire	111,994	£793.18	S. Philp	(b) B. Crown
North Kesteven, Lincs	79,942	£806.79	Mrs R. Marlow	(b) D. Dickinson
North Norfolk	90,461	£829.67	B. A. Barrell	(b) M. Gates
North Shropshire	52,873	£860.43	R. J. Hughes	(b) F. J. Udale
§North Warwickshire	60,747	£900.84	J. Hutchinson	C. Morson
North West Leicestershire	80,566	£865.11	M. J. Diaper	(b) J. Roberts
North Wiltshire	111,974	£567.78	R. Marshall	(b) Mrs L. M. Barber
NORWICH, Norfolk	120,895	£872.44	Ms A. Seex	(a) R. Borritt
§Nuneaton and Bedworth, Warks	117,052	£898.82	Ms C. Kerr	Ms D. Hawkes

Council	Population	Band D charge 2000	Chief Executive	Chairman (a) Mayor (b) Lord Mayor 2000–1
§Oadby and Wigston, Leics	51,547	£864.87	Mrs R. E. Hyde	Mrs S. Morris
§Oswestry, Salop	33,508	£851.25	P. Shevlin	D. Aldridge
OXFORD	134,800	£825.89	R. S. Block	(a) Ms M. Christian
§Pendle, Lancs	85,111	£991.72	S. Barnes	I. A. Gilhespy
Penwith, Cornwall	59,251	£738.46	J. A. R. McKenna	(b) Mrs S. M. Menadue
§Preston, Lancs	126,082	£1,010.04	J. E. Carr	J. Hood, CBE
Purbeck, Dorset	42,445	£874.37	P. B. Croft	(b) R. Anderson
§Redditch, Worcs	78,106	£829.31	Ms K. Kerswell	M. Shurmer
§Reigate and Banstead, Surrey	117,777	£817.34	M. Bacon	J. Lyndon Morgan
§Restormel, Cornwall	86,519	£791.04	Mrs P. Crowson	(b) T. H. Menear
§Ribble Valley, Lancs	51,767	£943.15	D. G. Morris	C. Holtom
Richmondshire, N. Yorks	44,179	£825.00	H. Tabiner	(b) M. Heseltine
Rochford, Essex	75,395	£849.46	P. Warren	(b) Mrs W. M.Stevenson
§Rossendale, Lancs	65,681	£991.44	J. S. Hartley	D. Hancock
Rother, E. Sussex	81,683	£838.84	D. F. Powell, FRICS	(b) C. N. Ramus
§Rugby, Warks	81,683	£900.09	Mrs D. M. Colley	I. G. Mistry
§Runnymede, Surrey	71,789	£727.50	T. N. Williams	G. B. Woodger
§Rushcliffe, Notts	97,567	£950.80	K. Beaumont	R. H. Butler
§Rushmoor, Hants	82,526	£821.34	J. A. Lloyd	J. E. C. White
Ryedale, N. Yorks	47,981	£819.74	H. W. Mosley	(b) D. E. Cussons
ST ALBANS, Herts	128,700	£809.49	E. A. Hackford	R. Mills
§St Edmundsbury, Suffolk	91,731	£790.65	G. R. N. Toft	J. R. Motton Wayman
Salisbury, Wilts	105,318	£827.95	R. Sheard	(b) Mrs B. Jay
§Scarborough, N. Yorks	106,221	£797.00	J. M. Trebble	Mrs D. Clegg
§Sedgefield, Co. Durham	90,530	£1,009.34	N. Vaulks	G. Morgan
Sedgemoor, Somerset	97,763	£811.24	K. Rickards	(b) D. S. Alder
Selby, N. Yorks	89,428	£813.42	M. Connor	(b) J. Duggan
Sevenoaks, Kent	109,742	£836.77	N. Howells	(b) J. Sandeford
Shepway, Kent	96,020	£845.47	R. J. Thompson	(b) Mrs S. Newlands
§Shrewsbury and Atcham, Salop	94,600	£821.50	R. Hooper	D. Moore
South Bedfordshire	108,941	£965.02	J. Ruddick	(b) R. Goodwin
South Bucks	62,482	£812.52	C. R. Furness	(b) J. R. A. Kennedy
South Cambridgeshire	124,500	£764.30	J. S. Ballantyne	(b) S. Kime
South Derbyshire	71,772	£908.00	F. McArdle	(b) Ms J. Mead
South Hams, Devon	77,565	£820.35	Miss R. E. Bagley	(b) P. J. Prudden
South Holland, Lincs	70,386	£833.22	C. J. Simpkins	(b) J. Clark
South Kesteven, Lincs	108,945	£635.04	C. Farmer	(b) R. Lovelock
South Lakeland, Cumbria	96,897	£900.00	P. J. Cunliffe	(b) Mrs J. S. Borer
South Norfolk	102,612	£840.29	G. Rivers	(b) K. Warman
South Northamptonshire	70,685	£844.77	R. Tinlin	(b) A. Wilkinson
South Oxfordshire	119,476	£847.00	R. W. Watson	(b) J. E. Stimson
§South Ribble, Lancs	102,001	£934.70	Ms J. Hunter	G. Davies
South Shropshire	38,230	£830.00	G. C. Biggs, MBE	(b) M. R. Williams
South Somerset	145,000	£836.62	Ms E. Peters	(b) N. Speakman, MBE, TD
South Staffordshire Council	105,487	£729.24	L. T. Barnfield	(b) A. R. Hood
§Spelthorne, Surrey	89,748	£800.27	M. B. Taylor	Ms J. Wood-Dow
Staffordshire Moorlands	95,072	£820.34	B. J. Preedy	(b) Ms L. Malyon
§Staffordshire	117,788	£808.70	D. Rawlings	P. Bruce
§Stevenage, Herts	75147	£804.18	I. Paske	P. D. Kissane
Stratford, Warks	109,400	£843.78	I. B. Prosser	(b) W. P. McCarthy
Stroud, Glos	106,300	£890.86	R. M. Ollin	(b) R. Eccles
Suffolk Coastal	107,970	£803.86	T. K. Griffin	(b) R. Gween
§Surrey Heath	80,800	£803.23	B. R. Catchpole	Mrs P. F. M. Pearce
§Swale, Kent	115,769	£810.69	C. Edwards	P. Salmon
§Tamworth, Staffs	70,065	£779.39	D. Weatherley	D. Foster
Tandridge, Surrey	76,316	£815.36	J. D. Thomas	(b) T. Servant
§Taunton Deane, Somerset	93,696	£635.60	vacant	T. Floyd
Teesdale, Co. Durham	24,068	£886.71	C. M. Anderson	(b) Mrs M. Bolden
Teignbridge, Devon	108,258	£828.33	B. T. Jones	(b) C. J. Brimblecombe
Tendring, Essex	130,900	£816.80	J. Hawkins	(b) B. Thomasson
§Test Valley, Hants	103,261	£751.74	A. Jones	A. Hope
§Tewkesbury, Glos	70,709	£796.83	vacant	M. D. Calway
Thanet, Kent	123,665	£841.03	D. Ralls, CBE, DFC	(b) C. Young
Three Rivers, Herts	78,457	£998.00	A. Robertson	(b) G. Williams
§Tonbridge and Malling, Kent	101,763	£828.60	T. Thompson	M. Dobson

Council	Population	Band D charge 2000	Chief Executive	Chairman (a) Mayor (b) Lord Mayor 2000–1
Torridge, Devon	52,129	£820.00	R. K. Brasington	(b) (until March 2001) R. Johns; (from April 2001) P. Waters
§Tunbridge Wells, Kent	99,538	£800.70	R. J. Stone	R. Morton
Tynedale, Northumberland	57,275	£932.90	P. A. Kemp	(b) W. Garrett
Uttlesford, Essex	67,500	£841.22	Ms E. Forbes	(b) D. M. Miller
Vale of White Horse, Oxon	109,922	£810.79	T. A. Stock	(b) V. Butt
§Vale Royal, Oxon	114,700	£903.40	J. W. Page	S. Gough
Wansbeck, Northumberland	63,171	£956.99	R. A. Stephenson	(b) J. J. Tyler
Warwick	116,299	£843.32	Miss J. M. Barrett	(b) J. Short
§Watford, Herts	74,566	£873.75	A. Clarke	I. Brown
Waveney, Suffolk	106,751	£790.34	Mrs M. McLean	(b) Ms R. Carter
§Waverley, Surrey	113,212	£818.60	Ms C. L. Pointer	J. R. Sandy
Wealden, E. Sussex	130,214	£886.05	Ms S. Douglas	(b) J. A. Fordham
Wear Valley, Co. Durham	62,746	£1,105.48	Mrs C. Hughes	(b) Mrs A. Newton
§Wellingborough	67,900	£746.50	A. D. W. McArdle	G. D. Ryan
Welwyn Hatfield Council, Herts	92,366	£813.36	M. Saminaden	(b) Ms L. Mendez
§West Devon	45,895	£879.29	D. J. Incoll	Mrs C. Grills
West Dorset	85,463	£882.59	R. C. Rennison	(b) Mrs N. M. Penfold
West Lancashire	107,978	£953.26	W. J. Taylor	(b) A. Johnson
West Lindsey	76,218	£847.54	R. W. Nelsey	(b) A. D. Caine
West Oxfordshire	90,251	£788.58	G. Bonner	(b) A. Walker
West Somerset	31,651	£831.85	T. Howes	(b) V. A. Brewer
West Wiltshire	107,803	£880.64	J. Ligo	(b) R. J. Brice
§Weymouth and Portland, Dorset	61,233	£886.50	T. Grainger	Mrs S. McGown
WINCHESTER, Hants	96,386	£816.11	D. H. Cowan	Ms G. Busher
§Woking, Surrey	86,765	£836.57	P. Russell	I. Eastwood
WORCESTER	89,481	£795.14	D. Wareing	Mrs M. Drinkwater
§Worthing, W. Sussex	96,157	£756.81	Miss S. Grady (acting)	Mrs A. Lynn
Wychavon, Worcs	101,716	£797.34	S. Pritchard	(b) D. Folkes
Wycombe, Bucks	162,000	£820.54	R. J. Cummins	(b) D. A. E. Cox
§Wyre, Lancs	101,818	£943.08	M. Brown	J. Lawrenson
Wyre Forest, Lancs	94,814	£826.86	W. Delin	(b) J. Gordon

Northumberland
Newcastle upon Tyne North Tyneside
Gateshead South Tyneside
Sunderland
Durham Hartlepool
Cumbria
Darlington 1 Redcar and Cleveland

North Yorkshire

York East Riding
of Yorkshire
Lancashire Bradford
Leeds
Kingston upon Hull
Calderdale Wake-
Sefton Wigan Kirklees field N Lincs
Barnsley Doncaster NE Lincs
Wirral Sheffield Rotherham
Cheshire
Derby-
shire Lincolnshire
Stoke-
on-
Trent Derby Nottinghamshire
Stafford-
shire
Shropshire Leicestershire
Leicester Rutland Norfolk

1 Stockton-on-Tees
2 Middlesbrough
3 Blackpool
4 Blackburn with Darwen
5 Bolton
6 Bury
7 Rochdale
8 Salford
9 Oldham
10 Liverpool
11 Knowsley
12 St Helens
13 Halton
14 Warrington
15 Trafford
16 Manchester
17 Tameside
18 Stockport
19 Nottingham
20 Telford and Wrekin
21 Wolverhampton
22 Walsall
23 Sandwell
24 Dudley
25 Birmingham
26 Solihull
27 Coventry
28 Peterborough
29 South Glos
30 Bristol
31 Bath and NE Somerset
32 Windsor and Maidenhead
33 Slough
34 Reading
35 Wokingham
36 Bracknell Forest
37 Thurrock
38 Southend
39 Medway
40 Plymouth
41 Torbay

Worcester-
shire Northants Cambridge-
shire
Warwickshire Suffolk
Herefordshire
Milton
Keynes Beds
Luton
Gloucestershire
Bucks Herts Essex
Oxfordshire
Swindon LONDON
NW (see box)
Somerset W Berks
Wiltshire Surrey Kent
Somerset Hampshire
Southampton West
Sussex East
Sussex
Devon Dorset Portsmouth
Poole Brighton and Hove
Cornwall Bournemouth Isle of Wight

LONDON

1 Hillingdon
2 Harrow
3 Barnet
4 Enfield
5 Waltham Forest
6 Redbridge
7 Barking and Dagenham
8 Havering
9 Ealing
10 Brent
11 Camden
12 Haringey
13 Islington
14 Hackney
15 Newham
16 Hounslow
17 Hammersmith and Fulham
18 Kensington and Chelsea
19 City of Westminster
20 City of London
21 Tower Hamlets
22 Richmond upon Thames
23 Wandsworth
24 Lambeth
25 Southwark
26 Lewisham
27 Greenwich
28 Bexley
29 Kingston upon Thames
30 Merton
31 Sutton
32 Croydon
33 Bromley

London

THE CORPORATION OF LONDON

The City of London is the historic centre at the heart of London known as 'the square mile' around which the vast metropolis has grown over the centuries. The City's residential population is 5,500. The civic government is carried on by the Corporation of London through the Court of Common Council.

The City is an international financial centre, generating over £20 billion a year for the British economy. It includes the head offices of the principal banks, insurance companies and mercantile houses, in addition to buildings ranging from the historic Roman Wall and the 15th century Guildhall, to the massive splendour of St Paul's Cathedral and the architectural beauty of Wren's spires.

The City of London was described by Tacitus in AD 62 as 'a busy emporium for trade and traders'. Under the Romans it became an important administration centre and hub of the road system. Little is known of London in Saxon times, when it formed part of the kingdom of the East Saxons. In 886 Alfred recovered London from the Danes and reconstituted it a burgh under his son-in-law. In 1066 the citizens submitted to William the Conqueror who in 1067 granted them a charter, which is still preserved, establishing them in the rights and privileges they had hitherto enjoyed.

THE MAYORALTY

The Mayoralty was probably established about 1189, the first Mayor being Henry Fitz Ailwyn who filled the office for 23 years and was succeeded by Fitz Alan (1212–14). A new charter was granted by King John in 1215, directing the Mayor to be chosen annually, which has ever since been done, though in early times the same individual often held the office more than once. A familiar instance is that of 'Whittington, thrice Lord Mayor of London' (in reality four times, 1397, 1398, 1406, 1419); and many modern cases have occurred. The earliest instance of the phrase 'Lord Mayor' in English is in 1414. It was used more generally in the latter part of the 15th century and became invariable from 1535 onwards. At Michaelmas the liverymen in Common Hall choose two Aldermen who have served the office of Sheriff for presentation to the Court of Aldermen, and one is chosen to be Lord Mayor for the following mayoral year.

LORD MAYOR'S DAY

The Lord Mayor of London was previously elected on the feast of St Simon and St Jude (28 October), and from the time of Edward I, at least, was presented to the King or to the Barons of the Exchequer on the following day, unless that day was a Sunday. The day of election was altered to 16 October in 1346, and after some further changes was fixed for Michaelmas Day in 1546, but the ceremonies of admittance and swearing in of the Lord Mayor continued to take place on 28 and 29 October respectively until 1751. In 1752, at the reform of the calendar, the Lord Mayor was continued in office until 8 November, the 'New Style' equivalent of 28 October. The Lord Mayor is now presented to the Lord Chief Justice at the Royal Courts of Justice on the second Saturday in November to make the final declaration of office, having been sworn in at Guildhall on the preceding day. The procession to the Royal Courts of Justice is popularly known as the Lord Mayor's Show.

REPRESENTATIVES

Aldermen are mentioned in the 11th century and their office is of Saxon origin. They were elected annually between 1377 and 1394, when an Act of Parliament of Richard II directed them to be chosen for life.

The Common Council, elected annually on the first Friday in December, was, at an early date, substituted for a popular assembly called the *Folkmote*. At first only two representatives were sent from each ward, but the number has since been greatly increased. The Corporation is reducing the number of Common Councilmen from 130 to 100 through natural wastage. The Government has introduced legislation to remove anomalies from the election system and to extend the non-resident franchise.

OFFICERS

Sheriffs were Saxon officers; their predecessors were the *wic-reeves* and *portreeves* of London and Middlesex. At first they were officers of the Crown, and were named by the Barons of the Exchequer; but Henry I (in 1132) gave the citizens permission to choose their own Sheriffs, and the annual election of Sheriffs became fully operative under King John's charter of 1199. The citizens lost this privilege, as far as the election of the Sheriff of Middlesex was concerned, by the Local Government Act 1888; but the liverymen continue to choose two Sheriffs of the City of London, who are appointed on Midsummer Day and take office at Michaelmas.

The office of Chamberlain is an ancient one, the first contemporary record of which is 1237. The Town Clerk (or Common Clerk) is mentioned in 1274.

ACTIVITIES

The work of the Corporation is assigned to a number of committees which present reports to the Court of Common Council. These Committees are: City Lands and Bridge House Grants Estates, Policy and Resources, Finance, Planning and Transportation, Central Markets, Billingsgate and Leadenhall Markets, Spitalfields Market, Police, Port and City of London Health and Social Services, Libraries, Art Galleries and Records, Board of Governors of City of London Freemen's School, Music and Drama (Guildhall School of Music and Drama), Establishment, Housing and Sports Development, Gresham (City side), Hampstead Health Management, Epping Forest and Open Spaces, West Ham Park, Privileges, Barbican Residential and Barbican Centre (Barbican Arts and Conference Centre).

The City's estate, in the possession of which the Corporation of London differs from other municipalities, is managed by the City Lands and Bridge House Grants Estates Committee, the chairmanship of which carries with it the title of Chief Commoner.

The Honourable Irish Society, which manages the Corporation's estates in Ulster, consists of a Governor and five other Aldermen, the Recorder, and 19 Common Councilmen, of whom one is elected Deputy Governor.

THE LORD MAYOR 1999–2000*

The Rt. Hon. the Lord Mayor, Alderman Clive Martin, OBE, TD
  Private Secretary, P. Tribe

---

* The Lord Mayor for 2000–1 was elected on Michaelmas Day. *See* Stop-press

THE SHERIFFS 2000–1

R. Agutter (*Alderman Castle Baynard*) and N. A. C. Brarsen, *elected* 26 June 2000; *assumed office* 28 September 2000

OFFICERS, ETC

Town Clerk, T. Simmons
Chamberlain, P. Derrick
Chief Commoner (2000), R. Eve
Clerk, The Honourable the Irish Society, S. Waley, The Irish Chamber, 1st Floor, 75 Watling Street, London EC4M 9BJ

THE ALDERMEN

Name and Ward	CC	Ald.	Shff.	Lord Mayor
Sir Christopher Leaver, GBE, *Dowgate*	1973	1974	1979	1981
Sir Alan Traill, GBE, *Langbourn*	1970	1975	1982	1984
Sir David Rowe-Ham, GBE, *Bridge* and *Bridge Wt.*	—	1976	1984	1986
Sir Christopher Collett, GBE, *Broad Street*	1973	1979	1985	1988
Sir Alexander Graham, GBE, *Queenhithe*	1978	1979	1986	1990
Sir Brian Jenkins, GBE, *Cordwainer*	—	1980	1987	1991
Sir Paul Newall, TD, *Walbrook*	1980	1981	1989	1993
Sir Christopher Walford, *Farringdon Wn.*	—	1982	1990	1994
Sir John Chalstrey, *Vintry*	1981	1984	1993	1995
Sir Roger Cork, *Tower*	1978	1983	1992	1996
Richard Nichols, *Candlewick*	1983	1984	1994	1997
Lord Levene of Portsoken, KBE, *Portsoken*	1983	1984	1995	1998
Clive Martin, OBE, TD, *Aldgate*	—	1985	1996	1999

All the above have passed the Civic Chair

David Howard, *Cornhill*	1972	1986	1997
Michael Oliver, *Bishopsgate*	1980	1987	1997
Anthony Bull, *Cheap*	1968	1984	
Gavyn Arthur, *Cripplegate*	1988	1991	1998
Robert Finch, *Coleman Street*	—	1992	1999
Richard Agutter, *Castle Baynard*	—	1995	2000
Michael Savory, *Bread Street*	1980	1996	
David Brewer, *Bassishaw*	1992	1996	
Nicholas Anstee, *Aldersgate*	1987	1996	
Michael Everard, CBE, *Lime Street*	—	1996	
John Hughesdon, *Billingsgate*	1991	1997	
vacant, *Farringdon Wt.*			

THE COMMON COUNCIL

Deputy: Each Common Councilman so described serves as deputy to the Alderman of her/his ward.

Absalom, J. D. (1994)	*Farringdon Wt.*
Altman, L. P., CBE (1996)	*Cripplegate Wn.*
Andrade, P. (1999)	*Farringdon Wt.*
Angell, E. H. (1991)	*Cripplegate Wt.*
Archibald, *Deputy* W. W. (1986)	*Cornhill*
Ayers, K. E. (1996)	*Bassishaw*
Balls, H. D. (1970)	*Castle Baynard*
Barker, *Deputy* J. A. (1981)	*Cripplegate Wn.*
Barnes-Yallowley, H. M. F. (1986)	*Coleman Street*
Barter, S. (1999)	*Langbourn*
Beale, *Deputy* M. J. (1979)	*Lime Street*
Bird, J. L., OBE (1977)	*Bridge*
Bowman, J. C. R. (1995)	*Aldgate*
Bradshaw, D. J. (1991)	*Cripplegate Wn.*
Bramwell, F. M. (1983)	*Langbourn*
Brewster, J. W., OBE (1994)	*Bassishaw*
Brighton, R. L. (1984)	*Portsoken*
Brooks, W. I. B. (1988)	*Billingsgate*
Byllam-Barnes, J. C. F. B. (1997)	*Cheap*
Caspi, D. R. (1994)	*Bridge*
Cassidy, *Deputy* M. J. (1989)	*Coleman Street*
Catt, B. F. (1982)	*Farringdon Wn.*
Chadwick, R. A. H. (1994)	*Tower*
Challis, *Deputy* G. H., CBE (1978)	*Langbourn*
Charkham, J. P. (1996)	*Farringdon Wt.*
Cohen, Mrs C. M. (1986)	*Lime Street*
Cole, Lt.-Col. Sir Colin, KCB, KCVO, TD (1964)	*Castle Baynard*
Cotgrove, D. (1991)	*Lime Street*
Currie, *Deputy* Miss S. E. M. (1985)	*Cripplegate Wt.*
Daily-Hunt, R. B. (1989)	*Cripplegate Wt.*
Darwin, G. E. (1995)	*Farringdon Wt.*
Davis, C. B. (1991)	*Bread Street*
Dove, W. H., MBE (1993)	*Bishopsgate*
Dunitz, A. A. (1984)	*Portsoken*
Eskenzi, *Deputy* A. N. (1970)	*Farringdon Wn.*
Eve, R. A. (1980)	*Cheap*
Everett, K. M. (1984)	*Candlewick*
Falk, F. A., TD (1997)	*Broad Street*
Farr, M. C. (1998)	*Walbrook*
Farrow, M. W. W. (1996)	*Farringdon Wt.*
Farthing, R. B. C. (1981)	*Aldgate*
FitzGerald, *Deputy* R. C. A. (1981)	*Bread Street*
Forbes, G. B. (1993)	*Bishopsgate*
Fraser, S. J. (1993)	*Coleman Street*
Fraser, W. B. (1981)	*Vintry*
Galloway, A. D. (1981)	*Broad Street*
Gillon, G. M. F. (1995)	*Cordwainer*
Ginsburg, S. (1990)	*Bishopsgate*
Gowman, *Deputy* Miss A. J. (1991)	*Dowgate*
Graves, A. C. (1985)	*Bishopsgate*
Green, C. (1994)	*Aldersgate*
Hall, B. R. H. (1995)	*Farringdon Wn.*
Halliday, Mrs P. (1992)	*Walbrook*
Hardwick, Dr P. B. (1987)	*Aldgate*
Harris, B. N. (1996)	*Broad Street*
Hart, *Deputy* M. G. (1970)	*Bridge*
Haynes, J. E. H. (1986)	*Cornhill*
Henderson-Begg, M. (1977)	*Coleman Street*
Holland, *Deputy* J., CBE (1972)	*Aldgate*
Holliday, Mrs E. H. L. (1987)	*Vintry*
Horlock, H. W. S. (1969)	*Farringdon Wn.*
Jackson, L. St J. T. (1978)	*Bread Street*
Kellett, Mrs M. W. F. (1986)	*Tower*
Kemp, D. L. (1984)	*Coleman Street*
King, A. (1999)	*Queenhithe*
Knowles, S. K. (1984)	*Candlewick*
Lawrence, G. A. (1994)	*Farringdon Wt.*
Lawson, G. C. H. (1971)	*Portsoken*
Leck, P. (1998)	*Aldersgate*
Littlechild, Mrs V. (1998)	*Cripplegate Wt.*
Luder, I. D. (1998)	*Farringdon Wn.*
McGuinness, C. (1997)	*Castle Baynard*
MacLellan, *Deputy* A. P. W. (1989)	*Walbrook*
McNeil, I. D. (1977)	*Lime Street*
Malins, *Deputy* J. H., QC (1981)	*Farringdon Wt.*
Martinelli, *Deputy* P. J. (1994)	*Bassishaw*
Mayhew, Miss J. (1986)	*Queenhithe*
Mayhew, J. P. (1996)	*Aldersgate*
Mead, Mrs W. (1997)	*Farringdon Wt.*
Mitchell, *Deputy* C. R. (1971)	*Castle Baynard*
Mobsby, *Deputy* D. J. L. (1985)	*Billingsgate*
Montgomery, B. (1999)	*Dowgate*
Mooney, B. D. F. (1998)	*Queenhithe*
Moss, A. D. (1989)	*Tower*

Nash, *Deputy* Mrs J. C. (1983)　　*Aldersgate*
Newman, Mrs P. B. (1989)　　*Aldersgate*
O'Ferrall, P. C. K., OBE (1996)　　*Aldgate*
Owen, Mrs J. (1975)　　*Langbourn*
Owen-Ward, J. R. (1983)　　*Bridge*
Parmley, A. C., PH.D. (1992)　　*Vintry*
Pembroke, *Deputy* Mrs A. M. F. (1978)　　*Cheap*
Platts-Mills, J. F. F., QC　　*Farringdon Wt.*
Price, E. E. (1996)　　*Farringdon Wt.*
Pulman, *Deputy* G. A. G. (1983)　　*Tower*
Punter, C. (1993)　　*Cripplegate Wn.*
Quilter, S. D. (1998)　　*Cripplegate Wt.*
Regan, R. D. (1998)　　*Farringdon Wn.*
Revell-Smith, *Deputy* P. A., CBE (1959)　　*Vintry*
Rigby, P. P., CBE (1972)　　*Farringdon Wn.*
Robinson, Mrs D. C. (1989)　　*Bishopsgate*
Roney, E. P. T., CBE (1974)　　*Bishopsgate*
Samuel, *Deputy* Mrs I., MBE (1971)　　*Portsoken*
Sargant, K. A. (1991)　　*Cornhill*
Saunders, *Deputy* R. (1975)　　*Candlewick*
Scott, J. (1999)　　*Broad Street*
Scriven, R. G., CBE (1984)　　*Candlewick*
Sellon, S. A., OBE, TD (1990)　　*Cordwainer*
Shalit, D. M. (1972)　　*Farringdon Wn.*
Sharp, *Deputy* Mrs I. M. (1974)　　*Queenhithe*
Sherlock, M. R. C. (1992)　　*Dowgate*
Snyder, *Deputy* M. J. (1986)　　*Cordwainer*
Spanner, J. H., TD (1984)　　*Broad Street*
Stevenson, F. P. (1994)　　*Cripplegate Wn.*
Taylor, J. A. F., TD (1991)　　*Bread Street*
Thorp, C. R. (1996)　　*Billingsgate*
Trotter, J. (1993)　　*Billingsgate*
Walsh, S. (1989)　　*Farringdon Wt.*
Warner, D. W. (1994)　　*Cripplegate Wn.*
Willoughby, P. J. (1985)　　*Bishopsgate*
Wilmot, R. T. D. (1973)　　*Cordwainer*
Wixley, G. R. A., CBE, TD (1964)　　*Coleman Street*

The City Guilds (Livery Companies)

The constitution of the livery companies has been unchanged for centuries. There are three ranks of membership: freemen, liverymen and assistants. A person can become a freeman by patrimony (through a parent having been a freeman); by servitude (through having served an apprenticeship to a freeman); or by redemption (by purchase).

Election to the livery is the prerogative of the company, who can elect any of its freemen as liverymen. Assistants are usually elected from the livery and form a Court of Assistants which is the governing body of the company. The Master (in some companies called the Prime Warden) is elected annually from the assistants.

As at June 1998, 22,923 liverymen of the guilds were entitled to vote at elections at Common Hall.

The order of precedence, omitting extinct companies, is given in parenthesis after the name of each company in the list below. In certain companies the election of Master or Prime Warden for the year does not take place until the autumn. In such cases the Master or Prime Warden for 1999–2000 is given.

THE TWELVE GREAT COMPANIES
In order of civic precedence

MERCERS (*1*). *Hall*, Ironmonger Lane, London EC2V 8HE. *Livery*, 253. *Clerk*, C. H. Parker. *Master*, R.C. Cunis
GROCERS (*2*). *Hall*, Princes Street, London EC2R 8AD. *Livery*, 320. *Clerk*, Brig. P. P. Rawlins. *Master*, T. W. N. Guinness
DRAPERS (*3*). *Hall*, Throgmorton Avenue, London EC2N 2DQ. *Livery*, 254. *Clerk*, A. L. Lang. *Master*, R. W. P. Beharrell
FISHMONGERS (*4*). *Hall*, London Bridge, London EC4R 9EL. *Livery*, 360. *Clerk*, K. S. Waters. *Prime Warden*, The Earl of Erroll
GOLDSMITHS (*5*). *Hall*, Foster Lane, London EC2V 6BN. *Livery*, 280. *Clerk*, R. D. Buchanan-Dunlop. *Prime Warden*, The Rt. Hon. Sir Adam Butler
MERCHANT TAYLORS (*6/7*). *Hall*, 30 Threadneedle Street, London EC2R 8JB. *Livery*, 300. *Clerk*, D. A. Peck. *Master*, Sir Geoffrey Holland
SKINNERS (*6/7*). *Hall*, 8 Dowgate Hill, London EC4R 2SP. *Livery*, 390. *Clerk*, Capt. D. Hart Dyke. *Master*, P. Attenborough
HABERDASHERS (*8*). *Hall*, 39–40 Bartholomew Close, London EC1A 7JN. *Livery*, 320. *Clerk*, Capt. R. J. Fisher. *Master*, (until 23 November) M. D. G. Wheldon, FRICS; (from 24 November) B. E. Shawcross
SALTERS (*9*). *Hall*, 4 Fore Street, London EC2Y 5DE. *Livery*, 165. *Clerk*, Col. M. P. Barneby. *Master*, The Rt. Hon. Lord Lloyd of Berwick
IRONMONGERS (*10*). *Hall*, Shaftesbury Place, Barbican, London EC2Y 8AA. *Livery*, 129. *Clerk*, J. A. Oliver. *Master*, S. D. Apsley
VINTNERS (*11*). *Hall*, Upper Thames Street, London EC4V 3BG. *Livery*, 290. *Clerk*, Brig. M. Smythe. *Master*, D. B. Butler-Adams
CLOTHWORKERS (*12*). *Hall*, Dunster Court, Mincing Lane, London EC3R 7AH. *Livery*, 200. *Clerk*, M. G. T. Harris. *Master*, J. C. Hutchins

OTHER CITY GUILDS
In alphabetical order

ACTUARIES (*91*). 81 Worrin Road, Shenfield, Brentwood, Essex CM15 8JN. *Livery*, 198. *Clerk*, Mrs J. V. Evans. *Master*, P. D. Esslemont
THE GUILD OF AIR PILOTS AND AIR NAVIGATORS (*81*). Cobham House, 9 Warwick Court, Gray's Inn, London WC1R 5DJ. *Livery*, 500. *Clerk*, Air Vice-Marshal R. G. Peters, CB. *Master*, A. G. Thorning
THE SOCIETY OF APOTHECARIES (*58*). *Hall*, 14 Black Friars Lane, London EC4V 6EJ. *Livery*, 1,200. *Clerk*, Lt.-Col. R. J. Stringer. *Master*, J. H. D. Briscoe
THE COMPANY OF ARBITRATORS (*93*). 13 Hall Gardens, Colney Heath, St Albans, Herts AL4 0QF. *Livery*, 160. *Clerk*, Mrs G. Duffy. *Master*, M. R. Ludlow
THE COMPANY OF ARMOURERS AND BRASIERS (*22*). *Hall*, 81 Coleman Street, London EC2R 5BJ. *Livery*, 120. *Clerk*, Cdr. T. J. K. Sloane, OBE, RN. *Master*, The Vernerable C. J. H. Wagstaff
BAKERS (*19*). *Hall*, Harp Lane, London EC3R 6DP. *Livery*, 370. *Clerk*, R. E. B. Sawyer. *Master*, J. W. Tompkins
BARBERS (*17*). *Hall*, Monkwell Square, Wood Street, London EC2Y 5BL. *Livery*, 200. *Clerk*, Brig. A. F. Eastburn. *Master*, G. G. Macdonald

BASKETMAKERS (*52*). 48 Seymour Walk, London SW10 9NF. *Livery*, 317. *Clerk*, Maj. G. J. Flint-Shipman, TD. *Prime Warden*, N. E. Woolley

BLACKSMITHS (*40*). 48 Upwood Road, London SE12 8AN. *Livery*, 210. *Clerk*, C. Jeal. *Prime Warden*, Col. Sir Neil Thorne

BOWYERS (*38*). 11 Aldermans Hill, London N13 4YD. *Livery*, 105. *Clerk*, J. R. Owen-Ward. *Master*, E. J. Burnett

BREWERS (*14*). *Hall*, Aldermanbury Square, London EC2V 7HR. *Livery*, 130. *Clerk*, Brig. D. J. Ross, CBE. *Master*, J. H. Wells, DL

BRODERERS (*48*). Ember House, 35–37 Creek Road, East Molesey, Surrey KT8 9BE. *Livery*, 167. *Clerk*, P. J. C. Crouch. *Master*, B. W. Pride

BUILDERS MERCHANTS (*88*). 4 College Hill, London EC4R 2RB. *Livery*, 185. *Clerk*, Miss S. M. Robinson, TD. *Master*, D. C. E. Ridgeon

BUTCHERS (*24*). *Hall*, 87 Bartholomew Close, London EC1A 7EB. *Livery*, 622. *Clerk*, G. J. Sharp. *Master*, J. F. Jackman

CARMEN (*77*). 35/37 Ludgate Hill, London EC4M 7JN. *Livery*, 430. *Clerk*, Cdr. R. M. H. Bawtree, OBE, RN. *Master*, B. H. Owen

CARPENTERS (*26*). *Hall*, 1 Throgmorton Avenue, London EC2N 2JJ. *Livery*, 150. *Clerk*, Maj.-Gen. P. T. Stevenson, OBE. *Master*, W. S. Haynes

CHARTERED ACCOUNTANTS IN ENGLAND AND WALES (*86*). The Rustlings, Valley Close, Studham, Dunstable LU6 2QN. *Livery*, 340. *Clerk*, C. Bygrave. *Master*, A. M. C. Staniforth

CHARTERED ARCHITECTS (*98*). 82A Muswell Hill Road, London N10 3JR. *Livery*, 160. *Clerk*, D. Cole-Adams. *Master*, Lady Williams, MBE

CHARTERED SECRETARIES AND ADMINISTRATORS (*87*). Sadler's Hall, 3rd Floor, 40 Gutter Lane, London EC2V 6BR. *Livery*, 230. *Clerk*, C. H. Grinsied. *Master*, W. C. Hammond, MBE

THE WORSHIPFUL COMPANY OF CHARTERED SURVEYORS (*85*). 16 St Mary-at-Hill, London EC3R 8EE. *Livery*, 350. *Clerk*, Mrs A. L. Jackson. *Master*, N. P. L. Baker

CLOCKMAKERS (*61*). Room 66–67 Albert Buildings, 49 Queen Victoria Street, London EC4N 4SE. *Livery*, 230. *Clerk*, Gp Capt. P. H. Gibson, MBE. *Master*, Sir George White, BT, FSA

COACHMAKERS AND COACH HARNESS MAKERS (*72*). 8 Chandlers Court, Burwell, Cambridge CB5 0AZ. *Livery*, 400. *Clerk*, Gp Capt. G. Bunn, CBE. *Master*, Hon. Roy Constantine

CONSTRUCTORS (*99*). 181 Fentiman Road, London SW8 1JY. *Livery*, 130. *Clerk*, L. L. Brace. *Master*, J. M. Burrell

COOKS (*35*). Registry Chambers, The Old Deanery, Deans Court, London EC4V 5AA. *Livery*, 75. *Clerk*, M. C. Thatcher. *Master*, P. D. Herbage

COOPERS (*36*). *Hall*, 13 Devonshire Square, London EC2M 4TH. *Livery*, 260. *Clerk*, J. A. Newton. *Master*, W. M. Heath

CORDWAINERS (*27*). 8 Warrick Court, Gray's Inn, London WC1R 5DJ. *Livery*, 163. *Clerk*, Lt.-Col. J. R. Blundell, RM. *Master*, Rear-Adm. J. F. T. G. Salt, CB

THE COMPANY OF CURRIERS (*29*). Kestrel Cottage, East Knoyle, Salisbury SP3 6AD. *Livery*, 94. *Clerk*, Gp Capt. F. J. Hamilton. *Master*, D. A. Stewart

CUTLERS (*18*). *Hall*, Warwick Lane, London EC4M 7BR. *Livery*, 100. *Clerk*, K. S. G. Hinde, OBE, TD. *Master*, The Hon. R. J. I. Mais

DISTILLERS (*69*). 71 Lincoln's Inn Fields, London WC2A 3JF. *Livery*, 270. *Clerk*, C. V. Hughes. *Master*, R. H. Nicholson

DYERS (*13*). *Hall*, 10 Dowgate Hill, London EC4R 2ST. *Livery*, 123. *Clerk*, J. R. Chambers, FCA. *Prime Warden*, R. A. Leuchars, FRACS, B.Sc.

ENGINEERS (*94*). Kiln Bank, Bodle Street Green, Hailsham, E. Sussex BN27 4UA. *Livery*, 290. *Clerk*, Cdr. B. D. Gibson, RN. *Master*, Dr L. J. Weaver, CBE

ENVIRONMENTAL CLEANERS (*97*). Woodside Cottage, 44 New Road, Bengeo, Herts SG14 3JL. *Livery*, 235. *Clerk*, J. C. M. Chapman. *Master*, R. D. G. Burtinshaw

FAN MAKERS (*76*). 2 Bolts Hill, Castle Camps, Cambridge CB1 6TL. *Livery*, 202. *Clerk*, Lt.-Col. I. R. P. Green. *Master*, R. M. Freeman

FARMERS (*80*). *Hall*, 3 Cloth Street, London EC1A 7LD. *Livery*, 300. *Clerk*, Miss M. L. Winter. *Master*, R. A. Brooks

FARRIERS (*55*). 19 Queen Street, Chipperfield, Kings Langley, Herts WD4 9BT. *Livery*, 375. *Clerk*, Mrs C. C. Clifford. *Master*, Lady Graham

FELTMAKERS OF LONDON (*63*). Providence Cottage, Chute Cadley, Andover, Hants SP11 9EB. *Livery*, 170. *Clerk*, Lt.-Col. C. J. Holroyd. *Master*, Cdre I. R. Welsey-Harding

FLETCHERS (*39*). *Hall*, 3 Cloth Street, London EC1A 7LD. *Livery*, 108. *Clerk*, J. R. Owen-Ward. *Master*, H. R. Vogt

FOUNDERS (*33*). *Hall*, Number One, Cloth Fair, London EC1A 7JA. *Livery*, 175. *Clerk*, A. J. Gillett. *Master*, Sir Ian Ley, BT

FRAMEWORK KNITTERS (*64*). Whitegarth Chambers, 37 The Uplands, Loughton, Essex IG10 1NQ. *Livery*, 211. *Clerk*, H. W. H. Ellis. *Master*, J. M. Dean

FRUTTERERS (*45*). Chapelstones, 84 High Street, Codford St Mary, Warminster BA12 0ND. *Livery*, 262. *Clerk*, Lt.-Col. L. G. French. *Master*, L. S. Olins

FUELLERS (*95*). 22 Broadfields, Headstone Lane, Hatch End, Middx HA2 6NH. *Livery*, 66. *Clerk*, R. A. Riley. *Master*, F. B. Harrison, CBE

FURNITURE MAKERS (*83*). *Hall*, 9 Little Trinity Lane, London EC4V 2AD. *Livery*, 296. *Clerk*, Mrs J. A. Wright. *Master*, S. F. Brown

GARDENERS (*66*). 25 Luke Street, London EC2A 4AR. *Livery*, 247. *Clerk*, Col. N. G. S. Gray. *Master*, V. Robinson

GIRDLERS (*23*). *Girdlers' Hall*, Basinghall Avenue, London EC2V 5DD. *Livery*, 80. *Clerk*, Lt.-Col. R. Sullivan. *Master*, J. M. Westall

GLASS SELLERS OF LONDON (*71*). 43 Aragon Avenue, Thames Ditton, Surrey KT7 0PY. *Livery*, 180. *Hon. Clerk*, B. J. Rawles. *Master*, The Rt. Revd J. Waine, KCVO

GLAZIERS AND PAINTERS OF GLASS (*53*). *Hall*, 9 Montague Close, London SE1 9DD. *Livery*, 240. *Clerk*, Col. D. W. Eking. *Master*, P. R. Batchelor

GLOVERS (*62*). 71 Ifield Road, London SW10 9AU. *Livery*, 270. *Clerk*, Mrs M. Hood. *Master*, J. D. Henderson Clarke, FRSA

GOLD AND SILVER WYRE DRAWERS (*74*). 'Twizzletwig', The Ballands South, Fetcham, Leatherhead, Surrey KT22 9EP. *Livery*, 310. *Clerk*, T. J. Waller. *Master*, Sir Peter G. Yarranton

GUNMAKERS (*73*). The Proof House, 48-50 Commercial Road, London E1 1LP. *Livery*, 250. *Clerk*, J. M. Riches. *Master*, R. M. Mitchell

HORNERS (*54*). Whitethorns, Rannoch Road, Crowborough, E. Sussex TN6 1RA. *Livery*, 244. *Clerk*, A. R. Layard. *Master*, L. P. Smith

INFORMATION TECHNOLOGISTS (*100*). 39A Bartholomew Close, London EC1A 7JN. *Livery*, 270. *Clerk*, Mrs G. Davies. *Master*, P. Cropper

INNHOLDERS (*32*). *Hall*, 30 College Street, London EC4R 2RH. *Livery*, 129. *Clerk*, D. E. Bulger. *Master*, G. M. Sayer, CBE

INSURERS (*92*). *Hall*, 20 Aldermanbury, London EC2V 7HY. *Livery*, 375. *Clerk*, L. J. Walters. *Master*, D. R. Losse

JOINERS AND CEILERS (*41*). 75 Meadway Drive, Horsell, Woking, Surrey GU21 4TF. *Livery*, 125. *Clerk*, Mrs A. L. Jackson. *Master*, M. J. Chapman

LAUNDERERS (*89*). *Hall*, 9 Montague Close, London Bridge, London SE1 9DD. *Livery*, 250. *Clerk*, Mrs J. Polek. *Master*, P. C. Crane

LEATHERSELLERS (*15*). *Hall*, 15 St Helen's Place, London EC3A 6DQ. *Livery*, 150. *Clerk*, Capt. J. G. F. Cooke, OBE, RN. *Master*, D. R. Curtis

LIGHTMONGERS (*96*). Crown Wharf, 11A Coldharbour, Blackwall Reach, London E14 9NS. *Livery*, 145. *Clerk*, D. B. Wheatley. *Master*, R. C. Oliver

LORINERS (*57*). 50 Cheyne Avenue, London E1W 2QR. *Livery*, 355. *Clerk*, G. B. Forbes. *Master*, J. R. A. Allison

MAKERS OF PLAYING CARDS (*75*). 6 The Priory, Godstone, Surrey RH9 8NL. *Livery*, 147. *Clerk*, M. J. Smyth. *Master*, W. G. Hunt, TD

MARKETORS (*90*). 13 Hall Gardens, Colney Heath, St Albans, Herts AL4 0PF. *Livery*, 220. *Clerk*, Mrs G. Duffy. *Master*, Dr J. A. P. Treasure

MASONS (*30*). 22 Cannon Hill, Southgate, London N14 6LG. *Livery*, 122. *Clerk*, P. F. Clark. *Master*, D. Ruffle

HONOURABLE COMPANY OF MASTER MARINERS (*78*). HQS Wellington, Temple Stairs, Victoria Embankment, London WC2R 2PN. *Livery*, 250. *Clerk*, J. A. V. Maddock. *Master*, Capt L. A. Holder

MUSICIANS (*50*). 75 Watling Street, London EC4M 9BJ. *Livery*, 365. *Clerk*, S. F. N. Waley. *Master*, D. R. Hill

NEEDLEMAKERS (*65*). 5 Staple Inn, London WC1V 7QH. *Livery*, 230. *Clerk*, M. G. Cook. *Master*, B. Hatfield

PAINTER-STAINERS (*28*). *Hall*, 9 Little Trinity Lane, London EC4V 2AD. *Livery*, 300. *Clerk*, Col. W. J. Chesshyre. *Master*, R. E. Millard

PATTENMAKERS (*70*). Vanguard House, Sutton Valence, Kent ME17 3JA. *Livery*, 200. *Clerk*, Lt. Col. R. W. Murfin, TD. *Master*, R. J. H. Edwards

PAVIORS (*56*). 3 Ridgemount Gardens, Enfield, Middx EN2 8QL. *Livery*, 230. *Clerk*, J. L. White. *Master*, J. H. Cruse

PEWTERERS (*16*). *Hall*, Oat Lane, London EC2V 7DE. *Livery*, 119. *Clerk*, Cdr. A. St J. Steiner, OBE. *Master*, M. G. C. Gibbs

THE COMPANY OF PLAISTERERS (*46*). *Hall*, 1 London Wall, London EC2Y 5JU. *Livery*, 213. *Clerk*, R. Vickers. *Master*, P. J. Cook

PLUMBERS (*31*). Room 28, 49 Queen Victoria Street, London EC4N 4SA. *Livery*, 347. *Clerk*, Lt.-Col. R. J. A. Paterson-Fox. *Master*, R. H. M. Moir

POULTERS (*34*). 23 Orchard Drive, Chorleywood, Herts WD3 5QN. *Livery*, 180. *Clerk*, Mrs G. W. Butcher. *Master*, P. C. Keevil

SADDLERS (*25*). *Hall*, 40 Gutter Lane, London EC2V 6BR. *Livery*, 75. *Clerk*, Gp Capt. W. S. Brereton Martin, CBE. *Master*, M. F. S. Bullen

SCIENTIFIC INSTRUMENT MAKERS (*84*). 9 Montague Close, London SE1 9DD. *Livery*, 235. *Clerk*, F. G. Everard. *Master*, Rear-Adm. J. M. T. Hilton

SCRIVENERS (*44*). HQS Wellington, Temple Stairs, Victoria Embankment, London WC2R 2PN. *Livery*, 170. *Clerk*, G. A. Hill. *Master*, P. H. Grove

SHIPWRIGHTS (*59*). *Hall*, Barbican, London EC2Y 8AA. *Livery*, 400. *Clerk*, Capt. R. F. Channon, RN. *Prime Warden*, Dr T. J. Parker

THE CITY OF LONDON SOLICITORS' COMPANY (*79*). 4 College Hill, London EC2R 2RB. *Livery*, 260. *Clerk*, Miss S. M. Robinson, TD. *Master*, R. Finch

SPECTACLE MAKERS (*60*). *Hall*, Black Friars Lane, London EC4V 6EL. *Livery*, 325. *Clerk*, Lt.-Col. J. A. B. Salmon, OBE, LLB. *Master*, B. J. Mitchell, FCA, FRSA

STATIONERS AND NEWSPAPER MAKERS (*47*). *Hall*, Ave Maria Lane, London EC4M 7DD. *Livery*, 462. *Clerk*, Brig. D. G. Sharp, AFC. *Master*, H. F. Chappell

TALLOW CHANDLERS (*21*). *Hall*, 4 Dowgate Hill, London EC4R 2SH. *Livery*, 180. *Clerk*, Brig. W. K. L. Prosser, CBE, MC. *Master*, C. R. Lambourne, FCA

TIN PLATE WORKERS ALIAS WIRE WORKERS (*67*). Bartholomew House, 66 Westbury Road, New Malden, Surrey KT3 5AS. *Livery*, 200. *Clerk*, M. Henderson-Begg. *Master*, M. J. Lawrence

TOBACCO PIPE MAKERS AND TOBACCO BLENDERS (*82*). Hackhurst Farm, Lower Dicker, Hailsham, E. Sussex BN27 4BP. *Livery*, 156. *Clerk*, N. J. Hallings-Pott. *Master*, I. M. Panto

TURNERS (*51*). 182 Temple Chambers, Temple Avenue, London EC4Y 0HP. *Livery*, 190. *Clerk*, E. A. Windsor Clive. *Master*, Maj.-Gen. C. Tyler, CENG

THE TYLERS AND BRICKLAYERS COMPANY (*37*). Hawthorns, Claygate Lane, Thames Ditton, Surrey KT7 0DT. *Livery*, 126. *Clerk*, J. A. Norris. *Master*, G. J. Bateman

UPHOLDERS (*49*). Hall in the Wood, 46 Quail Gardens, Selsdon Vale, Croydon CR2 8TF. *Livery*, 225. *Clerk*, J. P. Cody. *Master*, B. E. Chapman, CBE

WATER CONSERVATORS (*102*). *Hall*, 16 St Mary-at-Hill, London EC2R 8EF. *Livery*, 148. *Hon. Clerk*, R. A. Riley. *Master*, P. N. Paul

WAX CHANDLERS (*20*). *Hall*, Gresham Street, London EC2V 7AD. *Livery*, 125. *Clerk*, John Williams (*acting*). *Master*, R. B. Blaxland

WEAVERS (*42*). Saddlers' House, Gutter Lane, London EC2V 6BR. *Livery*, 125. *Clerk*, Mrs F. Newcombe. *Upper Bailiff*, R. D. B. Mynors

WHEELWRIGHTS (*68*). Ember House, 35–37 Creek Road, East Molesey, Surrey KT8 9BE. *Livery*, 212. *Clerk*, P. J. C. Crouch. *Master*, T. R. Sermon

WOOLMEN (*43*). Hollands, Hedsor Road, Bourne End, Bucks SL8 5EE. *Livery*, 135. *Clerk*, F. Allen. *Master*, Sir William Goring, Bt.

WORLD TRADERS (*101*). 36 Ladbroke Grove, London W11 2PA. *Livery*, 100. *Clerk*, N. R. Pullman. *Master*, Miss S. Hughes

THE COMPANY OF FIREFIGHTERS (*No livery*). The Insurance Hall, 20 Aldermanbury, London EC2V 7GF. *Freemen*, 130. *Clerk*, G. P. Ellis. *Master*, J. E. Lawrence, MBE

THE COMPANY OF PARISH CLERKS (*No livery*). c/o 1 Dean Trench Street, London SW1P 3HB. *Members*, 95. *Clerk*, Lt. Col. B. J. N. Coombes. *Master*, W. H. Dove, MBE

THE COMPANY OF WATERMEN AND LIGHTERMEN (*No livery*). *Hall*, 16 St Mary-at-Hill, London EC3R 8EF. *Craft Owning Freemen*, 365. *Clerk*, C. Middlemiss. *Master*, L. G. Burrow

LONDON BOROUGH COUNCILS

Council	Municipal offices	Population	Band D charge 2000	Chief Executive	Mayor (a) Lord Mayor 2000–1
Barking and Dagenham	°Dagenham, RM10 7BN	143,681	£784.42	G. Farrant	P. J. Manley
Barnet	†The Burroughs, Hendon, NW4 4BG	293,564	£814.89	*vacant*	Ms G. Sargeant
Bexley Council	‡Bexleyheath, Kent DA6 7LB	215,615	£802.29	C. Duffield	J. Wilkinson
Brent	†Forty Lane, Wembley HA9 9EZ	243,025	£739.81	G. Daniel	J. Bacchus
Bromley	°Bromley, BR1 3UH	290,609	£735.66	David Bartlett	D. Crowe
§Camden	†Judd Street, WC1H 9JE	170,444	£906.19	S. Bundred	Ms H. Johnson
§City of Westminster	City Hall, Victoria Street, SW1E 6QP	174,814	£375.00	P. Rogers	(a) M. Brahams
Croydon	Taberner House, Park Lane, Croydon, CR9 3JS	313,510	£807.72	D. Wechsler	Ms M. Walker
Ealing	†Uxbridge Road, W5 2HL	275,257	£756.15	Ms G. Guy	D. Bond
Enfield	°Enfield, EN1 3XA	257,417	£797.30	D. Plank	A. Constantinides
§Greenwich	†Wellington Street, SE18 6PW	207,650	£883.35	(until December) D. Brooks; (from January 2001) Ms M. Ney	J. Sekhon
§Hackney	†Mare Street, E8 1EA	181,248	£841.59	M. Caller	J. Lobenstein, MBE
§Hammersmith and Fulham	†King Street, W6 9JU	148,502	£878.40	R. Harbord	A. Slaughter
Haringey	°Wood Green, N22 4LE	202,204	£932.00	D. Warwick	H. Brown
Harrow	°Harrow, HA1 2UJ	200,100	£852.63	T. Redmond	K. Thammaiah
Havering	†Romford, RM1 3BD	229,492	£853.00	H. W. Tinworth	B. Eagling
Hillingdon	°Uxbridge, UB8 1UW	231,602	£824.11	D. Leatham	A. Kanjee
Hounslow	°Lampton Road, Hounslow, TW3 4DN	204,397	£860.15	D. Myers	D. Sandhu
§Islington	†Upper Street, N1 2UD	164,686	£887.00	Ms L. Fullick	Ms M. Powell
§Kensington and Chelsea (RB)	†Hornton Street, W8 7NX	138,394	£483.56	*vacant*	R. Walker-Arnott
Kingston upon Thames (RB)	Guildhall, Kingston upon Thames, KT1 1EU	132,996	£863.19	B. McDonald	S. Mirza
§Lambeth	†Brixton Hill, SW2 1RW	244,834	£656.00	Ms F. Boardman	Ms C. Whelan
§Lewisham	†Catford, SE6 4RU	230,983	£798.25	Dr B. Quirk	D. Sullivan
Merton	°London Road, Morden, SM4 5DX	168,470	£866.69	R. Paine	I. Munn
§Newham	†East Ham, E6 2RP	212,170	£768.13	D. Burbage	B. Collier
Redbridge	†Ilford, IG1 1DD	226,218	£811.00	R. Hampson	Ms M. Hoskins
Richmond upon Thames	°Richmond Road, Twickenham, TW1 3AA	160,732	£908.65	Mrs G. Norton	Ms B. Westmorland
§Southwark	†Peckham Road, SE5 8UB	218,541	£845.44	R. A. Coomber	H. Canagasebey
Sutton	‡St Nicholas Way, Sutton, SM1 1EA	168,880	£795.56	Mrs P. Hughes	L. Hussain
§Tower Hamlets	107A Commercial Street, E1 6BG	160,064	£726.52	Ms E. Kelly	S. Alom
Waltham Forest	†Forest Road, Walthamstow, E17 4JF	212,033	£877.59	A. Tobias	M. Nasim
§Wandsworth	†Wandsworth, SW18 2PU	252,425	£398.00	G. K. Jones	J. Garrett

§ Inner London Borough
RB Royal Borough
° Civic centre
† Town Hall
‡ Civic Offices

Wales

The Principality of Wales (Cymru) occupies the extreme west of the central southern portion of the island of Great Britain, with a total area of 20,758 sq. km (8,015 sq.miles): land 20,628 sq. km (7,965 sq. miles); inland water 130 sq. km (50 sq. miles). It is bounded on the north by the Irish Sea, on the south by the Bristol Channel, on the east by the English counties of Cheshire, Shropshire, Worcestershire and Gloucestershire, and on the west by St George's Channel.

Across the Menai Straits is the island of Anglesey (Ynys Mon) (276 sq. miles), communication with which is facilitated by the Menai Suspension Bridge (1,000 ft long) built by Telford in 1826, and by the tubular railway bridge (1,100 ft long) built by Stephenson in 1850. Holyhead harbour, on Holy Isle (north-west of Anglesey), provides accommodation for ferry services to Dublin (70 miles).

POPULATION

The population at the 1991 census was 2,835,073 (males 1,370,104; females 1,464,969). The average density of population in 1991 was 1.36 persons per hectare.

RELIEF

Wales is a country of extensive tracts of high plateau and shorter stretches of mountain ranges deeply dissected by river valleys. Lower-lying ground is largely confined to the coastal belt and the lower parts of the valleys. The highest mountains are those of Snowdonia in the north-west (Snowdon, 3,559 ft), Berwyn (Aran Fawddwy, 2,971 ft), Cader Idris (Pen y Gadair, 2,928 ft), Dyfed (Plynlimon, 2,467 ft), and the Black Mountain, Brecon Beacons and Black Forest ranges in the south-east (Carmarthen Van, 2,630 ft, Peny Fan, 2,906 ft, Waun Fâch, 2,660 ft).

HYDROGRAPHY

The principal river rising in Wales is the Severn, which flows from the slopes of Plynlimon to the English border. The Wye (130 miles) also rises in the slopes of Plynlimon. The Usk (56 miles) flows into the Bristol Channel, through Gwent. The Dee (70 miles) rises in Bala Lake and flows through the Vale of Llangollen, where an aqueduct (built by Telford in 1805) carries the Pontcysyllte branch of the Shropshire Union Canal across the valley. The estuary of the Dee is the navigable portion, 14 miles in length and about five miles in breadth, and the tide rushes in with dangerous speed over the 'Sands of Dee'. The Towy (68 miles), Teifi (50 miles), Taff (40 miles), Dovey (30 miles), Taf (25 miles) and Conway (24 miles), the last named broad and navigable, are wholly Welsh rivers.

The largest natural lake is Bala (Llyn Tegid) in Gwynedd, nearly four miles long and about one mile wide. Lake Vyrnwy is an artificial reservoir, about the size of Bala, and forms the water supply of Liverpool; Birmingham is supplied from reservoirs in the Elan and Claerwen valleys.

WELSH LANGUAGE

According to the 1991 census results, the percentage of persons of three years and over able to speak Welsh was:

Clwyd	18.2	Powys	20.2
Dyfed	43.7	S. Glamorgan	6.5
Gwent	2.4	W. Glamorgan	15.0
Gwynedd	61.0		
Mid Glamorgan	8.5	Wales	18.7

The 1991 figure represents a slight decline from 18.9 per cent in 1981 (1971, 20.8 per cent; 1961, 26 per cent).

FLAG

The flag of Wales, the Red Dragon (Y Ddraig Goch), is a red dragon on a field divided white over green (per fess argent and vert a dragon passant gules). The flag was augmented in 1953 by a royal badge on a shield encircled with a riband bearing the words *Ddraig Goch Ddyry Cychwyn* and imperially crowned, but this augmented flag is rarely used.

EARLY HISTORY

The earliest inhabitants of whom there is any record appear to have been subdued or exterminated by the Goidels (a people of Celtic race) in the Bronze Age. A further invasion of Celtic Brythons and Belgae followed in the ensuing Iron Age. The Roman conquest of southern Britain and Wales was for some time successfully opposed by Caratacus (Caractacus or Caradog), chieftain of the Catuvellauni and son of Cunobelinus (Cymbeline). South-east Wales was subjugated and the legionary fortress at Caerleon-on-Usk established by about AD 75–77; the conquest of Wales was completed by Agricola about AD 78. Communications were opened up by the construction of military roads from Chester to Caerleon-on-Usk and Caerwent, and from Chester to Conwy (and thence to Carmarthen and Neath). Christianity was introduced during the Roman occupation, in the fourth century.

ANGLO-SAXON ATTACKS

The Anglo-Saxon invaders of southern Britain drove the Celts into the mountain stronghold of Wales, and into Strathclyde (Cumberland and south-west Scotland) and Cornwall, giving them the name of *Waelisc* (Welsh), meaning 'foreign'. The West Saxons' victory of Deorham (AD 577) isolated Wales from Cornwall and the battle of Chester (AD 613) cut off communication with Strathclyde and northern Britain. In the eighth century the boundaries of the Welsh were further restricted by the annexations of Offa, King of Mercia, and counter-attacks were largely prevented by the construction of an artificial boundary from the Dee to the Wye (Offa's Dyke).

In the ninth century Rhodri Mawr (844–78) united the country and successfully resisted further incursions of the Saxons by land and raids of Norse and Danish pirates by sea, but at his death his three provinces of Gwynedd (north), Powys (mid) and Deheubarth (south) were divided among his three sons, Anarawd, Mervyn and Cadell. Cadell's son Hywel Dda ruled a large part of Wales and codified its laws but the provinces were not united again until the rule of Llewelyn ap Seisyllt (husband of the heiress of Gwynedd) from 1018 to 1023.

THE NORMAN CONQUEST

After the Norman conquest of England, William I created palatine counties along the Welsh frontier, and the Norman barons began to make encroachments into Welsh territory. The Welsh princes recovered many of their losses during the civil wars of Stephen's reign and in the early 13th century Owen Gruffydd, prince of Gwynedd, was the dominant figure in Wales. Under Llewelyn ap Iorwerth (1194–1240) the Welsh united in powerful resistance to English incursions and Llywelyn's privileges and *de facto* independence were recognised in Magna Carta. His grandson, Llywelyn ap Gruffydd, was the last native prince; he was killed in 1282 during hostilities between the Welsh and English, allowing Edward I of England to establish his authority over the country. On 7 February 1301, Edward of Caernarvon, son of Edward I, was created Prince of Wales, a title which has subsequently been borne by the eldest son of the sovereign.

Strong Welsh national feeling continued, expressed in the early 15th century in the rising led by Owain Glyndwr, but the situation was altered by the accession to the English throne in 1485 of Henry VII of the Welsh House of Tudor. Wales was politically assimilated to England under the Act of Union of 1535, which extended English laws to the Principality and gave it parliamentary representation for the first time.

EISTEDDFOD

The Welsh are a distinct nation, with a language and literature of their own, and the national bardic festival (Eisteddfod), instituted by Prince Rhys ap Griffith in 1176, is still held annually. These *Eisteddfodau* (sessions) form part of the *Gorsedd* (assembly), which is believed to date from the time of Prydian, a ruling prince in an age many centuries before the Christian era.

PRINCIPAL CITIES

CARDIFF

Cardiff, at the mouth of the Rivers Taff, Rhymney and Ely, is the capital city of Wales and a major administrative, commercial and business centre. The National Assembly for Wales was opened in Cardiff in 1999. It has many industries, including steel, and its flourishing port is within the Cardiff Bay area, subject of a major redevelopment continuing for many years.

The many fine buildings include the City Hall, the National Museum of Wales, University Buildings, Law Courts, Welsh Office, County Hall, Police Headquarters, the Temple of Peace and Health, Llandaff Cathedral, the Welsh National Folk Museum at St Fagans, Cardiff Castle, the New Theatre, the Sherman Theatre and the Welsh College of Music and Drama. More recent buildings include St David's Hall, Cardiff International Arena and World Trade Centre, and the Welsh National Ice Rink. The Millennium Stadium was ready for the 1999 Rugby World Cup and the Centre for Visual Arts opened in 1999.

SWANSEA

Swansea (*Abertawe*) is a city and a seaport. The Gower peninsula was brought within the city boundary under local government reform in 1974. The trade of the port includes coal, steel products, containerised goods, petroleum products and petrochemicals.

The principal buildings are the Norman Castle (rebuilt *c*. 1330), the Royal Institution of South Wales, founded in 1835 (including a library), the University of Wales Swansea at Singleton, and the Guildhall, containing Frank Brangwyn's British Empire panels. The Dylan Thomas Centre, formerly the old Guildhall, was restored in 1995. More recent buildings include the County Hall, the new Maritime Quarter and Marina and the leisure centre.

Swansea was chartered by the Earl of Warwick, *c.* 1158–84, and further charters were granted by King John, Henry III, Edward II, Edward III and James II, Cromwell (two) and the Marcher Lord William de Breos.

LOCAL COUNCILS

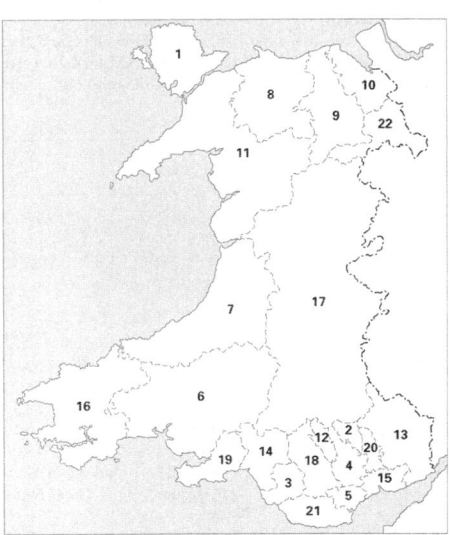

Key	Council
1	Anglesey
2	Blaenau Gwent
3	Bridgend
4	Caerphilly
5	Cardiff
6	Carmarthenshire
7	Ceredigion
8	Conwy
9	Denbighshire
10	Flintshire
11	Gwynedd
12	Merthyr Tydfil
13	Monmouthshire
14	Neath Port Talbot
15	Newport
16	Pembrokeshire
17	Powys
18	Rhondda, Cynon, Taff
19	Swansea
20	Torfaen
21	Vale of Glamorgan
22	Wrexham

LORD-LIEUTENANTS AND HIGH SHERIFFS

County/Shire	Lord-Lieutenant	High Sheriff, 2000–1
Clwyd	*vacant*	Dr M. Jones-Mortimer
Dyfed	Sir David Mansel Lewis, KCVO	D. G. Jones
Gwent	*vacant*	Brig. J. Hedley Hooper, OBE
Gwynedd	Prof. E. Sunderland	G. W. Hughes
Mid Glamorgan	M. A. McLaggan	W. H. Joseph
Powys	The Hon. Mrs E. S. Legge-Bourke, LVO	W. N. H. Legge-Bourke
S. Glamorgan	Capt. N. Lloyd-Edwards	M. C. Eddershaw
W. Glamorgan	R. C. Hastie, CBE	Mrs R. J. Harris

LOCAL COUNCILS

SMALL CAPITALS denote CITY status
§ Denotes Borough status

Council	Administrative headquarters	Population	Band D charge 2000	Chief Executive	Chairman 2000–1 (a) Mayor (b) Lord Mayor
Anglesey	Llangefni	67,055	£620.73	G. F. Edwards	T. L. Hughes
Blaenau Gwent	Ebbw Vale	73,200	£730.44	R. Leadbeter, OBE	(a) E. P. Jones
Bridgend	Bridgend	128,340	£702.01	I. K. Lewis	(a) I. Jones, MBE
Caerphilly	Hengoed	69,100	£670.22	M. Davies	Mrs M. Hughes
CARDIFF	Cardiff	315,040	£632.78	B. Davies	(b) R. Goodway
Carmarthenshire	Carmarthen	169,108	£723.86	B. Roynon	W. D. Thomas
Ceredigion	Aberaeron	69,545	£723.35	O. Watkin	J. D. Rowland Jones
§Conwy	Conwy	110,600	£551.20	C. D. Barker	Mrs C. Cooper
Denbighshire	Ruthin	90,400	£630.53	H. V. Thomas	L. Williams
Flintshire	Mold	144,900	£654.27	P. McGreevy	T. Jones
Gwynedd	Caernarfon	116,000	£672.95	G. R. Jones	G. Owen, MBE
§Merthyr Tydfil	Merthyr Tydfil	58,100	£797.60	G. W. Meredith	(a) B. Driscoll
Monmouthshire	Cwmbran	86,248	£586.43	Ms J. Redfearn	G. Robbins
§Neath Port Talbot	Port Talbot	139,459	£811.92	K. R. Sawyers	(a) J. Rogers
§Newport	Newport	136,800	£573.17	R. D. Blair	(a) G. Dally
Pembrokeshire	Haverfordwest	114,400	£609.00	B. Parry-Jones	B. Hitchings
Powys	Llandrindod Wells	124,400	£627.53	Miss J. Tonge	B. W. Davies
§Rhondda, Cynon, Taff	Tonypandy	240,117	£771.00	K. Ryley	Mrs R. Moses
SWANSEA	Swansea	230,200	£674.61	Ms V. Sugar	(b) W. J. F. Davies
§Torfaen	Pontypool	90,527	£549.11	Dr C. Grace	(a) B. Smith
Vale of Glamorgan	Barry	119,500	£569.79	J. Maitland (*acting*)	A. M. Ernest
§Wrexham	Wrexham	125,200	£697.61	D. Griffin	(a) N. Rogers

Scotland

The Kingdom of Scotland occupies the northern portion of the main island of Great Britain and includes the Inner and Outer Hebrides, and the Orkney, Shetland, and many other islands. It lies between 60°51′30″ and 54°38′ N. latitude and between 1°45′32″ and 6°14′ W. longitude, with England to the south, the Atlantic Ocean on the north and west, and the North Sea on the east.

The greatest length of the mainland (Cape Wrath to the Mull of Galloway) is 274 miles, and the greatest breadth (Buchan Ness to Applecross) is 154 miles. The customary measurement of the island of Great Britain is from the site of John o' Groats house, near Duncansby Head, Caithness, to Land's End, Cornwall, a total distance of 603 miles in a straight line and approximately 900 miles by road.

The total area of Scotland is 78,789 sq. km (30,420 sq. miles); land 77,097 sq. km (29,767 sq. miles), inland water 1,692 sq. km (653 sq. miles).

POPULATION

The population at the 1991 census was 4,998,567 (males 2,391,961; females 2,606,606). The average density of the population in 1991 was 0.65 persons per hectare.

RELIEF

There are three natural orographic divisions of Scotland. The southern uplands have their highest points in Merrick (2,766 ft), Rhinns of Kells (2,669 ft), and Cairnsmuir of Carsphairn (2,614 ft), in the west; and the Tweedsmuir Hills in the east (Hartfell 2,651 ft, Dollar Law 2,682 ft, Broad Law 2,756 ft).

The central lowlands, formed by the valleys of the Clyde, Forth and Tay, divide the southern uplands from the northern Highlands, which extend almost from the extreme north of the mainland to the central lowlands, and are divided into a northern and a southern system by the Great Glen.

The Grampian Mountains, which entirely cover the southern Highland area, include in the west Ben Nevis (4,406 ft), the highest point in the British Isles, and in the east the Cairngorm Mountains (Cairn Gorm 4,084 ft, Braeriach 4,248 ft, Ben Macdui 4,296 ft). The north-western Highland area contains the mountains of Wester and Easter Ross (Carn Eige 3,880 ft, Sgurr na Lapaich 3,775 ft).

Created, like the central lowlands, by a major geological fault, the Great Glen (60 miles long) runs between Inverness and Fort William, and contains Loch Ness, Loch Oich and Loch Lochy. These are linked to each other and to the north-east and south-west coasts of Scotland by the Caledonian Canal, providing a navigable passage between the Moray Firth and the Inner Hebrides.

HYDROGRAPHY

The western coast is fragmented by peninsulas and islands, and indented by fjords (sea-lochs), the longest of which is Loch Fyne (42 miles long) in Argyll. Although the east coast tends to be less fractured and lower, there are several great drowned inlets (firths), e.g. Firth of Forth, Firth of Tay, Moray Firth, as well as the Firth of Clyde in the west.

The lochs are the principal hydrographic feature. The largest in Scotland and in Britain is Loch Lomond (27 sq. miles), in the Grampian valleys; the longest and deepest is Loch Ness (24 miles long and 800 ft deep), in the Great Glen; and Loch Shin (20 miles long) and Loch Maree in the Highlands.

The longest river is the Tay (117 miles), noted for its salmon. It flows into the North Sea, with Dundee on the

estuary, which is spanned by the Tay Bridge (10,289 ft) opened in 1887 and the Tay Road Bridge (7,365 ft) opened in 1966. Other noted salmon rivers are the Dee (90 miles) which flows into the North Sea at Aberdeen, and the Spey (110 miles), the swiftest flowing river in the British Isles, which flows into Moray Firth. The Tweed, which gave its name to the woollen cloth produced along its banks, marks in the lower stretches of its 96-mile course the border between Scotland and England.

The most important river commercially is the Clyde (106 miles), formed by the junction of the Daer and Portrail water, which flows through the city of Glasgow to the Firth of Clyde. During its course it passes over the picturesque Falls of Clyde, Bonnington Linn (30 ft), Corra Linn (84 ft), Dundaff Linn (10 ft) and Stonebyres Linn (80 ft), above and below Lanark. The Forth (66 miles), upon which stands Edinburgh, the capital, is spanned by the Forth (Railway) Bridge (1890), which is 5,330 ft long, and the Forth (Road) Bridge (1964), which has a total length of 6,156 ft (over water) and a single span of 3,000 ft.

The highest waterfall in Scotland, and the British Isles, is Eas a'Chual Aluinn with a total height of 200 m (658 ft), which falls from Glas Bheinn in Sutherland. The Falls of Glomach, on a head-stream of the Elchaig in Wester Ross, have a drop of 370 ft.

GAELIC LANGUAGE

According to the 1991 census, 1.4 per cent of the population of Scotland, mainly in the Highlands and western coastal regions, were able to speak the Scottish form of Gaelic.

LOWLAND SCOTTISH LANGUAGE

Several regional Lowland Scottish dialects, known variously as Scots, Scotch, Lallans or Doric, are widely spoken. The General Register Office (Scotland) has estimated that 1.5 million people, or 30 per cent of the population, are Scots speakers.

FLAG

The flag of Scotland is known as the Saltire. It is a white diagonal cross on a blue field (saltire argent in a field azure) and represents St Andrew, the patron saint of Scotland.

THE SCOTTISH ISLANDS

ORKNEY

The Orkney Islands (total area 375½ sq. miles) lie about six miles north of the mainland, separated from it by the Pentland Firth. Of the 90 islands and islets (holms and skerries) in the group, about one-third are inhabited.

The total population at the 1991 census was 19,612; the 1991 populations of the islands shown here include those of smaller islands forming part of the same civil parish.

Mainland, 15,128	Rousay, 291
Burray, 363	Sanday, 533
Eday, 166	Shapinsay, 322
Flotta and Fara, 126	South Ronaldsay, 943
Graemsay and Hoy, 477	Stronsay, 382
North Ronaldsay, 92	Westray, 704
Papa Westray, 85	

The islands are rich in prehistoric and Scandinavian remains, the most notable being the Stone Age village of Skara Brae, the burial chamber of Maeshowe, the many brochs (towers) and the 12th century St Magnus Cathedral. Scapa Flow, between the Mainland and Hoy, was the war station of the British Grand Fleet from 1914 to 1919 and the scene of the scuttling of the surrendered German High Seas Fleet (21 June 1919).

Most of the islands are low-lying and fertile, and farming (principally beef cattle) is the main industry. Flotta, to the south of Scapa Flow, is the site of the oil terminal for the Piper, Claymore and Tartan fields in the North Sea.

The capital is Kirkwall (population 6,881) on Mainland.

SHETLAND

The Shetland Islands have a total area of 551 sq. miles and a population at the 1991 census of 22,522. They lie about 50 miles north of the Orkneys, with Fair Isle about half-way between the two groups. Out Stack, off Muckle Flugga, one mile north of Unst, is the most northerly part of the British Isles (60°51′30″ N. lat.).

There are over 100 islands, of which 16 are inhabited. Populations at the 1991 census were:

Mainland, 17,596	Muckle Roe, 115
Bressay, 352	Trondra, 117
East Burra, 72	Unst, 1,055
Fair Isle, 67	West Burra, 857
Fetlar, 90	Whalsay, 1,041
Housay, 85	Yell, 1,075

Shetland's many archaeological sites include Jarlshof, Mousa and Clickhimin, and its long connection with Scandinavia has resulted in a strong Norse influence on its place-names and dialect.

Industries include fishing, knitwear and farming. In addition to the fishing fleet there are fish processing factories, while the traditional handknitting of Fair Isle and Unst is supplemented now with machine-knitted garments. Farming is mainly crofting, with sheep being raised on the moorland and hills of the islands. Latterly the islands have become a centre of the North Sea oil industry, with pipelines from the Brent and Ninian fields running to the terminal at Sullom Voe, the largest of its kind in Europe. Lerwick is the main centre for supply services for offshore oil exploration and development.

The capital is Lerwick (population 7,901) on the Mainland.

THE HEBRIDES

Until the late 13th century the Hebrides included other Scottish islands in the Firth of Clyde, the peninsula of Kintyre (Argyll), the Isle of Man, and the (Irish) Isle of Rathlin. The origin of the name is stated to be the Greek *Eboudai*, latinised as *Hebudes* by Pliny, and corrupted to its present form. The Norwegian name *Sudreyjar* (Southern Islands) was latinised as *Sodorenses*, a name that survives in the Anglican bishopric of Sodor and Man.

There are over 500 islands and islets, of which about 100 are inhabited, though mountainous terrain and extensive peat bogs mean that only a fraction of the total area is under cultivation. Stone, Bronze and Iron Age settlement has left many remains, including those at Callanish on Lewis, and Norse colonisation influenced language, customs and place-names. Occupations include farming (mostly crofting and stock-raising), fishing and the manufacture of tweeds and other woollens. Tourism is also an important factor in the economy.

The Inner Hebrides lie off the west coast of Scotland and relatively close to the mainland. The largest and best-known is Skye (area 643 sq. miles; pop. 8,868; chief town, Portree), which contains the Cuillin Hills (Sgurr Alasdair 3,257 ft), the Red Hills (Beinn na Caillich 2,403 ft), Bla Bheinn (3,046 ft) and The Storr (2,358 ft). Skye is also famous as the refuge of the Young Pretender in 1746. Other islands in the Highland council area include Raasay (pop. 163), Rum, Eigg and Muck.

Further south the Inner Hebridean islands include Arran (pop. 4,474) containing Goat Fell (2,868 ft); Coll and Tiree (pop. 940); Colonsay and Oronsay (pop. 106); Islay (area 235 sq. miles; pop. 3,538); Jura (area 160 sq. miles; pop. 196) with a range of hills culminating in the Paps of Jura (Beinn-an-Oir, 2,576 ft, and Beinn Chaolais, 2,477 ft); and Mull (area 367 sq. miles; pop. 2,708; chief town Tobermory) containing Ben More (3,171 ft).

The Outer Hebrides, separated from the mainland by the Minch, now form the Eilean Siar/Western Isles Islands Council area (area 1,119 sq. miles; population at the 1991 census 29,600). The main islands are Lewis with Harris (area 770 sq. miles, pop. 21,737), whose chief town, Stornoway, is the administrative headquarters; North Uist (pop. 1,404); South Uist (pop. 2,106); Baleshare (55); Benbecula (pop. 1,803) and Barra (pop. 1,244). Other inhabited islands include Bernera (262), Berneray (141), Eriskay (179), Grimsay (215), Scalpay (382) and Vatersay (72).

EARLY HISTORY

There is evidence of human settlement in Scotland dating from the third millennium BC, the earliest settlers being Middle Stone Age hunters and fishermen. Early in the second millennium BC, New Stone Age farmers began to cultivate crops and rear livestock; their settlements were on the west coast and in the north, and included Skara Brae and Maeshowe (Orkney). Settlement by the Early Bronze Age 'Beaker folk', so-called from the shape of their drinking vessels, in eastern Scotland dates from about 1800 BC. Further settlement is believed to have occurred from 700 BC onwards, as tribes were displaced from further south by new incursions from the Continent and the Roman invasions from AD 43.

Julius Agricola, the Roman governor of Britain AD 77–84, extended the Roman conquests in Britain by advancing into Caledonia, culminating with a victory at Mons Graupius, probably in AD 84; he was recalled to Rome shortly afterwards and his forward policy was not pursued. Hadrian's Wall, mostly completed by AD 30, marked the northern frontier of the Roman empire except for the period between about AD 144 and 190 when the frontier moved north to the Forth–Clyde isthmus and a turf wall, the Antonine Wall, was manned.

After the Roman withdrawal from Britain, there were centuries of warfare between the Picts, Scots, Britons, Angles and Vikings. The Picts, believed to be a non-Indo-European race, occupied the area north of the Forth. The Scots, a Gaelic-speaking people of northern Ireland, colonised the area of Argyll and Bute (the kingdom of Dalriada) in the fifth century AD and then expanded eastwards and northwards. The Britons, speaking a Brythonic Celtic language, colonised Scotland from the south from the first century BC; they lost control of south-eastern Scotland (incorporated into the kingdom of Northumbria) to the Angles in the early seventh century but retained Strathclyde (south-western Scotland and Cumbria). Viking raids from the late eighth century were followed by Norse settlement in the western and northern isles, Argyll, Caithness and Sutherland from the mid-ninth century onwards.

UNIFICATION

The union of the areas which now comprise Scotland began in AD 843 when Kenneth mac Alpin, king of the Scots from c. 834, became also king of the Picts, joining the two lands to form the kingdom of Alba (comprising Scotland north of a line between the Forth and Clyde rivers). Lothian, the eastern part of the area between the

Forth and the Tweed, seems to have been leased to Kenneth II of Alba (reigned 971–95) by Edgar of England *c*. 973–4, and Scottish possession was confirmed by Malcolm II's victory over a Northumbrian army at Carham *c*. 1016. At about this time Malcolm II (reigned 1005–34) placed his grandson Duncan on the throne of the British kingdom of Strathclyde, bringing under Scots rule virtually all of what is now Scotland.

The Norse possessions were incorporated into the kingdom of Scotland from the 12th century onwards. An uprising in the mid-12th century drove the Norse from most of mainland Argyll. The Hebrides were ceded to Scotland by the Treaty of Perth in 1266 after a Norwegian expedition in 1263 failed to maintain Norse authority over the islands. Orkney and Shetland fell to Scotland in 1468–9 as a pledge for the unpaid dowry of Margaret of Denmark, wife of James III, though Danish claims of suzerainty were relinquished only with the marriage of Anne of Denmark to James VI in 1590.

From the 11th century, there were frequent wars between Scotland and England over territory and the extent of England's political influence. The failure of the Scottish royal line with the death of Margaret of Norway in 1290 led to disputes over the throne which were resolved by the adjudication of Edward I of England. He awarded the throne to John Balliol in 1292 but Balliol's refusal to be a puppet king led to war. Balliol surrendered to Edward I in 1296 and Edward attempted to rule Scotland himself. Resistance to Scotland's loss of independence was led by William Wallace, who defeated the English at Stirling Bridge (1297), and Robert Bruce, crowned in 1306, who held most of Scotland by 1311 and routed Edward II's army at Bannockburn (1314). England recognised the independence of Scotland in the Treaty of Northampton in 1328. Subsequent clashes include the disastrous battle of Flodden (1513) in which James IV and many of his nobles fell.

THE UNION

In 1603 James VI of Scotland succeeded Elizabeth I on the throne of England (his mother, Mary Queen of Scots, was the great-granddaughter of Henry VII), his successors reigning as sovereigns of Great Britain. Political union of the two countries did not occur until 1707.

THE JACOBITE REVOLTS

After the abdication (by flight) in 1688 of James VII and II, the crown devolved upon William III (grandson of Charles I) and Mary II (elder daughter of James VII and II). In 1689 Graham of Claverhouse roused the Highlands on behalf of James VII and II, but died after a military success at Killiecrankie.

After the death of Anne (younger daughter of James VII and II), the throne devolved upon George I (great-grandson of James VI and I). In 1715, armed risings on behalf of James Stuart (the Old Pretender, son of James VII and II) led to the indecisive battle of Sheriffmuir, and the Jacobite movement died down until 1745, when Charles Stuart (the Young Pretender) defeated the Royalist troops at Prestonpans and advanced to Derby (1746). From Derby, the adherents of 'James VIII and III' (the title claimed for his father by Charles Stuart) fell back on the defensive and were finally crushed at Culloden (16 April 1746).

PRINCIPAL CITIES

ABERDEEN

Aberdeen, 130 miles north-east of Edinburgh, received its charter as a Royal Burgh in 1179. Scotland's third largest city, Aberdeen is the second largest Scottish fishing port and the main centre for offshore oil exploration and production. It is also an ancient university town and distinguished research centre. Other industries include engineering, food processing, textiles, paper manufacturing and chemicals.

Places of interest include King's College, St Machar's Cathedral, Brig o' Balgownie, Duthie Park and Winter Gardens, Hazlehead Park, the Kirk of St Nicholas, Mercat Cross, Marischal College and Marischal Museum, Provost Skene's House, Art Gallery, Gordon Highlanders Museum, Satrosphere Hands-On Discovery Centre, and Aberdeen Maritime Museum in Provost Ross's House.

DUNDEE

Dundee, a Royal Burgh, is situated on the north bank of the Tay estuary. The city's port and dock installations are important to the offshore oil industry and the airport also provides servicing facilities. Principal industries include textiles, computers and other electronic industries, lasers, printing, tyre manufacture, food processing, carpets, engineering, clothing manufacture and tourism.

The unique City Churches – three churches under one roof, together with the 15th century St Mary's Tower – are the most prominent architectural feature. Dundee has two historic ships: the Dundee built RRS *Discovery* which took Capt. Scott to the Antarctic lies alongside Discovery Quay, and the frigate *Unicorn*, the only British-built wooden warship still afloat, is moored in Victoria Dock. Places of interest include Mills Public Observatory, the Tay road and rail bridges, McManus Galleries, Barrack Street Museum, Claypotts Castle, Broughty Castle and Verdant Works (Textile Heritage Centre).

EDINBURGH

Edinburgh is the capital of and seat of government in Scotland. The city is built on a group of hills and contains in Princes Street one of the most beautiful thoroughfares in the world.

The principal buildings are the Castle, which now houses the Stone of Scone and also includes St Margaret's Chapel, the oldest building in Edinburgh, and near it, the Scottish National War Memorial; the Palace of Holyroodhouse; Parliament House, the present seat of the judicature; three universities (Edinburgh, Heriot-Watt, Napier); St Giles' Cathedral; St Mary's (Scottish Episcopal) Cathedral (Sir George Gilbert Scott); the General Register House (Robert Adam); the National and the Signet Libraries; the National Gallery; the Royal Scottish Academy; the National Portrait Gallery; and the Edinburgh International Conference Centre, opened in 1995. A new Scottish Parliament building is under construction at Holyrood.

GLASGOW

Glasgow, a Royal Burgh, is the principal commercial and industrial centre in Scotland. The city occupies the north and south banks of the Clyde, formerly one of the chief commercial estuaries in the world. The principal industries include engineering, electronics, finance, chemicals and printing. The city has also developed recently as a tourism and conference centre.

The chief buildings are the 13th century Gothic Cathedral, the University (Sir George Gilbert Scott), the City Chambers, the Royal Concert Hall, St Mungo Museum of Religious Life and Art, Pollok House, the School of Art (Mackintosh), Kelvingrove Art Galleries, the Gallery of Modern Art, the Burrell Collection museum and the Mitchell Library. The city is home to the Scottish National Orchestra, Scottish Opera and Scottish Ballet.

LORD-LIEUTENANTS

Title	Name
Aberdeenshire	A. D. M. Farquharson, OBE
Angus	The Earl of Airlie, KT, GCVO, PC, LLD
Argyll and Bute	The Duke of Argyll
Ayrshire and Arran	Maj. R. Y. Henderson, TD
Banffshire	J. A. S. McPherson, CBE
Berwickshire	*vacant*
Caithness	Maj. G. T. Dunnett, TD
Clackmannan	Lt.-Col. R. C. Stewart, CBE, TD
Dumfries	Capt. R. C. Cunningham-Jardine
Dunbartonshire	Brig. D. D. G. Hardie, TD
East Lothian	Sir Hew Hamilton-Dalrymple, Bt., KCVO
Eilean Siar/ Western Isles	*vacant*
Fife	Mrs C. M. Dean
Inverness	The Lord Gray of Contin, PC
Kincardineshire	J. D. B. Smart
Lanarkshire	*vacant*
Midlothian	Capt. G. W. Burnet, LVO
Moray	Air Vice-Marshal G. A. Chesworth, CB, OBE, DFC
Nairn	Ewen J. Brodie
Orkney	G. R. Marwick
Perth and Kinross	Sir David Montgomery, Bt.
Renfrewshire	C. H. Parker, OBE
Ross and Cromarty	Capt. R. W. K. Stirling of Fairburn, TD
Roxburgh, Ettrick and Lauderdale	Dr J. Paterson-Brown, CBE
Shetland	J. H. Scott
Stirling and Falkirk	Lt.-Col. J. Stirling of Garden, CBE, TD
Sutherland	Maj.-Gen. D. Houston, CBE
The Stewartry of Kirkcudbright	Lt.-Gen. Sir Norman Arthur, KCB
Tweeddale	Capt. D. Younger
West Lothian	The Earl of Morton
Wigtown	Maj. E. S. Orr-Ewing

The Lord Provosts of the four city districts of Aberdeen, Dundee, Edinburgh and Glasgow are Lord-Lieutenants for those districts *ex officio*.

LOCAL COUNCILS

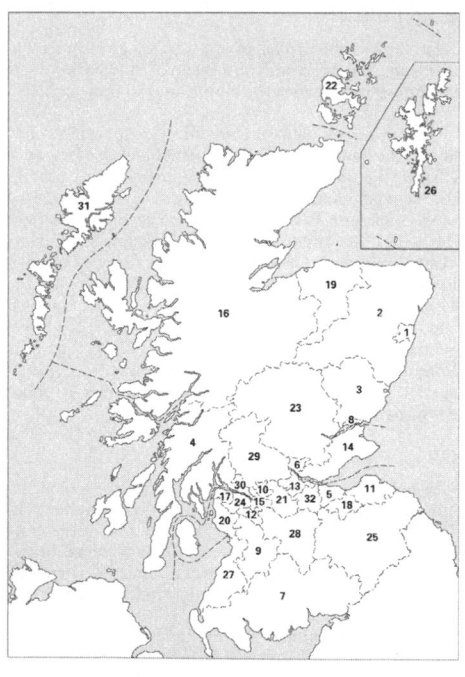

Key	Council
1	Aberdeen City
2	Aberdeenshire
3	Angus
4	Argyll and Bute
5	City of Edinburgh
6	Clackmannanshire
7	Dumfries and Galloway
8	Dundee City
9	East Ayrshire
10	East Dunbartonshire
11	East Lothian
12	East Renfrewshire
13	Falkirk
14	Fife
15	Glasgow City
16	Highland
17	Inverclyde
18	Midlothian
19	Moray
20	North Ayrshire
21	North Lanarkshire
22	Orkney
23	Perth and Kinross
24	Renfrewshire
25	Scottish Borders
26	Shetland
27	South Ayrshire
28	South Lanarkshire
29	Stirling
30	West Dunbartonshire
31	Western Isles (Eilean Siar)
32	West Lothian

LOCAL COUNCILS

Council	Administrative headquarters	Population (latest estimate)	Band D charge 2000	Chief Executive	Chairman (a) Convenor (b) Provost (c) Lord Provost
Aberdeen City	Aberdeen	213,070	£1,173.08	D. Paterson	(c) Ms M. Smith
Aberdeenshire	Aberdeen	228,610	£777.00	A. G. Campbell	(a) R. Bisset
Angus	Forfar	110,070	£771.00	A. B. Watson	(b) Mrs F. M. Duncan
Argyll and Bute	Lochgilphead	89,730	£938.00	J. A. McLellan	(a) D. C. Currie
City of Edinburgh	Edinburgh	452,806	£915.00	T. N. Aitchison	(c) Rt. Hon. Eric Milligan
Clackmannanshire	Alloa	48,560	£913.00	K. Bloom (acting)	(b) W. McAdam
Dumfries and Galloway	Dumfries	147,300	£817.00	P. N. Jones	(b) K. Cameron
Dundee City	Dundee	146,690	£1,054.34	A. Stephen	(b) Rt. Hon. Helen W. Wright
East Ayrshire	Kilmarnock	123,230	£1,101.60	D. Montgomery	(b) J. Boyd
East Dunbartonshire	Glasgow	110,000	£830.00	Dr V. Nash	(b) R. McSkimming
East Lothian	Haddington	90,430	£858.00	J. Lindsay	(b) P. O'Brien
East Renfrewshire	Giffnock	87,980	£810.00	P. Daniels	(b) A. Steele
Eilean Siar/Western Isles	Stornoway	27,940	£1,023.00	W. Howat	(a) A. A. Macdonald
Falkirk	Falkirk	143,400	£757.00	Mrs M. Pitcaithly	(b) D. Goldie
Fife	Glenrothes	348,900	£1,076.00	D. Sinclair	(a) J. MacDougall
Glasgow City	Glasgow	611,440	£1,094.00	J. Andrews	(c) A. Mosson
Highland	Inverness	208,700	£839.00	A. D. McCourt	(b) W. Smith
Inverclyde	Greenock	86,500	£933.00	R. Cleary	(b) R. Roach
Midlothian	Dalkeith	80,860	£936.00	T. Muir	(b) S. Campbell
Moray	Elgin	85,870	£786.00	A. Keddie	(a) E. Aldridge
North Ayrshire	Irvine	139,780	£1,050.20	B. Devine	(a) S. Taylor
North Lanarkshire	Motherwell	327,940	£1,099.20	G. Whitefield	(b) B. McCulloch
Orkney Islands	Kirkwall	19,550	£690.00	A. Buchan	(a) H. Halcro-Johnston
Perth and Kinross	Perth	133,040	£795.00	H. Robertson	(b) M. O'Malley
Renfrewshire	Paisley	177,830	£846.00	T. Scholes	(b) J. McDowell
Scottish Borders	Newtown St Boswells	106,200	£670.00	A. M. Croall	(a) A. L. Tulley
Shetland Islands	Lerwick	22,375	£621.00	M. Goodlad	(a) T. Stove
South Ayrshire	Ayr	114,000	£832.00	G. W. F. Thorley	(b) Ms E. Foulkes
South Lanarkshire	Hamilton	307,350	£1,124.20	M. Docherty	(b) A. Dick
Stirling	Stirling	83,130	£992.00	K. Yates	(b) T. Brookes
West Dunbartonshire	Dumbarton	94,980	£1,222.20	T. Huntingford	(b) A. Macdonald
West Lothian	Livingston	153,090	£1,115.00	A. M. Linkston	(b) J. Thomas

Northern Ireland

Northern Ireland has a total area of 14,144 sq. km (5,467 sq. miles): land, 13,532 sq. km (5,225 sq. miles); inland water and tideways, 628 sq. km (249 sq. miles).

The population of Northern Ireland at the 1991 census was 1,577,836 (males, 769,071; females, 808,765). The average density of population in 1991 was 1.11 persons per hectare.

In 1991 the number of persons in the various religious denominations (expressed as percentages of the total population) were: Roman Catholic, 38.4; Presbyterian, 21.4; Church of Ireland, 17.7; Methodist, 3.8; others 7.7; none, 3.7; not stated, 7.3.

FLAG

The official national flag of Northern Ireland is now the Union Flag. The flag formerly in use (a white, six-pointed star in the centre of a red cross on a white field, enclosing a red hand and surmounted by a crown) has not been used since the imposition of direct rule.

PRINCIPAL CITIES

BELFAST

Belfast, the administrative centre of Northern Ireland, is situated at the mouth of the River Lagan at its entrance to Belfast Lough. The city grew, owing to its easy access by sea to Scottish coal and iron, to be a great industrial centre.

The principal buildings are of a relatively recent date and include the Parliament Buildings at Stormont, the City Hall, Waterfront Hall, the Law Courts, the Public Library and the Museum and Art Gallery.

Belfast received its first charter of incorporation in 1613 and was created a city in 1888; the title of Lord Mayor was conferred in 1892.

LONDONDERRY

Londonderry (originally Derry) is situated on the River Foyle, and has important associations with the City of London. The Irish Society was created by the City of London in 1610, and under its royal charter of 1613 it fortified the city and was for long closely associated with its administration. Because of this connection the city was incorporated in 1613 under the new name of Londonderry.

The city is famous for the great siege of 1688–9, when for 105 days the town held out against the forces of James II until relieved by sea. The city walls are still intact and form a circuit of almost a mile around the old city.

Interesting buildings are the Protestant Cathedral of St Columb's (1633) and the Guildhall, reconstructed in 1912 and containing a number of beautiful stained glass windows, many of which were presented by the livery companies of London.

CONSTITUTIONAL DEVELOPMENTS

Northern Ireland is subject to the same fundamental constitutional provisions which apply to the rest of the United Kingdom. It had its own parliament and government from 1921 to 1972, but after increasing civil unrest the Northern Ireland (Temporary Provisions) Act 1972

transferred the legislative and executive powers of the Northern Ireland parliament and government to the UK Parliament and a Secretary of State. The Northern Ireland Constitution Act 1973 provided for devolution in Northern Ireland through an assembly and executive, but a power-sharing executive formed by the Northern Ireland political parties in January 1974 collapsed in May 1974; since then Northern Ireland has been governed by direct rule under the provisions of the Northern Ireland Act 1974. This allows Parliament to approve all laws for Northern Ireland and places the Northern Ireland department under the direction and control of the Secretary of State for Northern Ireland.

Attempts were made by successive governments to find a means of restoring a widely acceptable form of devolved government to Northern Ireland. In 1985 the governments of the United Kingdom and the Republic of Ireland signed the Anglo-Irish Agreement, establishing an inter-governmental conference in which the Irish government may put forward views and proposals on certain aspects of Northern Ireland affairs.

Discussions between the British and Irish governments and the main Northern Ireland parties began in 1991. It was agreed that any political settlement would need to address relationships within Northern Ireland, within the island of Ireland (north/south) and between the British and Irish governments (east/west). Although round table talks ended in 1992 the process continued from September 1993 as separate bilateral discussions with three of the Northern Ireland parties (the DUP declined to participate).

In December 1993 the British and Irish governments published the Joint Declaration complementing the political talks, and making clear that any settlement would need to be founded on principles of democracy and consent. The declaration also stated that all democratically mandated parties could be involved in political talks as long as they permanently renounced paramilitary violence.

The provisional IRA and loyalist paramilitary groups announced cease-fires on 31 August and 13 October 1994 respectively. The Government initiated exploratory meetings with Sinn Fein and loyalist representatives in December 1994.

In February 1995 the then Prime Minister (John Major) launched *A Framework for Accountable Government in Northern Ireland* and, with the Irish Prime Minister, *A New Framework for Agreement*. These outlined what a comprehensive political settlement might look like. The ideas were intended to facilitate multilateral dialogue involving the Northern Ireland parties and the British government.

In autumn 1995 the Prime Minister said that Sinn Fein would not be invited to all-party talks until the IRA had decommissioned its arms; the IRA ruled out any decommissioning of weapons in advance of a political settlement. An international body chaired by a former US senator, George Mitchell, reported in January 1996 that no weapons would be decommissioned before the start of all-party talks and that a compromise agreement was necessary under which weapons would be decommissioned during negotiations. The Prime Minister accepted the report and proposed the election of representatives to conduct all-party talks. On 9 February 1996 the IRA called off its cease-fire.

PEACE TALKS

Following elections on 30 May 1996, all-party talks opened at Stormont Castle on 10 June 1996 which included nine of the ten parties returned at the election; Sinn Fein representatives were turned away because the IRA had failed to reinstate its cease-fire. On 29 July 1996 the all-party talks were suspended after disagreements over the issue of decommissioning arms. An opening agenda for the talks was agreed in October 1996.

On 25 June 1997 the newly-elected Labour Government said that substantive negotiations should begin in September 1997 with a view to reaching conclusions by May 1998. The British and Irish governments issued a joint paper outlining their proposals for resolving the decommissioning issue. The Government also indicated that if the IRA were to call a cease-fire, it would assess whether it was genuine over a period of six weeks, and if satisfied that it was so, would then invite Sinn Fein to the talks. An IRA cease-fire was declared on 20 July 1997.

When the UK Government announced in August 1997 that Sinn Fein would be present when the substantive talks opened on 15 September, the Unionist and loyalist parties, unhappy at the terms on which Sinn Fein had been admitted, boycotted the opening session. The Ulster Unionist Party, the Progressive Unionist Party and the Ulster Democratic Party re-entered the negotiations on 17 September. Full-scale peace talks began on 7 October. The parties had agreed to concentrate on constitutional issues, with the issue of decommissioning terrorist weapons to be handled by a new independent commission.

On 12 January 1998 the British and Irish governments issued a joint document, *Propositions on Heads of Agreement*, proposing the establishment of various new cross-border bodies; further proposals were presented on 27 January. A draft peace settlement was issued by the talk's chairman, Sen. George Mitchell, on 6 April 1998 but was rejected by the Unionists the following day. On 10 April agreement was reached between the British and Irish governments and the eight Northern Ireland political parties still involved in the talks (the Good Friday/Belfast Agreement). The agreement provided for an elected New Northern Ireland Assembly; a North/South Ministerial Council, and a British-Irish Council comprising representatives of the British, Irish, Channel Islands and Isle of Man governments and members of the new assemblies for Scotland, Wales and Northern Ireland. Further points included the abandonment of the Republic of Ireland's constitutional claim to Northern Ireland; the decommissioning of weapons; the release of paramilitary prisoners; and changes in policing.

Referendums on the agreement were held in Northern Ireland and the Republic of Ireland on 22 May 1998. In Northern Ireland the turnout was 81 per cent, of which 71.12 per cent voted in favour of the agreement. In the Republic of Ireland, the turnout was about 55 per cent, of which 94.4 per cent voted in favour of both the agreement and the necessary constitutional change. In the UK, the Northern Ireland Act 1998, enshrining the provisions of the Agreement, received Royal Assent in November 1998.

For details of the Northern Ireland Assembly and the further political developments in Northern Ireland, *see* Regional Government section.

OTHER BODIES

Consultations between the First Minister and Deputy First Minister, the British and Irish Governments and the political parties concluded in early 1999 with an agreement to establish six areas for cross-border bodies and a further six areas for co-operation. Treaties between the British and Irish governments establishing the bodies and parallel domestic legislation to underpin them are now in place.

The intergovernmental conference established by the 1985 Anglo-Irish Agreement was replaced by a new British-Irish Intergovernmental Conference which will discuss all areas of mutual bilateral interest.

The British-Irish Council will operate on the basis of consensus and may reach agreements and pursue common policies in areas of mutual interest.

ECONOMY

FINANCE

Northern Ireland's expenditure is funded by the Northern Ireland Consolidated Fund (NICF). Up to date of devolution on 2 December 1999, the NICF was largely financed by Northern Ireland's attributed share of UK taxation and supplemented by a grant-in-aid. From devolution, these separate elements have been subsumed into a single Block Grant.

	1999–2000*	2000–1**
Public income	£7,629,735,880	£7,797,000,000
Public expenditure	6,940,392,596	7,797,000,000

*Outturn
**Estimate

PRODUCTION

The products of the engineering and allied industries, which employed 28,800 persons in 1997, were valued at £2,093 million. The textiles industry (manufacture of textiles and textile products), employing about 2,500 persons, produced goods valued at approximately £936 million. The food products, beverages and tobacco industry, employing about 20,700 persons, produced goods valued at £3,836 million.

In 1999, 1,724 persons were employed in mining and quarrying operations in Northern Ireland and the minerals raised (28,555,000 tonnes) were valued at £58,433,000.

COMMUNICATIONS

The total tonnage handled by Northern Ireland ports in 1999 was 18.5 million. Regular ferry, freight and container services operate to ports in Great Britain and Europe from a number of ports, with most trade passing through Belfast (65 per cent of the total), Larne and Warrenpoint.

The Northern Ireland Transport Holding Company is largely responsible for the supervision of the subsidiary companies, Ulsterbus and Citybus (which operate the public road passenger services) and Northern Ireland Railways (collectively known as Translink). Road freight services are also provided by a large number of hauliers operating competitively under licence.

Belfast International Airport, owned by TBI International, provides scheduled and chartered services on domestic and international routes. In 1998–9 the airport handled approximately 2.5 million passengers and 26,000 tonnes of freight. Scheduled services also operate from Belfast City Airport (BCA, owned by Shorts Bombardier Aerospace) to 16 UK destinations. In 1998–9 the airport handled approximately 1.3 million passengers. City of Derry Airport (Londonderry, owned and operated by Derry City Council) provides services to three UK and European destinations and to Belfast, providing links to many of the locations serviced by BCA. In 1998–9 City of Derry Airport served approximately 60,000 passengers.

NORTHERN IRELAND COUNTIES

County	Area* (sq. miles)	Lord-Lieutenant	High Sheriff, 2000
Antrim	1,093	The Lord O'Neill, TD	Mrs P. E. MacCarthy-Morragh
Armagh	484	The Earl of Caledon	A. T. Laughlin Gibson
‡Belfast City	25	Lady Carswell, OBE	T. Campbell
Down	945	W. J. Hall	D. Montgomery
Fermanagh	647	The Earl of Erne	J. Lendrum Dickey
†Londonderry	798	J. Thompson Eaton, CBE, TD	A. F. Danton
‡Londonderry City	3.4	D. F. Desmond, CBE	W. F. G. Hunter
Tyrone	1,211	The Duke of Abercorn, KG	R. R. T. Cummings

*Excluding inland waters and tideways
‡Denotes County Borough
†Excluding the City of Londonderry

DISTRICT COUNCILS

SMALL CAPITALS denotes CITY status
§ Denotes Borough Council

Council	Population (September 1998)	Net Annual Value	Council Clerk	Chairman †Mayor 2000
§Antrim, Co. Antrim	47,500	£31,789,387	S. J. Magee	†P. Marks
§Ards, Co. Down	67,800	29,102,892	D. J. Fallows	†A. J. McDowell
§Armagh, Co. Armagh	53,200	20,400,462	D. R. D. Mitchell	†T. Canavan
§Ballymena, Co. Antrim	58,200	33,802,740	M. G. Rankin	†J. Currie
§Ballymoney, Co. Antrim	24,900	8,820,057	J. Dempsey	†W. Logan
Banbridge, Co. Down	37,700	14,557,214	R. Gilmore	W. McFadden
BELFAST, Co. Antrim and Co. Down	297,200	288,307,383	B. Hanna	R.Stoker
§Carrickfergus, Co. Antrim	35,700	15,840,050	A. Cardwell	†T.Creighton
§Castlereagh, Co. Down	64,500	34,048,365	A. Donaldson	†M. Chambers
§Coleraine, Co. Londonderry	54,700	29,088,695	W. Moore	†N. Hillis
Cookstown, Co. Tyrone	31,800	15,034,494	M. J. McGuckin	W. Greer
§Craigavon, Co. Armagh	79,100	44,734,166	T. Reaney	†Mrs D. Kelly
DERRY, Co. Londonderry	104,700	58,849,009	C. Logue (acting)	†P. Ramsey
Down, Co. Down	61,200	23,278,028	J. McGrillen	P. Fitzpatrick
Dungannon, Co. Tyrone	47,100	24,174,044	W. J. Beattie	R. Mulligan
Fermanagh, Co. Fermanagh	55,500	28,134,863	Mrs A. McGinley	D. Nixon
§Larne, Co. Antrim	30,300	17,557,734	C. McGarry	†Mrs J. Drummond
§Limavady, Co. Londonderry	30,800	11,952,034	J. K. Stevenson	†J. McKinney
§Lisburn, Co. Antrim and Co. Down	106,600	57,952,077	N. Davidson	†P. O'Hagan
Magherafelt, Co. Londonderry	37,900	15,177,326	J. A. McLaughlin	F. McKendry
Moyle, Co. Antrim	15,000	4,852,987	R. G. Lewis	A. McIntosh
Newry and Mourne, Co. Down and Co. Armagh	84,900	35,048,562	T. McCall	J. O'Hare
§Newtownabbey, Co. Antrim	79,600	43,419,562	N. Dunn	†J. Bingham
§North Down, Co. Down	73,500	39,327,195	T. Polley	†M. Smith
Omagh, Co. Tyrone	47,000	22,421,564	J. P. McKinney	A. Rainey
Strabane, Co. Tyrone	36,800	13,176,333	D. McSorley	T. Murtagh

The Isle of Man

Ellan Vannin

The Isle of Man is an island situated in the Irish Sea, in latitude 54°3'–54°25'N. and longitude 4°18'–4°47' W., nearly equidistant from England, Scotland and Ireland. Although the early inhabitants were of Celtic origin, the Isle of Man was part of the Norwegian Kingdom of the Hebrides until 1266, when this was ceded to Scotland. Subsequently granted to the Stanleys (Earls of Derby) in the 15th century and later to the Dukes of Atholl, it was brought under the administration of the Crown in 1765. The island forms the bishopric of Sodor and Man.

The total land area is 572 sq. km (221 sq. miles). The report on the 1991 census showed a resident population of 69,788 (males, 33,693; females, 36,095). The main language in use is English. There are no remaining native speakers of Manx Gaelic but 643 people are able to speak the language.

CAPITAL – ΨDouglas; population (1991), 22,214.

ΨCastletown (3,152) is the ancient capital; the other towns are ΨPeel (3,829) and ΨRamsey (6,496)

FLAG – A red flag charged with three conjoined armoured legs in white and gold

TYNWALD DAY – 5 July

GOVERNMENT

The Isle of Man is a self-governing Crown dependency, having its own parliamentary, legal and administrative system. The British Government is responsible for international relations and defence. Under the UK Act of Accession, Protocol 3, the island's relationship with the European Union is limited to trade alone and does not extend to financial aid. The Lieutenant-Governor is The Queen's personal representative in the island.

The legislature, Tynwald, is the oldest parliament in the world in continuous existence. It has two branches: the Legislative Council and the House of Keys. The Council consists of the President of Tynwald, the Bishop of Sodor and Man, the Attorney-General (who does not have a vote) and eight members elected by the House of Keys. The House of Keys has 24 members, elected by universal adult suffrage. The branches sit separately to consider legislation and sit together, as Tynwald Court, for most other parliamentary purposes.

The presiding officer of Tynwald Court is the President of Tynwald, elected by the members, who also presides over sittings of the Legislative Council. The presiding officer of the House of Keys is Mr Speaker, who is elected by members of the House.

The principal members of the Manx Government are the Chief Minister and nine departmental ministers, who comprise the Council of Ministers.

Lieutenant-Governor, HE Sir Timothy Daunt, KCMG
ADC to the Lieutenant-Governor, C. J. Tummon
President of Tynwald, The Hon. N. Q. Cringle
Speaker, House of Keys, The Hon. J. D. Cannan
The First Deemster and Clerk of the Rolls, His Honour
  T. W. Cain
*Clerk of Tynwald, Secretary to the House of Keys and Counsel
  to the Speaker*, Prof. T. St J. N. Bates
Clerk of Legislative Council and Clerk Assistant of Tynwald,
  T. A. Bawden
Attorney-General, W. J. H. Corlett, QC
Chief Minister, The Hon. D. J. Gelling
Chief Secretary, J. F. Kissack
Chief Financial Officer, J. A. Cashen

ECONOMY

Most of the income generated in the island is earned in the services sector with financial and professional services accounting for just over half of the national income. Tourism and manufacturing are also major generators of income whilst the island's other traditional industries of agriculture and fishing now play a smaller role in the economy.

Under the terms of Protocol 3, the island has tariff-free access to EU markets for its goods.

The island's unemployment rate is approximately 0.5 per cent and price inflation is around 2.5 per cent per annum.

FINANCE

The budget for 2000–1 provided for net revenue expenditure of £317 million. The principal sources of government revenue are taxes on income and expenditure. Income tax is payable at a rate of 14 per cent on the first £10,000 of taxable income for single resident individuals and 20 per cent on the balance, after personal allowances of £7,535. These bands are doubled for married couples. The rate of income tax is 14 per cent on the first £125,000 of taxable income of companies, rising to 20 per cent on the balance. Non-residents are charged tax at the rate of 20 per cent. By agreement with the British Government, the island keeps most of its rates of indirect taxation (VAT and duties) the same as those in the United Kingdom, but this agreement may be terminated by either party. However, VAT on tourist accommodation, property, repairs and renovations is charged at five per cent. A reciprocal agreement on national insurance benefits and pensions exists between the governments of the Isle of Man and the United Kingdom. Taxes are also charged on property (rates), but these are comparatively low.

The major government expenditure items are health, social security and education, which account for 60 per cent of the government budget. The island makes a voluntary annual contribution to the United Kingdom for defence and other external services.

The island has a special relationship with the European Union and neither contributes money to nor receives funds from the EU budget.

The Channel Islands

The Channel Islands, situated off the north-west coast of France (at distances of from ten to 30 miles), are the only portions of the Dukedom of Normandy still belonging to the Crown, to which they have been attached since the Conquest. They were the only British territory to come under German occupation during the Second World War, following invasion on 30 June and 1 July 1940. The islands were relieved by British forces on 9 May 1945, and 9 May (Liberation Day) is now observed as a bank and public holiday.

The islands consist of Jersey (11,630 ha/28,717 acres), Guernsey (6,340 ha/15,654 acres), and the dependencies of Guernsey: Alderney (795 ha/1,962 acres), Brechou (30/74), Great Sark (419/1,035), Little Sark (97/239), Herm (130/320), Jethou (18/44) and Lihou (15/38) – a total of 19,474 ha/48,083 acres, or 194 sq. km/75 sq. miles. In 1991 the population of Jersey was 84,082; and of Guernsey, 58,867; Alderney, 2,297 and Sark, 575. The official languages are English and French but French is being supplanted by English, which is the language in daily use. In country districts of Jersey and Guernsey and throughout Sark a Norman-French *patois* is also in use, though to a declining extent.

GOVERNMENT

The islands are Crown dependencies with their own legislative assemblies (the States in Jersey, Guernsey and Alderney, and the Court of Chief Pleas in Sark), and systems of local administration and of law, and their own courts. Acts passed by the States require the sanction of The Queen-in-Council. The British Government is responsible for defence and international relations. The Channel Islands have trading rights alone within the European Union; these rights do not include financial aid.

In both Bailiwicks the Lieutenant-Governor and Commander-in-Chief, who is appointed by the Crown, is the personal representative of The Queen and the channel of communication between the Crown (via the Privy Council) and the island's government.

The government of each Bailiwick is conducted by committees appointed by the States. Justice is administered by the Royal Courts of Jersey and Guernsey, each consisting of the Bailiff and 12 elected Jurats. The Bailiffs of Jersey and Guernsey, appointed by the Crown, are President of the States and of the Royal Courts of their respective islands.

Each Bailiwick constitutes a deanery under the jurisdiction of the Bishop of Winchester (*see* Index).

ECONOMY

A mild climate and good soil have led to the development of intensive systems of agriculture and horticulture, which form a significant part of the economy. Equally important are invisible earnings, principally from tourism and banking and finance, the low rate of income tax (20p in the £ in Jersey and Guernsey; no tax of any kind in Sark) and the absence of super-tax and death duties making the islands a popular tax-haven.

Principal exports are agricultural produce and flowers; imports are chiefly machinery, manufactured goods, food, fuel and chemicals. Trade with the UK is regarded as internal.

British currency is legal tender in the Channel Islands but each Bailiwick issues its own coins and notes (*see* page 613). They also issue their own postage stamps; UK stamps are not valid.

JERSEY

Lieutenant-Governor and Commander-in-Chief of Jersey, HE Gen. Sir Michael Wilkes, KCB, CBE, *apptd* 1995
Secretary and ADC, Lt.-Col. A. J. C. Woodrow, OBE, MC
Bailiff of Jersey, Sir Philip Bailhache, Kt.
Deputy Bailiff, M. C. St J. Burt
Attorney-General, W. J. Bailhache, QC
Receiver-General, Gp Capt. R. Green, OBE
Solicitor-General, Miss S. C. Nicolle, QC
Greffier of the States, Miss C. M. Newcombe
States Treasurer, I. Black

FINANCE

Year to 31 Dec.	1998	1999
Revenue income	£442,434,776	£478,161,000
Revenue expenditure	357,773,876	405,162,000
Capital expenditure	82,380,488	85,018,000
Public debt	0	0

CHIEF TOWN – ΨSt Helier, on the south coast of Jersey
FLAG – A white field charged with a red saltire cross, and the arms of Jersey in the upper centre

GUERNSEY AND DEPENDENCIES

Lieutenant-Governor and Commander-in-Chief of the Bailiwick of Guernsey and its Dependencies, HE Lt.-Gen. Sir John Foley, KCB, OBE, MC, *apptd* 2000
Secretary and ADC, Col. R. H. Graham, MBE
Bailiff of Guernsey, V. G. Carey
Deputy Bailiff, A. C. K. Day, QC
HM Procureur and Receiver-General, G. R. Rowland, QC
HM Comptroller, H. E. Roberts, QC
States Supervisor, M. J. Brown

FINANCE

Year to 31 Dec.	1998	1999
Revenue	£217,424,000	£238,216,000
Expenditure	180,780,000	190,846,000

CHIEF TOWNS – ΨSt Peter Port, on the east coast of Guernsey; St Anne on Alderney
FLAG – White, bearing a red cross of St George, with a gold cross overall in the centre

ALDERNEY

President of the States, J. Kay-Mouat, OBE
Clerk of the States, D. V. Jenkins
Clerk of the Court, Mrs S. Kelly

SARK

Seigneur of Sark, J. M. Beaumont
The Seneschal, Lt.-Col. R. J. Guille, MBE
The Greffier, J. P. Hamon

OTHER DEPENDENCIES

Herm and Lihou are owned by the States of Guernsey; Herm is leased. Jethou is leased by the Crown to the States of Guernsey and is sub-let by the States. Brecqhou is within the legislative and judicial territory of Sark.

The Environment

INTERNATIONAL CONVENTIONS

Legislation and strategies to protect the environment in the UK are driven by the requirements of international conventions and protocols (of which there are over 50) and European Directives (of which there are over 300), as well as the desires of the UK government. The Environment Agency, the Scottish Environment Protection Agency and the Environment and Heritage Service for Northern Ireland are responsible for regulation.

EUROPEAN UNION MEASURES

The European Union's (EU) work is developed based on its Environmental Action Programme. The current Fifth Environmental Action Programme, 'Towards Sustainability', was adopted in 1992 and sets the programme to 2000. It advocates the use of a wide range of instruments: legislation, economic, support measures (information, education, research), and financial support.

The sixth action programme for adoption in 2001 is currently being prepared, taking into account discussion with member states, target groups, comments from the public, the 1999 State of the Environment Report from the European Environment Agency and the results of the 1999 Eurobarometer (a survey of the opinions and attitudes of Europeans). The document is due at the end of 2000.

SUSTAINABLE DEVELOPMENT AND LOCAL AGENDA 21

The environmental agenda in the UK, both at a business and government level, is moving forward to address sustainability which incorporates social, environmental and economic development. There is much debate over the definition of sustainable development, although the one most commonly used is 'development that meets the needs of the present without compromising the ability of future generations to meet their own needs'.

The UK published its first national sustainable development strategy in 1994 and its first set of sustainable development indicators in 1996. The latest strategy *A Better Quality of Life* was published in May 1999. It establishes a framework for integrating social, environmental and economic policies to meet four objectives: social progress, to protect the environment, prudent use of natural resources, and to maintain high and stable levels of economic growth and employment.

The strategy contains 15 headline indicators, which are backed by a further 150, against which progress in the UK will be measured. Leading businesses are beginning to use the indicators in assessing and reporting their own progress towards achieving sustainability.

Local authorities also have a role to play in sustainable development. Under Local Agenda 21, which came out of the UN Conference on Environment and Development in Rio, Brazil in 1992, local authorities are to draw up sustainable development strategies for their areas. Although not a statutory obligation, the government wants all councils to have adopted Local Agenda 21 by the end of 2000. Currently some 70 per cent have adopted it, with a further 20 per cent planning to do so by the end of the year. Work is under way to bring the other 40 or so on board.

WASTE

Waste policy in the UK follows a number of principles: the waste hierarchy of reduce, re-use, recycle, dispose; the proximity principle of disposing of waste close to its generation; and national self sufficiency.

Directives from Europe are playing an increasingly important role in driving UK policy particularly regarding commercial and industrial waste: the recent Landfill Directive sets stringent targets for reducing the amount of waste sent to landfill and the planned Producer Responsibility directives address the issue of a 'cradle to grave' approach with producers and others in the distribution chain taking greater responsibility for end of life goods. The first directive to be developed was for packaging waste. It came into force in the UK in 1997. Further directives on waste electrical and electronic goods, end-of-life vehicles and batteries are being developed. Meanwhile the UK is considering a producer responsibility initiative on junk mail.

In May 2000, the Waste Strategy for England and Wales was published. It aims to tackle the amount of waste produced; increase recycling rates through statutory targets for local authorities; reduce the amount of waste sent to landfill; and develop markets and end-uses for secondary materials.

A draft national waste strategy for Scotland was published in 1999 and the final version is expected imminently.

CLIMATE CHANGE AND AIR POLLUTION

The UK's response to climate change is driven by the Framework Convention on Climate Change. This is a binding agreement that has been signed and ratified by 181 countries. It was ratified in the UK in December 1993 and came into force in March 1994. It is intended to reduce the risks of global warming by limiting 'greenhouse' gas emissions.

Progress towards the convention's targets are assessed at regular conferences. At Kyoto, Japan in 1997, a protocol (the Kyoto Protocol) to the convention was adopted. So far this has been signed by 84 parties and ratified by 22. It covers the six main greenhouse gases – carbon dioxide, methane, nitrous oxide, hydrofluorocarbons (HFCs), perfluorocarbons (PFCs), and sulphur hexafloride. Under the protocol industrialised countries agreed to legally binding targets for cutting emissions of greenhouse gases by 5.2 per cent below 1990 levels by 2008–12. EU members agreed to an 8 per cent reduction and the UK's target is a 12.5 per cent cut.

The protocol set three ways (Kyoto mechanisms) for countries to increase the flexibility and reduce the cost of making emission cuts – the clean development mechanism, emissions trading and joint implementation. Decisions on the principles and guidelines for these mechanisms will be taken at the sixth Conference of the Parties (CoP-6) in The Hague, Netherlands in November 2000. This meeting will also clarify the methodology of using sinks (such as offsetting emissions by growing forests) and discuss a compliance regime to ensure countries meet their targets.

In March 2000, a draft climate change programme was published which sets out how the UK intends to meet its Kyoto target and progress towards its domestic goal of a 20 per cent cut in carbon dioxide emissions by 2010, some of the policies mentioned are already in place. The proposed measures include: a climate change levy which will come into effect in April 2001 applied to sales of electricity, coal, natural gas, and liquified petroleum gas to the business and public sectors; agreements with energy intensive sectors to meet targets; carbon trading; integrated pollution prevention and control (see below); cutting transport congestion and pollution; energy efficiency standards of performance requiring electricity and gas suppliers to help domestic consumers save energy; better countryside management; cuts in fertiliser use; and new targets for improving energy management of public buildings.

Scotland is currently consulting on its climate change programme.

Other conventions covering air pollution include the Convention on Long Range Transboundary Air Pollution which was adopted in 1979 and came into force in 1993. Protocols to this convention cover various pollutants, such as sulphur and nitrogen oxides. Others, such as the protocol on persistent organic pollutants are still under development.

The UK has also developed its own policy on air pollution. The Environmental Protection Act 1990 established two regimes: integrated pollution control (IPC) to regulate emissions to any environmental medium from certain industrial processes and local air pollution control to regulate emissions to air from smaller processes. The recent European Integrated Pollution Prevention and Control (IPPC) Directive was largely based on the UK's IPC regime. Although IPPC is very similar to the UK's IPC it will cover many more installations and will include returning sites to a satisfactory state on closure, using energy efficiently and noise and vibration regulation.

The Environment Agency is currently assessing ways to integrate a regulatory and voluntary approach to reduce the burden of regulation for those companies with good environmental management that is backed by certification to the ISO 14001 international environmental management standard.

The first National Air Quality Strategy was published in 1997 and was revised in January 2000. The strategy sets air quality objectives for the main pollutants (benzene, 1-3, butadiene, carbon monoxide, lead, nitrogen dioxide, sulphur dioxide, ozone, and particulates) to be met by 2003–8.

Under the strategy, all district and unitary authorities have a duty to review air quality, including likely future air quality, in their areas. This is accompanied by an assessment of whether air quality objectives (set in the strategy) are being, or are likely to be, met. If authorities find that any part of their area breaches the objectives, an air quality management area must be declared and an action plan drawn up for improvements. Councils are currently in the process of declaring such areas.

WATER

Water quality targets are set at both EU and UK levels for drinking water sources, wastewater discharges, rivers, coastal water and bathing water.

The EC Bathing Water Directive sets standards for bathing waters. This applies to 391 coastal and nine inland bathing waters in the UK. In 1999, 90 per cent met the standards, up from 65 per cent in 1988.

The Environment Agency sets river quality objectives for each stretch of river. In 1997, 82 per cent of rivers met their objectives.

Water quality is protected through licensing abstraction and regulating discharges. Consents to discharge sewage and industrial effluent are regulated under the Water Resources Act 1991 and the Environmental Protection Act 1990 through its IPC regime. Discharge consents are based on the river quality objectives and relevant EU directives and specify the concentration and quantity permitted.

The European Urban Waste Water Treatment Directive sets minimum standards for sewage treatment before discharge into coastal waters with the levels of treatment needed depending on the sensitivity of the receiving water. In 1999 the government set more stringent UK targets for all significant coastal discharges to have a minimum of secondary treatment by 2005.

SELECTED UK TARGETS

Global Atmosphere

- Reduce greenhouse gas emissions to 12.5 per cent below 1990 levels by 2010
- Reduce carbon dioxide emissions to 20 per cent below 1990 levels by 2010

Air Quality and Noise

- Reduce sulphur dioxide emissions by 63 per cent based on 1990 levels by 2010
- Reduce emissions of nitrogen oxides by 41 per cent based on 1990 levels by 2010
- Reduce emissions of volatile organic compounds by 40 per cent based on 1990 levels by 2010
- Reduce ammonia emissions by 17 per cent based on 1990 levels by 2010

Fresh Water and the Sea

- 97 per cent of bathing waters to meet European directive standards consistently by 2005
- Phase out use of untreated sewage sludge on agricultural land by the end of 2001
- Provide secondary treatment for discharges above 15,000 population equivalent by 31 March 2002
- Provide secondary treatment for all significant coastal discharges (over 2,000 population equivalent) by 2005

Waste

- Reduce industrial and commercial waste going to landfill by 85 per cent of 1998 levels by 2005
- Recover 40 per cent of municipal waste by 2005, 45 per cent by 2010 and 67 per cent by 2015
- Recycle or compost 25 per cent of household waste by 2005, 30 per cent by 2010 and 33 per cent by 2015
- Reduce biodegradable waste sent to landfill to 75 per cent of 1995 levels by 2010, 50 per cent by 2013 and 35 per cent by 2020
- Ensure 60 per cent of UK newspaper feedstock content is waste paper by end of 2001, 65 per cent by end of 2003 and 70 per cent by end of 2006
- Recover 50–65 per cent of packaging waste by June 2001, including at least 15 per cent of each material
- Recycle 25–45 per cent of packaging waste by June 2001
- Proposed re-use and recovery of 85 per cent for end-of-life vehicles with a minimum of 80 per cent recycling by 2006, 95 per cent and 85 per cent by 2015

Land

- Ensure 60 per cent of all new housing is built on re-used sites

Housing

- Reduce the proportion of homes lying empty to 3 per cent by 2005
- To ensure 60 per cent of all additional dwellings are built on previously developed land or are provided through conversions by 2008
- Reduce the number of government-owned empty names

CONTACTS

ADVISORY COMMITTEE ON BUSINESS AND THE ENVIRONMENT, Zone 6/D12, Ashdown House, 123 Victoria Street, London SW1E 6DE. Tel: 020-7890 6278. Web: http://www.environment.detr.gov.uk/acbe/index.htm

DEPARTMENT OF ENVIRONMENT, TRANSPORT AND THE REGIONS, Eland House, Bressenden Place, London SW1E 5DU. Tel: 020-7944 3000. Web: http://www.detr.gov.uk

ENVIRONMENT AENCY, Rivers House, Waterside Drive, Aztec West, Almondsbury, Bristol BS12 4UD. Tel: 01454 624400. Web: http://www.environment-agency.gov.uk

ENVIRONMENTAL TECHNOLOGY Best Practice Programme, The Environment and Energy Helpline. Tel: 0800 585794. Web: http://www.etbpp.netgates.co.uk

EUROPEAN ENVIRONMENT AGENCY, Kongens Nytorv 6, DK-1050 Copenhagen K, Denmark. Tel: 45-3336 7100. Web: http://www.eea.eu.int

GOVERNMENT PANEL ON SUSTAINABLE DEVELOPMENT, 5th Floor, Romney House, 43 Marsham Street, London SW1P 3PY. Tel: 020-7944 4964. Web: http://www.open.gov.uk/panel-sd/homesd.htm

LOCAL AGENDA 21, Improvement and Development Agency, Layden House, 76–78 Turnmill Street, London EC1M 5QU. Tel: 020-7296 6599. Web: http://www.la21-uk.org.uk

ROYAL COMMISSION ON ENVIRONMENTAL POLLUTION, Steel House, 11 Tothill Street, London SW1H 9RE. Tel: 020 7273 6635. Web: http://www.rcep.org.uk/contacts.html

SCOTTISH ENVIRONMENTAL PROTECTION AGENCY, Erskine Court, Castle Business Park, Stirling FK9 4TR. Web: http://www.sepa.gov.uk

UK ROUND TABLE ON SUSTAINABLE DEVELOPMENT, 5th Floor, Romney House, Tufton Street, London SW1P 3RA. Tel: 020-7944 4960.

UN COMMISSION ON SUSTAINABLE DEVELOPMENT, Division for Sustainable Development, 2 UN Plaza, Room DC2-2220, New York, NY 10017, USA. Tel: 212-963 3170. Web: http://www.un.org/esa/sustdev

World Heritage Sites

The Convention Concerning the Protection of the World Cultural and Natural Heritage was adopted by UNESCO in 1972 and ratified by the UK in 1984. By May 2000 the convention had been ratified by 156 states. The convention provides for the identification, protection and conservation of cultural and natural sites of outstanding universal value.

Cultural sites may be:
– monuments
– groups of buildings
– sites of historic, aesthetic, archaeological, scientific, ethnologic or anthropologic value
– historic areas of towns
– 'cultural landscapes', i.e. sites whose characteristics are marked by significant interactions between human populations and their natural environment

Natural sites may be:
– those with remarkable physical, biological or geological formations
– those with outstanding universal value from the point of view of science, conservation or natural beauty
– the habitat of threatened species and plants

Governments which are party to the convention nominate sites in their country for inclusion in the World Cultural and Natural Heritage List. Nominations are considered by the World Heritage Committee, an inter-governmental committee composed of 21 representatives of the parties to the convention. The committee is advised by the International Council on Monuments and Sites (ICOMOS) and the International Union for the Conservation of Nature (IUCN). ICOMOS evaluates and reports on proposed cultural sites and IUCN on proposed natural sites. The International Centre for the Study of the Preservation and Restoration of Cultural Property (ICCROM) provides the committee with expert advice on monument restoration. The Department for Culture, Media and Sport represents the UK government in matters relating to the convention.

A prerequisite for inclusion in the World Cultural and Natural Heritage List is the existence of an effective legal protection system in the country in which the site is situated (e.g. listing, conservation areas and planning controls in the United Kingdom) and a detailed management plan to ensure the conservation of the site. Inclusion in the list does not confer any greater degree of protection on the site than that offered by the national protection framework.

If a site is considered to be in serious danger of decay or damage the committee may add it to a complementary list, the World Heritage in Danger List. Sites on this list may benefit from particular attention or emergency measures. There were 27 sites on this list in November 1999.

Financial support for the conservation of sites on the World Cultural and Natural Heritage List is provided by the World Heritage Fund. This is administered by the World Heritage Committee, which determines the financial and technical aid to be allocated. The fund's income is derived from the obligatory contributions of the parties to the convention, amounting to 1 per cent of their contribution to UNESCO. The fund may also receive voluntary contributions from the parties to the convention, donations from institutions or individuals, and income from national and international promotional activities.

DESIGNATED SITES

As at December 1999 there were 630 sites in 118 countries on the World Cultural and Natural Heritage List. Of these, 16 were in the United Kingdom and two in British overseas territories; 14 were listed for their cultural significance (†) and four for their natural significance (*).

United Kingdom
†Bath – the city
†Blenheim Palace and park, Oxfordshire
†Canterbury Cathedral, St Augustine's Abbey, St Martin's Church, Kent
†Castle and town walls of King Edward I, north Wales – Beaumaris, Anglesey, Caernarfon Castle, Conwy Castle, Harlech Castle
†Durham Cathedral and Castle
†Edinburgh Old and New Towns
†Giant's Causeway and Causeway coast, Co. Antrim
†Greenwich, London – maritime Greenwich, including the Royal Naval College, Old Royal Observatory, Queen's House, town centre
†Hadrian's Wall, northern England
†Heart of Neouthic, Orkney
†Ironbridge Gorge, Shropshire – the world's first iron bridge and other early industrial sites
†St Kilda, Western Isles
†Stonehenge, Avebury and related megalithic sites, Wiltshire
†Studley Royal Park, Fountains Abbey, St Mary's Church, N. Yorkshire
†Tower of London
†Westminster Abbey, Palace of Westminster, St Margaret's Church, London

British Overseas Territories
*Henderson Island, Pitcairn Islands, South Pacific Ocean
*Gough Island wildlife reserve (part of Tristan da Cunha), South Atlantic Ocean

BUILDINGS, MONUMENTS AND SITES DIVISION, Department for Culture, Media and Sport, 2-4 Cockspur Street, London SW1Y 5DH. Tel: 020-7211 6909

WORLD HERITAGE CENTRE, UNESCO, 7 place de Fontenoy, 75352 Paris, France. Tel: Paris 4568 1876. Email: whinfo@unesco.org

INTERNATIONAL CENTRE FOR THE STUDY OF THE PRESERVATION AND RESTORATION OF CULTURAL PROPERTY (ICCROM), Via di San Michele 13, I-00153 Rome, Italy. Tel: Rome 585531

INTERNATIONAL COUNCIL ON MONUMENTS AND SITES (ICOMOS), 10 Barley Mow Passage, London W4 4PH. Tel: 020-8994 6477

INTERNATIONAL UNION FOR THE CONSERVATION OF NATURE (IUCN), UK Committee, c/o 36 Kingfisher Court, Hambridge Road, Newbury, Berks RG14 5SJ. Tel: 01635-522925

Conservation and Heritage

Conservation of the Countryside

NATIONAL PARKS

ENGLAND AND WALES

The ten National Parks of England and Wales were set up under the provisions of the National Parks and Access to the Countryside Act 1949 to conserve and protect scenic landscapes from inappropriate development and to provide access to the land for public enjoyment.

The Countryside Agency (established on 1 April 1999 from the merger of the Countryside Commission and the Rural Development Commission) is the statutory body which has the power to designate National Parks in England, and the Countryside Council for Wales is responsible for National Parks in Wales. Designations in England are confirmed by the Secretary of State for the Environment, Transport and the Regions and those in Wales by the National Assembly for Wales. The designation of a National Park does not affect the ownership of the land or remove the rights of the local community. The majority of the land in the National Parks is owned by private landowners (74 per cent) or by bodies such as the National Trust (7 per cent) and the Forestry Commission (7 per cent). The National Park Authorities own only 2.3 per cent of the land.

The Environment Act 1995 replaced the existing National Park boards and committees with free-standing National Park Authorities (NPAs). NPAs are the sole local planning authorities for their areas and as such influence land use and development, and deal with planning applications. Their duties include conserving and enhancing the natural beauty, wildlife and cultural heritage of the National Parks; promoting opportunities for public understanding and enjoyment of the National Parks; and fostering the economic and social well-being of the communities within National Parks. The NPAs publish management plans as statements of their policies and appoint their own officers and staff.

Membership of the NPAs differs slightly between England and Wales. In England membership is split between representatives of the constituent local authorities and members appointed by the Secretary of State (of whom one half minus one are nominated by the parish councils in the park), with the local authority representatives in a majority of one. The Countryside Agency advises the Secretary of State on appointments not nominated by the parish councils. In Wales two-thirds of NPA members are appointed by the constituent local authorities and one-third by the National Assembly for Wales, advised by the Countryside Council for Wales.

Central government provides 75 per cent of the funding for the parks through the National Park Grant. The remaining 25 per cent is supplied by the local authorities concerned. Approved net expenditure for all National Parks in 1999–2000 was £25,036,000 for England and £6,694,000 for Wales.

Two areas considered as having equivalent status are the Broads and the New Forest.

The National Parks (with date designation confirmed) are:

BRECON BEACONS (1957), Powys (66 per cent)/Carmarthenshire/Rhondda, Cynon and Taff/Merthyr Tydfil/Blaenau Gwent/Monmouthshire, 1,351 sq. km/522 sq. miles – The park is centred on the Beacons, Pen y Fan, Corn Du and Cribyn, but also includes the valley of the Usk, the Black Mountains to the east and the Black Mountain to the west. There are information centres at Brecon, Craig-y-nos Country Park, Abergavenny and Llandovery, a study centre at Danywenallt and a day visitor centre near Libanus. *Information Office*, 7 Glamorgan Street, Brecon, Powys LD3 7DP. Tel: 01874-624437. *National Park Officer*, M.Fitton

DARTMOOR (1951 and 1994), Devon, 954 sq. km/368 sq. miles – The park consists of moorland and rocky granite tors, and is rich in prehistoric remains. There are information centres at Newbridge, Tavistock, Bovey Tracey, Steps Bridge, Princetown and Postbridge. *Information Office*, Parke, Haytor Road, Bovey Tracey, Devon TQ13 9JQ. Tel: 01626-832093. *National Park Officer*, N. Atkinson

EXMOOR (1954), Somerset (71 per cent)/Devon, 693 sq. km/268 sq. miles – Exmoor is a moorland plateau inhabited by wild ponies and red deer. There are many ancient remains and burial mounds. There are information centres at Lynmouth, County Gate, Dulverton and Combe Martin. *Information Office*, Exmoor House, Dulverton, Somerset TA22 9HL. Tel: 01398-23665. *National Park Officer*, K.Bungay

LAKE DISTRICT (1951), Cumbria, 2,292 sq. km/885 sq. miles – The Lake District includes England's highest mountains (Scafell Pike, Helvellyn and Skiddaw) but it is most famous for its glaciated lakes. There are information centres at Keswick, Waterhead, Hawkshead, Seatoller, Bowness, Grasmere, Coniston, Glenridding and Pooley Bridge, an information van at Gosforth and a park centre at Brockhole, Windermere. *Information Office*, Brockhole, Windermere, Cumbria LA23 1LJ. Tel: 01539-446601. *National Park Officer*, P. Tiplady

NORTHUMBERLAND (1956), Northumberland, 1,049 sq. km/405 sq. miles – The park is an area of hill country stretching from Hadrian's Wall to the Scottish Border. There are information centres at Ingram, Once Brewed, Rothbury, Housesteads, Harbottle and Kielder, and an information caravan at Cawfields. *Information Office*, Eastburn, South Park, Hexham, Northumberland NE46 1BS. Tel: 01434-605555. *National Park Officer*, G. Taylor

NORTH YORK MOORS (1952), North Yorkshire (96 per cent)/Redcar and Cleveland, 1,436 sq. km/554 sq. miles – The park consists of woodland and moorland, and includes the Hambleton Hills and the Cleveland Way. There are information centres at Danby, Pickering, Sutton Bank, Ravenscar, Helmsley and Hutton-le-Hole, and a day study centre at Danby.

Information Office, The Old Vicarage, Bondgate, Helmsley, York YO6 5BP. Tel:01439-70657. *National Park Officer*, D.Arnold-Forster

PEAK DISTRICT (1951), Derbyshire (64 per cent)/ Staffordshire/South Yorkshire/Cheshire/West Yorkshire/Greater Manchester, 1,438 sq. km/ 555 sq. miles – The Peak District includes the gritstone moors of the 'Dark Peak' and the limestone dales of the 'White Peak'. There are information centres at Bakewell, Edale, Fairholmes and Castleton, and information points at Torside (in the Longdendale Valley) and at Hartington (former station). *Information Office*, Aldern House, Baslow Road, Bakewell, Derbyshire DE45 1AE. Tel: 01629-814321. *National Park Officer*, C. Harrison

PEMBROKESHIRE COAST (1952 and 1995), Pembrokeshire, 584 sq. km/225 sq. miles – The park includes cliffs, moorland and a number of islands, including Skomer. There are information centres at Tenby, St David's, Pembroke, Newport, Kilgetty, Haverfordwest and Broad Haven. *Information Office*, Winch Lane, Haverfordwest, Pembrokeshire SA61 1PY. Tel: 01437-764636. *National Park Officer*, N.Wheeler

SNOWDONIA (1951), Gwynedd/Conwy, 2,142 sq. km/827 sq. miles – Snowdonia is an area of deep valleys and rugged mountains. There are information centres at Aberdyfi, Bala, Betws y Coed, Blaenau Ffestiniog, Conwy, Harlech, Dolgellau and Llanberis. *Information Office*, Penrhyndeudraeth, Gwynedd LL48 6LF. Tel: 01766-770274. *National Park Officer*, I.Huws

YORKSHIRE DALES (1954), North Yorkshire (88 per cent)/Cumbria, 1,769 sq. km/683 sq. miles – The Yorkshire Dales are composed primarily of limestone overlaid in places by millstone grit. The three peaks of Ingleborough, Whernside and Pen-y-Ghent are within the park. There are information centres at Clapham, Grassington, Hawes, Aysgarth Falls, Malham and Sedbergh. *Information Office*, Yorebridge House, Bainbridge, Leyburn, N. Yorks DL8 3BP. Tel: 01969-50456. *National Park Officer*, H. Hancock

Two other areas considered to have equivalent status to national parks are the Broads and the New Forest. The Broads Authority, a special statutory authority, was established in 1989 to develop, conserve and manage the Norfolk and Suffolk Broads. The Government declared in 1992 its intention of giving the New Forest a status equivalent to that of a National Park by declaring it an 'area of national significance'.

THE BROADS (1989), Norfolk, 303 sq. km/117 sq. miles – The Broads are located between Norwich and Great Yarmouth on the flood plains of the five rivers flowing through the area to the sea. The area is one of fens, winding waterways, woodland and marsh. The 40 or so broads are man-made, and are connected to the rivers by dykes, providing over 200 km of navigable waterways. There are information centres at Beccles, Hoveton, North-west Tower (Yarmouth), Ranworth and Toad Hole. *Broads Authority*, Thomas Harvey House, 18 Colegate, Norwich NR3 1BQ. Tel: 01603-610734. *Chief Executive*, A.Clark

THE NEW FOREST, Hampshire, 376 sq. km/145 sq. miles – The forest has been protected since 1079 when it was declared a royal hunting forest. The area consists of forest, ancient woodland and heathland. Much of the Forest is managed by the Forestry Commission, which provides several camp-sites. The main villages are Brockenhurst, Burley and Lyndhurst, which has a visitor centre. *The Forestry Commission*, Office of the Deputy Surveyor of the New Forest and the New Forest Committee, The Queen's House, Lyndhurst, Hants SO43 7NH. Tel: 023-8028 4149

SCOTLAND AND NORTHERN IRELAND

The National Parks and Access to the Countryside Act 1949 dealt only with England and Wales and made no provision for Scotland or Northern Ireland. Although there are no national parks in these two countries, there is power to designate them in Northern Ireland under the Amenity Lands Act 1965 and the Nature Conservation and Amenity Lands Order (Northern Ireland) 1985. In 1998 Scottish Natural Heritage submitted proposals to the Government for the designation of National Parks in Scotland. It will be for the Scottish Parliament to legislate in this area.

AREAS OF OUTSTANDING NATURAL BEAUTY

ENGLAND AND WALES

Under the National Parks and Access to the Countryside Act 1949, provision was made for the designation of Areas of Outstanding Natural Beauty (AONBs) by the Countryside Commission. The Countryside Agency is now responsible for AONBs in England and since April 1991 the Countryside Council for Wales has been responsible for the Welsh AONBs. Designations in England are confirmed by the Secretary of State for the Environment, Transport and the Regions and those in Wales by the National Assembly for Wales.

Although less emphasis is placed upon the provision of open-air enjoyment for the public than in the national parks, AONBs are areas which are no less beautiful and require the same degree of protection to conserve and enhance the natural beauty of the countryside. This includes protecting flora and fauna, geological and other landscape features. In AONBs planning and management responsibilities are split between county and district councils; where unitary authorities exist in Wales, they have sole responsibility for planning and management. Several AONBs cross local authority boundaries. Finance for the AONBs is provided by grant-aid.

The 41 Areas of Outstanding Natural Beauty (with date designation confirmed) are:

ANGLESEY (1967), Anglesey, 221 sq. km/85 sq. miles
ARNSIDE AND SILVERDALE (1972), Cumbria/Lancashire, 75 sq. km/29 sq. miles
BLACKDOWN HILLS (1991), Devon/Somerset, 370 sq. km/143 sq. miles
CANNOCK CHASE (1958), Staffordshire, 68 sq. km/26 sq. miles
CHICHESTER HARBOUR (1964), Hampshire/West Sussex, 74 sq. km/29 sq. miles
CHILTERNS (1965; extended 1990), Bedfordshire/ Hertfordshire/Buckinghamshire/Oxfordshire, 833 sq. km/322 sq. miles
CLWYDIAN RANGE (1985), Denbighshire/Flintshire, 157 sq. km/60 sq. miles
CORNWALL (1959; Camel estuary 1983), 958 sq. km/370 sq. miles

COTSWOLDS (1966; extended 1990),
Gloucestershire/Wiltshire/Warwickshire/
Worcestershire/Somerset, 2,038 sq. km/787 sq. miles

CRANBORNE CHASE AND WEST WILTSHIRE DOWNS
(1983), Dorset/Hampshire/Somerset/Wiltshire,
983 sq. km/379 sq. miles

DEDHAM VALE (1970; extended 1978, 1991),
Essex/Suffolk, 90 sq. km/35 sq. miles

DORSET (1959), 1,129 sq. km/436 sq. miles

EAST DEVON (1963), 268 sq. km/103 sq. miles

EAST HAMPSHIRE (1962), 383 sq. km/148 sq. miles

FOREST OF BOWLAND (1964), Lancashire/North
Yorkshire, 802 sq. km/310 sq. miles

GOWER (1956), Swansea, 188 sq. km/73 sq. miles

HIGH WEALD (1983), Kent/Surrey/East Sussex/West
Sussex, 1,460 sq. km/564 sq. miles

HOWARDIAN HILLS (1987), North Yorkshire, 204
sq. km/79 sq. miles

ISLE OF WIGHT (1963), 189 sq. km/73 sq. miles

ISLES OF SCILLY (1976), 16 sq. km/6 sq. miles

KENT DOWNS (1968), 878 sq. km/339 sq. miles

LINCOLNSHIRE WOLDS (1973), 558 sq. km/215 sq. miles

LLEYNN (1957), Gwynedd, 161 sq. km/62 sq. miles

MALVERN HILLS (1959), Herefordshire/Worcestershire/
Gloucestershire, 105 sq. km/40 sq. miles

MENDIP HILLS (1972; extended 1989), Somerset,
198 sq. km/76 sq. miles

NIDDERDALE (1994), North Yorkshire, 603 sq. km/
233 sq. miles

NORFOLK COAST (1968), 451 sq. km/174 sq. miles

NORTH DEVON (1960), 171 sq. km/66 sq. miles

NORTH PENNINES (1988), Cumbria/Durham/
Northumberland, 1,983 sq. km/766 sq. miles

NORTHUMBERLAND COAST (1958), 135 sq. km/
52 sq. miles

QUANTOCK HILLS (1957), Somerset, 99 sq. km/
38 sq. miles

SHROPSHIRE HILLS (1959), 804 sq. km/310 sq. miles

SOLWAY COAST (1964), Cumbria, 115 sq. km/44 sq. miles

SOUTH DEVON (1960), 337 sq. km/130 sq. miles

SOUTH HAMPSHIRE COAST (1967), 77 sq. km/30 sq. miles

SUFFOLK COAST AND HEATHS (1970), 403 sq. km/
156 sq. miles

SURREY HILLS (1958), 419 sq. km/162 sq. miles

SUSSEX DOWNS (1966), 983 sq. km/379 sq. miles

TAMAR VALLEY (1995), Cornwall/Devon, 195 sq. km/
115 sq. miles

NORTH WESSEX DOWNS (1972), Berkshire/Hampshire/
Oxfordshire/Wiltshire, 1,730 sq. km/668 sq. miles

WYE VALLEY (1971), Monmouthshire/Gloucestershire/
Herefordshire, 326 sq. km/126 sq. miles

NORTHERN IRELAND

The Department of the Environment for Northern
Ireland, with advice from the Council for Nature
Conservation and the Countryside, designates Areas of
Outstanding Natural Beauty in Northern Ireland. At
present there are nine and these cover a total area of
approximately 284,948 hectares (704,121 acres).

ANTRIM COAST AND GLENS, Co. Antrim, 70,600 ha/
174,452 acres

CAUSEWAY COAST, Co. Antrim, 4,200 ha/10,378 acres

LAGAN VALLEY, Co. Down, 2,072ha/5,119 acres

LECALE COAST, Co. Down, 3,108 ha/7,679 acres

MOURNE, Co. Down, 57,012 ha/140,876 acres

NORTH DERRY, Co. Londonderry, 12,950 ha/
31,999 acres

RING OF GULLION, Co. Armagh, 15,353ha/37,938 acres

SPERRIN, Co. Tyrone/Co. Londonderry,
101,006 ha/249,585 acres

STRANGFORD LOUGH, Co. Down, 18,647 ha/46,077 acres

NATIONAL SCENIC AREAS

In Scotland, National Scenic Areas have a broadly
equivalent status to AONBs. Scottish Natural Heritage
recognises areas of national scenic significance. At mid
1999 there were 40, covering a total area of 1,001,800
hectares (2,475,448 acres).

Development within National Scenic Areas is dealt with
by local authorities, who are required to consult Scottish
Natural Heritage concerning certain categories of development. Disagreements between Scottish Natural Heritage and local authorities are referred to the Scottish
Executive. Land management uses can also be modified in
the interest of scenic conservation.

ASSYNT-COIGACH, Highland, 90,200 ha/222,884 acres

BEN NEVIS AND GLEN COE, Highland/Argyll and
Bute/Perth and Kinross, 101,600 ha/251,053 acres

CAIRNGORM MOUNTAINS, Highland/Aberdeenshire/
Moray, 67,200 ha/166,051 acres

CUILLIN HILLS, Highland, 21,900 ha/54,115 acres

DEESIDE AND LOCHNAGAR, Aberdeenshire/Angus,
40,000 ha/98,840 acres

DORNOCH FIRTH, Highland, 7,500 ha/18,532 acres

EAST STEWARTRY COAST, Dumfries and Galloway,
4,500 ha/11,119 acres

EILDON AND LEADERFOOT, Scottish Borders,
3,600 ha/8,896 acres

FLEET VALLEY, Dumfries and Galloway,
5,300 ha/13,096 acres

GLEN AFFRIC, Highland, 19,300 ha/47,690 acres

GLEN STRATHFARRAR, Highland, 3,800 ha/9,390 acres

HOY AND WEST MAINLAND, Orkney Islands,
14,800 ha/36,571 acres

JURA, Argyll and Bute, 21,800 ha/53,868 acres

KINTAIL, Highland, 15,500 ha/38,300 acres

KNAPDALE, Argyll and Bute, 19,800 ha/48,926 acres

KNOYDART, Highland, 39,500 ha/97,604 acres

KYLE OF TONGUE, Highland, 18,500 ha/45,713 acres

KYLES OF BUTE, Argyll and Bute, 4,400 ha/10,872 acres

LOCH NA KEAL, MULL, Argyll and Bute, 12,700
ha/31,382 acres

LOCH LOMOND, Argyll and Bute/Stirling/
West Dunbartonshire, 27,400 ha/67,705 acres

LOCH RANNOCH AND GLEN LYON, Perth and
Kinross/Stirling, 48,400 ha/119,596 acres

LOCH SHIEL, Highland, 13,400 ha/33,111 acres

LOCH TUMMEL, Perth and Kinross, 9,200 ha/22,733 acres

LYNN OF LORN, Argyll and Bute, 4,800 ha/11,861 acres

MORAR, MOIDART AND ARDNAMURCHAN, Highland,
13,500 ha/33,358 acres

NORTH-WEST SUTHERLAND, Highland, 20,500 ha/50,655
acres

NITH ESTUARY, Dumfries and Galloway, 9,300 ha/
22,980 acres

NORTH ARRAN, North Ayrshire, 23,800 ha/58,810 acres

RIVER EARN, Perth and Kinross, 3,000 ha/7,413 acres

RIVER TAY, Perth and Kinross, 5,600 ha/13,838 acres

ST KILDA, Western Isles, 900 ha/2,224 acres

SCARBA, LUNGA AND THE GARVELLACHS, Argyll and
Bute, 1,900 ha/4,695 acres

SHETLAND, SHETLAND ISLANDS, 11,600 ha/28,664 acres

SMALL ISLES, Highland, 15,500 ha/38,300 acres

SOUTH LEWIS, HARRIS AND NORTH UIST, Western Isles, 109,600 ha/270,822 acres
SOUTH UIST MACHAIR, Western Isles, 6,100 ha/ 15,073 acres
THE TROSSACHS, Stirling, 4,600 ha/11,367 acres
TROTTERNISH, Highland, 5,000 ha/12,355 acres
UPPER TWEEDDALE, Scottish Borders, 10,500 ha/ 25,945 acres
WESTER ROSS, Highland, 145,300 ha/359,036 acres

THE NATIONAL FOREST

The National Forest is being planted across 200 square miles of Derbyshire, Leicestershire and Staffordshire. About 30 million trees, of mixed species but mainly broadleaved, will be planted, and will eventually cover about one-third of the designated area. The project is funded by the Department of the Environment, Transport and the Regions. It was developed in 1992–5 by the Countryside Commission and is now run by the National Forest Company, which was established in April 1995. Since then 3.5 million trees have been planted on 1,998 hectares of land across 428 sites. Under the National Forest Tender Scheme, anybody wishing to undertake a project can submit a competitive bid to the National Forest Company.

NATIONAL FOREST COMPANY, Enterprise Glade, Bath Lane, Moira, Swadlincote, Derbys DE12 6BD. Tel: 01283-551211. *Chief Executive*, Miss S. Bell, OBE

Nature Conservation Areas

SITES OF SPECIAL SCIENTIFIC INTEREST

Site of Special Scientific Interest (SSSI) is a legal notification applied to land in England, Scotland or Wales which English Nature (EN), Scottish Natural Heritage (SNH), or the Countryside Council for Wales (CCW) identifies as being of special interest because of its flora, fauna, geological or physiographical features. In some cases, SSSIs are managed as nature reserves.

EN, SNH and CCW must notify the designation of a SSSI to the local planning authority, every owner/ occupier of the land, and the Secretary of State for the Environment, Transport and the Regions, the First Minister in Scotland or the National Assembly for Wales. Forestry and agricultural departments and a number of other bodies are also informed of this notification.

Objections to the notification of a SSSI can be made and ultimately considered at a full meeting of the Council of EN or CCW. In Scotland an objection will be dealt with by the appropriate area board or the main board of SNH, depending on the nature of the objection. Unresolved objections on scientific grounds must be referred to the Advisory Committee on SSSI.

The protection of these sites depends on the co-operation of individual landowners and occupiers. Owner/occupiers must consult EN, SNH or CCW and gain written consent before they can undertake certain listed activities on the site. Funds are available through management agreements and grants to assist owners and occupiers in conserving sites' interests. As a last resort a site can be purchased.

The number and area of SSSIs in Britain as at 31 March 2000 was:

	no.	hectares	acres
England*	4,088	1,053,796	2,603,930
Scotland	1,459	992,670	2,452,854
Wales	999	223,632	552,371

*Figures as on 30 September 1999

NORTHERN IRELAND

In Northern Ireland 161 Areas of Special Scientific Interest (ASSIs) have been established by the Department of the Environment for Northern Ireland. These cover a total area of 83,465.476 hectares (206,243.19 acres).

NATIONAL NATURE RESERVES

National Nature Reserves are defined in the National Parks and Access to the Countryside Act 1949 as land designated for the study and preservation of flora and fauna, or of geological or physiographical features.

English Nature (EN), Scottish Natural Heritage (SNH) or the Countryside Council for Wales (CCW) can designate as a National Nature Reserve land which is being managed as a nature reserve under an agreement with one of the statutory nature conservation agencies; land held and managed by EN, SNH or CCW; or land held and managed as a nature reserve by another approved body. EN, SNH or CCW can make by-laws to protect reserves from undesirable activities; these are subject to confirmation by the Secretary of State for the Environment, Transport and the Regions, the National Assembly for Wales or the First Minister in Scotland.

The number and area of National Nature Reserves in Britain as on 31 March 2000 was:

	no.	hectares	acres
England	202	81,433	201,221
Scotland	71	114,277	282,378
Wales	64	18,757	46,330

NORTHERN IRELAND

National Nature Reserves are established and managed by the Department of the Environment for Northern Ireland, with advice from the Council for Nature Conservation and the Countryside. There are 45 National Nature Reserves covering 4,322.1 hectares (10,676 acres).

LOCAL NATURE RESERVES

Local Nature Reserves are defined in the National Parks and Access to the Countryside Act 1949 as land designated for the study and preservation of flora and fauna, of geological or physiographical features. The Act gives local authorities in England, Scotland and Wales the power to acquire, declare and manage local nature reserves in consultation with English Nature, Scottish Natural Heritage and the Countryside Council for Wales. Conservation trusts can also own and manage non-statutory local nature reserves.

The number and area of designated Local Nature Reserves in Britain as at 31 March 2000 was:

	no.	hectares	acres
England	632	29,442	72,751
Scotland	29	9,297	22,973
Wales	49	4,671	11,537

An additional 38 km of linear trails are designated as Local Nature Reserves.

FOREST NATURE RESERVES

Forest Enterprise (an executive agency of the Forestry Commission) is responsible for the management of the Commission's forests. It has created 46 Forest Nature Reserves with the aim of protecting and conserving special forms of natural habitat, flora and fauna. There are about 300 SSSIs on the estates, some of which are also Nature Reserves.

Forest Nature Reserves extend in size from under 50 hectares (124 acres) to over 500 hectares (1,236 acres). The largest include the Black Wood of Rannoch, by Loch Rannoch; Cannop Valley Oakwoods, Forest of Dean; Culbin Forest, near Forres; Glen Affric, near Fort Augustus; Kylerhea, Skye; Pembrey, Carmarthen Bay; Starr Forest, in Galloway Forest Park; and Wyre Forest, near Kidderminster.

Forest Enterprise also manages 18 Caledonian Forest Reserves in Scotland. These reserves are intended to protect and expand 16,000 hectares of native oak and pine woods in the Scottish highlands.

NORTHERN IRELAND
There are 35 Forest Nature Reserves in Northern Ireland, covering 1,537 hectares (3,796 acres). They are designated and administered by the Forest Service, an agency of the Department of Agriculture and Rural Development for Northern Ireland. There are also 16 National Nature Reserves on Forest Service-owned property.

MARINE NATURE RESERVES

The Secretary of State for the Environment, Transport and the Regions, the National Assembly for Wales and the Scottish Executive have the power to designate Marine Nature Reserves. English Nature, Scottish Natural Heritage and the Countryside Council for Wales select and manage these reserves. Marine Nature Reserves may be established in Northern Ireland under a 1985 Order.

Marine Nature Reserves provide protection for marine flora and fauna, and geological and physiographical features on land covered by tidal waters or parts of the sea in or adjacent to the UK. Reserves also provide opportunities for study and research.

The three statutory Marine Nature Reserves are:

LUNDY (1986), Bristol Channel
SKOMER (1990), Dyfed
STRANGFORD LOUGH (1995), Northern Ireland

Two other areas proposed for designation as reserves are: the Menai Strait, and Bardsey Island and part of the Llyn peninsula, both in Wales.

A number of non-statutory marine reserves have been set up by conservation groups.

EUROPEAN MARINE SITES
The 1992 EC Habitats Directive and the 1979 Birds Directive allow the UK government to establish Special Areas of Conservation (SACs) on Special Protection Areas (SPA) for birds on land and at sea. Where the designated area includes sea or seashore it is described as a European marine site. The UK Marine SACs project is a demonstration initiative, funded partly by the EU, to establish management schemes for twelve of the marine SACs in the UK.

Conservation of wildlife and habitats

The UK is party to a number of international conventions.

RAMSAR CONVENTION

The 1971 Ramsar Convention on Wetlands of International Importance especially as Waterfowl Habitat, entered into force in the UK in May 1976. By June 2000 121 countries were party to the convention with another 20 on the way.

The aim of the convention is the conservation and wise use of wetlands and their flora and fauna, especially waterfowl. Governments that are party to the convention must designate wetlands and include wetland conservation considerations in their land-use planning. A total of 1,027 wetland sites, totalling 78.1 million hectares have been designated for inclusion in the List of Wetlands of International Importance. The UK currently has 150 designated sites covering 720,640 hectares.

The UK has set targets under its Ramsar Strategic Plan, 1997-2002. Progress towards these is monitored by the UK Ramsar Committee, known as the Joint Working Party. The UK and the Republic of Ireland have established a formal protocol to ensure common monitoring standards for waterbirds in the two countries.

RAMSAR CONVENTION BUREAU, Rue Mauverney 28, CH-1196 Gland, Switzerland. Tel: 99941-0170. Web: http://www.ramsar.org

BIODIVERSITY

There is much synergy between the Ramsar Convention and the 1992 Convention on Biological Diversity. In 1996 the Ramsar Secretariat became a lead partner in implementing activities under the Convention on Biological Diversity with joint work plans. The UK ratified the Convention on Biological Diversity in June 1994.

The objectives are the conservation of biological diversity, the sustainable use of its components and the fair and equitable sharing of the benefits arising out of the use of genetic resources.

The UK published its own Biodiversity Action Plan in 1994. A report from the UK Biodiversity Steering Group, published in 1995, identified some 400 priority species and 38 priority habitats, requiring urgent action.

THE BIODIVERSITY ACTION PLAN SECRETARIAT, European Wildlife Division, Department of the Environment Transport and the Regions, Room 902D, Tollgate House, Houlton Street, Bristol BS2 9DJ. Tel: 0117-987 8974. Web: http://www.jncc.gov.uk/ukbg

CITES

The 1973 Convention on International Trade in Endangered Species of Wild Fauna and Flora (CITES) came into force in the UK in July 1975. Currently 150 countries are members. The countries party to the convention ban commercial international trade in an agreed list of endangered species and regulate and monitor trade in others species that might become endangered. The convention covers around 30,000 species.

The Conference of the Parties to CITES meets every two to three years to review the convention's implementation.

The Global Wildlife Division at the Department of the Environment, Transport and the Regions carries out the government's responsibilities under CITES and the Bonn Convention on the Conservation of Migratory Species of Wild Animals.

CITES SECRETARIAT, 15 Chemin des Anemones, CH-1219 Châtelaine, Geneva, Switzerland. Tel: 41-917 8139/8140. Web: http://www.wcmc. org.uk:80/CITES/english/ index.shtml

BONN CONVENTION

The 1979 Convention on Conservation of Migratory Species of Wild Animals came into force in the UK in October 1979. By June 2000, 67 parties were party to the convention.

It requires the protection of listed endangered migratory species and encourages international agreements covering these and other threatened species. Seven agreements have been concluded to date under the convention. They aim to conserve: bats in Europe; cetaceans of the Mediterranean and Black Seas; small cetaceans of the Baltic and North Seas; seals in the Wadden Sea; African-Eurasian migratory waterbirds; the Siberian Crane; and the Slender-billed Curlew.

Further agreements are being developed for a wide range of migratory species, including Sahelo-Saharan ungulates, albatrosses of the southern hemisphere, bustards and marine turtles.

International agreements can range from legally-binding treaties to less formal memoranda of understanding.

UNEP/CMS SECRETARIAT, United Nations Premises in Bonn, Martin-Luther-King Strasse 8, D-53175 Bonn, Germany. Tel: 49-815 2401. Web: http://uncmc.org.uk/ cmg

BERN CONVENTION

The 1979 Bern Convention on the Conservation of European Wildlife and Natural Habitats came into force in the UK in June 1982. A total of 40 countries are party to the convention.

The aims are to conserve wild flora and fauna and their natural habitats, especially where this requires the co-operation of several countries, and to promote such co-operation. The convention gives particular emphasis to endangered and vulnerable species.

All parties to the convention must promote national conservation policies and take account of the conservation of wild flora and fauna when setting planning and development policies.

SECRETARIAT OF THE BERN CONVENTION STANDING COMMITTEE, Council of Europe, F-67075 Strasbourg Cedex, France. Tel: 33-8841 3476. Web: http:// zwww.nature.coe.int

EUROPEAN WILDLIFE TRADE REGULATION

The Council (EC) Regulation on the Protection of Species of Wild Fauna and Flora by Regulating Trade Therein came into force in the UK on 1 June 1997. It is intended to standardise wildlife trade regulations across Europe and to improve the application of CITES. Approximately 30,000 plant and animal species are protected under the regulation.

UK LEGISLATION

The Wildlife and Countryside Act 1981 gives legal protection to a wide range of wild animals and plants. Subject to parliamentary approval, the Secretary of State for the Environment, Transport and the Regions may vary the animals and plants given legal protection. The most recent variation of Schedules 5 and 8 came into effect in March and April 1998.

Under Section 9 and Schedule 5 of the Act it is illegal without a licence to kill, injure, take, possess or sell any of the listed animals (whether alive or dead) and to disturb its place of shelter and protection or to destroy that place.

Under Section 13 and Schedule 8 of the Act it is illegal without a licence to pick, uproot, sell or destroy any of the listed plants and, unless authorised, to uproot any wild plant.

The Act lays down a close season for wild birds (other than game birds) from 1 February to 31 August inclusive, each year. Exceptions to these dates are made for:

Capercaillie and (except Scotland) *Woodcock* – 1 February to 30 September

Snipe – 1 February to 11 August

Wild Duck and *Wild Goose* (below high water mark) – 21 February to 31 August

Birds which may be killed or taken outside the close season (except on Sundays and on Christmas Day in Scotland, and on Sundays in prescribed areas of England and Wales) are the above-named, plus coot, certain wild duck (gadwall, goldeneye, mallard, pintail, pochard, shoveler, teal, tufted duck, wigeon), certain wild geese (Canada, greylag, pink-footed, white-fronted (in England and Wales only)), moorhen, golden plover and woodcock.

Certain wild birds may be killed or taken subject to the conditions of a general licence at any time by authorised persons: crow, collared dove, gull (great and lesser black-backed or herring), jackdaw, jay, magpie, pigeon (feral or wood), rook, sparrow (house), and starling. Conditions usually apply where the birds pose a threat to agriculture, public health, air safety, other bird species, and to prevent the spread of disease.

All other British birds are fully protected by law throughout the year.

Animals

‡Adder (*Vipera berus*)
Anemone, Ivell's Sea (*Edwardsia ivelli*)
Anemone, Starlet Sea (*Nematosella vectensis*)
Apus, Tadpole shrimp (*Triops cancriformis*)
Bat, Horseshoe (*Rhinolophidae*, all species)
Bat, Typical (*Vespertilionidae*, all species)
Beetle (*Graphoderus zonatus*)
Beetle (*Hypebaeus flavipes*)
Beetle, Lesser Silver Water (*Hydrochara caraboides*)
§§Beetle, Mire Pill (*Curimopsis nigrita*)
Beetle, Rainbow Leaf (*Chrysolina cerealis*)
*Beetle, Stag (*Lucanus cervus*)
Beetle, Violet Click (*Limoniscus violaceus*)
Beetle, Water (*Graphoderus zonatus*)
Beetle, Water (*Paracymus aeneus*)
Burbot (*Lota lota*)
*Butterfly, Adonis Blue (*Lysandra bellargus*)
*Butterfly, Black Hairstreak (*Strymonidia pruni*)
*Butterfly, Brown Hairstreak (*Thecla betulae*)
*Butterfly, Chalkhill Blue (*Lysandra coridon*)
*Butterfly, Chequered Skipper
  (*Carterocephalus palaemon*)
*Butterfly, Duke of Burgundy Fritillary (*Hamearis lucina*)
*Butterfly, Glanville Fritillary (*Melitaea cinxia*)
Butterfly, Heath Fritillary (*Mellicta athalia*
  (or *Melitaea athalia*))
Butterfly, High Brown Fritillary (*Argynnis adippe*)
Butterfly, Large Blue (*Maculinea arion*)
Butterfly, Large Copper (*Lycaena dispar*)
*Butterfly, Large Heath (*Coenonympha tullia*)
*Butterfly, Large Tortoiseshell (*Nymphalis polychloros*)
*Butterfly, Lulworth Skipper (*Thymelicus acteon*)
Butterfly, Marsh Fritillary (*Eurodryas aurinia*)

*Butterfly, Mountain Ringlet (*Erebia epiphron*)
*Butterfly, Northern Brown Argus (*Aricia artaxerxes*)
*Butterfly, Pearl-bordered Fritillary (*Boloria euphrosyne*)
*Butterfly, Purple Emperor (*Apatura iris*)
*Butterfly, Silver Spotted Skipper (*Hesperia comma*)
*Butterfly, Silver-studded Blue (*Plebejus argus*)
*Butterfly, Small Blue (*Cupido minimus*)
Butterfly, Swallowtail (*Papilio machaon*)
*Butterfly, White Letter Hairstreak (*Stymonida w-album*)
*Butterfly, Wood White (*Leptidea sinapis*)
Cat, Wild (*Felis silvestris*)
Cicada, New Forest (*Cicadetta montana*)
**Crayfish, Atlantic stream (*Austropotamobius pallipes*)
Cricket, Field (*Gryllus campestris*)
Cricket, Mole (*Gryllotalpa gryllotalpa*)
Damselfly, Southern (*Coenagrion mercuriale*)
Dolphin (*Cetacea*)
Dormouse (*Muscardinus avellanarius*)
Dragonfly, Norfolk Aeshna (*Aeshna isosceles*)
*Frog, Common (*Rana temporaria*)
Goby, Couch's (*Gobius couchii*)
Goby, Giant (*Gobius cobitis*)
Grasshopper, Wart-biter (*Decticus verrucivorus*)
Hatchet Shell, Northern (*Thyasira gouldi*)
Hydroid, Marine (*Clavopsella navis*)
Lagoon Snail (*Paludinella littorina*)
Lagoon Snail, De Folin's (*Caecum armoricum*)
Lagoon Worm, Tentacled (*Alkmaria romijni*)
Leech, Medicinal (*Hirudo medicinalis*)
‡Lizard, Sand (*Lacerta agilis*)
Lizard, Viviparous (*Lacerta vivipara*)
Marten, Pine (*Martes martes*)
Moth, Barberry Carpet (*Pareulype berberata*)
Moth, Black-veined (*Siona lineata* (or *Idaea lineata*))
Moth, Essex Emerald (*Thetidia smaragdaria*)
Moth, Fiery clearwing (*Bembecia chrysidiformis*)
Moth, Fisher's estuarine (*Gortyna borelii*)
Moth, New Forest Burnet (*Zygaena viciae*)
Moth, Reddish Buff (*Acosmetia caliginosa*)
Moth, Sussex Emerald (*Thalera fimbrialis*)
††Mussel, Fan (*Atrina fragilis*)
†Mussel, Freshwater Pearl (*Margaritifera margaritifera*)
Newt, Great Crested (or Warty) (*Triturus cristatus*)
*Newt, Palmate (*Triturus helveticus*)
*Newt, Smooth (*Triturus vulgaris*)
Otter, Common (*Lutra lutra*)
Porpoise (*Cetacea*)
Sandworm, Lagoon (*Armandia cirrhosa*)
††Sea Fan, Pink (*Eunicella verrucosa*)
Sea-Mat, Trembling (*Victorella pavida*)
Sea Slug, Lagoon (*Tenellia adspersa*)
‡‡Shad, Allis (*alosa alosa*)
§§Shad, Twaite (*alosa fallax*)
Shark, Basking (*Cetorhinus maximus*)
Shrimp, Fairy (*Chirocephalus diaphanus*)
Shrimp, Lagoon Sand (*Gammarus insensibilis*)
‡Slow-worm (*Anguis fragilis*)
Snail, Glutinous (*Myxas glutinosa*)
Snail, Sandbowl (*Catinella arenaria*)
‡Snake, Grass (*Natrix natrix* (*Natrix helvetica*))
Snake, Smooth (*Coronella austriaca*)
Spider, Fen Raft (*Dolomedes plantarius*)
Spider, Ladybird (*Eresus niger*)
Squirrel, Red (*Sciurus vulgaris*)
Sturgeon (*Acipenser sturio*)
*Toad, Common (*Bufo bufo*)
Toad, Natterjack (*Bufo calamita*)
Turtle, Marine (*Dermochelyidae* and *Cheloniidae*,
  all species)
Vendace (*Coregonus albula*)

§§Vole, Water (*Arvicola terrestris*)
Walrus (*Odobenus rosmarus*)
Whale (*Cetacea*)
Whitefish (*Coregonus lavaretus*)
* The offence relates to 'sale' only
** The offence relates to 'taking' and 'sale' only
†The offence relates to 'killing and injuring' only
‡The offence relates to 'killing, injuring and sale'
§The offence relates to 'killing, injuring and taking'
§§The offence relates only to damaging, destroying or obstructing access to a shelter or protection
††The offence relates to killing, injuring, taking, possession and sale
‡‡The offence relates to killing, injuring, taking and damaging, etc., a shelter

Plants

Adder's tongue, Least (*Ophioglossum lusitanicum*)
Alison, Small (*Alyssum alyssoides*)
Blackwort (*Southbya nigrella*)
°Bluebell (*Hyacinthoides non-scripta*)
Broomrape, Bedstraw (*Orobanche caryophyllacea*)
Broomrape, Oxtongue (*Orobanche loricata*)
Broomrape, Thistle (*Orobanche reticulata*)
Cabbage, Lundy (*Rhynchosinapis wrightii*)
Calamint, Wood (*Calamintha sylvatica*)
Caloplaca, Snow (*Caloplaca nivalis*)
Catapyrenium, Tree (*Catapyrenium psoromoides*)
Catchfly, Alpine (*Lychnis alpina*)
Catillaria, Laurer's (*Catellaria laureri*)
Centaury, Slender (*Centaurium tenuiflorum*)
Cinquefoil, Rock (*Potentilla rupestris*)
Cladonia, Upright Mountain (*Cladonia stricta*)
Clary, Meadow (*Salvia pratensis*)
Club-rush, Triangular (*Scirpus triquetrus*)
Colt's-foot, Purple (*Homogyne alpina*)
Cotoneaster, Wild (*Cotoneaster integerrimus*)
Cottongrass, Slender (*Eriophorum gracile*)
Cow-wheat, Field (*Melampyrum arvense*)
Crocus, Sand (*Romulea columnae*)
Crystalwort, Lizard (*Riccia bifurca*)
Cudweed, Broad-leaved (*Filago pyramidata*)
Cudweed, Jersey (*Gnaphalium luteoalbum*)
Cudweed, Red-tipped (*Filago lutescens*)
Cut-grass (*Leersia oryzoides*)
Diapensia (*Diapensia lapponica*)
Dock, Shore (*Rumex rupestris*)
Earwort, Marsh (*Jamesoniella undulifolia*)
Eryngo, Field (*Eryngium campestre*)
Fern, Dickie's bladder (*Cystopteris dickieana*)
Fern, Killarney (*Trichomanes speciosum*)
Flapwort, Norfolk (*Leiocolea rutheana*)
Fleabane, Alpine (*Erigeron borealis*)
Fleabane, Small (*Pulicaria vulgaris*)
Fleawort, South stack (*Tephroseris integrifolia (ssp maritima)*)
Frostwort, Pointed (*Gymnomitrion apiculatum*)
Fungus, Hedgehog (*Hericium erinaceum*)
Fungus, Oak polypore (*Buglossoporus pulvinus*)
Fungus, Royal bolete (*Boletus regius*)
Fungus, Sandy stilt puffball (*Battarraea phalloides*)
Galingale, Brown (*Cyperus fuscus*)
Gentian, Alpine (*Gentiana nivalis*)
Gentian, Dune (*Gentianella uliginosa*)
Gentian, Early (*Gentianella anglica*)
Gentian, Fringed (*Gentianella ciliata*)
Gentian, Spring (*Gentiana verna*)
Germander, Cut-leaved (*Teucrium botrys*)
Germander, Water (*Teucrium scordium*)
Gladiolus, Wild (*Gladiolus illyricus*)
Goosefoot, Stinking (*Chenopodium vulvaria*)

Grass-poly (*Lythrum hyssopifolia*)
Grimmia, Blunt-leaved (*Grimmia unicolor*)
Gyalecta, Elm (*Gyalecta ulmi*)
Hare's-ear, Sickle-leaved (*Bupleurum falcatum*)
Hare's-ear, Small (*Bupleurum baldense*)
Hawk's-beard, Stinking (*Crepis foetida*)
Hawkweed, Northroe (*Hieracium northroense*)
Hawkweed, Shetland (*Hieracium zetlandicum*)
Hawkweed, Weak-leaved (*Hieracium attenuatifolium*)
Heath, Blue (*Phyllodoce caerulea*)
Helleborine, Red (*Cephalanthera rubra*)
Helleborine, Young's (*Epipactis youngiana*)
Horsetail, Branched (*Equisetum ramosissimum*)
Hound's-tongue, Green (*Cynoglossum germanicum*)
Knawel, Perennial (*Scleranthus perennis*)
Knotgrass, Sea (*Polygonum maritimum*)
Lady's-slipper (*Cypripedium calceolus*)
Lecanactis, Churchyard (*Lecanactis hemisphaerica*)
Lecanora, Tarn (*Lecanora archariana*)
Lecidea, Copper (*Lecidea inops*)
Leek, Round-headed (*Allium sphaerocephalon*)
Lettuce, Least (*Lactuca saligna*)
Lichen, Alpine sulphur-tresses (*Alectoria ochroleuca*)
Lichen, Arctic kidney (*Nephroma arcticum*)
Lichen, Ciliate strap (*Heterodermia leucomelos*)
Lichen, Convoluted cladonia (*Cladonia convoluta*)
Lichen, Coralloid rosette (*Heterodermia propagulifera*)
Lichen, Ear-lobed dog (*Peltigera lepidophora*)
Lichen, Forked hair (*Bryoria furcellata*)
Lichen, Goblin lights (*Catolechia wahlenbergii*)
Lichen, Golden hair (*Teloschistes flavicans*)
Lichen, New Forest beech-lichen (*Enterographa elaborata*)
Lichen, Orange fruited Elm (*Caloplaca luteoalba*)
Lichen, River jelly (*Collema dichotomum*)
Lichen, Scaly breck (*Squamarina lentigera*)
Lichen, Stary breck (*Buellia asterella*)
Lichen, upright mountain cladonia (*Cladonia convoluta*)
Lily, Snowdon (*Lloydia serotina*)
Liverwort, Leafy (*Petallophyllum ralfsi*)
Liverwort, Lindenberg's (*Adelanthus lindenbergianus*)
Marsh-mallow, Rough (*Althaea hirsuta*)
Marshwort, Creeping (*Apium repens*)
Milk-parsley, Cambridge (*Selinum carvifolia*)
Moss (*Drepanocladius vernicosus*)
Moss, Alpine copper (*Mielichoferia mielichoferi*)
Moss, Anomodon, long-leaved (*Anomodon longifolius*)
Moss, Baltic bog (*Sphagnum balticum*)
Moss, Blue dew (*Saelania glaucescens*)
Moss, Blunt-leaved bristle (*Orthotrichum obtusifolium*)
Moss, Bright green cave (*Cyclodictyon laetevirens*)
Moss, Cordate beard (*Barbula cordata*)
Moss, Cornish path (*Ditrichum cornubicum*)
Moss, Derbyshire feather (*Thamnobryum angustifolium*)
Moss, Dune thread (*Bryum mamillatum*)
Moss, Flamingo (*Desmatodon cernuus*)
Moss, Glaucous beard (*Barbula glauca*)
Moss, Green shield (*Buxbaumia viridis*)
Moss, Hair silk (*Plagiothecium piliferum*)
Moss, Knothole (*Zygodon forsteri*)
Moss, Large yellow feather (*Scorpidium turgescens*)
Moss, Millimetre (*Micromitrium tenerum*)
Moss, Multifruited river (*Cryphaea lamyana*)
Moss, Nowell's limestone (*Zygodon gracilis*)
Moss, Polar feather-moss (*Hygrohypnum polare*)
Moss, Rigid apple (*Bartramia stricta*)
Moss, Round-leaved feather (*Rhyncostegium rotundifolium*)
Moss, Schleicher's thread (*Bryum schleicheri*)
Moss, Threadmoss, long-leaved (*Bryum neodamense*)

Moss, Triangular pygmy (*Acaulon triquetrum*)
Moss, Vaucher's feather (*Hypnum vaucheri*)
Mudwort, Welsh (*Limosella australis*)
Naiad, Holly-leaved (*Najas marina*)
Naiad, Slender (*Najas flexilis*)
Orache, Stalked (*Halimione pedunculata*)
Orchid, Early spider (*Ophrys sphegodes*)
Orchid, Fen (*Liparis loeselii*)
Orchid, Ghost (*Epipogium aphyllum*)
Orchid, Lapland marsh (*Dactylorhiza lapponica*)
Orchid, Late spider (*Ophrys fuciflora*)
Orchid, Lizard (*Himantoglossum hircinum*)
Orchid, Military (*Orchis militaris*)
Orchid, Monkey (*Orchis simia*)
Panneria, Caledonia (*Panneria ignobilis*)
Parmelia, New Forest (*Parmelia minarum*)
Parmentaria, Oil stain (*Parmentaria chilensis*)
Pear, Plymouth (*Pyrus cordata*)
Penny-cress, Perfoliate (*Thlaspi perfoliatum*)
Pennyroyal (*Mentha pulegium*)
Pertusaria, Alpine moss (*Pertusaria bryontha*)
Physcia, Southern grey (*Physcia tribacioides*)
Pigmyweed (*Crassula aquatica*)
Pine, Ground (*Ajuga chamaepitys*)
Pink, Cheddar (*Dianthus gratianopolitanus*)
Pink, Childing (*Petroraghia nanteuilii*)
Pink, Deptford (*Dianthus armeria*) (England and
  Wales only)
Plantain, Floating water (*Luronium natans*)
Pseudocyphellaria, Ragged (*Pseudocyphellaria lacerata*)
Psora, Rusty Alpine (*Psora rubiformis*)
Ragwort, Fen (*Senecio paludosus*)
Ramping-fumitory, Martin's (*Fumaria martinii*)
Rampion, Spiked (*Phyteuma spicatum*)
Restharrow, Small (*Ononis reclinata*)
Rock-cress, Alpine (*Arabis alpina*)
Rock-cress, Bristol (*Arabis stricta*)
Rustwort, Western (*Marsupella profunda*)
Sandwort, Norwegian (*Arenaria norvegica*)
Sandwort, Teesdale (*Minuartia stricta*)
Saxifrage, Drooping (*Saxifraga cernua*)
Saxifrage, Marsh (*Saxifrage hirulus*)
Saxifrage, Tufted (*Saxifraga cespitosa*)
Solenopsora, Serpentine (*Solenopsora liparina*)
Solomon's-seal, Whorled (*Polygonatum verticillatum*)
Sow-thistle, Alpine (*Cicerbita alpina*)
Spearwort, Adder's-tongue (*Ranunculus
  ophioglossifolius*)
Speedwell, Fingered (*Veronica triphyllos*)
Speedwell, Spiked (*Veronica spicata*)
Spike rush, Dwarf (*Eleocharis parvula*)
Star-of-Bethlehem, Early (*Gagea bohemica*)
Starfruit (*Damasonium alisma*)
Stonewort, Bearded (*Chara canescens*)
Stonewort, Foxtail (*Lamprothamnium papulosum*)
Strapwort (*Corrigiola litoralis*)
Turpswort (*Geocalyx graveolens*)
Violet, Fen (*Viola persicifolia*)
Viper's-grass (*Scorzonera humilis*)
Water-plantain, Ribbon-leaved (*Alisma gramineum*)
Wood-sedge, Starved (*Carex depauperata*)
Woodsia, Alpine (*Woodsia alpina*)
Woodsia, Oblong (*Woodsia ilvenis*)
Wormwood, Field (*Artemisia campestris*)
Woundwort, Downy (*Stachys germanica*)
Woundwort, Limestone (*Stachys alpina*)
Yellow-rattle, Greater (*Rhinanthus serotinus*)

°The sale of plants taken from the wild is prohibited; the sale
  of cultivated plants is still permitted

MOST UNDER THREAT

The animals and birds considered to be most under threat
in Great Britain by the Joint Nature Conservation
Committee are the high brown fritillary butterfly; violet
click beetle; new forest burnet moth; corncrake; aquatic
warbler; tree sparrow; wryneck; water vole; red squirrel;
allis shad; and twaite shad.

Historic Buildings and Monuments

LISTING

Under the Planning (Listed Buildings and Conservation Areas) Act 1990, the Secretary of State for Culture, Media and Sport has a statutory duty to compile lists of buildings or groups of buildings in England which are of special architectural or historic interest. Under the Ancient Monuments and Archaeological Areas Act 1979 as amended by the National Heritage Act 1983, the Secretary of State is also responsible for compiling a schedule of ancient monuments. Decisions are taken on the advice of English Heritage (see page 331).

Listed buildings are classified into Grade I, Grade II* and Grade II. There are currently about 500,000 individual listed buildings in England, of which about 95 per cent are Grade II listed. Almost all pre-1700 buildings are listed, and most buildings of 1700 to 1840. English Heritage is carrying out thematic surveys of particular types of buildings with a view to making recommendations for listing, and members of the public may propose a building for consideration. The main purpose of listing is to ensure that care is taken in deciding the future of a building. No changes which affect the architectural or historic character of a listed building can be made without listed building consent (in addition to planning permission where relevant). Applications for listed building consent are normally dealt with by the local planning authority, although English Heritage is always consulted about proposals affecting Grade I and Grade II* properties. It is a criminal offence to demolish a listed building, or alter it in such a way as to affect its character, without consent.

There are currently about 22,500 scheduled monuments in England. English Heritage is carrying out a Monuments Protection Programme assessing archaeological sites with a view to making recommendations for scheduling, and members of the public may propose a monument for consideration. All monuments proposed for scheduling are considered to be of national importance. Where buildings are both scheduled and listed, ancient monuments legislation takes precedence. The main purpose of scheduling a monument is to preserve it for the future and to protect it from damage, destruction or any unnecessary interference. Once a monument has been scheduled, scheduled monument consent is required before any works are carried out. The scope of the control is more extensive and more detailed than that applied to listed buildings, but certain minor works, as detailed in the Ancient Monuments (Class Consents) Order 1994, may be carried out without consent. It is a criminal offence to carry out unauthorised work to scheduled monuments.

Under the Planning (Listed Buildings and Conservation Areas) Act 1990 and the Ancient Monuments and Archaeological Areas Act 1979, the Secretary of State for Wales is responsible for listing buildings and scheduling monuments in Wales on the advice of Cadw (see Regional Government section), the Historic Buildings Council for Wales (see page 335) and the Royal Commission on the Ancient and Historical Monuments of Wales (see page 337). The criteria for evaluating buildings are similar to those in England and the same listing system is used. There are approximately 19,200 listed buildings and approximately 3,000 scheduled monuments in Wales.

Under the Planning (Listed Buildings and Conservation Areas) (Scotland) Act 1997 and the Ancient Monuments and Archaeological Areas Act 1979, the Secretary of State for Scotland is responsible for listing buildings and scheduling monuments in Scotland on the advice of Historic Scotland (see Regional Government section), the Historic Buildings Council for Scotland (see page 335) and The Royal Commission on the Ancient and Historical Monuments of Scotland (see page 357). The criteria for evaluating buildings are similar to those in England but an A, B, C grading system is used. There are about 44,462 listed buildings and about 7,035 scheduled monuments in Scotland.

Under the Planning (Northern Ireland) Order 1991 and the Historic Monuments and Archaeological Objects (Northern Ireland) Order 1995, the Department of the Environment, now a newly formed department of the Northern Ireland Executive (see Regional Government section) is responsible for listing buildings and scheduling monuments in Northern Ireland on the advice of Historic Buildings Council for Northern Ireland and the Historic Monuments Council for Northern Ireland. The criteria for evaluating buildings are similar to those in England but no statutory grading system is used. In March 1999 there were 8,563 listed buildings and 1,365 scheduled monuments in Northern Ireland.

OPENING TO THE PUBLIC

The following is a selection of the many historic buildings and monuments open to the public. Admission charges and opening hours vary. Many properties are closed in winter and some are also closed in the mornings. Most properties are closed on Christmas Eve, Christmas Day, Boxing Day and New Year's Day, and many are closed on Good Friday. During the winter season, most English Heritage monuments are closed on Mondays and Tuesdays and monuments in the care of Cadw are closed on Sunday mornings. In Northern Ireland most monuments are closed on Mondays except on bank holidays. Information about a specific property should be checked by telephone.

*Closed in winter (usually November–March)
†Closed in winter, and in mornings in summer

ENGLAND

For more information on any of the English Heritage properties listed below, the official website is: http://www.english-heritage.org.uk
For more information on any of the National Heritage properties listed below, the official website is: http://www.nationaltrust.org.uk

EH English Heritage property
NT National Trust property

*A LA RONDE (NT), Summer Lane, Exmouth, Devon. Tel: 01395-265514. Unique 16-sided house completed c.1796

†ALNWICK CASTLE, Northumberland. Tel: 01665-510777. Seat of the Dukes of Northumberland since 1309; Italian Renaissance-style interior

ALTHORP, Northants. Tel: 01604-770107, ticket reservations 01604-592020. Spencer family seat. Diana, Princess of Wales memorabilia

†ANGLESEY ABBEY (NT), Cambs. Tel: 01223-811200. House built c.1600. Outstanding grounds with unique statuary

APSLEY HOUSE, London W1. Tel: 020-7499 5676. Built by Robert Adam 1771–8, home of the Dukes of Wellington since 1817 and known as 'No. 1 London'. Collection of fine and decorative arts

†ARUNDEL CASTLE, W. Sussex. Tel: 01903-883136. Castle dating from the Norman Conquest. Seat of the Dukes of Norfolk

AVEBURY (NT), Wilts. Tel: 01672-539250. Remains of stone circles constructed 4,000 years ago surrounding the later village of Avebury. Also *Alexander Keiller Museum*

BANQUETING HOUSE, Whitehall, London SW1. Tel: 020-7930 4179. Designed by Inigo Jones; ceiling paintings by Rubens. Site of the execution of Charles I

†BASILDON PARK (NT), Berks. Tel: 0118-984 3040. Palladian house built in 1776–83

BATTLE ABBEY (EH), E. Sussex. Tel: 01424-773792. Remains of the abbey founded by William the Conqueror on the site of the Battle of Hastings

BEAULIEU, Hants. Tel: 01590-612345. House and gardens, Beaulieu Abbey and exhibition of monastic life, National Motor Museum

BEESTON CASTLE (EH), Cheshire. Tel: 01829-260464. Thirteenth-century inner ward with gatehouse and towers, and remains of outer ward

†BELTON HOUSE (NT), Grantham, Lincs. Tel: 01476-566116. Fine 17th-century house in landscaped park

*BELVOIR CASTLE, nr Grantham, Lincs. Tel: 01476-870262. Seat of the Dukes of Rutland; 19th-century Gothic-style castle

*BERKELEY CASTLE, Glos. Tel: 01453-810332. Completed 1153; site of the murder of Edward II (1327)

*BLENHEIM PALACE, Woodstock, Oxon. Tel: 01993-811325. Seat of the Dukes of Marlborough and Winston Churchill's birthplace; designed by Vanbrugh

†BLICKLING HALL (NT), Norfolk. Tel: 01263-738030. Jacobean house with state rooms, temple and 18th-century orangery

BODIAM CASTLE (NT), E. Sussex. Tel: 01580-830436. Well-preserved medieval moated castle

BOLSOVER CASTLE (EH), Derbys. Tel: 01246-823349. Notable 17th-century buildings

BOSCOBEL HOUSE (EH), Shropshire. Tel: 01902-850244. Timber-framed 17th-century hunting lodge, refuge of fugitive Charles II

†BOUGHTON HOUSE, Northants. Tel: 01536-515731. A 17th-century house with French-style additions

*BOWOOD HOUSE, Wilts. Tel: 01249-812102. An 18th-century house in Capability Brown park, with lake, temple and arboretum

†BROADLANDS, Hants. Tel: 01794-505010. Palladian mansion in Capability Brown parkland. Mountbatten exhibition

BRONTË PARSONAGE, Haworth, W. Yorks. Tel: 01535-642323. Home of the Brontë sisters; museum and memorabilia

BUCKFAST ABBEY, Devon. Tel: 01364-642519. Benedictine monastery on medieval foundations

*BUCKINGHAM PALACE, London SW1. Tel: 020-7839 1377. Purchased by George III in 1762, and the Sovereign's official London residence since 1837. Eighteen state rooms, including the Throne Room, and Picture Gallery

BUCKLAND ABBEY (NT), Devon. Tel: 01822-853607. A 13th-century Cistercian monastery. Home of Sir Francis Drake

BURGHLEY HOUSE, Stamford, Lincs. Tel: 01780-752451. Late Elizabethan house; vast state apartments

†CALKE ABBEY (NT), Derbys. Tel: 01332-863822. Baroque 18th-century mansion

CARISBROOKE CASTLE (EH), Isle of Wight. Tel: 01983-522107. Norman castle; prison of Charles I 1647-8

CARLISLE CASTLE (EH), Cumbria. Tel: 01228-606000. Medieval castle, prison of Mary Queen of Scots

*CARLYLE'S HOUSE (NT), Cheyne Row, London SW3. Tel: 020-7352 7087. Home of Thomas Carlyle

CASTLE ACRE PRIORY (EH), Norfolk. Tel: 01760-755394. Remains include 12th-century church and prior's lodgings

*CASTLE DROGO (NT), Devon. Tel: 01647-433306. Granite castle designed by Lutyens

*CASTLE HOWARD, N. Yorks. Tel: 01653-648444. Designed by Vanbrugh 1699–1726; mausoleum designed by Hawksmoor

CASTLE RISING CASTLE (EH), Norfolk. Tel: 01553-631330. A 12th-century keep in a massive earthwork with gatehouse and bridge

*CHARTWELL (NT), Kent. Tel: 01732-866368. Home of Sir Winston Churchill

*CHATSWORTH, Derbys. Tel: 01246-582204. Tudor mansion in magnificent parkland

CHESTERS ROMAN FORT (EH), Northumberland. Tel: 01434-681379. Roman cavalry fort

*CHYSAUSTER ANCIENT VILLAGE (EH), Cornwall. Tel: 0831-757934. Romano-Cornish village, 2nd and 3rd century AD, on a probably late Iron Age site

CLIFFORD'S TOWER (EH), York. Tel: 01904-646940. A 13th-century tower built on a mound

†CLIVEDEN (NT), Berks. Tel: 01628-605069. House open Thurs. and Sun. only, gardens daily. Former home of the Astors, now an hotel set in garden and woodland

CORBRIDGE ROMAN SITE (EH), Northumberland. Tel: 01434-632349. Excavated central area of a Roman town and successive military bases

CORFE CASTLE (NT), Dorset. Tel: 01929-481294. Ruined former royal castle dating from 11th century

†CROFT CASTLE (NT), Herefordshire. Tel: 01568-780246. Pre-Conquest border castle with Georgian-Gothic interior

DEAL CASTLE (EH), Kent. Tel: 01304-372762. Largest of the coastal defence forts built by Henry VIII

DICKENS HOUSE, Doughty Street, London WC1. Tel: 020-7405 2127. House occupied by Dickens 1837–9; manuscripts, furniture and portraits

DR JOHNSON'S HOUSE, 17 Gough Square, London EC4. Tel: 020-7353 3745. E-mail: curator@drjh.co.uk. Web: http://www.drjh.dircon.co.uk. Home of Samuel Johnson

DOVE COTTAGE, Grasmere, Cumbria. Tel: 01539-435544. Wordsworth's home 1799–1808; museum

DOVER CASTLE (EH), Kent. Tel: 01304-201628. Castle with Roman, Saxon and Norman features; wartime operations rooms

DUNSTANBURGH CASTLE (EH), Northumberland. Tel: 01665-576231. A 14th-century castle on a cliff, with a substantial gatehouse-keep

ELTHAM PALACE (EH), Court Yard, Eltham, London SE9. Tel: 020-8294 2548. Combines a 1930s country house and remains of medieval palace set in moated gardens

FARLEIGH HUNGERFORD CASTLE (EH), Somerset. Tel: 01225-754026. Late 14th-century castle with two courts; chapel with tomb of Sir Thomas Hungerford

*FARNHAM CASTLE KEEP (EH), Surrey. Tel: 01252-713393. Large 12th-century shell-keep

FOUNTAINS ABBEY (NT), nr Ripon, N. Yorks. Tel: 01765-608888. Deer park visitor centre, deer park and St Mary's Church. Ruined Cistercian monastery; 18th-century landscaped gardens of Studley Royal estate

FRAMLINGHAM CASTLE (EH), Suffolk. Tel: 01728-724189.
Castle (c.1200) with high curtain walls enclosing an
almshouse (1639)
FURNESS ABBEY (EH), Cumbria. Tel: 01229-823420.
Remains of church and conventual buildings founded
in 1123
GLASTONBURY ABBEY, Somerset. Tel: 01458-832267.
Ruins of a 12th-century abbey rebuilt after fire. Site of an
early Christian settlement
GOODRICH CASTLE (EH), Herefordshire. Tel: 01600-
890538. Remains of 13th- and 14th-century castle
with 12th-century keep
GREENWICH, London SE10. *Royal Observatory.*
Tel: 020-8858 6575. Web: http://www.rof.nmm.ac.uk
Former Royal Observatory (founded 1675) housing the
time ball and zero meridian of longitude. *The Queen's
House.* Tel: 020-8858 4422. Designed for Queen Anne,
wife of James I, by Inigo Jones. *Painted Hall and Chapel*
(Royal Naval College). Visitors admitted to Sunday
service (11 a.m.) in the chapel during college term
GRIME'S GRAVES (EH), Norfolk. Tel: 01842-810656.
Neolithic flint Mines. One shaft can be descended
GUILDHALL, London EC2. Tel: 020-7332 1460.
Centre of civic government of the City. Built c.1441;
facade built 1788–9
*HADDON HALL, Derbys. Tel: 01629-812855.
Well-preserved 12th-century manor house
HAILES ABBEY (EH), Glos. Tel: 01242-602398.
Ruins of a 13th-century Cistercian monastery
†HAM HOUSE (NT), Richmond, Surrey. Tel: 020-8940
1950. Garden open all year except Thurs. and Fri.
Stuart house with fine interiors
HAMPTON COURT PALACE, East Molesey, Surrey.
Tel: 020-8781 9500. A 16th-century palace with
additions by Wren. Gardens with maze; Tudor tennis
court (summer only)
†HARDWICK HALL (NT), Derbys. Tel: 01246-850430.
Built 1591–7 for Bess of Hardwick; notable furnishings
*HARDY'S COTTAGE (NT), Dorset. Tel: 01305-262366.
Higher Bockhampton, Dorset. Birthplace of Thomas
Hardy
*HAREWOOD HOUSE, W. Yorks. Tel: 0113-288 6331.
An 18th-century house designed by John Carr and
Robert Adam; park by Capability Brown
†HATFIELD HOUSE, Herts. Tel: 01707-262823.
Jacobean house built by Robert Cecil; surviving wing
of Royal Palace of Hatfield (1497)
HELMSLEY CASTLE (EH), N. Yorks. Tel: 01439-770442.
A 12th-century keep and curtain wall with 16th-
century buildings. Spectacular earthwork defences
†HEVER CASTLE (EH), Kent. Tel: 01732-865224. A 13th-
century double-moated castle, childhood home of
Anne Boleyn
*HOLKER HALL, Cumbria. Tel: 015395-58328. Former
home of the Dukes of Devonshire; award-winning
gardens
†HOLKHAM HALL, Norfolk. Tel: 01328-710227. Fine
Palladian mansion
HOUSESTEADS ROMAN FORT (EH), Northumberland.
Tel: 01434-344363. Excavated infantry fort on
Hadrian's Wall with extra-mural civilian settlement
†HUGHENDEN MANOR (NT), High Wycombe. Tel:
01494-755565. Home of Disraeli; small formal garden
JANE AUSTEN'S HOUSE, Chawton, Hants. Tel: 01420-
83262. Jane Austen's home 1809–17
KEDLESTON HOUSE (NT), Derby. Tel: 01332-842191.
A classical Palladian mansion built 1759–65; complete
Robert Adam interiors.

*KELMSCOTT MANOR, nr Lechlade, Oxon. Tel: 01367-
252486. Summer home of William Morris, with
products of Morris and Co.
KENILWORTH CASTLE (EH), Warks. Tel: 01926-852078.
Castle with building styles from 1155 to 1649
KENSINGTON PALACE, London W8. Tel: 0207-937 7079.
Built in 1605 and enlarged by Wren; bought by
William and Mary in 1689. Birthplace of Queen
Victoria. Royal Ceremonial Dress Collection
KENWOOD (EH), Hampstead Lane, London NW3.
Tel: 020-8348 1286. Adam villa housing the Iveagh
bequest of paintings and furniture. Open-air concerts
in summer
*KEW, Surrey. Tel: 020-8332 5189. *Queen Charlotte's
Cottage*
†KINGSTON LACY HOUSE (NT), Dorset. Tel: 01202-
883402. A 17th-century house with 19th-century
alterations; important art collection
†KNEBWORTH HOUSE, Herts. Tel: 01438-812661.
Tudor manor house concealed by 19th-century
Gothic decoration; Lutyens gardens
*KNOLE (NT), Kent. Tel: 01732-450608. House dating
from 1456 set in parkland; fine art treasures
LAMBETH PALACE, London SE1. Tel: 020-7928 8282.
Official residence of the Archbishop of Canterbury.
A 19th-century house with parts dating from the 12th
century
*LANERCOST PRIORY (EH), Cumbria. Tel: 01697-73030.
The nave of the Augustinian priory church, c.1166, is
still used; remains of other claustral buildings
*LANHYDROCK (NT), Cornwall. Tel: 01208-73320.
House dating from the 17th century; 45 rooms,
including kitchen and nursery
LEEDS CASTLE, Kent. Tel: 01622-765400. Castle dating
from 9th century, on two islands in lake
†LEVENS HALL, Cumbria. Tel: 01539-560321.
Elizabethan house with unique topiary garden (1694).
Steam engine collection
LINCOLN CASTLE. Tel: 01522-511068. Built by William
the Conqueror in 1068
LINDISFARNE PRIORY (EH), Northumberland. Tel: 01289-
389200. Bishopric of the Northumbrian kingdom
destroyed by the Danes; re-established in the 11th
century as a Benedictine priory, now ruined
LITTLE MORETON HALL (NT), Cheshire. Tel: 01260-
272018. Timber-framed moated manor house with knot
garden
LONGLEAT HOUSE, Warminster, Wilts. Tel: 01985-
844400. Elizabethan house in Italian Renaissance style
LULLINGSTONE ROMAN VILLA (EH), Kent. Tel: 01322-
863467. Large villa occupied for much of the Roman
period; fine mosaics
MANSION HOUSE, London EC4. Tel: 020-7626 2500.
The official residence of the Lord Mayor of London
MARBLE HILL HOUSE (EH), Twickenham, Middx.
Tel: 020-8892 5115. English Palladian villa with
Georgian paintings and furniture
*MICHELHAM PRIORY, E. Sussex. Tel: 01323-844224.
Tudor house built onto an Augustinian priory
MIDDLEHAM CASTLE (EH), N. Yorks. Tel: 01969-623899.
A 12th-century keep within later fortifications. Child-
hood home of Richard III
†MONTACUTE HOUSE (NT), Somerset. Tel: 01935-
823289. Elizabethan house with National Portrait
Gallery portraits from period
MOUNT GRACE PRIORY (EH), N. Yorks. Tel: 01609-
883494. Carthusian monastery, with remains of
monastic buildings
NETLEY ABBEY (EH), Hants. Tel: 023-8045 3076. Remains
of Cistercian abbey, used as house in Tudor period

OLD SARUM (EH), Wilts. Tel: 01722-335398. Earthworks enclosing remains of the castle and the 11th-century cathedral

ORFORD CASTLE (EH), Suffolk. Tel: 01394-450472. Circular keep of *c.*1170 and remains of coastal defence castle built by Henry II

*OSBORNE HOUSE (EH), Isle of Wight. Tel: 01983-200022. Queen Victoria's seaside residence

†OSTERLEY PARK HOUSE (NT), Isleworth, Middx. Tel: 020-8568 7714. Elizabethan mansion set in parkland

PENDENNIS CASTLE (EH), Cornwall. Tel: 01326-316594. Well-preserved coastal defence castle built by Henry VIII

†PENSHURST PLACE, Kent. Tel: 01892-870307. House with medieval Baron's Hall and 14th-century gardens

†PETWORTH (NT), W. Sussex. Tel: 01798-343929. Late 17th-century house set in deer park

PEVENSEY CASTLE (EH), E. Sussex. Tel: 01323-762604. Walls of a 4th-century Roman fort; remains of an 11th-century castle

PEVERIL CASTLE (EH), Derbys. Tel: 01433-620613. A 12th-century castle defended on two sides by precipitous rocks

†POLESDEN LACEY (NT), Surrey. Tel: 01372-458203. Regency villa remodelled in the Edwardian era. Fine paintings and furnishings

PORTCHESTER CASTLE (EH), Hants. Tel: 023-9237 8291. Walls of a late Roman fort enclosing a Norman keep and an Augustinian priory church

*POWDERHAM CASTLE, Devon. Tel: 01626-890243. Medieval castle with 18th- and 19th-century alterations

†RABY CASTLE, Co. Durham. Tel: 01833-660202. A 14th-century castle with walled gardens

*RAGLEY HALL, Warks. Tel: 01789-762090. A 17th-century house with gardens, park and lake

RICHBOROUGH ROMAN FORT (EH), Kent. Tel: 01304-612013. Landing-site of the Claudian invasion in AD 43, with 3rd-century stone walls

RICHMOND CASTLE (EH), N. Yorks. Tel: 01748-822493. A 12th-century keep with 11th-century curtain wall and domestic buildings

RIEVAULX ABBEY (EH), N. Yorks. Tel: 01439-798228. Remains of a Cistercian abbey founded *c.*1131

ROCHESTER CASTLE (EH), Kent. Tel: 01634-402276. An 11th-century castle partly on the Roman city wall, with a square keep of *c.*1130

†ROCKINGHAM CASTLE, Northants. Tel: 01536-770240. Built by William the Conqueror

ROYAL PAVILION, Brighton. Tel: 01273-290900. Palace of George IV, in Chinese style with Indian exterior and Regency gardens

†RUFFORD OLD HALL (NT), Lancs. Tel: 01704-821254. A 16th-century hall with unique screen

ST AUGUSTINE'S ABBEY (EH), Canterbury, Kent. Tel: 01227-767345. Remains of Benedictine monastery, with Norman church, on site of abbey founded AD 598 by St Augustine

ST MAWES CASTLE (EH), Cornwall. Tel: 01326-270526. Coastal defence castle built by Henry VIII

ST MICHAEL'S MOUNT (NT), Cornwall. Tel: 01736-710507. A 12th-century castle with later additions, off the coast at Marazion

*SANDRINGHAM, Norfolk. Tel: 01553-772675. The Queen's private residence; a neo-Jacobean house built in 1870

SCARBOROUGH CASTLE (EH), N. Yorks. Tel: 01723-372451. Remains of 12th-century keep and curtain walls

†SHERBORNE CASTLE, Dorset. Tel: 01935-813182. Sixteenth-century castle built by Sir Walter Raleigh

*SHUGBOROUGH (NT), Staffs. Tel: 01889-881388. House set in 18th-century park with monuments, temples and pavilions in the Greek Revival style

SKIPTON CASTLE, N. Yorks. Tel: 01756-792442. D-shaped castle with six round towers and beautiful inner courtyard

†SMALLHYTHE PLACE (NT), Kent. Tel: 01580-762334. Half-timbered 16th-century house; home of Ellen Terry 1899-1928

†STANFORD HALL, Leics. Tel: 01788-860250. William and Mary house with Stuart portraits. Motorcycle museum

STONEHENGE (EH), Wilts. Tel: 01980-624715. Prehistoric monument consisting of concentric stone circles surrounded by a ditch and bank

†STONOR PARK, Oxon. Tel: 01491-638587. Medieval house with Georgian facade. Centre of Roman Catholicism after the Reformation

†STOURHEAD (NT), Wilts. Tel: 09001-335205. English Palladian mansion with famous gardens

*STRATFIELD SAYE HOUSE, Hants. Tel: 01256-882882. House built 1630-40; home of the Dukes of Wellington since 1817

STRATFORD-UPON-AVON, Warks. *Shakespeare's Birthplace* with Shakespeare Centre; *Anne Hathaway's Cottage*, home of Shakespeare's wife; *Mary Arden's House*, home of Shakespeare's mother; *Nash's House and New Place*, where Shakespeare died; and *Hall's Croft*, home of Shakespeare's daughter. Tel: 01789-204016. Also *Grammar School* attended by Shakespeare, *Holy Trinity Church*, where Shakespeare is buried, *Royal Shakespeare Theatre* (burnt down 1926, rebuilt 1932) and *Swan Theatre* (opened 1986)

*SUDELEY CASTLE, Glos. Tel: 01242-602308. Castle built in 1442; restored in the 19th century

SYON HOUSE, Brentford, Middx. Tel: 020-8560 0883. Built on the site of a former monastery; Adam interior

TILBURY FORT (EH), Essex. Tel: 01375-858489. A 17th-century coastal fort

TINTAGEL CASTLE (EH), Cornwall. Tel: 01840-770328. A 12th-century cliff-top castle and Dark Age settlement site

TOWER OF LONDON, London EC3N 4AB. Tel: 020-7709 0765. Web: http://www.hrp.org.uk. Royal palace and fortress begun by William the Conqueror in 1078. Houses the Crown Jewels

*TRERICE (NT), Cornwall. Tel: 01637-875404. Elizabethan manor house

TYNEMOUTH PRIORY AND CASTLE (EH), Tyne and Wear. Tel: 0191-257 1090. Remains of a Benedictine priory, founded *c.*1090, on Saxon monastic site

†UPPARK (NT), W. Sussex. Tel: 01730-825857. Late 17th-century house, completely restored after fire. Fetherstonhaugh art collection

WALMER CASTLE (EH), Kent. Tel: 01304-364288. One of Henry VIII's coastal defence castles, now the residence of the Lord Warden of the Cinque Ports

WALTHAM ABBEY (EH), Essex. Tel: 01992-702200. Ruined abbey including the nave of the abbey church, 'Harold's Bridge' and late 14th-century gatehouse. Traditionally the burial place of Harold II (1066)

WARKWORTH CASTLE (EH), Northumberland. Tel: 01665-711423. A 15th-century keep amidst earlier ruins, with 14th-century hermitage upstream

WARWICK CASTLE. Tel: 01926-406600. Medieval castle with Madame Tussaud's waxworks, in Capability Brown parkland

WHITBY ABBEY (EH), N. Yorks. Tel: 01947-603568. Remains of Norman church on the site of a monastery founded in AD 657

*WILTON HOUSE, Wilts. Tel: 01722-746720. A 17th-century house on the site of a Tudor house and Saxon abbey

WINDSOR CASTLE, Berks. Tel: 01753-831118. Official residence of The Queen; oldest royal residence still in regular use. Also *St George's Chapel*

*WOBURN ABBEY, Beds. Tel: 01525-290666. Built on the site of a Cistercian abbey; seat of the Dukes of Bedford. Important art collection; antiques centre

WROXETER ROMAN CITY (EH), Shropshire. Tel: 01743-761330. Second-century public baths and part of the forum of the Roman town of Viroconium

---

WALES

For more information on any of the National Trust properties listed below, the official website is:
http://www.nationaltrust.org.uk
For more information on any of the Cadw properties listed below, the official website is:
http://www.cadw.wales.gov.uk

(C) Property of Cadw: Welsh Historic Monuments
(NT) National Trust property

BEAUMARIS CASTLE (C), Anglesey. Tel: 01248-810361. Concentrically-planned castle, still almost intact

CAERLEON ROMAN BATHS AND AMPHITHEATRE (C), nr Newport. Tel: 01633-890104. Rare example of a legionary bath-house and late 1st-century arena surrounded by bank for spectators

CAERNARFON CASTLE (C). Tel: 01286-677617. Important Edwardian castle built, with the town wall, between 1283 and 1330

CAERPHILLY CASTLE (C). Tel: 029 2088 3143. Concentrically-planned castle (c.1270) notable for its scale and use of water defences

CARDIFF CASTLE. Tel: 029-2087 8100. Castle built on the site of a Roman fort; spectacular towers and rich interior

CASTELL COCH (C), nr Cardiff. Tel: 029-2081 0101. Rebuilt 1875-90 on medieval foundations

CHEPSTOW CASTLE (C). Tel: 01291-624065. Rectangular keep amid extensive fortifications

CONWY CASTLE (C). Tel: 01492-592358. Built by Edward I, 1283-7

*CRICCIETH CASTLE (C). Tel: 01766-522227. Native Welsh 13th-century castle, altered by Edward I

DENBIGH CASTLE (C). Tel: 01745-813385. Remains of the castle (begun 1282), including triple-towered gatehouse

HARLECH CASTLE (C). Tel: 01766-780552. Well-preserved Edwardian castle, constructed 1283-90, on an outcrop above the former shoreline

PEMBROKE CASTLE. Tel: 01646-681510. Castle founded in 1093; Great Tower built 1200; birthplace of King Henry VII

*PENRHYN CASTLE (NT), Bangor. Tel: 01248-353084. Neo-Norman castle built in the 19th century. Industrial railway museum

PORTMEIRION, Penrhyndeudraeth. Tel: 01766-770228. Village in Italianate style

†POWIS CASTLE (NT), nr Welshpool. Tel: 01938-557018. Medieval castle with interior in variety of styles; 17th-century gardens and Clive of India museum

RAGLAN CASTLE (C). Tel: 01291-690228. Remains of 15th-century castle with moated hexagonal keep

ST DAVIDS BISHOP'S PALACE (C), St Davids. Tel: 01437-720517. Remains of residence of Bishops of St Davids built 1328–47

TINTERN ABBEY (C), nr Chepstow. Tel: 01291-689251. Remains of 13th-century church and conventual buildings of a Cistercian monastery

*TRETOWER COURT AND CASTLE (C), nr Crickhowell. Tel: 01874-730279. Medieval house with remains of 12th-century castle nearby

---

SCOTLAND

For more information on any of the Historic Scotland properties listed below, the official website is:
http://www.historic-scotland.gov.uk
For more information on any of the National Trust For Scotland properties listed below, the official website is:
http://www.nts.org.uk

(HS) Historic Scotland property
(NTS) National Trust for Scotland property

ANTONINE WALL, between the Clyde and the Forth. Built about AD 142, consists of ditch, turf rampart and road, with forts every two miles

BALMORAL CASTLE, nr Braemar. Tel: 013397-42334. Baronial-style castle built for Victoria and Albert. The Queen's private residence

BLACK HOUSE, ARNOL (HS), Lewis, Western Isles. Tel: 01851-710395. Traditional Lewis thatched house

*BLAIR CASTLE, Blair Atholl. Tel: 01796-481207. Mid 18th-century mansion with 13th-century tower; seat of the Dukes of Atholl

*BONAWE IRON FURNACE (HS), Argyll and Bute. Tel: 01866-822432. Charcoal-fuelled ironworks founded in 1753

†BOWHILL, Selkirk. Tel: 01750-22204. Seat of the Dukes of Buccleuch and Queensberry; fine collection of paintings, including portrait miniatures

BROUGH OF BIRSAY (HS), Orkney. Remains of Norse church and village on the tidal island of Birsay

CAERLAVEROCK CASTLE (HS), nr Dumfries. Tel: 01387-770244. Fine early classical Renaissance building

CALANAIS STANDING STONES (HS), Lewis, Western Isles. Tel: 01851-621422. Standing stones in a cross-shaped setting, dating from 3000 BC

CATHERTUNS (BROWN AND WHITE) (HS), nr Brechin. Two large Iron Age hill forts

*CAWDOR CASTLE, Inverness. Tel: 01667-404615. A 14th-century keep with 15th- and 17th-century additions

CLAVA CAIRNS (HS), Highland. Late Neolithic or early Bronze Age cairns

*CRATHES CASTLE (NTS), nr Banchory. Tel: 01330-844525. A 16th-century baronial castle in woodland, fields and gardens

*CULZEAN CASTLE (NTS), S. Ayrshire. Tel: 01655-760274. An 18th-century Adam castle with oval staircase and circular saloon

DRYBURGH ABBEY (HS), Scottish Borders. Tel: 01835-822381. A 12th-century abbey containing tomb of Sir Walter Scott

*DUNVEGAN CASTLE, Skye. Tel: 01470-521206. A 13th-century castle with later additions; home of the chiefs of the Clan MacLeod; trips to seal colony

EDINBURGH CASTLE (HS). Tel: 0131-225 9846. Includes the Scottish National War Memorial, Scottish United Services Museum and historic apartments

EDZELL CASTLE (HS), nr Brechin. Tel: 01356-648631. Medieval tower house; unique walled garden

*EILEAN DONAN CASTLE, Wester Ross. Tel: 01599-555202. A 13th-century castle with Jacobite relics

ELGIN CATHEDRAL (HS), Moray. Tel: 01343-547171.
A 13th-century cathedral with fine chapterhouse

*FLOORS CASTLE, Kelso. Tel: 01573-223333. Largest
inhabited castle in Scotland; seat of the Dukes
of Roxburghe

FORT GEORGE (HS), Highland. Tel: 01667-462777.
An 18th-century fort

*GLAMIS CASTLE, Angus. Tel: 01307-840393. Seat of
the Lyon family (later Earls of Strathmore and
Kinghorne) since 1372

GLASGOW CATHEDRAL (HS). Tel: 0141-552 6891.
Medieval cathedral with elaborately vaulted crypt

GLENELG BROCH (HS), Highlands. Two broch towers with
well-preserved structural features

*HOPETOUN HOUSE, nr Edinburgh. Tel: 0131-331 2451.
House designed by Sir William Bruce, enlarged by
William Adam

HUNTLY CASTLE (HS). Tel: 01466-793191. Ruin of a
16th- and 17th-century house

*INVERARAY CASTLE, Argyll. Tel: 01499-302203.
Gothic-style 18th-century castle; seat of the Dukes of
Argyll

IONA ABBEY, Inner Hebrides. Tel: 01828-640411.
Monastery founded by St Columba in AD 563

*JARLSHOF (HS), Shetland. Tel: 01950-460112. Remains
from Stone Age

JEDBURGH ABBEY (HS), Scottish Borders. Tel: 01835-
863925. Romanesque and early Gothic church
founded c.1138

KELSO ABBEY (HS), Scottish Borders. Remains of great
abbey church founded 1128

LINLITHGOW PALACE (HS). Tel: 01506-842896. Ruin of
royal palace in park setting. Birthplace of
Mary, Queen of Scots

MAES HOWE (HS), Orkney. Tel: 01856-761606.
Neolithic tomb

*MEIGLE SCULPTURED STONES (HS), Angus. Tel: 01828-
640612. Celtic Christian stones

MELROSE ABBEY (HS), Scottish Borders. Tel: 01896-
822562. Ruin of Cistercian abbey founded c.1136

MOUSA BROCH (HS), Shetland. Finest surviving Iron Age
broch tower

NETHER LARGIE CAIRNS (HS), Argyll and Bute. Bronze
Age and Neolithic cairns

NEW ABBEY CORN MILL (HS), nr Dumfries. Tel: 01387-
850260. Water-powered mill

PALACE OF HOLYROODHOUSE, Edinburgh. Tel: 0131-
556-7371. The Queen's official Scottish residence.
Main part of the palace built 1671–9

RING OF BROGAR (HS), Orkney. Neolithic circle of
upright stones with an enclosing ditch

RUTHWELL CROSS (HS), Dumfries and Galloway.
Seventh-century Anglian cross

ST ANDREWS CASTLE AND CATHEDRAL (HS), Fife. Tel:
01334-477196 (castle); 01334-472563 (cathedral).
Ruins of 13th-century castle and remains of the
largest cathedral in Scotland

*SCONE PALACE, Perth. Tel: 01738-552300. House built
1802–13 on the site of a medieval palace

SKARA BRAE (HS), Orkney. Tel: 01856-841815. Stone-
Age village with adjacent 17th-century house

*SMAILHOLM TOWER (HS), Scottish Borders. Tel: 01573-
460365. Well-preserved tower-house

STIRLING CASTLE (HS). Tel: 01786-450000. Great Hall
and gatehouse of James IV, palace of James V, Chapel
Royal remodelled by James VI

TANTALLON CASTLE (HS), E. Lothian. Tel: 01620-
892727. Fortification with earthwork defences and a
14th-century curtain wall with towers

*THREAVE CASTLE (HS), Dumfries and Galloway. Tel:
0831-168512. Late 14th-century tower on an island;
reached by boat, long walk to castle

URQUHART CASTLE (HS), Loch Ness. Tel: 01456-450551.
Castle remains with well-preserved tower

NORTHERN IRELAND

For more information on any of the National Trust
properties listed below, the official website is:
http://www.nationaltrust.org.uk

DE Property in the care of the Northern Ireland
Department of the Environment

NT National Trust property

CARRICKFERGUS CASTLE (DE), Co. Antrim. Tel: 01960-
351273. Castle begun in 1180 and garrisoned until 1928

†CASTLE COOLE (NT), Enniskillen. Tel: 01365-322690.
An 18th-century mansion by James Wyatt in parkland

†CASTLE WARD (NT), Co. Down. Tel: 01396-881204.
An 18th-century house with Classical and Gothic
facades

*DEVENISH ISLAND (DE), Co. Fermanagh. Island
monastery founded in the 6th century by St Molaise

DOWNHILL CASTLE (NT), Co. Londonderry. Tel: 01265-
848728. Ruins of palatial house in landscaped estate
including Mussenden Temple. Opening times of
temple vary.

DUNLUCE CASTLE (DE), Co. Antrim. Tel: 012657-31938.
Ruins of 16th-century stronghold of the MacDonnells

†FLORENCE COURT (NT), Co. Fermanagh. Tel: 01365-
348249. Mid-18th-century house with rococo
plasterwork

*GREY ABBEY (DE), Co. Down. Tel: 01247-788585.
Substantial remains of a Cistercian abbey founded in
1193

HILLSBOROUGH FORT (DE), Co. Down. Built in 1650

†MOUNT STEWART (NT), Co. Down. Tel: 012477-88387.
An 18th-century house, childhood home of Lord
Castlereagh

NENDRUM MONASTERY (DE), Mahee Island, Co. Down.
Founded in the 5th century by St Machaoi

*TULLY CASTLE (DE), Co. Fermanagh. Fortified house
and bawn built in 1613

*WHITE ISLAND (DE), Co. Fermanagh. Tenth-century
monastery and 12th-century church. Access by ferry

Museums and Galleries

There are more than 2,500 museums and galleries in the United Kingdom. Over 1,800 are registered with Resource: The Council for Museums Archives and Libraries, formerly the Museums and Galleries Commission (*see* page 344), which indicates that they have an appropriate constitution, are soundly financed, have adequate collection management standards and public services, and have access to professional curatorial advice. Museums must achieve full or provisional registration status in order to be eligible for grants from Resource and from Area Museums Councils. Over 700 of the registered museums are run by a local authority.

The national museums and galleries receive direct government grant-in-aid. These are: British Museum; Imperial War Museum; National Army Museum; National Galleries of Scotland; National Gallery; National Maritime Museum; National Museums and Galleries on Merseyside; National Museum of Wales; National Museums of Scotland; National Portrait Gallery; Natural History Museum; RAF Museum; Royal Armouries; Science Museum; Tate Gallery; Ulster Folk and Transport Museum; Ulster Museum; Victoria and Albert Museum; Wallace Collection. An online art museum (Web: http://www.24hourmuseum.org.uk) has also been awarded national collection status.

Local authority museums are funded by the local authority and may also receive grants from Resource. Independent museums and galleries mainly rely on their own resources but are also eligible for grants from the Museums and Galleries Commission.

The former Museums and Galleries Commission identified 26 non-national museum bodies which have pre-eminent collections of more than local or regional importance. Some of those designated are museum services with a wide variety of collections; others are small and more focused in a particular field. Ten Area Museum Councils in the UK, which are independent charities give advice and support to the museums in their area and may offer improvement grants. They also circulate exhibitions and assist with training and marketing.

OPENING TO THE PUBLIC

The following is a selection of the museums and art galleries in the United Kingdom. Opening hours and admission charges vary. Most museums are closed on Christmas Eve, Christmas Day, Boxing Day and New Year's Day; many are closed on Good Friday, and some are closed on May Day Bank Holiday. Some smaller museums close at lunchtimes. Information about a specific museum or gallery should be checked by telephone.

ENGLAND

*Local authority museum/gallery
†Museum/gallery contains a collection designated pre-eminent

BARNARD CASTLE, Co. Durham – *†*The Bowes Museum*, Westwick Road. Tel: 01833-690606.
European art from the late medieval period to the 19th century; music and costume galleries; English period rooms from Elizabeth I to Victoria; local archaeology
BATH – *American Museum in Britain*, Claverton Manor. Tel: 01225-460503.
American decorative arts from the 17th to 19th century
Museum of Costume, Bennett Street. Tel: 01225-477752.
Fashion from the 16th century to the present day
Roman Baths Museum, Abbey Church Yard.
Tel: 01225-477774.
Museum adjoins the remains of a Roman baths and temple complex

Victoria Art Gallery, Bridge Street. Tel: 01225-477772.
European Old Masters and British art since the 18th century
BEAMISH, Co. Durham – *†*Beamish, The North of England Open Air Museum*. Tel: 01207-231811.
Recreated northern town *c*.1900, with rebuilt and furnished local buildings, colliery village, farm, railway station, tramway, Pockerley Manor and horse-yard (set *c*.1800)
BEAULIEU, Hants – †*National Motor Museum*.
Tel: 01590-612345.
Displays of over 250 vehicles dating from 1895 to the present day
BIRMINGHAM – *†*Aston Hall*, Trinity Road.
Tel: 0121-327 0062.
Jacobean House containing paintings, furniture and tapestries from 17th to 19th century
*†*Barber Institute of Fine Arts*, off Edgbaston Park Road. Tel: 0121-472 0962.
Fine arts, including Old Masters
Birmingham Nature Centre, Edgbaston.
Tel: 0121-472 7775.
Indoor and outdoor enclosures displaying wildlife, especially British and European
*†*City Museum and Art Gallery*, Chamberlain Square.
Tel: 0121-303 2834.
Includes notable collection of Pre-Raphaelites
*†*Museum of the Jewellery Quarter*, Vyse Street, Hockley.
Tel: 0121-554 3598.
Built around a real jewellery workshop
*†*Soho House*, Soho Avenue. Tel: 0121-554 9122. Eighteenth-century home of industrialist Matthew Boulton
BOVINGTON Camp, Dorset – †*Tank Museum*.
Tel: 01929-405096.
Collection of 300 tanks from the earliest days of tank warfare to the present
BRADFORD – *Cartwright Hall Art Gallery*, Lister Park.
Tel: 01274-493313.
British 19th- and 20th-century fine art
Industrial Museum and Horses at Work, Moorside Road.
Tel: 01274-631756.
Engineering, textiles, transport and social history exhibits, including recreated back-to-back cottages, shire horses and horse tram-rides
National Museum of Photography, Film and Television.
Tel: 01274-202030.
Photography, film and television interactive exhibits.
Features the UK's first IMAX cinema and the only public Cinerama screen in the world
BRIGHTON – *†*Booth Museum of Natural History*, Dyke Road.
Tel: 01273-292777.
Zoology, botany and geology collections; British birds in recreated habitats
*†*Brighton Museum and Art Gallery*, Church Street.
Tel: 01273-290900.
Includes fine art and design, fashion, non-Western art, Brighton history
BRISTOL – *Arnolfini Gallery*, Narrow Quay.
Tel: 0117-929 9191.
Contemporary visual arts, dance, performance, music, talks and workshops
*†*Blaise Castle House Museum*, Henbury.
Tel: 0117-950 6789.
Agricultural and social history collections in an 18th-century mansion
*†*Bristol Industrial Museum*, Prince Street.
Tel: 0117-925 1470.
Industrial, maritime and transport collections
*†*City Museum and Art Gallery*, Queen's Road.
Tel: 0117-922 3571.
Includes fine and decorative art, oriental art, Egyptology

and Bristol ceramics and paintings

CAMBRIDGE – *Duxford Airfield*, Duxford.
Tel: 01223-835000.
Displays of military and civil aircraft, tanks, guns and naval exhibits

†*Fitzwilliam Museum*, Trumpington Street.
Tel: 01223-332900.
Antiquities, fine and applied arts, clocks, ceramics, manuscripts, furniture, sculpture, coins and medals, temporary exhibitions

†*Sedgwick Museum of Geology*, Downing Street.
Tel: 01223-333456.
Extensive geological collection

†*University Museum of Archaeology and Anthropology*, Downing Street. Tel: 01223-333516. Archaeology and anthropology from all parts of the world

†*University Museum of Zoology*, Downing Street.
Tel: 01223-336650.
Extensive zoological collection

†*Whipple Museum of the History of Science*, Free School Lane.
Tel: 01223-330906.
Scientific instruments from the 14th century to the present

CARLISLE – *Tullie House Museum and Art Gallery*, Castle Street. Tel: 01228-534781.
Prehistoric archaeology, Hadrian's Wall, Viking and medieval Cumbria, and the social history of Carlisle; also British 19th- and 20th-century art and English porcelain

CHATHAM – *World Naval Base*. Tel: 01634-823800. Maritime attractions including HMS *Cavalier*, the UK's last World War II destroyer

†*Royal Engineers Museum*, Brompton Barracks.
Tel: 01634-406397.
Regimental history, ethnography, decorative art and photography

CHELTENHAM – *†Art Gallery and Museum*, Clarence Street.
Tel: 01242-237431.
Paintings, arts and crafts

CHESTER – *Grosvenor Museum*, Grosvenor Street.
Tel: 01244-321616.
Roman collections, natural history, art, Chester silver, local history and costume

CHICHESTER – †*Weald and Downland Open Air Museum*, Singleton. Tel: 01243-811348.
Rebuilt vernacular buildings from south-east England; includes medieval houses, agricultural and rural craft buildings and a working watermill

COLCHESTER – *†Colchester Castle Museum*, Castle Park. Tel: 01206-282931.
Largest Norman keep in Europe standing on foundations of roman Temple of Claudius; tours of the Roman vaults, castle walls and chapel with medieval and prison displays

COVENTRY – *Herbert Art Gallery and Museum*, Jordan Well.
Tel: 024-7683 2381.
Local history, archaeology and industry, and fine and decorative art

†Museum of British Road Transport, Hales Street.
Tel: 024-7683 2425.
Hundreds of motor vehicles and bicycles

CRICH, nr Matlock, Derbys – †*National Tramway Museum*.
Tel: 01773-852565.
Open-air working museum with tram rides

DERBY – *Derby Museum and Art Gallery*, The Strand.
Tel: 01332-716659.
Includes paintings by Joseph Wright of Derby and Derby porcelain

Industrial Museum, off Full Street. Tel: 01332-255308.
Rolls-Royce aero engine collection and a railway engineering gallery

DEVIZES – †*Devizes Museum*, Long Street.
Tel: 01380-727369.
Natural and local history, art gallery, archaeological finds

from Bronze Age, Iron Age, Roman and Saxon sites

DORCHESTER – *Dorset County Museum*, High West Street.
Tel: 01305-262735.
Includes a collection of Thomas Hardy's manuscripts, books, notebooks and drawings

ELLESMERE PORT – †*Boat Museum*, South Pier Road.
Tel: 0151-355 5017.
Craft and boating history

EXETER – *†Royal Albert Memorial Museum*, Queen Street.
Tel: 01392-265858.
Natural history, archaeology, worldwide fine and decorative art including Exeter silver

GATESHEAD – *†Shipley Art Gallery*, Prince Consort Road.
Tel: 0191-477 1495.
Contemporary crafts

GAYDON, Warwick – *British Motor Industry Heritage Trust*, Heritage Motor Centre, Banbury Road.
Tel: 01926-641188.
History of British motor industry from 1895 to present; classic vehicles; engineering gallery; Corgi and Lucas collections

GLOUCESTER, – †*National Waterways Museum*, Llanthony Warehouse, The Docks. Tel: 01452-318054.
Two-hundred-year history of Britain's canals and inland waterways

GOSPORT, Hants – *Royal Navy Submarine Museum*, Haslar Jetty Road. Tel: 023-9252 9217.
Underwater warfare, including the submarine *Alliance*; historical and nuclear galleries; and first Royal Navy submarine

GRASMERE, CUMBRIA – †*Dove Cottage* and the *Wordsworth Museum*

HALIFAX – *Eureka! The Museum for Children*, Discovery Road.
Tel: 01426-983191.
Hands-on museum designed for children up to age 12

HULL – *Ferens Art Gallery*, Queen Victoria Square.
Tel: 01482-613902.
European art, especially Dutch 17th-century paintings, British portraits from 17th to 20th century, and marine paintings

Town Docks Museum, Queen Victoria Square.
Tel: 01482-613902.
Whaling, fishing and navigation exhibits

HUNTINGDON – *Cromwell Museum*, Grammar School Walk.
Tel: 01480-375830.
Portraits and memorabilia relating to Oliver Cromwell

IPSWICH – *Christchurch Mansion and Wolsey Art Gallery*, Christchurch Park. Tel: 01473-253246.
Tudor house with paintings by Gainsborough, Constable and other Suffolk artists; furniture and 18th-century ceramics. Art gallery for temporary exhibitions

LEEDS – *†City Art Gallery*, The Headrow.
Tel: 0113-247 8248.
British and European paintings including English watercolours, modern sculpture, Henry Moore gallery, print room

Leeds Industrial Museum at Armley Mills, Canal Road, Armley. Tel: 0113-263 7861.
Largest woollen mill in world

†Lotherton Hall, Aberford. Tel: 0113-281 3259.
Costume and oriental collections in furnished Edwardian house; deer park and bird garden

Royal Armouries Museum, Armouries Drive.
Tel: 0990-106666.
National collection of arms and armour from BC to present; demonstrations of foot combat in museum's five galleries; falconry and mounted combat in the tiltyard

†Temple Newsam House. Tel: 0113-264 7321.
Old Masters and 17th- and 18th-century decorative art in furnished Jacobean/Tudor house

LEICESTER – *Jewry Wall Museum*, St Nicholas Circle.

Tel: 0116-247 3021.
Archaeology, Roman Jewry Wall and baths, and mosaics
New Walk Museum and Art Gallery, New Walk.
Tel: 0116-255 4100.
Natural history, geology, ancient Egypt gallery, European art and decorative arts
Snibston Discovery Park, Coalville. Tel: 01530-510851.
Open-air science and industry museum on site of a coal mine; country park with nature trail
LINCOLN – *Museum of Lincolnshire Life*, Burton Road.
Tel: 01522-528448.
Social history and agricultural collection
Usher Gallery, Lindum Road. Tel: 01522-527980. Watches, miniatures, porcelain, silver; collection of Peter de Wint works; Lincolnshire topography and Royal Lincs Regiment memorabilia
LIVERPOOL – *Lady Lever Art Gallery*, Wirral.
Tel: 0151-478 4136.
Paintings, furniture and porcelain
Liverpool Museum, William Brown Street.
Tel: 0151-478 4399.
Includes Egyptian mummies, weapons and classical sculpture; planetarium, aquarium, vivarium and natural history centre
Merseyside Maritime Museum, Albert Dock.
Tel: 0151-478 4499.
Floating exhibits, working displays and craft demonstrations; incorporates *HM Customs and Excise National Museum*
Museum of Liverpool Life, Mann Island.
Tel: 0151-478 4080. The history of Liverpool
Sudley House, Mossley Hill Road. Tel: 0151-724 3245.
Late 18th- and 19th-century British paintings in former shipowner's home
Tate Gallery Liverpool, Albert Dock. Tel: 0151-709 3223.
Twentieth-century painting and sculpture
Walker Art Gallery, William Brown Street.
Tel: 0151-478 4199.
Paintings from the 14th to 20th century
LONDON: GALLERIES – *Barbican Art Gallery*, Barbican Centre, EC2. Tel: 020-7382 7105.
Temporary exhibitions
† *Courtauld Gallery*, Somerset House, Strand, WC2.
Tel: 020-7848 2526.
The University of London galleries
† *Dulwich Picture Gallery*, College Road, SE21.
Tel: 020-8693 5254.
Built by Sir John Soane to house 17th- and 18th-century paintings
Hayward Gallery, Belvedere Road, SE1.
Tel: 020-7928 3144.
Temporary exhibitions
National Gallery, Trafalgar Square, WC2.
Tel: 020-7839 3321.
Western painting from the 13th to 20th century; early Renaissance collection in the Sainsbury wing
National Portrait Gallery, St Martin's Place, WC2.
Tel: 020-7306 0055.
Portraits of eminent people in British history
Percival David Foundation of Chinese Art, Gordon Square, WC1. Tel: 020-7387 3909.
Chinese ceramics from tenth to 18th century
Photographers Gallery, Great Newport Street, WC2.
Tel: 020-7831 1772.
Temporary exhibitions
The Queen's Gallery, Buckingham Palace, SW1.
Tel: 020-7839 1377.
Art from the Royal Collection
Royal Academy of Arts, Piccadilly, W1.
Tel: 020-7300 8000.
British art since 1750 and temporary exhibitions; annual Summer Exhibition

Saatchi Gallery, Boundary Road, NW8.
Tel: 020-7624 8299.
Contemporary art including paintings, photographs, sculpture and installations
Serpentine Gallery, Kensington Gardens, W2.
Tel: 020-7298 1515.
Temporary exhibitions of British and international contemporary art
Tate Gallery, Millbank, SW1. Tel: 020-7887 8000. British painting and 20th-century painting and sculpture. In 2000 the Millbank site became the Tate Gallery of British Art, and the Tate Gallery of Modern Art opened on the South Bank, London SE1
Wallace Collection, Manchester Square, W1.
Tel: 020-7935 0687.
Paintings and drawings, French 18th-century furniture, armour, porcelain, clocks and sculpture
Whitechapel Art Gallery, Whitechapel High Street, E1.
Tel: 020-7522 7878.
Temporary exhibitions of modern art
LONDON: MUSEUMS – *Bank of England Museum*, Threadneedle Street, EC2 (entrance from Bartholomew Lane). Tel: 020-7601 5545.
History of the Bank since 1694
Bethnal Green Museum of Childhood, Cambridge Heath Road, E2. Tel: 020-8983 5200.
Toys, games and exhibits relating to the social history of childhood
British Museum, Great Russell Street, WC1.
Tel: 020-7636 1555.
Antiquities, coins, medals, prints and drawings
Cabinet War Rooms, King Charles Street, SW1.
Tel: 020-7930 6961.
Underground rooms used by Churchill and the Government during the Second World War
Commonwealth Experience, Kensington High Street, W8.
Tel: 020-7603 4535.
Exhibitions on Commonwealth nations, visual arts and crafts; Interactive World
Cutty Sark, Greenwich, SE10. Tel: 020-8858 3445. Restored and re-rigged tea clipper with exhibits on board.
Design Museum, Shad Thames, SE1. Tel: 020-7378 6055.
The development of design and the mass-production of consumer objects
Estorick Collection, Canonbury Square, N12.
Tel: 020-7704 9522.
Stages the main Estorick Collection of modern Italian art together with temporary loan exhibitions.
Geffrye Museum, Kingsland Road, E2.
Tel: 020-7739 9893.
English urban domestic interiors from 1600 to present day; also paintings, furniture, decorative arts, walled herb garden and period garden rooms
Gilbert Collection, The Strand, WC2. Tel: 020-7240 4080.
The collection comprises some 800 works of art including European silver, gold snuff boxes and Italian mosaics.
HMS Belfast, Morgans Lane, Tooley Street, SE1.
Tel: 020-7940 6300.
Life on a warship, illustrated on World War II warship
† *Horniman Museum and Gardens*, London Road, SE23.
Tel: 020-8699 1872.
Museum of ethnography, musical instruments, natural history and aquarium; reference library; sunken, water and flower gardens
Imperial War Museum, Lambeth Road, SE1.
Tel: 020-7416 5000.
All aspects of the two world wars and other military operations involving Britain and the Commonwealth since 1914
† *Jewish Museum, Camden Town*, Albert Street, NW1.

Tel: 020-7284 1997.
Jewish life, history and religion
†*Jewish Museum, Finchley*, East End Road, N3.
Tel: 020-8349 1143.
Jewish life in London and Holocaust education
†*London Transport Museum*, Covent Garden, WC2.
Tel: 020-7379 6344.
Vehicles, photographs and graphic art relating to the
history of transport in London
MCC Museum, Lord's, NW8. Tel: 020-7289 1611. Cricket
museum. Conducted tours by appointment with Tours
Manager.
Museum of Garden History, Lambeth Palace Road SE1.
Tel: 020-7401 8865.
Exhibition of aspects of garden history and re-created
17th-century garden
†*Museum of London*, London Wall, EC2.
Tel: 020-7600 3699.
History of London from prehistoric times to present day
National Army Museum, Royal Hospital Road, SW3.
Tel: 020-7730 0717.
Five-hundred-year history of the British soldier;
exhibits include model of the Battle of Waterloo and *Army
for Today* gallery
National Maritime Museum, Greenwich, SE10.
Tel: 020-8858 4422.
Comprises the main building, the Royal Observatory and
the Queen's House. Maritime history of Britain; collections
include globes, clocks, telescopes and paintings
Natural History Museum, Cromwell Road, SW7.
Tel: 020-7938 9123.
Natural history collections
†*Petrie Museum of Egyptian Archaeology*, University College
London. Tel: 020-7504 2884. Egyptian archaeology
collection
Royal Air Force Museum, Colindale, NW9.
Tel: 020-8205 2266.
National museum of aviation with over 70 full-size aircraft;
aviation from before the Wright brothers to the present-day
RAF; flight simulator
Royal Mews, Buckingham Palace, SW1.
Tel: 020-7839 1377.
Carriages, coaches, stables and horses
Science Museum, Exhibition Road, SW7.
Tel: 020-7942 4454.
Science, technology, industry and medicine collections
Shakespeare Globe Exhibition, Bankside, SE1.
Tel: 020-7902 1500.
Recreation of Elizabethan theatre using 16th-century
techniques
Sherlock Holmes Museum, Baker Street, NW1.
Tel: 020-7935 8866.
Recreated rooms of the fictional detective
Sir John Soane's Museum, Lincoln's Inn Fields, WC2.
Tel: 020-7430 0175.
Art and antiques
Theatre Museum, Russell Street, WC2.
Tel: 020-7836 2330.
History of the performing arts
Tower Bridge Experience, SE1. Tel: 020-7378 1928.
History of the bridge and display of Victorian steam
machinery; panoramic views from walkways
Victoria and Albert Museum, Cromwell Road, SW7.
Tel: 020-7938 8500.
Includes National Art Library and Print Room. Fine and
applied art and design, including furniture, glass, textiles,
dress collections (British Galleries closed for refurbish-
ment)
Wellington Museum, Apsley House, W1

Wimbledon Lawn Tennis Museum, Church Road, SW19.
Tel: 020-8946 6131.
Tennis trophies, fashion and memorabilia; view of Centre
Court
MANCHESTER – *Gallery of Costume*, Rusholme.
Tel: 0161-224 5217.
Exhibits from the 16th to 20th century
†*Manchester Museum*, Oxford Road. Tel: 0161-275 2634.
Archaeology, archery, botany, Egyptology, entomology,
ethnography, geology, natural history, numismatics, or-
iental and zoology collections
†*Museum of Science and Industry*, Castlefield.
Tel: 0161-832 2244.
On site of world's oldest passenger railway station; galleries
relating to space, energy, power, transport, aviation, textiles
and social history; interactive science centre
†*Pump House People's History Museum*, for *National Museum of
Labour History*, Left Bank.
Tel: 0161-228 7212.
Political and working life history
†*Whitworth Art Gallery*, Oxford Road.
Tel: 0161-275 7450.
Watercolours, drawings, prints, textiles, wallpapers
and 20th-century British art
MONKWEARMOUTH – *†Monkwearmouth Station Museum*,
North Bridge Street. Tel: 0191-567 7075.
Victorian train station
NEWCASTLE UPON TYNE– *†Hancock Museum*, Barras Bridge.
Tel: 0191-222 7418.
Natural history
†Laing Art Gallery, New Bridge Street.
Tel: 0191-232 7734.
British and European art, ceramics, glass, silver, textiles and
costume; *Art on Tyneside* display
†Newcastle Discovery Museum, Blandford Square.
Tel: 0191-232 6789.
Science and industry, local history, fashion and Tyneside's
maritime history; *Turbinia*
(first steam-driven vessel) gallery
NEWMARKET – *National Horseracing Museum*, High Street.
Tel: 01638-667333.
The Essential Horse Millennium Exhibition, horseracing
exhibits and tours of local trainers' yards and studs
NORTHAMPTON – *†Central Museum and Art Gallery*, Guild-
hall Road. Tel: 01604-238548.
Boot and shoe collection
NORTH SHIELDS – †*Stephenson Railway Museum*, Middle
Engine Lane. Tel: 0191-200 7144.
Locomotive engines and rolling stock
NOTTINGHAM – *Brewhouse Yard Museum*, Castle Boulevard.
Tel: 0115-915 3600.
Daily life from the 17th to 20th century
Castle Museum and Art Gallery. Tel: 0115-915 3700.
Paintings, ceramics, silver and glass; history of Nottingham
Industrial Museum, Wollaton Park. Tel: 0115-915 3910.
Lacemaking machinery, steam engines and transport
exhibits
Museum of Costume and Textiles, Castle Gate.
Tel: 0115-915 3500.
Costume displays from 1790 to the mid-20th century
in period rooms
Natural History Museum, Wollaton Park.
Tel: 0115-915 3900.
Local natural history and wildlife dioramas
OXFORD – †*Ashmolean Museum*, Beaumont Street.
Tel: 01865-278000.
European and Oriental fine and applied arts, archaeology,
Egyptology and numismatics
Museum of Modern Art, Pembroke Street.
Tel: 01865-722733.
Temporary exhibitions
†*Museum of the History of Science*, Broad Street.

Tel: 01865-277280.
Displays include early scientific instruments, chemical apparatus, clocks and watches
†*Oxford University Museum of Natural History*, Parks Road. Tel: 01865-272950.
Entomology, geology, mineralogy and zoology
†*Pitt Rivers Museum*, South Parks Road. Tel: 01865-270927.
Ethnographic and archaeological artefacts
PLYMOUTH – *†*City Museum and Art Gallery*, Drake Circus. Tel: 01752-304774.
Local and natural history, ceramics, silver, Old Masters, temporary exhibitions
*The Dome, The Hoe. Tel: 01752-603300.
Maritime history museum
PORTSMOUTH – **Charles Dickens Birthplace Museum*, Old Commercial Road. Tel: 023-9282 7261.
Dickens memorabilia
*D-Day Museum, Clarence Esplanade. Tel: 023-9282 7261.
Includes the Overlord Embroidery
Flagship Portsmouth, HM Naval Base. Incorporates the *Royal Naval Museum* (Tel: 023-9272 7562), HMS *Victory* (Tel: 023-9282 2034), HMS *Warrior* (Tel: 023-9229 1379), the †*Mary Rose* (Tel: 023-9275 0521) and the *Dockyard Museum*. History of the Royal Navy and of the dockyard and the trades in it
PRESTON – **Harris Museum and Art Gallery*, Market Square. Tel: 01772-258248.
British art since the 18th century, ceramics, glass, costume and local history; also contemporary exhibitions
READING – †*Rural History Museum*, University of Reading. Tel: 0118-931 8660.
History of farming and the countryside over the last 200 years
ST ALBANS – **Verulamium Museum*, St Michael's. Tel: 01727-866100.
Iron Age and Roman Verulamium, including wall plasters, jewellery, mosaics and room reconstructions
ST IVES, Cornwall – *Tate Gallery St Ives*, Porthmeor Beach. Tel: 01736-796226.
Painting and sculpture by artists associated with St Ives
SALISBURY †*Salisbury and South Wiltshire Museum*, The Close. Tel: 01722-332151.
Archaeology collection
SHEFFIELD – **City Museum and Mappin Art Gallery*, Weston Park. Tel: 0114-276 8588.
Includes applied arts, natural history, Bronze Age archaeology and ethnography, 19th- and 20th-century art
*Graves Art Gallery, Surrey Street. Tel: 0114-273 5158.
Twentieth-century British art, Grice Collection of Chinese ivories
*Kelham Island Industrial Museum, off Alma Street. Tel: 0114-272 2106.
Local industrial and social history
*Ruskin Gallery and Ruskin Craft Gallery, Norfolk Street. Tel: 0114-273 5299/203 9416.
SOUTHAMPTON – *†*City Art Gallery, Civic Centre. Tel: 023-8083 2277.
Fine art, especially 20th-century British
*†*Maritime Museum*, Town Quay. Tel: 023-8022 3941.
Southampton maritime history
*†*Museum of Archaeology*, Town Quay. Tel: 023-8063 5904.
Roman, Saxon and medieval archaeology
*†*Tudor House Museum and Garden*, Bugle Street. Tel: 023-8033 2513.
Restored 16th century garden; social history exhibitions
SOUTH SHIELDS – *†*Arbeia Roman Fort*, Baring Street. Tel: 0191-456 6612.
Excavated ruins
*†*South Shields Museum and Art Gallery*, Ocean Road.

Tel: 0191-456 8740.
South Tyneside history, including reconstructed street
STOKE-ON-TRENT – **Etruria Industrial Museum*, Etruria. Tel: 01782-233144.
Britain's sole surviving steam-powered potter's mill
*Gladstone Pottery Museum, Longton. Tel: 01782-319232.
A working Victorian pottery
*†*Potteries Museum and Art Gallery*, Hanley. Tel: 01782-232323.
Pottery, china and porcelain collections and a Mark XVI Spitfire. Pottery factory tours are available by arrangement at the following: *Royal Doulton*, Burslem; *Spode*, Stoke; *Wedgwood*, Barlaston; *W. Moorcroft*, Cobridge; *H & R Johnson Tiles*, Tunstall; *Staffordshire Enamels*, Longton; *Royale Stratford China*, Fenton
STYAL, CHESHIRE – *Quarry Bank Mill*. Tel: 01625-527468.
Working mill illustrating history of cotton industry; costumed guides at restored Apprentice House
SUNDERLAND – *†*Sunderland Art Gallery*, Borough Road. Tel: 0191-565 0723.
Fine and decorative art
WASHINGTON – †*Washington F' Pit Museum*, Albany Way. Tel: 0191-565 0723.
Colliery-related collection
TELFORD – *†*Ironbridge Gorge Museums*. Tel: 01952-432166.
Includes first iron bridge; Blists Hill (late Victorian working town); Museum of Iron; Jackfield Tile Museum; Coalport China Museum; Tar Tunnel; Broseley Pipeworks
TRING, Herts – *Tring Zoological Museum*, Akeman Street. Tel: 01442-824181.
Display of more than 4,000 animal species
WAKEFIELD – *Yorkshire Sculpture Park*, West Bretton. Tel: 01924-830302.
Open-air sculpture gallery including works by Moore, Hepworth, Frink and others in 300 acres of parkland
WORCESTER – **City Museum and Art Gallery*, Foregate Street. Tel: 01905-25371.
Includes a military museum, River Severn Gallery and changing art exhibitions
Museum of Worcester Porcelain and Royal Worcester Visitor Centre, Severn Street. Tel: 01905-23221.
Factory tours
WROUGHTON, nr Swindon, Wilts – *Science Museum*, Wroughton Airfield. Tel: 01793-814466.
Aircraft displays and some of the Science Museum's transport and agricultural collection
YEOVIL, Somerset – *Fleet Air Arm Museum*, Royal Naval Air Station, Yeovilton. Tel: 01935-840565.
History of naval aviation; historic aircraft, including Concorde 002
Montacute House, Montacute. Elizabethan and Jacobean portraits from the National Portrait Gallery
YORK – *Beningbrough Hall*, Shipton-by-Beningbrough. Tel: 01904-470666.
Portraits from the National Portrait Gallery
*†*Castle Museum*. Tel: 01904-653611.
Reconstructed streets; costume and military collections
*†*City Art Gallery*, Exhibition Square. Tel: 01904-551861.
European and British painting spanning seven centuries; modern pottery
Jorvik Viking Centre, Coppergate. Tel: 01904-643211.
Reconstruction of Viking York
National Railway Museum, Leeman Road. Tel: 01904-621261.
Includes locomotives, rolling stock and carriages
*†*Yorkshire Museum*, Museum Gardens. Tel: 01904-629745. Yorkshire life from Roman to medieval times; geology gallery

WALES

BODELWYDDAN, Denbighshire – *Bodelwyddan Castle*.
Tel: 01745-584060.
Portraits from the National Portrait Gallery, furniture from
the Victoria and Albert Museum and sculptures from the
Royal Academy
CAERLEON – *Roman Legionary Museum*.
Tel: 01633-423134.
Material from the site of the Roman fortress of Isca and its
suburbs
CARDIFF – *National Museum and Gallery Cardiff*, Cathays Park.
Tel: 029-2039 7951.
Includes natural sciences, archaeology and Impressionist
paintings
Museum of Welsh Life, St Fagans. Tel: 029-2057 3500.
Open-air museum with re-erected buildings, agricultural
equipment and costume
DRE-FACH Felindre, nr Llandysul – *Museum of the Welsh
Woollen Industry*. Tel: 01559-370929.
Exhibitions, a working woollen mill and craft workshops
LLANBERIS, nr Caernarfon –*Welsh Slate Museum*.
Tel: 01286-870630.
Former slate quarry with original machinery and plant slate
crafts demonstrations
LLANDRINDOD WELLS – *National Cycle Exhibition*,
Automobile Palace, Temple Street. Tel: 01597-825531.
Over 200 bicycles on display, from 1818 to the present day
SWANSEA – *Glynn Vivian Art Gallery and Museum*, Alexandra
Road. Tel: 01792-655006.
Paintings, ceramics, Swansea pottery and porcelain, clocks,
glass and Welsh art
Swansea Maritime and Industrial Museum, Museum Square.
Tel: 01792-650351
Includes a working woollen mill and historic boats afloat
Swansea Museum, Victoria Road. Tel: 01792-653763.
Archaeology, social history, Swansea pottery

SCOTLAND

ABERDEEN – *Aberdeen Art Gallery*, Schoolhill.
Tel: 01224-523700.
Art from the 18th to 20th century
Aberdeen Maritime Museum, Shiprow.
Tel: 01224-337700.
Maritime history, incl. shipbuilding and North Sea oil
EDINBURGH – *Britannia*, Leith docks. Tel: 0131-555 5566.
Former royal yacht with royal barge and royal family picture
gallery. Tickets must be pre-booked
City Art Centre, Market Street. Tel: 0131-529 3993. Late
19th- and 20th-century art and temporary exhibitions
Huntly House Museum, Canongate. Tel: 0131-529 4143.
Local history, silver, glass and Scottish pottery
Museum of Childhood, High Street. Tel: 0131-529 4142.
Toys, games, clothes and exhibits relating to the social
history of childhood
Museum of Flight, East Fortune Airfield, nr North Berwick.
Tel: 01620-880308.
Display of aircraft
Museum of Scotland, Chambers Street.
Tel: 0131-247 4422.
Scottish history from prehistoric times to the present
National Gallery of Scotland, The Mound.
Tel: 0131-624 6200.
Paintings, drawings and prints from the 16th to 20th
century, and the national collection of Scottish art
The People's Story, Canongate. Tel: 0131-529 4057.
Edinburgh life since the 18th century
Royal Museum of Scotland, Chambers Street.
Tel: 0131-225 7534.

Scottish and international collections from prehistoric
times to the present
Scottish Agricultural Museum, Ingliston.
Tel: 0131-333 2674.
History of agriculture in Scotland
Scottish National Gallery of Modern Art, Belford Road.
Tel: 0131-624 6200.
Twentieth-century painting, sculpture and graphic art
Scottish National Portrait Gallery, Queen Street.
Tel: 0131-624 6200.
Portraits of eminent people in Scottish history, and the
national collection of photography
The Writers' Museum, Lawnmarket.
Tel: 0131-529 4901.
Robert Louis Stevenson, Walter Scott and Robert Burns
exhibits
FORT WILLIAM – *West Highland Museum*, Cameron Square.
Tel: 01397-702169.
Includes tartan collections and exhibits relating to
1745 uprising
GLASGOW – *Burrell Collection*, Pollokshaws Road.
Tel: 0141-649 7151.
Paintings, textiles, furniture, ceramics, stained glass and
silver from classical times to the 19th century
Gallery of Modern Art, Queen Street.
Tel: 0141-229 1996.
Collection of contemporary Scottish and world art
Glasgow Art Gallery and Museum, Kelvingrove.
Tel: 0141-287 2699.
Includes Old Masters, 19th-century French paintings and
armour collection
Hunterian Art Gallery, Hillhead Street.
Tel: 0141-330 5431.
Rennie Mackintosh and Whistler collections; Old Masters,
Scottish paintings and modern paintings, sculpture and
prints
McLellan Galleries, Sauchiehall Street.
Tel: 0141-331 1854.
Temporary exhibitions
Museum of Transport, Bunhouse Road.
Tel: 0141-287 2720.
Includes a reproduction of a 1938 Glasgow street, cars since
the 1930s, trams and a Glasgow subway station
People's Palace Museum, Glasgow Green.
Tel: 0141-554 0223.
History of Glasgow since 1175
St Mungo Museum of Religious Life and Art, Castle Street.
Tel: 0141-553 2557.
Explores universal themes through objects of all the main
world religions

NORTHERN IRELAND

BELFAST – *Ulster Museum*, Botanic Gardens.
Tel: 028-9038 3000.
Irish antiquities, natural and local history, fine and applied
arts
HOLYWOOD, Co. Down – *Ulster Folk and Transport Museum*,
Cultra. Tel: 028-9042 8428.
Open-air museum with original buildings from Ulster town
and rural life *c.* 1900; indoor galleries including Irish rail and
road transport and *Titanic* exhibitions
LONDONDERRY – *The Tower Museum*, Union Hall Place.
Tel: 028-7137 2411.
Tells the story of Ireland through the history of
Londonderry
OMAGH, Co. Tyrone – *Ulster American Folk Park*, Castletown.
Tel: 028-8224 3292.
Open-air museum telling the story of Ulster's emigrants to
America; restored or recreated dwellings and workshops;
ship and dockside gallery

Sights of London

For historic buildings and museums and galleries in London, *see* pages 594–9 and 602–3

ALEXANDRA PALACE, Alexandra Palace Way, Wood Green, London N22 7AY. Tel: 020-8365 2121. The Victorian Palace was severely damaged by fire in 1980 but was restored, and reopened in 1988. Alexandra Palace now provides modern facilities for exhibitions, conferences, banquets and leisure activities. There is an ice rink, open daily, a boating lake, the Phoenix Bar and a conservation area.

BARBICAN CENTRE, Silk Street, London EC2Y 8DS. Tel: 020-7638 4141. Owned, funded and managed by the Corporation of London, the Barbican Centre opened in 1982 and houses the 1,156-seat Barbican Theatre, a 200-seat studio theatre (The Pit), and the 1,989-seat Barbican Hall. There are also three cinemas, two art galleries, a sculpture court, a lending library, conference, trade and banqueting facilities, conservatory, shops, restaurants, cafés and bars.

BRIDGES. The bridges over the Thames (from east to west) are:

The Queen Elizabeth II Bridge, opened 1991, from Dartford to Thurrock

Tower Bridge, opened 1894

London Bridge, opened after rebuilding by Rennie, 1831; the new London Bridge opened 1973

Alexandra Bridge (railway bridge), built 1863–6

Southwark Bridge (Rennie), built 1814–19; rebuilt 1912–21

Millennium Bridge, opened June 2000.

Blackfriars Railway Bridge, completed 1864

Blackfriars Bridge, built 1760–9; rebuilt 1860–9; widened 1907–10

Waterloo Bridge (Rennie), opened 1817; rebuilt 1937–42

Hungerford Railway Bridge (Brunel), suspension bridge built 1841–5; replaced by present railway and foot-bridge 1863

Westminster Bridge (width 84ft), opened 1750; rebuilt 1854–62

Lambeth Bridge, built 1862; rebuilt 1929–32

Vauxhall Bridge, built 1811–16; rebuilt 1895–1906

Grosvenor Bridge (railway bridge), built 1859–60; rebuilt 1963–7

Chelsea Bridge, built 1851–8; replaced by suspension bridge 1934; widened 1937

Albert Bridge, opened 1873; restructured (Bazalgette) 1884; strengthened 1971–3

Battersea Bridge (Holland), opened 1772; rebuilt (Bazalgette) 1890

Battersea Railway Bridge, opened 1863

Wandsworth Bridge, opened 1873; rebuilt 1940

Putney Railway Bridge, opened 1889

Putney Bridge, built 1727–9; rebuilt (Bazalgette) 1882–6; starting point of Oxford and Cambridge Boat Race

Hammersmith Bridge, built 1824–7; rebuilt (Bazalgette) 1883–7; closed in 1997 for safety work

Barnes Railway Bridge (also pedestrian), built 1846–9; restructured 1893

Chiswick Bridge, opened 1933

Kew Railway Bridge, opened 1869

Kew Bridge, built 1758–9; rebuilt and renamed King Edward VII Bridge 1903

Richmond Lock; lock, weir and footbridge opened 1894

Twickenham Bridge, opened 1933

Richmond Railway Bridge, opened 1848; restructured 1906–8

Richmond Bridge, built 1774–7; widened 1937

Teddington Lock, footbridge opened 1889; marks the end of the tidal reach of the Thames

Kingston Bridge, built 1825–8; widened 1914

Hampton Court Bridge, built 1753; replaced by iron bridge 1865; present bridge built 1933.

A new footbridge is under construction; it is being constructed alongside the railway on Hungerford Bridge

CEMETERIES. *Abney Park*, Stamford Hill, N16 (35 acres), tomb of General Booth, founder of the Salvation Army, and memorials to many Nonconformist divines. *Brompton*, Old Brompton Road, SW10 (40 acres), graves of Sir Henry Cole, Emmeline Pankhurst, John Wisden. *City of London Cemetery and Crematorium*, Aldersbrook Road, E12 (200 acres). *Golders Green Crematorium*, Hoop Lane, NW11 (12 acres), with Garden of Rest and memorials to many famous men and women. *Hampstead*, Fortune Green Road, NW6 (36 acres), graves of Kate Greenaway, Lord Lister, Marie Lloyd. *Highgate*, Swains Lane, N6 (38 acres), tombs of George Eliot, Faraday and Marx; guided tours only, west side. *Kensal Green*, Harrow Road, W10 (70 acres), tombs of Thackeray, Trollope, Sydney Smith, Wilkie Collins, Tom Hood, George Cruikshank, Leigh Hunt, I. K. Brunel and Charles Kemble. Churchyard of the former *Marylebone Chapel*, Marylebone High Street, W1, Charles Wesley and his son Samuel Wesley buried; chapel demolished in 1949, now Garden of Rest. *Nunhead*, Linden Grove, SE15 (26 acres), closed in 1969, recently restored and opened for burials. *St Marylebone Cemetery and Crematorium*, East End Road, N2 (47 acres). *West Norwood Cemetery and Crematorium*, Norwood High Street, SE27 (42 acres), tombs of Sir Henry Bessemer, Mrs Beeton, Sir Henry Tate and Joseph Whitaker (*Whitaker's Almanack*).

CENOTAPH, Whitehall, London SW1. The word 'cenotaph' means 'empty tomb'. The monument, erected 'To the Glorious Dead', is a memorial to all ranks of the sea, land and air forces who gave their lives in the service of the Empire during the First World War. Designed by Sir Edwin Lutyens and erected as a temporary memorial in 1919, it was replaced by a permanent structure unveiled by George V on Armistice Day 1920. An additional inscription was made after the Second World War to commemorate those who gave their lives in that conflict.

CHARTERHOUSE, Charterhouse Square, London EC1M 6AN. Tel: 020-7253 9503. A Carthusian monastery from 1371 to 1537, purchased in 1611 by Thomas Sutton, who endowed it as a residence for aged men 'of gentle birth' and a school for poor scholars (removed to Godalming in 1872). *Registrar and Clerk to the Governors*, R. B. Heaton-Watson, BA, FRGS

CHELSEA PHYSIC GARDEN, 66 Royal Hospital Road, London SW3 4HS. Tel: 020-7352 5646. A garden of general botanical research and education, maintaining a wide range of rare and unusual plants. The garden was established in 1673 by the Society of Apothecaries. All enquiries to the Curator.

DOWNING STREET, London SW1. Number 10 Downing Street is the official town residence of the Prime

Minister, No. 11 of the Chancellor of the Exchequer and No. 12 is the office of the Government Whips. The street was named after Sir George Downing, Bt., soldier and diplomatist, who was MP for Morpeth from 1660 to 1684.

Chequers, a Tudor mansion in the Chilterns near Princes Risborough, was presented by Lord and Lady Lee of Fareham in 1917 to serve, from 1921, as a country residence for the Prime Minister of the day.

GEORGE INN, Borough High Street, London SE1. The last galleried inn in London, built in 1677. Now run as an ordinary public house.

GREENWICH, London SE10. *The Royal Naval College* was until 1873 the Greenwich Hospital. It was built by Charles II, largely from designs by John Webb, and by Queen Mary II and William III, from designs by Wren. It stands on the site of an ancient abbey, a royal house and Greenwich Palace which was constructed by Henry VII. Henry VIII, Mary I and Elizabeth I were born in the royal palace and Edward VI died there. *Greenwich Park* (196½ acres) was enclosed by Humphrey, Duke of Gloucester, and laid out by Charles II from the designs of Le Nôtre. On a hill in Greenwich Park is the Royal Observatory (founded 1675). Its buildings are now managed by the National Maritime Museum and the earliest building is named Flamsteed House, after John Flamsteed (1646–1719), the first Astronomer Royal. *The Cutty Sark*, the last of the famous tea clippers, has been preserved as a memorial to ships and men of a past era. Sir Francis Chichester's round-the-world yacht, *Gipsy Moth IV*, can also be seen. *The Millennium Dome, see* Millennium Experience

HORSE GUARDS, Whitehall, London SW1. Archway and offices built about 1753. The mounting of the guard takes place at 11a.m. (10a.m. on Sundays) and the dismounted inspection at 4p.m. Only those with the Queen's permission may drive through the gates and archway into *Horse Guards' Parade* (230,000 sq. ft), where the Colour is 'trooped' on The Queen's official birthday.

THE HOUSE OF COMMONS, Westminster, London SW1A 2TT. Tel: 020-7219 4272.
E-mail: hcinfo@parliament.uk. The royal palace of Westminster, originally built by Edward the Confessor, was the normal meeting place of Parliament from about 1340. St Stephen's Chapel was used from about 1550 for the meetings of the House of Commons, which had previously been held in the Chapter House or Refectory of Westminster Abbey. The House of Lords met in an apartment of the royal palace.

The fire of 1834 destroyed much of the palace and the present Houses of Parliament were erected on the site from the designs of Sir Charles Barry and Augustus Welby Pugin between 1840 and 1867. The chamber of the House of Commons was destroyed by bombing in 1941 and a new Chamber designed by Sir Giles Gilbert Scott was used for the first time in 1950.

Lord Chancellor's Residence, Lord Chancellor's Office, House of Lords, London, SW1A 0PW.
Tel: 020-7219 3107.

Westminster Hall and the Crypt Chapel was the only part of the old palace of Westminster to survive the fire of 1834. It was built by William Rufus (1097–9) and altered by Richard II (1394–9). The hammerbeam roof of carved oak dates from 1396–8. The Hall was the scene of the trial of Charles I.

The Victoria Tower of the House of Lords is about 330 ft high, and when Parliament is sitting the Union flag flies by day from its flagstaff. *The Clock Tower* of the House of Commons is about 320 ft high and contains

'Big Ben', the hour bell said to be named after Sir Benjamin Hall, First Commissioner of Works when the original bell was cast in 1856. This bell, which weighed 16 tons 11 cwt, was found to be cracked in 1857. The present bell (13½ tons) is a recasting of the original and was first brought into use in 1859. The dials of the clock are 23 ft in diameter, the hands being 9 ft and 14 ft long (including balance piece). A light is displayed from the Clock Tower at night when Parliament is sitting.

For security reasons tours of the Houses of Parliament are available only to those who have made advance arrangements through an MP or peer.

Admission to the Strangers' Gallery of the House of Lords is arranged by a peer or by queue via St Stephen's Entrance. Admission to the Strangers' Gallery of the House of Commons is by Members' order (Members' orders should be sought several weeks in advance), or by queue via St Stephen's Entrance. The House does not always sit on Fridays. Overseas visitors may write to the Parliamentary Education Unit to obtain a permit to tour the Houses of Parliament, or obtain cards of introduction from their Embassy or High Commission to attend the public gallery.

INNS OF COURT. The *Inner* and *Middle Temple*, Fleet Street/Victoria Embankment, London EC4. Have occupied since the early 14th century the site of the buildings of the Order of Knights Templars. *Inner Temple Hall* is open by appointment on application to the Treasurer's Office. *Middle Temple Hall* (1562–70) is open when not in use. In Middle Temple Gardens Shakespeare (Henry VI, Part I) places the incident which led to the 'Wars of the Roses' (1455–85).

Temple Church, London EC4, has a nave which forms one of five remaining round churches in England. *Master of the Temple*, Revd R. Griffith-Jones

Lincoln's Inn, Chancery Lane/Lincoln's Inn Fields, London WC2. Occupies the site of the palace of a former Bishop of Chichester and of a Black Friars monastery. The hall and library buildings are of 1845, although the library is first mentioned in 1474; the old hall (late 15th-century) and the chapel were rebuilt *c.* 1619–23. Halls open by appointment, chapel and gardens, Monday–Friday 12–2.30. Chapel services Sunday 11.30a.m. during law terms. *Lincoln's Inn Fields* (7 acres). The square was laid out by Inigo Jones.

Gray's Inn, Holborn/Gray's Inn Road, London WC1. Tel: 020-7458 7800. Early 14th century; Hall 1556–8. No other 'Inns' are active, but there are remains of *Staple Inn*, a gabled front on Holborn (opposite Gray's Inn Road). *Clement's Inn* (near St Clement Danes Church), *Clifford's Inn*, Fleet Street, and *Thavies Inn*, Holborn Circus, are all rebuilt. *Serjeants' Inn*, Fleet Street, and another (demolished 1910) of the same name in Chancery Lane, were composed of Serjeants-at-Law, the last of whom died in 1922.

LLOYD'S, Lime Street, London EC3M 7HA. E-mail: lloyds-external-enquiries@lloyds.com. Web: http://www.lloyds.com. International insurance market which evolved during the 17th-century from Lloyd's Coffee House. The present building was opened for business in May 1986, and houses the Lutine Bell. Underwriting is on three floors with a total area of 114,000 sq. ft.

LONDON EYE, The Thames South Bank. Opened in February 2000 as London's millennium landmark, this 450 ft observation wheel is the capital's fourth largest structure. The wheel provides a 30 minute ride offering spectacular panoramic views of the capital.

LONDON PARKS, ETC.

Royal Parks

Bushy Park (1,099 acres), Middx. Adjoining Hampton Court, contains avenue of horse-chestnuts enclosed in a fourfold avenue of limes planted by William III. 'Chestnut Sunday' (when the trees are in full bloom with their 'candles') is usually about 1 to 15 May

Green Park (49 acres), London W1. Between Piccadilly and St James's Park, with Constitution Hill leading to Hyde Park Corner

Greenwich Park (196½ acres), London SE10

Hyde Park (341 acres), London W1/W2. From Park Lane to Kensington Gardens, containing the Serpentine. Fine gateway at Hyde Park Corner, with Apsley House, the Achilles Statue, Rotten Row and the Ladies' Mile. To the north-east is the Marble Arch, originally erected by George IV at the entrance to Buckingham Palace and re-erected in the present position in 1851

Kensington Gardens (275 acres), London W2/W8. From the western boundary of Hyde Park to Kensington Palace, containing the Albert Memorial and Peter Pan statue

Kew, Royal Botanic Gardens, see page 357

Regent's Park and *Primrose Hill* (464 acres), London NW1. From Marylebone Road to Primrose Hill surrounded by the Outer Circle and divided by the Broad Walk leading to the Zoological Gardens

Richmond Park (2,469 acres), Middx

St James's Park (93 acres), London SW1. From Whitehall to Buckingham Palace. Ornamental lake of 12 acres. The original suspension bridge built in 1857 was replaced in 1957. The Mall leads from the Admiralty Arch to Buckingham Palace, Birdcage Walk from Storey's Gate to Buckingham Palace. Maintained by the Royal Parks Agency

Ashtead Common (500 acres), Surrey

Burnham Beeches and *Fleet Wood* (540 acres), Bucks. Purchased by the Corporation for the benefit of the public in 1880, Fleet Wood (65 acres) being presented in 1921

Coulsdon Common (133 acres), Surrey

Epping Forest (6,000 acres), Essex. Purchased by the Corporation and opened to the public in 1882. The present forest is 12 miles long by 1 to 2 miles wide, about one-tenth of its original area

Farthing Downs (121 acres), Surrey

Hampstead Heath (789 acres), London NW3. Including Golders Hill (36 acres) and Parliament Hill (271 acres)

Highgate Wood (70 acres), London N6/N10

Kenley Common (138 acres), Surrey

Queen's Park (30 acres), London NW6

Riddlesdown (90 acres), Surrey

Spring Park (51 acres), Kent

West Ham Park (77 acres), London E15

West Wickham Common (25 acres), Kent

Woodredon and Warlies Park Estate (740 acres), Waltham Abbey

Also smaller open spaces within the City of London, including *Finsbury Circus Gardens* which are maintained by Historic Royal Palaces

Hampton Court Gardens (54 acres), Middx

Hampton Court Green (17 acres), Middx

Hampton Court Park (622 acres), Middx

LONDON PLANETARIUM, Marylebone Road, London NW1 5LR. Tel: 0890 4003000. Star show and interactive exhibits.

LONDON ZOO, Regent's Park, London NW1. Tel: 020-7722 3333. Opened in 1828.

MADAME TUSSAUD'S, Marylebone Road, London NW1 5LR. Tel: 0870 400 3000. Waxwork exhibition.

MARKETS. The London markets are mostly administered by the Corporation of London. *Billingsgate* (fish), Thames Street site dating from 1875, a market site for over 1,000 years, moved to the Isle of Dogs in 1982. *Borough*, SE1 (vegetables, fruit, flowers, etc.), established on present site 1756, privately owned and run. *Covent Garden* (vegetables, fruit, flowers, etc.), established in 1661 under a charter of Charles II, moved in 1973 to Nine Elms. *Leadenhall*, EC3 (meat, poultry, fish, etc.), built 1881, part recently demolished. *London Fruit Exchange*, Brushfield Street, built by Corporation of London 1928–9 as buildings for Spitalfields market; not connected with the market since it moved in 1991. *Petticoat Lane*, Middlesex Street, E1, a market has existed on the site for over 500 years, now a Sunday morning market selling almost anything. *Portobello Road*, W11, originally for herbs and horse-trading from 1870; became famous for antiques after the closure of the Caledonian Market in 1948. *Smithfield, Central Meat, Fish, Fruit, Vegetable and Poultry Markets*, built 1851–66, the site of St Bartholomew's Fair from 12th to 19th century, new hall built 1963, market refurbished 1993–4. *Spitalfields*, E1 (vegetables, fruit, etc.), established 1682, modernised 1928, moved to Leyton in 1991.

MARLBOROUGH HOUSE, Pall Mall, London SW1A 5HX. Tel: 020-7839 3411. E-mail: info@commonwealth.int. Web: http://www.thecommonwealth.org. Built by Wren for the first Duke of Marlborough and completed in 1711, the house reverted to the Crown in 1835. In 1863 it became the London house of the Prince of Wales and was the London home of Queen Mary until her death in 1953. In 1959 Marlborough House was given by The Queen as the headquarters for the Commonwealth Secretariat and it was opened as such in 1965. The Queen's Chapel, Marlborough Gate was begun in 1623 from the designs of Inigo Jones for the Infanta Maria of Spain, and completed for Queen Henrietta Maria.

MILLENNIUM EXPERIENCE (The Dome, Greenwich). Tel: 020-8293 8600. E-mail: info@newmill.co.uk. Web: http://www.dome2000.co.uk

Open to the public from 1 January 2000. The Dome's circumference is over one km, it is over 80,000 m^2 and the roof is 50 m high. It is divided into 14 zones, Body, Faith, Home Planet, Journey, Learning, Living Island, Mind, Money, Play, Self Portrait, Shared Ground, Rest, Talk and Work. Visitors can also enjoy the latest Blackadder episode in the entertainment venue Skyscape, see over 200 performances by local communities on the Our Town stage and experience the spectacular Millennium Show in the dome's Central Arena. The Dome's future is currently being debated following the collapse of negotiations with Dome Europe to purchase the Dome.

LONDON MONUMENT (commonly called The Monument), Monument Street, London EC3. Built from designs of Wren, 1671–7, to commemorate the Great Fire of London, which broke out in Pudding Lane on 2 September 1666. The fluted Doric column is 120 ft high; the moulded cylinder above the balcony supporting a flaming vase of gilt bronze is an additional 42 ft; and the column is based on a square plinth 40 ft high (with fine carvings on the west face) making a total height of 202 ft. Splendid views of London from gallery at top of column (311 steps).

MONUMENTS (sculptor's name in parenthesis). *Albert Memorial* (Durham), Kensington Gore; *Royal Air Force* (Blomfield), Victoria Embankment; *Viscount*

Alanbrooke, Whitehall; *Beaconsfield*, Parliament Square; *Beatty* (Macmillan), Trafalgar Square; *Belgian Gratitude* (setting by Blomfield, statue by Rousseau), Victoria Embankment; *Boadicea* (or Boudicca), Queen of the Iceni (Thornycroft), Westminster Bridge; *Brunel* (Marochetti), Victoria Embankment; *Burghers of Calais* (Rodin), Victoria Tower Gardens, Westminster; *Burns* (Steel), Embankment Gardens; *Canada Memorial* (Granche), Green Park; *Carlyle* (Boehm), Chelsea Embankment; *Cavalry* (Jones), Hyde Park; *Edith Cavell* (Frampton), St Martin's Place; *Cenotaph* (Lutyens), Whitehall; *Charles I* (Le Sueur), Trafalgar Square; *Charles II* (Gibbons), South Court, Chelsea Hospital; *Churchill* (Roberts-Jones), Parliament Square; *Cleopatra's Needle* (68½ ft high, *c*.1500 BC, erected on the Thames Embankment in 1877–8; the sphinxes are Victorian); *Clive* (Tweed), King Charles Street; *Captain Cook* (Brock), The Mall; *Crimean*, Broad Sanctuary; *Oliver Cromwell* (Thornycroft), outside Westminster Hall; *Cunningham* (Belsky), Trafalgar Square; *Gen. Charles de Gaulle*, Carlton Gardens; *Lord Dowding* (Faith Winter), Strand; *Duke of Cambridge* (Jones), Whitehall; *Duke of York* (124 ft), Carlton House Terrace; *Edward VII* (Mackennal), Waterloo Place; *Elizabeth I* (1586, oldest outdoor statue in London; from Ludgate), Fleet Street; *Eros* (Shaftesbury Memorial) (Gilbert), Piccadilly Circus; *Marechal Foch* (Mallisard, copy of one in Cassel, France), Grosvenor Gardens; *Charles James Fox* (Westmacott), Bloomsbury Square; *George III* (Cotes Wyatt), Cockspur Street; *George IV* (Chantrey), riding without stirrups, Trafalgar Square; *George V* (Reid Dick), Old Palace Yard; *George VI* (Macmillan), Carlton Gardens; *Gladstone* (Thornycroft), Strand; *Guards'* (Crimea) (Bell), Waterloo Place; (Great War) (Ledward, figures, Bradshaw, cenotaph), Horse Guards' Parade; *Haig* (Hardiman), Whitehall; *Sir Arthur (Bomber) Harris* (Faith Winter), Strand; *Irving* (Brock), north side of National Portrait Gallery; *James II* (Gibbons and/or pupils), Trafalgar Square; *Jellicoe* (Wheeler), Trafalgar Square; *Samuel Johnson* (Fitzgerald), opposite St Clement Danes; *Kitchener* (Tweed), Horse Guards' Parade; *Abraham Lincoln* (Saint-Gaudens, copy of one in Chicago), Parliament Square; *Milton* (Montford), St Giles, Cripplegate; *The Monument* (*see* above); *Mountbatten*, Foreign Office Green; *Nelson* (170 ft 2 in), Trafalgar Square, with Landseer's lions (cast from guns recovered from the wreck of the *Royal George*); *Florence Nightingale* (Walker), Waterloo Place; *Palmerston* (Woolner), Parliament Square; *Peel* (Noble), Parliament Square; *Pitt* (Chantrey), Hanover Square; *Portal* (Nemon), Embankment Gardens; *Prince Consort* (Bacon), Holborn Circus; *Queen Elizabeth Gate*, Hyde Park Corner; *Raleigh* (Macmillan), Whitehall; *Richard I (Coeur de Lion)* (Marochetti), Old Palace Yard; *Roberts* (Bates), Horse Guards' Parade; *Franklin D. Roosevelt* (Reid Dick), Grosvenor Square; *Royal Artillery* (South Africa) (Colton), The Mall; (Great War), Hyde Park Corner; *Captain Scott* (Lady Scott), Waterloo Place; *Shackleton* (Sarjeant Jagger), Kensington Gore; *Shakespeare* (Fontana, copy of one by Scheemakers in Westminster Abbey), Leicester Square; *Smuts* (Epstein), Parliament Square; *Sullivan* (Goscombe John), Victoria Embankment; *Trenchard* (Macmillan), Victoria Embankment; *Victoria Memorial*, in front of Buckingham Palace; *Raoul Wallenberg* (Phillip Jackson), Great Cumberland Place; *George Washington* (Houdon copy), Trafalgar Square; *Wellington* (Boehm), Hyde Park Corner, (Chantrey) riding without stirrups, outside Royal Exchange; *John*

Wesley (Adams Acton), City Road; *William III* (Bacon), St James's Square; *Wolseley* (Goscombe John), Horse Guards' Parade.

PORT OF LONDON. Port of London Authority, Devon House, 58–60 St. Katherines Way, London E1W 1J2. Tel: 020-7265 2656. The Port of London covers the tidal section of the River Thames from Teddington to the seaward limit (the outer Tongue buoy at the Sunk light vessel), a distance of 150km. The governing body is the Port of London Authority (PLA). Each year over 52 million tonnes of cargo is handled at privately operated riverside terminals between Fulham and Canvey Island, including the enclosed dock at Tilbury, 40km below London Bridge. Passenger vessels and cruise liners can be handled at moorings at Greenwich, Tower Bridge and Tilbury.

ROMAN REMAINS. The city wall of Roman *Londinium* was largely rebuilt during the medieval period but sections may be seen near the White Tower in the Tower of London; at Tower Hill; at Coopers' Row; at All Hallows, London Wall, its vestry being built on the remains of a semi-circular Roman bastion; at St Alphage, London Wall, showing a succession of building repairs from the Roman until the late medieval period; and at St Giles, Cripplegate. Sections of the great forum and basilica, more than 165m^2, have been encountered during excavations in the area of Leadenhall, Gracechurch Street and Lombard Street. Traces of Roman activity along the river include a massive riverside wall built in the late Roman period, and a succession of Roman timber quays along Lower and Upper Thames Street. Finds from these sites can be seen at the Museum of London (*see* page 603).

Other major buildings are the amphitheatre at Guildhall; remains of bath-buildings in Upper and Lower Thames Street; and the temple of Mithras in Walbrook.

ROYAL ALBERT HALL, Kensington Gore, London SW7 2AP. Tel: 020-7589 3203. E-mail: sales@royalalberthall.com. Web: http://www.royalalberthall.com. The elliptical hall, one of the largest in the world, was completed in 1871, and since 1941 has been the venue each summer for the Promenade Concerts founded in 1895 by Sir Henry Wood. Other events include pop and classical music concerts, dance, opera, sporting events, conferences and banquets.

ROYAL HOSPITAL, CHELSEA, Royal Hospital Road, London SW3 4SR. Tel: 020-7730 0161. Founded by Charles II in 1682, and built by Wren; opened in 1692 for old and disabled soldiers. The extensive grounds include the former Ranelagh Gardens and are the venue for the Chelsea Flower Show each May. *Governor*, Gen. Sir Jeremy Mackenzie, GCB, OBE.

ROYAL OPERA House, Covent Garden, London WC2E 9DD. Home of The Royal Ballet (1931) and The Royal Opera (1946). The Royal Opera House is the third theatre to be built on the site, opening 1858; the first was opened in 1732.

ST JAMES'S PALACE, Pall Mall, London SW1. Tel: 020-7930 4832. Web: http://www.royal.gov.uk. Built by Henry VIII; the Gatehouse and Presence Chamber remain; later alterations were made by Wren and Kent. Representatives of foreign powers are still accredited 'to the Court of St James's'. *Clarence House* (1825) in the palace precinct is the home of The Queen Mother.

ST PAUL'S CATHEDRAL, St Paul's Churchyard, London EC4M 8AD. Tel: 020-7246 8348. E-mail: chapterhouse@stpaulscathedral.org.uk. Web: http://www.stpauls.co.uk. Built 1675–1710, cost £747,660. The cross on the dome is 365 ft above the ground level, the inner cupola 218 ft above the floor. 'Great Paul' in the south-west tower weighs nearly 17 tons. The organ by Father Smith (enlarged by Willis and rebuilt by Mander) is in a case carved by Grinling Gibbons, who also carved the choir stalls.

SOMERSET HOUSE, Strand and Victoria Embankment, London WC2. The river façade (600 ft long) was built in 1776–86 from the designs of Sir William Chambers; the eastern extension, which houses part of King's College, was built by Smirke in 1829. Somerset House was the property of Lord Protector Somerset, at whose attainder in 1552 the palace passed to the Crown, and it was a royal residence until 1692.

SOUTH BANK, London SE1. Tel: 020-7960 4242. E-mail: boxoffice@rfh.-org.uk. Web: http://www.sbc.org.uk. The arts complex on the south bank of the River Thames which consists of the 2,903-seat *Royal Festival Hall* (opened in 1951 for the Festival of Britain), the adjacent 1,056-seat *Queen Elizabeth Hall*, the 368-seat *Purcell Room*, and the 77-seat Voice Box.

The *National Film Theatre* (opened 1952), Tel: 020-7928 3232 administered by the British Film Institute, has three auditoria showing over 2,000 films a year. The London Film Festival is held here every November. There is an IMAX cinema with 500 seats.

The *Royal National Theatre* Tel: 020-7452 3000 opened in 1976 and stages classical, modern, new and neglected plays in its three auditoria: the 1,160-seat Olivier theatre, the 890-seat Lyttelton theatre and the Cottesloe theatre which seats up to 400.

SOUTHWARK CATHEDRAL, London SE1 9DA. Tel: 020-7367 6700. E-mail: cathedral@dswark.org.uk. Web: http://www.dswark.org. Mainly 13th century, but the nave is largely rebuilt. The tomb of John Gower (1330–1408) is between the Bunyan and Chaucer memorial windows in the north aisle; Shakespeare's effigy, backed by a view of Southwark and the Globe Theatre, is in the south aisle; the tomb of Bishop Andrewes (died 1626) is near the screen. The lady chapel was the scene of the consistory courts of the reign of Mary (Gardiner and Bonner) and is still used as a consistory court. John Harvard, after whom Harvard University is named, was baptised here in 1607, and the chapel by the north choir aisle is his memorial chapel.

THAMES EMBANKMENTS. The *Victoria Embankment*, on the north side from Westminster to Blackfriars, was constructed by Sir Joseph Bazalgette (1819–91) for the Metropolitan Board of Works, 1864–70; the seats, of which the supports of some are a kneeling camel, laden with spicery, and of others a winged sphinx, were presented by the Grocers' Company and by W. H. Smith, MP, in 1874; the *Albert Embankment*, on the south side from Westminster Bridge to Vauxhall, 1866–9; the *Chelsea Embankment*, 1871–4. The total cost exceeded £2,000,000. Bazalgette also inaugurated the London main drainage system, 1858–65. A medallion (*Flumini vincula posuit*) has been placed on a pier of the Victoria Embankment to commemorate the engineer.

THAMES FLOOD BARRIER. Officially opened in May 1984, though first used in February 1983, the barrier consists of ten rising sector gates which span 570 yards from bank to bank of the Thames at Woolwich Reach. When not in use the gates lie horizontally, allowing shipping to navigate the river normally; when the barrier is closed, the gates turn through 90 degrees to stand vertically more than 50 feet above the river bed. The barrier took eight years to complete and can be raised within about 30 minutes.

THAMES TUNNELS. The *Rotherhithe Tunnel*, opened 1908, connects Commercial Road, London E14, with Lower Road, Rotherhithe; it is 1 mile 332 yards long, of which 525 yards are under the river. The first *Blackwall Tunnel* (northbound vehicles only), opened 1897, connects East India Dock Road, Poplar, with Blackwall Lane, East Greenwich. The height restriction on the northbound tunnel is 13 ft 4 in. A second tunnel (for southbound vehicles only) opened 1967. The lengths of the tunnels measured from East India Dock Road to the Gate House on the south side are 6,215 ft (old tunnel) and 6,152 ft. *Greenwich Tunnel* (pedestrians only), opened 1902, connects the Isle of Dogs, Poplar, with Greenwich; it is 406 yards long. The *Woolwich Tunnel* (pedestrians only), opened 1912, connects North and South Woolwich below the passenger and vehicular ferry from North Woolwich Station, London E16, to High Street, Woolwich, London SE18; it is 552 yards long.

WALTHAM CROSS, Herts. At Waltham Cross is one of the crosses (partly restored) erected by Edward I to mark a resting place of the corpse of Queen Eleanor on its way to Westminster Abbey. Ten crosses were erected, but only those at Geddington, Northampton and Waltham survive; 'Charing' Cross originally stood near the spot now occupied by the statue of Charles I at Whitehall.

WESTMINSTER ABBEY, The Chapter Office, 20 Dean's Yard, London SW1 3PA. Tel: 020-7222 5152. E-mail: press@westminster-abbey.org. Web: http://www.west-minster-abbey.org. The original abbey was a Benedictine monastery founded around 960 by St Dunstan, and re-founded by Edward the Confessor in 1065. It has been the coronation church since 1066. The present structure was begun by Henry III in 1245 and contains Edward the Confessor s shrine, the tombs of kings and queens and several hundred monuments and memorials, including the Tomb of the Unknown Warrior. Numerous literary figures are buried or commemorated in Poet's Corner. Among its other treasures are the Coronation Chair and the 13th-century Cosmati pavement

WESTMINSTER CATHEDRAL, Ashley Place, London SW1P 1QW. Tel: 020-7798 9055. Web: http://www.westmin-stercathedral.org.uk. Roman Catholic cathedral built 1895–1903 from the designs of J. F. Bentley. The campanile is 283 feet high. Cathedral open 6.50 a.m.–7 p.m. Masses: Sundays, 7, 8, 9, 10.30 (sung), 12, 5.30 and 7; Solemn Vespers and Benediction 3.30; Monday–Friday, 7, 8, 8.30, 9, 10.30, 12.30, 1.05 and 5.30 (sung), Morning Prayer 7.40, Vespers 5; Saturdays 8, 8.30, 9, 10.30 (sung), 12.30 and 6, Morning Prayer 10.00, Rosary, Benediction 7.00. Holy days of Obligation, Low Masses 7, 8, 8.30, 9, 10.30, 12.30, 1.05, 5.30 (sung) and 7.

LONDON TOURIST BOARD AND CONVENTION BUREAU, Glen House, Stag Place, London, SW1E 5LT. Tourist information: 0839-123456

Hallmarks

Hallmarks are the symbols stamped on gold, silver or platinum articles to indicate that they have been tested at an official Assay Office and that they conform to one of the legal standards. With certain exceptions, all gold, silver or platinum articles are required by law to be hallmarked before they are offered for sale. Hallmarking was instituted in England in 1300 under a statute of Edward I.

MODERN HALLMARKS

Since 1 January 1999, UK hallmarks have consisted of three compulsory symbols – the sponsor's mark, the fineness (standard) mark and the assay office mark. Traditional marks such as the year date letter, the Britannia for 958 silver, the lion passant for 925 silver (lion rampant in Scotland) and the orb for 950 platinum may be added voluntarily. The distinction between UK and foreign articles has been removed, and more finenesses are now legal, reflecting the more common finenesses elsewhere in Europe.

SPONSOR'S MARK

Instituted in England in 1363, the sponsor's mark was originally a device such as a bird or fleur-de-lis. Now it consists of the initial letters of the name or names of the manufacturer or firm. Where two or more sponsors have the same initials, there is a variation in the surrounding shield or style of letters.

FINENESS (STANDARD) MARK

The fineness (standard) mark indicates that the content of the precious metal in the alloy from which the article is made, is not less than the legal standard. The legal standard is the minimum content of precious metal by weight in parts per thousand, and the standards are:

Gold	999	
	990	
	916.6	(22 carat)
	750	(18 carat)
	585	(14 carat)
	375	(9 carat)
Silver	999	
	958.4	(Britannia)
	925	(sterling)
	800	
Platinum	999	
	950	
	900	
	850	

ASSAY OFFICE MARK

This mark identifies the particular assay office at which the article was tested and marked. The British assay offices are:

LONDON, Goldsmiths' Hall, London EC2V 8AQ.
Tel: 020-7606 8975

BIRMINGHAM, Newhall Street, Birmingham B3 1SB.
Tel: 0121-236 6951

SHEFFIELD, 137 Portobello Street, Sheffield S1 4DS.
Tel: 0114-275 5111

EDINBURGH, 24A Broughton Street, Edinburgh EH1 3RH.
Tel: 0131-226 1122

Assay offices formerly existed in other towns, e.g. Chester, Exeter, Glasgow, Newcastle, Norwich and York, each having its own distinguishing mark.

DATE LETTER

The date letter shows the year in which an article was assayed and hallmarked. Each alphabetical cycle has a distinctive style of lettering or shape of shield. The date letters were different at the various assay offices and the particular office must be established from the assay office mark before reference is made to tables of date letters. Date letter marks became voluntary from 1 January 1999.

The table on page 612 shows specimen shields and letters used by the London Assay Office on silver articles in each period from 1498. The same letters are found on gold articles but the surrounding shield may differ. Since 1 January 1975, each office has used the same style of date letter and shield for all articles.

OTHER MARKS

FOREIGN GOODS

Foreign goods imported into the UK are required to be hallmarked before sale, unless they already bear a convention mark (*see* below) or a hallmark struck by an independent assay office in the European Economic Area which is deemed to be equivalent to a UK hallmark.

The following are the assay office marks used for gold until the end of 1998. For silver and platinum the symbols remain the same but the shields differ in shape.

 London

 Birmingham

 Sheffield

 Edinburgh

CONVENTION HALLMARKS

Special marks at authorised assay offices of the signatory countries of the International Convention on Hallmarking (Austria, the Czech Republic, Denmark, Finland, Ireland, the Netherlands, Norway, Portugal, Sweden, Switzerland and the UK) are legally recognised in the United Kingdom as approved hallmarks. These consist of a sponsor's mark, a common control mark, a fineness mark (arabic numerals showing the standard in parts per thousand), and an assay office mark. There is no date letter.

The fineness marks are:

Gold	750	(18 carat)
	585	(14 carat)
	375	(9 carat)
Silver	925	(sterling)
Platinum	950	

The common control marks are:

 Gold (18 carat)

 Silver

 Platinum

DUTY MARKS

In 1784 an additional mark of the reigning sovereign's head was introduced to signify that the excise duty had been paid. The mark became obsolete on the abolition of the duty in 1890.

COMMEMORATIVE MARKS

There are three other marks to commemorate special events: the silver jubilee of King George V and Queen Mary in 1935, the coronation of Queen Elizabeth II in 1953, and her silver jubilee in 1977. During 1999 and 2000 there is a voluntary additional Millennium Mark.

LONDON (GOLDSMITHS' HALL) DATE LETTERS FROM 1498

	Black letter, small	1498–9	1517–8
	Lombardic	1518–9	1537–8
	Roman and other capitals	1538–9	1557–8
	Black letter, small	1558–9	1577–8
	Roman letter, capitals	1578–9	1597–8
	Lombardic, external cusps	1598–9	1617–8
	Italic letter, small	1618–9	1637–8
	Court hand	1638–9	1657–8
	Black letter, capitals	1658–9	1677–8
	Black letter, small	1678–9	1696–7
	Court hand	1697	1715–6
	Roman letter, capitals	1716–7	1735–6
	Roman letter, small	1736–7	1738–9
	Roman letter, small	1739–40	1755–6
	Old English, capitals	1756–7	1775–6
	Roman letter, small	1776–7	1795–6
	Roman letter, capitals	1796–7	1815–6
	Roman letter, small	1816–7	1835–6
	Old English, capitals	1836–7	1855–6
	Old English, small	1856–7	1875–6
	Roman letter, capitals [A to M square shield N to Z as shown]	1876–7	1895–6
	Roman letter, small	1896–7	1915–6
	Black letter, small	1916–7	1935–6
	Roman letter, capitals	1936–7	1955–6
	Italic letter, small	1956–7	1974
	Italic letter, capitals	1975	

Economic Statistics

The Budget 2000

GOVERNMENT RECEIPTS   £ billion

	Outturn 1998–9	Estimate 1999–2000	Forecast 2000–2001
Inland Revenue	127.7	138.2	143.8
Income tax (gross)	88.4	95.2	101
Income tax credits	−2.0	−2.9	−5.1
Corporation tax[1]	30.0	34.1	33.8
Windfall tax	2.6	—	
Petroleum revenue tax	0.5	0.9	1.2
Capital gains tax	1.8	2.4	3.4
Inheritance tax	1.8	2.0	2.3
Stamp duties	4.6	6.6	7.2
Customs and Excise	94.0	97.4	103.3
Value added tax	52.3	56.7	59.6
Fuel duties	21.6	22.3	23.3
Tobacco duties	8.2	5.7	7.4
Spirits duties	1.6	1.8	1.8
Wine duties	1.5	1.6	1.7
Beer and cider duties	2.8	2.9	3.1
Betting and gaming duties	1.5	1.5	1.4
Air passenger duty	0.8	0.9	1.0
Insurance premium tax	1.2	1.4	1.6
Landfill tax	0.3	0.4	0.4
Customs duties and levies	2.1	2.0	2.0
Vehicle excise duties	4.7	4.9	4.9
Oil royalties	0.3	0.4	0.5
Business rates[2]	15.3	15.5	16.2
Social security contributions	55.1	56.4	58.8
Council tax	12.1	12.8	13.6
Other taxes and royalties[3]	8.3	8.0	8.2
Net taxes and social security contributions[4]	17.7	333.6	349.4
Interest and dividends	4.3	3.2	4.4
Accrual adjustments on taxes	1.2	3.8	3.0
Less own resources contribution to EU budget	−6.2	−5.5	−5.4
Less PC corporation tax payments	−0.4	−0.4	−0.4
Income tax credits[5]	2.0	2.9	5.1
Other receipts[6]	−35.6	−37.1	—
CURRENT RECEIPTS	335.9	356.2	375.6
North Sea revenues[7]	2.5	2.5	4.3

1. Includes advance corporation tax (net of payment). Also includes North Sea corporation tax after ACT set-off and corporation tax on gains
2. Includes district council rates in Northern Ireland
3. Includes money paid into the National Lottery Distribution Fund
4. Includes VAT and 'traditional own resources' contributions to EU budget. Net of income tax credits. Cash basis

5. Excludes Children's Tax Credit, which scores as a tax repayment in the national accounts
6. Main gross operating surpluses and rent.
7. North Sea corporation tax (before ACT set-off), petroleum revenue tax and royalties
Source: The Stationery Office – *Budget 2000*

GOVERNMENT EXPENDITURE

The Economic and Fiscal Strategy Report in June 1998 introduced changes to the public expenditure control regime. Three-year departmental expenditure limits (DELs) now apply to most government departments. Spending which cannot easily be subject to three-year planning is reviewed annually in the Budget as annually managed expenditure (AME). Current and capital expenditure are treated separately.

DEPARTMENTAL EXPENDITURE LIMITS

CURRENT BUDGET   £ billion

	Outturn 1998–99	Estimate 1999–2000	Plans 2000–2001
Education and Employment	13.6	14.8	16.6
Health	37.5	40.5	44.2
of which NHS	36.8	39.9	43.5
DETR – main programmes	4.0	4.6	4.7
DETR – local government and regional policy	32.4	33.9	35.3
Home Office	6.5	7.3	7.6
Legal departments[1]	2.6	2.7	2.8
Defence	20.8	21.6	21.3
Foreign and Commonwealth Office	1.0	1.1	1.0
International Development	2.1	2.2	2.5
Trade and Industry[2]	2.6	3.0	3.2
Agriculture, Fisheries and Food[3]	1.2	1.2	1.1
Culture, Media and Sport	0.8	0.9	0.9
Social Security (administration)	3.3	3.3	3.2
Scotland[1,4]	11.6	12.3	13.0
Wales[4]	5.9	6.4	6.9
Northern Ireland[4]	5.1	5.5	5.5
Chancellor of the Exchequer's departments	3.1	3.5	3.6
Cabinet Office	1.0	1.1	1.1
Welfare to Work[5]	0.3	0.5	0.8
Invest to save budget	0	0	0
Reserve[6]	0	0	2.0
Allowance for shortfall	0	−1.4	0
TOTAL CURRENT BUDGET	155.3	165.1	177.3

1. The Crown Office is included with the Legal Departments up to 1998–9 and thereafter with the Scotland figures

2. Including capital expenditure of the Export Credits Guarantee Department
3. Includes spending on BSE related programmes
4. For Scotland and Wales, the split between current and capital budgets is decided by the respective Executives. For Northern Ireland, during any period when the assembly ceases to operate, this is a matter for the Secretary of State
5. Expenditure financed by the Windfall Tax
6. Reserve has been arbitrarily apportioned between current and capital, with 10 per cent allocated to capital
Source: The Stationery Office – *Budget 2000*

ANNUALLY MANAGED EXPENDITURE
(FORECASTS) £ *billion*

	1999–2000	2000–2001	2001–02
Departmental expenditure limits	178.9	193.7	202.6
Social security benefits	97.1	99.6	104.5
Housing revenue account subsidies	3.4	3.3	3.3
Common agricultural policy	2.6	2.5	2.6
Export Credits Guarantee Department	0.9	0.3	0.4
Net payment to EC institutions	2.6	2.7	2.5
Self-financing public corporations	−0.2	−0.2	−0.1
Locally financed expenditure	17.2	18.1	19.1
Net public service pensions	5.6	5.7	5.6
National Lottery	2.0	2.3	2.0
Central government gross debt interest	25.5	27.8	27.1
Accounting and other adjustments	9.3	13.7	14.5
AME margin	0.0	1.0	2.0
Annually managed expenditure	166.3	177.2	183.6

Source: The Stationery Office – *Budget 2000*

SUMMARY OF LOCAL AUTHORITY 1998/99 BUDGETS (OUTTURN PRICES) AND 1999/2000 BUDGETS (OUTTURN PRICES) £ *billion*

	Budget Estimates 1998–9	Budget Estimates 1999–2000	Change %
	£m	£m	
Total Service Expenditure	50,882	53,936	6.0
Manadatory Student Awards, Rent Allowances, Levies & Other Adjustments	7,702	7,644	−0.8
Net Current Expenditure	58,584	61,580	5.1
Capital Financing, Interest Receipts, Dividends And Other Items	4,788	4,761	−0.6
Gross Revenue Expenditure	63,372	66,341	4.7
Funded By:			
Specific Grants outside Aggregate External Finance	(9,190)	(9,129)	−0.7
Specific Grants inside Aggregate External Finance	(2,145)	(2,450)	14.2
Net Revenue Expenditure (all services)	52,037	54,762	5.2
Met From:			
Reserves	(848)	(878)	3.2
Budget Requirement	51,189	53,884	5.3
SSA Reduction Grant/ Council Tax Reduction Grant	(133)	(90)	−32.3
Police Grant	(3,549)	(3,686)	3.9
Revenue Support Grant	(21,278)	(21,765)	2.3
Revenue Support Protection Grant	—	(51)	—
Council Tax Benefit Subsidy Limitation Scheme	—	31	—
National Non-Domestic Rates	(13,136)	(14,268)	8.6
Council Tax	(10,724)	(11,708)	9.2
Gross Expenditure on Council Tax Benefits and Expenditure funded by Council Tax Transitional Reduction Scheme Grant	(2,151)	(2,166)	0.7
Other Items	(218)	(181)	−17.0

Source: CIPFA – *Finance and General Statistics 1999–2000*

PUBLIC SECTOR FINANCES £ *billion*

	Outturn 1998–9	Estimate 1999–2000	Forecast 2000–2001
Current receipts	335.9	356.2	376.0
Current expenditure	312.5	325.6	348.0
Depreciation	13.6	14.1	14.0
Surplus on current budget*	7.5	17.1	14.0
Net investment	5.0	5.5	8.0
Public sector net borrowing	−2.8	−11.9	−6.0

AS A PERCENTAGE OF GDP

	Outturn 1998–9	Estimate 1999–2000	Forecast 2000–2001
Current receipts	39.2	39.6	39.7
Current expenditure	36.5	36.2	36.8
Depreciation	1.6	1.6	1.5
Surplus on current budget*	−0.5	1.9	1.4
Net investment	0.6	0.6	1.5
Public sector net borrowing	0.3	−1.3	−0.7
Public sector net debt	39.7	37.1	35.1

* Excluding windfall tax receipts and associated spending
Source: The Stationery Office – *Budget 2000*

GROSS VALUE ADDED AT BASIC PRICES BY INDUSTRY 1998 *£ million*

Agriculture, hunting, forestry and fishing	9,656
Mining and quarrying, including oil and gas extraction	12,748
Manufacturing (revised definition)	147,306
Electricity, gas and water supply	16,737
Construction	39,262

Wholesale and retail trade	113,070
Transport and communication	63,340
Financial intermediation	206,347
Adjustment for financial services	−29,370
Public administration, defence	40,495
Education; health; social work	89,041
Other services	38,912
ALL INDUSTRIES	747,544

*At basic prices, not market prices, and excluding taxes on
 products
Source: The Stationery Office – Annual Abstract of Statistics
1999 (Crown copyright)

BALANCE OF PAYMENTS 1998 £ million

CURRENT ACCOUNT
Trade in goods	
Exports	164,132
Imports	184,897
Trade in goods balance	−20,765
Services balance	12,253
Investment income	15,174
Transfers balance	−6,526
CURRENT BALANCE	−402

Source: The Stationery Office – Annual Abstract of Statistics 2000
(Crown copyright)

UK TRADE ON A BALANCE OF PAYMENTS BASIS
£ million

	Exports	Imports	Balance
1988	80,711	102,264	−21,553
1989	92,611	117,335	−24,724
1990	102,313	121,020	−18,707
1991	103,939	114,162	−10,223
1992	107,863	120,913	−13,050
1993	122,039	135,358	−13,319
1994	135,260	146,351	−11,091
1995	153,725	165,449	−11,724
1996	167,403	180,489	−13,086
1997	171,798	183,590	−11,792
1998	164,132	184,897	−20,765

Source: The Stationery Office – Annual Abstract of Statistics 2000
(Crown copyright)

VALUE OF UK EXPORTS 1999
BY DESTINATION £ million

European Community	96,851.8
Other western Europe	6,695.8
Eastern Europe	4,257.8
North America	27,953.8
Other America	2,623.9
Middle East and North Africa	7,399.7
Sub-Saharan Africa	2,956.8
Asia and Oceania	16,997.3
Low-value exports	494.2
Total non-EC exports	69,407.2
Total exports	166,259.0

Source: HM Customs and Excise

VALUE OF UK IMPORTS 1999
BY SOURCE £ million

European Community	104,918.5
Other western Europe	11,225.4
Eastern Europe	4,751.1
North America	29,022.9
Other America	3,088.3
Middle East and North Africa	4,247.5
Sub-Saharan Africa	3,237.5
Asia and Oceania	36,819.7
Low-value imports	554.5
Total non-EC imports	93,018.7
Total imports	197,937.2

Source: HM Customs and Excise

EMPLOYMENT

LABOUR FORCE BY AGE 1997 (UK)

Age	Male	Female
16–24	2,400,000	2,000,000
25–44	8,100,000	6,400,000
45–59	4,500,000	3,700,000
60–64	700,000	400,000
65 and over	300,000	200,000
Total	16,000,000	12,700,000

Source: The Stationery Office – Social Trends 30 (Crown copyright)

ECONOMIC STATUS OF PEOPLE OF WORKING AGE
(UK) as at spring 1998

	Male	Female
All in employment	14,700,000	11,700,000
Working full-time	11,400,000	6,200,000
Working part-time	900,000	4,600,000
Self-employed	2,200,000	700,000
Others in employment	100,000	100,000
Unemployed	1,100,000	600,000
All economically active	15,800,000	12,300,000
Economically inactive	3,000,000	4,800,000
TOTAL	18,800,000	17,100,000

Source: The Stationery Office – Social Trends 30 (Crown copyright)

THE WORKFORCE IN EMPLOYMENT (UK)
SEASONALLY ADJUSTED, AT DECEMBER 1999

Employees in employment	24,252,000
Self-employed	3,433,000
*HM Forces	208,000
*Work-related government-supported	
training	93,000
Total workforce in employment	27,986,000

*not seasonally adusted

EMPLOYEES IN EMPLOYMENT, BY MAIN SECTOR
(UK) SEASONALLY ADJUSTED, AT DECEMBER 1999

Service industries	21,156,000
Manufacturing industries	4,289,000
Energy and water supply	219,000
Other industries	2,322,000
Total employees in employment	27,986,000

AVERAGE GROSS WEEKLY EARNINGS OF EMPLOYEES
(GREAT BRITAIN) *as at April 1999*

	Full-time	*Part-time*
All adults	£400	£132
All men	£442	£155
Men, manual	£335	—
Men, non-manual	£526	
All women	£327	£128
Women, manual	£222	—
Women, non-manual	£347	—

Source: Office for National Statistics

UNEMPLOYMENT BY REGIONS SEASONALLY
ADJUSTED, DECEMBER 1999 TO FEBRUARY 2000

	Total	*% of total economically active*
United Kingdom	1,715,000	5.8
England:	1,385,000	5.6
Eastern	110,000	3.9
East Midlands	111,000	5.2
London	268,000	7.3
Merseyside	68,000	11.6
North East	100,000	8.5
North West	212,000	6.4
South East	158,000	3.7
South West	103,000	4.2
West Midlands	165,000	6.3
Yorkshire and the Humber	157,000	6.4
Wales	90,000	6.7
Scotland	189,000	7.5
Northern Ireland	50,000	6.7

Source: Office for National Statistics

UNEMPLOYMENT RATES BY AGE 1999 (UK)

Percentages

Age	*Male*	*Female*
16–17	21.6	14.0
18–24	12.5	9.3
25–44	5.6	4.8
45–54	4.9	3.2
55–59	6.4	3.6
60–64	6.4	—
60 and over	—	1.9
All ages	6.8	5.1

Source: The Stationery Office – *Social Trends 30* (Crown copyright)

INDUSTRIAL STOPPAGES 1998 (UK)

Duration

Not more than 5 days	130,000
6–10 days	21,000
11–20 days	3,000
21–30 days	4,000
31–50 days	3,000
More than 50 days	5,000
Total number of stoppages	166,000

Source: The Stationery Office – *Annual Abstract of Statistics 2000*
(Crown copyright)

TRADE UNIONS (UK)

Year	*No. of unions at end of year*	*Total membership at end of year*
1970	543	11,187,000
1975	470	12,026,000
1980	438	12,947,000
1985	370	10,821,000
1990	287	9,947,000
1995	238	8,089,000
1997*	233	7,795,000

*Figures for Great Britain only
Source: Office for National Statistics; Department of Trade and
Industry; Certification Office for Trade Unions and Employers'
Associations

HOUSEHOLDS AND THEIR EXPENDITURE 1998–9[1]

NUMBER OF HOUSEHOLDS

SUPPLYING DATA	6,630
Total number of persons	16,218
Total number of adults[2]	11,886

DISTRIBUTION BY TENURE

Rented unfurnished	28%
Rented furnished	3%
Rent-free	2%
Owner-occupied	67%

AVERAGE NUMBER OF PERSONS PER HOUSEHOLD

All persons	2.4
Males	1.2
Females	1.2
Adults[2]	1.8
Persons under 65	1.5
Persons 65 and over	0.4
Children[2]	0 5
Children under 2	0.1
Children 2 and under 5	0.1
Children 5 and under 18	0.4
Persons economically active	1.2
Persons not economically active	1.2
Men 65 and over, women 60 and over	0.4
Others	0.8

HOUSEHOLD EXPENDITURE ON COMMODITIES AND
SERVICES – WEEKLY AVERAGE

	£	*As % of total*
Housing[3]	57.20	16.2
Fuel and power	11.70	3.3
Food	58.90	16.7
Alcoholic drink	14.00	4.0
Tobacco	5.80	1.6
Clothing and footwear	21.70	6.2
Household goods	29.60	8.4
Household services	18.90	5.4
Personal goods and services	13.30	3.8
Motoring expenditure	51.70	14.7
Fares and other travel costs	8.30	2.4
Leisure goods	17.80	5.1
Leisure services	41.90	11.9
Miscellaneous	1.20	0.3
Total	352.20	100.0

1. Information derived from the Family Expenditure Survey;
relates to the UK
2. Adults = all persons 18 and over and married persons under 18;
Children = all unmarried persons under 18
3. Includes interest element of mortgage payments
Source: The Stationery Office – *Annual Abstract of Statistics 2000*
(Crown copyright)

SOURCES OF HOUSEHOLD INCOME 1998–9*

AVERAGE WEEKLY INCOME BY SOURCE (£)

Wages and salaries	309.20
Self-employment	37.20
Investments	18.80
Annuities and pensions (other than social security benefits)	30.30
Social security benefits	55.80
Other sources	5.70
Total	457.00

SOURCES AS A PERCENTAGE OF
TOTAL HOUSEHOLD INCOME (%)

Wages and salaries	68.0
Self-employment	8.0
Investments	4.0
Annuities and pensions (other than social security benefits)	7.0
Social security benefits	12.0
Other sources	1.0
Total	100.0

*Information derived from the Family Expenditure Survey; relates to the UK. Number of households supplying data, 6,630
Source: The Stationery Office – *Annual Abstract of Statistics 2000* (Crown copyright)

AVAILABILITY OF CERTAIN DURABLE GOODS 1997–8*

	% of households
Car	72
One	44
Two	23
Three or more	5
Central heating, full or partial	89
Washing machine	92
Fridge/freezer or deep freezer	92
Refrigerator	52
Television	98[†]
Telephone	95
Home computer	33
Video recorder	85

*Information derived from the Family Expenditure Survey; relates to the UK. Number of households supplying data, 6,630
[†] 1992 figure
Source: The Stationery Office – *Annual Abstract of Statistics 2000* (Crown copyright)

Cost of Living and Inflation Rates

The first cost of living index to be calculated took July 1914 as 100 and was based on the pattern of expenditure of working-class families in 1914. The cost of living index was superseded in 1947 by the general index of retail prices (RPI), although the older term is still popularly applied to it.

GENERAL INDEX OF RETAIL PRICES

The general index of retail prices measures the changes month by month in the average level of prices of goods and services purchased by most households in the United Kingdom. The spending pattern on which the index is based is revised each year, mainly using information from the Family Expenditure Survey. The expenditure of certain higher income households and of households mainly dependent on state pensions is excluded.

The index is compiled using a selection of over 600 goods and services, and the prices charged for these items are collected at regular intervals in about 146 locations throughout the country. For the index, the price changes are weighted in accordance with the pattern of consumption of the average family.

INFLATION RATE

The twelve-monthly percentage change in the 'all items' index of the RPI is usually referred to as the rate of inflation. The percentage change in prices between any two months/years can be obtained using the following formula:

$$\frac{\text{Later date RPI} - \text{Earlier date RPI}}{\text{Earlier date RPI}} \times 100$$

e.g. to find the rate of inflation for 1988, using the annual averages for 1987 and 1988:

$$\frac{106.9 - 101.9}{101.9} \times 100 = 4.9\%$$

PURCHASING POWER OF THE POUND

Changes in the internal purchasing power of the pound may be defined as the 'inverse' of changes in the level of prices; when prices go up, the amount which can be purchased with a given sum of money goes down. To find the purchasing power of the pound in one month or year, given that it was 100p in a previous month or year, the calculation would be:

$$100p \times \frac{\text{Earlier month/year RPI}}{\text{Later month/year RPI}}$$

Thus, if the purchasing power of the pound is taken to be 100p in 1975, the comparable purchasing power in 1997 would be:

$$100p \times \frac{34.2}{157.5} = 21.71p$$

For longer term comparisons, it has been the practice to use an index which has been constructed by linking together the RPI for the period 1962 to date; an index derived from the consumers expenditure deflator for the period from 1938 to 1962; and the prewar 'cost of living' index for the period 1914 to 1938. This long-term index enables the internal purchasing power of the pound to be calculated for any year from 1914 onwards. It should be noted that these figures can only be approximate.

	Long-term index of consumer goods and services (Jan. 1987 = 100)	Comparable purchasing power of £1 in 1998	Rate of inflation (annual average)
1914	2.8	58.18	
1915	3.5	46.54	
1920	7.0	23.27	
1925	5.0	32.58	
1930	4.5	36.20	
1935	4.0	40.72	
1938	4.4	37.02	
There are no official figures for 1939–45			
1946	7.4	22.01	
1950	9.0	18.10	
1955	11.2	14.54	
1960	12.6	12.93	
1965	14.8	11.00	
1970	18.5	8.80	
1975	34.2	4.76	
1980	66.8	2.44	18.0
1981	74.8	2.18	11.9
1982	81.2	2.01	8.6
1983	84.9	1.92	4.6
1984	89.2	1.83	5.0
1985	94.6	1.72	6.1
1986	97.8	1.67	3.4
1987	101.9	1.60	4.2
1988	106.9	1.52	4.9
1989	115.2	1.41	7.8
1990	126.1	1.29	9.5
1991	133.5	1.22	5.9
1992	138.5	1.18	3.7
1993	140.7	1.16	1.6
1994	144.1	1.13	2.4
1995	149.1	1.09	3.5
1996	152.7	1.07	2.4
1997	157.5	1.03	3.1
1998	162.9	1.00	3.4
1999	165.4	0.98	1.5

The RPI figures are published around the middle of each month. They are available as a recorded message which can be heard by telephoning 020-7533 5866. Each month an updated Consumer Price Indices bulletin is published by the Office of National Statistics.

OFFICE OF NATIONAL STATISTICS, 1 Drummond Gate, London SW1V 2QQ.

PUBLIC ENQUIRIES LINE: 020-7533 5874
WEB: http://www.ons.gov.uk

Lotteries and Gaming

Gaming and lotteries in the UK are officially regulated and may only be run by licensed operators or in licensed premises. Responsibility for policy and the laws on gaming and lotteries rests with the Home Secretary. The National Lottery is regulated by the National Lottery Commission, which replaced the Office of the National Lottery in April 1999. Supervision of other lottery operations and gaming is mostly the responsibility of the Gaming Board of Great Britain.

Most betting is on horseracing and greyhound racing, and may take place at racecourses and greyhound tracks, or at off-course betting offices. The amount spent on on-course betting is estimated to be about 10 per cent of the figures for off-course betting.

OFF-COURSE BETTING (UK)

	£ million
1996–7	6,718
1997–8	6,851p
1998–9	7,109p
1999–2000	7,293p

p provisional
Source: Horserace Totalisator Board

Other forms of gaming and lotteries include the following:

Number of casinos operating	116
Total drop (1998–9)	£2,670m
Bingo clubs holding gaming licences	751
Amount staked (1998–9)	£1,004m
Gaming machines licensed	250,000+
Society lottery schemes registered	634
Total ticket sales (£ million)	c.£161m

In 1998–9 sales of society lottery tickets increased by 23 per cent to £161 million. Of this, £55.5 million (34.4 per cent) was spent on prizes, £43.5 million (27 per cent) on expenses and £62 million (38.6 per cent) went to good causes.
Source: Report of the Gaming Board for Great Britain 1998–9

THE NATIONAL LOTTERY

The National Lottery is currently run by a private company, Camelot Group PLC. The seven-year licence granted to Camelot expires in 2001. It is expected that the successful bidder for the next licence will be appointed by autumn 2000.

The National Lottery Commission is responsible for the granting, varying and enforcing of licences to run the National Lottery. The Commission's duties are to ensure that the National Lottery is run with all due care and attention, that the interests of players are protected, and subject to these two points, to maximise the money raised for good causes.

The first National Lottery tickets draw was made on 19 November 1994, with a mid-week draw introduced on Wednesday 5 February 1997. Instants (scratchcards) were introduced on 21 March 1995 and on 12 June 1999 Thunderball was introduced, providing players with another way of playing the National Lottery. Tickets for the main lottery game cost £1. If the jackpot prize is not won, it is 'rolled over' to the next draw. The highest win on a single ticket to date was £22,590,829 on 10 June 1995. By June 2000, 1,000 millionaires had been created.

SALES 1999–2000

Average number of tickets (on-line and instants) sold per week	c.96.7m
Average number of people playing weekly	c.30m
% of adult population buying tickets regularly	c.65%
Amount raised by ticket sales, 1994 to June 2000	c.£27.9 billion

Sources: Camelot, Oflot

DISTRIBUTION OF PROCEEDS
over the seven-year licence period

Allocated to:	%
Prize money	50
Tax	13
Retailer commission	5
Camelot (operating costs and profit)	4
Good causes	28

The 'good causes' originally benefiting from lottery funds were the arts, sport, heritage, charities and the Millennium Commission. In July 1998 the National Lottery Act created a sixth good cause, the New Opportunities Fund, to fund health, education and environmental initiatives. The New Opportunities Fund announced its first awards in summer 1999. The Act also created a National Endowment for Science, Technology and the Arts (NESTA), a non-departmental public body whose objectives are: to help talented individuals; to enable inventions and ideas to be commercially exploited; and to promote public knowledge of science, technology and the arts. NESTA received an initial £200 million from the New Opportunities Fund but thereafter is to generate its own income.

From October 1997 the percentage of all the funds allocated to the good causes received by each cause is as follows: the arts, sport, heritage and charities 16.66 per cent each; the Millennium Commission 20 per cent; and the New Opportunities Fund 13.33 per cent. From October 1999 the share going to the Millennium Commission will be reduced to 13.33 per cent and that going to the New Opportunities Fund will rise to 20 per cent.

The cumulative amount allocated to the good causes from November 1994 to March 1999 was £7,304 million.

AWARDS 1999–2000

Most awards are conditional on partnership funding being obtained from other sources.

	Number	Total value £
Total	12,932	3,192,005,425
Arts, total	1,200	354,198,747
Arts Council of England	372	152,948,348
Arts Council of Wales	529	17,855,921
Scottish Arts Council	190	17,514,563
Arts Council of Northern Ireland	109	8,879,915
Millennium Commission		
awards to projects	187	1,256,437,474
awards to schemes funding individuals	81	79,056,834
Heritage Lottery Fund	675	127,814,392
National Lottery Charities Board	11,643	453,918,077
Sport, total	1,526	148,024,803
Sport England	260	82,374,611
Sports Council for Wales	58	3,304,018
Sport Scotland	1,024	32,505,458
Sports Council for Northern Ireland	916	41,850,301

Finance

British Currency

The unit of currency is the pound sterling (£) of 100 pence. The decimal system was introduced on 15 February 1971.

COIN

Gold Coins	‡*Bi-colour Coins*
*One hundred pounds £100	Two pounds £2
*Fifty pounds £50	*Nickel-Brass Coins*
*Twenty-five pounds £25	§Two pounds £2
*Ten pounds £10	One pound £1
Five pounds £5	
Two pounds £2	*Cupro-Nickel Coins*
Sovereign £1	Crown £5 (since 1990)
Half-Sovereign 50p	50 pence 50p
	Crown 25p (pre-1990)
Silver Coins	20 pence 20p
(*Britannia coins)	10 pence 10p
Two pounds £2	5 pence 5p
One pound £1	
50 pence 50p	*Bronze Coins*
Twenty pence 20p	2 pence 2p
(†*Maundy Money*)	1 penny 1p
Fourpence 4p	
Threepence 3p	*Copper-plated Steel Coins*
Twopence 2p	2 penny 2p
Penny 1p	1 penny 1p

*Britannia coins: gold bullion coins introduced 1987; silver coins introduced 1997

†Gifts of special money distributed by the Sovereign annually on Maundy Thursday to the number of aged poor men and women corresponding to the Sovereign's own age

‡Cupro-nickel centre and nickel-brass outer ring

§Commemorative coins; not intended for general circulation

GOLD COIN

Gold ceased to circulate during the First World War. Since then controls on buying, selling and holding gold coin have been imposed at various times but subsequently have been revoked. Under the Exchange Control (Gold Coins Exemption) Order 1979, gold coins may now be imported and exported without restriction, except gold coins which are more than 50 years old and valued at a sum in excess of £8,000; these cannot be exported without specific authorisation from the Department of Trade and Industry.

In 1982 the Government introduced VAT on sales of all gold coin.

SILVER COIN

Prior to 1920 silver coins were struck from sterling silver, an alloy of which 925 parts in 1,000 were silver. In 1920 the proportion of silver was reduced to 500 parts. From 1 January 1947 all 'silver' coins, except Maundy money, have been struck from cupro-nickel, an alloy of copper 75 parts and nickel 25 parts, except for the 20p, composed of copper 84 parts, nickel 16 parts. Maundy coins continue to be struck from sterling silver.

BRONZE COIN

Bronze, introduced in 1860 to replace copper, is an alloy of copper 97 parts, zinc 2.5 parts and tin 0.5 part. These proportions have been subject to slight variations in the past. Bronze was replaced by copper-plated steel in September 1992 and reintroduced in April 1997.

LEGAL TENDER

Gold (dated 1838 onwards, if not below least current weight)	to any amount
£5 (Crown since 1990)	to any amount
£2	to any amount
£1	to any amount
50p	up to £10
25p (Crown pre-1990)	up to £10
20p	up to £10
10p	up to £5
5p	up to £5
2p	up to 20p
1p	up to 20p

The £1 coin was introduced in 1983 to replace the £1 note.

These coins ceased to be legal tender on the following dates:

Farthing	31 December 1960
Halfpenny (½d)	1 August 1969
Half-crown	1 January 1970
Threepence	31 August 1971
Penny (1d)	31 August 1971
Sixpence	30 June 1980
Halfpenny (½p)	31 December 1984
old 5 pence	31 December 1990
old 10 pence	30 June 1993
old 50 pence	28 February 1998

Since 1982 the word 'new' in 'new pence' displayed on decimal coins has been dropped.

The Channel Islands and the Isle of Man issue their own coinage, which are legal tender only in the island of issue. For denominations, *see* page 621.

	Metal	Standard weight (g)	Standard diameter (cm)
Penny	bronze	3.564	2.032
Penny	copper-plated steel	3.564	2.032
2 pence	bronze	7.128	2.591
2 pence	copper-plated steel	7.128	2.591
5p	cupro-nickel	3.25	1.80
10p	cupro-nickel	6.5	2.45
20p	cupro-nickel	5.0	2.14
25p Crown	cupro-nickel	28.28	3.861
50p	cupro-nickel	13.5	3.0
50p	cupro-nickel	8.00	2.73
£1	nickel-brass	9.5	2.25
£2	nickel-brass	15.98	2.84
‡£2	cupro-nickel, nickel-brass	12.00	2.84
£5 Crown	cupro-nickel	28.28	3.861

The 'remedy' is the amount of variation from standard permitted in weight and fineness of coins when first issued from the Mint.

The Trial of the Pyx is the examination by a jury to ascertain that coins made by the Royal Mint, which have been set aside in the pyx (or box), are of the proper weight, diameter and composition required by law. The trial is held annually, presided over by the Queen's Remembrancer (the Senior Master of the Supreme Court), with a jury of freemen of the Company of Goldsmiths.

BANKNOTES

Bank of England notes are currently issued in denominations of £5, £10, £20 and £50 for the amount of the fiduciary note issue, and are legal tender in England and Wales. No £1 notes have been issued since 1984 and in March 1998 the outstanding notes were written off in accordance with the provision of the Currency Act 1983.

The current E series of notes was introduced from June 1990, replacing the D series (*see* below). The historical figures portrayed in this series are:

£5	June 1990–	George Stephenson
£10	April 1992–	Charles Dickens*
£20	June 1991–	Michael Faraday
£20	June 1999–	Sir Edward Elgar
£50	April 1994–	Sir John Houblon

*A new version of the Bank of England £10 banknote will be issued in the autumn of 2000, bearing a portrait of Charles Darwin

NOTE CIRCULATION

Note circulation is highest at the two peak spending periods of the year, around Christmas and during the summer holiday period. The total value of notes in circulation at 22 December 1999 was £29,048 million, compared to £25,991 million at 23 December 1998.

The value of notes in circulation at end February 1999 and 2000 was:

	1999	2000
£5	£1,111m	£1,045m
£10	£5,966m	£5,684m
£20	£11,414m	£13,197m
£50	£3,962m	£4,195m
Other notes†	£2,339m	£1,014m
Total	£24,792m	£25,135m

†Includes higher value notes used internally in the Bank of England, e.g. as cover for the note issues of banks in Scotland and Northern Ireland in excess of their permitted issue

LEGAL TENDER

Banknotes which are no longer legal tender are payable when presented at the head office of the Bank of England in London.

The white notes for £10, £20, £50, £100, £500 and £1,000, which were issued until April 1943, ceased to be legal tender in May 1945, and the white £5 note in March 1946.

The white £5 note issued between October 1945 and September 1956, the £5 notes issued between 1957 and 1963 (bearing a portrait of Britannia) and the first series to bear a portrait of The Queen, issued between 1963 and 1971, ceased to be legal tender in March 1961, June 1967 and September 1973 respectively.

The series of £1 notes issued during the years 1928 to 1960 and the 10 shilling notes issued from 1928 to 1961 (those without the royal portrait) ceased to be legal tender in May and October 1962 respectively. The £1 note first issued in March 1960 (bearing on the back a representation of Britannia) and the £10 note first issued in February 1964 (bearing a lion on the back), both bearing a portrait

of The Queen on the front, ceased to be legal tender in June 1979. The £1 note first issued in 1978 ceased to be legal tender on 11 March 1988. The 10 shilling note was replaced by the 50p coin in October 1969, and ceased to be legal tender on 21 November 1970.

The D series of banknotes was introduced from 1970 and ceased to be legal tender from the dates shown below. The predominant identifying feature of each note was the portrayal on the back of a prominent figure from British history:

£1	Feb. 1978–March 1988	Sir Isaac Newton
£5	Nov. 1971–Nov. 1991	The Duke of Wellington
£10	Feb. 1975–May 1994	Florence Nightingale
£20	July 1970–March 1993	William Shakespeare
£50	March 1981–Sept. 1996	Sir Christopher Wren

The £1 coin was introduced on 21 April 1983 to replace the £1 note.

OTHER BANKNOTES

SCOTLAND – Banknotes are issued by three Scottish banks. The Royal Bank of Scotland issues notes for £1, £5, £10, £20 and £100. The Bank of Scotland and the Clydesdale Bank issue notes for £5, £10, £20, £50 and £100. Scottish notes are not legal tender in Scotland but they are an authorised currency and enjoy a status comparable to that of Bank of England notes.

NORTHERN IRELAND – Banknotes are issued by four banks in Northern Ireland. The Bank of Ireland, the Northern Bank and the Ulster Bank issue notes for £5, £10, £20, £50 and £100. The First Trust Bank issues notes for £10, £20, £50 and £100. Northern Ireland notes are not legal tender in Northern Ireland but they circulate widely and enjoy a status comparable to that of Bank of England notes.

CHANNEL ISLANDS – The States of Guernsey issues its own currency notes and coinage. The notes are for £1, £5, £10, £20 and £50, and the coins are for 1p, 2p, 5p, 10p, 20p, 50p, £1, £2 and £5. The States of Jersey issues its own currency notes and coinage. The notes are for £1, £5, £10, £20 and £50, and the coins are for 1p, 2p, 5p, 10p, 20p, 50p, £1 and £2.

THE ISLE OF MAN – The Isle of Man Government issues notes for £1, £5, £10, £20 and £50. Although these notes are only legal tender in the Isle of Man, they are accepted at face value in branches of the clearing banks in the UK. The Isle of Man issues coins for 1p, 2p, 5p, 10p, 20p, 50p, £1, £2 and £5.

Although none of the series of notes specified above is legal tender in the UK, they are generally accepted by the banks irrespective of their place of issue. At one time the banks made a commission charge for handling Scottish and Irish notes but this was abolished some years ago.

Banking

Deposit-taking institutions may be broadly divided into two sectors: the monetary sector, which is predominantly banks, and those institutions outside the monetary sector, of which the most important are the building societies and National Savings. Both sectors are supervised by the Financial Services Authority. As a result of the conversion of several building societies into banks in recent years, the size of the banking sector, which was already substantially greater than the non-bank deposit-taking sector, has increased further.

The main institutions within the British banking system are the Bank of England (the central bank), the retail banks, the merchant banks and the overseas banks. In its role as the central bank, the Bank of England acts as banker to the Government and as a note-issuing authority; it also oversees the efficient functioning of payment and settlement systems.

Since May 1997, the Bank of England has had operational responsibility for monetary policy. At monthly meetings of its monetary policy committee the Bank sets the interest rate at which it will lend to the money markets.

OFFICIAL INTEREST RATES 1999–2000

10 June 1999	5.00%
8 September 1999	5.25%
4 November 1999	5.50%
13 January 2000	5.75%
10 February 2000	6.00%

RETAIL BANKS

The major retail banks are Abbey National, Alliance and Leicester, Bank of Scotland, Barclays, Halifax, Lloyds/TSB, HSBC (formerly Midland), National Westminster, Northern Rock, Royal Bank of Scotland and the Woolwich.

Retail banks offer a wide variety of financial services to companies and individuals, including current and deposit accounts, loan and overdraft facilities, automated teller (cash dispenser) machines, cheque guarantee cards, credit cards and debit cards. Several banks also now offer telephone and Internet banking facilities.

The Banking Ombudsman scheme provides independent and impartial arbitration in disputes between a bank and its customer (*see also* page 642).

Banking hours differ throughout the UK. Many banks now open longer hours and some at weekends, and hours vary from branch to branch. Current core opening hours are:

ENGLAND AND WALES: Monday–Friday, 9.30–4.30
SCOTLAND: Monday–Friday, 9.00–5.00
NORTHERN IRELAND: Monday–Friday, 9.30–4.30 (Wednesdays 10.00–4.30, except Ulster Bank Ltd); Northern Bank, 10.00–3.30, Saturdays 9.30–12.30

PAYMENT CLEARINGS

The Association for Payment Clearing Services (APACS) is an umbrella organisation for payment clearings in the UK. It operates three clearing companies:

–BACS Ltd is the UK's automated clearing house for bulk clearing of electronic debits and credits (e.g. direct debits and salary credits)
–the Cheque and Credit Clearing Company Ltd operates bulk clearing systems for inter-bank cheques and paper credit items in Great Britain
–CHAPS Clearing Company Ltd provides same-day clearing for electronic funds transfers throughout the UK in sterling and globally in euro

Membership of APACS and the clearing companies is open to any appropriately regulated financial institution providing payment services and meeting the relevant membership criteria. As at May 2000, APACS had 29 members, comprising the major banks, building societies and the Post Office.

ASSOCIATION FOR PAYMENT CLEARING SERVICES (APACS), Mercury House, Triton Court, 14 Finsbury Square, London EC2A 1LQ. Tel: 020-7711 6200.
Head of Public Affairs, R. Tyson-Davies
BACS LTD, De Havilland Road, Edgware, Middx HA8 5QA. Tel: 0870 165 0019. *Chief Executive*, G. Younger.
CHEQUE AND CREDIT CLEARING COMPANY LTD, Mercury House, Triton Court, 14 Finsbury Square, London EC2A 1LQ. Tel: 020-7711 6200
CHAPS Clearing Company Ltd, Mercury House, Triton Court, 14 Finsbury Square, London EC2A 1LQ. Tel: 020-7711 6200

MAJOR RETAIL BANKS: FINANCIAL RESULTS 1999

Bank Group	Profit before taxation £m	Profit after taxation £m	Total assets £m	Number of UK branches
Abbey National	1,520	1,105	177,800	793
Alliance and Leicester	500	354	30,500	315
Bank of Scotland	1,242	654	71,813	330
Barclays	2,460	1,811	254,793	1,899
Halifax	1,705	1,171	138,000	910
Lloyds/TSB Group	3,015	2,133	167,997	2,700
*Midland	1,522	1,043	104,846	1,700
*NatWest Group	2,142	1,641	185,993	1,727
Northern Rock	215.1	143.5	20,125	76
Royal Bank of Scotland Group	1,211	776	88,852	650
Woolwich	520.4	354.7	33,758	405

*1998 figures

Stamp Duties and Stamp Duty Reserve Tax

Stamp duty is a tax on documents; Stamp duty reserve tax is charged upon agreements for the sale of shares and securities where there is no stamped stock transfer form.

Where stamp duty is not paid or deposited with the Stamp Office within 30 days after execution, interest accrues. This applies where the instrument is executed offshore. For agreements for lease the interest commences from 30 days after the execution of the lease. A stampable instrument may be stamped without penalty if presented for stamping within 30 days after its date of first execution. Where wholly executed abroad, the period begins to run from the date of arrival in the UK.

Instruments presented after the proper time may be subject to a penalty which is equal to:
(a) where presented within 12 months after execution, the lower of £300 or the amount of the duty;
(b) where presented after 12 months from execution, the higher of £300 or the amount of the duty

Under the Finance Act 1999, a person dissatisfied with a decision of the Commissioners as to the issuing or the appropriate level of stamp duty may appeal within 30 days of their decision.

AGREEMENT FOR SALE OF PROPERTY

Charged with *ad valorem* duty as if an actual conveyance on sale, with certain exceptions, e.g. agreements for the sale of legal interests in land, stocks and shares, goods, wares or merchandise, a ship or foreign property (*see* s59 (1), Stamp Act 1891). If *ad valorem* duty is paid on an agreement in accordance with this provision, the subsequent conveyance or transfer is not chargeable with any *ad valorem* duty and the Commissioners will upon application either place a denoting stamp on such conveyance or transfer or will transfer the *ad valorem* duty thereto. Further, if such an agreement is not performed the *ad valorem* duty paid will be returned.

BEARER INSTRUMENT

Inland or Overseas bearer instrument, 1.5 per cent

CONVEYANCE OR TRANSFER ON SALE

"Sale" includes transfers for cash, shares and debt and in the case of land exchanges, any other property.
Value not exceeding £60,000, *nil*
Value of £60,001–£250,000, 1 per cent
Value of £250,001–£500,000, 2.5 per cent
Value exceeding £500,000, 3.5 per cent
Rates are now decimalised and rounded up to £5.
Rates apply to conveyance or transfer on sale of any property except for shares and marketable securities where the rate is 0.5 per cent.

CONVEYANCE OR TRANSFER OF ANY OTHER KIND

Fixed duty, £5

However, under the Stamp Duty (Exempt Instruments) Regulations 1987, instruments which would otherwise fall under this head are exempt from stamp duty provided that the document is duly certified.

COVENANT, for original creation and sale of any annuity, *see* Conveyance on Sale, above

DECLARATION OF TRUST

Not being a conveyance on sale, will or settlement, £5

DUPLICATE OR COUNTERPART

Same duty as original, but not to exceed £5

LEASES (INCLUDING AGREEMENTS FOR LEASES)

Lease or tack for any definite term less than a year of any furnished dwelling-house or apartments where the rent for such term exceeds £500, £5

Of any lands, tenements etc. in consideration of any rent, according to the following:
[†]Term not exceeding seven years (and rent not exceeding £500 p.a.), *nil*
Term not exceeding seven years (and rent not exceeding £500 p.a.), 1 per cent
Term not exceeding 35 years, 2 per cent
Term not exceeding 100 years, 12 per cent
Term exceeding 100 years, 24 per cent
[†]If the term is indefinite the same duty is payable as if the term did not exceed seven years.

Where a consideration other than rent is payable e.g. a premium in cash or other property, the same rule applies where the consideration does not exceed £60,000 as under conveyance or transfer on sale (except stock or marketable securities), provided that any rent payable does not exceed £600 a year and a certificate of value is included in the conveyance or transfer and the reduced rates of 1 per cent and 2.5 per cent for consideration not exceeding £500,000 apply.

Where a lease is granted pursuant to a prior written agreement for lease, the agreement itself is liable to duty. Credit for any duty paid on the agreement will be given against the duty payable on the lease and the Commissioners will place a denoting stamp on the lease.

Where there is no prior written agreement for lease, the lease must contain a certificate that it has not been made in pursuance of such an agreement.

STAMP DUTIES

UNIT TRUST INSTRUMENT

Duty was abolished in the Finance Act 1988. Transfer of property to a unit trust or agreement to transfer units is generally subject to Conveyance on Sale duty or Stamp Duty Reserve Tax. By the Finance Act 1989, the transfer of units in certain authorised unit trusts is no longer subject to duty.

VOLUNTARY DISPOSITION, *inter vivos*

Fixed duty, £5

However, under the Stamp Duty (Exempt Instruments) Regulations 1987, instruments which would otherwise fall under this head are exempt provided that the document is certified as falling within category L in the schedule to the Regulations. *See* Conveyance or Transfer of Any Other Kind, above.

STAMP DUTY RESERVE TAX

This is charged where there is a contract for the transfer of chargeable securities unless the charge is cancelled. The tax is payable by or on behalf of the buyer who is required to report the transaction and pay the tax on the seventh day of the month following that in which the contract is made or becomes unconditional. Penalties and interest are imposed for late payment or reporting.

Mutual Societies

In July 1997 the Government announced that responsibility for regulation of mutual societies would be transferred to a single new regulatory organisation, since named Financial Services Authority (FSA).

On 1 January 1999 the staff of the Registry of Friendly Societies (RFS), which had supported the functions of the Building Societies Commission, the Friendly Societies Commission and (in relation to Credit Unions) the Chief Registrar, were transferred to FSA. The new organisation provides services and support to the commissions and Chief Registrar under Service Level Agreements. These agreements will operate until the responsibilities are subsumed into those of the FSA following passage of the secondary legislation, expected around June 2001, to bring into force the transitional provisions in the Financial Services and Markets Act, which received Royal Assent on 14 June 2000. The registration and records work of RFS, on which a decision had earlier been deferred, is now also expected to transfer to the FSA in 2001.

FRIENDLY SOCIETIES IN BRITAIN

Friendly societies are voluntary mutual organisations, whose main purposes are assisting members during sickness, unemployment or retirement, and the provision of life assurance. Many of the older traditional societies complement their business activities by social activity and a general care for individual members in ways normally outside the scope of a purely commercial organisation. There are three main categories of friendly societies: societies with separately registered branches, commonly called orders; centralised societies, which conduct business directly with members (having no separately registered branches); and collecting societies which conduct industrial assurance business (commonly known as home service assurance). Collecting societies will benefit from a number of deregulatory measures included in the Financial Services and Markets Act 2000 involving relaxations for the future administration of existing contracts and by the removal of special requirements, in the industrial assurance legislation, concerning the selling of future contracts. Such business will be subject to the general conduct of business rules governing the marketing and selling of investment products.

The Friendly Societies Act 1992 created a new legislative framework for friendly societies, enabling them to provide a wider range of services to their members and allowing them to compete on more equal terms with other financial institutions. At the same time it provided for more flexible prudential supervision to safeguard members of societies.

The Act enables friendly societies to incorporate and establish subsidiaries to provide various financial and other services to their members and the public. The activities which subsidiaries are able to conduct include those to establish and manage unit trust schemes and personal equity plans; to arrange for the provision of credit, whether as agents or providers; to carry on long-term or general insurance business; to provide insurance intermediary services; to provide fund management services for trustees of pension funds; to administer estates and execute trusts of wills; and to establish and manage sheltered housing, residential homes for the elderly, hospitals and nursing homes.

The Act established a new framework to oversee friendly societies, including a Friendly Societies Commission, whose principal functions are to regulate the activities of friendly societies, promote their financial stability and protect members' funds. All friendly societies carrying on insurance or non-insurance business require authorisation by the Commission, which has a broad range of prudential powers. Friendly societies were also to be brought within the scope of the Policyholders Protection Act 1975, the statutory investor protection scheme covering insurance policyholders.

At the end of May 2000 there were 108 societies authorised to write new business. Forty societies had taken advantage of the 1992 Act to incorporate and 20 of them had established subsidiary companies providing a wide range of services. More than half the friendly societies on the register were not authorised to transact new business, many being small and with a declining membership.

At the end of March 2000 there were 259 friendly societies on the register compared to 271 a year earlier. The 42 Life Directive and Incorporated Societies accounted for 97 per cent of the total funds of the movement. Statistics for those societies are set out in the table below.

Life Directive and Incorporated Societies

	1998	1997
No. of societies	42	40
Membership ('000s)	4,681	4,698
Contribution income (£'000s)	787,305	768,309
Investment income (£'000s)	1,137,073	1,059,216
Benefits paid (£'000s)	945,789	792,022
Management expenses (£'000s)	314,920	222,860
Total assets (£'000s)	12,894,769	11,716,427

The Friendly Societies Act 1974 allowed three other main classes of society to be registered: benevolent societies, working men's clubs and specially authorised societies. Benevolent societies are established for any charitable or benevolent purpose, to provide the same type of benefits as would be permissible for a friendly society, but in contrast the benefits must be for persons who are not members instead of, or in addition to, members. Working men's clubs provide social and recreational facilities for members. Specially authorised societies are registered for any purpose authorised by the Treasury as a purpose to which some or all of the provisions of the 1974 Act ought to be extended. Examples are societies for the promotion of science, literature and the fine arts, or to enable members to pursue an interest in sports and games. No new societies of any type may now be registered under this Act.

The numbers of the various types of bodies registered under the Friendly Societies Acts at the end of 1998 were:

FRIENDLY SOCIETIES
Orders*	14
Collecting societies	15
Other centralised societies	249

INDUSTRIAL AND PROVIDENT SOCIETIES IN BRITAIN

The familiar 'Co-op' societies are amongst the wide variety which are registered under the Industrial and Provident Societies Act 1965. This consolidating Act, which is principally administered by the Central Office of the Registry of Friendly Societies (*see* below for credit unions), provides for the registration of societies and lays down the broad framework within which they must operate. Internal relations of societies are governed by their registered rules.

Registration under the Act confers upon a society corporate status by its registered name with perpetual succession and a common seal, and limited liability. A society qualifies for registration if it is carrying on an industry, business or trade, and it satisfies the Registrar either (a) that it is a bona fide co-operative society, or (b) that in view of the fact that its business is being, or is intended to be, conducted for the benefit of the community, there are special reasons why it should be registered under the Act rather than as a company under the Companies Act.

The Credit Unions Act 1979 added a new class of society registrable under the 1965 Act. It also made provision for the supervision of these savings and loan bodies. Unlike other classes, where the role of the Registry remains solely that of a registration authority, it became for credit unions the financial regulator, a role now carried out for it by the Financial Services Authority.

During 1998 the number of registered societies of all classes decreased by 120 to 10,420 but the number of credit unions again increased – by 34 during the year. The number of new credit unions has been growing steadily at an average rate in excess of 50 registrations a year since 1988. There were 666 by end September 1999. Assets of all industrial and provident societies totalled £53,774 million at the end of 1998. The principal statistics at the end of 1998 are given in the table below.

	No. of societies	No. of mem-bers 000s	Funds of members £000s	Total assets £000s
Retail	87	6,101	2,034,429	3,643,410
Wholesale and productive	150	5	645,779	1,611,246
Agricultural	919	240	211,863	617,647
Fishing	79	4	6,279	14,374
Clubs	3,651	2,199	354,167	518,872
General service	1,181	561	2,285,111	21,726,124
Housing	3,723	175	9,753,404	25,494,428
Credit unions	630	256	140,472	147,940
TOTAL	10,420	9,541	15,431,504	53,774,041

BUILDING SOCIETIES IN THE UK

The Building Societies Act 1997, which received royal assent on 21 March 1997, makes substantive amendments to, but does not replace, the Building Societies Act 1986. It liberalises the statutory regime for building societies to enable them to compete on more level terms with other financial institutions without having to forego their mutual status.

The Building Societies Act 1986 gave building societies a completely new legal framework for the first time since the initial comprehensive building society legislation in 1874. The 1986 Act sets out detailed provisions in relation to:

– the constitution of building societies
– building societies' powers in relation to raising funds, advances, loans, other assets and the provision of services
– the powers of control of the Building Societies Commission
– protection of investors, and complaints and disputes
– management of building societies, accounts and audit
– mergers and transfers of business

The 1986 Act was prescriptive in respect of building societies' powers and the way in which they were exercised. However, it gave numerous powers to the Building Societies Commission and/or the Treasury to make statutory instruments which, subject to parliamentary approval, can amend, extend and supplement the provisions of the Act. Since it came into force on 1 January 1987 the Act had been amended and extended considerably, especially in respect of building societies' powers.

The main purposes of the Building Societies Act 1997 are:

– remove the prescriptive powers' regime relating to building societies and to replace it with a permissive regime with appropriately revised balance-sheet 'nature limits', thus increasing the commercial freedom of societies and allowing increased competition and wider choice for customers
– enhance the powers of control of the Building Societies Commission
– introduce a package of measures to enhance the accountability of building societies' boards to their members
– make changes to the provisions relating to the transfer of a building society's business to a company

The Act came fully into force on 21 October 1997. Under it a building society may pursue any activities set out in its memorandum, subject only to:

– principal purpose: its purpose or principal purpose must be that of making loans which are secured on residential properties and are funded substantially by its members
– lending limit: at least 75 per cent of its business assets must be loans fully secured on residential property
– funding limit: at least 50 per cent of its funds must be raised in the form of shares held by individual members
– restrictions: subject to certain exceptions, it must not act as a market maker in securities, commodities or currencies; trade in commodities or currencies; enter into transactions involving derivatives, except in relation to hedging; nor create a floating charge over its assets
– prudential: it must comply with the criteria of prudential management

All authorised building societies, after making the necessary changes to their memoranda and rules, are now operating under the more liberal statutory regime set out in the 1997 Act.

CONVERSIONS AND TAKE-OVERS

During the year ending 31 March 2000 two building societies transferred their business to other societies.

The transfer of the Standard Building Society to the Mercantile became effective on 27 September 1999 and the Nottingham Imperial to the Newcastle on 1 February 2000. More recently, Bradford and Bingley Building Society confirmed the process of change to PLC status. At a Special Meeting on 17 July 2000 members passed resolutions covering the transfer of its business to Bradford and Bingley PLC. The following table shows how the number of societies has reduced, through merger, conversion and takeover, over the five years 1995–2000 and the amount of assets involved.

Year	Authorised societies		Societies transferring their engagements within the sector		Societies transferring their business out of the sector	
	No.	Assets £bn	No.	Assets £bn	No.	Assets £bn
1995	82	295	1	20.97	1	19.39
1996	80	292	2	0.14	1	13.89
1997	77	297	1	0.18	5	176.80
1998	71	131	–	–	–	–
1999	71	148	1	0.02	1	7.83
2000 (first half)	69	155	1	0.06	–	–

OMBUDSMAN SCHEME

Complaints about the actions of building societies may be resolved through societies' own internal complaints procedures. All authorised building societies are, in addition, members of the Building Societies Ombudsman scheme which provides an independent service to consider and determine complaints which are within its remit. In the year to 31 March 2000 the Ombudsman received 5,929 complaints, of which 1,256 were against former building societies, now for consideration by the Banking Ombudsman. The Financial Services and Markets Act 2000 will bring together the Building Societies Ombudsman and seven others including the Banking Ombudsman and the Insurance Ombudsman, in a single Financial Ombudsman Service. This new complaints-handling organisation will provide consumers with a free, informal and independent service for resolving disputes with most providers of financial products and services. From 1 April 2000 this new body is providing a complaints handling service on behalf of each of the existing schemes. The arrangements will continue until the Financial Ombudsman Service receives powers in its own right when the legislation is brought into force in the course of 2001. As a result, the Building Societies Ombudsman is now at South Quay Plaza, 183 Marsh Wall, London EC14 9SR. Tel: 020-7931 0044.

BUILDING SOCIETIES 1998–9

	1998	1999
No. of societies – total	78	72
– authorised	71	69
No. of shareholders (000s)	21,195	21,774
No. of depositors (000s)	909	722
No. of borrowers (000s)	3,136	3,044
Share balances (£m)	103,290	109,138
Deposit balances (£m)	33,453	34,579
Mortgage balances (£m)	116,285	120,410
Total assets (£m)	156,014	157,141
Advances during year		
No. (000s)	521	519
Amount (£m)	24,244	26,555

INTEREST RATES: MORTGAGE AND SHARE 1995–2000

The interest rates prevailing on mortgage lending and share investment vary from society to society and in relation to the type or amount of loan or investment.

The interval between the payments or compounding of interest is crucial in determining the competitiveness of particular societies' accounts. In order to make a true comparison of interest rates, the annual percentage rate or APR, which should appear in all advertisements and leaflets, must be used.

	1995	1996	1997	1998	1999	2000 1st quarter
Average bank base rate	6.70	5.96	6.56	7.24	5.34	5.86
Building societies average mortgage rate	7.84	6.72	7.03	7.76	6.47	6.69
Building societies average share rate	5.62	4.54	5.49	6.34	4.89	5.19

AUTHORISED SOCIETIES at end of August 2000

Name of Building Society (a) and principal office address	Members (b)	Total assets (c)
		£'000
Barnsley, Regent Street, Barnsley, S. Yorks S70 2EH	51,713	252,439
Bath Investment, 20 Charles Street, Bath BA1 1HY	21,700	92,518
Beverley, 57 Market Place, Beverley, E. Yorks HU17 8AA	9,000	55,577
Bradford and Bingley, Crossflatts, Bingley, W. Yorks BD16 2UA (converting to PLC)	3,532,380	23,885,200
Britannia, Britannia House, Cheadle Road, Leek, Staffs ST13 5RG	2,162,542	13,366,495
Buckinghamshire, High Street, Chalfont St Giles, Bucks HP8 4QB	10,043	97,772
Cambridge, 51 Newmarket Road, Cambridge CB5 8FF	99,060	494,473
Catholic, 7 Strutton Ground, London SW1P 2HY	4,875	31,180
Century, 21 Albany Street, Edinburgh EH1 3QW	2,806	15,006
Chelsea, Thirlestaine Hall, Thirlestaine Road, Cheltenham, Glos GL53 7AL	501,000	4,752,510
Chesham, 12 Market Square, Chesham, Bucks HP5 1ER	21,080	153,656
Cheshire, Castle Street, Macclesfield, Cheshire SK11 6AF	360,996	2,286,500
Chorley and District, Key House, Foxhole Road, Chorley, Lancs PR7 1NZ	17,154	91,002
Clay Cross, Eyre Street, Clay Cross, Chesterfield S45 9NS	5,049	18,867
Coventry, PO Box 9, High Street, Coventry CV1 5QN	820,000	5,681,689
Cumberland, Cumberland House, Castle Street, Carlisle CA3 8RX	175,000	781,989
Darlington, Sentinel House, Lingfield Way, Darlington, Co. Durham DL1 4PR	92,258	391,048
Derbyshire, Duffield Hall, Duffield, Derby DE56 1AG	375,600	2,777,016
Dudley, Dudley House, Stone Street, Dudley DY1 1NP	26,500	106,123
Dunfermline, Caledonia House, Carnegie Avenue, Dunfermline, Fife KY11 8PJ	343,000	1,547,622
Earl Shilton, 22 The Hollow, Earl Shilton, Leicester LE9 7NB	11,867	67,061
Ecology, 18 Station Road, Cross Hills, Keighley, W. Yorks BD20 7EH	5,699	28,999
Furness, 51–55 Duke Street, Barrow-in-Furness LA14 1RT	110,653	480,874
Gainsborough, 9 Lord Street, Gainsborough, Lincs DN21 2DD	5,478	31,688
Hanley Economic, Granville House, Festival Park, Hanley, Stoke-on-Trent, Staffs ST1 5TB	42,000	246,329
Harpenden, 14 Station Road, Harpenden, Herts AL5 4SE	16,450	71,870
Hinckley and Rugby, Upper Bond Street, Hinckley, Leics LE10 1DG	94,000	435,495
Holmesdale, 43 Church Street, Reigate, Surrey RH2 0AE	9,611	97,501
Ilkeston Permanent, 3 South Street, Ilkeston, Derby DE7 5HQ	3,668	17,130
Ipswich, 44 Upper Brook Street, Ipswich IP4 1DP	31,161	251,309
Kent Reliance, Reliance House, Manor Road, Chatham, Kent ME4 6AF	69,000	342,849
Lambeth, 118–120 Westminster Bridge Road, London SE1 7XE	68,121	680,084
Leeds and Holbeck, 105 Albion Street, Leeds LS1 5AS	267,000	3,548,823
Leek United, 50 St Edward Street, Leek, Staffs ST13 5DH	70,810	477,206
Londonderry Provident, 31A Carlisle Road, Londonderry BT48 6JJ	1,386	12,780
Loughborough, 6 High Street, Loughborough, Leics LE11 2QB	29,292	157,821
Manchester, 24 Queen Street, Manchester M2 5AH	21,563	208,835
Mansfield, Regent House, Regent Street, Mansfield, Notts NG18 1SS	27,233	141,201
Market Harborough, Welland House, The Square, Market Harborough, Leics LE16 7PD	57,684	282,576
Marsden, 6–20 Russell Street, Nelson, Lancs BB9 7NJ	76,376	283,661
Melton Mowbray, 39 Nottingham Street, Melton Mowbray, Leics LE13 1NR	62,158	250,878
Mercantile, Mercantile House, Silverlink Business Park, Wallsend, Tyne and Wear NE28 9NY	34,972	179,951
Monmouthshire, John Frost Square, Newport, Gwent NP20 1PX	41,293	270,910
National Counties, National Counties House, Church Street, Epsom, Surrey KT17 4NL	40,458	605,148
Nationwide, Nationwide House, Pipers Way, Swindon SN38 1NW	10,000,000	64,010,000
Newbury, 17–20 Bartholomew Street, Newbury, Berks RG14 5LY	53,192	341,751
Newcastle, Portland House, New Bridge Street, Newcastle upon Tyne NE1 8AL	390,899	2,151,674
Norwich and Peterborough, Peterborough Business Park, Lynch Wood, Peterborough PE2 6WZ	357,658	2,228,821
Nottingham, 5–13 Upper Parliament Street, Nottingham NG1 2BX	163,614	1,391,013
Penrith, 7 King Street, Penrith, Cumbria CA11 7AR	7,186	56,715
Portman, Portman House, Richmond Hill, Bournemouth, Dorset BH2 6EP	1,219,723	6,321,600
Principality, PO Box 89, Principality Buildings, Queen Street, Cardiff CF10 1UA	300,000	2,088,500
Progressive, 33–37 Wellington Place, Belfast BT1 6HH	95,652	651,959
Saffron Walden, Herts and Essex, 1A Market Street, Saffron Walden, Essex CB10 1HX	67,931	338,787
Scarborough, Prospect House, PO Box 6, Scarborough, N. Yorks YO12 6EQ	148,120	1,072,245
Scottish, 23 Manor Place, Edinburgh EH3 7XE	28,554	149,482
Shepshed, Bull Ring, Shepshed, Loughborough, Leics LE12 9QD	9,920	42,556
Skipton, The Bailey, Skipton, N. Yorks BD23 1DN	465,000	5,139,147
Stafford Railway, 4 Market Square, Stafford ST16 2JH	12,878	69,216
Staffordshire, Jubilee House, PO Box 66, 84 Salop Street, Wolverhampton WV3 0SA	230,000	1,349,747
Stroud and Swindon, Rowcroft, Stroud, Glos GL5 3BG	193,580	1,289,081
Swansea, 11 Cradock Street, Swansea SA1 3EW	4,908	32,541
Teachers, Allenview House, Hanham Road, Wimborne, Dorset BH21 1AG	20,364	172,081

Name of Building Society (a) and principal office address	Members (b)	Total assets (c)
		£'000
Tipton and Coseley, 70 Owen Street, Tipton, W. Midlands DY4 8HG	34,750	166,758
Universal, Universal House, Kings Manor, Newcastle upon Tyne NE1 6PA	50,000	365,941
Vernon, 19 St Petersgate, Stockport, Cheshire SK1 1HF	37,921	167,464
West Bromwich, 374 High Street, West Bromwich, W. Midlands B70 8LR	499,353	2,797,100
Yorkshire, Yorkshire House, Yorkshire Drive, Bradford BD5 8LJ	1,875,524	10,354,400

(a) 'Building Society' are the last words in every society's name
(b) Includes both investing and borrowing members. Some totals are estimated or the latest available
(c) At 31 December 1999

National Savings

INVESTMENT AND ORDINARY ACCOUNTS

Interest is earned at 1.85 per cent per year on each ordinary account for every complete calendar month in which the balance is £500 or more. The minimum deposit is £10; maximum balance £10,000 plus interest credited.

The investment account pays a higher rate of interest depending on the account balance (the current rate can be found at any post office). The minimum deposit is £20; maximum balance £100,000 plus interest credited.

Since April 1999 Individual Savings Accounts (ISAs) have been offered by National Savings. An ISA can be opened with £10. Interest is calculated daily on balances of over £1 and is free of tax. The same regulations apply as for ISAs offered by all companies.

PREMIUM BONDS

Premium Bonds are a government security which were first introduced in 1956. Premium Bonds enable savers to enter a regular draw for tax-free prizes, while retaining the right to get their money back. A sum equivalent to interest on each bond is put into a prize fund and distributed by monthly prize draws. (The rate of interest is 4.25 per cent a year from 1 June 2000.) The prizes are drawn by ERNIE (electronic random number indicator equipment) and are free of all UK income tax and capital gains tax.

Bonds are in units of £1, with a minimum purchase of £100; above this, purchases must be in multiples of £10, up to a maximum holding limit of £20,000 per person. The scheme offers a facility to reinvest prize wins automatically. Upon completion of an automatic prize reinvestment mandate, holders receive new bonds which are immediately eligible for future prize draws. Bonds can only be held in the name of an individual and not by organisations.

Bonds become eligible for prizes once they have been held for one clear calendar month following the month of purchase. Each £1 unit can win only one prize per draw, but it will be awarded the highest for which it is drawn. Bonds remain eligible for prizes until they are repaid. When a holder dies, bonds remain eligible for prizes up to and including the twelfth monthly draw after the month in which the holder dies.

By May 2000 bonds to the value of over £13,700 million had been sold. By the May 2000 prize draw, 77 million prizes totalling £4,930 million had been distributed since the first prize draw in June 1957.

INCOME BONDS

National Savings Income Bonds were introduced in 1982. They are suitable for those who want to receive regular monthly payments of interest while preserving the full cash value of their capital. The bonds are sold in multiples of £500. The minimum holding is £500 and the maximum £1,000,000 (sole or joint holding).

Interest is calculated on a day-to-day basis and paid monthly. Interest is taxable but is paid without deduction of tax at source. The bonds have a guaranteed life of ten years, but may be repaid at par before maturity on giving three months' notice. Repayment is also possible without giving notice but incurs a penalty. If the sole or sole surviving holder dies, however, no fixed period of notice is required and there is no loss of interest for repayment made within the first year.

PENSIONERS GUARANTEED INCOME BONDS

Pensioners Guaranteed Income Bonds were introduced in January 1994 and are designed for people aged 60 and over who wish to receive regular monthly payments with a rate of interest that is fixed for a five-year period whilst preserving the full cash value of their investment. A new two-year fixed rate term bond was introduced in May 1999.

The minimum limit for each purchase is £500. The maximum holding is £1,000,000 (sole or joint holding); within those limits bonds can be bought for any amount in pounds and pence. The rate of interest is fixed and guaranteed for the first two or five years, depending on the term invested in. Interest is taxable but is paid without deduction of tax at source.

Holders can apply for repayment (or part repayment of a bond subject to the minimum holding limits) by giving 60 days' notice (if repayment is before the fifth anniversary date). No interest is earned during the notice period. If repayment is requested within two weeks of any fifth anniversary of purchase, there is no formal period of notice. Repayment is possible without giving notice but a penalty is incurred. On the death of a holder or sole surviving investor in a joint holding, repayment will be made without notice. Interest will be paid in full up to the date of repayment.

CHILDREN'S BONUS BONDS

Children's Bonus Bonds were introduced in 1991. The latest issue, Issue R, was introduced in January 2000. They can be bought for any child under 16 and will go on growing in value until he or she is 21. The bonds are sold in multiples of £25. The minimum holding is £25. The maximum holding in Issue R is £1,000 per child. This is in addition to holdings of earlier issues of the bond (excluding interest and bonuses). Bonds for children under 16 must be held by a parent or guardian.

Children's Bonus Bonds (Issue R) earn 3.5 per cent a year over five years. A bonus (12.84 per cent) of the purchase price is added at the fifth anniversary. This is equal to 5.65 per cent a year compound. All returns are totally exempt from UK income tax. No interest is earned on bonds cashed in before the first anniversary of purchase. Bonuses are only payable if the bond is held until the next bonus date. Bonds over five years old continue to earn interest and bonuses until the holder is 21, when they should be cashed in. If bonds are not cashed in on the holder's 21st birthday, they earn no interest after that birthday.

FIXED RATE SAVINGS BOND

Fixed Rate Savings Bonds are lump sum investments that earn guaranteed rates of interest over set periods of time from six months to three years. Interest, from which basic rate tax is deducted at source, can be paid out or reinvested into the bond monthly, annually or at the end of the term. Holders can also choose where the interest is paid.

CAPITAL BONDS

National Savings Capital Bonds were introduced in 1989. The latest series, Series U, was introduced in January 2000. Capital Bonds offer capital growth over five years with guaranteed returns at fixed rates. The interest is taxable each year (for those who pay income tax) but is not deducted at source. The minimum purchase is £100. There is a maximum holding limit of £250,000 from Series B onwards.

Capital Bonds will be repaid in full with all interest gained at the end of five years. No interest is earned on bonds repaid in the first year. Reinvestment or extension terms may also be available.

NATIONAL SAVINGS TREASURER'S ACCOUNT

The Treasurer's Account, introduced in September 1996, offers attractive rates and security to non-profit making organisations such as charities, friendly societies, clubs, etc. The minimum holding is £10,000 and the maximum is £2 million. Interest is paid at the rate of 5.0 per cent a year on holdings of £10,000 to £24,999, 5.3 per cent a year on holdings of £25,000 to £99,999, and 5.7 per cent a year on holdings of £100,000 and above.

NATIONAL SAVINGS CERTIFICATES

RECENT ISSUES

Interest, index-linked increase, bonus or other sum payable is free of UK income tax (including investment income surcharge) and capital gains tax.

From June 1982, savings certificates of the 7th to 54th Issues have been extended on general extension rates as they reach the end of their existing extension periods. The percentage interest rate is determined by the Treasury and any change in this general extension rate will be applicable from the first of the month following its announcement. Under the system, a certificate earns interest for each complete period of three months beyond the expiry of the previous extension terms. Within each three-month period, interest is calculated separately for each month at the rate applicable from the beginning of that month. The interest for each month is one-twelfth of the annual rate (i.e. it does not vary with the number of days in the month) and is capitalised annually on the anniversary of the date of purchase. The current rate of interest under the general extension rate is given in leaflets available at post offices.

By June 2000 there had been seventeen issues of index-linked certificates, 54 issues of fixed-interest certificates and three issues of two-year index-linked certificates.

Insurance

The Insurance Companies Act 1982 initially empowered the Department of Trade and Industry Insurance Division to authorise corporate bodies to transact insurance in the United Kingdom provided they comply with the financial and other regulations detailed in the Act. In January 1998 an interim transfer of this function to the Insurance Directorate of HM Treasury was completed. When the Financial Services and Markets Act is fully implemented this function will transfer to the Financial Services Authority. In practice, this has already happened as from 1 January 1999 the Treasury contracted out most of the Insurance Supervision and authorisation functions to the FSA.

At the end of 1999 there were over 800 insurance companies with authorisation from the Treasury to transact one or more classes of insurance business. However, with the establishment of the single European insurance market on 1 July 1994 an insurer authorised in any of the European Union (EU) countries can now transact insurance in the UK without further formality; this creates a potential market of over 5,000 insurance companies.

REGULATION

Over 23,000 firms are authorised to conduct a wide variety of investment business in the UK. The overall regulator for investment business of any kind is the Financial Services Authority (FSA), 25 The North Colonade, London E14 5HS. Web: http://www.fsa.gov.uk.

The FSA does not undertake all the regulatory work itself. Instead it recognises a number of specialist bodies to carry out the frontline regulation. The bulk of this work is undertaken by three Self-Regulating Organisations (SROs).

The main regulator of firms advising on and arranging deals in life insurance and pensions, friendly society investments, unit trusts and investment trusts is one of the SROs, the Personal Investment Authority (PIA). (25 The North Colonade, Canary Wharf, London E14 5HS).

Disputes between policyholders and life or general insurers have, in the past, been referred to the Insurance Ombudsman. In common with many other sections of the Financial Services industry, the Insurance Ombudsman Bureau became part of the Financial Ombudsman Service administered by the FSA. During 1999 Walter Merricks was appointed Chief Ombudsman.

Private policyholders with a complaint against an insurer who subscribes to the scheme can refer their problem, free of charge, to the Ombudsman who examines the facts of a complaint and delivers a decision which is binding on the insurer (but not the policyholder). When the Financial Services Ombudsman Scheme is finalised it is expected that small businesses with a turnover of up to £1m and third parties, who cannot currently use the service, will have access to the scheme. It is proposed that all authorised firms – banks and building societies, insurance companies and investment firms – will be covered by the new service on a compulsory basis.

ASSOCIATION OF BRITISH INSURERS

Over 98 per cent of the world-wide business of UK insurance companies is transacted by the 405 members of the Association of British Insurers (ABI), 51 Gresham Street, London EC2V 7HQ. Web: http://www.abi.org.uk. ABI is a trade association which represents both life and general insurers. On general insurance (motor, household, holiday, etc.), ABI currently acts as a non-statutory regulator for insurance intermediaries but this function will pass to the General Insurance Standards Council when its formation is complete. The General Insurance Standards Council is located at: 110 Cannon Street, London EC4N 6EU. Web: http://www.gisc.co.uk.

INSURANCE BROKERS AND INTERMEDIARIES

In July 1998 the Economic Secretary to the Treasury confirmed that the Financial Services and Markets Act will repeal the Insurance Brokers (Registration) Act 1977. This will end the statutory status of the Insurance Brokers Registration Council (IBRC) (Higham Business Centre, Midland Road, Higham Ferrers, Northants NN10 8DW). Until the Act is implemented the IBRC remains in existence.

BALANCE OF PAYMENTS

The insurance industry contributes nearly 2 per cent to the UK's Gross Domestic Product (GDP). In 1998 the overseas earnings of the UK insurance sector was around £7,000m, which was roughly the same level as 1997.

TAKE-OVERS AND MERGERS

1999 saw more activity on take-overs and mergers as the larger players in the UK attempted to expand to a size that would enable them to compete in global markets. Overseas companies have also purchased UK operations and smaller companies have recognised the need to merge if they are to continue to offer any realistic competition. During the year the AXA group made purchases of both life and general (including private medical) insurance companies. A number of mutual insurers have also consulted policyholders (in effect, their shareholders) about de-mutualisation. For Norwich Union and Scottish Widows policyholders the result was a vote to lose their mutual status (with a cash or shares "windfall") followed in each case by a take-over or merger. It is expected that take-over and merger activity in the UK market will continue.

GENERAL INSURANCE

The issue that dominated the headlines and much of the insurers' attention at the end of 1999 was the possibility of problems following the millennium date change. Insurers were interested in the issue as they had a financial interest in any potential claims but also as major users of information technology. In the event, there were few major problems in the UK, which initially led the media to speculate that it had been over-hyped. Most insurers, however, have pointed to the serious problems, albeit not on the scale predicted, that occurred in other parts of the world which suggest that the preparations and publicity were justified.

With no startling movements in claims figures on the general insurance side and a reasonable winter, general insurers' attention turned to legal liability insurances and the Law Commission's review of the law of damages which was due to report in a number of areas. The Court of Appeal's decision on damages for pain and suffering was also significant. The worry was that premiums for employers' and public liability and motor insurances would need to rise significantly to enable insurers to meet the increased compensation awards. In the event, the reviews did not propose retrospective measures and the increases in the level of damages proposed will not put undue pressure on premium rates.

Fraud and uninsured driving continue to be concerns for insurers and in each case IT-based solutions have been proposed. For motor insurers the year saw final agreement on the establishment of an industry-wide database of all insured drivers. This will be a major step forward in combatting uninsured driving and from the middle of 2000 all motor insurances being renewed or taken out were included in the database.

Claims statistics were, on the whole, encouraging with most types of claim showing small falls. Overall, theft claims fell by 5 per cent to £675m. Weather damage claims fell by 14 per cent to £788m. Domestic fire costs were the exception with a 3.9 per cent rise to £271m; however the inclusion of commercial fire claims made the overall total for fire claims £850m, which is a fall of 1.5 per cent on 1998.

LONDON INSURANCE MARKET

The London Insurance Market is a distinct, separate sector of the UK insurance and reinsurance industry. It is the world's leading market for internationally traded insurances and reinsurance, its business comprising mainly overseas non-life large and high-exposure risks. The market is centred on the City of London, which provides the required international financial, banking, legal and other support services. Currently there are 139 Lloyd's syndicates, about 120 insurance companies and 39 Marine Protection and Indemnity Clubs active in the market. In 1998 the market had a written gross premium income of £14,400 million. Most of the business is brought to the market by the 201 firms of Lloyd's brokers.

The trade association for the international insurance and reinsurance companies writing primarily non-marine insurance and all classes of reinsurance business in the London Market is the International Underwriting Association (IUA), London Underwriting Centre, 3 Minster Court, Mincing Lane, London EC3R 7DD; web: http://www.iua.co.uk.

BRITISH INSURANCE COMPANIES

The following insurance company figures refer to members and certain non-members of the ABI.

CLAIMS STATISTICS (£ million)

	1998	1999
Domestic claims		
Theft	532	503
Fire	261	271
Weather	664	541
Subsidence	375	324
Business interruption	n/a	n/a
Total	1,832	1,639
Commercial claims		
Theft	178	172
Fire	602	579
Weather	256	247
Subsidence	n/a	n/a
Business interruption	235	124
Total	1,271	1,122

WORLD-WIDE GENERAL BUSINESS TRADING RESULT

	1997 £m	1998 £m
Net written premiums	34,973	35,804
Underwriting profit (loss) for one year account business	(1,083)	(2,362)
Transfer to profit and loss account for other business		
Marine, Aviation, Transport	(72)	(198)
Other	(60)	(56)
Total underwriting result	(1,095)	(2,617)
Net investment income	4,831	5,685
Overall trading profit	3,042	1,188
Profit as % of premium income	8.7	3.3

WORLD-WIDE GENERAL BUSINESS UNDERWRITING RESULT

	1997					1998				
	UK	Other EU	USA	Other	Total	UK	Other EU	USA	Other	Total
Motor										
Premiums: £m	6,092	1,689	1,533	1,753	11,067	6,490	1,915	1,591	1,786	11,782
Profit (loss): £m	(1,163)	(223)	(66)	(46)	(1,498)	(1,472)	(332)	(198)	(88)	(2,090)
% of premiums	(19.1)	(13.2)	(4.3)	(2.62)	(13.5)	(22.7)	(17.3)	(12.4)	(4.9)	(17.7)
Non-motor										
Premiums: £m	12,424	2,321	1,864	1,982	18,591	12,953	2,413	2,008	1,821	19,195
Profit (loss): £m	119	(100)	(173)	(31)	(185)	(723)	(17)	(859)	(218)	(1,817)
% of premiums	1	4.3	9.28	1.56	9.95	5.58	0.7	42.77	11.9	9.5

NET PREMIUM INCOME BY TERRITORY 1998

	UK £m	Other EU £m	USA £m	Other £m	Total £m
Motor	6,507	1,915	1,591	1,786	11,799
Non-motor	13,691	2,413	2,008	1,821	19,932
Marine, Aviation and Transport	931	244	253	162	1,590
Non-MAT reinsurance	1,589	443	43	126	2,201
Other funded business	272	9	0	0	281
Total general business	22,990	5,145	3,895	3,895	35,803
Ordinary long-term	71,429	7,188	3,690	5,024	87,331
Industrial long-term	972	—	—	—	972
Total long-term business	72,401	7,188	3,690	5,024	88,303

LLOYD'S OF LONDON

Lloyd's of London is an international market for almost all types of general insurance. Lloyd's currently has a capacity to accept insurance premiums of over £10,000 million. Much of this business comes from outside Great Britain and makes a valuable contribution to the balance of payments.

A policy is underwritten at Lloyd's by a mixture of private and corporate members, corporate members having been admitted for the first time in 1992. Specialist underwriters accept insurance risks at Lloyd's on behalf of members (referred to as 'Names') grouped in syndicates. There are currently around 165 syndicates of varying sizes, some with up to 2,000 names, each managed by an underwriting agent approved by the Council of Lloyd's.

Individual members are still in the majority at Lloyd's with a total of 3,317 individuals as opposed to 853 corporate members. In 1999 the market capacity of the corporate sector was £8,042 while individuals represented £2,003 million of capacity.

Lloyd's is incorporated by an Act of Parliament (Lloyd's Acts 1971 onwards) and is governed by a council of 19 members. Market management is handled by a Market Board of 18 members (comprising three working members and three external members of the Council, three Corporation executives (including the chief executive officer), eight additional market practitioners and one external member. Regulation is supervised by a Board of 14 members, comprising four nominated members of the Council, two external members of the Council, four appointed working members, two other appointed external members and the Director, Regulatory Division.

The Corporation is a non-profit making body chiefly financed by its members' subscriptions. It provides the premises, administrative staff and services enabling Lloyd's underwriting syndicates to conduct their business. It does not, however, assume corporate liability for the risks accepted by its members, who remain responsible to the full extent of their personal means for their underwriting affairs.

At present, Lloyd's syndicates have no direct contact with the public. All business is transacted through insurance brokers accredited by the Corporation of Lloyd's. In addition, non-Lloyd's brokers in the UK, when guaranteed by Lloyd's brokers, are able to deal directly with Lloyd's motor syndicates, a facility which has made the Lloyd's market more accessible to the insuring public.

Lloyd's also provides the most comprehensive shipping intelligence service in the world. The shipping and other information received from Lloyd's agents, shipowners, news agencies and other sources throughout the world is collated and distributed to the media as well as to the maritime and commercial sectors in general. *Lloyd's List* is London's oldest daily newspaper and contains news of general commercial interest as well as shipping information. *Lloyd's Shipping Index*, also published daily, lists some 25,000 ocean-going vessels in alphabetical order and gives the latest known report of each.

DEVELOPMENTS IN 1999

The 1997 year of account saw a steep drop from the 1996 profit of £748m to a whole account loss of £176m. This was composed of an underwriting loss of £79m, personal expenses of £341m and releases from prior reserves of £244m. The majority of the losses for 1997 came from the motor market which suffered from strong competition and a series of legal decisions which saw increased claims or the need to reserve for them.

In 1997 only 75 of the 165 syndicates trading made a profit and it is expected that 1998 will see this figure deteriorate still further. Optimists in the Lloyd's market hope that the 1998 and 1999 results will see the bottom of the current severe loss cycle but natural disasters can often upset trends. In 1998 Hurricane Georges and the Canadian ice storms meant an end to the relatively quiet period that had been seen up until that date. Some analysts believe it will not be until at least 2002 before the market sees a profit again.

The litigation, which has been a feature of the market since the 1980s, continued during 1999. Notable among the lawsuits is one which, instead of alleging negligence, alleges fraud. The common feature is the allegation that Lloyd's knew that the market was facing serious levels of claims from asbestosis and related diseases in the 1970s but did not make this fact public. Many cases remain to be heard and the subject is likely to keep re-appearing in the media.

In June 1999 the Financial Services Authority published the result of their consultation exercise on the regulation of the Lloyd's market. In May 1997 a regulatory Review Group set up by Lloyd's recommended that wider statutory oversight of its regulatory activities should be sought. The FSA's conclusion was largely in line with this and, in common with the rest of the financial services industry, Lloyd's will be regulated by the FSA as soon as the Financial Services and Markets Act is implemented. However, in situations where Lloyd's internal regulatory and compensation arrangements are deemed to be more far-reaching, as for example with the Lloyd's Central Fund, which safeguards claim payments to policyholders, the existing arrangements will remain in force.

Chairman, M. Taylor
Chief Executive, R. Sandler

LLOYD'S MEMBERSHIP

	1997	1998	1999
Total no. of underwriting members participating			
Individuals	9,958	6,825	4,503
Corporate	202	435	668

TOTAL MARKET CAPACITY

	1997	1998	1999
	£m	£m	£m
Individual	5,824	4,105	2,700
Corporate	4,500	6,064	7,170
Total	10,324	10,169	9,870

LLOYD'S PURE YEAR RESULTS 1996/7

	Marine Energy		Non-marine		Aviation		Motor	
	1996	1997	1996	1997	1996	1997	1996	1997
	£m	£m	£m	£m	£m	£m	£m	£m
Pure year result	193	(25)	523	101	136	8	(104)	(163)

LLOYD'S GLOBAL ACCOUNTS
as at 31 December 1997

	1996 and prior years of account £m	1997 pure year result £m
Gross premiums written (net of brokerage)	6,718	6,820
Outward reinsurance premiums	1,922	2,116
Net premiums	4,796	4,704
Reinsurance to close premiums received from earlier years of account	3,554	—
Amounts retained to meet all known and unknown outstanding liabilities brought forward	136	—
	8,486	4,704
Gross claims paid	4,424	4,098
Reinsurers' share	1,126	1,274
Net claims	3,298	2,824
Other reinsurance premiums paid to close the year of account	4,391	1,760
Amounts retained to meet all known and unknown outstanding liabilities carried forward	62	116
	7,751	4,700
Underwriting result	735	4
Other profit (loss) on exchange	(6)	8
Syndicate operating expenses	(316)	(421)
Balance on technical account	413	(409)
Investment income	528	406
Investment expenses and charges	(9)	(7)
Investment gains less losses	63	(69)
Result before personal expenses	995	(79)
Personal expenses	(389)	(341)
Result after personal expenses	606	(420)

1999 was dominated by fears that the industry faced another mis-selling scandal over mortgage endowment policies. The allegation was that policyholders had not been adequately advised when taking out endowment policies for the repayment of mortgages and that the returns on these policies may not reach the amount required to fully repay the mortgage. In December the FSA announced the conclusion of a study of the problem which noted that policyholders would not have financially been any better off had they opted for a repayment mortgage. However, life companies were criticised for their past selling and record keeping practices. A new code of practice has now been introduced.

STAKEHOLDER PENSIONS

At the end of 1998 the Government published a Green Paper proposing a new pension system known as 'Stakeholder Pensions'. The intention is to provide a framework in which people would be encouraged to make provision for themselves and in which state assistance would be concentrated on the poorest. During the course of the year the Department of Social Security and the Inland Revenue published a number of consultative documents and the work towards formulating a workable system continues.

REVIEW OF PENSIONS MIS-SELLING

The regulators' review of personal pensions continued throughout 1999. The pensions concerned were contracts sold between April 1988 and July 1994 to up to 1,500,000 people who were advised to take out a personal pension plan; in many cases this was in preference to remaining in a company pension scheme. The review began in late 1994 and because of the number of cases involved, cases involving those closer to retirement were given higher priority and dealt with first. During 1999 the attention turned to the phase two cases which involved widespread advertising and publicity to encourage victims to come forward. All potential victims of mis-selling have now been identified and contacted.

LIFE AND LONG-TERM INSURANCE AND PENSIONS

The total individual long-term new business in the UK rose by 3.5 per cent in 1999 to £3,728 million for annual contracts and by 22.3 per cent to £46,660 for single premium business.

NEW NON-LINKED PERSONAL PENSION BUSINESS

	Regular premium policies		Single premium policies	
	No. new policies	New premiums £m	No. new policies	New premiums £m
1995	320,000	365	98,000	1,598
1996	307,000	391	114,000	1,865
1997	330,000	424	144,000	2,173
1998	417,000	556	129,000	1,456

NEW LINKED PERSONAL PENSION BUSINESS

1995	528,000	467	132,000	1,638
1996	573,000	582	165,000	2,169
1997	693,000	768	196,000	2,913
1998	728,000	919	181,000	2,960

NET PREMIUM INCOME FOR WORLDWIDE LONG-TERM INSURANCE BUSINESS

	1997 £m	1998 £m
Ordinary Branch		
Business written in UK		
Annual premiums		
Life	12,606	12,546
Annuities	67	50
Pensions	11,518	11,960
Income Protection	673	715
Industrial Business	1,015	942
Single premiums		
Life	14,022	17,720
Annuities	346	373
Pensions	21,104	28,008
Income protection	45	56
Business written overseas		
Annual premiums	4,966	4,866
Single premiums	9,471	10,064
Total	66,546	74,849

PAYMENTS TO POLICYHOLDERS

	1997 £m	1998 £m
Payments to UK policyholders	48,399	54,547
Payments to overseas policyholders	10,042	10,280
Total	58,441	64,827

INVESTMENTS OF INSURANCE COMPANIES 1998

Investment of funds	Long-term business £m	General business £m
Index-linked British Government securities	17,936	2,202
Non-index-linked British Government securities	102,767	13,559
Other UK public sector debt securities	5,099	527
Overseas government, provincial and municipal securities	31,299	16,853
Debentures, loan shares, preference and guaranteed stocks and shares		
UK	65,696	7,169
Overseas	40,753	8,675
Ordinary stocks and shares		
UK	309,735	14,646
Overseas	78,590	10,973
Unit trusts		
Equities	55,075	1,314
Fixed interest	4,179	161
Loans secured on property	13,509	2,256
Real property and ground rents	47,483	4,158
Other invested assets	54,881	30,794
Total invested assets	827,002	113,289
Net investment income	34,905	5,685

DIRECTORY OF INSURANCE COMPANIES

Classes of insurance undertaken		*Group membership*	
G	General	(CGNU)	CGNU
L	Life	(Z)	Zurich Financial Group
M	Marine	(A)	AXA Group
Re	Reinsurance	(RSA)	Royal and SunAlliance

Nature of business	*Name of company*	*Head Office address*
L	Abbey Life	Abbey Life House, PO Box 33, Bournemouth BH8 8AL
L	Abbey National Life	287 St Vincent Street, Glasgow, G2 5NB
G	Ace Insurance SANV	CIGNA House, 8 Lime Street, London EC3M 7NA
L	AIG Life (UK)	Alico House, 22 Addiscombe Road, Croydon CR9 5AZ
L	Alba LifeLimited	Britannia Court, 50 Bothwell Street, Glasgow G2 6HR
GM Re	Albion	Whittaker House, Whittaker Ave, Richmond, TW9 1EH
L	Alico	Alico House, 22 Addiscombe Road, Croydon CR9 5AZ
GL	Alliance & Leicester Insurance	Carlton Park, Narborough, LE9 5XX
L	Allied Dunbar (Z)	UK Life Centre, Swindon SN1 1EL
G	Ansvar	31 St Leonards Road, Eastbourne BN21 3UR
L	Australian Mutual Provident	Spectrum, Bond Street, Bristol BS1 3AL
LGM	Avon Insurance	Arden Street, Stratford-upon-Avon CV37 6WA
G	AXA Insurance (A)	Royal Exchange, London EC3V 3LS
G	AXA Provincial (A)	107 Cheapside, London EC2V 6DU
L	AXA Sun Life (A)	Sun Life Centre, PO Box 1810, Bristol BS99 5SN
G	Baptist	1 Merchant Street, London E3 4LY
L	Barclays Life	9 Fleetway House, 25 Farringdon Street, London EC4A 4JA
M	Bradford (RSA)	Bowling Mill, Dean Clough, Halifax HX3 5WA
GL	Britannic Assurance	1 Wythall Green Way, Wythall, Birmingham B47 6WG
L	British Life Office	Reliance House, Mount Ephraim, Tunbridge Wells, Kent TN4 8BL
Medical	BUPA	BUPA House, 15–19 Bloomsbury Way, London WC1A 2BA
L	Caledonian (A)	Royal Exchange, London EC3V 3LS

Nature of business	Name of company	Head Office address
GM	Cambrian (A)	Royal Exchange, London EC3V 3LS
L	Canada Life	Canada Life House, Potters Bar EN6 5BA
L	Century Life	Century House, 5 Old Bailey, London EC4M 7BA
G	CGNU Insurance (CGNU)	St Helens, 1 Undershaft, London EC3P 3DQ
L	CGNU Life	2 Rougier Street, York YO90 1UU
L	CIGNA Healthcare & Group Life	PO Box 42, Greenock PA15 1AB
L	Clerical, Medical Group	Narrow Plain, Bristol BS2 0JH
L	Colonial	Colonial House, Chatham Maritime ME14 4YY
L	Confederation Life	Lytton Way, Stevenage SG1 2NN
G	Congregational and General	Currer House, Currer Street, Bradford BD1 5BA
GLM Re	Co-operative	Miller Street, Manchester M60 0AL
GLM Re	Cornhill	57 Ladymead, Guildford GU1 1DB
GL	Direct Line Insurance	3 Edridge Road, Croydon CR9 1AG
GLM Re	Eagle Star (Z)	60 St Mary Axe, London EC3A 8JQ
GL Re	Ecclesiastical	Beaufort House, Brunswick Road, Gloucester GL1 1JZ
G	Equine and Livestock	PO Box 100, Ouseburn, York YO5 9SZ
L	Equitable Life	Walton Street, Aylesbury HP21 7QW
L	Friends' Provident	Pixham End, Pixham Lane, Dorking RH4 1QA
L	GE Life	Stalwart House, Station Road, Dorking, RH4 1HL
G	Gresham Fire and Accident	11 Queen Victoria Street, London EC4N 4XP
G	Groupama Insurance	Groupama House, Arthur Street, London EC4R 9AT
G	Groupama General Insurance	Groupama House, Arthur Street, London EC4R 9AT
GLM Re	Guardian Insurance (A)	Civic Drive, Ipswich IP1 2AN
GLM Re	Guardian Royal Exchange (A)	Civic Drive, Ipswich IP1 2AN
GLM Re	Hibernian	Haddington Road, Dublin 4, Republic of Ireland
L	Hill Samuel Life	NLA Tower, 12–16 Addiscombe Road, Croydon CR9 6DR
G	Hiscox Insurance Co.	52 Leadenhall Street, London EC3A 2BJ
GL	Ideal	Pitmaston, Moseley, Birmingham B13 8NG
L	Irish Life	Irish Life Centre, Victoria Street, St Albans AL1 5TS
GF	Iron Trades	Iron Trades House, 21–24 Grosvenor Place, London SW1X 7JA
GLM Re	Legal and General	Temple Court, 11 Queen Victoria Street, London EC4N 4TP
L	Lincoln	Barnett Way, Barnwood, Gloucester, GL4 3RZ
GM	Liverpool Marine and General (RSA)	1 Bartholomew Lane, London EC2N 2AB
GL	Liverpool Victoria Friendly	135 Poole Road, Bournemouth BH4 9BG
GM	Local Government Guarantee (A)	Royal Exchange, London EC3V 3LS
G	MMA Insurance	Norman Insurance House, Kings Road, RG1 4LL
L	M and G Life	Three Quays, Tower Hill, London EC3R 6BQ
L	Manulife	Broadstreet House, 55 Old Broad Street, London EC2N 1TL
M	Marine (RSA)	1 Cornhill, London EC3V 3QR
M Re	Maritime (CGNU)	PO Box 6, Surrey Street, Norwich NR1 3NS
L	Medical Sickness Society	Colmore Circus, Birmingham B4 6AR
Re	Mercantile and General	Moorfields House, Moorfields, London EC4R 9BJ
L	Merchant Investors	St Bartholomew's House, Lewins Mead, Bristol BS1 2NH
G Re	Methodist	Brazennose House, Brazennose Street, Manchester M2 5AS
L	MGM Assurance	MGM House, Heene Road, Worthing BN11 2DY
L	National Mutual Life	The Priory, Hitchin SG5 2DW
GM	Navigators and General (Z)	Lanchester House, Trafalgar Place, Trafalgar Street, Brighton BN1 4DA
GL Re	NFU Mutual	Tiddington Road, Stratford-upon-Avon CV37 7BJ
G	NIG	Crown House, 145 City Road, London EC1V 1LP
L	NM Financial Management	Enterprise House, Isambard Brunel Road, Portsmouth PO1 2AW
L	NPI	NPI House, 55 Calverley Road, Tunbridge Wells TN1 2UE
GLM Re	Pearl	The Pearl Centre, Lynchwood, Peterborough PE2 6FY
L Sickness	Permanent	Pynes Hill House, Rydon Lane, Exeter EX2 5SP
GLM	Phoenix (RSA)	1 Bartholomew Lane, London EC2N 2AB
Medical	PPP Healthcare (A)	PPP House, Vale Road, Tunbridge Wells TN1 1BJ
L	Property Growth (RSA)	Phoenix House, Redcliff Hill, Bristol BS1 6SX
GLM Re	Prudential	Laurence Pountney Hill, London EC4R 0EU
GL	Refuge	Refuge House, Alderley Road, Wilmslow, Cheshire SK9 1PF
L	Reliance Mutual	Reliance House, Mount Ephraim, Tunbridge Wells, Kent TN4 8BL
G	Road Transport and General (CGNU)	Pitheavlis, Perth PH2 0NH
G	Royal Exchange (A)	Royal Exchange, London EC3V 3LS
L	Royal Heritage Life (RSA)	Royal Insurance House, Business Park, Peterborough PE2 6GG
GLM Re	Royal and SunAlliance (RSA)	30 Berkeley Square, London, W1X 5AN
Engineering	Royal and SunAlliance Engineering (RSA)	17 York Street, Manchester M2 3RS
L	Royal Liver	Royal Liver Building, Pier Head, Liverpool L3 1HT

Nature of business	*Name of company*	*Head Office address*
GL	Royal London	Royal London House, 27 Middleborough, Colchester CO1 1RA
L	Royal National Pension Fund for Nurses	Burdett House, 15 Buckingham Street, Strand, London WC2N 6ED
F	Salvation Army	117–121 Judd Street, London WC1H 9NN
L	Save and Prosper	Hexagon House, 28 Western Road, Romford RM1 3LB
L	Scottish Amicable	Craigforth, PO Box 25, Stirling FK9 4UE
Engineering	Scottish Boiler (CGNU)	PO Box 131, 825 Wilmslow Road, Didsbury, Manchester M20 8GS
L	Scottish Equitable	28 St Andrew Square, Edinburgh EH2 2QZ
L	Scottish Friendly	16 Blythswood Square, Glasgow G2 6HJ
M	Scottish General (CGNU)	PO Box 896, 103 Westerhill Road, Bishopbriggs, Glasgow G64 2QX
L	Scottish Legal Life	95 Bothwell Street, Glasgow G2 7HY
L	Scottish Life	19 St Andrew Square, Edinburgh EH2 1YE
L	Scottish Mutual	301 St Vincent Street, Glasgow G2 5HN
L	Scottish Provident Life	6 St Andrew Square, Edinburgh EH2 2YA
L	Scottish Widows'	15 Dalkeith Road, Edinburgh EH16 5BU
GM	Sea (RSA)	1 Bartholomew Lane, London EC2N 2AB
L	Standard Life	30 Lothian Road, Edinburgh EH1 2DH
GLM	Sun Alliance (RSA)	1 Bartholomew Lane, London EC2N 2AB
GM	Sun Insurance Office (RSA)	1 Bartholomew Lane, London EC2N 2AB
L Re	Sun Life of Canada	Basing View, Basingstoke RG21 2DZ
L	Swiss Life	Swiss Life House, South Park, Sevenoaks TN13 1BG
GL	Teacher's Provident Soc	Deansleigh Road, Bournemouth BH7 7DT
L	Tunstall Assurance	Station Chambers, The Boulevard, Tunstall, Stoke-on-Trent ST6 6DU
M	Ulster Marine (CGNU)	Pitheavlis, Perth PH2 0NH
GL	UIA Insurance	Kings Court, London Road, Stevenage SG1 2TP
GM	Union Insurance Society of Canton (CGNU)	Royal Exchange, London EC3V 3LS
L	United Friendly	Refuge House, Alderley Road, Wilmslow SK9 1PF
GL Re	Wesleyan Assurance	Colmore Circus, Birmingham B4 6AR
L	Windsor Life	Windsor House, Telford TF3 4NB
L	Winterthur Life	Winterthur Way, Basingstoke RG21 6SZ
GM Re	Zurich (Z)	Zurich House, Stanhope Road, Portsmouth PO1 1DU
L	Zurich Life (Z)	The Zurich Centre, 3000 Parkway, Whiteley, Fareham PO15 7JY

The London Stock Exchange

The London Stock Exchange Ltd serves the needs of government, industry and investors by providing facilities for raising capital and a central market-place for securities trading. This market-place covers government stocks (called gilts), UK and overseas company shares (called equities and fixed interest stocks), and traditional options.

PRIMARY MARKETS

The Exchange enables companies to raise capital for development and growth through the issue of securities. For a company entering the market for the first time there is a choice of Exchange markets, depending upon the size, history and requirements of the company. The first is the main market, which exists for well-established companies; these must comply with stringent criteria relating to all aspects of their operations. A company's securities are admitted to the Official List by the UK Listing Authority (UKLA), a division of the Financial Services Authority, and also admitted to trading by the Exchange. In parallel to the UKLA's listing process, the Exchange has its own set of admission and disclosure standards which are designed to sit alongside the UKLA's listing rules.

The Alternative Investment Market (AIM) began trading in June 1995. It enables small, young and growing companies to raise capital, widen their investor base and have their shares traded on a regulated market without the expense of a full Exchange listing. Many companies use AIM as a stepping-stone to a full listing.

Once admitted to the Exchange, all companies are obliged to keep their shareholders informed of their progress, making announcements of a price-sensitive nature through the Exchange's company announcement department.

At the end of 1999 there were 1,945 UK companies listed on the London Stock Exchange; their equity capital had a total market value of £1,820,100 million. In addition, 499 international companies were listed, with a total equity market value of £3,577,500 million. By the end of 1999 AIM had attracted 347 companies, with a total capitalisation of £13,500 million.

UK equity turnover in 1999 was £1,410,590 million with an average 83,637 bargains and £5,597.6 million value a day. International equity turnover in 1999 totalled £2,240,134.3 million.

BIG BANG

During 1986 the London Stock Exchange went through the greatest period of change in its 200-year history. In March 1986 it opened its doors for the first time to overseas and corporate membership of the Exchange, allowing banks, insurance companies and overseas securities houses to become members of the Exchange and to buy existing member firms. On 27 October 1986, three major reforms took place, changes which became known as 'Big Bang':

- the abolition of scales of minimum commissions, allowing clients to negotiate freely with their brokers about the charge for their services
- the abolition of the separation of member firms into brokers and jobbers: firms are now broker/dealers, able to act as agents on behalf of clients; to act as principals buying and selling shares for their own account; and to become registered market makers, making continuous buying and selling prices in specific securities
- the introduction of the Stock Exchange automated quotations (SEAQ) system

Since the introduction of SEAQ in 1986, dealing in stocks and shares has taken place by telephone in the firms' own dealing rooms, rather than face to face on the floor of the Exchange. The Stock Exchange Electronic Trading Service (SETS), launched in 1997, introduced over-driven trading in which deals are executed electronically on an electronic order book. SETS runs alongside SEAQ and allows remote control access to the Exchange. The new systems also provide increased investor protection. All deals taking place via the Exchange systems are recorded on a database which can be used to resolve disputes or to carry out investigations.

Members of the London Stock Exchange buy and sell shares on behalf of the public, as well as institutions such as pension funds or insurance companies. In return for transacting the deal, the broker will charge a commission, which is usually based upon the value of the transaction. The market makers, or wholesalers, in each security do not charge a commission for their services, but will quote the broker two prices, a price at which they will buy and a price at which they will sell. It is the middle of these two prices which is published in lists of Stock Exchange prices in newspapers.

iX

On 3 May 2000 the London Stock Exchange and the Deutsche Börse announced plans to merge and create a new company called iX. iX will be based in and managed from London with major operations in Frankfurt.

iX will offer trading and information products for equities, commodities and derivatives, together with the core exchange systems technology and an increasing emphasis on new e-commerce businesses. The electronic trading platform will be the Deutsche Börse Xetra system. iX will provide the largest European stock market, with 53 per cent of traded volume and, through Eurex, the biggest derivatives market worldwide.

In addition, iX and Nasdaq have agreed to create a pan-European, high growth market. The joint venture will bring together London's techMARK and Germany's Neuer Market. It will represent Europe's biggest high growth market with a market share of around 80 per cent of traded volume. iX and Nasdaq will be equal shareholders in the venture, incorporated in and managed from London and operated in Frankfurt. At the time of going to press there was speculation as to whether the merger with Deutsche Börse would take place (*see* Events of the Year).

REGULATORY BODIES

The London Stock Exchange and the Securities and Futures Authority are the two regulatory bodies (*see* pages 635–6). They were formed under the provisions of the Financial Services Act 1986, which requires investment businesses to be authorised and regulated by a self-regulating organisation (SRO), of which the Securities and Futures Authority is one. The Act also requires business to be conducted through a recognised investment exchange (RIE). The London Stock Exchange is an RIE, regulating three main markets: UK equities, international equities and gilts. In May 2000 the UKLA, which regulates the flotation of UK companies on public markets, transferred to the Financial Services Authority.

THE GOVERNING BOARD

The London Stock Exchange has its headquarters in London, and representative offices around the UK. On 15

March 2000, the 298 members voted to become share-holders in a demutualised London Stock Exchange, making possible the formation of iX (*see* above) .

The governing board is responsible for overall policy and the strategic direction of the Exchange. The board consists of representatives drawn from listed companies, investors and other major users, elected at the annual general meeting, and the Government Broker, the Chief Executive and up to five senior executives of the Stock Exchange.

LONDON STOCK EXCHANGE LTD, Old Broad Street, London EC2N 1HP. Tel: 020-7797 1000
http://www.londonstockexchange.com

Chairman, D. Cruickshank
Chief Executive, G. Casey
Government Broker, I. Plenderleith
Other Board members, G. Allen, CBE; J. Howell; M. Marks; P. Meinertzhagen; S. Robertson; I. Salter; H. Sants; N. Sherlock; M. Wheatley

Financial Services Regulation

In May 1997 the Government decided to establish a new single statutory financial regulator responsible for the supervision of banks, building societies, insurance companies, investment firms and markets. The new regulator is the Financial Services Authority (FSA) which is in corporate and legal terms the Securities and Investments Board (SIB) renamed. The FSA replaces earlier regulatory bodies, established under a number of different statutes.

The FSA is acquiring its full range of responsibilities in two stages. The first stage was completed on 1 June 1998 when the FSA acquired responsibility, under the Bank of England Act 1998, for supervising banks, listed money market institutions and related clearing houses; the Bank of England had previously exercised this responsibility. The majority of functions previously carried out by the Insurance Directorate of HM Treasury has now been taken over by the FSA, including Lloyd's of London. The second stage follows the enactment of the Financial Services and Markets Act, which received Royal Assent on 14 June 2000. When this is implemented, a date commonly referred to as N2 which is expected to be in 2001, the FSA will acquire its full range of powers. The additional organisations whose responsibilities will be absorbed into the FSA are as follows:

SELF-REGULATING ORGANISATIONS
INVESTMENT MANAGEMENT REGULATORY
    ORGANISATION (IMRO)
PERSONAL INVESTMENT AUTHORITY (PIA)
SECURITIES AND FUTURES AUTHORITY LTD (SFA)

OTHERS
BUILDING SOCIETIES COMMISSION
FRIENDLY SOCIETIES COMMISSION
REGISTRY OF FRIENDLY SOCIETIES
RECOGNISED PROFESSIONAL BODIES (RPBs)

All the above organisations are based at the FSA's offices in Canary Wharf (see below).

The FSA also supervises the recognised professional bodies and recognised clearing houses, ensuring that they continue to fulfil their regulatory responsibilities. On 1 May 2000 the FSA took over from the London Stock Exchange the role of the UK's listing authority.

Under the new legislation the FSA will have four statutory objectives including the:

– promotion of market confidence
– raising of public awareness
– protection of consumers
– reduction of financial crime

The legislation will require the FSA to carry out its general functions, whilst having regard to:

– the need to use its resources in the most efficient way
– the responsibilities of those who manage the affairs of authorised persons
– the principle that a burden or restriction that is imposed on a person, or on the carrying of an activity, should be proportionate to the benefits expected to result.
– the desirability of facilitating innovation in connection with regulated activities
– the international character of financial services and markets and the desirability of maintaining the competitive position of the United Kingdom
– the need to minimise the adverse effects on competition that may arise from anything done in the discharge of those functions

– the desirability of facilitating competition between those who are subject to any form of regulation by the Authority

The FSA is preparing its policies, the details of regulatory approach and a single set of rules. As part of this process it is issuing a series of consultation papers and policy statements. It has also established a Practitioner Panel and Consumer Panel to advise on how its work affects the industry and consumers and various advisory groups on specific topics.

It is also the intention that, under the new legislation, there will be one compensation scheme and one Ombudsman scheme to deal with complaints.

FSA CENTRAL REGISTER/CONSUMER HELPLINE

The FSA maintains a Central Register of all firms that are, or were, authorised to carry on investment business and authorised deposit takers. The entry for each firm gives its name, address and telephone number; a reference number; its authorisation status; and states which organisation regulates it; and whether it can handle client money.

The Consumer Helpline is available to members of the public seeking information about firms listed on the Register as well as booklets or other information and assistance on financial services issues.
CONSUMER HELPLINE: 0845-606 1234

PUBLICATIONS FOR CONSUMERS

The FSA has issued a series of booklets aimed at providing generic advice to consumers and providing contact points for help and further information. These are also available on the FSA website.

THE FINANCIAL SERVICES COMPENSATION SCHEME

The Financial Services and Markets Bill will simplify the current arrangements for compensating investors where a firm authorised to carry on regulated activity is unable to meet claims against it. The six existing schemes covering depositors, policyholders and investors will be replaced by a single scheme. A new company, the Financial Services Compensation Scheme Ltd, has been set up to manage the scheme from N2. The new scheme will take over from the following existing organisations:

THE DEPOSIT PROTECTION BOARD, 25 The North
    Colonnade, Canary Wharf, London E14 5HS.
    Tel: 020-7676 0808 Fax: 020-7676 0973
THE BUILDING SOCIETIES INVESTOR PROTECTION
    SCHEME, 25 The North Colonnade, Canary Wharf,
    London E14 5HS. Tel: 020-7676 0808
    Fax: 020-7676 0973
THE INVESTORS COMPENSATION SCHEME, Cottons
    Centre, Cottons Lane, London SE1 2QB.
    Tel: 020-7367 6000 Fax: 020-7367 6001
THE S43 SCHEME, 25 North Colonnade, Canary Wharf,
    London E14 5HS. Tel: 020-7676 0808
    Fax: 020-7676 0973
THE POLICYHOLDERS PROTECTION BOARD, 5 Gresham
    Street, London EC2V 7HQ. Tel: 020-7600 3333
THE FRIENDLY SOCIETIES INVESTOR PROTECTION
    SCHEME, 10–13 Lovat Lane, London EC3R 8DT.
    Tel: 020-7937 9550

These schemes will continue to operate until N2 and will respectively deal with claims relating to deposits held by insolvent banks; claims against persons authorised under the Financial Services Act 1986 to carry on investment business and claims on protected policies of insurance where the insurer is insolvent.

FINANCIAL SERVICES AUTHORITY, 25 The North Colonnade, Canary Wharf, London E14 5HS. Tel: 020-7676 1000. Web: http://www.fsa.gov.uk
Chairman, H. Davies

AUTHORISED DEPOSIT-TAKING INSTITUTIONS

For deposit-taking institutions, *see* Banking

RECOGNISED PROFESSIONAL BODIES

Under the current legislation the FSA is empowered to recognise professional bodies (RPBs) which, as a result, can authorise their members to conduct investment business. Such business must not form the whole or main part of the total business undertaken by the firm. The RPBs are:

INSTITUTE OF CHARTERED ACCOUNTANTS IN ENGLAND AND WALES, Chartered Accountants' Hall, PO Box 433, Moorgate Place, London EC2P 2BJ. Tel: 020-7920 8100
INSTITUTE OF CHARTERED ACCOUNTANTS OF SCOTLAND, 27 Queen Street, Edinburgh EH2 1LA. Tel: 0131-225 5673
THE ULSTER SOCIETY OF THE INSTITUTE OF CHARTERED ACCOUNTANTS IN IRELAND, 11 Donegall Square South, Belfast BT1 5JE. Tel: 028-9032 1600
ASSOCIATION OF CHARTERED CERTIFIED ACCOUNTANTS, 29 Lincoln's Inn Fields, London WC2A 3EE. Tel: 020-7242 6855
INSTITUTE OF ACTUARIES, Staple Inn Hall, High Holborn, London WC1V 7QJ. Tel: 020-7242 0106
THE LAW SOCIETY, 113 Chancery Lane, London WC2A 1PL. Tel: 020-7242 1222
LAW SOCIETY OF NORTHERN IRELAND, Law Society House, 98 Victoria Street, Belfast BT1 3JZ. Tel: 028-9023 1614
LAW SOCIETY OF SCOTLAND, Law Society's Hall, 26 Drumsheugh Gardens, Edinburgh EH3 7YR. Tel: 0131-226 7411

RECOGNISED INVESTMENT EXCHANGES

Investment exchanges are exempt from needing authorisation under the Financial Services Act. A recognised investment exchange (RIE) must fulfil the following requirements: adequate financial resources; proper conduct of business rules; a proper market in its products; procedures for recording transactions; effective monitoring and enforcement of rules; proper arrangements for the clearing and performance of contracts.

TRADEPOINT STOCK EXCHANGE, 35 King Street, London WC2E 8JD. Tel: 020-7240 8000
INTERNATIONAL PETROLEUM EXCHANGE (IPE), International House, 1 St Katharine's Way, London E1 9UN. Tel: 020-7481 0643
LONDON STOCK EXCHANGE (LSE), Old Broad Street, London EC2N 1HP. Tel: 020-7623 0444
LONDON INTERNATIONAL FINANCIAL FUTURES AND OPTIONS EXCHANGE (LIFFE), Cannon Bridge, London EC4R 3XX. Tel: 020-7623 0444
LONDON METAL EXCHANGE LTD (LME), 56 Leadenhall Street, London EC3V 5AF. Tel: 020-7264 5555
THE LONDON SECURITIES AND DERIVATIVES EXCHANGE LTD (OM LONDON EXCHANGE LTD), 107 Cannon Street, London EC4N 5AF. Tel: 020-7283 0678

COREDEAL, Seven Limeharbour, Docklands, London E14 9NQ. Tel: 020-7510 2730

Following the implementation of the EC Investment Services Directive, recognition by the UK authorities is no longer required for exchanges within the European Economic Area (with certain exceptions).

RECOGNISED CLEARING HOUSES

A recognised clearing house (RCH) must satisfy similar criteria to those which apply to be an RIE. There are two RCHs which act as clearing houses for some of the above RIEs. In addition, Crest also operates a system for dematerialised settlement of share transactions.

CREST CO LTD, 33 Cannon Street, London EC4M 5SB. Tel: 020-7849 0000
LONDON CLEARING HOUSE LTD (LCH), Roman Wall House, 1–2 Crutched Friars, London EC3N 2AN. Tel: 020-7265 2000

DESIGNATED INVESTMENT EXCHANGES

The FSA has drawn up a list of 52 designated overseas investment exchanges. These are deemed to provide protection for investors of an equivalent standard to that provided by RIEs.

OMBUDSMAN SCHEMES

Independent ombudsman schemes have been set up for banks, building societies, insurance companies, financial institutions and independent financial advisers. They provide an independent and impartial method of resolving disputes that arise between a company and a customer. In most ombudsman schemes there is a council which appoints and supervises the Ombudsman. The Ombudsman Council is composed of people representing public and consumer interests and member companies. The schemes are funded in various ways: annual subscription from member companies, a levy on member companies according to the size of their assets, a charge for each complaint handled against a particular company, or a combination of these.

The Investment Ombudsman is responsible for resolving disputes that arise between a customer and a company regulated by IMRO. The Personal Investment Authority (PIA) Ombudsman is primarily responsible for resolving complaints against PIA members about personal investments.

The Pensions Ombudsman is appointed and operates under the Pension Schemes Act 1993 as amended by the Pensions Act 1995; he is responsible to Parliament. He investigates and decides complaints and disputes concerning occupational pension schemes, primarily alleged maladministration by the persons responsible for managing an occupational pension scheme. Personal pension complaints are normally dealt with only if outside the jurisdiction of the Personal Investment Authority.

The Financial Services and Markets Act will simplify the current arrangement by providing one Ombudsman to handle customers disputes, the Financial Ombudsman Service (FOS). The FOS has now been established but the existing Ombudsman schemes continue to operate until N2.

FINANCIAL OMBUDSMAN SERVICE, South Quay Plaza, 183 Marsh Wall, London E14 9SR. Tel: 020-7964 1000. Fax: 020-7964 1001. Web: http://www.financial-ombudsman.org.uk

THE OFFICE OF THE BANKING OMBUDSMAN,
70 Gray's Inn Road, London WC1X 8NB.
Tel: 020-7404 9944. *Banking Ombudsman*,
D. Thomas
THE OFFICE OF THE BUILDING SOCIETIES OMBUDSMAN,
Millbank Tower, Millbank, London SW1P 4XS.
Tel: 020-7931 0044. *Building Societies Ombudsman*,
B. Murphy
THE INSURANCE OMBUDSMAN BUREAU, City Gate One,
135 Park Street, London SE1 9EA. Tel: 020-7928 4488.
Insurance Ombudsman, W. Merricks
THE OFFICE OF THE INVESTMENT OMBUDSMAN,
6 Frederick's Place, London EC2R 8BT.
Tel: 020-7796 3065. *Investment Ombudsman*,
P. Dean, CBE
THE PENSIONS OMBUDSMAN, 6th Floor, 11 Belgrave
Road, London SW1V 1RB. Tel: 020-7834 9144. *Pensions
Ombudsman*, Dr J.T. Farrand
THE PIA OMBUDSMAN BUREAU, Hertsmere House,
Hertsmere Road, London E14 4AB. Tel: 020-7216 0016.
Principal Ombudsman, A. J. Holland; *Ombudsmen*,
R. Prior; M. Thomas

THE TAKEOVER PANEL

The Takeover Panel was set up in 1968 in response to
concern about practices unfair to shareholders in take-
over bids for public and certain private companies. Its
principal objective is to ensure equality of treatment, and
fair opportunity for all shareholders to consider on its
merits an offer that would result in the change of control of
a company. It is a non-statutory body that operates the
City code on take-overs and mergers.

The chairman, deputy chairmen and three lay members
of the panel are appointed by the Bank of England. The
remainder are representatives of the banking, insurance,
investment, pension fund and accountancy professional
bodies, the CBI, IMRO and the Stock Exchange.

THE TAKEOVER PANEL, PO Box 226, The Stock Exchange
Building, London, EC2P 2JX. Tel: 020-7382 9026.
Web: http://www.takeoverpanel.org.uk *Chairman*,
Sir David Calcutt, QC

Taxation

INCOME TAX

Income tax is charged on the taxable income of individuals for a year of assessment commencing on 6 April and ending on the following 5 April. Substantial changes have been introduced during recent years which affect both the calculation of income chargeable to tax and the rate or rates at which the amount of tax due must be determined. In view of these changes the following information is confined to the year of assessment 2000–1 ending on 5 April 2001 and has only limited application to earlier years. However, some changes affecting future years are also noted where the information is available.

An individual's liability to satisfy income tax for 2000–1 is determined by establishing the level of taxable income for the year. This income must then be allocated between three different headings, namely: (a) all income excluding that arising from savings and dividends; (b) income from savings; (c) company dividends, including distributions.

Once this allocation has been completed the first calculation must be limited to taxable income excluding that arising from both savings and dividends. This income will be reduced by an individual's personal allowance and other available allowances. The first £1,520 of taxable income remaining is assessed to income tax at the starting rate of ten per cent. The next £26,880 is taxable at the basic rate of 22 per cent. Should any excess over £28,400 (£1,520 plus £26,880) remain, this will be taxable at the higher rate of 40 per cent.

The second calculation is limited to income from savings, if any. Liability may arise at the starting rate of ten per cent, the lower rate of 20 per cent or the higher rate of 40 per cent. There is no liability to income tax at the basic rate of 22 per cent. The appropriate rate which must be used is determined by adding income from savings to other taxable income, excluding dividends. To the extent that the addition does not increase taxable income above £1,520, income from savings is taxed at the starting rate of ten per cent. Should this level be exceeded but total income does not reach £28,400 any excess remains taxable at the lower rate of 20 per cent. In those situations where the addition of savings extends total income above £28,400 the excess is taxed at the higher rate of 40 per cent.

Finally, any company dividends are taxed at either the Schedule F ordinary rate of ten per cent or the Schedule F upper rate of 32.5 per cent. The amount of dividends (with the addition of any tax credit) must be added to taxable income comprising general income together with income from savings. If this addition does not increase total taxable income above £28,400 dividends remain taxable at the ordinary rate of ten per cent only. However, if or to the extent that the addition discloses dividends exceeding the £28,400 level the excess is taxed at the upper rate of 32.5 per cent.

Trustees administering settled property and personal representatives dealing with the estate of a deceased person are chargeable to income tax at the basic rate of 22 per cent. Where trustees retain discretionary powers or income from settled property is accumulated, liability may be increased to 34 per cent. Companies residing in the UK are not liable to income tax but suffer corporation tax on income, profits and gains (see page 653).

Income arising overseas will often incur liability to foreign taxation. If that income is also chargeable to UK income tax, excessive liability could arise. The UK has concluded double taxation agreements with the governments of many foreign countries and these ensure that the same slice of income is not doubly taxed.

HUSBAND AND WIFE

A husband and wife are separately taxed, with each entitled to his or her personal allowance. A married man 'living with' his wife can only obtain a married couple's allowance, but only if, one party to the marriage was over the age of 64 years before 6 April 2000. In the absence of any claim, this allowance must be used by the husband but where any balance remains the surplus may be transferred to the wife. It is possible for a married woman to claim half the basic married couple's allowance as of right. In addition, the entire basic allowance may be claimed by the wife, if her husband so agrees.

Each spouse may obtain other allowances and reliefs where the required conditions are satisfied. Income must be accurately allocated between the couple by reference to the individual beneficially entitled to that income. Where income arises from jointly-held assets, this must be apportioned equally between husband and wife. However, in those cases where the beneficial interests in jointly-held assets are not equal, a special declaration can be made to apportion income by reference to the actual interests in that income.

SELF-ASSESSMENT

Self-assessment affects individuals, trustees and personal representatives. Central to self-assessment is the requirement to deliver a completed tax return. This must normally be submitted by 31 January following the end of the year of assessment to which the return relates. In addition to completing the return, the taxpayer must calculate the amount of income tax due. If a taxpayer wishes the Inland Revenue to calculate the tax due, the return must be forwarded to the Inland Revenue not later than the previous 30 September.

It is the responsibility of the taxpayer to submit payments of income tax on time. There are three different dates on which payments may fall due:

(a) an interim payment due on 31 January in the year of assessment itself
(b) a second interim payment due on the following 31 July
(c) a balancing payment, or possibly a repayment, on the following 31 January

The two interim payments will be based on tax payable for the previous year of assessment but liability may be reduced where income has fallen or even avoided entirely where the amounts are not substantial.

The impact of self-assessment is largely restricted to some nine million persons receiving tax returns. These comprise self-employed individuals, those receiving income from the exploitation of land in the UK, company directors, others with investment income liable to higher rate income tax, trustees and personal representatives. Elderly persons receiving small amounts of untaxed income may be excluded from the need to complete a tax return. Separate tax return forms are issued to a husband and wife, where such forms are needed.

Failure to submit completed tax returns by 31 January or to discharge payments of income tax on time will incur a liability to interest, surcharges and penalties.

INCOME TAXABLE

Income tax is assessed under several Schedules. Each Schedule determines the extent of liability and establishes the amount to be included in taxable income. In some instances the actual income arising in a year of assessment will be charged to income tax for that year.

A different basis of assessment may be used for income taxable under Cases I to V of Schedule D. For many years income was assessed under these Cases on a 'preceding year' basis. This involved measuring income for the year by reference to that arising in a previous year or period but there were special rules where a new source was acquired or an existing source discontinued. The 'preceding year' basis has been replaced by a 'current year' basis of assessment. This requires that business profits assessable under Case I or Case II of Schedule D will be those for the accounting period ending in the year of assessment, with special adjustments for the opening and closing years of a business. Other income assessable under Schedule D will be that which arises in the actual year of assessment.

Following the withdrawal of income tax liability for most commercial woodlands in the UK, Schedule B no longer applies. Schedule C has also been withdrawn as the result of further changes. The contents of the remaining schedules are shown below.

Schedule A

Tax is charged under Schedule A on the annual profits or gains arising from a business carried on for the exploitation of land in the UK. The determination of profits from a Schedule A business adopts principles identical to those used when establishing the profits or gains of a trade, profession or vocation. Rents and other income from the exploitation of land are included in the calculation, and outgoings incurred wholly and exclusively for the purposes of the Schedule A business may be deducted from income.

Schedule A does not extend to profits from farming, market gardening or woodlands, nor does it apply to mineral rents and royalties. Premiums arising on the grant of a lease for a period not exceeding 50 years in duration are treated as rents. However, the amount of the taxable premium may be reduced by two per cent for each complete year, after the first 12 months, of the leasing period. Income arising from the provision of certain furnished holiday accommodation attracts a number of tax advantages not otherwise available for most income chargeable under Schedule A.

Receipts not exceeding £4,250 annually and accruing to an individual from letting property furnished in his or her own home are usually excluded from liability to income tax.

Schedule D

This Schedule is divided into six Cases:

Cases I and II – profits arising from trades, professions and vocations, including farming and market gardening. Profits must now be calculated on an accounting basis which provides 'a true and fair view' of business results. This remains subject to any statutory adjustment which may be required. For example, only sums laid out 'wholly and exclusively' for the purposes of a business may be subtracted from receipts, notwithstanding that those outgoings may reflect a proper accounting charge. Capital expenditure incurred on assets used for business purposes will often produce an entitlement to capital allowances which reduce the profits chargeable. These profits may also be reduced by claims for loss relief and other matters.

Case III – interest on government stocks not taxed at source, interest on National Savings Bank deposits and discounts. Interest up to £70 on ordinary National Savings Bank deposits is exempt from income tax. The exemption applies to both husband and wife separately. Interest on National Savings Bank special investment accounts is not exempt. Interest and other items of savings income incur liability at the starting rate, lower rate or the higher rate depending on the level of the recipients income.

Cases IV and V – interest from overseas securities, rents, dividends and all other income accruing outside the UK. Assessment is based on the full amount of income arising, whether remitted to the UK or retained overseas, but individuals who are either not domiciled in the UK or who are ordinarily resident overseas may be taxed on a remittance basis. Overseas pensions are taxable but the amount arising may be reduced by ten per cent for assessment purposes. Interest received on most overseas investments is chargeable at the rates as those which apply to interest from sources within the UK. Overseas dividends are usually taxed at ten per cent or 32.5 per cent.

Case VI – sundry profits and annual receipts not assessed under any other Case or Schedule. These may include insurance commissions, post-cessation receipts from a discontinued business and numerous other receipts specifically charged under Case VI.

Schedule E

All earnings from an office or employment are assessable under this Schedule. There are three Cases:

Case I – applies to all earnings of an individual resident and ordinarily resident in the UK.

Case II – of application where the individual is not resident or not ordinarily resident and extends to earnings for duties undertaken in the UK.

Case III – applies in rare situations to other earnings remitted to the UK.

A 'receipts basis' applies for determining the year of assessment in which earnings must be taxed. Where earnings are assessable under Case I or Case II, the date of receipt will comprise the earlier of the date of payment, or the date entitlement arises. In the case of company directors it is the earlier of these two dates, with the addition of the following three which establish the time of receipt: the date earnings are credited in the company's books; where earnings for a period are determined after the end of that period, the date of determination; where earnings for a period are determined in that period, the last day of that period.

The earnings assessable under Schedule E include all salaries, wages, director's fees and other money sums. In addition, the value of a wide range of benefits must be added to taxable earnings. These include the provision of living accommodation on advantageous terms and advantages arising from the use of vouchers.

Further taxable benefits accrue to directors and also to employees receiving earnings of £8,500 or more in the year of assessment. Such benefits include the reimbursement of expenses, the availability of motor cars for private motoring, the provision of petrol or other fuel for private motoring, the use of vans, the provision of interest-free loans, and other benefits provided at the employer's expense. The cost of providing a limited range of child care facilities may be excluded.

In arriving at the amount to be assessed under Schedule E, all expenses incurred wholly, exclusively and necessarily in the performance of the duties, together with the cost of business travel, may be deducted. Fees and subscriptions paid to certain professional bodies and learned societies may also be deducted. Fees paid to managers by entertainers, actors and others assessable under Schedule E may be deducted, up to a maximum of 17.5 per cent of earnings.

Compensation for loss of office and other sums received on the termination of an office or employment are assessable to tax. However, the first £30,000 may be excluded with only the balance remaining chargeable, unless the compensatory payment is linked with the retirement of the recipient.

Schedule F

This Schedule is concerned with dividends and distributions received from a UK resident company.

INCOME FROM SAVINGS

Many payments of interest made by building societies and banks are received after the deduction of income tax at the lower rate of 20 per cent. However, investors not liable to income tax may arrange to receive interest gross with no tax being deducted on payment.

Interest of this nature represents 'income from savings'; an expression which also extends to interest on government securities, interest on a restricted range of National Savings products and the income element of purchased life annuities. In addition, 'income from savings'; may extend to other income of a similar nature arising outside the United Kingdom. Not all forms of investment income are included in the list, notable exceptions comprising income from letting property and company dividends.

A great deal of interest arising from sources in the United Kingdom will be received after deduction of income tax at the lower rate of 20 per cent. Although this interest is not taxable at the basic rate it remains chargeable at the starting rate of ten per cent, the lower rate of 20 per cent or the higher rate of 40 per cent. Where such interest when added to other income, excluding dividends, falls within the starting rate band tax will be due at ten per cent. As tax will have been suffered by deduction at the lower rate of 20 per cent a repayment of the excess may well be obtained from the Inland Revenue. To the extent that interest from savings when added to other income exceeds £1,520 but does not exceed £26,880 liability arises at the lower rate of 20 per cent. In those situations where, or to the extent that, income from savings when added to other income exceeds £26,880 liability arises at the higher rate of 40 per cent. As income tax will usually have been deducted at source at the rate of 20 per cent higher rate liability arises at a further 20 per cent (40 per cent less 20 per cent).

DIVIDENDS

Dividends and other distributions paid by a UK resident company have a tax credit attached equal to one-ninth of the sum received in 2000–1. Therefore a recipient shareholder also residing in the UK who receives a cash dividend of £90 will have a tax credit of £10. The gross dividend or distribution (sum received plus tax credit) is regarded as having suffered income tax, equal to the tax credit, at the rate of ten per cent. Where the shareholder is not liable, or not fully liable, to income tax it is not possible to claim a repayment of the tax credit. However, for 2000–1 dividends are taxed at the Schedule F ordinary rate of ten per cent or the Schedule F upper rate of 32.5 per cent. Where the total income of an individual is not unduly substantial the amount of the tax credit, namely ten per cent, will be offset against the Schedule F ordinary rate of

income tax, which is also ten per cent, leaving no further liability. Should the gross amount of dividends or distributions when added to other taxable income exceed £28,400 the excess is chargeable at the Schedule F upper rate of 32.5 per cent. The amount of the tax credit will then reduce tax otherwise payable at the upper rate. Although the rates of ten per cent and 32.5 per cent apply to dividends and distributions from United Kingdom companies, they also extend to income of a similar nature arising outside the UK.

INCOME NOT TAXABLE

Income which is not taxable in 2000–1 includes interest on National Savings certificates, most scholarship income, bounty payments to members of the armed services and annuities payable to the holders of certain awards. Dividend income arising from qualifying investments in personal equity plans (PEPs) and venture capital trusts is exempt from tax. Although tax credits on dividends from such trusts can no longer be recovered it is possible for PEP managers to obtain repayment of credits during the five year period ending on 5 April 2004. Income received under maintenance agreements and court orders will not be liable to tax. Nor will payments made under many deeds of covenant be recognised for tax purposes, unless the recipient is a charity. Interest arising on a tax exempt special savings account (TESSA) opened with a building society or bank will be exempt from tax if the account is maintained throughout a five-year period.

A popular investment, the individual savings account (ISA), is available to United Kingdom resident individuals aged 18 years or over. The ISA may have three components, namely cash, stocks and shares and life assurance. Interest on the cash component, usually comprising bank or building society deposits, is exempt from income tax. Dividends on most quoted buildings in the stocks and shares component are also immune from liability to income tax, with tax credits being repaid for years up to and including that ending on 5 April 2004. Income and gains accruing to the provider of the life assurance component will be free of all liability to taxation.

A maximum subscription of £7,000 can be made by an individual to an ISA during 2000–1. Of this sum no more than £3,000 can be allocated to the cash component and £1,000 to the life assurance component. Potential investors are provided with the choice whether to invest in a maxi-ISA or in mini-ISAs. Should a maxi-ISA be selected the entire £7,000 can be invested in stocks and shares, but the use of a mini-ISA limits such an investment to £3,000 with the balance of £4,000 capable of being used to invest in the cash and life assurance components.

Although no new TESSA accounts can now be opened, where an existing TESSA matures at the end of a five-year period the capital (but not the income) proceeds can be separately invested in the cash component of an ISA.

SOCIAL SECURITY BENEFITS

Many social security benefits are not liable to income tax. These include income support, maternity allowance, child benefit, war widow's pension and disability living allowance. The benefits which are taxable include the retirement pension, widow's pension, widowed mother's allowance and jobseeker's allowance. Short-term sick pay and maternity pay payable by an employer are also chargeable to tax. Incapacity benefit is chargeable to tax but no liability arises on most short term benefit.

A working families' tax credit system replaced family credit in October 1999 (*see* Social Welfare section).

PAY AS YOU EARN

The Pay As You Earn (PAYE) system is not an independent form of taxation but is designed to collect income tax by deduction from most earnings. When paying earnings to employees, an employer is usually required to deduct income tax and account for that tax to the Inland Revenue. In many cases this deduction procedure will fully exhaust the individual's liability to income tax, unless there is other income. The date of 'receipt' used for assessment purposes also identifies the date of 'payment' when establishing liability for PAYE.

The PAYE system is used to collect tax on certain payments made 'in kind'. The system is also used when collecting tax on many pensions.

ALLOWANCES

Several allowances which were available to individuals for the tax year ended on 5 April 2000 have been withdrawn entirely or modified for the following year. Those allowances which remain for 2000–1 are shown below.

Personal allowance

Basic personal allowance	£4,385
Those over 64 on 5 April 2001	£5,790
Those over 74 on 5 April 2001	£6,050

The increased allowance is available for those who died during the year of assessment but who would otherwise have achieved the appropriate age not later than 5 April 2001.

The amount of the increased personal allowance for older taxpayers will be reduced by one-half of total income in excess of £17,000. This reduction in the allowance will continue until it has been reduced to the basic personal allowance of £4,385.

The personal allowance is given as a deduction in calculating taxable income and may therefore produce relief at the rate of ten, 23 or 40 per cent, as appropriate.

Married couple's allowance

A married man who was 'living with' his wife at any time in the year ending on 5 April 2001 may be entitled to a married couple's allowance. It is a requirement before this allowance can be obtained that at least one party to the marriage reached the age of 65 years before 6 April 2000. The allowance cannot be obtained where both parties were below this age on that date, nor will it be forthcoming where a husband or wife reaches 65 on some future date.

The allowance is £5,185 if the husband or the wife satisfies the 65 year requirement. It may, however, be increased to £5,255 where either party to the marriage was 75 or over on 5 April 2001. Where an individual would otherwise have reached the age of 75 by 5 April 2001 but who died earlier in the year the increased allowance is given.

The amount of the married couple's allowance will be reduced where the income of the husband (excluding the income of the wife) exceeds £17,000. The deduction will comprise:

(a) one-half of the husband's total income in excess of £17,000, less

(b) the amount of any reduction made when calculating the husband's increased personal allowance.

This reduction in the married couple's allowance cannot reduce that allowance below the basic allowance of £2,000.

If husband and wife were married during 2000–1 the married couple's allowance must be reduced by one-twelfth for each complete month commencing on 6 April 2000 and preceding the date of marriage.

Unlike the personal allowance, the married couple's allowance does not reduce taxable income. Relief is granted by reducing the tax otherwise payable by ten per cent of the allowance. Should the amount of the reduction exceed tax otherwise payable, no tax will be due, nor will any repayment arise.

In the absence of any further action, the married couple's allowance will be given to the husband. If he is unable to utilise all or any part of that allowance due to an absence of income, the husband may transfer the unused portion to his wife. The decision whether or not to transfer remains at the discretion of the husband.

However, a wife may file an election to obtain one-half of the basic married couple's allowance of £2,000 as of right, leaving the husband with the balance of that allowance. Alternatively, the couple may jointly elect that the entire basic allowance should be allocated to the wife only. Should either spouse be unable to utilise his or her share of the total married couple's allowance the unused part may be transferred to the other spouse.

Widow's bereavement allowance

For the year of assessment in which a husband died his surviving widow could previously obtain a widow's bereavement allowance. It remained a requirement that the parties were 'living together' immediately before the husband's death. A similar allowance was available in the year following death unless the widow remarried in the year of the death.

The widow's bereavement allowance has been withdrawn for deaths occurring on and after 6 April 2000. However, where a husband died during 1999–2000 and the surviving widow remains unmarried she will be entitled to a widow's bereavement allowance of £2,000 for 2000–1.

Blind person's allowance

An allowance of £1,400 is available to an individual if at any time during the year ending on 5 April 2001, he or she was registered as blind on a register maintained by a local authority. If the individual is 'living with' a wife or husband, any unused part of the blind person's allowance can be transferred to the other spouse. The allowance reduces taxable income and may therefore give rise to relief at the taxpayer's highest rate of tax suffered.

Children's tax credit

A new allowance, the children's tax credit, is being introduced for 2001–2 and future years. This allowance will be available to a husband and wife 'living together' or a man and woman 'living together' as husband and wife. In both situations it is necessary that the couple have a qualifying child resident with them. Where these requirements are satisfied an allowance of £4,420 will be available and given at the rate of ten per cent as a deduction from income tax otherwise payable. Where the income of both members of the 'family' is insufficient to incur liability to income tax at the higher rate no further adjustments will be required. However, where one or both family members is liable to income tax at the higher rate the allowance will be allocated to the higher earner. It then becomes necessary to reduce the allowance of £4,420 by two-thirds of the higher earner's income chargeable at the higher rate.

MAINTENANCE PAYMENTS

Maintenance payments made to a separated spouse, a divorced former spouse or for the benefit of a child could previously enable the payer to obtain a range of tax reliefs. However, for payments made in 2000–1 relief is limited to £2,000 or the amount of payment, whichever is smaller.

A further requirement is that at least one of the parties to the transaction has reached his or her 65th birthday before 6 April 2000. No relief is available to younger parties. Relief is given at the rate of ten per cent and subtracted from the amount of tax otherwise due by the payer.

The maintenance payment is exempt from liability to income tax in the hands of the recipient.

INTEREST

Further reliefs may be available to an individual including payments of interest.

In some instances, interest paid by a business proprietor may be included when calculating profits chargeable to income tax under Case I or Case II of Schedule D. In addition, relief for interest paid on a loan applied to acquire or develop land and buildings for letting may be obtained by including the outlay in the calculation of income chargeable under Schedule A. However, many private individuals cannot obtain relief in this manner and must satisfy stringent requirements before relief will be forthcoming. In general terms it is a requirement that before interest can qualify for relief it must be paid for a qualifying purpose. Relief will not be available to the extent that interest exceeds a reasonable commercial rate and no relief is forthcoming for interest on an overdraft.

At earlier times many individuals could obtain relief for mortgage interest paid on loans applied to acquire a private home. However, relief of this nature ceased to apply for interest paid on or after 6 April 2000.

For 2000–1 relief for interest is restricted to the following payments:

(a) Interest on a loan used to acquire an interest in a close company or in a partnership, or to advance money to such a person

(b) Interest on a loan to a member of a partnership to acquire machinery or plant for use in the partnership business

(c) Interest on a loan to an employed person to acquire machinery or plant for the purposes of his or her employment

(d) Interest on a loan made for the purpose of contributing capital to an industrial co-operative

(e) Interest on a loan applied for investment in an employee-controlled company

(f) Interest on a loan to personal representatives to provide funds for the payment of inheritance tax

(g) Interest on a loan made to elderly persons for the purchase of an annuity where the loan is secured on land. If the loan exceeds £30,000, relief is limited to interest on this amount. This relief is restricted to income tax at the basic rate of 22 per cent. Whilst the relief remains for existing borrowers, it cannot be obtained for interest only new loans taken out after 8 March 1999

Relief under headings (a) to (f) (but not (g)) are given by deducting interest from taxable income. This enables the taxpayer to obtain relief at his or her top rate of tax suffered.

OTHER OUTGOINGS

Many employees pay contributions to an approved occupational pension scheme. The amount of their contributions may be deducted when calculating earnings assessable under Schedule E. Relief should also be available for any additional voluntary contributions paid.

Self-employed individuals and those receiving earnings not covered by an occupational pension scheme may contribute under personal pension scheme arrangements or perhaps under stakeholder schemes to be introduced shortly. Individuals may also pay premiums under retirement annuity schemes if the arrangements were concluded before 1 July 1988. Contributions paid under all headings and which do not exceed upper limits may obtain income tax relief by deduction from taxable income.

Subject to a maximum of £150,000 in 2000–1, the cost of subscribing for shares in an unquoted trading company or companies may qualify for relief under the Enterprise Investment Scheme. Many requirements must be satisfied before this relief can be obtained, but a husband and wife may each take advantage of the £150,000 maximum. Relief is given by reducing tax payable at the rate of 20 per cent of the share subscription cost. Further relief, up to a maximum of £100,000 and also given at the rate of 20 per cent, is available for a subscription of shares in a venture capital trust company.

CAPITAL GAINS TAX

An individual is potentially chargeable to capital gains tax on chargeable gains which accrue from disposals made during a year of assessment ending on 5 April. The application of the tax and the calculation of liability has been the subject of numerous changes in recent years. In recognition of these changes the following information is largely confined to the year of assessment 2000–1, ending on 5 April 2001.

Liability extends to individuals who are either resident or ordinarily resident for the year but special rules apply where a person permanently leaves the UK or comes to this territory for the purpose of acquiring residence. Non-residents are not usually liable to capital gains tax unless they carry on a business in the UK through a branch or agency. However, individuals who leave the UK after 16 March 1998 and who have been resident or ordinarily resident in at least four of the seven years preceding departure may remain liable to capital gains tax unless they reside overseas throughout a period of five complete tax years. Exceptions from this liability may apply where there is a disposal of assets acquired in the period of absence.

Trustees residing in the UK, together with personal representatives, are chargeable to capital gains tax at the rate of 34 per cent but chargeable gains accruing to companies are assessable to corporation tax.

For 1997–8 and earlier years, capital gains tax was chargeable on the net chargeable gains accruing to a person in a year of assessment after subtracting the annual exemption for that year. Net chargeable gains represented capital gains less capital losses arising from disposals carried out during the year. Unused losses brought forward from an earlier year could be offset against current net chargeable gains, but in the case of individuals were not to reduce the net gains below the annual exemption limit. It was possible to utilise trading losses against chargeable gains where those losses had not been offset against income.

TAPER RELIEF

The calculation of net gains chargeable to capital gains tax for 1998–9 and future years is now affected by taper relief. The purpose of this relief, which replaced the former indexation allowance, is to require that only a percentage of gains become chargeable to capital gains tax.

Taper relief draws a distinction between business assets and non-business assets. The expression 'business asset' broadly identifies an asset used for business purposes in addition to some holdings of shares in trading companies. Where the nature of an asset has changed during the period of ownership from a business asset to a non-business asset, or vice versa, the asset must be effectively broken down into two parts. This may be particularly relevant where the period overlaps 5 April 2000 when some non-business assets were re-classified as business assets.

The percentage which must be used to calculate taper relief is governed by the number of complete years of ownership falling after 5 April 1998. Initially an additional 'bonus year' could be added for most assets acquired before 17 March 1998. This 'bonus year' continues to apply to non-business assets but has been withdrawn where the disposal of a business asset takes place after 5 April 2000.

The maximum percentage attributable to business assets was previously achieved after an ownership period extending throughout ten years. This was reduced to one of four years only where the disposal takes place after 5 April 2000. No corresponding change was made in the percentages attributable to non-business assets. The percentages which must be used for disposals taking place after 5 April 2000 are as follows:

| No. of whole years of ownership | Percentage of gain chargeable | |
	Business assets	Non-business assets
	%	%
1	87.5	100
2	75.0	100
3	50.0	95
4	25.0	90
5	25.0	85
6	25.0	80
7	25.0	75
8	25.0	70
9	25.0	65
10	25.0	60

If only chargeable gains arise from disposals carried out in 2000–1, the taper relief, if any, must be calculated by reference to each disposal. The aggregate sum will then be subtracted from the total chargeable gains and the net sum remained reduced, or perhaps eliminated, by the annual exemption of £7,200.

Where disposals in 2000–1 produce both gains and losses, the losses must be subtracted from the gains and taper relief calculated on the net sum remaining. It is necessary to allocate the losses between the gains where there are two or more disposals, with the allocation being carried out in the most tax efficient manner. Losses brought forward from an earlier year must also be subtracted when calculating the net gains qualifying for taper relief. However, losses brought forward are not to reduce the net gains below the annual exemption of £7,200.

RATES OF TAX

The net gains remaining, if any, calculated after subtracting taper relief and the annual exemption, incur liability to capital gains tax for 2000–1. Although income tax rates are used for this purpose, liability arises only at the starting rate of ten per cent, the lower rate of 20 per cent, the higher rate of 40 per cent, or a combination of the three rates. Unlike some income tax commitments, there is no liability at the basic rate of 22 per cent.

The first step is to calculate the amount of taxable income chargeable to income tax. This will include income from savings, company dividends and all other forms of taxable income. The second step is to add the amount of net chargeable gains to the taxable income

chargeable to income tax. To the extent that this does not increase the aggregate total above £1,520, capital gains tax will be charged at the rate of ten per cent. If the aggregate total exceeds £1,520 but does not exceed £28,400 any balance needed to reach £1,520 is chargeable at ten per cent and the excess at 20 per cent. If, or to the extent that, any part of the chargeable gains exceed the limit of £28,400 the excess is chargeable at 40 per cent. Although some income tax rates are used, capital gains tax remains an entirely separate tax.

Capital gains tax for 2000–1 falls due for payment in full on 31 January 2002. If payment is delayed beyond that date, interest or surcharges may be imposed.

HUSBAND AND WIFE

Independent taxation requires that a husband and wife 'living together' are separately assessed to capital gains tax. Each spouse must independently calculate his or her gains and losses, with each entitled to the benefit of taper relief, if any, and the annual exemption of £7,200 for 2000–1. No liability to capital gains tax arises from the transfer of assets between husband and wife 'living together'.

DISPOSAL OF ASSETS

Before chargeable gains potentially liable to capital gains tax can arise, a disposal or deemed disposal of an asset must take place. This occurs not only where assets are sold or exchanged but applies on the making of a gift. There is also a disposal of assets where any capital sum is derived from assets, e.g. where compensation is received for loss or damage to an asset.

The date on which a disposal must be treated as having taken place will determine the year of assessment into which the chargeable gain or allowable loss falls. In those cases where a disposal is made under an unconditional contract, the time of disposal will be that when the contract was entered into and not the subsequent date of conveyance or transfer. A disposal under a conditional contract or option is treated as taking place when the contract becomes unconditional or the option is exercised. Disposals by way of gift are undertaken when the gift becomes effective.

VALUATION OF ASSETS

The amount actually received as consideration for the disposal of an asset will be the sum from which very limited outgoings must be deducted for the purpose of establishing the gain or loss. In cases where the consideration does not accurately reflect the value of the asset, a different basis must be used. This applies, in particular, where an asset is transferred by way of gift or otherwise than by a bargain made at arm's length. Such transactions are deemed to take place for a consideration representing market value, which will determine both the disposal proceeds accruing to the transferor and the cost of acquisition to the transferee.

Market value represents the price which an asset might reasonably be expected to fetch on a sale in the open market. In the case of unquoted shares or securities, it is to be assumed that the hypothetical purchaser in the open market would have available all the information which a prudent prospective purchaser of shares or securities might reasonably require if that person were proposing to purchase them from a willing vendor by private treaty and at arm's length. The market value of unquoted shares or securities will often be established following negotiations with the Shares Valuation Division of the Capital Taxes Office. The valuation of land and interests in land in the UK will be dealt with by the District Valuer. Special rules apply to determine the market value of shares quoted on the Stock Exchange.

DEDUCTION FOR OUTGOINGS

Once the actual or notional disposal proceeds have been determined, it only remains to subtract eligible outgoings for the purpose of computing the gain or loss. There is the general rule that any outgoings deducted, or which are available to be deducted, when calculating income tax liability must be ignored. Subject to this, deductions will usually be limited to:

(a) the cost of acquiring the asset, together with incidental costs wholly and exclusively incurred in connection with the acquisition

(b) expenditure incurred wholly and exclusively on the asset in enhancing its value, being expenditure reflected in the state or nature of the asset at the time of the disposal, and any other expenditure wholly and exclusively incurred in establishing, preserving or defending title to, or a right over, the asset

(c) the incidental costs of making the disposal

Where the disposal concerns a leasehold interest having less than 50 years to run, any expenditure falling under (a) and (b) must be written off throughout the duration of the lease.

INDEXATION ALLOWANCE

For many years an indexation allowance could be inserted when calculating a gain on the disposal of an asset. The allowance was based on percentage increases in the retail prices index between the month of March 1982, or the month in which expenditure was incurred if later, and the month of disposal. The indexation allowance calculated on this basis entered into the calculation of chargeable gain arising on the disposal of an asset. It was not possible to use the allowance to increase or to create an allowable loss.

Taper relief has largely replaced the indexation allowance for disposal made after 5 April 1998. However, where an asset was acquired before this date, the indexation allowance will be calculated to the month of April 1998 and frozen. The frozen allowance then enters into the calculation of chargeable gain, if any, when the asset is disposed of at some later date. The adjustment for the indexation allowance must be made before calculating taper relief on the net sum remaining.

EXEMPTIONS

There is a general exemption from liability to capital gains tax where the net gains of an individual for 2000–1 do not exceed £7,200. This general exemption applies separately to a husband and wife whether or not the parties are 'living together'.

The disposal of many assets will not give rise to chargeable gains or allowable losses and these assets include:

(a) private motor cars

(b) government securities

(c) loan stock and other securities (but not shares)

(d) options and contracts relating to securities within (b) and (c)

(e) National Savings Certificates, Premium Bonds, Defence Bonds and National Development Bonds

(f) currency of any description acquired for personal expenditure outside the UK

(g) decorations awarded for valour

(h) betting wins and pools, lottery or games prizes

(i) compensation or damages for any wrong or injury suffered by an individual in his/her person, profession or vocation

(j) life assurance and deferred annuity contracts where the person making the disposal is the original beneficial owner

(k) dwelling-houses and land enjoyed with the residence which is an individual's only or main residence

(l) tangible movable property, the consideration for the disposal of which does not exceed £6,000

(m) certain tangible movable property which is a wasting asset having a life not exceeding 50 years

(n) assets transferred to charities and other bodies

(o) works of art, historic buildings and similar assets

(p) assets used to provide maintenance funds for historic buildings

(q) assets transferred to trustees for the benefit of employees

(r) assets held in a Personal Equity Plan or Individual Savings Account

DWELLING-HOUSES

Exemption from capital gains tax will usually be available for any gain which accrues to an individual from the disposal of, or of an interest in, a dwelling-house or part of a dwelling-house which has been his/her only or main residence. The exemption extends to land which has been occupied and enjoyed with the residence as its garden or grounds. Some restriction may be necessary where the land exceeds half a hectare.

The gain will not be chargeable to capital gains tax if the dwelling-house, or part, has been the individual's only or main residence throughout the period of ownership, or throughout the entire period except for all or any part of the last three years. A proportionate part of the gain will be exempt in other cases if the dwelling-house has been the individual's only or main residence for part only of the period of ownership. In the case of property acquired before 31 March 1982, the period of ownership is treated as commencing on this date.

Where part of the dwelling-house has been used exclusively for business purposes, that part of the gain attributable to business use will not be exempt.

In those cases where part of a qualifying dwelling-house has been used to provide rented residential accommodation, this non-personal use may frequently be ignored when calculating exemption from capital gains tax, unless relatively substantial sums are involved.

Dwellings occupied by dependent relatives, separated spouses or divorced former spouses, may also qualify for the exemption, but only where occupation commenced before 6 April 1988.

ROLL-OVER RELIEF

Persons carrying on business will often undertake the disposal of an asset and use the proceeds to finance the acquisition of a replacement asset. Where this situation arises, a claim for roll-over relief may be available. The broad effect of such a claim is that all or part of the gain arising on the disposal of the old asset may be disregarded. The gain or part is then subtracted from the cost of acquiring the replacement asset. As this cost is reduced, any gain arising from the future disposal of the replacement asset will be correspondingly increased, unless a further roll-over situation then develops.

It remains a requirement that both the old and the replacement asset must be used for the purpose of the taxpayer's business. Relief will only be available if the acquisition of the replacement asset takes place within a period commencing 12 months before, and ending three years after, the disposal of the old asset, although the Inland Revenue retain a discretion to extend this period where the circumstances were such that it was impossible for the taxpayer to acquire the replacement asset before the expiration of the normal time limit.

Whilst many business assets qualify for roll-over relief there are exceptions.

Roll-over relief may also be available where a gain arises on the disposal of land or buildings to an authority capable to exercising compulsory purchase powers. Similar relief may be forthcoming where shares in a company are transferred to trustees administering an employees' share ownership plan for the benefit of persons employed by that company or group of companies.

Deferral Relief

A form of roll-over relief enables gains arising on the disposal of an asset to be matched, in whole or in part, with a subscription for shares in a restricted range of unquoted companies, including certain companies whose shares are dealt in on the Alternative Investment Market. Where matching can be achieved any part of the gain arising on disposal, not exceeding the cost of the qualifying share subscription, may become the subject of a claim. Unlike the usual form of roll-over relief, this claim does not eliminate or reduce the chargeable gain. It has the effect of deferring that gain until the time of some future event, which will usually be identified by the disposal of the newly acquired shares or the loss of UK residential status. The relief, referred to as deferral relief, applied also to transactions taking place before 6 April 1998 but was limited to a subscription for shares qualifying for enterprise investment scheme income tax relief.

A similar form of deferral relief is available for gains arising on other disposals which are matched with a qualifying share investment in a venture capital trust company. To the extent of the gain arising, which must not exceed the amount of the investment qualifying for income tax relief, that gain is deferred until the time of a future event, which will normally comprise the disposal of shares in the venture capital trust or the loss of UK residential status.

Hold-over Relief – Gifts

The gift of an asset is treated as a disposal made for a consideration equal to market value, with a corresponding acquisition by the transferee at an identical value. In the case of gifts made by individuals and a limited range of trustees to a transferee resident in the UK, a form of hold-over relief may be available. Relief, which must be claimed, is limited to the transfer of certain assets, including the following:

(a)   assets used for the purposes of a trade or similar activity carried on by the transferor or his/her personal company
(b)   shares or securities of a trading company which is not listed on a stock exchange
(c)   shares or securities of a trading company which is listed but which is the transferor's personal company
(d)   many interests in agricultural property qualifying for agricultural property relief for inheritance tax purposes
(e)   assets involved in transactions which are lifetime transfers for inheritance tax purposes, other than potentially exempt transfers

The transfer of shares or securities to a company is precluded from obtaining relief is made after 8 November 1999. The effect of a valid claim for hold-over relief is similar to that following a claim for roll-over relief on the disposal of business assets, but adjustments may be necessary where some consideration is given for the transfer, the asset has not been used for business purposes throughout the period of ownership, or not all assets of a company are used for business purposes.

Retirement Relief

Retirement relief is available to an individual who disposes by way of sale or gift of the whole or part of a business. The isolated disposal of assets used for the purpose of a business will not necessarily represent the disposal of the whole or part of a business. The main condition for granting this relief is that throughout a period of at least one year the business has been owned either by the individual or by a trading company in which the individual retained a sufficient shareholding interest. The relief extends also to cases where an individual disposes by way of sale or gift of shares or securities of a company. It must be demonstrated that the company was a trading company, that the individual retained a sufficient shareholding interest, and that he/she was engaged as a full-time working officer or employee.

An individual who has attained the age of 50 years at the time of a disposal may obtain substantial retirement relief which shelters gains from liability to capital gains tax. Maximum relief was available for disposals taking place not later than 5 April 1999. The amount of relief then reduces on an annual basis before being abolished entirely for disposals taking place on and after 6 April 2003.

No retirement relief will be forthcoming if the disposal occurs before the individual's 50th birthday, except where an individual is compelled to retire early on the grounds of ill-health.

Retirement relief must be subtracted from the net gains arising on disposal, leaving the balance, if any, chargeable to capital gains tax in the normal manner. Taper relief applies only to this balance of net gains and not to the calculation of gains eliminated by retirement relief.

Death

No capital gains tax is chargeable on the value of assets retained at the time of death. However, the personal representatives administering the deceased's estate are deemed to acquire those assets for a consideration representing market value on death. This ensures that any increase in value occurring before the date of death will not be chargeable to capital gains tax. If a legatee or other person acquires an asset under a will or intestacy no chargeable gain will accrue to the personal representatives, and the person taking the asset will also be treated as having acquired it at the time of death for its then market value.

INHERITANCE TAX

Liability to inheritance tax may arise on a limited range of lifetime gifts and other dispositions and also on the value of assets retained, or deemed to be retained, at the time of death. An individual's domicile at the time of any gift or on death is an important matter. Domicile will generally be determined by applying normal rules, although special considerations may be necessary where an individual was previously domiciled in the UK but subsequently acquired a domicile of choice overseas. In addition, individuals who have been resident in the UK for at least 17 of the previous 20 years at the time of an event are treated as domiciled in the UK for this purpose.

Where a person was domiciled, or treated as domiciled, in the UK at the time of a disposition or on death the location of assets is immaterial and full liability to inheritance tax arises. Individuals domiciled outside the UK are, however, chargeable to inheritance tax only on transactions affecting assets located in the UK.

The assets of husband and wife are not merged for inheritance tax purposes. Each spouse is treated as a separate individual entitled to receive the benefit of his or her exemptions, reliefs and rates of tax. Where husband and wife retain similar assets, e.g. shares in the same family company, special 'related property' provisions may require the merger of those assets for valuation purposes only.

LIFETIME GIFTS AND DISPOSITIONS

Gifts and dispositions made during lifetime fall under four broad headings, namely:
(a) dispositions which are not transfers of value
(b) exempt transfers
(c) potentially exempt transfers
(d) chargeable transfers

Dispositions which are not transfers of value

Several lifetime transactions are not treated as transfers of value and may be entirely disregarded for inheritance tax purposes. These include transactions not intended to confer gratuitous benefit, the provision of family maintenance, the waiver of the right to receive remuneration or dividends, and the grant of agricultural tenancies for full consideration.

Exempt transfers

Certain transfers are treated as exempt transfers and incur no liability to inheritance tax. The main exempt transfers are listed below:

Transfers between spouses – Transfers between husband and wife are usually exempt. However, if the transferor is, but the transferee spouse is not, domiciled in the UK, transfers will be exempt only to the extent that the total does not exceed £55,000. Unlike the requirement used for income tax and capital gains tax purposes, it is immaterial whether husband and wife are living together.

Annual exemption – The first £3,000 of gifts and other dispositions made in a year ending on 5 April is exempt. If the exemption is not used, or not wholly used, in any year the balance may be carried forward to the following year only. The annual exemption will only be available for a potentially exempt transfer if that transfer becomes chargeable by reason of the donor's subsequent death.

Small gifts – Outright gifts of £250 or less to any person in one year ending on 5 April are exempt.

Normal expenditure – A transfer made during lifetime and comprising normal expenditure is exempt. To obtain this exemption it must be shown that:
(a) the transfer was made as part of the normal expenditure of the transferor;
(b) taking one year with another, the transfer was made out of income; and
(c) after allowing for all transfers of value forming part of normal expenditure the transferor was left with sufficient income to maintain his or her usual standard of living

Gifts in consideration of marriage – These are exempt if they satisfy certain requirements. The amount allowed will be governed by the relationship between the donor and a party to the marriage. The allowable amounts comprise:
(a) gifts by a parent, £5,000
(b) gifts by a grandparent, £2,500
(c) gifts by a party to the marriage, £2,500
(d) gifts by other persons, £1,000

Gifts to charities – These are exempt from liability.

Gifts to political parties – Gifts which satisfy certain requirements are generally exempt.

Gifts for national purposes – Gifts made to certain bodies are exempt from liability. These bodies include, among others, the National Gallery, the British Museum, the National Trust, the National Art Collections Fund, the National Heritage Memorial Fund, the Historic Buildings and Monuments Commission for England (English Heritage), any local authority, and any university or university college in the UK.

A number of other gifts made for the public benefit are also exempt.

Potentially exempt transfers

Lifetime gifts and dispositions which are neither to be ignored nor comprise exempt transfers incur possible liability to inheritance tax. However, relief is available for a range of potentially exempt transfers. These comprise gifts made by an individual to:
(a) a second individual
(b) trustees administering an accumulation and maintenance trust
(c) trustees administering a disabled person's trust

The accumulation and maintenance trust mentioned in (b) must provide that on reaching a specified age, not exceeding 25 years, a beneficiary will become absolutely entitled to trust assets or obtain an interest in possession in the income from those assets.

Additions to the above list affect settled property administered by trustees where an individual, or individuals, retain an interest in possession. The transfer of assets to, the removal of assets from, or the rearrangement of interests in such property comprise potentially exempt transfers if the person transferring an interest and the person benefiting from the transfer are both individuals.

No immediate liability to inheritance tax will arise on the making of a potentially exempt transfer. Should the donor survive for a period of seven years, immunity from liability will be confirmed. However, the donor's death within the seven-year *inter vivos* period produces liability if the amounts involved are sufficiently substantial (*see* below).

Chargeable transfers

Any remaining lifetime gifts or dispositions which are neither to be ignored nor represent exempt transfers or potentially exempt transfers, incur liability to inheritance tax.

GIFTS WITH RESERVATION

A lifetime gift of assets made at any time after 17 March 1986 may incur additional liability to inheritance tax if the donor retains some interest in the subject matter of the gift. This may arise, for example, where a parent transfers a dwelling-house to a son or daughter and continues to occupy the property or to enjoy some benefit from that property. The retention of a benefit may be ignored where it is enjoyed in return for full consideration, perhaps a commercial rent, or where the benefit arises from changed circumstances which could not have been foreseen at the time of the original gift. The gift with reservation provisions will not usually apply to most exempt transfers.

There are three possibilities which may arise where the donor reserves or enjoys some benefit from the subject matter of a previous gift and subsequently dies, namely:
(a) if no benefit is enjoyed within a period of seven years before death there can be no further liability
(b) if the benefit ceased to be enjoyed within a period of seven years before the date of death, the original donor is deemed to have made a potentially exempt transfer representing the value of the asset at the time of cessation
(c) if the benefit is enjoyed at the time of death, the value of the asset must be included in the value of the deceased's estate on death

It must be emphasised that the existence of a benefit enjoyed at any time within a period of seven years before death will establish liability to tax on gifts with reservation, notwithstanding that the gift may have been made many years earlier, providing it was undertaken after 17 March 1986.

DEATH

Immediately before the time of death an individual is deemed to make a transfer of value. This transfer will comprise the value of assets forming part of the deceased's estate after subtracting most liabilities. Any exempt transfers may, however, be excluded. These include transfers for the benefit of a surviving spouse, a charity and a qualifying political party, together with bequests to approved bodies and for national purposes.

Death may also trigger three additional liabilities:

(a) A potentially exempt transfer made within the period of seven years ending on death loses its potential status and becomes chargeable to inheritance tax

(b) The value of gifts made with reservation may incur liability if any benefit was enjoyed within a period of seven years preceding death

(c) Additional tax may become payable for chargeable lifetime transfers made within seven years before death

VALUATIONS

The valuation of assets establishes the value transferred for lifetime dispositions and also the value of a person's estate at the time of death. The value of property will represent the price which might reasonably be expected from a sale in the open market.

In some cases it may be necessary to incorporate the value of 'related property'. This will include property comprised in the estate of the transferor's spouse and certain property previously transferred to charities. The purpose of the related property valuation rules is not to add the value of the property to the estate of the transferor. Related property must be merged to establish the aggregate value of the respective interests and this value is then apportioned, usually on a *pro rata* basis, to the separate interests.

The value of shares and securities listed on the Stock Exchange will be determined by extracting figures from the daily list of official prices.

Where quoted shares and securities are sold or the quotation is suspended within a period of 12 months following the date of death, a claim may be made to substitute the proceeds or subsequent value for the value on death. This claim will only be beneficial if the gross proceeds realised are lower or the value has fallen below market value at the time of death. A similar claim may be available for interests in land sold within a period of four years following death.

RELIEF FOR SELECTED ASSETS

Special relief is made available for certain assets, notably:

Woodlands

Where woodlands pass on death the value will usually be included in the deceased's estate. However, an election may be made in respect of land in the UK on which trees or underwood is growing to delete the value of those assets. Relief is confined to the value of trees or underwood and does not extend to the land on which they are growing. Liability to inheritance tax will arise if and when the trees or underwood are sold.

Agricultural property

Relief is available for the agricultural value of agricultural property. Such property must be occupied and used for agricultural purposes and relief is confined to the agricultural value only.

The value transferred, either on a lifetime gift or on death, must be determined. This value may then be reduced by a percentage. For events taking place after 9 March 1992, a 100 per cent deduction will be available if the transferor retained vacant possession or could have obtained that possession within a period of 12 months following the transfer. In other cases, notably including land let to tenants, a lower deduction of 50 per cent is usually available. However, this lower deduction may be increased to 100 per cent if the letting was made after 31 August 1995.

It remains a requirement that the agricultural property was either occupied by the transferor for the purposes of agriculture throughout a two-year period ending on the date of the transfer, or was owned by him/her throughout a period of seven years ending on that date and also occupied for agricultural purposes.

Business property

Where the value transferred is attributable to relevant business property, that value may be reduced by a percentage. The reduction in value applies to:

(a) property consisting of a business or an interest in a business (i.e. a partnership)

(b) shares or securities of an unquoted company which provided the transferor with more than 25 per cent of voting rights

(c) other unquoted shares or securities

(d) shares or securities of a quoted company which provided the transferor with control

(e) any land, building, machinery or plant which, immediately before the transfer, was used wholly or mainly for the purposes of a business carried on by a company of which the transferor had control

(f) any land, building, machinery or plant which, immediately before the transfer, was used wholly or mainly for the purposes of a business carried on by a partnership of which the transferor was a partner

(g) any land, building, machinery or plant which, immediately before the transfer, was used wholly or mainly for the purposes of a business carried on by the transferor and was then settled property in which he/she retained an interest in possession

For events occurring after 9 March 1992, a deduction of 100 per cent is available for assets falling within (a) and (b). The deduction for unquoted shares in (c) is 100 per cent for events taking place after 5 April 1996. A deduction of 50 per cent remains for assets within (d) to (g).

It is a general requirement that the property must have been retained for a period of two years before the transfer or death and restrictions may be necessary if the property has not been used wholly for business purposes. The same property cannot obtain both business property relief and the relief available for agricultural property.

CALCULATION OF TAX PAYABLE

The calculation of inheritance tax payable adopts the use of a cumulative total. Each chargeable lifetime transfer is added to the total with a final addition made on death. The top slice added to the total for the current event determines the rate at which inheritance tax must be paid. However, the cumulative total will only include transfers made within a period of seven years before the current event and those undertaken outside this period must be excluded.

Lifetime chargeable transfers

The value transferred by the limited range of lifetime chargeable transfers must be added to the seven-year cumulative total to calculate whether any inheritance tax is due. Should the nil rate band be exceeded, tax will be imposed on the excess at the rate of 20 per cent. However, if the donor dies within a period of seven years from the date of the chargeable lifetime transfer, additional tax may be due. This is calculated by applying tax at the full rate or 40 per cent in substitution for the rate of 20 per cent previously used. The amount of tax is then reduced to a percentage by applying tapering relief. This percentage is governed by the number of years from the date of the lifetime gift to the date of death, as follows:

Period of years before death	
Not more than 3	100%
More than 3 but not more than 4	80%
More than 4 but not more than 5	60%
More than 5 but not more than 6	40%
More than 6 but not more than 7	20%

Should this exercise produce liability greater than that previously paid at the 20 per cent rate on the lifetime transfer, additional tax, representing the difference, must be discharged. Where the calculation shows an amount falling below tax paid on the lifetime transfer, no additional liability can arise nor will the shortfall become repayable.

Tapering relief will, of course, only be available if the calculation discloses a liability to inheritance tax. There can be no liability to the extent that the lifetime transfer falls within the nil rate band.

Potentially exempt transfers

Where a potentially exempt transfer loses immunity from liability due to the donor's death within the seven-year *inter vivos* period, the value transferred by that transfer enters into the cumulative total. Any liability to inheritance tax will be calculated by applying the full rate of 40 per cent, reduced to the percentage governed by tapering relief if the original transfer occurred more than three years before death. Liability can only arise to the extent, if any, that the nil rate band is exceeded.

Death

The final addition to the seven-year cumulative total will comprise the value of an estate on death. Inheritance tax will be calculated by applying the full rate of 40 per cent to the extent the nil rate band is exceeded. No tapering relief can be obtained.

RATES OF TAX

In earlier times there were several rates of inheritance tax which progressively increased as the value transferred grew in size. However, since 1988 there have been only three rates, namely:

(a) a nil rate
(b) a lifetime rate of 20 per cent
(c) a full rate of 40 per cent

The nil rate band usually changes on an annual basis and for events taking place after 5 April 2000 applies to the first £234,000. Any excess over this level is taxable at 20 per cent or 40 per cent as the case may be.

PAYMENT OF TAX

Inheritance tax usually falls due for payment six months after the end of the month in which the chargeable transaction takes place. Where a transfer other than that made on death occurs after 5 April and before the following 1 October, tax falls due on the following 30 April, although there are some exceptions to this.

Inheritance tax attributable to the transfer of certain land, controlling shareholding interests, unquoted shares, businesses and interests in businesses, together with agricultural property, may usually be satisfied by instalments spread over ten years. Except in the case of non-agricultural land, where interest is charged on outstanding instalments, no liability to interest arises where tax is paid on the due date. In all cases, delay in the payment of tax may incur as liability to discharge interest.

SETTLED PROPERTY

Complex rules apply to establish inheritance tax liability on settled property. Where a person is beneficially entitled to an interest in possession, that person is effectively deemed to own the property in which the interest subsists. It follows that where the interest comes to an end during the beneficiary's lifetime and some other person becomes entitled to the property or interest, the beneficiary is treated as having made a transfer of value. However, this will usually comprise a potentially exempt transfer. In addition, no liability will arise where the property vests in the absolute ownership of the previous beneficiary. The death of a person entitled to an interest in possession will require the value of the underlying property to be added to the value of the deceased's estate.

In the case of other settled property where there is no interest in possession (e.g. discretionary trusts), liability to tax will arise on each ten-year anniversary of the trust. There will also be liability if property ceases to be held on discretionary trusts before the first ten-year anniversary date is reached or between anniversaries. The rate of tax suffered will be governed by several considerations, including previous dispositions made by the settlor of the trust, transactions concluded by the trustees, and the period throughout which property has been held in trust.

Accumulation and maintenance settlements which require assets to be distributed, or interests in income to be created, not later than a beneficiary's 25th birthday may be exempt from any liability to inheritance tax.

CORPORATION TAX

Profits, gains and income accruing to companies resident in the UK incur liability to corporation tax. Non-resident companies are immune from this tax unless they carry on a trade in the UK through a permanent establishment, branch or office. Companies residing outside the UK may be liable to income tax at the basic rate on other income arising in the UK, perhaps from letting property. The following comments are confined to companies resident in the UK.

Liability to corporation tax is governed by the profits, gains or income for an accounting period. This is usually the period for which financial accounts are made up, and in the case of companies preparing accounts to the same accounting date annually will comprise successive periods of 12 months.

RATE OF TAX

The amount of profits or income for an accounting period must be determined on normal taxation principles. The special rules which apply to individuals where a source of income is acquired or discontinued are ignored and consideration is confined to the actual profits or income for an accounting period.

The rate of corporation tax is fixed for a financial year ending on 31 March. Where the accounting period of a company overlaps this date and there is a change in the rate of corporation tax, profits and income must be apportioned.

The full rate of corporation tax for each of the financial years ending on 31 March 1998 and 31 March 1999 was 31 per cent. This reduced to 30 per cent for each of the years ending on 31 March 2000 and 31 March 2001.

SMALL COMPANIES' RATE

Where the profits of a company do not exceed stated limits, corporation tax becomes payable at the small companies' rate. This may be replaced by a lower starting rate where profits are very small, as discussed later. It is the amount of profits and not the size of the company which governs the application of both the small companies' rate and the starting rate.

For each of the financial years ending on 31 March 1998 and 31 March 1999 the small companies' rate was 21 per cent. It then reduced to 20 per cent for each of the years ending on 31 March 2000 and 31 March 2001.

The level of profits which a company may derive without losing the benefit of the small companies' rate is £300,000 for each of the four years. However, if profits exceed £300,000 but fall below £1,500,000, marginal small companies' rate relief applies. The effect of marginal relief is that the average rate of corporation tax imposed on all profits steadily increases from the lower small companies' rate to the full rate of 31 or 30 per cent, with tax being imposed on profits in the margin at an increased rate. Where a change in the rate of tax is introduced and the accounting period of a company overlaps 31 March, profits must be apportioned to establish the appropriate rate for each part of those profits.

The lower limit of £300,000 and the upper limit of £1,500,000 apply to a period of 12 months and must be proportionally reduced for shorter periods. Some restriction in the small companies' rate and the marginal rate may be necessary if there are two or more associated companies, namely companies under common control. The small companies' rate is not available for close investment-holding companies.

COMPANIES' STARTING RATE

A new companies' starting rate was introduced for the financial year commencing on 1 April 2000 and ending on 31 March 2001. This requires that where profits of a 12 month period do not exceed £10,000 a starting rate of ten per cent will apply. Marginal relief is available where profits exceed £10,000 but do not exceed £50,000. Here also restrictions apply where the accounting period is less than 12 months, there are associated companies or a company retains close investment-holding status.

PAYMENT OF TAX

Corporation tax charged on profits for an accounting period usually falls due for payment in a single lump sum nine months after the end of that period. Most companies discharge corporation tax on this basis but other arrangements concern large companies for accounting periods ending on or after 1 July 1999. These companies must discharge their liability by four instalments. The receipt of annual profits amounting to £1,500,000 or more is sufficient to identify a large company. Where a company is a member of a group the profits of the entire group must be merged to establish whether the company is large.

CAPITAL GAINS

Chargeable gains arising to a company are calculated in a manner similar to that used for individuals. However, the withdrawal of the indexation allowance after April 1998 and the introduction of taper relief have no application to companies. Nor are companies entitled to the annual exemption of £7,200. Companies do not suffer capital gains tax on chargeable gains but incur liability to corporation tax. Tax is due on the full chargeable gain of an accounting period after subtracting relief for losses, if any.

DISTRIBUTIONS

Dividends and other qualifying distributions made by a UK resident company on or after 6 April 1999 are not satisfied after deduction of income tax. Similar outgoings made by a company previously required the payment of advance corporation tax but this obligation no longer applies. The only effect which the payment of a dividend or the making of a distribution now has on a company is that the outlay cannot form an ingredient in the calculation of profits.

INTEREST

On making many payments of interest a company is required to deduct income tax at the lower rate of 20 per cent and account for the tax deducted to the Inland Revenue. The gross amount of interest paid will usually be included in the calculation of profits on which corporation tax becomes payable.

GROUPS OF COMPANIES

Each company within a group is separately charged to corporation tax on profits, gains and income. However, where one group member realises a loss, other than a capital loss, a claim may be made to offset the deficiency against profits of some other member of the same group.

Claims are also available to deduction of income tax on the payment of interest, for transactions between members of a group of companies. The transfer of capital assets from one member of a group to a fellow member will usually incur no liability to tax on chargeable gains.

COMPLIANCE

For several years a 'pay and file' system affected all companies. A feature of this system required that tax should be payable nine months following the end of the accounting period involved with accounts and returns being submitted three months later. Failure to satisfy corporation tax or to submit documents within these time limits could result in a liability to discharge interest and penalties. This system has been replaced following the introduction of self-assessment which extends to all companies for accounting periods ending after 30 June 1999.

VALUE ADDED TAX

Value added tax (VAT) is charged on the value of the supplies made by a registered trader and extends to both the supply of goods and the supply of services. It is administered by Customs and Excise.

Liability to account for VAT arises on the value of goods imported into the UK from sources outside the European Community. In contrast goods imported by a trader from a second trader in a member state of the European Community attract no VAT on importation. Instead there is an acquisition tax whereby a trader who acquires goods must include the acquisition in his normal VAT return and account for the tax due. A UK trader who exports goods to a member state will not be required to account for VAT on the supply, if that trader observes the requirements laid down by regulations.

REGISTRATION

All traders, including professional men and women and companies, making taxable supplies of a value exceeding stated limits are required to register for VAT purposes. Taxable supplies represent the supply of goods and services potentially chargeable with VAT. The limits which govern mandatory registration are amended periodically, and from 1 April 2000 an unregistered trader must register:

(a) at any time, if there are reasonable grounds for believing that the value of taxable supplies in the next 30 days will exceed £52,000

(b) at the end of any month if the value of taxable supplies in the 12 months then ending has exceeded £52,000.

Liability to register under (b) may be avoided if it can be shown that the value of supplies in the period of 12 months then beginning will not exceed £50,000. There may, however, be liability to register immediately where a business is taken over from another trader as a 'going concern'. Other limits apply where goods are acquired from within the European Community.

Where the limits governing mandatory registration have been exceeded, the trader must notify Customs and Excise. In the event of failure to provide prompt notification, the person concerned will be required to account for VAT from the proper registration date.

A trader whose taxable supplies do not reach the mandatory registration limits may apply for voluntary registration. This step may be thought advisable to recover input tax or to compete with other registered traders.

A registered trader may submit an application for deregistration if the value of taxable supplies subsequently falls. From 1 April 2000, an application for deregistration can be made if the value of taxable supplies for the year beginning on the application date is not expected to exceed £50,000.

INPUT TAX

A registered trader will both suffer tax (input tax) when obtaining goods or services for the purposes of his business and also become liable to account for tax (output tax) on the value of goods and services which he/she supplies. Relief can usually be obtained for input tax suffered, either by setting that tax against output tax due or by repayment. Most items of input tax can be relieved in this manner but there are exceptions, including the prohibition of relief for the cost of business entertaining. Where a registered trader makes both exempt supplies and taxable supplies to his customers or clients, there may be some restriction in the amount of input tax which can be recovered.

OUTPUT TAX

When making a taxable supply of goods or services, a registered trader must account for output tax, if any, on the value of the supply. Usually the price charged by the registered trader will be increased by adding VAT but failure to make the required addition will not remove liability to account for output tax.

The liability to account for output tax, and also relief for input tax, may be affected where a trader is using a special second-hand goods scheme.

EXEMPT SUPPLIES

No VAT is chargeable on the supply of goods or services which are treated as exempt supplies. These include the provision of burial and cremation facilities, insurance, finance and education. The granting of a lease to occupy land or the sale of land will usually comprise an exempt supply, but there are numerous exceptions. In particular, the sale of new non-domestic buildings or certain buildings used by charities cannot be treated as exempt supplies.

A taxable person may elect to tax rents and other supplies relating to buildings and agricultural land not used for residential or charitable purposes.

Exempt supplies do not enter into the calculation of taxable supplies which governs liability to mandatory registration. Such supplies made by a registered trader may, however, limit the amount of input tax which can be relieved. It is for this reason that the election may be useful.

RATES OF TAX

Two rates of VAT have applied since 1 April 1991, namely:
(a) a zero, or nil, rate
(b) a standard rate of 17.5 per cent

In addition, a special reduced rate of eight per cent applied to supplies of domestic fuel after March 1994. This rate was reduced to five per cent for supplies made after 1 September 1997. On 1 July 1998 a reduced rate of five per cent was introduced for the installation of some energy saving materials in certain homes. This rate was extended to such installations in all homes on 1 April 2000.

ZERO-RATING

A large number of supplies are zero-rated. The following list is not exhaustive but indicates the wide range of supplies which may be included under this heading:

(a) the supply of many items of food and drink for human consumption. This does not include ice creams, chocolates, sweets, potato crisps and alcoholic drinks. Nor does it extend to supplies made in the course of catering or to items supplied for consumption in a restaurant or café. Whilst the supply of cold items, e.g. sandwiches for consumption away from the supplier's premises, is zero-rated, the supply of hot food, e.g. fish and chips, is not

(b) animal feeding stuffs

(c) sewerage and water, unless for industrial purposes

(d) books, brochures, pamphlets, leaflets, newspapers, maps and charts

(e) talking books for the blind and handicapped, and wireless sets for the blind

(f) supplies of services, other than professional services, when constructing a new domestic building or a building to be used by a charity. The supply of materials for such a building is zero-rated, together with the sale or the grant of a long lease. Alterations to some protected buildings are zero-rated

(g) the transportation of persons in a vehicle, ship or aircraft designed to carry not less than 12 persons

(h) supplies of drugs, medicines and other aids for the handicapped

(i) supplies of clothing and footwear for young persons

(j) exports

Although no tax is due on a zero-rated supply, this does comprise a taxable supply which must be included in the calculation governing liability to register.

COLLECTION OF TAX

Registered traders submit VAT returns for accounting periods usually of three months duration but arrangements can be made to submit returns on a monthly basis. Very large traders must account for tax on a monthly basis but this does not affect the three-monthly return. The return will show both the output tax due for supplies made by the trader in the accounting period and also the input tax for which relief is claimed. If the output tax exceeds input tax the balance must be remitted with the VAT return. Where input tax suffered exceeds the output tax due the registered trader may claim recovery of the excess from Customs and Excise.

This basis for collecting tax explains the structure of VAT. Where supplies are made between registered traders the supplier will account for an amount of tax which will usually be identical to the tax recovered by the person to whom the supply is made. However, where the supply is made to a person who is not a registered trader there can be no recovery of input tax and it is on this person that the final burden of VAT eventually falls.

Where goods are acquired by a UK trader from a supplier within a member state of the European Community, the trader must also account for the tax due on acquisition.

An optional scheme is available for registered traders having an annual turnover of taxable supplies not exceeding £300,000. Such traders may render returns annually. Nine interim payments of VAT will be made on account, with a final balancing payment accompanying submission of the return. The number of interim payments may be reduced if turnover does not exceed £100,000.

BAD DEBTS

Many retailers operate special retail schemes for calculating the amount of VAT due. These schemes are based on the volume of consideration received in an accounting period. Should a customer fail to pay for goods or services supplied, there will be no consideration on which to calculate VAT .

To avoid the problem of bad debts incurred by traders not operating a special retail scheme, an optional system of cash accounting is available. This scheme, confined to traders with annual taxable supplies not exceeding £350,000, enables returns to be made on a cash basis, in substitution for the normal supply basis. Traders using such a scheme will not include bad debts in the calculation of cash receipts.

Where neither the cash accounting arrangements nor a special retail scheme applies, output tax falls due on the value of the supply and liability is not affected by failure to receive consideration. However, where a debt is more than six months old, relief for bad debts will be forthcoming. The calculation of the six-month period commences from the date on which payment for the supply falls due.

In those cases where a supplier obtains relief for a bad debt, the person to whom the supply has been made must refund to Customs and Excise any input tax relief which may have been granted.

OTHER SPECIAL SCHEMES

In addition to the schemes for retailers, there are several special schemes applied to calculate the amount of VAT due and which also limit the ability to recover input tax. The supply of virtually all second-hand goods has now been brought with special margin schemes.

FARMERS

Farmers may elect to apply a special flat rate scheme. This scheme is available to farmers who are not registered traders. Under the scheme a flat-rate addition of four per cent may be made on sales, with the amount of the addition being retained by the farmer. Registered traders to whom such a supply is made may treat the four per cent as recoverable input tax.

Legal Notes

IMPORTANT

These notes outline certain aspects of the law as they might affect the average person. They are intended only as a broad guideline and are by no means definitive. The law is constantly changing so expert advice should always be taken. In some cases, sources of further information are given in these notes.

It is always advisable to consult a solicitor without delay; timely advice will set your mind at rest but sitting on your rights can mean that you lose them. Anyone who does not have a solicitor already can contact the Citizens' Advice Bureau, the Community Legal Service (http://www.legalservices.gov.uk), the Law Society of England and Wales (113 Chancery Lane, London WC2A 1PL) or the Law Society of Scotland (26 Drumsheugh Gardens, Edinburgh EH3 7YR) for assistance in finding one.

The community legal service fund and legal aid and assistance schemes exist to make the help of a lawyer available to those who would not otherwise be able to afford one. Entitlement depends on an individual's means but a solicitor or Citizens' Advice Bureau will be able to advise about entitlement.

ADOPTION OF CHILDREN

In England and Wales the adoption of children is mainly governed by the Adoption Act 1976 and the Children Act 1989.

Anyone over 21 can legally adopt a child. Married couples must adopt 'jointly', unless one partner cannot be found, is incapable of making an application, or if a separation is likely to be permanent. Unmarried couples may not adopt 'jointly' although one partner in that couple may adopt. The only organisations allowed to arrange adoptions are the social services departments of local authorities or voluntary agencies which are registered with the local authorities.

Once an adoption has been arranged, a court order is necessary to make it legal. These are obtained from the High Court (Family Division) or from a county or family proceedings court. The child's natural parents (or guardians) must consent to the adoption, unless the court dispenses with the consent, e.g. where the natural parent has neglected the child or is incapable of giving consent. Once adopted, the child has the same status as a child born to the adoptive parents and the natural parents cease to have any rights or responsibilities where the child is concerned. The adopted child will be treated as the natural child of the adoptive parents for the purposes of intestate succession, national insurance, family allowances, etc. The adopted child ceases to have any rights to the estates of his/her natural parents.

REGISTRATION AND CERTIFICATES

All adoptions in England and Wales are registered in the Adopted Children Register kept by the Office of National Statistics, and by the General Register Office for Scotland. Certificates from the registers can be obtained in a similar way to birth certificates.

TRACING NATURAL PARENTS OR CHILDREN WHO HAVE BEEN ADOPTED

An adult adopted person may apply to the Registrar-General for information to enable him/her to obtain a full birth certificate. For those adopted before 12 November 1975 it is obligatory to receive counselling services before this information is given; for those adopted after that date counselling services are optional. There is also an Adoption Contact Register (created after the 1989 Act) in which details of adult adopted people and of their relatives may be recorded. The BAAF can provide addresses of organisations which offer advice, information and counselling to adopted people, adoptive parents and people who have had their children adopted.

SCOTLAND

The relevant legislation is the Adoption (Scotland) Act 1978 (as amended by the Children Act 1995) and the provisions are similar to those described above. In Scotland, petitions for adoption are made to the Sheriff Court or the Court of Session.

Further information can be obtained from:
BRITISH AGENCIES FOR ADOPTION AND FOSTERING (BAAF), Skyline House, 200 Union Street, London SE1 0LX. Tel: 020-7593 2000
SCOTTISH ADOPTION ADVICE SERVICE
16 Sandyford Place, Glasgow G3 7NB
Tel: 0141-339 0772

BIRTHS (REGISTRATION)

The birth of a child must be registered within 42 days of birth at the register office of the district in which the baby was born. In England and Wales it is possible to give the particulars to be registered at any other register office. Responsibility for registering the birth rests with the parents, except in the case of an illegitimate child, when the mother is responsible for registration. Responsibility rests firstly with the parents (in Scotland, if the father of the child is not married to the mother and has not been married to her since the child's conception, the mother alone is responsible for registration) but if they fail, particulars may be given to the registrar by:
– a relative of either parent (in Scotland only)
– the occupier of the house in which the baby was born
– a person present at the birth
– the person having charge of the child
Failure to register the birth within 42 days without reasonable cause may leave the parents liable to a penalty in England and Wales and may lead to a court decree being granted by a sheriff in Scotland.

If the parents were married at the time of the birth, either parent may register the birth and details about both parents will be entered on the register. If the parents were unmarried at the time of the birth, the father's details are entered only if both parents attend or if the parents have made a statutory declaration confirming the identity of the father. Copies of the forms necessary to make such a declaration are available at the register offices. A short birth certificate is issued free when the birth is registered.

STILL BIRTHS

If a baby is stillborn, i.e. born dead after the 24th week of pregnancy, the birth must be registered. The doctor or midwife who attends the birth or afterwards examines the body of the child will issue a Medical Certificate of Stillbirth and this must be presented at the register office.

RE-REGISTRATION

In certain circumstances it may be necessary to re-register a birth, e.g. where the birth of an illegitimate child is legitimated by the subsequent marriage of the parents. It is also possible to re-register the birth of an illegitimate child so that the father's name is entered on the register.

BIRTH ABROAD

Births of British subjects occurring abroad are registered with consular officers and certificates of birth are subsequently available from the Registrar-General. The registration of births among members of the armed forces that occur abroad or on military ships or aircraft is governed by the Registration of Births, Deaths and Marriages (Special Provisions) Act 1957.

SCOTLAND

In Scotland the birth of a child must be registered within 21 days at the register office of either the district in which the baby was born or the district in which the mother was resident at the time of the birth.

If the child is born, either in or out of Scotland, on a ship, aircraft or land vehicle that ends its journey at any place in Scotland, the child, in most cases, will be registered as if born in that place.

CERTIFICATES OF BIRTHS, DEATHS OR MARRIAGES

Certificates of births, deaths or marriages that have taken place in England and Wales since 1837 can be obtained from the Office of National Statistics (General Register Office). Applications can be made:

– by a personal visit
– by postal application

Certificates are also available from the Superintendent Registrar for the district in which the event took place or, in the case of marriage certificates, from the minister of the church in which the marriage took place. Any register office can advise about the best way to obtain certificates. The fees for certificates (from 1 April 2000) are:

Obtained from Registrar who registered the birth, death or marriage
Standard certificate, £3.50
Short certificate of birth (other than the first issued at the time of birth registration), death, marriage and adoption, £3.50

Obtained from Superintendent Registrar
Standard certificate, £6.50
Short certificate of birth, death, marriage and adoption, £5.00

From the Family Records Centre, London/by post from the General Register Office, Southport
Standard certificate of birth, death or marriage
Personal application, £6.50
Standard certificate of adoption
Personal application, £6.50
Short certificate of birth
Personal application, £5.00
Short certificate of adoption
Personal application, £3.50
for postal application fees, please contact the General Register Office

Indexes prepared from the registers are available for searching by the public at the Family Records Centre in London or at a Superintendent Registrar's Office; indexes at the latter relate only to births, deaths and marriages

which occurred in that registration district. There is no charge for searching the indexes in the Public Search Room at the Family Records Centre but a general search fee is charged for searches at a Superintendent Registrar's Office. A fee is charged for verifying index references against the records.

The Society of Genealogists has many records of baptisms, marriages and deaths prior to 1837.

SCOTLAND

Certificates of births, deaths or marriages that have taken place in Scotland since 1855 can be obtained from the General Register Office for Scotland or from the appropriate local registrar. The General Register Office for Scotland also keeps the Register of Divorces (including decrees of declaration of nullity of marriage), and holds parish registers dating from before 1855.

Fees for certificates (from 1 April 1999) are:

Certificates (full or abbreviated) of birth, death, marriage or adoption, £8.00
A priority service is available for an additional fee of £10.00

Particular search for each period of five years or part thereof, whether specified entry is traced or not:
Personal application, £5.00
Postal application, £5.00

General search in the indexes to the statutory registers and parochial registers, per day or part thereof:
Full day (i.e. 9 a.m. to 4.30 p.m.) search with payment being made not less than 14 days in advance, £13.00
Full day search in any other case, £17.00
Afternoon (i.e. 1 p.m. to 4.30 p.m.) search £10.00
One week search, £65.00

Further information can be obtained from:

THE GENERAL REGISTER OFFICE, Office for National Statistics, Smedley Hydro, Trafalgar Road, Birkdale, Southport, Merseyside PR8 2HH. Tel: 01704-569824

FAMILY RECORDS CENTRE, 1 Myddelton Street, London EC1R 1UW. Opens 9 a.m. on Monday, Wednesday, Thursday, Friday, 10 a.m. Tuesday, 9.30 a.m. Saturday. Closes 5 p.m. Monday, Wednesday, Friday, Saturday, 7 p.m. Tuesday, Thursday

THE GENERAL REGISTER OFFICE FOR SCOTLAND, New Register House, Edinburgh EH1 3YT. Tel: 0131-334 0380

THE SOCIETY OF GENEALOGISTS, 14 Charterhouse Buildings, Goswell Road, London EC1M 7BA. Tel: 020-7251 8799

BRITISH CITIZENSHIP

The British Nationality Act 1981 which came into force on 1 January 1983 established three types of citizenship to replace the single form of Citizenship of the UK and Colonies created by the British Nationality Act 1948. The three forms of citizenship are: British Citizenship; British Dependent Territories Citizenship; and British Overseas Citizenship. Three residual categories were created: British Subjects; British Protected Persons; and British Nationals (Overseas).

BRITISH CITIZENSHIP

Almost everyone who was a citizen of the UK and colonies and had a right of abode in the UK prior to the 1981 Act became British citizens when the Act came into force. British citizens have the right to live permanently in the UK and are free to leave and re-enter the UK at any time.

A person born on or after 1 January 1983 in the UK (including, for this purpose, the Channel Islands and the Isle of Man) is entitled to British citizenship if he/she falls into one of the following categories:
- he/she has a parent who is a British citizen
- he/she has a parent who is settled in the UK
- he/she is a newborn infant found abandoned in the UK
- his/her parents subsequently settle in the UK
- he/she lives in the UK for the first ten years of his/her life and is not absent for more than 90 days in each of those years
- he/she is adopted in the UK and one of the adopters is a British Citizen

A person born outside the UK may acquire British citizenship if he/she falls into one of the following categories:
- he/she has a parent who is a British citizen otherwise than by descent, e.g. a parent who was born in the UK
- he/she has a parent who is a British citizen serving the Crown overseas
- the Home Secretary consents to his/her registration while he/she is a minor
- he/she is a British Dependent Territories citizen, a British Overseas citizen, a British subject or a British protected person and has been lawfully resident in the UK for five years
- he/she is a British Dependent Territories citizen who acquired that citizenship from a connection with Gibraltar
- he/she is adopted or naturalised

Where parents are married, the status of either may confer citizenship on their child. If a child is illegitimate, the status of the mother determines the child's citizenship.

Under the 1981 Act, Commonwealth citizens and citizens of the Republic of Ireland were entitled to registration as British citizens before 1 January 1988. In 1985 citizens of the Falkland Islands were granted British citizenship.

Renunciation of British citizenship must be registered with the Home Secretary and will be revoked if no new citizenship or nationality is acquired within six months. If the renunciation was required in order to retain or acquire another citizenship or nationality, the citizenship may be reacquired once.

British Dependent Territories Citizenship

Under the 1981 Act, this type of citizenship was conferred on citizens of the UK and colonies by birth, naturalisation or registration in British Dependent Territories. British Dependent Territories citizens may be entitled to registration as British citizens on completion of five years' legal residence in the UK.

On 1 July 1997 citizens of Hong Kong who did not qualify to register as British citizens under the British Nationality (Hong Kong) Act 1990 lost their British Dependent Territories citizenship on the handover of sovereignty to China; they may, however, have applied to register as British Nationals (Overseas).

Eligibility for British Dependent Territories citizenship is determined by similar rules to those for acquiring British citizenship, except that the connection is with the dependent territory rather than with the UK.

British Overseas Citizenship

Under the 1981 Act, this type of citizenship was conferred on any UK and colonies citizens who did not qualify for British citizenship or citizenship of the British Dependent Territories. British Overseas citizenship may be acquired by the wife and minor children of a British Overseas citizen in certain circumstances. British Overseas citizens may be entitled to registration as British citizens on completion of five years' legal residence in the UK.

Residual Categories

British subjects, British protected persons and British Nationals (Overseas) may be entitled to registration as British citizens on completion of five years' legal residence in the UK.

Citizens of the Republic of Ireland who were also British subjects before 1 January 1949 can retain that status if they fulfil certain conditions.

European Union Citizenship

British citizens (including Gibraltarians who are registered as such) are also EU citizens and are entitled to travel freely to other EU countries to work, study, reside and set up a business. EU citizens have the same rights with respect to the United Kingdom.

Naturalisation

Naturalisation is granted at the discretion of the Home Secretary. The basic requirements are five years' residence (three years if the applicant is married to a British citizen), good character, adequate knowledge of the English, Welsh or Scottish Gaelic language, and an intention to reside permanently in the UK.

Status of Aliens

Aliens may not hold public office or vote in Britain and they may not own a British ship or aircraft. Citizens of the Republic of Ireland are not deemed to be aliens.

CONSUMER LAW

Sale of Goods

A sale of goods contract is the most common type of contract. It is governed by the Sale of Goods Act 1979 (as amended by the Sale and Supply of Goods Act 1994). The Act provides protection for buyers by implying terms into every sale of goods contract. These terms are:
- a condition that the seller will pass good title to the buyer (unless the seller agrees to transfer only such title as he has)
- where the seller sells goods by reference to a description, a condition that the goods will match that description and, where the sale is by sample and description, a condition that the bulk of the goods will correspond with such sample and description
- where goods are sold by a business seller, a condition that the goods will be of satisfactory quality if they meet the standard that a reasonable person would regard as satisfactory taking into account any description of the goods, the price, and all other relevant circumstances. The quality of the goods includes their state and condition, relevant aspects being whether they are suitable for their common purpose, their appearance and finish, freedom from minor defects and their safety and durability. This term will not be implied, however, if a buyer has examined the goods and should have noticed the defect or if the seller specifically drew the buyer's attention to the defect
- where goods are sold by a business seller, a condition that the goods are reasonably fit for any purpose made known to the seller by the buyer, unless the buyer does not rely on the seller's judgement, or it is not reasonable for him/her to do so

– where goods are sold by sample, conditions that the bulk of the sample will correspond with the sample in quality, that the buyer will have a reasonable opportunity of comparing the two and that the goods are free from any defect rendering them unsatisfactory which would not be obvious from the sample

Some of the above terms can be excluded from contracts by the seller. The seller's right to do this is, however, restricted by the Unfair Contract Terms Act 1977. The Act offers more protection to a buyer who 'deals as a consumer', that is where the sale is a business sale, the goods are of a type ordinarily bought for private use and the goods are bought by a buyer who is not a business buyer. In a sale by auction or competitive tender, a buyer never deals as consumer. Also, a seller can never exclude the implied term as to title mentioned above.

HIRE-PURCHASE AGREEMENTS

Terms similar to those implied in contracts of sales of goods are implied into contracts of hire-purchase, under the Supply of Goods (Implied Terms) Act 1973. The 1977 Act limits the exclusion of these implied terms as before.

SUPPLY OF GOODS AND SERVICES

Under the Supply of Goods and Services Act 1982, similar terms are also implied in other types of contract under which ownership of goods passes, e.g. a contract for 'work and materials' such as supplying new parts while servicing a car, and contracts for the hire of goods. These types of contracts have additional implied terms:
– that the supplier will use reasonable care and skill
– that the supplier will carry out the service in a reasonable time (unless the time has been agreed)
– that the supplier will make a reasonable charge (unless the charge has already been agreed)
The 1977 Act limits the exclusion of these implied terms in a similar manner as before.

UNFAIR TERMS

The Unfair Terms in Consumer Contracts Regulations 1999 apply to contracts between business sellers (or suppliers of goods and services) and consumers, where the terms have not been individually negotiated, i.e where the terms were drafted in advance so that the consumer was unable to influence those terms. An unfair term is one which operates to the detriment of the consumer. An unfair term does not bind the consumer but the contract will continue to bind the parties if it is capable of existing without the unfair term. The regulations contain a non-exhaustive list of terms which are regarded as unfair. Whether a term is regarded as fair or not will depend on many factors, including the nature of the goods or services, the surrounding circumstances (such as the bargaining strength of both parties) and the other terms in the contract.

TRADE DESCRIPTIONS

It is a criminal offence under the Trade Descriptions Act 1968 for a business seller to apply a false trade description of goods or to supply or offer to supply any goods to which a false description has been applied. A 'trade description' includes descriptions of quality, size, composition, fitness for purpose and method, and place and date of manufacture of the goods. It is also an offence to give a false indication of the price of goods.

FAIR TRADING

The Fair Trading Act 1973 is designed to protect the consumer. It provides for the appointment of a Director-General of Fair Trading, one of whose duties is to review commercial activities in the UK relating to the supply of goods and services to consumers. An example of a practice which has been prohibited by a reference made under this Act is that of business sellers posing in advertisements as private sellers.

CONSUMER PROTECTION

Under the Consumer Protection Act 1987, producers of goods are liable for any injury or for any damage exceeding £275 caused by a defect in their product (subject to certain defences).

The Consumer Protection (Cancellation of Contracts Concluded Away from Business Premises) Regulations 1987 allow consumers a seven-day period in which to cancel contracts for the supply of goods and services, where the contracts were made during an unsolicited visit to the consumer's home or workplace. This only applies to contracts where the cost exceeds £35.

CONSUMER CREDIT

In matters relating to the provision of credit (or the supply of goods on hire or hire-purchase), consumers are also protected by the Consumer Credit Act 1974. Under this Act a licence, issued by the Director-General of Fair Trading, is required to conduct a consumer credit or consumer hire business or to deal in credit brokerage, debt adjusting, counselling or collecting. Any 'fit' person may apply to the Director-General of Fair Trading for a licence, which is normally renewable after ten years. A licence is not necessary if such types of business are only transacted occasionally, or if only exempt agreements are involved. The provisions of the Act only apply to 'regulated' agreements, i.e. those that are with individuals or partnerships, those that are not exempt (such as certain local authority and building society loans), and those where the total credit does not exceed £25,000. Provisions include:
– the terms of the regulated agreement can be altered by the creditor provided the agreement gives him/her the right to do so; in such cases the debtor must be given proper notice of this
– in order for a creditor to enforce a regulated agreement, the agreement must comply with certain formalities and must be properly executed. The debtor must also be given specified information by the creditor or his/her broker or agent during the negotiations which take place before the signing of the agreement. The agreement must state certain information such as the amount of credit, the annual interest rate, the amount and timing of repayments
– if an agreement is signed other than at the creditor's (or credit broker's or negotiator's) place of business and oral representations were made in the debtor's presence during discussions pre-agreement, the debtor has a right to cancel the agreement. Time for cancellation expires five clear days after the debtor receives a second copy of the agreement. The agreement must inform the debtor of his right to cancel and how to cancel
– if the debtor is in arrears (or otherwise in breach of the agreement), the creditor must serve a default notice before taking any action such as repossessing the goods
– if the agreement is a hire-purchase or conditional sale agreement, the creditor cannot repossess the goods without a court order if the debtor has paid one-third of the total price of the goods
– in agreements where the debtor is required to make grossly exorbitant payments or where the agreement grossly contravenes the ordinary principles of fair trading, the debtor may request that the court alter or set aside some of the terms of the agreement. The

agreement can also be reopened during enforcement proceedings by the court itself

Where a credit reference agency has been used to check the debtor's financial standing, the creditor must give the agency's name to the debtor, who is entitled to see the agency's file on him. A fee of £1 is payable to the agency.

SCOTLAND

The legislation governing the sale and supply of goods applies to Scotland as follows:
- the Sale of Goods Act 1979 applies with some modifications and it has been amended by the Sale and Supply of Goods Act 1994
- the Supply of Goods (Implied Terms) Act 1973 applies
- the Supply of Goods and Services Act 1982 does not extend to Scotland but some of its provisions were introduced by the Sale and Supply of Goods Act 1994
- only Parts II and III of the Unfair Contract Terms Act 1977 apply
- the Trade Descriptions Act 1968 applies with minor modifications
- the Consumer Credit Act 1974 applies

PROCEEDINGS AGAINST THE CROWN

Until 1947, proceedings against the Crown were generally possible only by a procedure known as a petition of right, which put the litigant at a considerable disadvantage. The Crown Proceedings Act 1947 placed the Crown (not the Sovereign in his/her private capacity, but as the embodiment of the State) largely in the same position as a private individual. The Act did not, however, extinguish or limit the Crown's prerogative or statutory powers, and it granted immunity to HM ships and aircraft. It also left certain Crown privileges unaffected. The Act largely abolished the special procedures which previously applied to civil proceedings by and against the Crown. Civil proceedings may be instituted against the appropriate government department or against the Attorney-General.

In Scotland proceedings against the Crown founded on breach of contract could be taken before the 1947 Act and no special procedures applied. The Crown could, however, claim certain special pleas. The 1947 Act applies in part to Scotland and brings the practice of the two countries as closely together as the different legal systems permit. Civil proceedings may be instituted against the Lord Advocate where proceedings are against the Scottish Administration of the Scottish Parliament or against the Advocate General for Scotland representing the appropriate government department in any other case.

DEATHS

WHEN A DEATH OCCURS

If the death was expected, the doctor who attended the deceased during their final illness should be contacted. If the death was sudden or unexpected, the family doctor (if known) and police should be contacted.

If the cause of death is quite clear the doctor will provide:
- a medical certificate that shows the cause of death (this will be in a sealed envelope, addressed to the registrar)
- a formal notice that states that the doctor has signed the medical certificate and that explains how to get the death registered

If the death was known to be caused by a natural illness but the doctor wishes to know more about the cause of death, he/she may ask the relatives for permission to carry out a post-mortem examination. This should not delay the funeral.

In England and Wales a coroner is responsible for investigating deaths occurring in the following circumstances:
- when no doctor has treated the deceased during his or her last illness or when the doctor attending the patient did not see him or her within 14 days before death, or after death; or
- when the death occurred during an operation or before recovery from the effect of an anaesthetic; or
- when the death was sudden and unexplained or attended by suspicious circumstances; or
- when the death might be due to an industrial injury or disease, or to accident, violence, neglect or abortion, or to any kind of poisoning; or
- the death occurred in prison or in police custody

The doctor will write on the formal notice that the death has been referred to the coroner; if the post mortem shows that death was due to natural causes, the coroner may issue a notification which gives the cause of death so that the death can be registered. If the cause of death was violent or unnatural, the coroner is obliged to hold an inquest.

In Scotland the office of coroner does not exist. The local procurator fiscal inquires into sudden or suspicious deaths. A fatal accident inquiry will be held before the sheriff where the death has resulted from an accident during the course of the employment of the person who has died, or where the person who has died was in legal custody, or where the Lord Advocate deems it in the public interest that an inquiry be held.

REGISTERING A DEATH

In England and Wales the death must be registered by the registrar of births and deaths for the district in which it occurred; details can be obtained from the telephone directory (under registration of births and deaths and marriages), from the doctor or local council, or at a post office or police station. From April 1997, information concerning a death can be given before any registrar of births and deaths in England and Wales. The registrar will pass the relevant details to the registrar for the district where the death occurred, who will then register the death or, if different in the registration district in which the death took place.

In England and Wales the death must normally be registered within five days; in Scotland it must be registered within eight days. If the death has been referred to the coroner/local procurator fiscal it cannot be registered until the registrar has received authority from the coroner/local procurator fiscal to do so. Failure to register a death involves a penalty in England and Wales and may lead to a court decree being granted by a sheriff in Scotland.

If the death occurred at a house, the death may be registered by:
- any relative of the deceased present at the death or in attendance during the last illness
- any relative of the deceased residing or being in the sub-district where the death occurred
- any person present at the death
- the occupier or any inmate of the house if he/she knew of the occurrence of the death
- any person causing the disposal of the body

The person registering the death should take the medical certificate of the cause of death with them; it is

also useful, though not essential, to take the deceased's birth and marriage certificates, medical card (if possible), pension documents and life assurance details. The registrar will issue a certificate for burial or cremation and a certificate of registration of death; both are free of charge. A death certificate is a certified copy of the entry in the death register; these can be provided on payment of a fee and may be required for the following purposes:
– the will
– bank and building society accounts
– savings bank certificates and premium bonds
– insurance policies
– pension claims
If the death occurred abroad or on a foreign ship or aircraft, the death should be registered according to the local regulations of the relevant country and a death certificate should be obtained. The death can also be registered with the British Consul in that country and a record will be kept at the General Register Office. This avoids the expense of bringing the body back.

After 12 months of death or the finding of a dead body, no death can be registered without the consent of the Registrar-General.

BURIAL AND CREMATION

In most circumstances in England and Wales a certificate for burial or cremation must be obtained from the registrar before the burial or cremation can take place. If the death has been referred to the coroner, an order for burial or a certificate for cremation must be obtained. In Scotland a body may be buried (but not cremated) before the death is registered.

Funeral costs can normally be repaid out of the deceased's estate and will be given priority over any other claims. If the deceased has left a will it may contain directions concerning the funeral; however, these directions need not be followed by the executor.

The deceased's papers should also indicate whether a grave space had already been arranged. Most town churchyards and many suburban churchyards are no longer open for burial because they are full. Most cemeteries are non-denominational and may be owned by local authorities or private companies; fees vary.

If the body is to be cremated, an application form, two cremation certificates (for which there is a charge) or a certificate for cremation if the death was referred to the coroner, and a certificate signed by the medical referee must be completed in addition to the certificate for burial or cremation (the form is not required if the coroner has issued a certificate for cremation). All the forms are available from the funeral director or crematorium. Most crematoria are run by local authorities; the fees usually include the medical referee's fee and the use of the chapel. Ashes may be scattered, buried in a churchyard or cemetery, or kept.

The registrar must be notified of the date, place and means of disposal of the body within 96 hours (England and Wales) or three days (Scotland).

If the death occurred abroad or on a foreign ship or aircraft, a local burial or cremation may be arranged. If the body is to be brought back to England or Wales, a death certificate from the relevant country or an authorisation for the removal of the body from the country of death from the coroner or relevant authority will be required. To arrange a funeral in England or Wales an authenticated translation of a foreign death certificate or a death certificate issued in Scotland or Northern Ireland which must show the cause of death, is needed, together with a certificate of no liability to register from the registrar in England and Wales in whose sub-district it is intended to bury or cremate the body. If it is intended to cremate the body a cremation order will be required from the Home Office or a certificate for cremation.

Further information can be obtained from:
THE GENERAL REGISTER OFFICE, Office for National Statistics, Smedley Hydro, Trafalgar Road, Birkdale, Southport, Merseyside PR8 2HH. Tel: 01704-569824
THE GENERAL REGISTER OFFICE FOR SCOTLAND, NEW Register House, Edinburgh EH1 3YT. Tel: 0131-334 0380

DIVORCE AND RELATED MATTERS

ENGLAND AND WALES

There are two types of matrimonial suit: those seeking the annulment of a marriage, and those seeking a judicial separation or divorce. To obtain an annulment, judicial separation or divorce in England and Wales, one or both of the parties must have their permanent home in England and Wales when the petition is started, or have been living in England and Wales for at least a year on the day the petition is started. All cases are commenced in divorce county courts or in the Divorce Registry in London. If a suit is defended it may be transferred to the High Court.

NULLITY OF MARRIAGE

Various circumstances will render a marriage invalid from the beginning including if: the parties were within the prohibited degrees of consanguinity, affinity or adoption; the parties were not male and female; either of the parties was already married; either of the parties was under the age of 16; the formalities of the marriage were defective, e.g. the marriage did not take place in an authorised building, and both parties knew of the defect. Declarations of nullity are sought in very few cases.

SEPARATION

A couple may enter into an agreement to separate by consent but for the agreement to be valid it must be followed by an immediate separation; a solicitor should be contacted.

Judicial separation does not dissolve a marriage and it is not necessary to prove that the marriage has irretrievably broken down. Either party can petition for a judicial separation at any time; the grounds listed below as grounds for divorce are also grounds for judicial separation.

DIVORCE

Neither party can petition for divorce until at least one year after the date of the marriage. The sole ground for divorce is the irretrievable breakdown of the marriage; this must be proved on one or more of the following grounds:
– the respondent has committed adultery and the petitioner finds it intolerable to live with him/her; however the petitioner cannot rely on an act of adultery by the other party if they have lived together for more than six months after the discovery that adultery had been committed
– the respondent has behaved in such a way that the petitioner cannot reasonably be expected to continue living with him/her
– the respondent deserted the petitioner for two years immediately before the petition. Desertion may be defined as a voluntary withdrawal from cohabitation by the respondent without just cause and against the wishes of the petitioner; where one party is guilty of serious misconduct which forces the other party to

leave, the party at fault is said to be guilty of constructive desertion
- the respondent and the petitioner have lived separately for two years immediately before the petition and the respondent consents to the decree
- the respondent and the petitioner have lived separately for five years immediately before the petition

A total period of less than six months during which the parties have resumed living together is disregarded in determining whether the prescribed period of separation or desertion has been continuous (but cannot be included as part of the period of separation).

The Matrimonial Causes Act 1973 requires the solicitor for the petitioner in certain cases to certify whether the possibility of a reconciliation has been discussed with the petitioner.

The Decree Nisi

A decree nisi does not dissolve or annul the marriage but must be obtained before a divorce or annulment can take place.

Where the suit is undefended, the evidence normally takes the form of a sworn written statement made by the petitioner which is considered by a district judge. If the judge is satisfied that the petitioner has proved the contents of the petition, he/she will set a date for the pronouncement of the decree nisi in open court; neither party need attend.

If the judge is not satisfied that the petitioner has proved the contents of the petition, or if the suit is defended, the petition will be heard in open court with the parties giving oral evidence.

The Decree Absolute

The decree nisi is usually made absolute after six weeks and on the application of the petitioner. If the judge thinks it may be necessary to exercise any of his/her powers under the Children Act 1989, he/she can in exceptional circumstances delay the granting of the decree absolute. The decree absolute dissolves or annuls the marriage.

Children

Neither parent is now awarded 'custody' of any children of the marriage in England and Wales. Both parents, if married, have 'parental responsibility'. Either parent can exercise this, independently of the other. Any dispute between the parents can be resolved by the courts. In all court cases concerning children, whether connected to a matrimonial suit or not, the welfare of the child is the paramount consideration.

Maintenance, etc.

Either party may be liable to pay maintenance to their former spouse. If there were any children of the marriage, both parents have a legal responsibility to support them financially if they can afford to do so. These so-called ancillary matters, including any property settlements, may be settled before the divorce goes through but currently can go on long after the marriage is dissolved.

The courts are responsible for assessing maintenance for the former spouse, taking into account each party's income and essential outgoings and other aspects of the case. The court also deals with any maintenance for a child which has been treated by the spouses as a 'child of the family', e.g. a stepchild, and any property settlements.

The Child Support Agency (CSA) was set up under the Child Support Act 1991 and is now responsible for assessing the maintenance that absent parents should pay for their natural or adopted children (whether or not a marriage has taken place). The CSA accepts applications only when all the people involved are habitually resident in the UK; the courts will continue to deal with cases where one of the people involved lives abroad. The CSA deals with all new cases, and is gradually taking on cases where the parent with care (or his/her new partner) was already receiving income support, family credit or disability working allowance before 5 April 1993. People with existing court orders or written maintenance agreements made before 5 April 1993 should continue to use the courts. Where it is already collecting child maintenance, the CSA has the power to offer a collection and enforcement service for certain other payments of maintenance.

A formula is used to work out how much child maintenance is payable. The formula ensures that after the payment of child maintenance the absent parent's income, and that of any second family he/she may now have, remains significantly above basic income support rates. Also, no absent parent will normally be assessed to pay more than 30 per cent of his/her net income in current child maintenance, or more than 33 per cent if he/she is also liable for any arrears. Absent parents are normally expected to pay at least a minimum amount of child maintenance (currently about £2.50 a week).

A scheme has begun to be introduced since the end of 1996 which allows departures from the formula in certain tightly defined circumstances, e.g. the high costs of travel to maintain contact with a child, or to have a property and capital transfer ('clean break' settlement) entered into before April 1993 taken into account; there will also be some additional grounds which may result in liability being increased.

Some cases involving unusual circumstances are treated as special cases and the assessment is modified. Where there is financial need (e.g. because of disability or continuing education), maintenance may be ordered by the court for children even beyond the age of 18.

The level of maintenance is reviewed automatically every two years. Either parent can report a change of circumstances and request a review at any time. An independent complaints examiner for the CSA was appointed in early 1997.

If the absent parent does not pay the child maintenance, the CSA may make an order for payments to be deducted directly from his/her salary or wages; if all other methods fail, the CSA may take court action to enforce the payment.

Court Orders

Magistrates' courts used for domestic proceedings are now called family proceedings courts. A spouse can apply to the family proceedings court for a court order on the ground that the other spouse:
- has failed to pay reasonable maintenance for the applicant
- has failed to make a proper contribution towards the reasonable maintenance of a 'child of the family'
- has deserted the applicant
- has behaved in such a way that the applicant cannot reasonably be expected to live with the respondent
If the case is proved, the court can order:
- periodical payments for the applicant and/or a 'child of the family'
- a lump sum payment (not exceeding £1,000) to the applicant and/or a 'child of the family'
In deciding what orders (if any) to make, the court must consider guidelines which are similar to those governing financial orders in divorce cases. There are also special provisions relating to consent orders and separation by agreement. An order may be enforceable even if the parties are living together, but in some cases it will cease to have effect if they continue to do so for six months.

DOMESTIC VIOLENCE

If one spouse has been subjected to violence at the hands of the other, it is now possible to obtain a court order very quickly to restrain further violence and if necessary to have the other spouse excluded from the home. Such orders may also relate to unmarried couples and to a range of other relationships.

SCOTLAND

Although there is separate legislation for Scotland covering nullity of marriage, judicial separation, divorce and ancillary matters, the provisions are in most respects the same as those for England and Wales. The following is confined to major points on which the law in Scotland differs.

An action for 'declarator of nullity' can be brought only in the Court of Session. Where a spouse is capable of sexual intercourse but refuses to consummate the marriage, this is not a ground of nullity in Scots law, though it could be a ground for divorce. The fact that a spouse was suffering from venereal disease at the time of marriage and the other spouse did not know this is not a ground of nullity in Scots law, neither is the fact that a wife was pregnant by another man at the time of marriage and her husband did not know this.

An action for judicial separation or divorce may be raised in the Court of Session; it may also be raised in the Sheriff Court if either party was resident in the sheriffdom for 40 days immediately before the date of the action or for 40 days ending not more than 40 days before the date of the action. The fee for starting a divorce petition in the Sheriff Court is £72.

When adultery is cited as proof that the marriage has broken down irretrievably, it is not necessary in Scotland to prove also that it is intolerable for the pursuer to live with the defender. In the case of desertion, irretrievable breakdown is not established if, after the two year desertion period has expired, the parties resume living together at any time after the end of three months from the date when they first resume living together.

Where a divorce action has been raised, it may be sisted or put on hold for a variety of reasons.

If the parties do cohabit during such postponement, no account is taken of the cohabitation if the action later proceeds.

In actions for divorce and separation, the court has the power to award a residence order in respect of any children of the marriage. The welfare of the children is of paramount importance, and the fact that a spouse has caused the breakdown of the marriage does not in itself preclude him/her from being awarded residence.

A simplified procedure for 'do-it-yourself' divorce was introduced in 1983 for certain divorces. If the action is based on two or five years' separation and will not be opposed, and if there are no children under 16 and no financial claims, and there is no sign that the applicant's spouse is unable to manage his or her affairs through mental illness or handicap, the applicant can write directly to the local sheriff court or to the Court of Session for the appropriate forms to enable him or her to proceed. The fee is £57, unless the applicant receives income support, family credit or legal advice and assistance, in which case there is no fee.

An extract decree, which dissolves or annuls marriage, will be made available 14 days after the divorce has been granted.

Further information can be obtained from any divorce county court, solicitor or Citizens' Advice Bureau, the Lord Chancellor's Department or the Lord Advocate's Office, or the following:

THE PRINCIPAL REGISTRY, First Avenue House, 42–49 High Holborn, London WC1V 6NP. Tel: 020-7936 6000

THE COURT OF SESSION, Parliament House, Parliament Square, Edinburgh EH1 1HQ. Tel: 0131-225 2595

THE CHILD SUPPORT AGENCY, Longbenton, Newcastle upon Tyne NE98 1YX. Tel: 0191-213 5000

EMPLOYMENT LAW

PAY AND CONDITIONS

The Employment Rights Act 1996 consolidates the statutory provisions relating to employees' rights. Employers must give each employee employed for more than one month a written statement containing the following information:

- names of employer and employee
- date when employment began
- remuneration and intervals at which it will be paid
- job title or description of job
- hours and place(s) of work
- holiday entitlement and holiday pay
- entitlement to sick leave and sick pay
- details of pension scheme(s)
- length of notice period that employer and employee need to give to terminate employment, or the end date for a fixed-term contract
- details of any collective agreement which affects the terms of employment
- details of disciplinary and grievance procedures
- if the employee is to work outside the UK for more than one month, the period of such work and the currency in which payment is made

This must be given to the employee within two months of the start of their employment. The Working Time Regulation 1998, the National Minimum Wage Act 1998 and the Employment Relations Act 1999 now supplement the 1996 Act.

SICK PAY

Employees absent from work through illness or injury are entitled to receive Statutory Sick Pay (SSP) from the employer for a maximum period of 28 weeks in any three-year period. This applies to all employees, both men and women, up to the age of 65.

DEDUCTIONS FROM PAY

Employers may not make deductions from an employee's wages without the employee's prior written consent or unless authorised by statute (e.g. deductions for national insurance or tax).

SUNDAY TRADING

The Sunday Trading Act 1994 gave new rights to shop workers. They have the right not to be dismissed, selected for redundancy or to suffer any detriment (such as the denial of overtime, promotion or training) if they refuse to work on Sundays. This does not apply to those who, under their contracts, are employed to work on Sundays.

TRADE UNION MEMBERSHIP

Under employment legislation, employees or potential employees may not be penalised because they are or are not a member of a trade union.

DISPUTES

Where it has not been possible to settle a dispute in the workplace, it may be possible for employees to make a complaint to an industrial tribunal. ACAS offers advice and conciliation in employment disputes.

TERMINATION OF EMPLOYMENT

An employee may be dismissed without notice if guilty of gross misconduct but in other cases a period of notice must be given by the employer. The minimum periods of notice specified in the Employment Rights Act 1996 are:
– at least one week if the employee has been continuously employed for one month or more but for less than two years
– at least two weeks if the employee has been continuously employed for two years or more. A week is added for every complete year of continuous employment up to 12 years
– at least 12 weeks for those who have been continuously employed for 12 years or more
– longer periods apply if these are specified in the contract of employment
If an employee is dismissed with less notice than he/she is entitled to, the employer is generally liable to pay wages for the period of proper notice (or for the period of the contract for those on fixed-term contracts). Generally, no notice needs to be given of the expiry of a fixed-term contract.

REDUNDANCY

An employee dismissed because of redundancy may be entitled to a lump sum. This applies if:
– the employee has at least two years' continuous service
– the employee is actually dismissed by the employer (even in cases of voluntary redundancy)
– dismissal is due to a reduction in the work force
An employee may not be entitled to a redundancy payment if offered a new job by the same employer. The amount of payment depends on the length of service, the salary and the age of the employee. The redundancy payment is guaranteed by the State in cases where the employer becomes insolvent (subject to the conditions above).

UNFAIR DISMISSAL

Complaints about unfair dismissal are dealt with by an employment tribunal. Any employee, with one years' continuous service subject to exceptions, regardless of their hours of work, can make a complaint to the tribunal. At the tribunal the employer must prove that the dismissal was due to one or more of the following reasons:
– the employee's capability for the job
– the employee's conduct
– redundancy
– a legal restriction preventing the continuation of the employee's contract
– some other substantial reason
If so, the tribunal must decide whether the employer acted reasonably in dismissing the employee for that reason. If the employee is found to have been unfairly dismissed, the tribunal can order that he/she be reinstated or compensated.

DISCRIMINATION

Discrimination in employment on the grounds of sex, race or (subject to wide exceptions) disability is unlawful. The following legislation applies to those employed in Great Britain but not to employees in Northern Ireland or (subject to EC exceptions) to those who work mainly abroad:
– The Equal Pay Act 1970 (as amended) entitles men and women to equality in matters related to their contracts of employment. Those doing like work for the same employer are entitled to the same pay and conditions regardless of their sex
– The Sex Discrimination Act 1975 (as amended by the Sex Discrimination Act 1986) makes it unlawful to discriminate on grounds of sex or marital status. This covers all aspects of employment, including advertising for recruits, terms offered, opportunities for promotion and training, and dismissal procedures
– The Race Relations Act 1976 gives individuals the right not to be discriminated against in employment matters on the grounds of race, colour, nationality, or ethnic or national origins. It applies to all aspects of employment
– The Disability Discrimination Act 1995 makes discrimination against a disabled person in all aspects of employment unlawful. Unlike sex and race discrimination, an employer may show that the treatment is justified and that the employer acted reasonably. Employers with fewer than 20 employees are exempt
The Equal Opportunities Commission, the Commission for Racial Equality and the Disability Rights Commission (for entries, *see* Index) have the function of eliminating such discriminations in the workplace and can provide further information and assistance.

In Northern Ireland like provisions exist but are constituted in separate legislation which also provides protection against religious discrimination.

RECENT CHANGES

The Employment Relations Act 1999 has made a number of important changes to the existing law. The main changes are:
– a right of accompaniment. A worker attending a serious disciplinary or grievance hearing will have a right to be accompanied by a trade union representative or co-worker of their choice
– a new scheme of compulsory trade union recognition following a workplace ballot
– greater protection from dismissal for striking employees
– more 'family friendly' measures, including greater rights to maternity leave and parental leave
– the maximum compensatory award in unfair dismissal cases is £50,000.

HUMAN RIGHTS

On 2 October 2000 the Human Rights Act 1998 came into force. This Act incorporates the European Convention on Human Rights into the law of the United Kingdom and it is expected to have a wide impact.

The main principles of the Act are as follows:
– all legislation must be interpreted by the courts as compatible with the Convention so far as it is possible to do so
– subordinate legislation (e.g. statutory instruments) which are incompatible with the Convention can be struck down by the courts
– primary legislation (e.g. Acts of Parliament) which is incompatible with the Convention cannot be struck down by a court, but the higher courts can make a declaration of incompatibility which is a signal to Parliament to change the law

– all public authorities (including courts and tribunals) must not act in a way which is incompatible with the Convention

– individuals whose Convention rights have been infringed by a public authority may bring proceedings against that authority, but the Act is not intended to create new rights as between individuals.

The main human rights protected by the Convention are the right to life (article 2); protection from torture and inhuman or degrading treatment (article 3); protection from slavery or forced labour (article 4); the right to liberty and security of the person (article 5); right to a fair trial (article 6); the right not to be subject to retrospective criminal offences (article 7); right to private and family life (article 8); freedom of thought, conscience and religion (article 9); freedom of expression (article 10); freedom of association and assembly (article 11); right to marry and found a family (article 12); protection from discrimination (article 14); the right to property (article 1 Protocol No.1) and the right to education (article 2 Protocol No.1). Most of the Convention rights are subject to limitations which are 'necessary in a democratic society'.

ILLEGITIMACY AND LEGITIMATION

The Children Act 1989 gives the mother parental responsibility for the child when she is not married to the father. The unmarried father can acquire parental responsibility either by agreement with her (in prescribed form) or by applying to the court. If an illegitimate child is to be adopted, the father's consent is required only where he has been awarded parental rights by the court.

Every child born to a married woman during marriage is presumed to be legitimate, unless the couple are separated under court order when the child is conceived, in which case the child is presumed not to be the husband's child. It is possible to challenge the presumption of legitimacy or illegitimacy through civil proceedings.

In Scotland, the relevant legislation is the Children (Scotland) Act 1995, which also gives the mother parental responsibility for her child when she is not married to the child's father. The Act also provides that a father has no automatic parental rights when unmarried to the mother, but can acquire parental responsibility by applying to the court.

LEGITIMATION

Under the Legitimacy Act 1976, an illegitimate person automatically becomes legitimate when his/her parents marry. This applies even where one of the parents was married to a third person at the time of the birth. In such cases it is necessary to re-register the birth of the child. In Scotland, the relevant legislation is the Legitimation (Scotland) Act 1968.

RIGHTS OF ILLEGITIMATE PEOPLE

For the purposes of most legislation, illegitimate and legitimate people have the same rights and responsibilities. In particular, under the Family Law Reform Acts 1969 and 1987, legitimate and illegitimate children have broadly the same rights on an intestacy. Furthermore, in any will made after 31 December 1969, it is assumed that any reference to children or relatives will include those who are illegitimate and those related through another person who is illegitimate. In Scotland, illegitimate and legitimate people are given equal status under the Law Reform (Parent and Child) Scotland Act 1986.

JURY SERVICE

In England and Wales a person charged with any but the most minor offences is entitled to be tried by jury (However the right to trial by jury will be restricted if the Criminal Justice (Mode of Trial) (No.2) Bill presently before Parliament becomes law). No such right exists in Scotland, although more serious offences are heard before a jury. In England and Wales there are 12 members of a jury in a criminal case and eight members in a civil case. In Scotland there are 12 members of a jury in a civil case in the Court of Session (the civil jury being confined to the Court of Session and a restricted number of actions), and 15 in a criminal trial. Jurors are normally asked to serve for ten working days, although jurors selected for longer cases are expected to sit for the duration of the trial.

Every parliamentary or local government elector between the ages of 18 and 70 who has lived in the UK (including, for this purpose, the Channel Islands and the Isle of Man) for any period of at least five years since reaching the age of 13 is qualified to serve on a jury unless he/she is ineligible or disqualified.

ENGLAND AND WALES

Those ineligible for jury service include:

– those who have at any time been judges, magistrates or senior court officials

– those who have within the previous ten years been concerned with the administration of justice

– priests of any religion and vowed members of religious communities

– certain sufferers from mental illness

Those disqualified from jury service include:

– those who have at any time been sentenced by a court in the UK (including, for this purpose, the Channel Islands and the Isle of Man) to a term of imprisonment or custody of five years or more

– those who have within the previous ten years served any part of a sentence of imprisonment, youth custody or detention, been detained in a young offenders' institution, received a suspended sentence of imprisonment or order for detention, or received a community service order

– those who have within the previous five years been placed on probation

– those who are on bail in criminal proceedings

Those who may be excused as of right from jury service include:

– persons over the age of 65

– members and officers of the Houses of Parliament

– members of the National Assembly for Wales

– representatives to the European Parliament

– full-time serving members of the armed forces

– registered and practising members of the medical, dental, nursing, veterinary and pharmaceutical professions

– those who have served on a jury in the previous two years

The court has the discretion to excuse a juror from service, or defer the date of service, if the service would be a hardship to the juror. If a person serves on a jury knowing himself/herself to be ineligible or disqualified, he/she is liable to be fined up to £5,000 if disqualified and up to £1,000 for all other offences. The defendant can object to any juror if he/she can show cause.

A juror may claim travelling expenses, a subsistence allowance and an allowance for other financial loss (e.g. loss of earnings or benefits, fees paid to carers or child-minders) up to a stated limit.

It is an offence for a juror to disclose what happened in the jury room even after the trial is over. A jury's verdict must normally be unanimous, but if no verdict has been reached after two hours' consideration (or such longer period as the court deems to be reasonable) a majority verdict is acceptable if ten jurors agree to it.

SCOTLAND

Qualification criteria for jury service in Scotland are similar to those in England and Wales, except that the maximum age for a juror is 65, members of the judiciary are ineligible for ten years after ceasing to hold their post, and others concerned with the administration of justice are only eligible for service five years after ceasing to hold office. Ministers of religion, persons in holy orders and those who have served on a jury in the previous five years are excusable as of right.

The maximum fine for a person serving on a jury knowing himself/herself to be ineligible is £1,000. The maximum fine for failing to attend without good cause is also £1,000.

Further information can obtained from:

THE COURT SERVICE, Southside, 105 Victoria Street, London SW1E 6QT. Tel: 020-7210 2266

THE CLERK OF JUSTICIARY, High Court of Justiciary, Parliament House, Parliament Square, Edinburgh EH1 1HQ. Tel: 0131-225 2595

LANDLORD AND TENANT

When a property is rented to a tenant, the rights and responsibilities of the landlord and the tenant are determined largely by the tenancy agreement but also by statutory provisions. Some of the main provisions are outlined below but it is advisable to contact the Citizens' Advice Bureau or the local authority housing department for further information.

RESIDENTIAL LETTINGS

The provisions outlined here apply only where the tenant lives in a separate dwelling from the landlord and where the dwelling is the tenant's only or main home. It does not apply to licensees such as lodgers, guests or service occupiers.

The 1996 Housing Act radically changes certain aspects of the legislation referred to below, in particular the grant of assured and assured shorthold tenancies under Housing Act 1988. It is advisable to check whether the new legislation has come into force before relying on the provisions set out below.

ASSURED SHORTHOLD TENANCIES

If a tenancy was granted on or after 15 January 1989 and before 28 February 1997, the tenant may have an assured tenancy giving that tenant greater rights. The tenant could, for example, stay in possession of the dwelling for as long as the tenant observed the terms of the tenancy. The landlord cannot obtain possession from such a tenant unless the landlord can establish a specific ground for possession (set out in the Housing Act 1988) and obtains a court order. The rent payable is that agreed with the landlord unless the rent has been fixed by the rent assessment committee of the local authority. The tenant or the landlord may request that the committee set the rent in line with open market rents for that type of property. Any rent increases that are to take place should be written into the agreement but failing that, the landlord must give advance notice of the increase.

Under the Housing Act 1996, most new lettings entered into on or after 28 February 1997 will be assured shorthold tenancies. This means that tenants are given limited rights. The landlord must obtain a court order, however, to obtain possession if the tenant refuses to vacate at the end of the tenancy.

REGULATED TENANCIES

Before the Housing Act 1988 came into force (15 January 1989) there were regulated tenancies; some are still in existence and are protected by the Rent Act 1977. Under this Act it is possible for the landlord or the tenant to apply to the local rent officer to have a 'fair' rent registered. The fair rent is then the maximum rent payable.

SECURE TENANCIES

Secure tenancies are generally given to tenants of local authorities, housing associations and certain other bodies. This gives the tenant lifelong tenure unless the terms of the agreement are broken by the tenant. In certain circumstances those with secure tenancies may have the right to buy their property. In practice this right is generally only available to council tenants.

AGRICULTURAL PROPERTY

Tenancies in agricultural properties are governed by the Agricultural Holdings Act 1986 and the Rent (Agricultural) Act 1976, which give similar protections to those described above, e.g. security of tenure, right to compensation for disturbance, etc. The Agricultural Holdings (Scotland) Act 1991 applies similar provisions to Scotland.

EVICTION

Under the Protection from Eviction Act 1977 (as amended by the Housing Act 1988), a landlord must give reasonable notice that he/she is to evict the tenant, and in most cases a possession order, granted in court, is necessary. Notice is generally to be at least four weeks and in prescribed statutory form (notices are available from law stationers). It is illegal for a landlord to evict a person by putting their belongings onto the street, by changing the locks and so on. It is also illegal for a landlord to harass a tenant in any way in order to persuade him/her to give up the tenancy.

LANDLORD RESPONSIBILITIES

Under the Landlord and Tenant Act 1985, where the term of the lease is less than seven years the landlord is responsible for maintaining the structure and exterior of the property and all installations for the supply of water, gas and electricity, for sanitation, and for heating and hot water.

LEASEHOLDERS

Legally leaseholders have bought a long lease rather than a property and in certain limited circumstances the landlord can end the tenancy. Under the Leasehold Reform Act 1967 (as amended by the Housing Acts 1969, 1974 and 1980), leaseholders of houses may have the right to buy the freehold or to take an extended lease for a term of 50 years. This applies to leases where the term of the lease is over 21 years and where the leaseholder has occupied the house as his/her main residence for the last three years, or for a total of three years over the last ten.

The Leasehold Reform, Housing and Urban Development Act came into force in 1993 and allows the leaseholders of flats in certain circumstances to buy the freehold of the building in which they live.

Responsibility for maintenance of the structure, exterior and interior of the building should be set out in the lease. Usually the upkeep of the interior of his/her part of the property is the responsibility of the leaseholder, and responsibility for the structure, exterior and common interior areas is shared between the freeholder and the leaseholder(s).

BUSINESS LETTINGS

The Landlord and Tenant Acts 1927 and 1954 (as amended) give security of tenure to the tenants of most business premises. The landlord can only evict the tenant on one of the grounds laid down in the 1954 Act, and in some cases where the landlord repossesses the property the tenant may be entitled to compensation.

SCOTLAND

In Scotland assured and short assured tenancies exist for lettings after 2 January 1989 and are similar to assured tenancies in England and Wales. The relevant legislation is the Housing (Scotland) Act 1988.

Most tenancies created before 2 January 1989 were regulated tenancies and the Rent (Scotland) Act 1984 still applies where these exist. The Act defines, among other things, the circumstances in which a landlord can increase the rent when improvements are made to the property. The provisions of the Rent Act do not apply to tenancies where the landlord is the Crown, a local authority, the development corporation of a new town or a housing corporation.

The Housing (Scotland) Act 1987 and its provisions relate to local authority responsibilities for housing, the right to buy, and local authority secured tenancies. The provisions are broadly similar to England and Wales.

In Scotland, business premises are not controlled by statute to the same extent as in England and Wales, although the Shops (Scotland) Act 1949 gives some security to tenants of shops. Tenants of shops can apply to the sheriff for a renewal of tenancy if threatened with eviction. This application may be dismissed on various grounds including where the landlord has offered to sell the property to the tenant at an agreed price or, in the absence of agreement as to price, at a price fixed by a single arbiter appointed by the parties or the sheriff. The Act extends to properties where the Crown or government departments are the landlords or the tenants.

Under the Leases Act 1449 the landlord's successors (either purchasers or creditors) are bound by the agreement made with any tenants so long as the following conditions are met:
– the lease, if for more than one year, must be in writing
– there must be a rent
– there must be a term of expiry
– the tenant must have entered into possession
Many leases contain references to term and quarter days.

LEGAL AID

The Access to Justice Act 1999 has transformed what used to known as the Legal Aid system. The Legal Aid Board has been abolished and replaced from 1 April 2000 with the Legal Services Commission (85 Gray's Inn Road, London WC1X 8TX. Tel: 020-7759 0000). The changeover from the Legal Aid system is set to continue until 2002 with the next major change being the introduction of the Criminal Defence Service in April 2001 to replace the old system of criminal legal aid. Up-to-date information and further guidance can be obtained from the Legal Services Commission website http://www.legalservices.gov.uk.

The Legal Services Commission administers the Community Legal Service fund under which (like the former legal aid) people on low or moderate incomes may qualify for help with the costs of legal advice or representation. Further advice about entitlement to assistance should be sought from a solicitor or Citizens' Advice Bureau. A key element of the reforms has been the introduction of the Community Legal Service which is designed to increase access to legal information and advice by involving a much wider network of funders and providers in giving publicly funded legal services. In Scotland, provision of legal aid is governed by the Legal Aid (Scotland) Act 1986.

CIVIL LEGAL AID

From 1 January 2000, only organisations (solicitors or Citizens' Advice Bureau) with a contract with the Legal Services Commission have been able to give initial help in any civil matter. Moreover, from that date decisions about funding were devolved from the Legal Services Commission to contracted organisations in relation to any level of publicly funded service in family and immigration cases. For other types of case, applications for public funding are made through a solicitor (or other contracted legal services provider) in much the same way as the former Legal Aid. From 1 April 2001 the so-called civil contracting scheme will be extended to cover all levels of service for all types of cases.

Under the new civil funding scheme there are broadly seven levels of service available:
– legal help
– help at court (the first two types of service are limited to advice and assistance with preparing a case, but do not include representation)
– approved family help – either general family help or help with mediation (special levels of service for family cases)
– legal representation – either investigative help or full representation (this covers assistance with representation in court)
– support funding – either investigative support or litigation support (this is a new type of assistance which allows the costs of a privately funded case to be topped up from public funds. It is only available for personal injury claims)
– family mediation
– such other services as are specifically authorised by the Lord Chancellor

In general, public funding is not available for the following type of cases:
– personal injury (except for the availability of support funding and clinical negligence claims)
– allegations of negligent damage to property
– conveyancing
– boundary disputes
– the making of wills
– matters of trust law
– defamation proceedings
– partnership disputes and company law
– other matters arising out of the carrying on of a business.

ELIGIBILITY

Eligibility for funding from the Community Legal Service depends broadly on 5 factors:
– the level of service sought (see above)
– whether the applicant qualifies financially
– the merits if the applicant's case (cases with less than a 50% chance of success will not usually be supported)
– a costs-benefits analysis (if the costs are likely to outweigh any benefit that might be gained from the proceedings, funding may be refused)

– whether there is any public interest in the case being litigated (i.e. whether the case has a wider public interest beyond that of the parties involved – for example, a human rights case)

The limits on capital and income above which a person is not entitled to public funding vary with the type of service sought.

CONTRIBUTIONS

Some of those who qualify for Community Legal Service funding will have to contribute towards their legal costs:
– if in receipt of income support or income-based job seeker's allowance, no contributions are due
– if annual disposable income is between £2,723 and £8,067, a contribution must be made from disposable income
– if disposable capital is over £3,000, all disposable capital in excess of £3,000 must be paid as a contribution

Contributions from disposable income are paid monthly. The amount of the contribution depends on the amount of disposable income in excess of £2,723; the greater the excess income, the greater the contribution. Contributions from capital are payable immediately. There are extra allowances for people over 60.

STATUTORY CHARGE

A statutory charge is made if a person receives money or property in a case for which they have received legal aid. This means that the amount paid by the Community Legal Service fund on their behalf is deducted from the amount that the person receives. This does not apply if the court has ordered that the costs be paid by the other party (unless the amount paid by the other party does not cover all of the costs) or if the payments are for maintenance. In family proceedings cases, the first £2,500 is exempt and the statutory charge is taken from anything in excess of that.

CONTINGENCY OR CONDITIONAL FEES

This system was introduced by the Courts and Legal Services Act 1990. It offers legal representation on a "no win, no fee" basis. It provides an alternative form of assistance, especially for those cases which are ineligible for funding by the Community Legal Service. The main area for such work is in the field of personal injuries which claims are now largely exempt from public finding (except for clinical negligence claims).

Not all solicitors offer such a scheme and different solicitors may well have different terms. The effect of the agreement is that solicitors will not make any charges until the case is concluded successfully. The charges are usually linked to a percentage of the amount recovered. The merits of a case are usually assessed before the scheme is offered to potential litigants. Should the case be accepted, then the percentage charges will be linked to the risks involved: the higher the risks, the higher the percentage. Any agreement should be in writing and set out the exact terms of the agreement and the effects of success and failure.

SCOTLAND

Civil legal aid is available for cases in the following:
– the House of Lords
– the Court of Session
– the Lands Valuation Appeal Court
– the Scottish Land Court
– sheriff courts
– the Lands Tribunal for Scotland
– the Employment Appeal Tribunals
– the Restrictive Practices Court

Eligibility for civil legal aid is assessed in a similar way to that in England and Wales, though the financial limits differ in some respects and are as follows:
– a person is eligible if disposable income is £8,571 or less and disposable capital is £8,560 or less
– if disposable income is between £2,625 and £8,571, contributions are payable
– if disposable capital exceeds £3,000, contributions are payable

CRIMINAL LEGAL AID

Criminal legal aid is now administered by the Legal Services Commission. As part of the changes under the Access to Justice Act 1999, in April 2001 the Criminal Defence Service will be introduced to replace the old system of criminal legal aid under the Legal Aid Act 1988 (which continues in force until then). Up-to-date information and further guidance can be obtained from the Legal Services Commission website http://www.legalservices.gov.uk or from a solicitor or Citizens' Advice Bureau.

The courts will grant criminal legal aid if it is desirable in the interests of justice (e.g. if there are important questions of law to be argued or the case is so serious that if found guilty the person may go to prison) and the person needs help to pay their legal costs.

Criminal legal aid covers the cost of preparing a case and legal representation (including the cost of a barrister) in criminal proceedings. It is also available for appeals against verdicts or sentences in magistrates' courts, the Crown Court or the Court of Appeal. It is not available for bringing a private prosecution in a criminal court.

If granted criminal legal aid, either the person may choose their own solicitor or the court will assign one. Contributions to the legal costs must be paid by anyone who has a disposable income of over £53 a week or disposable capital of over £3,000. These contributions are payable each month and will probably be returned to the person if they are acquitted. If the payments are not made, the legal aid order may be revoked.

DUTY SOLICITORS

The Legal Aid Act 1988 also provides free advice and assistance to anyone questioned by the police (whether under arrest or helping the police with their enquiries). No means test or contributions are required for this. The advice or assistance can be from the duty solicitor at the police station, from a person's own solicitor or from any local solicitor (a list is available at police stations).

Duty solicitors are usually available at the magistrates' court, in criminal cases, for advice and/or representation on first appearances. This assistance is not means-tested.

SCOTLAND

Legal advice and assistance operates in a similar way in Scotland. A person is eligible:
– if disposable income does not exceed £180 a week. If disposable income is between £76 and £180 a week, contributions are payable
– if disposable capital does not exceed £1,000 (£1,335 if the person has one dependant, £1,535 if two dependants with an additional £100 for every other dependant). There are no contributions from capital

SCOTLAND

The procedure for application for criminal legal aid depends on the circumstances of each case. In solemn cases (more serious cases, such as homicide) heard before a jury, a person is automatically entitled to criminal legal aid until they are given bail or placed in custody. Thereafter, it is for the court to decide whether to grant legal aid. The court will do this if the person accused cannot meet the expenses of the case without undue hardship on him or his dependants. In less serious cases the procedure depends on whether the person is in custody:

- anyone taken into custody has the right to free legal aid from the duty solicitor up to and including the first court appearance
- if the person is not in custody and wishes to plead guilty, they are not entitled to criminal legal aid but may be entitled to legal advice and assistance, including assistance by way of representation
- if the person is not in custody and wishes to plead not guilty, they can apply for criminal legal aid. This must be done within 14 days of the first court appearance at which they made the plea

The criteria used to assess whether or not criminal legal aid should be granted is similar to the criteria for England and Wales.

MARRIAGE

Any two persons may marry provided that:

- they are at least 16 years old on the day of the marriage (in England and Wales persons under the age of 18 must generally obtain the consent of their parents; if consent is refused an appeal may be made to the High Court, the county court or a court of summary jurisdiction)
- they are not related to one another in a way which would prevent their marrying (*see* below)
- they are unmarried (a person who has already been married must produce documentary evidence that the previous marriage has been ended by death, divorce or annulment)
- they are not of the same sex
- they are capable of understanding the nature of a marriage ceremony and of consenting to marriage
- the marriage would be regarded as valid in any foreign country of which either party is a citizen

DEGREES OF RELATIONSHIP

A marriage between persons within the prohibited degrees of consanguinity, affinity or adoption is void.

A man may not marry his mother, daughter, grandmother, granddaughter, sister, aunt, niece, great-grandmother, great-granddaughter, adoptive mother, former adoptive mother, adopted daughter or former adopted daughter. In some circumstances he may now be allowed to marry his former wife's daughter, former wife's granddaughter, father's former wife or grandfather's former wife.

A woman may not marry her father, son, grandfather, grandson, brother, uncle, nephew, great-grandfather, great-grandson, adoptive father, former adoptive father, adopted son or former adopted son. In some circumstances she may now be allowed to marry her former husband's son, former husband's grandson, mother's former husband or grandmother's former husband.

ENGLAND AND WALES

TYPES OF MARRIAGE CEREMONY

It is possible to marry by either religious or civil ceremony. A religious ceremony can take place at a church or chapel of the Church of England or the Church in Wales, or at any other place of worship which has been formally registered by the Registrar-General.

A civil ceremony can take place at a register office, a registered building or any other premises approved by the local authority.

An application for an approved premises licence must be made by the owners or trustees of the building concerned; it cannot be made by the prospective marriage couple. Approved premises must be regularly open to the public so that the marriage can be witnessed; the venue must be deemed to be a permanent and immovable structure. Open-air ceremonies are prohibited.

Non-Anglican marriages may also be solemnised following the issue of a Registrar-General's licence in unregistered premises where one of the parties is seriously ill, is not expected to recover, and cannot be moved to registered premises. Detained and housebound persons may be married at their place of residence.

MARRIAGE IN THE CHURCH OF ENGLAND OR THE CHURCH IN WALES

Marriage by banns

The marriage must take place in a parish in which one of the parties lives, or in a church in another parish if it is the usual place of worship of either or both of the parties. The banns must be called in the parish in which the marriage is to take place on three Sundays before the day of the ceremony; if either or both of the parties lives in a different parish the banns must also be called there. After three months the banns are no longer valid.

Marriage by common licence

The vicar who is to conduct the marriage will arrange for a common licence to be issued by the diocesan bishop; this dispenses with the necessity for banns. One of the parties must have lived in the parish for 15 days immediately before the issuing of the licence or must usually worship at the church. Affidavits are prepared from the personal instructions of one of the parties and the licence will be given to the applicant in person.

Marriage by special licence

A special licence is granted by the Archbishop of Canterbury in special circumstances for the marriage to take place at any place, with or without previous residence in the parish, or at any time. Application must be made to the Faculty Office of the Archbishop of Canterbury, 1 The Sanctuary, London SW1P 3JT. Tel: 020-7222 5381.

Marriage by certificate

The marriage can be conducted on the authority of the superintendent registrar's certificate, provided that the vicar's consent is obtained. One of the parties must live in the parish or must usually worship at the church.

MARRIAGE BY OTHER RELIGIOUS CEREMONY

One of the parties must normally live in the registration district where the marriage is to take place. In addition to giving notice to the superintendent registrar it may also be necessary to book a registrar to be present at the ceremony.

CIVIL MARRIAGE

A marriage may be solemnised at any register office, registered building or approved premises in England and Wales. The superintendent registrar of the district should be contacted, and, if the marriage is to take place at approved premises, the necessary arrangements at the venue must also be made.

NOTICE OF MARRIAGE

Unless it is to take place by banns or under common or special licence in the Church of England or the Church in Wales, a notice of the marriage must be given in person to the superintendent registrar. Notice of marriage may be given in the following ways:
– by certificate. Both parties must have lived in a registration district in England or Wales for at least seven days immediately before giving notice at the local register office. If they live in different registration districts, notice must be given in both districts. The marriage can take place in any register office in England and Wales 21 days after notice has been given
– by licence (often known as 'special licence'). One of the parties must have lived in a registration district in England or Wales for at least 15 days before giving notice at the register office; the other party need only be a resident of, or be physically in, England and Wales on the day notice is given. The marriage can take place one clear day (other than a Sunday, Christmas Day or Good Friday) after notice has been given

A notice of marriage is valid for 12 months. It is not therefore possible to give formal notice of a marriage more than three months before it is to take place, but it should be possible to make an advance (provisional) booking 12 months before the ceremony. In this case it is still necessary to give formal notice three months before the marriage. When giving notice of the marriage it is necessary to produce official proof, if relevant, that any previous marriage has ended in divorce or death by producing a decree absolute or death certificate; it is also useful, but not necessary, to take birth certificates or passports as proof of age and identity.

SOLEMNISATION OF THE MARRIAGE

On the day of the wedding there must be at least two other people present who are prepared to act as witnesses and sign the marriage register. A registrar of marriages must be present at a marriage in a register office or at approved premises, but an authorised person may act in the capacity of registrar in a registered building.

If the marriage takes place at approved premises, the room must be separate from any other activity on the premises at the time of the ceremony, and no food or drink can be sold or consumed in the room during the ceremony or for one hour beforehand.

The marriage must be solemnised between 8 a.m. and 6 p.m., with open doors. At some time during the ceremony the parties must make a declaration that they know of no legal impediment to the marriage and they must also say the contracting words; the declaratory and contracting words may vary according to the form of service in use.

A civil marriage cannot contain any religious aspects, but it may be possible for non-religious music and/or poetry readings to be included. It may also be possible to embellish the marriage vows taken by the couple.

If both parties are Jewish, they may be married in a synagogue, in a private house or elsewhere. The wedding may take place at any time of day and must be registered by the secretary of the synagogue of which the man is a member. The presence of a registrar of marriages is not necessary.

If both parties are members of the Society of Friends (Quakers), they may be married in a Friends' meeting-house. The marriage must be registered by the registering officer of the Society appointed to act for the district in which the meeting-house is situated. The presence of a registrar of marriages is not necessary.

CIVIL FEES *from 1 April 2000*

Marriage at a Register Office (the fees below include a fee of £34.00 for the registrar's attendance on the day of the wedding)

By superintendent registrar's certificate where the partners live in the same registration district, £59.00
By superintendent registrar's certificate where the partners live in different registration districts, £84.00
By superintendent registrar's licence, £105.50

Marriage on Approved Premises (in addition to the fees below a fee will also be payable for the superintendent registrar's and registrar's attendance at the marriage which is set locally by the local authority responsible. A further charge is likely to be made by the owners of the building for the use of the premises) AND Marriage in a religious building other than in the Church of England or Church in Wales (in addition to the fees below a fee of £40.00 will also be payable for the registrar's attendance at the marriage unless an "Authorised Person" appointed by the trustees of the building has agreed to register to marriage. Additional fees may also be charged by the trustees of the building for the wedding, and by the person who performs the ceremony)

By superintendent registrar's certificate where the partners live in the same registration district, £25.00
By superintendent registrar's certificate where the partners live in different registration districts, £50.00
By superintendent registrar's licence, £71.50

ECCLESIASTICAL FEES *since 1 April 2000*

(Church of England and Church in Wales*)
Marriage by banns
For publication of banns, £15.00
For certificate of banns issued at time of publication, £8.00
For marriage service, £132.00
Marriage by common licence
Fee for licence, £57.00
Marriage by special licence
Fee for licence, £125.00
Further fees may be payable for additional facilities at the marriage, e.g. the organist's fee.

*Some of these fees may not apply to the Church in Wales

SCOTLAND

REGULAR MARRIAGES

A regular marriage is one which is celebrated by a minister of religion or authorised registrar or other celebrant. Each of the parties must complete a marriage notice form and return it to the district registrar for the area in which they are to be married, irrespective of where they live, at least 15 days before the ceremony is due to take place. The district registrar must then enter the date of receipt and certain details in a marriage book kept for this purpose, and must also enter the names of the parties and the proposed date of marriage in a list which is displayed in a conspicuous place at the registration office until the date of the marriage has passed. All persons wishing to enter into a regular marriage in Scotland must follow the same preliminary procedure regardless of whether they intend to have a religious or civil ceremony.

A marriage schedule, which is prepared by the registrar, will be issued to one or both of the parties in person up to seven days before a religious marriage; for a civil marriage the schedule will be available at the ceremony. The schedule must be handed to the celebrant before the ceremony starts; it must be signed immediately after the wedding and the marriage must be registered within three days.

The authority to conduct a religious marriage is deemed to be vested in the authorised celebrant rather than the building in which it takes place; open-air religious ceremonies are therefore permissible in Scotland.

MARRIAGE BY COHABITATION WITH HABIT AND REPUTE

If two people live together constantly as husband and wife and are generally held to be such by the neighbourhood and among their friends and relations, there may arise a presumption from which marriage can be inferred. Before such a marriage can be registered, however, a decree of declarator of marriage must be obtained from the Court of Session.

CIVIL FEES *from 1 April 1998*

The basic statutory fee is £77.00, comprising a £12.00 per person fee for a statutory notice of intention to marry, a £45.00 fee for solemnisation of the marriage in a register office, and an £8.00 fee for a copy of the marriage certificate.

Further information can be obtained from:
THE GENERAL REGISTER OFFICE, Office for National Statistics, Smedley Hydro, Trafalgar Road, Birkdale, Southport, Merseyside PR8 2HH. Tel: 01704-569824
THE GENERAL REGISTER OFFICE FOR SCOTLAND, New Register House, Edinburgh EH1 3YT. Tel: 0131-334 0380

TOWN AND COUNTRY PLANNING

The principal legislation governing the development of land and buildings in England and Wales is the Town and Country Planning Act 1990 (as amended by the Planning and Compensation Act 1991). The equivalent legislation in Scotland is the Town and Country Planning (Scotland) Act 1997. The uses of buildings are classified by the Town and Country Planning (Use Classes) Order 1987 (as amended) in England and Wales, and in Scotland by the Town and Country Planning (Use Classes) (Scotland) Order 1997. It is advisable in all cases to contact the planning department of the local authority to check whether planning or other permission is needed.

PLANNING PERMISSION

Planning permission is needed if the work involves:
– making a material change in use, such as dividing off part of the house so that it can be used as a separate home or dividing off part of the house for commercial use, e.g. for a workshop
– going against the terms of the original planning permission, e.g. there may be a restriction on fences in front gardens on an open-plan estate
– building, engineering for mining, except for the permissions below
– new or wider access to a main road
– additions or extensions to flats or maisonettes
Planning permission is not needed to carry out internal alterations or work which does not affect the external appearance of the building.

There are certain types of development for which the Secretary of State for the Environment has granted general permissions. These include:
– house extensions and additions (including conservatories, loft conversions, garages and dormer windows). Up to 10 per cent or up to 50 cubic metres (whichever is the greater) can be added to the original house for terraced houses. Up to 15 per cent or 70 cubic metres (whichever is the greater) to other kinds of houses. The

maximum that can be added to any house is 115 cubic metres
– buildings such as garden sheds and greenhouses so long as they are no more than 3 metres high (or 4 metres if the roof is ridged), are no nearer to a highway than the house, and at least half the ground around the house remains uncovered by buildings
– adding a porch with a ground area of less than 3 square metres and that is less than 3 metres in height
– putting up fences, walls and gates of under 1 metre in height if next to a road and under 2 metres elsewhere
– laying patios, paths or driveways for domestic use

OTHER RESTRICTIONS

It may be necessary to obtain other types of permissions before carrying out any development. These permissions are separate from planning permission and apply regardless of whether or not planning permission is needed, e.g.:
– building regulations will probably apply if a new building is to be erected, if an existing one is to be altered or extended, or if the work involves building over a drain or sewer. The building control department of the local authority will advise on this
– any alterations to a listed building or the grounds of a listed building must be approved by the local authority
– local authority approval is necessary if a building (or, in some circumstances, gates, walls, fences or railings) in a conservation area is to be demolished; each local authority keeps a register of all local buildings that are in conservation areas
– many trees are protected by tree preservation orders and must not be pruned or taken down without local authority consent
– bats and other species are protected and English Nature, the Countryside Council for Wales or Scottish Natural Heritage (for entries, *see* Index) must be notified before any work is carried out that will affect the habitat of protected species, e.g. timber treatment, renovation or extensions of lofts
– any development in areas designated as a National Park, an Area of Outstanding Natural Beauty, a National Scenic Area or in the Norfolk or Suffolk Broads is subject to greater restrictions. The local planning authority will advise or refer enquirers to the relevant authority

VOTERS' QUALIFICATIONS

Those entitled to vote at parliamentary, European Union (EU) and local government elections are those who are:
– resident in the constituency or ward on the qualifying date i.e. 10 October in the year before the electoral register (*see* below) comes into effect; in Northern Ireland the qualifying date is 15 September and voters must have been resident in Northern Ireland for the three months leading up to that date
– over 18 years old
– Commonwealth (which includes British) citizens or citizens of the Republic of Ireland
British citizens resident abroad are entitled to vote, for 20 years after leaving Britain, as overseas electors in parliamentary and EU elections in the constituency in which they were last resident. Members of the armed forces, Crown servants and employees of the British Council who are overseas and their spouses are entitled to vote regardless of how long they have been abroad.

European Union citizens resident in the UK may vote in EU and local government elections.

The main categories of people who are not entitled to vote are:
- patients detained under mental health legislation
- voluntary mental patients (unless they make a prescribed declaration)
- those serving prison sentences
- those convicted within the previous five years of corrupt or illegal election practices

REGISTERING TO VOTE

Voters must be entered on an electoral register, which runs from 16 February in one year to 15 February in the following year. The registration officer for each constituency is responsible for preparing and publishing the register. A registration form is sent to all households in the autumn of each year and the householder is required to provide details of all occupants who are eligible to vote, including ones who will reach their 18th birthday in the year covered by the register. Those who fail to give the required information or who give false information are liable to be fined.

VOTING

Voting is not compulsory in the UK. Those who wish to vote must generally vote in person at the allotted polling station. Those who will be away at the time of the election, those who will not be able to attend in person due to physical incapacity or the nature of their occupation, and those who have changed address during the period for which the register is valid, may apply for a postal vote or nominate a proxy to vote for them. Overseas electors who wish to vote must do so by proxy.

Further information can be obtained from the local authority's electoral registration officer in England and Wales or the electoral registration office in Scotland, or the Chief Electoral Officer in Northern Ireland.

WILLS AND INTESTACY

In a will a person leaves instructions as to the disposal of their property after they die. A will is also used to appoint executors (who will administer the estate), give directions as to the disposal of the body, appoint guardians for children and, for larger estates, can operate to reduce the level of inheritance tax. It is best to have a will drawn up by a solicitor but if a solicitor is not employed, the following points must be taken into account:
- if possible the will must not be prepared on behalf of another person by someone who is to benefit from it or who is a close relative of a major beneficiary
- the language used must be clear and unambiguous and it is better to avoid the use of legal terms where the same thing can be expressed in plain language
- it is better to rewrite the whole document if a mistake is made. If necessary, alterations can be made by striking through the words with a pen, and the signature or initials of the testator and the witnesses must be put in the margin opposite the alteration. No alteration of any kind should be made after the will has been executed
- if the person later wishes to change the will or part of it, it is better to write a new will revoking the old. The use of codicils (documents written as supplements or containing modifications to the will) should be left to a solicitor
- the will should be typed or printed, or if handwritten be legible and preferably in ink. Commercial will forms can

be obtained from some stationers

The form of a will varies to suit different cases; the following is an example of how a will might be written. The notes after this example explain the terms used and procedures that need to be followed in drawing up a will.

This is the last will and testament of me [*Thomas Smith*] of [*Heather Cottage, Prospero Road, Manchester* M1 4DK] which I make this [*seventeenth*] day of [*May 1999*] and I revoke all previous wills and testamentary dispositions.
1. I appoint as my executors and trustees [*Ann Green of_____ and Richard Brown of_____*]. In my will the expression 'my Trustees' means any executors and trustees for the time being of my will and of any trust arising under it.
2. I give all my property to [*such of my children as shall survive me by 28 days and if more than one in equal shares* or as the case may be].
or
2. I give to [*Pamela Henderson of_____*] the sum of [£_____] and to [*Michael Broadbent of_____*] the sum of [£_____] and to [*Ruth Walker of_____*] all of my [*jewellery, books* or as the case may be]
and
3. I give everything not otherwise disposed of to [*Richard Black of_____*]
Signed by the testator in our joint presence and then by us in his.
Thomas Smith
[*Signature of the person making the will*]
Elizabeth Wall
[*Signature of witness*] of 67 Beatrice Lane, Manchester M1 4DK, journalist
William Jones
[*Signature of witness*] of 17 Paris Road, Manchester M1 4EN, tailor

SPECIFIC GIFTS AND LEGACIES

Gifts of specific items usually fail if the property is not owned by the person making the will on their death. This problem can be avoided by making a gift of any property fulfilling a particular description, e.g. a car, which is owned at the date of death. It is better in all cases where such gifts are made, to insert a clause which reads 'I give everything not otherwise disposed of to [*Richard Black of_____*], even if it seems that all property has been disposed of in the will.

LAPSED LEGATEES

If a person who has been left property in a will dies before the person who made the will, the gift fails and will pass to the person entitled to everything not otherwise disposed of (the residuary estate).

If the person left the residuary estate dies before the person who made the will, their share will generally pass to the closest relative(s) of the person who made the will (as in intestacy) unless the will names a beneficiary such as a charity who will take as a 'long stop' if this gift is unable to take effect for any reason.

It is always better to draw up a new will if a beneficiary predeceases the person who made the will.

EXECUTORS

It is usual to appoint two executors, although one is sufficient. No more than four persons can deal with the estate of the person who has died. The name and address of each executor should be given in full (the addresses are not essential but including them adds clarity to the document).

Executors should be 18 years of age or over. An executor may be a beneficiary of the will.

WITNESSES

A person who is a beneficiary of a will, or the spouse of a beneficiary at the time the will is signed, must not act as a witness or else he/she will be unable to take his/her gift. Husband and wife can both act as witnesses provided neither benefits from the will.

It is better that a person does not act as an executor and as a witness, as he/she can take no benefit under a will to which he/she is witness. The identity of the witnesses should be made as explicit as possible.

EXECUTION OF A WILL

The person making the will should sign his/her name at the foot of the document, in the presence of the two witnesses. The witnesses must then sign their names while the person making the will looks on. If this procedure is not adhered to, the will will be considered invalid. There are certain exceptional circumstances where these rules are relaxed, e.g. where the person may be too ill to sign, and in these cases the attestation clause which normally reads 'signed by the testator in our joint presence and then by us in his/hers' should be reworded as follows:

'The will was read over to Thomas Smith in our presence when he stated that he understood it. It was then signed on his behalf by Thomas Brown in the presence of the testator and by his direction in our joint presence and then by us in his'.

CAPACITY TO MAKE A WILL

Anyone aged 18 or over can make a will. However, if there is any suspicion that the person making the will is not, through reasons of infirmity or age, fully in command of his/her faculties, it is advisable to arrange for a medical practitioner to examine the person making the will at the time it is to be executed to verify his/her mental capacity and to record that medical opinion in writing, and to ask the examining practitioner to act as a witness. If a person is not mentally able to make a will, the Court may do this for him/her by virtue of the Mental Health Act 1983.

REVOCATION

A will may be revoked or cancelled in a number of ways:
- a later will revokes an earlier one if it says so; otherwise the earlier will is impliedly revoked by the later one to the extent that it contradicts or repeats the earlier one
- a will is also revoked if the physical document on which it is written is destroyed by the person whose will it is. There must be an intention to revoke the will. It may not be sufficient to obliterate the will with a pen
- a will is revoked when the person marries, unless it is clear from the will that the person intended the will to stand after the marriage
- where a marriage ends in divorce or is annulled or declared void, gifts to the spouse and the appointment of the spouse as executor fail unless the will says that this is not to happen. A former spouse is treated as having predeceased the testator. A separation does not change the effect of a married person's will.

PROBATE AND LETTERS OF ADMINISTRATION

Probate is granted to the executors named in a will and once granted, the executors are obliged to carry out the instructions of the will. Letters of administration are granted where no executor is named in a will or is willing or able to act or where there is no will or no valid will; this gives a person, often the next of kin, similar powers and duties to those of an executor.

Applications for probate or for letters of administration can be made to the Principal Registry of the Family Division, to a district probate registry or to a probate sub-registry. Applicants will need the following documents: the original will (if any); a certificate of death; oath for executors or administrators; particulars of all property and assets left by the deceased; a list of debts and funeral expenses. Certain property, up to the value of £5,000, may be disposed of without a grant of probate or letters of administration.

WHERE TO FIND A PROVED WILL

Since 1858 wills which have been proved, that is wills on which probate or letters of administration have been granted, must have been proved at the Principal Registry of the Family Division or at a district probate registry. The Lord Chancellor has power to direct where the original documents are kept but most are filed where they were proved and may be inspected there and a copy obtained. The Principal Registry also holds copies of all wills proved at district probate registries and these may be inspected at Somerset House. An index of all grants, both of probate and of letters of administration, is compiled by the Principal Registry and may be seen either at the Principal Registry or at a district probate registry.

It is also possible to discover when a grant of probate or letters of administration is issued by requesting a standing search. In response to a request and for a small fee, a district probate registry will supply the names and addresses of executors or administrators and the registry in which the grant was made, of any grant in the estate of a specified person made in the previous 12 months or following six months. This is useful for applicants under the Inheritance (Provision for Family and Dependants) Act 1975 (*see* Intestacy, page 675) and for creditors of the deceased.

SCOTLAND

In Scotland any person over 12 and of sound mind can make a will. The person making the will can only freely dispose of the heritage and what is known as the 'dead's part' of the estate because:
- the spouse has the right to inherit one-third of the moveable estate if there are children or other descendants, and one-half of it if there are not
- children are entitled to one-third of the moveable estate if there is a surviving spouse, and one-half of it if there is not

The remaining portion is the dead's part, and legacies and bequests are payable from this. Debts are payable out of the whole estate before any division.

From August 1995, wills no longer needed to be 'holographed' and it is now only necessary to have one witness. The person making the will still needs to sign each page. It is better that the will is not witnessed by a beneficiary although the attestation would still be sound and the beneficiary would not have to relinquish the gift.

Subsequent marriage does not revoke a will but the birth of a child who is not provided for may do so. A will may be revoked by a subsequent will, either expressly or by implication, but in so far as the two can be read together both have effect. If a subsequent will is revoked, the earlier will is revived.

Wills may be registered in the sheriff court Books of the Sheriffdom in which the deceased lived or in the Books of Council and Session at the Registers of Scotland.

CONFIRMATION

Confirmation (the Scottish equivalent of probate) is obtained in the sheriff court of the sheriffdom in which the deceased was resident at the time of death. Executives are either 'nominate' (named by the deceased in the will) or 'dative' (appointed by the court in cases where no executor is named in a will or in cases of intestacy). Applicants for confirmation must first provide an inventory of the deceased's estate and a schedule of debts, with an affidavit. In estates under £25,000 gross, confirmation can be obtained under a simplified procedure at reduced fees. The local sheriff clerk's office can provide assistance.

INTESTACY

Intestacy occurs when someone dies without leaving a will or leaves a will which is invalid or which does not take effect for some reason. In such cases the person's estate (property, possessions, other assets following the payment of debts) passes to certain members of the family. The relevant legislation is the Administration of Estates Act 1925, as amended by various legislation including the Intestates Estates Act 1952, the Law Reform (Succession) Act 1995, and the Trusts of Land and Appointment of Trustees Act 1996 and Orders made there under. Some of the provisions of this legislation are described below. If a will has been written that disposes of only part of a person's property, these rules apply to the part which is undisposed of.

If the person (intestate) leaves a spouse who survives for 28 days and children (legitimate, illegitimate and adopted children and other descendants), the estate is divided as follows:

- the spouse takes the 'personal chattels' (household articles, including cars, but nothing used for business purposes), £125,000 free of tax (with interest payable at 6 per cent from the time of the death until payment) and a life interest in half of the rest of the estate (which can be capitalised by the spouse if he/she wishes)
- the rest of the estate goes to the children*

If the person leaves a spouse who survives for 28 days but no children:

- the spouse takes the personal chattels, £200,000 free of tax (interest payable as before) and full ownership of half of the rest of the estate
- the other half of the rest of the estate goes to the parents (equally, if both alive) or, if none, to the brothers and sisters of the whole blood*
- if there are no parents or brothers or sisters of the whole blood or their children, the spouse takes the whole estate

If there is no surviving spouse, the estate is distributed among those who survive the intestate as follows:

- to surviving children*, but if none to
- parents (equally, if both alive), but if none to
- brothers and sisters of the whole blood*, but if none to
- brothers and sisters of the half blood*, but if none to
- grandparents (equally, if more than one), but if none to
- aunts and uncles of the whole blood*, but if none to
- aunts and uncles of the half blood*, but if none to
- the Crown, Duchy of Lancaster or the Duke of Cornwall (*bona vacantia*)

* To inherit, a member of these groups must survive the intestate and attain 18, or marry under that age. If they die under 18 (unless married under that age), their share goes to others, if any, in the same group. If any member of these groups predeceases the intestate leaving children, their share is divided equally among their children.

In England and Wales the provisions of the Inheritance (Provision for Family and Dependants) Act 1975 may allow other people to claim provision from the deceased's assets. This Act also applies to cases where a will has been made and allows a person to apply to the Court if they feel that the will or rules of intestacy or both do not make adequate provision for them. The Court can order payment from the deceased's assets or the transfer of property from them if the applicant's claim is accepted. The application must be made within six months of the grant of probate or letters of administration and the following people can make an application:

- the spouse
- a former spouse who has not remarried
- a child of the deceased
- someone treated as a child of the deceased's family
- someone maintained by the deceased
- someone who has cohabited for two years before the death in the same household as the deceased and as the husband or wife of the deceased

SCOTLAND

Under the Succession (Scotland) Act 1964, no distinction is made between 'moveable' and 'heritable' property in intestacy cases.

A surviving spouse is entitled to 'prior rights'. This means that from 1 April 1999 the spouse has the right to inherit:

- the matrimonial home up to a value of £130,000, or one matrimonial home if there is more than one, or, in certain circumstances, the value of the matrimonial home
- the furnishings and contents of that home, up to the value of £22,000
- £35,000 if the deceased left children or other descendants, or £58,000 if not

These figures are increased from time to time by regulations.

Once prior rights have been satisfied, what remains of the estate is generally divided between the surviving spouse and children (legitimate and illegitimate) according to 'legal' rights. Legal rights are:

Jus relicti(ae) – the right of a surviving spouse to one-half of the net moveable estate, after satisfaction of prior rights, if there are no surviving children; if there are surviving children, the spouse is entitled to one-third of the net moveable estate

Legitim – the right of surviving children to one-half of the net moveable estate if there is no surviving spouse; if there is a surviving spouse, the children are entitled to one-third of the net moveable estate after the satisfaction of prior rights

Where there are no surviving spouse or children, half of the estate is taken by the parents and half by the brothers and sisters. Failing that, the lines of succession, in general, are:

- to descendants
- if no descendants, then to collaterals (i.e. brothers and sisters) and parents
- surviving spouse
- if no collaterals or parents or spouse, then to ascendants collaterals (i.e. aunts and uncles), and so on in an ascending scale
- if all lines of succession fail, the estate passes to the Crown

Relatives of the whole blood are preferred to relatives of the half blood. The right of representation, i.e. the right of the issue of a person who would have succeeded if he/she had survived the intestate, also applies.

Intellectual Property

COPYRIGHT

Copyright protects all original literary, dramatic, musical and artistic works (including photographs, maps and plans), published editions of works, computer programs, sound recordings, films (including video), broadcasts (including satellite broadcasts) and cable programmes (including on-line information services). Under copyright the creators of these works can control the various ways in which their material may be exploited, the rights broadly covering copying, adapting, issuing (including renting and lending) copies to the public, performing in public, and broadcasting the material.

Copyright protection in the United Kingdom is automatic and there is no registration system. The main legislation is the Copyright, Designs and Patents Act 1988, which has been amended by other Acts and by Statutory Instrument to take account of EC Directives. As a result of an EC Directive effective from January 1996, the term of copyright protection for literary, dramatic, musical and artistic works lasts until 70 years after the death of the author, and for film now lasts for 70 years after the death of the last to survive of the director, author of the screenplay, author of the dialogue and composer of music specially created for the film. Sound recordings are protected for 50 years after their publication, and broadcasts and cable programmes for 50 years from the end of the year in which the first broadcast/transmission is made. Published editions remain under copyright protection for 25 years from the end of the year in which the edition was published. An EC Directive effective from January 1998 created a 15-year non-copyright called 'database right' to protect substantial investment in obtaining, verifying or presenting the contents of a database.

The main international treaties protecting copyright are the Bern Convention for the Protection of Literary and Artistic Works, the Rome Convention for the Protection of Performers, Producers of Phonograms and Broadcasting Organisations, and the Universal Copyright Convention (UCC); the UK is a signatory to these conventions. Copyright material created by UK nationals or residents is protected in each country which is a member of the conventions by the national law of that country. A list of participating countries may be obtained from the Patent Office. The World Trade Organisation Trade-Related Aspects of Intellectual Property Agreement (TRIPS) also confers reciprocal obligations on signatory states to protect copyright works.

Two new treaties were agreed in December 1996, but have yet to enter into force. These are WIPO (World Intellectual Property Organisation) Copyright Treaty, and the WIPO Performance and Phonograms Treaty, which strengthen and update international standards of protection, particularly in relation to new technologies.

LICENSING

Reproduction of copyright material without seeking permission in each instance may be permitted under licence. The International Federation of Reproduction Rights Organisations facilitates agreements between its member licensing agencies and on behalf of its members with organisations such as the WIPO, UNESCO, the European Union and the Council of Europe.

PATENTS

A patent is a document issued by the Patent Office relating to an invention and giving the proprietor monopoly rights, effective within the United Kingdom (including the Isle of Man). In return the patentee pays a fee to cover the costs of processing the patent and publicly discloses details of the invention.

To qualify for a patent an invention must be new, must exhibit an inventive step, and must be capable of industrial application. The patent is valid for a maximum of 20 years from the date on which the application was filed, subject to payment of annual fees from the end of the fourth year.

The Patent Office, established in 1852, is responsible for ensuring that all stages of an application comply with the Patents Act 1977, and that the invention meets the criteria for a patent. Patent Office Examiners check that the invention is new and innovative by searching previously published documents on the Patent Office databank, which contains details of some two million British patents, together with published international and European applications. The contents of the databank and of the Science Reference Library, which developed from the library established at the Patent Office, are available to the public.

The WIPO is responsible for administering many of the international conventions on intellectual property. The Patent Co-operation Treaty allows inventors to file a single application for patent rights in some or all of the 101 contracting states. This application is searched by an International Searching Authority and published by the International Bureau of WIPO. It may also be the subject of an (optional) international preliminary examination. Applicants must then deal directly with the patent offices in the countries where they are seeking patent rights.

The European Patent Convention, linked to the Patent Co-operation Treaty, allows inventors to obtain patent rights in all 19 contracting states by filing a single European patent application which is processed by the European Patent Office (EPO). Once granted, the patent is subject to national laws in each signatory country. To comply with security requirements, an applicant resident in the UK must file a European patent application with the UK Patent Office unless the Patent Office gives permission for it to be filed directly with the EPO.

TRADE MARKS

Trade marks are a means of identification, whether a word or device or a combination of both, a logo, or the shape of goods or their packaging, which enable traders to make their goods or services readily distinguishable from those supplied by other traders. Registration prevents other traders using the same or a similar trade mark for similar products or services for which the mark is registered.

In the UK trade marks are registered at the Trade Marks Registry in the Patent Office. In order to qualify for registration a mark must be capable of distinguishing its proprietor's goods or services from those of other undertakings. It should be non-deceptive and not easily confused with a mark that has already been registered for the same or similar goods or services. The relevant current legislation is the Trade Marks Act 1994.

It is possible to obtain an international trade mark registration, effective in 61 countries, under the Madrid Agreement. UK companies cannot take advantage of this because the UK is not a party to this agreement. Following revision of UK trade marks law, however, the UK has ratified the protocol to the Madrid Agreement, and British companies can now obtain international trade mark registration through a single application to WIPO in those countries party to the protocol.

EC trade mark regulation is now in force and is administered by the Office for Harmonisation in the Internal Market (Trade Marks and Designs) in Alicante, Spain. The office registers EC trade marks, which are a unitary right valid throughout the European Union. The national registration of trade marks in member states is continuing in parallel with the EC trade mark.

DESIGN PROTECTION

Design protection covers the outward appearance of an article and takes two forms in the UK, registered design and design right, which are not mutually exclusive. Registered design protects the aesthetic appearance of an article, including shape, configuration, pattern or ornament, although artistic works such as sculptures are excluded, being generally protected by copyright. In order to qualify for protection, a design must be new and materially different from earlier UK published designs. The owner of the design must apply to the Designs Registry at the Patent Office. Initial registration lasts for five years and is extendible in five-yearly steps to a maximum of 25 years. The current legislation is the Registered Designs Act 1949 (as amended).

There is no international design registry currently available to UK applicants; in general, separate applications must be made in each country in which protection is sought. However, the EC Directive for the Legal Protection of Designs was adopted in 1998 to harmonise laws on certain aspects of design protection throughout the European Union. Member states are to amend their laws to comply with the Directive by 28 October 2001.

Design right is an automatic right which applies to the shape or configuration of articles and does not require registration. Unlike registered design, two-dimensional designs do not qualify for protection but designs of semiconductor chips (topographies) are protected by design right. Designs must be original and non-commonplace. The term of design right is ten years from first marketing of the design and the right is effective only in the UK. The current legislation is Part 3 of the Copyright, Designs and Patents Act 1988.

LEGAL DEPOSIT

Publishers are legally obliged to send one copy of a new publication to each of the legal deposit libraries within one month of publication. The aim of legal deposit is to keep a complete national archive of published works as a current reference and information source. The legal deposit libraries are the British Library, the Bodleian Library in Oxford, Cambridge University Library, the National Library of Scotland, the National Library of Wales, and Trinity College Library in Dublin.

The British Library's Legal Deposit Office is split between two locations; books and other publications are deposited at Boston Spa, and newspapers and periodicals at the Newspaper Legal Deposit Office in London. All publications for the other four copyright libraries in the UK are dealt with by the Agent for the Copyright Libraries.

In 1998 the Report of the Working Party on Legal Deposit recommended that legislation should be introduced establishing legal deposit for certain electronically published materials (mainly CD-ROMs). The Government agreed in principle, but called for a voluntary scheme to be established first. In mid-1999 negotiations between publishers and the copyright libraries to agree a code of practice were still under way.

INTELLECTUAL PROPERTY ORGANISATIONS

AGENT FOR THE COPYRIGHT LIBRARIES, 100 Euston Street, London NW1 2HQ. Tel: 020-7380 0240. *Agent*, A. T. Smail

CHARTERED INSTITUTE OF PATENT AGENTS, Staple Inn Buildings, High Holborn, London WC1V 7PZ. Tel: 020-7405 9450

DESIGNS REGISTRY, The Patent Office, Cardiff Road, Newport NP10 8QQ. Tel: 0845-950 0505

EUROPEAN PATENT OFFICE, *Headquarters*, Erhardtstrasse 27, D-8000, Munich 2, Germany. Tel: 49-399 4538

INTERNATIONAL FEDERATION OF REPRODUCTION RIGHTS ORGANISATIONS (IFRRO), rue du Prince Royal 87, B-1050 Brussels, Belgium. Tel: 32-551 0899

LEGAL DEPOSIT OFFICE, The British Library, Boston Spa, Wetherby, W. Yorks LS23 7BY. Tel: 01937-546267

NEWSPAPER LEGAL DEPOSIT OFFICE, The British Library, Newspaper Library, Colindale Avenue, London NW9 5LF. Tel: 020-7412 7378

OFFICE FOR HARMONISATION IN THE INTERNAL MARKET (Trade Marks and Designs), 20 Avenida de la Aguilera, 03080 Alicante, Spain. Tel: 34-139459

THE PATENT OFFICE, Cardiff Road, Newport NP10 8QQ. Tel: 0845-950 0505

SCIENCE REFERENCE LIBRARY, 96 Euston Road, London NW1 2DB. Tel: 020-7412 7494

STATIONERS' HALL REGISTRY LTD, The Registrar, Stationers' Hall, Ave Maria Lane, London EC4M 7DD. Tel: 020-7248 2934

TRADE MARKS REGISTRY, The Patent Office, Cardiff Road, Newport NP10 8QQ. Tel: 0845-950 0505

WORLD INTELLECTUAL PROPERTY ORGANISATION (WIPO), 34 chemin des Colombettes, 1211 Geneva 20, Switzerland. Tel: 41-338 9111

COPYRIGHT LICENSING/COLLECTING AGENCIES

AUTHORS' LICENSING AND COLLECTING SOCIETY, Marlborough Court, 14–18 Holborn, London EC1N 2LE. Tel: 020-7395 0600

CHRISTIAN COPYRIGHT LICENSING (EUROPE) LTD, PO Box 1339, Eastbourne, E. Sussex BN21 4YF. Tel: 01323-417711

COPYRIGHT LICENSING AGENCY LTD, 90 Tottenham Court Road, London W1P 0LP. Tel: 020-7631 5555

DESIGN AND ARTISTS COPYRIGHT SOCIETY, Parchment House, 13 Northburgh Street, London EC1V 0JP. Tel: 020-7336 8811

EDUCATIONAL RECORDING AGENCY LTD, New Premier House, 150 Southampton Row, London WC1B 5AL. Tel: 020-7837 3222

INTERNATIONAL FEDERATION OF THE PHONOGRAPHIC INDUSTRIES, 54 Regent Street, London W1R 5PJ. Tel: 020-7878 7900

MCPS-PRS ALLIANCE, Copyright House, 29–33 Berners Street, London W1P 4AA. Tel: 020-7580 5544

NEWSPAPER LICENSING AGENCY, Lonsdale Gardens, Tunbridge Wells, Kent TN1 1NL. Tel: 01892-525274

PERFORMING RIGHT SOCIETY (PRS), *see* MCPS-PRS ALLIANCE

PHONOGRAPHIC PERFORMANCE LTD, 1 Upper James Street, London W1R 3HG. Tel: 020-7534 1000

PUBLISHERS LICENSING SOCIETY, 5 Dryden Street, London WC2E 9NW. Tel: 020-7829 8486

VIDEO PERFORMANCE LTD, 1 Upper James Street, London W1R 3HG. Tel: 020-7534 1400

The Media

CROSS-MEDIA OWNERSHIP

There are rules on cross-media ownership to prevent undue concentration of ownership. These were amended by the Broadcasting Act 1996. Radio companies are now permitted to own one AM, one FM and one other (AM or FM) service; ownership of the third licence is subject to a public interest test. Local newspapers with a circulation under 20 per cent in an area are also allowed to own one AM, one FM and one other service, and may control a regional Channel 3 television service subject to a public interest test. Local newspapers with a circulation between 20 and 50 per cent in an area may own one AM and one FM service, subject to a public interest test, but may not control a regional Channel 3 service. Those with a circulation over 50 per cent may own one radio service in the area (provided that more than one independent local radio service serves the area) subject to a public interest test.

Ownership controls on the number of television or radio licences have been removed; holdings are now restricted to 15 per cent of the total television audience or 15 per cent of the total points available in the radio points scheme. Ownership controls on cable operators have also been removed. National newspapers with less than 20 per cent of national circulation may apply to control any broadcasting licences, subject to a public interest test. National newspapers with more than 20 per cent of national circulation may not have more than a 20 per cent interest in a licence to provide a Channel 3 service, Channel 5 or national and local analogue radio services.

Broadcasting

The British Broadcasting Corporation (*see* page 322) is responsible for public service broadcasting in the UK. Its constitution and finances are governed by royal charter and agreement. On 1 May 1996 a new royal charter came into force, establishing the framework for the BBC's activities until 2006.

The Independent Television Commission (*see* page 337) and the Radio Authority (*see* page 354) were set up under the terms of the Broadcasting Act 1990. The ITC is the regulator and licensing authority for all commercially-funded television services, including cable and satellite services. The Radio Authority is the regulator and licensing authority for all independent radio services.

COMPLAINTS

The Broadcasting Standards Commisson was set up in April 1997 under the Broadcasting Act 1996 and was formed from the merger of the Broadcasting Complaints Commission and the Broadcasting Standards Council. The Commission considers and adjudicates upon complaints of unfair treatment or unwarranted infringement of privacy in all broadcast programmes and advertisements on television, radio, cable, satellite and digital services. It also monitors the portrayal of violence and sex, and matters of taste and decency. Its new code of practice came into force on 1 January 1998.

BROADCASTING STANDARDS COMMISSION, 7 The Sanctuary, London SW1P 3JS. Tel: 020-7808 1000. *Chairman*, Lord Holme; *Deputy Chairmen*, Ms J. Leighton, Mrs S. Warner; *Director*, S. Whittle

TELEVISION

All channels are broadcast in colour on 625 lines UHF from a network of transmitting stations. The BBC's transmission network was sold to the Castle Tower Consortium in February 1997; ITV transmission services are owned and operated by National Transcommunications Ltd. Transmissions are available to more than 99 per cent of the population.

The total number of receiving television licences in the UK at July 1999 was 22,274,792, of which 98.8 per cent were for colour televisions. Annual television licence fees are: monochrome £34.50; colour £104.00.

No overall statistics are available for subscriptions in the UK to satellite television services; British Sky Broadcasting had 8.6 million subscribers at June 2000 (4.1 million via digital and analogue satellite, 3.8 million via cable and 647,000 via digital terrestrial television).

DIGITAL TELEVISION

Digital broadcasting will increase the number and quality of television channels. It uses digital modulation to improve reception and digital compression to make more effective use of the frequency channels available than PAL, the analogue system currently used.

The Broadcasting Act 1996 provided for the licensing of 20 or more digital terrestrial television channels (on six frequency channels or 'multiplexes'). Analogue broadcasting will eventually be discontinued, with the frequencies being sold to mobile telephone companies.

In June 1997 the licences to run the remaining digital multiplexes were awarded by the ITC to British Digital Broadcasting (now called ONdigital), a consortium led by Carlton Communications and Granada. The first digital services went on air in autumn 1998. A set-top digital decoder or an integrated digital television set is required to convert the digital signals into analogue sound and picture waves in order to watch the digital channels. Digital television services are also offered by cable and satellite companies.

ESTIMATED AUDIENCE SHARE *for 12 months to 31 March 2000*

	Percentage (rounded)
ITV companies	29.4
BBC 1	28.2
BBC 2	10.8
Cable, satellite and digital channels	12.8
Channel 4	10
Channel 5	5.6
S4C Wales	0.3

Source: Independent Television Commission

BBC TELEVISION

Television Centre, Wood Lane, London W12 7RJ.
Tel: 020-8743 8000

The BBC's experiments in television broadcasting started in 1929 and in 1936 the BBC began the world's first public service of high-definition television from Alexandra Palace. The BBC broadcasts two UK-wide television services, BBC 1 and BBC 2; outside England these services are designated BBC Scotland on 1, BBC Scotland on 2, BBC 1 Northern Ireland, BBC 2 Northern Ireland, BBC Wales on 1 and BBC Wales on 2.

BBC WORLDWIDE LTD
Woodlands, 80 Wood Lane, London W12 0TT
Tel: +44 (0)20 8433 2000; Fax: +44 (0)20 8749 0538
Web: www.bbcworldwide.com

BBC Worldwide Limited is the main commercial arm, and a wholly owned subsidiary, of the British Broadcasting Corporation. The company was formed in 1994 to develop a co-ordinated approach to the BBC's commercial activities: television, publishing, product licensing, internet and interactive media. BBC Worldwide exists to maximise the value of the BBC's programme and publishing assets for the benefit of the licence payer, and re-invest in public service programming.

INDEPENDENT TELEVISION

The ITV franchises for the 15 regional companies and for breakfast television were allocated new ten-year licences from January 1993. Since 1998 licensees have had several opportunities to apply for renewal of their licence; the last such opportunity will be in early 2001. The ITC received bids for the licence for a new independent national television channel in May 1995. The winner was Channel 5 Broadcasting Ltd and the new channel was launched on 30 March 1997.

ITV NETWORK CENTRE/ITV ASSOCIATION
200 Gray's Inn Road, London WC1X 8HF.
Tel: 020-7843 8000

The ITV Network Centre is wholly owned by the ITV companies and undertakes the commissioning and scheduling of those television programmes which are shown across the ITV network. Through its sister organisation, the ITV Association, it also provides a range of services to the ITV companies where a common approach is required.

In December 1998 ITV launched an addition digital channel called ITV2.
Chairman, Leslie Hill

INDEPENDENT TELEVISION NETWORK
COMPANIES

ANGLIA TELEVISION LTD (owned by United Broadcasting and Entertainment) (*eastern England*), Anglia House, Norwich NR1 3JG. Tel: 01603-615151
Web: http://www.anglia.tv.co.uk
BORDER TELEVISION PLC (*the Borders*), The Television Centre, Carlisle CA1 3NT. Tel: 01228-525101
Web: http://www.border-tv.com
CARLTON UK TELEVISION (*London (weekdays)*), 101 St Martin's Lane, London WC2N 4AZ. Tel: 020-7240 4000
Web: http://www.carlton.com
CENTRAL INDEPENDENT TELEVISION LTD (owned by Carlton Communications) (*the Midlands*), Central Court, Gas Street, Birmingham B1 2JT. Tel: 0121-643 9898
CHANNEL TELEVISION LTD (*Channel Islands*), The Television Centre, St Helier, Jersey JE1 3ZD.
Tel: 01534-816816 Web: http://www.channeltv.co.uk
GMTV LTD (*breakfast television*), The London Television Centre, Upper Ground, London SE1 9TT.
Tel: 020-7827 7000 Web: http://www.gmtv.co.uk
GRAMPIAN TELEVISION PLC (owned by Scottish Media) (*northern Scotland*), Queen's Cross, Aberdeen AB15 2XJ. Tel: 01224-846846
Web: http://www.grampiantv.co.uk

GRANADA TELEVISION LTD (owned by Granada Media) (*north-west England*), Quay Street, Manchester M60 9EA. Tel: 0161-832 7211
Web: http://www.granadatv.co.uk
HTV GROUP PLC (owned by United Broadcasting and Entertainment) (*Wales and western England*), HTV Wales, The Television Centre, Culverhouse Cross, Cardiff CF5 6XJ. Tel: 029-2059 0590; HTV West, The Television Centre, Bath Road, Bristol BS4 3HG. Tel: 0117-977 8366
LONDON WEEKEND TELEVISION LTD (owned by Granada Media) (*London (weekends)*), The London Television Centre, Upper Ground, London SE1 9LT. Tel: 020-7620 1620
Web: http://www.lwt.co.uk
MERIDIAN BROADCASTING LTD (owned by United Broadcasting and Entertainment) (*south and south-east England*), The Television Centre, Southampton SO14 0PZ. Tel: 023-8022 2555
Web: http://www.meridian.co.uk
SCOTTISH TELEVISION PLC (owned by Scottish Media) (*central Scotland*), Cowcaddens, Glasgow G2 3PR. Tel: 0141-300 3000
Web: http://www.scottishtv.co.uk
TYNE TEES TELEVISION LTD (owned by Granada Media) (*north-east England*), The Television Centre, City Road, Newcastle upon Tyne NE1 2AL. Tel: 0191-261 0181
ULSTER TELEVISION PLC (*Northern Ireland*), Havelock House, Ormeau Road, Belfast BT7 1EB.
Tel: 028-9032 8122
Web: http://www.utvlive.com
WESTCOUNTRY TELEVISION LTD (owned by Carlton Communications) (*south-west England*), Langage Science Park, Plymouth PL75BG. Tel: 01752-333333
YORKSHIRE TELEVISION LTD (owned by Granada Media) (*Yorkshire*), The Television Centre, Kirkstall Rd, Leeds LS3 1JS. Tel: 0113-243 8283

OTHER INDEPENDENT TELEVISION COMPANIES

CHANNEL 5 BROADCASTING LTD, 22 Long Acre, London WC2E 9LY. Tel: 020-7550 5555
CHANNEL FOUR TELEVISION CORPORATION, 124 Horseferry Road, London SW1P 2TX. Tel: 020-7396 4444. Provides a service to the UK except Wales and is charged to cater for interests under-represented by the ITV network companies. Channel 4 sells its own advertising
INDEPENDENT TELEVISION NEWS LTD, 200 Gray's Inn Road, London WC1X 8XZ. Tel: 020-7833 3000
TELETEXT LTD, 101 Farm Lane, London SW6 1QJ.
Tel: 020-7386 5000. Provides teletext services for the ITV companies and Channel 4
WELSH FOURTH CHANNEL AUTHORITY (Sianel Pedwar Cymru), Parc Ty Glas, Llanishen, Cardiff CF4 5DU. Tel: 029-2074 7444. S4C schedules Welsh language and most Channel 4 programmes

DIRECT BROADCASTING BY SATELLITE TELEVISION

BRITISH SKY BROADCASTING LTD, 6 Centaurs Business Park, Grant Way, Isleworth, Middx TW7 5QD. Tel: 020-7705 3000. British Sky Broadcasting is the UK's broadband entertainment company, distributing sports, movies, entertainment and news to 8.6 million households throughout the UK and Eire (4.1m via digital and analogue satellite, 3.8m via cable and 647,000 via digital terrestrial television)

SKY DIGITAL, which was launched on 1 October 1998, offers 200 channels, pay-per-view services and interactive entertainment. It has attracted 3.4 million customers to date

BRITISH SKY BROADCASTING is one of the largest private sector employers in Scotland with more than 6000 individuals, the majority employed at Sky's call centres in Livingston and Dumfermline

RADIO

UK domestic radio services are broadcast across three wavebands: FM (or VHF), medium wave (also referred to as AM) and long wave (used by BBC Radio 4). In the UK the FM waveband extends in frequency from 87.5 MHz to 108 MHz and the medium wave band extends from 531 kHz to 1602 kHz. Some radios are still calibrated in wavelengths rather than frequency. To convert frequency to wavelength, divide 300,000 by the frequency in kHz.

DIGITAL RADIO

Digital radio allows more services to be broadcast to a higher technical quality and provides the data facility for text or pictures associated with sound programmes. It improves the robustness of high fidelity radio services, especially compared with current FM and AM radio transmissions. It was developed in a collaborative research project under the pan-European EUREKA initiative and has been adopted as a world standard for new digital radio systems. The frequencies allocated for terrestrial digital radio in the UK are 217.5 to 230 MHz.

The Broadcasting Act 1996 provided for the licensing of digital radio services (on seven frequency channels or 'multiplexes'). The BBC has been allocated a multiplex capable of broadcasting six to eight national stereo services; BBC digital broadcasts began in the London area in September 1995. A national digital multiplex has also been made available, on which the three independent national radio stations have a guaranteed place, and local and regional services (BBC and commercial) will use the remaining five multiplexes. The Radio Authority is responsible for awarding licences for capacity on the non-BBC multiplexes. The first national independent radio digital licence was awarded in October 1998 to Digital One, a company owned by GWR Digital Radio, NTL Digital Radio and Talk Radio UK. Broadcasting began in October 1999. The first local multiplex licence was awarded in May 1999 (to CE Digital, for Birmingham) and commenced broadcasting in May 2000. Analogue services will eventually be discontinued. It is necessary to have a radio set with a digital decoder in order to receive digital radio broadcasts.

ESTIMATED AUDIENCE SHARE

January to March 2000

	Percentage
BBC Radio 1	9.1
BBC Radio 2	13.1
BBC Radio 3	6.6
BBC Radio 4	12.5
BBC Radio 5 Live	7.4
BBC Local/Regional	10.9
Atlantic 252	4.5
Classic FM	7.3
Talk Radio	6
Virgin Radio (AM only)	6.3
Local commercial	14.8
Other	7.6

Source: RAJAR/RSL

BBC RADIO

Broadcasting House, Portland Place, London W1A 1AA. Tel: 020-7580 4468

BBC Radio broadcasts five network services to the UK, Isle of Man and the Channel Islands. There is also a tier of national services in Wales, Scotland and Northern Ireland and 39 local radio stations in England and the Channel Islands. In Wales and Scotland there are also dedicated language services in Welsh and Gaelic respectively.

BBC NETWORK RADIO SERVICES

RADIO 1 (Contemporary pop music, social action campaigns and entertainment news) – 24 hours a day. *Frequencies:* 97.6–99.8 FM, coverage 99%

RADIO 2 (Popular music, entertainment, comedy and the arts) – 24 hours a day. *Frequencies:* 88–90.2 FM, coverage 99%

RADIO 3 (Classical music, classic drama, documentaries and features) – 24 hours a day. *Frequencies:* 90.2–92.4 FM, coverage 99%

RADIO 4 (News, documentaries, drama, entertainment, and cricket on long wave in season) – 5.55a.m.–1.00a.m. daily, with BBC World Service overnight. *Frequencies:* 94.6–96.1 FM and 103.5–105 FM, coverage 99%; 1449 AM, plus eight local fillers on AM

RADIO 5 Live (News and sport) – 24 hours a day. *Frequencies:* 693 AM and 909 AM, plus one local filler

BBC NATIONAL RADIO SERVICES

RADIO SCOTLAND *Frequencies:* 810 MW plus two local fillers; 92.4–94.7 FM, coverage 99%. Local programmes on FM as above: HIGHLANDS; NORTH-EAST BORDERS; SOUTH-WEST (also 585 MW); ORKNEY: SHETLAND

RADIO NAN GAIDHEAL (Gaelic service) *Frequencies:* 103.5–105 FM, 990 MW in Aberdeen, coverage 90%

RADIO ULSTER *Frequencies:* 1341 MW (873 MW Enniskillen), plus two local fillers; 92.4–95.4 FM, coverage 96%

RADIO WALES *Frequencies:* 882 MW plus two local fillers; 95.1 FM, 95.9 FM (*Gwent*), 103.9 FM (Cardiff), 95.4 FM (Wrexham), coverage 97%

RADIO Cymru (Welsh-language) *Frequencies:* 92.4–94.6 FM, 95.7 FM (*Llanfyllin*), 96.1 FM (*Llandinam*), 96.8 FM and 103.5–105 FM, coverage 97%

BBC LOCAL RADIO STATIONS

There are 40 local stations serving England and the Channel Islands:

ASIAN NETWORK, Epic House, Charles Street, Leicester LE1 3SH. Tel: 0116-251 6688. *Frequencies:* 828/837/1458 MW

BERKSHIRE, BBC Radio Berkshire, PO Box 1044, Reading RG94 8FH. Tel: 0645-311444. *Frequencies:* 94.6/95.4/104.1/104.4 FM

BRISTOL/SOMERSET SOUND, PO Box 194, Bristol BS99 7QT. Tel: 0117-974 1111; *Frequencies:* 1323 AM, 1548 MW, 94.9/95.5/104.6 FM

CAMBRIDGESHIRE, PO Box 96, Hills Road, Cambridge CB2 1LD. Tel: 01223-259696. *Frequencies:* 95.7/96.0 FM, 1026/1449 MW

CLEVELAND, PO Box 95-FM, Newport Road, Middlesbrough TS1 5DG. Tel: 01642-225211. *Frequencies:* 95.0/95.8 FM

CORNWALL, Phoenix Wharf, Truro, Cornwall TR1 1UA. Tel: 01872-275421. *Frequencies:* 95.2/96.0/103.9 FM, 630/657 MW

COVENTRY AND WARWICKSHIRE, Holt Court, 1 Greyfriars Road, Coventry CV1 2WR. Tel: 024-7623 1231. *Frequencies:* 94.8/103.7/104.0 FM

CUMBRIA, Annetwell Street, Carlisle CA3 8BB.
Tel: 01228-592444. *Frequencies:* 95.2/95.6/96.1/104.1
FM, 756/837/1458 MW
DERBY, PO Box 269, Derby DE1 3HL. Tel: 01332-361111.
Frequencies: 94.2/95.3/104.5 FM, 1116 MW
DEVON, PO Box 5, Plymouth PL1 1XT. Tel: 01752-260323.
Frequencies: 103.4/96.0/95.8/94.8 FM, 801, 855, 990,
1458 MW
ESSEX, 198 New London Road, Chelmsford CM2 9XB.
Tel: 01245-616000. *Frequencies:* 95.3/103.5 FM, 729/
765/1530 MW
GLOUCESTERSHIRE, London Road, Gloucester GL1 1SW.
Tel: 01452-308585. *Frequencies:* 95/95.8/104.7 FM
GLR (GREATER LONDON RADIO), 35C Marylebone
High Street, London W1A 4LG. Tel: 020-7224 2424.
Frequency: 94.9 FM
GMR (GREATER MANCHESTER RADIO), PO Box 951,
Oxford Road, Manchester M60 1SD. Tel: 0161-200 2000.
Frequencies: 95.1/104.6 FM
GUERNSEY, Commerce House, Les Banques, St Peter
Port, Guernsey GY1 2HS. Tel: 01481-728977.
Frequencies: 1116 AM, 93.2 FM
HEREFORD AND WORCESTER, Hylton Road, Worcester
WR2 5WW. Tel: 01905-748485. *Frequencies:* 94.7/104.0/
104.6 FM, 818/738 MW
HUMBERSIDE, 9 Chapel Street, Hull HU1 3NU. Tel: 01482-
323232. *Frequency:* 95.9 FM, 1485 MW
JERSEY, 18 Parade Road, St Helier, Jersey JE2 3PL.
Tel: 01534-870000. *Frequencies:* 1026 AM, 88.8 FM
KENT, Sun Pier, Chatham, Kent ME4 4EZ. Tel: 01634-
830505. *Frequencies:* 96.7/97.6/104.2 FM,
774/1602 MW
LANCASHIRE, 26 Darwen Street, Blackburn BB2 2EA.
Tel: 01254-262411. *Frequencies:* 95.5/103.9/104.5 FM,
855/1557 MW
LEEDS, Broadcasting House, Woodhouse Lane, Leeds
LS2 9PN. Tel: 0113-244 2131. *Frequencies:* 774 AM,
92.4/95.3/103.9 FM, 774 MW
LEICESTER, Epic House, Charles Street, Leicester LE1 3SH.
Tel: 0116-251 6688. *Frequency:* 104.9 FM
LINCOLNSHIRE, PO Box 219, Newport, Lincoln LN1 3XY.
Tel: 01522-511411. *Frequencies:* 94.9 FM, 1368 MW
LONDON, BBC London Live, 35C Marylebone High
Street, London W1A 4LG. Tel: 020-7224 2424.
Frequency: 94.9 FM
MERSEYSIDE, 55 Paradise Street, Liverpool L1 3BP.
Tel: 0151-708 5500. *Frequency:* 95.8 FM, 1485 MW
NEWCASTLE, Broadcasting Centre, Barrack Road,
Newcastle upon Tyne NE99 1RN. Tel: 0191-232 4141.
Frequencies: 95.4/96.0/103.7/104.4 FM, 206 MW
NORFOLK, Norfolk Tower, Surrey Street, Norwich NR1
3PA. Tel: 01603-617411. *Frequencies:* 95.1/104.4 FM,
855/873 MW
NORTHAMPTON, Broadcasting House, Abington Street,
Northampton NN1 2BH. Tel: 01604-239100. *Frequencies:*
103.6/104.2 FM, 1107 MW
NOTTINGHAM, York House, Mansfield Road,
Nottingham NG1 3JB. Tel: 0115-955 0500. *Frequencies:*
95.5/103.8 FM, 1584 MW
OXFORD, BBC Radio Oxford, 269 Banbury Road, Oxford
OX2 7DW. Tel: 01865-311444. *Frequency:* 95.2 FM
SHEFFIELD, Ashdell Grove, 60 Westbourne Road,
Sheffield S10 2QU. Tel: 0114-268 6185. *Frequencies:*
88.6/94.7/104.1 FM
SHROPSHIRE, 2–4 Boscobel Drive, Shrewsbury SY1 3TT.
Tel: 01743-248484. *Frequencies:* 95.0/96.0 FM,
1584 MW
SOLENT, Broadcasting House, Havelock Road,
Southampton SO14 7PW. Tel: 023-8063 1311.
Frequencies: 96.1 FM, 999 MW

SOMERSET SOUND, 14–15 Paul Street, Taunton TA1 3PF.
Tel: 01823-252437. *Frequency:* 1323 MW
SOUTHERN COUNTIES, Broadcasting Centre, Guildford
GU2 5AP. Tel: 01483-306306. *Frequencies:* 95–95.3/104–
104.8 FM
STOKE, Cheapside, Hanley, Stoke-on-Trent ST1 1JJ. Tel:
01782-208080. *Frequencies:* 94.6/104.1 FM, 1503 MW
SUFFOLK, Broadcasting House, St Matthew's Street,
Ipswich IP1 3EP. Tel: 01473-250000. *Frequencies:*
95.5/103.9/104.6 FM
THREE COUNTIES RADIO, PO Box 3CR, Luton,
Beds LU1 5XL. Tel: 01582-637400. *Frequencies:*
95.5/103.8/104.5 FM, 630/1161 MW
WILTSHIRE SOUND, Broadcasting House, Prospect Place,
Swindon SN1 3RW. Tel: 01793-513626. *Frequencies:*
103.5/103.6/104.3/104.9 FM, 1332/1368 MW
WM (WEST MIDLANDS), Pebble Mill Road, Birmingham
B5 7SD. Tel: 0121-432 8484. *Frequency:* 95.6 FM.
YORK, 20 Bootham Row, York YO3 7BR.
Tel: 01904-641351. *Frequencies:* 95.5/103.7/104.3 FM,
666/1260 MW

BBC WORLD SERVICE

Bush House, Strand, London WC2B 4PH.
Tel: 020-7240 3456

The BBC World Service broadcasts over 1,000 hours of
programmes a week in 43 languages including English.
It has a weekly audience of 151 million globally, of whom
40 million listen to English language services. Many
services are also available by satellite and on the internet.
UK frequencies: 648 AM in Southern England and on BBC
Radio 4 at night.
   The World Service is organised into five world regions,
each responsible for programmes in English as well as
regional languages.
AFRICA AND THE MIDDLE EAST, Arabic, French, Hausa,
Kinyarwanda/Kirundi, Portuguese, Somali and Swahili;
English programmes including *Network Africa* and
Focus on Africa
ASIA AND THE PACIFIC, Bengali, Burmese, Cantonese,
Hindi, Indonesian, Mandarin, Nepali, Sinhala, Tamil,
Thai, Urdu and Vietnamese; English programmes
including *East Asia Today*
EUROPE, Albanian, Bulgarian, Croatian, Czech, Greek,
Hungarian, Macedonian, Polish, Romanian, Serbian,
Slovak and Slovene; English programmes including
The World Today
FORMER SOVIET UNION AND SOUTH-WEST ASIA, Azeri,
Kazakh, Kyrgyz, Pashto, Persian, Russian, Turkish,
Ukrainian and Uzbek
THE AMERICAS, Portuguese for Brazil, Spanish; English
programmes including *The World* (a global news
magazine for American listeners), *Caribbean Report*
and *Calling the Falklands*
BBC ENGLISH teaches English world-wide through radio,
television and a wide range of published courses
BBC MARKET INTELLIGENCE carries out audience
research and sells printed publications and data
BBC MONITORING supplies news and information from
the output of overseas radio and television stations and
news agency sources
BBC MPM (MARSHALL PLAN OF THE MIND TRUST)
makes programmes about business, democracy and
management for countries of the former Soviet
Union, Eastern Europe and the Far East
BBC WORLD SERVICE TRAINING runs journalism,
management and skills training courses for overseas
broadcasters

INDEPENDENT RADIO

The Radio Authority began advertising new licences for the development of commercial radio in January 1991. Since then it has awarded three national licences, 101 new local radio licences (including ten regional licences) and one additional service licence (to use the spare capacity in an existing channel which is not used by the programme service). The Authority has also issued about 2,000 restricted service licences (for temporary low-powered radio services). In 1999–2000 the Authority advertised one new analogue licence a month. It also advertised one digital multiplex licence a month and re-advertise existing analogue licences.

COMMERCIAL RADIO COMPANIES ASSOCIATION, 77 Shaftesbury Avenue, London W1V 7AD.
Tel: 020-7306 2603.
Chief Executive, P. Brown

INDEPENDENT NATIONAL RADIO STATIONS

CLASSIC FM, 7 Swallow Place, London W1R 7AA. Tel: 020-7343 9000. 24 hours a day. *Frequencies:* 99.9/101.9 FM
TALK SPORT, 18 Hatfields, London SE1 8DJ. Tel: 020-7959 7900. 24 hours a day. *Frequencies:* 1053/1089 AM
VIRGIN RADIO, 1 Golden Square, London W1R 4DJ. Tel: 020-7434 1215. 24 hours a day. *Frequencies:* 1215/1197/1233/1242/1260 AM

INDEPENDENT REGIONAL LOCAL RADIO STATIONS

100.7 HEART FM (*west Midlands*), 1 The Square, 111 Broad Street, Birmingham B15 1AS. Tel: 0121-626 1007. *Frequency:* 100.7 FM
CENTURY 105 (*north-west*), Century House, Waterfront Quay, Salford Quays, Manchester M5 2XW. Tel: 0161-400 0105. *Frequency:* 105.4 FM
CENTURY 106 (*east Midlands*), City Link, Nottingham NG2 4NG. Tel: 0115-910 6100. *Frequency:* 106.0 FM
CENTURY RADIO (*north-east*), Century House, PO Box 100, Gateshead NE8 2YX. Tel: 0191-477 6666. *Frequencies:* 100.7/101.8/96.2/96.4 FM
GALAXY 101 (*Severn estuary*), Millennium House, 26 Baldwin Street, Bristol BS1 1SE. Tel: 0117-901 0101. *Frequencies:* 101.0/97.2 FM (Bristol)
GALAXY 105 (*Yorkshire*), Joseph's Well, Westgate, Leeds LS3 1AB. Tel: 0113-213 0105. *Frequencies:* 105.1 FM (Leeds); 105.6 FM (Bradford and Sheffield); 105.8 FM (Hull)
GALAXY 105–106 (*north-east*), Kingfisher Way, Silverlink Business Park, Tyne and Wear NE28 9ND. Tel: 0191-206 8000. *Frequencies:* 105.3/105.6/106.4 FM
JAZZ FM 100.4 (*north-west*), The World Trade Centre, Exchange Quay, Manchester M5 3EJ. Tel: 0161-877 1004. *Frequency:* 100.4 FM
SCOT FM (*central Scotland*), 1 Albert Quay, Leith EH6 7DN. Tel: 0131-554 6677. *Frequencies:* 100.3/101.1 FM
VIBE FM (*east*), Reflection House, The Anderson Centre, Olding Road, Bury St Edmunds, Suffolk IP33 3TA. Tel: 01284-718800. *Frequencies:* 107.7 FM (Peterborough); 105.6 FM (Cambridge); 106.1 FM (Norwich); 106.4 FM (Ipswich)
WAVE 105 FM (*Solent*), 5 Manor Court, Barnes Wallis Road, Segensworth East, Fareham, Hants PO15 5TH. Tel: 01489-481050. *Frequencies:* 105.2 FM (Solent); 105.8 FM (Poole)

INDEPENDENT LOCAL RADIO STATIONS

England
2-TEN FM, PO Box 2020, Reading RG31 7FG. Tel: 0118-945 4400. *Frequencies:* 97.0/102.9/103.4 FM
2BR FM, Imex Lomeshaye Business Village, Nelson, Lancs BB9 7DR. Tel: 01282 690000. Expected on air summer 2000. *Frequency:* 99.8 FM
2CR FM, 5 Southcote Road, Bournemouth BH1 3LR. Tel: 01202-259259. *Frequency:* 102.3 FM
96 TRENT FM 29–31 Castle Gate, Nottingham NG1 7AP. Tel: 0115-952 7000. *Frequencies:* 96.2/96.5 FM
96.3 AIRE FM, 51 Burley Road, Leeds LS3 1LR. Tel: 0113-283 5500. *Frequency:* 96.3 FM
96.4 FM BRMB, Nine Brindleyplace, 4 Oozells Square, Birmingham B1 2DJ. Tel: 0121-245 5000. *Frequency:* 96.4 FM
96.4 THE EAGLE, Dolphin House, North Street, Guildford, Surrey GU1 4AA. Tel: 01483-300964. *Frequency:* 96.4 FM
96.9 VIKING FM, Commercial Road, Hull HU1 2SG. Tel: 01482-325141. *Frequency:* 96.9 FM
97.2 STRAY FM, PO Box 972, Station Parade, Harrogate HG1 5YF. Tel: 01423-522972. *Frequency:* 97.2 FM
97.4 VALE FM, Longmead, Shaftesbury, Dorset SP7 8QQ. Tel: 01747-855711. *Frequency:* 97.4 FM
100.7 HEART FM, 1 The Square, 111 Broad Street, Birmingham B15 1AS. Tel: 0121-695 0000. *Frequency:* 100.7 FM
102.4 WISH FM, Orrell Lodge, Orrell Road, Orrell, Wigan WN5 8HJ. Tel: 01942-761024. *Frequency:* 102.4 FM
102.7 HEREWARD FM, PO Box 225, Queensgate Centre, Peterborough PE1 1XJ. Tel: 01733-460460. *Frequency:* 102.7 FM
103.2 POWER FM, Radio House, Whittle Avenue, Segensworth West, Fareham, Hants PO15 5SH. Tel: 01489-589911. *Frequency:* 103.2 FM
103.4 THE BEACH, PO Box 103.4, Lowestoft, Suffolk NR32 2TL. Tel: 07000-001035. *Frequency:* 103.4 FM
106 CTFM RADIO, 16 Lower Bridge Street, Canterbury, Kent CT1 2HQ. Tel: 01227-789106. *Frequency:* 106.0 FM
106.9 SILK FM, Radio House, Bridge Street, Macclesfield, Cheshire SK11 6DJ. Tel: 01625-268000. *Frequency:* 106.9 FM
107 OAK FM, 7 Waldron Court, Prince William Road, Loughborough, Leics LE11 5GD. Tel: 01509-211711. *Frequency:* 107.0 FM
107.2 WIRE FM, Warrington Business Park, Long Lane, Warrington WA2 8TX. Tel: 01925-445545. *Frequency:* 107.2 FM
107.3 THE EAGLE, Bristol Evening Post Building, Temple Way, Bristol BS99 7HD. Tel: 0117-910 6600. *Frequency:* 107.3 FM
107.4 TELFORD FM, PO Box 1074, Telford TF3 3WG. Tel: 01952-280011. *Frequency:* 107.4 FM
107.5 CAT FM, Regent Arcade, Cheltenham, Glos GL50 1JZ. Tel: 01242-699555. *Frequency:* 107.5 FM
107.6 KESTREL FM, 2nd Floor, Paddington House, The Walks Shopping Centre, Basingstoke, Hants RG21 7LJ. Tel: 01256-694000. *Frequency:* 107.6 FM
107.7 CHELMER FM, Cater House, High Street, Chelmsford, Essex CM1 1AL. Tel: 01245-259400. *Frequency:* 107.7 FM
107.7 THE WOLF, 10th Floor, Mander House, Wolverhampton WV1 3NB. Tel: 01902-571070. *Frequency:* 107.7 FM
107.7 WFM, 11 Beaconsfield Road, Weston-super-Mare, Somerset BS23 1YE. Tel: 01934-624455. *Frequency:* 107.7 FM

107.8 ARROW FM, Priory Meadow Centre, Hastings, E. Sussex TN34 1PJ. Tel: 01424-461177. *Frequency:* 107.8 FM

107.8 FM THAMES RADIO, Brentham House, 45c High Street, Hampton Wick, Kingston upon Thames KT1 4DG. Tel: 020-8288 1300. *Frequency:* 107.8 FM

107.9 THE EAGLE, Radio House, Sturton Street, Cambridge CB1 2QF. Tel: 01223-722300. *Frequency*: 107.9 FM

963/972 LIBERTY RADIO, 7th Floor, Trevor House, 100 Brompton Road, London SW3 1ER. Tel: 020-7893 8966. *Frequency:* 963/972 AM

1458 LITE AM, PO Box 1458, Quay West, Trafford Park, Manchester M17 1FL. Tel: 0161-872 1458. *Frequency:* 1458 AM

ACTIVE 107.5 FM, Lambourne House, 7 Western Road, Romford, Essex RM1 3LD. Tel: 01708-731643. *Frequency:* 107.5 FM

ALPHA 103.2, Radio House, 11 Woodland Road, Darlington DL3 7BJ. Tel: 01325-255552. *Frequency:* 103.2 FM

ASIAN SOUND RADIO, Globe House, Southall Street, Manchester M3 1LG. Tel: 0161-288 1000. *Frequencies:* 1377/963 AM

B97 CHILTERN FM, 55 Goldington Road, Bedford MK40 3LT. Tel: 01234-272400. *Frequency:* 96.9 FM

BATH FM, Station House, Ashley Avenue, Lower Weston, Bath BA1 3DS. Tel: 01225-471571. *Frequency:* 107.9 FM

THE BAY, PO Box 969, St George's Quay, Lancaster LA1 3LD. Tel: 01524-848747. *Frequencies:* 96.9/102.3/ 103.2 FM

BCR FM, 33 Manor Road, Bridgwater, Somerset TA6 4RJ. Tel: 01278 444211. *Frequencies*: to be announced.

BEACON FM, 267 Tettenhall Road, Wolverhampton WV6 0DQ. Tel: 01902-461300. *Frequencies:* 97.2 FM (Wolverhampton and Black Country); 103.1 FM (Shrewsbury and Telford)

BIG AM, Forster Square, Bradford, W. Yorks BD1 5NE. Tel: 01274 203040. *Frequencies:* 1278/1530 AM

BIG 1170, Stoke Road, Stoke-on-Trent ST4 2SR. Tel: 01782-747047. *Frequency:* 1170 AM

BIG 1458 AM, 4th Floor, Quay West, Trafford Park, Manchester M17 1FL. Tel: 0161-607 0420. *Frequency:* 1458 AM

THE BREEZE, Radio House, Clifftown Road, Southend-on-Sea, Essex SS1 1SX. Tel: 01702-333711. *Frequencies:* 1359 AM (Chelmsford); 1431 AM (Southend)

BREEZE 1521, The Stanley Centre, Kelvin Way, Crawley, W. Sussex RH10 2SE. Tel: 01293-519161. *Frequency:* 1521 AM

BROADLAND 102, St George's Plain, 47–49 Colegate, Norwich NR3 1DB. Tel: 01603-630621. *Frequency:* 102.4 FM

THE BUZZ 97.1, Media House, Claughton Road, Birkenhead CH41 6EY. Tel: 0151-650 1700. *Frequency:* 97.1 FM

CAPITAL FM, 30 Leicester Square, London WC2H 7LA. Tel: 020-7766 6000. *Frequency:* 95.8 FM

CAPITAL GOLD (1152), Nine Brindleyplace, 4 Oozells Square, Birmingham B1 2DJ. Tel: 0121-245 5000. *Frequency:* 1152 AM

CAPITAL GOLD (1170 and 1557), Radio House, Whittle Avenue, Segensworth West, Fareham, Hants PO15 5SH. Tel: 01489-589911. *Frequencies:* 1170/1557 AM

CAPITAL GOLD (1242 and 603), Radio House, John Wilson Business Park, Whitstable, Kent CT5 3QX. Tel: 01227-772004. *Frequencies:* 603 AM (East Kent); 1242 AM (Maidstone and Medway)

CAPITAL GOLD (1323 and 945), Radio House, PO Box 2000, Brighton BN41 2SS. Tel: 01273-430111. *Frequencies:* 945/1323 AM

CAPITAL GOLD (1548), 30 Leicester Square, London WC2H 7LA. Tel: 020-7766 6000. *Frequency:* 1548 AM

CENTRE FM, 5–6 Aldergate, Tamworth, Staffs B79 7DJ. Tel: 01827-318000. *Frequencies:* 101.6/102.4 FM

CENTURY (105), Century House, Waterfront Quay, Salford Quays, Manchester M5 2XW. Tel: 0161-400 0105. *Frequency:* 105.4 FM

CENTURY (106), City Link, Nottingham NG2 4NG. Tel: 0115-910 6100. *Frequency:* 106 FM

CENTURY RADIO, Century House, PO Box 100, Gateshead NE8 2YY. Tel: 0191-477 6666. *Frequencies:* 96.2/96.4/100.7/101.8 FM

CFM, PO Box 964, Carlisle, Cumbria CA1 3NG. Tel: 01228-818964. *Frequencies:* 96.4 FM (Penrith); 102.5 FM (Carlisle); 102.2 FM (Workington); 103.4 FM (Whitehaven)

CHANNEL (103), 6 Tunnell Street, St Helier, Jersey JE2 4LU. Tel: 01534-888103. *Frequency:* 103.7 FM

CHANNEL TRAVEL RADIO, Main Control Building, Folkestone, Kent CT18 8XY. Tel: 01303-283873. *Frequency:* 107.6 FM

CHELMER FM (107.7), Cater House, High Street, Chelmsford CM1 1AL. Tel: 01245-259400. *Frequency:* 107.7FM

CHILTERN FM (96.9), 55 Goldington Road, Bedford, Beds MK40 3LT. Tel: 01234-272400. *Frequency:* 96.9 FM

CHILTERN FM (97.6), Chiltern Road, Dunstable, Beds LU6 1HQ. Tel: 01582-676200. *Frequency:* 97.6 FM

CHOICE FM, 291–299 Borough High Street, London SE1 1JG. Tel: 020-7378 3969. *Frequency:* 96.9 FM

CHOICE (107.1), 291–299 Borough High Street, London SE1 1JG. Tel: 020-8348 1033. *Frequency:* 107.1 FM

RADIO CITY 96.7, 8–10 Stanley Street, Liverpool L1 6AF. Tel: 0151-227 5100. *Frequency:* 96.7 FM

CLASSIC GOLD 666/954, Hawthorn House, Exeter Business Park, Exeter EX1 3QS. Tel: 01392-444444. *Frequencies:* 666/954 AM

CLASSIC GOLD 774, Bridge Studios, Eastgate Centre, Gloucester GL1 1SS. Tel: 01452-313200. *Frequency:* 774 AM

CLASSIC GOLD 792/828, Chiltern Road, Dunstable, Beds LU6 1HQ. Tel: 01582-676200. *Frequencies:* 792 AM (Bedford); 828 AM (Luton)

CLASSIC GOLD 828, 5 Southcote Road, Bournemouth, Dorset BH1 3LR. Tel: 01202-259259. *Frequency:* 828 AM

CLASSIC GOLD 936/1161 AM, PO Box 2000, Swindon SN4 7EX. Tel: 01793-842600. *Frequencies:* 936 AM (West Wilts); 1161 AM (Swindon)

CLASSIC GOLD RADIO 954/1530, The Old Smithy, Post Office Lane, Kempsey, Worcs WR5 3NS. Tel: 01905-820659. *Frequencies:* 954 AM (Hereford); 1530 AM (Worcester)

CLASSIC GOLD 1260, PO Box 2020, Watershed, Canons Road, Bristol BS99 7SN. Tel: 0117-984 3200. *Frequency:* 1260 AM

CLASSIC GOLD 1332 AM, PO Box 2020, Queensgate Centre, Peterborough PE1 1LL. Tel: 01733-460460. *Frequency:* 1332 AM

CLASSIC GOLD 1359, Hertford Place, Coventry CV1 3TT. Tel: 024-7686 8200. *Frequency:* 1359 AM

CLASSIC GOLD 1431/1485, PO Box 2020, Reading RG31 7FG. Tel: 0118-945 4400. *Frequencies:* 1431/1485 AM

CLASSIC GOLD 1557, 19–21 St Edmunds Road, Northampton NN1 5DY. Tel: 01604-795600. *Frequency:* 1557 AM

CLASSIC GOLD AMBER, St George's Plain, 47–49 Colegate, Norwich NR3 1DB. Tel: 01603-630621. *Frequency:* 1152 AM

CLASSIC GOLD AMBER (Suffolk), Alpha Business Park, 6–12 White House Road, Ipswich IP1 5LT. Tel: 01473-461000. *Frequency:* 1170 AM (Ipswich); 1251 AM (Bury St Edmunds)

CLASSIC GOLD GEM, 29–31 Castle Gate, Nottingham NG1 7AP. Tel: 0115-952 7000. *Frequencies:* 945/999 AM

CLASSIC GOLD WABC, 267 Tettenhall Road, Wolverhampton WV6 0DQ. Tel: 01902-461300. *Frequencies:* 990 AM (Wolverhampton); 1017 AM (Shrewsbury and Telford)

CONNECT FM, Unit 1, Centre 2000, Kettering, Northants, NN16 8PU. Tel: 01536-412413. *Frequency:* 97.2 FM/107.4 FM

COUNTY SOUND RADIO 1566 MW, Dolphin House, North Street, Guildford GU1 4AA. Tel: 01483-300964. *Frequency:* 1566 MW

DELTA FM 97.1, 65 Weyhill, Haslemere, Surrey GU27 1HN. Tel: 01428-651971. *Frequency:* 97.1/101.6/102 FM

DREAM 100 FM, Northgate House, St Peter's Street, Colchester, CO1 1HT. Tel: 01206-764466. *Frequency:* 100.2 FM

DUNE FM, The Power Station, Victoria Way, Southport PR8 1RR. Tel: 01704-502500. *Frequency:* 107.9 FM

ELEVEN SEVENTY, PO Box 1170, High Wycombe, Bucks HP13 6YT. Tel: 01494-446611. *Frequency:* 1170 FM

ESSEX FM, Radio House, Clifftown Road, Southend-on-Sea, Essex SS1 1SX. Tel: 01702-333711. *Frequencies:* 96.3 FM (Southend); 97.5 FM (Southend Centre); 102.6 FM (Chelmsford)

FLR 107.3, Astra House, Arklow Road, London SE14 6EB. Tel: 020-8691 9202. *Frequency:* 107.3 FM

FM 102 – THE BEAR, The Guard House Studios, Banbury Road, Stratford-upon-Avon, Warks CV37 7HX. Tel: 01789-262636. *Frequency:* 102.0 FM

FM 107 THE FALCON, Brunel Mall, London Road, Stroud, Glos GL5 2BP. Tel: 01453-767369. *Frequency:* 107.2/107.9 FM

FOSSEWAY RADIO, PO Box 107, Hinckley, Leics LE10 1WR. Tel: 01455-614151. *Frequency:* 107.9 FM

FOX FM, Brush House, Pony Road, Oxford OX4 2XR. Tel: 01865-871000. *Frequencies:* 102.6/97.4 FM

FRESH AM, Gargrave Road, Skipton, N. Yorks BD23 1YD. Tel: 01756-799991. *Frequencies:* 936 MW (Hawes); 1413 MW (Skipton)

GALAXY 101, Millennium House, 26 Baldwin Street, Bristol BS1 1SE. Tel: 0117-901 0101. *Frequencies:* 97.2 FM (Bristol); 101 FM (Severn Estuary)

GALAXY 102, 127–129 Portland Street, Manchester M1 6ED. Tel: 0161-228 0102. *Frequency:* 102.0 FM

GALAXY 102.2, 1 The Square, 111 Broad Street, Birmingham B15 1AS. Tel: 0121-695 0000. *Frequency:* 102.2 FM

GALAXY 105, Joseph's Well, Westgate, Leeds LS3 1AB. Tel: 0113-213 0105. *Frequencies:* 105.1 FM (Leeds); 105.6 FM (Bradford and Sheffield); 105.8 FM (Hull)

GALAXY 105–106, Kingfisher Way, Silverlink Business Park, Tyne and Wear NE28 9ND. Tel: 0191-206 8000. *Frequencies:* 105.3/105.6/106.4 FM

GEMINI FM, Hawthorn House, Exeter Business Park, Exeter EX1 3QS. Tel: 01392-444444. *Frequencies:* 96.4/97.0/103.0 FM

GWR FM (BRISTOL AND BATH), PO Box 2000, Watershed, Canon's Road, Bristol BS99 7SN. Tel: 0117-984 3200. *Frequencies:* 96.3 FM (Bristol); 103.0 FM (Bath)

GWR FM (SWINDON AND WEST WILTSHIRE), PO Box 2000, Swindon SN4 7EX. Tel: 01793-842600. *Frequencies:* 97.2 FM (Swindon); 102.2 FM (West Wilts); 96.5 FM (Marlborough)

HALLAM FM, Radio House, 900 Herries Road, Sheffield S6 1RH. Tel: 0114-285 3333. *Frequencies:* 97.4 FM (Sheffield); 102.9 FM (Barnsley); 103.4 FM (Doncaster)

HEART 106.2, The Chrysalis Building, Bramley Road, London W10 6SP. Tel: 020-7468 1062. *Frequency:* 106.2 FM

HEARTBEAT 106.9 FM, PO Box 299, Hertford, Herts SG14 3XN. Tel: 01992-505362. *Frequencies:* 106.7/106.9 FM

HOME, The Old Stableblock, Lockwood Park, Huddersfield HD1 3UR. Tel: 01484-321107. *Frequency:* 107.9 FM

HORIZON FM 103, The Broadcast Centre, Vincent Avenue, Crownhill, Milton Keynes MK8 0AB. Tel: 01908-269111. *Frequency:* 103.3 FM

IMAGINE FM, Regent House, Heaton Lane, Stockport SK4 1BX. Tel: 0161-285 4545. *Frequencies:* 96.4 FM (Cheshire); 104.9 FM (Stockport)

INVICTA FM, Radio House, John Wilson Business Park, Whitstable, Kent CT5 3QX. Tel: 01227-772004. *Frequencies:* 103.1 FM (Maidstone and Medway); 102.8 FM (Canterbury); 95.9 FM (Thanet); 97.0 FM (Dover); 96.1 FM (Ashford)

ISLAND FM, 12 Westerbrook, St Sampsons, Guernsey GY2 4QQ. Tel: 01481-242000. *Frequencies:* 93.7 FM (Alderney); 104.7 FM (Guernsey)

ISLE OF WIGHT RADIO, Dodnor Park, Newport, Isle of Wight PO30 5XE. Tel: 01983-822557. *Frequencies:* 102.0/107.0 FM

JAZZ FM 102.2, 26–27 Castlereagh Street, London W1H 6DJ. Tel: 020-7706 4100. *Frequency:* 102.2 FM

JAZZ FM 100.4, The World Trade Centre, Exchange Quay, Manchester M5 3EJ. Tel: 0161-877 1004. *Frequency:* 100.4 FM

JUICE 107.6, 27 Fleet Street, Liverpool L1 4AR. Tel: 0151-707 3107. *Frequency:* 107.6 FM

KCR, PO Box 106, Prescot, Merseyside L35 0RN. Tel: 07808-179999. Expected on air early 2001. *Frequency:* to be announced

KICK FM, The Studios, 42 Bone Lane, Newbury, Berks RG14 5SD. Tel: 01635-841600. *Frequencies:* 105.6/107.4 FM

KISS 100 FM, Kiss House, 80 Holloway Road, London N7 8JG. Tel: 020-7700 6100. *Frequency:* 100.0 FM

KIX 96, Watch Close, Spon Street, Coventry CV1 3LN. Tel: 024-7652 5656. *Frequency:* 96.2 FM

KL.FM 96.7, PO Box 77, 18 Blackfriars Street, King's Lynn, Norfolk PE30 1NN. Tel: 01553-772777. *Frequency:* 96.7 FM

LANTERN FM, 2B Lauder Lane, Roundswell Business Park, Barnstaple EX31 3TA. Tel: 01271-340340. *Frequency:* 96.2 FM

LBC 1152 AM, 200 Gray's Inn Road, London WC1X 8XZ. Tel: 020-7973 1152. *Frequency:* 1152 AM

LEICESTER SOUND, Granville House, Granville Road, Leicester LE1 7RW. Tel: 0116-256 1300. *Frequency:* 105.4 FM

LINCS FM, Witham Park, Waterside South, Lincoln LN5 7JN. Tel: 01522-549900. *Frequencies:* 102.2 /96.7 FM (Grantham Relay)/97.6 FM (Scunthorpe Relay)

LITE FM, 5 Church Street, Peterborough PE1 1XJ. Tel: 01733-898106. *Frequency:* 106.8 FM

LONDON GREEK RADIO, Florentia Village, Vale Road, London N4 1TD. Tel: 020-8800 8001. *Frequency:* 103.3 FM

LONDON TURKISH RADIO LTR, 185B High Road, Wood Green, London N22 6BA. Tel: 020-8881 0606. *Frequency:* 1584 AM

MAGIC 105.4 FM, The Network Building, 97 Tottenham Court Road, London W1P 9HF. Tel: 020-7504 7000. *Frequency:* 105.4 FM

MAGIC 828, 51 Burley Road, Leeds LS3 1LR. Tel: 0113-283 5500. *Frequency:* 828 AM

MAGIC 999, PO Box 999, Preston, Lancs PR1 1XR. Tel: 01772-556301. *Frequency:* 999 AM

MAGIC 1152, Castle Quay, Castlefield, Manchester M15 4PR. Tel: 0161-288 5000. *Frequency:* 1152 AM

MAGIC 1152 AM, Newcastle upon Tyne NE99 1BB. Tel: 0191-420 3040. *Frequency:* 1152 AM

MAGIC 1161 AM, Commercial Road, Hull HU1 2SG. Tel: 01482-325141. *Frequency:* 1161 AM

MAGIC 1170, Radio House, Yales Crescent, Thornaby, Stockton-on-Tees, Cleveland TS17 6AA. Tel: 01642-888222. *Frequency:* 1170 AM

MAGIC 1548, 8–10 Stanley Street, Liverpool L1 6AF. Tel: 0151-227 5100. *Frequency:* 1548 AM

MAGIC AM, Radio House, 900 Herries Road, Sheffield S6 1RH. Tel: 0114-285 2121. *Frequencies:* 990/1305/1548 AM

MANCHESTER'S MAGIC (1152), Castle Quay, Castlefield, Manchester M15 4PR. Tel: 0161-288 5000. *Frequency:* 1152 AM

MANSFIELD 103.2, The Media Suite, Brunts Business Centre, Samuel Brunts Way, Mansfield, Notts NG18 2AH. Tel: 01623-646666.. *Frequency:* 103.2 FM

MARCHER GOLD, The Studios, Mold Road, Wrexham LL11 4AF. Tel: 01978-752202. *Frequency:* 1260 AM

MEDWAY FM, Berkeley House, 186 High Street, Rochester ME1 1EY. Tel: 01634-841111. *Frequencies:* 107.9/100.4 FM

MERCIA FM, Hertford Place, Coventry CV1 3TT. Tel: 024-7686 8200. *Frequencies:* 97.0/102.9 FM

MERCURY 96.2 FM, 1 East Street, Tonbridge, Kent TN9 1AR. Tel: 01732-369200. *Frequencies:* 96.2 FM (South); 101.6 FM (North)

MERCURY 96.6 FM, 9 Christopher Place, Shopping Centre, St Albans, Herts AL3 5DQ. Tel: 01727-831966. *Frequency:* 96.6 FM

MERCURY 102.7 FM, The Stanley Centre, Kelvin Way, Crawley, W. Sussex RH10 2SE. Tel: 01293-519161. *Frequencies:* 97.5/102.7 FM

MERCURY 107.9 FM, Berkeley House, 186 High Street, Rochester ME1 1EY. Tel: 01634-841111. *Frequencies:* 100.4/107.9 FM

METRO RADIO, Newcastle upon Tyne NE99 1BB. Tel: 0191-420 0971. *Frequencies:* 97.1 FM (Northumberland, Tyne and Wear, Durham); 103.0 FM (Tyne Valley); 102.6 FM (Alnwick); 103.2 FM (Hexham)

MFM 103.4, The Studios, Mold Road, Gwersyllt, Nr Wrexham LL11 4AF. Tel: 01978-752202. *Frequency:* 103.4 FM

MILLENNIUM RADIO, Harrow Manor Way, Thamesmead, London SE2 9XH. Tel: 020-8311 3112. *Frequency:* 106.8 FM

MINSTER FM, PO Box 123, Dunnington, York YO1 5ZX. Tel: 01904-488888. *Frequencies:* 104.7 FM (York); 102.3 FM (Thirsk)

MIX 96, Friars Square Studios, 11 Bourbon Street, Aylesbury, Bucks HP20 2PZ. Tel: 01296-399396. *Frequency:* 96.2 FM

NEPTUNE RADIO, PO Box 1068, Dover CT16 1GB; PO Box 964, Folkestone CT18 8GG. Tel: 01304-202505. *Frequencies:* 96.4 FM (Folkestone); 106.8 FM (Dover)

NEWS DIRECT 97.3 FM, 200 Gray's Inn Road, London WC1X 8XZ. Tel: 020-7973 1152. *Frequency:* 97.3 FM

NORTHANTS 96, 19–21 St Edmunds Road, Northampton NN1 5DY. Tel: 01604-795601. *Frequency:* 96.6 FM

THE NRG, PO Box 1234, Bournemouth BH1 3YH. Tel: 01202-318100. *Frequency:* 107.6 FM

OCEAN FM, Radio House, Whittle Avenue, Segensworth West, Fareham, Hants PO15 5SH. Tel: 01489-589911. *Frequencies:* 96.7/97.5 FM

ORCHARD FM, Haygrove House, Taunton, Somerset TA3 7BT. Tel: 01823-338448. *Frequencies:* 96.5 FM (Taunton); 97.1 FM (Yeovil); 102.6 FM (Somerset)

Oxygen 107.9 FM, Suite 41, Westgate Centre, Oxford OX1 1PD. Tel: 01865-724442. *Frequency:* 107.9 FM

PEAK 107 FM, Radio House, Foxwood Road, Chesterfield, Derbys S41 9RF. Tel: 01246-269107. *Frequencies:* 107.4 FM (Chesterfield and NE Derbyshire); 102.0 FM (Matlock and Bakewell)

PICCADILLY KEY, Castle Quay, Castlefield, Manchester M15 4PR. Tel: 0161-288 5000. *Frequency:* 103 FM

PIRATE FM 102, Carn Brea Studios, Wilson Way, Redruth, Cornwall TR15 3XX. Tel: 01209-314400. *Frequencies:* 102.2 FM (East Cornwall and West Devon); 102.8 FM (West Cornwall and Isles of Scilly)

PLYMOUTH SOUND FM, Earl's Acre, Plymouth PL3 4HX. Tel: 01752-227272. *Frequencies:* 96.6/97.0 FM

PREMIER CHRISTIAN RADIO, Glen House, Stag Place, London SW1E 5AG. Tel: 020-7316 1300. *Frequencies:* 1305/1332/1413 AM

THE PULSE, Pennine House, Forster Square, Bradford BD1 5NE. Tel: 01274-203040. *Frequencies:* 97.5 FM (Bradford); 102.5 FM (Huddersfield and Halifax)

Q103 FM, Enterprise House, The Vision Park, Chivers Way, Histon, Cambridge CB4 4WW. Tel: 01223-235255. *Frequencies:* 103.0 FM (Cambridge); 97.4 FM (Newmarket)

QUAY WEST RADIO, Harbour Studios, The Esplanade, Watchet, Somerset TA23 0AJ. Tel: 01984-634900. *Frequency:* 102.4 FM

RADIO XL 1296 AM, KMS House, Bradford Street, Birmingham B12 0JD. Tel: 0121-753 5353. *Frequency:* 1296 AM

RAM FM, 35–36 Irongate, Derby DE1 3GA. Tel: 01332-205599. *Frequency:* 102.8 FM

REVOLUTION, PO Box 962, Oldham OL1 1FE. Tel: 0161-628 8787. *Frequency:* 96.2 FM

RIDINGS FM, 2 Thornes Office Park, Monckton Road, Wakefield WF2 7AN. Tel: 01924-367177. *Frequency:* 106.8 FM

RITZ 1035 AM, 33–35 Wembley Hill Road, London HA9 8RT. Tel: 020-8733 1300. *Frequency:* 1035 AM

ROCK FM, PO Box 974, Preston PR1 1XS. Tel: 01772-556301. *Frequency:* 97.4 FM

RUTLAND RADIO, Rutland Business Centre, Gaol Street, Oakham, Rutland LE15 6AY. Tel: 01572-757868. *Frequency:* 107.2 FM (Rutland); 97.4 FM (Stamford)

SABRAS RADIO, Radio House, 63 Melton Road, Leicester LE4 6PN. Tel: 0116-261 0666. *Frequency:* 1260 AM

SEVERN SOUND FM, Bridge Studios, Eastgate Centre, Gloucester GL1 1SS. Tel: 01452-313200. *Frequencies:* 103.0/102.4 FM

SGR COLCHESTER, Abbeygate Two, 9 Whitewell Road, Colchester CO2 7DE. Tel: 01206-575859. *Frequency:* 96.1 FM

SGR-FM, Radio House, Alpha Business Park, White House Road, Ipswich IP1 5LT. Tel: 01473-461000. *Frequencies:* 97.1 FM (Ipswich); 96.4 FM (Bury St Edmunds)

SIGNAL ONE FM, Stoke Road, Stoke-on-Trent ST4 2SR. Tel: 01782-747047. *Frequencies:* 102.6/96.9 FM

SOUTH CITY FM, City Studios, Marsh Lane, Southampton, SO14 3ST. Tel: 023-8022 0020. *Frequency:* 107.8 FM

SOUTHERN FM, Radio House, PO Box 2000, Brighton BN41 2SS. Tel: 01273-430111. *Frequencies:* 102.0 FM (Hastings); 102.4 FM (Eastbourne); 96.9 FM (Newhaven); 103.5 FM (Brighton)

SOUTH HAMS RADIO, Unit 9, South Hams Business Park, Churchstow, Knightsbridge, Devon TQ7 3QR. Tel: 01548-854595. *Frequency:* 100.5 FM (Totnes); 100.8 FM (Dartmouth); 101.2 FM (South Hams); 101.9 FM (Ivybridge)

SOVEREIGN RADIO, 14 St Mary's Walk, Hailsham, E. Sussex BN27 1AF. Tel: 01323-442700. *Frequency:* 107.5 FM

SPECTRUM INTERNATIONAL RADIO, International Radio Centre, 204–206 Queenstown Road, London SW8 3NR. Tel: 020-7627 4433. *Frequency:* 558 AM

SPIRE FM, City Hall Studios, Malthouse Lane, Salisbury, Wilts SP2 7QQ. Tel: 01722-416644. *Frequency:* 102.0 FM

SPIRIT FM, Dukes Court, Bognor Road, Chichester, W.Sussex PO19 2FX. Tel: 01243-773600. *Frequencies:* 96.6/102.3 FM

STAR FM, The Observatory Shopping Centre, Slough, Berks SL1 1LH. Tel: 01753-551066. *Frequency:* 106.6 FM

SUN FM, PO Box 1034, Sunderland SR5 2YL. Tel: 0191-548 1034. *Frequency:* 103.4 FM

SUNRISE FM, Sunrise House, 30 Chapel Street, Little Germany, Bradford BD1 5DN. Tel: 01274-735043. *Frequency:* 103.2 FM

SUNRISE RADIO, Sunrise House, Sunrise Road, Southall, Middx UB2 4AU. Tel: 020-8574 6666. *Frequency:* 1458 AM

SUNSHINE 855, Sunshine House, Waterside, Ludlow, Shropshire SY8 1PE. Tel: 01584-873795. *Frequency:* 855 AM

SURF 107, PO Box 107, Brighton BN1 1QG. Tel: 01273-386107. Frequency: 107.2 FM

TEN 17, Latton Bush Centre, Southern Way, Harlow, Essex CM18 7BU. Tel: 01279-431017. *Frequency:* 101.7 FM

TFM, Radio House, Yale Crescent, Thornaby, Stockton-on-Tees TS17 4AA. Tel: 01642-888222. *Frequency:* 96.6 FM

TLR, Imperial House, 2–14 High Street, Margate, Kent CT9 1DH. Tel: 01843-220222. *Frequency:* 107.2 FM

TOWER FM, The Mill, Brownlow Way, Bolton BL1 2RA. Tel: 01204-387000. *Frequency:* 107.4 FM

TRAX FM, PO Box 444, Worksop, Notts S81 9YW. Tel: 01909-500611. *Frequency:* 107.9AM

TRAX FM, PO Box 444, Doncaster DN3 3GB. Tel: 01302-341166. *Frequency:* 107.1 FM

VIBE FM, Reflection House, The Anderson Centre, Olding Road, Bury, St Edmunds IP33 3TA. Tel: 01284-718800. *Frequencies:* 105.6 FM (Cambridge); 106.1 FM (Norwich); 106.4 FM (Ipswich); 107.7 FM (Peterborough)

VICTORY 107.4, Media House, Tipner Wharf, Twyford Avenue, Portsmouth PO2 8PE. Tel: 023-9263 9922. *Frequency:* 107.4 FM

VIRGIN 105.8, 1 Golden Square, London W1R 4DJ. Tel: 020-7434 1215. *Frequency:* 105.8 FM

THE WAVE 96.5, 965 Mowbray Drive, Blackpool FY3 7JR. Tel: 01253-304965. *Frequency:* 96.5 FM

WAVE 105 FM, 5 Manor Court, Barnes Wallis Road, Segensworth East, Fareham, Hampshire PO15 5TH. Tel: 01489-481050. *Frequencies:* 105.2 FM (Solent); 105.8 FM (Poole)

WESSEX FM, Radio House, Trinity Street, Dorchester DT1 1DJ. Tel: 01305-250333. *Frequencies:* 97.2/96.0 FM

WIN 107.2, PO Box 1072, The Brooks, Winchester SO23 8FT. Tel: 01962-841071. *Frequency:* 107.2 FM

WYVERN FM, 5–6 Barbourne Terrace, Worcester WR1 3JZ. Tel: 01905-612212. *Frequencies:* 97.6 FM (Hereford); 102.8 FM (Worcester); 96.7 FM (Kidderminster)

X-CEL FM, 46 Camel Road, Littleport, Cambs CB6 1EW. Tel: 01353-865102. *Frequencies:* 107.1/107.5 FM

XFM, 30 Leicester Square, London WC2H 7LA. Tel: 020-7766 6600. *Frequency:* 104.9 FM

YORKSHIRE COAST RADIO, PO Box 962, Scarborough, N. Yorks YO12 5YX. Tel: 01723-500962. *Frequencies:* 96.2/103.1 FM

YORKSHIRE COAST RADIO BRIDLINGTON'S BEST, Old Harbour Master's Office, Harbour Road, Bridlington, E. Yorks YO15 2NR. Tel: 01262-404400. *Frequency:* 102.4 FM

Wales

106.3 BRIDGE FM, 25 Wyndham Street, Bridgend CF31 1EB. Tel: 01656-647777. *Frequency:* 106.3 FM

CAPITAL GOLD, West Canal Wharf, Cardiff CF10 5XL. Tel: 029-2023 7878. *Frequencies:* 1359 AM (Cardiff); 1305 AM (Newport)

CHAMPION FM, Llys y Dderwen, Parc Menai, Bangor LL57 4BN. Tel: 01248-671888. *Frequency:* 103.0 FM

COAST FM, 41 Conwy Road, Colwyn Bay LL28 5AB. Tel: 01492-533733. *Frequency:* 96.3 FM

RADIO CEREDIGION, Yr Hen Ysgol Gymraeg, Ffordd Alexandra, Aberystwyth SY23 1LF. Tel: 01970-627999. *Frequencies:* 96.6/97.4/103.3/FM

RADIO MALDWYN, The Studios, The Park, Newtown, Powys SY16 2NZ. Tel: 01686-623555. *Frequency:* 756 AM

REAL RADIO, PO Box 6105, Ty-Nant Court, Cardiff CF15 8YF. Tel: 029-2023 1863. Expected air date Autumn 2000. *Frequency:* to be arranged.

RED DRAGON FM, Radio House, West Canal Wharf, Cardiff CF10 5XL. Tel: 029-2038 4041. *Frequencies:* 103.2 FM (Cardiff); 97.4 FM (Newport)

SWANSEA SOUND, PO Box 1170, Victoria Road, Gowerton, Swansea SA4 3AB. Tel: 01792-511170. *Frequency:* 1170 AM

VALLEYS RADIO, Festival Park, Victoria, Ebbw Vale NP3 6XW. Tel: 01495-301116. *Frequencies:* 999/1116 AM

THE WAVE 96.4 FM, PO Box 964, Victoria Road, Gowerton, Swansea SA4 3AB. Tel: 01792-511964. *Frequency:* 96.4 FM

Scotland

96.3 QFM, 26 Lady Lane, Paisley PA1 2LG. Tel: 0141-887 9630. *Frequency:* 96.3 FM

ARGYLL FM, 27–29 Longrow, Campbeltown, Argyll PA28 6ER. Tel: 01586-551800. Expected on air Summer 2000. *Frequency:* 107.1/107.7/106.5 FM

BEAT 106, Four Winds Pavilion, Pacific Quay, Glasgow G51 1EB. Tel: 0141-566 6106 *Frequencies:* 105.7/106.1 FM

CENTRAL FM, 201 High Street, Falkirk FK1 1DU. Tel: 01324-611164. *Frequency:* 103.1 FM

CLAN FM, Radio House, Rowantree Avenue, Newhouse Industrial Estate, Newhouse ML1 5RX. Tel: 01689-733107. *Frequency:* 107.5/107.9 FM

CLYDE 1 (FM) AND 2 (AM), Clydebank Business Park, Clydebank, Glasgow G81 2RX. Tel: 0141-565 2200. *Frequencies:* 102.5 FM; 103.3 FM (Firth of Clyde); 97.0 FM (Vale of Leven); 1152 AM

FORTH AM AND FM, Forth House, Forth Street, Edinburgh EH1 3LF. Tel: 0131-556 9255. *Frequencies:* 1548 AM, 97.3/97.6/102.2 FM

HEARTLAND FM, Atholl Curling Rink, Lower Oakfield, Pitlochry, Perthshire PH16 5HQ. Tel: 01796-474040. *Frequency:* 97.5 FM

ISLES FM, PO Box 333, Stornoway, Isle of Lewis HS1 2PU. Tel: 01851-703333. *Frequency:* 103.0 FM

KINGDOM FM, Haig House, Haig Business Park, Markinch, Fife KY7 6AQ. Tel: 01592-753753. *Frequencies:* 95.2/96.1 FM

LOCHBROOM FM, Radio House, Mill Street, Ullapool, Wester Ross IV26 2UN. Tel: 01854-613131. *Frequency:* 102.2 FM

MORAY FIRTH RADIO, Scorguie Place, Inverness IV3 8UJ. Tel: 01463-224433. *Frequencies:* 97.4 FM, 1107 AM; *local opt-outs:* MFR Speysound 96.6 FM, MFR Keith Community Radio 102.8 FM; MFR Kinnaird Radio 96.7 FM; MFR Caithness 102.5 FM

NECR (NORTH-EAST COMMUNITY RADIO), Town House, Kintore, Inverurie AB51 0US. Tel: 01467-632909. *Frequencies:* 97.1 FM (Braemar); 102.1 FM (Meldrum and Inverurie); 102.6 FM (Kildrummy); 103.2 FM (Colpy)

NEVIS RADIO, Inverlochy, Fort William, Inverness-shire PH33 6LU. Tel: 01397-700007. *Frequencies:* 96.6 FM (Fort William); 97.0 FM (Glencoe); 102.3 FM (Skye); 102.4 FM (Loch Leven)

NORTH SOUND ONE (FM) and TWO (AM), 45 Kings Gate, Aberdeen AB15 4EL. Tel: 01224-337000. *Frequencies:* 1035 AM, 96.9/97.6/103.0 FM

OBAN FM, 132 George Street, Oban, Argyll PA34 5NT. Tel: 01631-570057. *Frequency:* 103.3 FM

RADIO BORDERS, Tweedside Park, Galashiels TD1 3TD. Tel: 01896-759444. *Frequencies:* 96.8/97.5/103.1/103.4 FM

RADIO TAY AM AND TAY FM, 6 North Isla Street, Dundee DD3 7JQ. Tel: 01382-200800. *Frequencies:* 1161 AM, 102.8 FM (Dundee); 1584 AM, 96.4 FM (Perth)

RNA FM, Arbroath Infirmary, Rosemount Road, Arbroath, Angus DD11 2AT. Tel: 01241-879660. *Frequency:* 96.6 FM

SCOT FM, 1 Albert Quay, Leith EH6 7DN. Tel: 0131-625 8400. *Frequencies:* 100.3 FM (West); 101.1 FM (East)

SIBC, Market Street, Lerwick, Shetland ZE1 0JN. Tel: 01595-695299. *Frequencies:* 96.2/102.2 FM

SOUTH WEST SOUND, Campbell House, Bankend Road, Dumfries DG1 4TH. Tel: 01387-250999. *Frequencies:* 96.5/97.0/103.0 FM

WAVE 102, 8 South Tay Street, Dundee DD1 1PA. Tel: 01382-901000. *Frequency:* 102 FM

WAVES RADIO PETERHEAD, Unit 2, Blackhouse Industrial Estate, Peterhead AB42 1BW. Tel: 01779-491012. *Frequency:* 101.2 FM

WEST SOUND AM AND WEST FM, Radio House, 54A Holmston Road, Ayr KA7 3BE. Tel: 01292-283662. *Frequencies:* 1035 AM, 96.7 FM (Ayr); 97.5 FM (Girvan)

Northern Ireland

CITY BEAT 96.7, Lamont Buildings, Stranmillis Embankment, Belfast BT9 5FN. Tel: 028-9020 5967. *Frequency:* 96.7 FM

COOL FM, PO Box 974, Belfast BT1 1RT. Tel: 028-9081 7181. *Frequency:* 97.4 FM

DOWNTOWN RADIO, Newtownards, Co. Down BT23 4ES. Tel: 028-9181 5555. *Frequencies:* 1026 AM (Belfast); 96.4 FM (Limavady); 96.6 FM (Enniskillen); 97.1 FM (Larne); 102.3 FM (Ballymena); 102.4 FM (Londonderry); 103.1 FM (Newry); 103.4 FM (Newcastle); 1026 AM (Belfast)

Q97.2 FM, 24 Clafin Road, Coleraine BT52 2NU. Tel: 028-7035 9100. *Frequency:* 97.2 FM

Q102.9 FM, The Riverside Suite, Old Waterside Railway Station, Duke Street, Londonderry BT47 6DH. Tel: 028-7134 4449. *Frequency:* 102.9 FM

Channel Islands

104.7 ISLAND FM, 12 Westerbrook, St Sampsons, Guernsey GY2 4QQ. Tel: 01481-242000. *Frequencies:* 104.7 FM (Guernsey); 93.7 FM (Alderney)

CHANNEL 103 FM, 6 Tunnell Street, St Helier, Jersey JE2 4LU. Tel: 01534-888103. *Frequency:* 103.7FM

The Press

The newspaper and periodical press in the UK is large and diverse, catering for a wide variety of views and interests. There is no state control or censorship of the press, though it is subject to the laws on publication and the Press Complaints Commission was set up by the industry as a means of self-regulation.

The press is not state-subsidized and receives few tax concessions. The income of most newspapers and periodicals is derived largely from sales and from advertising; the press is the largest advertising medium in Britain.

SELF-REGULATION

The Press Complaints Commission was founded by the newspaper and magazine industry in January 1991 to replace the Press Council (established in 1953). It is a voluntary, non-statutory body set up to operate the press's self-regulation system following the Calcutt report in 1990 on privacy and related matters, when the industry feared that failure to regulate itself might lead to statutory regulation of the press. The performance of the Press Complaints Commission was reviewed after 18 months of operation (the *Calcutt Review of Press Self-Regulation*, presented to Parliament in January 1993) to determine whether statutory measures were required. No proposals for replacing the self-regulation system have been made to date.

The Commission is funded by the industry through the Press Standards Board of Finance.

COMPLAINTS

The Press Complaints Commission's objects are to consider, adjudicate, conciliate, and resolve complaints of unfair treatment by the press; and to ensure that the press maintains the highest professional standards with respect for generally recognized freedoms, including freedom of expression, the public's right to know, and the right of the press to operate free from improper pressure. The Commission judges newspaper and magazine conduct by a code of practice drafted by editors, agreed by the industry and ratified by the Commission.

Seven of the Commission's members are editors of national, regional and local newspapers and magazines, and nine, including the chairman, are drawn from other fields. One member has been appointed Privacy Commissioner with special powers to investigate complaints about invasion of privacy.

PRESS COMPLAINTS COMMISSION, 1 Salisbury Square, London EC4Y 8JB. Tel: 020-7353 1248. Fax: 020-7353 8355. *Chairman*, Lord Wakeham, PC; *Director*, G. Black

NEWSPAPERS

Newspapers are usually financially independent of any political party, though most adopt a political stance in their editorial comments, usually reflecting proprietorial influence. Ownership of the national and regional daily newspapers is concentrated in the hands of large corporations whose interests cover publishing and communications. The rules on cross-media ownership, as amended by the Broadcasting Act 1996, limit the extent to which newspaper organisations (with over 20 per cent of national circulation) may become involved in broadcasting.

There are about 15 daily and 17 Sunday national papers, about 84 regional daily papers, and several hundred local papers that are published weekly or twice-weekly. Scotland, Wales and Northern Ireland all have at least one daily and one Sunday national paper.

Newspapers are usually published in either broadsheet or tabloid format. The 'quality' daily papers, e.g. those providing detailed coverage of a wide range of public matters, have a broadsheet format. The tabloid papers take a more popular approach and are more illustrated.

CIRCULATION
(as at April 2000)

National Daily Newspapers

Daily Mail	2,354,517
Daily Sport	210,000
Daily Star	521,387
Daily Telegraph	1,030,493
The Express	1,086,169
Financial Times	456,706
The Guardian	387,442
The Independent	224,534
The Mirror	2,255,916
Racing Post	83,854
The Scotsman	78,973
The Sun	3,559,146
The Times	711,457

National Sunday Newspapers

Express on Sunday	1,003,186
Independent on Sunday	252,304
Mail on Sunday	2,242,802
News of the World	4,002,952
The Observer	409,295
The People	1,514,798
Scotland on Sunday	84,265
Sunday Mirror	1,888,710
Sunday Sport	191,058
Sunday Telegraph	805,069
Sunday Times	1,391,784

Source: Audit Bureau of Circulations Ltd, May 2000. For further information please see http://www.abc.org.uk

NATIONAL DAILY NEWSPAPERS

DAILY MAIL, Northcliffe House, 2 Derry Street, London W8 5TT. Tel: 020-7938 6000. Fax: 020-7937 3745

DAILY SPORT, 19 Great Ancoats Street, Manchester M60 4BT. Tel: 0161-236 4466. Fax: 0161-236 4535. Email: sport@globalnet.co.uk; Web: http://www.dailysport.co.uk

DAILY STAR, Ludgate House, 245 Blackfriars Road, London SE1 9UX. Tel: 020-7928 8000. Fax: 020-7633 0244. Web: http://www.megastar.co.uk

DAILY TELEGRAPH, 1 Canada Square, Canary Wharf, London E14 5DT. Tel: 020-7538 5000. Fax: 020-7513 2506. Web: http://www.telegraph.co.uk

THE EXPRESS, Ludgate House, 245 Blackfriars Road, London SE1 9UX. Tel: 020-7928 8000. Fax: 020-7633 0244. Web: http://www.express.co.uk

FINANCIAL TIMES, 1 Southwark Bridge, London SE1 9HL. Tel: 020-7873 3000. Fax: 020-7407 5700. Email: readerenquiries@ft.com; Web: http://www.ft.com

THE GUARDIAN, 119 Farringdon Road, London EC1R 3ER.
Tel: 020-7278 2332. Fax: 020-7837 2114.
Email: letters@guardian.co.uk;
Web: http://www.guardian.co.uk
THE HERALD, 195 Albion Street, Glasgow G1 1QP.
Tel: 0141-552 6255. Fax: 0141-552 1344.
Email: heraldmail@cims.co.uk;
Web: http://www.theherald.co.uk
THE INDEPENDENT, 1 Canada Square, Canary Wharf,
London E14 5DL. Tel: 020-7293 2000. Fax: 020-
7293 2435. Email: letters@independent.co.uk;
Web: http://www.independent.co.uk
THE MIRROR, 1 Canada Square, Canary Wharf,
London E14 5AP. Tel: 020-7293 3000.
Fax: 020-7293 3405. Email: ic24@mgn.co.uk;
Web: http://www.mirror.co.uk
MORNING STAR, Cape House, 787 Commercial Road,
London E14 7HG. Tel: 020-7538 5181. Fax:
020-7538 5125. Email: morsta@geo2.poptel.org.uk;
Web: http://www.poptel.org.uk/morning-star/
RACING POST, 1 Canada Square, Canary Wharf,
London E14 5AP. Tel: 020-7293 3000.
Fax: 020-7293 3758. Email: editor@racingpost.co.uk;
Web: http://www.racingpost.co.uk
THE SCOTSMAN, Barclay House, 108 Holyrood Road,
Edinburgh EH8 8AS. Tel: 0131-620 8620.
Fax: 0131-620 8615/6. Email: newsdesk_ts@scots-
man.com; Web: http://www.scotsman.com
THE SUN, 1 Virginia Street, London E1 9XR.
Tel: 020-7782 4000. Fax: 020-7583 9504.
Web: http://www.lineone.net
THE TIMES, 1 Pennington Street, London E98 1TT.
Tel: 020-7782 5000. Fax: 020-7782 5988.
Email: home.news@the-times.co.uk;
Web: http://www.the-times.co.uk

REGIONAL DAILY NEWSPAPERS

BERKSHIRE

READING EVENING POST, 8 Tessa Road, Reading RG1 8NS.
Tel: 0118-918 3000. Fax: 0118-959 9363.
Email: editorial@reading-epost.co.uk;
Web: http://www.getreading.co.uk

CAMBRIDGESHIRE

CAMBRIDGE EVENING NEWS, Winship Road, Milton,
Cambridge CB4 6PP. Tel: 01223-434434.
Fax: 01223-434415.
Email: colingrant@cambridge-news.co.uk;
Web: http://www.cambridge-news.co.uk
PETERBOROUGH EVENING TELEGRAPH, New Priestgate
House, 57 Priestgate, Peterborough PE1 1JW.
Tel: 01733-555111. Fax: 01733-555188

CUMBRIA

NEWS AND STAR, Newspaper House, Dalston Road,
Carlisle CA2 5UA. Tel: 01228-612600.
Fax: 01228-612601
NORTH-WEST EVENING MAIL, Newspaper House,
Abbey Road, Barrow-in-Furness LA14 5QS.
Tel: 01229-821835. Fax: 01229-840164.
Email: news@cumbrian-newspapers.co.uk;
Web: http://www.news-and-star.co.uk

DERBYSHIRE

DERBY EVENING TELEGRAPH, Northcliffe House,
Meadow Road, Derby DE1 2DW. Tel: 01332-291111.
Fax: 01332-253011.
Web: http://www.thisisderbyshire.co.uk

DEVON

EXPRESS AND ECHO, Heron Road, Sowton, Exeter
EX2 7NF. Tel: 01392-442211. Fax: 01392-442295
EVENING HERALD, 17 Brest Road, Derriford Business
Park, Plymouth PL6 5AA. Tel: 01752-765500.
Fax: 01752-765515.
Email: news@westcountrypublications.co.uk;
Web: http://www.thisisplymouth.co.uk
HERALD EXPRESS, Harmsworth House, Barton
Hill Road, Torquay TQ2 8JN. Tel: 01803-676000.
Fax: 01803-676228
WESTERN MORNING NEWS, 17 Brest Road, Derriford
Business Park, Plymouth PL6 5AA. Tel: 01752-765500.
Fax: 01752-765515

DORSET

DORSET ECHO, Fleet House, Hampshire Road,
Granby Industrial Estate, Weymouth Dorset DT4 9XD.
Tel: 01305-830930. Fax: 01305-830802.
Web: http://www.dorsetecho.co.uk
THE DAILY ECHO, Richmond Hill, Bournemouth
BH2 6HH. Tel: 01202-554601. Fax: 01202-293676.
Email: newsdesk@bournemouthecho.co.uk;
Web: http://www.daily-echo.co.uk

DURHAM

NORTHERN ECHO, Priestgate, Darlington DL1 1NF.
Tel: 01325-381313. Fax: 01325-380539.
Email: echo@nen.co.uk;
Web: http://www.thisisthenortheast.co.uk

EAST SUSSEX

THE ARGUS/EVENING ARGUS, Argus House,
Crowhurst Road, Hollingbury, Brighton BN1 8AR.
Tel: 01273-544544. Fax: 01273-566114

ESSEX

EVENING ECHO, Newspaper House,
Chester Hall Lane, Basildon SS14 3BL.
Tel: 01268-522792. Fax: 01268-532060
EVENING GAZETTE, Wickham House, 1 Northgate
Street, Colchester CO1 1HA. Tel: 01206-506000.
Fax: 01206-508274

GLOUCESTERSHIRE

THE CITIZEN, St John's Lane, Gloucester GL1 2AY.
Tel: 01452-424442. Fax: 01452-505596
GLOUCESTERSHIRE ECHO, 1–3 Clarence Parade,
Cheltenham GL50 3NZ. Tel: 01242-271900.
Fax: 01242-271792

HAMPSHIRE

THE NEWS, The News Centre, Hilsea, Portsmouth
PO2 9SX. Tel: 023-9266 4488. Fax: 023-9267 3363
SOUTHERN DAILY ECHO, Newspaper House,
Test Lane, Retbridge, Southampton SO16 9JX.
Tel: 023-8042 4777. Fax: 023-8042 4770

KENT

KENT TODAY, Messenger House, New Hythe Lane,
Larkfield, Aylesford ME20 6SG. Tel: 01622-717880.
Fax: 01622-719637

LANCASHIRE

BOLTON EVENING NEWS, Newspaper House,
Churchgate, Bolton BL1 1DE. Tel: 01204-522345.
Fax: 01204-365068.
Email: ben_editorial@newsquest.co.uk;
Web: http://www.thisisbolton.co.uk

THE GAZETTE, Avroe House, Avroe Crescent, Blackpool FY4 2DP. Tel: 01253-400888. Fax: 01253-694152

LANCASHIRE EVENING POST, Oliver's Place, Fulwood, Preston PR2 9ZA. Tel: 01772-254841. Fax: 01772-880173

LANCASHIRE EVENING TELEGRAPH, Newspaper House, High Street, Blackburn BB1 1HT. Tel: 01254-678678. Fax: 01254-682185

MANCHESTER EVENING NEWS, 164 Deansgate, Manchester M60 2RD. Tel: 0161-832 7200. Fax: 0161- 832 5351.
Email: newsdesk@mcr-evening-news.co.uk;
Web: http://www.manchesteronline.co.uk

WIGAN EVENING POST, Oliver's Place, Fulwood, Preston PR2 9ZA. Tel: 01772-254841. Fax: 01772-880173

LEICESTERSHIRE

LEICESTER MERCURY, St George Street, Leicester LE1 9FQ. Tel: 0116-251 2512. Fax: 0116-262 4687

LINCOLNSHIRE

GRIMSBY EVENING TELEGRAPH, 80 Cleethorpe Road, Grimsby DN31 3EH. Tel: 01472-360360. Fax: 01472-352272

LINCOLNSHIRE ECHO, Brayford Wharf East, Lincoln LN5 7AT. Tel: 01522-820000. Fax: 01522-804492.
Email: editor@thisislincolnshire.co.uk;
Web: http://www.thisislincolnshire.co.uk

SCUNTHORPE EVENING TELEGRAPH, Telegraph House, Doncaster Road, Scunthorpe DN15 7RE. Tel: 01724-273273. Fax: 01724-853495

LONDON

THE Evening STANDARD, Northcliffe House, 2 Derry Street, London W8 5TT. Tel: 020-7938 6000. Fax: 020-7937 3745

MERSEYSIDE

DAILY POST, AND LIVERPOOL ECHO, PO Box 48, Old Hall Street, Liverpool L69 3EB. Tel: 0151-227 2000. Fax: 0151-236 4682

NORFOLK

EASTERN DAILY PRESS, AND EVENING NEWS, Prospect House, Rouen Road, Norwich NR1 1RE. Tel: 01603-628311. Fax: 01603-612930

NORTHAMPTONSHIRE

CHRONICLE AND ECHO, Upper Mounts, Northampton NN1 3HR. Tel: 01604-467000. Fax: 01604-467190

NORTHAMPTONSHIRE EVENING TELEGRAPH, Newspaper House, Ise Park, Rothwell Road, Kettering NN16 8GA. Tel: 01536-506100. Fax: 01536-506196

NOTTINGHAMSHIRE

NOTTINGHAM EVENING POST, Castle Wharf House, Nottingham NG1 7EU. Tel: 0115-948 2000. Fax: 0115-964 4032.
Email: nep.editorial@dial.pipex.com;
Web: http://www.thisisnottingham.co.uk

OXFORDSHIRE

THE OXFORD MAIL, Newspaper House, Osney Mead, Oxford OX2 0EJ. Tel: 01865-244988. Fax: 01865-790423

SHROPSHIRE

SHROPSHIRE STAR, Ketley, Telford TF1 4HU. Tel: 01743-248428. Fax: 01743-222451

SOMERSET

THE BATH CHRONICLE, Windsor House, Windsor Bridge, Bath BA2 3AU. Tel: 01225-322322. Fax: 01225-322291

BRISTOL EVENING POST, AND WESTERN DAILY PRESS, Temple Way, Bristol BS99 7HD. Tel: 0117-934 3000. Fax: 0117-934 3571

STAFFORDSHIRE

BURTON MAIL, 65–68 High Street, Burton on Trent DE14 1LE. Tel: 01283-512345. Fax: 01283-510075

THE SENTINEL, Sentinel House, Etruria, Stoke-on-Trent ST1 5SS. Tel: 01782-289800. Fax: 01782-280781

SUFFOLK

EAST ANGLIAN DAILY TIMES, AND EVENING STAR, 30 Lower Brook Street, Ipswich IP4 1AN. Tel: 01473-230023. Fax: 01473-211391.
Email: eadt@ecng.co.uk;
Web: http://www.suffolk-now.co.uk

TYNE AND WEAR

NEWCASTLE EVENING CHRONICLE, AND THE JOURNAL, Thomson House, Groat Market, Newcastle upon Tyne NE1 1ED. Tel: 0191-232 7500. Fax: 0191-230 4144

SHIELDS GAZETTE, Chapter Row, South Shields NE33 1BL. Tel: 0191-455 4661. Fax: 0191-456 8270

SUNDERLAND ECHO, Echo House, Pennywell, Sunderland SR4 9ER. Tel: 0191-534 3011. Fax: 0191-534 3807

WARWICKSHIRE

HEARTLAND EVENING NEWS, Newspaper House, 11–15 Newtown Road, Nuneaton CV11 4HP. Tel: 01203-353534. Fax: 01203-353481

WEST MIDLANDS

COVENTRY EVENING TELEGRAPH, Corporation Street, Coventry CV1 1FP. Tel: 024-7663 3633. Fax: 024-7663 1736

EXPRESS AND STAR, 51–53 Queen Street, Wolverhampton WV1 1ES. Tel: 01902-313131. Fax: 01902-710106

THE BIRMINGHAM POST, AND BIRMINGHAM EVENING MAIL, 28 Colmore Circus, Queensway, Birmingham B4 6AX. Tel: 0121-236 3366. Fax: 0121-233 3958

WILTSHIRE

SWINDON EVENING ADVERTISER, Newspaper House, 100 Victoria Road, Swindon SN1 3BE. Tel: 01793-528144. Fax: 01793-523883.
Web: http://www.thisiswiltshire.co.uk

YORKSHIRE

EVENING GAZETTE, Gazette Buildings, Borough Road, Middlesbrough TS1 3AZ. Tel: 01642-245401. Fax: 01642-232014

EVENING PRESS, PO Box 29, 76–86 Walmgate, York YO1 9YN. Tel: 01904-653051. Fax: 01904-612853.
Email: editor@ycp.co.uk;
Web: http://www.thisisyork.co.uk

HALIFAX EVENING COURIER, PO Box 19, Courier Buildings, King Cross Street, Halifax HX1 2SF. Tel: 01422-260200. Fax: 01422-260341.
Email: editor@halifaxcourier.co.uk;
Web: http://www.halifaxcourier.co.uk

HUDDERSFIELD DAILY EXAMINER, PO Box A26, Queen Street South, Huddersfield HD1 2TD. Tel: 01484-430000. Fax: 01484-423722

HULL DAILY MAIL, Blundell's Corner, Beverley Road, Hull HU3 1XS. Tel: 01482-327111. Fax: 01482-584353. Email: news@hulldailymail.co.uk; Web: http://www.thisishull.co.uk

SCARBOROUGH EVENING NEWS, 17–23 Aberdeen Walk, Scarborough YO11 1BB. Tel: 01723-363636. Fax: 01723-354092. Email: editorial@scarboroughveningnews.co.uk; Web: http://www.scarboroughveningnews.co.uk

SHEFFIELD STAR, York Street, Sheffield S1 1PU. Tel: 0114-276 7676. Fax: 0114-272 5978. Web: http://www.sheffweb.co.uk

TELEGRAPH AND ARGUS, Hall Ings, Bradford BD1 1JR. Tel: 01274-729511. Fax: 01274-723634

YORKSHIRE EVENING POST, PO Box 168, Wellington Street, Leeds LS1 1RF. Tel: 0113-243 2701. Fax: 0113-244 3430. Email: eped@ypn.co.uk; Web: http://www.thisisleeds.co.uk

YORKSHIRE POST, PO Box 168, Wellington Street, Leeds LS1 1RF. Tel: 0113-243 2701. Fax: 0113-238 8525 Email: yp.editor@ypn.co.uk; Web: http://www.yorkshirepost.co.uk

WALES

EVENING LEADER, Mold Business Park, Wrexham Road, Mold CH7 1XY. Tel: 01352-707707. Fax: 01352-700048

SOUTH WALES ARGUS, Cardiff Road, Maesglas, Newport NP9 1QW. Tel: 01633-810000. Fax: 01633-462121

SOUTH WALES ECHO, Thomson House, Havelock Street, Cardiff CF1 1XR. Tel: 029-2058 3583. Fax: 029-2058 3451

SOUTH WALES EVENING POST, PO Box 14, Adelaide Street, Swansea SA1 1QT. Tel: 01792-510000. Fax: 01792-514697. Email: postbox@swwp.co.uk; Web: http://www.thisissouthwales.co.uk

WESTERN MAIL, Thomson House, Havelock Street, Cardiff CF1 1XR. Tel: 029-2058 3583. Fax: 029-2058 3451

SCOTLAND

COURIER AND ADVERTISER, 80 Kingsway East, Dundee DD4 8SL. Tel: 01382-223131. Fax: 01382-454590. Email: courier@dcthomson.co.uk; Web: http://www.thecourier.co.uk

DAILY RECORD, 40 Anderston Quay, Glasgow G3 8DA. Tel: 0141-248 7000. Fax: 0141-242 3340. Web: http://www.record-mail.co.uk

EDINBURGH EVENING NEWS, 108 Holyrood Road, Edinburgh EH8 8AS. Tel: 0131-620 8620. Fax: 0131-225 7302. Web: http://www.scotsman.com

EVENING EXPRESS, PO Box 43, Lang Stracht, Mastrick, Aberdeen AB15 6DF. Tel: 01224-690222. Fax: 01224-344106. Email: ee.editor@ajl.co.uk; Web: http://www.thisisnorthscotland.co.uk

EVENING TELEGRAPH AND POST, 2 Albert Square, Dundee DD1 9QJ. Tel: 01382-223131. Fax: 01382-201264. Email: general@eveningtelegraph.co.uk; Web: http://www.eveningtelegraph.co.uk

EVENING TIMES, 195 Albion Street, Glasgow G1 1QP. Tel: 0141-552 6255. Fax: 0141-552 1344. Email: times@eveningtimes.co.uk; Web: http://www.eveningtimes.co.uk

GREENOCK TELEGRAPH, Pitreavie Business Park, Dunfermline KY11 8QS. Tel: 01383-728201. Fax: 01383-737040

PAISLEY DAILY EXPRESS, 1 Woodside Terrace, Glasgow G3 7UY. Tel: 0141-353 3366. Fax: 0141-353 1066

PRESS AND JOURNAL, PO Box 43, Lang Stracht, Mastrick, Aberdeen AB15 6DF. Tel: 01224-690222. Fax: 01224-694613

NORTHERN IRELAND

BELFAST TELEGRAPH, 124–144 Royal Avenue, Belfast BT1 1EB. Tel: 028-9026 4000. Fax: 028-9055 4506

CHANNEL ISLANDS

JERSEY EVENING POST, PO Box 582, Five Oaks, St Saviour Jersey JE4 8XQ. Tel: 01534-611611. Fax: 01534-611622

GUERNSEY PRESS AND STAR, PO Box 57, Guernsey GY1 3BW. Tel: 01481-240240. Fax: 01481-240235. Email: newsroom@guernsey-press.com; Web: http://www.guernsey-press.com

WEEKLY NEWSPAPERS

THE EXPRESS ON SUNDAY, Ludgate House, 245 Blackfriars Road, London SE1 9UX. Tel: 020-7928 8000. Fax: 020-7633 0244

INDEPENDENT ON SUNDAY, 1 Canada Square, Canary Wharf, London E14 5DL. Tel: 020-7293 2000. Fax: 020-7293 2043. Email: sundayletters@independent.co.uk; Web: http://www.independent.co.uk

INDIA TIMES, Global House, 90 Ascot Gardens, Southall Middx UB1 2SB. Tel: 020-8575 0151. Fax: 020-8575 5661

THE MAIL ON SUNDAY, Northcliffe House, 2 Derry Street, London W8 5TS. Tel: 020-7938 6000. Fax: 020-7937 7896. Web: http://www.smos.co.uk

NEWS OF THE WORLD, 1 Virginia Street, London E1 9XR. Tel: 020-7782 1000. Fax: 020-7583 9504

THE OBSERVER, 119 Farringdon Road, London EC1R 3ER. Tel: 020-7278 2332. Fax: 020-7837 2114. Email: newmedia@guardian.co.uk; Web: http://www.guardian.co.uk

SCOTLAND ON SUNDAY, 108 Holyrood Road, Edinburgh EH8 8AS. Tel: 0131-620 8620. Fax: 0131-523 0313. Email: letters-sos@scotlandonsunday.com; Web: http://www.scotlandonsunday.com

SUNDAY BUSINESS, The Isis Building, 193 Marsh Wall, London E14 5DT. Tel: 020-7418 9600. Fax: 020-7418 9655

THE SUNDAY HERALD, 195 Albion Street, Glasgow G1 1QP. Tel: 0141-552 6255. Fax: 0141-552 1344. Web: http://www.sundayherald.com

SUNDAY MAIL, 40 Anderston Quay, Glasgow G3 8DA. Tel: 0141-248 7000. Fax: 0141-242 3340. Web: http://www.record-mail.co.uk

Sunday MIRROR, 1 Canada Square, Canary Wharf, London E14 5AP. Tel: 020-7293 3000. Fax: 020-7293 3405. Web: http://www.mirror.co.uk

SUNDAY PEOPLE, 1 Canada Square, Canary Wharf, London E14 5AP. Tel: 020-7293 3000. Fax: 020-7293 3405. Web: http://www.mirror.co.uk

SUNDAY POST, Courier Place, Dundee DD1 9QJ. Tel: 01382-223131. Fax: 01382-201064. Email: mail@sundaypost.com; Web: http://www.sundaypost.com

SUNDAY SPORT, 848B Melton Road, Thurmaston, Leicester LE4 8BJ. Tel: 0116-269 4892. Fax: 0116-264 0948. Email: sport@globalnet.co.uk; Web: http://www.dailysport.co.uk

THE SUNDAY TELEGRAPH, 1 Canada Square, Canary Wharf, London E14 5DT. Tel: 020-7538 5000. Fax: 020-7512 2504. Web: http://www.telegraph.co.uk

THE SUNDAY TIMES, 1 Pennington Street, London E1 9XN.
Tel: 020-7782 5000. Fax: 020-7782 5988.
Web: http://www.the-times.co.uk
WALES ON SUNDAY, Thomson House, Havelock Street,
Cardiff CF1 1XR, Wales. Tel: 029-2058 3721.
Fax: 029-2058 3725. Email: wosmail@wme.co.uk
WEEKLY NEWS, Courier Place, Dundee DD1 9QJ.
Tel: 01382-223131. Fax: 01382-201390.
Email: weeklynews@dcthomson.co.uk;
Web: http://www.dcthomson.co.uk

RELIGIOUS PAPERS

CHALLENGE - THE GOOD NEWS PAPER, 50 Loxwood
Avenue, Worthing W. Sussex BN14 7RA.
Tel: 01903-824174. Fax: 01903-824376
THE CHURCH OF ENGLAND NEWSPAPER, 10 Little
College Street, London SW1P 3SH. Tel: 020-7878 1545.
Fax: 020-7976 0783. Email: cen@parlicom.com;
Web: http://www.churchnewspaper.com
CHURCH TIMES, 33 Upper Street, London N1 0PN.
Tel: 020-7359 4570. Fax: 020-7226 3073.
Email: editor@churchtimes.co.uk;
Web: http://www.churchtimes.co.uk
THE FRIEND, New Premier House, 150 Southampton
Row, London WC1B 5BQ. Tel: 020-7387 7549.
Fax: 020-7387 9382
JEWISH TELEGRAPH, Telegraph House, 11 Park Hill,
Bury Old Road, Prestwich Manchester M25 0HH.
Tel: 0161-740 9321. Fax: 0161-740 9325.
Email: mail@jewishtelegraph.com;
Web: http://www.jewishtelegraph.com
LIFE AND WORK, Church of Scotland, 121 George Street,
Edinburgh EH2 4YN. Tel: 0131-225 5722. Fax: 0131-240
2207
METHODIST RECORDER, 122 Golden Lane, London
EC1Y 0TL. Tel: 020-7251 8414. Fax: 020-7608 3490.
Email: editorial@methodistrecorder.co.uk;
Web: http://www.methodistrecorder.co.uk
MIDDLE WAY, Buddhist Society, 58 Eccleston Square,
London SW1V 1PH. Tel: 020-7834 5858.
Fax: 020-7976 5238. Web: http://www.buddsoc.org.uk
ORTHODOX OUTLOOK, 42 Withens Lane, Wallasey
Wirral CH45 7NN. Tel: 0151-639 6509. Fax: 0151-200
6359. Email: pancratios.outlook@mcmail.com
PRESBYTERIAN HERALD, Church House, Fisherwick
Place, Belfast BT1 6DW. Tel: 028-9032 2284.
Fax: 028-9024 8377.
Email: herald@presbyterianireland.org;
Web: http://www.presbyterianireland.org
REFORM, United Reformed Church, 86 Tavistock Place,
London WC1H 9RT. Tel: 020-7916 8630.
Fax: 020-7916 2021. Email: reform@urc.org.uk;
Web: http://www.urc.org.uk
THE SIKH COURIER INTERNATIONAL, World Sikh
Foundation, 33 Wargrave Road, Harrow Middx
HA2 8LL. Tel: 020-8864 9228
THE SIKH MESSENGER, 43 Dorset Road, London
SW19 3EZ. Tel: 020-8540 4148
The TABLET, 1 King Street Cloisters, Clifton Walk,
London W6 0QZ. Tel: 020-8748 8484.
Fax: 020-8748 1550. Email: publisher@thetablet.co.uk;
Web: http://www.thetablet.co.uk
The UNIVERSE, 1st Floor, St James Building, Oxford
Street, Manchester M1 6FP. Tel: 0161-236 8856.
Fax: 0161-236 8530
THE WAR CRY, 101 Newington Causeway, London
SE1 6BN. Tel: 020-7367 4900. Fax: 020-7367 4710.
Email: warcry@salvationarmy.org.uk;
Web: http://www.salvationarmy.org.uk/warcry

PERIODICALS

There are about 6,500 periodicals published in Britain.
These are classified as consumer, e.g. general interest, or
as trade, professional or academic.

CONSUMER PERIODICALS

19, King's Reach Tower, Stamford Street, London SE1 9LS.
Tel: 020-7261 6410. Fax: 020-7261 7634
ANGLING TIMES, Bushfield House, Orton Centre,
Peterborough PE2 5UW. Tel: 01733-232600.
Fax: 01733-465844. Email: richard.lee@ecm.emap.com
ARENA, 3rd Floor, Block A, Exmouth House,
Pine Street, London EC1R 0JL. Tel: 020-7689 9999.
Fax: 020-7689 0901. Email: editorial@arenamag.co.uk
ART MONTHLY, Suite 17, 26 Charing Cross Road,
London WC2H 0DG. Tel: 020-7240 0389.
Fax: 020-7240 0389. Email: info@artmonthly.co.uk;
Web: http://www.artmonthly.co.uk
ASTRONOMY NOW, PO Box 175, Tonbridge, Kent
TN10 4ZY. Tel: 01903-266165. Fax: 01732-356230
AUTOCAR, 60 Waldegrave Road, Teddington, Middx
TW11 8LG. Tel: 020-8267 5630. Fax: 020-8267 5776.
Email: autocar@haynet.com
BBC GOOD FOOD MAGAZINE, Woodlands, 80 Wood
Lane, London W12 0TT. Tel: 020-8433 2000.
Fax: 020-8433 3931.
Email: good.food.magazine@bbc.co.uk
BBC HOMES AND ANTIQUES, Woodlands,
80 Wood Lane, London W12 0TT. Tel: 020-8433 3490.
Fax: 020-8433 3867
BBC TOP GEAR, Woodlands, 80 Wood Lane, London
W12 0TT. Tel: 020-8433 3716. Fax: 020-8433 3753.
Email: hayley.day@bbc.co.uk;
Web: http://www.topgear.com
BELFAST GAZETTE (OFFICIAL), The Stationery Office,
16 Arthur Street, Belfast BT1 4GD. Tel: 0289-089 5135.
Fax: 0289-023 5401. Email: roy.dubois@theso.co.uk;
Web: http://www.ukstate.com
THE BIG ISSUE, 236–240 Pentonville Road, London N1 9JY.
Tel: 020-7526 3200. Fax: 020-7526 3201. Email:
london@bigissue.com; Web: http://www.bigissue.com
BIKE, Bushfield House, Orton Centre, Peterborough
PE2 5UW. Tel: 01733-237111. Fax: 01733-465858.
Email: bike@ecm.emap.com
BIRDS, RSPB, The Lodge, Sandy, Beds SG19 2DL.
Tel: 01767-680551. Fax: 01767-683262.
Web: http://www.rspb.org.uk
BRIDES, Vogue House, Hanover Square, London W1R 0AD.
Tel: 020-7499 9080. Fax: 020-7460 6369.
Email: ccurry@msmail.condenast.co.uk;
Web: http://www.bridesuk.net
BRITISH PHILATELIC BULLETIN, Royal Mail, 2–14 Bunhill
Row, London EC1Y 8HQ. Tel: . Fax: 020-7847 3359
CAMPING AND CARAVANNING, Greenfields House,
Westwood Way, Coventry CV4 8JH.
Tel: 024-7669 4995. Fax: 024-7685 6722.
Email: pa.comms@campandcaravan.co.uk;
Web: http://www.campingandcaravanningclub.co.uk
CAR, Angel House, 338–346 Goswell Road, London
EC1V 7QP. Tel: 020-7477 7399. Fax: 020-7477 7279.
Email: car@ecm.emap.com
CLASSIC & SPORTS CAR, Somerset House, Somerset Road,
Teddington, Middx TW11 8RT. Tel: 020-8267 5399.
Fax: 020-8267 5318.
Email: letters.classicandsportscar@haynet.com
COARSE FISHERMAN, 67 Tyrrell Street, Leicester LE3 5SB.
Tel: 0116-251 1277. Fax: 0116-251 1335

COSMOPOLITAN, National Magazine House, 72 Broadwick Street, London W1V 2BP. Tel: 020-7439 5000. Fax: 020-7439 5016. Email: cosmo.mail@natmags.co.uk; Web: http://www.natmags.co.uk

COUNTRY LIFE, King's Reach Tower, Stamford Street, London SE1 9LS. Tel: 020-7261 7058. Fax: 020-7261 5139. Web: http://www.countrylife.co.uk

COUNTRY LIVING MAGAZINE, National Magazine House, 72 Broadwick Street, London W1V 2BP. Tel: 020-7439 5000. Fax: 020-7439 5093. Web: http://www.natmags.co.uk

CYCLING WEEKLY, Link House, Dingwall Avenue, Croydon CR9 2TA. Tel: 020-8774 0811. Fax: 020-8686 0947. Email: cycling@ipc.co.uk

DALTONS WEEKLY, CI Tower, St George's Square, New Malden, Surrey KT3 4JA. Tel: 020-8949 6199. Fax: 020-8949 2718. Email: daltons@daltons.co.uk; Web: http://www.daltons.co.uk

DANCING TIMES, Clerkenwell House, 45–47 Clerkenwell Green, London EC1R 0EB. Tel: 020-7250 3006. Fax: 020-7253 6679. Email: DT@dancing-times.co.uk; Web: http://www.dt-ltd.dircon.co.uk

DOGS TODAY, Pankhurst Farm, Bagshot Road, West End, Woking, Surrey GU24 9QR. Tel: 01276-858880. Fax: 01276-858860. Email: dogstoday@dial.pipex.com; Web: http://www.dial-a-dog.com

THE ECOLOGIST, Unit 18, Chelsea Wharf, 15 Lots Road, London SW10 0QJ. Tel: 020-7351 3578. Fax: 020-7351 3617. Email: sally@theecologist.org; Web: http://www.theecologist.org

ELLE, Endeavour House, 189 Shaftesbury Avenue, London WC2H 8JG. Tel: 020-7437 9011. Fax: 020-7208 3599

EMPIRE, Mappin House, 4 Winsley Street, London W1N 7AR. Tel: 020-7436 1515. Fax: 020-7323 0276. Email: empire@ecm.emap.com; Web: http://www.empireonline.co.uk

ESSENTIALS, King's Reach Tower, Stamford Street, London SE1 9LS. Tel: 020-7261 6970. Fax: 020-7261 5262. Email: essentials@ipc.co.uk; Web: http://www.ipc.co.uk

FAMILY CIRCLE, King's Reach Tower, Stamford Street, London SE1 9LS. Tel: 020-7261 6195. Fax: 020-7261 5929. Email: familycircle@ipc.co.uk

THE FIELD, King's Reach Tower, Stamford Street, London SE1 9LS. Tel: 020-7261 5198. Fax: 020-7261 5358. Web: http://www.thefield.co.uk

FILM REVIEW, 9 Blades Court, Deodar Road, London SW15 2NU. Tel: 020-8875 1520. Fax: 020-8875 1588. Email: filmreview@visimag.com; Web: http://www.visimag.com

GEOGRAPHICAL JOURNAL, Royal Geographical Society, 1 Kensington Gore, London SW7 2AR. Tel: 020-7591 3026. Fax: 020-7591 3001. Email: g.lowman@rgs.org; Web: http://www.rgs.org

GOLF WORLD, Bretton Court, Bretton, Peterborough PE3 8DZ. Tel: 01733-264666. Fax: 01733-465248

GQ, Vogue House, Hanover Square, London W1R 0AD. Tel: 020-7499 9080. Fax: 020-7493 1345

GUIDING MAGAZINE, 17–19 Buckingham Palace Road, London SW1W 0PT. Tel: 020-7834 6242. Fax: 020-7828 5791. Email: guiding@guides.org.uk; Web: http://www.guides.org.uk

HANSARD, The Stationery Office, PO Box 29, Norwich NR3 1GN. Tel: 0870-600 5522. Fax: 0870-600 5533

HAVING A BABY, National Magazine House, 72 Broadwick Street, London W1V 2BP. Tel: 020-7439 5000. Fax: 020-7439 5337. Email: hab@natmags.co.uk; Web: http://www.natmags.co.uk

HEALTH AND FITNESS MAGAZINE, Nexus House, Azalea Drive, Swanley, Kent BR8 8HU. Tel: 01322-660070. Fax: 01322-616319. Email: editorial@hfonline.co.uk; Web: http://www.hfonline.co.uk

HELLO!, 69–71 Upper Ground, London SE1 9PQ. Tel: 020-7667 8700. Fax: 020-7667 8716

HISTORY TODAY, 20 Old Compton Street, London W1V 5PE. Tel: 020-7534 8000. Email: editorial@historytoday.com; Web: http://www.historytoday.com

HOMES AND GARDENS, King's Reach Tower, Stamford Street, London SE1 9LS. Tel: 020-7261 5678. Fax: 020-7261 6247

HOUSE AND GARDEN, Vogue House, Hanover Square, London W1R 0AD. Tel: 020-7499 9080. Fax: 020-7629 2907

HOUSE BEAUTIFUL, National Magazine House, 72 Broadwick Street, London W1V 2BP. Tel: 020-7439 5000. Fax: 020-7439 5595

IRISH POST, Cambridge House, Cambridge Grove, London W6 0LE. Tel: 020-8741 0649. Fax: 020-8741 3382. Email: info@irishpost.co.uk; Web: http://www.irishpost.co.uk

LABOUR RESEARCH, 78 Blackfriars Road, London SE1 8HF. Tel: 020-7928 3649. Fax: 020-7928 0621. Email: info@lrd.org.uk; Web: http://www.lrd.org.uk

THE LADY, 39–40 Bedford Street, London WC2E 9ER. Tel: 020-7379 4717. Fax: 020-7497 2137

LONDON GAZETTE (OFFICIAL), The Stationery Office, PO Box 7923, London SE1 5ZH. Tel: 020-7394 4580. Fax: 020-7394 4581. Web: http://www.london-gazette.co.uk

LONDON REVIEW OF BOOKS, 28 Little Russell Street, London WC1A 2HN. Tel: 020-7209 1141. Fax: 020-7209 1151. Email: subs@lrb.co.uk; Web: http://www.lrb.co.uk

MAJESTY, 26–28 Hallam Street, London W1N 6NP. Tel: 020-7436 4006. Fax: 020-7436 3458. Email: majestymagazine@aol.com

MELODY MAKER (MM), King's Reach Tower, Stamford Street, London SE1 9LS. Tel: 020-7261 6229. Fax: 020-7261 6706. Email: your_shout@ipc.co.uk; Web: http://www.melodymaker.com

METEOROLOGICAL MAGAZINE, The Stationery Office, PO Box 276, London SW8 5DT. Tel: 0870 600 5522. Fax: 020-7873 8200

MY WEEKLY, 80 Kingsway East, Dundee DD4 8SL. Tel: 01382-223131. Fax: 01382-452491. Email: myweekly@dcthomson.co.uk

NEEDLECRAFT, Future Publishing, 30 Monmouth Street, Bath BA1 2BW. Tel: 01225-442244. Fax: 01225-732398. Email: needlecraft@futurenet.co.uk; Web: http://www.futurenet.co.uk

NEW INTERNATIONALIST, 55 Rectory Road, Oxford OX4 1BW. Tel: 01865-728181. Fax: 01865-793152. Email: ni@newint.org; Web: http://www.newint.org

NEW SCIENTIST, 151 Wardour Street, London W1V 4BN. Tel: 020-7331 2735. Fax: 020-7331 2777. Email: enquiries@newscientist.com; Web: http://www.newscientist.com

NEW WOMAN, Endeavour House, 189 Shaftesbury Avenue, London WC2H 8JG. Tel: 020-7437 9011. Fax: 020-7434 0656

NEWSWEEK, 18 Park Street, London W1Y 4HH. Tel: 020-7629 8361. Fax: 020-7408 1403. Web: http://www.newsweek.com

OK!, Northern and Shell Tower, City Harbour, London E14 9GL. Tel: 020-7308 5090. Fax: 020-7308 5078

OPERA, 36 Black Lion Lane, London W6 9BE.
Tel: 020-8563 8893. Fax: 020-8563 8635.
Email: operamag@clara.co.uk;
Web: http://www.opera.co.uk
PARLIAMENTARY DEBATES (COMMONS) (HANSARD),
The Stationery Office, PO Box 29, Norwich NR3 1GN.
Tel: 0870-600 5522. Fax: 0870-600 5533
PARLIAMENTARY DEBATES (LORDS) (HANSARD),
The Stationery Office, PO Box 29, Norwich NR3 1GN.
Tel: 0870-600 5522. Fax: 0870-600 5533
POETRY REVIEW, 22 Betterton Street, London WC2H 9BU.
Tel: 020-7420 9880. Fax: 020-7240 4818.
Email: poetrysoc@dial.pipex.com;
Web: http://www.poetrysoc.com
PONY MAGAZINE, Haslemere House, Lower Street,
Haslemere, Surrey GU27 2PE. Tel: 01428-651551.
Fax: 01428-653888. Email: pony@djmurphy.co.uk;
Web: http://www.ponymag.com
PROSPECT, 4 Bedford Square, London WC1B 3RA.
Tel: 020-7255 1281. Fax: 020-7255 1279.
Email: publishing@prospect-magazine.co.uk;
Web: http://www.prospect-magazine.co.uk
Q, Mappin House, 4 Winsley Street, London W1M 7AR.
Tel: 020-7312 8182. Fax: 020-7312 8247
RADIO TIMES, 80 Wood Lane, London W12 0TT.
Tel: 0870-608 4455. Fax: 020-8433 3923.
Email: radio.times@bbc.co.uk;
Web: http://www.radiotimes.com
THE RAILWAY MAGAZINE, King's Reach Tower,
Stamford Street, London SE1 9LS. Tel: 020-7261 5821.
Fax: 020-7261 5269. Email: railway@ipc.co.uk;
Web: http://www.ipc.co.uk
READER'S DIGEST, 11 Westferry Circus,
Canary Wharf, London E14 4HE. Tel: 020-7715 8000.
Fax: 020-7715 8181
RIDE, Bushfield House, Orton Centre, Peterborough
PE2 5UW. Tel: 01733-465692. Fax: 01733-465804.
Email: ride@ecm.emap.com
RUGBY WORLD, King's Reach Tower, Stamford Street,
London SE1 9LS. Tel: 020-7261 6810. Fax: 020-7261
5419. Email: Paul_Morgan@ipc.co.uk;
Web: http://www.rugbyworld.com
SEA ANGLER, Emap Active, Bushfield House, Orton
Centre, Peterborough PE2 5UW. Tel: 01733-237111.
Fax: 01733-465658
SKY MAGAZINE, 5th Floor, Mappin House, 4 Winsley
Street, London W1N 7AR. Tel: 020-7436 1515.
Fax: 020-7637 0948
SLIMMING MAGAZINE, Endeavour House,
189 Shaftesbury Avenue, London WC2H 8JG.
Tel: 020-7437 9011. Fax: 020-7208 3302.
Email: slimming@ecm.emap.com
SMASH HITS, Mappin House, 4 Winsley Street,
London W1N 7AR. Tel: 020-7436 1515.
Fax: 020-7636 0276
THE SPECTATOR, 56 Doughty Street, London WC1N 2LL.
Tel: 020-7405 1706. Fax: 020-7242 0603
THE STRAD, 7 St John's Road, Harrow Middx HA1 2EE.
Tel: 020-8863 2020. Fax: 020-8863 2444.
Email: thestrad@orpheuspublications.com;
Web: http://thestrad.com
TATLER, Vogue House, Hanover Square, London
W1R 0AD. Tel: 020-7499 9080
THIS ENGLAND, Alma House, 73 Rodney Road,
Cheltenham, Glos GL50 1HT. Tel: 01242-537900.
Fax: 01242-537901. Email: sales@thisengland.co.uk;
Web: http://www.thisengland.co.uk
THOROUGBRED & CLASSIC CARS, Bushfield House, Orton
Centre, Peterborough PE2 5UW. Tel: 01733-465798.
Fax: 01733-465857. Email: classic.cars@ecm.emap.com

TIME MAGAZINE, Brettenham House, Lancaster Place,
London WC2E 7TL. Tel: 020-7490 4080.
Fax: 020-7322 1213. Web: http://www.timeinc.com
TIME OUT, Universal House, 251 Tottenham Court
Road, London W1P 0AB. Tel: 020-7813 3000.
Fax: 020-7813 6001
THE TIMES EDUCATIONAL SUPPLEMENT, Admiral
House, 66–68 East Smithfield, London E1W 1BX.
Tel: 020-7782 3000. Fax: 020-7782 3200.
Web: http://www.tes.co.uk
THE TIMES LITERARY SUPPLEMENT, Admiral House,
66–68 East Smithfield, London E1W 1BX.
Tel: 020-7782 3000. Fax: 020-7782 3100.
Email: letters@the-tls.co.uk
TRIBUNE, 308 Gray's Inn Road, London WC1X 8DY.
Tel: 020-7278 0911. Fax: 020-7833 0385.
Email: george@tribpub.demon.co.uk;
Web: http://www.tribuneuk.co.uk
TROUT AND SALMON, Bushfield House, Orton Centre,
Peterborough PE2 5UW. Tel: 01733-237111.
Fax: 01733-231137.
Email: sandy.leventon@ecm.emap.com
VACHER'S PARLIAMENTARY COMPANION, PO Box 3700,
London SW1E 5NP. Tel: 020-7828 7256.
Fax: 020-7828 7269. Email: politics@vacherdod.co.uk;
Web: http://www.politicallinks.co.uk
THE VOICE, 370 Coldharbour Lane, London SW9 8PL.
Tel: 020-7737 7377. Fax: 020-7274 8994.
Email: thevoicenewspaper@the-voice.co.uk;
Web: http://www.voice-online.co.uk
WEATHER, 104 Oxford Road, Reading RG1 7LL.
Tel: 0118-956 8500. Fax: 0118-956 8571.
Email: weather@royal-met-soc.org.uk;
Web: http://www.royal-met-soc.org.uk
THE WEEKLY TELEGRAPH, 1 Canada Square, Canary
Wharf, London E14 5DT. Tel: 020-7538 6704.
Fax: 020-7513 2509. Email: weeklyt@telegraph.co.uk
WHAT CAR?, 60 Waldegrave Road, Teddington, Middx
TW11 8LG. Tel: 020-8267 5688. Fax: 020-8267 5750.
Email: whatcar@haynet.com;
Web: http://www.whatcar.co.uk
WHICH?, 2 Marylebone Road, London NW1 4DF.
Tel: 020-7770 7000. Fax: 020-7770 7485. Email:
editor@which.net; Web: http://www.which.net
WOMAN'S OWN, King's Reach Tower, Stamford Street,
London SE1 9LS. Tel: 020-7261 5500.
Fax: 020-7261 5346
WOMAN'S REALM, King's Reach Tower, Stamford Street,
London SE1 9LS. Tel: 020-7261 6033
ZEST, National Magazine House, 72 Broadwick Street,
London W1V 2BP. Tel: 020-7439 5000.
Fax: 020-7312 3750

TRADE, PROFESSIONAL AND ACADEMIC PERIODICALS

ACCOUNTANCY AGE, VNU House, 32–34 Broadwick
Street, London W1A 2HG. Tel: 020-7316 9000.
Fax: 020-7316 9003
ANTIQUARIAN BOOK MONTHLY (ABM), PO Box 97,
High Wycombe, Bucks HP14 4GH. Tel: 01494-562266.
Fax: 01494-565533. Email: editor@abmr.co.uk;
Web: http://www.abmr.co.uk
ANTIQUE DEALER AND COLLECTORS GUIDE,
PO Box 805, London SE10 8TD. Tel: 020-8691 4820.
Fax: 020-8691 2489. Email:
antiquedealercollectorsguide@ukbusiness.com;
Web: http://www.antiquecollectorsguide.co.uk

ANTIQUES TRADE GAZETTE, 115 Shaftesbury Avenue, London WC2H 8AD. Tel: 020-7420 6600.
Fax: 020-7420 6605.
Email: editorial@antiquestradegazette.com;
Web: http://www.antiquestradegazette.com

THE ARCHITECTURAL REVIEW, 151 Rosebery Avenue, London EC1R 4GB. Tel: 020-7505 6725.
Fax: 020-7505 6701. Web: http://www.arplus.com

THE AUTHOR, SOCIETY OF AUTHORS, 84 Drayton Gardens, London SW10 9SB. Tel: 020-7373 6642.
Fax: 020-7373 5768. Email: authorsoc@writers.org.uk;
Web: http://www.writers.org.uk/society

BIOLOGIST, Institute of Biology, 20–22 Queensberry Place, London SW7 2DZ. Tel: 020-7581 8333.
Fax: 020-7823 9409. Email: biologist@iob.org;
Web: http://www.iob.org

THE BOOKSELLER, 12 Dyott Street, London WC1A 1DF.
Tel: 020-7420 6000. Fax: 020-7420 6103.
Email: letters.to.editor@bookseller.co.uk;
Web: http://www.thebookseller.com

BREWING AND DISTILLING INTERNATIONAL, 52 Glenhouse Road, London SE9 1JQ.
Tel: 020-8859 4300. Fax: 020-8859 5813.
Email: bdilondon@dial.pipex.com;
Web: http://www.bdinews.com

BRITISH BAKER, Quantum House, 19 Scarbrook Road, Croydon CR9 1LX. Tel: 020-8565 4285.
Fax: 020-8565 4302. Email: britishbaker@qpp.co.uk;
Web: http://www.britishbaker.net

BRITISH FOOD JOURNAL, 60–62 Toller Lane, Bradford, W. Yorks BD8 9BY. Tel: 01274-777700.
Fax: 01274-785200. Web: http://www.mcb.co.uk

BRITISH JOURNAL OF PSYCHOLOGY, British Psychological Society, St Andrews House, 48 Princess Road East, Leicester LE1 7DR. Tel: 0116-252 9580.
Fax: 0116-247 0787. Email: journals@bps.org.uk;
Web: http://www.bps.org.uk

BRITISH MEDICAL JOURNAL, British Medical Association, BMA House, Tavistock Square, London WC1H 9JR.
Tel: 0800-056 1424. Fax: 020-7383 6556

BRITISH TAX REVIEW, 100 Avenue Road, London NW3 3PF. Tel: 020-7393 7000. Fax: 020-7393 7010.
Web: http://www.sweetandmaxwell.co.uk

CHEMIST AND DRUGGIST, Miller Freeman House, Sovereign Way, Tonbridge Kent TN9 1RW.
Tel: 01732-377487. Fax: 01732-367065.
Email: chemdrug@unmf.com;
Web: http://www.dotpharmacy.com

CHEMISTRY AND INDUSTRY, 15 Belgrave Square, London SW1X 8PS. Tel: 020-7235 3681. Fax: 020-7235 9410.
Email: enquiries@chemind.demon.co.uk;
Web: http://www.ci.mond.org

COMPUTING, VNU House, 32–34 Broadwick Street, London W1A 2HG. Tel: 020-7316 9000.
Fax: 020-7316 9160. Email: computing@vnu.co.uk;
Web: http://www.vnunet.com

CONTRACT JOURNAL, Quadrant House, The Quadrant, Sutton, Surrey SM2 5AS. Tel: 020-8652 3500.
Fax: 020-8652 8958

CONTROL AND INSTRUMENTATION, St Giles House, 50 Poland Street, London W1V 4AX. Tel: 020-7970 4119.
Fax: 020-7970 4191.
Web: http://www.e4engineering.com

CRAFTS MAGAZINE, Crafts Council, 44A Pentonville Road, London N1 9BY. Tel: 020-7806 2538. Fax: 020-7837 6891. Email: crafts@craftscouncil.org.uk;
Web: http://www.craftscouncil.org.uk

DAIRY INDUSTRIES INTERNATIONAL, Wilmington House, Church Hill, Dartford DA2 7EF. Tel: 01322-394710.
Fax: 01322-289188

THE DIRECTOR, (MAGAZINE OF THE INSTITUTE OF DIRECTORS), 116 Pall Mall, London SW1Y 5ED.
Tel: 020-7766 8950. Fax: 020-7766 8840. Email: director-ed@iod.co.uk; Web: http://www.iod.co.uk

EDUCATION TODAY, Datateam Publishing Ltd, London Road, Maidstone, Kent ME16 8LY. Tel: 01622-687031.
Fax: 01622-757646. Email: education@datateam.co.uk;
Web: http://www.datateam.co.uk

ELECTRICAL AND RADIO TRADING, Queensway House, 2 Queensway, Redhill, Surrey RH1 1QS.
Tel: 01737-855271. Fax: 01737-855460. Email: ert@dmg.co.uk; Web: http://www.dmg.co.uk

THE ENGINEER, St Giles House, 50 Poland Street, London W1V 4AX. Tel: 020-7970 4100.
Fax: 020-7970 4189. Email: pcarslake@centaur.co.uk;
Web: http://www.e4engineering.com

ENGINEERING, Chester Court, High Street, Knowle, Solihull, W. Midlands B93 0LL. Tel: 01564-771772.
Fax: 01564-774776

FAIRPLAY INTERNATIONAL SHIPPING WEEKLY, 20 Ullswater Crescent, Ullswater Business Park, Coulsdon, Surrey CR5 2HR. Tel: 020-8645 2820.
Fax: 020-8660 2824. Email: sales@fairplay.co.uk;
Web: http://www.fairplay.co.uk

FARMERS WEEKLY, Quadrant House, The Quadrant, Sutton, Surrey SM2 5AS. Tel: 020-8652 4911.
Fax: 020-8652 4005. Email: famers.weekly@rbi.co.uk;
Web: http://www.fwi.co.uk

FIRE PREVENTION, Fire Protection Association, Bastille Court, 2 Paris Garden, London SE1 8ND.
Tel: 020-7902 5308. Fax: 020-7902 5301. Email: fpa@thefpa.co.uk; Web: http://www.thefpa.co.uk

FLIGHT INTERNATIONAL, Quadrant House, The Quadrant, Sutton, Surrey SM2 5AS.
Tel: 020-8652 3842. Fax: 020-8652 3840.
Email: flight.international@rbi.co.uk;
Web: http://www.flightinternational.com

FOOD TRADE REVIEW, Station House, Hortons Way, Westerham, Kent TN16 1BZ.
Tel: 01959-563944. Fax: 01959-561285.
Email: foodtradereview@aol.com

FOUNDRY TRADE JOURNAL, Queensway House, 2 Queensway, Redhill, Surrey RH1 1QS.
Tel: 01737-855164. Fax: 01737-855469.
Web: http://www.dmg.co.uk/castings/

FROZEN AND CHILLED FOODS, Queensway House, 2 Queensway, Redhill, Surrey RH1 1QS.
Tel: 01737-768611. Fax: 01737-855470

GEOGRAPHY, Geographical Association, 160 Solly Street, Sheffield S1 4BF. Tel: 0114-296 0088.
Fax: 0114-296 7176. Email: ga@geography.org.uk;
Web: http://www.geography.org.uk

THE GROCER, Broadfield Park, Crawley, W. Sussex RH11 9RT. Tel: 01293-613400. Fax: 01293-610333.
Email: grocer.editorial@william.reed.co.uk;
Web: http://www.foodanddrink.co.uk

HEATING, VENTILATING AND PLUMBING, Hereford House, Bridle Path, Croydon, Surrey CR9 4NL.
Tel: 020-8680 4200. Fax: 020-8681 5049.
Email: hvp@bmpublications.co.uk;
Web: http://www.hvpmag.co.uk

JANE'S DEFENCE WEEKLY, Sentinel House, 163 Brighton Road, Coulsdon, Surrey CR5 2YH. Tel: 020-8700 3700.
Fax: 020-8763 1007. Email: jdw@janes.co.uk;
Web: http://www.jdw.janes.com

JUSTICE OF THE PEACE REPORTS, Tolley House, 2 Addiscombe Road, Croydon CR9 5AF.
Tel: 020-8686 9141. Fax: 020-8686 3155.
Email: jpr@tolley.co.uk

THE LANCET, 84 Theobalds Road, London WC1X 8RR.
Tel: 020-7611 4046. Fax: 020-7611 4466
Web: http://www.thelancet.com
THE LAW REPORTS, Megarry House, 119 Chancery Lane,
London WC2A 1PP. Tel: 020-7242 6741.
Fax: 020-7831 5247. Email: postmaster@iclr.co.uk;
Web: http://www.lawreports.co.uk
LAW SOCIETY'S GAZETTE, 6th Floor, Newspaper House,
8–16 Great New Street, London EC4A 3BN.
Tel: 020-7230 5853. Fax: 020-7831 0869.
Email: gazette-editorial@lawsociety.org.uk;
Web: http://www.lawgazette.co.uk
LEATHER: The International Journal, Tubs Hill House,
London Road, Sevenoaks TN13 1BY. Tel: 01732-470024.
Fax: 01732-470046. Email: leather@wilmington.co.uk
LIBRARY ASSOCIATION RECORD, 7 Ridgmount Street,
London WC1E 7AE. Tel: 020-7636 7543.
Fax: 020-7255 0581. Email: record@la-hq.org.uk;
Web: http://www.la-hq.org.uk/record
MANAGEMENT ACCOUNTING, Chartered Institute of
Management Accountants, 63 Portland Place, London
W1N 4AB. Tel: 020-7637 2311. Fax: 020-7580 6916
MANAGING INFORMATION, ASLIB, Staple Hall, Stone
House Court, London EC3A 7PB. Tel: 020-7903 0000.
Fax: 020-7903 0011. Email: pubs@aslib.com;
Web: http://www.aslib.com
MANUFACTURING CHEMIST, Tubs Hill House, London
Road, Sevenoaks, Kent TN13 1BY. Tel: 01732-470025.
Fax: 01732-470047
MATERIALS RECYCLING WEEK, 19th Floor,
Leon House, 233 High Street, Croydon, Surrey
CR0 9XT. Tel: 020-8277 5540. Fax: 020-8277 5560.
Email: recycling@maclaren.emap.co.uk
MEDIA WEEK, Quantum House, 19 Scarbrook Road,
Croydon, Surrey CR9 1LX. Tel: 020-8565 4323.
Fax: 020-8565 4394. Email: mweeked@qpp.co.uk;
Web: http://www.mediaweek.co.uk
MUSIC JOURNAL, Incorporated Society of Musicians,
10 Stratford Place, London W1N 9AE.
Tel: 020-7629 4413. Fax: 020-7408 1538. Email:
membership@ism.org; Web: http://www.ism.org
MUSICIAN, 241 Shaftesbury Avenue, London WC2H 8EH.
Tel: 020-7333 1733. Fax: 020-7333 1736.
Web: http://www.musiciansunion.org.uk
PACKAGING MAGAZINE, Miller Freeman House,
Sovereign Way, Tonbridge Kent TN9 1RW.
Tel: 01732-377486. Fax: 01732-353328.
Email: packagingmagazine@unmf.com;
Web: http://www.dotpackaging.com
PEOPLE MANAGEMENT, Institute of Personnel and
Development, 17 Britton Street, London EC1M 9NQ.
Tel: 020-7880 6200. Fax: 020-7336 7635
PHARMACEUTICAL JOURNAL, Royal Pharmaceutical
Society of Great Britain, 1 Lambeth High Street,
London SE1 7JN. Tel: 020-7735 9141.
Fax: 020-7582 7327. Email: editor@pharmj.org.uk;
Web: http://www.pharmj.com
PHILOSOPHY (JOURNAL OF THE ROYAL INSTITUTE OF
PHILOSOPHY), The Royal Institute of Philosophy,
14 Gordon Square, London WC1H 0AG.
Tel: 020-7387 4130. Fax: 020-7383 4061.
Email: l.purkiss@mailbox.ulcc.ac.uk
PRIMARY GEOGRAPHER, Geographical Association, 160
Solly Street, Sheffield S1 4BF. Tel: 0114-296 0088.
Fax: 0114-296 7176. Email: ga@geography.org.uk;
Web: http://www.geography.org.uk
PRINTING WORLD, Miller Freeman House, Sovereign
Way, Tonbridge, Kent TN9 1RW. Tel: 01732-377391.
Fax: 01732-377552. Email: printing.world@unmf.com;
Web: http://www.dotprint.com

PROBATION JOURNAL, 217A Balham High Road, London
SW17 7BP. Tel: 020-8671 0640. Fax: 020-8671 0640.
Email: prbjournal@aol.com
PROFESSIONAL CARE OF MOTHER AND CHILD,
PO Box 100, Chichester, W. Sussex PO18 8HD.
Tel: 01243-576444. Fax: 01243-576456. Email:
admin@pmh.uk.com; Web: http://www.phm.uk.com
THE PSYCHOLOGIST, British Psychological Society,
St Andrews House, 48 Princess Road East, Leicester
LE1 7DR. Tel: 0116-254 9568. Fax: 0116-247 0787.
Email: psychologist@bps.org.uk;
Web: http://www.bps.org.uk
QUARRY MANAGEMENT, 7 Regent Street, Nottingham
NG1 5BS. Tel: 0115-941 1315. Fax: 0115-948 4035.
Email: mail@qmj.co.uk; Web: http://www.qmj.co.uk
RAILWAY GAZETTE INTERNATIONAL, Quadrant House,
The Quadrant, Sutton, Surrey SM2 5AS.
Tel: 020-8652 8608. Fax: 020-8652 3738.
Web: http://www.railwaygazette.com
SOLICITORS JOURNAL, 100 Avenue Road, London
NW3 3PG. Tel: 020-7393 7000. Fax: 020-7393 7789.
Email: solicitors.journal@sweetandmaxwell.co.uk
THE STAGE, 47 Bermondsey Street, London SE1 3XT.
Tel: 020-7403 1818. Fax: 020-7357 9287.
Email: editorial-listings@thestage.co.uk;
Web: http://www.thestage.co.uk
SURVEYOR, 32 Vauxhall Bridge Road, London SW1V 2SS.
Tel: 020-7973 6400. Fax: 020-7973 6677.
Email: editorial.surveyor@hemming-group.co.uk;
Web: http://www.hemming-group.co.uk
TAX ADVISER (THE CHARTERED INSTITUTE OF
TAXATION), 12 Upper Belgrave Street, London
SW1X 8BB. Tel: 020-7235 9381. Fax: 020-7235 2562.
Email: post@tax.org.uk; Web: http://www.tax.org.uk
TAXI, Taxi House, 7–11 Woodfield Road, London W9 2BA.
Tel: 020-7432 1429. Fax: 020-7266 2297.
Email: spessok@comcab.co.uk
TEACHING GEOGRAPHY, Geographical Association,
160 Solly Street, Sheffield S1 4BF. Tel: 0114-296 0088.
Fax: 0114-296 7176. Email: ga@geography.org.uk;
Web: http://www.geography.org.uk
TELEVISION, Royal Television Society, Holborn Hall,
100 Gray's Inn Road, London WC1X 8AL.
Tel: 020-7430 1000. Fax: 020-7430 0924. Email:
publications@rts.org.uk; Web: http://www.rts.org.uk
TEXTILE MONTH, Perkin House, 1 Longlands Street,
Bradford, W. Yorks BD1 2TB. Tel: 01274-378800.
Fax: 01274-378811. Email: awilson@worldtextile.com;
Web: http://www.worldtextile.com
TIMBER AND WOOD PRODUCTS, Tubs Hill House,
London Road, Sevenoaks, Kent TN13 1BY.
Tel: 01732-470042. Fax: 01732-470049.
Email: adixon@wilmington.co.uk;
Web: http://www.worldwidewood.com
THE TRADER, Link House, 25 West Street, Poole, Dorset
BH15 1LL. Tel: 01202-445301. Fax: 01202-445309.
Email: trader@unitedadvertising.co.uk;
Web: http://www.the-trader.co.uk
WOODCARVING, Castle Place, 166 High Street,
Lewes, E. Sussex BN7 1XU. Tel: 01273-477374.
Fax: 01273-487606
WORLD'S FAIR, 2 Daltry Street, Oldham, Lancs OL1 4BB.
Tel: 0161-624 3687. Fax: 0161-785 3131.
Email: wfair@worldsfair.co.uk;
Web: http://www.worldsfair.co.uk

Book Publishers

The following list is one comprising publishers whose names are most familiar to the general public.

AA PUBLISHING
Fanum House, Basingstoke, Hants RG21 4EA
Tel: 0990-448866
Web: http://www.theaa.co.uk

AGE CONCERN ENGLAND
Astral House, 1268 London Road, London SW16 4ER
Tel: 020-8765 7200
Web: http://www.ageconcern.org.uk

IAN ALLAN
Riverdene Business Park, Molesey Road,
Hersham KT12 4RG
Tel: 01932-266600
Web: http://www.ianallanpub.com

ALLISON & BUSBY
114 New Cavendish Street, London W1M 7FD
Tel: 020-7636 2942
Web: http://www.allisonandbusby.ltd.uk

APPLE PRESS
The Old Brewery, 6 Blundell Street, London N7 9BH
Tel: 020-7700 2929

ARNOLD
338 Euston Road, London NW1 3BH
Tel: 020-7873 6000
Web: http://www.arnoldpublishers.com

ARROW BOOKS
20 Vauxhall Bridge Road, London SW1V 2SA
Tel: 020-7840 8400
Web: http://www.randomhouse.co.uk

ASLIB, THE ASSOCIATION FOR INFORMATION
MANAGEMENT
Staple Hall, Stone House Court, London EC3A 7PB
Tel: 020-7903 0000
Web: http://www.aslib.com

AURUM PRESS
25 Bedford Avenue, London WC1B 3AT
Tel: 020-7637 3225
Web: http://www.aurumpress.co.uk

BARRIE & JENKINS
20 Vauxhall Bridge Road, London SW1V 2SA
Tel: 020-7840 8400
Web: http://www.randomhouse.co.uk

A. & C. BLACK
35 Bedford Row, London WC1R 4JH
Tel: 020-7242 0946
Web: http://www.acblack.co.uk

BLACKWELL PUBLISHERS
108 Cowley Road, Oxford OX4 1JF
Tel: 01865-791100
Web: http://www.blackwellpublishers.co.uk

BLOOMSBURY PUBLISHING
38 Soho Square, London W1V 5DF
Tel: 020-7494 2111
Web: http://www.bloomsbury.com

MARION BOYARS
24 Lacy Road, London SW15 1NL
Tel: 020-8788 9522
Web: http://www.marionboyars.co.uk

BRIMAX BOOKS
2–4 Heron Quays, London E14 4JP
Tel: 020-7531 8598

BUTTERWORTHS LTD
Halsbury House, 35 Charcey Lane,
London WC2A 1EL
Tel: 020-7400 2500

CADOGAN BOOKS
Morris Communications, West End House,
11 Hills Place, London W1R 1AH
Tel: 020-7287 6555

CANONGATE BOOKS
14 High Street, Edinburgh EH1 1TE
Tel: 0131-557 5111
Web: http://www.canongate.net

JONATHAN CAPE
20 Vauxhall Bridge Road, London SW1V 2SA
Tel: 020-7840 8400
Web: http://www.randomhouse.co.uk

CASSELL & CO.
Wellington House, 125 Strand, London WC2R 0BB
Tel: 020-7420 5555

CAVENDISH PUBLISHING
The Glass House, Wharton Street, London WC1X 9PX
Tel: 020-7278 8000
Web: http://www.cavendishpublishing.com

CENTURY
Random House Group Ltd, 20 Vauxhall Bridge Road,
London SW1V 2SA
Tel: 020-7840 8400
Web: http://www.randomhouse.co.uk

CHAMBERS HARRAP PUBLISHERS LTD
7 Hopetoun Crescent, Edinburgh EH7 4AY
Tel: 0131-556 5929
Web: http://www.chambersharrap.com

CHIVERS PRESS
Windsor Bridge Road, Bath BA2 3AX
Tel: 01225-335336
Web: http://www.chivers.co.uk

CHURCH HOUSE PUBLISHING
Church House, Great Smith Street, London SW1P 3NZ
Tel: 020-7898 1451
Web: http://www.chpublishing.co.uk

CRONER PUBLICATIONS LTD
Croner House, 145 London Road, Kingston upon
Thames, Surrey KT2 6SR
Tel: 020-8547 3333

DARTON, LONGMAN & TODD
1 Spencer Court, 140–142 Wandsworth High Street,
London SW18 4JJ
Tel: 020-8875 0155

DEBRETT'S PEERAGE LTD
Kings Court, 2–16 Goodge Street, London W1P 1FF
Tel: 020-7240 1515
Web: http://www.debretts.co.uk

ANDRE DEUTSCH
76 Dean Street, London W1V 5HA
Tel: 020-7316 4450

DUN & BRADSTREET LTD
50–100 Holmers Farm Way, High Wycombe,
Bucks HP12 4UL
Tel: 01494-422000
Web: http://www.dnb.com/uk

EBURY PRESS
20 Vauxhall Bridge Road, London SW1V 2SA
Tel: 020-7840 8400
Web: http://www.randomhouse.co.uk

ELSEVIER SCIENCE
Oxford Spires, The Boulevard, Kidlington,
Oxon OX5 1GB
Tel: 01865-843000

ENCYCLOPAEDIA BRITANNICA INTERNATIONAL
12 Golden Square, London W1R 3AF
Tel: 020-7862 4000
Web: http://www.britannica.co.uk
EPWORTH PRESS
SCM Press, 9–17 St Albans Place, London N1 0NX
Tel: 020-7359 8033
FABER & FABER
3 Queen Square, London WC1N 3AU
Tel: 020-7465 0045
Web: http://www.faber.co.uk
G. T. FOULIS
Sparkford, Yeovil, Somerset BA22 7JJ
Tel: 01963-440635
Web: http://www.haynes.com
W. FOULSHAM & CO.
The Publishing House, Bennetts Close,
Cippenham, Slough SL1 5AP
Tel: 01753-526769
Web: http://www.foulsham.com
FOURTH ESTATE
6 Salem Road, London W2 4BU
Tel: 020-7727 8993
Web: http://www.4thestate.co.uk
SAMUEL FRENCH LTD
52 Fitzroy Street, London W1P 6JR
Tel: 020-7387 9373
Web: http://www.samuelfrench-london.co.uk
GALE RESEARCH INTERNATIONAL
PO Box 699, Cheriton House, North Way,
Andover SP10 5YE
Tel: 01264-342962
Web: http://www.galegroup.com
GINN & CO.
Linacre House, Jordan Hill, Oxford OX2 8DP
Tel: 01865-888000
GOWER PUBLISHING LTD
Gower House, Croft Road, Aldershot, Hants GU11 3HR
Tel: 01252-331551
Web: http://www.gowerpub.com
ROBERT HALE
45 Clerkenwell Green, London EC1R 0HT
Tel: 020-7251 2661
HAMLYN
2–4 Heron Quays, London E14 4JP
Tel: 020-7531 8400
HARLEQUIN MILLS & BOON LTD
Eton House, 18–24 Paradise Road, Richmond,
Surrey TW9 1SR Tel: 020-8288 2800
Web: http://www.eharlequin.com
HARPERCOLLINS PUBLISHERS
77–85 Fulham Palace Road, London W6 8JB
Tel: 020-8741 7070
Web: http://www.fireandwater.com
J. H. HAYNES & CO. LTD
Sparkford, Yeovil, Somerset BA22 7JJ
Tel: 01963-440635
Web: http://www.haynes.com
R. HAZELL & CO.
PO Box 39, Henley on Thames, Oxfordshire RG9 5UA
Tel: 01491-641018
HERBERT PRESS
35 Bedford Row, London WC1R 4JH
Tel: 020-7242 0946
JARROLD PUBLISHING
Whitefriars, Norwich NR3 1TR
Tel: 01603-763300
Web: http://www.jarrold-publishing.co.uk

JORDAN PUBLISHING
21 St Thomas Street, Bristol BS1 6JS
Tel: 0117-923 0600
Web: http://www.jordanpublishing.co.uk
KEGAN PAUL INTERNATIONAL
PO Box 256, London WC1B 3SW
Tel: 020-7580 5511
KINGFISHER PUBLICATIONS PLC
New Penderel House, 283–288 High Holborn,
London WC1V 7HZ
Tel: 020-7903 9999
KINGSWAY PUBLICATIONS
Lottbridge Drove, Eastbourne BN23 6NT
Tel: 01323-437700
KOGAN PAGE
120 Pentonville Road, London N1 9JN
Tel: 020-7278 0433
Web: http://www.kogan-page.co.uk
LETTS EDUCATIONAL
Aldine House, 9–15 Aldine Street, London W12 8AW
Tel: 020-8740 2266
Web: http://www.letts-education.com
FRANCES LINCOLN
4 Torriano Mews, Torriano Avenue, London NW5 2RZ
Tel: 020-7284 4009
LION PUBLISHING
Sandy Lane West, Oxford OX4 6HG
Tel: 01865-747550
LITTLE, BROWN & CO.
Brettenham House, Lancaster Place, London WC2E 7EN
Tel: 020-7911 8000
LUND HUMPHRIES
Mecklenburgh House, 11 Mecklenburgh Square,
London WC1N 2AD
Tel: 020-7841 9800
LUTTERWORTH PRESS
PO Box 60, Cambridge CB1 2NT
Tel: 01223-350865
Web: http://www.lutterworth.com
MACMILLAN PUBLISHERS,
25 Eccleston Place, London SW1W 9NF
MAINSTREAM PUBLISHING CO.
7 Albany Street, Edinburgh EH1 3UG
Tel: 0131-557 2959
Web: http://www.mainstreampublishing.com
MCGRAW-HILL
Shoppenhangers Road, Maidenhead, Berks SL6 2QL
Tel: 01628-502500
Web: http://www.mcgraw-hill.co.uk
METAL BULLETIN JOURNALS LTD
Park House, Park Terrace, Worcester Park,
Surrey KT4 7HY
Tel: 020-8827 9977
Web: http://www.metalbulletin.com
METHUEN PUBLISHING LTD
215 Vauxhall Bridge Road, London SW1V 1EJ
Tel: 020-7798 1600
Web: http://www.methuen.co.uk
JOHN MURRAY
50 Albemarle Street, London W1X 4BD
Tel: 020-7493 4361
OCTOPUS PUBLISHING GROUP
2–4 Heron Quays, London E14 4JP
Tel: 020-7531 8400
MICHAEL O'MARA BOOKS LTD
9 Lion Yard, Tremadoc Road, London SW4 7NQ
Tel: 020-7720 8643
Web: http://www.mombooks.com

PETER OWEN
73 Kenway Road, London SW5 0RE
Tel: 020-7373 5628
Web: http://www.peterowen.com

OXFORD UNIVERSITY PRESS
Great Clarendon Street, Oxford OX2 6DP
Tel: 01865-556767
Web: http://www.oup.co.uk

PAVILION BOOKS LTD
London House, Great Eastern Wharf, Parkgate Road,
London SW11 4NQ
Tel: 020-7350 1230
Web: http://www.pavilionbooks.co.uk

PERGAMON
Oxford Spires, The Boulevard, Langford Lane,
Kidlington, Oxon OX5 1GB
Tel: 01865-843000

PHAIDON PRESS
Regent's Wharf, All Saints Street, London N1 9PA
Tel: 020-7843 1234

GEORGE PHILIP
2–4 Heron Quays, London E14 4JP
Tel: 020-7531 8400
Web: http://www.philips.maps.co.uk

PITKIN UNICHROME LTD
Healey House, Dene Road, Andover, Hants SP10 2AA
Tel: 01264-409200
Web: http://www.britguides.com

QUARTET BOOKS
27 Goodge Street, London W1P 2LD
Tel: 020-7636 3992

QUILLER PRESS
46 Lillie Road, London SW6 1TN
Tel: 020-7499 6529

REED BUSINESS INFORMATION
Quadrant House, The Quadrant, Sutton,
Surrey SM2 5AS
Tel: 020-8652 3500
Web: http://www.reedbusiness.com

ROUGH GUIDES
62–70 Shorts Gardens, London WC2H 9AB
Tel: 020-7556 5000
Web: http://www.roughguides.com

SAINT ANDREW PRESS
121 George Street, Edinburgh EH2 4YN
Tel: 0131-225 5722

SCHOLASTIC CHILDREN'S BOOKS
Commonwealth House, 1–19 New Oxford Street,
London WC1A 1NU
Tel: 020-7421 9000
Web: http://www.scholastic.co.uk/zone

SCM PRESS
9-17 St Albans Place, London N1 0NX
Tel: 020-7359 8033

SECKER & WARBURG
20 Vauxhall Bridge Road, London SW1V 2SA
Tel: 020-7840 8400
Web: http://www.randomhouse.co.uk

SERPENT'S TAIL
4 Blackstock Mews, London N4 2BT
Tel: 020-7354 1949

SEVERN HOUSE
9 Sutton High Street, Sutton SM1 1DF
Tel: 020-8770 3930
Web: http://www.severnhouse.com

SOUVENIR PRESS
43 Great Russell Street, London WC1B 3PA
Tel: 020-7580 9307

SPCK
Holy Trinity Church, Marylebone Road,
London NW1 4DU
Tel: 020-7387 5282
Web: http://www.spck.org.uk

THE STATIONERY OFFICE LTD
PO Box 29, Norwich NR3 1GN
Tel: 0870-600 5522
Web: http://www.ukstate.com

PATRICK STEPHENS LTD
Sparkford, Yeovil BA22 7JJ
Tel: 01963-440635
Web: http://www.haynes.com

SWEET & MAXWELL
100 Avenue Road, London NW3 3PS
Tel: 020-7393 7000
Web: http://www.sweetandmaxwell.co.uk

TAYLOR & FRANCIS
11 New Fetter Lane, London EC4P 4EE

THAMES & HUDSON
181A High Holborn, London WC1V 7QX
Tel: 020-7845 5000
Web: http://www.thamesandhudson.com

TOLLEY PUBLISHING
Tolley House, 2 Addiscombe Road, Croydon CR9 5AF
Tel: 020-8686 9141

UNITED BUSINESS MEDIA INFORMATION SERVICES
Riverbank House, Angel Lane, Tonbridge,
Kent TN9 1SE
Tel: 01732-377591

UNIVERSITY OF WALES PRESS
6 Gwennyth Street, Cathays, Cardiff CF24 4YD
Tel: 029-2023 1919
Web: http://www.wales.ac.uk/press

USBORNE PUBLISHING
Usborne House, 83–85 Saffron Hill, London EC1N 8RT
Tel: 020-7430 2800
Web: http://www.usborne.com

VIRAGO PRESS
Brettenham House, Lancaster Place, London WC2E 7EN
Tel: 020-7911 8000
Web: http://www.virago.co.uk

WALKER BOOKS
87 Vauxhall Walk, London SE11 5HJ
Tel: 020-7793 0909

WARD LOCK EDUCATIONAL CO.
Bic Ling Kee House, 1 Christopher Road,
East Grinstead, W. Sussex RH19 3BT
Tel: 01342-318980

J. WHITAKER
Woolmead House West, Bear Lane, Farnham GU9 7LG
Tel: 01252-742500
Web: http://www.whitaker.co.uk

Annual Reference Books

This list comprises a selection of popular reference books and their price.

ANNUAL ABSTRACT OF STATISTICS (£39.50)
PO Box 29, Norwich NR3 1GN
Tel: 0870-600 5522

ASTRONOMICAL ALMANAC (£32.50)
PO Box 29, Norwich NR3 1GN
Tel: 0870-600 5522

ATHLETICS: ASSOCIATION OF TRACK AND FIELD STATISTICIANS YEAR BOOK (£14.95)
Vine House Distribution Ltd, Waldenbury, North Chailey, Lewes, E. Sussex BN8 4DR
Tel: 01825-723398; Fax: 01825-724188
Email: sales@vinehouseuk.co.uk;
Web: http://www.vinehouseuk.co.uk

BAILY'S HUNTING DIRECTORY (£34.95)
Chesteton Mill, French's Road, Cambridge CB4 3NP
Tel: 01223-350555

BANKER'S ALMANAC (£498.00)
East Grinstead House, Windsor Court, East Grinstead, W. Sussex RH19 1XA
Tel: 01342-335946; Fax: 01342-335969

BENEDICTINE AND CISTERCIAN MONASTIC YEAR BOOK (£2.50)
Ampleforth Abbey, York YO62 4EN
Tel: 01257-463248; Fax: 01257-462495
Email: osbyearbook@hotmail.com

BRITAIN: THE OFFICIAL HANDBOOK OF THE UNITED KINGDOM (£37.50)
PO Box 29, Norwich NR3 1GN
Tel: 0870-600 5522

BROWN'S NAUTICAL ALMANAC DAILY TIDE TABLES (£42.00)
4–10 Darnley Street, Glasgow G41 2SD
Tel: 0141-429 1234; Fax: 0141-420 1694
Email: info@skipper.co.uk;
Web: http://www.skipper.co.uk

CHRISTIES' REVIEW OF THE YEAR (£45.00)
1 Langley Lane, London SW8 1TH
Tel: 020-7389 2242; Fax: 020-7820 9659
Email: christiesbooks@christies.com

CHURCH OF ENGLAND YEARBOOK (£25.00)
Church House Publishing, Church House, Great Smith Street, London SW1P 3NZ
Tel: 020-7898 1451; Fax: 020-7898 1449
Email: publishing@c-of-e.org.uk;
Web: http://www.chpublishing.co.uk

CHURCH OF SCOTLAND YEAR BOOK (£11.00)
121 George Street, Edinburgh EH2 4YN
Tel: 0131-225 5722; Fax: 0131-220 3113
Email: cofs.standrew@dial.pipex.com

CIVIL SERVICE YEAR BOOK (£40.00)
PO Box 29, Norwich NR3 1GN
Tel: 0870-600 5522

COMMONWEALTH UNIVERSITIES YEARBOOK (£165.00)
36 Gordon Square, London WC1H 0PF
Tel: 020-7380 6700; Fax: 020-7387 2655
Email: acusales@acu.ac.uk;
Web: http://www.acu.ac.uk

DIRECTORY OF DIRECTORS (£255.00)
Windsor Court, East Grinstead House, East Grinstead, W. Sussex RH19 1XA
Tel: 01342-336172; Fax: 01342-335547
Email: kflint@reedinfo.co.uk;
Web: http://www.reedinfo.co.uk

THE EDUCATION AUTHORITIES' DIRECTORY AND ANNUAL (£78.00; £66.00)
Darby House, Bletchingley Road, Merstham, Redhill, Surrey RH1 3DN
Tel: 01737-642223; Fax: 01737-644283
Email: info@schoolgovernment.co.uk;
Web: http://www.schoolgovernment.co.uk

HISTORIC HOUSES, CASTLES AND GARDENS (£4.99)
Johansens, 5th Floor, Therese House, Glasshouse Yard, London EC1A 4JN
Tel: 020-7566 9700; Fax: 020-7490 2538
Email: info@johansens.com;
Web: http://www.johansens.com

HOLLIS UK PRESS AND PR ANNUAL (£125.00)
Harlequin House, 7 High Street, Teddington TW11 8EL
Tel: 020-8977 7711; Fax: 020-8977 1133
Email: prannual@hollis-pr.co.uk;
Web: http://www.hollis-pr.co.uk

INSURANCE DIRECTORY (£262.00)
39 Earlham Street, London WC2H 9LD
Tel: 020-7306 7000; Fax: 020-7306 7141
Email: data@benn.co.uk

INTERNATIONAL WHO'S WHO (£210.00)
11 New Fetter Lane, London EC4P 4EE
Tel: 020-7822 4300; Fax: 020-7842 2249
Email: sales@europapublications.co.uk;
Web: http://www.europapublications.co.uk

JANE'S ARMOUR AND ARTILLERY (£340.00)
Sentinel House, 163 Brighton Road, Coulsdon, Surrey CR5 2YH
Tel: 020-8700 3803; Fax: 020-8700 3908

JEWISH YEAR BOOK (£26.00)
Vallentine Mitchell & Co. Ltd, Newbury House, 890–900 Eastern Avenue, Ilford, Essex IG2 7HH
Tel: 020-8599 8866; Fax: 020-8599 0984

LIBRARY ASSOCIATION YEAR BOOK (£37.50)
39 Milton Park, Abingdon, Oxon OX14 4TD

MEDICAL REGISTER (£110.00)
178 Great Portland Street, London W1N 6JE
Tel: 020-7580 7642; Fax: 020-7915 3641
Email: gmc@gmc-uk.org;
Web: http://www.gmc-uk.org

MOTOR INDUSTRY OF GREAT BRITAIN WORLD AUTOMOTIVE STATISTICS (£145.00)
Forbes House, Halkin Street, London SW1X 7DS
Tel: 020-7235 7000; Fax: 020-7235 7112
Email: vpatterson@smmt.co.uk;
Web: http://www.smmt.co.uk

MUNICIPAL YEAR BOOK (£173.00)
32 Vauxhall Bridge Road, London SW1V 2SS
Tel: 020-7973 6402; Fax: 020-7233 5057
Email: newmans@hemming-group.co.uk;
Web: http://www.newmanbooks.co.uk

MUSEUMS AND GALLERIES IN GREAT BRITAIN AND IRELAND (£8.95)
Johansens, 5th Floor, Therese House, Glasshouse Yard, London EC1A 4JN
Tel: 020-7566 9700; Fax: 020-7490 2538
Email: info@johansens.com;
Web: http://www.johansens.com

NAUTICAL ALMANAC (£28.00)
PO Box 29, Norwich NR3 1GN
Tel: 0870-600 5522

REGIONAL TRENDS (£39.50)
PO Box 29, Norwich NR3 1GN
Tel: 0870-600 5522

RIBA DIRECTORY OF PRACTICES (£65.00)
Construction House, 56–64 Leonard Street,
London EC2A 4LT
Tel: 020-7251 0791; Fax: 020-7608 2375
Email: riba.publications@ribabooks.com;
Web: http://www.ribabookshop.com
ROTHMAN'S FOOTBALL YEAR BOOK (£30.00, £18.99)
39 Milton Park, Abingdon, Oxon OX14 4TD
ROTHMAN'S RUGBY LEAGUE YEAR BOOK (£17.99)
39 Milton Park, Abingdon, Oxon OX14 4TD
ROTHMAN'S RUGBY UNION YEAR BOOK (£18.99)
39 Milton Park, Abingdon, Oxon OX14 4TD
ROYAL AND ANCIENT GOLFER'S HANDBOOK
(£50.00, £25.00)
Macmillan Publishers Ltd, 25 Eccleston Place,
London SW1W 9NF
Tel: 020-7881 8000; Fax: 020-7881 8001
Web: http://www.panmacmillan.com
SALVATION ARMY YEAR BOOK (£5.50)
101 Queen Victoria Street, London EC4P 4EP
Tel: 020-7332 0101; Fax: 020-7236 4981
Web: http://www.salvationarmy.org
SPINK STANDARD CATALOGUE OF BRITISH COINAGE
(£15.00)
69 Southampton Row, Bloomsbury, London WC1B 4ET
Tel: 020-7563 4045; Fax: 020-7563 4068
Email: info@spinkandson.com;
Web: http://www.spink-online.com
SOCIAL TRENDS (£39.50)
PO Box 29, Norwich NR3 1GN
Tel: 0870-600 5522
STATESMAN'S YEARBOOK (£59.99)
25 Eccleston Place, London SW1W 9NF
Tel: 020-7881 8038; Fax: 020-7881 8001
Web: http://www.macmillan-reference.co.uk
UNITED REFORMED CHURCH YEAR BOOK (£22.50)
86 Tavistock Place, London WC1H 9RT
Tel: 020-7916 2020; Fax: 020-7916 2021
Email: urc@urc.org.uk;
Web: http://www.urc.org.uk
WHITAKER'S RED BOOK – THE DIRECTORY OF
PUBLISHERS (£25.00)
Woolmead House West, Bear Lane, Farnham, Surrey
Tel: 01252-742500; Fax: 01252-742501
Email: custserv@whitaker.co.uk;
Web: http://www.whitaker.co.uk
WILLING'S PRESS GUIDE (£225.00)
Harlequin House, 7 High Street, Teddington,
Middx TW11 8EY
Tel: 020-8977 7711; Fax: 020-8977 1133
Email: willings@hollis-pr.co.uk;
Web: http://www.hollis-pr.co.uk
WISDEN CRICKETERS' ALMANACK (£29.99)
25 Down Road, Merrow, Guildford, Surrey GU1 2PY
Tel: 01483-570358
Email: wisden@ndirect.co.uk;
Web: http://www.wisden.com
UNITED KINGDOM MINERALS YEARBOOK (£35.00)
Onshore Mineral and Energy Resources, British
Geological Survey, Keyworth, Notts NG12 5GG
Tel: 0115-936 3100; Fax: 0115-936 3200
Email: minerals@bgs.ac.uk;
Web: http://www.mineralsuk.com
WORLD OF LEARNING (£280.00)
11 New Fetter Lane, London EC4P 4EE
Tel: 020-7822 4300; Fax: 020-7842 2249
Email: sales@europapublications.co.uk;
Web: http://www.europapublications.co.uk

WRITERS' AND ARTISTS' YEARBOOK (£12.99)
PO Box 19, Huntingdon, Cambs PE19 3SF
Tel: 01480-212379; Fax: 01480-405014
Email: orders@acblack.co.uk

PRESIDENTS OF THE USA

Name (*with Native State*)	Party	Born	Inaugura-tion	Died	Age
George Washington, *Va.*	Federation	22 February 1732	1789	14 December 1799	67
John Adams, *Mass.*	Federation	30 October 1735	1797	4 July 1826	90
Thomas Jefferson, *Va.*	Republican	13 April 1743	1801	4 July 1826	83
James Madison, *Va.*	Republican	16 March 1751	1809	28 June 1836	85
James Monroe, *Va.*	Republican	28 April 1758	1817	4 July 1831	73
John Quincy Adams, *Mass.*	Republican	11 July 1767	1825	23 February 1848	80
Andrew Jackson, *SC*	Democrat	15 March 1767	1829	8 June 1845	78
Martin Van Buren, *NY*	Democrat	5 December 1782	1837	24 July 1862	79
William Henry Harrison[†], *Va.*	Whig	9 February 1773	1841	4 April 1841	68
John Tyler (*a*), *Va.*	Whig	29 March 1790	1841	17 January 1862	71
James Knox Polk, *NC*	Democrat	2 November 1795	1845	15 June 1849	53
Zachary Taylor[†], *Va.*	Whig	24 November 1784	1849	9 July 1850	65
Millard Fillmore (*a*), *NY*	Whig	7 January 1800	1850	8 March 1874	74
Franklin Pierce, *NH*	Democrat	23 November 1804	1853	8 October 1869	64
James Buchanan, *Pa.*	Democrat	23 April 1791	1857	1 June 1868	77
Abraham Lincoln[†][§], *Ky.*	Republican	12 February 1809	1861	15 April 1865	56
Andrew Johnson (*a*), *NC*	Republican	29 December 1808	1865	31 July 1875	66
Ulysses Simpson Grant, *Ohio*	Republican	27 April 1822	1869	23 July 1885	63
Rutherford Birchard Hayes, *Ohio*	Republican	4 October 1822	1877	17 January 1893	70
James Abram Garfield[†][§], *Ohio*	Republican	19 November 1831	1881	19 September 1881	49
Chester Alan Arthur (*a*), *Vt.*	Republican	5 October 1830	1881	18 November 1886	56
Grover Cleveland, *NJ*	Democrat	18 March 1837	1885	24 June 1908	71
Benjamin Harrison, *Ohio*	Republican	20 August 1833	1889	13 March 1901	67
Grover Cleveland, *NJ*	Democrat	18 March 1837	1893	24 June 1908	71
William McKinley[†][§], *Ohio*	Republican	29 January 1843	1897	14 September 1901	58
Theodore Roosevelt (*a*), *NY*	Republican	27 October 1858	1901	6 January 1919	60
William Howard Taft, *Ohio*	Republican	15 September 1857	1909	8 March 1930	72
Woodrow Wilson, *Va.*	Democrat	28 December 1856	1913	3 February 1924	67
Warren Gamaliel Harding[†], *Ohio*	Republican	2 November 1865	1921	2 August 1923	57
Calvin Coolidge (*a*), *Vt.*	Republican	4 July 1872	1923	5 January 1933	60
Herbert Clark Hoover, *Iowa*	Republican	10 August 1874	1929	20 October 1964	90
Franklin Delano Roosevelt[†][‡], *NY*	Democrat	30 January 1882	1933	12 April 1945	63
Harry S. Truman (*a*), *Missouri*	Democrat	8 May 1884	1945	26 December 1972	88
Dwight David Eisenhower, *Texas*	Republican	14 October 1890	1953	28 March 1969	78
John Fitzgerald Kennedy[†][§], *Mass.*	Democrat	29 May 1917	1961	22 November 1963	46
Lyndon Baines Johnson (*a*), *Texas*	Democrat	27 August 1908	1963	22 January 1973	64
Richard Milhous Nixon, *California*	Republican	9 January 1913	1969	22 April 1994	81
Gerald Rudolph Ford (*b*), *Nebraska*	Republican	14 July 1913	1974		
James Earl Carter, *Georgia*	Democrat	1 October 1924	1977		
Ronald Wilson Reagan, *Illinois*	Republican	6 February 1911	1981		
George Herbert Walker Bush, *Mass.*	Republican	12 June 1924	1989		
William Jefferson Blythe IV Clinton, *Ark.*	Democrat	19 August 1946	1993		

[†] Died in office
[‡] Re-elected 5 November 1940, the first case of a third term; re-elected for a fourth term 7 November 1944
[§] Assassinated
(*a*) Elected as Vice-President
(*b*) Appointed under the provisions of the 25th Amendment

Employers' and Trade Associations

Most national employer's associations are members of the Confederation of British Industry (CBI).

CONFEDERATION OF BRITISH INDUSTRY
Centre Point, 103 New Oxford Street, London WC1A 1DU
Tel: 020-7379 7400

The Confederation of British Industry was founded in 1965 and is an independent non-party political body financed by industry and commerce. It exists primarily to ensure that the Government understands the intentions, needs and problems of British business. It is the recognised spokesman for the business viewpoint and is consulted as such by the Government.

The CBI represents, directly and indirectly, some 250,000 companies, large and small, from all sectors.
President, Sir Clive Thompson
Director-General, J. Adair Turner
Secretary, P. Forder
WALES 3 Columbus Walk, Atlantic Wharf, Cardiff CF10 4WW Tel: 029-2045 3710. *Regional Director*, Ms E. Haywood
SCOTLAND Beresford House, 5 Claremont Terrace, Glasgow G3 7XT. Tel: 0141-332 8661 *Regional Director*, I. McMillan
NORTHERN IRELAND Fanum House, 108 Great Victoria Street, Belfast BT2 7PD. Tel: 028-9032 6658 *Regional Director*, N. Smyth

ADVERTISING ASSOCIATION, Abford House, 15 Wilton Road, London SW1V 1NJ. Tel: 020-7828 2771; Fax: 020-7931 0376; Email: aa@adassoc.org.uk; Web: http://www.adassoc.org.uk
ASSOCIATION OF BRITISH INSURERS, 51 Gresham Street, London EC2V 7HQ. Tel: 020-7600 3333; Fax: 020-7696 8996; Email: info@abi.org.uk; Web: http://www.abi.org.uk
ASSOCIATION OF PRIVATE MARKET OPERATORS, 4 Worrygoose Lane, Rotherham, S. Yorks S60 4AD. Tel: 01709-700072; Fax: 01709-703648; Email: market-planuk@lineone.net
BLC LEATHER TECHNOLOGY CENTRE, Leather Trade House, Kings Park Road, Moulton Park, Northampton NN3 6JD. Tel: 01604-679999; Fax: 01604-679998; Email: info@blcleathertech.com; Web: http://www.blcleathertech.com
BOSS FEDERATION, 6 Wimpole Street, London W1M 8AS. Tel: 020-7637 7692; Fax: 020-7436 3137; Email: info@bossfed.co.uk; Web: http://www.bossfed.co.uk
BREWERS AND LICENSED RETAILERS ASSOCIATION, 42 Portman Square, London W1H 0BB. Tel: 020-7486 4831; Fax: 020-7935 3991; Email: mailbox@blra.co.uk; Web: http://www.blra.co.uk
BRF (BRITISH ROAD FEDERATION), Pillar House, 194–202 Old Kent Road, London SE1 5TG. Tel: 020-7703 9769; Fax: 020-7701 0029; Email: brf@brf.uk.com; Web: http://www.brf.co.uk
BRITISH APPAREL AND TEXTILE CONFEDERATION LTD, 5 Portland Place, London W1N 3AA. Tel: 020-7636 7788; Fax: 020-7636 7515; Email: batc@dial.pipex.com; Web: http://www.batc.co.uk

BRITISH BANKERS' ASSOCIATION, Pinners Hall, 105–108 Old Broad Street, London EC2N 1EX. Tel: 020-7216 8800; Fax: 020-7216 8811; Web: http://www.bba.org.uk
BRITISH CLOTHING INDUSTRY ASSOCIATION LTD, 5 Portland Place, London W1N 3AA. Tel: 020-7636 7788; Fax: 020-7636 7515; Email: bcia@dial.pipex.com
BRITISH MARINE INDUSTRIES FEDERATION, Marine House, Thorpe Lea Road, Egham, Surrey TW20 8HE. Tel: 01784-223600; Fax: 01784-439678; Email: bmif@bmif.co.uk; Web: http://www.bmif.co.uk
BRITISH PLASTICS FEDERATION, 6 Bath Place, Rivington Street, London EC2A 3JE. Tel: 020-7457 5000; Fax: 020-7457 5045
BRITISH PORTS ASSOCIATION, Africa House, 64–78 Kingsway, London WC2B 6AH. Tel: 020-7242 1200; Fax: 020-7405 1069; Email: info@britishports.org.uk; Web: http://www.britishports.org.uk
BRITISH PRINTING INDUSTRIES FEDERATION, 11 Bedford Row, London WC1R 4DX. Tel: 020-7915 8300; Fax: 020-7405 7784; Email: info@bpif.org.uk; Web: http://www.bpif.org.uk
BRITISH PROPERTY FEDERATION, 7th Floor, 1 Warwick Row, London SW1E 5ER. Tel: 020-7828 0111; Fax: 020-7834 3442; Email: info@bpf.org.uk; Web: http://www.bpf.org.uk
BRITISH RETAIL CONSORTIUM, 5 Grafton Street, London W1X 3LB. Tel: 020-7647 1500; Fax: 020-7647 1599; Email: info@brc.org.uk
BRITISH RUBBER MANUFACTURERS' ASSOCIATION LTD, 6 Bath Place, Rivington Street, London EC2A 3JE. Tel: 020-7457 5040; Fax: 020-7972 9008; Email: mail@brma.co.uk
THE CHAMBER OF SHIPPING LTD, Carthusian Court, 12 Carthusian Street, London EC1M 6EZ. Tel: 020-7417 8400; Fax: 020-7726 2080; Email: postmaster@british-shipping.org; Web: http://www.british-shipping.org
CHEMICAL INDUSTRIES ASSOCIATION LTD, Kings Buildings, Smith Square, London SW1P 3JJ. Tel: 020-7963 6701; Fax: 020-7834 4470; Email: finere@cia.org.uk
COMMERCIAL RADIO COMPANIES ASSOCIATION (CRCA), 77 Shaftesbury Avenue, London W1D 5DU. Tel: 020-7306 2603; Fax: 020-7470 0062; Email: info@crca.co.uk; Web: http://www.crca.co.uk
CONFEDERATION OF PASSENGER TRANSPORT UK, Imperial House, 15–19 Kingsway, London WC2B 6UN. Tel: 020-7240 3131; Fax: 020-7240 6565; Email: info@cpt-uk.org; Web: http://www.cpt-uk.org/cpt
CONSTRUCTION CONFEDERATION, Construction House, 56–64 Leonard Street, London EC2A 4JX. Tel: 020-7608 5000; Fax: 020-7608 5001; Email: enquiries@constructionconfederation.co.uk; Web: http://www.constructionconfederation.co.uk
CONSTRUCTION PRODUCTS ASSOCIATION, 26 Store Street, London WC1E 7BT. Tel: 020-7323 3770; Fax: 020-7323 0307; Email: enquiries@constprod.org.uk; Web: http://www.constprod.org.uk
DAIRY INDUSTRY FEDERATION, 19 Cornwall Terrace, London NW1 4QP. Tel: 020-7486 7244; Fax: 020-7935 3920; Email: mailbox@dif.org.uk

ENGINEERING EMPLOYERS' FEDERATION, Broadway
House, Tothill Street, London SW1H 9NQ.
Tel: 020-7222 7777; Fax: 020-7222 0792;
Email: enquiries@eef-fed.org.uk;
Web: http://www.eef.org.uk

FEDERATION OF BAKERS, 6 Catherine Street, London
WC2B 5JW. Tel: 020-7420 7190; Fax: 020-7379 0542;
Email: info@bakersfederation.org.uk;
Web: http://www.bakersfederation.org.uk

FEDERATION OF BRITISH ELECTROTECHNICAL AND
ALLIED MANUFACTURERS' ASSOCIATIONS (BEAMA),
Westminster Tower, 3 Albert Embankment, London
SE1 7SL. Tel: 020-7793 3000; Fax: 020-7793 3003;
Email: info@beama.org.uk;
Web: http://www.beama.org.uk

FEDERATION OF MASTER BUILDERS, Gordon Fisher
House, 14–15 Great James Street, London WC1N 3DP.
Tel: 020-7242 7583; Fax: 020-7404-0296;
Email: ian@fmb.org.uk; Web: http://www.fmb.org.uk

FINANCE AND LEASING ASSOCIATION, 15–19 Imperial
House, Kingsway, London WC2B 6UN.
Tel: 020-7836 6511; Fax: 020-7420 9600;
Email: info@fla.org.uk; Web: http://www.fla.org.uk

FOOD AND DRINK FEDERATION, 6 Catherine Street,
London WC2B 5JJ. Tel: 020-7836 2460;
Fax: 020-7836 0580;
Web: http://www.foodanddrink.org

FREIGHT TRANSPORT ASSOCIATION LTD, Hermes House,
St John's Road, Tunbridge Wells, Kent TN4 9UZ.
Tel: 01892-526171; Fax: 01892-534989;
Email: inquiries@fta.org.uk;
Web: http://www.fta.co.uk

KNITTING INDUSTRIES' FEDERATION LTD, 53 Oxford
Street, Leicester LE1 5XY. Tel: 0116-254 1608;
Fax: 0116-254 2273; Email: directorate@knitfed.co.uk

LEATHER PRODUCERS' ASSOCIATION, 8 Queensberry
Road, Kettering, Northants NN15 7HL.
Tel: 01536-483668; Fax: 01536-416771;
Email: jaklpa@globalnet.co.uk

MANAGEMENT CONSULTANCIES ASSOCIATION, 11 West
Halkin Street, London SW1X 8JL. Tel: 020-7235 3897;
Fax: 020-7235 0825; Email: bruce@mca.org.uk;
Web: http://www.mca.org.uk

THE NATIONAL FARMERS' UNION (NFU), 164 Shaftesbury
Avenue, London WC2H 8HL. Tel: 020-7331 7200;
Fax: 020-7331 7313; Email: nfu@nfu.org.uk;
Web: http://www.nfu.org.uk

NATIONAL FEDERATION OF RETAIL NEWSAGENTS,
Yeoman House, Sekforde Street, London EC1R 0HD.
Tel: 0171-253 4225; Fax: 0171-250 0927;
Email: info@nfrn.org.uk;
Web: http://www.nfrn.org.uk

NATIONAL MARKET TRADERS' FEDERATION, Hampton
House, Hawshaw Lane, Hoyland, Barnsley S74 0HA.
Tel: 01226-749021; Fax: 01226-740329;
Email: enquiries@nmtf.co.uk;
Web: http://www.nmtf.co.uk

NEWSPAPER PUBLISHERS ASSOCIATION LTD, 34
Southwark Bridge Road, London SE1 9EU. Tel: 020-
7207 2200; Fax: 020-7928 2067

NEWSPAPER SOCIETY, Bloomsbury House, 74–77 Great
Russell Street, London WC1B 3DA.
Tel: 020-7636 7014; Fax: 020-7580 1972;
Email: neweu@newspapersoc.org.uk;
Web: http://www.newspapersoc.org.uk

THE PAPER FEDERATION OF GREAT BRITAIN,
Papermakers House, Rivenhall Road, Swindon SN5 7BD.
Tel: 01793-889600; Fax: 01793-878700;
Email: fedn@paper.org.uk
Web: http://www.paper.org.uk

THE PUBLISHERS ASSOCIATION, 1 Kingsway, London
WC2B 6XF. Tel: 020-7565 7474; Fax: 020-7836 4543;
Email: mail@publishers.org.uk;
Web: http://www.publishers.org.uk

ROAD HAULAGE ASSOCIATION LTD, Roadway House,
35 Monument Hill, Weybridge, Surrey KT13 8RN.
Tel: 01932-841555; Fax: 01932-852516;
Email: weybridge@rha.net;
Web: http://www.rha.net

SOCIETY OF BRITISH AEROSPACE COMPANIES LTD,
Duxbury House, 60 Petty France, London SW1H 9EU.
Tel: 020-7227 1000; Fax: 020-7227 1067;
Email: post@-sbac.co.uk; Web: www.sbac.co.uk

SOCIETY OF MOTOR MANUFACTURERS AND TRADERS
LTD, Forbes House, Halkin Street, London
SW1X 7DS. Tel: 020-7235 7000; Fax: 020-7235 7112;
Email: membership@smmt.co.uk;
Web: http://www.smmt.co.uk

THE SPORT INDUSTRIES FEDERATION, Federation House,
National Agricultural Centre, Stoneleigh Park,
Kenilworth, Warks CV8 2RF. Tel: 01203-414999;
Fax: 01203-414990; Email: admin@sportslife.org.uk;
Web: http://www.sportslife.org.uk

THE TIMBER TRADE FEDERATION, Clareville House,
26–27 Oxendon Street, London SW1Y 4EL.
Tel: 020-7839 1891; Fax: 020-7930 0094;
Email: ttf@ttf.co.uk; Web: http://www.ttf.co.uk

UK OFFSHORE OPERATORS ASSOCIATION LTD, First
Floor, 30 Buckingham Gate, London SW1E 6NN.
Tel: 020-7802 2400; Fax: 020-7802 2401;
Email: info@ukooa.co.uk;
Web: http://www.oilandgas.org.uk

UK PETROLEUM INDUSTRY ASSOCIATION LTD, 9
Kingsway, London WC2B 6XF. Tel: 020-7240 0289;
Fax: 020-7379 3102; Email: ukpia@aol.com;
Web: http://www.ukpia.com

ULSTER FARMERS' UNION, 475 Antrim Road, Belfast
BT15 3DA. Tel: 028-9037 0222; Fax: 028-9037 1231;
Email: info@ufuhq.com

Trade Unions

Nearly 80 per cent of trade union members belong to unions affiliated to the TUC.

The Central Arbitration Committee arbitrates on trade disputes, adjudicates on disclosure of information complaints, determines claims for statutory recognition under the Employment Relations Act 1999 and certain issues relating to the implementation of the European Works Council Directive.

THE CENTRAL ARBITRATION COMMITTEE, 3rd Floor, Discovery House, 28–42 Banner Street, London EC1Y 8QE Tel: 020-7251 9747, Fax: 020-7251 3114, Web: http://www.cac.gov.uk

Chairman, Sir Michael Burton, *Secretary*, C. Johnston

TRADES UNION CONGRESS (TUC)

Congress House, 23–28 Great Russell Street, London WC1B 3LS Tel: 020-7636 4030; Fax: 020-7636 0632
Web: http://www.tuc.org.uk

The Trades Union Congress, founded in 1868, is an independent association of trade unions. The TUC promotes the rights and welfare of those in work and helps the unemployed. It helps its member unions promote membership in new areas and industries, and campaigns for rights at work for all employees, including part-time and temporary workers, whether union members or not TUC representatives sit on many public bodies at national and international level. It makes representations to government, political parties, employers and international bodies such as the European Union.

The governing body of the TUC is the annual Congress Between Congresses, business is conducted by a General Council, which meets five times a year, and an Executive Committee, which meets monthly. The full-time staff is headed by the General Secretary who is elected by Congress and is a permanent member of the General Council.

Affiliated unions in 1999–2000 totalled 76 with a total membership of nearly 6,800,000.
President (1999–2000), Ms R Donaghy (UNISON)
(The President for 2000–1 was elected in September 2001, *see* Stop-press)
General Secretary, J. Monks, *elected* 1993

SCOTTISH TRADES UNION CONGRESS

333 Woodlands Road, Glasgow G3 6NG Tel: 0141–337 8100, Fax: 0141-337 8101
Email: info@stuc.org.uk

The Congress was formed in 1897 and acts as a national centre for the trade union movement in Scotland. In 2000 it consisted of 46 unions with a membership of 634,797 and 34 directly affiliated Trade Councils.

The Annual Congress in April elects a 38-member General Council on the basis of six industrial sections.
Chairperson, Ms. L. Elkind
General Secretary, B. Spems

AFFILIATED UNIONS AS AT AUGUST 2000

(Number of Members in parenthesis)
AMALGAMATED ENGINEERING AND ELECTRICAL UNION (AEEU) (750,000), Hayes Court, West Common Road, Bromley, Kent BR2 7AU. Tel: 020-8462 7755; Fax: 020-8315 8215; Web: http://www.aeeu.org.uk

ANSA (INDEPENDENT UNION FOR ABBEY NATIONAL STAFF) (8,645), 2nd Floor, 16–17 High Street, Tring, Herts HP23 5AH. Tel: 01442-891122; Fax: 01442-891133; Email: info@ansa.org.uk; Web: http://www.ansa.org.uk

ASSOCIATED METALWORKERS UNION (AMU) (500), 92 Worsley Road North, Worsley, Manchester M28 5QW. Tel: 01204-793245; Fax: 01204-793245

ASSOCIATED SOCIETY OF LOCOMOTIVE ENGINEERS AND FIREMEN (ASLEF) (16,000), 9 Arkwright Road, London NW3 6AB. Tel: 020-7317 8600; Fax: 020-7794 6406; Email: info@ascef.org.uk

ASSOCIATION OF EDUCATIONAL PSYCHOLOGISTS (2,264), 26 The Avenue, Durham DH1 4ED. Tel: 0191-384 9512; Fax: 0191-386 5287.

ASSOCIATION OF FIRST DIVISION CIVIL SERVANTS (10,627), 2 Caxton Street, London SW1H 0QH. Tel: 020-7343 1111; Fax: 020-7343 1105; Email: head-office@fda.org.uk; Web: http://www.fda.org.uk

ASSOCIATION OF FLIGHT ATTENDANTS – COUNCIL 7 (847), United Airlines Cargo Centre, Shoreham Road East, Heathrow Airport, Hounslow TW6 3UA. Tel: 020-8276 6723; Fax: 020-8276 6706; Email: 75452.2427@compuserve.com; Web: http://www.unitedafa.org/councils/7-london.html

ASSOCIATION OF MAGISTERIAL OFFICERS (6,849), 231 Vauxhall Bridge Road, London SW1V 1EG. Tel: 020-7630 5455; Fax: 020-7630 1989; Email: helen@amo.org.uk

ASSOCIATION OF TEACHERS AND LECTURERS (150,000), 7 Northumberland Street, London WC2N 5RD. Tel: 020-7930 6441; Fax: 020-7930 1359; Email: info@atl.org.uk; Web: http://www.atl.org.uk

ASSOCIATION OF UNIVERSITY TEACHERS (42,500), Egmont House, 25–31 Tavistock Place, London WC1H 9UT. Tel: 020-7670 9700; Fax: 020-7670 9799; Email: hq@aut.org.uk; Web: http://www.aut.org.uk

BAKERS, FOOD AND ALLIED WORKERS' UNION (31,028), Stanborough House, Great North Road, Stanborough, Welwyn Garden City, Herts AL8 7TA. Tel: 01707-260150; Fax: 01707-261570; Email: bfawu@aol.com

BRITANNIA STAFF UNION (2,172), Court Lodge, Leonard Street, Leek, Staffs ST13 5JP. Tel: 01538-399627; Fax: 01538-371342

BRITISH ACTORS' EQUITY ASSOCIATION (36,500), Guild House, Upper St Martin's Lane, London WC2H 9EG. Tel: 0171-379 6000; Fax: 0171-379 7001

BRITISH AIR LINE PILOTS ASSOCIATION (BALPA) (6,700), 81 New Road, Harlington, Hayes, Middx UB3 5BG. Tel: 020-8476 4000; Fax: 020-8476 4077; Email: balpa@balpa.org; Web: http://www.balpa.org

BRITISH ASSOCIATION OF COLLIERY MANAGEMENT – TECHNICAL ENERGY AND ADMINISTRATIVE MANAGEMENT (BACM-TEAM) (4,315), 17 South Parade, Doncaster, S. Yorks DN1 2DR. Tel: 01302-815551; Fax: 01302-815552; Email: bacmteam@aol.com

BRITISH DIETETIC ASSOCIATION (4,900), 5th Floor, Elizabeth House, 22 Suffolk Street, Queensway, Birmingham B1 1LS. Tel: 0121-616 4900; Fax: 0121-616 4901

BRITISH ORTHOPTIC SOCIETY (1,300), Tavistock House North, Tavistock Square, London WC1H 9HX. Tel: 020-7387 7992; Fax: 020-7383 2584

BROADCASTING ENTERTAINMENT, CINEMATOGRAPH AND THEATRE UNION (BECTU) (26,000), 111 Wardour Street, London W1V 4AY. Tel: 020-7437 8506; Fax: 020-7437 8268; Web: http://www.bectu.org.uk

CARD SETTING MACHINE TENTERS' SOCIETY (88), 48 Scar End Lane, Staincliffe, Dewsbury, W. Yorks WF13 4NY. Tel: 01924-400206

CERAMIC AND ALLIED TRADES UNION (20,000), Hillcrest House, Garth Street, Hanley, Stoke-on-Trent. ST1 2AB. Tel: 01782-272755; Fax: 01782-284902

THE CHARTERED SOCIETY OF PHYSIOTHERAPY (30,000), 14 Bedford Row, London WC1R 4ED. Tel: 020-7306 6666; Fax: 020-7306 6611; Email: ceo@csphysio.org.uk; Web: http://www.csp.org.uk

COMMUNICATION WORKERS UNION (300,000), 150 The Broadway, Wimbledon, London SW19 1RX. Tel: 020-8971 7200; Fax: 020-8971 7300; Email: cproctor@cwu.org; Web: http://www.cwu.org

COMMUNITY AND DISTRICT NURSING ASSOCIATION (5,750), Thames Valley University, 32–38 Uxbridge Road, Ealing, London W5 2BS. Tel: 020-8280 5342; Fax: 020-8280 5341; Email: cdna@tvu.ac.uk; Web: http://www.cdna.tvu.ac.uk

COMMUNITY AND YOUTH WORKERS UNION (4,500), Unit 302, The Argent Centre, 60 Frederick Street, Birmingham B1 3HS. Tel: 0121-244 3344; Fax: 0121-244 3345; Email: dougnic@email.msn.com

CONNECT THE UNION FOR PROFESSIONALS IN COMMUNICATIONS (18,000), 30 St George's Road, London SW19 4BD. Tel: 020-8971 6000; Fax: 020-8971 6002; Email: union@connectuk.org; Web: http://www.connectuk.org
Birmingham Field Office, 22A Caroline Street, St Paul's Square, Birmingham B3 1UE. Tel: 0121-236 0596; Fax: 0121-233 2616; Email: birmingham1@connectuk.org

ENGINEERING AND FASTENER TRADE UNION (150), 42 Galton Road, Warley, West Midlands B67 5JU. Tel: 0121-429 2594; Fax: 0121-429 2594

ENGINEERS' AND MANAGERS' ASSOCIATION (30,000), Flaxman House, Gogmore Lane, Chertsey, Surrey KT16 9JS. Tel: 01932-577007; Fax: 01932-567166; Email: gs@ema.org.uk

THE FIRE BRIGADES UNION (57,654), Bradley House, 68 Coombe Road, Kingston upon Thames, Surrey KT2 7AE. Tel: 020-8541 1765; Fax: 020-8546 5187; Email: office@fbu-ho.org.uk; Web: http://www.fbu-ho.org.uk

GENERAL UNION OF LOOM OVERLOOKERS (310), 9 Wellington Street, St Johns, Blackburn, Lancs BB1 8AF. Tel: 01254-51760; Fax: 01254-51760

GMB (700,000), 22–24 Worple Road, London SW19 4DD. Tel: 020-8947 3131; Fax: 020-8944 6552

GRAPHICAL, PAPER AND MEDIA UNION (204,822), 63–67 Bromham Road, Bedford. MK40 2AG. Tel: 01234-351521; Fax: 01234-270580; Email: general@gpmu.org.uk; Web: http://www.gpmu.org.uk

GUINNESS STAFF ASSOCIATION (604), Sun Works Cottage, Park Royal Brewery, London NW10 7RR. Tel: 020-8965 7700; Fax: 020-8963 5184

HOSPITAL CONSULTANTS AND SPECIALISTS ASSOCIATION (2,259), 1 Kingsclere Road, Overton, Basingstoke, Hants RG25 3JA. Tel: 01256-771777; Fax: 01256-770999; Email: conspec@hcsa.com; Web: http://www.hcsa.com

INDEPENDENT UNION OF HALIFAX STAFF (26,000), Simmons House, 46 Old Bath Road, Charvil, Reading RG10 9QR. Tel: 0118-934 1808; Fax: 0118-932 0208; Email: 101670.3051@compuserve.com

INSTITUTION OF PROFESSIONALS MANAGERS AND SPECIALISTS (74,261), 75–79 York Road, London SE1 7AQ. Tel: 020-7902 6600; Fax: 020-7902 6667; Email: ipmshq@ipms.org.uk; Web: http://www.ipms.org.uk

IRON AND STEEL TRADES CONFEDERATION (50,000), Swinton House, 324 Gray's Inn Road, London WC1X 8DD. Tel: 020-7837 6691; Fax: 020-7278 8378

MANAGERIAL AND PROFESSIONAL OFFICERS UNION (10,160), Terminus House, The High, Harlow, Essex CM20 1TZ3. Tel: 01279-434444; Fax: 01279-451176

MANUFACTURING SCIENCE AND FINANCE UNION (MSF) (416,000), MSF Centre, 33–37 Moreland Street, London EC1V 8BB. Tel: 020-7505 3000; Fax: 020-7505 3020; Email: bradyf@msf.org.uk; Web: http://www.msf.org.uk

MILITARY AND ORCHESTRAL MUSICAL INSTRUMENT MAKERS TRADE SOCIETY (57), 2 Whitehouse Avenue, Borehamwood, Herts WD6 1HD

MUSICIANS' UNION (31,000), 60–62 Clapham Road, London SW9 0JJ. Tel: 020-7582 5566; Fax: 020-7582 9805; Email: info@musiciansunion.org.uk; Web: http://www.musiciansunion.org.uk

NASUWT (NATIONAL ASSOCIATION OF SCHOOLMASTERS/UNION OF WOMEN TEACHERS) (185,000), Hillscourt Education Centre, Rednal, Birmingham B45 8RS. Tel: 0121-453 6150; Fax: 0121-457 6208; Email: nasuwt@nasuwt.org.uk; Web: http://www.teachersunion.org.uk

NATFHE (UNIVERSITY AND COLLEGE LECTURERS UNION) (66,000), 27 Britannia Street, London WC1X 9JP. Tel: 020-7837 3636; Fax: 020-7837 4403; Email: hq@natfhe.org.uk; Web: http://www.natfhe.org.uk

NATIONAL ASSOCIATION OF CO-OPERATIVE OFFICIALS (2,750), Coronation House, Arndale Centre, Manchester M4 2HW. Tel: 0161-834 6029; Fax: 0161-832 0671

NATIONAL ASSOCIATION OF PROBATION OFFICERS (7,100), 4 Chivalry Road, London SW11 1HT. Tel: 020-7223 4887; Fax: 020-7223 3503; Email: nopo@ukonline.co.uk

NATIONAL LEAGUE OF THE BLIND AND DISABLED (2,200), 2 Tenterden Road, London N17 8BE. Tel: 020-8808 6030; Fax: 020-8885 3235

NATIONAL UNION OF DOMESTIC APPLIANCES AND GENERAL OPERATIVES (2,500), 7–8 Imperial Buildings, Corporation Street, Rotherham, S. Yorks S60 1PB. Tel: 01709-382820; Fax: 01709-362826

NATIONAL UNION OF JOURNALISTS (NUJ) (20,000), Acorn House, 314–320 Gray's Inn Road, London WC1X 8DP. Tel: 020-7278 7916; Fax: 020-7837 8143; Email: acorn.house@nuj.org.uk

NATIONAL UNION OF KNITWEAR FOOTWEAR AND APPAREL TRADES (28,000), 55 New Walk, Leicester LE1 7EA. Tel: 0116-255 6703; Fax: 0116-254 4406; Email: head-office@kfat.org.uk; Web: http://www.kfat.org.uk

NATIONAL UNION OF LOCK AND METAL WORKERS (3,716), Bellamy House, Wilkes Street, Willenhall, W. Midlands WV13 2BS. Tel: 01902-366651; Fax: 01902-368035

NATIONAL UNION OF MARINE AVIATION AND SHIPPING TRANSPORT OFFICERS (18,600), Oceanair House, 750-760 High Road, London E11 3BB. Tel: 020-8989 6677; Fax: 020-8530 1015; Email: info@numast.org; Web: http://www.numast.org

NATIONAL UNION OF MINEWORKERS (NUM) (5,000), Miners' Offices, 2 Huddersfield Road, Barnsley, S. Yorks S70 2LS. Tel: 01226-215555; Fax: 01226-215561

NATIONAL UNION OF RAIL MARITIME AND TRANSPORT WORKERS (RMT) (60,000), Unity House, 205 Euston Road, London NW1 2BL. Tel: 020-7387 4771; Fax: 020-7387 4123; Email: jknapp@rmt-hq.demon.co.uk; Web: http://www.rmt.org.uk

NATIONAL UNION OF TEACHERS (NUT) (286,503), Hamilton House, Mabledon Place, London WC1H 9BD. Tel: 020-7388 6191; Fax: 020-7387 8458; Web: http://www.teachers.org.uk

NORTHERN CARPET TRADES' UNION (600), 22 Clare Road, Halifax HX1 2HX. Tel: 01422-360492; Fax: 01422-321146

POWER LOOM CARPET WEAVERS' AND TEXTILE WORKERS' UNION (1,300), 148 Hurcott Road, Kidderminster, Worcs DY10 2RL. Tel: 01562-823192; Fax: 01562-861469; Email: gensec@carpetunion-gem.freeserve.co.uk

PRISON OFFICERS' ASSOCIATION (29,000), Cronin House, 245 Church Street, London N9 9HW. Tel: 020-8803 0255; Fax: 020-8803 1761.

PROFESSIONAL FOOTBALLERS' ASSOCIATION (4,000), 20 Oxford Court, Bishopsgate, Manchester M2 3WQ. Tel: 0161-236 0575; Fax: 0161-228 7229; Email: info@thepfa.co.uk; Web: http://www.thepfa.co.uk

PUBLIC AND COMMERCIAL SERVICES UNION (PCS) (252,000), 160 Falcon Road, London SW11 2LN. Tel: 020-7924 2727; Fax: 020-7924 1847; Email: pauld@pcs.org.uk; Web: http://www.pcs.org.uk

SCOTTISH PRISON OFFICERS' ASSOCIATION (3,200), 21 Calder Road, Edinburgh EH11 3PF. Tel: 0131-443 8105; Fax: 0131-444 0657

SHEFFIELD WOOL SHEAR WORKERS' UNION (15), 17 Galsworthy Road, Sheffield S5 8QX. Tel: 0114-233 8262

SOCIETY OF CHIROPODISTS AND PODIATRISTS (8,500), 53 Welbeck Street, London W1M 7HE. Tel: 020-7486 3381; Fax: 020-7935 6359; Email: eng@scpod.org; Web: http://www.feetforlife.org

THE SOCIETY OF RADIOGRAPHERS (13,000), 207 Providence Square, Mill Street, London SE1 2EW. Tel: 020-7740 7200; Fax: 020-7740 7204; Email: info@sor.org; Web: http://www.sor.org

TRANSPORT AND GENERAL WORKERS' UNION (TGWU) (881,357), Transport House, 128 Theobalds Road, London WC1X 8TN. Tel: 020-7611 2500; Fax: 020-7611 2555; Email: tgwu@tgwu.org.uk; Web: http://www.tgwu.org.uk

TRANSPORT SALARIED STAFFS' ASSOCIATION (31,000), Walkden House, 10 Melton Street, London NW1 2EJ. Tel: 020-7387 2101; Fax: 020-7383 0656

UNDEB CENEDLAETHOL ATHRAWON CYMRU (NATIONAL ASSOCIATION OF TEACHERS OF WALES) (3,600), Pen Roc, Rhodfa'r Môr, Aberystwyth, Ceredigion SY23 2AZ. Tel: 01970-615577; Fax: 01970-626765; Email: swyddfa@ucac.cymru.org; Web: http://www.ucac.cymru.org

UNIFI (164000), Sheffield House, 1B Amity Grove, London SW20 0LG. Tel: 020-8946 9151; Fax: 020-8879 7916; Email: amity@bifu.org.uk

UNION FOR BRADFORD AND BINGLEY STAFF (2,600), 18D Market Place, Malton, N. Yorks YO17 7LX. Tel: 01653-697634; Fax: 01653-695222

UNION OF CONSTRUCTION ALLIED TRADES AND TECHNICIANS (UCATT) (114,000), UCATT House, 177 Abbeville Road, London SW4 9RL. Tel: 020-7622 2362; Fax: 020-7720 4081; Email: sstevenson@ucatt.org.uk; Web: http://www.ucatt.org.uk

UNION OF SHOP DISTRIBUTIVE AND ALLIED WORKERS (USDAW) (315,000), Oakley, 188 Wilmslow Road, Fallowfield, Manchester M14 6LJ. Tel: 0161-224 2804; Fax: 0161-257 2566; Email: usdaw-co@mcrl.poptel.org.uk; Web: http://www.poptel.org.uk/usdaw/

UNION OF TEXTILE WORKERS (1,550), Foxlowe, Market Place, Leek, Staffs ST13 6AD. Tel: 01538-382068; Fax: 01538-382068.

UNISON (130, 0000), 1 Mabledon Place, London. WC1H 9AJ. Tel: 020-7388 2366; Fax: 020-7387 6692; Web: http://www.unison.org.uk

WRITERS' GUILD OF GREAT BRITAIN (2,200), 430 Edgware Road, London W2 1EH. Tel: 020-7723 8074; Fax: 020-7706 2413; Email: postie@wggb. demon.co.uk; Web: http://www.writers.org.uk/guild

National Academies of Scholarship

THE BRITISH ACADEMY (1901)
10 Carlton House Terrace, London SW1Y 5AH
Tel 020-7969 5200

The British Academy is an independent, self-governing learned society for the promotion of the humanities and social sciences. It supports advanced academic research and is a channel for the Government's support of research in those disciplines.

The Fellows are scholars who have attained distinction in one of the branches of study that the Academy exists to promote. Candidates must be nominated by existing Fellows. At 5 May 2000 there were 708 Fellows, 15 Honorary Fellows and 320 Corresponding Fellows overseas.

President, Sir Tony Wrigley, PBA
Vice-President, Prof. J. L. Nelson; Prof. J. D. Y. Peel
Treasurer, J. S. Flemming, FBA
Foreign Secretary, Prof. C. N. J. Mann, FBA
Publications Secretary, Prof. F. G. B. Millar, FBA
Chair, Committee on Academy Research Projects, Prof. R. R. Davies, FBA
Secretary, P. W. H. Brown, CBE

ROYAL ACADEMY (1768)
Burlington House, London W1V 0DS
Tel 020-7300 8000

The Royal Academy of Arts is an independent, self-governing society devoted to the encouragement and promotion of the fine arts.

Membership of the Academy is limited to 80 Royal Academicians, all being painters, engravers, sculptors or architects. Candidates are nominated and elected by the existing Academicians. There is also a limited class of honorary membership.

President, Sir Phillip King, CBE, PRA
Treasurer, P. Huxley, RA
Keeper, B. Neiland, RA
Secretary, D. Gordon

THE ROYAL ACADEMY OF ENGINEERING (1976)
29 Great Peter Street, London SW1P 3LW
Tel 020-7222 2688

The Royal Academy of Engineering was established as the Fellowship of Engineering in 1976. It was granted a royal charter in 1983 and its present title in 1992. It is an independent, self-governing body whose object is the pursuit, encouragement and maintenance of excellence in the whole field of engineering, in order to promote the advancement of the science, art and practice of engineering for the benefit of the public.

Election to the Fellowship is by invitation only from nominations supported by the body of Fellows. Fellows are chosen from among chartered engineers of all disciplines. At July 2000 there were 1,150 Fellows, 22 Honorary Fellows and 80 Foreign Members. The Duke of Edinburgh is the Senior Fellow and the Duke of Kent is a Royal Fellow.

President, Sir David Davies, CBE, FRS, FREng
Senior Vice-President, Dr J. R. Forrest, FREng
Vice-Presidents, Sir Alec Broers, FREng, FRS;
Prof. A. P. Dowling, FREng; Prof. P. J. Dowling,
FREng, FRS; B. V. George, CBE, FREng;
Dr D. Michael, FREng; Prof. R. W. E. Shannon, FREng
Hon. Treasurer, J. W. Herbert, FREng
Hon. Secretaries, Prof. J. M. Brady, FRS, FREng
(*Electrical Engineering*); Prof. P. Braiden, FREng
(*Mechanical Engineering*); J. R. Darley, FREng
(*Process Engineering*); Prof. R. W. E. Shannon,
FREng (*International Activities*); Prof. G. F. Hewitt,
FREng, FRS (*Education and Training*)
Executive Secretary, J. Burch

THE ROYAL SCOTTISH ACADEMY (1838)
The Mound, Edinburgh EH2 2EL
Tel 0131-225 6671

The Scottish Academy was founded in 1826 to arrange exhibitions of contemporary paintings and to establish a society of fine art in Scotland. The Academy was granted a royal charter in 1838.

Members are elected from the disciplines of painting, sculpture, architecture and printmaking. Elections are from nominations put forward by the existing membership. At mid-2000 there were seven Senior Academicians, five Senior Associates, 36 Academicians, 41 Associates, four non-resident Associates and 22 Honorary Members.

President, Ian McKenzie Smith, OBE, PRSA
Secretary, W. Scott, RSA
Treasurer, I. Metzstein, RSA
Librarian, P. Collins, RSA
Administrative Secretary, B. Laidlaw

ROYAL SOCIETY (1660)
6 Carlton House Terrace, London SW1Y 5AG
Tel 020-7839 5561

The Royal Society is the United Kingdom academy of science. It is an independent, self-governing body under a royal charter, promoting and advancing all fields of physical and biological sciences, of mathematics and engineering, medical and agricultural sciences, their applications and place in society.

Election to Fellowship of the Royal Society is limited to those distinguished for original scientific work. Each year up to 40 new Fellows and six Foreign Members are elected from the most distinguished scientists. In addition, the Council can recommend for election members of the royal family and, on average, one person each year for conspicuous service to the cause of science. At July 2000, there were 1,210 Fellows and 115 Foreign Members. The patron is HM Queen Elizabeth II and there are five Royal Fellows or Patrons.

President, Sir Aaron Klug, OM, PRS (until November 2000);
Sir Robert May (from November 2000)
Treasurer, Prof. Sir Eric Ash, Kt., CBE, FRS, FREng
Biological Secretary, Prof. P. Bateson, FRS
Physical Secretary, Prof. J. Enderby, CBE, FRS
Foreign Secretary, Prof. B. Heap, CBE, FRS
Executive Secretary, S. Cox, CVO

THE ROYAL SOCIETY OF EDINBURGH (1783)
22–26 George Street, Edinburgh EH2 2PQ
Tel 0131-240 5000

The Royal Society of Edinburgh is Scotland's premier learned society. The Society was founded by royal charter in 1783 for 'the advancement of learning and useful knowledge', and its principal role is the promotion of scholarship in all its branches. It provides a forum for broadly-based interdisciplinary activity in Scotland, including organising public lectures, conferences and specialist research seminars; providing advice to Parliament and government; administering a range of research fellowships held in Scotland; and publishing learned journals.

Fellows are elected by ballot after being nominated by at least four existing Fellows. At July 2000 there were 1,174 Ordinary Fellows and 67 Honorary Fellows.

President, Prof. Sir William Stewart, Kt., FRS, FRSE

Vice-Presidents, Sir James Armour, CBE, FRSE;
    Prof. R. J. Donovan, FRSE; The Rt. Hon. Lord Ross, FRSE

Treasurer, Prof. Sir Laurence Hunter, Kt., CBE, FRSE

General Secretary, Prof. P. N. Wilson, CBE

Executive Secretary, Dr W. Duncan

The Research Councils

The Government funds basic and applied civil science research, mostly through the seven research councils, which are supported by the Department of Trade and Industry. The councils support research and training in universities and other higher education establishments. They also receive income for research commissioned by government departments and the private sector. In July 1998, the Government announced additional funding for research of £1,100 million over the three years 1999–2002.

In addition to scientific research, the establishment of an Arts and Humanities Research Council was proposed by the National Committee of Inquiry into Higher Education (the Dearing Committee) in 1997. The Arts and Humanities Research Board was established in 1998 with the intention of becoming a Research Council in due course. It is supported by the British Academy, the Higher Education Funding Councils for England, Scotland and Wales and the Department of Education for Northern Ireland. ARTS AND HUMANITIES RESEARCH BOARD, Northavon House, Coldharbour Lane, Bristol BS16 1QD. Tel: 0117-931 7317, *Chairman and Chief Executive*, Prof. P. Langford, D.Phil., FBA

The total government science budget as through the Office of Science and Technology in the 2000–2001 financial year is 1,603,820 million.

	1999–2000	2000–01
		Appropriation
	Actual	(Budget)
	£ 000	£ 000
BBSRC	195,545	202,420
ESCR	70,872	71,300
EPSRC	404,796	412,026
MRC	304,538	319,151
NERC	176,715	181,450
PPARC	186,680	205,774
CCLRC	2,000	2,000
Pensions	21,295	23,639
Royal Society	23,850	24,622
Royal Academy of Engineering	3,706	4,025
OST Initiatives	3,071	8,522
Joint Infrastructure Fund	1,571	100,000
University Challenge Fund	0	10,000
Science Enterprise Challenge	13,150	0
Cambridge/Massachusetts Institute of Technology	0	14,000
Synchrotron Radiation Source	0	14,084

BIOTECHNOLOGY AND BIOLOGICAL SCIENCES RESEARCH COUNCIL (BBSRC)
Polaris House, North Star Avenue, Swindon SN2 1UH
Tel 01793-413200

The BBSRC promotes and supports research and postgraduate training relating to the understanding and exploitation of biological systems; advances knowledge and technology; provides trained scientists to meet the needs of biotechnological-related industries; and provides advice, disseminates knowledge, and promotes public understanding of biotechnology and the biological sciences.
Chairman, Dr P. Doyle, CBE, FRSE
Chief Executive, Prof. R. Baker, FRS

INSTITUTES

BABRAHAM INSTITUTE
Director, Dr R. G. Dyer, Babraham Hall, Babraham, Cambridge CB2 4AT. Tel: 01223-496000
INSTITUTE FOR ANIMAL HEALTH
Director, Dr C. J. Bostock, Compton, Newbury, Berks RG20 7NN. Tel: 01635-578411
BBSRC AND MRC NEUROPATHOGENESIS UNIT, Ogston Building, West Mains Road, Edinburgh EH9 3JF. Tel: 0131-667 5204/5.
COMPTON LABORATORY, Compton, Newbury, Berks RG20 7NN. Tel: 01635-578411.
PIRBRIGHT LABORATORY, Ash Road, Pirbright, Woking, Surrey GU24 0NF. Tel: 01483-232441. *Head*, Dr A. I. Donaldson

INSTITUTE OF ARABLE CROPS RESEARCH
Director, Prof. I. R. Crute, Rothamsted, Harpenden, Herts AL5 2JQ. Tel: 01582-763133
IACR – BROOM'S BARN, Higham, Bury St Edmunds, Suffolk IP28 6NP. Tel: 01284-812200. *Director*, Dr J. D. Pidgeon
IACR – LONG ASHTON RESEARCH STATION, Long Ashton, Bristol BS41 9AF. Tel: 01275-392181. *Director*, Prof. P. R. Shewry
IACR – ROTHAMSTED, Harpenden, Herts AL5 2JQ. Tel: 01582-763133. *Director*, Prof. I. R. Crute

INSTITUTE OF FOOD RESEARCH
Norwich Research Park, Colney Lane, Norwich NR4 7UA. Tel: 01603-255000. *Director*, Dr A. Robertson

INSTITUTE OF GRASSLAND AND ENVIRONMENTAL RESEARCH
Director, Prof. C. J. Pollock, Plas Gogerddan, Aberystwyth, Ceredigion SY23 3EB. Tel: 01970-828255
ABERYSTWYTH RESEARCH CENTRE, Plas Gogerddan, Aberystwyth, Ceredigion SY23 3EB. Tel: 01970-828255
BRONYDD MAWR RESEARCH STATION, Trecastle, Brecon, Powys LD3 8RD. Tel: 01874-636480
NORTH WYKE RESEARCH STATION, Okehampton, Devon EX20 2SB. Tel: 01837-82558. *Head*, Prof. R. J. Wilkins
TRAWSGOED RESEARCH FARM, Trawsgoed, Aberystwyth, Ceredigion SY23 4LL. Tel: 01974-261615

JOHN INNES CENTRE
Director, Prof. C. Lamb, Norwich Research Park, Colney, Norwich NR4 7UH. Tel: 01603-452571

ROSLIN INSTITUTE
Director, Prof. G. Bulfield, FRSE, Roslin, Midlothian EH25 9PS. Tel: 0131-527 4200

SILSOE RESEARCH INSTITUTE
Director, Prof. B. Day, Wrest Park, Silsoe, Bedford MK45 4HS. Tel: 01525-860000

SCOTTISH AGRICULTURAL AND BIOLOGICAL RESEARCH INSTITUTES

HANNAH RESEARCH INSTITUTE, Ayr KA6 5HL. Tel: 01292-674000. *Director*, Prof. M. Peaker, FRS
MACAULAY LAND USE RESEARCH INSTITUTE, Craigiebuckler, Aberdeen AB15 8QH. Tel: 01224-318611. *Director*, Prof. T. J. Maxwell, FRSE

MOREDUN RESEARCH INSTITUTE, Pentlands Science Park, Bush Loan, Penicuik, Midlothian EH26 0PZ. Tel: 0131-445 5111. *Director*, Prof. Q. A. McKellar
ROWETT RESEARCH INSTITUTE, Greenburn Road, Bucksburn, Aberdeen AB21 9SB. Tel: 01224-712751. *Director*, Prof. P. J. Morgan
SCOTTISH CROP RESEARCH INSTITUTE (SCRI), Invergowrie, Dundee DD2 5DA. Tel: 01382-562731. *Director*, Prof. J. Hillman, FRSE
BIOMATHEMATICS AND STATISTICS SCOTLAND (BioSS) (administered by SCRI), University of Edinburgh, James Clerk Maxwell Building, The King's Buildings, Mayfield Road, Edinburgh EH9 3JZ. Tel: 0131-650 4901. *Director*, R. A. Kempton

---

CENTRAL LABORATORY OF THE RESEARCH COUNCILS (CLRC)
Chilton, Didcot, Oxon OX11 0QX
Tel 01235-821900

The CLRC was formed in April 1995. CLRC comprises Daresbury, Chilbolton and Rutherford Appleton Laboratories, which provide advanced facilities and specialist expertise to support academic and industrial research in the physical and life sciences. It is operated by the Council for the Central Laboratory of the Research Councils (CCLRC), an independent, non-departmental public body of the Office of Science and Technology, which is itself part of the Department of Trade and Industry.
Chairman, Prof. B. Eyre, CBE
Chief Executive, Dr Gordon Walker, OBE

DARESBURY LABORATORY, Daresbury, Warrington, Cheshire WA4 4AD. Tel: 01925-603000
RUTHERFORD APPLETON LABORATORY, Chilton, Didcot, Oxon OX11 0QX. Tel: 01235-821900
CHILBOLTON OBSERVATORY, Stockbridge, Hampshire SO20 6BJ. Tel: 01264-860391

ECONOMIC AND SOCIAL RESEARCH COUNCIL (ESRC)
Polaris House, North Star Avenue, Swindon SN2 1UJ
Tel 01793-413000

The purpose of the ESRC is to promote and support research and postgraduate training in the social sciences; to advance knowledge and provide trained social scientists; to provide advice on, and disseminate knowledge and promote public understanding of, the social sciences.
Chairman, Dr B. Smith, OBE
Chief Executive, Dr G. Marshall

RESEARCH CENTRES

CAMBRIDGE GROUP FOR THE HISTORY OF POPULATION AND SOCIAL STRUCTURE, 27 Trumpington Street, Cambridge CB2 1QA. Tel: 01223-333181. *Director*, Prof. R. Smith
CENTRE FOR THE ANALYSIS OF SOCIAL EXCLUSION, London School of Economics, Houghton Street, London WC2A 2AE. Tel: 020-7955 7419. *Director*, Prof. J. Hills
CENTRE FOR BUSINESS RESEARCH, Department of Applied Economics, University of Cambridge, Sidgwick Avenue, Cambridge CB3 9DE. Tel: 01223-335248. *Director*, A. Hughes
CENTRE FOR ECONOMIC LEARNING AND SOCIAL EVOLUTION, Department of Economics, University College London, Gower Street, London WC1E 6BT.

Tel: 020-7387 7050. *Research Director*, Prof. K. Binmore
CENTRE FOR ECONOMIC PERFORMANCE, London School of Economics, Houghton Street, London WC2A 2AE. Tel: 020-7955 7048. *Director*, Prof. R. Layard
CENTRE FOR FISCAL POLICY, Institute for Fiscal Studies, 7 Ridgmount Street, London WC1E 7AE. Tel: 020-7636 3784. *Director*, Prof. R. Blundell
CENTRE FOR INTERNATIONAL EMPLOYMENT RELATIONS RESEARCH, School of Industrial and Business Studies, University of Warwick, Coventry CV4 7AL. Tel: 024-7652 4265. *Director*, Prof. K. Sisson
CENTRE FOR ORGANISATION AND INNOVATION, Institute of Work Psychology, University of Sheffield, Sheffield S10 2TN. Tel: 0114-222 3287. *Director*, Prof. T. Wall
CENTRE FOR RESEARCH IN DEVELOPMENT, INSTRUCTION AND TRAINING, Department of Psychology, University of Nottingham, Nottingham NG7 2RD. Tel: 0115-951 5312. *Director*, Prof. D. J. Wood
CENTRE FOR RESEARCH INTO ELECTIONS AND SOCIAL TRENDS, Social and Community Planning Research, 35 Northampton Square, London EC1V 0AX. Tel: 020-7250 1866. *Director*, Prof. R. Jowell
CENTRE FOR RESEARCH ON INNOVATION AND COMPETITION, Faculty of Economic and Social Studies, University of Manchester M13 9PL. Tel: 0161-275 2000. *Director*, Prof. S. Metcalfe; Manchester School of Management, UMIST, Manchester M60 1QD. Tel: 0161-236 3311. *Director*, Prof. R. Coombs
CENTRE FOR SOCIAL AND ECONOMIC RESEARCH ON THE GLOBAL ENVIRONMENT, School of Environmental Sciences, University of East Anglia, Norwich NR4 7TJ. Tel: 01603-593176. *Director*, Prof. K. Turner
CENTRE FOR THE STUDY OF AFRICAN ECONOMIES, Institute of Economics and Statistics, University of Oxford, St Cross Building, Manor Road, Oxford OX1 3UL. Tel: 01865-271084. *Director*, Prof. P. Collier
CENTRE FOR THE STUDY OF GLOBALISATION AND REGIONALISATION, Department of Political Science, University of Warwick, Coventry CV4 7AL. Tel: 024-7652 3916. *Directors*, Prof. R. Higgott, Prof. J. Whalley
COMPLEX PRODUCT SYSTEM INNOVATION CENTRE, SPRU, Mantell Building, University of Sussex, Brighton BN1 9RF. Tel: 01273-686758. *Director*, Dr M. Hobday; CENTRIM, University of Brighton, Brighton BN1 9PH. Tel: 01273-642188. *Director*, H. Rush
FINANCIAL MARKETS CENTRE, London School of Economics, Houghton Street, London WC2A 2AE. Tel: 020-7955 7002. *Director*, Prof. D. Webb
HUMAN COMMUNICATION RESEARCH CENTRE, University of Edinburgh, 2 Buccleuch Place, Edinburgh EH8 9LW. Tel: 0131-650 4444. *Director*, Prof. K. Stenning
RESEARCH CENTRE ON MICRO-SOCIAL CHANGE, University of Essex, Wivenhoe Park, Colchester, Essex CO4 3SQ. Tel: 01206-872957. *Director*, Prof. J. Gershuny
TRANSPORT STUDIES UNIT, Centre for Transport Studies, University College London, Gower Street, London WC1E 6BT. Tel: 020-7380 7009. *Director*, Dr P. Goodwin

RESOURCE CENTRES

BUSINESS PROCESS RESOURCE CENTRE, Warwick Manufacturing Group, University of Warwick, Coventry CV4 7AL. Tel: 024-7652 4173. *Director*, Prof. K. Bhattacharrya

CENTRE FOR APPLIED SOCIAL SURVEYS, Social and
Community Planning Research, 35 Northampton
Square, London EC1V 0AX. Tel: 020-7250 1866.
Director, R. Thomas
CENTRE FOR ECONOMIC POLICY RESEARCH, 90–98
Goswell Road, London EC1V 7DB. Tel: 020-7878 2900.
Director, Prof. R. Portes
ESRC DATA ARCHIVE, University of Essex, Wivenhoe
Park, Colchester, Essex CO4 3SQ. Tel: 01206-872006.
Director, Dr S. Musgrave
INTERNATIONAL BIBLIOGRAPHY OF THE SOCIAL
SCIENCES, British Library of Political and Economic
Science, London School of Economics, Houghton
Street, London WC2A 2AE. Tel: 020-7955 7000.
Director, Ms J. Sykes
QUALITATIVE DATA ARCHIVAL RESOURCE CENTRE,
Department of Sociology, University of Essex,
Wivenhoe Park, Colchester, Essex CO4 3SQ.
Tel: 01206-873333. *Director*, Prof. P. Thompson
RESOURCE CENTRE FOR ACCESS TO DATA IN EUROPE,
Department of Geography, University of Durham,
Durham DH1 3HP. Tel: 0191-374 7350.
Director, Prof. R. Hudson

ENGINEERING AND PHYSICAL SCIENCES RESEARCH COUNCIL (EPSRC)
Polaris House, North Star Avenue, Swindon SN2 1ET
Tel 01793-444000

The EPSRC promotes and supports basic, strategic and
applied research and training in UK higher education
institutions in the physical sciences and engineering.
Chairman, Prof. A. Ledwith, CBE, FRS
Chief Executive, Prof. R. Brook, OBE, FREng.

MEDICAL RESEARCH COUNCIL (MRC)
20 Park Crescent, London W1N 4AL
Tel 020-7636 5422; Fax 020-7436 2663;
Web http://www.mrc.ac.uk

The purpose of the MRC is to promote medical and
related biological research. The council employs its own
research staff and funds research by other institutions and
individuals, complementing the research resources of the
universities and hospitals.
Chairman, Sir Anthony Cleaver
Chief Executive, Prof. G. K. Radda, CBE, D.Phil., FRS
Chairman, Neurosciences and Mental Health Board,
Prof. E. Johnston, MD, FRCP, FRCPsych
Chairman, Molecular and Cellular Medicine Board,
Prof. L. K. Borysiewicz
Chairman, Physiological Medicine and Infections Board, Prof.
A. M. McGregor, MD, FRCP
Chairman, Health Services and Public Health Research Board,
Prof. R. Fitzpatrick, Ph.D.

NATIONAL INSTITUTE FOR MEDICAL RESEARCH,
The Ridgeway, Mill Hill, London NW7 1AA.
Tel: 020-8959 3666.
Director, Prof. Sir John Skehel, Ph.D., FRS
CLINICAL SCIENCES CENTRE, Imperial College School
of Medicine, Du Cane Road, London W12 0NN.
Tel: 020-8383 1000.
Director, Prof. C. Higgins, Ph.D., FRSE
LABORATORY OF MOLECULAR BIOLOGY, Hills Road,
Cambridge CB2 2QH. Tel: 01223-248011.
Director, Dr R. Henderson, FRS

RESEARCH UNITS
ANATOMICAL NEUROPHARMACOLOGY UNIT, Mansfield
Road, Oxford OX1 3TH. Tel: 01865-271865.
Director, Prof. P. Somogyi, Ph.D.
BIOCHEMICAL AND CLINICAL MAGNETIC RESONANCE
UNIT, Magnetic Resonance Spectroscopy,
John Radcliffe Hospital, Headington, Oxford OX3 9DU.
Tel: 01865-221111. *Hon. Director*, P. Styles, D.Phil.
BIOSTATISTICS UNIT, Institute of Public Health,
University Forvie Site, Robinson Way, Cambridge
CB2 2SR. Tel: 01223-330366.
Hon. Director, Prof. N. E. Day, Ph.D.
CELL MUTATION UNIT, University of Sussex, Falmer,
Brighton BN1 9RR. Tel: 01273-678123.
Director, Prof. B. A. Bridges, Ph.D., FIBiol.
CELLULAR IMMUNOLOGY UNIT, Sir William Dunn
School of Pathology, Oxford OX1 3RE.
Tel: 01865-275594. *Director (acting)*, D. W. Mason
CENTRE FOR BRAIN REPAIR (MRC CAMBRIDGE),
Ed Brian Building, University Forvie Site, Robinson
Way, Cambridge CB2 2PY. Tel: 01223-331160.
Chairman, Prof. D. A. S. Compston, MD, FRCP
CENTRE FOR COGNITIVE NEURO-SCIENCE (MRC IRC),
Department of Experimental Psychology, University of
Oxford, Oxford OX1 3UD. Tel: 01865-271444.
Director, Prof. C. Blakemore, FRS
CENTRE FOR MECHANISMS OF HUMAN TOXICITY,
Hodgkin Building, University of Leicester,
PO Box 138, Lancaster Road, Leicester LE1 9HN.
Tel: 0116-252 5600.
Director, Prof. G. C. K. Roberts, Ph.D.
CENTRE FOR PROTEIN ENGINEERING, MRC Centre,
Hills Road, Cambridge CB2 2QH. Tel: 01223-248011.
Director, Prof. A. Fersht, Ph.D., FRS
CLINICAL TRIALS UNIT, University College London
Medical School, Mortimer Market Centre, Mortimer
Market (off Capper Street), London WC1E 6AU.
Tel: 020-7380 9991. *Director*, Prof. J. H. Darbyshire
COGNITION AND BRAIN SCIENCES UNIT, 15 Chaucer
Road, Cambridge CB2 2EF. Tel: 01223-355294.
Director, Prof. W. Marslen-Wilson, FBA
CYCLOTRON UNIT, MRC Clinical Sciences Centre,
RPMS Hammersmith Hospital, Du Cane Road,
London W12 0NN. Tel: 020-8383 3161.
Director, Prof. C. Higgins, Ph.D., FRSE
DUNN HUMAN NUTRITION UNIT, The Wellcome
Trust, MRC Building, Addenbrooks Site, Hill Road,
Cambridge CB2 2XY. Tel: 01223-415695.
Director, Prof. Sir John Walker, D.Phil., FRS
ENVIRONMENTAL EPIDEMIOLOGY UNIT, Southampton
General Hospital, Southampton SO16 6YD.
Tel: 023-8077 7624.
Director, Prof. D. J. P. Barker, MD, Ph.D., FRCP, FRCOG
EPIDEMIOLOGY AND MEDICAL CARE UNIT, Wolfson
Institute of Preventive Medicine, St Bartholomew's
and the Royal London Hospital School of Medicine
and Dentistry, Charterhouse Square, London
EC1M 6BQ. Tel: 020-7982 6253.
Director, Prof. T. W. Meade, CBE, DM, FRCP
HEALTH SERVICES RESEARCH COLLABORATION,
University of Bristol, Canynge Hall, Whiteladies
Road, Bristol BS8 2PR. Tel: 0117-928 7343.
Director, Prof. P. Dieppe, MD, FRCP
HUMAN GENETICS UNIT, Western General Hospital,
Crewe Road, Edinburgh EH4 2XU. Tel: 0131-322 2471.
Director, Prof. N. D. Hastie, Ph.D., FRSE
HUMAN GENOME MAPPING PROJECT RESOURCE
CENTRE, Hinxton Hall, Hinxton, Cambridge
CB10 1RQ. Tel: 01223-494500.
Director, D. Campbell, Ph.D.

HUMAN IMMUNOLOGY UNIT, John Radcliffe Hospital, Headington, Oxford OX3 9DU. Tel: 01865-222443. *Director*, Prof. A. McMichael

HUMAN MOVEMENT AND BALANCE UNIT, Institute of Neurology, National Hospital for Neurology and Neurosurgery, Queen Square, London WC1 3BG. Tel: 020-7837 3611. *Hon. Director*, Dr J. C. Rothwell

IMMUNOCHEMISTRY UNIT, University Department of Biochemistry, South Parks Road, Oxford OX1 3QU. Tel: 01865-275354. *Director*, Prof. K. B. M. Reid, PH.D.

INSTITUTE FOR ENVIRONMENT AND HEALTH, University of Leicester, 94 Regent Road, Leicester LE1 7DD. Tel: 0116-223 1600. *Director (acting)*, Dr P. Harrison

INSTITUTE OF HEARING RESEARCH, University of Nottingham, Nottingham NG7 2RD. Tel: 0115-922 3431. *Director*, Prof. M. P. Haggard, PH.D.

INSTITUTE OF MOLECULAR MEDICINE, John Radcliffe Hospital, Headington, Oxford OX3 9DU. Tel: 01865-222359. *Director*, Prof. Sir David Weatherall, MD, FRCP, FRCPath., FRS

INTERDISCIPLINARY RESEARCH CENTRE IN CELL BIOLOGY, MRC Laboratory for Molecular Cell Biology, University College London, Gower Street, London WC1E 6BT. Tel: 020-7380 7806. *Director*, Dr Jane Cope

MAMMALIAN GENETICS UNIT, Harwell Site, Chilton, Didcot, Oxon OX11 0RD. Tel: 01235-834393. *Director*, Prof. S. Brown, PH.D.

MOLECULAR HAEMATOLOGY UNIT, Institute of Molecular Medicine, John Radcliffe Hospital, Headington, Oxford OX3 9DS. Tel: 01865-222359. *Hon. Director*, Prof. Sir David Weatherall, MD, FRCP, FRCPath., FRS

MRC CENTRE, CAMBRIDGE, Hills Road, Cambridge CB2 2QH. Tel: 01223-248011. *Head of Centre*, M. B. Davies, PH.D.

MRC CENTRE, OXFORD, Manor House, John Radcliffe Hospital, Headington, Oxford OX3 9DU. Tel: 01865-222124. *Head of Centre*, D. McLaren, PH.D.

MRC HUMAN REPRODUCTION SCIENCE UNIT, Centre for Reproductive Biology, 37 Chalmers Street, Edinburgh EH3 9EW. Tel: 0131-229 2575. *Director*, Prof. R. P. Millar, PH.D., FRCPath.

MRC LABORATORIES, THE GAMBIA, PO Box 273, Banjul, The Gambia, W. Africa. *Director*, Prof. K. McAdam, FRCP

MRC LABORATORIES, JAMAICA, University of the West Indies, Mona, Kingston 7, Jamaica. *Director*, Prof. G. R. Serjeant, CMG, MD, FRCP

MUSCLE AND CELL MOTILITY UNIT, New Hants House, GKT School of Biomedical Sciences, London Bridge, London SE1 1HL. Tel 020-7848 6434. *Hon. Director*, Prof. R. M. Simmons, PH.D., FRS

PRION UNIT, Imperial College School of Medicine at St Mary's, Norfolk Place, London W2 1PG. Tel: 020-7594 3760. *Director*, Prof. J. Collinge

PROTEIN PHOSPHORYLATION UNIT, Department of Biochemistry, Medical Sciences Institute, University of Dundee, Dundee DD1 4HN. Tel: 01382-344241. *Hon. Director*, Prof. Sir Philip Cohen, PH.D., FRS, FRSE

RADIATION AND GENOME STABILITY UNIT, Harwell Site, Chilton, Didcot, Oxon OX11 0RD. Tel: 01235-834393. *Director*, Prof. D. Goodhead, D.Phil.

RESOURCE CENTRE FOR HUMAN NUTRITION RESEARCH, Downhams Lane, Milton Road, Cambridge CB4 1XJ. Tel: 01223-426356. *Director*, Dr A. Prentice

SOCIAL AND PUBLIC HEALTH SCIENCES UNIT, 6 Lilybank Gardens, Glasgow G12 8QQ. Tel: 0141-357 3949. *Director*, Prof. S. Macintyre, OBE, PH.D., FRSE

SOCIAL, GENETIC AND DEVELOPMENTAL PSYCHIATRY RESEARCH CENTRE, Institute of Psychiatry, De Crespigny Park, Denmark Hill, London SE5 8AF. Tel: 020-7919 3873. *Director*, Prof. P. McGuffin

SYNAPTIC PLASTICITY CENTRE, School of Medical Sciences, University of Bristol, University Walk, Bristol BS8 1TD. Tel: 0117-928 7420. *Director*, Prof. G. L. Collingridge

TOXICOLOGY UNIT, Hodgkin Building, University of Leicester, PO Box 138, Lancaster Road, Leicester LE1 9HN. Tel: 0116-252 5600. *Director (acting)*, Prof. G. Cohen

UK MOUSE GENOME CENTRE, Harwell Site, Chilton, Didcot, Oxon OX11 0RD. Tel: 01235-834393. *Director*, Prof. S. Brown, PH.D.

VIROLOGY UNIT, Institute of Virology, Church Street, Glasgow G11 5JR. Tel: 0141-330 4017. *Director*, Prof. D. J. McGeoch

---

NATURAL ENVIRONMENT RESEARCH COUNCIL (NERC)
Polaris House, North Star Avenue, Swindon SN2 1EU
Tel 01793-411500

The purpose of the NERC is to promote and support research, survey, long-term environmental monitoring and related postgraduate training in terrestrial, marine and freshwater biology, and Earth atmospheric, hydrological, oceanographic and polar sciences and Earth observation; to advance knowledge and technology, and to provide services and trained scientists and engineers; to provide advice, disseminate knowledge and promote public understanding in these fields.
Chairman, J. C. Smith, CBE, FREng, FRSE
Chief Executive, Prof. J. Lawton, CBE, FRS

CENTRES/SURVEYS

BRITISH ANTARCTIC SURVEY, High Cross, Madingley Road, Cambridge CB3 0ET. Tel: 01223-221400. *Director*, Dr C. Rapley

BRITISH GEOLOGICAL SURVEY, Kingsley Dunham Centre, Keyworth, Nottingham NG12 5GG. Tel: 0115-936 3100. *Director*, Dr D. Falvey

CENTRE FOR COASTAL AND MARINE SCIENCE *Acting Director*, Dr G. Shimmield

PLYMOUTH MARINE LABORATORY, Prospect Place, West Hoe, Plymouth PL1 3DH. Tel: 01752-633100. *Director*, Prof. N. Owens

PROUDMAN OCEANOGRAPHIC LABORATORY, Bidston Observatory, Birkenhead L43 7RA. Tel: 0151-653 8633. *Director CCMS*, Dr E. Hill

DUNSTAFFNAGE MARINE LABORATORY, PO Box 3, Oban, Argyll PA34 4AD. Tel: 01631-562244. *Director*, Dr G. B. Shimmield

CENTRE FOR ECOLOGY AND HYDROLOGY *Director*, Prof. T. M. Roberts (based at CEH Monks Wood) CEH Windermere, The Ferry House, Far Sawrey, Ambleside, Cumbria LA22 0LP. Tel: 015394-42468. *Director*, Prof. A. D. Pickering CEH Wallingford, Maclean Building, Crowmarsh Gifford, Wallingford, Oxon OX10 8BB. Tel: 01491-838800. *Director*, Prof. J. Wallace Monks Wood, Abbots Ripton, Huntingdon PE17 2LS. Tel: 01487-773381. *Director*, Prof. T. M. Roberts

CEH Oxford, Mansfield Road, Oxford OX1 3SR. Tel: 01865-281630. *Director*, Dr P. Nuttall

SOUTHAMPTON OCEANOGRAPHY CENTRE, European way, Southampton SO14 3ZH. Tel: 023-8059 6888. *Director*, Dr H. Roe

UNITS

ATMOSPHERIC CHEMISTRY MODELLING SUPPORT UNIT, University Chemical Laboratory, University of Cambridge, Lensfield Road, Cambridge CB2 1EP. Tel: 01223-336473. *Director*, Dr J. A. Pyle

CENTRE FOR GLOBAL ATMOSPHERIC MODELLING, Department of Meteorology, University of Reading, 2 Earley Gate, Whiteknights, Reading RG6 2AU. Tel: 0118-931 8315. *Director*, Prof. A. O'Neill

CENTRE FOR POPULATION BIOLOGY, Imperial College, Silwood Park, Ascot, Berks SL5 7PY. Tel: 020-7594 2349. *Director*, Prof. C. Godfray

ENVIRONMENTAL SYSTEMS SCIENCE CENTRE, Gatty PittBuilding, Reading University, Whiteknights, Reading RG6 6AL. Tel: 0118-931 8741. *Director*, Prof. R. Gurney

SEA MAMMAL RESEARCH UNIT, Gatty Marine Laboratory, University of St Andrews, St Andrews, Fife KY16 8LB. Tel: 01334-462630. *Head*, Dr. P. Hammond

---

PARTICLE PHYSICS AND ASTRONOMY RESEARCH COUNCIL (PPARC)
Polaris House, North Star Avenue, Swindon SN2 1SZ
Tel 01793-442000; Fax 01793-442002;
Email pr.pus@pparc.ac.uk

The Particle Physics and Astronomy Research Centre (PPARC) is the UK's strategic science investment agency. It funds research, education and public understanding in four broad areas of science – particle physics, astronomy, cosmology and space sciences.

PPARC is government funded and provides research grants and studentships to scientists in British universities, gives researchers access to world-class facilities and funds the UK membership of international bodies such as the European Laboratory for Particle Physics (CERN) and the European Space Agency. It also contributes money to the UK telescopes overseas on La Palma and in Hawaii, Australia and Chile, the UK Astronomy Technology Centre at the Royal Observatory, Edinburgh and the MERLIN/VLBI National Facility.

Chairman, Dr R. Hawley, CBE, FRSE, FREng
Chief Executive, Prof. I. Halliday

ISAAC NEWTON GROUP OF TELESCOPES, Apartado de Coreos 321, Santa Cruz de la Palma, Tenerife 38780, Canary Islands. Tel: 00 3422-411048. *Director*, R. Rutten

JOINT ASTRONOMY CENTRE, 660 N A'ohoku Place, University Park, Hilo, Hawaii 96720. Tel: Hawaii 961 3756. *Head*, Prof. I. Robson

UK ASTRONOMY TECHNOLOGY CENTRE, Blackford Hill, Edinburgh EH9 3HJ. Tel: 0131-668 8100. *Director*, Dr A. Russell

Research and Technology Organisations

The following industrial and technological research bodies are members of the Association of Independent

Research and Technology Organisations (AIRTO). Members' activities span a wide range of disciplines from life sciences to engineering. Their work includes basic research, development and design of innovative products or processes, instrumentation testing and certification, and technology and management consultancy. AIRTO publishes a directory to help clients identify the organisations which might be able to assist them.

AIRTO, PO Box 85, Leatherhead, Surrey KT22 7YG. Tel: 01372-802260. *President*, Dr B. Blunden, OBE

ADVANCED MANUFACTURING TECHNOLOGY RESEARCH INSTITUTE, Hulley Road, Macclesfield, Cheshire SK10 2NE. Tel: 01625-425421. *Managing Director*, D. Palethorpe

AIRCRAFT RESEARCH ASSOCIATION LTD, Manton Lane, Bedford MK41 7PF. Tel: 01234-350681. *Chief Executive*, B. Timmins

BHR GROUP LTD (*Fluid mechanics and process technology*), The Fluid Engineering Centre, Cranfield, Bedford MK43 0AJ. Tel: 01234-750422. *Chief Executive*, I. Cooper

BIBRA INTERNATIONAL (*Assessment of toxicity of food and chemicals to humans*), Woodmansterne Road, Carshalton, Surrey SM5 4DS. Tel: 020-8652 1000. *Director*, Dr S. E. Jaggers

BLC (THE LEATHER TECHNOLOGY CENTRE), Leather Trade House, Kings Park Road, Moulton Park, Northants NN3 6JD. Tel: 01604-679999. *Chief Executive*, Dr K. Alexander

BRITISH GLASS, Northumberland Road, Sheffield S10 2UA. Tel: 0114-268 6201. *Director-General*, Dr W. Cook

BRITISH MARITIME TECHNOLOGY LTD, Orlando House, 1 Waldegrave Road, Teddington, Middx TW11 8LZ. Tel: 020-8943 5544. *Chief Executive*, D. Goodrich

BREWING RESEARCH INTERNATIONAL (*Alcoholic beverages*), Lyttel Hall, Coopers Hill Road, Nutfield, Surrey RH1 4HY. Tel: 01737-822272. *Director-General*, Prof. R. Righelato

BRITISH TEXTILE TECHNOLOGY GROUP, Wira House, West Park Ring Road, Leeds LS16 6QL. Tel: 0113-259 1999; Shirley House, Wilmslow Road, Didsbury, Manchester M20 2RB. Tel: 0161-445 8141. *Chief Executive*, A. King

BUILDING RESEARCH ESTABLISHMENT, Garston, Watford WD2 7JR. Tel: 01923-664000. *Managing Director*, Dr. M. Wyatt

BUILDING SERVICES RESEARCH AND INFORMATION ASSOCIATION, Old Bracknell Lane West, Bracknell, Berks RG12 7AH. Tel: 01344-426511. *Chief Executive*, G. J. Baker

CAMBRIDGE REFRIGERATION TECHNOLOGY (CRT), 140 Newmarket Road, Cambridge CB5 8HE. Tel: 01223-365101. *Managing Director*, A. Robertson

CAMPDEN AND CHORLEYWOOD FOOD RESEARCH ASSOCIATION, Chipping Campden, Glos GL55 6LD. Tel: 01386-842000. *Director-General*, Prof. C. Dennis

CENTRE FOR MARINE AND PETROLEUM TECHNOLOGY, Exploration House, Offshore Technology Park, Aberdeen AB23 8GX. Tel: 01224-853400; 19 Buckingham Street, London WC2N 6EF. Tel: 020-7321 0674; Research Park North, Riccarton, Edinburgh EH14 4AP. Tel: 0131-451 5231. *Chief Executive*, R. Lane-Nott, CB

CERAM RESEARCH (BRITISH CERAMIC RESEARCH LTD), Queen's Road, Penkhull, Stoke-on-Trent ST4 7LQ. Tel: 01782-764444. *Chief Executive*, Dr N. E. Sanderson

CIRIA (CONSTRUCTION INDUSTRY RESEARCH AND INFORMATION ASSOCIATION), 6 Storey's Gate, London SW1P 3AU. Tel: 020-7222 8891. *Director-General*, Dr P. L. Bransby

CRL (*Specialist products, technology licences, research and development*), Dawley Road, Hayes, Middx UB3 1HH. Tel: 020-8848 9779. *Managing Director*, Dr J. White

EA TECHNOLOGY (*Use and distribution of electricity*), Capenhurst, Chester CH1 6ES. Tel: 0151-339 4181. *Chief Executive*, Dr S. F. Exell

ERA TECHNOLOGY LTD (*Electronic, electrical, materials and structural engineering*), Cleeve Road, Leatherhead, Surrey KT22 7SA. Tel: 01372-367000. *Managing Director and Chief Executive*, Prof. M. J. Withers

FIRA INTERNATIONAL LTD (FURNITURE INDUSTRY RESEARCH ASSOCIATION), Maxwell Road, Stevenage, Herts SG1 2EW. Tel: 01438-313433. *Managing Director*, H. Davies

HR WALLINGFORD GROUP LTD (*Hydroinformatics and engineering*), Howbery Park, Wallingford, Oxon OX10 8BA. Tel: 01491-835381. *Chief Executive*, Dr. J. Weare, OBE

LABORATORY OF THE GOVERNMENT CHEMIST, Queens Road, Teddington, Middx TW11 0LY. Tel: 020-8943 7300. *Chief Executive and Government Chemist*, Dr R. Worswick

LEATHERHEAD FOOD RESEARCH ASSOCIATION, Randalls Road, Leatherhead, Surrey KT22 7RY. Tel: 01372-376761. *Director*, Dr M. P. J. Kierstan

LUCAS VARITY, Stratford Road, Solihull, W. Midlands B90 4GW. Tel: 0121-627 4141. *General Manager*, R. Tribe

MATERIALS ENGINEERING RESEARCH LABORATORY LTD, Tamworth Road, Hertford SG13 7DG. Tel: 01992-500120. *Managing Director*, Dr A. Stevenson

MINERAL INDUSTRY RESEARCH ORGANISATION, Expert House, Sandford Street, Lichfield, Staffs WS13 6QA. Tel: 01543-262957. *Director*, N. Roberts

MOTOR INDUSTRY RESEARCH ASSOCIATION, Watling Street, Nuneaton, Warks CV10 0TU. Tel: 024-7635 5000. *Managing Director*, J. R. Wood

MOTOR INSURANCE REPAIR RESEARCH CENTRE, Colthorp Lane, Thatcham, Berks RG19 4NP. Tel: 01635-868855. *Chief Executive*, M. Smith

THE NATIONAL COMPUTING CENTRE LTD, Oxford House, Oxford Road, Manchester M1 7ED. Tel: 0161-228 6333. *Managing Director*, C. Pearse

NATIONAL PHYSICAL LABORATORY, Queens Road, Teddington, Middx TW11 0LW. Tel: 020-8977 3222. *Deputy Director*, Dr A. Wallard

PAINT RESEARCH ASSOCIATION, 8 Waldegrave Road, Teddington, Middx TW11 8LD. Tel: 020-8977 4427. *Managing Director*, J. A. Bernie

PERA GROUP (*Multi-disciplinary research, design, development and consultancy*), Middle Aston House, Middle Aston, Oxon OX6 3PT. Tel: 01869-347755. *Chief Executive*, R. A. Armstrong

PIRA INTERNATIONAL (*Paper and board, printing, publishing and packaging*), Randalls Road, Leatherhead, Surrey KT22 7RU. Tel: 01372-802000. *Managing Director*, M. Hancock

RAPRA TECHNOLOGY LTD (*Rubber and plastics*), Shawbury, Shrewsbury SY4 4NR. Tel: 01939-250383; North East Centre, 18 Belasis Court, Belasis Technology Park, Billingham TS23 4AZ. Tel: 01642-370406. *Chief Executive*, Dr P. Extance

SATRA TECHNOLOGY CENTRE (*Footwear, apparel, safety products and furniture*), Satra House, Rockingham Road, Kettering, Northants NN16 9JH. Tel: 01536-410000. *Chief Executive*, Dr R. E. Whittaker

SIRA LTD (*Measurement, instrumentation, control and optical systems technology*), South Hill, Chislehurst, Kent BR7 5EH. Tel: 020-8467 2636. *Managing Director*, Prof. R. A. Brook

SMITH INSTITUTE (*Mathematics and computing*), PO Box 183, Guildford, Surrey GU2 5GG. Tel: 01483-579108. *Director*, Dr L. Wallen

SPORTS TURF RESEARCH INSTITUTE, St Ives Estate, Bingley, W. Yorks BD16 1AU. Tel: 01274-565131. *Chief Executive*, Dr M. Canaway

STEEL CONSTRUCTION INSTITUTE, Silwood Park, Ascot, Berks SL5 7QN. Tel: 01344-623345. *Director*, Dr G. Owens

TRADA TECHNOLOGY LTD (*Timber and wood-based products*), Chiltern House, Stocking Lane, Hughenden Valley, High Wycombe, Bucks HP14 4ND. Tel: 01494-563091. *Managing Director*, A. Abbott

TRANSPORT RESEARCH LABORATORY, Old Wokingham Road, Crowthorne, Berks RG45 6AU. Tel: 01344-773131. *Chief Executive*, G. Clarke

TWI (*Welding*), Abington Hall, Abington, Cambridge CB1 6AL. Tel: 01223-891162. *Chief Executive*, A. B. M. Braithwaite, OBE

Sports Bodies

Sports Councils
CENTRAL COUNCIL OF PHYSICAL RECREATION, Francis
House, Francis Street, London SW1P 1DE.
Tel: 020-7828 3163; Fax: 020-7630 8820; *General
Secretary*, M. Denton
SPORT ENGLAND, 16 Upper Woburn Place, London
WC1H 0QP. Tel: 020-7273 1500; Fax: 020-7383 5740;
Email: info@english.sports.gov.uk;
Web: http://www.english.sports.gov.uk
Chief Executive, D. Casey. *Chairman*, T. Brooking
SPORTSCOTLAND, Caledonia House, South Gyle,
Edinburgh EH12 9DQ. Tel: 0131-317 7200; Fax:
0131-317 7202; Email: library@sportscotland.org.uk;
Web: http://www.sportscotland.org.uk
Chief Executive, F. A. L. Alstead, CBE. *Chairman*,
A. Dempster
SPORTS COUNCIL FOR NORTHERN IRELAND, House of
Sport, Upper Malone Road, Belfast BT9 5LA.
Tel: 028-9038 1222; Fax: 028-9068 2757;
Web: http://www.sportni.com *Chief Executive*,
E. McCartan. *Chairman*, Prof. E. Saunders
SPORTS COUNCIL FOR WALES, Sophia Gardens, Cardiff
CF11 9SW. Tel: 029-2030 0500; Fax: 029-2030 0600;
Email: scw@scw.co.uk;
Web: http://www.sports-council-wales.co.uk
Chief Executive, Dr H. Jones. *Chairman*, G. Davies
UK SPORTS COUNCIL, 40 Bernard Street, London
WC1N 1LE. Tel: 020-7841 9500; Fax: 020-7841 8850;
Web: http://www.uksport.gov.uk *Chief Executive*,
R. Callicott. *Chairman*, Sir Rodney Walker

Angling
NATIONAL FEDERATION OF ANGLERS, Halliday House,
Egginton Junction, Derbys DE65 6GU.
Tel: 01283-734735; Fax: 01283-734799;
Email: office@nfahq.freeserve.co.uk;
Web: http://www.the.nfa.org.uk *Administration
Manager*, Mrs J. A. Price. *President*, K. W. Ball

Archery
GRAND NATIONAL ARCHERY SOCIETY, Lilleshall National
Sports Centre, Newport, Shropshire TF10 9AT.
Tel: 01952-677888; Fax: 01952-606019. *Chief
Executive*, D. Sherratt. *Chairman*, D. V. Whiteman.
President. M. Shepherd

Association Football
THE FOOTBALL ASSOCIATION, 25 Soho Square, London
W1D 4FA. Tel: 020-7402 7151; Fax: 020-7402 0486.
Chief Executive, A. Crozier. *Chairman*, G. Thompson
FOOTBALL ASSOCIATION OF WALES, Plymouth Chambers,
3 Westgate Street, Cardiff CF10 1DP. Tel: 029-2037
2325; Fax: 029-2034 3961; Email: hburlace@faw.co.uk;
Web: http://www.faw.org.uk *Secretary-General*,
D. G. Collins. *President*, D. W. Shantlin
THE FOOTBALL LEAGUE LTD, Edward VII Quay,
Navigation Way, Preston, Lancs PR2 2YF.
Tel: 01772-325800; Fax: 01772-325801;
Email: fl@football-league.co.uk;
Web: http://www.football-league.co.uk
Secretary, J. D. Dent
IRISH FOOTBALL ASSOCIATION, 20 Windsor Avenue,
Belfast BT9 6EE. Tel: 028-9066 9458; Fax: 028-
9066 7620; Email: enquiries@irishfa.com;
Web: http://www.irishfa.com
General Secretary, D. I. Bowen

IRISH FOOTBALL LEAGUE, 96 University Street, Belfast
BT7 1HE. Tel: 028-9024 2888; Fax: 028-9033 0773;
Email: irishleague@talk21.com.
Secretary, H. Wallace. *President*, J. Semple
SCOTTISH FOOTBALL ASSOCIATION, 6 Park Gardens,
Glasgow G3 7YF. Tel: 0141-332 6372; Fax: 0141-332
7559; Email: info@scottishfa.co.uk;
Web: http://www.scottishfa.co.uk
Chief Executive, D. Taylor. *President*, J. McGinn
SCOTTISH FOOTBALL LEAGUE, 188 West Regent Street,
Glasgow G2 4RY. Tel: 0141-248 3844; Fax: 0141-
221 7450; Email: sfl@sol.co.uk;
Web: http://www.scottishfootball.com
Secretary, P. Donald

Athletics
ATHLETICS ASSOCIATION OF WALES, Catsash Road,
Catsash, Newport NP18 1WA. Tel: 01633-423833;
Fax: 01633-430654; Email: walesathletics@lineone.net;
Chairman, Ms L. Harries
NORTHERN IRELAND ATHLETIC FEDERATION, Athletics
House, Old Coach Road, Belfast BT9 5PR. Tel: 028-9060
2707; Fax: 028-9030 9939; Email: info@niathletics.org;
Web: http://www.niathletics.org *Secretary*, J. Allen.
Chairman, Mrs A. Smyth. *President*. J. McColgan, MBE
SCOTTISH ATHLETICS FEDERATION, Caledonia House,
South Gyle, Edinburgh EH12 9DQ. Tel: 0131-317 7320;
Fax: 0131-317 7321; Web: http://www.saf.org.uk
General Manager, N. F. Park. *President*, Mrs J. Watt.
Chief Executive, D. Joy
UK ATHLETICS, Athletics House, 10 Harborne Road,
Edgbaston, Birmingham B15 3AA. Tel: 0121-456 5098;
Fax: 0121-456 8752;
Email: information@ukathletics.org.uk;
Web: http://www.ukathletics.org
Information Officer, W. Adcocks

Badminton
BADMINTON ASSOCIATION OF ENGLAND LTD, National
Badminton Centre, Bradwell Road, Loughton Lodge,
Milton Keynes MK8 9LA. Tel: 01908-268400;
Fax: 01908-268412; Email: enquiries@baofe.co.uk;
Web: http://www.baofe.co.uk *Chief Executive*,
S. Baddeley. *Chairman*, J. Havers. *President*, W. Andrew
SCOTTISH BADMINTON UNION, Cockburn Centre,
40 Bogmoor Place, Glasgow G51 4TQ.
Tel: 0141-445 1218; Fax: 0141-425 1218;
Email: name@scotbadminton.demon.co.uk;
Web: http://www.scotbadminton.demon.co.uk
Chief Executive, Miss A. Smillie. *Hon. Secretary*,
I. E. Brown
WELSH BADMINTON UNION, Fourth Floor, 3 Westgate
Street, Cardiff CF10 1DP. Tel: 029-2022 2082;
Fax: 029-2039 4282;
Email: welsh@welshbadminton.force9.co.uk;
Web: http://www.welshbadminton.force9.co.uk
Director of Badminton, L. Williams

Baseball
BASEBALLSOFTBALL UK, Ariel House, 74A Charlotte
Street, London W1P 1LR. Tel: 020-7453 7055;
Fax: 020-7453 7007;
Email: info@baseballsoftballuk.com;
Web: http://www.baseballsoftballuk.com
Chief Executive, B. Fromer

Basketball

ENGLISH BASKETBALL ASSOCIATION, 48 Bradford
Road, Stanningley, Leeds LS28 6DF.
Tel: 0113-236 1166; Fax: 0113-236 1022;
Email: ebba@basketballengland.net;
Web: http://www.basketballengland.org.uk
Chief Executive, S. Kirkland. *President*, K. Mitchell, OBE

BASKETBALL SCOTLAND, Caledonia House, South Gyle,
Edinburgh EH12 9DQ. Tel: 0131-317 7260; Fax: 0131-
317 7489; Email: sba@basketball-scotland.com;
Web: http://www.basketball-scotland.com
Chief Executive Officer, Mrs S. F. E. Mason.
Chairman, W. D. McInnes

Billiards

WORLD LADIES BILLIARDS AND SNOOKER ASSOCIATION,
27 Oakfield Road, Clifton, Bristol BS8 2AT. Tel: 0117-
974 4491; Fax: 0117-974 4931. *Company Secretary*,
Ms E. Walker. *Chairman*, M. Wildman

WORLD PROFESSIONAL BILLIARDS AND SNOOKER
ASSOCIATION, 27 Oakfield Road, Clifton, Bristol
BS8 2AT. Tel: 0117-974 4491; Fax: 0117-974 4931;
Email: wsa@wpbsa.com; Web: http://www.wpbsa.com
Chief Executive, P. Middleton. *Chairman*, M. Wildman

Bobsleigh

BRITISH BOBSLEIGH ASSOCIATION, Albany House, 5 New
Street, Salisbury, Wilts SP1 2PH. Tel: 01722-340014;
Fax: 01722-340014; Email: bba@dial.pipex.com;
Web: http://www.british-bobsleigh.com
General Secretary, Ms H. Alderman. *Chairman*,
Maj.-Gen. R. McAgee

Bowls

BRITISH ISLES BOWLS COUNCIL, 2 Pentland Avenue,
Gowkshill, Gorebridge, Midlothian EH23 4PG.
Tel: 01875-821105; Fax: 01875-821105. *Hon. Secretary*,
J. P. Darling. *President*, I. G. Jones

BRITISH ISLES WOMEN'S BOWLING COUNCIL, 2 Case
Gardens, Seaton, Devon EX12 2AP. Tel: 01297-21317;
Fax: 01297-21317. *Hon. Secretary*, Mrs N. Colling, MBE

BRITISH ISLES WOMEN'S INDOOR BOWLS COUNCIL,
Hillcrest Villa, Tynewydd, Treorchy, Rhonda,
Mid Glam. CF42 5LV. Tel: 01443-771618;
Fax: 01443-771618. *Hon. Secretary*, Mrs H. King

ENGLISH BOWLING ASSOCIATION, Lyndhurst Road,
Worthing, W. Sussex BN11 2AZ. Tel: 01903-820222;
Fax: 01903-820444. *Secretary*, G. D. Shaw

ENGLISH INDOOR BOWLING ASSOCIATION, David
Cornwell House, Bowling Green, Leicester Road,
Melton Mowbray, Leics LE13 0DA. Tel: 01664-481900;
Fax: 01664-481901; Email: indoorbowl@aol.com
Secretary, D. N. Brown. *President*, A. E. Horobin

ENGLISH WOMEN'S BOWLING ASSOCIATION, 2 Case
Gardens, Seaton, Devon EX12 2AP. Tel: 01297-21317;
Fax: 01297-21317. *Hon. Secretary*, Mrs N. Colling, MBE.
President, Mrs J. Janes

ENGLISH WOMEN'S INDOOR BOWLING ASSOCIATION,
3 Scirocco Close, Moulton Park, Northampton NN3 6AP.
Tel: 01604-494163; Fax: 01604-494434. *Secretary*,
Mrs M. E. Ruff. *President*, R. Williams

Boxing

THE AMATEUR BOXING ASSOCIATION OF ENGLAND LTD,
Crystal Palace National Sports Centre, London SE19 2BB.
Tel: 020-8778 0251; Fax: 020-8778 9324;
Email: ne@abae.org.uk *General Secretary*, T. Collier.
Chairman, J. Smart

BRITISH AMATEUR BOXING ASSOCIATION, 96 High Street,
Lochee, Dundee DD2 3AY. Tel: 01382-611412;
Chief Executive, F. Hendry

BRITISH BOXING BOARD OF CONTROL LTD, Jack Petersen
House, 52A Borough High Street, London SE1 1XN.
Tel: 020-7403 5879; Fax: 020-7378 6670;
Web: http://www.bbbofc.com
General Secretary, S. J. Block. *President*, L. Read,
QPM. *Chairman*, Lord Brooks of Tremorfa, DL

Canoeing

BRITISH CANOE UNION, John Dudderidge House,
Adbolton Lane, West Bridgford, Nottingham NG2 5AS.
Tel: 0115-982 1100; Fax: 0115-982 1797; Email:
info@bcu.org.uk; Web: http://www.bcu.org.uk
Chief Executive, P. Owen. *Chairman*, D. Gent

Chess

BRITISH CHESS FEDERATION, The Watch Oak, Chain
Lane, Battle, E. Sussex TN33 0YD. Tel: 01424-775222;
Fax: 01424-775904; Email: office@bcf.org.uk;
Web: http://www.bcf.indirect.co.uk
Manager, Mrs G. White

Cricket

ENGLAND AND WALES CRICKET BOARD, Lord's Cricket
Ground, London NW8 8QZ. Tel: 020-7432 1200;
Fax: 020-7289 5619; Web: http://www.ecb.co.uk
Chief Executive, T. Lamb

MCC, Lord's Cricket Ground, London NW8 8QN.
Tel: 020-7289 1611; Fax: 020-7289 9100.
Secretary, R. D. V. Knight. *President*, The Rt. Hon.
The Lord Alexander of Weedon, QC

Croquet

CROQUET ASSOCIATION, c/o The Hurlingham Club,
Ranelagh Gardens, London SW6 3PR.
Tel: 020-7736 3148; Fax: 020-7736 3148;
Email: caoffice@croquet.org.uk;
Web: http://www.croquet.org.uk
Secretary, N. R. Graves. *Chairman*,
D. L. Gaunt. *President*, W. Solomon

Cycling

BRITISH CYCLING FEDERATION, National Cycling Centre,
Stuart Street, Manchester M11 4DQ. Tel: 0161-230 2301;
Fax: 0161-231 0591; Email: info@bcf.uk.com;
Web: http://www.bcf.uk.com
Chief Executive, P. King. *President*, B. Cookson

ROAD TIME TRIALS COUNCIL, 77 Arlington Drive,
Pennington, Leigh, Lancs WN7 3QP.
Tel: 01942-603976; Fax: 01942-262326;
Email: nationalsecretary@rttchq.freeserve.co.uk;
Web: http://www.rttc.org.uk *National Secretary*,
P. Heaton. *Chairman*, P. McGrath

Darts

BRITISH DARTS ORGANISATION, 2 Pages Lane, Muswell
Hill, London N10 1PS. Tel: 020-8883 5544; Fax: 020-
8883 0109; Email: 101776.666@compuserve.com;
Web: http://www.bdodarts.com
General Secretary, O. A. Croft

Equestrianism

BRITISH EQUESTRIAN FEDERATION, National Agricultural
Centre, Stoneleigh Park, Kenilworth, Warks CV8 2RH.
Tel: 024-7669 8871; Fax: 024-7669 8484; Email:
win.shortland@bef.co.uk; Web: http://www.bef.co.uk
Secretary-General, A. Finding. *Chairman and President*,
J. Tulloch

BRITISH HORSE TRIALS ASSOCIATION, National
Agricultural Centre, Stoneleigh Park, Kenilworth,
Warks CV8 2RN. Tel: 024-7669 8856;
Fax: 024-7669 7235; Email: eventing@bhta.co.uk;
Web: http://www.bhta.co.uk
Commercial Director, P. Durrant

Eton Fives
ETON FIVES ASSOCIATION, 3 Bourchier Close, Sevenoaks,
Kent TN13 1PD. Tel: 01732-458775; Fax: 01732-743112;
Email: mike.fenn@etonfives.co.uk;
Web: http://www.etonfives.co.uk *Secretary*,
M. R. Fenn. *Chairman*, M. D. Constantinidi.
President, J. Shortland-Jones

Fencing
BRITISH FENCING ASSOCIATION, 1 Baron's Gate,
33–35 Rothschild Road, London W4 5HT.
Tel: 020-8742 3032; Fax: 020-8742 3033;
Email: british_fencing@compuserve.com;
Web: http://www.britishfencing.com
General Secretary, Miss G. Kenneally

Gliding
BRITISH GLIDING ASSOCIATION, Kimberley House,
Vaughan Way, Leicester LE1 4SE. Tel: 0116-253 1051;
Fax: 0116-251 5939; Email: bga@gliding.co.uk;
Web: http://www.gliding.co.uk *Secretary*, B. Rolfe

Golf
LADIES' GOLF UNION, The Scores, St Andrews, Fife
KY16 9AT. Tel: 01334-475811; Fax: 01334-472818;
Web: http://www.lgu.org *Secretary*, Mrs J. Hall
THE ROYAL AND ANCIENT GOLF CLUB OF ST ANDREWS,
Golf Place, St Andrews, Fife KY16 9JD.
Tel: 01334-472112; Fax: 01334-477580;
Email: thesecretary@randagc.org;
Web: http://www.randa.org *Secretary*, P. Dawson

Greyhound Racing
NATIONAL GREYHOUND RACING CLUB LTD, Twyman
House, 16 Bonny Street, London NW1 9QD. Tel: 020-
7267 9256; Fax: 020-7482 1023; Email: ngrc@clara.net;
Web: http://www.thedogs.co.uk *Chief Executive*,
F. Melville. *Chairman*, J. H. C. Nicholson

Gymnastics
BRITISH GYMNASTICS, Ford Hall, Lilleshall National
Sports Centre, Newport, Shropshire TF10 9NB.
Tel: 01952-820330; Fax: 01952-820621;
Email: info@baga.co.uk; Web: http://www.baga.co.uk
General Secretary, D. Minnery

Hockey
ENGLISH HOCKEY ASSOCIATION, The National Hockey
Stadium, The Stadium, Silbury Boulevard, Milton
Keynes MK9 1HA. Tel: 01908-544644; Fax:
01908-241106; Email: info@englishhockey.org;
Web: http://www.hockeyonline.co.uk *Chief Executive*,
R. F. Wyatt. *President*, Mrs M. Pickersgill
SCOTTISH HOCKEY UNION, 34 Cramond Road North,
Edinburgh EH4 6JD. Tel: 0131-312 8870; Fax: 0131-
312 7829; Email: info@scottish-hockey.org.uk;
Web: http://www.scottish-hockey.org.uk.
Chairman, G. Ralph
WELSH HOCKEY UNION, 80 Woodville Road, Cathays,
Cardiff CF24 4ED. Tel: 029-2023 3257; Fax: 029-
2023 3258; Email: welsh.hockey@whu.softnet.co.uk;
Chairman, A. J. Rookes

Horse-racing
BRITISH HORSERACING BOARD, 42 Portman Square,
London W1H 0EN. Tel: 020-7396 0011; Fax: 020-
7935 3626; Email: info@bhb.co.uk;
Web: http://www.bhb.co.uk *Chief Executive*,
T. Ricketts. *Chairman*, P. Savill
THE JOCKEY CLUB, 42 Portman Square, London W1H 0EN.
Tel: 020-7486 4921; Fax: 020-7935 8703; Email:
info@thejockeyclub.co.uk;
Web: http://www.thejockeyclub.co.uk
Senior Steward, C. Spence.

Ice Hockey
ICE HOCKEY UK, The Galleries of Justice, Shire Hall,
High Pavement, The Lace Market, Nottingham
NG1 1HN. Tel: 0115-915 9204; Fax: 0115-915 1376;
Email: hockey@ukhockey.freeserve.co.uk;
Web: http://www.icehockeyuk.co.uk *Directors*,
J. Anderson; J. Fisher; N. Moraloe; G. Stofan; R. Stirling

Ice Skating
NATIONAL ICE SKATING ASSOCIATION OF THE UK LTD,
First Floor, 114–116 Curtain Road, London EC2A 3AH.
Tel: 020-7613 1188; Fax: 020-7739 2445;
Email: nisa@iceskating.org.uk;
Web: http://www.iceskating.org.uk *Chief Executive*,
R. Gordon. *President*, Ms S. A. Stapleford, OBE

Judo
BRITISH JUDO ASSOCIATION, 7A Rutland Street, Leicester
LE1 1RB. Tel: 0116-255 9669; Fax: 0116-255 9660;
Email: britjudo@aol.com;
Web: http://www.britishjudo.org.uk
Office Manager, Mrs S. Startin

Lacrosse
ENGLISH LACROSSE ASSOCIATION, 4 Western Court,
Bromley Street, Digbeth, Birmingham B9 4AN.
Tel: 0121-773 4422; Fax: 0121-753 0042;
Email: info@englishlacrosse.co.uk;
Web: http://www.englishlacrosse.co.uk
Chief Executive Officer, D. Shuttleworth.
Chair of Executive Committee, Prof. A. Dyer

Lawn Tennis
LAWN TENNIS ASSOCIATION, The Queen's Club, London
W14 9EG. Tel: 020-7381 7000; Fax: 020-7381 3773.
Secretary, J. C. U. James

Martial Arts
MARTIAL ARTS DEVELOPMENT COMMISSION, No 3,
Brockley Cross Business Centre, Endwell Road,
London SE4 2PD. Tel: 020-7639 5005; Fax: 020-
7639 5065; Email: office@madec.org;
Web: http://www.madec.org. *Office Administrator*,
Mrs E. Jewell. *Chairman*, R. Thomas

Motor Sports
BRITISH MOTORCYCLE SPORT LEISURE, ACU House,
Wood Street, Rugby, Warks CV21 2YX. Tel: 01788-
566400; Fax: 01788-573585; Email: admin@acu.org.uk;
Web: http://www.acu.org.uk *Chief Executive*,
G. Wilson. *Chairman*, E. P. Bartlett
BRITISH SUPERBIKES RACE ORGANISATION, Nene House,
Drayton Fields Industrial Estate, Daventry NN11 5PB.
Tel: 01327-876000; Fax: 01327-878114. *Manager*,
D. R. Barnfield
THE MOTOR SPORTS ASSOCIATION, Motor Sports House,
Riverside Park, Colnbrook, Slough SL3 0HG. Tel: 01753-
681736; Fax: 01753-682938;
Email: msa_mail@compuserve.com;
Web: http://www.msauk.org
Chief Executive, J. Quenby
SCOTTISH AUTO CYCLE UNION LTD, Block 2, Unit 6,
Whiteside Industrial Estate, Bathgate, W. Lothian
EH48 2RX. Tel: 01506-630262; Fax: 01506-634972.
Secretary, G. Anderson

Mountaineering

BRITISH MOUNTAINEERING COUNCIL, 177–179 Burton Road, West Didsbury, Manchester M20 2BB. Tel: 0161-445 4747; Fax: 0161-445 4500; Email: members@thebmc.co.uk; Web: http://www.thebmc.co.uk *General Secretary*, R. Payne. *President*, D. Walker

Multi-Sport Bodies

BRITISH OLYMPIC ASSOCIATION, 1 Wandsworth Plain, London SW18 1EH. Tel: 020-8871 2677; Fax: 020-8871 9104; Email: firstname.surname@boa.org.uk; Web: http://www.olympics.org.uk *Chief Executive*, S. Clegg. *Chairman*, C. Reedie
BRITISH UNIVERSITIES SPORTS ASSOCIATION, 8 Union Street, London SE1 1SZ. Tel: 020-7357 8555; Fax: 020-7403 0127; Web: http://www.busa.org.uk *Chief Executive*, G. Gregory-Jones. *Chairman*, A. Odell
COMMONWEALTH GAMES COUNCIL FOR ENGLAND, Tavistock House South, Tavistock Square, London WC1H 9JZ. Tel: 020-7388 6643; Fax: 020-7388 6744; Email: info@cgce.org. Web: http://www.cgce.co.uk *Chief Executive*, Miss A. Hogbin. *Chairman*, I. Emmerson, OBE
COMMONWEALTH GAMES FEDERATION, Walkden House, 3–10 Melton Street, London NW1 2EB. Tel: 020-7383 5596; Fax: 020-7383 5506; Email: commonwealthgamesfederation@btinternet.com; Web: http://www.commonwealthgames-fed.org *Hon. Secretary*, Ms L. Martin. *Chairman*, M. Fennell

Netball

ALL ENGLAND NETBALL ASSOCIATION LTD, Netball House, 9 Paynes Park, Hitchin, Herts SG5 1EH. Tel: 01462-442344; Fax: 01462-442343. *Chief Executive*, Miss C. Alcock. *President*, Mrs J. Jack
NORTHERN IRELAND NETBALL ASSOCIATION, House of Sport, Upper Malone Road, Belfast BT9 5LA. Tel: 028-9038 1222. *Secretary*, Ms K. Harrup
NETBALL SCOTLAND, 24 Ainslie Road, Hillington Business Park, Hillington, Glasgow G52 4RU. Tel: 0141-570 4016; Fax: 0141-570 4017; Email: netballscotland@btinternet.com *Administrator*, D. McLaughlan
WELSH NETBALL ASSOCIATION, 2nd Floor, 33–35 Cathedral Rd, Cardiff CF11 9HB. Tel: 029-2023 7048; Fax: 029-2022 6430; Email: welshnetball@mcmail.com; Web: http://www.welshnetball.org.uk *Chief Executive Officer*, Mrs S. J. Holvey. *President*, Miss P. Nicholas

Orienteering

BRITISH ORIENTEERING FEDERATION, Riversdale, Dale Road North, Darley Dale, Matlock, Derbys DE4 2HX. Tel: 01629-734042; Fax: 01629-733769; Email: bof@bof.cix.co.uk; Web: http://www.cix.co.uk/bof *Secretary-General*, D. Locke

Polo

THE HURLINGHAM POLO ASSOCIATION, Manor Farm, Little Coxwell, Faringdon, Oxfordshire SN7 7LW. Tel: 01367-242828; Fax: 01367-242829; Email: enquiries@hpa-polo.co.uk; Web: http://www.hpa-polo.co.uk *Chief Executive*, D. J. B. Woodd

Rackets and Real Tennis

TENNIS AND RACKETS ASSOCIATION, c/o The Queen's Club, Palliser Road, London W14 9EQ. Tel: 020-7386 3447/8; Fax: 020-7385 7424; Email: cpo@tennis-rackets.net *Chief Executive and Secretary*, Brig. A. D. Myrtle, CB, CBE. *Chairman*, C. J. Swallow. *President*, The Rt. Hon. Lord Aberdare, KBP DL

Rifle Shooting

NATIONAL RIFLE ASSOCIATION, Bisley Camp, Brookwood, Woking, Surrey GU24 0PB. Tel: 01483-797777; Fax: 01483-797285; Email: info@nra.org.uk; Web: http://www.nra.org.uk *Chief Executive*, Col. C. C. C. Cheshire, OBE. *Chairman*, J. A. de Havilland
NATIONAL SMALL-BORE RIFLE ASSOCIATION, Lord Roberts House, Bisley Camp, Brookwood, Woking, Surrey GU24 0NP. Tel: 01483-485500; Fax: 01483-476392; Email: info@nsra.co.uk; Web: http://www.nsra.co.uk *Secretary*, Lt.-Col. J. D. Hoare. *Chairman*, G. D. Pound

Rowing

AMATEUR ROWING ASSOCIATION LTD, The Priory, 6 Lower Mall, London W6 9DJ. Tel: 020-8748 3632; Fax: 020-8741 4658; Web: http://www.ara-rowing.org *National Manager*, Mrs R. Napp
HENLEY ROYAL REGATTA, Regatta Headquarters, Henley-on-Thames, Oxon RG9 2LY. Tel: 01491-572153; Fax: 01491-575509; Web: http://www.hrr.co.uk *Secretary*, R. S. Goddard
SCOTTISH AMATEUR ROWING ASSOCIATION, 71 Gillbrae Crescent, Georgetown, Dumfries DG1 4DJ. Tel: 01387-264233. *Secretary*, G. West

Rugby Fives

RUGBY FIVES ASSOCIATION, The Old Forge, Sutton Valence, Maidstone, Kent ME17 3AW. Tel: 01622-842278; Email: michael.beaman@which.net; Web: http://www.rfa.org.uk *General Secretary*, M. F. Beaman. *President*, P. W. Dunscombe

Rugby League

BRITISH AMATEUR RUGBY LEAGUE ASSOCIATION, West Yorkshire House, 4 New North Parade, Huddersfield HD1 5JP. Tel: 01484-544131; Fax: 01484-519985; Email: info@barla.org.uk; Web: http://www.barla.org.uk *General Manager*, I. Cooper. *Chairman*, T. Parle
THE RUGBY FOOTBALL LEAGUE, Red Hall, Red Hall Lane, Leeds LS17 8NB. Tel: 0113-232 9111; Fax: 0113-232 3666; Email: rfl@rfl.uk.com; Web: http://www.rfl.uk.com *Chief Executive*, P. Haworth. *Chairman*, Sir Rodney Walker

Rugby Union

IRISH RUGBY FOOTBALL UNION, 62 Lansdowne Road, Ballsbridge, Dublin 4. Tel: 00 353-1-647 3800; Fax: 00 353-1-647 3801; Web: http://www.irfu.ie *Chief Executive*, P. R. Browne. *President*, E. J. Coleman
RUGBY FOOTBALL UNION, Rugby House, Rugby Road, Twickenham TW1 1DS. Tel: 020-8892 2000; Fax: 020-8892 9816; Web: www.rfu.com *Chief Executive*, F. Baron. *Chairman of the Management Board*, B. Baister
RUGBY FOOTBALL UNION FOR WOMEN, Newbury Sports Arena, Monks Lane, Newbury RG14 7RW. Tel: 01635-42333; Fax: 01635-43016. *Secretary*, Ms D. Lintonbon

SCOTTISH RUGBY UNION, Murrayfield, Roseburn
Street, Edinburgh EH12 5PJ. Tel: 0131-346 5000;
Fax: 0131-346 5001; Email: feedback@sru.org.uk;
Web: http://www.sru.org.uk
Chief Executive, W. S. Watson. *Secretary*, I. A. L. Hogg
SCOTTISH WOMEN'S RUGBY UNION, Flat 3, 108 Comiston
Road, Edinburgh EH10 5QL. Tel: 0131-557 5663; Fax:
0131-556 7379; Email: barb@shawltd.demon.co.uk
Chairwoman, Miss B. Wilson
WELSH RUGBY UNION, Custom House, Custom House
Street, Cardiff CF10 1RF. Tel: 029-2078 1700;
Fax: 029-2022 5601; Web: http://www.wru.co.uk
Secretary, D. Gethin. *Chairman*, G. S. Griffiths.
President IR Tasker Watkins, VCP GBE DL

Shooting
CLAY PIGEON SHOOTING ASSOCIATION LTD, Earlstrees
Court, Earlstrees Road, Corby, Northants NN17 4AX.
Tel: 01536-443566; Fax: 01536-443438. *Director*,
E. G. Orduna

Skiing
BRITISH SKI AND SNOWBOARD FEDERATION, Hillend,
Biggar Road, Midlothian EH10 7EF. Tel: 0131-445 7676;
Fax: 0131-445 7722; Email: britski@easynet.co.uk;
Web: http://www.complete-skier.com
Operations Director, Ms F. McLean

Snooker
WORLD LADIES BILLIARDS AND SNOOKER ASSOCIATION,
27 Oakfield Road, Clifton, Bristol BS8 2AT. Tel: 0117-
974 4491; Fax: 0117-974 4931; Email: wsa@wpbsa.com;
Web: http://www.wpbsa.com *Company Secretary*,
Ms E. Walker. *Chairman*, Ms M. Fisher
WORLD PROFESSIONAL BILLIARDS AND SNOOKER
ASSOCIATION, 27 Oakfield Road, Clifton, Bristol
BS8 2AT. Tel: 0117-974 4491; Fax: 0117-974 4931;
Email: wsa@wpbsa.com; Web: http://www.wpbsa.com
Chief Executive, P. Middleton

Speedway
SPEEDWAY CONTROL BOARD LTD, ACU Headquarters,
Wood Street, Rugby, Warks CV21 2YX. Tel: 01788-
565603; Fax: 01788-552308. *General Secretary*, R. Allan.
Chairman, J. Quenby

Squash Rackets
SCOTTISH SQUASH, Caledonia House, South Gyle,
Edinburgh EH12 9DQ. Tel: 0131-317 7343; Fax: 0131-
317 7734. *Secretary*, N. Brydon. *President*, A. McCue
SQUASH RACKETS ASSOCIATION, Ground Floor, Bellevue
Athletics Centre, Pink Bank Lane, Manchester M12 5GL.
Tel: 0161-231 4499; Fax: 0161-231 4231; Email:
sra@squash.uk.com; Web: http://www.squash.co.uk
Chief Executive, S. H. Courtney. *President*, J. Barrington
SQUASH WALES, St Mellons Country Club, St Mellons,
Cardiff CF3 2XR. Fax: 01633-680998; Email:
squash.wales@tesco.net *Administrator*, Ms D. Selley.
Chairman, D. Jenkins. *President*. James

Sub-Aqua
BRITISH SUB-AQUA CLUB, Telfords Quay, South Pier
Road, Ellesmere Port, Cheshire CH65 4FL.
Tel: 0151-350 6200; Fax: 0151-350 6215;
Email: postmaster@bsac.com;
Web: http://www.bsac.com
Chairman, P. Harrison

Swimming
AMATEUR SWIMMING ASSOCIATION, Harold Fern House,
Derby Square, Loughborough, Leics LE11 5AL.
Tel: 01509-618700; Fax: 01509-618701;
Email: cserv@asagb.org.uk *Chief Executive*,
D. Sparkes

SCOTTISH AMATEUR SWIMMING ASSOCIATION, Holmhills
Farm, Greenlees Road, Cambuslang, Glasgow
G72 8DT. Tel: 0141-641 8818; Fax: 0141-641 4443;
Email: scotswim@aol.com *Chief Executive*, P. Bush
WELSH AMATEUR SWIMMING ASSOCIATION, Roath Park
House, Ninian Road, Cardiff CF23 5ER.
Tel: 029-2048 8820; Fax: 029-2048 8820;
Email: brynwilliams@welshasa.co.uk;
Web: http://www.welshasa.co.uk
Director of Swimming, B. Williams. *Chairman*,
G. Robins

Table Tennis
ENGLISH TABLE TENNIS ASSOCIATION, Queensbury
House, Havelock Road, Hastings, E. Sussex TN34 1HF.
Tel: 01424-722525; Fax: 01424-422103;
Email: admin@ettahq.freeserve.co.uk;
Web: http://www.etta.co.uk
Chief Executive, R. Yule. *Chairman*, A. E. Ransome OBE

Volleyball
ENGLISH VOLLEYBALL ASSOCIATION, 27 South Road,
West Bridgford, Nottingham NG2 7AG.
Tel: 0115-981 6324; Fax: 0115-981 5429;
Email: general@eng-volleyball.demon.co.uk
Chief Executive Officer, T. Ojasoo
SCOTTISH VOLLEYBALL ASSOCIATION, 48 The Pleasance,
Edinburgh EH8 9TJ. Tel: 0131-556 4633; Fax: 0131-
557 4314; Email: sva@callnetuk.com
Director, N. S. Moody

Walking
RACE WALKING ASSOCIATION, Hufflers, Heard's Lane,
Shenfield, Brentwood, Essex CM15 0SF.
Tel: 01277-220687; Fax: 01277-212380;
Email: peter.cassidy@btinternet.com; *Hon. General
Secretary*, P. J. Cassidy. *President*, R. Holland

Water Skiing
BRITISH WATER SKI FEDERATION, 390 City Road,
London EC1V 2QA. Tel: 020-7833 2855;
Fax: 020-7837 2855; Email: info@bwsf.co.uk;
Web: http://www.britishwaterski.co.uk
Executive Officer, Ms G. Hill

Weightlifting
BRITISH AMATEUR WEIGHTLIFTERS ASSOCIATION
(BAWLA), 131 Hurst Street, Oxford OX4 1HE.
Tel: 01865-200339; Fax: 01865-790096;
Email: jane@bawla.com; Web: http://www.bawla.com
Chief Executive, S. Cannon. *President*, H. Binder.
Chairman. Barton

Wrestling
BRITISH AMATEUR WRESTLING ASSOCIATION, 41 Great
Clowes Street, Salford, Manchester M7 1RQ.
Tel: 0161-832 9209; Fax: 0161-833 1120;
Web: http://www.britishwrestling.org
Chairman, M. Morley. *Treasurer*, S. McNeil

Yachting
ROYAL YACHTING ASSOCIATION, RYA House, Romsey
Road, Eastleigh, Hants SO50 9YA. Tel: 023-8062 7400;
Fax: 023-8062 9924; Email: admin@rya.org.uk;
Web: http://www.rya.org.uk
Acting Secretary-General, W. Anderson.
Chairman, K. Ellis

Clubs

LONDON CLUBS

ALPINE CLUB (1857), 55 Charlotte Road, London
EC2A 3QF. Tel: 020-7613 0755; Fax: 020-7613 0755;
Email: sec@alpine-club.org.uk;
Web: http:// www.alpine-club.org.uk; *Hon. Secretary*,
G. D. Hughes

AMERICAN WOMEN'S CLUB (1899), 68 Old Brompton
Road, London SW7 3LQ. Tel: 020-7589 8292; Fax: 020-
7283 9006; Email: mail@awc-london.demon.co.uk;
Web: http://www.london.fawco.org;
President, T. Erzmoneit

ANGLO-BELGIAN CLUB (1955), 60 Knightsbridge,
London SW1X 7LF. Tel: 020-7235 2121; Fax: 020-7245
9470; *Secretary*, P. Bresnan

ARMY AND NAVY CLUB (1837), 36 Pall Mall, London
SW1Y 5JN. Tel: 020-7930 9721; Fax: 020-7930 9720;
Email: secretary@therag.co.uk;
Web: http://www.armynavyclub.co.uk;
Secretary, Cdr. J. A. Holt, BE, RN

ARTS CLUB (1863), 40 Dover Street, London W1X 3RB.
Tel: 020-7499 8581; Fax: 020-7409 0913; *Secretary*,
I. Campbell

THE ATHENAEUM (1824), 107 Pall Mall, London
SW1Y 5ER. Tel: 020-7930 4843; Fax: 020-7839 4114;
Acting Secretary, J. Ford

AUTHORS' CLUB (1892), 40 Dover Street, London
W1X 3RB. Tel: 020-7499 8581; Fax: 020-7409 0913;
Club Secretary, Mrs A. de la Grange

BEEFSTEAK CLUB (1876), 9 Irving Street, London WC2H
7AT. Tel: 020-7930 5722; Fax: 020-7925 2325; *Secretary*,
Sir John Lucas-Tooth, Bt.

BROOKS'S (1764), St James's Street, London SW1A 1LN.
Tel: 020-7493 4411; Fax: 020-7499 3736; *Secretary*,
G. Snell

BUCK'S CLUB (1919), 18 Clifford Street, London
W1X 1RG. Tel: 020-7734 6896; Fax: 020-7287 2097;
Email: secretary@bucksclub.co.uk; *Secretary*,
Capt. P. G. J. Murison, RN

CALEDONIAN CLUB (1891), 9 Halkin Street, London
SW1X 7DR. Tel: 020-7235 5162; Fax: 020-7235 4635;
Email: secy@caledonian-club.org.uk;
Web: http://www.caledonian-club.org.uk;
Secretary, P. J. Varney

CANNING CLUB (1910), 4 St James's Square, London
SW1Y 4JU. Tel: 020-7827 5757; Fax: 020-7827 5758;
Email: canningclub@compuserve.com;
Secretary, T. M. Harrington

CARLTON CLUB (1832), 69 St James's Street, London
SW1A 1PJ. Tel: 020-7493 1164; Fax: 020-7495 4090;
Email: secretary@carltonclub.co.uk; Web: http://
www.carltonclub.co.uk; *Secretary*, A. E. Telfer

CAVALRY AND GUARDS CLUB (1893), 127 Piccadilly,
London W1V 0PX. Tel: 020-7499 1261; Fax: 020-7495
5956; *Secretary*, Cdr. I. R. Wellesley-Harding, RN

CHELSEA ARTS CLUB (1891), 143 Old Church Street,
London SW3 6EB. Tel: 020-7376 3311; Fax: 020-7351
5986; *Secretary*, D. Winterbottom

CITY LIVERY CLUB (1914), 20 Aldermanbury, London
EC2V 7HP. Tel: 020-7814 0200; Fax: 020-7814 0201;
Hon. Secretary, W. C. Hammond

CITY OF LONDON CLUB (1832), 19 Old Broad Street,
London EC2N 1DS. Tel: 020-7588 7991; Fax: 020-7374
2020; Email: cityclub@dial.pipex.com; *Secretary*,
G. Jones

CITY UNIVERSITY CLUB (1895), 50 Cornhill, London
EC3V 3PD. Tel: 020-7626 8571; Fax: 020-7626 8572;
Email: secretary@city-university-club.demon.co.uk;
Web: http://www.city-university-club.demon.co.uk;
Secretary, Miss R. C. Graham

DEN NORSKE KLUB LTD (1887), In Out, 4 St James's
Square, London SW1Y 4JU. Tel: 020-7839 6242;
Fax: 020-7930 7946;
Web: http://www.dennorskeklub.co.uk;
Secretary, M. Børud Kamark

EAST INDIA CLUB (1849), 16 St James's Square, London
SW1Y 4LH. Tel: 020-7930 1000; Fax: 020-7321 0217;
Email: eastindi@globalnet.co.uk; *Secretary*, M. Howell

FARMERS CLUB (1842), 3 Whitehall Court, London
SW1A 2EL. Tel: 020-7930 3751; Fax: 020-7839 7864;
Secretary, Gp Capt. G. P. Carson

FLYFISHERS' CLUB (1884), 69 Brook Street, London
W1Y 2ER. Tel: 020-7629 5958; *Secretary*,
Cdr. T. H. Boycott, OBE, RN

GARRICK CLUB (1831), 15 Garrick Street, London
WC2E 9AY. Tel: 020-7379 6478; Fax: 020-7379 5966;
Secretary, M. J. Harvey

GREEN ROOM CLUB (1877), 17 Mercer Street, London
WC2H 9QR. Tel: 020-7836 7453; Fax: 020-7836 8073;
Email: greenroom1878@netscapeonline.co.uk;
Secretary, D. Lamden

HURLINGHAM CLUB (1869), Ranelagh Gardens, London
SW6 3PR. Tel: 020-7736 8411; Fax: 020-7731 1289;
Email: membership@hurlinghamclub.org.uk;
Secretary, P. H. Covell

THE KENNEL CLUB (1873), 1–5 Clarges Street, London
W1Y 8AB. Tel: 0870-606 6750; Fax: 020-7518 1058;
Email: info@the-kennel-club.org.uk; Web: http://
www.the-kennel-club.org.uk; *Chief Executive*,
R. French

LANSDOWNE CLUB (1934), 9 Fitzmaurice Place, London
W1X 6JD. Tel: 020-7629 7200; Fax: 020-7408 0246;
Email: info@lansdowne-club.co.uk;
Web: http://www.lansdowne-club.co.uk;
Secretary, M. Anderson

LONDON ROWING CLUB (1856), Embankment, Putney,
London SW15 1LB. Tel: 020-8788 1400; Fax: 020-8874
9056; Email: metregatta@compuserve.com;
Web: http://www.londonrc.org.uk;
Hon. Secretary, N. A. Smith

MCC (MARYLEBONE CRICKET CLUB) (1787), Lord's
Cricket Ground, London NW8 8QN. Tel: 020-7289 1611;
Fax: 020-7289 9100; Web: http://www.lords.org;
Secretary, R. D. V. Knight

THE NATIONAL CLUB (1845), c/o Carlton Club, 69
St James's Street, London SW1A 1PJ. Tel: 020-7493 1164;
Hon. Secretary, I. A. Sowton

NATIONAL LIBERAL CLUB (1882), Whitehall Place,
London SW1A 2HE. Tel: 020-7930 9871; Fax:
020-7839 4768; Web: http://www.nlc.org.uk;
Secretary, S. J. Roberts

NAVAL AND MILITARY CLUB (1862), 4 St James's Square,
London SW1Y 4JU. Tel: 020-7827 5757;
Fax: 020-7827 5758; *Secretary*, M. G. G. Ebbitt

NAVAL CLUB (1946), 38 Hill Street, London W1X 8DP.
Tel: 020-7493 7672; Fax: 020-7629 7995;
Email: reservations@navalclub.co.uk;
Web: http://www.navalclub.co.uk;
Chief Executive, Cdr. J. L. L. Prichard
NEW CAVENDISH CLUB (1920), 44 Great Cumberland
Place, London W1H 8BS. Tel: 020-7723 0391; Fax: 020-
7262 8411; *General Manager*, J. P. Dauvergne
ORIENTAL CLUB (1824), Stratford House, Stratford Place,
London W1N 0ES. Tel: 020-7629 5126; Fax: 020-7629
0494; Email: sec@orientalclub.org.uk; *Secretary*,
S. C. Doble
PORTLAND CLUB (1816), 69 Brook Street, London
W1Y 2ER. Tel: 020-7499 1523; *Secretary*, J. Burns, CBE
PRATT'S CLUB (1841), 14 Park Place, London SW1A 1LP.
Tel: 020-7493 0397; Fax: 020-7499 3736; *Secretary*,
G. Snell
THE QUEEN'S CLUB (1886), Palliser Road, London
W14 9EQ. Tel: 020-7385 3421; Fax: 020-7386 3425;
Email: admin@queensclub.co.uk;
Web: http://www.queensclub.co.uk; *Secretary*,
J. A. S. Edwardes
RAILWAY CLUB (1899), Room 208, 25 Marylebone Road,
London NW1 5JS. Tel: 01737-812175; *Hon. Secretary*,
A. G. Wells
REFORM CLUB (1836), 104–105 Pall Mall, London
SW1Y 5EW. Tel: 020-7930 9374; Fax: 020-7930 1857;
Email: reform.club@msn.com; *Secretary*,
R. A. M. Forrest
ROYAL AIR FORCE CLUB (1918), 128 Piccadilly, London
W1V 0PY. Tel: 020-7399 1000; Fax: 020-7355 1516;
Email: admin@rafclub.org.uk;
Web: http://www.rafclub.org.uk;
Secretary, P. N. Owen
ROYAL OCEAN RACING CLUB (1925), 20 St James's Place,
London SW1A 1NN. Tel: 020-7493 2248; Fax: 020-7493
5252; Email: rorc@saintjames.demon.co.uk;
Web: http://www.rorc.org;
General Manager, D. J. Minords, OBE
ROYAL OVER-SEAS LEAGUE (1910), Over-Seas House,
Park Place, St James's Street, London SW1A 1LR.
Tel: 020-7408 0214; Fax: 020-7499 6738;
Email: info@rosl.org.uk; Web: http://www.rosl.org.uk;
Director-General, R. F. Newell
SAVAGE CLUB (1857), 1 Whitehall Place, London
SW1A 2HD. Tel: 020-7930 8118; Fax: 020-7839 4768;
Hon. Secretary, The Ven. B. H. Lucas, CB
SAVILE CLUB (1868), 69 Brook Street, London W1Y 2ER.
Tel: 020-7629 5462; Fax: 020-7499 7087;
Email: admin@savileclub.co.uk;
Web: http://www.savileclub.co.uk;
Secretary, N. Storey
SKI CLUB OF GREAT BRITAIN (1903), The White House,
57–63 Church Road, Wimbledon SW19 5DQ.
Tel: 020-8410 2000; Fax: 020-8410 2001; Email:
skiers@skiclub.co.uk; Web: http:// www.skiclub.co.uk;
Managing Director, Ms C. Stuart-Taylor
THAMES ROWING CLUB (1860), Embankment, Putney,
London SW15 1LB. Tel: 020-8788 0798; Fax: 020-8788
0798; Email: info@thamesrc.demon.co.uk; Web:
http://www.thamesrc.demon.co.uk; *Hon. Secretary*,
J. R. Elder
TRAVELLERS CLUB (1819), 106 Pall Mall, London
SW1Y 5EP. Tel: 020-7930 8688; Fax: 020-7930 2019;
Email: secretary@thetravellersclub.org.uk;
Web: http://www.csma.org.uk; *Secretary*, M. S. Allcock
TURF CLUB (1868), 5 Carlton House Terrace, London
SW1Y 5AQ. Tel: 020-7930 8555; *Secretary*, Lt. Col. O. R.
StJ Breakwell, MBE

UNIVERSITY WOMEN'S CLUB (1886), 2 Audley Square,
South Audley Street, London W1Y 6DB.
Tel: 020-7499 2268; Fax: 020-7499 7046;
Email: uwc@globalnet.co.uk;
Web: http://www.the-university-womens-club.co.uk;
Acting Secretary, Ms S. McCue
VICTORY SERVICES CLUB (1907), 63–79 Seymour Street,
London W2 2HF. Tel: 020-7723 4474; Fax: 020-7402
9496; Email: res@vsc.co.uk; Web: http://
www.vsc.co.uk; *General Manager*, G. F. Taylor
WHITE'S (1693), 37–38 St James's Street, London
SW1A 1JG. Tel: 020-7493 6671; Fax: 020-7495 6674;
Secretary, D. A. Anderson

CLUBS OUTSIDE LONDON AND YACHT CLUBS

THE ATHENAEUM (1797), Church Alley, Liverpool
L1 3DD. Tel: 0151-709 7770; Fax: 0151-709 0418;
Email: library@athena.force9.net; *Secretary*,
B. H. Denton
BATH AND COUNTY CLUB (1858), Queen's Parade,
Bath BA1 2NJ. Tel: 01225-423732; Fax: 01225-423732;
Email: secretary@bathandcountyclub.com;
Web: http://www.bathandcountyclub.com;
Secretary, R. M. Lockert
BEMBRIDGE SAILING CLUB (1886), Embankment Road,
Bembridge, IOW PO35 5NR. Tel: 01983-872237;
Fax: 01983-874950; Email: bsc@clara.net;
Web: http://home.clara.net/bsc/index.html;
Secretary, Lt.-Col. M. J. Samuelson, RM
CARDIFF AND COUNTY CLUB (1866), Westgate Street,
Cardiff CF1 1DA. Tel: 029-2022 0846; Fax: 029-2037
3393; *Hon. Secretary*, Cdr J. E. Payn, RD
CHICHESTER YACHT CLUB (1965), Chichester Yacht
Basin, Birdham, Chichester, W. Sussex PO20 7EJ.
Tel: 01243-512918; Fax: 01243-512627; Email:
secretary@cyc.co.uk; Web: http://www.cyc.co.uk;
Secretary, I. M. Clarke
CLIFTON CLUB (1882), 22 The Mall, Clifton, Bristol BS8
4DS. Tel: 0117-973 5527; Fax: 0117-974 3910;
Email: cliftonclub@hotmail.com; *Secretary*,
M. G. M. Henry
THE COUNTY CLUB, 158 High Street, Guildford
GU1 3HJ. Tel: 01483-560677; Fax: 01483-560677;
Hon. Secretary, R. W. D. Hemingway
ESSEX YACHT CLUB (1890), HQS Bembridge, Foreshore,
Leigh-on-Sea, Essex SS9 1BD. Tel: 01702-478404;
Email: peter.brooker@virgin.net; Web:
http://www.sailinginleigh.com; *Hon. Secretary*,
Ms L. Kelly
FREWEN CLUB (1869), 98 St Aldate's, Oxford OX1 1BT.
Tel: 01865-243816; *Hon. Secretary*, B. R. Boyt
HOVE CLUB (1882), 28 Fourth Avenue, Hove, E. Sussex
BN3 2PJ. Tel: 01273-730872; Fax: 01273-732481;
Secretary, G. J. L. Gordon
THE KINGSWAY CLUB (1868), Lightfoot Institute,
Kingsway, Bishop Auckland, Co. Durham DL14 7JN.
Tel: 01388-603219; *Hon. Secretary*, D. McAvoy
THE LEEDS CLUB (1849), 3 Albion Place, Leeds LS1 6JL.
Tel: 0113-242 1591; Fax: 0113-245 0755;
Administrator, Mrs I. Sigsworth
NEW CLUB (1874), 2 Montpellier Parade, Cheltenham
GL50 1UD. Tel: 01242-523285; *Hon. Secretary*,
N. S. Parrack
THE NORFOLK CLUB (1770), 17 Upper King Street,
Norwich NR3 1RB. Tel: 01603-610652; *Secretary*,
G. G. Hardaker

NORTH BAILEY CLUB (1842), 24 North Bailey, Durham DH1 3EW. Tel: 0191-384 3724; Fax: 0191-384 7060; Email: Durham-Union.Society@durham.ac.uk; Web: http://www.dur.ac.uk/DUS/; *Permanent Secretary*, Mrs E. M. Hardcastle

NORTHAMPTON AND COUNTY CLUB (1873), George Row, Northampton NN1 1DF. Tel: 01604-632962; *Secretary*, D. J. Harrop

NORTHERN CONSTITUTIONAL CLUB (1882), 37 Pilgrim Street, Newcastle upon Tyne NE1 6QE. Tel: 0191-232 0884; *Hon. Secretary*, D. Blake

NORTHERN COUNTIES CLUB (1880), 24 Bishop Street, Londonderry BT48 6PP. Tel: 028-7126 2012; *Hon. Secretary*, N. Dykes

OLD BOYS' AND PARK GREEN CLUB (1771), 7 Churchside, Macclesfield, Cheshire SK10 1HG. Tel: 01625-423292; *Hon. Secretary*, J. G. P. van der Feltz

PAIGNTON CLUB (1882), The Esplanade, Paignton, Devon TQ4 6ED. Tel: 01803-559682; Fax: 01803-559043; Email: pgrafton@freenet.co.uk; *Hon. Secretary*, P. Grafton

PARKSTONE YACHT CLUB (1895), Pearce Avenue, Poole, Dorset BH14 8EH. Tel: 01202-743610; Fax: 01202-716394; Email: office@parkstoneyc.co.uk; Web: http://www.parkstoneyc.co.uk; *General Manager*, M. Simms

PENARTH YACHT CLUB (1880), The Esplanade, Penarth, Vale of Glam CF64 3AU. Tel: 029-2070 8196; *Hon. Secretary*, R. S. McGregor

PHYLLIS COURT CLUB (1906), Marlow Road, Henley-on-Thames, Oxon RG9 2HT. Tel: 01491-570500; Fax: 01491-570528; Email: phyllis@globalnet.co.uk; Web: http://www.phylliscourt.co.uk; *Secretary*, R. Edwards

THE POOLE YACHT CLUB (1865), New Harbour Road West, Hamworthy, Poole, Dorset BH15 4AQ. Tel: 01202-672687; Fax: 01202-661174; *Secretary/ Manager*, Miss L. Clark

REGNUM CLUB (1862), 45A South Street, Chichester, W. Sussex PO19 1DS. Tel: 01243-780219; *Hon. Secretary*, A. H. Murray

ROYAL CANOE CLUB (1866), Trowlock Island, Teddington, Middx TW11 9QZ. Tel: 020-8977 5269; Fax: 020-8977 5269; Email: dawdy@btinternet.com; *Hon. Secretary*, Mrs J. S. Evans

ROYAL CHANNEL ISLANDS YACHT CLUB (1862), Le Mont du Boulevard, St Aubin, Jersey JE3 8AD. Tel: 01534-745783; Fax: 01534-490042; Email: rciyc@localdial.com; *Hon. Secretary*, B. Murray

ROYAL CORINTHIAN YACHT CLUB (1872), The Quay, Burnham-on-Crouch, Essex CM0 8AX. Tel: 01621-782105; Fax: 01621-784965; *Hon. Secretary*, D. Horn

ROYAL DART YACHT CLUB (1866), Priory Street, Kingswear, Dartmouth, Devon TQ6 0AB. Tel: 01803-752272; Fax: 01803-752496; *Hon. Secretary*, J. Crozier

ROYAL HARWICH YACHT CLUB (1843), Woolverstone, Ipswich IP9 1AT. Tel: 01473-780319; Email: secretary@rhyc.demon.co.uk; Web: http://www.rhyc.demon.co.uk; *Secretary*, Cdr. J. A. Adams, RD

ROYAL LYMINGTON YACHT CLUB (1922), Bath Road, Lymington, Hants SO41 3SE. Tel: 01590-672677; Fax: 01590-671642; Email: sail@rlymyc.org.uk; Web: http://www.rlymyc.org.uk; *Secretary*, I. Gawn

ROYAL MERSEY YACHT CLUB (1844), Bedford Road East, Rock Ferry, Birkenhead, Merseyside CH42 1LS. Tel: 0151-645 3204; *Hon. Secretary*, P. A. Bastow

ROYAL NAVAL CLUB AND ROYAL ALBERT YACHT CLUB (1867), 17 Pembroke Road, Portsmouth PO1 2NT. Tel: 023-9282 4491; Fax: 023-9287 5009; *Secretary*, Cdr. P. Bolas

ROYAL NORFOLK AND SUFFOLK YACHT CLUB (1859), Royal Plain, Lowestoft, Suffolk NR33 0AQ. Tel: 01502-566726; Fax: 01502-517981; Email: rnsyc@ctc-net.co.uk; *Manager and General Secretary*, B. Falat

ROYAL PLYMOUTH CORINTHIAN YACHT CLUB (1877), Madeira Road, Plymouth PL1 2NY. Tel: 01752-664327; Fax: 01752-256140; Email: secretary@rpcyc.demon.co.uk; Web: http://www.rpcyc.demon.co.uk

ROYAL SOLENT YACHT CLUB (1878), Yarmouth, IOW PO41 0NS. Tel: 01983-760256; Fax: 01983-761172; Email: royal_solentyc@compuserve.com; *Secretary*, Mrs S. Tribe

ROYAL SOUTHAMPTON YACHT CLUB, 1 Channel Way, Ocean Village, Southampton SO14 3QF. Tel: 023-8022 3352; Fax: 023-8033 0613; Email: rsyc@rsyc.org.uk; *Secretary*, A. M. Paterson

ROYAL SOUTHERN YACHT CLUB (1837), Rope Walk, Hamble, Southampton; SO31 4HB. Tel: 023-8045 0300; Fax: 023-8045 0210; *Secretary*, M. G. Long, TD

ROYAL TEMPLE YACHT CLUB (1857), 6 Westcliff Mansions, Ramsgate, Kent CT11 9HY. Tel: 01843-591766; Fax: 01843-583211; Email: info@rtyc.com; Web: http://www.rtyc.com; *Hon. Secretary*, Maj. B. A. Cook

ROYAL THAMES YACHT CLUB (1775), 60 Knightsbridge, London SW1X 7LF. Tel: 020-7235 2121; Fax: 020-7245 9470; Email: club@royalthames.com; Web: http://www.royalthames.com; *Secretary*, Capt. D Goldson, RN

ROYAL TORBAY YACHT CLUB (1863), 12 Beacon Terrace, Torquay, Devon TQ1 2BH. Tel: 01803-292006; Fax: 01803-200297; Email: admin@royaltorbayyc.org.uk; Web: http://www.royaltorbayyc.org.uk/royaltorbayyc; *Secretary*, R. M. Porteous

ROYAL ULSTER YACHT CLUB (1866), 101 Clifton Road, Bangor, Co. Down BT20 5HY. Tel: 028-9127 0568; Fax: 028-9127 3525; Email: ruyc@btinternet.com; *Secretary and Manager*, Ms J. S. Wilson

ROYAL WELSH YACHT CLUB (1847), Porth-Yr-Aur, Caernarfon, LL55 1SN. Tel: 01286-672599; *Commodore*, Mrs C. Sotherland

ROYAL WINDERMERE YACHT CLUB (1860), Fallbarrow Road, Bowness-on-Windermere, Windermere, Cumbria LA23 3DJ. Tel: 015394-43106; *Hon. Secretary*, Mrs F. Bentley

ROYAL YACHT SQUADRON (1815), The Castle, Cowes, IOW PO31 7QT. Tel: 01983-292191; Fax: 01983-200253; Email: rys@btinternet.com; Web: http://www.rys.org.uk; *Secretary*, Maj. R. P. Rising, RM

STOURBRIDGE OLD EDWARDIAN CLUB (1898), Drury Lane, Stourbridge, W. Midlands DY8 1BL. Tel: 01384-395635; *Hon. Secretary*, Dr P. M. Mason

THAMES ESTUARY YACHT CLUB (1895), 3 The Leas, Westcliff-on-Sea, Essex SS0 7ST. Tel: 01702-345967; Email: djb64b@aol.com; Web: http://www.dowden.demon.co.uk/teyc/; *Hon. Secretary*, D. G. Brown

VICTORIA CLUB (1853), Beresford Street, St Helier, Jersey JE2 4WN. Tel: 01534-723381; Fax: 01534-874700; Email: victoriaclub@jerseymail.co.uk; *Secretary*, C. J. Blackstone

PRESIDENTS OF THE ROYAL SOCIETY

The Royal Society received a charter from Charles II on 22 April 1662, when it was incorporated as a body politic and corporate under the appellation of The President, Council and Fellowship of the Royal Society of London, for improving Natural Knowledge.

Year appointed	Name	Year appointed	Name
1662	Viscount Brouncker (?1620–84)	1871	Sir George Biddell Airy (1801–92)
1677	Sir Joseph Williamson (1633–1701)	1873	Sir Joseph Dalton Hooker (1817–1911)
1680	Sir Christopher Wren (1632–1723)	1878	William Spottiswoode (1825–83)
1682	Sir John Hoskins, Bt. (1634–1705)	1883	Thomas Henry Huxley (1825–95)
1683	Sir Cyril Wyche (?1632–1707)	1885	Sir George Stokes, Bt. (1819–1903)
1684	Samuel Pepys (1633–1703)	1890	Lord Kelvin (1824–1907)
1686	Earl of Carbery (1640–1712/13)	1895	Lord Lister (1827–1912)
1689	Earl of Pembroke (1656–1732/3)	1900	Sir William Huggins (1824–1910)
1690	Sir Robert Southwell (1635–1702)	1905	Lord Rayleigh (1842–1919)
1695	Earl of Halifax (1661–1715)	1908	Sir Archibald Geikie (1835–1924)
1698	Lord Somers (1652–1716)	1913	Sir William Crookes (1832–1919)
1703	Sir Isaac Newton (1642–1727)	1915	Sir Joseph John Thomson (1856–1940)
1727	Sir Hans Sloane, Bt. (1660–1753)	1920	Sir Charles Scott Sherrington (1857–1952)
1741	Martin Folkes (1690–1754)	1925	Lord Rutherford (1871–1937)
1752	Earl of Macclesfield (1697–1764)	1930	Sir Frederick Gowland Hopkins (1861–1947)
1764	Earl of Morton (1702–68)	1935	Sir William Henry Bragg (1862–1942)
1768	Sir James Burrow (1701–82)	1940	Sir Henry Dale (1875–1968)
1768	James West (?1704–72)	1945	Sir Robert Robinson (1886–1975)
1772	Sir John Pringle, Bt. (1707–82)	1950	Lord Adrian (1889–1977)
1778	Sir Joseph Banks, Bt. (1743–1820)	1955	Sir Cyril Hinshelwood (1897–1967)
1820	William Hyde Wollaston (1766–1828)	1960	Lord Florey (1898–1968)
1820	Sir Humphrey Davy, Bt. (1778–1829)	1965	Lord Blackett (1897–1974)
1827	Davies Gilbert (1767–1839)	1970	Sir Alan Hodgkin (1914–)
1830	Duke of Sussex (1773–1843)	1975	Lord Todd (1907–97)
1838	Marquess of Northampton (1790–1851)	1980	Sir Andrew Huxley (1917–)
1848	Earl of Rosse (1800–1867)	1985	Lord Porter of Luddenham (1920–)
1854	Lord Wrottesley (1798–1867)	1990	Sir Michael Atiyah (1929–)
1858	Sir Benjamin Brodie, Bt. (1783–1862)	1996	Sir Aaron Klug (1926–)
1861	Sir Edward Sabine (1788–1883)	2000	Sir Robert May (from November 2000)

Societies and Institutions

This list is in alphabetical order and contains a selection of societies and institutions. The date in parenthesis is the year of foundation.

ABBEYFIELD SOCIETY (1956), Abbeyfield House, 53 Victoria Street, St Albans, Herts AL1 3UW. Tel: 01727-857536; Fax: 01727-846166; E-mail: post@abbeyfield.com; Web: http://www.abbeyfield.com

ACE STUDY TOURS (1958), Babraham, Cambridge CB2 4AP. Tel: 01223-835055; Fax: 01223-837394; E-mail: ace@study-tours.org; Web: http://www.study-tours.org

ACTION FOR BLIND PEOPLE (1857), 14–16 Verney Road, London SE16 3DZ. Tel: 020-7635 4800; Fax: 020-7635 4900; E-mail: central@afbp.org; Web: http://www.afbp.org

ACTION RESEARCH (1952), Vincent House, Horsham, W. Sussex RH12 2DP. Tel: 01403-210406; Fax: 01403-210541; E-mail: info@actionresearch.co.uk; Web: http://www.actionresearch.co.uk

ACTORS' CHARITABLE TRUST (1896), 255–256 Africa House, 64–78 Kingsway, London WC2B 6BD. Tel: 020-7242 0111; Fax: 020-7242 0234; E-mail: tact.actors@virgin.net

ADAM SMITH INSTITUTE (1977), 23 Great Smith Street, London SW1P 3BL. Tel: 020-7222 4995; Fax: 020-7222 7544; E-mail: info@adamsmith.org.uk; Web: http://www.adamsmith.org.uk

ADVERTISING STANDARDS AUTHORITY (1962), 2 Torrington Place, London WC1E 7HW. Tel: 020-7580 5555; Fax: 020-7631 3051; Web: http://www.asa.org.uk

AFRICAN MEDICAL AND RESEARCH FOUNDATION (1961), 4 Grosvenor Place, London SW1X 7HJ. Tel: 020-7201 6070; Fax: 020-7201 6170; E-mail: amref.uk@amref.org; Web: http://www.amref.org

AGE CONCERN CYMRU, 4th Floor, 1 Cathedral Road, Cardiff CF11 9SD. Tel: 029-2037 1566; Fax: 029-2039 9562; E-mail: enquiries@accymru.org.uk

AGE CONCERN ENGLAND (1940), Astral House, 1268 London Road, London SW16 4ER. Tel: 020-8765 7200; Helpline: 0800-009966; Fax: 020-8765 7211; E-mail: ace@ace.org.uk; Web: http://www.ageconcern.org.uk/

AGE CONCERN SCOTLAND, 113 Rose Street, Edinburgh EH2 3DT. Tel: 0131-220 3345; Fax: 0131-220 2779; E-mail: enquiries@ascinfo3.freeserve.co.uk

AGRICULTURAL ENGINEERS ASSOCIATION (1875), Samuelson House, Paxton Road, Orton Centre, Peterborough PE2 5LT. Tel: 01733-371381; Fax: 01733-370664; E-mail: dg@aea.uk.com; Web: http://www.aea.uk.com

THE AIR LEAGUE (1909), Broadway House, Tothill Street, London SW1H 9NS. Tel: 020-7222 8463; Fax: 020-7222 8462; E-mail: exec@airleague.co.uk; Web: www.airleague.co.uk

ALCOHOLICS ANONYMOUS (1947), PO Box 1, Stonebow House, Stonebow, York YO1 2NJ. Tel: 01904-644026; National Helpline: 0845-769 7555; Fax: 01904-629091; Web: http://www.alcoholics-anonymous.org.uk

ALEXANDRA ROSE DAY (1912), 2A Ferry Road, Barnes, London SW13 9RX. Tel: 020-8748 4824; Fax: 020-8748 3188

ALLIANCE PARTY OF NORTHERN IRELAND (1970), 88 University Street, Belfast BT7 1HE. Tel: 028-9032 4274; Fax: 028-9033 3147; E-mail: alliance@allianceparty.org; Web: http://www.allianceparty.org

ALZHEIMER'S SOCIETY (1979), Gordon House, 10 Greencoat Place, London SW1P 1PH. Tel: 020-7306 0608; Helpline: 0800-300 0336; Fax: 020-7306 0608; E-mail: info@alzheimers.org.uk; Web: http://www.alzheimers.org.uk

AMNESTY INTERNATIONAL UNITED KINGDOM (1961), 99–119 Rosebery Avenue, London EC1R 4RE. Tel: 020-7814 6200; Fax: 020-7833 1510; E-mail: info@amnesty.org.uk; Web: http://www.amnesty.org.uk

ANCIENT MONUMENTS SOCIETY (1924), St Ann's Vestry Hall, 2 Church Entry, London EC4V 5HB. Tel: 020-7236 3934; Fax: 020-7329 3677; E-mail: ancientmonuments@talk21.com

ANGLO-ARAB ASSOCIATION (1961), The Arab British Centre, 21 Collingham Road, London SW5 0NU. Tel: 020-7373 8414; Fax: 020-7835 2088

ANGLO-BELGIAN SOCIETY (1982), 5 Hartley Close, Bickley, Kent BR1 2TP. Tel/Fax: 020-8467 8442

ANTHROPOSOPHICAL SOCIETY IN GREAT BRITAIN (1923), Rudolf Steiner House, 35 Park Road, London NW1 6XT. Tel: 020-7723 4400; Fax: 020-7724 4364; E-mail: rsh@cix.compulink.co.uk; Web: http://www.anth.org.uk

ANTIQUARIAN HOROLOGICAL SOCIETY (1953), New House, High Street, Ticehurst, Wadhurst, E. Sussex TN5 7AL. Tel: 01580-200155; Fax: 01580-201323; E-mail: secretary@ahsoc.demon.co.uk

ANTI-SLAVERY INTERNATIONAL (1839), Thomas Clarkson House, The Stableyard, Broomgrove Road, London SW9 9TL. Tel: 020-7501 8920; Fax: 020-7738 4110; E-mail: antislavery@antislavery.org; Web: http://www.antislavery.org

APOSTLESHIP OF THE SEA (1920), Stella Maris, Herald House, Lamb's Passage, Bunhill Row, London EC1Y 8LE. Tel: 020-7588 8285; Fax: 020-7588 8280; E-mail: england_wales@stellamaris.net; Web: http://www.stellamaris.net/england_wales

ARCHITECTS BENEVOLENT SOCIETY (1850), 43 Portland Place, London W1N 3AG. Tel: 020-7580 2823; Fax: 020-7580 7075; E-mail: mail@theabs.org.uk

ARCHITECTS REGISTRATION BOARD (1931 and 1997), 8 Weymouth Street, London W1N 3FB. Tel: 020-7580 5861; Fax: 020-7436 5269; E-mail: info@arb.org.uk; Web: http://www.arb.org.uk

ARCHITECTURAL ASSOCIATION INC. (1847), 34–36 Bedford Square, London WC1B 3ES. Tel: 020-7887 4000; Fax: 020-7414 0782; E-mail: arch-assoc@arch-assoc.org.uk; Web: http://www.aaschool.ac.uk

ARCHITECTURAL HERITAGE FUND (1976), Clareville House, 26–27 Oxendon Street, London SW1Y 4EL. Tel: 020-7925 0199; Fax: 020-7930 0295; E-mail: ahf@ahfund.org.uk; Web: http://www.ahfund.org.uk

ARCHITECTURE AND SURVEYING INSTITUTE (1926), St Mary House, 15 St Mary Street, Chippernham, Wilts SN15 3WD. Tel: 01249-444505; Fax: 01249-443602; E-mail: mail@asi.org.uk; Web: http://www.asi.org.uk

ARLIS/UK AND IRELAND (THE ART LIBRARIES SOCIETY) (1969), 18 College Road, Bromsgrove, Worcs B60 2NE. Tel: 01527-579298; Fax: 01527-579298; E-mail: sfrench@arlis.demon.co.uk; Web: http://www.arlis.nal.vam.ac.uk

ARMY BENEVOLENT FUND (1944), 41 Queen's Gate, London SW7 5HR. Tel: 020-7591 2000; Fax: 020-7589 0889

ARMY CADET FORCE ASSOCIATION (1930), E Block, Duke of York's HQ, London SW3 4RR. Tel: 020-7730 9733; Fax: 020-7730 8264; E-mail: acfa@armycadets.com; Web: http://www.armycadets.com

ARTHRITIS CARE (1949), 18 Stephenson Way, London NW1 2HD. Tel: 020-7380 6500; Fax: 020-7380 6505; Web: http://www.arthritiscare.org.uk

ARTHRITIS RESEARCH CAMPAIGN (1936), Copeman House, St Mary's Court, St Mary's Gate, Chesterfield, Derbys S41 7TD. Tel: 01246-558033; Fax: 01246-558007; E-mail: info@arc.org.uk; Web: http://www.arc.org.uk

ASIAN FAMILY COUNSELLING SERVICE, 76 Church Road, London W7 1LB. Tel: 020-8567 5616; Fax: 020-8567 5616; E-mail: afcs99@hotmail.com

ASLIB (THE ASSOCIATION FOR INFORMATION MANAGE-MENT) (1924), Staple Hall, Stone House Court, London EC3A 7PB. Tel: 020-7903 0000; Fax: 020-7903 0011; E-mail: aslib@aslib.com; Web: http://www.aslib.com

ASSOCIATION FOR LANGUAGE LEARNING (1990), 150 Railway Terrace, Rugby CV21 3HN. Tel: 01788-546443; Fax: 01788-544149; E-mail: langlearn@languagelearn.co.uk; Web: http://www.languagelearn.co.uk

ASSOCIATION FOR SCIENCE EDUCATION (1901), College Lane, Hatfield, Herts AL10 9AA. Tel: 01707-283000; Fax: 01707-266532; E-mail: davidmoore@ase.org.uk; Web: http://www.ase.org.uk/

ASSOCIATION FOR SPINA BIFIDA AND HYDROCEPHALUS (ASBAH) (1966), ASBAH House, 42 Park Road, Peterborough PE1 2UQ. Tel: 01733-555988; Fax: 01733-555985; E-mail: postmaster@asbah.demon.co.uk; Web: http://www.asbah.demon.co.uk

ASSOCIATION FOR THE PROTECTION OF RURAL SCOTLAND (1926), 3rd Floor, Gladstone's Land, 483 Lawnmarket, Edinburgh EH1 2NT. Tel: 0131-225 7012/3; Fax: 0131-225 6592; E-mail: aprs@aprs.org.uk; Web: http://www.aprs.org.uk

ASSOCIATION OF ACCOUNTING TECHNICIANS (1980), 154 Clerkenwell Road, London EC1R 5AD. Tel: 020-7837 8600; Fax: 020-7837 6970; E-mail: aatuk@dial.pipex.com; Web: http://www.aat.co.uk

ASSOCIATION OF BRITISH CORRESPONDENCE COLLEGES (1955), PO Box 17926, London SW19 3WB. Tel: 020-8544 9559; Fax: 020-8540 7657; E-mail: abcc@msn.com; Web: http://www.homestudy.org.uk

ASSOCIATION OF BRITISH DISPENSING OPTICIANS (1925), 6 Hurlingham Business Park, Sulivan Road, London SW6 3DU. Tel: 020-7736 0088; Fax: 020-7731 5531; E-mail: general@abdo.org.uk

ASSOCIATION OF BRITISH INSURERS (1985), 51 Gresham Street, London EC2V 7HQ. Tel: 020-7600 3333; Fax: 020-7696 8999; E-mail: info@abi.org.uk; Web: http://www.abi.org.uk

ASSOCIATION OF BRITISH TRAVEL AGENTS (1950), 68–71 Newman Street, London W1P 4AH. Tel: 020-7637 2444; Fax: 020-7637 0713; E-mail: abta@abta.co.uk; Web: http://www.abtanet.com

ASSOCIATION OF BUILDING ENGINEERS (1925), Lutyens House, Billing Brook Road, Weston Favell, Northampton NN3 8NW. Tel: 01604-404121; Fax: 01604-784200; E-mail: building.engineers@abe.org.uk

ASSOCIATION OF BUSINESS RECOVERY PROFESSIONALS, Halton House, 20–23 Holborn, London EC1N 2JE. Tel: 020-7831 6563; Fax: 020-7405 7047; E-mail: rmstancombe@r3.org.uk; Web: http://www.r3.org.uk

ASSOCIATION OF CHARTERED CERTIFIED ACCOUNTANTS (1904), 29 Lincoln's Inn Fields, London WC2A 3EE. Tel: 020-7242 6855; Fax: 020-7831 8054; Web: http://www.acca.org.uk

ASSOCIATION OF CONSULTING ENGINEERS (1913), Alliance House, 12 Caxton Street, London SW1H 0QL. Tel: 020-7222 6557; Fax: 020-7222 0750; E-mail: consult@acenet.co.uk; Web: http://www.acenet.co.uk

ASSOCIATION OF CONVENIENCE STORES (1890), Federation House, 17 Farnborough Street, Farnborough, Hants GU14 8AG. Tel: 01252-515001; Fax: 01252-515002; E-mail: acs@acs.org.uk

ASSOCIATION OF CORPORATE TREASURERS (1979), Ocean House, 10–12 Little Trinity Lane, London EC4V 2DJ. Tel: 020-7213 9728; Fax: 020-7248 2591; E-mail: enquiries@treasurers.co.uk; Web: http://www.treasurers.org

ASSOCIATION OF CORPORATE TRUSTEES (1974), The Glen House, 43 Surrey Road, Westbourne, Bournemouth, Dorset BR4 9HR. Tel: 01202-765559; Fax: 01202-765559; E-mail: tactglen@lineone.net; Web: http://www.trustee.org.uk

ASSOCIATION OF COUNCIL SECRETARIES AND SOLICITORS (1974, merged 1996), Foxcroft, Gill Lane, Longton, Preston PR4 4SR. Tel: 01772-611167; Fax: 01772-611167; E-mail: acssny@globalnet.co.uk; Web: http://www.acses.org.uk

ASSOCIATION OF DIRECTORS OF PUBLIC HEALTH (1982), Walsall Health Authority, Lichfield House, 27–31 Lichfield Street, Walsall, W. Mids WS1 1TE. Tel: 01922-720255; Fax: 01922-722051; E-mail: ramaiahs@ha.walsall-ha.wmids.nhs.uk

ASSOCIATION OF DRAINAGE AUTHORITIES (1937), The Mews, 3 Royal Oak Passage, High Street, Huntingdon, Cambs PE29 3EA. Tel: 01480-411123; Fax: 01480-431107; E-mail: drainage@ada.org.uk; Web: http://www.ada.org.uk

ASSOCIATION OF FRIENDLY SOCIETIES (1995), 10–13 Lovat Lane, London EC3R 8DT. Tel: 020-7397 9550; Fax: 020-7397 9551; E-mail: friendly@afs.org.uk

ASSOCIATION OF INTER VARSITY CLUBS (1946), 2nd Floor, Grosvenor House, 94–96 Grosvenor Square, Manchester M1 7HL. Tel: 0161-273 2316; E-mail: aivc_secretary@bigfoot.com; Web: http://www.ivc.org.uk

ASSOCIATION OF LONDON GOVERNMENT (2000), 36 Old Queen Street, London SW1H 9JF. Tel: 020-7222 7799; Fax: 020-7799 2339; E-mail: reception@alg.gov.uk

ASSOCIATION OF MANAGEMENT AND PROFESSIONAL STAFFS (1972), Parkgates, Bury New Road, Prestwich, Manchester M25 0JW. Tel: 0161-773 8621; Fax: 0161-798 6182; E-mail: sec@amps.demon.co.uk; Web: http://www.amps.demon.co.uk

ASSOCIATION OF ROYAL NAVY OFFICERS (1920), 70 Porchester Terrace, London W2 3TP. Tel: 020-7402 5231; Fax: 020-7402 5533; E-mail: ARNO@eurosurf.com; Web: http://www.eurosurf.com/ARNO

ASSOCIATION OF SPEAKERS CLUBS (1971), Beanlands Chase, 20 Rivermead Drive, Garstang, Preston, Lancashire PR3 1JJ. Tel: 01995-602560; Fax: 01995-602560; E-mail: natsecasc@lineone.net

ASSOCIATION OF SPORTS HISTORIANS, Ground Floor Offices, 13–16 Faro Close, Bromley, Kent BR1 2RR. Tel: 020-8467 1951

ASSOCIATION OF TEACHERS OF MATHEMATICS (1952), 7 Shaftesbury Street, Derby DE23 8YB. Tel: 01332-346599; Fax: 01332-204357; E-mail: atm_maths@compuserve.com; Web: http://www.atm.org.uk

ATS AND WRAC BENEVOLENT FUND (1944), AGC Centre, Worthy Down, Winchester, Hants SO21 2RG. Tel: 01962-887612; Fax: 01962-887612

AUDIT BUREAU OF CIRCULATIONS LTD (1931), Saxon House, 211 High Street, Berkhamsted, Herts HP4 1AD. Tel: 01442-870800; Fax: 01442-877407; E-mail: abcpost@abc.org.uk; Web: http://www.abc.org.uk

AYRSHIRE ARCHAEOLOGICAL AND NATURAL HISTORY SOCIETY (1947), 10 Longlands Park, Ayr KA7 4RJ. Tel: 01292-441915

AYRSHIRE CATTLE SOCIETY OF GREAT BRITAIN AND IRELAND (1877), 1 Racecourse Road, Ayr KA7 2DE. Tel: 01292-267123; Fax: 01292-611973; E-mail: society@ayrshires.org; Web: http://www.ayrshires.org

BACKCARE, 16 Elmtree Road, Teddington, Middx TW11 8ST. Tel: 020-8977 5474; Fax: 020-8943 5318; E-mail: Back_Pain@compuserve.com; Web: http://www.backpain.org

BALTIC AIR CHARTER ASSOCIATION (1949), The Baltic Exchange, St Mary Axe, London EC3A 8BH. Tel: 020-7623 5501; Fax: 020-7369 1623; Web: http://www.baca.org.uk

BALTIC EXCHANGE CHARITABLE SOCIETY (1978), 13 Norton Folgate, London E1 6DB. Tel: 020-7247 6863; Fax: 020-7247 6863

BAPTIST MISSIONARY SOCIETY (1792), Baptist House, PO Box 49, 129 Broadway, Didcot, Oxon OX11 8XA. Tel: 01235-517700; Fax: 01235-517601; E-mail: mail@bms.org.uk; Web: http://www.bms.org.uk

BAR ASSOCIATION FOR LOCAL GOVERNMENT AND THE PUBLIC SERVICE (1945), c/o Birmingham City Council, Ingleby House, 11–14 Cannon Street, Birmingham B2 5EN. Tel: 0121-303 9991; Fax: 0121-303 1312; E-mail: chairman@balgps.freeserve.co.uk; Web: http://www.balgps.freeserve.co.uk

BARNARDO'S (1866), Tanners Lane, Barkingside, Ilford, Essex IG6 1QG. Tel: 020-8550 8822; Fax: 020-8551 6870; Web: http://www.barnardos.org.uk

BARRISTERS' BENEVOLENT ASSOCIATION (1873), 14 Gray's Inn Square, London WC1R 5JP. Tel: 020-7242 4761; Fax: 020-7831 5366; E-mail: linda@thebba.swinternet.co.uk

BERKSHIRE ARCHAEOLOGICAL SOCIETY (1871), 43 Laburnham Road, Maidenhead, Berks SL6 4DE. Tel: 01628-631225

BEVIN BOYS ASSOCIATION (1989), 28 Sir Christopher Court, Hythe, Southampton, Hampshire SO45 6JR. Tel/Fax: 023-8087 9766

BI – BRITISH INVISIBLES (1968), Windsor House, 39 King Street, London EC2V 8DQ. Tel: 020-7600 1198; Fax: 020-7606 4248; E-mail: enquiries@bi.org.uk; Web: http://www.bi.org.uk

BIBLIOGRAPHICAL SOCIETY (1892), c/o The Wellcome Library, 183 Euston Road, London NW1 2BE. Tel: 020-7611 7244; Fax: 020-7611 8703; E-mail: jm93@dial.pipex.com

THE BIOCHEMICAL SOCIETY (1911), 59 Portland Place, London W1N 3AJ. Tel: 020-7580 5530; Fax: 020-7637 3626; E-mail: Alison.McWhinnie@biochemistry.org; Web: http://www.biochemistry.org

BIRMINGHAM AND MIDLAND INSTITUTE AND LIBRARY (1954), Margaret Street, Birmingham B3 3BS. Tel: 0121-236 3591; Fax: 0121-212 4577

BIRMINGHAM AND WARWICKSHIRE ARCHAEOLOGICAL SOCIETY (1870), c/o Birmingham and Midland Institute, Margaret Street, Birmingham B3 3BS; Web: http://www.bwas.swinternet.co.uk

BMI HEALTH SERVICES, 46 Wimpole Street, London W1M 7DG. Tel: 020-7569 5000; Fax: 020-7569 5001; E-mail: sales@bmihs.co.uk; Web: http://www.bmihs.co.uk

BOOK AID INTERNATIONAL (1954), 39–41 Coldharbour Lane, London SE5 9NR. Tel: 020-7733 3577; Fax: 020-7978 8006; E-mail: info@bookaid.org; Web: http://www.bookaid.org

BOOK TRUST, Book House, 45 East Hill, London SW18 2QZ. Tel: 020-8516 2977; Fax: 020-8516 2978; Web: http://www.booktrust.org.uk

BOOKSELLERS ASSOCIATION OF THE UK AND IRELAND LTD, Minster House, 272 Vauxhall Bridge Road, London SW1V 1BA. Tel: 020-7834 5477; Fax: 020-7834 8812; E-mail: mail@booksellers.org.uk; Web: http://www.booksellers.org.uk

BORN FREE FOUNDATION (1984), 3 Grove House, Foundry Lane, Horsham, W. Sussex RH13 5PL. Tel: 01403-240170; Fax: 01403-327838; E-mail: wildlife@bornfree.org.uk; Web: http://www.bornfree.org.uk

BOTANICAL SOCIETY OF THE BRITISH ISLES (1836), c/o Department of Botany, The Natural History Museum, Cromwell Road, London SW7 5BD. Tel: 020-7942 5002; E-mail: bsbihgs@aol.com; Web: http://www.members.aol.com/bsbihgs

BOY'S BRIGADE (1883), Felden Lodge, Hemel Hempstead, Herts HP3 0BL. Tel: 01442-231681; Fax: 01442-235391; E-mail: bbhq@boys-brigade.org.uk; Web: http://www.boys-brigade.org.uk

BRIDEWELL ROYAL HOSPITAL (1553), Witley, Godalming, Surrey GU8 5SG. Tel: 01428-686700; Fax: 01428-682850; Web: http://www.kesw.surrey.sch.uk

BRISTOL AND GLOUCESTERSHIRE ARCHAEOLOGICAL SOCIETY (1976), 22 Beaumont Road, Gloucester GL2 0EJ. Tel: 01452-302610; Web: http://www.ihr.sas.ac.uk/ihr.bg/

BRITAIN–RUSSIA CENTRE – BRITISH EAST WEST CENTRE, 1 Nine Elms Lane, London SW8 5NQ. Tel: 020-7498 6640; Fax: 020-7498 4660; Web: http://www.briteastwest.org.uk

BRITISH ACADEMY OF COMPOSERS AND SONGWRITERS, 2nd Floor, 25–27 Berners Street, London W1P 3DB. Tel: 020-7636 2929; Fax: 020-7636 2212; E-mail: info@britishacademy.com; Web: http://www.britishacademy.com

BRITISH AND FOREIGN BIBLE SOCIETY (1804), Stonehill Green, Westlea, Swindon SN5 7DG. Tel: 01793-418100; Fax: 01793-418118; E-mail: info@bfbs.org.uk; Web: http://www.biblesociety.org.uk

BRITISH AND FOREIGN SCHOOL SOCIETY (1808), Croudace House, Godstone Road, Caterham, Surrey CR3 6RE. Tel: 01883-331177

BRITISH AND INTERNATIONAL SAILORS' SOCIETY (1818), 3 Orchard Place, Southampton SO14 3AT. Tel: 023-8033 7333; Fax: 023-8033 8333; E-mail: admin@biss.org.uk; Web: http://www.biss.org.uk

BRITISH ANTIQUE DEALERS' ASSOCIATION (1918), 20 Rutland Gate, London SW7 1BD. Tel: 020-7589 4128; Fax: 020-7581 9083; E-mail: enquiry@bada.demon.co.uk; Web: http://www.bada.org

BRITISH ASSOCIATION FOR EARLY CHILDHOOD EDUCATION (1923), 136 Cavell Street, London E1 2JA. Tel: 020-7539 5400; Fax: 020-7539 5409; E-mail: office@early-education.org.uk; Web: http://www.early-education.org.uk

BRITISH ASSOCIATION FOR LOCAL HISTORY (1952), PO Box 1576, Salisbury, Wilts SP2 8SY. Tel: 01722-322158; Fax: 01722-413242. Web: http://www.balh.co.uk

BRITISH ASSOCIATION FOR THE ADVANCEMENT OF SCIENCE (1831), 23 Savile Row, London W1X 2NB. Tel: 020-7973 3500; Fax: 020-7973 3051; E-mail: admin@britassoc.org.uk; Web: http://www.britassoc.org.uk

BRITISH ASSOCIATION OF COMMUNICATORS IN BUSINESS (1949), 42 Borough High Street, London SE1 1XW. Tel: 020-7378 7139; Fax: 020-7378 7140; E-mail: bacb@globalnet.co.uk; Web: http://www.bacb.org

BRITISH ASTRONOMICAL ASSOCIATION, Burlington House, Piccadilly, London

BRITISH BEE-KEEPERS' ASSOCIATION, National Beekeeping Centre, Stoneleigh Park, Kenilworth, Warks CV8 2LG. Tel: 024-7669 6679; Fax: 024-7669 0682; E-mail: information@bbka.demon.co.uk; Web: http://www.bbka.demon.co.uk

BRITISH BOARD OF FILM CLASSIFICATION (1912), 3 Soho Square, London W1V 6HD. Tel: 020-7440 1570; Fax: 020-7287 0141; E-mail: webmaster@bbfc.co.uk; Web: http://www.bbfc.co.uk

BRITISH CHAMBERS OF COMMERCE, Manning House, 22 Carlisle Place, London SW1P 1JA. Tel: 020-7565 2000; Fax: 020-7565 2049; E-mail: info@britishchambers.org.uk; Web: http://www.britishchambers.org.uk

BRITISH CHESS FEDERATION (1904), The Watch Oak, Chain Lane, Battle, E. Sussex TN33 0YA. Tel: 01424-775222; E-mail: office@bcf.org.uk; Web: http://www.bcf.mdirect.co.uk

BRITISH COMMONWEALTH EX-SERVICES LEAGUE (1921), 48 Pall Mall, London SW1Y 5JG. Tel: 020-7973 7263; Fax: 020-7973 7308

BRITISH COMPUTER SOCIETY (1957), 1 Sanford Street, Swindon SN1 1HJ. Tel: 01793-417417; Fax: 01793-480270; E-mail: beshq@hq.bcs.org.uk; Web: http://www.bcs.org.uk

BRITISH CONSULTANTS BUREAU (1965), 1 Westminster Palace Gardens, 1–7 Artillery Row, London SW1P 1RJ. Tel: 020-7222 3651; Fax: 020-7222 3664; E-mail: mail@bcb.co.uk; Web: http://www.bcbforum.demon.co.uk

BRITISH COPYRIGHT COUNCIL (1965), 29–33 Berners Street, London W1P 4AA. Tel: 01986-788122; Fax: 01986-788847; E-mail: copyright@bcc2.demon.co.uk

BRITISH DEAF ASSOCIATION (1890), 1 Worship Street, London EC2A 2AB. Tel: 020-7588 3520; Fax: 020-7588 3527; E-mail: info@bda.org.uk; Web: http://www.bda.org.uk

BRITISH DENTAL ASSOCIATION (1880), 64 Wimpole Street, London W1M 8AL. Tel: 020-7935 0875; Fax: 020-7487 5232; E-mail: enquiries@bda-dentistry.org.uk; Web: http://www.bda-dentistry.org.uk

BRITISH DRIVING SOCIETY (1957), 27 Dugard Place, Barford, War CV35 8DX. Tel: 01926-624420; Fax: 01926-624633; E-mail: brit.driving.soc@care4free.net; Web: http://www.carriage-driving.com

BRITISH EPILEPSY ASSOCIATION, New Anstey House, Gate Way Drive, Yeadon, Leeds LS19 7XY. Tel: 0113-210 8800; Helpline: 0808-800 5050; Fax: 0113-391 0300; E-mail: epilepsy@bea.org.uk; Web: http://www.epilepsy.org.uk

BRITISH EQUESTRIAN FEDERATION, National Agricultural Centre, Stoneleigh Park, Kenilworth, Warks CV8 2RH. Tel: 0247-669 8871; Fax: 0247-669 6484; E-mail: mary.kelly@bef.co.uk; Web: http://www.bef.co.uk

BRITISH FALSE MEMORY SOCIETY (1993), Bradford on Avon, Wilts BA15 1NF. Tel: 01225-868682; Fax: 01225-862251; E-mail: BFMS@compuserve.com; Web: http://www.bfms.org.uk

BRITISH FEDERATION OF WOMEN GRADUATES (1907), 4 Mandeville Courtyard, 142 Battersea Park Road, London SW11 4NB. Tel/Fax: 020-7498 8037; E-mail: bfwg@bfwg.demon.co.uk; Web: http://homepages.wyenet.co.uk/bfwg

BRITISH GLIDING ASSOCIATION (1929), Kimberley House, Vaughan Way, Leicester LE1 4SE. Tel: 0116-253 1051; Fax: 0116-251 5939; E-mail: bga@gliding.co.uk; Web: http://www.gliding.co.uk

BRITISH GOAT SOCIETY, 34–36 Fore Street, Bovey Tracey, Newton Abbot, Devon TQ13 9AD. Tel/Fax: 01626-833168

BRITISH HEALTH CARE ASSOCIATION (1930), 24A Main Street, Garforth, Leeds LS25 1AA. Tel: 0113-232 0903; Fax: 0113-232 0404; E-mail: cbell@bhca.org.uk; Web: http://www.bhca.org.uk

BRITISH HEART FOUNDATION, 14 Fitzhardinge Street, London W1H 4DH. Tel: 020-7487 7186; Fax: 020-7486 5820; E-mail: directorate@bhf.org.uk; Web: http://www.bhf.org.uk

BRITISH HEDGEHOG PRESERVATION SOCIETY (1982), Knowbury House, Knowbury, Ludlow, Shropshire SY8 3LQ. Tel: 01584-890801

BRITISH HOROLOGICAL INSTITUTE (1858), Upton Hall, Upton, Newark, Notts NG23 5TE. Tel: 01636-813795; Fax: 01636-812258; E-mail: clocks@bhi.co.uk; Web: http://www.bhi.co.uk

BRITISH HORSE SOCIETY (1947), Stoneleigh Deer Park, Kenilworth, Warks CV8 2XZ. Tel: 01926-707700; Fax: 01926-707800; E-mail: enquiry@bhs.org.uk; Web: http://www.bhs.org.uk

BRITISH HUMANIST ASSOCIATION, 47 Theobald's Road, London WC1X 8SP. Tel: 020-7430 0908; Fax: 020-7430 1271; E-mail: info@humanism.org.uk; Web: http://www.humanism.org.uk

BRITISH INSTITUTE IN EASTERN AFRICA (1959), 10 Carlton House Terrace, London SW1Y 5AH. Tel: 020-7969 5201; Fax: 020-7969 5401; E-mail: biea@britac.ac.uk; Web: http://www.britac.ac.uk/institutes/eafrica

BRITISH INSTITUTE OF ARCHAEOLOGY AT ANKARA, 10 Carlton House Terrace, London SW1Y 5AH. Tel: 020-7969 5204; Fax: 020-7969 5401; E-mail: biaa@britac.ac.uk

BRITISH INSTITUTE OF GRAPHOLOGISTS, 24–26 High Street, Hampton Hill, Hampton, Middx TW12 1PD. Tel: 01753-891241; E-mail: text@virgin.net

BRITISH INSTITUTE OF HUMAN RIGHTS (1970), 8th Floor, Kings College London, 75–79 York Road, London SE17AW. Tel: 020-7401 2712; Fax: 020-7401 2695; E-mail: bihr@kcl.ac.uk; Web: http://www.kcl.ac.uk/kis/schools/law/research/bihr/index.html

BRITISH INSTITUTE OF PROFESSIONAL PHOTOGRAPHY (1901), Fox Talbot House, Amwell End, Ware, Herts SG12 9HN. Tel: 01920-464011; Fax: 01920-487056; E-mail: bipp@compuserve.com; Web: http://www.bipp.com

BRITISH INSTITUTE OF RADIOLOGY, 36 Portland Place, London W1N 4AT. Tel: 020-7307 1400; Fax: 020-7307 1414; E-mail: admin@bir.org.uk; Web: http://www.bir.org.uk

BRITISH INSURANCE BROKERS' ASSOCIATION, BIBA House, 14 Bevis Marks, London EC3A 7NT. Tel: 020-7623 9043; Fax: 020-7626 9676; E-mail: enquiries@biba.org.uk; Web: http://www.biba.org.uk

BRITISH INTERPLANETARY SOCIETY (1933), 27–29 South Lambeth Road, London SW8 1SZ. Tel: 020-7735 3160; Fax: 020-7820 1504; E-mail: bis.bis@virgin.net; Web: http://www.bis-spaceflight.com

BRITISH ISRAEL WORLD FEDERATION (1919), 8 Blades Court, Deodar Road, London SW15 2NU. Tel: 020-8877 9010; Fax: 020-8871 4770; E-mail: admin@britishisrael.co.uk; Web: http://www.britishisrael.co.uk

BRITISH LUNG FOUNDATION (1984), 78 Hatton Garden, London EC1N 8LD. Tel: 020-7831 5831; Fax: 020-7831 5832; E-mail: blf@britishlungfoundation.com; Web: http://www.lunguk.org

BRITISH MEDICAL ASSOCIATION (1832), BMA House, Tavistock Square, London WC1H 9JP. Tel: 020-7387 4499; Fax: 020-7383 6400. Web: http://www.bma.org.uk

BRITISH MENSA LTD (1946), St John's House, St Johns Square, Wolverhampton WV2 4AH. Tel: 01902-772771; Fax: 01902-392500; E-mail: enquiries@mensa.org.uk; Web: http://www.mensa.org.uk

BRITISH MUSIC HALL SOCIETY, 82 Fernlea Road, London, SW12 9RW. Tel: 020-8673 2175

BRITISH NATIONAL PARTY, PO Box 14, Welshpool, Powys SY21 0WE. Tel: 0700-900 2671; E-mail: letters@bnp.net; Web: http://www.bnp.net

BRITISH NATIONAL TEMPERANCE LEAGUE, Westbrook Court, 2 Sharrow Vale Road, Sheffield S11 8YZ. Tel: 0114-267 9976; Fax: 0114-267 9976; E-mail: info@bntl.org; Web: http://www.bntl.org

BRITISH NATURALISTS' ASSOCIATION (1905), 1 Bracken Mews, London E4 7UT. Web: http://www.bna-naturalists.org

BRITISH NUCLEAR ENERGY SOCIETY, 1–7 Great George Street, London SW1P 3AA. Tel: 020-7665 2241; Fax: 020-7799 1325; E-mail: andrew.tillbrook@ice.org.uk; Web: http://www.bnes.org.uk

BRITISH PHARMACOLOGICAL SOCIETY (1931), 16 Angel Gate, City Road, London EC1V 2SG. Tel: 020-7417 0110; Fax: 020-7417 0114; E-mail: admin@bps.ac.uk; Web: http://www.bps.ac.uk

BRITISH PIG ASSOCIATION, Scotsbridge House, Scots Hill, Rickmansworth, Herts WD3 3BB. Tel: 01923-695295; Fax: 01923-695347; E-mail: bpa@britishpigs.org; Web: http://www.britishpigs.org

BRITISH PSYCHOLOGICAL SOCIETY (1901), St Andrews House, 48 Princess Road East, Leicester LE1 7DR. Tel: 0116-254 9568; Fax: 0116-247 0787; E-mail: mail@bps.org.uk; Web: http://www.bps.org.uk

BRITISH RECORDS ASSOCIATION, 40 Northampton Road, London EC1R 0HB. Tel: 020-7833 0428; Fax: 020-7833 0416; E-mail: britishrecordsassn@charity.vfree.com

BRITISH RED CROSS (1870), 9 Grosvenor Crescent, London SW1X 7EJ. Tel: 020-7235 5454; Fax: 020-7245 6315; E-mail: information@redcross.org.uk; Web: http://www.redcross.org.uk

BRITISH REFUGEE COUNCIL, Bondway House, 3 Bondway, London SW8 1SJ. Tel: 020-7820 3000; Fax: 020-7582 9929; E-mail: info@refugeecouncil.demon.co.uk; Web: http://www.refugeecouncil.org.uk

BRITISH SOCIETY OF DOWSERS (1933), Sycamore Barn, Hastingleigh, Ashford, Kent TN25 5HW. Tel: 01233-750253; Fax: 01233-750253; E-mail: bsd@dowsers.demon.co.uk; Web: http://www.dowsers.demon.co.uk

BRITISH TRUST FOR ORNITHOLOGY, The Nunnery, Thetford, Norfolk IP24 2PU. Tel: 01842-750050; Fax: 01842-750030; E-mail: general@bto.org

BRITISH UNION FOR THE ABOLITION OF VIVISECTION (1898), 16A Crane Grove, London N7 8NN. Tel: 020-7700 4888; Fax: 020-7700 0252; E-mail: info@buav.org

BRITISH VETERINARY ASSOCIATION (1883), 7 Mansfield Street, London W1M 0AT. Tel: 020-7636 6541; Fax: 020-7436 2970; E-mail: bvahq@bva.co.uk; Web: http://www.bva.co.uk and http://www.vetrecord.co.uk

BRITISH WOOD PRESERVING AND DAMP-PROOFING ASSOCIATION (1930), 6 The Office Village, 4 Romford Road, London E15 4EA. Tel: 020-8519 2588; Fax: 020-8519 3444; E-mail: info@bwpda.co.uk; Web: http://www.bwpda.co.uk

BTBS THE BOOK TRADE CHARITY (1837), Dillon Lodge, The Retreat, Kings Langley, Herts WD4 8LT. Tel: 01923-263128; Fax: 01923-270732; E-mail: btbs@booktradecharity.demon.co.uk; Web: http://www.booktradecharity.demon.co.uk

BTCV, 36 St Mary's Street, Wallingford, Oxon OX10 0EU. Tel: 01491-821600; Fax: 01491-839646; E-mail: information@btcv.org.uk; Web: http://www.btcv.org

BUCKINGHAMSHIRE ARCHAEOLOGICAL SOCIETY (1847), County Museum, Church Street, Aylesbury, Bucks HP20 2QP

BUDDIST SOCIETY, 58 Eccleston Square, London SW1V 1PH. Tel: 020-7834 5858; Fax: 020-7976 5238. Web: http://www.buddsoc.org.uk

THE BUDGERIGAR SOCIETY (1925), Spring Gardens, Northampton NN1 1DR. Tel: 01604-624549; Fax: 01604-627108. Web: http://www.budgerigarsociety.com

BUILDING SOCIETIES ASSOCIATION, 3 Savile Row, London W1X 1AF. Tel: 020-7437 0655; Fax: 020-7734 6416; Web: http://www.bsa.org.uk

BUSINESS IN THE COMMUNITY (1981), 44 Baker Street, London W1M 1DH. Tel: 020-7224 1600; Fax: 020-7486 1700; E-mail: information@bitc.org.uk; Web: http://www.bitc.org.uk

CAFOD (CATHOLIC FUND FOR OVERSEAS DEVELOPMENT) (1962), Romero Close, Stockwell Road, London SW9 9TY. Tel: 020-7733 7900; E-mail: reception@cafod.org.uk; Web: http://www.cafod.org.uk

CALOUSTE GULBENKIAN FOUNDATION (1956), 98 Portland Place, London W1N 4ET

CAMBRIDGE ANTIQUARIAN SOCIETY, 30 Fen Road, Milton, Cambridge

CAMBRIDGE PRESERVATION SOCIETY (1928), Wandlebury Ring, Gog Magog Hills, Babraham, Cambridge CB2 4AE. Tel: 01223-243830; Fax: 01223-243830; E-mail: admin@cpswandlebury.org.uk; Web: http://www.cpswandlebury.org.uk

CAMERON FUND, Tavistock House North, Tavistock Square, London WC1H 9HR. Tel: 020-7388 0796

CAMPAIGN FOR AN INDEPENDENT BRITAIN, 81 Ashmole Street, London SW8 1NF. Tel: 020-8340 0314; Fax: 020-7582 7021; E-mail: info@cibhq.co.uk; Web: http://www.cibhq.co.uk

CAMPAIGN FOR FREEDOM OF INFORMATION (1984), Suite 102, 16 Baldwin Gardens, London EC1N 7RJ. Tel: 020-7831 7477; Fax: 020-7831 7461; E-mail: admin@cfoi.demon.co.uk; Web: http://www.cfoi.org.uk

CAMPAIGN FOR NUCLEAR DISARMAMENT (CND) (1958), 162 Holloway Road, London N7 8DQ. Tel: 020-7700 2393; Fax: 020-7700 2357; E-mail: cnd@gn.apc.org; Web: http://www.cnduk.org

CAMPAIGN FOR THE PROTECTION OF RURAL WALES (1928), Tŷ Gwyn, 31 High Street, Welshpool, Powys SY21 7YD. Tel: 01938-552525; Fax: 01938-552741; E-mail: info@cprw.org.uk; Web: http://www.cprw.org.uk

CANADA–UNITED KINGDOM CHAMBER OF COMMERCE, 38 Grosvenor Street, London W1X 0DP. Tel: 020-7258 6572; Fax: 020-7258 6594; E-mail: info@canada-uk.org; Web: http://www.canada-uk.org

CANCER RESEARCH CAMPAIGN (1923), 10 Cambridge Terrace, London NW1 4JL. Tel: 020-7224 1333; Fax: 020-7487 4310; E-mail: cancerinfo@crc.org.uk; Web: http://www.crc.org.uk

CARERS NATIONAL ASSOCIATION (1988), Ruth Pitter House, 20–25 Glasshouse Yard, London EC1A 4JT. Tel: 020-7490 8818; Fax: 020-7490 8824; E-mail: info@ukcarers.org; Web: http://www.carersuk.demon.co.uk

CARNEGIE DUNFERMLINE TRUST (1903), Abbey Park House, Dunfermline, Fife KY12 7PB. Tel: 01383-723638; Fax: 01383-721862

CARNEGIE HERO FUND TRUST (1908), Abbey Park House, Dunfermline, Fife KY12 7PB. Tel: 01383-723638; Fax: 01383-721862

CARNEGIE UNITED KINGDOM TRUST, Comely Park House, Dunfermline, Fife KY12 7EJ. Tel: 01383-721445; Fax: 01383-620682

CATHEDRALS FABRIC COMMISSION FOR ENGLAND (1991), Fielden House, 13 Little College Street, London SW1P 3SH. Tel: 020-7898 1863; Fax: 020-7898 1881; E-mail: enquiries@cfce.c-of-e.org.uk

CATHOLIC ENQUIRY OFFICE (1902), The Chase Centre, 114 West Heath Road, London NW3 7TX. Tel: 020-8458 3316; Fax: 020-8905 5780; E-mail: coe@cms.org.uk; Web: http://www.epinet.co.uk/go/ceo

CATHOLIC HOUSING AID SOCIETY, 209 Old Marylebone Road, London NW1 5QT. Tel: 020-7723 7273; Fax: 020-7723 5943; E-mail: info@chasnat.demon.co.uk; Web: http://www.chasnat.demon.co.uk

CATHOLIC TRUTH SOCIETY (1868), 40–46 Harleyford Road, London SE11 5AY. Tel: 020-7640 0042; Fax: 020-7640 0046; E-mail: info@cts-online.org.uk; Web: http://www.cts-online.org.uk

CATHOLIC UNION OF GREAT BRITAIN (1872), St Maxmilian Kolbe House, 63 Jeddo Road, London W12 9EE. Tel: 020-8749 1321; Fax: 020-8735 0816

CENTRAL AND CECIL HOUSING TRUST (1926), 2 Priory Road, Kew, Richmond, Surrey TW9 3DG. Tel: 020-8940 9828; Fax: 020-8332 1044

CENTRAL BUREAU FOR EDUCATIONAL VISITS AND EXCHANGES, 10 Spring Gardens, London SW1A 2BN. Tel: 020-7389 4487; Fax: 020-7389 4497; E-mail: peter.upton@britishcouncil.org; Web: http://www.britishcouncil.org/cbeve

CENTRAL COUNCIL OF CHURCH BELL RINGERS, 50 Cramhurst Lane, Witley, Godalming, Surrey GU8 5QZ. Tel: 01428-682790; Fax: 01428-682790; Web: http://www.cccbr.org.uk

CENTREPOINT, Neil House, 7 Whitechapel Road, London E1 1DU. Tel: 020-7426 5300; Fax: 020-7426 5301; Web: http://www.centrepoint.org.uk

CEREDIGION ANTIQUARIAN SOCIETY, Henllys, Lô Tyllwyd, Llanfarian, Aberystwyth SY23 4UH. Tel: 01970-625818

CHARITIES AID FOUNDATION (1924), Kings Hill, West Malling, Kent ME19 4TA. Tel: 01732-520000; Fax: 01732-520001; E-mail: enquiries@caf.charitynet.org; Web: http://www.cafonline.org

CHARTER88 (1988), 16–24 Underwood Street, London N1 7JQ. Tel: 020-7684 3888; Fax: 020-7684 3889; E-mail: info@charter88.org.uk

CHARTERED INSTITUTE OF ARBITRATORS, 24 Angel Gate, City Road, London EC1V 2RS. Tel: 020-7387 4483; Fax: 020-7837 4185; E-mail: 71411,2735@compuserve.com; Web: http://www.arbitrators.org

THE CHARTERED INSTITUTE OF BANKERS (1879), 90 Bishopsgate, London EC2N 4AS. Tel: 020-7444 7111; Fax: 020-7444 7115; E-mail: institute@cib.org.uk; Web: http://www.cib.org.uk

CHARTERED INSTITUTE OF BANKERS IN SCOTLAND (1875), Drumsheugh House, 38B Drumsheugh Gardens, Edinburgh EH3 7SW. Tel: 0131-473 7777; Fax: 0131-473 7788; E-mail: info@ciobs.org.uk; Web: http://www.ciobs.org.uk

CHARTERED INSTITUTE OF ENVIRONMENTAL HEALTH, Chadwick Court, 15 Hatfields, London SE1 8DJ. Tel: 020-7928 6006; Fax: 020-7827 5866; E-mail: cieh@dial.pipex.com; Web: http://www.cieh.org.uk/

CHARTERED INSTITUTE OF HOUSING, Octavia House, Westwood Business Park, Westwood Way, Coventry CV4 8JP. Tel: 024-7685 1700; Fax: 024-7669 5110; E-mail: customer.services@cih.org; Web: http://www.cih.org

CHARTERED INSTITUTE OF JOURNALISTS, 2 Dock Offices, Surrey Quays Road, London SE16 2XU. Tel: 020-7252 1187; Fax: 020-7232 2302

CHARTERED INSTITUTE OF PATENT AGENTS (1882), Staple Inn Buildings, High Holborn, London WC1V 7PZ. Tel: 020-7405 9450; Fax: 020-7430 0471; E-mail: mail@cipa.org.uk; Web: http://www.cipa.org.uk

CHARTERED INSTITUTE OF PUBLIC FINANCE AND ACCOUNTANCY (1885), 3 Robert Street, London WC2N 6BH. Tel: 020-7543 5600; Fax: 020-7543 5700; Web: http://www.cipfa.org.uk

CHARTERED INSTITUTE OF PURCHASING AND SUPPLY (1932), Easton House, Easton on the Hill, Stamford, Lincs PE9 3NZ. Tel: 01780-756777; Fax: 01780-751610; E-mail: info@cips.org; Web: http://www.cips.org

THE CHILDREN'S SOCIETY, Edward Rudolf House, Margery Street, London WC1X 0JL. Tel: 020-7841 4000; Fax: 020-7841 4500. Web: http://www.the-childrens-society.org.uk

CHINA ASSOCIATION (1891), Swire House,
59 Buckingham Gate, London SW1E 6AJ.
Tel: 020-7821 3220; Fax: 020-7630 0353

CHRISTIAN AID SCOTLAND, 41 George IV Bridge,
Edinburgh EH1 1EL. Tel: 0131-220 1254; Fax: 0131-225
8861; E-mail: edinburgh@christian-aid.org;
Web: http://www.christian-aid.org.uk

CHRISTIAN EDUCATION MOVEMENT (1965), Royal
Buildings, Victoria Street, Derby DE1 1GW.
Tel: 01332-296655; Fax: 01332-343253; E-mail:
cem@cem.org.uk; Web: http://www.cem.org.uk

CHURCH ARMY (1882), Independents Road, London
SE3 9LG. Tel: 020-8318 1226; Fax: 020-8318 5258;
E-mail: information@churcharmy.org.uk;
Web: http://www.churcharmy.org.uk

CHURCH LADS' AND CHURCH GIRLS' BRIGADE (1891),
2 Barnsley Road, Wath upon Dearne, Rotherham,
S. Yorks S63 6PY. Tel: 01709-876535; Fax: 01709-878089;
E-mail: general-secretary@church-brigade.syol.com;
Web: http://www.church-brigade.syol.com

CHURCH MISSION SOCIETY, Partnership House, 157
Waterloo Road, London SE1 8UU. Tel: 020-7928-8681;
Fax: 020-7401 3215; E-mail: info@cms-uk.org;
Web: http://www.cms-uk.org

CHURCH MONUMENTS SOCIETY, c/o Society of
Antiquaries, Burlington House, Piccadilly, London
W1V 0HS. Tel: 020-7734 0193; Fax: 020-7287 6967

CHURCH OF ENGLAND PENSIONS BOARD (1926), 29 Great
Smith Street, London SW1P 3PS. Tel: 020-7898 1800;
Fax: 020-7898 1801

CHURCH UNION, Faith House, 7 Tufton Street, London
SW1P 3QN. Tel: 020-7222 6952; Fax: 020-7976 7180;
E-mail: faithhouse@thechurchunion.demon.co.uk;
Web: http://www.churchunion.care4free.net

CHURCHES MAIN COMMITTEE (1941), Fielden House,
13 Little College Street, London SW1P 3SH. Tel: 020-7222
4984; Fax: 020-7898 1899; E-mail: cmc@c-of-e.org.uk

CHURCH'S MINISTRY AMONG JEWISH PEOPLE, 30C
Clarence Road, St Albans, Herts AL1 4JJ.
Tel: 01727-833114; Fax: 01727-848312; E-mail:
enquiries@cmj.org.uk; Web: http://www.cmj.org.uk

THE CHURCHILL SOCIETY - LONDON (1990),
c/o 18 Grove Lane, Ipswich, Suffolk IP4 1NR.
Tel: 01473-413533; Fax: 01473-413533;
E-mail: secretary@churchill-society-london.org.uk;
Web: http://www.churchill-society-london.org.uk/
index.htm

CITY BUSINESS LIBRARY, Brewers Hall Garden
(off Aldermanbury Square), London EC2V 5BX.
Tel: 020-7332 1812; Fax: 020-7332 1847

CITY OF COVENTRY FREEMEN'S GUILD, 47 Brownshill
Green Road, Coventry CV6 2AP. Tel: 024-7633 3980

CITY OF STOKE-ON-TRENT MUSEUM ARCHAEOLOGICAL
SOCIETY (1959), The Potteries Museum and Art Gallery,
Hanley, Stoke-on-Trent ST1 3DW. Tel: 01782-232323

CITY PAROCHIAL FOUNDATION, 6 Middle Street, London
EC1A 7PH. Tel: 020-7606 6145; Fax: 020-7600 1866

THE CIVIC TRUST (1957), 17 Carlton House Terrace,
London SW1Y 5AW. Tel: 020-7930 0914;
Fax: 020-7321 0180; E-mail: pride@civictrust.org.uk;
Web: http://www.civictrust.org.uk

CLASSICAL ASSOCIATION (1903), Senate House, Malet
Street, London WC1E 7HU. Tel: 020-7862 8706;
Fax: 020-7862 8729; E-mail: croberts@sas.ac.uk;
Web: http://www.sas.ac.uk/icls/ClassAss

CLERGY ORPHAN CORPORATION, 1 Dean Trench
Street, London SW1P 3HB. Tel: 020-7799 3696;
Fax: 020-7233 1913

COLLEGE OF OPTOMETRISTS (1980), 42 Craven Street,
London WC2N 5NG. Tel: 020-7839 6000; Fax: 020-7839
6800; E-mail: optometry@college-optometrists.org;
Web: http://www.college-optometrists.org

COMMERCIAL TRAVELLERS' BENEVOLENT INSTITUTION
(1849), Regent Farm Estate, 54 Rothbury Avenue,
Gosforth, Newcastle upon Tyne NE3 3HL.
Tel: 0191-284 9100; Fax: 0191-284 9100;
E-mail: gill.tate@ctb.swinternet.co.uk

COMMONWEALTH FORESTRY ASSOCIATION, c/o Oxford
Forestry Institute, South Parks Road, Oxford OX1 3RB. Tel:
01865-271037; Fax: 01865-275074;
E-mail: cfa_oxford@hotmail.com

COMMONWEALTH SOCIETY FOR THE DEAF 'SOUND
SEEKERS', 34 Buckingham Palace Road, London
SW1W 0RE. Tel: 020-7233 5700; Fax: 020-7233 5800;
E-mail: sound.seekers@btinternet.com

CONSUMERS' ASSOCIATION (1957), c/o The Association
for Consumer Research, 2 Marylebone Road, London
NW1 4DF. Tel: 020-7770 7000; Fax: 020-7770 7220.
Web: http://www.which.net

CONTEMPORARY APPLIED ARTS (1948), 2 Percy Street,
London W1P 9FA. Tel: 020-7436 2344; Fax: 020-7436
2446. Web: http://www.caa.org.uk

CO-OPERATIVE UNION LTD (1869), Holyoake House,
Hanover Street, Manchester M60 0AS.
Tel: 0161-246 9200; Fax: 0161-831 7684;
E-mail: pgreen.coopunion@co-op.co.uk; Web:
http://www.co-op.co.uk/UKCOM/Union/index.html

CO-OPERATIVE WHOLESALE SOCIETY LTD (1863), PO Box
53, New Century House, Manchester M60 4ES.
Tel: 0161-834 1212; Web: http://www.co-op.co.uk

CORAM FAMILY (1739), 49 Mecklenburgh Square, London
WC1N 2QA. Tel: 020-7520 0300; Fax: 020-7520 0301;
E-mail: reception@coram.org.uk;
Web: http://www.coram.org.uk

CORONER'S SOCIETY OF ENGLAND AND WALES (1846),
44 Ormond Avenue, Hampton, Middx TW12 2RX

CORPORATION OF CHURCH HOUSE (1888), Church
House, Dean's Yard, London SW1P 3NZ.
Tel: 020-7898 1310; Fax: 020-7898 1321

COUNCIL FOR BRITISH ARCHAEOLOGY (1944), Bowes
Morrell House, 111 Walmgate, York YO1 9WA.
Tel: 01904-671417; Fax: 01904-671384;
E-mail: info@britarch.ac.uk;
Web: http://www.britarch.ac.uk

COUNCIL FOR BRITISH RESEARCH IN THE LEVANT, 29 The Walk, Southport, Merseyside PR8 4GB. Tel/Fax: 01704-569664; E-mail: cm@cbrluk.demon.co.uk; Web: http://www.britac.ac.uk/institutes/cbrl/index.html

COUNCIL FOR PROFESSIONS SUPPLEMENTARY TO MEDICINE, Park House, 184 Kennington Park Road, London SE11 4BU. Tel: 020-7582 0866; Fax: 020-7820 9684

COUNCIL FOR THE CARE OF CHURCHES (1921), Church House, Great Smith Street, London SW1P 3NZ. Tel: 020-7898 1866; Fax: 020-7898 1881; E-mail: enquiries@ccc.c-of-e.org.uk

COUNCIL OF CHRISTIANS AND JEWS (1942), 5th Floor, Camelford House, 87–89 Albert Embankment, London SE1 7TP. Tel: 020-7820 0090; Fax: 020-7820 0504; E-mail: cckuk@aol.com; Web: http://www.ccj.org.uk

COUNSEL AND CARE (1954), Twyman House, 16 Bonny Street, London NW1 9PG. Tel: 020-7485 1550; Fax: 020-7267 6877; E-mail: advice@counselandcare.demon.co.uk

COUNTRY HOUSES ASSOCIATION (1955), Suite 10, Synhoe Park, Aynhoe, Banbury, Oxon OX17 3BQ. Tel: 01869-812800; Fax: 01869-812819

COUNTRY LANDOWNERS ASSOCIATION, 16 Belgrave Square, London SW1X 8PQ. Tel: 020-7235 0511; Fax: 020-7235 4696; E-mail: mail@cla.org.uk; Web: http://www.cla.org.uk

COUNTRYSIDE ALLIANCE (1998), Old Town Hall, 367 Kennington Road, London SE11 4PT. Tel: 020-7582 5432; Fax: 020-7793 8484; E-mail: info@countryside-alliance.org; Web: http://www.countryside-alliance.org

COVENTRY AND DISTRICT ARCHAEOLOGICAL SOCIETY (1965), 1 Holloway Field, Coventry CV6 2DA. Tel: 024-7659 1078

CRAFTS COUNCIL (1971), 44A Pentonville Road, London N1 9BY. Tel: 020-7278 7700; Fax: 020-7837 6891; Web: http://www.craftscouncil.org.uk

CRISIS (1967), 1st Floor, Challenger House, 42 Adler Street, London E1 1EE. Tel: 020-7655 8300; Fax: 020-7247 1525; E-mail: crisis.uk@easynet.co.uk; Web: http://www.crisis.org.uk

CROSSLINKS (1922), 251 Lewisham Way, London, SE4 1XF. Tel: 020-8691 6111; Fax: 020-8694 8023; E-mail: mail@crosslinks.org

CTC (CYCLISTS' TOURING CLUB), Cotterell House, 69 Meadrow, Godalming, Surrey GU7 3HS. Tel: 01483-417217; Fax: 01483-426994; E-mail: cycling@ctc.org.uk; Web: http://www.ctc.org.uk

CUMBERLAND AND WESTMORLAND ANTIQUARIAN AND ARCHAEOLOGICAL SOCIETY (1866), 2 High Tenterfell, Kendal, Cumbria LA9 4PG. Tel: 01539-773542; Fax: 01539-773538; E-mail: info@cwaas.org.uk; Web: http://www.cwaas.org.uk

CWMNI URDD GOBAITH CYMRU (1922), Swyddfa'r Urdd, Aberystwyth, Dyfed SY23 1EN. Tel: 01970-613100; Fax: 01970-626120; E-mail: urdd@urdd.org; Web: http://www.urdd.org

CYSTIC FIBROSIS TRUST (1964), 11 London Road, Bromley, Kent BR1 1BY. Tel: 020-8464 7211; Fax: 020-8313 0472; E-mail: enquiries@cftrust.org.uk; Web: http://www.cftrust.org.uk

DATA (DESIGN AND TECHNOLOGY ASSOCIATION) (1989), 16 Wellesbourne House, Walton Road, Wellesbourne, Warks CV35 9JB. Tel: 01789-470007; Fax: 01789-841955; E-mail: data@data.org.uk; Web: http://www.data.org.uk

DEMOS (1993), Panton House, 25 Haymarket, London SW1Y 4EN. Tel: 020-7321 2200; Fax: 020-7321 2342; E-mail: mail@demos.co.uk; Web: http://www.demos.co.uk

DESIGN AND INDUSTRIES ASSOCIATION, 11 St Gabriel's Manor, Cormont Road, Lambeth, London SE5 9RH. Tel: 020-7735 8661; Fax: 020-7582 0160; E-mail: dia@bibdes.demon.co.uk

DIABETES UK (1934), 10 Queen Anne Street, London W1M 0BD. Tel: 020-7323 1531; Fax: 020-7637 3644; E-mail: info@diabetes.org.uk; Web: http://www.diabetes.org.uk

DIANA, PRINCESS OF WALES MEMORIAL FUND (1997), County Hall, Westminster Bridge Road, London SE1 7PB. Tel: 020-7902 5500; Fax: 020-7902 5511; E-mail: memorial.fund@memfund.org.uk; Web: http://www.theworkcontinues.org.uk

DICKENS FELLOWSHIP (1902), Dickens House, 48 Doughty Street, London WC1N 2LF. Tel: 020-7405 2127; Fax: 020-7831 5175; E-mail: arwilliams33@compuserve.com; Web: http://www.dickens.fellowship.btinternet.co.uk

DIRECTORY & DATABASE PUBLISHERS ASSOCIATION, PO Box 23034, London W6 0RJ. Tel: 020-8846 9707; E-mail: RosemaryPettit@msn.com; Web: http://www.directory-publisher.co.uk

DITCHLEY FOUNDATION, Ditchley Park, Enstone, Chipping Norton, Oxon OX7 4ER. Tel: 01608-677346; Fax: 01608-677399; E-mail: mail@ditchley.co.uk; Web: http://www.ditchley.co.uk

DORSET NATURAL HISTORY AND ARCHAEOLOGICAL SOCIETY, Dorset County Museum, Dorchester, Dorset DT1 1XA. Tel: 01305-262735; Fax: 01305-257180; E-mail: dorsetcountymuseum@dor-mus.demon.co.uk; Web: http://www.dorset.museum.clara.net

DOWNS SYNDROME ASSOCIATION (1970), 155 Mitcham Road, London SW17 9PG. Tel: 020-8682 4001; Fax: 020-8682 4012; E-mail: info@downs-syndrome.org.uk; Web: http://www.downs-syndrome.org.uk

DRUGSCOPE, 32–36 Loman Street, London SE1 0EE. Tel: 020-7928 1211; Fax: 020-7928 1771; E-mail: services@drugscope.org.uk; Web: http://www.drugscope.org.uk

EAST HERTFORDSHIRE ARCHAEOLOGICAL SOCIETY (1898), 1 Marsh Lane, Stanstead Abbots, Ware, Herts SG12 8HH. Tel: 01920-870664

EATING DISORDERS ASSOCIATION, First Floor, Wensum House, 103 Prince of Wales Road, Norwich NR1 1DW. Helpline: 01603-621414; Youthline: 01603-765050; E-mail: info@edauk.com; Web: http://www.edauk.com

ECCLESIOLOGICAL SOCIETY, Underedge, Back Lane, Hathersage, Sheffield S32 1AR. Tel: 01433-650833

EDINBURGH CHAMBER OF COMMERCE AND ENTERPRISE (1786), Conference House, The Exchange, 152 Morrison Street, Edinburgh EH3 8EB. Tel: 0131-477 7000; Fax: 0131-477 7002; E-mail: info@ecce.org; Web: http://www.ecce.org

EDITH CAVELL AND NATION'S FUND FOR NURSES (1920), Flints, Petersfield Road, Winchester, Hants SO23 0JID. Tel: 01962-860900; Fax: 01962-860900; E-mail: natnurses.fund@virgin.net

EDWINA MOUNTBATTEN TRUST (1960), Estate Office, Broadlands, Romsey, Hants SO51 9ZE. Tel: 01794-518885

EGYPT EXPLORATION SOCIETY, 3 Doughty Mews, London WC1N 2PG. Tel: 020-7242 1880; Fax: 020-7404 6118; E-mail: eeslondon@talk21.com; Web: htttp://www.ees.ac.uk

ELECTORAL REFORM SOCIETY (1884), 6 Chancel Street, London SE1 0UU. Tel: 020-7928 1622; Fax: 020-7401 7789; E-mail: ers@reform.demon.co.uk; Web: http://www.electoral-reform.org.uk

ELGAR FOUNDATION, The Elgar Birthplace Museum, Lower Broadheath, Worcester WR2 6RH. Tel: 01905-333224; Fax: 01905-333224

ELGAR SOCIETY (1951), c/o 29 Van Diemens Close, Chinnor, Oxon OX9 4QE. Tel: 01844-354096; Fax: 01844-354459; E-mail: elgar@music.com; Web: http://www.elgar.org

EMERGENCY PLANNING SOCIETY, Northumberland House, 11 The Pavement, Popes Lane, London W5 4NG. Tel: 020-8579 7971; Fax: 020-8579 7972; E-mail: headquarters@emergplansoc.org.uk; Web: http://www.emergplansoc.org.uk

ENABLE (SCOTTISH SOCIETY FOR THE MENTALLY HANDICAPPED), 7 Buchanan Street, Glasgow G1 3HL. Tel: 0141-226 4541; Fax: 0141-204 4398; E-mail: enable@enable.org.uk

ENGINEERING INDUSTRIES ASSOCIATION (1940), Broadway House, Tothill Street, London SW1H 9NS. Tel: 020-7222 2367; Fax: 020-7799 2206; E-mail: head.office@eia.co.uk; Web: http://www.eia.co.uk

THE ENGLISH ASSOCIATION (1906), University of Leicester, University Road, Leicester LE1 7RH. Tel: 0116-252 3982; Fax: 0116-252 2301; E-mail: engassoc@le.ac.uk; Web: http://www.le.ac.uk/engassoc/

ENGLISH FOLK DANCE AND SONG SOCIETY, Cecil Sharp House, 2 Regent's Park Road, London NW1 7AY. Tel: 020-7485 2206; Fax: 020-7284 0534; Web: http://www.efdss.org.com

ENGLISH NATIONAL BOARD FOR NURSING, MIDWIFERY AND HEALTH VISITING, Victory House, 170 Tottenham Court Road, London W1P 0HA. Tel: 020-7391 6229; Fax: 020-7383 4031. Web: http://www.enb.org.uk

ENGLISH-SPEAKING UNION OF THE COMMONWEALTH (1918), Dartmouth House, 37 Charles Street, London W1X 8AB. Tel: 020-7493 3328; Fax: 020-7495 6108; E-mail: esu@esu.org; Web: http://www.esu.org

ENGLISH TOURIST COUNCIL, Thames Tower, Black's Road, London W6 9EL. Tel: 020-8563 3000; Web: http://www.englishtourism.org.uk

ERSKINE HOSPITAL (1916), Bishopton, Renfrewshire PA7 5PU. Tel: 0141-812 1100; Fax: 0141-812 3733; Web: http://www.erskine.org/welcome.htm

ESPERANTO ASSOCIATION OF BRITAIN, 201 Felixstowe Road, Ipswich IP3 9BJ. Tel: 01473-727221; Fax: 01473-274531; E-mail: eabo@esperanto.demon.co.uk; Web: http://www.esperanto.demon.co.uk

ESSEX SOCIETY FOR ARCHAEOLOGY AND HISTORY (1852), Hollytrees Museum, High Street, Colchester CO1 1UG. Tel: 01206-271458

EVANGELICAL LIBRARY, 78A Chiltern Street, London W1M 2HB. Tel: 020-7935 6997; E-mail: stlibrary@aol.com; Web: http://www.elib.org.uk

EX-SERVICES MENTAL WELFARE SOCIETY (1919), Hollybush House, Hollybush, nr Ayr KA6 7EA. Tel: 01292-560214; Fax: 01292-560871; Web: http://www.combatstress.com

F.A.N.Y. (PRINCESS ROYAL'S VOLUNTEER CORPS), Right Wing, Duke of York's HQ, Turks Row, London SW3 4RY. Tel: 020-7730 2058; Fax: 020-7414 5399; E-mail: fanyhq@cwcom.net

FABIAN SOCIETY, 11 Dartmouth Street, London SW1H 9BN. Tel: 020-7227 4900; Fax: 020-7976 7153; E-mail: info@fabian-society.org.uk; Web: http://www.fabian-society.org.uk

FACULTY OF ACTUARIES IN SCOTLAND (1856), 18 Dublin Street, Edinburgh EH1 3PP. Tel: 0131-240 1300; Fax: 0131-240 1313; E-mail: faculty@actuaries.org.uk; Web: http://www.actuaries.org.uk

FAIR ISLE BIRD OBSERVATORY TRUST (1948), Fair Isle Bird Observatory, Fair Isle, Shetland ZE2 9JU. Tel/Fax: 01595-760258; E-mail: fairisle.birdobs@zetnet.co.uk; Web: http://www.fairislebirdobs.co.uk

FAMILY WELFARE ASSOCIATION (1869), 501–505 Kingsland Road, London E8 4AU. Tel: 020-7254 6251; Fax: 020-7245 5443; E-mail: fwa.headoffice@fwa.org.uk

FAUNA AND FLORA INTERNATIONAL, Great Eastern House, Tenison Road, Cambridge CB1 2TT. Tel: 01223-571000; Fax: 01223-461481; E-mail: info@fauna-flora.org; Web: http://www.fauna-flora.org

FEDERATION OF BRITISH ARTISTS (1961), 17 Carlton House Terrace, London SW1Y 5BD. Tel: 020-7930 6844; Fax: 020-7839 7830; Web: http://www.mallgalleries.org.uk

FEDERATION OF FAMILY HISTORY SOCIETIES (1974), PO Box 8684, Shirley, Solihull B90 4JU. Tel: 07041-492032; E-mail: info@ffhs.org.uk; Web: http://www.ffhs.org.uk

FIRE PROTECTION ASSOCIATION, Bastille Court, 2 Paris Garden, London SE1 8ND. Tel: 020-7902 5300; Fax: 020-7902 5301; E-mail: fpa@thefpa.co.uk; Web: http://www.thefpa.co.uk

FIRE SERVICES NATIONAL BENEVOLENT FUND (1943), Fund Headquarters, Marine Court, Fitzalan Road, Littlehampton, W. Sussex BN17 5NF. Tel: 01903-736062; Fax: 01903-731095

FLEET AIR ARM OFFICERS' ASSOCIATION (1957), 4 St James's Square, London SW1Y 4JU. Tel: 020-7930 7722; Fax: 020-7930 7728; E-mail: faaoa@fleetairarmoa.org; Web: http://www.fleetairarmoa.org

FOOD FROM BRITAIN, 123 Buckingham Palace Road, London SW1W 9SA. Tel: 020-7233 3111; Fax: 020-7233 9515; E-mail: jfletcher@foodfrombritain.co.uk; Web: http://www.foodfrombritain.com

FOREIGN PRESS ASSOCIATION IN LONDON (1888), 11 Carlton House Terrace, London SW1Y 5AJ. Tel: 020-7930 0445; Fax: 020-7925 0469; E-mail: secretariat@foreign-press.org.uk; Web: http://www.foreign-press.org.uk

FORENSIC SCIENCE SOCIETY (1959), Clarke House, 18A Mount Parade, Harrogate, N. Yorks HG1 1BX. Tel: 01423-506068; Fax: 01423-566391; E-mail: president@fscisoc.demon.co.uk; Web: http://forensic-science-society.org.uk

FOUNDATION FOR SPORT AND THE ARTS, PO Box 20, Liverpool L13 1HB. Tel: 0151-259 5505; Fax: 0151-230 0664

FREEMEN OF ENGLAND AND WALES, Glenrise, Churchfields, Stonesfield, Witney, Oxon OX8 8PP. Tel: 01993-891414

FRIENDS OF CATHEDRAL MUSIC, Aeron House, Llangeitho, Tregaron, Ceredigion SY25 6SU. E-mail: info@fcm.org.uk; Web: http://www.fcm.org.uk

FRIENDS OF FRIENDLESS CHURCHES, St Ann's Vestry Hall, 2 Church Entry, London EC4V 5HB. Tel: 020-7236 3934; Fax: 020-7329 3677; E-mail: ancientmonuments@talk21.com

FRIENDS OF THE BODLEIAN (1925), Bodleian Library, Oxford OX1 3BG. Tel: 01865-277022/277234; Fax: 01865-277182/277187; E-mail: fob@bodley.ox.ac.uk; Web: http://www.bodley.ox.ac.uk/friends

FRIENDS OF THE EARTH SCOTLAND, 72 Newhaven Road, Edinburgh EH6 5QG. Tel: 0131-554 9977; Fax: 0131-554 8656; E-mail: info@foe-scotland.org.uk; Web: http://www.foe-scotland.org.uk

FRIENDS OF THE ELDERLY (1905), 40–42 Ebury Street, London SW1W 0LZ. Tel: 020-7730 8263; Fax: 020-7259 0154

FRIENDS OF THE NATIONAL LIBRARIES, c/o Department of Manuscripts, The British Library, 96 Euston Road, London NW1 2DB. Tel: 020-7412 7559

FURNITURE HISTORY SOCIETY (1964), 1 Mercedes Cottages, St John's Road, Haywards Heath, W. Sussex RH16 4EH. Tel: 01444-413845; Fax: 01444-413845

GALLIPOLI ASSOCIATION (1969), Earleydene Orchard, Earleydene, Ascot, Berks SL5 9JY. Tel: 01344-626523; E-mail: webmaster@gallipoli-association.org; Web: http://www.gallipoli-association.org

GALTON INSTITUTE, 19 Northfields Prospect, London SW18 1PE

GAME CONSERVANCY TRUST, Fordingbridge, Hants SP6 1EF. Tel: 01425-652381; Fax: 01425-655848; E-mail: admin@gct.org.uk; Web: http://www.gct.org.uk

GARDENERS' ROYAL BENEVOLENT SOCIETY (1839), Bridge House, 139 Kingston Road, Leatherhead, Surrey KT22 7NT. Tel: 01372-373962; Fax: 01372-362575; E-mail: info@gardeners-grbs.org.uk

GEMMOLOGICAL ASSOCIATION AND GEM TESTING LABORATORY OF GREAT BRITAIN (1931), 27 Greville Street (Saffron Hill entrance), London EC1N 8TN. Tel: 020-7404 3334; Fax: 020-7404 8843; E-mail: gagtl@btinternet.com; Web: http://www.gagtl.ac.uk/gagtl

GENERAL DENTAL COUNCIL, 37 Wimpole Street, London W1M 8DQ. Tel: 020-7887 3800; Fax: 020-7224 3294

GENERAL MEDICAL COUNCIL (1858), 178 Great Portland Street, London W1N 6JE. Tel: 020-7580 7642; Fax: 020-7915 3641; E-mail: gmc@gmc-uk.org; Web: http://www.gmc-uk.org

GENERAL OPTICAL COUNCIL (1959), 41 Harley Street, London W1N 2DJ. Tel: 020-7580 3898; Fax: 020-7436 3525; E-mail: goc@optical.org; Web: http://www.optical.org

GENERAL OSTEOPATHIC COUNCIL (1993), Osteopathy House, 176 Tower Bridge Road, London SE1 3LU. Tel: 020-7357 6655; Fax: 020-7357 0011; E-mail: info@osteopathy.org.uk; Web: http://www.osteopathy.org.uk

GEOLOGICAL SOCIETY (1807), Burlington House, Piccadilly, London W1V 0JU. Tel: 020-7434 9944; Fax: 020-7439 8975; E-mail: enquiries@geolsoc.org.uk; Web: http://www.geolsoc.org.uk

GEORGIAN GROUP (1937), 6 Fitzroy Square, London W1P 6DX. Tel: 020-7387 1720; Fax: 020-7387 1721; E-mail: office@georgian-group.org.uk

GILBERT AND SULLIVAN SOCIETY, 1 Nethercourt Avenue, London N3 1PS

GUILD OF FREEMEN OF THE CITY OF YORK (1953) 29 Albermarle Road, York YO23 1EW. Tel: 01904-653698; Fax: 0870-052 9911; E-mail: gild@bedern.demon.co.uk; Web: http://www.bedern.demon.co.uk

GINGERBREAD, 16–17 Clerkenwell Close,
London EC1R 0AN. Tel: 020-7336 8183.
Helpline: 0800-018 4318; Fax: 020-7336 8185;
E-mail: office@gingerbread.org.uk;
Web: http://www.gingerbread.org.uk

GIRLS' FRIENDLY SOCIETY IN ENGLAND AND WALES
(1875), 126 Queens Gate, London SW7 5LQ.
Tel: 020-7589 9628; Fax: 020-7225 1458;
E-mail: platform@gfs.u-net.com;
Web: http://www.tabor.co.uk/gfs/

GIRLS' VENTURE CORPS AIR CADETS (1964), Redhill
Aerodrome, Kings Mill Lane, South Nutfield, Redhill
RH1 5JY. Tel: 01737-823345; Fax: 01737-823345;
Web: http://www.gvcac.org.uk

GLASGOW CHAMBER OF COMMERCE AND MANUFACTURES
(1783), 30 George Square, Glasgow G2 1EQ.
Tel: 0141-204 2121; Fax: 0141-221 2336;
E-mail: chamber@glasgowchamber.org;
Web: http://www.glasgowchamber.org

GRAND LODGE OF ANCIENT FREE AND ACCEPTED
MASONS OF SCOTLAND (1736), Freemasons' Hall,
96 George Street, Edinburgh EH2 3DH.
Tel: 0131-225 5304; Fax: 0131-225 3953;
Web: http://www.grandlodgescotland.com

GREEK INSTITUTE, 34 Bush Hill Road, London N21 2DS.
Tel/Fax: 020-8360 7698

THE GREEN PARTY, 1A Waterlow Road, London N19 5NJ.
Tel: 020-7272 4474; Fax: 020-7272 6653;
E-mail: office@greenparty.org.uk;
Web: http://www.greenparty.org.uk

GREENPEACE UK, Canonbury Villas, London N1 2PN.
Tel: 020-7865 8100; Fax: 020-7865 8200

THE GUIDE ASSOCIATION, 17–19 Buckingham Palace
Road, London SW1W 0PT. Tel: 020-7834 6242;
Fax: 020-7828 8317; E-mail: chq@guides.org.uk;
Web: http://www.guides.org.uk

THE GUIDE DOGS FOR THE BLIND ASSOCIATION (1934),
Hillfields, Burghfield Common, Reading, Berks RG7 3YG.
Tel: 0118-983 5555; Fax: 0118-983 5433;
E-mail: guidedogs@gdba.org.uk;
Web: http://www.gdba.org.uk

GUILD OF AID FOR GENTLEPEOPLE, 10 St Christopher's
Place, London W1M 6HY. Tel: 020-7935 0641

GUILD OF GLASS ENGRAVERS (1975), 35 Ossulton Way,
London N2 0JY. Tel/Fax: 020-8731 9352

GURKHA WELFARE TRUST (1969), 2nd Floor, 1 Old
Street, London EC1V 9XB. Tel: 020-7251 5234;
Fax: 020-7251 5248; E-mail: gwt@charity.vfree.com

HAEMOPHILIA SOCIETY, Chesterfield House, 385
Euston Road, London NW1 3AU. Tel: 020-7380 0600;
Fax: 020-7387 8220; E-mail: info@haemophilia.org.uk;
Web: http://www.haemophilia.org.uk

HAIG HOMES, Alban Dobson House, Green Lane,
Morden, Surrey SM4 5NS. Tel: 020-8685 5777;
Fax: 020-8685 5778; E-mail: haig@haighomes.org.uk;
Web: http://www.haighomes.org.uk

THE HAKLUYT SOCIETY, c/o Map Library,
The British Library, 96 Euston Road, London NW1 2DB.
Tel: 01986-788359; Fax: 01986-788181;
E-mail: office@hakluyt.com;
Web: http://www.hakluyt.com

HALIFAX ANTIQUARIAN SOCIETY (1900), 7 Hyde Park
Gardens, Haugh Shaw Road, HaliFax, W. Yorks HX1 3AH.
Tel: 01422-250780

HAMPSHIRE FIELD CLUB AND ARCHAEOLOGICAL SOCIETY,
Hyde Historic Resources Centre, 75 Hyde Street,
Winchester SO23 7DW. Tel: 01962-848269; Fax:
01962-848299; Web: http://www.fieldclub.hants.org.uk

HEARING CONCERN (BRITISH ASSOCIATION FOR THE
HARD OF HEARING) (1947), 7–11 Armstrong Road,
London W3 7JL. Tel: 020-8743 1110;
Helpline: 0845-0744600; Fax: 020-8742 9043;
E-mail: hearingconcern@hearingconcern.com;
Web: http://www.hearingconcern.com

HELP THE AGED (1961), St James's Walk, Clerkenwell
Green, London EC1R 0BE. Tel: 020-7253 0253;
Fax: 020-7251 0747; E-mail: info@helptheaged.org.uk;
Web: http://www.helptheaged.org.uk

THE HERALDRY SOCIETY, PO Box 32, Maidenhead,
Berks, SL6 3FD. Tel/Fax: 0118-932 0210;
E-mail: heraldry-society@cwcom.net

HISPANIC AND LUSO BRAZILIAN COUNCIL (1943),
Canning House, 2 Belgrave Square, London SW1X 8PJ.
Tel: 020-7235 2303; Fax: 020-7235 3587;
E-mail: enquiries@canninghouse.com;
Web: http://www.canninghouse.com

HISTORIC HOUSES ASSOCIATION, 2 Chester Street,
London SW1X 7BB. Tel: 020-7259 5688;
Fax: 020-7259 5590; E-mail: hha@compuserve.com;
Web: http://www.hha.org.uk

THE HISTORICAL ASSOCIATION (1906), 59A Kennington
Park Road, London SE11 4JH. Tel: 020-7735 3901;
Fax: 020-7582 4989; E-mail: enquiry@history.org.uk;
Web: http://www.history.org.uk

THE HOME FARM TRUST (1962), Merchants House,
Wapping Road, Bristol BS1 4RW. Tel: 0117-927 3746

HONOURABLE SOCIETY OF CYMMRODORION (1751), 30
Eastcastle Street, London W1N 7PD. Tel: 020-7631 0502;
E-mail: cymmrodorion@tinyworld.co.uk

THE HOSPITAL SATURDAY FUND (1873), 24 Upper
Ground, London SE1 9PD. Tel: 020-7928 6662;
Fax: 020-7928 0446; E-mail: sales@hsf.co.uk;
Web: http://www.hsf.co.uk

HOSTELLING INTERNATIONAL NORTHERN IRELAND,
22–32 Donegall Road, Belfast BT12 5JN.
Tel: 028-9032 4733; Fax: 028-9043 9699;
E-mail: info@hini.org.uk; Web: http://www.hini.org.uk

HOUSE OF ST BARNABAS-IN-SOHO, 1 Greek Street, London
W1V 6NQ. Tel: 020-7434 1846; Fax: 020-7434 1746

THE HOWARD LEAGUE FOR PENAL REFORM, 1
Ardleigh Road, London N1 4HS.
Tel: 020-7249 7373; Fax: 020-7249 7789;
E-mail: howard.league@ukonline.co.uk;
Web: http://www.howardleague.org

HUGUENOT SOCIETY OF GREAT BRITAIN AND IRELAND, The Huguenot Library, University College, Gower Street, London WC1E 6BT. Tel: 020-7380 7094; E-mail: s.massil@ucl.ac.uk; Web: http://www.ucl.ac.uk/UCL-INFO/Divisions/Library/Huguenot.htm

HYDROGRAPHIC SOCIETY, c/o University of East London, Longbridge Road, Dagenham, Essex RM8 2AS. Tel: 020-8597 1946; Fax: 020-8590 9730; E-mail: hydrosoc@compuserve.com; Web: http://www.hydrographicsociety.org

HYMN SOCIETY OF GREAT BRITAIN AND IRELAND (1936), 7 Paganel Road, Minehead, Somerset TA24 5ET. Tel: 01643-703530; Fax: 01643-703530; E-mail: g.wrayford@breathemail.net

ICAN (THE NATIONAL EDUCATIONAL CHARITY FOR CHILDREN WITH SPEECH AND LANGUAGE DIFFICULTIES), 4 Dyers Buildings, Holborn, London EC1N 2QP. Tel: 0870-010 4066; Fax: 0870-010 4067; E-mail: ican@ican.btinternet.com

IMMIGRATION ADVISORY SERVICE (1970), County House, 190 Great Dover Street, London SE1 4YB. Tel: 020-7357 7511; Fax: 020-7403 5875; E-mail: advice@iasuk.org; Web: http://www.iasuk.org

INCORPORATED COUNCIL OF LAW REPORTING FOR ENGLAND AND WALES (1865), Megarry House, 119 Chancery Lane, London WC2A 1PP. Tel: 020-7242 6471; Fax: 020-7831 5247; E-mail: postmaster@iclr.co.uk; Web: http://www.lawreports.co.uk

INCORPORATED SOCIETY OF MUSICIANS, 10 Stratford Place, London W1N 9AE. Tel: 020-7629 4413; Fax: 020-7408 1538; E-mail: membership@ism.org; Web: http://www.ism.org

INDEPENDENT SCHOOLS' BURSARS ASSOCIATION (1932), 5 Chapel Close, Old Basing, Basingstoke, Hants RG24 7BZ. Tel: 01256-330369; Fax: 01256-330376; E-mail: office@isba.uk.com

INDEPENDENT SCHOOLS CAREERS ORGANISATION (1973), 12A Princess Way, Camberley, Surrey GU15 3SP. Tel: 01276-21188; Fax: 01276-691833; E-mail: info@isco.org.uk; Web: http://www.isco.org.uk

INDEPENDENT SCHOOLS INFORMATION SERVICE (1972), Grosvenor Gardens House, 35–37 Grosvenor Gardens, London SW1W 0BS. Tel: 020-7798 1500; Fax: 020-7798 1501; E-mail: national@isis.org.uk; Web: http://www.isis.org.uk

INDUSTRIAL CHRISTIAN FELLOWSHIP, c/o St Matthews House, 100 George Street, Croydon CR0 1PE. Tel/Fax: 020-8656 1644; E-mail: yrq86@dial.pipex.com

INDUSTRY AND PARLIAMENT TRUST (1977), 1 Buckingham Place, London SW1E 6HR. Tel: 020-7630 3700; Fax: 020-7630 3701; E-mail: admin@ipt.org.uk; Web: http://www.ipt.org.uk

INSTITUTE FOR PUBLIC POLICY RESEARCH (1988), 30–32 Southampton Street, London WC2E 7RA. Tel: 020-7470 6100; Fax: 020-7470 6111; E-mail: postmaster@ippr.org.uk; Web: http://www.ippr.org.uk

INSTITUTE OF ACTUARIES (1848), Staple Inn Hall, High Holborn, London WC1V 7QJ. Tel: 020-7632 2100; Fax: 020-7632 2111; E-mail: institute@actuaries.org.uk; Web: http://www.actuaries.org.uk

INSTITUTE OF ADMINISTRATIVE MANAGEMENT (1915), 40 Chatsworth Parade, Petts Wood, Orpington, Kent BR5 1RW. Tel: 01689-875555; Fax: 01689-891541; E-mail: enquiries@instam.org; Web: http://www.instam.org

INSTITUTE OF BIOLOGY (1950), 20–22 Queensberry Place, London SW7 2DZ. Tel: 020-7581 8333; Fax: 020-7823 9409; E-mail: info@iob.org; Web: http://www.iob.org

INSTITUTE OF CANCER RESEARCH: ROYAL CANCER HOSPITAL, 123 Old Brompton Road, London SW7 3RP. Tel: 020-7352 8133; Fax: 020-7225 2574; Web: http://www.icr.ac.uk

INSTITUTE OF CHARTERED ACCOUNTANTS IN ENGLAND AND WALES (1880), Chartered Accountants' Hall, PO Box 433, Moorgate Place, London EC2P 2BJ. Tel: 020-7920 8100; Fax: 020-7920 0547

INSTITUTE OF CHARTERED FORESTERS (1926), 7A St Colme Street, Edinburgh EH3 6AA. Tel: 0131-225 2705; Fax: 0131-220 6128; E-mail: icf@charteredforesters.org; Web: http://www.charteredforesters.org

INSTITUTE OF CHARTERED SECRETARIES AND ADMINISTRATORS (1891), 16 Park Crescent, London W1N 4AH. Tel: 020-7580 4741; Fax: 020-7323 1132; E-mail: icsa@dial.pipex.com; Web: http://www.icsa.org.uk

INSTITUTE OF CHARTERED SHIPBROKERS, 3 St Helen's Place, London EC3A 6EJ. Tel: 020-7628 5559; Fax: 020-7628 5445; E-mail: icslon@dial.pipex.com; Web: http://www.ics.org.uk

INSTITUTE OF CLERKS OF WORKS OF GREAT BRITAIN (1882), 41 The Mall, London W5 3TJ. Tel: 020-8579 2917; Fax: 020-8579 0554; E-mail: icwgb@sagehost.co.uk

INSTITUTE OF COMPANY ACCOUNTANTS (1928), 40 Tyndalls Park Road, Bristol BS8 1PL. Tel: 0117-973 8261; Fax: 0117-923 8292

INSTITUTE OF COMPLEMENTARY MEDICINE (1982), PO Box 194, London SE16 7QZ. Tel: 020-7237 5165; Fax: 020-7237 5175; E-mail: icm@icmedicine.co.uk; Web: http://www.icmedicine.co.uk

INSTITUTE OF ECONOMIC AFFAIRS (1955), 2 Lord North Street, London SW1P 3LB. Tel: 020-7799 3745; Fax: 020-7799 2137; E-mail: iea@iea.org.uk; Web: http://www.iea.org.uk

THE INSTITUTE OF ENERGY (1927), 18 Devonshire Street, London W1N 2AU. Tel: 020-7580 7124; Fax: 020-7580 4420; E-mail: info@instenergy.org.uk; Web: http://www.instenergy.org.uk

INSTITUTE OF EXPORT (1935), Export House, 64 Clifton Street, London EC2A 4HB. Tel: 020-7247 9812; Fax: 020-7377 5343; E-mail: institute@export.org.uk; Web: http://www.export.org.uk

INSTITUTE OF FIELD ARCHAEOLOGISTS (1982), University of Reading, PO Box 239, Reading RG6 6AU. Tel: 0118-931 6446; Fax: 0118-931 6448; E-mail: admin.ifa@virgin.net; Web: http://www.archaeologists.net

INSTITUTE OF FINANCIAL ACCOUNTANTS (1916), Burford House, 44 London Road, Sevenoaks, Kent TN13 1AS. Tel: 01732-458080; Fax: 01732-455848; E-mail: mail@ifa.org.uk; Web: http://www.ifa.org.uk

INSTITUTE OF FOOD SCIENCE AND TECHNOLOGY (1964), 5 Cambridge Court, 210 Shepherd's Bush Road, London W6 7NJ. Tel: 020-7603 6316; E-mail: info@ifst.org; Web: http://www.ifst.org

INSTITUTE OF HEALTH PROMOTION AND EDUCATION, Department of Oral Health and Development, University Dental Hospital, Higher Cambridge Street, Manchester M15 6FH. Tel/Fax: 0161-275 6610; Web: http://www.ihpe.org.uk

INSTITUTE OF HEALTHCARE MANAGEMENT, 7–10 Chandos Street, London W1M 9DE. Tel: 020-7460 7654; Fax: 020-7460 7655

INSTITUTE OF HERALDIC AND GENEALOGICAL STUDIES (1961), 79–82 Northgate, Canterbury, Kent CT1 1BA. Tel: 01227-768664; Fax: 01227-765617; E-mail: ihgs@ihgs.ac.uk; Web: http://www.ihgs.ac.uk

INSTITUTE OF INFORMATION SCIENTISTS, 39–41 North Road, London N7 9DP. Tel: 020-7619 0624/5; Fax: 020-7619 0627

INSTITUTE OF LEGAL EXECUTIVES (1963), Kempston Manor, Kempston, Bedford MK42 7AB. Tel: 01234-841000; Fax: 01234-840373; E-mail: jburns@ilex.org.uk; Web: http://www.ilex.org.uk

INSTITUTE OF LINGUISTS (1910), Saxon House, 48 Southwark Street, London SE1 1UN. Tel: 020-7940 3100; Fax: 020-7940 3101; E-mail: info@iol.org.uk; Web: http://www.iol.org.uk

INSTITUTE OF LOGISTICS AND TRANSPORT (1926), 80 Portland Place, London W1N 4DP. Tel: 020-7467 9400; Fax: 020-7467 9440; E-mail: enquiry@iolt.org.uk; Web: http://www.iolt.org.uk

INSTITUTE OF MANAGEMENT, Management House, Cottingham Road, Corby, Northants NN17 1TT. Tel: 01536-204222; Fax: 01536-201651

INSTITUTE OF MARINE ENGINEERS (1889), 80 Coleman Street, London EC2R 5BJ. Tel: 020-7382 2600; Fax: 020-7382 2670; E-mail: imare@imare.org.uk; Web: http://www.imare.org.uk

INSTITUTE OF MEASUREMENT AND CONTROL (1944), 87 Gower Street, London WC1E 6AA. Tel: 020-7387 4949; Fax: 020-7388 8431; E-mail: education@instmc.org.uk; Web: http://www.instmc.org.uk

INSTITUTE OF PATENTEES AND INVENTORS (1919), Suite 505A, Triumph House, 189 Regent Street, London W1R 7WF. Tel: 020-7434 1818; Fax: 020-7434 1727; E-mail: ipi@invent.org.uk; Web: http://www.invent.org.uk

INSTITUTE OF PETROLEUM (1913), 61 New Cavendish Street, London W1M 8AR. Tel: 020-7467 7100; Fax: 020-7255 1472; E-mail: ip@petroleum.co.uk; Web: http://www.petroleum.co.uk

INSTITUTE OF PHYSICS, 76 Portland Place, London W1N 3DH. Tel: 020-7470 4800; Fax: 020-7470 4848; E-mail: physics@iop.org; Web: http://www.iop.org

INSTITUTE OF PHYSICS AND ENGINEERING IN MEDICINE, Fairmount House, 230 Tadcaster Road, York YO24 1ES. Tel: 01904-610821; Fax: 01904-612279; E-mail: office@ipem.org.uk

INSTITUTE OF PRACTITIONERS IN ADVERTISING (1917), 44 Belgrave Square, London SW1X 8QS. Tel: 020-7235 7020; Fax: 020-7245 9904; Web: http://www.ipa.co.uk

INSTITUTE OF PRINTING (1980), The Mews, Hill House, Clanricarde Road, Tunbridge Wells, Kent TN1 1PJ. Tel: 01892-538118; Fax: 01892-518028; E-mail: iop@globalprint.com; Web: http://www.globalprint.com/uk/iop

INSTITUTE OF QUALITY ASSURANCE, 12 Grosvenor Crescent, London SW1X 7EE. Tel: 020-7245 6722; Fax: 020-7245 6788; E-mail: iqa@iqa.org; Web: http://www.iqa.org

INSTITUTE OF QUARRYING (1917), 7 Regent Street, Nottingham NG1 5BS. Tel: 0115-941 1315; Fax: 0115-948 4035; E-mail: iq@qmj.co.uk; Web: http://www.inst-of-quarrying.org/iq

INSTITUTE OF ROAD TRANSPORT ENGINEERS, 22 Greencoat Place, London SW1P 1PR. Tel: 020-7630 1111; Fax: 020-7630 6677; E-mail: irte@irte.org; Web: http://www.irte.org

INSTITUTE OF SPORTS MEDICINE (1965), 2nd Floor, Charles Bell House, University College of London Medical School, 67–73 Riding House Street, London W1P 7LD. Tel: 020-7813 2832; Fax: 020-7813 2832; E-mail: m.hobsley@ucl.ac.uk

INSTITUTE OF TRADE MARK ATTORNEYS (1934), Canterbury House, 2–6 Sydenham Road, Croydon CR0 9XE. Tel: 020-8686 2052; Fax: 020-8680 5723; E-mail: tm@itma.org.uk; Web: http://www.itma.org.uk

INSTITUTE OF TRADING STANDARDS ADMINISTRATION (1881), 3–5 Hadleigh Business Centre, 351 London Road, Hadleigh, Essex SS7 2BT. Tel: 01702-559922; Fax: 01702-551161; E-mail: itsa@itsa.org.uk; Web: http://www.tradingstandards.gov.uk

INSTITUTE OF TRANSLATION AND INTERPRETING (1986), 377 City Road, London EC1V 1ND. Tel: 020-7713 7600; Fax: 020-7713 7650; E-mail: info@iti.org.uk; Web: http://www.iti.org.uk

INSTITUTE OF WASTES MANAGEMENT, 9 Saxon Court, St Peter's Gardens, Northampton NN1 1SX. Tel: 01604-620426; Fax: 01604-621339; E-mail: technical@iwm.co.uk; Web: http://www.iwm.co.uk

INSTITUTION OF CHEMICAL ENGINEERS (1922), Davis Building, 165–189 Railway Terrace, Rugby, Warks CV21 3HQ. Tel: 01788-578214; Fax: 01788-560833; Web: http://www.icheme.org.uk

INSTITUTION OF ELECTRICAL ENGINEERS, Savoy Place, London WC2R 0BL. Tel: 020-7240 1871; Fax: 020-7240 7735; E-mail: postmaster@iee.org.uk; Web: http://www.iee.org.uk

INSTITUTION OF ENGINEERING DESIGNERS (1945), Courtleigh, Westburgh Leigh, Westbury, Wilts BA13 3TA. Tel: 01373-822801; Fax: 01373-858085; E-mail: ied@inst-engg-design.demon.co.uk; Web: http://www.ied.org.uk

INSTITUTION OF GAS ENGINEERS, 21 Portland Place, London W1N 3AF. Tel: 020-7636 6603; Fax: 020-7636 6602; E-mail: general@igaseng.demon.co.uk; Web: http://www.igaseng.com

INSTITUTION OF MECHANICAL ENGINEERS (1847), 1 Birdcage Walk, London SW1H 9JJ. Tel: 020-7222 7899; Fax: 020-7222 8553; Web: http://www.imeche.org.uk

INSTITUTION OF STRUCTURAL ENGINEERS (1908), 11 Upper Belgrave Street, London SW1X 8BH. Tel: 020-7235 4535; Fax: 020-7235 4294; E-mail: mail@istructe.org.uk; Web: http://www.istructe.org.uk

INTERCONTINENTAL CHURCH SOCIETY, 1 Athena Drive, Tachbrook Park, War CV34 6NL. Tel: 01926-430347; Fax: 01926-330238; E-mail: enquiries@ics-uk.org; Web: http://www.ics-uk.org

INTERNATIONAL AFRICAN INSTITUTE (1926), SOAS, Thornhaugh Street, Russell Square, London WC1H 0XG. Tel: 020-7898 4420; Fax: 020-7898 4419; E-mail: iai@soas.ac.uk; Web: http://www.oneworld.org/iai

INTERNATIONAL BALZAN FOUNDATION (1961), Piazzetta Giordano 4, Milan, Italy 20122. Tel: 00-39-02-7600 2212; Fax: 00-39-02-7600 9457; E-mail: balzan@balzan.it; Web: http://www.balzan.it

INTERNATIONAL CHURCHILL SOCIETY (1968), PO Box 1257, Melksham, Wilts SN12 6GQ. Tel: 01380-828609; Fax: 01380-828609; Web: http://www.winstonchurchill.org

INTERNATIONAL CONSULTING ECONOMISTS' ASSOCIATION (1986), c/o Capricorn Business Services, 50–52 London End, Beaconsfield, Bucks HP9 2JH. Tel: 01494-670372; Fax: 01494-675426; E-mail: capricorn_business@compuserve.com

INTERNATIONAL FRIENDSHIP LEAGUE, 3 Creswick Road, London W3 9HE

INTERNATIONAL INSTITUTE FOR CONSERVATION OF HISTORIC AND ARTISTIC WORKS, 6 Buckingham Street, London WC2N 6BA. Tel: 020-7839 5975; Fax: 020-7976 1564; E-mail: iicon@compuserve.com; Web: http://www.iiconservation.org

INTERNATIONAL INSTITUTE FOR STRATEGIC STUDIES (1958), Arundel House, 13–15 Arundel Street, Temple Place, London WC2R 3DX. Tel: 020-7379 7676; Fax: 020-7836 3108; E-mail: iiss@iiss.org.uk; Web: http://www.isn.ethz.ch/iiss

INTERNATIONAL Pen (1921), 9–10 Charterhouse Buildings, Goswell Road, London EC1M 7AT. Tel: 020-7253 4308; Fax: 020-7253 5711; E-mail: intpen@dircon.co.uk; Web: http://oneworld.org/internatpen

INTERNATIONAL POLICE ASSOCIATION (BRITISH SECTION), 1 Fox Road, West Bridgford, Nottingham NG2 6AJ. Tel: 0115-981 3638; E-mail: mail@ipa-uk.org; Web: http://www.ipa-uk.org

INTERNATIONAL TREE FOUNDATION, Sandy Lane, Crawley Down, W. Sussex RH10 4HS. Tel: 01342-712536; Fax: 01342-718282; E-mail: hq.itf@tree-foundation.org.uk; Web: http://www.tree-foundation.org.uk

INTERSERVE, 325 Kennington Road, London SE11 4QH. Tel: 020-7735 8227; Fax: 020-7587 5362; Web: http://www.interserve.org/ew

INVALIDS-AT-HOME (1965), 17 Lapstone Gardens, Kenton, Harrow, Middx HA3 0EB. Tel: 020-8907 1706

INVERNESS FIELD CLUB, 6 Drumblair Crescent, Inverness, IV2 4RG

IRAN SOCIETY, 2 Belgrave Square, London SW1X 8PJ. Tel: 020-7235 5122; Fax: 020-7259 6771

IRISH GENEALOGICAL RESEARCH SOCIETY (1936), c/o The Irish Club, 82 Eaton Square, London SW1W 9AJ. Tel: 020-7235 4164

ISLE OF WIGHT NATURAL HISTORY AND ARCHAEOLOGICAL SOCIETY, Island Countryside Centre, Rylstone Gardens, Shanklin, Isle of Wight PO37 6RG. Tel: 01983-867016

ITRI LTD, Kingston Lane, Uxbridge, Middx UB8 3PJ. Tel: 01895-272406; Fax: 01895-251841; E-mail: postmaster@itri.co.uk; Web: http://www.itri.co.uk

JACQUELINE DU PRÉ MUSIC BUILDING LTD, St Hilda's College, Oxford OX4 1DY. Tel: 01865-276821; Fax: 01865-286674; E-mail: jdp@st-hildas.ox.ac.uk; Web: http://www.sthildas.ox.ac.uk/jdp

JERUSALEM AND THE MIDDLE EAST CHURCH ASSOCIATION, 1 Hart House, The Hart, Farnham, Surrey GU9 7HJ. Tel: 01252-726994; Fax: 01252-735558; E-mail: jmeca@lineone.net

JOHN CURWEN SOCIETY, 5 Bigbury Close, Styvechale, Coventry CV3 5AJ. Tel: 024-7641 3010

JOHN STUART MILL INSTITUTE (1992), 1 Whitehall Place, London SW1A 2HE. Tel: 01582-615067; Fax: 01582-615087; E-mail: julian.wates@net.ntl.com; Web: http://www.jsminstitute.org.uk

JUSTICE (1957), 59 Carter Lane, London EC4V 5AQ. Tel: 020-7329 5100; Fax: 020-7329 5055; E-mail: admin@justice.org.uk

JUSTICES' CLERKS' SOCIETY, The Magistrates' Court, 107 Dale Street, Liverpool L2 2JQ. Tel: 0151-255 0790; Fax: 0151-236 4458; E-mail: honsec@jc-society.co.uk; Web: http://www.jc-society.co.uk

KENT ARCHAEOLOGICAL SOCIETY, Three Elms, Woodlands Lane, Shorne, Gravesend, Kent DA12 3HH. E-mail: secretary@kentarchaeology.org.uk; Web: http://ourworld.compuserve.com/homepages/ai_moffat

KING GEORGE'S FUND FOR SAILORS (1917), 8 Hatherley Street, London SW1P 2YY. Tel: 020-7932 0000; Fax: 020-7932 0095; E-mail: seafarers@kgfs.org.uk; Web: http://www.kgfs.org.uk

KING'S FUND (1897), 11–13 Cavendish Square, London W1M 0AN. Tel: 020-7307 2400; Fax: 020-7307 2801; Web: http://www.kingsfund.org.uk

KIPLING SOCIETY (1927), 6 Clifton Road, London W9 1SS. Tel: 020-7286 0194; Fax: 020-7286 0194; E-mail: sharadkeskar@hotmail.com; Web: http://www.kipling.org.uk

LANDSCAPE INSTITUTE (1929), 6–8 Barnard Mews, London SW11 1QU. Tel: 020-7350 5200; Fax: 020-7350 5201; E-mail: mail@l-i.org.uk; Web: http://www.l-i.org.uk

THE LEAGUE (1893), 119–133 Limekiln Lane, Liverpool L5 8SN. Tel: 0151-207 1984; Fax: 0151-207 1984; E-mail: info@theleague.liv.org.uk

LEAGUE OF THE HELPING HAND, Petersham Hollow, 226 Petersham Road, Petersham, Richmond, Surrey TW10 7AL. Tel: 020-8940 7303; Fax: 020-8940 7303

LEATHER AND HIDE TRADES' BENEVOLENT INSTITUTION (1860), 60 Wickham Hill, Hurstpierpoint, Hassocks, W. Sussex BN6 9NP. Tel: 01273-843488; Fax: 01273-843488

LEPROSY MISSION (ENGLAND AND WALES) (1874), Goldhay Way, Orton Goldhay, Peterborough PE2 5GZ. Tel: 01733-370505; Fax: 01733-404880; E-mail: post@tlmew.org.uk; Web: http://www.leprosymission.org

LEUKAEMIA RESEARCH FUND (1960), 43 Great Ormond Street, London WC1N 3JJ. Tel: 020-7405 0101; Fax: 020-7405 3139; E-mail: info@lrf.org.uk; Web: http://www.lrf.org.uk

THE LIBERAL PARTY (1877), PO Box 263, Southport, Lancs PR9 9WS. Tel: 01704-500115; Fax: 01704-500115; E-mail: libparty@libparty.demon.co.uk; Web: http://www.liberal.org.uk

LIBERTY (NATIONAL COUNCIL FOR CIVIL LIBERTIES) (1934), 21 Tabard Street, London SE1 4LA. Tel: 020-7403 3888; Fax: 020-7407 5354; E-mail: info@liberty-human-rights.org.uk; Web: http://www.liberty-human-rights.org.uk

LINNEAN SOCIETY OF LONDON, Burlington House, Piccadilly, London W1V 0LQ. Tel: 020-7434 4479; Fax: 020-7287 9364; E-mail: john@linnean.org; Web: http://www.linnean.org

LIONS CLUBS INTERNATIONAL (BRITISH ISLES AND IRELAND), 257 Alcester Road South, Kings Heath, Birmingham B14 6DT. Tel: 0121-441 4544; Fax: 0121-441 4510

LISTENING BOOKS, 12 Lant Street, London SE1 1QH. Tel: 020-7407 9417; Fax: 020-7403 1377; E-mail: info@listening-books.org.uk; Web: http://www.listening-books.org.uk

LLOYD'S REGISTER OF SHIPPING, 71 Fenchurch Street, London EC3M 4BS. Tel: 020-7709 9166; Fax: 020-7488 4796; E-mail: mipg@lr.org; Web: http://www.lr.org

LOCAL GOVERNMENT ASSOCIATION, Local Government House, Smith Square, London SW1P 3HZ. Tel: 020-7664 3000; Fax: 020-7664 3030; E-mail: info@lga.gov.uk; Web: http://www.lga.gov.uk

LONDON AND MIDDLESEX ARCHAEOLOGICAL SOCIETY, 34 Alexandra Road, Wimbledon, London SW19 7JZ. Tel: 020-8879 7109

LONDON APPRECIATION SOCIETY (1932), 7–20 Hampden Gurney Street, London W1H 5AL. Tel: 020-7724 0221

LONDON ASSOCIATION IN AID OF MORAVIAN MISSIONS, Moravian Church House, 5–7 Muswell Hill, London N10 3TJ. Tel: 020-8883 3409; Fax: 020-8365 3371; E-mail: moravianchurchhouse@btinternet.com; Web: http://www.moravian.org.uk

LONDON CHAMBER OF COMMERCE AND INDUSTRY, 33 Queen Street, London EC4R 1AP. Tel: 020-7248 4444; Fax: 020-7203 1570; E-mail: lc@londonchamber.co.uk; Web: http://www.londonchamber.co.uk

LONDON COLLEGE OF OSTEOPATHIC MEDICINE, 8–10 Boston Place, London NW1 6QH. Tel: 020-7262 5250; Fax: 020-7723 7492

LONDON COURT OF INTERNATIONAL ARBITRATION (LCIA), 6th Floor, Hulton House, 161–166 Fleet Street, London EC4A 2DY. Tel: 020-7936 3530; Fax: 020-7936 3533; E-mail: ib@lcia-arbitration.com; Web: http://www.icia-arbitration.com/lcia/

LONDON FLOTILLA (1937), 40 Endlesham Road, London SW12 8JL. Tel: 020-8673 1879; Fax: 020-8673 1879

THE LONDON LIBRARY, 14 St James's Square, London SW1Y 4LG. Tel: 020-7930 7705; Fax: 020-7766 4766; E-mail: membership@londonlibrary.co.uk; Web: http://webpac.londonlibrary.co.uk

LONDON MAGISTRATES' CLERKS' ASSOCIATION (1889), c/o South Western Magistrates' Court, 176A Lavender Hill, Battersea, London SW11 1JU. Tel: 020-7805 1413; Fax: 020-7805 1409

LONDON PLAYING FIELDS SOCIETY (1890), Fraser House, 29 Albermarle Street, London W1X 3FA. Tel: 020-7493 3211; Fax: 020-7409 3405; E-mail: lonplayingfields@aol.com

THE LONDON SOCIETY (1912), 4th Floor, Senate House, Malet Street, London WC1E 7HU. Tel: 020-7580 5537

LORD'S DAY OBSERVANCE SOCIETY (1831), 3 Epsom Business Park, Kiln Lane, Epsom, Surrey KT17 1JF. Tel: 01372-728300; Fax: 01372-722400; E-mail: info@dayone.co.uk; Web: http://www.lordsday.co.uk

THE LOTTERIES COUNCIL (1979), Woodlands, High Grove Road, Grasscroft, Saddleworth OL4 4HG. Tel: 01457-872988; Fax: 01457-872988; E-mail: sue@lotco.freeserve.co.uk; Web: http://www.lotteriescouncil.co.uk

MACA – PARTNERS IN MENTAL HEALTH (1859), 2T Bedford Square, London WC1B 3HW. Tel: 020-7436 6194; Fax: 020-7637 1980; E-mail: maca-bs@maca.org.uk; Web: http://www.maca.org.uk

MACMILLAN CANCER RELIEF, Anchor House, 15–19 Britten Street, London SW3 3TZ. Tel: 020-7351 7811; Fax: 020-7376 8098; Web: http://www.macmillan.org.uk

MAGISTRATES' ASSOCIATION, 28 Fitzroy Square, London W1P 6DD. Tel: 020-7387 2353; Fax: 020-7383 4020; E-mail: secretariat@magistrates-association.org.uk; Web: http://www.magistrates-association.org.uk/mags.assn/

MAIL USERS' ASSOCIATION (1976), 70 Main Road, Hermitage, Near Emsworth, W. Sussex PO10 8AX. Tel: 0976-710315; Fax: 01243-370840; E-mail: jeremypartridge@compuserve.com

MANIC DEPRESSION FELLOWSHIP, Castle Works, 21 St George's Road, London SE1 6ES. Tel: 020-7793 2600; Fax: 020-7793 2639 E-mail: mdf@mdf.org.uk; Web: http://www.mdf.org.uk

MANORIAL SOCIETY OF GREAT BRITAIN (1906), 104 Kennington Road, London SE11 6RE. Tel: 020-7735 6633; Fax: 020-7582 7022; E-mail: msgb@manor.net

MANPOWER SOCIETY LTD (1970), 34 Downview Road, Felpham, Bognor Regis, W. Sussex PO22 8HH. Tel: 01243-837355; Fax: 01243-837355; E-mail: heather@mansoc.org.uk; Web: http://www.mansoc.demon.co.uk

MARIE CURIE CANCER CARE (1948), 89 Albert Embankment, London SE1 7TP. Tel: 020-7599 7777; Fax: 020-7599 7788; E-mail: info@mariecurie.org.uk; Web: http://www.mariecurie.org.uk

MARINE BIOLOGICAL ASSOCIATION OF THE UK (1884), Citadel Hill, Plymouth PL1 2PB. Tel: 01752-633100; Fax: 01752-633102; E-mail: sec@mba.ac.uk; Web: http://www1.npm.ac.uk/mba

THE MARINE SOCIETY (1756), 202 Lambeth Road, London SE1 7JW. Tel: 020-7261 9535; Fax: 020-7401 2537; E-mail: enq@marine-society.org; Web: http://www.marine-society.org

MARIO LANZA EDUCATIONAL FOUNDATION (1976), 646 Portway, Avonmouth, Bristol BS11 9NZ

MATHEMATICAL ASSOCIATION, 259 London Road, Leicester LE2 3BE. Tel: 0116-221 0013; Fax: 0116-212 2835

ME ASSOCIATION, 4 Corringham Road, Stanford-le-Hope, Essex SS17 0AH. Tel: 01375-642466; Fax: 01375-360256; E-mail: enquiries@meassociation.org.uk; Web: http://www.meassociation.org.uk

MEDICAL SOCIETY FOR THE STUDY OF VENEREAL DISEASES, 1 Wimpole Street, London W1M 8AE. Tel: 020-7290 2968; Fax: 020-7290 2989; E-mail: mssvd@roysocmed.ac.uk; Web: http://www.mssvd.org.uk

MEDICAL SOCIETY OF LONDON (1773), Lettsom House, 11 Chandos Street, London W1M 0EB. Tel: 020-7580 1043; Fax: 020-7580 5793

MEDICAL WOMEN'S FEDERATION, Tavistock House North, Tavistock Square, London WC1H 9HX. Tel: 020-7387 7765; Fax: 020-7387 7765; E-mail: lyn@m-w-f.demon.co.uk

MEDIC-ALERT FOUNDATION, 1 Bridge Wharf, 156 Caledonian Road, London N1 9UU. Tel: 020-7833 3034; Fax: 020-7278 0647; E-mail: info@medicalert.co.uk; Web: http://www.medicalert.co.uk

MENCAP (ROYAL SOCIETY FOR MENTALLY HANDICAPPED CHILDREN AND ADULTS), 123 Golden Lane, London EC1Y 0RT. Tel: 020-7454 0454; Fax: 020-7608 3254; E-mail: info@mencap.org.uk; Web: http://www.mencap.co.uk

MERCHANT NAVY WELFARE BOARD, 19–21 Lancaster Gate, London W2 3LN. Tel: 020-7723 3642; Fax: 020-7723 3643; E-mail: enquiries@mnwb.org.uk; Web: http://www.merchantnavywelfare.org.uk

METROPOLITAN HOSPITAL-SUNDAY FUND (1873), 45 Westminster Bridge Road, London SE1 7JB. Tel: 020-7922 0200; Fax: 020-7401 3641; E-mail: mhsf@peabody.org.uk; Web: http://www.mhsf.org.uk

MIGRAINE ACTION ASSOCIATION (1958), 178A High Road, Byfleet, West Byfleet, Surrey KT14 7ED. Tel: 01932-352468; Fax: 01932-351257; E-mail: info@migraine.org.uk; Web: http://www.migraine.org.uk

THE MIGRAINE TRUST, 45 Great Ormond Street, London WC1N 3HZ. Tel: 020-7831 4818; Fax: 020-7831 5174; Web: http://www.migrainetrust.org

MILITARY HISTORICAL SOCIETY, National Army Museum, Royal Hospital Road, London SW3 4HT. Tel: 01980-615689; Fax: 01980-618746

MINERALOGICAL SOCIETY, 41 Queen's Gate, London SW7 5HR. Tel: 020-7584 7516; Fax: 020-7823 8021

THE MISSION TO SEAFARERS, The Michael Paternoster Royal, College Hill, London EC4R 2RL. Tel: 020-7248 5202; Fax: 020-7248 4761; E-mail: general@missiontoseafarers.org; Web: http://www.missiontoseafarers.org

MODERN CHURCHPEOPLE'S UNION (1898), MCU Office, 25 Birch Grove, London W3 9SP. Tel: 020-8932 4379; Fax: 020-8993 5812; E-mail: modchurchunion@btinternet.com; Web: http://www.mcm.co.uk/modchurchunion

THE MOTHERS' UNION (1876), Mary Sumner House, 24 Tufton Street, London SW1P 3RB. Tel: 020-7222 5533; Fax: 020-7222 1591; E-mail: mu@themothersunion.org; Web: http://www.themothersunion.org

MOUNTBATTEN MEMORIAL TRUST (1979), Estate Office, Broadlands, Romsey, Hants SO51 9ZE. Tel: 01794-518885

MULTIPLE SCLEROSIS SOCIETY, 25 Effie Road, London SW6 1EE. Tel: 020-7610 7171; Fax: 020-7736 8861. Web: http://www.mssociety.org.uk

MUSEUMS ASSOCIATION, 42 Clerkenwell Close, London EC1R 0PA. Tel: 020-7608 2933; Fax: 020-7250 1929; E-mail: info@museumassociation.org; Web: http://www.museumsassociation.org

MUSICIANS BENEVOLENT FUND (1921), 16 Ogle Street, London W1P 8JB. Tel: 020-7636 4481; Fax: 020-7637 4307; E-mail: hfaulkner@mbf.org.uk; Web: http://www.mbf.org.uk

NACRO, THE CRIME REDUCATION CHARITY (1966), 169 Clapham Road, London SW9 0PU. Tel: 020-7582 6500; Fax: 020-7735 4666; E-mail: office@narco.org.uk; Web: http://www.narco.org

NATIONAL ADULT SCHOOL ORGANISATION (1899), Riverton, 370 Humberstone Road, Leicester LE5 0SA. Tel: 0116-253 8333; Fax: 0116-251 3626; E-mail: gensec@naso.org.uk; Web: http://www.naso.org.uk

NATIONAL ART COLLECTIONS FUND (1903), Mallais House, 7 Cromwell Place, London SW7 2JN. Tel: 020-7225 4800; Fax: 020-7225 4848; E-mail: info@art-fund.org; Web: http://www.art-fund.org

NATIONAL ASSOCIATION FOR COLITIS AND CROHN'S DISEASE (1979), 4 Beaumont House, Sutton Road, St Albans, Herts AL1 5HH. Tel: 01727-830038; Fax: 01727-862550; E-mail: nacc@nacc.org.uk; Web: http://www.nacc.org.uk

NATIONAL ASSOCIATION FOR GIFTED CHILDREN (1967), Elder House, Milton Keynes MK9 1LR. Tel: 01908-673677; Fax: 01908-673679; E-mail: nagc@rmplc.co.uk; Web: http://www.rmplc.co.uk/orgs/nagc/index.html

NATIONAL ASSOCIATION OF BRITISH MARKET AUTHORITIES (1919), 13 Moor Road, Orrell Post, Wigan, WN5 8ND. Tel: 01942-203797; Fax: 01942-205885; E-mail: nabma@aol.com; Web: http://members.aol.com/nabma/nabma.html

NATIONAL ASSOCIATION OF CITIZENS' ADVICE BUREAUX (1939), Myddelton House, 115–123 Pentonville Road, London N1 9LZ. Tel: 020-7833 2181; Fax: 020-7833 4371; Web: http://www.nacab.org.uk

NATIONAL ASSOCIATION OF CLUBS FOR YOUNG PEOPLE, 371 Kennington Lane, London SE11 5QY. Tel: 020-7793 0787; Fax: 020-7820 9815; E-mail: office@nacyp.org.uk; Web: http://www.nacpy.org.uk

NATIONAL ASSOCIATION OF ESTATE AGENTS (1962), Arbon House, 21 Jury Street, Warwick CV34 4EH. Tel: 01926-496800; Fax: 01926-400953; E-mail: info@naea.co.uk; Web: http://www.naea.co.uk

NATIONAL ASTHMA CAMPAIGN (1990), Providence House, Providence Place, London N1 0NT. Tel: 020-7226 2260; Fax: 020-7704 0740; Web: http://www.asthma.org.uk

NATIONAL BENEVOLENT INSTITUTION (1812), 61 Bayswater Road, London W2 3PG. Tel: 020-7723 0021; Fax: 020-7706 7035

NATIONAL BLOOD AUTHORITY, Oak House, Reeds Crescent, Watford, Herts WD1 1QH. Tel: 01923-486800; Fax: 01923-486801

NATIONAL BOARD FOR NURSING, MIDWIFERY AND HEALTH VISITING FOR NORTHERN IRELAND (1979 and 1983), Centre House, 79 Chichester Street, Belfast BT1 4JE. Tel: 028-9023 8152; Fax: 028-9033 3298; E-mail: enquiries@nbni.n-i.nhs.uk; Web: http://www.n-i.nhs.uk/NBNI/index.htm

NATIONAL CAMPAIGN FOR THE ARTS LTD (1985), Pegasus House, 37–43 Sackville Street, London W1X 1DB. Tel: 020-7333 0375; Fax: 020-7333 0660; E-mail: nca@artscampaign.org.uk

NATIONAL CHILDBIRTH TRUST (1956), Alexandra House, Oldham Terrace, London W3 6NH. Tel: 020-8992 2616; Enquiries: 020-8992 8637; Fax: 020-8992 5929; Web: http://www.nct-online.org

NATIONAL COUNCIL FOR ONE-PARENT FAMILIES (1918), 255 Kentish Town Road, London NW5 2LX. Tel: 020-7428 5400; Fax: 020-7482 4851; E-mail: info@oneparentfamilies.org.uk

NATIONAL COUNCIL FOR VOLUNTARY ORGANISATIONS (1919), Regents Wharf, 8 All Saints Street, London N1 9RL. Tel: 020-7713 6161; Fax: 020-7713 6300

NATIONAL EXTENSION COLLEGE, 18 Brooklands Avenue, Cambridge CB2 2HN. Tel: 01223-450200; Fax: 01223-313586; E-mail: info@nec.ac.uk; Web: http://www.nec.ac.uk

NATIONAL FEDERATION OF MUSIC SOCIETIES (1935), 7–15 Rosebery Avenue, London EC1R 4SP. Tel: 020-7841 0110; Fax: 020-7841 0115; E-mail: nfms@nfms.org.uk; Web: http://www.nfms.org.uk

NATIONAL FEDERATION OF RETIREMENT PENSIONS ASSOCIATIONS (1940), Thwaites House, Railway Road, Blackburn BB1 5AX. Tel: 01254-52606; Fax: 01254-52606

NATIONAL FEDERATION OF WOMEN'S INSTITUTES, 104 New Kings Road, London SW6 4LY. Tel: 020-7371 9300; Fax: 020-7736 3652; E-mail: cs@nfwi.org.uk; Web: http://www.nfwi.org.uk

NATIONAL FOUNDATION FOR EDUCATIONAL RESEARCH IN ENGLAND AND WALES (1946), The Mere, Upton Park, Slough SL1 2DQ. Tel: 01753-574123; Fax: 01753-691632; E-mail: enquiries@nfer.ac.uk; Web: http://www.nfer.ac.uk

NATIONAL GARDENS SCHEME CHARITABLE TRUST (1927), Hatchlands Park, East Clandon, Guildford, Surrey GU4 7RT. Tel: 01483-211535; Fax: 01483-211537; E-mail: ngs@ngs.org.uk; Web: http://www.ngs.org.uk

NATIONAL LIBRARY FOR THE BLIND (1828), Far Cromwell Road, Bredbury, Stockport, Cheshire SK6 2SG. Tel: 0161-355 2000; Fax: 0161-355 2098; E-mail: enquiries@nlbuk.org; Web: http://www.nlbuk.org

NATIONAL MISSING PERSONS HELPLINE (1992), PO Box 28908, London SW14 7ZU. Tel: 020-8392 4545; Freefone: 0500-700700; Fax: 020-8878 7752; E-mail: nmph.press@virgin.net; Web: http://www.missingpersons.com

NATIONAL OPERATIC AND DRAMATIC ASSOCIATION (1899), NODA House, 1 Crestfield Street, London WC1H 8AU. Tel: 020-7837 5655; Fax: 020-7833 0609; E-mail: everyone@noda-hq.org; Web: http://www.noda-hq.org

NATIONAL PLAYING FIELDS ASSOCIATION (1925), 25 Ovington Square, London SW3 1LQ. Tel: 020-7584 6445; Fax: 020-7581 2402; E-mail: npfa@npfa.co.uk; Web: http://www.npfa.co.uk

NATIONAL SCHIZOPHRENIA FELLOWSHIP SCOTLAND (1985), Claremont House, 130 East Claremont Street, Edinburgh EH7 4LB. Tel: 0131-557 8969; Fax: 0131-557 8968; E-mail: info@nsfscot.org.uk; Web: http://www.nsfscot.org.uk

NATIONAL SECULAR SOCIETY LTD (1866), 25 Red Lion Square, London WC1R 4RL. Tel: 020-7404 3126; Fax: 020-7404 3126; E-mail: kpw@secularism.org.uk; Web: http://www.secularism.org.uk

THE NATIONAL SOCIETY (1811), Church House, Great Smith Street, London SW1P 3NZ. Tel: 020-7898 1518; Fax: 020-7898 1493; E-mail: info@natsoc.c-of-e.org.uk; Web: http://www.natsoc.org.uk

THE NATIONAL TRUST FOR SCOTLAND (1931), 28 Charlotte Square, Edinburgh EH2 4ET. Tel: 0131-243 9300; Fax: 0131-243 9301; E-mail: information@nts.org.uk; Web: www.nts.org.uk

NATIONAL UNION OF STUDENTS (1922), Nelson Mandela House, 461 Holloway Road, London N7 6LJ. Tel: 020-7272 8900; Fax: 020-7263 5713; E-mail: nusuk@nus.org.uk; Web: http://www.nus.org.uk

NATIONAL VIEWERS' AND LISTENERS' ASSOCIATION, 3 Willow House, Kennington Road, Ashford, Kent TN24 0NR. Tel: 01233-633936; Fax: 01233-633836; Web: http://www.nvala.org

NATIONAL WOMEN'S REGISTER, 3A Vulcan House, Vulcan Road North, Norwich NR6 6AQ. Tel: 01603-406767; Fax: 01603-407003; E-mail: office@nwr.org; Web: http://www.nwr.org

NAVAL, MILITARY AND AIR FORCE BIBLE SOCIETY (1780), Radstock House, 3 Eccleston Street, London SW1W 9LZ. Tel: 020-7463 1468; Fax: 020-7730 0240; E-mail: nma@sgm.org

NAVY RECORDS SOCIETY, c/o Department of War Studies, King's College, The Strand, London WC2R 2LS

NEW TIMES NETWORK, 6 Cynthia Street, London N1 9JF. Tel: 020-7278 4443; Fax: 020-7278 4425; E-mail: info@newtimesnetwork.org.uk; Web: http://www.newtimesnetwork.org.uk

NEWCOMEN SOCIETY (1920), The Science Museum, London SW7 2DD. Tel: 020-7371 4445; Fax: 020-7371 4445; E-mail: thomas@newcomen.com; Web: http://www.nmsl.ac.uk/researchers/newchome.htm

NEWSPAPER PRESS FUND, Dickens House, 35 Wathen Road, Dorking, Surrey RH4 1JY. Tel: 01306-887511; Fax: 01306-888212

THE NHS CONFEDERATION, 26 Chapter Street, London SW1P 4ND. Tel: 020-7233 7388; Fax: 020-7233 7390; Web: http://www.nhsconfed.net

NORFOLK AND NORWICH ARCHAEOLOGICAL SOCIETY, 30 Brettingham Avenue, Norwich NR4 6XG. Tel: 01603-455913

NORTH OF ENGLAND ZOOLOGICAL SOCIETY (1934), Chester Zoo, Upton by Chester, Chester CH2 1LH. Tel: 01244-380280; Fax: 01244-371273; E-mail: marketing@chesterzoo.co.uk; Web: http://www.demon.co.uk/chesterzoo

THE NOTARIES SOCIETY (1882), 23 New Street, Woodbridge, Suffolk IP12 1DN. Tel: 01394-384134; Fax: 01394-382906; E-mail: 100407.3230@compuserve.com; Web: http://www.netlink.co.uk/users/notaries

THE NUFFIELD FOUNDATION, 28 Bedford Square, London WC1B 3EG. Tel: 020-7631 0566; Fax: 020-7323 4877; Web: http://www.nuffieldfoundation.org

NUFFIELD TRUST (1940), 59 New Cavendish Street, London W1M 7RD. Tel: 020-7631 8450; Fax: 020-7631 8451; E-mail: mail@nuffieldtrust.org.uk; Web: http://www.nuffieldtrust.org.uk

THE OFFICERS' ASSOCIATION, 48 Pall Mall, London SW1Y 5JY. Tel: 020-7930 0125; Fax: 020-7930 9053; E-mail: postmaster@oaed.org.uk; Web: http://www.theplanet.net/oaed/

OFFICERS' PENSIONS SOCIETY (1946), 68 South Lambert Road, London SW8 1RL. Tel: 020-7820 9988; Fax: 020-7820 9948; E-mail: memsec@officerspensionsoc.co.uk; Web: http://www.officerspensionsoc.co.uk

OMBUDSMAN FOR ESTATE AGENTS (1998), Beckett House, 4 Bridge Street, Salisbury, Wilts SP1 2LX. Tel: 01722-333306; Fax: 01722-332296; E-mail: admin@oea.co.uk; Web: http://www.oea.co.uk

OPEN SPACES SOCIETY (1865), 25A Bell Street, Henley-on-Thames, Oxon RG9 2BA. Tel: 01491-573535; E-mail: hq@aol.com; Web: http://www.oss.org.uk

THE OPEN-AIR MISSION (1853), 19 John Street, London WC1N 2DL. Tel: 020-7405 6135; Fax: 020-7405 6135; E-mail: oamission@btinternet.com; Web: http://www.btinternet.com/ oamission

OPSIS (1992), c/o Queen Alexandra College, Court Oak Road, Birmingham B17 9TG. Tel: 0121-428 5037; Fax: 0121-428 5048; E-mail: opsis@dircon.co.uk

ORDERS AND MEDALS RESEARCH SOCIETY (1942), 123 Turnpike Link, Croydon CR0 5NU. Tel: 020-8680 2701; Web: http://www.omrs.org.uk

THE ORIENTAL CERAMIC SOCIETY (1921), 30B Torrington Square, London WC1E 7LJ. Tel: 020-7636 7985; Fax: 020-7580 6749; E-mail: ocs-london@beeb.net

OVERSEAS SERVICE PENSIONERS' ASSOCIATION (1960), 138 High Street, Tonbridge, Kent TN9 1AX. Tel: 01732-363806

OXFAM GREAT BRITAIN (1943), 274 Banbury Road, Oxford OX2 7DZ. Tel: 01865-311311; E-mail: oxfam@oxfam.org.uk; Web: http://www.oxfam.org.uk

OXFORD PRESERVATION TRUST (1927), 10 Turn Again Lane, St Ebbes, Oxford OX1 1QL. Tel: 01865-242918; Fax: 01865-251022

OXFORD SOCIETY, 41 Wellington Square, Oxford OX1 2JF. Tel: 01865-280720; Fax: 01865-270280; E-mail: oxford.society@virginnet.co.uk

OXFORDSHIRE ARCHITECTURAL AND HISTORICAL SOCIETY (1839), 53 Radley Road, Abingdon, Oxon OX14 3PN. Tel: 01235-525960; Fax: 0870-056 0773; E-mail: tony@oahs.org.uk; Web: http://www.oahs.org.uk

PARLIAMENTARY AND SCIENTIFIC COMMITTEE, 48 Westminster Palace Gardens, 1–7 Artillery Row, London, SW1P 1RR. Tel: 020-7222 7085; Fax: 020-7222 5355

PATIENTS ASSOCIATION, PO Box 935, Harrow, Middx HA1 3YJ. Tel: 020-8423 9111; Helpline: 020-8423 8999; Fax: 020-8423 9119; E-mail: mailbox@patients-association.com; Web: http://www.patients-association.com

PEARSON'S HOLIDAY FUND (1892), PO Box 3017, South Croydon, Surrey CR2 9PN. Tel: 020-8657 3053; Fax: 020-8657 3053

THE PEDESTRIANS ASSOCIATION (1929), 31–33 Bondway, London SW8 1SJ. Tel: 020-7820 1010; Fax: 020-7820 8208; E-mail: info@pedestrians.org.uk; Web: http://www.pedestrians.org.uk

PESTALOZZI CHILDREN'S VILLAGE TRUST (1957), Sedlescombe, Battle, E. Sussex TN33 0RR. Tel: 01424-870444; Fax: 01424-870655; E-mail: director@pestalozzi.org.uk; Web: http://www.pestalozzi.org.uk

PHILOLOGICAL SOCIETY (1842), School of Oriental and African Studies, University of London, Thornhaugh Street, London WC1H 0XG

THE PHYSIOLOGICAL SOCIETY (1876), PO Box 11319, London WC1E 7JF. Tel: 020-7631 1458; Fax: 020-7631 1462; E-mail: admin@physoc.org; Web: http://www.physoc.org

THE PILGRIM TRUST, Fielden House, Little College Street, London SW1P 3SH. Tel: 020-7222 4723; Fax: 020-7976 0461

THE PILGRIMS OF GREAT BRITAIN (1902), Allington Castle, Maidstone, Kent ME16 0NB. Tel: 01622-606404; Fax: 01622-606402; E-mail: sec@pilgrimsoc.freeserve.co.uk

PLAIN ENGLISH CAMPAIGN (1979), PO Box 3, New Mills, High Peak SK22 4QP. Tel: 01663-744409; Fax: 01663-747038; E-mail: info@plainenglish.co.uk; Web: http://www.plainenglish.co.uk

PLUNKETT FOUNDATION (1919), 23 Hanborough Business Park, Long Hanborough, Oxford OX8 8LH. Tel: 01993-883636; Fax: 01993-883576; E-mail: info@plunkett.co.uk; Web: http://www.co-op.uk/UKCM/plunkett/index.html

THE POETRY SOCIETY, 22 Betterton Street, London WC2H 9BU. Tel: 020-7420 9880; E-mail: info@poetrysoc.com; Web: http://www.poetrysoc.com

POLICY STUDIES INSTITUTE, 100 Park Village East, London NW1 3SR. Tel: 020-7468 0468; Fax: 020-7388 0914; Web: http://www.psi.org.uk

THE PONY CLUB, National Agricultural Centre, Stoneleigh Park, Kenilworth, Warks CV8 2RW. Tel: 0247-669 8300; Fax: 0247-669 6836; E-mail: enquiries@pony-club.org.uk; Web: http://www.pony-club.org.uk

POWYSLAND CLUB (1867), Llygad y Dyffryn, Llanidloes, Powys SY18 6JD. Tel: 01686-412277

THE PRAYER BOOK SOCIETY (1975), St James Garlickhythe, Garlick Hill, London, EC4V 2AF. Tel: 01923-824278; Web: http://www.churchnet.ucsm.ac.uk/prayerbook

PRE-SCHOOL LEARNING ALLIANCE (1961), 69 Kings Cross Road, London WC1X 9LL. Tel: 020-7833 0991; Fax: 020-7837 4942; E-mail: pla@pre-school.org.uk; Web: http://www.pre-school.org.uk

THE PRINCE'S TRUST (1976), 18 Park Square East, London NW1 4LH. Tel: 0800-842842; E-mail: info@princes-trust.org.uk; Web: http://www.princes-trust.org.uk

PRINTERS' CHARITABLE CORPORATION (1827), 7 Cantelupe Mews, Cantelupe Road, East Grinstead, W. Sussex RH19 3BG. Tel: 01342-318882; Fax: 01342-318887; E-mail: printerscharitablecorporation@compuserve.com

PRISONERS ABROAD, 89–93 Fonthill Road, London N4 3JH. Tel: 020-7561 6820; Fax: 020-7561 6821; E-mail: info@prisonersabroad.org.uk; Web: http://www.prisonersabroad.org.uk

PRIVATE LIBRARIES ASSOCIATION, Ravelston, South View Road, Pinner, Middx HA5 3YD; Web: http://www.praxis.co.uk/ppuk/pla.htm

PROFESSIONAL FOOTBALLERS' ASSOCIATION, 20 Oxford Court, Bishopsgate, Manchester M2 3WQ. Tel: 0161-236 0575; Fax: 0161-228 7229; E-mail: info@thepfa.co.uk; Web: http://www.thepfa.co.uk

THE PROTESTANT ALLIANCE, 77 Ampthill Road, Flitwick, Bedford MK45 1BD. Tel/Fax: 01525-712348

PSORIASIS ASSOCIATION, 7 Milton Street, Northampton NN2 7JG. Tel: 01604-711129; Fax: 01604-792894; E-mail: mail@psoriasis.demon.co.uk

QUAKER SOCIAL RESPONSIBILITY AND EDUCATION, Friends House, 173–177 Euston Road, London NW1 2BJ. Tel: 020-7663 1000; Fax: 020-7663 1001; Web: http://www.quaker.org.uk

QUEEN VICTORIA SCHOOL (1908), Dunblane, Perthshire FK15 0JY. Tel: 01786-822288; Fax: 0131-310 2955; E-mail: enquiries@qvs.pkc.sch.uk; Web: http://www.qvs.pkc.sch.uk

THE QUEEN'S ENGLISH SOCIETY (1973), 20 Jessica Road, London SW18 2QN. Tel: 020-8874 2200; Web: http://www.queens-english-society.co.uk

QUEEN'S NURSING INSTITUTE (1887), 3 Albemarle Way, London EC1V 4RQ. Tel: 020-7490 4227; Fax: 020-7490 1269; E-mail: qni1@aol.com; Web: http://www.qni.org.uk

RADAR (ROYAL ASSOCIATION FOR DISABILITY AND REHABILITATION) (1977), 12 City Forum, 250 City Road, London EC1V 8AF. Tel: 020-7250 3222; Fax: 020-7250 0212; E-mail: radar@radar.org.uk; Web: http://www.radar.org.uk

RAIL PASSENGERS COUNCIL, Clements House, 14–18 Gresham Street, London EC2V 7NL. Tel: 020-7505 9090; Fax: 020-7505 9004; E-mail: rpc@gtnet.gov.uk

RAILWAY AND CANAL HISTORICAL SOCIETY (1954), 3 West Court, West Street, Oxford OX2 0NP. Tel: 01865-240514; E-mail: ms@bodley.ox.ac.uk; Web: http://www.bodley.ox.ac.uk/external/rchs/index.html

RAILWAY BENEVOLENT INSTITUTION, 7–11 Macon Court, Herald Drive, Crewe, Cheshire CW1 6WA. Tel: 01270-251316; Fax: 01270-251316

RAMBLERS' ASSOCIATION (1935), 2nd Floor, Camelford House, 87–90 Albert Embankment, London SE1 7TW. Tel: 020-7339 8500; Fax: 020-7339 8501; E-mail: ramblers@london.ramblers.org.uk; Web: http://www.ramblers.org.uk

RARE BREEDS SURVIVAL TRUST (1973), National Agricultural Centre, Stoneleigh Park, Kenilworth, Warks CV8 2LG. Tel: 024-7669 6551; Fax: 024-7669 6706; E-mail: postmaster@rare-breeds.com; Web: http://www.rare-breeds.com

RED POLL CATTLE SOCIETY (1888), The Market Hill, Woodbridge, Suffolk IP12 4LU. Tel: 01394-380643; Fax: 01394-610058; E-mail: sec@redpollcattlesociety.co.uk

REGIONAL STUDIES ASSOCIATION (1965), PO Box 2058, Seaford BN25 4QU. Tel: 01323-899698; Fax: 01323-899798; E-mail: rsa@mailbox.ulcc.ac.uk; Web: http://www.regional.studies.assoc.ac.uk

REGULAR FORCES EMPLOYMENT ASSOCIATION LTD (1885), 49 Pall Mall, London SW1Y 5JG. Tel: 020-7321 2011; Fax: 020-7839 0970; E-mail: rfea@primex.co.uk; Web: http://www.rfea.org.uk

RELATE (1938), Herbert Gray College, Little Church Street, Rugby, Warks CV21 3AP. Tel: 01788-753241; Fax: 01788-535007; E-mail: info@national.relate.org.uk; Web: http://www.relate.org.uk

RESEARCH INTO AGEING (1976), Baird House, 15–17 St Cross Street, London EC1N 8UW. Tel: 020-7404 6878; Fax: 020-7404 6816; E-mail: ria@ageing.org; Web: http://www.ageing.org

RESERVE FORCES ASSOCIATION (1972), Duke of York's HQ, London SW3 4SG. Tel: 020-7414 5588; Fax: 020-7414 5589

RETIRED NURSES' NATIONAL HOME, Riverside Avenue, Bournemouth BH7 7EE. Tel: 01202-396418; Fax: 01202-302530

RICHARD III SOCIETY (1924), 4 Oakley Street, London SW3 5NN; E-mail: info@rimms.co.uk; Web: http://www.richardiii.net

ROOM: THE NATIONAL COUNCIL FOR HOUSING AND PLANNING (1900), 14–18 Old Street, London EC1V 9BH. Tel: 020-7251 2363; Fax: 020-7608 2830

ROTARY INTERNATIONAL IN GREAT BRITAIN AND IRELAND (1905), Kinwarton Road, Alcester, Warks B49 6BP. Tel: 01789-765411; Fax: 01789-765570; E-mail: secretary@ribi.org; Web: http://www.ribi.org

ROYAL AGRICULTURAL SOCIETY OF THE COMMONWEALTH (1957), 2 Grosvenor Gardens, London SW1W 0DH. Tel: 020-7259 9678; Fax: 020-7259 9675; E-mail: rasc@commagshow.org; Web: http://www.commagshow.org

ROYAL AIR FORCE BENEVOLENT FUND (1919), 67 Portland Place, London W1N 4AR. Tel: 020-7580 8343; Fax: 020-7656 7005; E-mail: mail@rafbf.org.uk; Web: http://www.raf-benfund.org

ROYAL ALEXANDRA AND ALBERT SCHOOL, Gatton Park, Reigate, Surrey RH2 0TW. Tel: 01737-642576; Fax: 01737-642294

ROYAL ALFRED SEAFARERS' SOCIETY, SBC House, Restmor Way, Wallington, Surrey SM6 7AH. Tel: 020-8401 2889; Fax: 020-8401 2592

ROYAL ANTHROPOLOGICAL INSTITUTE (1843), 50 Fitzroy Street, London W1P 5HS. Tel: 020-7387 0455; Fax: 020-7383 4235; E-mail: rai@cix.compulink.co.uk; Web: http://www.lucy.ukc.ac.uk/rai

ROYAL ARCHAEOLOGICAL INSTITUTE (1844), c/o Society of Antiquaries of London, Burlington House, Piccadilly, London W1V 0HS. Tel: 020-7479 7092

ROYAL ARMOURED CORPS WAR MEMORIAL BENEVOLENT FUND, c/o RHQ RTR, Bovington Camp, Wareham, Dorset BH20 6JA. Tel: 01929-403331; Fax: 01929-403488

ROYAL ARTILLERY ASSOCIATION, Artillery House, Front Parade, Royal Artillery Barracks, Woolwich, London SE18 4BH. Tel: 020-8781 3003; Fax: 020-8854 3617; Web: http://www.raa.uk.com

ROYAL ASSOCIATION FOR DEAF PEOPLE, Centre for Deaf People, Walsingham Road, Colchester, Essex CO2 7BP. Tel: 01206-509509; Fax: 01206-769755; E-mail: info@royaldeaf.org.uk; Web: http://www.royaldeaf.org.uk/royaldeaf/

ROYAL BRITISH LEGION SCOTLAND (1921), New Haig House, Logie Green Road, Edinburgh EH7 4HR

ROYAL CALEDONIAN SCHOOLS TRUST (1815), 80A High Street, Bushey, Watford, Herts WD2 3DE. Tel: 020-8421 8845; Fax: 020-8421 8845; E-mail: rcst@caleybushey.demon.co.uk

ROYAL CAMBRIAN ACADEMY OF ARTS (1882), Crown Lane, Conwy LL32 8AN. Tel: 01492-593413; Fax: 01492-593413; E-mail: rca@nol.com; Web: http://www.rcaconwy.co.uk

ROYAL CAMBRIDGE HOME FOR SOLDIERS' WIDOWS (1851), 82–84 Hurst Road, East Molesey, Surrey KT8 9AH. Tel: 020-8979 3788

ROYAL CELTIC SOCIETY (1820), 23 Rutland Street, Edinburgh EH1 2RN. Tel: 0131-228 6449; Fax: 0131-229 6987; E-mail: gcameron@stuartandstuard.co.uk

ROYAL COLLEGE OF GENERAL PRACTITIONERS (1952), 14 Princes Gate, London SW7 1PU. Tel: 020-7581 3232; Fax: 020-7225 3047; E-mail: info@rcgp.org.uk; Web: http://www.rcgp.org.uk

ROYAL COLLEGE OF NURSING, 20 Cavendish Square, London W1M 0AB. Tel: 020-7409 3333; Fax: 020-7647 3435; E-mail: corpaffairs.dept@rcn.org.uk; Web: http://www.rcn.org.uk

ROYAL COLLEGE OF OBSTETRICIANS AND GYNAECOLOGISTS (1929), 27 Sussex Place, London NW1 4RG. Tel: 020-7772 6200; Fax: 020-7723 0575; E-mail: coll.sec@rcog.org.uk; Web: http://www.rcog.org.uk

ROYAL COLLEGE OF PHYSICIANS (1518), 11 St Andrews Place, Regent's Park, London NW1 4LE. Tel: 020-7935 1174; Fax: 020-7487 5218; Web: http://www.rcplondon.ac.uk

ROYAL COLLEGE OF PSYCHIATRISTS (1841), 17 Belgrave Square, London SW1X 8PG. Tel: 020-7235 2351; Fax: 020-7245 1231; E-mail: rcpsych@rcpsych.ac.uk; Web: http://www.rcpsych.ac.uk

ROYAL COLLEGE OF RADIOLOGISTS (1975), 38 Portland Place, London W1N 4JQ. Tel: 020-7636 4432; Fax: 020-7323 3100; E-mail: enquiries@rcr.ac.uk; Web: http://www.rcr.ac.uk

ROYAL COLLEGE OF SURGEONS OF ENGLAND, 35–43 Lincoln's Inn Fields, London WC2A 3PN. Tel: 020-7405 3474; Web: http://www.rcseng.ac.uk

ROYAL COLLEGE OF VETERINARY SURGEONS (1844), Belgravia House, 62–64 Horseferry Road, London SW1P 2AF. Tel: 020-7222 2001; Fax: 020-7222 2004; E-mail: admin@rcvs.org.uk; Web: http://www.rcvs.org.uk

ROYAL ENGINEERS ASSOCIATION (1869), RHQ Royal Engineers, Brompton Barracks, Chatham, Kent ME4 4UG. Tel: 01634-822394; Fax: 01634-822397; Web: http://www.reahq.org.uk

ROYAL FACULTY OF PROCURATORS IN GLASGOW, 12 Nelson Mandela Place, Glasgow G2 1BT. Tel: 0141-331 0533; Fax: 0141-333 9104; E-mail: i.c.pearson@btinternet.com; Web: http://www.rfpg.org

ROYAL FORESTRY SOCIETY OF ENGLAND, WALES AND NORTHERN IRELAND (1882), 102 High Street, Tring, Herts HP23 4AF. Tel: 01442-822028; Fax: 01442-890395; E-mail: rfshq@rfs.org.uk; Web: http://www.rfs.org.uk

ROYAL GEOGRAPHICAL SOCIETY (WITH THE INSTITUTE OF BRITISH GEOGRAPHERS) (1830), 1 Kensington Gore, London SW7 2AR. Tel: 020-7591 3000; Fax: 020-7591 3001; E-mail: info@rgs.org; Web: http://www.rgs.org

ROYAL HIGHLAND AND AGRICULTURAL SOCIETY OF SCOTLAND (1784), Royal Highland Centre, Ingliston, Edinburgh EH28 8NF. Tel: 0131-335 6200; Fax: 0131-333 5236; E-mail: rayj@rhass.org.uk; Web: http://www.rhass.org.uk

ROYAL HISTORICAL SOCIETY (1868), University College London, Gower Street, London WC1E 6BT. Tel/Fax: 020-7387 7532; E-mail: royalhistsoc@ucl.ac.uk; Web: http://www.rhs.ac.uk

ROYAL HUMANE SOCIETY (1774), Brettenham House, Lancaster Place, London WC2E 7EP. Tel: 020-7836 8155; Fax: 020-7836 8155

ROYAL INCORPORATION OF ARCHITECTS IN SCOTLAND (1916), 15 Rutland Square, Edinburgh EH1 2BE. Tel: 0131-229 7545; Fax: 0131-228-2188; E-mail: stombs@rias.org.uk; Web: http://www.rias.org.uk

ROYAL INSTITUTE OF BRITISH ARCHITECTS, 66 Portland Place, London W1N 4AD. Tel: 020-7580 5533; Information: 0906-302 0400; Fax: 020-7255 1541; E-mail: bal@inst.riba.org; Web: http://www.architecture.com

ROYAL INSTITUTE OF INTERNATIONAL AFFAIRS, Chatham House, 15 St James's Square, London SW1Y 4LE. Tel: 020-7957 5700; Fax: 020-7957 5710; E-mail: contact@riia.org; Web: http://www.riia.org

ROYAL INSTITUTE OF NAVIGATION (1947), 1 Kensington Gore, London SW7 2AT. Tel: 020-7591 3130; Fax: 020-7591 3131; E-mail: info@rin.org.uk; Web: http://www.rin.org.uk

ROYAL INSTITUTE OF OIL PAINTERS (1882), 17 Carlton House Terrace, London SW1Y 5BD; Tel: 020-7930 6844; Fax: 020-7839 7830; Web: http://www.mallgalleries.org.uk

ROYAL INSTITUTE OF PAINTERS IN WATER COLOURS (1831), 17 Carlton House Terrace, London SW1Y 5BD. Tel: 020-7930 6844; Fax: 020-7839 7830; Web: http://www.mallgalleries.org.uk

ROYAL INSTITUTION OF CHARTERED SURVEYORS, 12 Great George Street, London SW1P 3AD. Tel: 020-7222 7000; Fax: 020-7222 5074; E-mail: info@rics.org.uk; Web: http://www.rics.org

THE ROYAL INSTITUTION OF GREAT BRITAIN (1799), 21 Albemarle Street, London W1X 4BS. Tel: 020-7409 2992; Fax: 020-7629 3569; E-mail: ri@ri.ac.uk; Web: http://www.ri.ac.uk

THE ROYAL LIFE SAVING SOCIETY UK (1891), River House, High Street, Broom, Warks B50 4HN. Tel: 01789-773994; Fax: 01789-773995; E-mail: mail@rlss.org.uk

ROYAL LITERARY FUND, 3 Johnson's Court, off Fleet Street, London EC4A 3EA. Tel: 020-7353 7150; Fax: 020-7353 1300; E-mail: egunnflf@globalnet.co.uk

ROYAL MASONIC BENEVOLENT INSTITUTION, 20 Great Queen Street, London WC2B 5BG. Tel: 020-7405 8341; Fax: 020-7404 0724; E-mail: enquiries@rmbi.org.uk

ROYAL MEDICAL BENEVOLENT FUND, 24 King's Road, London SW19 8QN. Tel: 020-8540 9194; Fax: 020-8542 0494; E-mail: rm.bf@virgin.net; Web: http://www.rmbf.co.uk

ROYAL METAL TRADES BENEVOLENT SOCIETY, Brooke House, 4 The Lakes, Bedford Road, Northampton NN4 7YD. Tel: 01604-622023; Fax: 01604-631252

ROYAL MUSICAL ASSOCIATION (1874), Royal Academy of Music, Marylebone Road, London NW1 5HT. Web: http://www.soton.ac.uk./ stilwell/RMA/

ROYAL NATIONAL COLLEGE FOR THE BLIND (1872), College Road, Hereford HR1 1EB. Tel: 01432-265725; Fax: 01432-353478; E-mail: ss@rncb.ac.uk; Web: http://www.rncb.ac.uk

ROYAL NATIONAL INSTITUTE FOR THE BLIND, 224 Great Portland Street, London W1N 6AA. Tel: 0845-669999; Fax: 020-7388 2034; E-mail: helpline@rnib.org.uk; Web: http://www.rnib.org.uk

ROYAL NATIONAL LIFEBOAT INSTITUTION (1824), West Quay Road, Poole, Dorset BT15 1HZ. Tel: 01202-663000; Fax: 01202-663167; E-mail: info@rnli.org.uk; Web: http://www.rnli.org.uk

ROYAL NATIONAL MISSION TO DEEP SEA FISHERMEN
(1881), 43 Nottingham Place, London W1M 4BX.
Tel: 020-7487 5101; Fax: 020-7224 5240;
E-mail: rnmdsf@charity.vfree.com;
Web: http://www.fishing-news.co.uk/rnmdsf/

ROYAL NAVAL ASSOCIATION, 82 Chelsea Manor Street,
London SW3 5QJ. Tel: 020-7352 6764;
Fax: 020-7351 0610; E-mail: rna@netcomuk.co.uk

ROYAL NAVAL BENEVOLENT SOCIETY FOR OFFICERS
(1739), 1 Fleet Street, London EC4Y 1BD.
Tel: 020-7427 7471; Fax: 020-7427 7471

ROYAL NAVAL BENEVOLENT TRUST (1922), Castaway
House, 311 Twyford Avenue, Portsmouth PO2 8PE.
Tel: 023-9269 0112/9266 0296; Fax: 023-9266 0852;
E-mail: rnbt@rnbt.org.uk

ROYAL OVER-SEAS LEAGUE (1910), Over-Seas House,
Park Place, St James's Street, London SW1A 1LR.
Tel: 020-7408 0214; Fax: 020-7499 6738;
E-mail: info@rosl.org.uk;
Web: http://www.rosl.org.uk

ROYAL PATRIOTIC FUND CORPORATION (1854),
40 Queen Anne's Gate, London SW1H 9AP.
Tel: 020-7233 1894; Fax: 020-7233 1799

ROYAL PHARMACEUTICAL SOCIETY OF GREAT BRITAIN
(1841), 1 Lambeth High Street, London SE1 7JN.
Tel: 020-7735 9141; Fax: 020-7735 7629; E-mail:
enquiries@rpsgb.org.uk; Web: http://www.rpsgb.org.uk

ROYAL PHILATELIC SOCIETY LONDON (1869), 41
Devonshire Place, London W1N 1PE. Tel: 020-7486 1044;
Fax: 020-7486 0803; Web: http://www.rpsl.org.uk

ROYAL PHOTOGRAPHIC SOCIETY (1853), The Octagon,
Milsom Street, Bath BA1 1DN. Tel: 01225-462841;
Fax: 01225-448688; E-mail: rps@rps.org;
Web: http://www.rps.org

ROYAL SCHOOL FOR DEAF CHILDREN (1792),
Victoria Road, Margate, Kent CT9 1NB.
Tel: 01843-227561; Fax: 01843-227637;
E-mail: enquiries@royalschoolfordeaf.kent.sch.uk;
Web: http://www.royalschoolfordeaf.kent.sch.uk

ROYAL SCHOOL OF CHURCH MUSIC (1927), Cleveland
Lodge, Westhumble, Dorking, Surrey RH5 6BW.
Tel: 01306-872800; Fax: 01306-887260;
E-mail: cl@rscm.com; Web: http://www.rscm.com

ROYAL SCHOOL OF NEEDLEWORK, Apartment 12A,
Hampton Court Palace, East Molesey, Surrey KT8 9AU.
Tel: 020-8943 1432; Fax: 020-8943 4910;
Web: http://www.royal-needlework.co.uk

ROYAL SCOTTISH AGRICULTURAL BENEVOLENT
INSTITUTION (1897), Ingliston, Edinburgh EH28 8NB.
Tel: 0131-333 1023/1027; Fax: 0131-333 1027;
E-mail: rsabi@argonet.co.uk;
Web: http://www.argonet.co.uk/users/rsabi/

THE ROYAL SOCIETY FOR ASIAN AFFAIRS (1901),
2 Belgrave Square, London SW1X 8PJ.
Tel: 020-7235 5122; Fax: 020-7259 6771;
E-mail: sec@rsaa.org.uk;
Web: http://www.rsaa.org.uk

ROYAL SOCIETY FOR THE ENCOURAGEMENT OF ARTS,
MANUFACTURES AND COMMERCE (RSA) (1754),
8 John Adam Street, London WC2N 6EZ.
Tel: 020-7930 5115; Fax: 020-7839 5805;
E-mail: general@rsa-uk.demon.co.uk;
Web: http://www.rsa.org.uk

ROYAL SOCIETY FOR THE PREVENTION OF ACCIDENTS,
ROSPA House, Edgbaston Park, 353 Bristol Road,
Birmingham B5 7ST. Tel: 0121-248 2000;
Fax: 0121-248 2001; E-mail: help@rospa.co.uk;
Web: http://www.rospa.co.uk

ROYAL SOCIETY FOR THE PREVENTION OF CRUELTY TO
ANIMALS (1824), Causeway, Horsham, W. Sussex
RH12 1HG. Tel: 01403-264181; Fax: 01403-241048;
Web: http://www.rspca.org.uk

THE ROYAL SOCIETY FOR THE PROMOTION OF HEALTH
(1876), 38 St George's Drive, London SW1V 4BH.
Tel: 020-7630 0121; Fax: 020-7976 6847; E-mail:
rshealth@rshealth.org.uk; Web: http://www.rsph.org

ROYAL SOCIETY FOR THE PROTECTION OF BIRDS (RSPB)
(1889), The Lodge, Sandy, Beds SG19 2DL.
Tel: 01767-680551; Fax: 01767-692365;
Web: http://www.rspb.org.uk

ROYAL SOCIETY OF CHEMISTRY (1841), Burlington
House, Piccadilly, London W1V 0BN.
Tel: 020-7437 8656; Fax: 020-7437 8883;
E-mail: rsc@rsc.org;
Web: http://www.rsc.org and http://www.chemsoc.org

ROYAL SOCIETY OF LITERATURE (1820),
Somerset House, Strand, London WC2R 0RN.
Tel: 020-7845 4676; Fax: 020-7845 4679;
E-mail: rslit@aol.com;
Web: http://www.rslit.org

ROYAL SOCIETY OF MARINE ARTISTS (1945),
17 Carlton House Terrace, London SW1Y 5BD.
Tel: 020-7930 6844; Fax: 020-7839 7830;
Web: http://www.mallgalleries.org.uk

THE ROYAL SOCIETY OF MEDICINE, 1
Wimpole Street, London W1M 8AE.
Tel: 020-7290 2900; Fax: 020-7290 2992;
E-mail: membership@roysocmed.ac.uk;
Web: http://www.roysocmed.ac.uk

ROYAL SOCIETY OF MINIATURE PAINTERS, SCULPTORS
AND GRAVERS (1895), 1 Knapp Cottages,
Wyke, Gillingham, Dorset SP8 4NQ. Tel: 01747-825718;
Fax: 01747-826835; E-mail: hendersons@dial.pipex.com;
Web: http://www.royal-miniature-society.org.uk

THE ROYAL SOCIETY OF MUSICIANS OF GREAT BRITAIN
(1738), 10 Stratford Place, London W1N 9AE.
Tel: 020-7629 6137; Fax: 020-7629 6137

ROYAL SOCIETY OF PAINTER-PRINTMAKERS, Bankside
Gallery, 48 Hopton Street, London SE1 9JH.
Tel: 020-7928 7521; Fax: 020-7928 2820;
E-mail: bankside@freeuk.com

ROYAL SOCIETY OF PORTRAIT PAINTERS (1891),
17 Carlton House Terrace, London SW1Y 5BD.
Tel: 020-7930 6844; Fax: 020-7839 7830;
Web: http://www.mallgalleries.org.uk

ROYAL SOCIETY OF TROPICAL MEDICINE AND HYGIENE (1907), Manson House, 26 Portland Place, London W1N 4EY. Tel: 020-7580 2127; Fax: 020-7436 1389; E-mail: mail@rstmh.org; Web: http://www.rstmh.org

ROYAL STATISTICAL SOCIETY (1834), 12 Errol Street, London EC1Y 8LX. Tel: 020-7638 8998; Fax: 020-7256 7598; E-mail: rss@rss.org.uk; Web: http://www.rss.org.uk

ROYAL TANK REGIMENT BENEVOLENT FUND, RHQ RTR, Bovington Camp, Wareham, Dorset BH20 6JA. Tel: 01929-403331; Fax: 01929-403488

ROYAL TELEVISION SOCIETY, Holborn Hall, 100 Gray's Inn Road, London WC1X 8AL. Tel: 020-7430 1000; Fax: 020-7430 0924; E-mail: info@rts.org.uk; Web: http://www.rts.org.uk

ROYAL THEATRICAL FUND, 11 Garrick Street, London WC2E 9AR. Tel: 020-7836 3322; Fax: 020-7379 8273; E-mail: admin@trtf.co.uk; Web: http://www.trtf.co.uk

ROYAL ULSTER AGRICULTURAL SOCIETY, The King's Hall, Balmoral, Belfast BT9 6GW. Tel: 028-9066 5225; Fax: 028-9066 1264; E-mail: general@kingshall.co.uk; Web: http://www.balmoralshow.co.uk

THE ROYAL UNITED KINGDOM BENEFICIENT ASSOCIATION (1863), 6 Avonmore Road, London W14 8RL. Tel: 020-7605 4200; Fax: 020-7605 4201; E-mail: charity@rukba.org.uk; Web: http://www.rukba.org.uk

ROYAL UNITED SERVICES INSTITUTE FOR DEFENCE STUDIES, Whitehall, London SW1A 2ET. Tel: 020-7930 5854; Fax: 020-7321 0943; E-mail: defence@rusi.org; Web: http://www.rusi.org

ROYAL WATERCOLOUR SOCIETY (1804), Bankside Gallery, 48 Hopton Street, London SE1 9JH. Tel: 020-7928 7521; Fax: 020-7928 2820; E-mail: bankside@freeuk.com

ST ALBANS AND HERTFORDSHIRE ARCHITECTURAL AND ARCHAEOLOGICAL SOCIETY (1845), 24 Rose Walk, St Albans, Herts AL4 9AF. Tel: 01727-853204

ST DUNSTAN'S (CARING FOR BLIND EX-SERVICE MEN AND WOMEN), 12–14 Harcourt Street, London W1A 4XB. Tel: 020-7723 5021; Fax: 020-7262 6199

ST JOHN AMBULANCE (1099), 1 Grosvenor Crescent, London SW1X 7EF. Tel: 020-7235 5231; Fax: 020-7235 0796; E-mail: pr@nhq.sja.org.uk; Web: http://www.sja.org.uk

SAILORS' FAMILIES' SOCIETY, Newland, Hull HU6 7RJ. Tel: 01482-342331; Fax: 01482-447868; E-mail: info@sailors-families.org.uk; Web: http://www.sailors-families.org.uk

SALTIRE SOCIETY (1936), 9 Fountain Close, 22 High Street, Edinburgh EH1 1TF. Tel: 0131-556 1836; Fax: 0131-557 1675; E-mail: saltire@saltire.org.uk; Web: http://www.saltire-society.demon.co.uk

THE SAMARITANS (1953), 10 The Grove, Slough SL1 1QP. Tel: 01753-216500; Fax: 01753-819004; E-mail: admin@samaritans.org.uk; Web: http://www.samaritans.org.uk

SANE (1986), 1st Floor, Cityside House, 40 Alder Street, London E1 1EE. Tel: 020-7375 1002; Fax: 020-7375 2162. Web: http://mhn.co.uk/help/charity/sane/index

SARGENT CANCER CARE FOR CHILDREN, Griffin House, 161 Hammersmith Road, London W6 8SG. Tel: 020-8752 2800; Fax: 020-8752 2806

SAVE BRITAIN'S HERITAGE (1975), 70 Cowcross Street, London EC1M 6EJ. Tel: 020-7253 3500; Fax: 020-7253 3400; E-mail: save@btinternet.com; Web: http://www.savebritainsheritage.org

THE SCHOOL OF PUBLIC POLICY, University College London, 29 Tavistock Square, London WC1H 9EZ. Tel: 020-7679 4999; Fax: 020-7679 4969; E-mail: spp@ucl.ac.uk; Web: http://www.ucl.ac.uk/spp/

SHOOL LIBRARY ASSOCIATION (1937), Unit 1, Lotmead Business Nillage, Lotmead Farm, Wanborough, nr Swindon SN3 4AJ. Tel: 01793-617838; Fax: 01793-537374; E-mail: info@SLA.org.uk; Web: http://www.sla.org.uk

SCHOOLMISTRESSES AND GOVERNESSES BENEVOLENT INSTITUTION, Queen Mary House, Manor Park Road, Chislehurst, Kent BR7 5PY. Tel: 020-8468 7997

SCOPE (1952), 6 Market Road, London N7 9PW. Tel: 020-7619 7100; Fax: 020-7619 7399; E-mail: cphelpline@scope.org.uk; Web: http://www.scope.org.uk/

SCOTTISH CHAMBERS OF COMMERCE (1948), Conference House, The Exchange, 152 Morrison Street, Edinburgh EH3 8EB. Tel: 0131-477 8025; Fax: 0131-477 7002; E-mail: mail@scottishchambers.org.uk; Web: http://www.scottishchambers.org.uk

SCOTTISH CHURCH HISTORY SOCIETY (1927), Crown House, 39 Southside Road, Inverness IV2 4XA. Tel: 01463-231140; Fax: 01463-230537

SCOTTISH COUNCIL FOR VOLUNTARY ORGANISATIONS, 18–19 Claremont Crescent, Edinburgh EH7 4QD. Tel: 0131-556 3882; Fax: 0131-556 0279; E-mail: enquiries@scvo.org.uk; Web: http://www.scvo.org.uk

SCOTTISH GENEALOGY SOCIETY (1953), Library and Family History Centre, 15 Victoria Terrace, Edinburgh EH1 2JL. Tel: 0131-220 3677; Fax: 0131-220 3677; E-mail: scotgensoc@sol.co.uk; Web: http://www.scotsgenealogy.com

SCOTTISH LANDOWNERS' FEDERATION, Stuart House, Eskmills Business Park, Musselburgh EH21 7PB. Tel: 0131-653 5400; Fax: 0131-653 5401; E-mail: slfinfo@slf.org.uk

SCOTTISH NATIONAL INSTITUTION FOR THE WAR BLINDED (1915), PO Box 500, Gillespie Crescent, Edinburgh EH10 4HZ. Tel: 0131-229 1456; Fax: 0131-229 4060; E-mail: enquiries@rbas.org.uk

SCOTTISH NATIONAL WAR MEMORIAL, The Castle, Edinburgh EH1 2YT. Tel: 0131-226 7393; Fax: 0131-225 8920

SCOTTISH NATURAL HISTORY LIBRARY (1970), Foremount House, Kilbarchan, Renfrewshire PA10 2EZ. Tel: 01505-702419

SCOTTISH SOCIETY FOR THE PROTECTION OF WILD BIRDS (1928), Foremount House, Kilbarchan, Renfrewshire PA10 2EZ. Tel: 01505-702419

SCOTTISH TOURIST BOARD, 23 Ravelston Terrace, Edinburgh EH4 3TP. Tel: 0131-332 2433; Fax: 0131-315 3906; E-mail: tom.buncle@stb.gov.uk; Web: http://www.visitscotland.com

SCOTTISH WILDLIFE TRUST (1964), Cramond House, Kirk Cramond, Cramond Glebe Road, Edinburgh EH4 6NS. Tel: 0131-312 7765; Fax: 0131-312 8705; Web: http://www.swt.org.uk

THE SCOUT ASSOCIATION (1907), Baden-Powell House, Queen's Gate, London SW7 5JS. Tel: 020-7584 7030; Fax: 020-7590 5103; E-mail: baden.powell.house@scout.org.uk; Web: http://www.scoutbase.org.uk/

SCRIPTURE GIFT MISSION INCORPORATED (1888), Radstock House, 3 Eccleston Street, London SW1W 9LZ. Tel: 020-7730 2155; Fax: 020-7730 0240; E-mail: int@sgm.org

SCRIPTURE UNION (1867), 207–209 Queensway, Bletchley, Milton Keynes MK2 2EB. Tel: 01908-856000; Fax: 01908-856111; E-mail: info@scriptureunion.org.uk; Web: http://www.scripture.org.uk

THE SEA CADET ASSOCIATION, 202 Lambeth Road, London SE1 7JF. Tel: 020-7928 8978; Fax: 020-7928 8914

SEEABILITY (1799), 56–66 Highlands Road, Leatherhead, Surrey KT22 8NR. Tel: 01372-373086; Fax: 01372-361508; E-mail: reception@seeability.org

SELDEN SOCIETY (1887), Faculty of Laws, Queen Mary and Westfield College, Mile End Road, London E1 4NS. Tel: 020-7882 5136; Fax: 020-8981 8733; E-mail: selden-society@qmw.ac.uk; Web: http://www.selden-society.qmw.ac.uk

SENSE (THE NATIONAL DEAFBLIND AND RUBELLA ASSOCIATION), 11–13 Clifton Terrace, London N4 3SR. Tel: 020-7272 7774; Fax: 020-7272 6012; E-mail: enquiries@sense.org.uk; Web: http://www.sense.org.uk

SHELTER (NATIONAL CAMPAIGN FOR HOMELESS PEOPLE), 88 Old Street, London EC1V 9HU. Tel: 020-7505 2000; Shelterline: 0808-800 4444; Fax: 020-8505 2169; E-mail: info@shelter.org.uk; Web: http://www.shelter.org.uk

SHERLOCK HOLMES SOCIETY OF LONDON (1934), 13 Crofton Avenue, Orpington, Kent BR6 8DU. Tel: 01689-811314; E-mail: shsl221b@aol.com; Web: http://www.sherlock-holmes.org.uk

SHIRE HORSE SOCIETY, East of England Showground, Peterborough PE2 6XE. Tel: 01733-234451; Fax: 01733-370038; E-mail: info@eastofengland.org.uk; Web: http://www.shire-horse.org.uk

SHROPSHIRE ARCHAEOLOGICAL AND HISTORICAL SOCIETY (1877), Westcott Farm, Pontesbury, Shrewsbury SY5 0SQ. Tel: 01743-790531; E-mail: jlwestcott@aol.com

SIGHT SAVERS INTERNATIONAL (ROYAL COMMON-WEALTH SOCIETY FOR THE BLIND), Grosvenor Hall, Bolnore Road, Haywards Heath, W. Sussex RH16 4BX. Tel: 01444-446600; Fax: 01444-446688; Web: http://www.sightsavers.org.uk

SIMPLIFIED SPELLING SOCIETY (1908), Tailours, High Road, Chigwell, Essex IG7 6DL. Web: http://www.les.aston.ac.uk/simplspel.html

SIR OSWALD STOLL FOUNDATION, 446 Fulham Road, London SW6 1DT. Tel: 020-7385 2110; Fax: 020-7381 8274

THE SOCIALIST PARTY (1904), 52 Clapham High Street, London SW4 7UN. Tel: 020-7622 3811; Fax: 020-7720 3665; E-mail: spgb@worldsocialism.org; Web: http://www.worldsocialism.org/spgb

SOCIETY FOR LINCOLNSHIRE HISTORY AND ARCHAEOLOGY, Jew's Court, Steep Hill, Lincoln LN2 1LS. Tel/Fax: 01522-521337

SOCIETY FOR PROMOTING CHRISTIAN KNOWLEDGE (SPCK) (1698), Holy Trinity Church, Marylebone Road, London NW1 4DU. Tel: 020-7387 5282; Fax: 020-7388 2352; E-mail: spck@spck.org.uk; Web: http://www.spck.org.uk

SOCIETY FOR PROMOTING THE TRAINING OF WOMEN (1859), Meadowbrook, Carlby Road, Greatford, Stamford, Lincs PE9 4PR. Tel: 01778-560978

SOCIETY FOR PSYCHICAL RESEARCH (1882), 49 Marloes Road, London W8 6LA. Tel/Fax: 020-7937 8984; Web: http://www.moebius.psy.ed.ac.uk

SOCIETY FOR THE ASSISTANCE OF LADIES IN REDUCED CIRCUMSTANCES (1886), Lancaster House, 25 Hornyold Road, Malvern, Worcs WR14 1QQ. Tel: 01684-574645

SOCIETY FOR THE PROMOTION OF HELLENIC STUDIES (1879), Senate House, Malet Street, London WC1E 7HU. Tel: 020-7862 8730; Fax: 020-7862 8731; E-mail: hellenic@sas.ac.uk; Web: http://www.sas.ac.uk/icls/hellenic/

SOCIETY FOR THE PROMOTION OF ROMAN STUDIES (1910), Senate House, Malet Street, London WC1E 7HU. Tel: 020-7862 8727; Fax: 020-7862 8728; E-mail: romansoc@sas.ac.uk; Web: http://www.sas.ac.uk/icls/roman/

SOCIETY FOR THE PROTECTION OF ANCIENT BUILDINGS (1877), 37 Spital Square, London E1 6DY. Tel: 020-7377 1644; Fax: 020-7247 5296; E-mail: info@spab.org.uk; Web: http://www.spab.org.uk

SOCIETY FOR THE PROTECTION OF UNBORN CHILDREN, Phyllis Bowman House, 5–6 St Matthew Street, London SW1P 2JT. Tel: 020-7222 5845; Fax: 020-7222 0630; E-mail: enquiry@spuc.org.uk; Web: http://www.spuc.org.uk

SOCIETY FOR THEATRE RESEARCH (1948), c/o The Theatre Museum, 1E Tavistock Street, London WC2E 7PA; E-mail: e.cottis@btinternet.com; Web: http://www.blot.co.uk/str

SOCIETY OF ANTIQUARIES OF LONDON (1707), Burlington House, Piccadilly, London W1V 0HS. Tel: 020-7734 0193; Fax: 020-7287 6967; E-mail: admin@sal.org.uk; Web: http://www.sal.org.uk

SOCIETY OF ANTIQUARIES OF SCOTLAND, Royal Museum of Scotland, Chambers Street, Edinburgh EH1 1JF. Tel: 0131-247 4115/4133; Fax: 0131-247 4163

SOCIETY OF APOTHECARIES OF LONDON (1617), 14 Black Friars Lane, London EC4V 6EJ. Tel: 020-7236 1189; Fax: 020-7329 3177; E-mail: clerk@apothecaries.org; Web: http://www.apothecaries.org

SOCIETY OF ARCHIVISTS (1947 and 1954), 40 Northampton Road, London EC1R 0HB. Tel: 020-7278 8630; Fax: 020-7278 2107; E-mail: societyofarchivists@archives.org.uk; Web: http://www.archives.org.uk

SOCIETY OF AUTHORS, 84 Drayton Gardens, London SW10 9SB. Tel: 020-7373 6642; Fax: 020-7373 5768; E-mail: authorsoc@writers.org.uk; Web: http://www.writers.org.uk/society

SOCIETY OF COUNTY TREASURERS, Buckinghamshire County Council, Finance Division, County Hall, Aylesbury, Bucks HP20 1UD. Tel: 01296-383119; Fax: 01296-382960; E-mail: snolan@buckcc.gov.uk

SOCIETY OF EDITORS, University Centre, Granta Place, Mill Lane, Cambridge CB2 1RU. Tel: 01223-304080; Fax: 01223-304090; E-mail: society@ukeditors.com; Web: http://www.ukeditors.com

SOCIETY OF EDUCATION OFFICERS (1972), Manchester House, 84–86 Princess Street, Manchester M1 6NG. Tel: 0161-236 5766; Fax: 0161-236 6742; E-mail: seo-office@rmplc.co.uk

THE SOCIETY OF ENGINEERS (1854), Guinea Wiggs, Nayland, Colchester, Essex CO6 7NF. Tel: 01206-263332; Fax: 01206-262624; E-mail: secretary@society-of-engineers.org.uk

SOCIETY OF GENEALOGISTS ENTERPRISES LTD (1911 and 1999), 14 Charterhouse Buildings, Goswell Road, London EC1M 7BA. Tel: 020-7251 8799; Fax: 020-7250 1800; E-mail: enterprises@sog.org.uk; Web: http://www.sog.org.uk

SOCIETY OF GLASS TECHNOLOGY, Don Valley House, Savile Street East, Sheffield S4 7UQ. Tel: 0114-263 4455; Fax: 0114-263 4411; E-mail: sgt@glass.demon.co.uk; Web: http://www.sgt.org

SOCIETY OF INDEXERS (1957), Globe Centre, Penistone Road, Sheffield S6 3AE. Tel: 0114-281 3060; Fax: 0114-281 3061; E-mail: admin@socind.demon.co.uk; Web: http://www.socind.demon.co.uk

SOCIETY OF PUBLIC TEACHERS OF LAW (1908), School of Law, Kings College London, Strand, London WC2R 2LS. Tel: 020-7848 2849; Fax: 020-7848 2465; E-mail: peter.niven@kcl.ac.uk; Web: http://www.law.warwick.ac.uk

SOCIETY OF SCRIBES AND ILLUMINATORS (1922), 6 Queen Square, London WC1N 3AR. Tel: 01524-251534; Fax: 01524-251534; E-mail: scribe@calligraphy.org; Web: http://www.calligraphy.org

SOCIETY OF SOLICITORS IN THE SUPREME COURT OF SCOTLAND (1784), SSC Library, Parliament House, 11 Parliament Square, Edinburgh EH1 1RF. Tel: 0131-225 6268; Fax: 0131-225 2270; E-mail: ssc.library@dial.pipex.com

THE SOCIETY OF WOMEN ARTISTS (1855), 1 Knapp Cottages, Wyke, Gillingham, Dorset SP8 4NQ. Tel: 01747-825718; Fax: 01747-826835; E-mail: hendersons@dial.pipex.com; Web: http://www.society-women-artists.org.uk

SOCIETY OF WRITERS TO HM SIGNET (1594), Signet Library, Parliament Square, Edinburgh EH1 1RF. Tel: 0131-220 3426; Fax: 0131-220 4016; E-mail: wssoc@dial.pipex.com; Web: http://www.signetlibrary.co.uk

SOIL ASSOCIATION (1946), Bristol House, 40–56 Victoria Street, Bristol BS1 6BY. Tel: 0117-929 0661; Fax: 0117-925 2504; E-mail: info@soilassociation.org; Web: http://www.soilassociation.org

SOMERSET ARCHAEOLOGICAL AND NATURAL HISTORY SOCIETY (1849), Taunton Castle, Taunton, Somerset TA1 4AD. Tel: 01823-272429; Fax: 01823-272429

SOROPTIMIST INTERNATIONAL OF GREAT BRITAIN AND IRELAND, 127 Wellington Road South, Stockport SK1 3TS. Tel: 0161-480 7686; Fax: 0161-477 6152; E-mail: hq@soroptimistgbi.prestel.co.uk

SOUTH AMERICAN MISSION SOCIETY (1844), Allen Gardiner Cottage, Pembury Road, Tunbridge Wells, Kent TN2 3QU. Tel: 01892-538647; Fax: 01892-525797; E-mail: SAMSGB@compuserve.com; Web: http://ourworld.compuserve.com/homepages/samsgb

THE SOUTH WALES INSTITUTE OF ENGINEERS, 2nd Floor, Empire House, Mount Stuart Square, Cardiff CF10 5PN. Tel: 029-2048 1726; Fax: 029-2045 1953; E-mail: swie@celtic.co.uk; Web: http://www.celtic.co.uk/swie

SPORT HORSE BREEDING OF GREAT BRITAIN (1885), 96 High Street, Edenbridge, Kent TN8 5AR. Tel: 01732-866277; Fax: 01732-867464; E-mail: office@sporthorsegb.co.uk; Web: http://www.sporthorsegb.co.uk

SPURGEON'S CHILD CARE (1867), 74 Wellingborough Road, Rushden, Northants NN10 9TY. Tel: 01933-412412; Fax: 01933-412010; E-mail: scc@spurgeons.org; Web: http://www.spurgeonschildcare.org

SSAFA FORCES HELP, 19 Queen Elizabeth Street, London SE1 2LP. Tel: 020-7403 8783; Fax: 020-7403 8815; E-mail: public-awareness@ssafa-forces-help.org.uk; Web: http://www.ssafa.org.uk

STANDING COUNCIL OF THE BARONETAGE (1903), 3 Eastcroft Road, West Ewell, Epsom, Surrey KT19 9TX. Tel: 020-8393 6620; Fax: 020-8393 6620

THE STEWART SOCIETY (1899), 53 George Street, Edinburgh EH2 2HT. Tel: 0131-220 4512; Fax: 0131-220 4512; E-mail: member@stewartsociety.org; Web: http://www.stewartsociety.org

THE STRATEGIC PLANNING SOCIETY, 17 Portland Place, London W1N 3AF. Tel: 020-7636 7737; Fax: 020-7323 1692; E-mail: enquiry@sps.org.uk; Web: http://www.sps.org.uk

STUDENT CHRISTIAN MOVEMENT (1889), Westhill College, 14–16 Weoley Park Road, Selly Oak, Birmingham B29 6LL. Tel: 0121-471 2404; Fax: 0121-415 5399; E-mail: scm@movement.org.uk; Web: http://www.movement.org.uk

SUFFOLK HORSE SOCIETY, The Market Hill, Woodbridge, Suffolk IP12 4LU. Tel: 01394-380643; Fax: 01394-610058; E-mail: sec@suffolkhorsesociety.org.uk

SUFFOLK INSTITUTE OF ARCHAEOLOGY AND HISTORY (1848), Roots, Church Lane, Playford, Ipswich IP6 9DS

SUNDERLAND ANTIQUARIAN SOCIETY (1900), 16 Grizedale Court, Seaburn Dene, Sunderland SR6 8JP. Tel: 0191-548 7541

SURREY ARCHAEOLOGICAL SOCIETY (1854), Castle Arch, Guildford, Surrey GU1 3SX. Tel: 01483-532454; Fax: 01483-532454; E-mail: surreyarch@compuserve.com; Web: http://ourworld.compuserve.com/homepages/surreyarch/

SURVIVAL INTERNATIONAL (1969), 11–15 Emerald Street, London WC1N 3QT. Tel: 020-7242 1441; Fax: 020-7424 1771; E-mail: info@survival-international.org; Web: http://www.survival-international.org

SUSSEX ARCHAEOLOGICAL SOCIETY (1846), Bull House, 92 High Street, Lewes, E. Sussex BN7 1XH. Tel: 01273-486260; Fax: 01273-486990; E-mail: admin@sussexpast.co.uk; Web: http://www.sussexpast.co.uk

SUZY LAMPLUGH TRUST (1986), 14 East Sheen Avenue, London SW14 8AS. Tel: 020-8392 1839; Fax: 020-8392 1830; E-mail: trust@suzylamplugh.org; Web: http://www.suzylamplugh.org

SWEDENBORG SOCIETY, 20–21 Bloomsbury Way, London WC1A 2TH. Tel: 020-7405 7986; Fax: 020-7831 5848; E-mail: swed.soc@netmatters.co.uk; Web: http://www.swedenborg.org.uk

TELECOMMUNICATIONS USERS' ASSOCIATION (1965), Woodgate Studios, 2–8 Games Road, Cockfosters, Barnet, Herts EN4 9HN. Tel: 020-8449 8844; Fax: 020-8447 4901; E-mail: tua@dial.pipex.com; Web: http://www.tua.co.uk

TEMPLETON FOUNDATION (1970), 18 Eastgate Gardens, Taunton, Somerset TA1 1RD. Tel: 01823-324500; Fax: 01823-324522

THE TEXTILE INSTITUTE (1925), 4th Floor, St James's Building, Oxford Street, Manchester M1 6FQ. Tel: 0161-237 1188; Fax: 0161-236 1991

THE THEATRES TRUST (1976), 22 Charing Cross Road, London WC2H 0HR. Tel: 020-7836 8591; Fax: 020-7836 3302; E-mail: info@theatrestrust.org.uk

THEOSOPHICAL SOCIETY IN ENGLAND (1875), 50 Gloucester Place, London W1H 4EA. Tel: 020-7935 9261; Fax: 020-7935 9543

THOMAS PAINE SOCIETY (1963), 43 Wellington Gardens, Selsey, W. Sussex PO20 0RF. Tel: 01243-605730; E mail: paineeric@netscape.net

THORESBY SOCIETY (1889), Claremont, 23 Clarendon Road, Leeds LS2 9NZ

THE TIDY BRITAIN GROUP, Elizabeth House, The Pier, Wigan WN3 4EX. Tel: 01942-824620; Fax: 01942-824778; E-mail: enquiries@tidybritain.org.uk; Web: http://www.tidybritain.org.uk

TOWN AND COUNTRY PLANNING ASSOCIATION (1899), 17 Carlton House Terrace, London SW1Y 5AS. Tel: 020-7930 8903/4/5; Fax: 020-7930 3280; E-mail: tcpa@tcpa.org.uk; Web: http://www.tcpa.org.uk

TOWNSWOMEN'S GUILDS, Chamber of Commerce House, 75 Harborne Road, Birmingham B15 3DA. Tel: 0121-456 3435; Fax: 0121-452 1890; E-mail: tghq@townswomen.org.uk; Web: http://www.townswomen.org.uk

THE TREE COUNCIL (1974), 51 Catherine Place, London SW1E 6DY. Tel: 020-7828 9928; Fax: 020-7828 9060; Web: http://www.treecouncil.org.uk

TURNER SOCIETY (1975), BCM Box Turner, London WC1N 3XX. E-mail: turner@equinox.demon.co.uk; Web: http://www.turnersociety.org.uk

UFAW (1926), The Old School, Brewhouse Hill, Wheathampstead, Herts AL4 8AN. Tel: 01582-831818; Fax: 01582-831414; E-mail: ufaw@ufaw.org.uk; Web: http://www.ufaw3.dircon.co.uk

UK CENTRAL COUNCIL FOR NURSING, MIDWIFERY AND HEALTH VISITING (1983), 23 Portland Place, London W1N 4JT. Tel: 020-7637 7181; Fax: 020-7436 2924; Web: http://www.ukcc.org.uk

UK INDEPENDENCE PARTY, Triumph House, 189 Regent Street, London W1R 7WF. Tel: 020-7434 4559; Fax: 020-7439 4659; E-mail: enquiries@independenceuk.org.uk; Web: http://www.independenceuk.org.uk

ULSTER TEACHERS' UNION (1919), 94 Malone Road, Belfast BT9 5HP. Tel: 028-9066 2216; Fax: 028-9066 3055; E-mail: office@utu.edu; Web: http://www.utu.edu/home.html

UNITED GRAND LODGE OF ENGLAND (1717), Freemasons' Hall, Great Queen Street, London WC2B 5AZ. Tel: 020-7831 9811; Fax: 020-7831 6021; E-mail: ugle@compuserve.com; Web: http://www.grand-lodge.org

UNITED KINGDOM ALLIANCE (1853), 176 Blackfriars Road, London SE1 8ET. Tel: 020-7928 1538

UNITED REFORMED CHURCH HISTORY SOCIETY (1972), Westminster College, Madingley Road, Cambridge CB3 0AA. Tel: 01223-741300; E-mail: mt212@cam.ac.uk

UNITED SOCIETY FOR CHRISTIAN LITERATURE (1964), Albany House, 67 Sydenham Road, Guildford, Surrey GU1 3RY. Tel: 01483-888580; Fax: 01483-888581; E-mail: feedtheminds@gn.apc.org; Web: http://www.feedtheminds.org

UNITED SOCIETY FOR THE PROPAGATION OF THE GOSPEL (1701), Partnership House, 157 Waterloo Road, London SE1 8XA. Tel: 020-7928 8681; Fax: 020-7928 2371; E-mail: enquiries@uspg.org.uk; Web: http://www.uspg.org.uk

THE VEGAN SOCIETY, Donald Watson House, 7 Battle Road, St Leonards-on-Sea, E. Sussex TN37 7AA. Tel: 01424-427393; Fax: 01424-717064; E-mail: info@vegansociety.com; Web: http://www.vegansociety.com

VEGETARIAN SOCIETY OF THE UNITED KINGDOM LTD (1847), Parkdale, Dunham Road, Altrincham, Cheshire WA14 4QG. Tel: 0161-925 2000; Fax: 0161-926 9182; E-mail: info@vegsoc.org; Web: http://www.vegsoc.org

THE VERNACULAR ARCHITECTURE GROUP (1952), 'Ashley', Willows Green, Chelmsford, Essex CM3 1QD. Tel: 01245-361408

VICTIM SUPPORT (NATIONAL ASSOCIATION OF VICTIMS SUPPORT SCHEMES) (1979), National Office, Cranmer House, 39 Brixton Road, London SW9 6DZ. Tel: 020-7735 9166; Helpline: 0845-3030 900; Fax: 020-7582 5712

VICTIM SUPPORT SCOTLAND, 15–23 Hardwell Close, Edinburgh EH8 9RX. Tel: 0131-668 4486; Fax: 0131-662 5400; E-mail: info@victimsupportsco.demon.co.uk; Web: http://www.victimsupportsco.demon.co.uk

VICTORIA CROSS AND GEORGE CROSS ASSOCIATION, Room 028, The Old War Office, London SW1A 2EU. Tel: 020-7930 3506

THE VICTORIA INSTITUTE (PHILOSOPHICAL SOCIETY OF GREAT BRITAIN), 41 Marne Avenue, Welling, Kent DA16 2EY. Tel/Fax: 020-8303 0465

THE VICTORIAN SOCIETY (1958), 1 Priory Gardens, Bedford Park, London W4 1TT. Tel: 020-8994 1019; Fax: 020-8995 4895; E-mail: admin@victorian-society.org; Web: http://www.victorian-society.org.uk

VICTORY (SERVICES) ASSOCIATION LTD AND CLUB, 63–79 Seymour Street, London W2 2HF. Tel: 020-7723 4474; Fax: 020-7402 9496; E-mail: res@vsc.co.uk; Web: http://www.vsc.co.uk

VIKING SOCIETY FOR NORTHERN RESEARCH, Department of Scandinavian Studies, University College, Gower Street, London WC1E 6BT. Tel: 020-7380 7176; Fax: 020-7380 7750; E-mail: s.rust@ucl.ac.uk; Web: http://www.nott.ac.uk/ aezjj/homepage.html

VSO (VOLUNTARY SERVICE OVERSEAS) (1958), 317 Putney Bridge Road, London SW15 2PN. Tel: 020-8780 7200; Fax: 020-8780 7300. Web: http://www.vso.org.uk

WELLBEING – THE HEALTH RESEARCH CHARITY FOR WOMEN AND BABIES (1965), 27 Sussex Place, Regent's Park, London NW1 4SP. Tel: 020-7262 5337; Fax: 020-7724 7725; E-mail: wb239281@aol.com; Web: http://www.wellbeing.demon.co.uk

THE WELLCOME TRUST (1936), The Wellcome Building, 183 Euston Road, London NW1 2BE. Tel: 020-7611 8888; Fax: 020-7611 8545; E-mail: contact@wellcome.ac.uk; Web: http://www.wellcome.ac.uk

WELSH NATIONAL BOARD FOR NURSING, MIDWIFERY AND HEALTH VISITING (1983), 2nd Floor, Golate House, 101 St Mary Street, Cardiff CF10 1DX. Tel: 029-2026 1400; Fax: 029-2026 1499; E-mail: info@wnb.org.uk; Web: http://www.wnb.org.uk

WES WORLD WIDE EDUCATION SERVICE LTD, Canada House, 272 Field End Road, Eastcote, Ruislip, Middx HA4 9NA. Tel: 020-8582 0317; Fax: 020-8429 4838; E-mail: wes@wesworldwide.com; Web: http://www.wesworldwide.com

WEST LONDON MISSION, 19 Thayer Street, London W1M 5LJ. Tel: 020-7935 6179; Fax: 020-7487 3965; E-mail: office@westlondonmission.freeserve.co.uk; Web: http://www.methodist.org.uk/west.london.mission

WESTMINSTER FOUNDATION FOR DEMOCRACY (1992), 2nd Floor, 125 Pall Mall, London SW1Y 5EA. Tel: 020-7930 0408; Fax: 020-7930 0449; E-mail: wfd@wfd.org; Web: http://www.wfd.org

THE WILDFOWL AND WETLANDS TRUST (1947), The New Grounds, Slimbridge, Glos GL2 7BT. Tel: 01453-890333; Fax: 01453-890827; E-mail: enquiries@wwt.org.uk; Web: http://www.wwt.org.uk

WILLIAM MORRIS SOCIETY AND KELMSCOTT FELLOWSHIP, Kelmscott House, 26 Upper Mall, London W6 9TA. Tel: 020-8741 3735; Fax: 0707-801730; E-mail: wmsoc@compuserve.com; Web: http://www.ccny.cnny.edu/wmorris/morris.html

WILTSHIRE ARCHAEOLOGICAL AND NATURAL HISTORY SOCIETY (1853), Wiltshire Heritage Museum, 41 Long Street, Devizes, Wilts SN10 1NS. Tel: 01380-727369; Fax: 01380-722150; E-mail: wanhs@wiltshireheritage.org.uk

THE WINE AND SPIRIT ASSOCIATION (1824), Five Kings House, 1 Queen Street Place, London EC4R 1XX. Tel: 020-7248 5377; Fax: 020-7489 0322; E-mail: wsa@wsa.org.uk; Web: http://www.wsa.org.uk

WOMEN'S ENGINEERING SOCIETY (1919), 2 Queen Anne's Gate Buildings, Dartmouth Street, London SW1H 9BP. Tel: 020-7233 1974; E-mail: info@wes.org.uk; Web: http://www.cant.ac.uk/misc/wes/weshome

WOMEN'S NATIONWIDE CANCER CONTROL CAMPAIGN, 128–130 Suna House, Curtain Road, London EC2A 3AQ. Tel: 020-7729 4688; Fax: 020-7613 0771; E-mail: admin@wnccc.org.uk; Web: http://www.wnccc.org.uk

WOMEN'S ROYAL VOLUNTARY SERVICE (1938), Milton Hill House, Milton Hill, Abingdon, Oxfordshire OX13 6AF. Tel: 01235-442900; Fax: 01235-861166

THE WOODLAND TRUST (1972), Autumn Park, Dysart Road, Grantham, Lincs NG31 6LL. Tel: 01476-581111; Fax: 01476-590808; E-mail: enquiries@woodland-trust.org.uk; Web: http://www.woodland-trust.org.uk

WOOLHOPE NATURALISTS' FIELD CLUB (1851), Chy an Whyloryon, Wigmore, Leominster, Herefordshire HR6 9UD. Tel: 01568-770356

WORLD EDUCATION FELLOWSHIP (1921), International Headquarters, 54 Fox Lane, London N13 3AL. Tel: 020-8245 4561; Fax: 020-8245 4561; E-mail: daturner@glam.ac.uk

WORLD ENERGY COUNCIL, Regency House, 1–4 Warwick Street, London W1R 6LE. Tel: 020-7734 5996; Fax: 020-7734 5926; E-mail: info@worldenergy.org; Web: http://www.worldenergy.org

YEOMANRY BENEVOLENT FUND, 10 Stone Buildings, Lincoln's Inn, London WC2A 3TG. Tel: 020-7831 6727

YORKSHIRE AGRICULTURAL SOCIETY (1837), Great Yorkshire Showground, Harrogate, N. Yorks HG2 8PW. Tel: 01423-541000; Fax: 01423-541414; E-mail: info@yas.co.uk; Web: http://www.yas.co.uk

YORKSHIRE ARCHAEOLOGICAL SOCIETY (1863), Claremont, 23 Clarendon Road, Leeds LS2 9NZ. Tel: 0113-245 7910; Fax: 0113-244 1979; E-mail: j.heron@shef.ac.uk; Web: http://www.yas.org.uk

THE YORKSHIRE SOCIETY (1835), 35 Waldorf Heights, Camberley, Surrey. Tel: 01276-36342; Fax: 01276-36342

YOUNG MEN'S CHRISTIAN ASSOCIATION (YMCA), National Council of YMCAs, 640 Forest Road, London E17 3DZ. Tel: 020-8520 5599; Fax: 020-8509 3190; E-mail: national.secretary@england.ymca.org.uk; Web: http://www.ymca.org.uk

YOUNG WOMEN'S CHRISTIAN ASSOCIATION OF GREAT BRITAIN (1855), Clarendon House, 52 Cornmarket Street, Oxford OX1 3EJ. Tel: 01865-304200; Fax: 01865-204805

YOUTH CLUBS UK (1911), 2nd Floor, Kirby House, 20–24 Kirby Street, London EC1N 8TS. Tel: 020-7242 4045; Fax: 020-7242 4125; E-mail: info@youthclubs.org.uk; Web: http://www.youthclubs.org.uk

YOUTH HOSTELS ASSOCIATION (ENGLAND & WALES), Trevelyan House, 8 St Stephen's Hill, St Albans, Herts AL1 2DY. Tel: 01727-855215; Fax: 01727-844126; E-mail: customerservices@yha.org.uk; Web: http://www.yha.org.uk

YOUTHACTION NORTHERN IRELAND (1944), Hampton, Glenmachan Park, Belfast BT4 2PJ. Tel: 028-9076 0067; Fax: 028-9076 8799

ZOOLOGICAL SOCIETY OF LONDON (1826), Regent's Park, London NW1 4RY. Tel: 020-7722 3333; Fax: 020-7586 5743; Web: http://www.zsl.org

International Organisations

ANDEAN COMMUNITY

General Secretariat, Paseo de la República 3895,
San Isidro, Lima, Peru.
Tel: (00 51) (1) 221 2222;
fax: (00 51) (1) 221 3329
E-mail: contacto@comunidadandina.org
Web: http://www.comunidadandina.org

The Andean Community came into being on 1 August 1997. It facilitates the development of the member countries through economic and social integration and co-operation, acceleration of the economic growth of the Andean countries, the promotion of job creation, furthering the aim of creating a Latin American common market, strengthening the position of the member states in the international economic context, and reducing the differences in development that exist between the member states.

It aims to achieve its objectives by a programme of complete trade liberalisation, a common external tariff, the reduction of border controls, the progressive harmonisation of economic and social policies, the co-ordination of national legislation in relevant fields, promoting industrialisation and agricultural development, and supporting technological development programmes.

It comprises the five member states, Bolivia, Colombia, Ecuador, Peru and Venezuela, and the bodies of the Andean Integration System (AIS). The General Secretariat of the Andean Community is its executive body, which is responsible for administration, ensuring that member states comply with their obligations, and resolving disputes.

The Andean Presidential Council is the highest-level body of the AIS and comprises the presidents of the member states; it meets at least once a year and decides on new policies, evaluates the integration process and makes decisions on reports and suggestions from other bodies. The chairmanship is rotated among the members of the council on a calendar year basis.

Other AIS bodies include the Andean Council of Foreign Ministers, which co-ordinates the positions of the member states in international issues, signs international agreements on behalf of its member states and can issue decisions that are legally binding in the member states. The Commission of the Andean Community is composed of a plenipotentiary representative from each member state and makes, implements and evaluates policies in the field of trade and investment in the region. The Court of Justice of the Andean Community comprises one judge from each member state. It ensures the uniform implementation of decisions and settles disputes. The Andean Development Corporation aims to support the sustainable development of the member states by promoting trade and investment. The Andean Parliament is presently composed of representatives of the national legislatures of the member states, but is due to become directly elected in 2003. It submits proposals to other bodies and promotes the harmonisation of legislation.
Secretary-General, Sebastián Alegrett

ARAB MAGHREB UNION

27 Avenue Okba, Rabat, Morocco
Tel: (00 212) (7) 777 2668; fax: (00 212) (7) 777 2693
E-mail: uma@mtds.com
Web: http://www.maghrebarabe.org

The treaty establishing the Arab Maghreb Union (AMU) was signed on 17 February 1989 by the heads of state of the five member states, Algeria, Libya, Mauritania, Morocco and Tunisia. The AMU aims to strengthen ties between the member states, who share strong historical, cultural and linguistic affinities, by developing agriculture and commerce, introducing the free circulation of goods and services, and establishing joint projects and economic co-operation programmes.

Decisions are made by the Council of Heads of State, which meets annually, and must be unanimous. A Council of Foreign Affairs Ministers meets regularly to prepare for the sessions of the Council of Heads of State. The Secretariat is based in Rabat and there is a Consultative Assembly, which consists of 30 representatives from each member state based in Algiers, and a Court of Justice, with two judges from each country, based in Nouakchott, Mauritania.
Secretary-General, Mohamed Amamou

ASIA-PACIFIC ECONOMIC CO-OPERATION

438 Alexandra Road, #14–00 Alexandra Point,
Singapore 119958
Tel: (00 65) 276 1880; fax: (00 65) 276 1775
E-mail: info@mail.apecsec.org.sg
Web: http://www.apecsec.org.sg

Asia-Pacific Economic Co-operation (APEC) was founded in 1989 in response to the growing interdependence among Asia-Pacific economies. The 1994 Declaration of Common Resolve envisaged a free trade zone, to be established by 2010 by the industrialised countries and by 2020 by the developing member states. In 1995, APEC leaders adopted the Osaka Action Agenda, which established three pillars of APEC activities: trade and investment liberalisation, business facilitation, and economic and technical co-operation. The Manila Action Plan for APEC, adopted in 1996, established a programme for developing human capital, capital markets, economic infrastructure, technologies of the future, environmentally sustainable growth and small and medium-sized enterprises. The 1997 meeting in Vancouver agreed to liberalise trade in certain sectors and to harmonise and simplify customs clearances.

The members are: Australia, Brunei, Canada, Chile, China (Hong Kong), Indonesia, Japan, Republic of Korea, Malaysia, Mexico, New Zealand, Papua New Guinea, Peru, the Philippines, Russia, Singapore, Taiwan, Thailand, the USA and Vietnam.

The APEC chairman is responsible for hosting the annual ministerial meeting of foreign and economic ministers. The chairmanship rotates annually among member states. Senior officials of the organisation make recommendations to the ministers and carry out their decisions. They oversee and co-ordinate budgets and work programmes. In addition, there are many advisory groups.

ASSOCIATION OF SOUTH EAST ASIAN NATIONS

70 A. Jalan Sisingamangaraja, Jakarta 12110, Indonesia
Tel: (00 62) (21) 726 2991; fax: (00 62) (21) 739 8234
E-mail: public@asean.or.id
Web: http://www.asean.or.id

The Association of South East Asian Nations (ASEAN) was formed in 1967 with the aims of accelerating economic growth, social progress and cultural development, and ensuring regional stability. The founding members are Indonesia, Malaysia, the Philippines, Singapore and Thailand. Brunei and Vietnam joined in 1984 and 1995 respectively. Laos and Myanmar were admitted in July 1997. Cambodia was admitted on 30 April 1999.

The ASEAN Summit, a meeting of the heads of government, which convenes every three years, is ASEAN's highest authority, but informal summits are held annually. The ASEAN Ministerial Meeting (AMM) is an annual meeting of ASEAN foreign ministers and is responsible for the formulation of policy guidelines and the co-ordination of activities, although other relevant ministers are included in the AMM depending on the subject under discussion. The ASEAN Economic Ministers (AEM) meet annually to co-ordinate economic policy. The AMM and AEM usually hold a joint ministerial meeting before an ASEAN summit.

The 1992 Summit agreed to set up the ASEAN Free Trade Area (AFTA), which is to be implemented by 2003, with Vietnam likely to join by 2006. A common preferential tariff was introduced in 1993. At the annual summit in 1995, a South East Asia nuclear weapon-free zone was declared by ASEAN, Cambodia, Laos and Myanmar.

The Secretary-General of ASEAN is appointed on merit by the heads of government and can initiate, advise on, co-ordinate and implement ASEAN activities. In addition to the ASEAN Secretariat based in Jakarta, each member state has a national secretariat in its foreign ministry which organises and implements activities at national level.

Secretary-General, Rodolfo C. Severino (Philippines)
ASEAN COMMITTEE IN THE UK, Indonesian Embassy,
    38 Grosvenor Square, London W1X 9AD
    Tel 020-7499 7661; fax 020-7491 4993
Chairman, HE Nana S. Sutresna

BALTIC ASSEMBLY

Basteja bulvaris 12, LV-1050 Riga, Latvia
Tel: (00 371) 770 1795; fax: (00 371) 770 1796
E-mail: baltasam@parks.lv
Web: http://www.lrs.lt/baltasm/ba_en.htm

The Baltic Assembly (BA) is an international organisation for co-operation between the parliaments of Estonia, Latvia and Lithuania, established in November 1991.

The legislature of each member state appoints 20 parliamentarians to the BA, including a head and deputy head of the national delegation. The BA holds two sessions per year, which are held in each of the member states in rotation.

The Presidium of the BA comprises the head and deputy head of each national delegation. It selects a Chairman, who is the head of the delegation of the member state which will host the following session, and the heads of the two other delegations become Vice Chairmen. The Presidium is responsible for co-ordinating the activities of BA institutions, and organises the sessions, supervises the budget and maintains relations with international organisations and the member states' national legislatures. In addition, there are permanent and ad-hoc committees.

The Baltic Assembly meets once a year with the Baltic Council of Ministers, which comprises the heads of government and ministers of the Baltic states and which carries out intergovernmental and regional co-operation between the Baltic States; the joint sessions are known as the Baltic Council.

BANK FOR INTERNATIONAL SETTLEMENTS

Centralbahnplatz 2, CH-4002 Basel, Switzerland
Tel: (00 41) (61) 280 8080; fax: (00 41) (61) 280 9100
E-mail: EMAILMASTER@bis.org
Web: http://www.bis.org

The objectives of the Bank for International Settlements (founded in 1930) are to promote co-operation between central banks; to provide facilities for international finanial operations; and to act as trustee or agent in international financial settlements entrusted to it. There are 45 members. The London agent is the Bank of England, and the Governor of the Bank of England is a member of the Board of Directors, in which administrative control is vested.

Chairman of the Board of Directors and President of the Bank for International Settlements, Urban Bäckström (Sweden)

CAB INTERNATIONAL

Wallingford, Oxon OX10 8DE
Tel: 01491-832111; fax: 01491-833508
E-mail: cabi@cabi.org
Web: http://www.cabi.org

CAB International (formerly the Commonwealth Agricultural Bureaux) was founded in 1929. It generates, disseminates and applies scientific knowledge in support of sustainable development, with an emphasis on agriculture, forestry and natural resources, and the needs of developing countries. The organisation is owned and governed by its 40 member governments, each represented on an Executive Council. A Governing Board provides guidance to management on policy issues.

CABI has three divisions: bioscience, information and publishing. These undertake research and consultancy aimed at raising agricultural productivity, conserving biological resources, protecting the environment and controlling disease. The organisation publishes books, journals and newsletters and produces bibliographic databases on agriculture, health and allied disciplines. It also undertakes contracted scientific research and provides consultancy services and information support to developing countries.

Director-General, James H. Gilmore

CARIBBEAN COMMUNITY AND COMMON MARKET

PO Box 10827, Georgetown, Guyana
Tel: (00 592) (2) 69281; fax: (00 592) (2) 67816
E-mail: carisec2@caricom.org
Web: http://www.caricom.org

The Caribbean Community and Common Market (CARICOM) was established in 1973 with three objectives: economic co-operation through the Caribbean

Common Market, the co-ordination of member states' foreign policy, and the provision of common services and co-operation in health, education, culture, communications and industrial relations.

The supreme organ is the Conference of Heads of Government, which determines policy, takes strategic decisions and is responsible for resolving conflicts and all matters relating to the founding treaty. The Community Council of Ministers consists of ministers of government responsible for CARICOM affairs and any other ministers designated by member states, and is responsible for strategic planning in the areas of economic integration, functional co-operation and external relations. The principal administrative arm is the Secretariat, based in Guyana. The Bureau of the Conference of Heads of Government is the executive body. It comprises the Chairman of the Conference, the outgoing Chairman and the Secretary-General, who are authorised to initiate proposals and to secure the implementation of CARICOM decisions.

The 14 member states are Antigua and Barbuda, the Bahamas (which is not a member of the Common Market), Barbados, Belize, Dominica, Grenada, Guyana, Jamaica, Montserrat, St Christopher and Nevis, St Lucia, St Vincent and the Grenadines, Suriname, and Trinidad and Tobago. Anguilla, the British Virgin Islands and the Turks and Caicos Islands are associate members. Aruba, Bermuda, the Cayman Islands, Colombia, the Dominican Republic, Mexico, the Netherlands' Antilles, Puerto Rico and Venezuela have observer status. Following a successful application for membership, Haiti is to be admitted as a full member of the Caribbean Community upon depositing an instrument of accession.

Secretary-General, Edwin W. Carrington

THE COMMONWEALTH

The Commonwealth is a voluntary association of 54 sovereign independent states together with their associated states and dependencies. All of the states were formerly parts of the British Empire or League of Nations (later UN) mandated territories, except for Mozambique which was admitted as a unique case because of its history of co-operation with neighbouring Commonwealth nations.

The status and relationship of member nations were first defined by the Inter-Imperial Relations Committee of the 1926 Imperial Conference, when the six existing dominions (Australia, Canada, the Irish Free State, Newfoundland, New Zealand and South Africa) were described as 'autonomous Communities within the British Empire, equal in status, in no way subordinate one to another in any aspect of their domestic or external affairs, though united by a common allegiance to the Crown and freely associated as Members of the British Commonwealth of Nations'. This formula was given legal substance by the Statute of Westminster 1931.

This concept of a group of countries owing allegiance to a single Crown changed in 1949 when India decided to become a republic. Her continued membership of the Commonwealth was agreed by the other members on the basis of her 'acceptance of The King as the symbol of the free association of its independent member nations and as such the head of the Commonwealth'. This paved the way for other republics to join the association in due course. Member nations agreed at the time of the accession of Queen Elizabeth II to recognise Her Majesty as the new Head of the Commonwealth. However, the position is not vested in the British Crown.

THE MODERN COMMONWEALTH

As the UK's former colonies joined, initially with India and Pakistan in 1947, the Commonwealth was transformed from a grouping of all-white dominions into a multi-racial association of equal, sovereign nations. It increasingly focused on promoting development and racial equality and effectively expelled South Africa in 1961 over its policy of apartheid.

The new goals of advocating democracy, the rule of law, good government and social justice were enshrined in the Harare Commonwealth Declaration (1991), which formed the basis of new membership guidelines agreed in Cyprus in 1993. Following the adoption of measures at the New Zealand summit in 1995 against serious or persistent violations of these principles, Nigeria was suspended in 1995 and Sierra Leone was suspended in 1997 for anti-democratic behaviour. Sierra Leone's suspension was revoked in March 1998 when the legitimate government was returned to power. Similarly, Nigeria's suspension was lifted on 29 May 1999, the day a newly elected civilian president took office. The heads of government meeting in Edinburgh in 1997 established a set of economic principles for the Commonwealth, promoting economic growth whilst protecting smaller member states from the negative effects of globalisation.

MEMBERSHIP

Membership of the Commonwealth involves acceptance of the association's basic principles and is subject to the approval of existing members. There are 54 members at present. (The date of joining the Commonwealth is shown in parenthesis.)

*Antigua and Barbuda (1981)	Nauru (1968)
*Australia (1931)	*New Zealand (1931)
*The Bahamas (1973)	Nigeria (1960)
Bangladesh (1972)	†Pakistan (1947)
*Barbados (1966)	*Papua New Guinea (1975)
Botswana (1966)	*St Christopher and Nevis (1983)
Brunei (1984)	*St Lucia (1979)
Cameroon (1995)	*St Vincent and the Grenadines (1979)
*Canada (1931)	Samoa (1970)
Cyprus (1961)	Seychelles (1976)
Dominica (1978)	Sierra Leone (1961)
Fiji (1970, 1997)	Singapore (1965)
The Gambia (1965)	*Solomon Islands (1978)
Ghana (1957)	South Africa (1931)
*Grenada (1974)	Sri Lanka (1948)
Guyana (1966)	Swaziland (1968)
India (1947)	Tanzania (1961)
*Jamaica (1962)	Tonga (1970)
Kenya (1963)	Trinidad and Tobago (1962)
Kiribati (1979)	*Tuvalu (1978)
Lesotho (1966)	Uganda (1962)
Malawi (1964)	*United Kingdom
Malaysia (1957)	Vanuatu (1980)
The Maldives (1982)	Zambia (1964)
Malta (1964)	Zimbabwe (1980)
Mauritius (1968)	
Mozambique (1995)	
Namibia (1990)	

*Realms of Queen Elizabeth II; †Suspended 18 October 1999

Tuvalu is a special member, with the right to participate in all functional Commonwealth meetings and activities, but not to attend meetings of Commonwealth heads of government. Nauru was also a special member until

1 May 1999, when it became a full member. Pakistan's membership was suspended on 18 October 1999, following a military coup.

Countries which have left the Commonwealth
Fiji (1987, rejoined 1997)
Republic of Ireland (1949)
Pakistan (1972, rejoined 1989, suspended 1999)
South Africa (1961, rejoined 1994)

Of the 54 member states, 16 have Queen Elizabeth II as head of state, 33 are republics, and five have national monarchies.

In each of the realms where Queen Elizabeth II is head of state (except for the UK), she is personally represented by a Governor-General, who holds in all essential respects the same position in relation to the administration of public affairs in the realm as is held by Her Majesty in Britain. The Governor-General is appointed by The Queen on the advice of the government of the state concerned.

INTERGOVERNMENTAL AND OTHER LINKS

The main forum for consultation is the Commonwealth heads of government meetings held biennially to discuss international developments and to consider co-operation among members. Decisions are reached by consensus, and the views of the meeting are set out in a communiqué. There are also annual meetings of finance ministers and frequent meetings of ministers and officials in other fields, such as education, health, women's affairs, agriculture, and science. Intergovernmental links are complemented by the activities of some 300 Commonwealth non-governmental organisations linking professionals, sportsmen and sportswomen, and interest groups, forming a 'people's Commonwealth'. The Commonwealth Games take place every four years.

Assistance to other Commonwealth countries normally has priority in the bilateral aid programmes of the association's developed members (Australia, Britain, Canada and New Zealand), who direct about 30 per cent of their aid to other member countries. Developing Commonwealth nations also assist their poorer partners, and many Commonwealth voluntary organisations promote development.

COMMONWEALTH SECRETARIAT

The Commonwealth has a secretariat, established in 1965 in London, which is funded by all member governments. This is the main agency for multilateral communication between member governments on issues relating to the Commonwealth as a whole. It promotes consultation and co-operation, disseminates information on matters of common concern, organises meetings including the biennial summits, co-ordinates Commonwealth activities, and provides technical assistance for economic and social development through the Commonwealth Fund for Technical Co-operation.

The Commonwealth Foundation was established by Commonwealth governments in 1966 as an autonomous body with a board of governors representing Commonwealth governments that fund the Foundation. It promotes and funds exchanges and other activities aimed at strengthening the skills and effectiveness of professionals and non-governmental organisations. It also promotes culture, rural development, social welfare and the role of women.

COMMONWEALTH SECRETARIAT, Marlborough House, Pall Mall, London SW1Y 5HX. Tel: 020-7839 3411; fax: 020-7839 9081
E-mail: info@commonwealth.int
Web: http://www.thecommonwealth.org
Secretary-General, Rt. Hon. Don McKinnon (New Zealand)
COMMONWEALTH FOUNDATION, Marlborough House, Pall Mall, London SW1Y 5HY. Tel: 020-7930 3783
Director, Colin Ball (UK)
COMMONWEALTH INSTITUTE, Kensington High Street, London W8 6NQ. Tel: 020-7603 4535.
Director-General, David French

COMMONWEALTH OF INDEPENDENT STATES

Ul. Kirova 17, Minsk, Belarus
Tel: (00 375) (17) 223517 fax: (00 375) (17) 272339
Web: http://www.cis.minsk.by

The Commonwealth of Independent States (CIS) is a multilateral grouping of 12 sovereign states which were formerly constituent republics of the USSR. It was formed by Russia, Ukraine and Belarus on 8 December 1991, with the remaining republics, apart from the Baltic states and Georgia, joining on 21 December. Georgia joined in December 1993. The CIS charter, signed in 1993 by seven states (Armenia, Belarus, Kazakhstan, Kyrgyzstan, Russia, Tajikistan, Uzbekistan) and open for signing by the other states, formally established the functions of the organisation and the obligations of its member states.

The CIS acts as a co-ordinating mechanism for foreign, defence and economic policies, and is a forum for addressing problems which have specifically arisen from the break-up of the USSR. These matters are addressed in more than 50 inter-state, intergovernmental co-ordinating and consultative statutory bodies. However, member states have criticised the CIS for operating ineffectively, and for failing to carry through decisions made by CIS organs.

STRUCTURE

The two supreme CIS bodies are the Council of Heads of State and the Council of Heads of Government. The Council of Heads of State is the highest organ of the CIS and meets not less than twice yearly, with every member having the right of veto. It is chaired by the heads of state of the members in (Russian) alphabetical order. The Council of Heads of Government meets not less than once every three months to co-ordinate military and economic activity. Other important bodies are the Council of Heads of Collective Security (defence ministers), the Joint Staff for Co-ordinating Military Co-operation, the CIS Inter-Parliamentary Assembly, the Economic Arbitration Court and the Co-ordinating Consultative Committee. Administrative support is provided by the Executive Committee based in Minsk.

DEFENCE CO-OPERATION

On becoming member states of the CIS, the 11 original states agreed to recognise their existing borders, respect one another's territorial integrity and reject the use of military force or other forms of coercion to settle disputes between them. Agreement was also reached on fulfilling all the international treaty obligations of the former USSR, together with the establishment of CIS joint armed forces.

The members agreed on a central CIS command for all nuclear weapons, the control over which was passed to CIS commander-in-chief Marshal Shaposhnikov in December

1991. All tactical nuclear weapons had been transferred to Russia by May 1992. An agreement was reached with the USA in May 1992 by the four republics with strategic nuclear weapons (Russia, Ukraine, Belarus, Kazakhstan) on implementing the strategic arms reduction talks (START) treaty previously signed by the USA and USSR, and the START I treaty was ratified by the five parties between October 1992 and February 1994. Under this agreement Ukraine, Belarus and Kazakhstan agreed to eliminate all their strategic nuclear weapons over a seven-year period and Russia has agreed to reduce its strategic nuclear weapons arsenal.

A CIS high command and a joint conventional force were created in 1992 to operate in parallel with member states' own armed forces. In the same year, a Treaty on Collective Security was signed by six states and a joint peacemaking force, to intervene in CIS conflicts, was agreed upon by nine states. Russia concluded bilateral and multilateral agreements with other CIS states under the supervision of the Council of Heads of Collective Security (established 1993). These were gradually upgraded into CIS agreements under the umbrella of the Treaty on Collective Security, enabling Russia to station troops in nine of the other 11 CIS states (not Moldova, Turkmenistan or Ukraine), and giving Russian forces *de facto* control of virtually all of the former USSR's external borders. Only Ukraine and Moldova remained outside the defence co-operation framework and did not sign the Treaty on Collective Security, from which Azerbaijan, Georgia and Uzbekistan withdrew in 1999, forming a new defensive grouping with Moldova and Ukraine. Russian border guards were also withdrawn from Georgia, Kyrgyzstan and Turkmenistan in 1999.

ECONOMIC CO-OPERATION

In 1991, 11 republics signed a treaty forming an economic community. The principles of the treaty were embodied within the CIS and formed the basis of its economic co-operation. Members agreed to refrain from economic actions that would damage each other and to co-ordinate economic and monetary policies. A Co-ordinating Consultative Committee, an economic arbitration court and an inter-state bank were established. A single monetary unit, the rouble, was originally agreed upon by all member states, and the members recognised that the basis of recovery for their economies was private ownership, free enterprise and competition.

Russia effectively forced the collapse of the rouble zone in July 1993 by withdrawing all pre-1993 roubles and forcing the remaining states using roubles to accept Russian monetary control or introduce their own currencies, which all did apart from Tajikistan. The resulting economic collapse of the non-Russian economies led to renewed interest in economic co-operation and the signing of a Treaty on Economic Union in September 1993. The 11 CIS members who have signed the Treaty (Ukraine is an associate member of the economic union) are committed to a common market without internal barriers to trade, common fiscal policies and an eventual currency union with currencies semi-fixed against the rouble. Belarus has withdrawn its currency and rejoined Russia and Tajikistan in the rouble zone. A treaty creating a common market was signed by Kazakhstan, Kyrgyzstan, Russia and Belarus in March 1996, with other CIS states originally excluded from membership, although Tajikistan has since joined. An Economic Committee was established in 1999.

Executive Secretary, Yuri Yarov

COUNCIL OF THE BALTIC SEA STATES
Secretariat, Strömsborg, PO Box 2010, S-103 11 Stockholm, Sweden
Tel: (00 46) (8) 440 1920; fax: (00 46) (8) 440 1944
E-mail: cbss@baltinfo.org
Web: http://www.baltinfo.org

The Council of the Baltic Sea States (CBSS) was founded in March 1992 with the aim of creating a regional forum to increase co-operation and co-ordination among the states which border on the Baltic Sea in assisting new democratic institutions, economic and technical development, humanitarian aid and health, energy and environmental issues, cultural programmes, education, tourism, transportation and communication.

There are 12 members: Denmark, Estonia, Finland, Germany, Iceland, Latvia, Lithuania, Norway, Poland, Russia, Sweden and the European Union.

The Council consists of the foreign ministers of each member state, the EU being represented by a member of the European Commission. Chairmanship of the Council rotates on an annual basis, and the annual session is held in the country currently in the chair. The foreign minister of the presiding country is responsible for co-ordinating activities between the sessions.

Chairmanship 2000–1, Germany

THE COUNCIL OF EUROPE
F-67075 Strasbourg, France
Tel: (00 33) (3) 8841 2000; fax: (00 33) (3) 8841 2781/2/3
E-mail: information.point@seddoc.coe.fr
Web: http://www.coe.fr

The Council of Europe was founded in 1949. Its aim is to achieve greater unity between its members, to safeguard their European heritage and to facilitate their progress in economic, social, cultural, educational, scientific, legal and administrative matters, and in the furtherance of pluralist democracy, human rights and fundamental freedoms.

The 41 members are Albania, Andorra, Austria, Belgium, Bulgaria, Croatia, Cyprus, Czech Republic, Denmark, Estonia, Finland, France, Georgia, Germany, Greece, Hungary, Iceland, Republic of Ireland, Italy, Latvia, Liechtenstein, Lithuania, Luxembourg, Macedonia, Malta, Moldova, the Netherlands, Norway, Poland, Portugal, Romania, Russia, San Marino, Slovakia, Slovenia, Spain, Sweden, Switzerland, Turkey, the UK and Ukraine. 'Special guest status' has been granted to Armenia, Azerbaijan and Bosnia-Hercegovina. Turkey's membership was suspended from April 1995 to September 1996 over its military offensive against Kurdish guerrillas in northern Iraq.

The organs are the Committee of Ministers, consisting of the foreign ministers of member countries, who meet twice yearly, and the Parliamentary Assembly of 291 members, elected or chosen by the national parliaments of member countries in proportion to the relative strength of political parties. There is also a Joint Committee of Ministers and Representatives of the Parliamentary Assembly.

The Committee of Ministers is the executive organ. The majority of its conclusions take the form of international agreements (known as European Conventions) or recommendations to governments. Decisions of the Ministers may also be embodied in partial agreements to which a limited number of member governments are party. Member governments accredit Permanent Representatives to the Council in Strasbourg, who are also the Ministers' Deputies. The Committee of Deputies meets every month to transact business and to take decisions on behalf of Ministers.

The Parliamentary Assembly holds three week-long sessions a year. Its 13 permanent committees meet once or twice between each public plenary session of the Assembly. The Congress of Local and Regional Authorities of Europe each year brings together mayors and municipal councillors in the same numbers as the members of the Parliamentary Assembly.

One of the principal achievements of the Council of Europe is the European Convention on Human Rights (1950) under which was established the European Commission and the European Court of Human Rights, which were merged in 1993. The reorganised European Court of Human Rights sits in chambers of seven judges or exceptionally as a grand chamber of 17 judges. Litigants must exhaust legal processes in their own country before bringing cases before the court.

Among other conventions and agreements are the European Social Charter, the European Cultural Convention, the European Code of Social Security, the European Convention on the Protection of National Minorities, and conventions on extradition, the legal status of migrant workers, torture prevention, conservation, and the transfer of sentenced prisoners. Most recently, the specialised bodies of the Venice Commission and Demosthenes have been set up to assist in developing legislative, administrative and constitutional reforms in central and eastern Europe.

Non-member states take part in certain Council of Europe activities on a regular or *ad hoc* basis; thus the Holy See participates in all the educational, cultural and sports activities. The European Youth Centre is an educational residential centre for young people. The European Youth Foundation provides youth organisations with funds for their international activities.

Secretary-General, Daniel Tarschys (Sweden)
Permanent UK Representative, HE Andrew Carter, CMG, apptd 1997

THE ECONOMIC COMMUNITY OF WEST AFRICAN STATES
Secretariat Building, 60 Yakubu Gowon Crescent, PMB 401, Abuja, Nigeria
Tel: (00 234) (9) 314 7427 9; fax: (00 234) (9) 314 3005
E-mail: ecosummit@hotmail.com
Web: http://www.cedeao.org

The Economic Community of West African States (ECOWAS) was founded in 1975 and came into operation in 1977. It aims to promote the cultural, economic and social development of West Africa through mutual co-operation. A revised ECOWAS Treaty was signed in 1993 and came into effect in July 1995. It makes the prevention and control of regional conflicts an aim of ECOWAS and provides for the imposition of a community tax and for the establishment of a regional parliament, an economic and social council, and a court of justice.

The supreme authority of ECOWAS is vested in the annual summit of heads of government of all 16 member states. A Council of Ministers, two from each member state, meets biannually to monitor the organisation and make recommendations to the summit. ECOWAS operates through a Secretariat, headed by the Executive

Secretary. In addition there is a financial controller, an external auditor, the Disputes Tribunal and the Defence Council.

A Fund for Co-operation, Compensation and Development, situated at Lomé, Togo, finances development projects and provides compensation to member states who have suffered losses as a result of ECOWAS's policies, particularly trade liberalisation.

An ECOWAS Monitoring Group (ECOMOG) peacekeeping force has been involved in attempts to restore peace in Liberia (1990–6) and in Sierra Leone since 1997.

Executive Secretary, Lansana Kouyate (Guinea)

THE EUROPEAN BANK FOR RECONSTRUCTION AND DEVELOPMENT
One Exchange Square, London EC2A 2JN
Tel: 020-7338 6000; fax: 020-7338 6100
Web: http://www.ebrd.com

The European Bank for Reconstruction and Development (EBRD), established in 1991, is an international institution with 60 members (58 countries, the European Union and the European Investment Bank).

The aim of the EBRD is to facilitate the transition of the countries of central and eastern Europe and the former USSR from centrally planned to free-market economies, and to promote multi-party democracy, entrepreneurial initiative, and environmentally sound development.

The EBRD finances projects in both the private and public sectors, providing direct funding for financial institutions, infrastructure, and industry and commerce. The main forms of EBRD financing are loans, equity investments and guarantees. No more than 40 per cent of the EBRD's investment can be made in state-owned concerns. The bank is the largest foreign investor in the region's private sector, paying particular attention to strengthening the financial sector and to promoting small and medium-sized enterprises. It works in co-operation with its members, private companies, and international organisations such as the OECD, the IMF, the World Bank and the UN specialised agencies.

The EBRD has a subscribed capital of €20,000 billion. The EBRD is also able to borrow on world capital markets. Its major subscribers are the USA, 10 per cent; Britain, France, Germany, Italy and Japan, 8.5 per cent each. As of 31 December 1999, the EBRD had signed 624 projects with a total net value of €10.8 billion.

The highest authority is the Board of Governors; each member appoints one Governor and one Alternate. The Governors delegate most powers to a 23-member Board of Directors; the Directors are responsible for the EBRD's operations and budget, and are elected by the Governors for three-year terms. The Governors also elect the President of the Board of Directors, who acts as the Bank's president for a four-year term.

President of the Board of Directors, Charles Frank (USA) (*acting*)
Chairman of the Board of Governors, Sauli Niinistö (Finland)

EUROPEAN FREE TRADE ASSOCIATION
Headquarters: 9–11 rue de Varembé, CH-1211
Geneva 20, Switzerland
Tel: (00 41) (22) 749 1111; fax: (00 41) (22) 733 9291
Web: http://www.efta.int
EEA matters: Trierstraat 74, B-1040 Brussels, Belgium
Tel: (00 32) (2) 286 1711; fax: (00 32) (2) 286 1750
E-mail: efta-mailbox@secrbru.efta.be

The European Free Trade Association (EFTA) was established in 1960 by Austria, Denmark, Norway, Portugal, Sweden, Switzerland and the UK, and was subsequently joined by Finland (associate member 1961, full member 1986), Iceland (1970) and Liechtenstein (1991). Six members have left to join the European Union: Denmark and the UK (1972), Portugal (1985), Austria, Finland and Sweden (1995). The existing members are Iceland, Liechtenstein, Norway and Switzerland.

The first objective of EFTA was to establish free trade in industrial products between members; this was achieved in 1966. Its second objective was the creation of a single market in western Europe and in 1972 EFTA signed free trade agreements with the EC covering trade in industrial goods; the remaining tariffs on industrial products were abolished in 1977 and the Luxembourg Declaration on broader co-operation between EFTA and the European Community was signed in 1984.

An agreement on the creation of the European Economic Area (EEA), an extension of the EC single market to the EFTA states, was signed in 1992 and entered into force on 1 January 1994. Switzerland rejected EEA membership in a referendum in 1992 and Liechtenstein joined on 1 May 1995 after adapting its customs union with Switzerland. The implementation of the agreement is supervised by the EEA Council, composed of EFTA and EU ministers, and the EFTA Surveillance Authority. The three EFTA EEA members also participate in a wide range of other EC programmes including research and development, environmental matters, and education and training.

EFTA has expanded its relations with other non-EU states in recent years, signing free trade agreements with Turkey (1991), Israel, Poland and Romania (1992), Bulgaria, the Czech Republic, Hungary and Slovakia (1993), Estonia, Latvia, Lithuania and Slovenia (1995), Morocco (1997), and the PLO (1998). In addition, EFTA has signed declarations of economic co-operation with Albania (1992), Egypt and Tunisia (1995), Macedonia (1996), and Jordan and Lebanon (1997).

The EFTA Council is the principle organ of the Association. It meets regularly at the level of heads of the permanent national delegations to the EFTA Secretariat in Geneva.
Secretary-General, Kjartan Jóhannsson (Iceland)
Deputy Secretary-General (Geneva), Aldo Matteucci (Switzerland)
Deputy Secretary-General (Brussels), Guttorm Vik (Norway)

EUROPEAN ORGANISATION FOR NUCLEAR RESEARCH (CERN)
CH-1211 Geneva 23, Switzerland
Tel: (00 41) (22) 767 4101; fax: (00 41) (22) 785 0247
Web: http://www.cern.ch

The Convention establishing the European Organisation for Nuclear Research (CERN) came into force in 1954. CERN promotes European collaboration in high energy physics of a scientific, rather than a military nature.

The member countries are Austria, Belgium, Bulgaria, Czech Republic, Denmark, Finland, France, Germany, Greece, Hungary, Italy, Netherlands, Norway, Poland, Portugal, Slovakia, Spain, Sweden, Switzerland and the UK. Israel, Japan, Russia, Turkey, the USA, the EU Commission and UNESCO have observer status.

The Council is the highest policy-making body and comprises two delegates from each member state. There is also a Committee of the Council comprising a single delegate from each member state (who is also a Council member) and the chairmen of the scientific policy and finance advisory committees. The Council is chaired by the President who is elected by the Council in Session. The Council also elects the Director-General, who is responsible for the internal organisation of CERN. The Director-General heads a workforce of approximately 3,000, including physicists, craftsmen, technicians and administrative staff. At present over 6,500 physicists use CERN's facilities.

The member countries contribute to the budget in proportion to their net national revenue. The 2000 budget was SFr 931 million.
President of the Council, Hans Eschelbacher (Germany)
Director-General (1999–2004), Prof. Luciano Maiani (Italy)

EUROPEAN SPACE AGENCY
8–10 rue Mario Nikis, F-75738 Paris Cedex 15, France
Tel: (00 33) (1) 5369 7654; fax: (00 33) (1) 5369 7560
Web: http://www.esa.int

The European Space Agency (ESA) was created in 1975 by the merger of the European Space Research Organisation (ESRO) and the European Launcher Development Organisation (ELDO). Its aims include the advancement of space research and technology and the implementation of a long-term European space policy.

The member countries are Austria, Belgium, Denmark, Finland, France, Germany, Republic of Ireland, Italy, the Netherlands, Norway, Portugal, Spain, Sweden, Switzerland and the UK. Canada is a co-operating state.

The agency is directed by a Council composed of the representatives of the member states; its chief officer is the Director-General.
Director-General, Antonio Rodotà, *apptd* 1997

FOOD AND AGRICULTURE ORGANISATION OF THE UNITED NATIONS
Viale delle Terme di Caracalla, I-00100 Rome, Italy
Tel: (00 39) (6) 57051; fax: (00 39) (6) 5705 3152
E-mail: fao-hq@fao.org
Web: http://www.fao.org

The Food and Agriculture Organisation (FAO) is a specialised UN agency, established in 1945. It assists rural populations by raising levels of nutrition and living standards, and by encouraging greater efficiency in food production and distribution. It analyses and disseminates information on agriculture and natural resources. The FAO also advises governments on national agricultural policy and planning; its Investment Centre, together with the World Bank and other financial institutions, helps to prepare development projects. The FAO's field programme covers a range of activities, including strengthening crop production, rural and livestock development, and conservation.

The FAO's top priorities are sustainable agriculture, rural development and food security. The Organisation attempts to ensure the availability of adequate food supplies, stability in the flow of supplies and the securing of access to food by the poor. The FAO monitors potential famine areas. The Special Relief Operations Service channels emergency aid from governments and other agencies, and assists in rehabilitation. The Technical Co-operation Programme provides schemes for countries facing agricultural crises.

The FAO had 181 members (180 states and the EU) as at May 2000. It is governed by a biennial conference of its members which sets a programme and budget. The budget for 1998–9 was US$650 million, funded by member countries in proportion to their gross national products. The FAO is also funded by the UN Development Programme, donor governments and other institutions.

The Conference elects a Director-General and a 49-member Council which governs between conferences. The Regular and Field Programmes are administered by a Secretariat, headed by the Director-General. Five regional, five sub-regional and 80 national offices help administer the Field Programme.

Director-General, Jacques Diouf (Senegal)
UK Representative, Anthony Beattie, British Embassy, Rome

INMARSAT
99 City Road, London EC1Y 1AX
Tel: 020-7728 1000; fax: 020-7728 1044
E-mail: information@inmarsat.org
Web: http://www.inmarsat.org

Inmarsat (formerly the International Mobile Satellite Organisation) was founded in 1979 as the International Maritime Satellite Organisation and began operations in 1982. Inmarsat was an internationally owned co-operative, but became a private company in April 1999. It now comprises two entities: a two-tier private company, (Inmarsat Holdings and Inmarsat Ltd), and an intergovernmental body, the International Mobile Satellite Organisation (IMSO), to oversee Inmarsat's delivery of its public service obligations. It operates a system of satellites to provide global mobile communications. Inmarsat satellite terminals are used world-wide on ships, aircraft and on land for telecommunications, as well as maritime safety, position reporting and distress communications.

Inmarsat comprises three bodies: the Assembly, the Council and the Directorate. The Assembly is composed of representatives of the 80 member countries, each having one vote. It meets every two years to review activities and objectives, and to make recommendations to the Council. The Council is the main decision-making body and consists of representatives of the 18 members with the largest investment shares, and four members representing the interests of developing countries who are elected to the Council on the basis of geographical representation. Members have voting powers equal to their investment shares. The Council meets at least three times a year and oversees the activities of the Directorate, the permanent staff of Inmarsat.

Director-General, Warren Grace (Australia)

INTERNATIONAL ATOMIC ENERGY AGENCY
Vienna International Centre, Wagramerstrasse 5,
PO Box 100, A-1400 Vienna, Austria
Tel: (00 43) (1) 26000; fax: (00 43) (1) 26007
E-mail: Official.Mail@iaea.org
Web: http://www.iaea.org/worldatom

The International Atomic Energy Agency (IAEA) was established in 1957. It is an intergovernmental organisation that reports to, but is not a specialised agency of, the UN.

The IAEA aims to enhance the contribution of atomic energy to peace, health and prosperity, and to ensure that any assistance that it provides is not used for military purposes. It establishes atomic energy safety standards and offers services to its member states for the safe operation of their nuclear facilities and for radiation protection. It is the focal point for international conventions on the early notification of a nuclear accident, assistance in the case of such an accident, civil liability for nuclear damage, physical protection of nuclear material, nuclear safety and the safety of spent fuel and radioactive waste management. The IAEA also encourages research and training in nuclear power. It is additionally charged with drawing up safeguards and verifying their use in accordance with the Nuclear Non-Proliferation Treaty (NPT) 1968, the Treaty for the Prohibition of Nuclear Weapons in Latin America (Tlatelolco Treaty) 1968, the Treaty on a South Pacific Nuclear-Free Zone (Rarotonga Treaty), the South East Asia Nuclear Weapon-Free Zone Treaty (Bangkok Treaty) and the African Nuclear Weapon-Free Zone Treaty (Pelindaba Treaty) 1996. Together with the Food and Agriculture Organisation and the World Health Organisation, the IAEA established an International Consultative Group on Food Irradiation in 1983.

The IAEA concluded a safeguards agreement with North Korea in April 1992 and began inspections to verify that its nuclear programme was for peaceful purposes only. In 1993 the IAEA informed the UN Security Council that North Korea had violated its NPT obligations and all technical aid to North Korea was suspended. North Korea resigned from the IAEA in 1994, but permitted IAEA inspections under the terms of an agreement with the USA which enabled the IAEA to resume safeguards inspections.

The IAEA had 130 members as at May 2000. A General Conference of all its members meets annually to decide policy, a programme and a budget (2000, US$226.3 million), as well as electing a Director-General and a 35-member Board of Governors. The Board meets four times a year to formulate policy which is implemented by the Secretariat under a Director-General.

Director-General, Mohamed El Baradei (Egypt)
Permanent UK Representative, Dr John Freeman, Jaurèsgasse 12, A-1030 Vienna, Austria

INTERNATIONAL CIVIL AVIATION ORGANISATION
999 University Street, Montréal, Québec, Canada H3C 5H7
Tel: (00 1) (514) 954 8219; fax: (00 1) (514) 954 6077
E-mail: icaohq@icao.int; Web: http://www.icao.int

The International Civil Aviation Organisation (ICAO) was founded with the signing of the Chicago Convention on International Civil Aviation in 1944, and became a specialised agency of the United Nations in 1947. It sets international technical standards and recommended practices for all areas of civil aviation, including airworthiness, air navigation, traffic control and pilot licensing. It encourages uniformity and simplicity in ground regulations and operations at international airports, including immigration and customs control. The ICAO also promotes regional air navigation, plans for ground facilities, and collects and distributes air transport statistics world-wide. It is dedicated to improving safety and to the orderly development of civil aviation throughout the world.

The ICAO had 185 members as at 14 April 2000. It is governed by an assembly of its members which meets at least once every three years. A Council of 33 members is elected, which represents leading air transport nations as well as less developed countries. The Council elects the President, appoints the Secretary-General and supervises the organisation through subsidiary committees, serviced by a Secretariat.

President of the Council, Dr Assad Kotaite (Lebanon)
Secretary-General, R. C. Costa Pereira (Brazil)
UK Representative, D. S. Evans, CMG, 999 University Street, Montréal, Québec, Canada H3C 5H7

INTERNATIONAL CONFEDERATION OF FREE TRADE UNIONS
Boulevard Emile Jacqmain 155 B1, B-1210 Brussels, Belgium
Tel: (00 32) (2) 224 0211; fax: (00 32) (2) 201 5815/ 224 0297
E-mail: internetpo@icftu.org
Web: http://www.icftu.org

The International Confederation of Free Trade Unions (ICFTU) was created in 1949. It aims to establish, maintain and promote free trade unions, and to promote peace with economic security and social justice.

Affiliated to the ICFTU are 215 individual unions and representative bodies in 145 countries and territories. There were 125 million members in May 2000.

The Congress, the supreme authority of the ICFTU, convenes at least every four years. It is composed of delegates from the affiliated trade union organisations. The Congress elects an Executive Board of 53 members, including five nominated by the Women's Committee and one representing young workers, which meets not less than once a year. The Board establishes the budget and receives suggestions and proposals from affiliates as well as acting on behalf of the Confederation. The Congress also elects the General Secretary.

General Secretary, Bill Jordan (UK)
UK Affiliate, TUC, Congress House, 23–28 Great Russell Street, London WC1B 3LS. Tel: 020-7636 4030

INTERNATIONAL CRIMINAL POLICE ORGANISATION
200 Quai Charles de Gaulle, F-69006 Lyon, France
Tel: (00 33) (4) 7244 7000; fax: (00 33) (4) 7244 7163
Web: http://www.interpol.com

The International Criminal Police Commission (Interpol) was set up in 1923 to establish an international criminal records office and to harmonise extradition procedures. As of 1 April 2000, the organisation comprised 178 member states.

Interpol's aims are to promote co-operation between criminal police authorities, and to support government agencies concerned with combating crime, whilst respecting national sovereignty. It is financed by annual contributions from the governments of member states.

Interpol's policy is decided by the General Assembly which meets annually; it is composed of delegates appointed by the member states. The 13-member Executive Committee is elected by the General Assembly from among the member states' delegates, and is chaired by the President, who has a four-year term of office. The permanent administrative organ is the General Secretariat, headed by the Secretary-General, who is appointed by the General Assembly.

Secretary-General, Raymond Kendall, QPM (UK)
UK OFFICE, NCIS Interpol, PO Box 8000, London SE11 5EN. Tel: 020-7238 8000. *UK Representative*, J. M. Abbott, QPM

INTERNATIONAL ENERGY AGENCY
9 rue de la Fédération, F-75739 Paris Cedex 15, France
Tel: (00 33) (1) 4057 6554; fax: (00 33) (1) 4057 6559
Web: http://www.iea.org

The International Energy Agency (IEA), founded in 1974, is an autonomous agency within the framework of the Organisation for Economic Co-operation and Development (OECD). The IEA had 25 member countries as at May 2000.

The IEA's objectives include improvement of energy co-operation world-wide, increased efficiency, development of alternative energy sources and the promotion of relations between oil producing and oil consuming countries. The IEA also maintains an emergency system to alleviate the effects of severe oil supply disruptions.

The main decision-making body is the Governing Board, composed of senior energy officials from member countries. Various standing groups and special committees exist to facilitate the work of the Board. The IEA Secretariat, with a staff of energy experts, carries out the work of the Governing Board and its subordinate bodies. The Executive Director is appointed by the Board.

Executive Director, Robert Priddle (UK)

INTERNATIONAL FRANCOPHONE ORGANISATION
Cabinet du Secrétaire général, 28 rue de Bourgogne, F-75007 Paris, France
Tel: (00 33) (1) 4411 1250; fax: (00 33) (1) 4411 1276
E-mail: webmaitre@francophonie.org
Web: http://www.francophonie.org

The International Francophone Organisation (known as La Francophonie) is an intergovernmental organisation founded in 1970 by 21 French-speaking countries. It aims to prevent conflict and promote development and co-operation between the Francophone countries, to represent its member states internationally and to promote French culture and the use of the French language.

The Conference of Heads of State and Heads of Government of Countries using French as a Common Language, also known as the Francophone Summit, takes place biennially. Other institutions include the Ministerial Conference of La Francophonie, the Permanent Council of La Francophonie and the Secretariat.

The Ministerial Conference of La Francophonie, which consists of the foreign minister or the minister responsible for Francophone affairs of each member state, implements decisions made at the summits and makes preparations for the following summit. It also puts forward prospective new members.

The Permanent Council of La Francophonie, which is chaired by the Secretary-General and consists of representatives of the member states, oversees the execution of decisions made by the Ministerial Conference, allocates funds, and reviews and approves projects. It has 18 members, chosen in advance of each summit, in rotation from among the member states.

La Francophonie has a current membership of 55 member states and regional governments (Albania (observer), Belgium, the Francophone Community of Belgium, Benin, Bulgaria, Burkina Faso, Burundi, Cambodia, Cameroon, Canada, Canada (New Brunswick), Canada (Québec), Cape Verde, Central African Republic, Chad, the Comoros, Czech Republic (observer), Democratic Republic of Congo, Republic of Congo-Brazzaville, Côte d'Ivoire, Djibouti, Dominica, Egypt, Equatorial Guinea, France, Gabon, Guinea, Guinea-Bissau, Haiti, Laos, Lebanon, Lithuania (observer), Luxembourg, Macedonia (observer), Madagascar, Mali, Mauritania, Mauritius, Moldova, Monaco, Morocco, Niger, Poland (observer), Romania, Rwanda, St Lucia, São Tomé e Príncipe, Senegal, Seychelles, Slovenia (observer), Switzerland, Togo, Tunisia, Vanuatu and Vietnam).

Secretary-General, Boutros Boutros-Ghali

INTERNATIONAL FUND FOR AGRICULTURAL DEVELOPMENT
107 Via del Serafico, I-00142 Rome, Italy
Tel: (00 39) (6) 54591; fax: (00 39) (6) 504 3463
E-mail: ifad@ifad.org
Web: http://www.ifad.org

The establishment of the International Fund for Agricultural Development (IFAD) was proposed by the 1974 World Food Conference and IFAD began operations as a UN specialised agency in 1977. Its purpose is to mobilise additional funds for agricultural and rural development projects in developing countries that benefit the poorest rural populations; provide employment and additional income for poor farmers; reduce malnutrition; and improve food distribution systems.

IFAD had 161 members as at May 2000. Membership is divided into three lists: List A (OECD countries), List B (OPEC countries), and List C (developing countries) which is subdivided into C1 (Africa), C2 (Africa, Asia and the Pacific) and C3 (Latin America and the Caribbean). All powers are vested in a Governing Council of all member countries. It elects an 18-member Executive Board (with 18 alternate members) responsible for IFAD's operations. The Council meets annually and elects a President who is also chairman of the Board. He is assisted by a Vice-President and three Assistant Presidents.

Between 1978 and 1999, IFAD has committed a total of US$6.4 billion in loans and grants for 550 approved projects in 115 developing countries.

President, Fawzi H. Al-Sultan (Kuwait)

INTERNATIONAL LABOUR ORGANISATION
4 route des Morillons, CH-1211 Geneva 22, Switzerland
Tel: (00 41) (22) 799 6111; fax: (00 41) (22) 798 8685
Web: http://www.ilo.org

The International Labour Organisation (ILO) was established in 1919 as an autonomous body of the League of Nations and became the UN's first specialised agency in 1946. The ILO aims to increase employment, improve working conditions, raise living standards and encourage democratic development. It sets minimum international labour standards through the drafting of international conventions. Member countries are obliged to submit these to their domestic authorities for ratification, and thus undertake to bring their domestic legislation in line with the conventions. Members must report to the ILO periodically on how these regulations are being implemented. The ILO plays a major role in helping developing countries achieve economic stability and job expansion through its wide-ranging programme of technical co-operation. The ILO is also the world's principal resource centre for information, analysis and guidance on labour and employment. The organisation aims to improve working and living conditions throughout the world and to support the transition to democracy and market economics under way in many states.

The ILO had 175 members as at March 2000. It is composed of the International Labour Conference, the Governing Body and the International Labour Office. The Conference of members meets annually, and is attended by national delegations comprising two government delegates, one worker delegate and one employer delegate. It formulates international labour conventions and recommendations, provides a forum for discussion of world employment and social issues, and approves the ILO's programme and budget (2000–1, US$467 million).

The 56-member Governing Body, composed of 28 government, 14 worker and 14 employer members, acts as the ILO's executive council. Ten governments, including the UK, hold permanent seats on the Governing Body because of their industrial importance. There are also various regional conferences and advisory committees. The International Labour Office acts as a secretariat and as a centre for operations, publishing and research.

Director-General, Juan Somavia (Chile)

UK OFFICE, Millbank Tower, 21-24 Millbank, London SW1P 4QP. Tel: 020-7828 6401; fax: 020-7233-5925. E-mail: london@ilo-london.org.uk

INTERNATIONAL MARITIME ORGANISATION
4 Albert Embankment, London SE1 7SR
Tel: 020-7735 7611; fax: 020-7587 3210
E-mail: info@imo.org
Web: http://www.imo.org

The International Maritime Organisation (IMO) was established as a UN specialised agency in 1948. Owing to delays in treaty ratification it did not commence operations until 1958. Originally it was called the Inter-Governmental Maritime Consultative Organisation (IMCO) but changed its name in 1982.

The IMO fosters intergovernmental co-operation in technical matters relating to international shipping, especially with regard to safety at sea. It is also charged with preventing and controlling marine pollution caused by shipping and facilitating marine traffic. The IMO is responsible for convening maritime conferences and drafting marine conventions. It also provides technical aid to countries wishing to develop their activities at sea.

The IMO had 158 members and two associate members as at May 2000. It is governed by an Assembly comprising delegates of all its members. It meets biennially to formulate policy, set a budget (1998–9, £36.6 million), vote on specific recommendations on pollution and maritime safety and elect the Council. The Council fulfils the functions of the Assembly between sessions and appoints the Secretary-General. It consists of 32 members: eight from the world's largest shipping nations, eight from the nations most dependent on seaborne trade, and 16 other members to ensure a fair geographical representation. The Maritime Safety Committee, through its sub-committees, makes reports and recommendations to the Council and the Assembly. There are a number of other specialist subsidiary committees, including one for marine environmental protection.

The IMO acts as the secretariat for the London Convention (1972) which regulates the disposal of land-generated waste at sea.

Secretary-General, William A. O'Neil (Canada)

INTERNATIONAL MONETARY FUND
700 19th Street NW, Washington DC 20431, USA
Tel: (00 1) (202) 623 7300; fax: (00 1) (202) 623 6278
E-mail: publicaffairs@imf.org
Web: http://www.imf.org

The International Monetary Fund (IMF) was established in 1944, at the UN Monetary and Financial Conference held at Bretton Woods, New Hampshire. Its Articles of Agreement entered into force in 1945 and it began operations in 1947.

The IMF exists to promote international monetary co-operation, the expansion of world trade, and exchange stability. It advises members on their economic and financial policies; promotes policy co-ordination among the major industrial countries; and gives technical assistance in central banking, balance of payments accounting, taxation, and other financial matters. The IMF serves as a forum for members to discuss important financial and monetary issues and seeks the balanced growth of international trade and, through this, high levels of employment, income and productive capacity. As at March 1999 the IMF had 182 members.

Upon joining the IMF, a member is assigned a 'quota', based on the member's relative standing in the world economy and its balance of payments position, that determines its capital subscription to the Fund, its access to IMF resources, its voting power, and its share in the allocation of Special Drawing Rights (SDRs). Quotas are reviewed every five years and adjusted accordingly. Since the 11th General Review of quotas in 1999, total Fund quotas stand at SDR 212 billion. The SDR, an international reserve asset issued by the IMF, is calculated daily on a basket of usable currencies and is the IMF's unit of account; on 30 April 1999, SDR 1 equalled US$1.35123. SDRs are allocated at intervals to supplement members' reserves and thereby improve international financial liquidity.

IMF financial resources derive primarily from members' capital subscriptions, which are equivalent to their quotas. In addition, the IMF is authorised to borrow from official lenders. It may also draw on a line of credit of SDR 18.5 billion from various countries under the so-called General Arrangements to Borrow (GAB). Periodic charges are also levied on financial assistance. At the end of April 1999, total outstanding IMF credits amounted to SDR 67.2 billion.

The IMF is not a bank and does not lend money; it provides temporary financial assistance by selling a member's SDRs or other members' currencies in exchange for the member's own currency. The member can then use the purchased currency to alleviate its balance of payments difficulties. The IMF's credit under its regular facilities is made available to members in tranches or segments of 25 per cent of quota. For first credit tranche purchases, members are required to demonstrate reasonable efforts to overcome their balance of payments difficulties. There are no performance criteria. Upper credit tranche purchases are normally associated with stand-by arrangements and are aimed at overcoming balance of payment difficulties and are required to meet certain performance criteria. Repurchases are made in three and a quarter to five years.

The IMF supports long-term efforts at economic reform and transformation as well as medium-term programmes under the extended Fund facility, which runs for three to four years and is aimed at overcoming balance of payments difficulties stemming from macroeconomic and structural problems. Members experiencing a temporary balance of payments shortfall have access to the compensatory and contingency financing facility. The IMF also offers credits to low-income countries engaged in economic reform through its enhanced structural adjustment facility (ESAF). As at 28 February 1999, SDR 7.0 billion in ESAF loans is outstanding.

The IMF is headed by a Board of Governors, comprising representatives of all members, which meets annually. The Governors delegate powers to 24 Executive Directors, who are appointed or elected by member countries. The Executive Directors operate the Fund on a daily basis under a Managing Director, whom they elect.

Managing Director, Michel Camdessus (France)

UK Executive Director, Gus O'Donnell, Room 11-120, IMF, 700 19th Street NW, Washington DC 20431, USA

INTERNATIONAL RED CROSS AND RED CRESCENT MOVEMENT
17 avenue de la Paix, CH-1211 Geneva, Switzerland
Web: http://www.icrc.org

The International Red Cross and Red Crescent Movement is composed of three elements. The International Committee of the Red Cross (ICRC), the organisation's founding body, was formed in 1863. It aims to negotiate between warring factions and to protect and assist victims of armed conflict. It also seeks to ensure the application of the Geneva Conventions with regard to prisoners of war and detainees.

The International Federation of Red Cross and Red Crescent Societies was founded in 1919 to contribute to the development of the humanitarian activities of national societies, to co-ordinate their relief operations for victims of natural disasters, and to care for refugees outside areas of conflict. There are Red Cross and Red Crescent Societies in 175 countries, with a total membership of 250 million.

The International Conference of the Red Cross and Red Crescent meets every four years, bringing together delegates of the ICRC, the International Federation and the national societies, as well as representatives of nations bound by the Geneva Conventions.

President of the ICRC, Jakob Kellenberger

BRITISH RED CROSS, 9 Grosvenor Crescent, London SW1X 7EJ. Tel: 020-7235 5454; fax: 020-7245 6315.

E-mail: information@redcross.org.uk

Web: http://www.redcross.org.uk/vauxhall.htm.

Director-General, Sam Younger

INTERNATIONAL TELECOMMUNICATIONS SATELLITE ORGANISATION

3400 International Drive NW, Washington DC 20008, USA

Tel: (00 1) (202) 944 6800; fax: (00 1) (202) 944 7898

E-mail: customer.service@intelsat.int

Web: http://www.intelsat.int

The International Telecommunications Satellite Organisation (Intelsat) was formed in 1964. It owns and operates the world-wide commercial communications satellite system which is composed of 20 satellites and more than 4,000 antennas which connect over 200 countries, territories and dependencies. Intelsat provides international and domestic voice/data and video services.

Each of the 143 member states contributes to the capital costs of the organisation in proportion to its investment share, which is based on its relative usage of the system.

There is a four-tier hierarchy. The Assembly of Parties to the agreement meets every two years to consider long-term objectives and is composed of representatives of the member governments. The Meeting of Signatories; annually considers the financial, technical and operational aspects of the system. The Board of Governors has 28 members; Intelsat Management is the permanent staff of the organisation and is headed by a Director-General who reports to the Board of Governors.

Director-General, Conny Kullman (Sweden)

INTERNATIONAL TELECOMMUNICATION UNION

Place des Nations, CH-1211 Geneva 20, Switzerland

Tel: (00 41) (22) 730 5111; fax: (00 41) (22) 733 7256

E-mail: itumail@itu.org

Web: http://www.itu.org

The International Telecommunication Union (ITU) was founded in Paris in 1865 as the International Telegraph Union and became a UN specialised agency in 1947. It promotes international co-operation and sets standards and regulations for the interconnection of telecommunications systems of all kinds. It assists the development of telecommunications in developing countries by providing technical assistance, management, investment financing and network installation. The ITU adopts international regulations and treaties to allocate the radio frequency spectrum and registers radio frequency assignments in order to avoid harmful interference between radio stations of different countries. It also governs and allocates the use of the geostationary-satellite orbit and collects and disseminates telecommunications information.

The ITU had 189 member states and over 600 members (scientific and industrial companies, broadcasters, public and private operators, and international organisations) as at April 2000. The supreme authority is the Plenipotentiary Conference, composed of representatives of all the members, which meets once every four years. It elects the Administrative Council of 46 members which meets annually to supervise the Union and set the budget (1996–7, SFr 295 million). The Conference also elects the Secretary-General, who heads the General Secretariat. The ITU is structured into three sectors: the radiocommunication sector, including world and regional radiocommunication conferences, radiocommunication assemblies and the Radio Regulations Board; the telecommunication standardisation sector; and the telecommunication development sector.

Secretary-General, Yoshio Utsumi (Japan)

LEAGUE OF ARAB STATES

Maidane Al-Tahrir, Cairo, Egypt

Tel: (00 20) (2) 575 0511; fax: (00 20) (2) 574 0331

The purpose of the League of Arab States, founded in 1945, is to ensure co-operation among member states and protect their independence and sovereignty, to supervise the affairs and interests of Arab countries, to control the execution of agreements concluded among the member states, and to promote the process of integration among them. The League considers itself a regional organisation and has observer status at the United Nations.

Member states are Algeria, Bahrain, the Comoros, Djibouti, Egypt, Iraq, Jordan, Kuwait, Lebanon, Libya, Mauritania, Morocco, Oman, Palestine, Qatar, Saudi Arabia, Somalia, Sudan, Syria, Tunisia, the UAE and Yemen.

Member states participate in various specialised agencies of the League whose role is to develop specific areas of co-operation between Arab states. These include: the Arab Organisation for Mineral Resources; the Arab Monetary Fund; the Arab Satellite Communications Organisation; the Arab Academy of Maritime Transport; the Arab Bank for Economic Development in Africa; the Arab League Educational, Cultural and Scientific Organisation; and Council of Arab Economic Unity.

Secretary-General, Dr Ahmed Esmat Abdul-Maguid (Egypt)

UK OFFICE, 52 Green Street, London W1Y 3RH. Tel: 020-7629 0044; fax: 020-7493 7943

MERCOSUR

Rincón 575 P 12, 11000-Montevideo, Uruguay

Tel: (00 598) (2) 96 45 90 fax: (00 598) (2) 96 45 91

Web: http://www.mercosur.org

Brazil and Argentina signed a Treaty for Integration, Co-operation and Development in 1988 which aimed to create a common market between the two countries within ten years, with the elimination of all tariff barriers and harmonisation of macroeconomic policies; the agreement was to be open to other Latin American countries. Paraguay and Uruguay expressed their interest and MERCOSUR (the Southern Common Market) was created by the Treaty of Asunción, which was signed by the four countries on 26 March 1991. Chile became an associate member in 1996 and Bolivia in 1997.

The Common Market Council (CMC) is the highest-level agency of MERCOSUR, with authority to conduct its policy, and responsibility for compliance with the objects and time frames set forth in the Asunción Treaty. It comprises the ministers of foreign affairs and the economy of the member states. Each country presides over the council for a period of six months, in rotating alphabetical order. The CMC meets at least once a year. The presidents of the member states can take part whenever possible.

The Common Market Group (CMG) is the executive body of MERCOSUR and is co-ordinated by the foreign ministries of the member states. Its function is to ensure compliance with the Asunción Treaty and to implement decisions made by the CMC, and where necessary, to help resolve disputes. It can establish work subgroups to work on particular issues. It is composed of four permanent members and four substitutes from each country. It normally meets at least four times a year.

Other bodies include a Joint Parliamentary Committee, a Trade Commission and a Socioeconomic Advisory Forum.

THE NORDIC COUNCIL

The Nordic Council was established in March 1952 as an advisory body on economic and social co-operation, comprising parliamentary delegates from Denmark, Iceland, Norway and Sweden. It was subsequently joined by Finland (1956), and representatives from the Faröes (1970), the Åland Islands (1970), and Greenland (1984).

Co-operation is regulated by the Treaty of Helsinki signed in 1962. This was amended in 1971 to create the Nordic Council of Ministers, which discusses all matters except defence and foreign affairs. Matters are given preparatory consideration by a Committee of Co-operation Ministers' Deputies and joint committees of officials. Decisions of the Council of Ministers, which are taken by consensus, are binding, although if ratification by member parliaments is required, decisions only become effective following parliamentary approval. The Council of Ministers is advised by the Nordic Council, to which it reports annually. There are Ministers for Nordic Co-operation in every member government.

The Nordic Council, comprising 87 voting delegates nominated from member parliaments and about 80 non-voting government representatives, meets at least once a year in plenary sessions. The full Council chooses a 13-member Praesidium, which conducts business between sessions. A Secretariat, headed by a Secretary-General, liaises with the Council of Ministers and provides administrative support. The Council of Ministers has a separate Secretariat.

SECRETARIAT OF THE NORDIC COUNCIL, PO Box 3043, DK-1021 Copenhagen K, Denmark.
Tel: (00 45) 3396 0400; fax: (00 45) 3311 1870.
Web: http://www.norden.org. *Secretary-General*, Frida Nokken (Norway)
SECRETARIAT OF THE NORDIC COUNCIL OF MINISTERS, Store Strandstræede 18, DK-1255 Copenhagen K, Denmark. Tel: (00 45) 3396 0400; fax: (00 45) 3311 1870. E-mail: nordisk-rad@nordisk-rad.dk; Web: http://www.norden.org. *Secretary-General*, Søren Christensen (Denmark)

NORTH AMERICAN FREE TRADE AGREEMENT

NAFTA Secretariat, Canadian Section, 90 Sparks Street, Suite 705, Ottawa, Ontario K1P 5B4, Canada
Tel: (00 1) (613) 992 9388; fax: (00 1) (613) 992 9392
NAFTA Secretariat, Mexican Section, Blvd. Adolfo López Mateos 3025, 2° Piso, Col. Héroes de Padierna, C.P. 10700, Mexico, D.F.
Tel: (00 52) (5) 629 9630; fax: (00 52) (5) 629 9637
NAFTA Secretariat, US Section, 14th Street and Constitution Avenue NW, Room 2061, Washington DC, 20230, USA
Tel: (00 1) (202) 482 5438; fax: (00 1) (202) 482 0148
E-mail: webmaster@nafta-sec-alena.org
Web: http://www.nafta.net

The leaders of Canada, Mexico and the USA signed the North American Free Trade Agreement (NAFTA) on 17 December 1992 in their respective capitals; it came into force on 1 January 1994 after being ratified by the legislatures of the three member states.

NAFTA aims to eliminate barriers to trade in goods and services, promote fair competition within the free trade area, protect and enforce intellectual property rights and create a framework for further co-operation. To achieve these aims, import tariffs and quotas are being removed, with the aim of achieving a free trade zone by 2008 at the latest.

The NAFTA Secretariat is composed of Canadian, Mexican and US sections. It is responsible for the administration of the dispute settlement provisions of the agreement, provides assistance to the Free Trade Commission and support for various committees and working groups, and facilitates the operation of the agreement. Under the NAFTA agreement, each member state has an identical national section.

NORTH ATLANTIC TREATY ORGANISATION

Brussels B-1110, Belgium
Tel: (00 32) (2) 707 4111; fax: (00 32) (2) 707 4579
E-mail: natodoc@hq.nato.int
Web: http://www.nato.int

The North Atlantic Treaty (Treaty of Washington) was signed in 1949 by Belgium, Canada, Denmark, France, Iceland, Italy, Luxembourg, the Netherlands, Norway, Portugal, the UK and the USA. Greece and Turkey acceded to the Treaty in 1952, the Federal Republic of Germany in 1955 (the reunited Germany acceded in October 1990), Spain in 1982, and the Czech Republic, Hungary and Poland in 1999.

The North Atlantic Treaty Organisation (NATO) is the structural framework for a defensive political and military alliance designed to provide common security for its members through co-operation and consultation in political, military and economic as well as scientific and other non-military fields.

STRUCTURE

The North Atlantic Council (NAC), chaired by the Secretary-General, is the highest authority of the Alliance and is composed of permanent representatives of the 19 member countries. It meets at ministerial level (foreign and/or defence ministers) at least twice a year. The permanent representatives (ambassadors) head national delegations of advisers and experts. The Defence Planning Committee (DPC), composed of representatives of all member countries, deals with defence matters. The DPC also meets at ministerial level (defence ministers) at least twice a year. Nuclear matters are dealt with in the Nuclear Planning Group (NPG), composed of representatives of all countries except for France. The NPG meets regularly at Permanent Representative level and twice a year at ministerial level (defence ministers). The NATO Secretary-General chairs the Council, the DPC and the NPG.

The Council and DPC are forums for constant inter-governmental consultation and are the main decision-making bodies within the Alliance. They are assisted by an International Staff, divided into five divisions: political affairs; defence planning and operations; defence support; security investment, logistics and civil emergency planning; scientific and environmental affairs.

The senior military authority in NATO, under the Council and DPC, is the Military Committee composed of the Chief of Defence Staffs of each member country except Iceland, which has no military and may be represented by a civilian. The Military Committee, which is assisted by an integrated international military staff, also meets in permanent session with permanent military representatives and is responsible for making recommendations to the Council and DPC on measures considered necessary for the common defence of the NATO area and for supplying guidance on military matters to the major NATO commanders. The Chairman of the Military Committee, elected for a period of two to three years, represents the committee on the Council.

The strategic area covered by the North Atlantic Treaty is divided between two major NATO commands (MNCs), European and Atlantic; and three major subordinate commands (MSCs) within Allied Command Europe, South, Central and North-West. There is also a Regional Planning Group (Canada and the United States).

The major NATO commanders are responsible for the development of defence plans for their respective areas, for the determination of force requirements and for the deployment and exercise of the forces under their command. The major NATO commanders report to the Military Committee. The integrated military structure of the Alliance has been reorganised. The new structure, based on reduced numbers of permanent headquarters and more flexible and mobile forces, is expected to be fully in place by 2003.

POST-COLD WAR DEVELOPMENTS

In response to the new security environment arising from the demise of the Warsaw Pact and the end of the Cold War in 1990, NATO issued a Declaration on Peace and Co-operation in 1991, and published a new strategic concept which introduced organisational changes and force reductions of around 30 per cent. The strategic concept was subsequently revised and updated and a new edition was published in April 1999.

The Euro-Atlantic Partnership Council (EAPC), which was established in 1997 as a replacement for the North Atlantic Co-operation Council (NACC), was formed to develop closer security links with eastern European and former Soviet states. It focuses on defence planning, defence industry conversion, defence management and force structuring, and the democratic concepts of civilian-military relations. The EAPC provides the framework for consultations and co-operation under the Partnership for Peace (PFP) programme, a form of association with NATO launched in 1994. NATO will consult with any PFP partner that perceives a direct threat to its territorial integrity, political independence or security. Most of the 27 PFP partners send liaison officers to NATO head-quarters in Brussels and to the Partnership Co-ordination Cell in Mons, Belgium, and participate in joint military exercises co-ordinated by NATO. EAPC membership is open to all former NACC members and PFP participants. It meets monthly at ambassadorial level in Brussels and twice a year at foreign minister and defence minister level.

In 1994, NATO announced that it would consider admitting new members, and in March 1999, Poland, the Czech Republic and Hungary acceded to the Treaty. The NATO-Ukraine Charter, signed in July 1997, recognised the importance to European security of a democratic and independent Ukraine, and set up a programme for further co-operation in the future. Russian opposition to NATO's enlargement was tempered by the signing of a Founding Act on Mutual Relations, Co-operation and Security in May 1997, which provided for the creation of a Permanent Joint Council. Russian participation was suspended in March 1999 as a result of NATO's stance on the conflict in Kosovo.

In 1996 the NAC proposed the creation of combined joint task forces which would provide European NATO members with a framework for operations without US involvement, under the auspices of the Western Europe Union. The strengthening of the European Defence Identity was one of several objectives developed in the new strategic concept issued by the Alliance at the Washington summit.

From 1992 until the end of 1995, NATO provided support for UN peacekeeping efforts in the former Yugolavia. With the signing of the Bosnian peace agreement in 1995, a NATO-led multinational Implementation Force (IFOR) embarked on Operation Joint Endeavur to implement the peace accord; IFOR was replaced by the Sustaining Force (SFOR) in December 1996.

In March 1999, NATO began air operations against military and industrial targets in Yugoslavia following the repression and ethnic cleansing of ethnic Albanians in Kosovo. Yugoslavia accepted a peace plan drawn up by NATO and Russia on 3 June 1999 and the withdrawal of Yugoslav forces from Kosovo took place between 10–20 June. NATO ended its air operations on 10 June and on 12 June 1999, the NATO-led security force (KFOR) entered Kosovo to oversee the demilitarisation of the Kosovo Liberation Army, facilitate the return of refugees and provide humanitarian support. By May 2000, KFOR had overseen the disbanding and demilitarisation of the Kosovo Liberation Army and the return of over 850,000 refugees.

Secretary-General and Chairman of the North Atlantic Council, of the DPC and of the NPG, Lord Robertson (UK)

UK Permanent Representative on the North Atlantic Council, Sir John Goulden, KCMG

Chairman of the Military Committee, Adm. Guido Venturoni (Italy)

Supreme Allied Commander, Europe, Gen. Joseph Ralston (USA)

Supreme Allied Commander, Atlantic, Lt. Gen. William F. Kernan (USA)

ORGANISATION FOR ECONOMIC CO-OPERATION AND DEVELOPMENT

2 rue André-Pascal, F-75116 Paris
Tel: (00 33) (1) 4524 8200; fax: (00 33) (1) 4524 8500
Web: http://www.oecd.org

The Organisation for Economic Co-operation and Development (OECD) was formed in 1961 to replace the Organisation for European Economic Co-operation. It is the instrument for international co-operation among industrialised member countries on economic and social policies. Its objectives are to assist its member governments in the formulation and co-ordination of policies designed to achieve high, sustained economic growth while maintaining financial stability, to contribute to world trade on a multilateral basis and to stimulate members' aid to developing countries.

The members are Australia, Austria, Belgium, Canada, Czech Republic, Denmark, Finland, France, Germany, Greece, Hungary, Iceland, Republic of Ireland, Italy, Japan, Republic of Korea, Luxembourg, Mexico, the Netherlands, New Zealand, Norway, Poland, Portugal, Spain, Sweden, Switzerland, Turkey, the UK and the USA.

The Council is the supreme body of the organisation. It is composed of one representative for each member country and meets at permanent representative level under the chairmanship of the Secretary-General, and at ministerial level (usually once a year) under the chairmanship of a minister elected annually. Decisions and recommendations are adopted by the unanimous agreement of all members. Most of the OECD's work is undertaken in over 200 specialised committees and working parties. Five autonomous or semi-autonomous bodies are associated in varying degrees to the Organisation: the Nuclear Energy Agency, the International Energy Agency, the Development Centre, the Centre for Educational Research and Innovation, and the European Conference of Ministers of Transport. These bodies, the committees and the Council are serviced by an international Secretariat headed by the Secretary-General.

Secretary-General, Donald J. Johnston (Canada)
UK Permanent Representative, HE Christopher Crabbie, 19 rue de Franqueville, Paris F-75116

ORGANISATION FOR SECURITY AND CO-OPERATION IN EUROPE

Kärntner Ring 5–7, A-1010 Vienna, Austria
Tel: (00 43) (1) 514 36 180; fax: (00 43) (1) 514 36 105
E-mail: info@osce.org
Web: http://www.osce.org

The Organisation for Security and Co-operation in Europe (OSCE) was launched in 1975 (as the Conference on Security and Co-operation in Europe (CSCE)) under the Helsinki Final Act. This established agreements between NATO members, Warsaw Pact members, and neutral and non-aligned European countries covering security in Europe; economic, scientific, technological and environmental co-operation; and humanitarian principles. Further conferences were held at Belgrade (1977–8), Madrid (1980–3) and Vienna (1986–9).

With the end of the Cold War, it was decided that the CSCE should be institutionalised to provide a new security framework for Europe. The Charter of Paris for a New Europe, signed on 21 November 1990, committed members to support multi-party democracy, free-market economics, the rule of law, and human rights. The signatories also agreed to regular meetings of heads of government, ministers and officials. The first institutionalised heads of state and government summit was held in Helsinki in December 1992, at which the Helsinki Document was adopted. This declared the CSCE to be a regional organisation and defined the structures of the organisation. The summit also appointed a High Commissioner on National Minorities. At its December 1994 summit the CSCE was renamed the Organisation for Security and Co-operation in Europe.

Three structures have been established: the Ministerial Council, which comprises the foreign ministers of participating states and is the central decision-making and governing body, and which meets at least once a year; the Senior Council, which prepares work for the Ministerial Council, carries out its decisions and is responsible for the overview, management and co-ordination of OSCE activities and meets at least three times a year; and the Permanent Council, which is responsible for the day-to-day operational tasks of the OSCE and is the regular body for political consultation, meeting weekly. The chairmanship of the Ministerial Council, Senior Council and Permanent Council rotates among participating states with the Senior Council meeting in Prague and the Permanent Council in Vienna.

The OSCE is also underpinned by five permanent institutions: a Secretariat (Vienna); a Forum for Security Co-operation (Vienna), which meets weekly to discuss arms control, disarmament and security-building measures; an Office for Democratic Institutions and Human Rights (Warsaw), which is charged with furthering human rights, democracy and the rule of law; an office of the High Commissioner on National Minorities (The Hague), which identifies ethnic tensions that might endanger peace and promotes their resolution; and a Representative on Freedom of the Media (Vienna), which is responsible for assisting governments in the furthering of free, independent and pluralistic media. There is also a documentation and conference centre in Prague, an OSCE Parliamentary Assembly with a secretariat based in Copenhagen, and a Court of Conciliation and Arbitration in Geneva.

In June 1991 the CSCE agreed upon new crisis prevention mechanisms to prevent or manage violent conflict between and within member countries. The OSCE has monitoring missions in ten OSCE countries, and has sent an assistance group to Chechnya. It is also organising a peacekeeping force in Nagorno-Karabakh. The OSCE supervised all elections in Bosnia-Hercegovina between 1996 and 2000. A Joint Consultative Group of the OSCE promotes the objectives and implementation of the Conventional Armed Forces in Europe (CFE) Treaty (1990) which limits conventional ground and air forces. In November 1999, the Charter on European Security committed the OSCE to co-operate with other organisations and institutions concerned with the promotion of security within the OSCE area.

The OSCE has 55 participating states: Albania, Andorra, Armenia, Austria, Azerbaijan, Belarus, Belgium, Bosnia-Hercegovina, Bulgaria, Canada, Croatia, Cyprus, Czech Republic, Denmark, Estonia, Finland, France, Georgia, Germany, Greece, Hungary, Iceland, Republic of Ireland, Italy, Kazakhstan, Kyrgyzstan, Latvia, Liechtenstein, Lithuania, Luxembourg, Macedonia, Malta, Moldova, Monaco, the Netherlands, Norway, Poland, Portugal, Romania, Russia, San Marino, Slovakia, Slovenia, Spain, Sweden, Switzerland, Tajikistan, Turkey,

Turkmenistan, the UK, Ukraine, the USA, Uzbekistan, the Vatican and Yugoslavia (suspended from activities July 1992).

Chair of the OSCE, Austria (2000); Romania (2001)
Secretary-General of the OSCE, Ján Kubiš (Slovakia)
Director of the Office for Democratic Institutions and Human Rights, Gérard Stoudmann (Switzerland)
OSCE High Commissioner on National Minorities, Max van der Stoel (Netherlands)
Representative on Freedom of the Media, Freimut Duve (Germany)

ORGANISATION OF AFRICAN UNITY
PO Box 3243, Addis Ababa, Ethiopia
Tel: (00 251) (1) 517700; fax: (00 251) (1) 513036
Web: http://www.oau-oua.org

The Organisation of African Unity (OAU) was established in 1963 and has 53 members; Morocco suspended its participation in 1985 in protest at the Polisario-proclaimed Saharan Arab Democratic Republic (SADR), representing Western Sahara, being admitted as a member. The OAU aims to further African unity and solidarity, to co-ordinate political, economic, social and defence policies, and to eliminate colonialism in Africa.

The chief organs are the Assembly of heads of state or government, which is the supreme organ of the OAU and meets once a year to consider matters of common African concern and to co-ordinate the Organisation's policies; the Council of foreign ministers, which is the Organisation's executive body responsible for the implementation of the Assembly's policies, and which meets twice a year; and the Commission of Mediation, Conciliation and Arbitration which promotes the peaceful settlement of disputes between member countries. The main administrative body is the General Secretariat, based in Addis Ababa, headed by a Secretary-General who is elected by the Assembly for a four-year term.

Substantial budgetary arrears due to delays in the payment of national contributions has meant that the OAU continually faces difficulties in furthering its aims. Its budget for 1997–8 was set at US$30.85 million; several OAU programmes have been suspended since November 1994 after unpaid contributions reached US$77 million, although by June 1995 arrears had dropped to US$38.3 million. In June 1991 the Assembly adopted an African Economic Community Treaty which envisages establishment of the Economic Community after ratification by two-thirds of the OAU's membership. In June 1993 a mechanism was created for conflict prevention, management and resolution, and a peace fund was established.
Secretary-General, Salim Ahmed Salim (Tanzania)

ORGANISATION OF AMERICAN STATES
17th Street and Constitution Avenue NW, Washington DC 20006, USA
Tel: (00 1) (202) 458 3000; fax: (001) (202) 458 6421
E-mail: pi@oas.org
Web: http://www.oas.org

Originally founded in 1890 for largely commercial purposes, the Organisation of American States (OAS) adopted its present name and charter in 1948. The charter entered into force in 1951 and was amended in 1967, 1985, 1996 and 1997.

The OAS aims to strengthen the peace and security of the continent; to promote and consolidate representative democracy with due respect for the principle of non-intervention; to prevent possible causes of difficulties and to ensure the peaceful resolution of disputes arising among its member states; to provide for common action on the part of those states in the event of aggression; to seek the resolution of political, judicial and economic problems that may arise among them; to promote, by co-operative action, their economic, social and cultural development; and to achieve an effective limitation of conventional weapons so that resources can be devoted to economic and social development.

The Declaration of Principles and the Plan of Action resulting from the 1994 Miami summit and signed by all the members except Cuba, envisage the establishment of a free trade area, in which barriers to trade and investment will be progressively eliminated.

Policy is determined by the annual General Assembly, which is the supreme authority and elects the Secretary-General for a five-year term. The Meeting of Consultation of ministers of foreign affairs considers urgent problems on an *ad hoc* basis. The Permanent Council, comprising one representative from each member state, promotes friendly inter-state relations, acts as an intermediary in case of disputes arising between states and oversees the General Secretariat, the main administrative body. The Inter-American Council for Integral Development was created in 1996 by the ratification of the Protocol of Managua to promote sustainable development.

The 35 member states are Antigua and Barbuda, Argentina, the Bahamas, Barbados, Belize, Bolivia, Brazil, Canada, Chile, Colombia, Costa Rica, Cuba, Dominica, Dominican Republic, Ecuador, El Salvador, Grenada, Guatemala, Guyana, Haiti, Honduras, Jamaica, Mexico, Nicaragua, Panama, Paraguay, Peru, St Christopher and Nevis, St Lucia, St Vincent and the Grenadines, Suriname, Trinidad and Tobago, Uruguay, the USA and Venezuela. The European Union and 39 non-American states have permanent observer status.
Secretary-General, Dr César Gaviria Trujillo (Colombia)

ORGANISATION OF ARAB PETROLEUM EXPORTING COUNTRIES
PO Box 20501, Safat 13066, Kuwait
Tel: (00 965) 484 4500; fax: (00 965) 481 5747
E-mail: oapec@qualitynet.net
Web: http://www.oapecorg.org

The Organisation of Arab Petroleum and Exporting Countries (OAPEC) was founded in 1968. Its objectives are to promote co-operation in economic activities, to safeguard members' interests, to unite efforts to ensure the flow of oil to consumer markets, and to create a favourable climate for the investment of capital and expertise.

The Ministerial Council is composed of oil ministers from the member countries and meets twice a year to determine policy and to approve the budgets and accounts of the General Secretariat and the Judicial Tribunal. The Judicial Tribunal is composed of seven part-time judges who rule on disputes between member countries and disputes between countries and oil companies. The executive organ of OAPEC is the General Secretariat.

The members are Algeria, Bahrain, Egypt, Iraq, Kuwait, Libya, Qatar, Saudi Arabia, Syria and the UAE. Tunisia's membership has been inactive since 1987.
Secretary-General, Abdel-Aziz A. Al-Turki

ORGANISATION OF THE BLACK SEA ECONOMIC CO-OPERATION

International Secretariat, Istinye Caddesi, Müsir Fuad Pasa Yalisi, Eski Tersane, 80860 Istinye-Istanbul, Turkey
Tel: (00 90) (212) 229 6330/6335;
fax: (00 90) (212) 229 6336
E-mail: bsec@turk.net
Web: http://www.bsec.gov.tr

The Black Sea Economic Co-operation (BSEC) resulted from the Istanbul Summit Declaration and the adoption of the Bosporus Statement on 25 June 1992. BSEC acquired a permanent secretariat in 1994. Following the Yalta Summit of the Heads of State or Government in June 1998, a charter was drawn up to found the Organisation of the Black Sea Economic Co-operation, which was inaugurated on 1 May 1999.

The organisation aims to promote closer political and economic co-operation in the context of the European integration process between the countries in the Black Sea region and to foster security, regional initiatives, social justice, economic liberty and respect for human rights.

The Council of the Ministers of Foreign Affairs, the highest decision-making authority, meets twice yearly. The meetings rotate among the member states and the chairman is the foreign minister of the state in which the meeting is held. There is also a Committee of Senior Officials and 15 working groups, which deal with specific areas of co-operation.

There are 11 member states: Albania, Armenia, Azerbaijan, Bulgaria, Georgia, Greece, Moldova, Romania, Russia, Turkey and Ukraine.

ORGANISATION OF THE ISLAMIC CONFERENCE

PO Box 178, Jeddah 21411, Saudi Arabia
Tel: (00 966) (2) 680 0800; fax: (00 966) (2) 687 3568

The Organisation of the Islamic Conference (OIC) was established in 1971 with the purpose of promoting solidarity and co-operation between Islamic countries. It also has the specific aims of co-ordinating efforts to safeguard the Muslim holy places, supporting the formation of a Palestinian state, assisting member states to maintain their independence, co-ordinating the views of member states in international forums such as the UN, and improving co-operation in the economic, cultural and scientific fields.

The OIC has three central organs, supreme among them the Conference of the Heads of State which meets once every three years to discuss issues of importance to Islamic states. The Conference of Foreign Ministers meets annually to prepare reports for the Conference of Heads of State. The General Secretariat carries out administrative tasks. It is headed by a Secretary-General who is elected by the Conference of Foreign Ministers for a non-renewable four-year term.

In addition to this structure, the OIC has several subsidiary bodies and specialised bodies. These include the Islamic Solidarity Fund, to aid Islamic institutions in member countries, and the Islamic Development Bank, to finance development projects in poorer member states. An Islamic Court of Justice is planned. The OIC runs various offices to organise the economic boycott of Israel.

The achievement of the OIC's aims has often been prevented by political rivalry and conflicts between member states, such as the Iran-Iraq war and the Iraqi invasion of Kuwait. Egypt's membership was suspended from 1979 to 1984 because of its peace treaty with Israel. Saudi Arabia, the main source of funding, exercises great influence within the OIC. Since 1991 the OIC has become more united and has spoken out against violence against Muslims in India, the Occupied Territories and Bosnia-Hercegovina. From 1993 to 1995 the OIC co-ordinated the offering of troops to the UN by Muslim states to protect Muslim areas of Bosnia-Hercegovina.

The Organisation has 55 members (54 sovereign Muslim states in Africa, the Middle East, central and south-east Asia and Europe, plus the Palestine Liberation Organisation) and three observers, the Central African Republic, Turkish Northern Cyprus and Côte d'Ivoire. It has an annual budget of £5 million.
Secretary-General, Azzedine Laraki (Morocco)

ORGANISATION OF THE PETROLEUM EXPORTING COUNTRIES

Obere Donaustrasse 93, A-1020 Vienna, Austria
Tel: (00 43) (1) 211 120; fax: (00 43) (1) 214 9827
E-mail: prid@opec.org
Web: http://www.opec.org

The Organisation of the Petroleum Exporting Countries (OPEC) was created in 1960 as a permanent intergovernmental organisation with the principal aims of unifying and co-ordinating the petroleum policies of its members, determining ways of protecting their interests individually and collectively, and ensuring the stabilisation of prices in international oil markets with a view to eliminating unnecessary fluctuations. Since 1982 OPEC has attempted (only partially successfully) to impose overall production limits and production quotas in an attempt to maintain stable oil prices. In March 1999, OPEC and some non-OPEC producers agreed to cut output by a total of 2.1 million barrels per day, which raised the price of petroleum. In March 2000, the member states, with the exception of Iran and Iraq, agreed to boost output by 1.452 million barrels per day.

The supreme authority is the Conference of Ministers of oil, mines and energy of member countries, which meets at least twice a year to formulate policy. The Board of Governors, nominated by member countries, directs the management of OPEC and implements conference resolutions. The Secretariat carries out executive functions under the direction of the Board of Governors.

The member states are Algeria, Indonesia, Iran, Iraq, Kuwait, Libya, Nigeria, Qatar, Saudi Arabia, the UAE and Venezuela. Ecuador withdrew in 1992 and Gabon in 1995.
Secretary-General, HE Dr Rilwanu Lukman (Nigeria)

THE PACIFIC COMMUNITY

BP D5, 98848 Nouméa Cedex, New Caledonia
Tel: (00 687) 262000; fax: (00 687) 263818
E-mail: spc@spc.org.nc
Web: http://www.spc.org.nc

The Pacific Community (formerly the South Pacific Commission) was established in 1947 by Australia, France, the Netherlands, New Zealand, the UK and the USA with the aim of promoting the economic and social stability of the islands in the region. The Community now numbers 26 member states and territories: the four remaining founder states (the Netherlands and the UK have withdrawn), in which no programmes are run, and the other 22 states and territories of Melanesia, Micronesia and Polynesia.

The Secretariat of the Pacific Community (SPC) is a technical assistance agency with programmes in agriculture and plant protection, fisheries and marine resources, community health, socio-economic and statistical services, and community education services.

The governing body is the Conference of the Pacific Community, which meets every two years. The Director-General is the chief executive.

Director-General, Bob Dun (Australia)
Deputy Directors-General, Jimmie Rodgers (Solomon Islands); Lourdes Pangelinan (Guam)

SOUTH ASIAN ASSOCIATION FOR REGIONAL CO-OPERATION
PO Box 4222, Kathmandu, Nepal
Tel: (00 977) (1) 221794; fax: (00 977) (1) 227033
E-mail: saarc@mos.com.np
Web: http://www.south-asia.com

The South Asian Association for Regional Co-operation (SAARC) was established in 1985 by Bangladesh, Bhutan, India, the Maldives, Nepal, Pakistan and Sri Lanka to promote the acceleration of economic growth and mutual assistance in the region by fostering co-operation in the fields of agriculture, telecommunications, health, arts and culture. A preferential trade agreement was adopted in 1993, designed to reduce tariffs on trade between SAARC member states, and in 1997 it was agreed to establish a regional free trade zone by 2001.

The highest decision-making body is the Summit, an annual meeting of the heads of state or government. The Council of Ministers, which meets twice a year, is made up of the foreign ministers of the member states; it is responsible for formulating policy, reviewing progress and deciding on new areas of co-operation. The Standing Committee is composed of the foreign secretaries of the member states and monitors and co-ordinates SAARC programmes and their financing; it normally meets twice a year. Technical Committees are responsible for individual areas of SAARC's activities. The Secretariat co-ordinates, monitors, facilitates and promotes SAARC's activities.

Secretary General, Nadeem U. Hasan

SOUTHERN AFRICAN DEVELOPMENT COMMUNITY
Private Bag 0095, Gaborone, Botswana
Tel: (00 267) 351 863; fax: (00 267) 372 848
Web: http://www.saep.org/sadc/sadc.html

The Southern African Development Community (SADC) was formed in August 1992 by the members of its predecessor, the Southern African Development Co-ordination Conference, founded in 1979 to harmonise economic development among the countries in Southern Africa and reduce their dependence on South Africa. The SADC now comprises 14 countries, including South Africa, and works on a regional basis to increase economic integration and regional security.

It aims to evolve common political values, systems and institutions, to promote development and economic growth, regional security, self-sustaining development and the interdependence of member states, and to maximise production and strengthen and consolidate the historical, social and cultural links among the peoples of the region.

The original ten members, Angola, Botswana, Lesotho, Malawi, Mozambique, Namibia, Swaziland, Tanzania, Zambia and Zimbabwe, were joined by South Africa in 1994, Mauritius in 1995 and the Democratic Republic of Congo and the Seychelles in 1997.

The headquarters of the SADC are in Gaborone, Botswana, but member states each have a responsibility for an area of economic activity.

Executive Secretary, Dr Kaire Mbuende

THE UNITED NATIONS
UN Plaza, New York, NY 10017, USA
Tel: (00 1) (212) 963 1234
Web: http://www.un.org

The United Nations (UN) is an intergovernmental organisation of member states, dedicated through signature of the UN Charter to the maintenance of international peace and security and the solution of economic, social and political problems through international co-operation.

The UN was founded as a successor to the League of Nations and inherited many of its procedures and institutions. The name 'United Nations' was first used in the Washington Declaration 1942 to describe the 26 states that had allied to fight the Axis powers. The UN Charter developed from discussions at the Moscow Conference of the foreign ministers of China, the UK, the USA and the Soviet Union in 1943. Further progress was made at Dumbarton Oaks, Washington, in 1944 during talks involving the same states. The role of the Security Council was formulated at the Yalta Conference in 1945. The Charter was formally drawn up by 50 allied nations at the San Francisco Conference between April and 26 June 1945, when it was signed. Following ratification the UN came into effect on 24 October 1945, which is celebrated annually as United Nations Day. The UN flag is light blue with the UN emblem centred in white.

The principal organs of the UN are the General Assembly, the Security Council, the Economic and Social Council, the Trusteeship Council, the Secretariat and the International Court of Justice. The Economic and Social Council and the Trusteeship Council are auxiliaries, charged with assisting and advising the General Assembly and Security Council. The official languages used are Arabic, Chinese, English, French, Russian and Spanish. Deliberations at the International Court of Justice are in English and French only.

MEMBERSHIP
Membership is open to all countries which accept the Charter and its principle of peaceful co-existence. New members are admitted by the General Assembly on the recommendation of the Security Council. The original membership of 51 states has grown to 188:

Afghanistan, Albania, Algeria, Andorra, Angora, Antigua and Barbuda, *Argentina, Armenia, *Australia, Austria, Azerbaijan, The Bahamas, Bahrain, Bangladesh, Barbados, *Belarus, *Belgium, Belize, Benin, Bhutan, *Bolivia, Bosnia-Hercegovina, Botswana, *Brazil, Brunei, Bulgaria, Burkina Faso, Burundi, Cambodia (suspended), Cameroon, *Canada, Cape Verde, Central African Republic, Chad, *Chile, *China, *Colombia, The Comoros, Congo-Democratic Republic, Congo Republic of, *Costa Rica, Cte d Ivoire, Croatia, *Cuba, Cyprus, *Czech Republic, *Denmark, Djibouti, Dominica, *Dominican Republic, *Ecuador, *Egypt, *El Salvador, Equatorial Guinea, Eritrea, Estonia,

*Ethiopia, Federated States of Micronesia, Fiji, Finland, *France, Gabon, Gambia, Georgia, Germany, Ghana, *Greece, Grenada, *Guatemala, Guinea, Guinea-Bissau, Guyana, *Haiti, *Honduras, Hungary, Iceland, *India, Indonesia, *Iran, *Iraq, Ireland – Republic of, Israel, Italy, Jamaica, Japan, Jordan, Kazakhstan, Kenya, Korea Democratic Peoples Republic, Korea – Republic of, Kuwait, Kyrgystan, Laos, Latvia, *Lebanon, Lesotho, *Liberia, Libya, Liechtenstein, Lithuania, *Luxembourg, Macedonia, Madagascar, Malawi, Malaysia, Maldives, Mali, Malta, Marshall Islands, Mauritania, Mauritius, *Mexico, Moldova, Monaco, Mongolia, Morocco, Mozambique, Myanmar, Namibia, Nepal, *Netherlands, *New Zealand, *Nicaragua, Niger, Nigeria, *Norway, Oman, Pakistan, Palau, *Panama, Papua New Guinea, *Paraguay, *Peru, *Philippines, *Poland, Portugal, Qatar, Romania, *Russian Federation, Rwanda, St Christopher and Nevis, St Lucia, St Vincent and the Grenadines, Samoa, San Marino, São Tomé and Príncipe, *Saudi Arabia, Senegal, Seychelles, Sierra Leone, Singapore, *Slovakia, Slovenia, Solomon Islands, Somalia, *South Africa, Spain, Sri Lanka, Sudan, Suriname, Swaziland, Sweden, *Syria, Tajikistan, Tanzania, Thailand, Togo, Trinidad and Tobago, Tunisia, Turkey, Turkmenistan, Tuvalu, Uganda, *Ukraine, United Arab Emirates, *United Kingdom, *United States of America, *Uruguay, Uzbekistan, Vanuatu, *Venezuela, Vietnam, Yemen, *Yugoslavia (suspended), Zambia, Zimbabwe

*Original member (i.e. from 1945)

From 25 October 1971 'China' was taken to mean the People's Republic of China. Czechoslovakia was an original member in 1945 and a member until 31 December 1992; the successor states of the Czech Republic and Slovakia were admitted as members in January 1993.

The Russian Federation took over the membership of the Soviet Union in the Security Council and all other UN organs on 24 December 1991. Belarus (formerly Belorussia) and Ukraine on becoming independent sovereign states continued their existing memberships of the UN, both having been granted separate UN membership in 1945 as a concession to the Soviet Union.

OBSERVERS

Permanent observer status is held by the Holy See and Switzerland. The Palestine Liberation Organisation has special observer status.

NON-MEMBERS

A number of countries are not members, usually due to their small size and limited financial resources. Notable exceptions include Switzerland, which follows a policy of absolute neutrality, and Taiwan, which was replaced by the People's Republic of China in 1971. The others are Kiribati, Nauru, Tonga and the Holy See.

THE GENERAL ASSEMBLY
UN Plaza, New York, NY 10017, USA

The General Assembly is the main deliberative organ of the UN. It consists of all members, each entitled to five representatives but having only one vote. The annual session begins on the third Tuesday of September, when the President is elected, and usually continues until mid-December. Special sessions are held on specific issues and emergency special sessions can be called within 24 hours.

The Assembly is empowered to discuss any matter within the scope of the Charter, except when it is under consideration by the Security Council, and to make recommendations. Under the 'uniting for peace' resolu-tion, adopted in 1950, the Assembly may also take action to maintain international peace and security when the Security Council fails to do so because of a lack of unanimity of its permanent members. Important de-cisions, such as those on peace and security, the election of officers, the budget, etc., need a two-thirds majority. Others need a simple majority. The Assembly has effective power only over the internal operations of the UN itself; external recommendations are not legally binding.

The work of the General Assembly is divided among six main committees, on each of which every member has the right to be represented: disarmament and international security; economic and financial; social, humanitarian and cultural; special political issues and decolonisation (in-cluding non-self governing territories); administrative and budgetary; and legal. In addition, the General Assembly appoints *ad hoc* committees to consider special issues, such as human rights, peacekeeping, disarmament and inter-national law. All committees consider items referred to them by the Assembly and recommend draft resolutions to its plenary meeting.

The Assembly is assisted by a number of functional committees. The General Committee co-ordinates its proceedings and operations, while the Credentials Com-mittee verifies the credentials of representatives. There are also two standing committees, the Advisory Committee on Administration and Budgetary Questions and the Committee on Contributions, which suggests the scale of members' payments to the UN.
President of the General Assembly (1997), Hennadiy Udovenko (Ukraine)

The Assembly has created a large number of specialised bodies over the years, which are supervised jointly with the Economic and Social Council. They are supported by UN and voluntary contributions from governments, non-governmental organisations and individuals. These organisations include:

THE CONFERENCE ON DISARMAMENT (CD)
Palais des Nations, CH-1211 Geneva 10, Switzerland
Established by the UN as the Committee on Disarmament in 1962, the CD is the single multilateral disarmament negotiating forum. The present title of the organisation was adopted in 1984. There were 40 members as at June 1994.

A Chemical Weapons Convention was agreed in Paris in 1993 and came into force in April 1997 after being ratified by 87 countries. It bans the use, production, stockpiling and transfer of all chemical weapons. All US and Russian weapons must be destroyed within 15 years of the Convention entering into force and all other states' weapons must be destroyed within ten years.
Secretary-General, Vladimir Petrovsky (Russia)
UK Representative, I. Soutar, 37–39 rue de Vermont, CH-1211 Geneva 20, Switzerland

THE UNITED NATIONS CHILDREN'S FUND (UNICEF)
3 UN Plaza, New York, NY 10017, USA
Established in 1947 to assist children and mothers in the immediate post-war period, UNICEF now concentrates on developing countries. It provides primary health-care and health education. In particular, it conducts pro-grammes in oral hydration, immunisation against leading diseases, child growth monitoring, and the encourage-ment of breast-feeding. Its operations are often conducted in co-operation with the World Health Organisation (WHO).
Executive Director, Carol Bellamy (USA)

THE UNITED NATIONS DEVELOPMENT PROGRAMME (UNDP)

1 UN Plaza, New York, NY 10017, USA
Established in 1966 from the merger of the UN Expanded Programme of Technical Assistance and the UN Special Fund, UNDP is the central funding agency for economic and social development projects around the world. Much of its annual expenditure is channelled through UN specialised agencies, governments and non-governmental organisations.
Administrator, James G. Speth (USA)

THE UNITED NATIONS HIGH COMMISSIONER FOR REFUGEES (UNHCR)

Centre William Rappard, 154 rue de Lausanne, PO Box 2500, CH-1211 Geneva 2, Switzerland
Established in 1951 to protect the rights and interests of refugees, UNHCR organises emergency relief and longer-term solutions, such as voluntary repatriation, local integration or resettlement.
High Commissioner, Sadako Ogata (Japan)
UK OFFICE, 76 Westminster Palace Gardens, London SW1P 1RL. Tel: 020-7828 9191

THE UN RELIEF AND WORKS AGENCY FOR PALESTINE REFUGEES IN THE NEAR EAST (UNRWA)

Vienna International Centre, Wagramerstrasse 5, PO Box 100, A-1400 Vienna, Austria
Established in 1949 to bring relief to the Palestinians displaced by the Arab-Israeli conflict.
Commissioner-General, Ilter Turkman (Turkey)

THE UNITED NATIONS HIGH COMMISSIONER FOR HUMAN RIGHTS

Established in 1993 to secure respect for, and prevent violations of human rights by engaging in dialogue with governments and international organisations. Responsible for the co-ordination of all UN human rights activities.
High Commissioner, Mary Robinson (Ireland)

Other bodies include:

THE UN CENTRE FOR HUMAN SETTLEMENTS (Habitat), PO Box 30030, Nairobi, Kenya
THE UN CONFERENCE ON TRADE AND DEVELOPMENT (UNCTAD), Palais des Nations, CH-1211 Geneva 10, Switzerland
THE DEPARTMENT OF HUMANITARIAN AFFAIRS (DHA), Palais des Nations, CH-1211 Geneva 10, Switzerland
THE INTERNATIONAL SEABED AUTHORITY, Kingston, Jamaica
THE UN ENVIRONMENT PROGRAMME (UNEP), PO Box 30552, Nairobi, Kenya
THE UN POPULATION FUND (UNFPA), 220 East 42nd Street, New York, NY 10017, USA
THE UN INSTITUTE FOR THE ADVANCEMENT OF WOMEN (INSTRAW), PO Box 21747, Santo Domingo, Dominican Republic
THE UN UNIVERSITY (UNU), Toho Seimei Building,15-1, Shibuya, 2-Chome, Shibuya-ku, Tokyo 150, Japan
THE WORLD FOOD COUNCIL (WFC), Via delle Terme di Caracalla, I-00100 Rome, Italy
THE WORLD FOOD PROGRAMME (WFP), Via delle Terme di Caracalla, I-00100 Rome, Italy

BUDGET OF THE UNITED NATIONS

The budget adopted for the biennium 1998–9 was US$2,387 million. The scale of assessment contributions of 88 UN members is set at the minimum 0.01 per cent.

The ten largest assessments are: USA, 25 per cent; Japan, 12.45; Germany, 8.93; Russia, 6.91; France, 6.00; UK, 5.02; Italy, 4.29; Canada, 3.11; Spain, 1.98; Australia, 1.51.

THE SECURITY COUNCIL

UN Plaza, New York, NY 10017, USA

The Security Council is the senior arm of the UN and has the primary responsibility for maintaining world peace and security. It consists of 15 members, each with one representative and one vote. There are five permanent members, China, France, Russia, the UK and the USA, and ten non-permanent members. Each of the non-permanent members is elected for a two-year term by a two-thirds majority of the General Assembly and is ineligible for immediate re-election. Five of the elective seats are allocated to Africa and Asia, one to eastern Europe, two to Latin America and two to western Europe and remaining countries. Procedural questions are determined by a majority vote. Other matters require a majority inclusive of the votes of the permanent members; they thus have a right of veto. The abstention of a permanent member does not constitute a veto. The presidency rotates each month by state in (English) alphabetical order. Parties to a dispute, other non-members and individuals can be invited to participate in Security Council debates but are not permitted to vote.

The Security Council is empowered to settle or adjudicate in disputes or situations which threaten international peace and security. It can adopt political, economic and military measures to achieve this end. Any matter considered to be a threat to or breach of the peace or an act of aggression can be brought to the Security Council's attention by any member state or by the Secretary-General. The Charter envisaged members placing at the disposal of the Security Council armed forces and other facilities which would be co-ordinated by the Military Staff Committee, composed of military representatives of the five permanent members. The Security Council is also supported by a Committee of Experts, to advise on procedural and technical matters, and a Committee on Admission of New Members.

Owing to superpower disunity, the Security Council rarely played the decisive role set out in the Charter; the Military Staff Committee was effectively suspended from 1948 until 1990, when a meeting was convened during the Gulf Crisis on the formation and control of UN-supervised armed forces. However, at an extraordinary meeting of the Security Council in January 1992, heads of government laid plans to transform the UN in light of the changed post-Cold War world. The Secretary-General was asked to draw up a report on enhancing the UN's preventive diplomacy, peacemaking and peacekeeping ability. The report, *An Agenda for Peace*, was produced in June 1992 and centred on the establishment of a UN army composed of national contingents on permanent standby, as envisaged at the time of the UN's formation.

PEACEKEEPING FORCES

The Security Council has established a number of peacekeeping forces since its foundation, comprising contingents provided mainly by neutral and non-aligned UN members. Current forces include: the UN Truce Supervision Organisation (UNTSO), Israel, 1948; the UN Military Observer Group in India and Pakistan (UNMOGIP), 1949; the UN Peacekeeping Force in Cyprus (UNFICYP), 1964; the UN Disengagement Observer Force (UNDOF), Golan Heights, Syria, 1974; the UN Interim Force in Lebanon (UNIFIL), 1978; the UN Iraq-Kuwait Observation Mission (UNIKOM), 1991; the UN Mission for the Referendum in Western

Sahara (MINURSO), 1991; the UN Observer Mission in Georgia (UNOMIG), 1993; the UN Observer Mission in Liberia (UNOMIL), 1993; the UN Observer Mission in Guatemala (MINUGA), 1994; the UN Observer Mission in Tajikistan (UNMOT), 1994; the UN Preventive Deployment Force (UNPREDEP), Macedonia, 1995; the UN Mission in Bosnia-Hercegovina (UNMIBH), 1995; the UN Mission of Observers in Prevlaka (UNMOP), 1996.

THE ECONOMIC AND SOCIAL COUNCIL
UN Plaza, New York, NY 10017, USA

The Economic and Social Council is responsible under the General Assembly for the economic and social work of the UN and for the co-ordination of the activities of the 15 specialised agencies and other UN bodies. It makes reports and recommendations on economic, social, cultural, educational, health and related matters, often in consultation with non-governmental organisations, passing the reports to the General Assembly and other UN bodies. It also drafts conventions for submission to the Assembly and calls conferences on matters within its remit.

The Council consists of 54 members, 18 of whom are elected annually by the General Assembly for a three-year term. Each has one vote and can be immediately re-elected on retirement. A President is elected annually and is also eligible for re-election. One substantive session is held annually and decisions are reached by simple majority vote of those present.

The Council has established a number of standing committees on particular issues and several commissions. Commissions include: Statistical, Human Rights, Social Development, Sustainable Development, Status of Women, Crime Prevention and Criminal Justice, Narcotic Drugs, Science and Technology for Development, and Population; and Regional Economic Commissions for Europe, Asia and the Pacific, Western Asia, Latin America and Africa.

THE TRUSTEESHIP COUNCIL
UN Plaza, New York, NY10017, USA

The Trusteeship Council supervised the administration of territories within the UN Trusteeship system inherited from the League of Nations. It consists of the five permanent members of the Security Council. With the independence of the Republic of Palau in October 1994, all eleven trusteeships have now progressed to independence or merged with neighbouring states and the Trusteeship Council suspended its operations on 1 November 1994.

THE SECRETARIAT
UN Plaza, New York, NY 10017, USA

The Secretariat services the other UN organs and is headed by a Secretary-General elected by a majority vote of the General Assembly on the recommendation of the Security Council. He is assisted by an international staff, chosen to represent the international character of the organisation. The Secretary-General is charged with bringing to the attention of the Security Council any matter which he considers poses a threat to international peace and security. He may also bring other matters to the attention of the General Assembly and other UN bodies and may be entrusted by them with additional duties. As chief administrator to the UN, the Secretary-General is present in person or via representatives at all meetings of the other five main organs of the UN. He may also act as an impartial mediator in disputes between member states.

The power and influence of the Secretary-General has been determined largely by the character of the office-holder and by the state of relations between the superpowers. The thaw in these relations since the mid-1980s has increased the effectiveness of the UN, particularly in its attempts to intervene in international disputes. It helped to end the Iran-Iraq war and sponsored peace in Central America. Following Iraq's invasion of Kuwait in 1990 the UN took its first collective security action since the Korean War. UN action to protect the Kurds in northern Iraq has widened its legal authority by breaching the prohibition on its intervention in the essentially domestic affairs of states. Currently the UN is involved in peacekeeping, aid distribution and negotiations in the former Yugoslavia; and is addressing the global problems of AIDS and environmental destruction.
Secretary-General, Kofi Annan, apptd 1996 (Ghana)
Deputy Secretary-General, Louise Frechette, apptd 1998 (Canada)

UNDER-SECRETARIES-GENERAL
Administration and Management, Joseph Connor (USA)
Chef de Cabinet, Iqbqal Riza (Pakistan)
Development Support and Management Services, Jin Yongjian (China)
Humanitarian Affairs, Sergio Vieira de Mello (Brazil)
Legal Affairs and UN Legal Counsel, Hans Corell (Sweden)
Peacekeeping Operations, Bernard Miyet (France)
Policy Co-ordination and Sustainable Development, Nitin Desai (India)
Political Affairs, Sir Kieran Prendergast (UK)

FORMER SECRETARIES-GENERAL
1946–53	Trygve Lie (Norway)
1953–61	Dag Hammarskjöld (Sweden)
1961–71	U Thant (Burma)
1971–81	Kurt Waldheim (Austria)
1981–91	Javier Pérez de Cuéllar (Peru)
1991–6	Boutros Boutros-Ghali (Egypt)

INTERNATIONAL COURT OF JUSTICE
The Peace Palace, NL-2517 KJ The Hague, The Netherlands

The International Court of Justice is the principal judicial organ of the UN. The Statute of the Court is an integral part of the Charter and all members of the UN are *ipso facto* parties to it. The Court is composed of 15 judges, elected by both the General Assembly and the Security Council for nine-year terms which are renewable. Judges may deliberate over cases in which their country is involved. If no judge on the bench is from a country which is a party to a dispute under consideration, that party may designate a judge to participate *ad hoc* in that particular deliberation. If any party to a case fails to adhere to the judgement of the Court, the other party may have recourse to the Security Council.
President, Gilbert Guillaume (France) (2009)
Vice-President, Shi Jiuyong (China) (2003)
Judges, Awn Shawkat Al-Khasawneh (Jordan) (2009); Thomas Buergenthal (USA) (2009); Mohammed Bedjaoui (Algeria) (2006); Carl-August Fleischhauer (Germany) (2003); Géza Herczegh (Hungary) (2003); Rosalyn Higgins (UK) (2009); Pieter H. Kooijmans (Netherlands) (2006); Abdul G. Koroma (Sierra Leone) (2003); Shigeru Oda (Japan) (2003); Gonzalo Parra-Aranguren (Venezuela) (2009); Raymond Ranjeva (Madagascar) (2009); José Francisco Rezek (Brazil) (2006); Vladlen S. Vereshchetin (Russia) (2006)

INTERNATIONAL WAR CRIMES TRIBUNAL FOR THE FORMER YUGOSLAVIA

Churchill Plein 1, PO Box 13888, NL-2501 EW The Hague, The Netherlands

In February 1993, the Security Council voted to establish a war crimes tribunal for the former Yugoslavia to hear cases covering grave breaches of the Geneva Conventions and crimes against humanity. The Court was inaugurated in November 1993 in The Hague with 11 judges elected by the UN General Assembly from 11 states, divided into two trial chambers of three judges each and an appeal chamber of five judges. The court is unable to force suspects to stand trial but is empowered to pass verdicts in the absence of suspects and can put suspects under an 'act of accusation' which prevents them from leaving their own country.

In October 1995, the tribunal formally charged the Bosnian Serb leaders Radovan Karadzić and Gen. Ratko Mladić, and the Croatian Serb President Milan Martić and 21 others with genocide and crimes against humanity. In May 1999, the tribunal formally charged the Yugoslav president Slobodan Milošević, the Serbian president Milan Milutinović, two other Serb politicians and the Yugoslav armed forces chief of staff Dragoljub Ojdanić.

President, Antonio Cassese (Italy)

Chief Prosecutor, Louise Arbour (Canada)

INTERNATIONAL CRIMINAL TRIBUNAL FOR RWANDA

In November 1994, the UN Security Council voted to establish a tribunal to try those responsible for genocide and other violations of international humanitarian law in Rwanda between 1 January and 31 December 1994. The tribunal, based in Arusha, Tanzania, is empowered to try the most senior people responsible for the massacre. It formally opened in November 1995 to consider 463 indictments.

Chief Prosecutor, Louise Arbour (Canada)

UNITED NATIONS MONITORING, VERIFICATION AND INSPECTION COMMITTEE

Room S-3120G, New York, NY 10017, USA

Tel: (00 1) (212) 963 3022; fax: (00 1) (212) 963 3922

Web: http://www.un.org/peace

The former United Nations Special Commission for the Elimination of Iraq's Weapons of Mass Destruction (UNSCOM), which had been created in April 1991 by Resolution 687 of the UN Security Council, was replaced by the United Nations Monitoring, Verification and Inspection Committee (UNMOVIC), created by UN Security Council Resolution 1284, adopted in December 1999. This resolution committed Iraq to destroy, dismantle or make safe its atomic, biological or chemical weapons of mass destruction, together with ballistic missiles with a target distance of more than 150 km, to destroy all research, development and production facilities and to desist from the future development or acquisition of such weapons and operate a monitoring and verification programme to ensure that prohibited items and programmes are not reactivated.

The lifting of sanctions on the export of goods to Iraq was linked to its co-operation with UNMOVIC.

Executive Chairman, Dr. Hans Blix (Sweden)

SPECIALISED AGENCIES

Fifteen independent international organisations, each with its own membership, budget and headquarters, carry out their responsibilities in co-ordination with the UN under agreements made with the Economic and Social Council. An entry for each appears elsewhere in the International Organisations section. They are: the Food and Agriculture Organisation of the UN; International Civil Aviation Organisation; International Fund for Agricultural Development; International Labour Organisation; International Maritime Organisation; the International Monetary Fund; International Telecommunications Union; UN Educational, Scientific and Cultural Organisation; UN Industrial Development Organisation; Universal Postal Union; World Bank (International Bank for Reconstruction and Development, International Development Agency, International Finance Corporation); World Health Organisation; World Intellectual Property Organisation; and World Meteorological Organisation. The International Atomic Energy Agency and the World Trade Organisation are linked to the UN but are not specialised agencies.

UK MISSION TO THE UNITED NATIONS

1 Dag Hammarskjöld Plaza, 885 Second Avenue, New York, NY 10017, USA

Tel: (00 1) (212) 745 9200; fax: (00 1) (212) 745 9316

Web: http://www.britain-info.org/ukmis/ukmis.htm

Permanent Representative to the United Nations and Representative on the Security Council, Sir Jeremy Greenstock, KCMG, *apptd* 1998

Deputy Permanent Representative, S. G. Eldon, CMG, OBE

UK MISSION TO THE OFFICE OF THE UN AND OTHER INTERNATIONAL ORGANISATIONS IN GENEVA

37–39 rue de Vermont, CH-1211 Geneva 20, Switzerland

Tel: (00 41) (22) 198 2300; fax: (00 41) (22) 918 2333

E-mail: trade.uk@ties.itu.int

Permanent UK Representative, S. W. J. Fuller, *apptd* 2000

Deputy Permanent Representative, P. R. Jenkins

UK MISSION TO THE INTERNATIONAL ATOMIC ENERGY AGENCY, THE UN INDUSTRIAL DEVELOPMENT ORGANISATION AND THE UN IN VIENNA

Jaurèsgasse 12, A-1030 Vienna, Austria

Permanent UK Representative, Dr J. P. G. Freeman, *apptd* 1997

Deputy Permanent Representative, M. R. Etherton

UN OFFICE AND INFORMATION CENTRE

Millbank Tower, 21–24 Millbank, London, SW1P 4QH

Tel: 020-7630 1981; fax: 020-7976 6478

UNITED NATIONS EDUCATIONAL, SCIENTIFIC AND CULTURAL ORGANISATION

7 place de Fontenoy, F-75352 Paris 07 SP, France

Tel: (00 33) (1) 4568 1000; fax: (00 33) (1) 4567 1690

Web: http://www.unesco.org

The United Nations Educational, Scientific and Cultural Organisation (UNESCO) was established in 1946. It promotes collaboration among its member states in education, science, culture and communication. It aims to further a universal respect for human rights, justice and the rule of law, without distinction of race, sex, language or religion, in accordance with the UN Charter.

UNESCO runs a number of programmes to improve education and extend access to it. It provides assistance to ensure the free flow of information and its wider and better balanced dissemination without any obstacle to freedom of expression, and to maintain cultural heritage in the face of development. It fosters research and study in all areas of the social and environmental sciences.

UNESCO had 188 member states as at May 2000. The General Conference, consisting of representatives of all the members, meets biennially to decide the programme and the budget (2000–1, US$544). It elects the 58-member Executive Board, which supervises operations, and appoints a Director-General who heads a Secretariat responsible for carrying out the organisation's programmes. In most member states national commissions liaise with UNESCO to execute its programme.

The UK withdrew from UNESCO in 1985; it rejoined on 1 July 1997.

Director-General, Koichiro Matsuura (Japan)

UNITED NATIONS INDUSTRIAL DEVELOPMENT ORGANISATION

Vienna International Centre, Wagramerstrasse 5,
PO Box 300, A-1400 Vienna, Austria
Tel: (00 43) (1) 26026 0; fax: (00 43) (1) 269 2669
E-mail: unido-pinfo@unido.org
Web: http://www.unido.org

The United Nations Industrial Development Organisation (UNIDO) was established in 1966 by the UN General Assembly to act as the central co-ordinating body for industrial activities within the UN. It became a UN specialised agency in 1985. UNIDO's mission is to improve living conditions and promote prosperity by providing technical assistance and advice, investment promotion and planning. UNIDO aims to develop sustainable industrialisation by concentrating on economic competitiveness, environmental awareness and employment issues. To this end, it assists both public and private sectors and has made its services available to former centrally planned economies in transition to a market economy.

UNIDO had 168 members as at May 2000. It is funded by the UN, member states and non-governmental organisations. A General Conference of all the members meets biennially to discuss strategy and policy, approve the budget (2000–1,US$132.9 million) and elect the Director-General. The Industrial Development Board is composed of members from 53 member states and reviews implementation of the regular work programme and the budget, which is prepared by the Programme and Budget Committee.

Director-General, Carlos Magariños (Argentina)
Permanent UK Representative, Dr John Freeman, British Embassy, Vienna

UNIVERSAL POSTAL UNION

Weltpoststrasse 4, CH-3000 Bern 15, Switzerland
Tel: (00 41) (31) 350 3111; fax: (00 41) (31) 350 3110
E-Mail: info@upu.int
Web: http://www.upu.int

The Universal Postal Union (UPU) was established by the Treaty of Bern 1874, taking effect from 1875, and became a UN specialised agency in 1948. The UPU is an intergovernmental organisation that exists to form and regulate a single postal territory of all member countries for the reciprocal exchange of correspondence without discrimination. It also assists and advises on the improvement of postal services.

The UPU had 189 members as at May 2000. A Universal Postal Congress of all its members is the UPU's supreme authority and meets every five years to review the Treaty. A Council of Administration composed of 41 members was established by the 1994 Congress. It meets annually to ensure continuity between congresses, study regulatory developments and broad policies, approve the budget and examine proposed Treaty changes. A Postal Operations Council also meets annually to deal with specific technical and operational issues. The three UPU bodies are served by the International Bureau, a secretariat headed by a Director-General.

Funding is provided by members according to a scale of contributions drawn up by the Congress. The Council sets the annual budget (2000, SFr35,700,000) within a five-year figure decided by the Congress.

Director-General, Thomas E. Leavey (USA)

UNREPRESENTED NATIONS AND PEOPLES ORGANISATION

40A Javastraat, NL-2585 AP, The Hague,
The Netherlands
Tel: (00 31) (70) 360 3318; fax: (00 31) (70) 360 3346
Web: http://www.unpo.org

The Unrepresented Nations and Peoples Organisation (UNPO) was founded in 1991 to offer an international forum for occupied nations, indigenous peoples and national minorities who are not represented in other international organisations.

UNPO does not aim to represent these nations and peoples, but rather to assist and empower them to represent themselves more effectively, and provides professional services and facilities as well as education and training in the fields of diplomacy, international and human rights law, democratic processes, institution building, conflict management and resolution, and environmental protection.

Participation is open to all nations and peoples who are inadequately represented at the United Nations and who declare allegiance to five principles relating to the right of self-determination of all peoples, human rights, democracy, non-violence and the rejection of terrorism, and protection of the natural environment. Applicants must show that they constitute a 'nation or people' and that the organisation applying for membership is representative of that nation or people.

As at December 1999, there were 52 full members and five supporting members, who are all former full members who have achieved full independence.

Interim General Secretary, Erkin Alptekin (Eastern Turkestan)

WESTERN EUROPEAN UNION

Regentschapsstraat 4, B-1000 Brussels, Belgium
Tel: (00 32) (2) 500 4411; fax: (00 32) (2) 511 3270
E-mail: ueo.presse@skynet.be
Web: http://www.weu.int

The Western European Union (WEU) originated as the Brussels Treaty Organisation (BTO) established under the Treaty of Brussels, signed in 1948 by Belgium, France, Luxembourg, the Netherlands and the UK, to provide collective self-defence and economic and social collaboration amongst its signatories. With the collapse of European Defence Community and the decision of NATO to incorporate the Federal Republic of Germany into the Western security system, the BTO was modified to become the WEU in 1954 with the admission of West Germany and Italy. However, owing to the overlap with

NATO and the Council of Europe, the Union became largely defunct.

From the late 1970s onwards efforts were made to add a security dimension to the EC's European Political Co-operation. Opposition to these efforts from Denmark, Greece and Ireland led the remaining EC countries, all WEU members, to decide to reactivate the Union in 1984. Members committed themselves to harmonising their views on defence and security and developing a European security identity, while bearing in mind the importance of transatlantic relations. Portugal and Spain joined the WEU in 1988, and Greece became a full member in 1995.

In 1991, the EU Maastricht Treaty committed the European Community to the establishment of a Common Foreign and Security Policy (CFSP). The WEU was designated as the future defence component of the European Union and member states of the EU who were not already members of the WEU were invited to join or become observers. WEU foreign ministers agreed in the Petersberg Declaration 1992 to make available units of their conventional armed forces to WEU command for military tasks including humanitarian and rescue missions, peacekeeping, and crisis management. In November 1992 the WEU's role as the common security dimension of the EU was enhanced when WEU ministers signed a declaration with remaining European NATO members to give them various forms of WEU membership. Iceland, Norway and Turkey became associate members; the Republic of Ireland, Denmark, Austria, Finland and Sweden became observer members. In 1994 the WEU reached agreements with Estonia, Latvia, Lithuania, Poland, the Czech Republic, Slovakia, Hungary, Romania and Bulgaria, under which they all became associate partners; Slovenia became an associate partner in 1996. The Czech Republic, Hungary and Poland, who had been associate partners, became associate members in 1999, following their accession to NATO.

The WEU works in close co-operation with the Atlantic Alliance, and relations between the WEU and NATO are developing on the basis of transparency and complementarity. The 1993 Luxembourg Declaration states that the WEU is ready to participate in the future work of the NATO Alliance as its European pillar, and at the Atlantic Alliance summit in January 1994, NATO expressed its readiness to make Alliance assets and capabilities available for WEU operations. In June 1996, NATO foreign and defence ministers approved the Combined Joint Task Force (CJTF) concept and the elaboration of multinational European command arrangements for WEU-led operations.

The formation of a 'Eurocorps' based on the Franco-German brigade as a force answerable to the WEU was announced in 1992. The 'Eurocorps' was inaugurated in 1993 and became fully operational in 1995 with 60,000 troops comprising French, German, Belgian, Luxembourg and Spanish forces.

A Council of Ministers (foreign and defence) meets biannually in the capital of the presiding country; the presidency rotates biannually, and from 1999 the sequence of WEU presidencies has been harmonised with those of the EU Council of Ministers. A Permanent Council of the member states' permanent representatives meets weekly in Brussels. The Permanent Council is chaired by the Secretary-General and serviced by the Secretariat. The WEU military staff is responsible for the implementation of policies and decisions as directed by the council and the military committee. It prepares plans, carries out studies and recommends policy on matters of an operational nature for the WEU. It comprises a planning cell and a situation centre.

In 1999, NATO and the EU decided to establish a direct relationship; the EU committed itself to ensuring that it was able to take decisions on conflict prevention and crisis management and NATO agreed to give the EU access to its collective assets and capabilities for operations in which NATO as a whole was not engaged. The WEU will continue its present role until the NATO and EU decisions are implemented.

The Assembly of the WEU is composed of 115 parliamentarians of member states and meets twice annually in Paris to debate matters within the scope of the revised Brussels Treaty.

Presidency (2000) Portugal, France; (2001) Netherlands, Belgium
Secretary-General, Javier Solana Madariaga (Spain)
UK Representative on the Permanent Council, Sir John Goulden, KCMG
Assembly, 43 avenue du Président Wilson, F-75775 Paris Cedex 16, France

---

THE WORLD BANK
1818 H Street NW, Washington DC 20433, USA
Tel: (00 1) (202) 477 1234; fax: (00 1) (202) 477 6391
Web: http://www.worldbank.org

The World Bank, more formally known as the International Bank for Reconstruction and Development (IBRD), is a specialised agency of the UN. It developed from the international monetary and financial conference held at Bretton Woods, New Hampshire, in 1944 and was established by 44 nations in 1945 to encourage economic growth in developing countries through the provision of loans and technical assistance to their respective governments. The IBRD now has 181 members.

The Bank is owned by the governments of member countries and its capital is subscribed by its members. It finances its lending primarily from borrowing in world capital markets, and derives a substantial contribution to its resources from its retained earnings and the repayment of loans. The interest rate on its loans is calculated in relation to its cost of borrowing. Loans generally have a grace period of five years and are repayable within 20 years. The loans made by the Bank since its inception to 30 June 1997 totalled US$295,263.9 million to 131 countries. Total capital is US$182,426 million.

Originally directed towards post-war reconstruction in Europe, the Bank has subsequently turned towards assisting less-developed countries with the establishment of two affiliates, the International Finance Corporation (IFC) in 1956 and the International Development Association (IDA) in 1960. The IFC promotes the growth of the private sector in developing member countries by mobilising domestic and foreign capital. The IFC's subscribed share capital was US$2.36 million at 30 June 1997. It is also empowered to borrow up to two and a half times the amount of its unimpaired subscribed capital and accumulated earnings for use in its lending programme. At 30 June 1997, the IFC had committed financing totalling more than US$6.7 billion in 129 countries.

The IDA performs the same function as the World Bank but primarily to less-developed countries and on terms that bear less heavily on their balance of payments than IBRD loans. Eligible countries typically have a per capita gross national product of less than US$925 (1996). Funds (called credits to distinguish them from IBRD loans) come mostly in the form of subscriptions and contributions from the IDA's richer members and transfers from the net income of the IBRD. The terms for IDA credits, which bear no interest and are made to governments only, are ten-year grace periods and 35- or 40-year maturities. By 30 June 1997, the IDA had extended development credits totalling US$101,563.4 million to 100 countries.

The IBRD and its affiliates are financially and legally distinct but share headquarters. The IBRD is headed by a Board of Governors, consisting of one Governor and one alternate Governor appointed by each member country. Twenty-four Executive Directors exercise all powers of the Bank except those reserved to the Board of Governors. The President, elected by the Executive Directors, conducts the business of the Bank, assisted by an international staff. Membership in both the IFC (162 members) and the IDA (160 members) is open to all IBRD countries. The IDA is administered by the same staff as the Bank; the IFC has its own personnel but draws on the IBRD for administrative and other support. All share the same President.

In 1988 a third affiliate, the Multilateral Investment Guarantee Agency (MIGA) was formed. MIGA encourages foreign investment in developing states by providing investment guarantees to potential investors and advisory services to developing member countries. At 30 December 1994, 128 countries were members of MIGA.

President (IBRD, IFC, IDA, MIGA), James D. Wolfensohn (USA)

UK Executive Director, A. O'Donnell, Room 11-120, IMF, 700 19th Street NW, Washington DC 20431

EUROPEAN OFFICE, 66 avenue d'Iéna, F-75116 Paris, France

JAPAN OFFICE, 10F, Fukoku Seimei Building, 2-2-2 Uchisaiwai-cho, Chiyoda-ku, Tokyo 100-0011, Japan

UK OFFICE, New Zealand House, Haymarket, London SW1Y 4TQ. Tel: 020-7930 8511; fax: 020-7930 8515

THE WORLD COUNCIL OF CHURCHES
PO Box 2100, CH-1211 Geneva 2, Switzerland
Tel: (00 41) (22) 791 6111; fax: (00 41) (22) 791 0361
E-mail: info@mail.wcc-coe.org
Web: http://www.wcc-coe.org

The World Council of Churches (WCC) was constituted in 1948 to promote unity among Christian churches. The 336 member churches have adherents in more than 100 countries. With the exception of Roman Catholicism, virtually all Christian traditions are represented.

The policies of the Council are determined by delegates of the member churches meeting in Assembly, roughly every seven years; the seventh Assembly was held in Canberra, Australia, in February 1991 and the eighth Assembly was held in Harare, Zimbabwe, in December 1998. More detailed decisions are taken by a 156-member Central Committee which is elected by the Assembly and meets, with the eight WCC Presidents, annually. The Central Committee in turn appoints a smaller Executive Committee and also nominates commissions to guide the various programmes.

General Secretary, Dr Konrad Raiser (Germany)

WORLD HEALTH ORGANISATION
20 avenue Appia, CH-1211 Geneva 27, Switzerland
Tel: (00 41) (22) 791 2111; fax: (00 41) (22) 791 0746
E-mail: info@who.ch
Web: http://www.who.ch

The UN International Health Conference, held in 1946, established the World Health Organisation (WHO) as a UN specialised agency, with effect from 1948. It is dedicated to attaining the highest possible level of health for all. It collaborates with member governments, UN agencies and other bodies to improve health standards, control communicable diseases and promote all aspects of family and environmental health. It seeks to raise the standards of health teaching and training, and promotes research through collaborating research centres worldwide. Its other services include the *International Pharmacopoeia*, epidemiological surveillance, and the collation and publication of statistics. WHO activities are orientated to achieving 'Health for All'.

WHO had 191 members as at May 2000. It is governed by the annual World Health Assembly of members which meets to set policy, approve the budget (1997–8, US$1,800 million), appoint a Director-General, and adopt health conventions and regulations. It also elects 32 members who designate one expert to serve on the Executive Board. The Board effects the programme, suggests initiatives and is empowered to deal with emergencies. A Secretariat, headed by the Director-General, supervises the activities of six regional offices.

Director-General, Gro Harlem Bruntland (Norway)

WORLD INTELLECTUAL PROPERTY ORGANISATION
34 chemin des Colombettes, CH-1211 Geneva 20, Switzerland
Tel: (00 41) (22) 338 9111; fax: (00 41) (22) 733 5428
E-mail: publicinf.mail@wipo.int
Web: http://www.wipo.int

The World Intellectual Property Organisation (WIPO) was established in 1967 by the Stockholm Convention, which entered into force in 1970. In addition to that Convention, WIPO administers 19 treaties, the principal ones being the Paris Convention for the Protection of Industrial Property and the Bern Convention for the Protection of Literary and Artistic Works. WIPO became a UN specialised agency in 1974.

WIPO promotes the protection of intellectual property throughout the world through co-operation among states, and the administration of various 'Unions', each founded on a multilateral treaty and dealing with the legal and administrative aspects of intellectual property.

Intellectual property comprises two main branches: industrial property (inventions, trademarks, industrial designs and appellations of origin); and copyright (literary, musical, photographic, audiovisual and artistic works, etc.). WIPO also assists creative intellectual activity and facilitates technology transfer, particularly to developing countries.

WIPO had 173 members as at January 2000. The biennial session of all its governing bodies sets policy, a programme and a budget (1998–9, SFr400 million). WIPO has three governing bodies: the General Assembly, composed of WIPO members who are also members of the Paris or Bern conventions; the Conference, composed of all WIPO members; and the Co-ordination Committee, composed of member states elected by members of WIPO and the Paris and Bern conventions. The General Assembly elects a Director-General, who heads the International Bureau (secretariat).

A separate International Union for the Protection of New Varieties of Plants (UPOV), established by convention in 1961, is linked to WIPO. It has 40 members.

Director-General, Dr Kamil Idris (Sudan)

...

WORLD METEOROLOGICAL ORGANISATION

7 bis, avenue de la Paix, PO Box 2300, CH-1211 Geneva 2, Switzerland
Tel: (00 41) (22) 730 8315; fax: (00 41) (22) 733 2829
Web: http://www.wmo.ch

The World Meteorological Organisation (WMO) was established in 1950 and became a UN specialised agency in 1951, succeeding the International Meteorological Organisation founded in 1873. It facilitates co-operation in the establishment of networks for making meteorological, climatological, hydrological and geophysical observations, as well as their exchange, processing and standardisation, and assists technology transfer, training and research. It also fosters collaboration between meteorological and hydrological services, and furthers the application of meteorology to aviation, shipping, environment, water problems, agriculture, etc.

The WMO had 179 member states and six member territories as at 19 May 2000. The supreme authority is the World Meteorological Congress of member states and member territories, which meets every four years to determine general policy, make recommendations and set a budget (2000-3, SFr252.3 million). It also elects 26 members of the 36-member Executive Council, the other members being the President and three Vice-Presidents of the WMO, and the Presidents of the six regional associations, who are ex-officio members. The Council supervises the implementation of Congress decisions, initiates studies and makes recommendations on matters needing international action. The WMO functions through six regional associations and eight technical commissions. Each of the regional associations has responsibility for co-ordinating meteorological activities within its region. The technical commissions study meteorological and hydrological problems, lay down the necessary methodologies and procedures, and make recommendations to the Executive Council and Congress. The Secretariat is headed by a Secretary-General, appointed by the Congress.

Secretary-General, G. O. P. Obasi (Nigeria)

WORLD TRADE ORGANISATION

Centre William Rappard, 154 rue de Lausanne, 1211 CH-Geneva 21, Switzerland
Tel: (00 41) (22) 739 5111; fax: (00 41) (22) 739 5458
E-mail: enquiries@wto.org
Web: http://www.wto.org

The World Trade Organisation was established on 1 January 1995 as the successor to the General Agreement on Tariffs and Trade (GATT). GATT was established in 1948 as an interim agreement until the charter of a new international trade organisation could be drafted by a committee of the UN Economic and Social Council and ratified by member states. The charter was never ratified and GATT became the only regime for the regulation of world trade, evolving its own rules and procedures.

GATT was dedicated to the expansion of non-discriminatory international trade and progressively extended free trade via 'rounds' of multilateral negotiations. Eight rounds were concluded: Geneva (1947), Annecy (1948), Torquay (1950), Geneva (1956), Dillon (1960-1), Kennedy (1964-7), Tokyo (1973-9) and Uruguay (1986-94). By the time the measures of the Uruguay Round are fully implemented in 2002, the average duties on manufactured goods will have been reduced from 40 per cent in the 1940s to 3 per cent. The Final Act of the Uruguay Round was signed by trade ministers from the 128 GATT negotiating states and the EU in Marrakesh, Morocco, on 15 April 1994. It established the World Trade Organisation (WTO) to supersede GATT and implement the Uruguay Round agreements. A summit held in Seattle, USA, in December 1999 was unable to reach agreement on further integration of the international trading system.

The WTO is the legal and institutional foundation of the multilateral trading system. It provides the contractual obligations determining how governments frame and implement trade policy and provides the forum for the debate, negotiation and adjudication of trade problems. The WTO's principal aims are to liberalise world trade and place it on a secure basis, and it seeks to achieve this partly by an agreed set of trade rules and market access agreements and partly through further trade liberalisation negotiations. The WTO also administers and implements a further 29 multilateral agreements in fields such as agriculture, textiles and clothing, services, government procurement, rules of origin and intellectual property.

The highest authority of the WTO is the Ministerial Conference composed of all members, which meets at least once every two years. The General Council meets as required and acts on behalf of the Ministerial Conference in regard to the regular working of the WTO. Composed of all members, the General Council also convenes in two particular forms: as the Dispute Settlement Body, dealing with disputes between members arising from the Uruguay Round Final Act; and as the Trade Policy Review Body, conducting regular reviews of the trade policies of members. A secretariat of 500 staff headed by a Director-General services WTO bodies and provides trade performance and trade policy analysis.

As at May 1999 there were 134 WTO members, and a further 31 governments had applied to join. The WTO budget for 1998 was SFr115 million, with members' contributions calculated on the basis of their share of the total trade conducted by WTO members. The official languages of the WTO are English, French and Spanish.

Acting Director-General, David Hartridge
Permanent UK Representative, R. M. J. Lyne, 37-39 rue de Vermont, CH-1211 Geneva 20

The European Union

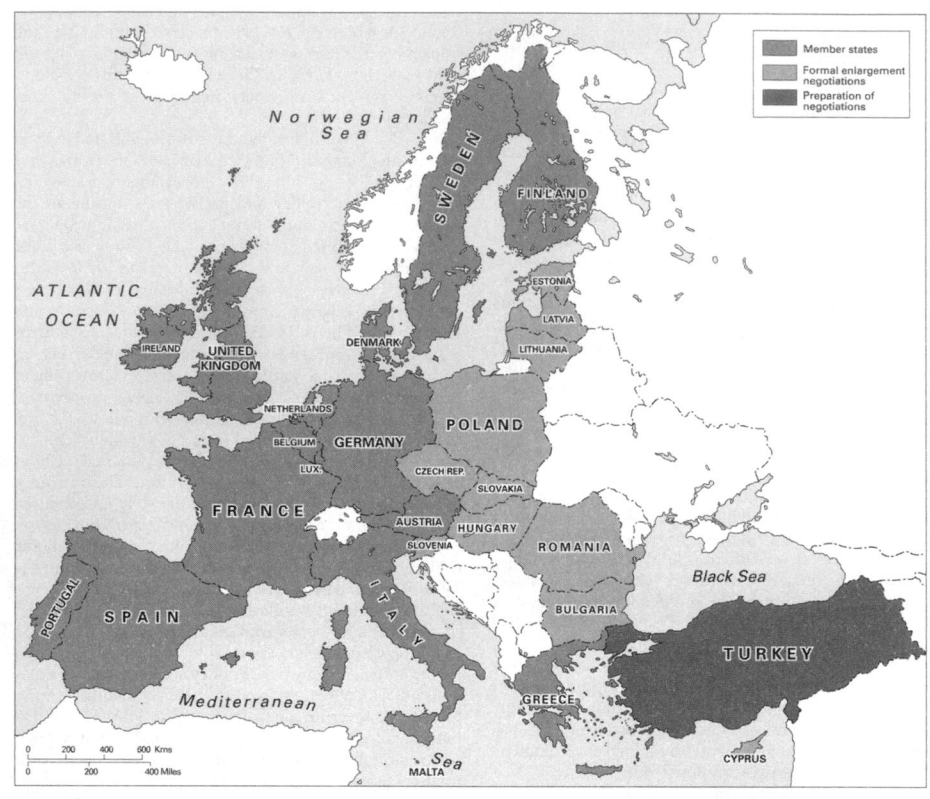

MEMBERS

STATE	ACCESSION DATE	POPULATION (million)	GNP (US$ million) (1998)	GDP PER HEAD IN PPP (ECU)(1998)	COUNCIL VOTES	EP SEATS
Austria	1 January 1995	8.11	216,697	22,432	4	21
Belgium	1 January 1958*	10.16	258,968	22,542	5	25
Denmark	1 January 1973	5.26	175,160	24,082	3	16
Finland	1 January 1995	5.13	125,091	20,522	3	16
France	1 January 1958*	58.38	1,465,399	19,956	10	87
Germany	1 January 1958*†	81.91	2,179,802	21,797	10	99
Greece	1 January 1981	10.48	123,394	13,330	5	25
Ireland	1 January 1973	3.63	69,322	21,668	3	15
Italy	1 January 1958*	57.34	1,157,001	20,286	10	87
Luxembourg	1 January 1958*	0.41	19,239	35,489	2	6
Netherlands	1 January 1958*	15.52	389,055	22,754	5	31
Portugal	1 January 1986	9.92	106,391	14,986	5	25
Spain	1 January 1986	39.27	555,244	16,289	8	64
Sweden	1 January 1995	8.84	226,454	20,575	4	22
UK	1 January 1973	58.78	1,264,262	20,613	10	87
TOTAL		373.14	8,331,479		87	626

Sources: Eurostat Yearbook: A Statistical Eye on Europe 2000–2001, World Bank Atlas 2000
*Acceded to the European Coal and Steel Community (ECSC) on its formation in 1952
†Federal Republic of Germany (West) 1952/1958; German Democratic Republic (East) acceded on German reunification (3 October 1990)
EP – European Parliament   PPP – purchasing power parities

DEVELOPMENT

1950 Robert Schuman (French foreign minister) proposes that France and West Germany pool their coal and steel industries under a supranational authority (Schuman Plan)

1951 Paris Treaty signed by France, West Germany, Belgium, Italy, Luxembourg and the Netherlands establishes the European Coal and Steel Community (ECSC)

1952 ECSC treaty enters into force

1957 25 March: Treaty of Rome signed by the six, establishes the European Economic Community (EEC) and the European Atomic Energy Authority (EURATOM). Treaty aims to create a customs union; remove obstacles to free movement of capital, goods, people and services; establish common external trade policy and common agricultural and fisheries policies; co-ordinate economic policies; harmonise social policies; promote co-operation in nuclear research

1958 1 January: EEC and EURATOM begin operation. Joint Parliament and Court of Justice established for all three communities, and the Commission, Council of Ministers, Economic and Social Committee and Investment Bank for the EEC

1962 Common Agricultural Policy (CAP) agreed (see page 785)

1967 EEC, ECSC and EURATOM merge to form the European Communities (EC), with a single Council of Ministers and Commission

1968 EEC customs union completed Implementation of CAP completed

1974 Regular heads of governments summits begin

1975 'Own resources' funding of EC budget introduced (see page 785) UK renegotiates its terms of accession European Regional Development Fund created

1979 European Monetary System (EMS) comes into operation (see page 786) First direct elections to European Parliament (June)

1984 Fontainebleau summit settles UK annual budget rebate and agrees first major CAP reform

1986 Single European Act (SEA) signed (see page 785) European Political Co-operation (EPC) established

1988 Second major CAP reform

1991 Maastricht Treaty agreed (see page 786)

1992 31 December: Single internal market programme completed

1993 September: the exchange rate mechanism (ERM) of the EMS effectively suspended 1 November: The Maastricht Treaty enters into force, establishing the European Union (EU)

1994 1 January: European Economic Area (EEA) agreement comes into operation (see page 786) Norway rejects EU membership in referendum

1997 Amsterdam Treaty agreed

1998 11 states chosen to enter first round of EMU European Central Bank replaces European Monetary Institute

1999 1 January: Euro launched March: 'Agenda 2000' financial and policy reform agreed 1 May: The Amsterdam Treaty enters into force

ENLARGEMENT AND EXTERNAL RELATIONS

The procedure for accession to the EU is laid down in the Treaty of Rome; states must be stable European democracies governed by the rule of law with free market economies. A membership application is studied by the Commission, which produces an Opinion. If the Opinion is positive, negotiations may be opened leading to an Accession Treaty which must be approved by all member state governments and parliaments, the European Parliament, and the applicant state's government and parliament.

Applicants: Morocco (applied 1987/rejected 1987), Turkey (applied 1987/negative Opinion 1989/offered accession partnership 1999), Cyprus (applied 1990/negotiations begun 1998), Malta (applied 1990/reapplied following a change of government 1998/negotiations begun 2000), Switzerland (applied 1992/no Opinion yet), Hungary (applied 1994/negotiations begun 1998), Poland (applied 1994/negotiations begun 1998), Bulgaria (applied 1995/offered partnership 1998/negotiations begun 2000), Estonia (applied 1995/negotiations begun 1998), Latvia (applied 1995/offered partnership 1998/ negotiations begun 2000), Lithuania (applied 1995/offered partnership 1998/ negotiations begun 2000), Romania (applied 1995/offered partnership 1998/negotiations begun 2000), Slovakia (applied 1995/offered partnership 1998/ negotiations begun 2000), the Czech Republic (applied 1996/negotiations begun 1998), Slovenia (applied 1996/ negotiations begun 1998).

Apart from the EEA Agreement (see page 778), the EU has three types of agreements with other European and CIS states. 'Europe' Agreements commit the EU and signatory states to long-term political and economic integration, a free trade zone (apart from agriculture and labour movement) and eventual EU membership. Government representatives from the signatory states are entitled to attend one summit and two finance and foreign council meetings a year. Agreements have been signed with Bulgaria (1993), the Czech Republic (1993), Estonia (1995), Hungary (1991), Latvia (1995), Lithuania (1995), Poland (1991), Romania (1993), Slovakia (1993) and Slovenia (1996). Association agreements include a commitment to EU financial aid and to eventual membership; agreements have been signed with Malta (1970), Cyprus (1972) and Turkey (1963). Partnership and co-operation agreements are based on regulating and improving political and economic relations and mutual trade concessions but exclude any possibility of membership. Agreements have been signed with Ukraine, Russia, Moldova (1994), Kazakhstan, Kyrgyzstan and Belarus (1995), and Armenia, Azerbaijan, Georgia and Uzbekistan (1996).

Agenda 2000, a document submitted by the Commission in 1997, addressed both the challenges posed by further enlargement of the Union, the institutional reforms that would be required to enable the Union to function effectively with additional members, and it also evaluated each applicant in relation to the accession criteria, and established a new financial framework for the period 2000–2006.

In March 1998, formal accession negotiations were begun with Hungary, Poland, Estonia, the Czech Republic, Slovenia and Cyprus; they were begun with Bulgaria, Romania, Latvia, Lithuania, Malta and Slovakia in 2000, following the Helsinki Summit in December 1999, when it was also agreed that an accession partnership should be offered to Turkey. The European Commission reports each year on the progress towards accession of all current applicants.

THE COUNCIL OF THE EUROPEAN UNION
Wetstraat 175, B-1048 Brussels, Belgium

The Council of the European Union (Council of Ministers) formally comprises the foreign ministers of the member states but in practice the ministers attending depend on the subject under discussion. Council decisions are taken by qualified majority vote (in which members' votes are weighted), by a simple majority, or by unanimity. The Council is assisted by a General Secretariat, whose head has since 1999 been the High Representative for the Common Foreign and Security Policy.

Unanimity votes are taken on sensitive issues such as taxation and constitutional matters; in preparation for an expanded Union, the Amsterdam Treaty extended areas where qualified majority votes may be taken, to areas such as Single Market laws and harmonisation, environment policy, health and safety, transport policy, overseas aid, research and development, culture, consumer protection, education and training, the development of a single currency and some aspects of social policy. Member states have weighted votes in the Council loosely proportional to their relative population sizes (*see* introductory table), with a total of 87 votes. For a proposal from the Commission to pass, it must receive 62 votes; 26 votes are necessary to block a proposal, and 23 votes constitute a temporary blocking minority. For other proposals to be passed they must receive 62 votes cast by at least ten member states.

An Intergovernmental Conference (IGC) was opened in February 2000 with the aim of agreeing amendments to the treaties in relation to the size and composition of the European Commission, the weighting of votes and the extension of qualified majority voting in the Council of Ministers and other issues relating to the Treaty of Amsterdam.

The European Council, comprising the heads of state or government of the member states and the President of the European Commission, meets twice a year to provide overall policy direction. The presidency of the EC is held in rotation for six-month periods, setting the agenda for and chairing all Council meetings. The European Council holds a summit in the country holding the presidency at the end of its period in office. The holders of the presidency for the years 2000–2002 are:
2000 Portugal, France
2001 Sweden, Belgium
2002 Spain, Denmark

GENERAL SECRETARIAT OF THE COUNCIL OF THE EUROPEAN UNION

Wetstraat 175, B-1048 Brussels, Belgium
Secretary-General of the Council of the European Union and High Representative for the Common Foreign and Security Policy, Javier Solana Madariaga (Spain)
Deputy Secretary-General of the Council of the European Union, Pierre de Boissieu (France)

OFFICE OF THE UNITED KINGDOM PERMANENT REPRESENTATIVE TO THE EUROPEAN COMMUNITIES

Oudergemse–laan 10, B-1040 Brussels, Belgium
Ambassador and UK Permanent Representative, HE Nigel Schinewald, *apptd* 2000
Deputy Permanent Representative, W. Stow

THE EUROPEAN COMMISSION
Wetstraat 200, B-1049 Brussels, Belgium

The Commission consists of 20 Commissioners, two each from France, Germany, Italy, Spain and the UK, and one each from the remaining member states. The members of the Commission are appointed for five-year renewable terms by the agreement of the member states; the terms run concurrently with the terms of the European Parliament. The President and the other Commissioners are nominated by the governments of the Member States, and, under the terms of the Amsterdam Treaty, the appointments are approved by the European Parliament. The Commissioners pledge sole allegiance to the EC. The Commission initiates and implements EC legislation and is the guardian of the EC treaties. It is the exponent of Community-wide interests rather than the national preoccupations of the Council. Each Commissioner is supported by advisers and oversees whichever of the departments, known as Directorates-General (DGs), is assigned to him. Each Directorate-General is headed by a Director-General.

President Romano Prodi was nominated by the governments of the member states on 24 March 1999, and under the terms of the Amsterdam Treaty, his appointment was approved by the European Parliament on 15 September 1999, having already announced his new Commission in June. The previous commission had resigned *en masse* on 16 March 1999 after a committee of experts appointed by the European Parliament had concluded that lax management had allowed fraud and nepotism in the Commission's services; they remained in office in a caretaker capacity until the new commission was appointed, a process which was delayed until autumn 1999 by the European Parliament elections. The new Commission has restructured the Directorates-General to reflect the priorities of the new administration.

The Commission has a total staff of around 16,000 permanent civil servants.

COMMISSIONERS *as at March 2000*

President
Secretariat General; Legal Service; Media and Communication Service, Romano Prodi (Italy)
Vice-President for Administration Reform; Overall Co-ordination of Administrative Reform; Personnel and Administration; Linguistic Services; Protocol and Security, Neil Kinnock (UK)
Vice-President for Relations with the European Parliament, and for Transport and Energy; Relations with the European Parliament; Relations with the Committee of the Regions, the Economic and Social Committee, and the Ombudsman; Transport (including Trans-European Networks); Energy, Loyola de Palacio (Spain)

Members
Agriculture and Rural Development, Fisheries, Franz Fischler (Austria)
Budget, Financial Control, Fraud Prevention, Michaele Schreyer (Germany)
Citizens' Europe, Transparency, Education and Culture, Publications Office, Viviane Reding (Luxembourg)
Competition, Mario Monti (Italy)
Development Aid and Co-operation, Humanitarian Aid, Poul Nielson (Denmark)
Economic and Financial Affairs, Monetary Matters, Statistical Office, Pedro Solbes Mira (Spain)

Education, Training and Youth, Culture, Viviane Reding (Luxembourg)
Employment, Social Affairs, Equal Opportunities, Anna Diamantopoulou (Greece)
Enlargement Process including the Pre-Accession Strategy, Günter Verheugen (Germany)
Enterprise, Competitiveness, Innovation, Information Society, Erkki Liikanen (Finland)
Environment, Nuclear Safety, Margot Wallström (Sweden)
External Relations, Common Foreign and Security Policy, Delegations in Non-Member Countries, Common Service for External Relations, Chris Patten (UK)
Freedom, Security, and Justice, António Vitorino (Portugal)
Internal Market, Financial Services, Customs, Taxation, Frits Bolkestein (Netherlands)
Public Health, Consumer Protection, David Byrne (Ireland)
Regional Policy, Cohesion Fund, Inter-Governmental Conference, Michel Barnier (France)
Science, Research and Development, Joint Research Centre, Philippe Busquin (Belgium)
Trade Policy and Instruments of Trade Policy, Pascal Lamy (France)

THE EUROPEAN PARLIAMENT
E-mail: civis@europarl.eu.int
Web: http://www.europarl.eu.int

The European Parliament (EP) originated as the Common Assembly of the ECSC; it acquired its present name in 1962. Members (MEPs) were initially appointed from the membership of national parliaments; direct elections to the Parliament were first held in 1979 and take place at five-year intervals. Elections to the Parliament are held on differing bases throughout the EC; in June 1999, British MEPs were elected for the first time by a 'regional list' system of proportional representation. The Parliament comprises 626 seats. The most recent elections were held in June 1999. For total number of seats per member and political groupings, *see* table below. MEPs serve on committees which scrutinise draft EC legislation and the activities of the Commission. A minimum of 12 plenary sessions a year are held in Strasbourg and Brussels, committees meet in Brussels, and the Secretariat's headquarters is in Luxembourg.

EUROPEAN PARLIAMENT POLITICAL GROUPINGS

	PES	EPP-ED	UEN	ELDR	EUL/NGL	Green/EFA	TGI	EDD	Ind.	Total
Austria	7	7	–	–	–	2	–	–	5	21
Belgium	5	6	–	5	–	7	2	–	–	25
Denmark	3	1	1	6	1	–	–	4	–	16
Finland	3	5	–	5	1	2	–	–	–	16
France	22	21	12	–	11	9	5	6	1	87
Germany	33	53	–	–	6	7	–	–	–	99
Greece	9	9	–	–	7	–	–	–	–	25
Ireland	1	5	6	1	–	2	–	–	–	15
Italy	17	34	9	8	6	2	11	–	–	87
Luxembourg	2	2	–	1	–	1	–	–	–	6
Netherlands	6	9	–	8	1	4	–	3	–	31
Portugal	12	9	2	–	2	–	–	–	–	25
Spain	24	28	–	3	4	4	–	–	1	64
Sweden	6	7	–	4	3	2	–	–	–	22
UK	30	37	–	10	–	6	–	3	1	87
TOTAL	180	233	30	51	42	48	18	16	8	626

PES	Party of European Socialists (including the British, Irish and Dutch Labour Parties, Northern Ireland Social Democratic and Labour Party, Austrian, Danish, Finnish, German, Italian and Swedish Social Democrats, Belgian, French, Greek, Portuguese, and Spanish Socialists, Italian Democratic Left Party, Luxembourg Socialist Workers Party) Socialist, Social Democratic and Labour parties
EPP-ED	European People's Party and European Democrats (including British and Danish Conservative Parties, Spanish Popular Party, French Nouvelle UDF, RPR and DL, Irish Fine Gael, Swedish Moderate Party, Finnish National Coalition Party, Austrian People's Party, Greek New Democracy, Belgian Christian Socialists, Italian Christian Democrats, Pensioners' Party and People's Party, Luxembourg Christian Socialists, Portuguese Social Democrats), Christian Democrats, Christian Socialists and Conservatives
UEN	Union for a Europe of Nations
ELDR	European Liberal Democratic and Reformist Group (including British Liberal Democratic Party, Danish Left and Radical Left Parties, Dutch Democrats' 66 and People's Party for Freedom and Democracy, Belgian Liberals, Italian and Luxembourg Democrats, Swedish Liberal People's Party, the Finnish Swedish People's Party and Centre Party) centre and liberal parties

EUL/NGL	Confederal Group of the European United Left/Nordic Green Left (French, Greek, Italian and Portuguese Communist Parties, Italian Refounded Communist Party, Danish, Dutch, Swedish, Finnish, Greek and Spanish Socialist/Left parties)
Green/EFA	Greens/European Free Alliance Group (Austrian, British, Danish, Finnish, French, German, Greek, Irish, Italian, Luxembourg, Portuguese, Spanish and Swedish Green Parties, Dutch Green Left Party, Belgian Ecological Parties, Plaid Cymru and Scottish National Parties) green and nationalist parties
TGI	Technical Group of Independents (Belgian Flemish Block, Italian National Alliance, French National Front) technical group allowing independents group privileges
EDD	Europe of Democracies and Diversities (French Hunting, Fishing, Nature and Traditions, Dutch Calvinists and Christians, UK Independence Party, Danish June Movement and Movement against the EU) anti-EU, anti-federalist and religious parties
Ind	Independents (Austrian Freedom Party, Northern Ireland Democratic Unionist Party)

The EP has gradually expanded its influence within the EU through the Single European Act, which introduced the co-operation procedure, the Maastricht Treaty, which extended the co-operation procedure and introduced the co-decision procedure (*see* Legislative Process), and the Amsterdam Treaty, which effectively extended co-decision to all areas except economic and monetary union. It has general powers of supervision over the Commission, and consultation and co-decision with the Council; it votes to approve a newly appointed Commission and can dismiss it at any time by a two-thirds majority (as it threatened to do in January 1999). Under the Maastricht Treaty it has the right to be consulted on the appointment of the new Commission and can veto its appointment. It can reject the EU budget as a whole, alter non-compulsory expenditure not specified in the EU primary legislation, and can question the Commission's management of the budget and call in the Court of Auditors. Although the EP cannot directly initiate legislation, its reports can spur the Commission into action. In accordance with the Maastricht Treaty the EP appointed an ombudsman in October 1995, to provide citizens with redress against maladministration by EU institutions.

The Parliament's organisation is deliberately biased in favour of multi-national political groupings, recognition of a political grouping in the parliament entitling it to offices, funding, representation on committees and influence in debates and legislation. A political grouping with members from only one country needs a minimum of 29 members for recognition, whereas one with members from two countries needs 23 members, a grouping with members from three countries needs 18 members, and a grouping with members from four or more countries needs only 14 members.

PARLIAMENT, Palais de l'Europe, Alleé du Printemps,
  BP 1024/F, F-67070 Strasbourg Cedex, France;
  Wiertzstraat, Postbus 1047, B-1047 Brussels, Belgium
SECRETARIAT, Centre Européen, Plateau du Kirchberg,
  BP 1601 L-2929 Luxembourg
President, Nicole Fontaine (France)
Ombudsman, Jacob Söderman (Finland), 1 avenue du
  Président Robert Schuman, BP 403, F-67001,
  Strasbourg, France.
  E-mail: euro-ombudsman@europarl.eu.int.
  Web: http://www.euro-ombudsman.eu.int
(For a full list of British MEPs, *see* European Parliament
Section)

THE LEGISLATIVE PROCESS

The core of the EU policymaking process is a dialogue between the Commission, which initiates and implements policy, and the Council of Ministers, which takes policy decisions. An increasing degree of democratic control is exercised by the European Parliament.

The original legislative process is known as the consultative procedure. The Commission drafts a proposal which it submits to the Council and to the Parliament. The Council then consults the Economic and Social Committee (ESC), the Parliament and the Committee of the Regions; the Parliament may request that amendments are made. With or without these amendments, the proposal is then adopted by the Council and becomes law.

Under the Single European Act (SEA), the role of the Parliament was strengthened by the introduction of the co-operation procedure. The Parliament now has a second reading of proposals in some fields, and after the second reading its rejection of a proposal can only be overturned by a unanimous decision of the Council. The

Maastricht Treaty extended the scope of the co-operation procedure, which was applied to Single Market laws and harmonisation, trans-European networks, development policy, the social fund, and some aspects of transport, environment, research, social policy and competition policy.

The SEA introduced the assent procedure, whereby an absolute majority of the Parliament must vote to approve laws in certain fields before they are passed. Issues covered by the assent procedure include foreign treaties, accession treaties, international agreements with budgetary implications, citizenship, residence rights, the CAP, and regional and structural funds.

The Maastricht Treaty introduced the co-decision procedure; if, after the Parliament's second reading of a proposal, the Council and Parliament fail to agree, a conciliation committee of the two will reach a compromise. If a compromise is not reached, the Parliament can reject the legislation by the vote of an absolute majority of its members. The Amsterdam Treaty extended co-decision to all areas covered by qualified majority voting, with the exception of measures related to European Monetary Union (EMU).

The Council issues the following legislation:
– Regulations, which are binding in their entirety and directly applicable to all member states; they do not need to be incorporated into national law to come into effect
– Directives, which are less specific, binding as to the result to be achieved but leaving the method of implementation open to member states; a directive thus has no force until it is incorporated into national law
– Decisions, which are also binding but are addressed solely to one or more member states or individuals in a member state
– Recommendations
– Opinions, which are merely persuasive

The Council also has certain budgetary powers, including the power to reject the budget as a whole and to increase expenditure or redistribute money within sectors. However, the final decision on whether the budget should be adopted or rejected lies with the Parliament.

The Council may delegate legislative powers to the Commission. These consist of implementing powers and technical updating of existing legislation.

The European Central Bank has legislative powers within its field of competence. The Commission also has limited legislative powers, where it has been delegated the power to implement or revise legislation by the Council.

THE COMMUNITY BUDGET

The principles of funding the European Community budget were established by the Treaty of Rome and remain with modifications to this day. There is a legally binding limit on the overall level of resources (known as 'own resources') that the Community can raise from its member states; this limit is defined as a percentage of gross national product (GNP). Budget revenue and expenditure must balance and there is therefore no deficit financing. The own resources decision, which came into effect in 1975 and has been regularly updated, states that there are four sources of Community funding under which each member state makes contributions: levies charged on agricultural imports into the Community from non-member states; customs duties on imports from non-member states; contributions based on member states' shares of a notional Community harmonised VAT base; and contributions based on member states' shares of Community GNP. The latter is the budget-balancing item and covers the difference between total expenditure and the revenue from the other three sources. Since 1984 the UK has had an annual rebate equivalent to 66 per cent of the difference between what the UK contributes to the budget and what it receives. This was introduced to compensate the UK for disproportionate contributions caused by its high proportion of agricultural and non-agricultural imports from non-member states and its relatively small receipts from the Common Agricultural Policy, the most important portion of Community expenditure.

BUDGET 2000

	Billion ECU*	As % of total
Agriculture	41.0	44.0
Regional and Social	32.7	35.1
External Action	4.8	5.1
Pre-accession Aid	3.2	3.4
Research and Technology	3.6	3.9
Other internal policies	2.4	2.6
Administration	4.7	5.0
Reserves	0.9	1.0
TOTAL	92.7	100.1

Source: General Budget of the European Union for the Financial Year 2000

EC BUDGET BY MEMBER STATE 1998 (billion ECU*)

	Contributions	Receipts	Net gain‡
Germany	20.63 (25.1%)	10.17	−10.46
France	13.58 (16.5%)	11.87	−1.71
UK	12.54 (15.2%)	6.88	−8.32
Italy	10.58 (12.9%)	8.47	−2.11
Netherlands	5.10 (6.2%)	2.06	−3.04
Spain	5.75 (7.0%)	12.24	+6.49
Belgium	3.13 (3.8%)	1.70	−1.43
Austria	2.01 (2.4%)	1.26	−0.75
Sweden	2.38 (2.9%)	1.26	−1.12
Denmark	1.69 (2.1%)	1.50	−0.19
Greece	1.31 (1.6%)	5.88	+4.57
Finland	1.14 (1.4%)	0.92	−0.22
Portugal	1.10 (1.3%)	3.93	+2.83
Ireland	0.98 (1.2%)	3.12	+2.83
Luxembourg	0.22 (0.3%)	0.08	−0.14
TOTAL	82.25 (100%)	76.49	—

Source: General Budget of the European Union for the Financial Year 2000

*1 ECU = £0.658 as at 31 August 1999
‡Net contributor (−)/net recipient (+)

Under the Edinburgh summit agreement (December 1992) the EC budget will rise in stages from 1.2 per cent of Community (Union) GNP in 1992 to a maximum of 1.27 per cent in 1999. The agreed budget for 2000–2006 will keep the 1.27 per cent ceiling, but resources devoted to the existing member states will fall to 0.98 per cent, with the remaining resources devoted to enlargement.

THE COMMON AGRICULTURAL POLICY

The Common Agricultural Policy (CAP) was established to increase agricultural production, provide a fair standard of living for farmers and ensure the availability of food at reasonable prices. This aim was achieved by a number of mechanisms:
– import levies
– intervention purchase
– export subsidies

These measures stimulated production but also placed increasing demands on the EC budget which were exacerbated by the increase in EC members and yields enlarged by technological innovation; CAP now accounts for over 40 per cent of EC expenditure. To surmount these problems reforms were agreed in 1984, 1988, 1992, 1997 and 1999.

REFORMS

The 1984 reforms created the system of co-responsibility levies: farm payments to the EC by volume of product sold. This system was supplemented by national quotas for particular products, such as milk. The 1988 reforms emphasised 'set-aside', whereby farmers are given direct grants to take land out of production as a means of reducing surpluses. The set-aside reforms were extended in 1993 for another five years and to every farm in the EC. The 1999 reforms will further reduce surpluses of cereals, beef and milk by cutting the intervention prices by up to 20 per cent and compensating producers by making area payments. Under the reforms, CAP rules will also be simplified, eliminating inconsistencies between policies.

Under the Uruguay round agreement of GATT concluded in 1993, the EU must, over a six-year period from 1 January 1995, reduce its import levies by 36 per cent, reduce its domestic subsidies by 20 per cent, reduce its export subsidies by 36 per cent in value, and reduce its subsidised exports by 21 per cent in volume. Agenda 2000, the programme to overhaul the policies of the EU and prepare it for the accession of new member states, will temporarily increase the cost of the CAP by €1,000 million a year in compensation payments, but leave it broadly stable by the end of the current planning period in 2006.

THE SINGLE MARKET

Even after the removal of tariffs and quotas between member states in the 1970s and 1980s, the EC was still separated into a number of national markets by a series of non-tariff barriers. It was to overcome these internal barriers to trade that the concept of the Single Market was developed. The measures to be undertaken were codified in the Commission's 1995 White Paper on completing the internal market.

The White Paper included articles removing obstacles that distorted the internal market: the elimination of frontier controls; the mutual recognition of professional qualifications; the harmonisation of product specifications, largely by the mutual recognition of national standards; open tendering for public procurement contracts; the free movement of capital; the harmonisation of VAT and excise duties; and the reduction of state aid to particular industries. The target date for the completion of this process was 31 December 1992. The Single European Act aided the completion of the Single Market by changing the legislative process within the EC, particularly with the introduction of qualified majority voting in the Council of Ministers for some policy areas, and the introduction of the assent procedure in the European Parliament. The SEA also extends EC competence into the fields of technology, the environment, regional policy, monetary policy and external policy. The Single Market came into effect on 1 January 1993. The full implementation of the elimination of frontier controls and the harmonisation of taxes have, however, been repeatedly delayed.

THE EUROPEAN ECONOMIC AREA (see also EFTA, page 760)

The EC Single Market programme spurred European non-member states to open negotiations with the EC on preferential access for their goods, services, labour and capital to the Single Market. Principal among these states were European Free Trade Association (EFTA) members who opened negotiations on extending the Single Market to EFTA by the formation of the European Economic Area (EEA) encompassing all 19 EC and EFTA states. Agreement was reached in May 1992 but the operation of the EEA was delayed by its rejection in a Swiss referendum, necessitating an additional protocol agreed by the remaining 18 states. The EEA came into effect on 1 January 1994 after ratification by 17 member states (Liechtenstein joined on 1 May 1995 after adapting its customs union with Switzerland).

Austria, Finland and Sweden joined the EU itself on 1 January 1995, leaving only Norway, Iceland and Liechtenstein as the non-EU EEA members. Under the EEA agreement, the three states are to adopt the EU's *acquis communautaire*, apart from in the fields of agriculture, fisheries, and coal and steel.

The EEA is controlled by regular ministerial meetings and by a joint EU-EFTA committee which extends relevant EU legislation to EEA states. Apart from single market measures, there is co-operation in education, research and development, consumer policy and tourism. An EFTA Court of Justice has been established in Luxembourg and an EFTA Surveillance Authority in Brussels to supervise the implementation of the EEA Agreement.

THE EUROPEAN MONETARY SYSTEM AND THE SINGLE CURRENCY

The European monetary system (EMS) began operation in March 1979 with three main purposes. The first was to establish monetary stability in Europe, initially in exchange rates between EC member state currencies through the exchange rate mechanism (ERM), and in the longer term to be part of a wider stabilisation process, overcoming inflation and budget and trade deficits. The second purpose was to overcome the constraints resulting from the interdependence of EC economies, and the third was to aid the long-term process of European monetary integration.

The Maastricht Treaty set in motion timetables for achieving economic and monetary union (EMU) and a single currency (the euro). At the Brussels summit in May 1998, 11 member states were judged to fulfil or be close to fulfilling the necessary criteria for participation in the first stage of EMU: Austria, Belgium, Finland, France, Germany, Ireland, Italy, Luxembourg, the Netherlands, Portugal and Spain.

The criteria were that:
– the budget deficit should be 3 per cent or less of gross domestic product (GDP)
– total national debt must not exceed 60 per cent of GDP
– inflation should be no more than 1.5 per cent above the average rate of the three best performing economies in the EU
– long-term interest rates should be no more than 2 per cent above the average of the three best performing economies in the EU in the previous 12 months
– applicants must have been members of the ERM for two years without having realigned or devalued their currency

Under the terms of a growth and stability pact agreed in Dublin in December 1996, penalties may be imposed on EMU members with high budget deficits. Governments with deficits exceeding 3 per cent of GDP will receive a warning and will be obliged to pay up to 0.5 per cent of their GDP into a fund after ten months. This will become a fine if the budget deficit is not rectified within two years. A member state with negative growth will be allowed to apply for an exemption from the fine in exceptional circumstances , e.g. a recession whereby GDP had fallen by 0.75 per cent or more during one year.

On 1 January 1999, the qualifying member states adopted the euro at irrevocably fixed exchange rates (see table below), the European Central Bank (ECB) took charge of the single monetary policy, and the euro replaced the ECU on a one-for-one basis. The euro is now the legal currency in the participating states. Euro notes and coins will be introduced from 1 January 2002 and will circulate alongside national currencies for a maximum of six months, after which time national notes and coins will cease to be legal tender.

THE CONVERSION RATES BETWEEN THE EURO AND THE CURRENCIES OF THE MEMBER STATES ADOPTING THE EURO ARE:

1 euro =	
13.7603	Austrian Schillings
40.3399	Belgian Francs
2.20371	Dutch Gulden
5.94573	Finnish Markka
6.55957	French Francs
1.95583	German Deutsche Mark
0.787564	Irish Punts
1,936.27	Italian Lire
40.3399	Luxembourg Francs
200.482	Portuguese Escudos
166.386	Spanish Pesetas

Source: The Official Journal of the European Communities

The ECB (see also page 788) meets every two weeks to set interest rates for the countries participating in the euro. Its governing council has 17 members, being the six members of the ECB's executive board and the 11 governors of the national central banks of the participating states.

The UK, Denmark and Sweden chose not to take part in the first stage of EMU; Greece was unable to meet the criteria. With the advent of EMU, the ERM was revised and Denmark and Greece became members of ERM II, which requires them to maintain their currencies within set margins of the euro. Membership of ERM II is voluntary, although all member states outside the euro zone are encouraged to take part. Sweden and the UK are currently not members.

Greece reapplied for membership of EMU on 9 March 2000 and the Danish government announced that a referendum on membership would be held in September 2000. Greece was judged to have met the criteria necessary for membership on 20 June 2000.

THE MAASTRICHT TREATY

The Treaty on European Union was agreed at a meeting of the European Council in Maastricht, the Netherlands, in December 1991. It came into effect in November 1993 following ratification by the member states.

Three 'pillars' formed the basis of the new treaty:
– the European Community with its established institutions and decision-making processes
– a Common Foreign and Security Policy (see below) with the Western European Union as the potential defence component of the EU

– co-operation in justice and home affairs, with the Council of Ministers to co-ordinate policies on asylum, immigration, conditions of entry, cross-border crime, drug trafficking and terrorism

The Treaty established a common European citizenship for nationals of all member states and introduced the principle of subsidiarity whereby decisions are taken at the most appropriate level: national, regional or local. It extended EC competency into the areas of environmental and industrial policies, consumer affairs, health, and education and training, and extended qualified majority voting in the Council of Ministers to cover areas which had previously required a unanimous vote. The powers of the European Parliament over the budget and over the Commission were also enhanced and a co-decision procedure enabled the Parliament to override decisions made by the Council of Ministers (*see* page 782). A separate protocol to the Maastricht Treaty on social policy was adopted by 11 states and was incorporated into the Amsterdam Treaty in 1997 following adoption by the UK.

THE AMSTERDAM TREATY

The treaties of Rome and Maastricht were again amended through the Treaty of Amsterdam, which came into effect on 1 May 1999. It extends the scope of qualified majority voting and the powers of the European Parliament.

COMMON FOREIGN AND SECURITY POLICIES

The Common Foreign and Security Policy (CFSP) was created as a pillar of the EU by the Maastricht Treaty (*see* above). It adopted the machinery of the European Political Co-operation (EPC) framework which it replaced and was charged with providing a forum for member states and EU institutions to consult on foreign affairs.

The CFSP system is headed by the Council of the European Union, which provides general lines of policy. Specific policy decisions are taken by the Council of Foreign Ministers, which meets at least four times a year to determine areas for joint action. The High Representative of the CFSP initiates action, manages the CFSP and represents it abroad. The Council of Ministers is supported by the Political Committee which meets monthly, or within 48 hours if there is a crisis, to prepare for ministerial discussions. A group of correspondents, designated diplomats in each member's foreign ministry, provides day-to-day contact.

The Amsterdam Treaty introduced qualified majority voting for foreign affairs and created a high representative on CFSP to act as a spokesperson. It also established a new policy planning and early warning unit to monitor international developments. The unit is to consist of specialists from the member states, the Council and the Commission, as well as from the WEU.

THE SCHENGEN AGREEMENT

The Schengen Agreement was signed by France, Germany, Belgium, Luxembourg and the Netherlands in 1990 to replace an accord on border controls agreed in Schengen, Luxembourg, in 1985. The Agreement committed the five states to abolishing internal border controls and erecting external frontiers against illegal immigrants, drug traffickers, terrorists and organised crime.

Subsequently signed by Spain and Portugal, the Agreement was ratified by the seven signatory states and entered into force in March 1995 with the removal of internal frontier, passport, customs and immigration controls. Italy and Austria became full members in April 1998 and Greece achieved full membership on 1 January 2000. Provisional agreement was reached in June 1995 between the signatory states and the Nordic Union on a merger of the two frontier-free zones, but Denmark, Finland, Sweden, Iceland and Norway are not yet full members, although all five have signed the Schengen Agreement. The UK and the Republic of Ireland have not signed the agreement, but have expressed their intention to join in some aspects of its work.

The Schengen Agreement originated as an intergovernmental agreement but became part of the EU following the signing of the Amsterdam Treaty.

COURT OF JUSTICE OF THE EUROPEAN COMMUNITIES
Boulevard Konrad Adenauer, L–2925 Luxembourg
Web: http://curia.eu.int

The Court of Justice is common to the three European Communities. It exists to safeguard the law in the interpretation and application of the Community treaties, to decide on the legality of decisions of the Council of Ministers or the Commission, and to determine infringements of the treaties. Cases may be brought to it by the member states, the Community institutions, firms or individuals. Its decisions are directly binding in the member countries, and the Maastricht Treaty enhanced the Court's powers by permitting it to impose fines on member states. The 15 judges and eight advocates-general of the Court are appointed for renewable six-year terms by the member governments in concert. During 1999, 543 new cases were lodged at the court, 382 cases were concluded and 234 judgments were delivered.

Composition of the Court, in order of precedence, with effect from 15 December 1999:
G. C. Rodríguez Iglesias (*President*); J. C. Moitinho de Almeida (*President of the 3rd and 6th Chambers*); D. A. O. Edward (*President of the 4th and 5th Chambers*); L. Sevón (*President of the 1st Chamber*); N. Fennelly (*First Advocate-General*); R. Schintgen (*President of the 2nd Chamber*); F. G. Jacobs (*Advocate-General*); P. J. G. Kapteyn (*Judge*); C. Gulmann (*Judge*); A. M. La Pergola (*Judge*); G. Cosmas (*Advocate-General*); J.-P. Puissochet (*Judge*); P. Léger (*Advocate-General*); G. Hirsch (*Judge*); P. Jann (*Judge*); H. Ragnemalm (*Judge*); D. Ruiz-Jarabo Colomer (*Advocate-General*); M. Wathelet (*Judge*); S. Alber (*Advocate-General*); J. Mischo (*Advocate-General*); A. Saggio (*Advocate-General*); V. Skouris (*Judge*); F. Macken (*Judge*); R. Grass (*Registrar*)

COURT OF FIRST INSTANCE
L-2925 Luxembourg

Established under powers conferred by the Single European Act, the Court of First Instance has jurisdiction to hear and determine all actions brought by natural or legal persons. It is composed of 15 judges, appointed for renewable six-year terms by the governments of the member states. During 1999, 644 new cases were lodged at the court and 322 cases were concluded.

Composition of the Court, in order of precedence, for the judicial year 1999–2000:
B. Vesterdorf (*President of the Court of First Instance*); R. García-Valdecasas y Fernández (*President of Chamber*); K. Lenaerts (*President of Chamber*); V. Tiili (*President of Chamber*); J. Pirrung (*President of Chamber*); P. Lindh (*Judge*); J. Azizi (*Judge*); A. Potocki (*President of Chamber*); R. Moura Ramos (*President of Chamber*); J. D. Cooke (*President of Chamber*); M. Jaeger (*President of Chamber*);

P. Mengozzi (*Judge*); A. Meij (*Judge*); M. Vilaras (*Judge*);
N. Forwood (*Judge*); H.Jung (*Registrar*)

THE COMMITTEE OF THE REGIONS
Belliardstraat 79, B-1040 Brussels, Belgium
E-mail: info@cdr.be
Web: http://www.cor.eu.int

The Committee of the Regions (COR) is an advisory and
consultative body established to redress the lack of a role
for regional and local authorities in the EU democratic
system. The COR is composed of 222 appointed and
indirectly elected members, of whom half are from large
regions and half are from small local authorities, who meet
five times each year for two days. The COR has seven
commissions which deliver opinions on policies affecting
regions, such as trans-border transport links, economic
and social cohesion, education and training, social policy,
culture and regional policy.
President, Jos Chabert (Belgium)

THE ECONOMIC AND SOCIAL COMMITTEE
Ravensteinstraat 2, B-1000 Brussels, Belgium
Web: http://ces.eu.int

The Economic and Social Committee (ESC) is an advisory
and consultative body. It has 222 members, nominated by
member states, and is divided into three groups: employers, workers, and other interest groups such as consumers,
farmers and the self-employed. It issues opinions on draft
EC legislation and can bring matters to the attention of
the Commission, Council and Parliament. Consultation
of the ESC by the Parliament is enshrined in the
Amsterdam Treaty, formally recognising the importance
of the opinions of the EU s economic and social partners.
President, Beatrice Rangoni Machiavelli (Italy)

THE EUROPEAN CENTRAL BANK
29 Kaiserstrasse, D-60311 Frankfurt-am-Main, Germany
E-mail: info@ecb.int
Web: http://www.ecb.int

The European Central Bank (ECB), which superseded the
European Monetary Institute, was established on 1 July
1998. Its governing bodies are the Executive Board and the
Governing Council. The Executive Board consists of the
President, the Vice-President and four other members,
who are appointed by the governments of the participating
states, from people with recognised standing and professional experience; the Governing Council comprises the
six members of the Executive Board and the 11 governors
of the national central banks of the participating states.
The ECB is independent of national governments and of
all other EU institutions. It became fully operational on
1 January 1999, and defines and implements the single
monetary policy necessary for EMU. It operates as part
of the European System of Central Banks (ESCB), which
consists of the ECB and the national central banks of
the participating states.
President, Willem Duisenberg (Netherlands)
Vice-President, Christian Noyer (France)

THE EUROPEAN COURT OF AUDITORS
12 rue A. De Gasperi, L-1615 Luxembourg
E-mail: euradu@eca.eu.int
Web: http://www.eca.eu.int

The European Court of Auditors, established in 1977, is
responsible for the audit of the budgets of the European
Communities and Community bodies and evaluates
whether their expenditure is in accordance with the
principles of sound financial management. The Court
issues an annual report and a statement of assurance as to
the reliability of the accounts and the legality and
regularity of the underlying transactions. It also publishes
special reports on specific topics and delivers opinions on
financial matters. The Maastricht Treaty designated the
Court of Auditors as a full institution of the European
Union, enabling it to take other institutions to the Court
of Justice. It has 15 members appointed for six-year terms
by the Council of Ministers following consultation with
the European Parliament.
President, Jan Karlsson (Sweden)

THE EUROPEAN INVESTMENT BANK
100 boulevard Konrad Adenauer, L-2950 Luxembourg
E-mail: info@eib.org
Web: http://www.eib.org

The European Investment Bank (EIB) was set up in 1958
under the terms of the Treaty of Rome to finance capital
investment projects promoting the balanced development
of the European Community.

It grants long-term loans to private and public enterprises, public authorities and financial institutions, to
finance projects which further the economic development
of less advanced regions (Assisted Areas); improvement
of European transport and telecommunications infrastructure; environmental protection; attainment of the
EU's energy policy objectives; modernisation of enterprises, and promotion of industrial competitiveness and
integration at EU level.

EIB activities have also been extended outside member
countries as part of the EU's development co-operation
policy, under the terms of different association or co-
operation agreements with countries in the Mediterranean region, in central and eastern Europe, in Latin
America, Asia and South Africa, and, under the Lomé
Conventions, with 71 countries in Africa, the Caribbean
and the Pacific.

The Bank's total financing operations in 1999
amounted to €31,800 million, of which €27,800 million
was for investment within the EU.

In June 2000, the EIB launched the Innovation 2000
Initiative, under which €12,000–15,000 million would be
available over a three-year period to invest in the provision
of new technologies in education, co-finance research and
development, finance information and communications
technology networks, make use of information technology
to increase access to public services and assist SMEs to
acquire and use information technologies.

The members of the EIB are the 15 member states of the
EU, who have all subscribed to the Bank's capital of
€100,000 billion. The bulk of the funds required by the
Bank to carry out its tasks are borrowed on the capital
markets of the EU and non-member countries, and on the
international market.

As it operates on a non-profit-making basis, the interest
rates charged by the EIB reflect the cost of the Bank's

borrowings and closely follow conditions on world capital markets.

The Board of Governors of the EIB consists of one government minister nominated by each of the member countries, usually the finance minister, who lay down general directives on the policy of the Bank and appoint members to the Board of Directors (24 nominated by the member states, one by the European Commission), which takes decisions on the granting and raising of loans and the fixing of interest rates. A Management Committee, composed of the Bank's President and eight Vice-Presidents, also appointed by the Board of Governors, is responsible for the day-to-day operations of the Bank. The President and Vice-Presidents also preside as Chairman and Vice-Chairmen at meetings of the Board of Directors.

President, Philippe Maystadt
Vice-Presidents, Wolfgang Roth; Panagiotis-
Loukas Gennimatas; Massimo Ponzellini; Louis Martí; Rudolf de Korte; Ewald Nowotny; Francis Mayer; Peter Sedgwick
UK OFFICE: 68 Pall Mall, London SW1Y 5ES.
Tel: 020-7343 1200

THE EUROPEAN POLICE OFFICE
PO Box 90850, NL-2509 LW The Hague,
The Netherlands
E-mail: info@europol.eu.int
Web: http://www.europol.eu.int

The European Police Office (Europol), came into being on 1 October 1998 and assumed its full powers on 1 July 1999. It superseded the Europol Drugs Unit and exists to improve police co-operation between member states and to combat terrorism, illicit traffic in drugs and other serious forms of international crime. It is ultimately responsible to the Council. Each member state has set up a national unit to liaise with Europol, and the units send at least one liaison officer to represent its interests at Europol headquarters. Europol maintains a computerised information system, designed to facilitate the exchange of information between member states; the system is maintained by the national units and may be consulted by Europol agents. The computerised database may contain both personal and non-personal data; individuals are entitled to request access to data concerning themselves. Europol has a Management Board comprising one senior police representative from each member state. All Europol activities are monitored by an independent joint supervisory body, to ensure the rights of the individual are upheld.

Director, Jürgen Storbeck (Germany)
Deputy Directors, Willy Bruggeman (Belgium); Gilles Leclair (France); Emanuele Marotta (Italy); Georges Rauchs (Luxembourg); David Valls-Russell (UK)

Other bodies:
THE EUROPEAN MEDICINE EVALUATION AGENCY (EMEA), 7 Westferry Circus, London E14 4HB; E-mail: mail@emea.eudra.org
THE EUROPEAN ENVIRONMENT AGENCY (EEA), Kongens Nytorv 6, DK-1050, København, Denmark; E-mail: info@eea.dk
THE EUROPEAN TRAINING FOUNDATION, Villa Gualino, Viale Settimio Sever 65, I-10133 Torn, Italy; E-mail: info@etf.eu.int
THE EUROPEAN CENTRE FOR THE DEVELOPMENT OF VOCATIONAL TRAINING (CEDEFOP), PO Box 27, GR-55102 Thessaloniki (Finikas), Greece; E-mail: webmaster@cedefop.gr

THE EUROPEAN MONITORING CENTRE FOR DRUGS AND DRUG ADDICTION, Palacete Mascarenhas, Rua da Cruz de Santa Apolónia 23–25, P-1100 Lisboa, Portugal; E-mail: info@emcdda.org
THE EUROPEAN FOUNDATION FOR THE IMPROVEMENT OF LIVING AND WORKING CONDITIONS, Wyattville Road, Loughlinstown, Co. Dublin, Ireland; E-mail: postmaster@eurofound.ie
THE OFFICE FOR HARMONISATION IN THE INTERNAL MARKET (OHIM), Avenida de Aguilera 20, AC 77, E-03080 Alicante, Spain; E-mail: information@oami.eu.int
THE COMMUNITY PLANT VARIETY RIGHTS OFFICE (CPVO), BP 2141, F- 49021 Angers Cedex 02, France; E-mail: cpvo@cpvo.fr
THE EUROPEAN AGENCY FOR SAFETY AND HEALTH AT WORK, Gran Vía 33, E-48009 Bilbao, Spain; E-mail: information@osha.eu.int
THE TRANSLATION CENTRE FOR BODIES IN THE EUROPEAN UNION, Nouvel Hémicycle, niveau 4, 1 rue du Fort Thüngen, L-1499 Luxembourg; E-mail: cdt.eu.int
THE EUROPEAN MONITORING CENTRE ON RACISM AND XENOPHOBIA, Rahlgasse 3, A-1060 Wien, Austria; E-mail: office@eumc.at

---

EUROPEAN COMMUNITY INFORMATION

EUROPEAN COMMISSION REPRESENTATIVE OFFICES
ENGLAND, 8 Storey's Gate, London SW1P 3AT.
Tel: 020-7973 1992
WALES, 4 Cathedral Road, Cardiff CF1 9SG.
Tel: 029-2037 1631
SCOTLAND, 9 Alva Street, Edinburgh EH2 4HP.
Tel: 0131-225 2058
NORTHERN IRELAND, Windsor House, 9–15 Bedford Street, Belfast BT2 7EG. Tel: 028-9024 0708
REPUBLIC OF IRELAND, 39 Molesworth Street, Dublin 2
AUSTRALIA, 18 Alakana Street, Yarralumla, ACT 2600, and a number of other cities
CANADA, Inn of the Provinces, Office Tower (Suite 1110), 350 Sparks Street, Ottawa, Ontario K1R 7SA
USA, 2100 M Street NW (Suite 707), Washington DC 20037; 1 Dag Hammarskjöld Plaza, 254 East 47th Street, New York, NY 10017

UK EUROPEAN PARLIAMENT INFORMATION OFFICE
2 Queen Anne's Gate, London SW1H 9AA.
Tel: 020-7227 4300

There are European Information Centres, set up to give information and advice to small businesses, in 25 British towns and cities. A number of universities maintain European Documentation Centres. Many local authorities also maintain European Public Information Centres, which provide information to the general public.

Countries of the World

WORLD AREA AND POPULATION

The total population of the world in mid-1990 was estimated at 5,292 million, compared with 3,019 million in 1960 and 2,070 million in 1930.

Continent, etc.	Area sq. miles '000	sq. km '000	Estimated population mid-1990
Africa	11,704	30,313	642,000,000
North America[1]	8,311	21,525	276,000,000
Latin America[2]	7,933	20,547	448,000,000
Asia[3]	10,637	27,549	3,113,000,000
Europe[4]	1,915	4,961	498,000,000
Former USSR	8,649	22,402	289,000,000
Oceania[5]	3,286	8,510	26,500,000
TOTAL	52,435	135,807	5,292,000,000

[1]Includes Greenland and Hawaii
[2]Mexico and the remainder of the Americas south of the USA
[3]Includes European Turkey, excludes former USSR
[4]Excludes European Turkey and former USSR
[5]Includes Australia, New Zealand and the islands inhabited by Micronesian, Melanesian and Polynesian peoples
Source UN Demographic Yearbook 1990 (pub. 1992)

A United Nations report *The Sex and Age Distribution of the World Populations* (revised 1994) puts the world's population in the late 20th and the 21st centuries at the following levels (medium variant data):

1995	5,176.4m	2030	8,670.6m
2000	6,158.0m	2040	9,318.2m
2010	7,032.3m	2050	9,833.2m
2020	7,887.8m		

The population forecast for the years 2000 and 2050 is:

Continent, etc.	Estimated population (million) 2000	2050
Africa	831.596	2,140.844
North America[1]	306.280	388.997
Latin America[2]	523.875	838.527
Asia	3,753.846	5,741.005
Europe	729.803	677.764
Oceania	30.651	46.070
TOTAL	6,158.051	9,833.207

[1]Includes Bermuda, Greenland, and St Pierre and Miquelon
[2]Mexico and the remainder of the Americas south of the USA

AREA AND POPULATION BY CONTINENT

No complete survey of many countries has yet been achieved and consequently accurate area figures are not always available. Similarly, many countries have not recently, or have never, taken a census. The areas of countries given below are derived from estimated figures published by the United Nations. The conversion factors used are:

(i) to convert square miles to square km, multiply by 2.589988
(ii) to convert square km to square miles, multiply by 0.3861022

Population figures for countries are derived from the most recent estimates available. Accurate and up-to-date data for the populations of capital cities are scarce, and definitions of cities' extent differ. The figures given below are the latest estimates available.

Ψ seaport

AFRICA

COUNTRY/TERRITORY	AREA sq. miles	sq. km	POPULATION	CAPITAL	POPULATION OF CAPITAL
Algeria	919,595	2,381,741	29,050,000	ΨAlgiers (El Djazaïr)	1,507,241
Angola	481,354	1,246,700	11,569,000	ΨLuanda	475,328
Benin	43,484	112,622	5,828,000	ΨPorto Novo	179,138
Botswana	224,607	581,730	1,533,000	Gaborone	286,779
Burkina Faso	105,792	274,000	11,087,000	Ouagadougou	634,479
Burundi	10,747	27,834	6,194,000	Bujumbura	235,440
Cameroon	183,569	475,442	13,937,000	Yaoundé	653,670
Cape Verde	1,557	4,033	406,000	ΨPraia	61,644
Central African Republic	240,535	622,984	3,245,000	Bangui	473,817
Chad	495,755	1,284,000	6,702,000	N'Djaména	179,000
Comoros	863	2,235	651,000	Moroni	17,267
Congo, Dem. Rep. of	905,355	2,344,858	48,040,000	Kinshasa	2,664,309
Congo – Brazzaville, Rep. of	132,047	342,000	2,745,000	Brazzaville	596,200
Côte d'Ivoire	124,504	322,463	14,300,000	Yamoussoukro	126,191
Djibouti	8,958	23,200	634,000	ΨDjibouti	62,000
Egypt	386,662	1,001,449	62,011,000	Cairo	6,800,000
Equatorial Guinea	10,831	28,051	420,000	ΨMalabo	30,418
Eritrea	45,406	117,600	3,409,000	Asmara	358,100
Ethiopia	426,373	1,104,300	60,148,000	Addis Ababa	2,084,588
Gabon	103,347	267,668	1,138,000	ΨLibreville	251,000
Gambia	4,361	11,295	1,169,000	ΨBanjul	109,986

COUNTRY/TERRITORY	AREA sq. miles	sq. km	POPULATION	CAPITAL	POPULATION OF CAPITAL
Ghana	92,098	238,533	18,885,616	ΨAccra	1,445,515
Guinea	94,926	245,857	7,614,000	ΨConakry	763,000
Guinea-Bissau	13,948	36,125	1,112,000	ΨBissau	109,214
Kenya	224,081	580,367	33,141,000	Nairobi	1,400,000
Lesotho	11,720	30,355	2,131,000	Maseru	367,000
Liberia	43,000	111,369	2,879,000	ΨMonrovia	421,053
Libya	679,362	1,759,540	4,389,739	ΨTripoli (Tarābulus)	1,000,000
Madagascar	226,658	587,041	15,845,000	Antananarivo	1,052,835
Malawi	45,747	118,484	10,441,000	Lilongwe	233,973
Mali	478,841	1,240,192	11,480,000	Bamako	809,552
Mauritania	395,956	1,025,520	2,392,000	Nouakchott	850,000
Mauritius	788	2,040	1,160,000	ΨPort Louis	146,499
Mayotte (Fr.)	144	372	94,410	Mamoudzou	12,000
Morocco	172,414	446,550	27,310,000	ΨRabat	1,220,000
Western Sahara	102,703	266,000	265,000	El-Aaiūn	20,010
Mozambique	309,494	801,590	16,916,600	ΨMaputo	1,039,700
Namibia	318,261	824,292	1,613,000	Windhoek	147,056
Niger	489,191	1,267,000	9,788,000	Niamey	392,169
Nigeria	356,669	923,768	118,369,000	Abuja	378,671
Réunion (Fr.)	969	2,510	673,000	St Denis	121,999
Rwanda	10,169	26,338	5,883,000	Kigali	116,227
St Helena (UK)	47	122	6,000	ΨJamestown	884
Ascension Island (UK)	34	88	1,051	ΨGeorgetown	—
Tristan da Cunha (UK)	38	98	288	ΨEdinburgh of the Seven Seas	—
São Tomé And Príncipe	372	964	138,000	ΨSão Tomé	43,420
Senegal	75,955	196,722	8,802,000	ΨDakar	1,641,358
Seychelles	176	455	78,846	ΨVictoria	24,324
Sierra Leone	27,699	71,740	4,428,000	ΨFreetown	469,776
Somalia	246,201	637,657	10,217,000	ΨMogadishu	230,000
South Africa	471,445	1,221,037	43,336,000	Pretoria	822,925
				ΨCape Town	1,911,521
				Bloemfontein	300,150
Sudan	967,500	2,505,813	27,889,000	Khartoum (Al-Khartūm)	947,483
Swaziland	6,704	17,364	906,000	Mbabane	38,290
Tanzania	341,216	883,749	31,507,000	Dodoma	85,000
Togo	21,925	56,785	4,317,000	ΨLomé	366,476
Tunisia	63,170	163,610	9,215,000	ΨTunis	1,830,634
Uganda	93,065	241,038	20,438,000	Kampala	750,000
Zambia	290,587	752,618	8,478,000	Lusaka	982,362
Zimbabwe	150,872	390,757	12,294,000	Harare	1,189,103

AMERICA

North America

Canada	3,849,674	9,970,610	30,491,294	Ottawa	1,010,498
Greenland (Den.)	840,004	2,175,600	56,000	ΨGodthåb (Nuuk)	12,483
Mexico	756,066	1,958,201	96,400,000	Mexico City	15,047,685
St Pierre and Miquelon (Fr.)	93	242	6,316	ΨSt Pierre	5,416
United States of America	3,536,382	9,156,119	274,520,000	Washington DC	7,285,206

Central America and the West Indies

Anguilla (UK)	37	96	12,394	The Valley	2,400
Antigua and Barbuda	171	442	67,000	ΨSt John's	22,342
Aruba (Neth.)	75	193	87,000	ΨOranjestad	25,000
Bahamas	5,358	13,878	289,000	ΨNassau	172,196
Barbados	166	430	262,000	ΨBridgetown	108,000
Belize	8,763	22,696	230,000	Belmopan	44,087
Bermuda (UK)	20	53	60,000	ΨHamilton	2,277
Cayman Islands (UK)	102	264	38,000	ΨGeorge Town	20,000
Costa Rica	19,730	51,100	3,464,000	San José	1,220,412
Cuba	42,804	110,861	11,059,000	ΨHavana	2,184,990
Dominica	290	751	71,000	ΨRoseau	16,243
Dominican Republic	18,730	48,511	8,097,000	ΨSanto Domingo	2,134,779

Country/Territory	Area sq. miles	sq. km	Population	Capital	Population of Capital
El Salvador	8,124	21,041	5,928,000	San Salvador	1,200,000
Grenada	133	344	93,000	ΨSt George's	4,788
Guadeloupe (Fr.)	658	1,705	437,000	ΨBasse Terre	29,522
Guatemala	42,042	108,889	10,517,000	Guatemala City	1,675,589
Haiti	10,714	27,750	7,492,000	ΨPort-au-Prince	884,472
Honduras	43,277	112,088	6,338,000	Tegucigalpa	670,100
Jamaica	4,243	10,990	2,590,400	ΨKingston	524,638
Martinique (Fr.)	425	1,102	388,000	ΨFort de France	133,920
Montserrat (UK)	39	102	4,500	ΨPlymouth	1,478
Netherlands Antilles (Neth.)	309	800	207,333	ΨWillemstad	50,000
Nicaragua	50,193	130,000	4,351,000	Managua	608,020
Panama	29,157	75,517	2,719,000	ΨPanama City	464,928
Puerto Rico (USA)	3,427	8,875	3,771,000	ΨSan Juan	1,222,316
St Kitts – Nevis	101	261	41,000	ΨBasseterre	14,161
St Lucia	240	622	146,000	ΨCastries	51,994
St Vincent and the Grenadines	150	388	112,000	ΨKingstown	15,466
Trinidad and Tobago	1,981	5,130	1,307,000	ΨPort of Spain	43,396
Turks and Caicos Islands (UK)	166	430	23,000	ΨGrand Turk	3,691
Virgin Islands					
British (UK)	58	151	20,000	ΨRoad Town	3,983
US (USA)	134	347	114,483	ΨCharlotte Amalie	11,842
South America					
Argentina	1,073,518	2,780,400	35,672,000	ΨBuenos Aires	11,298,030
Bolivia	424,165	1,098,581	8,140,000	La Paz	739,453
Brazil	3,300,171	8,547,403	159,884,000	Brasília	1,737,813
Chile	292,135	756,626	14,622,000	Santiago	4,640,635
Colombia	439,737	1,138,914	36,162,000	Bogotá	5,398,998
Ecuador	109,484	283,561	11,937,000	Quito	1,444,363
Falkland Islands (UK)	4,700	12,173	2,221	ΨStanley	1,636
French Guiana (Fr.)	34,749	90,000	159,000	ΨCayenne	41,164
Guyana	83,000	214,969	847,000	ΨGeorgetown	250,000
Paraguay	157,048	406,752	5,085,000	Asunción	718,690
Peru	496,225	1,285,216	25,015,000	Lima	6,321,173
South Georgia (UK)	1,580	4,092	—	—	—
Suriname	63,037	163,265	437,000	ΨParamaribo	265,000
Uruguay	67,574	175,016	3,221,000	ΨMontevideo	1,303,182
Venezuela	352,145	912,050	22,777,000	Caracas	3,672,779

ASIA

Country/Territory	Area sq. miles	sq. km	Population	Capital	Population of Capital
Afghanistan	251,773	652,090	22,132,000	Kābol (Kabul)	1,424,400
Bahrain	268	694	620,000	ΨManama (Al-Manāmah)	140,401
Bangladesh	55,598	143,998	122,013,000	Dhaka	3,397,187
Bhutan	18,147	47,000	1,862,000	Thimphu	15,000
Brunei Darussalam	2,226	5,765	307,000	Bandar Seri Begawan	49,902
Cambodia	69,898	181,035	10,516,000	ΨPhnom Penh	832,000
China[1]	3,705,408	9,596,961	1,243,738,000	Beijing	7,362,426
Hong Kong (China)	415	1,075	6,687,200	—	—
India	1,269,213	3,287,263	970,930,000	New Delhi	301,297
Indonesia	735,358	1,904,569	199,867,000	ΨJakarta	9,160,500
Iran	630,574	1,633,188	60,694,000	Tehrān	6,750,043
Iraq	169,235	438,317	21,177,000	Baghdad	3,841,268
Israel[2]	8,130	21,056	6,100,000	Tel Aviv	1,919,700
West Bank and Gaza Strip	2,406	6,231	1,635,000	Gaza City	120,000
Japan	145,880	377,829	125,638,000	Tokyo	11,680,296
Jordan	37,738	97,740	5,774,000	Ammān	1,270,000
Kazakhstan	1,052,085	2,724,900	15,671,000	Astana	275,100
Korea, Democratic People's Republic	46,540	120,538	22,082,000	Pyongyang	2,741,260
Korea, Republic of	38,327	99,268	46,858,460	Seoul	10,321,000
Kuwait	6,880	17,818	1,866,104	ΨKuwait City (Al-Kuwayt)	388,663
Kyrgyzstan	77,181	199,900	4,856,000	Bishkek	589,400
Laos	91,429	236,800	5,035,000	Vientiane	132,253
Lebanon	4,015	10,400	3,144,000	ΨBeirut	1,500,000
Macao (China)	7	18	440,000	ΨMacao	241,413

COUNTRY/TERRITORY	AREA sq. miles	sq. km	POPULATION	CAPITAL	POPULATION OF CAPITAL
Malaysia	127,320	329,758	21,667,000	Kuala Lumpur; Putrajaya	1,145,342; 3,000
Maldives	115	298	273,000	ΨMalé	62,973
Mongolia	604,829	1,566,500	2,313,000	Ulaanbaatar	515,100
Myanmar	261,228	676,578	46,402,000	ΨYangon (Rangoon)	2,513,023
Nepal	56,827	147,181	22,591,000	Kathmandu	421,258
Oman	82,030	212,457	2,302,000	ΨMuscat (Masqat)	400,000
Pakistan	307,374	796,095	138,150,000	Islamabad	350,000
Philippines	115,831	300,000	73,527,000	ΨManila	8,594,150
Qatar	4,247	11,000	569,000	ΨDoha (Ad-Dawhah)	217,294
Saudi Arabia	830,000	2,149,690	19,494,000	Riyadh (Ar-Riyād)	1,800,000
Singapore	239	618	3,737,000	—	—
Sri Lanka	25,332	65,610	18,552,000	ΨColombo	615,000
Syria	71,498	185,180	14,951,000	Damascus	1,549,000
Taiwan	13,800	35,742	21,854,273	Taipei	2,638,565
Tajikistan	55,251	143,100	5,919,000	Dushanbe	528,600
Thailand	198,115	513,115	60,206,000	ΨBangkok	5,882,000
Turkey[3]	299,158	774,815	63,745,000	Ankara	3,258,026
Turkmenistan	188,456	488,100	4,569,000	Ashgabat	407,000
United Arab Emirates	32,278	83,600	2,580,000	Abu Dhabi (Abū Żaby)	450,000
Uzbekistan	172,742	447,400	24,000,000	Tashkent	2,200,000
Vietnam	128,066	331,689	76,548,000	Hanoi	1,073,760
Yemen	203,850	527,968	15,919,000	Sana'ā'	926,595

[1]Including Tibet
[2]Including East Jerusalem, the Golan Heights and Israeli citizens on the West Bank
[3]Including Turkey in Europe

EUROPE

Albania	11,099	28,748	3,731,000	Tirana	244,153
Andorra	181	468	65,877	Andorra la Vella	21,721
Armenia	11,506	29,800	3,798,400	Yerevan	1,254,400
Austria	32,378	83,859	8,072,000	Vienna	1,806,737
Azerbaijan	33,436	86,600	7,625,000	ΨBaku	1,149,000
Belarus	80,155	207,600	10,179,000	Minsk	1,708,308
Belgium	11,787	30,528	10,188,000	Brussels	953,175
Bosnia-Hercegovina	19,767	51,197	3,784,000	Sarajevo	529,021
Bulgaria	42,823	110,912	8,306,000	Sofia	1,192,735
Croatia	21,824	56,538	4,498,000	Zagreb	867,717
Cyprus	3,572	9,251	766,000	Nicosia	193,000
Czech Republic	30,450	78,866	10,304,000	Prague	1,200,458
Denmark	16,639	43,094	5,284,000	ΨCopenhagen	1,362,264
Faroe Islands	540	1,399	48,000	ΨTórshavn	16,218
Estonia	17,413	45,100	1,453,844	Tallinn	415,299
Finland	130,559	338,145	5,140,000	ΨHelsinki	905,555
France	212,935	551,500	58,607,000	Paris	9,319,367
Georgia	26,911	69,700	5,434,000	Tbilisi	1,268,000
Germany	137,846	357,022	82,071,000	Berlin	3,472,009
Gibraltar (UK)	2.3	6	28,000	ΨGibraltar	—
Greece	50,949	131,957	10,522,000	Athens	3,072,922
Hungary	35,920	93,032	10,153,000	Budapest	1,896,507
Iceland	39,769	103,000	275,277	ΨReykjavík	107,764
Ireland, Republic of	27,132	70,273	3,626,087	ΨDublin	952,692
Italy	116,339	301,318	57,523,000	Rome	2,648,843
Latvia	24,942	64,600	2,474,000	Riga	805,997
Liechtenstein	62	160	32,015	Vaduz	5,106
Lithuania	25,174	65,200	3,701,300	Vilnius	580,099
Luxembourg	998	2,586	417,000	Luxembourg	77,400
Macedonia	9,928	25,713	2,190,000	Skopje	429,964
Malta	122	316	378,518	ΨValletta	7,100
Moldova	13,070	33,700	4,335,000	Chişinău	655,940
Monaco	0.4	1	32,000	Monaco	27,063
Netherlands	16,033	41,526	15,604,000	ΨAmsterdam	1,102,323
Norway[1]	125,050	323,877	4,445,460	ΨOslo	499,693
Poland	124,808	323,250	38,650,000	Warsaw	1,632,534
Portugal[2]	35,514	91,982	9,920,760	ΨLisbon	2,561,225

COUNTRY/TERRITORY	AREA sq. miles	sq. km	POPULATION	CAPITAL	POPULATION OF CAPITAL
Romania	92,043	238,391	22,520,000	Bucharest	2,027,500
Russia[3]	6,592,850	17,075,400	146,100,000	Moscow	8,598,896
San Marino	24	61	26,000	San Marino	4,357
Slovakia	18,923	49,012	5,383,000	Bratislava	452,278
Slovenia	7,821	20,256	1,987,000	Ljubljana	273,000
Spain[4]	195,365	505,992	39,270,000	Madrid	3,084,673
Sweden	173,732	449,964	8,846,000	ΨStockholm	1,148,953
Switzerland	15,940	41,284	7,114,600	Bern	321,932
Ukraine	233,090	603,700	51,094,000	Kiev (Kyiv)	2,630,000
United Kingdom[5]	93,784	242,900	58,784,000	ΨLondon	7,074,265
England	50,351	130,410	48,903,000	—	—
Wales	8,015	20,758	2,917,000	ΨCardiff (Caerdydd)	315,040
Scotland	30,420	78,789	5,137,000	ΨEdinburgh	448,850
Northern Ireland	5,467	14,160	1,649,000	ΨBelfast	297,300
Vatican City State	0.2	0.44	1,000	Vatican City	766
Yugoslavia	39,449	102,173	10,597,000	Belgrade	1,338,856

[1]Excludes Svalbard and Jan Mayen Islands (approx. 24,101 sq. miles (62,422 sq. km) and 3,000 population)
[2]Includes Madeira (314 sq. miles) and the Azores (922 sq. miles)
[3]Includes Russia in Asia
[4]Includes Balearic Islands, Canary Islands, Ceuta and Melilla
[5]Excludes Isle of Man (221 sq. miles (572 sq. km), 69,788 population), and Channel Islands (75 sq. miles (194 sq. km), 142,949 population)

OCEANIA

American Samoa (*USA*)	77	199	58,000	ΨPago Pago	3,519
Australia	2,988,902	7,741,220	19,080,-800	Canberra	309,500
Norfolk Island (*Aust.*)	14	36	1,772	ΨKingston	—
Fiji	7,056	18,274	809,000	ΨSuva	141,273
French Polynesia (*Fr.*)	1,544	4,000	227,000	ΨPapeete	36,784
Guam (*USA*)	212	549	145,780	Agana	1,139
Kiribati	280	726	81,000	Tarawa	17,921
Marshall Islands	70	181	61,000	Dalap-Uliga-Darrit	20,000
Micronesia, Federated States of	271	702	130,000	Palikir	—
Nauru	8	21	11,000	ΨNauru	—
New Caledonia (*Fr.*)	7,172	18,575	193,000	ΨNoumea	97,581
New Zealand	104,454	270,534	3,811,0-00	ΨWellington	346,700
Cook Islands	91	236	20,000	Rarotonga	9,281
Niue	100	260	2,000	Alofi	—
Ross Dependency[1]	175,000	453,248	—	—	—
Tokelau	5	12	2,000	—	—
Northern Mariana Islands (*USA*)	179	464	49,000	Saipan	52,706
Palau (*USA*)	177	459	17,000	Koror	10,493
Papua New Guinea	178,704	462,840	4,500,0-00	ΨPort Moresby	173,500
Pitcairn Islands (*UK*)	2	5	54	—	—
Samoa	1,093	2,831	168,000	ΨApia	36,000
Solomon Islands	11,157	28,896	404,000	ΨHoniara	40,000
Tonga	288	747	99,000	ΨNuku'alofa	29,018
Tuvalu	10	26	10,000	ΨFongafale	2,856
Vanuatu	4,706	12,189	178,000	ΨPort Vila	26,100
Wallis And Futuna Islands (*Fr.*)	77	200	15,000	ΨMata–Utu	—

[1]Includes permanent shelf ice

Time Zones

Standard time differences from the Greenwich meridian

+   hours ahead of GMT
−   hours behind GMT
*   may vary from standard time at some part of the year (Summer Time or Daylight Saving Time)
h   hours
m   minutes

	h	*m*
Afghanistan	+4	30
*Albania	+1	
Algeria	+1	
*Andorra	+1	
Angola	+1	
Anguilla	−4	
Antigua and Barbuda	−4	
Argentina	−3	
*Armenia	+4	
Aruba	−4	
Ascension Island	0	
*Australia	+10	
ACT, NSW (except Broken Hill area) Qld, Tas., Vic, Whitsunday Islands		
*Broken Hill area (NSW)	+9	30
*Lord Howe Island	+10	30
Northern Territory	+9	30
*South Australia	+9	30
Western Australia	+8	
*Austria	+1	
*Azerbaijan	+4	
*Bahamas	−5	
Bahrain	+3	
Bangladesh	+6	
Barbados	−4	
*Belarus	+2	
*Belgium	+1	
Belize	−6	
Benin	+1	
*Bermuda	−4	
Bhutan	+6	
Bolivia	−4	
*Bosnia-Hercegovina	+1	
Botswana	+2	
Brazil		
Acre	−5	
central states	−4	
N. and NE coastal states	−3	
*S. and E. coastal states, including Brasilia	−3	
Fernando de Noronha Island	−2	
western states	−5	
British Antarctic Territory	−3	
British Indian Ocean Territory	+5	
Diego Garcia	+6	
British Virgin Islands	−4	
Brunei	+8	
*Bulgaria	+2	
Burkina Faso	0	
Burundi	+2	
Cambodia	+7	
Cameroon	+1	
Canada		
*Alberta	−7	
*British Columbia	−8	

	h	*m*
*Labrador	−4	
*Manitoba	−6	
*New Brunswick	−4	
*Newfoundland	−3	30
*Northwest Territories		
east of 85°W.	−5	
85W.–102°W.	−6	
*Nunavut	−7	
*Nova Scotia	−4	
*Ontario		
east of 90° W.	−5	
west of 90° W.	−6	
*Prince Edward Island	−4	
Québec		
east of 63° W.	−4	
*west of 63° W.	−5	
Saskatchewan	−6	
*Yukon	−8	
Cape Verde	−1	
Cayman Islands	−5	
Central African Republic	+1	
Chad	+1	
*Chatham Islands	+12	45
*Chile	−4	
China (inc. Hong Kong and Macao)	+8	
Christmas Island (Indian Ocean)	+7	
Cocos (Keeling) Islands	+6	30
Colombia	−5	
Comoros	+3	
Congo (Dem. Rep.)		
east	+2	
west	+1	
Congo-Brazzaville	+1	
Cook Islands	−10	
Costa Rica	−6	
Côte d'Ivoire	0	
*Croatia	+1	
*Cuba	−5	
*Cyprus	+2	
*Czech Republic	+1	
*Denmark	+1	
*Faroe Islands	0	
*Greenland	−3	
Danmarkshavn	0	
Mesters Vig	0	
*Scoresby Sound	−1	
*Thule area	−4	
Djibouti	+3	
Dominica	−4	
Dominican Republic	−4	
East Timor	+8	
Ecuador	−5	
Galápagos Islands	−6	
*Egypt	+2	
El Salvador	−6	
Equatorial Guinea	+1	
Eritrea	+3	
*Estonia	+2	
Ethiopia	+3	
*Falkland Islands	−4	
Fiji	+12	
*Finland	+2	
*France	+1	
French Guiana	−3	
French Polynesia	−10	
Guadeloupe	−4	

	h	*m*
Martinique	−4	
Réunion	+4	
Marquesas Islands	−9	30
Gabon	+1	
The Gambia	0	
*Georgia	+3	
*Germany	+1	
Ghana	0	
*Gibraltar	+1	
*Greece	+2	
Grenada	−4	
Guam	+10	
Guatemala	−6	
Guinea	0	
Guinea-Bissau	0	
Guyana	−4	
*Haiti	−5	
Honduras	−6	
*Hungary	+1	
Iceland	0	
India	+5	30
Indonesia		
Java, Kalimantan (west and central), Sumatra	+7	
Bali, Flores, Kalimantan (south and east), Sulawesi, Sumbawa, West Timor	+8	
Irian Jaya, Maluku, Tanimbar	+9	
*Iran	+3	30
*Iraq	+3	
*Ireland, Republic of	0	
*Israel	+2	
*Italy	+1	
Jamaica	−5	
Japan	+9	
*Jordan	+2	
*Kazakhstan		
western (Aktau)	+4	
central (Atyrau)	+5	
eastern	+6	
Kenya	+3	
Kiribati	+12	
Line Islands	+14	
Phoenix Islands	+13	
Korea, North	+9	
Korea, South	+9	
Kuwait	+3	
*Kyrgyzstan	+5	
Laos	+7	
*Latvia	+2	
*Lebanon	+2	
Lesotho	+2	
Liberia	0	
*Libya	+2	
*Liechtenstein	+1	
Line Islands not part of Kiribati	−10	
*Lithuania	+1	
*Luxembourg	+1	
*Macedonia	+1	
Madagascar	+3	
Madeira	0	
Malaŵi	+2	
Malaysia	+8	
Maldives	+5	

	h	m		h	m
Mali	0		St Vincent and the		
*Malta	+1		Grenadines	−4	
Marshall Islands	+12		Samoa	−11	
Ebon Atoll	−12		Samoa, American	−11	
Mauritania	0		*San Marino	+1	
Mauritius	+4		São Tomé and Princípe	0	
*Mexico	−6		Saudi Arabia	+3	
Nayarit, Sinaloa, Sonora,	−7		Senegal	0	
S. Baja California			Seychelles	+4	
N. Baja California	−8		Sierra Leone	0	
Micronesia			Singapore	+8	
Caroline Islands	+10		*Slovakia	+1	
Kosrae	+11		*Slovenia	+1	
Pingelap	+11		Solomon Islands	+11	
Pohnpei	+11		Somalia	+3	
*Moldova	+2		South Africa	+2	
*Monaco	+1		South Georgia	−2	
*Mongolia	+8		*Spain	+1	
Montserrat	−4		*Canary Islands	0	
Morocco	0		Sri Lanka	+6	
Mozambique	+2		Sudan	+2	
Myanmar	+6	30	Suriname	−3	
*Namibia	+1		Swaziland	+2	
Nauru	+12		*Sweden	+1	
Nepal	+5	45	*Switzerland	+1	
*Netherlands	+1		*Syria	+2	
Netherlands Antilles	−4		Taiwan	+8	
New Caledonia	+11		Tajikistan	+5	
*New Zealand	+12		Tanzania	+3	
Nicaragua	−6		Thailand	+7	
Niger	+1		Togo	0	
Nigeria	+1		Tonga	+13	
Niue	−11		Trinidad and Tobago	−4	
Norfolk Island	+11	30	Tristan da Cunha	0	
Northern Mariana Islands	+10		Tunisia	+1	
*Norway	+1		*Turkey	+2	
Oman	+4		Turkmenistan	+5	
Pakistan	+5		*Turks and Caicos Islands	−5	
Palau	+9		Tuvalu	+12	
Panama	−5		Uganda	+3	
Papua New Guinea	+10		*Ukraine	+2	
*Paraguay	−4		United Arab Emirates	+4	
Peru	−5		*United Kingdom	0	
Philippines	+8		*United States of America		
*Poland	+1		Alaska	−9	
*Portugal	0		Aleutian Islands,	−9	
*Azores	−1		east of 169° 30′W.		
Puerto Rico	−4		Aleutian Islands,	−10	
Qatar	+3		west of 169° 30′W.		
Réunion	+4		eastern time	−5	
*Romania	+2		central time	−6	
*Russia			Hawaii	−10	
Zone 1	+2		mountain time	−7	
Zone 2	+3		Pacific time	−8	
Zone 3	+4		Uruguay	−3	
Zone 4	+5		Uzbekistan	+5	
Zone 5	+6		Vanuatu	+11	
Zone 6	+7		*Vatican City State	+1	
Zone 7	+8		Venezuela	−4	
Zone 8	+9		Vietnam	+7	
Zone 9	+10		Virgin Islands (US)	−4	
Zone 10	+11		Yemen	+3	
Zone 11	+12		*Yugoslavia (Fed. Rep. of)	+1	
Rwanda	+2		Zambia	+2	
St Helena	0		Zimbabwe	+2	
St Christopher and Nevis	−4				
St Lucia	−4				
*St Pierre and Miquelon	−3				

Source: reproduced with permission from data produced by HM Nautical Almanac Office

THE ANTARCTIC

The Antarctic is generally defined as the area lying within the Antarctic Convergence, the zone where cold north-ward-flowing Antarctic sea water sinks below warmer southward-flowing water. This zone is at about latitude 50° S. in the Atlantic Ocean and latitude 55°–62° S. in the Pacific Ocean. The continent itself lies almost entirely within the Antarctic Circle, an area of about 13.66 million sq. km (5.3 million sq. miles), 99.67 per cent of which is permanently ice-covered. The average thickness of the ice is 2,450 m (7,100 ft) but in places exceeds 4,500 m (14,500 ft). Some mountains protrude, the highest being Vinson Massif, 4,897 m (16,067 ft). The ice amounts to some 30 million cubic km (7.2 million cubic miles) and represents more than 90 per cent of the world's fresh water. Much of the sea freezes in winter, forming fast ice which breaks up in summer and drifts north as pack ice.

The most conspicuous physical features of the continent are its high inland plateau (much of it over 3,000 m (10,000 ft)), the Transantarctic Mountains and the mountainous Antarctic Peninsula and off-lying islands which extend northwards towards South America.

CLIMATE

On land, summer temperatures range from just above freezing around the coast to −34°C (about −30°F) on the plateau, and in winter from −20°C (about −4°F) on the coast to −65°C (about −85°F) inland. Over a large area the maxima do not exceed −15°C (+5°F).

Precipitation is scant over the plateau but amounts to 25–76 cm (10–30 in) (water equivalent) along the coast and some scientific stations are permanently buried by snow. Some rain falls over the more northerly areas in summer. Gravity winds on the plateau slopes and cyclonic storms further north can both exceed 160 km/h (100 m.p.h.) and visibility can be reduced to zero in blizzards.

FLORA AND FAUNA

Although a small number of flowering plants, ferns and clubmosses occur on the sub-Antarctic islands, only two (a grass and a pearlwort) extend south of 60° S. Antarctic vegetation is dominated by lichens and mosses, with a few liverworts, algae and fungi. Most of these occur around the coast or on islands.

The only land animals are tiny insects and mites with nematodes, rotifers, and tardigrades in the mosses, but large numbers of seals, penguins and other sea-birds go ashore to breed in the summer. The emperor penguin is the only species which breeds ashore throughout the winter. By contrast, the Antarctic seas abound with life, a wide variety of invertebrates (including krill) and fish providing food for the seals, penguins and other birds, and a residual population of whales.

In 1994 the International Whaling Commission agreed to establish a whale sanctuary around Antarctica in which commercial whaling will be banned for ten years.

POTENTIAL RESOURCES

Minerals may be present in great variety but not in commercially exploitable concentrations in accessible localities. There are indications that off-shore hydrocarbons may be present but mostly below great depths of stormy, ice-infested seas. A 50-year ban on Antarctic mineral exploitation came into effect in January 1998 (see below).

Currently, the chief interest is in marine protein, including the shrimp-like krill already fished commercially by Japan and Poland. It is estimated that these could sustain a yield equal to the present total annual world fish catch.

THE ANTARCTIC TREATY

The co-operative 12 nations (Argentina, Australia, Belgium, Chile, France, Japan, New Zealand, Norway, South Africa, the Soviet Union, the UK and the USA) pledged themselves to promote scientific and technical co-operation unhampered by politics, and the Antarctic Treaty was signed by the 12 states in 1959. The signatories agreed to establish free use of the Antarctic continent for peaceful scientific purposes; to freeze all territorial claims and disputes in the Antarctic; to ban all military activities in the area; and to prohibit nuclear explosions and the disposal of radioactive waste. Since then additional agreements have been reached to promote conservation and regulate tourism, waste disposal and pollution.

The Antarctic Treaty was defined as covering areas south of latitude 60°S., excluding the high seas but including the ice shelves, and came into force in 1961. It has since been signed by a further 31 states, 14 of which are active in the Antarctic and have therefore been accorded consultative status, bringing the number of consultative parties to 26. In 1998 an extension to the treaty came into effect, placing a 50-year ban on mining, oil exploration and mineral extraction in Antarctica. Furthermore, all tourists, explorers and expeditions will now need permission to enter the Antarctic.

TERRITORIAL CLAIMS

Under the provisions of the Antarctic Treaty all territorial claims and disputes were frozen without the acceptance or denial of the claims of the various claimants. The US and Soviet governments also made it clear that although they had not made any specific territorial claims, they did not relinquish the right to make such claims.

Seven states have made claims in the Antarctic: Argentina claims the part of Antarctica between 74°W. and 25°W.; Chile that part between 90°W. and 53°W.; Britain claims the British Antarctic Territory, an area of 1,709,340 sq. km (660,000 sq. miles) between 20° and 80°W. longitude; France claims Terre Adélie, 432,000 sq. km (166,800 sq. miles) between 136° and 142°E.; Australia claims the Australian Antarctic Territory, 6,120,000 sq. km (2,330,000 sq. miles) between 160° and 45°E. longitude excluding Terre Adélie; Norway claims Queen Maud Land between 20°W. and 45°E.; and New Zealand claims the Ross Dependency, 450,000 sq. km (175,000 sq. miles) between 160°E. and 150°W. longitude. The Argentinian, British and Chilean claims overlap; the part of the continent between 90°W. and 150°W. is unclaimed by any state.

SCIENTIFIC RESEARCH

There were 36 permanently occupied stations in 1999–2000 operated by the following nations: Argentina (6), Australia (3), Brazil (1), Chile (3), China (2), France (1), Germany (1), India (1), Japan (2), New Zealand (1), Poland (1), Russia (4), South Africa (1), South Korea (1), UK (2), Ukraine (1), Uruguay (2), USA (3, including one at the South Pole).

The staff of these stations and summer field-workers are the only people present on the continent and off-lying islands. There are no indigenous inhabitants.

Countries of the World: A–Z

AFGHANISTAN
*Dι Afğānistān Islāmī Dawlat (Pushtu)/
Dowlat-e Eslamî-ye Afqânestân (Dari) –
The Islamic Republic of Afghanistan*

AREA – 251,773 sq. miles (652,090 sq. km). Neighbours: Iran (west), Pakistan (south), Tajikistan, Uzbekistan and Turkmenistan (north), Pakistan and China (east)
POPULATION – 22,132,000 (1997 UN estimate): Pushtuns (38 per cent) predominate in the south and west; Tajiks (25 per cent); Hazaras (19 per cent) in the centre; Uzbeks (6 per cent) in the north; Aimaqs (4 per cent); Baluchis (0.5 per cent). The principal languages are Dari (a form of Persian) and Pushtu
CAPITAL – Kābol (Kabul) (population, 1,424,400, 1988)
MAJOR CITIES – Herāt (177,300); Jalālābād (55,000); Qandahār (225,500); Mazār-i-Sharīf (130,600) (1988 UN estimates)
CURRENCY – Afghani (Af) of 100 puls
NATIONAL ANTHEM – Sorūd-e-Melli
NATIONAL DAY – 19 August
NATIONAL FLAG – Three horizontal stripes of green, white, black with the national arms in the centre in gold
LIFE EXPECTANCY (years) – male 43.00; female 44.00
POPULATION DENSITY – 34 per sq. km (1997)

Mountains, chief among which are the Hindu Kush, cover three-quarters of the country. There are three great river basins, the Oxus, Helmand, and Kābol. The climate is dry, with extreme temperatures.

HISTORY AND POLITICS

In December 1979 Soviet troops invaded Afghanistan and installed Babrak Karmal as head of state. Armed Islamic resistance groups, the Mujahidin, fought against Soviet and Afghan forces until the withdrawal of Soviet troops in 1988. Mujahidin opposition to the Homeland Party government continued until the government collapsed in April 1992. Mujahidin forces overran Kabul bringing an end to the war, and declared an Islamic state.

The new government appointed Burhanuddin Rabbani as interim President, but infighting between factions of the Mujahidin resumed in December 1992. A cease-fire and power sharing agreement between them collapsed in October 1993. In the winter of 1994–5, divided Mujahidin forces suffered heavy defeats at the hands of the Taliban (armed Islamic students), which extended its power across half of the country. In March 1996, the Mujahidin agreed to combine their forces against the Taliban but failed to prevent the Taliban from seizing Kābol in September 1996. The forces of the former government were forced northwards. The United Islamic Front for the Salvation of Afghanistan (UIFSA) or Northern Alliance was formed by the four main Mujahidin factions which together controlled one-third of Afghanistan. The Taliban, thought to be backed by Pakistan and Saudi Arabia, imposed strict Sharia law.

Peace talks between the Taliban and UIFSA resumed in March 1999, but soon collapsed; a further round was conducted in May 2000. Fighting continues throughout the country.

The United Nations imposed limited sanctions on Afghanistan on 14 November 1999 for refusing to hand over Osama bin Laden, an Islamic terrorist, to US authorities.

POLITICAL SYSTEM
There are 29 provinces, 20 of which are under Taliban control and governed through an interim council (*shura*).

EMBASSY OF THE ISLAMIC STATE OF AFGHANISTAN
31 Prince's Gate, London SW7 1QQ
Tel: 020-7589 8891
Ambassador Extraordinary and Plenipotentiary,
  new appointment awaited
Minister-Counsellor and Chargé d'Affaires,
  Ahmad Wali Masud

BRITISH EMBASSY
Karte Parwan, Kābol
Staff were withdrawn from post in February 1989. Ambassador is now resident in Islamabad.

ECONOMY
The economy has been devastated by the political upheavals of the last 20 years. Traditional industries have diminished as the narcotics trade has grown. Afghanistan is the world's largest producer of opium; in 1999 around 4,600 tonnes of opium were produced, more than twice as much as in the previous year. The Taliban impose a 10 per cent tax on opium sales.

Agriculture and sheep raising were traditionally the principal industries. Silk, woollen and hair cloths and carpets were manufactured. Salt, silver, copper, coal, iron, lead, rubies, lapis lazuli, gold, chrome, barite, uranium, and talc are found.

There are thought to be considerable fuel reserves. US and Saudi Arabian companies have attempted to negotiate with the Taliban and Mujahidin for permission to construct an oil pipeline from Pakistan to Turkmenistan crossing Afghanistan.
GDP – US$1,467 million (1996); US$70 per capita (1996)
ANNUAL AVERAGE GROWTH OF GDP – 6.0 per cent (1996)
INFLATION RATE – 56.7 per cent (1991); estimated to be 400 per cent in 1996

TRADE
Trade is now largely limited to narcotics, but in the past exports have been Persian lambskins (Karakul), dried fruits, nuts, cotton, raw wool, carpets, spice and natural gas, while the imports are chiefly oil, cotton yarn and piece goods, tea, sugar, machinery and transport equipment.

In 1995 imports totalled US$50 million and exports US$26 million.

Trade with UK	1998	1999
Imports from UK	£10,565,000	£3,624,000
Exports to UK	2,535,000	1,769,000

COMMUNICATIONS
Main roads run from Kābol to Qandahār, Herāt, Maimana via Mazār-i-Sharīf and Faizabad via Khanabad. Roads cross the border with Pakistan at Chaman and via the Khyber Pass, and there are roads from Herāt to the borders of Central Asia and Iran. Much of the country's road system has been damaged during the fighting.

In 1982 the Afghan and Uzbek shores of the River Oxus were linked by a road and rail bridge which joins the Afghan port of Hairatan and the Uzbek port of Termez.

EDUCATION

Education is free and nominally compulsory, elementary schools having been established in most centres; there are secondary schools in large urban areas and four universities, in Kābol (established 1932), Jalālābād (established 1962), Balkh and Herāt (both established 1988). Kābol's 26 newspapers were closed by the Taliban and women were prohibited from teaching or studying at schools and universities; in late 1999, the Taliban allowed schooling for girls under the age of 12.

ILLITERACY RATE – 63.7 per cent
ENROLMENT (percentage of age group) – primary 29 per cent (1993); secondary 14 per cent (1993); tertiary 1.8 per cent (1990)

ALBANIA
Republika e Shqipërisë

AREA – 11,099 sq. miles (28,748 sq. km). Neighbours: Montenegro (north), Serbia and Macedonia (east), Greece (south)
POPULATION – 3,731,000 (1997 UN estimate). Muslim (70 per cent), Greek Orthodox (20 per cent), Roman Catholic (10 per cent). The language is Albanian
CAPITAL – Tirana (population, 244,153, 1990)
CURRENCY – Lek (Lk) of 100 qindarka
NATIONAL ANTHEM – Rreth flamurit të për bashkuar (The flag that united us in the struggle)
NATIONAL DAY – 28 November
NATIONAL FLAG – Black two-headed eagle on a red field
LIFE EXPECTANCY (years) – male 69.60; female 75.50
POPULATION GROWTH RATE – 1.9 per cent (1997)
POPULATION DENSITY – 130 per sq. km (1997)
URBAN POPULATION – 36.7 per cent (1991)
ENROLMENT (percentage of age group) – primary 100 per cent (1995); tertiary 12 per cent (1996)

HISTORY AND POLITICS

Albania was under Turkish suzerainty from 1468 until 1912, when independence was declared. After a period of unrest, a republic was declared in 1925, and in 1928 a monarchy. The King went into exile in 1939 when the country was occupied by the Italians; Albania was liberated in November 1944. Elections in 1945 resulted in a Communist-controlled Assembly; the King was deposed in absentia and a republic declared in January 1946.

From 1946 to 1991 Albania was a one-party, Communist state. In March 1991 multiparty elections took place. Rioting broke out in January 1997 following the collapse of several pyramid investment schemes. Anti-government protests, taking the form of armed rebellion, spread throughout the country. A state of emergency was declared in March, and an interim government held power until elections could take place. Legislative elections were held in June 1997 and were won by a Socialist-led coalition. President Berisha resigned following the announcement of the result and was replaced by Rexhep Mejdani.

Following the abandonment of the Rambouillet peace talks on the future of Kosovo, NATO commenced air operations against Yugoslavia in March 1999. Yugoslavia responded by actively expelling hundreds of thousands of Kosovar Albanians, with the majority fleeing to Albania. In April 1999, Albania granted NATO unrestricted access to Albania's airspace, ports and military infrastructure. There were several incursions into Albanian territory by Serb troops who captured some border villages and set fire to homes before withdrawing. By mid-May 1999, over 400,000 Kosovar Albanians had taken refuge in Albania and over 10,000 NATO troops were stationed there.

In June 1999 the refugees began returning home following the end of air operations and the entry of NATO forces into Kosovo. By the end of 1999, nearly all of the refugees had left Albania and the number of NATO troops stationed in the country had fallen to 2,000.

HEAD OF STATE
President, Prof. Rexhep Mejdani, elected by parliament 24 July 1997

COUNCIL OF MINISTERS as at September 2000
Prime Minister, Ilir Meta (SP)
Deputy PM, Labour and Social Affairs, Makbule Ceco
Agriculture and Food, Lufter Xhuveli (AP)
Culture, Youth and Sport, Edi Rama
Defence, Ilir Gjoni (SP)
Economic Co-operation and Trade, Ermelinda Meksi (SP)
Education and Science, Et' hem Ruka (SP)
Finance, Anastas Angjeli (SP)
Foreign Affairs, Paskal Milo (SDP)
Health, Leonard Solis (HRUP)
Justice, Arben Imami
Local Government, Bashkim Fino
Minister of State to the Prime Minister, Ndre Legisi
Public Economy and Privatization, Mustafa Muci
Public Order, Spartak Poci (SP)
Public Works, Ilir Zela
Transport, Sokol Nako (Ind.)

AP Agrarian Party; HRUP Human Rights Union Party; SP Socialist Party; SDP Social Democratic Party; Ind. Independent

EMBASSY OF THE REPUBLIC OF ALBANIA
4th Floor, 38 Grosvenor Gardens, London SW1W 0EB
Tel: 020-7730 5709
Ambassador Extraordinary and Plenipotentiary, HE Agim Besim Fagu, apptd 1997

BRITISH EMBASSY
Rruga Skenderbeg 12, Tirana
Tel: (00 355) (42) 34973/4/5
Ambassador Extraordinary and Plenipotentiary, HE Dr Peter January, apptd 1999
BRITISH COUNCIL REPRESENTATIVE, E. Berisha, c/o The British Embassy; e-mail: evis@icc.al.eu.org

DEFENCE

The Army has 859 main battle tanks, 103 armoured personnel carriers and 823 artillery pieces. The Navy has 21 patrol and coastal combatant vessels at four bases. The Air Force has 98 combat aircraft.
MILITARY EXPENDITURE – 6.6 per cent of GDP (1998)
MILITARY PERSONNEL – Armed Forces yet to be reconstituted following civil unrest

ECONOMY

Much of the country is mountainous and nearly a half is covered by forest. The main crops are wheat, maize, sugar beet, potatoes and fruit. There are large chromium deposits. The principal industries are agricultural product processing, textiles, oil products and cement.

Since April 1992, the government has imposed austerity measures in an attempt to reduce the budget deficit and to cut inflation. Up to US$1,200 million worth of personal savings were lost in the collapse of several fraudulent pyramid savings schemes in January 1997, and the value of the lek fell heavily.

Remittances from 500,000 overseas workers remain an important source of revenue. Albania has received US$1 billion in aid from Western donors and was pro-

mised £2,800 million in food and medical aid by the EU in March 1997. An international donors' conference in October 1997 approved a US$600 million aid package dependent on the closure of all remaining pyramid schemes, and in November 1997, the IMF approved credit of approximately US$12 million.
GNP – US$2,718 million (1998); US$810 per capita (1998)
GDP – US$1,667 million (1996); US$490 per capita (1996)
ANNUAL AVERAGE GROWTH OF GDP – 9.1 per cent (1996)
INFLATION RATE – 20.6 per cent (1998)
UNEMPLOYMENT – 9.1 per cent (1991)
TOTAL EXTERNAL DEBT – US$821 million (1998)

TRADE

Exports include crude oil, minerals (bitumen, chrome, nickel, copper), tobacco, fruit and vegetables. In 1996 imports totalled US$842 million and exports US$207 million. In 1998 Albania had a trade deficit of US$604 million and a current account deficit of US$65 million.

Trade with UK	1998	1999
Imports from UK	£7,176,000	£12,062,000
Exports to UK	529,000	793,000

ALGERIA
Al-Jumhūriyya al-Jazā'iriyya ad-Dimuqratiyya ash-Sha'biyya

AREA – 919,595 sq. miles (2,381,741 sq. km). Neighbours: Morocco and Western Sahara (west), Mauritania and Mali (south-west), Niger (south-east), Libya and Tunisia (east)
POPULATION – 29,050,000 (1997 UN estimate); 22,971,558 (1987 census). Arabic is the official language although French and Berber are also spoken. The state religion is Sunni Islam
CAPITAL – ΨAlgiers (El Djazaïr) (population, 1,507,241, 1987). It is one of the principal ports of the Mediterranean
MAJOR CITIES – ΨAnnaba; ΨBejaia; Blida (El Boulaida); Constantine (Qacentina); ΨMestaghanem; ΨOran (Wahran); Setif; Sidi-Bel-Abbès; ΨSkikda; Tizi Ouzou; Tilimsen
CURRENCY – Algerian dinar (DA) of 100 centimes
NATIONAL ANTHEM – Qassaman bin nazilat il-mahiqat (We swear by the lightning that destroys)
NATIONAL DAY – 1 November
NATIONAL FLAG – Divided vertically green and white with a red crescent and star over all in the centre
LIFE EXPECTANCY (years) – male 65.75; female 66.34
POPULATION GROWTH RATE – 2.1 per cent (1997)
POPULATION DENSITY – 12 per sq. km (1997)
ILLITERACY RATE – 36.7 per cent
ENROLMENT (percentage of age group) – primary 94 per cent (1996); secondary 56 per cent (1996); tertiary 12 per cent (1995)

HISTORY AND POLITICS

Algeria was annexed to France in 1842, with the departments of Algiers, Oran and Constantine forming an integral part of France. Algeria gained its independence in July 1962 following an eight-year armed liberation struggle by the Front de Libération Nationale (FLN). Ben Bella was elected president in 1963, but was deposed in 1965 by Col. Houari Boumediène, who was formally elected president in 1976. Boumediène died in 1978 and was succeeded by Chadli Bendjedid.
A new constitution agreed by referendum in 1988

moved Algeria towards pluralism. However, the 1991 legislative elections were abandoned in anticipation of the success of the opposition Islamic Salvation Front (FIS), which had campaigned on a radical 'Islamist' platform. President Bendjedid resigned and a Higher Committee of State (HCS), headed by former FLN veteran Mohammed Boudiaf, took power.
A national reconciliation conference in January 1994 was boycotted by the FIS but nevertheless it appointed Gen. Liamine Zeroual as president to replace the HCS, which disbanded itself. Zeroual was elected president for a five-year term in November 1995, but announced his intention to stand down from office in September 1998. Abdelaziz Bouteflika was elected president on 15 April 1999. The other candidates decided to boycott the election some days before it took place, saying that the military had intervened to rig the vote in his favour.
Multiparty elections on 5 June 1997 were won by a newly-formed pro-Zeroual party, National Democratic Rally (RND), which captured 155 seats. Hamas (Movement for a Society of Peace) (MSP) won 69 seats; the FLN 64 seats; Annahda (Renaissance Movement) 34; Rally for Culture and Democracy 19; Socialist Forces Front 19. Elections to the National Council (the upper house) took place in December 1997 and were dominated by RND, which won 80 of the 96 elected seats.

INSURGENCY

Since the abortive elections in 1992, the FIS-backed Islamic Salvation Army (AIS) and the more extreme Armed Islamic Group (GIA) have waged an armed campaign against the military regime in favour of an Islamic state. The two groups have targeted the military and security forces, their secular supporters in the population, and foreign expatriates, resulting in up to 100,000 deaths since 1992. The FAIS announced in June 1999 that it was renouncing the armed struggle following negotiations with the government; the resulting peace plan was approved by 98 per cent of the electorate in a referendum which was held on 16 September 1999. On 5 January 2000, the AIS announced that it had agreed to disband.

POLITICAL SYSTEM

The legislature is bicameral. The National Assembly (the lower chamber) has 380 members, directly elected for a five-year term. The *Majlis el-Umma* (Council of the Nation) is the upper chamber, with a third of its 144 members appointed by the president; two-thirds are indirectly elected for six-year terms, of which half are re-elected every three years.

HEAD OF STATE

President, Abdelaziz Bouteflika, *elected* April 1999

COUNCIL OF MINISTERS *as at September 2000*
Head of Government, Ali Benflis
Agriculture, Said Berkat
Budget, Ali Brahiti (RND)
Commerce, Mourad Medlci
Communications and Culture, Mohieddine Amimour
Defence, The President
Energy and Mines, Chakib Khelil
Finance, Abedellatif Benachenhou
Fisheries and Marine Resources, Omar Ghoul
Foreign Affairs, Abdelaziz Belkhadem
Health, Mohamed Moumene
Higher Education and Scientific Research, Ammar Sakhri
Housing, Abdelkader Bounekraf (FLN)
Industry and Restrucuturing, Abdelmajid Menasra (MSP)
Interior, Local Authorities, Noureddine Zerhouni
Justice, Ahmed Ouyahia
Labour and Social Protection, Soltani Bouguerra (MSP)
National Community Abroad and Regional Co-operation,
    Abdelaziz Ziari
National Education, Boubakeur Benbouzid (RND)
National Solidarity, Djamel ould Abbes
Participation and Co-ordination of Reforms, Hamid Temmar
Post and Telecommunications, Mohamed Maghlaoui
Prime Minister's Office, Youcef Yousfi (RND)
Public Works, Amara Benyounes
Relations with Parliament, Abdelwahab Derbal
Religious Affairs and Endowments, Bouabdellah Ghlamallah
    (RND)
Secretary-General, Ahmed Noui (RND)
Small and Medium-sized Enterprises, Noureddine
    Boukrouh
Tourism and Traditional Industries, Lakhdar Dorbani
    (MSP)
Transport, Hamid Lounaouci
Urban Planning and Environment, Cherif Rahmani
Vocational Training, Karim Younes (FLN)
War Veterans, Mohamed Cherif Abbes
Water Resources, Salim Saadi
Youth and Sports, Abdelmalek Sellal (RND)

ALGERIAN EMBASSY

54 Holland Park, London W11 3RS
Tel: 020-7221 7800
Ambassador Extraordinary and Plenipotentiary,
    HE Ahmed Benyamina, apptd 1996

BRITISH EMBASSY

7 Chemin des Glycines,
BP 08, Alger-Gare 16000, Algiers
Tel: (00 213) (2) 230092
Ambassador Extraordinary and Plenipotentiary,
    HE William Sinton, OBE, apptd 1999
BRITISH COUNCIL, c/o The British Embassy;
e-mail: Hafida.Gabouze@algiers.mail.fco.gov.uk

DEFENCE

The Army has 951 main battle tanks, 680 armoured
personnel carriers and 416 artillery pieces. The Navy has
two submarines, three frigates and 19 patrol and coastal
vessels. The Air Force has 181 combat aircraft and 65
armed helicopters.
MILITARY EXPENDITURE – 4.8 per cent of GDP (1998)
MILITARY PERSONNEL – 303,200: Army 105,000,
    Navy 7,000, Air Force 10,000; Paramilitaries 181,200
CONSCRIPTION DURATION – 18 months

ECONOMY

The main industry is the hydrocarbons industry. Oil and
natural gas are pumped from the Sahara to terminals on
the coast before being exported; the gas is first liquefied at
liquefaction plants at Skikda and Arzew, although
pipelines serve Libya and Italy direct. In November
1996 a 750-mile gas pipeline to Spain was opened,
enabling Algeria to double its gas exports to Morocco,
Spain, Germany and France. Its initial annual capacity of
8,000 million cubic metres was projected to rise to 20,000
million cubic metres a year by 2000.
    Other major industries include a steel industry, motor
vehicles, building materials, paper making, chemical
products and metal manufactures. Most major industrial
enterprises are still under state control.
    Prior to 1989 the economy was centrally planned and
state-controlled in most sectors. Economic reform, begun
in 1987, was speeded up in 1988 and now includes
industrial and financial sectors. In 1994 the government
finally accepted full economic reform and liberalisation
under a reform programme agreed with the IMF. The
government has cut the budget deficit, devalued the
currency and freed price controls. The first stock exchange
in Algiers opened on 15 December 1997.
GNP – US$46,389 million (1998); US$1,550 per capita
    (1998)
GDP – US$44,167 million (1996); US$1,534 per capita
    (1996)
ANNUAL AVERAGE GROWTH OF GDP – 4.0 per cent (1996)
INFLATION RATE – 3.8 per cent (1997)
UNEMPLOYMENT – 28.7 per cent (1997)
TOTAL EXTERNAL DEBT – US$30,665 MILLION (1998)

TRADE

Export earnings come mainly from crude oil and liquefied
natural gas sales. Algeria's main trading partners are
France, Italy, USA, Spain and Germany.
    In 1991 Algeria had a trade surplus of US$5,468 million
and a current account surplus of US$2,367 million. In
1996 imports totalled US$8,327 million and exports
US$12,620 million.

Trade with UK	1998	1999
Imports from UK	£112,731,000	£110,780,000
Exports to UK	82,128,000	162,388,000

ANDORRA

Principat d'Andorra

AREA – 175 sq. miles (453 sq. km). Neighbours: Spain
    and France
POPULATION – 65,877 (1998); less than one-quarter of
    the population are native Andorrans. The official
    language is Catalan, but French and Spanish (Castilian)
    are also spoken. The established religion is Roman
    Catholicism
CAPITAL – Andorra la Vella (population, 21,721, 1996)
CURRENCY – French and Spanish currencies in use
NATIONAL ANTHEM – El gran Carlemany, mon pare
    (Great Charlemagne, my father)
NATIONAL DAY – 8 September
NATIONAL FLAG – Three vertical bands, blue, yellow, red;
    Andorran coat of arms frequently imposed on central
    (yellow) band but not essential
POPULATION GROWTH RATE – 4.9 per cent (1997)
POPULATION DENSITY – 158 per sq. km (1997)
URBAN POPULATION – 95.6 per cent (1991)

HISTORY AND POLITICS

Andorra is a small, neutral principality formed by a treaty in 1278. The first elections under the new constitution were held in December 1993, and on 20 January 1994 the first sovereign government of Andorra took office.

POLITICAL SYSTEM

Under a new constitution promulgated in May 1993, Andorra became an independent, democratic parliamentary co-principality, with sovereignty vested in the people rather than in the two co-princes, as had previously been the case. The constitution enables Andorra to establish an independent judiciary and to carry out its own foreign policy, whilst its people may now join trade unions and political parties. The two co-princes, the President of the French Republic and the Spanish Bishop of Urgel, remain heads of state but now only have the power to veto treaties with France and Spain which affect the state's borders and security. The co-princes are represented by Permanent Delegates of whom one is the French Prefect of the Pyrénées Orientales department at Perpignan and the other is the Spanish Vicar-General of the diocese of Urgel.

Andorra has a unicameral legislature of 28 members known as the *Consell General de las Valls d'Andorra* (Valleys of Andorra General Council). Fourteen members are elected on a national list basis and 14 in seven dual-member constituencies based on Andorra's seven parishes. The Council appoints the head of the executive government, who designates the members of his government.

Permanent French Delegate, Pierre Steinmetz
Permanent Episcopal Delegate, Nemesi Marqués Oste

EXECUTIVE GOVERNMENT *as at September 2000*
Prime Minister, Marc Forné Molné
Agriculture and the Environment, Olga Adellach Coma
Economy, Enric Casadevall Medrano
Education, Youth and Sports, Pere Cervos Cardona
Finance, Susagna Arasanz Serra
Foreign Affairs, Albert Pintat Santolària
Health and Social Security, Josep Maria Goicoechea Utrillo
Home Affairs, Estanislau Sangrà Cardona
Secretary-General, Joaquima Sol Ordis
Territorial Planning, Candid Naudi Mora
Tourism and Culture, Enric Pujal Areny

ANDORRAN DELEGATION, 63 Westover Road, London SW18 2RF. Tel: 020-8874 4806
BRITISH AMBASSADOR – HE Peter Torry, resident at Madrid

ECONOMY

Potatoes are produced in the highlands and tobacco in the valleys. The economy is largely based on tourism, banking, commerce, tobacco, construction and forestry; a third of the country is classified as forest. Andorra has negotiated a customs union with the European Union which came into force in 1991. The economy is now diversifying rapidly into offshore financial services.
GDP – US$1,040 million (1996); US$14,641 per capita (1996)
ANNUAL AVERAGE GROWTH OF GDP – 2.3 per cent (1996)

Trade with UK	1998	1999
Imports from UK	£15,488,000	£10,966,000
Exports to UK	33,000	340,000

COMMUNICATIONS

A road into the valleys from Spain is open all year round, and that from France is closed only occasionally in winter.

There are two radio stations in Andorra, one privately owned and Radio Andorra, operated by the government, as well as a state-owned television station.

ANGOLA
República de Angola

AREA – 481,354 sq. miles (1,246,700 sq. km). Neighbours: Democratic Republic of Congo (north and east), Zambia (east), Namibia (south). The enclave of Cabinda is separated from the rest of Angola by the Democratic Republic of Congo and also borders on the Republic of Congo–Brazzaville
POPULATION – 11,569,000 (1997 UN estimate). Main ethnic groups are Ovimbundu (37 per cent); Kimbundu (25 per cent); Bakongo (13 per cent). The official language is Portuguese
CAPITAL – ΨLuanda (population, 475,328, 1970; now estimated at 3,000,000)
CURRENCY – Readjusted kwanza (Kzrl) of 100 lwei
NATIONAL ANTHEM – Angola Avante (Advance Angola)
NATIONAL DAY – 11 November (Independence Day)
NATIONAL FLAG – Red and black with a yellow star, machete and cog-wheel
LIFE EXPECTANCY (years) – male 44.90; female 48.10
POPULATION GROWTH RATE – 2.1 per cent (1997)
POPULATION DENSITY – 9 per sq. km (1997)
ENROLMENT (percentage of age group) – tertiary 0.7 per cent (1991)

HISTORY AND POLITICS

After a Portuguese presence of five centuries, and an anti-colonial war since 1961, Angola became independent on 11 November 1975 in the midst of civil war. The Popular Movement for the Liberation of Angola (MPLA) took control early in 1976, but remained under pressure from the National Union for the Total Independence of Angola (UNITA). Following a 1988 cease-fire, a peace agreement was signed between the government and UNITA in 1991 and foreign forces withdrew; multiparty legislative and presidential elections took place in 1992, and were won by the MPLA and its leader, José Eduardo dos Santos. UNITA refused to accept the results and the civil war resumed in 1993.

UNITA and the MPLA government signed a peace agreement (the Lusaka Protocol) under UN mediation in November 1994. A government of national reconciliation was formed in April 1997 and 70 UNITA legislators took up their seats in parliament, although UNITA's leader, Dr Jonas Savimbi, rejected an offer of the vice-presidency and refused to enter Luanda. UNITA also refused to allow central state administration to be restored in key areas, and following the fall from power of Zaïre's President Mobutu (one of UNITA's key supporters), fighting resumed in May 1997.

On 31 October 1997 the UN Security Council ordered sanctions against UNITA for failing to meet its obligations under the Lusaka Protocol. UNITA returned much of its territory to government control in December, and in March UNITA became a legitimate political party. Three of its representatives were appointed governors of provinces of Angola.

Fighting continued and the UN Security Council adopted a resolution in September 1998 which urged the rejection of military force by all parties and named UNITA as 'the primary cause of the crisis in Angola'. In February 1999 the UN Security Council voted to withdraw the UN Observer Mission in Angola, the UN Secretary-General Kofi Annan having declared that the country was on the verge of a catastrophic breakdown and that there was no more peace to keep. In December 1999 Namibia allowed the Angolan government to use its territory and armed forces for a joint operation against the UNITA rebels. The UN Security Council adopted a further resolution on 13 April 2000, which called for an investigation into allegations that several countries had violated sanctions imposed on UNITA.

SECESSION

In the northern enclave of Cabinda, the Front for the Liberation of the Cabinda Enclave (FLEC) fought a 20-year war of independence until the signing of a cease-fire with the government in September 1995, which was followed by the initialling of a peace agreement in April 1996.

POLITICAL SYSTEM

The MPLA, formerly a Marxist-Leninist party, was the sole legal party until early 1991 when a multiparty system was adopted. The constitution declares Angola to be a democratic state and provides for a president, who appoints a Council of Ministers to assist him, and a 220-member National Assembly. In November 1996 the National Assembly adopted a constitutional amendment extending its mandate for between two and four years.

HEAD OF STATE

President, José Eduardo dos Santos, *re-elected* 30 September 1992

COUNCIL OF MINISTERS *as at September 2000*

Prime Minister, vacant
Agriculture and Rural Development, Gilberto Buta Lutuuta (MPLA)
Assistance and Social Reintegration, Albino Malungo (MPLA)
Commerce, Victorino Domingos Hossi (UNITA)
Defence, Gen. Kundi Paihama (MPLA)
Education and Culture, Antonio Burity da Silva Neto (MPLA)
Energy and Water, Luis Felipe da Silva (MPLA)
Ex-Servicemen and War Veterans, Pedro José van Dúnem (MPLA)
Family and Women's Advancement, Cándida Celeste da Silva (MPLA)
Finance, Joaquim Duarte da Costa David (MPLA)
Fisheries and Environment, Maria de Fatima Monteiro Jardim (MPLA)
Foreign Affairs, João Bernardo de Miranda (MPLA)
Geology and Mines, Manuel Antonio Africano (MPLA)
Governor of the National Bank, Aguinaldo Jaime (MPLA)
Health, Albertina Julia Hamukuya (UNITA)
Hotel Industry and Tourism, Jorge Alicerces Valentim (UNITA)
Industry, Albina Faria de Assis (MPLA)
Information, Pedro Hendrick vaal Neto (MPLA)
Interior, Fernando Dias dos Santos da Piedade (MPLA)
Justice, Paulo Tjipilica (FDA)
Oil, José Maria Botelho de Vasconcelos (MPLA)
Planning, Ana Dias Lourenço (MPLA)
Posts and Telecommunications, Licinio Tavares Ribeiro (MPLA)
Public Administration, Employment and Social Welfare, Antonio Pitra Costra Neto (MPLA)
Public Works and Town Planning, António Henriques da Silva (MPLA)
Science and Technology, João Baptista Ngandagina (MPLA)
Territorial Administration, Fernando Faustino Muteka (MPLA)
Transport, André Luis Brandão (MPLA)
Youth and Sports, José Marcos Barrica (MPLA)
FDA Angolan Democratic Forum; MPLA Popular Movement for the Liberation of Angola; UNITA National Union for the Total Independence of Angola

EMBASSY OF THE REPUBLIC OF ANGOLA

98 Park Lane, London W1Y 3TA
Tel: 020-7495 1752
Ambassador Extraordinary and Plenipotentiary, HE Antonio da Costa Fernandes, apptd 1993

BRITISH EMBASSY

Rua Diogo Cão 4 (Caixa Postal 1244), Luanda
Tel: (00 244) (2) 334582
Ambassador Extraordinary and Plenipotentiary, HE Caroline Elmes, apptd 1998

DEFENCE

The Army has 100 main battle tanks, 100 armoured personnel carriers and 300 artillery pieces. The Navy has seven patrol vessels. The Air Force has 85 combat aircraft and 28 armed helicopters.
MILITARY EXPENDITURE – 11.7 per cent of GDP (1998)
MILITARY PERSONNEL – 127,500: Army 100,000, Navy 1,500, Air Force 11,000; Paramilitaries 15,000

ECONOMY

Angola has valuable oil and diamond deposits and exports of these two commodities account for over 90 per cent of total exports. Principal agricultural crops are cassava, maize, bananas, coffee, palm oil and kernels, cotton and sisal. Coffee, sisal, maize and palm oil are exported; exports also include mahogany and other hardwoods from the tropical rain forests in the north of the country.

The government is attempting to reform the socialist economy by free market reforms but is making little progress, with high inflation and a collapsing economy.

The government raised fuel prices by 1,600 per cent in February 2000 in response to IMF demands to remove state subsidies on petroleum products.

In 1996 Angola had a trade surplus of US$3,055 million and a current account surplus of US$3,266 million.
GNP – US$4,578 million (1998); US$380 per capita (1998)
GDP – US$3,280 million (1996); US$293 per capita (1995)
ANNUAL AVERAGE GROWTH OF GDP – 8.6 per cent (1996)
TOTAL EXTERNAL DEBT – US$12,173 million (1998)

Trade with UK	1998	1999
Imports from UK	£41,481,000	£66,353,000
Exports to UK	7,499,000	10,818,000

ANTIGUA AND BARBUDA
State of Antigua and Barbuda

AREA – 171 sq. miles (442 sq. km); Antigua 108 sq. miles (279 sq. km); Barbuda 62 sq.miles (160 sq. km); Redonda $\frac{1}{2}$ sq. mile (1.2 sq. km)
POPULATION – 67,000 (1997 UN estimate); 65,962, Antigua 64,562, Barbuda 1,400 (official census 1991); the official language is English
CAPITAL – ΨSt John's (population, 22,342, 1991)
MAJOR TOWNS – The town of Barbuda is Codrington
CURRENCY – East Caribbean dollar (EC$) of 100 cents
NATIONAL ANTHEM – Fair Antigua and Barbuda
NATIONAL DAY – 1 November (Independence Day)
NATIONAL FLAG – Red with an inverted triangle divided black over blue over white, with a rising gold sun on the white band
POPULATION GROWTH RATE – 0.7 per cent (1997)
POPULATION DENSITY – 152 per sq. km (1997)
MILITARY EXPENDITURE – 0.6 per cent of GDP (1998)
MILITARY PERSONNEL – 150: Army 125, Navy 25

Antigua is part of the Leeward Islands in the eastern Caribbean. It is distinguished from the rest of the Leeward group by its absence of high hills and forest, and a drier climate than most of the West Indies. Barbuda is very flat with a large lagoon.

HISTORY AND POLITICS

Antigua was first settled by the English in 1632, and was granted to Lord Willoughby by Charles II. It became internally self-governing in 1967 and fully independent on 1 November 1981.

The Antigua Labour party won the general election of 9 March 1999 and a sixth successive term of office with 12 seats in the House of Representatives compared to four seats for the United Progressive Party.

POLITICAL SYSTEM

Antigua and Barbuda is a constitutional monarchy with Queen Elizabeth II as Head of State, represented by the Governor-General. There is a Senate of 17 appointed members and a House of Representatives of 17 members elected every five years. The Attorney-General may be appointed.

Governor-General, HE Sir James Carlisle, GCMG

CABINET *as at September 2000*

Prime Minister, Foreign Affairs, Lester Bird
Agriculture, Lands and Fisheries, Vere Bird Jr
Commerce, Industry and Business Development, Hilroy Humphreys
Education, Culture and Technology, Dr Rodney Williams
Finance, John E. St Luce
Health and Social Improvementt, Bernard Percival
Justice, Legal Affairs and Attorney-General, Dr L. Errol Cort
Labour, Home Affairs and Co-operatives, Steadroy Benjamin
Planning, Implementation and Public Service Affairs, Gaston Browne
Public Utilities, Housing, Transportation and Aviation, Robin Yearwood
Tourism and Environment, Molwyn Joseph
Youth Affairs, Sports, Carnivals and Community Development, Guy Yearwood

HIGH COMMISSION FOR ANTIGUA AND BARBUDA
15 Thayer Street, London W1M 5LD
Tel: 020-7486 7073
High Commissioner, HE Ronald Sanders, CMG, apptd 1995

BRITISH HIGH COMMISSION
11 Old Parham Road (PO 483), St John's
Tel: (00 1 268) 462 0008/9
High Commissioner, HE Gordon Baker, resident at Bridgetown, Barbados
Resident Acting High Commissioner, Sandra Murphy

ECONOMY

The economy is largely based on tourism and related services, and offshore financial services. Agricultural production includes livestock, sea island cotton, mixed market gardening and fishing.

In 1996 Antigua and Barbuda had a trade deficit of US$263 million and a current account deficit of US$40 million. Imports totalled US$314 million and exports US$30 million.

GNP – US$565 million (1998); US$8,450 per capita (1998)
GDP – US$560 million (1996); US$8,484 per capita (1996)
ANNUAL AVERAGE GROWTH OF GDP – 6.0 per cent (1996)
INFLATION RATE – 1.0 per cent (1985)

Trade with UK	1998	1999
Imports from UK	£30,572,000	£32,387,000
Exports to UK	1,161,000	1,628,000

ARGENTINA
República Argentina

AREA – 1,073,518 sq. miles (2,780,400 sq. km).
Neighbours: Bolivia (north), Paraguay, Brazil and Uruguay (north-east), Chile (west) from which it is separated by the Cordillera de los Andes
POPULATION – 35,672,000 (1997 UN estimate); 32,370,298 (1991 census). The language is Spanish
CAPITAL – ΨBuenos Aires (population, 11,298,030, 1991); metropolitan area 2,965,403
MAJOR CITIES – Córdoba (1,208,554); ΨLa Plata (642,979); ΨMar del Plata (512,880); Mendoza (773,113); ΨRosario (1,118,905); San Miguel de Tucumán (622,324)
CURRENCY – Peso of 10,000 australes
NATIONAL ANTHEM – ¡Oid Mortales! (Hear, oh mortals!)
NATIONAL DAY – 25 May
NATIONAL FLAG – Horizontal bands of blue, white, blue; gold sun in centre of white band
LIFE EXPECTANCY (years) – male 68.17; female 73.09
POPULATION GROWTH RATE – 1.3 per cent (1997)
POPULATION DENSITY – 13 per sq. km (1997)
URBAN POPULATION – 88.9 per cent (1997)

Argentina occupies the greater portion of the southern part of the South American continent, and extends from Bolivia to Cape Horn.

HISTORY AND POLITICS

The estuary of La Plata was discovered in 1515 by Juan Díaz de Solís and the region was subsequently colonised by the Spanish. Spain ruled the territory from the 16th century until 1810. In 1816, after a long campaign of liberation conducted by General José de San Martín, independence was declared by the Congress of Tucumán.

President Juan Domingo Perón was overthrown in 1955, and there followed 18 years of instability until 1973 when he was recalled from exile. Perón died within a year and was succeeded by his widow, Vice-President María Estela Martínez de Perón. A coup led to the establishment of a military junta in 1976. Following the Falkland Islands defeat in 1982, the President, Gen. Galtieri, resigned and the Army appointed Gen. Bignone. A civilian president was elected in 1983. Presidential elections in 1989 were won by the Justicialist Party (Perónist) candidate Carlos Menem. In the October 1997 elections, the Justicialist Party lost its overall majority and in the October 1999 elections, the Radical Civic Union-National Solidarity Front (UCR-Frepaso) Alliance became the largest party in the Chamber of Deputies and took office on 10 December 1999.

POLITICAL SYSTEM

The 1853 constitution was amended in 1994. Power is vested in the president who appoints the Cabinet and is directly elected for a once-renewable four-year term. A presidential candidate must win at least 45 per cent of the vote, or 40 per cent with a 10 per cent lead over the nearest challenger, to gain victory. The legislature consists of a 72-member (three for each province) Senate and a 257-member Chamber of Deputies. A half of the Chamber of Deputies is elected every two years. Deputies serve for a four-year term. Senators have served for a nine-year term, with a third being elected every three years but the terms of all sitting senators will end in December 2001, after which all members will be directly elected by the provinces for a six-year term, with one-third renewable every two years.

FEDERAL STRUCTURE

The republic is divided into 23 provinces, each with an elected Governor and legislature, and one federal district (Buenos Aires), with an elected mayor and autonomous government.

Province	Area (sq. km)	Population (1991 census)	Capital
Buenos Aires	307,571	12,594,974	La Plata
Catamarca	102,602	264,234	Catamarca
Chaco	99,633	839,677	Resistencia
Chubut	224,686	357,189	Rawson
Córdoba	165,321	2,766,683	Córdoba
Corrientes	88,199	795,594	Corrientes
Entre Ríos	78,781	1,020,257	Paraná
Federal Capital	200	2,965,403	Buenos Aires
Formosa	72,066	398,413	Formosa
Jujuy	53,219	512,329	San Salvador de Jujuy
La Pampa	143,440	259,996	Santa Rosa
La Rioja	89,680	229,729	La Rioja
Mendoza	148,827	1,412,481	Mendoza
Misiones	29,801	788,915	Posadas
Neuquén	94,078	388,833	Neuquén
Rio Negro	203,013	506,772	Viedma
Salta	155,488	866,153	Salta
San Juan	89,651	528,715	San Juan
San Luis	76,748	286,458	San Luis
Santa Cruz	243,943	159,839	Rio Gallegos
Santa Fé	133,007	2,798,422	Santa Fé
Santiago del Estero	136,351	671,988	Santiago del Estero
Tierra del Fuego	21,571	69,369	Ushuaia
Tucumán	22,524	1,142,105	San Miguel de Tucumán

HEAD OF STATE

President, Fernando de la Rúa, *elected* 24 October 1999, *sworn in* 10 December 1999
Vice-President, Carlos Alvárez

CABINET *as at September 2000*

Cabinet Chief, RodolfoTerragno
Defence, Ricardo López Murphy
Economy and Finance, José Luis Machinea
Education, Juan José Llach
Foreign Affairs, International Trade, Culture, Adalberto Rodríguez Giavarini
Infrastructure and Housing, Nicolás Gallo
Interior, Federico Storani
Justice, Ricardo Gil Lavedra
Labour, Alberto Flamarique
Public Health, Héctor Lombardo
Social Affairs, Graciela Fernández Meijide

EMBASSY OF THE ARGENTINE REPUBLIC

65 Brook Street, London W1Y 1YE
Tel: 020-7318 1300
Ambassador Extraordinary and Plenipotentiary, HE Rogelio Pfirter, apptd 1995
Defence Attaché, Gp Capt. Jorge Oscar Ratti
Counsellor (Economic and Commercial Affairs), Gustavo Martino

BRITISH EMBASSY

Dr Luis Agote 2141/52, 1425 Buenos Aires
Tel: (00 54) (11) 4576 2222
Ambassador Extraordinary and Plenipotentiary, HE William Marsden, CMG, apptd 1997
Deputy Head of Mission and Minister, Dominic Asquith
Defence and Air Attaché, Gp Capt. T. Brewer, OBE

Naval and Military Attaché, Col. H. Massey
First Secretary (Commercial), H. Deas
Cultural Attaché and British Council Representative, K. Board, OBE, Marcelo T. de Alvear 590, 1058 Buenos Aires; e-mail: britcoun@britcoun.int.ar

BRITISH CHAMBER OF COMMERCE, Av. Corrientes 457, 10 piso, 1043 Buenos Aires

DEFENCE

The Army has 200 main battle tanks, 826 armoured infantry fighting vehicles and armoured personnel carriers and 38 helicopters. The Navy has three submarines, six destroyers, seven frigates, 14 patrol and coastal vessels, 31 combat aircraft and eight armed helicopters. The Air Force has 125 combat aircraft and 27 armed helicopters.
MILITARY EXPENDITURE – 1.8 per cent of GDP (1998)
MILITARY PERSONNEL – 101,740: Army 40,000, Navy 20,000, Air Force 10,500; Paramilitaries 31,240

ECONOMY

A large proportion of the land is still held in large estates devoted to cattle-raising but the number of small farms is increasing. The principal crops are wheat, maize, oats, barley, rye, linseed, sunflower seed, alfalfa, sugar, fruit and cotton. Argentina is pre-eminent in the production of beef, mutton and wool. There is an oil refinery in San Lorenzo (Santa Fé province). Natural gas is also produced. Coal, lead, zinc, tungsten, iron ore, sulphur, mica and salt are the other chief minerals being exploited. There are small worked deposits of beryllium, manganese, bismuth, uranium, antimony, copper, kaolin, arsenate, gold, silver and tin. Coal is produced at the Rio Turbio mine in the province of Santa Cruz.

Meat-packing is one of the principal industries; flour-milling, sugar-refining, and the wine industry are also important. In recent years progress has been made by the textile, plastic and machine tool industries and engineering, especially in the production of motor vehicles and steel manufactures.

The Menem government introduced an economic reform programme in 1991 involving the privatisation of most state-owned industries, widespread deregulation, exchange-rate stabilisation and lower trade barriers. This led to economic growth, increased foreign investment and much lower inflation.

The de la Rúa government has taken measures to reduce the fiscal deficit to US$4,700 million in 2000 and pledged to eliminate it by 2003.
GNP – US$290,261 million (1998); US$8,030 per capita (1998)
GDP – US$297,460 million (1996); US$8,446 per capita (1996)
ANNUAL AVERAGE GROWTH OF GDP – 4.3 per cent (1996)
INFLATION RATE – 0.9 per cent (1998)
UNEMPLOYMENT – 16.3 per cent (1996)
TOTAL EXTERNAL DEBT – US$144,050 million (1998)

TRADE

The chief imports are machinery, industrial and transport equipment, chemicals, metals and plastics. The chief exports are vegetable products, processed foods, minerals, live animals and oils. Argentina's main trading partners are Brazil and the USA.

In 1998 Argentina had a trade deficit of US$3,223 million and a current account deficit of US$14,730 million. In 1998 imports totalled US$31,402 million and exports US$25,227 million.

Trade with UK	1998	1999
Imports from UK	£469,077,000	£295,880,000
Exports to UK	207,986,000	196,977,000

COMMUNICATIONS

The 25,386 miles of railway are state-owned. The combined national and provincial road network totals approximately 137,000 miles of which 23,180 miles are surfaced.

CULTURE AND EDUCATION

The literature of Spain is part of the culture. There is little indigenous literature before the break from Spain, but all branches have flourished since the latter half of the 19th century. About 450 daily newspapers are published in Argentina, including seven major ones in the city of Buenos Aires. The English language newspaper is the *Buenos Aires Herald* (daily).

Education is compulsory for the seven grades of primary school (six to 13). Secondary schools (14 to 17+) are available in and around Buenos Aires and in most of the important towns in the interior of the country. Most secondary schools are administered by the Central Ministry of Education in Buenos Aires, while primary schools are administered by the Central Ministry or by Provincial Ministries of Education. Private schools, of which there are many, are also loosely controlled by the Central Ministry. The total number of universities is over 50 with 24 national, 25 private and a small number of provincial universities.

ILLITERACY RATE – 3.1 per cent

ENROLMENT (percentage of age group) – primary 95 per cent (1991); secondary 59 per cent (1991); tertiary 41.8 per cent (1996)

ARMENIA
Hayastany Hanrapetoutioun

AREA – 11,506 sq. miles (29,800 sq. km). Neighbours: Azerbaijan (east and south-west), Georgia (north), Iran (south), Turkey (west)

POPULATION – 3,798,400 (1999). Armenians 93.8 per cent, Kurds 1.7 per cent and Russians 1.6 per cent. Azeris formed 2.6 per cent of the population, but most fled or were expelled after the outbreak of war with Azerbaijan. There are also Ukrainians, Greeks and Assyrians. The Armenian diaspora numbers some 5,300,000.

Armenian is the official language, though Russian is widely spoken and understood. The main religion is Armenian Orthodox Christian (Armenian Church centred in Etchmiadzin). Armenia adopted Christianity as its official religion in AD 301, the first state in the world to do so

CAPITAL – Yerevan (population, 1,254,400, 1990)

CURRENCY – Dram of 100 louma

NATIONAL ANTHEM – Mer Hayrenik azat, ankakh (Land of our fathers)

NATIONAL DAY – 21 September (Independence Day)

NATIONAL FLAG – Three horizontal stripes of red, blue and orange

LIFE EXPECTANCY (years) – male 67.88; female 74.36

POPULATION GROWTH RATE – 0.4 per cent (1997)

POPULATION DENSITY – 122 per sq. km (1997)

URBAN POPULATION – 67.6 per cent (1994)

Armenia lies between the Black and Caspian Seas, occupying the south-western part of the Caucasus region of the former Soviet Union. It is very mountainous, consisting of several vast tablelands surrounded by ridges. The climate is continental, dry and cold, but the Ararat valley has a long, hot and dry summer.

HISTORY AND POLITICS

Armenia was first unified in 95 BC but was divided between the Persian and Byzantine Empires in AD 387 and then conquered in the 11th century by the Seljuk Turks and the Mongols. In the 16th century most of Armenia was incorporated into the Ottoman Empire. In 1639 the country was divided again, the easternmost portions, now the republic of Armenia, becoming part of the Persian Empire. In 1828 eastern Armenia became part of the Russian Empire while western Armenia remained under Ottoman rule. The Ottomans launched pogroms against the Armenians from 1894 onwards, and in 1915 to 1918 massacred 1,500,000 Armenians.

Armenia declared its independence on 28 May 1918, but was crushed and divided between Turkish and Soviet forces in 1920, with the area under Soviet control proclaimed a Soviet Socialist Republic on 29 November 1920. The Soviet government was overthrown by a nationalist revolt in 1921 but reinstated by the Red Army a few months later. In early 1922 Armenia acceded to the USSR.

An Armenian nationalist movement swept to power in national elections in mid-1990. In a referendum in 1991, 99 per cent of the electorate voted for independence, which was declared on 21 September 1991.

Prime Minister Vazgen Sarkissian and six other politicians were shot dead in the National Assembly during an attempted coup on 27 October 1999; Aram Sarkissian, the younger brother of Vazgen Sarkissian, was appointed prime minister on 5 November 1999.

FOREIGN RELATIONS

The dispute between the (ethnic Armenian) Nagorno-Karabakh forces supported by Armenia and the Azeri government over Nagorny-Karabakh erupted into all-out war in May 1992, when Nagorno-Karabakh forces breached Azerbaijan's defences to form a land bridge to Armenia. By the end of summer 1992 all of Nagorny-Karabakh was under Armenian control, and by the end of 1993 all Azeri territory that separated Nagorny-Karabakh from Armenia and all mountainous Azeri territory around Nagorny-Karabakh was under the control of Nagorno-Karabakh Armenians. Armenia claims this territory as historically Armenian land arbitrarily given to Azerbaijan by Stalin in 1921–2. A cease-fire agreement between Armenia, Azerbaijan and Nagorny-Karabakh was reached in May 1994, and talks mediated by the OSCE continue to seek a peaceful resolution to the dispute.

In August 1997 Armenia and Russia renewed a Treaty of Friendship, Co-operation and Mutual Assistance in effect since 1991.

POLITICAL SYSTEM

There is a 131-member unicameral National Assembly (*Azgayin Joghov*), directly elected every four years. A new constitution was approved by a referendum in July 1995. Armenia is divided into 11 Administrative Regions.

Since the 1999 election, Unity, an alliance of the Republican Party and the People's Party, has been the dominant grouping in the National Assembly.

HEAD OF STATE

President, Robert Kocharian, *elected* 30 March 1998, *sworn in* 9 April 1998

CABINET *as at September 2000*

Prime Minister, Andranik Markarian
Agriculture and Ecology, Zaven Gevorkyan
Culture, Youth and Sport, Roland Sharoian
Defence, Serge Sarkissian
Ecology, Murad Muradian
Education and Science, Eduard Kazarian
Energy, Karen Galustyan

Finance and Economy, Levon Barkhudarian
Foreign Affairs, Vardan Oskanian
Health, Ararat Mkrtchyan
Internal Affairs, Haik Arutiunian
Justice, David Haroutiounian
National Security, Karlos Petrosian
Post and Communications, Ruben Tonoian
Prime Minister's Chief of Staff, Karine Kirakosian
Privatisation, David Vardanyan
Production Infrastructures, David Zadoyan
Social Security, Razmik Martirosian
State Commission for Statistics and Data,
  Stepan Mnatsakanian
State Income, Gagik Pogosyan
*Territorial Administration and Co-ordinating Town
  Planning*, Leonid Akopyan
Trade, Services, Tourism and Industry, Karen Chshmaritian
Transport and Communications, Eduard Madatian

EMBASSY OF THE REPUBLIC OF ARMENIA
25A Cheniston Gardens, London W8 6TG
Tel: 020-7938 5435
Ambassador Extraordinary and Plenipotentiary,
  HE Dr Armen Sarkissian, apptd 1998

BRITISH EMBASSY
28 Charents Street, Yerevan
Tel: (00 374) (2) 151 841/2
Ambassador Extraordinary and Plenipotentiary,
  HE Dr John Mitchiner, apptd 1996

DEFENCE

The Army has 102 main battle tanks, 218 armoured
infantry fighting vehicles and armoured personnel carriers, six combat aircraft and 13 armed helicopters.
  Russia maintains 3,100 army personnel in Armenia. An
agreement on military co-operation with Russia was
signed in 1996 which paved the way for joint military
exercises. A protocol was also signed on the establishment
of coalition troops in Transcaucasia and the planned use of
Russian and Armenian armed forces as part of coalition
troops in cases of mutual interest.
MILITARY EXPENDITURE – 8.4 per cent of GDP (1998)
MILITARY PERSONNEL – 53,000: Army 52,000,
  Paramilitaries 1,000
CONSCRIPTION DURATION – 18 months

ECONOMY

The Armenian economy has been badly affected by the
Azeri and Turkish economic embargoes which have been
in place since 1988. The main trade and transportation
routes now lie via Georgia and Iran.
  Armenia has a strong agricultural sector in low-lying
areas, where industrial and fruit crops are grown. Grain
is grown in the hills and the country is also noted for
its wine and brandy. There are large copper ore and
molybdenum deposits and other minerals. The country
also has developed chemicals, industrial vehicles and
textiles industries.
  The government introduced a programme of economic
reforms in November 1994 with IMF support, including
the liberalisation of prices, stabilisation of the currency
and privatisation.
  In 1998 Armenia had a trade deficit of US$578 million
and a current account deficit of US$390 million. Imports
totalled US$896 million and exports US$223 million.
GNP – US$1,728 million (1998); US$460 per capita
  (1998)
GDP – US$1,595 million (1996); US$438 per capita
  (1996)
ANNUAL AVERAGE GROWTH OF GDP – 4.1 per cent (1996)
INFLATION RATE – 8.7 per cent (1998)

UNEMPLOYMENT – 9.3 per cent (1998)
TOTAL EXTERNAL DEBT – US$800 million (1998)

Trade with UK	1998	1999
Imports from UK	£4,533,000	£4,571,000
Exports to UK	1,111,000	871,000

CULTURE AND EDUCATION

The Armenian alphabet was established in AD 405. Major
cultural figures include the poets Narekatsi (10th century),
Frick (13th century), Nahapet Kuchak (16th century) and
Sayat-Nova (18th century), the composer Aram Khacha-
turian (1903–78), and the film director Sergei Parajanov.
ILLITERACY RATE – 0.4 per cent
ENROLMENT (percentage of age group) – tertiary 12
  per cent (1996)

AUSTRALIA
The Commonwealth of Australia

AREA – 2,988,902 sq. miles (7,741,220 sq. km)
POPULATION – 18,871,800 (1999 estimate): 386,049 of
  Aboriginal and Torres Strait Islander origin (1996
  estimate). The language is English
CAPITAL – Canberra, in the Australian Capital Territory
  (population, 309,500, 1997 estimate). It has been the
  seat of government since 1927
MAJOR CITIES – Adelaide (1,088,400); Brisbane
  (1,574,600); Hobart (195,000); Melbourne
  (3,371,3000); Perth, including Fremantle (1,341,900);
  Sydney (3,986,700), 1998 estimates
CURRENCY – Australian dollar ($A) of 100 cents
NATIONAL ANTHEM – Advance Australia Fair
NATIONAL DAY – 26 January (Australia Day)
NATIONAL FLAG – The British Blue Ensign with five
  stars of the Southern Cross in the fly and the white
  Commonwealth Star of seven points beneath the
  Union Flag
LIFE EXPECTANCY (years) – male 75.22; female 81.05
POPULATION GROWTH RATE – 1.2 per cent (1997)
POPULATION DENSITY – 2 per sq. km (1997)
URBAN POPULATION – 85.4 per cent (1986)

Australia is a continent in the southern hemisphere. The
highest point is Mt. Kosciusko (2,228 m) and the lowest,
Lake Eyre (–15 m). Climatic conditions range from the
alpine to the tropical. Two-thirds of the continent is arid
or semi-arid although good rainfalls (over 800mm
annually) occur in the northern monsoonal belt and along
the eastern and southern highland regions.

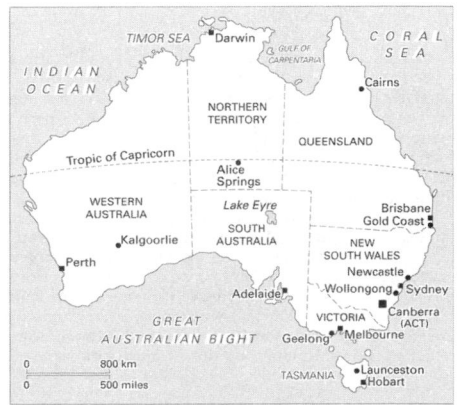

HISTORY AND POLITICS

Australia was discovered by Europeans in the 17th century. Its eastern coast was claimed by Capt. James Cook on behalf of Britain in 1770 and became a penal colony; Tasmania, Western Australia, South Australia, Victoria and Queensland were established as colonies between 1825 and 1859. The colonies were federated as the Commonwealth of Australia on 1 January 1901, at which time Australia gained dominion status within the British Empire. Australia became independent within the British Commonwealth by the 1931 Statute of Westminster. Following a referendum in 1967, the Aboriginal population was granted full political rights. In 1986, the Australia Act was passed, which abolished the remaining legislative, executive and judicial links to the UK, while retaining the British monarch as head of state.

On 13 February 1998, the Constitutional Convention voted by 89 votes to 52 to sever constitutional links with the United Kingdom monarchy. A national referendum was held on the issue on 6 November 1999; the proposition to make Australia a republic was defeated, with 45.3 per cent voting in favour and 54.7 per cent against.

The general election in October 1998 was won by the ruling Liberal-National Party coalition, though with a much reduced majority.

POLITICAL SYSTEM

The government is that of a federal commonwealth within the Commonwealth, the executive power being vested in the Sovereign (through the Governor-General), assisted by a federal government. Under the constitution the federal government has acquired and may acquire certain defined powers as surrendered by the states, residuary legislative power remaining with the states. The right of a state to legislate on any matter is not abrogated except in connection with matters exclusively under federal control, but where a state law is inconsistent with a law of the Commonwealth the latter prevails to the extent of the inconsistency.

Parliament consists of Queen Elizabeth II, the Senate and the House of Representatives. The constitution provides that the number of members of the House of Representatives shall be, as nearly as practicable, twice the number of senators. Members of the Senate are elected for six years by universal suffrage, half the members retiring every third year, except in the Australian Capital Territory and the Northern Territory, where members are elected for a three-year term. Each of the six states returns 12 senators, and the Australian Capital Territory and the Northern Territory two each. The House of Representatives, elected for a maximum of three years, contains members proportionate to the population, with a minimum of five members for each state. There are now 148 members in the House of Representatives, including one member for the Northern Territory and two for the Australian Capital Territory.

The High Court exercises jurisdiction over all matters arising under the constitution, all matters arising between the states and between residents of different states, matters to which the Commonwealth of Australia is a party, matters arising under any treaty, and matters affecting foreign representatives in Australia. The High Court also hears appeals from the Federal Court and from the Supreme Courts of states and territories.

The Federal Court of Australia has jurisdiction over important industrial, trade practices, intellectual property, administrative law, admiralty law and bankruptcy matters. It also acts as a court of appeal for decisions from the Australian Capital Territory Supreme Court and certain decisions of state Supreme Courts exercising federal jurisdiction. Each state has its own judicature of supreme, superior and minor courts for criminal and civil cases.

FEDERAL STRUCTURE

In the states, executive authority is vested in a Governor (appointed by the Crown), assisted by a Council of Ministers or Executive Council. Each state has a legislature comprising a Legislative Council and a Legislative Assembly or House of Assembly which are elected for four-year terms, except Queensland, which has a Legislative Assembly only.

Administration of the Northern Territory became a federal responsibility in 1911. Since 1978 Northern Territory ministers have had responsibility for Territory finances and administration.

GOVERNOR-GENERAL

Governor-General, HE The Hon. Sir William Deane, AC, KBE, *assumed office* 16 February 1996

CABINET *as at September 2000*

Prime Minister, John Howard
Deputy Prime Minister, Transport and Regional Development, John Anderson
Agriculture, Fisheries and Forestry, Warren Truss
Arts and the Centenary of Federation, Peter McGauran
Attorney-General, Daryl Williams
Communications, Information Technology and the Arts, Sen. Richard Alston
Defence, John Moore
Education, Training and Youth Affairs, David Kemp
Employment, Workplace Relations and Small Business, Leader of the House, Peter Reith
Environment and Heritage, Leader of the Government in the Senate, Sen. Robert Hill
Family and Community Services, Sen. Jocelyn Newman
Finance and Administration, John Fahey
Foreign Affairs, Alexander Downer
Health and Aged Care, Dr Michael Wooldridge
Immigration and Multicultural Affairs, Philip Ruddock
Industry, Science and Resources, Sen. Nick Minchin
Trade, Mark Vaile
Treasurer, Peter Costello

President of the Senate, Sen. Kerry Sibraa
Speaker, House of Representatives, Neil Andrew

AUSTRALIAN HIGH COMMISSION

Australia House, Strand, London WC2B 4LA
Tel: 020-7379 4334
High Commissioner, HE Philip Flood, apptd May 1998
Deputy High Commissioner, D. Ritchie
Minister, M. B. Jenkins *(Commercial)*
Head of Defence Staff, Air Cdre Gary Waters

NEW SOUTH WALES GOVERNMENT OFFICE, The Australia Centre, Strand, London WC2B 4LG. Tel: 020-7887 5871. *Director*, Gary Offner
AGENT-GENERAL FOR QUEENSLAND, 392 Strand, London WC2R 0LZ. Tel: 020-7836 1333. *Agent-General*, Dermot A. McManus
AGENT-GENERAL FOR SOUTH AUSTRALIA, Australia Centre, Strand, London WC2B 4LG. Tel: 020-7836 3455. *Agent-General*, Maurice de Rohan
AGENT-GENERAL FOR VICTORIA, Victoria House, Melbourne Place, Strand, London WC2B 4LG. Tel: 020-7836 2656. *Agent-General*, Alan J. Brown
AGENT-GENERAL FOR WESTERN AUSTRALIA, Australia Centre, Strand, London WC2B 4LG. Tel: 020-7240 2881. *Agent-General*, Clive E. Griffiths

BRITISH HIGH COMMISSION
Commonwealth Avenue, Yarralumla, Canberra, ACT 2600 Tel: (00 61) (2) 6270 6666
High Commissioner, HE Sir Alistair Goodlad, KCMG, apptd 1999
Deputy High Commissioner, Dr A. J. Pocock

STATES AND TERRITORIES

	Area (sq. km)	Resident population 31 December 1999p	Capital	Governor	Premier
Australian Capital Territory (ACT)	2,360	311,200	Canberra	—	Kate Carnell‡
New South Wales (NSW)	800,640	6,451,700	Sydney	HE Gordon Samuels, AC, CVO	Bob Carr
Northern Territory (NT)	1,349,130	194,300	Darwin*	Dr Neil Conn, AO†	Denis Burke‡
Queensland (Qld)	1,730,650	3,539,500	Brisbane	HE Maj.-Gen. Peter Arnison, AO	Peter Beattie
South Australia (SA)	983,480	1,495,800	Adelaide	HE Sir Eric Neal, AC, CVO	John Olsen
Tasmania (Tas.)	68,400	469,900	Hobart	HE Sir Guy Green, AC, KBE, CVO	Jim Bacon
Victoria (Vic.)	227,420	4,741,500	Melbourne	HE Sir James Gobbo, AC, KT	Steve Bracks
Western Australia (WA)	2,529,880	1,873,800	Perth	HE Maj.-Gen. Philip Michael Jeffery, AC, AO, MC	Richard Court

p preliminary
* Seat of administration
† Administrator
‡ Chief Minister

First Secretary, B. J. Davidson *(Political)*
First Secretary (Defence/Research) and Head of British Defence Research and Supply Staff, Dr G. Stott
Consuls-General, S. J. Hiscock *(Brisbane)*; P. M. Innes *(Melbourne)*; M. J. Horne, OBE *(Perth)*; P. Beckingham *(Sydney)*
Cultural Adviser and British Council Director, Simon Gammell, Suite 401, Edgecliff Centre, 203–233 New South Head Road (PO Box 88), Edgecliff, Sydney, NSW 2027; e-mail: ecs@bc.org.au

DEFENCE

The Army has 71 main battle tanks, 620 armoured personnel carriers and armoured infantry fighting vehicles, six aircraft and 125 armed helicopters. The Navy has four submarines, three destroyers, eight frigates, 16 patrol and coastal vessels and 16 armed helicopters. There are bases at Sydney, Garden Island, Cairns and Darwin. The Air Force has 126 combat aircraft.
MILITARY EXPENDITURE – 1.9 per cent of GDP (1998)
MILITARY PERSONNEL – 55,200: Army 25,200,
Navy 14,200, Air Force 15,800

ECONOMY

The wide range of climatic and soil conditions has resulted in a diversity of crops. Generally, cereal crops (excluding rice and sorghum) are widely grown, while other crops are confined to specific locations in a few states. However, scant or erratic rainfall, limited potential for irrigation and unsuitable soils or topography have restricted intensive agriculture.

Significant mineral resources include bauxite, coal, copper, crude petroleum, gems, gold, ilmenite, iron ore, lead, limestone, manganese, nickel, rutile, salt, silver, tin, tungsten, uranium, zinc and zircon. In 1998 287,620,000 tonnes of coal, 28,000,000 tonnes of crude oil, 30,361,000 cubic metres of natural gas, 153,243,000 tonnes of iron ore, 618,000 tonnes of lead, and 309,600 kilograms of gold were produced.
GNP – US$387,006 million (1998); US$20,640 per capita (1998)
GDP – US$401,504 million (1996); US$22,235 per capita (1996)
ANNUAL AVERAGE GROWTH OF GDP – 3.4 per cent (1996)
INFLATION RATE – 0.9 per cent (1998)
UNEMPLOYMENT – 8.0 per cent (1998)

TRADE

In 1998–9 the main exports were metalliferous ores and metal scrap (12.35 per cent); coal, coke and briquettes (10.80 per cent); gold (7.37 per cent); non-ferrous metals (6.33 per cent); and cereals and cereal preparations (5.87 per cent). The major imports were motor vehicles and parts (12.20 per cent); computer technology (7.28 per cent); electrical machinery (6.01 per cent); manufactured articles (5.94 per cent); general industrial machinery and parts (5.91 per cent); and telecommunications equipment (5.05 per cent).

Australia's main trading partners are Japan, the USA, New Zealand, China, Korea, Germany and the UK.

In 1998 Australia had a trade surplus of US$5,397 million and a current account deficit of US$17,484 million. In 1998 imports totalled US$64,668 million and exports US$55,895 million.

Trade with UK	1998	1999
Imports from UK	£2,260,308,000	£2,163,073,000
Exports to UK	1,429,807,000	1,399,032,000

COMMUNICATIONS

There are six government-owned railway systems, operated by the State Rail Authority of NSW, VicRail, Queensland Government Railways, Western Australian Government Railways, the State Transport Authority of Southern Australia, and the National Rail Corporation (NRC). The NRC incorporates the former Commonwealth Railways system, and the Tasmanian and non-metropolitan South Australian railways (urban rail services in Southern Australia remain the responsibility of the State Transport Authority).

The Northern Territory has three main ports: Darwin, and the private mining ports of Gove and Groote Eylandt. Most freight in the Territory is moved by road trains. These are massive trucks hauling two or three trailers, having a net capacity of about 100 tonnes and measuring up to 45 metres in length.

EDUCATION

Education is administered by the state governments and is compulsory between the ages of five or six and 15 years. It is available at government schools controlled by the state education department and at private or independent schools, some of which are denominational. Tertiary education is available through universities, and technical and further education colleges. There are 39 universities

in Australia; the Australian Capital Territory has two universities, New South Wales 11, Queensland seven, Northern Territory one, South Australia three, Tasmania one, Victoria nine and Western Australia five.
ENROLMENT (percentage of age group) – primary 95 per cent (1997); secondary 89 per cent (1996); tertiary 80 per cent (1997)

EXTERNAL TERRITORIES

ASHMORE AND CARTIER ISLANDS

Ashmore Islands (known as Middle, East and West Islands) and Cartier Island are situated in the Indian Ocean 850 km and 790 km west of Darwin respectively. The islands are uninhabited. The territory has been administered by the Australian Government since 1933.

THE AUSTRALIAN ANTARCTIC TERRITORY

The Australian Antarctic Territory was established in 1933 and comprises all the islands and territories, other than Adélie Land, which are situated south of the latitude 60°S. and lying between 160°E. longitude and 45°E. longitude. The territory is administered by the Antarctic Division of the Department of the Environment. There are nine scientific research stations.

CHRISTMAS ISLAND

AREA – 52 sq. miles (135 sq. km)
POPULATION – 1,906 (1996 census)

Christmas Island is situated in the Indian Ocean about 1,408 km NW of North West Cape in Western Australia. The island became an Australian territory in 1958 and is managed by the Department of Transport and Regional Services. The Shire of Christmas Island (SOCI) has nine elected members. SOCI is responsible for municipal functions and services on the island.
Administrator, W. Taylor

COCOS (KEELING) ISLANDS

AREA – 5.4 sq. miles (14 sq. km)
POPULATION – 655 (1996 census)

The Cocos (Keeling) Islands are two separate atolls (North Keeling Island and, 24 km to the south, the main atoll) comprising some 27 small coral islands, situated in the Indian Ocean. The main islands of the southern atoll are West Island (about 9km in length); Home Island, where the Cocos Malay community lives; Direction Island, Horsburgh and South Island.
The islands were declared a British possession in 1857. All land in the islands was granted to George Clunies-Ross and his heirs by Queen Victoria in 1886. In 1978 the Australian Government purchased all Clunies-Ross land and property interests except for the family home and grounds; the last of the remaining grounds were purchased in 1993. Between 1979 and 1984 most of the land was transferred to trusts with the Cocos (Keeling) Islands Council as trustee, the local government body established in 1979 which was replaced by the Shire of the Cocos (Keeling) Islands in July 1992.
On 6 April 1984 the Cocos community, in a UN-supervised Act of Self-Determination, chose to integrate with Australia. The islands are managed by the Australian Government through the Department of Transport and Regional Services.
Administrator, W. Taylor

CORAL SEA ISLANDS TERRITORY

The Coral Sea Islands Territory lies east of Queensland between the Great Barrier Reef and longitude 156° 06′E., and between latitudes 12° and 24°S. It comprises scattered islands, spread over a sea area of 780,000 sq. km. The islands are formed mainly of coral and sand, and most are extremely small. There is a manned meteorological station in the Willis Group but the remaining islands are uninhabited.
The territory is managed by the Department of Transport and Regional Services.

HEARD ISLAND AND MCDONALD ISLANDS

The Heard and McDonald islands, about 4,100 km south-west of Perth, comprise all the islands and rocks lying between 52°30′ and 53°30′S. latitude and 72° and 74°30′E. longitude. The islands are administered by the Antarctic Division of the Department of the Environment.

NORFOLK ISLAND

AREA – 13.3 sq. miles (34.5 sq. km)
POPULATION – 1,772 (1996 census)
SEAT OF GOVERNMENT – Kingston

Norfolk Island is situated in the South Pacific Ocean. It is about 8 km long by 5 km wide. The climate is mild and subtropical.
The island, discovered by Captain Cook in 1774, served as a penal colony from 1788 to 1814 and 1825 to 1855. In 1856, 194 descendants of the *Bounty* mutineers accepted an invitation to leave Pitcairn and settle on Norfolk Island. Norfolk Island is an Australian external territory.
In 1979 Norfolk Island gained a substantial degree of self-government. Wide powers are exercised by a nine-member Legislative Assembly. The Administrator is responsible to the Australian Minister for Regional Services, Territories and Local Government.
Administrator, A. J. Messner
Source: for demographic, economic and education statistics, Australian Bureau of Statistics

---

AUSTRIA
Republik Österreich

AREA – 32,378 sq. miles (83,859 sq. km). Neighbours: the Czech Republic and Slovakia (north), Italy and Slovenia (south), Hungary (east), Germany (north-west), Switzerland and Liechtenstein (west)
POPULATION – 8,072,000 (1997 estimate); 7,813,000 (1991 census). The language is German, but the rights of the Slovene- and Croat-speaking minorities in Carinthia, Styria and Burgenland are protected.
The predominant religion is Roman Catholicism
CAPITAL – Vienna, on the Danube (population, 1,806,737, 1995 estimate)
MAJOR CITIES – Graz (271,017); Innsbruck (136,516); Klagenfurt (89,415); Linz (281,566); Salzburg (162,908)
CURRENCY – Euro (€) of 100 cents/Schilling of 100 Groschen
NATIONAL ANTHEM – Land der Berge, Land am Strome (Land of mountains, land on the river)
NATIONAL DAY – 26 October
NATIONAL FLAG – Three equal horizontal stripes of red, white, red
LIFE EXPECTANCY (years) – male 73.93; female 80.19
POPULATION GROWTH RATE – 0.6 per cent (1997)
POPULATION DENSITY – 96 per sq. km (1997)
URBAN POPULATION – 64.6 per cent (1991)

HISTORY AND POLITICS

The Austrian state dates back to the eighth century AD when Emperor Charlemagne conquered the territory and founded the *Ostmark*, the eastern march of the Holy Roman Empire. The Habsburg dynasty established an empire which united much of central Europe, including present-day Austria and Hungary. The Republic of Austria was established in 1918 on the break-up of the Austro-Hungarian Empire. In March 1938 Austria was incorporated into Nazi Germany under the name *Ostmark*. After the liberation of Vienna in 1945, the Republic of Austria was reconstituted within the 1937 frontiers and a freely-elected government took office in December 1945. The country was divided into four zones occupied respectively by the UK, USA, USSR and France, while Vienna was jointly occupied by the four Powers. In 1955 the Austrian State Treaty was signed by the foreign ministers of the four Powers and of Austria. This treaty recognized the re-establishment of Austria as a sovereign, independent and democratic state, having the same frontiers as on 1 January 1938. Austria acceded to the European Union on 1 January 1995.

After the general election of 17 December 1995 the Social Democrats and the People's Party formed a coalition government. In the general election of 3 October 1999, the Social Democrats won 65 seats and the People's Party and the Freedom Party won 52 seats each. Attempts to form a coalition between the Social Democrats and the People's Party were unsuccessful. A coalition government between the People's Party and the Freedom Party, which had stood on an anti-immigration platform and whose leader, Jörg Haider, had expressed support for some aspects of the wartime Nazi regime, was sworn in on 5 February 2000 after the signing by both parties of a document expressing the commitment of the new government to the European Union and condemning discrimination and intolerance. International opposition to the inclusion of the Freedom Party in the government resulted in the suspension of bilateral relations between the governments of the other EU members and Austria. On 1 May, Jörg Haider resigned as leader of the Freedom Party in an attempt to calm the situation.

POLITICAL SYSTEM

There is a bicameral national assembly; the lower house (*Nationalrat*) has 183 members and the upper house (*Bundesrat*) has 64 members. There is a 4 per cent qualification for parliamentary representation.

FEDERAL STRUCTURE

There are nine provinces:

Provinces	Area (sq. km)	Population	Capital
Burgenland	3,965	274,334	Eisenstadt
Carinthia	9,533	560,994	Klagenfurt
Lower Austria	19,174	1,518,254	St Pölten
Salzburg	7,154	506,850	Salzburg
Styria	16,388	1,206,317	Graz
Tirol	12,648	658,312	Innsbruck
Upper Austria	11,980	1,385,769	Linz
Vienna	415	1,592,596	Vienna
Vorarlberg	2,601	343,109	Bregenz

HEAD OF STATE

President of the Republic of Austria, Dr Thomas Klestil, *took office* 8 July 1992, *re-elected* 19 April 1998

CABINET *as at September 2000*

Chancellor, Wolfgang Schüssel (ÖVP)
Vice-Chancellor, Public Affairs and Sports, Susanne Riess-Passer (FPÖ)

Agriculture and Environment, Wilhelm Molterer (ÖVP)
Economic Affairs, Martin Bartenstein (ÖVP)
Education, Science and Cultural Affairs, Elisabeth Gehrer (ÖVP)
Finance, Karl-Heinz Grasser (FPÖ)
Foreign Affairs, Benita Ferrero-Waldner (ÖVP)
Infrastructure, Michael Schmid (FPÖ)
Interior, Ernst Strasser (ÖVP)
Justice, Dieter Böhmdorfer (Ind.)
Labour, Health and Social Affairs, Dr Elisabeth Sickl (FPÖ)
National Defence, Herbert Scheibner (FPÖ)

ÖVP People's Party; FPÖ Freedom Party; Ind. Independent

AUSTRIAN EMBASSY

18 Belgrave Mews West, London SW1X 8HU
Tel: 020-7235 3731
Ambassador Extraordinary and Plenipotentiary, vacant
Minister and Chargé d'Affaires, Brigitte Öppinger-Walchshofer
Defence Attaché, Brig.-Gen. Wolfgang Plasche
Consul-General, Hella Naumann
Commercial Counsellor and Trade Commissioner, Dr Rudolf Engel

BRITISH EMBASSY

Jaurèsgasse 12, 1030 Vienna
Tel: (00 43) (1) 716130
Ambassador Extraordinary and Plenipotentiary, HE Sir Anthony Figgis, KCVO, CMG, apptd 1996
Deputy Head of Mission, Counsellor and Consul-General, I. Cliffe, OBE
Defence Attaché, Lt.-Col. A. Manton
First Secretaries, P. J. Seymour; H. D. Marcelin; J. Hall; B. H. S. Critchley

BRITISH CONSULAR OFFICES – There is a consular office at Vienna, and Honorary Consulates at Bregenz, Graz, Innsbruck and Salzburg.

BRITISH COUNCIL DIRECTOR, M. Evans, CVO, Schenkenstrasse 4, A-1010 Vienna; e-mail: bc.vienna@bc-vienna.at

DEFENCE

The Army has 283 main battle tanks and 734 armoured personnel carriers. The Air Force has 53 combat aircraft.

Women were permitted to join the army for the first time in February 1998.

MILITARY EXPENDITURE – 0.8 per cent of GDP (1998)
MILITARY PERSONNEL – Army 40,500, of which Air Force 4,250
CONSCRIPTION DURATION – Seven to eight months plus refresher training

ECONOMY

Austria produces wheat, rye, barley, oats, maize, potatoes, sugar beet and turnips. Timber forms a valuable source of Austria's indigenous wealth, about 47 per cent of the total land area consisting of forest areas. Foreign exchange receipts from tourism were a major contribution to the balance of payments.

GNP – US$216,697 million (1998); US$26,830 per capita (1998)
GDP – US$228,735 million (1996); US$28,218 per capita (1996)
ANNUAL AVERAGE GROWTH OF GDP – 1.6 per cent (1996)
INFLATION RATE – 0.9 per cent (1998)
UNEMPLOYMENT – 4.2 per cent (1998)

TRADE

Main exports are processed goods (iron and steel, other metal goods, textiles, paper and cardboard products), machinery and transport equipment, other finished goods (including clothing), raw materials, chemical products and foodstuffs. Main imports are machinery and transport equipment, processed goods, chemical products, foodstuffs, fuel and energy. Austria's main trading partners are Germany, Italy, France and Switzerland.

In 1998, Austria had a trade deficit of US$4,072 million and a current account deficit of US$4,425 million. Imports totalled US$68,277 million and exports US$62,767 million.

Trade with UK	1998	1999
Imports from UK	£1,124,600,000	£1,092,800,000
Exports to UK	1,364,900,000	1,392,900,000

COMMUNICATIONS

Internal communications are partly restricted because of the mountainous nature of the country, although there is now a network of 1,567 km of *Autobahn* between major cities which also links up with the German and Italian networks. The railways are state-owned and in 1993 had 5,605 km of track, 58.8 per cent of which is electrified. Of the 425 km of waterways, 350 km are navigable and there is considerable trade through the Danube ports by both local and foreign shipping. There are six commercial airports catering for 5,527,600 passengers in 1995.

There are four national radio and two national television channels, together with three national and twelve regional newspapers.

EDUCATION

Education is free and compulsory between the ages of six and 15 and there are good facilities for secondary, technical and professional education. There are 12 state-maintained universities and six colleges of art.
ENROLMENT (percentage of age group) – primary
87 per cent (1996); secondary 88 per cent (1996); tertiary 48 per cent (1996)

AZERBAIJAN
Azarbaijchan Respublikasy

AREA – 33,436 sq. miles (86,600 sq. km). Neighbours: Iran (south), Armenia (west), Georgia and Russia (north)
POPULATION – 7,625,000 (1998): 83 per cent Azeri, 6 per cent Russian and 6 per cent Armenian. There are also Kurds, Jews, Georgians and Turks. There are more Azeris in Iran than in Azerbaijan. The population is predominantly Shia Muslim although it was heavily secularised during the Soviet era. The language is Azeri
CAPITAL – ΨBaku (population, 1,149,000, 1990)
CURRENCY – Manat of 100 gopik
NATIONAL ANTHEM – Azerbaijan! Azerbaijan!
NATIONAL DAY – 28 May (Independence Day)
NATIONAL FLAG – Three horizontal stripes of blue, red and green with a white crescent and eight-pointed star in the centre
LIFE EXPECTANCY (years) – male 66.50; female 74.00
POPULATION GROWTH RATE – 0.9 per cent (1997)
POPULATION DENSITY – 88 per sq. km (1997)
URBAN POPULATION – 53.0 per cent (1995)

Azerbaijan occupies the eastern part of the Caucasus region of the former Soviet Union, on the shore of the Caspian Sea. The north-eastern part of the republic is taken up by the south-eastern end of the main Caucasus ridge, its south-western part by the smaller Caucasus hills, and its south-eastern corner by the spurs of the Talysh Ridge. Its central part is a depression irrigated by the River Kura and the lower reaches of its tributary the Araks. Azerbaijan has a continental climate.

Azerbaijan has 64 administrative districts and also includes the Nakhichevan Autonomous Republic, which is geographically separated from the rest of Azerbaijan by Armenia and borders on Iran and Turkey, and the Nagorno-Karabakh Autonomous Province.

HISTORY AND POLITICS

The Turkic Azeri people formed an independent state in the first century BC. This was invaded by the Arab Caliphates in the seventh century AD and under their 300-year rule Islam was introduced and became the dominant religion. In the 16th century Azerbaijan was again invaded by Persia and became a Persian province. The country was divided during the Russo-Persian wars of the early 19th century, the northern portion (the present-day Azerbaijan) becoming part of the Russian Empire and the southern portion remaining Persian and subsequently Iranian.

In 1918 the Azerbaijan Democratic Republic was established. It was overthrown by Communists in 1918 and Azerbaijan acceded to the USSR in 1922.

In January 1990, the Azeri Popular Front took power from the local Communist Party and declared independence from the Soviet Union. Soviet troops overthrew the Popular Front and restored the Communist regime under President Ayaz Mutalibov. This government declared Azerbaijan's independence in August 1991. Mutalibov won the presidential election held in September 1991, but widespread civil unrest forced him to resign. At the presidential election in June 1992 the Popular Front leader Abulfaz Elchibey was elected.

Popular discontent at military defeats caused Elchibey to flee Baku in June 1993 and the former Azeri Communist Party First Secretary Heydar Aliyev took over the presidency. The new regime was confirmed in office in a referendum in August and Aliyev won the presidential election in October 1993.

In November 1995, elections were held to the *Milli Majlis* (parliament), which had been increased to 125 seats: 100 directly elected and 25 allocated by proportional representation. The New Azerbaijan party, founded by Aliyev, won 70 per cent of the vote and a majority of seats. Presidential elections were held on 11 October 1998. The incumbent President Aliyev won 76.1 per cent of the vote, but the elections were criticized by the OSCE and other international monitoring groups.

SECESSION

In 1988 fighting broke out in the predominantly Armenian-populated region of Nagorny-Karabakh between Soviet Azeri forces and ethnic Armenians demanding unification with Armenia. In late 1993 Nagorno-Karabakh forces captured all of the region, together with all Azeri territory separating the region from Armenia (20 per cent of Azeri territory). Azeri forces pushed back the Nagorno-Karabakh forces in early 1994 before a cease-fire agreement was signed in May 1994. Between 500,000 and one million Azeris have been displaced by the fighting, which briefly flared up again along the Azeri-Armenian border in April and May 1997. Peace talks, held under the auspices of the OSCE, have yet to yield any significant results, although both sides reaffirmed their commitment to finding a peaceful solution at a meeting in October 1997, in which both sides rejected the idea of full independence for Nagorny-Karabakh as "unrealistic".

POLITICAL SYSTEM

A new constitution was approved by a referendum in November 1995, which created a presidential republic with executive power to be exercised by the president and with legislative power vested in the *Milli Majlis*.

HEAD OF STATE

President, Heydar Aliyev, *assumed office* 18 June 1993, *elected* 3 October 1993, *re-elected* 11 October 1998

GOVERNMENT *as at September 2000*

Prime Minister, Artur Rasizade
Deputy Prime Ministers, Ali Gasanov (*Chair of State Refugee Committee*); Yagub Abdulla oglu Eyyubov; Izzet Rustamov
Agriculture, Irshad Aliyev
Communications, Nadir Akhmedov
Defence, Lt.-Gen. Safar Abiyev
Economy, Namik Nasrullayev
Education, Misir Mardanov
Finance, Avaz Alekperov
Foreign Affairs, Vilayat Mukhtar oglu Guliyev
Interior, Ramil Usubov
Justice, Fikrat Farrukh Mammadov
Media and Information, Siruz Tebrizli
National Security, Namig Abbasov
Trade, Huseyngulu Bagirov
Youth and Sports, Abdulfaz Karayev

EMBASSY OF THE AZERBAIJAN REPUBLIC

4 Kensington Court, London W8 5DL
Tel: 020-7938 3412
Ambassador Extraordinary and Plenipotentiary, HE Mahmud Mamed-Kuliyev, apptd 1994

BRITISH EMBASSY

2 Izmir Street, AZ-370065 Baku
Tel: (00 994) (12) 924813
E-mail: office@britemb.baku.az
Ambassador Extraordinary and Plenipotentiary, HE David R. Thomas, apptd 1997

BRITISH COUNCIL DIRECTOR, Dr A. Thomas, 1 Vali Mammadov Street, AZ-370004 Baku; e-mail: enquiries@britishcouncil.az

DEFENCE

The Army has 259 main battle tanks, 254 armoured infantry fighting vehicles and 74 armoured personnel carriers. The Navy is based at Baku, with a share of the former Soviet Caspian Fleet Flotilla, comprising one frigate and nine patrol and coastal vessels. The Air Force has 49 combat aircraft and 15 attack helicopters.
MILITARY EXPENDITURE – 4.6 per cent of GDP (1998)
MILITARY PERSONNEL – 80,910: Army 55,600, Navy 2,200, Air Force 8,110; Paramilitaries 15,000
CONSCRIPTION DURATION – 17 months

ECONOMY

Azerbaijan was heavily industrialised as part of the Russian Empire. Industry is dominated by oil and natural gas extraction and related industries centred on Baku and Sumgait and the large oil deposits in the Caspian Sea, estimated at more than 6,000 million barrels. Five contracts to explore and exploit oilfields in the Caspian Sea have been signed since 1994.
The republic is also rich in mineral resources, with iron, copper, lead and salt, and is important as a cotton-growing area and a silkworm-breeding area.
The Azeri economy was devastated by the war although it is now showing signs of recovery.
In 1998 Azerbaijan had a trade deficit of US$1,046 million and a current account deficit of US$1,365 million.
GNP – US$3,821 million (1998); US$480 per capita (1998)
GDP – US$3,193 million (1996); US$420 per capita (1996)
TOTAL EXTERNAL DEBT – US$693 million (1998)

Trade with UK	1998	1999
Imports from UK	£56,191,000	£27,756,000
Exports to UK	8,207,000	9,566,000

CULTURE AND EDUCATION

Azerbaijan was the birthplace of the prophet Zoroaster, who founded one of the first monotheistic religions in the world. The country has witnessed a succession of three religions: Zoroastrianism, Christianity and Islam.
Azeri is one of the Turkic languages. Previously written in the Russian script, Azeri in the Latin script was adopted as the official language in December 1992. In the 18th and 19th centuries Azerbaijani literature produced the poets and dramatists Vagif, Vazekhi, Zakir, Akhundov and Vezirov.
ILLITERACY RATE – 0.4 per cent
ENROLMENT (percentage of age group) – tertiary 17.5 per cent (1996)

THE BAHAMAS
The Commonwealth of The Bahamas

AREA – 5,358 sq. miles (13,878 sq. km)
POPULATION – 289,000 (1997 UN estimate). The language is English
CAPITAL – ΨNassau (population, 172,196, 1996 estimate)
CURRENCY – Bahamian dollar (B$) of 100 cents
NATIONAL ANTHEM – March on, Bahamaland
NATIONAL DAY – 10 July (Independence Day)
NATIONAL FLAG – Horizontal stripes of aquamarine, gold and aquamarine, with a black equilateral triangle on the hoist
LIFE EXPECTANCY (years) – male 68.32; female 75.28
POPULATION GROWTH RATE – 1.8 per cent (1997)
POPULATION DENSITY – 21 per sq. km (1997)
URBAN POPULATION – 83.5 per cent (1990)

The Bahamas extend from the coast of Florida on the north-west almost to Haiti on the south-east. The group consists of 700 islands, of which 30 are inhabited, and 2,400 cays. The principal islands include: Abaco, Acklins, Andros, Berry Islands, Bimini, Cat Island, Crooked Island, Eleuthera, Exuma, Grand Bahama, Harbour Island, Inagua, Long Island, Mayaguana, New Providence (on which is located the capital, Nassau), Ragged Island, Rum Cay, San Salvador and Spanish Wells. San Salvador was the first landfall in the New World of Christopher Columbus on 12 October 1492.

HISTORY AND POLITICS

The Bahamas were settled by the British and became a Crown colony in 1717. Taken over in 1782 by the Spanish, the Treaty of Versailles in 1783 restored them to the British. The Bahamas gained independence on 10 July 1973.
A general election held in March 1997 was won by the Free National Movement which defeated the Progressive Liberal Party. The Free National Movement holds 35 seats in the House of Assembly and the Progressive Liberal Party five seats.

POLITICAL SYSTEM

The head of state is Queen Elizabeth II who is represented in the islands by a Governor-General. There is an appointed Senate of 16 members and an elected House of Assembly of 40 members.

Governor-General, HE Sir Orville Turnquest, GCMG, QC, apptd 1994

CABINET *as at September 2000*
Prime Minister, Hubert Ingraham
Deputy Prime Minister, National Security, Frank Watson
Agriculture and Fisheries, Earl Deveaux
Attorney-General, Justice, Tennyson Wells
Consumer Welfare and Aviation, Pierre Dupuch
Education, Dame Ivy Dumont, DCMG
Finance and Planning, William Allen, KCMG
Foreign Affairs, Janet Bostwick
Health and Environment, Ronald Knowles
Labour, Immigration and Training, Theresa
   Moxey-Ingraham
Public Works, Orville Turnquest
Social Development and Housing, Algernon Allen
Tourism, Cornelius Smith
Transport, James Knowles

President of the Court of Appeal, Sir Joaquim
   Gonsalves-Sabola, KCMG
Chief Justice, Dame Joan Sawyer

BAHAMAS HIGH COMMISSION
Bahamas House, 10 Chesterfield Street, London W1X 8AH
Tel: 020-7408 4488
High Commissioner, HE Basil O'Brien, apptd 1999

BRITISH HIGH COMMISSION
PO Box N-7516, Nassau
Tel: (00 1 242) 325 7471
High Commissioner, HE Peter Young, OBE, apptd 1996

DEFENCE
The Navy has seven patrol and coastal vessels, four harbour patrol units and four light aircraft.
MILITARY EXPENDITURE – 0.6 per cent of GDP (1998)
MILITARY PERSONNEL – 860: Navy

ECONOMY
Tourism employs about 40 per cent of the labour force and provides more than 60 per cent of the country's GDP. International banking and trust business is also important. The absence of direct taxation coupled with internal stability have enabled the country to become one of the world's leading offshore financial centres. In February 1998, Finance Minister William Allen announced that regulations were in place for the establishment of a stock exchange, which was scheduled to start operating by the end of 1998.
   Manufacturing and agriculture account for less than 10 per cent of GDP. Agricultural production is mainly of fresh vegetables, fruit, meat and eggs for the domestic market, and crawfish, mostly for export. Reserves of aragonite, limestone and salt are being commercially exploited. Freeport is the country's leading industrial centre, with a pharmaceutical and chemicals plant, an oil trans-shipment and storage terminal, and port and bunkering facilities. There are also a brewery and a rum distillery on New Providence.
GNP – US$3,297 million (1995); US$11,940 per capita
   (1995)
GDP – US$3,548 million (1996); US$12,493 per capita
   (1996)
ANNUAL AVERAGE GROWTH OF GDP – 5.2 per cent (1996)
INFLATION RATE – 1.3 per cent (1998)
UNEMPLOYMENT – 9.8 per cent (1997)

TRADE
The imports are chiefly foodstuffs, manufactured articles, building materials, vehicles and machinery, chemicals and petroleum. The chief exports are rum, petroleum, hormones, salt, crawfish and aragonite.
   In 1998 the Bahamas had a trade deficit of US$1,061 million and a current account deficit of US$594 million. In 1998, imports totalled US$1,872 million and exports US$300 million.

Trade with UK	1998	1999
Imports from UK	£42,461,000	£31,498,000
Exports to UK	62,705,000	66,724,000

COMMUNICATIONS
The main ports are Nassau (New Providence), Freeport (Grand Bahama) and Matthew Town (Inagua). International air services are operated from Abaco, Bimini, Eleuthera, Exuma, Grand Bahama and New Providence. More than 60 smaller airports and landing strips facilitate services between the islands, the services being mainly provided by Bahamasair, the national carrier. In 1997 there were 2,693 km of roads. There are no railways.

EDUCATION
Education is compulsory between the ages of five and 16. More than 60,000 students are enrolled in Ministry of Education and independent schools in New Providence and the Family Islands.
ILLITERACY RATE – 3.9 per cent
ENROLMENT (percentage of age group) – primary 98 per cent (1993); secondary 86 per cent (1993); tertiary 17.7 per cent (1985)

BAHRAIN
Dawlat al-Bahrayn

AREA – 268 sq. miles (694 sq. km)
POPULATION – 620,000 (1997 UN estimate); about 70 per cent are Bahraini; about 40 per cent of the Bahrainis are Sunni Muslims, the remaining 60 per cent being Shias; the ruling family and many of the most prominent merchants are Sunnis. The official language is Arabic; English is often used for business, and Farsi, Hindi and Urdu are also spoken
CAPITAL – ΨManama (Al-Manāmah) (population, 140,401, 1991 census)
CURRENCY – Bahraini dinar (BD) of 1,000 fils
NATIONAL ANTHEM Bahrayn ona, baladolaman (Our Bahrain, secure)
NATIONAL DAY – 16 December
NATIONAL FLAG – Red, with vertical serrated white bar next to staff
LIFE EXPECTANCY (years) – male 66.83; female 69.43
POPULATION GROWTH RATE – 3.0 per cent (1997)
POPULATION DENSITY – 894 per sq. km (1997)
URBAN POPULATION – 88.4 per cent (1991)
ILLITERACY RATE – 12.4 per cent
ENROLMENT (percentage of age group) – primary 98 per cent (1996); secondary 83 per cent (1996); tertiary 20.2 per cent (1993)

Bahrain consists of a group of low-lying islands situated about half-way down the Gulf, some 20 miles off the east coast of Saudi Arabia. The largest of these, Bahrain Island, is about 30 miles long and 10 miles wide at its broadest, with the capital, Manama, situated on the north shore. The second largest, Al-Muharraq, with the town and Bahrain International Airport, is connected to Manama by a causeway 1½ miles long.

INSURGENCIES
Since 1994 Shi'ite protestors demanding the re-establishment of the National Assembly have regularly clashed with

security forces and Shi'ite leaders have been detained. Opponents of the government have engaged in a sustained bombing campaign.

POLITICAL SYSTEM

Bahrain is a constitutional monarchy and has been fully independent since 1971, when British protectorate status was ended. The 1973 constitution provides for a National Assembly but this was dissolved in 1975. A 40-member Consultative Council was appointed in September 1996; it is an advisory body with no legislative powers.

HEAD OF STATE

HH The Amir of Bahrain, C.-in-C., Bahrain Defence Force, Shaikh Hamad bin Isa al-Khalifa, KCMG

CABINET as at September 2000

Prime Minister, HH Shaikh Khalifa bin Sulman al-Khalifa
Agriculture and Public Works, HE Ali Ibrahim Al-Mahrus
Cabinet Affairs and Information, HE Mohammed Ibrahim Al-Mutawwa
Commerce, HE Ali Saleh Abdulla Al-Saleh
Defence, HE Maj.-Gen. Shaikh Khalifa bin Ahmed Al-Khalifa
Education, HE Brig.-Gen. Abdul Aziz Mohammed Al-Fadhil
Finance and National Economy, HE Abdulla Hassan Seif
Foreign Affairs, HE Shaikh Mohammed bin Mubarak Al-Khalifa
Health, HE Faisal Radhi Al-Mousawi
Housing, Municipalities, Shaikh Khalid bin Abdullah Al-Khalifa
Interior, HE Shaikh Mohammed bin Khalifa Al-Khalifa
Justice and Islamic Affairs, HE Shaikh Abdullah bin Khalid Al-Khalifa
Labour and Social Affairs, HE Abdul-Nabi Abdullah Al-Shu'la
Ministers of State, HE Jawad Salim Al-Arrayedh; Majed Jawad Al-Jeshi
Oil and Industry, HE Shaikh Isa bin Ali bin Hamad Al-Khalifa
Power and Water, HH Shaikh Duaij bin Khalifa bin Mohammed Al-Khalifa
Transport, Civil Aviation, HH Shaikh Ali bin Khalifa bin Sulman Al-Khalifa

EMBASSY OF THE STATE OF BAHRAIN

98 Gloucester Road, London SW7 4AU
Tel: 020-7370 5132
Ambassador Extraordinary and Plenipotentiary, HE Shaikh Abdul-Aziz bin Mubarak Al-Khalifa, apptd 1996

BRITISH EMBASSY

21 Government Avenue, Manama 306, PO Box 114
Tel: (00 973) 534404
E-mail: britem@batelco.com.bh
Ambassador Extraordinary and Plenipotentiary, P. Ford

BRITISH COUNCIL DIRECTOR, J. Shorter, AMA Centre, 146 Shaikh Salman Highway, PO Box 452, Manama 356; e-mail: bc.manama@bc-bahrain.bcouncil.org

DEFENCE

The Army has 106 main battle tanks and, 340 armoured personnel carriers. The Navy, based at Mina Sulman, has one frigate and 12 patrol and coastal vessels. The Air Force has 24 combat aircraft and 26 armed helicopters.
MILITARY EXPENDITURE – 6.7 per cent of GDP (1998)
MILITARY PERSONNEL – 21,150: Army 8,500, Navy 1,000, Air Force 1,500; Paramilitaries 10,150

ECONOMY

The largest sources of revenue are oil production and refining. The Bahrain field, discovered in 1932, is wholly owned by the Bahrain National Oil Co. The Sitra refinery derives about 70 per cent of its crude oil by submarine pipeline from Saudi Arabia. Bahrain also has a half share with Saudi Arabia in the profits of the offshore Abu Sa'afa field. A reservoir of unassociated gas has recently been developed on Bahrain Island.

There is some heavy industry on the islands and a number of small to medium-sized industrial units.

The state has developed as a financial centre. Apart from several commercial banks, many international banks have been licensed as offshore banking units; there are also money brokers and merchant banks.
GNP – US$4,909 million (1998); US$7,640 per capita (1998)
GDP – US$5,306 million (1996); US$9,309 per capita (1996)
ANNUAL AVERAGE GROWTH OF GDP – 3.8 per cent (1996)
INFLATION RATE – –0.2 per cent (1996)

TRADE

In 1998 the government had a trade surplus of US$71 million and a current account deficit of US$1,090 miilion. In 1997 imports totalled US$4,026 million and exports US$4,384 million.

Trade with UK	1998	1999
Imports from UK	£144,168,000	£118,133,000
Exports to UK	67,466,000	39,076,000

COMMUNICATIONS

Bahrain International airport is one of the main air traffic centres of the Gulf; it is the headquarters of Gulf Air, and a stopping point on routes between Europe and Australia and the Far East for other airlines. A causeway links Bahrain to Saudi Arabia.

A worldwide telephone and telex service, by satellite and cable, is operated by Bahrain Telecommunications Company.

BANGLADESH
Ghana Praja Tantri Bangladesh

AREA – 55,598 sq. miles (143,998 sq. km). Neighbours: India (west, north and east), Myanmar (east)
POPULATION – 122,013,000 (1997 UN estimate). The state language is Bengali. Use of Bengali is compulsory in all government departments. English is understood and is used widely as an unofficial second language. The faith of 88 per cent of the population is Islam and 10.5 per cent Hinduism. Islam has been declared the state religion
CAPITAL – Dhaka (population, 3,397,187, 1991 census)
CURRENCY – Taka (Tk) of 100 poisha
NATIONAL ANTHEM – Amar Sonar Bangla (My golden Bengal)
NATIONAL DAY – 26 March (Independence Day)
NATIONAL FLAG – Red circle on a bottle-green ground
LIFE EXPECTANCY (years) – male 58.65; female 58.25
POPULATION GROWTH RATE – 1.5 per cent (1997)
POPULATION DENSITY – 847 per sq. km (1997)
URBAN POPULATION – 13.8 per cent (1986)

The country is crossed by a network of rivers, including the eastern arms of the Ganges, the Jamuna (Brahmaputra) and the Meghna, flowing into the Bay of Bengal. The climate is tropical and monsoon; hot and extremely humid during the summer, and mild and dry during the short winter.

HISTORY AND POLITICS

Prior to becoming East Pakistan, Bangladesh had been the province of East Bengal and the Sylhet district of Assam of British India. The territory acceded to Pakistan in August 1947, which became a republic on 23 March 1956. Bangladesh achieved its independence from Pakistan on 16 December 1971, following the conclusion of the Indo-Pakistan war. Pakistan and Bangladesh accorded one another mutual recognition in 1974.

In 1975 a one-party presidential system was introduced. A presidential election in 1978 was won by Maj.-Gen. Zia Rahman, who introduced a multiparty presidential system of government. Zia was assassinated in 1981. His replacement, Justice Abdus Sattar, was overthrown in 1982 in a coup led by the then Chief of Army Staff, Gen. Ershad. Following parliamentary elections in 1986, Gen. Ershad was elected president. Popular unrest forced his resignation in December 1990; the Bangladesh National-ist Party (BNP) won the subsequent parliamentary elections. In August 1991 a constitutional amendment returned Bangladesh to parliamentary rule.

In December 1994, the opposition parties resigned from parliament, demanding fresh elections. Public disorder persisted despite a general election in February 1996 which was won by the BNP, although turnout was a mere five per cent. In March 1996, Prime Minister Zia agreed to new elections; these elections in June 1996 produced a majority for the Awami League under Prime Minister Sheikh Hasina Wajed. In November 1997, the BNP walked out of parliament, accusing the government of repression. They returned in March 1998 after signing a memorandum of understanding with the government. A series of nationwide general strikes, organized by the seven-party opposition alliance led by the BNP, began in December 1998 in an effort to oust the government. A conference organised by business leaders in January 2000 failed to bring about an end to the strikes.

POLITICAL SYSTEM

There is a unicameral parliament (*Jatiya Sangshad*) of 330 members, of whom 300 are directly elected and 30 reserved for women, which can amend the constitution by a two-thirds majority. The country is divided into six administrative divisions, sub-divided into 64 districts.

HEAD OF STATE

President, Shahabuddin Ahmed, *sworn in* 9 October 1996

CABINET *as at September 2000*

Prime Minister, Armed Forces Division, Cabinet Division, Special Affairs, Defence, Establishment, Energy and Minerals, Shaikh Hasina Wajed
Agriculture, Matia Choudhry
Chittagong Hill Tracts Affairs, Kalpa Ranjan Chakma
Civil Aviation, Tourism, Housing, Public Works, Mosharraf Hossain
Commerce, Abdul Jalil
Communications, Anwar Hossain
Education, Primary and Mass Education Division, A. S. H. K. Sadek
Environment and Forests, Syeda Sajeda Chowdhury
Finance, Shah A. M. S. Kibria
Fisheries and Livestock, A. S. M. Abdur Rab
Food, Amir Hossain Amu
Foreign Affairs, Abdus Samad Azad
Health and Family Welfare, Sheikh Fazlul Karim Selim
Home Affairs, Post and Telecommunications, Mohammad Nasim
Industry, Tofael Ahmed
Labour and Manpower, Abdul Mannan
Law, Justice and Parliamentary Affairs, Abdul Matin Khasru
Local Government, Mohammad Zillur Rahman
Science and Technology, Lt.-Gen. Nooruddin Khan
Water Resources, Irrigation and Flood Control, Abdur Razzak

Without Portfolio, Salahuddin Yousuf
There are 22 Ministers of State.

BANGLADESH HIGH COMMISSION
28 Queen's Gate, London SW7 5JA
Tel: 020-7584 0081
High Commissioner, HE Mahmood Ali, apptd 1996
Defence Adviser, Brig. M. A. Yusuf Farazi
First Secretary (Commerce), Mohammed Mahmud Reza Khan

BRITISH HIGH COMMISSION
United Nations Road, Baridhara, Dhaka
PO Box 6079, Dhaka-1212
Tel: (00 880) (2) 882 2705
E-mail: combhcbd@citechco.net
High Commissioner, HE Dr D. Carter, CVO
Deputy High Commissioner, S. E. Turner
Defence Adviser, Brig. S. M. A. Lee, OBE

BRITISH COUNCIL DIRECTOR, T. Cowin, OBE, 5 Fuller Road, PO Box 161, Dhaka 1000; e-mail: britcoun@TheBritishCouncil.net. There is a regional director in Chittagong

DEFENCE

The army has 200 main battle tanks and 130 armoured personnel carriers. The Navy has four frigates and 45 patrol and coastal vessels. The Air Force has 65 combat aircraft.
MILITARY EXPENDITURE – 1.9 per cent of GDP (1998)
MILITARY PERSONNEL – 192,200: Army 120,000, Navy 10,500, Air Force 6,500; Paramilitaries 55,200

ECONOMY

Between 1991–5, the government implemented an IMF economic reform plan which delivered stable prices and inflation, and reduced the budget deficit. In November 1997, the Paris Club promised US$1.9 billion of aid.

Bangladesh is self-sufficient in food production. Agri-cultural products include rice, wheat, tobacco, tea, oil seeds, pulses and sugar cane. The chief industries are jute, cotton, tea, leather, pharmaceuticals, fertilizer, sugar, prawn fishing and natural gas. Garment manufacturing is the main export. Remittances sent home by Bangladeshis abroad are of considerable significance to the economy.

Heavy flooding during the summer of 1998 left 23 million people homeless and killed 1,500; two-thirds of the country was under water and 800,000 hectares of farmland was destroyed.

International donors agreed in April 2000 to provide around US$2,000 million in additional aid over a 20-year period dependent on the introduction of free-market economic reforms.
GNP – US$44,224 million (1998); US$350 per capita (1998)
GDP – US$33,559 million (1996); US$279 per capita (1996)
ANNUAL AVERAGE GROWTH of GDP – 5.6 per cent (1996)
INFLATION RATE – 5.6 per cent (1997)
TOTAL EXTERNAL DEBT – US$16,376 million (1998)

TRADE
In 1997 Bangladesh had a current account deficit of US$327 million and a trade deficit of US$1,748 million. In 1998 imports totalled US$7,042 million and exports US$3,831 million.

Trade with UK	1998	1999
Imports from UK	£87,031,000	£63,685,000
Exports to UK	252,857,000	272,266,000

COMMUNICATIONS

Principal seaports are Chittagong and Mongla. The Bangladesh Shipping Corporation was set up by the Government to operate the Bangladesh merchant fleet. The principal airports are Dhaka (Zia International) and Chittagong. The international airline, Bangladesh Biman, serves Europe, the Middle East, South and South-East Asia, and an internal network.

EDUCATION

Primary education is free and planned to be universal by 2000. There are 11 universities.

ILLITERACY RATE – 59.2 per cent
ENROLMENT (percentage of age group) – primary 64 per cent (1990); secondary 18 per cent (1990); tertiary 4.4 per cent (1990)

BARBADOS

AREA – 166 sq. miles (430 sq. km); nearly 21 miles long by 14 miles broad
POPULATION – 262,000 (1997 UN estimate). The official language is English
CAPITAL – ΨBridgetown in the parish of St Michael (population, 108,000, 1990)
MAJOR TOWNS – Holetown in St James, Oistins in Christ Church and Speightstown in St Peter
CURRENCY – Barbados dollar (BD$) of 100 cents
NATIONAL ANTHEM – In Plenty and in Time of Need
NATIONAL DAY – 30 November (Independence Day)
NATIONAL FLAG – Three vertical stripes, dark blue, gold and dark blue, with a trident head on gold stripe
LIFE EXPECTANCY (years) – male 67.15; female 72.46
POPULATION GROWTH RATE – 0.3 per cent (1997)
POPULATION DENSITY – 609 per sq. km (1997)
MILITARY EXPENDITURE – 0.5 per cent of GDP (1998)
MILITARY PERSONNEL – 610: Army 500, Navy 110

Barbados is the most easterly of the Caribbean islands. The land rises in a series of terraced tablelands to the highest point, Mt Hillaby (1,116 ft). The annual average temperature is 26.6°C (79.8°F) with rainfall varying from a yearly average of 75 inches in the high central district to 50 inches in the low-lying coastal areas.

HISTORY AND POLITICS

The first inhabitants of Barbados were Arawak Indians but the island was uninhabited when first settled by the British in 1627. It was a Crown Colony from 1652 until it became an independent state within the Commonwealth on 30 November 1966.

The last general election took place on 20 January 1999 and seats in the House of Assembly were distributed as follows: Barbados Labour Party 26, Democratic Labour Party 2.

POLITICAL SYSTEM

The head of state is the British sovereign. The legislature consists of the Governor-General, a Senate and a House of Assembly. The Senate comprises 21 Senators appointed by the Governor-General, of whom 12 are appointed on the advice of the prime minister, two on the advice of the Leader of the Opposition and seven by the Governor-General at his/her discretion to represent religious, economic or social interests. The House of Assembly comprises 28 members elected every five years by adult suffrage.

There are 11 administrative areas (parishes): St Michael, Christ Church, St Andrew, St George, St James, St John, St Joseph, St Lucy, St Peter, St Philip and St Thomas.

Governor-General, HE Sir Clifford Husbands, GCMG, KA, apptd 1996

CABINET *as at September 2000*
Prime Minister, Defence and Security, Finance and Economic Affairs, Owen Arthur
Deputy Prime Minister, Foreign Affairs, Foreign Trade, Billie Miller
Agriculture and Rural Development, Anthony Wood
Attorney-General and Home Affairs, David Simmons, QC
Consumer Affairs and Business Development, Ronald Toppin
Education, Youth and Culture, Mia Mottley
Environment, Energy and Natural Resources, Rawle Eastmond
Health, Philip Goddard
Housing and Lands, Gline Clarke
Industry and International Business, Reginald Farley
Labour, Sports and Public Sector Reform, Rudolph Greenidge
Minister of State, Prime Minister's Office, Glyne Murray
Public Works and Transport, Rommel Marshall
Social Transformation, Hamilton Lashley
Tourism and International Transport, Noel Anderson Lynch

BARBADOS HIGH COMMISSION
1 Great Russell Street, London WC1B 3JY
Tel: 020-7631 4975
High Commissioner, HE Peter Simmons, apptd 1995
Deputy High Commissioner, Herbert Yearwood
First Secretary (Commercial), Kenneth Campbell

BRITISH HIGH COMMISSION
Lower Collymore Rock, PO Box 676, Bridgetown
Tel: (00 1 246) 430 7800
E-mail: Postmaster@bridgetown.mail.fco.gov.uk
High Commissioner, HE Gordon Baker, apptd 1998
Deputy High Commissioner, M. J. E. Mayhew
Defence Adviser, Capt. P. Jackson
First Secretary, P. Curwen

ECONOMY

The economy is based on tourism, sugar and light manufacturing. In 1995, 442,107 tourists visited Barbados and 484,670 cruise ship passengers. Chief exports are sugar, chemicals, electronic components and clothing.
GNP – US$1,745 million (1995); US$6,560 per capita (1995)
GDP – US$1,994 million (1996); US$7,639 per capita (1996)
ANNUAL AVERAGE GROWTH of GDP – 5.5 per cent (1996)
INFLATION RATE – –1.3 per cent (1998)
UNEMPLOYMENT – 14.5 per cent (1997)
TOTAL EXTERNAL DEBT – US$608 million (1998)

TRADE

In 1997 Barbados had a current account surplus of US$7 million and a trade deficit of US$592 million. In 1998 exports totalled US$251 million and imports US$1,009 million.

Trade with UK	1998	1999
Imports from UK	£42,470,000	£43,407,000
Exports to UK	28,295,000	21,526,000

COMMUNICATIONS

Barbados has some 965 miles of roads, of which about 917 miles are asphalted. The Grantley Adams International airport is situated at Seawell, 12 miles from Bridgetown. Bridgetown, the only port of entry, has a deep-water harbour with berths for eight ships; oil is pumped ashore at Spring Garden and at an Esso installation on the West Coast.

EDUCATION

Education is free in government schools. There are 105 primary schools, 22 government secondary schools and 15 approved government secondary schools.

ILLITERACY RATE – 2.6 per cent
ENROLMENT (percentage of age group) – primary 78 per cent (1991); secondary 75 per cent (1989); tertiary 29.4 per cent (1995)

BELARUS
Respublika Belarus

AREA – 80,155 sq. miles (207,600 sq. km). Neighbours: Latvia and Lithuania (north), Russia (east), Ukraine (south), Poland (west)
POPULATION – 10,179,000 (1999): 78 per cent Belarusian, 13 per cent Russian, 4 per cent Polish and 3 per cent Ukrainian, with smaller numbers of Jews and Lithuanians. Belarusian and Russian have equal official language status. Most of the population are Belarusian Orthodox with a minority of Roman Catholics
CAPITAL – Minsk (population, 1,708,308, 1997 UN estimate); the administrative centre of the CIS
MAJOR CITIES – Brest (294,620); Gomel (500,986); Grodno (303,606); Mogilev (367,710); Vitebsk (356,007), 1997 estimates
CURRENCY – Rouble of 100 kopeks
NATIONAL ANTHEM – The former Soviet national anthem but with the words omitted
NATIONAL DAY – 3 July (Independence Day)
NATIONAL FLAG – Red with a green strip along the lower edge, and in the hoist a vertical red and white ornamental pattern
LIFE EXPECTANCY (years) – male 62.98; female 74.29
POPULATION GROWTH RATE – –0.1 per cent (1997)
POPULATION DENSITY – 49 per sq. km (1997)
URBAN POPULATION – 69.1 per cent (1996)

Belarus is situated in the western part of the European area of the former USSR. The main rivers are the upper reaches of the Dnieper, of the Niemen and of the Western Dvina. Much of the land is a plain, with many lakes, swamps and marshy areas. The climate is continental with mild, humid winters and relatively cool and rainy summers.

HISTORY AND POLITICS

After being absorbed into Lithuania in the 13th and 14th centuries, the Belarusian nationality, language and culture flourished until Belarus came under Polish rule in the mid-16th century. Two hundred years of Polish rule followed until Belarus was re-absorbed into the Russian Empire.

Western Belarus was ceded to Poland after the Soviet defeat in the Polish-Soviet war of 1919–20, and was not recovered until Soviet forces occupied the area under the 1939 Nazi-Soviet Pact. Belarus was devastated by the German invasion in the Second World War; 25 per cent of the population was killed and thousands deported.

Belarus issued a Declaration of State Sovereignty on 27 July 1990 and declared its independence from the Soviet Union after the failed coup in Moscow in August 1991. Stanislav Shuskevich became Belarusian leader at the head of a coalition of Communists and democrats. Until 1994, however, parliament and the government remained under the control of former Communists, who thwarted all attempts at economic and political reform. Shuskevich was forced to resign in January 1994 and was replaced by Gen. Mecheslav Grib who pursued closer political, economic and trade relations with Russia. The presidential election in June 1994 was won by Alexandr Lukashenka.

FOREIGN RELATIONS

An agreement was signed with Russia in April 1996 to form a Commonwealth of Independent States (CIS). In April 1997 a treaty of union was signed with Russia. It provided for the creation of a supreme council, chaired by the state presidents on a two-year rotating basis, which will co-ordinate foreign affairs and economic and defence co-operation. The presidents of Belarus and Russia signed documents in December 1998 which called for the adoption of a common budget and single currency and for joint defence and security policies. On 8 December 1999, they signed the Treaty on the Creation of a Union State, which committed the two countries to eventually becoming a confederal state.

POLITICAL SYSTEM

The president's term of office is five years, although two referendums in 1996 and 1997 extended Lukashenka's term until 2001; the president has authority to appoint half the members of the constitutional court and the electoral commission. The legislature is the bicameral National Assembly, comprising a 110-member House of Representatives (lower chamber) and a 64-member Council of the Republic (upper chamber). Eight members of the upper chamber are appointed by the president, the rest are indirectly elected by members of the local soviets in each region.

The republic is divided into six regions (*oblasts*): Brest, Gomel, Grodno, Minsk, Mogilev and Vitebsk.

HEAD OF STATE
President, Aleksandr Lukashenka, *elected* 10 July 1994

COUNCIL OF MINISTERS *as at September 2000*
Prime Minister, Vladimir Yermoshin
First Deputy Prime Minister, Andrey Kobyakov
Deputy Prime Ministers, Mikhail Dzyamchuk (*Science, Education and Healthcare*); Valeriy Kokarau (*Industrial Development, Fuel and Energy*); Uladzimir Zamyatalin (*Social and Cultural Policy*); Ural Latypov (*Foreign Affairs*); Leanid Kozik (*Taxation, State Property, Privatization*); Aleksandr Popkov (*Agroindustrial Complex*)
Agriculture and Food, Vadzim Papou
Architecture and Construction, Genadz Kurachkin
Communications and Information Technology, Mikalai Krokovski
Culture, Aleksandr Sasnouski
Defence, Lt.-Gen. Aleksandr Chumakow
Economy, Uladzimir Shymow
Education, Vasil Strazhau
Emergency Situations, Valery Astapov
Enterprise and Investments, Aleksandr Sazonau
Finance, Nikolai Korbut
Forestry, Valentin Zorin
Health, Igor Zelenkevich
Housing and Municipal Services, Boris Batura
Industry, Anatol Kharlap
Internal Affairs (acting), Mikhail Udovikov
Justice, Genadz Varantsou
Labour, Ivan Lyakh
Natural Resources and Environmental Protection, Mikhail Rusy
Social Protection, Volga Dargel
Sport and Tourism, Yawhen Vorsin
State-owned Property and Privatization, Vasil Novak
Statistics and Analysis, Vladimir Zinovsky
Trade, Pyotr Kazlou
Transport, Aleksandr Lukashou

EMBASSY OF THE REPUBLIC OF BELARUS
6 Kensington Court, London W8 5DL
Tel: 020-7937 3288
Chargé d'Affaires, Valery Kurdyukov

BRITISH EMBASSY
37 Karl Marx Street, BY-220030 Minsk
Tel: (00 375) (17) 2105920
E-mail: pia@bepost.belpak.minsk.by
Ambassador Extraordinary and Plenipotentiary, HE Iain Kelly, apptd 1999

BRITISH COUNCIL REPRESENTATIVE,
N. Demchenko, English Teachers', Resource Centre,
Institute of Foreign Languages, Ulitsa Zakharova 21,
BY-220662 Minsk; e-mail: bc.minsk@bc-minsk.bcouncil.org

DEFENCE

The Army has 1,778 main battle tanks, 1,583 armoured infantry fighting vehicles and 930 armoured personnel carriers. The Air Force has 152 combat aircraft and 44 armed helicopters.

MILITARY EXPENDITURE – 3.2 per cent of GDP (1998)
MILITARY PERSONNEL – 73,800: Army 43,350, Air Force 22,450; Paramilitaries 8,000
CONSCRIPTION DURATION – 18 months

ECONOMY

Agricultural productivity was severely affected by nuclear fallout from the Chernobyl disaster in 1986 although Belarus is now self-sufficient in the production of foodstuffs. As a result of the collapse of the Soviet centrally planned economic system, the country lost cheap supplies of energy and raw materials. Energy from Russia is still the largest import.

Economic reform and privatisation have been introduced and in May 1995 a customs union agreement with Russia took effect. A treaty was signed with Kazakhstan, Kyrgyzstan and Russia in March 1996 aimed at the establishment of a single customs territory. In December 1997 the first Russia-Belarus joint budget was endorsed, with projects estimated to cost US$100 billion. Industrial output increased by 9.7 per cent in 1999.

In 1998 Belarus had a trade deficit of US$1,447 million and a current account deficit of US$945 million. Imports totalled US$8,509 million and exports US$7,016 million. GDP increased by 8 per cent in 1998.

GNP – US$22,332 million (1998); US$2,180 per capita (1998)
GDP – US$11,601 million (1996); US$1,121 per capita (1996)
INFLATION RATE – 72.9 per cent (1998)
UNEMPLOYMENT – 2.3 per cent (1998)
TOTAL EXTERNAL DEBT – US$1,120 million (1998)

Trade with UK	1998	1999
Imports from UK	£32,853,000	£26,946,000
Exports to UK	20,433,000	21,104,000

CULTURE AND EDUCATION

Belarusian is an Eastern Slavonic language, closely related to Russian and Ukrainian and written in the Cyrillic script. Important cultural figures include the poet Yanka Kupala (1882–1942), the writer Yakub Kolas (1882–1956) and the painter Marc Chagall (1887–1985).

The national education system comprises pre-school, general secondary, out-of-school, vocational training and trade schools, secondary specialized and higher education. General secondary education begins at the age of six. There are also 22 private educational institutions.

ILLITERACY RATE – 0.6 per cent
ENROLMENT (percentage of age group) – primary 85 per cent (1994); tertiary 44 per cent (1996)

BELGIUM
Koninkrijk België

AREA – 11,783 sq. miles (30,528 sq. km). Neighbours: the Netherlands (north), France (south), Germany and Luxembourg (east)
POPULATION – 10,188,000 (1997 UN estimate). Greater

Brussels 954,460; Flanders 5,926,838; Wallonia 3,332,454, of whom 70,472 are German-speaking. Roman Catholicism is the religion of 86 per cent of the population. The official languages are Flemish, French and German

CAPITAL – Brussels (population, 953,175, 1998 estimate)
MAJOR CITIES – ΨAntwerp, the chief port (931,718); Bruges (269,158); Charleroi (424,515); ΨGhent (493,329); Liège (588,312); Leuven (453,772); Mons (250,748); Namur (279,675)
CURRENCY – Euro (€) of 100 cents/Belgian franc (or frank) of 100 centimes (centiemen)
NATIONAL ANTHEM – O Vaderland, o edel land der Belgen (Oh Fatherland, oh noble land of the Belgians)
NATIONAL DAY – 21 July (Accession of King Leopold I, 1831)
NATIONAL FLAG – Three vertical bands, black, yellow, red
LIFE EXPECTANCY (years) – male 73.88; female 80.61
POPULATION GROWTH RATE – 0.3 per cent (1997)
POPULATION DENSITY – 334 per sq. km (1997)

The Maas and its tributary, the Sambre, divide Belgium into two distinct regions, that in the west being generally level and fertile, while the tableland of the Ardennes, in the east, has mostly poor soil. The polders near the coast, which are protected by dykes against floods, cover an area of 193 sq. miles. The principal rivers are the Schelde and the Maas.

Belgium is divided between those who speak Dutch (the Flemings) and those who speak French (the Walloons). Dutch is recognised as the official language in the northern areas and French in the southern (Walloon) area and there are guarantees for the respective linguistic minorities. Brussels is officially bilingual. There is a small German-speaking area (Eupen and Malmédy) along the German border, east of Liège.

HISTORY AND POLITICS

The kingdom formed part of the Low Countries (Netherlands) from 1815 until 14 October 1830, when a National Congress proclaimed its independence. Belgium was invaded by Germany in 1914 and Eupen and Malmédy were ceded to Belgium by Germany under the Versailles Treaty of 1919. The kingdom was again invaded by Germany in 1940 and was occupied by Nazi troops until liberated by the Allies in September 1944. In 1977 Belgium was divided into three administrative regions: Flanders, Wallonia and Brussels. The last general election was held on 13 June 1999. The results were as follows (seats):

Chamber of Deputies: Christian Social Party (CVP) (Flemish) 22; Socialist Party (PS) (Francophone) 19; Flemish Liberals and Democrats (VLD) 23; Socialist Party (SP) (Flemish) 14; Liberal Reform Party-Democratic Front (PRL-FDF) (Francophone) 18; Christian Social Party (PSC) (Francophone) 10; Vlaams Blok (Flemish Nationalist Party) 15; Ecolo (Francophone Ecology Party) 11; Agalev (Flemish Environmental Party) 9; Flemish People's Union (VU) 8; Front National (FN) 1.

Senate: Of the 40 seats directly elected, CVP 6; SP 4; VLD 6; PRL-FDF 5; PS 4; PSC 3; Vlaams Blok 4; VU 2; Ecolo 3; Agalev 3. A further 31 Senators are indirectly elected or co-opted (*see* below).

POLITICAL SYSTEM

Belgium is a constitutional representative and hereditary monarchy with a bicameral legislature, consisting of the King, the Senate and the Chamber of Deputies. The parliamentary term is four years. Amendments to the constitution enacted since 1968 have devolved power to the regions. The national government retains competence only in foreign and defence policies, the national budget and monetary policy, social security, and the judicial, legal and penal systems. The Senate has 71 seats, of which 40 are directly elected, 21 indirectly elected and ten co-opted by the Flemish and Francophone Communities. The Chamber of Deputies has 150 seats. There are four levels of sub-national government: community, regional, provincial, and communal.

FEDERAL STRUCTURE

There are three communities: Flemish; Francophone; Germanophone. Each community has its own assembly, which elects the community government. At this level, Flanders is covered by the Flemish Community Assembly; most of Wallonia is covered by the Francophone Community Assembly, and the areas of Wallonia in the German-speaking communities of Eupen and Malmédy are covered by the Germanophone Community Assembly; Brussels is covered by a Joint Community Commission of the Flemish and Francophone Community Assemblies.

At regional level, Belgium is divided into the three regions of Wallonia, Brussels and Flanders. Each region has its own assembly and government.

There are ten provinces; five French-speaking in Wallonia (Hainaut, Liège, Luxembourg, Namur and French Brabant); and five Dutch-speaking in Flanders (Antwerp, East Flanders, West Flanders, Limburg and Flemish Brabant). In addition, Belgium has 589 communes as the lowest level of local government.

Minister-President of the Flemish Government, Patrick Dewael (VLD)
Minister-President of the Walloon Regional Government, Elio Di Rupo (PS)
Head of City Government in Brussels, Jacques Simonet (PRL)

HEAD OF STATE

HM *The King of the Belgians*, King Albert II, *born* 6 June 1934; *succeeded* 9 August 1993; *married* 2 July 1959, Donna Paola Ruffo di Calabria, and has *issue* Prince Philippe (*see* below); Princess Astrid, *b.* 5 June 1962; Prince Laurent, *b.* 19 October 1963
Heir, HRH Prince Philippe Léopold Louis Marie, *born* 15 April 1960

CABINET *as at September 2000*

Prime Minister, Guy Verhofstadt (VLD)
Deputy PM, Budget, Social Integration and Social Economy, Johan Vande Lanotte (SP)
Deputy PM, Foreign Affairs, Louis Michel (PRL)
Deputy PM, Labour and Equal Opportunities, Laurette Onkelinx (PS)
Deputy PM, Mobility and Transport, Isabelle Durant (Ecolo)
Agriculture and Small and Medium-sized Enterprises, Jaak Gabriels (VLD)
Civil Service and Modernisation of Public Administration, Luc Van Den Bossche (SP)
Consumer Protections, Public Health and Environment, Magda Aelvoet (Agalev)
Defence, André Flahaut (PS)
Economic Affairs and Scientific Research, Charles Picqué (PS)
Finance, Didier Reynders (PRL)
Interior, Antoine Duquesne (PRL)
Justice, Mark Verwilghen (VLD)
Social Affairs and Pensions, Frank Vandenbroucke (SP)
Telecommunications and Public Enterprises, Rik Daems (VLD)

Agalev Green Party (Flemish); Ecolo Green Party (Francophone); PS Socialist Party (Francophone); SP Socialist Party (Flemish); PRL Liberal Reform Party (Francophone); VLD Liberal Democrats (Flemish)

BELGIAN EMBASSY
103–105 Eaton Square, London SW1W 9AB
Tel: 020-7470 3700
Ambassador Extraordinary and Plenipotentiary, HE Lode Willems, apptd 1997
Minister-Counsellors, M. Vanherk (*Political*); F. De Sutter (*Economic*)
Defence Attaché, Capt. A. Kockx

BRITISH EMBASSY
Aarlenstraat 85, B-1040 Brussels
Tel: (00 32) (2) 287 6211
Ambassador Extraordinary and Plenipotentiary, HE David Colvin, CMG, apptd 1993
Deputy Head of Mission, Counsellor (Commercial and Economic) and Consul-General, S. Smith
Defence Attaché, Col. T. E. Hall, CBE
There are British Consular Offices at Brussels, Antwerp and Liège.

BRITISH COUNCIL REPRESENTATIVE TO BELGIUM AND LUXEMBOURG M. Rose, Liefdadigheidstraat 15, B-1210 Brussels; e-mail:

Province	Area (sq. km)	Population (1999)	Main Town	Population (1998)
FLANDERS				
Antwerp	2,867	1,640,966	Antwerp	931,718
East Flanders	2,982	1,359,702	Ghent	493,329
Flemish Brabant	2,106	1,011,588	Leuven	453,772
Limburg	2,422	787,491	Hasselt	67,456
West Flanders	3,144	1,127,091	Bruges	269,158
WALLONIA				
Hainaut	3,786	1,280,427	Mons	92,260
Liège	3,862	1,018,259	Liège	588,312
Luxembourg	4,440	245,140	Arlon	15,000
Namur	3,666	441,205	Namur	279,675
Walloon Brabant	1,091	347,423	Wavre	27,000

bc.brussels@be.britcoun.org
BRITISH CHAMBER OF COMMERCE FOR BELGIUM AND
LUXEMBOURG (INC.), Egmontstraat 15,
B-1000 Brussels

DEFENCE

The Army has 155 main battle tanks, 497 armoured
personnel carriers, 272 armoured infantry fighting vehicles and 78 helicopters. The Navy is based at Ostend and
Zeebrugge and has three frigates. The Air Force has 90
combat aircraft.

The headquarters of NATO, SHAPE and the Western
European Union Military Planning Cell are in Belgium;
1,570 US personnel are stationed in the country.
MILITARY EXPENDITURE – 1.5 per cent of GDP (1998)
MILITARY PERSONNEL – 41,750: Army 26,400, Navy
2,600, Air Force 11,500, Medical Service 1,250

ECONOMY

The service sector accounts for more than half of
Belgium's GDP. With no natural resources except coal,
production of which has now ceased, industry is based
largely on the processing for re-export of imported raw
materials. Principal industries are steel and metal products, chemicals and petrochemicals, textiles, glass, and
foodstuffs.

On 1 May 1998, it was announced that Belgium had
satisfied the convergence criteria and would be one of 11
countries to participate in the European Single Currency
from 1 January 1999.

In 1999 there was a budget deficit of 0.9 per cent of GDP
and public debt was 112.5 per cent of GDP.
GNP – US$258,968 million (1998); US$25,380 per capita
(1998)
GDP – US$268,232 million (1996); US$26,403 per capita
(1996)
ANNUAL AVERAGE GROWTH OF GDP – 1.5 per cent (1996)
INFLATION RATE – 1.0 per cent (1998)
UNEMPLOYMENT – 9.1 per cent (1998)

TRADE

External trade figures relate to Luxembourg as well as
Belgium since the two countries formed an economic
union in 1921. The main trading partners are Germany,
France, the Netherlands and the UK.

In 1998 Belgium and Luxembourg had a trade surplus
of US$7,561 million and a current account surplus of
US$12,111 million. In 1998 exports from Belgium totalled
US$176,668 million and imports US$162,651 million.

Trade with UK (Belgium and Luxembourg)

	1998	1999
Imports from UK	£7,987,700,000	£8,680,100,000
Exports to UK	9,074,100,000	9,022,000,000

COMMUNICATIONS

The railways are operated by the Belgian National
Railways. Major ports include Antwerp, Zeebrugge,
Ghent and Ostend. There are 1,586 km of inland water-
ways; ship canals link Ghent with Terneuzen in the
Netherlands, Willebroek Rupel with Brussels, Zeebrugge
with Bruges, Liège with Antwerp and Charleroi with
Brussels. The rivers Maas, Sambre and Schelde form an
integral part of the network.

There are 14,421 km of trunk road, of which 1,631 km
are motorways. The Belgian national airline Sabena
operates regular services between Brussels and European
centres, as well as intercontinental services worldwide.

CULTURE AND EDUCATION

The literature of France and the Netherlands is supplemented by an indigenous Belgian literary activity in both
French and Dutch. Maurice Maeterlinck (1862–1949) was
awarded the Nobel Prize for Literature in 1911. Emile
Verhaeren (1855–1916) was a poet of international
standing. Of contemporary Belgian writers, the most
celebrated was Georges Simenon (1903–89).

Nursery schools provide free education for children
from two and a half to six years. There are over 4,000
primary schools (6 to 12 years), more than 1,000 secondary
schools offering a general academic education slightly
over half of which are free institutions (predominantly
Roman Catholic but subsidised by the state) and the
remainder official institutions. The official school-leaving
age is 18.
ENROLMENT (percentage of age group) – primary
98 per cent (1995); secondary 88 per cent (1995); tertiary
56 per cent (1995)

BELIZE

AREA – 8,763 sq. miles (22,696 sq. km). Neighbours:
Mexico (north and north-west), Guatemala (west and
south)
POPULATION – 230,000 (1997 UN estimate): 44 per cent
Mestizo (Maya-Spanish); 26 per cent Creole; 11 per cent
Maya; plus a number of East Indian and Spanish descent.
The races are now inter-mixed. The majority of the
population is Christian, about 58 per cent Catholic and
34 per cent Protestant. The official language and
language of instruction is English. Spanish is also widely
spoken and English Creole is the vernacular. There are
also Garifuna and Maya speakers
CAPITAL – Belmopan (population, 44,087, 1991)
MAJOR CITIES – ΨBelize City (1993 census 46,342), the
former capital; Corozal (7,420); Dangriga (6,761);
Orange Walk (11,573); San Ignacio (9,417)
CURRENCY – Belize dollar (BZ$) of 100 cents. The Belize
dollar is tied to the US dollar, BZ$2=US$1
NATIONAL ANTHEM – Land of the Free
NATIONAL DAY – 21 September (Independence Day)
NATIONAL FLAG – Blue ground with red band along top
and bottom edges, and in centre a white disc containing
the coat of arms surrounded by a green garland
LIFE EXPECTANCY (years) – male 69.95; female 74.07
POPULATION GROWTH RATE – 2.8 per cent (1997)
POPULATION DENSITY – 10 per sq. km (1997)
URBAN POPULATION – 50.4 per cent (1997)
MILITARY EXPENDITURE – 2.6 per cent of GDP (1998)
MILITARY PERSONNEL – 1,050: Army

The coastal areas are mostly flat and swampy with many
islets but the country rises gradually towards the interior,
which is mainly forest. The northern and western districts
are hilly, and in the south the Maya Mountains and the
Cockscombs form the backbone of the country, reaching
a height of 3,700 feet at Victoria Peak. The climate is
sub-tropical.

HISTORY AND POLITICS

Numerous ruins in the area indicate that Belize was heavily
populated by the Maya Indians. The first British settlement was established in 1638 but was subject to repeated
attacks by the Spanish, who claimed sovereignty until
defeated by the Royal Navy and settlers in 1798. In 1871
the area was recognised by Britain as a colony and called
British Honduras. The colony became self-governing in
1964, with the UK retaining control of foreign policy,
internal security and defence. In 1973 the colony was
renamed Belize, and was granted independence on 21
September 1981.

The 1998 elections were won by the People's United

Party, who took 26 out of the 29 seats in the House of Representatives.

FOREIGN RELATIONS

A long-standing territorial dispute with Guatemala was provisionally resolved in 1992 when the Guatemalan Congress and Supreme Court voted to recognise Belize and establish diplomatic relations. Guatemala still retains its claim, subject to arbitration by the International Court of Justice.

POLITICAL SYSTEM

Queen Elizabeth II is head of state, represented in Belize by a Governor-General. There is a National Assembly, comprising a House of Representatives (29 members elected for five years) and a Senate (eight members appointed by the Governor-General on the advice of the prime minister and the leader of the opposition). Executive power is vested in the Cabinet, which is responsible to the National Assembly.

Governor-General, HE Sir Colville Norbert Young, GCMG, apptd 17 November 1993

CABINET *as at September 2000*

Prime Minister, Finance and Foreign Affairs, Said Musa
Deputy PM, Natural Resources, Environment and Industry; John Briceño
Senior Minister, George Price
Agriculture, Fisheries and Co-operatives, Daniel Silva
Attorney-General, Information; Godfrey Smith
Budget Planning, Investment and Trade, Ralph Fonseca
Education and Sports, Cordel Hyde
Health and Public Service, José Coye
Housing, Urban Renewal and Home Affairs, Dickie Bradley
Human Development, Women and Civil Society, Dolores Balderamos García
National Security and Economic Development, Jorge Espat
Public Utilities, Energy, Communications and Immigration, Maxwell Samuels
Rural Development and Culture, Marcial Mes
Sugar Industry, Local Government and Labour, Valdemar Castillo
Tourism and Youth, Mark Espat
Works, Transport, Citrus and Banana Industries, Henry Canton

BELIZE HIGH COMMISSION
22 Harcourt House, 19 Cavendish Square,
London W1M 9AD
Tel: 020-7499 9728
High Commissioner, HE Assad Shoman, apptd 1999

BRITISH HIGH COMMISSION
PO Box 91, Belmopan
Tel: (00 501) (8) 22146/7
E-mail: brithicom@btl.net
High Commissioner, HE Timothy David, apptd 1998

ECONOMY

About 30 per cent of the population is engaged in agriculture. The country is more or less self-sufficient in fresh beef, pork and poultry, but processed meat and dairy products are imported. About 25 per cent of timber production (mostly mahogany) is exported, and there is a large US market for lobster, conch and scale fish. Tourism is also a valuable source of income.

In 1997 Belize had a trade deficit of US$78 million and a current account deficit of US$40 million. In 1998 imports totalled US$325 million and exports US$154 million.
GNP – US$635 million (1998); US$2,660 per capita (1998)
GDP – US$588 million (1996); US$2,685 per capita (1996)

ANNUAL AVERAGE GROWTH OF GDP – 3.5 per cent (1996)
INFLATION RATE – –0.9 per cent (1998)
UNEMPLOYMENT – 12.7 per cent (1997)
TOTAL EXTERNAL DEBT – US$338 million (1998)

Trade with UK	1998	1999
Imports from UK	£11,604,000	£11,658,000
Exports to UK	33,553,000	43,229,000

COMMUNICATIONS

There is a government-operated radio service and six privately-owned radio stations but no official television service in the country. An automatic telephone service operated by Belize Telecommunications Ltd covers the whole country.

The principal airport is at Belize City and various airlines operate international flights to the USA and other Central American states. The main port is also Belize City, which has deep water quays. Several inland waterways are also navigable. There are 1,865 miles of road, including four main highways, but there is no railway system.

EDUCATION

Education is compulsory from six to 14 years of age. In 1992 primary education was provided by 241 schools, most of which are government-aided. Secondary education is provided by 40 secondary and post-secondary institutions. A University College of Belize has been established. There is an extra-mural faculty of the University of the West Indies, with a resident tutor.
ENROLMENT (percentage of age group) – primary 99 per cent (1994); secondary 36 per cent (1992)

BENIN
République du Benin

AREA – 43,484 sq. miles (112,622 sq. km). Neighbours: Togo (west), Burkina Faso and Niger (north), Nigeria (east)
POPULATION – 5,828,000 (1997 UN estimate). The official language is French
CAPITAL – ΨPorto Novo (population, 179,138, 1992)
MAJOR TOWNS – ΨCotonou (487,020, 1992) is the principal commercial town and port
CURRENCY – Franc CFA of 100 centimes
NATIONAL ANTHEM – L'aube nouvelle (The new dawn)
NATIONAL DAY – 30 November
NATIONAL FLAG – Two horizontal stripes of yellow over red with a vertical green band in the hoist
LIFE EXPECTANCY (years) – male 51.30; female 56.24
POPULATION GROWTH RATE – 3.0 per cent (1997)
POPULATION DENSITY – 52 per sq. km (1997)
URBAN POPULATION – 37.5 per cent (1997)
MILITARY EXPENDITURE – 1.4 per cent of GDP (1998)
MILITARY PERSONNEL – 7,300: Army 4,500, Navy 150, Air Force 150; Paramilitaries 2,500
CONSCRIPTION DURATION – 18 months (selective)
ILLITERACY RATE – 62.5 per cent
ENROLMENT (percentage of age group) – primary 63 per cent (1996); tertiary 3 per cent (1996)

Benin (formerly known as Dahomey) has a short coastline of 78 miles on the Gulf of Guinea but extends northwards inland for 437 miles. The four main regions, running horizontally, are a narrow sandy coastal strip, a succession of inter-communicating lagoons, a clay belt and a sandy plateau in the north.

HISTORY AND POLITICS

Benin was placed under French administration in 1892 and became an independent republic within the French Community in December 1958; full independence outside the Community was proclaimed on 1 August 1960. Between 1963 and 1972 successive governments were overthrown by the military until a coup d'état in 1972 brought to power a Marxist-Leninist military government headed by Lt.-Col. Kérékou.

The government dropped Marxism-Leninism as the official ideology in 1989, revoked the constitution in March 1990 and changed the country's official name from the People's Republic of Benin to the Republic of Benin. The Revolutionary National Assembly (legislature) was replaced by a High Council of the Republic (HCR).

A pluralistic constitution was adopted in December 1990 and legislative and presidential elections were held in 1991. Nicéphore Soglo was sworn in as president and appointed a Benin Renaissance Party (PRB)-dominated provisional government. He was defeated by Gen. Kérékou in a presidential election in March 1996. Legislative elections to the 83-seat National Assembly in March 1999 gave the PRB and allies 27 seats and opposition parties 42 seats.

POLITICAL SYSTEM

The president is head of government as well as head of state, and is directly elected for a five-year term, renewable once only. The president appoints and presides over the Council of Ministers. The National Assembly has 83 members, directly elected for a maximum of four years.

HEAD OF STATE
President and Head of the Armed Forces, HE Gen. Mathieu Kérékou, *sworn in* 4 April 1996

CABINET *as at September 2000*

State Minister in charge of Co-ordination of Government Action, Planning, Employment Promotion and Expansion, Bruno Amoussou
Minister Designate to the Presidency, Defence, Pierre Osho
Civil Service, Administrative Reform, Ousmane Batoko
Culture and Communications, Government Spokesman, Gaston Zossou
Environment, Housing and Town Planning, Luc-Marie Constant Gnancadja
Finance and Economy, Abdoulaye Bio Tchane
Foreign Affairs and Co-operation, Antoine Idji Kolawole
Health, Marina d'Almeida-Massougbodji
Industry, Small and Medium-sized Enterprises, John Igue
Interior, Security and Territorial Administration, Daniel Tawema
Justice, Legislation and Human Rights, Joseph Gnonlonfou
Mines, Energy and Water Resources, Félix Essou Dansou
National Education and Scientific Research, Damien Alahassa
Public Works and Transport, Joseph Attin
Relations with Institutions, Civilian Society and Benin Nationals Abroad, Adekpedjou Sylvain Akindes
Rural Development, Théophile Nata
Social Welfare and Women's Affairs, Ramatou Baba-Moussa
Trade, Tourism and Handicrafts, Séverin Adjovi
Youth, Sports and Leisure, Valentin Aditi House

EMBASSY OF THE REPUBLIC OF BENIN

87 Avenue Victor Hugo, F-75116 Paris, France
Tel: (00 33) (1) 4500 9882
Ambassador Extraordinary and Plenipotentiary, HE Andres Ologoudou, apptd 1998

HONORARY CONSULATE, 16 The Broadway, Stanmore, Middx HA7 4DW. Tel: 020-8954 8800. *Honorary Consul*, Lawrence Landau

BRITISH AMBASSADOR, HE Sir Graham Burton, KCMG, resident at Lagos, Nigeria

BRITISH CONSULATE, Lot 24, Patte d'Oie, Contonou, Benin. Tel: (00 229) 301120. *Honorary Consul*, C. Barnes

ECONOMY

The principal exports are cotton, palm products, ground-nuts, shea-nuts, and coffee. Small deposits of gold, iron and chrome have been found. Oil production started in 1983.

In 1994 Benin had a trade deficit of US$65 million and a current account surplus of US$36 million. 1997 imports totalled US$641 million and exports US$407 million.

GNP – US$2,252 million (1998); US$380 per capita (1998)
GDP – US$2,297 million (1996); US$413 per capita (1996)
ANNUAL AVERAGE GROWTH OF GDP – 5.5 per cent (1996)
INFLATION RATE – 5.8 per cent (1998)
TOTAL EXTERNAL DEBT – US$1,647 million (1998)

Trade with UK	1998	1999
Imports from UK	£42,275,000	£59,394,000
Exports to UK	1,238,000	1,049,000

BHUTAN
Druk-yul

AREA – 18,147 sq. miles (47,000 sq. km). Neighbours: Tibet (north), India (west, south and east)
POPULATION – 1,862,000 (1997 UN estimate): about 80 per cent are Buddhists, the remainder (mostly the Nepali Bhutanese) are Hindu. The official language, for administrative and religious purposes, is Dzongkha, a variant of Tibetan, which functions as a lingua franca amongst a variety of languages and dialects. Nepali remains a recognised language and English remains the medium of instruction and the working language of the administration
CAPITAL – Thimphu (population, 15,000, 1987 estimate)
CURRENCY – Ngultrum of 100 chetrum (Indian currency is also legal tender)
NATIONAL ANTHEM – Druk tsendhen koipi gyelknap na (In the Thunder Dragon Kingdom)
NATIONAL DAY – 17 December
NATIONAL FLAG – Saffron yellow and orange-red divided diagonally, with dragon device in centre
LIFE EXPECTANCY (years) – male 49.10; female 52.40
POPULATION GROWTH RATE – 1.8 per cent (1997)
POPULATION DENSITY – 40 per sq. km (1997)
MILITARY EXPENDITURE – 4.5 per cent of GDP (1998)
ILLITERACY RATE – 52.7 per cent

There is a mountainous northern region which is infertile and sparsely populated, a central zone of upland valleys where most of the population and cultivated land is found, and in the south the densely forested foothills of the Himalayas, which are mainly inhabited by Nepalese settlers and indigenous tribespeople.

INSURGENCIES

In January 1989 the King introduced a code of national etiquette designed to protect the national culture and language from Nepali encroachment. These measures, together with the granting of citizenship only to Nepalis settled in Bhutan before 1958, led to an exodus of ethnic Nepalis to Nepal, where about 80,000 live in camps.

A low-level insurgency has been waged in the south of the country against the King's policies by ethnic Nepalis since 1990. Talks between the Nepali and Bhutan governments continue in an attempt to resolve the fate of the refugees.

FOREIGN RELATIONS

Under a 1949 treaty Bhutan is guided by the advice of India in regard to its external relations. It retains its own diplomatic representatives and is a member of the UN. It also receives from India an annual payment of Rs 500,000 as compensation for portions of its territory annexed by the British Government in India in 1864.

POLITICAL SYSTEM

Bhutan has a 154-member unicameral *Tsogdu* (National Assembly), 105 of whom are directly elected and serve three-year terms, 12 are representatives of religious bodies and 37 are nominated by the government. The National Assembly meets twice a year. The ten-member Royal Advisory Council, nominated by the King and the National Assembly, acts as a consultative body when the National Assembly is not in session. The King is also assisted by the *Lhengyal Sgungtsog* (Cabinet). There are no political parties.

In July 1998 the King introduced reforms giving the legislature the right to dismiss the King and to nominate the members of the cabinet, although the King retains the right to assign their portfolios.

HEAD OF STATE

HM The King of Bhutan, Jigme Singye Wangchuk, *born* 11 November 1955; *succeeded his father* July 1972; *crowned* 2 June 1974

Heir, Crown Prince Jigme Gesar Namgyal Wangchuk, *designated* 31 October 1988

CABINET *as at September 2000*

Chair of the Royal Advisory Council, Kungang Tsangbi
Chair of the Third Committee (*Social, Humanitarian, Cultural*), Ugyen Tsering
Agriculture, Kinzang Dorji
Cabinet Chairman, Education and Health, Sangay Ngedup
Finance, Hishey Zimba
Foreign Affairs, Jigme Thinley
Home Affairs, Thinley Gyamtsho
Law, Sonam Tobgye
Trade and Industry, Khandu Wangchuk

ECONOMY

The economy is based on industry, which in 1997 accounted for 38 per cent of GDP, and agriculture (37 per cent of GDP). Agriculture and animal husbandry engage around 94 per cent of the workforce in what is largely a self-sufficient rural society. The principal food crops are rice, wheat, maize and barley. Vegetables and fruit are also produced. Bhutan is the world's largest producer of cardamom, which forms its principal export to countries other than India. Agriculture is, however, limited by the country's mountainous topography and 60 per cent forest cover.

The mountains contain rich deposits of limestone, gypsum, dolomite and graphite and small amounts of coal, which are exported to India. A distillery and cement, chemicals and food-processing plants are in production; a forestry industries complex is being expanded. Tourism and postage stamps are increasingly important sources of foreign exchange.

The government budget deficit was equivalent to 0.26 per cent of GDP in 1993. In 1997 imports totalled US$137 million and exports US$118 million.
GNP – US$354 million (1998); US$470 per capita (1998)
GDP – US$320 million (1996); US$176 per capita (1996)

ANNUAL AVERAGE GROWTH of GDP – 6.4 per cent (1996)
INFLATION RATE – 8.5 per cent (1998)
TOTAL EXTERNAL DEBT – US$120 million (1998)

TRADE

Trade with India accounted for 65 per cent of imports and 91 per cent of exports in 1996. Principal exports are electricity, calcium carbide and timber; main imports are rice, machinery and diesel oil. Bhutan's airline, Druk Air, flies between Paro, New Delhi and Calcutta.

Trade with UK	1998	1999
Imports from UK	£1,563,000	£1,876,000
Exports to UK	1,206,000	534,000

BOLIVIA
República de Bolivia

AREA – 424,165 sq. miles (1,098,581 sq. km). Neighbours: Brazil (north and east), Paraguay and Argentina (south), Chile and Peru (west)
POPULATION – 8,140,000 (1999 estimate): 12 per cent is of white European descent, 30 per cent Mestizo (mixed European-Indian), 25 per cent Quechua Indian and 17 per cent Aymará Indian. The official language is Spanish; Quechua and Aymará are also spoken. Roman Catholicism was the state religion until disestablishment in 1961
CAPITAL – La Paz (population, 784,976, 1995 estimate)
MAJOR CITIES – Cochabamba (772,000); El Alto (446,189); Oruro (253,000); Potosí (252,000); Santa Cruz (1,265,000); Sucre, the legal capital and seat of the judiciary (184,000)
CURRENCY – Boliviano ($b) of 100 centavos
NATIONAL ANTHEM – Bolivianos, El Hado Propicio (Oh Bolivia, our long-felt desires)
NATIONAL DAY – 6 August (Independence Day)
NATIONAL FLAG – Three horizontal bands, red, yellow, green
LIFE EXPECTANCY (years) – male 59.80; female 63.16
POPULATION GROWTH RATE – 2.4 per cent (1997)
POPULATION DENSITY – 7 per sq. km (1997)
URBAN POPULATION – 61.1 per cent (1997)

The chief topographical feature is the great central plateau over 500 miles in length, at an average altitude of 12,500 feet above sea level, between the two great chains of the Andes, which traverse the country from south to north. The total length of the navigable rivers is about 12,000 miles, the principal rivers being the Itenez, Beni, Mamore and Madre de Dios.

HISTORY AND POLITICS

Bolivia won its independence from Spain in 1825 after a war of liberation led by Simon Bolivar (1783–1830), from whom the country derives its name. From 1964 to 1982 Bolivia was ruled by military juntas until civilian rule was restored.

Congressional and presidential elections were held in June 1997. No party won an outright majority in Congress and a multiparty government was formed. Following a period of protests and strikes which had been prompted by proposed increases in water rates, a state of emergency was declared between 8–20 April 2000. The Cabinet resigned on 24 April 2000; a new Cabinet, which included most of the members of the previous one, was appointed on 25 April 2000.

POLITICAL SYSTEM

The constitution provides for a directly elected executive president who appoints the Cabinet. The legislature (Congress) consists of a 27-member Senate and a 130-member Chamber of Deputies; both chambers are elected for five-year terms, and the president also for five years.

HEAD OF STATE

President of the Republic, Gen. (retd) Hugo Bánzer Suárez, *inaugurated* 6 August 1997
Vice-President, Jorge Quiroga Ramírez

CABINET *as at September 2000*

Agriculture and Rural Development, Oswaldo Antezana Vacadíez
Defence, Gen. Oscar Vargas Lorenzetti
Economic Development, José Luis Lupo Flores
Education, Culture and Sport, Tito Hoz de Vila
Finance, Ronald MacLean
Foreign Affairs and Worship, Javier Murillo de la Rocha
Housing and Services, Rubén Poma Rojas
Interior, Guillermo Fortún
International Trade and Investment, Carlos Saavedra Bruno
Justice and Human Rights, Juan Chahín
Labour and Small Businesses, Luis Vásquez Villamor
Presidency, Walter Guiteras Dennis
Social Welfare and Health, Guillermo Cuentas Yanez
Sustainable Development, José Luis Carvajal

BOLIVIAN EMBASSY
106 Eaton Square, London SW1W 9AD
Tel: 020-7235 2257/4248
Ambassador Extraordinary and Plenipotentiary, Jaime Quiroga Matos, apptd 1998

BRITISH EMBASSY
Avenida Arce 2732, (Casilla 694) La Paz
Tel: (00 591) (2) 433424
E-mail: pp@mail.rds.org.bo
Ambassador Extraordinary and Plenipotentiary,
HE Graham Minter, apptd 1998
Deputy Head of Mission, J. Gardner

BRITISH COUNCIL DIRECTOR, E. Lawrie, Avenida Arce 2708 (esq. Campos), Casilla 15047, La Paz; e-mail: information@britishcouncil.org.bo

DEFENCE

The Army has 72 armoured personnel carriers. The Navy has 18 patrol vessels. The Air Force has 50 combat aircraft and 10 armed helicopters.
MILITARY EXPENDITURE – 1.8 per cent of GDP (1998)
MILITARY PERSONNEL – 70,600: Army 25,000, Navy 4,500, Air Force 4,000; Paramilitaries 37,100
CONSCRIPTION DURATION – 12 months (selective)

ECONOMY

Mining, natural gas, petroleum and agriculture are the principal industries. The ancient silver mines of Potosí are now worked chiefly for tin, but gold is obtained on the Eastern Cordillera of the Andes. Tin output, together with other minerals (copper, tungsten, antimony, lead, zinc, asbestos, wolfram, bismuth salt and sulphur), provides over one-third of exports. Following a decline in the price of tin, many workers have taken to growing coca, which has become a significant export. A government plan to reduce coca production by offering growers alternative means of support has only been of limited success. Small quantities of oil are produced for internal consumption, and gas (currently providing about a quarter of export income) is piped to Argentina; in December 1997 the World Bank approved financing for the 3,150 km Bolivia–Brazil gas pipeline, estimated to cost around US$2 billion.

The economy deteriorated badly in the late 1970s and early 1980s; in the mid-1980s economic reforms were introduced with privatisation of some state-owned firms and the encouragement of foreign investment. The peso was replaced in 1987 with the Boliviano of 1,000,000 old pesos in a successful effort to stem hyperinflation. The economy and currency have stabilised.

In 1996 the government signed an agreement with the South American Common Market (Mercosur) to create a free trade zone within 18 years.
GNP – US$8,013 million (1998); US$1,010 per capita (1998)
GDP – US$7,132 million (1996); US$939 per capita (1996)
ANNUAL AVERAGE GROWTH OF GDP – 3.9 per cent (1996)
INFLATION RATE – 7.7 per cent (1998)
UNEMPLOYMENT – 4.2 per cent (1996)
TOTAL EXTERNAL DEBT – US$6,078 million (1998)

TRADE

Mineral exports represent about 40 per cent of total trade. Bolivia has now developed its own smelters and is exporting metals. The chief imports are wheat and flour, iron and steel products, machinery, vehicles and textiles.

In 1998 Bolivia had a trade deficit of US$655 million and a current account deficit of US$673 million. In 1998 imports totalled US$1,983 million and exports US$1,103 million.

Trade with UK	1998	1999
Imports from UK	£15,305,000	£9,755,000
Exports to UK	22,689,000	21,010,000

COMMUNICATIONS

There are 2,200 miles of railways in operation. Communication with Peru is by road from La Paz via Copacabana and thence to the railhead at Puno. In 1993 Bolivia and Peru signed an agreement granting Bolivia a concession of 162 hectares at the southern Peruvian port of Ilo for 98 years to construct a free trade zone.

Commercial aviation is conducted by the national airline, Lloyd Aereo Boliviano and Transporte Aereo Militar between the major towns; Lloyd Aereo Boliviano and a number of foreign airlines provide international flights to the USA, South and Central America and Europe.

Most towns have radio, telephone or telegraph communication with the main cities. There are 16 principal daily newspapers.

EDUCATION

Elementary education is compulsory and free and there are secondary schools in urban centres. Provision is also made for higher education; in addition to St Francisco Xavier's University at Sucre, founded in 1624, there are seven other universities, the largest being the University of San Andrés at La Paz, and ten private universities.
ILLITERACY RATE – 14.4 per cent
ENROLMENT (percentage of age group) – primary 91 per cent (1990); secondary 29 per cent (1990); tertiary 22 per cent (1991)

BOSNIA-HERCEGOVINA

AREA – 19,735 sq. miles (51,197 sq. km). Neighbours: Serbia (east), Montenegro (south-east), Croatia (north and west)
POPULATION – 3,784,000 (1997 UN estimate); 4.4 million (1991 census): 44 per cent Bosniac, 33 per cent Serbs and 17 per cent Croats. The languages are Bosnian (spoken

by Bosniacs and written in the Latin script), Serbian
(spoken by Serbs and written in the Cyrillic alphabet)
and Croatian (spoken by Croats and written in the Latin
script)
CAPITAL – Sarajevo (population, 529,021, 1991 estimate)
MAJOR CITIES – Banja Luka (195,994); Mostar (127,034);
Tuzla (131,866); Zenica (145,837)
CURRENCY – Convertible marka
NATIONAL DAY – 1 March (anniversary of 1992 declara-
tion of independence)
NATIONAL FLAG – Blue, bearing a yellow triangle above a
line of white stars
LIFE EXPECTANCY (years) – male 69.24; female 74.59
POPULATION GROWTH RATE – –2.4 per cent (1997)
POPULATION DENSITY – 74 per sq. km (1997)
URBAN POPULATION – 39.5 per cent (1991)
MILITARY EXPENDITURE – 8.1 per cent of GDP (1998)
MILITARY PERSONNEL – Bosniac Army (BiH): 40,000;
Croat Defence Council (HVO): 16,000; Bosnian Serb
Army: 30,000
GDP – US$1,829 million (1996); US$504 per capita
(1996)

HISTORY AND POLITICS

The country was settled by Slavs in the seventh century
and conquered by the Ottoman Turks in 1463. Ruled by
the Turks for over 400 years, the country came under
Austro-Hungarian control in 1878. The assassination of
the heir to the Austro-Hungarian throne in Sarajevo by an
ethnic Serb precipitated the First World War, after which
Bosnia-Hercegovina became part of the 'Kingdom of
Serbs, Croats and Slovenes' (renamed Yugoslavia in 1929).
It was occupied by German and Axis forces between 1941
and 1945. At the end of the war Bosnia-Hercegovina
became part of the Socialist Federal Republic of Yugoslavia, which eventually collapsed with the secession of
Slovenia and Croatia in 1991.
  The Bosnia-Hercegovina government issued a declaration of sovereignty in October 1991 against the wishes
of the ethnic Serb Democratic Party. Independence was
declared on 1 March 1992 following a referendum which
was boycotted by the Bosnian Serbs. Bosnia-Hercegovina
was recognised as an independent state by the EC and USA
in April 1992 and admitted to UN membership in May
1992.

THE WAR

Fighting broke out in March 1992 between the pro-
independence Muslims and Bosnian Serbs who wanted to
merge with the Serbian republic to form a Greater Serbia.
The Bosnian Serbs, assisted by the Serb-dominated
Federal Yugoslav Army (JNA) rapidly gained control of
70 per cent of Bosnia and in August 1992 declared
their own 'Republika Srpska' with its capital at Pale.
International pressure eventually forced the JNA to
withdraw but it handed over its weapons to the Bosnian
Serb forces.
  The Bosnian government (Muslim) forces formed an
alliance with Bosnian Croat and Croat forces in early 1992
which collapsed in 1993. The Muslims then came under
fire from both Bosnian Serb and Bosnian Croat forces. In
January 1993 the UN and EU attempted to negotiate an
end to the war but the Vance-Owen plan was rejected by
the Bosnian Serb parliament and the fighting continued.
  In August 1993 the Bosnian Croats declared a 'Republic
of Herceg-Bosna', with its capital in Mostar, and following
a cease-fire in February 1994 joined the government forces
in a Muslim-Croat Federation.
  NATO galvanised the USA, Britain, France, Germany
and Russia to form the Contact Group (CG) to co-
ordinate peace efforts. The CG brought about a cease-fire
in June 1994 and presented a peace plan, proposing a 51:49

division of territory between the Muslim-Croat Federation and the Bosnian Serbs. The Bosnian Serbs rejected
the plan and the CG attempted to isolate them, with the
support of Serbia, which had agreed to blockade Bosnian
Serb forces in exchange for a relaxation of sanctions.
  Fighting intensified in 1995, climaxing in a land-grab
during the final months of the war. Bosnian Serb forces
overran the UN safe areas of Zepa and Srebrenica in July,
allegedly massacring thousands of fleeing Muslims, and
then laid siege to the Bihac 'safe area' together with
Croatian Serbs and rebel Muslims. Bosnian government
and Croatian forces lifted the siege of Bihac in August,
enabling a joint attack on Serb-held central Bosnia.
  The foreign ministers of Bosnia, Croatia and Serbia
(rump Yugoslavia) met in Geneva in September 1995 and
agreed to a US-sponsored peace accord. A cease-fire
agreement was signed on 5 October and observed from
22 October, delayed by a Federation advance in the west
and north-west, and Bosnian Serbs overrunning Tuzla.

THE PEACE AGREEMENT

The Presidents of Bosnia, Serbia and Croatia met in
Dayton, Ohio, USA, for negotiations which culminated in
an agreement on 21 November 1995. The Dayton Peace
Treaty was signed in Paris on 14 December. It was agreed
to preserve Bosnia as a single state with a 51:49 division
of territory between the Bosnian and Croat Federation
and the Republika Srpska (Bosnian Serbs). A Republican
(national) government, presidency and democratically
elected institutions, based in Federation-controlled
Sarajevo, were provided for.
  The Dayton agreement provided for the deployment
of a 60,000-strong NATO-led Peace Implementation
Force (IFOR) which took over from UNPROFOR on
20 December 1995 and was mandated until December
1996. IFOR was replaced by a 31,000-strong, NATO-led
Stabilisation Force (SFOR), mandated until June 1998.
SFOR in turn was replaced by a Dissuasion Force (DFOR)
with no formal end date.
  Mostar, which had been divided during the war between
the Muslims and Croats of the Federation and administered by the EU, held elections in June 1996. The EU
withdrew in December 1996, when the Bosnian Croat
state of Herceg-Bosna ceased to exist. Following a
decision by international arbitrators, the northern town
of Brčko, which had been under Bosnian Serb control, was
merged into a self-governing neutral district in March
1999.

The Dayton peace agreement uses the term 'Bosniac' to refer to Bosnian Muslims.

POLITICAL SYSTEM

Under the Dayton peace agreement, the Bosnian republican (national) government was made responsible for foreign affairs, currency, citizenship and immigration. Executive authority was vested in a democratically elected rotating presidential triumvirate comprising a representative from each community.

Legislative authority is vested in a bicameral parliament, the Assembly of Bosnia-Hercegovina, comprising a House of Peoples and a House of Representatives. Both houses have two-year terms. The House of Peoples has 15 members, five from each community, who are selected by the House of Representatives. The House of Representatives has 42 members who are directly elected to the two constituent chambers, the Chamber of Deputies of the Federation, which has 28 members, and the Chamber of Deputies of the Republica Srpska, which has 14 members. Within the Bosniac-Croat Federation there is a 140-member House of Representatives and ten cantonal assemblies; in the Republika Srpska there is an 83-member People's Assembly.

HEADS OF STATE (FOR ALL BOSNIA)
Current President, Alija Izetbegović (Bosniac); *Presidency Members*, Ante Jelavić (Croat); Živko Radišic (Serb), *elected* 12/13 September 1998

HEAD OF THE FEDERATION
President, Ejup Ganić (Bosniac)
Vice-President, Ivo Andrić Lužanski (Croat)

HEAD OF REPUBLIKA SRPSKA
President, vacant
Vice-President, Mirko Sarović

COUNCIL OF MINISTERS (FOR ALL BOSNIA)
as at September 2000

Prime Minister, Treasury, Spasoje Tusevljak (Serb)
Communications and Civilian Affairs, Tihomir Gligorić (Serb)
Foreign Affairs, Jadranko Prlić (Croat)
European Integration, Bisera Turković (Bosniac)
Foreign Trade and Economic Relations, Mirsad Kurtović (Bosniac)

FEDERATION CABINET *as at September 2000*

Prime Minister, Edhem Bicakcić (Bosniac)
Deputy PM, Finance, Dragan Čović (Croat)
Agriculture, Water-power and Forestry, vacant
Defence, Miroslav Prce (Croat)
Education, Science, Culture and Sport, Fahrudin Rizvanbegović (Bosniac)
Energy, Mining and Industry, Mirsad Salkić (Bosniac)
Environment and Urban Planning, Ramiz Mehmedović (Bosniac)
Health, Bozo Ljubić (Croat)
Interior, Mehmed Zilić (Bosniac)
Justice, Ignjac Dodik (Croat)
Social Welfare, Displaced Persons and Refugees, Sulejman Garib (Bosniac)
Trade, Branko Ivković (Croat)
Transport and Communications, Besim Mehmedić (Bosniac)
Without Portfolio, Nikola Antunović (Croat); Nedeljko Despotović (Serb)

REPUBLIKA SRPSKA GOVERNMENT *as at September 2000*

Prime Minister, Milorad Dodik
Deputy PMs, Djuradj Banjac *(Industry and Technology)*; Ostoja Kremenović *(Administration and Local Govern-*

ment); Savo Loncar *(Foreign Trade Relations)*; Nenad Suzić *(Education)*
Agriculture, Waterways and Forestry, Dusıko Komarcević
Defence, Col.-Gen. (retd) Manojlo Milovanović
Energy and Mining, Vladimir Dokić
Finance, Novak Kondić
Health and Social Welfare, Zeljko Rodić
Information, vacant
Interior, Sredoje Nović
Justice, Cedo Vrzina
Refugees, vacant
Religion, Jovo Turanjanin
Science and Culture, Zivojin Erić
Sport and Youth, Milorad Karalić
Trade and Tourism, Nikola Kragulj
Transport and Communications, Marko Pavić
Urban Planning, Construction, Housing, Public Services and Environment, Jovo Basić
War Veterans and War Victims, Slobodan Zupljanin

EMBASSY OF BOSNIA-HERCEGOVINA
4th Floor, Morley House, 320 Regent Street, London W1R 5AB
Tel: 020-7255 3758
Ambassador Extraordinary and Plenipotentiary, HE Osman Topcagić, apptd 1998

BRITISH EMBASSY
8 Tina Ujevica, Sarajevo
Tel: (00 387) (71) 204781/2/3
Ambassador Extraordinary and Plenipotentiary, HE Graham Hand, apptd 1998

BRITISH COUNCIL DIRECTOR, C. Newton, 2nd Floor, Obala Kulina Bana 4, Sarajevo 71000;
e-mail: British.Council@ba.britcoun.org

ECONOMY

Wheat, maize, potatoes and cabbage are among the major crops; crude steel and lignite are among the principal mineral products. In 1990 exports totalled US$2,876 million and imports US$2,548 million.

Trade with UK	1998	1999
Imports from UK	£13,366,000	£16,077,000
Exports to UK	2,281,000	5,321,000

BOTSWANA
The Republic of Botswana

AREA – 224,607 sq. miles (581,730 sq. km). Neighbours: South Africa (south and east), Zimbabwe (north and north-east), Namibia (west)
POPULATION – 1,533,000 (1997 UN estimate): Batswana (95 per cent); the remainder are Kalanga, Basarwa, Kgalagadi and Europeans. The national language is Setswana and the official language is English
CAPITAL – Gaborone (population, 286,779, 1994 UN estimate)
MAJOR CITIES – Francistown (55,244); Lobatse (26,052); Selebi-Phikwe (39,772)
CURRENCY – Pula (P) of 100 thebe
NATIONAL ANTHEM – Fatshe La Rona (Blessed be this noble land)
NATIONAL DAY – 30 September
NATIONAL FLAG – Light blue with a horizontal black stripe fimbriated in white across the centre
LIFE EXPECTANCY (years) – male 52.32; female 59.70
POPULATION GROWTH RATE – 2.4 per cent (1997)
POPULATION DENSITY – 3 per sq. km (1997)
URBAN POPULATION – 48.2 per cent (1996)

A plateau at a height of about 4,000 feet divides Botswana into two main topographical regions. To the east of the plateau streams flow into the Marico, Notwani and Limpopo rivers; to the west lies a flat region comprising the Kgalagadi Desert, the Okavango Swamps and the Northern State Lands area. The climate is generally sub-tropical.

HISTORY AND POLITICS

The Tswana people were dominant in the area now known as Botswana from the 17th century. In 1885, at the request of indigenous chiefs fearing invasion by the Boers, Britain formally took control of Bechuanaland, and the northern part of the territory was formally declared a British protectorate, while land to the south of the Molopo river became British Bechuanaland, which was later incorporated into the Cape Colony. On 30 September 1966 the British Protectorate of Bechuanaland became a republic within the Commonwealth under the name Botswana.

The last general election on 16 October 1999 was won by the Botswana Democratic Party with 33 seats to the Botswana National Front's 7 seats.

POLITICAL SYSTEM

The president is head of state and is elected by an absolute majority in the National Assembly. He appoints as vice-president a member of the National Assembly who is leader of government business in the National Assembly. The Assembly consists of the president, 40 members elected on a basis of universal adult suffrage, four co-opted members, and the Attorney-General (non-voting). Presidential and legislative elections are held every five years. There is also a 15-member House of Chiefs which considers legislation affecting the constitution and chieftaincy matters. In August 1997 the minimum voting age was lowered from 21 to 18.

HEAD OF STATE
President, HE Festus Mogae, *sworn in* 2 April 1998
Vice-President, Lt.-Gen. Ian Khama

CABINET *as at September 2000*
The President
Vice-President, Minister for Presidential Affairs and Public Administration, vacant
Agriculture, Johnny Swartz
Assistant Ministers, Pelokgale Seloma *(Agriculture)*; Boyce Sebetela *(Finance and Development Planning)*; Gladys Kokorwe *(Local Government, Lands and Housing)*; Tebekelo Seretse *(Office of the President)*
Commerce and Industry, Daniel Kwelagobe
Education, George Kgoroba
Finance and Development Planning, Baledzi Gaolathe
Foreign Affairs, Lt.-Gen. Mompati Merafhe
Health, Joy Phumaphi
Labour and Home Affairs, Thebe Mogami
Lands and Housing, Jacob Nkate
Local Government, Margaret Nasha
Mineral Resources, Energy and Water Affairs, Boometswe Mokgothu
Works, Transport and Communications, David Magang

BOTSWANA HIGH COMMISSION
6 Stratford Place, London W1N 9AE
Tel: 020-7499 0031
High Commissioner, HE Roy Warren Blackbeard, apptd 1999

BRITISH HIGH COMMISSION
Private Bag 0023, Gaborone
Tel: (00 267) 352841/2/3
E-mail: british@bc.bw
High Commissioner, HE J. Wilde, apptd 1998

BRITISH COUNCIL DIRECTOR, Dr. P. Mitchell, British High Commission Building, Queen's Road,

The Mall, PO Box 439, Gaborone;
e-mail: general.enquiries@bc.bw

DEFENCE

The Army has 30 armoured personnel carriers. The Air Wing has 32 combat aircraft.
MILITARY EXPENDITURE – 6.5 per cent of GDP (1998)
MILITARY PERSONNEL – 10,000: Army 8,500, Air Wing 500; Paramilitaries 1,000

ECONOMY

Agriculture is predominantly pastoral and accounts for around 3 per cent of GDP. The national herd is around 2.2 million cattle and one million sheep and goats. Cattle rearing accounts for about 85 per cent of agricultural output.

Mineral extraction and processing is now the major source of income following the opening of large mines for diamonds, copper and nickel. Botswana is one of the largest producers of diamonds in the world, with diamonds accounting for 74 per cent of export revenue. Large deposits of coal have been discovered and are now being mined.

Service industries account for nearly half of GDP. Tourism is the third largest industry, generating about 7 per cent of GDP. Main imports are motor vehicles, machinery and electrical equipment and foodstuffs; main exports are diamonds, motor vehicles and cupro-nickel.

In 1997 the government had a trade surplus of US$895 million and a current account surplus of US$721 million. In 1998 imports totalled US$1,120 million and exports US$1,122 million.
GNP – US$4,795 million (1998); US$3,070 per capita (1998)
GDP – US$4,401 million (1996); US$2,966 per capita (1996)
ANNUAL AVERAGE GROWTH OF GDP – 7.0 per cent (1996)
INFLATION RATE – 6.7 per cent (1998)
TOTAL EXTERNAL DEBT – US$548 million (1998)

Trade with UK	1998	1999
Imports from UK	£19,757,000	£21,874,000
Exports to UK	77,430,000	177,638,000

COMMUNICATIONS

The railway from Cape Town to Zimbabwe passes through eastern Botswana. The main roads are the north-south road, which closely follows the railway, and the road running east-west that links Francistown and Maun. Air services are provided on a scheduled basis between the main towns.

EDUCATION

There are 657 primary schools, 163 community junior secondary schools and 23 government and government-aided senior secondary schools. Total enrolment in the tertiary sector (teacher training establishments, colleges of education and the University of Botswana) numbers 6,923.
ILLITERACY RATE – 22.8 per cent
ENROLMENT (percentage of age group) – primary 81 per cent (1996); secondary 44 per cent (1995); tertiary 6 per cent (1996)

BRAZIL
República Federativa do Brasil

AREA – 3,300,171 sq. miles (8,547,403 sq. km).
Neighbours: Guyana, Suriname, French Guiana,

Colombia and Venezuela (north), Peru, Bolivia, Paraguay and Argentina (west), Uruguay (south)
POPULATION – 159,884,000 (1997 UN estimate); 157,070,163 (1996 census). Portuguese is the national language but Italian, Spanish, German, Japanese and Arabic are also spoken
CAPITAL – Brasília (population, 1,737,813, 1995 estimate)
MAJOR CITIES – Belo Horizonte (2,097,311); ΨFortaleza (1,917,236); ΨRecife (1,329,768); ΨRio de Janeiro (5,606,497), the former capital; ΨSalvador (2,262,731); São Paulo (10,017,821)
CURRENCY – Real of 100 centavos
NATIONAL ANTHEM – Ouviram do Ipirangas às Margens Placidas (From peaceful Ypiranga's banks)
NATIONAL DAY – 7 September (Independence Day)
NATIONAL FLAG – Green with a yellow lozenge containing a blue sphere studded with white stars, and crossed by a white band with the motto *Ordem e Progresso*
LIFE EXPECTANCY (years) – male 64.12; female 70.64
POPULATION GROWTH RATE – 1.4 per cent (1997)
POPULATION DENSITY – 19 per sq. km (1997)
URBAN POPULATION – 75.6 per cent (1991)

The north is mainly wide, low-lying, forest-clad plains. The central areas are principally plateau land and the east and south are traversed by successive mountain ranges interspersed with fertile valleys. The principal ranges are the Serra do Mar, the Serra da Mantiqueira and the Serra do Espinhaco along the east coast. The River Amazon flows from the Peruvian Andes to the Atlantic.

HISTORY AND POLITICS

Brazil was discovered by the Portuguese navigator Pedro Alvares Cabral in 1500 and colonised by Portugal in the early 16th century. In 1822 it became independent under Dom Pedro, son of King João VI of Portugal, who had been forced to flee to Brazil during the Napoleonic Wars. In 1889, Dom Pedro II was dethroned and a republic was proclaimed. In 1985 Brazil returned to democratic rule after two decades of military government.

Fernando Cardoso of the Social Democratic Party, part of the Liberal Front coalition, won the presidential election of October 1994 and was returned for a second term on 4 October 1998. In simultaneous legislative elections, the five-party coalition which supported him won 377 seats in the Chamber of Deputies and 21 state governorships. The coalition currently holds 68 seats in the Senate.

POLITICAL SYSTEM

The Federative Republic of Brazil is composed of the federal district and 26 states. Under the 1988 constitution the president, who heads the executive, is directly elected for a four-year term; in June 1997 the constitution was amended to allow the president to stand for a second term. The Congress consists of an 81-member Senate (three senators per state elected for an eight-year term) and a 513-member Chamber of Deputies which is elected every four years; the number of deputies per state depends upon the state's population. Each state has a Governor, and a Legislative Assembly with a four-year term.

FEDERAL STRUCTURE

Federal Unit	Area (sq. km)	Population (1996)	Capital
Central west		10,500,579	
Distrito Federal	5,822	1,821,946	Brasília
Goiás	341,290	4,514,967	Goiãnia
Matto Grosso	906,807	2,235,832	Cuiabá
Matto Grosso do Sul	358,159	1,927,834	Campo Grande
North		11,288,259	

Federal Unit	Area (sq. km)	Population (1996)	Capital
Acre	153,150	483,593	Rio Branco
Amapá	143,454	379,459	Macapá
Amazonas	1,577,820	2,389,279	Manaus
Pará	1,253,165	5,510,849	Belém
Rondnia	238,513	1,229,306	Pôrto Velho
Roraima	225,116	247,131	Boa Vista
Tocantins	278,421	1,048,642	Palmas
North-east		44,766,851	
Alagoas	27,933	2,633,251	Maceió
Bahia	567,295	12,541,675	Salvador
Ceará	146,348	6,809,290	Fortaleza
Maranhão	333,366	5,222,183	São Luís
Paraíba	56,585	3,305,616	João Pessoa
Pernambuco	98,938	7,399,071	Recife
Piaui	252,378	2,673,085	Teresina
Rio Grande do Norte	53,307	2,558,660	Natal
Sergipe	22,050	1,624,020	Aracajú
South		23,513,736	
Paraná	199,709	9,003,804	Curitiba
Rio Grande do Sul	282,062	9,634,688	Pórto Alegre
Santa Catarina	95,443	4,875,244	Florianópolis
South-east		67,000,738	
Espírito Santo	46,184	2,802,707	Vitória
Minas Gerais	588,384	16,672,613	Belo Horizonte
Rio de Janeiro	43,910	13,406,308	Rio de Janeiro
São Paulo	248,809	34,119,110	São Paulo

HEAD OF STATE
President, Fernando Henrique Cardoso, *sworn in* 1 January 1995
Vice-President, Marco Maciel

CABINET *as at September 2000*
Agriculture and Supply, Marcus Vinicius Pratini de Moraes
Armed Forces Chief of Staff, Gen. Benedito Bezerra Leonel
Civilian Household of the Presidency, Pedro Parente
Communications, João Pimenta da Veiga
Culture, Francisco Correa Weffort
Defence, Geraldo Magela Quintão
Development, Industry and Foreign Trade, Alcides Tapias
Education, Paulo Renato de Souza
Energy and Mines, Rodolfo Tourinho
Environment, José Sarney Filho
Finance, Pedro Malan
Foreign Affairs, Luiz Felipe Lampreia
Government Communication, Andrea Matarazzo
Health, José Serra
Justice, José Gregori
Labour and Employment, Francisco Dornelles
Land Reform, Raúl Jungmann
Military Household of the Presidency, Gen. Alberto Cardoso
National Integration, Fernando Bezerra
Planning, Budget and Co-ordination, Martus Tavares
Science and Technology, Ronaldo Sardenberg
Secretariatry of the Presidency, Aloysio Nunes Ferreira
Secretary of State for Administration and Patrimony (Budget and Management), Claudia Costin
Secretary of State for Human Rights (Justice), Gilberto Saboia
Secretary of State for Special Urban Policies, Ovídio Antonio de Angelis
Social Security and Welfare, Waldeck Vieira Ornelas
Sports and Tourism, Raphael Grecca
Transport, Eliseu Padilha

BRAZILIAN EMBASSY
32 Green Street, London W1Y 4AT
Tel: 020-7499 0877
Ambassador Extraordinary and Plenipotentiary, HE Sergio

Silva Do Amaral, KBE, apptd 1999
Military Attachés, Col. Paulo Chagas, Capt. Arlei Caetano
Franco, Gp. Capt. Flavio Neri Hadmann Jasper
Counsellor (Commercial Affairs), João de Mendonça
Lima Neto

There is also a Brazilian Consulate-General in London
and honorary consular offices at Cardiff and Glasgow.

BRITISH EMBASSY
Setor de Embaixadas Sul, Quadra 801, Conjunto K, CEP
70.408–900, Brasília DF
Tel: (00 55) (61) 225 2710
E-mail: britemb@zaz.com.br
Ambassador Extraordinary and Plenipotentiary, HE Roger
Bone, CMG, apptd 1999
*Deputy Head of Mission, Consul-General, Minister/
Counsellor*, S. Gillett, MVO
Defence Attaché, Col. J. M. Bowles, MBE
First Secretary, J. F. Jarvine

There are British Consulates-General at Rio de Janeiro
and São Paulo.

BRITISH COUNCIL DIRECTOR, Howard Thompson, OBE,
Edificio Morro Vermelho, Quadra 1. Bloco H, SCS,
70399–900, Brasília DF; e-mail:
brasilia@britishcouncil.org.br. Regional directors in
Curitiba, Recife, Rio de Janeiro and São Paulo

BRITISH AND COMMONWEALTH CHAMBER OF COMMERCE
IN SÃO PAULO, Rua Barão de Itapetininga 275, 7th
Floor, 01042 São Paulo (*Postal Address*, PO Box 1621,
01000 São Paulo) and Rua Real Grandeza 99,
22281 Rio de Janeiro

DEFENCE

The Army has 178 main battle tanks, 803 armoured
personnel carriers and 73 helicopters. The Navy has bases
at Rio de Janeiro, Salvador, Recife, Belém, Florianópolis,
Ladario and Manaus. It is equipped with four submarines,
one aircraft carrier, 14 frigates and 37 patrol and coastal
vessels. Naval aviation has 22 combat aircraft and 54
armed helicopters, the Marines have 33 armoured
personnel carriers. The Air Force has 274 combat aircraft
and 29 armed helicopters.

MILITARY EXPENDITURE – 3.2 per cent of GDP (1998)
MILITARY PERSONNEL – 291,000: Army 189,000, Navy
52,000, Air Force 50,000
CONSCRIPTION DURATION – 12 months (can be
extended to 18)

ECONOMY

There are large mineral deposits including iron ore
(hematite), manganese, bauxite, beryllium, chrome, nickel,
tungsten, cassiterite, lead, gold, monazite (containing rare
earths and thorium) and zirconium. Diamonds and
precious and semi-precious stones are also found. Brazil
is the world's largest producer of coffee; the other main
agricultural products are cassava, maize, soya, rice, wheat,
black beans, potatoes, cotton, cocoa, tobacco and peanuts.
Successive governments have attempted to curb high
inflation and large budget deficits. A new, supposedly non-
inflationary currency, the real, was introduced in 1994, but
had to be devalued by nearly 9 per cent in January 1999 as a
result of the effects of the global financial crisis on the
Brazilian economy, which had resulted in the government
announcing an austerity package in 1997. The plan
doubled interest rates, increased taxes and cut budgets.
The IMF agreed a US$41.5 billion rescue package in
November 1998 and in March 1999 made the reduction of
inflation and overall public debt preconditions of the loan.
The economic crisis, high unemployment, and the

government's austerity programme led to increasing
criticism of the government in 1999 from both opponents
and allies, who demanded changes in the management of
the economy; inflation fell as a result of the government's
programme and by April 2000 was estimated at 7 per cent.
GNP – US$767,568 million (1998); US$4,630 per capita
(1998)
GDP – US$748,696 million (1996); US$4,648 per capita
(1996)
ANNUAL AVERAGE GROWTH OF GDP – 0.3 per cent (1996)
INFLATION RATE – 3.2 per cent (1998)
UNEMPLOYMENT – 7.8 per cent (1997)
TOTAL EXTERNAL DEBT – US$232,004 million (1998)

TRADE

Principal imports are machinery, fuel and lubricants,
mineral products, transport equipment and chemicals.
Principal exports are industrial goods, coffee, iron ore and
soya. In 1994 the Brazilian automobile industry produced
1,400,000 vehicles. Of these, 374,000 vehicles were
exported. The main trading partners are the USA,
Argentina and the EU.
In 1997 Brazil had a trade deficit of US$8,364 million
and a current account deficit of US$33,840 million.
Imports totalled US$65,007 million and exports
US$52,990 million.

Trade with UK	1998	1999
Imports from UK	£921,300,000	£744,930,000
Exports to UK	928,961,000	948,956,000

COMMUNICATIONS

There are 1,670,148 km of highways, of which 161,503 km
are paved, and the route-length of railways is 30,129 km, of
which 2,150 km are electrified. There are ten international
airports and internal air services are highly developed.
There are some 50,000 km of navigable inland waterways.
Rio de Janeiro and Santos are the two leading ports. A
3,415 km gas pipeline running from Santa Cruz, Bolivia, to
São Paolo, was opened in 2000.

EDUCATION

The education system includes both public and private
institutions. Public education is free at all levels.
ILLITERACY RATE – 14.7 per cent
ENROLMENT (percentage of age group) – primary
90 per cent (1994); secondary 19 per cent (1994); tertiary
15 per cent (1996)

BRUNEI
Negara Brunei Darussalam

AREA – 2,226 sq. miles (5,765 sq. km). Neighbour:
Malaysia
POPULATION – 307,000 (1997 UN estimate): 66.9 per cent
Malay, 15.2 per cent Chinese, 5.9 per cent indigenous
races and 12 per cent European, Indian and other races.
The majority are Sunni Muslims. The official language
is Malay; English and dialects of Chinese are also spoken
CAPITAL – Bandar Seri Begawan (population, 49,902,
1994 estimate)
CURRENCY – Brunei dollar (B$) of 100 sen (fully
interchangeable with Singapore currency)
NATIONAL ANTHEM – Allah Peliharakan Sultan (God
Bless His Majesty)
NATIONAL DAY – 23 February
NATIONAL FLAG – Yellow with diagonal stripes of white
over black and the arms in red all over the centre
LIFE EXPECTANCY (years) – male 70.13; female 72.69

POPULATION GROWTH RATE – 2.7 per cent (1997)
POPULATION DENSITY – 53 per sq. km (1997)
URBAN POPULATION – 66.6 per cent (1991)
ILLITERACY RATE – 8.4 per cent
ENROLMENT (percentage of age group) – primary
91 per cent (1994); secondary 68 per cent (1994); tertiary
6.6 per cent (1996)

Brunei is situated on the north-west coast of the island of Borneo. It has a humid tropical climate.

HISTORY AND POLITICS

Formerly a powerful Muslim sultanate, Brunei was reduced to its present size by the mid-19th century and became a British Protectorate in 1888. In 1959 the Sultan promulgated the first written constitution, and on 1 January 1984 Brunei resumed full independence from Britain.

POLITICAL SYSTEM
Supreme executive authority rests with the Sultan, who presides over and is advised by the Privy Council, the Religious Council and the Council of Ministers. The Sultan effectively rules by decree as a state of emergency has been in effect since a revolt in 1962; there are no political parties and no elections.

HEAD OF STATE
HM The Sultan of Brunei, HM Sultan Haji Hassanal Bolkiah Mu'izzaddin Waddaullah, Sultan and Yang Di-Pertuan, GCB, *acceded* 1967, *crowned* 1 August 1968

COUNCIL OF MINISTERS *as at September 2000*
Prime Minister, Defence, Finance, HM The Sultan
Communications, Pehin Dato Zakaria
Development, Pengiran Dato Haji Ismail
Education; Health (acting), Pehin Dato Haji Abdul Aziz
Foreign Affairs, Prince Mohamed Bolkiah
Home Affairs, Special Adviser to the Sultan,
Pehin Dato Haji Isa
Industry and Primary Resources, Pehin Dato Haji
Abdul Rahman
Law, Pengiran Haji Bahrin
Religious Affairs, Pehin Dato Haji Mohammad Zain
Youth, Sports and Culture, Pehin Dato Haji Hussein

BRUNEI DARUSSALAM HIGH COMMISSION
19–20 Belgrave Square, London SW1X 8PG
Tel: 020-7581 0521
High Commissioner, HE Dato Haji Yusof Hamid, apptd 1999

BRITISH HIGH COMMISSION
2/01 2nd Floor Block D, Kompleks Bangunan Yayasan, Sultan Haji Hassanal Bolkiah, Jalan Pretty, PO Box 2197, Bandar Seri Begawan 1921
Tel: (00 673) (2) 222231
High Commissioner, Stuart Laing, apptd 1998

BRITISH COUNCIL DIRECTOR, T. Walsh, 45 Simpang 100, Gadong BE3619, Bandar Seri Begawan 3192;
e-mail: bcbrunei@brunet.bn

DEFENCE

The Army has 50 armoured personnel carriers. The Navy, based in Muara, has six patrol and coastal vessels. The Air Force has six armed helicopters.
MILITARY EXPENDITURE – 6.9 per cent of GDP (1998)
MILITARY PERSONNEL – 8,750: Army 3,900, Navy 700, Air Force 400, Paramilitaries 3,750

ECONOMY

The economy is based on the production of oil and natural gas, which accounted for about 36 per cent of GDP in 1996

and 90 per cent of exports. Royalties and taxes from these operations form the bulk of government revenue and have enabled the construction of free health, education and welfare services. However, the Asian economic slump coupled with a 40 per cent drop in the price of oil have damaged the economy.

The country has eight hospitals, 350 schools and one university. Royal Brunei Airlines operates scheduled flights to the UK, Australia and throughout the Far East. Radio Television Brunei broadcasts one television and three radio channels from the capital.

In 1998 Brunei produced 7,800,000 tonnes of crude petroleum and 10,700 million cubic metres of natural gas. In 1994 imports totalled US$1,634 million and exports US$2,215 million.
GNP – US$3,975 million (1994); US$14,240 per capita (1994)
GDP – US$5,450 million (1996); US$18,167 per capita (1996)
ANNUAL AVERAGE GROWTH OF GDP – 4.6 per cent (1996)

Trade with UK	1998	1999
Imports from UK	£257,197,000	£132,042,000
Exports to UK	183,564,000	76,118,000

BULGARIA
Republika Bålgarija

AREA – 42,823 sq. miles (110,912 sq. km). Neighbours: Romania (north), Serbia and the Former Yugoslav Republic of Macedonia (west), Greece and Turkey (south)
POPULATION – 8,306,000 (1997 estimate): 85.7 per cent Bulgarian, 9.4 per cent Turkish, 3.7 per cent Roma, 1.2 per cent others. The language is Bulgarian, a Southern Slavonic tongue closely allied to Serbo-Croat and Russian with local admixtures of modern Greek, Albanian and Turkish words. The alphabet is Cyrillic. The predominant religion is the Bulgarian Orthodox Church (85.7 per cent of the population); Islam is the second largest religion (13.1 per cent).
CAPITAL – Sofia (population, 1,191,743, 1996 estimate)
MAJOR CITIES – ΨBurgas (214,830); Dobrich (103,532); Pleven (154,140); Plovdiv (344,326); Ruse (184,445); Sliven (144,492); Stara Zagora (174,688); ΨVarna (307,394), 1996 estimates
CURRENCY – Lev of 100 stotinki
NATIONAL ANTHEM – Gorda stara planina (Proud and ancient mountains)
NATIONAL DAY – 3 March
NATIONAL FLAG – Three horizontal bands, white, green, red
LIFE EXPECTANCY (years) – male 67.11; female 74.85
POPULATION GROWTH RATE – –1.1 per cent (1997)
POPULATION DENSITY – 75 per sq. km (1997)
URBAN POPULATION – 67.7 per cent (1994)

HISTORY AND POLITICS

A principality of Bulgaria was created by the Treaty of Berlin in 1878, and in 1908 the country was declared an independent kingdom. A coup d'état in September 1944 gave power to the Fatherland Front, a coalition of Communists, Agrarians and Social Democrats. In August 1945, the main body of Agrarians and Social Democrats left the government. A referendum in September 1946 led to the abolition of the monarchy and the establishment of a republic.

The post-war period was dominated by the Communist Party (BCP), led by Todor Zhivkov. He was forced to resign in November 1989, and in January 1990 the National Assembly voted to abolish the BCP's constitutional guarantee of power. Multiparty elections to a Grand National Assembly (parliament) were held in June 1990 and won by the BCP, renamed the Bulgarian Socialist Party (BSP). This government lasted only two months, and in December 1990 a multiparty government was formed which began to implement a programme of economic and political reform.

After legislative elections in October 1991 a coalition government of the Union of Democratic Forces (UDF) and the Turkish Movement for Rights and Freedom Party (MRF) was formed. This government was replaced in December 1992 by a weak government of non-party technocrats which also collapsed. The BSP won the ensuing general election in December 1994 and formed a government with the Agrarian National Union (ANU). In November 1996 the UDF candidate, Petar Stoyanov, became president. The following month the BSP Prime Minister Jan Videnov resigned following protests about falling standards of living. The UDF won the resulting elections in April 1997. In April 2000, the Bulgarian media alleged that corruption was widespread among government officials following the resignation of a government spokesman who had been accused of accepting bribes.

POLITICAL SYSTEM

A new constitution enshrining democracy and the free market was adopted in 1991. It provides for a directly-elected president who serves for no more than two five-year terms. The chief executive is the prime minister who is appointed by the president, and is usually the leader of the largest party in the legislature. There is a unicameral National Assembly of 240 members who are directly elected by proportional representation for four-year terms.

HEAD OF STATE
President, Petar Stoyanov, *elected* 3 November 1996

COUNCIL OF MINISTERS *as at September 2000*
Prime Minister; State Administration, Ivan Kostov
Deputy PM, Economy, Peter Zhotev
Agriculture, Forests and Land Reform,
   Ventsislav Vurbanov
Culture, Emma Moskova
Defence, Boiko Noev
Education and Science, Dimiter Dimitrov
Environment and Waters, Evdokia Maneva
Finance, Mouravei Radev
Foreign Affairs, Nadezhda Mihailova
Health, Ilko Semerdjiev
Interior, Emanuil Yordanov
Justice, Teodossiy Simeonov
Labour and Social Policy, Ivan Neikov
Regional and Urban Development, Evgeni Chachev
Transport and Communications, Antoni Slavinski
Without Portfolio, Alexander Pramatarski

EMBASSY OF THE REPUBLIC OF BULGARIA
186–188 Queen's Gate, London SW7 5HL
Tel: 020-7584 9400
Ambassador Extraordinary and Plenipotentiary,
   HE Valentin Dobrev, apptd 1998
Counsellor (Commercial), Christo Charenkov
Military, Air and Naval Attaché, Lt.-Gen. Anu Anguelov

BRITISH EMBASSY
38 Boulevard Vassil Levski, Sofia
Tel: (00 359) (2) 2980 1220
E-mail: britembsof@mbox.cit.bg
Ambassador Extraordinary and Plenipotentiary,
   HE Richard Stagg, apptd 1998
Deputy Head of Mission and First Secretary, J. H. Kidner
Defence Attaché, Col. R. E. Fielding
First Secretary (Commercial), M. J. Carbine

BRITISH COUNCIL DIRECTOR, K. Lewis, 7 Tulovo Street, BG-1504, Sofia; e-mail: bc.sofia@britcoun.ttm.bg

DEFENCE

The Army has 1,475 main battle tanks, 214 armoured infantry fighting vehicles, and 1,772 armoured personnel carriers. The Navy has one submarine, one frigate, 23 patrol and coastal vessels, and nine armed helicopters. The Air Force has 227 combat aircraft and 43 armed helicopters.
MILITARY EXPENDITURE – 3.7 per cent of GDP (1998)
MILITARY PERSONNEL – 10,960: Army 43,400, Navy
   5,260, Air Force 18,300, Paramilitaries 34,000
CONSCRIPTION DURATION – 12 months

ECONOMY

The principal crops are wheat, maize, beet, tomatoes, tobacco, oleaginous seeds, fruit, vegetables and cotton. Around 24 per cent of the population is engaged in agriculture, which accounted for 26.2 per cent of GDP in 1997. Cadmium, coal, copper, pig iron, kaolin, lead, silver and zinc are produced.

The lack of radical economic reform has hampered economic development; in 1996, the value of the lev plummeted by 70 per cent. The government responded by adopting a radical reform package, but inflation exceeded 100 per cent in 1997.

The lev was pegged to the Deutsche Mark from 1 July 1997, at a rate of DM1=1,000 leva. Following the implementation of fiscal reforms, Bulgaria received some US$385 million in loans from the EU and the World Bank to help economic recovery. The World Bank agreed a further loan of US$275 million in April 1999.
GNP – US$10,085 million (1998); US$1,220 per capita
   (1998)
GDP – US$9,333 million (1996); US$1,102 per capita
   (1996)
ANNUAL AVERAGE GROWTH OF GDP – –10.9 per cent
   (1996)
INFLATION RATE – 22.3 per cent (1998)
UNEMPLOYMENT – 14.4 per cent (1997)
TOTAL EXTERNAL DEBT – US$9,907 million (1998)

TRADE

The principal imports are fuels, industrial equipment, chemicals, textiles and clothing, and foodstuffs and beverages. The principal exports are chemicals, textiles and clothing, iron and steel products, foodstuffs and beverages, industrial equipment and non-ferrous metals.

In 1993 Bulgaria signed an Association Agreement with the EU, and EU duties on many Bulgarian industrial goods were abolished by 1995 and levies on agricultural goods significantly lowered.

In 1998 Bulgaria had a trade deficit of US$316 million and a current account deficit of US$252 million. Imports totalled US$4,979 million and exports US$4,300 million. The principal trading partners are Russia, Germany and Italy.

Trade with UK	1998	1999
Imports from UK	£80,417,000	£78,032,000
Exports to UK	78,160,000	68,567,000

EDUCATION

Education is free and compulsory for children from seven to 15 years inclusive. There are three universities (at Sofia, Plovdiv and Veliko Turnovo), an American University and 21 higher education establishments.
ILLITERACY RATE – 1.5 per cent
ENROLMENT (percentage of age group) – primary
   92 per cent (1996); secondary 74 per cent (1996); tertiary
   41.2 per cent (1996)

BURKINA FASO
République Démocratique du Burkina Faso

AREA – 105,792 sq. miles (274,000 sq. km). Neighbours: Mali (west), Niger and Benin (east), Togo, Ghana and Côte d'Ivoire (south)
POPULATION – 11,087,000 (1997 UN estimate). The official language is French. Mossi, More, Dioula and Gourmantché are indigenous languages
CAPITAL – Ouagadougou (population, 634,479, 1991 estimate)
MAJOR CITIES – Bobo-Dioulasso (228,668); Koudougou (30,000)
CURRENCY – Franc CFA of 100 centimes
NATIONAL ANTHEM – Ditanyé
NATIONAL DAY – 11 December
NATIONAL FLAG – Equal bands of red over green, with a yellow star in centre
LIFE EXPECTANCY (years) – male 45.38; female 47.59
POPULATION GROWTH RATE – 3.0 per cent (1997)
POPULATION DENSITY – 40 per sq. km (1997)
URBAN POPULATION – 15.0 per cent (1995)
MILITARY EXPENDITURE – 2.5 per cent of GDP (1998)
MILITARY PERSONNEL – 10,000: Army 5,600, Air Force 200; Paramilitaries 4,200
ILLITERACY RATE – 77.0 per cent
ENROLMENT (percentage of age group) – primary 31 per cent (1994); secondary 7 per cent (1993); tertiary 0.9 per cent (1996)

Burkina Faso (formerly Upper Volta) is an inland savannah state in West Africa. The largest tribe is the Mossi whose king, the Moro Naba, still wields a certain moral influence.

HISTORY AND POLITICS

Burkina Faso was annexed by France in 1896 and between 1932 and 1947 was administered as part of the Colony of the Ivory Coast. It decided on 11 December 1958 to remain an autonomous republic within the French Community; full independence outside the Community was proclaimed on 5 August 1960.

In 1966 the Army assumed power; a constitution allowing for a partial return to civilian rule was adopted in 1970, but was suspended in 1974. Full legislative and presidential elections were held again in 1978.

Following a number of military coups, Capt. Blaise Compaoré seized power in 1987. A new constitution was adopted in 1991. Presidential elections were held in November 1998 and won by Compaoré in the face of a boycott by the opposition parties.

HEAD OF STATE

President, Capt. Blaise Compaoré, *assumed office* October 1987, *elected* December 1991, *re-elected* November 1998

COUNCIL OF MINISTERS *as at September 2000*

Prime Minister, Economy and Finance, Kadré Désiré Ouédraogo
Agriculture, Issa Martin Bikenga
Animal Resources, Alassane Seré
Civil Service and Institutional Development, Paramanga Ernest Yonli
Communications, Théodore Kilimité Hien
Culture and Arts, Mahmadou Ouédraogo
Defence, Government Spokesman, Albert D. Millogo
Economy and Finance, Tertius Zongo
Employment, Labour, Social Security, Sané Mohammed Topan
Energy and Mines, Elie Ouédraogo
Health, Alain Ludovic Tou
Infrastructure, Housing, Urban Planning, Hyppolite Lingani
Justice, Keeper of the Seals, Boureima Badini
Ministers of State, Capt. Bongnessan Arsène Yé (*Environment and Water*); Youssouf Ouédraogo (*Foreign Affairs*); Ram Ouédraogo (*Without Portfolio*)
National Education, Basic Training and Literacy, Baworo Seydou Sanou
Presidential Affairs, Pierre Tapsoba
Regional Integration, Bernadette Sanou
Relations with Parliament, Cyril Goungounga
Secondary and Higher Education, Scientific Research, Christophe Dabiré
Social Affairs and Family, Nayatigungou Kongo Kaboré
Territorial Administration and Security, Yéro Boly
Trade, Industry and Crafts, Kader Cissé
Transport and Tourism, Bédouma Alain Yoda
Women's Promotion, Gisèle Guigma
Youth and Sports, René Emile Kaboré

EMBASSY OF THE REPUBLIC OF BURKINA FASO
16 Place Guy d'Arezzo, B-1180 Brussels, Belgium
Tel: (00 32) (2) 345 9912
Ambassador Extraordinary and Plenipotentiary, vacant

HONORARY CONSULATE, Cinnamon Row, Plantation Wharf, London SW11 3TW. Tel: 020-7738 1800.
Honorary Consul-General, S. G. Singer

BRITISH AMBASSADOR, HE Haydon Warren-Gash, CMG, resident at Abidjan. Côte d'Ivoire

ECONOMY

The principal industry is cattle and sheep rearing. Agriculture employs over 90 per cent of the workforce and contributes 35 per cent of GDP. The chief exports are cotton, livestock and animal feed, and gold. The chief imports are capital goods, foodstuffs and fuel oils.

In 1994 Burkina Faso had a trade deficit of US$129 million and a current account surplus of US$15 million. In 1997 imports totalled US$530 million and exports US$186 million.
GNP – US$2,575 million (1998); US$240 per capita (1998)
GDP – US$1,916 million (1996); US$178 per capita (1996)
ANNUAL AVERAGE GROWTH OF GDP – 5.6 per cent (1996)
INFLATION RATE – 5.1 per cent (1998)
TOTAL EXTERNAL DEBT – US$1,399 million (1998)

Trade with UK	1998	1999
Imports from UK	£5,149,000	£6,711,000
Exports to UK	1,182,000	824,000

COMMUNICATIONS

There are 12,349 km of roads, of which 1,988 km are bituminised, and 617 km of railway track in operation. There are two main airports, Ouagadougou and Bobo-Dioulasso.

BURUNDI
République du Burundi

AREA – 10,747 sq. miles (27,834 sq. km). Neighbours: Rwanda (north), Tanzania (east and south), Democratic Republic of Congo (west)
POPULATION – 6,194,000 (1997 UN estimate): 83 per cent Hutu, 15 per cent Tutsi. The official languages are Kirundi, a Bantu language, and French. Kiswahili is also used
CAPITAL – Bujumbura (formerly Usumbura) (population, 235,440, 1990)

MAJOR CITIES – Kitega (18,000)
CURRENCY – Burundi franc of 100 centimes
NATIONAL DAY – 1 July
NATIONAL FLAG – Divided diagonally by a white saltire into red and green triangles; on a white disc in the centre three red six-pointed stars edged in green
NATIONAL ANTHEM – Burundi Bwacu (Dear Burundi)
LIFE EXPECTANCY (years) – male 42.96; female 46.15
POPULATION GROWTH RATE – 1.8 per cent (1997)
POPULATION DENSITY – 223 per sq. km (1997)
URBAN POPULATION – 5.0 per cent (1990)
MILITARY EXPENDITURE – 7.2 per cent of GDP (1998)
MILITARY PERSONNEL – 45,500: Army 40,000, Paramilitaries 5,500
ILLITERACY RATE – 51.9 per cent
ENROLMENT (percentage of age group) – primary 52 per cent (1992); secondary 5 per cent (1992); tertiary 0.9 per cent (1995)

HISTORY AND POLITICS

Formerly a Belgian trusteeship under the United Nations, Burundi became independent as a constitutional monarchy on 1 July 1962. However, the monarchy was overthrown in 1966 and the country became a republic. After a coup in 1987 the Military Committee of National Redemption came to power, led by Maj. Pierre Buyoya, a Tutsi.

Although most of the population is Hutu, political and military power has traditionally rested with the Tutsi minority. Since the 1960s, Hutu attempts to overthrow Tutsi rule have resulted in ethnic massacres. The Tutsi-dominated army attempted a coup in 1993 in which President Melchior Ndadaye was killed. The government regained control in December but two months of inter-racial fighting left more than 50,000 dead and 500,000 refugees.

The Front for Democracy in Burundi (FRODEBU) and the National Unity and Progress Party (UPRONA) agreed to form a coalition government in 1994 with a Tutsi prime minister and Hutu president. However, the government was unable to halt attacks by the Tutsi-dominated army and Hutu militias on each other's communities. The fighting claimed 200,000 lives in 1993–5.

In July 1996 the army again seized power and installed Maj. Buyoya as president. Political parties were banned and the National Assembly was suspended until October 1996 when fewer than half its deputies attended. A multi-ethnic government of national unity was formed in August 1996. Clashes between the army and Hutu militias, and massacres of civilians have continued, despite talks aimed at finding a peaceful solution. More than 300,000 refugees remain in camps in Tanzania and the Democratic Republic of Congo. In April 2000, President Buyoya promised to dismantle the 'regroupment camps' into which over 800,000 Hutus had been placed to stabilise the security situation.

A new transitional constitution, designed to provide for a political partnership between Hutus and Tutsis, came into being in June 1998 and a 117-member Transitional National Assembly was inaugurated in July 1998.

HEAD OF STATE

President, Maj. Pierre Buyoya, *appointed* 25 July 1996, *sworn in* 11 June 1998
Vice-Presidents, Frédéric Bamvunginyumvira; Mathias Sinamenye

COUNCIL OF MINISTERS *as at September 2000*
Agriculture and Livestock, Salvator Ntihabose
Communal Development and Handicrafts, Denis Nshimirimana
Defence, Lt.-Col. Cyrille Ndayirukiye
Development Planning and Reconstruction, Léon Nimbona
Education, Prosper Mpawenayo

Energy and Mines, Bernard Barandereka
External Relations and Co-operation, Séverin Ntahomvukiye
Finance, Charles Nihangaza
Health, Stanislas Ntahobari
Human Rights, Institutional Reforms and Relations with National Assembly, Eugène Nindorera
Information and Government Spokesman, Luc Rukingama
Internal Affairs and Public Security, Col. Ascension Twagiramungu
Justice, Térence Sinunguruza
Labour, Civil Service and Professional Training, Emmanuel Tungamwese
Land and Environment, Jean-Pacifique Nsengiyumva
Peace Process, Ambroise Niyonsaba
Public Works and Housing, Gaspard Ntirampeba
Reintegration and Resettlement of Displaced Persons and Repatriates, Pascal Nkurunziza
Trade, Industry and Tourism, Joseph Ntanyotora
Transport, Posts and Telecommunications, Cyprien Mbonigaba
Women, Welfare and Social Affairs, Romaine Ndorimana
Youth, Sports and Culture, Gérard Nyamwiza

EMBASSY OF THE REPUBLIC OF BURUNDI
Marie Louise-square 46, B-1040 Brussels, Belgium
Tel: (00 32) (2) 2304535
Ambassador Extraordinary and Plenipotentiary, HE Jonathas Niyungeko, apptd 1999

BRITISH AMBASSADOR, HE G. Loten, resident at Kigali, Rwanda

ECONOMY

The chief crops are coffee and tea, accounting for around 98 per cent of export earnings. Mineral, hide and skin exports are also important. Agriculture accounted for 58 per cent of GDP and employed over 90 per cent of the workforce in 1997.

In 1997 there was a trade deficit of US$11 million and a current account surplus of US$4 million. In 1998 imports totalled US$158 million and exports US$65 million.
GNP – US$911 million (1998); US$140 per capita (1998)
GDP – US$1,030 million (1996); US$166 per capita (1996)
ANNUAL AVERAGE GROWTH OF GDP – –3.6 per cent (1996)
INFLATION RATE – 12.5 per cent (1998)
TOTAL EXTERNAL DEBT – US$1,119 million (1998)

Trade with UK	1998	1999
Imports from UK	£2,296,000	£2,110,000
Exports to UK	188,000	973,000

CAMBODIA
Preăh Réachéanachăkr Kămpŭchéa – The Kingdom of Cambodia

AREA – 69,898 sq. miles (181,035 sq. km). Neighbours: Laos (north), Thailand (north and west), Vietnam (east)
POPULATION – 10,516,000 (1997 UN estimate). The language is Khmer. Chinese, Vietnamese and French are also spoken
CAPITAL – ΨPhnom Penh (population, 832,000, 1997)
CURRENCY – Riel of 100 sen
NATIONAL ANTHEM – Nokoreach
NATIONAL DAY – 9 November (Independence Day)
NATIONAL FLAG – Three horizontal stripes of blue, red, blue, with the blue of double width and containing a representation of the temple of Angkor in white
LIFE EXPECTANCY (years) – male 50.10; female 52.90
POPULATION GROWTH RATE – 2.9 per cent (1997)

POPULATION DENSITY – 58 per sq. km (1997)
URBAN POPULATION – 14.4 per cent (1996)
ILLITERACY RATE – 34.7 per cent
ENROLMENT (percentage of age group) – primary 100
    per cent (1997); tertiary 1 per cent (1997)

HISTORY AND POLITICS

Cambodia became a French protectorate in 1863 and was
granted independence within the French Union as an
Associate State in 1949. Full independence was proclaimed in 1953, and Prince Norodom Sihanouk became
head of state. In 1970 Prince Sihanouk was deposed and a
Khmer Republic was declared.

In 1975, Phnom Penh fell to the North Vietnamese-
backed Khmer Rouge. During Khmer Rouge rule
hundreds of thousands of Cambodians fled into exile and
an estimated two million were killed.

In 1978, Vietnamese troops invaded Cambodia and the
state was renamed The People's Republic of Kampuchea
(PRK); in 1989 it became the State of Cambodia (SOC).
Following the Vietnamese withdrawal in 1989, the
resistance forces regained ground.

In September 1990, the government and the resistance
forces established a Supreme National Council and peace
agreements were signed in October 1991. In March 1992
the United Nations Transitional Authority for Cambodia
(UNTAC) assumed authority from the government in the
run-up to the multiparty elections, which were held in
May 1993. Prince Sihanouk brokered a coalition government agreement under which he became head of state
and Prince Ranariddh and Hun Sen, became co-prime
ministers. In September 1993 a new constitution was
adopted under which Cambodia became a pluralist
liberal democracy with a constitutional monarchy. Prince
Sihanouk was elected king and he appointed a new
government.

Prince Ranariddh was ousted from power following a
coup by soldiers loyal to Hun Sen in July 1997, and armed
conflicts between the rival factions broke out throughout
the country. On 27 February 1998, both sides declared a
cease-fire in a Japanese-brokered peace plan. Under the
terms of the deal Prince Ranariddh was tried by the Hun

Sen government and unconditionally pardoned after
being found guilty; he then returned to the country for
democratic elections in July 1998.

In November 1998 a coalition government was formed
with Hun Sen as prime minister and Prince Ranariddh as
chairman of the National Assembly.

INSURGENCIES

In July 1994 the Royal Government outlawed the Khmer
Rouge, which responded by declaring a provisional
government. Large numbers of Khmer Rouge defected
to the Royal Government including more than 2,500 led
by Ieng Sary, who formally joined the Royal Cambodian
Armed Forces in November 1996. Khmer Rouge leader
Pol Pot was captured by a group of defectors in June 1997
and died in captivity on 15 April 1998. The remaining
4,332 Khmer Rouge soldiers surrendered on 9 February
1999.

POLITICAL SYSTEM

Legislative power is vested in the National Assembly, which
has 122 members elected for five-year terms, and
the Senate, which has 61 appointed members and was
formed on 25 March 1999, following an amendment to the
constitution by the National Assembly. Executive power
rests in the Royal Government, with the King having the
power only to make appointments and declare a state of
emergency, in consultation with the government.

HEAD OF STATE

HM The King of Cambodia, Norodom Sihanouk, *elected by
    the Council of the Throne* 24 September 1993

ROYAL GOVERNMENT OF CAMBODIA *as at September
2000*

Prime Minister, Hun Sen (CPP)
Deputy Prime Minister, Co-Minister of Interior, Sar Kheng
    (CPP)
Deputy Prime Minister, Education, Youth and Sports,
    Tol Loah (F)
Agriculture, Forestry and Fishing, Chhea Song (CPP)
Co-Minister of National Defence, Prince Sisowath
    Sereiroat (F)
Commerce, Cham Prasit (CPP)
Culture and Fine Arts, Princess Norodom Bophadevi (F)
Environment, Mok Maret (CPP)
Foreign Affairs and International Co-operation,
    Hor Namhong (CPP)
Health, Hong Sun-huot (F)
Industry, Mines and Energy, Suy Sem (CPP)
Information and Press, Loe Laysreng (F)
Justice, Uk Vithun (F)
Landscaping, Urbanism and Construction, Im Chhunlim
    (CPP)
Planning, Chhay Than (CPP)
Post and Telecommunications, So Khun (CPP)
Public Works and Transport, Khi Tanglim (F)
Relations with National Assembly and Inspection,
    Khun Hang (F)
Religious Affairs, Chea Savoeun (F)
Rural Development, Chhim Siekleng (F)
*Social Affairs, Labour, Vocational Training and Youth
    Rehabilitation*, It Sam-heng (CPP)
State Minister, Co-Minister of Interior, Yu Hokkri (F)
State Minister, Co-Minister of National Defence,
    Gen. Tie Banh (CPP)
State Minister, Economy and Finance, Keat Chong (CPP)
State Minister, Office of the Council of Ministers, Sok An
    (CPP)
State Ministers, Loe Laysreng (F); Hor Namhong (F)
Tourism, Veng Sereivut (F)
Water Resources, Lim Kean-hao (CPP)
Women's and Veterans' Affairs, Mu Sok-huo (F)

CPP Cambodian People's Party; F United National Front

for an Independent, Neutral, Peaceful and Co-operative Cambodia (FUNCINPEC)

BRITISH EMBASSY
29, Street 75, Phnom Penh
Tel: (00 855) (23) 427124
Ambassador Extraordinary and Plenipotentiary,
   HE George Edgar, apptd 1997

DEFENCE

The Army has 100 main battle tanks and 240 armoured personnel carriers. The Navy has 10 patrol and coastal vessels. The Air Force has 24 combat aircraft.
MILITARY EXPENDITURE – 4.2 per cent of GDP (1998)
MILITARY PERSONNEL – 140,000: Army 90,000, Navy 3,000, Air Force 2,000, Provincial Forces 45,000
CONSCRIPTION DURATION – Not implemented since 1993

ECONOMY

The economy is largely based on agriculture, fishing and forestry. Agriculture employs over 70 per cent of the workforce and produced 51 per cent of GDP in 1997. In addition to rice, which is the staple crop, the major products are rubber, livestock, maize, timber, pepper, palm sugar, fresh and dried fish, kapok, beans, soya and tobacco. Textiles, leather goods, furnishings, timber and rubber are the main exports; the main imports are cigarettes, gold, diesel and oil.

Under the Khmer Rouge, the urban population was forced to work on the land, and re-establish plantations producing such crops as cotton, rubber and bananas. Following the Vietnamese invasion of 1978 the towns were repopulated and factories, in particular textile mills, iron smelting works and cement works, were put back in production.

In 1998 there was a trade deficit of US$387 million and a current account deficit of US$219 million.
GNP – US$2,945 million (1998); US$260 per capita (1998)
GDP – US$1,469 million (1996); US$143 per capita (1996)
ANNUAL AVERAGE GROWTH OF GDP – 6.5 per cent (1996)
INFLATION RATE – 14.8 per cent (1998)
TOTAL EXTERNAL DEBT – US$2,210 million (1998)

Trade with UK	1998	1999
Imports from UK	£6,083,000	£4,184,000
Exports to UK	24,039,000	42,798,000

COMMUNICATIONS

The country has about 34,100 kilometres of roads, although most are now in a state of disrepair. There are two railways, one from Phnom Penh to the Thai border, the other from Phnom Penh to Kampot and Sihanoukville (Kompong Som). Phnom Penh is on a river capable of receiving ships of up to 2,500 tons all the year round. The deep water port at Sihanoukville (Kompong Som) on the Gulf of Thailand can receive ships of up to 10,000 tons. The port is linked to Phnom Penh by a modern highway.

CAMEROON
République du Cameroun

AREA – 183,569 sq. miles (475,442 sq. km). Neighbours: Nigeria (north and west), Chad and Central African Republic (east), Republic of Congo-Brazzaville, Gabon and Equatorial Guinea (south)
POPULATION – 13,937,000 (1997 UN estimate). French and English are both official languages and enjoy equal status
CAPITAL – Yaoundé (population, 653,670, 1986 estimate)
MAJOR CITIES – ΨDouala (1,029,731) is the commercial centre
CURRENCY – Franc CFA of 100 centimes
NATIONAL ANTHEM – O Cameroun, Berceau de Nos Ancêtres (O Cameroon, thou cradle of our forefathers)
NATIONAL DAY – 20 May
NATIONAL FLAG – Vertical stripes of green, red and yellow with single five-pointed yellow star in centre of red stripe
LIFE EXPECTANCY (years) – male 53.28; female 56.17
POPULATION GROWTH RATE – 2.8 per cent (1997)
POPULATION DENSITY – 29 per sq. km (1997)
MILITARY EXPENDITURE – 2.9 per cent of GDP (1998)
MILITARY PERSONNEL – 22,100: Army 11,500, Navy 1,300, Air Force 300, Paramilitaries 9,000
ILLITERACY RATE – 24.6 per cent
ENROLMENT (percentage of age group) – secondary 15 per cent (1980); tertiary 3.3 per cent (1990)

HISTORY AND POLITICS

The German colony of the Cameroons, established in 1884, was captured by British and French forces in 1916 and divided into the League of Nations-mandated territories (later UN trusteeships) of East (French) and West (British) Cameroon. On 1 January 1960 East Cameroon became independent as the Republic of Cameroon. This was joined on 1 October 1961 by the southern part of West Cameroon after a plebiscite held under United Nations auspices; the northern part joined Nigeria. Cameroon became a federal republic with separate East and West Cameroon state governments. After a plebiscite held in 1972, Cameroon became a unitary republic and a one-party state.

After extensive unrest, multiparty elections were held in March 1992. The ruling People's Democratic Movement formed a coalition government with a small opposition party, the Movement for the Defence of the Republic.

A legislative election held in May 1997 was dominated by the ruling Cameroon People's Democratic Movement (CPDM) which won 109 of the 180 seats, though Commonwealth observers reported widespread fraud and voter intimidation.

INSURGENCIES

Secessionists in the largely Anglophone Northwest and Southwest provinces declared independence as the Federal Republic of Southern Cameroon in December 1999 and appointed a president in April 2000.

INTERNATIONAL RELATIONS

There have been armed clashes with Nigeria over the disputed Bakassi peninsula. The dispute is under consideration at the International Court of Justice.

POLITICAL SYSTEM

The president is directly elected for a seven-year term, and appoints the prime minister and Cabinet. The National Assembly comprises 180 members, directly elected for a five-year term. Under the 1995 constitutional amendments a Senate is to be created.

HEAD OF STATE
President and Commander-in-Chief of the Armed Forces,
   Paul Biya, *acceded* 6 November 1982, *elected*
   14 January 1984, *re-elected* 24 April 1988,
   10 October 1992, 12 October 1997

CABINET *as at September 2000*
Prime Minister, Peter Mafany Musonge

Agriculture, Zacharie Perevet
City Affairs, Claude Joseph Mbafou
Civil Service and Administrative Reform, René Ze Nguele
Communication, Jacques Famé Ndongo
Culture, Ferdinand Leopold Oyono
Defence and National Police Force, Rémi Zé Meka
Delegate at the Foreign Ministry in charge of Commonwealth Relations, Joseph Ndion Ngute
Delegate at the Foreign Ministry in charge of Islamic Relations, Adoum Gargoum
Delegate at the Ministry of Finance in charge of Budget, Roger Melingui
Delegate at the Ministry of Finance in charge of the Plan for Stability, Jean-Marie Gankou
Delegate at the Presidency in charge of Relations with the Assemblies, Grégoire Owona
Delegate at the Presidency in charge of Supreme State Audit, Lucy Gwanmesia
Economy and Finance, Edouard Akame Mfoumdou
Employment, Labour and Social Causes, Pius Ondoua
Environment and Forests, Sylvester Naah Ondoua
Foreign Affairs, Augustin Kontchou Kouemegni
Higher Education, Jean-Marie Atangana Mebara
Industrial and Commercial Development, Bello Bouba Maigari; Edmond Moampea Mbio
Justice, Keeper of the Seals, Robert Mbella Mbappe
Livestock, Fisheries and Animal Industries, Ajoudji Hamadjoda
Mines, Water Resources and Energy, Yves Mbelle
National Education, Joseph Owona; Joseph Yunga Teghen; Haman Adama
Post and Telecommunications, Mounchipou Seydou; Denis Oumarou
Public Health, Laurent Esso; Alim Hayatou
Public Investment and Regional Planning, Martin Okouda; Shey Johnes Yembe
Public Works, Jérome Etah; Emmanuel Bonde
Scientific and Technical Research, Henri Hogbe Nlend
Social Affairs, Madeleine Fouda
Special Duties at the Presidency, Peter Abety; Justin Ndioro; Raphael Onambele; Elvis Ngole Ngole; Baba Hamadou
Territorial Administration, Ferdinand Koungou; Adama Modi Bakari
Tourism, Pierre Hele
Town Planning and Housing, Boubakary Yerima Halilou; Tsala Messi
Transport, Joseph Tsanga Abanda; Nana Aboubakar Djalloh
Women's Affairs, Julienne Ngo Som
Youth and Sports, Bidoung Mkpatt

HIGH COMMISSION FOR THE REPUBLIC OF CAMEROON
84 Holland Park, London W11 3SB
Tel: 020-7727 0771
Ambassador Extraordinary and Plenipotentiary, HE Samuel Libock Mbei, apptd 1995

BRITISH HIGH COMMISSION
Avenue Winston Churchill, BP 547 Yaoundé
Tel: (00 237) 220545
High Commissioner, HE Peter Boon, MBE, apptd 1998
There is also a British Consulate at Douala.

BRITISH COUNCIL DIRECTOR, J. Rollinson, Avenue Charles de Gaulle, BP 818, Yaoundé;
e-mail: bc.yaounde@bc-yaounde.iccnet.cm

ECONOMY

Principal products are cocoa, coffee, bananas, cotton, timber, groundnuts, aluminium, rubber and palm products. Crude petroleum is also one of Cameroon's principal products.
France, Italy and other European Union states are

Cameroon's main trading partners. In 1995 there was a trade surplus of US$627 million and a current account surplus of US$90 million. In 1997 exports totalled US$1,860 million and imports US$1,359 million.
GNP – US$8,736 million (1998); US$610 per capita (1998)
GDP – US$9,112 million (1996); US$672 per capita (1996)
ANNUAL AVERAGE GROWTH OF GDP – 5.1 per cent (1996)
INFLATION RATE – 1.5 per cent (1997)
TOTAL EXTERNAL DEBT – US$9,829 million (1998)

Trade with UK	1998	1999
Imports from UK	£37,118,000	£23,866,000
Exports to UK	42,543,000	42,854,000

CANADA

AREA – 3,849,674 sq. miles (9,970,610 sq. km).
  Neighbours: USA (south), Alaska (USA) (west)
POPULATION – 30,491,294 (1999). The languages are English and French
CAPITAL – Ottawa (population, 1,010,498, 1996 census).
MAJOR CITIES – Calgary (853,711); Edmonton (890,771); Halifax (344,135); Hamilton (657,230); Kitchener (404,216); London (420,614); ΨMontréal (3,365,160); Toronto (4,410,269); ΨVancouver (1,883,679); Winnipeg (680,285), 1996 estimates
CURRENCY – Canadian dollar (C$) of 100 cents
NATIONAL ANTHEM – O Canada
NATIONAL DAY – 1 July (Canada Day)
NATIONAL FLAG – Red maple leaf with 11 points on white square, flanked by vertical red bars one-half the width of the square
LIFE EXPECTANCY (years) – male 74.55; female 80.89
POPULATION GROWTH RATE – 1.1 per cent (1997)
POPULATION DENSITY – 3 per sq. km (1997)
URBAN POPULATION – 76.7 per cent (1995)

Canada occupies the whole of the northern part of the North American continent, with the exception of Alaska. In eastern Canada, the southernmost point is Middle Island in Lake Erie. Canada has six main physiographic divisions: the Appalachian-Acadian region, the Canadian shield, which comprises more than half the country, the St Lawrence-Great Lakes lowland, the interior plains, the Cordilleran region and the Arctic archipelago.
  The climate of the eastern and central portions presents greater extremes than in corresponding latitudes in Europe, but in the south-western portion of the prairie region and the southern portions of the Pacific slope the climate is milder.

HISTORY AND POLITICS

Canada was originally discovered by Cabot in 1497 but its history dates from 1534, when the French took possession of the country. The first permanent settlement at Port Royal (now Annapolis), Nova Scotia, was founded in 1605, and Québec was founded in 1608. In 1759 Québec was captured by British forces under General Wolfe and in 1763 the whole territory of Canada became a possession of Great Britain by the Treaty of Paris 1763. Nova Scotia was ceded in 1713 by the Treaty of Utrecht, the provinces of New Brunswick and Prince Edward Island being subsequently formed out of it. British Columbia was formed into a Crown colony in 1858, having previously been a part of the Hudson Bay Territory, and was united to Vancouver Island in 1866.

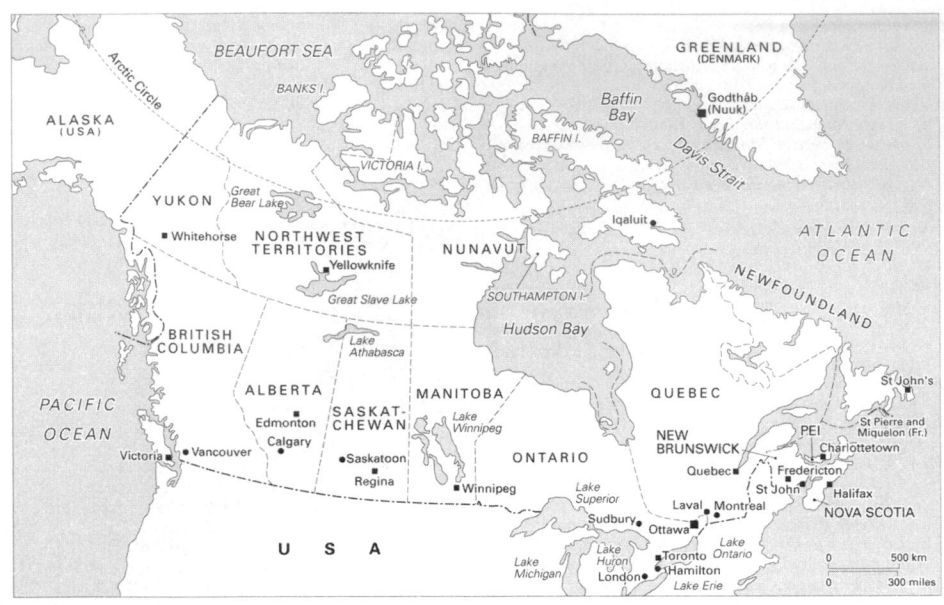

FEDERAL STRUCTURE

Provinces or Territories (with official contractions)	Area (sq. kilometres)	Population 1999	Capital	Lieutenant-Governor	Premier
Alberta (AB)	661,190	2,964,689	Edmonton	Lois Hole	Ralph Klein
British Columbia (BC)	947,800	4,023,100	ΨVictoria	Garde Gardom	Ujjal Dosanjh
Manitoba (MB)	649,950	1,143,509	Winnipeg	Peter Liba	Gary Doer
New Brunswick (NB)	73,440	754,969	Fredericton	Marilyn Trenholme Counsell	Bernard Lord
Newfoundland and Labrador (NF)	405,720	541,000	ΨSt John's	A. M. House	Brian Tobin
Nova Scotia (NS)	55,490	939,791	ΨHalifax	Myra Freeman	John Hamm
Ontario (ON)	1,068,580	11,513,808	ΨToronto	Hilary Weston	Michael Harris
Prince Edward Island (PE)	5,660	137,980	ΨCharlottetown	Gilbert Clements	Patrick Binns
Québec (QC)	1,540,680	7,345,390	ΨQuébec	Lise Thibeault	Lucien Bouchard
Saskatchewan (SK)	652,330	1,027,780	Regina	Dr Lynda Haverstock	Roy John Romanow
Yukon Territory (YT)	483,450	30,633	*Whitehorse	†Judy Gingell	‡Pat Duncan
Northwest Territories (NT)	3,426,320	41,606	*Yellowknife	†Daniel Marion	‡Stephen Kakfwi
Nunavut (NT)§		27,039	*Iqaluit	†Peter Irniq	‡Paul Okalik

Area figures include land and water area   †Commissioner
*seat of government   ‡Government Leader
§Nunavut was created in 1999 from the Northwest Territories; area figures given are for both territories

The constitution of Canada has its source in the British North America Act of 1867 which formed a Dominion, under the name of Canada, of the four provinces of Ontario, Québec, New Brunswick and Nova Scotia. To this federation the other provinces and territories have subsequently been admitted: Manitoba and Northwest Territories (1870), British Columbia (1871), Prince Edward Island (1873), Yukon (1898), Alberta and Saskatchewan (1905) and Newfoundland (1949). In 1982, the constitution was patriated (severed from the British parliament) with the approval of all provinces except Québec. In 1985, the federal prime minister and the provincial premiers concluded the Meech Lake Accord which provided for Québec to be recognised as a distinct society within Canada. However, two provincial legislatures withheld approval and the accord did not come into force. In Québec, a referendum calling for sovereignty and

a new political and economic partnership was defeated in October 1995. In September 1997 Québec was recognised as having a 'unique character' by leaders of the other provinces and territories. A new territory, Nunavut, which means 'our land' in the Inuit language of Inuktitut, was created on 1 April 1999 by partitioning the Northwest Territories. It comprises approximately 2.2 million square kilometres, but has a population of only 27,039, about 85 per cent of whom are Inuit.

In the federal election on 2 June 1997 the Liberal Party was returned to power. The state of parties in the House of Commons following the election was Liberals 155, Reform Party 60, Bloc Québécois 44, New Democrats 21, Progressive Conservatives 20, Independent 1.

POLITICAL SYSTEM

Executive power is vested in a Governor-General appointed by the Sovereign on the advice of the Canadian government.

Parliament consists of a Senate and a House of Commons. The Senate consists of 105 members, nominated by the Governor-General on the advice of the prime minister, the seats being distributed between the various provinces. The House of Commons has 301 members directly elected for a five-year term. Representation is proportional to the population of each province.

The judicature is administered by judges following the civil law in Québec province and common law in other provinces. Each province has a Court of Appeal. All superior, county and district court judges are appointed by the Governor-General, the others by the Lieutenant-Governors of the provinces.

The highest federal court is the Supreme Court of Canada, which exercises general appellate jurisdiction throughout Canada in civil and criminal cases. There is one other federally constituted court, the Federal Court of Canada, which has jurisdiction on appeals from its trial division, from federal tribunals and reviews of decisions and references by federal boards and commissions.

GOVERNOR-GENERAL

Governor-General and Commander-in-Chief, HE Adrienne Clarkson

FEDERAL CABINET *as at September 2000*

Prime Minister, Jean Chrétien
Deputy Prime Minister, Herbert Gray
Agriculture and Agri-Food, Lyle Vanclief
Citizenship and Immigration, Elinor Caplan
Environment, David Anderson
Finance, Paul Martin
Fisheries and Oceans, Herb Dhaliwal
Foreign Affairs, Lloyd Axworthy
Health, Allan Rock
Heritage, Sheila Copps
Human Resources Development, Jane Stewart
Indian Affairs and Northern Development, Robert Noult
Industry, John Manley
Infrastructure, President of the Treasury Board, Lucienne Robillard
Intergovernmental Affairs, President of the Privy Council, Stéphane Dion
International Co-operation, Maria Minna
International Trade, Pierre Pettigrew
Justice and Attorney-General, Anne McLellan
Labour and the Homeless, Claudette Bradshaw
Leader of the Government in the House of Commons, Don Boudria
Leader of the Government in the Senate, Bernard Boudreau
National Defence, Arthur C. Eggleton
National Revenue, Secretary of State (Economic Development Agency of Canada for the Regions of Québec), Martin Cauchon
Natural Resources, Canadian Wheat Board, Ralph Goodale
Public Works and Government Services, Alfonso Gagliano
Solicitor-General, Lawrence MacAulay
Transport, David Collenette
Veterans' Affairs, George Baker

CANADIAN HIGH COMMISSION
Macdonald House, 1 Grosvenor Square, London W1X 0AB
Tel: 020-7258 6600
Canada House, Pall Mall East, London SW1Y 5BJ
High Commissioner, HE Roy MacLaren, apptd 1996
Deputy High Commissioner, J. Bilodeau
Minister, T. MacDonald (*Commercial/Economic*)
Defence Adviser, Brig.-Gen. R. Bastien

BRITISH HIGH COMMISSION
80 Eigin Street, Ottawa K1P 5K7

Tel: (00 1) (613) 237 1530
High Commissioner, HE Sir Anthony Goodenough, KCMG, apptd 1996
Deputy High Commissioner, R. Codrington
Counsellor, M. Uden (*Economic*)
Defence and Military Adviser, Brig. E. Springfield, CBE
CONSULATES-GENERAL – Montréal, Toronto, Vancouver
CONSULATES – Halifax/Dartmouth, Québec City, St John's, Winnipeg

BRITISH COUNCIL DIRECTOR, Dr S. Lewis, c/o British High Commission; e-mail: af572@freenet.carleton.ca

BRITISH COUNCIL REPRESENTATIVE IN QUEBEC, S. Dawbarn, 1000 ouest rue de La Gauchetière, Montréal, Québec H3B 4W5; e-mail: britcnl@alcor.concordia.ca

DEFENCE

The Canadian armed forces are unified and organised into three functional commands: Land Force Command; Maritime Command; Air Command.

The Army (Land Forces) has 114 main battle tanks and, 1,743 armoured personnel carriers. The Navy (Maritime Forces) has one submarine, four destroyers, 12 frigates and 14 patrol and coastal vessels. The Air Force has 140 combat aircraft and 30 armed helicopters.

MILITARY EXPENDITURE – 1.1 per cent of GDP (1998)
MILITARY PERSONNEL – 60,600: Army 20,900, Navy 9,000, Air Force 15,000; Other 15,700

ECONOMY

About 7.3 per cent of the total land area is farmed. Over 60 per cent of this is under cultivation, the remainder being predominantly classified as unimproved pasture. More than 80 per cent of the cultivated land is in the prairie region of western Canada. In 1996, there were 274,955 farms in Canada, with a total land area of 168 million acres. The farm sector accounts for less than 2 per cent of GDP and employs about 3 per cent of the labour force.

Almost half of Canada's land area is forest, making it the world's largest exporter of timber, pulp and newsprint.

Canada produced agricultural goods to the value of C$12,184 million in 1997 and fishing, trapping, logging and forestry contributed a further C$5,005 million.

In 1997, Canada was the world's largest producer of potash and uranium, the second largest of nickel, asbestos, cadmium, zinc and elemental sulphur. The country is also rich in gold, copper, lead, molybdenum, platinum group metals, gypsum, cobalt, titanium concentrates, and aluminium. The total value of mineral production in 1996 was C$49,171.8 million.

Production of gold was 157,790 kg in 1999 and of silver 1,173,000 kg. Uranium production in 1999 was 9,892 tonnes.

GNP – US$580,872 million (1998); US$19,170 per capita (1998)
GDP – US$579,201 million (1996); US$19,515 per capita (1996)
ANNUAL AVERAGE GROWTH OF GDP – 1.2 per cent (1996)
INFLATION RATE – 1.0 per cent (1998)
UNEMPLOYMENT – 8.3 per cent (1998)

TRADE

The main exports in 1999 were automotive products, including cars, trucks and parts, machinery and equipment, industrial products and raw materials, forestry products, including wood, wood pulp and paper products, agricultural products (chiefly wheat), fishery products, and energy products, including crude petroleum and natural gas.

Trade with the USA accounts for about 85 per cent of Canada's exports and 75 per cent of its imports.

In 1998 imports totalled US$206,233 million and exports US$214,327 million. There was a trade surplus of US$12,625 million and a current account deficit of US$11,213 million.

Trade with UK	1998	1999
Imports from UK	£2,189,409,000	£2,556,271,000
Exports to UK	2,604,232,000	3,137,050,000

COMMUNICATIONS

In 1991 there were 290,194 km of federal and provincial territorial roads and highways and 85,563 km of railway track in operation.

The registered shipping on 1 January 1991 including inland vessels, was 43,787 vessels with gross tonnage 4,956,845. The bulk of canal shipping in Canada is handled through the two sections of the St Lawrence Seaway, which provide access to the Great Lakes for ocean-going ships.

EDUCATION

Education is under the control of the provincial governments, the cost of the publicly controlled schools being met by local taxation, aided by provincial grants. Education is compulsory between the ages of five or six and fifteen or sixteen.

In 1995–6 there were 16,096 elementary and secondary schools with 5,899,943 pupils. There were 70 degree-granting universities.

ENROLMENT (percentage of age group) – primary 95 per cent (1995); secondary 91 per cent (1995); tertiary 88 per cent (1995)

CAPE VERDE
República de Cabo Verde

AREA – 1,557 sq. miles (4,033 sq. km). Comprising the Windward Islands (Santo Antão, São Vicente, Santa Luzia, São Nicolau, Boa Vista and Sal) and Leeward Islands (Maio, São Tiago, Fogo and Brava)

POPULATION – 406,000 (1997 estimate), the majority of whom are Roman Catholic. The official language is Portuguese; a creole is spoken by most of the population

CAPITAL – ΨPraia (population, 61,644, 1995 estimate)

CURRENCY – Escudo Caboverdiano of 100 centavos

NATIONAL ANTHEM – É patria amada (This is our beloved country)

NATIONAL DAY – 5 July (Independence Day)

NATIONAL FLAG – Blue with three horizontal stripes of white, red, white near the bottom; over all on these near the hoist a ring of ten yellow stars

LIFE EXPECTANCY (years) – male 63.53; female 71.33

POPULATION GROWTH RATE – 2.5 per cent (1997)

POPULATION DENSITY – 101 per sq. km (1997)

URBAN POPULATION – 44.1 per cent (1990)

MILITARY EXPENDITURE – 1.6 per cent of GDP (1998)

MILITARY PERSONNEL – 1,150: Army 1,000, Air Force 100; Coast Guard 50

CONSCRIPTION DURATION – Selective conscription

ILLITERACY RATE – 26.5 per cent

ENROLMENT (percentage of age group) – primary 100 per cent (1993); secondary 48 per cent (1997)

HISTORY AND POLITICS

The islands, colonised *c*.1460, achieved independence from Portugal on 5 July 1975 under the Partido Africano da Independência da Guiné e Cabo Verde (PAIGC). A federation of the islands with Guinea Bissau was planned but this was dropped following the 1980 coup in Guinea Bissau.

The republic was a one-party state under the African Party for the Independence of Cape Verde (PAICV) until the constitution was amended in 1990. Multiparty elections, held in January 1991, were won by the opposition Movement for Democracy (MPD). The MPD government was re-elected in December 1995 with 50 of the 72 seats in the National Assembly. President António Mascarenhas Monteiro was re-elected unopposed in February 1996.

HEAD OF STATE
President, António Mascarenhas Monteiro, *assumed office* 22 March 1991, *re-elected* 18 February 1996

COUNCIL OF MINISTERS *as at September 2000*
Prime Minister, António Gualberto de Rosario
Agriculture, Food, Supply and the Environment, José António Pinto Monteiro
Culture, António Jorge Delgado
Defence, Ulpio Napoleão Fernandes
Employment, Training and Social Integration, Orlanda Santos Ferreira
Finance, José Ulysses Correia Silva
Foreign Affairs and Communities, Rui Figueiredo Soares
Health, João Baptista Medina
Infrastructure and Housing, Education, Science, Youth and Sport, António Joaquim Rocha Fernandes
Justice and Internal Administration, Januaria Moreira
Minister of the Presidency of the Council of Ministers, Orlando Dias
Secretary of State for Cape Verdeans Abroad, Marly Meneses Vicente
Secretary of State for Decentralisation, vacant
Secretary of State for the Fight Against Poverty, Manuela Teresa Silva Gomes
Secretary of State for Public Administration, Anna Paula Almeida
Tourism, Transport and Marine Affairs, Maria Helena Semedo
Trade, Industry and Energy, Alexandre Dias Monteiro

EMBASSY OF THE REPUBLIC OF CAPE VERDE
Burgemeester Patijnlaan 1930, NL-2585 CB, The Hague, The Netherlands
Tel: (00 31) (70) 355 3651/78
Ambassador Extraordinary and Plenipotentiary, HE Julio Vasco DeSousa Lobo, apptd 1998

BRITISH AMBASSADOR, HE David Snoxell, resident at Dakar, Senegal
There is a British Consulate on São Vicente.

ECONOMY

The islands have little rain and agriculture is mostly confined to irrigated inland valleys. The chief products are bananas and coffee (for export), maize, sugar cane and nuts. Fish and shellfish are important exports. Salt is obtained on Sal, Boa Vista and Maio; volcanic rock is also mined for export.

In 1993 the government announced a programme of reform to institute a change to a market economy and to privatise most industry within four years. In 1997 there was a trade deficit of US$172 million and a current account deficit of US$30 million. In 1995 imports totalled US$252 million and exports US$9 million.

The main ports are Praia and Mindelo, and there is an international airport on Sal.

GNP – US$499 million (1998); US$1,200 per capita (1997)

GDP – US$390 million (1996); US$985 per capita (1996)
TOTAL EXTERNAL DEBT – US$244 million (1998)

Trade with UK	1998	1999
Imports from UK	£4,088,000	£5,498,000
Exports to UK	3,097,000	2,424,000

CENTRAL AFRICAN REPUBLIC
République Centrafricaine/Ködrö tî Bê-Afrîka

AREA – 240,535 sq. miles (622,984 sq. km). Neighbours: Chad (north), Sudan (east), Democratic Republic of Congo and Congo-Brazzaville (south), Cameroon (west)
POPULATION – 3,245,000 (1997 UN estimate). French is the official language; the national language is Sangho.
CAPITAL – Bangui (population, 473,817, 1984 estimate)
CURRENCY – Franc CFA of 100 centimes
NATIONAL ANTHEM– La Renaissance
NATIONAL DAY – 1 December
NATIONAL FLAG – Four horizontal stripes, blue, white, green, yellow, crossed by central vertical red stripe with a yellow five-pointed star in top left-hand corner
LIFE EXPECTANCY (years) – male 45.85; female 50.90
POPULATION GROWTH RATE – 2.2 per cent (1996)
POPULATION DENSITY – 5 per sq. km (1997)
MILITARY EXPENDITURE – 4.7 per cent of GDP (1998)
MILITARY PERSONNEL – 4,950: Army 2,500, Air Force 150, Paramilitaries 2,300
CONSCRIPTION DURATION – Two years (selective)
ILLITERACY RATE – 53.5 per cent
ENROLMENT (percentage of age group) – primary 53 per cent (1991); tertiary 1.4 per cent (1991)

HISTORY AND POLITICS

In December 1958 the French colony of Ubanghi Shari elected to remain within the French Community and adopted the title of the Central African Republic. It became fully independent on 17 August 1960. The first president, David Dacko, was overthrown in 1966 by the then Col. Bokassa, who in 1976 proclaimed himself Emperor and renamed the country the Central African Empire. In 1979 Bokassa was deposed by Dacko in a bloodless coup and the country reverted to a republic. President Dacko surrendered power in 1981 to Gen. André Kolingba, who instituted military rule until 1985, when a civilian-dominated Cabinet was appointed. In November 1986 a referendum was held which approved a new constitution and the establishment of a one-party state.

Multiparty presidential and legislative elections were held in October 1992 but were annulled due to irregularities. President Kolingba formed a coalition government in February 1993. Presidential elections held in 1993 were won by Ange-Félix Patasse of the Central African People's Liberation Party (MLPC); he was re-elected in September 1999. Legislative elections were held on 22 November and 13 December 1998. The MLPC emerged as the largest party with 47 of 109 seats and formed a multiparty coalition government.

POLITICAL SYSTEM

Constitutional reforms were passed in a national referendum in December 1994 which created a constitutional court, introduced elected local assemblies, extended the presidential mandate to a maximum of two six-year terms and subordinated the government to the president.

INSURGENCY

The army is divided between southerners loyal to former President Gen. Kolingba and northerners loyal to President Patasse. The 1,100 French troops stationed near Bangui have been called upon to quell frequent mutinies by Gen. Kolingba's supporters; in March 1998 the French troops were replaced by the UN MINURCA peacekeeping force, which withdrew on 15 February 2000.

HEAD OF STATE
President, Ange-Félix Patasse, *elected* 19 September 1993, *re-elected* 19 September 1999

COUNCIL OF MINISTERS *as at September 2000*
Prime Minister, Economy, Planning and International Co-operation, Anicet Georges Doleguele (MLPC)
Agriculture and Livestock, Daniel Emèry Dédé (PLD)
Civic Culture, Parliamentary Relations, Agba Otikpo Mézodé
Commerce, Industry and Private Sector Promotion, Jean-Baptiste Koyassambia
Communications, Francis-Albert Ouakanga (MLPC)
Education, Eloi Anguimaté (CN)
Employment, Civil Service and Training, Godeffroy Mokamanédé
Environment, Water, Forestry, Hunting and Fishing, Jean-Baptiste Nouganga (PSD)
Equipment, Territorial Administration and Urban Planning, Aristide Sokambi (PLD)
Family, Social, and Handicapped Affairs, Rachel Dea Nambona (MLPC)
Foreign and Francophone Affairs, Marcel Metefara (MLPC)
Higher Education and Scientific Research, Timoléon Mbaikoua (MLPC)
Housing and Public Building, Armand Sana (MDD)
Interior, Security, Security, Maurice Régonessa
Justice, Denis Wangao-Kizimalé
Mines and Energy, André Latou (MLPC)
Minister-Delegates, Jacob Mbaitadjimp (*Economy, Planning and International Co-operation*); Théodore Dabanga (*Finance and Budget*); Bello Mamadou (*Relations with the Arab World*)
National Defence, War Veterans and War Victims, Jean-Jacques Demafourth (MLPC)
Posts and Telecommunications, Jean Bruno Vickos (PUN)
Presidential Affairs, Michel Gbezera-Bria
Public Health and Population, Richard Lakoué
Tourism, Nathalie Constance Gounébana (PLD)
Transport and Civil Aviation, Désiré Pendémon (MLPC)
Youth and Sports, Bernard Yoro (PLD)

CN National Convention; MDD Movement for Democracy and Development; MLPC Central African People's Liberation Party; PLD Liberal Democratic Party; PSD Social Democratic Party; PUN National Unity Party

EMBASSY OF THE CENTRAL AFRICAN REPUBLIC
30 rue des Perchamps, F-75016, Paris
Tel: (00 33) (1) 4224 4256
Ambassador Extraordinary and Plenipotentiary, vacant
BRITISH AMBASSADOR, HE Peter Boon, resident at Yaoundé, Cameroon

ECONOMY

Cotton, diamonds, coffee and timber are the major exports. Industrial goods, machinery and transport equipment, foodstuffs and fuels are the main imports.

In 1994 there was a trade surplus of US$15 million and a current account deficit of US$25 million. In 1995 exports totalled US$171 million and imports US$174 million.
GNP – US$1,053 million (1998); US$300 per capita (1998)
GDP – US$1,313 million (1996); US$393 per capita (1996)

INFLATION RATE – –1.9 per cent (1998)
TOTAL EXTERNAL DEBT – US$921 million (1998)

Trade with UK	1998	1999
Imports from UK	£569,000	£748,000
Exports to UK	206,000	576,000

CHAD
République du Tchad

AREA – 495,755 sq. miles (1,284,000 sq. km). Neighbours: Niger, Nigeria and Cameroon (west), Libya (north), Sudan (east), Central African Republic (south)
POPULATION – 6,702,000 (1997 UN estimate); French and Arabic are the official languages; there are more than 50 indigenous languages, of which the most widely spoken is Sara
CAPITAL – N'Djaména (population, 179,000, 1972 estimate)
CURRENCY – Franc CFA of 100 centimes
NATIONAL ANTHEM – Peuple tchadien, debout et à l'ouvrage (People of Chad, arise and to work)
NATIONAL DAY – 1 December
NATIONAL FLAG – Vertical stripes, blue, yellow and red
LIFE EXPECTANCY (years) – male 45.06; female 48.32
POPULATION GROWTH RATE – 2.3 per cent (1997)
POPULATION DENSITY – 5 per sq. km (1997)
URBAN POPULATION – 21.7 per cent (1993)
MILITARY EXPENDITURE – 5.6 per cent of GDP (1998)
MILITARY PERSONNEL – 29,850: Army 25,000, Air Force 350, Paramilitaries 4,500
ILLITERACY RATE – 46.4 per cent
ENROLMENT (percentage of age group) – primary 46 per cent (1996); secondary 6 per cent (1995); tertiary 0.6 per cent (1995)

HISTORY AND POLITICS

Chad became a member state of the French Community in 1958, and was proclaimed fully independent on 11 August 1960. The constitution was suspended in 1975 when President Tombalbaye was killed in a coup by Gen. Félix Malloum; following a succession of further coups, Idriss Déby came to power in 1990 and announced the adoption of a multiparty system, allowing the legalisation of political parties in 1991 and 1992. A Higher Transitional Council (CST) was elected in 1993 to serve as the transitional legislature and appointed a transitional government in conjunction with President Déby. The CST has twice extended the transitional period by one year to allow sufficient time to organise elections. In March 1996, the government concluded the Franceville agreement with opposition parties which provided for a national cease-fire and an independent commission to oversee the election. A new constitution, establishing a unified, democratic state, was confirmed by a referendum. Déby won the first multiparty presidential elections in 1996. Elections to the 125-member National Assembly in January and February 1997 were won by the pro-Déby Patriotic Salvation Movement (MPS).

FOREIGN RELATIONS

The Aouzou strip was claimed by Libya, which occupied the area from 1973 to 1994. A war over the territory ended in 1987. In 1990 Chad and Libya presented their claims to the International Court of Justice, which in 1994 awarded jurisdiction over the whole of the strip to Chad.

INSURGENCIES

Three rebel movements, the Movement for Unity and the Republic (MUR), the Movement for Democracy and Justice in Chad (MDJT), and the Democratic Revolutionary Council (DRC), announced that they had formed an alliance in February 2000.

HEAD OF STATE

President, Idriss Déby, *took power* December 1990, *elected* 3 July 1996

GOVERNMENT *as at September 2000*
Prime Minister, Nagoum Yamassoum
Agriculture, Minister of State, Saleh Kebzabo
Civil Service, Labour, Employment, Promotion and Modernisation, Gen. Routouang Yoma Golom
Communications, Parliamentary Affairs, Government Spokesman, Mahamat Loani
Culture, Youth and Sport, Mahamat Ahmat Choukou
Development and Economic Promotion, Ahmat Lamine Ali
Education, Abderahim Breme Hamid
Environment and Water, Nadjo Abdel Kerim
Finance, Mahamat Ali Hassane
Foreign Affairs, Oumar Boukar Kadjallami
Higher Education, Laoukissam Nissala
Industry, Commerce and Handicrafts, Salibou Garba
Interior, Security and Decentralisation, Abderrahmane Moussa
Justice, Guardian of the Seals, Mahamat Hamat Alabo
Livestock, Mahamat Nouri
Mines, Energy and Oil, Moctar Moussa
National Defence and Reinsertion, Col. Weiding Assi-Assoue
Posts and Telecommunications, Mouadjidibayé Titingar
Public Health, Nadjo Abdel Karim
Public Works, Transport and Urban Development, Bichara Cherif Daoussa
Secretary-General to the Government, David Houdeingar
Social Action and Family, Fatime Kimto
Tourism, Abba Koi Djouassab

EMBASSY OF THE REPUBLIC OF CHAD
Boulevard Lambermont 52, B-1030 Brussels, Belgium
Tel: (00 32) (2) 215 1975
Ambassador Extraordinary and Plenipotentiary, vacant

BRITISH AMBASSADOR, HE Peter Boon, resident at Yaoundé, Cameroon
Honorary Consulate, BP877, Avenue Charles de Gaulle, N'Djaména

ECONOMY

About 90 per cent of the workforce is occupied in agriculture, fishing and forestry. There is an oilfield in Kanem and salt is mined around Lake Chad, but the most important activities are cotton growing and animal husbandry. Raw cotton, meat and groundnuts are the main exports. Chad's main trading partners are France and Cameroon.

On 7 January 2000 the IMF approved a loan facility of about US$26.5 million to support the government's 1999–2002 economic programme.

In 1994 Chad had a trade deficit of US$77 million and a current account deficit of US$38 million. In 1997 imports totalled US$242 million and exports US$246 million.
GNP – US$1,658 million (1998); US$230 per capita (1998)
GDP – US$1,111 million (1996); US$171 per capita (1996)
ANNUAL AVERAGE GROWTH OF GDP – 2.7 per cent (1996)
INFLATION RATE – 5.6 per cent (1997)
TOTAL EXTERNAL DEBT – US$1,091 million (1998)

Trade with UK	1998	1999
Imports from UK	£1,050,000	£917,000
Exports to UK	369,000	259,000

CHILE
República de Chile

AREA – 292,135 sq. miles (756,626 sq. km). Neighbours: Peru (north), Bolivia and Argentina (east)
POPULATION – 14,622,000 (1997 UN estimate). The main groups are: indigenous Araucanian Indians, Fuegians, Rapanui and Changos; Spanish settlers and their descendants; mixed Spanish Indians; and European immigrants. Because of extensive intermarriage only a few indigenous Indians are racially separate. The language is Spanish, with admixtures of local words of Indian origin. The main religion is Roman Catholicism
CAPITAL – Santiago (population, 4,640,635, 1997 UN estimate)
MAJOR CITIES – ΨAntofagasta (243,038); Concepción (362,589); Puente Alto (363,012); Temuco (253,451); ΨValparaíso (283,489); ΨPunta Arenas (120,148), on the Straits of Magellan, is the southernmost city in the world (1997 UN estimates)
CURRENCY – Chilean peso of 100 centavos
NATIONAL ANTHEM – Canción Nacional de Chile
NATIONAL DAY – 18 September (National Anniversary)
NATIONAL FLAG – Two horizontal bands, white, red; in top sixth a white star on blue square, next staff
LIFE EXPECTANCY (years) – male 72.13; female 78.10
POPULATION GROWTH RATE – 1.6 per cent (1997)
POPULATION DENSITY – 19 per sq. km (1997)
URBAN POPULATION – 84.9 per cent (1997)

Chile lies between the Andes (5,000 to 15,000 feet above sea level) and the shores of the South Pacific, extending coastwise from the arid north around Arica to Cape Horn. The extreme length of the country is about 2,800 miles, with an average breadth, north of 41°, of 100 miles.

Island possessions include the Juan Fernández group (three islands) about 360 miles from Valparaíso; one of these islands is the reputed scene of Alexander Selkirk's (Robinson Crusoe) shipwreck. Easter Island, about 2,000 miles away in the South Pacific Ocean, contains stone platforms and hundreds of stone figures.

HISTORY AND POLITICS

Chile was discovered by Spanish adventurers in the 16th century and remained under Spanish rule until 1810, when the first autonomous government was established. Full independence was consolidated in 1818 after a revolutionary war.

A Marxist, Salvador Allende, was elected president in 1970, but was overthrown in a military coup in 1973. Gen. Pinochet, who led the coup, assumed the presidency until presidential and congressional elections were held in 1989, beginning the transition to full democracy. Gen. Pinochet retired as commander-in-chief of the Army but took up an unelected seat for life in the Senate, despite public protests and government attempts to prevent it. He was arrested in London on 16 October 1998 following a request by the Spanish government for his extradition, but extradition proceedings were dropped on the grounds of poor health on 2 March 2000, and he was freed and allowed to return to Chile.

Presidential and legislative elections were held in 1993. Eduardo Frei won the presidential election and his ruling Coalition for Democracy (CPD) (centre and centre-left parties) won 70 seats in the Chamber of Deputies and 22 in the Senate. In the 1997 legislative elections the CPD

maintained its 70-seat majority in the Chamber of Deputies. Presidential elections held in December 1999 and January 2000 were won by Ricardo Lagos Escobar.

POLITICAL SYSTEM
Executive power is held by the president. Legislative power is exercised by a Congress which comprises a Senate of 47 Senators (38 elected and nine appointed) and a Chamber of Deputies of 120 elected members. Senators serve eight-year terms and deputies serve four-year terms. The presidential term is six years with no possibility of re-election.

Chile is divided into 12 regions and the Metropolitan Area.

HEAD OF STATE
President of the Republic, Ricardo Lagos Escobar,
   elected 16 January 2000, *sworn in* 11 March 2000

CABINET *as at September 2000*
Agriculture, Jaime Campos (PRSD)
Defence, Mario Fernández (PDC)
Economy, Energy and Mining, José de Gregorio (PDC)
Education, Mariana Aylwin (PDC)
Finance, Nicolás Eyzaguirre (PPD)
Foreign Affairs, María Soledad Alvear (PDC)
Health, Michelle Bachelet (PS)
Housing and Social Assets, Claudio Orrego (PDC)
Interior, José Miguel Insulza (PS)
Justice, José Antonio Gómez (PRSD)
Labour, Ricardo Solari (PS)
National Women's Secretariat, Adriana Delpiano (PPD)
Planning, Alejandra Krauss (PDC)
Public Works, Transport and Telecommunications,
   Carlos Cruz (PS)
Secretary-General of the Government, Claudio Huepe
   (PDC)
Secretary-General of the Presidency, Alvaro García Hurtado
   (PPD)

PDC Christian Democratic Party; PS Socialist Party; PPD Party for Democracy; PRSD Social Democratic Radical Party

EMBASSY OF CHILE
12 Devonshire Street, London W1N 2DS
Tel: 020-7580 6392
Ambassador Extraordinary and Plenipotentiary, HE
   Pablo Cabrera, apptd 1999

BRITISH EMBASSY
Avenida El Bosque 0125 Casilla 72-D, Santiago
Tel: (00 56) (2) 370 3737
E-mail: consulate@santiago.mail.fco.gov.uk
Ambassador Extraordinary and Plenipotentiary, HE
   Greg Faulkner, apptd 2000
Deputy Head of Mission, Counsellor and Consul-General,
   D. Roberts
Defence Attaché, Capt. P. Ellis
First Secretary (Commercial), T. Torlot

CONSULAR OFFICES – Antofagasta, Arica, Concepción,
   Punta Arenas, Valparaíso.

BRITISH COUNCIL DIRECTOR, D. Stokes
   (*Cultural Attaché*), Eliodoro Yáñez 832, Providencia,
   Santiago; e-mail: info@britcoun.cl
British-Chilean Chamber of Commerce, Av. Suecia 155-C,
   Casilla 536, Santiago

DEFENCE

The Army has 227 main battle tanks, 20 armoured infantry fighting vehicles, and 565 armoured personnel carriers. The Navy has four submarines, three destroyers, three frigates, 29 patrol and coastal vessels, eight combat aircraft

and 20 armed helicopters. The Air Force has 90 combat aircraft.
MILITARY EXPENDITURE – 3.7 per cent of GDP (1998)
MILITARY PERSONNEL – 122,500: Army 51,000, Navy 29,000, Air Force 13,000; Paramilitaries 29,500
CONSCRIPTION DURATION – 12–22 months

ECONOMY

Economic reforms during the late 1970s and the 1980s, with large-scale privatisation and deregulation, have made Chile one of the most successful economies in Latin America. Cereals, vegetables, fruit, tobacco, hemp and vines are grown extensively and livestock accounts for nearly 40 per cent of agricultural production. Sheep farming predominates in the extreme south. There are large timber tracts in the central and southern zones which produce timber, cellulose and wood for export. Fishing is also a major industry.

Chile is rich in copper-ore, iron-ore and nitrates, and has the only commercial production of nitrate of soda (Chile saltpetre) from natural resources in the world. There are large deposits of high grade sulphur. Oil and natural gas are produced in the Magallanes area, but domestic production is now declining.

In 1998 there was a trade deficit of US$2,494 million and a current account deficit of US$4,552 million.
GNP – US$73,935 million (1998); US$4,990 per capita (1998)
GDP – US$71,906 million (1996); US$4,986 per capita (1996)
ANNUAL AVERAGE GROWTH OF GDP – 7.2 per cent (1996)
INFLATION RATE – 5.1 per cent (1998)
UNEMPLOYMENT – 7.2 per cent (1998)
TOTAL EXTERNAL DEBT – US$36,302 million (1998)

TRADE

The principal exports are minerals, timber and metal products, fish products and vegetables. The principal imports are food products, industrial raw materials, machinery, and equipment and spares. The main trade partners are Japan and the USA; in 1996 Chile joined the Mercosur Free Trade Zone, and in March 1998 signed an extension to a free trade agreement with Mexico. In 1998 imports totalled US$18,828 million and exports US$14,895 million.

Trade with UK	1998	1999
Imports from UK	£172,774,000	£113,884,000
Exports to UK	346,308,000	342,730,000

COMMUNICATIONS

With the improvement of the roads an increasing share of internal transportation is moving by road and rail, although shipping is still important. The road system is about 80,000 km in length, of which around 11,000 km is paved.

There are 6,782 km of railway track. A railway line runs from Valparaíso through La Calera and Santiago to Puerto Montt. With the completion of a section of 435 miles from Corumba, Brazil, to Santa Cruz, Bolivia, the Trans-Continental Line will link the Chilean Pacific port of Arica with Rio de Janeiro on the Atlantic. A line runs from Antofagasta to Salta (Argentina).

Domestic air traffic is carried by Línea Aérea Nacional (LAN) and LADECO, which also operate internationally, and smaller regional carriers.

CULTURE AND EDUCATION

Chilean Nobel Prize winners include the writers Gabriela Mistral (1945) and Pablo Neruda (1971).

Elementary education is free and compulsory. There are eight state universities (three in Santiago, two in Valparaíso, one each in Antofagasta, Concepción and Valdivia), and many private universities.
ILLITERACY RATE – 4.3 per cent
ENROLMENT (percentage of age group) – primary 89 per cent (1996); secondary 58 per cent (1996); tertiary 31 per cent (1997)

CHINA
Zhonghua Renmin Gongheguo – The People's Republic of China

AREA – 3,705,408 sq. miles (9,596,961 sq. km).
Neighbours: Russia and Mongolia (north), North Korea (east), Vietnam, Laos, Myanmar, India, Bhutan and Nepal (south), India, Pakistan, Afghanistan, Tajikistan, Kyrgyzstan and Kazakhstan (west)
POPULATION – 1,243,738,000 (1997 UN estimate). A census (the fourth) was held in 1990 and recorded a total population of 1,130 million. About 6 per cent of the population belong to around 55 ethnic minorities. Among the largest are the Zhuang of Guangxi, the Hui of Ningxia, the Miao of southern China, the Manchu of Heilongjiang, the Uygurs and Kazakhs of Xinjiang, the Tibetans and the Mongols. The indigenous religions are Confucianism, Taoism and Buddhism. There are also Muslims (officially estimated at about 12 million) and Christians (unofficially estimated at about 50 million). The official language is Mandarin Chinese; of the many local dialects the largest are Cantonese, Fukienese, Xiamenhua and Hakka. The autonomous regions of Mongolia, Tibet and Xinjiang have their own languages
CAPITAL – Beijing (population, 7,362,426, 1990)
MAJOR CITIES – Chengdu (2,954,872); Chongqing (3,172,178); Dalian (2,483,776); Guangzhou (Canton) (3,935,193); Harbin (2,990,921); Qingdo (2,101,808); ΨShanghai (8,214,384); Shenyang (4,669,737); Tianjin (5,855,044); Wuhan (4,040,113); Wuxi (1,013,606); Yantai (847,285); Zaozhuang (1,793,103)
CURRENCY – Renminbi Yuan of 10 jiao or 100 fen
NATIONAL ANTHEM – March of the Volunteers
NATIONAL DAY – 1 October (Founding of People's Republic)
NATIONAL FLAG – Red, with large gold five-point star and four small gold stars in crescent, all in upper quarter next staff
LIFE EXPECTANCY (years) – male 66.85; female 70.49
POPULATION GROWTH RATE – 1.1 per cent (1997)
POPULATION DENSITY – 130 per sq. km (1997)
URBAN POPULATION – 26.2 per cent (1990)

HISTORY AND POLITICS

China was ruled by imperial dynasties for over 20 centuries until revolutionaries led by Sun Yat-sen forced the Emperor to abdicate on 10 October 1911. Neither the new Nationalist Party (Kuomintang (KMT)) government nor the emergent Chinese Communist Party (CCP) were able to unify China, or to agree on the basis for further reform. Warlord infighting rendered China weak, enabling Japan to occupy Manchuria and all the important northern and coastal areas of China by 1939. Japan's occupation was ended by its defeat by the allies in 1945.

The Communists established control over large areas of China in the early 1940s, seizing the territory abandoned by Japan in 1945. Civil war lasted until 1949 when the CCP, led by Mao Zedong (Mao Tse-tung), inaugurated the People's Republic of China (PRC), and the KMT under Chiang Kai-shek went into exile in Taiwan. The

USA continued to recognise the Chiang Kai-shek regime as the rightful government of China until 1971, when the PRC took over China's membership of the United Nations from Taiwan.

Under Mao Zedong China was ruled on the basis of four 'cardinal principles': Marxist–Leninist–Maoist thought, the Socialist Road, the dictatorship of the proletariat, and the leadership of the CCP. Mao's 'Great Leap Forward' (1958–61) was an attempt to industrialise rural areas which resulted in a famine in which 30–40 million people died. China was plunged into chaos during the Cultural Revolution (1966–70) when the Red Guards were used to rid the country of 'rightist elements'.

Following the death of Mao Zedong in 1976, the disgraced Deng Xiaoping was recalled. In 1977 he was elected Vice-Chairman of the CCP, becoming the dominant force within the party by eliminating leftist influence, rehabilitating fallen leaders and promoting an 'open door' policy of economic liberalisation. The Congresses of 1982 and 1987 reaffirmed Deng's policies, and in 1987 most of the revolutionary generation were replaced in the top posts by younger, more liberal supporters of reform.

Student-led pro-democracy demonstrations in April and May 1989, centred on Tiananmen Square in Beijing, ended on 3–4 June when the army took control of Beijing, killing thousands of protesters. This strengthened the position of hardliners within the leadership, who re-adopted policies of centralisation based on Marxist ideology. Deng retired from his last official post in November 1989 but retained effective control until late 1994.

At Deng's instigation during 1992 the emphasis switched back to economic reform and the power of the hardliners waned. The 14th Party Congress in 1992 endorsed Deng's calls for faster, bolder economic reforms and his 'socialist market economy'. Deng died on 19 February 1997 and Jiang Zemin assumed the mantle of leader.

In addition to continuing economic reforms, Jiang has sought to improve China's standing in the international community. In June 1998, President Clinton became the first US president to visit China since the 1989 Tiananmen Square massacre; he was followed in October 1998 by UK Prime Minister, Tony Blair, who visited Beijing and Hong Kong and became the first foreign leader to have an article published in the *People's Daily*.

INSURGENCIES

Separatists from the Uygur Muslim minority group in Xinjiang Autonomous Region have demonstrated against Han rule. They have claimed responsibility for bomb attacks in the provincial capital, Ürümqi, and in Beijing. Two Muslim separatists were executed in January 1999 as part of an effort to tighten control of the region. It was reported that separatists had clashed with Chinese troops in February 2000.

The government banned the Falun Gong cult on 22 July 1999, which had claimed to have 70 million followers; the government had become worried after it was revealed that a large number of Chinese Communist Party officials and senior officers in the People's Liberation Army had joined the cult.

POLITICAL SYSTEM

Under the 1982 constitution, the National People's Congress is the highest organ of state power. It is elected for a term of five years and is supposed to hold one session a year. It is empowered to amend the constitution, make laws, select the president and vice-president and other leading officials of the state, approve the national economic plan, the state budget and the final state accounts, and to decide on questions of war and peace. The State Council is the highest organ of the state administration. It is composed of the Premier, the Vice-Premiers, the State Councillors, heads of Ministries and Commissions, the Auditor-General and the Secretary-General. Command over the armed forces is vested in the Central Military Commission.

Deputies to Congresses at the primary level are 'directly elected' by the voters 'through a secret ballot after democratic consultation'. This is now extended to county level. These Congresses elect the deputies to the Congress at the next higher level. Deputies to the National People's Congress are elected by the People's Congresses of the provinces, autonomous regions and municipalities directly under the central government, and by the armed forces.

Local government is conducted through People's Governments at provincial, municipal and county levels. Autonomous regions, prefectures and counties exist for national minorities and are described as self-governing.

HEAD OF STATE

President of the People's Republic of China, Jiang Zemin, elected April 1993, re-elected 16 March 1998
Vice-President, Hu Jintao
Chairman of the Standing Committee of the National People's Congress, Li Peng
Chairman of the Central Military Committee, Jiang Zemin
Deputy Chairmen of the Central Military Committee, Chi Haotian; Hu Jintao; Zhang Wannian

STATE COUNCIL *as at September 2000*
Premier, Zhu Rongji
Vice-Premiers, Qian Qichen; Li Lanqing; Wen Jiabao; Wu Bangguo
State Councillors, Gen. Chi Haotian; Ismail Amat; Luo Gan; Wu Yi; Wang Zhongyu

MINISTERS

Agriculture, Chen Yaobang
Civil Affairs, Doje Cering
Communications, Huang Zhendong
Construction, Yu Zhengsheng
Culture, Sun Jiazheng
Defence, Gen. Chi Haotian
Education, Chen Zhili
Finance, Xiang Huaicheng
Foreign Affairs, Tang Jiaxuan
Foreign Trade and Economic Co-operation, Shi Guansheng
Health, Zhang Wenkang
Information Industry, Wu Jichuan
Justice, Gao Changli
Labour and Social Security, Zhang Zuoji
Land and Natural Resources, Zhou Yongkang
Personnel, Song Defu
Public Security, Jia Chunwang
Railways, Fu Zhihuan
Science and Technology, Zhu Lilan
State Security, Xu Yongyue
Supervision, He Yong
Water Resources, Wang Shucheng

MINISTERS IN CHARGE OF STATE COMMISSIONS
Development Planning, Zeng Peiyan
Economics and Trade, Sheng Huaren
Ethnic Affairs, Li Dezhu

Family Planning, Zhang Weiqing
Legislative Affairs, Yang Jingyu
Science, Technology and Industry for National Defence, Liu Jibin
Auditor-General, Li Jinhua

President of the People's Bank of China, Liu Mingkang

CHINESE PEOPLE'S POLITICAL CONSULTATIVE CONFERENCE
Chair, Li Ruihan

THE CHINESE COMMUNIST PARTY
General Secretary, Jiang Zemin
Politburo Standing Committee, Jiang Zemin; Li Peng; Zhu Rongji; Li Ruihuan; Hu Jintao; Wei Jianxing; Li Lanqing
Politburo of the Central Committee, Tian Jiyun; Jiang Zemin; Li Tieying; Li Ruihuan; Zhu Rongji; Hu Jintao; Ding Guangen; Qian Qichen; Li Lanqing; Wei Jiangxing; Wu Bangguo; Li Peng; Huang Ju; Wen Jiabao; Li Changchun; Wu Guanzheng; Chi Haotian; Zhang Wannian; Luo Gan; Jia Qinglin; Jiang Chunyun (*full members*); Zeng Qinghong; Wu Yi (*alternate members*)
Secretariat of the Central Committee, Zeng Qinghong (*Director*); Ding Guangen; Hu Jintao; Wei Jiangxing; Wen Jiabao; Luo Gan (*full members*)
Membership, 52,000,000 (1993)

EMBASSY OF THE PEOPLE'S REPUBLIC OF CHINA
49-51 Portland Place, London WIN 4JL
Tel: 020–7636 5726
Ambassador Extraordinary and Plenipotentiary, HE Ma Zhengang, apptd 1997
Minister-Counsellor, Yang Zucheng (*Commercial*)
Defence Attaché, Maj.-Gen. Yan Kunsheng

BRITISH EMBASSY
11 Guang Hua Lu, Jian Guo Men Wai, Beijing 100 600
Tel: (00 86) (10) 6532 1961/2/3/4
E-mail: beinfo@public.bta.net.cn
Ambassador, HE Anthony Galsworthy, KCMG, apptd 1997
Minister, Consul-General and Deputy Head of Mission, A. D. Sprake
Counsellors, J. V. Everard (*Political and Economic*); C. Segar (*Commercial*); M. Davidson (*Cultural, and British Council Director*)
Defence, Military and Air Attaché, Brig. J. G. Kerr, OBE, QGM

BRITISH CONSULATES-GENERAL – Shanghai and Guangzhou

BRITISH COUNCIL DIRECTOR M. Davidson (*Cultural Counsellor*), Cultural and Education Section, British Embassy, Landmark Building, 8 North Dongsanhuan Road, Chaoyang District, Beijing 100004; e-mail: enquiry@bc-beijing.sprint.com. Regional directors in Chengdu, Guangzhou and Shanghai.

DEFENCE

All three military arms are parts of the People's Liberation Army (PLA). China has 15–20 intercontinental and 66 intermediate range land-based, and 13 submarine-launched nuclear ballistic missiles. The Army has about 8,300 main battle tanks and, 5,500 armoured personnel carriers and armoured infantry fighting vehicles.

The Navy has 71 submarines, 18 destroyers, 35 frigates, 676 patrol and coastal vessels, 541 combat aircraft and 25 armed helicopters. The Air Force has 3,520 combat aircraft.
MILITARY EXPENDITURE – 5.3 per cent of GDP (1998)
MILITARY PERSONNEL – 3,580,000: Army 1,830,000, Navy 230,000, Air Force 420,000; Paramilitaries 1,100,000
CONSCRIPTION DURATION – Two years (selective)

ECONOMY

Economic liberalisation in the early 1980s reduced central planning and broadened the role of the market, which led to an explosion in manufacturing, concentrated in China's coastal regions. Foreign direct investment, especially from Hong Kong and Taiwan, has enabled the construction of a significant industrial base and transport infrastructure. In the coastal regions the economy has become a free market in all but name, with several stock markets and Shanghai's emergence as a financial centre. Since 1980, special economic zones have been established in Guangdong, Fujian and Hainan provinces. In addition, there are free trade and development zones throughout the country, designed to stimulate both foreign trade and internal economic development.

Agriculture remains of great importance, with 70 per cent of the population still living in rural areas. Agricultural policies have devolved responsibility for agricultural production to individual households. Cereals, with peas and beans, are grown in the northern provinces, and rice, tea and sugar in the south. Rice is the staple food of the inhabitants. Cotton (mostly in valleys of the Yangtze and Yellow Rivers), tea (in the west and south), with hemp, jute and flax, are the most important crops. Livestock is raised in large numbers. Sericulture is one of the oldest industries. Cottons, woollens and silks are manufactured in large quantities.

Coal, iron ore, tin, antimony, wolfram, bismuth and molybdenum are abundant. Oil is produced in several northern provinces, particularly in Heilongjiang and Shandong, and off-shore deposits are being sought in co-operation with western and Japanese companies. In November 1997, a deal was reached with Russia over the construction of a US$12 billion liquefied natural gas (LNG) pipeline to take LNG from Siberia to China's Pacific coast. In March 1998, China announced the construction of a US$2.3 billion 1,875-mile oil pipeline along the Silk Road to Kazakhstan.

In January 1998, reforms of the banking sector were announced in response to the south-east Asian financial crisis. The reforms introduce stricter controls on loan management, increased competition in the banking sector, and the dropping of import duties to encourage foreign investment. China's refusal to devalue the yuan has helped restore a degree of stability to the region.

GNP – US$923,560 million (1998); US$750 per capita (1998)
GDP – US$812,386 million (1996); US$671 per capita (1996)
ANNUAL AVERAGE GROWTH OF GDP – 9.7 per cent (1996)
INFLATION RATE – – 0.8 per cent (1998)
UNEMPLOYMENT – 3.1 per cent (1998)
TOTAL EXTERNAL DEBT – US$154,599 million (1998)

TRADE

Foreign trade and external economic relations have grown enormously since 1978. In 1995, import tariffs were cut to an average 23 per cent in line with China's attempts to join the World Trade Organisation. The principal exports are animals and animal products, oil, textiles, ores, metals, tea, electronics and manufactured goods. The principal imports are motor vehicles, machinery, chemical fertiliser, plants, aircraft, books, paper and paper-making materials, chemicals, metals and ores, and dyes.

In 1997 China had a trade surplus of US$46,222 million and a current account surplus of US$29,718 million. In 1998 imports totalled US$140,305 million and exports US$183,589 million.

Trade with UK	1998	1999
Imports from UK	£868,952,000	£1,216,253,000
Exports to UK	2,960,661,000	3,530,789,000

COMMUNICATIONS

There are 57,600 km of railway lines and 1,278,000 km of highway (1998). In addition, internal civil aviation has been developed, with routes totalling more than 1,506,000 km.

In the past the principal means of communication east to west was by the rivers, the most important of which are the Yangtze (Changjiang) (3,400 miles), the Yellow River (Huanghe) (2,600 miles) and the West River (Xihe) (1,650 miles). These, together with the network of canals connecting them, are still much used but their overall importance has declined. Coastal port facilities are being improved and the merchant fleet expanded.

Postal services and telecommunications have developed in recent years and it is claimed that 95 per cent of all rural townships are on the telephone and that postal routes reach practically every production brigade headquarters.

EDUCATION

Primary education lasts six years and secondary education lasts six years (three years in junior middle school and three years in senior middle school). There are over 1,000 universities, colleges and institutes.
ILLITERACY RATE – 15.0 per cent
ENROLMENT (percentage of age group) – primary 100 per cent (1996); tertiary 6 per cent (1997)

CULTURE

The Chinese language has many dialects, notably Cantonese, Hakka, Amoy, Foochow, Changsha, Nanchang, Wu (Shanghai) and the northern dialect. The Common Speech or *putonghua* (often referred to as Mandarin) is based on the northern dialect. The Communists have promoted it as the national language and it is taught throughout the country. As *putonghua* encourages the use of the spoken language in writing, the old literary style and ideographic form of writing has fallen into disuse. Since 1956 simplified characters have been introduced to make reading and writing easier. In 1958 the National People's Congress adopted a system of romanisation known as pinyin.

Chinese literature is one of the richest in the world. Paper has been employed for writing and printing for nearly 2,000 years. The Confucian classics which formed the basis of traditional Chinese culture date from the Warring States period (fourth to third centuries BC), as do the earliest texts of Taoism. Histories, philosophical and scientific works, poetry, literary and art criticism, novels and romances survive from most periods.

Important newspapers and magazines include the *People's Daily* and the twice-monthly *Qiushi*, which replaced *Red Flag* as the CCP's mouthpiece in 1989.

TIBET

AREA – 463,000 sq. miles (1,199,164 sq. km)
POPULATION – 2,260,000 (1993)
CAPITAL – Lhasa

Tibet is a plateau seldom lower than 10,000 feet, which forms the northern frontier of India (boundary imperfectly demarcated), from Kashmir to Myanmar, but is separated therefrom by the Himalayas.

From 1911 to 1950, Tibet was virtually an independent country though its status was never officially so recognised. In 1950 Chinese Communist forces invaded eastern Tibet. In 1951 an agreement was reached whereby the Chinese army was allowed entry into Tibet, and a Communist military and administrative headquarters was set up. A series of revolts against Chinese rule culminated in 1959 in a rising in Lhasa, the capital. Fighting continued for several days before the rebellion was crushed and military rule was imposed. The Dalai Lama fled to India where he and his followers were granted political asylum and established a government in exile.

In 1964 the Dalai Lama and the Panchen Lama were dismissed, marking the end of co-operation between the Chinese government and the traditional religious authorities. Tibet became an Autonomous Region of China in 1965. Martial law was declared in Tibet in 1989 after serious unrest, and sporadic outbursts of unrest continue. The Panchen Lama died in 1989. China rejected the Dalai Lama's choice of successor, who is believed to have been executed, and enthroned its own candidate.

In December 1997, the International Commission of Jurists issued a report declaring that Tibet was 'under alien subjugation' and called for a UN-managed referendum to decide its future status. China contested that the report failed to acknowledge its historical claims to the region.

The 17th Karmapa Lama, the first reincarnation of a living Buddha to be recognised by both China and the Dalai Lama, defected from Tibet in late December 1999 and fled to India, where he appealed for political asylum. On 16 January 2000, the 7th Reting Lama was ordained in Tibet; the Dalai Lama had refused to recognise him as the reincarnation of the previous Reting Lama.

COLOMBIA
República de Colombia

AREA – 439,737 sq. miles (1,141,748 sq. km). Neighbours: Venezuela (north and east), Brazil (south-east), Peru (south), Ecuador (south-west), Panama (north-west)

POPULATION – 36,162,000 (1997 UN estimate): 58 per cent mestizo, 20 per cent white, 14 per cent mulatto, 4 per cent black, 3 per cent mixed black-Amerindian, 1 per cent Amerindian. The language is Spanish.

Roman Catholicism is the established religion

CAPITAL – Bogotá (population, 5,398,998, 1993)

MAJOR CITIES – ΨBarranquilla (1,328,833), the major port on the Caribbean; Bucaramanga (759,651); ΨBuenaventura (227,478), the major port on the Pacific; Cali (2,063,867); ΨCartagena (656,632); Medellín (2,556,357)

CURRENCY – Colombian peso of 100 centavos

NATIONAL ANTHEM – Oh gloria inmarcesible (Oh glory unfading!)

NATIONAL DAY – 20 July (National Independence Day)

NATIONAL FLAG – Broad yellow band in upper half, surmounting equal bands of blue and red

LIFE EXPECTANCY (years) – male 66.36; female 72.26

POPULATION GROWTH RATE – 1.6 per cent (1997)

POPULATION DENSITY – 32 per sq. km (1997)

URBAN POPULATION – 71 per cent (1993)

Colombia lies in the extreme north-west of South America, having a coastline on both the Caribbean Sea and Pacific Ocean.

The country is divided by the Cordillera de los Andes into a coastal region in the north and west and extensive plains in the east. The eastern range of the Colombian Andes is a series of vast tablelands. This temperate region is the most densely peopled portion of the country. The principal rivers are the Magdalena, Guaviare, Cauca, Atrato, Caquetá, Putumayo and Patia.

HISTORY AND POLITICS

The Colombian coast was visited in 1502 by Columbus, and in 1536 a Spanish expedition penetrated the interior and established a government. The country remained under Spanish rule until 1819 when Simón Bolivar established the Republic of Colombia, consisting of the territories now known as Colombia, Panama, Venezuela and Ecuador. In 1829–30 Venezuela and Ecuador withdrew, and in 1831 the remaining territories formed the Republic of New Granada. The name was changed to the Granadine Confederation in 1858, to the United States of Colombia in 1861 and to the Republic of Colombia in 1866. Panama seceded in 1903.

From 1957 to 1974 the country was governed under the 'National Front' agreement with an alternating presidency and equal numbers of ministerial posts. The alternation of the presidency ended in 1974 and parity in appointments in 1978.

A new constitution was promulgated in 1991. In the 1994 presidential election the Liberal candidate Ernesto Samper narrowly defeated the Social Conservative Party (PSC) candidate. President Samper appointed a Liberal–PSC coalition government in August 1994. The March 1998 legislative elections were won by the Liberal Party, but some of its members defected to join the Great Alliance for Change (GAC), a Conservative-led coalition which now commands an overall majority in the House of Representatives. The presidential election in June 1998 was won by the PSC candidate Andrés Pastrana Arango, who swore in a cabinet which includes members of the GAC coalition on 7 August 1998.

INSURGENCIES

Colombia is dogged by insurgency from left-wing guerrillas. The main active guerrilla factions are the Revolutionary Armed Forces of Colombia (FARC) and the National Liberation Army (ELN). Formal peace talks began on 6 May 1999, but fighting has continued. The FARC movement called a truce between 20 December 1999 and 10 January 2000 after the army sent Christmas cards to rebels urging them to put down their guns for the holiday season; ELN guerrillas refused to call a truce. On 30 April 2000, FARC launched a political party, the Bolivarian Movement for the New Colombia. On 20 April the government agreed to grant the ELN a demilitarised zone; FARC already had such a zone.

POLITICAL SYSTEM

The Congress is a bicameral legislature. The lower house (the House of Representatives) has 161 members directly elected for a four-year term. The upper house (the Senate) has 102 members, 100 of whom are directly elected for four years; two seats are reserved for representatives of indigenous people. The president, who appoints the Cabinet, is directly elected for a four-year term.

HEAD OF STATE

President, Andrés Pastrana Arango, *elected* 21 June 1998
Vice-President, Gustavo Bell

CABINET *as at September 2000*

Agriculture and Rural Development, Rodrigo Villalba
Communications, María del Rosario Sintes Ulloa
Culture, Consuelo Aravjo Naguera
Defence, Luis Fernando Ramírez Acuna
Economic Development, Jaime Alberto Cabal
Education, Francisco José Lloreda Mera
Environment, Juan Mayr (Ind.)
Finance, Joan Manuel Santos Calderon (LP)
Foreign Affairs, Guillermo Fernández de Soto (PSC)
Foreign Trade, Marta Lucia Ramírez (LP)
Health, Sara Ordonez Noriega
Interior, Humberto de la Calle
Justice, Rómulo González
Labour and Social Welfare, Angelino Garzon
Mines and Energy, Carlos Caballero Argaez (PSC)
Planning, Claudia de Francisco
Transport, Gustavo Canal

LP Liberal Party; PSC Social Conservative Party; Ind. Independent

COLOMBIAN EMBASSY
Flat 3A, 3 Hans Crescent, London SW1X 0LN
Tel: 020-7589 9177/5037
Ambassador Extraordinary and Plenipotentiary, HE Victor
G. Ricardo, apptd 2000

BRITISH EMBASSY
Edificio Ing Barings, Carrera 9 No 76-49 Piso 9, Bogotá
Tel: (00 57) (1) 317 6690/6310/6321
E-mail: britain@cable.net.co
Ambassador Extraordinary and Plenipotentiary,
HE Jeremy Thorp, apptd 1998

BRITISH CONSULAR OFFICES – Barranquilla,
Bogotá, Cali and Medellín

BRITISH COUNCIL DIRECTOR, J. Docherty, Calle 87
No. 12–79, Santa Fé de Bogotá;
e-mail: brit.council@bc-bogota.bcouncil.org.
Regional directors in Cali and Medellín

COLOMBO-BRITISH CHAMBER OF COMMERCE, Apartado
Aereo 054 728, Av. 39 No. 13–62, Bogotá

DEFENCE

The Army has 30 light tanks and, 160 armoured personnel
carriers. The Navy has four submarines, four frigates, 104
patrol and coastal vessels, six aircraft and two helicopters
at nine bases. The Air Force has 72 combat aircraft and
72 armed helicopters.
MILITARY EXPENDITURE – 3.2 per cent of GDP (1998)
MILITARY PERSONNEL – 231,000: Army 121,000, Navy
15,000, Air Force 8,000; Paramilitaries 87,000
CONSCRIPTION DURATION – 12–18 months

ECONOMY

Coal, natural gas and hydroelectricity resources are largely
unexploited, although development of coal is being given
priority. The hydrocarbon sector accounts for over half of
the mining output, precious metals (gold, platinum and
silver) and iron ore accounting for the remainder. Other
mineral deposits include nickel, bauxite, copper, gypsum,
limestone, phosphates, sulphur and uranium. Colombia is
also the world's largest producer of emeralds.

Major cash crops are coffee, sugar, bananas, cut flowers
and cotton. Cattle are raised in large numbers, and meat
and cured skins and hides are also exported.

The government has encouraged diversification to
reduce dependence on coffee as the major export and this
has led to the growth of new export-orientated industries,
particularly textiles, paper products and leather goods.
Stimulus to the economy has been provided by loans from
the World Bank and IADB for project development.

Since the late 1980s the government has introduced
trade liberalisation and privatisation measures which have
effectively freed foreign exchange transactions, increased
foreign competition, ended protectionism and reduced
inflation.

In 1997 there was a trade deficit of US$2,728 million
and a current account deficit of US$5,682 million. In 1996
and 1997 Colombia was blacklisted by the USA for failing to curb levels of drug production sufficiently. These
sanctions were ended in March 1998.
GNP – US$100,667 million (1998); US$2,470 per capita
(1998)
GDP – US$84,733 million (1996); US$2,325 per capita
(1996)
ANNUAL AVERAGE GROWTH OF GDP – 2.2 per cent (1996)
INFLATION RATE – 20.7 per cent (1998)
TOTAL EXTERNAL DEBT – US$33,263 million (1998)

TRADE

Principal exports are petroleum and derivatives, coffee,
bananas, cut flowers, clothing and textiles, ferro-nickel
and coal. Principal trading partners are the USA, the EU
and Latin America.

In 1997 imports totalled US$15,378 million and exports
US$11,522 million.

Trade with UK	1998	1999
Imports from UK	£179,744,000	£106,961,000
Exports to UK	208,520,000	200,008,000

COMMUNICATIONS

The Andes make surface transport difficult so air transport
is used extensively. There are daily air services between
Bogotá and all the principal towns, as well as frequent
services to other countries. The 'Atlantic Railway' links
the departmental lines running down to the River
Magdalena, and completes the connection between
Bogotá and Santa Marta. Although the railways are in a
poor state, there are about 3,386 km of rail in use at
present. The road network consists of 106,600 km of roads
of all types, of which 21,800 km are classified as main trunk
and transversal roads. A canal to link the Pacific Ocean and
the Caribbean Sea has been planned.

There are three national television channels.

CULTURE AND EDUCATION

There is a flourishing press in urban areas and a national
literature supplements the rich inheritance from the time
of Spanish colonial rule. State education is free.
ILLITERACY RATE – 8.2 per cent
ENROLMENT (percentage of age group) – primary
85 per cent (1996); secondary 46 per cent (1995);
tertiary 17 per cent (1996)

THE COMOROS
République Fédérale Islamique des Comores

AREA – 863 sq. miles (2,235 sq. km). The Comoro
archipelago includes the islands of Great Comoro,
Anjouan, Mayotte and Moheli and certain islets in the
Indian Ocean
POPULATION – 651,000 (1997 UN estimate), mostly
Muslim. French and Arabic are the official languages;
the majority of the population speak Comoran, a blend
of Arabic and Swahili
CAPITAL – Moroni (population, 17,267, 1980 estimate),
on Great Comoro
CURRENCY – Comorian franc (KMF) of 100 centimes.
The Franc CFA of 100 centimes is also used
NATIONAL ANTHEM – Udzima wa ya Masiwa
(The union of the islands)
NATIONAL DAY – 6 July (Independence Day)
NATIONAL FLAG – Green ground, with a white crescent
and four white stars, horns towards the fly. The name of
Allah, in Arabic script in the upper fly and the name of
Mohammed in the lower hoist
LIFE EXPECTANCY (years) – male 55.00; female 56.00
POPULATION GROWTH RATE – 3.1 per cent (1997)
POPULATION DENSITY – 291 per sq. km (1997)
URBAN POPULATION – 28.5 per cent (1991)
ILLITERACY RATE – 43.8 per cent
ENROLMENT (percentage of age group) – primary
52 per cent (1993); tertiary 0.6 per cent (1995)

HISTORY AND POLITICS

The islanders voted for independence from France in
December 1974 and three islands became independent on
6 July 1975. The island of Mayotte opposed independence

and has remained under French administration.

An election in 1993 brought President Djohar's National Rally for Development party (RND) to power. Djohar was temporarily ousted in a coup in 1995 which was thwarted by French troops. While Djohar was abroad for medical attention, Prime Minister Caabiel Yachroutou declared himself interim president and refused to acknowledge Djohar's authority, resulting in the formation of a rival government. Djohar returned to the Comoros in January 1996 but was prohibited from contesting the March 1996 presidential election, which was won by Mohammad Taki Abdoulkarim of the National Union for Democracy in the Comoros. Taki dissolved the National Assembly and legislative elections were held in December 1996 although boycotted by the opposition Forum for National Recovery party (FRN).

President Taki died in office on 6 November 1998 and Tajiddine Ben Said Massonde took over as interim president. He and the government he had appointed were deposed in a coup on 30 April 1999 by Col. Assoumani Azzali, who was sworn in as president on 6 May. On 2 September 1999, an unsuccessful coup was launched while Col. Azzali was overseas. He announced that he would retain power until a presidential election was held, which was due to take place by 14 April 2000; twelve opposition parties held a protest march when no election had taken place by that date.

INSURGENCIES

In August 1997 separatists on the islands of Anjouan and Moheli demanded independence from the Comoros and a return to French rule. Following a failed attempt to resolve the situation by force, President Taki assumed absolute power and established a State Transition Commission to function as a Cabinet. In a referendum in October 1997, the inhabitants of Anjouan voted overwhelmingly for independence. Talks mediated by the OAU began in December 1997 and an agreement drawn up with OAU support, which would have given each island considerable autonomy, was signed by Grand Comore and Moheli, but was rejected by Anjouan. Anjouan citizens voted by a large majority against reincorporation into the Comoros in a referendum held on 23 January 2000.

In March 1998, Anjouan's self-proclaimed President Abdallah Ibrahim appointed a prime minister and Cabinet, though their legitimacy has not been recognised internationally. Fighting broke out between President Ibrahim's forces and those of a previous Anjouan prime minister, Chamassi Said Omar, on 5 December 1998. On 1 August, President Ibrahim resigned and transferred most of his powers to Col. Said Abeid. A general election was held in Anjouan in August 1999.

POLITICAL SYSTEM

In October 1996 a new constitution was approved by referendum. The president may be elected for an unlimited number of six-year terms and has the authority to appoint a prime minister and Governors, and reports to the Federal Assembly.

Each island is administered by a Governor, assisted by up to four Commissioners whom he appoints, and has an elected Legislative Council.

HEAD OF STATE

President, Defence, Col. Assoumani Azzali

COUNCIL OF MINISTERS *as at September 2000*

Prime Minister, Bianrifi Tarmidi
Civil Service, Employment and Labour, Milisaani Hamdia
Culture, Youth, Sport and Information, Ahmed Sidi
Economy, Commerce, Industry and Crafts, Assumani Abdou
Equipment and Energy, Djaffar Mmadi
Finance and Budget, Soundi Abdou Toybou

Foreign Affairs, Soeuf Mohamed Elamine
Interior and Establishment of Institutions, Mohamed Abdou Soimadou
Justice and Islamic Affairs, Abdoulbar Youssouf
National Education, Professional Training and Francophone Issues, Moinaecha Cheikh Yahaya
Production and Environment, Charif Abdallah
Public Health, Population and Women's Affairs, Mlahali Mistoihi
Tourism, Transport, Posts and Telecommunications, Said Dhoifir Bounou

EMBASSY OF THE FEDERAL ISLAMIC REPUBLIC OF THE COMOROS
20 rue Marbeau, F-75016 Paris, France
Tel: (00 33) (1) 4067 9054

BRITISH AMBASSADOR, HE C. F. Mochan, resident at Antananarivo, Madagascar

ECONOMY

The most important products are vanilla, copra, cloves and essential oils, which are the principal exports; cacao, sisal and coffee are also cultivated. Great Comoro is well forested and produces some timber.

GNP – US$197 million (1998); US$370 per capita (1998)
GDP – US$227 million (1996); US$359 per capita (1996)
TOTAL EXTERNAL DEBT – US$203 million (1998)

Trade with UK	1998	1999
Imports from UK	£790,000	£1,008,000
Exports to UK	229,000	74,000

DEMOCRATIC REPUBLIC OF CONGO
République Démocratique du Congo

AREA – 905,355 sq. miles (2,344,858 sq. km). Neighbours: Central African Republic (north), Sudan (north-east), Uganda, Rwanda, Burundi and Tanzania (east), Zambia (south), Angola (south-west), Republic of Congo-Brazzaville (north-west)

POPULATION – 48,040,000 (1997 UN estimate). The population was 34,671,607 at the 1985 census, composed almost entirely of Bantu groups, divided into roughly 300 semi-autonomous tribes. Minorities include Sudanese, Nilotes, Pygmies and Hamites, as well as refugees from Angola. Swahili, a Bantu dialect

with an admixture of Arabic, is the nearest approach to a common language in the east and south, while Lingala is the language of a large area along the river and in the north, and Kikongo of the region between Kinshasa and the sea. French is the language of administration
CAPITAL – Kinshasa (population, 2,664,309, 1984)
MAJOR CITIES – Kananga (298,693); Kisangani (317,581); Likasi (213,862); Lubumbashi (564,830); ΨMatadi (138,798); Mbandaka (137,291)
CURRENCY – Congolese franc
NATIONAL DAY – 24 November
NATIONAL FLAG – Blue with a large yellow five-pointed star in the centre and five small yellow five-pointed stars in a vertical line down the hoist
LIFE EXPECTANCY (years) – male 50.30; female 53.72
POPULATION GROWTH RATE – 4.3 per cent (1997)
POPULATION DENSITY – 20 per sq. km (1997)
URBAN POPULATION – 39.5 per cent (1985)
MILITARY EXPENDITURE – 6.6 per cent of GDP (1998)
MILITARY PERSONNEL – 55,900: Army 55,000, Navy 900
ILLITERACY RATE – 22.7 per cent
ENROLMENT (percentage of age group) – primary 61 per cent (1994); secondary 23 per cent (1994); tertiary 2.3 per cent (1994)

The Democratic Republic of Congo (formerly Zaïre) is Africa's third largest state. Apart from the coastal district in the west which is fairly dry, the rainfall averages between 60 and 80 inches a year. The average temperature is about 27°C, but in the south the winter temperature can fall nearly to freezing point. Extensive forest covers the central districts.

HISTORY AND POLITICS

The state of the Congo, founded in 1885, became a Belgian colony in 1908 and was administered by Belgium until independence in 1960. Mobutu Sésé Seko, formerly commander-in-chief of the Congolese National Army, came to power in a coup in 1965 and was elected president in 1970. Legislative power was vested in a unicameral National Legislative Council, with candidates proposed by the sole legal political party, Mouvement Populaire de la Révolution (MPR).

Political reforms were announced in April 1990 and President Mobutu accepted an opposition-dominated government under Prime Minister Etienne Tshisekedi in October 1991.

In January 1994 President Mobutu dissolved the government and on 9 April 1994 promulgated a Transitional Constitutional Act which regulated a 15-month period of transition to democracy. In July 1995 the transition period was extended by a further two years.

In October 1996 fighting broke out between Zaïrean Tutsis (Banyamulenge) and the Zaïrean army in North and South Kivu provinces which had received an influx of Hutu refugees from Rwanda. The pro-Hutu army attempted to expel the Tutsis from the region but found themselves outgunned by the rebels, under the leadership of Laurent Kabila, who were backed by the Rwandan and Ugandan governments. Kabila's Alliance of Democratic Forces for the Liberation of Congo-Zaïre (AFDL) captured Kinshasa in May 1997 and President Mobutu fled. Zaïre was renamed the Democratic Republic of Congo.

A rebellion against the government of Laurent Kabila began in Kivu on 2 August 1998 and by the end of the month the rebels had seized large areas in the east and west of the country. Angola, Chad, Kenya, Namibia and Zimbabwe promised President Kabila military support. The Angolan army quickly recaptured several towns in the south-west, but the rebels maintained their grip on the eastern regions. The rebel movement, the Congolese Democratic Rally (RCD), was supported by Uganda and Rwanda. On 17 May 1999, Ernest Wamba dia Wamba, the RCD leader, was ousted, splitting the movement into two distinct factions, that led by Wamba dia Wamba being called the Congolese Democratic Rally – Liberation Movement (RCD-LM). A cease-fire signed on 31 August 1999 between the government and the two rebel groups has remained largely intact, although localised clashes have been frequent. The main rebel groups, the RCD, the RCD-LM and the Congolese Liberation Movement (MLC) reached agreement on 20 December 1999 to form an umbrella organisation to defeat the government.

POLITICAL SYSTEM

A Constituent Council was set up to draft a new constitution. Political parties have been banned.

There are 11 regions, each under a Governor and provincial administration: Bas-Zaïre (provincial capital, Matadi); Bandundu (Bandundu); Equateur (Mbandaka); Haut-Zaïre (Kisangani); Kinshasa (Kinshasa); Maniema (Kindu); North Kivu (Goma); South Kivu (Bukavu); Shaba (Katanga) (Lubumbashi); East Kasai (Mbuji-Mayi); West Kasai (Kananga).

HEAD OF STATE

President and Minister of Defence, Laurent Désiré Kabila, *sworn in* 29 May 1997

CABINET *as at September 2000*
Agriculture and Animal Husbandry, Etienne Kikanga Shima Musebo
Civil Service, Labour and Social Welfare, Paul-Gabriel Kapita Shabanga
Culture and Arts, Juliana Lumumba
Economy and Industry, Bemba Saolona
Energy, Dabi Mbaye
Finance and State Enterprises, Ferdinand Mawapanga Mwananga
Foreign Affairs and International Co-operation, Abdoulaye Yerodia Ndombasi
Health, Machako Mamba
Human Rights, Leonard Okitundu
Information and Tourism, Didier Mumengi
Interior, Gaetan Kakudji
Justice, Mwenze Kongolo
Land Affairs, Environment, Fisheries and Forest Resources, Anatole Bisikwabo Tshiumbaka
Mines, Frederic Kibassa-Maliba
National Education, Kamara Rwakaikara
Oil Development, Pierre-Victor Mpoyo
Planning and Trade, Badimani Bilembo Mulumba
Post and Telecommunications, Prosper Kibue Molambo
Public Works, Yagi Sitolo
Reconstruction, Maj. Denis Kalume Nunde
Social Affairs, Moleko Moliwa
Transport and Communications, Odette Babandoya Etowa
Youth, Sports and Leisure, Vincent Mutomb Tshibal

EMBASSY OF THE DEMOCRATIC REPUBLIC OF CONGO
26 Chesham Place, London SW1X 8HG
Tel: 020-7235 6137
Chargé d'Affaires, Henri N'Swana

BRITISH EMBASSY
Avenue de Lemera 83, BP 8049, Kinshasa
Tel: (00 243) 34775
E-mail: ambrit@ic.cd
Ambassador Extraordinary and Plenipotentiary, HE Douglas Scrafton, apptd 1996

CONSULATE – Kisangani

ECONOMY

Palm oil is the most important agricultural cash product though it is no longer exported. Coffee, rubber, cocoa and timber are the most important agricultural exports. The production of cotton, pyrethrum and copal is increasing. Copper is widely exploited, and industrial diamonds and cobalt are also produced. Oil deposits are exploited off the Zaïre estuary and reef-gold is mined in the north-east of the country.

The main industrial products are foodstuffs, beverages, tobacco, textiles, leather, wood products, cement and building materials, metallurgy, small river craft and bicycles. There are reserves of hydroelectric power and the Inga dam on the river Zaïre supplies electricity to Matadi, Kinshasa and Shaba.

Rampant hyperinflation and corruption have left the economy and the state's finances in a parlous state. In 1993 the government had a budget deficit equivalent to 13.72 per cent of GDP.

GNP – US$5,433 million (1998); US$110 per capita (1998)
GDP – US$4,207 million (1996); US$90 per capita (1996)
ANNUAL AVERAGE GROWTH OF GDP – 1.3 per cent (1996)
INFLATION RATE – 175.5 per cent (1997)
TOTAL EXTERNAL DEBT – US$12,929 million (1998)

TRADE

The chief exports are copper, crude oil, coffee, diamonds, rubber, cobalt, gold, zinc and other metals.

In 1996 imports totalled US$424 million and exports US$592 million.

Trade with UK	1998	1999
Imports from UK	£5,905,000	£2,657,000
Exports to UK	4,129,000	3,359,000

COMMUNICATIONS

There are approximately 20,500km of roads (earth-surfaced) of national importance, and 6,000 km of railways. The country has four international and 40 principal airports.

REPUBLIC OF CONGO-BRAZZAVILLE
République du Congo-Brazzaville

AREA – 132,047 sq. miles (342,000 sq. km). Neighbours: Gabon (west), Cameroon and Central African Republic (north), Angola (Cabinda) (south-west), the Democratic Republic of Congo (east and south)
POPULATION – 2,745,000 (1997 UN estimate). The official language is French; Lingala, Monokutuba and Kikongo are widely spoken
CAPITAL – Brazzaville (population, 596,200, 1984)
MAJOR CITIES – ΨPointe Noire (298,014), the main commercial centre
CURRENCY – Franc CFA of 100 centimes
NATIONAL ANTHEM – La Congolaise
NATIONAL DAY – 15 August
NATIONAL FLAG – Divided diagonally into green, yellow and red bands
LIFE EXPECTANCY (years) – male 48.87; female 54.14
POPULATION GROWTH RATE – 3.0 per cent (1997)
POPULATION DENSITY – 8 per sq. km (1997)
MILITARY EXPENDITURE – 3.9 per cent of GDP (1998)
MILITARY PERSONNEL – 12,000: Army 8,000, Navy 800, Air Force 1,200; Paramilitaries 2,000
ILLITERACY RATE – 19.3 per cent
ENROLMENT (percentage of age group) – primary 96 per cent (1980); tertiary 7 per cent (1992)

HISTORY AND POLITICS

Formerly the French colony of Middle Congo, Congo-Brazzaville became a member state of the French Community on 28 November 1958 and fully independent on 17 August 1960.

In 1968, a National Council of army officers took power and created the Parti Congolais du Travail (PCT) and the People's Republic of the Congo. After popular pressure, the PCT abandoned its monopoly of power and renounced Marxism in 1990. In 1992 the country adopted a new multiparty constitution with a directly elected president and a bicameral parliament.

The lack of a parliamentary majority forced President Lissouba to call fresh elections in 1993. These were won by the Pan-African Union for Social Democracy (UPADS) but the results were disputed by opposition groups and violence broke out between rival parties. A new UPADS-dominated government was appointed in January 1995. In June 1997, fighting broke out between forces of President Lissouba and followers of former president Sassou-Nguesso, who was reinstalled as president in October 1997. Elections scheduled for July 1997 were called off and a National Forum for Unity and Democracy was set up to schedule legislative elections. It declared a three-year transition period after which democratic elections will be held. A constitutional committee was inaugurated on 19 November 1998, charged with drafting a constitution to be approved by referendum in 1999.

Supporters of Bernard Kolelas, who had briefly been prime minister in 1997, were thought to be responsible for a wave of killings in the Pool region close to Brazzaville, which began in November 1998. In April 1999, they formed themselves into a political party, the Patriotic Union of Ninja Forces. Following a period of intense fighting, negotiations between the government and the rebels began on 13 November 1999; an accord was reached in which the two sides agreed to an unconditional end to hostilities and the demilitarisation of political parties. President Omar Bongo of Gabon was appointed as mediator on 29 December.

HEAD OF STATE

President, Denis Sassou-Nguesso, *sworn in* 25 October 1997

CABINET *as at September 2000*

Agriculture and Livestock, Nkoua Celestin Gongara
Civil Service, Administrative Reform and Women's Affairs, Jeanne Dambenze
Commerce, Small and Medium-sized Enterprises, Pierre Damien Boussoukou Boumba
Communication and Government Spokesman, François Ibovi
Culture and Tourism, Mambou Elie Niamy
Energy and Water Resources, Jean-Marie Tassoua
Finance and Budget, Mathias Dzon
Foreign Affairs and Co-operation, Rodolphe Adada
Forestry, Henri Djombo
Health and National Solidarity, Leon Alfred Opimba
Industrial Development, Alphonse Mbamba
Industry and Mines, Michel Mampoya
Interior, Security and Territorial Administration, Col. Pierre Oba
Keeper of the Seals, Justice, Jean-Martin M'bemba
Labour and Social Security, Lambert Ndouane
Minister in the President's Office in charge of Defence, Itihi Lekounzou Ossetoumba
Petroleum Affairs, Jean-Baptiste Taty-Loutard
Posts and Telecommunications, Jean-Félix Demba Delo
Primary and Secondary Education, Pierre Tsiba
Reconstruction and Urban Development, Martin Mberi
Social Amenities and Public Works, Col. Florent Tsiba
Technical Education and Vocational Training, André Okombi Salissan
Territorial and Regional Development, Pierre Moussa
Transport, Civil Aviation and Merchant Navy, Isidore Mvouba

EMBASSY OF THE REPUBLIC OF CONGO-BRAZZAVILLE
37 bis rue Paul Valéry, F-75116 Paris, France
Tel: (00 33) (1) 4500 6057
Ambassador Extraordinary and Plenipotentiary,
HE Henri Marie Joseph Lopes, apptd 1999

HONORARY CONSULATE, 4 Wendle Court, 131–137
Wandsworth Road, London SW8 2LH.
Tel: 020-7622 0419. *Honorary Consul,* L. Muzzu

BRITISH AMBASSADOR, HE Douglas Scrafton, CMG,
resident at Kinshasa, Democratic Republic of Congo

HONORARY CONSULATE – Brazzaville

ECONOMY

Congo-Brazzaville has its own oil deposits, producing
about 9 million tonnes annually. It also produces lead,
zinc and gold. The principal agricultural products
are timber, cassava and yams. Imports are mainly of
machinery.

In 1997 Congo-Brazzaville had a trade surplus of
US$941 million and a current account deficit of US$252
million. Imports in 1996 totalled US$1,551 million and
exports US$1,555 million. In 1996 the UN approved a
three-year loan of US$100 million and the Paris Club
cancelled 67 per cent of the debt owed to it by Congo-
Brazzaville.

GNP – US$1,899 million (1998); US$680 per capita
(1998)
GDP – US$3,367 million (1996); US$1,262 per capita
(1996)
ANNUAL AVERAGE GROWTH OF GDP – 6.8 per cent (1996)
INFLATION RATE – –0.2 per cent (1996)
TOTAL EXTERNAL DEBT – US$5,119 million (1998)

Trade with UK	1998	1999
Imports from UK	£21,512,000	£12,230,000
Exports to UK	6,943,000	8,463,000

COSTA RICA
República de Costa Rica

AREA – 19,730 sq. miles (51,100 sq. km). Neighbours:
Nicaragua, Panama
POPULATION – 3,464,000 (1997 UN estimate), mainly of
European origin. The language is Spanish
CAPITAL – San José (population, 1,220,412, 1996 estimate)
MAJOR CITIES – Alajuela (175,129); Cartago (120,420),
1996 UN estimates
CURRENCY – Costa Rican colón (₡) of 100 céntimos
NATIONAL ANTHEM – Himno Nacional de Costa Rica
NATIONAL DAY – 15 September
NATIONAL FLAG – Five horizontal bands, blue, white, red,
white, blue (the red band twice the width of the others
with emblem near staff)
LIFE EXPECTANCY (years) – male 72.89; female 77.60
POPULATION GROWTH RATE – 3.0 per cent (1997)
POPULATION DENSITY – 68 per sq. km (1997)
URBAN POPULATION – 41.4 per cent (1994)
MILITARY EXPENDITURE – 0.7 per cent of GDP (1998)
MILITARY PERSONNEL – 8,400: Paramilitaries
ILLITERACY RATE – 4.4 per cent
ENROLMENT (percentage of age group) – primary
89 per cent (1997); secondary 40 per cent (1996);
tertiary 30 per cent (1994)

The coastal lowlands have a tropical climate but the
interior plateau, with a mean elevation of 4,000 feet, enjoys
a temperate climate.

HISTORY AND POLITICS

For nearly three centuries (1530–1821) Costa Rica was
under Spanish rule. In 1821 the country obtained its
independence, although from 1824 to 1839 it was one of
the United States of Central America.

In 1948 the Army was abolished, the President declaring
it unnecessary. The main political parties are the Social
Christian Unity Party (PUSC) and the National Liberation Party (PLN). The last presidential and legislative
elections were held on 1 February 1998, when PUSC
candidate Miguel Angel Rodríguez won the presidential
election, and the PUSC won 27 seats in the Legislative
Assembly.

POLITICAL SYSTEM

Executive power is vested in the president, who is head of
state and government, with legislative power vested in the
57-member Legislative Assembly. Under the constitution
both the president and the members of the Legislative
Assembly are elected for a single four-year term and may
not be re-elected.

HEAD OF STATE

President, Miguel Angel Rodríguez, *elected*
1 February 1998
First Vice-President, Astrid Fischel
Second Vice-President, Minister of Environment,
Elizabeth Odio

CABINET *as at September 2000*
Agriculture and Livestock, Alberto Dent
Culture, Enrique Granados
Economy and Foreign Trade, Tomás Dueñas
Finance, Leonel Baruch
Foreign Affairs, Roberto Rojas
Health, Rogelio Pardo
Housing, Alexander Salas
Justice, Mónica Nágel
Labour and Social Security, Victor Morales
Presidency and Planning, Danilo Chaverri
President of the Central Bank, Eduardo Lizano
Public Education, Guillermo Vargas
Public Security, Rogelio Ramos
Public Works and Transport, Rodolfo Mendez
Women's Affairs, Gloria Valerín

COSTA RICAN EMBASSY

Flat 1, 14 Lancaster Gate, London W2 3LH
Tel: 020-7706 8844
Ambassador Extraordinary and Plenipotentiary,
HE Rodolfo Gutiérrez, apptd 1998

BRITISH EMBASSY

Apartado 815, Edificio Centro Colón (Eleventh Floor),
San José 1007
Tel: (00 506) 258 2025
E-mail: britemb@sol.racsa.co.cr
*Ambassador Extraordinary and Plenipotentiary and Consul-
General,* HE Peter Spiceley, MBE, apptd 1998

ECONOMY

Tourism is the largest single industry, with ecotourism a
growing area; one third of the country is national parkland
or nature reserve. In 1999, there were more than one
million foreign visitors. Industrial activity is principally in
the manufacturing sector and manufactured goods include
computer components, foodstuffs, textiles and clothing,
plastic goods and pharmaceuticals. The principal agricultural products are coffee, bananas, sugar and cattle (for
meat).

GNP – US$9,771 million (1998); US$2,770 per capita
(1998)

GDP – US$9,225 million (1996); US$2,636 per capita (1996)
ANNUAL AVERAGE GROWTH OF GDP – –0.5 per cent (1996)
INFLATION RATE – 11.7 per cent (1998)
UNEMPLOYMENT – 5.6 per cent (1998)
TOTAL EXTERNAL DEBT – US$3,971 million (1998)

TRADE

The chief exports are manufactured goods, bananas, coffee, fish and shellfish, machinery and tropical fruits. The chief imports are raw materials for industry, consumer goods, capital equipment, and fuel and mineral oils. In 1997 there was a trade deficit of US$560 million and a current account deficit of US$254 million. In 1998 imports totalled US$6,230 million and exports US$5,511 million.

Trade with UK	1998	1999
Imports from UK	£38,381,000	£37,561,000
Exports to UK	174,414,000	359,671,000

COMMUNICATIONS

The chief ports are Limón on the Atlantic coast, through which passes most of the coffee exported, and Caldera on the Pacific coast. LACSA is the national airline, operating flights throughout Central and South America, the Caribbean and the USA, besides internal flights to local airports by SANSA.

CÔTE D'IVOIRE
République de la Côte d'Ivoire

AREA – 124,504 sq. miles (322,463 sq. km). Neighbours: Guinea and Liberia (west), Mali and Burkina Faso (north), Ghana (east)
POPULATION – 14,300,000 (1997 UN estimate): 39 per cent Muslim, 28 per cent Christian (mainly Roman Catholic) and 17 per cent maintain traditional beliefs. The official language is French, but Agni, Baoulé, Dioula, Senoufo and Yacouba are spoken
CAPITAL – Yamoussoukro (population, 126,191, 1988), the political and administrative capital since 1983
MAJOR CITIES – ΨAbidjan (1,929,079), the economic and financial centre
CURRENCY – Franc CFA of 100 centimes
NATIONAL ANTHEM – L'Abidjanaise
NATIONAL DAY – 7 August
NATIONAL FLAG – Three vertical stripes, orange, white and green
LIFE EXPECTANCY (years) – male 50.85; female 53.57
POPULATION GROWTH RATE – 3.9 per cent (1996)
POPULATION DENSITY – 44 per sq. km (1997)
URBAN POPULATION – 45.6 per cent (1993)
MILITARY EXPENDITURE – 0.9 per cent of GDP (1998)
MILITARY PERSONNEL – 15,400: Army 6,800, Navy 900, Air Force 700, Paramilitaries 7,000
CONSCRIPTION DURATION – Six months (selective)
ILLITERACY RATE – 53.2 per cent
ENROLMENT (percentage of age group) – primary 55 per cent (1996); tertiary 6 per cent (1994)

The climate is equatorial in the south and west, which are mainly forested; tropical in the centre and east, which are savannah regions with trees; dry and tropical in the north, which is a grassy savannah region.

HISTORY AND POLITICS

Although French contact was made in the first half of the 19th century, Côte d'Ivoire became a colony only in 1893

and was finally pacified in 1912. It decided on 5 December 1958 to remain an autonomous republic within the French Community; full independence outside the Community was proclaimed on 7 August 1960.

After having been president since independence in 1960, President Houphouët-Boigny died in December 1993 and was replaced by the parliamentary speaker Henri Konan-Bédié. Konan-Bédié was elected by an overwhelming majority following an opposition party boycott in the October 1995 presidential election. The Democratic Party of Côte d'Ivoire (PDCI) won 148 of the 175 seats in the November 1995 elections to the National Assembly. The President was deposed by Gen. Robert Guëi in a military coup on 24–25 December 1999, who announced a transitional government on 4 January 2000; a general election was planned for 1 October 2000.

POLITICAL SYSTEM

Côte d'Ivoire has a presidential system of government and a single-chamber National Assembly of 175 members, directly elected for a five-year term. It has been a multiparty system since 1990. In May 1998, the president's term of office was increased from five to seven years.

HEAD OF STATE

President, Chairman of the National Committee of Public Salvation, Defence, Gen. Robert Guëi, *took office* 25 December 1999

CABINET as at September 2000
Agriculture and Animal Resources, Ahmed Timite
Budget, Mamadou Koulibaly
Communications and Culture, Maj. Henri-César Sama
Construction and Environment, Honoré Zohin
Economy and Finance, N'Golo Coulibaly
Education, N'Guessan Michel Amani
External Relations, Charles Providence Gomis
Family and Women's Promotion, Constance Yai
Foreign Affairs and Francophone Affairs, Charles Gomis
Higher Education and Scientific Research, Zacharie Bailly Seri
Industry and Tourism, Affi N' Guessan
Infrastructure, Michel Yoro
Interior and Decentralisation, Col. Mouassi Grena
Justice and Keeper of the Seals, N'Guetta Essy
Labour and Civil Service, Hubert Oulaye
Mines and Energy, Moussa Touré
Planning, Development and Government Co-ordination, Seydou Diarra
Public Health and Social Protection, Jeanine Tagliante
Secretary-General to the Government, Albert Agré
Security, Gen. Lassana Palenfo
Technical Education and Professional Training, Léon Emmanuel Monnet
Trade, Capt. Saint-Cyr Djikalou
Youth and Sports, Col.-Maj. Mathias Doué

EMBASSY OF THE REPUBLIC OF CÔTE D'IVOIRE

2 Upper Belgrave Street, London SW1X 8BJ
Tel: 020-7235 6991
Ambassador Extraordinary and Plenipotentiary, HE Kouadio Adjoumani, apptd 1997

BRITISH EMBASSY

Immeuble 'Les Harmonies', 01 BP 2581 01, Abidjan
Tel: (00 225) 226850
E-mail: britemb.a@africaonline.co.ci
Ambassador Extraordinary and Plenipotentiary, HE Haydon Warren-Gash

ECONOMY

Côte d'Ivoire became wealthy in the 1970s because of the high prices of its two principal export earners, coffee and cocoa. In the late 1980s the economy contracted considerably as its exports deteriorated in competitiveness and its rivals devalued their currencies while the franc CFA remained pegged to the French franc. An economic reform and stabilisation programme began in 1989 under IMF auspices and has brought down inflation, increased investment and led to GDP growth. The devaluation of the CFA franc in January 1994 has increased exports considerably and restored a trade surplus. In February 1998 a further economic reform programme began, aided by a US$385 million loan from the IMF. Foreign debt repayments were suspended in January 2000 owing to economic difficulties.

The principal exports are coffee, cocoa, timber, palm oil, sugar, rubber, pineapples, bananas, and cotton. There are a few deposits of diamonds and minerals including manganese and iron. Oil and gas deposits began to be exploited in 1995.

There was a trade surplus of US$1,805 million in 1997 and a current account surplus of US$35 million. In 1997 imports totalled US$2,741 million and exports US$4,134 million.

GNP – US$10,196 million (1998); US$700 per capita (1998)
GDP – US$10,699 million (1996); US$763 per capita (1996)
ANNUAL AVERAGE GROWTH OF GDP – 6.8 per cent (1996)
INFLATION RATE – 4.7 per cent (1998)
TOTAL EXTERNAL DEBT – US$14,852 million (1998)

Trade with UK	1998	1999
Imports from UK	£49,574,000	£47,733,000
Exports to UK	74,801,000	80,025,000

CROATIA
Republika Hrvatska

AREA – 21,824 sq. miles (56,538 sq. km). Neighbours: Slovenia, Hungary (north), the rump Federal Yugoslav state (east), Bosnia-Hercegovina (south, and east of Adriatic coastal strip)
POPULATION – 4,498,000 (1997 UN estimate); 4,784,265 (1991 census): 78 per cent Croat, 12 per cent Serb, 2 per cent Yugoslav; also Hungarians, Italians, Albanians, Czechs, Ukrainians and Jews. Roman Catholic 76.5 per cent, Eastern Orthodox 11.1 per cent, Protestant 1.4 per cent, Muslim 1.2 per cent. The language is Croatian in the Latin script
CAPITAL – Zagreb (population, 867,717, 1991)
MAJOR CITIES – Osijek (129,792); Rijeka (167,964); Split (200,459), 1991
CURRENCY – Kuna of 100 lipa
NATIONAL ANTHEM – Lijepa naša domovina (Our Beautiful Homeland)
NATIONAL DAY – 30 May (Statehood Day)
NATIONAL FLAG – Three horizontal stripes of red, white, blue, with the national arms over all in the centre
LIFE EXPECTANCY (years) – male 68.59; female 75.95
POPULATION GROWTH RATE – –0.9 per cent (1997)
POPULATION DENSITY – 80 per sq. km (1997)
URBAN POPULATION – 54.3 per cent (1991)
ILLITERACY RATE – 1.7 per cent
ENROLMENT (percentage of age group) – primary 82 per cent (1994); secondary 66 per cent (1994); tertiary 27.9 per cent (1996)

Croatia is divided into three major geographic regions: the Pannonian region in the north, the central mountain belt, and the Adriatic coast region of Istria and Dalmatia which has 1,185 islands and islets and 1,104 miles (1,778 km) of coastline.

HISTORY AND POLITICS

Croatia was part of the Austro-Hungarian Empire from 1526 to 1918. On 29 October 1918 the Croatian parliament declared Croatia independent and soon after Croatia joined with Slovenia, Bosnia-Hercegovina, Serbia and Montenegro to form the 'Kingdom of Serbs, Croats and Slovenes' (renamed Yugoslavia in 1929). From 1941 to 1945 Yugoslavia was occupied by the Axis powers, with Italy and Hungary annexing parts of Croatia and a pro-Nazi Croat puppet state being established in the remainder of Croatia and Bosnia-Hercegovina. The armed extremists of this state (Ustashe) engaged in fierce fighting with Serbian royalists, Communist partisans and pro-Allied Croat partisans.

At the end of the war Yugoslavia was re-established as a federal republic under Communist rule but gradually disintegrated following the death of the wartime partisan leader Josep Tito in 1980.

In April and May 1990 Croatia's first free, democratic elections were won by the Croatian Democratic Union (HDZ) of Dr Franjo Tudjman. A new constitution was adopted by parliament in December 1990 and a referendum in May 1991 backed independence from Yugoslavia. Croatia declared its independence on 30 May 1991. The Federal Yugoslav Army (JNA) intervened against local defence forces to prevent the disintegration of the federation. Croatia's ethnic Serb minority, which rejected Croatia's independence, began fighting with the Croat defence forces. By September 1991 this had escalated into war between Croatia and Serbia, which had assumed control of the JNA.

The war in Croatia continued until January 1992 when a cease-fire was declared. The JNA and Serb forces had secured control of virtually all ethnic Serb areas in Croatia.

The HDZ won a majority of seats in the 1995 elections to the Chamber of Representatives and in the April 1997 elections to the Chamber of Districts. President Tudjman was re-elected in June 1997 but was temporarily replaced by Vlatko Pavletić on 26 November 1999 after he fell ill; he died on 10 December. Stipe Mesić was elected in presidential elections held on 7 February 2000. In the general election held on 4 January 2000, the opposition coalition of the Social Democratic Party of Croatia (SPH) and the Croatian Social Liberal Party (HSLS) scored a decisive victory, winning a total of 68 seats.

SECESSION

Croatia's ethnic Serbs voted to establish a Republic of Serbian Krajina (RSK) in 1993 and elected Milan Martić as president in January 1994.

The government seized Western Slavonia in May 1995 and the whole of Krajina in August 1995 prompting the withdrawal of 10,000 UNCRO peacekeepers and the flight of 150,000 Serbs. The last Croatian Serb-held area of Eastern Slavonia agreed in November 1995 to its eventual reintegration into Croatia. A 5,000-strong UN force was dispatched to the area in 1996 to oversee the formation of a two-year transitional government. On 15 January 1998, the UN pulled out of Eastern Slavonia and Croatia resumed full control of the territory.

FOREIGN RELATIONS

An agreement to normalise relations with Yugoslavia was signed in August 1996. Croatia was sworn in as a member of the Council of Europe in November 1996.

POLITICAL SYSTEM

Executive power is vested in a president and government. The president is directly elected for five-year terms. Legislative power is vested in the bicameral parliament (*Sabor*), comprising the 68-member Chamber of Counties, 63 of whom are directly elected and five appointed by the president, and the 151-member Chamber of Representatives, who are directly elected for a four-year term.

Croatia is divided into 21 counties; each county elects three members to the Chamber of Counties. Counties are composed of groups of districts and function both as units of local government and as regional offices for the central administration. There are 102 districts.

HEAD OF STATE

President, Stipe Mesić, *elected* 7 February 2000

CABINET *as at September 2000*

Prime Minister, Ivica Racan (SPH)
First Deputy Prime Minister, Goran Granić (HSLS)
Deputy PMs, Slavko Linić (SPH); Zeljka Antunović
  (SPH)
Agriculture and Forestry, Bozidar Pankretić (HSS)
Croatian Homeland War Defenders, Ivica Pandić
Culture, Anton Vujić (SPH)
Defence, Jozo Rados (HSLS)
Economy, Goranko Fizulić (HSLS)
Education and Sport, Vladimir Strugar (HSS)
Environmental Protection and Zoning, Bozo Kovacević
  (LS)
European Integration, Ivan Jaković (IDS)
Finance, Mato Crkvenac (SPH)
Foreign Affairs, Tonino Picula (SPH)
Health, Maja Stavljević-Rukavina
Interior, Sime Lucin (SPH)
Justice, Administration and Local Self-Government,
  Stjepan Ivanisević (SPH)
Labour and Social Welfare, Davorko Vidović (SPH)
Public Works, Reconstruction and Construction,
  Radimir Cacić (HNS)
Science and Technology, Hrvoje Kraljević (HSLS)
Tourism, Pave Zupan Rusković
Trade, Small and Medium Businesses, Zeljko Pecek (HSLS)
Transport and Telecommunications, Alojz Tusek (HSLS)

HNS Croatian People's Party; HSLS Croatian Social Liberal Party; HSS Croatian Peasants' Party; IDS Istrian Democratic Assembly; LS Liberal Party; SPH Social Democratic Party of Croatia

EMBASSY OF THE REPUBLIC OF CROATIA

21 Conway Street, London W1P 5HL
Tel: 020-7387 2022
Ambassador Extraordinary and Plenipotentiary,
  HE Andrija Kojaković, apptd 1997

BRITISH EMBASSY

Vlaska 121/III Floor, PO Box 454, 10000 Zagreb
Tel: (00 385) (1) 455 5310
E-mail: british-embassy@zg.tel.hr
Ambassador Extraordinary and Plenipotentiary,
  HE Colin Munro, apptd 1997
BRITISH CONSULATES – Split and Dubrovnik

BRITISH COUNCIL DIRECTOR, R. Evans, PO Box 55, 10000
Zagreb; e-mail: bc.zagreb@bc.tel.hr

DEFENCE

The Army has 300 main battle tanks, 45 armoured personnel carriers and 109 armoured infantry fighting vehicles. The Air Force has 44 combat aircraft and 15 armed helicopters. The Navy has one submarine and 13 patrol and coastal combatants at five bases.
MILITARY EXPENDITURE – 8.3 per cent of GDP (1998)
MILITARY PERSONNEL – 101,000: Army 53,000, Navy 3,000, Air Force 5,000; Paramilitaries 40,000
CONSCRIPTION DURATION – Ten months

ECONOMY

Production was severely hampered during the conflict in

1991–5; the material damage was estimated by the government to be US$27 billion, with the loss of 13,583 lives. Large areas of farmland were destroyed and the tourist industry, which provided one third of total foreign exchange earnings in 1990, was decimated.

Shipbuilding and fishing are major industries on the Adriatic coast. Inland there is a light manufacturing sector, food-processing industries, bauxite deposits, thermal mineral springs, hydroelectric potential, and agriculture based on grain, horticulture, livestock and tobacco. Textiles is one of the most important industries employing more than 17 per cent of the population. In April 1996, Croatia agreed to pay 29.5 per cent of Yugoslavia's debt, totalling US$1.45 billion.

In 1998 Croatia had a trade deficit of US$4,169 million and a current account deficit of US$1,554 million. Imports totalled US$8,384 million and exports US$4,540 million.
GNP – US$20,786 million (1998); US$4,620
  per capita (1998)
GDP – US$19,067 million (1996); US$4,236
  per capita (1996)
INFLATION RATE – 6.4 per cent (1998)
UNEMPLOYMENT – 11.4 per cent (1998)
TOTAL EXTERNAL DEBT – US$8,297 million (1998)

TRADE

Trade with UK	1998	1999
Imports from UK	£105,867,000	£79,413,000
Exports to UK	42,532,000	41,630,000

CUBA
República de Cuba

AREA – 42,804 sq. miles (110,861 sq. km)
POPULATION – 11,059,000 (1997 UN estimate).
  The language is Spanish
CAPITAL – ΨHavana (population, 2,184,990, 1995 UN
  estimate)
MAJOR CITIES – Camagüey (296,601); Guantánamo
  (204,903); Holguín (243,240); Santa Clara (206,900);
  ΨSantiago (432,396), 1995 UN estimates
CURRENCY – Cuban peso of 100 centavos
NATIONAL ANTHEM – Al Combate, Corred Bayameses
  (To battle, men of Bayamo)
NATIONAL DAY – 1 January (Day of Liberation)
NATIONAL FLAG – Five horizontal bands, blue and white
  (blue at top and bottom) with red triangle, close to staff,
  charged with five-point star
LIFE EXPECTANCY (years) – male 72.89; female 76.80
POPULATION GROWTH RATE – 0.6 per cent (1997)
POPULATION DENSITY – 100 per sq. km (1997)
URBAN POPULATION – 74.5 per cent (1995)

HISTORY AND POLITICS

The island was visited by Columbus in 1492. Early in the 16th century the island was conquered by the Spanish, and for almost four centuries remained under Spanish rule. Separatist agitation culminated in the closing years of the 19th century in open warfare. In 1898 the USA intervened and demanded the evacuation of Cuba by Spanish forces. The Spanish–American war led to the abandonment of the island, which came under American military rule from 1899 until 1902, when an autonomous government was inaugurated with an elected president, and bicameral legislature.

A revolution led by Dr Fidel Castro overthrew the government of Gen. Batista in 1959. In 1965 the Communist Party of Cuba (PCC) was formed to succeed the United Party of the Socialist Revolution; it is the only authorised political party. A new Socialist constitution came into force in 1976 and indirect elections to the National Assembly of People's Power were subsequently held. The first direct elections to the National Assembly were held in February 1993; all candidates were officially approved by the Communist Party and ran for election unopposed. The 14 provincial assemblies were elected in the same manner. The fifth congress of the PCC was held in October 1997. At the election of deputies to the National Assembly in January 1998, all 601 PCC candidates received the required 50 per cent of the vote, and in February the National Assembly confirmed Dr Castro as president for a further five-year term.

HEAD OF STATE

President of Council of State and Council of Ministers,
   Dr Fidel Castro Ruz, *appointed* 2 November 1976,
   re-elected 15 March 1993, 24 February 1998

COUNCIL OF STATE *as at September 2000*

President, Dr Fidel Castro Ruz
First Vice-President, Gen. Raúl Castro Ruz
Vice-Presidents, Carlos Lage Dávila; Juan Almeida Bosque;
   Abelardo Colomé Ibarra; Esteban Lazo Hernández;
   José Ramón Machado Ventura
Secretary, José Miyar Barrueco

COUNCIL OF MINISTERS *as at September 2000*

President, Dr Fidel Castro Ruz
First Vice-President, Revolutionary Armed Forces,
   Gen. Raúl Castro Ruz
Vice-Presidents, Dr Carlos Rafael Rodríguez Rodríguez;
   Pedro Miret Prieto; José Ramón Fernández Alvárez;
   Jaime Crombet Hernández Baquero; Adolfo Diaz
   Suárez
Secretary, Carlos Lage Dávila

Ministers, Alfredo Jordán Morales (*Agriculture*); Gen.

Silvano Colás Sánchez (*Communications*); Juan Mario Junco del Pino (*Construction*); vacant (*Construction Materials Industry*); Abel Prieto Jiménez (*Culture*); Barbara Castillo Cuesta (*Domestic Trade*); José Luis Rodríguez García (*Economy and Planning*); Luís Ignacio Gómez Gutiérrez (*Education*); Manuel Millares Rodríguez (*Finance and Prices*); Orlando Felipe Rodríguez Romay (*Fishing Industry*); Alejandro Rocas Iglesias (*Food Industry*); Marta Lomas Morales (*Foreign Investment and Economic Co-operation*); Felipe Pérez Roque (*Foreign Relations*); Raúl de la Nuez Ramirez (*Foreign Trade*); Marcos J. Portal León (*Heavy Industries*); Fernando Vecino Alegret (*Higher Education*); Gen. Abelardo Colomé Ibarra (*Interior*); Roberto Díaz Sotolongo (*Justice*); Alfredo Morales Cartaya (*Labour and Social Security*); Jesús Pérez Othon (*Light Industry*); Roberto Ignacio González Planas (*Metal working and Electronics Industries*); Carlos Dotres Martínez (*Public Health*); Rosa Eleana Simeón Negrín (*Science, Technology and Environment*); Div.-Gen. Ulises Rosales del Toro (*Sugar Industry*); Ibrahim Ferradaz García (*Tourism*); Alvaro Pérez Morales (*Transport*); Wilfredo López Rodríguez; Ricardo Cabrisas Ruíz (*Without Portfolio*)

EMBASSY OF THE REPUBLIC OF CUBA
167 High Holborn, London WC1V 6PA
Tel: 020-7240 2488
Ambassador Extraordinary and Plenipotentiary,
   HE Rodney Alejandro López Clemente, apptd 1995

BRITISH EMBASSY
Calle 34 No. 702/4, entre 7ma Avenida y 17, Miramar,
   Havana.
Tel: (00 53) (7) 241 771
Ambassador Extraordinary and Plenipotentiary,
   HE David Ridgeway, OBE, apptd 1998
BRITISH COUNCIL REPRESENTATIVE, M. White,
   Calle 34 No 702, 4 entre 7ma Avenida y 17,
   Miramar, Havana; e-mail: britcoun@ip.etecsa.cu

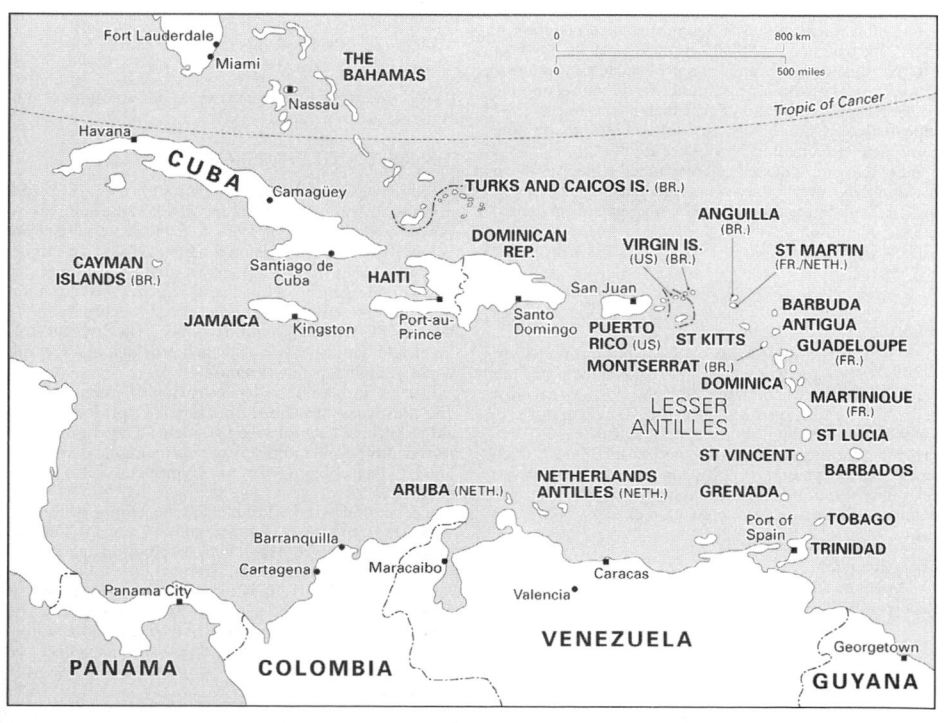

DEFENCE

The Army has 1,500 main battle tanks and 700 armoured personnel carriers. The Navy has one submarine, two frigates and five patrol and coastal vessels at six bases. The Air Force has 130 combat aircraft and 45 armed helicopters.

The last former Soviet combat personnel left Cuba in 1993, but 810 Russian military advisers remain to operate military intelligence facilities. The United States has 1,080 naval personnel at Guantánamo Bay Naval Base, which has been leased since before the 1959 revolution.
MILITARY EXPENDITURE – 5.2 per cent of GDP (1998)
MILITARY PERSONNEL – 86,500: Army 45,000, Navy 5,000, Air Force 10,000; Paramilitaries 26,500
CONSCRIPTION DURATION – Two years

ECONOMY

After the revolution virtually all land and industrial and commercial enterprises were nationalised. Following the curtailing of Cuba's privileged trading relationships with the Soviet bloc in 1989, the economy deteriorated sharply. GDP fell by 75 per cent between 1989 and 1994, and the government was forced to introduce reforms. Since 1993, the government has legalised the holding of US dollars by private individuals, permitted private enterprise, cut subsidies to loss-making state industries, allowed prices for some goods and services to rise, and introduced income tax. State farms have been transformed into co-operatives run by private individuals and permitted to sell 20 per cent of produce on the open market, but remain relatively unproductive. In 1995, foreign investors were permitted to buy property and own Cuban-based companies, with British and Canadian firms becoming involved in the oil and mining industries.

Following austerity measures imposed in 1993, the economy has slowly started to grow; output has risen by 15 per cent since 1994. Sugar is still the mainstay of the economy and the principal source of foreign exchange; production dropped from 8.04 million tons in 1989–90 to 4.4 million tons in 1996–7. Domestic oil production is rising and reached 1,680,000 tonnes in 1998. Lack of external finance has been a major obstacle to economic recovery, as has the long-standing trade and economic embargo imposed by the USA, which has been criticised repeatedly by the UN and was condemned by the European Parliament in November 1998.

The tourism industry has expanded since 1986 to become the country's largest foreign exchange earner. In 1997 1.2 million tourists visited Cuba, generating some US$1,500 million.
GDP – US$22,815 million (1996); US$2,071 per capita (1996)
ANNUAL AVERAGE GROWTH OF GDP – 7.8 per cent (1996)

TRADE

Cuba's exports dropped from US$8.1 billion in 1989 to US$1.7 billion in 1993 while imports declined by 73 per cent. Trade between Cuba and the former socialist economies of Europe is now less than 10 per cent of pre-1989 levels. A trade deal was signed with Russia in 1995 providing for the exchange of sugar for oil. The US trade and economic embargo remains in force, though it was relaxed in March 1998 to allow food and medicine into the country. Principal exports are sugar, nickel, seafood, citrus fruits, tobacco and rum.

Trade with UK	1998	1999
Imports from UK	£33,641,000	£21,825,000
Exports to UK	15,798,000	16,671,000

COMMUNICATIONS

There are 12,700 km of railway track, of which 5,000 km are in public service. In 1986 there were 13,247 km of road. Scheduled international air services run to Central and South American countries and Europe. In March 1998 the ban on direct flights between Cuba and the USA was lifted.

CULTURE AND EDUCATION

The press and broadcasting are under the control of the government. Education is compulsory and free. In 1964 illiteracy was officially declared to be eliminated.
ILLITERACY RATE – 3.6 per cent
ENROLMENT (percentage of age group) – primary 100 per cent (1996); secondary 59 per cent (1993); tertiary 12.4 per cent (1996)

CYPRUS
Kypriaki Dimokratia/Kibris Çumhuriyeti

AREA – 3,572 sq. miles (9,251 sq. km)
POPULATION – 766,000 (1997 UN estimate): 85 per cent Greek, 12 per cent Turkish. Greek and Turkish are official languages
CAPITAL – Nicosia (Lefkosia) population, 193,000, 1996 estimate)
MAJOR CITIES – ΨFamagusta; ΨLarnaca; ΨLimassol; Paphos
CURRENCY – Cyprus pound (C£) of 100 cents
NATIONAL ANTHEM – Ode to Freedom
NATIONAL DAY – 1 October (Independence Day)
NATIONAL FLAG – White with a gold map of Cyprus above a wreath of olive
LIFE EXPECTANCY (years) – male 75.31; female 79.75
POPULATION GROWTH RATE – 1.7 per cent (1997)
POPULATION DENSITY – 83 per sq. km (1997)
URBAN POPULATION – 67.7 per cent (1992)
ENROLMENT (percentage of age group) – primary 96 per cent (1995); secondary 93 per cent (1995); tertiary 23 per cent (1996)

The climate is Mediterranean, with a hot dry summer and a variable warm winter.

HISTORY AND POLITICS

Cyprus came under British administration from 1878, and was formally annexed to Britain in 1914 on the outbreak of war with Turkey. From 1925 to 1960 it was a Crown Colony. Following the launching in 1955 of an armed campaign by EOKA in support of union with Greece, a state of emergency was declared which lasted for four years. An agreement was signed on 19 February 1959 between the United Kingdom, Greece, Turkey, and the Greek and Turkish Cypriots which provided that Cyprus would be an independent republic.

The island became independent on 16 August 1960. The constitution provided for a Greek Cypriot president and a Turkish Cypriot vice-president. The constitution proved unworkable and led to intercommunal trouble. The UN Peacekeeping Force in Cyprus (UNFICYP) was set up in 1964.

A general election was held for the House of Representatives (56 Greek Cypriot and 24 vacant Turkish Cypriot seats) on 26 May 1996, resulting in the parties gaining the following seats: Democratic Rally-Liberal Party 20; AKEL (Left-wing) 19; Democratic Party (DIKO) 10; EDEK (Socialist) 5; Free Democrats 2. In February 1998, Glafcos Clerides of the Democratic Rally-Liberal Party was re-elected president with 51 per cent of the vote. On 30 March 1998, formal accession talks with the EU began.

HEAD OF STATE
President, Glafcos Clerides, *elected* 14 February 1993, re-elected 15 February 1998

COUNCIL OF MINISTERS *as at September 2000*
Agriculture, Environment and Natural Resources, Costas Themistocleous
Commerce, Industry and Tourism, Nicos Rolandis
Communications and Works, Averof Neophytou
Defence, Socrates Hasikos
Education and Culture, Ouranios Ioannides
Finance, Takis Klerides
Foreign Affairs, Ioannis Kasoulides
Health, Frixos Savvides
Interior, Christodoulos Christodoulou
Justice and Public Order, Nicos Koshis
Labour and Social Insurance, Andreas Moushouttas

CYPRUS HIGH COMMISSION
93 Park Street, London W1Y 4ET
Tel: 020-7499 8272
Acting High Commissioner, Dr George Kasoulides
First Counsellor, Consul-General, Yannis Iacovou
Counsellors, K. Avgoustinos *(Cultural Affairs)*; A. Georgiades *(Commerce)*, S. Georgiallis *(Press Counsellor)*

BRITISH HIGH COMMISSION
Alexander Pallis Street (PO Box 1978), CY-1587 Nicosia
Tel: (00 357) (2) 861100
High Commissioner, HE Edward Clay, CMG, apptd May 1999
Counsellor and Deputy High Commissioner, J. S. Buck
Defence Adviser, Col. C. S. Wakelin, OBE
First Secretary (Commercial), W. Preston

BRITISH COUNCIL DIRECTOR, P. Skelton, 3 Museum Street, CY-1097 Nicosia;
e-mail: enquiries@britishcouncil.org.cy

BRITISH SOVEREIGN AREAS
The UK retained full sovereignty and jurisdiction over two areas of 99 square miles in all: Akrotiri–Episkopi–Paramali and Dhekelia–Pergamos–Ayios Nicolaos–Xylophagou. The British Administrator of these areas is appointed by The Queen and is responsible to the Secretary of State for Defence. The combined total of army and RAF personnel stationed in the areas is 5,000.
Administrator of the British Sovereign Areas, Air Vice-Marshal P. Millar

DEFENCE

The National Guard has 145 main battle tanks, 70 armoured infantry fighting vehicles and 402 armoured personnel carriers. Turkey has 30–33,000 troops in northern Cyprus.
In January 1998, a military airfield in Paphos was completed. It is intended to provide a base for Greek military aircraft, as Cyprus does not possess its own air force.
MILITARY EXPENDITURE – 5.5 per cent of GDP (1998)
MILITARY PERSONNEL – 10,000 National Guard, Northern Cyprus Army 4,500
CONSCRIPTION DURATION – 26 months

ECONOMY

In 1997, 9.9 per cent of the workforce were employed in agriculture, 23.5 per cent in industry and 66.6 per cent in the services sector. Main products are citrus fruits, grapes and vine products, meat, milk, potatoes and other vegetables. Manufacturing, construction, distribution and other service industries are other major employers. Tourism is the main growth industry with over two

million tourists producing C£878 million in foreign exchange earnings in 1998, accounting for 18.9 per cent of GDP. 1,055 foreign firms were registered as offshore companies in Cyprus in 1998, and 20 per cent of the world's ships are Cypriot registered.
GNP – US$8,983 million (1998); US$11,920 per capita (1998)
GDP – US$8,694 million (1996); US$11,500 per capita (1996)
ANNUAL AVERAGE GROWTH OF GDP – 4.1 per cent (1996)
INFLATION RATE – 2.2 per cent (1998)
UNEMPLOYMENT – 3.3 per cent (1998)

TRADE
The UK is the main trading partner, taking 15 per cent of exports in 1998 and supplying 11 per cent of imports. In 1998 there was a trade deficit of US$2,490 million and a current account deficit of US$600 million. Imports totalled US$3,685 million and exports US$1,061 million.

Trade with UK	1998	1999
Imports from UK	£259,990,000	£259,513,000
Exports to UK	170,127,000	190,550,000

TURKISH REPUBLIC OF
NORTHERN CYPRUS

In 1974, mainland Greek officers under instructions from the military junta in Athens launched a coup and installed a former EOKA member, Nikos Sampson, as president. Turkey invaded northern Cyprus and occupied over a third of the island. In 1975 a 'Turkish Federated State of Cyprus' under Rauf Denktaş was declared in this area and in 1983 a 'Declaration of Statehood' was issued which purported to establish the 'Turkish Republic of Northern Cyprus'. The declaration was condemned by the UN Security Council and only Turkey has recognised the new 'state'. In 1985, Denktaş was elected president and a general election was held. Denktaş was re-elected in 1990, 1995 and on 15 April 2000. A UN plan for the reunification of the island was formally rejected by him on 31 August 1998. On 6 December 1998, elections to the 50-seat Republican Assembly resulted in a coalition government between the National Unity Party, who gained 24 seats, and the Democrat Party, who gained 13 seats. UN-sponsored proximity talks were held on 3–14 December 1999 between representatives of the Greek and Turkish communities, but no agreement was reached; a further round was planned.

CZECH REPUBLIC
Česká Republika

AREA – 30,450 sq. miles (78,866 sq. km). Neighbours: Poland (north-east), Germany (west and north-west), Austria (south), Slovakia (east)
POPULATION – 10,304,000 (1997 UN estimate), 10,302,000 (1991 census): 95 per cent Czech, 3 per cent Slovak. Czech is the official language. The majority of the population is Roman Catholic, with a small Protestant minority
CAPITAL – Prague (Praha) on the Vltava (Moldau) (population, 1,200,458, 1997 UN estimate)
MAJOR CITIES – Brno (Brünn) (385,866); Ostrava (323,177); Plzeň (Pilsen); (169,391),1997 UN estimates
CURRENCY – Koruna (Kčs) of 100 haléřu
NATIONAL ANTHEM – Kde Domov Můj (Where is my Motherland)
NATIONAL DAY – 28 October

NATIONAL FLAG – White over red horizontally with a blue
triangle extending from the hoist to the centre of the flag
LIFE EXPECTANCY (years) – male 70.37; female 77.27
POPULATION GROWTH RATE – –0.1 per cent (1997)
POPULATION DENSITY – 131 per sq. km (1997)
URBAN POPULATION – 74.7 per cent (1996)

The Czech Republic is composed of Bohemia and
Moravia. Bohemia is surrounded by mountain ranges
while Moravian land stretches to the Danubian basin.

HISTORY AND POLITICS

The area which is now the Czech Republic came under the
rule of the Habsburg dynasty in 1526 and remained part
of the Austro-Hungarian Empire until 1918. The rise of
Czech nationalism in the late 19th century led to the
proclamation of the independence of Czechoslovakia on
28 October 1918 following an amalgamation of Bohemia,
Moravia, Slovakia and Ruthenia and was confirmed by the
Versailles Peace Conference in 1919.

Czechoslovakia was forced to cede the ethnic German
Sudetenland to Nazi Germany in 1938 after the Munich
Agreement. German forces invaded the Czech Republic in
March 1939 and incorporated it into Germany while
Slovakia became a puppet state. The Czech Republic was
liberated by Soviet and American forces in May 1945. The
pre-war democratic Czechoslovak state was re-established
in 1945, having ceded Ruthenia to the Soviet Union. The
Communists took power in a coup in 1948 and remained
in power until 1989.

In 1968 the Communist Party under Alexander
Dubček embarked on a political and economic reform
programme (the Prague Spring). The reforms were
suppressed following an invasion by Warsaw Pact troops
on the night of 20 August 1968, and were abandoned when
Gustáv Husák became leader of the Communist Party
in 1969.

Mass protests in November 1989 led to the resignation
of the Communist Party Central Committee. The Party
was forced to concede its monopoly of power and on 10
December a new government was appointed in which only
half the ministers were Communists. Husák resigned as
president and was replaced by the dissident writer Václav
Havel. Free elections were held in June 1990 in which the
Communist Party was defeated.

In late 1992 the leaders of the Czech and Slovak
republics agreed to dissolve the federation and form two
sovereign states; this took effect on 1 January 1993.

The elections of June 1992 had returned the Civil
Democratic Party (ODS) as the largest party in the Czech
parliament, and it formed a coalition government with
three other centre-right parties. The former federal
President Havel was elected president. Following the
general election of 31 May 1996, the ODS and its coalition
partners, two seats short of a majority, agreed to slow the
rate of privatisation in return for support from the
opposition Social Democrats. The general election in
June 1998 produced no outright winner. Miloš Zeman,
leader of the Czech Social Democratic Party (CSSD),
formed a coalition government; all ministers are
members of the CSSD except the Justice Minister, who
is non-partisan.

POLITICAL SYSTEM

The constitution vests legislative power in the bicameral
parliament, comprising a 200-member Chamber of
Deputies elected for a four-year term and an 81-member
Senate elected for a six-year term, one-third being
renewed every two years. The president is elected by
parliament for a five-year term. Executive power is held by
the prime minister and Council of Ministers. A two-thirds
majority in parliament is necessary to amend the
constitution, and federal laws remain in place unless
superseded by Czech ones. A Constitutional Court has

been established comprising 15 judges nominated by the
president for ten-year terms with Senate approval.

HEAD OF STATE

President, Václav Havel, *elected* 26 January 1993,
re-elected 20 January 1998

COUNCIL OF MINISTERS *as at September 2000*
Prime Minister, Miloš Zeman
Deputy Prime Minister, Finance, Pavel Mertlík, (CSSD)
*Deputy Prime Minister in charge of Foreign Affairs and
Security Policy*, Jan Kavan (CSSD)
Deputy Prime Minister in charge of Legislative Affairs,
Pavel Rychetský (CSSD)
Deputy Prime Minister, Labour and Social Affairs,
Vladimir Spidla (CSSD)
Agriculture, Jan Fencl (CSSD)
Culture, Pavel Dostál (CSSD)
Defence, Vladimír Vetchý (CSSD)
Education, Eduard Zeman (CSSD)
Environment, Miloš Kužvart (CSSD)
Health, Bohumil Fišer
Interior, Stanislav Gross (CSSD)
Justice, Otakar Motejl (Ind.)
Regional Development, Petr Lachnit
Trade and Industry, Miroslav Grégr (CSSD)
Transport and Communications, Jaromír Schling
Without Portfolio, Karel Březina; Jan Mueller
    (*Intelligence Services and Romany Affairs*)

CSSD Czech Social Democratic Party; Ind. Independent

EMBASSY OF THE CZECH REPUBLIC
26 Kensington Palace Gardens, London W8 4QY
Tel: 020-7243 1115
Ambassador Extraordinary and Plenipotentiary,
    HE Pavel Seifter, apptd 1998
Minister-Counsellor, Milan Čoupek
Military Attaché, Col. Milan Skalický

BRITISH EMBASSY
Thunovská 14, CZ-11800 Prague 1
Tel: (00 420) (2) 5732 0355
E-mail: info@britain.cz
Ambassador Extraordinary and Plenipotentiary,
    HE David Broucher, apptd 1997
Counsellor and Deputy Head of Mission, D. E. P. P. Keefe
Defence Attaché, Col. A. F. Davidson, MBE
First Secretary (Commercial), M. L. Connor
BRITISH COUNCIL DIRECTOR, M. O'Neill (*Cultural
    Attaché*), Narodni 10, CZ-12501 Prague 1; e-mail:
info@britcoun.cz. Regional offices in Brno, České
Budějovice, Olomouc, Ostrava, Pardubice, Plzeň and
Usti Nad Labem

DEFENCE

The army has 938 main battle tanks, 804 armoured
infantry fighting vehicles, and 415 armoured personnel
carriers. The Air Force has 94 combat aircraft and 34
attack helicopters. The Czech Republic became a member
of NATO on 12 March 1999.
MILITARY EXPENDITURE – 2.1 per cent of GDP (1998)
MILITARY PERSONNEL – 58,200: Army 25,300, Air Force
    15,400, Paramilitaries 5,600, Others 11,900
CONSCRIPTION DURATION – 12 months

ECONOMY

Under Communist rule industry and most agricultural
land was state-owned. An economic reform programme
began in 1990 to produce a free-market economy, and
the government of the Czech Republic has continued to
follow the policies of the former federal government. This

has necessitated a restrictive monetary policy to stem inflation and a restructuring of industry to be competitive, and these were major reasons for the break with Slovakia. As a result, foreign investment (US$4,000 million in 1989–94) and private enterprises have grown and reliance on trade with the former Soviet bloc countries has ended. By late 1995 over 90 per cent of the economy had been privatised, with two-thirds of the population owning shares.

A trade-liberalising association agreement with the EU is in operation, and formal EU accession talks began in March 1998.

A customs union between the Czech and Slovak Republics is in place but separate currencies were introduced in February 1993 following speculation. The Koruna was made fully convertible in October 1995.

Principal agricultural products are sugar beet, potatoes and cereal crops; the timber industry is also very important. Having been the major industrial area of the Austro-Hungarian Empire, the country has long been industrialised, and machinery, industrial consumer goods and raw materials are major exports.

In 1994 the government had a budget surplus equivalent to 0.88 per cent of GDP. In 1997 there was a trade deficit of US$4,588 million and a current account deficit of US$3,271 million. In 1998 imports totalled US$30,239 million and exports US$26,337 million.

GNP – US$53,034 million (1998); US$5,150 per capita (1998)
GDP – US$50,422 million (1996); US$4,919 per capita (1996)
ANNUAL AVERAGE GROWTH OF GDP – 9.7 per cent (1996)
INFLATION RATE – 10.7 per cent (1998)
UNEMPLOYMENT – 6.5 per cent (1998)
TOTAL EXTERNAL DEBT – US$25,301 million (1998)

Trade with UK	1998	1999
Imports from UK	£714,866,000	£739,158,000
Exports to UK	576,520,000	597,354,000

EDUCATION

Education is compulsory and free for all children from the ages of six to 15. There are nine universities of which the oldest and most famous is Charles University in Prague (founded 1348).
ENROLMENT (percentage of age group) – primary 87 per cent (1995); secondary 87 per cent (1995); tertiary 24 per cent (1996)

CULTURE

The Reformation gave a widespread impetus to Czech literature, the writings of Jan Hus (martyred in 1415 as a religious and social reformer) familiarising the people with Wyclif's teaching. This lasted until the close of the 17th century when Jan Amos Komenský or Comenius (1592–1670) was expelled from the country. There was a period of stagnation until the national revival in the 19th century. Authors of international reputation include Jaroslav Hašek (1883–1923), Jaroslav Seifert (1901–86, Nobel Prize for Literature, 1985), Václav Havel (b. 1936) and Milan Kundera (b. 1929).

DENMARK
Kongeriget Danmark

AREA – 16,639 sq. miles (43,094 sq. km). Neighbour: Germany (south)
POPULATION – 5,284,000 (1997 UN estimate). The majority of the population is Lutheran. The language is Danish
CAPITAL – ΨCopenhagen (population, 1,362,264, 1996 UN estimate)
MAJOR CITIES – ΨÅlborg (159,980); ΨÅrhus (279,759); ΨOdense (183,564), 1996 UN estimates
CURRENCY – Danish krone of 100 øre
NATIONAL ANTHEMS – Kong Kristian stod ved højen mast (King Christian stood by the lofty mast); Det er et yndigt land (There is a lovely land)
NATIONAL DAY – 5 June (Constitution Day)
NATIONAL FLAG – Red, with white cross
LIFE EXPECTANCY (years) – male 72.62; female 77.82
POPULATION GROWTH RATE – 0.4 per cent (1997)
POPULATION DENSITY – 123 per sq. km (1997)

Denmark is a kingdom, consisting of the islands of Zealand, Funen, Lolland, etc., the peninsula of Jutland, the outlying island of Bornholm in the Baltic, and the Farøes and Greenland.

HISTORY AND POLITICS

The Danes were at the forefront of Viking expansionism and briefly united England and Scandinavia under Knut (Canute) (995–1035).

The Union of Kalmar (1397) brought Norway and Sweden (including Finland) under Danish rule. Danish power waned during the 16th century, however, enabling Sweden to re-establish its independence in 1523. In the 19th century Norway was ceded to Sweden under the Treaty of Kiel (1814) and both Schleswig and Holstein, which had been subsumed in 1460, were surrendered to Germany.

Denmark remained neutral during the First World War, and in a plebiscite held in accordance with the Versailles Treaty (1919), northern Schleswig voted to return to Danish sovereignty. In 1939 Denmark signed a non-aggression pact with Germany but was invaded on 9 April 1940 and coerced into contributing to the German war effort. Iceland declared its independence from Denmark in 1944 and the Farøe Islands were granted home rule in 1948. Greenland, which had had the status of a colony, was integrated into Denmark in 1953 and granted home rule in 1979. Social Democrat-led coalitions dominated the post-war era until 1982 when a right-wing government was elected. Denmark joined the European Community in 1973.

On 21 September 1994, a new coalition government of the Social Democrat, Social Liberal and Centre Democrat parties was formed. On 12 March 1998, Poul Nyrop Rasmussen's centre-left coalition was re-elected, winning 90 of the 179 seats in the parliament, giving a majority of a single seat.

A referendum is to be held on 28 September 2000 on membership of the European single currency.

POLITICAL SYSTEM

The legislature consists of one chamber, the *Folketing*, of not more than 179 members, including two for the Faroes and two for Greenland, which is elected for a four-year term. The voting age is 18 with voting based on a proportional representation system with a 2 per cent threshold for parliamentary representation.

HEAD OF STATE

HM The Queen of Denmark, Queen Margrethe II, KG, *born* 16 April 1940, *succeeded* 14 January 1972, *married* 10 June 1967, Count Henri de Monpezat (Prince Henrik of Denmark), and *has issue* Crown Prince Frederik (*see* below); Prince Joachim, *born* 7 June 1969, *married* 18 November 1995, Miss Alexandra Manley (Princess Alexandra of Denmark)

Heir, HRH Crown Prince Frederik, *born* 26 May 1968

CABINET *as at September 2000*

Prime Minister, Poul Nyrup Rasmussen (SD)
Culture, Elsebeth Gerner Nielsen (RV)
Defence, Hans Hækkerup (SD)
Development Co-operation, Jan Trøjborg (SD)
Economic Affairs and Nordic Co-operation,
   Marianne Jelved (RV)
Education and Ecclesiastical Affairs, Margrethe Vestager
   (RV)
Environment and Energy, Svend Auken (SD)
Finance, Mogens Lykketoft (SD)
Food, Agriculture and Fisheries, Ritt Bjerregaard (SD)
Foreign Affairs, Niels Helveg Petersen (RV)
Health, Sonja Mikkelsen (SD)
Interior, Karen Jespersen (SD)
Justice, Frank Jensen (SD)
Labour, Ove Hygum (SD)
Research and Information Technology, Birte Weiss (SD)
Social Affairs, Henrik Dam Kristensen (SD)
Taxation, Ole Stavad (SD)
Trade and Industry, Pia Gjellerup (SD)
Transport and Communications, Jacob Buksti (SD)
Urban Affairs and Housing, Gender Equality,
   Jytte Andersen (SD)

SD Social Democrat Party; RV Social Liberal Party

ROYAL DANISH EMBASSY
55 Sloane Street, London SW1X 9SR
Tel: 020-7333 0200
Ambassador Extraordinary and Plenipotentiary,
   HE Ole Lønsmann Poulsen, apptd 1996
Counsellor (Commercial), Gunner Tetler
Defence Attaché, Capt. Uffe Haagen Olsen

BRITISH EMBASSY
36–40 Kastelsvej, DK-2100 Copenhagen Ø
Tel: (00 45) 3544 5200
E-mail: www.brit-emb@post6.tele.dk
Ambassador Extraordinary and Plenipotentiary,
   HE Philip Astley, LVO, apptd 1999
Counsellor and Deputy Head of Mission, P. B. Yaghmourian
Defence Attaché, Cmdr. A. Gordon-Lennox, RN
First Secretary (Commercial), F. J. Martin

BRITISH CONSULATES – Åbenrå, Ålborg, Århus, Esbjerg,
   Fredericia, Herning, Odense, Rønne (Bornholm),
   Tórshavn (Faroe Islands)

BRITISH COUNCIL DIRECTOR, Dr M. Sørensen-Jones,
   Gammel Mønt 12.3, DK-1117 Copenhagen K;
   e-mail: british.council@britcoun.dk

DEFENCE

The Army has 337 main battle tanks, 50 armoured infantry fighting vehicles, 486 armoured personnel carriers and 12 attack helicopters. The Navy has five submarines, three frigates and 38 patrol and coastal vessels at two bases. The Air Force has 69 combat aircraft.

MILITARY EXPENDITURE – 1.6 per cent of GDP (1998)
MILITARY PERSONNEL – 24,300: Army 15,300, Navy
   4,300, Air Force 4,700
CONSCRIPTION DURATION – Four to 12 months

ECONOMY

Of the labour force in 1996, 45 per cent was employed in the professional services and administration; 18 per cent in commerce; 19 per cent in manufacturing and 5 per cent in agriculture. The chief agricultural products are pigs, dairy products, poultry and eggs, seeds and cereals; manufactures are mostly based on imported raw materials but there are also considerable imports of finished goods. Denmark is self-sufficient in oil and natural gas.

GNP – US$175,160 million (1998); US$33,040 per capita
   (1998)
GDP – US$174,845 million (1996); US$33,387 per capita
   (1996)
ANNUAL AVERAGE GROWTH OF GDP – 2.7 per cent
   (1996); forecast to be 2.9 per cent in 1997
INFLATION RATE – 1.8 per cent (1998)
UNEMPLOYMENT – 5.5 per cent (1998)

TRADE

The principal imports are industrial raw materials, consumer goods, construction inputs, machinery, raw materials, vehicles and textile products. The chief exports are manufactured articles, and agricultural and dairy products. Germany and Sweden are Denmark's main trading partners.

In 1997 Denmark had a trade surplus of US$5,553 million and a current account surplus of US$883 million. In 1998 imports totalled US$44,994 million and exports US$47,070 million.

Trade with UK	1998	1999
Imports from UK	£1,934,100,000	£1,913,700,000
Exports to UK	2,067,300,000	2,125,300,000

COMMUNICATIONS

In 1996, the Danish mercantile fleet numbered 584 ships of more than 100 gross tonnage. There were 3,000 km of railway, 85 per cent of which belonged to the state and 15 per cent to privately-owned companies. A rail tunnel and bridge linking the islands of Sjælland and Fyn was opened in 1997.

CULTURE AND EDUCATION

The Danish language is akin to Swedish and Norwegian. Danish literature, ancient and modern, embraces all forms of expression, familiar names being Hans Christian Andersen (1805–75), Søren Kierkegaard (1813–55), Karen Blixen (1885–1962) and Peter Høeg (b. 1957). Some 38 newspapers are published in Denmark; eight daily papers are published in Copenhagen.

Education is free and compulsory. Special schools are numerous, commercial, technical and agricultural predominating. There are universities at Copenhagen (founded in 1479), Århus (1928), Odense (1966), Roskilde (1972) and Ålborg (1974).

ENROLMENT (percentage of age group) – primary
99 per cent (1995); secondary 88 per cent (1995);
tertiary 48 per cent (1995)

THE FARØE ISLANDS

AREA – 540 sq. miles (1,399 sq. km)
POPULATION – 48,000 (1997 UN estimate)
CAPITAL – Tórshavn (population, 16,218, 1992)

Since 1948 the Faroes or Sheep Islands have had a degree
of home rule. The islands are governed by a *Løgting* of
between 27 and 32 members and a *Landsstýri* of three to
six members which deals with special Faroes affairs, and
send two representatives to the *Folketing* at Copenhagen.
The Faroes are not part of the EU.

Prime Minister, Anfinn Kallsberg

Trade with UK	1998	1999
Imports from UK	£7,533,000	£7,050,000
Exports to UK	90,285,000	85,132,000

GREENLAND

AREA – 840,004 sq. miles (2,175,600 sq. km) of which
about 16 per cent is ice-free
POPULATION – 56,000 (1997)
CAPITAL – Godthåb (Nuuk) (population, 12,483, 1997
estimate)

Greenland attained a status of internal autonomy in
May 1979 and a government (*Landsstyret*) was established.
It has a *Landsting* (parliament) of 31 members and sends
two representatives to the *Folketing* at Copenhagen.
Greenland negotiated its withdrawal from the EU, without discontinuing relations with Denmark, and left on
1 February 1985.
  The USA has acquired certain rights to maintain air
bases in Greenland.

Prime Minister, Jonathan Motzfeldt

Trade with UK	1998	1999
Imports from UK	£1,909,000	£2,087,000
Exports to UK	1,707,000	1,171,000

DJIBOUTI
Jumhūriyya Jībūtī

AREA – 8,958 sq. miles (23,200 sq. km). Neighbours:
Eritrea (north), Ethiopia (west and south), Somalia
(south-east)
POPULATION – 634,000 (1997 UN estimate), 520,000
(1991 census), mostly Afar or Issas. The official
languages are Arabic and French; Afar and Somali are
also spoken
CAPITAL – ΨDjibouti (population, 62,000, 1991)
CURRENCY – Djibouti franc of 100 centimes
NATIONAL ANTHEM – Hinjinne u sara kaca (Arise with
strength)
NATIONAL DAY – 27 June (Independence Day)
NATIONAL FLAG – Blue over green with white triangle in
the hoist containing a red star
LIFE EXPECTANCY (years) – male 46.72; female 50.00
POPULATION GROWTH RATE – 2.9 per cent (1997)
POPULATION DENSITY – 27 per sq. km (1997)
MILITARY EXPENDITURE – 5.1 per cent of GDP (1998)
MILITARY PERSONNEL – 11,400: Army 8,000, Navy 200,
Air Force 200; Paramilitaries 3,000
GDP – US$536 million (1996); US$868 per capita (1996)
ANNUAL AVERAGE GROWTH OF GDP – –0.2 per cent
(1996)
TOTAL EXTERNAL DEBT – US$288 million (1998)

ILLITERACY RATE – 48.6 per cent
ENROLMENT (percentage of age group) – primary 32
per cent (1996); secondary 12 per cent (1996); tertiary
0.3 per cent (1996)

The climate is harsh and much of the country is semi-arid
desert.

HISTORY AND POLITICS

Formerly French Somaliland and then the French
Territory of the Afars and the Issas, the Republic of
Djibouti became independent on 27 June 1977. A multiparty constitution was adopted by referendum in 1992 and
subsequent multiparty elections held in December 1992
were won by the *Rassemblement Populaire pour le Progrès*
(RPP, the Popular Rally for Progress). President Aptidon
was re-elected for a fourth six-year term in 1993. However,
less than half the electorate voted in either election and the
Front for the Restoration of Unity and Democracy
(FRUD) boycotted both. In December 1997, in the first
elections since the 1994 peace accord, the RPP and the
FRUD formed an alliance and won all 65 seats in the
Chamber of Deputies. On 9 April 1999, President Ismael
Omar Guelleh was elected, gaining approximately three-
quarters of the votes cast; about 60 per cent of the
electorate were estimated to have voted. On 7 February
2000, the government signed a peace agreement with a
breakaway faction of the FRUD, which had continued its
armed opposition to the government after the 1994 peace
accord.

HEAD OF STATE
President, Ismael Omar Guelleh, *elected* 9 April 1999

COUNCIL OF MINISTERS *as at September 2000*
Prime Minister, National and Regional Development, Barkat
  Gourad Hamadou
Agriculture, Livestock and Marine Affairs, Ali Muhammad
  Daoud
*Communication and Culture, Posts and Telecommunications,
  Government Spokesman*, Rifki Abdoulkader Bamakhrama
Defence, Ougoure Kifle Ahmed
Economy, Finance and Privatisation, Yacin Elmi Bouh
Energy and Natural Resources, Muhammad Ali Muhammad
*Foreign Affairs and International Co-operation, Relations with
  Parliament*, Ali Abdi Farah
*Housing, Town Planning, Environment and Regional
  Development*, Saleiban Omar Oudine
Interior, Abdallah Abdillahi Miguil
Justice, Human Rights, Islamic Affairs and Prisons,
  Ibrahim Idriss Djibril
Labour and Vocational Training, Mohamed
  Barkat Abdillahi
Minister-Delegates, Ahmed Guirreh Waberi
  (*Decentralisation*); Hawa Ahmad Yousouf (*Women,
  Families and Social Welfare*); Cheikh Mogueh Dirir
  Samatar (*Religious Affairs and Islamic Affairs*)
National Education, Abdi Ibrahim Absieh
Presidential Affairs and Promotion of Investments, Osman
  Ahmad Moussa
Public Health, Mohamed Dini Farah
Trade, Industry and Handicrafts, Elmi Obsieh Waiss
Transport and Equipment, Osman Idriss Djama
Youth, Sport, Leisure and Tourism, Dini Abdallah Bililis

EMBASSY OF THE REPUBLIC OF DJIBOUTI
26 rue Emile Ménier, F-75116 Paris, France
Tel: (00 33) (1) 4727 4922
Ambassador Extraordinary and Plenipotentiary,
  HE Djama Omar Idleh, apptd 1998

BRITISH AMBASSADOR, HE Gordon Wetherell, resident at Addis Ababa, Ethiopia

BRITISH CONSULATE
PO Box 81, 9–11 Rue de Genève, Djibouti
Honorary Consul, P. Lambrecht

The French continue to maintain army, navy and air force bases in Djibouti, with a total strength of 2,600 personnel. Djibouti has an excellent port, an international airport, and a railway line runs to Addis Ababa. In 1995 Djibouti had a trade deficit of US$171 million and a current account deficit of US$23 million.

Trade with UK	1998	1999
Imports from UK	£17,027,000	£19,971,000
Exports to UK	235,000	386,000

DOMINICA
The Commonwealth of Dominica

AREA – 290 sq. miles (751 sq. km)
POPULATION – 71,000 (1997 UN estimate). English is the official language although Creole French is more commonly used
CAPITAL – ΨRoseau (population, 16,243, 1991)
CURRENCY – East Caribbean dollar (EC$) of 100 cents
NATIONAL ANTHEM – Isle of Beauty
NATIONAL DAY – 3 November (Independence Day)
NATIONAL FLAG – Green ground with a cross overall of yellow, black and white stripes, and in the centre a red disc charged with a Sisserou parrot in natural colours within a ring of ten green stars
POPULATION GROWTH RATE – –0.1 per cent (1997)
POPULATION DENSITY – 95 per sq. km (1997)

Dominica, in the Lesser Antilles, lies in the Windward Islands group 95 miles south of Antigua. It is about 29 miles long and 16 miles wide. The island is of volcanic origin and very mountainous, and the soil is very fertile. The temperature varies, according to the altitude, from 13° to 29°C.

HISTORY AND POLITICS

The island was discovered by Columbus in 1493, when it was a stronghold of the Caribs, who remained virtually the sole inhabitants until the French established settlements in the 18th century. It was captured by the British in 1759 but passed back and forth between France and Britain until 1805, after which British possession was not challenged. From 1871 to 1939 Dominica was part of the Leeward Islands Colony, then from 1940 the island was a unit of the Windward Islands group. Internal self-government from 1967 was followed on 3 November 1978 by independence as a republic.

The most recent general election was held on 31 January 2000 and won by the Dominica Labour Party, which captured 10 seats, with nine seats going to the United Workers' Party and two seats to the Dominica Freedom Party.

POLITICAL SYSTEM

Executive authority is vested in the president, who is elected by the House of Assembly for not more than two terms of five years. Parliament consists of the president and the House of Assembly (21 representatives elected by universal adult suffrage for a five-year term) and nine senators, five of whom are appointed on the advice of the prime minister and the other four on the advice of the Leader of the Opposition.

HEAD OF STATE
President, HE Vernon Shaw, *elected* 2 October 1998, *took office* 6 October 1998

CABINET *as at September 2000*
Prime Minister, Foreign Affairs, Labour, Carib Affairs, Banana Industry, Roosevelt Douglas
Agriculture and the Environment, Lloyd Pascal
Communications and Works, Pierre Charles
Community Development and Women's Affairs, Matthew Walter
Education, Science and Technology, Herbert Sabaroche
Finance, Ambrose George
Health and Social Security, John Toussaint
Housing, Vince Henderson
Tourism, Ports and Employment, Charles Savarin
Trade, Industry and Marketing, Osborne Rivière
Youth and Sports, Roosevelt Skerrit

HIGH COMMISSION FOR THE COMMONWEALTH OF DOMINICA
1 Collingham Gardens, London SW5 0HW
Tel: 020-7370 5194/5
High Commissioner, HE George Williams, apptd 1996

BRITISH HIGH COMMISSIONER, HE Gordon Baker, resident at Bridgetown, Barbados

BRITISH CONSULATE
PO Box 2269, Roseau
Honorary Consul, P. Fletcher

ECONOMY

Agriculture is the principal occupation, with tropical and citrus fruits the main crops. Products for export are bananas, fruit juices, lime oil, bay oil, copra and rum. Forestry, fisheries and agro-processing are being encouraged. The only commercially exploitable mineral is pumice, used chiefly for building purposes. Manufacturing consists largely of the processing of agricultural products although there have been attempts to diversify into light industry. In 1997 imports totalled US$125 million and exports US$53 million.

GNP – US$230 million (1998); US$3,150 per capita (1998)
GDP – US$230 million (1996); US$3,242 per capita (1996)
ANNUAL AVERAGE GROWTH OF GDP – 3.2 per cent (1996)
INFLATION RATE – 1.0 per cent (1999)
TOTAL EXTERNAL DEBT – US$109 million (1998)

Trade with UK	1998	1999
Imports from UK	£10,982,000	£13,294,000
Exports to UK	14,943,000	15,556,000

DOMINICAN REPUBLIC
República Dominicana

AREA – 18,816 sq. miles (48,511 sq. km). Neighbour: Haiti (west)
POPULATION – 8,097,000 (1997 UN estimate). The language is Spanish
CAPITAL – ΨSanto Domingo (population, 2,134,779, 1993)
MAJOR CITIES – Duarte (272,227); La Vega (335,140); Puerto Plata (255,061); San Cristóbal (409,381); San Juan (247,029); Santiago de los Caballeros (690,458), 1993 UN estimates

CURRENCY – Dominican Republic peso (RD$) of 100 centavos
NATIONAL FLAG – Divided into blue and red quarters by a white cross
NATIONAL ANTHEM – Quisqueyanos Valientes, Alcemos (Brave men of Quisqueya, let's raise our song)
NATIONAL DAY – 27 February (Independence Day 1844)
LIFE EXPECTANCY (years) – male 67.63; female 71.69
POPULATION GROWTH RATE – 1.7 per cent (1997)
POPULATION DENSITY – 167 per sq. km (1997)
URBAN POPULATION – 61.7 per cent (1995)
MILITARY EXPENDITURE – 1.1 per cent of GDP (1998)
MILITARY PERSONNEL – 24,500: Army 15,000, Navy 4,000, Air Force 5,500, Paramilitaries 15,000
ILLITERACY RATE – 16.2 per cent
ENROLMENT (percentage of age group) – primary 81 per cent (1994); secondary 22 per cent (1994); tertiary 23 per cent (1996)

The Dominican Republic, the eastern part of the island of Hispaniola (Haiti is the western part), is the oldest European settlement in America. The climate is tropical in the lowlands and semi-tropical to temperate in the higher altitudes.

HISTORY AND POLITICS

Santo Domingo was discovered by Columbus in 1492, and was a Spanish colony until 1797, when it passed to France. It was restored to Spanish rule in 1809. Independence was proclaimed in 1821, but in 1822 it was subjugated by the neighbouring Haitians who remained in control until 1844, when the Dominican Republic was proclaimed. The country was occupied by American marines from 1916 until 1924, and ruled by, Gen. Rafael Trujillo from 1930 until 1961.

A presidential election in May 1994 was won by the incumbent President Balaguer. Balaguer was replaced by opposition Dominican Liberation Party (PLD) candidate, Leonel Fernández, who defeated the ruling Christian Social Reform Party (PRSC) candidate, Jacinto Peynado, in a run-off election on 30 June 1996. The presidential election on 16 May 2000 was won by Hipólito Mejía.

POLITICAL SYSTEM

Executive power is vested in the president, who is directly elected for a single four-year term and appoints the Cabinet. Legislative power is exercised by the Congress, which has a term of four years concurrent with the presidency. The Congress comprises the Senate of 30 senators, one for each province and one for Santo Domingo, and the 149-member Chamber of Deputies.

HEAD OF STATE

President, Hipólito Mejía, *elected* 16 May 2000
Vice-President, Milagros Bosh

CABINET *as at September 2000*

Agriculture, Eligio Jaquez
Defence, José Miguel Soto Jiménez
Education, Milagros Ortiz
Environment, Frank Moya Pons
Finance, Fernando Álvarez Bogaert
Foreign Affairs, Hugo Tolentino Dipp
Health, José Rodríguez Soldevilla
Industry and Commerce, Angel Lockward
Interior, Rafael Suberví Bonilla
Labour, Rafael Albuquerque de Castro
Public Works, Miguel Vargas
Sports, Cesar Cedeno
Tourism, Ramón Alfredo Borgas
Without Portfolio, Angel Molan
Youth, António Peña Guaba

EMBASSY OF THE DOMINICAN REPUBLIC
139 Inverness Terrace, London, W2 6JF
Tel: 020-7727 6285
Ambassador Extraordinary and Plenipotentiary,
HE Dr Pedro Padilla Tonos, apptd 1997

BRITISH EMBASSY
Edificio Corominas Pepin, Ave 27 de Febrero No 233, Santo Domingo
Tel: (00 1 809) 472 7111/7905
Ambassador Extraordinary and Plenipotentiary,
HE David Ward, apptd 1999

BRITISH CONSULAR OFFICE – Puerto Plata

ECONOMY

Since 1990 the government has successfully reduced inflation and increased output. Large amounts of foreign debt have been paid off but unemployment remains high. State subsidies were ended in 1995 in an attempt to reduce the budget deficit.

Sugar, cocoa, coffee, bananas, rice and tobacco are the most important crops. Other products are maize, molasses, beans, tomatoes, cement, ferro-nickel, gold, silver and cattle. Light industry produces beer, tinned foodstuffs, glass products, textiles, soap, cigarettes, construction materials, plastic articles, paint, rum, matches and peanut oil. Tourism is an important part of the economy, with 2.2 million foreign visitors to the Dominican Republic in 1995.

GNP – US$14,629 million (1998); US$1,770 per capita (1998)
GDP – US$13,040 million (1996); US$1,638 per capita (1996)
ANNUAL AVERAGE GROWTH OF GDP – 7.0 per cent (1996)
INFLATION RATE – 8.3 per cent (1997)
TOTAL EXTERNAL DEBT – US$4,451 million (1998)

TRADE

The chief imports are fuel oils, foodstuffs, motor vehicles, pharmaceuticals and machinery components. The chief exports are minerals, sugar and sugar by-products, coffee and cocoa. The USA is the main trading partner.

In 1997 there was a trade deficit of US$1,995 million and a current account deficit of US$163 million. Imports totalled US$4,821 million and exports US$882 million.

Trade with UK	1998	1999
Imports from UK	£43,854,000	£36,900,000
Exports to UK	24,861,000	26,621,000

COMMUNICATIONS

There are over 4,000 miles of roads and a direct road from Santo Domingo to Port-au-Prince, the capital of Haiti, but that part of it in the border area has fallen into disuse. The frontier has been closed since 1967, except for the section crossed by the main road linking the two capitals. A telephone system connects all the principal towns. There are more than 90 commercial broadcasting stations and six television stations.

ECUADOR
República del Ecuador

AREA – 109,484 sq. miles (283,561 sq. km). Neighbours: Colombia (north), Peru (east and south)
POPULATION – 11,937,000 (1997 UN estimate), descendants of the Spanish, Amerindians, and mestizos. Spanish is the principal language but

Quechua is also a recognised language and is spoken by most Indians

CAPITAL – Quito (population, 1,444,363, 1996 estimate)

MAJOR CITIES – Cuenca (255,028); ΨGuayaquil (1,973,880), the chief port (1997 UN estimates)

CURRENCY – Sucre of 100 centavos

NATIONAL ANTHEM – Salve, oh patria, mil veces, oh patria (Hail, oh fatherland, a thousand times, oh fatherland)

NATIONAL DAY – 10 August (Independence Day)

NATIONAL FLAG – Three horizontal bands, yellow, blue and red (the yellow band twice the width of the others); emblem in centre

LIFE EXPECTANCY (years) – male 67.32; female 72.49

POPULATION GROWTH RATE – 2.2 per cent (1997)

POPULATION DENSITY – 42 per sq. km (1997)

URBAN POPULATION – 62.0 per cent (1997)

MILITARY EXPENDITURE – 2.6 per cent of GDP (1998)

MILITARY PERSONNEL – 57,370: Army 50,000, Navy 4,100, Air Force 3,000; Paramilitaries 270

CONSCRIPTION DURATION – 12 months (selective)

Ecuador is an equatorial state of South America. It extends across the Western Andes, the highest peaks being Chimborazo (20,408 ft) and Ilinza (17,405 ft) in the Western Cordillera; and Cotopaxi (19,612 ft) and Cayambe (19,160 ft) in the Eastern Cordillera. Ecuador is watered by the Upper Amazon, and by the rivers Guayas, Mira, Santiago, Chone and Esmeraldas on the Pacific coast. There are extensive forests.

HISTORY AND POLITICS

The former kingdom of Quito was conquered by the Incas of Peru in the 15th century. Early in the 16th century Pizarro's conquests led to the inclusion of the present territory of Ecuador in the Spanish viceroyalty of Quito. Independence was achieved in a revolutionary war which culminated in the battle of Mount Pichincha (1822).

After seven years of military rule, Ecuador returned to democracy in 1979. In the 1992 legislative election a loose coalition of parties enabled President Ballén to introduce a programme of economic reform, financial liberalisation and privatisation. This, together with reductions in state spending, caused social unrest in 1992–4 and led to the government's defeat in the May 1994 legislative elections. In the July 1996 elections the ruling Social Christian Party (PSC) won a majority of seats. Abdala Bucaram was elected president in July 1996, and appointed a coalition government. Bucaram was ousted by the legislature on the grounds of insanity and replaced firstly by Vice-President Arteaga and then by the Speaker of the National Congress Fabián Alarcón. The presidential elections in July 1998 were won by Jamil Mahaud, the former Mayor of Quito, who gained 51 per cent of the vote. A series of strikes and protests caused disruption throughout July 1999 and led to mass demonstrations calling for the removal of the president. Proposed tax increases led to another wave of protest in November, which again called for the removal of the president. On 18 January 2000, Quito and most provincial capitals were occupied by thousands of Indians. President Mahaud was deposed in a coup by a military junta on 21 January 2000, which was dissolved by the military just five hours after taking office and Vice-President Noboa was elevated to the presidency.

FOREIGN RELATIONS

The border with Peru was demarcated by a 1942 treaty that was partly revoked by Ecuador in 1960 in relation to a disputed 50-mile stretch. An inconclusive four-week border war was fought with Peru in February 1995 until a cease-fire was signed on 1 March 1995. A 54-mile demilitarised zone was agreed in July 1995. An agreement was signed on 26 October 1998 by the presidents of the two countries formally ending the territorial dispute after mediation by Argentina, Brazil, Chile and the USA.

POLITICAL SYSTEM

The 1979 constitution provides for an elected president and vice-president who serve for a single four-year term. There is a unicameral National Congress which meets for two months a year and has 121 members, 20 of whom are elected on a national basis every four years and 101 on a provincial basis every two years. Voting is compulsory for all literate and voluntary for all illiterate citizens over the age of 18. The republic is divided into 21 provinces.

HEAD OF STATE

President, Gustavo Noboa Bejarano, *sworn in* 22 January 2000

Vice-President, Pedro Pinto Rubianes

CABINET *as at September 2000*

Agriculture and Livestock, Mauricio Davalos Guevara

Education, Roberto Hanze Salem

Energy and Mines, Pablo Terán

Finance, Luís Yturralde

Foreign Relations, Heinz Moeller

Foreign Trade, Roberto Pena Durini

Interior, Juan Manrique Martínez

Labour, Martin Insua

National Defence, Adm. Hugo Unda

Public Health, Fernando Bustamante Riofrio

Public Works, José Machiavello Almeida

Secretary-General of the Administration, Marcelo Santos

Social Welfare, Raúl Patino Aroca

Tourism and Environment, Rocío Vázquez

Urban Development and Housing, Nelson Murgueytio Penaherrera

EMBASSY OF ECUADOR

Flat 3B, 3 Hans Crescent, London SW1X 0LS

Tel: 020-7584 1367/2648/8084

Ambassador Extraordinary and Plenipotentiary, HE Osvaldo Ramírez-Landázuri

BRITISH EMBASSY

Citiplaza Building, Naciones Unidas Ave and República de El Salvador, PO Box 17-17-830, Quito

Tel: (00 593) (2) 970 800

e-mail: britemcom@impsat.net.ec

Ambassador Extraordinary and Plenipotentiary, HE Ian Gerken, LVO, apptd 2000

BRITISH CONSULAR OFFICES – Cuenca, Galápagos and Guayaquil

BRITISH COUNCIL DIRECTOR, J. Knagg, OBE

Av. da Amazonas 1646 y La Niña, Casilla 17-07-8829, Quito; e-mail: erey@britcoun.org.ec

ECONOMY

Agriculture is the most important sector of the economy. The main products for export are fish, bananas, which provide a third of agricultural exports, cocoa and coffee. Other important crops are sugar, soya, rice, cotton, African palm, vegetables, fruit and timber. The main imports are manufactured goods and machinery.

The economy was transformed by the discovery in 1972 of major oil fields in the Oriente area.

In March 1999, the sucre fell in value by 38 per cent, causing panic withdrawing of deposits which forced the government to close all banks for seven days. A state of emergency was declared following a two-day general strike, and an austerity programme, which included limiting bank withdrawals, tax increases and privatisation of state enterprises, was introduced.

The sucre fell by 65 per cent against the US dollar in 1999, GDP fell by 7 per cent and inflation was 61 per cent. In response, President Noboa introduced proposals for economic restructuring, substituted the US dollar for the sucre and agreed terms on an IMF US$1,700 million loan for the country.

In 1997 there was a trade surplus of US$598 million and a current account deficit of US$743 million. In 1998 imports totalled US$5,503 million and exports US$4,141 million.

GNP – US$18,450 million (1998); US$1,520 per capita (1998)
GDP – US$19,040 million (1996); US$1,627 per capita (1996)
ANNUAL AVERAGE GROWTH OF GDP – 2.0 per cent (1996)
INFLATION RATE – 36.1 per cent (1998)
UNEMPLOYMENT – 11.5 per cent (1998)
TOTAL EXTERNAL DEBT – US$15,140 million (1998)

Trade with UK	1998	1999
Imports from UK	£40,275,000	£25,929,000
Exports to UK	41,221,000	29,644,000

COMMUNICATIONS

There are 23,256 km of permanent roads and 5,044 km of roads which are only open during the dry season. Ten commercial airlines operate international flights and there are internal services between all important towns. Two daily newspapers are published at Quito and four at Guayaquil.

EDUCATION

Elementary education is free and compulsory. There are ten universities (three at Quito, three at Guayaquil, and one each at Cuenca, Machala, Loja and Portoviejo), polytechnic schools at Quito and Guayaquil and eight technical colleges in other provincial capitals.
ILLITERACY RATE – 8.1 per cent
ENROLMENT (percentage of age group) – primary 97 per cent (1996); tertiary 20.0 per cent (1990)

GALÁPAGOS ISLANDS

The Galápagos (Giant Tortoise) Islands, forming the province of the Archipelago de Colón, were annexed by Ecuador in 1832. The archipelago lies in the Pacific, about 500 miles from the mainland. There are 12 large and several hundred smaller islands with a total area of about 3,000 sq. miles and an estimated population (1982) of 6,119. The capital is Puerto Baquerizo Moreno, on San Cristóbal Island. Although the archipelago lies on the equator, the temperature of the surrounding water is well below equatorial average owing to the Humboldt current. The province consists for the most part of National Park Territory, where unique marine birds, iguanas, and the giant tortoises are conserved. There is some local subsistence farming; the main industry, apart from tourism, is tuna and lobster fishing.

EGYPT
Al-Jumhūriyya al-Miṣriyya al-'Arabiyya

AREA – 386,662 sq. miles (1,001,449 sq. km). Neighbours: Sudan (south), Libya (west), Gaza Strip and Israel (east)
POPULATION – 62,011,000 (1997 UN estimate). The largest, or 'Egyptian' element, is a Hamito-Semite race. A second element is the *Bedouin*, or nomadic Arabs of the Western and Eastern deserts, who are now mainly semi-sedentary tent-dwellers. The third element is the *Nubian* of the Nile Valley of mixed Arab and Negro blood. Over 90 per cent of the population are Muslims of the Sunni denomination, and most of the rest are Coptic Christians. Arabic is the official language
CAPITAL – Cairo (Al-Qāhirah) (population, 6,800,000, 1994 estimate) stands on the Nile about 14 miles from the head of the delta
MAJOR CITIES – Ψ Alexandria (Al-Iskandariya) (3,328,196, 1997 estimate), founded 332 BC by Alexander the Great, was the capital for over 1,000 years; Asyūt (2,802,185); Faiyūm (1,989,881); Ismailia (715,009); ΨPort Said (Būr Sa'īd) (469,533); ΨSuez (As-Suways) (417,610)
CURRENCY – Egyptian pound (£E) of 100 piastres or 1,000 millièmes
NATIONAL ANTHEM – Biladi (My homeland)
NATIONAL DAY – 23 July (Anniversary of Revolution in 1952)
NATIONAL FLAG – Horizontal bands of red, white and black, with an eagle in the centre of the white band
LIFE EXPECTANCY (years) – male 65.15; female 69.00
POPULATION GROWTH RATE – 2.2 per cent (1997)
POPULATION DENSITY – 62 per sq. km (1997)
URBAN POPULATION – 44.0 per cent (1997)
ILLITERACY RATE – 44.7 per cent
ENROLMENT (percentage of age group) – primary 93 per cent (1996); secondary 67 per cent (1996); tertiary 20.3 per cent (1995)

Egypt comprises Egypt proper, the peninsula of Sinai and a number of islands in the Gulf of Suez and Red Sea, of which the principal are Jubal, Shadwan, Gafatin and Zeberged (or St John's Island).

The country is mainly flat but there are mountainous areas in the south-west, along the Red Sea coast and in the south of the Sinai peninsula; the highest peak is Mt Catherina (8,668 ft). Most of the land is desert and the Nile valley and delta were the only fertile areas until the opening of the Aswan Dam allowed areas of desert to be reclaimed. West of the Nile Valley is the Western Desert, containing some depressions whose springs irrigate oases. The Eastern Desert between the Nile and the mountains along the Red Sea coast is mostly plateaux dissected by wadis (dry water-courses).

HISTORY AND POLITICS

The unification of the kingdoms of Lower and Upper Egypt under the Pharaohs c.3100 BC marked the establishment of the Egyptian state, with Memphis as its capital. Egypt was ruled for nearly 2,800 years by a succession of 31 Pharaonic dynasties which built the pyramids at Gizeh. A period of Hellenic rule began in 332 BC, followed by a period of rule by Rome (30 BC to AD 324) and then by the Byzantine Empire. In AD 640 Egypt was subjugated by Arab Muslim invaders. In 1517 the country was incorporated in the Ottoman Empire, under which it remained until the early 19th century. A British Protectorate over Egypt lasted from 1914 to 1922, when Sultan Ahmed Fuad was proclaimed King of Egypt. In 1953 the monarchy was deposed and Egypt became a republic.

In 1956, President Nasser seized the assets of the Suez Canal Company. Egyptian occupation of the Canal Zone was used as a pretext for military action by Britain and France in support of their Suez Canal Company interests. A cease-fire and Anglo-French withdrawal were negotiated by the UN.

The Israeli invasion of 1956 overran the Sinai peninsula but six months later Israel withdrew. However, mounting tension culminated in a second invasion of Sinai (the Six Day War in June 1967) and occupation of the peninsula by Israel. Sinai was returned to Egypt in 1982 under the treaty of 1979 which resulted from the Camp David talks and formally terminated a 31-year-old state of war between the two countries.

The ruling National Democratic Party won the general election held in November and December 1995. President Mubarak was nominated by the legislature to run unopposed for a fourth six-year term in June 1999, and was endorsed by a national referendum held on 26 September. A general election is due by November 2000.

INSURGENCY

Militant Islamist fundamentalists re-emerged in 1992, carrying out attacks on tourists, Coptic Christians, government ministers, civil servants and the security forces. Attacks are concentrated in Upper Egypt and the Cairo area. The government has reacted vigorously to the armed campaign with the arrest of 20,000 militants.

On 27 March 1999, the largest fundamentalist organisation, Gamaat-i-Islamiya, announced that it had given up its violent campaign to overthrow the government.

POLITICAL SYSTEM

The constitution of 1971 provides for an executive president who appoints the Council of Ministers and determines government policy. The president is elected by the legislature every six years. The legislature is the People's Assembly which has 454 members, 444 of whom are elected, the remaining ten nominated by the president. The Shura Council or Consultative Assembly (210 members) has an advisory role. A state of emergency, which was first introduced following the assassination of President Sadat in 1981, remains in force.

HEAD OF STATE

President, Mohammed Hosni Mubarak, *elected* 1981, *re-elected* 1987, 1993, 2 June 1999, *confirmed by national referendum* 26 September 1999

COUNCIL OF MINISTERS *as at September 2000*

Prime Minister, Atef Mohammad Obeid
Deputy PM, Agriculture and Land Reclamation, Yousef Amin Wali
Communications and Information Technology, Ahmed Muhammad Nazif
Culture, Farouk Hosni Abdel Aziz
Defence and Military Production, Field Marshal Mohammad Hussein Tantawi
Economy and Foreign Trade, Yussef Boutros Ghali
Education, Hussein Kamel Bahaeddin
Electricity and Energy, Ali Fahmi Ibrahim al-Sa'idi
Finance, Mohammed Midhat Hasanayn
Foreign Affairs, Amr Mahmoud Moussa
Health and Population, Ismail Awadallah Sallam
Higher Education and Scientific Research, Mufid Shehab
Information, Muhammad Safwat El-Sherif
Interior, Maj.-Gen. Habib al-Adli
Justice, Farouk Seif El-Nasr
Labour and Emigration, Ahmed al-Amawi
Ministers of State, Mahmoud Zaki Abu Amer
  (Administrative Development); Nadia Makram Obeid
  (Environment); Gen. Sayyid Abduh Mustafa Mash'al
  (Military Production); Kamal Mohammed Al Shazli
  (People's National Assembly and Consultative Council Affairs); Mustafa Abdel Qader *(Rural Development)*
Oil and Mineral Resources, Amin Sameh Fahmi
Planning and International Co-operation, Ahmed Mahrus al-Darsh
Public Enterprise, Mukhtar Khattab
Public Works and Irrigation, Mahmoud Abdul Halim Abu Zaid
Reconstruction, New Urban Zones and Environment, Mohammed Ibrahim Soliman
Religious Affairs and Wakfs (Endowments), Mahmoud Hamdi Zakzouk
Secretary-General to the Council of Ministers,

Ahmed Hassan Abu Taleb
Social Insurance and Social Affairs, Amina Hamzah al-Jundi
Supply and Internal Trade, Hassan Ali Khedr
Technological Development and Industry, Mustafa al-Rifai
Tourism, Mamdouh Ahmed Al-Beltagui
Transport, Ibrahim al-Dumeiri
Youth, Ali al-Din Hilal al-Dasuqi

EMBASSY OF THE ARAB REPUBLIC OF EGYPT

26 South Street, London W1Y 6DD
Tel: 020-7499 2401/3304
Ambassador Extraordinary and Plenipotentiary, HE Abdel El-Gazzar, apptd 1997
Ministers Plenipotentiary, Mohamed Abdel Hamid Higazy *(Deputy Chief of Mission)*; Abdallah El Arnosy
Defence Attaché, Col. Mahmoud Hegab
Cultural Counsellor, Mohamed A. El-Sharkawy

BRITISH EMBASSY

Ahmed Ragheb Street, Garden City, Cairo
Tel: (00 20) (2) 354 0852/8
e-mail: britemb@idsc.gov.eg
Ambassador Extraordinary and Plenipotentiary, HE Graham Boyce, CMG, apptd 1999
Counsellor and Deputy Head of Mission, G. D. Adams
Defence and Military Attaché, Col. P. Dennison, OBE
First Secretaries, P. Byrde *(Consul)*; D. G. Reader *(Commercial/Aid)*

BRITISH CONSULAR OFFICES – *Consulate-General*, Alexandria; *Consulates*, Luxor, Suez

BRITISH COUNCIL DIRECTOR, D. Marler, OBE *(Cultural Counsellor)*, 192 Sharia el Nil, Agouza, Cairo; e-mail: britcoun@eg.britishcouncil.org.
Regional directors in Alexandria and Heliopolis

DEFENCE

The Army has 3,855 main battle tanks, 790 armoured infantry fighting vehicles, and 4,280 armoured personnel carriers. The Navy has one destroyer, ten frigates, four submarines, 39 patrol and coastal vessels and 24 armed helicopters at six bases. The Air Force has 583 combat aircraft and 129 armed helicopters.
MILITARY EXPENDITURE – 4.1 per cent of GDP (1998)
MILITARY PERSONNEL – 680,000: Army 320,000, Navy 20,000, Air Force 30,000, Air Defence Command 80,000 Paramilitaries 230,000
CONSCRIPTION DURATION – Three years (selective)

ECONOMY

Despite increasing industrialisation, agriculture remains the most important economic activity, employing 35 per cent of the labour force and producing 22 per cent of GDP in 1995. Egypt is still a net importer of foodstuffs, especially grain, and a food security programme has been set up with the aim of achieving self-sufficiency. The main cash crop is cotton, of which Egypt is one of the world's main producers. Other important crops are maize, rice, sugar cane, wheat and potatoes. Other fruits and vegetables are also grown.

With its considerable reserves of petroleum and natural gas, and the hydroelectric power produced by the Aswan and High Dams, Egypt is self-sufficient in energy. The major manufacturing industries are food processing, motor cars, electrical goods, steel, chemical products, yarns and textiles. In 1996 more than two million tourists visited Egypt, though in 1997 the tourism industry was badly affected following attacks on foreign tourists by Islamist militants.

In 1998 the government had a trade deficit of US$10,215 million and a current account deficit of US$2,552 million.

GNP – US$79,185 million (1998); US$1,290 per capita (1998)
GDP – US$67,385 million (1996); US$1,065 per capita (1996)
ANNUAL AVERAGE GROWTH OF GDP – 4.9 per cent (1996)
INFLATION RATE – 4.2 per cent (1998)
UNEMPLOYMENT – 11.3 per cent (1995)
TOTAL EXTERNAL DEBT – US$31,964 million (1998)

TRADE

The main imports are wheat, maize, chemicals and motor vehicles and parts. The main exports are crude petroleum, cotton, cotton yarn, oranges, rice and cotton textiles.
In 1996 Egypt's imports totalled US$13,019 million and exports US$3,535 million.

Trade with UK	1998	1999
Imports from UK	£510,246,000	£540,790,000
Exports to UK	291,114,000	266,940,000

COMMUNICATIONS

There are international airports at Cairo and Luxor. The road and rail networks link the Nile valley and delta with the main development areas east and west of the river. The Suez Canal was reopened in 1975 and a two-stage development project begun to widen and deepen the canal to allow the passage of larger shipping and to permit two-way traffic. Port Said and Suez have been reconstructed and the port of Alexandria is being improved.

EL SALVADOR
República de El Salvador

AREA – 8,124 sq. miles (21,041 sq. km). Neighbours: Guatemala (north-west), Honduras (north-east and east)
POPULATION – 5,928,000 (1997 UN estimate): 94 per cent mestizo, 5 per cent Amerindian, 1 per cent European. The language is Spanish
CAPITAL – San Salvador (population, 1,200,000, 1998)
MAJOR CITIES – San Miguel (127,696); Santa Ana (139,389)
CURRENCY – El Salvador colón (₡) of 100 centavos
NATIONAL ANTHEM – Saludemos La Patria Orgullosos (Let us proudly hail the Fatherland)
NATIONAL DAY – 15 September
NATIONAL FLAG – Three horizontal bands, sky blue, white, sky blue; coat of arms on white band
LIFE EXPECTANCY (years) – male 50.74; female 63.89
POPULATION GROWTH RATE – 2.3 per cent (1997)
POPULATION DENSITY – 282 per sq. km (1997)
URBAN POPULATION – 50.4 per cent (1992)
MILITARY EXPENDITURE – 1.7 per cent of GDP (1998)
MILITARY PERSONNEL – 36,600: Army 22,300, Navy 700, Air Force 1,600; Paramilitaries 12,000
CONSCRIPTION DURATION – 12 months (selective)

El Salvador extends along the Pacific coast of Central America for 160 miles. The surface of the country is very mountainous, many of the peaks being extinct volcanoes. Much of the interior has an average altitude of 2,000 feet. The climate varies from tropical to temperate. There is a wet season from May to October, and a dry season from November to April. Earthquakes are frequent, the most recent being in October 1986.

HISTORY AND POLITICS

El Salvador was conquered in 1526 by Pedro de Alvarado, and formed part of the Spanish viceroyalty of Guatemala until 1821. It is divided into 14 Departments.
Decades of military rule ended in October 1979; a Constituent Assembly was elected in 1982. Subsequent presidential and parliamentary elections were boycotted by the FMLN (Farabundo Martí National Liberation Front) guerrilla movement. Conflict between the guerrillas and the government continued throughout the 1980s until negotiations culminated in a peace plan signed in January 1992. In December 1992 the FMLN disarmed and became a political party.
On 7 March 1999, Francisco Flores of the ruling right-wing National Republican Alliance (ARENA) party won the presidential election; he took office on 1 June. ARENA won 29 of the Legislative Assembly's 84 seats and formed a government with other right-wing parties in legislative elections on 12 March 2000; the FMLN became the largest party, winning 31 seats.

HEAD OF STATE

President, Francisco Flores Pérez, *elected* 7 March 1999, *took office* 1 June 1999
Vice-President, Minister of the Presidency, Carlos Quintanilla Schmidt
Secretary of the Presidency, Juan José Daboub

COUNCIL OF STATE *as at September 2000*
Agriculture and Livestock, Salvador Urrutia Loucel
Defence, Gen. Juan Antonio Martínez Varela
Director of the Salvadorean Institute of Tourism, Arturo Morales
Economy, Miguel Lacayo
Education, Ana Evelyn Jacir de Lovo
Environment and Natural Resources, Ana María Majano Guerrero
Foreign Affairs, María Eugenia Brizuela de Avila
Interior, Mario Acosta Oertel
Justice and Public Security, Francisco Bertrand Galindo
Labour and Social Security, Jorge Nieto Menéndez
Public Health, José López Beltrán
Public Works, José Angel Quiroz
Treasury, José Luis Trigueros

EMBASSY OF EL SALVADOR
Tennyson House, 159 Great Portland Street, London WIN 5FD
Tel: 020-7436 8282
Ambassador Extraordinary and Plenipotentiary, HE Mauricio Castro-Aragón, apptd 1999

BRITISH EMBASSY
PO Box 1591, San Salvador
Tel: (00 503) 263 6527
Ambassador Extraordinary and Plenipotentiary, HE Patrick Morgan, apptd 1999

ECONOMY

The principal agricultural products are coffee, cotton, sugar cane, maize, shrimps and balsam. In the lower altitudes towards the east, sisal is produced and used in the manufacture of coffee and cereal bags. The Salvadorean Coffee Company and the banking system have now been privatised.
Existing factories make textiles, clothing, constructional steel, furniture, cement and household items.
GNP – US$11,207 million (1998); US$1,850 per capita (1998)
GDP – US$10,380 million (1996); US$1,791 per capita (1996)
ANNUAL AVERAGE GROWTH OF GDP – 2.5 per cent (1998)
INFLATION RATE – 2.5 per cent (1998)
UNEMPLOYMENT – 8.0 per cent (1997)
TOTAL EXTERNAL DEBT – US$3,633 million (1998)

TRADE

Chief exports are coffee, cotton, sugar, shrimps, sisal, balsam, meat, towels, hides and skins. The chief imports are chemicals, petroleum, manufactured goods, industrial and electronic machinery, pharmaceutical goods, vehicles and consumer goods.

In 1997 there was a trade deficit of US$1,107 million and a current account surplus of US$96 million. In 1998 imports totalled US$3,112 million and exports US$1,263 million.

Trade with UK	1998	1999
Imports from UK	£18,647,000	£12,727,000
Exports to UK	85,400,000	12,044,000

COMMUNICATIONS

The principal ports are Cutuco, La Unión and Acajutla. There are more than 12,000 km of roads and 600 km of railways. The Pan-American Highway from the Guatemalan frontier passes through San Salvador and Santa Ana, and continues to the Honduran frontier. Comalapa international airport has daily flights to other Central American capitals, Mexico and the USA. There are 100 broadcasting stations and nine television stations. Five daily newspapers are published in San Salvador.

EDUCATION

Primary education is free and compulsory. There are 38 universities.

ILLITERACY RATE – 21.3 per cent
ENROLMENT (percentage of age group) – primary 78 per cent (1995); secondary 22 per cent (1995); tertiary 18 per cent (1996)

EQUATORIAL GUINEA
República de Guinea Ecuatorial

AREA – 10,831 sq. miles (28,051 sq. km). Neighbours: Cameroon (north), Gabon (east and south)
POPULATION – 420,000 (1997 UN estimate). The official languages are Spanish and French; Bubi, Fang, Ibo and pidgin English are also spoken
CAPITAL – ΨMalabo on the island of Bioko (population, 30,418, 1983 estimate)
MAJOR TOWN – ΨBata is the principal town and port of Rio Muni
CURRENCY – Franc CFA of 100 centimes
NATIONAL ANTHEM – Himno Nacional
NATIONAL DAY – 12 October
NATIONAL FLAG – Three horizontal bands, green over white over red; blue triangle next staff; coat of arms in centre of white band
LIFE EXPECTANCY (years) – male 44.86; female 47.78
POPULATION GROWTH RATE – 2.7 per cent (1997)
POPULATION DENSITY – 15 per sq. km (1997)
URBAN POPULATION – 37.0 per cent (1991)
MILITARY EXPENDITURE – 1.5 per cent of GDP (1998)
MILITARY PERSONNEL – 1,320: Army 1,100, Navy 120, Air Force 100
ILLITERACY RATE – 16.8 per cent

Equatorial Guinea consists of the island of Bioko, in the Bight of Biafra about 20 miles from the west coast of Africa, Annonbón Island in the Gulf of Guinea, the Corisco Islands (Corisco, Elobey Grande and Elobey Chico), and Rio Muni, a mainland area between Cameroon and Gabon.

HISTORY AND POLITICS

Formerly colonies of Spain, the territories now forming Equatorial Guinea were constituted as two provinces of Metropolitan Spain in 1959, became autonomous in 1963 and fully independent in 1968.

In 1979 President Macias was deposed by a revolu-
tionary military council headed by Col. Obiang Nguema. Constitutional amendments in 1982 provided for legislative elections, which were held in 1983 and 1988, but all candidates were chosen by the president.

A multiparty political system under a new constitution was approved by a referendum in 1991 and ten opposition parties have been legalised, operating alongside the ruling Equatorial Guinea Democratic Party (PDGE). A National Pact was agreed and signed in March 1993 but legislative elections in November, which were won by the PDGE, were boycotted by most of the electorate and opposition parties. In the February 1996 election, the president claimed to have won more than 99 per cent of the vote. Most opposition parties boycotted the ballot. In June 1997 the Progress Party, the largest opposition party, was banned by the government, and in February 1998 opposition party coalitions were deemed illegal. The PDGE won 75 of the 80 seats in the National Assembly elections on 7 March 1999 amid allegations of electoral malpractice.

HEAD OF STATE
President of the Supreme Military Council and Minister of Defence, Brig.-Gen. Teodoro Obiang Nguema Mbasogo, *took office* August 1979, *re-elected* June 1989, 25 February 1996

MINISTERS *as at September 2000*
Prime Minister, Angel Serafín Dougan
First Deputy PM, Minister of State for Agriculture, Livestock and Rural Development, Miguel Oyono Ndong Mifumu
Second Deputy PM, Minister of State for Interior and Local Corporations, Demetrio Elo Ndong Nze Fumu
Minister of State, Forestry, Fisheries and Environment, Teodoro Nguema Obiang
Minister of State, Information, Tourism and Culture, Lucas Nguema Esono
Minister of State, Labour and Social Security, Ricardo Mangue Obama Nfube
Minister of State, Presidency, Alejandro Evuna Owono Asangono
Minister of State, Relations with Assemblies and Legal Affairs, Government Spokesman, Antonio Fernando Nve Ngu
Minister of State, Secretary-General of the Government, Marcelino Nguema Onguene
Minister of State, Transport and Communications, Marcelino Oyono Ntutumu
Civil Service and Administrative Reform, Fernando Mabale Mba Nnomo
Economic Affairs and Finance, Miguel Abia Biteo
Education, Science and Francophone Affairs, Santiago Ngua Nfumu
Health and Social Welfare, Juan Antonio Nchuchumu
Industry, Commerce, Small and Medium-sized Enterprises, Constantino Ekong Nsue
Justice and Religious Affairs, Rubén Mye Nsue
Mines and Energy, Cristóbal Menana Ela
Ministers-Delegate: Carlos Eyi Obama *(Agriculture, Livestock and Rural Development)*; Clemente Engonga Nguema Andeme *(Interior and Local Corporations)*; Melanio Ebendeng Somo *(National Defence)*
Planning and Economic Development, Fortunato Ofa Mbo
Public Works, Housing and Urban Affairs, Florentino Nkongo Ndong
Social Affairs, Women's Affairs, Teresa Efua Asangono
Youth and Sports, Vidal Choni Bekoba

EMBASSY OF THE REPUBLIC OF EQUATORIAL GUINEA
6 rue Alfred de Vigny, F-75008 Paris
Tel: (00 33) (1) 4766 4433
Ambassador Extraordinary and Plenipotentiary, HE Lino-Sima Ekua Avomo, apptd 1997

BRITISH AMBASSADOR, HE Peter Boon, resident at Yaoundé, Cameroon

ECONOMY

The chief products are cocoa, coffee and wood. Production has declined and except for cocoa there is little commercial agriculture. The economy is heavily dependent on outside aid, principally from Spain. Oil and gas production is increasing. Equatorial Guinea entered the 'franc zone' in 1985.

In 1996, there was a trade deficit of US$117 million and a current account deficit of US$344 million. Imports totalled US$292 million and exports US$175 million.
GNP – US$478 million (1998); US$1,110 per capita (1998)
GDP – US$246 million (1995); US$601 per capita (1996)
ANNUAL AVERAGE GROWTH OF GDP – 5.0 per cent (1996)
INFLATION RATE – 4.0 per cent (1993)
TOTAL EXTERNAL DEBT – US$306 million (1998)

Trade with UK	1998	1999
Imports from UK	£9,134,000	£6,386,000
Exports to UK	7,969,000	781,000

ERITREA

AREA – 45,406 sq. miles (117,600 sq. km). Neighbours: Sudan (north and north-west), Ethiopia (south and south-west), Djibouti (south-east)
POPULATION – 3,409,000 (1997 UN estimate), roughly half Coptic Christian (mainly highlanders) and half Muslim (mainly lowlanders). Arabic and Tigrinya are official languages, but English and Italian are widely spoken. There are nine indigenous language groups: Afar; Bilen; Hadareb; Kunama; Nara; Rashida; Saho; Tigre; Tigrinya
CAPITAL – Asmara (population, 358,100, 1990 estimate)
MAJOR TOWNS – ΨAssab; ΨMassawa
CURRENCY – Nakfa
NATIONAL DAY – 24 May (Independence Day)
NATIONAL FLAG – Divided into three triangles; the one based on the hoist is red and bears a gold olive wreath; the upper triangle is green and the lower one light blue
LIFE EXPECTANCY (years) – male 48.03; female 51.16
POPULATION GROWTH RATE – 2.4 per cent (1997)
POPULATION DENSITY – 29 per sq. km (1997)
ENROLMENT (percentage of age group) – primary 30 per cent (1996); secondary 16 per cent (1996); tertiary 1 per cent (1997)

HISTORY AND POLITICS

Eritrea was colonised by Italy in the late 19th century and was the base for the 1936 Italian invasion of Abyssinia (Ethiopia). After the Italian defeat in East Africa in 1941 by British and Commonwealth forces, Eritrea became a British protectorate. This lasted until 15 September 1952 when Eritrea was federated with Ethiopia. The Ethiopian Emperor Haile Selassie incorporated Eritrea as a province of Ethiopia in 1962. An armed campaign for independence began in the 1970s, first against Emperor Haile Selassie's forces and from 1974 against the Mengistu regime.

In 1991 the Mengistu government was overthrown by the Eritrean People's Liberation Front (EPLF) and the Ethiopian People's Revolutionary Democratic Front (EPRDF). The new EPRDF-led government in Ethiopia agreed to an Eritrean referendum on independence which was held in April 1993 and recorded a 99 per cent vote in favour. Independence was declared on 24 May 1993.

FOREIGN RELATIONS

Eritrea had claimed the Hanish and Mohabaka Islands in the Red Sea, which they seized from Yemen in December 1995; however, on 9 October 1998, the International Court of Justice ruled that the Hanish Islands belonged to Yemen and Eritrea formally handed them over to Yemen on 1 November 1998. The land border with Djibouti is also disputed.

In May 1998 sporadic fighting flared up on the border with Ethiopia, with both countries accusing the other of sending troops across the border. Proposals for a resolution of the conflict drawn up by a special mediation committee meeting of the Organisation for African Unity (OAU) held on 7–8 November 1998, which called on Eritrea to hand back the disputed town of Badme pending adjudication, were rejected by Eritrea. Full-scale fighting broke out on 6 February 1999 and Ethiopia had recaptured the town by 28 February. Eritrea accepted the OAU's proposals on 9 March, but fighting continues. A further proposal to end the fighting was brokered by the OAU in July 1999, which envisaged a return to the original borders and was provisionally accepted by both sides, but Ethiopia later rejected some of the provisions. Fighting resumed on 23 February 2000. A further OAU-sponsored summit in April 2000 failed to produce an agreement. On 12 May, Ethiopia launched a full-scale invasion, which ended in early June after Ethiopian forces had captured much of Eritrea's western lowlands. An interim peace plan was signed by both countries on 18 June, which envisages the international demarcation of the border and, in the interim period, a UN force to monitor the border in a 25 km-wide buffer zone in Eritrean territory.

POLITICAL SYSTEM

Under the 1997 constitution, the head of state is the president, elected for a five-year term by the National Assembly, of which he is chair. The 150-member unicameral legislature (the *Hagerawi Baito*) is directly elected for four years. The president is head of government and presides over a State Council.

HEAD OF STATE

President, Chairman of the National Assembly, Issaias Afewerki, *elected by National Assembly* 22 May 1993

STATE COUNCIL *as at September 2000*
Chairman, The President
Agriculture, Arefaine Berhe
Defence, Efrem Sebhat
Education, Osman Saleh
Energy and Mines, Tesfai Gebreselassie
Eritrean Relief, Refugee Commission, Worku Tesfamichael
Finance and Development, Ghebreselassie Yoseph
Fisheries, Petros Solomon
Foreign Affairs, Haile Woldetensae
Health, Saleh Meki
Industry and Trade, Ali Said Abdella
Information, Beraki Gebreselassie
Justice, Foazia Hashim
Labour and Human Welfare, Mekerios Askalu
Land, Water and Environment, Tesfaye Ghirmazion
Local Government, Mahmoud Ahmed Sherifo
Public Works, Abraha Asfaha
Tourism, Ahmed Haj Ali
Transport, Saleh Idris Kekia

EMBASSY OF THE STATE OF ERITREA
96 White Lion Street, London N1 9PF
Tel: 020-7713 0096
Ambassador Extraordinary and Plenipotentiary, HE
Ghirmai Ghebremariam, apptd 2000

BRITISH AMBASSADOR, HE Gordon Wetherell, resident
at Addis Ababa, Ethiopia

BRITISH EMBASSY
Emperor Yohannes Avenue, House no 24,
PO Box 5584, Asmara
Tel: (00 291) (1) 120145
Honorary Consul, T. Thodensen

BRITISH COUNCIL DIRECTOR, Dr Negusse Araya, PO Box
997, Asmara; e-mail: britcoun@eol.com.er

DEFENCE

The Navy has ten patrol and coastal combatants. The Air
Force has 19 combat aircraft.
MILITARY EXPENDITURE – 35.8 per cent of GDP (1998)
MILITARY PERSONNEL – 182,100: Army 180,000, Navy
1,100, Air Force 1,000
CONSCRIPTION DURATION – 18 months

ECONOMY

Since 1991 the government has attempted to rebuild
industry, agriculture and infrastructure which were
devastated by the war of independence. The rebuilding
programme has focused on the ports of Massawa and
Assab, the roads from the ports to Ethiopia, and the
railway from Massawa to Sudan via Asmara. Before 1962
Eritrea was one of the most industrialised areas of Africa
and some industry remains, producing textiles and footwear. The government hopes to base the rebuilding of the
economy on the return of well-educated exiles, international aid and investment, the development of tourism
along the coast, and the diversification of the economy
away from agriculture.
GNP – US$781 million (1998); US$200 per capita
(1998)
GDP – US$572 million (1996); US$174 per capita
(1996)
ANNUAL AVERAGE GROWTH OF GDP – 3.9 per cent
(1996)
TOTAL EXTERNAL DEBT – US$149 million (1998)

Trade with UK	1998	1999
Imports from UK	£9,179,000	£5,737,000
Exports to UK	189,000	314,000

ESTONIA
The Republic of Estonia

AREA – 17,413 sq. miles (45,100 sq. km). Neighbours:
Russia (east), Latvia (south)
POPULATION – 1,453,844 (1998): 65 per cent Estonian,
28 per cent Russian, 2.5 per cent Ukrainian, 1.5 per cent
Belarusian, 1 per cent Finnish, others 2 per cent. The
majority religion is Lutheran, with Russian Orthodox
and Baptist minorities. Estonian is the first language
of 64.2 per cent and Russian of 28.7 per cent
CAPITAL – Tallinn (population, 415,299, 1998 estimate)
MAJOR TOWNS AND CITIES – Kohtla-Järve (70,800);
Narva (80,300); Tartu (109,100)
CURRENCY – Kroon of 100 sents
NATIONAL ANTHEM – Mu Isamaa, mu onn ja rõõm
(My Native Land, My Joy, Delight)
NATIONAL DAY – 24 February (Independence Day)
NATIONAL FLAG – Three horizontal stripes of blue,
black, white
LIFE EXPECTANCY (years) – male 64.47; female 75.48
POPULATION GROWTH RATE – –1.1 per cent (1997)
POPULATION DENSITY – 32 per sq. km (1997)
URBAN POPULATION – 69.6 per cent (1996)
MILITARY EXPENDITURE – 1.3 per cent of GDP (1998)
MILITARY PERSONNEL – 7,600: Army 4,320, Navy 340, Air
Force 140; Paramilitiaries 2,800
CONSCRIPTION DURATION – 12 months

Estonia includes 1,500 islands in the Baltic Sea and the
Gulf of Riga. Forests cover roughly 20 per cent of the
country, which also has many lakes. The climate is mild
and maritime.

HISTORY AND POLITICS

Estonia, a former province of the Russian Empire,
declared its independence on 24 February 1918. A war of
independence was fought against the German army until
November 1918, and then against Soviet forces until the

peace treaty of Tartu was signed in 1920. By this treaty the Soviet Union recognised Estonia's independence.

The Soviet Union annexed Estonia in 1940 under the terms of the Molotov-Ribbentrop pact with Germany. Estonia was occupied when Germany invaded the Soviet Union during the Second World War. In 1944 the Soviet Union recaptured the country from Germany and confirmed its annexation.

The Estonian Supreme Soviet in November 1989 declared the republic to be sovereign and its 1940 annexation by the Soviet Union to be illegal. In February 1990 the leading role of the Communist Party was abolished, and following multiparty elections in March 1990 a period of transition to independence was inaugurated. Independence was declared on 20 August 1991.

Presidential and legislative elections were held in September 1992 on the basis of special provisions different from the 1992 constitution. The president was directly elected for a four-year term and the Riigikogu for a three-year term. A radical right-wing coalition government was elected which held power until September 1994. At the legislative election of March 1995 a centre-right government of the Coalition Party and Rural People's Union (KMÜ) and the Centre Party was formed; the government collapsed in October 1995. A new coalition government formed by the KMÜ and the Reform Party (R) lasted until the withdrawal of the Reform Party in November 1996, after which the KMÜ formed a minority government. After legislative elections held on 7 March 1999, a centre-right coalition government of the Pro Patria Union (I), the Mõõdukad Party (M) and the Reform Party was formed.

POLITICAL SYSTEM

Legislative power is exercised by the unicameral *Riigikogu* of 101 members elected by proportional representation every four years. The president is elected for a five-year term by the Riigikogu by a two-thirds majority or, if no candidate receives this majority after three rounds of voting, by an electoral body composed of Riigikogu members and local government officials. Executive authority is vested in a prime minister who is nominated by the president and who forms a government. Members of the government need not be members of the Riigikogu.

Estonia is divided into 46 towns and 15 districts for local administration purposes.

HEAD OF STATE

President, Lennart Meri, *elected* 5 October 1992, *re-elected* 20 September 1996

GOVERNMENT *as at September 2000*

Prime Minister, Mart Laar (I)
Agriculture, Ivari Padar (M)
Culture, Signe Kivi (R)
Defence, Jüri Luik (I)
Economics, Mihkel Pärnoja (M)
Education, Tõnis Lukas (I)
Environment, Heiki Kranich (R)
Ethnic Affairs, Katrin Saks (M)
Finance, Siim Kallas (R)
Foreign Affairs, Toomas Hendrik Ilves (M)
Interior, Tarmo Loodus (I)
Justice, Märt Rask (R)
Regional Affairs, Toivo Asmer (R)
Social Affairs, Eiki Nestor (M)
Transport and Communications, Toivo Jürgenson (I)

EMBASSY OF THE REPUBLIC OF ESTONIA

16 Hyde Park Gate, London SW7 5DG
Tel: 020-7589 3428
Ambassador Extraordinary and Plenipotentiary, HE Raul Mälk, apptd 1996

BRITISH EMBASSY

Wismari 6, EE-10136 Tallinn
Tel: (00 372) 667 4700
Ambassador Extraordinary and Plenipotentiary, HE Timothy Craddock, apptd 1997

BRITISH COUNCIL DIRECTOR, I. Stewart, Resource Centre, Vana Posti 7, EE-0001 Tallinn;
e-mail: british.council@bctallinn.ee

ECONOMY

Since 1992 the government has introduced free-market reforms, privatisation and restructuring. Estonia is still dependent on Russian natural gas supplies.

Ten per cent of the workforce are engaged in agriculture, which accounts for 7 per cent of GDP, the main products being rye, oats, barley, flax, potatoes, meat, milk, butter and eggs.

Industry accounts for 34 per cent of employment and 28 per cent of GDP, concentrating on textiles, clothing and footwear, forestry, wood and paper products, and food and fish processing. Some heavy industry exists, mostly chemicals and the manufacture of power equipment.

The kroon is pegged to the euro.
GNP – US$4,878 million (1998); US$3,360 per capita (1998)
GDP – US$4,376 million (1996); US$2,975 per capita (1996)
ANNUAL AVERAGE GROWTH OF GDP – 4.0 per cent (1996)
INFLATION RATE – 10.7 per cent (1998)
UNEMPLOYMENT – 9.6 per cent (1998)
TOTAL EXTERNAL DEBT – US$782 million (1998). The IMF approved a stand-by credit of US$22 million in December 1997

TRADE

Although Estonia signed a free trade deal with Russia in 1992, it has greatly reduced its trade with the former Soviet states. Its main trading partners are Finland, Sweden, Russia and Germany. The main imports are machinery and equipment, transport vehicles, foodstuffs and metals. Exports consist mainly of machinery and equipment, foodstuffs, textiles and clothing, and timber and wood products. Free trade and association agreements with the EU came into effect in 1995; Estonia has a partnership agreement with the EU with a view to becoming a full member at a future date.

In 1998 there was a trade deficit of US$1,115 million and a current account deficit of US$478 million. Imports totalled US$4,611 million and exports US$3,123 million.

Trade with UK	1998	1999
Imports from UK	£66,650,000	£53,126,000
Exports to UK	158,471,000	188,464,000

COMMUNICATIONS

Freedom of the press is guaranteed in the constitution, and the state monopoly on television and radio ended soon after independence. All newspapers have been privatised and broadcasting channels are in the process of being privatised. Russian-language news and programmes are provided on Estonian Television. There are five Estonian- and three Russian-language daily newspapers.

EDUCATION

Estonia has a three-tier education system, consisting of primary level (four years), secondary level (six years) and university level (four to six years). Primary- and secondary-level education is compulsory.
ILLITERACY RATE – 0.2 per cent
ENROLMENT (percentage of age group) – primary 87

per cent (1995); secondary 83 per cent (1995); tertiary 41.8 per cent (1996)

ETHIOPIA
Federal Democratic Republic of Ethiopia

AREA – 426,373 sq. miles (1,104,300 sq. km). Neighbours: Sudan (west), Kenya (south), Djibouti and Somalia (east), Eritrea (north)
POPULATION – 60,148,000 (1997 UN estimate). About one-third are of Semitic origin (Amharas and Tigreans) and the remainder mainly Oromos (40 per cent), Somalis (6 per cent) and Afar (4 per cent). Amharas, Tigreans and many Oromos are Ethiopian Orthodox Christians. The Afar people in the north and the Somalis in the south-east, as well as some Oromos, are Muslim. Amharic is the most widely used of the 70 languages
CAPITAL – Addis Ababa (population, 2,084,588, 1994 estimate)
MAJOR CITIES – Dire Dawa (population, 194,587, 1994 estimate)
CURRENCY – Ethiopian birr (EB) of 100 cents
NATIONAL ANTHEM – Ityopya, Ityopya Kidemi
NATIONAL DAY – 28 May
NATIONAL FLAG – Three horizontal bands: green, yellow, red; in the centre a blue disc, containing a yellow pentagram
LIFE EXPECTANCY (years) – male 45.93; female 49.06
POPULATION GROWTH RATE – 3.1 per cent (1997)
POPULATION DENSITY – 54 per sq. km (1997)
URBAN POPULATION – 15.7 per cent (1996)

HISTORY AND POLITICS

The Hamitic culture was heavily influenced by Semitic immigration from Arabia at about the time of Christ. Christianity was introduced in the fourth century. The empire attained its zenith in the sixth century under the Axum rulers but was checked by Islamic expansion from the east. Modern Ethiopia dates from 1855 when Theodore established supremacy over the various tribes. The last emperor was Haile Selassie who reigned from 1930 until 1974, when he was deposed by the armed forces. After ten years of military rule, a Workers' Party on the Soviet model was formed with Lt.-Col. Mengistu Haile Mariam as General Secretary. The People's Democratic Republic of Ethiopia was established under a new constitution in 1987 with Lt.-Col. Mengistu as president. Armed insurgencies by the Eritrean People's Liberation Front (EPLF) and the Ethiopian People's Revolutionary Democratic Front (EPRDF), originating in Tigre, brought down Mengistu's government in May 1991.

A transitional administration comprising the EPRDF and other opposition groups formed a Council of Representatives which governed until 1995 under President Meles Zenawi. In 1994, the Council agreed on a draft federal constitution, which was adopted by an elected Constituent Assembly on 8 December 1994. Multiparty elections in May and June 1995 were won by the EPRDF, which gained 80 per cent of the seats in the newly-created Council of People's Representatives, which has 548 seats; a 108-member Federal Council to represent the nine states which comprise the federation was also created. The Council of People's Representatives elected Dr Negaso Gidada to the non-executive office of president and Meles Zenawi as prime minister. The Federal Democratic Republic of Ethiopia was proclaimed on 22 August 1995.

Famine broke out in southern and eastern areas of the country in early 2000 as a result of prolonged drought.

FOREIGN RELATIONS

Eritrea, which since 1962 had been a province of Ethiopia, seceded and became independent on 24 May 1993. Relations between the two countries had been good until fighting broke out along the border in June 1998, with each side accusing the other of sending troops across the border. Ethiopia launched an attack on Eritrea in May 2000, capturing much of the west of the country. An interim peace plan was signed in June, but Ethiopian troops remained in the captured areas pending the formation and arrival of a UN monitoring force (see Eritrea).

POLITICAL SYSTEM

The constitution provides for a federal government responsible for foreign affairs, defence and economic policy, and for nine regional administrations (Tigre, Afar, Amara, Oromia, Somai, Benshangui, Gambela, Harer and Southern), with a degree of autonomy and the right to secede.

HEAD OF STATE
President, Dr Negaso Gidada, *elected by the Council of People's Representatives* 22 August 1995

COUNCIL OF MINISTERS *as at September 2000*
Prime Minister, Meles Zenawi
Deputy Prime Minister, Economic Affairs, Kassu Illala
Deputy Prime Minister, National Defence, Adisu Legese
Agriculture, Desta Hamito
Commerce and Industry, Kasahun Ayele
Education, Genet Zewdie
Finance, Sufyan Ahmad
Foreign Affairs, Seyoum Mesfin
Health, Adem Ibrahim
Information and Culture, Wolde Mikael Chamo
Justice, Worede-Wold Wolde
Labour and Social Affairs, Hassan Abdella
Mines and Energy, Ezaddin Ali
Transport and Communications, Mohammed Dirir
Water Resources, Shiferaw Jarso
Works and Urban Development, Haile Aseged

EMBASSY OF ETHIOPIA
17 Prince's Gate, London SW7 1PZ
Tel: 020-7589 7212/3/4/5
Ambassador Extraordinary and Plenipotentiary, HE Dr Beyene Negewo, apptd 1999
Counsellor, Osman Imam Bashir (*Commercial*)

BRITISH EMBASSY
Fikre Mariam Abatechan Street (PO Box 858), Addis Ababa
Tel: (00 251) (1) 612354
e-mail: b.emb4@telecom.net.et
Ambassador Extraordinary and Plenipotentiary, HE Gordon Wetherell, apptd 1997
Deputy Head of Mission and First Secretary, F. Guy

BRITISH COUNCIL DIRECTOR, R. Arnott, PO Box 1043, Artistic Building, Adwa Avenue, Addis Ababa; e-mail: bc.addisababa@bc-addis.bcouncil.org

DEFENCE

The Army has 500 main battle tanks and 200 armoured infantry fighting vehicles and armoured personnel carriers. The Air Force has 71 combat aircraft and 24 armed helicopters.
MILITARY EXPENDITURE – 6.0 per cent of GDP (1998)
MILITARY PERSONNEL – 352,500: Army 350,000, Air Force 2,500

ECONOMY

The post-Mengistu government implemented a programme of free-market economic reform which reduced government spending and inflation.

Agriculture accounts for approximately 50 per cent of GDP and employs around 80 per cent of the workforce. The major food crops are teff, maize, barley, sorghum, wheat, pulses and oil seeds. Famine conditions in 1984–5 recurred to a lesser extent in 1992, 1997 and 2000. However, agricultural liberalisation has led to dramatic progress in food production.

Manufacturing industry accounts for less than 9 per cent of GDP and is heavily dependent on agriculture. Ethiopia's known, but as yet largely unexploited, natural resources include gold, platinum, copper and potash. Traces of oil and natural gas have been found.

In 1997 there was a trade deficit of US$417 million and a current account deficit of US$8 million.

GNP – US$6,169 million (1998); US$100 per capita (1998)
GDP – US$5,871 million (1996); US$101 per capita (1996)
Annual Average Growth of GDP – 6.5 per cent (1996)
Inflation Rate – –3.7 per cent (1997)
Total External Debt – US$10,352 million (1998)

Trade

The chief imports by value are machinery and transport equipment, manufactured goods and chemicals; the principal exports by value are coffee, oil seeds, hides and skins, and pulses. In 1996 imports totalled US$1,119 million and in 1998 exports totalled US$560 million.

Trade with UK	1998	1999
Imports from UK	£44,178,000	£33,091,000
Exports to UK	14,202,000	9,989,000

COMMUNICATIONS

A network of roads in rural areas links the major cities with each other, with the Sudanese and Kenyan borders and through Eritrea to the Red Sea coast.

There is a railway link from Addis Ababa to Djibouti. Ethiopian Airlines maintains regular services from Addis Ababa to many provincial towns, throughout Africa and to Europe.

EDUCATION

Elementary and secondary education are provided by government schools in the main centres of population; there are also mission schools. The National University (founded 1961) co-ordinates the institutions of higher education. There is a separate university at Alemaya (agricultural).

Illiteracy Rate – 61.3 per cent
Enrolment (percentage of age group) – primary 32 per cent (1996); tertiary 0.8 per cent (1996)

FIJI
Matanitu ko Viti – Republic of Fiji

Area – 7,056 sq. miles (18,274 sq. km)
Population – 809,000 (1997 UN estimate), 715,373 (1986 census): 48.6 per cent Indians, 46.2 per cent Fijians, and 5.2 per cent other races. Since the 1987 coup many ethnic Indians have left and by 1994 Melanesian Fijians formed the largest population group. The main languages are Fijian and Hindi
Capital – ΨSuva (population, 141,273, 1986), on the island of Viti Levu

Currency – Fiji dollar (F$) of 100 cents
National Anthem – God Bless Fiji
National Day – 10 October (Fiji Day)
National Flag – Light blue ground with Union flag in top left quarter and the shield of Fiji in the fly
Life Expectancy (years) – male 60.72; female 63.87
Population Growth Rate – 1.4 per cent (1997)
Population Density – 44 per sq. km (1997)
Urban Population – 38.7 per cent (1987)
Military Expenditure – 1.6 per cent of GDP (1998)
Military Personnel – 3,500: Army 3,200, Navy 300
Illiteracy Rate – 7.1 per cent
Enrolment (percentage of age group) – primary 99 per cent (1992); tertiary 11.9 per cent (1991)

Fiji is composed of roughly 332 islands (about 100 permanently inhabited) and over 500 islets in the South Pacific, about 1,100 miles north of New Zealand. The group extends 300 miles from east to west and 300 miles north to south. The International Date Line has been diverted to the east of the island group. The largest islands are Viti Levu and Vanua Levu. The main groups of islands are Lomaiviti, Lau and Yasawas. The climate is tropical without extremes of heat.

HISTORY AND POLITICS

Fiji was a British colony from 1874 until 10 October 1970 when it became an independent state and a member of the Commonwealth.

The constitution was changed in 1990 to give greater power to indigenous Melanesian Fijians at the expense of the Indian community. The Fijian Political Party led by Lt.-Col. Sitiveni Rabuka won the general elections in May 1992 and February 1994 and formed a coalition government. In the general election on 8–15 May 1999, the Fijian Political Party was swept from power by a coalition of parties led by the Fiji Labour Party. Its leader, Mahendra Chaudhry, became Fiji's first ethnic Indian prime minister.

On 19 May 2000 a group of indigenous Fijian rebels, led by George Speight, stormed parliament and took Prime Minister Mahendra Chaudhry and most of the Cabinet hostage. The army declared martial law on 29 May following the resignation of President Ratu Sir Kamisese Mara. An interim administration was set up on 28 June, following unsuccessful negotiations between the military government and the rebels. The military named an all-indigenous government to replace the multiracial coalition of the deposed premier. The interim government was to rule for two years and prepare for fresh elections. Following the release of the last hostages on 13 July, the Great Council of Chiefs announced the appointment of Ratu Josefa Iloilo as president.

Fiji's membership of the Commonwealth was suspended following the coup.

Interim Head of State

President, Ratu Josefa Iloilo *appointed* 13 July 2000
Vice-President, Ratu Jope Naucabalavu Seniloii

Interim Cabinet *as at September 2000*

Prime Minister, National Reconciliation, Laisenia Qarase
Deputy Prime Minister, Fijian Affairs, Ratu Epeli Nailatikau
Agriculture, Fisheries, Forests and ALTA, Apisai Tora
Assistant Minister for Fijian Affairs, Ratu Suliano Matanitobua
Attorney-General, Alipate Qetaki
Education, Nelson Delailomaloma
Finance, National Planning and Public Enterprise, Ratu Jone Kubuabola
Foreign Affairs, External Trade and Sugar, Kaliopate Tavola
Health, Pita Nacuva
Home Affairs and Immigration, Ratu Talemo Ratakele
Information and Communications, Ratu Inoke Kubuabola

Labour and Industrial Relations, Ratu Tevita Moemoedono
Lands and Mineral Resources, Mitieli Bulanauca
Local Government, Housing and Urban Development,
  John Teaiwa
Public Enterprises and Public Sector Reform, Hector Hatch
Regional Development and Multi-ethnic Affairs, Ratu Inoke
  Takiveikata
Tourism, Transport, Civil Aviation and Communication, Jone
  Koroitamana
Trade, Commerce, Business Development and Investment,
  Tomasi Vuetilovoni
Women, Culture and Social Welfare, Ro Teimomu Kepa
Works and Energy, Joketani Cokanasiga
Youth, Sports and Employment Opportunities, Keni
  Dakuidreketi

HIGH COMMISSION OF THE REPUBLIC OF FIJI

34 Hyde Park Gate, London SW7 5DN
Tel: 020-7584 3661
Ambassador Extraordinary and Plenipotentiary, HE
  Filimone Jitoko, apptd 1996

BRITISH HIGH COMMISSION

Victoria House, 47 Gladstone Road, PO Box 1355, Suva
Tel: (00 679) 311033
e-mail: ukconsular@bhc.org.fj
Ambassador Extraordinary and Plenipotentiary, HE
  Michael Dibben, apptd 1997

ECONOMY

Agriculture accounts for 18 per cent of GDP and employs
44 per cent of the workforce. The economy is primarily
agrarian. The principal cash crop is sugar cane, which is
the main export, followed by coconuts, ginger and copra.
A variety of other fruit, vegetables and root crops are also
grown, and self-sufficiency in rice is a major aim. Forestry,
fishing and beef production are being encouraged in order
to diversify the economy. The processing of agricultural,
marine and timber products are the main industries, along
with gold mining and textiles. Tourism is second only to
sugar as a money-earner.
GNP – US$1,748 million (1998); US$2,210 per capita
  (1998)
GDP – US$2,104 million (1996); US$2,639 per capita
  (1996)
ANNUAL AVERAGE GROWTH OF GDP – 3.1 per cent (1996)
INFLATION RATE – 5.7 per cent (1998)
UNEMPLOYMENT – 5.4 per cent (1995)
TOTAL EXTERNAL DEBT – US$193 million (1998)

TRADE

The chief imports are foodstuffs, machinery, mineral
fuels, chemicals, beverages, tobacco and manufactured
articles. Chief exports are sugar, coconut oil, fish, lumber,
molasses and ginger.
  In 1996 there was a trade deficit of US$182 million
and a current account surplus of US$10 million. In 1997
imports totalled US$957 million and exports US$576
million.

Trade with UK	1998	1999
Imports from UK	£6,777,000	£7,312,000
Exports to UK	65,203,000	66,244,000

COMMUNICATIONS

Fiji is one of the main aerial crossroads in the Pacific,
providing services to New Zealand, Australia, Tonga,
Samoa, Vanuatu, the Solomon Islands, Kiribati, Tuvalu,
New Caledonia and American Samoa. Fiji has three ports
of entry, at Suva, Lautoka and Levuka. There are 5,100 km
of roads.

FINLAND
Suomen Tasavalta

AREA – 130,559 sq. miles (338,145 sq. km). Neighbours:
  Norway (north-west and north), Russia (east),
  Sweden (west)
POPULATION – 5,140,000 (1997 UN estimate). Finnish
  and Swedish are both official languages, 93.6 per cent
  speaking Finnish as their first language and 6.2 per cent
  Swedish. Lapp is spoken by the 2,500 Lapps who live
  in the far north. The population is predominantly
  Lutheran
CAPITAL – ΨHelsinki (Helsingfors) (population,
  1,056,495, 1996 estimate)
MAJOR CITIES – Espoo (Esbo) (200,834); ΨOulu
  (Uleåborg) (113,567); Tampere (Tammerfors)
  (188,726); ΨTurku (Åbo) (168,772); Vantaa (Vanda)
  (171,297), 1997 estimates
CURRENCY – Euro (€) of 100 cents/Markka (Mk) of
  100 penniä
NATIONAL ANTHEM – Maame/Vårt land (Our land)
NATIONAL DAY – 6 December (Independence Day)
NATIONAL FLAG – White with blue cross
LIFE EXPECTANCY (years) – male 73.02; female 80.52
POPULATION GROWTH RATE – 0.4 per cent (1997)
POPULATION DENSITY – 15 per sq. km (1997)
URBAN POPULATION – 64.8 per cent (1996)

The Åland archipelago (Ahvenanmaa), a group of small
islands at the entrance to the Gulf of Bothnia, covers about
572 square miles, with a population (1994) of 25,158
(95.2 per cent Swedish-speaking). The islands have semi-
autonomous status.

HISTORY AND POLITICS

Finland was part of the Swedish Empire from the Middle
Ages until it was ceded to Russia in 1809 and became an
autonomous grand duchy of the Russian Empire. Finland
became independent after the Russian revolution of 1917,
but was forced to cede around one-tenth of its land to the
Soviet Union and to resettle 10 per cent of its population

under the Treaty of Paris (1947). A Soviet-Finnish Co-operation Treaty forced Finland to demilitarise its Soviet border, to enter into a barter trade agreement and to adopt a stance of neutrality. These terms lasted until the demise of the Soviet Union in 1991.

Finland joined the European Union on 1 January 1995 following a referendum in October 1994.

The present government took office in April 1999. The five parties in the ruling coalition are the Social Democratic Party, the National Coalition Party (conservative), the Left-wing Alliance, the Swedish People's Party, and the Greens, with a total of 139 out of 200 seats.

POLITICAL SYSTEM

Under the constitution there is a unicameral legislature, the *Eduskunta*, composed of 200 members elected by universal suffrage for a four-year term. The highest executive power is held by the president who is directly elected for a period of six years. The first direct elections for the presidency were held in 1994, the president having previously been elected by an electoral college.

HEAD OF STATE

President, Tarja Kaarina Halonen, *elected* 6 February 2000, *inaugurated* 1 March 2000

CABINET as at September 2000

Prime Minister, Paavo Lipponen (SDP)
Deputy PM, Finance, Sauli Niinistö (NCP)
Agriculture and Forestry, Kalevi Hemilä (Ind.)
Cultural Affairs, Suvi Lindén (NCP)
Defence, Jan-Erik Enestam (SPP)
Education, Maija Rask (SDP)
Environment, Satu Hassi (Greens)
Finance, Suvi-Anne Siimes (LA)
Foreign Affairs, Erkki Tuomioja (SDP)
Foreign Trade, Kimmo Sasi (NCP)
Health and Social Services, Osmo Soininvaara (Greens)
Interior, Kari Häkämies (NCP)
Justice, Johannes Koskinen (SDP)
Labour, Tarja Filatov (SDP)
Minister at the Ministry of Finance, Suvi-Anne Siimes (LA)
Regional and Municipal Affairs, Martti Korhonen (LA)
Social Affairs and Health, Maija Perho (NCP)
Trade and Industry, Sinikka Mönkäre (SDP)
Transport and Communications, Olli-Pekka Heinonen (NCP)

SDP Social Democratic Party; NCP National Coalition Party; LA Left-wing Alliance; SPP Swedish People's Party; Ind. Independent

EMBASSY OF FINLAND

38 Chesham Place, London SW1X 8HW
Tel: 020-7838 6200
Ambassador Extraordinary and Plenipotentiary, HE Pertti Salolainen, apptd 1996
Minister, Kirsti Eskelinen
Counsellor (Commercial), Marcus Moberg
Defence Attaché, Cmdr Ilpo Eerik Bergholm

BRITISH EMBASSY

Itäinen Puistotie 17, FIN-00140 Helsinki
Tel: (00 358) (9) 2286 5100
Ambassador Extraordinary and Plenipotentiary, HE Gavin Hewitt, CMG, apptd 1997
Deputy Head of Mission and Counsellor, R. A. Cambridge
First Secretary (Commercial), M. Towsey
Defence Attaché, Lt.-Col. G. A. B. Grant

BRITISH CONSULAR OFFICES – Helsinki, Jyväskylä, Kotka, Kuopio, Oulu, Pori, Tampere, Turku, Vaasa, Mariehamn

BRITISH COUNCIL DIRECTOR, T. Talvitie, Hakaniemenkatu 2, FIN-00530 Helsinki; e-mail: office@britcoun.fi

DEFENCE

The Army has 230 main battle tanks, 273 armoured infantry fighting vehicles, and 790 armoured personnel carriers. The Navy has 15 patrol and coastal vessels. The Air Force has 85 combat aircraft.

MILITARY EXPENDITURE – 1.5 per cent of GDP (1998)
MILITARY PERSONNEL – 35,100: Army 24,000, Navy 5,000, Air Force 2,700, Paramilitaries 3,400
CONSCRIPTION DURATION – Six to 12 months

ECONOMY

Finland produces a wide range of capital and consumer goods. The glass, ceramics and furniture industries enjoy international reputations. Other important industries are mobile phones, rubber, plastics, chemicals and pharmaceuticals, footwear, foodstuffs and shipbuilding.

The markka joined the ERM in August 1996, and on 1 May 1998 it was announced that Finland had satisfied the convergence criteria and would be one of the 11 countries to participate in the European Single Currency from January 1999.

In 1997 the budget deficit was equivalent to 4.5 per cent of GDP, and public debt was 67.7 per cent of GDP.

GNP – US$125,091 million (1998); US$24,280 per capita (1998)
GDP – US$125,126 million (1996); US$24,410 per capita (1996)
ANNUAL AVERAGE GROWTH OF GDP – 6.7 per cent (1997)
INFLATION RATE – 1.4 per cent (1998)
UNEMPLOYMENT – 11.3 per cent (1998)

TRADE

The principal imports are raw materials, machinery and manufactured goods. The main exports are electronic and electrical goods, paper and wood pulp, machinery, and metal products. Trade with EU countries accounts for more than half of Finland's total trade.

In 1998 there was a trade surplus of US$12,304 million and a current account surplus of US$7,324 million. Imports totalled US$31,364 million and exports US$42,104 million.

Trade with UK	1998	1999
Imports from UK	£1,363,000,000	£1,267,100,000
Exports to UK	2,250,600,000	2,246,100,000

COMMUNICATIONS

There are 5,859 km of railroad, railway connections with Russia, and passenger boat connections with Sweden, Germany, Poland, Russia and the Baltic states. There are also passenger/cargo services between Britain and Helsinki, Kotka and other Finnish ports. External air services are maintained by most European airlines.

CULTURE AND EDUCATION

Newspapers, books, plays and films appear in both Finnish and Swedish. There is a vigorous modern literature. F. E. Sillanpää, who died in 1964, was awarded the Nobel Prize for Literature in 1939. Jean Sibelius (1865–1957) is the most famous composer. In 1999 there were 56 daily newspapers.

Primary education (co-educational comprehensive school) is free and compulsory for children from seven to 16 years.

ENROLMENT (percentage of age group) – primary 98 per cent (1996); secondary 93 per cent (1996); tertiary 74 per cent (1996)

FRANCE
La République Française

AREA – 212,935 sq. miles (551,500 sq. km). Neighbours: Belgium and Luxembourg (north-east), Germany, Switzerland and Italy (east), Spain and Andorra (south-west)
POPULATION – 58,607,000 (1997 UN estimate); 57,218,000 (Metropolitan France), and 58,745,000 including overseas departments (1992 official estimate): 72 per cent Catholic, 8 per cent Muslim, 2 per cent Jewish. The language is French; there are several regional languages including Basque, Breton, Catalan, Corsican, Dutch, German and Provençal.
CAPITAL – Paris (population, 9,319,367, 1990), on the Seine
MAJOR CITIES – ΨBordeaux (696,819); Grenoble (404,837); Lille (959,433); Lyon (1,262,342); ΨMarseille (1,230,871); Nantes (495,229); Nice (517,291); Strasbourg (388,466); Toulon (437,825); Toulouse (650,311). The chief towns of Corsica are ΨAjaccio (58,315) and ΨBastia (52,446)
CURRENCY – Euro (€) of 100 cents/Franc of 100 centimes
NATIONAL ANTHEM – La Marseillaise
NATIONAL DAY – 14 July (Bastille Day 1789)
NATIONAL FLAG – The tricolour, three vertical bands, blue, white, red (blue next to flagstaff)
LIFE EXPECTANCY (years) – male 73.92; female 81.86
POPULATION GROWTH RATE – 0.5 per cent (1997)
POPULATION DENSITY – 106 per sq. km (1997)
URBAN POPULATION – 73.8 per cent (1993)

HISTORY AND POLITICS

Gaul, the area which is now France, was conquered by Julius Caesar in the 1st century BC and remained a part of the Roman Empire until the Frankish invasions in the 5th and 6th centuries. The Treaty of Verdun (AD 843) divided the Frankish Empire into three parts, of which the western part, *Francia Occidentalis*, became the basis for modern France.

France established itself as the dominant country in Europe in the 17th century. As a result of the French Revolution, a republic was declared in 1792 and the king, Louis XVI, was executed. The republic was overthrown by Napoléon Bonaparte, who established the first French Empire, which ended in 1815. The ensuing Congress of Vienna restored the monarchy, but in 1848 the Second Republic was declared, which lasted only until 1852, when the Second Empire was proclaimed under Napoléon III. He was forced to abdicate after the defeat of France in the Franco-Prussian war (1870–1871) and the Third Republic was established.

In 1940, Germany invaded France, occupying most of the country and establishing a pro-German government in the south. France was liberated in 1944, a provisional government was established under Gen. Charles de Gaulle, and the Fourth Republic was declared in 1946. In 1958, the threat of a military coup following a rebellion in Algeria resulted in the assembly inviting Gen. de Gaulle to return as premier; a new constitution which strengthened the powers of the president was adopted, the Fifth Republic was proclaimed, and Gen. de Gaulle was elected president. France granted its colonies independence between 1954 and 1962.

The state of the parties in the Senate at August 2000 was: Rassemblement pour la République (RPR) 99; Socialist Party (PS) 77; Centrist Union (UDC) 52; Republican and Independent Union (RI) 46; Democratic and European Rally (RDE) 23; Communists (PCF) 17; Independents 7.

In the last elections to the National Assembly in May and June 1997 the PS won 241 seats, the Gaullist RPR 134,

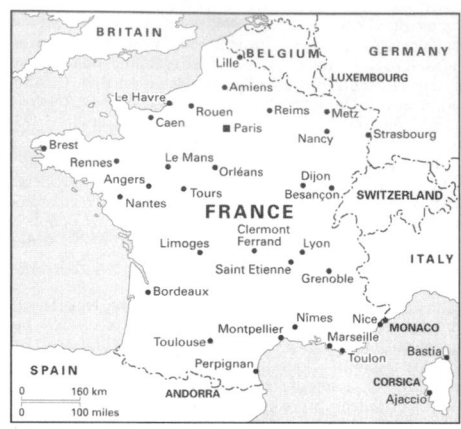

Union pour la Démocratie Française (UDF) 108, PCF 38, Independent Left 21, Independent Right 14, Radical Socialist Party 12, Green Party 7, National Front 1, Independent 1.

POLITICAL SYSTEM

The legislature consists of the National Assembly of 577 deputies (555 for Metropolitan France and 22 for the overseas departments and territories) and the Senate of 321 Senators (296 for Metropolitan France, 13 for the overseas departments and territories and 12 for French citizens abroad). Deputies in the National Assembly are directly elected for a five-year term. One-third of the Senate is indirectly elected every three years.

The prime minister is appointed by the president, as is the Council of Ministers on the prime minister's recommendation. They are responsible to the legislature, but as the executive is constitutionally separate from the legislature, ministers may not sit in the legislature and must hand over their seats to a substitute.

France is divided into 22 metropolitan regions and 96 metropolitan and four overseas departments, which are also regions. There are also four overseas territories and two territorial collectivities.

HEAD OF STATE

President of the French Republic, Jacques Chirac, *elected* 7 May 1995, *took office* 17 May 1995

COUNCIL OF MINISTERS *as at September 2000*
Prime Minister, Lionel Jospin
Agriculture and Fisheries, Jean Glavany
Capital Works, Transport and Housing, Jean-Claude Gayssot
Civil Service, Administrative Reform and Decentralisation, Michel Sapin
Culture and Communications, Government Spokesperson, Cathérine Tasca
Defence, Alain Richard
Economy, Finance and Industry, Laurent Fabius
Employment and Solidarity, Martine Aubry
Foreign Affairs, Hubert Vedrine
Interior, Daniel Vaillant
Justice, Keeper of the Seals, Elisabeth Guigou
National Education, Research and Technology, Jack Lang
Relations with Parliament, Jean-Jack Queyranne
Research, Roger-Gérard Schwartzenberg
Town and Country Planning and the Environment, Dominique Voynet
Youth and Sport, Marie-George Buffet

FRENCH EMBASSY

58 Knightsbridge, London SW1X 7JT
Tel: 020-7201 1000
Ambassador Extraordinary and Plenipotentiary, HE Daniel
Bernard, CMG, CBE, apptd 1998
Minister-Counsellor, S. Gompertz
Defence Attaché, Contre-Amiral P. Sabatie-Garat
Cultural Counsellor, X. North
Minister-Counsellor (Economic and Commercial Affairs),
P. O'Quin

BRITISH EMBASSY

35 rue du Faubourg St Honoré, F-75383 Paris Cédex 08
Tel: (00 33) (1) 4451 3100
Ambassador Extraordinary and Plenipotentiary, HE
Sir Michael Jay, KCMG, apptd 1996
Minister, S. F. Howarth
Defence and Air Attaché, Air Cdre D. N. Adams
Counsellor, V. Caton (*Finance and Economic*)
First Secretary and Consul-General, K. C. Moss

BRITISH CONSULAR OFFICES – Amiens, Biarritz,
Bordeaux, Boulogne, Calais, Cherbourg, Dunkirk,
Le Havre, Lille, Lorient, Lyon, Marseille, Montpellier,
Nantes, Nice, Paris, Perpignan, St Malo-Dinard,
Saumur, Toulouse; overseas in Cayenne (French
Guiana), Nouméa (New Caledonia), Papeete
(French Polynesia), Fort de France (Martinique),
Pointe à Pitre (Guadeloupe) and St Denis (Réunion)

BRITISH COUNCIL DIRECTOR, J. Tod, OBE, 9/11 rue de
Constantine, F-75340 Paris Cédex 07;
e-mail: information@bc-paris.bcouncil.org.
Regional office in Bordeaux

FRANCO-BRITISH CHAMBER OF COMMERCE, 8 rue
Cimarosa, F-75116 Paris. *President*, R. Lyon.
Vice-President, B. Cordery, OBE

DEFENCE

The Army has 1,207 main battle tanks, 3,820 armoured
personnel carriers, 713 armoured infantry fighting vehicles and 518 helicopters.
The Navy has 12 submarines, one aircraft carrier, one
cruiser, four destroyers, 35 frigates and 40 patrol and
coastal vessels, 61 combat aircraft and 25 armed helicopters. The Navy has four domestic and five overseas bases.
The Air Force has 531 combat aircraft including 45
short-range nuclear attack aircraft and 15 strategic
bombers, and 18 intermediate-range ballistic missiles.
France deploys 30,297 armed forces personnel abroad;
3,300 in Germany; 11,550 in French Overseas Depart-
ments and Territories; 5,970 in former French colonies in
Africa; and 9,477 on UN and peacekeeping duties.
MILITARY EXPENDITURE – 2.8 per cent of GDP (1998)
MILITARY PERSONNEL – 420,300: Army 178,300, Strategic
Nuclear Forces 8,700, Navy 62,600, Air Force 76,400,
Paramilitaries 94,300
CONSCRIPTION DURATION – Ten months. Conscription
is to be phased out over six years, beginning in 1997

ECONOMY

Viniculture is extensive, regions famous for their wines
including Bordeaux, Burgundy and Champagne. Production of wine in 1995 was 5,300,000 tonnes. Cognac,
liqueurs and cider are also produced. Other important
agricultural products include sugar beet, dairy products,
cereals and oilseeds.
Oil is produced from fields in the Landes area, but
France is a net importer of crude oil, for processing by its
important oil-refining industry. Natural gas is produced in
the foothills of the Pyrenees.
Heavy industries include oil-refining and the production of iron and steel, and aluminium. In 1997 production

of pig iron was 13,315,344 tonnes and steel 19,767,457
tonnes. Other important industries produce chemicals,
tyres, aluminium, textiles, paper products and processed
food. Engineering products include motor vehicles, and
television and radio sets.
The Banque de France was made independent in
1994 with the formation of a nine-member monetary
policy council to define and implement monetary policy
independent of the government.
In 1995–6, the government introduced austerity measures to enable France to meet the Maastricht criteria
for European monetary union. Cost-cutting reforms targeted the welfare budget, provoking a series of strikes by
public-sector workers in December 1995 and early 1996.
On 1 May 1998 it was announced that France would
participate in the European Single Currency from January
1999.
GNP – US$1,465,399 million (1998); US$24,210
per capita (1998)
GDP – US$1,538,481 million (1996); US$26,374
per capita (1996)
ANNUAL AVERAGE GROWTH OF GDP – 2.3 per cent (1997)
INFLATION RATE – 0.7 per cent (1998)
UNEMPLOYMENT – 11.8 per cent (1998)

TRADE

The principal imports are raw materials for the heavy
and manufacturing industries (e.g. oil, minerals, chemicals), machinery and precision instruments, agricultural
products, chemicals and vehicles. Agricultural products,
chemicals, pharmaceuticals and vehicles are also the
principal exports. Most of France's trade is done with
other EU countries. There are around 45 million hectares
of farmland.
In 1998 there was a trade surplus of US$26,174 million
and a current account surplus of US$40,161 million.
Imports totalled US$287,687 million and exports
US$305,384 million.

Trade with UK	1998	1999
Imports from UK	£15,559,300,000	£15,834,700
Exports to UK	16,829,400,000	17,235,800,000

COMMUNICATIONS

The length of roads in 1998 was 965,916 km, of which
9,011 km were motorways.
The railroad system is extensive. The length of lines
open for traffic in 1998 was 31,852 km.
The French mercantile marine consisted in 1998 of 210
ships of a total of 4,100,000 tonnes which transported
91,500,000 tonnes of freight.

CULTURE AND EDUCATION

French is the official language. The work of the French
Academy, founded in 1635, has established *le bon usage*,
equivalent to 'The Queen's English' in Britain. French
authors have been awarded the Nobel Prize for Literature
on 12 occasions and include R. F. A. Sully-Prudhomme
(1901), Anatole France (1921), André Gide (1947),
François Mauriac (1952), Albert Camus (1957), Jean-Paul
Sartre (1964) and Claude Simon (1985).
Education is compulsory, free and secular from six to
16. Schools may be single-sex or co-educational. Primary
education is given in nursery schools, primary schools
and *collèges d'enseignement général* (four-year secondary
modern course); secondary education in *collèges d'enseignement technique*, *collèges d'enseignement secondaire* and *lycées*
(seven-year course leading to one of the five *baccalauréats*).
Special schools are numerous.
There are many *grandes écoles* in France which award
diplomas in many subjects not taught at university,
especially applied science and engineering. Most of these
are state institutions but have a competitive system of

entry, unlike universities. There are universities in 24 towns including 13 in Paris and the immediate area.

In 1993 the government gave German official parity with French in Alsace schools.

ENROLMENT (percentage of age group) – primary 100 per cent (1996); secondary 95 per cent (1996); tertiary 51 per cent (1996)

OVERSEAS DEPARTMENTS

Greater powers of self-government were granted to French Guiana, Guadeloupe, Martinique and Réunion in 1982. These former colonies had enjoyed departmental status since 1946. Their directly elected Assemblies operate in parallel with the existing, indirectly constituted Regional Councils. The French government is represented by a Prefect in each.

FRENCH GUIANA

AREA – 34,749 sq. miles (90,000 sq. km)
POPULATION - 157,213 (1999)
CAPITAL – ΨCayenne (50,594)

Situated on the north-eastern coast of South America, French Guiana is flanked by Suriname on the west and by Brazil on the south and east. Under the administration of French Guiana is a group of islands (St Joseph, Île Royal and Île du Diable), known as Îles du Salut.

Prefect, P. Dartout

GUADELOUPE

AREA – 658 sq. miles (1,704 sq. km)
POPULATION – 422,496 (1999)
CAPITAL – ΨBasse-Terre (12,410) on Guadeloupe

A number of islands in the Leeward Islands group of the West Indies, consisting of the two main islands of Guadeloupe (or Basse-Terre) and Grande-Terre, with the adjacent islands of Marie-Galante, La Désirade and Îles des Saintes, and the islands of St-Barthélemy and the part of St-Martin under French administration, which lie over 150 miles to the north-west. The main towns are ΨLes Abymes (63,054); ΨSt-Martin (29,078); ΨPointe à Pitre (20,948) in Grande-Terre and ΨGrand Bourg (6,611) in Marie-Galante.

Prefect, M. Diefenbacher

MARTINIQUE

AREA – 425 sq. miles (1,102 sq. km)
POPULATION – 381,427 (1999)
CAPITAL – ΨFort-de-France (94,049)

An island situated in the Windward Islands group of the West Indies, between Dominica in the north and St Lucia in the south. The main towns are ΨLe Lamentin (35,460) and ΨSchoelcher (20,845).

Prefect, J.-F. Cordet

RÉUNION

AREA – 969 sq. miles (2,507 sq. km)
POPULATION – 706,300 (1999)
CAPITAL – St-Denis (131,557)

Réunion, which became a French possession in 1638, lies in the Indian Ocean, about 569 miles east of Madagascar and 110 miles south-west of Mauritius. Other towns are Saint-Paul (87,712) and Saint-Pierre (68,915). The smaller, uninhabited islands of Bassas da India, Europa, Îles Glorieuses, Juan de Nova and Tromelin are administered from Réunion.

Prefect, H. Fournier

TERRITORIAL COLLECTIVITIES

MAYOTTE

AREA – 144 sq. miles (372 sq. km)
POPULATION – 94,410 (1991 census)
CAPITAL – Mamoudzou (12,000)

Part of the Comoros Islands group, Mayotte remained a French dependency when the other three islands became independent as the Comoros Republic in 1975. Since 1976 the island has been a *collectivité territoriale*, an intermediate status between Overseas Department and Overseas Territory.

Prefect, P. Boisadam

Trade with UK	1998	1999
Imports from UK	£3,427,000	£5,549,000
Exports to UK	201,000	476,000

ST PIERRE AND MIQUELON

AREA – 93 sq. miles (242 sq. km)
POPULATION – 6,316 (1999)
CAPITAL – ΨSt-Pierre (5,580)

These two small groups of islands off the coast of Newfoundland became a *collectivité territoriale* in 1985.

Prefect, R. Thuau

Trade with UK	1998	1999
Imports from UK	£547,000	£311,000
Exports to UK	—	6,000

OVERSEAS TERRITORIES

FRENCH POLYNESIA

AREA – 1,544 sq. miles (4,000 sq. km)
POPULATION - 227,000 (1997 UN estimate)
CAPITAL – ΨPapeete (36,784), in Tahiti

Five archipelagos in the south Pacific, comprising the Society Islands (Windward Islands group includes Tahiti, Moorea, Makatea, Mehetia, Tetiaroa, Tubuai Manu; Leeward Islands group includes Huahine, Raiatea, Tahaa, Bora-Bora, Maupiti), the Tuamotu Islands (Rangiroa, Hao, Turéia, etc.), the Gambier Islands (Mangareva, etc.), the Tubuai Islands (Rimatara, Rurutu, Tubuai, Raivavae, Rapa, etc.) and the Marquesas Islands (Nuku-Hiva, Hiva-Oa, Fatu-Hiva, Tahuata, Ua Huka, etc.).

High Commissioner, P. Roncière

Trade with UK	1998	1999
Imports from UK	£4,796,000	£3,816,000
Exports to UK	69,000	96,000

NEW CALEDONIA

AREA – 7,172 sq. miles (18,575 sq. km)
POPULATION – 193,000 (1997 UN estimate)
CAPITAL – ΨNouméa (97,581)

New Caledonia is a large island in the western Pacific, 700 miles east of Queensland. Dependencies are the Isles of Pines, the Loyalty Islands (Mahé, Lifou, Urea, etc.), the Bélep Archipelago, the Chesterfield Islands, the Huon Islands and Walpole.

New Caledonia was discovered in 1774 and annexed by France in 1854; from 1871 to 1896 it was a convict settlement. In 1995, the territory was divided into three provinces, each with a provincial assembly which combined to form the Territorial Assembly. In elections in July 1995, Kanaks won majorities in North province and the Loyalty Islands, whereas pro-French settlers won a majority in the South province.

A referendum in 1987 on the question of independence was boycotted by the indigenous Kanaks, and New Caledonia therefore voted to remain French. In April 1998 an agreement was reached between the pro-independence Kanak Socialist National Liberation Front, the anti-independence Rally for Caledonia in the Republic and the French government to hold a referendum on independence in 15–20 years' time, and for greater autonomy for the indigenous people in the intervening period. A referendum on the agreement, the Nouméa Accord, was held on 8 November 1998. It was supported by 71.9 per cent of voters; more than 74 per cent of registered voters took part.

High Commissioner, D. Bur

Trade with UK	1998	1999
Imports from UK	£9,564,000	£9,924,000
Exports to UK	1,855,000	94,000

SOUTHERN AND ANTARCTIC TERRITORIES

Created in 1955 from former Réunion dependencies, the territory comprises the islands of Amsterdam (25 sq. miles) and St Paul (2.7 sq. miles), the Kerguelen Islands (2,700 sq. miles) and Crozet Islands (116 sq. miles) archipelagos and Adélie Land (116,800 sq. miles) in the Antarctic continent. The only population are members of staff of the scientific stations.

WALLIS AND FUTUNA ISLANDS

AREA – 77 sq. miles (200 sq. km)
POPULATION – 15,000 (1997 UN estimate)
CAPITAL – Mata-Utu on Uvea, the main island of the Wallis group

Two groups of islands (the Wallis Archipelago and the Îles de Hoorn) in the central Pacific, north-east of Fiji.

Prefect, L. Legrand

Trade with UK	1998	1999
Imports from UK	£43,000	£120,000
Exports to UK	—	—

THE FRENCH COMMUNITY

The constitution of the Fifth French Republic, promulgated in 1958, envisaged the establishment of a French Community of States. A number of the former French states in Africa have seceded from the Community but for all practical purposes continue to enjoy the same close links with France as those that remain formally members. Most former French African colonies are closely linked to France by financial, technical and economic agreements.

GABON
République Gabonaise

AREA – 103,347 sq. miles (267,668 sq. km). Neighbours: Equatorial Guinea and Cameroon (north), Republic of Congo-Brazzaville (east and south)
POPULATION – 1,138,000 (1997 UN estimate). The official language is French; Fang is widely spoken
CAPITAL – ΨLibreville (population, 251,000)
CURRENCY – Franc CFA of 100 centimes
NATIONAL ANTHEM – La Concorde
NATIONAL DAY – 17 August
NATIONAL FLAG – Horizontal bands, green, yellow and blue
LIFE EXPECTANCY (years) – male 51.86; female 55.18
POPULATION GROWTH RATE – 2.8 per cent (1997)
POPULATION DENSITY – 4 per sq. km (1997)

URBAN POPULATION – 73.1 per cent (1993)
MILITARY EXPENDITURE – 2.2 per cent of GDP (1998)
MILITARY PERSONNEL – 9,500: Army 3,200, Navy 500, Air Force 1,000; Paramilitaries 4,800
ILLITERACY RATE – 29.2 per cent

HISTORY AND POLITICS

The first Europeans to visit the region were the Portuguese in the 15th century, and Dutch, French and English traders arrived over the following decades. In 1849 a slave ship was captured by the French, and the freed slaves formed a settlement which they called Libreville, the current capital. The territory was annexed to French Congo in 1888.

Gabon elected on 28 November 1958 to remain an autonomous republic within the French Community and gained full independence on 17 August 1960.

Multiparty elections held in autumn 1990 were won by the ruling Parti Démocratique Gabonais (PDG), amid allegations of fraud. The PDG formed a coalition government, although the other parties left the government in 1991 in protest at PDG domination. In September 1994, the government and opposition parties signed the Paris Agreement, which provided for a new coalition government and parliamentary elections. The elections, held in December 1996, returned the PDG to power. President Bongo of the PDG, who first took office in 1967, was re-elected for a fifth term of office in December 1998.

POLITICAL SYSTEM

The constitution provides for an executive president, directly elected for a seven-year term, who appoints the Council of Ministers. There is a 120-member National Assembly, directly elected for a five-year term, and a 91-member Senate, elected by municipal and regional councillors for a six-year term.

HEAD OF STATE

President, El Hadj Omar Bongo, *assumed office* December 1967, *re-elected* 1973, 1979, 1986, 1993 and 6 December 1998
Vice-President, Didjob Divungi-di-Ndinge

COUNCIL OF MINISTERS *as at September 2000*

Prime Minister, Jean-François Ntoutoume-Emane
Deputy Prime Minister, National Unity, Social Affairs, Emmanuel Ondo Metgoho
Minister of State, Communications, Posts and Information Technology, Jean-Rémy Pendy-Bouyiki
Minister of State, Equipment and Construction, Zacharie Myboto
Minister of State, Foreign Affairs, Co-operation and Francophone Affairs, Jean Ping
Minister of State, Housing, Urban Affairs, Land Survey, Welfare and Cities, Jacques Adiahénot
Minister of State, Interior, Public Security, Decentralisation, Antoine Mboumbou-Miyakou
Minister of State, Labour, Employment, Professional Training, Paulette Moussavou Missambo
Minister of State, Planning, Development, Regional Development, Casimir Oyé Mba
Agriculture, Livestock and Rural Development, Fabien Owono-Essono
Civil Service, Administrative Reform and Modernisation of the State, Patrice Nziengui
Commerce, Tourism, Handicrafts and Industrial Development, Alfred Mabicka
Culture, Art, Mass Education, Youth, Sport and Leisure, Daniel Ona-Ondo
Defence, Ali Bongo
Family and the Advancement of Women, Angélique Ngoma
Finance, Economy, Budget and Privatisation, Émile Doumba

Higher Education, Scientific Research and Technology,
André Dieudonné Berre
Justice, Keeper of the Seals, Human Rights, Pascal Désiré
Missongo
Mines, Energy, Oil and Hydraulic Resources, Paul Toungui
National Education, Government Spokesperson,
André Mba-Obame
Public Health and Population, Faustin Boukoubi
Small and Medium-sized Enterprises and Industries,
Paul Biyighe-Mba
Transport and Merchant Marine, Gen. Idriss Ngari
*Water, Forests, Fishing, Re-afforestation, Environment and
Protection of Nature,* Richard Onouviet

EMBASSY OF THE REPUBLIC OF GABON
27 Elvaston Place, London SW7 5NL
Tel: 020-7823 9986
Ambassador Extraordinary and Plenipotentiary, HE
Honorine Dossou-Naki, apptd 1996

BRITISH AMBASSADOR, HE Peter Boon, OBE, resident at
Yaoundé, Cameroon

ECONOMY

The economy is heavily dependent on oil and, to a lesser
extent, other mineral resources, including manganese
and uranium. Gabon has considerable timber reserves
with 80 per cent of the country still forested, although
production has stagnated in recent years.

France and the USA are the main trading partners. In
1995 there was a trade surplus of US$1,744 million and
a current account surplus of US$100 million. Imports
totalled US$882 million and exports US$2,713 million.
GNP – US$4,922 million (1998); US$4,180 per capita
(1998)
GDP – US$4,761 million (1996); US$4,305 per capita
(1996)
ANNUAL AVERAGE GROWTH OF GDP – 3.3 per cent
(1996)
INFLATION RATE – 4.0 per cent (1997)
TOTAL EXTERNAL DEBT – US$4,425 million (1998)

Trade with UK	1998	1999
Imports from UK	£21,512,000	£16,080,000
Exports to UK	5,034,000	4,768,000

THE GAMBIA
The Republic of the Gambia

AREA – 4,361 sq. miles (11,295 sq. km). Neighbour:
Senegal, which surrounds the Gambia except at the
coast
POPULATION – 1,169,000 (1997 UN estimate), mainly
Wollof, Mandinka and Fula peoples who originally
migrated from the north and east. The official language
is English; Fula, Jola, Mandinka, Serahule and Wollof
are indigenous languages
CAPITAL – ΨBanjul (population, 109,986, 1980 estimate)
CURRENCY – Dalasi (D) of 100 butut
NATIONAL ANTHEM – For The Gambia, Our Homeland
NATIONAL DAY – 18 February (Independence Day)
NATIONAL FLAG – Horizontal stripes of red, blue and
green, separated by narrow white stripes
LIFE EXPECTANCY (years) – male 43.41; female 46.63
POPULATION GROWTH RATE – 3.4 per cent (1997)
POPULATION DENSITY – 103 per sq. km (1997)
MILITARY EXPENDITURE – 3.6 per cent of GDP (1998)
MILITARY PERSONNEL – Army 800

The Gambia is named after the Gambia River, which it
straddles for over 200 miles inland from the west coast of
Africa. There is a dry season between October and May
and heavy rainfall in July and August.

HISTORY AND POLITICS

The Gambia River basin was part of the region dominated
in the tenth to 16th centuries by the Songhai and Mali
kingdoms centred on the upper Niger. The Portuguese
reached the Gambia River in 1447; English merchants
began to trade along the river from 1588. Merchants from
France, Courland (now Latvia) and the Netherlands also
established trading posts. In 1816 the British stationed a
garrison on an island at the river mouth which became the
capital of a small British-administered colony. In 1889
France agreed that the British rights along the upper river
should extend to 10 km from the river on either bank.
British administration was extended from the Colony to
this Protectorate. The Gambia became independent
within the Commonwealth on 18 February 1965, and a
republic on 24 April 1970.

In July 1994 junior army officers launched a coup which
ousted the president and the government, and a military
council was formed. The coup leader, Lt. (later Capt.)
Jammeh, assumed the presidency, the constitution was
suspended and a civilian-military government was formed
to rule in conjunction with the Ruling Military Council.
A referendum approved a new constitution in August
1996, Jammeh was elected president the following
month and the Ruling Military Council was dissolved.
A pro-presidential party won 33 of the 49 seats in the new
parliament in a legislative election in January 1997.

FOREIGN RELATIONS

The relationship with Senegal remains an important
factor in political and economic policy. Moves towards a
closer association were accelerated after an abortive coup
in 1981 was put down with the help of Senegalese troops.
In 1982 the Senegambia Confederation was instituted but
following disagreements it was dissolved in 1989. A treaty
of friendship and co-operation was signed with Senegal
in 1991.

POLITICAL SYSTEM

The constitution gives enhanced powers to the president
who is elected for an indefinite term. The National
Assembly has 49 members, of whom 45 are directly
elected, and four appointed by the president.

HEAD OF STATE
President, Defence, Capt. Yahya Jammeh, *took power*
23 July 1994, *elected* 26 September 1996
Vice-President, Health and Social Affairs, Isatou Njie-Saidy

CABINET *as at September 2000*
Agriculture, Abdoulif Sallah
Education, Thérèse Ndong-Jatta
External Affairs, Lamine Sedat Jobe
Finance and Economic Affairs, Famara Jatta
Interior, Ousman Badjie
Justice, Attorney-General, Pap Cheyassin Secka
*Presidency, National Assembly, Fisheries and Natural
Resources,* Capt. Edward Singhateh
Public Works, Communications, Information, Sarjo Jallow
Territorial Administration, Nai Ceesay
Tourism and Culture, Susan Ogoo
Trade, Industry and Employment, Musa Sillah
Youth and Sports, Capt. Yankouba Touray

GAMBIA HIGH COMMISSION
57 Kensington Court, London W8 5DG
Tel: 020-7937 6316/7/8
Acting High Commissioner, Bala Garba Jahumpa

BRITISH HIGH COMMISSION
48 Atlantic Road, Fajara (PO Box 507), Banjul
Tel: (00 220) 495133
e-mail: bhcbanjul@commet.gm
High Commissioner, HE John Perrott, apptd 2000

ECONOMY

Agriculture accounts for 79.9 per cent of employment and contributes 29.1 per cent of GDP. The chief product, groundnuts, also forms over 80 per cent of domestic exports. Other crops are cotton, rice, millet, sorghum and maize.

Manufactures are limited to groundnut processing, minor metal fabrications, paints, furniture, soap and bottling. Tourism is developing quickly with more than 80,000 visitors in 1996–7. Trade through the Gambia, re-exporting imported goods to neighbouring countries, is an important element in the economy. The main exports are groundnuts, cotton, and fish and fish products. The main imports are foodstuffs and live animals, industrial goods, machinery and transport equipment, and fuels. In 1997 there was a trade deficit of US$87 million and a current account deficit of US$24 million. Imports in 1998 totalled US$245 million and exports US$19 million.

GNP – US$408 million (1998); US$340 per capita (1998)
GDP – US$346 million (1996); US$303 per capita (1996)
ANNUAL AVERAGE GROWTH OF GDP – 3.2 per cent (1996)
INFLATION RATE – 1.1 per cent (1998)
TOTAL EXTERNAL DEBT – US$477 million (1998)

Trade with UK	1998	1999
Imports from UK	£14,417,000	£16,654,000
Exports to UK	2,904,000	2,844,000

COMMUNICATIONS

There is an international airport at Yundum, 17 miles from Banjul, with scheduled services flying to other West African states and to the UK and Belgium. Banjul is the main port. Internal communication is by road and river. In 1996 there were 2,700 km of roads, of which 956 km were paved. There are seven radio broadcasting stations and a UHF telephone service linking Banjul with the principal towns in the provinces. There is one television station.

EDUCATION

There are 24 secondary schools (eight high and 16 technical). Two high schools provide A-level education. Gambia College provides post-secondary courses in education, agriculture, public health and nursing. There are seven vocational training institutions. Higher education and advanced training courses are taken outside the Gambia, currently by over 200 students.

ILLITERACY RATE – 63.5 per cent
ENROLMENT (percentage of age group) – primary 65 per cent (1995); secondary 20 per cent (1992); tertiary 1.7 per cent (1994)

GEORGIA
Sakartvelos Respublikis

AREA – 26,911 sq. miles (69,700 sq. km). Neighbours: Russia (north), Azerbaijan (south-east), Armenia (south), Turkey (south-west)
POPULATION – 5,411,000 (1998 estimate): 70 per cent Georgian, 8 per cent Armenian, 6 per cent Russian, 6 per cent Azerbaijani, 3 per cent Ossetian and 2 per cent Abkhazian, with smaller groups of Greeks, Ukrainians, Jews and Kurds. The majority religion is the Georgian Orthodox Church. There is also a small Muslim minority. Georgian, Russian and Armenian are the most commonly used languages. Georgian is one of the oldest languages in the world to have been continually in use, the alphabet having emerged in the third century BC

CAPITAL – Tbilisi (population, 1,268,000, 1990 estimate)
MAJOR CITIES – Batumi (137,000); Kutaisi (236,000); Rustavi (160,000); Sukhumi (capital of Abkhazia) (122,000), 1990 UN estimates
CURRENCY – Lari of 100 tetri
NATIONAL ANTHEM – Dideba zetsit kurtheuls (Praise be to the Heavenly Bestower of Blessings)
NATIONAL DAY – 26 May (Independence Day)
NATIONAL FLAG – Cherry red with a canton in the upper hoist divided black over white
LIFE EXPECTANCY (years) – male 68.10; female 75.70
POPULATION GROWTH RATE – –0.1 per cent (1997)
POPULATION DENSITY – 78 per sq. km (1997)
URBAN POPULATION – 55.6 per cent (1995)
MILITARY EXPENDITURE – 2.5 per cent of GDP (1998)
MILITARY PERSONNEL – 22,250: Army 12,600, Navy 750, Air Force 2,400; Paramilitaries 6,500
CONSCRIPTION DURATION – Two years
ILLITERACY RATE – 0.5 per cent
ENROLMENT (percentage of age group) – primary 87 per cent (1996); secondary 74 per cent (1996); tertiary 42 per cent (1996)

Georgia occupies the north-western part of the Caucasus region of the former Soviet Union. It contains the two autonomous republics of Abkhazia and Adjaria and the disputed region of South Ossetia (Tskhinvali).

Georgia is mountainous, with the Greater Caucasus in the north and the Lesser Caucasus in the south. Western Georgia has a mild and damp climate, eastern Georgia is more continental and dry. The Black Sea shore and the Rioni lowland are subtropical.

HISTORY AND POLITICS

The Georgians formed two states, Colchis and Iberia, on the edge of the Black Sea around 1000 BC. After centuries of invasions by Arabs, Turks and Khazars, Georgia entered its 'Golden Age' in the 12th century AD when trade, irrigation and communications were developed. Invasions by the Khazars and Mongols led to the division of Georgia into several states. These struggled against the Turkish and the Persian empires from the 16th to the 18th centuries, gradually turning to the Russian Empire for protection and support. Eastern Georgia signed a treaty of alliance with Russia which recognised Russian supremacy in 1783 and joined the Russian Empire in 1801, followed soon after by Western Georgia.

In the late 19th century, nationalist and Marxist movements competed for limited political influence under autocratic Russian rule. One of the most prominent Marxist activists was Iosif Dzhugashvili (Josef Stalin). After the Russian revolution of 1917, a nationalist government came to power in Georgia supported by allied intervention forces. In 1921 Soviet forces occupied Tbilisi, and in 1922 Georgia joined the Soviet Union as part of the Transcaucasian Soviet Socialist Republic.

In March 1990 the Georgian Supreme Soviet declared illegal the treaties of 1921–2 by which Georgia had joined the Soviet Union. The Communist Party's monopoly on power was abolished and in multiparty elections held in October and November 1990 the nationalist leader Zviad Gamsakhurdia was elected president. Georgia declared its independence from the Soviet Union in May 1991 and was admitted to UN membership on 31 July 1992.

Gamsakhurdia's government faced armed opposition from 1991 onwards. Defeat in the ensuing civil war in

Tbilisi led to Gamsakhurdia's overthrow in January 1992, and in March 1992 a state council was appointed with the former Soviet foreign minister Eduard Shevardnadze as chairman. Fighting continued throughout 1992 and 1993. In October 1992 Shevardnadze was elected head of state and Chairman of the Parliament, and a loose alliance of pro-Shevardnadze parties formed a government.

Gamsakhurdia returned to western Georgia in September 1993. President Shevardnadze failed to prevent the advance of Gamsakhurdia's rebels as most government forces were engaged in Abkhazia. Shevardnadze was forced to accept Russian armaments and troops to defeat the rebellion and in return agreed to join the CIS. Georgia rescinded its participation in the CIS Collective Security treaty in February 1999 and Russian troops, who had been guarding Georgia's frontier with Turkey, began to withdraw. The legislative election held on 31 October 1999 was won by the Union of Citizens of Georgia, which gained 130 of the 235 seats. In the presidential election held on 9 April 2000, President Shevardnadze was re-elected, gaining 78.8 per cent of the votes cast.

SECESSION

In late 1990 the South Ossetians took up arms against Georgian rule in an attempt to join North Ossetia, itself part of Russia. The South Ossetian provincial parliament voted in November 1992 to secede from Georgia and join Russia. Fighting ceased in June 1992 and a joint Russian-Georgian-Ossetian peacekeeping force was dispatched. Representatives of the South Ossetian and Georgian governments met in April 1996 to agree security and confidence-building measures. South Ossetia was renamed Tskhinvali under Georgia's 1995 constitution. Presidential elections in South Ossetia were won by Ludvig Chibirov, the chair of the Supreme Council, in November 1996. Legislative elections were held in May 1999.

In July 1992 the Abkhazian republican parliament declared Abkhazia independent. Fighting broke out between Georgian forces and Abkhazian separatists supported by Russian arms and irregulars; Georgian forces were defeated and were forced to withdraw in September 1993. Negotiations under Russian auspices led to an Abkhaz-Georgian cease-fire and separation of forces agreement being signed in May 1994 and the deployment of 2,500 Russian UN peacekeepers on the Abkhaz-Georgian border. In November 1994 the Abkhaz Supreme Soviet declared Abkhazia's independence again and elected Vladislav Ardzinba as president. Abkhazia was given autonomous republic status under the 1995 constitution; this was rejected by the republican parliament. Elections to the self-declared Abkhaz People's Assembly were held in November 1996. Following a guarantee of security from President Ardzinba, ethnic Georgians who had fled Abkhazia during the fighting began returning in March 1999.

FOREIGN RELATIONS

In September 1997, President Shevardnadze signed an accord with President Maskhadov of Chechnya, calling for closer co-operation between the two states. In October 1997, a Georgian-Ukrainian declaration was signed, promising a development of co-operation with NATO within the framework of the Partnership for Peace programme. Georgia and Russia agreed on 18 November 1999 that two of the four remaining Russian military bases on Georgian territory would close by 1 July 2000 and that the Russian military presence in Georgia would be reduced by 31 December 2000. Georgia has signed a Partnership and Co-operation Agreement with the European Union.

POLITICAL SYSTEM

The 1995 constitution provides for a federal republic with a unicameral legislature, to become bicameral 'following the creation of appropriate conditions'; and a popularly elected president who serves a maximum of two five-year terms. The present parliament has 235 members, directly elected for a four-year term.

HEAD OF STATE

President, Eduard Shevardnadze, elected 11 October 1992, re-elected 1995, 9 April 2000

CABINET as at September 2000
Minister of State, Head of Chancellery, Giorgi Arsenishvili
Deputy Minister of State, Economics and Banking Issues, Levan Dzneladze
Agriculture and Food, Davit Kirvalidze
Culture, Sesili Goaiberidze
Defence, Maj.-Gen. Davit Tevzadze
Economy, Industry and Trade, Vano Chakhartishvili Vladimer Papava
Education, Alexandre Kartozia
Finance, Zurab Noghaideli
Foreign Affairs, Irakli Menagarishvili
Fuel and Energy, Davit Mirtskhulava
Health and Social Security, Avtandil Jorbenadze
Industry, Badri Shoshitaishvili
Internal Affairs, Kakha Targamadze
Justice, Joni Khetsuriani
Natural Resources and Environment, Nino Chkobadze
Refugees and Accommodation, Valeri Vashakidze
Social Security, Labour, Employment, Tengiz Gazdeliani
State Property Management, Michael Ukleba
State Security, Vakhtang Kutateladze
Tax Revenue, Mikheil Machavariani
Trade, Foreign Economic Relations, Tamar Beruchasvili
Transport and Communications, Merab Adeishvili
Urban Planning and Construction, Merab Chkhenkeli
Without Portfolio, Malkhaz Kakabadze

EMBASSY OF THE REPUBLIC OF GEORGIA
3 Hornton Place, London, W8 4LZ
Tel: 020-7937 8233
Ambassador Extraordinary and Plenipotentiary, HE Teimuraz Mamatsashvili, apptd 1995

BRITISH EMBASSY
Metechi Palace Hotel, GE-380003 Tbilisi
Tel: (00 995) (32) 955497
Ambassador Extraordinary and Plenipotentiary, HE Richard Jenkins, OBE, apptd 1997

BRITISH COUNCIL REPRESENTATIVE, M. Kiasahvili,
13 Chavcharaze Avenue, University VIII Building, GE-380079 Tbilisi; e-mail: office.bc@britcoun.org.ge

ECONOMY

The economy was brought to the brink of collapse by civil and secessionist wars and the ending of former Soviet trading relationships. Although Georgia has deposits of coal, they have not been exploited and it is desperately short of energy supplies. A large proportion of production is stolen by black marketeers, whilst the tourist industry on the Black Sea coast has been destroyed by the fighting. The only productive sector of the economy is agriculture, which employs 30 per cent of the workforce and generates 38 per cent of GDP, with a concentration on viniculture, tea and tobacco-growing and citrus fruits. The main exports are iron alloys, wine, nuts, chemical fertilisers, and oil and oil products. The main imports are oil and oil products, gas, automobiles, pharmaceuticals and wheat.

GNP – US$5,281 million (1998); US$970 per capita (1998)

GDP – US$3,236 million (1996); US$595 per capita (1996)
ANNUAL AVERAGE GROWTH OF GDP – 10.8 per cent (1996)
TOTAL EXTERNAL DEBT – US$1,674 million (1998)

Trade with UK	1998	1999
Imports from UK	£20,991,000	£14,681,000
Exports to UK	3,222,000	3,665,000

CULTURE

Famous Georgians include the 12th-century writer Shota Rustaveli, who composed the epic poem *Knight in a Tiger's Skin*, and the film director Tengiz Abuladze (b. 1924), who directed the film *Repentance*.

GERMANY
Bundesrepublik Deutschland – Federal Republic of Germany

AREA – 137,735 sq. miles (357,022 sq. km). Neighbours: Denmark (north), Poland (east), Czech Republic (east and south-east), Austria (south-east and south), Switzerland (south), France, Luxembourg, Belgium and the Netherlands (west)
POPULATION – 82,071,000 (1997 UN estimate). Approximately 80 per cent of the population live in the former West Germany. In 1994 there were 28,197,000 Protestants, 27,909,797 Roman Catholics, 2,700,000 Muslims and 53,797 Jews. The language is German; there are Danish- and Frisian-speaking minorities in Schleswig-Holstein and a Sorbian-speaking minority in Saxony
CAPITAL – Berlin (population, 3,472,009, 1996).
MAJOR CITIES – Bremen (546,968); Cologne (964,311); Dortmund (594,866); Dresden (459,222); Duisburg (529,062); Düsseldorf (570,969); Essen (608,732); Frankfurt am Main (643,469); Hamburg (1,704,731); Hannover (520,670); Leipzig (446,491); Munich (1,205,923); Nuremberg (489,758); Stuttgart (585,274), 1998 estimates
CURRENCY – Euro (€) of 100 cents/Deutsche Mark (DM) of 100 Pfennig
NATIONAL ANTHEM – Einigkeit und Recht und Freiheit (Unity and right and freedom)
NATIONAL DAY – 3 October (Anniversary of 1990 Unification)
NATIONAL FLAG – Horizontal bars of black, red and gold

LIFE EXPECTANCY (years) – male 73.29; female 79.72
POPULATION GROWTH RATE – 0.5 per cent (1997)
POPULATION DENSITY – 230 per sq. km (1997)
URBAN POPULATION – 76.3 per cent (1990)

HISTORY AND POLITICS

The first German realm was the Holy Roman Empire, established in AD 962 when Otto I of Saxony was crowned Emperor. The Empire endured until 1806, but the achievement of a national state was prevented by fragmentation into small principalities and dukedoms.

The Empire was replaced by a loose association of sovereign states known as the German Confederation, which was dissolved in 1866 and replaced by the Prussian-dominated North German Federation. The south German principalities united with the northern federation to form a second German Empire in 1871 and the King of Prussia was proclaimed Emperor.

Defeat in the First World War led to the abdication of the Emperor, and the country became a republic. The

Land	Area (sq. km)	Population (1998)	Capital	Minister-President (May 2000)
Baden-Württemberg	35,752	10.4m	Stuttgart	Erwin Teufel (CDU)
Bavaria	70,548	12.1m	Munich	Dr Edmund Stoiber (CSU)
Berlin	891	3.4m	—	Eberhard Diepgen (CDU)*
Brandenburg	29,476	2.6m	Potsdam	Dr Manfred Stolpe (SPD)
Bremen	404	0.7m	—	Dr Henning Scherf (SPD)*
Hamburg	755	1.7m	—	Ortwin Runde (SPD)*
Hesse	21,115	6.0m	Wiesbaden	Roland Koch (CDU)
Lower Saxony	47,613	7.9m	Hannover	Sigmar Gabriel (SPD)
Mecklenburg-Western Pomerania	23,170	1.8m	Schwerin	Dr Harald Ringstorff (SPD)
North Rhine-Westphalia	34,079	18.0m	Düsseldorf	Wolfgang Clement (SPD)
Rhineland-Palatinate	19,847	4.0m	Mainz	Kurt Beck (SPD)
Saarland	2,570	1.1m	Saarbrücken	Peter Müller (SPD)
Saxony	18,412	4.5m	Dresden	Prof. Kurt Biedenkopf (CDU)
Saxony-Anhalt	20,447	2.7m	Magdeburg	Dr Reinhard Höppner (SPD)
Schleswig-Holstein	15,770	2.8m	Kiel	Heide Simonis (SPD)
Thuringia	16,172	2.5m	Erfurt	Dr Bernhard Vogel (CDU)

*Berlin, *Governing Mayor*; Bremen, *Mayor*; Hamburg, *First Mayor*
CDU Christian Democratic Union; CSU Christian Social Union; SPD Social Democratic Party

Treaty of Versailles (1919) ceded Alsace-Lorraine to France, and large areas in the east were lost to Poland. The world economic crisis of 1929 contributed to the collapse of the Weimar Republic and the subsequent rise to power of the National Socialist movement of Adolf Hitler, who became Chancellor in 1933.

After concluding a Treaty of Non-Aggression with the Soviet Union in August 1939, Germany invaded Poland (1 September 1939), precipitating the Second World War, which lasted until 1945. Hitler committed suicide on 30 April 1945. On 8 May 1945, Germany unconditionally surrendered.

THE POST-WAR PERIOD

Germany was divided into American, French, British and Soviet zones of occupation. The territories to the east of the Oder and Neisse rivers were placed under Polish and Russian administration and some 7.75 million Germans were deported.

The Federal Republic of Germany (FRG) was created out of the three western zones in 1949. A Communist government was established in the Soviet zone (henceforth the German Democratic Republic (GDR)). In 1961 the Soviet zone of Berlin was sealed off, and the Berlin Wall was built along the zonal boundary, partitioning the western sectors of the city from the eastern.

Soviet-initiated reform in eastern Europe during the late 1980s led to unrest in the GDR, culminating in the opening of the Berlin Wall in November 1989 and the collapse of Communist government. The 'Treaty on the Final Settlement with Respect to Germany', concluded between the FRG, GDR and the four former occupying powers in September 1990, unified Germany with effect from 3 October 1990 as a fully sovereign state. Economic and monetary union preceded formal union on 1 July 1990. Unification is constitutionally the accession of Berlin and the five reformed *Länder* of the GDR to the FRG, which remains in being. The first government of the new Germany took office in January 1991 following all-German elections on 2 December 1990. Berlin was declared to be the capital of the unified Germany and arrangements to transfer parliament and government departments from Bonn were drawn up. The transfer began in November 1998 and the process was due to be completed during 2000.

The distribution of seats following the last election for the Bundestag on 27 September 1998 was: Social Democrats, 298; Christian Democratic Union, 198; Christian Social Union, 47; The Greens, 47; Free Democrats, 44; Democratic Socialists, 35. A coalition of Social Democrats and Greens forms the present government.

POLITICAL SYSTEM

The Basic Law provides for a president, elected by a Federal Convention (electoral college) for a five-year term, a lower house (*Bundestag*) of 669 members elected by direct universal suffrage for a four-year term of office, and an upper house (*Bundesrat*) composed of 69 members appointed by the governments of the *Länder* in proportion to *Länder* populations, without a fixed term of office.

Judicial authority is exercised by the Federal Constitutional Court, the federal courts provided for in the Basic Law and the courts of the *Länder*.

FEDERAL STRUCTURE

Germany is a federal republic composed of 16 states (*Länder*) (ten from the former West, five from the former East and Berlin). Each *Land* has its own directly elected legislature and government led by Minister-Presidents (prime ministers) or equivalents. The 1949 Basic Law vests executive power in the *Länder* governments except in those areas reserved for the federal government.

HEAD OF STATE
Federal President, Johannes Rau, *elected* 24 May 1999
CABINET *as at September 2000*
Federal Chancellor, Gerhard Schröder (SPD)
Federal Vice-Chancellor, Foreign Affairs, Joschka Fischer (Greens)
Defence, Rudolf Scharping (SPD)
Economic Co-operation and Development, Heidemarie Wieczorek-Zeul (SPD)
Economics and Technology, Werner Müller (Ind.)
Education and Research, Edelgard Bulmahn (SPD)
Environment, Nature Conservation and Reactor Safety, Jürgen Trittin (Greens)
Family, Pensioners, Women and Youth, Dr Christine Bergmann (SPD)
Finance, Hans Eichel (SPD)
Food, Agriculture and Forestry, Karl-Heinz Funke (SPD)
Head of Chancellory, Frank-Walter Steinmeier (SPD)
Health, Andrea Fischer (Greens)
Interior, Otto Schily (SPD)
Justice, Herta Däubler-Gmelin (SPD)
Labour and Social Affairs, Walter Riester (SPD)
Minister Delegate for Culture, Michael Naumann (Ind.)
Minister Delegate for East Germany, Rolf Schwanitz (SPD)
Ministers Delegate for Foreign Affairs, Günter Verheugen (SPD); Ludger Vollmer (Greens)
Transport, Construction and Housing, Reinhard Klimmt (SPD)
CDU Christian Democratic Union; CSU Christian Social Union; Ind. Independent

EMBASSY OF THE FEDERAL REPUBLIC OF GERMANY
23 Belgrave Square, London SW1X 8PZ
Tel: 020-7824 1300
Ambassador Extraordinary and Plenipotentiary, HE Dr Hans-Friedrich von Ploetz, apptd 1999
Minister, Peter von Butler
Minister-Counsellor, Co-ordinator of EU Affairs, Paul von Maltzahn, CVO
Counsellors, C. Gläser (*Cultural Affairs*); E. P. Fischer (*Economic Affairs*)
Defence Attaché, Rear-Adm. Hubert Hass

BRITISH EMBASSY
Unter den Linden 32/34, D-10117 Berlin
Tel: (00 49) (30) 201 840
Ambassador Extraordinary and Plenipotentiary, HE Sir Paul Lever, KCMG, apptd 1997
Deputy Head of Mission, A. Charlton, CMG
Defence and Military Attaché, Brig. B. R. Isbell, MBE
Counsellor (Economic), R. L. Turner

BRITISH EMBASSY, COMMERCIAL, ENVIRONMENT AND MANAGEMENT SECTIONS
Friedrichstrasse 79/80, D-10117 Berlin
Tel: (00 49) (30) 201 840

BRITISH CONSULATES-GENERAL – Düsseldorf, Frankfurt, Hamburg, Munich, Stuttgart
BRITISH CONSULATES – Bremen, Hannover, Kiel and Nuremberg
BRITISH COUNCIL DIRECTOR, K. Dobson, OBE, Hahnenstrasse 6, D-50667 Köln; e-mail: bc.cologne@britcoun.de. Offices at Berlin, Hamburg, Leipzig and Munich
BRITISH CHAMBER OF COMMERCE, Neumarkt 14, D-5000 Köln 1. *Director*, Herr Heumann

DEFENCE
The Army has 3,136 main battle tanks, 3,306 armoured

personnel carriers, 2,461 armoured infantry fighting vehicles, and 204 attack helicopters. The Navy has 14 submarines, two destroyers, 12 frigates, 28 patrol and coastal vessels, 52 combat aircraft and 39 armed helicopters. The Air Force has 451 combat aircraft.

There remain 98,020 NATO personnel in Germany (USA 68,820; UK 20,800; Belgium 2,100; France 3,300; Netherlands 3,000).

During 1993 both the Constitutional Court and the Bundestag agreed that German armed forces may operate outside Germany and the NATO area in UN and other peacekeeping operations for the first time since 1945. In 1994 the Constitutional Court ruled that German forces could serve in armed peacekeeping missions.

MILITARY EXPENDITURE – 1.5 per cent of GDP (1998)
MILITARY PERSONNEL – 332,800: Army 228,300, Navy 28,100, Air Force 76,400. Under the terms of the Treaty of Unification, the German armed forces have been limited to 370,000 active personnel since the end of 1994
CONSCRIPTION DURATION – Ten months

ECONOMY

Germany has a predominantly industrial economy. Principal industries are coal mining, iron and steel production, machine construction, the electrical industry, the manufacture of steel and metal products, chemicals, automobile production, electronics, textiles and the processing of foodstuffs.

In 1998, Germany produced 207,642,000 tonnes of coal and 2,895,446 tonnes of crude petroleum. The government announced in June 2000 that it was to abolish all 19 of Germany's nuclear power stations over a 32-year period, which currently supplied over 30 per cent of the energy generated in the country.

After a mini-boom generated by new East German demand in 1990 and 1991, Germany entered its most severe recession since the war induced by the costs of reunification. In 1993 a 'Solidarity Pact' was agreed, which lays down the basis of future funding transfers to the East based on a 5.5 per cent rise in income taxes, wage restraint in the West, more private investment in the East, and the distribution of the funding burden between the federal and *Länder* governments. The government was forced to make spending cuts in order to meet the criteria for European monetary union. In November 1998, the government announced that it would double investment in research over its five-year term. An austerity package was approved in August 1999, which cut DM30,000 million from public spending in 2000, and in December 1999 it was announced that the basic rate of company tax would fall from 40 per cent to 25 per cent from 1 January 2001. The rate of economic growth increased in 1999 and the first quarter of 2000, aided by the weakness of the euro.

In 1998 there was a trade surplus of US$77,937 million and a current account deficit of US$3,104 million. Imports totalled US$467,315 million and exports US$540,554 million.

GNP – US$2,179,802 million (1998); US$26,570 per capita (1998)
GDP – US$2,353,469 million (1996); US$28,728 per capita (1996)
ANNUAL AVERAGE GROWTH OF GDP – 2.0 per cent (1997)
INFLATION RATE – 1.0 per cent (1998)
UNEMPLOYMENT – 9.7 per cent (1998)

Trade with UK	1998	1999
Imports from UK	£19,453,500,000	£19,217,6400,000
Exports to UK	24,063,000,000	25,131,000,000

COMMUNICATIONS

In 1995 the state-owned railways measured 40,209 km of which 17,054 km were electrified, and the privately owned

railways totalled approximately 2,807 km. Classified roads measured 228,860 km in 1996, of which motorways were 11,190 km. Merchant shipping under the German flag in 1994 amounted to 5,696,088 tonnes gross. Inland waterways are 6,929 km long.

EDUCATION

School attendance is compulsory between the ages of six and 18 and comprises nine years of full-time education at primary and main schools and three years of vocational education on a part-time basis. The secondary school leaving examination (*Abitur*) entitles the holder to a place of study at a university or another institution of higher education.

Children below the age of 18 who are not attending a general secondary or a full-time vocational school have compulsory day-release at a vocational school.

The largest universities are in Munich, Berlin, Hamburg, Bonn, Frankfurt and Cologne.

ENROLMENT (percentage of age group) – primary 86 per cent (1996); secondary 88 per cent (1996); tertiary 47 per cent (1996)

CULTURE

Modern (or New High) German has developed from the time of the Reformation to the present day, with differences of dialect in Austria, Alsace, Luxembourg, Liechtenstein and the German-speaking cantons of Switzerland.

The literary language is usually regarded as having become fixed by Luther and Zwingli at the Reformation, since which time many great names occur in all branches, notably philosophy, from Leibnitz (1646–1716) to Kant (1724–1804), Schelling (1775–1854) and Hegel (1770–1831); drama, from Goethe (1749–1832) and Schiller (1759–1805) to Gerhart Hauptmann (1862–1946); and poetry, Heine (1797–1856). Eight German authors have received the Nobel Prize for Literature: Theodor Mommsen (1902), R. Eucken (1908), P. Heyse (1909), Gerhart Hauptmann (1912), Thomas Mann (1929), N. Sachs (1966) Heinrich Böll (1972), and Günther Grass (1999).

GHANA
The Republic of Ghana

AREA – 92,098 sq. miles (238,533 sq. km). Neighbours: Burkina Faso (north), Côte d'Ivoire (west), Togo (east)
POPULATION – 18,885,616 (1998 estimate); most are Sudanese Negroes, although Hamitic strains are common in the north. The official language is English. The principal indigenous language group is Akan, of which Twi and Fanti are the most commonly used. Ga, Ewe and languages of the Mole-Dagbani group are common in certain regions. Most Ghanaians are Christians, although there is a substantial Muslim minority in the north
CAPITAL – ΨAccra (population, 1,445,515, 1998), Greater Accra Region (including Tema) 2,384,753 (1998 estimate)
MAJOR CITIES – Koforidua (81,378); Kumasi (577,878); Ψ Takoradi (96,897); Tamale (228,827)
CURRENCY – Cedi of 100 pesewas
NATIONAL FLAG – Equal horizontal bands of red over gold over green; five-point black star on gold stripe
NATIONAL ANTHEM – God Bless our Homeland Ghana
NATIONAL DAY – 6 March (Independence Day)
LIFE EXPECTANCY (years) – male 54.22; female 57.84
POPULATION GROWTH RATE – 2.9 per cent (1997)
POPULATION DENSITY – 77 per sq. km (1997)
MILITARY EXPENDITURE – 1.4 per cent of GDP (1998)

MILITARY PERSONNEL – 7,000. Army 5,000, Navy 1,000, Air Force 1,000
ILLITERACY RATE – 29.8 per cent
ENROLMENT (percentage of age group) – tertiary 1.4 per cent (1990)

HISTORY AND POLITICS

First reached by Europeans in the 15th century, the constituent parts of Ghana came under British administration at various times, the original Gold Coast Colony being constituted in 1874, and Ashanti and the Northern Territories Protectorate in 1901. Trans-Volta-Togoland, part of the former German colony of Togo, was mandated to Britain by the League of Nations after the First World War, and became a United Nations Trusteeship under British administration after the Second World War. After a plebiscite in 1956, the territory was integrated with the Gold Coast Colony. The former Gold Coast Colony and associated territories became the independent state of Ghana on 6 March 1957 and became a republic in 1960.

Since 1966, Ghana has experienced long periods of military rule interspersed with short-lived civilian governments. A coup in 1979 led to the formation of an Armed Forces Revolutionary Council chaired by Flt. Lt. Jerry Rawlings. Civilian rule was restored in 1979 but another coup in December 1981 brought Rawlings back to power.

A referendum in 1992 approved a new multiparty constitution and the legalisation of political parties. The National Democratic Congress (NDC) was established as a political party from the ruling Provisional National Defence Council. The presidential and parliamentary elections in late 1992 were won by Rawlings and the NDC, following a boycott by most opposition parties and most of the electorate. The Fourth Republic was declared on 7 January 1993 and a new government nominated by the president took office in March 1993. In legislative elections in December 1996, the NDC retained its absolute majority; President Rawlings was also re-elected. Presidential and legislative elections are scheduled for December 2000.

POLITICAL SYSTEM

The head of state is an executive president elected for a four-year term, renewable only once. The president appoints the Council of Ministers. The unicameral legislature, the Parliament, has 200 members directly elected for a four-year term.

For political and administrative purposes Ghana is divided into ten regions, each headed by a Regional Minister who is the representative of the central government.

HEAD OF STATE

President, Flt. Lt. (retd) Jerry John Rawlings, took power 31 December 1981, elected 3 November 1992, re-elected 7 December 1996
Vice-President, John Evans Mills
Presidential Adviser on Governmental Affairs, Mahama Iddrissu

COUNCIL OF MINISTERS as at September 2000

Communications, John Mahama
Defence, Lt. Col. (retd) E. K. T. Donkoh
Education, Ekwow Spio-Garbrah
Employment and Social Welfare, Alhaji Mohammed Mumuni
Environment, Science and Technology, Cletus Avoka
Finance, Richard Kwame Peprah
Food and Agriculture, J. H. Owusu-Acheampong
Foreign Affairs, James Victor Gbeho
Health, Kwame Danso Buafo
Interior, Nii Okaija Adamafio
Justice and Attorney-General, Obed Asamoah
Lands and Forestry, Christine Amoako-Nuamah

Local Government and Rural Development, Cecilia Johnson
Mines and Energy, John Ebu
National Security, Kofi Totobi-Quakyi
Parliamentary Affairs, Kwabena Brobbey
Planning and Regional Economic Co-operation and Integration, Kwamena Ahwoi
Presidency, Chieftaincy Affairs and State Protocol, D. O. Agyekum
Roads and Transport, Edward Salia
Tourism, Mike Gizo
Trade and Industry, Dan Abodakpi
Without Portfolio, Margaret Clarke-Kwesie
Works and Housing, Isaac Adjei-Mensah
Youth and Sports, E. T. Mensah

GHANA HIGH COMMISSION
13 Belgrave Square, London SW1X 8PN
Tel: 020-7235 4142
High Commissioner, HE James E. K. Aggrey-Orleans, apptd 1997
Defence Adviser, Cdre C. B. Puplampu
Minister-Counsellor, E. K. Amenuvor (Trade)

BRITISH HIGH COMMISSION
PO Box 296, Osu Link, Accra
Tel: (00 233) (21) 221665
e-mail: High.Commission@accra.mail.fco.gov.uk
High Commissioner, HE Ian Mackley, CMG, CVO, apptd 1996
Deputy High Commissioner, C. Murray
Defence Adviser, Lt.-Col. E. Glover
First Secretary (Commercial), M. A. Ives

BRITISH COUNCIL DIRECTOR, T. Humphreys, 11 Liberia Road, PO Box 771, Accra;
e-mail: bcaccra@bcgha.africaonline.com.gh.
There is also an office in Kumasi.

ECONOMY

Agriculture is the basis of the economy, employing 57.6 per cent of the workforce and generating 47 per cent of GDP in 1997. Crops include cocoa, the largest single source of revenue, rice, cassava, plantains, oranges and pineapples, groundnuts, corn, millet, oil palms, yams, maize and vegetables. Livestock is raised in uncultivated areas. Fishing is important in coastal areas and in the Volta lake and river system.

Manganese production ranks among the world's largest, with 384,173 tonnes of ore being produced in 1998; diamonds, gold and bauxite are also produced.

Small-scale traditional industries include tailoring, goldsmithing and carpentry. Priority has been given in recent years to establishing manufacturing industries and a modern industrial complex has developed in the Accra-Tema area. In 1997, 325,000 tourists visited Ghana.

Since 1966 the Volta Dams at Akosombo and Kpong have generated hydroelectric power for the processing of bauxite and fed a power transmission network for most of Ghana, Togo and Benin. There is considerable foreign investment in Ghana, and its economy has grown consistently. Gold production rose by 40 per cent in 1998.

In 1998 there was a trade deficit of US$384 million and a current account deficit of US$502 million. Imports in 1998 totalled US$2,214 million and exports US$1,885 million.

GNP – US$7,269 million (1998); US$390 per capita (1998)
GDP – US$6,770 million (1996); US$380 per capita (1996)
ANNUAL AVERAGE GROWTH OF GDP – 5.2 per cent (1996)
INFLATION RATE – 14.6 per cent (1998)
TOTAL EXTERNAL DEBT – US$6,884 million (1998)

TRADE

Principal exports are gold, cocoa, and timber. Principal

imports are capital goods, semi-manufactures, consumables and energy.

Trade with UK	1998	1999
Imports from UK	£222,202,000	£174,842,000
Exports to UK	155,160,000	153,559,000

COMMUNICATIONS

The Kotoka Airport at Accra is an international airport and Ghana Airways is the national airline. There are also internal airports at Takoradi, Kumasi, Sunyani, and Tamale.

There are more than 20,000 miles of motorable roads. There are 600 miles of railway, linking Accra and the principal ports of Takoradi and Tema with their hinterlands, the mining centres and with each other.

Takoradi Harbour consists of seven quay berths: one is leased specially for manganese exports. Tema Harbour has ten berths for larger ocean-going vessels and the largest dry dock on the West African coast. An oil berth has also been built to serve the refinery at Tema.

GREECE
Elliniki Dimokratia

AREA – 50,949 sq. miles (131,957 sq. km). Neighbours: Albania, Bulgaria and Macedonia (north), Turkey (east)
POPULATION – 10,522,000 (1997 UN estimate), 10,256,464 (1991 census): 98 per cent Greek Orthodox, 1 per cent Catholic, 1 per cent Muslim. The language is Greek
CAPITAL – Athens (population 3,072,922, 1991); including ΨPiraeus and suburbs, 3,096,775 (1991 census)
MAJOR CITIES – ΨIráklion (Heraklion) (132,117); Lárisa (113,090); ΨPátrai (Patras) (170,452); ΨThessaloníki (Salonika) (749,048) ΨVólos (116,031), 1991
CURRENCY – Drachma of 100 leptae
NATIONAL ANTHEM – Imnos Eis Tin Eleftherian (Hymn to Freedom)
NATIONAL DAY – March 25 (Independence Day)
NATIONAL FLAG – Blue and white stripes with a white cross on a blue field in the canton
LIFE EXPECTANCY (years) – male 75.02; female 80.20
POPULATION GROWTH RATE – 0.5 per cent (1997)
POPULATION DENSITY – 80 per sq. km (1997)
URBAN POPULATION – 58.9 per cent (1991)

The main areas are: Macedonia (which includes Mt Athos and the island of Thasos), Thrace (including the island of Samothrace), Epirus, Thessaly, Continental Greece (which includes the island of Euboea and the Sporades), Crete and the Peloponnese. The main island groups are the Sporades (of which the largest is Skyros), the Dodecanese or Southern Sporades (Rhodes, Astypalaia, Karpathos, Kassos, Nisyros, Kalymnos, Leros, Patmos, Kos, Symi, Khalki, Tilos), the Cyclades (about 200, including Syros, Andros, Tinos, Mykonos, Naxos, Paros, Santorini, Milos and Serifos), the Ionian Islands (Corfu, Paxos, Levkas, Ithaca, Cephalonia, Zante and Cerigo), and the Aegean Islands (Chios, Lesbos, Limnos and Samos). In Crete from about 3000 to 1400 BC a civilisation flourished which spread its influence throughout the Aegean, and the ruins of the palace of Minos at Knossos afford evidence of astonishing comfort and luxury.

HISTORY AND POLITICS

Greece was under Turkish rule from the mid-15th century until a war of independence (1821–7) led to the establishment of a Greek kingdom in the Peloponnese in 1829. The remainder of Greece gradually became independent until the Dodecanese were returned by Italy in 1947. After the Nazi German occupation of 1941–4, a civil war between monarchist and Communist groups lasted from 1946 to 1949, and tension between right-wing and radical groups continued after 1949. In 1967 right-wing elements in the army seized power and established a military regime (the 'Greek Colonels'). The King went into voluntary exile in 1967. Unrest in Athens in 1973–4 intensified after the government was involved in the overthrow of President Makarios of Cyprus in July 1974, and led the Colonels to surrender power. Konstantinos Karamanlis (prime minister 1955–63) returned from exile to form a provisional government, and the first elections for ten years were held in 1974. The restoration of the monarchy was rejected by referendum on 8 December 1974 and Greece became a republic.

The most recent general election was held on 9 April 2000 with the Panhellenic Socialist Party (PASOK) winning 158 seats, the New Democracy Party (Christian Democrats) 125 seats, the Communist Party 11 seats, and the Coalition of the Left and Progress six seats.

POLITICAL SYSTEM

In 1986 most executive power was transferred from the president to the government. The unicameral 300-member Chamber of Deputies (*Vouli*) is elected for a four-year term by universal adult suffrage under a system of proportional representation, with a three per cent threshold for parliamentary representation.

HEAD OF STATE

President of the Hellenic Republic, Constantine Stephanopoulos, *elected by parliament* 1995, *re-elected* 10 March 2000

CABINET *as at September 2000*

Prime Minister, Costas Simitis
Aegean, Nicos Sifounakis
Agriculture, Georgios Anomeritis
Culture, Theodoros Pangalos
Development, Nikos Christodoulakis
Education and Religious Affairs, Petros Ephthimiou
Environment, Town Planning and Public Works, Costas Laliotis
Foreign Affairs, George Papandreou
Health and Welfare, Alekos Papadopoulos
Interior, Public Administration and Decentralisation, Vasso Papandreou
Justice, Michalis Stathopoulos
Labour and Social Security, Athanasios Yiannitsis
Macedonia and Thrace, George Paschalidis

Merchant Marine, Christos Papoutsis
National Defence, Akis Tsochatzopoulos
National Economy and Finance, Yiannos Papandoniou
Press and Media, Government Spokesman, Dimitris Reppas
Public Order, Michalis Chrysochoidis
Transport and Communications, Christos Verelis
Without Portfolio, Miltiades Papaioannou

EMBASSY OF GREECE
1A Holland Park, London W11 3TP
Tel: 020-7229 3850
Ambassador Extraordinary and Plenipotentiary, vacant
Defence Attaché, Capt. N. Louloudis
First Counsellor and Chargé d'Affaires, C. Bitsios

HONORARY CONSULATES – Belfast, Birmingham,
Edinburgh, Falmouth, Glasgow, Leeds and
Southampton

BRITISH EMBASSY
1 Ploutarchou Street, GR-10675 Athens
Tel: (00 30) (1) 727 2600
e-mail: britania@hol.gr
Ambassador Extraordinary and Plenipotentiary, HE
David C. A. Madden, CMG, apptd 1999
Deputy Head of Mission, Counsellor and Consul-General,
P. J. Millett
Defence and Military Attaché, Brig. S. W. J. Saunders
First Secretary (Commercial), G. G. Thomas

BRITISH CONSULAR OFFICES – Athens, Corfu, Iráklion
(Crete), Kos, Pátrai, Rhodes, Thessaloníki, Syros and
Zakynthos

BRITISH COUNCIL DIRECTOR, P. Chenery, 17 Kolonaki
Square, Athens GR-10673;
e-mail: British.Council@britcoun.gr.
There is also an office at Thessaloníki.

BRITISH-HELLENIC CHAMBER OF COMMERCE,
25 Vas. Sofias Avenue, GR-10674 Athens.
Tel: (00 30) (1) 721 0361

DEFENCE

The Army has 1,735 main battle tanks, 1,977 armoured
personnel carriers and 500 armoured infantry fighting
vehicles. The Navy has eight submarines, four destroyers,
13 frigates, 42 patrol and coastal vessels, six combat
aircraft and 15 armed helicopters. The Air Force has a total
of 458 combat aircraft.
Greece maintains 1,250 army personnel in Cyprus.
There are 420 US military personnel stationed in Greece.
MILITARY EXPENDITURE – 4.8 per cent of GDP (1998)
MILITARY PERSONNEL – 169,670; Army 116,000, Navy
19,500, Air Force 30,170; Paramilitaries 4,000
CONSCRIPTION DURATION – Up to 21 months

ECONOMY

The principal minerals are nickel, bauxite, iron ore, iron
pyrites, manganese magnesite, chrome, lead, zinc and
emery. The chief industries are textiles (cotton, woollen
and synthetics), chemicals, cement, glass, metallurgy,
shipbuilding, domestic electrical equipment and footwear, the production of aluminium, nickel, iron and steel
products, tyres, chemicals, fertilisers and sugar (from
locally-grown beet). Food processing and ancillary
industries are also growing.
The development of the country's electric power
resources, irrigation and land reclamation schemes, and
the exploitation of lignite resources for fuel and industrial
purposes are continuing. Tourism is also a major industry,
with over 10 million visitors in 1995.
Though there has been substantial industrialisation,
agriculture still employs about a fifth of the working
population and contributes 8.1 per cent of GDP. The

most important agricultural products are tobacco, wheat,
cotton, sugar, rice, fruit (olives, peaches, vines, oranges,
lemons, figs, almonds and currant-vines). Exports of fresh
fruit, currants and vegetables are an important contributor to the economy.
In March 1998 the drachma was devalued by 14 per cent
and admitted to the ERM. In March 2000, Greece applied
to participate in EMU; its application was approved on
19 June 2000 and it is to become a member on 1 January
2001.
In 1997 there was a trade deficit of US$15,375 million
and a current account deficit of US$4,860 million.
Imports totalled US$27,799 million and exports totalled
US$8,626 million.
GNP – US$123,394 million (1998); US$11,740 per capita
(1998)
GDP – US$122,446 million (1996); US$11,673 per capita
(1996)
ANNUAL AVERAGE GROWTH OF GDP – 2.6 per cent (1996)
INFLATION RATE – 4.8 per cent (1998)
UNEMPLOYMENT – 10.3 per cent (1997)

Trade with UK	1998	1999
Imports from UK	£987,900,000	£1,069,800,000
Exports to UK	344,100,000	382,400,000

COMMUNICATIONS

The 2,650 km of railways are state-owned, with the
exception of the Athens–Piraeus Electric Railway. Roads
total over 38,500 km, of which about 25 per cent are
national highways and just under 30,000 km are provincial
roads. The Greek mercantile fleet numbers 1,864 ships
over 100 tons gross with a total tonnage of 53,778,128 tons
gross. Athens has direct airline links with Australasia,
North America, most countries in Europe, Africa and the
Middle East.

EDUCATION

Education is free and compulsory from the age of six to
15 and is maintained by state grants. There are eighteen
universities and several other institutes of higher learning.
ILLITERACY RATE – 2.8 per cent
ENROLMENT (percentage of age group) – primary
90 per cent (1996); secondary 87 per cent (1996);
tertiary 47 per cent (1996)

CULTURE

Greek civilisation emerged *c.*1300 BC and the poems of
Homer, which were probably current *c.*800 BC, record
the struggle between the Achaeans of Greece and the
Phrygians of Troy (1194 to 1184 BC).
The spoken language of modern Greece is descended
from the Common Greek of Alexander the Great's
empire. *Katharevousa*, a conservative literary dialect
evolved by Adamantios Corais (Diamant Coray) (1748–
1833) and used for official and technical matters, has been
phased out. Novels and poetry are mostly in *dimotiki*, a
progressive literary dialect which owes much to John
Psycharis (1854–1929). The poets Solomos, Palamas,
Cavafy and Sikelianos have won a European reputation.
George Seferis (1963) and Odysseus Elytis (1979) have
won the Nobel Prize for Literature.

GRENADA
The State of Grenada

AREA – 133 sq. miles (344 sq. km)
POPULATION – 93,000 (1997 UN estimate), 95,000
(1992 census), of which about 75 per cent are of African

descent; there are minorities of Europeans and Indians. The language is English

CAPITAL – ΨSt George's (population, 4,788, 1981)
CURRENCY – East Caribbean dollar (EC$) of 100 cents
NATIONAL ANTHEM – Hail Grenada, land of ours
NATIONAL DAY – 7 February (Independence Day)
NATIONAL FLAG – Divided diagonally into yellow and green triangles within a red border containing six yellow stars, a yellow star on a red disc in the centre and a nutmeg on the green triangle in the hoist
POPULATION GROWTH RATE – 0.3 per cent (1997)
POPULATION DENSITY – 270 per sq. km (1997)

The island is about 21 miles long and 12 miles wide. Also a part of Grenada are some of the Grenadines islets, the largest of which is Carriacou, 13 square miles in area.

HISTORY AND POLITICS

Discovered by Columbus in 1498, and named Concepción, Grenada was originally colonised by France and was ceded to Great Britain by the Treaty of Versailles in 1783. It became a Crown colony in 1877, an Associated State in 1967 and an independent nation within the Commonwealth on 7 February 1974.

The government was overthrown in 1979 by the New Jewel Movement and a People's Revolutionary Government was set up. In October 1983 disagreements within the PRG led to the death of Prime Minister Maurice Bishop, whose government was replaced by a Revolutionary Military Council. These events prompted the intervention of Caribbean and US forces. The Governor-General installed an advisory council to act as an interim government until a general election was held in December 1984. A phased withdrawal of US forces was completed by June 1985.

The general election held on 18 January 1999 was won by the New National Party led by Dr Keith Mitchell. They won all 15 seats in the House of Representatives.

POLITICAL SYSTEM

Queen Elizabeth II is head of state and is represented by a Governor-General. Legislative power is vested in a bicameral parliament consisting of an elected 15-member House of Representatives and a 13-member Senate appointed by the Governor-General.

Governor-General, HE Sir Daniel Williams, GCMG, QC, apptd 1996

CABINET *as at September 2000*

Prime Minister, National Security, and Information, Keith Mitchell
Agriculture, Lands, Forestry and Fisheries, Claris Charles
Communications, Works and Public Utilities, Gregory Bowen
Culture, Co-operatives, Housing and Social Services, Brian McQueen
Education, Augustine John
Finance, Trade, Industry and Planning, Anthony Boatswain
Foreign Affairs, Mark Isaac
Health and Environment, Clarise Modeste-Curwen
Labour, Attorney-General, Lawrence Joseph
Legal Affairs, Labour, Local Government, Carriacou and Petit Martinique Affairs, Elvin Nimrod
Ministers of State, Laurina Waldron (*Communications, Works and Public Utilities*); Michael Baptiste (*Co-operatives*); Joslyn Whiteman (*Information*)
Parliamentary Secretaries, Einstein Louison (*Agriculture, Forestry, Lands and Fisheries*); Eleuthan Noel (*Carriacou and Petit Martinique Affairs*); Richard McPhail (*Health and Environment*)
Tourism, Civil Aviation, Social Security and Women's Affairs, Brenda Hood
Youth, Sports, Community Development, Adrian Mitchell

GRENADA HIGH COMMISSION
1 Collingham Gardens, London SW5 0HW
Tel: 020-7373 7809
High Commissioner, HE Ruth Elizabeth Rouse, apptd 1999

BRITISH HIGH COMMISSION
14 Church Street, St George's
Tel: (00 1 473) 440 3536/440 3222
e-mail: bhcgrenada@caribsurf.com
High Commissioner, HE Gordon Baker, resident at Bridgetown, Barbados
Resident Acting High Commissioner, D. R. Miller

ECONOMY

The economy is principally agrarian, with cocoa, nutmegs and bananas the major crops. Fruit and vegetables are grown and livestock raised for domestic consumption. The fishing industry is being developed. Manufacturing consists of processing agricultural products and the production of textiles, concrete, aluminium and handicrafts. Tourism is the main foreign exchange earner. In 1996 there were 386,013 tourists.
GNP – US$313 million (1998); US$3,250 per capita (1998)
GDP – US$252 million (1996); US$2,738 per capita (1996)
ANNUAL AVERAGE GROWTH OF GDP – 3.0 per cent (1996)
INFLATION RATE – 1.2 per cent (1997)
TOTAL EXTERNAL DEBT – US$183 million (1998)

TRADE

In 1996 there was a trade deficit of US$123 million and a current account deficit of US$58 million. Imports totalled US$152 million and exports US$21 million.

Trade with UK	1998	1999
Imports from UK	£8,508,000	£7,232,000
Exports to UK	744,000	1,266,000

GUATEMALA
República de Guatemala

AREA – 42,042 sq. miles (108,889 sq. km). Neighbours: Mexico (north and west), El Salvador, Honduras and Belize (east)
POPULATION – 10,517,000 (1997 UN estimate): 56 per cent mestizo, 44 per cent Amerindian. The language is Spanish, but 40 per cent of the population speak an Indian language
CAPITAL – Guatemala City (population, 1,675,589, 1990 estimate)
MAJOR CITIES – Antigua (30,000); Mazatenango (21,000); ΨPuerto Barrios (23,000); Quezaltenango (100,000)
CURRENCY – Quetzal (Q) of 100 centavos
NATIONAL ANTHEM – Guatemala Feliz (Guatemala be praised)
NATIONAL DAY – 15 September
NATIONAL FLAG – Three vertical bands, blue, white, blue; coat of arms on white stripe
LIFE EXPECTANCY (years) – male 62.41; female 67.33
POPULATION GROWTH RATE – 1.9 per cent (1997)
POPULATION DENSITY – 97 per sq. km (1997)
URBAN POPULATION – 38.7 per cent (1995)
MILITARY EXPENDITURE – 1.2 per cent of GDP (1998)
MILITARY PERSONNEL – 38,400: Army 29,200, Navy 1,500, Air Force 700; Paramilitaries 7,000
CONSCRIPTION DURATION – 30 months (selective)
ILLITERACY RATE – 31.3 per cent
ENROLMENT (percentage of age group) – primary 72 per cent (1997); secondary 13 per cent (1980); tertiary 8.1 per cent (1995)

Guatemala is traversed from west to east by mountains containing volcanic summits rising to 13,000 feet above sea level; earthquakes are frequent. There are numerous rivers. The climate is hot and malarial near the coast, temperate in the higher regions.

HISTORY AND POLITICS

Guatemala was under Spanish rule from 1524 until gaining independence in 1821. It formed part of the Confederation of Central America from 1823 to 1839.

After a series of military coups, civilian rule was restored with the election of a Constituent Assembly in 1984 and the promulgation of a new constitution in 1985. In May 1993 President Serrano partially suspended the constitution and attempted to rule by decree but was effectively ousted by the army on 1 June. Ramiro de León Carpio was elected president by Congress to serve out Serrano's term to January 1996.

President de León continued attempts to curb political corruption and in November 1993 forced Congress and the Supreme Court to dissolve themselves and to agree to constitutional changes, including reducing the presidential term to four years, which were ratified by a referendum in January 1994. The legislative election to the National Congress on 7 November 1999 was won by the Guatemalan Republican Front (FRG) which obtained 63 seats; the National Advancement Party (PAN) won 37 seats. The presidential election on 26 December 1999 was won by Alfonso Portillo of the FRG.

INSURGENCY

Since 1960 the armed forces have been fighting insurgency by the left-wing, mainly Mayan Indian, guerrillas of the Guatemalan Revolutionary National Unity Movement (URNG). Some 200,000 have been killed in the fighting. Government–URNG negotiations began in 1991 and have continued since, leading to a reduction in fighting and agreements in 1993. In March 1994 a human rights accord was reached under which a 300-strong UN Observer Mission (MINUGUA) was established in November 1994 to supervise the implementation of government–URNG accords. An accord recognising the rights of the indigenous population was signed in March 1995, but in a referendum held on 16 May 1999, constitutional reforms which would have recognised the rights of the majority indigenous population and limited the powers of the military were rejected. Representatives of the four rebel groups comprising the URNG signed a peace treaty with the government in December 1996; an independent commission into the 36-year civil war, set up under the 1996 peace treaty, published a report on 25 February 1999 which concluded that the army had committed acts of genocide against the indigenous Mayan population.

POLITICAL SYSTEM

Executive power is vested in the president, who is directly elected for a single four-year term. He appoints the Cabinet. Legislative authority is vested in the National Congress, whose 113 members are directly elected for a four-year term.

The republic is divided into 22 departments.

HEAD OF STATE

President, Alfonso Portillo Cabrera, *elected* 26 December 1999, *sworn in* 14 January 2000
Vice-President, Juan Francisco Reyes López

GOVERNMENT *as at September 2000*

Agriculture, Livestock and Food, Roger Valenzuela
Communications, Transport and Public Works, Luis Rabbe
Culture and Sport, Otilia Lux de Coti
Defence, Col. Juan de Dios Estrada Velásquez

Economy, Eduardo Weymann
Education, Mario Torres
Energy and Mines, Raúl Archila
Foreign Affairs, Gabriel Orellana Rojas
Interior, Byron Barrientos
Labour and Social Security, Juan Francisco Alfaro
Public Finance, Manuel Maza Castellanos
Public Health and Social Welfare, Mario Bolaños

EMBASSY OF GUATEMALA

13 Fawcett Street, London SW10 9HN
Tel: 020-7351 3042
Ambassador Extraordinary and Plenipotentiary, vacant
Minister-Counsellor and Chargé d' Affaires, Dr M. A. Toledo

BRITISH EMBASSY

Avenida La Reforma 16–00, Zona 10, Edificio Torre
Internacional, Nivel 11, Guatemala City
Tel: (00 502) (2) 367 5425/6/7/8/9
Ambassador Extraordinary and Plenipotentiary, HE
Andrew Caie, apptd 1998

ECONOMY

Agriculture provides 25 per cent of GDP and employs nearly two thirds of the workforce. The principal export is coffee, other articles being manufactured goods, sugar, bananas and cardamom. The chief imports are petroleum, vehicles, machinery and foodstuffs.

The chief seaports are San José de Guatemala on the Pacific and Santo Tomás de Castilla and Puerto Barrios on the Atlantic side.

In 1998 there was a trade deficit of US$1,409 million and a current account deficit of US$1,039 million. Imports totalled US$4,651 million and exports US$2,582 million.
GNP – US$17,759 million (1998); US$1,640 per capita (1998)
GDP – US$15,805 million (1996); US$1,446 per capita (1996)
ANNUAL AVERAGE GROWTH OF GDP – 4.1 per cent (1997)
INFLATION RATE – 7.0 per cent (1998)
TOTAL EXTERNAL DEBT – US$4,565 million (1998)

Trade with UK	1998	1999
Imports from UK	£38,701,000	£34,145,000
Exports to UK	23,740,000	24,807,000

GUINEA
République de Guinée

AREA – 94,926 sq. miles (245,857 sq. km). Neighbours: Guinea-Bissau (east), Senegal and Mali (north), Côte d'Ivoire (west), Sierra Leone and Liberia (south)
POPULATION – 7,614,000 (1997 UN estimate); the official language is French; Fullah, Malinké and Soussou are indigenous languages
CAPITAL – ΨConakry (population, 763,000)
MAJOR CITIES – Kankan; Kindia; Labé; Mamou; N'Zérékoré; Siguiri
CURRENCY – Guinea franc of 100 centimes
NATIONAL ANTHEM – Liberté
NATIONAL DAY – 2 October (Anniversary of Proclamation of Independence)
NATIONAL FLAG – Three vertical stripes of red, yellow and green
LIFE EXPECTANCY (years) – male 44.00; female 45.00
POPULATION GROWTH RATE – 4.0 per cent (1997)
POPULATION DENSITY – 31 per sq. km (1997)
MILITARY EXPENDITURE – 1.8 per cent of GDP (1998)
MILITARY PERSONNEL – 12,300: Army 8,500, Navy 400, Air Force 800; Paramilitaries 2,600

CONSCRIPTION DURATION – Two years
ILLITERACY RATE – 58.9 per cent
ENROLMENT (percentage of age group) – primary
42 per cent (1997); secondary 9 per cent (1985);
tertiary 1 per cent (1996)

HISTORY AND POLITICS

Guinea was separated from Senegal in 1891 and administered by France as a separate colony. On 2 October 1958
Guinea became an independent republic.
M. Sékou Touré assumed office as head of the new
government, and was elected president in 1961. His death
in 1984 was followed by a military coup. Guinea was ruled
by a military government directed by a Military Committee for National Recovery (CMRN). A new constitution,
providing for the end of military rule, was approved by
referendum in 1990.
   In January 1991 the CMRN was dissolved and a mixed
civilian-military Transitional Committee for National
Recovery (CTRN) was established which appointed a new
government. Civil disturbances in 1991 caused the
government to introduce a full multiparty system in April
1992, since when 40 opposition parties have been
legalised. Legislative elections in June 1995 were won by
President Conté's Party of Unity and Progress (PUP),
which gained 71 of the 114 National Assembly seats. A
presidential election held on 14 December 1998 was
won by the incumbent President Conté with 54 per cent of
the vote. Legislative elections were due by June 2000 but
were postponed.

HEAD OF STATE

President, Maj.-Gen. Lansana Conté, *took power* 3 April
1984, *elected* 19 December 1993, *re-elected*
14 December 1998

COUNCIL OF MINISTERS *as at September 2000*

Prime Minister, Lamine Sidime
Agriculture and Animal Husbandry, Jean-Paul Sarr
Commerce, Industry and Small and Medium-sized Enterprises,
   Madikaba Camara
Communication, Alpha Ibrahima Mongo Diallo
Defence, Assifat Dorank Diasseny
Economic Affairs, Finance, Sheik Amadou Camara
Employment and Civil Service, Lamine Camara
Fishing and Aquaculture, Mocktar Moussa Sidibé
Foreign Affairs, Camara Hadja Mahawa Bangoura
Higher Education and Scientific Research, Eugène Camara
Justice, Keeper of the Seals, Abou Camara
Mines, Geology and Environment, Facinet Fofana
Pre-University Teaching and Civil Education,
   Germain Doualamou
Public Health, Mamadou Saliou Diallo
Public Works, Transport, Cellou Dalen Diallo
Secretary-General to the Government, El Hadj Ousmane
   Sanoko
Secretary-General to the President, El Hadj Fodé Bangoura
Social Affairs, Promotion of Women and Children,
   Mariame Aribot
Technical Education and Vocational Training, Almane
   Fodé Sylla
Territorial Administration and Decentralisation, Moussa
   Solana
Tourism, Hotels and Handicrafts, Kozo Zoumanigui
Urbanisation and Housing, Alpha Ousmane Diallo
Water Resources and Energy, Fassou Niancoye Fanny
Youth, Sports and Culture, Sylla Koumba Diakité

EMBASSY OF THE REPUBLIC OF GUINEA

51 rue de la Faisanderie, F-75016 Paris, France
Tel: (00 33) (1) 4704 8148
Ambassador Extraordinary and Plenipotentiary, HE
   Ibrahima Sylla, apptd 1998

BRITISH CONSULATE

BP 834 Conakry, Guinea
Tel: (00 224) 461 680/446 982/403 523
British Ambassador, HE David Snoxell, resident at Dakar,
   Senegal
Honarary Consul, V. A. Treitlein, MBE

ECONOMY

The principal products are bauxite, alumina, palm kernels,
millet, cassava, bananas, plantains and rubber. Deposits of
iron ore, gold, diamonds and uranium have been
discovered. Principal imports are cotton goods, petroleum
products, sugar, flour and salt; exports, bauxite, alumina,
iron ore, diamonds, coffee, bananas, palm kernels and
pineapples.
   In 1997 there was a trade surplus of US$118 million and
a current account deficit of US$91 million.
GNP – US$3,777 million (1998); US$530 per capita
   (1998)
GDP – US$3,963 million (1996); US$527 per capita
   (1996)
ANNUAL AVERAGE GROWTH OF GDP – 4.5 per cent
   (1996)
TOTAL EXTERNAL DEBT – US$3,546 million (1998)

Trade with UK	1998	1999
Imports from UK	£10,684,000	£16,923,000
Exports to UK	2,191,000	4,546,000

GUINEA–BISSAU
República da Guiné-Bissau

AREA – 13,948 sq. miles (36,125 sq. km). Neighbours:
   Senegal (north), Guinea (east and south)
POPULATION – 1,112,000 (1997 UN estimate). The
   main ethnic groups are the Balante, Malinké, Fulani,
   Mandjako and Pepel. The official language is
   Portuguese; most of the population speak
   Guinean Creole
CAPITAL – ΨBissau (population, 109,214, 1979)
CURRENCY – Franc CFA
NATIONAL ANTHEM – É patria amada (This is our beloved
country)
NATIONAL DAY – 24 September (Independence Day)
NATIONAL FLAG – Horizontal bands of yellow over
   green with vertical red band in the hoist charged with
   a black star
LIFE EXPECTANCY (years) – male 41.31; female 44.43
POPULATION GROWTH RATE – 2.0 per cent (1997)
POPULATION DENSITY – 31 per sq. km (1997)
MILITARY EXPENDITURE – 5.5 per cent of GDP (1998)
MILITARY PERSONNEL – 9,250: Army 6,800, Navy 350,
   Air Force 100; Paramilitaries 2,000
CONSCRIPTION DURATION – Selective conscription
ILLITERACY RATE – 63.2 per cent
ENROLMENT (percentage of age group) – primary
   46 per cent (1986); secondary 3 per cent (1980);
   tertiary 0.5 per cent (1988)

HISTORY AND POLITICS

Guinea-Bissau, formerly Portuguese Guinea, achieved
independence on 24 September 1974. Following a coup
led by Maj. (now Brig.-Gen.) Vieira in 1980, a Revolutionary Council was established. Under a new constitution
adopted in 1984, the Revolutionary Council became a
15-member Council of State and an Assembly of 150
members was set up. The ruling African Party for the
Independence of Guinea and Cape Verde (PAIGC)

introduced a multiparty system in January 1991. Ten opposition parties have been legalised since November 1991. Elections to a new 100-seat legislature were held in July 1994; the PAIGC won 64 seats. Brig.-Gen. Vieira won the second round of the presidential election in August 1994 with 52 per cent of the vote.

In June 1998, several hundred people were killed when fighting broke out in Bissau between troops loyal to President Vieira and supporters of the sacked army chief Ansumane Mane. Guinea and Senegal sent in troops to support Vieira, and a peace agreement was signed on 1 November, which promised legislative and presidential elections in March 1999. On 27 November, the National Assembly called on Vieira to resign, but he refused. A government of national unity was formed in February 1999 and Guinean and Senegalese troops withdrew in March in accordance with the peace agreement, but no elections took place. Fighting resumed in May 1999, and the government was overthrown on 7 May by rebels loyal to Gen. Mane, who appointed the Speaker of the National Assembly as acting president. Legislative elections held on 28 November 1999 resulted in the Social Renewal Party (PRS) gaining 38 seats in the 102-seat National Assembly. The PRS's ally, the Guinea-Bissau Resistance-Batafa Movement (RGB-Batafa), gained 28 seats. In presidential elections, the founder of the PRS, Kumba Yalla, was elected on 16 January 2000. He resigned his chairmanship of the PRS on 11 May 2000.

POLITICAL SYSTEM

A new constitution, which limited the tenure of the presidency to two terms, was adopted in July 1999. Under the constitution, the president is the head of government and appoints the Council of Ministers. There is a unicameral legislature, the Assembleia Nacional Popular (National People's Assembly), composed of 102 members elected by universal suffrage for a four-year term.

HEAD OF STATE

President, Chairman of the Council of State, C.-in-C. of the Armed Forces, Kumba Yalla, *elected* 16 January 2000, *took office* 17 February 2000

COUNCIL OF MINISTERS *as at September 2000*

Prime Minister, Caetano N'Tchama
Deputy Prime Minister, Economic and Social Reconstruction, Faustino Fadut Imbali
Administration and Labour, Dauda Sow
Agriculture and Forestry, Alamara Niasse
Defence and Freedom Fighters, Fernando Correia
Economy, Helder Vaz Lopez
Education, Science and Technology, João José Silva Monteiro
Finance, Purna Bia
Foreign Affairs and International Co-operation, Yaia Djallo
Health, Antonio Bamba
Interior, Antonio Artur Sanha
Justice, Antonieta Roa Gomes
Natural Resources and the Environment, Francisco José Ferando Jr
Social Infrastructure, Carlito Barai
War Veterans, Solidarity, Integration of Former Fighters and the Fight against Poverty, Iancuba Indjai

EMBASSY OF THE REPUBLIC OF GUINEA-BISSAU
94 rue St Lazare, Paris F-75009, France
Tel: (00 33) (1) 4526 1851
Chargé d' Affaires, Maria Filomena Araujo Vieira

HONORARY CONSULATE
Flat 5, 8 Palace Gate, London W8 5NF
Tel: 020-7589 5253
Honorary Consul, Raja Makarem

BRITISH CONSULATE
Mavegro Int., CP100, Bissau

British Ambassador, HE David Snoxell, resident at Dakar, Senegal

ECONOMY

Guinea-Bissau produces rice, coconuts, groundnuts and plantains. Cattle are raised, and there are bauxite and phosphate deposits. In May 1997 Guinea-Bissau joined the French Franc Zone, and the CFA Franc replaced the peso as currency.

In 1995 there was a trade deficit of US$35 million and a current account deficit of US$41 million. In 1996 imports totalled US$87 million and exports US$27 million.

GNP – US$184 million (1998); US$160 per capita (1998)
GDP – US$188 million (1996); US$172 per capita (1996)
ANNUAL AVERAGE GROWTH OF GDP – 5.0 per cent (1996)
INFLATION RATE – 49.1 per cent (1997)
TOTAL EXTERNAL DEBT – US$964 million (1998)

Trade with UK	1998	1999
Imports from UK	£722,000	£1,830,000
Exports to UK	17,000	—

GUYANA
The Co-operative Republic of Guyana

AREA – 83,000 sq. miles (214,969 sq. km). Neighbours: Venezuela (west), Brazil (west and south), Suriname (east)
POPULATION – 847,000 (1997 UN estimate): 51 per cent East Indian (mainly rural), 30 per cent African (mainly urban), Amerindians, Europeans, Chinese and people of mixed descent; 50 per cent Christian, 35 per cent Hindu, less than 10 per cent Muslim. Guyana is the only English-speaking country in South America
CAPITAL – ΨGeorgetown (population, 250,000)
MAJOR TOWNS – Corriverton (24,000); Linden (35,000); ΨNew Amsterdam (25,000)
CURRENCY – Guyana dollar (G$) of 100 cents
NATIONAL ANTHEM – Dear Land of Guyana
NATIONAL DAYS – 26 May (Independence Day); 23 February (Republic Day)
NATIONAL FLAG – Green with a yellow, white-bordered triangle based on the hoist and surmounted by a red, black-bordered triangle
LIFE EXPECTANCY (years) – male 59.80; female 66.41
POPULATION GROWTH RATE – 0.9 per cent (1997)
POPULATION DENSITY – 4 per sq. km (1997)
MILITARY EXPENDITURE – 1.0 per cent of GDP (1998)
MILITARY PERSONNEL – 1,600: Army 1,400, Navy 100, Air Force 100

HISTORY AND POLITICS

Guyana (formerly British Guiana) became independent on 26 May 1966, with a Governor-General appointed by Queen Elizabeth II. It became a republic on 23 February 1970.

Elections were held in October 1992 after voter registration lists and electoral machinery had finally been established after many years. In the presidential election Dr Cheddi Jagan defeated the incumbent Desmond Hoyte and in the legislative election Jagan's People's Progressive Party (PPP) defeated the People's National Congress (PNC) which had governed since independence. Jagan died in March 1997 and was replaced by former Prime Minister Samuel Hinds. In the December 1997 election, Janet Jagan (who had previously served as prime minister and was the widow of the late president) was elected president and the PPP returned to power. The PNC claimed the result was fixed and their demonstrations against the government became violent; in January 1998 an agreement was reached between the PNC and the PPP whereby the constitution would be reviewed within 18 months and new elections would be held within three years rather than five. President Janet Jagan resigned on 11 August 1999 on the grounds of ill health and was succeeded by Bharrat Jagdeo, who had previously been the vice-president.

POLITICAL SYSTEM

The 1980 constitution provides for an executive president who serves a five-year term, and a National Assembly of 65 members, of which 53 are elected nationally by proportional representation and 12 are regional representatives.

HEAD OF STATE

President, Bharrat Jagdeo
Vice-president, vacant

CABINET as at September 2000
Prime Minister, Public Works, Sam Hinds
Agriculture and Parliamentary Affairs, Reepu
  Daman Persaud
Amerindian Affairs, Vibert de Souza
Attorney-General, Legal Affairs, Charles Ramson
Education, Ramnauth Bisnauth
Finance, Sasenarine Kowlessar
Foreign Affairs, Clement Rohee
Forestry, Fisheries, Crops and Livestock, Satyadeow Sawh
Home Affairs, Ronald Gajraj
Housing and Water, Shaik Baksh
Human Services, Social Security, Indranie Chandarpal
Information, Moses Nagamootoo
Labour, Health, Henry Jeffrey
Local Government, Harripersaud Nokta; Clinton
  Collymore
Presidential Secretariat, Roger Luncheon
Public Service, George Fung-on
Trade, Tourism and Industry, Geoffrey da Silva
Transport and Hydraulics, Carl Anthony Xavier
Youth, Sport and Culture, Gail Teixeira

GUYANA HIGH COMMISSION

3 Palace Court, Bayswater Road, London W2 4LP
Tel: 020-7229 7684/5/6/7/8
High Commissioner, HE Laleshwar Singh, apptd 1993

BRITISH HIGH COMMISSION

44 Main Street (PO Box 10849), Georgetown
Tel: (00 592) (2) 65881/2/3/4
High Commissioner, HE Edward Glover, MVO, apptd 1998

ECONOMY

Agriculture is the principal economic activity, accounting for 39 per cent of GDP and employing 19 per cent of the workforce. Main export items include Demerara sugar, gold, rice and bauxite. Diamonds are also mined. There is some cattle ranching in the savanna country, and oil deposits have been found there. Industry is fairly small-scale. Much emphasis is now being placed on eco-tourism. Foreign aid covers much of the government deficit.
  In 1995 there was a trade deficit of US$41 million and a current account deficit of US$135 million. In 1997 exports totalled US$596 million and imports US$630 million.
GNP – US$661 million (1998); US$780 per capita (1998)
GDP – US$687 million (1996); US$820 per capita (1996)
ANNUAL AVERAGE GROWTH OF GDP – 7.9 per cent
  (1996)
INFLATION RATE – 4.6 per cent (1998)
TOTAL EXTERNAL DEBT – US$1,653 million (1998)

Trade with UK	1998	1999
Imports from UK	£23,282,000	£21,540,000
Exports to UK	71,895,000	74,136,000

COMMUNICATIONS

Georgetown and New Amsterdam are the principal ports, though bauxite ships also sail to Linden, on the Demerara, and Everton, on the Berbice. The few roads are confined mainly to the coastal areas. Paved roads total about 571 km out of a total network of 7,820 km. Air transport is the easiest form of communication between the coast and the interior. The state-owned national airline is called Guyana Airways.
  There is a state-owned radio broadcasting station which operates two channels and a fledgling television service.

EDUCATION

Education is compulsory between the ages of five and 14; nursery, primary and secondary schooling are free. The government assumed total control of the education system in 1976 and made education free. The government instituted fees for study at the University of Guyana in 1994.
  There are several technical and vocational institutions, as well as some 30 adult education schools. There are also a number of technical and vocational institutions not under the aegis of the Ministry of Education.
ILLITERACY RATE – 1.5 per cent
ENROLMENT (percentage of age group) – primary
  87 per cent (1995); secondary 66 per cent (1995);
  tertiary 11 per cent (1996)

HAITI
République d'Haiti

AREA – 10,714 sq. miles (27,750 sq. km). Neighbour:
  Dominican Republic (east)
POPULATION – 7,492,000 (1997 UN estimate) of which
  90 per cent are black and 10 per cent mulatto (mixed
  race). Both French and Creole are regarded as official
  languages. French is the language of government and
  the press but it is only spoken by the educated mulatto
  minority. The usual language is Creole
CAPITAL – ΨPort-au-Prince (population, 884,472, 1996
  estimate)
MAJOR CITIES – ΨCap Haitien (102,233); Carrefour
  (290,204); Delmas (240,429), 1996 UN estimates
CURRENCY – Gourde of 100 centimes
NATIONAL ANTHEM – La Dessalinienne
NATIONAL DAY – 1 January
NATIONAL FLAG – Horizontally blue over red
LIFE EXPECTANCY (years) – male 52.69; female 56.07
POPULATION GROWTH RATE – 2.1 per cent (1997)
POPULATION DENSITY – 270 per sq. km (1997)
URBAN POPULATION – 33.8 per cent (1997)
MILITARY EXPENDITURE – 2.4 per cent of GDP (1998)
ILLITERACY RATE – 51.4 per cent
ENROLMENT (percentage of age group) – primary 22
  per cent (1990); tertiary 1.1 per cent (1985)

The Republic of Haiti occupies the western third of the Caribbean island of Hispaniola. The climate is tropical with high humidity and an almost constant temperature.

HISTORY AND POLITICS

Haiti was a French slave colony under the name of Saint-Domingue from 1697 until 1791, when French rule was overthrown in a revolt led by Toussaint L'Ouverture. French rule was restored by Napoleon in 1802 but in 1803 French forces surrendered to a British naval blockade and on 1 January 1804 the colony was declared independent as Haiti by Jean Jacques Dessalines. Dessalines became Emperor of Haiti but was assassinated in 1806.

Haiti was under US military occupation from 1915 to 1934. Dr François 'Papa Doc' Duvalier was elected in 1957 and became life president in 1964. He was succeeded in 1971 by his son Jean-Claude 'Baby Doc' Duvalier who fled to France in 1986 in the face of sustained popular unrest. Five years of military government followed until Father Jean-Bertrand Aristide, leader of the National Front for Change and Democracy, won a free presidential election in 1990.

Aristide fled to the USA following a military coup in September 1991. The UN and OAS imposed an oil and arms embargo and froze the military élite's foreign assets, forcing the regime to negotiate the Governor's Island Agreement in July 1993, which provided for Aristide's return. In September 1993, the military reneged on the agreement and the UN imposed a naval blockade and a total economic, trade and travel ban. In September 1994, an agreement was reached on President Aristide's return and the flight of the military junta members abroad. Sanctions were lifted and Aristide returned on 15 October to appoint a new government. Forces of the UN Mission in Haiti (UNMIH) took over responsibility for internal security and retraining Army personnel on 31 March 1995. At the expiration of the UNMIH peacekeeping mandate in November 1997, the UN Security Council agreed to establish a civilian police mission (MIPONUH), which was replaced by an International Civilian Support Mission (MICAH) in March 2000.

The presidential election in December 1995 was won by Lavalas candidate René Préval. Following the resignation of Prime Minister Rosny Smarth in October 1997, the President and the legislature were unable to agree on a successor and Haiti had no prime minister until 12 January 1999, when the appointment of Jacques Édouard Alexis was confirmed by a presidential decree, after the Senate but not the Chamber of Deputies had approved the appointment. Elections to the 27-member Senate and 83-member Chamber of Deputies on 21 May and 9 July 2000 were won by the pro-Aristide Lavalas party, although there was much international criticism of the manner in which they had been conducted.

POLITICAL SYSTEM

The head of state is a president, directly elected for a five-year term that may not be renewed immediately. The National Assembly is the bicameral legislature; the lower house, the Chamber of Deputies, has 83 members directly elected for four years. The upper house or Senate has 27 members elected for six years; one third of the senators are elected every two years. The president appoints the prime minister, who must be approved by the National Assembly. The prime minister chooses the Cabinet.

HEAD OF STATE

President, René Préval, sworn in 7 February 1996

CABINET as at September 2000
Prime Minister, Interior, Territorial Communities, Jacques Édouard Alexis
Agriculture, Natural Resources and Rural Development, François Severin
Commerce and Industry, Gerald Germain
Culture, Jean-Robert Vaval
Economy and Finance, Fred Joseph
Environment, Yves Cadet
Foreign Affairs, Emmanuel Fritz Longchamp
Haitians Living Abroad, Jean Geneus
Justice and Public Security, Camille Leblanc
National Education, Youth and Sport, Paul Antoine Bien-Aimé
Planning and External Co-operation, Antony Dessources
Public Health, Michaelle Amede Gedeon

Public Works, Transport and Communications, Serge Raphael
Social Affairs, Mathilde Flambert
Women's Affairs and Rights, Nonie Mathieu

BRITISH AMBASSADOR, HE David Ward, resident at Santo Domingo, Dominican Republic
BRITISH CONSULATE, Hotel Montana (PO Box 1302), Port-au-Prince
Tel: (00 509) 257 3969
Vice-Consul, M. Guercy, MBE

ECONOMY

Light industrial products account for over 80 per cent of total exports. Coffee is the second largest export earner. Corn, sorghum and rice are also grown. Increased production of tropical fruits and vegetables is being encouraged.

Leather goods, textiles, electronic components and sports equipment are manufactured, using imported raw materials, for re-export. Principal imports are foodstuffs, machinery and transport equipment, and fuels.

In 1996 Haiti had a trade deficit of US$416 million and a current account deficit of US$138 million. In 1998 imports totalled US$797 million and exports US$175 million.

GNP – US$3,163 million (1998); US$410 per capita (1998)
GDP – US$2,772 million (1996); US$382 per capita (1996)
ANNUAL AVERAGE GROWTH OF GDP – 1.1 per cent (1997)
INFLATION RATE – 10.6 per cent (1998)
TOTAL EXTERNAL DEBT – US$1,048 million (1998)

Trade with UK	1998	1999
Imports from UK	£8,254,000	£7,003,000
Exports to UK	979,000	591,000

COMMUNICATIONS

There are more than 4,000 km of roads. Air services are maintained between the capital and the principal provincial towns and to the USA and Caribbean and South American countries. The principal towns and villages are connected by telephone and/or telegraph. There are several commercial radio stations and two television stations at Port-au-Prince.

HOLY SEE, see VATICAN CITY STATE

HONDURAS
República de Honduras

AREA – 43,277 sq. miles (112,088 sq. km). Neighbours: Guatemala (north-west), El Salvador (south-west), Nicaragua (south)
POPULATION – 6,338,000 (1997 UN estimate) of mixed Spanish and Indian blood. The Garifunas in the north are of West Indian origin. The language is Spanish, although English is the first language of many in the islands and on the north coast
CAPITAL – Tegucigalpa (population, 670,100, 1991 estimate)
MAJOR CITIES – Choluteca (63,200); ΨLa Ceiba (77,100); ΨPuerto Cortés (32,500); San Pedro Sula (325,900); ΨTela (24,000)
CURRENCY – Lempira of 100 centavos
NATIONAL ANTHEM – Tu Bandera Es Un Lampo De Cielo (Your flag is a heavenly light)
NATIONAL DAY – 15 September
NATIONAL FLAG – Three horizontal bands, blue, white, blue (with five blue stars on white band)
LIFE EXPECTANCY (years) – male 65.43; female 70.06

POPULATION GROWTH RATE – 3.1 per cent (1997)
POPULATION DENSITY – 57 per sq. km (1997)
URBAN POPULATION – 49.1 per cent (1997)
MILITARY EXPENDITURE – 2.0 per cent of GDP (1998)
MILITARY PERSONNEL – 14,300: Army 5,500, Navy 1,000,
Air Force 1,800, Paramilitaries 6,000

The country is mountainous, being traversed by the
Cordilleras, with peaks rising to 1,500 and 2,400 metres
above sea level. Rainfall is seasonal, May to October being
wet and November to April dry.

HISTORY AND POLITICS

Discovered and settled by the Spanish in the 16th century,
Honduras formed part of the Spanish American dominions until 1821 when independence was proclaimed.
Under military government from 1972, Honduras returned to civilian rule in 1981 with an executive
presidency, a 128-seat unicameral Congress, and a multiparty system. The most recent legislative elections were
held on 30 November 1997 and won by the Liberal Party.
In October 1997, Congress approved a constitutional
amendment reducing the legislature to 80 members. The
amendment must also be ratified by the current session of
Congress before it becomes law.
The country is divided into 18 departments.

HEAD OF STATE

President of the Republic, Carlos Roberto Flores (Liberal),
elected 30 November 1997

CABINET *as at September 2000*

Agriculture and Livestock, Guillermo Alvarado
Culture, Arts and Sports, Herman Allan Padgett
Director of the National Agrarian Institute, Anibal
Delgado Fiallos
Education, Ramón Calix Figueroa
Finance, Gabriela Nuñez López
Foreign Affairs, Roberto Flores Bermúdez
Government and Justice, Enrique Flores Valeriano
Health, Plutarco Castellanos
Industry, Commerce, Oscar Kafati
Labour and Social Security, Rosa America de Galo
Ministers Without Portfolio, Jorge Arturo Reina; Nahum
Valladares; Roberto Leiva
National Defence and Public Security, Edgardo Dumas
Rodríguez
Natural Resources and Environment, Xiomara Gómez
Presidential Office, Gustavo Alfaro
Public Works, Transport and Housing, Tomás Lozano Reyes
Security, Elizabeth Chiuz Sierra
Social Investment Fund, Manuel Zelaya Rosales
Technical and International Co-operation Secretariat,
Moises Starkman
Tourism, Norman García

EMBASSY OF HONDURAS
115 Gloucester Place, London W1H 3PJ
Tel: 020-7486 4880
Ambassador Extraordinary and Plenipotentiary, HE
Hernán Antonio Bermúdez-Aguilar, apptd 1999

BRITISH EMBASSY
Edificio Palmira, 3er Piso, Colonia Palmira, Apartado
Postal 290, Tegucigalpa
Tel: (00 504) 232 0612/18
Ambassador Extraordinary and Plenipotentiary, HE David
Osborne, apptd 1998

BRITISH CONSULATE – San Pedro Sula

ECONOMY

Three-quarters of the country is covered by pine forests.
Agriculture and cattle raising is mainly confined to the
fertile coastal plain on the Caribbean and the extensive

valleys in the Comayagua and Olancho regions of the
interior. The Mosquitia tropical forest covers the area
from the coast to the border with Nicaragua and provides
valuable reserves of timber. Lead, zinc and silver are mined
on a small scale.
The chief exports are coffee, bananas, frozen meat,
shrimps, lobsters and timber, the most important woods
being pine, mahogany and cedar. The main imports are
machinery and electrical equipment, industrial chemicals
and lubricants.
In October 1998 Hurricane Mitch devastated
Honduras, killing an estimated 6,500 people and wrecking
Tegucigalpa. The cost of repairing the damage was
estimated at US$4 billion.
In 1997 Honduras had a trade deficit of US$294 million
and a current account deficit of US$272 million. In 1998
imports totalled US$2,500 million and exports US$1,533
million.
GNP – US$4,564 million (1998); US$740 per capita
(1998)
GDP – US$4,064 million (1996); US$699 per capita
(1996)
ANNUAL AVERAGE GROWTH OF GDP – 4.5 per cent (1997)
INFLATION RATE – 13.7 per cent (1998)
UNEMPLOYMENT – 3.9 per cent (1998)
TOTAL EXTERNAL DEBT – US$5,002 million (1998)

Trade with UK	1998	1999
Imports from UK	£18,074,000	£10,043,000
Exports to UK	33,785,000	27,214,000

COMMUNICATIONS

There are about 595 km of railway in operation, chiefly to
serve the banana plantations and the Caribbean ports.
There are 15,100 km of roads, of which 3,050 km are
paved. There are over 80 smaller airstrips and four international airports, Tegucigalpa, San Pedro Sula, La Ceiba
and Roatún (Bay Island).
The chief ports are Puerto Cortés, Tela and Puerto
Castilla on the north coast, through which passes the bulk
of the trade with the USA and Europe. Puerto Castilla is
being developed as a deep-water container port, and San
Lorenzo is also experiencing rapid growth.

EDUCATION

Primary and secondary education is free, primary education being compulsory from the age of seven to 12, and the
government has launched a campaign to eradicate
illiteracy.
ILLITERACY RATE – 27.8 per cent
ENROLMENT (percentage of age group) – primary
90 per cent (1993); secondary 21 per cent (1991);
tertiary 10.0 per cent (1994)

HONG KONG

AREA – 415 sq. miles (1,075 sq. km)
POPULATION – 6,687,200 (1998)
CURRENCY – Hong Kong dollar (HK$) of 100 cents
FLAG – Red, with a white bauhinia flower of five petals each
containing a red star
LIFE EXPECTANCY (years) – male 76.34; female 81.82
POPULATION GROWTH RATE – 1.9 per cent (1997)
POPULATION DENSITY – 6,048 per sq. km (1997)
URBAN POPULATION – 93.1 per cent (1986)

Hong Kong, consisting of more than 230 islands and of a
portion of the mainland (Kowloon and the New Territories) on the south-east coast of China, is situated at the
eastern side of the mouth of the Pearl River. Hong Kong
Island is about 11 miles (18 km) long and from two to five
miles (three to eight km) broad. It is separated from the
mainland by a narrow strait.

The climate is sub-tropical, tending towards the temperate for nearly half the year. The mean monthly temperature ranges from 16°C to 29°C. The average annual rainfall is 2,214 mm, of which nearly 80 per cent falls between May and September. Tropical cyclones occur between May and November, causing high winds and heavy rain.

HISTORY AND POLITICS

Hong Kong Island was first occupied by Great Britain in 1841 and formally ceded by the Treaty of Nanking in 1842. Kowloon was acquired by the Beijing Convention of 1860 and the New Territories, consisting of a peninsula in the southern part of the Guangdong province together with adjacent islands, by a 99-year lease signed on 9 June 1898.

On 19 December 1984 the UK and China signed a Joint Declaration in which it was agreed that China would resume sovereignty over Hong Kong on 1 July 1997. In the run-up to the 1997 handover, the Chinese government's insistence on a greater say in the running of the colony and Governor Patten's plan for an extension of democracy prompted acrimonious disputes. The Chinese government refused to accept the reforms and replaced the Legislative Council.

Hong Kong became, with effect from 1 July 1997, a Special Administrative Region (SAR) of the People's Republic of China.

The Joint Declaration which took effect in May 1985 guarantees: the free movement of goods and capital; the retention of Hong Kong's free port status, separate customs territory and freely convertible currency; the protection of property rights and foreign investment; the right of free movement to and from Hong Kong; Hong Kong's autonomy in the conduct of its external commercial relations and its own monetary and financial policies; and judicial independence. Hong Kong's constitution is the Basic Law which was passed by China's National People's Congress in 1990 and guarantees that the SAR's social and economic systems will remain unchanged for 50 years.

POLITICAL SYSTEM

Hong Kong is administered by the Hong Kong government, headed by the Chief Executive, who is aided by an Executive Council and a Legislative Council. The Executive Council consists of three ex-officio members (the Chief Secretary, the Financial Secretary and the Attorney-General) together with ten other members.

The Legislative Council consists of 60 members. Both the Chief Executive and the Legislative Council were elected by a 400-strong committee which in turn was chosen by a 150-member Preparatory Committee, headed by the Chinese foreign minister, from a shortlist drawn up by China. The President of the Legislative Council is elected by the members. Legislative elections in May 1998 used a proportional representation system in five geographical constituencies, each with three to five seats. Thirty members were elected in functional constituencies and ten more from a committee. A legislative election is due to take place on 10 September 2000, in which 24 members will be returned by five geographical constituencies, 30 members by 28 functional constituencies and six members by the election committee.

The Urban Council provides services relating to public health and sanitation, culture and recreation in the urban area. A Regional Council was set up in 1986 to provide similar services in the New Territories. There are also 18 district boards (nine in the urban areas and nine in the New Territories) which are statutory bodies that provide a forum for public consultation and participation in the administration of the districts.

Chief Executive, Tung Chee-hwa, *sworn in* 1 July 1997

EXECUTIVE COUNCIL *as at July 2000*

Non-official Members, Leung Chun-ying (*convenor*); Dr Raymond Ch'ien; Chung Shui-ming; Nellie Fong Wong; Charles Lee; Antony Leung; Tam Yiu-chung; Henry Tang; Rosanna Wong; Yang Ti-liang
Ex-officio Members, Anson Chan; Donald Tsang; Elsie Leung

GOVERNMENT SECRETARIAT *as at February 2000*

Administrative Secretary, Anson Chan
Financial Secretary, Donald Tsang
Justice, Elsie Leung
Civil Service, Joseph Wong
Constitutional Affairs, Michael Suen
Corruption, Li Nian
Economic Services, Sandra Lee
Education and Manpower, Fanny Law
Financial Services, Stephen Ip
Health and Welfare, Yong Yong-qiang
Home Affairs, Lam Woon-kwong
Housing, Dominic Wong
Information, Technology and Broadcasting, Carrie Yau
Planning, Environment and Lands, Gordon Siu
Security, Regina Ip
Trade and Industry, Chau Tak-hay
Transport, Nicholas Ng
Treasury, Denise Yue
Works, Li Cheng-shi
President of the Legislative Council, Rita Fan

CONSUL-GENERAL, Sir Andrew Burns, KCMG, 1 Supreme Court Road, Central, (PO Box 528), Hong Kong. Tel: (00 852) 2901 3000
BRITISH COUNCIL DIRECTOR, D. Lauder, 3 Supreme Court Road, Admiralty, Hong Kong; e-mail: bc.hongkong@britcoun.org.hk
HONG KONG ECONOMIC AND TRADE OFFICE, 6 Grafton Street, London W1X 3LB. Tel: 020-7499 9821.
Commissioner, Sandra Lee, apptd 1999

ECONOMY

The main economic sector is the services industry, especially financial services. It employed 85 per cent of the workforce and contributed 84.7 per cent of GDP in 1998. Principal exports are clothing, electrical machinery and apparatus, and textiles.

Diversification in terms of products and markets continues to be the main feature of recent industrial development, as are industrial partnerships with overseas companies. The economy is based on export rather than the domestic market. Tourism is very important to the economy; 10.7 million people visited Hong Kong in 1999.

In October 1997, the financial crisis in south-east Asia reached Hong Kong. The Hong Kong Monetary Authority used its foreign exchange reserves to fend off speculators and preserve the Hong Kong currency's peg to the US dollar, which stabilised the currency. GDP declined throughout 1998, the result of falling government and consumer spending, property prices and exports, but achieved modest growth in 1999, although unemployment rose to 6.2 per cent.

GNP – US$158,238 million (1998); US$23,660 per capita (1998)
GDP – US$154,170 million (1996); US$24,902 per capita (1996)
ANNUAL AVERAGE GROWTH OF GDP – 5.0 per cent (1996)
INFLATION RATE – 2.8 per cent (1998)

TRADE

In 1998 imports totalled US$184,503 million and exports US$173,990 million. Hong Kong's principal customers for its domestic products, in order of value of trade, were China, USA, Japan and Germany. China was its principal supplier. About 40 per cent of China's foreign trade passes through Hong Kong.

Trade with UK	1998	1999
Imports from UK	£2,699,855,000	£2,319,999,000
Exports to UK	4,614,388,000	5,121,330,000

COMMUNICATIONS

Hong Kong has one of the world's finest natural harbours, and it is the busiest container port in the world, with eight terminals, as well as large modern cargo and liner terminals. Dockyard facilities include eight floating dry-docks, the largest being capable of docking vessels up to 150,000 tonnes deadweight. A new 17-berth container port will open in stages between 1997 and 2003.

An international airport built on reclaimed land at Chek Lap Kok opened in July 1998. When fully operational, it will be capable of handling 35 million passengers and 1.5 million tonnes of cargo annually.

EDUCATION

Free education for children up to the age of 15 is compulsory. Post-secondary education is provided by six universities and one college. The Open Learning Institute of Hong Kong provides university education. There are also seven technical institutes and the Hong Kong Institute of Education.

ILLITERACY RATE – 6.6 per cent
ENROLMENT (percentage of age group) – primary
    90 per cent (1995); secondary 69 per cent (1995);
    tertiary 21.9 per cent (1993)

HUNGARY
Magyar Köztársaság

AREA – 35,920 sq. miles (93,032 sq. km). Neighbours: Slovakia (north), Ukraine and Romania (east), the rump Yugoslav Federal state and Croatia (south), Slovenia and Austria (west)
POPULATION – 10,153,000 (1997 UN estimate). There are minorities of Romanies (4 per cent), ethnic Germans (3 per cent), Serbs (2 per cent), Romanians (1 per cent) and Slovaks (1 per cent). About two-thirds of the population are Roman Catholic and the remainder mostly Calvinist. The language is Hungarian (Magyar)
CAPITAL – Budapest (population, 2,002,121, 1996 estimate)
MAJOR CITIES – Debrecen (209,296); Miskolc (178,975); Pécs (161,617); Szeged (166,663), 1996 UN estimates
CURRENCY – Forint of 100 fillér
NATIONAL ANTHEM – Isten Aldd Meg A Magyart (God Bless the Hungarians)
NATIONAL DAYS – 15 March, 20 August, 23 October
NATIONAL FLAG – Red, white, green (horizontally)
LIFE EXPECTANCY (years) – male 66.06; female 74.70
POPULATION GROWTH RATE – –0.3 per cent (1997)
POPULATION DENSITY – 109 per sq. km (1997)
URBAN POPULATION – 63.2 per cent (1996)

HISTORY AND POLITICS

The Hungarians settled the Danube basin in 896 AD and in 1000, King Istvan (Stephen) adopted Roman Catholicism and received a crown from the Pope. The Turks invaded Hungary in 1526; the Austrians finally succeeded in expelling them in 1699. Following nationalist unrest, the *Ausgleich* (compromise) of 1867 created the Dual Monarchy of Austria-Hungary, giving Hungary internal autonomy. The defeat of Austria-Hungary in the First World War led to the declaration of Hungarian independence in November 1918.

Hungary joined the Anti-Comintern Pact in February 1939 and entered the Second World War on the side of Germany in 1941. On 20 January 1945 a Hungarian provisional government of liberation signed an armistice under the terms of which the frontiers of Hungary were withdrawn to the 1937 limits.

After the liberation, a coalition of parties carried out land reform and nationalisation. By 1949 the Communists had succeeded in gaining a monopoly of power and by 1952 practically the entire economy had been 'socialised'.

Divisions within the Communist Party and popular demand for free elections and Soviet troop withdrawals grew. An uprising on 23 October 1956 was quelled by Soviet forces the following morning. But a reformist all-party coalition government under Imre Nagy was formed which declared Hungary's withdrawal from the Warsaw pact. This government was suppressed by a renewed attack by Soviet forces on Budapest on 4 November and a new Communist government under János Kádár was announced the same day.

From 1968 the government gradually introduced economic reforms and some political liberalisation. Kádár was forced to resign in May 1989. In October 1989 the National Assembly (*Országgyülés*) approved an amended constitution which described Hungary as an independent, democratic state. The 386-seat National Assembly is elected on a mixed first past the post and proportional representation basis with a 5 per cent threshold for representation. The first free multiparty elections took place in March and April 1990 and were won by the (conservative) Hungarian Democratic Forum.

In the legislative elections in May 1998, no party won an overall majority. The Federation of Young Democrats-Hungarian Civic Party (Fidesz-MPP) won the largest number of seats and its leader, Viktor Orbán, was asked by President Göncz to form a coalition government. The composition of the National Assembly in June 1998 was: Fidesz-MPP 147, Hungarian Socialist Party (HSP) 134, Independent Smallholders Party (FKGP) 48, Alliance of Free Democrats (AFD) 24, Hungarian Democratic Forum (MDF) 18, Hungarian Justice and Life Party 14, others 1. On 6 June 2000, Ferenc Madl, an independent candidate, was elected as president by parliament.

HEAD OF STATE
President, Ferenc Madl, *elected* 6 June 2000, *sworn in* 4 August 2000

CABINET *as at September 2000*

Prime Minister, Telecommunications, Viktor Orbán (F)
Agriculture and Regional Development, József Torgyán (FKGP)
Defence, János Szabó (FKGP)
Economic Affairs, György Matolcsi (F)
Education, Zoltán Pokorni (F)
Environmental Protection, Ferenc Ligetvári (FKGP)
Finance, Zsigmond Járai (F)
Foreign Affairs, János Martonyi (F)
Health, Árpád Gógl (F)
Home Affairs, Sándor Pintér (F)
Justice, Ibolya Dávid (MDF)
National Cultural Heritage, Zoltán Rockenbauer (F)
Social and Family Affairs, Péter Harrach (F)
Transport, and Water Management, László Nogradi (F)
Without Portfolio, Ervin Demeter (F) (*Civilian Intelligence Services*); Imre Boros (FKGP) (*Relations with the EU*); István Stumpf (F) (*Prime Minister's Office, Privatisation*)
Youth and Sports, Tamás Deutsch (F)

F Fidesz-MPP; FKGP Independent Smallholders Party; MDF Hungarian Democratic Forum

EMBASSY OF THE REPUBLIC OF HUNGARY
35 Eaton Place, London SW1X 8BY
Tel: 020-7235 5218
Ambassador Extraordinary and Plenipotentiary, HE Gábor
Szentiványi, apptd 1997
Minister Plenipotentiary, Sándor Juhász
Counsellor and Consul-General, Dr László Takács
Commercial Counsellor, András Hirschler
Defence and Military Attaché, Col. István Lakatos

BRITISH EMBASSY
Harmincad Utca 6, H-1051 Budapest
Tel: (00 36) (1) 266-2888
E-mail: info@britemb.hu
Ambassador Extraordinary and Plenipotentiary, HE Nigel
Thorpe, CVO, RCDS, apptd 1998
Counsellor and Deputy Head of Mission, G. B. Reid
Defence Attaché, Col. A. T. B. Kimber
First Secretary (Commercial), S. C. Martin
First Secretary (Management) and Consul, B. Halliwell, MBE

BRITISH COUNCIL DIRECTOR, P. Dick, OBE, Benczúr Utca
26, H-1068 Budapest; e-mail: hungary@britcoun.hu.
Resource centres in Debrecen, Miskolc, Pécs,
Szombathely and Veszprém

DEFENCE

The Army has 807 main battle tanks, 572 armoured
infantry fighting vehicles and 786 armoured personnel
carriers. The Air Force has 136 combat aircraft and 86
attack helicopters. Hungary became a member of NATO
in March 1999.
MILITARY EXPENDITURE – 1.4 per cent of GDP (1998)
MILITARY PERSONNEL – 49,29: Army 23,500, Army
Maritime Wing 290, Air Force 11,500, Paramilitaries
14,000
CONSCRIPTION DURATION – Nine months

ECONOMY

Agriculture accounts for around 6 per cent of GDP and
employs 8 per cent of the workforce. Production is concentrated on maize, wheat, sugar beet, barley, rye and oats.
Industry is mainly based on imported raw materials but
Hungary has its own coal, bauxite, considerable deposits
of natural gas, some iron ore and oil. Output figures in
1998 were: coal 14,494,299 tonnes; aluminium 33,700
tonnes; crude steel 1,939,784 tonnes; crude petroleum
1,257,830 tonnes. Natural gas production totalled 4,345
million cubic metres.
The economy suffered from the loss of export markets
in the Soviet Union and the former Yugoslavia, and
the transition to a market economy, but now exports the
majority of its goods to the countries of the EU. The
economy has benefited from a strong inflow of foreign
direct investment.
Some 40 per cent of state enterprises have been
privatised. Hungary joined the OECD in March 1996.
In February 1998, the IMF announced its decision not to
renew Hungary's stand-by credit arrangement, on the
basis that the Hungarian economy was now strong enough
to operate without outside assistance.
The main exports are machinery and equipment,
manufactures, foodstuffs, beverages and tobacco products, raw materials and energy transmission equipment.
In 1998 Hungary had a trade deficit of US$2,123
million and a current account deficit of US$2,304 million.
In 1997 imports totalled US$20,758 million and exports
US$18,732 million.
GNP – US$45,660 million (1998); US$4,510 per capita
(1998)
GDP – US$44,845 million (1996); US$4,463 per capita
(1996)
ANNUAL AVERAGE GROWTH OF GDP – 1.3 per cent
(1996); estimated to be 3.2 per cent in 1997

INFLATION RATE – 14.4 per cent (1998)
UNEMPLOYMENT – 7.8 per cent (1998)
TOTAL EXTERNAL DEBT – US$28,580 million (1998)

Trade with UK	1998	1999
Imports from UK	£500,190,000	£489,481,000
Exports to UK	558,095,000	686,250,000

EDUCATION

There are five types of schools under the Ministry of
Education: kindergartens for age three to six, general
schools for age six to 14 (compulsory), vocational schools
(15–18), secondary schools (15–18), universities and adult
training schools (over 18).
ILLITERACY RATE – 0.6 per cent
ENROLMENT (percentage of age group) – primary
97 per cent (1995); secondary 86 per cent (1995);
tertiary 23.8 per cent (1995)

CULTURE

Magyar, or Hungarian, is one of the Finno-Ugrian
languages. Hungarian literature began to flourish in the
second half of the 16th century. Among the greatest
writers of the 19th and 20th centuries are Mihály
Vörösmarty (1800–55), Sándor Petöfi (1823–49), János
Arany (1817–82), Imre Madách (1823–64), Kálmán
Mikszáth (1847–1910), Endre Ady (1877–1918), Attila
József (1905–37), Mihály Babits (1883–1941), Dezsö
Kosztolányi (1885–1936), Gyula Illyes (1902–83), János
Pilinszky (1921–81) and Sándor Weöres (1913–89).

ICELAND
Lýðveldið Ísland

AREA – 39,769 sq. miles (103,000 sq. km)
POPULATION – 278,702 (1999). Some 89.4 per cent of the
population are members of the (Lutheran) Church of
Iceland. The language is Icelandic
CAPITAL – ΨReykjavík (population, 115,193, 1999)
MAJOR CITIES – Akranes; ΨAkureyri; ΨEgilsstaðir;
ΨHafnarfjörður; Isafjörður; Kópavogur; Reykjanesbær;
ΨSiglufjörður
CURRENCY – Icelandic króna (Kr) of 100 aurar
NATIONAL ANTHEM – Lofsöngur (Song of praise)
NATIONAL DAY – 17 June
NATIONAL FLAG – Blue, with white-bordered red cross
LIFE EXPECTANCY (years) – male 76.20; female 80.59
POPULATION GROWTH RATE – 0.9 per cent (1997)
POPULATION DENSITY – 3 per sq. km (1997)
URBAN POPULATION – 91.8 per cent (1996)
MILITARY PERSONNEL – 120 Paramilitaries

HISTORY AND POLITICS

Iceland was uninhabited before the ninth century, when
settlers came from Norway. For several centuries a form of
republican government prevailed, with an annual assembly of leading men called the *Alþingi (Althingi)*, but in 1262
Iceland became subject to Norway, and later to Denmark.
During the colonial period, Iceland maintained its cultural
integrity but a deterioration in the climate, together with
frequent volcanic eruptions and outbreaks of disease, led
to a serious drop in living standards and to a decline in the
population to little more than 40,000. In the 19th century a
struggle for independence led to home rule in 1918 and to
independence as a republic in 1944.
The parliamentary (*Althingi*) elections on 9 May 1999
gave the Independence Party 26 seats, Unified Left 17,
Progressives 12, Left-Green Alliance 6 and Liberals 2. A
coalition government of the Independence Party and the
Progressive Party was formed after the election.

HEAD OF STATE
President, Ólafur Ragnar Grímsson, *elected* 29 June 1996

CABINET *as at September 2000*

Prime Minister, Statistical Bureau of Iceland, Davið Oddsson (IP)
Agriculture, Gudni Ágústsson (PP)
Education, Culture and Science, Björn Bjarnason (IP)
Environment, Siv Fridleifsdóttir (PP)
Finance, Geir Haarde (IP)
Fisheries, Árni Mathiesen (IP)
Foreign Affairs, Halldór Ásgrímsson (PP)
Health and Social Security, Ingibjörg Pálmadóttir (PP)
Justice and Ecclesiastical Affairs, Sólveig Pétursdóttir (IP)
Social Affairs, Páll Pétursson (PP)
Trade and Industry, Valgerdur Sverrisdóttir (PP)
Transport, Sturla Bödvarsson (IP)

IP Independence Party; PP Progressive Party

EMBASSY OF ICELAND
1 Eaton Terrace, London SW1W 8EY
Tel: 020-7590 1100
Ambassador Extraordinary and Plenipotentiary, HE Þorsteinn Pálsson, apptd 1999

BRITISH EMBASSY
Laufásvegur 31, IS-101 Reykjavík
Tel: (00 354) 550 5100/1/2
E-mail: britemb@centrum.is
Ambassador Extraordinary and Plenipotentiary and Consul-General, HE James McCulloch, apptd 1996

CONSULATE – Akureyri

ECONOMY

Iceland has considerable resources of hydroelectric and geothermal energy. Heavy industry includes an aluminium smelter, a nitrogen fertiliser factory, a cement factory, a diatomite plant and a ferro-silicon plant.

The major sectors of the economy are fishing and fish processing, manufacturing, agriculture, energy production and tourism, which is of growing importance with 232,219 visitors in 1998.

As a member of the European Free Trade Association (EFTA), Iceland has become a member of the European Economic Area (EEA) which extends most of the provisions of the EU's single market to EFTA states.

In 1997 Iceland had a trade surplus of US$3 million and a current account deficit of US$133 million. In 1998 imports totalled US$2,489 million and exports US$2,050 million.
GNP – US$7,626 million (1998); US$27,830 per capita (1998)
GDP – US$7,296 million (1996); US$26,922 per capita (1996)
ANNUAL AVERAGE GROWTH OF GDP – 5.0 per cent (1997)
INFLATION RATE – 1.7 per cent (1998)
UNEMPLOYMENT – 2.7 per cent (1998)

TRADE

The principal exports are fish and fish products, ferro-silicon and aluminium; the chief imports are consumer durables, petroleum products, transport equipment, textiles, foodstuffs, animal feeds and timber.

Trade with UK	1998	1999
Imports from UK	£163,158,000	£164,751,000
Exports to UK	264,829,000	299,319,000

COMMUNICATIONS

At 1 January 1999, the mercantile marine consisted of 955 registered vessels (237,379 gross tons). There are regular shipping services between Reykjavík and Felixstowe, Humber ports, Europe and the USA.

A regular air service is maintained by Icelandair between Glasgow and London and Reykjavík. There are also air services to Scandinavia, USA, Germany, France, the Netherlands and Canada.

Road communications are adequate in summer but greatly restricted by snow in winter. Only roads in town centres and key highways are metalled, the rest being of gravel, sand and lava dust. The climate and terrain make first-class surfaces for highways out of the question. There are no railways.

There are four television channels (one public, three private) and several private and public radio stations.

CULTURE

The ancient Norræna (or Northern tongue) has close affinities to Anglo-Saxon and as spoken and written in Iceland today differs little from that introduced into the island in the ninth century. There is a rich literature with two distinct periods of development, from the mid-11th to the late 13th century and from the early 19th century to the present.
ENROLMENT (percentage of age group) – primary 98 per cent (1996); secondary 87 per cent (1995); tertiary 37 per cent (1996)

INDIA
The Republic of India/Bhāratīya Ganarajya

AREA – 1,269,346 sq. miles (3,287,263 sq. km). Neighbours: Pakistan (north-west), China, Tibet, Nepal and Bhutan (north), Myanmar (east), Bangladesh
POPULATION – 970,930,000 (1998 estimate); 846,302,688 (1991 census): Hindu (82.41 per cent), the rest being Muslim (11.67 per cent), Christian (2.32 per cent), Sikh (1.99 per cent), Buddhist (0.77 per cent) and Jain (0.41 per cent). The official languages are Hindi in the Devanagari script and English, though 17 regional languages also are recognised for adoption as official state languages
CAPITAL – New Delhi (population, 301,297; 8,419,084 including Delhi/Dilli), 1991
MAJOR CITIES – Ahmedabad (3,312,216); Bangalore (4,130,288); ΨBombay/Mumbai (12,596,243); ΨCalcutta/Kolkata (11,021,918); Hyderabad (4,344,437); Kanpur (2,029,889); Lucknow (1,669,204); ΨMadras/Chennai (5,421,985); Pune (2,493,987) (1991 figures)
CURRENCY – Indian rupee (Rs) of 100 paisa
NATIONAL ANTHEM – Jana-gana-mana
NATIONAL DAY – 26 January (Republic Day)
NATIONAL FLAG – A horizontal tricolour with bands of deep saffron, white and dark green in equal proportions. In the centre of the white band appears an Asoka wheel in navy blue
LIFE EXPECTANCY (years) – male 59.00; female 59.70
POPULATION GROWTH RATE – 1.9 per cent (1997)
POPULATION DENSITY – 291 per sq. km (1997)
URBAN POPULATION – 27.6 per cent (1997)
ILLITERACY RATE – 44.2 per cent
ENROLMENT (percentage of age group) – tertiary 6.9 per cent (1996)

India has three well-defined regions: the mountain range of the Himalayas, the Indo–Gangetic plain, and the southern peninsula. The main mountain ranges are the Himalayas (over 29,000 feet) and the Western and Eastern Ghats (over 8,000 feet). Major rivers include the Ganges, Indus, Krishna, Godavari and Mahanadi. Temperatures vary over the country between averages of about 10°C and 33°C, reaching over 38°C in some parts during the hot season. There are similar variations in rainfall, from only a few inches a year falling in the western Thar Desert to over 400 inches in Meghalaya.

HISTORY AND POLITICS

The Indus civilisation was fully developed by *c*.2500 BC but collapsed *c*.1750 BC, and was replaced by an Aryan civilisation from the west. Arab invasions of the north-west began in the seventh century and Muslim, Hindu and Buddhist states developed until the establishment of the Mughal dynasty in 1526. The British East India Company established settlements throughout the 17th century; clashes with the French and native princes led to the British government taking control of the company in 1784 and gradually extending sovereignty over the whole subcontinent. The separate dominions of India and Pakistan became independent within the Commonwealth on 15 August 1947 and India became a republic in 1950.

Between 1947 and 1996, India was ruled by the Congress (I) Party for all but four years (March 1977–January 1980, November 1989–June 1991). Congress (I) has been led by members of the Nehru-Gandhi dynasty for most of the post-independence period: Prime Ministers Jawaharlal Nehru (1947–64), Indira Gandhi (1966–1977, 1980–84) and Rajiv Gandhi (1984–89). Indira Gandhi was assassinated by Sikh extremists seeking an independent Sikh state in Punjab; her son Rajiv was assassinated by Sri Lankan Tamils.

In November 1997, the United Front government (a coalition of Communist and low-caste parties) collapsed after Congress (I) withdrew its support. The parliamentary elections in February 1998 produced no outright winner; in March 1998, the BJP formed a coalition government under Atal Bihari Vajpayee, which collapsed following the loss of a confidence motion on 17 April 1999. The opposition parties were unable to form a majority government and parliament was dissolved on 26 April 1999 by President Narayanan. The BJP-led 24-party National Democratic Alliance won elections on 3 October 1999 with a majority of 296 seats.

SECESSION

The Hindu Maharaja of Kashmir signed his state's instrument of accession to India in October 1947, two months after India and Pakistan became independent. This was disputed by Pakistan, on the basis that the majority of the state's population was Muslim. After three Indian-Pakistani wars, a line of control was agreed under the 1972 Simla agreement (China has also occupied some of Kashmir since the 1962 Sino-Indian war). Kashmir was placed under direct rule in 1990 but state assembly elections, held in September 1996, were won by Jammu and Kashmir National Conference. The Islamic militant groups *Hizbul Mujaheddin* and *Lashkar-e-Tayyeba* continued to launch attacks on Hindu civilians, government officials and security forces.

FOREIGN RELATIONS

India and Pakistan have fought three major wars since independence, in 1947–8, 1965 and 1971. Since 1985 they have continued a low-level war at altitude for control of the Siachen glacier in Kashmir.

In May 1998, India conducted five underground nuclear tests, confirming its status as a nuclear power. The tests were condemned by the international community. Within three weeks, Pakistan had conducted its own nuclear tests, leading to fears that border confrontations between the two countries could escalate into nuclear conflict.

On 20 May 1999 the Indian Air Force launched air attacks on Muslim insurgents who had occupied mountainous areas within Indian-controlled Kashmir; the Indian government accused Pakistan of sending more than 500 Islamist militants into Indian territory. Much of the lost

territory was quickly recovered by the Indian Army; following mediation by the USA's President Clinton, on 9 July 1999, the Pakistani government asked the insurgents to withdraw. Small-scale incidents between the Indian and Pakistani troops stationed along the line of control dividing Kashmir continue to occur on a regular basis.

POLITICAL SYSTEM

Executive power is vested in the president, elected for a five-year term by an electoral college consisting of the elected members of the Union and State legislatures. The president appoints the prime minister and, on the latter's advice, the ministers, and can dismiss them. The Council of Ministers is collectively responsible to the *Lok Sabha* (lower house). The vice-president is ex-officio chairman of the *Rajya Sabha* (upper house).

Legislative power rests with the president, the Rajya Sabha (245 members serving six-year terms) and the Lok Sabha (545 members). Twelve members of the Rajya Sabha are presidential nominees, the rest are indirectly elected representatives of the State and Union Territories. The 530 members of the Lok Sabha representing the States are directly elected by universal adult franchise, and 15 representatives of the Union Territories are chosen, for a maximum term of five years.

The Supreme Court consists of the Chief Justice and not more than 25 other judges, appointed by the president. It is the highest court in respect of all constitutional matters and the final Court of Appeal and is situated in New Delhi. Each state or group of states also has a High Court with a hierarchy of subordinate courts. The judges of the High Court of a state are appointed by the president.

FEDERAL STRUCTURE

There are 25 States and seven Union Territories. Each state is headed by a Governor, who is appointed by the president and holds office for five years, and by a Council of Ministers. All states have a Legislative Assembly, and some have also a Legislative Council, elected directly by adult suffrage for a maximum period of five years.

The Union Territories are administered, except where otherwise provided by Parliament, by the president acting through an Administrator or Lieutenant-Governor, or other authority appointed by him.

	Area (sq. km)	Population (1998 estimate)	Capital
STATES			
Andhra Pradesh	275,100	74,170,000	Hyderabad
Arunachal Pradesh	83,700	1,130,000	Itanagar
Assam	78,400	25,650,000	Dispur
Bihar	173,900	96,960,000	Patna
Goa	3,700	1,510,000	Panaji
Gujarat	196,000	47,100,000	Gandhinagar
Haryana	44,200	19,340,000	Chandigarh
Himachal Pradesh	55,700	6,420,000	Shimla
Jammu and Kashmir*	222,200	9,530,000	Srinagar/ Jammu
Karnataka	191,800	50,980,000	Bangalore
Kerala	38,900	31,780,000	Trivandrum (Thiruvananthapuram)
Madhya Pradesh	443,500	77,400,000	Bhopal
Maharashtra	307,700	89,410,000	Bombay (Mumbai)
Manipur	22,300	2,390,000	Imphal
Meghalaya	22,400	2,310,000	Shillong
Mizoram	21,100	900,000	Aizawl
Nagaland	16,600	1,590,000	Kohima
Orissa	155,700	35,300,000	Bhubaneswar
Punjab	50,400	23,100,000	Chandigarh
Rajasthan	342,200	52,010,000	Jaipur
Sikkim	7,100	530,000	Gangtok
Tamil Nadu	130,100	60,880,000	Madras (Chennai)
Tripura	10,500	3,580,000	Agartala
Uttar Pradesh	294,400	164,040,000	Lucknow
West Bengal	88,800	77,250,000	Calcutta (Kolkata)
UNION TERRITORIES			
Andaman and Nicobar Is.	8,200	370,000	Port Blair
Chandigarh	114	840,000	
Dadra and Nagar Haveli	500	180,000	Silvassa
Daman and Diu	112	130,000	
Delhi/Dilli	1,500	13,040,000	
Lakshadweep	30	70,000	Kavaratti
Pondicherry	500	1,050,000	

*The figures include those parts occupied by Pakistan and China, which are claimed by India. The state's capital is at Srinagar in summer and Jammu in winter.

HEAD OF STATE

President of the Republic of India, Kocheril Raman Narayanan, *elected* 14 July 1997
Vice-President, Krishan Kant, *elected* 16 August 1997

CABINET *as at September 2000*

Prime Minister, Atomic Energy, Personnel, Public Grievances and Pensions, Space, Atal Bihari Vajpayee (BJP)
Agriculture, Nitish Kumar
Chemicals and Fertilisers, Suresh Prabhu
Civil Aviation, Sharad Yadav
Commerce and Industry, Murasoli Maran
Communications, Ram Vilas Paswan
Consumer Affairs and Public Distribution, Shanta Kumar
Culture and Tourism, Ananth Kumar (BJP)
Defence, George Fernandes (SP)
Environment and Forests, T. R. Baalu
External Affairs, Jaswant Singh (BJP)
Finance, Yashwant Sinha (BJP)
Health and Family Welfare, C. P. Thakur; Rita Verma

Heavy Industries and Public Enterprises, Manohar Joshi
Home Affairs, Lal Krishna Advani (BJP)
Human Resource Development, Science and Technology, Murli Manohar Joshi (BJP)
Information Technology, Parliamentary Affairs, Pramod Mahajan (BJP)
Labour, Satynarayan Jatiya (BJP)
Law Justice and Company Affairs, Information and Broadcasting, Arun Jairley (BJP)
Petroleum and Natural Gas, Ram Naik (BJP)
Power, Vacant
Railways, Mamata Banerjee
Rural Development, Sunder Lal Patwa
Surface Transport, Rajnath Singh
Textiles, Kashi Ram Rana (BJP)
Tribal Affairs, Juel Oram (BJP)
Urban Development and Poverty Alleviation, Jagmohan (BJP)
Water Resources, Arun Sethi
Youth Affairs and Sports, Mines, Sukhdev Singh Dhindsa

BJP Bharatiya Janata Party; SP Samta (Equality) Party; Ind. Independent

INDIAN HIGH COMMISSION

India House, Aldwych, London WC2B 4NA
Tel: 020-7836 8484
High Commissioner, HE Nareshwar Dayal, apptd 2000
Deputy High Commissioner, H. S. Puri
Ministers, S. K. Mandal *(Political)*; G. Singh *(Consular)*; G. R. Karnad *(Culture)*
Counsellor (Economic); R. Panday
Military Adviser, Brig. S. Sharma
CONSULATES-GENERAL – Birmingham, Edinburgh

BRITISH HIGH COMMISSION

Chanakyapuri, New Delhi 1100021
Tel: (00 91) (11) 687 2161
High Commissioner, HE Sir Rob Young, KCMG, apptd 1998
Deputy High Commissioner and Minister, T. T. Macan
Deputy High Commissioners, M. C. Bates, OBE *(Bombay/ Mumbai)*; S. M. Scaddan *(Calcutta/Kolkata)*; M. E. J. Herridge *(Madras/Chennai)*
Defence and Military Adviser, Brig. S. M. A. Lee, OBE
Counsellor (Economic and Commercial), G. C. Gillham

BRITISH COUNCIL MINISTER – C. Perchard OBE, CVO, 17 Kasturba Gandhi Marg, New Delhi 110 001; e-mail: delhi@bc-delhi.bcindia.sprintsmx.ems.vsnl.net.in. Offices at Bombay/Mumbai, Calcutta/Kolkata and Madras/Chennai. British Council libraries at these four centres and British libraries at Ahmedabad, Bangalore, Bhopal, Bhubaneswar, Hyderabad, Lucknow, Patna, Pune and Trivandrum/Thiruvananthapuram

DEFENCE

The Army has 3,414 main battle tanks, 1,350 armoured infantry fighting vehicles and 157 armoured personnel carriers. The Navy has 16 submarines, one aircraft carrier, seven destroyers, 13 frigates, 40 patrol and coastal vessels, 79 combat aircraft and 83 armed helicopters. It has nine bases including one under construction. The Air Force has 774 combat aircraft and 34 armed helicopters.

India exploded its first nuclear weapon in 1974 and is since believed to have acquired a stockpile of nuclear arms. It conducted further nuclear tests in May 1998. In 1993–4 India successfully test-fired its intermediate-range 'Agni' and 'Prithvi' ballistic missiles, and the latter went into production in September 1997.

MILITARY EXPENDITURE – 3.0 per cent of GDP (1998)
MILITARY PERSONNEL – 2,263,000: Army 980,000, Navy 53,000, Air Force 140,000; Paramilitaries 1,090,000

ECONOMY

Agriculture supports about 64 per cent of the population, and contributes nearly 27.4 per cent of GDP. Production has grown by 2.67 per cent each year since 1951, remaining slightly ahead of the 2 per cent increase necessary to keep pace with the rising population. Food crops occupy three-quarters of the total cultivated area. The main food crops are rice, cereals (principally wheat) and pulses. The major cash crops include sugar cane, jute, cotton and tea. Other products include oil seeds, spices, groundnuts, soya bean, tobacco, rubber and coffee. Livestock is raised, principally for dairy purposes or for the hides.

Industry is based on the exploitation and processing of mineral resources, principally coal, oil and iron, and on the production of textiles. The coal industry reached an output in 1998 of 316,574,000 tonnes; production of crude petroleum was 32,893,000 tonnes. Steel production is mainly in the hands of the public sector, with five public and one private sector integrated steel plants producing 23,863,000 tonnes of ingot steel in 1998. The engineering industry, heavy and light, is increasingly being privatised.

The manufacture of paper, cement, pharmaceuticals, chemicals, fertilisers, petrochemicals, motor vehicles and commercial vehicles has been expanded. Other principal manufactures are those derived from agricultural products, textiles, jute goods, sugar and leather, which along with tea, tobacco, rubber, fish and iron ore are major exports.

Tourism is a major industry, with 167 million domestic tourists and 2,358,609 overseas visitors in 1998, employing 9.8 million people.

The main exports are textiles, gemstones and jewellery, chemical products, agricultural produce, engineering products, leather goods, marine products and ores and minerals.

GDP has been rising by about 6 per cent per annum, but growth has been concentrated in the more prosperous western and southern states, increasing regional inequalities.

Orissa was devastated by a cyclone on 29 October 1999, which left at least 1.5 million people homeless and caused widespread destruction of crops.

In 1998 there was a trade deficit of US$10,973 million and a current account deficit of US$7,147 million. Imports totalled US$42,201 million and exports US$32,881 million.

GNP – US$427,407 million (1998); US$440 per capita (1998)

GDP – US$354,637 million (1996); US$375 per capita (1996)

Annual Average Growth of GDP – 6.8 per cent (1996)

Inflation Rate – 13.2 per cent (1998)

Total External Debt – US$98,232 million (1998)

Trade with UK	1998	1999
Imports from UK	£1,255,370,000	£1,454,036,000
Exports to UK	1,453,908,000	1,482,350,000

COMMUNICATIONS

The International Airports Authority manages five international airports: Indira Gandhi (Delhi/Dilli), Dum Dum (Calcutta/Kolkata), Meenambakkam (Madras/Chennai) and Thiruvananthapuram. The other 88 aerodromes are controlled and operated by the Civil Aviation Department of the government. The national airlines are Indian Airlines (internal) and Air India (international).

The railways are grouped into nine administrative zones, Southern, Central, Western, Northern, North-Eastern, North-East Frontier, Eastern, South-Eastern and South-Central; there is also the Konkan Railway which links Bombay/Mumbai and Mangalore. The total track length is 62,495 km, of which 13,490 km is electrified. The total length of the road network is about 3,319,644 km of which 1,334,078 km is surfaced. The national highway system comprises 51,966 km of roads.

The chief seaports are Bombay/Mumbai, Calcutta/Kolkata, Haldia, Madras/Chennai, Mormugao, Cochin, Visakhapatnam, Kandla, Paradip, Mangalore and Tuticorin; these handled a cargo of 179.3 million tonnes in 1993–4. There are 139 minor working ports with varying capacity.

INDONESIA
Republik Indonesia

Area – 735,358 sq. miles (1,904,569 sq. km). Indonesia shares borders with Malaysia (on Borneo) and Papua New Guinea (on New Guinea)

Population – 199,867,000 (1997 UN estimate): 87 per cent Muslim, with Christian, Buddhist, Hindu and Animist minorities. Bahasa Indonesian, a variant of Malay, is the national language, although more than 250 dialects are spoken

Capital – ΨJakarta (population, 9,160,500)

Major Cities – (Irian Jaya) Jayapura (180,400); (Java) Bandung (2,368,200), ΨSemarang (1,366,500), ΨSurabaya (2,701,300); (Kalimantan) Banjarmasin (534,600), ΨPontianak (449,100); (Maluku) Ambon (313,100); (Sulawesi) ΨUjung Pandang (1,091,800); (Sumatra) Medan (1,909,700), Palembang (1,352,300)

Currency – Rupiah (Rp) of 100 sen

National Anthem – Indonesia Raya (Great Indonesia)

National Day – 17 August (Anniversary of Proclamation of Independence)

National Flag – Equal bands of red over white

Life Expectancy (years) – male 61.00; female 64.50

Population Growth Rate – 1.5 per cent (1997)

Population Density – 105 per sq. km (1997)

Urban Population – 37.7 per cent (1997)

Illiteracy Rate – 13.0 per cent

Enrolment (percentage of age group) – primary 95 per cent (1996); secondary 42 per cent (1994); tertiary 11 per cent (1996)

Indonesia comprises the islands of Java, Madura, Sumatra, the Riouw-Lingga archipelago, Bangka and Billiton, part of the island of Borneo (Kalimantan), Sulawesi (formerly Celebes), Maluku (formerly Moluccas), the islands of Bali, Lombok, Sumbawa, Sumba, Flores, and others comprising the provinces of East and West Nusa Tenggara and the western half of the islands of New Guinea (Irian Jaya) and Timor.

HISTORY AND POLITICS

From the early part of the 17th century much of the Indonesian archipelago was under Dutch rule. Following the Second World War, during which the archipelago was occupied by the Japanese, a strong nationalistic movement formed and after sporadic fighting all the former Dutch East Indies except western New Guinea became independent as Indonesia on 27 December 1949. Western New Guinea became part of Indonesia in 1963 under the name West Irian (now Irian Jaya), this interpretation being confirmed in an 'Act of Free Choice' in July 1969.

The Army Minister Gen. Suharto assumed effective political power in March 1966. Gen. Suharto was appointed president in 1968 and was reappointed by the People's Consultative Assembly at every subsequent presidential election. The military effectively ruled through its political organisation Golkar.

Following the imposition of austerity measures, as a result of the Asian economic crisis in 1997, there was widespread ill-feeling towards Suharto and his family, many of whom had amassed large personal fortunes presiding over state businesses. Rampant inflation and

high food and fuel prices provoked civil unrest, and by April 1998 riots and protests calling for Suharto's resignation were frequent. On 21 May 1998, he announced he would step down. He was replaced by his deputy B. J. Habibie.

In January 1999 the House of Representatives passed a number of liberalising reforms to the country's political system, under which the next president was to be chosen in November 1999 by a joint assembly of MPs and representatives of the armed forces, regional legislatures and professional groups.

The Golkar party was defeated in the general election of 7 June 1999, in which the Indonesian Democratic Struggle Party (DSP) led by Megawati Sukarnoputri, daughter of Indonesia's first president, gained 37.4 per cent of the vote and won the greatest number of seats. The new government elected Abdurrahman Wahid, the leader of the National Awakening Party (NAP), as president and Megawati Sukarnoputri was voted vice-president. A coalition government was formed, consisting of the DSP, NAP, and the National Mandate Party.

INSURGENCIES

There are two armed secessionist movements based on ethnic and nationalist groups, which are fighting perceived Javanese domination. In Irian Jaya government forces are fighting the Papua Independent Organisation (OPM) guerrillas who claim the 1969 referendum was rigged and oppose Indonesian settlement. In northern Sumatra the Free Aceh Movement (GAM) is active. On 7–8 November 1999, a crowd of at least 500,000 people demonstrated in the provincial capital Banda Aceh calling for independence for Aceh. President Wahid promised the province a referendum on increased autonomy within Indonesia. Following a series of violent incidents between separatists and the armed forces, a three-month cease-fire, beginning on 2 June 2000, was signed by GAM and Indonesia, to allow negotiations on the future of the province.

Periodic outbursts of violence between Christians and Muslims in Maluku province occurred in 1999 and early 2000; more than 750 people were estimated to have died and 100,000 to have fled in 1999. The violence intensified in May 2000, following the arrival in Maluku of over 2,000 militant Islamic fighters from other parts of Indonesia. *See also* East Timor, page 906

HEAD OF STATE

President, Abdurrahman Wahid (Gus Dur) *sworn in* 20 October 1999
Vice-President, Megawati Sukarnoputri

CABINET *as at September 2000*

Prime Minister (Acting), The Vice-President
Co-ordinating Minister for the Economy and Industry; Rizal Ramli
Co-ordinating Minister for Politics and Security (Lt. Gen. Susilo Bambang Yodhoyono),
Agriculture, Bungaran Saragih
Communications, Lt.-Gen.Agum Gumelar
Culture and Tourism, Gede Ardhika
Defence, H. Moh Mahfud
Economy, Finance and Industry, Kwik Kian Gie
Exploration of Marine Resources, Sarwono Kusumaatmaja
Finance, Prijadi praptosohardjo
Foreign Affairs, Alwi Shihab
Forestry and Plantations, Nur Mahmudi Ismail
Health, Ahmad Suyudi
Home Affairs Gen. (retd) Suryadi Sudirja
Industry and Trade, Lt.-Gen. (retd) Luhut Pandjaitan
Law and Legal Affairs, Yusril Ihza Mahendra
Manpower and Transmigration, Al Hilal Hamdi
Mining and Energy, Lt.-Gen. Susilo Bambang Yudhoyono
National Education, Yahya Muhaimin
People's Welfare and the Eradication of Poverty, Basri Husanuddin

Religious Affairs, K. H. Muhammad Tholchah Hasan
Settlement and Regional Development, Erna Witular

INDONESIAN EMBASSY

38 Grosvenor Square, London W1X 9AD
Tel: 020-7499 7661
Ambassador Extraordinary and Plenipotentiary, HE
 Nana Sutresna, apptd 1999
Minister, Deputy Chief of Mission, R. R. Siahaan
Commercial Attaché, A. Anugerah

BRITISH EMBASSY

Jalan M. H. Thamrin 75, Jakarta 10310
Tel: (00 62) (21) 315 6264
Ambassador Extraordinary and Plenipotentiary, HE Robin
 Christopher, CMG, apptd 1997
Deputy Head of Mission and Consul-General, A. J. Sparkes
Counsellor (Commercial/Development), A. Godson
Defence Attaché, Col. D. S. MacFarlane
BRITISH CONSULAR OFFICES – Jakarta, Medan, Surabaya

BRITISH COUNCIL DIRECTOR, Dr N. Kemp, S. Widjojo
 Centre, Jalan Jenderal Sudirman 71, Jakarta 12190;
 e-mail: bc.jakarta@britcoun.org.id. Offices in Medan
 and Surabaya

DEFENCE

The Army has 461 armoured personnel carriers and 32
aircraft. The Navy has two submarines, 17 frigates, 58
patrol and coastal vessels, 49 combat aircraft and 21 armed
helicopters. There are five principal naval bases. The Air
Force has 91 combat aircraft.
MILITARY EXPENDITURE – 2.6 per cent of GDP (1998)
MILITARY PERSONNEL – 504,000: Army 230,000, Navy
 47,000, Air Force 21,000; Paramilitaries 206,000
CONSCRIPTION DURATION – Two years (selective)

ECONOMY

Nearly 70 per cent of the population is engaged in
agriculture and related production. Copra, nutmeg,
pepper, palm oil, sugar, fibres, rubber, tea, coffee and
tobacco are produced. Rice is a staple food and Java,
Sulawesi and Sumatra are important producers.
 Oil and liquefied natural gas are the most important
assets. Timber is the second largest foreign exchange
earner after oil. Indonesia is rich in minerals, particularly
tin, of which the country is the world's third biggest
producer; coal, nickel and bauxite are the other principal
mineral products. There are also considerable deposits of
gold, silver, manganese phosphates and sulphur.
 Principal exports are petroleum, textiles and clothing,
timber, natural gas and rubber. Principal imports are
machinery and transport equipment, electrical equipment
and chemicals.
 Indonesia was one of the countries worst affected by the
Asian economic crisis, which began in the latter half of
1997; GNP fell by 20 per cent in 18 months and the
ensuing high unemployment and inflation have led to
widespread political and inter-ethnic unrest. The econo-
my began to recover in early 1999.
 In 1998 there was a trade surplus of US$18,429 million
and a current account surplus of US$3,972 million.
Imports totalled US$27,337 million and exports
US$48,847 million.
GNP – US$130,600 million (1998); US$640 per capita
 (1998)
GDP – US$204,085 million (1996); US$1,018 per capita
 (1996)
ANNUAL AVERAGE GROWTH OF GDP – 4.6 per cent (1997)
INFLATION RATE – 57.6 per cent (1998)
TOTAL EXTERNAL DEBT – US$150,875 million (1998)

Trade with UK	1998	1999
Imports from UK	£379,118,000	£398,679,000
Exports to UK	967,484,000	1,038,564,000

COMMUNICATIONS

There are railway systems in Java and Sumatra linking the
main towns. There are about 137,060 km of roads.
 Sea communications are maintained by the state-run
shipping companies Jakarta-Lloyd (ocean-going) and
PELNI (coastal and inter-island) and other small concerns. Transport by small craft on the rivers of the larger
islands plays an important part in trade.
 Air services are operated by Garuda Indonesian Airways
and other local airlines, and Jakarta is served by various
international services.

EAST TIMOR

East Timor was a Portuguese colony from 1702 until
Portuguese control collapsed following the 1974 coup in
Portugal. An independence war waged by the Marxist
Fretilin (Revolutionary Front for an Independent East
Timor) developed into a civil war between Fretilin and
local conservative forces in 1975. After gaining control,
Fretilin declared East Timor independent on 27 November 1975 and this was recognised by Portugal. Indonesian
forces invaded East Timor on 7 December 1975 and
declared East Timor Indonesia's 27th province.
 Since 1975 Fretilin waged an armed campaign for
independence; resistance left 200,000 East Timorese
dead. About 150,000 Muslims were settled in East Timor
alongside the predominantly Roman Catholic population
(80 per cent in 1975). The UN did not recognise the
annexation.
 Following negotiations between Indonesia and
Portugal, an agreement was reached to conduct a
plebiscite on 30 August 1999, which would offer East
Timor autonomy within Indonesia or independence. The
plebiscite resulted in a turnout of 98.6 per cent of the
electorate, with 78.5 per cent voting for independence for
East Timor.
 After extensive violence and intimidation by pro-
Indonesian militias and Indonesian troops against the
civilian population, and the forcible evacuation of many
towns and villages, the UN voted to send in peacekeeping
troops after having gained the agreement of the
Indonesian government; the first UN peacekeepers
arrived on 20 September and Indonesian troops began to
withdraw. On 19 October 1999, the Indonesian Consultative Assembly unanimously ratified the result of the
referendum on the independence of East Timor. By early
October, the UN-established International Force for
East Timor (INTERFET) had managed to install its
forces on the border with West Timor with the aim of
preventing cross-border attacks by pro-Indonesia militias. INTERFET also managed to land troops in the
East Timorese enclave of Ocussi. The commander of
Indonesian forces in West Timor signed an agreement
with INTERFET on the repatriation of refugees on 22
November 1999.
 The UN Security Council voted unanimously on 25
October 1999 to replace INTERFET with a UN force of
up to 8,950 troops and 1,600 police to support the
establishment of a UN Transitional Administration in
East Timor (UNTAET). On 27 November, the pro-
independence activist José Xanana Gusmão visited Jakarta
to establish relations with the Indonesian government.
The National Consultative Council (NCC), which was
established to make policy recommendations to UN-
TAET, held its first meeting on 11 December.
 In December 1999, international donors pledged
US$520 million in aid for the reconstruction of East
Timor.
 Two reports which were published on 31 January
2000 concluded that the Indonesian authorities had

co-operated with the pro-Indonesian militias in wide-ranging human rights abuses and called for the establishment of an international war crimes tribunal.

The NCC adopted the US dollar as the country's transitional currency on 24 January 2000.

President Wahid signed a memorandum of understanding with UNTAET on 29 February, to allow the resumption of cross-border trade and transport between East Timor and Indonesia.

Transitional Administrator, Sergio Vieira de Mello

IRAN
Jomhuri-ye-Eslami-ye-Iran

AREA – 634,293 sq. miles (1,633,188 sq. km). Neighbours: Armenia, Azerbaijan, Turkmenistan (north), Afghanistan (north-east), Pakistan (south-east), Iraq (south-west), Turkey (north-west)

POPULATION – 61,128,000 (1996 census): 99 per cent Muslims (Shia 91 per cent and Sunni 8 per cent) with small minorities of Zoroastrians, Jews, and Armenian and Assyrian Christians. The official language is Persian (Farsi). Minority languages are Turkic (26 per cent), Kurdish (9 per cent), Luri (2 per cent), Arabic, Baluchi and Turkish (1 per cent each)

CAPITAL – Tehrān, (population 6,750,043, 1994 estimate)

MAJOR CITIES – Ahwaz (828,380); Esfahan (1,220,595); Mashhad (1,964,489); Qom (780,453); Shiraz (1,042,801); Tabriz (1,166,203), 1994

CURRENCY – Rial

NATIONAL ANTHEM – Soru-e Jomhuri-ye Eslami (Anthem of the Islamic Republic of Iran)

NATIONAL DAY – 11 February

NATIONAL FLAG – Three horizontal stripes of green, white, red, with the slogan *Allahu Akbar* repeated 22 times along the edges of the green and red stripes, and the national emblem in the centre

LIFE EXPECTANCY (years) – male 58.38; female 59.70

POPULATION GROWTH RATE – 1.5 per cent (1997)

POPULATION DENSITY – 37 per sq. km (1997)

URBAN POPULATION – 58.1 per cent (1994)

Iran is mostly an arid tableland, encircled, except in the east, by mountains, which the highest in the north rising to 18,934 ft. The central and eastern portion is a vast salt desert.

HISTORY AND POLITICS

Iran was ruled from the end of the 18th century by Shahs of the Qajar dynasty. In 1925 the last of the dynasty, Sultan Ahmed Shah, was deposed in his absence by the National Assembly, which handed executive power to Prime Minister Reza Khan. Reza Khan was elected Shah as Reza Shah Pahlavi by the Constituent Assembly in December 1925. In 1941 Reza Shah abdicated in favour of the Crown Prince, who ascended the throne as Mohammed Reza Shah Pahlavi.

In January 1979, the Shah left Iran, handing over power to the Prime Minister, who was ousted by Ayatollah Khomeini, the spiritual leader of the Shia Muslims, on his return from exile. Following a national referendum, an Islamic Republic was declared on 1 April 1979. A new constitution, providing for a president, prime minister, Consultative Assembly, and leadership by Ayatollah Khomeini, was approved by referendum in December 1979. In June 1989 Khomeini died and President Khamenei was appointed Leader of the Islamic Republic. Rafsanjani was elected president in July 1989, and the post of prime minister was abolished. The 1997 presidential election was won by Mohammad Khatami, leader of a centre-left coalition. He was seen as a moderate, and following his election has pursued reformist policies,

including calling for 'a thoughtful dialogue with the American people'. Iran and the UK re-established full diplomatic relations in May 1999. The three rounds of elections to the Majlis held on 18 February, 5 May and 30 May 2000 gave a large majority to reformist candidates.

FOREIGN RELATIONS

Iran was at war with Iraq following the Iraqi invasion of Iran in September 1980. International efforts to end the fighting resulted in a cease-fire in August 1988. In August 1990 Iraq accepted Iran's conditions for settling the conflict, including a return to the 1975 border, but a formal peace treaty has not been signed.

Following the murder of nine Iranian diplomats in August 1998 by Taliban militia forces in Afghanistan, Iran held large-scale military manoeuvres on the Afghan frontier. There were border skirmishes on 8 October 1998.

POLITICAL SYSTEM

The leader of the republic is elected by the Council of Experts whose 83 members are popularly elected every eight years. The president, who is the chief executive, is directly elected for a four-year term, renewable once. Ministers are nominated by the president and must obtain a vote of confidence in the Majlis. The Majlis comprises 290 representatives who are directly elected for a four-year term. Laws passed by the Majlis must be approved by the 12-member Guardian Council. In November 1997, President Khatami announced the establishment of the Committee for the Implementation and Supervision of the Constitution, a five-member body to ensure the constitution was abided by and that people's rights were respected.

Leader of the Islamic Republic, Ayatollah Seyed Ali Khamenei, *appointed* June 1989

President, Seyed Mohammad Khatami, *elected* 23 May 1997

First Vice-President, Hassan Ebrahim Habibi

COUNCIL OF MINISTERS *as at September 2000*

Vice-Presidents, Mohammad Bagerian; Mohammas Ali Najafi (*Advisers to the President*) Gholamreza Aqazadeh (*Atomic Energy*); Abdollah Nouri (*Development and Social Affairs*); Masoumeh Ebtekar (*Environmental Protection*); Mohammad Hashemi (*Executive Affairs*); Mohammad Ali Saduqi (*Legal and Parliamentary Affairs*); Mostafa Hashemi-Taba (*Physical Education*); Mohammad Ali Najafi (*Planning and Budget*)

Administration and Planning, Mohammad Reza Aref

Agriculture and Rural Affairs, Isa Kalantari

Commerce, Mohammad Shariatmadari

Co-operatives, Morteza Hajji

Culture and Islamic Guidance, Ataollah Mohajerani

Defence and Logistics, Adm. Ali Shamkhani

Economic Affairs and Finance, Hossain Namazi

Education, Hossain Mozafar

Energy, Habibollah Bitaraf

Foreign Affairs, Kamal Kharrazi

Health, Mohammad Farhadi

Higher Education, Mostafa Moin

Housing and Urban Development, Ali Abdol-Alizadeh

Industries, Gholamreza Shafei

Information, Ali Yunesi

Interior, State Security Council, Abdulvahed Moussavi-Lari

Jihad for Reconstruction, Mohammad Saidi Kya

Justice, Hojjatolislam Ismail Shoshtari

Labour and Social Affairs, Hossein Kamali

Mines and Metals, Eshaq Jahangiri

Oil, Bijan Namdar Zanganeh

Posts, Telephones and Telegraphs, Mohammad Reza Aref

Roads and Transport, Mahmoud Hojjati

EMBASSY OF THE ISLAMIC REPUBLIC OF IRAN

16 Prince's Gate, London SW7 1PT

Tel: 020-7225 3000

Ambassador Extraordinary and Plenipotentiary,
HE Gholamreza Ansari

BRITISH EMBASSY
143 Ferdowsi Avenue, PO Box 11365–4474, Tehran
11344
Tel: (00 98) (21) 670 5011
Ambassador Extraordinary and Plenipotentiary, HE Nicholas
W. Browne, CMG
First Secretary (Commercial), E. Jenkinson

DEFENCE

The Army has around 1,345 main battle tanks, 550
armoured personnel carriers, 440 armoured infantry
fighting vehicles, 77 aircraft and 100 attack helicopters.
The Navy has five submarines, three frigates, 64 patrol and
coastal vessels, eight combat aircraft and nine armed
helicopters. There are six naval bases. The Air Force has
some 304 combat aircraft, of which about 60–80 per cent
are serviceable.
MILITARY EXPENDITURE – 6.5 per cent of GDP (1998)
MILITARY PERSONNEL – 585,600: Army 350,000,
    Revolutionary Guard Corps 125,000, Navy 20,600,
    Air Force 50,000; Paramilitaries 40,000
CONSCRIPTION DURATION – 21 months

ECONOMY

Iran's alleged support for international terrorism and its
suspected nuclear weapons programme prompted the
USA to impose a full trade and investment embargo in
June 1995. On 17 March 2000, the USA announced that it
would lift sanctions on the importation of certain goods,
including carpets, caviar and pistachio nuts.
    Wheat is the principal agricultural crop; other im-
portant crops are barley, rice, cotton, sugar beet, fruit, nuts
and vegetables. Wool is also a major product.
    The oilfields, which lie in south-western Iran, were
nationalised in 1951. In 1979, the National Iranian Oil
Company assumed control of the production, refining and
sale of oil. Oil production was 187,700,000 tonnes in 1998.
    Apart from oil, the principal industrial products are
carpets, textiles, sugar, cement and other construction
materials, ginned cotton, vegetable oil and other food
products, leather and shoes, metal manufactures, pharmaceuticals, motor vehicles, fertilisers and plastics. Privatisation began in 1991.
    It was announced in April 2000 that reserves of gas had
been found in the Gavband region with an estimated value
of US$16,500 million. Natural gas production was 50,000
million cubic metres in 1998.
    In 1997 there was a trade surplus of US$4,258 million
and a current account surplus of US$2,213 million. In
1996 imports totalled US$16,274 million and exports
US$22,391 million.
GNP – US$102,242 million (1998); US$1,650 per capita
    (1998)
GDP – US$132,938 million (1996); US$1,900 per capita
    (1996)
ANNUAL AVERAGE GROWTH OF GDP – 5.9 per cent (1996)
INFLATION RATE – 19.4 per cent (1998)
TOTAL EXTERNAL DEBT – US$14,391 million (1998)

TRADE

Imports are mainly industrial and agricultural machinery,
motor vehicles and components for assembly, iron and
steel, electrical machinery and goods, foodstuffs and
certain textile fabrics and yarns. The principal exports,
apart from oil and gas, are carpets and fruit. Japan,
Germany, France, the UAE and Italy are Iran's main
trading partners.

Trade with UK	1998	1999
Imports from UK	£330,860,000	£244,817
Exports to UK	36,123,000	36,456,000

COMMUNICATIONS

Tehran is the centre of a network of highways linking the
major towns, ports, the Caspian Sea and the national
frontiers; there are 156,507 km of roads.
    The Trans-Iranian Railway runs from Bandar
Turcoman, on the Caspian Sea, via Tehran to Bandar
Khomeini, on the Persian Gulf. Other lines link Tehran
with Tabriz and Mashhad; Tabriz to Julfa; Zahedan to
Quetta; Ahvaz to Khorramshahr; Qom to Kerman; and
Bandar Turcoman to Gorgan. The rail system is linked to
the Turkish system via Van. A track between Mashhad
and Tedzhen in Turkmenistan, opened in May 1996, has
re-established the ancient Silk Road between China and
the Mediterranean; there are 5,612 km of railway track.
    There is an international airport at Tehran (Mehrabad),
and airports at all the major provincial centres.
The national airline, Iranair, is government-owned and
operates international and domestic routes.

EDUCATION AND CULTURE

Since 1943 primary education has been compulsory and
free. There are 74 universities in Iran. The educational
system has been reformed following the revolution.
    Persian or Farsi is an Indo-European language with
many Arabic elements added; the alphabet is mainly
Arabic, with writing from right to left. Among the great
names in Persian literature are those of Abu'l Kásim
Mansúr, or Firdausi (AD 939–1020), Omar Khayyám, the
astronomer-poet (died AD 1122), Muslihu'd-Din, known
as Sa'di (born AD 1184), and Shems-ed-Din Muhammad,
or Hafiz (died AD 1389).
ILLITERACY RATE – 23.1 per cent
ENROLMENT (percentage of age group) – primary
    90 per cent (1996); secondary 71 per cent (1996);
    tertiary 18 per cent (1996)

IRAQ
Al-Jumhūriyya al-'Iraqiyya

AREA – 169,235 sq. miles (438,317 sq. km). Neighbours:
    Iran (east), Saudi Arabia, Kuwait (south), Jordan (west),
    Syria (north-west), Turkey (north)
POPULATION – 21,177,000 (1997 UN estimate),
    16,278,316 (1987 census). The official language is
    Arabic. Minority languages include Kurdish (about 15
    per cent), Turkic and Aramaic
CAPITAL – Baghdād (population, 3,841,268, 1987)
MAJOR CITIES – ΨAl-Başra (406,296); Kirkūk (418,624);
    Al-Mawşil (664,221)
CURRENCY – Iraqi dinar (ID) of 1,000 fils
NATIONAL ANTHEM-Land of two rivers
NATIONAL DAY – 17 July (Revolution Day)
NATIONAL FLAG – Three horizontal stripes of red, white,
    black; on the white stripe three stars and the slogan
    Allahu Akbar all in green
LIFE EXPECTANCY (years) – male 77.43; female 78.22
POPULATION GROWTH RATE – 2.3 per cent (1997)
POPULATION DENSITY – 48 per sq. km (1997)
URBAN POPULATION – 69.9 per cent (1990)
ILLITERACY RATE – 29.2 per cent
ENROLMENT (percentage of age group) – primary
    76 per cent (1995); secondary 37 per cent (1992); tertiary
    11.2 per cent (1995)

In 1993 the border between Iraq and Kuwait was
formally demarcated, moving a few hundred metres
northwards and giving part of the port of Umm Qasr to
Kuwait. The rivers Euphrates (1,700 miles) and Tigris
(1,150 miles) rise in Turkey and traverse Iraq to their

junction at Qurna, from where the Euphrates flows the 70 miles to the Gulf.

HISTORY AND POLITICS

Iraq is the site of the remains of several ancient civilisations: one site at Tel Hassuna, near Shura, dates back to 5000 BC; Tel Abu Shahrain near 'Ur of the Chaldees' is the site of the Sumerian city of Eridu; the ancient city of Hillah, 70 miles south of Baghdād, is near the site of Babylon and the Tower of Babel. Al-Mawşil governorate covers a great part of the ancient kingdom of Assyria, the ruins of Nineveh, the Assyrian capital, being visible on the banks of the Tigris, opposite Al-Mawşil. Qurna, at the junction of the Tigris and Euphrates, is traditionally supposed to be the site of the Garden of Eden.

Iraq was part of the Ottoman empire from 1534 until it was captured by British forces in 1916. A provisional government was set up in 1920, and in 1921 the Emir Faisal was elected King of Iraq. The country was a monarchy until July 1958, when King Faisal II was assassinated. From 1958 Iraq has been under the rule of the Ba'ath Party.

The Arab Ba'ath Socialist Party held 165 of the 250 Assembly seats following the most recent election, held on 27 March 2000; the remaining seats were held by independents.

FOREIGN RELATIONS

Iraq invaded Iran in September 1980 and was at war until the August 1988 cease-fire. In 1990 Iraq accepted Iran's conditions for peace, including a return to the 1975 border, but a formal peace treaty has not been signed.

Iraq invaded Kuwait on 2 August 1990 and declared Kuwait a province of Iraq. The UN Security Council declared the annexation void. After months of diplomatic attempts to secure an Iraqi withdrawal from Kuwait, an alliance of NATO and Middle East countries launched an offensive in January 1991 and liberated Kuwait in February 1991.

A United Nations Special Committee (UNSCOM), charged with securing Iraq's full nuclear, biological and chemical disarmament, has frequently been hindered in its task by Iraqi officials. In October 1998, the Iraqi government announced that it was suspending all co-operation with UNSCOM officials in protest at the continuing sanctions; the USA and the UK began to increase their military presence in the region and emphasised that they were prepared to use military force

to enable the UNSCOM mission to continue; on 15 November, the Iraqi regime agreed to allow UNSCOM officials to resume operations.

In December 1999, the UN Security Council created a new weapons inspection body, the UN Monitoring, Verification and Inspection Commission (UNMOVIC), to replace UNSCOM. UNMOVIC was to monitor the elimination of Iraq's nuclear, chemical and biological weapons arsenal and was empowered to suspend all sanctions for four-month renewable phases if the Iraqi authorities co-operated fully with UNMOVIC and the IAEA within a whole 120-day period.

INSURGENCIES

Following the allied victory in Kuwait in February 1991, rebellion broke out in the Kurdish north and the Shi'ite south. Although the revolt was quickly suppressed, Iraqi attacks on Kurdish civilians led to the setting up of a UN safe haven in northern Iraq to protect them. An air exclusion zone north of the 36th parallel was also established.

Although the Shi'ite revolt in southern Iraq was defeated in April 1991, a low-level insurgency continued in the southern marshlands. Since then the Iraqi regime has systematically drained the southern marshes by canal construction and river diversion; with continued ground offensives, this had effectively ended the Shi'ite rebellion by late 1994.

Iraqi aircraft have frequently violated the air exclusion zones; allied forces have responded by attacking Iraqi air defence installations.

POLITICAL SYSTEM

According to the provisional constitution, the highest state authority is the Revolutionary Command Council (RCC), which elects the president from among its members. A constitutional amendment approved in September 1995 provided for the confirmation of the RCC's choice of president by the National Assembly and by a popular referendum. The president appoints the Council of Ministers. Legislative authority is shared by the RCC and the 250-member National Assembly, which is elected every four years by universal adult suffrage. Following the amendment to the constitution, a referendum on a further seven-year term for President Saddam was approved by a claimed 99.96 per cent of voters on 15 October 1995.

HEAD OF STATE

President, Saddam Hussein, *assumed office* 16 July 1979, *reappointed* 17 October 1995
Vice-Presidents, Taha Mohieddin Maarouf, Taha Yassin Ramadan

REVOLUTIONARY COMMAND COUNCIL

Chairman, The President
Vice-Chairman, Izzat Ibrahim
Secretary-General, Khaled Abdel-Moneim Rasheed
Members, Taha Yassin Ramadan; Sa'adoun Shaker; Tariq Aziz; Taha Mohieddin Maarouf; Mohammad Hamzah al-Zubaydi; Mizban Khader Hadi

COUNCIL OF MINISTERS *as at September 2000*

The President
Deputy Prime Ministers, Tariq Aziz; Taha Yassin Ramadan; Mohammad Hamzah al-Zubaydi; Hikmat Mizban Ibrahim al-Azzawi (*Finance*)
Agriculture, Abd al-Ilah Hamid Muhammad Salih
Defence, Lt.-Gen. Sultan Hashim Ahmad al-Jabburi Tai
Education, Higher Education and Scientific Research (*acting*), Fahd Salem al-Shaqra
Foreign Affairs, Muhammad Said Kazim al-Sahhaf
Health, Umid Midhat Mubarak
Housing and Reconstruction, Ma'n Abdullah al-Sarsam
Industry, Minerals, Adnan abd al Majid Jasim al-Ani

Information and Culture, Humam abd al-Khaliq
abd al-Ghafur
Interior, Muhammad Ziman Abd al-Razzaq
Irrigation, Mahmud Dhiyab al-Ahmad
Justice, Mondher Ibrahim al-Shawi
Labour and Social Affairs, Staff Gen. Sa'di Tu'mah Abbas
Military Industrialisation, Abd al-Tawwab al-Mulla
Huwaysh
Oil, Lt.-Gen. Amir Muhammad Rashid al-Ubaydi
Religious Endowments and Religious Affairs, Abd al-Munim
Ahmad Salih
Trade, Mohammad Mehdi Salih
Transport and Communications, Ahmad Murtada Khalil

IRAQI DIPLOMATIC MISSION IN LONDON

Since Iraq's breach of diplomatic relations with Britain in
February 1991, the Jordanian Embassy has handled Iraqi
interests in the UK.
Minister/Head of Interests Section, vacant

BRITISH DIPLOMATIC REPRESENTATION

The British Embassy was closed in January 1991. The
Russian Embassy has since handled British interests in
Iraq.

DEFENCE

The Army has roughly 2,200 main battle tanks, 2,000
armoured personnel carriers, 900 armoured infantry
fighting vehicles, and 120 armed helicopters. The Navy
has two frigates and six patrol and coastal vessels at two
bases.

In 1991, the UN demanded the destruction of all
weapons of mass destruction and their means of production as a prerequisite for the lifting of sanctions. By mid-
1995 it was believed that most of these weapons had been
destroyed and a long-term monitoring operation was
under way to ensure production did not restart. In late
1995, evidence of a ballistic missile programme and large
biological weapons stockpiles was discovered; in 1997
evidence of further Iraqi chemical weapons, including
missiles loaded with VX gas, was discovered.
MILITARY EXPENDITURE – 7.3 per cent of GDP (1998)
MILITARY PERSONNEL – 479,000: Army 375,000, Navy
2,000, Air Force 35,000, Air Defence Force 17,000,
Paramilitaries 50,000
CONSCRIPTION DURATION – 18–24 months

ECONOMY

Increasing industrialisation is taking place but production
has been hampered by war damage and sanctions. Iraq's
major industry is oil production which was nationalised in
1972. Production was 105,300,000 tonnes in 1998.

Agricultural production is important, with two harvests
usually gathered in a year, depending on rainfall. Salinity
and soil erosion limit productivity.

The UN imposed economic sanctions and a world-wide
ban on Iraqi oil exports in August 1990. In May 1996, Iraq
agreed to a UN-proposed 'oil-for-food' deal, permitting
the sale of oil to buy food and medicine. Limited oil
exports resumed in December 1996. Thirty per cent of the
revenue will pay for reparations to Gulf War victims, and
up to 15 per cent will provide aid to Iraqi Kurds.
GDP – US$286,024 million (1996); US$13,880 per capita
(1996)
ANNUAL AVERAGE GROWTH OF GDP – 0.7 per cent (1996)

TRADE

The principal imports are normally iron and steel, military
equipment, building materials, mechanical and electrical
machinery, motor vehicles, textiles and clothing, essential
foodstuffs and raw industrial materials. The chief exports
are normally crude petroleum, dates, raw wool, raw hides

and skins and raw cotton.

Trade with UK	1998	1999
Imports from UK	£25,644,000	£35,488,000
Exports to UK	21,481,000	412,000

COMMUNICATIONS

The port of Al-Başra has not been used since the outbreak
of hostilities with Iran in 1980. Continuous dredging of
the Shatt-al-Arab has also been suspended by hostilities
and the channel has seriously silted. The port of Umm
Qasr on the Kuwaiti border, which was developed for
freight and sulphur handling and includes a container
terminal, was opened in late 1993. All external borders,
except that of Jordan, are closed to Iraqi traffic.

There is an international airport at Baghdād. Iraqi
Airways provided flights between Baghdād and London,
and other international airlines operated to Europe. Iraqi
Republican Railways provided regular passenger and
goods services between Al-Başra, Baghdād and Al-Mawşil.
There is also a metre gauge rail line connecting Baghdād
with Khanaqin, Kirkūk and Arbil.

Iraqi communications were greatly affected by the Gulf
War; large numbers of bridges were destroyed and the
railway system extensively disrupted.

REPUBLIC OF IRELAND
Poblacht Na hÉireann

AREA – 27,137 sq. miles (70,273 sq. km). Neighbour:
Northern Ireland (north)
POPULATION – 3,626,087 (1996 census). At the 1991
census religious adherence was: Roman Catholic,
3,228,327; Church of Ireland, 89,187; Presbyterians,
13,199; Methodists, 5,037; others, 189,969. Irish is the
first official language; English is recognised as a second
official language, but is more commonly used
CAPITAL – ΨDublin (*Baile Átha Cliath*) (population,
952,700, 1996 census)
MAJOR CITIES – ΨCork (*Corcaigh*) (180,000); ΨGalway
(*Gaillimh*) (57,400); ΨLimerick (*Luimheach*) (79,100);
Waterford (*Port Láirge*) (44,200), 1996 census
CURRENCY – Euro (€) of 100 cents/Punt (IR£)
of 100 pence
NATIONAL ANTHEM – Amhrán na BhFiann (The Soldier's
Song)
NATIONAL DAY – 17 March (St Patrick's Day)
NATIONAL FLAG – Equal vertical stripes of green, white
and orange
LIFE EXPECTANCY (years) – male 72.30; female 77.87
POPULATION GROWTH RATE – 0.6 per cent (1997)
POPULATION DENSITY – 52 per sq. km (1997)
URBAN POPULATION – 58.1 per cent (1996)
MILITARY EXPENDITURE – 1.0 per cent of GDP (1998)
MILITARY PERSONNEL – 11,46: Army 9,300, Navy 1,100,
Air Force 1,060

Ireland is separated from Scotland by the North Channel
and from England and Wales by the Irish Sea and St
George's Channel. The greatest length of the island, from
north-east to south-west (Torr Head to Mizen Head), is
302 miles, and the greatest breadth, from east to west
(Dundrum Bay to Annagh Head), is 174 miles. On the
north coast of Achill Island (Co. Mayo) are the highest
cliffs in the British Isles, 2,000 feet sheer above the sea.

The highest point is Carrantuohill (3,414 ft). The
principal river is the Shannon (240 miles), which drains
the central plain. The Slaney flows into Wexford
Harbour, the Liffey to Dublin Bay, the Boyne to
Drogheda, the Lee to Cork Harbour, the Blackwater to
Youghal Harbour, and the Suir, Barrow and Nore to
Waterford Harbour.

The principal hydrographic feature is the loughs; the Shannon chain of Allen, Boderg, Forbes, Ree and Derg, and the Erne chain of Gowna, Oughter, Lower Erne, and Erne; Melvin, Gill, Gara and Conn in the north-west; and Corrib and Mask (joined by a hidden channel) in the west.

The Republic of Ireland is divided into four provinces of 26 counties: Leinster (Carlow, Dublin, Kildare, Kilkenny, Laoighis, Longford, Louth, Meath, Offaly, Westmeath, Wexford and Wicklow); Munster (Clare, Cork, Kerry, Limerick, Tipperary and Waterford); Connacht (Galway, Leitrim, Mayo, Roscommon and Sligo); and part of Ulster (Cavan, Donegal and Monaghan).

HISTORY AND POLITICS

The first inhabitants of Ireland, hunters from mainland Britain, arrived in 7,000 BC, and were joined by Celts from central Europe from the sixth century BC until about the time of Christ. The introduction of Christianity in the fifth century is traditionally associated with St Patrick and inspired 300 years of rich cultural achievements. The Vikings, who established most of the major towns, including Dublin and Cork, invaded around AD 800 and controlled Ireland until their defeat at the Battle of Clontarf (1014) by Brian Boru, who had become king of all Ireland in 1002.

In the 12th century the Norman English invaded at the invitation of Dermod MacMurrough, the deposed king of Leinster, and established feudal control over most of the island; this lasted for 300 years. King Henry VIII of England reconquered Ireland and in 1541 declared himself king of Ireland, the first English monarch to do so. Protestantism was introduced but failed to take root, except in Ulster where English and Scottish Presbyterians settled during the reign of James I (1603–25). A rebellion initiated by Ulster Catholics in 1641 was ruthlessly crushed by Oliver Cromwell's army. Catholicism was repressed and further Protestant colonisation encouraged. Following the abdication of the Catholic King James II in 1688, Irish Protestants supported William of Orange's accession to the throne. James II was defeated in Ireland, most famously at the Battle of the Boyne (1690), and

Protestant ascendancy was restored, enduring throughout the 18th century.

The Irish parliament was granted independence in 1782, although the Dublin administration was still appointed by the king. The parliament was abolished by the Act of Union in 1801 following a rebellion by the Society of the United Irishmen in 1798, and subsequently Irish MPs sat at Westminster. Demands for the restoration of the Irish parliament and home rule for Ireland were successful in 1914, but were delayed when World War I broke out. A rebellion, the Easter Rising of 1916, was suppressed by the British, fuelling support for the *Sinn Féin* party, which won the 1918 election in Ireland and withdrew from the British parliament to form a legislature in Dublin under the leadership of Éamon de Valera. The resulting two-year war of independence between the Irish Republican Army and British forces ended in a truce, followed by negotiations leading to the signing of the Anglo-Irish Treaty in December 1921. The island was partitioned, the 26 counties of the Irish Free State accepting dominion status within the British Empire, while six of the nine counties of Ulster, where the majority Protestant population opposed home rule, remained part of the United Kingdom, governed by a Northern Ireland parliament.

Civil war broke out between the new Irish government and opponents of the treaty until a truce was reached in May 1923. Constitutional links between the Irish Free State and the UK were gradually removed by the Irish parliament and a new constitution enacted in 1937 declared the Irish Free State a sovereign, independent state with a republican government. However, it continued in association with the states of the British Commonwealth until 1949, when constitutional links with Britain were severed and the state was renamed the Republic of Ireland.

Under the terms of the 1998 Belfast Agreement, the Irish Republic gave up its territorial claim to the six counties of Northern Ireland. Additionally, a North-South Ministerial Council, comprising officials from both countries, would meet to regulate areas of common interest.

The presidential election in October 1997 was won by Mary McAleese with almost 59 per cent of second-round votes. The composition of the Dáil Eireann as of July 1999 was: Fianna Fáil 76; Fine Gael 54; Labour 16; Democratic Left 4; Progressive Democrats 4; Green Party 2; Sinn Fein 1; Socialist 1; others 6. Fianna Fail and the Progressive Democrats formed a coalition government.

POLITICAL SYSTEM

The president (*Uachtarán na hÉireann*) is directly elected for a term of seven years, and is eligible for a second term. The president is aided and advised by a Council of State.

The National Parliament (*Oireachtas*) consists of the president, House of Representatives (*Dáil Éireann*) and Senate (*Seanad Éireann*). Dáil Éireann is composed of 166 members elected for a five-year term on a basis of proportional representation by means of the single transferable vote. Seanad Éireann is composed of 60 members, of whom 11 are nominated by the prime minister (*Taoiseach*) and 49 are elected, six by institutions of higher education and 43 from panels of candidates established on a vocational basis.

Executive power is vested in the government subject to the constitution. The government is responsible to the Dáil. The taoiseach is appointed by the president on the nomination of the Dáil. The other members of the government are appointed by the president on the nomination of the taoiseach with the previous approval of the Dáil. The taoiseach appoints a member of the government to be his deputy (the *tánaiste*).

The judicial system comprises courts of first instance and a court of final appeal called the Supreme Court (*Cúirt*

Uachtarach). The courts of first instance include a High Court (*Ard-Chúirt*) and courts of local and limited jurisdiction, with a right of appeal as determined by law. The High Court alone has original jurisdiction to consider the question of the validity of any law having regard to the provisions of the constitution. The Supreme Court has appellate jurisdiction from decisions of the High Court.

HEAD OF STATE

President, Mary McAleese, *elected* 30 October 1997, *sworn in* 11 November 1997

CABINET *as at September 2000*

Taoiseach (PM), Bertie Ahern
Tánaiste (Deputy PM), Enterprise, Trade and Employment, Mary Harney
Agriculture and Food, Joe Walsh
Arts, Heritage, Gaeltachta and Islands, Síle de Valera
Defence and European Affairs, Michael Smith
Education and Science, Michael Woods
Environment and Local Government, Noel Dempsey
Finance, Charlie McCreevy
Foreign Affairs, Brian Cowen
Health and Children, Michael Martin
Justice and Equality, Law Reform, John O'Donoghue
Marine and Natural Resources, Frank Fahey
Public Enterprise, Mary O'Rourke
Social, Community and Family Affairs, Dermot Ahern
Tourism, Sport and Recreation, Jim McDaid

IRISH EMBASSY

17 Grosvenor Place, London SW1X 7HR
Tel: 020-7235 2171
Ambassador Extraordinary and Plenipotentiary, HE Edward Barrington, apptd 1995
Counsellor, E. Carey (*Economic*)

BRITISH EMBASSY

29 Merrion Road, IE-Dublin 4
Tel: (00 353) (1) 205 3700
E-mail: bembassy@internet-ireland.ie
Ambassador Extraordinary and Plenipotentiary, HE Ivor Roberts, CMG, apptd 1998
Counsellor and Deputy Head of Mission, J. Rankin
Defence Attaché, Col. J. D. Wilson
First Secretary (Commercial), R. N. J. Baker

BRITISH COUNCIL DIRECTOR, Harold Fish, OBE, Newmount House, 22/24 Lower Mount Street, IE-Dublin 2; e-mail: helen@bcdublin.iol.ie

ECONOMY

Although industry has expanded greatly since Ireland's entry into the European Community in 1973, agriculture remains important; in 1999, 8.5 per cent of the workforce was employed in agriculture, forestry and fisheries. The main crops are wheat, barley, oats, potatoes and sugar beet. Agriculture has benefited considerably from the EU Common Agricultural Policy and support funds but has suffered from the drift of the rural population to urban areas and abroad.

Industry accounted for about 39 per cent of GDP and about 28.7 per cent of employment in 1998. The traditional brewing, spirits and food-processing sectors have expanded and have been joined by the manufacture of textiles, chemicals, pharmaceuticals, electronics, office machinery and transportation equipment. The services sector is currently the fastest-growing sector of the economy and accounted for 56 per cent of GDP and 62.2 per cent of employment in 1998. Tourism is the most important part of the service sector and in recent years has provided substantial revenue, with 6,068,000 visitors in 1999.

The Kinsale gas field off the south coast provided 27 per cent of Ireland's gas needs in 1999, with 63 per cent coming via an undersea pipeline from Moffat, Scotland. There are six government-funded milled peat power-generating stations. Hydroelectric power from the Shannon barrage and other schemes is also important but Ireland still imports 54 per cent of oil and coal for power generation. Metal content of ores raised (1999) was lead, 42,208 tonnes; zinc, 223,814 tonnes; silver 15,533 kg.

Computer equipment and organic chemicals are the main exports. The UK, USA, Germany, France and the Netherlands are Ireland's main trading partners.

Having satisfied the Maastricht convergence criteria, Ireland participates in the European Single Currency.

In 1998 Ireland had a trade surplus of US$24,142 million and a current account surplus of US$1,503 million. Imports totalled US$44,355 million and exports US$63,959 million.

GNP – US$69,322 million (1998); US$18,710 per capita (1998)

GDP – US$70,731 million (1996); US$19,902 per capita (1996)

ANNUAL AVERAGE GROWTH OF GDP – 9.8 per cent (1997)
INFLATION RATE – 2.4 per cent (1998)
UNEMPLOYMENT – 7.8 per cent (1998)

Trade with UK	1998	1999
Imports from UK	£9,026,600,000	£10,100,600,000
Exports to UK	7,426,400,000	8,014,100,000

COMMUNICATIONS

In 1999 there were 1,945 km of railway operated by *Iarnród Eirann*. In 1998 the number of ships with cargo which arrived at Irish ports was 16,669 (176,228,000 net registered tons), with a total weight of goods handled of 40 million tonnes.

Shannon Airport, Co. Clare, is on the main transatlantic air route. In 1999 the airport handled 2.2 million passengers. Dublin Airport serves the cross-channel and European services operated by the Irish national airline Aer Lingus and other airlines. In 1999 the airport handled 12.8 million passengers. In 1999 Cork Airport handled 1.5 million passengers.

EDUCATION

Primary education is directed by the state, with the exception of 37 private primary schools. There were 3,181 state-aided primary schools in 1998–9.

In 1998–9 there were 432 recognised secondary schools under private management (mainly religious orders), and 245 vocational schools. There were 16 state comprehensive schools and 66 community schools.

Third-level education is catered for by seven university colleges, 13 Institutes of Technology, seven teacher training colleges and a number of other third-level institutions.

ENROLMENT (percentage of age group) – primary 92 per cent (1996); secondary 86 per cent (1996); tertiary 41 per cent (1996)

ISRAEL
Medinat Yisra'el/Dawlat Isrā'īl

AREA – 8,130 sq. miles (21,056 sq. km). Neighbours: Lebanon (north), Syria (north-east), Jordan and the West Bank (east), the Gaza Strip and the Egyptian province of Sinai (south-west)

POPULATION – 6,100,000 (1999 estimate): roughly 82 per cent Jewish, 14 per cent Arab Muslims, 2.5 per cent Christians of which 90 per cent are Arab,

and 2 per cent Druze. Since independence Israel has had a policy of granting an immigration visa to every Jew who expresses a desire to settle in Israel. Between 1948 and 1992, 2.3 million immigrants had entered Israel from over 100 different countries. Hebrew and Arabic are the official languages. Arabs are entitled to transact all official business with government departments in Arabic

CAPITAL – Most of the government departments are in Jerusalem, population 662,700 (1995 estimate). A resolution proclaiming Jerusalem as the capital of Israel was adopted by the *Knesset* in 1950. It is not, however, recognised as the capital by the UN because East Jerusalem is part of the Occupied Territories captured in 1967. The UN and international law continues to reject the Israeli annexation of East Jerusalem and considers the pre-1950 capital Tel Aviv (population, 1,919,700) to be the capital

MAJOR CITIES – Beersheba (and district 122,000); ΨHaifa (and district 491,000); Rishon Le'Zion (178,000)
CURRENCY – Shekel of 100 agora
NATIONAL ANTHEM – Hatikvah (The Hope)
NATIONAL FLAG – White, with two horizontal blue stripes, the Shield of David in the centre
LIFE EXPECTANCY (years) – male 75.49; female 79.38
POPULATION GROWTH RATE – 3.2 per cent (1997)
POPULATION DENSITY – 277 per sq. km (1997)
URBAN POPULATION – 89.6 per cent (1996)

Israel comprises the hill country of Galilee and parts of Judea and Samaria, rising to heights of nearly 4,000 ft; the coastal plain from the Gaza strip to north of Acre, including the plain of Esdraelon running from Haifa Bay to the south-east which divides the hill region; the Negev, a semi-desert triangular-shaped region, extending from a base south of Beersheba, to an apex at the head of the Gulf of Aqaba; and parts of the Jordan valley, including the Hula region, Tiberias and the south-western extremity of the Dead Sea.

The principal river is the Jordan, which rises from three main sources in Israel, the Lebanon and Syria, and flows through the Hula valley, Lake Tiberias/Kinneret (Sea of Galilee) and the Jordan Valley into the Dead Sea, falling 1,517 ft from Hulata to the Dead Sea. The other principal rivers are the Yarkon and Kishon. The Dead Sea is a lake (shared between Israel, the West Bank and Jordan), 1,286 ft below sea-level; it has no outlet, the surplus being carried off by evaporation.

The climate is variable, modified by altitude and distance from the sea, with hot summers and rainy winters.

HISTORY AND POLITICS

The Ottoman Empire province of Palestine was captured by British forces in 1917, the same year that the British Government issued the Balfour Declaration which 'viewed with favour the establishment of a national home for the Jewish people in Palestine'. The Balfour Declaration's terms were enshrined in Britain's League of Nations mandate over Palestine, leading to steady Jewish immigration in the inter-war years and a post-1945 flood by Nazi concentration camp survivors. The Arab Palestinian population revolted against Jewish immigration from 1936 onwards, while Jewish groups conducted a terrorist campaign against the British administration from 1945 onwards.

In 1947 Britain announced its withdrawal from Palestine with effect from May 1948, handing over to the UN responsibility for resolving the conflict between Arabs and Jews. Both sides ignored the UN partition plan; on the withdrawal of British forces on 14 May 1948 the State of Israel was proclaimed and the first Arab-Israeli war began. By the time of the January 1949 cease-fire Israeli forces controlled all of the former mandate territory apart from the West Bank (and East Jerusalem) and the Gaza Strip, which had come under Jordanian and Egyptian control respectively.

During the 1967 Six-Day War Israel captured the West Bank and the Gaza Strip, together with Sinai from Egypt and the Golan Heights from Syria, and annexed East Jerusalem. Israel held on to its gains in the 1973 Yom Kippur War. The Golan Heights were annexed in 1981; Sinai was returned to Egypt in 1982 in accordance with the 1979 Israeli–Egyptian peace treaty, and the South Lebanon Security Zone was established after the 1982–5 invasion of Lebanon. The annexations of East Jerusalem and the Golan Heights remain unrecognised internationally.

The Labour leader of the coalition government formed after the 1992 general election, Yitzhak Rabin, was assassinated by a Jewish extremist on 4 November 1995, and was replaced by Foreign Minister Shimon Peres. A general election on 29 May 1996, the first to have separate ballots for the prime minister and legislature, was won by Likud leader Binyamin Netanyahu, who formed an eight-party coalition government which commanded 66 seats in the Knesset. Ehud Barak, leader of the Labour Party and the One Israel electoral alliance of the Labour, Gesher and Meymad parties, was elected prime minister on 17 May 1999 and formed a six-party coalition government which held 70 of the 120 seats in the Knesset. A police investigation into allegations of fraud against President Weizman concluded in April 2000 that the President could not be indicted for the crimes because a statute of limitations had expired. On 28 May 2000, President Weizman announced that he would resign from office on 10 July. On 31 July, Moshe Katsav was elected president.

FOREIGN RELATIONS

A peace process, started in October 1991 in Madrid, led to agreements with the Palestine Liberation Organisation, and with Jordan on 14 September 1993. A full peace agreement with Jordan was signed on 26 October 1994 and provides for the return to Jordan of land occupied by Israel since 1967 in the southern Araba valley (completed 9 February 1995).

POLITICAL SYSTEM

Israel is a sovereign democratic republic with executive power vested in a prime minister and Cabinet, and legislative power in a unicameral legislature (*Knesset*) of 120 members elected by proportional representation for a maximum term of four years. The prime minister is elected separately from the legislature. The president is head of state and is elected by the Knesset. Previous presidents have been elected for a maximum of two five-year terms, but under a bill approved by the Knesset in December 1998, the president is to be elected for a seven-year non-renewable term.

HEAD OF STATE

President of Israel, Moshe Katsav, *elected* 31 July 2000, *sworn in* 1 August 2000

CABINET *as at September 2000*

Prime Minister, Defence, Agriculture, Education, Industry and Trade
   Ehud Barak (OI-L)
Deputy Prime Minister, Communications, Housing and Construction, Benjamin Ben-Eliezer (OI-L)
Agriculture and Rural Development, vacant
Environment, Dalia Itzik (OI-L)
Finance, National Infrastructure, Avraham Shochat (OI-L)
Health (*acting*), Roni Milo (Centre)
Immigration Absorption, Yuli Tamir
Interior, Haim Ramon (OI-L)
Justice, Religious Affairs, Yossi Beilin (OI-L)
Labour and Social Affairs, Ra'anan Cohen
Minister in the Office of the Prime Minister, Mikhael Malchior (OI) (*Diaspora and Social Affairs*)
PM's Office, Jerusalem Affairs, Haim Ramon (OI-L)
Public Security, Foreign Affairs (*acting*), *Internal Security*, Shlomo Ben-Ami (OI-L)
Regional Co-operation, Shimon Peres (OI-L)
Science, Culture and Sport, Matan Vilnai (OI)
Tourism, Transport, Amnon Lipkin-Shahaq (Centre)

OI One Israel; OI-L One Israel-Labour

EMBASSY OF ISRAEL

2 Palace Green, Kensington, London W8 4QB
Tel: 020-7957 9500
Ambassador Extraordinary and Plenipotentiary, HE Dror Zeigerman, apptd 1998
Minister Plenipotentiary, A. Magid
Defence and Armed Forces Attaché, Col. I. Yaar
Minister, M. Bar-On (*Consular*)
Counsellor, R. Kan (*Commercial*)

BRITISH EMBASSY

192 Hayarkon Street, Tel Aviv 63405
Tel: (00 972) (3) 524 9171
Ambassador Extraordinary and Plenipotentiary, HE Francis Cornish, CMG, LVO, apptd 1998
Counsellor, Consul-General and Deputy Head of Mission, S. Pease
Defence and Military Attaché, Col. E. Houstoun, OBE
First Secretary (*Commercial*), W. W. Magor
CONSULATES – Tel Aviv, Eilat

BRITISH COUNCIL DIRECTOR, D. Elliot, 140 Hayarkon Street, PO Box 3302, Tel Aviv 61032;
e-mail: bc.telaviv@britcoun.org.il. Regional offices in Jerusalem and Nazareth
ISRAEL-BRITISH CHAMBER OF COMMERCE, 76 IBN Guirol Street, Tel Aviv 64162

DEFENCE

Israel is believed to have a nuclear capacity of around 100 warheads which could be delivered by aircraft or Jericho I and II missiles.
   The Army has 3,800 main battle tanks and around 9,900 armoured personnel carriers. The Navy has four submarines and 53 patrol and coastal vessels at three bases. The Air Force has 459 combat aircraft and 133 armed helicopters.
MILITARY EXPENDITURE – 11.6 per cent of GDP (1998)
MILITARY PERSONNEL – 179,550: Army 130,000, Navy 6,500, Air Force 37,000, Paramilitaries 6,050
CONSCRIPTION DURATION – 21–48 months (Jews and Druze only)

ECONOMY

The country is generally fertile although water supply for irrigation restricts production. Agriculture accounts for 4 per cent of GDP.
   The 'Jaffa' orange is produced in large quantities for export, along with other summer fruits, seasonal vegetables, flowers and glasshouse crops. Olives are cultivated, mainly for the production of oil. The main winter crops are wheat, barley and various kinds of pulses, while in summer sorghum, millet, maize, sesame and summer pulses are grown. Beef, cattle and poultry farming have been developed. Tobacco and cotton are now grown.
   Polished diamonds account for about 27.5 per cent of total exports. Amongst the most important industries are textiles, foodstuffs and chemicals (mainly fertilisers and pharmaceuticals). Metal-working and science-based industries are sophisticated and technologically advanced and include the aircraft and military industries. Other important manufacturing industries include plastics, rubber, cement, glass, paper and oil refining. Industry accounts for 38 per cent and services for 58 per cent of GDP.
GNP – US$96,483 million (1998); US$16,180 per capita (1998)
GDP – US$91,137 million (1996); US$16,091 per capita (1996)
ANNUAL AVERAGE GROWTH OF GDP – 1.9 per cent (1997)
INFLATION RATE – 5.4 per cent (1998)
UNEMPLOYMENT – 8.6 per cent (1998)

TRADE

The principal imports are machinery and transport equipment, semi-manufactures, uncut diamonds, chemicals and chemical products, crude oil, and foodstuffs. The principal exports are semi-manufactures, machinery, polished diamonds, chemicals and chemical products, foodstuffs and uncut diamonds.
   In 1998 Israel had a trade deficit of US$3,265 million and a current account deficit of US$2,297 million. Imports totalled US$29,342 million and exports totalled US$23,286 million.

Trade with UK	1998	1999
Imports from UK	£1,089,247,000	£1,297,788,000
Exports to UK	918,911,000	1,040,915,000

COMMUNICATIONS

Israel State Railways serves Haifa, Tel Aviv, Jerusalem, Lod, Nahariya, Beersheba, Dimona, Ashdod and intermediate stations with a network of 609km. There were 15,464 km of paved road in 1997. A major road building programme has been underway in the West Bank since 1992.
   The chief ports are Haifa and Ashdod on the Mediterranean, and Eilat on the Red Sea; Acre has an anchorage for small vessels. The chief international airport is Ben Gurion between Tel Aviv and Jerusalem.

EDUCATION

Education from five to 16 years is free and compulsory. The law also provides for working youth aged 16–18, who for some reason have not completed their education, to be exempted from work in order to do so. There are seven universities including two engineering and technological institutes.

ILLITERACY RATE – 3.9 per cent

ENROLMENT (percentage of age group) – tertiary 41.1 per cent (1995)

CULTURE

Important historic sites in Israel include: *Jerusalem* – the Church of the Holy Sepulchre, the Al Aqsa Mosque and Dome of the Rock standing on the remains of the Temple Mount of Herod the Great of which the Western (wailing) Wall is a fragment, the Church of the Dormition and the Coenaculum on Mount Zion, Ein Karem, Church of the Visitation, Church of St John the Baptist; *Galilee* – the Sea, Church and Mount of the Beatitudes, ruins of Capernaum and other sites connected with the life of Christ; *Mount Tabor* – Church of the Transfiguration; *Nazareth* – Church of the Annunciation, and other Christian shrines associated with the childhood of Christ; there are also numerous sites dating from biblical and medieval days, such as Ascalon, Caesarea, Atlit, Massada, Megiddo and Hazor.

PALESTINIAN AUTONOMOUS AREAS

AREA – The total area is 2,406 sq. miles (6,231 sq. km). The area which is fully autonomous is 159 sq. miles (412 sq. km), of which the Gaza Strip is 136 sq. miles (352 sq. km) and the Jericho enclave 23 sq. miles (60 sq. km). The partially autonomous area is the remainder of the West Bank, some 2,247 sq. miles (5,819 sq. km). The UN and the international community also recognise East Jerusalem as part of the Occupied Territories

POPULATION – 2,920,454 (1998 census), of whom 210,209 live in East Jerusalem. In addition there are 141,000 Jewish settlers in the West Bank and 4,000 in the Gaza Strip who remain under Israeli administration and jurisdiction. Some 90 per cent of Palestinians are Muslim (the vast majority Sunni) and 10 per cent are Christians

CAPITAL – Although Palestinians claim East Jerusalem as their capital, the administrative capital has been established in Gaza City (population 120,000)

MAJOR TOWNS – Khan Yunis, Rafah in the Gaza Strip; Nablus, Hebron, Jericho, Ramallah and Bethlehem on the West Bank

FLAG – Three horizontal stripes of black, white, green with a red triangle based on the hoist (the PLO flag)

NATIONAL ANTHEM – Fidai, Fidai (Freedom Fighter, Freedom Fighter)

HISTORY AND POLITICS

Israel captured the Gaza Strip, East Jerusalem and the West Bank during the 1967 Six-Day War and annexed East Jerusalem. After the war the Israeli government began to establish settlements in the Occupied Territories. Palestinian resistance to Israeli rule was led by the Palestine Liberation Organisation (PLO) which was established in 1964. Frustration at continued Israeli occupation led to the start of the *intifada*, a campaign of sustained unrest, in 1987. When the 1991 Madrid peace process stalled, Israeli and PLO officials engaged in secret negotiations in Norway which led to the signing of the 'Declaration of Principles on Interim Self-Government Arrangements' on 13 September 1993. Under this agreement the PLO renounced terrorism and recognised

Israel's right to exist in secure borders, while Israel recognised the PLO as the legitimate representative of the Palestinian people.

The Declaration of Principles established a timetable for progress towards a final settlement: negotiations leading to an Israeli military withdrawal from the Gaza Strip and Jericho by 13 April 1994, when power was to be transferred to a nominated Palestinian National Authority (PNA); elections to a new Palestinian Council, which would also exercise control over six policy areas in the rest of the West Bank (culture, tourism, health, education, social welfare, direct taxation), and the Israeli military administration dissolved by 13 July 1994; negotiations on a permanent settlement, including Jewish settlers and East Jerusalem, to begin by 13 April 1996; and a permanent settlement to be in place by 13 April 1999.

The timetable has slipped, with the Israeli military not finally redeploying in the Gaza Strip and withdrawing from Jericho until 18 May 1994, when the five-year period of interim self-government under the PNA began.

Israel and the Palestinians struggled to reach agreement on the extension of self-rule until 28 September 1995, when the 'Oslo B' or Taba Accord was signed which provided for Israeli withdrawal from six towns and 85 per cent of Hebron; the extension of self-rule to most of the West Bank by 1998; the release of 5,300 Palestinian prisoners; and the striking out of the demand for Israel's destruction from the PLO's charter. On 29 December 1995 an agreement was reached on the transfer of 17 areas of civilian power to the PNA in Hebron.

Implementation of the agreement began with the release of 1,100 Palestinian prisoners in October 1995; Israeli troops left Ramallah, the last of the six West Bank towns, on 27 December 1995 and the inaugural Palestinian National Council meeting on 23 April 1996 voted to amend the PLO charter. The final element of the Declaration of Principles, the 'final status talks' opened in Taba, Egypt, on 5 May 1996 to decide the final status of the West Bank, Gaza and Jerusalem. The election of a Likud-led government opposed to the establishment of a Palestinian state resulted in a deadlock in negotiations in 1997 and delays in the withdrawal of Israeli troops from Hebron.

Legislative elections on 20 January 1996 were won by the mainstream al-Fatah faction of the PLO, with its leader Yasser Arafat winning 88.1 per cent of the vote to become the president of the Palestinian National Authority.

Talks between the Palestinians and Israelis continued intermittently throughout 1997, but little of substance was achieved. Yasser Arafat and Binyamin Netanyahu met separately with American diplomats in London in May 1998, but talks broke down over the precise extent of Israeli troop withdrawals.

Yasser Arafat had planned to declare an independent Palestinian state on 4 May 1999, the end of the five-year transitional period which had been agreed in the 1993 Oslo peace accords, but the announcement was postponed in the hope that talks with the new Israeli government would lead to a negotiated settlement.

On 15 May 2000, widespread violence erupted during protests marking al-Nakba (the Catastrophe), the anniversary of the founding of the state of Israel in 1948, including exchanges of fire between Palestinian police and Israeli troops. In July, President Clinton hosted talks between Yasser Arafat and Ehud Barak, which aimed to resolve issues which had thwarted a comprehensive peace settlement, but no agreement was reached.

POLITICAL SYSTEM

The Oslo B accord laid down the political structure of the nascent Palestinian state. Executive authority is vested in the Palestinian National Authority which is headed by a popularly elected leader (rais). Legislative authority is vested in the 88-member Palestinian Council which is directly elected by means of a first-past-the-post system, and itself elects the four-fifths of the PNA not appointed by the leader.

PALESTINIAN NATIONAL AUTHORITY *as at September 2000*

Leader, Yasser Arafat
Agriculture, Hikmet Zeid
Bethlehem 2000 project; Dr Nabi Qsies
Civil Affairs, Jamil al-Tarifi
Culture and Arts, Information, Yassir Abd ar-Rabbuh
Detainees' and Freed Detainees' Affairs, Hisham Abdul Razeq
Economy and Trade, Mahir al-Masri
Education, vacant
Environment, Yusuf Abu-Safiyah
Finance, Muhammad Zuhdi al-Nashashibi
Health, Riyad al-Za'nun
Higher Education, Dr Munther Salah
Housing, Dr Abd al-Rahman Hamad
Industry, Dr Saad al-Karnaz
Interior, vacant
Justice, Furayh Abu Middayn
Labour, Rafiq al-Natshe
Local Government, Dr Sa'ib Urayqat
Non-governmental Organisations, Hassan Asfour
Parliamentary Affairs, Nabil Amr
Planning, International Co-operation, Dr Nabil Sha'ath
Post and Telecommunications, Imad al-Faluji
Public Works, Azzam al-Ahmad
Religious Affairs and Waqf, vacant
Social Affairs, vacant
Supply, Abd al-Aziz Shahin
Tourism and Archaeology, Mitri Abu Ayta
Transport, Dr Ali al-Qawasmi
Youth and Sport, vacant

BRITISH CONSULATE-GENERAL

19 Nashashibi Street, PO Box 19690, East Jerusalem 97200
Consul-General, R. A. Kealy, CMG

BRITISH COUNCIL DIRECTOR, D. Martin (*Cultural Attaché*), Al-Nuzha Building, 4 Abu Obeida Street, PO Box 19136, Jerusalem;
e-mail: bc.ejerusalem@bc-ejerusalem.bcouncil.org.
Regional offices in Gaza, Hebron, Nablus and Ramallah

Trade with UK	1998	1999
Imports from UK	£86,000	£302,000
Exports to UK	—	40,000

ITALY
Repubblica Italiana

AREA – 116,320 sq. miles (301,318 sq. km). Neighbours: Switzerland and Austria (north), Slovenia (east), France (west)
POPULATION – 57,523,000 (1997 UN estimate): 83 per cent Catholic. The language is Italian, a Romance language derived from Latin. There are several regional languages including Sardinian and Catalan in Sardinia, Friulian in Friuli, German and Ladin in the South Tyrol, French in the Valle d' Aosta, and Slovene in parts of Gorizia
CAPITAL – Rome (population, 2,648,843, 1995 estimate). The Eternal City was founded, according to legend, by Romulus in 753 BC. It was the centre of Latin civilisation and capital of the Roman Republic and Roman Empire

MAJOR CITIES – Bologna (404,322); Florence (402,316); ΨGenoa (675,659); Milan (1,371,008); ΨNaples (1,054,601); Turin (961,916); *Sicily*, ΨPalermo (697,162); *Sardinia*, ΨCagliari (203,254), 1991 census
CURRENCY – Euro (€) of 100 cents/Lira of 100 centesimi
NATIONAL ANTHEM – Inno di Mameli
NATIONAL DAY – 2 June
NATIONAL FLAG – Vertical stripes of green, white and red
LIFE EXPECTANCY (years) – male 74.34; female 80.74
POPULATION GROWTH RATE – 0.0 per cent (1997)
POPULATION DENSITY – 191 per sq. km (1997)
URBAN POPULATION – 96.6 per cent (1991)

Italy consists of a peninsula, the islands of Sicily, Sardinia, Elba and about 70 other small islands. The peninsula is for the most part mountainous, but between the Apennines, which form its spine, and the eastern coastline are two large fertile plains: Emilia-Romagna in the north and Apulia in the south. The Alps divide Italy from France, Switzerland, Austria and Slovenia. Partly within the Italian borders are Monte Rosa (15,217 ft), the Matterhorn (14,780 ft) and several peaks from 12,000 to 14,000 ft. The chief rivers are the Po (405 miles), flowing through Piedmont, Lombardy and the Veneto; the Adige (Trentino and Veneto); the Arno (Florentine plain); and the Tiber (flowing through Rome to Ostia).

HISTORY AND POLITICS

Italian unity was accomplished under the House of Savoy after a struggle from 1848 to 1870 in which Mazzini (1805–72), Garibaldi (1807–82) and Cavour (1810–61) were the principal figures. It was completed when Lombardy was ceded by Austria in 1859 and Venice in 1866, and through the evacuation of Rome by the French in 1870. In 1871 the King of Italy entered Rome, and that city was declared to be the capital.
A fascist regime came to power in 1922 under Benito Mussolini, known as *Il Duce* (The Leader), who was prime minister from 1922 until 25 July 1943, when the regime was abolished. Mussolini was captured by Italian partisans while attempting to escape across the Swiss frontier and killed on 28 April 1945.
A referendum on the future of the monarchy was held in June 1946, in which a majority favoured a republic, and the royal family left the country.
Political instability and corruption led to public disenchantment with the major political parties, whose support collapsed in the 1992 general election. The so-called 'clean hands' investigation into corruption and

Mafia links that began in 1992 has led to the arrest by magistrates of thousands of politicians and businessmen.

The independent Treasury minister Lamberto Dini formed a government of technocrats in January 1995. Dini resigned in January 1996 and a general election on 21 April 1996 was won by the left-wing Olive Tree alliance led by the Democratic Party of the Left, whose leader, Romano Prodi, became prime minister. The government won 157 seats in the Senate and 284 seats in the Chamber of Deputies where it required the support of the Communist Refoundation (RC) to win a vote of confidence. In October 1997, the RC refused to support the government budget and Prodi offered his resignation. President Scalfaro refused to accept the resignation and after negotiations Prodi and the RC signed a one-year agreement, but on 9 October 1998, the government collapsed after the RC refused to support the 1999 budget. Prodi lost the confidence motion and was forced to resign. Massimo D'Alema was invited by the president to form a new government on 20 October. On 19 December 1999, the government collapsed, but Massimo d'Alema was asked to form a new government the following day; he resigned as prime minister on 17 April 2000 following the defeat of his centre-left coalition in regional elections on 16 April. President Ciampi invited Giuliano Amato to form a new government and Amato was sworn in as prime minister on 26 April 2000.

POLITICAL SYSTEM

The constitution provides for the election of the president for a seven-year term by an electoral college which consists of the two houses of the parliament (the Chamber of Deputies and the Senate) sitting in joint session, together with three delegates from each region (one in the case of the Valle d'Aosta). The president, who must be over 50 years of age, has the right to dissolve one or both houses after consultation with the Speakers. Members of both houses were elected wholly by proportional representation until 1993. Now 75 per cent (232) of the 315 elected seats in the Senate are elected on a first-past-the-post basis and the remaining elected seats are filled by proportional representation. There is a variable number of life senators, who are past presidents and senators appointed by incumbent presidents. In the Chamber of Deputies 75 per cent (472) of seats are elected on a first-past-the-post basis, and 25 per cent (158) by proportional representation, with a 4 per cent threshold for parliamentary representation. A referendum on 18 April 1999 on abolishing the seats elected by proportional representation foundered when less than the required 50 per cent of the electorate participated.

HEAD OF STATE

President, Carlo Azeglio Ciampi, *elected by electoral college* 13 May 1999

COUNCIL OF MINISTERS *as at September 2000*

Prime Minister, Giuliano Amato (Ind.)
Agriculture, Alfonso Pecoraro Scanio (Green)
Culture, Giovanna Melandri (DPL)
Defence, Sergio Mattarella (IPP)
Education, Tullio De Mauro (Ind.)
Employment and Social Welfare, Cesare Salvi (DPL)
Environment, Willer Bordon (Dem.)
Equal Opportunities, Katia Bellillo (PIC)
European Affairs, Gianni Mattioli (Green)
Finance, Ottaviano Del Turco (IS)
Foreign Affairs, Lamberto Dini (IR)
Health, Umberto Veronesi (Ind.)
Industry, Foreign Trade and Tourism, Enrico Letta (IPP)
Institutional Reforms, Antonio Maccanico (Dem.)
Interior, Enzo Bianco (Dem.)
Justice, Piero Fassino (DPL)

Public Administration, Franco Bassanini (DPL)
Public Works, Nerio Nesi (PIC)
Regional Affairs, Agazio Loiero (DUR)
Relations with Parliament, Patrizia Toia (IPP)
Social Solidarity, Livia Turco (DPL)
Telecommunications, Salvatore Cardinale (DUR)
Transport, Pierluigi Bersani (DPL)
Treasury and Budget, Vicenzo Visco (DPL)
University and Scientific Research, Ortensio Zecchino (IPP)

Dem. Democrats; DPL Democratic Party of the Left; DUR Democratic Union for the Republic; Green Green Party; IPP Italian People's Party; IR Italian Renewal; ISD Italian Social Democrats; PIC Party of Italian Communists; Ind. Independent

ITALIAN EMBASSY

14 Three Kings Yard, Davies Street, London W1Y 2EH
Tel: 020-7312 2200
Ambassador Extraordinary and Plenipotentiary, HE Luigi Amaduzzi, apptd 1999
Minister-Counsellor, Dr A. d' Andria
Defence and Naval Attaché, Rear-Admr. A. Campregher
Cultural Attaché, Prof. B. Abruzzese
Minister (Consular Affairs), L. Savoia
CONSULAR OFFICES – Bedford, Edinburgh, Manchester

BRITISH EMBASSY

Via XX Settembre 80A, I-00187 Rome
Tel: (00 39) (6) 482-5441/5551
Ambassador Extraordinary and Plenipotentiary, HE Thomas L. Richardson, CMG, apptd 1996
Deputy Head of Mission, A. M. Leslie
Defence and Military Attaché, Brig. J. A. Anderson
Director-General for British Trade Development in Italy and Consul-General, C. De Chassiron (*Milan*)
Counsellor (Economic and Commercial), M. A. Hatfull

CONSULATE-GENERAL – Milan

CONSULATES – Rome, Bari, Brindisi, Cagliari, Catania, Florence, Genoa, Messina, Naples, Palermo, Trieste, Turin, Venice,

BRITISH COUNCIL DIRECTOR, R. Alford, OBE, Via Quattro Fontane 20, I-00184 Rome; e-mail: Enquiry.BCRome@britcoun.it
There are British Council Offices at Milan, Bologna, Naples and Turin

BRITISH CHAMBER OF COMMERCE, Via San Paolo 7, I-20121Milan

DEFENCE

The Army has 1,322 main battle tanks and 3,107 armoured personnel carriers. The Navy has eight submarines, one aircraft carrier, one cruiser, four destroyers, 24 frigates, 16 patrol and coastal vessels, 18 combat aircraft and 80 armed helicopters. There are ten naval bases. The Air Force has 321 combat aircraft.
MILITARY EXPENDITURE – 2.0 per cent of GDP (1998)
MILITARY PERSONNEL – 521,200: Army 165,600, Navy 38,000, Air Force 61,900, Paramilitaries 255,700
CONSCRIPTION DURATION – Ten months

ECONOMY

Deposits of natural methane gas and oil have been discovered, mainly south of Sicily, and have been rapidly exploited. Production of lignite has also increased. Other minerals include iron ores and pyrites, mercury (over one-quarter of the world production), lead, zinc and aluminium. Rich gold veins were discovered in Sardinia in 1996. Marble is a traditional product of the Massa Carrara district.

Agricultural production is concentrated in Tuscany, Emilia-Romagna, Sicily and the whole of the southern third of the country. The principal products are wine, tobacco, citrus fruits, tomatoes, almonds, sugar beet, wheat and maize.

Tourism is a major contributor to the economy; in 1997, around 57 million people visited Italy. The commercial and banking services are concentrated in Rome and in Milan, where the stock market is located.

The state-owned sector of Italian industry is still important, dominated by the holding companies IRI (mechanical, steel, airlines), ENI (petrochemicals), and ENEL (electricity), although in November 1999, the government sold 34.5 per cent of ENEL, and in February 2000 agreed to the liberalisation of the gas market over which ENI had previously had a virtual monopoly. Industry is centred around Milan (steel, machine tools, motor cars), Turin (motor cars, steel, roller bearings, textiles), Rome (light industries), Venice (shipbuilding, paper, mechanical equipment, electrical goods, woollens), Bologna/Florence (food industry, footwear and textiles, reproduction furniture, glassware, pottery, ceramics), Naples, Bari (valves, vehicle bodies, tyres), Taranto (steel, oil refining), Trieste (shipbuilding) and Cagliari (aluminium production, petrochemicals).

Following a programme of severe austerity measures, Italy satisfied the convergence criteria and participated in the European Single Currency from 1 January 1999.

In 1998 there was a trade surplus of US$35,631 million and a current account surplus of US$19,998 million. Imports totalled US$215,887 million and exports US$242,332 million.

Italy's chief exports are industrial and agricultural machinery, textiles and clothing, electrical equipment and chemicals. Chief imports are chemicals, motor vehicles and metals. Italy's main trading partners are Germany, France, the UK and the USA.

GNP – US$1,157,001 million (1998); US$20,090 per capita (1998)
GDP – US$1,214,268 million (1996); US$21,219 per capita (1996)
ANNUAL AVERAGE GROWTH OF GDP – 1.5 per cent (1997)
INFLATION RATE – 2.0 per cent (1998)
UNEMPLOYMENT – 12.3 per cent (1997)

Trade with UK	1998	1999
Imports from UK	£8,140,000,000	£7,374,410,000
Exports to UK	9,273,700,000	8,875,600,000

COMMUNICATIONS

The main railway system is state-run by the *Ferrovia dello Stato*. There are 19,527 km of railway track. A network of motorways (*autostrade*) covers the country, built and operated mainly by the IRI state holding company and ANAS, the state highway authority. There are 306,445 km of roads. Alitalia, the principal international and domestic airline, is also state-controlled by the IRI group. Other smaller companies, including ATI (an Alitalia subsidiary) and Air Mediterranea, operate on domestic routes. Genoa is the major port, handling about one-third of Italy's foreign trade.

EDUCATION

Education is free and compulsory between the ages of six and 14; this comprises five years at primary school and three in 'middle school', of which there are 9,215. Pupils who obtain the middle school certificate may seek admission to any 'senior secondary school', which may be a lyceum with a classical or scientific or artistic bias, or an institute directed at technology (of which there are eight different types), trade or industry (including vocational schools), or teacher-training. Courses at the lyceums and technical institutes usually last for five years

and success in the final examination qualifies for admission to university.

There are 62 universities, some of ancient foundation; those at Bologna, Modena, Parma and Padua were started in the 12th century. University education is not free, but entrants with higher qualifications are charged reduced fees according to a sliding scale.

In general, schools, lyceums and universities are financed by local taxation and central government grants.
ILLITERACY RATE – 1.5 per cent
ENROLMENT (percentage of age group) – primary 100 per cent (1996); tertiary 47 per cent (1996)

CULTURE

Florence, the capital of Tuscany, was one of the greatest cities in Europe from the 11th to the 16th centuries, and the cradle of the Renaissance. Under the Medici family in the 15th century flourished many of the greatest names in Italian art, including Filippo Lippi, Botticelli, Donatello and Brunelleschi, and in the 16th century Michelangelo and Leonardo da Vinci.

Italian literature (in addition to Latin literature, which is the common inheritance of western Europe) is one of the richest in Europe, particularly in its golden age (Dante, 1265–1321; Petrarch, 1304–74; Boccaccio, 1313–75) and in the Renaissance (Ariosto, 1474–1533; Machiavelli, 1469–1527; Tasso, 1544–95). Notable in modern Italian literature are Manzoni (1785–1873), Carducci (1835–1907) and Gabriele d'Annunzio (1864–1938). The Nobel Prize for Literature has been awarded to Italian authors on six occasions: G. Cariducci (1906), Signora G. Deledda (1926), Luigi Pirandello (1934), Salvatore Quasimodo (1959), Eugenio Montale (1975) and Dario Fo (1997).

ISLANDS

CAPRI, in the Bay of Naples; area 4 sq. miles (10 sq. km); population 12,000
EOLIAN ISLANDS, including Lipari; area 45 sq. miles (116 sq. km); population 18,636
FLEGREAN ISLANDS, including Ischia; area 23 sq. miles (60 sq. km); population 51,883
PANTELLERIA ISLAND (part of Trapani Province) in the Sicilian Narrows; area 31 sq. miles (80 sq. km); population 9,601
THE PELAGIAN ISLANDS (Lampedusa, Linosa and Lampione) are part of the province of Agrigento; area 8 sq. miles (21 sq. km); population 4,811
PONTINE ARCHIPELAGO, including Ponza; area 4 sq. miles (10 sq. km); population 2,515
TREMITI ISLANDS; area 1 sq. mile (3 sq. km); population 426
THE TUSCAN ARCHIPELAGO (including Elba); area 113 sq. miles (293 sq. km); population 31,861

JAMAICA

AREA – 4,243 sq. miles (10,990 sq. km)
POPULATION – 2,590,400 (1999 estimate). The official language is English; a local patois is also spoken
CAPITAL – ΨKingston (population, 524,638, 1991)
MAJOR CITIES – Mandeville; May Pen; ΨMontego Bay; Ocho Rios; Spanish Town
CURRENCY – Jamaican dollar (J$) of 100 cents
NATIONAL ANTHEM – Jamaica, Land We Love
NATIONAL DAY – 6 August (Independence Day)
NATIONAL FLAG – Gold diagonal cross forming triangles of green at top and bottom, triangles of black at hoist and in fly
LIFE EXPECTANCY (years) – male 72.20; female 75.82
POPULATION GROWTH RATE – 0.7 per cent (1999)
POPULATION DENSITY – 232 per sq. km (1997)

URBAN POPULATION – 43.3 per cent (1999)
MILITARY EXPENDITURE – 0.9 per cent of GDP (1998)
MILITARY PERSONNEL – 2,830: Army 2,500, Coast Guard 190, Air Wing 140
ILLITERACY RATE – 13.3 per cent
ENROLMENT (percentage of age group) – primary 100 per cent (1999); secondary 69 per cent (1999); tertiary 12.7 per cent (1999)

Jamaica is divided into three counties (Surrey, Middlesex and Cornwall) and 14 parishes. The island consists mainly of coastal plains, divided by the Blue Mountain range in the east and the hills and limestone plateaux in the central and western areas of the interior. The central chain of the Blue Mountains is over 6,000 feet above sea level, and the Blue Mountain Peak is 7,402 feet.

HISTORY AND POLITICS

The island was discovered by Columbus in 1494, and occupied by Spain from 1509 until 1655 when an English expedition under Admiral Penn and General Venables captured the island. In 1670 it was formally ceded to England by the Treaty of Madrid. Jamaica became an independent state within the Commonwealth on 6 August 1962.

At the general election of 18 December 1997, the People's National Party won 50 out of a total of 60 seats, securing a third term for the party and a second term for Prime Minister Percival Patterson.

POLITICAL SYSTEM

Queen Elizabeth II is the head of state, represented by the Governor-General. The legislature consists of a Senate of 21 nominated members and a House of Representatives consisting of 60 members elected by universal adult suffrage for a five-year term. The prime minister is the leader of the majority party in the House.

Governor-General, HE Sir Howard Felix Hanlon Cooke, GCMG, GCVO, apptd 1991

CABINET *as at September 2000*

Prime Minister, Defence, Percival J.Patterson, QC
Deputy PM, Land and the Environment, Seymour Mullings
Agriculture, Roger Clarke
Education and Culture, Burchel Whiteman
Finance and Planning, Omar Davies
Foreign Affairs, Paul Robertson
Foreign Trade, Anthony Hylton
Health, John Archbald Junor
Industry, Commerce and Technology, Phillip Paulwell
Information, Maxine Henry-Wilson
Labour, and Social Security, Donald Buchanan
Legal Affairs, Attorney-General, Arnold Nicholson
Local Government, Youth and Community Development, Arnold Bertram
Mining and Energy, Robert Pickersgill
National Security and Justice, Keith Desmond Knight
Tourism and Sports, Entertainment, Portia Simpson-Miller
Transportation and Works, Peter Phillips
Water and Housing, Karl Blythe

JAMAICAN HIGH COMMISSION

1–2 Prince Consort Road, London SW7 2BZ
Tel: 020-7823 9911
High Commissioner, HE David Muirhead, apptd 1999
Deputy High Commissioners, A. Rodriques; J. K. Pringle, CBE, OJ (*Trade*)
Minister-Counsellor, K. Hamilton (*Consular Affairs*)
Defence Adviser, Col. B. Blake

BRITISH HIGH COMMISSION

PO Box 575, Trafalgar Road, Kingston 10
Tel: (00 1 876) 926 9050
E-mail: bhckingston@cw.com

High Commissioner, HE A. F. Smith, apptd 1999
Deputy High Commissioner, J. Malcolm, OBE
Defence Adviser, Col. A. Moorby
First Secretary (Management/Consular), P. Duffy
BRITISH COUNCIL MANAGER, N. Johnson, British High Commission, Trafalgar Road, PO Box 235, Kingston 5; e-mail: bcjamaica@bc-caribbean.org

ECONOMY

Alumina, bananas, bauxite and sugar are the main exports. Other exports include garments, processed food products, limestone and horticultural products.

Since 1989 the PNP government has abolished price subsidies, removed foreign exchange controls and introduced a 10 per cent consumption tax. Jamaica is a popular tourist resort, attracting 2,012,738 visitors in 1999.

In February 2000 parliament approved the liberalisation of telecommunications, to be phased in over a three-year period.

The economy has faced many problems, including a GDP which has been falling since 1996, interest repayments on debt which accounted for 41 per cent of government revenue in 1999, low market prices for many of Jamaica's exports and interest rates of over 30 per cent.

In 1999 Jamaica had a trade deficit of US$1,140 million and a current account deficit of US$273 million. Imports totalled US$2,631 million and exports US$1,490 million.
GNP – US$4,280 million (1999); US$1,740 per capita (1998)
GDP – US$5,475 million (1996); US$2,198 per capita (1996)
ANNUAL AVERAGE GROWTH OF GDP – –0.4 per cent (1999)
INFLATION RATE – 6.8 per cent (1999)
UNEMPLOYMENT – 15.7 per cent (1999)
TOTAL EXTERNAL DEBT – US$3,024 million (1999)

Trade with UK	1998	1999
Imports from UK	£68,277,000	£92,279,000
Exports to UK	114,683,000	112,995,000

COMMUNICATIONS

There are several excellent harbours, Kingston being the principal port. The island has 2,944 miles of main roads and 7,264 miles of subsidiary roads.

There are two international airports, the Norman Manley International Airport on the south coast serving Kingston, and Sangster Airport on the north coast serving the major tourist areas. In addition there are licensed aerodromes at Port Antonio, Ocho Rios, Mandeville and Negril. There are 16 privately owned, seven public and two military airstrips. Air Jamaica, the national airline, operates international services.

JAPAN
Nihon Koku – Land of the Rising Sun

AREA – 145,870 sq. miles (377,829 sq. km)
POPULATION – 125,638,000 (1997 UN estimate). The principal religions are Mahayana Buddhism and Shinto. About 1 per cent of Japanese are Christians. The language is Japanese
CAPITAL – Tokyo (population, 11,680,296, 1993 estimate)
MAJOR CITIES – ΨFukuoka (1,284,795); ΨKobé (1,423,792); Kyoto, the ancient capital (1,463,822); ΨNagoya (2,152,184); ΨOsaka (2,602,421); Sapporo (1,757,025); ΨYokohama (3,307,136), 1995
CURRENCY – Yen
NATIONAL ANTHEM – Kimigayo (His Majesty's reign)

NATIONAL FLAG – White, charged with sun (red)
LIFE EXPECTANCY (years) – male 77.01; female 83.59
POPULATION GROWTH RATE – 0.2 per cent (1997)
POPULATION DENSITY – 333 per sq. km (1997)
URBAN POPULATION – 78.1 per cent (1995)

Japan consists of four large islands: *Honshu* (or Mainland) 88,839 sq. miles (230,448 sq.km), *Shikoku*, 7,231 sq. miles (18,757 sq.km), *Kyushu*, 16,170 sq. miles (42,079 sq.km), *Hokkaido*, 30,265 sq. miles (78,508 sq.km), and many small islands (including Okinawa).

The interior is very mountainous, and crossing the mainland from the Sea of Japan to the Pacific is a group of volcanoes, mainly extinct or dormant. Mount Fuji, the most sacred mountain of Japan, is 12,370 ft high and has been dormant since 1707, but volcanoes which are active include Mount Aso in Kyushu. There are frequent earthquakes, mainly along the Pacific coast near the Bay of Tokyo. The climate varies from sub-tropical in the south to cool temperate in the north.

HISTORY AND POLITICS

According to tradition, Jimmu, the first Emperor of Japan, ascended the throne on 11 February 660 BC. Under the *Meiji* constitution (1889), the monarchy is hereditary in the male heirs of the Imperial house.

After the unconditional surrender to the Allied nations (14 August 1945), Japan was occupied by Allied forces under General MacArthur. A Japanese peace treaty became effective on 28 April 1952. Japan then resumed her status as an independent power.

The (conservative) Liberal Democratic Party (LDP) governed Japan almost without interruption from the Second World War until 1993.

The LDP returned to power in June 1994 in coalition with the SDPJ and Sakigake parties, with SDPJ leader Tomiichi Murayama becoming Japan's first socialist prime minister. Murayama resigned in January 1996 and was replaced by LDP leader Ryutaro Hashimoto. In March 1998 four opposition parties merged to form the Democratic Party of Japan.

Hashimoto was elected to a second term as prime minister, but resigned in July 1998 following a heavy defeat for the LDP in the upper house elections, seen as largely due to his handling of the economic crisis. He was replaced as prime minister and leader of the LDP by Foreign Minister Keizo Obuchi, who suffered a stroke on 1 April 2000 and died on 14 May. Cabinet Secretary Mikio Aoki took over as acting prime minister on 3 April and the LDP Secretary-General Yoshiro Mori was elected

prime minister by the House of Representatives on 5 April. The LDP have 263 seats in the House of Representatives. The standing of the other parties is: Democratic Party 91; Heiwa Kaikaku 47; Liberal Party 40; Japan Communist Party 26; SDP 14; Sakigake 2; Independent 10.

POLITICAL SYSTEM

Legislative authority rests with the bicameral *Diet*, which comprises a 480-member House of Representatives, and a 252-member House of Councillors. The House of Representatives chooses the prime minister from among its ranks, ratifies treaties and passes budget bills. Since January 2000, 180 of its members are elected by proportional representation in 11 regional blocks and 300 in single-member, first-past-the-post constituencies. All members serve four-year terms. The House of Councillors elects half its members every three years for six-year terms. Unlike the lower House it cannot be dissolved by the prime minister. Executive authority is vested in the Cabinet which is responsible to the legislature.

HEAD OF STATE

His Imperial Majesty The Emperor of Japan, Emperor Akihito, *born* 23 December 1933; *succeeded* 8 January 1989; *enthroned* 12 November 1990; *married* 10 April 1959, Miss Michiko Shoda, and has *issue*: the Crown Prince (*see* below); Prince Fumihito, *born* 30 November 1965; and Princess Sayako, *born* 18 April 1969

Heir, HRH Crown Prince Naruhito Hironomiya, *born* 23 February 1960, *married* 9 June 1993 Miss Masako Owada

CABINET *as at September 2000*

Prime Minister, Yoshiro Mori (LDP)
Agriculture, Forestry and Fisheries, Yoichi Tani (LDP)
Construction, National Land Agency, Chikage Ogi
Education, Science and Technology Agency, Tadamori Ohshima
Finance, Kiichi Miyazawa (LDP)
Foreign Affairs, Yohei Kono (LDP)
Health and Welfare, Yuji Tsushima (LDP)
Home Affairs, Mamoru Nishida (LDP)
International Trade and Industry, Takashi Hiranuma (LDP)
Justice, Okiharu Yasuoka (LDP)
Labour, Yoshio Yoshikawa (LDP)
Post and Telecommunications, Kozo Hirabayashi (LDP)
State Ministers, Hidenao Nakagawa (LDP) (*Chief Cabinet Secretary, Okinawa Development Agency*); Tsutomu Kawara (LDP) (*Defence Agency*); Taichi Sakaiya (Ind.) (*Economic Planning Agency*); Yorkio Kawaguchi (Ind.) (*Environment Agency*); Hideyuki Aizawa (LDP) (*Financial Reconstruction Commission*); Kunihiro Tsuzuki (NK) (*Management and Co-ordination Agency*)
Transport, Hokkaido Development Agency, Hajime Morita (LDP)

LDP Liberal Democratic Party; NCP New Conservative Party; NK New Komeito; Ind. Independent

EMBASSY OF JAPAN

101–104 Piccadilly, London W1V 9FN
Tel: 020-74656500
Ambassador Extraordinary and Plenipotentiary, HE Sadayuki Hayashi, apptd 1997
Ministers, K. Shimanouchi (*Plenipotentiary*); S. Nakamura (*Consul-General*); H. Kuramochi (*Commercial*); K. Monji; S. Nishimiya; T. Uranishi

BRITISH EMBASSY

No. 1 Ichiban-cho, Chiyoda-ku, Tokyo 102-8381
Tel: (00 81) (3) 5211-1100
E-mail: bejapan@crisscross.com
Ambassador Extraordinary and Plenipotentiary, HE

Stephen Gomersall, CMG, apptd 1999
Chargé d'Affaires, C. T. W. Humfrey, CMG
Counsellors, P. Bateman (Commercial); R. R. Hoggard
(Management and Consul-General)
Defence and Naval Attaché, Capt. J. A. Boyd

CONSULATES-GENERAL – Tokyo, Osaka
HONORARY CONSULATES – Fukuoka, Hiroshima,
Nagoya, Sapporo
BRITISH COUNCIL DIRECTOR, T. Toney, 2 Kagurazaka
1-Chome, Shinjuku-ku, Tokyo 162-0825;
e-mail: bctokyo@britishcouncil.org.jp
Regional offices in Fukuoka, Kyoto, Nagoya and Osaka

BRITISH CHAMBER of COMMERCE, No. 16 Kowa Building,
1–9–20 Akasaka, Minato-ku, Tokyo 107

DEFENCE

The constitution prohibits the maintenance of armed
forces, although internal security forces were created in
the 1950s and their mission was extended in 1954 to
include the defence of Japan against aggression. In the
1990s legislation was passed permitting the armed forces
limited participation in UN peacekeeping missions and
allowing them to enter foreign conflicts in order to rescue
Japanese nationals. A revision to the USA–Japan defence
co-operation guidelines agreed in 1997 permits Japan to
play a supporting role in US military operations in areas
surrounding Japan.

The Ground Self-Defence Force (GSDF) has 1,080
main battle tanks, around 840 armoured personnel
carriers, 60 infantry fighting vehicles, 10 aircraft and 90
attack helicopters. The Maritime Self-Defence Force
(MSDF) has 16 submarines, nine destroyers, 46 frigates,
90 combat aircraft and 90 armed helicopters at five bases.
The Air Self-Defence Force (ASDF) has 330 combat
aircraft.

The USA has 40,100 personnel stationed in Japan.
Following an agreement in December 1996 the USA is due
to vacate 21 per cent of the land it occupies in Japan and
close part or all of 11 military facilities.
MILITARY EXPENDITURE – 1.0 per cent of GDP (1998)
MILITARY PERSONNEL – 246,900: Army 145,900, Navy
43,800, Air Force 45,200; Paramilitaries 12,000

ECONOMY

Owing to the mountainous nature of the country less than
20 per cent of its area can be cultivated and only 14 per cent
is used for agriculture; 67 per cent is wooded. The soil is
only moderately fertile but intensive cultivation secures
good crops. Tobacco, tea, potatoes, rice, maize, wheat and
other cereals are all cultivated. Rice is the staple food of the
people. Fruit is abundant and pigs and chickens are widely
reared.

Mineral resources include gold, silver, copper, lead,
zinc, iron chromite, white arsenic, coal, sulphur, petroleum, salt and uranium. However, iron ore, coal and crude
oil are among the principal imports.

Japan is one of the most highly industrialised nations in
the world, with the whole range of modern light and heavy
industries, including steel, aerospace, computers, office
machinery, motor vehicles, electronics, metals, machinery, chemicals, textiles (cotton, silk, wool and synthetics),
cement, pottery, glass, rubber, lumber, paper, oil refining
and shipbuilding.

Japan's economy was severely affected by the financial
crisis in Asia. Its banks had made loans totalling
some US$200 billion to tiger economies, and following
widespread economic collapse in the region, Japan's
financial institutions have suffered. Emergency measures
announced by the government were perceived by the

markets as inadequate. Japan's economy contracted in
1998; GDP fell by 2.8 per cent. The economy showed
signs of recovery in the first half of 1999, but the second
half of the year was disappointing. Unemployment
reached 4.8 per cent, the highest level since the Second
World War. In November 1999, the government
announced an economic stimulus package, which was
designed to aid economic recovery and restructuring.
GNP – US$4,089,140 million (1998); US$32,350 per
capita (1998)
GDP – US$4,595,155 million (1996); US$36,658 per
capita (1996)
ANNUAL AVERAGE GROWTH OF GDP – 0.9 per cent (1997)
INFLATION RATE – 0.6 per cent (1998)
UNEMPLOYMENT – 4.1 per cent (1998)

TRADE

Being deficient in natural resources, Japan has had to
develop a complex foreign trade. Principal imports
include mineral fuels, food, raw materials and metal ores.
Principal exports include machinery, transport equipment, chemicals, metal products and textiles.

In 1998 Japan had a trade surplus of US$122,389
million and a current account surplus of US$120,696
million. Imports totalled US$280,484 million and exports
US$387,927 million. The USA, China, Australia, Hong
Kong, South Korea, Taiwan and Singapore are Japan's
main trading partners.

Trade with UK	1998	1999
Imports from UK	£3,222,587,000	£3,304,346,000
Exports to UK	9,548,786,000	9,542,821,000

COMMUNICATIONS

There are 27,258 km of railway track and 1,142,308 km of
roads. Japan National Railways was privatised in 1987 and
is known as Japan Railways (JR). There are six regional
companies and one goods company. Shinkansen (bullet
train) tracks are currently being expanded. The opening in
1988 of the Seikan rail tunnel and the Seto Ohashi rail
bridge means that the four major islands are now linked for
the first time. There are six international airports.

EDUCATION

Education at elementary (six-year course) and lower
secondary (three-year course) schools is free, compulsory
and co-educational. The (three-year) upper secondary
schools are attended by 96.7 per cent of the age group.

There are two- or three-year colleges and four-year
universities. Some of the universities have graduate
schools. In 1999 there were 622 universities and colleges,
most of which are privately maintained. The most
prominent universities are the seven state universities of
Tokyo, Kyoto, Tohoku (Sendai), Hokkaido (Sapporo),
Kyushu (Fukuoka), Osaka and Nagoya, and the two
private universities of Keio and Waseda.
ENROLMENT (percentage of age group) – primary 100
per cent (1994); secondary 98 per cent (1994); tertiary
41 per cent (1994)

CULTURE

Japanese is said to be one of the Ural-Altaic group of
languages and remained a spoken tongue until the fifth to
seventh centuries AD, when Chinese characters came into
use. Japanese who have received school education can read
and write the Chinese characters in current use (about
1,800) and also the syllabary characters called Kana.

JORDAN
Al-Mamlaka al-Urdunniyya al-Hashimiyya

AREA – 37,738 sq. miles (97,740 sq. km). Neighbours: Syria (north), Israel and the West Bank (west), Saudi Arabia (south and east), Iraq (east)
POPULATION – 5,774,000 (1997 UN estimate); 4,095,579 (1994 census). The majority are Sunni Muslims and Islam is the religion of the state; however, freedom of belief is guaranteed by the constitution
CAPITAL – 'Ammān (population, 1,270,000, 1994)
MAJOR CITIES – Irbid (216,000); Az-Zarqā (359,000), 1991
CURRENCY – Jordanian dinar (JD) of 1,000 fils
NATIONAL ANTHEM – Asha al Malik (Long Live the King)
NATIONAL DAY – 25 May (Independence Day)
NATIONAL FLAG – Three horizontal stripes of black, white, green and a red triangle based on the hoist, containing a seven-pointed white star
LIFE EXPECTANCY (years) – male 66.16; female 69.84
POPULATION GROWTH RATE – 4.3 per cent (1997)
POPULATION DENSITY – 59 per sq. km (1997)
ILLITERACY RATE – 10.2 per cent
ENROLMENT (percentage of age group) – primary 89 per cent (1992); secondary 42 per cent (1989); tertiary 24.5 per cent (1989)

HISTORY AND POLITICS

After the defeat of Turkey in the First World War, the Amirate of Transjordan was established in the area east of the River Jordan as a state under British mandate. The mandate was terminated after the Second World War and the Amirate, still ruled by its founder the Amir Abdullah, became the Hashemite Kingdom of Jordan. Following the 1948–9 war between Israel and the Arab states, that part of Palestine remaining in Arab hands (the West Bank and East Jerusalem, but excluding Gaza) was, with Palestinian agreement, incorporated into the Hashemite Kingdom. King Abdullah was assassinated in 1951; his son Talal ruled briefly but abdicated in favour of King Hussein in 1952.

The West Bank has been under Israeli occupation since its capture from Jordan in the 1967 war, and East Jerusalem was annexed by Israel in 1967. In 1988 Jordan severed its legal and administrative ties with the occupied West Bank, but did not formally renounce sovereignty over the area. As a result of the wars of 1948–9 and 1967 there are about one million Palestinian refugees and displaced persons living in East Jordan, about 200,000 of whom live in refugee and displaced persons camps established by the UN Relief and Works Agency (UNRWA). In addition there are 300,000 self-supporting Palestinians in East Jordan.

In 1993, multiparty parliamentary elections were held for the first time since 1956. In the most recent elections, held on 4 November 1997, pro-government candidates won 62 out of 80 seats; the main opposition parties boycotted the elections.

FOREIGN RELATIONS

The Middle East peace process begun in 1991 led to Jordan signing an agreement on a 'common agenda' for peace with Israel in 1993. On 25 July 1994 King Hussein and the Israeli Prime Minister signed a framework agreement for peace which ended the state of war existing since 1948. The first Israeli–Jordanian border crossing was opened between Eilat and Aqaba in August 1994. A full peace treaty was signed on 26 October 1994 which established full diplomatic and economic relations between the two states. It included agreements on sharing water from the Jordan and Yarmouk rivers; co-operating in the fields of commerce, transport, tourism, communications, energy and agriculture; and granted King Hussein custodianship of Islamic holy sites in Jerusalem. Israeli forces completed their withdrawal from Jordanian land in the Arava valley on 9 February 1995.

On 25 January 1999, King Hussein signed a decree naming his eldest son, Abdullah ibn al-Hussein, as his new heir, in place of his youngest brother, Prince Hassan; Prince Abdullah became King following the death of King Hussein on 7 February 1999.

Jordan and Kuwait re-established full diplomatic relations on 3 March 1999, which had been broken off following the 1990 Gulf War.

POLITICAL SYSTEM

The constitution provides for a Senate of 40 members (all appointed by the King for a four-year term) and an elected House of Representatives which has 80 members, directly elected for a four-year term.

The King appoints the members of the Council of Ministers. In 1991 a new national charter was formulated which lifted the ban on political parties, imposed in 1957.

HEAD OF STATE
His Majesty The King of the Jordan, Abdullah II, *born* 30 January 1962, *succeeded* 7 February 1999
Crown Prince, Hamzeh ibn al-Hussein, *born* 29 March 1982, son of King Hussein of Jordan
Chief of the Royal Court, Fayez Tarawneh

COUNCIL OF MINISTERS *as at September 2000*
Prime Minister, Defence, Ali Abu-al-Raghib
Deputy PM, Cabinet Affairs, Salih Irshaydat
Deputy PM, Economic Affairs, Mohammed Halayka
Deputy PM, Interior, Awad Khulayfat
Deputy PM, Justice, Faris al-Nabulsi
Administrative Development, Muhammad Dhunaybat
Agriculture, Zuhayr Zannunah
Culture, Mahmud al-Kayid
Education, Higher Education, Khalid Tuqan
Energy and Mineral Resources, Wael Sabri
Finance, Michel Martu
Foreign Affairs, Abdul Illah al-Khatib
Health, Tariq Suhaymat
Industry and Trade, Wasif Azar
Information, Taleb Rifai
Labour, Eid Fayez
Ministers of State, Adil al-Shuraydah; Dayfallah al-Masaidah (*Legal Affairs*); Yusuf al-Dalabih (*Parliamentary Affairs*)
Municipal, Rural and Environmental Affairs, Abd-al-Rahim al-Ukur
Planning, Jawad Hadid
Post and Telecommunications, Fawwaz Hatim al-Zubi
Public Works and Housing, Hosni Abu Ghida
Religious Endowments (Waqfs), Islamic Affairs, Abdul Salam al-Abbadi
Social Development, Tamam al-Ghul
Tourism and Antiquities, Aqel Biltaji
Transport, Muhammad al-Kalalidah
Water and Irrigation, Hatim al-Halawani
Youth and Sport, Said Shuqum

EMBASSY OF THE HASHEMITE KINGDOM OF JORDAN
6 Upper Phillimore Gardens, London W8 7HB
Tel: 020-7937 3685
Ambassador Extraordinary and Plenipotentiary, HE Timoor Daghistani, apptd 1999
Defence Attaché, Brig. Mohammad Quda'h

BRITISH EMBASSY
Abdoun (PO Box 87), 'Ammān
Tel: (00 962) (6) 592 3100/6592
Ambassador Extraordinary and Plenipotentiary,
  HE Christopher Battiscombe, CMG, apptd 1997
Counsellor, S. P. Collis (*Deputy Head of Mission and Consul General*)
Defence Attaché, Col. R. J. Sandy
First Secretary, R. Leadbeater (*Consul and Management*)
BRITISH COUNCIL DIRECTOR, R. Walton, Rainbow Street, Jabal 'Ammān, (PO Box 634), 'Ammān 11118; e-mail: bcamman@britishcouncil.org.jo

DEFENCE

The Army has 1,204 main battle tanks, 1,400 armoured personnel carriers and 35 armoured infantry fighting vehicles. The Navy has three patrol and coastal vessels at its base at Aqaba. The Air Force has 93 combat aircraft and 16 armed helicopters.
MILITARY EXPENDITURE – 7.7 per cent of GDP (1998)
MILITARY PERSONNEL – 113,980: Army 90,000, Navy 480, Air Force 13,500, Paramilitaries 10,000

ECONOMY

The main agricultural areas are the Jordan valley, the hills overlooking the valley, and the flatter country to the south of 'Ammān and around Madaba and Irbid. However, several large farms, which depend for irrigation on water pumped from deep aquifers, have been established in the southern desert area. The rest of the country is desert and semi-desert. The principal crops are wheat, barley, vegetables, olives and fruit. Agricultural production has increased considerably in recent years due to improvements in production and irrigation techniques.

Important industrial products are raw phosphates (1998, 5,925,000 tonnes) and potash (1998, 916,169 tonnes), most of which is exported, together with fertilisers and pharmaceuticals. The Trans-Arabian oil pipeline (Tapline) runs through north Jordan from Saudi Arabia to the Lebanese port of Sidon. A branch pipeline, together with oil trucked by road from Iraq, feeds a refinery at Zerqa, which meets most of Jordan's requirements for refined petroleum products. Sufficient reserves of natural gas have been discovered in the north-east to produce electricity for the national grid since 1989.

Tourism has developed, principally in 'Ammān, Aqaba, Zerka Ma'in and on the shores of the Dead Sea. In 1996, Jordan had 2,800,000 visitors.

In 1998 there was a trade deficit of US$1,613 million and a current account surplus of US$3 million. In 1997 imports totalled US$4,095 million and exports US$1,843 million.
GNP – US$5,252 million (1998); US$1,150 per capita (1998)
GDP – US$7,259 million (1996); US$1,301 per capita (1996)
ANNUAL AVERAGE GROWTH OF GDP – 5.2 per cent (1996)
INFLATION RATE – 4.4 per cent (1998)
TOTAL EXTERNAL DEBT – US$8,485 million (1998)

Trade with UK	1998	1999
Imports from UK	£124,879,000	£121,280,000
Exports to UK	27,045,000	24,263,000

COMMUNICATIONS

'Ammān is linked to Aqaba, Damascus, Baghdād and Jiddah by roads which are of considerable importance in the overland trade of the Middle East.

The former Hejaz Railway runs from Syria through Jordan, and is used mainly for freight between 'Ammān and Damascus. The Aqaba railway carries phosphate rock from the mines of al-Hasa and al-Abiad to Aqaba.

The Royal Jordanian Airline operates from 'Ammān to Aqaba and has an extensive network of routes to the Middle East, Europe, North America and the Far East.

KAZAKHSTAN
Kazakstan Respublikasy

AREA – 1,049,156 sq. miles (2,724,900 sq. km).
  Neighbours: Russia (north and west), Turkmenistan, Uzbekistan and Kyrgyzstan (south), China (east)
POPULATION – 15,700,000 (2000 estimate): Kazakhs (44 per cent), Russians (36 per cent), Ukrainians (5 per cent) and ethnic Germans (4 per cent), with smaller numbers of Tatars, Uzbeks, Koreans and Belarusians. The Russian population is concentrated in the north of the country, where it forms a significant majority, and in Almaty. The majority of ethnic Kazakhs are Sunni Muslims, and this is the main religion of the republic. Kazakh (one of the Turkic languages) became the official language in 1993; a law passed in July 1997 decreed Kazakh as the language of state administration; Russian has a special status as the 'social language between peoples'. Otherwise each ethnic group uses its own language
CAPITAL – Astana (population, 275,100, 1997 estimate. Known as Akmola until May 1998). The capital was moved from Alma-Ata (Almaty) in December 1997
MAJOR CITIES – Almaty (1,198,000); Karaganda (596,000); Pavlograd (367,000); Shimkent (447,000), 1993 estimates
CURRENCY – Tenge
NATIONAL DAY – 25 October (Republic Day)
NATIONAL FLAG – Dark blue with a sun and a soaring eagle in the centre all in gold, and a red vertical ornamentation stripe near the hoist
LIFE EXPECTANCY (years) – male 58.47; female 69.95
POPULATION GROWTH RATE – 0.4 per cent (1997)
POPULATION DENSITY – 6 per sq. km (1997)
URBAN POPULATION – 55.2 per cent (1996)
ILLITERACY RATE – 2.5 per cent
ENROLMENT (percentage of age group) – tertiary 32.7 per cent (1995)

Kazakhstan occupies the northern part of what was Soviet Central Asia. It stretches from the Volga and the Caspian Sea in the west to the Altai and Tienshan mountains in the east. The country consists of arid steppes and semi-deserts, flat in the west, hilly in the east and mountainous in the south-east (Southern Altai and Tienshan mountains). The main rivers are the Irtysh, the Ural, the Syr-Darya and the Ili. The climate is continental and very dry.

HISTORY AND POLITICS

Kazakhstan was inhabited by nomadic tribes before being invaded by Ghenghiz Khan and incorporated into his empire in 1218. After his empire disintegrated, feudal towns emerged based on large oases. These towns affiliated and established a Kazakh state in the late 15th century which engaged in almost continuous warfare with the marauding Khanates on its southern border. After appealing to Russia for aid and protection, in 1731 Kazakhstan acceded to the Russian Empire under a voluntary act of accession.

The First World War brought privation to Kazakhstan, leading to an uprising in 1916 against the conscription of male Kazakhs. After the 1917 Russian revolution, Kazakhstan came under the control of White Russian forces until 1919. On 26 August 1920 a constitution was signed under which Kazakhstan became a Soviet Socialist Republic. Under Soviet rule in the 1920s and 1930s there was rapid industrial development and the traditional nomadic way of life disappeared. The Kazakhs suffered greatly in the Stalinist purges, the merchant and religious classes being murdered and thousands dying in the desert on collective farms. Other nationalities, such as Tatars and Germans, were forcibly transported to Kazakhstan by Stalin. Kazakhstan was the last of the former USSR republics to declare its independence (16 December 1991).

The Communist-derived Congress of People's Unity of Kazakhstan (SNEK) won the March 1994 legislative elections which were ruled invalid by the Constitutional Court. The President responded by dissolving the Supreme Kenges (the bicameral legislature) in March 1995. Elections to the new legislature were held in December 1995; the requirement for candidates to achieve an absolute majority made run-offs necessary. A referendum on 29 April 1995 extended President Nazarbayev's term until 2000, but constitutional changes unanimously agreed by the Kenges brought forward presidential elections to 10 January 1999. Elections to the upper chamber of the legislature were held on 17 September 1999 and to the lower house on 10 and 24 October 1999 and were won by the Fatherland Republican Party.

INSURGENCY

A group of ethnic Russians was arrested in the east of the country in November 1999 who had been planning an armed rebellion in the predominantly ethnic Russian North and East oblasts of the country, with the aim of establishing an independent Russian state in the region.

POLITICAL SYSTEM

Executive power is vested in the president and government. The president must be a Kazakh speaker and has the power to appoint the prime minister, other senior ministers and all ambassadors. The parliament does not have the power to impeach the president but the president can dissolve parliament.

A new constitution approved by referendum on 30 August 1995 granted the president the power to dissolve the legislature and to rule by decree. It also nominated Kazakh as the sole official language; prohibited dual citizenship; and created a new bicameral legislature composed of a 39-member Senate, of whom 32 are indirectly elected and seven appointed, and a 77-member directly elected Majlis (lower house of the legislature). The Constitutional Court, which opposed the new constitution, was replaced by a Constitutional Council which was made subject to presidential veto.

HEAD OF STATE

President, Nursultan Nazarbayev, *elected* 1 December 1991, *confirmed in office by referendum* 29 April 1995, *re-elected* 10 January 1999

GOVERNMENT *as at September 2000*

Prime Minister, Kasymzhomart Tokayev
First Deputy PM, Alexander Pavlov
Deputy PMs, Yerzhan Utembayev; Daniyal Akhmetov
Agriculture, Sauat Mynbayev
Culture, Information and Social Harmony, Altynbek Sarsenbayev
Defence, Sat Tokpakbayev.
Director of the Strategic Planning Agency, Kairat Kelimbetov
Economy, Zhaksubek Kulyekeyev
Energy, Trade and Industry, Vladimir Shkolnik
Finance, Mazhit Yesenbayev
Foreign Affairs, Yerlan Idrisov
Head of Prime Minister's Office, Kanat Saudabayev
Interior, Lt. Gen. Kairbek Suleymenov
Justice, Baurzhan Mukhamedzhanov
Labour and Social Security, Alikhan Baymenov
National Security, The President

Natural Resources and Environmental Protection, Serikbek Daukeyev
Revenues, Zeynulla Kakimzhanov
Science and Education, Kyrymbek Kusherbayev
Transport and Communications, Karim Masimov
Without Portfolio, Aitkul Samakova

EMBASSY OF THE REPUBLIC OF KAZAKHSTAN
33 Thurloe Square, London SW7 2SD
Tel: 020-7581 4646
Ambassador Extraordinary and Plenipotentiary, HE Dr Adil Akhmetov, apptd 2000

BRITISH EMBASSY
Ul. Furmanova 173, Almaty
Tel: (00 7) (3272) 506191
E-mail: british-embassy@kaznet.kz
Ambassador Extraordinary and Plenipotentiary, HE Richard Lewington, apptd 1999

BRITISH COUNCIL DIRECTOR, L. Biglou, Panfilova 158-1, KZ-480091 Almaty; e-mail: bc@britcoun.almaty.kz

DEFENCE

In 1993-4 Kazakhstan established its own armed forces from forces that were formerly under joint CIS control with Russia. An agreement signed with Russia in January 1995 provides for eventual reunification of the two states' armed forces. The CIS mutual defence treaty of 1993, to which Kazakhstan is a signatory, retains a common air defence force, while Kazakh forces also take part in the CIS peacekeeping force along the Tajikistan-Afghanistan border. A military union with a joint staff is being formed in co-operation with Kyrgyzstan and Uzbekistan. Kazakhstan ratified the Start 1 Treaty in 1992 and signed the Nuclear Non-Proliferation Treaty in December 1994. By 1996, all nuclear warheads had been returned to Russia although Kazakhstan retained 48 SS-18 intercontinental ballistic missiles. Kazakhstan participates in the NATO Partnership for Peace programme.

The Army has 630 main battle tanks. The Caspian Sea Flotilla, which Kazakhstan shares with Russia and Turkmenistan, operates under Russian command. The Air Force has 131 combat aircraft.
MILITARY EXPENDITURE – 2.2 per cent of GDP (1998)
MILITARY PERSONNEL – 100,300: Army 46,800, Air Force 19,000; Paramilitaries 34,500
CONSCRIPTION DURATION – 31 months

ECONOMY

Kazakhstan is rich in minerals, with copper, lead, gold, uranium, chromium, silver, zinc, iron ore, coal, oil and natural gas. In 1998 production of coal was 68,700,000 tonnes and of iron ore was 18,000,000 tonnes. The oil and gas industry, concentrated in the west of the country, has been expanded by foreign investment, which is also being used to explore the Karachaganak (gas) and Tengiz (oil) fields in the Caspian Sea. In November 1997, a deal was signed with the USA that provided for a US$26 billion investment in the energy sector.

The Tengiz-Novorossiisk pipeline between Russia and Kazakhstan is due to be completed in 2001. A pipeline to Turkey is in operation and a further pipeline to China is under consideration. Oil production in 1998 was 25.9 million tonnes and gas output was 8.3 billion cubic metres. Industry is dominated by food processing and mining and metals production; textiles, steel and tractors are also produced. The main centres of the metal industry are in the Altai mountains, in Shimkent, north of Lake Balkhash and in central Kazakhstan.

Agriculture, including stock-raising, is highly developed, particularly in the central and south-west of the republic. Grain is grown in the north and north-east, and cotton and wool produced in the south and south-east.

12.5 million tonnes of wheat and 3.5 million tonnes of barley were grown in 1999.

In 1993 the government announced a privatisation programme under which most state-owned enterprises were to be sold. The economy was weakened by the ending of preferential trading links to other CIS states at the break-up of the Soviet Union although a single market was formed with Kyrgyzstan and Uzbekistan in 1994. A treaty on further economic and humanitarian co-operation, as well as a customs union, was signed with Belarus, Kyrgyzstan and Russia in March 1996. A treaty of economic co-operation for 1998–2007 was signed with Russia in October 1998. The tenge was floated on 5 April 1999 in a bid to reduce the trade deficit.

In 1998 the trade deficit was US$750 million and the current account deficit US$1,201 million. Imports totalled US$4,242 million and exports US$5,339 million.

GNP – US$20,856 million (1998); US$1,340 per capita (1998)
GDP – US$21,036 million (1996); US$1,251 per capita (1996)
ANNUAL AVERAGE GROWTH OF GDP – 0.4 per cent (1996)
INFLATION RATE – 7.1 per cent (1998)
UNEMPLOYMENT – 3.7 per cent (1998)
TOTAL EXTERNAL DEBT – US$5,714 million (1998)

Trade with UK	1998	1999
Imports from UK	£95,792,000	£65,782,000
Exports to UK	40,456,000	51,278,000

KENYA
Jamhuri ya Kenya

AREA – 224,081 sq. miles (580,367 sq. km). Neighbours: Somalia (east), Ethiopia (north), Sudan (north-west), Uganda (west), Tanzania (south)
POPULATION – 33,144,000 (1997 UN estimate). The main tribal groups are the Kikuyu, Luhya, Luo, Kalenjin, Kamba and Masai. The official languages are Swahili, which is generally understood throughout Kenya, and English; numerous indigenous languages are also spoken
CAPITAL – Nairobi (population, 1,400,000, 1989 estimate)
MAJOR CITIES –ΨKisumu (192,733); ΨMombasa (461,753); Nakuru (163,927), 1989 estimates
CURRENCY – Kenya shilling (Ksh) of 100 cents
NATIONAL ANTHEM – Wimbo wa Taifa (National Anthem)
NATIONAL DAY – 12 December (Independence Day)
NATIONAL FLAG – Horizontally black, red and green with the red fimbriated in white, and with a shield and crossed spears all over in the centre
LIFE EXPECTANCY (years) – male 57.50; female 61.40
POPULATION DENSITY – 57 per sq. km (1997)
MILITARY EXPENDITURE – 3.1 per cent of GDP (1998)
MILITARY PERSONNEL – 29,200: Army 20,500, Navy 1,200, Air Force 2,500; Paramilitaries 5,000
ILLITERACY RATE – 17.5 per cent
ENROLMENT (percentage of age group) – primary 91 per cent (1980); tertiary 1.6 per cent (1990)

HISTORY AND POLITICS

Kenya became an independent state and a member of the British Commonwealth on 12 December 1963 and a republic in 1964. In 1982 the government introduced amendments to the constitution making the country a one-party state, with the Kenya African National Union (KANU) as the ruling party. In December 1991, the government yielded to internal and international pressure and introduced a multiparty democracy.

Multiparty presidential and legislative elections were held in December 1992 and were won by President Moi and KANU respectively. KANU formed a new government in January 1993. In July and August 1997, pro-democracy rallies were violently broken up by police and 14 demonstrators were killed, provoking outrage at home and abroad. In November 1997, Moi responded to pressure and granted limited reforms, repealing laws suppressing political debate, and granting equal media access to all parties. On 29 December 1997, in elections hampered by heavy flooding and marred by allegations of electoral malpractice, KANU won 109 out of 210 seats in the National Assembly, and Moi won just over 40 per cent of the vote to win a fifth term in office.

Following the elections, fighting broke out in the Rift Valley; by April 1998, more than 100 people had died and 300,000 had been driven from their homes. The victims were mainly from the Kikuyu tribe, and the perpetrators appeared to be members of Moi's Kalenjin tribe. The army was sent into the area to confiscate weapons and end the conflict in May 1998, but a further outbreak of attacks began in 1999.

The country is divided into eight provinces (Central, Coast, Eastern, Nairobi, Nyanza, North Eastern, Rift Valley, Western).

POLITICAL SYSTEM

The head of state is a president, directly elected for a five-year term, who is head of government and appoints the Cabinet. The unicameral legislature, the *Bunge* (National Assembly), has 224 members, of whom 210 are directly elected for a five-year term, 12 appointed by the president, and two ex-officio members, the attorney-general and the speaker. In November 1999, an amendment to the constitution was passed which limited the powers of the president over the National Assembly and affirmed the Bunge's supremacy.

HEAD OF STATE

President and C.-in-C. Armed Forces, Daniel T. arap Moi (KANU), *took office* 14 October 1978, *re-elected* 1979, 1983, 1988, 1992 and 29 December 1997
Vice-President, George Saitoti

CABINET *as at September 2000*

The President
The Vice-President
Agriculture, Chris Obure
Attorney-General, Amos Wako
Education, Stephen Kalonzo Musyoka
Energy, Francis Lotodo; Yekoyada Masakhalia
Environment, Francis Nyenze
Finance, Chrysanthus Okemo
Foreign Affairs and International Co-operation, Bonaya Godana
Home Affairs, Heritage and Sport, Noah Ngala
Information, Transport and Communications, Musalia Mudavadi
Labour, Joseph Kimen Ngutu
Lands and Settlement, Joseph Nyagah
Local Government, Joseph Kamotho
Medical Services, Amukowa Anangwe
Mineral Exploration, Jackson Kalweo
Ministers of State in the President's Office, Marsden Madoka; Shariff Nassir Taib; William ole Ntimana; Julius Sunkuli
Planning, Gideon Ndambuki
Public Health, Samson Ongeri
Roads and Public Works, William Morogo
Rural Development, Hussein Maalim Mohammed
Science and Technology, Henry Kosgey
Tourism, Trade and Industry, Kipyator Biwott
Vocational Training, Isaac Ruto
Water, Kipng'eno arap Ng'eny

KENYA HIGH COMMISSION
45 Portland Place, London WIN 4AS
Tel: 020-7636 2371/5
High Commissioner, HE Nancy Kirui, apptd 2000
Defence Adviser, Col. G. L. Okanga
Commercial Attaché, D. Mbugua

BRITISH HIGH COMMISSION
Upper Hill Road, PO Box 30465 Nairobi
Tel: (00 254) (2) 714699
E-mail: bhcinfo@africaonline.co.ke
High Commissioner, HE Jeffrey James, CMG, apptd 1997
Deputy High Commissioner, A. Tucker
Defence Adviser, Col. T. Merritt, OBE
First Secretary (Commercial), J. Chandler
First Secretary (Consular), D. Levoir

CONSULAR OFFICES – Nairobi, Mombasa, Malindi

BRITISH COUNCIL DIRECTOR, P. Skelton, ICEA Building, Kenyatta Avenue, PO Box 40751, Nairobi; e-mail: bc.nairobi@bc-nairobi.bcouncil.org. There are offices at Kisumu and Mombasa

ECONOMY

Agriculture provides about 30 per cent of GDP. The great variation in altitude and ecology provides conditions under which a wide range of crops can be grown. These include wheat, barley, pyrethrum, coffee, tea, sisal, coconuts, cashew nuts, cotton, maize and a wide variety of tropical and temperate fruits and vegetables. The total area of well-farmed land on which concentrated mixed farming can be practised is small and the remainder is arid or semi-arid country but population pressure and the need to increase agricultural production for export has led to attempts to develop such areas.

Mineral production consists of soda ash, salt and limestone. Hydroelectric power has been developed, particularly on the Upper Tana River, and Kenya is now almost self-sufficient in electric power generation.

There has been considerable industrial development over the last 15 years and Kenya has a variety of industries processing agricultural produce and manufacturing products from local and imported raw materials. New industries are steel, textile mills, dehydrated vegetable processing and motor tyre manufacture. Smaller schemes have added to the country's consumer goods manufacturing base. There is an oil refinery in Mombasa supplying both Kenya and Uganda, and a fuel pipeline now connects Mombasa and Nairobi. Tourism generates some US$400 million per year.

GNP – US$10,201 million (1998); US$350 per capita (1998)
GDP – US$9,170 million (1996); US$330 per capita (1996)
ANNUAL AVERAGE GROWTH OF GDP – 2.1 per cent (1997)
INFLATION RATE – 5.8 per cent (1998)
TOTAL EXTERNAL DEBT – US$7,010 million (1998)

TRADE

Principal exports are coffee and tea, which account for roughly a third of total export earnings. Also exported are fruit, vegetables, and crude animal and vegetable material. Industrial machinery is the largest single import; other imports are transport equipment, petroleum and petroleum products, metals, pharmaceuticals and chemicals.

In 1997 Kenya had a trade deficit of US$883 million and a current account deficit of US$454 million. In 1997 imports totalled US$3,280 million and exports US$1,993 million.

Trade with UK	1998	1999
Imports from UK	£224,417,000	£196,942,000
Exports to UK	214,975,000	196,733,000

COMMUNICATIONS

The Kenya Railways Corporation has 2,506 km of railway open to traffic. There are also 67,000 km of road, of which 8,900 km are bitumen surfaced.

The principal port is Mombasa, operated by the Kenya Ports Authority. International air services operate from airports at Nairobi and Mombasa. The national airline is Kenya Airways.

KIRIBATI
Ribaberikin Kiribati – Republic of Kiribati

AREA – 280 sq. miles (726 sq. km)
POPULATION – 81,000 (1997 UN estimate): predominantly Christian. The languages are I-Kiribati and English
CAPITAL – Tarawa (population, 17,921, 1978)
CURRENCY – Australian dollar ($A) of 100 cents
NATIONAL ANTHEM – Teirake Kain Kiribati (Stand Kiribati)
NATIONAL DAY – 12 July (Independence Day)
NATIONAL FLAG – Red, with blue and white wavy lines in base, and in the centre a gold rising sun and a flying frigate bird
POPULATION GROWTH RATE – 1.7 per cent (1997)
POPULATION DENSITY – 112 per sq. km (1997)

Kiribati (pronounced Kiribas) comprises 36 islands: the Gilberts Group (17) including Banaba (formerly Ocean Island), the Phoenix Islands (8), and the Line Islands (11), which are situated in the south-west central Pacific around the point at which the International Date Line cuts the Equator. The total land area is spread over some 2 million square miles of ocean. Few of the atolls are more than half a mile in width or more than 12 feet high. The vegetation consists mainly of coconut palms, breadfruit trees and pandanus.

HISTORY AND POLITICS

The Gilbert and Ellice Islands were proclaimed a British protectorate in 1892 and annexed as the Gilbert and Ellice Islands Colony on 10 November 1915 (taking effect 12 January 1916). The Gilbert Islands were occupied by the Japanese army during World War II. Nuclear tests were carried out by the British off Kiritimati (Christmas Island) in 1957. In October 1975 the Ellice Islands seceded to become the independent state of Tuvalu. The Gilbert Islands achieved independence on 12 July 1979 as the Republic of Kiribati.

Legislative elections were held on 23 September 1998 and presidential elections held on 27 November 1998 were won by Teburoro Tito. There are no formal political parties.

POLITICAL SYSTEM

The president is head of state as well as head of government and is directly elected. There is a House of Assembly of 41 members (39 elected members, the Attorney-General and a representative of the Banaban community from Rabi Island). Executive authority is vested in the Cabinet.

HEAD OF STATE

President, Foreign Affairs, Teburoro Tito, *sworn in* 1 October 1994, *re-elected* 27 November 1998
Vice-President, Home Affairs, Rural Development, Tewareka Tentoa

CABINET *as at September 2000*
The President
The Vice-President
Commerce, Industry and Tourism, Teaiwa Tenieu

Education, Training and Technology, Teambo Keariki
Environment, Social Development, Kataotika Tekee
Finance and Economic Planning, Beniamina Tinga
Health and Family Planning, Baraniko Mooa
Labour, Employment and Co-operatives, Teiraoi Tetabea
Line and Phoenix Islands, Tim Taekiti
Natural Resources Development, Emile Schutz
Transport, Communications and Information, Willie
  Tokataake
Works and Energy, Manraoi Kaiea

HIGH COMMISSION
c/o Office of the President, P.O Box 68, Bairiki,
Tarawa, Kiribati
High Commissioner, vacant
Acting High Commissioner, Peter Timeon

BRITISH HIGH COMMISSIONER, HE Michael Dibben,
apptd 1998, resident at Suva, Fiji

ECONOMY

Many people still practise a semi-subsistence economy,
the main staples of their diet being coconuts and fish.
  The principal imports are foodstuffs, consumer goods,
machinery and transport equipment. The principal
exports are copra and fish.
  In May 2000, Japanese-funded improved port facilities
at Betio were opened.
  In 1994 there was a trade deficit of US$21 million and a
current account surplus of US$1 million.
GNP – US$101 million (1998); US$1,170 per capita
(1998)
GDP – US$46 million (1996); US$573 per capita (1996)

Trade with UK	1998	1999
Imports from UK	£106,000	£149,000
Exports to UK	—	7,000

COMMUNICATIONS

Air communication exists between most of the islands
and is operated by Air Kiribati, a statutory corporation.
Air Marshall Islands operates a weekly service between
Majuro, Tarawa, Funafuti and Nadi, and Air Nauru
between Tarawa, Nauru and Nadi. Inter-island shipping
is operated by a statutory corporation, the Shipping
Corporation of Kiribati.

EDUCATION AND SOCIAL WELFARE

There are 104 primary schools, eight secondary schools
and one high school. There is a teacher training college, a
technical institute and a marine training centre.
  There is a general hospital at Tarawa. The other
inhabited islands have dispensaries.

KOREA

Korea's southern and western coasts are fringed with
innumerable islands, of which the largest, forming a
province of its own, is Cheju. The Korean language is of
the Ural-Altaic Group. Its script, Hangul, was invented in
the 15th century; prior to this Chinese characters alone
were used. Despite the great cultural influence of the
Chinese, Koreans have developed and preserved their own
cultural heritage.

HISTORY

The Korean peninsula was first unified in AD 668 when
Shilla, having emerged as the dominant tribal state,
conquered Koguryo and Paekche. The Koryo dynasty
ruled from 912 until 1392 and was succeeded by the
Choson dynasty, who ruled from 1392 until 1910 when
Japan formally annexed Korea. The country remained part
of the Japanese Empire until the defeat of Japan in 1945,
when it was occupied by troops of the USA and the USSR,
the 38th parallel being fixed as the boundary between the
two zones of occupation.
  Attempts to reunite Korea failed and the issue was
referred to the UN General Assembly. The UN in
November 1947 resolved that elections should be held
for a National Assembly which, when elected, should set
up a government. The Soviet government refused to
comply and a UN commission was only allowed to operate
south of the 38th parallel.
  A general election was held on 10 May 1948, and the first
National Assembly met in Seoul on 31 May. The Assembly
passed a constitution on 12 July and on 15 August 1948 the
republic was formally inaugurated and American military
government came to an end. Meanwhile, in the Soviet-
occupied zone north of the 38th parallel the Democratic
People's Republic had been established with its capital at
Pyongyang. A Supreme People's Soviet was elected in
September 1948, and a Soviet-style constitution adopted.

THE KOREAN WAR

Korea remained divided along the 38th parallel until June
1950, when North Korean forces invaded South Korea. In
response to Security Council recommendations, 16
nations, including the USA and the UK, came to the aid
of the Republic of Korea. China entered the war on the
side of North Korea in November 1950. The fighting was
ended by an armistice agreement signed on 27 July 1953.
By this agreement (which was not signed by the Republic
of Korea), the line of division between North and South
Korea remained close to the 38th parallel, and a Military
Armistice Commission (MAC) was established to monitor
the cease-fire. North Korea and China withdrew from the
MAC in 1994.
  Talks between North and South Korea on the
reunification of the country have taken place intermittently. A non-aggression accord was signed between the
North and South in 1991 and an agreement on the
denuclearisation of the Korean peninsula was reached in
1992. A summit of North and South Korean presidents
was scheduled for July 1994 but Kim Il-sung died before it
could take place. Four-party talks between China, the
USA and the two Koreas took place in December 1997 and
again in March 1998, but no new agreements were
reached. A summit meeting between the presidents of
North and South Korea took place on 13–15 June 2000 at
which a communiqué was signed agreeing to promote
economic co-operation, achieve reconciliation and eventually reunify the two countries.

DEMOCRATIC PEOPLE'S REPUBLIC OF
KOREA
Chosun Minchu-chui Inmin Kongwa-guk

AREA – 46,540 sq. miles (120,538 sq. km). Neighbours:
  China, Russia (north), Republic of Korea (south)
POPULATION – 22,082,000 (1999 estimate). The language
  is Korean
CAPITAL – Pyongyang (approximate population,
  2,741,260)
CURRENCY – Won of 100 chon
NATIONAL ANTHEM – Aegukka (The song of love of
  country)
NATIONAL DAY – 16 February (Kim Jong-il's birthday)
NATIONAL FLAG – Red with white fimbriations and blue
  borders at top and bottom; a large red star on a white disc
  near the hoist
LIFE EXPECTANCY (years) – male 59.80; female 64.50

POPULATION GROWTH RATE – 1.4 per cent (1998)
POPULATION DENSITY – 189 per sq. km (1997)

POLITICAL SYSTEM

The constitution of the Democratic People's Republic of Korea provides for a Supreme People's Assembly, presently consisting of 687 deputies, which is elected every five years by universal suffrage. The Assembly elects a president for a five-year term, and the Central People's Committee. In turn, the Central People's Committee directs the Administrative Council which implements the policy formulated by the Committee.

The Administrative Council (36 members), the government of North Korea, includes the prime minister and various ministers. In practice, however, the country is ruled by the Korean Workers' Party which elects a Central Committee; this in turn appoints a Politburo. The senior ministers of the Administrative Council are all members of the Communist Party Central Committee and the majority are also members of the Politburo. Kim Il-sung, who had been head of the state, party and military since the country's inception in 1948, died on 8 July 1994, but was declared the eternal president in September 1998. His son Kim Jong-il, who had been party general secretary since October 1997, became chair of the National Defence Committee, which is now de facto the highest office.

HEAD OF STATE

Eternal President, Kim Il-sung (deceased)
Chair of the National Defence Committee, General Secretary, Korean Workers' Party; Member of Presidium, Kim Jong-il
Chair of the Standing Committee of the Supreme People's Assembly, Kim Yong-nam

SPA STANDING COMMITTEE

Chairman, Kim Yong-nam
Vice-Chairmen, Yang Hyong-sop; Kim Yong-tae
Secretary-General, Kim Yun-hyok
Honorary Vice-Chairmen, Pak Song-chol; Kim-yong Chu
Members, Yu Mi-yong; Kang Yong-sop; Yi Kil-song; Yi Chol-pong; Yi Il-hwan; Song Sang-sop

ADMINISTRATIVE COUNCIL as at September 2000

Prime Minister, Hong Song-nam
Deputy Prime Ministers, Kwak Pom-ki; Cho Chang-tok
Foreign Affairs, Paek Nam-sun

MINISTERS

Agriculture, Yi Ha-sop
Chair, Physical Culture and Sports Guidance Committee, Pak Myong-chol
Chair, State Planning Committee, Pak Nam-ki
Chemical Industry, Pak Pong-chu
City Management, Choe Chong-kon
Commerce, Yi Yong-son
Construction and Building Materials Industry, Cho Yun-hui
Culture, Kang Nung-su
Director of the Central Statistics Bureau, Kim Chang-su
Director of the Secretariat and State Administration Council, Chong Mun-sang
Education, Byun Yong-ryp
Electronics, Oh Su-ryong
Finance, Yim Kyong-suk
Fisheries, Yi Song-ung
Foreign Affairs, Paek Nam-sun
Forestry, Yi Sang-mu
Labour, Yi Won-il
Land and Maritime Transport, Kim Yong-il
Land Environmental Protection, Chang il-son
Light Industry, Yi Yon-su
Metal and Machine Industry, Chon Sung-hun
Mining Industry, Son Chong-o

People's Armed Forces, Vice-Marshall Kim Il-chol
Posts and Telecommunications, Yi Kun-pom
Power and Coal Industry, Sin Tae-nok
President of the Academy of Sciences, Yi Kwang-ho
President of the Central Bank, Chong Song-taek
Procurement and Food Administration, Paek Chang-yong
Public Health, Kim Su-hak
Public Security, Lt.-Gen. Paek Hak-nim
Railways, Kim Yong-san
State Construction Commission, Pae Tal-chun
State Inspection, Kim Ui-sun
Trade, Kang Chong-mo

Full Members of the Politburo, Kim Jong-il; Pak Son-chol; Kim Yong-nam; Kye Ung-tae; Han Song-yong; Kim Yong-ju; Jun Byung-ho

DEFENCE

The Army has about 3,500 main battle tanks and 2,500 armoured personnel carriers. The Navy has 26 submarines, three frigates and about 309 patrol and coastal vessels at 15 bases. The Air Force has 593 combat aircraft.

Between 1992 and 1994 North Korea embarked on a clandestine nuclear weapons programme despite being a signatory of the Nuclear Non-Proliferation Treaty (NPT). North Korea withdrew from the NPT following an International Atomic Energy Authority (IAEA) report that the country was attempting to reprocess plutonium for use in nuclear weapons. An agreement was signed with the USA on 21 October 1994 under which North Korea vowed to remain a party to the NPT; to permit IAEA inspections; and to switch to light-water reactors unsuitable for plutonium production. In return the USA agreed to establish diplomatic and economic relations and to pay for interim energy requirements. The IAEA verified the halting of North Korea's nuclear programme in November 1994 although a final settlement was only achieved in June 1995.

MILITARY EXPENDITURE – 14.3 per cent of GDP (1998)
MILITARY PERSONNEL – 1,271,000: Army 950,000, Navy 46,000, Air Force 86,000, Paramilitaries 189,000
CONSCRIPTION DURATION – Three to ten years

ECONOMY

North Korea is rich in minerals and industry was developed, but the economy has stagnated owing to poor planning and a shortage of foreign exchange. The current economic crisis was precipitated by the curtailment of barter trade with the Soviet Union after 1991, and the end of subsidised oil and grain from China. Industrial output has collapsed, with industry operating at one-third of capacity. The economy has been sustained by foreign exchange sent by ethnic Koreans in Japan. In April 1998, South Korea lifted its ban on investment in North Korea, allowing South Koreans to send money to their relatives in the north.

In 1995–8, a slump in agricultural production was exacerbated by widespread flooding which devastated the rice harvest. A North Korean survey quoted by South Korean security services stated that up to three million people had died as a result of famine between 1995 and 1998. In January 1998, the UN World Food Programme launched a food aid operation to provide 658,000 tonnes of food to North Korea. The USA increased food aid to North Korea in May 1999.

GDP – US$4,381 million (1996); US$195 per capita (1996)
ANNUAL AVERAGE GROWTH OF GDP–3.7 per cent (1996)

Trade with UK	1998	1999
Imports from UK	£10,769,000	£13,624,000
Exports to UK	765,000	1,518,000

REPUBLIC OF KOREA
Taehanminguk

AREA – 38,368 sq. miles (99,268 sq. km). Neighbour: Democratic People's Republic of Korea (north)
POPULATION – 46,858,460 (1999 estimate). The largest religions are Buddhism (10.3 million) and Christianity (8.8 million Protestants, 2.9 million Roman Catholics). The language is Korean
CAPITAL – Seoul (population, 10,321,000, 1999 estimate)
MAJOR CITIES – ΨInchon (2,524,000); ΨPusan (3,831,000); Taegu (2,517,000)
CURRENCY – Won
NATIONAL ANTHEM – Aegukka (The Song of Love of country)
NATIONAL DAY – 15 August (Liberation Day)
NATIONAL FLAG – White with a red and blue yin-yang symbol in the centre, surrounded by four black trigrams
LIFE EXPECTANCY (years) – male 70.60; female 78.10
POPULATION GROWTH RATE – 0.9 per cent (1999)
POPULATION DENSITY – 471 per sq. km (1999)
URBAN POPULATION – 91.0 per cent (1999)

HISTORY AND POLITICS

The Republic of Korea was not officially recognised by any former Communist bloc country until 1989, and not by the People's Republic of China until 1992.

The most recent elections to the National Assembly in April 2000 produced no outright majority. The Millennium Democratic Party won 115 seats and formed a coalition with the United Liberal Democrats, who won 17 seats; the opposition Grand National Party won 133 seats. Lee Han-dong was appointed prime minister on 22 May 2000. In the most recent presidential election of 18 December 1997, Kim Dae-jung of the National Congress for New Politics was elected president with just over 40 per cent of the vote.

POLITICAL SYSTEM

A new constitution was adopted in 1988 following a year of political unrest. The president, who is head of state, chief of the executive and commander-in-chief of the armed forces, is directly elected for a single term of five years. He appoints the prime minister with the consent of the National Assembly, and members of the State Council (Cabinet) on the recommendation of the prime minister. The president is also empowered to take wide-ranging measures in an emergency, including the declaration of martial law, but must obtain the agreement of the National Assembly. The National Assembly of 273 members is directly elected for a four-year term.

HEAD OF STATE

President, Kim Dae-jung, *elected* 18 December 1997, *sworn in* 25 February 1998

CABINET *as at September 2000*
Prime Minister, Lee Han-dong
Deputy PM, Finance and Economy, Jin Nyum
Agriculture and Forestry, Han Kap-soo
Construction and Transportation, Kim Yoon-ki
Culture and Tourism, Park Jie-won
Defence, Cho Seong-tae
Education, Lee Don-hee
Environment, Kim Myung-ja
Finance and Economy, Lee Hun-jai
Foreign Affairs, Trade, Lee Joung-binn
Government Administration, Home Affairs, Choi In-kee
Health and Welfare, Choi Sun-jung
Information and Communications, Ahn Byung-yub

Justice, Kim Jung-kil
Labour, Kin Ho-jin
Legislation, Kim Hong-dae
Maritime Affairs and Fisheries, Noh Mu-hyun
National Unification, Park Jae-kyu
Planning and Budget, Jeon Yun-churl
Science and Technology, Seo Jung-uck
Trade, Industry and Energy, Shin Kook-hwan

EMBASSY OF THE REPUBLIC OF KOREA
60 Buckingham Gate, London SW1E 6AJ
Tel: 020-7227 5500/2
Ambassador Extraordinary and Plenipotentiary, HE Choi Sung-hong, apptd 1999
Defence Attaché, Capt. Lee Byung-moon
Consul, Chin-Ki-hoon
First Secretary (Commercial), Cheong Seung-il

BRITISH EMBASSY
No. 4, Chung-dong, Chung-Ku, Seoul 100–120
Tel: (00 82) (2) 735-7341/3;
E-mail: britemb@kotis.net
Ambassador Extraordinary and Plenipotentiary, HE Stephen Brown, KCVO, apptd 1997
Consul-General and Deputy Head of Mission, D. R. Marsh, CVO
Defence and Military Attaché, Brig. J. G. Baker, MBE
First Secretary (Commercial), D. F. Graham

There is a Trade Office and an Honorary British Consul at Pusan.

BRITISH COUNCIL DIRECTOR, M. Baumfield, Joongwhoo Building, 61–21, Taepyungro1-ka, Choong-ku, Seoul 100–101; e-mail: info@britcoun.or.kr

BRITISH CHAMBER OF COMMERCE, 2nd Floor, Joong hoo Building, 61–21, Seoul 100–101

DEFENCE

The Army has 2,130 main battle tanks, 2,500 armoured personnel carriers and 143 armed helicopters. The Navy has 19 submarines, six destroyers, 33 frigates, 84 patrol and coastal vessels, 23 combat aircraft, 47 armed helicopters, 60 main battle tanks and 63 armoured personnel carriers. There are eight naval bases. The Air Force has 488 combat aircraft.

The USA maintains 36,530 personnel in the country.
MILITARY EXPENDITURE – 3.1 per cent of GDP (1998)
MILITARY PERSONNEL – 676,500: Army 560,000, Navy 60,000, Air Force 52,000, Paramilitaries 4,500
CONSCRIPTION DURATION – 26–30 months

ECONOMY

Land redistribution and US aid (US$6,000 million from 1945 to 1978) enabled the rapid industrialisation of South Korea in the 1950s and 1960s. Former land owners formed *chaebols* (industrial conglomerates) which benefited from a highly-educated workforce and import substitution policies. From 1961 to 1979 exports increased by an average of 10 per cent a year. From 1985 to 1997, GDP grew strongly, but fell by 5.8 per cent during 1998; it recovered to grow by 10.7 per cent during 1999.

Major industries include shipbuilding, construction, iron and steel, textiles, electrical and electronic goods, semiconductors, passenger vehicles and petrochemicals.

The soil is fertile but arable land is limited by the mountainous nature of the country. Staple agricultural products are rice, barley and other cereals, beans and potatoes. Fruit-growing, sericulture and the growing of the medicinal root ginseng are also practised. The fishing industry is a major contributor to both food supply and exports.

Korea is deficient in mineral resources, except for deposits of coal on the east coast and tungsten. There are some prospects of discovering oil in the sea between Korea and Japan.

In 1999 there was a trade surplus of US$23,933 million and a current account surplus of US$25,000 million; imports totalled US$119,752 million and exports US$143,685 million.

GNP – US$402,100 million (1999); US$8,581 per capita (1999)

GDP – US$406,700 million (1999); US$8,679 per capita (1999)

ANNUAL AVERAGE GROWTH OF GDP – 10.7 per cent (1999)

INFLATION RATE – 0.8 per cent (1999)

UNEMPLOYMENT – 6.3 per cent (1999)

Trade with UK	1998	1999
Imports from UK	£684,269,000	£949,771,000
Exports to UK	2,304,934,000	2,912,110,000

COMMUNICATIONS

There are international airports in Seoul (Kimpo), Kimhae (near Pusan), Taegu and Cheju city. Korean Air and Asiana Airlines operate regular flights to Europe, the USA, the Middle East and south-east Asia. In 1999, 29 foreign airlines operated services to Seoul. Pusan and Inchon are the major ports with Pusan serving the industrial areas of the south-east. Inchon, 28 miles from Seoul, serves the capital, but development and operation at Inchon are hampered by a tidal variation of 9–10 metres.

EDUCATION

Primary education is compulsory for six years from the age of six. Secondary and higher education is extensive with the option of middle school to age 15 and high school to age 18.

ILLITERACY RATE – 2.2 per cent

ENROLMENT (percentage of age group) – primary 93 per cent (1997); secondary 97 per cent (1996); tertiary 68 per cent (1997)

KUWAIT
Dawlat al-Kuwayt

AREA – 6,880 sq. miles (17,818 sq. km). Neighbours: Iraq (north and west); Saudi Arabia (south and south-west)

POPULATION – 1,866,104 (1998 estimate): 41.6 per cent were Kuwaiti citizens, the remainder being other Arabs, Iranians, Indians and Pakistanis. The total Western population was 14,240. Islam is the official religion, though religious freedom is constitutionally guaranteed. The official language is Arabic, and English is widely spoken as a second language

CAPITAL – ΨKuwait City (Al-Kuwayt) (population, 388,663, 1998)

CURRENCY – Kuwaiti dinar (KD) of 1,000 fils

NATIONAL DAY – 25 February

NATIONAL FLAG – Three horizontal stripes of green, white and red, with black trapezoid next to staff

LIFE EXPECTANCY (years) – male 71.77; female 73.32

POPULATION GROWTH RATE – –2.4 per cent (1997)

POPULATION DENSITY – 102 per sq. km (1997)

In 1993 the UN settled the dispute between Kuwait and Iraq, moving the border some few hundred metres northwards. Kuwait has since completed a 130-mile ditch, sand wall and barbed wire system along its border.

Kuwait has a dry, desert climate with summer extending from April to September. The mean temperature varies between 29–45°C in summer, and 8–18°C in winter. Humidity rarely exceeds 60 per cent except in July and August.

HISTORY AND POLITICS

Although Kuwait had been independent for some years, the 'exclusive agreement' of 1899 between the Sheikh of Kuwait and the British government was formally abrogated by an exchange of letters dated 19 June 1961. Iraq invaded Kuwait on 2 August 1990 and it was liberated on 26 February 1991 by an alliance of Western and Arab forces. Iraq built up its armed forces on Kuwait's border in October 1994, until it was deterred by the arrival of US and British forces. Iraq formally recognised the sovereignty and territorial integrity of Kuwait as well as the UN-demarcated border in November 1994. Roughly 600 Kuwaitis are still held in Iraq.

The Amir dissolved the National Assembly on 4 May 1999; elections were held on 3 July 1999. Opposition Liberals won 16 and Islamists won 20 of the 50 seats.

POLITICAL SYSTEM

Under the constitution legislative power is vested in the Amir and the 50-member National Assembly, and executive power in the Amir and the Cabinet. Following popular pressure after the liberation, elections for the National Assembly were held in October 1992. The electorate consists of all Kuwaiti male nationals over 21 whose families have lived in the Emirate since before 1921.

There are five governorates: Capital, Hawallī, Ahmadī, Al-Jahrah and Al Farwaniya.

HEAD OF STATE

HH The Amir of Kuwait, Shaikh Jabir al-Ahmad al-Jabir al-Sabah, born 1928, acceded 31 December 1977

Crown Prince, HH Shaikh Saad al-Abdullah al-Salim al-Sabah

CABINET as at September 2000

Prime Minister, HH The Crown Prince

First Deputy PM, Foreign Affairs, Shaikh Sabah al-Ahmed al-Jabir al-Sabah

Deputy PM, Cabinet Affairs, National Assembly Affairs, Mohammad Dhaif Allah Sharar

Deputy PM, Defence, Shaikh Salem Sabah al-Salem al-Sabah

Communications, Finance, Shaikh Ahmed Abdullah al-Ahmed al-Sabah

Education and Higher Education, Dr Yousif Hamad al-Ibrahim

Electricity and Water, Minister of State for Housing Affairs, Dr Adel Khalid al-Subeeh

Health, Dr Mohammad Ahmad al-Jara' Allah

Information, Dr Sa'ad Mohammad bin Tifla al-Ajmi

Interior, Shaikh Mohammad Khaled al-Hamad al-Sabah

Justice, Awqaf and Islamic Affairs, Dr Sa'ad Jassem Youssef al-Hashil

Minister of State for Amiri Diwan Affairs, Nasir Mohammad Ahmed al-Sabah

Minister of State for Foreign Affairs, Suleiman Majid al-Shaheen

Oil, Shaikh Sa'ud Nasir al-Sabah

Planning, Minister of State for Administrative Development Affairs, Dr Mohammad Bteihan al-Dawaihees

Public Works, Eid Haddal Sa'ud al-Risheedi

Trade and Industry, Labour and Social Affairs, Abdul Wahab Mohammad al-Wazzan

EMBASSY OF THE STATE OF KUWAIT

2 Albert Gate, London SW1X 7JU

Tel: 020-7590 3400

Ambassador Extraordinary and Plenipotentiary, HE Khaled
al-Duwaisan, GCVO, apptd 1993
Cultural Attaché, Dr Salah al-Mazidi

BRITISH EMBASSY

PO Box 2 Safat, 13001 Safat, Kuwait
Tel: (00 965) 240 3334/5/6
Ambassador Extraordinary and Plenipotentiary, HE Richard
Muir, CMG, apptd 1999
Counsellor and Deputy Head of Mission, B. E. Stewart
First Secretaries, J. Francis (*Management and Consul*);
M.Hurley (*Commercial*)
Defence Attaché, Col. Hon. A. J. C. Campell
BRITISH COUNCIL DIRECTOR, C. Reuter, 2 Al Arabi
Street, Block 2, PO Box 345, 13004 Safat, Mansouriya,
Kuwait City; e-mail: britcoun@kuwait.net

DEFENCE

The Army has 385 main battle tanks, 140 armoured
personnel carriers and 355 armoured infantry fighting
vehicles. The Navy has 11 patrol and coastal vessels, based
at Ras al-Qalaya. The Air Force has 76 combat aircraft and
20 armed helicopters.
The USA and UK station aircraft and support units in
the country to patrol the air exclusion zone in southern
Iraq.
MILITARY EXPENDITURE – 12.9 per cent of GDP (1998)
MILITARY PERSONNEL – 20,300: Army 11,000, Navy
1,800, Air Force 2,500; Paramilitaries 5,000
CONSCRIPTION DURATION – Two years

ECONOMY

Despite the desert terrain, 8.4 per cent of land is under
cultivation; tomatoes, onions, melons and dates are the
main crops. Shrimp fishing has declined through oil
pollution of coastal waters.
The oil industry was brought into government ownership in 1975. Since reorganisation in 1980, the national
industry has been run by the Kuwait Petroleum Corporation. Oil installations were extensively damaged when
Iraqi forces set light to oil wells prior to their retreat. Oil
production was 107,600,000 tonnes in 1998.
There are four power stations capable of generating
almost 7,000 MW of electricity. The country depends on
desalination plants for its water supply. Both water and
power facilities were heavily damaged during the war,
although electricity and water distillation capacity were
restored to pre-invasion levels in 1995.
GDP – US$28,498 million (1996); US$16,893 per capita
(1996)
ANNUAL AVERAGE GROWTH OF GDP – 4.9 per cent (1996)
INFLATION RATE – 0.1 per cent (1998)

TRADE

Oil is the major export. Non-oil exports, mainly to Asian
countries and the Indian sub-continent, have included
chemical fertilisers, ammonia and other chemicals, metal
pipes, shrimps and building materials. Re-exports to
neighbouring states traditionally accounted for a major
proportion of non-oil exports but were brought to a halt
by the Iraqi invasion. Major trading partners are Japan,
the USA, the UAE, Saudi Arabia and Western Europe.
In 1998 Kuwait had a trade surplus of US$2,254 million
and a current account surplus of US$2,940 million.
Imports totalled US$6,130 million and exports
US$9,529 million.

Trade with UK	1998	1999
Imports from UK	£334,825,000	£301,971,000
Exports to UK	185,736,000	134,689,000

COMMUNICATIONS

There is a network of dual-carriageway roads and more are
under construction; there are 4,741 km of roads. Telecommunications and postal services are conducted by the
government.

SOCIAL WELFARE

The government invested its considerable oil revenues in
comprehensive social services. Medical services are free to
all residents. Education is free and compulsory from six to
14 years.
ILLITERACY RATE – 17.7 per cent
ENROLMENT (percentage of age group) – primary
62 per cent (1996); secondary 61 per cent (1996);
tertiary 19 per cent (1996)

KYRGYZSTAN
Kyrgyz Respublikasy

AREA – 76,641 sq. miles (199,900 sq. km). Neighbours:
Kazakhstan (north), China (east), Tajikistan (south and
south-west), Uzbekistan (west)
POPULATION – 4,856,000 (1998 estimate): 52.4 per cent
Kyrgyz (Turkic origin), 21.5 per cent Russian and 12.9
per cent Uzbek, with smaller numbers of Ukrainians,
Germans, Tatars and Kazakhs. Islam is the main
religion. Kyrgyz, the official language since indepen-
dence, is a Turkic language, written in the Roman
alphabet since 1992. Russian is an equal official
language.
CAPITAL – Bishkek (population, 589,400, 1997 estimate;
616,000, 1989 census)
CURRENCY – Som of 100 tyin (introduced on 10 May 1993
at rate of 1:200 against the rouble)
NATIONAL DAY – 31 August (Independence Day)
NATIONAL FLAG – Red with a rayed sun containing a
representation of a yurt, all in gold
LIFE EXPECTANCY (years) – male 61.41; female 70.38
POPULATION GROWTH RATE – 0.8 per cent (1997)
POPULATION DENSITY – 23 per sq. km (1997)
URBAN POPULATION – 34.6 per cent (1996)
MILITARY EXPENDITURE – 3.6 per cent of GDP (1998)
MILITARY PERSONNEL – 12,200: Army 6,800, Air Force
2,400; Paramilitaries 3,000
CONSCRIPTION DURATION – 18 months

Kyrgyzstan (formerly Kyrgyzia) is mountainous, the
major part being covered by the ridge of the Central
Tienshan, while the Pamir-Altai system occupies its
southern part. There are a number of spacious mountain
valleys, the Alai, Susamyr and others. Kyrgyzstan is
divided into six administrative regions.

HISTORY AND POLITICS

The Kyrgyz people were first mentioned in Chinese
chronicles in the second millennium BC. They are a merger
of two ethnic groups, a Turkic-speaking people driven
into the area by the Mongols from the River Yenisei area of
Central Asia, and indigenous peoples. After a long period
under Mongol, Chinese and Persian rule, the Kyrgyz
became part of the Russian Empire in the 1860s and 1870s.
Kyrgyzstan became part of the Soviet Union in 1920 and
underwent some industrialisation.
Kyrgyzstan declared independence just after the failed
Moscow coup on 31 August 1991.
Ethnic tensions between the rural nomadic Kyrgyz, the
urban Russians and the wealthy Uzbeks who own many
businesses and form the majority in the second largest
town of Osh, are never far from the surface.

President Akayev had difficulty in introducing economic reforms because of obstruction by the bureaucracy and the *Uluk Kenesh* (parliament) over the reforms enshrined in the constitution. The president won a referendum on his plans for greater economic reform in January 1994.

A referendum on amendments to the constitution was held on 17 October 1998, which introduced private ownership of land.

Legislative elections were held on 20 February and 12 March 2000. The largest opposition parties were not allowed to take part on the grounds of supposed minor infractions of the electoral procedures, a decision which was criticised by observers from the Organisation for Security and Co-operation in Europe; their leaders were allowed to stand as independent candidates. The Communist party and the pro-government Union of Democratic Forces emerged as the largest parties. The results were widely condemned by opposition groups amid allegations of widespread electoral fraud.

POLITICAL SYSTEM

The head of state is a president directly elected for a five-year term. There is a bicameral legislature composed of a 60-member Legislative Assembly and a 45-member People's Assembly, both of which serve five-year terms. The president appoints the prime minister and the other members of the government. The Assembly of the People of Kyrgyzstan, which comprises the leaders of the republic's ethnic communities, was designated a consultative body in January 1997.

HEAD OF STATE

President, Askar Akayev, *elected* 12 October 1991, *re-elected* 24 December 1995

GOVERNMENT *as at September 2000*

Prime Minister, Amangeldy Muraliyev
First Deputy PM, Boris Silayev
Deputy PM, Trade and Industry, Esenbek Omuraliyev
Agriculture and Water Resources, Aleksandr Kostyuk
Chair, State Property Fund, Tashkul Kereksizov
Chair, State Social Fund, Roza Uchkempirova
Defence, Lt.-Gen. Esen Topoyev
Education, Science and Culture, Tursunbek Bekbolotov
Emergencies and Civil Defence, Sultan Urmanyev
Environmental Protection, Tynybek Alykulov
Finance, Sultan Mederov
Foreign Affairs, Muratbek Imanaliyev
Health, Tilekbek Meinenaliev
Interior, Maj.-Gen. Omurbek Kutuyev
Justice, Neliya Beyshenaliyeva
Labour and Social Security, Imankadyr Rysaliyev
National Security, Tashtemir Aitbaev
Prime Minister's Office, Orozbek Eshmambetov
Transport and Communications, Jantoro Satybaldiyev

EMBASSY OF THE KYRGYZ REPUBLIC

Ascot House, 119 Crawford Street, London W1H 1AF
Tel: 020-7935 1462
Ambassador Extraordinary and Plenipotentiary, HE Roza Otunbayeva, apptd 1997

BRITISH AMBASSADOR, HE Richard Lewington, resident at Almaty, Kazakhstan
BRITISH COUNCIL, 237 Panfilova, Room 2026, KS-720000 Bishkek; e-mail: bc@britcoun.elcat.kg

ECONOMY

Agriculture is the main sector of the economy, with sugar beet, grain and sheep the main products. Private ownership of land was legalised in 1998. Industry is concentrated in the food-processing, textiles, timber and mining fields. Since 1992, some 60 per cent of state-owned enterprises have been privatised. Hydroelectric power is abundant and Kyrgyzstan has reserves of gold, coal, mercury and uranium, although only gold has so far been exploited and is the country's largest export. In 1997, industry grew by 47 per cent and agriculture by 10 per cent.

The government introduced the som in May 1993 to break the link with the depreciating rouble, the cause of high inflation in 1992 and early 1993. The president and government have also made the Central Bank independent of government and parliamentary control. In March 1996, a treaty was signed with Belarus, Kazakhstan and Russia enhancing economic co-operation and working towards a single customs territory.

In 1997 there was a trade deficit of US$15 million and a current account deficit of US$139 million. Imports totalled US$709 million and exports US$604 million.
GNP – US$1,771 million (1998); US$380 per capita (1998)
GDP – US$1,827 million (1996); US$409 per capita (1996)
ANNUAL AVERAGE GROWTH OF GDP – 3.6 per cent (1998)
INFLATION RATE – 13.6 per cent (1998)
TOTAL EXTERNAL DEBT – US$1,148 million (1998)

Trade with UK	1998	1999
Imports from UK	£2,735,000	£2,494,000
Exports to UK	2,654,000	10,000

CULTURE AND EDUCATION

Until the 1930s the Kyrgyz language had an oral tradition of literature which included the epic poem *Manas*, which tells the history of the Kyrgyz people. Internationally, one of the best-known writers of the former Soviet Union is the Kyrgyz writer Chingiz Aitmatov (1928–).
ILLITERACY RATE – 3.0 per cent
ENROLMENT (percentage of age group) – primary 95 per cent (1995); tertiary 12.2 per cent (1995)

LAOS
Satharanarath Pasathipatai Pasason Lao

AREA – 91,429 sq. miles (236,800 sq. km). Neighbours: China (north), Vietnam (north-east and east), Cambodia (south), Thailand (west), Myanmar (north-west)
POPULATION – 5,035,000 (1995 census): 68 per cent Lao Loum (lowland Lao), 22 per cent Lao Theung (upland Lao), 9 per cent Lao Soung (highland Lao, including Hmong and Yau). Lao is the official language; French and English are spoken
CAPITAL – Vientiane (population, 132,253, 1966; 120,000, 1984 estimate)
CURRENCY – Kip (K) of 100 at
NATIONAL ANTHEM – Pheng xat Lao (Laos national anthem)
NATIONAL DAY – 2 December
NATIONAL FLAG – Blue background with a central white circle, framed by two horizontal red stripes
LIFE EXPECTANCY (years) – male 49.50; female 52.50
POPULATION GROWTH RATE – 3.0 per cent (1997)
POPULATION DENSITY – 22 per sq. km (1997)
MILITARY EXPENDITURE – 3.7 per cent of GDP (1998)
MILITARY PERSONNEL – 129,100: Army 25,000, Navy 600, Air Force 3,500; Paramilitaries 100,000
CONSCRIPTION DURATION – 18 months minimum
ILLITERACY RATE – 38.2 per cent
ENROLMENT (percentage of age group) – primary 72 per cent (1996); secondary 22 per cent (1996); tertiary 2.8 per cent (1996)

HISTORY AND POLITICS

The kingdom of Lane Xang, the Land of a Million Elephants, was founded in the 14th century but broke up at the beginning of the 16th century into the separate kingdoms of Luang Prabang and Vientiane and the principality of Champassac, which together came under French protection in 1893. In 1945 the Japanese staged a coup and suppressed the French administration. In 1947 Laos became a constitutional monarchy under King Sisvang Vong, and an independent sovereign state in 1953. The next 22 years in Laos were marked by power struggles and civil war, eventually won by the North Vietnamese-backed Pathet Lao, a Communist-dominated organisation.

The Lao People's Democratic Republic was proclaimed in December 1975 following victory by the Pathet Lao and the abdication of the King. A president and Council of Ministers were installed, and a 45-member Supreme People's Council was appointed to draft a constitution, which was approved in 1991. The Lao People's Revolutionary Party (LPRP) is the sole legal political organisation. A general election to the enlarged 99-member National Assembly was held on 21 December 1997; all the candidates were approved by the LPRP. The president, prime minister and Council of Ministers were confirmed in their posts by the National Assembly on 24 February 1998.

HEAD OF STATE

President, Gen. Khamtay Siphandone, *elected by the National Assembly* 24 February 1998

COUNCIL OF MINISTERS *as at September 2000*

Prime Minister, Gen. Sisavat Keobounphanh
Deputy PMs, Boungnang Vorachith (*Finance and Domestic Affairs*); Somsavat Lengsavad (*Foreign Affairs*); Gen. Choumaly Sayasone (*National Defence*);
Agriculture and Forestry, Siene Saphangthong
Commerce and Tourism, Phoumy Thipphavone
Communications, Transport, Posts and Construction, Phao Bounnaphol
Education, Phimmasone Leuangkhamma
Governor of the State Bank, Soukhan Maharaj
Industry and Handicrafts, Soulivong Daravong
Information and Culture, Sileua Bounkham
Interior, Gen. Asang Laoly
Justice, Khamouane Boupha
Labour and Social Welfare, Somphan Phengkhammy
National Economic Institute, Minister attached to Prime Minister, Khamxay Souphanouvong
Public Health, Ponemek Daraloy
State Planning Committee, Bouathong Vonglokham

EMBASSY OF THE LAO PEOPLE'S DEMOCRATIC REPUBLIC
74 Avenue Raymond-Poincaré, F-75116 Paris
Tel: (00 33) (1) 4553 0298
Ambassador Extraordinary and Plenipotentiary, HE Kamphan Simmalavong, apptd 1996

BRITISH AMBASSADOR, HE Sir James Hodge, KCVO, CMG, resident at Bangkok, Thailand

ECONOMY

A 'new economic mechanism' programme was introduced in 1986 which began the liberalisation of the economy. These reforms have produced a market-orientated economic system which has increased growth and reduced inflation. The economy is dominated by the agricultural sector, which contributed 53 per cent of real GDP in 1997. Laos is a major producer of opium.

Although Laos is one of the poorest states in the world, there is potential for increased hydroelectric power exports to Thailand and there are deposits of coal, tin, iron ore, gold, bauxite and lignite. Foreign capital investment in infrastructure began with the 1994 opening of the Friendship Bridge over the Mekong river border with Thailand which links road routes from Singapore to China. Clothing, wood and wood products, electricity, coffee and agricultural products are the main exports.

In 1998 Laos had a trade deficit of US$165 million and a current account deficit of US$150 million. Imports totalled US$553 million and exports US$370 million.
GNP – US$1,583 million (1998); US$320 per capita (1998)
GDP – US$1,868 million (1996); US$371 per capita (1996)
ANNUAL AVERAGE GROWTH OF GDP – 6.9 per cent (1996)
INFLATION RATE – 91.0 per cent (1998)
TOTAL EXTERNAL DEBT – US$2,437 million (1998)

Trade with UK	1998	1999
Imports from UK	£5,117,000	£4,840,000
Exports to UK	1,907,000	8,514,000

LATVIA
Latvijas Republika

AREA – 24,942 sq. miles (64,600 sq. km). Neighbours: Estonia (north), Lithuania and Belarus (south), the Russian Federation (east)
POPULATION – 2,474,000 (1997 UN estimate): 55.3 per cent Latvian, 32.5 per cent Russian, 4.0 per cent Belarusian, with small Ukrainian and Polish minorities. The main religions are Lutheran, Roman Catholic and Russian Orthodox. The official language is Latvian; Russian is also spoken. Education is in Latvian and Russian. Public sector employees must pass language tests in Latvian to a level commensurate with the nature of their employment. The right of minorities to use their mother tongue has been acknowledged
CAPITAL – Riga (population, 805,997, 1998)
MAJOR CITIES – Daugavpils (117,502); Jelgava (70,962); Jūrmala (58,977); Liepāja (97,278); Ventspils (46,564)
CURRENCY – Lats of 100 santims
NATIONAL ANTHEM – Dievs, svet Latviju (God bless Latvia)
NATIONAL DAY – 18 November (Independence Day 1918)
NATIONAL FLAG – Crimson, with a white horizontal stripe across the centre
LIFE EXPECTANCY (years) – male 63.94; female 75.62
POPULATION GROWTH RATE – –1.1 per cent (1997)
POPULATION DENSITY – 38 per sq. km (1997)
URBAN POPULATION – 69.0 per cent (1996)

HISTORY AND POLITICS

Latvia came under the control of the German Teutonic Knights at the end of the 13th century. During the next few centuries the country endured sporadic invasions by the Swedes, Poles and Russians. By 1795 Latvia was entirely under Russian control. On 18 November 1918, Latvia declared its independence, but was annexed by the Soviet Union in 1940 under the terms of the Molotov–Ribbentrop pact with Germany. Latvia was invaded and occupied when Germany invaded the Soviet Union during the Second World War but recaptured by the Soviet Union in 1944.

In 1988 the Popular Front of Latvia was formed to campaign for greater sovereignty and democracy for Latvia. It won the elections to the Supreme Council in 1989, and on 4 May 1990 the Supreme Council declared the independent republic of Latvia to be, *de jure*, still in existence. A national referendum was held in March 1991 in which 73 per cent voted in favour of independence, and this was declared on 21 August 1991. The State Council of the Soviet Union recognised the independence of Latvia on 10 September 1991.

The last Russian military base in the Baltic states at Skrunda was handed back to Latvian control in 1999.

The general election of 3 October 1998 resulted in the People's Party gaining the most seats, but a coalition of Latvia's Way, the Union for Fatherland and Freedom and the New Party formed a government on 26 November. The Latvian Social Democratic Union joined the coalition on 4 February 1999.

POLITICAL SYSTEM

Executive authority is vested in a prime minister and Cabinet of Ministers. Legislative power is exercised by the unicameral parliament (*Saeima*), which comprises 100 deputies elected for four-year terms by proportional representation, with a 5 per cent threshold for parliamentary representation. The deputies elect a president of state, serving for four years, who in turn appoints the prime minister. The prime minister appoints, and the Saeima approves, the Cabinet of Ministers.

The electorate and citizenship had been restricted to descendants of Latvian citizens before the 1940 Soviet occupation and to those who could pass the required Latvian language tests, until 1994 when a law was passed enabling naturalisation of long-term residents. In October 1998 a referendum to amend the citizenship law was passed which granted citizenship to those children born in Latvia after Latvian independence if their parents requested it and provided for simpler language tests for older residents.

HEAD OF STATE

President, Vaira Vīķe-Freiberga, *elected* 17 June 1999, *sworn in* 8 July 1999

CABINET *as at September 2000*

Prime Minister, Andris Berzins (LC)
Agriculture, Atis Slakteris (TP)
Culture, Karīna Pētersone (LC)
Defence, Ģirts Valdis Kristovskis (TB)
Economy, Aigars Kalvitis (TP)
Education and Science, Karlis Greiskalns (TP)
Environment and Regional Development, Vladimirs Makarovs (TB)
Finance, Gundars Bērziņš (TP)
Foreign Affairs, Indulis Bērziņš (LC)
Interior, Mareks Segliņš (TP)
Justice, Ingrida Labucka
Special Tasks Minister for Co-operation with International Financial Institutions, Roberts Zīle (TB)
Special Tasks Minister for State Administration and Local Government, Janis Krumins (LC)
Transport, Anatolijs Gorbunovs (LC)
Welfare, Andrejs Pozarnovs (TB)

TB Union For Fatherland and Freedom; LC Latvia's Way; TP People's Party

EMBASSY OF THE REPUBLIC OF LATVIA

45 Nottingham Place, London W1M 3FE
Tel: 020-7312 0040
Ambassador Extraordinary and Plenipotentiary,
HE Normans Penke, apptd 1997

BRITISH EMBASSY

5, J. Alunana Street, Riga LV-1010
Tel: (00 371) 733 8126-31
E-mail: british.embassy@apollo.lv
Ambassador Extraordinary and Plenipotentiary, HE Stephen Nash, apptd 1999

BRITISH COUNCIL DIRECTOR, I. Stewart, 5A Blaumana iela 3, Riga LV-1011; e-mail: mail@bcriga.lv

DEFENCE

The Army has 13 armoured personnel carriers, the Navy has 12 patrol craft at three bases and the Air Force has two aircraft and three helicopters.

Russian forces withdrew from Latvia in 1994.

MILITARY EXPENDITURE – 2.5 per cent of GDP (1998)
MILITARY PERSONNEL – 7,320: Army 2,550, Navy 840, Air Force 210, Paramilitaries 3,720
CONSCRIPTION DURATION – 12 months

ECONOMY

Attempts to move from a command economy to a market economy resulted in low growth and high unemployment in the early 1990s, though economic reforms have begun to show results. The government has initiated a privatisation process which has made many industrial facilities available for purchase both by Latvian and foreign private investors. The privatisation of small and medium-sized enterprises has been completed, along with most large enterprises. A number of energy and telecommunications enterprises were due to be privatised in 2000.

Latvia is an agricultural exporter, specialising in cattle and pig breeding, dairy farming and crops, including sugar beet, flax, cereals and potatoes. In 1996, 13.6 per cent of the population were employed in agriculture. Natural resources include limestone, gypsum, peat and timber.

Industry is specialised in certain areas including the production of food and beverages, motor vehicles, textiles and timber and paper products.

Tourism is being developed, capitalising on Latvia's beach resorts, nature reserves and parks. Latvia is also geographically well-placed for the development of transport services.

GNP – US$5,917 million (1998); US$2,420 per capita (1998)
GDP – US$5,024 million (1996); US$2,007 per capita (1996)
ANNUAL AVERAGE GROWTH OF GDP – 0.1 per cent (1999)
INFLATION RATE – 2.4 per cent (1999)
UNEMPLOYMENT – 9.1 per cent (1999)
TOTAL EXTERNAL DEBT – US$850 million (1999)

TRADE

In 1996, a free trade regime was agreed with the EU and EFTA. The main imports are machinery, chemical goods and transport vehicles, and the main exports are wood and wood products, textiles and base metals and metallic products. The most important import partners are Germany, Russia, Finland, Lithuania and Sweden. The most important export partners are Germany, the UK, Sweden, Lithuania and Russia.

In 1998 there was a trade deficit of US$1,130 million and a current account deficit of US$713 million. Imports totalled US$3,189 million and exports US$1,801 million.

Trade with UK	1998	1999
Imports from UK	£87,172,000	£71,153,000
Exports to UK	296,471,000	269,511,000

COMMUNICATIONS

Latvia has 2,413 km of railways and some 20,400 km of roads. Many of the exports from former CIS states are transported to Western Europe via Latvia. Latvia is also being developed as a transportation route from Scandinavia to central and southern Europe. Several warm-water ports exist, of which three, Riga, Ventspils and Liepaja, are developed for commercial transport. The national airline, Air Baltic, operates regular flights to Scandinavia and Europe.

CULTURE AND EDUCATION

The Latvian language belongs to the Baltic branch of the Indo-European languages. The Latin alphabet is used. Latvian literature appeared in the 19th century and played a role in the fight for independence in 1918.

There are 27 higher education institutions, of which five are universities.

ILLITERACY RATE – 0.3 per cent

ENROLMENT (percentage of age group) – primary 89 per cent (1996); secondary 79 per cent (1996); tertiary 33.3 per cent (1996)

LEBANON
Al-Jumhūriyya al-Lubnāniyya

AREA – 4,015 sq. miles (10,400 sq. km). Neighbours: Syria (north and east), Israel (south)

POPULATION – 3,144,000 (1997 UN estimate): 32 per cent Shi'ite Muslim; 21 per cent Sunni Muslim, 40 per cent Christian, 7 per cent Druze. Arabic is the official language, and French and English are also widely used

CAPITAL – ΨBeirut (Bayrūt) (population, 1,500,000, 1991)

MAJOR CITIES – ΨSaydā (Sidon) (100,000); ΨTarābulus (Tripoli) (200,000); ΨSūr (Tyre) (70,000)

CURRENCY – Lebanese pound (L£) of 100 piastres

NATIONAL ANTHEM – Kulluna Lil Watan Lilula Lil'alam (We all belong to the homeland)

NATIONAL DAY – 22 November

NATIONAL FLAG – Horizontal bands of red, white and red with a green cedar of Lebanon in the centre of the white band

LIFE EXPECTANCY (years) – male 66.60; female 70.50

POPULATION GROWTH RATE – 3.0 per cent (1997)

POPULATION DENSITY – 302 per sq. km (1997)

HISTORY AND POLITICS

Lebanon became an independent state in 1920, administered under French mandate until 22 November 1943. Powers were transferred to the Lebanese government from January 1944 and French troops were withdrawn in 1946.

In 1975, fighting broke out in Beirut between Maronite, Sunni and Shia factions, the latter supported by Palestinian guerrillas based in Lebanon; fighting continued until the end of the civil war in 1990. In 1982 Israeli forces invaded and, in 1985 established a buffer zone along the Israeli–Lebanon border controlled by the South Lebanon Army (SLA), a Christian militia.

A new government incorporating the main militia leaders was formed in December 1990. Since then the government has attempted to clear the militias from the Greater Beirut area and restore its authority throughout most of the country. Since 1993 the Lebanese Army has deployed in southern villages alongside UNIFIL forces but has not disarmed Hezbollah forces, who are financed, armed and trained by Syria and Iran.

Low-level fighting continued throughout 1993–9. In April 1996, Israel began a two-week missile bombardment of Hezbollah targets in Beirut and southern Lebanon. The mission, code-named 'Grapes of Wrath', was in retaliation for suicide attacks and Hezbollah strikes against Israel's northern cities.

The Israeli Prime Minister Ehud Barak had committed himself to the withdrawal of Israeli forces from the buffer zone during his election campaign in May 1999 and Israel began its withdrawal in mid-May 2000, initially handing over their positions to the SLA, but a mass movement of exiled civilians, led by Hezbollah forces, effectively routed the SLA. The last Israeli troops left on 24 May 2000 and the SLA troops surrendered to the Lebanese authorities or fled to Israel.

Syrian forces remain in west Beirut and in the north and the east of the country.

The first parliamentary elections since 1972 were held between August and October 1992. The 128-seat National Assembly was directly elected by universal suffrage and divided equally between Christians and Muslims. The polls were widely boycotted in Christian areas because of the continuing presence of Syrian troops. National Assembly elections were held in August and September 2000, and the first local elections for 35 years were held in May and June 1998.

Salim al-Hoss was appointed prime minister by President Lahoud on 2 December 1998, pledging himself to continue with the reconstruction programmes initiated by his predecessor, along with a programme of fiscal austerity to cut the budget deficit.

POLITICAL SYSTEM

The National Covenant (1943) is characterised by the division of power between the religious communities. The executive comprises the president, prime minister and Cabinet. The president is elected by the National Assembly for a non-renewable term of six years and must be a Maronite Christian. The prime minister is appointed following consultation between the president and National Assembly and must be a Sunni Muslim. The 128-member unicameral National Assembly comprises equal numbers of Christians and Muslims although the speaker must be a Shia Muslim. Political parties are banned. There are six governorates divided into 26 districts.

The constitution was amended on 15 October 1998 to allow the election of Gen. Lahoud as president. Serving state officials had previously been prohibited from standing for the presidency.

HEAD OF STATE

President of the Republic of Lebanon, Gen. Émile Lahoud, *elected* 15 October 1998, *sworn in* 24 November 1998

CABINET *as at September 2000*

Prime Minister, Foreign Affairs, Expatriates' Affairs, Salim al-Hoss

Deputy PM, Interior, Municipal and Rural Affairs, Michel al-Murr

Agriculture, Housing and Co-operatives, Soleiman Franjieh

Economy and Trade, Industry, Nasir al-Sa'idi

Finance, Georges Qurum

Hydroelectric Resources, Oil, Soleiman Trabulsi

Information, Displaced Persons' Affairs, Anwar al-Khalil

Justice, Joseph Shaoul

Labour, Social Affairs, Michel Musa

Minister of State for Administrative Reform, Hassan Shalaq

National Defence, Ghazi Zu'aytar

National Education, Youth and Sports, Vocational and Technical Education, Culture and Higher Education, Muhammad Yusuf Baydun

Post and Telecommunications, Isam Nu'man

Public Health, Karam Karam

Public Works, Transport, Najib Miqati

Speaker of the National Assembly, Nabi Berri

Tourism, Environment, Artur Nazarian

LEBANESE EMBASSY
21 Kensington Palace Gardens, London W8 4QM
Tel: 020-7229 7265/7727 6696
Ambassador Extraordinary and Plenipotentiary, HE Jihad Mortada, apptd 1999

BRITISH EMBASSY
Autostrade Jal El Dib, Coolrite Building (PO Box 60180), Beirut
Tel: (00 961) (4) 715 900-034
E-mail: britemb@cyberia.net.lb
Ambassador Extraordinary and Plenipotentiary,

HE David MacLennan, apptd 1996

BRITISH COUNCIL DIRECTOR, A. Malamah-Thomas, MBE,
Sidani Street, Fawzi Azar Building, Ras Beirut;
e-mail: general.enquiries@bc-beirut.sprint.com

DEFENCE

The Army has 304 main battle tanks, and 1,281 armoured
personnel carriers. The Navy has seven patrol and coastal
vessels at two bases.

There are a 4,4964-strong UN peacekeeping force,
22,000 Syrian troops and 150 Iranian Revolutionary
Guards operating in Lebanon.

MILITARY EXPENDITURE – 3.6 per cent of GDP (1998)
MILITARY PERSONNEL – 67,900: Army 65,000, Navy
1,200, Air Force 1,700; Paramilitaries 13,000
CONSCRIPTION DURATION – 12 months

ECONOMY

Fruits are the most important products and include citrus
fruit, apples, grapes, bananas and olives. There is some
light industry, mostly for the production of consumer
goods, but most factories are still in need of reconstruction
because of the civil war.

A ten-year plan has been initiated to repair war damage
and to restore Lebanon's position as a regional financial
services and light industrial centre. The 1993–2002
reconstruction plan is estimated to cost US$12,900
million, of which US$7,600 million is to come from
foreign loans and grants and US$5,300 million from
budget surpluses. It is to concentrate on rebuilding
housing, transport, services, education and health services,
and aiding industry and agriculture.

GNP – US$14,975 million (1998); US$3,560 per capita
(1998)
GDP – US$12,814 million (1996); US$4,155 per capita
(1996)
ANNUAL AVERAGE GROWTH OF GDP – 4.0 per cent
(1996)
INFLATION RATE – 6.8 per cent (1994)
TOTAL EXTERNAL DEBT – US$6,725 million (1998)

TRADE

Principal imports are foodstuffs, machinery and electrical
equipment, vehicles, chemical products, mineral ores, and
metals and metal products. There is a free trade agreement
with Syria.

Principal exports include foodstuffs, chemical products,
jewellery, machinery and electrical goods, textiles, metals
and metal products, paper and paper products, and
vehicles.

At one time there was a considerable transit trade
through Beirut into the Arab hinterland. Lebanon is the
terminal for two oil pipelines, one formerly belonging to
the Iraq Petroleum Company, debouching at Tripoli, the
other belonging to the Trans Arabian Pipeline Company,
at Sidon. These lines have not functioned for some years.

In 1996 imports totalled US$7,582 million and exports
US$1,017 million.

Trade with UK	1998	1999
Imports from UK	£180,160,000	£157,023,000
Exports to UK	21,502,000	17,121,000

COMMUNICATIONS

There are 7,370 km of roads, of which 6,265km are paved;
there is 222 km of railway track. There is an international
airport at Beirut, served by the national carrier Middle
East Airlines and other airlines. An internal service
operates from Beirut to Tripoli.

EDUCATION

There are 13 universities in Lebanon, among them the
American and the French universities, and the Lebanese
National University, the Beirut University College, the
Kaslik Saint Esprit University and the Arab University in
Beirut, with the University of Balamand situated near
Tripoli. There are also ten other institutions of higher
education and an Academy of Fine Arts. There are several
institutions for vocational training, and there is a good
provision throughout the country of primary and secondary schools, among which are a great number of private
schools.

ILLITERACY RATE – 13.9 per cent
ENROLMENT (percentage of age group) – primary
76 per cent (1996); tertiary 27.0 per cent (1995)

LESOTHO
'Muso oa Lesotho

AREA – 11,720 sq.miles (30,355 sq. km). Neighbour: South
Africa, which completely surrounds Lesotho
POPULATION – 2,131,000 (1997 UN estimate).
The languages are Sesotho and English
CAPITAL – Maseru (population, 367,000, 1992 estimate)
CURRENCY – Loti (M) of 100 lisente. The South African
rand is also legal tender
NATIONAL ANTHEM – Pina ea Sechaba
NATIONAL DAY – 4 October (Independence Day)
NATIONAL FLAG – Diagonally white over blue over green
with the white of double width, and an assegai and
knobkerrie on a Basotho shield in brown in the upper
hoist
LIFE EXPECTANCY (years) – male 56.38; female 58.99
POPULATION GROWTH RATE – 2.5 per cent (1997)
POPULATION DENSITY – 70 per sq. km (1997)
MILITARY EXPENDITURE – 3.5 per cent of GDP (1998)
MILITARY PERSONNEL – 2,000 Army

HISTORY AND POLITICS

Lesotho (formerly Basutoland) became a constitutional
monarchy within the Commonwealth on 4 October 1966.
The constitution was suspended in 1970 and the country
was governed by a Council of Ministers until the
establishment of a National Assembly in 1974.

Leabua Jonathan's government was overthrown in
1986, and executive and legislative powers were conferred
on the King. Elections were held in March 1993 and the
Basotho Congress Party (BCP) won all 65 seats in the new
National Assembly. A BCP government led by Ntsu
Mokhele was formed, and King Letsie III swore allegiance
to a new multiparty democratic constitution.

On 17 August 1994 King Letsie III and sections of the
military mounted a coup attempt, but after mediation, the
government, which had refused to leave office, was
restored by the King. King Letsie also announced his
intention to abdicate in favour of his father, Moshoeshoe
II, who was restored on 25 January 1995. When King
Moshoeshoe II died in a car crash on 15 January 1996,
King Letsie III again ascended to the throne.

At the last legislative elections in May 1998, the Lesotho
Congress for Democracy won 78 of the 80 seats in the
National Assembly. Allegations of electoral fraud, later
confirmed by an investigation which said that the election
had been marred by irregularities, but that there were
insufficient grounds to annul the poll, led to violent
protests, which began in August; there were also reports of
an alleged army mutiny. The deteriorating situation led to
the intervention of South African and Botswanan military
forces on 22 September to restore order after a request by
the prime minister, Bethuel Pakalitha Mosisili; they
withdrew in May 1999.

An Interim Political Authority (IPA) was created in 1998 to enable a new election to be held, free of irregularities. It announced in September 1999 that the first-past-the-post electoral system would be replaced by a new system incorporating a degree of proportional representation and that the number of seats in the National Assembly would be increased by 50 to 130. The IPA announced in May 2000 that the general election, which had been expected in April 2000, would be held in May 2001.

On 3 April 2000, the government announced the establishment of a commission of enquiry into the political unrest that had followed the May 1998 general election. Several opposition parties announced that they would boycott the commission.

The country is divided into ten administrative districts. In each district there is a district secretary who co-ordinates all government activity in the area, working in co-operation with hereditary chiefs.

HEAD OF STATE

HM The King of Lesotho, King Letsie III, *acceded* February 1996, *crowned* 31 October 1997

COUNCIL OF MINISTERS *as at September 2000*

Prime Minister, Defence, Public Service, Bethuel Pakalitha Mosisili
Deputy Prime Minister, Finance and Development Planning, Kelebone Albert Maope
Agriculture, Vova Bulane
Education and Manpower Development, Lesao Lehohla
Environment, Women, Youth Affairs, Mrs Mathabiso
Foreign Affairs, Motsoahae Thomas Thabane
Health and Social Welfare, Tefo Mabote
Home Affairs, Local Government, Mopshatla Mabitle
Industry, Trade and Marketing, Mpho Malie
Information, Boradcasting, Post and Telecommunications, Nyane Mphafi
Justice, Human Rights, Law and Constitutional Affairs, Shakhane Robong Mokhehle
Labour and Employment, Not'si Molopo
Natural Resources, Monyane Moleleki
Prime Minister's Office, Sephiri Motanyane
Tourism, Sports and Culture, Hlalele Motaung
Works and Transport, Mofelehetsi Moerane

HIGH COMMISSION FOR THE KINGDOM OF LESOTHO
7 Chesham Place, London SW1 8HN
Tel: 020-7235 5686
High Commissioner, HE Benjamin Masilo, apptd 1996

BRITISH HIGH COMMISSION
PO Box Ms 521, Maseru 100
Tel: (00 266) 313961
E-mail: hcmaseru@lesoff.co.za
High Commissioner, HE Kaye Oliver, OBE, apptd 1999

BRITISH COUNCIL DIRECTOR, S. Bush, Hobson's Square, PO Box 429, Maseru 100; e-mail: general.enquiries@ bc-lesotho.bcouncil.org

ECONOMY

The economy is based on agriculture and animal husbandry, and the adverse balance of trade (mainly consumer and capital goods) is offset by the earnings of the large numbers of the population who work in South Africa. Apart from some diamonds, Lesotho has few natural resources. Agriculture contributes 13.9 per cent of GDP and the main crops are maize, sorghum and vegetables. Industry contributes 40.1 per cent and services 46.1 per cent of GDP. The Lesotho National Development Corporation was set up to promote the development of industry, mining, trade and tourism; a number of light manufacturing and processing industries have recently been established. The main sources of revenue are customs and excise duty.

In 1994 Lesotho had a trade deficit of US$667 million and a current account surplus of US$108 million.
GNP – US$1,167 million (1998); US$570 per capita (1998)
GDP – US$804 million (1996); US$387 per capita (1996)
ANNUAL AVERAGE GROWTH OF GDP – 10.0 per cent (1996)
TOTAL EXTERNAL DEBT – US$692 million (1998)

Trade with UK	1998	1999
Imports from UK	£1,041,000	£755,000
Exports to UK	15,000	—

COMMUNICATIONS

A tarred road links Maseru to several of the main low-land towns, and this is being extended in the south of the country. The mountainous areas are linked by tarred, gravelled and earth roads and tracks. Roads link border towns in South Africa with the main towns in Lesotho. Maseru is also connected by rail with the main Bloemfontein–Natal line of the South African Railways. Scheduled international air services are operated daily between Maseru and Johannesburg, and other scheduled international flights are to Gaborone, Harare, Manzini and Maputo. There are around 30 airstrips. Internal scheduled services are operated by the Lesotho Airways Corporation.

The telephone network is fully automated in all urban centres. Radio telephone communication is used extensively in the remote rural areas.

EDUCATION

Most schools are mission-controlled, the government providing grants for salaries and buildings. There are over 1,200 primary and over 180 secondary schools, with emphasis being laid on agricultural and vocational education. The National University of Lesotho at Roma was established as a university in 1975.
ILLITERACY RATE – 16.1 per cent
ENROLMENT (percentage of age group) – primary 70 per cent (1996); secondary 18 per cent (1996); tertiary 2.4 per cent (1996)

LIBERIA
Republic of Liberia

AREA – 43,000 sq. miles (111,369 sq. km). Neighbours: Guinea (north), Côte d'Ivoire (east), Sierra Leone (north-west)
POPULATION – 2,879,000 (1997 UN estimate). The official language is English. The main African languages are Bassa, Kpelle and Kru, though some 16 ethnic languages are spoken
CAPITAL – ΨMonrovia (population, 1,000,000, 1993 estimate)
MAJOR CITIES – ΨBuchanan (Grand Bassa); ΨGreenville (Sinoe); ΨHarper (Cape Palmas)
CURRENCY – Liberian dollar (L$) of 100 cents
NATIONAL ANTHEM – All Hail, Liberia, Hail
NATIONAL DAY – 26 July
NATIONAL FLAG – Alternate horizontal stripes (five white, six red), with five-pointed white star on blue field in upper corner next to flagstaff
LIFE EXPECTANCY (years) – male 45.80; female 44.00
POPULATION GROWTH RATE – 2.6 per cent (1997)
POPULATION DENSITY – 26 per sq. km (1997)
URBAN POPULATION – 45.4 per cent (1997)

MILITARY EXPENDITURE – 3.9 per cent of GDP (1998)
MILITARY PERSONNEL – 14,000
ILLITERACY RATE – 46.6 per cent

HISTORY AND POLITICS

Liberia was founded by the American Colonisation Society in 1822 as a colony for freed American slaves, and has been recognised since 1847 as an independent state.

William V. S. Tubman, President since 1944, died in 1971 and was succeeded by Dr Tolbert. The constitution was suspended following a military coup in 1980 during which Tolbert was killed. M/Sgt. Samuel Doe assumed power as chairman of a military council. A new constitution was endorsed by a referendum in 1984. Doe and his party, the National Democratic Party of Liberia (NDPL) won the elections held in 1985, amid allegations of electoral fraud, and a civilian government was formally installed in 1986.

CIVIL WAR

A rebel incursion in 1989 by the National Patriotic Front of Liberia (NPFL) led by Charles Taylor developed into a full-scale civil war in 1990. A five-nation Economic Community of West African States (ECOWAS) peace-keeping force (known as ECOMOG) landed in Monrovia in an effort to end the conflict but in September 1990 President Doe was killed, having refused to step down.

The Interim Government of National Unity (IGNU) was formed in August 1990. A peace agreement was signed by the IGNU, NPFL and another rebel group, ULIMO, on 25 July 1993, which brought about a cease-fire on 1 August.

In August 1999, President Taylor ordered a state of emergency after rebels from the Joint Forces for the Liberation of Liberia crossed the border from Guinea and briefly seized several towns. In September 1999, Guinea accused Liberia of attacking three Guinean villages, a charge that the Liberian authorities denied. Following talks arranged by Nigeria in September, a commission was established to consider the security problems between Liberia and Guinea.

In July 2000, the USA threatened Liberia with international sanctions if it continued to support insurgency in Sierra Leone.

Legislative elections held in July 1997 were won by the NPFL, and Charles Taylor was elected president with 75 per cent of the vote in elections deemed free and fair by international observers.

POLITICAL SYSTEM

The head of state is an executive president, directly elected for a six-year term, who appoints the Cabinet. There is a bicameral legislature consisting of a 64-member lower chamber, the House of Representatives, which is directly elected for a six-year term, and a 26-member Senate, elected for a nine-year term.

HEAD OF STATE

President, Charles Taylor, *elected* 19 July 1997, *inaugurated* 3 August 1997
Vice-President, Moses Z. Blah

CABINET *as at September 2000*

Agriculture, Roland Massaquoi
Commerce, Enieh Reward
Defence, Daniel Chea
Director of the Cabinet, Blamo Nelson
Education, Evelyne Kandakai
Finance, Nathaniel Barnes
Foreign Affairs, Monie Captan
Health and Social Welfare, Peter Coleman
Information, Culture and Tourism, Joe Mulbah

Interior, Maxwell Poe
Justice, Eddington Varmah
Labour, Christian Neufville
Ministers of State, Wisseh McClain (*Planning and Economic Affairs*); Jonathan Taylor (*Presidential Affairs*); Augustine Zayzay (Without Portfolio)
National Security, Philip Kamah
Planning and Economic Affairs, Larmin Kawah
Post and Telecommunications, Charles Bright
Public Works, Emmet Taylor
Rural Development, Hezekiah Bowen
Transport, Francis Carbah
Youth and Sports, Francis Massaquoi

EMBASSY OF THE REPUBLIC OF LIBERIA
2 Pembridge Place, London W2 4XB
Tel: 020-7221 1036
Ambassador Extraordinary and Plenipotentiary, vacant
Minister-Counsellor (Head of Chancery) and Chargé d'Affaires, Jeff Gongoer Dowana Sr

BRITISH AMBASSADOR, HE Haydon Warren-Gash, resident at Abidjan, Côte d'Ivoire

ECONOMY

Before the civil war began principal exports were iron ore, crude rubber, timber, uncut diamonds, palm kernels, cocoa and coffee, but the civil war has resulted in the suspension of most economic activity.
GDP – US$2,695 million (1996); US$1,200 per capita (1996)
ANNUAL AVERAGE GROWTH OF GDP – 2.7 per cent (1996)
INFLATION RATE – 9.1 per cent (1989)
TOTAL EXTERNAL DEBT – US$2,103 million (1998)

Trade with UK	1998	1999
Imports from UK	£7,818,000	£15,273,000
Exports to UK	1,906,000	1,323,000

COMMUNICATIONS

The artificial harbour and free port of Monrovia was opened in 1948. There are 10,300 km of roads, of which 628 km are paved, and 490 km of railway track. There are nine ports of entry, including three river ports. Robertsfield International Airport is under NPFL control and not yet in use. Spriggs Payne airfield, on the outskirts of Monrovia, normally used for internal flights, is currently being used for flights to other West African countries.

LIBYA
Al-Jamāhīriyya Al-Arabiyya
Al-Lībiyya Ash-Sha'biyya Al-Ishtirākiyya

AREA – 679,362 sq. miles (1,759,540 sq. km). Neighbours: Egypt and Sudan (east), Chad and Niger (south), Algeria and Tunisia (west)
POPULATION – 4,389,739 (1995 census). The people of Libya are principally Arab with some Berbers in the west and some Tuareg tribesmen in the Fezzan. Islam is the official religion but other religions are tolerated. The official language is Arabic
CAPITAL – ΨTripoli (population, 1,000,000, 1991 estimate)
MAJOR CITIES – ΨBangāzī (500,000); ΨMisrāta (200,000); Sirte (100,000)
CURRENCY – Libyan dinar (LD) of 1,000 dirhams
NATIONAL DAY – 1 September
NATIONAL FLAG – Libya uses a plain emerald green flag

LIFE EXPECTANCY (years) – male 61.58; female 65.00
POPULATION DENSITY – 3 per sq. km (1997)
ILLITERACY RATE – 20.2 per cent
ENROLMENT (percentage of age group) – primary 96 per cent (1992); secondary 62 per cent (1980); tertiary 18.4 per cent (1992)

Vast sand and rock deserts, almost completely barren, occupy the greater part of Libya. The southern part of the country lies within the Sahara Desert. There are few rivers and as rainfall is irregular outside parts of Cyrenaica and Tripolitania, good harvests are rare.

The ancient ruins in Cyrenaica, at Cyrene, Ptolemais (Tolmeta) and Apollonia, are outstanding, as are those at Leptis Magna, 70 miles east, and at Sabratha, 40 miles west of Tripoli. An Italian expedition found in the south-west of the Fezzan a series of rock-paintings more than 5,000 years old.

HISTORY AND POLITICS

From the 16th century Libya was dominated by the Ottoman Empire, until occupied by Italy in 1911–12 in the course of the Italo-Turkish War. Under the 1912 Treaty of Ouchy, sovereignty over the province was transferred by Turkey to Italy, and in 1939 the four provinces of Libya (Tripoli, Misurata, Banghāzī and Derna) were incorporated in the national territory of Italy as *Libia Italiana*. After the Second World War Tripolitania and Cyrenaica were placed provisionally under British and the Fezzan under French administration, and in conformity with a resolution of the UN General Assembly in 1949, Libya became on 24 December 1951 the first independent state to be created by the UN. The monarchy was overthrown by a revolution in 1969 and the country was declared a republic. It was ruled by the Revolutionary Command Council (RCC) under the leadership of Col. Muammar al-Gadhafi.

In 1977, a new form of direct democracy, the 'Jamahiriya' (state of the masses) was promulgated and the official name of the country was changed to Socialist People's Libyan Arab Jamahiriya. Since a reorganisation in 1979, neither Col. Gadhafi nor his former RCC colleagues have held formal posts in the administration. Gadhafi continues to hold the ceremonial title 'Leader of the Revolution'.

POLITICAL SYSTEM

At local level authority is vested in about 1,500 Basic and 14 Municipal People's Congresses which appoint Popular Committees to execute policy. Officials of these congresses and committees, together with representatives from unions and other organisations, form the General People's Congress, which normally meets twice each year. In addition, a number of extraordinary sessions are held throughout the year. This is the highest policy-making body in the country.

The General People's Congress appoints its own General Secretariat and the General People's Committee, whose members head the government departments which execute policy at national level. The Secretary of the General People's Committee has functions similar to those of a prime minister.

On 1 March 2000 it was announced that 12 of the ministries run by the General People's Committee had been abolished and that their powers had been devolved to provincial committees.

Leader of the Revolution and Supreme Commander of the Armed Forces, Col. Muammar al-Gadhafi

SECRETARIAT OF THE GENERAL PEOPLE'S CONGRESS *as at September 2000*

Secretary-General, Mubarak Abdallah al-Shamikh
Deputy Secretary for Production, Beshir Bujeneh

Deputy Secretary for Services, Bagdadi Mahmudi
Secretary, African Unity, Ali Abdel Salam Turayki
Secretary, Finance, Mohammad Abdallah Beit al-Mal
Secretary, Foreign Liaison and International Co-operation, Abdel Rahman Muhammad Shalgam
Secretary, Information, Culture and Tourism, Fawziya Basheer Shalabi
Secretary, Justice and Public Security, Mohamed Abu al-Gasem al-Zowi
Co-ordinator of the General Provisional Committee for Defence, Abu Bakr Jaber Yunes
Speaker of the General People's Congress, Mohammad al-Zenati

LIBYAN PEOPLE'S BUREAU
61– 62 Ennismore Gardens, London SW7 1NH
Tel: 020-7589 6120
Chargé d'Affaires, Isa Baruni Edaeki
Financial Attaché, Mustafa Mansour Tantoush

BRITISH EMBASSY
Sharia Uahran 1, PO Box 4206, Tripoli
Tel: (00 218) (21) 333 1191/2/3
Ambassador Extraordinary and Plenipotentiary, HE R. Dalton, CMG

DEFENCE

The Army has about 2,210 main battle tanks, 1,000 armoured infantry fighting vehicles, and 990 armoured personnel carriers. The Navy has four submarines, two frigates, 32 patrol and coastal vessels, and 32 armed helicopters at seven bases. The Air Force has 420 combat aircraft and 52 armed helicopters.

Libya is alleged to have built at least one chemical weapons plant. The USA claims that a plant at Rabta, closed in 1990, was reopened in 1995, and that a plant has been constructed near Tahunah, south of Tripoli.

As part of the UN economic sanctions imposed in April 1992, there is a total embargo on arms sales to Libya.
MILITARY EXPENDITURE – 5.3 per cent of GDP (1998)
MILITARY PERSONNEL – 65,000: Army 35,000, Navy 8,000, Air Force 22,000
CONSCRIPTION DURATION – One to two years (selective)

ECONOMY

Economic sanctions were imposed on Libya in April 1992 by the UN Security Council following Libya's failure to hand over two suspects in the bombing of Pan-Am flight 103 over Lockerbie, Scotland, in 1988, in which 270 people were killed. The UN imposed additional sanctions in December 1993, including freezing assets abroad and restricting imports of spare parts and equipment for the oil and aviation sectors. The sanctions were suspended in April 1999, following mediation by President Mandela of South Africa in March 1999, which led to the extradition in April of the two suspects to the Netherlands to stand trial.

Agriculture is confined mainly to the coastal areas of Tripolitania and Cyrenaica, where barley, wheat, olives, citrus fruits and livestock are produced, and to the areas of the oases.

The main industry is oil and gas production. There are pipelines from Zaltan to the terminal at al-Burayqah, from Dahra to as-Sidrah, from Amal to Ras Lanuf, and from the Intisar field to az-Zuwaytīnah. In 1998, 69.2 million tonnes of crude oil was produced. Cement, construction materials and textiles are also produced. Economic constraints have delayed some projects, particularly since Libya decided in 1983 to go ahead with a major irrigation scheme, the 'Great Man-Made River'.

Libya has technical assistance agreements with a number of countries, and also employs large numbers of foreign labourers and experts.
GDP – US$20,925 million (1996); US$3,741 per capita (1996)

ANNUAL AVERAGE GROWTH OF GDP – 2.0 per cent (1996)

TRADE

Exports are dominated by crude oil, but some wool, cattle, sheep and horses, olive oil, and hides and skins are also exported. Principal imports are machinery and transport equipment, foodstuffs, livestock, and most construction materials and consumer goods. After the revolution the private sector was virtually eliminated and Libya became a state trading country with imports controlled by state monopolies. Since reforms in 1988, however, a small private sector has been re-established.

Trade with UK	1998	1999
Imports from UK	£237,386,000	£177,050,000
Exports to UK	149,114,000	115,940,000

COMMUNICATIONS

There are 25,675 km of roads; the coastal road running from the Tunisian frontier through Tripoli to Bangāzī, Tubruk and the Egyptian border serves the main population centres. Main roads also link the provincial centres, and the oil-producing areas of the south with the coastal towns.

There are airports at Tripoli and Bangāzī (Benina), Kufra, Labrag, Misrātah and Tubruk. Since April 1992 a UN embargo on air links with Libya has been in force.

LIECHTENSTEIN
Fürstentum Liechtenstein

AREA – 62 sq. miles (160 sq. km). Neighbours: Austria, Switzerland
POPULATION – 32,015 (1998). The language of the principality is German
CAPITAL – Vaduz (population, 5,106, 1998)
CURRENCY – Swiss franc of 100 rappen (or centimes)
NATIONAL ANTHEM – Oben am Jungen Rhein (Up on the young Rhine)
NATIONAL DAY – 15 August
NATIONAL FLAG – Equal horizontal bands of blue over red; gold crown on blue band near staff
LIFE EXPECTANCY (years) – male 66.07; female 72.94
POPULATION GROWTH RATE – 1.4 per cent (1997)
POPULATION DENSITY – 200 per sq. km (1997)

HISTORY AND POLITICS

The Principality of Liechtenstein was established by Emperor Charles VI in 1719. Following the First World War, Liechtenstein severed its ties with Austria and began its association with Switzerland, taking up the Swiss currency in 1921.

In November 1999, the European Court of Human Rights fined Prince Hans Adam II for abusing his subjects' freedom of speech, a development which prompted a constitutional crisis in the principality.

In February 2000, Prince Hans Adam announced that he wished to hold a referendum on constitutional reform, and threatened to abdicate if his proposals were rejected by the electorate.

There is a threshold of 8 per cent for parties to gain representation in the 25-member *Landtag*, the unicameral parliament. The Patriotic Union and Progressive Citizens' parties governed the country in coalition from 1938 until March 1997. At the general election on 31 January and 2 February 1997 the Patriotic Union won 13 seats, Progressive Citizens' Party 10, and Free List 2. The Patriotic Union formed a government which took office in April 1997.

HEAD OF STATE

HSH The Prince of Liechtenstein, Hans Adam II, *born* 14 February 1945; *succeeded* 13 November 1989; *married* 30 July 1967, Countess Marie Kinsky; and has *issue:* Prince Alois (*see* below); Prince Maximilian, *b.* 16 May 1969; Prince Constantin, *b.* 15 March 1972; Princess Tatjana, *b.* 10 April 1973
Heir, HSH Prince Alois, *b.* 11 June 1968, *married* 1993 Duchess Sophie of Bavaria; and has *issue:* Prince Wenzel, *b.* 24 May 1995; Princess Marie, *b.* 17 October 1996; Prince Georg, *b.* 20 April 1999

MINISTRY *as at September 2000*

Prime Minister, Finance, Construction, Mario Frick
Education, Environment, Transport, Norbert Marxer
Foreign Affairs, Family and Equal Opportunities, Culture and Sport, Andrea Willi
Interior, Health and Welfare, Economy, Michael Ritter
Justice, Heinz Frommelt

DIPLOMATIC REPRESENTATION
Liechtenstein is represented in diplomatic and consular matters in the United Kingdom by the Swiss Embassy.

BRITISH AMBASSADOR, Christopher Hulse, CMG, OBE, resident at Bern, Switzerland

ECONOMY

The main industries are high and ultra-high vacuum engineering, the semiconductor industry, roller bearings, artificial teeth, heating equipment, synthetic fibres, woollen and homespun fabrics.

In 1991 Liechtenstein became a member of the European Free Trade Association, and joined the European Economic Area on 1 May 1995.

In 1999, imports from the UK totalled £4,824,000, and exports to the UK £21,776,000.
GDP – US$1,263 million (1996); US$40,746 per capita (1996)
ANNUAL AVERAGE GROWTH OF GDP – 0.2 per cent (1996)

LITHUANIA
Lietuva

AREA – 25,174 sq. miles (65,200 sq. km). Neighbours: Latvia (north), Belarus (east and south), Poland and the Kaliningrad region of the Russian Federation (south-west)
POPULATION – 3,701,300 (1998): 81.6 per cent Lithuanian, 8.2 per cent Russian, 6.9 per cent Polish, 1.5 per cent Belarusian, 1 per cent Ukrainian. The majority are Roman Catholic, with Russian Orthodox and Lutheran minorities. Lithuanian is the state language
CAPITAL – Vilnius (population, 578,412, 1999)
MAJOR CITIES – Kaunas (414,199); Klaipėda ((202,545), 1999
CURRENCY – Litas, pegged to the dollar, US$1= 4 litas
NATIONAL ANTHEM – Tautiška Giesmė (The National Song)
NATIONAL DAY – 16 February (Independence Day)
NATIONAL FLAG – Three horizontal stripes of yellow, green, red
LIFE EXPECTANCY (years) – male 63.59; female 75.19
POPULATION GROWTH RATE – –0.1 per cent (1997)
POPULATION DENSITY – 57 per sq. km (1999)
URBAN POPULATION – 68.1 per cent (1999)

Lithuania lies in the middle and lower basin of the river Nemunas. Along the coast is a lowland plain which rises inland to form uplands in east and central Lithuania.

These uplands, the Middle Lowlands, give way to the Baltic Highlands in east and south-east Lithuania; the highest point is 294 m (965 ft). There is a network of rivers and over 2,800 lakes, which mainly lie in the east of the country. The climate varies between maritime and continental.

HISTORY AND POLITICS

The first independent Lithuanian state emerged as the Kingdom of Lithuania in 1251. After forming a joint Commonwealth and Kingdom with Poland in 1569, Lithuania was taken over by the Russian Empire in the partitions of Poland that occurred in 1772, 1793 and 1795.

Lithuania declared its independence from the Russian Empire on 16 February 1918 and signed a peace treaty with the Soviet Union on 12 July 1920. The Soviet Union annexed Lithuania in 1940 under the terms of the Molotov–Ribbentrop pact with Germany. Lithuania was invaded and occupied when Germany invaded the Soviet Union during the Second World War. In 1944, the Soviet Union recaptured the country and confirmed its annexation.

In December 1989, public pressure forced the Lithuanian Communist Party to agree to multiparty elections, which were held in February 1990. These were won by the nationalist Sajudis movement, and the Supreme Council (parliament) declared the restoration of independence on 11 March 1990. Over 90 per cent of the population voted for independence in a referendum in February 1991. The Soviet Union recognised the independence of Lithuania on 10 September 1991.

The ruling Lithuanian Democratic Labour Party (former Communist Party) was defeated in a legislative election in October and November 1996. The Homeland Union (Conservative Party) and the Christian Democratic Party formed a coalition government. On 4 January 1998, the independent candidate Valdas Adamkus won the presidential election with 50.3 per cent of the vote. A legislative election is due to be held on 8 October 2000.

FOREIGN RELATIONS

Lithuania applied for membership of the EU in December 1995; a treaty of association with the EU entered into force on 1 February 1998.

POLITICAL SYSTEM

Under the 1992 constitution, the head of state is a directly elected president, whose five-year term of office is renewable once only. Executive authority is vested in the government, consisting of the prime minister, who is appointed by the president with the approval of the *Seimas*, and ministers appointed upon the recommendation of the prime minister.

Legislative power is exercised by the Seimas, a unicameral parliament of 141 members directly elected for four-year terms. Seventy-one members are elected in first-past-the-post constituencies and 70 by proportional representation, with a 5 per cent threshold for representation. The constitution bans an alignment of Lithuania with any post-Soviet eastern alliance.

HEAD OF STATE

President, Valdas Adamkus, *inaugurated* 25 February 1998

GOVERNMENT *as at September 2000*

Prime Minister, Andrius Kubilius (HU)
Administration Reforms and Local Authorities,
   Jonas Rudarevičius (Ind.)
Agriculture, Edvardas Makelis (Ind.)
Culture, Arūnas Bėkšta (Ind.)
Defence, Česlovas Stankevičius (CD)
Economy, Valentinas Milaknis (Ind.)
Education and Science, Kornelijus Platelis (Ind.)

Environment, Danius Lygis (HU)
Finance, Vytautas Dudėnas (HU)
Foreign Affairs, Algirdas Saudargas (CD)
Health, Raimundas Alekna (HU)
Interior, Česlovas Blažys (Ind.)
Justice, Gintaras Balčiūnas (Ind.)
Social Welfare and Labour, Irena Deguticnė (HU)
Transport, Rimantas Didžiokas (HU)

HU Homeland Union; CD Christian Democrats; Ind. Independent

EMBASSY OF LITHUANIA
84 Gloucester Place, London W1H 3HN
Tel: 020-7486 6401/2
Ambassador Extraordinary and Plenipotentiary, HE
   Justas Paleckis, apptd 1996

BRITISH EMBASSY
2 Antakalnio, LT-2055 Vilnius
Tel: (00 370) (2) 222 2070
Ambassador Extraordinary and Plenipotentiary,
   HE Christopher Robbins, apptd 1998

BRITISH COUNCIL REPRESENTATIVE, L. Balenaite,
   Vilniaus 39/6, LT-2001 Vilnius;
   e-mail: Lina@britishcouncil.lt

DEFENCE

The Army has 27 armoured personnel carriers; the Navy has two frigates and four patrol and coastal vessels based at Klaipėda; the Air Force has eight helicopters. The last Russian troops withdrew in 1993.

MILITARY EXPENDITURE – 1.7 per cent of GDP (2000)
MILITARY PERSONNEL – 12,130: Army 7,840,
   Navy 1,320, Air Force 970, Paramilitaries 3,900
CONSCRIPTION DURATION – 12 months

ECONOMY

The economy was largely agricultural prior to rapid industrialisation during the Soviet era. A privatisation programme began in 1991 and progress in the sale of small enterprises has been quick and successful. In 1997, the privatisation of communication, energy and transport companies was begun.

In 1998, agriculture and forestry accounted for 10 per cent of GDP, mining and manufacturing industry 19 per cent, construction 8 per cent and transport and communications 10 per cent.. The main industries are chemicals and petrochemicals, food processing, wood products, textiles, leather goods, machinery, machine tools and household appliances.

GNP – US$9,411 million (1998); US$2,540 per capita (1998)
GDP – US$9,585 million (1997); US$1,510 per capita (1996)
ANNUAL AVERAGE GROWTH OF GDP – 5.7 per cent (1997)
INFLATION RATE – 0.3 per cent (1999)
UNEMPLOYMENT – 6.9 per cent (1999)
TOTAL EXTERNAL DEBT – US$3,000 million (1999)

TRADE

Lithuania's main trading partners are Germany, Latvia, Russia, Denmark and Belarus. In 1999, total foreign investment in Lithuania reached US$1.9 billion.

In 1998 there was a trade deficit of US$1,518 million and a current account deficit of US$1,298 million. Imports totalled US$5,765 million and exports US$3,693 million.

Trade with UK	1998	1999
Imports from UK	£116,743,000	£95,636,000
Exports to UK	146,974,000	163,125,000

COMMUNICATIONS

There are 45,340 km of surfaced roads; there is a relatively well-developed railway system of 2,898 km running east-west and north-south and linking the major towns with Vilnius and Klaipèda, the main international port. Vilnius has an international airport and there are smaller ones at Kaunas, Palanga and Šiauliai.

CULTURE AND EDUCATION

Lithuanian culture and literature are closely linked to the national liberation movements of the 19th and early 20th centuries, and the literature of Lithuanians who went into exile during the Soviet era.

Lithuania re-established a national education system in 1990. Education is free and compulsory from seven to 16 years, with the system comprising elementary schools (four years), nine-year schools (five years), and secondary schools (three years). The language of instruction is predominantly Lithuanian, but there are also Russian and Polish schools. There are 105 vocational schools and 65 colleges. Lithuania has eight universities and seven other institutes of higher education. Vilnius University, founded in 1579, is one of the oldest universities in eastern Europe.

ILLITERACY RATE – 0.5 per cent
ENROLMENT (percentage of age group) – secondary 80 per cent (1994); tertiary 31.4 per cent (1996)

LUXEMBOURG
Groussherzogtom Lëtzebuerg

AREA – 998 sq. miles (2,586 sq. km). Neighbours: Germany (east), Belgium (west and north), France (south)
POPULATION – 417,000 (1997 UN estimate), nearly all Roman Catholic. The officially designated 'national language' is Lëtzebuergesch (Luxembourgish), a mainly spoken language. French and German are the official languages for written purposes, and French is the language of administration
CAPITAL – Luxembourg (population, 77,400, 1996)
CURRENCY – Euro (€) of 100 cents/Luxembourg franc (LF) of 100 centimes (Belgian currency is also legal tender)
NATIONAL ANTHEM – Ons Hémécht (Our homeland)
NATIONAL DAY – 23 June
NATIONAL FLAG – Three horizontal bands, red, white and blue
LIFE EXPECTANCY (years) – male 70.61; female 77.87
POPULATION GROWTH RATE – 1.3 per cent (1997)
POPULATION DENSITY – 161 per sq. km (1997)
ENROLMENT (percentage of age group) – primary 81 per cent (1985); secondary 64 per cent (1994); tertiary 10 per cent (1996)

HISTORY AND POLITICS

Established as an independent state under the sovereignty of the King of the Netherlands as Grand Duke by the Congress of Vienna in 1815, Luxembourg formed part of the Germanic Confederation from 1815 to 1866, and was included in the German 'Zollverein'. In 1867 the Treaty of London declared it a neutral territory. On the death of the King of the Netherlands in 1890 it passed to the Duke of Nassau.

The territory was invaded and overrun by the Germans at the beginning of the war in 1914 but was liberated in 1918. By the Treaty of Versailles (1919), Germany renounced its former agreements with Luxembourg and in 1921 an economic union was formed with Belgium. The Grand Duchy was again invaded and occupied by Germany in 1940, and liberated in 1944.

FOREIGN RELATIONS

The constitution was modified in 1948 and the stipulation of permanent neutrality was abandoned. Luxembourg is now a signatory of the Brussels and North Atlantic treaties, and also a member of the EU. Luxembourg is a member of the Belgium-Netherlands-Luxembourg Customs Union (Benelux 1960).

POLITICAL SYSTEM

There is a Chamber of 60 deputies, elected by universal suffrage for five years. Legislation is submitted to the Council of State. The last general election was held on 13 June 1999 and a coalition government was installed. In March 1998, Grand Duke Jean passed certain constitutional powers on to his son and heir, Prince Henri, and announced on 25 December 1999 that he would abdicate in favour of Prince Henri in September 2000.

HEAD OF STATE

HRH The Grand Duke of Luxembourg, HRH Grand Duke Henri, *born* 16 April 1955; *succeeded* (on the abdication of his father) 28 September 2000; *married* 14 February 1981, Maria Teresa Mestre, and has *issue*, Prince Guillaume (*see* below); Prince Felix, *b.* 3 June 1984; Prince Louis, *b.* 3 August 1986; Princess Alexandra, *b.* 2 February 1991; Prince Sébastien, *b.* 16 April 1992, Princess Gabriella, *b.* 26 March 1994
Heir, HRH Prince Guillaume, *born* 11 November 1981

CABINET *as at September 2000*
Prime Minister, Finance, Jean-Claude Juncker (CSP)
Deputy P.M., Foreign Affairs, Trade, Civil Service and Administrative Reform, Lydie Polfer (DP)
Agriculture, Viticulture, Rural Development, Small Businesses, Housing and Tourism, Fernand Boden (CSP)
Culture, Higher Education and Research, Public Works, Erna Hennicot-Schoepges (CSP)
Development Aid and Defence, Environment, Charles Goerens (DP)
Economy, Transport, Henri Grethen (DP)
Employment, Religion, Parliamentary Relations, François Biltgen (CSP)
Family, Social Solidarity and Youth, Advancement of Women, Marie-Josée Jacobs (CSP)
Health and Social Security, Carlo Wagner (DP)
Home Affairs, Michel Wolter (CSP)
National Education, Vocational Training and Sport, Anne Brasseur (DP)
Secretaries of State, Joseph Schaack (DP) (*Civil Service and Administrative Reform*); Eugène Berger (DP) (*Environment*)
Treasury and Budget, Justice, Luc Frieden (CSP)
CSP Christian Social Party; DP Democratic Party

EMBASSY OF LUXEMBOURG
27 Wilton Crescent, London SW1X 8SD
Tel: 020-7235 6961
Ambassador Extraordinary and Plenipotentiary, HE Joseph Weyland, apptd 1993

BRITISH EMBASSY
14 Boulevard F. D. Roosevelt, L-2450 Luxembourg Ville
Tel: (00 352) 229864/5/6
Ambassador Extraordinary and Plenipotentiary, HE William Ehrman, apptd 1998

DEFENCE

For legal reasons, NATO's squadron of E-3A Sentry airborne early warning aircraft is registered in Luxembourg.
MILITARY EXPENDITURE – 0.9 per cent of GDP (1998)
MILITARY PERSONNEL – Army 768, Paramilitaries 612

ECONOMY

The country has an important iron and steel industry and is an important financial centre. In 1998, 727,000 tourists visited Luxembourg.

The chief exports are metal goods, manufactures, machinery, chemicals, transport equipment, and foodstuffs and livestock. The chief imports are machinery, transport equipment, metal goods, manufactures, chemicals, and foodstuffs and livestock.

GNP – US$19,239 million (1998); US$45,100 per capita (1998)
GDP – US$16,969 million (1996); US$41,187 per capita (1996)
ANNUAL AVERAGE GROWTH OF GDP – 3.0 per cent (1996)
INFLATION RATE – 1.0 per cent (1998)
UNEMPLOYMENT – 3.1 per cent (1998)

TRADE WITH UK
(Belgium and Luxembourg)

Trade with UK	1998	1999
Imports from UK	£7,987,700,000	£8,801,300,000
Exports to UK	9,047,100,000	9,090,300,000

MACAO

AREA – 7 sq. miles (18 sq. km)
POPULATION –419,000 (1997)
Macao, situated at the mouth of the Pearl River, comprises a peninsula and the islands of Coloane and Taipa.

Macao became a Portuguese colony in 1557; in a Sino-Portuguese treaty of 1887 China recognised Portugal's sovereignty over Macao. An agreement to transfer the administration of Macao to the Chinese authorities was signed on 13 April 1987. Macao became the Macao Special Administrative Region (MSAR) of China when power was transferred by the outgoing Portuguese governor Vasco Rocha Vieira to the new chief executive on 19 December 1999. The final session of the Macao SAR Basic Law Drafting Committee had been held in Beijing in January 1993 and had approved the Basic Law which was to serve as Macao's constitution after 1999.

On 10 April 1999, a 200-member committee of Macao residents was established to determine the composition of the first government of the Macao SAR. They elected Edmund Ho Hao Wah to be its first chief executive. The Chief Executive announced in September 1999 that he had appointed the 10 members of his Executive Council, a body intended to assist the chief executive in policy-making. In addition, he appointed seven legislators to the 23-member MSAR First Legislative Council, which included 15 members of the previous 16-member Legislative Assembly; a replacement was chosen for the member who had not wished to continue.

Chief Executive, Edmund Ho Hao Wah

EXECUTIVE COUNCIL *as at September 1999*

Victor Ng; Ma Iao Lai; Tong Chi Kin;
   Leong Heng Teng; Fernando Chui Sai On;
   Florinda da Rosa Silver Chan;
   Cheong Kuok Va; Liu Chak Wan;
   Ao Man Long; Francis Tam Pak Un
CONSUL-GENERAL, Sir Andrew Burns, KCMG,
   resident at Hong Kong

Trade with UK	1998	1999
Imports from UK	£31,029,000	£19,598,000
Exports to UK	53,697,000	42,636,000

MACEDONIA
Republika Makedonija

AREA – 9,928 sq. miles (25,713 sq. km). Neighbours: Federal Republic of Yugoslavia (north), Bulgaria (east), Greece (south), Albania (west)
POPULATION – 2,190,000 (1997 UN estimate); 1,936,877 (1994 census): 66.5 per cent Macedonian, 22.9 per cent Albanian, 4.0 per cent ethnic Turks, 2.3 per cent Romanies, 2.0 per cent Serbs and 0.4 per cent Vlachs. The census results are disputed by the ethnic Albanians and Serbs. Macedonian Orthodox Christianity is the majority religion, with a Muslim minority. The main language is Macedonian (a south Slavic language), which is written in the Cyrillic script
CAPITAL – Skopje (population, 429,964, 1994)
MAJOR CITIES – Bitola (84,002); Kumanov (69,231); Prilep (70,152)
CURRENCY – Dinar of 100 paras
NATIONAL ANTHEM – Denes nad Makedonija se radja novo sonce na slobodata (Today a new sun of liberty appears over Macedonia)
NATIONAL FLAG – Red with an eight-rayed sun displayed over the whole field
LIFE EXPECTANCY (years) – male 69.27; female 73.65
POPULATION GROWTH RATE – 1.1 per cent (1997)
POPULATION DENSITY – 85 per sq. km (1997)
URBAN POPULATION – 58.1 per cent (1991)
MILITARY EXPENDITURE – 9.9 per cent of GDP (1998)
MILITARY PERSONNEL – 16,000: Army 15,000, Paramilitaries 7,500
CONSCRIPTION DURATION – Nine months
ENROLMENT (percentage of age group) – primary 95 per cent (1996); secondary 56 per cent (1996); tertiary 20 per cent (1996)

HISTORY AND POLITICS

From the ninth to the 14th centuries AD Macedonia was ruled alternately by the Bulgars and the Byzantine Empire. In the middle of the 14th century the area was conquered by the Turks and remained under the Ottoman Empire for over 500 years. After the defeat of Turkey in the two Balkan wars of 1912–13 the geographical area of Macedonia was divided, the major part becoming Serbian (the areas of the present-day Macedonia) and the remainder given to Greece and Bulgaria. In 1918 Serbian Macedonia was incorporated into Serbia as South Serbia. When Yugoslavia was reconstituted in 1944 as a Communist federal republic under President Tito, Macedonia became a constituent republic.

Multiparty elections for the 120-seat assembly held in November and December 1990 produced the first non-Communist government since the Second World War. The electorate overwhelmingly approved Macedonian sovereignty and independence in a referendum and independence was declared on 8 September 1991.

In elections to the *Sobranje* (National Assembly) held on 18 October and 1 November 1998, the coalition of the Internal Macedonian Revolutionary Organisation-Democratic Party for Macedonian National Unity and the Democratic Alternative won 62 of the 120 seats. It invited the National Democratic Party, an ethnic Albanian party, to join the coalition. Presidential elections on 14 November and 5 December 1999 were won by Boris Trajkovski of the Internal Macedonian Revolutionary Organisation-Democratic Party for Macedonian National Unity (RO-DP).

FOREIGN RELATIONS

A new constitution was adopted in November 1991 and then amended at the EC's request to make it clear that Macedonia had no territorial claim on its neighbours. Macedonia applied for EC recognition in December 1991 but was refused because of Greece's objections to the state's name, flag and currency which, according to the Greek government, amounted to a territorial claim on the Greek province of Macedonia. The peaceful withdrawal of the Yugoslav Army (JNA) from Macedonia was completed in April 1992.

Macedonia gained UN membership on 8 April 1993 following a compromise with Greece by which it is temporarily known as the 'Former Yugoslav Republic of Macedonia' (FYROM).

The Federal Republic of Yugoslavia began forcibly expelling Kosovo's ethnic Albanian population following the outbreak of hostilities between Yugoslavia and NATO forces on 24 March 1999, which resulted in an exodus of refugees; by early June, some 300,000 had sought sanctuary in Macedonia. The refugees began to return when the conflict ended on 9 June 1999.

HEAD OF STATE

President, Boris Trajkovski, *elected* 5 December 1999
Vice-Presidents, Dosta Dimovska (RO-DP); Radmila Kiprijanova Radovanovik (RO-DP); Bedredin Ibrahimi (DPA) (*Labour and Social Policy*)

CABINET *as at September 2000*

Prime Minister, Ljubčo Georgievski (RO-DP)
Deputy Prime Minister, Vasil Turpurkovski (DA)
Deputy Prime Minister, Interior, Dosta Dimovska (RO-DP)
Deputy Prime Minister, Labour and Social Policy, Bedredin Ibrahami (DPA)
Agriculture, Forestry and Water Resources Management, Marjan Gjorcev (RO-DP)
Culture, Ganka Samiolovska-Cvetano (RO-DP)
Defence, Ljuben Paunovski (RO-DP)
Development, Trajko Slaveski (RO-DP)
Economy, Borko Andreev (DA)
Education and Science, Gale Galev (DA)
Emigration, Martin Trenevski (RO-DP)
Environment, Toni Popovski (DA)
Finance, Nikola Gruevski (RO-DP)
Foreign Affairs, Aleksander Dimitrov (DA)
Health, Dragan Danailovski (RO-DP)
Information, Vehbi Bexheti (DPA)
Justice, Dxevded Nasufi (DPA)
Local Self-government, Xhemaili Saiti (DPA)
Trade, Milijana Danevska (RO-DP)
Transport and Communications, Ljubčo Balkovski (DA)
Urban Planning and Construction, Dusko Kadiyevski (RO-DP)
Without Portfolio, Adnan Klahil (DA); Ernad Fejzulahu (DPA)
Youth and Sport, Georgi Boev (RO-DP)

DA Democratic Alternative; DPA Democratic Party of Albanians; RO-DP Internal Macedonian Revolutionary Organisation-Democratic Party for Macedonian National Unity

EMBASSY OF THE REPUBLIC OF MACEDONIA
10 Harcourt House, 19A Cavendish Square, London W1M 9AD
Tel: 020-7499 5152/1854
Ambassador Extraordinary and Plenipotentiary, HE Stevo Crvenkovski, apptd 1997

BRITISH EMBASSY
Veljko Vlahović 26, MK-9100 Skopje
Tel: (00 389) (91) 116772/237637
Ambassador Extraordinary and Plenipotentiary, HE Mark Dickinson, apptd 1997

BRITISH COUNCIL, British Information Centre, Bulevar Goce Delcev 6, PO Box 562, MK-91000 Skopje; e-mail: britcoun@nic.mpt.com.mk

ECONOMY

The economy was decimated by the UN trade sanctions against the rump Yugoslavia (from May 1992 until November 1995), with which Macedonia had conducted 60 per cent of its trade. The Greek economic blockade (from February 1994 until October 1995) deprived Macedonia of most of its oil supplies and industry survived on imports from Turkey and Bulgaria. Macedonia is attempting to transform its economy to a market-orientated one and to introduce privatisation; by 1997, 45 per cent of the economy was in private hands. In April 2000, the government sold 65 per cent of Macedonia's largest bank, the Stopanska bank, and parliament voted to return property expropriated during the period under Communist rule. An economic co-operation agreement was signed by Macedonia and Albania in July 1999, covering energy, mining and trade.

In 1996 58.3 per cent of GDP was produced by service industries, 28.3 per cent by industry, and 13.4 per cent by agriculture.

The main exports are textiles, tobacco, zinc, wine, iron ore and iron products. The main imports are oil, energy, telecommunications equipment, metal manufactures, foodstuffs and medicines.

In 1998 there was a trade deficit of US$398 million and a current account deficit of US$288 million. In 1995 imports totalled US$1,719 million and exports US$1,204 million.

GNP – US$2,584 million (1998); US$1,290 per capita (1998)
GDP – US$3,590 million (1996); US$1,651 per capita (1996)
ANNUAL AVERAGE GROWTH OF GDP – 1.7 per cent (1996)
INFLATION RATE – 0.5 per cent (1998)
UNEMPLOYMENT – 38.8 per cent (1996)
TOTAL EXTERNAL DEBT – US$2,392 million (1998)

Trade with UK	1998	1999
Imports from UK	£23,962,000	£33,736,000
Exports to UK	14,027,000	18,404,000

MADAGASCAR
Repoblikan'i Madagasikara

AREA – 226,658 sq. miles (587,041 sq. km)
POPULATION – 15,845,000 (1997 UN estimate). The people are of mixed Malayo-Polynesian, Arab and African origin. There are sizeable French, Chinese and Indian communities. The official languages are Malagasy and French
CAPITAL – Antananarivo (population, 1,052,835, 1993 census)
MAJOR CITIES – ΨAntsiranana (942,410); Fianarantsoa (2,671,150); ΨMahajanga (100,807); ΨToamasina (127,441), the chief port
CURRENCY – Franc malgache (FMG) of 100 centimes
NATIONAL ANTHEM – Ry tanindrazanay malala o (O, our beloved country)
NATIONAL DAY – 26 June (Independence Day)
NATIONAL FLAG – Equal horizontal bands of red (above) and green, with vertical white band by staff
LIFE EXPECTANCY (years) – male 55.00; female 58.00
POPULATION DENSITY – 27 per sq. km (1997)
MILITARY EXPENDITURE – 0.9 per cent of GDP (1998)

MILITARY PERSONNEL – 21,000: Army 20,000, Navy 500, Air Force 500; Paramilitaries 7,500
CONSCRIPTION DURATION – 18 months
ILLITERACY RATE – 54.3 per cent
ENROLMENT (percentage of age group) – primary 61 per cent (1995); tertiary 2 per cent (1996)

Madagascar lies 240 miles off the east coast of Africa and is the fourth largest island in the world.

HISTORY AND POLITICS

Madagascar (known from 1958 to 1975 as the Malagasy Republic) became a French protectorate in 1895, and a French colony in 1896 when the former queen was exiled. Republican status was adopted on 14 October 1958, and independence was proclaimed on 26 June 1960.
  The post-independence civilian government was replaced by a military government in 1975 and martial law was declared. A Supreme Council of the Revolution under Didier Ratsiraka was established.
  In November 1991, President Ratsiraka relinquished executive power to a new prime minister, Guy Razanamasy. However, the president retained his official position and the main opposition grouping, the *Forces Vives*, established a rival government led by Albert Zafy. In December 1991 a transitional government including Forces Vives and Razanamasy supporters was formed to draft a new constitution, approved by referendum in August 1992. Presidential elections were held in two rounds in November 1992 and February 1993, Albert Zafy emerging victorious with 67 per cent of the vote. He became the first president of the Third Republic, which came into being at the same time.
  President Zafy was impeached in September 1996 and defeated in a presidential election in November and December 1996 by former president Ratsiraka. Following legislative elections held in May 1998, Ratsiraka's *Avant-garde de la révolution malgache* (AREMA) party became the largest party in the 150-member National Assembly. The constitution also envisages an upper chamber, but this has yet to be established.

HEAD OF STATE

President, Didier Ratsiraka, *elected* 29 December 1996, *inaugurated* 9 February 1997

COUNCIL OF MINISTERS *as at September 2000*

Prime Minister, Finance and Economy, Tantely Andrianarivo
Deputy PM, Budget, Development of Autonomous Provinces, Pierrot Rajaonarivelo
Agriculture, Marcel Raveloarijaona
Armed Forces, Maj.-Gen. Marcel Ranjeva
Civil Service, Labour and Social Legislation, Alice Razafinakanga
Energy and Mines, Charles Rasoja
Environment, M. Alphonse
Fishing and Marine Resources, Abdallah Houssene
Foreign Affairs, Lila Ratsifandrihamanana
Health, Henriette Ratsimbazafimahefa
Higher Education, Joseph Sydson
Industrialisation and Cottage Industry, Mamy Ratovomalala
Information, Culture and Communications, Fredo Betsimifira
Interior, Brig.-Gen. Jean-Jacques Rasolondraibe
Justice, Keeper of the Seals, Anaclet Imbiki
Livestock, M. Rakotondrasoa
Population, Women's Affairs and Childhood, Noëline Jaotody
Posts and Telecommunications, Ny Hasina Andriamanjato
Primary and Secondary Education, Simon Jacquit Rosat
Private Sector Development and Privatisation, Horace Constant
Public Works, Col. Jean Emile Tsaranazy

Regional and Town Planning, Herivelona Ramanantsoa
Scientific Research, Solay Rakotonirainy
Secretaries of State, Maj.-Gen. Jean-Paul Bory (*Gendarmerie*); Marofo Azaly Ben (*Public Security*)
Technical Education and Vocational Training, Boniface Levelo
Tourism, Blandin Razafimanjato
Trade and Consumption, Alphonse Randrianambinina
Transport and Meteorology, Charles Rasolonay
Water and Forests, Rija Rajohnson
Youth and Sports, Cdr. Ndrianasolo

EMBASSY OF THE REPUBLIC OF MADAGASCAR
4 avenue Raphael, F-75016 Paris, France
Tel: (00 33) (1) 4504 6211
Ambassador Plenipotentiary and Extraordinary, HE Malala zo Raolison, apptd 1998

HONORARY CONSULATE OF THE REPUBLIC OF MADAGASCAR
16 Lanark Mansions, Pennard Road, London W12 8DT
Tel: 020-8746 0133
Honorary Consul, Stephen Hobbs

BRITISH EMBASSY
1st Floor, Immeuble 'Ny Havana', Cité de 67 Ha, BP 167, Antananarivo
Tel: (00 261) (2) 27749
Ambassador Extraordinary and Plenipotentiary, HE C. F. Mochan, apptd 1999

ECONOMY

The economy is still largely based on agriculture, which employs more than 80 per cent of the workforce. The main products are rice, cassava, sugar cane and sweet potatoes. Development plans have placed emphasis on improving communications, the exploitation of mineral deposits and the creation of small industries. Madagascar was hit by three cyclones in February and April 2000, which caused widespread flooding, resulting in the destruction of much of the rice crop.
  In 1996 there was a trade deficit of US$120 million and a current account deficit of US$291 million. In 1998, imports totalled US$514 million and exports US$241 million.
GNP – US$3,741 million (1998); US$260 per capita (1998)
GDP – US$2,020 million (1996); US$132 per capita (1996)
ANNUAL AVERAGE GROWTH OF GDP – 3.6 per cent (1997)
INFLATION RATE – 6.2 per cent (1998)
TOTAL EXTERNAL DEBT – US$4,394 million (1998)

Trade with UK	1998	1999
Imports from UK	£5,982,000	£6,263,000
Exports to UK	20,783,000	21,675,000

MALAŴI
Dziko La Malaŵi

AREA – 45,747 sq. miles (118,484 sq. km). Neighbours: Tanzania (north-east), Zambia (west), Mozambique (south)
POPULATION – 10,441,000 (1997 UN estimate). The official languages are Chichewa and English
CAPITAL – Lilongwe (population, 233,973, 1987)
MAJOR CITIES – Blantyre (331,588), incorporating Blantyre and Limbe, the major commercial and industrial centre; Mzuzu (44,238); Zomba (42,878), the former capital
CURRENCY – Kwacha (K) of 100 tambala

NATIONAL ANTHEM – O God Bless Our Land of Malaŵi
NATIONAL DAY – 6 July (Independence Day)
NATIONAL FLAG – Horizontal stripes of black, red and
  green, with rising sun in the centre of the black stripe
LIFE EXPECTANCY (years) – male 43.51; female 46.75
POPULATION GROWTH RATE – 3.3 per cent (1997)
POPULATION DENSITY – 88 per sq. km (1997)
URBAN POPULATION – 19.6 per cent (1996)
MILITARY EXPENDITURE – 1.2 per cent of GDP (1998)
MILITARY PERSONNEL – 5,000: Army 5,000;
  Paramilitaries 1,000

Malaŵi lies in south-eastern Africa. Much of the eastern
border of Malaŵi is formed by Lake Malaŵi (formerly
Lake Nyasa), which covers nearly half of the north of the
country. The valley of the River Shire runs south from the
lake, its watershed with the Zambezi lying on the western
border with Mozambique and its tributary, the Ruo, with
lakes Chinta and Chirwa, lying on the eastern border with
Mozambique. The north and centre are plateaux, and the
south highlands.

HISTORY AND POLITICS

Malaŵi (formerly Nyasaland) assumed internal self-
government on 1 February 1963, and became independent
on 6 July 1964. It became a republic on 6 July 1966.
  In 1991–2 Life President Hastings Banda, who had
ruled since independence, came under increasing pressure
to introduce a multiparty democratic system of government. In May 1992 aid donors tied new loans to
improvements in the human rights record and moves to
multiparty democracy. A referendum was held on the
adoption of a multiparty democracy in June 1993 and
approved by 63 per cent of voters. President Banda and the
Malaŵi Congress Party refused to resign but parliament
passed a law to amend the constitution to allow multiparty
politics and Banda announced a political amnesty to allow
exiles to return. Multiparty presidential and legislative
elections held in May 1994 were won by Bakili Muluzi and
the United Democratic Front (UDF) respectively. Foreign and multilateral aid has since been restored. Former
President Banda died on 25 November 1997. Presidential
and legislative elections were due to be held on 25 May
1999, but were delayed until 15 June; they were won by
the UDF, who won 93 seats. President Muluzi was also
re-elected.

POLITICAL SYSTEM

There is a Cabinet consisting of the president and
ministers. The unicameral National Assembly, which
usually meets three times a year, consists of 193 members
elected by universal suffrage for a five-year term of office.

HEAD OF STATE

President, Defence, Bakili Muluzi, elected 17 May 1994,
  sworn in 21 May 1994, re-elected 15 June 1999
Vice-President, Privatisation, Justin Malewezi

CABINET as at September 2000
The President
The Vice-President
Agriculture and Irrigation Development, Leonard
  Mangulama
Attorney-General, Justice, Peter Fachi
Commerce and Industry, Samuel Phumisa
Education, Science and Technology, Cassim Chilumpha
Finance and Economic Planning, Mathews Chikaonda
Foreign Affairs and International Co-operation, Lilian Patel
Health and Population, Aleke Banda
Home Affairs and Internal Security, Mangeza Maloza
Information, Clement Stambuli
Labour and Vocational Training, Peter Chupa
Lands, Housing, Physical Planning and Services, Thengo
  Maloya

Ministers of State, Rodwell Munyenyembe (Defence);
  Patrick Mbewe (District and Local Government Adminis-
  tration); George Claver (Persons with Disabilities); Ken
  Lipenga (Presidential Affairs); Bob Khamisa (Statutory
  Corporations)
Natural Resources and Environmental Affairs, Harry
  Thomson
Sports and Culture, Moses Dossi
Tourism, National Parks and Wildlife, George Mtafa
Transport and Public Works, Brown Mpinganjira
Water Development, Yusufu Mwawa
Without Portfolio, Uladi Mussa
Women, Youth and Community Services, Mary Banda

MALAŴI HIGH COMMISSION
33 Grosvenor Street, London W1X 0DE
Tel: 020-7491 4172/7
High Commissioner, Bright Msaka, apptd 1998

BRITISH HIGH COMMISSION
PO Box 30042, Lilongwe 3
Tel: (00 265) 782400
E-mail: britcom@malawi.net
High Commissioner, George Finlayson, apptd 1998

BRITISH COUNCIL DIRECTOR, D. Higgs, Head Office
  and Library, PO Box 30222, Lilongwe 3; e-mail:
  bc.lilongwe@bc-lilongwe.bcouncil.org

ECONOMY

The economy is largely agricultural, providing 90 per cent
of export earnings; maize is the main subsistence crop, and
tobacco, cassava, millet and rice are the main cash crops
and principal exports. There are two sugar mills. A
number of light manufacturing industries have been
established, mainly in agricultural processing, clothing/
textiles and building materials.
  In 1994 there was a trade deficit of US$276 million and
a current account deficit of US$450 million. In 1996
imports totalled US$624 million and exports US$481
million.
GNP – US$2,168 million (1998); US$210 per capita
  (1998)
GDP – US$2,186 million (1996); US$222 per capita
  (1996)
ANNUAL AVERAGE GROWTH OF GDP – 6.4 per cent
  (1997)
INFLATION RATE – 29.7 per cent (1998)
TOTAL EXTERNAL DEBT – US$2, 444 million (1998)

Trade with UK	1998	1999
Imports from UK	£13,066,000	£17,511,000
Exports to UK	10,550,000	10,855,000

COMMUNICATIONS

A single-track railway runs from Mchinji on the Zambian
border, through Lilongwe and Salima on Lake Malaŵi
(itself served by two passenger and a number of cargo
boats) through to Blantyre. The route south to the
Mozambique port of Beira was severed by the Mozambican civil war, but the route to Nacala in Mozambique is
open again; there are 797 km of railway track. There are
14,594 km of roads in Malaŵi of which 2,849 km are
bituminised. There is an international airport 26 km from
Lilongwe, which handles regional and intercontinental
flights, and another airport at Chileka.

EDUCATION

The Ministry of Education and Culture is responsible for
secondary schools, technical education and primary
teacher training. Religious bodies, with government
assistance, still play an important part in these fields.
The University of Malaŵi was opened in 1965; there are
also four colleges and one polytechnic.

ILLITERACY RATE – 39.7 per cent
ENROLMENT (percentage of age group) – primary 100
per cent (1994); secondary 2 per cent (1994); tertiary
0.6 per cent (1995)

MALAYSIA
Persekutuan Tanah Malaysia

AREA – 127,320 sq. miles (329,758 sq. km). Thailand
borders the Malay peninsula to the north. On Borneo,
Malaysia (Sarawak and Sabah) borders Indonesia to the
south, and surrounds Brunei to the north
POPULATION – 21,667,000 (1997 UN estimate);
16,921,300 (1988 census): Malays (58 per cent), Chinese
(27 per cent), and those of Indian and Sri Lankan origin,
as well as the indigenous races of Sarawak and Sabah.
Bahasa Malaysia (Malay) is the official language, but
English, various dialects of Chinese, and Tamil are also
widely spoken. There are a few indigenous languages
widely spoken in Sabah and Sarawak. Islam is the official
religion of Malaysia, each ruler being the head of
religion in his state (except in Sabah and Sarawak). The
Yang di-Pertuan Agong is the head of religion in Melaka
and Penang. The constitution guarantees religious
freedom
CAPITAL – Kuala Lumpur (population, 1,145,342, 1991);
Putrajaya (Administrative Capital) (population 3,000,
1999 estimate)
MAJOR CITIES – Ipoh (382,853); Johor Baharu (328,436);
Petaling Jaya (254,350), 1991
CURRENCY – Malaysian dollar (ringgit) (M$) of 100 sen
NATIONAL ANTHEM –Negara-Ku
NATIONAL DAY –31 August (*Hari Kebangsaan*)
NATIONAL FLAG – Equal horizontal stripes of red (seven)
and white (seven); 14-point yellow star and crescent in
blue canton
LIFE EXPECTANCY (years) – male 69.34; female 74.08
POPULATION GROWTH RATE – 2.8 per cent (1997)
POPULATION DENSITY – 66 per sq. km (1997)
URBAN POPULATION – 54.7 per cent (1995)
ILLITERACY RATE – 12.5 per cent
ENROLMENT (percentage of age group) – primary
100 per cent (1994); tertiary 12 per cent (1995)

Malaysia comprises the 11 states of peninsular Malaya plus
Sabah and Sarawak. It occupies two distinct regions, the
Malay peninsula which extends from the isthmus of Kra to
the Singapore Strait, and the north-western coastal area of
the island of Borneo. Each is separated from the other by
the South China Sea.

The year is commonly divided into the south-west and
north-west monsoon seasons. Rainfall averages about 100
inches throughout the year. The average daily temperature varies from 21°C to 32°C, though in higher areas
temperatures are lower and vary widely.

HISTORY AND POLITICS

The Federation of Malaya became an independent
country within the Commonwealth on 31 August 1957.
On 16 September 1963 the federation was enlarged by
the accession of the states of Singapore, Sabah (formerly
British North Borneo) and Sarawak, and the name of
Malaysia was adopted from that date. On 9 August 1965
Singapore seceded from the federation.

The National Front (Barisan Nasional) Coalition led
by Dr Mahathir Mohamed won a fifth term in office in
a general election held on 29 November 1999, winning
148 of the 193 seats.

POLITICAL SYSTEM

The constitution provides for a strong federal government
and a degree of autonomy for the state governments. It
created a constitutional Supreme Head of the Federation
(HM the *Yang di-Pertuan Agong*) and a Deputy Supreme
Head (HRH *Timbalan Yang di-Pertuan Agong*) to be
elected for a term of five years by the rulers from among
their number. The Malay rulers are either chosen or
succeed to their position in accordance with the custom of
the particular state. In other states of Malaysia, choice of
the head of state is at the discretion of the Yang di-Pertuan
Agong after consultation with the Chief Minister of the
state.

The Federal Parliament consists of two houses, the
Senate and the House of Representatives. The Senate
(*Dewan Negara*) consists of 69 members who serve a six-
year term, 26 being elected by the Legislative Assemblies
of the states (two from each) and 43 appointed by the Yang
di-Pertuan Agong. The House of Representatives (*Dewan
Rakyat*) consists of 193 members elected for a five-year
term by universal adult suffrage with a common electoral roll.

The judicial system consists of a Federal Court and two
High Courts, one in peninsular Malaysia and one for
Sabah and Sarawak. The Federal Court comprises a
president, the two Chief Justices of the High Courts and
other judges. It possesses appellate, original and advisory
jurisdiction. Each of the High Courts consists of a Chief
Justice and not less than four other judges.

FEDERAL STRUCTURE

According to the constitution, each state shall have its own
constitution not inconsistent with the federal constitution,
with the ruler or governor acting on the advice of an
Executive Council appointed on the advice of the Chief
Minister and a single-chamber Legislative Assembly. The
Legislative Assemblies are fully elected on the same basis
as the federal parliament.

State	Area (sq. km)	Population (1997 estimate)	Main Town
Johore	18,986	2,554,100	ΨJohor Baharu
Kedah	9,426	1,530,100	Alor Setar
Kelantan	14,943	1,447,000	Kota Baharu
Melaka	1,650	582,000	ΨMelaka
Negeri Sembilan	6,643	810,500	Seremban
Pahang	35,965	1,239,000	ΨKuantan
Penang	1,031	1,222,100	ΨGeorgetown
Perak	21,005	2,094,800	Ipoh
Perlis	795	217,400	Kangar
Sabah	73,711	2,593,400	ΨKota Kinabalu
Sarawak	124,449	1,954,300	ΨKuching
Selangor	7,956	2,999,800	ΨShah Alam
Terengganu	12,955	975,800	ΨKuala Terengganu

Federal Territories

| Kuala Lumpur | | |
| Labuan | } 1,231,500 | |

HEAD OF STATE

Supreme Head of State, HM Salehuddin Abdul Aziz ibni
al-Marhum Hisamuddin Alam (Yang di-Pertuan Agong
of Selangor), *sworn in* 26 April 1999

CABINET *as at September 2000*

Prime Minister, Dr Mahathir Mohamed
Deputy PM, Home Affairs, Abdullah Ahmad Badawi
Agriculture, Mohamed Effendi Norwani
Culture, Arts and Tourism, Abdul Kadir Sheikh Fadzir
Defence, Mohamed Najib Tun Razak
Domestic Trade and Consumer Affairs, Muhyuddin Yasin
Education, Musa Mohamad

Energy, Telecommunications and Posts, Leo Moggie Anak Irok
Entrepreneurial Development, Mohamed Nazri Abdul Aziz
Finance, Special Functions, Daim Zainuddin
Foreign Affairs, Hamid Albar
Health, Chua Jui Meng
Housing and Local Government, Ong Ka Ting
Human Resources, Fong Chan Ong
Information, Mohamad Khalil Yaakdo
International Trade and Industry, Seri Rafidah Aziz
Lands and Co-operative Development, Kasitah Gaddam
National Unity and Social Development, Siti Zaharah Sulaiman
Primary Industries, Dr Lim Keng Yaik,
Prime Minister's Department, Bernard Dompok; Pandikar Amin Musa; Abdul Hamid Osman; Rais Yatim
Public Works, S. Samy Vellu
Rural Development, Azmi Khalid
Science, Technology and Environment, Law Hieng Ding
Transport, Dr Ling Liong Sik
Youth and Sports, Hishamuddin Hussein

MALAYSIAN HIGH COMMISSION
45 Belgrave Square, London SW1X 8QT
Tel: 020-7235 8033
High Commissioner, HE Dato Mohamad Amir bin Ja'afar, apptd 1998
Deputy High Commissioner, Mohamad Daud M. Yusoff
Defence Adviser, Col. Kamaruddin Mattan

BRITISH HIGH COMMISSION
185 Jalan Ampang (PO Box 11030), 50450 Kuala Lumpur
Tel: (00 60) (3) 248 2122
High Commissioner, HE G. Fry, apptd 1998
Deputy High Commissioner, R. J. Wildash, LVO
Counsellor (Commercial/Economic), H. Parkinson, CVO
Defence Adviser, Col. R. J. Little

BRITISH COUNCIL DIRECTOR, E. Edmundson, Jalan Bukit Aman, PO Box 10539, 50916 Kuala Lumpur; e-mail: kualalumpur@britishcouncil.org.my. There are also offices at Penang, Kota Kinabalu (Sabah) and Kuching (Sarawak).

DEFENCE

The Army has 816 armoured personnel carriers. The Royal Malaysian Navy has four frigates, 41 patrol and coastal vessels and 17 armed helicopters at five bases. The Royal Malaysian Air Force has 87 combat aircraft. Australia maintains an infantry company and an air force detachment in Malaysia.
MILITARY EXPENDITURE – 3.7 per cent of GDP (1998)
MILITARY PERSONNEL – 105,000: Army 80,000, Navy 12,500, Air Force 12,500; Paramilitaries 20,100

ECONOMY

From being an agriculturally-based economy reliant on raw materials exports at independence, Malaysia has undergone an industrialisation programme and now produces clothing, textiles, rubber goods, electronics, office equipment, cars, household appliances, semi-conductors, food processing and chemicals. Under the New Economic Policy of 1970–90, the economy grew at an average rate of 6.7 per cent a year. The National Development Policy 1990–2000 is seen as the second stage in making Malaysia a fully-developed industrial state by 2020; it aims for GDP growth of 8 per cent per year. There are extensive privatisation programmes involving telecommunications, railways, airports, electricity and shipping. In 1997 40.8 per cent of GDP was produced by services, 47.6 per cent by manufacturing and 11.7 per cent by agriculture.

Malaysia has been severely affected by the economic crisis in Asia. The crisis was to some extent exacerbated by sudden policy changes by the government, though austerity measures and economic reforms averted the need to apply for IMF assistance.
GNP – US$81,311 million (1998); US$3,670 per capita (1998)
GDP – US$99,282 million (1996); US$4,824 per capita (1996)
ANNUAL AVERAGE GROWTH OF GDP – 7.8 per cent (1997)
INFLATION RATE – 5.3 per cent (1998)
UNEMPLOYMENT – 2.5 per cent (1997)
TOTAL EXTERNAL DEBT – US$44,773 million (1998)

TRADE
Malaysia is the largest exporter of natural rubber, tin, palm oil and tropical hardwoods. Other major export commodities are manufactured and processed products, petroleum, oil and other minerals, palm kernel oil, tea and pepper. Imports consist mainly of machinery and transport equipment, manufactured goods, foods, consumer durables and metal products. Japan, the USA and Singapore are the main trading partners.
In 1997 Malaysia had a trade surplus of US$3,876 million and a current account deficit of US$4,792 million. In 1998 imports totalled US$58,326 million and exports US$73,304 million.

Trade with UK	1998	1999
Imports from UK	£683,186,000	£940,269,000
Exports to UK	1,990,744,000	2,039,770,000

MALDIVES
Divehi Rājjē ge Jumhūriyyā

AREA – 115 sq. miles (298 sq. km)
POPULATION – 273,000 (1997 UN estimate). The people are Sunni Muslims and the Maldivian (Dhivehi) language is akin to Elu or old Sinhalese
CAPITAL – ΨMalé (population, 62,973, 1995)
CURRENCY – Rufiyaa of 100 laaris
NATIONAL ANTHEM – Gavmī ekuverikan matī tibegen kurīme salām (In national unity we salute our nation)
NATIONAL DAY – 26 July
NATIONAL FLAG – Green field bearing a white crescent, with wide red border
LIFE EXPECTANCY (years) – male 67.15; female 66.60
POPULATION GROWTH RATE – 3.4 per cent (1997)
POPULATION DENSITY – 916 per sq. km (1997)
URBAN POPULATION – 25.9 per cent (1990)
MILITARY EXPENDITURE – 11.1 per cent of GDP (1998)
ILLITERACY RATE – 3.7 per cent

The Maldives are a chain of coral atolls 400 miles to the south-west of Sri Lanka, stretching north for about 600 miles from just south of the Equator. There are about 19 coral atolls comprising over 1,200 islands, 198 of which are inhabited. No point in the entire chain of islands is more than eight feet above sea-level.

HISTORY AND POLITICS

Until 1952 the islands were a sultanate under the protection of the British Crown. Internal self-government was achieved in 1948 and full independence in 1965. The Maldives became a special member of the Commonwealth in 1982 and a full member in 1985.
The Maldives form a republic which is elective. The legislature, the Citizens' Assembly (*Majlis*), has 42 representatives elected from all the atolls, and eight

appointed by the president, for a five-year term. The government consists of a Cabinet, which is responsible to the Majlis. There are no political parties. Under the 1998 constitution, the president is elected by the Majlis and confirmed by a referendum.

The most recent legislative election took place on 19 November 1999.

HEAD OF STATE

President, Defence, National Security, Finance and Treasury, HE Maumoon Abdul Gayoom, *elected* 1978, *re-elected* 1983, 1989, 1993, 16 October 1998

CABINET *as at September 2000*

The President
Atolls Administration, Speaker of the Majlis, Abdullah Hameed
Attorney-General, Mohamed Munnawwar
Chief Justice, President of the Supreme Council on Islamic Affairs, Mohamed Rashid Ibrahim
Construction and Public Works, Umar Zahir
Education, Dr Mohamed Latheef
Fisheries and Agriculture, Abdul Rasheed Hussain
Foreign Affairs, Fathullah Jameel
Health, Ahmed Abdulla
Home Affairs, Housing and Environment, Ismail Shafeeu
Human Resources, Employment and Labour, Abdullah Kamaaludheen
Information, Arts and Culture, Ibrahim Manik
Justice, Ahmed Zahir
Minister at the President's Office, Abdullah Jameel
Ministers of State, Maj.-Gen. Anbaree Abdul Sattar (*Defence and National Security*); Mohamed Jaleel (*Finance and Treasury*); Mohamed Hussain (*Presidential Affairs*); Ismail Fathy
Mustashaaru of the Supreme Council on Islamic Affairs, Moosa Fathuhy
Planning and National Development, Ibrahim Hussain Zaki
Tourism, Hassan Sobir
Trade and Industry, Abdulla Yameen
Transport and Civil Aviation, Ilyas Ibrahim
Women's Affairs and Social Welfare, Rashida Yoosuf
Youth and Sports, Mohamed Zahir Hussain

HIGH COMMISSION OF THE REPUBLIC OF MALDIVES
22 Nottingham Place, London W1M 3FB
Tel: 020-7224 2135
Acting High Commissioner, Adam Hassan

BRITISH HIGH COMMISSIONER, HE Linda Duffield, resident at Colombo, Sri Lanka

ECONOMY

The vegetation of the islands is coconut palms with some scrub. Hardly any cultivation of crops is possible and nearly all food to supplement the basic fish diet has to be imported. Tourism is expanding rapidly (395,700 visitors in 1998). The principal industry is fishing, which together with tourism accounts for about 30 per cent of GDP. The Maldives National Ship Management Ltd (MNSML) has a fleet of nine merchant ships. There is an international airport at Malé.

In 1997 the Maldives had a trade deficit of US$199 million and a current account deficit of US$16 million. In 1998 imports totalled US$354 million and exports US$76 million.
GNP – US$296 million (1998); US$1,130 per capita (1998)
GDP – US$307 million (1996); US$1,166 per capita (1996)
ANNUAL AVERAGE GROWTH OF GDP – 6.2 per cent (1997)
INFLATION RATE — 2.2 per cent (1998)
TOTAL EXTERNAL DEBT – US$180 million (1998)

Trade with UK	1998	1999
Imports from UK	£4,538,000	£4,907,000
Exports to UK	11,159,000	5,460,000

MALI
République du Mali

AREA – 478,841 sq. miles (1,240,192 sq. km). Neighbours: Senegal (west), Mauritania (north-west), Algeria (north-east), Niger (east), Burkina Faso and Côte d'Ivoire (south), Guinea (south-west)
POPULATION – 11,480,000 (1997 UN estimate): 50 per cent Mande (Bambara, Malinke, Sarakole), 17 per cent Peul, 12 per cent Voltaic, 6 per cent Songhai, 10 per cent Tuareg and Moor. The official language is French; Bambara is the largest local language
CAPITAL – Bamako (population, 809,552, 1987)
MAJOR CITIES – Gao; Kayes; Mopti; Ségou; Sikasso; Timbuktu (all regional capitals)
CURRENCY – Franc CFA of 100 centimes
NATIONAL ANTHEM – A ton appel, Mali (At your call, Mali)
NATIONAL DAY – 22 September
NATIONAL FLAG – Vertical stripes of green (by staff), yellow and red
LIFE EXPECTANCY (years) – male 55.24; female 58.66
POPULATION DENSITY – 9 per sq. km (1997)
URBAN POPULATION – 22.0 per cent (1987)
MILITARY EXPENDITURE – 2.0 per cent of GDP (1998)
MILITARY PERSONNEL – 12,150: Army 7,350, Paramilitaries 4,800
CONSCRIPTION DURATION – Two years (selective)
ILLITERACY RATE – 59.7 per cent
ENROLMENT (percentage of age group) – primary 31 per cent (1995); secondary 5 per cent (1990); tertiary 1 per cent (1997)

HISTORY AND POLITICS

Formerly the French colony of Soudan, the territory elected on 24 November 1958 to remain an autonomous republic within the French Community. It associated with Senegal in the Federation of Mali, which was granted full independence on 20 June 1960. The Federation was effectively dissolved in August 1960 by the secession of Senegal. The title of the Republic of Mali was adopted in September 1960.

A new constitution was approved by referendum in January 1992. The new constitution provided for a multiparty political system, and legislative elections were held in February and March 1992 with the Alliance for Democracy in Mali (ADEMA) emerging victorious. Alpha Konaré, the ADEMA leader, won the presidential elections in April 1992 and was re-elected in May 1997. In legislative elections in July and August 1997, ADEMA won 129 out of 147 seats in the National Assembly. On 14 February 2000, the government resigned and a new prime minister and government was formed the following day, comprising members of ADEMA and opposition parties.

HEAD OF STATE

President, Alpha Oumar Konaré, *elected* 1992, *re-elected* 11 May 1997

CABINET *as at September 2000*

Prime Minister, Mande Sidibé
Armed Forces and Veterans, Soumeylou Boubeye Maiga
Communications, Ascofaré Tamboura
Cottage Industry and Tourism, Zakyatou Oualett Halatine
Culture, Pascal Coulibaly
Economy and Finance, Bacari Koné

Education, Moustapha Dicko
Environment, Soumaila Cissé
Foreign Affairs, Malians Abroad, Maj. Modibo Sidibé
Health, Traore Fatoumata Nafo
Industry, Commerce, Transport, Toure Alimata Traoré
Justice and Keeper of the Seals, Abdoulaye Ogotembely
  Poudiougou
Labour and Professional Training, Makan Sissoko
Mines, Energy and Water Resources, Aboubacary
  Coulibaly
Rural Development, Ahamed El Madani Diallo
Security and Civil Protection, Gen. Tiecoura Doumbia
Social Development, Solidarity and the Elderly, Diakité
  Fatoumata N'Diayé
State Building and Housing, Bouare Fily Sissoko
Territorial Administration and Local Communities,
  Ousmane Sy
Women, Children and the Family, Diarra Afsata Thiero
Youth and Sports, Adama Koné

EMBASSY OF THE REPUBLIC OF MALI
Avenue Molière 487, B-1050 Brussels, Belgium
Tel: (00 32) (2) 345 7432
Ambassador Extraordinary and Plenipotentiary, vacant
Chargé d'Affaires, First Counsellor, Moussa Kouyate

BRITISH AMBASSADOR, HE David Snoxell, resident at
  Dakar, Senegal
BRITISH CONSULATE – Bamako

ECONOMY

Mali's principal exports are cotton and gold, Principal
imports include machinery and vehicles, petroleum, and
foodstuffs. Mali rejoined the CFA Franc Zone in 1984.
In 1997 Mali had a trade surplus of US$10 million and a
current account deficit of US$178 million. Imports
totalled US$689 million and exports US$560 million.
GNP – US$2,646 million (1998); US$250 per capita
  (1998)
GDP – US$2,618 million (1996); US$235 per capita
  (1996)
ANNUAL AVERAGE GROWTH OF GDP – 4.0 per cent (1996)
INFLATION RATE – 4.0 per cent (1998)
TOTAL EXTERNAL DEBT – US$3,202 million (1998)

Trade with UK	1998	1999
Imports from UK	£15,396,000	£15,965,000
Exports to UK	468,000	2,769,000

MALTA
Repubblika ta'Malta

AREA – 122 sq. miles (316 sq. km)
POPULATION – 378,518 (1998). The Maltese are mainly
  Roman Catholic. The Maltese language is of Semitic
  origin and held by some to be derived from the
  Carthaginian and Phoenician tongues. Maltese and
  English are the official languages
CAPITAL – ΨValletta (population, 7,100, 1998)
CURRENCY – Maltese lira (LM) of 100 cents or 1,000 mils
NATIONAL ANTHEM – L-Innu Malti
NATIONAL DAYS – 31 March (Freedom Day); 8 September
  (Our Lady of Victories); 7 June (Sette Giugno Riots);
  21 September (Independence Day); 13 December
  (Republic Day)
NATIONAL FLAG – Two equal vertical stripes, white at the
  hoist and red at the fly. A representation of the George
  Cross is carried edged with red in the canton of the white
  stripe
LIFE EXPECTANCY (years) – male 74.40; female 80.07
POPULATION GROWTH RATE – 0.9 per cent (1998)

POPULATION DENSITY – 1,198 per sq. km (1998)
MILITARY EXPENDITURE – 0.8 per cent of GDP (1998)
MILITARY PERSONNEL – Armed Forces 1,730

Malta lies in the Mediterranean Sea, 93 km (58 miles)
from Sicily and about 288 km (180 miles) from the
African coast. It is about 27 km (17 miles) in length and
14.5 km (9 miles) in breadth. Malta also includes the
islands of Gozo (area 67 sq. km (25.9 sq. miles)), Comino
and minor islets.

HISTORY AND POLITICS

Malta was in turn held by the Phoenicians, Carthaginians,
Romans and Arabs. In 1090 it was conquered by Count
Roger of Normandy and in 1530 handed over to the
Knights of St John. In 1565 it sustained the famous siege,
when the Turks were successfully withstood by Grand-
master La Valette. The Knights fortified the islands and
built Valletta before being expelled by Napoleon in 1798.
The Maltese rose against the French garrison soon
afterwards and the island was subsequently blockaded by
the British fleet. The Maltese people requested the
protection of the British Crown in 1802 on condition
that their rights would be respected. The islands were
finally annexed to the British Crown by the Treaty of
Paris in 1814.
Malta was again besieged during the Second World
War. From June 1940 to the end of the war, 432 members
of the garrison and 1,540 civilians were killed by enemy
aircraft. The island was awarded the George Cross for
gallantry on 15 April 1942.
On 21 September 1964 Malta became an independent
state within the Commonwealth, and on 13 December
1974 a republic within the Commonwealth.
Elections to the unicameral parliament of 65 members
are held every five years by a system of proportional
representation; to ensure that a party receiving more than
50 per cent of the votes cast obtains a parliamentary
majority, extra seats may be allocated to that party.
Elections held in September 1998 were won by the
Nationalist Party, who gained 35 seats; Eddie Fenech-
Adami, a strong supporter of Malta's accession to the
European Union, was appointed prime minister.

FOREIGN RELATIONS

Malta applied for EC membership in 1990, but in
October 1996 the Labour government announced its
intention to withdraw Malta's EU application and its
participation in NATO's Partnership for Peace programme. Following the election in 1998, the new
government immediately re-activated Malta's application for EU membership. Accession negotiations commenced in February 2000.

HEAD OF STATE

President, Guido de Marco, *took office* 4 April 1999

CABINET *as at September 2000*

Prime Minister, Dr Edward Fenech-Adami
Deputy P.M., Social Policy, Dr Lawrence Gonzi
Agriculture and Fisheries, Ninu Zammit
Economic Services, Prof. Josef Bonnici
Education, Dr Louis Galea
Environment, Dr Francis Zammit Dimech
Finance, John Dalli
Foreign Affairs, Dr Joe Borg
Gozo, Giovanna Debono
Health, Dr Louis Deguara
Home Affairs, Dr Tonio Borg
Justice and Local Government, Dr Austin Gatt
Tourism, Dr Michael Refalo
Transport and Communications, Censu Galea

MALTA HIGH COMMISSION

Malta House, 36–38 Piccadilly, London WIV 0PQ
Tel: 020-7292 4800
High Commissioner, HE George Bonello du Puis, apptd
1999

BRITISH HIGH COMMISSION

7 St Anne Street, Floriana (PO Box 506), Malta GC
Tel: (00 356) 233134/7
E-mail: bhc@dream.vol.net.mt
High Commissioner, HE Howard John Pearce, CVO, apptd
1999
BRITISH COUNCIL DIRECTOR A. Bradley, c/o British High
Commission; e-mail: britcoun@waldonet.net.mt

ECONOMY

Tourism has assumed primary importance, with
1,214,230 tourists visiting the island in 1999. In 1999 3
million passengers passed through Malta International
Airport.

Agriculture and fisheries are also important. Principal
products are potatoes, tomatoes, animal products, fruit,
and other vegetables.

In 1999 manufacturing employed 21.8 per cent of the
workforce and accounted for 22.8 per cent of GDP.
Industries include communications equipment, food
processing, textiles, footwear and clothing, plastics and
chemical products, electrical, machinery, medical equipment and furniture. Value Added Tax was re-introduced
in January 1999.

In 1999 there was a trade deficit of US$864 million
and a current account deficit of US$127 million. Imports
totalled US$2,844 million and exports US$1,980 million.
GNP – US$3,616 million (1999); US$9,335 per capita
(1999)
GDP – US$3,621 million (1999); US$9,350 per capita
(1999)
ANNUAL AVERAGE GROWTH OF GDP – 4.6 per cent
(1997)
INFLATION RATE – 2.1 per cent (1999)
UNEMPLOYMENT – 5.3 per cent (1999)
TOTAL EXTERNAL DEBT – US$1,034 million (1997)

TRADE

The principal imports are foodstuffs (mainly wheat, meats,
milk and fruit), fodder, beverages and tobacco, fuels,
chemicals, textiles and machinery (industrial, agricultural
and transport). The chief exports are processed food,
electronics, textiles, and other manufactures.

Trade with UK	1998	1999
Imports from UK	£192,469,000	£199,299,000
Exports to UK	85,974,000	126,184,000

EDUCATION

Education is compulsory between the ages of five and 16
and is free at all levels. Secondary education in state
schools is provided in secondary schools, junior lyceums
and trade schools. There are ten junior lyceums, 18
secondary schools and five centres catering for low
achievers.

A Junior College, administered by the University of
Malta, prepares students specifically for a university
course. Tertiary education is available at the University
of Malta. There are also schools administered by the
Catholic Church and other private schools.
ILLITERACY RATE – 11.24 per cent
ENROLMENT (percentage of age group) – primary
100 per cent (1999); secondary 100 per cent (1999);
tertiary 21 per cent (1999)

MARSHALL ISLANDS
Republic of the Marshall Islands

AREA – 70 sq. miles (181 sq. km)
POPULATION – 61,000 (1997 UN estimate): 99 per cent are
Micronesian. Over half the population is under 15.
About 60 per cent of the population is concentrated on
the two atolls of Majuro and Kwajalein. The population
is Christian, primarily Protestant but with a substantial
Catholic minority. Marshallese and English are the
official languages
CAPITAL – Dalap-Uliga-Darrit, on Majuro Atoll
(population, 20,000)
MAJOR TOWN – Ebeye (9,200)
CURRENCY – Currency is that of the USA
NATIONAL DAY – 1 May (Independence Day)
NATIONAL FLAG – Blue with a diagonal ray divided white
over orange running from the lower hoist to the upper
fly; in the canton a white sun
LIFE EXPECTANCY (years) – male 59.06; female 62.96
POPULATION GROWTH RATE – 3.9 per cent (1997)
POPULATION DENSITY – 336 per sq. km (1997)

The Republic of the Marshall Islands consists of 29 atolls
and five islands in the central Pacific. The islands and atolls
form two parallel chains running north-west to south-east:
the Ratak (Sunrise) chain and the Ralik (Sunset) chain. The
largest atoll is Kwajalein in the Ralik chain. The atolls are
coral and the islands are volcanic. None of the islands rises
more than a few metres above sea level. The climate is hot
and humid with little seasonal variation in temperature.

HISTORY AND POLITICS

The Marshall Islands were claimed by Spain in 1592 but
were left undisturbed by the Spanish Empire for 300 years.
In 1886 the Marshall Islands formally became a German
protectorate. On the outbreak of the First World War in
1914, Japan took control of the islands on behalf of the
Allied powers, and after the war administered the territory as a League of Nations mandate. During the
Second World War US armed forces seized the islands
from the Japanese after intense fighting. In 1947 the USA
entered into agreement with the UN Security Council
to administer the Micronesia area, of which the Marshall
Islands are a part, as the UN Trust Territory of the
Pacific Islands.

The islands became internally self-governing in 1979,
and the US Trusteeship administration came to an end on
21 October 1986, when a Compact of Free Association
between the USA and the Republic of the Marshall Islands
came into effect. By this agreement the USA recognised
the Republic of the Marshall Islands as a fully sovereign
and independent state. The UN Security Council
terminated the UN Trust Territory of the Pacific in
relation to the Marshall Islands and recognised its
independence in December 1990.

FOREIGN RELATIONS

The Republic of the Marshall Islands has no defence
forces. The Compact of Free Association places full
responsibility for defence of the Marshall Islands on the
USA. The US Department of Defense retains control of
islands within Kwajalein Atoll where it has a missile test
range.

POLITICAL SYSTEM

The republic is a democracy based on a parliamentary
system of government. The executive is headed by the
president, who is elected by the *Nitijela* from among
its members. The president serves for a four-year term.

The legislature has two chambers, the Council of Chiefs (*Iroij*) of 12 members and the Nitijela of 33 members. The Nitijela is the law-making chamber, to which the president and government are accountable. The Iroij has an advisory role.

There are 24 local government districts, each of which usually consists of an elected council, a mayor and appointed local officials.

In the general election which took place on 15 November 1999, the United Democratic Party won 18 seats.

HEAD OF STATE

President, Kessai Note, *elected* 4 January 2000

GOVERNMENT *as at September 2000*

The President
Education, Wilfred Kendall
Finance, Michael Konelios
Foreign Affairs, Trade, Alvin Jacklick
Health and Environment, Tadashi Lometo
Internal Affairs and Welfare, Nidel Lorak
Minister in Assistance to the President, Gerald Zackios
Public Works, Rien Morris
Resources and Development, John Silk
Transportation and Communications, Brenson Wase

BRITISH AMBASSADOR, HE Christopher Haslam, resident at Suva, Fiji

ECONOMY

The economy is a mixture of subsistence and a service-based sector. About half the working population is engaged in agriculture and fishing, with coconut oil and copra production comprising 90 per cent of total exports. Imports include oil, food and machinery. The service sector is based in Majuro and Ebeye and concentrated in banking and insurance, construction, transportation and tourism. Direct US aid under the Compact accounts for two-thirds of the islands' budget. The islands charge foreign fishing fleets licences for fishing tuna in the waters around the islands. Japanese fleets pay some US$3 million a year. The USA, Japan and Australia are the main trading partners.

GNP – US$96 million (1998); US$1,540 per capita (1998)
GDP – US$107 million (1996); US$1,872 per capita (1996)

Trade with UK	1998	1999
Imports from UK	£3,143,000	£2,606,000
Exports to UK	223,000	1,171,000

COMMUNICATIONS

Air Marshall Islands provides air services within the islands and to Hawaii. Continental Air Micronesia serves Majuro and Kwajalein with flights to Hawaii and Guam. Majuro also has shipping links to Hawaii, Australia, Japan and throughout the Pacific.

SOCIAL WELFARE

Majuro and Ebeye have hospitals run by the government with aid from the US Public Health Service. Each outer island community has a health assistant.

The state school system provides education up to age 18, but only 25 per cent of students proceed beyond elementary level because of inadequate resources.

MAURITANIA
Al-Jumhūriyya al-Islāmiyya al-Mawrītāniyya

AREA – 395,956 sq. miles (1,025,520 sq. km). Neighbours: Senegal (south-west), Mali (east and south), Algeria and Western Sahara (north)
POPULATION – 2,392,000 (1997 UN estimate). The official language is Arabic. Pulaar, Soninke, Wolof and French are also spoken
CAPITAL – Nouakchott (population, 850,000)
CURRENCY – Ouguiya (UM) of 5 khoums
NATIONAL DAY – 28 November
NATIONAL FLAG – Yellow star and crescent on green ground
LIFE EXPECTANCY (years) – male 49.90; female 53.10
POPULATION GROWTH RATE – 2.5 per cent (1997)
POPULATION DENSITY – 2 per sq. km (1997)
MILITARY EXPENDITURE – 2.2 per cent of GDP (1998)
MILITARY PERSONNEL – 15,650: Army 15,000, Navy 500, Air Force 150, Paramilitaries 5,000
CONSCRIPTION DURATION – Two years
ILLITERACY RATE – 60.1 per cent
ENROLMENT (percentage of age group) – primary 57 per cent (1995); tertiary 3.9 per cent (1995)

HISTORY AND POLITICS

Mauritania elected on 28 November 1958 to remain within the French Community as an autonomous republic. It became fully independent on 28 November 1960. In 1972 Mauritania left the Franc Zone.

Mauritania and Morocco occupied the Western Sahara territory in February 1976 when Spain formally relinquished it and in April 1976 agreed on a new frontier dividing the territory between them. In August 1979, Mauritania relinquished all claim to the southern sector of the Western Sahara after a three-year war against Polisario Front guerrillas.

After a military coup in 1978, Mauritania was ruled by a Military Committee for National Salvation. In April 1991 President ould Taya announced a political amnesty, followed by multiparty elections for a reconvened Senate and National Assembly. The constitution was approved by referendum in July 1991. Multiparty legislative elections were held in March 1992 and won by the Republican Democratic and Social Party (PRDS) led by President ould Taya.

Legislative elections in October 1996 were won by the PRDS after the opposition grouping, the Union of Democratic Forces (UDF) pulled out after the first round accusing the government of fraud. In presidential elections in December 1997, President ould Taya was re-elected following a boycott by opposition parties.

HEAD OF STATE

President, Col. Moaouia ould Sidi Mohammed Taya (PRDS), *took power* 12 December 1984, *elected* 17 January 1992, *re-elected* 12 December 1997

COUNCIL OF MINISTERS *as at September 2000*

Prime Minister, Cheik El-Avia ould Mohamed Khouna
Civil Service, Labour, Youth, Sports, Baba ould Sidi
Communications and Relations with Parliament, Rachid ould Saleh
Culture, Islamic Orientation, Salmou ould Sidi Moustaph
Defence, Kaba ould Elewa
Economic and Development Affairs, Mohamed ould Annai
Education, Sghair ould M'bareck
Equipment and Transport, N'gaide Lamine Gayou
Finance, Kamara Ali Gueladio
Fisheries and Marine Economy, Mohamed El-Moctar ould Zamel

Foreign Affairs and Co-operation, Ahmed ould Sid Ahmed
Health and Social Affairs, Dia Ba
Interior, Post and Telecommunications, Dah ould Abdeljalil
Justice, Mohamed Salem ould Marzouk
Mines and Industry, Ishagh ould Rajel
Rural Development and Environment, Col. Mohamed ould Sid'Ahmed Lekhal
Trade, Handicrafts and Tourism, Ahmed ould Hamadi
Water Power, Energy, Cheik Ahmed ould Ezzahaf

EMBASSY OF THE ISLAMIC REPUBLIC OF MAURITANIA

140 Bow Common Lane, London E3 4BH
Tel: 020-8980 4382
Ambassador Extraordinary and Plenipotentiary, Dr Diagana Youssouf, apptd 1999

BRITISH AMBASSADOR, HE Anthony M. Layden, resident at Rabat, Morocco

ECONOMY

The main source of potential wealth lies in rich deposits of iron ore around Zouérate, in the north of the country, and rich fishing grounds off the coast.

It was announced in February 2000 that Mauritania would qualify for debt relief of US$1,100 million under the IMF's Heavily Indebted Poor Countries initiative.

In 1995 Mauritania had a trade surplus of US$184 million and a current account surplus of US$22 million. In 1994 imports totalled US$403 million and exports US$487 million.

GNP – US$1,033 million (1998); US$410 per capita (1998)
GDP – US$1,010 million (1996); US$433 per capita (1996)
ANNUAL AVERAGE GROWTH OF GDP – 4.9 per cent (1996)
INFLATION RATE – 4.6 per cent (1997)
TOTAL EXTERNAL DEBT – US$2,589 million (1998)

Trade with UK	1998	1999
Imports from UK	£7,702,000	£4,964,000
Exports to UK	8,542,000	20,461,000

MAURITIUS
Republic of Mauritius

AREA – 788 sq. miles (2,040 sq. km)
POPULATION – 1,182,212 (1999 estimate): Asiatic races (Hindus 51.8 per cent, Muslims 16.5 per cent, Chinese 2.8 per cent), and persons of European (mainly French) extraction, mixed and African descent (28.6 per cent). English is the official language but French may be used in the National Assembly and lower law courts. Creole is the most commonly used language and several Asian languages are also used
CAPITAL – ΨPort Louis (population, 146,499, 1997 estimate)
MAJOR TOWNS – Beau Bassin-Rose Hill (99,562); Curepipe (78,892); Quatre Bornes (75,967); Vacoas-Phoenix (97,417), 1997 estimates
CURRENCY – Mauritius rupee of 100 cents
NATIONAL ANTHEM – Glory to thee, Motherland
NATIONAL DAY – 12 March
NATIONAL FLAG – Red, blue, yellow and green horizontal stripes
LIFE EXPECTANCY (years) – male 66.56; female 74.28
POPULATION GROWTH RATE – 1.2 per cent (1997)
POPULATION DENSITY – 579 per sq. km (1999)
URBAN POPULATION – 43.5 per cent (1996)
MILITARY EXPENDITURE – 2.1 per cent of GDP (1998)
MILITARY PERSONNEL – 1,500 Paramilitaries

Mauritius is an island group lying in the Indian Ocean, 550 miles east of Madagascar. The climate is sub-tropical and maritime, with a wide range of rainfall and temperature resulting from the mountainous nature of the island. Humidity is high throughout the year.

HISTORY AND POLITICS

Mauritius was discovered in 1511 by the Portuguese; the Dutch visited it in 1598 and named it Mauritius after Prince Maurice of Nassau. From 1638 to 1710 it was held as a Dutch colony; the French took possession in 1715 but did not settle it until 1721. Mauritius was taken by a British force in 1810 and became a Crown Colony. It became an independent state within the Commonwealth on 12 March 1968 and a republic on 12 March 1992.

The last general election was held on 20 December 1995. The present government was formed by the Parti des Travailleurs Mauricien – Mauritius Labour Party (PTM). A general election is due to be held by December 2000.

POLITICAL SYSTEM

The president is head of state and is elected by the National Assembly. The prime minister, appointed by the president, is the member of the National Assembly who appears to the president best able to command the support of the majority of members of the Assembly. Other ministers are appointed by the president acting on the advice of the prime minister.

The National Assembly has a five-year term and consists of 62 elected members (the island of Mauritius is divided into 20 three-member constituencies and Rodrigues returns two members), and eight specially-elected members. Of the latter, four seats go to the 'best loser' of whichever communities in the island are under-represented in the Assembly after the general election and the four remaining seats are allocated on the basis of both party and community.

HEAD OF STATE

President, Cassam Uteem, *elected* June 1992, *re-elected* 28 June 1997
Vice-President, Angidi Veeriah Chettiar

COUNCIL OF MINISTERS *as at September 2000*

Prime Minister, Defence and Home Affairs, External Communications and Outer Islands, Dr Navinchandra Ramgoolam
Deputy PM, Foreign Affairs and International Trade, Rajkeswur Purryag
Agriculture, Food Technology and Natural Resources, Arvind Boolell
Arts and Culture, Tsang Fan Hin Tsang Mang Kin
Attorney-General, Justice, Human Rights and Reform Institutions, Abdool Razack Mohamed Ameen Peeroo
Civil Service Affairs and Administrative Reform, Sachindev Mahess Kumar Soonarane
Economic Development, Productivity and Regional Development, Rundheersing Bheenick
Education and Scientific Research, Ramsamy Chedumbarum Pillay
Finance, Vasant Kumar Bunwaree
Fisheries and Co-operatives, Dhaneshwar Beeharry
Health and Quality of Life, Vacant
Housing and Lands, Satish Faugoo
Industry, Commerce, Corporate Affairs and Financial Services, Sathiamoorthy Sunassee
Labour and Industrial Relations, Human Resource Development and Employment, Mohummud Siddick Chady
Land Transport, Shipping and Port Development, Clarel Désiré Malherbe
Local Government, Outer Islands Development, SMEs and Handicrafts, Urban and Rural Development, Environment, James Burty David

Public Infrastructure, Devanand Virahsawmy
Public Utilities, Dr Ahmed Rashid Beebeejaun
Rodrigues Island, Joseph Bénoit Jolicoeur
Social Security and National Solidarity, vacant
Telecommunications and Information Technology, Sarat Dutt
Lallah
Tourism and Leisure, Marie Joseph Jacques Chasteau de
Balyon
Women, Family Welfare and Child Development, Indira
Savitree Thacoor-Sidaya
Youth and Sports, Marie Claude Arouff-Parfait

MAURITIUS HIGH COMMISSION
32–33 Elvaston Place, London SW7 5NW
Tel: 020-7581 0294/5
High Commissioner, HE Sir Satcam Boolell, QC, apptd
1996

BRITISH HIGH COMMISSION
Les Cascades Building, Edith Cavell Street, Port Louis
(PO Box 1063)
Tel: (00 230) 211 1361
E-mail: infobhc@bow.intnet.mu
High Commissioner, HE James Daly, CVO, apptd 1997

BRITISH COUNCIL DIRECTOR, S. Ponnappa,
Royal Road, PO Box 111, Rose Hill; e-mail:
bcouncil@bow.intnet.mu

ECONOMY

The major cash crop is sugar cane. Tea and tobacco are
grown commercially on a smaller scale. Production in
1999 was: sugar, 373,294 tonnes; tea (manufactured),
1,812 tonnes; tobacco (leaves), air cured 60,238 kg and
Virginia flue-cured 662,457 kg. In 1998 production of
molasses, mainly for export, was 168,891 tonnes. Other
products include alcohol, rum, denatured spirits, per-
fumed spirits and vinegar.

The bulk of the island's requirements in manufactured
products still has to be imported. However, the Mauritius
Export Processing Zone (MEPZ) Scheme has attracted
investment from overseas and the number of export-
orientated enterprises had risen from ten in 1971 to 486 in
1998. The biggest firms are in clothing manufacture,
particularly woollen knitwear, but the range of goods
produced includes toys, plastic products, leather goods,
diamond cutting and polishing, watches, television sets
and telephones.

Tourism is a major source of income, with an estimated
578,100 tourists in 1999. France is the most important
source of tourists, followed closely by the neighbouring
French island of Réunion.
GNP – US$4,329 million (1998); US$3,730 per capita
(1998)
GDP – US$4,291 million (1996); US$3,800 per capita
(1996)
ANNUAL AVERAGE GROWTH OF GDP – 5.4 per cent (1996)
INFLATION RATE – 6.8 per cent (1998)
TOTAL EXTERNAL DEBT – US$2,482 million (1998)

TRADE

Most foodstuffs and raw materials have to be imported
from abroad. Apart from local consumption (about 36,500
tonnes a year), the sugar produced is exported, mainly to
Britain.

In 1998 Mauritius had a trade deficit of US$280
million and a current account surplus of US$35
million. Imports totalled US$2,183 million and exports
US$1,734 million.

Trade with UK	1998	1999
Imports from UK	£68,527,000	£54,115,000
Exports to UK	329,201,000	307,638,000

COMMUNICATIONS

Port Louis, on the north-west coast, handles the bulk of
the island's external trade. A bulk sugar terminal capable
of handling the total crop began operating in 1980. The
international airport is located at Plaisance, about five
miles from Mahébourg. There are five daily newspapers
and 15 weeklies, mostly in French. The Mauritius Broadcasting Corporation operates television and radio broadcasting in the country.

EDUCATION

Primary and secondary education are free and primary
education is compulsory. There are a number of training
facilities offering vocational training. The Institute of
Education is responsible for training primary and
secondary school teachers and for curriculum development. The University of Mauritius had 3,718 students in
1998–9.
ILLITERACY RATE – 15.7 per cent
ENROLMENT (percentage of age group) – primary
98 per cent (1997); tertiary 6 per cent (1997)

RODRIGUES AND DEPENDENCIES

Rodrigues, formerly a dependency but now part of
Mauritius, is about 350 miles east of Mauritius, with an
area of 40 square miles. Population (1998) 35,332. Cattle,
salt fish, sheep, goats, pigs, maize and onions are the
principal exports. The island is administered by an Island
Secretary.
Island Secretary, B. Juggoo

The islands of Agalega and St Brandon are dependencies
of Mauritius. Total population (1996) 170.

MEXICO
Estados Unidos Mexicanos

AREA – 756,066 sq. miles (1,958,201 sq. km). Neighbours:
USA (north), Guatemala and Belize (south-east)
POPULATION – 97,361,711 (2000 census preliminary
results). Spanish is the official language and is spoken by
about 95 per cent of the population. There are five main
groups of Indian languages (Náhuatl, Maya, Zapotec,
Otomí, Mixtec) and 59 dialects derived from them
CAPITAL – Mexico City (population, 15,047,685, 1990)
MAJOR CITIES – Ciudad Juárez (797,679); Guadalajara
(2,846,000); León (956,070); Monterrey (2,521,697);
Puebla (1,454,526); Tijuana (742,686); Toluca
(827,339); Torreón (876,456), 1990 census
CURRENCY – Peso of 100 centavos
NATIONAL ANTHEM – Mexicanos, Al Grito De Guerra
(Mexicans, to the war cry)
NATIONAL DAY – 16 September (Proclamation of
Independence)
NATIONAL FLAG – Three vertical bands in green, white,
red, with the Mexican emblem (an eagle on a cactus
devouring a snake) in the centre
LIFE EXPECTANCY (years) – male 62.10; female 66.00
POPULATION GROWTH RATE – 2.2 per cent (1997)
POPULATION DENSITY – 49 per sq. km (1997)
URBAN POPULATION – 73.5 per cent
ILLITERACY RATE – 9.0 per cent
ENROLMENT (percentage of age group) – primary
100 per cent (1996); secondary 51 per cent (1995);
tertiary 16 per cent (1996)

The Sierra Nevada, known in Mexico as the Sierra Madre,
and Rocky Mountains continue south from the northern
border with the USA, running parallel to the west and east
coasts. The interior consists of an elevated plateau

between the two ranges. In the west is the peninsula of Lower California, separated from the mainland by the Gulf of California. The main rivers are the Rio Grande (Rio Bravo) del Norte, which forms part of the northern boundary and is navigable for about 70 miles from its mouth in the Gulf of Mexico, and the Rio Grande de Santiago, the Rio Balsas and Rio Papaloapan.

HISTORY AND POLITICS

Present-day Mexico and Guatemala were once the centre of a civilisation which flowered in the periods from AD 500 to 1100 and 1300 to 1500 and collapsed before the Spanish army in the years following 1519. Pre-Columbian Mexico was divided between different Indian cultures, most notably the Mayan, Teotihuacáno, Zapotec, Totonac and Toltec cultures. The last and most famous Indian culture, the Aztec, suffered more than the others at the hands of the Spanish and very few Aztec monuments remain.

After the conquest, the country was largely converted to Christianity and a distinctive colonial civilisation, representing a marriage of Indian and Spanish traditions, developed. In 1810 a revolt began against Spanish rule. This was finally successful in 1821, when a precarious independence was proclaimed.

Friction with the USA led to the war of 1845–8, at the end of which Mexico was forced to cede the northern provinces of Texas, California and New Mexico. In 1862 Mexican insolvency led to invasion by French forces which installed Archduke Maximilian of Austria as Emperor. The empire collapsed with the execution of the Emperor in 1867. In 1910 began the Mexican Revolution which reformed the social structure and the land system, curbed the power of foreign companies and ushered in the independent industrial Mexico of today.

There are 11 registered political parties; the Partido Revolucionario Institucional (PRI) which constituted the governing party for more than 60 years, until its defeat in July 2000, the Partido de Acción Nacional (PAN) and the Partido de la Revolución Democrática (PRD) are the largest.

In presidential and legislative elections on 2 July 2000, Vicente Fox, the PAN candidate, was elected as president and the PAN-led alliance gained 224 seats, the PRI 209 seats and the PRD 67 seats in the Chamber of Deputies.

INSURGENCIES

An armed revolt of Zapatista peasant Indians in the southern state of Chiapas in January 1994 highlighted continuing charges against the PRI of corruption, and these continued up to the August 1994 elections.

A further armed revolt by the Zapatista National Liberation Army (ZNLA) in Chiapas from December 1994 to February 1995 caused a political and economic crisis. Negotiations with the Zapatistas produced a preliminary agreement on indigenous rights in February 1996, but talks broke down and were suspended in September 1996. Further talks took place in November 1998.

New guerrilla groups, the People s Revolutionary Army (EPR) and the Popular Insurgency Revolutionary Army (ERIP), emerged in 1996. There were nationwide protests after the police and senior officials were implicated in the massacre of 45 Indians in Chiapas on 22 December 1997. There were renewed calls for the Army to withdraw from the province, and discussions over new peace talks resumed in February 1998. In May 2000, three people were sentenced to eight years' imprisonment for their part in the 1997 massacre.

POLITICAL SYSTEM

Congress consists of a Senate (*Cámara de Senadores*) of 128 members, elected for six years, and of a Chamber of Deputies (*Cámara de Diputados*), at present numbering 500, elected for three years. The chief executive of the government is the president, who is elected for a six-year term and may not be re-elected.

FEDERAL STRUCTURE

State	Area (sq. km)	Population (2000)	Capital
Federal District	1,499	8,591,309	Mexico City
Aguascalientes	5,589	943,506	Aguascalientes
Baja California	70,113	2,487,700	Mexicali
Baja California Sur	73,677	423,516	La Paz
Campeche	51,833	689,656	Campeche
Coahuila	151,571	2,295,808	Saltillo
Colima	5,455	540,679	Colima
Chiapas	73,887	3,920,515	Tuxtla Gutiérrez
Chihuahua	247,087	3,047,867	Chihuahua
Durango	119,648	1,445,922	Victoria de Durango
Guanajuato	30,589	4,656,761	Guanajuato
Guerrero	63,794	3,075,083	Chilpancingo
Hidalgo	20,987	2,231,392	Pachuca de Soto
Jalisco	80,137	6,321,278	Guadalajara
México	21,461	13,083,359	Toluca de Lerdo
Michoacán	59,864	3,979,177	Morelia
Morelos	4,941	1,552,878	Cuernavaca
Nayarit	27,621	919,739	Tepic
Nuevo León	64,555	3,826,240	Monterrey
Oaxaca	95,364	3,432,180	Oaxaca de Juárez
Puebla	33,919	5,070,346	Puebla de Zaragoza
Querétaro	11,769	1,402,010	Querétaro
Quintana Roo	50,350	873,804	Chetumal
San Luis Potosí	62,848	2,296,363	San Luis Potosí
Sinaloa	58,092	2,534,835	Culiacán Rosales
Sonora	184,934	2,213,370	Hermosillo
Tabasco	24,661	1,889,367	Villahermosa
Tamaulipas	79,829	2,747,114	Ciudad Victoria
Tlaxcala	3,914	961,912	Tlaxcala
Veracruz	72,815	6,901,111	Jalapa Enríquez
Yucatán	39,340	1,655,707	Mérida
Zacatecas	75,040	1,351,207	Zacatecas

HEAD OF STATE

President, Dr Ernesto Zedillo Ponce de León, *elected* August 1994, *took office* 1 December 1994 (until 1 December 2000); Vicente Fox, *elected* 2 July 2000, *takes office* 1 December 2000

CABINET *as at September 2000*

Agrarian Reform, Arturo Warman Gryj
Agriculture, Livestock and Rural Development, Romárico Arroyo Marroquín
Attorney-General, Jorge Madrazo Cuéllar
Communications and Transport, Carlos Ruiz Sacristan
Comptroller-General, Arsenio Farell Cubillas
Defence, Gen. Enrique Cervantes Aguirre
Education, Miguel Limón Rojas
Energy, Luis Téllez Kuenzler
Environment, Natural Resources and Fisheries, Julia Carabias Lillo
Finance and Public Credit, José Ángel Gurría Treviño
Foreign Affairs, Rosario Green Macias
Health, Juan Ramón de la Fuente Ramírez
Interior, Diódoro Carrasco
Labour and Social Welfare, Mariano Palacios Alcocer
Naval Affairs, Adm. José Ramón Lorenzo Franco
Social Development, vacant
Tourism, vacant
Trade and Industry, Herminio Blanco Mendoza

MEXICAN EMBASSY
42 Hertford Street, London W1Y 7TF
Tel: 020-7499 8586
Ambassador Extraordinary and Plenipotentiary, HE
Santiago Oñate, apptd 1997
Minister, Deputy Head of Mission, J. Brito-Moncada
Military Attaché, Col. E. L. Villegas-Meléndez
Consul-General, R. Xilótl-Ramírez

BRITISH EMBASSY
Calle Río Lerma 71, Colonia Cuauhtémoc,
06500 Mexico City
Tel: (00 52) (5) 207 2089
E-mail: infogen@mail.embajadabritanica.com.mx
Ambassador Extraordinary and Plenipotentiary, HE Adrian
Thorpe, KCMG, apptd 1999
*Deputy Head of Mission, Minister-Counsellor and Consul-
General*, Dr P. Tibber
Defence Attaché, Col. J. Watson
First Secretary (Commercial), A. Stephens

CONSULAR OFFICES – Mexico City, Acapulco, Cancun,
Ciudad Juárez, Guadalajara, Mérida, Monterrey,
Oaxaca, Tampico, Tijuana, Veracruz

BRITISH COUNCIL DIRECTOR, A. Curry, Lope de Vega
316, Col. Chapultepec Morales, 11570 Mexico DF;
e-mail: bc.mexico@mx.britcoun.org

BRITISH CHAMBER OF COMMERCE, British Trade Centre,
Rio de la Plata 30, Col. Cuauhtémoc, CP 06500, Mexico
City DF. *Manager*, Stephen Grant

DEFENCE

The Army has 862 armoured personnel carriers. The
Navy has three destroyers, six frigates, 105 patrol and
coastal vessels, and nine combat aircraft. There are 20
naval bases. The Air Force has 125 combat aircraft and
95 armed helicopters.
MILITARY EXPENDITURE – 1.0 per cent of GDP (1998)
MILITARY PERSONNEL – 178,770: Army 130,000, Navy
37,000, Air Force 11,770
CONSCRIPTION DURATION – 12 months (four hours per
week) by lottery

ECONOMY

The principal crops are maize, beans, sorghum, rice,
wheat, barley, sugar cane, coffee, cotton, tomatoes,
chillies, tobacco, chick-peas, groundnuts, cocoa and many
kinds of fruit. The maguey, or Mexican cactus, yields
several fermented drinks, mezcal and tequila (distilled) and
pulque (undistilled). Another species of the plant supplies
sisal-hemp (henequen). The forests contain mahogany,
rosewood, ebony and chicle trees. Agriculture employs an
estimated 20 per cent of the working population.

The principal industries are mining and petroleum,
although there has been considerable expansion of both
light and heavy industries; exports of manufactured goods
now average more than 85 per cent of total exports. The
steel industry expanded steadily until recently and current
production is around 5.8 million tons. More than one
million vehicles are exported annually, along with more
than two million automotive engines and six million
television sets.

The mineral wealth is great, and principal minerals are
gold, silver, copper, fluorspar, lead, zinc, quicksilver, iron
and sulphur. Substantial reserves of uranium have been
found.

Oil production was 164 million tonnes in 1998. Oil
reserves have increased substantially due to discoveries in
the Gulf of Campeche. A refinery at Tula is the nation's
largest; and new refineries in Monterrey, State of Nuevo
León, and Salina Cruz, State of Oaxaca, are under
construction.

In 2000, GDP was expected to grow by 5–6 per cent.
Mexico joined GATT in 1986 and the OECD in 1994.
GNP – US$368,059 million (1998); US$3,840 per capita
(1998)
GDP – US$329,475 million (1996); US$3,554 per capita
(1996)
ANNUAL AVERAGE GROWTH OF GDP – 7.0 per cent (1997)
INFLATION RATE – 15.9 per cent (1998)
UNEMPLOYMENT – 2.3 per cent (1998)
TOTAL EXTERNAL DEBT – US$159,959 million (1998)

TRADE

Major imports include computers, auto assembly material,
electrical parts, auto and truck parts, powdered milk, corn
and sorghum, transport, sound-recording and power-
generating equipment, chemicals, industrial machinery,
pharmaceuticals and specialised appliances. Principal
exports include oil, automobiles, auto engines, fruits and
vegetables, shrimps, coffee, computers, cattle, glass, iron
and steel pipes, and copper. The main trading partners are
the USA, EU, Latin America and Japan. The North
American Free Trade Agreement, to which Mexico is a
signatory, came into effect on 1 January 1994; trade
between Mexico, Canada and the USA rose by 17 per cent
per year. Mexico has free trade deals with the EU, Bolivia,
Chile, Colombia, Costa Rica, Nicaragua and Venezuela,
and negotiations are under way to create free trade
agreements with other South American countries.

In 1998 Mexico had a trade deficit of US$7,743 million
and a current account deficit of US$15,786 million.
Imports totalled US$130,811 million and exports
US$117,500 million.

Trade with UK	1998	1999
Imports from UK	£536,775,000	£585,016,000
Exports to UK	337,688,000	410,180,000

COMMUNICATIONS

Veracruz, Tampico and Coatzacoalcos are the chief ports
on the Atlantic, and Guaymas, Mazatlán, Puerto Lázaro
Cárdenas and Salina Cruz on the Pacific. Work is
proceeding on the reorganisation and re-equipment of
the whole rail system. There were 307,142 km of roads in
1994; total track length of the railways was 20,445 km.
Mexico City may be reached by at least three highways
from the USA, and from the south from Yucatán as well
as on two principal highways from the Guatemalan
border.

There are 50 international airports and 33 national
airports in Mexico. There are many airline companies,
including two major, now private, national airlines,
Mexicana de Aviación and Aeroméxico.

Teléfonos de México, now privatised, controls about
98 per cent of all telephone services.

FEDERATED STATES OF MICRONESIA

AREA – 271 sq. miles (702 sq. km)
POPULATION – 130,000 (1997 UN estimate). Pohnpei:
population, 31,000; capital, Kolonia; Chuuk (Truk):
population, 52,000; capital, Moen; Yap: population,
12,000; capital, Colonia; Kosrae: population, 6,500;
capital, Lelu. The population is Micronesian and
predominantly Christian. English (official) and eight
other languages are used in different parts of the
Federated States: Yapese, Ulithian, Woleaian,
Ponapean, Nukuoran, Kapingamarangi, Trukese and
Kosraen
FEDERAL CAPITAL – Palikir, on Pohnpei
CURRENCY – Currency is that of the USA

NATIONAL FLAG – United Nations blue with four white stars in the centre
POPULATION GROWTH RATE – 3.7 per cent (1997)
POPULATION DENSITY – 185 per sq. km (1997)

The Federated States of Micronesia comprise more than 600 islands extending 2,900 km (1,800 miles) across the archipelago of the Caroline Islands in the western Pacific Ocean. The islands vary geologically from mountainous islands to low coral atolls. The climate is tropical. Storms are common between August and December, and typhoons between July and November.

HISTORY AND POLITICS

The Spanish Empire claimed sovereignty over the Caroline Islands until 1899, when Spain withdrew from her Pacific territories and sold her possessions in the Caroline Islands to Germany. The Caroline Islands became a German protectorate until the outbreak of the First World War in 1914, when Japan took control of the islands on behalf of the Allied powers. After the war, Japan continued to administer the territory under a League of Nations mandate. During the Second World War, US armed forces took control of the islands from the Japanese. In 1947 the USA entered into agreement with the UN Security Council to administer the Micronesia area, of which the Federated States of Micronesia were a part, as the UN Trust Territory of the Pacific Islands.

The US Trusteeship administration came to an end on 3 November 1986, when a Compact of Free Association between the USA and the Federated States of Micronesia came into effect. By this agreement the USA recognised the Federated States of Micronesia as a fully sovereign and independent state. The independence of the Federated States of Micronesia was recognised by the UN in December 1990.

POLITICAL SYSTEM

The constitution separates the executive, legislative and judicial branches. There is a bill of rights and provision for traditional rights. The executive comprises a federal president and vice-president, both of whom must be chosen from amongst the four nationally-elected senators. There is a single-chamber Congress of 14 members, four members elected on a nation-wide basis and ten members elected from congressional districts apportioned by population.

The Compact of Free Association places full responsibility for the defence of the Federated States of Micronesia on the USA.

The judiciary is headed by the Supreme Court, which is divided into trial and appellate divisions. Below this, each state has its own judicial system.

FEDERAL STRUCTURE

The Federated States of Micronesia is a federal republic of four constituent states: Chuuk, Kosrae, Pohnpei and Yap. Each of the constituent states has its own government and legislative system.

State	Area (sq. km)	Population (1994)	Headquarters
Chuuk	127	52,870	Weno
Kosrae	109	7,354	Tofol
Pohnpei	344	33,372	Kolonia
Yap	119	11,128	Colonia

HEAD OF STATE

President, Leo Falcam
Vice-President, Redley Killian

CABINET *as at September 2000*
Economic Affairs, Sebastiau Braghis
Finance and Administration, John Ehsa

Foreign Affairs, Epel Ilion
Health, Education and Social Services, Eliuel Pretrick
Justice, Emilio Musrasrik
Public Defender, Joseph Philip
Transportation, Communications and Infrastructure, Lukner Weilbacher

BRITISH AMBASSADOR, HE Christopher Haslam, resident at Suva, Fiji

ECONOMY

The economy is dependent mainly on subsistence agriculture and foreign aid. Copra and fish are the two main exports. The majority of the working population is engaged in government administration, subsistence farming, fishing, copra production and the tourist industry. In 1994, there were 25,000 visitors.

GNP – US$204 million (1998); US$1,800 per capita (1998)
GDP – US$291 million (1996); US$2,311 per capita (1996)

Trade with UK	1998	1999
Imports from UK	£18,000	£102,000
Exports to UK	—	179,000

MOLDOVA
Republica Moldova

AREA – 13,012 sq. miles (33,851 sq. km). Neighbours: Ukraine (north, east and south-east), Romania (west)
POPULATION – 4,335,000 (2000 official estimate): 65 per cent are Moldovan, 14.2 per cent Ukrainian and 13 per cent Russian, together with smaller numbers of Gagauz (ethnic Turks), Jews and Bulgarians. Most of the population are adherents of the Moldovan Orthodox Church. Moldovan was made the official language (written in the Latin script) in 1989 but the use of Russian in official business is permitted
CAPITAL – Chişinău (population, 655,940)
CURRENCY – Leu (plural lei)
NATIONAL ANTHEM – Limbă noastră (Our language)
NATIONAL DAY – 27 August (Independence Day)
NATIONAL FLAG – Vertical stripes of blue, yellow, red, with the national arms in the centre
LIFE EXPECTANCY (years) – male 62.29; female 69.79
POPULATION GROWTH RATE – 0.2 per cent (1997)
POPULATION DENSITY – 127 per sq. km (1997)
URBAN POPULATION – 46.7 per cent (1995)
MILITARY EXPENDITURE – 4.3 per cent of GDP (1998)
MILITARY PERSONNEL – 10,650: Army 9,600, Air Force 1,050; Paramilitaries 3,400
CONSCRIPTION DURATION – Up to 18 months
ILLITERACY RATE – 1.1 per cent
ENROLMENT (percentage of age group) – tertiary 26.1 per cent (1996)

HISTORY AND POLITICS

In the 15th century a Moldovan principality was formed which entered into military and political alliances with Muscovy before being absorbed into the Turkish Empire in the 16th century. Moldova became the site of many Russo-Turkish battles and skirmishes in the 18th century before the area between the Dniester and Prut rivers (later known as Bessarabia) was annexed to the Russian Empire by the Bucharest Peace Treaty of 1812.

After the Russian Revolution in 1917, an independent Moldovan state was proclaimed in Bessarabia, which came under the control of White Russian forces and was annexed to Romania under the Versailles Peace Treaty

(1919). In 1924 the Moldavian Autonomous Soviet Socialist Republic (ASSR) was established on the east bank of the Dniester river as part of Soviet Ukraine. In August 1940 the Soviet Union forced Romania to cede Bessarabia and the Moldavian Soviet Socialist Republic was formed from the majority of Bessarabia (the southernmost parts were incorporated into the Ukraine) and the Moldavian ASSR.

Moldova (formerly Moldavia) declared its independence from the USSR in August 1991. Reunification with Romania was rejected in a referendum on 6 March 1994, following which the Moldovan parliament voted to join the CIS. In July 1994 the Moldovan parliament adopted a new constitution which defines Moldova as a 'presidential parliamentary republic' based on political pluralism. It also provides for autonomous status for the Gagauz and Transdniester regions, with the Gagauz region having its own elected National Assembly.

Parliament now has 101 seats and is elected by proportional representation for a four-year term. President Petru Lucinschi replaced president Mircea Snegur in presidential elections in November–December 1996. In legislative elections in March 1998, no party won an overall majority, and a right-wing coalition government under Ion Ciubuc was formed. Ciubuc resigned on 1 February 1999 and a new government led by Ion Sturza was sworn in on 12 March. On 9 November 1999, Sturza's government lost a vote of confidence and, after six weeks of political turmoil, Parliament approved Dumitri Barghis as prime minister on 21 December 1999.

A referendum in May 1999 on the introduction of a presidential system of government was declared invalid because less than the required 60 per cent of the electorate voted.

INSURGENCIES

After independence was declared, the majority ethnic Romanian (Moldovan) population expressed a wish to rejoin Romania. This alienated the ethnic Ukrainian and Russian populations, who formed a majority east of the Dniester, and they declared their independence from Moldova as the Transdniester republic in December 1991. The Moldovan government refused to recognise this and in 1992 a war was waged between government forces and Transdniester forces, who were supported by the former Soviet 14th Army stationed in Transdniester and by Cossack volunteers from Russia.

A mainly Russian CIS peacekeeping force (later changed to a joint Russian-Moldovan-Transdniester force) was deployed in July 1992 and a cease-fire has held since August 1992. Although no political solution has been finalised and a state of armed truce remains, the Moldovan government in February 1994 agreed to an OSCE plan for the Transdniester area to have a high degree of autonomy within Moldova but no independent or federal status. A memorandum of understanding on the normalisation of relations between the two sides was signed in May 1997, which committed both parties to hold further talks within 'the framework of a single state'.

A referendum in Transdniester on 24 December 1995 approved independence. President Igor Smirnov was re-elected in presidential elections in Transdniester in December 1996.

In June 2000, the Russian president announced the creation of a commission which would look at settling the Transdniester dispute. Russian troops are to be withdrawn from Transdniester in 2002.

HEAD OF STATE

President, Petru Lucinschi, *elected* 1 December 1996

GOVERNMENT *as at September 2000*

Prime Minister, Dumitru Braghis
First Deputy PM, Economy and Reform, Andrei Cucu

Deputy PMs, Lidia Gutu (*Social Affairs*); Valeriu Cosarciuc (*Without portfolio*)
Agriculture and Processing Industry, Ion Russu
Cabinet, Mihai Petrache
Culture, Ghenadie Ciobanu
Defence, Brig. Gen. Boris Gamurari
Education and Science, Ion Gutu
Environmental Protection and Territorial Development, vacant
Finance, Mihai Manoli
Foreign Affairs, Nicolae Tabacaru
Health, Vasile Parasca
Industry and Energy, Ion Lesanu
Interior, Vladimir Turcanu
Justice, Valeria Sterbet
Labour, Social Protection and Family Affairs, Valerian Revenco
Minister of State, Vladiamir Filat
Territorial Development, Construction and Communal Services, Mihai Severovan
Transport and Communications, Afanasie Smochin

EMBASSY OF THE REPUBLIC OF MOLDOVA
175 Avenue Emile Max, B-10340 Brussels, Belgium
Tel: (00 32) (2) 732 9659
Ambassador Extraordinary and Plenipotentiary, HE Ion Capatina

BRITISH AMBASSADOR, HE R. Ralph, CVO, CMG, resident at Bucharest, Romania

ECONOMY

The main sector is agriculture, especially viniculture, fruit-growing and market gardening. Industry is small and concentrated east of the Dniester. Severe drought in 1992, the severance of most trading ties with former Soviet republics, war damage and reductions in Russian fuel deliveries paralysed the economy from 1992 to 1994. An economic reform programme aiming to attract foreign investment began in summer 1993; a privatisation programme, completed in November 1995, sold off 1,132 large enterprises. In 1998, telecommunications, power and heating companies were privatised. Moldova is dependent on Russia for energy supplies and owes roughly US$6,000 million. In September 1997 the World Bank approved a US$100 million loan to aid structural reform of the economy.

In 1998 there was a trade deficit of US$399 million and a current account deficit of US$334 million. In 1996 imports totalled US$1,079 million and exports US$805 million.

GNP – US$1,652 million (1998); US$380 per capita (1998)
GDP – US$1,995 million (1996); US$440 per capita (1996)
ANNUAL AVERAGE GROWTH OF GDP – 7.9 per cent (1996)
UNEMPLOYMENT – 1.0 per cent (1995)
TOTAL EXTERNAL DEBT – US$1,035 million (1998)

Trade with UK	1998	1999
Imports from UK	£5,644,000	£5,926,000
Exports to UK	1,241,000	3,367,000

MONACO
Principauté de Monaco

AREA – 0.4 sq. miles (1 sq. km). Neighbour: France
POPULATION – 33,268 (1997 UN estimate). Only 6,944 residents have full Monégasque citizenship and thus the right to vote. The official language is French. Monégasque, a mixture of Provençal and Ligurian, is also spoken
CAPITAL – Monaco
CURRENCY – Euro (€) of 100 cents/French franc of 100

centimes
NATIONAL ANTHEM – Hymne Monégasque
NATIONAL DAY – 19 November
NATIONAL FLAG – Two equal horizontal stripes,
   red over white
POPULATION GROWTH RATE – 0.9 per cent (1997)
POPULATION DENSITY – 21,477 per sq. km (1997)

A small principality on the Mediterranean, with land
frontiers joining France at every point, Monaco is divided
into the districts of Monaco-Ville, La Condamine,
Fontvieille and Monte Carlo.

HISTORY AND POLITICS

The principality, ruled by the Grimaldi family since 1297,
was abolished during the French Revolution and re-
established in 1815 under the protection of the kingdom of
Sardinia. In 1861 Monaco came under French protection.
   The 1962 constitution, which can be modified only with
the approval of the National Council, maintains the
traditional hereditary monarchy and guarantees freedom
of association, trade union freedom and the right to strike.
Legislative power is held jointly by the Prince and a
unicameral, 18-member National Council elected by
universal suffrage. In the most recent legislative election
on 1 and 8 February 1998, all 18 seats were won by the
National and Democratic Union. Executive power is
exercised by the Prince and a four-member Council of
Government, headed by a Minister of State, who is
nominated by the Prince from a list of three French
diplomats submitted by the French government. The
judicial code is based on that of France.

HEAD OF STATE

HSH The Prince of Monaco, Prince Rainier III Louis-Henri-
Maxence Bertrand, *born* 31 May 1923, *succeeded* 9 May
1949; *married* 19 April 1956, Miss Grace Patricia Kelly
(died 14 September 1982) and *has issue* Prince Albert (*see*
below); Princess Caroline Louise Marguerite, *born* 23
January 1957; and Princess Stephanie Marie Elisabeth,
born 1 February 1965
Heir, HRH Prince Albert Alexandre Louis Pierre, *born* 14
March 1958

President of the Crown Council, Charles Ballerio
President of the National Council, Dr Jean-Louis Campora
Minister of State, Patrick Leclercq
Finance and Economy, Henri Fissore
Interior, Philippe Deslandes
Public Works and Social Affairs, Michel Sosso

CONSULATE-GENERAL OF MONACO
4 Cromwell Place, London SW7 2JE
Tel: 020-7225 2679
Consul-General, I. B. Ivanovic

BRITISH CONSULATE-GENERAL
33 Boulevard Princesse Charlotte, BP 265, MC-98005
   Monaco CEDEX
Tel: (00 377) 93 50 99 66
Consul-General, I. Davies, apptd 1997, resident at
Marseilles, France
Honorary Consul, E. Blair

ECONOMY

The whole available ground is built over so that there is no
cultivation, though there are some notable public and
private gardens. The economy is based on real estate
revenues, the financial sector and tourism. Monaco has a
small harbour (30 ft alongside quay) and the import duties
are the same as in France.
GDP – US$844 million (1996); US$26,374 per capita
(1996)

MONGOLIA
Mongol Uls

AREA – 604,829 sq. miles (1,566,500 sq. km). Neighbours:
   Russia (north), China (south)
POPULATION – 2,313,000 (1997 UN estimate). Mongo-
   lians also live in China and in the neighbouring regions
   of Russia, especially the Mongolian Buryat Autonomous
   Region. The official language is Khalkha Mongolian
CAPITAL – Ulaanbaatar (population, 515,100, 1987
   estimate)
CURRENCY – Tugrik of 100 möngö
NATIONAL DAY – 11 July
NATIONAL FLAG – Vertical tricolour red, blue, red and in
   the hoist the traditional Soyombo symbol in gold
LIFE EXPECTANCY (years) – male 62.28; female 65.01
POPULATION GROWTH RATE – 0.6 per cent (1997)
POPULATION DENSITY – 1 per sq. km (1997)
URBAN POPULATION – 57.1 per cent (1989)
MILITARY EXPENDITURE – 2.1 per cent of GDP (1998)
MILITARY PERSONNEL – 9,100: Army 7,500, Air Defence
   800, Paramilitaries 7,200
CONSCRIPTION DURATION – 12 months
ILLITERACY RATE – 0.7 per cent
ENROLMENT (percentage of age group) – primary
   81 per cent (1996); secondary 53 per cent (1996);
   tertiary 17.0 per cent (1996)

Mongolia, which is almost entirely at least 1,000 metres
above sea level, forms part of the central Asiatic plateau
and rises towards the west in the mountains of the
Mongolian Altai and Hangai ranges. The Hentai range,
situated to the north-east of the capital Ulaanbaatar, is
lower. The Gobi region covers much of the southern half
of the country and contains sand deserts interspersed with
semi-desert. There are several long rivers and many lakes
but good water is scarce as much of the lake water is salty.
The climate is harsh, with a short mild summer giving way
to a long winter when temperatures can drop as low as
−50°C.

HISTORY AND POLITICS

Mongolia, under Genghis Khan the conqueror of China
and much of Asia, was for many years a buffer state
between Tsarist Russia and China, although it was under
general Chinese suzerainty. The Chinese Revolution in
1911 led to a declaration of autonomy under Chinese
suzerainty which was confirmed by the Sino-Russian
Treaty of Kiakhta (1915) but cancelled by a unilateral
Chinese declaration in 1919. Later the country became a
battleground of the Russian civil war, and Soviet and
Mongolian troops occupied Ulaanbaatar in 1921; this was
followed by another declaration of independence. In 1924
the Soviet Union in a treaty with China again recognised
the latter's sovereignty over Mongolia, but this was never
properly exercised because of China's preoccupation with
internal affairs and later with the war with Japan. The
Mongolian People's Republic was formally established
in 1924. Under the Yalta Agreement, President Chiang
Kai-shek of China agreed to a plebiscite, held in 1945, in
which the Mongolians declared their desire for independence and this was formally recognised by China.
   The Mongolian People's Revolutionary Party (MPRP)
was the sole political party from 1924 to 1990. Demonstrations in favour of political and economic reform began
in December 1989 and led to changes in the MPRP
leadership in March 1990. The MPRP's constitutionally
guaranteed monopoly of power was subsequently relinquished, and the introduction of a multiparty system was
approved by the Great People's Hural (parliament). The
MPRP won the first multiparty elections, held in July 1990.

The country's first direct presidential election was held in 1993 and won by the incumbent Punsalmaagiyn Ochirbat, who stood as an opposition candidate after the MPRP refused to endorse him as its candidate; he was ousted in May 1997 by the leader of the MPRP, Natsagyn Bagabandi. The June 1996 election was won by the Democratic Union Coalition (Mongolian National Democratic Party and Mongolian Social Democratic Party). The legislative election held on 2 July 2000 resulted in a victory for the MRRP, who gained 72 seats.

The country and three city districts (Ulanbaatar, Darkhan and Erdenet) are divided into 21 *aimaks* (provinces) and beneath these into 258 *somons* (districts), and these form the basis of the state organizisation of the country. The last remaining former Soviet armed forces personnel were withdrawn in late 1992.

POLITICAL SYSTEM

A new constitution was approved in January 1992 which enshrines the concepts of democracy, a mixed economy, free speech and neutrality in foreign affairs. The Great and Little Hurals were abolished, and a new unicameral Great Hural (*Ulsyn Ikh Khural*) became the legislative body of the country. There are 76 members of the Great Hural, elected for four-year terms by a simple majority amounting to at least 25 per cent of the votes cast.

HEAD OF STATE

President, Natsagyn Bagabandi, *elected* 18 May 1997

CABINET *as at September 2000*
Prime Minister, Nambariin Enkhbayar
Cabinet Secretary Chief, (without portfolio),
    O. Enkhtuvshin
Defence, J. Gurragchaa
Education, Culture and Science, A. Tsanjid
Finance and Economy, Ch. Ulaan
Food and Agriculture, D. Nasanjargal
Foreign Affairs, L. Erdenechuluun
Industry and Commerce, Ch. Ganzorig
Infrastructure Development, B. Jigjid
Justice and Internal Affairs, Ts. Nyamdorj
Nature and the Environment, U. Barsbold
Social Welfare and Labour, Sh. Batbayar

EMBASSY OF MONGOLIA
7 Kensington Court, London W8 5DL
Tel: 020-7937 0150
Ambassador Extraordinary and Plenipotentiary, HE
    Tsedenjavyn Suhbaatar, apptd 1997

BRITISH EMBASSY
30 Enkh Taivny Gudamzh (PO Box 703), Ulaanbaatar 13
Tel: (00 976) (1) 458133
e-mail:britemb@magicnet.mn
Ambassador Extraordinary and Plenipotentiary, HE Kay
    Coombs, apptd 1999

ECONOMY

Traditionally the Mongolians led a nomadic life tending flocks of sheep, goats, horses, cows and camels. With the coming of the Communist regime, and especially after 1952, great efforts were made to settle the population but a proportion still live nomadically or semi-nomadically in the traditional *ger* (circular tent). Collectivisation at the end of the 1950s into huge *negdels* (co-operatives) and state farms hastened the process of settlement, but within these the herdsmen and their families still move with their *gers* from pasture to pasture as the seasons change.

The semi-desert areas of the Gobi region provide pasture for sheep, goats, camels, horses and some cattle. In the steppe areas to the north of the Gobi pasturage is better

and livestock more abundant. Even further north, in the better-watered provinces, grain, fodder and vegetable crops are grown.

Although the economy remains predominantly pastoral, factories have started up, coal, copper and molybdenum are mined and the electricity industry has been developed. Ulaanbaatar and Darkhan are the main seats of industry, which includes lime, cement and building materials, a flour mill and a power station. Choibalsan is also being developed industrially.

Communication is still difficult as there are only 1,185 km of surfaced roads and horses are still the characteristic means of transport for the rural population. The trans-Mongolian railway links Mongolia with both China and Russia; total track length is 1,928 km. All trade barriers were abolished in May 1997. In October 1997, the Mongolian Assistance Group pledged US$250 million in aid for 1998.

A prolonged drought and an exceptionally severe winter in 1999–2000 resulted in the deaths of an estimated two million livestock, affecting 800,000 herders.
GNP – US$995 million (1998); US$380 per capita (1998)
GDP – US$972 million (1996); US$386 per capita (1996)
ANNUAL AVERAGE GROWTH OF GDP – 2.6 per cent (1996)
INFLATION RATE – 9.5 per cent (1998)
UNEMPLOYMENT – 5.7 per cent (1998)
TOTAL EXTERNAL DEBT – US$739 million (1998)

TRADE

Foreign trade was formerly dominated by the Soviet Union and other Eastern bloc countries. Following the collapse of the COMECON trading system, trade with Western countries, Japan and South Korea is increasing. Since January 1991, trade has been in hard currency, causing particular strain. The principal exports are animal by-products (especially wool, hides and furs) and cattle.

In 1998 there was a trade deficit of US$62 million and a current account deficit of US$77 million. In 1997 imports totalled US$443 million and exports US$418 million.

Trade with UK	1998	1999
Imports from UK	£2,594,000	£3,078,000
Exports to UK	4,938,000	4,724,000

MOROCCO
Al-Mamlaka Al-Maghribiyya

AREA – 172,414 sq. miles (446,550 sq. km).
    Neighbours: Algeria (east and south-east),
    Western Sahara (south-west)
POPULATION – 27,310,000 (1997 UN estimate). Arabic is the official language. Berber is the vernacular, mainly in the mountain regions. French and Spanish are also spoken, mainly in the towns. Islam is the state religion.
CAPITAL – ΨRabat (population, 1,220,000, 1993 estimate)
MAJOR CITIES – ΨAgadir (923,000); ΨCasablanca (Ad-Dar-el-Beida) (3,100,000); Fez (554,000); Marrakesh (878,000); Meknès (614,000); Oujda (430,000), 1997 estimates
CURRENCY – Dirham (DH) of 100 centimes
NATIONAL DAY – 3 March (Anniversary of the Throne)
NATIONAL FLAG – Red, with green pentagram (the Seal of Solomon)
LIFE EXPECTANCY (years) – male 62.84; female 66.20
POPULATION GROWTH RATE – 1.6 per cent (1997)
POPULATION DENSITY – 61 per sq. km (1997)
URBAN POPULATION – 50.3 per cent (1996)

Morocco is traversed in the north by the Rif mountains and, in a south-west to north-east direction, by the Middle Atlas, the High Atlas, the Anti-Atlas and the Sarrho ranges. Much of the country is desert. The north-westerly

World Physical

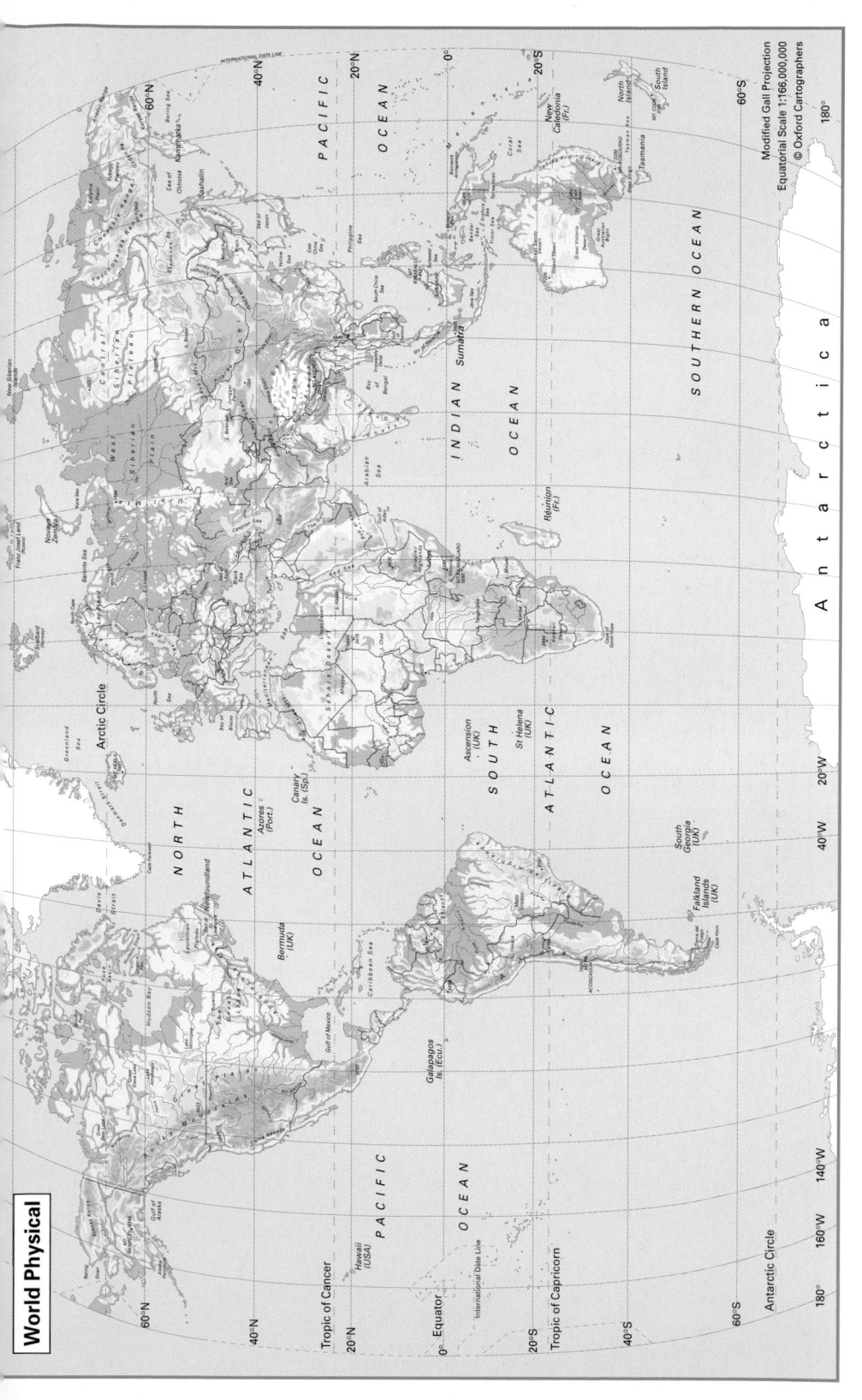

Modified Gall Projection
Equatorial Scale 1:166,000,000
© Oxford Cartographers

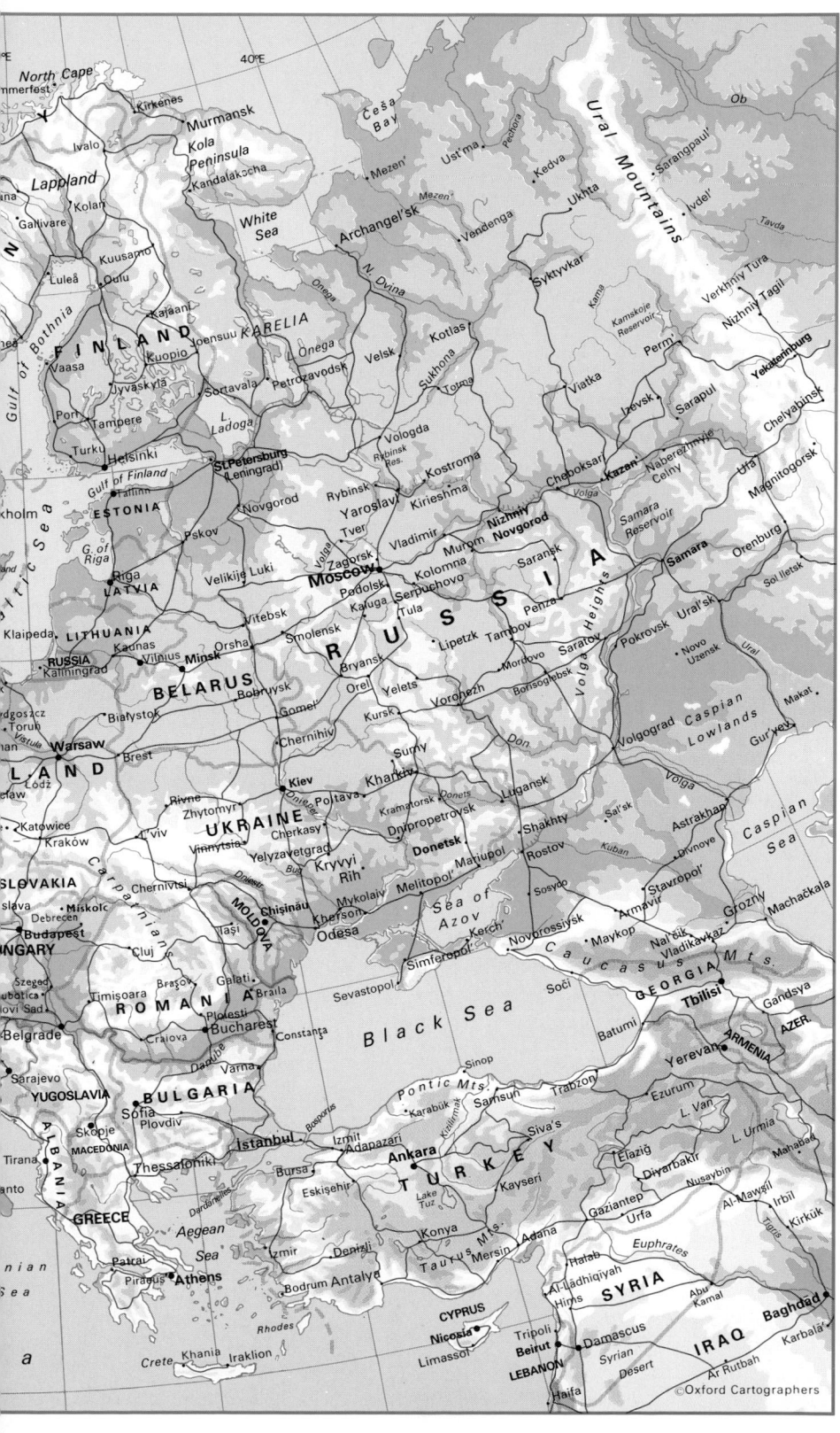
©Oxford Cartographers

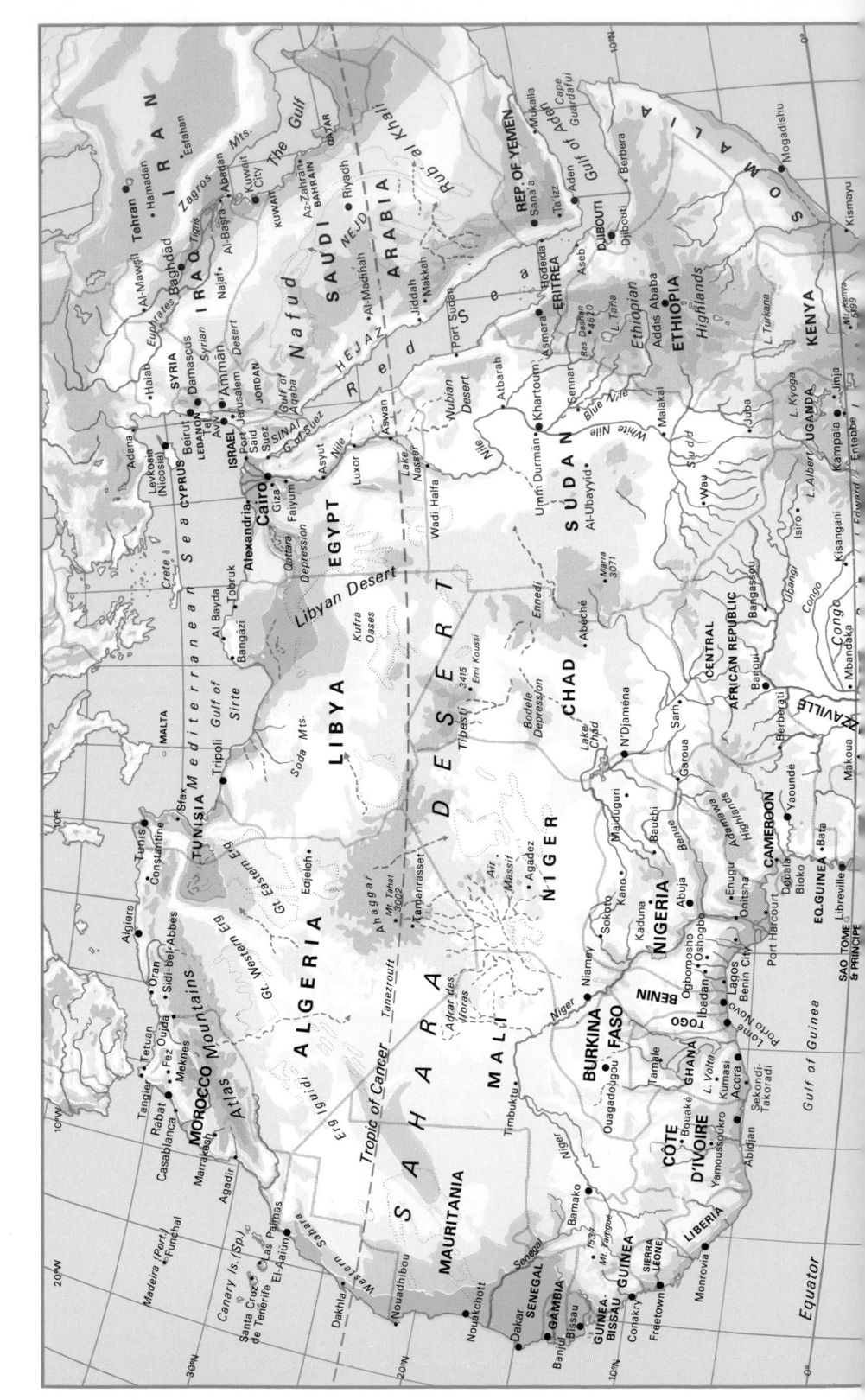

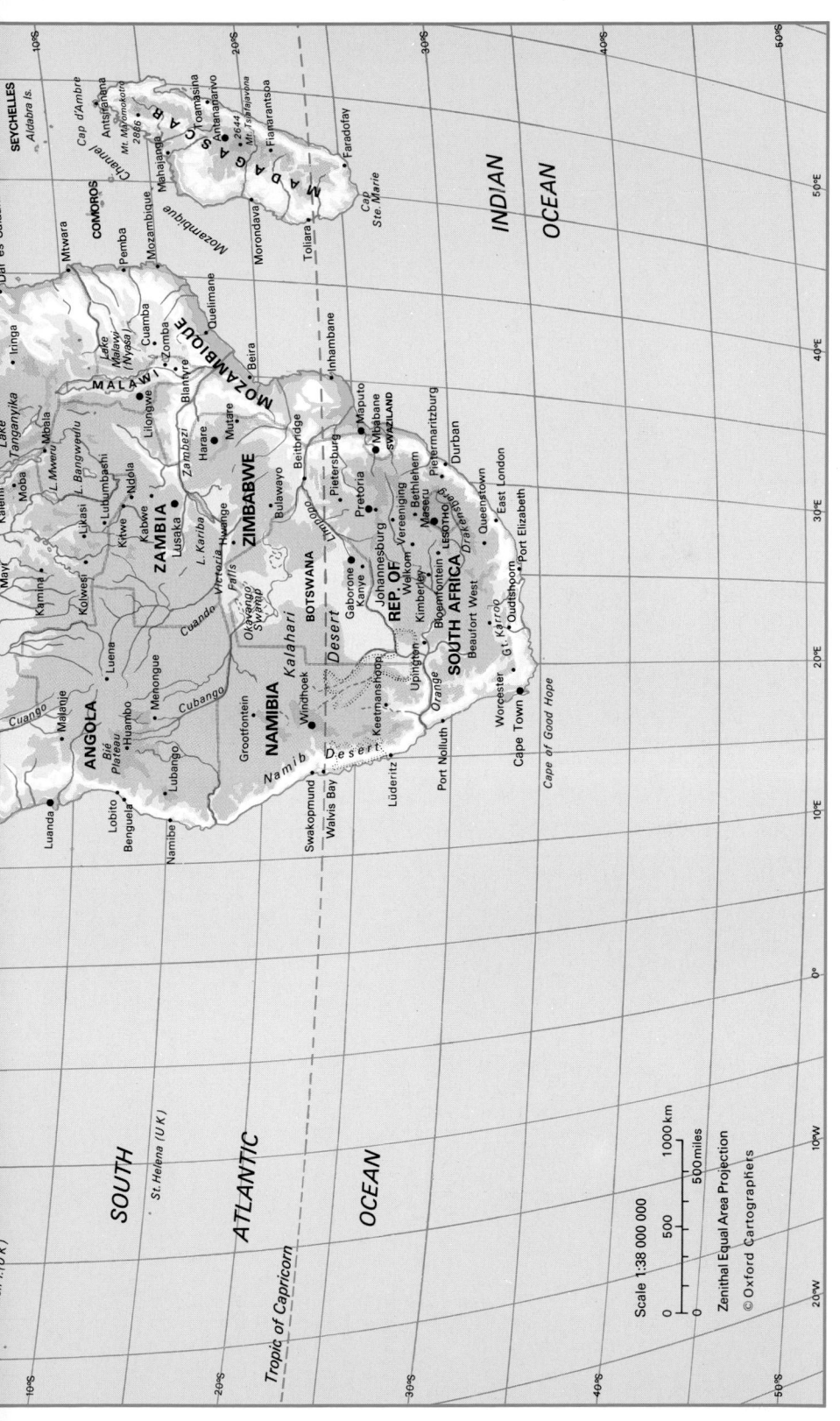

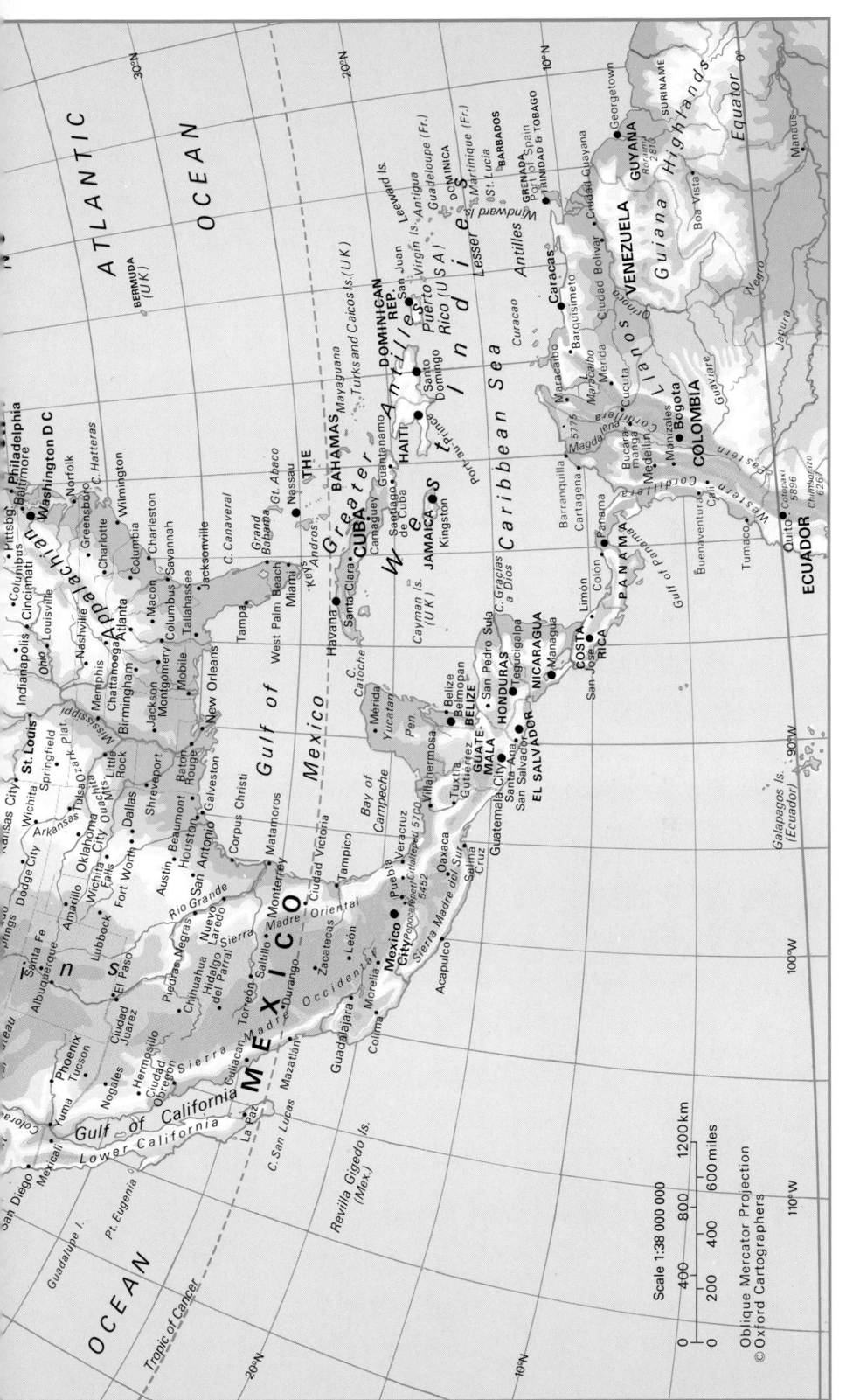

CUBA
Camaguey
Santa Clara
Santiago de Cuba
Guantanamo
JAMAICA
Kingston
Turks and Caicos Is.(UK)
DOMINICAN REP.
HAITI
Port-au-Prince
Santo Domingo
San Juan
Puerto Rico (USA)
Virgin Is.
Antigua (UK)
Guadeloupe (Fr.)
Lesser
DOMINICA
Martinique (Fr.)
St.Lucia
BARBADOS
GRENADA
Leeward Is.
Windward Is.
Antilles
Port of Spain
TRINIDAD & TOBAGO

Caribbean Sea
Curacao
Limón
Colón
Panama
PANAMA
Gulf of Panama
Buenaventura
Barranquilla
Cartagena
Maracaibo
Bucaramanga
Cúcuta
Mérida
6775
Manizales
Medellín
Bogotá
COLOMBIA
Cali
Llanos
Caracas
Barquisimeto
Ciudad Bolívar
Ciudad Guayana
VENEZUELA
Georgetown
Paramaribo
GUYANA
Roraima 2810
SURINAME
GUIANA
FR.
Cayenne
Guiana
Highlands
Boa Vista
Guaviare
Tumaco
Quito
Cotopaxi 5896
ECUADOR
Chimborazo 626?
Guayaquil
Cuenca
0°
Negro
Japurá
Equator

Sullana
Chiclayo
Cajamarca
Trujillo
PERU
Chimbote
Iquitos
Leticia
Marañón
Ucayali
Juruá
Pucalpa
Cruzeiro do Sol
Rio Branco
Purús
Porto Velho
Madeira
Selvas
Manaus
Santarém
Belém
Amazon
Tapajós
Marajó
São Luis
Bacabal
Teresina
Fortaleza
Mossoró
Natal
C. São Ro
Juazeiro do Norte
João Pe
Campina Grande
Caruaru
Recife

10°S
Callao
Lima
Huascarán 6768
La Oroya
Huánuco
Huancayo
Cuzco
Santa Ana
Trinidad
BRAZIL
Serra dos Parecis
Teles Pires
Xingu
Tocantins
Juazeiro
Barreiras
São Francisco
Paulo Alfonso
Aracaju
Maceió
Feira de Santana
Salvador
Ilhéus

Puno
Arequipa
Mollendo
Arica
Iquique
L.Titicaca
La Paz
BOLIVIA
Oruro
Cochabamba
Santa Cruz
Sucre
Potosí
L.Poopó
Mato Grosso
Cuiabá
Mato Grosso Plateau
Goiás
Goiânia
Brasília
Brazilian
Montes Claros
Diamantina
Governador Valadares
Caratinga

20°S
Tropic of Capricorn
Antofagasta
San Felix I. San Ambrosio I. (Chile)
Taltal
Copiapó
Salt Flat
Atacama Desert
Andes
Altiplano
Tarija
Salinas Grandes
Chaco
Gran Chaco
Pilcomayo
Corumba
Paraguay
Campo
Campo Grande
Marília
Uberlândia
Uberaba
Ribeirão Preto
Piraporo
Campinas
Londrina
Belo Horizonte
Juiz de Fora
Campos
Vitória
Highlands
São Paulo
Santos
Volta Redonda
Niterói
Rio de Janeiro

PARAGUAY
Concepción
Asunción
Villarrica
Formosa
San Salvador de Jujuy
Tucumán
Santiago del Estero
Catamarca
La Rioja
Resistencia
Corrientes
Posadas
Paraná
Uruguay
Passo Fundo
Florianopolis
Curitiba

30°S
La Serena
Juan Fernandez Is. (Chile)
Valparaíso
Santiago
Rancagua
Curicó
Talca
Córdoba
San Juan
Aconcagua 6960
Mendoza
San Luis
Santa Fe
Paraná
Rosario
Entre Rios
Santa Maria
Livramento
Tacuarembó
Pôrto Alegre
Pelotas
Mercedes
URUGUAY
Paysandú
Durazno
Rocha
Montevideo
Buenos Aires
La Plata
ARGENTINA
Pampas
SOUTH

40°S
Concepción
Chillán
Neuquén
Santa Rosa
Bolívar
Azul
Mar del Plata
Bahía Blanca
Colorado
Negro
Carmen de Patagones
Viedma

Valdivia
Osorno
Puerto Montt
Chiloé
Chubut
Valdés Peninsula
Rawson
Patagonia
Comodoro Rivadavia
Gulf of S. Jorge
Buenos Lago
Deseado

ATLANTIC
OCEAN

ATLANTIC
OCEAN

50°S
Taitao Pen.
L. Viedma
L. Argentino
Rio Gallegos
Puerto Natales
Punta Arenas
Strait of Magellan
Tierra del Fuego
Ushuaia
Cape Horn
Falkland Is. (UK)
Port Stanley
South Georgia (UK)

Scale 1:44 000 000
0   400   800   1200   1600 km
0   500   1000 miles

70°W   60°W   50°W   40°W   30°W

Oblique Mercator Projection
© Oxford Cartographer

Scale 1:40 000 000

Modified Zenithal Equidistant Projection

©Oxford Cartographers

0   500   1000km
0   500   miles

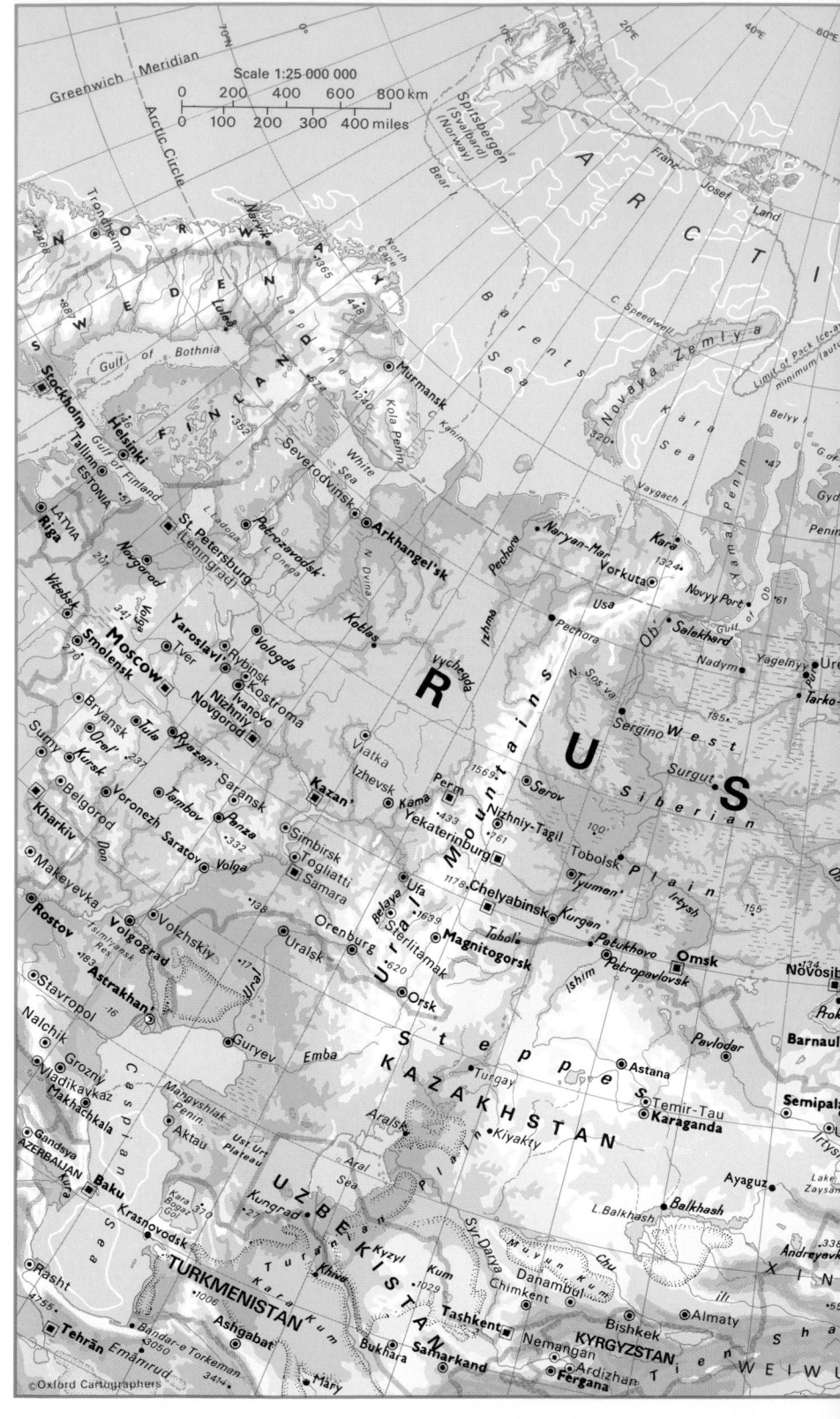

Scale 1:25 000 000

0 200 400 600 800km
0 100 200 300 400 miles

Greenwich Meridian

Arctic Circle

A R C T I

Spitsbergen
(Svalbard)
(Norway)

Bear I.

Franz
Josef
Land

C. Speedwell

Novaya Zemlya

Kara
Sea

Belyy I.

Gyda
Penin

•47

Barents
Sea

Vaygach I.

Yamal Penin

Gulf of Ob

•61

Novvy Port

N O R W A Y

Trondheim

•2468

North
C.

•3965

446

1240

Luleå

Murmansk

Kola Penin.

Kanin

White
Sea

Severodvinsk

Arkhangel'sk

Pechora

Naryan-Mar

Vorkuta

Kara

•1324

Usa

Salekhard

Ob'

Nadym

Yagelnyy

Ure

Tarko-

S W E D E N

•697

Gulf of Bothnia

F I N L A N D

352

Severodvinsk

L. Ladoga

L. Onega

N. Dvina

Pechora

Izhma

N. Sos'va

Ob'

Sergino

Surgut

•85

W e s t

Stockholm

Tallinn

Helsinki

Gulf of Finland

ESTONIA

St. Petersburg
(Leningrad)

Novgorod

Vologda

Vychegda

Vyatka

Perm

•1569

Serov

Nizhniy Tagil

•761

Tobolsk

Tyumen'

100°

S i b e r i a n

LATVIA

Riga

201

Vitebsk

341

Volga

Yaroslavl'

Tver

Rybinsk

Kostroma

Ivanovo

Nizhniy
Novgorod

Izhevsk

Kazan'

Kama

•433

Yekaterinburg

Chelyabinsk

Kurgan

Irtysh

155

S

R
U

Smolensk

276

Moscow

Bryansk

Tula

•237

Ryazan'

Saransk

Simbirsk

Ufa

•1178

•1639

Tobol'

Petukhovo

Omsk

Novosib

•734

Sumy

Orel'

Kursk

Voronezh

Tambov

Penza

•332

Togliatti

Samara

Belaya

Sterlitamak

Magnitogorsk

Petropavlovsk

Kharkiv

Belgorod

Saratov

Volga

•138

Orenburg

•620

Ishim

Proko

Barnaul

Makeyevka

Don

Rostov

Volgograd

Volzhskiy

Simlyansk
Res

•17

Uralsk

Orsk

Pavlodar

Semipala

U

Stavropol

•183

Astrakhan'

-16

Ural

Emba

S t e p p e s

Tungay

Astana

Temir-Tau

Irtysh

Nalchik

Grozny

Vladikavkaz

Makhachkala

Caspian

Manyshlak
Penin

Aktau

Ust Urt
Plateau

Guryev

K A Z A K H S T A N

Kiyakty

Karaganda

Ayaguz

Lake
Zaysan

•338

Andreyevka

Gandxa

AZERBAIJAN

Baku

Krasnovodsk

Kara
Bogaz
Gol

370

•27

Aral
Sea

Aralsk

U Z B E

Kungrad

Sea

L.Balkhash

Balkhash

Chu

Ili

X I N

•55

Rasht

TURKMENISTAN

4755

Bandar-e Torkeman

•1006

Ashgabat

Kara

Khiva

Turan

K I S T A N

Kyzyl
Kum

•1029

Muyun

Kum

Danambul

Chimkent

Syr Darya

Bishkek

KYRGYZSTAN

Almaty

Ili

S h a

Tehrān

Emāmrud

•3050

3414•

Mary

Bukhara

Samarkand

Tashkent

Nemangan

Ardizhan

Fergana

Tien

WEIWU

©Oxford Cartographers

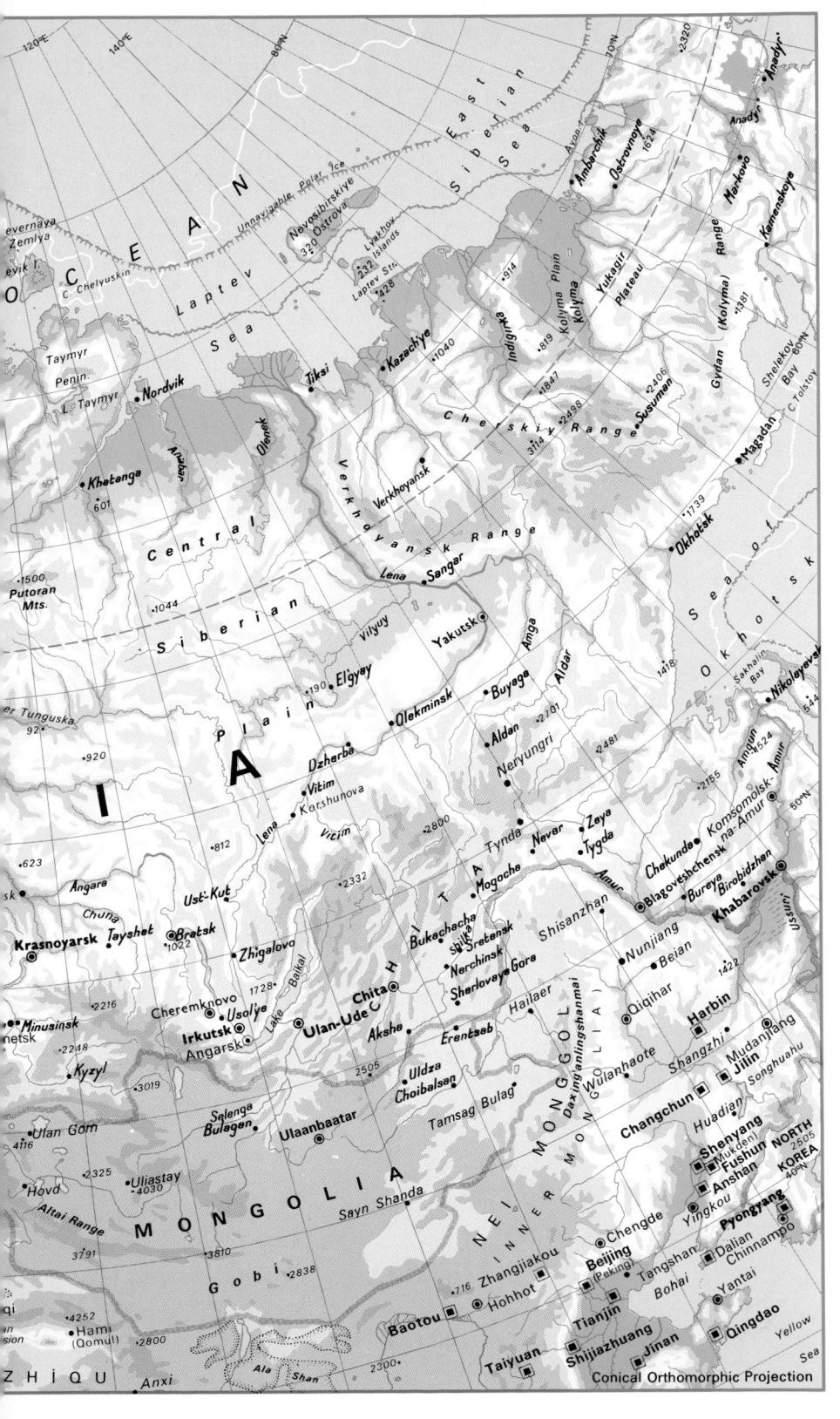

120°E   140°E   80°N   70°N   220

O C E A N

East Siberian Sea

Unnavigable, Polar Ice

evernaya Zemlya

evik I.

Novosibirskiye Ostrova

320

Lyakhov Islands

Laptev Str.

•428

•914

Kolyma Plain

Yukagir Plateau

(Kolyma) Range

Amarchik

Ostrovnoye 1624

Markovo

Anadyr

Komenskoye

Anadyr'

Anabar

C. Chelyuskin

Taymyr Penin.

L. Taymyr • Nordvik

Laptev Sea

• Tiksi

• Kazachye

•1040

Indigirka •819

•1847

•2498

3114

Chefskiy Range

•2416

Susuman

Shelekov Bay

BON

C. Tolstoy

• Magadan

•1381

Gydan

• Khatanga

601

Olenek

Verkhoyansk Range

• Verkhoyansk

Lena • Sangar

Central

Siberian

Plain

•1500

Putoran Mts.

•1044

Vilyuy

•190 El'gyey

• Yakutsk

Amga

• Buyaga

Aldan

•2101

•1739

• Okhotsk

S e a   o f

•1418

Sakhalin Bay

O k h o t s k

•514

er Tunguska

92

•920

• Olekminsk

Dzherba

• Aldan

• Neryungri

•2481

•2155

Amgun •524

• Nikolayevsk

I A

Lena Vitim • Korshunova

Vitim

•812

•2800

Tynda

• Never • Zeya

Tygda

•622

Chekunda

Bureya

Birobidzhan

Amur

• Khabarovsk

Ussuri

sk

Angara

Chuna

•623

•2332

Mogocha

Bukachacha

Shilka • Sretensk

Nerchinsk

Sherlovaya-Gora

Shisanzhan

Hailaer

• Blagoveshchensk

Komsomolsk-na-Amur

50°N

•422

Ust-Kut

• Zhigalova

•1022

• Bratsk

Tayshet

Krasnoyarsk

•2216

Cheremknovo

Usolye

Chita

Ulan-Ude

Aksha

•2505

Erentsab

Nunjiang

• Beian

• Qiqihar

Shangzhi

Harbin

Mudanjiang

Jilin

Songhuahu

•• Minusinsk

netsk

Irkutsk

Angarsk

Lake Baikal

1728

Uldza

Choibalsan

Tamsag Bulag

Daxinganlingshanmai

Wulanhaote

Changchun

Huadian

•2505

•2248

• Kyzyl

•3019

Selenga

Bulagen •

Ulaanbaatar

Sayn Shanda

Shenyang

Fushun

Mukden

Anshan

Yingkou

NORTH KOREA

40°N

• Ulan Gom

4116

•2325

• Uliastay •4030

• Hovd

Altai Range

3791

•3810

MONGOLIA

Gobi

•2838

Chengde

Pyongyang

Chinnampo

Dalian

• Zhangjiakou

• Hohhot

Beijing (Peking)

Tangshan

Bohai

Yantai

NEI MONGOL (INNER MONGOLIA)

•716

Hami (Qomul)

•4252

•2800

•2300

Baotou

ZHIQU

Anxi

Ala Shan

Taiyuan

Shijiazhuang

Tianjin

Jinan

Qingdao

Yellow Sea

Conical Orthomorphic Projection

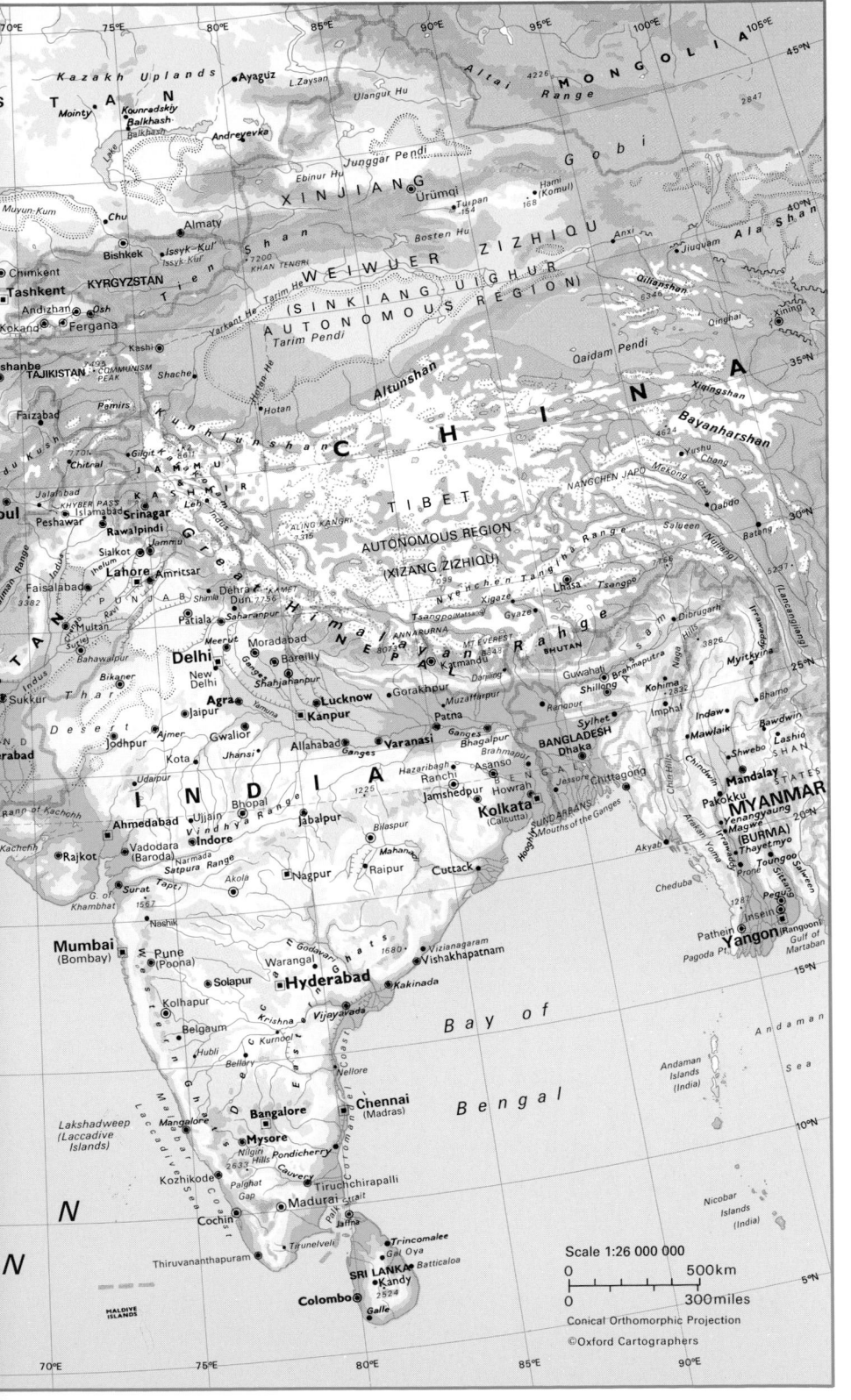

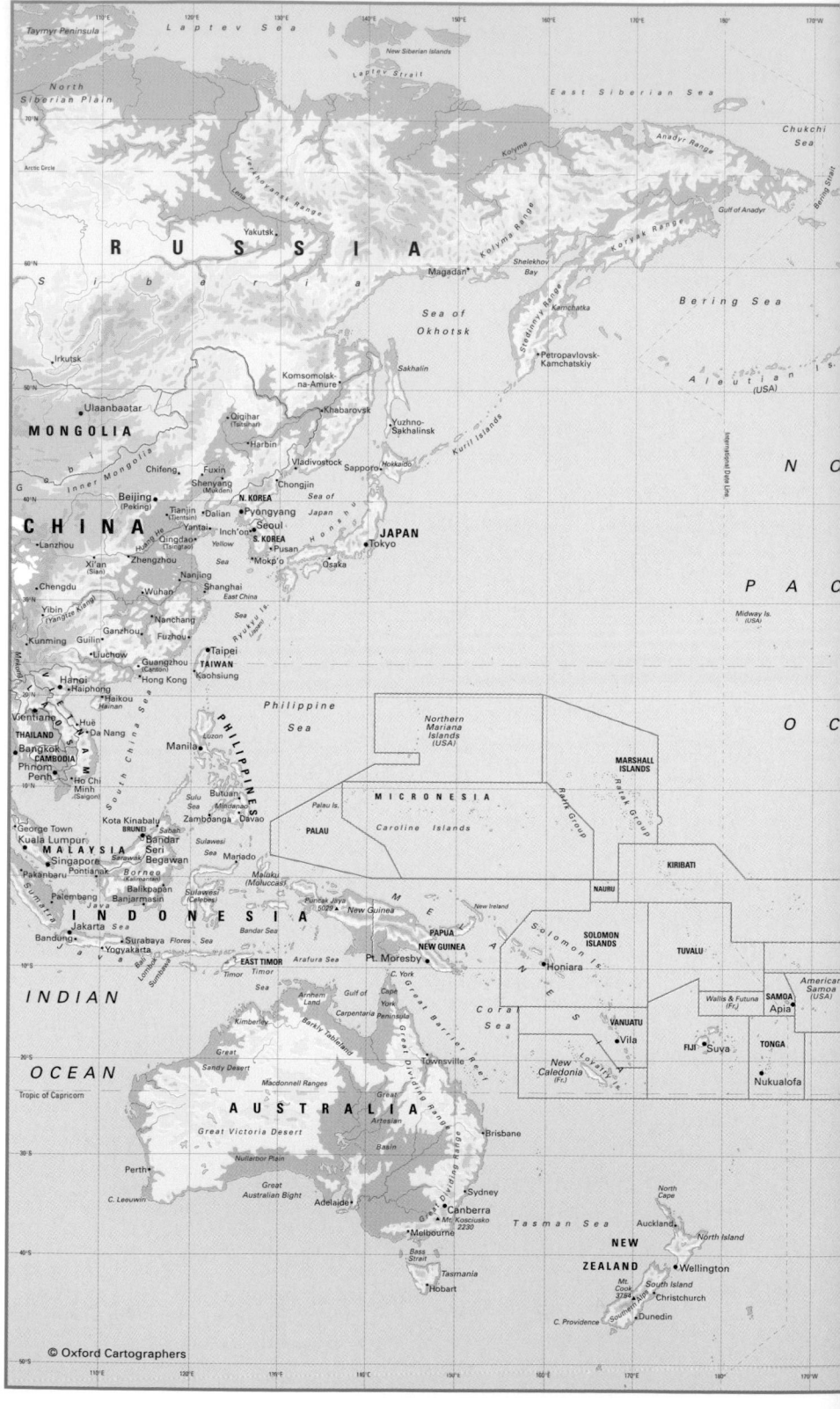

© Oxford Cartographers

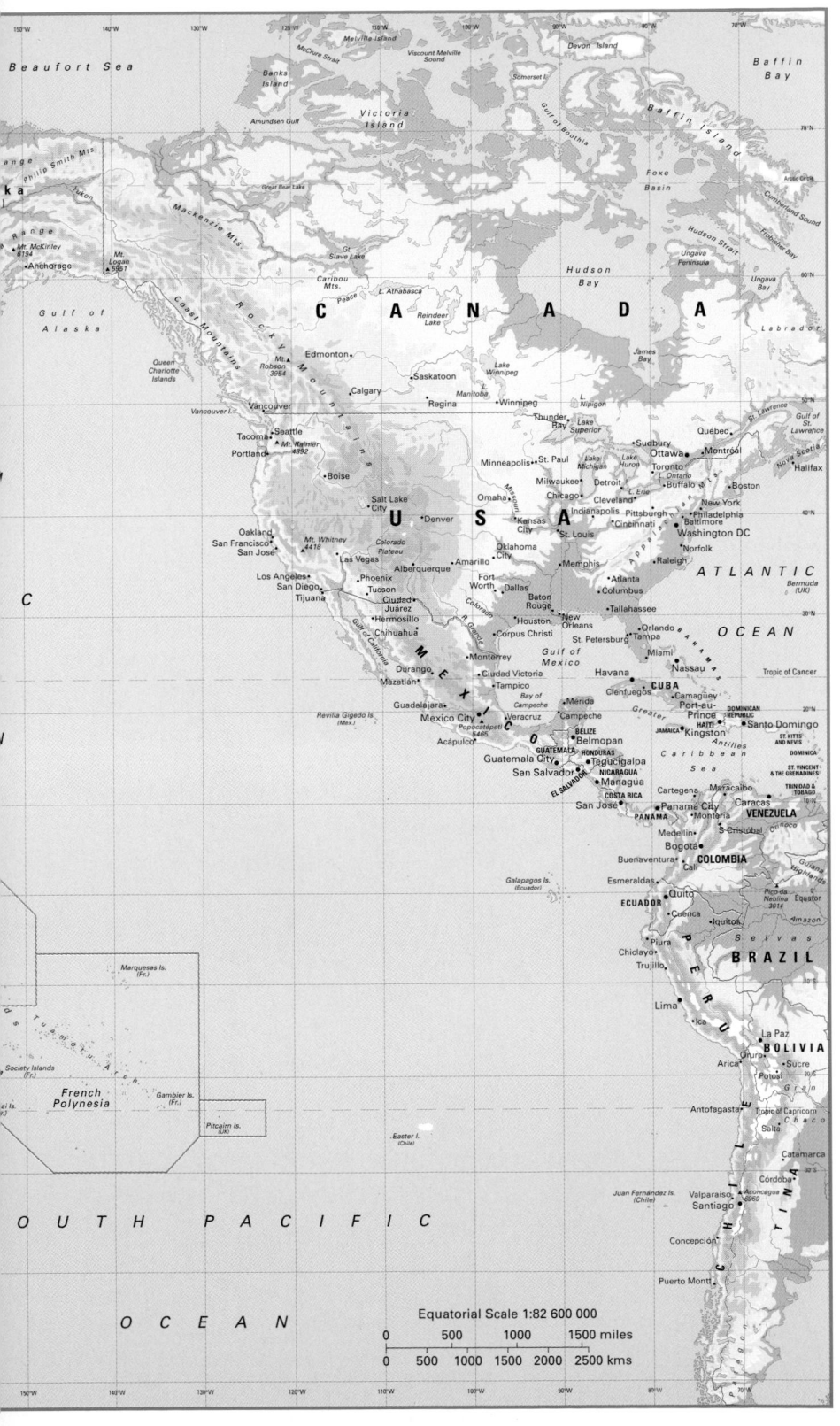

Beaufort Sea

Banks
Island

Melville Island

Viscount Melville
Sound

Devon Island

Baffin
Bay

Amundsen Gulf

Victoria
Island

Gulf of Boothia

Somerset I.

Baffin Island

Philip Smith Mts.
Range

Yukon

Mackenzie Mts.

Great Bear Lake

Foxe
Basin

Cumberland Sound

ka

Mt. McKinley
6194
Anchorage

Coast Mountains

Rocky Mountains

Gt.
Slave Lake

Caribou
Mts.

Peace

L. Athabasca

Hudson
Bay

Ungava
Peninsula

Ungava
Bay

Gulf of
Alaska

Mt.
Logan
5951

C A N A D A

Reindeer
Lake

James
Bay

Labrador

Queen
Charlotte
Islands

Edmonton

Saskatoon

Lake
Winnipeg

Manitoba

Lake
Nipigon

St. Lawrence

Gulf of
St.
Lawrence

Vancouver I.

Vancouver

Calgary

Regina

Winnipeg

Thunder
Bay

Lake
Superior

L.

Québec

Nova Scotia

Tacoma

Seattle

Mt. Rainier
4392

Portland

Boise

Salt Lake
City

Minneapolis

St. Paul

Lake
Michigan

Lake
Huron

Sudbury

Ottawa

Toronto

L. Ontario

Montréal

Halifax

Omaha

Milwaukee

Detroit

Chicago

Cleveland

L. Erie

Buffalo

Boston

New York

Oakland
San Francisco
San José

Mt. Whitney
4418

Colorado
Plateau

Denver

U S A

Kansas
City

St. Louis

Indianapolis

Cincinnati

Pittsburgh

Philadelphia
Baltimore
Washington DC

Las Vegas

Alberquerque

Oklahoma
City

Memphis

Norfolk

Raleigh

A T L A N T I C

Los Angeles
San Diego
Tijuana

Phoenix
Tucson

Fort
Worth

Dallas

Atlanta

Columbus

Bermuda
(UK)

Hermosillo

Chihuahua

R. Grande

Colorado

Baton
Rouge

Houston

New
Orleans

Tallahassee

O C E A N

Corpus Christi

Gulf of
California

M E X I C O

Monterrey

Durango

Ciudad Victoria

Tampico

Orlando
Tampa

St. Petersburg

Miami

Nassau

Tropic of Cancer

Mazatlán

Gulf of
Mexico

Bay of
Campeche

Havana

CUBA

Clenfuegos

Camaguey
Port-au-
Prince

DOMINICAN
REPUBLIC

Santo Domingo

Revilla Gigedo Is.
(Mex.)

Guadalajara

México City

Popocatépetl
5465

Veracruz

Mérida

Campeche

Greater

Antilles

JAMAICA

HAITI

Kingston

ST. KITTS
AND NEVIS

DOMINICA

Acápulco

GUATEMALA

BELIZE

Belmopan

Caribbean

Sea

ST. VINCENT
& THE GRENADINES

Guatemala City

San Salvador

HONDURAS

NICARAGUA

Tegucigalpa

Managua

EL SALVADOR

COSTA RICA

TRINIDAD &
TOBAGO

San José

PANAMA

Panama City

Cartagena

Montería

Maracaibo

Caracas

VENEZUELA

Medellín

Bogotá

S. Cristóbal

Orinoco

Guiana
Highlands

Buenaventura

Cali

COLOMBIA

Galapagos Is.
(Ecuador)

Esmeraldas

Quito

ECUADOR

Cuenca

Pico da
Neblina
3014

Equator

Amazon

Iquitos

Selvas

Marquesas Is.
(Fr.)

Piura

Chiclayo

Trujillo

P E R U

BRAZIL

Tuamotu Arch.

Society Islands
(Fr.)

Lima

Ica

La Paz

BOLIVIA

Arica

Oruro

Sucre

Potosí

Gran

French
Polynesia

Gambier Is.
(Fr.)

Pitcairn Is.
(UK)

Antofagasta

Tropic of Capricorn

Chaco

Salta

Easter I.
(Chile)

Catamarca

Córdoba

S O U T H   P A C I F I C

Juan Fernández Is.
(Chile)

Valparaíso
Santiago

Aconcagua
6960

CHILE

ARGENTINA

O C E A N

Concepción

Puerto Montt

Equatorial Scale 1:82 600 000

0   500   1000   1500 miles

0   500   1000   1500   2000   2500 kms

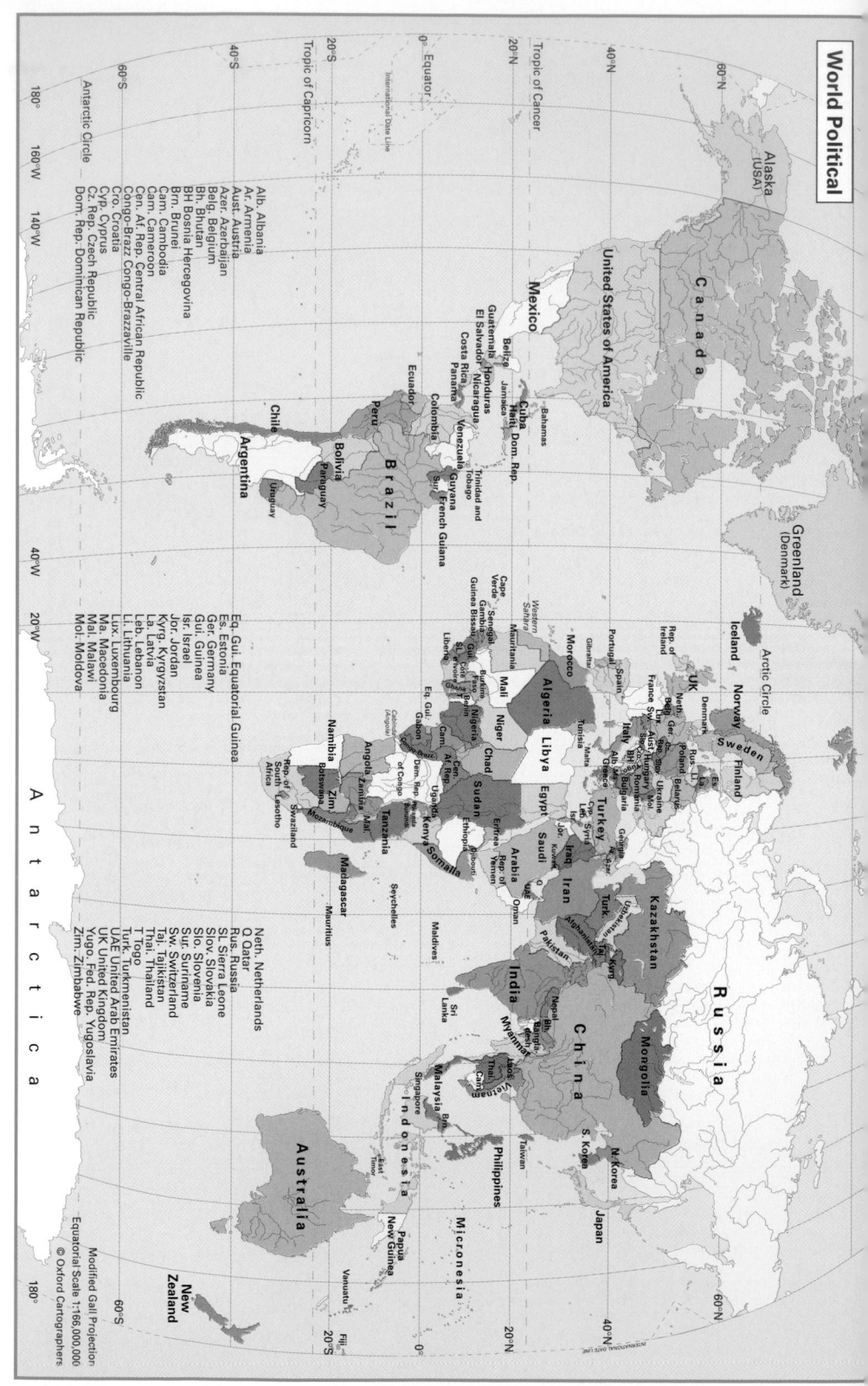

World Political

Alaska
(USA)

C a n a d a

Greenland
(Denmark)

Iceland

Arctic Circle

Norway

Sweden

Finland

R u s s i a

United States of America

Mexico

Belize
Guatemala
El Salvador
Honduras
Costa Rica
Panama
Nicaragua

Cuba
Jamaica
Dom. Rep.
Haiti
Bahamas

Rep. of
Ireland
UK
Denmark
Neth.
Belg.
Ger.
France Sw.
Port.
Spain
Gibraltar
Italy
Malta
Greece
Alb.
Mac.
Pol.
Cz. Rep. Ukraine
Aust. Hungary Mol.
Slov. Rom.
Bela.
Lith.
Lat.
Est.
Bul.
Bos.

Kazakhstan

Mongolia

Ecuador
Colombia
Venezuela
Guyana
Sur. French Guiana
Trinidad and
Tobago

Peru

B r a z i l

Bolivia
Paraguay

Chile
Argentina
Uruguay

Cape
Verde
Western
Sahara
Mauritania
Senegal
Gambia
Guinea Bissau Gui.
S. Leone
Liberia
Mali
Burkina
Côte
d'Ivoire
Ghana
Nigeria
Togo
Benin
Niger

Algeria
Tunisia
Morocco

Libya
Egypt

Turkey
Cyp.
Syria
Leb.
Isr.
Jor.
Geo.
Arm.
Azer.

Iraq
Iran

Turk.
Uzbekistan
Afghanistan
Kyr.
Taj.

C h i n a

S. Korea
N. Korea
Japan

Eq. Gui.
Gabon
Cam.
Cen.
Af. Rep.
Chad
Sudan
Eritrea
Djibouti
Ethiopia
Somalia

Saudi
Arabia
Rep. of
Yemen
Oman
UAE
Kuwait
Qatar

Pakistan

Nepal
Bhu.
Bang.

India
Myanmar
Laos
Thailand
Vietnam
Camb.

Angola
Rep. of
Congo
Dem. Rep.
of Congo
Uganda
Kenya
Tanzania

Namibia
Botswana
Zim.
Zambia
Mal.
Mozambique
Rep. of
South
Africa
Lesotho
Swaziland

Madagascar

Seychelles

Mauritius

Maldives

Sri
Lanka

Malaysia
Singapore
Bru.

I n d o n e s i a
East
Timor

Philippines

Taiwan

Micronesia

Papua
New Guinea

A u s t r a l i a

Vanuatu

Fiji

New
Zealand

A n t a r c t i c a

Alb. Albania
Ar. Armenia
Aust. Austria
Azer. Azerbaijan
Belg. Belgium
Bh. Bhutan
BH Bosnia Hercegovina
Brn. Brunei
Cam. Cambodia
Cam. Cameroon
Cen. Af. Rep. Central African Republic
Congo-Brazz Congo-Brazzaville
Cro. Croatia
Cyp. Cyprus
Cz. Rep. Czech Republic
Dom. Rep. Dominican Republic

Eq. Gui. Equatorial Guinea
Es. Estonia
Ger. Germany
Gui. Guinea
Isr. Israel
Jor. Jordan
Kyr. Kyrgyzstan
La. Latvia
Leb. Lebanon
Li. Lithuania
Lu. Luxembourg
Ma. Macedonia
Mal. Malawi
Mol. Moldova

Neth. Netherlands
Q. Qatar
Rus. Russia
Si. Sierra Leone
Slo. Slovakia
Slo. Slovenia
Sur. Suriname
Sw. Switzerland
Taj. Tajikistan
Tai. Thailand
T. Togo
Turk. Turkmenistan
UAE United Arab Emirates
UK United Kingdom
Yugo. Fed. Rep. Yugoslavia
Zim. Zimbabwe

Tropic of Cancer

Equator

Tropic of Capricorn

International Date Line

Antarctic Circle

Modified Gall Projection
Equatorial Scale 1:166,000,000
© Oxford Cartographers

point of Morocco is the peninsula of Tangier dominated by the Jebel Mousa which, with the rocky eminence of Gibraltar, was known to the ancients as the Pillars of Hercules, the western gateway of the Mediterranean.

HISTORY AND POLITICS

Morocco became an independent sovereign state in 1956, following joint declarations made with France on 2 March 1956 and with Spain on 7 April 1956. The Sultan of Morocco, Sidi Mohammad ben Youssef, adopted the title of King Mohammad V.

Elections were held on 14 November 1997 to the new House of Representatives; no party won an overall majority, but Abderrahmane El Youssoufi was appointed prime minister as the leader of the Socialist Union of Popular Forces, the largest party in the House of Representatives. On 5 December 1997, elections to the Chamber of Councillors were held. The pro-government *Wifaq* bloc and centre parties won 166 seats; the opposition *Koutla* bloc won 44 seats. The next legislative election is due by December 2000.

POLITICAL SYSTEM

The King nominates the prime minister and, on the latter's recommendation, appoints the members of the Council of Ministers. The government is responsible both to parliament and to the King. There is a bicameral legislature. The Chamber of Representatives (*Majlis an-Nuwab*) has 325 members elected by universal suffrage using a first-past-the-post system. The Chamber of Councillors (*Majlis al-Mustashareen*) has 270 members, 60 per cent of whom are elected by local councils, 20 per cent by employers' associations and 20 per cent by trade unions. One third of its members are elected every three years.

HEAD OF STATE

HM The King of Morocco, King Mohamed VI (Sidi Mohamed Ben Hassan), *born* 21 August 1963, *acceded* 23 July 1999

COUNCIL OF MINISTERS *as at September 2000*

Prime Minister, Abderrahmane El Youssoufi
Agriculture, Development, Maritime Fishing, Habib Malki
Communications, Larbi Messari
Cultural Affairs, Mohamed Achaari
Economy and Finance, Fathallah Oualalou
Energy and Mining, Youssef Tahiri
Equipment, Bouamar Tighouane
General Secretary of the Government, Abdessadek Rabii
Health, Abdelouahed El Fassi
Higher Education, Executive Training, Scientific Research, Najib Zerouali
Human Rights, Mohamed Aoujar
Industry, Commerce and Handicrafts, Alami Tazi
Justice, Omar Azziman
Minister of State for Foreign Affairs and Co-operation, Mohamed Ben Aissa
Minister of State for the Interior, Ahmed Midaoui
National Education, Ismail Alaoui
Public Sector and Privatisation, Rachid Filali
Public Service and Administrative Development, Aziz Hocine
Relations with Parliament, Mohamed Bouzoubaa
Social Development, Solidarity, Employment, Vocational Training, Government Spokesman, Khalid Alioua
Tourism, Hassan Sebbar
Town and Country Planning, Environment, Housing, Mohamed El Yazghi
Transport and Merchant Navy, Mustapha Mansouri
Waqf and Islamic Affairs, Abdelkebir M Daghri Alaoui
Youth and Sports, Ahmed Moussaoui

EMBASSY OF THE KINGDOM OF MOROCCO
49 Queen's Gate Gardens, London SW7 5NE
Tel: 020-7581 5001/4
Ambassador Extraordinary and Plenipotentiary, HE Mohammed Belmahi, apptd 1999

BRITISH EMBASSY
17 Boulevard de la Tour Hassan (BP 45), Rabat
Tel: (00 212) (7) 729696
E-mail: britemb@mtds.com
Ambassador Extraordinary and Plenipotentiary, HE Anthony Layden, apptd 1999
CONSULATE-GENERAL – Casablanca
CONSULATES – Agadir, Marrakesh, Tangier
BRITISH COUNCIL DIRECTOR, G. McCulloch, BP 427, 36 rue de Tanger, Rabat;
E-mail: britcoun.morocco@britishcouncil.org.ma
BRITISH CHAMBER OF COMMERCE, 1st Floor, 185 Boulevard Zerktouni, Casablanca.
Tel: (00 212) (2) 256920

DEFENCE

The Army has 524 main battle tanks, 115 armoured infantry fighting vehicles, and 785 armoured personnel carriers.

The Navy has one frigate and 27 patrol and coastal combatant vessels at five bases. The Air Force has 89 combat aircraft and 24 armed helicopters.

The UN has some 231 personnel in Western Sahara pending the referendum (*see* below). Polisario deploys 3,000–6,000 troops in Western Sahara with Algerian-supplied and captured Moroccan tanks, armoured personnel carriers, anti-tank and anti-aircraft weapons.
MILITARY EXPENDITURE – 4.7 per cent of GDP (1998)
MILITARY PERSONNEL – 196,300: Army 175,000, Navy 7,800, Air Force 13,500, Paramilitaries 42,000
CONSCRIPTION DURATION – 18 months

ECONOMY

Morocco's main sources of wealth are agricultural and mineral. A large-scale privatisation programme has attracted substantial foreign investment. It is planned to privatise the national airline, Royal Air Maroc, and liberalise the telecommunications, power and water sectors.

Agriculture contributed 17.7 per cent of GDP and employed 38.5 per cent of the workforce. The main agricultural exports are fruit and vegetables, with cereals and sugar beet produced and sheep reared for domestic consumption. Cork and wood pulp are the most important commercial forest products. Esparto grass is also produced. There is a fishing industry and substantial quantities of canned fish are exported.

For a developing country Morocco has a large industrial sector. The main sectors are chemicals, textiles and leather goods, food processing and cement production. Manufacturing industries are centred in Casablanca, Fez, Tangier and Safi.

Morocco's mineral exports are phosphates, fluorite, barite, manganese, iron ore, lead, zinc, cobalt, copper and antimony. Morocco possesses nearly three-quarters of the world's estimated reserves of phosphates. There are oil refineries at Mohammedia and Sidi Kacem handling about four million tonnes of crude oil a year.

Morocco has a high proportion of public employees; the salaries of its 750,000 civil servants consume about 12 per cent of the country's GDP.

Tourism is of great importance to the economy, with development concentrated in Agadir and Marrakesh. In 1998, about 2 million foreign tourists visited Morocco. GNP – US$34,421 million (1998); US$1,240 per capita (1998)

GDP – US$37,704 million (1996); US$1,395 per capita (1996)
ANNUAL AVERAGE GROWTH OF GDP – 12.0 per cent (1996)
INFLATION RATE – 2.9 per cent (1998)
UNEMPLOYMENT – 17.8 per cent (1996)
TOTAL EXTERNAL DEBT – US$20,687 million (1998)

TRADE

The main imports are petroleum products, machinery, chemical products, iron and steel, grain and textiles. The EU, with which an association agreement was signed in November 1995, is Morocco's largest trading partner and in May 1998 awarded Morocco grants totalling US$98 million. The main exports are, phosphates and phosphoric acid, textiles and leather, and fish and agricultural products.

In 1997 Morocco had a trade deficit of US$1,864 million and a current account deficit of US$87 million. In 1998 imports totalled US$10,262 million and exports US$7,219 million.

Trade with UK	1998	1999
Imports from UK	£353,572,000	£357,324,000
Exports to UK	637,237,000	400,219,000

COMMUNICATIONS

Railroads cover 1,907 km, linking the major towns. There are 60,449 km of roads; an extensive network of 30,374 km of surfaced roads covers all the main towns. There are air services between Casablanca, Tangier, Agadir (seasonal), Marrakesh and London, and also between Tangier and Gibraltar connecting with London. Royal Air Maroc is the national airline.

EDUCATION

Education is compulsory between the ages of seven and 16. There are government primary, secondary and technical schools. In 1991 there were 4,890 government schools. At Fez there is a theological university of great repute in the Muslim world. There is a secular university at Rabat. Schools for special denominations, Jewish and Catholic, are permitted and may receive government grants. American schools operate in Rabat and Casablanca. There is an English-language university in Ifrane.
ILLITERACY RATE – 51.1 per cent
ENROLMENT (percentage of age group) – primary 74 per cent (1996); secondary 20 per cent (1980); tertiary 11 per cent (1996)

WESTERN SAHARA

Formerly the Spanish Sahara, the territory was split between Morocco and Mauritania in 1976 after Spain withdrew in December 1975. In 1976 the Polisario Front (Frente Popular para la Liberación de Saguia y Río de Oro) declared Western Sahara to be an independent state, the Sahrawi Arab Democratic Republic, and formed a government which remains in exile. The Polisario Front has been recognised as the legitimate government of Western Sahara by over 70 states and the Organisation of African Unity. In 1979 Mauritania renounced its claim to its share of the territory, which was added by Morocco to its area.

In 1988, Morocco and the Polisario Front accepted a UN peace plan under which a cease-fire came into effect in September 1991. A referendum to determine the future of the area was to have been held in January 1992 but has not yet taken place because the Moroccan government and Polisario have not agreed on the referendum terms or voter eligibility. Voter identification began in August 1994 but the failure to agree on eligibility prompted the UN

to threaten the suspension of the UN Mission for the Referendum in Western Sahara (MINURSO), which had been deployed since 1991. A referendum is not expected before 2002, with MINURSO responsible for identifying voters.

Legislative elections to the National Assembly were held in 1995; President Mohamed Abdelaziz, who had been elected president since 1982 by the party congress of the Polisario Front, was re-elected by the National Assembly in 1995. Following a vote of no confidence in the previous incumbent, Bouchraya Hamoudi Bayoun was named Prime Minister on 10 February 1999.

MOZAMBIQUE
República de Moçambique

AREA – 309,496 sq. miles (801,590 sq. km).
    Neighbours: Swaziland (south), South Africa (south and west), Zimbabwe (west), Zambia and Malawi (north-west), Tanzania (north)
POPULATION – 16,916,600 (1998 census). The official language is Portuguese
CAPITAL – ΨMaputo (population, 1,039,700, 1998 census)
MAJOR CITIES – ΨBeira (264,202); ΨNacala (182,505), 1986 estimates
CURRENCY – Metical (MT) of 100 centavos
NATIONAL DAY – 25 June (Independence Day)
NATIONAL FLAG – Horizontally green, black, yellow with white fimbriations; a red triangle based on the hoist containing the national emblem
LIFE EXPECTANCY (years) – male 44.41; female 47.52
POPULATION GROWTH RATE – 3.6 per cent (1997)
POPULATION DENSITY – 23 per sq. km (1997)
MILITARY EXPENDITURE – 3.9 per cent of GDP (1998)
MILITARY PERSONNEL – 6,100: Army 5,000, Navy 100, Air Force 1,000
CONSCRIPTION DURATION – Two to three years
ILLITERACY RATE – 56.2 per cent
ENROLMENT (percentage of age group) – primary 40 per cent (1995); secondary 6 per cent (1995); tertiary 0.5 per cent (1996)

HISTORY AND POLITICS

Mozambique, discovered by Vasco da Gama in 1498 and colonised by Portugal, achieved independence on 25 June 1975. It was a Marxist one-party (Frelimo) state until a multiparty system was adopted in 1990. The legislative assembly has 250 members.

Following two years of negotiations, the Frelimo government and the rebel Mozambican National Resistance (Renamo) signed a peace agreement in October 1992 which ended 16 years of civil war. Under the peace agreement, demobilisation of government and Renamo troops was due to begin within one month of parliamentary ratification of the peace accord (which occurred on 9 October 1992) although the belated arrival of the UN Operation for Mozambique (ONUMOZ) delayed demobilisation until 1994.

Presidential and legislative elections were held on 3–5 December 1999. The incumbent, Joaquim Chissano of Frelimo, won the presidential election with 52.3 per cent of the vote. Frelimo also won the legislative election, gaining 133 seats to Renamo's 117. No other parties were able to secure the 5 per cent of the total vote necessary to obtain representation.

Mozambique was admitted to the Commonwealth on 12 November 1995 as a special case, because of its close links with Commonwealth countries.

HEAD OF STATE
President, Joaquim Alberto Chissano, *sworn in*
November 1986, *elected* 29 October 1994,
re-elected 5 December 1999

COUNCIL OF MINISTERS *as at September 2000*
Prime Minister, Pascoal Mocumbi
Agriculture and Rural Development, Helder Monteiro
Culture, Miguel Costa Mkaima
Education, Alcido Nguenha
Environmental Action Co-ordination, John Katchamila
Fisheries, Cadmiel Muthemba
Foreign Affairs and Co-operation, Leonardo Simão
Health, Francisco Songane
Higher Education, Science and Technology, Lidia Brito
Independence War Veterans,
    Gen. (retd) António Hama Thay
Industry and Commerce, Carlos Morgado
Justice, José Abudo
Labour, Mario Sevene
Mineral Resources and Energy, Castigo Langa
Ministers in the President's Office, Almerinho da Cruz
    Manhenje (*Defence, Security Affairs and Interior*);
    Francisco Madeira (*Parliamentary and Diplomatic Affairs*)
National Defence, Tobias Dai
Planning and Finance, Luisa Diogo
Public Works and Housing, Roberto White
Tourism, Fernando Sumbane Junior
Transport and Communications, Tomas Salomão
Women's Affairs and Social Welfare Action Co-ordination,
    Virginia Matabele
Youth and Sports, Joel Libombo

HIGH COMMISSION FOR THE REPUBLIC OF
MOZAMBIQUE
21 Fitzroy Square, London W1P 5HJ
Tel: 020-7383 3800
High Commissioner, HE Dr Eduardo José Baciao Koloma,
apptd 1996

BRITISH HIGH COMMISSION
Av. Vladimir I Lenine 310, CP 55, Maputo
Tel: (00 258) (1) 420111/2/5/6/7
e-mail: bhc.maputo@teledata.mz
High Commissioner, HE Bernard J. Everett, apptd 1996

BRITISH COUNCIL DIRECTOR, P. Woods, Rua John Issa
226, PO Box 4178, Maputo;
e-mail: general.enquiries@britishcouncil.org.mz

ECONOMY

The basis of the economy is subsistence agriculture, but
there is an industrial sector based mainly in Beira and
Maputo. There are substantial coal deposits in Tete province and an offshore gas field at Pande. Economic
subsidies have been removed and an IMF reform programme is being implemented. The economy is still
heavily dependent on aid. A five-year plan has been
launched with the priorities of rural development,
education, health and land reform.
    In July 1999, creditor countries cancelled US$2,200
million of Mozambique s external debt. In April 2000, the
IMF and the World Bank reduced the country's debt by
US$600 million, and granted the country a 12-month
interest-free period on its remaining debt.
    Severe flooding in February 2000 caused widespread
devastation, destroying a third of the maize crop and up to
one million homes.
GNP – US$3,478 million (1998); US$210 per capita
    (1998)
GDP – US$1,568 million (1996); US$88 per capita
    (1996)
ANNUAL AVERAGE GROWTH OF GDP – 6.4 per cent
    (1996)

INFLATION RATE – 5.5 per cent (1997)
TOTAL EXTERNAL DEBT – US$8,208 million (1998)

TRADE
The main exports are shellfish, cotton, sugar, cashew nuts,
copra, tea and sisal. Mozambique's main trading partners
are South Africa, Portugal, Spain and Japan.
    In 1996 Mozambique had a trade deficit of US$478
million and a current account deficit of US$359 million.
In 1995 imports totalled US$784 million and exports
US$168 million.

Trade with UK	1998	1999
Imports from UK	£10,968,000	£11,220,000
Exports to UK	3,675,000	2,550,000

MYANMAR
Pyidaungsu Myanmar Naingngandaw – Union of Myanmar

AREA – 261,228 sq. miles (676,578 sq. km).
    Neighbours: Bangladesh (west), India (north-west),
    China (north-east), Laos and Thailand (east)
POPULATION – 46,402,000 (1997 UN estimate). The
    indigenous inhabitants are of similar racial types and
    speak languages of the Tibeto-Burman, Mon-Khmer
    and Thai groups. The three significant non-indigenous
    elements are Indians, Chinese and those from
    Bangladesh. Burmese is the official language, but
    minority languages include Bamar, Chin, Kachin,
    Kayah, Kayin (Karen), Mon, Rakhine and Shan.
    English is spoken in educated circles. Buddhism is the
    religion of 89.5 per cent of the people, with 4.9 per cent
    Christians , 3.8 per cent Muslims, 1.3 per cent Animists
    and 0.05 per cent Hindus
CAPITAL – ΨYangon (Rangoon) (population, 2,513,023,
    1983)
MAJOR CITIES – Mandalay (532,949); Mawlamyine/
    Moulmein (219,961); Pathein/Bassein (144,096)
CURRENCY – Kyat (K) of 100 pyas
NATIONAL ANTHEM – Gba majay Bma
    (We shall love Burma for ever)
NATIONAL DAY – 4 January
NATIONAL FLAG – Red, with a canton of dark blue, inside
    which are a cogwheel and two rice ears surrounded by
    14 white stars
LIFE EXPECTANCY (years) – male 57.89; female 63.14
POPULATION GROWTH RATE – 1.6 per cent (1997)
POPULATION DENSITY – 69 per sq. km (1997)

HISTORY AND POLITICS

The Union of Burma (the name was officially changed to
the Union of Myanmar in 1989) became an independent
republic outside the British Commonwealth on 4 January
1948 and remained a parliamentary democracy for
14 years. In 1962 the army took power, suspended the
parliamentary constitution and instituted a socialist state.
    After months of popular demonstrations and a series of
presidents during 1988, Gen. Saw Maung, leader of the
armed forces, assumed power in September 1988. The
People's Assembly, the Council of State and the Council
of Ministers were abolished and replaced by the State
Law and Order Restoration Council (SLORC). The constitution was effectively abrogated.
    A People's Assembly Election Law was published in
1989 and multiparty elections were held on 27 May 1990,
resulting in a majority for the National League for
Democracy (NLD) even though its leader Aung San Suu
Kyi had been under house arrest since July 1989. The
SLORC refused to transfer power to a civilian government
and large numbers of NLD MPs and supporters were
detained or fled to Thailand where an exile government

was set up. A Constitutional Convention appointed by the SLORC to discuss a future constitution convened in January 1993 and has continued fitfully since, but with minimal progress. The SLORC released Aung San Suu Kyi (who won the Nobel Peace Prize in 1991) on 10 July 1995, although on several occasions subsequently she has been forcibly prevented from attending political meetings by government troops. Many other opposition figures remain in detention or under house arrest. In November 1997, the SLORC was renamed the State Peace and Development Council (SPDC).

The SPDC detained several hundred NLD members in September 1998 to thwart the NLD's plan to convene a 'People's Parliament' representing the assembly which would have resulted from the 1990 general election; most were released in October and November. Instead, the NLD set up an interim representation committee to act on behalf of the 'People's Parliament', which declared all laws and orders issued by the military government since the general election to be invalid.

Myanmar is comprised of seven states (Chin, Kachin, Kayin (Karen), Kayah, Mon, Rakhine, Shan) and seven divisions (Ayeyarwady (Irrawaddy), Magway (Magwe), Mandalay, Bago (Pegu), Yangon (Rangoon), Sagaing, Tanintharyi (Tenasserim)).

INSURGENCIES

Since independence in 1948 the government has fought various armed insurgent groups, the largest of which were derived from the Kachin, Kayin (Karen), Karenni, and Wa ethnic groups but the Shan, Mon, Arakan and Chin ethnic minorities have also formed armed groups.

Since 1992, as a result of government offensives, 15 ethnic groups have signed cease-fire agreements with the government. In 1995–6, government forces launched successful offensives against the Kayin (Karen) National Union (KNU), the Karenni National Progressive Party and the Mong Tai army. It was reported in May 1999 that 300,000 Shan had been forced out of their villages into resettlement camps close to army bases and that thousands more had fled to Thailand. In November 1999, the government launched a military offensive against KNU guerrillas and their allies in Karen state.

STATE PEACE AND DEVELOPMENT COUNCIL *as at September 2000*

Chairman, Senior Gen. Than Shwe
Vice-Chairman, Gen. Maung Aye
Members, Rear-Adml Nyunt Thein; Maj.-Gen. Kyaw Than; Maj.-Gen. Aung Htwe; Maj.-Gen. Ye Myint; Maj.-Gen. Khin Maung Than; Maj.-Gen. Kyaw Win; Maj.-Gen. Thein Sein; Maj.-Gen. Thura Thiha Thura Sit Maung; Brig.-Gen. Thura Shwe Mahn; Brig.-Gen. Myint Aung; Brig.-Gen. Maung Bo; Brig.-Gen. Thiha Thura Tin Aung Myint Oo; Brig.-Gen. Soe Win; Brig.-Gen. Tin Aye
Secretaries, Lt.-Gen. Khin Nyunt; Lt.-Gen. Tin Oo; Lt.-Gen. Win Myint

CABINET *as at September 2000*

Prime Minister, Defence, Senior Gen. Than Shwe
Deputy PMs, Vice-Adm. Maung Maung Khin
   Lt. -Gen. Tin Hla *(Military Affairs)*;
   Lt.-Gen. Tin Tun
Agriculture and Irrigation, Maj.-Gen. Nyunt Tin
Commerce, Brig. Gen. Pyi Sone
Construction, Maj.-Gen. Saw Tun
Co-operatives, U Aung San
Culture, U Win Sein
Education, U Than Aung
Electric Power, Maj.-Gen. Tin Htut
Energy, Brig.-Gen. Lun Thi
Finance and Revenue, U Khin Maung Thein
Foreign Affairs, U Win Aung

Forestry, U Aung Phone
Health, Maj.-Gen. Ket Sein
Home Affairs, Col. Tin Hlaing
Hotels and Tourism, Maj.-Gen. Saw Lwin
Immigration and Population, U Saw Tun
Industry, U Aung Thaung; Maj.-Gen. Saw Lwin
Information, Maj.-Gen. Kyi Aung
Labour, Maj.-Gen. Tin Ngwe
Livestock Breeding and Fisheries, Brig.-Gen. Maung Maung Thein
Mines, Brig.-Gen. Ohn Myint
Ministers in the Office of the SPDC Chairman, Lt.-Gen. Min Thein; Brig.-Gen. David Abel
National Planning and Economic Development, U Soe Tha
Prime Minister's Office, Brig.-Gen. Lun Maung; U Than Shwe; Lt.-Gen. Tin Ngwe
Progress of Border Area and National Races; Development Affairs, Col. Thein Nyunt
Rail Transport, U Pan Aung
Religious Affairs, U Aung Khin
Science and Technology, U Thaung
Social Welfare, Relief and Resettlement, Maj.-Gen. Sein Htwa
Sports, Brig.-Gen. Thura Aye Myint
Telecommunications, Posts and Telegraphs, Brig.-Gen. Win Tin
Transport, Maj.-Gen. Hla Myint Swe

EMBASSY OF THE UNION OF MYANMAR
19A Charles Street, Berkeley Square, London W1X 8ER
Tel: 020-7499 8841
Ambassador Extraordinary and Plenipotentiary, HE Dr Kyaw Win, apptd 1999

BRITISH EMBASSY
80 Strand Road (Box No. 638), Yangon
Tel: (00 95) (1)Yangon 295300
Ambassador Extraordinary and Plenipotentiary, HE Dr J Jenkins, LVO, apptd 1999

BRITISH COUNCIL DIRECTOR, C. Henning, OBE (*Cultural Attaché*), 78 Kanna Road, PO Box 638, Yangon; e-mail: admin@bc-burma.bcouncil.org

DEFENCE

The Army has some 100 main battle tanks and, 270 armoured personnel carriers. The Navy has 68 patrol and coastal vessels at six bases. The Air Force has 83 combat aircraft and 29 armed helicopters.
MILITARY EXPENDITURE – 6.8 per cent of GDP (1998)
MILITARY PERSONNEL – 429,000: Army 325,000, Navy 10,000, Air Force 9,000, Paramilitaries 85,250

ECONOMY

Agriculture remains the main sector of the economy, accounting for 58.5 per cent of GDP in 1997 and employing 63.4 per cent of the workforce; measures are being taken to increase productivity, promote crop diversification and increase agricultural exports. The chief products are rice, oilseeds (sesame and groundnut), maize, millet, cotton, beans, wheat, grain, tea, sugar cane, tobacco, jute and rubber.

Myanmar is rich in minerals, including petroleum, zinc, nickel, lead, silver, tungsten, wolfram and gemstones. Production of crude petroleum in 1998 totalled 1,177,000 tonnes. There are refineries at Chauk, the main oilfield, Syriam and Mann. Major reserves of natural gas have been discovered in the Martaban Gulf.

Since 1988, Myanmar has moved from a centrally planned economy to a market-oriented economy and has liberalised domestic and external trade, promoted the development of the private sector and encouraged foreign investment.

Myanmar is thought to be the world's leading producer of opium with an estimated annual output of 2,600 tons, although the government claimed to have destroyed 3,800 hectares of opium poppies between November 1998 and March 1999.

The principal exports are agricultural, forestry and fish products, minerals and precious stones. The principle imports are capital goods, chiefly transport equipment, machinery and plant, consumer goods and semi-manufactures.

In July 1997, Myanmar became a member of ASEAN. In 1997 the EU stripped Myanmar of trading privileges and the USA imposed economic sanctions.

In 1998 imports totalled US$2,666 million and exports US$1,067 million.

GDP – US$120,900 million (1996); US$2,633 per capita (1996)

ANNUAL AVERAGE GROWTH OF GDP – 5.8 per cent (1996)
INFLATION RATE – 51.5 per cent (1998)
TOTAL EXTERNAL DEBT – US$5,680 million (1998)

Trade with UK	1998	1999
Imports from UK	£12,571,000	£7,425,000
Exports to UK	17,278,000	23,835,000

COMMUNICATIONS

The Irrawaddy and its chief tributary, the Chindwin, are important waterways, the main stream being navigable 900 miles from its mouth and carrying much traffic. The chief seaports are Yangon (Rangoon), Mawlamyine (Moulmein), Akyab (Sittwe) and Pathein (Bassein).

The railway network covers 3,955 km, extending to Myitkyina on the Upper Irrawaddy. There are 2,452 miles of highways and 14,318 miles of other main roads. The airport at Mingaladon, about 13 miles north of Yangon (Rangoon), handles limited international air traffic.

EDUCATION

Most children attend primary school, and about six million are currently enrolled; in middle and high schools, enrolment is about two million. There are universities at Yangon (Rangoon), Mandalay, Taunggyi, Sagaing and Mawlamyine (Moulmein). Under the universities are three affiliated degree colleges and the Workers' College, Yangon.

Vocational training is provided at 17 teachers' training institutes and schools, 11 technical institutes, 17 technical high schools, 17 agricultural institutes and schools, and 41 vocational schools.

ILLITERACY RATE – 15.3 per cent
ENROLMENT (percentage of age group) – tertiary 5.4 per cent (1994)

NAMIBIA
The Republic of Namibia

AREA – 318,261 sq. miles (824,292 sq. km). Neighbours: Angola (north), South Africa (south), Botswana (east), Zambia and Zimbabwe (north-east)
POPULATION – 1,613,000 (1997 UN estimate). The main population groups are: Ovambo (587,000), Kavango (110,000), Damara (89,000), Herero (89,000), whites (78,000), Nama (57,000), coloured (48,000), Caprivians (44,000), Bushmen (34,000), Rehoboth Baster (29,000), Tswana (7,000). English is the official language, with Afrikaans, German and local languages also in use
CAPITAL – Windhoek (population, 147,056, 1995)
MAJOR TOWNS – Ondangwa (33,000); Oshakati (37,000); Rehoboth (21,500); Swakopmund (18,000); Walvis Bay (50,000), 1995

CURRENCY – Namibian dollar of 100 cents at parity to South African rand
NATIONAL ANTHEM – Namibia, land of the brave
NATIONAL DAY – 21 March (Independence Day)
NATIONAL FLAG – Divided diagonally blue, red and green with the red fimbriated in white; a gold twelve-rayed sun in the upper hoist
LIFE EXPECTANCY (years) – male 54.61; female 57.23
POPULATION GROWTH RATE – 2.5 per cent (1995)
POPULATION DENSITY – 2 per sq. km (1997)
URBAN POPULATION – 27.1 per cent (1991)
MILITARY EXPENDITURE – 3.6 per cent of GDP (1998)
MILITARY PERSONNEL – 9,100: Army 9,000, Coast Guard 100
ILLITERACY RATE – 17.9 per cent
ENROLMENT (percentage of age group) – primary 91 per cent (1996); secondary 36 per cent (1996); tertiary 8.1 per cent (1995)

HISTORY AND POLITICS

The German protectorate of South West Africa from 1884 to 1915, the territory was entrusted to South Africa by the 1919 Treaty of Versailles. The UN terminated South Africa's mandate in 1967.

An administrator-general was appointed in 1977 to govern the territory until independence; he began repealing all legislation based on racial discrimination. A transitional government was installed in 1985. Elections for 72 seats in Namibia's National Assembly took place under UN supervision on 7–11 November 1989. The South West Africa People's Organisation (SWAPO) won 41 seats. Independence was declared on 21 March 1990. Namibia joined the Commonwealth on independence.

Previously a British and South African colony separate from German South West Africa/Namibia, Walvis Bay was governed from August 1992 by the joint South African-Namibian Walvis Bay Administrative Body until 28 February 1994, when South Africa renounced its claim to sovereignty over the enclave and it became part of Namibia.

Presidential and legislative elections were held on 30 November–1 December 1999 and won by the incumbent, Sam Nujoma, and by SWAPO respectively. In the 72-seat National Assembly SWAPO has 55 seats, the Congress of Democrats and the Democratic Turnhalle Alliance 7 seats each, and other parties three seats.

INSURGENCIES

Government officials claimed to have uncovered a plot by Mishake Muyongo, a former leader of the opposition Democratic Turnhalle Alliance, and Mishake Boniface Mamili, a Mafwe chief, to launch a secessionist rebellion in the Caprivi strip in November 1998. An attempted uprising on 9 August 1999, believed to have been led by the Caprivi Liberation Army, was quickly quashed by government forces.

POLITICAL SYSTEM

Namibia has an executive president as head of state who exercises the functions of government with the assistance of a Cabinet headed by a prime minister. The president is directly elected for a maximum of two five-year terms. There is a bicameral legislature consisting of the 72-member National Assembly, elected for a five-year term, and the National Council, whose 26 members are indirectly elected by the regional councils from among their own members. The National Council is elected for a six-year term, and its main function is to review and consider legislation from the National Assembly. The constitution can only be changed by a two-thirds majority in the National Assembly.

HEAD OF STATE
President, Dr Sam Nujoma, *elected* 16 February 1990,
re-elected 8 December 1994, *re-elected* 1 December 1999

CABINET *as at July 2000*
Prime Minister, Hage Geingob
Deputy PM, Revd Hendrik Witbooi
Agriculture, Water and Rural Development,
    Helmut Angula
Attorney-General, Vekui Rukoro
Basic Education and Culture, John Mutorwa
Defence, Erikki Nghimtina
Environment and Tourism, Philemon Malima
Finance, Nangolo Mbumba
Fisheries and Marine Resources, Abraham Iyambo
Foreign Affairs, Theo-Ben Gurirab
Health and Social Services, Dr Libertine Amathila
Home Affairs, Jerry Ekandjo
Information and Broadcasting, Ben Amathila
Justice, Ngarikutuke Tjiriange
Labour and Manpower Development, Andimba
    Toivo ja Toivo
Lands, Resettlement, Rehabilitation, Pendukeni Ithana
Mines and Energy, Jesaya Nyamu
National Planning Council, Saara Kuugongelwa
Prisons and Correctional Services, Marco Hausiku
Regional and Local Government and Housing,
    Dr Nick Iyambo
Special Advisers, Gert Hanekom (*Economics*); Kanana
    Hishoono (*Political Matters*); Peter Tsheehama (*Security*)
Tertiary Education and Vocational Training, Nahas Angula
Trade and Industry, Hidipo Hamutenya
Without Portfolio, Hifikepunye Pohamba
Women's Affairs, Netumbo Ndaitwah
Works, Transport and Communication, Hampie Plichta
Youth and Sport, Richard Kapelwa-Kabajani

HIGH COMMISSION OF THE REPUBLIC OF NAMIBIA
6 Chandos Street, London W1M 0LQ
Tel: 020-7636 6244
High Commissioner, HE Monica Ndiliawike Nashandi,
    apptd 1999

BRITISH HIGH COMMISSION
116 Robert Mugabe Avenue, PO Box 22202, Windhoek
Tel: (00 264) (61) 223022
e-mail: bhc@iwwn.com.na
High Commissioner, HE Brian Donaldson, apptd 1999

BRITISH COUNCIL DIRECTOR, G. Belben, PO Box 24224,
    74 Bülowstrasse, Windhoek;
    e-mail: general.enquiries@britcoun.org.na

ECONOMY

Manufacturing contributes around 31 per cent of GDP,
with food production, metals and wooden products the
most important areas. Around 44 per cent of the population are engaged in agriculture, primarily livestock.
Guano is also exported. Deposits of diamonds along the
coast and offshore along the sea bed are estimated at
between 1,500 and 3,000 million carats; Namibia accounts
for roughly 8 per cent of world diamond production.
Walvis Bay and Lüderitz are the main ports. There are
41,815 km of roads, of which 4,572 km are surfaced; there
are 2,382 km of railway track.
    The principal imports are machinery and transport
equipment, foodstuffs, beverages and tobacco, and mineral fuels. The principal exports are diamonds and agricultural products.
    In 1998 there was a trade deficit of US$173 million and
a current account surplus of US$162 million. In 1994
imports totalled US$1,196 million and exports US$1,321
million.

GNP – US$3,217 million (1998); US$1,940 per capita
    (1998)
GDP – US$3,207 million (1996); US$2,036 per capita
    (1996)
ANNUAL AVERAGE GROWTH OF GDP – 2.6 per cent (1996)
INFLATION RATE – 8.8 per cent (1997)

Trade with UK	1998	1999
Imports from UK	£16,103,000	£16,172,000
Exports to UK	26,987,000	78,676,000

NAURU
The Republic of Nauru

AREA – 8 sq. miles (21 sq. km)
POPULATION – 11,000 (1997 UN estimate); 8,042 (1983
    census): Nauruans 4,964; other Pacific Islanders 2,134;
    Asians 682; Caucasians 262. About 43 per cent of
    Nauruans are adherents of the Nauruan Protestant
    Church and there is a Roman Catholic mission on the
    island. The main languages are English and Nauruan
CAPITAL – ΨNauru
CURRENCY – Australian dollar ($A) of 100 cents
NATIONAL DAY – 31 January (Independence Day)
NATIONAL FLAG – Twelve-point star (representing the
    12 original Nauruan tribes) below a gold bar
    (representing the Equator), all on a blue background
POPULATION GROWTH RATE – 1.4 per cent (1997)
POPULATION DENSITY – 524 per sq. km (1997)

HISTORY AND POLITICS

From 1888 until the First World War Nauru was
administered by Germany. In 1920 it became a British
Empire-mandated territory under the League of Nations,
administered by Australia. A trusteeship superseding the
mandate was approved in 1947 by the UN and Nauru
continued to be administered by Australia until it became
independent on 31 January 1968. Rene Harris was elected
president in April 1999 after his predecessor, Bernard
Dowiyogo, lost a vote of confidence. Harris resigned on
20 April 2000 and Dowiyogo was re-elected president on
24 April 2000. Nauru became a full member of the
Commonwealth on 1 May 1999; it had been an associate
member since 1968.

POLITICAL SYSTEM

Parliament has 18 members including the Cabinet and
Speaker. Voting is compulsory for all Nauruans over
20 years of age, except in certain specified instances. Elections are held every three years. The Cabinet is chosen by
the president, who is elected by the parliament from
amongst its members, and comprises not fewer than five
nor more than six members including the president.
    A Supreme Court of Nauru is presided over by the Chief
Justice. The District Court, which is subordinate to the
Supreme Court, is presided over by a Resident Magistrate.
Both the Supreme Court and the District Court are courts
of record. The Supreme Court exercises both original and
appellate jurisdiction.

HEAD OF STATE

President, Public Service, Foreign Affairs, Health,
    Island Development and Industry, the Nauru Phosphate
    Royalties Trust and the Republic of Nauru Finance
    Corporation, Bernard Dowiyogo, *elected by parliament*
    24 April 2000

CABINET *as at September 2000*
The President
Education and Vocational Training, Youth Development,
    Remy Namaduk

Home Affairs and Culture, Health, Women's Affairs,
Kinza Clodumar
Industry and Economic Development, Civil Aviation and
Transport, Anthony Audoa
Justice, Nauru Police Force, Customs and Immigration,
Vassal Gadoengin
Works, Planning and Housing Development, Sports,
Derog Gioura

BRITISH HIGH COMMISSIONER, HE Michael Dibben,
resident at Suva, Fiji

ECONOMY

The only fertile areas are in the narrow coastal belt and
local requirements of fruit and vegetables are mostly met
by imports. The economy is heavily dependent on the
extraction of phosphate, of which the island has one of the
world's richest deposits. In 1997, 541,050 tonnes of
phosphate rock was exported. Considerable investments
have been made abroad with the royalties on phosphate
exports to provide for a time when production declines. In
1993 an agreement was signed with Australia for
compensation to cover damage caused by phosphate
mining during the Australian mandate and trusteeship
periods. The compensation package is worth some £50
million (a portion of which will be paid by the UK and
New Zealand governments), composed of a £33 million
payment and a 20-year package of health and education
programmes.

Air Nauru operates air services throughout the Pacific
region and to Australia, New Zealand, Japan, Singapore
and the Philippines.

GDP – US$562 million (1996); US$51,053 per capita
(1996)
ANNUAL AVERAGE GROWTH OF GDP – 6.0 per cent
(1996)

Trade with UK	1998	1999
Imports from UK	£1,251,000	£1,464,000
Exports to UK	90,000	53,000

SOCIAL WELFARE

Nauru has a hospital service and other medical and dental
services. There is also a maternity and child welfare
service.

Education is compulsory between the ages of six and 17.
There are 10 infant and primary and two secondary
schools on the island with a total enrolment of about 2,707
pupils.

NEPAL

AREA – 56,827 sq. miles (147,181 sq. km). Neighbours:
China (north), India (south, west and east)
POPULATION – 22,591,000 (1997 UN estimate). The
inhabitants are of mixed stock, with Tibetan charac-
teristics prevailing in the north and Indian in the south.
The official religion is Hinduism; 87 per cent of the
population are Hindus, 8 per cent Buddhist and
3 per cent Muslim. Gautama Buddha was born in
Nepal. The official language is Nepali
CAPITAL – Kathmandu (population, 421,258, 1991)
MAJOR CITIES – Bhadgaon (61,122); Biratnagar (130,129);
Patan (117,023), 1991
CURRENCY – Nepalese rupee of 100 paisa
NATIONAL ANTHEM – Sri man gumbhira Nepali
prachanda pratapi bhupati (May Glory Crown
Our Illustrious Sovereign, the gallant Nepalese)
NATIONAL DAYS – 18 February (National Democracy
Day); 28 December (The King's Birthday)

NATIONAL FLAG – Double pennant of crimson with blue
border on peaks; white moon with rays in centre of top
peak; white quarter sun, recumbent in centre of bottom
peak
LIFE EXPECTANCY (years) – male 50.88; female 48.10
POPULATION GROWTH RATE – 3.2 per cent (1997)
POPULATION DENSITY – 153 per sq. km (1997)
URBAN POPULATION – 9.2 per cent (1991)
MILITARY EXPENDITURE – 0.7 per cent of GDP (1998)
MILITARY PERSONNEL – 86,000: Army 46,000,
Paramilitaries 40,000
ILLITERACY RATE – 58.6 per cent
ENROLMENT (percentage of age group) – tertiary
58.6 per cent (1996)

Nepal lies between India and the Tibet Autonomous
Region of China on the slopes of the Himalayas, and
includes Mount Everest (29,028 ft).

The southern region, the Terai, was covered with
jungle but has been more widely cultivated recently. It
forms about 23 per cent of the total land area and nearly
44 per cent of the population live there. The central belt
is hilly, but with many fertile valleys, leading up to the
snowline at about 16,000 feet. The hills account for 42 per
cent of the area and about 48 per cent of the population.
The remainder of the country, the Himalayan region,
consists of high mountains which are sparsely inhabited.
The country is drained by three great river systems rising
within and beyond the Himalayan mountain ranges and
eventually flowing into the Ganges in India.

HISTORY AND POLITICS

Nepal was originally divided into numerous hill clans
and petty principalities but emerged as a nation in the
middle of the 18th century when it was unified by the
warrior Raja of Gorkha, Prithvi Narayan Shah, who
founded the present Nepalese dynasty. In 1846 power was
seized by Jung Bahadur Rana after a massacre of nobles,
and he was the first of a line of hereditary Rana prime
ministers who ruled Nepal for 104 years. During this
time the role of the monarchs was mainly ceremonial.

In 1950–1 a revolutionary movement broke the hereditary power of the Ranas and restored the monarchy to
its former position. King Mahendra proscribed all political parties and assumed direct powers in 1960. In 1962
he introduced a new constitution embodying a tiered,
partyless system of panchyat (council) democracy.

Mass agitation for political reform led in April 1990
to the abolition of the panchyat system. A new constitution was promulgated in November 1990 establishing a
multiparty, parliamentary system of government and a
constitutional monarchy. Elections in May 1991 were won
by the Nepali Congress Party.

In October 1997 the government was brought down by
a vote of no confidence and several coalition governments ruled until a general election held on 3 and 17 May
1999 gave an absolute majority to the Nepali Congress
Party (NCP) who won 110 seats.

Prime Minister Krishna Prasad Bhattarai resigned on
16 March 2000, after a motion of no confidence in him was
signed by 58 NCP members in February and a day before
a vote was to be held in the House of Representatives on a
motion of no confidence signed by 69 NCP members;
he was replaced on 20 March by Girija Prasad Koirala.

INSURGENCIES

Maoist guerrillas from the Communist Party of Nepal,
who are opposed to the monarchy, began an armed
rebellion in 1996; they organised a campaign to boycott
the general election in May 1999 which involved strikes
and attacks on government and industrial targets. In
November 1999, the government offered an amnesty to
the guerrillas if they agreed to abandon violence and enter
into dialogue with the government.

POLITICAL SYSTEM

The King retains joint executive power with the Council of Ministers. The bicameral legislature consists of a 205-member House of Representatives and a 60-member National Council, including ten royal nominees.

HEAD OF STATE

HM The King of Nepal, King Birendra Bir Bikram Shah Dev, *born* 28 December 1945; *succeeded* 31 January 1972; *crowned* 24 February 1975; *married* February 1970, HM Queen Aishwatya Rajya Laxmi Devi Shah
Heir, HRH Crown Prince Dipendra Bir Bikram Shah Dev, *born* 27 June 1971

CABINET *as at September 2000*
Prime Minister, Defence, General Administration, Royal Palace Affairs, Women, Children and Social Welfare, Labour and Transport Managment, Girija Prasad Koirala
Deputy Prime Minister, Local Development, Ram Chandra Paudyel
Education and Sports, Tarini Dutta Chataut
Finance, Mahesh Acharya
Foreign Affairs, Chakara Prasad Bastola
Health, Ram Baran Yadav
Home Affairs, Govinda Raj Joshi
Industries, Commerce and Supplies, Ram Krishna Tamrakar
Information and Communications, Jaya Prakash Guptam
Land Reforms and Management, Sidha Raj Ojha
Law, Justice and Parliamentary Affairs, Mahanta Thakur
Ministers of State, Bal Dev Sharma Majgaiya (*Agriculture and Co-operatives*); Dilendra Prasad Badu (*Education and Sports*); Mohammad Aftab Allam (*Forest and Soil Conservation*); Tirtha Ram Dangol (*Health*); Narendra Bikram Nemwang (*Industries, Commerce and Supplies*); Surendra Hamal (*Labour and Transport Management*); Gopal Rai (*Land Reform and Management*); Suresh Malla (*Local Development*); Shiva Raj Joshi (*Population and Environment*); Ram Bahadur Gurung (*Water Resources*); Kamal Pant (*Women, Children and Social Welfare*)
Science and Technology, Surendra Prasad Chaudhary
Water Resources, Labour and Transport Management, vacant

ROYAL NEPALESE EMBASSY
12A Kensington Palace Gardens, London W8 4QU
Tel: 020-7229 1594/6231/5352
Ambassador Extraordinary and Plenipotentiary,
HE Dr Singha B. Basnyat, apptd 1997

BRITISH EMBASSY
Lainchaur Kathmandu, PO Box 106
Tel: (00 977) (1) 410583/411281/414588
e-mail: britemb@wlink.com.np
Ambassador Extraordinary and Plenipotentiary,
HE R. P. Nash, LVO, apptd 1999

BRITISH COUNCIL DIRECTOR, B. Wickham,
(PO Box 640), Kantipath, Kathmandu;
e-mail: bcnepal@bc-nepal.wlink.com.np

ECONOMY

In 1997, 93.3 per cent of the workforce were engaged in agriculture, which generated 41.6 per cent of GDP. The main exports are carpets, textiles and clothing, hides, jute, handicrafts and agricultural products. The main imports are machinery and transport equipment, and chemical and pharmaceutical products. Tourism is the single largest commercial earner of foreign exchange; 407,300 foreign tourists visited Nepal in 1997. Nepal's main trading partners are India, Germany and the USA.

In 1998 Nepal had a trade deficit of US$748 million and a current account deficit of US$58 million. Imports totalled US$1,239 million and exports US$474 million.

GNP – US$4,889 million (1998); US$210 per capita (1998)
GDP – US$4,408 million (1996); US$200 per capita (1996)
ANNUAL AVERAGE GROWTH OF GDP – 3.9 per cent (1997)
INFLATION RATE – 10.0 per cent (1998)
TOTAL EXTERNAL DEBT – US$2,646 million (1998)

Trade with UK	1998	1999
Imports from UK	£8,745,000	£6,988,000
Exports to UK	4,211,000	11,099,000

COMMUNICATIONS

The total length of roads is 9,933km, of which 3,421 km are paved. Kathmandu is connected by road with India and Tibet. Internally, the road network links Kathmandu to Kodari and Pokhara, and Pokhara to Sunauli. There are 155 km of railway track.

Royal Nepal Airlines operates an extensive network of domestic flights, and there are international flights to Europe, the Middle East and throughout Asia. There is an international airport at Kathmandu.

Telecommunication services, both domestic and international, are available. Television was introduced in 1984.

THE NETHERLANDS
Koninkrijk der Nederlanden

AREA – 15,770 sq. miles (41,526 sq. km). Neighbours: Belgium (south), Germany (east)
POPULATION – 15,604,000 (1997): 36 per cent Catholic, 27 per cent Reformed Church, 8 per cent Muslim. The language is Dutch, a West Germanic language of Frankish origin closely akin to Old English and Low German. It is spoken in the Netherlands and the northern part of Belgium (Flanders). Frisian is spoken in Friesland. Dutch is the official language in the Netherlands Antilles and Aruba; Papiamento, a mixture of Dutch and Spanish, is the vernacular
CAPITAL – ΨAmsterdam (population, 1,102,323, 1997 estimate)
SEAT OF GOVERNMENT – The Hague (Den Haag or, in full, 's-Gravenhage), population 694,572, 1995 estimate
MAJOR CITIES – Eindhoven (396,986); Groningen (210,101); Haarlem (211,885); ΨRotterdam (1,077,813); Tilburg (238,301); Utrecht (547,767), 1995 estimates
CURRENCY – Euro (€) of 100 cents/Gulden (guilder) or florin of 100 cents
NATIONAL ANTHEM – Wilhelmus van Nassouwe (William of Nassau)
NATIONAL FLAG – Three horizontal bands of red, white and blue
LIFE EXPECTANCY (years) – male 74.52; female 80.20
POPULATION GROWTH RATE – 0.6 per cent (1997)
POPULATION DENSITY – 376 per sq. km (1997)
URBAN POPULATION – 61.0 per cent (1996)

The Kingdom of the Netherlands is a maritime country of western Europe, situated on the North Sea, consisting of 12 provinces (Eastern and Southern Flevoland being amalgamated to form the twelfth province). The land is generally flat and low, intersected by numerous canals and connecting rivers. The principal rivers are the Rhine, Maas, IJssel and Schelde.

HISTORY AND POLITICS

The country was fragmented until the 16th century when, led by William (the Silent) of Orange, the Low Countries

1968; Prince Constantijn Christof, *b*. 11 October 1969
Heir, HRH Prince Willem Alexander, *b*. 27 April 1967

CABINET *as at September 2000*
Prime Minister, General Affairs, Wim Kok (PvdA)
Deputy PM, Economic Affairs, Annemarie Jorritsma-Lebbink (VVD)
Deputy PM, Health, Welfare and Sport, Dr Els Borst-Eilers (D66)
Agriculture, Nature Management and Fisheries, Laurens-Jan Brinkhorst (D66)
Defence, Frank de Grave (VVD)
Development Co-operation, Evelien Herfkens (PvdA)
Education, Cultural Affairs and Science, Loek Hermans (VVD)
Finance, Gerrit Zalm (VVD)
Foreign Affairs, Jozias van Aartsen (VVD)
Housing, Spatial Planning and Environment, Jan Pronk (PvdA)
Interior and Kingdom Relations, Klaas de Vries (PvdA)
Justice, Benk Korthals (VVD)
Major Cities and Integration Policy, Roger van Boxtel (D66)
Social Affairs and Employment, Willem VermeendKlaas de Vries (PvdA)
Transport and Public Works and Water Management, Tineke Netelenbos (PvdA)

VVD–People's Party for Freedom and Democracy;
D66–Democrats 66; PvdA–Labour Party

ROYAL NETHERLANDS EMBASSY
38 Hyde Park Gate, London SW7 5DP
Tel: 020-7590 3200
Ambassador Extraordinary and Plenipotentiary, HE Baron Willem Oswald Bentinck van Schoonheten, apptd 1999
Minister Plenipotentiary, G. C. M. van Pallandt
Consul-General, P. W. A. Bas Backer
Defence, Naval and Air Attaché, Capt. W. T. Lansink
First Secretaries (Economic Affairs), K. Huisman; T. Koster

BRITISH EMBASSY
Lange Voorhout 10, The Hague, NL-2514 ED
Tel: (00 31) (70) 427 0427
Ambassador Extraordinary and Plenipotentiary,
    HE Rosemary Spencer, CMG, apptd 1996
Counsellors, T. C. Holmes (*Deputy Head of Mission*);
    C. Bradley (*Commercial and Consul-General*);
    W. Jackson-Houlston, OBE
Defence and Naval Attaché, Capt. R. St J. S. Bishop, RN

CONSULATE-GENERAL – Amsterdam
CONSULATE – Willemstad (Curaçao); Vice-Consulate –
    Philipsburg (St Maarten) (both Netherlands Antilles)

BRITISH COUNCIL DIRECTOR, T. Butchard, Keizersgracht
    269, NL-1016 ED Amsterdam;
    e-mail: bc.amsterdam@britcoun.nl

NETHERLANDS – BRITISH CHAMBER OF COMMERCE,
    The Dutch House, 307–308 High Holborn, London
    WC1V 7LS

UK OFFICE IN THE HAGUE, Holland Trade House,
    Bezuidenhoutseweg 181, NL-2594 AH The Hague

DEFENCE

The Army has 359 main battle tanks, 448 armoured infantry fighting vehicles and 269 armoured personnel carriers. The Navy has four submarines, four destroyers, 12 frigates, 13 combat aircraft and 22 armed helicopters. The Air Force has 170 combat aircraft and 42 armed helicopters.
MILITARY EXPENDITURE – 1.8 per cent of GDP (1998)
MILITARY PERSONNEL – 56,380: Army 27,000, Navy

fought the Eighty Years' War (1568–1648) against Spanish rule. The Union of Utrecht (1579) united the northern provinces and in 1581 independence was declared. Dutch economic and military power flourished in the 17th and 18th centuries.

The Netherlands were overrun by French Revolutionary troops in the late 18th century, becoming part of the French Empire until 1814, when the northern and southern Netherlands were united into one kingdom. In 1830 the southern provinces seceded to form Belgium. The Duchy of Luxembourg was made an independent state in 1867.

The Netherlands remained neutral during the First World War but were invaded by Germany during the Second World War and occupied until the war ended. The Netherlands joined the Benelux economic union with Belgium and Luxembourg in 1948 and became a member of NATO in 1949. The Dutch East Indies gained independence as Indonesia in 1949.

The most recent election to the Second Chamber was held on 6 May 1998 and resulted in a centre-left coalition of the Labour Party, People's Party for Freedom and Democracy, and Democrats 66. The state of the parties as at May 1998 was: Labour Party (PvdA) 45; People's Party for Freedom and Democracy (VVD) 38; Christian Democratic Appeal (CDA) 29; Democrats 66 (D66) 14; Green Left 11; others 13.

POLITICAL SYSTEM

The States-General consists of the *Eerste Kamer* (First Chamber) of 75 members, elected for four years by the Provincial Council; and the *Tweede Kamer* (Second Chamber) of 150 members, elected for four years by voters of 18 years and upwards. Members of the *Tweede Kamer* are paid.

HEAD OF STATE

HM *The Queen of the Netherlands*, Queen Beatrix Wilhelmina Armgard, KG, GCVO, *born* 31 January 1938; *succeeded* 30 April 1980, upon the abdication of her mother Queen Juliana; *married* 10 March 1966, HRH Prince Claus George Willem Otto Frederik Geert of the Netherlands, Jonkheer van Amsberg; and has *issue*, Prince Willem; Prince Johan Friso, *b*. 25 September

13,800, Air Force 11,980, Paramilitaries 3,600
CONSCRIPTION DURATION – abolished in August 1996

ECONOMY

The chief agricultural products are potatoes, wheat, rye, barley, sugar beet, cattle, poultry, pigs, dairy products, vegetables, fruit, flower bulbs, plants and cut flowers and there is an important fishing industry.

Among the principal industries are engineering, electronics, nuclear energy, petrochemicals and plastics, road vehicles, aircraft and defence equipment, shipbuilding repair, steel, textiles of all types, electrical appliances, metal ware, furniture, paper, cigars, sugar, liqueurs, beer, clothing etc.

The majority of the workforce, 64 per cent, are engaged in service industries.
GNP – US$389,055 million (1998); US$24,780 per capita (1998)
GDP – US$396,014 million (1996); US$25,426 per capita (1996)
ANNUAL AVERAGE GROWTH OF GDP – 3.7 per cent (1997)
INFLATION RATE – 2.0 per cent (1998)
UNEMPLOYMENT – 4.4 per cent (1998)

TRADE
The Dutch are traditionally a trading nation. Trade, banking and shipping are of particular importance to the economy. The Netherlands is the sixth largest exporter and third largest agricultural exporter in the world. The geographical position of the Netherlands, at the mouths of the Rhine, Maas and Schelde, brings a large volume of transit trade to and from the interior of Europe to Dutch ports. Principal trading partners are Germany, Belgium/Luxembourg, the UK and France.

In 1997 the Netherlands had a trade surplus of US$18,994 million and a current account surplus of US$27,684 million. In 1998, imports totalled US$185,104 million and exports US$199,624 million.

Trade with UK	1998	1999
Imports from UK	£12,237,700,000	£12,711,000,000
Exports to UK	12,858,800,000	12,705,400,000

COMMUNICATIONS

There are 58,133 km of inter-urban roads, of which 2,207 km are motorways. The total extent of navigable rivers including canals is 5,046 km. The total length of the railway system is 2,739 km, of which 1,991 km are electrified. The mercantile marine in 1996 consisted of 379 ships of total 2,795,000 gross registered tons.

There are 64 daily newspapers.

EDUCATION

Primary and secondary education is given in both denominational and state schools and is compulsory.

The principal universities are at Leiden, Utrecht, Groningen, Amsterdam (two), Nijmegen, Maastricht and Rotterdam, and there are technical universities at Delft, Eindhoven, Enschede and Wageningen (agriculture).
ENROLMENT (percentage of age group) – primary 100 per cent (1996); secondary 90 per cent (1996); tertiary 47 per cent (1996)

OVERSEAS TERRITORIES

ARUBA

AREA – 75 sq. miles (193 sq. km)
POPULATION – 71,000 (1997)
CAPITAL – ΨOranjestad (population 25,000);
   and Sint Nicolaas (17,000)
CURRENCY – Aruban florin

The island of Aruba was from 1828 part of the Dutch West Indies and from 1845 part of the Netherlands Antilles. On 1 January 1986 it became a separate territory within the Kingdom of the Netherlands. The 1983 Constitutional Conference agreed that Aruba's separate status would last for ten years from 1986, after which the island would become fully independent. In 1994 this decision was changed and it was decided that Aruba will retain its separate status within the Kingdom of the Netherlands.

Governor, Olindo Koolman
Prime Minister, J. H. Eman

Trade with UK	1998	1999
Imports from UK	£56,033,000	£45,616,000
Exports to UK	682,000	13,899,000

NETHERLANDS ANTILLES

AREA – 309 sq. miles (800 sq. km)
POPULATION – 207,333 (1995), Curaçao 151,448, Bonaire 14,218, St Maarten 38,567, St Eustatius 1,900, Saba 1,200
CAPITAL – ΨWillemstad (on Curaçao) (pop. 50,000)
CURRENCY – Netherlands Antilles guilder of 100 cents

The Netherlands Antilles comprise the islands of Curaçao, Bonaire, part of St Maarten, St Eustatius, and Saba in the West Indies. The Netherlands Antilles, which have a 22-member federal parliament, are largely self-governing under the terms of the Realm Statute which took effect in 1954. The part of St Maarten belonging to the Netherlands voted in a non-binding referendum held on 23 June 2000 to secede from the Netherlands Antilles and become an independent state within the Kingdom of the Netherlands. This was rejected by the government of the Netherlands, which did not believe that St Maarten was large enough to be a viable state, but discussions on its future status continue.

Governor, Dr Jaime Saleh
Prime Minister, S. F. Camelia-Römer

Trade with UK	1998*	1999*
Imports from UK	£25,697,000	£40,500,000
Exports to UK	3,047,000	1,603,000

*Curaçuao

NEW ZEALAND

AREA – 104,454 sq. miles (270,534 sq. km)
POPULATION – 3,811,000 (1999 estimate): 79 per cent European stock, 13 per cent Māori, 5 per cent other Pacific Islanders. The main religion is Christianity. In 1991 the principal denominations were Anglican 22.1 per cent, Presbyterian 16.3 per cent, Roman Catholic 15 per cent, Methodist 4.2 per cent, Baptist 2.1 per cent. The official languages are English and Māori.

Islands	Area (sq. miles)	Population (census 1996)
North Island	44,281	2,749,788
South Island	58,093	930,824
Other islands	1,362	934
Total	103,736	3,681,546
Territories		
Tokelau	5	1,487
Niue	100	1,708 (a)
Cook Islands	93	18,008
Ross Dependency	175,000	—

(a) 1997 estimate

CAPITAL – ΨWellington (population, 346,700, 1999 estimate)
MAJOR CITIES – ΨAuckland (1,090,400); ΨChristchurch (341,000); ΨDunedin (112,000); Hamilton (169,100); Ψ Napier-Hastings (114,900), 1999 estimates
CURRENCY – New Zealand dollar (NZ$) of 100 cents
NATIONAL ANTHEM – God Save The Queen/God Defend New Zealand
NATIONAL DAY – 6 February (Waitangi Day)
NATIONAL FLAG – Blue ground, with Union Flag in top left quarter, four five-pointed red stars with white borders on the fly
LIFE EXPECTANCY (years) – male 73.44; female 79.11
POPULATION GROWTH RATE – 1.6 per cent (1997)
POPULATION DENSITY – 14 per sq. km (1997)
URBAN POPULATION – 85.4 per cent (1996)

New Zealand consists of a number of islands in the South Pacific Ocean, and also has administrative responsibility for the Ross Dependency in Antarctica. The two larger islands, North Island and South Island, are separated by a relatively narrow strait. The remaining islands are much smaller and widely dispersed.

Much of the North and South Islands is mountainous. The principal range is the Southern Alps, extending the entire length of the South Island and having its culminating point in Mount Cook/Mount Aoraki (3,754 m/12,349 ft). The North Island mountains include several volcanoes, two of which are active. Of the numerous glaciers in the South Island, the Tasman (18 miles long by 1 wide), the Franz Josef and the Fox are the best known. The more important rivers include the Waikato (425 km/270 miles in length), Wanganui (180 miles), and Clutha (210 miles) and lakes include Taupo, 234 sq. miles in area; Wakatipu, 113; and Te Anau, 133.

New Zealand includes, in addition to North and South Islands: Chatham Islands (Chatham, Pitt, South East Islands and some rocky islets, combined area, 965 sq. km (373 sq. miles), largely uninhabited); Stewart Island (area 1,746 sq. km (674 sq. miles), largely uninhabited); the Kermadec Group (Raoul or Sunday, Macaulay, Curtis Islands, L'Esperance, and some islets; population 9–10, all government employees at a meteorological station); Campbell Island, used as a weather station; the Three Kings (discovered by Tasman on the Feast of the Epiphany); Auckland Islands; Antipodes Group; Bounty Islands; Snares Islands and Solander.

New Zealand has a temperate marine climate, but with abundant sunshine. The mean temperature ranges from 15°C in the north to about 9°C in the south. Rainfall in the North Island ranges from 35 to 70 inches and in the South Island from 25 to 45 inches.

HISTORY AND POLITICS

The discoverers and first colonists of New Zealand were Polynesian people, ancestors of the modern-day Māori. The ninth century is generally considered to be the date of the first settlement; by the 13th or 14th century there were well-established settlements. The first European to discover New Zealand was a Dutch navigator, Abel Tasman, who sighted the coast in 1642 but did not land. It was the British explorer James Cook who circumnavigated New Zealand and landed in 1769. Largely as a result of increased British emigration, the country was annexed by the British government in 1840. The British Lieutenant-Governor, William Hobson, proclaimed sovereignty over the North Island by virtue of the Treaty of Waitangi, signed by him and many Māori chiefs, and over the South Island and Stewart Island by right of discovery.

In 1841 New Zealand was created a separate colony distinct from New South Wales. In 1907 the designation was changed to 'The Dominion of New Zealand'. The constitution rests upon the Constitution Act 1852 and other imperial statutes. A 1986 Constitution Act brought a number of statutory constitutional provisions. The Statute of Westminster was formally adopted by New Zealand in 1947.

Following the general election of 27 November 1999, the state of the parties in the House of Representatives was: Labour Party (LP) 49 seats, National Party 39, Alliance Party (AP) 10, Association of Consumers and Tax Payers 9, Green Party 7, New Zealand First 5, United Party 1. The Labour Party and the Alliance Party formed a minority administration with the support of the Green Party.

POLITICAL SYSTEM

The executive authority is entrusted to a Governor-General appointed by the Crown and aided by an Executive Council, within a unicameral legislature, the House of Representatives. The House of Representatives consists of 120 members elected for three-year terms. In the current parliament, 67 members were elected by the first-past-the-post system, of which six represented Māori electorates, and 53 by proportional representation on a party list basis. A referendum, held simultaneously with the general election in November 1999, approved a reduction in the number of members to 99 in future parliaments.

The judicial system comprises a High Court, a Court of Appeal and district courts having both civil and criminal jurisdiction.

GOVERNOR-GENERAL

Governor-General and Commander-in-Chief, HE Sir Michael Hardie Boys, KCMG, *sworn in* March 1996
from March 2001: HE Dame Silvia Cartwright

THE EXECUTIVE COUNCIL *as at September 2000*
The Governor-General
Prime Minister, Arts, Culture and Heritage, Helen Clark (LP)
Deputy PM, Economic Development, Industry, Regional Development, Jim Anderton (AP)
Agriculture, Trade Negotiations, Jim Sutton (LP)
Attorney-General, Labour, Treaty of Waitangi Negotiations, Margaret Wilson (LP)
Commerce, Communications, Information Technology, Land Information, Statistics, Paul Swain (LP)
Conservation, Local Government, Sandra Lee (AP)
Corrections, Courts, Disarmament and Arms Control, Matt Robson (AP)
Defence, Internal Affairs, State-owned Enterprises, Tourism, Veterans' Affairs, Mark Burton (LP)
Education, State Services, Sport, Fitness and Leisure, Trevor Mallard (LP)
Energy, Fisheries, Forestry, Research, Science and Technology, Crown Research Institutes, Pete Hodgson (LP)
Environment, Biosecurity, Broadcasting, Marian Hobbs (LP)
Foreign Affairs and Trade, Justice, Phil Goff (LP)
Health, Annette King (LP)
Immigration, Senior Citizens, Lianne Dalziel (LP)
Māori Affairs, Parekura Horomia
Police, Civil Defence, Ethnic Affairs, George Hawkins (LP)
Social Services, Employment, Steve Maharey (LP)
Transport, Housing, Pacific Island Affairs, Mark Gosche (LP)
Treasurer, Finance, Accident Insurance, Revenue, Michael Cullen (LP)
Women's Affairs, Youth Affairs, Laila Harré (AP)

NEW ZEALAND HIGH COMMISSION
New Zealand House, Haymarket, London SW1Y 4TQ
Tel: 020-7930 8422
High Commissioner, HE Paul Clayton East, QC, apptd 1999
Deputy High Commissioner, C. J. Seed
Minister, J. Waugh (*Commercial*)
Head, Defence Staff, Brig. R. Ottaway, MBE

BRITISH HIGH COMMISSION
44 Hill Street (PO Box 1812), Wellington 1
Tel: (00 64) (4) 472 6049

E-mail: bhc.wel@xtra.co.nz
High Commissioner, HE Martin Williams, CVO, OBE, apptd 1998
Deputy High Commissioner, C. H. Salvesen
Defence Adviser, Capt. D. A. Wines, RN
First Secretary, R. L. Foxwell (*Economic/Commercial*)
Consul-General and Director of Trade Promotion,
    T. N. Byrne; resident at Auckland

CONSULATE-GENERAL – Auckland
CONSULATE – Christchurch

BRITISH COUNCIL DIRECTOR, P. Atkins, c/o British High Commission; E-mail: enquiries@britishcouncil.org.nz. Regional office in Auckland

BRITISH CHAMBER OF COMMERCE FOR AUSTRALIA AND NEW ZEALAND, PO Box 141, Manuka, ACT 2603, Australia; UK OFFICE, Suite 615, 6th Floor, The Linen Hall, 162–168 Regent Street, London W1R 5TB

DEFENCE

The Army has 72 armoured personnel carriers. The Navy has three frigates, four patrol and coastal vessels and four armed helicopters. The Air Force has 42 combat aircraft.
MILITARY EXPENDITURE – 1.5 per cent of GDP (1998)
MILITARY PERSONNEL – 9,530: Army 4,400, Navy 2,080,
    Air Force 3,050

ECONOMY

Finance market and labour market deregulation, privatisation, VAT reform, the introduction of private sector principles in the civil service, health service and education, the ending of agricultural subsidies and the near elimination of import tariffs have all occurred. The Reserve Bank has been made independent, with a contract to keep inflation below 2 per cent.   Agricultural production is dominated by cattle- and sheep-rearing, for meat, wool, dairy products and other by-products, such as skins, leather, etc. Timber and wood pulp are also important.

Non-metallic minerals such as coal, clay, limestone and dolomite are more important than metallic ones. Coal output in 1997 was 3,664,034 tonnes. Of the metals, the most important are gold and ironsand. Natural gas deposits in the offshore Taranaki Maui field and onshore fields are increasingly being exploited and used for electricity generation and as a premium fuel. Energy use is dominated by oil (46 per cent), electricity (26 per cent), coal and gas (9 per cent each).

Manufacturing is based on food processing, machinery production, motor vehicle assembly, chemicals, electrical and electronic goods, and paper and printing. Tourism is the fastest growing sector of the economy, with 1,539,230 visitors in 1999.

In 1998 New Zealand had a trade surplus of US$923 million and a current account deficit of US$3,192 million.
GNP – US$55,356 million (1998); US$14,600 per capita
    (1998)
GDP – US$65,883 million (1996); US$18,291 per capita
    (1996)
ANNUAL AVERAGE GROWTH OF GDP – 2.4 per cent (1996)
INFLATION RATE – 1.2 per cent (1998)
UNEMPLOYMENT – 7.5 per cent (1998)

TRADE

New Zealand's largest trading partners are Australia, the USA, Japan, and the UK. Main exports include dairy products, meat, timber, fish, fruits and nuts, machinery and aluminium products. Imports include machinery, vehicles, petroleum and petroleum products, textiles, plastics and aircraft. In 1998 imports totalled US$12,496 million and exports US$12,070 million.

Trade with UK	1998*	1999*
Imports from UK	£348,078,000	£325,255,000
Exports to UK	542,427,000	591,058,000

*Includes Niue, Tokelau and Cook Islands

COMMUNICATIONS

The national railway system is owned and operated by the privately-owned Tranz Rail Ltd. There are 4,439 km of railway track .

In December 1995 there were 2,977 ships registered in New Zealand (gross tonnage 482,180).

There are international airports at Auckland, Christchurch and Wellington. Air New Zealand is the national carrier.

There are 91,864 km of maintained roads.

EDUCATION

Schools are free and attendance is compulsory between the ages of six and 15. There are 2,240 state and 61 private primary schools and 320 state secondary schools. There are seven universities and 25 polytechnics.
ENROLMENT (percentage of age group) – primary
    100 per cent (1997); secondary 90 per cent (1997);
    tertiary 63 per cent (1997)

TERRITORIES

TOKELAU (OR UNION ISLANDS)

Tokelau is a group of atolls, Fakaofo, Nukunonu and Atafu. It was proclaimed part of New Zealand as from 1 January 1949. A Council of Faipule, composed of one elected representative from each atoll, was established in August 1992 to govern Tokelau when the council of elders (General Fono) was not in session. The position of *Ulu-o-Tokelau* (leader) was also established in 1992 and is rotated among the three Faipule members annually. Administrative responsibility for Tokelau lies with the Administrator but in January 1994 his powers were delegated to the General Fono and Council of Faipule. The Tokelau Amendment Act, passed by the New Zealand Parliament in 1996, conferred legislative power on the General Fono. New Zealand provides substantial aid (NZ$6.5 million in year ended 30 June 2000).

Administrator, Lindsay Watt
Ulu-o-Tokelau (2000), Kolouei O'Brien

THE ROSS DEPENDENCY

The Ross Dependency, placed under the jurisdiction of New Zealand in 1923, is defined as all the Antarctic islands and territories between 160° E. and 150° W. longitude which are situated south of the 60° S. parallel, including Edward VII Land and portions of Victoria Land. Since 1957 a number of research stations have been established in the Dependency.

ASSOCIATED STATES

COOK ISLANDS

Included in the realm of New Zealand since June 1901, the Cook Islands group consists of the islands of Rarotonga, Aitutaki, Mangaia, Atiu, Mauke, Mitiaro, Manuae, Takutea, Palmerston, Penrhyn or Tongareva, Manihiki, Rakahanga, Suwarrow, Pukapuka or Danger, and Nassau. The population is mainly Māori; English and Cook Island Māori are the principal languages spoken.

Queen Elizabeth II has a representative on the islands, and there is a New Zealand High Commissioner. Since 1965 the islands have been in free association with New Zealand and enjoyed complete internal self-government, executive power being in the hands of a Cabinet consisting of a prime minister and eight other ministers. There is a

25-member Legislative Assembly. New Zealand has an obligation to assist with foreign affairs and defence if requested. The Cook Islanders are constitutionally guaranteed citizenship both of the Cook Islands and of New Zealand.

Agriculture remains the principle productive sector, but tourism, offshore banking and trade are of increasing importance to the economy.

HM Representative, Apenera Short, OBE
Prime Minister, Terepai Maoate
New Zealand High Commissioner, Rob Moore-Jones

NIUE

A New Zealand High Commissioner is stationed at Niue, which since 1974 has been self-governing in free association with New Zealand. New Zealand is responsible for external affairs and defence, and continues to give financial aid. Executive power is in the hands of a premier and a Cabinet of three drawn from the Assembly of 20 members. The Assembly is the supreme legislative body.

New Zealand High Commissioner, John Bryan

NICARAGUA
República de Nicaragua

AREA – 50,193 sq. miles (130,000 sq. km). Neighbours: Honduras (north), Costa Rica (south)
POPULATION – 4,351,000 (1997 estimate): three-quarters are of mixed blood, another 15 per cent are white, mostly of pure Spanish descent, and the remaining 10 per cent are West Indians or Indians. The latter group includes the Misquitos, who live on the Atlantic coast. The official language is Spanish and the majority are Roman Catholic, although the English language and the Moravian Church are widespread on the Atlantic coast
CAPITAL – Managua (population, 608,020, 1979 estimate)
MAJOR CITIES – Chinandega (144,291); Granada (72,640); León (158,577); Masaya (78,308)
CURRENCY – Córdoba (C$) of 100 centavos
NATIONAL ANTHEM – Salve A Tí Nicaragua (Hail, Nicaragua)
NATIONAL DAY – 15 September
NATIONAL FLAG – Horizontal stripes of blue, white and blue, with the Nicaraguan coat of arms in the centre of the white stripe
LIFE EXPECTANCY (years) – male 63.53; female 68.70
POPULATION GROWTH RATE – 1.7 per cent (1997)
POPULATION DENSITY – 33 per sq. km (1997)
URBAN POPULATION – 63.3 per cent (1995)
ILLITERACY RATE – 35.7 per cent
ENROLMENT (percentage of age group) – primary 77 per cent (1997); secondary 27 per cent (1993); tertiary 12 per cent (1997)

HISTORY AND POLITICS

Spanish colonisation of Nicaragua began in 1523. Independence was secured in 1838, Guerrillas of the Sandinista National Liberation Front (FSLN) overthrew the government in 1979, but after ten years in power and a civil war against US-backed Contra guerrillas, the Sandinistas lost their parliamentary majority in elections held in February 1990. A coalition of former opposition parties, the Unión Nacional de Opositora (UNO), formed a government. With the defeat of the Sandinistas, the civil war came to an end.

The Liberal Alliance won the legislative election in October 1996 although the Nationalist Liberal Party left the Alliance in May 1997.

FOREIGN RELATIONS

Following a long-running dispute between Nicaragua and Honduras concerning their maritime boundaries, the two countries signed a border accord on 7 March 2000, in which they agreed to conduct joint patrols in the Caribbean and the Gulf of Fonseca, and to withdraw all military forces from their mutual frontier.

POLITICAL SYSTEM

The head of government is the president, elected for a five-year term, not immediately renewable. The president appoints the Cabinet. There is a unicameral legislature, the National Assembly, with 90 members elected for a six-year term.

In January 2000, the President signed a package of constitutional changes, which would simplify the presidential electoral system, guarantee President Alemán a lifelong seat in the legislature and reform various government departments; an election for a constitutional assembly is due to be held in 2001.

HEAD OF STATE

President, Arnoldo Alemán Lacayo *sworn in* 10 January 1997
Vice-President, Enrique Bolanos

CABINET *as at September 2000*

Agriculture and Livestock, José Marenco Cardenal
Attorney-General, Julio Centeno Gómez
Defence, Ramón Kontorovski
Development, Industry and Commerce, Noel Sacasa
Education, Culture and Sports, Fernando Robleto
Environment and Natural Resources, Roberto Stadthagen
Family Affairs, Rosa Argentina López Prado
Finance, Estebán Duque-Estrada
Foreign Affairs, Eduardo Montealegre
Foreign Co-operation, Transport and Infrastructure, David Robleto Lang
Health, Mariangeles Arguello
Interior, René Herrera
Labour, Mario Montenegro
Presidential Adviser, Emilio Álvarez Montalbán
Presidential Secretary, David Castillo
Tourism, Lorenzo Guerrero

EMBASSY OF NICARAGUA
Suite 12, Vicarage House, 58–60 Kensington Church Street, London W8 4DP.
Tel: 020-7938 2373
Ambassador Extraordinary and Plenipotentiary,
HE Nora Campos de Lankes, apptd 1998

BRITISH EMBASSY
PO Box A-169, Plaza Churchill, Reparto 'Los Robles', Managua
Tel: (00 505) (2) 780014/7800887
Ambassador and Consul-General,
HE Roy Osbourne, apptd 1997

DEFENCE

The Army has 127 main battle tanks and, 166 armoured personnel carriers. The Navy has 5 patrol and coastal vessels at three bases. The Air Force has 15 armed helicopters.
MILITARY EXPENDITURE – 1.1 per cent of GDP (1998)
MILITARY PERSONNEL – 16,000: Army 14,000, Navy 800, Air Force 1,200
CONSCRIPTION DURATION – 18–36 months

ECONOMY

The country is mainly agricultural. The major crops are maize, sugar cane, rice, sorghum, beans, bananas and coffee; livestock and timber production are also important. Nicaragua possesses deposits of gold and silver. There were 358,400 tourists in 1997.

In 1998 there was a trade deficit of US$804 million and a current account deficit of US$607 million. Imports totalled US$1,492 million and exports US$573 million.
GNP – US$1,756 million (1998); US$370 per capita (1998)
GDP – US$2,044 million (1996); US$482 per capita (1996)
ANNUAL AVERAGE GROWTH OF GDP – 5.0 per cent (1997)
INFLATION RATE – 11.6 per cent (1996)
UNEMPLOYMENT – 13.3 per cent (1998)
TOTAL EXTERNAL DEBT – US$5,968 million (1998)

TRADE
Considerable quantities of foodstuffs are imported as well as cotton goods, jute, iron and steel, machinery and petroleum products. The chief exports are cotton, coffee, beef and sugar.

Trade with UK	1998	1999
Imports from UK	£5,740,000	£7,178,000
Exports to UK	6,201,000	3,811,000

COMMUNICATIONS
The Inter-American Highway runs between the Honduras and the Costa Rican borders; the inter-oceanic highway runs from Corinto on the Pacific coast via Managua to Rama, where there is a natural waterway to Bluefields on the Atlantic; there are 15,478 km of roads. The main airport is at Managua. The chief port is Corinto on the Pacific. There are 252 miles of railway, all on the Pacific side of the country. There are 51 radio stations and five television stations in Managua.

There are four daily newspapers published at Managua, apart from the official Gazette (*La Gaceta*). There are 5,251 primary schools, 203,962 secondary schools and 12 universities.

NIGER
République du Niger

AREA – 489,191 sq. miles (1,267,000 sq. km). Neighbours: Algeria and Libya (north), Chad (east), Nigeria and Benin (south), Mali and Burkina Faso (west). Apart from a small region along the Niger Valley in the south-west near the capital, the country is entirely savannah or desert
POPULATION – 9,788,000 (1997 UN estimate): Hausa (54 per cent) in the south, Songhai and Djerma in the south-west, Fulani, Beriberi–Manga, and nomadic Tuareg in the north. 95 per cent of the population are Muslims, with Christian and Animist minorities. The official language is French. Hausa, Djerma and Fulani are also spoken
CAPITAL – Niamey (population, 392,169, 1988 census)
CURRENCY – Franc CFA of 100 centimes
NATIONAL ANTHEM – Auprès du grand Niger Puissant (By the banks of the mighty great Niger)
NATIONAL DAY – 18 December
NATIONAL FLAG – Three horizontal stripes, orange, white and green with an orange disc in the middle of the white stripe
LIFE EXPECTANCY (years) – male 44.90; female 48.14
POPULATION GROWTH RATE – 3.4 per cent (1997)
POPULATION DENSITY – 8 per sq. km (1997)
URBAN POPULATION – 15.3 per cent (1988)
MILITARY EXPENDITURE – 1.5 per cent of GDP (1998)
MILITARY PERSONNEL – 5,300: Army 5,200, Air Force 100; Paramilitaries 5,400

CONSCRIPTION DURATION – Two years (selective)
ILLITERACY RATE – 84.3 per cent
ENROLMENT (percentage of age group) – primary 24 per cent (1996); secondary 6 per cent (1996); tertiary 0.7 per cent (1991)

HISTORY AND POLITICS
The first French expedition arrived in 1891 and the country was fully occupied by 1914. It decided on 18 December 1958 to remain an autonomous republic within the French Community; full independence outside the Community was proclaimed on 3 August 1960.

The president and government were overthrown in a military coup led by Col. Ibrahim Barre Mainassara on 27 January 1996, who suspended the constitution, appointed a civilian Cabinet and created a transitional legislature until presidential and parliamentary elections could be held. A new constitution was promulgated on 12 May 1996 and the ban on political parties was lifted. Brig.-Gen. Mainassara was elected president on 8 July 1996. The pro-Mainassara National Union of Independents for Democratic Renewal won the largest number of seats in legislative elections in November 1996, though these were boycotted by main opposition groups. On 24 November 1997, President Mainassara dismissed the government led by Prime Minister Amadou Boubacar Cissé on grounds of incompetence, and appointed a new government under Ibrahim Hassane Mayaki.

President Mainassara was assassinated on 9 April 1999. On 11 April Major Daouda Mallam Wanke, head of the presidential guard unit responsible for the assassination, was named as the country's new president and appointed head of a newly-created National Council for Reconciliation (CRN); he lifted the ban on political parties and announced that Ibrahim Hassane Mayaki would remain in post as prime minister until new elections could be held. In May, President Wanke established a Consultative Council which drafted a new constitution; it was approved by representatives of political groups in June and submitted to a national referendum in July; it was approved by 89.57 per cent of those who voted, only 31.6 per cent of the electorate. Presidential elections were held in November 1999 and won by Mamadou Tandja of the National Movement for Society in Development (MNSD), who took power on 6 December 1999 and was sworn in as president on 22 December. Hama Amadou was appointed prime minister on 3 January 2000; he announced his Cabinet on 5 January.

INSURGENCY
An ethnic Tuareg-based insurgency began in the north of Niger in November 1991; the Front for the Liberation of Aïr and Azawad (FLAA) aimed to gain greater local autonomy for the Tuaregs, a change to regional boundaries, the demilitarisation of the north and the teaching of the Tuareg language, Tamashek. In 1993 two groups split from the FLAA in protest at its entry into negotiations with the government. A peace accord ending the conflict and providing for a peace process was signed in April 1995. In November 1997, the remaining active Tuareg groups agreed to a cease-fire, and in March 1998, the National Assembly voted unanimously to grant an amnesty to all rebel groups representing the Tuareg and Toubou peoples. All rebel groups had been disarmed by June 1998.

HEAD OF STATE
President, Mamadou Tandja, *elected* 24 November 1999, *sworn in* 22 December 1999

COUNCIL OF MINISTERS *as at September 2000*
Prime Minister, Hama Amadou
Animal Resources, Korone Maoude
Commerce and Industry, Seini Oumarou

Communication, Amadou Elhadj Salifou
Environment and Desertification, Issoufou Assoumane
Equipment and Transport, Abdou Labo
Finance, Ali Badjo Gamatie
Foreign Affairs, Co-operation and African Integration,
     Nassirou Sabo
Higher Education, Research and Technology, Amadou Lawal
Interior and Territorial Administration, Mahama Manzo
Justice, Keeper of the Seals, Relations with Parliament, Ali Sirfi
Labour and Modernisation of the Administration,
     Mireille Ossey
Mines and Energy, Yahaya Bare
National Defence, Sabiou Dadi Gao
National Education, Ari Ibrahim
Planning, Baroumi Maliki
Privatisation and Restructuring of Enterprises,
     Alma Oumarou
Promotion of Small and Medium-sized Enterprises,
     Souley Hassane
Public Health, Assoumane Amadou
Rural Development, Wassalke Boukari
*Social Development, Population, Women's Promotion and
     Protection of Children*, Aissatou Foumakoye
Tourism and Cottage Industry, Rissa ag Boula
Water Resources, Government Spokesman, Akoli Dawel
Youth, Sports and Culture, Issa Lamine

EMBASSY OF THE REPUBLIC OF NIGER
154 rue de Longchamp, F-75116, Paris
Tel: (00 33) (1) 4504 8060
Ambassador Extraordinary and Plenipotentiary, HE Mariama
     Hima, apptd 1999

BRITISH AMBASSADOR, HE Haydon Warren-Gash,
     President at Abidjan, Côte d'Ivoire

ECONOMY

The cultivation of groundnuts and the production of
livestock are the main industries and provide two of the
main exports. Other agricultural products include millet,
cassava and sugar cane. In 1997, 88.5 per cent of the
workforce were engaged in agriculture. There are large
uranium deposits at Arlit and Akouta, and this is the main
export. Gold deposits exist north-west of Niamey. France
and Nigeria are the main trading partners.
   In 1995 Niger had a trade deficit of US$18 million and a
current account deficit of US$152 million. In 1997
imports totalled US$363 million and exports US$270
million.
GNP – US$2,023 million (1998); US$200 per capita
   (1998)
GDP – US$2,005 million (1996); US$212 per capita
   (1996)
ANNUAL AVERAGE GROWTH OF GDP – 3.5 per cent
   (1996)
INFLATION RATE – 4.5 per cent (1998)
TOTAL EXTERNAL DEBT – US$1,659 million (1998)

Trade with UK	1998	1999
Imports from UK	£2,239,000	£3,360,000
Exports to UK	7,883,000	2,270,000

NIGERIA
Federal Republic of Nigeria

AREA – 356,669 sq. miles (923,768 sq. km). Neighbours:
   Benin (west), Niger (north), Chad (north-east),
   Cameroon (east)
POPULATION – 118,369,000 (1997 UN estimate);
   88,514,501 (1991 census). The main ethnic groups are
   Hausa/Fulani, Yoruba and Ibo, and the principal
   languages are English, Hausa, Yoruba and Ibo. There

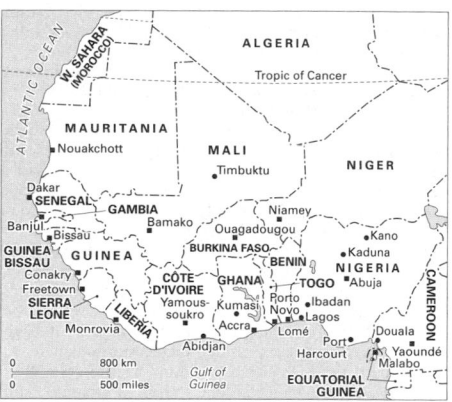

are some 250 ethnic groups, who speak over 500
different languages. Over half the population are
Muslim, these being concentrated in the north and west.
In the southern areas in particular there are many
Christians
CAPITAL – Abuja (population, 378,671), declared the
   federal capital in 1991
MAJOR CITIES – Ibadan (1,295,000); Kaduna (309,600);
   Kano (699,900); Lagos, the former capital (1,347,000);
   Ogbomosho (660,600); ΨPort Harcourt (371,000)
CURRENCY – Naira (N) of 100 kobo
NATIONAL ANTHEM – Arise, O Compatriots
NATIONAL DAY – 1 October (Independence Day)
NATIONAL FLAG – Three equal vertical bands, green,
   white and green
LIFE EXPECTANCY (years) – male 48.81; female 52.01
POPULATION GROWTH RATE – 3.0 per cent (1997)
POPULATION DENSITY – 128 per sq. km (1997)
URBAN POPULATION – 16.1 per cent (1988)
ILLITERACY RATE – 35.9 per cent
ENROLMENT (percentage of age group) – tertiary
   4.1 per cent (1993)

A belt of mangrove swamp forest lies along the entire
coastline. North of this there is a zone of tropical rain
forest and oil-palms. North of the rain forest, the country
rises and the vegetation changes to open woodland and
savannah. In the extreme north the country is semi-desert.
The Niger, Benue, and Cross are the main rivers. The
climate is tropical. The rainy season is from about April to
October. During the dry season the cool *harmattan* wind
blows from the desert.

HISTORY AND POLITICS

The Federation of Nigeria attained independence as a
member of the Commonwealth on 1 October 1960 and
became a republic in 1963. Originally comprising three
regions, the Federation is now divided into 36 states and
the Federal Capital Territory.
   In 1966 the military took power; in 1979 civil rule was
restored after elections at national and state level. The
administration was overthrown by the military in December 1983, this regime itself being overthrown in August
1985. An Armed Forces Ruling Council (AFRC) was
sworn in and governed until January 1993, when it was
replaced by a National Defence and Security Council
(NDSC) and a civilian Transitional Council respectively
to govern the country until a handover to civilian
government. A presidential election on 11 June was
declared invalid. The military government resigned on
26 August, handing power to the Transitional Council.

Continued instability led Defence Minister Gen. Sanni Abacha to launch a military coup on 17 November 1993 and install himself as head of state.

The military regime vowed to hand over power to an elected government in October 1998. In June 1998 Gen. Abacha died of a heart attack and was replaced by Gen. Abdulsalami Abubakar, who promised to continue with the handover to civilian rule and began the release of political prisoners. It was expected that Chief Abiola would be released, but in July he died of a heart attack while still in prison. News of his death prompted widespread rioting across the country. Gen. Abubakar announced that all elections held under Gen. Abacha's rule would be considered invalid and that fresh legislative and presidential elections would be held. A general election was held on 20 February 1999 in which the People's Democratic Party (PDP) won a majority in both houses of parliament; a presidential election was held on 27 February, in which Gen. Olusegun Obasanjo, the PDP candidate, was elected president. President Obasanjo and the civilian administration took office on 29 May 1999.

Following moves by several predominantly Muslim northern states to introduce the Islamic *sharia* legal system, President Obasanjo declared it unconstitutional on 1 November 1999, but Zamfara state introduced it on 27 January 2000 and was followed by Niger state on 22 February. On 29 March, President Obasanjo declared that he would not forbid Nigeria's states from introducing sharia, saying that it was the responsibility of individuals to challenge its legitimacy in the courts. The governors of 19 predominantly Muslim northern states met on 3 April to discuss the implementation of sharia and decided to establish a panel of Muslim and Christian leaders which would attempt to harmonise it with the federal penal code. Those states that had adopted sharia agreed on 2 May 2000 to revert back to the federal penal code, but on 21 June Kano state announced that it would implement sharia at the beginning of Ramadan in November 2000.

INSURGENCIES

Ethnic clashes between Muslim Hausas and Christian Yorubas have occurred in various parts of the country. The debate on sharia law has exacerbated the divisions between Muslims and Christians and there have been sporadic clashes in which hundreds have been killed.

Fighting has also occurred between Ijaw and Ilaje tribesmen in the Niger Delta region and the Isoko and Oleh tribes in Olomoro.

FEDERAL STRUCTURE

State	Population (1991)	Capital
Sokoto	4,392,391	Sokoto
*Zamfara		Gusau
Kebbi	2,062,226	Birnin-Kebbi
Niger	2,482,367	Minna
Kwara	1,566,469	Ilorin
Kogi	2,099,046	Lokoja
Benue	2,780,398	Makurdi
Plateau	3,283,704	Jos
*Nassarawa		Lafia
Taraba	1,480,590	Jalingo
Adamawa	2,124,049	Yola
Borno	2,596,589	Maiduguri
Yobe	1,411,481	Damaturu
Bauchi	4,294,413	Bauchi
*Gombe		Gombe
Jigawa	2,829,929	Dutse
Kano	5,632,040	Kano
Katsina	3,878,344	Katsina
Kaduna	3,969,252	Kaduna
Federal Capital Territory	378,671	Abuja
Oyo	3,488,789	Ibadan
Osun	2,203,016	Oshogbo
Ogun	2,338,570	Abeokuta
Lagos	5,685,781	Ikeja
Ondo	3,884,485	Akure
*Ekiti		Ado Ekiti
Edo	2,159,848	Benin City
Delta	2,570,181	Asaba
Rivers	3,983,857	Port-Harcourt
*Bayelsa		Yenagoa
Abia	2,297,978	Umuahia
Imo	2,485,499	Owerri
*Ebonyi		Abakaliki
Anambra	2,767,903	Awka
Enugu	3,161,295	Enugu
Cross River	1,865,604	Calabar
Akwa Ibom	2,359,736	Uyo

*New state, created on 1 October 1996 by dividing state immediately preceding it in list

HEAD OF STATE
President, Olusegun Obasanjo, elected 27 February 1999, sworn in 29 May 1999
Vice-President, Abubakar Atiku

FEDERAL EXECUTIVE COUNCIL *as at September 2000*
Agriculture and Rural Development, Hassan Adamu
Aviation, Dr Kema Chikwe
Commerce in Africa, Mustapha Bello
Communications, Alhaji Mohammed Arzika
Culture and Tourism, Chief Tonye Graham-Douglas
Defence, Gen. Theophilus Yakubu Danjuma
Education, Prof. Tunde Adeniran
Environment, Sani Zango Daura
Federal Capital Territory, Ibrahim Bunu
Finance, Mallam Adamu Ciroma
Foreign Affairs, Alhaji Sule Lamido
Health, Dr Tim Menakaya
Industry, Stephen Akiga
Information, Prof. Jerry Gana
Internal Affairs, Chief Sunday
Justice, Attorney-General, Chief Bola Ige
Labour, Musa Gwadabe
National Planning, Mohammed Shata
Police Affairs, Maj.-Gen. David Jemibewon
Power and Steel, Olusegun Agagu
Science and Technology, vacant
Solid Mineral Resources, Kanu Godwin Agabi
Sports and Social Development, Damisi Sango
Transport, Chief Ojo Maduekwe
Water Resources, Col. Muhammedu Bello Kaliel
Women and Youth, Aishat Ismail
Works and Housing, Chief Tony Anenih

NIGERIA HIGH COMMISSION
9 Northumberland Avenue, London WC2N 5BX
Tel: 020-7839 1244
High Commissioner, HE Prince Bola A. Ajibola, KBE, apptd 1999
Deputy High Commissioner, M. Sanusi
Minister, A. A. Ella

BRITISH HIGH COMMISSION
Shehu Shangari Way (North), Maitama, Abuja
Tel: (00 234) (9) 523 2010/2011
E-mail: consular@lagos.mail.fco.gov.uk
11 Walter Carrington Crescent, Victoria Island, Lagos
Tel: (00 234) (1) 261 9531
High Commissioner, HE Graham Burton, KCMG, apptd 1997
Deputy High Commissioner and Counsellor (Political), R. A. Pullen
First Secretary (Economic and Commercial), P. A. Stephenson
Defence Adviser, Col. G. G. Davies

LIAISON OFFICES – Ibadan, Kaduna, Kano, Port Harcourt

BRITISH COUNCIL DIRECTOR, C. Bruton,
11 Kingsway Road, Ikoyi (PO Box 3702), Lagos;
e-mail: bc.lagos@bc-lagos.bcouncil.org. Branch
offices at Abuja, Enugu, Ibadan, Kaduna and Kano

DEFENCE

The Army has 200 main battle tanks and 380 armoured
personnel carriers. The Navy has one frigate, 26 patrol and
coastal vessels and two helicopters at six bases. The Air
Force has 91 combat aircraft and 15 armed helicopters.
MILITARY EXPENDITURE – 4.3 per cent of GDP (1998)
MILITARY PERSONNEL – 94,000: Army 79,000, Navy
5,500, Air Force 9,500

ECONOMY

Nigeria was a predominantly agricultural country until the
early 1970s when oil became the principal source of export
revenue (over 90 per cent). Recent governments have
attempted to stimulate greater self-reliance by encouraging non-oil exports and the use of local rather than
imported raw materials.

Much of Nigeria's oil revenue has been squandered on
major projects which have failed to generate the predicted
returns. Nigeria has also suffered from endemic corruption, especially under Gen. Sani Abacha. Many state and
local governments have not published audited accounts
for many years. President Obasanjo has attempted to
tackle the problem by retiring many army officers
suspected of corruption and suspending government
contracts signed during the last three months of the
previous administration, pending investigations.

Agricultural production has fallen since 1970, largely as
a result of a system of marketing boards, with fixed prices
for agricultural commodities, often setting prices at levels
which were too high or low.

Three oil refineries are in operation at Port Harcourt,
Warri and Kaduna, and steel plants at Warri and Ajaokuta
(non-operational). Other projects include natural gas
liquefaction, petrochemicals, fertilisers, power stations
and irrigation schemes. Tin and calumbite mining on the
Jos plateau, textiles and coal mining are also important.
GNP – US$36,373 million (1998; US$300 per capita
(1998)
GDP – US$98,455 million (1996); US$856 per capita
(1996)
ANNUAL AVERAGE GROWTH OF GDP – 3.3 per cent
(1996)
INFLATION RATE – 10.3 per cent (1998)
TOTAL EXTERNAL DEBT – US$30,315 million (1998)

TRADE

The principal exports are oil, groundnuts, tin, cocoa,
rubber, fish and timber. In 1997 there was a trade surplus
of US$5,706 million and a current account surplus of
US$552 million. In 1998, imports totalled US$43,798
million and exports US$37,029 million.

Trade with UK	1998	1999
Imports from UK	£468,572,000	£462,060,000
Exports to UK	140,531,000	129,070,000

COMMUNICATIONS

There are 142,837 km of roads. The Nigerian railway
system, which is controlled by the Nigerian Railway
Corporation, has 3,505 route km of lines. The principal
international airlines operate from Lagos, Kano and Port
Harcourt. A network of internal air services connects the
main centres. The principal seaports are served by a
number of shipping lines, including the Nigerian National
Line. A nationwide television and radio network is being
developed, and ten states have their own television and
radio stations.

NORWAY
Kongeriket Norge

AREA – 125,050 sq. miles (323,877 sq. km) of which
Svalbard and Jan Mayen have a combined area of 24,355
sq. miles (63,080 sq. km). Neighbours: Sweden, Finland,
Russia (east)
POPULATION – 4,445,460 (1999 estimate). The language is
Norwegian and has two forms: Bokmål and Nynorsk.
Sami is spoken in the north of the country. The state
religion is Evangelical Lutheran
CAPITAL – ΨOslo (population, 499,693, 1998)
MAJOR CITIES – ΨBergen (225,439); ΨKristiansand
(70,640); ΨStavanger (106,858); ΨTrondheim
(145,778)
CURRENCY – Krone of 100 øre
NATIONAL ANTHEM – Ja, vi elsker dette landet (Yes, we
love this country)
NATIONAL DAY – 17 May (Constitution Day)
NATIONAL FLAG – Red, with white-bordered blue cross
LIFE EXPECTANCY (years) – male 75.37; female 81.07
POPULATION GROWTH RATE – 0.5 per cent (1997)
POPULATION DENSITY – 14 per sq. km (1997)
URBAN POPULATION – 72.0 per cent (1990)

The coastline is deeply indented with numerous fjords and
fringed with rocky islands. The surface is mountainous,
consisting of elevated and barren tablelands separated by
deep and narrow valleys. At the North Cape the sun does
not appear to set from about 14 May to 29 July, causing the
phenomenon known as the Midnight Sun; conversely,
there is no apparent sunrise from about 18 November to
24 January. During the long winter nights are seen the
Northern Lights or Aurora Borealis.

HISTORY AND POLITICS

Norway was unified under Harald I Fairhair c.AD 900 and
participated in the Viking expansion from the ninth to the
11th centuries. The accession of Magnus VII (1319)
unified the Norwegian and Swedish crowns until his son
became King Håkon VI of Norway in 1343. The
Norwegian and Danish crowns were united in 1380 and
confirmed by the Union of Kalmar (1397) which also
brought Sweden under the rule of Queen Margrethe of
Denmark. Norway remained a Danish province until
transferred to Sweden under the Treaty of Kiel (1814).
The union with Sweden was dissolved on 7 June 1905
when Norway regained complete independence.

Norway remained neutral during the First World War
and on the outbreak of the Second World War but was
invaded by Germany in 1940. Neutrality was abandoned
when Norway joined NATO in 1949. Norway became a
founder member of EFTA in 1960. The Labour Party
governed from 1945 to 1965 when the extensive welfare
state system was built. A referendum in 1972 rejected
membership of the EC.

The ruling centre-right coalition collapsed in October
1990 over the question of EC membership and was
replaced by a minority Labour government. This was
returned to power in the general election held on 13
September 1993. A general election was held on 15
September 1997, in which no party won an outright
majority. The Labour Party has the largest number of seats
(65) but a government was formed by a minority coalition
of the Christian Democratic People's Party, the Centre
Party and the Liberal Party, led by Kjell Magne Bondevik,
which resigned on 9 March 2000 after being defeated in a
confidence vote. The Labour Party was invited to form a

government the following day and appointed its Cabinet on 17 March.

FOREIGN RELATIONS

The Storting voted in November 1992 to apply to join the European Community. Negotiations with the EU concluded on 1 March 1994 with a proposed accession date of 1 January 1995, subject to parliamentary and national referendum ratifications. However, in a national referendum on 28 November 1994 the electorate voted against joining the EU by 52.4 per cent to 47.6 per cent.

POLITICAL SYSTEM

Under the 1814 constitution, the 165-member *Storting* elects one-quarter of its members to constitute the *Lagting* (Upper Chamber), the other three-quarters forming the *Odelsting* (Lower Chamber).

HEAD OF STATE

HM The King of Norway, King Harald V, GCVO, *born* 21 February 1937; *succeeded* 17 January 1991, on the death of his father King Olav V; *married* 29August 1968, Sonja Haraldsen, and has *issue*, Prince Håkon Magnus (*see* below), and Princess Martha Louise, *born* 22 September 1971
Heir, HRH Crown Prince Håkon Magnus, *born* 20 July 1973

CABINET *as at September 2000*
Prime Minister, Jens Stoltenberg
Agriculture, Bjarne Håkon Hanssen
Children and Family Affairs, Karita Bekkemellem Orheim
Cultural Affairs, Ellen Horn
Defence, Bjørn Tore Godal
Education, Research and Church Affairs, Trond Giske
Environment, Siri Bjerke
Finance, Karl Eirik Schjøtt-Pedersen
Fisheries, Otto Gregussen
Foreign Affairs, Thorbjørn Jagland
Health, Tore Tønne
Industry and Trade, Grete Knudsen
International Development, Anne Kristin Sydnes
Justice and Police, Hanne Harlem
Labour and Government Administration, Jørgen Kosmo
Local Government and Regional Development, Sylvia Brustad
Petroleum and Energy, Olav Akselsen
Social Affairs, Guri Ingebrigtsen
Transport, Communications, Terje Moe Gustavsen

ROYAL NORWEGIAN EMBASSY
25 Belgrave Square, London SW1X 8QD
Tel: 020-7591 5500
Ambassador Extraordinary and Plenipotentiary, HE Tarald Osnes Brautaset, apptd 2000
Defence Attaché, Col. P. Bærøy
First Secretary, R. Øverjordet (*Consular*)
Counsellor, S. Lindtvedt (*Commercial*)

BRITISH EMBASSY
Thomas Heftyesgate 8, N-0244 Oslo
Tel: (00 47) 2313 2700
Ambassador Extraordinary and Plenipotentiary, HE Richard Dales, CMG, apptd 1998
Counsellor, D. G. Blunt, LVO (*Deputy Head of Mission and Consul-General*)
First Secretary, M. Phelan (*Economic and Commercial*)
Defence and Naval Attaché, Cdr. D. L. Stanesby, RN

BRITISH CONSULAR OFFICES – Oslo; Honorary Consulates at Ålesund, Bergen, Harstad, Kristiansand (South), Kristiansund (North), Stavanger, Tromsø, Trondheim

BRITISH COUNCIL REPRESENTATIVE, R. Olsen, Fridtjof Nansens Plass 5, N-0160, Oslo 1; e-mail: british.council@britcoun.no

DEFENCE

Norway is a member of NATO. The Army has 170 main battle tanks, 103 armoured infantry fighting vehicles and 225 armoured personnel carriers. The Navy has 12 submarines, four frigates and 22 patrol and coastal vessels at three bases. The Air Force has 79 combat aircraft.
MILITARY EXPENDITURE – 2.2 per cent of GDP (1998)
MILITARY PERSONNEL – 31,000: Army 15,200, Navy 8,200, Air Force 6,700
CONSCRIPTION DURATION – 12 months

ECONOMY

The cultivated area is about 10,703 sq. km, 3.5 per cent of the total surface area. Forests cover 23 per cent; the rest consists of highland pastures or uninhabitable mountains. The chief agricultural products are grain, vegetables, milk, furs and timber.

The Gulf Stream causes the sea temperature to be higher than the average for the latitude, which brings shoals of herring and cod into the fishing grounds. In 1997 the catch totalled more than 9 million tonnes. In 1998, dried cod worth €352 million/US$400 million was produced.

The chief industries are oil production and transport, construction, electricity supply, manufactures, agriculture and forestry, fisheries, mining, metal and ferro-alloy production and shipping. Industries providing both manufactured products and services for the development of North Sea energy resources have become increasingly important. In 1998 150,006,000 tonnes of crude oil were produced. Norway produces large amounts of hydro-electric power. GDP was expected to grow by 3.3 per cent in 2000.
GNP – US$152,049 million (1998); US$34,300 per capita (1998)
GDP – US$157,802 million (1996); US$36,293 per capita (1996)
ANNUAL AVERAGE GROWTH OF GDP – 3.5 per cent (1997)
INFLATION RATE – 2.3 per cent (1998)
UNEMPLOYMENT – 4.1 per cent (1997)

TRADE

The chief imports are motor vehicles, ships and machinery, clothing, foods and textiles. Exports consist chiefly of crude oil and gas, machinery and transport equipment and manufactured goods.

In 1998 Norway had a trade surplus of US$1,566 million and a current account deficit of US$2,161 million. Imports totalled US$36,193 million and exports US$39,645 million.

Trade with UK	1998	1999
Imports from UK	£2,066,273,000	£2,120,383,000
Exports to UK	3,620,318,000	3,762,5744,000

COMMUNICATIONS

The total length of railways open at the end of 1997 was 4,021 km, excluding private lines. There are 91,254 km of public roads in Norway (including urban streets). Scheduled internal air services are operated by Scandinavian Airlines System (SAS) on behalf of Det Norske Luftfartselskap (DNL), by Braathens South American and Far East Airtransport (SAFE), and by Widerøes Flyveselskap AS. There are international airports at Oslo, Bergen and Stavanger. In 1996 there were 64 daily newspapers.

CULTURE AND EDUCATION

The Norwegian language in both its present forms is closely related to other Scandinavian languages. Independence from Denmark (1814) and resurgent nationalism led to the development of 'new Norwegian' based on dialects, which now has equal official standing with 'bokmål', in which Danish influence is more obvious. Ludvig Holberg (1684–1754) is regarded as the father of Norwegian literature, though the modern period begins with the writings of Henrik Wergeland (1808–45). Some of the famous names are Henrik Ibsen (1828–1906), Bjørnstjerne Bjørnson (1832–1910), Nobel Prizewinner in 1903, and the novelists Jonas Lie (1833–1908), Alexander Kielland (1849–1906), Knut Hamsun (1859–1952) and Sigrid Undset (1882–1949), the latter two are also Nobel Prizewinners. Old Norse literature is among the most ancient and richest in Europe.

Education from six to 16 is free and compulsory in the 'basic schools', and free from 16 to 19 years. The majority of the pupils receive post-compulsory schooling at 'upper secondary' schools, regional colleges akin to polytechnics, and 11 universities and other university-level specialist colleges.

ENROLMENT (percentage of age group) – primary 100 per cent (1996); secondary 97 per cent (1996); tertiary 62 per cent (1996)

TERRITORIES

SVALBARD, area 24,295 sq. miles (62,923 sq. km); population 3,700; inhabitants mainly engaged in coal-mining. The Svalbard archipelago consists of the main island, Spitsbergen (15,200 sq. miles), North East Land, the Wiche Islands, Barents and Edge Islands, Prince Charles Foreland, Hope Island, Bear Island and many islands in the neighbourhood of the main group. Glaciers cover 60 per cent of the land area. The sovereignty of Norway over the archipelago was recognised by other nations in 1920 and in 1925 Norway assumed sovereignty

JAN MAYEN ISLAND was joined to Norway by law in 1930

NORWEGIAN ANTARCTIC TERRITORIES

BOUVET ISLAND was declared a dependency of Norway in 1930
PETER THE FIRST ISLAND was declared a dependency of Norway in 1931
PRINCESS RAGNHILD LAND has been claimed as Norwegian since 1931
QUEEN MAUD LAND was declared Norwegian territory by the Norwegian government in 1939

OMAN
Saltanat 'Umān

AREA – 119,498 sq. miles (309,500 sq. km). Neighbours: Yemen, Saudi Arabia and the UAE (west)
POPULATION – 2,302,000 (1998 estimate). The official language is Arabic. Islam is the official religion. The majority of the population are Ibadhi Muslims; there is a large Sunni and a small Shia minority. Other religions are tolerated
CAPITAL – ΨMuscat (Masqat) (population, 400,000)
MAJOR CITIES – ΨBarka; ΨMutrah and Ruwi (the commercial centres); ΨSalālah (the main town of Dhofar); ΨSuhār; ΨSūr
CURRENCY – Rial Omani (OR) of 1,000 baisas
NATIONAL ANTHEM – Ya Rabbana elifidh lana jalalat al Saltan (O Lord, protect for us his majesty the Sultan)
NATIONAL DAY – 18 November
NATIONAL FLAG – Red with a white panel in the upper fly and a green one in the lower fly; in the canton the national emblem in white
LIFE EXPECTANCY (years) – male 67.70; female 71.80

POPULATION GROWTH RATE – 2.6 per cent (1997)
POPULATION DENSITY – 11 per sq. km (1997)

Oman lies at the eastern corner of the Arabian peninsula. Sharjah and Fujairah (UAE) separate the main part of Oman from the northernmost part of the state, a peninsula extending into the Strait of Hormuz.

The north and the south of Oman are divided by nearly 400 miles of desert. The Batinah, the coastal plain, is fertile. The Hajjar is a mountain spine running from north-west to south-east and for the most part barren, but valleys penetrate the central massif which are irrigated by wells or a system of underground canals called *falajs* which tap the water table. The two plateaus leading from the western slopes of the mountains descend to the Empty Quarter of the Arabian Desert. Dhofar, the southern province, is the only part of the Arabian peninsula to be touched by the south-west monsoon. Temperatures are more moderate than in the north.

HISTORY AND POLITICS

Oman became part of the Islamic empire in the seventh century. From the ninth to 16th centuries the area was governed by a succession of religious leaders, or imams of the Ibadhi branch of Islam. The Portuguese established trading posts on the coast in 1507 but were expelled in 1650.

In 1744 Ahmad bin Said Al bu Said established the current ruling dynasty. The country was divided between the sultan's stronghold in the coastal Muscat-Matrah region and the imam in the interior. The sultan cultivated close relations with Britain and the Sultanate of Muscat and Oman became a British protectorate in 1798. In the late 19th century Dhofar was annexed.

In the 1950s the imam proclaimed an independent state in a revolt which was put down with British assistance. A seven-year-long Marxist uprising was crushed in 1975. The current sultan ousted his father in a palace coup in 1970 and changed the state's name to the Sultanate of Oman. Dhofar is still governed as a separate province and Muscat has special status.

POLITICAL SYSTEM

A State Consultative Council established in 1981 was replaced by Sultanic decree in 1991 by a *Majlis al Shura*, or State Advisory Council. This body, meeting twice a year, consisted of representatives from each of the 59 wilayats, or governorates, of the Sultanate. The Council has the right to review legislation, question ministers and make policy proposals. Effective political power remains with the sultan, who rules by decree and is advised by the Cabinet, which he appoints.

In November 1996 the sultan decreed Oman to be a hereditary absolute monarchy. On 16 October 1997, elections were held to choose 164 people for a shortlist to the State Advisory Council; the sultan chose the 82 members of the Council from them. On 16 December 1997 the sultan appointed 41 members to the new *Majlis al-Dawla* (Council of State). Direct elections are due to take place by late 2000.

HEAD OF STATE
HM The Sultan of Oman, Sultan HM Qaboos bin Said al-Said, *succeeded* on deposition of Sultan Said bin Taimur, 23 July 1970

CABINET *as at September 2000*
Prime Minister, The Sultan
Personal Representative of HM The Sultan, HH Sayyid Thuwaini bin Shehab al-Said
Deputy PM for Cabinet Affairs, HH Sayyid Fahd bin Mamud al-Said
Agriculture and Fisheries, Dr Ahmed bin Khalfan bin Mohammed al-Rowahi
Civil Service, Shaikh Abdel Aziz bin Matar bin Salim al-Azizi

Commerce, Industry and Minerals, Maqbul bin Ali bin
Sultan
Communications, Suhail bin Mustahail bin Shamas
Defence, Sayyid Badr bin Saud bin Hareb al-Busaidi
Diwan of Royal Court, Sayyid Saif bin Hamad al-Busaidi
Education and Teaching, Sayyid Saud bin Ibrahim
al-Busaidi
Electricity and Water, Shaikh Mohammed bin Ali al-Qatabi
Foreign Affairs, Yusuf bin Alawi bin Abdullah
Health, Dr Ali bin Mohammed bin Mousa
Higher Education, Yehya bin Mahfuz al-Monzeri
Information, Abd al-Aziz bin Muhammad al Ruwas
Interior, Sayyid Ali bin Hamud al-Busaidi
Justice, Shaikh Mohammed bin Abdullah bin Zahir
al-Hinai
Legal Affairs, Mohammed bin Ali bin Nasir al-Alawi
Minister of State, Musalam bin Ali al-Busaidi
Minister of State and Governor of Muscat, Mutasim bin
Hamud al-Busaidi
National Economy, Ahmed bin Abdel-Nabi Meki
National Heritage and Culture, HH Sayyid Faisal bin
Ali al-Said
Oil and Gas, Dr Mohammed bin Hamad bin Saif al-Romhi
Palace Security, Gen. Ali bin Majed al-Mamari
Regional Administrative Areas and Environment, Dr Khamis
bin Mubarak bin Isa al-Alawi
Religious Property and Affairs, Shaikh Abdallah bin
Mahammed al-Salmi
Social Affairs, Labour, Vocational Training, Shaikh Amer bin
Shuwain al-Hosni
Special Adviser to the Sultan, Salim bin Abdullah al-Ghazali
Special Adviser to the Sultan on Economic Planning Affairs,
Muhammad bin Zubayr
Special Adviser to the Sultan on the Environment, Shahib ibn
Taymur al-Said
Special Adviser to the Sultan on External Liaison, Umar bin
Abd al-Munim al-Zawawi
Transport and Housing, Col. Maleik bin Sulaiman
al-Ma'mari
Water Resources, Lt.-Gen. Hamid bin Said al-Aufi

EMBASSY OF THE SULTANATE OF OMAN
167 Queen's Gate, London SW7 5HE
Tel: 020-7225 0001
Ambassador Extraordinary and Plenipotentiary, HE Hussain
Ali Abdullatif, apptd 1995
Minister Plenipotentiary, G. I. Shaker
Military Attaché, Brig. Said bin Salim bin Breikan Qahoor
al-Mahri

BRITISH EMBASSY
PO Box 300, Muscat, Postal Code 113
Tel: (00 968) 693077
e-mail: becomu@omantel.net.om
Ambassador Extraordinary and Plenipotentiary, HE Sir Ivan
Callan, KCVO, CMG, apptd 1999
Counsellor, A. J. N. Tansley (*Deputy Head of Mission*)
Defence and Military Attaché, Brig. M. Smith, CBE, MC
First Secretary (Commercial), R. MacKenzie
Consul, P. Smith

BRITISH COUNCIL DIRECTOR, C. Hepburn, Road One,
Medinat Qaboos West, PO Box 73, Muscat;
e-mail: bc.muscat@om.britishcouncil.org.
There is also an office in Seeb

DEFENCE

The Army has 141 main battle tanks and 103 armoured
personnel carriers. The Navy has 13 patrol and coastal
vessels at five bases. The Air Force has 40 combat aircraft.
MILITARY EXPENDITURE – 13.6 per cent of GDP (1998)
MILITARY PERSONNEL – 43,500: Army 25,000, Navy
4,200, Air Force 4,100, Royal Household 6,500,
Paramilitaries 4,400

ECONOMY

Although there is considerable cultivation in the fertile
areas and cattle are raised on the mountains, the backbone
of the economy is the oil industry, accounting for about 40
per cent of GDP. Petroleum Development (Oman) Ltd
(owned 60 per cent by the Oman Government) began
exporting oil in 1967. Concessions (off and on shore) are
held by several major international companies. Oil
production in 1998 was 44,788,000 tonnes. The government is actively encouraging the diversification of the
economy and private sector development. Tourism is also
an expanding area.

A gas turbine power station operates at Rusail, where
there is also a 200-plot industrial estate. There is a power
station and a desalination plant near Muscat and flour,
animal feed, cement and copper production facilities.

In 1997 there was a trade surplus of US$2,982 million
and a current account deficit of US$57 million.

GDP – US$14,728 million (1996); US$6,398 per capita
(1996)
ANNUAL AVERAGE GROWTH OF GDP – 5.2 per cent
(1996)
TOTAL EXTERNAL DEBT – US$3,629 million (1998)

TRADE

Trade is mainly with the UAE, UK, Japan, South Korea
and China. Chief imports are machinery and transport
equipment, industrial goods and foodstuffs. Oil accounts
for 79 per cent of exports.

In 1997 imports totalled US$5,026 million and exports
US$7,630 million.

Trade with UK	1998	1999
Imports from UK	£284,775,000	£231,359,000
Exports to UK	92,026,000	75,041,000

COMMUNICATIONS

Port Qaboos at Mutrah has eight deep-water berths which
have been constructed as part of the harbour facilities;
a new port is under construction at Suhār. A modern
telecommunications service to the main population
centres and an international service are operated by the
General Telecommunications Organisation. There are
some 6,000 km of tarmac roads linking most main
population centres of the country with the coast and with
the towns of the UAE, though only a trunk road links the
north and south of Oman. There are airports at Seeb,
Salālah, Sūr, Masirah, Khasab and Diba.

SOCIAL WELFARE AND EDUCATION

For many years the Sultanate was a poor country but the
advent of oil revenues and the change of regime in 1970
led to the initiation of a wide-ranging development
programme, especially concerned with health, education
and communications. There are now 47 hospitals and 115
health centres. Mass immunisation programmes have
eradicated poliomyelitis and diphtheria; 1,069 schools,
with 536,178 pupils, were in operation in 1998. There is
one university.
ENROLMENT (percentage of age group) – primary
69 per cent (1996); secondary 56 per cent (1996);
tertiary 8 per cent (1997)

PAKISTAN
Islāmī Jamhūriya-e-Pākistān

AREA – 307,374 sq. miles (796,095 sq. km). Neighbours:
Iran (west), Afghanistan (north and north-west), China
(north-east), the disputed territory of Kashmir, India
(east)

POPULATION – 138,150,000 (1997 UN estimate); 95 per cent Muslim, 3.5 per cent Christian, about 1 per cent Hindu, and 0.5 per cent Buddhist. Urdu is the national language, but is only spoken by a small minority of the population. The most widely used language is Punjabi, followed by Sindi and Pushto. English is used in business, government and higher education

CAPITAL – Islamabad (population, 350,000)

MAJOR CITIES – ΨKarachi (7,183,000); Lahore (4,072,000)

CURRENCY – Pakistan rupee of 100 paisa

NATIONAL ANTHEM – Quami Tarana

NATIONAL DAYS – 23 March (Pakistan Day), 14 August (Independence Day)

NATIONAL FLAG – Green with a white crescent and star, and a white vertical strip in the hoist

LIFE EXPECTANCY (years) – male 59.04; female 59.20

POPULATION GROWTH RATE – 2.9 per cent (1997)

POPULATION DENSITY – 174 per sq. km (1997)

URBAN POPULATION – 32.2 per cent (1995)

Running through Pakistan are five great rivers, the Indus, Jhelum, Chenab, Ravi and Sutlej. The upper reaches of these rivers are in Kashmir, and their sources in the Himalayas.

HISTORY AND POLITICS

Pakistan was constituted as a Dominion under the Indian Independence Act 1947, becoming a republic on 23 March 1956. Until 1972 Pakistan consisted of two geographical units, West and East Pakistan, separated by about 1,100 miles of Indian territory. East Pakistan's insistence on complete autonomy led to civil war, which broke out on 25 March 1971 and continued until December 1971 when a cease-fire was arranged. The independence of East Pakistan as Bangladesh was proclaimed in April 1972. Under the 1972 Simla Agreement with India, a line of control was established in Kashmir; Pakistan controls an area of 33,653 sq. miles (87,159 sq. km) to the north and west of the line.

Elections held in February 1997 were won by the Pakistan Muslim League with 134 seats. President Farooq Leghari resigned on 2 December 1997 following a dispute with Prime Minster Sharwaz. Muhammad Rafiq Tarar was subsequently elected president.

The government was overthrown by the military under Gen. Pervez Musharraf on 12 October 1999 after the Prime Minister, Nawaz Sharif, had tried to sack him. Gen. Musharraf declared himself chief executive and dissolved the legislature, but left the president in office. Gen. Musharraf established the National Security Council to run the country, comprising the chiefs of staff and civilian technocrats. Pakistan's membership of the Commonwealth was suspended on 18 October 1999.

In March 2000, Gen. Musharraf announced that elections for district councils and mayors were to be held between December 2000 and July 2001.

INSURGENCY

Since early 1994 there has been civil disorder in Sind province, especially in Karachi, in two conflicts: armed militants of the Mohajir Qaumi Movement (MQM) Party, which represents Urdu-speaking Indian Muslims who fled from India at partition and their descendants, are fighting for an autonomous Karachi province; and there is an armed conflict between Shia and Sunni fundamentalists.

POLITICAL SYSTEM

The legislature is bicameral, but was suspended following the coup in October 1999. Under the constitution, the *Majlis as-Shoora* (National Assembly) has a five-year term and comprises 237 members, of whom 207 are directly elected, 10 represent religious minorities and 20 are co-opted women. The Senate has 87 members, with a six-year

term; half of the seats are renewed every three years. In January 1997 the interim government set up a Council for Defence and National Security including members of the Cabinet and armed forces to advise on foreign, defence and economic policies. The four provinces each have a provincial assembly and are represented in both legislative chambers.

The National Assembly amended the constitution in April 1997 to remove from the president the power to dismiss the government and dissolve parliament.

FEDERAL STRUCTURE

Province	Area (sq. km)	Population (1981)	Capital
Baluchistan	347,190	4,332,000	Quetta
Federal Capital Territory Islamabad	907	340,000	—
Federally Administered Tribal Areas	27,219	2,199,000	—
North-West Frontier Province	74,521	11,061,000	Peshawar
Punjab	205,344	47,292,000	Lahore
Sind	140,914	19,029	Karachi

HEAD OF STATE

President, Muhammad Rafiq Tarar, *sworn in* 1 January 1998

NATIONAL SECURITY COUNCIL *as at September 2000*
Chief Executive, Chief of Army Staff, Gen. Pervez Musharraf
Chief of Air Staff, Air Chief Marshall, Pervez Mehdi
Chief of Naval Staff, Vice-Adm. Abdul Aziz Mirza
Commerce, Industry and Production, Abdul Razzak Dand
Foreign Affairs, Abdul Sattar
Interior and Narcotics Control, Captial Administration and Development Divisions, Lt.-Gen. (retd) Moeenuddin Haider

FEDERAL MINISTERS *as at September 2000*
Adviser to the Chief Executive for Foreign Affairs, Law, Justice and Human Rights, Sharifuddin Pirzada
Adviser to the Chief Executive for Food, Agriculture and Livestock, Shafi Nafiz
Adviser to the Chief Executive on National Affairs and Information, Javed Jabbar
Chair of the Federal Land Commision, Imtiaz Ahmad Ghazi
Communications and Railways, Lt-Gen, Javed Ashraf
Education, Science and Technology, Zubeda Jala
Food and Agriculture, Shafqat Ali Shah Jamot
Justice, Attorney General, Aziz A. Munshi
Kashmir Affairs, Northern Areas, States and Frontier Regions, Housing and Works, Abass Sarfraz Khan
Local Government and Rural Development, Labour, Environment, Overseas Pakistanis, Omar Asghar Khan
Patroleum and Natural Resources, Usman Aminuddin
Population, Welfare and Health, Adbul Malik Kansi
Religious Affairs, Mahmood Ahmed Ghazi
Science and Technology, Ataur Rahman
Sports, Culture and Minorities Affairs, S.K. Trassler
Women's Development, Attiya Inayatullah

HIGH COMMISSION FOR THE ISLAMIC REPUBLIC OF PAKISTAN
35–36 Lowndes Square, London SW1X 9JN
Tel: 020-7664 9200
High Commissioner, HE Kadir Jaffer, apptd 2000
Deputy High Commissioner, Javed Iqbal
Defence and Naval Adviser, Cdre Javed Ahmed Khan

BRITISH HIGH COMMISSION
Diplomatic Enclave, Ramna 5, PO Box 1122, Islamabad
Tel: (00 92) (51) 822131/5
E-mail: bhctrade@isb.comsats.net.pk
High Commissioner, HE Sir David Dain, KCVO, CMG,

apptd 1994
Deputy High Commissioners, M. Forbes-Smith (*Islamabad*);
D. B. Merry (*Karachi*)
First Secretary (*Commercial*), M. Pakes
Defence and Military Adviser, Brig. B. D. Wheelwright
DEPUTY HIGH COMMISSION – Karachi
HONORARY CONSULATE – Lahore

BRITISH COUNCIL DIRECTOR, P. Ellwood, Block 14, Civic
Centre G6, PO Box 1135, Islamabad
e-mail: bc-islamabad@bc-islamabad.bcouncil.org.
There are offices at Karachi, Lahore and Peshawar

DEFENCE

On 28 and 30 May 1998, Pakistan carried out six
underground nuclear tests, less than a month after India
had carried out its own nuclear tests. In doing so, it became
the world's seventh declared nuclear power.

The Army has some 2,320 main battle tanks, 850
armoured personnel carriers and 20 attack helicopters. The
Navy has ten submarines, eight frigates, 10 patrol
and coastal vessels, seven combat aircraft and 12 armed
helicopters based at Karachi. The Air Force has 389
combat aircraft.

MILITARY EXPENDITURE – 6.5 per cent of GDP (1998)
MILITARY PERSONNEL – 587,000: Army 520,000, Navy
22,000, Air Force 45,000; Paramilitaries 247,000

ECONOMY

Agriculture employs half the workforce and contributes
a quarter of GDP. The principal crops are cotton, rice,
wheat and sugar cane. Pakistan has one of the longest
irrigation systems in the world, irrigating 42.5 million
acres. There are large deposits of rock salt.

Pakistan also produces hides and skins, leather, wool,
fertilisers, paints and varnishes, soda ash, paper, cement,
fish, carpets, sports goods, surgical appliances and
engineering goods, including switchgear, transformers,
cables and wires.

In 1996 foreign exchange reserves fell below the
US$1,000 million floor decreed by the IMF and the
economy went into a severe recession. Attempts to impose
taxes resulted in industrial action and capital flight. The
Sharif government announced an economic revival
programme in March 1997 including tax and tariff
reductions. The IMF agreed a loan of more than US$1.5
billion to help finance economic reforms.

Following condemnation of Pakistan's nuclear tests
in May 1998, the international community imposed
economic sanctions. The government immediately
announced a series of spending cuts and severe austerity
measures to counteract the sanctions and protect the
economy. In January 1999, the government committed
itself to the continuation of financial reforms, trade
liberalisation and privatisation in return for the resumption of IMF loans; the World Bank also agreed a loan for
the reform of the banking and taxation systems and the
public utilities.

In December 1999, the chief executive announced the
economic strategy of the military government, which aims
to resume privatisation and prioritise certain key sectors of
the economy. There is also to be a reform of the taxation
system.

In 1997 there was a trade deficit of US$2,392 million
and a current account deficit of US$1,754 million.

GNP – US$61,451 million (1998); US$470 per capita
(1998)
GDP – US$70,480 million (1996); US$504 per capita
(1996)
ANNUAL AVERAGE GROWTH OF GDP – 3.4 per cent
(1997)
INFLATION RATE – 6.2 per cent (1998)

UNEMPLOYMENT – 6.1 per cent (1997)
TOTAL EXTERNAL DEBT – US$32,229 million (1998)

TRADE

Principal imports are petroleum products, machinery,
fertilisers, transport equipment, edible oils, chemicals and
ferrous metals. Principal exports are cotton yarn and cloth,
carpets, rice, petroleum products, textiles, leather and fish.

In 1998 imports totalled US$9,315 million and exports
US$8,501 million.

Trade with UK	1998	1999
Imports from UK	£234,572,000	£219,963,000
Exports to UK	357,254,000	333,228,000

COMMUNICATIONS

There are major seaports at Karachi and Port Qasim. The
main airports are at Karachi, Islamabad, Lahore, Peshawar
and Quetta. Pakistan International Airlines operates air
services between the principal cities as well as abroad.
There are 86,597 km of roads and 7,344 km of rail track.

EDUCATION

Education consists of five years of primary education (five
to nine years), three years of middle or lower secondary
(general or vocational), two years of upper secondary, two
years of higher secondary (intermediate) and two to five
years of higher education in colleges and universities.
Education is free to upper secondary level.

ILLITERACY RATE – 62.2 per cent
ENROLMENT (percentage of age group) – tertiary 3.0
per cent (1991)

PALAU
Belu'u era Belau/Republic of Palau

AREA – 177 sq. miles (459 sq. km)
POPULATION – 17,000 (1994 UN estimate); 15,122
(1990 census); 13,900 live on Koror and Babelthaup.
The population is Micronesian, and predominantly
Roman Catholic with a Protestant minority. Palauan
and English are official languages
CAPITAL – Koror (population, 10,493, 1994)
CURRENCY – Currency is that of the USA
NATIONAL FLAG – Light blue with a yellow disc set near
the hoist
POPULATION GROWTH RATE – 1.8 per cent (1997)
POPULATION DENSITY – 37 per sq. km (1997)

The Republic of Palau consists of 340 islands and islets in
the western Pacific Ocean, of which eight are inhabited.
Part of the Caroline Islands group, the Palau archipelago
stretches over 400 miles (644 km) between 2° and 8°N,
and 131° and 138°E. Koror island is about 810 miles
(1,300 km) south-west of Guam and about 530 miles
(852 km) south-east of Manila.

The islands vary in terrain from the highly mountainous
to low coral atolls. The climate is tropical with a rainy
season lasting from June to October; the average
temperature is 27°C (81°F).

HISTORY AND POLITICS

Spain acquired sovereignty over the Caroline Islands, of
which the Palau archipelago is part, in 1886. After defeat in
the Spanish-American war of 1898, Spain sold its remaining Pacific possessions, including Palau, to Germany
in 1899. On the outbreak of the First World War in 1914,
Japan took control of Palau on behalf of the Allied
powers, and Japanese administration was confirmed in a
League of Nations mandate in 1921. During the Second
World War Allied forces gained control of the archipelago

after intense fighting. In 1947 the USA entered into agreement with the UN Security Council to administer the Micronesia area, including Palau, as the UN Trust Territory of the Pacific Islands.

In July 1978, the Palau electorate voted in a referendum not to join the new Federated States of Micronesia and instead became a separate part of the UN Trust Territory. A Compact of Free Association was signed with the USA in 1982, giving Palau internal sovereignty whilst leaving foreign policy to be decided by the USA. The compact only came into effect in November 1993, however, as successive referendums refused to allow US nuclear waste and weapons into Palau. The Compact was finally implemented on 1 October 1994. Under this agreement the USA recognised the Republic of Palau as a fully sovereign and independent state and assumed responsibility for its defence for 50 years; the UN Trust Territory of the Pacific Islands was terminated. Palau was admitted to UN membership in December 1994.

The last presidential and legislative elections were held in November 1996. Presidential and legislative elections are due by November 2000.

POLITICAL SYSTEM

Executive power is vested in the president and vice-president, who are elected for four-year terms; the president appoints the Cabinet. There is a bicameral legislature (*Olbiil era Kelulau*) composed of the 16-member House of Delegates (one member elected from each of the 16 constituent states) and the 14-member Senate. There is also a Council of Chiefs to advise the president on matters concerning traditional law and customs. Each of the 16 component states have their own elected governors and legislatures.

HEAD OF STATE

President, Kuniwo Nakamura, *elected* 4 November 1992, *re-elected* 6 November 1996
Vice-President, Administration, Tommy Remengesau

CABINET *as at September 2000*

Commerce and Trade, George Ngirarsaol
Community and Cultural Affairs, Riosang Salvador
Education, Billy Kuartei
Health, Masao Ueda
Justice, Salvador Ingereklii
Minister of State, Sabias Anastacio
Resources and Development, Marcelino Melairei

BRITISH AMBASSADOR, HE Christopher Haslam, resident at Suva, Fiji

ECONOMY

The economy remains heavily dependent on US financial support, which the USA is committed to giving under the Compact. Fisheries, tourism, subsistence agriculture and government service are the main areas of employment. Agricultural products include coconuts and copra, and Palau earns significant revenue from the sale of fishing licences to foreign fleets fishing for tuna. The chief exports are fish, mussels, coconuts and copra. Tourism is being developed; there were 75,139 visitors in 1997. On 17 December 1997, Palau joined the International Monetary Fund, becoming its 182nd member. Its initial quota was set at 2.25 million special drawing rights.

The USA carried out an infrastructure improvement programme in the 1970s and 1980s. There are now three airports on Koror, Peleliu and Angaur which have daily flights from Guam operated by Continental Micronesia. Ocean freight services to Palau are provided by two shipping lines to the port at Koror. There are 61 km of roads, of which 36 km are paved. There is a privately owned television station and a government-operated radio station.

GDP – US$122 million (1996); US$7,184 per capita (1996)

EDUCATION AND SOCIAL WELFARE

There is a free public school system which, together with independent missionary schools, provides primary and secondary education. A tertiary technical school has been established on Koror since 1969. General medical and dental care is provided by a public hospital.

PANAMA
República de Panamá

AREA – 29,157 sq. miles (75,517 sq. km). Neighbours: Colombia (east), Costa Rica (west)
POPULATION – 2,719,000 (1997 UN estimate): 70 per cent mestizo, 14 per cent mixed Amerindian and black, 10 per cent European, 6 per cent Amerindian. Spanish is the official language
CAPITAL – ΨPanama City (population, 464,928, 1997 estimate)
CURRENCY – Balboa of 100 centésimos (US notes are also in circulation)
NATIONAL ANTHEM – Alcanzamos Por Fin La Victoria (Victory is ours at last)
NATIONAL DAY – 3 November
NATIONAL FLAG – Four quarters; white with blue star (top, next staff), red (in fly), blue (below, next staff) and white with red star
LIFE EXPECTANCY (years) – male 71.78; female 76.35
POPULATION GROWTH RATE – 1.8 per cent (1997)
POPULATION DENSITY – 36 per sq. km (1997)
URBAN POPULATION – 55.5 per cent (1997)
MILITARY EXPENDITURE – 1.3 per cent of GDP (1998)
MILITARY PERSONNEL – 11,800 Paramilitaries
ILLITERACY RATE – 8.1 per cent
ENROLMENT (percentage of age group) – primary 91 per cent (1990); secondary 51 per cent (1990); tertiary 32 per cent (1996)

HISTORY AND POLITICS

After a revolt in 1903, Panama declared its independence from Colombia and established a separate government.

An attempt in February 1988 by President Delvalle to remove Gen. Noriega as Commander of the Defence Forces failed. Noriega ousted Delvalle and replaced him with Manuel Solis Palma. Presidential elections were held in May 1989 but Noriega annulled the results and on 15 December he assumed power formally as head of state. On 20 December US troops invaded Panama to oust Noriega. Guillermo Endara, believed to have won the May elections, was installed as president. In December 1991 the Legislative Assembly approved a change to the constitution which abolished the armed forces.

The most recent presidential election, on 2 May 1999, was won by Mireya Elisa Moscoso de Gruber of the Union for Panama coalition. Simultaneous legislative elections were won by the New Nation coalition with 46 of the 71 contested seats.

POLITICAL SYSTEM

Legislative power is vested in a unicameral Legislative Assembly of 71 members; executive power is held by the president, assisted by two elected vice-presidents and an appointed Cabinet. Elections are held every five years under a system of universal and compulsory adult suffrage.

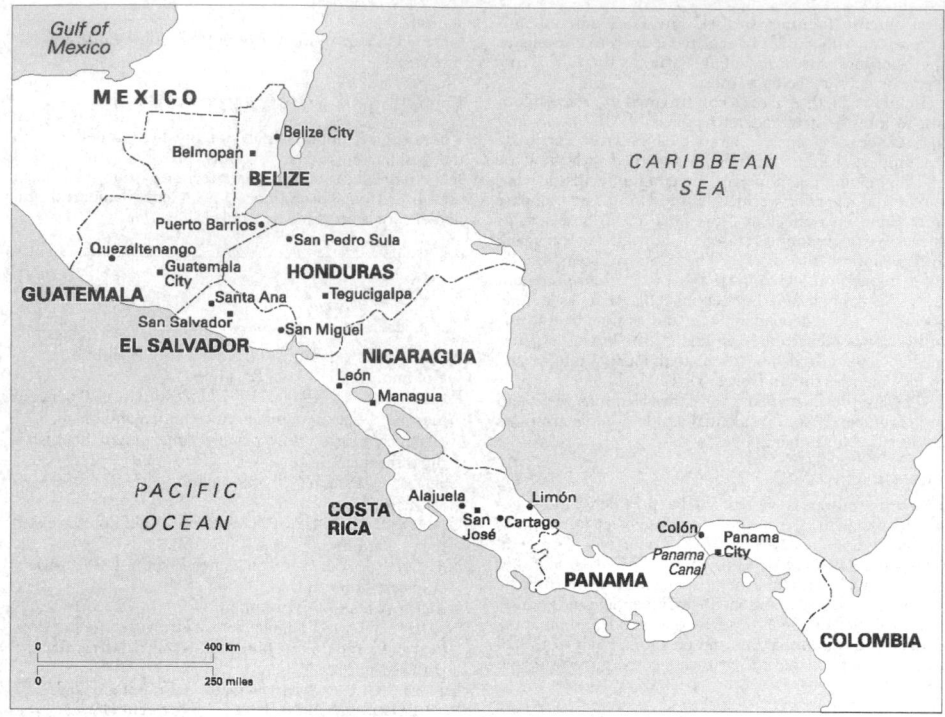

HEAD OF STATE

President, Mireya Elisa Moscoso de Gruber, *elected* 2 May 1999, *sworn in* 1 September 1999
First Vice-President, Arturo Vallarino
Second Vice-President, Dominador Kaiser Bazáan

CABINET *as at September 2000*
Agricultural Development, Pedro Adan Gordon
Canal Affairs, Ricardo Martinelli Berrocal
Commerce and Industry, Joaquín Jácome Diez
Education, Doris Rosas de Mata
Finance and Economy, Norberta Delgodo
Foreign Relations, José Miguel Alemán
Health, Dr José Manuel Terán Sittón
Housing, Miguel Cárdenas
Interior and Justice, Dr Winston Spadafora
Labour and Social Welfare, Joaquín José Vallarino III
Presidency, Ivonne Young Valdez
Public Works, Victor Julian
Women, Youth and Family, Alma Ester Tejada de Rolla

EMBASSY OF THE REPUBLIC OF PANAMA
48 Park Street, London W1Y 3PD
Tel: 020-7493 4646
Ambassador Extraordinary and Plenipotentiary, HE Ariadne Singares Robinson, apptd 2000
Counsellor (Financial and Commercial), S. Kheireddine

BRITISH EMBASSY
Torre Swiss Bank, Calle 53 (Apartado 889) Zona 1, Panama City
Tel: (00 507) 269 0866
Ambassador Extraordinary and Plenipotentiary, HE Glyn Davies, apptd 1999

ECONOMY

The soil is moderately fertile, but nearly one-half of the land is uncultivated. The chief crops are bananas, sugar, coconuts, coffee and cereals. Over 13,000 foreign ships are registered in Panama. The shrimping industry plays an important role in the economy. Tourism is the principal foreign currency earner. There are 547 km of railway track and 10,792 km of roads.

GNP – US$8,275 million (1998); US$2,990 per capita (1998)
GDP – US$8,110 million (1996); US$3,029 per capita (1996)
ANNUAL AVERAGE GROWTH OF GDP – 4.4 per cent (1997)
INFLATION RATE – 0.6 per cent (1998)
UNEMPLOYMENT – 13.9 per cent (1998)
TOTAL EXTERNAL DEBT – US$6,689 million (1998)

TRADE
Imports are mostly manufactured goods, machinery, lubricants, chemicals and foodstuffs. Exports are bananas, petroleum products, shrimps, sugar, meat, coffee and fishmeal.

In 1998 Panama had a trade deficit of US$1,338 million and a current account deficit of US$1,240 million. Imports totalled US$3,350 million and exports US$786 million.

Trade with UK†	1998	1999
Imports from UK	£82,822,000	£60,689,000
Exports to UK	6,452,000	7,975,000

†Including Coloôn Free Zone

THE PANAMA CANAL ZONE

The Panama Canal Zone was created in 1903 by a contract between Panama and the USA, under which the USA was given the right to build and operate the canal and administer the adjacent territory. With effect from 1 October 1979 the Canal Zone (1,442 sq. km/647 sq. miles) was disestablished, with all areas of land and water within the Zone reverting to Panama. By the 1977 treaty with the USA, the USA was allowed the use of operating bases for the Panama Canal, together with several military bases, but the Republic of Panama was sovereign in all such areas. Control of the Canal reverted to Panama at noon on 31 December 1999.

In the fiscal year 1998, the total number of transits by ocean-going commercial traffic was 13,025; canal net tons totalled 221,634,400; cargo tons totalled 192,091,000.

DEPENDENCIES

Taboga Island (area 4 sq. miles) is a popular tourist resort some 12 miles from the Pacific entrance to the Panama Canal.

Tourist facilities have also been developed in the Las Perlas Archipelago in the Gulf of Panama, particularly on the island of Contadora, as well as on the San Blas Islands in the Atlantic.

There is a penal settlement at Guardia on the island of Coiba (area 19 sq. miles) in the Gulf of Chiriqui.

PAPUA NEW GUINEA

AREA – 178,704 sq. miles (462,840 sq. km). Neighbour: Indonesia (west, on New Guinea)

POPULATION – 4,500,000 (1997 UN estimate). English is the official language; Hiri Motu and Neo-Melanesian are widely used

CAPITAL – ΨPort Moresby (population, 173,500, 1990)

MAJOR CITIES – Goroka; Lae; Madang; Mount Hagen; Rabaul; Wewak

CURRENCY – Kina (K) of 100 toea

NATIONAL ANTHEM – Arise All You Sons

NATIONAL DAY – 16 September (Independence Day)

NATIONAL FLAG – Divided diagonally red (fly) and black (hoist); on the red a soaring Bird of Paradise in yellow and on the black five white stars of the Southern Cross

LIFE EXPECTANCY (years) – male 55.16; female 56.68

POPULATION GROWTH RATE – 2.8 per cent (1998)

POPULATION DENSITY – 10 per sq. km (1997)

MILITARY EXPENDITURE – 1.0 per cent of GDP (1998)

MILITARY PERSONNEL – 4,300: Army 3,800, Navy 400, Air Force 100

ILLITERACY RATE – 24.0 per cent

ENROLMENT (percentage of age group) – tertiary 3.2 per cent (1995)

The country has many island groups, principally the Bismarck Archipelago, a portion of the Solomon Islands, the Trobriands, the D'Entrecasteaux Islands and the Louisade Archipelago. The main islands of the Bismarck Archipelago are New Britain, New Ireland and Manus. Bougainville is the largest of the Solomon Islands within Papua New Guinea.

Papua New Guinea lies within the tropics and has a typically monsoonal climate. Temperature and humidity are uniformly high throughout the year.

HISTORY AND POLITICS

In 1884 a British protectorate, British New Guinea, was proclaimed over the southern coast of New Guinea (Papua) and the adjacent islands, which were annexed outright in 1888. In 1906 the territory was placed under the authority of Australia.

In 1884 Germany had formally taken possession of certain northern areas. In 1914 these were occupied by Australian troops and in 1921, became a League of Nations mandate administered by Australia. New Guinea was administered under the mandate and Papua under the Papua Act until the invasion by the Japanese in 1942 when the civil administration was suspended until the Japanese surrendered in 1945.

From 1970 there was a gradual assumption of powers by the Papua New Guinea government, culminating in formal self-government in December 1973. Papua New Guinea achieved full independence within the Commonwealth on 16 September 1975.

Following elections in June 1997, a coalition government was formed by the Pangu Pati (PP), the People's Progress Party (PPP) and the People's National Congress, under Prime Minister Bill Skate. The PPP left the coalition in October 1998, but some PPP ministers joined the PNG First party formed in April 1998 by Bill Skate, who resigned as prime minister in July 1999; he was succeeded by Sir Mekere Morauta of the People's Democratic Movement (PDM) on 14 July 1999, who formed a multiparty coalition government.

In July 1998, the north coast of Papua New Guinea was devastated by a tidal wave that killed more than 1,600 people and washed away entire villages, leaving more than 6,000 people homeless.

INSURGENCIES

Following a 1989 insurrection, the Bougainville Revolutionary Army (BRA) declared an independent republic in May 1990. A peace accord was signed in January 1991, although the question of Bougainville's status was left unresolved. Government forces returned to the island in October 1992, subsequently capturing 90 per cent of rebel-held territory.

A permanent cease-fire came into effect on 30 April 1998, bringing to an end the nine-year civil war. A small group of rebels led by Francis Ona vowed to continue the armed campaign for an independent Bougainville. An interim Bougainville Reconciliation Government was established on 1 January 1999, which renamed itself the Bougainville People' Congress in April. Elections were held in early May. Joseph Kabui, a former rebel leader, was elected president.

An agreement signed on 23 March 2000 provides for an elected autonomous government, to be established by the end of 2000.

POLITICAL SYSTEM

Elections are held every five years. The National Parliament comprises 109 elected members, 20 from regional electorates, the remainder from open electorates. The Governor-General is appointed by parliament for a six-year term. Provincial governments were abolished in August 1995, and replaced with councils combining local and national politicians and headed by an appointed governor.

Governor-General, HE Sailas Atopare, GCMG, *appointed* 14 November 1997

NATIONAL EXECUTIVE COUNCIL *as at July 2000*

Prime Minister, National Executive Council, Finance and Treasury, Sir Mekere Morauta, KBE (PDM)

Deputy PM, Agriculture and Livestock, Mao Zeming (PDM)

Communication and Information, Peter Waieng (PDM)

Correctional Institution Services, Micah Wes (APNG)

Culture and, Tourism, Andrew Baing (PPP)

Defence, Muki Taranuki (PPP)

Education, Prof. John Waiko (PDM)

Environment and Conservation, Herowa Agiwa (PDM)

Fisheries and Marine Resources, Ron Ganarafo (PDM)

Foreign Affairs, Sir John Kaputin, KBE (Ind.)

Forests, Michael Ogio (PDM)

Health, Ludger Mond (PP)
Home Affairs, Andrew Kumbakor (PDM)
Housing and Urban Resettlement, John Kamb (PDM)
Justice, Kilroy Genia (APNG)
Labour and Employment, Charlie Benjamin (APNG)
Lands and Physical Planning, John Pundari (APNG)
Mining, Bougainville Affairs, Sir Michael Somare, KCMG (NAP)
Petroleum and Energy, Dr Fabian Pok (PDM)
Planning and Implementation, Moi Avei (NAP)
Police, Mathias Karani, OBE (PDM)
Privatisation, Vincent Auali (PDM)
Provincial and Local Government, Philemon Embel (PDM)
Public Service, Iairo Lasaro (PDM)
Rural Development, William Ebenosi (PDM)
Trade and Industry, Michael Nali (PPP)
Transport and Civil Aviation, Bart Philemon (NAP)
Works and Implementation, Alfred Pogo (PDM)

APNG Advance Papua New Guinea; NAP National Alliance Party; PDM People's Democratic Movement; PP Pangu Pati; PPP People's Progress Party; Ind. Independent

PAPUA NEW GUINEA HIGH COMMISSION
3rd Floor, 14 Waterloo Place, London SW1R 4AR
Tel: 020-7930 0922/7
High Commissioner, HE Sir Kina Bona, KBE, apptd 1995

BRITISH HIGH COMMISSION
PO Box 212, Waigani NCD 131, Port Moresby
Tel: (00 675) 325 1643/1645
E-mail: bhcpng@datec.com.pg
High Commissioner, HE Simon Mansfield Scadden, apptd 2000

ECONOMY

Until the 1970s the economy was based almost entirely on agriculture, principally copra, cocoa, tea, coffee, palm oil, rubber, groundnuts, spices and timber. A variety of commercial agricultural developments co-exist with the traditional rural economy. In 1995, the government initiated an austerity programme intended to reduce the budget deficit, privatise state assets and eliminate trade tariffs. Following prolonged drought and the financial crisis in south-east Asia, the country is facing its worst financial crisis since independence, with debt servicing amounting to a quarter of government spending.

There are extensive mineral deposits throughout Papua New Guinea, including copper, gold, silver, nickel, bauxite and commercial deposits of oil. The Bougainville copper mine closed indefinitely in 1989 because of the unrest on the island. It had provided more than 15 per cent of the country's annual revenue.

Industry includes processing of primary products, and brewing, packaging, paint, plywood, and metal manufacturing and the construction industries. A mini-budget was announced in August 1999, which aimed to raise revenue by raising taxes and reducing expenditure.

In 1997 there was a trade surplus of US$677 million and a current account deficit of US$192 million. In 1998 imports totalled US$1,189 million and exports US$1,677 million.

GNP – US$4,104 million (1998); US$890 per capita (1998)
GDP – US$5,196 million (1996); US$1,181 per capita (1996)
ANNUAL AVERAGE GROWTH OF GDP – 3.9 per cent (1999)
INFLATION RATE – 3.9 per cent (1997)
TOTAL EXTERNAL DEBT – US$2,692 million (1998)

Trade with UK	1998	1999
Imports from UK	£6,572,000	£7,498,000
Exports to UK	53,618,000	47,941,000

COMMUNICATIONS

Air Niugini operates regular air services to other countries in the region, as well as internal air services. Several shipping companies operate cargo services to Australia, Europe, the Far East and USA. There are very limited cargo and passenger services between Papua New Guinea main ports, outports, plantations and missions. There are 21,433 km of roads, the most important road being that linking Lae with the populous highlands. Papua New Guinea is linked by international cable to Australia, Guam, Hong Kong, the Far East and the USA.

PARAGUAY
República del Paraguay

AREA – 157,048 sq. miles (406,752 sq. km). Neighbours: Bolivia (north-west), Brazil (north-east and east), Argentina (south)
POPULATION – 5,085,000 (1997 UN estimate): 95 per cent mestizo. Spanish is the official language of the country but outside the larger towns Guaraní, the language of the largest single group of Amerindian inhabitants, is widely spoken, and is also an official language
CAPITAL – Asunción (population, 718,690)
MAJOR CITIES – Ciudad del Este (133,881); San Lorenzo (133,395)
CURRENCY – Guaraní (Gs) of 100 céntimos
NATIONAL ANTHEM – Paraguayos, República O Muerte (Paraguayans, republic or death)
NATIONAL DAY – 15 May
NATIONAL FLAG – Three horizontal bands, red, white, blue with the National seal on the obverse white band and the Treasury seal on the reverse white band
LIFE EXPECTANCY (years) – male 66.30; female 70.83
POPULATION GROWTH RATE – 2.7 per cent (1997)
POPULATION DENSITY – 13 per sq. km (1997)
URBAN POPULATION – 50.3 per cent (1992)
MILITARY EXPENDITURE – 1.4 per cent of GDP (1998)
MILITARY PERSONNEL – 20,200: Army 14,900, Navy 3,600, Air Force 1,700; Paramilitaries 14,800
CONSCRIPTION DURATION – One to two years

Paraguay is an inland subtropical state of South America, situated between Argentina, Bolivia and Brazil. It is a country of grassy plains and forested hills. In the angle formed by the Paraná-Paraguay confluence are marshes, one of which, known as Neembucú (or endless) is drained by Lake Ypoa, a large lagoon south-east of the capital. The Chaco, lying between the rivers Paraguay and Pilcomayo and bounded on the north by Bolivia, is a flat plain, rising uniformly towards its western boundary to a height of 1,140 feet; it suffers much from floods and still more from drought, but the building of dams and reservoirs has converted part of it into good pasture for cattle.

HISTORY AND POLITICS

Paraguay was settled as a Spanish possession in 1537 and became independent in 1811.

Gen. Alfredo Stroessner, dictator from 1954, was overthrown in February 1989 by Gen. Andrés Rodríguez, who was elected president in May 1989. In May 1991, the first free municipal elections were held, and elections to the parliament were held in December 1991. Amendments to the constitution came into effect in June 1992. The last presidential and legislative elections were held on 10 May 1998. The presidential election was won by Raúl Cubas Grau of the Colorado Party, after its original candidate Gen. Lino Oviedo was banned from standing in elections for his part in a failed coup in 1996. In the legislative election, the distribution of seats in the Senate was: Colorado Party (CP) 24; Democratic Alliance (DA) 20; Blanco Party 1. In the Chamber of Deputies, the CP won 45 seats and the DA 35.

Vice-President Luis María Argaña was assassinated on 23 March 1999, following a power struggle between his supporters and those of President Cubas Grau and Gen. Oviedo. Supporters of Argaña demanded the resignation of the president and an indefinite general strike was called. The Chamber of Deputies voted to initiate impeachment proceedings against President Cubas Grau. He resigned on 28 March and was granted asylum in Brazil. The president of the Senate, Luis González Macchi, was immediately sworn in as the new president. Gen. Oviedo fled to Argentina, where he was granted asylum, but in December fled to Brazil. An attempted coup, thought to be by supporters of Gen. Oviedo, was foiled by government forces on 18 May 2000. Gen. Oviedo was arrested in Brazil on 11 June 2000 pending extradition proceedings.

POLITICAL SYSTEM

The constitution provides for a two-chamber legislature consisting of a 45-member Senate and an 80-member Chamber of Deputies, both elected for five-year terms. Deputies are elected on a regional basis, the number of seats allocated to each regional department being directly proportional to the department's population. Voting is compulsory for all citizens over 18. The president is elected for a five-year term and may not be re-elected. The vice-president may only contest the presidency if he resigns his post six months before the election. The president appoints the Cabinet, which exercises all the functions of government.

HEAD OF STATE

President, Luis González Macchi, *sworn in* 28 March 1999
Vice-President, Julio Cesar Franco

CABINET *as at July 2000*

Agriculture and Livestock, Enrique Zuniga
Defence, Adm. José Ocampos Alfaro
Education and Culture, Nicanor Duarte Frutos
Finance, Federico Zayas Chirife
Foreign Affairs, Juan Estebán Aguirre
Industry and Commerce, Euclides Acevedo
Interior, Walter Bower
Justice and Labour, Silvio Ferreira
Health and Social Welfare, Martin Chiola
Public Health and Social Welfare, Martín Chiola
Public Works, Communications, José Alberto Planas
Secretary-General for the Presidency, Jaime Bestard

EMBASSY OF PARAGUAY

Braemar Lodge, Cornwall Gardens, London SW7 4AQ
Tel: 020-7937 1253/6629
Ambassador Extraordinary and Plenipotentiary, Raúl Dos Santos, apptd 1998

BRITISH EMBASSY

Avda. Boggiani 5848, C/R 16 Boqueron, Asunción
Tel: (00 595) (21) 612611
E-mail: brembasu@mail.pla.net.py
Ambassador Extraordinary and Plenipotentiary and Consul-General, HE Andrew George, apptd 1998

ECONOMY

President Rodríguez introduced an economic liberalisation programme which has been continued by subsequent governments. This has reduced foreign debt and attracted foreign investment, notably from Brazil. About half of the population are engaged in agriculture and cattle raising. Cassava, sugar cane, soya, cotton and wheat are the main agricultural products. The forests contain many varieties of timber which find a good market abroad.

Paraguay's rivers give it considerable hydroelectric capacity. There is a hydroelectric power station at Acaray which exports surplus power to Argentina and Brazil. Joint projects have been undertaken with Brazil, on a hydroelectric dam at Itaipú (the largest in the world), and with Argentina, at Yacyretá.

GNP – US$9,172 million (1998); US$1,760 per capita (1998)
GDP – US$9,650 million (1996); US$1,947 per capita (1996)
ANNUAL AVERAGE GROWTH OF GDP – 1.3 per cent (1996)
INFLATION RATE – 11.5 per cent (1998)
UNEMPLOYMENT – 8.2 per cent (1996)
TOTAL EXTERNAL DEBT – US$2,305 million (1998)

TRADE

The chief imports are machinery, fuels and lubricants, vehicles, drinks and tobacco. The chief exports are soya, cotton fibres, meat, timber and coffee. The main trading partners are Brazil, Argentina and the USA.

In 1994 Paraguay had a trade deficit of US$1,277 million and a current account deficit of US$749 million. In 1997 imports totalled US$3,403 million and exports US$1,089 million.

Trade with UK	1998	1999
Imports from UK	£42,859,000	£30,460,000
Exports to UK	1,547,000	672,000

COMMUNICATIONS

There are direct shipping services from Asunción to Europe and the USA, and river steamer services for internal transport. Eight airlines operate services from Asunción. There are 28,900 km of roads in Paraguay, connecting Asunción with São Paulo via the Bridge of Friendship and Foz de Yguazú, and with Buenos Aires via Puerto Pilcomayo. Many earth roads are liable to be closed or to become impassable in wet weather. There are 441 km of railway track. Rail services, with train ferries, provide internal and international links. Five daily and six weekly newspapers are published in Asunción.

EDUCATION

Education is free and compulsory. There are 11 universities and one institute of education.
ILLITERACY RATE – 6.7 per cent
ENROLMENT (percentage of age group) – primary 91 per cent (1996); secondary 38 per cent (1996); tertiary 10 per cent (1996)

PERU
República del Peru

AREA – 496,225 sq. miles (1,285,216 sq. km). Neighbours: Ecuador and Colombia (north), Brazil and Bolivia (east), Chile (south)
POPULATION – 25,015,000 (1999 estimate): 45 per cent Amerindian, 37 per cent mestizo, 15 per cent European, also Africans, Chinese and Japanese. The official languages are Spanish and Quechua
CAPITAL – Lima (including ΨCallao, population, 6,483,901, 1993 census)
MAJOR CITIES – Arequipa (624,500); Chiclayo (448,400); Chimbote (314,700); Trujillo (521,200)
CURRENCY – New Sol of 100 cénts
NATIONAL ANTHEM – Somos Libres, Seámoslo Siempre (We are free, let us remain so forever)
NATIONAL DAY – 28 July (Anniversary of Independence)
NATIONAL FLAG – Three vertical stripes of red, white, red
LIFE EXPECTANCY (years) – male 65.91; female 70.85
POPULATION GROWTH RATE – 1.7 per cent (1997)
POPULATION DENSITY – 19 per sq. km (1997)

URBAN POPULATION – 71.2 per cent (1995)
MILITARY EXPENDITURE – 1.6 per cent of GDP (1998)
MILITARY PERSONNEL – 115,000: Army 75,000, Navy
  25,000, Air Force 15,000; Paramilitaries 77,000
CONSCRIPTION DURATION – Two years (selective)

The country is traversed throughout its length by the Andes, running parallel to the Pacific coast. There are three main regions, the Costa, west of the Andes, the Sierra or mountain ranges of the Andes, which include the Punas or mountainous wastes below the region of perpetual snow, and the Montaña or Selva, which is the vast area of jungle stretching from the eastern foothills of the Andes to the eastern frontiers of Peru. The coastal area, lying upon and near the Pacific, is not tropical though close to the Equator, being cooled by the Humboldt Current.

HISTORY AND POLITICS

Peru was conquered in the early 16th century by Francisco Pizarro (1478–1541). He subjugated the Incas (the ruling caste of the Quechua Indians), who had started their rise to power some 500 years earlier, and for nearly three centuries Peru remained under Spanish rule. A revolutionary war of 1821–4 established its independence, declared on 28 July 1821. A military junta ruled Peru from 1968 until 1980 when civilian government was restored.

In April 1992 President Fujimori, faced with increasing terrorist violence, suspended the constitution, dissolved Congress and began to govern by decree. In November 1992 a legislative election was held to an 80-seat Democratic Constituent Congress (CCD) which was installed as an interim legislature and constituent assembly to write a new constitution. Parties supporting Fujimori's suspension of the constitution gained a majority in the CCD. In January 1993, the 1979 constitution was re-established and the CCD declared Fujimori constitutional head of state. The CCD produced a new constitution which was endorsed in a national referendum in October 1993.

Parliamentary and presidential elections were held on 9 April 1995, with President Fujimori winning the first round of the presidential election outright and his Cambio 90-Nueva Mayoría Party winning 67 out of 120 seats in the new *Congreso de la República* (Congress of the Republic).

President Fujimori announced in December 1999 that he would run for a third term of office. Following objections by the opposition, the National Elections Board ruled that Fujimori had been elected president only once since the introduction of the 1993 constitution and was therefore eligible to stand again. President Fujimori was unable to win the first round of the presidential election on 9 April 2000 outright, but polled the most votes. In the simultaneous legislative election, his Peru 2000 alliance won 51 seats, losing its absolute majority. The Peru Possible party won 28 seats and the Moralising Independent Front won nine seats. In the second round of the presidential election, President Fujimori was re-elected with 51.2 per cent of the vote after his opponent, Alejandro Toledo of the Peru Possible party refused to campaign, following accusations of widespread ballot rigging in the first round. Although voting was compulsory, Toledo asked his supporters to spoil their ballot papers; he gained 17.7 per cent of the vote and 31.1 per cent of ballot papers were spoiled. The chief of the Organisation of American States observer mission concluded that the entire electoral process had been irregular.

FOREIGN RELATIONS

A 78 km stretch of the border with Ecuador has been in dispute since 1960. In 1995 an inconclusive border war was fought between the two countries, and in July 1995 a demilitarised zone was established around the disputed area. Four guarantor countries (Argentina, Brazil, Chile and the USA) adjudicated the claims of both countries and produced an agreement which was signed on 26 October 1998 by the presidents of Ecuador and Peru, formally ending the dispute.

INSURGENCIES

Since the late 1970s the government has faced violence from drug organisations and insurgencies from two leftist guerrilla movements, the Maoist Sendero Luminoso (Shining Path) and the Movimiento Revolucionario Túpac Amaru (MRTA), with fighting having left 30,000 dead.

Security forces captured the leader of the MRTA in November 1998 and the leader of Shining Path in December 1998.

POLITICAL SYSTEM

The constitution, promulgated in December 1993, provides for the president to be able to serve two terms rather than one, as previously; the introduction of the death penalty for treason; and the formation of a new 120-member unicameral Congress. A constitutional panel approved a Bill in August 1996, allowing President Fujimori to stand for a third term in office.

HEAD OF STATE

President of the Republic, Alberto Fujimori, *assumed office* 28 July 1990, *re-elected* 9 April 1995, 28 May 2000
First Vice-President, Francisco Tudela
Second Vice-President, Ricardo Márquez Flores

CABINET *as at July 2000*

Presidency, Maria Luisa Alvarado
President of the Council of Ministers, Justice, Alberto Bustamante Belaúnde
Advancement of Women and Human Development, María Luisa Cuculiza Torres
Agriculture, Jose Chlimper
Defence, Gen. Carlos Bergamino Cruz
Economy and Finance, Carlos Bolona Behr
Education, Frederico Salas Guevara
Energy and Mines, Jorge Alfredo Chamot Sarmiento
Fisheries, Pablo Arturo Handabaka
Foreign Affairs, Dr Fernando de Trazegnies Granda
Health, Dr Alejandro Aguinaga Recuenco
Industry, Tourism, Commerce, Integration, Gonzalo Romero de la Puenta
Interior, Gen. Walter Chacon Malaga
Justice, Alberto Bustamante Belaunde
Labour and Social Promotion, Egardo Mosqueira Medina
Transport, Communications, Housing and Construction, Agusto Bedoya

EMBASSY OF PERU

52 Sloane Street, London SW1X 9SP
Tel: 020-7235 1917/2545/3802
Ambassador Extraordinary and Plenipotentiary,
  HE Gilbert Chauny De Porturas Hoyle, apptd 2000

BRITISH EMBASSY

Edificio El Pacifico Washington, Piso 12, Plaza Washington (PO Box 854), Lima 100
Tel: (00 51) (1) 433 4738/9
E-mail: britcom@cosapidata.com.pe
Ambassador Extraordinary and Plenipotentiary, HE Roger Hart, CMG, apptd 1999

CONSULAR OFFICE – Lima
HONORARY CONSULATES – Arequipa, Cusco, Iquitos, Piura, Trujillo

BRITISH COUNCIL DIRECTOR, G. Liesching,
  Calle Alberto Lynch 110, San Isidro, Lima 27;
  e-mail: bc.lima@bc-lima.org.pe

ECONOMY

The chief products of the coastal belt are cotton, sugar and petroleum. There are large tracts of land suitable for cultivation and stock-raising (cattle, sheep, llamas, alpacas and vicuñas) on the eastern slopes of the Andes, and in the mountain valleys maize, potatoes and wheat are grown. The jungle area is a source of timber and petroleum. Other major crops are fruit, vegetables, rice, barley, grapes and coffee. The mountains contain rich mineral deposits and mineral exports include lead, zinc, copper, iron ore and silver. Peru is normally the world's largest exporter of fishmeal.

Since 1990 the government has launched a radical free-market restructuring programme which has rebuilt the foreign exchange reserves, reduced inflation from 7,600 per cent a year in 1990 to four per cent in 1999, cut subsidies and import tariffs, freed interest rates and privatised most state firms. Foreign investment has been encouraged and has grown dramatically. The economic recovery has increased the gap between rich and poor.

Following a slowdown in economic growth, falling output, rising unemployment and a decline in the popularity of the government, further privatisation has been halted.

GNP – US$60,491 million (1998); US$2,440 per capita (1998)
GDP – US$60,951 million (1996); US$2,546 per capita (1996)
ANNUAL AVERAGE GROWTH OF GDP – 7.2 per cent (1997)
INFLATION RATE – 7.2 per cent (1998)
UNEMPLOYMENT – 7.7 per cent (1998)
TOTAL EXTERNAL DEBT – US$32,397 million (1998)

TRADE

The principal imports are machinery, chemicals and pharmaceutical products. The chief exports are minerals and metals, fishmeal, sugar, cotton and coffee.

In 1997 Peru had a trade deficit of US$1,739 million and a current account deficit of US$3,407 million. Imports totalled US$10,263 million and exports US$6,814 million.

Trade with UK	1998	1999
Imports from UK	£66,433,000	£48,677,000
Exports to UK	119,105,000	132,403,000

COMMUNICATIONS

There are 73,766 km of roads, of which 16,876 km are unsurfaced. The Andean Highway forms a link between the Pacific, the Amazon and the Atlantic. The Pan-American Highway runs along the Peruvian coast connecting it with Ecuador and Chile.

The railway is administered by the government. There are 1,992 km of railway track. There is also steam navigation on the Ucayali and Huallaga, and in the south on Lake Titicaca. Air services are maintained throughout Peru, and there is an international airport at Lima.

EDUCATION

Education is compulsory and free between seven and 16. There are 51 universities.
ILLITERACY RATE – 10.1 per cent
ENROLMENT (percentage of age group) – primary 91 per cent (1997); secondary 55 per cent (1997); tertiary 26 per cent (1997)

THE PHILIPPINES
Repúblika ng Pilipinas

AREA – 115,831 sq. miles (300,000 sq. km)

POPULATION – 73,527,000 (1997 UN estimate). The inhabitants are of Malay stock, with admixtures of Spanish and Chinese blood in many localities. The Chinese minority is estimated at 500,000, with smaller numbers of Spanish, American and Indian. About 90 per cent are Christian, predominantly Roman Catholics. Most of the remainder are Muslims or indigenous animists. The official languages are Filipino and English. Filipino is based on Tagalog, one of the Malay–Polynesian languages. English, the language of government, is spoken by at least 44 per cent of the population. Spanish is now spoken by a very small minority
CAPITAL – ΨManila (population, 8,594,150, 1994)
MAJOR CITIES – Bacolod (402,345); ΨCebu (662,299); ΨDavao (1,008,640); ΨIloilo (334,539); ΨZamboanga (511,139), 1995 UN estimates
CURRENCY – Philippine peso (P) of 100 centavos
NATIONAL ANTHEM – Lupang Hinirang
NATIONAL DAY – 12 June (Independence Day 1898)
NATIONAL FLAG – Equal horizontal bands of blue (above) and red; gold sun with three stars on a white triangle next staff
LIFE EXPECTANCY (years) – male 63.10; female 66.70
POPULATION GROWTH RATE – 2.6 per cent (1997)
POPULATION DENSITY – 245 per sq. km (1997)
URBAN POPULATION – 42.7 per cent (1990)

There are 11 larger islands and 7,079 other islands. The principal islands (area in sq. km) are: Luzon (104,688); Mindanao (94,630); Samar (13,080); Negros (12,710); Palawan (11,785); Panay (11,515); Mindoro (9,735); Leyte (7,214); Cebu (4,422); Bohol (3,865); Masbate (3,269). Other groups are the Sulu islands (capital, Jolo), Babuyanes and Batanes; the Calamian islands; and Kalayaan Islands.

HISTORY AND POLITICS

The Philippines were conquered by Spain in 1565 and named Filipinas after Philip II of Spain. Independence was declared on 12 June 1898. In the Spanish–American War of 1898, Manila was captured by American troops and remained under US control until 1946. The Republic of the Philippines came into existence on 4 July 1946.

Ferdinand Marcos was president from 1965 to 1986. Although he gained a majority of votes in the official count of a presidential election in February 1986, the election was marred by widespread electoral abuse and his rival, Mrs Corazón Aquino, launched a campaign of non-violent civil disturbance which gained wide support. On 25 February Marcos fled to Hawaii. Mrs Aquino took over as president and survived seven coup attempts.

Fidel Ramos was elected president in May 1992 and managed to overcome the attempted coups and legislative obstructiveness that had plagued President Aquino. The presidential election in May 1998 was won by the former Vice-President, Joseph Estrada.

Legislative elections were held on 11 May 1998. The coalition of the Lakas ng EDSA/National Union of Christian Democrats won a majority in the House of Representatives.

INSURGENCIES

On 2 September 1996, the government signed an agreement with the Moro National Liberation Front (MNLF) on the creation of an autonomous Muslim region in Mindanao, Palawan, Sulu and Basilan, ending a 24-year rebellion which had left more than 120,000 people dead. The Moro Islamic Liberation Front (MILF), a radical breakaway group, threatened to disrupt the agreement. The Communist New People's Army (NPA) maintains a presence in eastern Mindanao, Negros, Samar, Bicol, the mountains of northern Luzon and Bataan. The NPA signed a cease-fire agreement with the government in December 1993; peace talks were suspended in February 1999. MILF immediately announced that its forces would come to the aid of NPA rebels should they be attacked by government forces. Sporadic peace talks between the government and MILF began in October 1999, but collapsed in late April 2000.

On 23 April 2000, 21 people, including ten foreign tourists, were kidnapped on the Malaysian island of Sipadan and taken to the Philippine island of Jolo by Abu Sayyaf, an Islamic rebel group.

POLITICAL SYSTEM

A new constitution came into force in July 1987. Legislative authority is vested in a bicameral Congress. The House of Representatives has 250 members, of whom 204 are directly elected and 46 appointed by the President for a three-year term. The Senate has 24 members, of whom 12 are re-elected every three years.

The Autonomous Region of Mindanao consists of four provinces: Sulu, Tawitawi, Lanao del Sur and Maguinadanao. There is a 24-member regional assembly and a governor.

HEAD OF STATE

President, Joseph Ejercito Estrada, *assumed office* 30 June 1998
Vice-Presidentz, Social Welfare and Development, Gloria Macapagal Arroyo

CABINET *as at September 2000*
Agrarian Reform, Horacio Morales
Agriculture, Edgardo Angara
Budget and Management, Benjamin Diokno
Defence, Orlando Mercado
Education, Culture and Sport, Andrew Gonzales
Energy, Mario Tiaoque
Environment and Natural Resources, Antonio Cerilles
Executive Secretary, Ronaldo Zamora
Finance, José Pardo
Foreign Affairs, Domingo Siazon
Governor of the Central Bank, Rafael Buenventura Singson
Health, Alberto Romualdez
Interior and Local Government, Alfredo Lim
Justice, Artemio Tuquero
Labour and Employment, Bienvenido Laguesma
Public Works and Highways, Gregorio Vigilar
Science and Technology, Felimon Urierte
Socio-economic Planning, Director-General of the National Economic Development Agency, Felipe Medalla
Tourism, Gemma Cruz-Araneta
Trade and Industry, Manuel Roxas
Transportation and Communications, Vicente Rivera

EMBASSY OF THE PHILIPPINES
9A Palace Green, London W8 4QE
Tel: 020-7937 1600
Ambassador Extraordinary and Plenipotentiary, HE César Bautista, apptd 1999
Defence Attaché, Col. P. Inserto
Commercial Attaché, V. Casim

BRITISH EMBASSY
Floors 15–17 LV Locsin Building, 6752 Ayala Avenue, Corner Makati Avenue, 1226 Makati, Metro Manila (PO Box 2927 MCPO)
Tel: (00 63) (2) 816 7116
E-mail: bremb@skyin.net
Ambassador Extraordinary and Plenipotentiary, HE Alan Collins, CMG, apptd 1998
Deputy Head of Mission, M. Reilly
Defence Attaché, Capt. C. C. Peach, RN
First Secretary, E. McEvoy *(Commercial)*

BRITISH COUNCIL DIRECTOR, R. Bell, 10th Floor, Taipan Place, Emerald Avenue, Ortigas Business Centre, Pasig City 1605, Metro Manila; e-mail: britishcouncil@britishcouncil.org.ph

DEFENCE

The Army has 85 armoured infantry fighting vehicles, and 348 armoured personnel carriers. The Navy has one frigate, 67 patrol and coastal vessels and two combat aircraft at three bases. The Air Force has 42 combat aircraft and 97 armed helicopters.
MILITARY EXPENDITURE – 2.3 per cent of GDP (1998)
MILITARY PERSONNEL – 110,000: Army 73,000, Navy 20,500, Air Force 16,500; Paramilitaries 42,500

ECONOMY

In 1998, 39.8 per cent of the workforce were engaged in agriculture and in 1997, it accounted for 19.9 per cent of GDP. The chief products are rice, coconuts, sugar cane, bananas, maize and pineapples. There are an increasing number of manufacturing industries and it is the policy of the government to diversify the economy. There are also deposits of copper, coal, gold, silver, chromium, iron and nickel.

The Philippines has been bypassed by the economic growth of most of the rest of south-east Asia since the 1960s, mainly because of the incompetence and corruption of the Marcos regime. Recently, however, an economic reform programme of liberalisation, privatisation and deregulation has been put in place and has led to increased exports, increased foreign investment, and a reduction in inflation. In July 1998, the Bank of the Philippines effectively devalued the peso following attacks from speculators, prompted by the devaluation of the Thai baht. In December 1997, the government unveiled an austerity plan cutting spending by 25 per cent. Prompt and firm measures from the government are credited with limiting the damage caused by the regional economic crisis.
GNP – US$78,938 million (1998); US$1,050 per capita (1998)
GDP – US$83,532 million (1996); US$1,206 per capita (1996)
ANNUAL AVERAGE GROWTH OF GDP – 9.7 per cent (1997)
INFLATION RATE – 9.7 per cent (1998)
UNEMPLOYMENT – 9.6 per cent (1998)
TOTAL EXTERNAL DEBT – US$47,817 million (1998)

TRADE

Principal exports are electronic products, machinery and transport equipment, clothing, coconut oil and products, and minerals. Principal imports are fuelstuffs and oils, electronic goods and components, machinery, base metals, transport equipment, textiles and yarns, and cereals. The major trading partners are the USA, Japan, Singapore and Hong Kong.

In 1998 the Philippines had a trade deficit of US$28 million and a current account surplus of US$1,287 million. Imports totalled US$30,705 million and exports US$27,783 million.

Trade with UK	1998	1999
Imports from UK	£304,129,000	£241,165,000
Exports to UK	898,956,000	1,024,775,000

COMMUNICATIONS

The highway system covers about 187,000. The Philippine National Railway operates 429 km of track. There are 415 ports. There are 82 national airports and 137 privately operated airports. Philippine Airlines has regular flights throughout the Far East, to the USA and Europe, in addition to inter-island services.

EDUCATION

Secondary and higher education is extensive and there are 21 public and 53 private universities recognised by the government, including the Dominican University of Santo Tomás (founded in 1611). There are also 530 other institutions of higher education.

ILLITERACY RATE – 4.6 per cent
ENROLMENT (percentage of age group) – primary
100 per cent (1995); secondary 59 per cent (1995); tertiary 29 per cent (1995)

POLAND
Rzeczpospolita Polska

AREA – 124,808 sq. miles (323,250 sq. km). Neighbours: the Russian Federation (Kaliningrad) (north), Germany (west), the Czech Republic and Slovakia (south), Belarus, Ukraine and Lithuania (east)
POPULATION – 38,650,000 (1997). Roman Catholicism is the religion of 95 per cent of the inhabitants. The language is Polish; there are German, Ukrainian and Belarusian minorities
CAPITAL – Warsaw (population, 1,628,500, 1996 estimate), on the Vistula
MAJOR CITIES – Bydgoszcz (386,600); ΨGdańsk (Danzig) (462,300); Katowice (351,000); Kraków (740,700); Łódź (818,000); Poznań (580,800); ΨSzczecin (Stettin) (418,800); Wrocław (Breslau) (646,000), 1996 estimates
CURRENCY – Złoty of 100 groszy
NATIONAL ANTHEM – Jeszcze Polska Nie Zginęła (Poland has not yet perished)
NATIONAL DAY – 3 May
NATIONAL FLAG – Equal horizontal stripes of white (above) and red
LIFE EXPECTANCY (years) – male 68.12; female 76.57
POPULATION GROWTH RATE – 0.2 per cent (1997)
POPULATION DENSITY – 120 per sq. km (1997)
URBAN POPULATION – 62.0 per cent (1997)

HISTORY AND POLITICS

The Polish Commonwealth ceased to exist in 1795 after three successive partitions in 1772, 1793 and 1795 in which Prussia, Russia and Austria shared. The Republic of Poland was proclaimed at Warsaw in November 1918, and its independence guaranteed by the signatories of the Treaty of Versailles.

German forces invaded Poland on 1 September 1939; on 17 September, Russian forces invaded eastern Poland, and on 21 September 1939 Poland was declared by Germany and Russia to have ceased to exist. At the end of the war, its frontiers were redrawn; eastern Poland was ceded to the Soviet Union in return for the German territory east of the rivers Oder and Neisse. A coalition government was formed in which the Polish Workers' Party played a large part. In December 1948, the Polish Workers' Party and the Polish Socialist Party merged to form the Polish United Workers' Party (PUWP). A new constitution modelled on the Soviet constitution was adopted in 1952, and was modified in 1976.

Steep price rises in 1980 prompted strikes which forced the government to allow independent trade unions, including 'Solidarity' led by Lech Wałęsa. The unions agitated for further reforms although their activities were suspended when martial law was in force from December 1981 until July 1983.

A wave of strikes resulted in talks between Wałęsa and the PUWP early in 1989. Multiparty parliamentary elections were held in the summer of 1989, following which the PUWP ceased to be the ruling party. The post-Communist governments have introduced a market economy but economic difficulties and a fragmented parliament have led to a succession of short-lived governments.

Elections held on 21 September 1997 were won by the right-wing Solidarity Electoral Alliance (AWS), a group of 36 parties, which formed a government with the Freedom Union (UW). The AWS won 201 seats in the *Sejm* and 51 in the Senate; the UW won 60 seats in the *Sejm* and 8 in the Senate. On 6 June 2000, the UW withdrew from the government.

A presidential election is due on 8 October 2000.

FOREIGN RELATIONS

In July 1997, Poland was invited to join NATO. It has also been approved by the European Commission for membership of the EU, and formal accession talks began in March 1998.

POLITICAL SYSTEM

A new constitution came into effect on 16 October 1997. The President, directly elected for a maximum of two five-year terms, appoints the Prime Minister and has the right to be consulted over the appointment of the foreign, defence and interior ministers. The National Assembly is the bicameral legislature, comprising a 460-member *Sejm* (Diet) and a Senate of 100 members. Both houses have a four-year term. The Senate is elected on a provincial basis.

HEAD OF STATE

President, Aleksander Kwaśniewski, *elected* 19 November 1995, *sworn in* 23 December 1995

CABINET *as at September 2000*

Prime Minister, Jerzy Buzek (AWS)
Deputy P.M, Economy, Janusz Steinhoff (AWS)
Deputy P.M, Labour and Social Welfare, Longin Komołowski (AWS)
Agriculture and the Development of the Countryside, Artur Balazs (AWS)
Communications, Tomasz Szyszko (AWS)
Culture and National Heritage, Kazimierz Michal Ujazdowski (AWS)
Environmental Protection, Natural Resources and Forestry, Antoni Tokarczuk (AWS)
European Integration, Jacek Saryusz Wolski
Finance, Jarosław Bauc
Foreign Affairs, Władysław Bartoszewski
Health, Franciszka Cegielska (AWS)
Internal Affairs and Administration, Marek Biernacki (AWS)
Justice, Lech Kaczyński (UW)
National Defence, Bronislaw Komorowski (AWS)
National Education, Edmund Wittbrodt (AWS)
Regional Development and Housing, Jerzy Kropiwnicki (AWS)
Science, Andrzej Wiszniewski (AWS)
Transport and Maritime Economy, Jerzy Widzyk
Treasury, Andrzej Chronowski (AWS)
Without Portfolio, Janusz Palubicki (*Security Services*)
AWS Solidarity Electoral Alliance.

EMBASSY OF THE REPUBLIC OF POLAND
47 Portland Place, London W1N 3AG
Tel: 020-7580 4324/9
Ambassador Extraordinary and Plenipotentiary, HE Stanislaw Komorowski, apptd 1999
Commercial Counsellor, Minister Plenipotentiary, Piotr Kozerski
Defence Attaché, Col. Andrzej Adamowicz

BRITISH EMBASSY
No. 1 Aleje Róz, PL-00-556 Warsaw
Tel: (00 48) (22) 628 1001/5
E-mail: britemb@it.com.pl
Ambassador Extraordinary and Plenipotentiary, HE John
Macgregor, CVO, apptd 1998
Counsellor, R. A. Barnett (*Deputy Head of Mission*)
Defence and Air Attaché, Gp Capt. M. Mitchell
Director of Trade Promotion and Consul-General
M. H. Davenport

HONORARY CONSULATES – Gdańsk, Katowice, Kraków,
Poznań, Szczecin, Wrocław (Breslau)
BRITISH COUNCIL DIRECTOR, Dr J. Eyres,
Al. Jerozolimskie 59, PL-00–697 Warsaw; e-mail:
bc.warsaw@britcoun.org.pl. There is an office in
Kraków and libraries in Białystok, Gdańsk, Katowice,
Łódź, Lublin, Poznań, Szczecin, Torun and Wrocław

DEFENCE

The Army has 1,674 main battle tanks, 1,404 armoured
infantry fighting vehicles and 33 armoured personnel
carriers. The Navy has three submarines, one destroyer,
one frigate, 40 patrol and coastal vessels, 25 combat
aircraft and 11 armed helicopters at five bases. The Air
Force has 253 combat aircraft and 11 attack helicopters.
MILITARY EXPENDITURE – 2.2 per cent of GDP (1998) –
240,650: Army 142,500, Navy 17,100, Air Force 55,300,
Paramilitaries 23,400
CONSCRIPTION DURATION – 12 months

ECONOMY

Poland is well endowed with mineral resources; there are
large reserves of brown coal in central and south-western
Poland and hard coal in Upper Silesia and the Wałbrzych
and Lublin regions; sulphur, copper, zinc, lead, natural gas
and salt are also produced.
In 1990, the government embarked upon a series of
measures designed to introduce a free-market economy.
The transition to a market economy has been painful,
with unemployment doubling between 1990 and 1995 and
remaining high. Industrial output has improved and the
rate of growth of GDP has increased although inflation
remains high.
A programme is underway to modernise the agricultural
sector and adapt it to the EU's common agricultural
policy.
Poland's major imports are machinery and vehicles,
chemical products, leather and textiles, livestock, foodstuffs, luxury goods and metal products. Its major exports
are machinery and vehicles, leather and textiles, metal
goods, livestock, foodstuffs, luxury goods and chemical
products. Germany is Poland's main trading partner.
In 1997 there was a trade deficit of US$9,822 million
and a current account deficit of US$5,744 million.
Imports totalled US$42,308 million and exports
US$25,751 million.
GNP – US$151,285 million (1998); US$3,910 per capita
(1998)
GDP – US$134,570 million (1996); US$3,486 per capita
(1996)
ANNUAL AVERAGE GROWTH OF GDP – 6.1 per cent
(1996)
INFLATION RATE – 11.7 per cent (1998)
UNEMPLOYMENT – 10.5 per cent (1998)
TOTAL EXTERNAL DEBT – US$47,708 million (1998)

Trade with UK	1998	1999
Imports from UK	£1,213,416,000	£1,179,399,000
Exports to UK	684,035,000	692,886,000

EDUCATION

Elementary education (ages seven to 15) is compulsory
and free. Secondary education is optional and free. There
are 179 institutions of higher education, including
universities at Kraków, Warsaw, Poznań, Łódź, Wrocław,
Lublin and Toruń and a number of other towns.
ENROLMENT (percentage of age group) – primary
95 per cent (1995); secondary 85 per cent (1994); tertiary
24.7 per cent (1995)

CULTURE

Polish is a western Slavonic tongue, the Latin alphabet
being used. Major writers include Henryk Sienkiewicz
(1846–1916), Nobel Prizewinner for Literature in 1905;
Bolesław Prus (1847–1912); Stanisław Reymont (1867–
1925), Nobel Prizewinner in 1924; Czesław Miłosz,
Nobel Prize winner in 1980; and Wisława Szymborska,
Nobel Prize winner in 1996.

PORTUGAL
República Portuguesa

AREA – 35,514 sq. miles (91,982 sq. km). Neighbour: Spain
(north and east)
POPULATION – 9,920,760 (1995); 9,833,014 (excluding the
Azores and Madeira). 94 per cent of the population are
Catholic. The language is Portuguese
CAPITAL – ΨLisbon (population, 2,561,225, 1991)
MAJOR CITIES – ΨOporto (1,683,000)
CURRENCY – Euro (€) of 100 cents/Escudo (Esc) of 100
centavos
NATIONAL ANTHEM – A Portuguesa
NATIONAL DAY – 10 June
NATIONAL FLAG – Divided vertically into unequal parts of
green and red with the national emblem over all on the
line of division
LIFE EXPECTANCY (years) – male 71.27; female 78.57
POPULATION GROWTH RATE – 0.1 per cent (1997)
POPULATION DENSITY – 107 per sq. km (1997)
URBAN POPULATION – 48.2 per cent (1991)

HISTORY AND POLITICS

Portugal was a monarchy from the 12th century until
1910, when an armed rising in Lisbon drove King Manuel
II into exile and a republic was set up. A period of political
instability ensued until the military stepped in and
abolished political parties in 1926. The constitution of
1933 gave formal expression to the corporative 'Estado
Novo' (New State) which was personified by Dr Antonio
Salazar, Prime Minister 1932–68. Dr Caetano succeeded
Salazar as Prime Minister in 1968 but his failure to
liberalise the regime or to conclude the wars in the African
colonies resulted in his government's overthrow by a
military coup on 25 April 1974. There was great political
turmoil between April 1974 and July 1976, a period in
which most of the colonies gained their independence, but
with the failure of an attempted coup by the extreme left in
November 1975 the situation stabilised. Full civilian
government was restored in 1982.
In the general election held on 1 October 1995, the
Socialist Party (PS) won 112 seats, the Social Democrats
(PSD) 88 seats, the Christian Democrats (CDS/PP) 15
seats, and the Communist Coalition (CDU) 15 seats. The
Socialist candidate, Jorge Sampaio, won the January 1996
presidential election.
In the general elections held on 10 October 1999, the
Socialist Party was re-elected, winning 115 seats, just one
seat short of a majority.
Macao, which had been a Portuguese colony since
1557, and whose status was confirmed in an 1887

Sino-Portuguese treaty, was transferred to Chinese sovereignty on 19 December 1999, becoming the Macao Special Administrative Region, and maintaining a high degree of autonomy.

POLITICAL SYSTEM

Under the 1976 constitution, amended in 1982 and 1989, the President is elected for a five-year term by universal adult suffrage. The Prime Minister is designated by the largest party in the legislature. Legislative authority is vested in the 230-member Assembly of the Republic, elected by a system of proportional representation every four years. The President retains certain limited powers to dismiss the government, dissolve the Assembly or veto laws.

HEAD OF STATE

President of the Republic, Jorge Sampaio, *elected* 14 January 1996, *inaugurated* 9 March 1996

CABINET *as at September 2000*

Prime Minister, António Guterres
Deputy PM, Foreign Affairs, Jaime Gama
Agriculture, Rural Development and Fisheries, Luís Capoulas Santos
Cabinet Office, Public Works and Parliamentary Affairs, Jorge Coelho
Culture, José Sasportes
Defence, Julio Castro Caldas
Drug Addiction, Vitalino Canas
Economy, Finance, Joaquim Pina Moura
Education, Guilherme Oliveira Martins
Environment, Territorial Affairs and Urban Development, José Sócrates
Equality, Maria de Belém
Health, Maria Manuela Arcanjo
Interior, Prime Minister's Office, Fernando Gomes
Justice, António Costa
Planning, Maria Elisa Ferreira
Public Administration and Administrative Reform, Alberto Martins
Science and Technology, José Mariano Gago
Social Communication, Youth, Armando Vara
Solidarity, Social Security, Employment, Eduardo Ferro Rodrigues

PORTUGUESE EMBASSY
11 Belgrave Square, London SW1X 8PP
Tel: 020-7235 5331
Ambassador Extraordinary and Plenipotentiary, José Gregório Faria, apptd 1997
Minister-Plenipotentiary and Consul-General, António Sennfelt
Minister-Counsellor, J. Ataíde da Cámara
Commercial Counsellor, António Silva
Defence Attaché, Capt. C. Brites Nunes

BRITISH EMBASSY
Rua de S. Bernardo 33, P-1200 Lisbon
Tel: (00 351) (1) 392 4000
E-mail: britembassy@mail.telepac.pt
Ambassador Extraordinary and Plenipotentiary, HE Sir John Holmes, KBE, CMB, CVO, apptd 1999
Counsellor, R. M. Publicover (*Deputy Head of Mission*)
Defence Attaché, Cdr. A. J. Bull, RN
First Secretary, P. Sinkinson (*Commercial*)
CONSULATE – Oporto

HONORARY CONSULATES, – Portimão, Funchal (Madeira), Ribeira Grande (Azores)

BRITISH COUNCIL DIRECTOR, R. Ness,
Rua de São Marçal 174, P-1294 Lisbon;
e-mail: lisbon.enquiries@britcounpt.org.
There are also offices at Cascais, Coimbra, Oporto and Parede

BRITISH PORTUGUESE CHAMBER OF COMMERCE,
Rua da Estrela 8, P-1200 Lisbon and Rua Sa de Bandeira 784–20E, Frente, P-4000 Oporto

DEFENCE

The Army has 187 main battle tanks, and 374 armoured personnel carriers. The Navy has three submarines, six frigates and 30 patrol and coastal vessels at four bases. The Air Force has 60 combat aircraft.

Lisbon is the base of the NATO Iberian Atlantic Command and the USA maintains 1,020 personnel in mainland Portugal and on the Azores.
MILITARY EXPENDITURE – 2.3 per cent of GDP (1998)
MILITARY PERSONNEL – 49,700; Army 25,650, Navy 16,600, Air Force 7,445; Paramilitaries 40,900
CONSCRIPTION DURATION – Four to 12 months

ECONOMY

The chief agricultural products are wines, dairy products, potatoes, tomatoes, maize, meat, fruits, olives, wheat, fish, cork and rice. There are extensive forests of pine, cork, eucalyptus and chestnut covering about 38 per cent of the country. The principal mineral products are limestone, granite, marble, copper, coal, kaolin and wolframite.

The country is moderately industrialised. The principal manufactures are motor vehicle components, clothing and footwear, textiles, machinery, pulp and paper, pharmaceuticals, foodstuffs, chemicals, fertilisers, wood, cork, furniture, cement, glassware and pottery. There are a modern steelworks and large shipbuilding and repair yards at Lisbon and Setúbal, working mainly for foreign shipowners. There are several hydroelectric power stations and two thermal power stations.

Portugal was one of 11 states to adopt the European single currency on 1 January 1999.
GNP – US$106,391 million (1998); US$10,670 per capita (1998)
GDP – US$107,133 million (1996); US$10,923 per capita (1996)
ANNUAL AVERAGE GROWTH OF GDP – 3.0 per cent (1996)
INFLATION RATE – 2.8 per cent (1998)
UNEMPLOYMENT – 5.0 per cent (1998)

TRADE

The principal imports are machinery, vehicles, textiles, clothing and shoes, agricultural products, chemicals, oil, and base metals. The principal exports are textiles, clothing and shoes, machinery, vehicles and automobile parts, wood, pulp, paper and cork, and minerals.

In 1998 Portugal had a trade deficit of US$12,279 million and a current account deficit of US$7,253 million. Imports totalled US$37,049 million and exports US$24,220 million.

Trade with UK	1998	1999
Imports from UK	£1,620,700,000	£1,599,300,000
Exports to UK	1,695,800,000	1,732,200,000

COMMUNICATIONS

There are 3,072 km of railway track, of which 461 km are electrified. There are international airports at Lisbon, Oporto, Faro and Santa Maria and Lages (Azores) and Funchal (Madeira). There are 23 daily newspapers.

EDUCATION

Education is free and compulsory for nine years from the age of six. Secondary education is mainly conducted in state general unified schools, lyceums, technical and professional schools, but there are also private schools. There are also military, naval, polytechnic and other special schools. There are 17 public and private universities including those at Coimbra (founded in 1290),

Oporto, Lisbon, Braga, Aveiro, Vila Real, Faro, Evora and in the Azores.
ILLITERACY RATE – 7.8 per cent
ENROLMENT (percentage of age group) – primary 100 per cent (1994); secondary 78 per cent (1994); tertiary 39 per cent (1995)

AUTONOMOUS REGIONS

Madeira and The Azores are two administratively autonomous regions of Portugal, having locally elected assemblies and governments.
MADEIRA is a group of islands in the Atlantic Ocean about 520 miles south-west of Lisbon, and consists of Madeira, Porto, Santo and three uninhabited islands (Desertas). Total area is 300 sq. miles (779 sq. km); population, 257,290 (1995). ΨFunchal in Madeira, the largest island (270 sq. miles), is the capital (population 44,111)
THE AZORES are a group of nine islands (Flores, Corvo, Terceira, São Jorge, Pico, Faial, Graciosa, São Miguel and Santa Maria) in the Atlantic Ocean; area 895 sq. miles (2,330 sq. km); population, 241,490 (1995). ΨPonta Delgada, on São Miguel, is the capital (population, 137,700). Other ports are ΨAngra, in Terceira (55,900) and ΨHorta (16,300)

QATAR
Dawlat Qatar

AREA – 4,247 sq. miles (11,000 sq. km). Neighbours: United Arab Emirates (south), Saudi Arabia (south-west)
POPULATION – 569,000 (1997 UN estimate). Most of the population is concentrated in the urban district of Doha. Arabic is the official language. Islam is the religion of 95 per cent of the population
CAPITAL – ΨDoha (Ad-Dawhah) (population, 392,384; 1995 estimate)
MAJOR CITIES – Ar-Rayyān; Dukhāan; ΨMusay'īd Al-Wakrah
CURRENCY – Qatar riyal of 100 dirhams
NATIONAL DAY – 3 September
NATIONAL FLAG – White and maroon, white portion nearer the mast; vertical indented line comprising 17 angles divides the colours
LIFE EXPECTANCY (years) – male 68.75; female 74.20
POPULATION GROWTH RATE – 2.3 per cent (1997)
POPULATION DENSITY – 52 per sq. km (1997)
MILITARY EXPENDITURE – 12.0 per cent of GDP (1998)
MILITARY PERSONNEL – 11,800: Army 8,500, Navy 1,800, Air Force 1,500
ILLITERACY RATE – 18.7 per cent
ENROLMENT (percentage of age group) – primary 80 per cent (1993); secondary 69 per cent (1993); tertiary 27 per cent (1996)

The state of Qatar covers the peninsula of Qatar in the Gulf from approximately the northern shore of Khor al Odaid to the eastern shore of Khor al Salwa.

HISTORY AND POLITICS

Qatar was one of nine independent emirates in the Gulf in special treaty relations with the UK until 1971. On 2 April 1970, a provisional constitution for Qatar was proclaimed, providing for the establishment of a Council of Ministers and for the formation of a Consultative Council to assist the Council of Ministers in running the affairs of the state. There are no political parties or legislature; ministers are chosen by the Amir.
The Amir, who had ruled since 22 February 1972, was overthrown on 27 June 1995 by his son and heir, who

assumed power as Amir the same day. A coup attempt was thwarted in February 1996; 30 people who had been involved were sentenced to life imprisonment in February 2000.
The Amir announced in November 1998 that a committee of experts would be formed to draft a new constitution and that an elected National Assembly would be established. Municipal elections were held on 8 March 1999, the first in which women were allowed to vote and contest seats.

HEAD OF STATE
HH Amir of Qatar, Minister of Defence and Commander-in-Chief of Armed Forces, Shaikh Hamad bin Khalifa al-Thani, KCMG, *assumed power* 27 June 1995
Crown Prince, HH Shaikh Jassim bin Hamad al-Thani

COUNCIL OF MINISTERS *as at September 2000*
Prime Minister, Interior, HH Shaikh Abdulla bin Khalifa al-Thani
Deputy PM, Shaikh Mohammed bin Khalifa al-Thani
Awqaf (Religious Endowments) and Islamic Affairs, Ahmed Abdulla al-Marri
Civil Service Affairs and Housing, Shaikh Falah bin Jassim al-Thani
Communications and Transport, Shaikh Ahmed bin Nasser al-Thani
Education, Higher Education and Culture, Dr Mohammed Abdulrahim Kafoud
Energy and Industry, Electricity and Water, Abdulla bin Hamad al-Attiyah
Finance, Economy and Trade, Yousef Hussein Kamal
Foreign Affairs, Shaikh Hamad bin Jassem bin Jabr al-Thani
Justice, Hassan bin Abdulla al-Ghanem
Minister of State, Cabinet Affairs, Ali bin Saad al-Kawari
Minister of State, Foreign Affairs, Ahmed Abdulla al-Mahmoud
Minister of State, Internal Affairs, Shaikh Abdulla bin Khalid al-Thani
Ministers of State, Shaikh Mohammad bin Khalid al-Thani; Shaikh Hamad bin Suhaim al-Thani; Shaikh Ahmed bin Saif al-Thani; Shaikh Hamad bin Abdulla al-Thani; Shaikh Hasan bin Abdulla al-Thani
Municipal Affairs, Agriculture, Ali Mohammad al-Khater
Public Health, Dr Hajr bin Ahmed Hajr

EMBASSY OF THE STATE OF QATAR
1 South Audley Street, London W1Y 5DQ
Tel: 020-7493 2200
Ambassador Extraordinary and Plenipotentiary, HE Ali M. Jaidah, apptd 1993
Defence Attaché, S. S. S. S. Al Mansouri
Minister Plenipotentiary, A. S. Al Midhadi

BRITISH EMBASSY
PO Box 3, Doha
Tel: (00 974) 421991
E-mail: bembcomm@qatar.net.qa
Ambassador Extraordinary and Plenipotentiary, HE D. Wright, OBE, apptd 1997

BRITISH COUNCIL DIRECTOR, J. Gildea, 93 Al Sadd Street, (PO Box 2992), Doha, Qatar
e-mail: john.gildea@bc-doha.bcouncil.org

ECONOMY

Although Qatar is a desert country, there are gardens and smallholdings near Doha and to the north, and agriculture is being developed, with self-sufficiency an aim.
Oil accounts for over 70 per cent of Qatar's exports. The Qatar General Petroleum Corporation is the state-owned company controlling Qatar's interests in oil, gas and petrochemicals.

Current industries include a steel mill, a fertiliser plant, a cement factory, a petrochemical complex and two natural gas liquids plants. With the exception of the cement works at Umm Bāb, all these industries are at Musay'īd, about 30 miles south of Doha. Qatar is also expanding its infrastructure, including electrical generation and water distillation, roads, houses, and government buildings. The recent drop in demand for crude oil has slowed the economy considerably.

The chief imports are machinery and equipment, manufactures, foodstuffs and livestock, and chemicals. In 1994 imports totalled US$1,927 million.

GDP – US$8,107 million (1996); US$14,528 per capita (1996)

INFLATION RATE – 7.4 per cent (1996)

Trade with UK	1998	1999
Imports from UK	£293,104,000	£169,012,000
Exports to UK	29,971,000	24,665,000

COMMUNICATIONS

There are 1,210 km of roads, of which 1,089 km are surfaced. Regular air services provided by Gulf Air and Qatar Airways connect Qatar with the other Gulf states, the Middle East, the Indian sub-continent, Africa and Europe. The Qatar Broadcasting Service transmits on medium wave, shortwave and VHF.

ROMANIA
Romănia

AREA – 92,043 sq. miles (238,391 sq. km). Neighbours: Ukraine (north and east), Moldova (east), Bulgaria (south), Yugoslavia (south-west), Hungary (north-west)
POPULATION – 22,520,000 (1998 estimate); 22,810,035 (1992 census): 89.4 per cent Romanian, 7.1 per cent Hungarian, 1.7 per cent Romany, 0.5 per cent German, 0.3 per cent Ukrainian, 0.04 per cent Jews and others. Religious affiliation: Orthodox 86.8 per cent, Roman Catholic 5 per cent, Reformed 3.5 per cent, Greek Catholic 1 per cent. Romanian is a Romance language with many archaic forms and with admixtures of Slavonic, Turkish, Magyar and French words
CAPITAL – Bucharest (population, 2,027,500, 1997)
MAJOR CITIES – ΨBraşov (318,000); Constanţa (345,000); Cluj-Napoca (333,000); Craiova (313,000); ΨGalaţi (331,000); Iaşi (348,000); Oradea (222,994); Ploieşti (254,386); Timişoara (334,000), UN 1997
CURRENCY – Leu (Lei) of 100 bani
NATIONAL ANTHEM – Desteaptăte, romăne, din somnul cel de moarte (Awake ye, Romanians, from your deadly slumber)
NATIONAL DAY – 1 December
NATIONAL FLAG – Three vertical bands, blue, yellow, red
LIFE EXPECTANCY (years) – male 65.70; female 73.36
POPULATION GROWTH RATE – −0.4 per cent (1997)
POPULATION DENSITY – 95 per sq. km (1997)
URBAN POPULATION – 54.9 per cent (1996)

HISTORY AND POLITICS

Romania has its origin in the union of the Danubian principalities of Wallachia and Moldavia in 1859.

In 1918 Bessarabia, Bukovina, Transylvania and Banat were united with Romania, these additions being confirmed by the Versailles Treaty (1919). In 1940 the Soviet government compelled Romania to cede Bessarabia and northern Bukovina. In the same year north-western Transylvania was ceded to Hungary and southern Dobrogea to Bulgaria.

In 1947 King Michael was forced to abdicate and Romania became 'The Romanian People's Republic'. The leading political force from the Second World War until 1989 was the Romanian Communist Party. A revolution in December 1989 led to the overthrow of Nicolae Ceauşescu, president since 1965. A provisional government abolished the leading role of the Communist Party and held free elections in May 1990.

In the elections held in November 1996 the Romanian Democratic Convention (CDR) candidate, Prof. Emil Constantinescu, was elected President and three alliances (the CDR, the Social Democratic Union (USD), and the Democratic Union of the Romanian Magyars (UDMR)) combined to form a coalition government.

Prime Minister Radu Vasile resigned on 17 December 1999 following discontent with his leadership within both the ruling coalition and his own party, the Christian Democratic National Peasants' Party (PNTCD), which had culminated with his dismissal by President Constantinescu on 13 December 1999, which he had initially refused to accept. He was replaced as Prime Minister by Mugur Isarescu.

Presidential and legislative elections are due to be held by November 2000.

POLITICAL SYSTEM

The constitution of 1991 formally makes Romania a multiparty democracy and endorses human rights and a market economy. The parliament comprises the Chamber of Deputies with 341 seats, of which 15 are reserved for ethnic minorities, and the Senate with 143 seats. Both houses are elected for four-year terms.

HEAD OF STATE

President of the Republic, Prof. Emil Constantinescu, *elected* 17 November 1996

CABINET *as at September 2000*

Prime Minister, Mugur Isarescu (Ind.)
Minister of State, Foreign Affairs, Petre Roman (PD)
Minister of State, Health, Gábor Hajdu (UDMR)
Minister of State, Justice, Valeriu Stoica (PNL)
Minister of State, President of the Economic and Financial Co-ordination Council, Mircea Ciumara (PNTCD)
Culture, Ion Caramitru (PNTCD)
Education, Andrei Marga (PNTCD)
Finance, Decebal Traian Remeş (PNL)
Food and Agriculture, Ioan Avram Muresan (PNTCD)
Industry and Trade, Radu Berceanu (PD)
Interior, Constantin Dudu Ionescu (PNTCD)
Labour, Social Protection, Smaranda Dobrescu (PSDR)
Minister-Delegate, Ethnic Minorities, attached to the Prime Minister, Peter Ekstein-Kovacs (UDMR)
National Defence, Sorin Frunzaverde (PD)
Public Administration, Vlad Rosca (PNTCD)
Public Works and Territorial Planning, Nicolae Noica (PNTCD)
Secretary-General of the Government, Radu Stroe (PNL)
Transport, Anca Boangiu
Water, Forestry and Environmental Protection, Romulus Tomescu (PNTCD)
Youth and Sports, Crin Antonescu (PNL)

PNTCD Christian Democratic National Peasants' Party; PNL National Liberal Party; PD Democratic Party; PSDR Romanian Social Democratic Party; UDMR Democratic Union of Romanian Magyars; Ind. Independent

EMBASSY OF ROMANIA
Arundel House, 4 Palace Green, London W8 4QD
Tel: 020-7937 9666
Ambassador Extraordinary and Plenipotentiary, HE Radu Onofrei, apptd 1997

Defence Attaché, Col. Vasile Palcău
Minister-Counsellor, G. Moloşaga

BRITISH EMBASSY
24 Strada Jules Michelet, RO-70154 Bucharest
Tel: (00 40) (1) 312 0303
Ambassador Extraordinary and Plenipotentiary,
HE R. Ralph, CVO, CMG, apptd 1999
Counsellor, Deputy Head of Mission, E. A. Galves
Defence Attaché, Col. R. D. Shaw-Brown
First Secretary (Commercial), R. J. Cork

BRITISH COUNCIL DIRECTOR, H. Meixner, Calea
Dorobantilor 14, RO-71132 Bucharest; e-mail:
bc.romania@bc-bucharest.bcouncil.org. There are
libraries in Cluj-Napoca, Constanţa, Iaşi, Sibiu and
Timişoara

DEFENCE

The Army has 1,253 main battle tanks, 1,619 armoured
personnel carriers and 177 armoured infantry fighting
vehicles. The Navy has one submarine, one destroyer, six
frigates, 68 patrol and coastal vessels, seven helicopters,
and 120 main battle tanks at six bases. The Air Force has
367 combat aircraft and 16 attack helicopters.
MILITARY EXPENDITURE – 2.3 per cent of GDP (1998)
MILITARY PERSONNEL – 207,000: Army 106,000, Navy
20,800, Air Force 43,500, Paramilitaries 75,900
CONSCRIPTION DURATION – 12 months

ECONOMY

Agriculture employed 37.5 per cent of the workforce in
1997 and contributed 20 per cent of GDP in 1996. The
principal crops are cereals, vegetables, flax and hemp.
Vines and fruits are also grown. The forests of the
mountainous regions are extensive, and the timber
industry is important.

There are plentiful supplies of natural gas, together with
various mineral deposits including coal, iron ore, bauxite,
chromium and uranium in quantities which allow a
substantial part of the requirements of industry to be
met from local resources. Production of crude oil was
6,300,000 tonnes in 1998.

The economy inherited from the totalitarian regime
was characterised by state-owned and co-operative ownership, excessive centralisation, rigid planning and low
efficiency. After the revolution the government opted for a
slow pace of reform with subsidised production resulting
in budget and trade deficits, high inflation and currency
depreciation.

The government elected in 1996 vowed to accelerate
the restructuring and privatisation of state-owned
companies, reduce subsidies and liberalise prices. A
package of reforms designed to accelerate the pace of
privatisation was introduced in May 1999.

In order to meet the conditions imposed by the IMF to
gain access to the second tranche of a US$547 million
loan, a financial reform programme was announced in
January 2000, which aimed to cut public expenditure and
overhaul the taxation system. Agreement was reached with
the IMF in June after the government agreed to increase
gas and electricity prices and privatise the national oil
company.

Flooding on 5–10 April 2000 caused widespread
damage to agricultural land, buildings and transport links
in western areas of Romania.
GNP – US$30,596 million (1998); US$1,360 per capita
(1998)
GDP – US$35,508 million (1996); US$1,567 per capita
(1996)
ANNUAL AVERAGE GROWTH OF GDP – 4.1 per cent
(1996)
INFLATION RATE – 59.1 per cent (1998)

UNEMPLOYMENT – 6.3 per cent (1998)
TOTAL EXTERNAL DEBT – US$9,513 million (1998)

TRADE

The main imports are machines and equipment, minerals,
textiles, chemicals and metallurgical products. The main
exports are textiles, clothing, metallurgical products,
machinery components, minerals, chemicals, shoes and
transport equipment. Italy, Germany, Russia and France
are Romania's most important trading partners.

In 1998 Romania had a trade deficit of US$2,625
million and a current account deficit of US$2,918 million.
In 1997 imports totalled US$11,821 million and exports
US$8,300 million.

Trade with UK	1998	1999
Imports from UK	£235,552,000	£245,629,000
Exports to UK	232,742,000	260,633,000

COMMUNICATIONS

In 1996 there were 11,385 km of railway track, 34 per cent
of which was electrified, and 73,160 km of public roads.
The main national roads largely follow the railway lines
and almost all lead to the capital. The principal ports are
Constanţa (on the Black Sea), Sulina (on the Danube
Estuary), Galaţi, Brăila, Giurgiu and Drobeta-Turnu
Severin. The Danube and the Black Sea are linked by a
canal completed in 1984. In June 2000, an accord was
signed to build a bridge across the Danube carrying a road
and railway line linking the Romanian town of Calafat
with Vidin in Bulgaria.

EDUCATION

Education is free and primary and secondary education
are compulsory. There are state universities in seven
cities, 66 private universities, six polytechnics, two commercial academies, and five agricultural colleges.
ILLITERACY RATE – 1.8 per cent
ENROLMENT (percentage of age group) – primary
95 per cent (1996); secondary 73 per cent (1996);
tertiary 22.5 per cent (1996)

RUSSIA
Rossiiskaya Federatsiya – Russian Federation

AREA – 6,592,850 sq. miles (17,075,400 sq. km). Neigh-
bours: Norway, Finland, Estonia, Latvia, Belarus and
Ukraine (west), Georgia, Azerbaijan, Kazakhstan,
China, Mongolia and North Korea (south). The
Kaliningrad enclave borders Lithuania and Poland
POPULATION – 145,400,000 (2000 estimate): 87.5 per cent
Russian, 3.5 per cent Tatar, 2.7 per cent Ukrainian, 1.3
per cent ethnic German, 1.1 per cent Chuvash, 0.9 per
cent Bashkir, 0.7 per cent Belarusian and 0.7 per cent
Mordovian. There are another six minorities with
populations of over half a million and more than 130
nationalities in total. The Russian Orthodox Church is
the predominant religion, though the Tatars and many
in the north Caucasus are Muslims and there are Jewish
communities in Moscow and St Petersburg. The
language is Russian
CAPITAL – Moscow (population, 8,500,372, 2000
estimate), founded about 1147, became the centre of
the rising Moscow principality and in the 15th century
the capital of the whole of Russia (Muscovy). In 1325 it
became the seat of the Metropolitan of Russia. In 1703
Peter the Great transferred the capital to St Petersburg,
but on 14 March 1918 Moscow was again designated
as the capital

MAJOR CITIES – ΨSt Petersburg (4,660,800, 2000), from 1914 to 1924 Petrograd and from 1924 to 1991 Leningrad. Other cities: Chelyabinsk (1,143,000); Kazan (1,094,000); Nizhny-Novgorod/Gorky (1,438,000); Novosibirsk/Novonikolayevsk (1,436,000); Omsk (1,148,000); Perm/Molotov (1,091,000); Rostov-on-Don (1,020,000); Samara/Kuibyshev (1,257,000); Ufa (1,083,000); Yekaterinburg/Sverdlovsk (1,367,000), 1990
CURRENCY – New rouble of 100 kopeks
NATIONAL ANTHEM – The Patriotic Song
NATIONAL DAY – 12 June (Independence Day)
NATIONAL FLAG – Three horizontal stripes of white, blue, red
LIFE EXPECTANCY (years) – male 58.27; female 71.70
POPULATION GROWTH RATE – –0.1 per cent (1997)
POPULATION DENSITY – 9 per sq. km (1997)
URBAN POPULATION – 72.9 per cent (1995)
ILLITERACY RATE – 0.6 per cent
ENROLMENT (percentage of age group) – primary 93 per cent (1994); tertiary 42.9 per cent (1994)

Russia occupies three-quarters of the land area of the former Soviet Union.

The Russian Federation comprises 89 members: 49 regions (*oblast*) – Amur, Arkhangelsk, Astrakhan, Belgorod, Bryansk, Chelyabinsk, Chita, Irkutsk, Ivanovo, Kaliningrad, Kaluga, Kamchatka, Kemerovo, Kirov, Kostroma, Kurgan, Kursk, Leningrad, Lipetsk, Magadan, Moscow, Murmansk, Nizhny-Novgorod, Novgorod, Novosibirsk, Omsk, Orel, Orenburg, Penza, Perm, Pskov, Rostov, Ryazan, Sakhalin, Samara, Saratov, Smolensk, Sverdlovsk, Tambov, Tomsk, Tula, Tver, Tyumen, Ulyanovsk, Vladimir, Volgograd, Vologda, Voronezh, Yaroslavl; six autonomous territories (*krai*) – Altai, Khabarovsk, Krasnodar, Krasnoyarsk, Primorye, Stavropol; 21 republics – Adygeia, Altai, Bashkortostan, Buryatia, Chechnya, Chuvash, Daghestan, Ingush, Kabardino-Balkar, Kalmykia, Karachai-Cherkessia, Karelia, Khakassia, Komi, Mari-El, Mordovia, North Ossetia (Alania), Sakha, Tatarstan, Tyva, Udmurt; ten autonomous areas – Aga-Buryat, Chuckchi, Evenki, Khanty-Mansi, Komi-Permyak, Koryak, Nenets, Taimyr, Ust-Orda-Buryat, Yamal-Nenets; two cities of federal status – Moscow, St Petersburg; and one autonomous Jewish region, Birobijan.

There are three principal geographic areas: a low-lying flat western area stretching eastwards up to the Yenisei and divided in two by the Ural ridge; the eastern area between the Yenisei and the Pacific, consisting of a number of tablelands and ridges; and a southern mountainous area. Russia has a very long coastline, including the longest Arctic coastline in the world (about 17,000 miles).

The most important rivers are the Volga, the Northern Dvina and the Pechora, the Neva, the Don and the Kuban in the European part, and in the Asiatic part, the Ob, the Irtysh, the Yenisei, the Lena and the Amur, and, further north, Khatanga, Olenek, Yana, Indigirka, Kolyma and Anadyr. Lake Baikal in eastern Siberia is the deepest lake in the world.

HISTORY AND POLITICS

The Gregorian calendar was not introduced until 14 February 1918. For the events surrounding the 1917 revolutions the dates given here are the Gregorian calendar dates in use in the rest of the world at the time, with the dates in the Julian calendar (os) in parenthesis.

Russia was formally created from the principality of Muscovy and its territories by Tsar Peter I (The Great) (1682–1725), who initiated its territorial expansion, introduced Western ideas of government and founded St Petersburg. By the end of Peter the Great's reign, the Baltic territories (modern-day Estonia and Latvia) had been annexed from Sweden, and Russia had become the dominant military power of north-eastern Europe. In the 18th century the partitions of Poland and wars with Turkey brought the territories of modern-day Lithuania, Belarus, Ukraine and the Crimea under Russian control, and the colonisation of Siberia east of the Urals began in earnest. Russia overran the Caucasus region (modern-day Armenia, Azerbaijan and Georgia) in the early 19th century, seized Finland from Sweden in 1809 and Bessarabia from Turkey in 1812. Throughout the remainder of the 19th century Russia subdued and annexed the independent Muslim states which later formed the five Central Asian republics.

Discontent caused by autocratic rule, the poor conduct of the military in the First World War and wartime privation led to a revolution which broke out on 12 March (27 February OS) 1917. Tsar Nicholas II abdicated three days later and a provisional government was formed; a republic was proclaimed on 14 September (1 September OS) 1917. A power struggle ensued between the provisional government and the Bolshevik Party which controlled the Soviets (councils) set up by workers, soldiers and peasants. This led to a second revolution on 7 November (25 October OS) 1917 in which the Bolsheviks, led by Lenin, seized power.

The Bolshevik (Communist) Party withdrew from the First World War under the Treaty of Brest-Litovsk (March 1918), surrendering large areas of territory. Armed resistance to Communist rule developed into an all-out civil war between 'red' Bolshevik forces and 'white' monarchist and anti-Communist forces which lasted until the end of 1922. During the civil war, Russia had been declared a Soviet Republic and other Soviet republics had been formed in Ukraine, Byelorussia and Transcaucasia. These four republics merged to form the Union of Soviet Socialist Republics (USSR) on 30 December 1922.

The Nazi–Soviet pact of August 1939 and the Second World War resulted in further territorial expansion, regaining much of the territory lost in or after 1918, as well as extending Soviet influence to the countries of eastern Europe liberated by Soviet troops. The USSR lost 26 million combatants and civilians in the war.

Joseph Stalin emerged as the undisputed party leader in 1928. He introduced a policy of rapid industrialisation under a series of five-year plans, brought all sectors of industry under government control, abolished private ownership and enforced the collectivisation of agriculture. He eliminated potential political opponents through purges and show trials, and total political repression lasted until his death in 1953.

Repression lessened under Khrushchev and Brezhnev, but the Communist Party remained dominant in all walks of life. This was the state of affairs when Mikhail Gorbachev became Soviet leader in March 1985. Gorbachev introduced the policies of *perestroika* (complete restructuring) and *glasnost* (openness) in order to revamp the economy, which had stagnated since the 1970s, to root out corruption and inefficiency, and to end the Cold War and its attendant arms race. The retreat from total control by the Communist Party unleashed ethnic and nationalist tensions.

On 19 August 1991 a coup was attempted by hardline elements of the Communist Party, the armed forces and the state security service (KGB) in an attempt to reimpose Communist control on the USSR. The coup was defeated by reformist and democratic political groups under the leadership of Russian President Yeltsin. Mikhail Gorbachev returned to Moscow although it became clear that effective political power was in the hands of the republican leaders, especially Russian President Yeltsin, and the Soviet Union began to break up as the constituent republics declared their independence. Gorbachev resigned as Soviet President on 25 December 1991 and on 26 December 1991 the USSR formally ceased to exist.

Russia was recognised as an independent state by the EC and USA in January 1992; it took over the Soviet Union's seat at the UN in December 1991.

A new Russian Federal Treaty was signed on 13 March 1992 between the central government and the autonomous republics. Tatarstan refused to sign the Treaty and in April 1992 declared its 'independence'. In February 1994 Tatarstan signed its own agreement with the federal government on the basis of being a 'state united with Russia'. Similarly, after declaring its 'independence' in March 1992, Bashkortostan signed a treaty with the Federation in August 1994 giving it considerable legislative and economic autonomy.

A brief period of economic growth was followed by instability in the financial markets in early 1998. President Yeltsin dismissed the cabinet in March 1998, and appointed Sergei Kiriyenko, a little-known banker, to replace Viktor Chernomyrdin as Prime Minister. This did little to restore confidence in the economy and following a major collapse on the Russian stock exchange, Yeltsin once more dismissed the cabinet in August 1998. He nominated Chernomyrdin as Prime Minister but the *Duma* twice rejected the appointment. To avert a constitutional crisis, Yeltsin then nominated Foreign Minister Yevgeni Primakov, seen as a compromise candidate whose appointment as Prime Minister would appease all factions in the *Duma*. Although Primakov was successful in stabilising the economy and improving relations with the *Duma*, President Yeltsin ordered his dismissal on 12 May 1999 and appointed Sergei Stepashin as prime minister, but dismissed him also on 9 August 1999 and replaced him with Vladimir Putin, whose appointment was confirmed by the *Duma* on 16 August. Yeltsin resigned as President on 31 December 1999 and was replaced in an acting capacity by the Prime Minister, Vladimir Putin, until elections could be held.

The state of the parties in the State *Duma* following the election on 19 December 1999 was: Communist Party 113 seats; Unity 72; Fatherland-All Russia 67; Union of Rightist Forces 29; Yabloko 21; Zhirinovski's Bloc 17; Our Home is Russia 7; DPA 2; Russian All People Unity 2; others 5.

In the presidential election held on 26 March 2000, Vladimir Putin won 52.94 per cent of the vote, in which the turnout was 68.88 per cent, and was formally inaugurated on 7 May 2000.

POLITICAL SYSTEM

The 1993 constitution enshrines the right to private ownership and the freedoms of press, speech, association, worship and travel, and states that Russia is a multiparty democracy. The President is head of state and of government, head of the Security Council and commander-in-chief of the armed forces and may declare war or declare a state of emergency or martial law, subject to confirmation by the Federation Council. He may chair Cabinet meetings, determine basic government policy, veto legislation, issue decrees and directives, call referendums, dismiss the government, and nominate senior judges, the prosecutor-general and the Central Bank Governor. The President nominates the Prime Minister and Deputy Prime Ministers, who must be approved by the State *Duma*.

The President is directly elected for a maximum of two four-year terms, and may only be impeached on the grounds of treason or serious crime after rulings in both the Supreme and Constitutional Courts and two-thirds majorities in both houses of parliament. The Prime Minister takes over from the President in the event that he is unable to fulfil his duties.

Legislative power is vested in the Federal Assembly, comprising the Federation Council (upper house) of 178 members, two elected by each of the 89 members of the Russian Federation, and the State *Duma* (lower house) of 450 members, of which 225 are elected by constituencies on a first-past-the-post basis and 225 by proportional representation, with a five per cent threshold for representation. State *Duma* deputies may not serve as ministers. The Council is composed of two representatives from each constituent territory of the Federation: the head of the legislative and the head of the executive body.

The State *Duma*, elected for four-year terms, oversees government appointments, has the power to reject the government's fiscal and monetary policies, may pass votes of no confidence in the government (which the President may ignore on the first vote), and cannot be dissolved less than one year after its election.

President Putin announced plans to curtail the powers of the elected governors and in May 2000 he issued a decree forming seven federal districts, to each of which a presidential envoy would be appointed, who would ensure that local regions comply with Russian federal legislation; he also proposed extending his powers to remove incompetent governors and suggested that provincial governors should no longer have an automatic right to a seat in the Federation Council. These proposals were passed by the State *Duma* in May and June, but rejected by the Federation Council on 28 June and returned to the *Duma*, where a two-thirds majority will be required to override the Council's decision.

The judicial system consists of a Constitutional Court of 19 members appointed for a 12-year term which protects and interprets the constitution and decides if laws are compatible with it. The Supreme Court adjudicates in criminal and civil laws cases. The Arbitration Court deals with commercial disputes between companies. The new code of civil law came into force in January 1995.

INSURGENCIES

The Chechen republic declared its 'independence' in November 1991 after a nationalist coup in the republic Chechnya refused to sign the Russian Federal Treaty in March 1992. Civil war began in early 1994 between the Chechen government and armed opposition forces of the 'Provisional Chechen Council', tacitly supported by the Russian government. On 9 December 1994 President Yeltsin ordered the Russian military to retake the republic. Chechen forces were finally forced out of Grozny in early February 1995.

A peace accord was signed on 30 July 1995 which collapsed in October 1995. The Russian-approved candidate was elected head of state of Chechnya in December 1995 and concluded an autonomy accord with Russia giving the region autonomous status within the Federation. The rebels rejected the accord, and attacked Grozny in March 1996. President Yeltsin's new National Security Adviser, Gen. Lebed, resumed negotiations with the rebels in August 1996, reaching an agreement to end hostilities and to delay a decision on Chechnya's final status until 2001. The last Russian troops were withdrawn in January 1997 when presidential and legislative elections were also held in Chechnya. A treaty renouncing the use of force to resolve Chechnya's status was signed between Presidents Maskhadov and Yeltsin in May 1997. In September 1997, Chechnya introduced *Sharia* law, leading to public executions which were strongly criticised by Russia. A state of emergency was declared and a curfew imposed in June 1998 following an increase in serious criminal activity.

On 10 August 1999, Islamic rebels led by Shamil Basayev, a Chechen warlord, launched an incursion into Dagestan, declaring it to be an independent Islamic state. The Russian government immediately dispatched troops to the mountainous frontier region of Dagestan to quell the insurgency; a state of emergency was declared in Chechnya after Russia threatened to attack rebel bases located there.

Russian forces launched airstrikes against Chechnya on 23 September 1999 and on 30 September, Russian ground troops entered the territory. By 5 October, they had gained control of the area to the north of the Terek river. After several attempts, Russian forces captured the Chechen capital, Grozny, on 6 February 2000, forcing the rebels who had defended the city to flee to the southern mountains. Russian troops captured the last Chechen-held town on 29 February, but Chechen guerrilla attacks on Russian targets continued. On 8 June 2000, President Putin imposed temporary direct presidential rule on Chechnya.

Following allegations that the results of the second round of presidential elections on 16 May 1999 in the Karachai-Cherkess Republic were falsified, after a Cherkess candidate, Stanislav Derev, who had gained 40 per cent of the vote in the first round, only gained 12 per cent in the second round, a congress of the republic's Cherkess and Abazin ethnic groups resolved to seek re-integration into the neighbouring Russian region of Stavropol and ethnic Cherkess and Abazin deputies from the Karachai-Cherkess legislature formed a separate parliament on 28 September 1999.

FOREIGN RELATIONS

A union treaty was signed by the presidents of Russia and Belarus in April 1997. Both countries will retain sovereignty and territorial integrity although citizens of the two countries will also be citizens of the Union. The presidents of the two countries decided in December 1998 to effect a currency union.

A Founding Act was signed by Russia and NATO in May 1997 which lays down the principles of post-Cold War co-operation. A joint permanent council is to be set up.

HEAD OF STATE

President, Vladimir Putin, *elected* 26 March 2000, *inaugurated* 7 May 2000

GOVERNMENT *as at September 2000*

Chair, Mikhail Kasyanov
Deputy Chairs, Aleksey Gordeyev (*Agriculture and Foodstuffs*); Ilya Klebanov (*Defence*); Alexei Kudrin (*Finance*); Viktor Khristenko (*Presidential Envoy to International Financial Institutions; Regions*); Valentina Matviyenko (*Social Affairs*)
Anti-Monopoly and Entrepreneurial Affairs, Ilya Yuzhanov
Atomic Energy, Yevgeny Adamov
Communications and Information Support, Leonid Reyman
Culture, Mikhail Shvydkoi
Defence, Igor Sergeyev
Director of the Federal Security Services, Nikolai Patrushev
Economic Development and Trade, German Gref
Education, Vladimir Filippov
Emergencies, Civil Defence, Natural Disasters, Sergei Shoigu
Employment, Labour and Social Development, Alexander Pochinok
Energy, Aleksandr Gavrin
Federal Affairs and Nationalities, Aleksandr Blokhin
Foreign Affairs, Igor Ivanov
Head of Government Administration, Igor Shuvalov
Health, Yuri Shevchenko
Interior, Vladimir Rushailo
Justice, Yuri Chaika
Natural Resources, Boris Yatskevich
Press, Mikhail Lesin
Privatisation, Farid Gazizullin
Railways, Nikolai Aksenenko
Science, Industry and Technology, Aleksandr Dondukov
Tax and Levy Collection, Gennady Bukayev
Transport, Sergei Frank

EMBASSY OF THE RUSSIAN FEDERATION
13 Kensington Palace Gardens, London W8 4QX
Tel: 020-7229 2666/3628/6412
Ambassador Extraordinary and Plenipotentiary, HE Grigory B. Karasin, apptd 2000
Minister-Counsellor, A. M. Kramarenko
Defence and Air Attaché, Maj.-Gen. V. E. Glagolev
Counsellor and Consul-General, A. L. Prosvirkin

BRITISH EMBASSY
Sofiyskaya Naberezhnaya 14, RUS-109072 Moscow
Tel: (00 7) (095) 956 7200
E-mail: britembppas@glas.apc.org
Ambassador Extraordinary and Plenipotentiary, HE Sir Roderic Lyne, KBE, CMG, apptd 1999
Minister and Deputy Head of Mission, A. J. Longrigg, CMG
Defence and Air Attaché, Air Cdre J. C. Jarron
Counsellor (Commercial), S. J. M. Smith
Consuls-General: P. A. McDermott, MVO (Moscow); J. W. Guy, OBE (St Petersburg); S. T. Harrison (Yekaterinburg)
CONSULATES-GENERAL – St Petersburg, Yekaterinburg

HONORARY CONSULATES – Novorossiysk, Vladivostok
BRITISH COUNCIL DIRECTOR, A. Andrews, Ulitsa Nikoloyamskaya 1, RUS-109189 Moscow;
e-mail: bc.moscow@bc-moscow.bcouncil.org.
There are also offices at Nizhni Novgorod, St Petersburg and Yekaterinburg

DEFENCE

Since the demise of the Soviet Union the Russian armed forces have been considerably reduced. In July 1998 it was announced that the armed forces would be reduced to 1.2 million personnel.

Russia lowered the threshold at which nuclear weapons could be used in January 2000; this was thought to be due to fears about the capabilities of Russia's conventional forces.

The Strategic Nuclear Forces have 21 nuclear-powered ballistic missile submarines with 332 missiles, 771 intercontinental ballistic missiles and 100 anti-ballistic missiles.

The Army has about 15,500 main battle tanks, 26,300 armoured personnel carriers and armoured infantry fighting vehicles, and 2,300 helicopters. The Navy has about 70 submarines, one aircraft carrier, seven cruisers, 17 destroyers, ten frigates, 112 patrol and coastal vessels, 329 combat aircraft and 387 armed helicopters. The Air Force has 1,984 combat aircraft.

Russia deploys forces in Armenia (3,100), Georgia (5,000), Moldova (2,600) and Tajikistan (8,200). Russia is the world's third largest contributor to peacekeeping operations. An agreement with Ukraine on the division on the Black Sea Fleet was signed in May 1997.
MILITARY EXPENDITURE – 5.2 per cent of GDP (1998)
MILITARY PERSONNEL – 1,004,100: Strategic Nuclear Forces 149,000, Army 348,000, Navy 171,500, Air Force 184,600, Paramilitaries 478,000
CONSCRIPTION DURATION – 18–24 months.

ECONOMY

Under the Soviet regime, an essentially agrarian economy in 1917 was transformed by the early 1960s into the second strongest industrial power in the world. However, by the early 1970s the concentration of resources on the military-industrial complex was causing the civilian economy to stagnate. This was exacerbated by the bureaucratic inefficiency of the centrally planned economic system and the poor distribution system. It was in an attempt to solve these problems that Gorbachev introduced economic restructuring (*perestroika*). Free market reforms were introduced, including the legalisation of small private businesses, the reduction of state control over the economy, and denationalisation and privatisation. In May 1992 most state subsidies were abolished and price liberalisation was introduced. The first stage of mass privatisation of state industries began in October 1992 and the central distribution system was abolished with effect from 1 January 1993. By February 1996, 80 per cent of the economy had been privatised.

In January 1992 economic 'shock therapy' was introduced to end hyperinflation and restore government reserves by liberalising prices and restructuring firms to end their reliance on state subsidies. The policy was only partially implemented in 1992–4 due to parliamentary resistance. As a result industrial production declined (15.5 per cent in 1993), hyperinflation continued (900 per cent in 1993) and the rouble tumbled.

From 1994 to 1996, the economy began to stabilise with economic reforms judged to have become irreversible. Industrial output and GDP fell by three per cent and four per cent respectively in 1995, compared with 21 per cent and 18.6 per cent in 1994, a result of the government having finally gained control of the money supply. Russia has received considerable international aid since 1993. The G7 summit in Tokyo in April 1994 pledged aid of US$43 billion, in 1995 the IMF provided US$6,800 million and a further three-year credit of US$10,087 million was granted in February 1996.

In 1997, for the first time since economic reforms were introduced, Russian GDP grew by 0.4 per cent.

In May 1998 the Russian stock market went into steep decline, and interest rates were tripled to 150 per cent to avoid a devaluation of the currency. The IMF pledged US$13.7 billion to support the rouble, but in August, trading on the Russian stock exchange was suspended twice in a week after shares lost 15 per cent of their value. On 17 August, the central bank announced it was relaxing control of the rouble, in effect a *de facto* devaluation of 50 per cent, triggering panic selling of roubles, and prompting widespread fears that Russia would default on its loans. Western governments and financial institutions refused to pledge any more money to support the rouble, raising fears of hyperinflation and economic collapse.

A package of measures approved by the government in October 1998 included a state monopoly on alcohol sales and measures aimed at reducing inflation. The budget for 1999 increased military spending and allocated US$9.5 billion to servicing foreign debt, although US$17.5 billion of repayments were due. The IMF agreed in March 1999 to lend US$4.8 billion to enable Russia to restructure its debt; in April, it agreed a further loan of US$4.5 billion subject to reforms of banking laws, the relaxation of exchange controls and increases in indirect taxation.

The devaluation of the rouble in 1998 caused the return of growth in the Russian economy in 1999 and statistics showed a GDP increase of seven per cent at the end of 1999 with strong growth in industrial output, countering the 1998 fall. However, low productivity, overstaffing, and a lack of investment and entrepreneurship remained a problem. An OECD report issued in March 2000 said that Russia had made progress towards creating a market economy, but warned that structural reforms were required. A reform programme issued in June 2000 aims to increase the prices of energy, water and rents, simplify the taxation system and achieve an annual five per cent growth in GDP.

Russia has some of the richest mineral deposits in the world. Coal is mined in the Kuznetsk area, in the Urals, south of Moscow, in the Donets basin and in the Pechora area in the north. Oil is produced in the northern Caucasus, between the Volga and the Urals, and in western Siberia, which also has large deposits of natural gas. A pipeline to bring Caspian oil into Russia via Dagestan and North Ossetia is under construction. Coal and gas deposits in Siberia and the far east (especially Yakutia) are being developed. The Ural mountains contain high-quality iron ore, manganese, copper, aluminium, platinum, precious stones, salt, asbestos, pyrites, coal, oil, etc. Iron ore is also mined near Kursk, Tula, Lipetsk, in several areas in Siberia and in the Kola Peninsula. Non-ferrous metals are found in the Altai, in eastern Siberia, in the northern Caucasus, in the Kuznetsk basin, in the far east and in the far north. 106 tonnes of gold were produced in 1997.

The vast area and the great variety in climatic conditions are reflected in the structure of agriculture. In the far north reindeer breeding, hunting and fishing are predominant. Further south, timber industry is combined with grain growing. In the southern half of the forest zone and in the adjacent forest-steppe zone, the acreage under grain crops is larger and the structure of agriculture more complex. Between the Volga and the Urals cericulture is predominant (particularly summer wheat), followed by cattle breeding. Beyond the Urals is another important grain-growing and stock-breeding area in the southern part of the western Siberian plain. The southern steppe zone is the main wheat granary of Russia, containing also large acreages under barley, maize and sunflowers. In the extreme south cotton is cultivated. Vine, tobacco and other southern crops are grown on the Black Sea shore of the Caucasus.

Moscow and St Petersburg are still the two largest industrial centres in the country, but new industrial areas have been developed in the Urals, the Kuznetsk basin, in Siberia and the far east. Most of the oil produced in the former USSR came from Russia; half the annual output comes from Tyumen Oblast in western Siberia. All industries are represented in Russia, including iron and steel and engineering.

GNP – US$331,776 million (1998); US$2,260 per capita (1998)

GDP – US$440,563 million (1996); US$2,974 per capita (1996)

ANNUAL AVERAGE GROWTH OF GDP – −6.0 per cent (1996)

INFLATION RATE – 27.8 per cent (1998)

UNEMPLOYMENT – 13.3 per cent (1998)

TOTAL EXTERNAL DEBT – US$183,601 million (1998)

TRADE

Russia's main trading partners are Germany, the USA, Italy, China and the former Soviet states. In 1998 there was a trade surplus of US$17,306 million and a current account surplus of US$2,446 million. Imports totalled US$58,996 million and exports US$74,160 million.

Trade with UK	1998	1999
Imports from UK	£937,124,000	£537,069,000
Exports to UK	1,465,886,000	1,360,011,000

COMMUNICATIONS

The European area of Russia is well served by railways, St Petersburg and Moscow being the two main focal points of rail routes. The centre and south have a good system of north-south and east-west lines, but the eastern part (the Volga lands), traversed by trunk lines between Europe and Asia, lacks north-south routes. In Asia, there are still large areas, notably in the far north and Siberia, with few or no railways. In the northern part of European Russia, the North Pechora Railway has been completed, while in the far east a second Trans-Siberian line (the Baikal-Amur Railway) is partially in use; it follows a more northerly alignment than the earlier Trans-Siberian and terminates in the Pacific port of Sovetskaya Gavan.

The most important ports (Taganrog, Rostov and Novorossiisk) lie around the Black Sea and the Sea of Azov. The northern ports (St Petersburg, Murmansk and Arkhangelsk) are, with the exception of Murmansk, icebound during winter. Several ports have been built along the Arctic Sea route between Murmansk and Vladivostok and are in regular use every summer. The far eastern port of Vladivostok, the Pacific naval base of Russia, is kept open by icebreakers all the year round.

Inland waterways, both natural and artificial, are of great importance in the country, although some of them are icebound in winter (from two and a half months in the south to six months in the north). The great rivers of European Russia flow outwards from the centre, linking all parts of the plain with the chief ports, an immense system of navigable waterways which carried about 690 million tons of freight in 1988. They are supplemented by a system of canals which provide a through traffic between the White, Baltic, Black and Caspian Seas. The most notable are the White Sea-Baltic Canal, the Moscow-Volga Canal and the Volga-Don Canal linking the Baltic and the White Seas in the north to the Caspian Sea, the Black Sea and the Sea of Azov in the south.

CULTURE

Russian is a branch of the Slavonic family of languages and is written in the Cyrillic script.

Before the westernisation of Russia under Peter the Great (1682–1725), Russian literature consisted mainly of folk ballads (*byliny*), epic songs, chronicles and works of moral theology. The 18th and 19th centuries saw the development of poetry and fiction. Poetry reached its zenith with Alexander Pushkin (1799–1837), Mikhail Lermontov (1814–41), Alexander Blok (1880–1921), the 1958 Nobel Prize laureate Boris Pasternak (1890–1960), Vladimir Mayakovsky (1893–1930) and Anna Akhmatova (1888–1966). Fiction is associated with the names of Nikolai Gogol (1809–52), Ivan Turgenev (1818–83), Fyodor Dostoevsky (1821–81), Leo Tolstoy (1828–1910), Anton Chekhov (1860–1904), Maxim Gorky (1868–1936), Ivan Bunin (1870–1953), Mikhail Bulgakov (1891–1940), Mikhail Sholokhov (1905–84) and Alexander Solzhenitsyn (*b*.1918).

Great names in music include Glinka (1804–57), Borodin (1833–87), Mussorgsky (1839–81), Rimsky-Korsakov (1844–1908), Rubinstein (1829–94), Tchaikovsky (1840–93), Rachmaninov (1873–1943), Skriabin (1872–1915), Prokofiev (1891–1953), Stravinsky (1882–1971), Shostakovich (1906–75) and Alfred Schnittke (*b*.1934).

RWANDA
Republika y'u Rwanda

AREA – 10,169 sq. miles (26,338 sq. km). Neighbours: Burundi (south), Democratic Republic of Congo (west), Uganda (north), Tanzania (east)
POPULATION – 5,883,000 (1997 UN estimate): Hutus 90 per cent, Tutsis 9 per cent, Twa (pygmy) 1 per cent. Kinyarwanda, French and English are the official languages. Swahili is also spoken
CAPITAL – Kigali (population, 116,227)
CURRENCY – Rwanda franc of 100 centimes
NATIONAL ANTHEM – Rwanda rwacu, Rwanda gihugu cyambyage (My Rwanda, Rwanda who gave me birth)
NATIONAL DAY – 1 July
NATIONAL FLAG – Three vertical bands, red, yellow and green with letter R on yellow band
LIFE EXPECTANCY (years) – male 45.10; female 47.70
POPULATION GROWTH RATE – 2.8 per cent (1997)
POPULATION DENSITY – 223 per sq. km (1997)
URBAN POPULATION – 5.4 per cent (1991)
MILITARY EXPENDITURE – 6.9 per cent of GDP (1998)
MILITARY PERSONNEL – 47,000: Army 40,000, Paramilitaries 7,000

ILLITERACY RATE – 33.0 per cent
ENROLMENT (percentage of age group) – primary 75 per cent (1991); secondary 8 per cent (1991); tertiary 0.5 per cent (1990)

HISTORY AND POLITICS

The majority Hutu population rebelled against Tutsi feudal rule (under the Belgian colonial authority) in 1959–61, leading to the massacre of thousands of Tutsis. Large numbers fled into exile in Uganda. Rwanda became an independent republic on 1 July 1962, with Grégoire Kayibanda as Head of State. He was deposed in 1973 and replaced by a military government under Maj.-Gen. Juvénal Habyarimana, who established a one-party state.

Armed Tutsi exiles repeatedly attempted to invade Rwanda in the 1960s and 1970s but were defeated by the predominantly Hutu army. Continued Hutu-Tutsi conflict left thousands dead over a period of 30 years. In October 1990 Rwanda was invaded by the Rwandan Patriotic Front (RPF) of exiled Tutsis and moderate Hutus, who forced the one-party MRND (National Revolutionary Movement for Development) government to introduce a multiparty constitution in 1991. After the government reneged on a 1992 peace agreement, the RPF advanced on Kigali and forced the government to restart negotiations, which led to the August 1993 Arusha peace accord. The accord provided for a transitional period under a broad-based government including the RPF until the 1995 elections, with UN forces in the country throughout the period.

President Habyarimana, who had retained the interim presidency, died on 6 April 1994 in a plane crash widely believed to have been caused by a rocket attack by extremist sections of the Hutu army. The Hutu army and armed militia, the *interahamwe*, then carried out a preplanned act of genocide against the Tutsi minority and moderate Hutus; 500,000 people were massacred in three months. The civil war restarted and the RPF gradually re-established its control over the country, forcing the defeated government forces and two million Hutu refugees into exile. On 18 July 1994 the RPF declared victory and established a broad-based government of national unity in which moderate Hutus were given the presidency and premiership and the RPF took eight of the 22 seats. UN forces (UNAMIR II) were deployed to deter revenge attacks by Tutsis on Hutus.

In November 1994 the UN Security Council established the International Criminal Tribunal for Rwanda (ICTR) to prosecute those responsible for genocide and other international humanitarian law violations between 1 January and 31 December 1994. An estimated 200,000 Tutsi refugees who fled to Uganda in the 1960s and 1970s have returned to Rwanda. By December 1995, 500,000 refugees remained in Tanzania, and one million in Zaïre.

The 70-member Transitional National Assembly provided for by the Arusha agreement began operation on 12 December 1994 with the extremist Hutu MRND excluded. However, tensions between Tutsis and moderate Hutus in the government remain, with Prime Minister Twagiramungu and four other ministers being dismissed in August 1995 after criticising the lack of power-sharing by the RPF and the security situation in the country.

UN forces left the country in March 1996. Killings by both Hutu militia and government forces continued, and Hutu attacks in central and western Rwanda were frequent in the first half of 1998.

At the ICTR in May 1998, former Prime Minister Jean Kambanda pleaded guilty to charges of genocide, the first admission by a senior Hutu official that genocide had taken place. His admission may be used to implicate other officials who had denied that genocide was taking place.

Rwanda has supported a rebellion in the Democratic Republic of Congo led by the Congolese Democratic Rally, a Congolese Tutsi group. Rwandan troops have also been deployed in the Democratic Republic of Congo.

On 28 February 2000, Prime Minister Pierre-Célestin Rwigyema resigned and President Pasteur Bizimungu resigned on 23 March. Vice-President Paul Kagame became acting President, and was appointed as President by the Transitional National Assembly on 17 April. Bernard Makusa was appointed Prime Minister on 8 March.

Local elections took place on 29–31 March 1999, the first since 1994. The Transitional National Assembly was extended for four further years on 9 June 1999.

POLITICAL SYSTEM

The President is head of state and is elected by the Transitional National Assembly. The President appoints the Council of Ministers.

The Transitional National Assembly, which has 70 members, was appointed in 1994 for a five-year term, since extended for a further four years.

HEAD OF STATE

President, Defence, Maj.-Gen. Paul Kagame *appointed* 17 April 2000, *sworn in* 22 April 2000

GOVERNMENT *as at September 2000*

The President (FPR)
Prime Minister, Bernard Makusa (MDR)
Agriculture, Livestock, Environment and Rural Development, Ephraim Kabayija
Civil Service and Labour, Sylvie Zainab Kayitesi
Commerce, Industry and Tourism, Alexandre Byambabaje
Defence and National Security, Col. Emmanuel Habyarimana
Education, Emmanuel Mudidi
Energy, Water and Natural Resources, Bonaventure Niyibizi
Finance and Economic Planning, Donat Kaberuka
Foreign Affairs and Regional Co-operation, André Mumaya
Gender and Women's Promotion, Angeline Muganza
Health, Ezechias Rwabuhihi
Internal Affairs, Théobald Rwaka Gakwaya
Justice and Institutional Relations, Jean de Dieu Mucyo
Lands, Resettlement and Environmental Protection, Laurent Nkusi
Local Government and Social Affairs, Désiré Nyandwi
Ministers of State, Aaron Makuba (*Agriculture, Livestock, and Forestry*); (*Economic Planning*); Jean-Damascene Ntawukuriryayo (*Higher Education*); Célestin Kabanda; Odette Nyirmirimo (*Social Affairs*)
President's Office, Joseph Mutaboba
Public Works, Transport and Communications, Jean de Dieu Niruhungwa
Youth, Culture and Sports, François Ngarambe

FPR Rwandan Patriotic Front; MDR Republican Democratic Movement

EMBASSY OF THE REPUBLIC OF RWANDA
Uganda House, 58-59 Trafalgar Square, London WC2N 5DX
Tel: 020-7930 2570
Ambassador Extraordinary and Plenipotentiary, vacant
First Secretary, Hilary Byamugisha

BRITISH EMBASSY
Parcelle No. 1131, Blvd de 1 Umuganda, Kacyira-Sud, BP 576 Kigali
Tel: (00 250) 84098/85771/85773
Ambassador Extraordinary and Plenipotentiary, HE Graeme Loten, apptd 1998

ECONOMY

Coffee, tea and sugar are grown. Tin, hides, bark of quinine and extract of pyrethrum flowers are also exported.

In 1997 there was a trade deficit of US$152 million and a current account deficit of US$931 million. In 1998 imports totalled US$287 million and exports US$63 million.

GNP – US$1,864 million (1998); US$230 per capita (1998)
GDP – US$1,302 million (1996); US$241 per capita (1996)
ANNUAL AVERAGE GROWTH OF GDP – 13.3 per cent (1996)
INFLATION RATE – 9.1 per cent (1998)
TOTAL EXTERNAL DEBT – US$1,226 million (1998)

Trade with UK	1998	1999
Imports from UK	£2,848,000	£1,837,000
Exports to UK	610,000	653,000

ST CHRISTOPHER (ST KITTS) AND NEVIS
The Federation of St Christopher and Nevis

AREA – 101 sq. miles (261 sq. km)
POPULATION – 41,000 (1997 UN estimate). The language is English
CAPITAL – ΨBasseterre (population, 12,200, 1994 estimate 1980)
MAJOR TOWNS – ΨCharlestown (1,700, 1994 estimate), the chief town of Nevis
CURRENCY – East Caribbean dollar (EC$) of 100 cents
NATIONAL ANTHEM – Oh Land of Beauty
NATIONAL DAY – 19 September (Independence Day)
NATIONAL FLAG – Three diagonal bands, green, black and red; each colour separated by a stripe of yellow. Two white stars on the black band
LIFE EXPECTANCY (years) – male 67.41; female 70.36
POPULATION GROWTH RATE – 0.3 per cent (1997)
POPULATION DENSITY – 157 per sq. km (1997)

The state of St Christopher and Nevis is located at the northern end of the eastern Caribbean. It comprises the islands of St Christopher (St Kitts) (68 sq. miles) and Nevis (36 sq. miles). The central area of St Christopher is forest-clad and mountainous, rising to the 3,792 ft Mount Liamuiga. Nevis is separated from the southern tip of St Christopher by a strait two miles wide and is dominated by Nevis Peak, 3,232 ft.

HISTORY AND POLITICS

St Christopher was the first island in the British West Indies to be colonised (1623). The Territory of St Christopher and Nevis became a State in Association with Britain in 1967. The State of St Christopher and Nevis became an independent nation on 19 September 1983.

On 10 August 1998 a referendum was held in Nevis on the question of independence from St Christopher; although 61.8 per cent voted in favour of secession, it fell short of the two-thirds majority needed for independence.

In the legislative election held on 6 March 2000, the Labour Party won all eight of the seats on St Christopher. On Nevis, the Concerned Citizens' Movement won two seats and the Nevis Reformation Party one seat.

POLITICAL SYSTEM

Under the constitution, Queen Elizabeth II is Head of State, represented in the islands by the Governor-General. There is a central government with a ministerial system, the head of which is the Prime Minister of St Christopher and Nevis, and a National Assembly located on St Christopher. The National Assembly is composed of the Speaker, three senators (nominated by the Prime Minister and the Leader of the Opposition) and 11 directly elected representatives, who serve a five-year term. On Nevis there is a Nevis Island Administration, the head being styled Premier of Nevis, and a Nevis Island Assembly of five elected and three nominated members.

Governor-General, HE Sir Cuthbert Montraville Sebastian, GCMG, OBE, apptd 1996

CABINET *as at July 2000*

Prime Minister, Finance, National Security, Planning, Development, Dr Denzil Douglas
Deputy PM, Foreign Affairs, International Trade, and Caricom Affairs, Community and Social Development, Sam Condor
Agriculture, Fisheries, Co-operatives, Lands and Housing, Cedric Liburd
Attorney-General, Delano Bart
Communications, Works, and Public Utilities, Rupert Herbert
Culture, Youth Affairs and Sport, Jacinth Henry-Martin
Education, Labour and Social Security, Timothy Harris
Health, Environment, Dr Earl Asim Martin
Tourism, Information, Telecommunications, Commerce, Consumer Affairs, Dwyer Astaphan

HIGH COMMISSION FOR ST CHRISTOPHER AND NEVIS
2nd Floor, 10 Kensington Court, London W8 5DL
Tel: 020-7937 9522
Acting High Commissioner for St Christopher and Nevis, Shirley Vera Pemberton

BRITISH HIGH COMMISSIONER, HE G. M. Baker, resident at Bridgetown, Barbados

ECONOMY

The economy of the islands has been based on sugar for over three centuries. Tourism (172,000 visitors in 1996) and light industry, concentrating on distilling, food processing, clothing and electronics, are now being developed. The economy of Nevis centres on small peasant farmers, but a sea-island cotton industry is being developed for export.

The main exports are sugar, lobsters, beverages and electrical equipment. Foodstuffs, energy, machinery and transport equipment are the main imports.

About 70 per cent of homes on St Christopher were damaged by Hurricane Georges in September 1998.

In 1994 St Christopher and Nevis had a trade deficit of US$69 million and a current account deficit of US$26 million. In 1996 imports totalled US$149 million and exports US$22 million.

GNP – US$253 million (1998); US$6,190 per capita (1998)
GDP – US$210 million (1996); US$5,114 per capita (1996)
ANNUAL AVERAGE GROWTH OF GDP – 3.1 per cent (1996)
INFLATION RATE – 8.6 per cent (1997)
TOTAL EXTERNAL DEBT – US$115 million (1998)

Trade with UK	1998	1999
Imports from UK	£12,649,000	£6,355,000
Exports to UK	5,918,000	6,409,000

COMMUNICATIONS

Basseterre is a port of registry and has deep water harbour facilities. Golden Rock airport, on St Kitts, can take most large jet aircraft; Newcastle airstrip on Nevis can take small aircraft and has night landing facilities. The sea ferry route from Basseterre to Charlestown is 11 miles.

ST LUCIA

AREA – 240 sq. miles (622 sq. km)
POPULATION – 146,000 (1997 UN estimate). The official language is English. A French creole is spoken by most of the population
CAPITAL – ΨCastries (population, 59,788, 1997 estimate)
CURRENCY – East Caribbean dollar (EC$) of 100 cents
NATIONAL ANTHEM – Sons and Daughters of Saint Lucia
NATIONAL DAY – 22 February (Independence Day)
NATIONAL FLAG – Blue, bearing in centre a device of yellow over black over white triangles having a common base
LIFE EXPECTANCY (years) – male 68.00; female 74.80
POPULATION GROWTH RATE – 1.3 per cent (1997)
POPULATION DENSITY – 235 per sq. km (1997)

St Lucia, the second largest of the Windward group, is 27 miles in length, with an extreme breadth of 14 miles. It is mountainous, its highest point being Mt Gimie (3,145 ft) and for the most part it is covered with forest and tropical vegetation.

HISTORY AND POLITICS

Possession of St Lucia was fiercely disputed and it constantly changed hands between the British and the French until 1814 when it was ceded to Britain by the Treaty of Paris. It became independent within the Commonwealth on 22 February 1979.

The St Lucia Labour Party defeated the ruling United Workers' Party in a general election on 23 May 1997, winning all but one of the seats in the House of Assembly.

POLITICAL SYSTEM

The Head of State is Queen Elizabeth II, represented in the island by a St Lucian Governor-General, and there is a bicameral legislature. The Senate has 11 members, six appointed by the ruling party, three by the Opposition and two by the Governor-General. The House of Assembly, which has a life of five years, has 17 elected members and a Speaker, who may be appointed from outside the House.

Governor-General, HE Perlette Louisy, apptd 1997

CABINET *as at July 2000*

Prime Minister, Finance, Economic Affairs, Information, Kenny Anthony
Agriculture, Fisheries, Cassius Elias
Commerce, International Financial Services and Consumer Affairs, Phillip J. Pierre
Communications, Works, Transport and Public Utilities, Calixte George
Community Development, Culture, Local Government and Co-operatives, Damian Greaves
Development, Planning, Environment and Housing, Walter François.
Education, Human Resources Development, Youth and Sport, Mario Michel
Foreign Affairs, International Trade, George Odlum
Health, Human Services, Family Affairs and Women, Sarah Flood
Legal Affairs, Labour and Home Affairs, Velon John
Parliamentary Secretaries, Petrus Compton (*Attorney-General, Public Service*); Cyprian Lansiquot (*Communications, Works, Transport and Public Utilities*); Kenneth John (*Education, Human Resources Development, Youth and Sport*); Michael Gaspard (*Health, Human Services, Family Affairs and Gender Relations*)
Tourism, Civil Aviation, Menissa Rambally Pierre

HIGH COMMISSION FOR ST LUCIA
10 Kensington Court, London W8 5DL
Tel: 020-7937 9522

High Commissioner for St Lucia, HE Emmanuel Cotter, apptd 1998

OFFICE OF THE BRITISH HIGH COMMISSION
PO Box 227, Castries
Tel: (00 1 758) 452 2484
e-mail: postmaster@castries.mail.fco.gov.uk
High Commissioner, HE G. M. Baker, resident at Bridgetown, Barbados

ECONOMY

The economy is mainly agrarian, with manufacturing based on the processing of agricultural products. Principal crops are bananas, coconuts, cocoa, mangoes, breadfruit, yams and citrus fruit. Attempts are being made to increase industrialisation. There were 414,000 visitors to the island in 1998.
GNP – US$556 million (1998); US$3,660 per capita (1998)
GDP – US$576 million (1996); US$3,999 per capita (1996)
ANNUAL AVERAGE GROWTH OF GDP – 4.1 per cent (1996)
INFLATION RATE – 1.0 per cent (1996)
TOTAL EXTERNAL DEBT – US$184 million (1998)

TRADE

The principal exports are bananas, coconut products (copra, edible oils, soap), cardboard boxes, beer, and textile manufactures. The chief imports are flour, meat, machinery, building materials, motor vehicles, manufactured goods, petroleum and fertilisers.
In 1996 St Lucia had a trade deficit of US$184 million and a current account deficit of US$80 million. In 1997 imports totalled US$332 million and exports US$61 million.

Trade with UK	1998	1999
Imports from UK	£13,929,000	£17,502,000
Exports to UK	37,889,000	34,469,000

ST VINCENT AND THE GRENADINES

AREA – 150 sq. miles (388 sq. km)
POPULATION – 112,000 (1997 UN estimate). The language is English
CAPITAL – ΨKingstown (population, 15,466, 1991)
CURRENCY – East Caribbean dollar (EC$) of 100 cents
NATIONAL ANTHEM – St Vincent, Land So Beautiful
NATIONAL DAY – 27 October (Independence Day)
NATIONAL FLAG – Three vertical bands, of blue, yellow and green, with three green diamonds in the shape of a 'V' mounted on the yellow band
POPULATION GROWTH RATE – 0.8 per cent (1997)
POPULATION DENSITY – 288 per sq. km (1997)

The territory of St Vincent includes certain of the Grenadines, a chain of small islands stretching 40 miles across the Caribbean Sea between Grenada and St Vincent, some of the larger of which are Bequia, Canouan, Mayreau, Mustique, Union Island, Petit St Vincent and Prune Island.

HISTORY AND POLITICS

St Vincent was discovered by Christopher Columbus in 1498. It was granted by Charles I to the Earl of Carlisle in 1627 and after subsequent grants and a series of occupations alternately by the French and English, it was finally restored to Britain in 1783. St Vincent achieved full independence within the Commonwealth as St Vincent and the Grenadines on 27 October 1979.

The governing New Democratic Party won eight seats and the United Labour Party seven seats at the election held on 15 June 1998. As a consequence of opposition groups and trade unions pressing for the resignation of the government after the government had approved increased benefits for members of the legislature, the government and opposition agreed that the next election should be held before 31 March 2001.

POLITICAL SYSTEM

Queen Elizabeth II is Head of State, represented by a Governor-General. The House of Assembly consists of 15 elected members and four Senators appointed by the government and two by the Opposition. It is presided over by a Speaker elected by the House from within or without it.
Governor-General, HE Sir Charles Antrobus, GCMG, OBE, *sworn in* 15 October 1996

CABINET *as at September 2000*
Prime Minister, National Security and Home Affairs, Sir James Mitchell, KCMG
Agriculture and Labour, Jeremiah Scott
Attorney-General, Justice, Carl Joseph
Communications and Works, Glenford Stewart
Education, Culture, Women's and Ecclesiastical Affairs, Alpian Allen
Finance, Public Service, Arnhim Eustace
Foreign Affairs, Tourism and Information, Allan Cruickshank
Health and Environment, Joseph Bonadie
Housing and Local Government, Community Development, Youth and Sports, Monty Roberts
Trade and Consumer Affairs, John Horne

HIGH COMMISSION FOR ST VINCENT AND THE GRENADINES
10 Kensington Court, London W8 5DL
Tel: 020-7565 2874
High Commissioner for St Vincent and the Grenadines, HE Carlyle Dougan, QC, apptd 1998

BRITISH HIGH COMMISSION
Granby Street (PO Box 132), Kingstown
Tel: (00 1 784) 457 1701
High Commissioner, HE G. M. Baker, resident at Bridgetown, Barbados
Acting High Commissioner, B. Robertson

ECONOMY

This is based mainly on agriculture but tourism (218,000 visitors in 1995) and manufacturing industries have been expanding. The main products are bananas, arrowroot, coconuts, cocoa, spices and various kinds of food crops. The main imports are foodstuffs, textiles, lumber, chemicals, motor vehicles and fuel.
In 1996 St Vincent and the Grenadines had a trade deficit of US$75 million and a current account deficit of US$35 million. In 1998 imports totalled US$193 million and exports US$50 million.
GNP – US$290 million (1998); US$2,560 per capita (1998)
GDP – US$277 million (1996); US$2,448 per capita (1996)
ANNUAL AVERAGE GROWTH OF GDP – 3.6 per cent (1996)
INFLATION RATE – 2.1 per cent (1998)
TOTAL EXTERNAL DEBT – US$420 million (1998)

Trade with UK	1998	1999
Imports from UK	£7,462,000	£8,339,000
Exports to UK	19,531,000	20,304,000

SAMOA
Ole Malo Tutoatasi o Samoa – Independent State of Samoa

AREA – 1,093 sq. miles (2,831 sq. km)
POPULATION – 168,000 (1997 UN estimate); 162,000 (1989 census), the largest numbers being on Upolu (114,980) and Savai'i (43,150). The Samoans are a Polynesian people, though the population also includes other Pacific Islanders, Euronesians, Chinese and Europeans. The main languages are Samoan and English. The islanders are Christians of different denominations
CAPITAL – ΨApia (population, 36,000, 1989), on Upolu. Robert Louis Stevenson died and was buried at Apia in 1894
CURRENCY – Tala (S$) of 100 sene
NATIONAL ANTHEM – The Banner of Freedom
NATIONAL DAY – 1 June (Independence Day)
NATIONAL FLAG – Red with a blue canton bearing five white stars of the Southern Cross
LIFE EXPECTANCY (years) – male 61.00; female 64.30
POPULATION GROWTH RATE – 0.4 per cent (1997)
POPULATION DENSITY – 59 per sq. km (1997)

Samoa consists of the islands of Savai'i, Upolu, Apolima, Manono, Fanuatapu, Namua, Nuutele, Nuulua and Nuusafee. All the islands are mountainous. Upolu, the most fertile, contains the harbours of Apia and Mulifanua, and Savai'i the harbour of Salelologa.

HISTORY AND POLITICS

Formerly administered by New Zealand (latterly with internal self-government), Western Samoa became fully independent on 1 January 1962. The state was treated as a member country of the Commonwealth until its formal admission on 28 August 1970. A constitutional amendment came into effect on 4 July 1997 changing the state's name to the Independent State of Samoa.

Suffrage was made universal following a referendum held in 1990. After elections held on 26 April 1996, the seats in the *Fono* were: Human Rights Protection Party 26; Samoan National Development Party 13; Independents 10.

POLITICAL SYSTEM

The 1962 constitution provides for a head of state to be elected by the 49-member legislative assembly, the *Fono*, for a five-year term. Initially two of the four Paramount chiefs jointly held the office of head of state for life. When one of the chiefs died in April 1963, Susuga Malietoa Tanumafili II became Head of State for life. The head of state's functions are analogous to those of a constitutional monarch. Executive government is carried out by a Cabinet of Ministers.

HEAD OF STATE

Head of State for Life, HH Susuga Malietoa Tanumafili II, GCMG, CBE, *since* 15 April 1963

CABINET *as at September 2000*

Prime Minister, Foreign Affairs, Broadcasting, Police and Prisons, Internal Affairs, Finance, Tourism, Trade, Commerce and Industry, Customs, Audit, Tuilaepa Sailele Malielegaoi
Agriculture, Forestry, Fisheries and Meteorological Services, Molioo Teofilo
Education, Fiame Naomi Mata'afa
Health, Misa Telefoni
Justice, Solia Papu Vaai
Labour, Polataivao Fosi
Lands, Survey and Environment, Tuala Sale Tagaloa
Posts and Telecommunications, Electric Power Corporation, Gafa Ioelu Elisaia
Public Works, Matataualiitia Afa Lesa
Senior Minister without Portfolio, Tofilau Eti Alesana
Transport and Shipping, Hans Joachim Kell
Women's Affairs, Statistics, Leituala Tone Tuuaga Il
Youth, Sports and Culture, Leota Lu II

HIGH COMMISSION FOR THE INDEPENDENT STATE OF SAMOA
Avenue Franklin D. Roosevelt 123, B-1050 Brussels
Tel: (00 32) (2) 660 8454
High Commissioner for the Independent State of Samoa, HE Tau'ili'ili Meredith, apptd 1998

BRITISH HIGH COMMISSIONER, HE Martin Williams, CVO, OBE, resident at Wellington, New Zealand
HONORARY CONSULATE – PO Box 2029, Apia

ECONOMY

Agriculture is the basis of the economy, the principal cash crops (and exports) being coconuts (copra), cocoa and bananas. Efforts are being made to develop fishing on a commercial scale. Manufacturing is very small in scope and concerned largely with processing agricultural products, but is being encouraged by the government. There were over 60,000 visitors in 1995.

In June 1999, the World Bank approved funding of US$19.41 million to upgrade the international airport at Faleolo and improve the island's infrastructure.

Samoa and American Samoa signed a memorandum of understanding on trade, education, health, agriculture and law enforcement in January 2000.

In 1997 Samoa had a trade deficit of US$85 million and a current account surplus of US$9 million. In 1998 imports totalled US$97 million and exports US$15 million.
GNP – US$181 million (1998); US$1,070 per capita (1998)
GDP – US$173 million (1996); US$1,045 per capita (1996)
ANNUAL AVERAGE GROWTH OF GDP – 6.1 per cent (1996)
INFLATION RATE – 2.2 per cent (1998)
TOTAL EXTERNAL DEBT – US$180 million (1998)

Trade with UK	1998	1999
Imports from UK	£708,000	£1,222,000
Exports to UK	14,000	162,000

SAN MARINO
Repubblica di San Marino

AREA – 24 sq. miles (61 sq. km). Neighbour: Italy
POPULATION – 26,000 (1997 UN estimate). The official language is Italian and the religion is Roman Catholic
CAPITAL – San Marino (population, 4,357, 1994), on the slope of Monte Titano
CURRENCY – San Marino and Italian currencies are in circulation
NATIONAL DAY – 3 September
NATIONAL FLAG – Two horizontal bands, white, blue (with coat of arms of the republic in centre)
LIFE EXPECTANCY (years) – male 73.16; female 79.12
POPULATION GROWTH RATE – 1.7 per cent (1997)
POPULATION DENSITY – 426 per sq. km (1997)
URBAN POPULATION – 89.4 per cent (1995)
GDP – US$530 million (1996); US$21,219 per capita (1996)
ANNUAL AVERAGE GROWTH OF GDP – 0.7 per cent (1996)
UNEMPLOYMENT – 4.1 per cent (1998)

HISTORY AND POLITICS

San Marino is a small republic in the hills near Rimini, on the Adriatic, founded, it is said, by a pious stonecutter of Dalmatia in the fourth century. The republic resisted Papal claims and those of neighbouring dukedoms during the 15th to 18th centuries, and its integrity and sovereignty is recognised and respected by Italy.

A coalition government of the Christian Democratic Party and the Socialist Party was returned in the general elections of May 1998.

The principal products are wine, cereals and fruits, and the main industries are tourism, metals, machinery, textiles and food.

POLITICAL SYSTEM

Executive power is vested in the Congress of State composed of ten ministries under the presidency of the two heads of state, who are elected at six-monthly intervals (every April and October). Legislative power is exercised by the 60-member Great and General Council which is elected for a term of five years. A Council of Twelve forms in certain cases a Supreme Court of Justice.

HEADS OF STATE
Regents, Two 'Capitani Reggenti'

CONGRESS OF STATE *as at September 2000*
Education, Justice and Culture, Sante Canducci (PDCS)
Finance, Budget, Planning and Information, Clelio Galassi (PDCS)
Foreign and Political Affairs, Gabriele Gatti (PDCS)
Health and Social Security, Luciano Ciavatta (PSS)
Industry, Handicrafts, Economic Co-operation, Post and Telecommunications, Fiorenzo Stolfi (PSS)
Internal Affairs, Antonio Lazzaro Volpinari (PSS)
Labour and Co-operation, Romeo Morri (PDCS)
Relations with Municipal Authorities, Production, Services, Cesare Antonio Gasperoni (PDCS)
Territory, Environment and Agriculture, Augusto Casali (PSS)
Tourism, Commerce and Sport, Claudio Podeschi (PDCS)

PDCS Christian Democratic Party; PSS San Marino Socialist Party

BRITISH AMBASSADOR, HE John Shepherd, CMG, resident at Rome, Italy

BRITISH CONSULATE-GENERAL FOR SAN MARINO Lungarno Corsini 2, I-50123 Firenze, Italy.
Tel: (00 39) (55) 284133
Consul-General, R. J. Griffiths, OBE

SAN MARINO CONSULATE, Flat 51, 162 Sloane Street, London SW1X 9BS. Tel: 020-7823 4768.
Consul-General, M. de Camillo

Trade with UK	1998	1999
Imports from UK	£13,772,000	£13,009,000
Exports to UK	7,900,000	8,043,000

SÃO TOMÉ AND PRÍNCIPE
República Democrática de São Tomé e Príncipe

AREA – 372 sq. miles (964 sq. km)
POPULATION – 138,000 (1997 UN estimate). The official language is Portuguese
CAPITAL – ΨSão Tomé (population, 43,420, 1995 estimate)
CURRENCY – Dobra of 100 centavos
NATIONAL ANTHEM – Independência total (Total independence)
NATIONAL DAY – 12 July (Independence Day)

NATIONAL FLAG – Horizontal stripes of green, yellow, green, the yellow of double width and bearing two black stars; and a red triangle in the hoist
POPULATION GROWTH RATE – 2.6 per cent (1997)
POPULATION DENSITY – 143 per sq. km (1997)

The islands of São Tomé and Príncipe are situated in the Gulf of Guinea, off the west coast of Africa.

HISTORY AND POLITICS

The islands were first settled by the Portuguese in 1493. In 1951 they became an overseas province of Portugal, and gained full independence on 12 July 1975. A multiparty constitution was approved by referendum in August 1990. The Movement for the Liberation of São Tomé and Príncipe-Social Democratic Party (MLSTP-PSD), which had been the sole legal party since independence, was defeated by the opposition Democratic Convergence Party (PCD) in legislative elections held on 20 January 1991. Miguel Trovoada, an independent, was elected President on 3 March 1991. On 15 August 1995 five junior army officers launched a bloodless military coup, arrested the president and suspended parliament and the constitution. Following Angolan mediation and an EU threat to suspend all aid, the officers relinquished power on 21 August. The president, government, parliament and constitution were restored and the officers were granted an amnesty.

A government of national unity incorporating opposition party members was appointed on 5 January 1996. President Trovoada was re-elected in July 1996. In September 1996 the government lost a vote of confidence in the National Assembly and a coalition government was installed. Legislative elections were held on 8 November 1998, in which the MLSTP-PSD won 31 of the 55 seats in the National Assembly. Guilherme Posser da Costa was confirmed as Prime Minister by the President on 23 December; the Cabinet was sworn into office on 5 January 1999.

HEAD OF STATE
President and Commander-in-Chief of the Armed Forces, Miguel Trovoada, *elected* 3 March 1991, *re-elected* July 1996, *inaugurated* 3 September 1996

CABINET *as at September 2000*
Prime Minister, Guilherme Posser da Costa
Deputy PM, Justice and Parliamentary Affairs, Labour and Public Administration, Alberto Paulino
Defence, Maj. João Quaresma Viegas Bexigas
Economy, Maria das Neves Ceita Batista de Sousa
Education, Science and Culture, Youth, Peregrino do Sacramento da Costa
Foreign Affairs and São Toméan Communities Overseas, Rafael Branco
Health, Sports, Antonio Soares Marques de Lima
Infrastructure and Natural Resources, Luis Alberto Carneiro dos Prazeres
Interior, Manuel da Cruz Marcal Lima
Planning, Finance and Co-operation, Adelino Castelo David
Secretary of State for Youth, Sport and Professional Training, Luis Vaz de Sousa Bastos

EMBASSY OF THE DEMOCRATIC REPUBLIC OF SAO TOMÉ AND PRÍNCIPE
Square Montgomery, 175 avenue de Tervuren, B-1150 Brussels
Tel: (00 32) (2) 734 8966
Chargé d'Affaires, Antonio de Lima Viegas

BRITISH CONSULATE
Residencial Avenida, Av. Da Independencia CP 257, São Tomé
Tel: (00 239) (12) 21026/7

British Ambassador, HE Caroline Elmes, resident at
Luanda, Angola
Honorary Consul, J. Gomes

ECONOMY

The economy is heavily dependent on agriculture, with
cocoa accounting for 86 per cent of exports in 1997.

On 28 April 2000, the IMF approved a three-year credit
of US$8.7 million to support the government's 2000–2
economic programme.

In 1997 imports totalled US$16 million and exports
US$5 million.
GNP – US$38 million (1998); US$270 per capita (1998)
GDP – US$5 million (1996); US$40 per capita (1996)
ANNUAL AVERAGE GROWTH OF GDP – 2.2 per cent
(1996)
TOTAL EXTERNAL DEBT – US$246 million (1998)

Trade with UK	1998	1999
Imports from UK	£1,427,000	£3,911,000
Exports to UK	198,000	12,000

SAUDI ARABIA
Al-Mamlaka al-'Arabiyya as-Sa'ūdiyya

AREA – 830,000 sq. miles (2,149,690 sq. km).
Neighbours: UAE and Qatar (east), Jordan, Iraq
and Kuwait (north), Yemen and Oman (south)
POPULATION – 19,494,000 (1997 UN estimate);
16,929,294 (1992 census). Islam is the only
permitted religion. The language is Arabic
CAPITAL – Riyadh (Ar-Riyād) (population,
3,100,000, 1998 estimate)
MAJOR CITIES – Jiddah (1.5 million); Buraydah;
Ad-Dammām; Al-Hofūf; Makkah (Mecca);
Al-Madīnah; Tabūk
CURRENCY – Saudi riyal (SR) of 20 qursh or 100 halala
NATIONAL ANTHEM – Long live our beloved King
NATIONAL DAY – 23 September (proclamation and
unification of the Kingdom, 1932)
NATIONAL FLAG – Green oblong, white Arabic device in
centre: 'There is no God but God and Muhammad is
the Prophet of God', and a white scimitar beneath
the lettering
LIFE EXPECTANCY (years) – male 68.39; female 71.41
POPULATION GROWTH RATE – 3.9 per cent (1997)
POPULATION DENSITY – 9 per sq. km (1997)

Saudi Arabia comprises almost the whole of the Arabian
peninsula, with the exception of Yemen, Oman, the UAE
and Qatar. The Nejd ('plateau') extends over the centre of
the peninsula, including the Nafud and Dahna deserts.
The Hejaz ('the boundary') extends along the Red Sea
coast to Asir and contains the holy towns of Mecca
(Al-Makkah) and Medina (Al-Madīnah). Asir ('inaccessible') is so named for its mountainous terrain, and, with the
coastal plain of the Tihama, lies along the southern Red
Sea coast from the Hejaz to the border with Yemen. It is
the only region to enjoy substantial rainfall. The east and
south-east of the country are lower-lying and largely
desert.

Mecca (Al-Makkah), about 60 km east of Jeddah, is the
birthplace of the Prophet Muhammad, and contains the
Great Mosque, within which is the Kaaba (*Ka'abah*) or
sacred shrine of the Muslim religion. This is the focus of
the annual Hajj (pilgrimage'). Medina (Al-Madīnah)
Al Munawwarah ('The City of Light'), some 300 km north
of Al-Makkah, is celebrated as the first city to embrace
Islam and as the Prophet Muhammad's burial place.

HISTORY AND POLITICS

In the 18th century Nejd was an independent state
governed from Diriya. It subsequently fell under Turkish
rule; in 1913 Abdul Aziz ibn Saud threw off Turkish rule
and captured the Turkish province of Al Hasa. In 1920 he
captured the Asir and in 1921 the Jebel Shammar territory
of the Rashid family. In 1925 he completed the conquest of
the Hejaz. Great Britain recognised Abdul Aziz ibn Saud
as an independent ruler, King of the Hejaz and of Nejd and
its Dependencies, in 1927. The name was changed to the
Kingdom of Saudi Arabia in September 1932.

POLITICAL SYSTEM

Saudi Arabia is a hereditary monarchy, ruled by the sons
and grandsons of Abdul Aziz ibn Saud, in accordance with
the Islamic Sharia law. The line of succession passes from
brother to brother according to age, although several sons
of ibn Saud renounced their right to the throne. All
sons and grandsons of ibn Saud must be consulted before
a new king accedes to the throne.

In 1992 King Fahd announced a new Basic Law for the
system of government based on Sharia law and including
rules to protect personal freedoms. The constitution is
defined as the Holy Koran (*Qur'an*) and the *Sunnah* (the
teachings and sayings of the Prophet Muhammad). The
King and the Council of Ministers (established in 1953)
retain executive power. A consultative council (*Majlis-
ash-Shūra*) of a chairman and 90 members appointed by the
King was set up to share power with, and question, the
government and to make recommendations to the King.
The Majlis-ash-Shūra began meeting in December 1993
and debates government policy in the areas of the budget,
defence, foreign and social affairs. Members of the ruling
al Saud family are excluded from membership of the
Council, which has a four-year term and takes decisions by
majority vote. Cabinet ministers have terms of four years,
with the possibility of a two-year extension.

In 1993 the country was reorganised into 13 provinces:
Riyadh; (Makkah); (Al-Madīnah); Al Qasim; Eastern;
Asir; Tabūk; Hā'il; Northern Border; Jīzān; Najrān; Baha;
Al-Jawf. Each province has a governor appointed by the
King and a council of prominent local citizens to advise the
governor on local government, budgetary and planning
issues.

The judicial system is based on Sharia law, administered by the Justice Ministry through the Sharia courts:
general courts, courts of first instance, the High Sharia
Court and the Appeals Court. The highest court of appeal
is the Council of Ministers whose decision, signed by the
King, is final and absolute.

HEAD OF STATE

*Custodian of the Two Holy Mosques and HM The King of
Saudi Arabia*, King Fahd ibn Abdul Aziz al-Saud,
born 1923, ascended the throne 1 June 1982
HRH Crown Prince, Prince Abdullah ibn Abdul
Aziz al-Saud

CABINET *as at September 2000*

Prime Minister, HM The King
First Deputy PM, Commander of the National Guard,
HRH The Crown Prince
Second Deputy PM, Defence and Civil Aviation, HRH
Prince Sultan ibn Abdul Aziz al-Saud
Agriculture and Water Resources, Abdullah ibn Abdul Aziz
ibn Muammar
Civil Service, Mohammad ibn Ali al-Fayez
Commerce, Osama ibn Jaafar ibn Ibrahim al-Faqih
Consultative Council, Muhammad ibn Ibrahim ibn Jubair
(*Chairman*); Shaikh Abdullah Omar Naseef
(*Vice-Chairman*)
Education, Mohammad ibn Ahmad al-Rashid
Finance and National Economy, Ibrahim ibn Abdel
Aziz al-Assaf

Foreign Affairs, HRH Prince Saud al-Faisal ibn
Abdul Aziz al-Saud
Health, Osama ibn Abdul-Majid Shobokshi
Higher Education, Khalid ibn Muhammad al-Anqari
Industry and Electricity, Hashem ibn Abdullah
ibn Hashem Yamani
Information, Fouad ibn Abdul-Salam Mohammad Farisi
Intelligence Services, HRH Prince Saud ibn Fahd
(*Deputy Director*)
Interior, HRH Prince Nayef ibn Abdul Aziz al-Saud
Islamic Affairs, Religious Endowments, Call and Guidance,
Shaikh Saleh ibn Abdul-Aziz al-Shaikh
Justice, Abdullah ibn Muhammad ibn Ibrahim al-Shaikh
Labour and Social Affairs, Ali ibn Ibrahim al-Namlah
Minister of State, Ali ibn Talal al-Jehani
Municipal and Rural Affairs, Mohammad ibn Ibrahim
al-Jarallah
Oil and Mineral Resources, Ali Ibrahim al-Naimi
Pilgrimage Affairs, Ayad ibn Amin Madani
Planning, Posts, Telegraphs and Telecommunications,
Khaled ibn Mohammad al-Qussaibi
Public Works and Housing, HRH Prince Miteb ibn
Abdul Aziz al-Saud
Transport, Nasir ibn Muhammad al-Sallum

ROYAL EMBASSY OF SAUDI ARABIA
30 Charles Street, London W1X 7PM
Tel: 020-7917 3000
Ambassador Extraordinary and Plenipotentiary,
HE Dr Ghazi Algosaibi, apptd 1992
Defence Attaché, Brig.-Gen. B. F. al-Othman
Cultural Attaché, A. M. al-Nasser
Commercial Attaché, M. A. al-Sheddi
Information Attaché, Dr Fawaz al-Dakheel

BRITISH EMBASSY
PO Box 94351, Riyadh 11693
Tel: (00 966) (1) 488 0077
Ambassador Extraordinary and Plenipotentiary,
HE Sir Andrew F. Green, KCMG, apptd 1996
Counsellors, S. G. McDonald (*Deputy Head of Mission and
Consul-General*); R. Northern, MBE (*Commercial*)
Defence and Military Attaché, Brig. R. I. Talbot
First Secretary and Consul, S. J. Lovett

CONSULATE-GENERAL – PO Box 393, Jiddah 21411.
Consul-General, I. Rae, OBE
TRADE OFFICE – Az-Zahrān/Al- Khobar, PO Box 88,
Az-Zahrān Airport 31932

BRITISH COUNCIL DIRECTOR, D. Burton, Tower B,
2nd Floor, Al- Mousa Centre, Olaya Street,
PO Box 58012, Riyadh 11594; e-mail: enquiries@
bc-riyadh.bcouncil.org. There are also offices in
Jiddah and Ad-Dammām

DEFENCE

The Army has 1,055 main battle tanks, 1,900 armoured
personnel carriers, 970 armoured infantry fighting
vehicles and 55 helicopters. The Navy has eight frigates,
26 patrol and coastal vessels and 31 armed helicopters at
eight bases. The Air Force has 432 combat aircraft.
Saudi Arabia is base to the Gulf Co-operational Council
Peninsula Shield Force of 7,000 troops. The USA, UK
and France station aircraft and support units in the country to patrol the air exclusion zone in southern Iraq.
MILITARY EXPENDITURE – 15.7 per cent of GDP (1998)
MILITARY PERSONNEL – 105,500: Army 70,000, Navy
13,500, Air Force 18,000, Air Defence Force 4,000;
National Guard 77,000, Paramilitaries 15,500

ECONOMY

Saudi Arabia's revenue has been lower since the drop in
world oil prices from the mid-1980s onwards, and

financial reserves have been used up to meet budget
deficits.
Agriculture accounted for 6.1 per cent of GDP and
engaged 12.2 per cent of the workforce in 1997. The
productivity of traditional dryland farming is supplemented by extensive irrigation, desalination and use of
aquifers.
The principal industry is oil extraction and processing;
405,200,000 tonnes were produced in 1998. Oil was first
found in commercial quantities in 1938. Proven oil
reserves of 261,500 million barrels account for about
one-quarter of the world's proven reserves. The country is
the world's largest oil exporter. Recoverable gas reserves
of 190 trillion cubic feet, in fields associated with crude oil
and those separate from it, are beginning to be exploited;
production in 1998 was 46,820 million cubic metres.
Mineral exploitation of gold, silver, copper and other
minerals is also beginning, with gold production of
5.1 tonnes in 1998.
The government, in a series of five-year development
plans begun in 1970, has actively encouraged the
establishment of manufacturing industry. Industries have
developed in the fields of construction materials, metal
fabrication, simple machinery and electrical equipment,
food and beverages, textiles, chemicals and plastics.
Eight industrial centres have been established, the
principal ones at Al-Jubayl and Yanbū, financed by the
state agency Saudi Arabian Basic Industries Corporation.
Linked by gas and oil pipelines, both have petrochemical
complexes producing ethylene and methanol; six of the
seven plants on-stream are joint ventures with American
and Japanese companies.
A steep reduction in oil revenues in 1998 led to an
austere 1999 budget, which aimed to reduce government
expenditure by 12.6 per cent.
The government has taken measures during 1999 and
2000 to stimulate and diversify the economy with the
creation of a Higher Economic Council, which aims to
foster the role of the private sector in the economy and
encourage investment and job creation, and a Supreme
Petroleum and Mineral Affairs Council, which will
control policy, production quotas and pricing. In April
2000, a new foreign investment code was approved, which
permitted foreign investment in all sectors of the economy
and facilitated foreign ownership of local businesses.
Tourism is now being encouraged and the national
telecommunications and electricity companies are to be
privatised.
GNP – US$143,361 million (1998); US$6,910 per capita
(1998)
GDP – US$125,266 million (1996); US$6,650 per capita
(1996)
ANNUAL AVERAGE GROWTH OF GDP – 0.5 per cent
(1996)
INFLATION RATE – –0.4 per cent (1998)

TRADE

Oil remains the main source of receipts in the balance
of payments. The leading suppliers of imports are the
USA, the UK, Germany and Japan, and the chief customers for exports are Japan, the USA, South Korea and
Singapore. There is a total ban on the importation of
alcohol, pork products, firearms, and items regarded as
non-Islamic or pornographic.
In 1998 there was a trade surplus of US$12,238 million
and a current account deficit of US$12,880 million. In
1997 imports totalled US$28,742 million and exports
totalled US$62,381 million.

Trade with UK	1998	1999
Imports from UK	£2,690,207,000	£1,528,712,000
Exports to UK	891,959,000	874,684,000

COMMUNICATIONS

There is one railway line from Ad-Dammām to Riyadh, which was opened in 1951 and is operated by the Saudi Government Railway Organisation. The line is being extended to the port of Al-Jubayl on the Gulf. A network of 139,200 km of roads, including an expressway system, connects all the cities and main towns. There are 21 ports, of which the major ones are Ad-Dammām and Al-Jubayl (Gulf) and Jiddah, Yanbu and Jizan (Red Sea). The 15.5 mile-long King Fahd Causeway completed in 1986 connects the Eastern Province to the state of Bahrain and is the world's second longest causeway.

There are international airports at Az-Zahrān (King Fahd), Jiddah (King Abdul Aziz), and Riyadh (King Khalid).

Telecommunications are being rapidly expanded with 1.78 million telephone lines in 1995 and seven earth stations linked to the Intelsat system, allowing direct dialling to 185 countries.

EDUCATION

With the exception of a few schools for expatriate children, all schools are government-supervised and are segregated for boys and girls. There are universities in Jiddah, Makkah, Riyadh (branches in Abha and Qassim), Ad-Dammām (branch at Al-Hufūf) and Az-Zahrān, and there are Islamic universities in Al-Madīnah and Riyadh together with 83 tertiary colleges. There is great emphasis on vocational training, provided at literacy and artisan skill training centres and more advanced industrial, commercial and agricultural education institutes. Education from kindergarten to university is free, with more than 22,000 schools in 1996.

ILLITERACY RATE – 23.0 per cent

ENROLMENT (percentage of age group) – primary
61 per cent (1996); secondary 42 per cent (1996);
tertiary 16.3 per cent (1996)

SENEGAL
République du Sénégal

AREA – 75,955 sq. miles (196,722 sq. km). Neighbours: Mauritania (north), Mali (east), Guinea-Bissau and Guinea (south), the Gambia

POPULATION – 8,802,000 (1997 UN estimate), 94 per cent Muslim, 4 per cent Christian, 1 per cent Animist. The official language is French; the principal local language is Wolof. Fulani, Serer, Mandingo, Jola and Sarakole are also spoken

CAPITAL – ΨDakar (population, 1,641,358, 1994)

MAJOR CITIES – Kaolack (193,115), ΨSaint-Louis (132,499), Thiès (216,381), ΨZiguinchor (161,680)

CURRENCY – Franc CFA of 100 centimes

NATIONAL ANTHEM – Pincez tous vos koras, frappez les balafos (All pluck your koras, strike the balafos)

NATIONAL DAY – 4 April

NATIONAL FLAG – Three vertical bands, green, yellow and red; a green star on the yellow band

LIFE EXPECTANCY (years) – male 48.30; female 50.30

POPULATION GROWTH RATE – 2.7 per cent (1997)

POPULATION DENSITY – 45 per sq. km (1997)

URBAN POPULATION – 41.1 per cent (1997)

MILITARY EXPENDITURE – 1.7 per cent of GDP (1998)

MILITARY PERSONNEL – 11,000: Army 10,000, Navy 600, Air Force 400; Paramilitaries 5,800

CONSCRIPTION DURATION – Two years (selective)

ILLITERACY RATE – 62.7 per cent

ENROLMENT (percentage of age group) – primary
60 per cent (1997); tertiary 3.4 per cent (1994)

HISTORY AND POLITICS

Formerly a French colony, Senegal elected in 1958 to remain within the French Community as an autonomous republic. It became independent as part of the Federation of Mali in June 1960 and seceded to form the Republic of Senegal in September 1960.

Abdoulayé Wade, the leader of the Senegalese Democratic Party, was elected in the second round of the presidential election on 19 March 2000 with 58.49 per cent of the vote, thus becoming the first president not to belong to the Socialist Party. The legislative election in May 1998 was won by the ruling Socialist Party (PS), which secured 93 seats, with the Senegalese Democratic Party (PDS) winning 23 seats, and the Union for Democratic Renewal 11 seats.

INSURGENCY

A separatist civil war has been fought in the southern Casamance region for the past 17 years. The government and the Casamance Movement of Democratic Forces (MFDC) agreed a cease-fire on 26 December 1999. A meeting between the two sides in January 2000 agreed to establish a joint body to monitor progress, to withdraw army and rebel forces from occupied villages, and to co-operate on mine clearance and the refugee problem.

POLITICAL SYSTEM

In 1963 a new constitution was approved giving executive powers to the president. In August 1998 the National Assembly voted to remove the restriction which limited the president to two consecutive seven-year terms. A general election for the National Assembly of 140 seats is held every five years. An upper house, the Senate, was established in January 1999. It comprises 60 members, 45 chosen by a 14,000-member electoral college, three elected by overseas representatives and 12 appointed by the president, all of whom serve a five-year term.

A referendum on a new constitution is due to take place in late 2000, to be followed by a legislative election in 2001.

HEAD OF STATE

President, Abdoulayé Wade, *elected* 19 March 2000, *sworn in* 1 April 2000

CABINET *as at September 2000*

Prime Minister, Moustapha Niasse
African Integration, Amadou Sow
Agriculture and Livestock, Pape Diouf
Armed Forces, Youga Sambou
Budget, Abdoulayé Diop
Civil Service, Labour and Employment, Yero Deh
Culture and Communication, Mamadou Diop
Energy and Water Resources, Abdoulayé Bathily
Environment, Mamadou Lamine Ba
Equipment and Transportation, Madieyna Diouf
Finance and Economic Affairs, Moctar Diop
Fisheries, Oumar Sarr
Foreign Affairs and Senegalese Abroad, Cheikh Tidiane Gadio
Health, Abdou Fall
Higher Education, Madior Diouf
Interior, Maj.-Gen. Mamadou Niang
Justice and Keeper of the Seals, Mame Madior Boye
Mines, Handicrafts and Industry, Landing Savane
National Education, Technical and Vocational Training, Marie Lucienne Issa Gueye
National Solidarity and Family Affairs, Aminata Tall
Planning, Oumar Khassimou
Relations with Assemblies, Awa Dia
Sport and Leisure, Joseph Ndong

Territorial Administration and Decentralisation, Khady Fall
Tourism, Ndiawar Toure
Town Planning and Housing, Thierno Amath Dansokho
Trade, Khoureyssi Thiam
Youth, Modou Diagne Fada

EMBASSY OF THE REPUBLIC OF SENEGAL
39 Marloes Road, London W8 6LA
Tel: 020-7938 4048/7937 7237
Ambassador Extraordinary and Plenipotentiary,
HE Gabriel Alexandre Sar, apptd 1993

BRITISH EMBASSY
20 rue du Docteur Guillet (BP 6025), Dakar
Tel: (00 221) 823 7392/9971
E-mail: britemb@telecom-plus.sn
Ambassador Extraordinary and Plenipotentiary,
HE David Snoxell, apptd 1997

BRITISH COUNCIL DIRECTOR, S. McNulty, 34–36 Blvd
de la République, BP 6232, Dakar;
e-mail: Information@bc-dakar.enda.sn

ECONOMY

Around 75 per cent of the workforce are employed in agriculture. Senegal's principal exports are fish, groundnuts (raw and processed) and phosphates. Tourism is also of growing importance as a revenue earner; in 1997 there were 420,000 overseas visitors. Principal imports are food, machinery, fuel oils and transport equipment. Senegal exports fish, furniture, oilseeds and fruit, rubber, fertilisers and animal fodder to the UK, and imports foodstuffs, cigarettes, chemicals, machinery and transport equipment, vegetable fats and oils, and manufactured goods from the UK.

In 1996 there were 14,576 km of roads, of which 4,271 km were paved. There are 1,225 km of railway track.

In 1996 there was a trade deficit of US$276 million and a current account deficit of US$200 million. In 1997 imports totalled US$1,196 million and exports US$933 million.

GNP – US$4,683 million (1998); US$520 per capita (1998)
GDP – US$5,055 million (1996); US$592 per capita (1996)
ANNUAL AVERAGE GROWTH OF GDP – 5.6 per cent (1996)
INFLATION RATE – 1.2 per cent (1998)
TOTAL EXTERNAL DEBT – US$3,861 million (1998)

Trade with UK	1998	1999
Imports from UK	£27,093,000	£24,335,000
Exports to UK	9,007,000	10,272,000

SEYCHELLES
The Republic of Seychelles

AREA – 176 sq. miles (455 sq. km)
POPULATION – 78,846 (1998 UN estimate).
The languages are English, French and Créole
CAPITAL – ѰVictoria (population, 24,324, 1987), on Mahé
CURRENCY – Seychelles rupee of 100 cents
NATIONAL ANTHEM – Koste Seselwa (Seychellois Unite)
NATIONAL DAY – 18 June
NATIONAL FLAG – Five rays extending from the lower hoist over the whole field, coloured blue, yellow, green, white and red
LIFE EXPECTANCY (years) – male 65.26; female 74.05
POPULATION GROWTH RATE – 1.1 per cent (1997)
POPULATION DENSITY – 165 per sq. km (1997)
MILITARY EXPENDITURE – 2.9 per cent of GDP (1998)
MILITARY PERSONNEL – 450: Army 200,
    Paramilitaries 250

Seychelles, in the Indian Ocean, consists of 115 islands spread over 400,000 sq. miles of ocean. There is a relatively compact granitic group, 32 islands in all, with high hills and mountains (highest point about 2,972 ft), of which Mahé is the largest and most populated (90 per cent of the population live on Mahé); and the outlying coralline group, for the most part only a little above sea-level. Although only 4° S. of the Equator, the climate is pleasant though tropical.

HISTORY AND POLITICS

Proclaimed French territory in 1756, the Mahé group was settled as a dependency of Mauritius from 1770, was captured by a British ship in 1794, and changed hands several times between 1803 and 1814, when it was finally assigned to Great Britain. In 1903 these islands, together with the coralline group, were formed into a separate colony. On 29 June 1976, the islands became an independent republic within the Commonwealth. A coup d'état took place in 1977. Seychelles was a one-party state from 1979 until 1991, when a multiparty democratic system was proposed by President René.

In presidential and legislative elections held in March 1998, President René was re-elected with 67 per cent of the vote, and the Seychelles People's Progressive Front formed a government after winning 30 seats in the National Assembly.

POLITICAL SYSTEM

Under the constitution adopted in 1993, multiparty politics was institutionalised, a National Assembly of up to 34 members (23 elected by constituencies, up to 11 by proportional representation) was established and the presidential mandate was set at five years, renewable three times.

HEAD OF STATE

President, Commander-in-Chief of the Armed Forces, Defence, Interior, France-Albert René, *assumed office* 5 June 1977; *elected* 1979; *re-elected* 1984, 1989, 1993, 22 March 1998
Vice-President, Finance, Economic Planning, Information Technology and Communications, James Michel

CABINET *as at September 2000*

The President
The Vice-President
Administration, Noellie Alexander
Agriculture and Marine Resources, Dolor Ernesta
Culture and Information, Ronald Jumeau
Education, Danny Faure
Employment and Social Affairs, William Herminie
Foreign Affairs, Jérémie Bonnelame
Health, Jacquelin Dugasse
Industry and International Business, Patrick Pillay
Land Use and Environment, Joseph Belmont
Local Government, Sports and Youth, Sylvette Pool
Tourism and Civil Aviation, Simone de Comarmond

SEYCHELLES HIGH COMMISSION
BOX No. 4PE, 2nd Floor, Eros House, 111 Baker Street,
London W1M 1FE
Tel: 020-7224 1660
High Commissioner, HE Bertrand Rassool, apptd 1999

BRITISH HIGH COMMISSION
Oliaji Trade Centre, PO Box 161 Victoria, Mahé
Tel: (00 248) 225225/225356
e-mail: bhcsey@seychelles.net
High Commissioner, HE John Yapp, apptd 1997

ECONOMY

The economy is based on tourism, fishing, small-scale agriculture and manufacturing, and the re-export of fuel for aircraft and ships. Deep sea tuna fishing by foreign fleets under licence, improved port facilities at Victoria and exports from a tuna canning factory attract growing revenues. The government is attempting to reduce the reliance on tourism, which generates the majority of foreign exchange earnings, by promoting the country as an offshore haven for financial services. There were 128,258 foreign visitors in 1998.

GNP – US$505 million (1998); US$6,420 per capita (1998)
GDP – US$540 million (1996); US$7,294 per capita (1996)
ANNUAL AVERAGE GROWTH OF GDP – 2.8 per cent (1997)
INFLATION RATE – 0.6 per cent (1997)
TOTAL EXTERNAL DEBT – US$187 million (1998)

TRADE

Principal exports in 1998 were canned tuna, frozen prawns, fish and cinnamon bark. The principal imports were machinery and transport equipment, manufactures, foodstuffs and tobacco, fuel oils and chemicals.

In 1997 there was a trade deficit of US$188 million and a current account deficit of US$63 million. In 1995 imports totalled US$233 million and exports US$53 million.

Trade with UK	1998	1999
Imports from UK	£19,536,000	£14,215,000
Exports to UK	20,009,000	34,997,000

SIERRA LEONE
The Republic of Sierra Leone

AREA – 27,699 sq. miles (71,740 sq. km). Neighbours: Guinea (north, north-east), Liberia (south-east)
POPULATION – 4,428,000 (1997 UN estimate). The south is inhabited by peoples whose languages fall into the Mende group; the north by the Temne and smaller groups such as the Limba, Loko, Koranko and Susu
CAPITAL – ΨFreetown (population, 469,776, 1985)
CURRENCY – Leone (Le) of 100 cents
NATIONAL ANTHEM – High We Exalt Thee, Realm of the Free
NATIONAL DAY – 27 April (Independence Day)
NATIONAL FLAG – Three horizontal stripes of leaf green, white and cobalt blue
LIFE EXPECTANCY (years) – male 32.86; female 35.91
POPULATION GROWTH RATE – 1.5 per cent (1997)
POPULATION DENSITY – 62 per sq. km (1997)
MILITARY EXPENDITURE – 3.3 per cent of GDP (1998)
MILITARY PERSONNEL – 3,000: Army 2,800, Navy 200

HISTORY AND POLITICS

In the late 18th century a project was begun to settle destitute Africans from England on Freetown peninsula. In 1808 the settlement was declared a Crown colony and became the main base in West Africa for enforcing the 1807 Act outlawing the slave trade. Africans from North America and the West Indies, and Africans rescued from slave ships also settled there. In 1896 a Protectorate was declared over the hinterland.

In 1951 a new constitution was set up that united the colony of Freetown and the Protectorate and on 27 April 1961 Sierra Leone became a fully independent state within the Commonwealth. In 1971 a republican constitution was adopted and Dr Siaka Stevens became the first executive president. In 1978 Sierra Leone became a one-party state, following approval by Parliament and a referendum.

In September 1991 a new multiparty constitution was adopted and an interim government formed, which was overthrown by a military coup on 29 April 1992. Captain Valentine Strasser became head of state, but was ousted on 16 January 1996 in a bloodless coup by his deputy, Brig.-Gen. Julius Maada Bio. The military government surrendered power to a civilian government on 29 March 1996, following legislative elections on 26–27 February and a run-off election for the presidency on 15 March.

The Sierra Leone People's Party (SLPP) won 27 seats in the 68-member National Assembly and formed a government with the support of the People's Democratic Party and the Democratic Centre Party. The SLPP's candidate, Ahmad Tejan Kabbah, won the presidential contest, attracting 59.4 per cent of the vote.

In May 1997 army officers led by Major Johnny Koroma seized power. President Kabbah fled and a 20-member Armed Forces Revolutionary Council was set up with Koroma as chairman and Revolutionary United Front (RUF) leader Foday Sankoh as Vice-Chairman. In July 1997, a Nigerian-led ECOMOG force was sent to oust Koroma and restore the legitimate government. On 24 October 1997, a peace agreement was reached which provided for Kabbah to return to power within six months and granted immunity from prosecution to Koroma. There was renewed fighting in February 1998 with both sides accusing the other of breaking the cease-fire. ECOMOG troops gained control of Freetown on 12 February 1998, and ousted the Koroma regime. President Kabbah returned to Freetown on 10 March 1998.

INSURGENCY

Since May 1991 government forces have been fighting the RUF whose aim is to force all foreigners out of the country and to nationalise the mining sector. Attacks by the RUF intensified in December 1998 and on 6 January 1999 the RUF attacked Freetown. ECOMOG troops launched a counter-attack on 9–10 January, recapturing the city.

President Kabbah and Foday Sankoh signed a cease-fire agreement on 18 May 1999 and it was agreed in July 1999 that Sankoh would be appointed Vice-President and head the Mineral Resources Commission and that the RUF would be given four cabinet posts. A government of national unity was announced on 2 November 1999 and the RUF was registered as a political party on 22 November.

Violence continued, despite the efforts of a UN peacekeeping force, the UN Mission to Sierra Leone (UNAMSIL), which officially took over from ECOMOG on 29 April 2000. The cease-fire agreement collapsed when the RUF abducted 500 UNAMSIL peacekeepers between 30 April–6 May, and on 6 May the RUF used captured UNAMSIL weaponry to launch an advance on Freetown. A temporary UK military deployment was despatched to evacuate British, EU and Commonwealth nationals from Freetown. UNAMSIL troops, along with Sierra Leonean Army (SLA) and Nigerian Army troops, went on the offensive and drove the RUF back. RUF leader Foday Sankoh, who had been the Vice-President since November 1999, was arrested on 17 May 2000; three of the four RUF ministers were also reported to have been arrested on 17 June.

Following the withdrawal of British forces on 14 June 2000, the British government sent an army team to begin a three-year training programme to assist the SLA. UNANSIL troops managed to free 233 of the captured peacekeepers in June and it was announced on 21 August that the RUF had replaced Foday Sankoh as head of the organisation with the more moderate Issa Sesay.

HEAD OF STATE

President, Defence, Ahmad Tejan Kabbah,
elected 15 March 1996
Vice-President, Albert Joe Demby

CABINET *as at September 2000*
The President
The Vice-President
Agriculture, Forestry and Marine Resources, Okere Adams
Attorney-General, Justice, Solomon Berewa
Culture and Tourism, vacant
Development and Economic Planning, Kade Sesay
Education, Youth and Sport, Alpha Wurie
Energy and Power, vacant
Finance, James Jonah
Foreign Affairs, Sama Banya
Health and Sanitation, Ibrahim Tejan Jalloh
Information, Julius Spencer
Labour and Industrial Relations, Alpha Timbo
Lands, Housing and Environment, vacant
Mineral Resources, Alhaji Mohamed Deen
Political and Parliamentary Affairs, Abu Aiah Koroma
Rural Development and Local Government, James
    Banda Dauda
Safety and Security, Charles Magai
Social Welfare, Gender, Children's Affairs, Shirley Gbujama
Transport, Momoh Pujeh
Trade and Industry, vacant
Transport and Communications, Momoh Pujeh
Works and Maintenance, S. U. M. Jah

SIERRA LEONE HIGH COMMISSION
Oxford Circus House, 245 Oxford Street,
    London WIR 1LF
Tel: 020-7287 9884
Acting High Commissioner, Sulaiman Tejan-Jalloh

BRITISH HIGH COMMISSION
Spur Road, Freetown
Tel: (00 232) (22) 232563/4/5
e-mail: bhc@sierratel.sl
High Commissioner, HE Peter Penfold, CMG, OBE, apptd
    1997

BRITISH COUNCIL DIRECTOR, A. Thomas PO Box 124,
    Tower Hill, Freetown; e-mail: bcouncil@sierratel.sl

ECONOMY

On the Freetown peninsula, farming is largely confined to
the production of cassava and crops such as maize and
vegetables for local consumption. In the hinterland the
principal agricultural product is rice, which is the staple
food of the country, and cash crops such as cocoa, coffee,
palm kernels and ginger. Cattle production is also
important.

The economy depends largely on mineral exports,
mainly diamonds, gold and bauxite, although mineral
production has been disrupted by the insurgency.

In December 1999, the IMF approved US$21.31
million to assist the government's reconstruction and
economic recovery programme.

In 1995 there was a trade deficit of US$127 million
and a current account deficit of US$127 million. In 1997
imports totalled US$93 million and exports US$17
million.
GNP – US$703 million (1998); US$140 per capita (1998)
GDP – US$1,042 million (1996); US$243 per capita
    (1996)
ANNUAL AVERAGE GROWTH OF GDP – −3.6 per cent
    (1996)
INFLATION RATE – 35.5 per cent (1998)
TOTAL EXTERNAL DEBT – US$1,243 million (1998)

Trade with UK	1998	1999
Imports from UK	£21,909,000	£41,308,000
Exports to UK	3,944,000	3,141,000

COMMUNICATIONS

Since the phasing out of the railway system in 1974 the
road network has been developed considerably; there are
now 7,000 miles of roads in the country, 2,000 miles being
surfaced. A bridge has been constructed over the Mano
River linking Sierra Leone and Liberia.

The Freetown international airport is situated at Lungi.
The main port is Freetown, which has one of the largest
natural harbours in the world. There are smaller ports at
Pepel, Bonthe and Niti.

Radio is operated by the government. Broadcasts are
made in several of the indigenous languages, in addition to
English and French.

EDUCATION

Technical education is provided in the two government
technical institutes, situated in Freetown and Kenema, in
two trade centres and in the technical training establishments of the mining companies. Teacher training is
carried out at the University of Sierra Leone, six colleges
in the provinces and in the Milton Margai Training
College near Freetown.
ILLITERACY RATE – 63.7 per cent
ENROLMENT (percentage of age group) – tertiary
    1.3 per cent (1990)

SINGAPORE

AREA – 250 sq. miles (648 sq. km)
POPULATION – 3,865,600 (1998): Chinese 77 per cent,
    Malays 14 per cent, Indians (including those of
    Pakistani, Bangladeshi and Sri Lankan origin)
    7.6 per cent and 1.4 per cent from other ethnic groups.
    Malay, Mandarin, Tamil and English are the official
    languages. At least eight Chinese dialects are used.
    Malay is the national language and English is the
    language of administration. The religions are Buddhism
    31.9 per cent, Taoism 21.9 per cent, Islam 14.9 per cent,
    Christianity 12.9 per cent, Hinduism 3.3 per cent
CURRENCY – Singapore dollar (S$) of 100 cents
NATIONAL ANTHEM – Majullah Singapura (May
    Singapore progress)
NATIONAL DAY – 9 August
NATIONAL FLAG – Horizontal bands of red over white;
    crescent with five five-point stars on red band near staff
LIFE EXPECTANCY (years) – male 75.00; female 79.20
POPULATION GROWTH RATE – 3.1 per cent (1997)
POPULATION DENSITY – 6,046 per sq. km (1997)
MILITARY EXPENDITURE – 5.0 per cent of GDP (1998)
MILITARY PERSONNEL – 73,000: Army 50,000, Navy
    9,000, Air Force 13,500; Paramilitaries 108,000
CONSCRIPTION DURATION – 24–30 months
ILLITERACY RATE – 7.6 per cent
ENROLMENT (percentage of age group) – primary 93
    per cent (1995); tertiary 38.5 per cent (1996)

Singapore consists of the island of Singapore and 59 islets.
Singapore island is 26 miles long and 14 miles in breadth
and is situated just north of the Equator off the southern
extremity of the Malay peninsula, from which it is separated by the Straits of Johore. A causeway crosses the
three-quarters of a mile to the mainland. The climate is
hot and humid. Rainfall averages 240 cm a year and temperature ranges from 24° to 32°C (76°–89°F).

HISTORY AND POLITICS

Singapore, where Sir Stamford Raffles first established a
trading post under the East India Company in 1819, was
incorporated with Penang and Malacca to form the Straits
Settlements in 1826. The Straits Settlements became a

Crown colony in 1867. Singapore fell into Japanese hands in 1942 and civil government was not restored until 1946, when it became a separate colony. Internal self-government was introduced in 1959. Singapore became a state of Malaysia in September 1963, but left Malaysia and became an independent sovereign state within the Commonwealth on 9 August 1965. Singapore adopted a republican constitution from that date.

After the general election of 2 January 1997 the People's Action Party (PAP) had 81 seats in Parliament. S. R. Nathan became President of Singapore on 1 September 1999; no election was held as he was the sole candidate.

POLITICAL SYSTEM

The president is directly elected for a six-year term, and can veto government decisions relating to internal security, the budget, financial reserves and the appointment of senior civil servants. The President appoints the Prime Minister and, on his advice, the members of the Cabinet. There is a Parliament of 83 directly elected members, with up to six further non-constituency members from opposition parties (NCMPs), dependent on their share of the vote, directly elected for a five-year term. Up to nine members can also be nominated by the government for a two-year term (NMPs). In the present parliament, there is one NCMP and nine NMPs.

HEAD OF STATE

President, Sellapan Ramanathan Nathan, *took office* 1 September 1999

CABINET *as at September 2000*

Prime Minister, Goh Chok Tong
Senior Minister, PM's Office, Lee Kuan Yew
Deputy PM, Defence, Dr Tony Tan
Deputy PM, PM's Office, Lee Hsien Loong
Communications, Mah Bow Tan
Community Development, Muslim Affairs,
    Abdullah Tarmugi
Education, Defence, Rear-Adm. Teo Chee Hean
Finance, Dr Richard Hu Tsu Tau
Foreign Affairs and Law, Shanmugam Jayakumar
Health and Environment, Yeo Cheow Tong
Home Affairs, Wong Kan Seng
Information and the Arts, Trade and Industry,
    Brig.-Gen. George Yeo
Labour, Dr Lee Boon Yang
National Development, Foreign Affairs, Lim Hng Kiang
Trade and Industry, Finance, Lee Yock Suan
Without Portfolio, PM's Office, Lim Boon Heng

HIGH COMMISSION FOR THE REPUBLIC OF SINGAPORE
9 Wilton Crescent, London SW1X 8RW
Tel: 020-7235 8315
High Commissioner, HE Professor Pang Eng Fong, apptd 1999
Counsellor, Paul K. H. Koh
First Secretary, Kheng Hian Ho (*Commercial*)

BRITISH HIGH COMMISSION
Tanglin Road, Singapore 247919
Tel: (00 65) 473 9333
E-mail: brit_hc@pacific.net.sg/firecrest
High Commissioner, HE Alan Hunt, CMG, apptd 1997
Deputy High Commissioner, A. Gooch
Defence Adviser, Gp Capt. C. B. LeBas

BRITISH COUNCIL DIRECTOR, Dr J. Grote, OBE,
30 Napier Road, Singapore 258509;
e-mail: recept@britcoun.org.sg

ECONOMY

Historically Singapore's economy was based on the sale and distribution of raw materials from surrounding countries and on entrepôt trade in finished products. An industrialisation programme launched in 1968 has established a wide range of manufacturing industries, including shipbuilding, iron and steel, micro-electronics, electrical goods, telecommunications equipment, office machinery, scientific instruments, pharmaceuticals, etc. Singapore has also become an important financial services centre with significant insurance and foreign exchange markets, a stock exchange, 149 commercial banks and 79 merchant banks and an oil-refining centre. In February 1998 the government announced substantial liberalising reforms of the financial sector, aimed at allowing the country to compete more competitively with other financial sectors in the region. Singapore has not been as badly affected as its neighbours by the economic crisis in south-east Asia, due in part to currency reserves estimated at US$118 billion; it was praised by the IMF for its adroit response to the crisis, which included wage cuts.

There were 6,958,000 foreign visitors in 1999.

Singapore's major trading partners are the USA, Malaysia, the EU, Hong Kong and Japan.

In 1998 Singapore had a trade surplus of US$14,678 million and a current account surplus of US$17,614 million. Imports totalled US$104,719 million and exports US$109,895 million.

GNP – US$95,453 million (1998); US$30,170 per capita (1998)
GDP – US$93,712 million (1996); US$27,693 per capita (1996)
ANNUAL AVERAGE GROWTH OF GDP – 7.0 per cent (1996)
INFLATION RATE – –0.3 per cent (1998)
UNEMPLOYMENT – 3.2 per cent (1998)

Trade with UK	1998	1999
Imports from UK	£1,614,891,000	£1,604,085,000
Exports to UK	2,462,773,000	2,451,004,000

COMMUNICATIONS

Singapore is one of the largest and busiest seaports in the world, with six terminals, deep water wharves and ship repairing facilities. Ships also anchor in the roads, unloading into lighters. In 1999, the total volume of cargo handled was 325,902,200 tonnes. There were 141,523 ship arrivals in 1999.

The international airport is at Changi, in the east of the island, with Singapore Airlines operating flights to 43 countries and 24,500,000 passengers using the airport in 1996. There are 25.8 km of railway connected to the Malaysian rail system by the causeway across the Straits of Johore, and 3,027 km of roads.

There are 19 radio and four television channels operated by the Singapore Broadcasting Corporation in the four official languages, and three private broadcasting stations.

Singapore's government has prioritised information technology and telecommunications in its programme to transform the country into a knowledge-based economy by 2010. As at June 2000, there were 59 fixed line telephones, 58.5 mobile phones and 32.9 pagers per cent of population; access to the internet amounted to 54.6 per cent.

SLOVAKIA
Slovenská Republika – The Republic of Slovakia

AREA – 18,928 sq. miles (49,012 sq. km). Neighbours: Poland (north), Ukraine (east), Hungary (south), Austria (west), the Czech Republic (north-west)
POPULATION – 5,383,000 (1997 UN estimate): 87.7 per cent are ethnic Slovaks, 10.6 per cent ethnic Hungarians, 1.4 per cent Romany, 1 per cent Czech, with smaller numbers of Ruthenians, Ukrainians and Germans. The population is mainly Christian, some 60 per cent Roman Catholic and 8 per cent Protestant. Slovak is the official language, while Hungarian and Czech are also spoken
CAPITAL – Bratislava (population, 452,278, 1993), on the Danube
MAJOR CITIES – Košice (239,927); Žilina (86,373); Prešov (92,013); Banská Bystríca (88,390)
CURRENCY – Koruna (Sk) of 100 halierov
NATIONAL ANTHEM – Nad Tatrou sa blýska (Storm over the Tatras)
NATIONAL DAYS – 1 January (Establishment of Slovak Republic); 5 July (Day of the Slav Missionaries); 29 August (Slovak National Uprising); 1 September (Constitution Day)
NATIONAL FLAG – Three horizontal stripes of white, blue, red with the arms all over near the hoist
LIFE EXPECTANCY (years) – male 68.40; female 76.33
POPULATION GROWTH RATE – 0.2 per cent (1997)
POPULATION DENSITY – 110 per sq. km (1997)
URBAN POPULATION – 57.0 per cent (1995)
ENROLMENT (percentage of age group) – tertiary 22.1 per cent (1996)

The Tatry (Tatras) mountains in the centre and north of Slovakia reach heights of 2,655 m. The major river is the Váh which flows from the Tatry mountains to join the Danube at the Hungarian border. The climate is continental.

HISTORY AND POLITICS
(*see also* Czech Republic, Hungary)

At the end of the 11th century Slovakia became part of the Hungarian state when the Magyars gained control of the area. Following the dissolution of the Austro-Hungarian Empire, Slovakia was amalgamated into Czechoslovakia on 28 October 1918, but became independent in March 1939 as a Nazi puppet state when Germany invaded the Czech lands. Slovakia was liberated by Soviet forces in 1945 and returned to Czechoslovakia. The formation of a federal republic between the Czech lands and Slovakia was the only Prague Spring reform to survive the Soviet invasion of 1968. Following the collapse of Communist rule in 1989, the Czech and Slovak republics began to negotiate the dissolution of the federation into two sovereign states in 1992. Dissolution took effect on 1 January 1993.

A coalition government led by the Movement for a Democratic Slovakia (HZDS) was sworn in on 12 January 1993 but was brought down by a no-confidence vote in March 1994.

Legislative elections on 30 September and 1 October 1994 returned the HZDS to power at the head of a three-party coalition which took office on 13 December 1994.

Following the legislative elections on 25–26 September 1998, the HZDS remained the largest party, but a four-party coalition government led by the Slovak Democratic Coalition (SDK) was formed.

The number of seats held by each of the parties in the National Council following the 1998 election was: HZDS 43; SDK 42; Party of the Democratic Left (SDL) 23; Hungarian Coalition Party (SMK) 15; Slovak National

Party (SNS) 14; Party of Civic Understanding (SOP) 13. President Kováč's term of office ended on 2 March 1998. The presidential elections were not contested by the ruling HZDS, who were accused by opposition parties of trying to create a constitutional vacuum; since no president was elected by the end of Kováč's term, certain presidential powers were transferred to the prime minister. After the 1998 legislative elections, the National Council voted on 14 January 1999 for direct presidential elections, which were held on 29 May 1999 and won by Rudolf Schuster of the SOP.

POLITICAL SYSTEM
The constitution vests legislative power in the National Council of 150 members directly elected for a four-year term by proportional representation with a five per cent threshold for parliamentary representation. The president is elected for a five-year term, renewable only once, by direct election; executive power is held by the prime minister and Cabinet.

HEAD OF STATE
President, Rudolf Schuster, *elected* 29 May 1999, *sworn in* 15 June 1999

CABINET *as at September 2000*
Prime Minister, Mikuláš Dzurinda (SDK)
Deputy PMs, Ivan Mikloš (SDK) *(Economy)*; Pavol Hamik (SOP) *(European Integration)*; Pál Csáky (SMK) *(Human and Minority Rights and Regional Development)*; L'ubomír Foga (SDL) *(Legislation)*
Agriculture, Pavel Koncoš (SDL)
Construction and Public Works, István Harna (SMK)
Culture, Milan Kňazžko (SDK)
Defence, Pavol Kanis (SDL)
Economy, Lubomír Harach (SDK)
Education, Milan Ftáčnik (SDL)
Environment, László Miklós (SMK)
Finance, Brigita Schmögnerová (SDL)
Foreign Affairs, Eduard Kukan (SDK)
Health, Roman Kováč (SDK)
Interior, Ladislav Pittner (SDK)
Justice, Ján Čarnogurský (SDK)
Labour, Social Affairs and the Family, Peter Magvaši (SDL)
Privatizisation, Mária Machová (SOP)
Transport, Posts and Telecommunications, Jozef Macejko (SDK)

EMBASSY OF THE SLOVAK REPUBLIC
25 Kensington Palace Gardens, London W8 4QY
Tel: 020-7243 0803
Ambassador Extraordinary and Plenipotentiary, HE Frantiek Dlhopolček, apptd 2000

BRITISH EMBASSY
Panská 16, SK-811 01 Bratislava
Tel: (00 421) (7) 5441 9632/3
E-mail: bebra@internet.sk
Ambassador Extraordinary and Plenipotentiary, HE David Lyscom, apptd 1998
BRITISH COUNCIL DIRECTOR, J. McGrath, PO Box 68, Panská 17, SK-814 99 Bratislava;
e-mail: bc.bratislava@britishcouncil.sk

DEFENCE

The Army has 478 main battle tanks, 207 armoured personnel carriers, and 476 armoured infantry fighting vehicles. The Air Force has 102 combat aircraft and 19 attack helicopters.
MILITARY EXPENDITURE – 2.0 per cent of GDP (1998)
MILITARY PERSONNEL – 44,880: Army 23,800; Air Force 12,000; Paramilitaries 2,600
CONSCRIPTION DURATION – 12 months

ECONOMY

From independence until mid-1994 Slovakia faced economic difficulties because of the structure of its centrally-planned and inefficiently managed economy, reliant on state-subsidised heavy industries with low productivity, and because of the ambivalent attitude to reform of the HZDS government. In mid-1994 the economic situation stabilised as the Moravčik government implemented a second round of privatisation. The election of an HZDS-led government in October 1994 slowed the pace of reform. Following severe depreciation of the Koruna and the failure of the economy to achieve the anticipated growth targets, the SDK-led government introduced a package of austerity measures on 20 May 1999; the basic rate of VAT was raised, there were increases in energy, water, telecommunications and housing prices, and import taxes were reintroduced.

Natural resources include brown coal, natural gas, iron ore, antimony, lead, zinc and magnesite.

In 1998 Slovakia had a trade deficit of US$2,290 million and a current account deficit of US$2,066 million. Imports totalled US$13,611 million and exports US$9,048 million.

GNP – US$19,941 million (1998); US$3,700 per capita (1998)
GDP – US$18,963 million (1996); US$3,547 per capita (1996)
ANNUAL AVERAGE GROWTH OF GDP – 6.5 per cent (1997)
INFLATION RATE – 6.7 per cent (1998)
UNEMPLOYMENT – 11.9 per cent (1998)
TOTAL EXTERNAL DEBT – US$9,893 million (1998)

TRADE WITH UK	1998	1999
Imports from UK	£104,766,000	£113,518,000
Exports to UK	75,165,000	106,408,000

SLOVENIA
Republika Slovenija

AREA – 7,821 sq. miles (20,256 sq. km). Neighbours: Austria (north), Hungary (north-east), Croatia (east and south), Italy (west)
POPULATION – 1,987,000 (1997 UN estimate). The population is mostly Slovenian. There are small Hungarian (0.5 per cent) and Italian (0.1 per cent) minorities, together with a Romany population. The main religion is Roman Catholicism. Slovene is the official language, together with Hungarian and Italian in ethnically mixed regions
CAPITAL – Ljubljana (population, 273,000, 1996 estimate)
MAJOR CITIES – Maribor (103,113); Celje (39,782); Kranj (36,770); ΨKoper (24,495), the only port, 1994
CURRENCY – Tolar (SIT) of 100 stotin
NATIONAL ANTHEM – Zdravljica (A Toast)
NATIONAL DAY – 25 June (Statehood Day)
NATIONAL FLAG – Three horizontal stripes of white, blue, red, with the arms in the upper hoist
LIFE EXPECTANCY (years) – male 70.79; female 78.25
POPULATION GROWTH RATE – –0.1 per cent (1997)
POPULATION DENSITY – 98 per sq. km (1997)
URBAN POPULATION – 70.0 per cent (1999)
MILITARY EXPENDITURE – 1.7 per cent of GDP (1998)
MILITARY PERSONNEL – 9,550: Army 9,550; Paramilitaries 4,500
CONSCRIPTION DURATION – Seven months

Slovenia is a small mountainous state which is the most northerly of the former Yugoslav republics. The two major rivers are the Sava and the Drava. There is a short coastline in the south-west 29 miles (46 km) in length on the Adriatic. The climate is a mixture of Mediterranean, continental and alpine.

HISTORY AND POLITICS

The area that is now Slovenia came under the control of the Habsburg Empire in the 13th and 14th centuries and remained so until the defeat of the Austro-Hungarian Empire in 1918. On 27 October 1918 Slovenia became part of Yugoslavia. In 1941 German forces invaded Yugoslavia and Slovenia was divided between Germany, Italy and Hungary. Slovenia was reformed as a constituent republic of the federal Yugoslav state in May 1945. After a dispute with Italy and nine years of international administration, the Adriatic coast and hinterland were returned to Slovenia in 1954 and Italy retained Trieste.

Slovenian fears of Serbian dominance led the Slovene Assembly in 1989 to amend the republican constitution to lay the basis of a sovereign state. The first democratic elections, held in April 1990, were won by the pro-independence 'Demos' coalition. In a referendum in December 1990, 88 per cent of the electorate voted for independence, which was declared on 25 June 1991. A ten-day war with the Yugoslav National Army followed before the Army called off hostilities and withdrew under the mediation of the EU.

Legislative elections were held on 10 November 1996. Liberal Democracy of Slovenia (LDS) won the most seats and formed a coalition government with the Slovene People's Party (SLS) and the Democratic Party of the Pensioners of Slovenia (DeSUS). President Kučan was re-elected on 23 November 1997.

The SLS announced that it was leaving the coalition on 15 March 2000 (it later merged with the Slovene Christian Democrats (SKD)) and the government lost a vote of confidence on 8 April 2000. Andrej Bajuk was elected by the Assembly to lead a caretaker government, was approved on 8 June 2000. A legislative election is due to be held by November 2000.

FOREIGN RELATIONS

Slovenia signed an association agreement and applied for membership of the EU in June 1996. The EU began formal accession negotiations with Slovenia on 10 November 1998.

POLITICAL SYSTEM

The head of state is the president, elected for a five-year term. Executive power is vested in the prime minister and Cabinet of Ministers. The lower house of the legislature, the National Assembly, has 90 members directly elected for a four-year term. The upper house, the 40-member National Council, has an advisory role. The National Assembly is elected on a proportional representation basis, with one seat each reserved for the Italian and Hungarian minorities.

HEAD OF STATE

President, Milan Kučan, *elected* April 1990, *re-elected* December 1992, 23 November 1997

CARETAKER EXECUTIVE COUNCIL *as at September 2000*

President of the Executive Council (Prime Minister), Andrej Bajuk (SLS-SKD)
Agriculture and Forestry, Ciril Smrkolj (SLS-SKD)
Culture, Rudi Seligo (SDS)
Defence, Janez Jansa (SDS)
Economic Affairs, Joze Zagozen (SDS)
Economic Relations and Development, Marjan Senjur (Ind.)
Education and Sport, Lovro Sturm (Ind.)
Environmental and Physical Planning, Andrej Umek
Finance, Zvonko Ivanusić (Ind.)
Foreign Affairs, Lojze Peterle (SLS-SKD)
Health, Andrej Brucan (SDS)
Internal Affairs, Peter Jambrek (Ind.)
Justice, Barbara Brezigar (Ind.)
Labour, Family and Social Affairs, Miha Brejc (SDS)
Science and Technology, Lojze Marinček (SLS-SKD)

Small Enterprises and Tourism, Janko Razgoršsek (SLS-SKD)
Transport and Communications, Anton Bergauer (SLS-SKD)
Without Portfolio, Legislation, Tone Jerovšek (Ind.)

SLS-SKD Slovene People's Party/Slovene Christian Democrats; Ind. Independent

EMBASSY OF THE REPUBLIC OF SLOVENIA
11–15 Wigmore Street, London WIH 9LA
Tel: 020-7495 7775
Ambassador Extraordinary and Plenipotentiary,
 HE Marjan Setinc, apptd 1998

BRITISH EMBASSY
4th Floor, Trg Republike 3, SI-1000 Ljubljana
Tel: (00 386) (61) 200 3910
E-mail: info@british-embassy.si
Ambassador Extraordinary and Plenipotentiary,
 HE David Lloyd, OBE, apptd 1997

BRITISH COUNCIL DIRECTOR, S. Green, Cankarjevo nabrezje 27, SI-1000 Ljubljana;
e-mail: info@britishcouncil.si

ECONOMY

Slovenia's economy has emerged as the most stable of the former Yugoslav economies and the least affected by the end of central planning. Although it has lost its captive export market and cheap supplies of raw materials from other parts of the former Yugoslavia, Slovenia is one of the richest ex-Communist countries. It has successfully re-orientated its exports towards Western markets, its main trading partners being Germany, Italy and France. The privatisation process was completed in 1998.

In 1999 agriculture contributed 4 per cent to the total value of GDP, industry 38.5 per cent and services 59.9 per cent. The main agricultural products are potatoes, wheat, corn, sugar beet and wine. The major manufacturing sectors are metalworking, electronics, textiles, automotive parts, chemicals, glass products and food-processing. Tourism and transport are major export earners, with 1,400,000 tourists visiting in 1991.

In 1998 Slovenia had a trade deficit of US$775 million and a current account deficit of US$4 million. Imports totalled US$10,098 million and exports US$9,048 million.

GNP – US$19,385 million (1998); US$9,780 per capita (1998)
GDP – US$18,693 million (1996); US$9,716 per capita (1996); estimated to be US$20,294 million and US$10,248 per capita in 1999
ANNUAL AVERAGE GROWTH OF GDP – 3.9 per cent (1998); 4.9 per cent (1999 estimate)
INFLATION RATE – 8.6 per cent (1998); 6.1 per cent (1999 estimate)
UNEMPLOYMENT – 7.7 per cent (1998)
TOTAL EXTERNAL DEBT – US$4,762 million (1997); US$5,491 million (1999 estimate)

Trade with UK	1998	1999
Imports from UK	£136,308,000	£143,993,000
Exports to UK	103,527,000	108,685,000

COMMUNICATIONS

There are 14,810 km of roads and 1,201 km of rail track. Important road and rail communications cross the country from west to east (Milan–Ljubljana–Budapest), and north to south (Munich–Ljubljana–Zagreb–Belgrade–Athens). There are international airports at Ljubljana, Maribor and Portorož (Adriatic Coast). Koper is an important shipment point for goods from Austria, Hungary, the Czech Republic and Slovakia.

EDUCATION

Education is compulsory and free between the ages of six and 14. There are 821 primary schools (age six–14), 153 secondary or middle schools (age 14–19), 44 colleges and two universities (Ljubljana and Maribor).
ENROLMENT (percentage of age group) – primary 95 per cent (1996); tertiary 36.4 per cent (1996)

SOLOMON ISLANDS

AREA – 11,157 sq. miles (28,896 sq. km)
POPULATION – 408,358 (2000 estimate); 328,723 (1991 census). English is the official language; there are over 80 local languages
CAPITAL – ΨHoniara (population, 40,000, 1991)
CURRENCY – Solomon Islands dollar (SI$) of 100 cents
NATIONAL ANTHEM – God Bless our Solomon Islands
NATIONAL DAY – 7 July (Independence Day)
NATIONAL FLAG – Blue over green divided by a diagonal yellow band, with five white stars in the top left quarter
LIFE EXPECTANCY (years) – male 59.90; female 61.40
POPULATION GROWTH RATE – 3.3 per cent (1997)
POPULATION DENSITY – 14 per sq. km (1997)

Forming a scattered archipelago of mountainous islands and low-lying coral atolls, the Solomon Islands stretches about 900 miles in a south-easterly direction from the Shortland Islands to the Santa Cruz islands. The six biggest islands are Choiseul, New Georgia, Santa Isabel, Guadalcanal, Malaita and Makira. They are characterised by thickly-forested mountain ranges intersected by deep, narrow valleys.

HISTORY AND POLITICS

The origin of the present Melanesian inhabitants is uncertain. European interest in the islands began in the mid-16th century and continued intermittently for about 300 years, when the inauguration of sugar plantations in Queensland and Fiji (which created a need for labour) and the arrival of missionaries and traders led to increased European interest in the region. Great Britain declared a Protectorate in 1893 over the Southern Solomons, adding the Santa Cruz group in 1898 and 1899. The islands of the Shortland groups were transferred from Germany to Great Britain by treaty in 1900. The Solomon Islands achieved internal self-government in 1976, and became independent in July 1978.

Following legislative elections held on 6 August 1997, the Alliance for Change group, led by the Liberal Party, formed a government. Bartholomew Ulufa'alu, the Liberal Party leader, was elected prime minister on 27 August 1997. Following his resignation on 13 June 2000, Mannasseh Sogavare was elected prime minister on 30 June and appointed a government of national unity.

INSURGENCY

In late 1998 tension between the indigenous inhabitants of Guadalcanal and settlers from other parts of the country, chiefly Malaita, led to violent attacks on the settlers. On 28 June 1999, a peace agreement was signed by representatives of the national and provincial governments and the Isatabu Freedom Fighters (IFF), a local militant group, following mediation by the Commonwealth special envoy Sitiveni Rabuka.

Following further tension, on 28 February 2000 the government banned the IFF and their rivals the Malaita Eagles Force (MEF), but lifted the ban on 15 May to facilitate peace talks. MEF guerrillas took Prime Minister Ulufa'alu hostage on 5 June 2000 and took over the capital. The prime minister was freed on 10 June and the MEF and the IMF agreed to a two-week truce to allow mediation by a Commonwealth delegation. Further peace talks were held on 24–26 August 2000.

POLITICAL SYSTEM

The Solomon Islands is a constitutional monarchy. Queen Elizabeth II is represented locally by the Governor-General. Executive authority is exercised by the Cabinet. Legislative power is vested in a unicameral National Parliament of 50 members, elected for a four-year term.

Governor-General, HE John Lapli, GCMG, apptd 1999

CABINET *as at September 2000*

Prime Minister, Mannasseh Sogavare
Deputy PM, National Unity, Reconciliation and Peace, Allan Kemakeza
Deputy PM, Provincial Government and Rural Development, Nathaniel Waena
Agriculture and Primary Industries, Moon Pin Kwan
Commerce, Employment and Trade, David Holosivi
Culture, Tourism and Aviation, Johnson Koli
Education, William Gigini
Finance, Synder Rini
Fisheries and Marine Resources, George Luilamo
Foreign Affairs, Danny Philip
Forests, Environment and Conservation, Tommy Chan
Health and Medical Services, Allan Paul
Home and Ecclesiastical Affairs, Revd Reuben Mesepitu
Lands and Housing, Hilda Kari
Mines and Energy, David Vouza
National Planning and Human Resources Development, Michael Maina
Police and Justice, William Haomae
Transport, Works and Communication, Joses Saueha Tahua
Youth and Women's Affairs, Albert Laore

HIGH COMMISSION OF THE SOLOMON ISLANDS
Boulevard Saint Michel 28, Box 23, B-1040 Brussels
Tel: (00 32) (2) 2732 7085
High Commissioner, HE Robert Sisilo, apptd 1996

BRITISH HIGH COMMISSION
Telekom House, Mendana Avenue (PO Box 676), Honiara
Tel: (00 677)Honiara 21705/6
E-mail: bhc1@welkam.solomon.com.sb
High Commissioner, HE Alan Waters, apptd 1998

ECONOMY

The main imports are foodstuffs, consumer goods, machinery and transport materials. Principal exports are timber, fish, palm oil, copra and cocoa. In 1997 there was a trade deficit of US$29 million and a current account deficit of US$28 million. In 1995 imports totalled US$154 million and exports totalled US$168 million.
GNP – US$315 million (1998); US$760 per capita (1998)
GDP – US$370 million (1996); US$947 per capita (1996)
ANNUAL AVERAGE GROWTH OF GDP – 6.0 per cent (1996)

SOMALIA
Jamhuuriyadda Dimoqraadiya Soomaaliya

AREA – 246,201 sq. miles (637,657 sq. km). Neighbours: Djibouti, Ethiopia and Kenya (west)
POPULATION – 10,217,000 (1997 UN estimate). Somali and Arabic are the official languages. English and Italian are also spoken
CAPITAL – ΨMogadishu (Muqdisho) (population, 900,000, 1990 estimate)
MAJOR CITIES – ΨBerbera (15,000); Boroma (65,000); Burao (15,000); Hargeysa (20,000); ΨKismaayo (60,000)
CURRENCY – Somali shilling of 100 cents
NATIONAL DAY – under review

NATIONAL FLAG – Five-pointed white star on blue ground
LIFE EXPECTANCY (years) – male 45.41; female 48.60
POPULATION GROWTH RATE – 2.4 per cent (1997)
POPULATION DENSITY – 16 per sq. km (1997)
URBAN POPULATION – 23.5 per cent (1987)
ENROLMENT (percentage of age group) – primary 10 per cent (1985); secondary 3 per cent (1985); tertiary 2.1 per cent (1985)

HISTORY AND POLITICS

The British protectorate of Somaliland and the Italian trust territory of Somalia were joined and became independent on 1 July 1960. In 1969, the armed forces seized power and established a ruling Revolutionary Council under Siad Barre's leadership.

Siad Barre was overthrown by rebels in January 1991, sparking civil war between rival clan-based movements. The United Somali Congress (USC) seized control in Mogadishu, while the Somali National Movement formed a rival administration in the north. Fighting between the USC and supporters of the Somali National Alliance (SNA) of Gen. Mohammed Aideed devastated Mogadishu and large parts of the south, exacerbating famine conditions. The UN Operation in Somalia proved ineffective in securing aid distribution routes and was replaced on 9 December 1992 by a UN-approved, US-led, United Task Force (UNITAF).

On 4 May 1993, UNITAF handed over to a 28,000-strong UN force (UNOSOM).

The UN withdrew its troops in March 1995, enabling Gen. Aideed's militia to take control of the city's port and airport. On 12 June 1995, Gen. Aideed was ousted as SNA leader by a joint USC-SNA congress which nominated Osman Ali Ato as its leader. Gen. Aideed responded by declaring himself president on 15 June 1995. Gen. Aideed died of gunshot wounds in July 1996 and was replaced by his son, Hussein Aideed. Fighting between the factions continued in 1996–7 despite a brief cease-fire in October 1996.

On 22 December 1997, 26 out of the 28 factions signed the Cairo Declaration, an agreement aimed at establishing a cross-factional 13-member Presidential Council and a 189-member Council of Deputies in preparation for full elections to be held no later than 2003.

A peace plan proposed by Djibouti was overwhelmingly supported on 16 November 1999 by representatives of civil society and the armed factions at a forum in Nairobi. On 21 December, five faction leaders signed an agreement to establish a joint authority to govern the Mogadishu region, and then the southern region, as steps towards founding a national government. A Somali National Reconciliation Conference in Djibouti opened on 2 May 2000, which aimed to lay the foundations of the transitional institutions of the Somali state, but was opposed by the Rahawein Resistance Army, the Somali Patriotic Movement and the leaders of Puntland. The National Reconciliation Conference appointed a transitional national assembly on 13 August, which on 26 August appointed Abdiqassim Salad Hassan as president.

INSURGENCIES

Civil war broke out in May 1988 between the government and the opposition Somali National Movement (SNM) in the north of the country. With the downfall of Siad Barre, the SNM took control of the north-west (the former British Somaliland Protectorate) and in May 1991 declared unilateral independence as the 'Somaliland Republic'. A government and legislature was formed which elected Mohammed Ibrahim Egal as president in May 1993; he was re-elected in February 1997.

An autonomous administration was proclaimed in north-eastern Somalia on 23 July 1998. Col. Ahmed Abdullahi Yusuf was named as president of the region, calling itself Puntland, and a Cabinet was appointed. On 15 September 1998, a 69-member parliament was inaugurated.

SOMALI DIPLOMATIC REPRESENTATION
The Embassy closed in January 1992.

BRITISH DIPLOMATIC REPRESENTATION
The British Embassy in Mogadishu closed in January 1991.

ECONOMY

Livestock raising is the main occupation and there is a modest export trade in livestock, skins and hides, which accounted for 38 per cent of exports in 1988. Italy, the Gulf States and Saudi Arabia import the bulk of the banana crop, the biggest export, which accounted for 40 per cent of exports. The principal imports are machinery and transport equipment, industrial goods and foodstuffs.
GDP – US$811 million (1996); US$83 per capita (1996)
ANNUAL AVERAGE GROWTH OF GDP – –7.0 per cent (1996)
INFLATION RATE – 81.9 per cent (1988)
TOTAL EXTERNAL DEBT – US$2,635 million (1998)

Trade with UK	1998	1999
Imports from UK	£1,601,000	£3,079,000
Exports to UK	920,000	89,000

SOUTH AFRICA
Republic of South Africa

AREA – 471,445 sq. miles (1,221,037 sq. km).
   Neighbours: Namibia (north-west), Botswana and Zimbabwe (north), Mozambique and Swaziland (north-east), Lesotho, which is completely surrounded by South Africa
POPULATION – 43,336,000 (1997 UN estimate); 40,583,573 (1996 census): 76.7 per cent African, 10.9 per cent White, 8.9 per cent Coloured, 2.6 per cent Asian. The interim constitution designates 11 official languages: Afrikaans; English; IsiNdebele; IsiXosa; IsiZulu, Sepedi; Sosotho; SiSwati; Setswana; Tshivenda; Xitsonga. Afrikaans and English are to remain the languages of record although any citizen may correspond official business in his own language
CAPITAL –The seat of the government is Pretoria (population 2,341,000, 1995 estimate); the seat of the legislature is Cape Town (population, 2,279,000, 1995 estimate); the seat of the judiciary is Bloemfontein (300,150, 1991 census)
MAJOR CITIES – ΨDurban (3,215,000); ΨEast London (611,000); Johannesburg (4,247,360); Pietermaritzburg (519,000); ΨPort Elizabeth (1,015,000), 1995 estimates
CURRENCY – Rand (R) of 100 cents
NATIONAL ANTHEMS – Nkosi Sikelel' iAfrika (God Bless Africa); Die Stem Van Suid-Afrika (The Call of South Africa)
NATIONAL DAY – 27 April (Freedom Day)
NATIONAL FLAG – Divided red over blue by a horizontal white-fimbriated green Y; in the hoist a black triangle fimbriated in yellow
LIFE EXPECTANCY (years) – male 60.01; female 66.00
POPULATION GROWTH RATE – 2 per cent (1997)
POPULATION DENSITY – 35 per sq. km (1997)
URBAN POPULATION – 44.6 per cent (1996)
ILLITERACY RATE – 14.9 per cent
ENROLMENT (percentage of age group) – primary 94 per cent (1996); secondary 51 per cent (1996); tertiary 19 per cent (1995)

South Africa occupies the southernmost part of the African continent from the courses of the Limpopo, Marico, Molopo, Nosop and Orange Rivers to the Cape of Good Hope, with the exception of Lesotho, Swaziland and the extreme south of Mozambique. To the west, east and south lie the south Atlantic and southern Indian Oceans. Some 1,192 miles (1,920 km) to the south-east of Cape Town lie Prince Edward and Marion Islands, part of South Africa since 1947.
   The Orange, with its tributary the Vaal, is the principal river, rising in the Drakensberg and flowing into the Atlantic near the border with Namibia. The Limpopo, or Crocodile River, in the north, rises in North-West Province and flows into the Indian Ocean through Mozambique.
   The climate is subtropical, dry and sunny, moderated by the temperate winds from the Atlantic and Indian Oceans. Moist hot air masses from the Indian Ocean are the chief source of rainfall for most of the country.

HISTORY AND POLITICS

Hunter-gatherers, the San (Bushmen) and Khoikhoi (Hottentots) inhabited southern Africa from c.8,000 BC. Their descendants, and those of Bantu-speaking peoples who had migrated south, occupied the area when the Portuguese navigator Bartolomeu Días charted the coast in 1488.
   The colony of the Cape of Good Hope was founded by the Dutch at Cape Town in 1652 and remained a Dutch colony until Britain took possession of it in 1795. Restored to Dutch rule in 1803, it was again taken by Britain in 1806 and this was confirmed by the London Convention of 1814. A rejection of British liberalism and the desire to keep slaves led to the movement of large numbers of Boers (the descendants of Dutch settlers) north-eastwards in the years following 1834. This 'Great Trek' led to the foundation of the Orange Free State and Transvaal republics by the Boers, which were recognised by Britain in 1853–4. Natal was annexed to Cape Colony by the British in 1844 then formed as a separate colony in 1856, to which Zululand was added in 1897 after the British victory in the Zulu wars. Transvaal and the Orange Free State (renamed the Orange River Colony) became British colonies after the Boer defeat in the Second Boer War 1899–1902. The self-governing colonies of the Cape of Good Hope, Natal, the Transvaal and the Orange River Colony became united in 1910 under the name of the Union of South Africa. Independence within the Commonwealth was gained in 1931 under the Statute of Westminster. South Africa left the Commonwealth and became a republic on 31 May 1961, largely as a result of international condemnation of apartheid and of the Sharpeville massacre.
   From 1948, when the Afrikaner National Party came to power, South Africa's social and political structure was based on apartheid, a policy of racial segregation. Opposition protests culminated in the Sharpeville massacre in 1960; the African National Congress (ANC) and other opposition groups were subsequently banned. A new wave of opposition climaxed in 1976 with uprisings in Soweto, in which hundreds were shot dead. In 1984 renewed rioting in the black townships and continuing unrest led to the declaration of a state of emergency which was renewed annually until 1990.
   As part of its policy of apartheid, the government established a number of black 'homelands'. Six areas (Gazankulu, Lebowa, KwaNdebele, KaNgwane, Qwaqwa and KwaZulu) were designated as self-governing states. A further four (Bophuthatswana, Ciskei, Transkei and Venda) were regarded as independent republics by the South African government but never recognised as such by the UN.

MOVES TO DEMOCRACY

The first moves to reform apartheid came into effect in 1984, when a new constitution extended the franchise to the Coloured and Indian populations. However, whites retained effective political power and blacks remained excluded.

In 1989, F. W. de Klerk became president of South Africa and accelerated the process of reform. In 1990, the ban on the ANC and restrictions on other anti-apartheid groups were lifted; Nelson Mandela, the main ANC political detainee, was released. In 1991 the laws implementing apartheid were effectively abolished. In 1992 a referendum amongst the white electorate on continued political reform and a new constitution reached by negotiation was approved by 69 per cent to 31 per cent.

On 20 December 1991, the Convention on a Democratic South Africa (CODESA) talks between the government, ANC, Inkatha Freedom Party and other political, business and church groups, opened. CODESA reached agreement on the establishment of an inter-racial administration and the formation of a five-year coalition government following a multiracial election. An interim constitution was agreed on 17 November and adopted by parliament on 22 December.

In the country's first multiracial general election held on 26–29 April 1994 the ANC gained 252 seats in the 400-seat National Assembly with 62.7 per cent of the votes cast. In the 90-seat Senate the ANC gained 60 seats.

The parliament has passed two significant pieces of legislation to settle the legacy of the apartheid era. In November 1994 the Restitution of Land Rights Act was passed which established a Commission and a Court to restore the rights of those dispossessed of their land since the 1913 Land Act. In June 1995 the Promotion of National Unity and Reconciliation Act was passed which established a Truth Commission covering the apartheid era, with a remit to assess confessions, grant amnesties for political crimes and set compensation for victims. The first hearing opened on 15 April 1996.

In legislative and provincial elections held on 2 June 1999, the ANC gained 266 seats in the National Assembly with 66.4 per cent of votes cast, the Democratic Party (DP) 38 seats (9.6 per cent), the Inkatha Freedom Party (IFP) 34 seats (8.58 per cent), the New National Party (NNP) 28 seats (6.87 per cent), the United Democratic Movement 14 seats (3.42 per cent) and the African Christian Democratic Party 6 seats (1.43 per cent). Of parties who obtained less than 1 per cent of the vote, the Freedom Front, the United Christian Democratic Party and the Pan African Congress (PAC) gained three seats each, the Federal Alliance two seats and the Minority Front, the Afrikaner Eenheidsbeweging (Afrikaner Unity Movement) and the Azanian People's Organisation each gained one seat. In the provincial elections, the ANC retained an absolute majority in seven out of the nine provinces and formed a coalition government with the IFP in KwaZulu-Natal. In Western Cape, the ANC was the largest party, but a coalition was formed between the NNP and the DP.

On 9 June 1999 the ANC, being one seat short of the two-thirds majority required to amend the constitution, entered into a coalition with the Minority Front, which held just one seat in the National Assembly.

On 14 June 1999 the National Assembly met to select a new president. Thabo Mbeki was elected unopposed and was formally sworn in on 16 June 1999.

POLITICAL SYSTEM

The final constitution, which came into effect in 1997, retains the existing political structure but replaces the Senate with a National Council of Provinces, rejects the representation of minority parties in the Cabinet and incorporates a Bill of Rights.

Under the interim constitution the ten homelands had been reincorporated in South Africa. Executive power is vested in a president and Cabinet, with the president elected by the National Assembly. Legislative power is vested in a bicameral parliament, a directly elected 400-member National Assembly elected by proportional representation for a five-year term, and an indirectly elected 90-member National Council of Provinces composed of ten members elected by each of the nine regional legislatures for a five-year term.

The four former provinces (Cape Province, Natal, Orange Free State, Transvaal) have been replaced by nine new regions (Western Cape, Northern Cape, Eastern Cape, Free State, North-West, KwaZulu/Natal, Gauteng, Northern Province, Mpumalanga). Each region has its own premier, a legislature of between 30 and 100 seats elected by proportional representation, and its own constitution.

HEAD OF STATE

President, Commander-in-Chief of the Armed Forces, Thabo Mbeki (ANC), *elected by parliament* 14 June 1999, *sworn in* 16 June 1999

Executive Deputy President, Jacob Zuma (ANC)

CABINET *as at September 2000*

Agriculture and Land Affairs, Angela Didiza (ANC)
Arts, Culture, Science and Technology, Ben Ngubane (IFP)
Communications, Ivy Matsepe-Cassburri (ANC)
Correctional Services, Ben Skosana (IFP)
Defence, Patrick Lekota (ANC)
Education, Kader Asmal (ANC)
Environmental Affairs and Tourism, Mohammed Valli Moosa (ANC)
Finance, Trevor Manuel (ANC)
Foreign Affairs, Nkosazana Dlamini-Zuma (ANC)
Health, Mantombazana Tshabala-Msimang (ANC)
Home Affairs, Chief Mangosuthu Buthelezi (IFP)
Housing, Sankie Mthembi-Mahanyele (ANC)
Intelligence Service, Joseph Nhlanhla (ANC)
Justice and Constitutional Development, Penuell Maduna (ANC)
Labour, Membathisis Mdladlana (ANC)
Mineral and Energy Affairs, Phumzile Mlambo-Ncguka (ANC)
Minister, Office of the President, Essop Pahad (ANC)
Provincial and Local Government, Sidney Mufamadi (ANC)
Public Enterprises, Jeffrey Radebe (ANC)
Public Service and Administration, Geraldine Fraser-Moleketi (ANC)
Public Works, Stella Sigcua (ANC)
Safety and Security, Steve Tshwete (ANC)
Sports and Recreation, Ngconde Balfour (ANC)
Trade and Industry, Alec Erwin (ANC)
Transport, Dullah Omar (ANC)
Water Affairs and Forestry, Ronnie Kasrils (ANC)
Welfare and Population Development, Zola Skweyiya (ANC)

HIGH COMMISSION FOR THE REPUBLIC OF SOUTH AFRICA

South Africa House, Trafalgar Square, London WC2N 5DP
Tel: 020-7451 7299
High Commissioner, HE Cheryl Carolus, apptd 1998
Counsellors, G. Johannes
First Secretary (Economic), T. Gubevu
Defence Attaché, Brig.-Gen. S. Sijake

BRITISH HIGH COMMISSION

255 Hill Street, Arcadia 0083
Tel: (00 27) (12) 483 1200
E-mail: bhc@icon.co.za
91 Parliament Street, Cape Town 8001
Tel: (00 27) (21) 461 7220
E-mail: britain@icon.co.za
High Commissioner, HE Dame Maeve Fort, DCMG, DCVO, apptd 1996
Counsellor, Deputy High Commissioner, S. Gass, CMG, CVO
Counsellor (Political), D. Woods

Defence and Military Adviser, Brig. M. Raworth
Consul-General and Director of Trade Promotion (Johannesburg), N. McInnes
CONSULATES-GENERAL – Cape Town and Johannesburg
CONSULATE – Durban
HONORARY CONSULS – Port Elizabeth, East London

Cultural Attaché and British Council Director, L. T. Phillips, OBE, FSA, 76 Juta Street, (PO Box 30637), Braamfontein 2017, Johannesburg;
e-mail: enquiries.johannesburg@britcoun.org.za.
There are also offices in Cape Town and Durban

DEFENCE

The new South African National Defence Force (SANDF) was created from the merger of the South African Defence Forces (SADF), the Umkhonto we Sizwe (MK) armed wing of the ANC, the Azanian People's Liberation Army (APLA) of the PAC, and the defence forces of the four former independent homelands.

The Army has 124 main battle tanks, 974 armoured personnel carriers, and 1,240 armoured infantry fighting vehicles. The Navy has three submarines and nine patrol and coastal vessels at two bases. The Air Force has 116 combat aircraft and 3 armed helicopters.
MILITARY EXPENDITURE – 1.6 per cent of GDP (1998)
MILITARY PERSONNEL – 69,950: Army 37,970, Navy 5,150, Air Force 9,400

ECONOMY

Mining is of great importance, employing more than half a million people in 1996. It is the largest source of foreign exchange. The principal minerals produced are gold, coal, diamonds, copper, iron ore, manganese, lime and limestone, uranium, platinum, fluorspar, andalusite, zinc, zirconium, vanadium, titanium and chrome. South Africa is the world's largest producer of gold, platinum, diamonds, manganese, chrome and vanadium, and has the world's largest reserves of chrome ore, manganese, vanadium and andalusite.

Agriculture, forestry and fishing accounted for 4.1 per cent of GDP in 1998. Over 70 per cent of land is pasture so livestock farming is widespread and meat and wool important products. Principal crops are maize, sugar cane, fruits and vegetables, wheat, sorghum, sunflower seeds and groundnuts. Cotton is widely grown, and viticulture is also widespread.

Industries, concentrated most heavily around Johannesburg, Pretoria and the major ports, process foodstuffs, metals and non-metallic mineral products, produce oil from coal, and also produce beverages and tobacco, motor vehicles, chemicals and chemical products, machinery, textiles and clothing, and paper and paper products. Industry contributed 36.6 per cent of GDP in 1998.

Energy production is based upon coal and natural gas and the production of synthetic liquid fuel from coal. One nuclear power station is in operation and others are planned. South Africa exports electricity through its electric grid connections to all states in southern Africa.

The Minister of Public Enterprises announced in December 1999 that the bulk of the state industrial sector was to be sold off or floated on the stock exchange; the areas covered were Telkom, the telecommunication monopoly, Eskom, the state electricity provider, Deskom, the defence company and Transnet, the state transport company.

In 1998 there was a trade surplus of US$1,262 million and a current account deficit of US$2,265 million. Imports totalled US$29,268 million and exports US$26,322 million.

GNP – US$136,868 million (1998); US$3,310 per capita (1998)
GDP – US$126,301 million (1996); US$2,979 per capita (1996)
ANNUAL AVERAGE GROWTH OF GDP – 1.7 per cent(1997)
INFLATION RATE – 6.9 per cent (1998)
UNEMPLOYMENT – 5.1 per cent (1996)
TOTAL EXTERNAL DEBT – US$24,712 million (1998)

TRADE

Principal exports are gold, base metals and metal products, coal, diamonds, food (especially fruit) and wool. Principal imports are machinery, chemicals, motor vehicles, metals and metal products, food, inedible raw materials and textiles.

South Africa's main trading partners are Germany, the USA, the UK, Italy and Japan.

Trade with UK	1998	1999
Imports from UK	£1,541,813	£1,285,218,000
Exports to UK	1,421,675	1,707,061,000

COMMUNICATIONS

There are international airports at Johannesburg, Durban and Cape Town. South African Airways operates international services to Europe, South America, the Far East, Africa, Australia and the USA, and it is the principal operator of domestic flights. Durban is the largest seaport. Other major ports are Cape Town, Port Elizabeth, East London, Saldanha Bay, Mossel Bay and Richards Bay. The government announced in April 2000 that a new port was to be constructed at Coega, Eastern Cape province. The national railway system, and most long-distance passenger and freight road transport are run by independent companies. The six landlocked states of Botswana, Lesotho, Swaziland, Zimbabwe, Zambia and Malawi make extensive use of *Spoornet*, the South African rail freight and long-distance passenger carrier, for foreign trade.

SPAIN
España

AREA – 195,365 sq. miles (505,992 sq. km). Neighbours: Portugal (west), France (north)
POPULATION – 39,270,000 (1996 census): 96 per cent Catholic, 1 per cent Muslim. Castilian Spanish is the official language, although Basque, Catalan, Galician and Valencian, a dialect of Catalan, are spoken and have official status in the autonomous regions where they are spoken
CAPITAL – Madrid (population, 3,084,673, 1996)
MAJOR CITIES – ΨBarcelona (4,748,236); Ψ Valencia (2,200,319); Málaga (1,224,959); Sevilla (1,719,446); Zaragoza (852,332), 1995
CURRENCY – Euro (€) of 100 cents/Peseta of 100 céntimos
NATIONAL ANTHEM – Marcha Real Española (Spanish royal march)
NATIONAL DAY – 12 October
NATIONAL FLAG – Three horizontal stripes of red, yellow, red, with the yellow of double width
LIFE EXPECTANCY (years) – male 73.40; female 80.49
POPULATION GROWTH RATE – 0.1 per cent (1997)
POPULATION DENSITY – 78 per sq. km (1997)
URBAN POPULATION – 64.1 per cent (1991)

The interior of the Iberian peninsula consists of an elevated tableland surrounded and traversed by mountain ranges: the Pyrenees, the Cantabrian Mountains, the Sierra de Guadarrama, Sierra Morena, Sierra Nevada, Montes de Toledo, etc. The principal rivers are the Duero, the Tajo, the Guadiana, the Guadalquivir, the Ebro and the Miño.

HISTORY AND POLITICS

The kingdoms of Castile and Aragón were united in 1479; they captured Granada, the last region of Spain under Moorish rule, in 1492 and conquered Navarra in 1512. In 1492 Columbus reached the Americas on behalf of Spain and began the process of colonisation which led to most of central and south America coming under Spanish rule until their independence in the 19th century. A republic was proclaimed in 1931 and in February 1936 the Popular Front, a left-wing coalition, was elected. In July 1936 a counter-revolution broke out in military garrisons in Spanish Morocco and spread throughout Spain. Civil war ensued until March 1939, when the Popular Front governments in Madrid and Barcelona surrendered to the Nationalists (as Gen. Franco's followers were then named). Gen. Franco became president and ruled the country until his death in 1975, when, according to his wishes, he was succeeded as head of state by Prince Juan Carlos of Bourbon (grandson of Alfonso XIII) and Spain again became a monarchy. The first free election was held on 15 June 1977.

The general election of 12 March 2000 was won by the Popular Party (PP), which won 183 seats in the Congress of Deputies.

INSURGENCIES

The Basque separatist terrorist organisation ETA (*Euzkadi ta Azkatasuna* – Basque Nation and Liberty) has since its formation in 1959 carried out a terrorist campaign of bombings, shootings and kidnappings against the Spanish state and its security forces in an attempt to gain independence for the Basque country. ETA rejected regional autonomy for the Basque country in 1979 as insufficient and continued its campaign, but increased co-operation between French and Spanish security had greatly weakened ETA by the early 1990s. Most of its leaders were caught and jailed in 1992; the conflict has left 700–800 dead and 600 ETA members in jail. On 16 September 1998, ETA announced an indefinite truce, which was to begin the following day. On 28 November 1999, ETA announced that the truce was to end. On 23 January 2000, over a million people demonstrated in Madrid against the resumption of ETA terrorist attacks following a car bomb explosion in Madrid on 21 January, in which one person died.

POLITICAL SYSTEM

Under the 1978 constitution there is a bicameral *Cortes Generales* comprising a 350-member Congress of Deputies (*Congreso de los Diputados*) elected for a maximum term of four years, which elects the prime minister; and a Senate (*Senado*) consisting of 208 directly elected representatives and 48 representatives appointed by the assemblies of the autonomous regions.

Since the promulgation of the 1978 constitution, 19 autonomous regions have been established, with their own parliaments and governments. These are Andalucía, Aragón, Asturias, Balearics, the Basque country, Canaries, Cantabria, Castilla-La Mancha, Castilla y León, Catalunya, Ceuta, Extremadura, Galicia, Madrid, Melilla, Murcia, Navarra, La Rioja and Valencia.

HEAD OF STATE

HM The King of Spain, King Juan Carlos I de Borbón, KG, GCVO, *born* 5 January 1938, *acceded to the throne* 22 November 1975, *married* 14 May 1962, Princess Sophie of Greece *and has issue* Príncipe Felipe (*see* below); Infanta Elena Maria Isabel Dominga, *born* 20 December 1963; and Infanta Cristina Federica Victoria Antonia, *born* 13 June 1965

Heir, HRH The Prince of the Asturias (Príncipe Felipe Juan Pablo Alfonso y Todos los Santos), *born* 30 January 1968

CABINET *as at September 2000*

Prime Minister, José María Aznar López
First Deputy PM, Mariano Rajoy Brey
Second Deputy PMs, Economy, Rodrigo de Rato y Figaredo
Agriculture, Food and Fisheries, Miguel Arias Cañete
Defence, Federico Trillo-Figueroa y Martínez Conde
Development, Francisco Alvárez-Cascos Fernández
Education, Culture and Sport, Pilar del Castillo Vera
Environment, Jaume Matas Palou
Foreign Affairs, Josep Piqué i Camps
Government Spokesman, Pío Cabanillas Alonso
Health and Consumer Affairs, Celia Villalobos Talero
Interior, Jaime Mayor Oreja
Justice, Angel Acebes Paniagua
Labour and Social Affairs, Carlos Aparicio Pérez
Public Administration, Jesús Posadas Moreno
Science and Technology, Anna María Birulés y Bertrán
Treasury, Cristóbal Montoro Romero

SPANISH EMBASSY
39 Chesham Place, London SW1X 8SB
Tel: 020-7235 5555
Ambassador Extraordinary and Plenipotentiary, HE
   The Marqués de Tamarón, apptd 1999
Minister Counsellor, Don Pablo Barrios
Defence and Naval Attaché, Capt. Don José Carlos Iglesias
Counsellors, Don Antonio Lopez-Villares
   (*Commercial*); Don Ignacio Aguirre (*Consular*);
   Don Ramón Abaroa (*Cultural*)

BRITISH EMBASSY
Calle de Fernando el Santo 16, E-28010 Madrid
Tel: (00 34) (91) 700 8200
Ambassador Extraordinary and Plenipotentiary, HE
   Peter Torry, apptd 1998
Minister, Deputy Head of Mission, J. A. Dew
Counsellors, M. H. Conner (*Commercial*); E. A. Oakden
   (*EC and Economic Affairs*); M. Ramscar
Defence and Naval Attaché, Capt. P. Pacey
Consuls-General, J. Thomas (*Madrid*);
   D. Thomson (*Barcelona*); I. Lewis (*Bilbao*)

CONSULATES-GENERAL – Madrid, Barcelona, Bilbao
CONSULATES – Alicante, Málaga, Palma de Mallorca,
   Las Palmas, Seville, Tenerife
VICE-CONSULATES – Ibiza, Menorca
HONORARY CONSULATES – Santander, Vigo

BRITISH COUNCIL DIRECTOR, P. Sandiford, Paseo del
   General Martínez, Campos 31, E-28010 Madrid;
   e-mail: General.Enquiries@es.britcoun.org.
   There are offices in Seville and Valencia

BRITISH CHAMBER OF COMMERCE, Plaza de Santa
   Barbara 10, 1st Floor, E-28004 Madrid; Paseo de
   Gracia 11, Barcelona 7; Alameda de Mazarredo 5,
   Bilbao 1

DEFENCE

The Army has 660 main battle tanks, 1,997 armoured personnel carriers and 28 attack helicopters. The Navy has eight submarines, one aircraft carrier, 17 frigates, 32 patrol and coastal vessels, 18 combat aircraft and 25 armed helicopters at seven bases. The Air Force has 208 combat aircraft.

The USA maintains 1,760 naval and 240 air force personnel in Spain.

MILITARY EXPENDITURE – 1.3 per cent of GDP (1998)
MILITARY PERSONNEL – 186,500: Army 120,000, Navy
   36,950, Air Force 29,100, Paramilitaries 75,760
CONSCRIPTION DURATION – Nine months

ECONOMY

The expansion of the economy and accession to the EU have led to changes in Spanish agriculture. It accounted for

3.4 per cent of GDP in 1997 and employed 8.4 per cent of the working population. The country is generally fertile, and olives, oranges, lemons, almonds, pomegranates, bananas, apricots, tomatoes, peppers, cucumbers and grapes are cultivated. Other agricultural products include wheat, barley, oats, rice, hemp and flax. The vine is cultivated widely; in the south-west, around Jerez, sherry and tent wines are produced. Spain has one of Europe's largest fishing industries.

Spain's mineral resources of coal, iron, wolfram, copper, zinc, lead and iron ores are exploited. The principal industrial goods are cars, steel, ships, manufactured goods, textiles, chemical products, footwear and other leather goods. Tourism is a major industry with 47.7 million tourists visiting Spain in 1998.

Spain successfully met the convergence criteria laid down for EU economic and monetary union and was a participant in the European single currency, the euro, on 1 January 1999.

The centre-right government has withdrawn subsidies from uncompetitive industries, privatised the steel industry and reduced income tax. The economy has been performing well, with GDP growth of 4.1 per cent in the year preceding the first quarter of 2000; unemployment has been falling steadily, down to 14 per cent in early 2000.

In 1998 Spain had a trade deficit of US$18,707 million and a current account deficit of US$1,606 million. Imports totalled US$133,149 million and exports US$109,228 million.

GNP – US$555,244 million (1998); US$14,100 per capita (1998)
GDP – US$580,861 million (1996); US$14,641 per capita (1996)
ANNUAL AVERAGE GROWTH OF GDP – 3.6 per cent (1997)
INFLATION RATE – 1.8 per cent (1998)
UNEMPLOYMENT – 18.8 per cent (1998)

TRADE

The principal imports are manufactures, military hardware, semimanufactures, vehicles, consumer goods, foodstuffs and energy. The principal exports include manufactures, military hardware, vehicles, semimanufactures, foodstuffs, consumer goods and energy.

Trade with UK	1998	1999
Imports from UK	£6,756,800,000	£7,021,800,000
Exports to UK	5,513,400,000	5,622,300,000

EDUCATION

Education is free for those aged six to 18, and compulsory up to the age of 15. Private schools (30 per cent of primary and 60 per cent of secondary schools) have to fulfil certain criteria to receive government maintenance grants. There are 33 public sector universities, the oldest of which, Salamanca, was founded in 1218. Other ancient foundations are Valladolid (1346), Barcelona (1430), Zaragoza (1474), Santiago (1495), Valencia (1500), Seville (1505), Madrid (1508), Granada (1531), Oviedo (1604). Private universities are Deusto in Bilbao, Navarra in Pamplona, Carlos III in Madrid and one in Salamanca.
ILLITERACY RATE – 2.3 per cent
ENROLMENT (percentage of age group) – primary 100 per cent (1995); secondary 94 per cent (1994); tertiary 51 per cent (1996)

CULTURE

Castilian is the language of more than three-quarters of the population of Spain. Basque, said to have been the original language of Iberia, is spoken in Vizcaya, Guipúzcoa and Álava. Catalan is spoken in Provençal Spain, and Galician, spoken in the north-western provinces, is akin to Portuguese. The governments of these regions actively encourage use of their local languages.

The literature of Spain is one of the oldest and richest in the world, the *Poem of the Cid*, the earliest of the heroic songs of Spain, having been written about 1140. The outstanding writings of its golden age are those of Miguel de Cervantes Saavedra (1547–1616), Lope Felix de Vega Carpio (1562–1635) and Pedro Calderón de la Barca (1600–81). The Nobel Prize for Literature has five times been awarded to Spanish authors: J. Echegaray (1904), J. Benavente (1922), Juan Ramón Jiménez (1956), Vicente Aleixandre (1977) and Camilo José Cela (1989).

ISLANDS AND ENCLAVES

THE BALEARIC ISLES form an archipelago off the east coast of Spain. There are four large islands (Majorca, Minorca, Ibiza and Formentera), and seven smaller (Aire, Aucanada, Botafoch, Cabrera, Dragonera, Pinto and El Rey). Area 1,935 sq. miles (5,011 sq. km); population 685,088. The archipelago forms a province of Spain, the capital is ΨPalma in Majorca, population 323,138
THE CANARY ISLANDS are an archipelago in the Atlantic, off the African coast, consisting of seven islands and six islets. Area 2,807 sq. miles (7,270 sq. km); population 1,444,626. The Canary Islands form two provinces of Spain: Las Palmas, comprising Gran Canaria, Lanzarote (38,500), Fuerteventura (19,500) and the islets of Alegranza, Roque del Este, Roque del Oeste, Graciosa, Montaña Clara and Lobos, with seat of administration at ΨLas Palmas (373,772) in Gran Canaria; and Santa Cruz de Tenerife, comprising Tenerife, La Palma (76,000), Gomera (31,829), and Hierro (10,000), with seat of administration at ΨSanta Cruz in Tenerife, population estimate 204,948
ISLA DE FAISANES is an uninhabited Franco-Spanish condominium, at the mouth of the Bidassoa in La Higuera bay
ΨCEUTA is a fortified post on the Moroccan coast, opposite Gibraltar. Area 5 sq. miles (13 sq. km); population 70,864.
ΨMELILLA is a town on a rocky promontory of the Rif coast, connected with the mainland by a narrow isthmus. Population 58,449. Ceuta and Melilla are autonomous regions of Spain

OVERSEAS TERRITORIES

The following territories are Spanish settlements on the Moroccan seaboard.
PEÑÓN DE ALHUCEMAS is a bay including six islands; population 366
PEÑÓN DE LA GOMERA (or Peñón de Velez) is a fortified rocky islet; population 450
THE CHAFFARINAS (or Zaffarines) is a group of three islands near the Algerian frontier; population 610

SRI LANKA
Sri Lanka Prajatantrika Samajawadi Janarajaya

AREA – 25,332 sq. miles (65,610 sq. km)
POPULATION – 18,552,000 (1997 UN estimate): 74 per cent Sinhalese, 12.6 per cent Sri Lankan Tamils, 5.6 per cent Indian Tamils, 7.1 per cent Sri Lankan Moors, 0.7 per cent Burghers, Malays and others. The religion of the majority is Buddhism (69.3 per cent), then Hinduism (15.5 per cent), Islam (7.6 per cent), and Christianity (7.5 per cent). The national languages are Sinhala and Tamil
CAPITAL – ΨColombo (population, 615,000, 1993)
MAJOR CITIES – ΨGalle (971,000); ΨJaffna (879,000); Kandy (1,269,000); ΨTrincomalee (323,000)
CURRENCY – Sri Lankan rupee of 100 cents

NATIONAL ANTHEM – Namo Namo Matha
(We all stand together)
NATIONAL DAY – 4 February (Independence Day)
NATIONAL FLAG – On a dark red field, within a golden
border, a golden lion passant holding a sword in its
right paw, and a representation of a *bo*-leaf, issuing
from each corner; and to its right, two vertical stripes
of saffron and green also placed within a golden
border, to represent the minorities of the country
LIFE EXPECTANCY (years) – male 67.78; female 71.66
POPULATION GROWTH RATE – 1.3 per cent (1997)
POPULATION DENSITY – 283 per sq. km (1997)
ILLITERACY RATE – 8.4 per cent
ENROLMENT (percentage of age group) – tertiary
5.1 per cent (1995)

Sri Lanka (formerly Ceylon) is an island in the Indian
Ocean, off the southern tip of India and separated from it
by the narrow Palk Strait. Forests, jungle and scrub cover
the greater part of the island. In areas over 2,000 ft above
sea level grasslands (*patanas* or *talawas*) are found. One of
the highest peaks in the central massif is Adam's Peak
(7,360 ft), a place of pilgrimage for Buddhists, Hindus and
Muslims.
The climate is warm throughout the year, with a high
relative humidity. The two main monsoon seasons are
mid-May to September (south-west) and November to
March (north-east).

HISTORY AND POLITICS

The Portuguese landed in Ceylon in the early 16th century
and founded settlements, eventually conquering much of
the country. Portuguese rule lasted 150 years; in 1658 it
gave way to that of the Dutch East India Company until
1796. The maritime provinces of Ceylon were ceded by
the Dutch to the British in 1798, becoming a British Crown
Colony in 1802. With the annexation of the Kingdom of
Kandy in 1815, all Ceylon came under British rule. Ceylon
became a self-governing state and a member of the
British Commonwealth on 4 February 1948. A republican
constitution was adopted in 1972 and the country was
renamed Sri Lanka (meaning 'Resplendent Island').
Eight provincial councils were set up in 1988 under the
Indo-Sri Lankan peace accord in an attempt to diffuse
ethnic tension. Since then, except for the temporarily
merged North-East province, all provinces have had
elected provincial councils.
In the general election of 16 August 1994 the ruling
United National Party (UNP) was defeated by the
People's Alliance led by Chandrika Bandaranaike
Kumaratunga. The People's Alliance, a coalition of seven
parties, won 105 seats; the UNP 94 seats; and other
parties, mainly Muslim and moderate Tamils, 26 seats.
The People's Alliance formed a government with the
support of the Sri Lankan Muslim Congress and moderate Tamil parties. Prime Minister Kumaratunga won the
presidential election on 9 November 1994 with 62 per cent
of the vote after the UNP candidate Gamini Dissanayake
was assassinated by Tamil Tiger terrorists. President
Kumaratunga handed over the premiership to her mother,
the former Prime Minister Sirimavo Bandaranaike.
In August 1995 the government proposed constitutional changes intended to form a federal state with eight
autonomous regions (one covering the Tamil north-east).
Each region would have its own elected legislature,
executive and judicial branch of government, a police
force, and powers devolved from the central government.
Provincial elections were due to be held on 28 August
1998, but were delayed by a national state of emergency
declared on 5 August. The elections were held on 6 April
1999 in five of the eight provinces; the People's Alliance
won control of all five contested provincial legislatures.
Elections in Southern Province were held on 10 June 1999.
Presidential elections were held on 21 December 1999;

President Kumaratunga was elected for a second term,
gaining 51.37 per cent of the vote. Prime Minister
Sirimavo Bandaranaike resigned on 10 August 2000 and
was replaced by Ratnasiri Wickremanayake.

INSURGENCIES

The Liberation Tigers of Tamil Eelam (LTTE) guerrilla
group has been fighting Sri Lankan forces for control of
the Tamil majority areas in the north and east of the
country since 1983.
Peace negotiations in 1994, led to a formal cease-fire in
January 1995. Fighting resumed in April 1995 after the
LTTE had unilaterally broken the cease-fire and negotiations had broken down. A government offensive in
April 1996 gained control over almost the entire northern
Jaffna peninsula. A second government offensive in May
1997 to take control of a strategic highway on the Jaffna
peninsula resulted in losses for the LTTE.
Government gains in an offensive against the LTTE
which had begun in June 1999, but which came to a
standstill in September, were wiped out in only five days
in November, when LTTE forces launched an offensive
entitled 'Unceasing Waves III', capturing ten towns and
12 military camps. On 22 April 2000, LTTE forces
captured the Elephant Pass, the only land link to the
Jaffna peninsula. On 3 May 2000, President Kumaratunga
imposed a state of war, invoked an ordinance that gave
the police wide powers of arrest and confiscation, banned
strikes and political rallies and imposed censorship of
military, political and economic reporting. All non-
essential development projects were suspended and the
defence levy sales tax was raised to make more funds
available to the military.

POLITICAL SYSTEM

The 1978 constitution introduced a system of proportional representation. Legislative power is vested in the
parliament, whose 225 members are directly elected for a
six-year term. Executive power is exercised by the
president, elected for six years, and the Cabinet.

HEAD OF STATE

President, Buddha Sasana, Defence, Finance, Chandrika
Bandaranaike Kumaratunga, *elected* 9 November
1994, *re-elected* 21 December 1999, *sworn in*
22 December 1999

CABINET *as at September* 2000

The President
Prime Minister, Public Administration, Home Affairs,
Plantation Industries, Ratnasiri Wickremanayake (SLFP)
Agriculture and Land, D. M. Jayaratna (SLFP)
Co-operative Development, D. P. Wickremasinghe (SLFP)
Cultural and Religious Affairs, Buddhist Affairs, Lakshman
Jayakody (SLFP)
Education and Higher Education, Richard Pathirana (SLFP)
External Trade, Kingsley Wickremaratna (SLFP)
Foreign Affairs, Lakshman Kadirgamar (SLFP)
Forestry and Environment, Nandimitra Ekanayake (SLFP)
Health and Indigenous Medicine, Nimal Siripala De Silva
(SLFP)
Housing and Urban Development, Indika Gunawardena
(CPSL)
Industrial Development (acting), Athula Jayasinghe (SLFP)
Justice and Constitutional Affairs, G. L. Peiris (SLFP)
Labour, John Seneviratne (SLFP)
Livestock Development and Estates Infrastructure,
Arumugam Phondaman (SLWC)
Mahaweli Development, Maithripala Sirisena (SLFP)
Media, Posts and Telecommunications, Mangala
Samaraweera (SLFP)
Planning, Implementation and Parliamentary Affairs,
Jeyaraj Fernandopulle (SLFP)
Power, Irrigation, Gen. Anuruddha Ratwatte (SLFP)

Provincial Councils and Local Government, Alavi Maulana (SLFP)
Science and Technology, Bernard Soysa (LSSP)
Shipping, Ports, Rehabilitation of Eastern Provinces, vacant
Social Services, Berty Premanand Dissanayake (SLFP)
Tourism and Aviation, H. B. Semasinghe (SLFP)
Transport and Highways, A. H. M. Fowzie (SLFP)
Vocational Training and Rural Industries, Amarasiri Dodangoda (SLFP)
Welfare, Youth and Sport, S. B. Dissanayake (SLFP)
Women's Affairs, Hema Ratnayake (SLFP)

SLFP Sri Lanka Freedom Party; CPSL Communist Party of Sri Lanka; SLWC Sri Lanka Workers' Congress; LSSP Lanka Sama Samaja Party; SLMC Sri Lanka Muslim Congress

HIGH COMMISSION FOR THE DEMOCRATIC SOCIALIST REPUBLIC OF SRI LANKA
13 Hyde Park Gardens, London W2 2LU
Tel: 020-7262 1841/7
High Commissioner, HE Mangala Moonesinghe, apptd 2000
Deputy High Commissioner, J. Palipane
Ministers, A. Karunaratne *(Consular)*
First Secretary (Commercial), H. M. B. Herath

BRITISH HIGH COMMISSION
190 Galle Road, Kollupitiya, PO Box 1433, Colombo 3
Tel: (00 94) (1) 437336
E-mail: bhc@eureka.lk
High Commissioner, HE Linda Duffield, apptd 1999
Deputy High Commissioner, M. H. P. Hill
Defence Adviser, Lt.-Col. R. N. Kendell, MBE
First Secretary (Commercial and Economic), A. Madeley

BRITISH COUNCIL DIRECTOR, S. Maingay, 49 Alfred House Gardens, PO Box 753, Colombo 3;
e-mail: enquiries@britcoun.lk.
There is a regional office in Kandy

DEFENCE

The Army has 25 main battle tanks, 152 armoured personnel carriers, and 16 armoured infantry fighting vehicles. The Navy has 54 patrol and coastal vessels at seven bases. The Air Force has 22 combat aircraft and 15 armed helicopters.
MILITARY EXPENDITURE – 6.1 per cent of GDP (1998)
MILITARY PERSONNEL – 115,000: Army 95,000, Navy 10,000, Air Force 10,000; Paramilitaries 110,300

ECONOMY

The staple products are tea, rubber, copra, spices and gems. There is increasing emphasis on local production of food, especially rice, and plans for the large-scale production of sugar cane, cotton and citrus fruits.
The prinicipal exports are industrial goods, agricultural products (especially tea), and oil derivatives. Principal imports are manufactures, textiles and clothing, capital goods, consumer goods and oil. Tourism is an important industry, with 366,000 foreign visitors in 1997.
In 1998 there was a trade deficit of US$567 million and a current account deficit of US$288 million. Imports totalled US$5,917 million and exports US$4,732 million.
GNP – US$15,176 million (1998); US$810 per capita (1998)
GDP – US$13,957 million (1996); US$771 per capita (1996)
ANNUAL AVERAGE GROWTH OF GDP – 6.4 per cent (1997)
INFLATION RATE – 9.4 per cent (1998)
UNEMPLOYMENT – 10.6 per cent (1998)
TOTAL EXTERNAL DEBT – US$8,526 million (1998)

Trade with UK	1998	1999
Imports from UK	£136,948,000	£137,449,000
Exports to UK	295,877,000	343,567,000

COMMUNICATIONS

There are 25,952 km of roads in Sri Lanka, of which 11,077 km are surfaced, and a government-run railway system with 1,459 km of lines. A satellite earth station at Padukka provides telecommunication links world-wide. The principal airport is at Katunayake, north of Colombo. Sri Lankan Airlines operates 69 flights weekly to the Gulf States, the Maldives, western Europe and the Far East.

SUDAN
Al-Jūmhūriya as-Sūdān

AREA – 967,500 sq. miles (2,505,813 sq. km). Neighbours: Egypt (north), Eritrea and Ethiopia (east), Kenya, Uganda and the Democratic Republic of Congo (south), Central African Republic, Chad, and Libya (west)
POPULATION – 27,889,000 (1997 UN estimate). Arab and Nubian peoples populate the north and centre, Nilotic and Negro peoples the south. Arabic is the official language and Islam the state religion, although the Nilotics of the Bahr el Ghazal and Upper Nile valleys are generally Animists or Christians
CAPITAL – Khartoum (Al-Khartūm) (population, 947,483, 1994). The combined population of Khartoum, Khartoum North and Umm Durmān (excluding refugees and displaced people) is estimated at 3,000,000
MAJOR CITIES – Al-Ubayyid (228,096); Nyala (1,267,077); ΨPort Sudan (Būr Sūdān)(305,385); 1993 estimates
CURRENCY – Sudanese dinar (SD) of 10 pounds
NATIONAL ANTHEM – Nahnu Djundullah (We are the army of God)
NATIONAL DAY – 1 January (Independence Day)
NATIONAL FLAG – Three horizontal stripes of red, white and black with a green triangle next to the hoist
LIFE EXPECTANCY (years) – male 49.64; female 52.43
POPULATION GROWTH RATE – 2.1 per cent (1997)
POPULATION DENSITY – 11 per sq. km (1997)
URBAN POPULATION – 27.1 per cent (1994)
MILITARY EXPENDITURE – 4.3 per cent of GDP (1998)
MILITARY PERSONNEL – 94,700: Army 90,000, Navy 1,700, Air Force 3,000; Paramilitaries 15,000
CONSCRIPTION DURATION – Three years

The White Nile, as the Bahr el Jebel, flows through Sudan from Nimule to Wadi Halfa. The Blue Nile flows from Lake Tana on the Ethiopian plateau through Sudan to join the White Nile at Khartoum. The next confluence of importance is at Atbara where the main Nile is joined by the River Atbara. Between Khartoum and Wadi Halfa lie five of the six cataracts.

HISTORY AND POLITICS

The Anglo-Egyptian Condominium over Sudan was established in 1899 and ended when the Sudan House of Representatives, on 19 December 1955, declared Sudan a fully independent sovereign state. A republic was proclaimed on 1 January 1956, and was recognised by Great Britain and Egypt. Sudan was under military rule from 1958 to 1964, from 1969 to 1986, and from 1989 until Presidential and legislative elections were held in March 1996. President al-Bashir was elected with 75.7 per cent of the vote having faced no serious contender. Hassan al-Tourabi of the fundamentalist National Islamic Front (NIF) was elected president of the 400-member National Assembly, although political parties had officially been banned from contesting the elections. The founding of political parties was legalised on 1 January 1999. In early

January 1999, the voting age was lowered to 17 and a new dress code was imposed on women, requiring them to wear headscarves. In March 1999, the UN Children's Fund (UNICEF) asked the government of Sudan to investigate the continued existence of slavery in Sudan; the Foreign Ministry denied institutionalised slavery, but admitted that tribal kidnappings were commonplace. In December 1999, President al-Bashir suspended the National Assembly and declared a three-month state of emergency, shortly before a vote on constitutional changes, which included the reduction of the powers of the president, was due to be debated. In March 2000, the state of emergency was extended until the end of 2000.

INSURGENCIES

Nearly 17 years of insurrection in the southern provinces ended in 1972 with the signing of an agreement recognising southern regional autonomy within the Sudanese state. However, insurrection resumed in 1983 and since then there has been civil war in the south of the country between government forces and the Christian and Animist majority in the area, organised into the Sudan People's Liberation Army (SPLA).

The warfare has left an estimated 1.4 million dead, including 300,000 who died in the war-induced famine in 1988 and thousands in a similar situation in 1994. Some three million refugees have fled the fighting, either to the north, to neighbouring states or to the far south near the Ugandan border. The fighting has left large areas of the south desolate and uninhabitable.

In November 1999, the government and the opposition Ummah Party reached an accord to end the civil war and institute a four-year transitional period, at the end of which a referendum would be held, offering the south a choice of federalism or independence. However, the National Democratic Alliance (NDA), to which the Ummah Party belonged, denounced the accord, objecting to its lack of detail and condemned it for not mentioning a secular state. The Ummah Party left the NDA in March 2000.

FOREIGN RELATIONS

In 1995 Sudan's relations with its neighbours, notably Egypt, Eritrea and Uganda, deteriorated as they considered that Sudan was arming Islamic and insurgent groups in their states. On 2 May 1999 a peace agreement was signed with Eritrea. Sudan and the UK agreed to resume full diplomatic representation in June 1999. On 8 December 1999, Sudan and Uganda signed an agreement under which they agreed to cease supporting rebel groups in each other's countries, to disarm and disband such groups and to re-establish full diplomatic links. On 24 December, Sudan and Egypt agreed to normalise their relations and seek a solution to their dispute over the Hala'ib region.

HEAD OF STATE

President, Prime Minister, Lt.-Gen. Omar Hassan Ahmad al-Bashir, *appointed* 16 October 1993, *elected* 17 March 1996 *First Vice-President*, Maj.-Gen. Ali Osman Mohamad Taha
Vice-President, Gen. George Kongor

CABINET *as at September 2000*

The President
Agriculture and Forestry, Abdel Hamid Mussa Kasha
Animal Resources, Abdullah Muhammad Sid Ahmad
Aviation, Shambul Adland
Cabinet Affairs, Abdalla Hassan Ahmed; Lt.-Gen. Abd al-Rahman Sirr al-Khatim; Bedriya Suleiman
Defence, Maj.-Gen. Bakri Hassan Salih
Education, Abd al-Basit Abd al-Majid
Energy and Mining, Awad Ahmad al-Jaz
Federal Relations, Lt.-Gen. (retd) Ibrahim Sulayman
Finance and National Economy, Muhammad al-Kheir

al-Zubeir
Foreign Affairs, Mustapha Osman Ismail
Foreign Trade, Makki Ali Bilayl
Health, Abu al-Qasim Muhammad Ibrahim
Higher Education and Scientific Research, Zubayr Bashir Taha
Information and Culture, Ghazi Salah al-Din Atabani
Internal Affairs, Maj.-Gen. El-Hadi Abdallah
Irrigation and Water Resources, Kamal Ali Muhammad
Justice, Ali Mohammad Uthman Yassin
Manpower, Maj.-Gen. (retd) Allison Manani Magaya
National Industry and Investment, Abd al-Halim Isma'il al-Muta'afi
Presidential Advisor on Peace Affairs, Ahmed Ibrahim al-Tahir
Presidential Affairs, Maj.-Gen. Abd al-Rahim Muhammad Husayn
Roads and Telecommunications, Muhammad Tahir Ila
Social Planning, Qutbi al-Mahdi Ahmad
Surveys, Construction and Development, Joseph Malwal
Tourism and Environment, Maj.-Gen. Al-Tijani Adam al-Tahir
Transport, Lam Akol Ajawin

EMBASSY OF THE REPUBLIC OF THE SUDAN
3 Cleveland Row, London SW1A 1DD
Tel: 020-7839 8080
Ambassador Extraordinary and Plenipotentiary, HE Dr Hassan Abdeen, apptd 2000

BRITISH EMBASSY
PO Box 801, Khartoum East
Tel: (00 249) (11) 777105/780828
E-mail: british@sudanmail.net
Ambassador Extraordinary and Plenipotentiary, HE Richard Makepeace, apptd 1999

BRITISH COUNCIL DIRECTOR, D. Sloan, 14 Abu Sin Street (PO Box 1253), Khartoum;
e-mail: bc.khartoum@bc-khartoum.bcouncil.org

ECONOMY

Agriculture provides employment for over half the labour force and contributes nearly half of GDP. It is based on large and medium-sized public sector irrigation projects. Mechanised and traditional agriculture is practised in areas of sufficient rainfall. The principal grain crops are *dura* (great millet) and wheat, the staple food of the population. Sesame and groundnuts are other important food crops, which also yield an exportable surplus, and a promising start has been made with castor seed. Sudan still has to achieve self-sufficiency in its production.

In 1998 Sudan had a trade deficit of US$1,137 million and a current account deficit of US$957 million. Imports totalled US$1,915 million and exports US$596 million.
GNP – US$8,224 million (1998); US$290 per capita (1998)
GDP – US$1,079 million (1996); US$40 per capita (1996)
INFLATION RATE – 17.1 per cent (1998)
TOTAL EXTERNAL DEBT – US$16,843 million (1998)

TRADE

The principal exports are sesame, cotton and livestock. The chief imports are manufactures, machinery and transport equipment, and raw materials.

Trade with UK	1998	1999
Imports from UK	£72,281,000	£89,992,000
Exports to UK	10,985,000	6,127,000

COMMUNICATIONS

The railway system, adversely affected by the civil war, has a route length of about 5,516 km. There are 11,610 km of roads, of which 4,203 km are paved. Nile river services between Khartoum and Juba have been interrupted by the southern insurrection. Port Sudan is the country's main seaport. Sudan Airways flies services from Khartoum to other parts of Sudan and to other African states, Europe and the Middle East.

EDUCATION

School education is free for most children but not compulsory, beginning with six years of primary education, followed by three years of secondary education at general secondary schools, the more academic higher secondary schools or vocational schools. The medium of instruction is Arabic. English has not been taught in schools since new Arabisation legislation came into effect in 1991.

In addition to 20 universities there are various technical post-secondary institutes as well as professional and vocational training establishments.
ILLITERACY RATE – 42.9 per cent
ENROLMENT (percentage of age group) – tertiary
3.0 per cent (1990)

SURINAME
Republiek Suriname

AREA – 63,037 sq. miles (163,265 sq. km). Neighbours: French Guiana (east), Brazil (south), Guyana (west)
POPULATION – 437,000 (1997 UN estimate): 37 per cent Indians, 31 per cent creoles, 15 per cent Javanese, 10 per cent Africans, small numbers of Amerindians, Chinese and Europeans. The official language is Dutch, the native language is Sranang Tongo, and other widely-used languages are Hindustani and Javanese
CAPITAL – ΨParamaribo (population, 265,000, 1993)
CURRENCY – Suriname guilder of 100 cents
NATIONAL ANTHEM – God zij met ons Suriname (God be with our Suriname)
NATIONAL DAY – 25 November
NATIONAL FLAG – Horizontal stripes of green, white, red, white, green, with a five-pointed yellow star in the centre
LIFE EXPECTANCY (years) – male 64.71; female 70.09
POPULATION GROWTH RATE – 1.2 per cent (1997)
POPULATION DENSITY – 3 per sq. km (1997)
URBAN POPULATION – 69.9 per cent (1996)
MILITARY EXPENDITURE – 4.2 per cent of GDP (1998)
MILITARY PERSONNEL – 1,800: Army 1,400, Navy 240, Air Force 160
ILLITERACY RATE – 5.8 per cent

HISTORY AND POLITICS

Formerly known as Dutch Guiana, Suriname remained part of the Netherlands West Indies until 25 November 1975, when it achieved complete independence. The civilian government was ousted in 1980 by the military who appointed a predominantly civilian government in 1982.

The New Front for Democracy, a four-party bloc consisting of the National Party of Suriname (NPS), The Progressive Reform Party, Pertjajah Luhur and the Suriname Labour Party, won 32 of the 51 seats in the elections to the National Assembly on 25 May 2000 and appointed Ronald Venetiaan of the NPS as president on 4 August 2000.

POLITICAL SYSTEM

The unicameral legislature, the National Assembly, has 51 members, directly elected for a five-year term. The president is elected by a two-thirds majority in the National Assembly, or if the required majority cannot be achieved, by a specially convened United Peoples' Conference, including district and local council representatives, for a

five-year term of office.

HEAD OF STATE
President, Ronald Venetiaan, *inaugurated* 4 August 2000
Vice-President, Jules Ajodhia

COUNCIL OF MINISTERS *as at September 2000*
Agriculture, Animal Husbandry and Fisheries, Gangaram Panday
Defence, Ronald Assen
Education and Community Development, Walther Sandriman
Finance, Humphrey Hildenberg
Foreign Affairs, Marie Levens
Health, Rakieb Khudabux
Home Affairs, Urmilla Sewnundun-Joella
Justice and Police, Siegfried Gilds
Labour and Technological Sciences, Clifford Marica
Natural Resources, Rudi Demon
Planning and Development Co-operation, Stanley Raghoebarsingh
Public Works, Dewanand Balesar
Regional Development, Fred van Russel
Social Affairs and Housing, Salam Somohardjo
Trade and Industry, John Tjon Tjin Joe
Transport, Communication and Tourism, Guno Castelen

EMBASSY OF THE REPUBLIC OF SURINAME
Alexander Gogelweg 2, NL-2517 JH The Hague, The Netherlands
Tel: (00 31) (70) 365 0844
Ambassador Extraordinary and Plenipotentiary, HE Evert Guillaume Azimullah, apptd 1994
BRITISH AMBASSADOR, HE Edward Glover, MVO, resident at Georgetown, Guyana
BRITISH CONSULATE, c/o VSH United Buildings, Van't Hogerhuystraat, PO Box 1860, Paramaribo. *Honorary Consul*, J. J. Healy, MBE

ECONOMY

Suriname has large timber resources. Rice and sugar cane are the main crops. Bauxite is mined, and is the principal export. Principal trading partners are the Netherlands, the USA and Norway.

In 1995 Suriname had a trade surplus of US$123 million and a current account surplus of US$73 million.
GNP – US$684 million (1998); US$1,660 per capita (1998)
GDP – US$388 million (1996); US$898 per capita (1996)
ANNUAL AVERAGE GROWTH OF GDP – 3.0 per cent (1996)
INFLATION RATE – 7.1 per cent (1997)
UNEMPLOYMENT – 10.5 per cent (1997)

Trade with UK	1998	1999
Imports from UK	£12,728,000	£8,299,000
Exports to UK	16,528,000	19,476,000

SWAZILAND
Umbuso we Swatini

AREA – 6,704 sq. miles (17,364 sq. km). Neighbours: South Africa (north, west and south), Mozambique (east)
POPULATION – 906,000 (1997 UN estimate). The languages are English and Swazi
CAPITAL – Mbabane (population, 38,290, 1986)
MAJOR TOWNS – Manzini (30,000); Hlatikulu; Mhlume; Nhlangano; Pigg's Peak; Siteki
CURRENCY – Lilangeni (E) of 100 cents (South African currency is also in circulation). Swaziland is a member of the Common Monetary Area and its unit of currency *Emalangeni* (singular *Lilangeni*) has a par value with the South African rand

NATIONAL ANTHEM – Ingoma Yesive
NATIONAL DAY – 6 September (Independence Day)
NATIONAL FLAG – Blue with a wide crimson horizontal band bordered in yellow across the centre, bearing a shield and two spears horizontally
LIFE EXPECTANCY (years) – male 42.90; female 49.50
POPULATION GROWTH RATE – 2.3 per cent (1997)
POPULATION DENSITY – 52 per sq. km (1997)
URBAN POPULATION – 25.3 per cent (1996)
ILLITERACY RATE – 20.2 per cent
ENROLMENT (percentage of age group) – primary 91 per cent (1996); secondary 37 per cent (1996); tertiary 6.0 per cent (1996)

The broken mountainous Highveld along the western border, with an average altitude of 4,000 ft, is densely forested, mainly with conifers and eucalyptus; the Middleveld, averaging about 2,000 ft, is a mixed farming area including cotton and pineapples; and the Lowveld in the east was mainly scrubland until the introduction of large sugar-cane plantations. Four rivers, the Komati, Usutu, Mbuluzi and Ngwavuma, flow from west to east.

HISTORY AND POLITICS

The Kingdom of Swaziland came into being on 25 April 1967 under a self-government constitution and became an independent kingdom, headed by HM Sobhuza II, in membership of the Commonwealth on 6 September 1968.

POLITICAL SYSTEM

The King, assisted by his appointed Cabinet, holds considerable executive, legislative and judicial authority. There is a bicameral legislative body comprising a Senate and a House of Assembly. Each of the 55 *Tinkhundla* (administrative districts) directly elects one member to the House of Assembly. The King appoints ten members to the House of Assembly, making 65 in all, who then elect ten members of their own number to the Senate. To these are added 20 senators appointed by the King, bringing the full membership of the Senate to 30. In addition, the King appoints Commissions, who assess public opinion. There are also public gatherings, where any citizen can express an opinion. All political parties are banned.

A Constitutional Review Commission is due to report its conclusions by the end of 2000. Legislative elections to the House of Assembly were held on 16–24 October 1998. The members of the Senate were elected and appointed in November 1998.

HEAD OF STATE

King of Swaziland, HM King Mswati III, *inaugurated* 25 April 1986

CABINET *as at September 2000*

Prime Minister, Dr Barnabas Sibusiso Dlamini
Deputy PM, Arthur Khoza
Agriculture, Co-operatives, Roy Fanourakis
Economic Planning and Development, Majozi Sithole
Education, Revd Abednego Ntshangase
Enterprise and Employment, Lutfo Dlamini
Finance, John Carmichael
Foreign Affairs and Trade, Albert Shabangu
Health and Social Welfare, Dr Phetsile Dlamini
Home Affairs, Prince Sobandla Dlamini
Housing and Urban Development, Stella Lukhele
Justice and Constitutional Development, Chief Maweni Simelane
Natural Resources and Energy, Prince Guduza
Public Service and Information, Ephraim Magwagwa Mdluli
Public Works and Transport, vacant
Tourism and Communications, Soze Vilakazi

KINGDOM OF SWAZILAND HIGH COMMISSION

20 Buckingham Gate, London SW1E 6LB

Tel: 020-7630 6611
High Commissioner, HE Revd Percy Mngomezulu, apptd 1994

BRITISH HIGH COMMISSION

Allister Miller Street, Mbabane
Tel: (00 268) 404 2582/3/4
E-mail: general.enquiries@bc-swaziland.council.org
High Commissioner, HE Neil Hook, MVO, apptd 1999
BRITISH COUNCIL ACTING DIRECTOR, A. Rose, Ground and 3rd Floors, Lilunga House, Gilfillan Street, Mbabane; e-mail: general.enquiries@bcswaziland.bcouncil.org

ECONOMY

Manufacturing has replaced agriculture as the dominant sector, with timber, textiles and footwear the main products. Agricultural products include sugar cane and fruit. GDP growth rates have declined in the 1990s, partly as a result of lower growth rates in South Africa, on which the Swazi economy is strongly dependent. South Africa accounts for around 60 per cent of exports from Swaziland and about 85 per cent of imports.

In 1997 Swaziland had a trade deficit of US$212 million and a current account deficit of US$49 million. In 1996 imports totalled US$1,174 million and exports US$893 million.
GNP – US$1,384 million (1998); US$1,400 per capita (1998)
GDP – US$1,202 million (1996); US$1,365 per capita (1996)
ANNUAL AVERAGE GROWTH OF GDP – 2.3 per cent (1998)
INFLATION RATE – 8.1 per cent (1998)
TOTAL EXTERNAL DEBT – US$251 million (1998)

Trade with UK	1998	1999
Imports from UK	£3,844,000	£2,688,000
Exports to UK	41,469,000	30,843,000

COMMUNICATIONS

Swaziland's railway is 301 km long and connects with the Mozambique port of Maputo and the South African railway network to Richards Bay. A rail line to the north-west border provides a link to Komatipoort. There are 2,886 km of roads, of which 828 km are paved. Most passenger and goods traffic is carried by privately-owned motor transport services. There is an international airport at Manzini. Royal Swazi National Airways provides scheduled air services to southern and eastern Africa. International telecommunications and television services are provided through a satellite earth station.

SWEDEN
Konungariket Sverige

AREA – 173,732 sq. miles (449,964 sq. km). Neighbours: Norway (west), Finland (east)
POPULATION – 8,846,000 (1997 UN estimate); 8,745,109 (1993 census). The state religion is Lutheran Protestant, to which over 95 per cent officially adhere. The language is Swedish; in the north there are both Finnish- and Lapp-speaking communities
CAPITAL – ΨStockholm (population, 1,148,953, 1995)
MAJOR CITIES – ΨGothenburg (Göteborg) (480,839); ΨMalmö (234,599); Uppsala (119,979), 1995
CURRENCY – Swedish krona of 100 öre
NATIONAL ANTHEM – Du Gamla, Du Fria (Thou ancient, thou freeborn)
NATIONAL DAY – 6 June (Day of the Swedish Flag)
NATIONAL FLAG – Yellow cross on a blue ground

LIFE EXPECTANCY (years) – male 76.51; female 81.53
POPULATION GROWTH RATE – 0.5 per cent (1997)
POPULATION DENSITY – 20 per sq. km (1997)
URBAN POPULATION – 83.4 per cent (1990)

HISTORY AND POLITICS

Sweden takes its name from the Svear people who inhabited the region during the seventh century AD. The Swedes participated in the Viking expansion during the ninth to 11th centuries and established sovereignty over Finland in the 13th century. The Union of Kalmar (1397) brought Sweden and Norway under Danish rule. Northern Sweden regained its independence following a rebellion by noblemen in 1521 which resulted in the election to the Swedish throne of Gustav I of the house of Vasa.

Swedish influence burgeoned under the Vasa kings despite frequent wars with Denmark. Sweden's power climaxed in the 17th century under Gustavus II Adolf. The Danes were driven out of southern Sweden, the Baltic coast of Russia was seized and the Swedish army pushed into Germany after vanquishing the Catholic League. The Treaty of Westphalia (1648) confirmed Sweden's great power status. Swedish power waned in the 17th and 18th centuries. Finland was lost to Russia in 1809; Norway was ceded to Sweden under the Congress of Vienna (1814–5) but seceded in 1905.

Sweden remained neutral during both World Wars. Post-war party politics was dominated by Social Democrat-led coalitions which established a mixed economy and a generous welfare state. Right-wing and centrist parties held power from 1976–82 and 1991–4. Sweden applied for EU membership in July 1991 and acceded to the EU on 1 January 1995.

In the general election held on 20 September 1998 the Social Democrats remained the largest party in the legislature with 131 seats and formed a minority government.

POLITICAL SYSTEM

Sweden is a constitutional monarchy, with the monarch retaining purely ceremonial functions as head of state. Under the Act of Succession 1810 (with amendments) the throne is hereditary in the House of Bernadotte. The constitution is based upon the Instrument of Government 1974, which amended the 1810 Act and removed from the monarch the roles of appointing the prime minister and signing parliamentary bills into law. A 1979 amendment vested the succession in the monarch's eldest child irrespective of sex.

Executive power is vested in the prime minister and Council of Ministers. There is a unicameral legislature (*Riksdag*) of 349 members elected by universal suffrage on a proportional representation basis (with a 4 per cent threshold for representation) for four years. The Council of Ministers (*Statsråd*) is responsible to the *Riksdag*.

Sweden is divided into 24 counties (*län*) and 288 municipalities (*kommun*).

HEAD OF STATE

HM The King of Sweden, Carl XVI Gustaf, KG, *born* 30 April 1946, *succeeded* 15 September 1973, *married* 19 June 1976 Fräulein Silvia Renate Sommerlath and has *issue*, Crown Princess Victoria (*see* below); Prince Carl Philip Edmund Bertil, Duke of Värmland, *born* 13 May 1979; Princess Madeleine Thérèse Amelie Josephine, Duchess of Hälsingland and Gästrikland, *born* 10 June 1982
Heir, HRH Crown Princess Victoria Ingrid Alice Désirée, Duchess of Västergötland, *born* 14 July 1977

CABINET *as at September 2000*

Prime Minister, Göran Persson
Deputy Prime Minister, Lena Hjelm-Wallén
Agriculture, Food and Fisheries, Margareta Winberg
Culture, Marita Ulvskog
Defence, Björn von Sydow
Education and Science, Thomas Östros
Environment, Kjell Larsson
Finance, Bosse Ringholm
Foreign Affairs, Anna Lindh
Health and Social Affairs, Lars Engqvist
Industry and Commerce, Björn Rosengren
Justice, Laila Freivalds
Ministers-Delegate, Ulrica Messing (*Culture*); Ingegerd Wärnersson (*Education*); Lars-Erik Lövdén (*Finance*); Leif Pagrotsky, Pierre Schori (*Foreign Affairs*); Britta Lejon (*Justice*); Maj-Inger Klingvall (*Social Affairs*); Mona Sahlin (*Trade and Industry*)

EMBASSY OF SWEDEN

11 Montagu Place, London W1H 2AL
Tel: 020-7917 6400
Ambassador Extraordinary and Plenipotentiary, HE Mats Bergquist, CMG, apptd 1997
Minister (Economic), T. Rosander
Defence Attaché, Col. M. Engman
Consul-General, G. Dannerljung

BRITISH EMBASSY

Skarpögatan 6–8, S-115 93 Stockholm
Tel: (00 46) (8) 671 9000
Ambassador Extraordinary and Plenipotentiary, HE John Grant, CMG, apptd 1999
Counsellor, Consul-General and Deputy Head of Mission, M. Raven
Counsellor (Economic and Commercial), P. J. Mathers, LVO
Naval and Military Attaché, Cmdr. G. Bateman

CONSULAR OFFICES – Stockholm, Gothenburg
HONORARY CONSULATES – Malmö, Sundsvall

BRITISH COUNCIL DIRECTOR , Dr P. Spaven,
PO Box 27819, S-115 93 Stockholm;
e-mail: info@britishcouncil.se
BRITISH–SWEDISH CHAMBER OF COMMERCE,
Grevgatan 34, S-114 53 Stockholm

DEFENCE

The Army has 537 main battle tanks, 646 armoured personnel carriers and 1,210 armoured infantry fighting vehicles. The Navy has nine submarines, and 24 patrol and coastal vessels at four bases. The Air Force has 253 combat aircraft.

Sweden has a policy of non-alignment in peace and neutrality in war, and it maintains a 'total defence' which includes peacetime organisations for civil, economic and psychological defence.

It was announced in March 1999 that the size of the armed forces was to be reduced by about 50 per cent in line with budget cuts and the perceived diminished threat to Sweden's security.

MILITARY EXPENDITURE – 2.5 per cent of GDP (1998)
MILITARY PERSONNEL – 53,100: Army 35,100, Navy 9,200, Air Force 8,800, Paramilitaries 600
CONSCRIPTION DURATION – Seven to 15 months

ECONOMY

Less than 10 per cent of the land area is farmland and less than 3 per cent of the labour force is employed in farming, although Sweden is more than 80 per cent self-sufficient in food.

Industrial prosperity is based on natural resources: forests, mineral deposits and water power. The forests cover about half the total land surface and sustain timber, finished wood products, pulp and paper milling industries. The mineral resources include iron ore, lead, zinc, sulphur, granite, marble, precious and heavy metals (the latter not exploited) and extensive deposits of low-grade uranium ore. Industries based on mining are important but it is the general engineering industry that provides 80 per cent of Sweden's exports, especially specialised machinery and systems, motor vehicles, aircraft, electrical and electronic equipment, pharmaceuticals, plastics and chemical industries.

Hydroelectricity supplies 15 per cent of energy needs. Sweden has no significant indigenous resources of conventional hydrocarbon fuels and relies for 50 per cent of its energy needs upon imported oil and coal. Around half of Sweden's electricity is generated by nuclear power but as a result of a referendum in 1980 the nuclear programme is to be phased out by 2010. Small supplies of natural gas are imported from Denmark into southern Sweden, with the pipeline being extended to Gothenburg.

Sweden experienced a deep recession between 1992 and 1994. The centre-right government, elected in 1991, introduced austerity measures and free market economic reforms. In October 1997 Sweden decided not to join European economic and monetary union (EMU) at the first stage; however, a referendum on EMU membership is to be held, probably in 2002. Following an improvement in the economic situation, the budget for the year 2000 contained significant income and corporation tax reductions, together with increased spending on health care, education and social services.

In 1998 there was a trade surplus of US$17,536 million and a current account surplus of US$4,567 million. Imports totalled US$68,413 million and exports US$84,730 million.

GNP – US$226,454 million (1998); US$25,580 per capita (1998)
GDP – US$251,745 million (1996); US$28,546 per capita (1996)
ANNUAL AVERAGE GROWTH OF GDP – 1.8 per cent (1997)
INFLATION RATE – −0.1 per cent (1998)
UNEMPLOYMENT – 6.5 per cent (1998)

TRADE

About 45 per cent of industrial output is exported, mainly in the form of cars, trucks, machinery, and electrical and communications equipment. Sweden conducts 70 per cent of its trade with EFTA and the rest of the EU.

Trade with UK	1998	1999
Imports from UK	£4,153,900,000	£3,769,000,000
Exports to UK	4,213,900,000	4,397,700,000

COMMUNICATIONS

The total length of railroads is 10,939 km. The road network is about 210,000 km in length. The mercantile marine amounted in 1996 to 2,950,000 gross tonnage. Regular domestic air traffic is maintained by the Scandinavian Airlines System and by Malmö Aviation. Regular European and intercontinental air traffic is maintained by the Scandinavian Airlines System.

EDUCATION

The state system provides nine years' free and compulsory schooling from the age of seven to 16 in the comprehensive elementary schools. 95 per cent continue into further education of two to four years' duration in the upper secondary schools and a unified higher education system administered in six regional areas containing one of the universities: Uppsala (founded 1477); Lund (1668); Stockholm (1878); Gothenburg (1887); Umeå (1963) and Linköping (1967). There are 40 institutions of higher education including three technical universities in Stockholm, Gothenburg and Luleå.

ENROLMENT (percentage of age group) – primary 100 per cent (1996); secondary 99 per cent (1996); tertiary 50 per cent (1996)

CULTURE

Swedish belongs, with Danish and Norwegian, to the North Germanic language group. Swedish literature dates back to King Magnus Eriksson, who codified the old Swedish provincial laws in 1350. With his translation of the Bible, Olaus Petri (1493–1552) formed the basis for the modern Swedish language. Literature flourished during the reign of Gustavus III, who founded the Swedish Academy in 1786. Notable Swedish writers include Almquist (1795–1866), Strindberg (1849–1912) and Lagerlöf (1858–1940), Nobel Prizewinner in 1909. Contemporary authors include Lagerquist (1891–1974), Nobel Laureate in 1951, Martinson (1904–78) and Johnson (1900–76), Nobel Laureates jointly in 1974. The Swedish scientist Alfred Nobel (1833–96) founded the Nobel Prizes for literature, science and peace.

SWITZERLAND
Schweizerische Eidgenossenschaft – Confédération Suisse – Confederazione Svizzera – Confederaziun Svizra

AREA – 15,940 sq. miles (41,284 sq. km). Neighbours: France (west and north-west), Germany (north), Austria and Liechtenstein (east), Italy (south)
POPULATION – 7,114,600 (1998 estimate): 46.1 per cent Roman Catholic, 40 per cent Protestant, 5 per cent other religions and 8.9 per cent without religion. The official languages are German (the first language of 63.7 per cent), French (19.2 per cent), Italian (7.6 per cent) and Romansch (0.6 per cent). German is the dominant language in 19 of the 26 cantons; French in Fribourg, Jura, Geneva, Neuchâtel, Valais and Vaud; Italian in Ticino; and Romansch in parts of Graubünden
CAPITAL – Bern (population, 321,932, 1994)
MAJOR CITIES – Geneva (438,819); Lausanne (283,631); Lucerne (180,050); Winterthur (115,994); Zürich (921,446), 1994
CURRENCY – Swiss franc of 100 rappen (or centimes)
NATIONAL ANTHEM – Trittst im Morgenrot Daher (Radiant in the morning sky)
NATIONAL DAY – 1 August
NATIONAL FLAG – Square and red, bearing a couped white cross
LIFE EXPECTANCY (years) – male 75.70; female 81.90
POPULATION GROWTH RATE – 0.8 per cent (1997)
POPULATION DENSITY – 172 per sq. km (1997)
URBAN POPULATION – 67.6 per cent (1996)

Switzerland is the most mountainous country in Europe. The Alps, from 1,700 to 4,634 m (5,000 to 15,217 ft) in height, occupy its southern and eastern frontiers and the chief part of its interior; the Jura mountains rise in the north-west. The Alps occupy 61 per cent, and the Jura mountains 12 per cent of the country. The highest peak, Mont Blanc, Pennine Alps (4,807 m/15,782 ft) is partly in France and partly in Italy; Monte Rosa (4,634 m/15,217 ft) and Matterhorn (4,478 m/14,780 ft) are partly in Switzerland and partly in Italy. The highest wholly Swiss peaks are Finsteraarhorn (4,274 m/14,026 ft), Aletschhorn (4,195/13,711), Jungfrau (4,158/13,671), Mönch (4,099/13,456), Eiger (3,970/13,040), Schreckhorn (4,078/13,385), and Wetterhorn (3,701/12,150) in the Bernese Alps, and Dom (4,545/14,918), Weisshorn (4,506/14,803) and Breithorn (4,165/13,685). The Swiss lakes include Lakes Maggiore, Zürich, Lucerne, Neuchâtel, Geneva, Constance, Thun, Zug, Lugano, Brienz and the Walensee.

HISTORY AND POLITICS

The Romans invaded the area populated by Helvetii tribes in the first century BC and named the region Helvetia. The Roman Empire was overrun in the fifth century AD by Germanic tribes who are the ancestors of the modern Swiss.

The Swiss confederation achieved full independence under the Peace of Westphalia (1648), having been a province of the Holy Roman Empire since 1033. French Revolutionary forces seized Switzerland in 1789 and named it the Helvetic Republic. Independence was not restored until the Congress of Vienna (1815), which also joined Geneva and Valais to the confederation and instituted perpetual neutrality in foreign affairs. In 1847 a war broke out between the Protestant and Roman Catholic cantons, the latter being defeated. A new constitution was adopted in 1848 which enhanced the powers of the central government.

Proportional representation was introduced in 1919 and has ensured coalition governments throughout the 20th century. Women were given the vote in 1971.

On 24 October 1999, the ruling coalition, comprising the Social Democrats, the Swiss People's Party, the Radical Democratic Party and the Christian Democrats, in power since 1959, was re-elected with 173 of the 200 seats in the National Council.

FOREIGN RELATIONS

The Federal Council voted in 1992 to apply for European Community membership. The European Economic Area (EEA) Treaty between the EC and EFTA, which extends the provisions of the EC single internal market to EFTA states, was rejected in a national referendum on 6 December 1992. Switzerland is consequently the only EFTA state outside the EEA. Switzerland has observer status at the UN. On 21 May 2000, a referendum on seven bilateral agreements with the EU, which would progressively reduce trade barriers and allow the free movement of people between Switzerland and the EU, was passed, with 67.2 per cent of voters in favour.

POLITICAL SYSTEM

The federal government consists of the Federal Assembly of two chambers, a National Council (*Nationalrat*) of 200 members, and a States Council (*Ständerat*) of 46 members (two from each canton and one from each demi-canton). Members of the National Council are elected for four years, elections taking place in October. The executive power is in the hands of a Federal Council (*Bundesrat*) of seven members, elected for four years by the Federal Assembly and presided over by the president of the Confederation. Each year the Federal Assembly elects from the Federal Council the president and the vice-president. Not more than one person from the same canton may be elected a member of the Federal Council; however, there is a tradition that Italian- and French-speaking areas should between them be represented on the Federal Council by at least two members.

CONFEDERAL STRUCTURE

There are 23 cantons, three of which are subdivided, making 26 in all. Each canton has its own government. The main language in 19 of the cantons is German; in the others it is French (*) or Italian (†).

Canton	Area (sq. km)	Population (1998)
Aargau	1,404	536,700
Appenzell-Ausserrhoden	243	53,900
Appenzell-Innerrhoden	173	14,900
Basel-Country (Basel-Landschaft)	517	256,900
Basel-Town (Basel-Stadt)	37	190,700
Bern	5,961	936,600
*Fribourg	1,671	232,300
*Geneva	282	398,300
Glarus	685	38,400
Graubünden/Grischun	7,105	185,100
*Jura	837	69,000
Lucerne (Luzern)	1,493	343,200
*Neuchâtel	803	165,600
Nidwalden	276	37,600
Obwalden	491	32,100
St Gallen	2,026	444,600
Schaffhausen	299	73,500
Schwyz	909	126,400
Solothurn	791	242,300
Thurgau	991	225,700
†Ticino	2,812	306,200
Uri	1,077	35,700
*Valais	5,225	274,100
*Vaud	3,212	611,800
Zürich	1,729	1,186,300
Zug	239	96,600

FEDERAL COUNCIL *as at September 2000*

President of the Swiss Confederation (2000), *Defence, Civil Protection and Sports*, Adolf Ogi (SVP)
Vice-President (2000), *Transport, Energy and Communications*, Moritz Leuenberger (SPS)
Federal Chancellor, Annemarie Huber-Hotz
Economic Affairs, Pascal Couchepin (FDP)
Finance, Kaspar Villiger (FDP)
Foreign Affairs, Joseph Deiss (CVP)
Interior, Ruth Dreifuss (SPS)
Justice and Police, Ruth Metzler-Arnold (CVP)

CVP Christian Democratic People's Party; SPS Social Democratic Party; FDP Radical Democratic Party; SVP Swiss People's Party

EMBASSY OF SWITZERLAND
16–18 Montagu Place, London W1H 2BQ
Tel: 020-7616 6000
Ambassador Extraordinary and Plenipotentiary, HE Bruno Max Spinner, apptd 2000
Minister, R. Reich
Defence Attaché, Col. W. Knüsli
Consul-General, R. Müller
Counsellor, D. Furgler (*Economic and Financial*)

CONSULATE-GENERAL – Manchester
BRITISH EMBASSY
Thunstrasse 50, CH-3005 Bern
Tel: (00 41) (31) 359 7700
Ambassador Extraordinary and Plenipotentiary, HE Christopher Hulse, CMG, OBE, apptd 1997
Counsellor, Deputy Head of Mission and Director of Trade Promotion, J. Nichols
Commercial Attachés, B. Haessig, S. Valdettaro, H. Küpfer
Defence Attaché, Lt.-Col. E. J. Gould

CONSULATE – Geneva
CONSULAR OFFICES – Bern (at Embassy), Lugano, Montreux, Valais, Zürich

BRITISH COUNCIL DIRECTOR, C. Morrissey, Sennweg 2, PO Box 532, CH-3000 Bern 9;
e-mail: britishcouncil@britishcouncil.ch
BRITISH-SWISS CHAMBER OF COMMERCE, Freiestrasse 155, CH-8032 Zürich
SWISS-BRITISH SOCIETIES: Bern, *President*, Dr H. Beriger; Zürich, *President*, J.-P. Müller; Basel, *President*, Dr C. Grey

DEFENCE

The Army has 769 main battle tanks, 1,022 armoured

personnel carriers, 513 armoured infantry fighting vehicles, and 60 helicopters. The Air Force has 171 combat aircraft.

MILITARY EXPENDITURE – 1.4 per cent of GDP (1998)
MILITARY PERSONNEL – 3,470 active (384,900 to be mobilised: Army 352,860, Air Force 32,024)
CONSCRIPTION DURATION – 15 weeks, then ten refresher courses

ECONOMY

Agriculture is followed chiefly in the valleys and the central plateau, where cereals, flax, hemp, wine and tobacco are produced, and fruits and vegetables are grown. Dairying and stock-raising are the principal industries; there are 308,924 hectares of open arable land, 111,133 ha of cultivated grassland and 628,976 ha of natural grassland and pasture. The forests cover about 28 per cent of the whole surface.

The chief manufacturing industries comprise engineering and electrical engineering, metalworking, chemicals and pharmaceuticals, textiles, watchmaking, woodworking, foodstuffs, publishing and footwear. Banking, insurance and tourism are major industries. In 1997, 4.6 per cent of the workforce was employed in agriculture, 26.8 per cent in industry and 68.6 per cent in services.

GNP – US$284,119 million (1998); US$39,980 per capita (1998)
GDP – US$294,349 million (1996); US$40,746 per capita (1996)
ANNUAL AVERAGE GROWTH OF GDP – 1.1 per cent (1997)
INFLATION RATE – 0.1 per cent (1998)
UNEMPLOYMENT – 3.6 per cent (1998)

TRADE

The principal imports are machinery, chemicals, vehicles, metals, textiles, precision instruments, watches and jewellery. The principal exports are machinery, chemicals, precision instruments, watches and jewellery, and metals.

In 1997 Switzerland had a trade surplus of US$2,414 million and a current account surplus of US$23,714 million. In 1998 imports totalled US$73,877 million and exports US$75,431 million.

Trade with UK	1998	1999
Imports from UK	£2,982,711,000	£2,827,403,000
Exports to UK	5,025,776,000	5,629,363,000

COMMUNICATIONS

There were in 1995, 5,041 km of railway tracks and 70,975 km of roads, of which 1,540 km were national highways. The merchant marine consisted in 1995 of 174 vessels with a total gross tonnage of 4.36 million tonnes. Goods handled at Basel Rhine ports amounted to 13 million tonnes. Swissair, the national airline, flies to and from the airports at Zürich, Geneva and Basel.

EDUCATION

Education is controlled by cantonal and communal authorities. Primary education is free and compulsory. School age varies, generally seven to 14, with secondary education from age 12 to 15. Special schools make a feature of commercial and technical instruction. University sites are Basel (founded 1460), Bern (1834), Fribourg (1889), Geneva (1873), Lausanne (1890), Zürich (1832), and Neuchâtel (1909), the technical universities of Lausanne and Zürich and the economics university of St Gall.

ENROLMENT (percentage of age group) – primary 100 per cent (1993); secondary 79 per cent (1990); tertiary

32.9 per cent (1995)

CULTURE

Modern authors who have achieved international fame include Karl Spitteler (1845–1924) and Hermann Hesse (1877–1962), awarded the Nobel Prize for Literature in 1919 and 1946 respectively.

In 1993 there were 96 daily newspapers published (76 German, 16 French, four Italian).

SYRIA
Al-Jumhūriyya Al-Arabiyya as-Sūriyya

AREA – 71,498 sq. miles (185,180 sq. km). Neighbours: Lebanon (west), Israel and Jordan (south-west), Iraq (east), Turkey (north)
POPULATION – 14,951,000 (1997 UN estimate): mostly Muslim. Arabic is the principal language, but Kurdish, Turkish and Armenian are spoken among significant minorities and a few villages still speak Aramaic, the language spoken by Christ and the Apostles. English has taken over from French as the main foreign language
CAPITAL – Damascus (Dimashq) (population, 1,549,000, 1994)
MAJOR CITIES – Halab (Aleppo) (1,542,000); Hamāha (273,000); Hims (558,000); ΨAl-Lādhiqīyah, the principal port (303,000), 1994 estimates
CURRENCY – Syrian pound (S$) of 100 piastres
NATIONAL ANTHEM – Humata al Diyari alaykum salaam (Defenders of the Realm on you be peace)
NATIONAL DAY – 17 April
NATIONAL FLAG – Red over white over black horizontal bands, with two green stars on central white band
LIFE EXPECTANCY (years) – male 64.42; female 68.05
POPULATION GROWTH RATE – 3.0 per cent (1997)
POPULATION DENSITY – 81 per sq. km (1997)
URBAN POPULATION – 51.4 per cent (1995)

The Orontes flows northwards from the Lebanon range across the northern boundary to Antakya (Antioch, Turkey). The Euphrates crosses the northern boundary near Jerablus and flows through north-eastern Syria to the boundary of Iraq.

The region is rich in historical remains. Damascus (Dimashq ash-Sham) is said to be the oldest continuously inhabited city in the world (although Halab disputes this claim), having existed as a city for over 4,000 years. The city contains the Omayed Mosque, the Tomb of Saladin, and the 'street which is called Straight' (Acts 9:11), while to the north-east is the Roman outpost of Dmeir and further east is Palmyra. On the Mediterranean coast at Amrit are ruins of the Phoenician towns of Marath, and Crusaders' fortresses at Markab, Sahyoun, and Krak des Chevaliers. One of the oldest alphabets in the world has been discovered at Ugarit (Ras Shamra), a Phoenician village near Al-Lādhiqīyah. Hittite cities dating from 2000 to 1500 BC, have been explored on the west bank of the Euphrates at Jerablus and Kadesh.

HISTORY AND POLITICS

Once part of the Ottoman Empire, Syria came under French mandate after the First World War. Syria became an independent republic during the Second World War; the first independently elected parliament met in August 1943, but foreign troops were in occupation until April 1946. Syria remained an independent republic until 1958, when it became part, with Egypt, of the United Arab Republic. It seceded from the United Arab Republic in

September 1961.

Elections to the 250-seat People's Council in November 1998 resulted in the National Progressive Front retaining all of its 167 seats unchallenged. This seven-party bloc is dominated by the Ba'ath Party, its allies being the Arab Socialist Union, Socialist Unionist Party, Arab Socialist Movement, Syrian Communist Party and Socialist Unionist Democratic Party. Independents, who are predominantly businessmen, won 83 seats. Mahmoud Zubi, who had been prime minister since 1987, resigned on 7 March 2000 and was replaced by Mustafa Mohamad Miro on 13 March. Zubi committed suicide on 21 May following his expulsion from the Ba'ath Party amid allegations of corruption.

President Hafez al-Assad, who had seized power in a military coup in 1970 and been elected president in 1971 and re-elected in 1978, 1985, 1992 and 1999, died on 10 June 2000. On 18 June, his son, Bashar al-Assad, was unanimously elected as leader by the Ba'ath Party, on 27 June the legislature nominated him for the presidency, and on 10 July he was elected president, gaining 97.29 per cent of the votes cast.

POLITICAL SYSTEM

The constitution promulgated in 1973 declares that Syria is a democratic, popular socialist state, and that the Arab Socialist Renaissance (Ba'ath) Party, which has been the ruling party since 1963, is the leading party in the state and society. The president is head of state and is elected by parliament for a seven-year term. The legislature, the *Majlis al-Chaab* (People's Council) has 250 members directly elected for a four-year term.

HEAD OF STATE

President, Bashar al-Assad, *elected by parliament* 27 June 2000, *approved by referendum* 10 July 2000
Vice-Presidents, Abdel Halim Khaddam, Zuheir Masharqa

CABINET *as at September 2000*

Prime Minister, Mustafa Mohamad Miro
Deputy PM, Defence, First Lt.-Gen. Mustafa Tlass
Deputy PM, Economic Affairs, Khaled Raed
Deputy PM, Service Affairs, Mohamad Naji Utree
Agriculture and Agrarian Reform, Assa'ad Mustafa
Assistant Secretary-General, Abdullah al-Ahmar
Awqaf (Religious Endowments), Mohamad Abd ar-Ra'uf Ziyadah
Communications, Radwan Martini
Construction and Building, Nihad Mushantat
Culture, Maha Kannoot
Economy and Foreign Trade, Mohamad al-Imadi
Education, Mahmood as-Sayed
Electricity, Munib bin Assa'ad Saem al-Daher
Finance, Khalid al-Mahayni
Foreign Affairs, Farouk al-Shara'
Health, Mohamad Iyad al-Shatti
Higher Education, Hassan Reesha
Housing and Utilities, Husam al-Safadi
Industry, Ahmad Hamo
Information, Adnan Omran
Interior, Mohamad Harba
Irrigation, Taha al-Atrash
Justice, Nabil al-Khatib
Labour and Social Affairs, Baria al-Qodsi
Local Administration, Salam el-Yaseen
Ministers of State, Mohamad Mufdi Safo (*Cabinet Affairs*); Farouk al-Adly (*Environment Affairs*); Nasser Qaddur (*Foreign Affairs*); Issam az-Zaim (*Planning Affairs*); Makhul Abu Hamida; Hassan an-Noori; Ihsan Shreiteh
Petroleum and Mineral Resources, Mohamad Maher Husni Jamal
Presidential Affairs, Haytham Dweihi
Supply and Internal Trade, Usama Ma'a al-Barid

Tourism, Kasim Mikdad
Transport, Makram Obeid

EMBASSY OF THE SYRIAN ARAB REPUBLIC
8 Belgrave Square, London SW1X 8PH
Tel: 020-7245 9012
Charge' d'Affaires, Dr Sami Glaiel

BRITISH EMBASSY
Kotob Building, 11 Mohammad Kurd Ali Street, Malki, Damascus (PO Box 37)
Tel: (00 963) (11) 373 9241/2/3/7
Ambassador Extraordinary and Plenipotentiary, HE Basil Eastwood, CMG, apptd 1996
CONSULATE – Halab
BRITISH COUNCIL DIRECTOR, D. Baldwin, Al Jala'a, Abu Rumaneh, PO Box 33105, Damascus;
e-mail: Britcoun@bc-damascus.bcouncil.org

DEFENCE

The Army has 4,650 main battle tanks, 1,500 armoured personnel carriers and 2,350 armoured infantry fighting vehicles. The Navy has three submarines, two frigates, 20 patrol and coastal vessels and 24 armed helicopters at three bases. The Air Force has 589 combat aircraft and 72 armed helicopters.

Syria maintains a force of some 22,000 men in Lebanon; 1,029 UN troops are deployed on the Golan Heights.
MILITARY EXPENDITURE – 7.3 per cent of GDP (1998)
MILITARY PERSONNEL – 316,000: Army 215,000, Navy 6,000, Air Force 40,000, Air Defence Command 55,000; Paramilitaries 108,000
CONSCRIPTION DURATION – 30 months

ECONOMY

Agriculture accounted for 25.9 per cent of GDP in 1997; fruit, vegetables, wheat and barley are the main crops, but the cotton crop is the highest in value. Large areas are coming under cultivation in the north-east of the country as a result of irrigation from the Thawra dam. Industry accounted for 27.2 per cent of GDP in 1997. There are an increasing number of light assembly plants as Syria's industrialisation programme develops. Leather goods, wool and silk, textiles, vegetable oil, soap, sugar, plastics and metal utensils are produced. Oil production is proceeding in the region of Deir ez Zor. A pipeline has been built to the Mediterranean port of Banias, via Hims. Two oil refineries are in production at Hims and Banias. Oil production in 1998 was 29,300,000 tonnes. Syria also has gas reserves, deposits of phosphate and rock salt, and produces asphalt.
GNP – US$15,532 million (1998); US$1,020 per capita (1998)
GDP – US$55,079 million (1996); US$3,779 per capita (1996)
ANNUAL AVERAGE GROWTH OF GDP – 5.9 per cent (1996)
INFLATION RATE – – 1.2 per cent (1998)
UNEMPLOYMENT – 6.8 per cent (1991)
TOTAL EXTERNAL DEBT – US$22,435 million (1998)

TRADE

The principal imports are manufactures, metals and metal goods, machinery, foodstuffs and transport equipment. Principal exports include oil and oil derivatives, agricultural products (chiefly fruit and vegetables, cotton and wheat) and textiles.

In 1998 Syria had a trade deficit of US$172 million and a current account surplus of US$59 million. Imports totalled US$3,895 million and exports US$2,890 million.

Trade with UK	1996	1999
Imports from UK	£84,191,000	81,499,000
Exports to UK	26,620,000	83,664,000

COMMUNICATIONS

Although railway lines run from Damascus to both Beirut and 'Ammān, train services go only to 'Ammān as much of the Lebanese line has been dismantled. A track has been opened connecting Hims with Damascus. A track links Hims, Hamāh, Halab, Deir ez Zor and Qamishliye to the Iraqi frontier. There are 2,750 km of rail track. All the principal towns in the country are connected by roads which vary from modern dual carriageways to narrow country lanes. There are 39,333 km of roads, of which 11,564 km are unpaved. An internal air service operates between all major towns. The main international airport is at Damascus and there are also flights from Halab, Al-Kamishli, Al-Lādhiqīyah and Deir ez-Zor.

There are eight national daily newspapers.

EDUCATION

Education is under state control and although a few of the schools are privately owned, they all follow a common syllabus. Elementary education is free at state schools and is compulsory from the age of seven. Secondary education is not compulsory and is free only at the state schools. There are universities at Damascus, Halab, Tishrin, Al-Lādhiqīyah and the Ba'ath University, Hims.

ILLITERACY RATE – 25.6 per cent

ENROLMENT (percentage of age group) – primary
91 per cent (1996); secondary 38 per cent (1996); tertiary 15.7 per cent (1994)

TAIWAN
Chung-hua Min-kuo – Republic of China

AREA – 13,800 sq. miles (35,742 sq. km)

POPULATION – 21,854,273 (1998). Mandarin Chinese has been the official language since 1949. Now Taiwanese, spoken by 85 per cent of the population, is growing in importance

CAPITAL – Taipei (population, 2,638,565, 1998)

MAJOR CITIES – ΨKaohsiung (1,461,996); ΨKeelung (381,695), Taichung (916,279); Tainan (721,264), 1998

CURRENCY – New Taiwan dollar (NT$) of 100 cents

NATIONAL ANTHEM – San min chu i (Our Aim Shall Be to Found a Free Land)

NATIONAL DAY – 10 October

NATIONAL FLAG – Red, with blue quarter at top next staff, bearing a 12-point white sun

An island in the China Sea, Taiwan, formerly Formosa, lies 90 miles east of the Chinese mainland. The eastern part of the main island is mountainous and forested. Mt Morrison (Yu Shan) (13,035 ft) and Mt Sylvia (Tz'ukaoshan) (12,972 ft) are the highest peaks. The western plains are watered by many rivers.

Territories include the Pescadores Islands (50 sq. miles), some 35 miles west of Taiwan, as well as Quemoy (68 sq. miles) and Matsu (11 sq. miles) which are only a few miles from mainland China.

HISTORY AND POLITICS

Settled for centuries by the Chinese, the island was ceded by China to Japan in 1895 and remained part of the Japanese empire until Japan's defeat in 1945. Nationalist Kuomintang (KMT) leader Gen. Chiang Kai-shek with-drew to Taiwan in 1949, towards the end of the war against the Communist regime in mainland China, after which the territory continued under his presidency until his death in 1975. He was succeeded as president by his son Gen. Chiang Ching-kuo who ruled until his death in 1988, when Vice-President Lee Teng-hui was appointed president. Martial law was lifted in 1987 after 38 years.

In 1991, President Lee announced that the 'period of Communist rebellion' on the Chinese mainland was over, recognising *de facto* the People's Republic of China. The announcement also ended emergency measures which had frozen political life on Taiwan since 1949. In 1991–2 power shifted away from mainlanders to native Taiwanese with the forcible retirement of the 'Senior Parliamentarians' who had retained their seats since being elected on the mainland in 1948. The new parliament, the Legislative Yuan, gained control of the budget, of law-making and of the appointment of the prime minister. A general election to the Legislative Yuan on 5 December 1998 was won by the KMT with 123 of the 225 seats; the pro-independence Democratic Progressive Party (DPP) won 70 seats; the pro-reunification New Party won 11 seats; independents and minor parties won 21 seats.

President Chen Shui-bian, won the presidential election on 18 March 2000 with 39 per cent of the vote, ahead of two KMT candidates, and took office on 20 May.

FOREIGN RELATIONS

Taiwan (Nationalist China) held China's seat on the UN Security Council until 25 October 1971 when it was replaced by the People's Republic of China. The Republic of China is recognised by less than 40 states.

POLITICAL SYSTEM

The legislature is bicameral. The Legislative Yuan has 225 members, 176 elected and 49 appointed proportionally by party, and serves a three-year term. Constitutional reforms passed by the Legislative Yuan in 1994 provide for the president and vice-president to be directly elected for four-year terms (previously the president was elected by parliament). The National Assembly, which had previously been an elected upper chamber, voted on 24 April 2000 to transform itself into a largely ceremonial body, to be convened when necessary to consider constitutional amendments, the impeachment of a president, or territorial changes. Members will be appointed proportionally by the parties in the Legislative Yuan.

HEAD OF STATE

President, Chen Shui-bian, *elected* 18 March 2000, *sworn in* 20 May 2000
Vice-President, Annette Lu

EXECUTIVE YUAN *as at July 2000*

Prime Minister, Gen. Tang Fei

Deputy PM, Without Portfolio, Chair of Consumer Protection Commission, Yu Hsi-kun

Administrator, Environmental Protection Administration, Lin Chun-yi

Chairs of Commissions, Youharni Yisicacafute (*Aboriginal Affairs*); Hsia Teh-yu (*Atomic Energy Commission*); Hsu Cheng-kuang (*Mongolian and Tibetan Affairs*); Lin Feng-mei (*National Youth Commission*); Chang Fu-mei (*Overseas Chinese Affairs, State Minister*); Hsu Hsin-yi (*Physical Education*); Lin Chia-cheng (*Research, Development and Evaluation Commission*); Yang Teh-chih (*Veterans' Affairs*)

Chairs of Councils, Chen Hsi-huang (*Agriculture*); Huang Hsih-cheng (*Central Election Commission*); Chen Yu-hsiu (*Cultural Affairs*); Chen Po-chih (*Economic Planning and Development*); Chen Chu (*Labour Affairs*); Tsing Ying-wen (*Mainland Affairs*); Chen Tang-shan (*National Science Council*)

Directors, Wang Chun (*Coast Guard Administration*);
Tu Cheng-sheng (*National Palace Museum*)
Directors-General, Lin Chuan (*Budget, Accounting and Statistics*); Chu Wu-hsien (*Central Personnel Administration*); Lee Ming-liang (*Department of Health*);
Chung Ching (*Government Information Office, Government Spokesman*)
Economic Affairs, Lin Hsin-yi
Education, Tseng Chih-lang
Finance, Shea Jia-dong
Foreign Affairs, Tien Hung-mao
Interior, Chang Po-ya
Justice, Chen Ding-nan
National Defence, Wu Hsih-wen
Secretary-General of the Executive Yuan, Wei Chi-lin
Transport and Communications, Yeh Chu-lan
Without Portfolio, Lin Neng-pai (*Chair of Public Construction Commission*); Chen Ching-huang; Chang Yu-hui, Tsai Ching-yen; Hu Ching-piao

TAIPEI REPRESENTATIVE OFFICE, 50 Grosvenor Gardens, London, SW1W 0EB

BRITISH COUNCIL DIRECTOR, C. Bell, 7F-1, British Trade and Cultural Office, 99 Jen Ai Road, Section 2, Taipei 10625; e-mail: inquiries@britishcouncil.org.tw. There is a regional office in Kaohsiung

DEFENCE

The Army has 719 main battle tanks, 950 armoured personnel carriers, 225 armoured infantry fighting vehicles, and 20 aircraft. The Navy has four submarines, 16 destroyers, 21 frigates, 104 patrol and coastal vessels, 31 combat aircraft and 21 armed helicopters at four bases. The Air Force has 598 combat aircraft.
MILITARY EXPENDITURE – 4.6 per cent of GDP (1998)
MILITARY PERSONNEL – 376,000: Army 240,000, Navy 68,000, Air Force 68,000; Paramilitaries 26,650
CONSCRIPTION DURATION – Two years

ECONOMY

Taiwan has transformed itself from a mainly agricultural country to a highly developed industrial economy. The industrial base has expanded to include steel, shipbuilding, chemicals, cement, machinery, electrical equipment and textiles. In 1997 agriculture contributed 3.5 per cent of GDP, manufacturing 36.3 per cent and services 60.2 per cent. Continued trade surpluses have led to one of the largest foreign exchange reserves of any country in the world. Direct shipping between Taiwan and China, which had been suspended in 1949, resumed in April 1997.
The principal seaports are ΨKeelung and ΨKaohsiung situated in the north and south of the island respectively.

TRADE

The principal exports are electronic goods, machinery, metal goods, textiles, plastic products, and toys and games. The main imports are oil, chemicals, machinery and natural resources. The main trading partners are the USA, Japan, Hong Kong and Germany.
In 1998 imports totalled US$104,946 million and exports US$110,454 million.

Trade with UK	1998	1999
Imports from UK	£878,292,000	£867,643,000
Exports to UK	2,328,940,000	2,737,748,000

TAJIKISTAN
Respublika i Tojikiston

AREA – 55,251 sq. miles (143,100 sq. km). Neighbours: Uzbekistan (north-west), Kyrgyzstan (north-east),
China (east), Afghanistan (south)
POPULATION – 5,513,400 (2000): 62 per cent Tajik, 23 per cent Uzbek and 8 per cent Russian, with smaller numbers of Tatars, Kyrgyz, Germans and Ukrainians. The people are predominantly Sunni Muslim. The main languages are Tajik, Uzbek and Russian. Tajik is close to the Farsi spoken in Iran
CAPITAL – Dushanbe (population, 528,600, 1993 estimate)
CURRENCY – Tajik rouble (TJR) of 100 tanga
NATIONAL DAY – 9 September (Independence Day)
NATIONAL FLAG – Three horizontal stripes of red, white and green with the white of double width and charged with a crown and seven stars, all in gold
LIFE EXPECTANCY (years) – male 65.40; female 71.10
POPULATION GROWTH RATE – 1.9 per cent (1997)
POPULATION DENSITY – 42 per sq. km (1997)
URBAN POPULATION – 28.4 per cent (1994)
MILITARY EXPENDITURE – 8.3 per cent of GDP (1998)
MILITARY PERSONNEL – 7,000: Army 7,000; Paramilitaries 1,200
CONSCRIPTION DURATION – Two years
ILLITERACY RATE – 0.8 per cent
ENROLMENT (percentage of age group) – tertiary 19.9 per cent (1996)

The republic includes the Gorno-Badakhstan Autonomous Province and the Kulyab, Kurgan-Tyubinsk and Khodzhent Provinces. The country is mountainous with the Pamir highlands in the east and the high ridges of the Pamir-Altai system in the centre. Plains are formed by wide stretches of the Syr-Darya valley in the north and of the Amu-Darya in the south. The country has areas prone to earthquakes, and a continental climate.

HISTORY AND POLITICS

The area that is now Tajikistan was conquered by Alexander the Great in the fourth century BC and remained under Greek and Greco-Persian rule for 200 years. Tajikistan was invaded by both the Arabs and the Samanid Persians between the seventh and ninth centuries AD. The cities of Bukhara and Samarkand were two of the most important cultural and educational centres in the Islamic world.
Soviet power was established in northern Tajikistan by 1 April 1918, when the Turkestan Soviet Socialist Republic was formed, and the Bukhara emirate was overthrown by Soviet forces in 1920. In 1924 the Tajikistan Autonomous Soviet Socialist Republic was formed as part of the Uzbek Republic before Tajikistan was given full republican status within the Soviet Union in 1929.
Tajikistan declared independence from the Soviet Union on 9 September 1991. Tension between the government and the opposition Islamic and democratic groups led to armed clashes in 1992 and President Nabiev was forced to resign on 7 September 1992. The Islamic-Democratic alliance formed a government in September but civil war broke out as forces loyal to the former Communist regime rebelled against the new government. By early November, pro-Communist forces controlled virtually all the country and the Supreme Soviet installed Emomaly Rakhmnov as its Speaker and head of state.
Fighting resumed in July, leading to the establishment of a CIS peacekeeping force on the Tajik-Afghan border to contain the rebel attacks. A cease-fire in October 1994 allowed presidential and parliamentary elections to be held, which were won by Emomaly Rakhmonov and the ruling (former Communist) People's Democratic Party of Tajikistan (HDKT), although the elections were boycotted by most opposition groups and were condemned as undemocratic by the OSCE monitoring team. Fighting restarted in early 1995. A peace agreement was signed in December 1996 which provided for the formation of a

National Reconciliation Commission (NRC), a general amnesty and an exchange of prisoners. The agreement has held, although there have been sporadic outbreaks of violence since it was signed. In June 1999, following complaints by the opposition, the NRC announced that opposition armed forces would be integrated into government forces by August 1999, that a timetable would be drawn up for assigning 30 per cent of government posts to the opposition and that a referendum would be held on constitutional amendments demanded by the opposition. The referendum was held on 26 September 1999 and was approved by the electorate. It amended the 1994 constitution to create a bicameral legislature, extended the president's term of office from five to seven years and allowed the formation of religious political parties. Legislation to allow the formation of a bicameral legislature was passed in December 1999.

Presidential elections which took place on 6 November 1999 resulted in a landslide victory for the incumbent President Rakhmonov, who gained over 96 per cent of the vote in a poll which the Organisation for Security and Co-operation in Europe had refused to monitor due to restrictions imposed on candidates and political parties. Oqil Oqilov was named as prime minister on 20 December when President Rakhmonov announced a new government. An election to the Assembly of Representatives took place on 27 February 2000, with a run-off election on 12 March in districts where no candidate had gained a majority. The HDKT won 30 of the 63 seats, gaining 64.5 per cent of the vote; the Communist Party won 13 seats, the Islamic Renaissance Party won 2 and independent candidates won 15 seats, with three seats remaining vacant. An election to the National Assembly was held on 23 March.

Under the new constitutional arrangements, the president serves a single seven-year term. The new bicameral legislature consists of a 63-seat *Majlisi Mamoyandogan* (Assembly of Representatives), which is directly elected and serves a five-year term, and the *Majlisi Milli* (National Assembly), which has 33 members, 25 of which are elected for a five-year term by five regional assemblies and eight are appointed by the president. Administratively Tajikistan is divided into two regions and one autonomous region.

HEAD OF STATE

President, Emomaly Sharipovich Rakhmonov, *elected by Supreme Soviet* 19 November 1992, *elected* 6 November 1994, *re-elected* 6 November 1999

COUNCIL OF MINISTERS *as at September 2000*

Prime Minister, Oqil Oqilov
First Deputy PM, Relations with CIS States, Haji Akbar Turajonzoda
Deputy PMs, Kozidavlat Koimdodov; Nigina Sharapova; Zokir Vazirov; Maj.-Gen. Saidamin Zuhurov
Agriculture, Shodi Kabirov
Chairs of State Committees, Matlubkhon Davlatov (*Administration of Affairs of State*); Ismat Eshmirzoyev (*Construction and Architecture*); Ayub Aliyev (*Industry and Mining*); Khayrulloyev Sadullo (*Land Resources and Reclamation*); Salomsho Muhabbatov (*Oil and Gas*); Muhammadjon Davlatov (*Precious Metals*); Rahimov Sayfullo (*Radio and Television*); Hakim Soliyev (*Trade and Contracts*)
Culture and Information, Bobokohon Mahmadov
Defence, Lt.-Gen. Sherali Khayrulloyev
Economics and Foreign Economic Relations, Yahya Azimov
Education, Munira Inoyatova Abdulloyevna
Emergency Situations and Civil Defence, Maj.-Gen. Mirzo Ahmadovoch Zieyoev
Environmental Protection and Water Resources, Ismail Davlatov
Finance, Anvarsho Muzaffurov

Foreign Affairs, Talbak Nazarov
Grain, Bekmurod Urokov
Health, Alamkhon Ahmedov
Interior, Lt.-Gen. Homiddin Sharipov
Justice, Shavkot Ishmoilov
Labour, Khudoiberdi Kholiknazarov
Security, Khayruddin Abdurahimov
Social Security, Abdusattor Jabborov
Transport and Roads, Abdujalol Salimov

ECONOMY

The Tajik rouble replaced the Russian rouble in May 1995. The economy is being reformed and privatizisation undertaken in order to attract foreign investment. In 1997 GDP grew by 1.7 per cent and industry grew by 9 per cent.

Agriculture is the major sector of the economy, concentrating on cotton-growing and cattle-breeding. Tajikistan also has rich mineral deposits of mercury, lead, zinc, oil, gold and uranium. Industry specializises in the production of clothing and textiles. In November 1997 and May 1998, donor conferences pledged loans totalling US$340 million to help stabilise the economic and political situation in Tajikistan.

GNP – US$2,256 million (1998); US$370 per capita (1998)
GDP – US$1,053 million (1996); US$177 per capita (1996)
ANNUAL AVERAGE GROWTH OF GDP – 3.7 per cent (1999)
INFLATION RATE – 26.3 per cent (1999)
TOTAL EXTERNAL DEBT – US$1,070 million (1998)

Trade with UK	1998	1999
Imports from UK	£1,763,000	£3,038,000
Exports to UK	2,372,000	2,696,000

TANZANIA
Jamhuri ya Muungano wa Tanzania – United Republic of Tanzania

AREA – 362,162 sq. miles (883,749 sq. km). Neighbours: Kenya and Uganda (north), Mozambique (south), Malawi and Zambia (south-west), Rwanda, Burundi and the Democratic Republic of Congo (west)
POPULATION – 31,507,000 (1997 UN estimate). Africans form a large majority, with European, Asian, and other non-African minorities. The African population consists mostly of tribes of mixed Bantu race. The official languages are Swahili and English
CAPITAL – Dodoma (population, 85,000, 1988)
MAJOR CITIES – ΨDar es Salaam (1,096,000), the economic and administrative centre; Mbeya (194,000); Mwanza (252,000); ΨTanga (172,000), 1985 estimates
CURRENCY – Tanzanian shilling of 100 cents
NATIONAL ANTHEM – Mungu Ibariki Afrika (God Bless Africa)
NATIONAL DAY – 26 April (Union Day)
NATIONAL FLAG – Green (above) and blue; divided by diagonal black stripe bordered by gold, running from bottom (next staff) to top (in fly)
LIFE EXPECTANCY (years) – male 47.00; female 50.00
POPULATION GROWTH RATE – 2.9 per cent (1997)
POPULATION DENSITY – 36 per sq. km (1997)
URBAN POPULATION – 20.8 per cent (1990)
MILITARY EXPENDITURE – 3.7 per cent of GDP (1998)
MILITARY PERSONNEL – 34,000: Army 30,000, Navy 1,000, Air Force 3,000; Paramilitaries 1,400
CONSCRIPTION DURATION – Two years

Tanzania comprises Tanganyika, on the mainland of east Africa, and the island of Zanzibar. The greater part of the country is occupied by the central African plateau from which rise, among others, Mt Kilimanjaro (19,340 ft), the highest point on the continent of Africa, and Mt Meru (14,974 ft). The Serengeti National Park covers an area of 6,000 sq. miles in the Arusha, Mwanza and Mara Regions.

HISTORY AND POLITICS

Tanganyika became an independent state and a member of the British Commonwealth on 9 December 1961, and a republic within the Commonwealth on 9 December 1962. Zanzibar, comprising the islands of Zanzibar, Pemba and Mafia, was formerly ruled by the Sultan of Zanzibar and was a British Protectorate until 10 December 1963 when it became an independent state within the Commonwealth. On 26 April 1964 Tanganyika united with Zanzibar to form the United Republic of Tanzania.

The sole legal political party from 1977 to 1992 was the Chama Cha Mapinduzi – the Revolutionary Party of Tanzania (CCM). The constitution was amended in 1992 to allow multiparty politics, with the stipulation that all parties must be active in both the mainland and in Zanzibar and that parties must not be formed on regional, religious, tribal or racial grounds.

The first multiparty presidential and parliamentary elections were held in October and November 1995. The CCM's candidate, Salmin Amour, was elected president of Zanzibar and his party won 26 seats in the Zanzibar House of Representatives. The Civic United Front gained 24 seats. Benjamin Mkapa of the CCM was elected Union president. The CCM won 186 of the 232 elected seats in the National Assembly. Legislative and presidential elections are due to be held on 29 October 2000.

POLITICAL SYSTEM

The president is directly elected and may serve two terms. The National Assembly contains 275 members, of whom 182 are elected from mainland constituencies and 50 from Zanzibar, 37 seats are reserved for women and are distributed to parties in ratio to their share of seats, five are nominated by the Zanzibar government and one is reserved for the Attorney-General. Constituency members are elected at a general election held at a maximum of five-yearly intervals.

Although Zanzibar has its own president, government and 60-member House of Representatives, Tanganyika is governed by the government of the Union. The president of Zanzibar is also a member of the Union Cabinet.

HEAD OF STATE

President of the United Republic, Benjamin Mkapa, elected 29 October 1995
Vice-President, President of Zanzibar, Salmin Amour

CABINET *as at September 2000*
The President
The Vice-President
Prime Minister, Frederick Sumaye
Agriculture and Co-operatives, William Kusila
Communications and Transport, Ernest Nyanda
Community Development, Women's Affairs and Children, Mary Nagu
Defence, Edgar Maokola Majogo
Education, Prof. Juma Athumani Kapuya
Energy and Mineral Resources, Dr Abdalla Kigoda
Foreign Affairs and International Co-operation, Jakaya Kikwete
Health, Dr Aaron Chiduo
Home Affairs, Mohammed Seif Khatib
Justice and Constitutional Affairs, Harith Bakari Mwapachu
Labour and Youth Development, Paul Kimiti
Land, Housing and Urban Development, Gideon Cheyo
Minister of State in the Vice-President's Office, Edward Lowassa

Ministers of State in the President's Office, Mateo Karesi (*Cabinet Affairs*); Jackson Makweta (*Civil Service*); Daniel Yona Ndhiwa (*Finance*); Nasoro Maloche (*Planning and Sector Reform*); Wilson Masilingi (*Security*)
Ministers of State in the Prime Minister's Office, Bakari Mbonde (*Information and Policy*); Ali Amer Mohammed
Natural Resources, Tourism and Environment, Zakia Meghji
Regional Administration and Local Government, Kingunge Ngombare Mwiru
Science, Technology and Higher Education, Pius Ng'wandu
Trade and Industry, Iddi Simba
Water and Livestock Development, Mussa Nkhangaa
Works, Anna Abdallah

HIGH COMMISSION FOR THE UNITED REPUBLIC OF TANZANIA
43 Hertford Street, London W1Y 8DB
Tel: 020-7499 8951/4
High Commissioner, HE Dr Abdul-kader Shareef, apptd 1995

BRITISH HIGH COMMISSION
Social Security House, Samora Avenue (PO Box 9200), Dar es Salaam
Tel: (00 255) (51) 117659/64
E-mail: bhc.dar@dar.mail.fco.gov.uk
High Commissioner, HE Bruce Dinwiddy, apptd 1998

BRITISH COUNCIL DIRECTOR, R. Hilhorst, Samora Avenue/Ohio Street, (PO Box 9100), Dar es Salaam; e-mail: bc.tanzania@ics-dar.sprint.com

ECONOMY

In 1997, 81.7 per cent of the workforce were employed in agriculture and agricultural produce accounted for 52 per cent of GDP in 1996. The islands of Zanzibar and Pemba produce a large part of the world's supply of cloves and clove oil; coconuts, coconut oil and copra are also produced. Tanzania's chief exports are coffee, cotton and cashew nuts. The chief imports are capital equipment, oil and oil derivatives, and consumer goods. Industry, which accounts for 14 per cent of GDP, is largely concerned with the processing of raw material for export or local consumption; secondary manufacturing industries include factories for the manufacture of leather and rubber footwear, knitwear, razor blades, cigarettes and textiles, and a wheat flour mill.

A debt-service relief package, worth about US$3 million, was announced by the International Development Association and the IMF in April 2000.

In 1997 Tanzania had a trade deficit of US$449 million and a current account deficit of US$707 million. In 1998, imports totalled US$1,454 million and exports US$674 million.

GNP – US$7,154 million (1998); US$220 per capita (1998)
GDP – US$5,150 million (1996); US$167 per capita (1996)
ANNUAL AVERAGE GROWTH OF GDP – 4.2 per cent (1996)
INFLATION RATE – 12.8 per cent (1998)
TOTAL EXTERNAL DEBT – US$7,603 million (1998)

Trade with UK	1998	1999
Imports from UK	£63,732,000	£63,431,000
Exports to UK	29,089,000	18,397,000

COMMUNICATIONS

The main ports are Dar es Salaam, Tanga, Mtwara, Zanzibar, Mkoani and Wete, in addition to Mwanza, Musoma and Bukoba on Lake Victoria and Kigoma on

Lake Tanganyika. Coastal shipping services connect the mainland to Zanzibar, and lake services are operated on Lake Tanganyika and Lake Malawi with neighbouring countries. The principal international airports are Dar es Salaam, Kilimanjaro and Zanzibar. There are two railway systems; one connecting Dar es Salaam to Zambia, and the second having two main lines running from Dar es Salaam, one to northern Tanzania and Kenya and the other to Lakes Tanganyika and Victoria. There are more than 3,000 km of railtrack.

EDUCATION

The school system is administered in Swahili but the government is making efforts to improve English standards for the purposes of secondary and higher education. All Tanzanian secondary schools are expected to include practical subjects in the basic course. There are three institutes of higher education: the University of Dar es Salaam, Sokoine University of Agriculture in Morogoro and an open university.

ILLITERACY RATE – 24.8 per cent
ENROLMENT (percentage of age group) – primary 48 per cent (1997); tertiary 0.6 per cent (1997)

THAILAND
Prathes Thai – Kingdom of Thailand

AREA – 198,115 sq. miles (513,115 sq. km). Neighbours: Malaysia (south), Myanmar (west), Laos and Cambodia (east)
POPULATION – 60,206,000 (1997 census). The principal language is Thai, a monosyllabic, tonal language of the Indo-Chinese linguistic family, with a vocabulary strongly influenced by Sanskrit and Pali. It is written in an alphabetic script derived from ancient Indian scripts. Significant minorities speak Chinese (in urban areas), Lao (in the north-east), Khmer (in the east) and Malay (in the far south). The principal religion is Buddhism (94.37 per cent), with Muslim and Christian minorities
CAPITAL – ΨBangkok (population, 5,882,000, 1993)
MAJOR CITIES – Chiang Mai (167,000); Chon Buri (187,000); Muang Khon Kaen (206,000); Nakhon Ratchasima (278,000); Songkhla (243,000)
CURRENCY – Baht of 100 satang
NATIONAL ANTHEM – Pleng Chart
NATIONAL DAY – 5 December (The King's Birthday)
NATIONAL FLAG – Five horizontal bands, red, white, dark blue, white, red (the blue band twice the width of the others)
LIFE EXPECTANCY (years) – male 63.82; female 68.85
POPULATION GROWTH RATE – 1.2 per cent (1997)
POPULATION DENSITY – 118 per sq. km (1997)
URBAN POPULATION – 18.7 per cent (1990)
  Thailand, formerly known as Siam, is divided geographically into four: the centre is a plain; to the north-east there is a plateau area and to the north-west mountains. The south of Thailand consists of a narrow mountainous peninsula. The principal rivers are the Chao Phraya in the central plains, and the Mekong on the northern and north-eastern borders.

HISTORY AND POLITICS

The Thai nation was founded in the 13th century. Although occupied by Burma in the 18th century, Thailand is the only country in the region not to have been colonised by a European power.
  Following a revolution in 1932, Thailand became a constitutional monarchy. After a military coup in February

1991, a new constitution was approved under which the military would have significant political power. Parties aligned with the military won the general election in March 1992, but mass demonstrations held in Bangkok, with the help of the King, forced the government from power. Military power was curbed, the 1978 constitution was restored and the interim government sacked military chiefs.
  Parliamentary elections in September 1992 resulted in a majority for those parties not allied with the military. Chuan Leekpai became prime minister at the head of a coalition which implemented a number of reforms. In a general election on 17 November 1996, New Aspiration became the largest party in the House of Representatives and formed a six-party coalition government. As a result of the economic crisis in Asia, the government resigned in November 1997, and a new eight-party coalition government was formed under Chuan Leekpai.
  The first election to the Senate was held on 4 March 2000. A re-run was held in 78 seats on 29 April following evidence of fraud. Further re-runs were necessary for some seats. An election to the House of Representatives is due by November 2000.

POLITICAL SYSTEM

The amended 1978 constitution provides for a National Assembly consisting of a 200-member Senate, formerly appointed, but now directly elected on a non-party basis, and a 393-member House of Representatives elected by universal adult suffrage for a term of four years.
  Following the election to the House of Representatives due to be held in November 2000, the House of Representatives will comprise 400 MPs from single constituencies and 100 from party lists.

HEAD OF STATE

HM The King of Thailand, King Bhumibol Adulyadej, *born* 1927; *succeeded his brother* 9 June 1946; *married* 28 April 1950 Princess Sirikit Kitiyakara; *crowned* 5 May 1950; and has *issue*, Princess Ubolratana, *born* 6 April 1951; Crown Prince Vajiralongkorn (*see* below); Princess Maha Chaki Sirindhorn, *born* 2 April 1955; Princess Chulabhorn, *born* 4 July 1957
Heir, HRH Crown Prince Vajiralongkorn, *born* 28 July 1952; *married* 3 January 1977 Soamsawali Kitiyakra

CABINET *as at September 2000*

Prime Minister, Defence, Chuan Leekpai (DP)
Deputy PMs, Phichai Rattakun (DP) ; Suwannakhiri Trairong (DP); Suphachai Phanitchaphak (DP) (*Commerce*); Banyat Bantadtan (*Interior*); Kon Thappharangsi (CP) (*Public Health*)
Ministers to the Prime Minister's Office, Suphattra Matsadit (DP); Adisai Photharamik; Sawit Phothiwihok (DP); Aphisit Wetchachiwa (DP); Paveena Honsakul (CP); Pinyo Nirote (CP)
Agriculture and Co-operatives, Praphat Phothasuthon (CT)
Education, Pritsananthakun Somsak (CT)
Finance, Tharin Nimmanhemin (DP)
Foreign Affairs, Surin Phitsuwan (DP)
Industry, Suwat Liptaphanlop (CP)
Justice, Suthat Ngoenmun (DP)
Labour and Social Welfare, Pracha Phromnok
Science, Technology and Environment, Urairat Athit (DP)
State University Bureau, Prachuap Chaiyasan
Transport and Communications, Suthep Thuaksuban (DP)

CP Chart Pattana; CT Chart Thai; DP Democrat Party; E Ekkaparb; PT Prakachakorn Thai

ROYAL THAI EMBASSY
29–30 Queen's Gate, London SW7 5JB
Tel: 020-7589 2944
Ambassador Extraordinary and Plenipotentiary, HE Sir Vidhya Rayanononda, KCVO, apptd 1994

Minister and Deputy Head of Mission, A. Manasvanich
Defence Attaché, Capt. S. Pruksa
Minister, S. Sarayudh (*Commercial*)

BRITISH EMBASSY
Wireless Road, Bangkok 10330
Tel: (00 66) (2) 2530 1919
Ambassador Extraordinary and Plenipotentiary, HE Lloyd
Barnaby Smith apptd 2000
Deputy Ambassador and Counsellor, P. Sizeland
Defence Attaché, Col. J. H. Thoyts
Counsellor (Commercial), D. Wyatt
Consul, B. P. Kelly

CONSULATE – Chiang Mai

BRITISH COUNCIL DIRECTOR, Dr J. Richards, OBE,
254 Chulalongkorn Soi 64, Siam Square, Phayathai
Road, Pathumwan, Bangkok 10330;
e-mail: bc.bangkok@britcoun.or.th. There is also
an office in Chiang Mai

BRITISH CHAMBER OF COMMERCE, BP Building 18th
Floor, Unit 1810, 54 Asoke Road (Sukhumvit 21),
Bangkok 10110

DEFENCE

The Army has 289 main battle tanks, 970 armoured
personnel carriers and four attack helicopters. The Navy
has one aircraft carrier, 14 frigates, 88 patrol and coastal
vessels, 67 combat aircraft and five armed helicopters at
five bases. The Air Force has 162 combat aircraft.
MILITARY EXPENDITURE – 1.5 per cent of GDP (1998)
MILITARY PERSONNEL – 306,000: Army 190,000, Navy
73,000, Air Force 43,000; Paramilitaries 71,000

ECONOMY

Thailand was one of the countries worst affected by the
economic crisis in south-east Asia. Many Thai banks had
borrowed heavily to finance the booming property
market, and suffered when the market collapsed. In May
1997 the stock market fell to an eight-year low. In July
1997 the government allowed the currency to float freely,
resulting in a *de facto* devaluation of 20 per cent and trig-
gering a currency crisis throughout south-east Asia. On
5 August 1997, an IMF loan of US$16.7 billion was
announced, in return for emergency financial reforms.
However, these reforms were only implemented after a
delay and were seen by the markets as inadequate, further
damaging economic confidence. The government resigned on 3 November 1997, and was replaced by an eight-
party coalition. The Thai economy contracted by about
8 per cent in 1998. In March 1999, the government
announced a package of tax cuts and increased spending
designed to stimulate the economy.

The banking system remains in crisis with nearly half of
all loans non-performing, as many businesses had become
heavily indebted during the financial crisis and are now
unable to repay their loans.

The agricultural sector employs around half of the
labour force. In 1997 it contributed 11 per cent of GDP.
Rice remains the most important crop; other main crops
are sugar, maize, sorghum, cassava, rubber, tobacco, kenaf
and jute. In recent years fishing and livestock production
have gained importance. There are reserves of oil, natural
gas and lignite; mineral resources include tin, tungsten,
lead and iron.

Important industrial sectors include textiles, transportation vehicles and equipment, construction materials,
brewing, petroleum refining, electrical appliances, plastics, computers and parts, and integrated circuits. In 1997,
industry contributed 39.8 per cent of GDP. Since 1982
tourism has been the main foreign exchange earner. In

1998, there were 7.8 million foreign visitors.
GNP – US$131,916 million (1998); US$2,160 per capita
(1998)
GDP – US$184,092 million (1996); US$3,136 per capita
(1996)
ANNUAL AVERAGE GROWTH OF GDP – 6.0 per cent
(1996)
INFLATION RATE – 8.1 per cent (1998)
UNEMPLOYMENT – 3.4 per cent (1998)
TOTAL EXTERNAL DEBT – US$86,172 million (1998)

TRADE

Thailand's main exports are computers and parts, cars,
integrated circuit boards, precious stones, rice, maize,
canned sea food, fabrics, sugar and tin. Main imports
are crude oil, chemicals, electrical goods, industrial
machinery, iron, steel and transport equipment.

In 1997 Thailand had a trade surplus of US$16,234
million and a current account surplus of US$14,230
million. Imports totalled US$42,971 million and exports
US$54,456 million.

Trade with UK	1998	1999
Imports from UK	£391,119,000	£465,796,000
Exports to UK	1,329,084,000	1,346,599,000

COMMUNICATIONS

The road network, totalling 56,903 km in 1993, reaches all
parts of the country. Navigable waterways have a length
of about 1,100 km in the dry season and 1,600 km in the
wet season. There are 4,600 km of state-owned railways.
Main lines run from Bangkok to the Cambodian border,
the ferry terminal on the River Mekong opposite
Vientiane, Chiang Mai and to Hat Yai, whence lines run
down both sides of the Malay peninsula to Singapore. A
new line to Sattahip on the east coast is being constructed.
Bangkok is the international airport, though airports at
Chiang Mai, Phuket and Hat Yai also receive international
flights. Most major provincial towns have airports. A mass
transit system has been planned for Bangkok.

There are two important ports in the country. Bangkok,
which is a river port, can serve vessels up to 27 ft draught.
The deep-sea port at Sattahip caters for larger vessels.
Phuket and Songkhla deep-water ports have already been
completed and are the first to be managed privately under
a ten-year concession.

In September 1999, the government approved a plan to
build a 350 km gas pipeline from the Gulf of Thailand to
Songkhla province, where it would link with the Malaysian
network.

EDUCATION

Primary education is compulsory and free, and secondary
education in government schools is free. Private universities and colleges are playing an increasing role in
higher education. Out of 43 universities and other similar
higher institutes of learning, 21 are private.

ILLITERACY RATE – 4.4 per cent
ENROLMENT (percentage of age group) – tertiary
22 per cent (1996)

TOGO
République Togolaise

AREA – 21,925 sq. miles (56,785 sq. km). Neighbours:
Ghana (west), Burkina Faso (north), Benin (east)
POPULATION – 4,317,000 (1997 UN estimate). The
official language is French; Ewe, Watchi and Kabiyé
are the main indigenous languages
CAPITAL – ΨLomé (population, 366,476, 1983)

CURRENCY – Franc CFA of 100 centimes
NATIONAL ANTHEM – Écartons tous mauvais esprit qui gêne l unité nationale (Let us discard all ill feelings which harm national unity)
NATIONAL DAY – 27 April
NATIONAL FLAG – Five alternating green and yellow horizontal stripes; a quarter in red at top next staff bearing a white star
LIFE EXPECTANCY (years) – male 49.46; female 52.59
POPULATION GROWTH RATE – 2.9 per cent (1997)
POPULATION DENSITY – 76 per sq. km (1997)
MILITARY EXPENDITURE – 2.4 per cent of GDP (1998)
MILITARY PERSONNEL – 6,950: Army 6,500 Navy 200, Air Force 250; Paramilitaries 750
CONSCRIPTION DURATION – Two years (selective)
ILLITERACY RATE – 42.9 per cent
ENROLMENT (percentage of age group) – primary 81 per cent (1996); secondary 18 per cent (1990); tertiary 3.6 per cent (1996)

HISTORY AND POLITICS

The first president of Togo, Sylvanus Olympio, was assassinated in 1963. In 1967, there was an army coup d'état and the army commander Lt.-Col. (later Gen.) Eyadéma named himself president. President Eyadéma came under increasing popular pressure to introduce reforms in 1990 and the *Rassemblement du peuple togolais* (RPT), the sole legal party, approved plans for a new constitutional conference after pro-democracy riots. In April the government was forced to concede a political amnesty, the introduction of a multiparty constitution and a national conference. In August 1991 the national conference stripped President Eyadéma of all powers, banned the RPT and elected Kokou Koffigoh as prime minister of an interim government. The national conference set a date of 9 February 1992 for a referendum on a new constitution.

Troops loyal to President Eyadéma three times attempted to overthrow Koffigoh (in October, November and December 1991) but were frustrated by pro-democracy supporters. Continued violence in 1992 between the army and pro-democracy groups and among rival opposition parties forced the postponement of the referendum until September 1992, when a new multiparty constitution was agreed. In November, Eyadéma, who had regained the position of head of state in August 1992, ordered the Army to crush civil unrest and a general strike against his rule. In February 1993, as violence continued, Koffigoh and Eyadéma agreed on the formation of a crisis government, which the national conference and the Collective Democratic Opposition-2 (COD-2) declared illegal.

The presidential election of 21 June 1998 was won by Gen. Eyadéma. Opposition politicians and EU observers expressed serious doubts over the conduct of the election.

Legislative elections to the 81-seat National Assembly were held on 21 March 1999. Opposition parties, who had refused to accept the results of the presidential election in 1998, boycotted the election, with the result that the ruling RPT gained 79 seats, the remaining two seats being won by independents. Eugene Koffi Adoboli was appointed prime minister on 22 May 1999 and a new Cabinet was appointed on 18 June. The government and opposition parties reached an agreement in July 1999 that a fresh election would be held in March 2000 and President Eyadéma agreed not to run in the 2003 presidential elections. The legislative election has been postponed.

HEAD OF STATE

President, Gen. Gnassingbé Eyadéma, *assumed office* 14 April 1967 *re-elected* 1986, 1993, 21 June 1998

GOVERNMENT *as at September 2000*

Prime Minister, Kodjo Agbeyomé
Agriculture, Livestock and Fisheries, Komikpine Bamenante
Civil Service and Labour, Biossey Kokou Tozoun
Communication and Civic Education, Koffi Panou
Defence, Brig.-Gen. Assani Tidjani
Economic Affairs, Finance and Privatizisation, Abdoul-Hamid Segoun Tidjani Dourodjaye
Environment and Forest Resources, Koffi Adade
Health, Kondi Charles Agba
Industry, Commerce and Development of Free Zone, Rudolph Kossivi Osseyi
Interior, Security and Decentralisation, Col. Sizing Akawilou Walla
Justice and Keeper of the Seals, Brig.-Gen. Séyi Méeméene
Mines, Energy, Posts and Telecommunications, Tchamdja Andjo
Minister Delegate at the Prime Minister's Office, Relations with Parliament and the European Union, Hodeminou Devo
Minister of State, Foreign Affairs and Co-operation, Kokou Joseph Koffigoh
National Education and Research, Koffi Sama
Planning and Development, Simnféeïitchéeou Prée
Secretary of State to the Prime Minister, Private Sector, Samarou Saïbou
Social Affairs, National Solidarity and the Promotion of Women, Irène Ashira Aissah
Special Adviser to the President, Barry Moussa Barque
Technical Education, Professional Training and Cottage Industry, Edo Kodjo Maurille Agbobli
Town Planning and Housing, Hope Agboli
Tourism and Leisure, Tankpadja Lalle
Transport and Water Resources, Dama Dramani
Youth, Sports and Culture, Horatio Freitas

EMBASSY OF THE REPUBLIC OF TOGO
35 rue Jouffroy d'Abbaus, F-75017 Paris, France
Tel: (00 33) (1) 4440 4853
Ambassador Extraordinary and Plenipotentiary, vacant

BRITISH AMBASSADOR, HE Ian Mackley, CMG, resident at Accra, Ghana
There is a Consulate (BP 20050) and a Commercial Office (BP 60958 BE) in Lomé.

ECONOMY

Although the economy remains largely agricultural, exports of phosphates have superseded agricultural products as the main source of export earnings. Other exports include palm kernels, copra and manioc.

In December 1998 the EU announced that it would not resume developmental aid to Togo following irregularities in the country's election process.

In 1994 Togo had a trade deficit of US$37 million and a current account deficit of US$63 million. In 1997 imports totalled US$374 million and exports US$237 million.
GNP – US$1,453 million (1998); US$330 per capita (1998)
GDP – US$1,382 million (1996); US$329 per capita (1996)
ANNUAL AVERAGE GROWTH OF GDP – 6.0 per cent (1996)
INFLATION RATE – 1.0 per cent (1998)
TOTAL EXTERNAL DEBT – US$1,448 million (1998)

Trade with UK	1998	1999
Imports from UK	£18,777,000	£19,556,000
Exports to UK	1,630,000	1,361,000

TONGA
Pule'anga Tonga/Kingdom of Tonga

AREA – 288 sq. miles (747 sq. km)
POPULATION – 99,000 (1997 UN estimate).

The languages are Tongan and English
CAPITAL – ΨNuku'alofa (population, 29,018, 1986), on
 Tongatapu
CURRENCY – Pa'anga (T$) of 100 seniti
NATIONAL ANTHEM – E, 'Otua Mafimafi (Oh, Almighty
 God Above)
NATIONAL DAY – 4 June (Emancipation Day)
NATIONAL FLAG – Red with a white canton containing a
 couped red cross
POPULATION GROWTH RATE – 0.4 per cent (1997)
POPULATION DENSITY – 133 per sq. km (1997)
URBAN POPULATION – 30.7 per cent (1986)

Tonga, or the Friendly Islands, comprises a group of
islands situated in the southern Pacific some 450 miles
east-south-east of Fiji. The largest island, Tongatapu,
was discovered by Tasman in 1643. Most of the islands
are of coral formation, but some are volcanic (Tofua, Kao
and Niuafoou or 'Tin Can' Island).

HISTORY AND POLITICS

The Kingdom of Tonga is an independent constitutional
monarchy within the Commonwealth. Prior to 4 June
1970 it had been a British-protected state for 70 years. The
constitution provides for a government consisting of the
Sovereign, an appointed privy council which functions
as a Cabinet, a legislative assembly and a judiciary. The
30-member legislative assembly comprises the King, the
11-member privy council, nine hereditary nobles elected
by their peers, and nine popularly elected representatives
who hold office for three years. The most recent election
took place on 12 March 1999.

HEAD OF STATE
King of Tonga, HM King Taufa'ahau Tupou IV, GCMG,
 GCVO, KBE, *born* 4 July 1918, *acceded* 16 December 1965
Heir, HRH Crown Prince Tupouto'a

CABINET *as at September 2000*
*Prime Minister, Agriculture, Forestry, Fisheries, Marine
 Affairs, Foreign Affairs and Defence*, HRH Prince
 'Ulukalala Lavaka Ata
Deputy P.M., Education and Civil Aviation, Dr S. Langi
 Kavaliku
Finance, Tutoatosi Fakafanua
Governor of Ha'apali, Fielakepa
Governor of Vava'u, Capt. S. M. Tuita
Health, Viliami Tangi
Justice, Tevita Tupou
Labour, Commerce and Industries, Masaso Paunga
Lands, Survey, and Natural Resources, Tu'i'afitu
Police, Prisons and Fire Services, Immigration, Clive Edwards
Works and Disaster Relief, Cecil Cocker

TONGA HIGH COMMISSION
36 Molyneux Street, London W1H 6AB
Tel: 020-7724 5828
High Commissioner, HE Col. Fetu'utolu Tupou,
 apptd 2000

BRITISH HIGH COMMISSION
PO Box 56, Nuku'alofa
Tel: (00 676) 24285/24395
E-mail: britcomt@candw.to
High Commissioner, HE Brian Connelly, apptd 1998

ECONOMY

The economy is primarily agricultural; the main crops are
coconuts, vanilla, yams, taro, cassava, groundnuts, squash
pumpkins and other fruits. Fish is an important staple
food, though recent shortfalls have led to canned fish
being imported. Industry is based on the processing of
agricultural produce, and the manufacture of foodstuffs,

clothing and sports equipment.
GNP – US$173 million (1998); US$1,750 per capita
 (1998)
GDP – US$178 million (1996); US$1,819 per capita
 (1996)
ANNUAL AVERAGE GROWTH OF GDP – 1.6 per cent (1996)
INFLATION RATE – 2.1 per cent (1997)
TOTAL EXTERNAL DEBT – US$65 million (1998)

TRADE
The principal exports are fish and vanilla. The principal
imports are manufactures, foodstuffs, machinery and
transport equipment and combustible fuels.
 In 1996 imports totalled US$75 million and exports
US$10 million.

Trade with UK	1998	1999
Imports from UK	£1,205,000	£1,467,000
Exports to UK	17,000	260,000

TRINIDAD AND TOBAGO
The Republic of Trinidad and Tobago

AREA – 1,981 sq. miles (5,130 sq. km)
POPULATION – 1,307,000 (1997 UN estimate). The
 language is English. Roman Catholicism,
 Protestantism, Hinduism and Islam are all practised
CAPITAL – ΨPort of Spain (population, 43,396, 1994)
MAJOR CITIES – San Fernando (55,784); ΨScarborough,
 the main town of Tobago
CURRENCY – Trinidad and Tobago dollar (TT$) of
 100 cents
NATIONAL ANTHEM – Forged from the love of liberty
NATIONAL DAY – 31 August (Independence Day)
NATIONAL FLAG – Black diagonal stripe bordered with
 white stripes, running from top by staff, all on a red field
LIFE EXPECTANCY (years) – male 68.39; female 73.20
POPULATION GROWTH RATE – 1.0 per cent (1997)
POPULATION DENSITY – 255 per sq. km (1997)
MILITARY EXPENDITURE – 0.7 per cent of GDP (1998)
MILITARY PERSONNEL – 2,700: Army 2,000,
 Coast Guard 700

Trinidad, the most southerly of the West Indian islands,
lies seven miles off the north coast of Venezuela. The
island is about 50 miles in length by 37 miles in width. Two
mountain systems, the Northern and Southern Ranges,
stretch across almost its entire width and a third, the
Central Range, lies diagonally across its middle portion;
otherwise the island is mostly flat.
 Tobago lies 19 miles north-east of Trinidad. The island
is 32 miles long at its widest point, and 11 miles wide.
 Corozal Point and Icacos Point, the north-west and
south-west extremities of Trinidad, enclose the Gulf of
Paria. West of Corozal Point lie several islands, of which
Chacachacare, Huevos, Monos and Gaspar Grande are
the most important.
 The climate is tropical. There is a dry season
from December to May, and a wet season from June to
November broken by a short dry season (the *Petit Carême*)
in September and October.

HISTORY AND POLITICS

Trinidad was discovered by Columbus in 1498, was
colonised in 1532 by the Spaniards, capitulated to the
British in 1797, and was ceded to Britain under the Treaty
of Amiens (1802). Tobago was discovered by Columbus
in 1498. Dutch colonists arrived in 1632; Tobago subsequently changed hands numerous times until it was
ceded to Britain by France in 1814 and amalgamated with
Trinidad in 1888. The Territory of Trinidad and Tobago
became an independent state and a member of the British

Commonwealth on 31 August 1962, and a republic in 1976.

The most recent general election on 6 November 1995 produced 17 seats each for the ruling People's National Movement (PNM) and the United National Congress (UNC). The UNC formed a coalition government with the National Alliance for Reconstruction (NAR) which held the remaining two seats. A general election is due by November 2000.

POLITICAL SYSTEM

The president is elected for five years by all members of the Senate and the House of Representatives. The House of Representatives has 36 members, directly elected for a five-year term, and the Senate has 31, of whom 16 are appointed on the advice of the prime minister, six on the advice of the Leader of the Opposition and nine at the discretion of the president. Legislation was passed in September 1980 which afforded Tobago a degree of self-administration through the 15-member Tobago House of Assembly, of whom 12 are directly elected and three chosen by the House for a four-year term.

HEAD OF STATE

President, HE Arthur N. Robinson, *elected* 14 February 1997

CABINET *as at September 2000*

Prime Minister, Communications and Information, Basdeo Panday
Agriculture, Lands and Marine Resources, Trevor Sudama
Attorney-General, Legal Affairs, Ramesh Lawrence Maharaj
Culture and Women's Affairs, Daphne Phillips
Education, Kamla Persad-Bissessar
Energy and Energy Industries, Finbar Ganga
Environment, Dr Reeza Mohammed
Finance, Planning and Development, Brian Kuei Tung
Foreign Affairs, Ralph Maraj
Health, Dr Hamza Rafeeq
Housing and Settlements, John Humphrey
Labour and Co-operatives, Harry Partrap
Local Government, Dhanraj Singh
Minister in the Ministry of Finance, Planning and Development, Vincent Lasse
National Security, Joseph Theodore
Prime Minister's Office, Lindsay Gillette
Public Administration, Wade Mark
Public Utilities, Ganga Singh
Social and Community Development, Sport and Youth Affairs, Manohar Ramsaran
Tobago Affairs, Minister in the Ministry of Finance, Planning and Development, Morgan Job
Tourism, Dr Adesh Nanan
Trade, Industry and Consumer Affairs, Mervyn Assam
Training and Distance Learning, Rupert Griffith
Works and Transport, Carlos John

HIGH COMMISSION OF THE REPUBLIC OF TRINIDAD AND TOBAGO

42 Belgrave Square, London SW1X 8NT
Tel: 020-7245 9351
High Commissioner, HE Sheelagh de Osuna, apptd 1996

BRITISH HIGH COMMISSION

19 St Clair Ave, St Clair, Port of Spain
Tel: (00 1 868) 622 2748/8960
High Commissioner, HE P. G. Harborne, apptd 1999

BRITISH COUNCIL, c/o British High Commission; e-mail: shereen@opus.co.tt

ECONOMY

Trinidad and Tobago's main source of revenue is from oil.

Production of domestic crude was 6.3 million tonnes in 1998. Trinidad has large reserves of natural gas, and in March 2000, an agreement was signed to expand significantly the production of liquefied natural gas. In May, it was announced that an additional natural gas deposit of some 56,600 million cubic metres had been discovered. An integrated steel plant, two anhydrous ammonia plants, four methanol plants, one urea plant and one iron carbide plant have been constructed at Point Lisas. An industrial complex, including an iron and steel production plant, is developing around San Fernando.

Fertilisers, tyres, clothing, soap, furniture and foodstuffs are manufactured locally while motor vehicles, radios, TV sets, and electro-domestic equipment are assembled from parts, mainly from Japan. The main agricultural products are sugar, cocoa, coffee, horticultural products and teak. There were 265,900 tourists in 1996.

In 1995 Trinidad and Tobago had a trade surplus of US$588 million and a current account surplus of US$294 million. In 1997 imports totalled US$2,990 million and exports US$2,542 million.

GNP – US$5,811 million (1998); US$4,520 per capita (1998)
GDP – US$5,418 million (1996); US$4,178 per capita (1996)
ANNUAL AVERAGE GROWTH OF GDP – 3.1 per cent (1996)
INFLATION RATE – 5.6 per cent (1998)
UNEMPLOYMENT – 14.2 per cent (1998)
TOTAL EXTERNAL DEBT – US$2,193 million (1998)

Trade with UK	1998	1999
Imports from UK	£94,177,000	£143,339
Exports to UK	39,274,000	53,433,000

COMMUNICATIONS

There are some 9,586 km of roads in Trinidad and Tobago. The three main ports are Scarborough (Tobago), Port of Spain and Point Lisas where new industries powered by local natural gas are located. The national airline is International Trinidad and Tobago Airways (BWIA), and the international airport, Piarco, is at Port of Spain. Air Caribbean flies between Trinidad and Tobago.

EDUCATION

Education is free at all state-owned and government-assisted denominational schools and certain faculties at the University of the West Indies. Attendance is compulsory for children aged six to 12 years, after which attendance at free secondary schools is determined by success in the common entrance examination at 11 years. There are three technical institutes, two teachers' training colleges, and one of the three branches of the University of the West Indies is located in Trinidad. A medical teaching complex at Mt Hope operates in collaboration with the University of the West Indies.

ILLITERACY RATE – 1.8 per cent
ENROLMENT (percentage of age group) – primary 88 per cent (1996); secondary 65 per cent (1992); tertiary 7.8 per cent (1996)

TUNISIA
Al-Jumhūriyya at-Tūisiyya

AREA – 62,592 sq. miles (163,610 sq. km). Neighbours: Algeria (west), Libya (south)
POPULATION – 9,215,000 (1997). Arabic is the official language
CAPITAL – ΨTunis (population, 918,000, 1997)
MAJOR CITIES – ΨBizerte (484,250); ΨSfax (732,865); ΨSousse (435,075), 1996
CURRENCY – Tunisian dinar of 1,000 millimes

NATIONAL ANTHEM – Himat Al Hima (Defenders of the homeland)
NATIONAL DAY – 20 March
NATIONAL FLAG – Red with a white disc containing a red crescent and star
LIFE EXPECTANCY (years) – male 69.55; female 73.14
POPULATION GROWTH RATE – 1.7 per cent (1997)
POPULATION DENSITY – 56 per sq. km (1997)
URBAN POPULATION – 61.0 per cent (1994)
MILITARY EXPENDITURE – 1.8 per cent of GDP (1998)
MILITARY PERSONNEL – 35,000: Army 27,000, Navy 4,500, Air Force 3,500; Paramilitaries 12,000
CONSCRIPTION DURATION – 12 months (selective)
ILLITERACY RATE – 29.2 per cent
ENROLMENT (percentage of age group) – primary 98 per cent (1996); secondary 43 per cent (1991); tertiary 13.7 per cent (1996)

HISTORY AND POLITICS

A French Protectorate from 1881 to 1956, Tunisia became an independent sovereign state on 20 March 1956. In 1957 the Constituent Assembly abolished the monarchy and elected M. Bourguiba president of the Republic. In March 1975 the National Assembly proclaimed M. Bourguiba as president for life. He was deposed on 7 November 1987 and succeeded by President Zine el-Abidine Ben Ali, who was subsequently elected in 1989 and re-elected in 1994.

President Ben Ali was elected for a third term of office on 24 October 1999, gaining 99.4 per cent of the vote; there were two other candidates. A parallel legislative election was won by the Democratic Constitutional Rally (RCD), who gained 91.6 per cent of the vote, winning 148 of the 182 seats in the National Assembly (*Majlis al-Nuwaab*). The Movement of Social Democrats (MDS) won 13 seats, the Unionist Democratic Union (UDU) and the Party of People's Unity (PUP) won 7 seats each, the Movement for Renewal (MR) won 5 seats and the Social-Liberal Party won 2 seats.

The country is divided into 23 regions (*gouvernorats*) each administered by a governor.

HEAD OF STATE

President, Gen. Zine el-Abidine Ben Ali, *took office* 7 November 1987, *elected* 2 April 1989, *re-elected* 20 March 1994, 24 October 1999

CABINET *as at September 2000*
Prime Minister, Mohammed Ghannouchi
Agriculture, Sadok Rabah
Communications, Ahmed Friaa
Culture, Abdelbaki Hermassi
Economic Development, Abdellatif Saddam
Education, Ahmed Eyadh Ouederni
Environment and Land Development, Faiza Kefi
Finance, Taoufik Baccar
Foreign Affairs, Habib Ben Yahia
Higher Education, Sadok Chaabane
Industry, Moncef Ben Abdallah
Interior, Abduallah Kallel
International Co-operation and Foreign Investment, Fethi Merdassi
Justice, Bechir Takali
Minister-Delegate to the Prime Minister in charge of Human Rights, Communications and Relations with the National Assembly, Afif Hendaoui
Minister of State, Special Adviser to the President, Abdelaziz Ben Dhia
National Defence, Mohammed Jegham
Public Health, Hedi Mhenni
Public Works and Housing, Slaheddine Belaid
Religious Affairs, Jelloul Jribi
Secretary-General to the Government, Abdallah Kaabi
Secretary-General to the Presidential Office, Slaheddine Ben Cherif

Social Affairs, Chedli Neffati
State Property, Real Estate Affairs, Ridha Grira
Tourism and Handicrafts, Slaheddine Maaouia
Trade, Mondher Zenaidi
Transport, Hassine Chouk
Vocational Training and Employment, Moncer Rouissi
Women and the Family, Neziha Zarrouk
Youth, Childhood and Sport, Raouf Najar

TUNISIAN EMBASSY

29 Prince's Gate, London SW7 1QG
Tel: 020-7584 8117
Ambassador Extraordinary and Plenipotentiary, HE Khemaies Jhinaoui, apptd 1999

BRITISH EMBASSY

5 Place de la Victoire, Tunis 1000 RP
Tel: (00 216) (1) 341444
E-mail: british.emb@planet.tn
Ambassador Extraordinary and Plenipotentiary, HE Ivor Rawlinson, OBE, apptd 1998
Consul, B. Bennett (*Deputy Head of Mission*)

HONORARY CONSULATE – Sfax

BRITISH COUNCIL DIRECTOR, J. Mackenzie (*Cultural Attaché*), c/o British Embassy;
e-mail: general.enquiries@bc-tunis.bcouncil.org

ECONOMY

Agriculture employed 25.7 per cent of the workforce in 1997 and in 1996 accounted for 15.9 per cent of GDP. The valleys of the northern region support large flocks and herds and contain rich agricultural areas in which cereal crops, citrus fruits, dates, melons and tomatoes are grown. Vines and olives are extensively cultivated. Crude oil production in 1998 was 3 million tonnes. Gas has also been discovered off the east coast but is only exploited in small quantities. Tourism is the main foreign exchange earner and there were 4.7 million visitors in 1998.

In 1998 Tunisia had a trade deficit of US$2,151 million and a current account deficit of US$675 million. Imports totalled US$8,338 million and exports US$5,750 million.
GNP – US$19,193 million (1998); US$2,060 per capita (1998)
GDP – US$19,634 million (1996); US$2,144 per capita (1996)
ANNUAL AVERAGE GROWTH OF GDP – 5.4 per cent (1997)
INFLATION RATE – 3.1 per cent (1998)
TOTAL EXTERNAL DEBT – US$11,078 million (1998)

TRADE

The chief exports are manufactures, textiles and leather goods, phosphates, mechanical and electronic products, agricultural products and energy. The chief imports are manufactures, raw materials and semi-manufactures, consumer goods, capital goods, and foodstuffs. France remains the main trading partner.

Tunisia became an associate of the EC in 1969. In July 1995 a new EU-Tunisian partnership agreement was signed which aims to modernise Tunisia's economy and improve its competitiveness with a view to creating a trade zone with the EU by 2008.

Trade with UK	1998	1999
Imports from UK	£101,387,000	£107,398,000
Exports to UK	77,024,000	83,873,000

TURKEY
Türkiye Cumhuriyeti

AREA – 314,508 sq. miles (814,578 sq. km). Neighbours: Greece (west), Bulgaria (north), Georgia, Armenia,

Population at least 75% Kurd

Nakhichevan (Azerbaijan) and Iran (east), Syria and Iraq (south)

POPULATION – 63,745,000 (1997 UN estimate); 56,473,035 (1990 census). Islam ceased to be the state religion in 1928 but 98.99 per cent of the population are Muslim. The main religious minorities, which are concentrated in Istanbul and on the Syrian frontier, are Greek Orthodox, Armenian, Syrian Christian, and Jewish. The language is Turkish; Kurdish is widely spoken in the south-east of the country

CAPITAL – Ankara (Angora), in Asia (population, 3,258,026, 1997 estimate). Ankara (or Ancyra) was the capital of the Roman Province of *Galatia Prima*, and a marble temple (now in ruins), dedicated to Augustus, contains the *Monumentum (Marmor) Ancyranum*, inscribed with a record of the reign of Augustus Caesar

MAJOR CITIES – Adana (1,519,800); Bursa (1,381,300); Gaziantep (973,800); ΨIstanbul (7,784,100); ΨIzmir (2,411,500); Konya (1,069,400), 1994 estimates. Istanbul, in Europe, is the former capital. The Roman city of Byzantium, it was selected by Constantine the Great as the capital of the Roman Empire about AD 328 and renamed Constantinople. Istanbul contains the celebrated church of St Sophia, which, after becoming a mosque, was made a museum in 1934. It also contains Topkapi, former palace of the Ottoman Sultans, which is also a museum

CURRENCY – Turkish lira (TL) of 100 kurus

NATIONAL ANTHEM – Istiklal Mari (The Independence March)

NATIONAL DAY – 29 October (Republic Day)

NATIONAL FLAG – Red, with white crescent and star

LIFE EXPECTANCY (years) – male 66.80; female 71.40

POPULATION GROWTH RATE – 1.4 per cent (1999)

POPULATION DENSITY – 83 per sq. km (1999)

URBAN POPULATION – 64.7 per cent (1997)

Turkey lies partly in Europe and partly in Asia. Turkey in Europe consists of Eastern Thrace, including the cities of Istanbul and Edirne, and is separated from Asia by the Bosporus at Istanbul and by the Dardanelles (about 40 miles in length with a width varying from one to four miles). Turkey in Asia comprises the whole of Asia Minor or Anatolia.

HISTORY AND POLITICS

On 29 October 1923 the National Assembly declared Turkey a republic and elected Gazi Mustafa Kemal (later known as Kemal Atatürk) president. In 1945 a multiparty system was introduced but in 1960 the government was overthrown by the armed forces. A new constitution was adopted in 1961 and a civilian government took office. Civilian governments remained in power until September 1980 when mounting problems with the economy and terrorism led to a military takeover.

Following the general election in November 1983 the military leadership handed over power to a civilian government.

Following elections on 18 April 1999, the Democratic Left Party (DSP) won the most seats and formed a coalition with the Nationalist Action Party (MHP) and the Motherland Party (ANAP). The MHP, a right-wing nationalist organisation, became the second biggest party in the Grand National Assembly, having not been represented in the previous parliament as it had not managed to secure the necessary 10 per cent of the vote. Hadep, the pro-Kurdish People's Democracy Party, failed to obtain the necessary 10 per cent of the vote, but won control of several towns in south-eastern Turkey in simultaneous local elections.

INSURGENCIES

Since 1984 Turkey has been fighting armed guerrillas of the Marxist Kurdistan Workers' Party (PKK) in the south-east of the country where Kurds are the majority population. The PKK has an estimated strength of 10,000 operating from bases in Lebanon, northern Iraq and Syria, with the latter giving tacit support and finance. The south-east remains under martial law. Since May 1993 the Turkish army has attempted to destroy the PKK by launching land and air raids against PKK bases in northern Iraq. Tension rose between Turkey and Syria in September 1998 when Turkey mobilised its troops on its southern border with Syria and threatened to bomb Kurdish bases in Syria and Lebanon. Egyptian and Iranian mediation secured an agreement by Syria not to offer support to the PKK, The leader of the PKK. Abdullah Öcalan, left Syria in October 1998 and was captured by Turkish authorities in February 1999 in Kenya and returned to Turkey to stand trial, where he was found guilty of treason on 31 May and sentenced to death on 29 June 1999. The sentence was upheld by the Supreme Court of Appeals in November, but the Turkish government announced on 12 January 2000 that it would suspend the execution, pending an appeal. The PKK announced on 8 February 2000 that it had renounced violence and removed the word 'Kurdistan', which is illegal in Turkey, from its title.

POLITICAL SYSTEM

A new constitution, extending the powers of the president, was approved in 1982. It provided for the separation of powers between the legislature, executive and judiciary, and the holding of free elections to the unicameral Grand National Assembly, which now has 550 members elected every five years.

Turkey is divided for administrative purposes into 81 *il* with subdivisions into *ilçe* and *nahiye*. Each *il* has a governor (*vali*) and elective council.

HEAD OF STATE

President, Ahmet Necdet Sezer, *elected by parliament for a seven-year term* 5 May 2000, *took office* 16 May 2000

CABINET *as at September 2000*

Prime Minister, Bülent Ecevit (DSP)

Deputy PM, EU Affairs, Mesut Yilmaz

Deputy PMs, Ministers of State, Devlet Bahçeli (MHP); Hasan Hüsamettin Özkan (DSP)

Deputy PM, Energy and Natural Resources, Cumhur Ersümer (ANAP)

Ministers of State, Mustafa Yilmaz (DSP); Şükrü Sina Gürel (DSP); Fikret Ünlü (DSP); Hasan Gemici (DSP); Mehmet Keçeciler (ANAP); Yüksel Yalova (ANAP);

Rüştü Kazim Yücelen (ANAP); Tunca Toskay (MHP); Faruk Bal (MHP); Ramazan Mirzaoğlu (MHP); Edip Safter Gaydalïi (ANAP); Şuayip Üşenmez (MHP); Abdulhaluk Çay (MHP); Recep Önal (DSP) (Economy)
Agriculture and Village Affairs, Hüsnü Yusuf Gökalp (MHP)
Culture, Mustafa Istemihan Talay (DSP)
Education, Metin Bostancıoglu (DSP)
Energy and Natural Resources, Cumhur Ersümer
Environment, Fevzi Aytekin (DSP)
Finance, Sümer Oral (ANAP)
Foreign Affairs, İsmail Cem (DSP)
Forestry, İbrahim Nami Çagan (DSP)
Health, Osman Durmus (MHP)
Interior, Saadettin Tantan (ANAP)
Justice, Hikmet Sami Türk (DSP)
Labour and Social Security, Yasan Okuyan (ANAP)
National Defence, Sabahattin Cakmakoglu (MHP)
Public Works, Koray Aydın (MHP)
Tourism, Erkan Mumcu (ANAP)
Trade and Industry, Ahmet Kenan Tanrïkulu (MHP)
Transport, Enis Öksüuz (MHP)

ANAP Motherland Party; DSP Democratic Left Party; MHP Nationalist Action Party

TURKISH EMBASSY

43 Belgrave Square, London SW1X 8PA
Tel: 020-7393 0202
Ambassador Extraordinary and Plenipotentiary,
HE Korkmaz Haktanır, apptd 2000
Minister Counsellor, Meih Mehmet Akat

BRITISH EMBASSY

Şehit Ersan Caddesi 46/A, Çankaya, Ankara
Tel: (00 90) (312) 468 6230/42
E-mail: britembank@superonline.com
Ambassador Extraordinary and Plenipotentiary,
HE David Logan, CMG, apptd 1997
Counsellor, Deputy Head of Mission, H. Mortimer
First Secretary, J. Macpherson (Commercial)
Defence and Military Attache', Brig. K. Winfield
Consul-General (Istanbul), P. Hunt
CONSULATE-GENERAL – Istanbul
CONSULATE – Izmir
HONORARY CONSULATES – Antalya, Bodrum, Bursa, Marmaris, Mersin

BRITISH COUNCIL DIRECTOR, C. Gobby, Esat Caddesi
No:41, Kucukesat, TR-06660 Ankara;
e-mail: bc.ankara@britcoun.org.tr.
Regional offices in Istanbul and Izmir

BRITISH CHAMBER OF COMMERCE OF TURKEY INC.,
Mesrutiyet Caddessi No. 34, Tepebasi Beyoglu,
Istanbul (postal address, PO Box 190 Karaköy, Istanbul)

DEFENCE

The Army has 4,205 main battle tanks, 3,643 armoured personnel carriers, 450 armoured infantry fighting vehicles and 37 attack helicopters. The Navy has 15 submarines, 21 frigates, 50 patrol and coastal vessels and 13 armed helicopters at eight bases. The Air Force has 440 combat aircraft.

Between 150,000 and 200,000 troops are stationed in the south-east of the country fighting Kurdish guerrillas.

Since its invasion of Cyprus in 1974, Turkey has maintained forces in the north of the island and at present has about 30,000 men stationed there.

As a member of NATO, Turkey is host to the Headquarters Allied Land Forces South-Eastern Europe and the Sixth Allied Tactical Air Force Headquarters. US (2,420 personnel) and UK (160 personnel) air force detachments are based at Incirlik air base in southern Turkey to patrol the air exclusion zone over northern Iraq.

MILITARY EXPENDITURE – 4.4 per cent of GDP (1998)
MILITARY PERSONNEL – 639,000: Army 525,000, Navy 51,000, Air Force 63,000; Paramilitaries 202,200
CONSCRIPTION DURATION – 18 months

ECONOMY

Agricultural production accounted for 15.8 per cent of GDP in 1999. About 50 per cent of the working population are in the rural sector. The principal crops are wheat, barley, rice, tobacco, sugar beet, tea, olives, grapes, figs and hazelnuts. Most of the crops are grown on the fertile littoral. Tobacco, sultana and fig cultivation is centred around Izmir, where substantial quantities of cotton are also grown. The main cotton area is in the Cukurova plain around Adana. The forests which lie between the littoral plain and the Anatolian plateau contain beech, pine, oak, elm, chestnut, lime, plane, alder, box, poplar and maple.

After agriculture, Turkey's most important industry is based on the considerable mineral wealth which is, however, relatively unexploited. The main export minerals are chromite and boron. Tourism is a major industry, with over 7.5 million visitors in 1999.

The bulk of the country's requirements in sugar, cotton, woollen and silk textiles, and cement, is produced locally. Other industries include vehicle assembly, paper, glass and glassware, iron and steel, leather and leather goods, sulphur refining, canning and rubber goods, soaps and cosmetics, pharmaceutical products, and prepared foodstuffs.

A customs union with the EU came into force on 1 January 1996 which was expected to boost the economy, although Greece has managed to suspend EU aid packages. A gas deal worth £14,800 million was signed with Iran in August 1996 which provided for a 20-year supply of Iranian gas.

Turkey was accepted as a candidate for EU membership in December 1999.

GNP – US$185,171 million (1999); US$2,879 per capita (1999)
GDP – US$183,314 million (1999); US$2,814 per capita (1995)
ANNUAL AVERAGE GROWTH OF GDP – 7.4 per cent (1996)
INFLATION RATE – 64.9 per cent (1999)
UNEMPLOYMENT – 7.3 per cent (1999)
TOTAL EXTERNAL DEBT – US$111,215 million (1999)

TRADE

The main imports are machinery, crude oil and petroleum products, iron and steel, vehicles, medicines, chemicals and electrical appliances. Agricultural commodities (cotton, tobacco, fruits, nuts, livestock) represented 16.7 per cent of total exports in 1999. Other exports are minerals, textiles, glass and cement. Germany, the USA and Italy are the main trading partners.

In 1997 Turkey had a trade deficit of US$14,099 million and a current account deficit of US$2,928 million. Imports totalled US$40,687 million and exports US$26,587 million.

Trade with UK	1998	1999
Imports from UK	£1,630,709,000	£1,253,992,000
Exports to UK	1,164,664,000	1,279,905,000

COMMUNICATIONS

The rail network is run by the State Railways Administration. There are about 8,800 km of railway track and 62,672 km of state highways, including 1,749 km of motorways. There are 156 ports. The Bosporus is spanned by two bridges; plans are being drawn up for a third fixed link between the two continents. The state airline (THY) operates all internal services and has services to Europe, the Far East, Africa, North America and the Middle East.

Most of the leading European airlines operate services to Istanbul and some also to Ankara.

EDUCATION

Education is free and secular, and since August 1997, compulsory from the ages of six to 14. There are elementary, secondary and vocational schools. There are 69 universities in Turkey.

ILLITERACY RATE – 15.8 per cent

ENROLMENT (percentage of age group) – primary 91 per cent (1998); secondary 50 per cent (1998); tertiary 21 per cent (1998)

CULTURE

Turkish was written in Arabic script until 1926 when a version of the Roman alphabet reflecting Turkish phonetics was substituted for use in official correspondence and in 1928 for universal use, with Arabic numerals as used throughout Europe. The revolution of 1908 led to the introduction of native literature free from foreign influences and adapted to the understanding of the people.

TURKMENISTAN
Turkmenostan Respublikasy

AREA – 188,456 sq. miles (488,100 sq. km). Neighbours: Iran and Afghanistan (south), Uzbekistan (east and north), Kazakhstan (north-west)

POPULATION – 3,808,900 (2000 estimate); 4,483,000 (1996 census): 77 per cent Turkmen, 9.2 per cent Uzbek, 6.7 per cent Russian, together with smaller numbers of Kazakhs, Tatars, Ukrainians and Armenians. Most of the population are Sunni Muslims. The main languages are Turkmen (72 per cent), Russian (9 per cent), Uzbek (9 per cent). Turkmen is one of the Turkic languages

CAPITAL - Ashgabat (population, 407,000, 1990)

MAJOR CITIES – Chardzhou (164,000), Tashauz (114,000), 1990

CURRENCY – Manat of 100 tenesi

NATIONAL DAY – 27–28 October (Independence Day)

NATIONAL FLAG – Green with a vertical carpet pattern near the hoist in black, white and wine-red; and in the lower part of the carpet design two laurel branches; in the upper hoist a crescent and five stars, all in white

LIFE EXPECTANCY (years) – male 61.80; female 68.40

POPULATION GROWTH RATE – 2.0 per cent (1997)

POPULATION DENSITY – 9 per sq. km (1997)

URBAN POPULATION – 45.2 per cent (1989)

MILITARY EXPENDITURE – 2.8 per cent of GDP (1998)

MILITARY PERSONNEL – 19,000: Army 16,000, Air Force 3,000

CONSCRIPTION DURATION – 24 months

ILLITERACY RATE – 2.3 per cent

ENROLMENT (percentage of age group) – tertiary 21.7 per cent (1990)

The republic comprises five regions: Ashgabat; Chardzhou; Krasnovodsk; Mary; and Tashauz. The country is a low-lying plain fringed by hills in the south. Ninety per cent of the plain is taken up by the Obe Kara-Kum (Black Sands) desert. The climate is hot and dry.

HISTORY AND POLITICS

Situated at the crossroads of Central Asia, the area that is now Turkmenistan has been invaded and occupied by many empires: Persian; Greek under Alexander the Great; Parthian; Mongol. From the early 19th century until 1886 Turkmenistan was gradually incorporated into the Russian Empire. Soviet control over Turkmenistan was established on 30 April 1918 when it became an Autonomous Soviet Socialist Republic. The banks, cotton refineries and oil and gas fields were nationalised before a civil war broke out in July 1918, sparked by the intervention of British troops from Iran and India. The war ended in 1920 with the withdrawal of the interventionist forces; Turkmenistan became a full republic of the Soviet Union in February 1925.

Turkmenistan declared its independence from the Soviet Union on 27 October 1991 and gained UN membership on 2 March 1992.

The autocratic government of President Niyazov has prevented any effective political opposition or free press through harassment and the continuation of authoritarianism. The political leadership has rejected political pluralism and instead a cult of personality has developed around President Niyazov. The Supreme Soviet voted on 30 December 1993 to extend the term of President Niyazov to 2002 and this was confirmed by a 99.99 per cent vote in a referendum on 15 January 1994. The Communist Party, renamed the Democratic Party (DP), remains in power. Legislative elections to the *Khalk Maslakhaty* were won by the Democratic Party. General elections were held on 12 December 1999, in which all 50 seats in the *Majlis* were won by candidates of the DP, the sole legal party.

FOREIGN RELATIONS

In 1992 joint Turkmen–Russian armed forces of 34,000 army and air force personnel were established and remain in operation. In late 1993 Turkmen–Russian agreements were signed allowing Russian troops to protect the borders with Iran and Afghanistan; Russian citizens to undergo military training in Turkmenistan; Turkmen officers to train in Russia; and Turkmenistan to bear the cost of Russian forces in the country. Agreement on dual citizenship for ethnic Russians in Turkmenistan was also reached. In December 1993 Turkmenistan signed the CIS charter to become a full CIS member and in January 1994 became a member of the CIS economic union.

POLITICAL SYSTEM

The 1992 constitution declares the president head of state and government. The legislature is the 50-member *Majlis* (formerly the Supreme Soviet). The *Khalk Maslakhaty* (People's Council) is a supervisory body with no legislative powers. The *Majlis* approved an amendment to the constitution on 28 December 1999, allowing President Niyazov to remain in power indefinitely.

HEAD OF STATE

President, Saparmurad Niyazov, *elected* 27 October 1990, *re-elected* 21 June 1992, *appointed head of government* 18 May 1992, *elected by referendum for an eight-year term* 15 January 1994, *term extended indefinitely* 28 December 1999

COUNCIL OF MINISTERS *as at September 2000*

Prime Minister, The President

Deputy PMs, Orazgeldi Aydogdiyev (*Culture*); Amangeldi Atayev (*Energy and Industry*); Rejep Saparov (*Foreign Economic Activity*); Yolly Gurbanmuradov (*Foreign Investment, Chair of State Bank Council on Foreign Economic Activity*); Khudaikuli Orazov (*Interbank Council*); Batyr Sarjayev (*Oil and Gas, Defence*); Chary Yazliev (*Science and Education*); Djamal Geklenova (*Textile Industry*); Khudaykuli Khalykov (*Transport*)

Chairmen, Muhamed Nazarov (*Committee for National Security*); Tirkish Tyrmyev (*State Border Service*); Seyitguly Chareyev (*State Committee for Land Use and Land Reform*); Ilyas Mahtumovich Chariyev (*State Commodity and Raw Materials Exchange*); Ovezgeldy Atayev (*Supreme Court*)

Agriculture, Ananmuhammed Ataev

Communications, Rovshan Kerkavov

Construction Materials Industry, Mukhammetnazar
Khudaygulyyev
Economy and Finance, Matkarim Rajapov
Education, Abat Ryzayeva
Foreign Affairs (acting), Batyr Berdyyev
General Public Prosecutor, Kurbanbibi Atadjanova
Health and the Pharmaceutical Industry, Gurbanguli
Berdymuhamedov
Interior, Poran Berdiev
Justice, Gen. Gurbanmuhamed Kasimov
Natural Resources and Environmental Protection, Pirdjan
Kurbanov
Oil and Gas Industry and Mineral Resources, Rejapbay
Arazov
Social Security, Eylaman Shikhiev
Trade and Foreign Economic Relations, Dortguly Aidogdyev
Transport, Senakuly Rakhmonov
Water Resources, Sahetmurad Gurbanov

EMBASSY OF TURKMENISTAN
2nd Floor South, St George's House, 14/17 Wells Street,
London W1P 3FP
Tel: 020-7255 1071
Ambassador Extraordinary and Plenipotentiary, HE Chary
Babaev, apptd 1999

BRITISH EMBASSY
3rd Floor, Office Building, Four Points Ak Altin Plaza
Hotel, Ashgabat
Tel: (00 993) (1) 510616/510861/510862
E-mail: postmaster@beasb.cat.glasnet.ru
Ambassador Extraordinary and Plenipotentiary, HE Fraser
Wilson, MBE, apptd 1998

ECONOMY

The large reserves of natural gas and the foreign revenue
that they earn make the country economically viable and
have enabled the government to maintain low stable prices
for basic commodities and utilities.

The principal industries are cotton cultivation, stock-
raising and mineral extraction, together with natural gas
production and the long-established silk industry. Some
fisheries exist along the Caspian Sea coast. Arable land is
irrigated by the Niyazov canal, which cuts through the
Kara Kum desert. There are estimated reserves of some
700 million tonnes of oil and 8,000,000 million cubic
metres of natural gas. Natural gas is exported by pipeline
to Ukraine and western Europe. A pipeline through Iran
and Turkey was opened in December 1997, and a pipeline
to Pakistan is under construction. Agreement on building
a further pipeline under the Caspian Sea, through
Azerbaijan and Georgia, to supply gas to Turkey was
reached in November 1999. The European Bank for
Reconstruction and Development announced in April
2000 that it would no longer grant loans to the public
sector in Turkmenistan, as the country had failed to make
any progress in democratisation or market reform. In 1997
there was a trade deficit of US$231 million and a current
account deficit of US$580 million.
GNP – US$2,987 million (1997); US$640 per capita
(1997)
GDP – US$983 million (1996); US$237 per capita (1996)
TOTAL EXTERNAL DEBT – US$2,266 million (1998)

Trade with UK	1998	1999
Imports from UK	£10,155,000	£16,139,000
Exports to UK	554,000	2,763,000

TUVALU

AREA – 10 sq. miles (26 sq. km)
POPULATION – 10,000 (1997 UN estimate). About 1,500

Tuvaluans work overseas, mostly in Nauru, or as
seamen. The people are almost entirely Polynesian.
The principal languages are Tuvaluan and English.
A large majority of the population is Christian,
predominantly Protestant
CAPITAL – ΨFunafuti (population, 2,856)
CURRENCY – The Australian dollar ($A) of 100 cents is
legal tender. In addition there are Tuvalu dollar and cent
coins in circulation
NATIONAL ANTHEM – Tuvalu Mo Te Atua (Tuvalu for the
Almighty)
NATIONAL DAY – 1 October (Independence Day)
NATIONAL FLAG – Light blue ground with Union flag in
top left quarter and nine five-pointed gold stars in the fly
POPULATION GROWTH RATE – 1.5 per cent (1997)
POPULATION DENSITY – 385 per sq. km (1997)

Tuvalu comprises nine coral atolls situated in the south-
west Pacific around the point at which the International
Date Line cuts the Equator. Few of the atolls are more
than 12 ft above sea level or more than half a mile in width.
The vegetation consists mainly of coconut palms.

HISTORY AND POLITICS

Tuvalu, formerly the Ellice Islands, formed part of the
Gilbert and Ellice Islands Colony until 1 October 1975,
when separate constitutions came into force. Separation
from the Gilbert Islands was implemented on 1 January
1976. On 1 October 1978 Tuvalu became a fully independent state within the Commonwealth.

In April 1998, Prime Minister Bikenibeu Paeniu was
sworn in for a second term of office; he was forced to
resign following his defeat in a motion of no confidence on
15 April 1999 and on 27 April was succeeded by Ionatana
Ionatana.

Tuvalu became a full member of the UN on 17 February
2000.

POLITICAL SYSTEM

The constitution provides for a prime minister and four
other ministers, who must be members of the 13-member
parliament, 12 of whom are directly elected. The prime
minister presides at meetings of the Cabinet, which consists of the five Ministers and is attended by the Attorney-
General. Local government services are provided by
elected Island Councils.
Governor-General, Sir Tomasi Puapua

CABINET *as at September 2000*
Prime Minister, Foreign Affairs, Tourism, Trade, Commerce,
Ionatana Ionatana
Deputy PM, Finance and Economic Planning, Lagitupu
Tuilimu
Attorney-General, Teleti Teo
*Education, Sports and Culture, Health, Women's and
Community Affairs*, Teagai Esekia
*Home Affairs and Rural Development, Natural Resources and
Environment*, Faimalaga Luka
Works, Energy and Communications, Samuelu Penitala Teo
BRITISH HIGH COMMISSIONER, HE M. Dibben,
resident at Suva, Fiji

ECONOMY

Most people still practise a subsistence economy, the main
staples of the diet being coconuts and fish. The main
imports are foodstuffs, semi-manufactures, machinery
and transport equipment and fuels. The main exports are
copra and fish, though philatelic sales provide a major
source of revenue and handicraft sales are increasing.
However, Tuvalu is almost entirely dependent on foreign
aid. In August 1998, Tuvalu signed a deal worth about

US$50 million over ten years with a US media company, granting rights to use the country's internet suffix of ".tv".

Funafuti has an airfield from which a service operates regularly to Fiji and Kiribati, and is also the only port.

GDP – US$13 million (1996); US$1,315 per capita (1995)

Trade with UK	1997	1996
Imports from UK	£306,000	£51,000
Exports to UK	584,000	33,000

SOCIAL WELFARE

All islands are served by a dispensary and a primary school. A maritime training school caters for 60 boys a year. There is a 30-bed hospital at Funafuti.

UGANDA
Republic of Uganda

AREA – 93,065 sq. miles (241,038 sq. km). Neighbours: Democratic Republic of Congo (west), Sudan (north), Kenya (east), Tanzania and Rwanda (south)

POPULATION – 20,438,000 (1997 UN estimate): 17 per cent Baganda, 12 per cent Karamojong; many other ethnic groups including Basogo, Iteso, Langi, Rwanda, Bagisu, Acholi, Lugbara, Bunyoro and Batobo. The official language is English. The main local vernaculars are of Bantu, Nilotic and Hamitic origins. Ki-Swahili is generally understood

CAPITAL – Kampala (population, 750,000, 1990)

MAJOR CITIES – Jinja (45,000); Masaka (29,000); Mbale (28,000)

CURRENCY – Uganda shilling of 100 cents

NATIONAL ANTHEM – Oh Uganda

NATIONAL DAY – 9 October (Independence Day)

NATIONAL FLAG – Six horizontal stripes of black, yellow, red, with a white disc in the centre containing the badge of a crested crane

LIFE EXPECTANCY (years) – male 39.97; female 42.03

POPULATION GROWTH RATE – 2.9 per cent (1997)

POPULATION DENSITY – 85 per sq. km (1997)

URBAN POPULATION – 14.5 per cent (1997)

MILITARY EXPENDITURE – 3.1 per cent of GDP (1998)

MILITARY PERSONNEL – 40,000: Ugandan People's Defence Force 40,000; Paramilitaries 600

Large parts of Lakes Victoria, Edward and Albert (Mobuto) are within Uganda's boundaries, as are Lakes Kyoga, Kwania, George and Bisina (formerly Salisbury) and the course of the River Nile from its outlet from Lake Victoria to the Sudan border at Nimule.

Despite its tropical location, the climate is tempered by its situation some 3,000 ft above sea level, and well over that altitude in the highlands of the Western and Eastern Regions. Uganda has three National Parks and a fourth (Lake Mburo) has been designated.

HISTORY AND POLITICS

Uganda became an independent state within the Commonwealth on 9 October 1962, after some 70 years of British rule. A republic was instituted in 1967, under an executive president assisted by a Cabinet of Ministers.

In 1971 an army coup took place and Maj.-Gen. Idi Amin, the army commander, proclaimed himself head of state. In 1979, following uprisings and military intervention by Tanzania, President Amin was overthrown. Dr Milton Obote became president in 1980 but was ousted by a military coup in 1985. A military council was installed but the National Resistance Movement led by Yoweri Museveni captured Kampala in January 1986, securing control of the rest of the country in the following few months. Yoweri Museveni was sworn in as president in January 1986.

President Museveni won the first direct presidential election on 9 May 1996. Supporters of the president won a majority of seats in legislative elections on 27 June. The ban on political party activity introduced by President Museveni in 1986, was endorsed in a referendum held on 29 June 2000, in which 90.7 per cent of those voting backed the continuation of the no party 'Movement' system, in which political parties were allowed to exist, but not to contest elections.

POLITICAL SYSTEM

A Constituent Assembly was elected in March 1994 to draft a new constitution. The constitution, promulgated on 8 October 1995, endorsed the existing non-party political system. The president, who is head of government, is directly elected for a five-year term. The legislature, the 276-seat National Assembly, is also directly elected for a five-year term; 214 members are elected by constituencies and 62 are elected indirectly to represent particular groups.

HEAD OF STATE

President, Yoweri Museveni, *sworn in* 29 January 1986, *elected* 9 May 1996

Vice-President, Specioza Wandira Kazibwe

CABINET *as at September 2000*

The President

The Vice-President

Prime Minister, Apolo Nsibambi

First Deputy PM, Foreign Affairs, Eriya Kategaya

Second Deputy PM, Tourism, Trade and Industry, Brig. Moses Ali

Ministers in the Office of the President, Kweronda Ruhemba (*Economic Monitoring*); Miria Matembe (*Ethics and Integrity*); Basoga Nsadhu (*Information*); Elizabeth Okwir (*Office of the Vice-President*); Ruhakana Rugunda (*Presidency*); Wilson Muruli Mukasa (*Security*)

Agriculture, Animal Industry and Fisheries, Kisamba Mugwera

Attorney-General, Bart Katureebe

Disaster Preparedness and Refugees, Maj. Tom Butiime

Education and Sports, Kiddu Makubuya

Energy and Minerals, Syda Bbumba

Finance, Planning and Economic Development, Gerald Sendawula

Gender, Labour and Social Development, Janet B. Mukwaya

Health, Dr Crispus W. C. B. Kiyonga

Internal Affairs, Edward Rugumayo

Justice and Constitutional Affairs, Joshua Mayanja-Nkangi

Local Government, Jaberi Bidandi-Ssalli

Parliamentary Affairs, Rebecca Kadaga

Public Service, Amanya Mushega

Water, Lands and Environment, Henry Muganwa Kajura

Works, Housing and Communications, John Nassasira

UGANDA HIGH COMMISSION

Uganda House, 58–59 Trafalgar Square, London WC2N 5DX

Tel: 020-7839 5783

High Commissioner, HE Prof. George Kirya, apptd 1990

Deputy High Commissioner, D. Ssozi

First Secretary, D. Nyakairu *(Commercial)*

Financial Attaché, A. Bamweyana

BRITISH HIGH COMMISSION

10–12 Parliament Avenue, PO Box 7070, Kampala

Tel: (00 256) (41) 257054/9

E-mail: bhcinfo@starcom.co.ug

High Commissioner, HE Michael Cook, apptd 1997

Deputy High Commissioner, P. Rouse, MBE

Defence Adviser, Lt.-Col. C. Thom, OBE

BRITISH COUNCIL DIRECTOR, S. Beaumont *(First*

Secretary), c/o British High Commission;
e-mail: bc.kampala@bc-kampala.swiftuganda.com

ECONOMY

Since 1988 the government has been successfully implementing an IMF recovery programme. In April 1998 the IMF and the World Bank agreed to grant Uganda debt relief totalling some US$360 million. In December 1998, the IMF pledged US$2.2 billion in economic assistance over a three-year period. On 8 February 2000, the IMF pledged a further US$139 million in debt relief, and the International Development Association (IDA) announced that it would give assistance of US$629 million over 20 years. In March, donor countries pledged at least US$2,000 million over three years to support economic development.

The principal export earners are coffee, tobacco, cotton and tea. Hydroelectricity is produced from the Owen Falls power station, some of which is exported to Kenya, Tanzania and Rwanda. The principal food crops are plantains, sugar cane, cassava, maize and sorghum; livestock raising and inshore fishing are also important.

In 1997 Uganda had a trade deficit of US$467 million and a current account deficit of US$388 million. In 1998 imports totalled US$1,409 million and exports US$512 million.

GNP – US$6,566 million (1998); US$310 per capita (1998)
GDP – US$6,170 million (1996); US$305 per capita (1996)
ANNUAL AVERAGE GROWTH OF GDP – 5.9 per cent (1996)
INFLATION RATE – 7.0 per cent (1997)
Total EXTERNAL DEBT – US$3,935 million (1998)

Trade with UK	1998	1999
Imports from UK	£45,643,000	£37,192,000
Exports to UK	16,453,000	10,706,000

COMMUNICATIONS

There is an international airport at Entebbe, and eight other airfields around the country. Having no sea coast, Uganda is dependent upon rail and road links to Mombasa and Dar es Salaam for its trade. There are more than 27,000 km of roads. A railway network joins the capital to the western, eastern and northern centres.

EDUCATION

Education is a joint undertaking by the government, local authorities and voluntary agencies. In 1995 Uganda had an estimated 7,905 primary schools, 774 secondary schools, and various technical training institutions and universities. In 1996, the Universal Primary Programme was launched, under which four children per family are entitled to receive free primary education.
ILLITERACY RATE – 32.7 per cent
ENROLMENT (percentage of age group) – tertiary
2 per cent (1996)

UKRAINE
Ukraïna

AREA – 233,090 sq. miles (603,700 sq. km). Neighbours: Belarus (north), Russia (north and east), Romania and Moldova (south-west), Hungary, Slovakia and Poland (west)
POPULATION – 50,500,000 (2000 estimate); 51,471,000 (1989 census): 73 per cent Ukrainian, 22 per cent Russian, with smaller numbers of Jews, Belarusians, Moldovans, Tatars, Poles, Hungarians and Greeks. The majority religion is Orthodox Christianity. There are also large numbers of Uniates and Reformed Protestants in the Transcarpathian region and a sizeable Jewish community in Kiev. The official language is Ukrainian. Russian is the language of 22 per cent of the population
CAPITAL – Kiev (population, 2,622,000, 1997 estimate)
MAJOR CITIES – Dnipropetrovsk (1,134,000); Donetsk (1,075,000); Kharkiv (1,536,000); Lviv (797,000), ΨOdesa (1,037,000), Zaporizhzhya (871,000), 1997 estimates
CURRENCY – Hryvna of 100 kopiykas
NATIONAL ANTHEM – Shche ne vmerla, Ukraïna (Thou hast not perished, Ukraine)
NATIONAL DAY – 24 August (Independence Day)
NATIONAL FLAG – Two horizontal stripes of blue over yellow
LIFE EXPECTANCY (years) – male 62.78; female 73.15
POPULATION GROWTH RATE – –0.3 per cent (1997)
POPULATION DENSITY – 84 per sq. km (1997)
URBAN POPULATION – 67.6 per cent (1995)
ILLITERACY RATE – 1.2 per cent
ENROLMENT (percentage of age group) – tertiary
42 per cent (1995)

The area of the present Ukraine is larger than that of the Ukrainian Soviet Republic formed in 1917–19 because of the westward territorial expansion of the former Soviet Union in the 1939–45 period and the addition of the Crimea from Russia in 1954. Ukraine now consists of 25 regions: Cherkasy, Chernihiv, Chernivtsi, Crimea, Dnipropetrovsk, Donetsk, Ivano-Frankivsk, Kharkiv, Kherson, Khmelnytsky, Kiev, Kirovohrad, Luhansk, Lviv, Mykolaïv, Odesa, Poltava, Rivne, Sumy, Ternopil, Transcarpathia, Vinnitsa, Volhynia, Zaporizhya and Zhytomyr.

Most of Ukraine forms a plain with small elevations. The Carpathian mountains lie in the south-western part of the republic. The main rivers are the Dnieper with its tributaries, the Southern Bug and the Northern Donets (a tributary of the Don). The climate is moderate with relatively mild winters (particularly in the south-west) and hot summers.

HISTORY AND POLITICS

The earliest Russian state was formed in the middle reaches of the Dnieper River with its capital at Kiev in the ninth century AD. The state lasted until Kiev fell to the Mongols in 1240. For the next four centuries Ukraine was invaded and ruled by Tatars, Turks, Poles, Hungarians and Lithuanians. During the reign of Catherine the Great of Russia (1763–96) Ukraine and the Crimea came under Russian control.

Ukraine became a battleground in the Russian civil war before the imposition of Soviet rule in 1922. Ukraine became a constituent republic of the USSR on 30 December 1922.

Ukraine declared itself independent of the Soviet Union, subject to a referendum, after the failed Moscow coup in August 1991. The referendum was held on 1 December 1991 and 90 per cent of the electorate voted for independence.

Political power in Ukraine in 1991–4 rested with the former Communists, led by President Leonid Kravchuk, in loose alliance with the Rukh nationalist party.

In the June 1994 presidential election Leonid Kuchma defeated President Kravchuk. A new constitution was adopted in June 1996. Following a constitutional amendment in September 1997, half of the 450 Supreme Council seats are to be elected from single-seat constituencies by a simple majority, and the other 225 are to be filled by proportional representation from party lists, with a 4 per cent barrier for representation.

In legislative elections held in March 1998, the Communist Party of Ukraine won 119 seats, well short of an overall majority, but making it the largest party in the legislature. The Popular Democratic Party won 84 seats, and the People's Movement of Ukraine 46. OSCE observers noted serious shortcomings in the electoral process, including violence and discrimination against certain candidates that 'raise[d] questions about the neutrality of the state apparatus in the election'.

President Kuchma won a second term of office in presidential elections on 14 November 1999, receiving 56.25 per cent of the vote.

In January 2000, the Supreme Council split into two factions following a failed attempt by the pro-government faction to remove the Speaker, Oleksandr Tkachenko, from office. The minority left-wing faction remained in control of the Supreme Council building, while the pro-government majority faction met in a different building until 8 February when they forcibly took control of the Supreme Council building.

A constitutional referendum was held on 16 April 2000, in which a large majority of those who voted approved changes to the constitution which would allow the dissolution of the Supreme Council if it failed to form a majority administration or adopt a budget, limit deputies' immunity, reduce the number of deputies from 450 to 300 and introduce a bicameral legislature.

INSURGENCIES

The Crimean parliament voted to make Crimea an autonomous republic in September 1991, which was accepted by Kiev, but then voted for independence in May 1992, which was not accepted, and was suspended. A constitutional and political crisis in Crimea caused by a power struggle between the Russian Nationalist President Meshkov and the Crimean parliament from September 1994 onwards was resolved by Ukrainian intervention in March 1995. Direct presidential rule over Crimea was imposed in April 1995, to be lifted in August following elections to the Crimean parliament which saw a dramatic drop in support for pro-Russian parties. Arkady Demydenko was appointed Prime Minister of Crimea on 26 February 1996. A new constitution, which gave Crimea property and budget rights, came into effect in January 1999.

A referendum in June 1994 in the Donbass region of eastern Ukraine in favour of closer economic ties with Russia and making Russian an official language was overwhelmingly passed, as was one in the Crimea in favour of dual Russian–Ukrainian citizenship.

FOREIGN RELATIONS

Since the demise of the Soviet Union, Russia and Ukraine have clashed over defence issues. All strategic nuclear weapons were placed under a central CIS command in December 1991, but on the abolition of the central command in July 1993 the government claimed possession of all nuclear weapons on its territory. Despite international pressure, the Supreme Council only ratified the START I Treaty in February 1994 and the Nuclear Non-Proliferation Treaty in November 1994.

Under a January 1994 USA–Russia–Ukraine Treaty, Ukraine agreed to transfer its nuclear arsenal to Russia for dismantling over a seven-year period. This was completed in May 1996. In return Ukraine has received a territorial guarantee from Russia, a cancellation of a large part of its debt to Russia, and nuclear security guarantees from Russia and the USA. Ukraine will also receive low-grade uranium from Russia for use in its power stations; and economic and technical aid from the USA.

In May 1997, a treaty of friendship and co-operation was signed with Russia. Agreement was also reached over the division of the former Soviet Black Sea Fleet. Russia is to gain four-fifths of the fleet and will rent most of the port of Sevastopol. The rent will be used to pay off part of Ukraine's debt to Russia.

In February 1998, a treaty on economic co-operation was signed between Ukraine and Russia which will increase trade between them by up to US$2 billion. It was announced in September 1997 that there would be annual summits for EU–Ukraine relations.

HEAD OF STATE

President, Leonid Kuchma, *elected* 10 July 1994, *sworn in* 19 July 1994, *re-elected* 14 November 1999

CABINET *as at September 2000*

Prime Minister, Viktor Yushchenko
First Deputy PM, Mykhaylo Hladiy
Deputy PMs, Yuri Yekhanurov *(Economic Issues)*; Yuliya Tymoshenko *(Fuel and Energy Complex)*; Mykola Zhulynskyy
Agriculture, Ivan Kyrylenko
Culture and Art, Bohdan Stupka
Defence, Gen. Oleksandr Kuzmuk
Economy, Vasyl Rohovyy
Education and Science, Vasyl Kremen
Emergency Situations and Protection of the Population from the aftermath of Chernobyl, Vasyl Durdanynets
Energy and Fuel, Serhiy Yermilov
Environment and Natural Resources, vacant
Finance, Ihor Mityukov
Foreign Affairs, Boris Tarasyuk
Health Protection, Vitaliy Moskalenko
Interior, Yurii Kravchenko
Justice, Syuzanna Stanik
Labour and Social Policy, Ivan Sakhan
Transport, Leonid Kostyuchenko

There are also 11 heads of state committees.

UKRAINIAN EMBASSY

60 Holland Park, London W11 3SJ
Tel: 020-7727 6312
Ambassador Extraordinary and Plenipotentiary, HE Volodymyr Vassylenko, apptd 1998
Minister Plenipotentiary, Y. Kyrylenko

BRITISH EMBASSY

UA-252025 Kiev Desyatinna 9
Tel: (00 380) (44) 462 0011/2/4
E-mail: ukembinf@sovam.com
Ambassador Extraordinary and Plenipotentiary, HE Roland Smith, CMG, apptd 1999
Consul-General and Deputy Head of Mission, S. Butt
Defence Attaché, Capt. M. Littleboy
First Secretary (Commercial), R. Cook

BRITISH COUNCIL DIRECTOR – M. Bird, 9/1 Besarabska Ploshcha, Flat 9, UA-252004 Kiev;
e-mail: bc.ukraine@bc.kiev.ua.
There are regional offices in Donetsk, Kharkiv, Lviv and Odesa

DEFENCE

The Army has 4,014 main battle tanks, 1,823 armoured personnel carriers, 3,079 armoured infantry fighting vehicles and 236 attack helicopters. The Navy has one submarines, eight principal surface combat vessels and eight patrol and coastal vessels at six bases. The Air Force has 521 combat aircraft.
MILITARY EXPENDITURE – 2.9 per cent of GDP (1998)
MILITARY PERSONNEL – 311,400: Army 154,900, Navy 13,000, Air Force 100,00; Paramilitaries 116,600
CONSCRIPTION DURATION – 18 months to two years

ECONOMY

The Communist-led government of 1991–4 was characterised by economic mismanagement and opposition to economic reforms. The economy came close to collapse because of hyperinflation, industrial output and GDP fell dramatically, and Russia threatened to cut all oil and gas supplies as Ukraine could not pay in hard currency. Ukraine has joined the CIS economic union as an associate member and is likely to seek full membership for access to better trading relations with Russia.

President Kuchma has introduced a wide-ranging economic reform programme. Ukraine has received large amounts of foreign aid in support of this programme and for the closure of the Chernobyl nuclear plant which suffered a partial meltdown in 1986 and which, it was announced in June 2000, would finally close on 15 December 2000. Continuing economic difficulties led to the devaluation of the hryvna in February 1999. In March 2000, the IMF issued an interim statement about the alleged misuse of foreign currency reserves, saying that Ukraine had received IMF funds in 1997–8 that it would not have received had the true state of the country's reserves been known. The IMF has suspended its loan programme to Ukraine until investigations are completed.

Ukraine is still in disagreement with Russia over the division of assets and debts of the former Soviet Union. A large proportion of Ukraine's debt to Russia has been paid by granting Russian enterprises shares in Ukrainian firms which are to be privatised; the remainder of the debt has been rescheduled. Russia accounts for 40 per cent of Ukraine's trade turnover and supplies all its oil needs and more than half of its industrial raw materials and components. Agreement was reached with Turkey in June 1997 to build an oil pipeline which will reduce Ukraine's dependence on Russia. In May 1998 Ukraine signed an agreement with the USA allowing it to import the technology necessary to modernise its nuclear power industry.

The southern part of the country contains a coal-mining and iron and steel industrial area. Ukraine also contains engineering and chemical industries and ship-building yards on the Black Sea coast. Ukrainian agricultural production is good with large areas under cultivation with wheat, cotton, flax and sugar beet; stock-raising is very important. There are large deposits of coal and salt in the Donets Basin, of iron ore in Kryvyi Rih and near Kerch in the Crimea, of manganese in Nikopol, and of quicksilver in Nikitovka.

The major ports are Odesa, Mykolaïv, Kerch and Sevastopol.

In 1997 there was a trade deficit of US$2,584 million and a current account deficit of US$1,296 million. In 1996, imports totalled US$18,639 million and exports US$14,441 million.

GNP – US$49,207 million (1998); US$980 per capita (1998)
GDP – US$44,007 million (1996); US$853 per capita (1996)
INFLATION RATE – 15.9 per cent (1997)
TOTAL EXTERNAL DEBT – US$12,718 million (1998)

Trade with UK	1998	1999
Imports from UK	£168,821,000	£145,449,000
Exports to UK	50,762,000	48,494,000

UNITED ARAB EMIRATES
Dawlat Al-Amārat Al-'Arabiyya Al-Muttahida

AREA – 32,278 sq. miles (83,600 sq. km) approximately.
  Neighbours: Oman (north-east and east), Saudi Arabia (south and west), Qatar (north-west)
POPULATION – 2,940,000 (1999 estimate), of which 75 per cent are expatriates. The official language is Arabic, and English is widely spoken. The established religion is Islam
CAPITAL – Abu Dhabi (Abū aby) (population, 450,000)
CURRENCY – UAE dirham (Dh) of 100 fils
NATIONAL DAY – 2 December
NATIONAL FLAG – Horizontal stripes of green over white over black with vertical red stripe in the hoist

LIFE EXPECTANCY (years) – male 72.95; female 75.27
POPULATION GROWTH RATE – 6.5 per cent (1999)
POPULATION DENSITY – 31 per sq. km (1997)

The United Arab Emirates is situated in the south-east of the Arabian peninsula. Six of the emirates lie on the shore of the Gulf between the Musandam peninsula in the east and the Qatar peninsula in the west while the seventh, Fujairah, lies on the Gulf of Oman. The climate varies between hot and humid in May to September and mild with erratic rainfall in October to April.

HISTORY AND POLITICS

The United Arab Emirates (formerly the Trucial States) is composed of seven emirates (Abu Dhabi, Ajman, Dubai, Fujairah, Ras al-Khaimah, Sharjah and Umm al-Qaiwain) which came together as an independent state on 2 December 1971 when they ended their individual special treaty relationships with the British government (Ras al-Khaimah joined the other six on 10 February 1972). On independence, the Union Government assumed full responsibility for all internal and external affairs apart from some internal matters that remained the prerogative of the individual emirates.

FOREIGN RELATIONS

Relations with Iran remain strained over Iran's illegal occupation of three UAE islands in the Gulf (Abu Musa and the Two Tunbs).

POLITICAL SYSTEM

Overall authority lies with the Supreme Council of the seven emirate rulers, each of whom also governs in his own territory. The president and vice-president are elected every five years by the Supreme Council from among its members. The Supreme Council appoints the Council of Ministers. A 40-member Federal National Council, drawn proportionately from each emirate and composed of appointees of the rulers, studies draft laws referred to it by the Council of Ministers.

The legal system consists of both secular and religious courts guided by the Islamic philosophy of justice. Individual emirates retain their own penal codes and courts alongside a federal court system and penal code.

FEDERAL STRUCTURE

Each emirate has its separate government, with Abu Dhabi having an executive council chaired by the Crown Prince.

Emirate	Area (sq. km)	Population (1997)
Abu Dhabi (Abū Żaby)	80,000	1,017,000
Ajman ('Ujman)	259	137,000
Dubai (Dubayy)	3,900	757,000
Fujairah (Al-Fujayrah)	1,300	83,000
Ras al-Khaimah (Ra's al-Khaymah)	1,700	152,000
Sharjah (Ash-Shariqah)	2,600	439,000
Umm al-Qaiwain (Umm al-Qaywayn)	777	39,000

HEAD OF STATE

President, HH Sheikh Zayed bin Sultan al-Nahyan (*Abu Dhabi*), *elected* 1971, *re-elected* 1976, 1981, 1986, 1991, October 1996
Vice-President, Prime Minister, HH Sheikh Maktoum bin Rashid al-Maktoum (*Dubai*)

SUPREME COUNCIL

The President
The Vice-President
HH Sheikh Sultan bin Mohammed al-Qassimi (*Sharjah*)
HH Sheikh Saqr bin Mohammed al-Qassimi (*Ras Al-Khaimah*)
HH Sheikh Hamad bin Mohammed al-Sharqi (*Fujairah*)
HH Sheikh Humaid bin Rashid al-Nuaimi (*Ajman*)

HH Sheikh Rashid bin Ahmad al-Mualla (*Umm al-Qaiwain*)

COUNCIL OF MINISTERS *as at September 2000*

The Vice-President
Deputy PM, Sheikh Sultan bin Zayed al-Nahyan
Agriculture and Fisheries, Saeed Mohammed al-Raqabani
Communications, Ahmed Humaid al-Tayir
Defence, HH Gen. Sheikh Mohammed bin Rashid al-Maktoum
Economy and Commerce, HH Sheikh Fahim bin Sultan al-Qassimi
Education and Youth, Ali Abd al-Aziz al-Sharhan
Electricity and Water, Humaid bin Nasir al-Uways
Finance and Industry, HH Sheikh Hamdan bin Rashid al-Maktoum
Economy and Commerce, HH Sheikh Fahim bin Sultan al-Qassimi
Education and Youth, Ali Abd al-Aziz al-Sharhan
Electricity and Water, Humaid bin Nasir al-Uways
Finance and Industry, HH Sheikh Hamdan bin Rashid al-Maktoum
Foreign Affairs, Rashid Abdullah al-Nuaimi
Health, Hamad Abdul Rahman al-Madfa
Higher Education and Scientific Research, HH Sheikh Nahyan bin Mubarak al-Nahyan
Information and Culture, HH Sheikh Abdullah bin Zayed al-Nahyan
Interior, Lt.-Gen. Mohammed Saeed al-Badi
Justice, Islamic Affairs and Awqaf (Religious Endowments), Mohammed Nakhira al-Dhahiri
Labour and Social Affairs, Matar Humaid al-Tayir
Minister of State for Cabinet Affairs, Saeed Khalfan al-Ghaith
Minister of State for Finance and Industrial Affairs, Dr Mohammed Khalfan bin Kharbash
Minister of State for Foreign Affairs, HH Sheikh Hamdan bin Zayed al-Nahyan
Minister of State for Supreme Council Affairs, HH Sheikh Majid bin Saeed al-Nuaimi
Petroleum and Mineral Resources, Ubayd bin Sayf al-Nasiri
Planning, HH Sheikh Humaid bin Ahmed al-Mualla
Public Works and Housing, Rakadh bin Salem al-Rakadh

EMBASSY OF THE UNITED ARAB EMIRATES
30 Princes Gate, London SW7 1PT
Tel 020-75811281
Ambassador Extraordinary and Plenipotentiary, HE Easa Saleh al-Gurg, CBE, apptd 1991
Military Attaché, Col. M. K. S. al-Hamadi
Cultural Attaché, A. al-Marri

BRITISH EMBASSIES
PO Box 248, Abu Dhabi
Tel: (00 971) (2) 326600
Ambassador Extraordinary and Plenipotentiary, HE Patrick Nixon, CMG, OBE, apptd 1998
Counsellor and Deputy Head of Mission, G. Pirnie
Defence and Military Attaché, Col. T. Dumas, OBE

PO Box 65, Dubai
Tel: (00 971) (4) 397 1070
Counsellor and Consul-General, N. Armour
Deputy Head of Mission, N. E. Cole, OBE

BRITISH COUNCIL DIRECTOR, R. Sykes, Villa no. 7, Al-Nasr Street, Khalidiya, PO Box 46523, Abu Dhabi; e-mail: information@ae.britcoun.org.
There is also an office in Dubai

DEFENCE

The Army has 237 main battle tanks, 570 armoured personnel carriers and 433 armoured infantry fighting vehicles. The Navy has 19 patrol and coastal vessels. The Air Force has 99 combat aircraft and 49 armed helicopters.

MILITARY EXPENDITURE – 2.9 per cent of GDP (1998)
MILITARY PERSONNEL – 64,500: Army 59,000, Navy 1,500, Air Force 4,000

ECONOMY

The UAE is the Gulf's third largest oil producer after Saudi Arabia and Iran, with oil reserves of 98,200 million barrels and gas reserves of 5,800 million cubic metres. Oil production in 1998 accounted for 21.7 per cent of GDP. Other important sectors of the economy are manufacturing (aluminium, cement, chemicals, fertilisers, ship repair), government services, construction, transport, communications and financial services. Tourism is growing in importance, with 1,919,000 visitors in 1994. Agricultural production (vegetables, dates, fruit, eggs, flowers, olives, animal husbandry) has increased due to large-scale water desalination and irrigation projects, with 250,000 hectares of agricultural land in 1996. There is no personal or corporate taxation apart from on oil companies and foreign banks. There are several free zones, where overseas companies can trade tax-free.

Fifteen major ports, of which nine are modern container terminals, handled 35 million tonnes of cargo in 1993. Six international airports (Dubai, Abu Dhabi, Sharjah, Ras al-Khaimah, Fujairah, Al Ain) are in operation.

Oil revenues over the past 30 years have enabled the government to invest heavily in education, health and social services, housing, transport and communications infrastructure, and agriculture, and enabled the UAE's citizens to have one of the highest GDPs per capita in the world.
GDP – US$44,607 million (1996); US$19,738 per capita (1996)
ANNUAL AVERAGE GROWTH OF GDP – 9.9 per cent (1996)

Trade with UK	1998	1999
Imports from UK	£1,562,540,000	£1,402,947,000
Exports to UK	459,111,000	666,536,000

EDUCATION AND SOCIAL WELFARE

In 1997 there were 668 government schools, where education is free; and 400 private schools. There are five universities. There were 41 hospitals in 1997.
ILLITERACY RATE – 23.5 per cent
ENROLMENT (percentage of age group) – primary 78 per cent (1996); secondary 71 per cent (1996); tertiary 11.9 per cent (1996)

UNITED STATES OF AMERICA

AREA – 3,536,338 sq. miles (9,159,116 sq. km).
Neighbours: Canada (north), Mexico (south)
POPULATION – 274,520,000 (2000 estimate). The language is English. There is a significant Spanish-speaking minority
CAPITAL – Washington DC (population, 7,285,206, 1998 estimate). The area of the District of Columbia (with which the City of Washington is considered co-extensive) is 61 sq. miles, with a resident population (1998 estimate) of 523,124. The District of Columbia is governed by an elected mayor and City Council
MAJOR CITIES –ΨChicago (2,802,079); Dallas (1,075,894); ΨDetroit (970,196); ΨHouston (1,786,691); ΨLos Angeles (3,597,556); ΨNew York (7,420,166); ΨPhiladelphia (1,436,287); Phoenix (1,198,064); San Antonio (1,114,130); ΨSan Diego (1,220,666), 1998 estimates
CURRENCY – US dollar (US$) of 100 cents
NATIONAL ANTHEM – The Star-Spangled Banner
NATIONAL DAY – 4 July (Independence Day)

NATIONAL FLAG – Thirteen horizontal stripes, alternately red and white, with blue canton in the hoist showing 50 white stars in nine horizontal rows of six and five alternately (known as the Star-Spangled Banner)
LIFE EXPECTANCY (years) – male 72.50; female 78.90
POPULATION GROWTH RATE – 1.0 per cent (1997)
POPULATION DENSITY – 29 per sq. km (1997)
URBAN POPULATION – 75.2 per cent (1990)

The coastline has a length of about 2,069 miles on the Atlantic, 7,623 miles on the Pacific, 1,060 miles on the Arctic, and 1,631 miles on the Gulf of Mexico.

The principal river is the Mississippi-Missouri-Red (3,710 miles long), traversing the whole country to its mouth in the Gulf of Mexico; its main affluents are the Yellowstone, Platte, Arkansas, and Ohio rivers. The chain of the Rocky Mountains separates the western portion of the country from the remainder. West of these, bordering the Pacific coast, the Cascade Mountains and Sierra Nevada form the outer edge of a high tableland, consisting in part of stony and sandy desert and partly of grazing land and forested mountains, and including the Great Salt Lake, which extends to the Rocky Mountains. In the eastern states large forests still exist, the remnants of the forests which formerly extended over all the Atlantic slope. The highest point is Mount McKinley (20,320 ft) in Alaska, and the lowest point of dry land is in Death Valley (Inyo, California), 282 ft below sea level.

AREA AND POPULATION

	Total land area 1990 (sq. km)	Population census 1990
The United States (a)	9,159,116	248,709,873
Outlying areas under US jurisdiction	10,929	3,862,431
Territories	10,888	3,862,238
Puerto Rico	8,875	3,522,037
Guam	544	133,152
US Virgin Islands	346	101,809
American Samoa	200	46,773
Northern Mariana Is.	464	43,345
Other US possessions	41	193
Population abroad (b)	–	925,845
TOTAL	9,170,045	253,498,149

(a) the 50 states and the Federal District of Columbia
(b) excludes US citizens temporarily abroad on business

RESIDENT POPULATION BY RACE 2000 ESTIMATE (Thousands)

White	225,825
Black	35,197
*American Indian	2,425
Asian and Pacific Islanders	11,073
†Hispanic origin	32,166
Total	274,520

*Includes Eskimo and Aleut
†Persons of Hispanic origin may be of any race

IMMIGRATION

From 1820 to 1998, 64,599,082 immigrants were admitted to the United States. Total number of immigrants in 1998 was 660,477, of which 298,390 came from North and South America (131,575 from Mexico), 219,696 from Asia and 90,793 from Europe.

HISTORY AND POLITICS

The area which is now the USA was first inhabited by nomadic hunters who probably arrived from Asia c.30,000 BC. The first (failed) European colony was founded by Sir Walter Raleigh in 1585. By 1733 there were 13 British colonies, composed largely of religious non-conformists who had left Britain to escape persecution; the French and Spanish had also founded colonies. Relations between the colonies reflected tensions and conflicts between the European powers in the 17th and 18th centuries; from 1689 to 1763 the French, with native Indians, frequently attacked British settlements. In accordance with the Peace of Paris (1763) Britain returned Cuba and the Philippines to Spain and received Florida in return and France ceded New Orleans and (until 1800) Louisiana to Spain.

The War of Independence broke out in 1775 largely because of the colonists' objection to being taxed by, but having no representation in, the British Parliament. The forces of the British government were defeated with French, Spanish and Dutch assistance. The Declaration of Independence which inaugurated the United States of America was signed on 4 July 1776; Britain recognised American sovereignty in 1783. The first federal constitution was drawn up in 1787; ten amendments, termed the Bill of Rights, were added in 1791. The 13 original states of the Union ratified the constitution between 1787 and 1790. Vermont, Kentucky and Tennessee were admitted in the 1790s but most of the states acceded in the 19th century as the opening up of the centre and west led to the creation of new states and European or neighbouring countries ceded or sold their territories to the USA.

The Civil War (1861–5) was fought over the issue of slavery, which was integral to the economy of the southern states but was opposed by the northern states. The northern states defeated the Confederacy of southern states (South Carolina, Georgia, Alabama, Florida, Mississippi, Louisiana), all of which had seceded from the Union between 1860 and 1861; they all re-entered the Union by 1870.

The USA emerged as a world economic and military superpower in the 20th century and played a decisive role in the two world wars, in which it was engaged between 1917 and 1918, and between 1941 and 1945. Its economic and military (including nuclear) supremacy gave the USA a key role in shaping the post-war world. The USA facilitated the rebuilding of Europe through the Marshall Plan, oversaw the creation of the United Nations, the International Monetary Fund and the International Bank for Reconstruction and Development, and underpinned the new liberal world economy. The USA contended for global supremacy with the USSR and the two superpowers engaged in a costly arms race and 'cold war' fought by proxy in the Third World. The USA's opposition to communism led it into wars in Korea (1950–3) and Vietnam (1964–73). President Richard Nixon initiated détente with Russia and China in the early 1970s but was forced to resign in 1974 over corruption allegations (Watergate).

POLITICAL SYSTEM

By the constitution of 17 September 1787 (to which amendments were added in 1791, 1798, 1804, 1865, 1868, 1870, 1913, 1920, 1933, 1951, 1961, 1964, 1967, 1971 and 1992), the government of the United States is entrusted to three separate authorities: the executive (the president and Cabinet), the legislature (Congress) and the judicature.

The president is indirectly elected by an electoral college every four years. There is also a vice-president, who, should the president die, becomes president for the remainder of the term. The tenure of the presidency is limited to two terms.

The president, with the consent of the Senate, appoints the Cabinet officers and all the chief officials. He makes recommendations of a general nature to Congress, and when laws are passed by Congress he may return them to Congress with a veto. But if a measure so vetoed is again passed by both Houses of Congress by two-thirds majority

in each House, it becomes law, notwithstanding the objection of the president. The president must be at least 35 years of age and a native citizen of the United States.

Presidential elections

Each state elects (on the first Tuesday after the first Monday in November of the year preceding the year in which the presidential term expires) a number of electors (members of the electoral college), equal to the whole number of Senators and Representatives to which the state may be entitled in the Congress. The electors for each state meet in their respective states on the first Monday after the second Wednesday in December following, and vote for a president by ballot. The ballots are then sent to Washington, and opened on 6 January by the President of the Senate in the presence of Congress. The candidate who has received a majority of the whole number of electoral votes cast is declared president for the ensuing term. If no one has a majority, then from the highest on the list (not exceeding three) the House of Representatives elects a president, the votes being taken by states, the representation from each state having one vote. A presidential term begins at noon on 20 January.

Presidential and legislative elections are due to take place on 7 November 2000.

HEAD OF STATE

President of the United States, William Jefferson Blythe IV Clinton, *born* 19 August 1946, *elected* 1992, *re-elected* 5 November 1996, *sworn in* 20 January 1997. Democrat
Vice-President, Albert Gore, jun., *born* 31 March 1948

THE CABINET *as at September 2000*

Agriculture, Daniel Glickman
Attorney-General, Janet Reno
Commerce, William Daley
Defence, William Cohen
Education, Richard Riley
Energy, Bill Richardson
Health and Human Services, Donna Shalala
Housing and Urban Development, Andrew Cuomo
Interior, Bruce Babbitt

Labour, Alexis Herman
Secretary of State, Madeleine Albright
Transportation, Rodney Slater
Treasury, Lawrence Summers
Veterans' Affairs, Togo West

Other senior positions:
Permanent Representative to the UN, Richard Holbrooke
Chair, Council of Economic Advisers, Martin Baily
White House Chief of Staff, John Podesta
National Security Adviser, Samuel Berger
Environmental Protection Agency, Carol Browner
Director, National Economic Council, Gene Sperling
Director, Office of Management and Budget, Jacob Lew
Director, Small Business Administration, Aida Alvarez
Trade Representative, Charlene Barshefsky
Director of CIA, George Tenet
Director of FBI, Louis Freeh
Chairman, Federal Reserve Board of Governors, Alan Greenspan

UNITED STATES EMBASSY
24 Grosvenor Square, London W1A 1AE
Tel: 020-7499 9000
Ambassador Extraordinary and Plenipotentiary, HE Philip Lader, apptd 1997
Deputy Chief of Mission, G. Davies
Defence and Naval Attaché, Capt. S. Barnett
Minister-Counsellors, L. A. Lohman (*Administrative*); D. Katz (*Commercial*); W. G. Griffith (*Consular*); J. Johnson (*Political*)

BRITISH EMBASSY
3100 Massachusetts Avenue NW, Washington DC 20008
Tel: (00 1) (202) 588 6500
Ambassador Extraordinary and Plenipotentiary, HE Sir Christopher Meyer, KCMG, apptd 1997
Ministers, M. A. Arthur, CMG; S. J. Pickford (*Economic*); J. C. Taylor (*Defence Material*)
Head of British Defence Staff and Defence Attaché, Maj.-Gen. C. Vyvyan, CBE
Counsellor, R. French (*Management and Consul-General*)
Consul-General (New York) and Director-General of Trade and Investment, T. Harris, CMG

BRITISH CONSULATES-GENERAL – Atlanta, Boston, Chicago, Houston, Los Angeles, New York and San Francisco
BRITISH VICE-CONSULATE – Orlando
BRITISH CONSULATES – Anchorage, Charlotte, Dallas Kansas City, Miami, Minneapolis, Nashville, New Orleans, Philadelphia, Phoenix, Pittsburgh, Portland, St Louis, Salt Lake City, San Diego, Seattle and Puerto Rico

BRITISH COUNCIL DIRECTOR, D. Blagbrough (*Cultural Attache*), c/o British Embassy; e-mail: enquiries@britishcouncil-usa.org

BRITISH–AMERICAN CHAMBER OF COMMERCE, 275 Madison Avenue, New York 10016; UK OFFICE, Suite 201, High Holborn, London WCIV 6RR

THE CONGRESS

Legislative power is vested in two houses, the Senate and the House of Representatives. The Senate has 100 members, two Senators from each state, elected for the term of six years, and each Senator has one vote.

The House of Representatives consists of 435 Representatives, directly elected in each state for a two-year term, a resident commissioner from Puerto Rico and a delegate each from American Samoa, the District of Columbia, Guam and the Virgin Islands.

Members of the 106th Congress were elected on 3 November 1998. The 106th Congress is constituted as follows:

Senate – Republicans 54; Democrats 46; total 100
House of Representatives – Republicans 223; Democrats 211; Independent 1; total 435

President of the Senate, The Vice-President
Senate Majority Leader, Trent Lott (*R*), *Mississippi*
Speaker of the House of Representatives, J. Dennis Hastert (*R*), *Illinois*
Secretary of the Senate, Gary Sisco
Clerk of the House of Representatives, Jeff Trandahl

THE JUDICATURE

The federal judiciary consists of three sets of federal courts: the Supreme Court at Washington DC, consisting of a Chief Justice and eight Associate Justices, with original jurisdiction in cases where a state is a party to the suit, and with appellate jurisdiction from inferior federal courts and from the judgments of the highest courts of the states; the United States Courts of Appeals, dealing with appeals from district courts and from certain federal administrative agencies, and consisting of 168 circuit judges within 13 circuits; the 94 United States district courts served by 575 district court judges.

THE SUPREME COURT
US Supreme Court Building, Washington DC 20543

Chief Justice, William H. Rehnquist, *Arizona*, apptd 1986

Associate Justices
John Paul Stevens, *Illinois*, apptd 1975
Sandra Day O'Connor, *Arizona*, apptd 1981
Antonin Scalia, *Virginia*, apptd 1986
Anthony M. Kennedy, *California*, apptd 1988
David H. Souter, *New Hampshire*, apptd 1990
Clarence Thomas, *Georgia*, apptd 1991
Ruth Bader Ginsburg, *New York*, apptd 1993
Stephen Breyer, *Massachusetts*, apptd 1994

Clerk of the Supreme Court, William K. Suter
In 1997 there were 13,175,070 recorded offences: murder and non-negligent manslaughter 18,210; forcible rape 96,120; robbery 497,950; aggravated assault 1,022,490; burglary 2,461,100; larceny-theft 7,725,500; motor vehicle theft 1,353,700.

DEFENCE

Each military department is separately organised and functions under the direction, authority and control of the Secretary of Defence. The Air Force has primary responsibility for the Department of Defence space development programmes and projects.

Under strategic command the USA has 432 submarine-launched ballistic missiles, 550 inter-continental ballistic missiles, 178 heavy nuclear-capable bombers and 90 strategic defence interceptor aircraft together with multiple intelligence satellites, radars and early warning systems throughout the world.

The Army has 7,684 main battle tanks, 6,715 armoured infantry fighting vehicles, 17,800 armoured personnel carriers, 249 aircraft and 1,437 armed helicopters.

The Navy has 18 strategic submarines, 57 tactical submarines, 12 aircraft carriers, 27 cruisers, 54 destroyers, 37 frigates, 21 patrol and coastal vessels, 290 amphibious and support ships, 1,510 combat aircraft and 506 armed helicopters.

The Marine Corps has 403 main battle tanks, and 1,321 amphibious armoured vehicles. The Air Force has 208 long-range strike aircraft, 2,598 tactical combat aircraft and 216 helicopters.

The major deployments of US personnel overseas are: Germany (67,640); South Korea (36,530); Japan (40,100); Italy (10,400); UK (11,170); Turkey (2,430).
MILITARY EXPENDITURE – 3.2 per cent of GDP (1998)
MILITARY PERSONNEL – 1,371,500: Army 469,300, Navy 369,800, Marine Corps 171,000, Coast Guard 41,100, Air Force 361,400

Chairman, Joint Chiefs of Staff, Gen. Henry Shelton

ECONOMY AND FINANCE

In 1999 central government budget receipts totalled US$1,827.3 billion and outlays US$1,704.6 billion. The largest items of expenditure were: defence US$276.8 billion; social security US$390.0 billion, income security US$237.2 billion, debt interest US$230.3 billion. In the year to the end of September 1999, US$57,438 million was spent on education, US$140,803 million on health, US$190,448 million on Medicare, US$237,180 million on income security, US$390,043 million on social security and US$43,210 million on veterans benefits and services.

At the end of the 1997 financial year the total gross federal debt stood at US$5,369,707 million; it was estimated to be US$5,915,719 million at the end of the 2000 financial year.
GNP – US$7,902,976 million (1998); US$29,240 per capita (1998)
GDP – US$7,388,100 million (1996); US$27,420 per capita (1996)
ANNUAL AVERAGE GROWTH OF GDP – 3.8 per cent (1997)
INFLATION RATE – 1.6 per cent (1998)
UNEMPLOYMENT – 4.2 per cent (1998)

GROSS DOMESTIC PRODUCT BY INDUSTRY 1997

	US$ millions
Private industries	7,083,258
Agriculture, forestry, fisheries	131,745
Mining	120,515
Construction	328,806
Manufacturing	1,378,869
Transportation and public utilities	676,313
Wholesale trade	562,755
Retail trade	712,890
Finance, insurance, and real estate	1,570,308
Services	1,656,849
Government and government enterprises	1,027,639
Statistical discrepancy	–55,792
TOTAL	8,110,897

THE STATES OF THE UNION

The United States of America is a federal republic consisting of 50 states and the federal District of Columbia and of organised territories. Of the present 50 states, 13 are original states, seven were admitted without previous organisation as territories, and 30 were admitted after such organisation.

STATE (with date and *order* of admission)	LAND AREA sq. km	POPULATION (1999 estimate)	CAPITAL	GOVERNOR (end of term in office)	
Alabama (AL) (1819) (*22*)	131,443	4,369,862	Montgomery	Don Siegelman (*D*)	(2002)
Alaska (AK) (1959) (*49*)	1,477,268	619,500	Juneau	Tony Knowles (*D*)	(2002)
Arizona (AZ) (1912) (*48*)	294,333	4,778,332	Phoenix	Jane Dee Hull (*R*)	(2002)
Arkansas (AR) (1836) (*25*)	134,875	2,551,373	Little Rock	Mike Huckabee (*R*)	(2002)
California (CA) (1850) (*31*)	403,971	33,145,121	Sacramento	Gray Davis (*D*)	(2002)
Colorado (CO) (1876) (*38*)	268,658	4,056,133	Denver	Bill Owens (*R*)	(2002)
Connecticut (CT)§ (1788) (*5*)	12,550	3,282,031	Hartford	John Rowland (*R*)	(2002)
Delaware (DE)§ (1787) (*1*)	5,063	753,538	Dover	Tom Carper (*D*)	(2000)
Florida (FL) (1845) (*27*)	139,853	15,111,244	Tallahassee	Jeb Bush (*R*)	(2002)
Georgia (GA)§ (1788) (*4*)	150,010	7,788,240	Atlanta	Roy Barnes (*D*)	(2002)
Hawaii (HI) (1959) (*50*)	16,637	1,185,497	Honolulu	Ben Cayetano (*D*)	(2002)
Idaho (ID) (1890) (*43*)	214,325	1,251,700	Boise	Dirk Kempthorne (*R*)	(2002)
Illinois (IL) (1818) (*21*)	143,987	12,128,370	Springfield	George Ryan (*R*)	(2002)
Indiana (IN) (1816) (*19*)	92,904	5,942,901	Indianapolis	Frank O'Bannon (*D*)	(2000)
Iowa (!A) (1846) (*29*)	144,716	2,869,413	Des Moines	Tom Vilsack (*D*)	(2002)
Kansas (KS) (1861) (*34*)	211,922	2,654,052	Topeka	Bill Graves (*R*)	(2002)
Kentucky (KY) (1792) (*15*)	102,907	3,960,825	Frankfort	Paul Patton (*D*)	(2003)
Louisiana (LA) (1812) (*18*)	112,836	4,372,035	Baton Rouge	M. J. Mike Foster (*R*)	(2004)
Maine (ME) (1820) (*23*)	79,939	1,253,040	Augusta	Angus King (*I*)	(2002)
Maryland (MD)§ (1788) (*7*)	25,316	5,171,634	Annapolis	Parris Glendening (*D*)	(2002)
Massachusetts (MA)§ (1788) (*6*)	20,300	6,175,169	Boston	Argeo Paul Cellucci (*R*)	(2002)
Michigan (MI) (1837) (*26*)	147,136	9,863,775	Lansing	John Engler (*R*)	(2002)
Minnesota (MN) (1858) (*32*)	206,207	4,775,508	St Paul	Jesse Ventura (*Reform*)	(2002)
Mississippi (MS) (1817) (*20*)	121,506	2,768,619	Jackson	David Ronald Musgrove (*D*)	(2004)
Missouri (MO) (1821) (*24*)	178,446	5,468,338	Jefferson City	Mel Carnahan (*D*)	(2000)
Montana (MT) (1889) (*41*)	376,991	882,779	Helena	Marc Racicot (*R*)	(2000)
Nebraska (NE) (1867) (*37*)	199,113	1,660,028	Lincoln	Mike Johanns (*R*)	(2002)
Nevada (NV) (1864) (*36*)	284,396	1,809,253	Carson City	Kenny Guinn (*R*)	(2002)
New Hampshire (NH)§ (1788) (*9*)	23,231	1,201,134	Concord	Jeanne Shaheen (*D*)	(2000)
New Jersey (NJ)§ (1787) (*3*)	19,215	8,143,412	Trenton	Christine Whitman (*R*)	(2002)
New Mexico (NM) (1912) (*47*)	314,334	1,739,844	Santa Fé	Gary Johnson (*R*)	(2002)
New York (NY)§ (1788) (*11*)	122,310	18,196,601	Albany	George Pataki (*R*)	(2002)
North Carolina (NC)§ (1789) (*12*)	126,180	7,650,789	Raleigh	James B. Hunt, jun. (*D*)	(2000)
North Dakota (ND) (1889) (*39*)	178,695	633,666	Bismarck	Edward Schafer (*R*)	(2000)
Ohio (OH) (1803) (*17*)	106,067	11,256,654	Columbus	Bob Taft (*R*)	(2002)
Oklahoma (OK) (1907) (*46*)	177,877	3,358,044	Oklahoma City	Frank Keating (*R*)	(2002)
Oregon (OR) (1859) (*33*)	248,646	3,316,154	Salem	John Kitzhaber (*D*)	(2002)
Pennsylvania (PA)§ (1787) (*2*)	116,083	11,994,016	Harrisburg	Tom Ridge (*R*)	(2002)
Rhode Island (RI)§ (1790) (*13*)	2,707	990,819	Providence	Lincoln Almond (*R*)	(2002)
South Carolina (SC)§ (1788) (*8*)	77,988	3,885,736	Columbia	Jim Hodges (*D*)	(2002)
South Dakota (SD) (1889) (*40*)	196,571	733,133	Pierre	William Janklow (*R*)	(2002)
Tennessee (TN) (1796) (*16*)	106,759	5,483,535	Nashville	Don Sundquist (*R*)	(2002)
Texas (TX) (1845) (*28*)	678,358	20,044,141	Austin	George W. Bush (*R*)	(2002)
Utah (UT) (1896) (*45*)	212,816	2,129,836	Salt Lake City	Mike Leavitt (*R*)	(2000)
Vermont (VT) (1791) (*14*)	23,956	593,740	Montpelier	Howard Dean (*D*)	(2000)
Virginia (VA)§ (1788) (*10*)	102,558	6,872,912	Richmond	James Gilmore (*R*)	(2002)
Washington (WA) (1889) (*42*)	172,445	5,756,361	Olympia	Gary Locke (*D*)	(2000)
West Virginia (WV) (1863) (*35*)	62,384	1,806,928	Charleston	Cecil Underwood (*R*)	(2000)
Wisconsin (WI) (1848) (*30*)	140,672	5,250,446	Madison	Tommy Thompson (*R*)	(2002)
Wyoming (WY) (1890) (*44*)	251,501	479,602	Cheyenne	Jim Geringer (*R*)	(2002)
Dist. of Columbia (DC) (1791)	159	519,000	—	Anthony Williams (*D*) (*Mayor*)	

OUTLYING TERRITORIES AND POSSESSIONS

American Samoa	200	62,093*	Pago Pago	Tauese Pita Sunia (*D*)	(2000)
Guam	544	149,101*	Hagatna	Carl Gutierrez (*D*)	(2002)
Northern Mariana Islands	464	66,611*	Saipan	Pedro P. Tenorio (*R*)	(2002)
Puerto Rico	8,875	3,860,091*	San Juan	Dr Pedro J. Rossello (*D*)	(2000)
US Virgin Islands	346	118,382*	Charlotte Amalie	Charles Wesley Turnbull (*D*)	(2002)

§ The 13 original states
* 1998 estimates
D Democratic Party; *I* Independent; *R* Republican Party

AGRICULTURE

The total number of farms in 1999 was 2,194,070 with a total area of land in farms of 947,340,000 acres, and an average acreage per farm of 432 acres. Principal crops are maize for grain, soybeans, wheat, hay, cotton, tobacco, grain sorghums, potatoes, oranges and barley. Gross income from farming in 1998 was US$223 billion. Cash receipts from all crops in 1998 was US$102 billion and from livestock and livestock products US$95 billion.

MINERALS

The value of non-fuel raw mineral production in 1997 totalled an estimated US$39 billion. Mineral exports in 1997 were valued at US$37 billion, and imports at US$58 billion. In 1998 the following quantities of minerals were produced: iron ore 62,931,000 tonnes; marketable phosphate rock 44,200,000 tonnes; copper 1,858,900 tonnes; zinc 755,000 tonnes; lead 415,000 tonnes.

ENERGY

Production in 1998 was 72.90 quadrillion BTU, principally coal, natural gas and crude oil. Coal accounted for almost half of energy exports at 4.32 quadrillion BTU. Net imports were 22.513 quadrillion BTU, of which crude oil was 18.68 quadrillion BTU, to meet consumption of 94.23 quadrillion BTU (quadrillion10^{15}).

TRADE

In 1998 the USA had a trade deficit of US$246,027 million and a current account deficit of US$233,762 million. Imports totalled US$944,353 million and exports US$682,497 million.

Trade with UK	1998	1999
Imports from UK	£21,614,472,000	£24,373,101,000
Exports to UK	25,614,472,000	25,212,005,000

COMMUNICATIONS

In 1998 there were 3.91 million miles of public roads and streets, of which 3.07 million miles were in rural areas and 0.84 million miles were in urban areas. Surfaced roads and streets account for 61.3 per cent of the total. An estimated total of US$101,953 million was spent in 1998 on public roads in the United States.

The ocean-going merchant marine on 1 January 1999 consisted of 29,827 vessels with a capacity of 73.7 million tonnes, of which 508 privately engaged in foreign trade. There were 189 ships in the National Defense Reserve Fleet of inactive government-owned vessels.

According to preliminary figures, US domestic and international scheduled airlines in 1999 carried 635,187,271 passengers over 651,466,236 revenue passenger miles. Operating revenues of all US scheduled airlines were US$117,946,780,445 in 1999. Total operating expenses rose to US$110,122,448,247 in 1999. Scheduled operations showed an operating profit of US$7,824,332,198 and a net profit of US$5,573,493,150 in 1999.

EDUCATION

All the states and the District of Columbia have compulsory school attendance laws. In general, children are obliged to attend school from seven to 16 years of age.

Most of the revenue for public elementary and secondary school purposes comes from federal, state, and local governments. Less than three per cent comes from gifts and from tuition and transportation fees.

Among the better-known universities are: Harvard, founded at Cambridge, Mass. in 1636, and named after John Harvard of Emmanuel College, Cambridge, England, who bequeathed to it his library and a sum of money in 1638; Yale, founded at New Haven, Connecticut, in 1701; Princeton, NJ, founded 1746.

ILLITERACY RATE – 0.5 per cent
ENROLMENT (percentage of age group) – primary 95 per cent (1995); secondary 90 per cent (1995); tertiary 81.0 per cent (1995)

US TERRITORIES, ETC

Responsibility within the federal government for the United States insular areas other than Puerto Rico and Kingman Reef lies with the United States Department of the Interior, either the Office of Insular Affairs (for American Samoa, Guam, the Northern Mariana Islands, the United States Virgin Islands, Navassa Island (3 sq. miles), Palmyra Atoll (1.56 sq. miles) and Wake Atoll (2.5 sq. miles) (shared with the United States Army Space and Missile Defense Command)) or the United States Fish and Wildlife Service (for Baker Island (0.59 sq. miles), Howland Island (1 sq. mile) and Jarvis Island (1.66 sq. miles), Midway Atoll (2 sq. miles) and Johnston Atoll (0.98 sq. miles) (shared with the Defense Special Weapons Agency)). Four of the eight populated insular areas are represented in the United States House of Representatives, Puerto Rico by a resident commissioner and American Samoa, Guam and the United States Virgin Islands each by a delegate. Although represented in the United States House of Representatives by a delegate, the District of Columbia was an incorporated territory for only three years, from 21 February 1871 to 20 June 1874.

THE COMMONWEALTH OF PUERTO RICO

AREA – 3,427 sq. miles (8,875 sq. km)
POPULATION – 3,860,091 (1998 estimate); 3,522,037 (1990 census). The majority of the inhabitants are of Spanish descent, and Spanish and English are the official languages
CAPITAL – ΨSan Juan, population of the municipality (1998 estimate), 439,427. Other major towns are: Bayamón (233,797); Carolina (190,469); ΨPonce (191,469)

Puerto Rico (Rich Port) is an island of the Greater Antilles group in the West Indies.

Puerto Rico was discovered in 1493 by Columbus and explored by Ponce de León in 1508. It was a Spanish possession until 1898, when the USA took formal possession as a result of the Spanish-American War.

The 1952 constitution establishes the Commonwealth of Puerto Rico with full powers of local government. The Legislative Assembly consists of two elected houses: the Senate of 27 members and the House of Representatives of 51 members. The term of the Legislative Assembly is four years. The Governor is popularly elected for a term of four years. Residents of Puerto Rico are US citizens. Puerto Rico is represented in Congress by a resident commissioner, elected for a term of four years, who has a seat in the House of Representatives but not a vote, although he has a right to vote on those committees of which he is a member. A plebiscite on the future constitutional status of Puerto Rico was held on 14 November 1993 in which 48 per cent voted to maintain the existing Commonwealth status, 46 per cent voted for full US statehood and 4 per cent for independence.

Principal agricultural products are milk, poultry, coffee, plantains, meat, ornamental plants, eggs, fish and seafood, and fruits and vegetables. Most valuable areas of manufacturing are chemicals and allied products, metal products and machinery, and food processing.

Governor, Dr Pedro J. Rossello

Trade with UK	1998	1999
Imports from UK	£349,400,000	£437,008,000
Exports to UK	148,963,000	262,520,000

GUAM

AREA – 212 sq. miles (549 sq. km)
POPULATION – 156,000 (1997 estimate): 43 per cent
Chamorro stock mingled with Filipino and Spanish
blood. The Chamorro language belongs to the Malayo-
Polynesian family, but with considerable admixture of
Spanish. Chamorro and English are the official
languages; most Chamorro residents are bilingual
CAPITAL – Hagatna. Port of entry, ΨApra

Guam is the largest of the Mariana Islands, in the north
Pacific Ocean.

Guam was occupied by the Japanese in December 1941
but was recaptured by US forces in 1944. Under the
Organic Act of Guam 1950, Guam has statutory powers of
self-government, and any person born in Guam is a US
citizen. A 21-member unicameral legislature is elected
biennially. The Governor and Lieutenant-Governor are
popularly elected. There is also a District Court of Guam,
with original jurisdiction in cases under federal law.

Guam's two main sources of revenue are tourism and
US military spending.

Governor, Carl Gutierrez
Lt.-Governor, Frank Blas

AMERICAN SAMOA

AREA – 77 sq. miles (199 sq. km)
POPULATION – 58,000 (1997 estimate)
CAPITAL – ΨPago Pago (population, 3,519)

American Samoa consists of the islands of Tutuila, Aunu'u,
Ofu, Olesega, Ta'u, Rose and Swains Islands. Tutuila, the
largest of the group, has an area of 52 sq. miles and a
magnificent harbour at Pago Pago. The remaining islands
have an area of about 24 sq. miles. Tuna and copra are the
chief exports.

Those born in American Samoa are US non-citizen
nationals, but some have acquired citizenship through
service in the United States armed forces or other
naturalisation procedure. The 1960 constitution grants
American Samoa a measure of self-government, with
certain powers reserved to the US Secretary of the
Interior. There is a bicameral legislature with popularly
elected representatives and traditionally elected senators,
and a popularly elected Governor.

Governor, Tauese Pita Sunia
Lt.-Governor, Togiola Tulafo

THE UNITED STATES VIRGIN ISLANDS

AREA – 134 sq. miles (347 sq. km)
POPULATION – 114,483 (1997 estimate)
CAPITAL – ΨCharlotte Amalie (population, 12,331, 1990),
on St Thomas

The US Virgin Islands were purchased from Denmark
and came under US sovereignty in 1917. There are three
main islands, St Thomas (28 sq. miles), St Croix (84
sq. miles), St John (20 sq. miles) and about 50 small islets
or cays, mostly uninhabited.

Under the provisions of the Revised Organic Act of
the Virgin Islands 1954, legislative power is vested in the
Legislature, a unicameral body composed of 15 senators
popularly elected for two-year terms. The Governor is
popularly elected. Those born in the US Virgin Islands are
US citizen nationals. A referendum is to take place at a
future date to determine the future political status of the
islands.

Governor, Charles Wesley Turnbull
Lt.-Governor, Kenneth E. Mapp

Trade with UK	1998	1999
Imports from UK	£18,488,000	£5,881,000
Exports to UK	11,682,000	591,000

NORTHERN MARIANA ISLANDS

AREA – 179 sq. miles (464 sq. km)
POPULATION – 63,763 (1997 estimate)
SEAT OF GOVERNMENT – Saipan (population, 52,706,
1995 census)

The USA administered the Northern Mariana Islands
as part of a UN Trusteeship until the trusteeship agreement was terminated in 1986, bringing fully into effect
a 1976 congressional law establishing the Northern
Mariana Islands as a Commonwealth under US sovereignty. Most of the then residents became US citizens.
Those born subsequently in the Northern Mariana Islands
are US citizen nationals. There is a popularly elected
bicameral legislature and a popularly elected Governor.

Governor, Pedro P. Tenorio
Lt.-Governor, Jesus Sablan

THE PANAMA CANAL

As a result of the Panama Canal Treaty 1977, the Canal
Zone was disestablished, with all jurisdiction over the
former Canal Zone reverting to Panama with effect from
1 October 1979. Under the treaty, the United States
was allowed the use of operating areas for the Panama
Canal, together with several military bases, although
the Republic of Panama was sovereign in all such areas.
The Panama Canal Commission, an arm of the US
Government, continued to operate the canal until noon
on 31 December 1999. The Panama Canal Authority, a
Panama government agency, then assumed administration
of the waterway.

URUGUAY

República Oriental del Uruguay

AREA – 68,500 sq. miles (175,016 sq. km). Neighbours:
Argentina (west), Brazil (north and east)
POPULATION – 3,221,000 (1997 UN estimate):
predominantly of Spanish and Italian descent. Spanish is
the official language. Many Uruguayans are Roman
Catholics. There is no established church
CAPITAL – ΨMontevideo (population, 1,378,705, 1996)
MAJOR CITIES – Melo; Mercedes; Minas; ΨPaysandú;
Punta del Este; Rivera; Salto
CURRENCY – Uruguayan peso of 100 centésimos
NATIONAL ANTHEM – Orientales, La Patria O La Tumba
(Uruguayans, the fatherland or death)
NATIONAL DAY – 25 August (Declaration of
Independence, 1825)
NATIONAL FLAG – Four blue and five white horizontal
stripes surcharged with sun on a white ground in the top
corner, next flagstaff
LIFE EXPECTANCY (years) – male 68.43; female 74.88
POPULATION GROWTH RATE – 0.6 per cent (1997)
POPULATION DENSITY – 18 per sq. km (1997)
URBAN POPULATION – 90.5 per cent (1997)
MILITARY EXPENDITURE – 2.3 per cent of GDP (1998)
MILITARY PERSONNEL – 25,600: Army 17,600,
Navy 5,000, Air Force 3,000; Paramilitaries 920

The country consists mainly of undulating grassy plains.
The principal river is the Rio Negro (with its tributary the
Yi), flowing from north-east to south-west into the Rio
Uruguay. The climate is temperate.

HISTORY AND POLITICS

Uruguay (or the *Banda Oriental*, as the territory lying on
the eastern bank of the Uruguay River was then called)
resisted all attempted invasions of the Portuguese and
Spanish until the early 17th century; 100 years later the

Portuguese settlements were captured by the Spanish. From 1726 to 1814 the country formed part of Spanish South America. In 1814 the armies of the Argentine Confederation captured the capital and annexed the province; afterwards it was annexed by Portugal and became a province of Brazil. In 1825, the country threw off Brazilian rule. This action led to war between Argentina and Brazil which was settled by the mediation of the UK, Uruguay being declared an independent state in 1828. In 1830 a republic was inaugurated.

General elections held in 1984 marked the return to civilian rule after 11 years of presidential rule with military support. The first fully free presidential and legislative elections since 1971 were held in 1989, and were won by the National (Blanco) Party (NP).

The presidential election on 31 October and 28 November 1999 was won by Jorge Batlle Ibáñez of the Colorado Party (CP), who gained 51.5 per cent of the vote in the second round of the election. The legislative elections for both houses of the General Assembly, which were held simultaneously with the first round of the presidential election, resulted in the Progressive Encounter-Broad Front (EP-FA) winning 40 seats, the CP 33 seats, the NP 22 seats and the New Space party (NE) four seats in the House of Representatives, with the EP-FA winning 12 seats, the CP ten seats, the NP seven seats and the NE one seat in the Senate. A coalition government of the CP and the NP was formed.

POLITICAL SYSTEM

Under the constitution the president (who may serve only a single term of five years) appoints a council of ministers and a Secretary (Planning and Budget Office), and the vice-president presides over Congress. The Congress consists of a Chamber of 99 deputies and a Senate of 30 members (plus the vice-president), elected for five years by proportional representation.

The republic is divided into 19 Departments, each with an elected governor and legislature.

HEAD OF STATE

President, Jorge Batlle Ibáñez, *elected* 28 November 1999, *took office* 1 March 2000
Vice-President, Luis Hierro López

COUNCIL OF MINISTERS *as at September 2000*

The President
Economy and Finance, Alberto Bensión (CP)
Education and Culture, Antonio Mercador (NP)
Foreign Relations, Didier Opertti (CP)
Health, Horacio Fernández Ameglio (CP)
Housing, Territorial Regulation and Environment, Carlos Cat (NP)
Industry, Energy and Mines, Sergio Abreu (NP)
Interior, Guillermo Sterling (CP)
Labour and Social Security, Álvaro Alonso (NP)
Livestock, Agriculture and Fisheries, Gonzalo González (NP)
National Defence, Luis Brezzo (CP)
Planning and Budget, Ariel Davrieux (NP)
Tourism, Alfonso Varela (CP)
Transport and Works, Lucio Cáceres (CP)

CP Colorado Party; NP National (Blanco) Party

EMBASSY OF THE ORIENTAL REPUBLIC OF URUGUAY
2nd Floor, 140 Brompton Road, London SW3 1HY
Tel: 020-7589 8835
Ambassador Extraordinary and Plenipotentiary, HE Dr Agustín Espinosa-Lloveras, apptd 1998

BRITISH EMBASSY

Calle Marco Bruto 1073, 11300 Montevideo (PO Box 16024)

Tel: (00 598) (2) 622 3650
Ambassador Extraordinary and Plenipotentiary, HE Andrew Murray, apptd 1998

BRITISH-URUGUAYAN CHAMBER OF COMMERCE, Avenida Labertador Brig. Gen., Lavalleja 1641, P2-OF 201, Montevideo

ECONOMY

Agriculture accounted for 8.2 per cent of GDP in 1998 and employed 13.1 per cent of the workforce in 1997. Beef, mutton and wool are produced and rice, wheat, barley, linseed and sunflower seed are cultivated. Other foodstuffs (citrus, wine, beer), fishing and textile industries are also of importance.

Industry accounted for 26.5 per cent of GDP in 1998. Textiles, tyres, sheet-glass, three-ply wood, cement, leather-curing, beet-sugar, plastics, household consumer goods and edible oils are produced. Exploited minerals include clinker, dolomite, marble and granite.

GNP – US$19,960 million (1998); US$6,070 per capita (1998)
GDP – US$18,687 million (1996); US$5,832 per capita (1996)
ANNUAL AVERAGE GROWTH OF GDP – 5.1 per cent (1997)
INFLATION RATE – 10.8 per cent (1998)
UNEMPLOYMENT – 10.1 per cent (1998)
TOTAL EXTERNAL DEBT – US$7,600 million (1998)

TRADE

The major exports are meat, meat by-products and livestock, agricultural products and textiles. The principal imports are machinery and transport equipment and chemical products. Principal trading partners are Brazil, Argentina, the USA and Germany.

In 1998 Uruguay had a trade deficit of US$762 million and a current account deficit of US$400 million. Imports totalled US$3,808 million and exports US$2,769 million.

Trade with UK	1998	1999
Imports from UK	£70,191,000	£66,430,000
Exports to UK	53,643,000	41,566,000

COMMUNICATIONS

There are over 50,000 km of roads, including 12,000 km of national highways, and over 2,000 km of standard gauge railway in use. A state-owned airline, PLUNA, provides international services, and internal passenger and limited freight services are provided by TAMU, a branch of the Uruguayan Air Force. The international airport of Carrasco lies 12 miles outside Montevideo. The River Uruguay is navigable from its estuary to Salto, 200 miles north, and the Negro is also navigable as far as Mercedes. In December 1998, the Senate approved the construction of a 45-km bridge across the River Plate, linking Uruguay and Argentina.

EDUCATION

Primary and secondary education is compulsory and free, and technical and trade schools and evening courses for adult education are state controlled. The university at Montevideo (founded in 1849) has ten faculties and a new university has been built at Salto.

ILLITERACY RATE – 2.2 per cent
ENROLMENT (percentage of age group) – primary 93 per cent (1996); tertiary 30 per cent (1996)

UZBEKISTAN
O'zbekiston Respublikasy

AREA – 172,742 sq. miles (447,400 sq. km). Neighbours: Kazakhstan (north and west), Kyrgyzstan and Tajikistan

(east), Afghanistan and Turkmenistan (south)
POPULATION – 21,206,800 (2000 estimate): 72 per cent
Uzbek, 8 per cent Russian, 5 per cent Tajik and 4 per
cent Kazakh, with smaller numbers of Tatars,
Kara-Kalpaks, Koreans, Ukrainians and Kyrgyz. The
predominant religion is Sunni Muslim. Islam is
tolerated within strict bounds; it is allowed to play no
part in politics. The official language is Uzbek (72 per
cent). Russian (8 per cent), Tajik (5 per cent) and Kazakh
(4 per cent) are also spoken. Uzbek is one of the Turkic
group of languages. In 1994 the government approved a
six-year programme for the transfer of the Uzbek
language to a Latin script
CAPITAL – Tashkent (population, 2,200,000,
1998 estimate)
MAJOR CITIES – Samarkand (370,000), which contains the
Gur-Emir (Tamerlane's Mausoleum); Bukhara
(228,000), which contains the Samanid Mausoleum
and the Ulughbek Madrassah
CURRENCY – Soum of 100 tiyin
NATIONAL DAY – 1 September (Independence Day)
NATIONAL FLAG – Three horizontal stripes of blue, white,
green, with the white fimbriated in red; on the blue near
the hoist a crescent and twelve stars, all in white
LIFE EXPECTANCY (years) – male 66.00; female 72.10
POPULATION GROWTH RATE – 2.1 per cent (1997)
POPULATION DENSITY – 53 per sq. km (1997)
URBAN POPULATION – 38.0 per cent (1997)
MILITARY EXPENDITURE – 5.4 per cent of GDP (1998)
MILITARY PERSONNEL – 74,000: Army 50,000, Air Force
4,000, Paramilitaries 20,000
CONSCRIPTION DURATION – 18 months
ILLITERACY RATE – 2.8 per cent
ENROLMENT (percentage of age group) – tertiary 32.9
per cent (1992)

Uzbekistan occupies the south-central part of former
Soviet Central Asia, lying between the high Tienshan
Mountains and the Pamir highlands in the east and south-
east and sandy lowlands in the west and north-west, in the
basin of the Amudarya and Syrdarya rivers. Uzbekistan
consists of the Republic of Karakalpakstan and 12
regions: Andijan, Bukhara, Jizak, Fergana, Kashka-Darya,
Khorezm, Namanghan, Navoi, Samarkand, Surhan-
Darya, Syr-Darya and Tashkent. Most of the country is
a plain with huge waterless deserts, and several large oases
which form the main centres of population and economic
life. The climate is hot, continental and dry.

HISTORY AND POLITICS.

In the 13th century the area that is now Uzbekistan became
the centre of a great Muslim empire under Amir Timur
(Tamerlane), with its capital at Samarkand. By the beginning of the 19th century three independent Khanates,
Khiva, Kokand and Bukhara, existed in what is now
Uzbekistan. These were annexed to the Russian Empire in
the second half of the 19th century. In November 1917
a Communist revolution broke out in Tashkent and
by 1921, all of Uzbekistan had been absorbed into the
Turkestan Soviet Republic: Under Soviet rule a massive
land irrigation programme was implemented to allow the
cultivation of cotton.

Uzbekistan declared its independence from the Soviet
Union on 1 September 1991. Its independence was
confirmed in a referendum on 29 December and recognised internationally. Elections to the new *Oliy Majlis*
were held on 25 December 1994 and won by the ruling
People's Democratic Party (PDP) and its allies.

The government of President Karimov is formed by the
People's Democratic Party. Despite the constitutionally
guaranteed freedom of religion and thought, and respect
for human rights and multiparty democracy, censorship is
still widely used and little political opposition is tolerated.
The main opposition parties, Erk (Freedom) and Birlik
(Unity) nationalist parties, have been continually banned
since the introduction of the multiparty constitution in
December 1992, but five political parties are legally registered. In March 1995 President Karimov's term of office
was extended to 2000 by a national referendum and he
won a further five-year term in a presidential election held
on 9 January 2000, gaining 91.9 per cent of the vote. The
election result attracted criticism from the Organisation
for Security and Co-operation in Europe, who claimed no
real opposition candidate had been allowed to stand. Legislative elections were held on 5 and 19 December 1999; the
People's Democratic Party and its allies won 123 seats.
The remaining seats were won by independent candidates
and citizens' groups.

FOREIGN RELATIONS

Uzbekistan has actively supported international efforts to
resolve the conflict in Afghanistan. It was announced in
February 1999 that Uzbekistan was to withdraw from the
collective security treaty of the Commonwealth of
Independent States. Uzbekistan is a member of the UN,
OSCE, UNESCO, WHO and many other international
organisations.

POLITICAL SYSTEM

Under the constitution of December 1992, the president
and government hold executive power. The president may
serve a maximum of two five-year terms and has the power
to dissolve the 250-member unicameral Supreme Assembly (*Oliy Majlis*), which may not remove or impeach the
president.

HEAD OF STATE

President, Islam Karimov, *elected* 29 December 1991,
   elected by referendum for a five-year term 26 March 1995,
   re-elected 9 January 2000

CABINET *as at September 2000*

Chairman of the Cabinet, The President
Prime Minister, Utkur Sultanov
Deputy PMs, Bakhtiyor Alimjanov; Valery Ataev (*Power
   and Electrification*); Rustam Azimov (*Finance*); Dilbar
   Ghulomova; Rustam Junusov; Bakhter Khamidov;
   Mirabror Usmanov, Turop Kholtaev (*Agriculture and
   Water Resources*)
Chairman, National Parliament, Erkin Khalilov
Communications, Abduwahid Djurabaev
Cultural Affairs, Khairulla Djurabaev
Defence, Lt.-Gen. Yuriy Agzamov
Education, R. Djuraev
Foreign Affairs, Abdulaziz Kamilov
Foreign Economic Relations, Alyar Majidovich Ganiev
Health, Feruz Nazirov
Higher and Secondary Specialised Education, Saidahror
   Gulamov
Interior, Zakir Almatov
Justice, Abdusamad Polvonzoda
Labour, vacant
Macroeconomics and Statistics, Rustam Shoabdurakhmanov
Municipal Economy, Gafurjan Mukhamedov
Social Security, Akildjon Abidov

EMBASSY OF THE REPUBLIC OF UZBEKISTAN

41 Holland Park, London W11 2RP
Tel: 020-7229 7679
Ambassador Extraordinary and Plenipotentiary, HE Alisher
   Faizullaev, apptd 1999

BRITISH EMBASSY

Ul. Gulyamova 67, UZ-700000 Tashkent
Tel: (00 998712) 1206822
Ambassador Extraordinary and Plenipotentiary, HE

Christopher Ingham, apptd 1998

BRITISH COUNCIL DIRECTOR, M. Moore,
11 Kounoev Street, Tashkent;
e-mail: bc-tashkent@ bc-tashkent.sprint.com

ECONOMY

Uzbekistan signed an economic agreement with Kazakhstan in 1994 to allow the free circulation of goods, services and capital and the co-ordination of credit and finance policies, budgets, taxation and customs duties. Uzbekistan is also a member of the CIS economic union and in 1994 signed an economic treaty with Russia to provide for mutually convertible currencies and to enhance private business links. Peasant farmers have been granted private plots of land and inflation has been reduced.

Uzbekistan's economy is based on intensive agricultural production, which accounted for 29.1 per cent of GDP in 1997 and engaged 46 per cent of the workforce in 1995. Cotton production is approximately 4 million tonnes per year, made possible by extensive irrigation schemes. Textile manufacture, silk production and leather goods are also important. Wheat, potatoes and rice are widely grown. In addition there are some agricultural and textile machinery plants and several chemical combines. Uzbekistan possesses extensive mineral deposits. Copper, uranium, oil, gold and many other metals are extracted. In 1998 oil output was 8.0 million tonnes, and gas production was 55 billion cubic metres. The Muruntao mine is the largest open-cast gold mine in the world; in 1998, 81 tonnes of gold were produced.

Foreign direct investment exceeds US$9 billion. South Korea, the USA, Japan, Turkey and the UK are the main investors.

GNP – US$22,900 million (1998); US$950 per capita (1998)
GDP – US$7,694 million (1996); US$332 per capita (1996)
ANNUAL AVERAGE GROWTH OF GDP – 4.8 per cent (1999)
UNEMPLOYMENT – 4.8 per cent (2000)
TOTAL EXTERNAL DEBT – US$3,162 million (1998)

Trade with UK	1998	1999
Imports from UK	£35,709,000	£30,555,000
Exports to UK	7,413,000	23,678,000

VANUATU
Ripablik Blong Vanuatu

AREA – 4,706 sq. miles (12,189 sq. km)
POPULATION – 178,000 (1997 UN estimate). About 95 per cent are Melanesian, the rest being mostly Micronesian, Polynesian and European. The national language is Bislama, but English and French are also official languages
CAPITAL – ΨPort Vila (population, 26,100, 1993), on Efate
MAJOR TOWN – Luganville (8,800, 1993), on Espiritu Santo
CURRENCY – Vatu of 100 centimes
NATIONAL ANTHEM – Nasonal sing sing blong Vanuatu
NATIONAL DAY – 30 July (Independence Day)
NATIONAL FLAG – Red over green with a black triangle in the hoist, the three parts being divided by fimbriations of black and yellow, and in the centre of the black triangle a boar's tusk overlaid by two crossed fern leaves
LIFE EXPECTANCY (years) – male 63.48; female 67.34
POPULATION GROWTH RATE – 3.0 per cent (1997)
POPULATION DENSITY – 15 per sq. km (1997)
URBAN POPULATION – 18.4 per cent (1989)
ENROLMENT (percentage of age group) – primary 74 per cent (1989); secondary 17 per cent (1991)

Vanuatu is situated in the South Pacific Ocean. It includes 13 large and some 70 small islands, of coral and volcanic origin, including the Banks and Torres Islands in the north. The principal islands are Vanua Lava, Espiritu Santo, Maewo, Pentecost, Ambae, Malekula, Ambrym, Epi, Efate, Erromango, Tanna and Aneityum. Most islands are mountainous and there are active volcanoes on several. The climate is oceanic tropical, moderated by the south-east trade winds which blow between May and October. At other times winds are variable and cyclones may occur.

HISTORY AND POLITICS

Vanuatu, the former Anglo-French Condominium of the New Hebrides, became an independent republic within the Commonwealth on 30 July 1980. Parliament consists of 52 members, directly elected for a term of four years. A Council of Chiefs advises on matters of custom. Executive power is held by the prime minister (elected from and by parliament) and a Council of Ministers who are responsible to parliament. The president is elected for a five-year term by the presidents of the six provincial governments and the members of parliament. The most recent legislative election took place on 6 March 1998. The government is a multiparty coalition. The most recent presidential election took place on 24 March 1999 and was won by Fr John Bani.

HEAD OF STATE
President, HE Fr John Bani, *elected* 24 March 1999
COUNCIL OF MINISTERS *as at September 2000*
Prime Minister, Barak Sope
Deputy PM, Infrastructure and Public Utilities, Stanley Reginald
Agriculture, Forestry and Fisheries, Albert Ravutia
Comprehensive Reform Programme, Sato Kilman
Education, Jacques Sese
Finance, Mokin Steven
Foreign Affairs, Serge Vohor
Health, Jean Keasipai Song
Infrastructure, Public Utilities, vacant
Internal Affairs, Banabas Tabi
Lands and Mineral Resources, Maxime Carlot Korman
Ni-Vanuatu Business Development, John Robert Alick
Youth and Sports, Willy Posen

HIGH COMMISSIONER TO GREAT BRITAIN, vacant, resident at Port Vila, Vanuatu

BRITISH HIGH COMMISSION
KPMG House, Rue Pasteur, PO Box 567, Port Vila
Tel: (00 678) 23100
e-mail: bhcvila@vanuatu.com.vu
High Commissioner, HE Malcolm Hilson, apptd 1997

ECONOMY

Most of the population is employed on plantations or in subsistence agriculture. Subsistence crops include yams, taro, manioc, sweet potato and breadfruit; principal cash crops are copra, cocoa and coffee. Cattle are kept on the plantations and beef is the second largest export. Principal exports are copra, meat (frozen, tinned and chilled), timber and cocoa.

There were 46,000 tourists in 1996. The absence of direct taxation has led to growth in the finance and associated industries.

In 1998 Vanuatu had a trade deficit of US$42 million and a current account surplus of US$5 million. In 1997 imports totalled US$94 million and exports totalled US$35 million.

GNP – US$231 million (1998); US$1,260 per capita (1998)
GDP – US$248 million (1996); US$1,424 per capita (1996)
ANNUAL AVERAGE GROWTH OF GDP – 3.0 per cent (1996)

INFLATION RATE – 2.8 per cent (1997)
TOTAL EXTERNAL DEBT – US$63 million (1998)

Trade with UK	1998	1999
Imports from UK	£206,000	£153,000
Exports to UK	25,000	307,000

VATICAN CITY STATE
Status Civitatis Vaticanae/Stato della Città del Vaticano

AREA – 0.2 sq. miles (0.44 sq. km). Neighbour: Italy
POPULATION – 1,000 (1994 UN estimate). The languages
are Latin and Italian
CAPITAL – Vatican City (population, 766, 1988)
CURRENCY – Italian currency is legal tender
NATIONAL DAY – 22 October (Inauguration of present
Pontiff)
NATIONAL FLAG – Square flag; equal vertical bands of
yellow (next staff), and white; crossed keys and triple
crown device on white band
POPULATION GROWTH RATE – 0.0 per cent (1997)
POPULATION DENSITY – 2,273 per sq. km (1997)
GDP – US$21 million (1996); US$21,219 per capita
(1996)

The office of the ecclesiastical head of the Roman Catholic
Church (Holy See) is vested in the Pope, the Sovereign
Pontiff. For many centuries the Sovereign Pontiff
exercised temporal power but by 1870 the Papal States
had become part of unified Italy. The temporal power of
the Pope was in suspense until the treaty of 1929 which
recognised the full and independent sovereignty of the
Holy See in the City of the Vatican.
Sovereign Pontiff, His Holiness Pope John Paul II (Karol
Wojtyla), *born* at Wadowice (Kraków, Poland), 18 May
1920, *elected* Pope in succession to Pope John Paul I,
16 October 1978
SECRETARIAT OF STATE *as at July 2000*
Secretary of State, Cardinal Angelo Sodano, *apptd* December 1990
Assistant Secretary of State, Archbishop Giovanni
Battista Re
Secretary for Relations with States, Archbishop Jean-Louis
Tauran

APOSTOLIC NUNCIATURE

54 Parkside, London SW19 5NE
Tel: 020-8946 1410/7971
Apostolic Nuncio, HE Archbishop Pablo Puente, apptd 1997

BRITISH EMBASSY TO THE HOLY SEE

91 Via dei Condotti, I–00187 Rome
Tel: (00 39) (6) 6992 3561
Ambassador Extraordinary and Plenipotentiary, HE Mark
Pellew, LVO, apptd 1997

Trade with UK	1998	1999
Imports from UK	£1,469,000	£847,000
Exports to UK	105,000	–

VENEZUELA
República Bolivariana de Venezuela

AREA – 352,145 sq. miles (912,050 sq. km). Neighbours:
Colombia (west), Guyana (east), Brazil (south)
POPULATION – 22,777,000 (1997 UN estimate): 67 per
cent mestizo, 21 per cent white, 10 per cent black and
2 per cent Amerindian. The language is Spanish. 96 per
cent of the population is Roman Catholic
CAPITAL – Caracas (population, 3,672,779, 1996 estimate)

MAJOR CITIES – Barquisimeto (793,565); ΨMaracaibo
(1,660,233); Maracay (449,180); Valencia (1,225,342),
1997 estimates
CURRENCY – Bolívar (Bs) of 100 céntimos
NATIONAL ANTHEM – Gloria Al Bravo Pueblo (Glory to
the brave people)
NATIONAL DAY – 5 July
NATIONAL FLAG – Three horizontal stripes of yellow, blue,
red with an arc of seven white stars on the blue stripe
LIFE EXPECTANCY (years) – male 68.31; female 74.73
POPULATION GROWTH RATE – 2.3 per cent (1997)
POPULATION DENSITY – 25 per sq. km (1997)
URBAN POPULATION – 86.1 per cent (1997)
ILLITERACY RATE – 7.0 per cent
ENROLMENT (percentage of age group) – primary
84 per cent (1996); secondary 22 per cent (1996);
tertiary 28.5 per cent (1991)

Included in the area of the South American republic of
Venezuela are 72 islands off the coast, with a total area of
about 14,650 sq. miles, the largest being Margarita (area,
about 400 sq. miles), which is politically associated with
Tortuga, Cubagua and Coche to form the state of Nueva
Esparta.
The mountains are the Eastern Andes and Maritime
Andes, running south-west to north-east. The main range
is known as the Sierra Nevada de Mérida, and contains
Pico Bolivar (16,411 ft) and Picacho de la Sierra (15,420 ft).
The principal river is the Orinoco, with innumerable
affluents, the main river exceeding 1,600 miles in length.
The upper waters of the Orinoco are united with those of
the Rio Negro (a Brazilian tributary of the Amazon) by a
natural river or canal, known as the Casiquiare. The coastal
regions contain many lagoons and lakes, of which Maracaibo
(area 8,296 sq. miles) is the largest lake in South America.
The climate is tropical, except where modified by
altitude or tempered by sea breezes.

HISTORY AND POLITICS

The first Spanish settlement was established at Cumaná in
1520. During the 18th century there were a number of
uprisings against Spanish rule, and troops led by Simón
Bolívar finally defeated the Spanish in 1823. Venezuela
became an independent republic in 1830.
Legislative elections were held on 8 November 1998
and were won by the Patriotic Front movement (PF), a
coalition of 14 minor parties led by the Fifth Republic
Movement. Hugo Chávez Frías of the PF was elected
president on 6 December 1998. On 25 April 1999, a referendum on convening a constituent assembly to rewrite
the constitution was passed and an election to decide the
members of the constituent assembly was held on 25 July
1999. The new constitution was approved in a referendum held on 15 December and was proclaimed on 20
December.
The National Congress was dissolved on 4 January 2000
pending elections to the new National Assembly, which
were due to be held on 28 May, but were postponed. In
the presidential election held on 30 July 2000, President
Chávez was re-elected, winning 59 per cent of the vote. In
the simultaneous election for the National Assembly, the
Fifth Republic Movement (MVR) won 76 seats, Democratic Action 29 seats, Movement towards Socialism 21
seats, and other parties 39 seats.

POLITICAL SYSTEM

Under the 1999 constitution, the country was renamed
the Bolivarian Republic of Venezuela, a unicameral
legislature, the National Assembly, was created, and the
post of vice-president instituted. The president, who is
directly elected, serves a six-year term, which is renewable
once only. The vice-president is appointed by the
president. Legislative power is exercised by the 165-
member *Asamblea Nacional* (National Assembly), which is

directly elected for a five-year term.

FEDERAL STRUCTURE

Venezuela is divided into 22 states and two federal districts.

State	Area (sq. km)	Population (1995 estimate)	Capital
Amazonas	175,750	94,590	Puerto Ayacucho
Anzoátegui	43,300	1,034,311	Barcelona
Apure	76,500	382,572	San Fernando
Aragua	7,014	1,344,099	Maracay
Barinas	35,200	519,197	Barinas
Bolívar	238,000	1,142,210	Ciudad Bolívar
Carabobo	4,650	1,823,767	Valencia
Cojedes	14,800	227,741	San Carlos
Delta Amacuro	40,200	114,390	Tucupita
Falcón	24,800	699,232	Coro
Federal District	1,930	2,279,677*	Caracas
Federal Dependencies	120	–	–
Guárico	64,986	583,221	San Juan
Lara	19,800	1,430,96	Barquisimeto
Mérida	11,300	680,503	Mérida
Miranda	7,950	2,303,302	Los Teques
Monagas	28,900	555,705	Maturín
Nueva Esparta	1,150	330,307	La Asunción
Portuguesa	15,200	720,865	Guanare
Sucre	11,800	781,756	Cumaná
Táchira	11,100	946,949	San Cristóbal
Trujillo	7,400	562,752	Trujillo
Yaracuy	7,100	466,132	San Felipe
Zulia	63,100	2,820,250	Maracaibo

*Includes Federal Dependencies

HEAD OF STATE

President, Hugo Chávez Frías, *elected* 6 December 1998, *sworn in* 2 February 1999
Vice-President, Isaías Rodríguez

COUNCIL OF MINISTERS *as at September 2000*
Co-ordination and Planning, Jorge Giordani
Defence, Gen. Eliecer Hurtado Sucre
Education, Héctor Navarro
Energy and Mines, Alí Rodríguez Araque
Environment and Renewable Natural Resources, Ana Elisa Osorio
Finance, José Rojas
Foreign Relations, José Vicente Rangel
Health, Gilberto Rodríguez Ochoa
Industry and Commerce, Luisa Romero
Infrastructure, Alberto Esqueda Torres
Interior and Justice, Col. Luís Alfonso Davila
Labour, Blancanieves Portocarrero
President, Corporación Venezolana de Guayana, Clemente Scotto
Production and Commerce, Juan Jesús Montilla
Science and Technology, Carlos Genatios
Secretary of the Presidency, Francisco Rangel

VENEZUELAN EMBASSY

1 Cromwell Road, London SW7 2HR
Tel: 020-7584 4206/7
Ambassador Extraordinary and Plenipotentiary, HE Roy Chaderton-Matos, apptd 1996
Defence Attaché, Capt. C. Briceño-Corales

BRITISH EMBASSY

Edificio Torre Las Mercedes (Piso 3), Avenida La Estancia, Chuao (Apartado 1246), Caracas 1010–A
Tel: (00 58) (2) 993 4111/4224
e-mail: embcarac@ven.net
Ambassador Extraordinary and Plenipotentiary, HE Richard Wilkinson, CVO, apptd 1997
Deputy Head of Mission, Donald Maclaren of Maclaren
Defence Attaché, Col. P. A. Reynolds, RM
First Secretary (Commercial), A. Goodworth

CONSULAR OFFICES – Caracas, Maracaibo, Margarita, Mérida, San Cristobal, Valencia

BRITISH COUNCIL DIRECTOR, J. Greenwood, Piso 3, Torre Creditcard, Av. Principal El Bosque, El Bosque, Caracas;
e-mail: caracas@britishcouncil.org.ve
BRITISH-VENEZUELAN CHAMBER OF COMMERCE, Apartado 5713, Caracas 1010. Torre Británica, Piso 10, Letra E, Av. José Félix Sosa, Altamira Sur, Caracas 1060

DEFENCE

The Army has 81 main battle tanks, 290 armoured personnel carriers and five attack helicopters. The Navy has two submarines, six frigates, six patrol and coastal vessels, seven combat aircraft and eight armed helicopters at nine bases. The Air Force has 124 combat aircraft and 31 armed helicopters.
MILITARY EXPENDITURE – 1.5 per cent of GDP (1998)
MILITARY PERSONNEL – 79,000: Army 34,000, Navy 15,000, Air Force 7,000, National Guard 23,000
CONSCRIPTION DURATION – 30 months (selective)

ECONOMY

President Hugo Chávez Frías pledged in December 1998 that his government would cut public spending and tackle tax evasion and corruption.

Products of the tropical forest region include orchids, wild rubber, timber, mangrove bark, balata gum and tonka beans. Agricultural products include corn, bananas, cocoa beans, coffee, cotton, rice, maize, sugar, sesame, groundnuts, potatoes, tomatoes, other vegetables, sisal and tobacco. There is an extensive beef and dairy farming industry.

The principal industry is petroleum and gas, which together account for 78 per cent of exports. There are eight refineries. The Orinoco heavy oil belt is being developed; estimates put recoverable resources at 73,000 million barrels in 1996.

Aluminium is abundant. Rich iron ore deposits in eastern Venezuela have been developed. Other industry includes a wide variety of manufacturing and component assembly, principally petrochemicals, gold, diamonds and foodstuffs.

On 2 February 2000, President Chávez announced reductions in the rate of value-added tax, a reduction in personal taxes, the abolition of bank debit tax, and tax exemptions in certain key areas of the economy.
GNP – US$82,096 million (1998); US$3,530 per capita (1998)
GDP – US$67,311 million (1996); US$3,017 per capita (1996)
ANNUAL AVERAGE GROWTH OF GDP – – 1.6 per cent (1996)
INFLATION RATE – 35.8 per cent (1998)
UNEMPLOYMENT – 11.4 per cent (1997)
TOTAL EXTERNAL DEBT – US$37,003 million (1998)

TRADE

Apart from oil, the main exports are bauxite, iron ore, agricultural products and basic manufactures. The main imports are machinery and transport equipment, chemicals and foodstuffs. The USA and Colombia are the major trading partners.

In 1997 Venezuela had a trade surplus of US$10,773 million and a current account surplus of US$4,684 million. Imports totalled US$14,606 million and exports US$21,624 million.

Trade with UK	1998	1999
Imports from UK	£245,004,000	£203,201,000
Exports to UK	122,568,000	149,992,000

COMMUNICATIONS

There are about 62,000 km of roads, some 24,000 km of them paved. Road and river communications have made railways of negligible importance in Venezuela except for carrying iron ore in the south-east, though the government is expanding the network, and there are now some 336 km of railway lines.

The Orinoco is navigable for ocean-going ships (up to 40 ft draught) for 150 miles upstream, by large steamers for 700 miles, and by smaller vessels some 900 miles upstream. There are seven Venezuelan airlines which between them have a comprehensive network of internal and international flights. There is an international airport at Caracas.

VIETNAM
Công Hòa Xã Hội Chu Nghī Việt Nam

AREA – 128,066 sq. miles (331,689 sq. km). Neighbours: China (north), Laos and Cambodia (west)
POPULATION – 76,548,000 (1997 UN estimate). The language is Vietnamese. French, English and Khmer are also spoken
CAPITAL – Hanoi (population, 3,056,146, 1992 estimate)
MAJOR CITIES – Hai Phong (1,447,523); Ho Chi Minh City (3,924,435)
CURRENCY – Dông of 10 hào or 100 xu
NATIONAL ANTHEM – Tien Quan Ca (The troops are advancing)
NATIONAL DAY – 2 September
NATIONAL FLAG – Red, with yellow five-point star in centre
LIFE EXPECTANCY (years) – male 63.66; female 67.89
POPULATION GROWTH RATE – 2.1 per cent (1997)
POPULATION DENSITY – 231 per sq. km (1997)
URBAN POPULATION – 19.5 per cent (1994)
ILLITERACY RATE – 6.7 per cent
ENROLMENT (percentage of age group) – primary 95 per cent (1980); tertiary 7 per cent (1996)

HISTORY AND POLITICS

Vietnam became a unified state at the end of the 18th century, with the assistance of France, whose influence on the region grew. In 1899 the Indo-Chinese Union was proclaimed, uniting Vietnam with Cambodia and Laos under French rule. Vietnam was under Japanese occupation from 1940–1945; insurrection by Communist, Nationalist and Revolutionary forces led to a French withdrawal in 1954 and the division of the country into Communist North Vietnam and non-communist South Vietnam. War broke out between the two countries in 1961, which lasted until 1975. North and South Vietnam were reunified in 1976 under the name of the Socialist Republic of Vietnam. The national flag, anthem and capital of North Vietnam were adopted, and Saigon was renamed Ho Chi Minh City.

POLITICAL SYSTEM

Effective power lies with the Vietnamese Communist Party (VCP), its highest executive body being the Central Committee, elected by a Party Congress on a national basis. The Politburo and the Secretariat of the Central Committee exercise the real power.

The constitution of 1992 reaffirmed Communist Party rule but also formalised free market economic reforms.

A new National Assembly (*Quoc-Hoi*) was elected on 20 July 1997; the VCP holds 384 of the 450 seats. The president is elected for a five-year term by the members of the National Assembly.

HEAD OF STATE
President, Tran Duc Luong, *elected* 25 September 1997
Vice-President, Nguyen Thi Binh

POLITBURO
Secretary-General of the VCP, Le Kha Phieu
Politburo Standing Board, Le Kha Phieu; Nong Duc Manh; Phan Van Khai; Pham The Duyet; Tran Duc Luong

COUNCIL OF MINISTERS *as at September* 2000
Prime Minister, Phan Van Khai
Deputy PMs, Nguyen Tan Dzung (*Co-ordinator for Deputy PMs, Economy, Industry, Combating Smuggling and Trade Fraud, Renovation of Enterprise Management*); Nguyen Manh Cam (*Foreign Affairs, Foreign Trade*); Nguyen Cong Tan (*Agriculture, Food Production, Forestry, Aquaculture, Capital Construction, Rural Development, Poverty Alleviation and Agricultural Industrialisation*); Pham Gia Khiem (*Science, Technology, Environment, Hydro-meteorology, Posts, Education, Training, Culture, Arts, Press and Information, Public Health and Sports*)
Agriculture and Rural Development, Le Huy Ngo
Aquatic Resources, Ta Quang Ngoc
Child Protection and Care, Tran Thi Thanh Thanh
Construction, Nguyen Manh Kiem
Culture and Information, Nguyen Khoa Diem
Education and Training, Nguyen Minh Hien
Ethnic Minorities and Mountain Regions, Hoang Duc Nghi
Finance, Nguyen Sinh Hung
Foreign Affairs, Nguyen Dy Nien
Government Personnel and Organisation, Do Quang Trung
Government Secretariat, Lai Van Cu
Governor, State Bank, Le Duc Thuy
Industry, Dang Vu Chu
Interior, Le Minh Huong
Justice, Nguyen Dinh Loc
Labour, War Invalids and Social Affairs, Tran Dinh Hoan
National Defence, Gen. Pham Van Tra
Physical Training and Sports, Ha Quang Du
Planning and Investment, Tran Xuan Gia
Population Activities and Family Planning, Tran Thi Trung Chien
Public Health, Do Nguyen Phuong
Science, Technology and Environment, Chu Tuan Nha
State Inspectorate, Ta Huu Thanh
Trade, Vu Khoan
Transport, Le Ngoc Hoan

EMBASSY OF THE SOCIALIST REPUBLIC OF VIETNAM
12–14 Victoria Road, London W8 5RD
Tel: 020-7937 1912
Ambassador Extraordinary and Plenipotentiary, HE Vuong Thua Phong, apptd 1998
Minister-Counsellor, Nguyen Trung Thanh
Commercial Counsellor, Dinh Van Hoi

BRITISH EMBASSY
Central Building, 31 Hai Ba Trung, Hanoi
Tel: (00 84) (4) 825 2510
e-mail: behanoi@fpt.vn
Ambassador Extraordinary and Plenipotentiary, HE David Fall, apptd 1997
Deputy Head of Mission, Consul, C. J. Owen
Second Secretary (Commercial), J. Wales

CONSULATE-GENERAL – Ho Chi Minh City

BRITISH COUNCIL DIRECTOR, Dr I. Simm (*Cultural Attaché*), 18B Cao Ba Quat, Ba Dinh District, Hanoi; e-mail: bc.hanoi@britcoun.org.vn. There is a regional office in Ho Chi Minh City

DEFENCE

The Army has 1,315 main battle tanks, 1,100 armoured personnel carriers and 300 armoured infantry fighting vehicles. The Navy has six frigates and 40 patrol and coastal vessels at seven principal bases. The Air Force has 189 combat aircraft and 43 armed helicopters.
MILITARY EXPENDITURE – 3.4 per cent of GDP (1998)
MILITARY PERSONNEL – 484,000: Army 412,000, Navy 42,000, Air Force 15,000, Air Defence Force 15,000; Paramilitaries 40,000
CONSCRIPTION DURATION – Two to three years

ECONOMY

Vietnam experienced economic difficulties following the imposition of socialist reforms in the south after 1975. However, economic reforms, known as 'Doi Moi' liberalisation, were instituted in 1986 and have had significant success. The state's share of control has been greatly reduced in most sectors, leading to significant improvement in agricultural production, with Vietnam becoming a major rice exporter. Industry has grown and now contributes 30 per cent of GDP. Building materials, chemicals, machinery and foodstuffs are the main products.

Foreign investment has been actively encouraged and was further boosted by the US decision in 1995 to establish full diplomatic and economic relations and by Vietnam's accession to ASEAN in August 1995, but the level of foreign investment has begun to fall in response to the lack of economic reform and the difficult local business environment, which includes foreign companies being charged premiums for all goods and services, corruption and inefficiency. Oil production has increased and large natural gas reserves have been found offshore, though these are also claimed by China.

Vietnam largely escaped 1998 regional financial crisis, due to its non-convertible currency, lack of a stock market and socialist banking system. An agreement in principle on the establishment of normal trade relations between Vietnam and the USA was reached in July 1999. A 1,690 km highway is under construction connecting Ho Chi Minh City and Hanoi.

In 1997 imports totalled US$11,271 million and exports US$8,900 million.
GNP – US$26,535 million (1998); US$350 per capita (1998)
GDP – US$23,440 million (1996); US$312 per capita (1996)
TOTAL EXTERNAL DEBT – US$22,359 million (1998)

Trade with UK	1998	1999
Imports from UK	£67,987,000	£79,245,000
Exports to UK	243,729,000	305,508,000

YEMEN
Al-Jumhūriyya Al-Yamaniyya

AREA – 203,850 sq. miles (527,968 sq. km). Neighbours: Saudi Arabia (north), Oman (east)
POPULATION – 15,919,000 (1995 census). The language is Arabic
CAPITAL – Sana'ā' (population, 926,595, 1995)
MAJOR CITIES – ΨAden ('Adan) (400,783), the former capital of South Yemen; Al-Hudaydah (246,068); (290,107), Ta'izz (290,107) 1993 estimates
CURRENCY – Riyal of 100 fils
NATIONAL ANTHEM – Raddidi Ayyatuha ad Dunya nashidi (Repeat, O World, my song)
NATIONAL DAY – 22 May
NATIONAL FLAG – Horizontal bands of red, white and black

LIFE EXPECTANCY (years) – male 54.90; female 55.90
POPULATION GROWTH RATE – 5.4 per cent (1997)
POPULATION DENSITY – 31 per sq. km (1997)
URBAN POPULATION – 23.5 per cent (1994)
ENROLMENT (percentage of age group) – tertiary 4.2 per cent (1996)

Included in the state of Yemen are the offshore islands of Perim and Kamarān in the Red Sea, and Suqutrā in the Gulf of Aden. The border with Saudi Arabia, except for the north-west corner, is unclear and is being delineated following an agreement between the two countries signed on 12 June 2000. The highlands and central plateau, and the highest portions of the maritime range in the south, form the most fertile part of Arabia, with abundant but irregular rainfall. The north is largely composed of mountains and desert, and rainfall is generally scarce.

HISTORY AND POLITICS

Turkish occupation of North Yemen (1872–1918) was followed by the rule of the Hamid al-Din dynasty until a revolution in 1962 overthrew the monarchy and the Yemen Arab Republic was declared. The People's Republic of South Yemen was set up in 1967 when the British government ceded power to the National Liberation Front, bringing to an end 129 years of British rule in Aden and some years of protectorate status in the hinterland. Negotiations towards merging the two states began in 1979 and unification was proclaimed on 22 May 1990. The constitution was approved by referendum in May 1991.

Continued political tensions and a power struggle between the former Northern and Southern Yemen élites in mid-1993 led to civil war on 5 May 1994 between the unmerged Northern and Southern forces. The Southern leadership declared secession on 20 May but fled when Aden was captured by victorious Northern forces on 7 July, ending the civil war.

After the war a coalition government of the General People's Congress and the Islamic Islah was formed, an amnesty for the secessionists declared (with the exception of key secessionist leaders) and the constitution amended. Gen. Saleh was elected president by the House of Representatives for a five-year term. Multiparty democracy, a free market economy and Sharia law are enshrined in the constitution.

A general election in April 1997 was won by the ruling General People's Congress. President Ali Abdullah Saleb was re-elected in the first direct presidential elction held on 23 September 1999, winning 96.3 per cent of the value.

HEAD OF STATE

President, Field Marshal Ali Abduallah Saleh, *took office* 22 May 1999, *elected* 1 October 1994, *re-elected* 23 Septermber 1999
Vice-President, Maj.-Gen. Abd Rabbah Mansar Hadi
COUNCIL OF MINISTERS *as at September 2000*
Prime Minister, Abd al-Karim Ali al-Iryani
Deputy PM, Foreign Affairs, Abd al-Qadir Abd al-Rahman Bajammal
Agriculture and Irrigation, Ahmad Salim al-Jabali
Awqaf (Religious Endowments) and Guidance, Ahmad al-Shami
Civil Service and Administrative Reform, Muhammad Ahmad al-Junayd
Construction, Housing and Urban Planning, Abdullah Husayn al-Daf i
Culture and Tourism, Abd al-Malik Mansur
Defence, Maj.-Gen. Muhammad Dayfallah Muhammad
Education, Yahya Muhammad Abdullah al-Shu'aybi
Finance, Alawi Salih al-Salami
Fisheries, Ahmad Musa id Husayn
Industry, Abd al-Rahman Muhammad Ali Uthman

Information, Abd al-Rahman Muhammad al-Akwa
Interior, Maj.-Gen. Husayn Muhammad Arab
Justice, Ismael Ahmed al-Wazir
Labour and Vocational Training, Muhammad Muhammad al-Tayyib
Legal and Parliamentary Affairs, Abdullah Ahmad Ghanim
Local Administration, Sadiq Amin Abu Ra's
Ministers of State, Mutahhar al-Sa'idi (*Affairs of the Council of Ministers*); Faysal Mahmud Hasan Ali (Council of Ministers); Ahmad Ali al-Bishari (*Expatriate Affairs*)
Oil and Mineral Resources, Muhammad al-Khadim al-Wajih
Planning and Development, Ahmad Muhammad Sufan
Power and Water, Ali Hamid Sharaf
Public Health, Abdullah Abd al-Wali Nashir
Social Security and Social Affairs, Muhammad Abdullah al-Batani
Telecommunications, Ahmad Muhammad al-Ansi
Trade and Supply, Abd al-Aziz al-Kumaym
Transport, Brig.-Gen. Abd al-Malik Sayyani
Youth and Sport, Abd al-Wahhab Rawih

EMBASSY OF THE REPUBLIC OF YEMEN
57 Cromwell Road, London SW7 2ED
Tel: 020-7584 6607
Ambassador Extraordinary and Plenipotentiary, HE Dr Hussein Abdullah Al-Amri, apptd 1995

BRITISH EMBASSY
129 Haddah Road, PO Box 1287, Sana'ā'
Tel: (00 967) (1) 264081/2/3/4
Ambassador Extraordinary and Plenipotentiary, HE Victor Henderson, apptd 1997
Deputy Head of Mission and Consul, D. Pearce

BRITISH COUNCIL DIRECTOR, B. McSharry, MBE,
As-Sabain Street No. 7, PO Box 2157, Sana'ā';
e-mail: bc.sanaa@bc-sanaa.bcouncil.org

DEFENCE

The Army has 1,320 main battle tanks, 640 armoured personnel carriers, and 300 armoured infantry fighting vehicles. The Navy has 13 patrol and coastal vessels at two bases. The Air Force has 49 combat aircraft and eight attack helicopters.
MILITARY EXPENDITURE – 6.6 per cent of GDP (1998)
MILITARY PERSONNEL – 66,300: Army 61,000, Navy 1,800, Air Force 3,500; Paramilitaries 70,000
CONSCRIPTION DURATION – Three years

ECONOMY

The economy has been seriously damaged by the civil war. However, the war had little effect on oil production, which amounted to 18.3 million tonnes in 1998 and accounted for 94 per cent of exports in 1995. An agreement was signed with the French oil company Total in September 1995 for the exploitation of liquefied natural gas over a 25-year period and the construction of a gas liquefaction plant by 2000. Despite the production of oil Yemen remains one of the poorest states in the world. Tourism has been hampered by the prevalence of kidnapping. The principal imports are machinery and transport equipment, raw materials, and foodstuffs and livestock.
Agriculture is the main occupation of the inhabitants, accounting for 54 per cent of the workforce in 1997 and 15 per cent of GDP in 1995. This is largely of a subsistence nature, sorghum, sesame, millet, wheat and barley being the chief crops. Exports include cotton, coffee, fruit, vegetables and hides. Imports include food and animals.
In 1998 Yemen had a trade deficit of US$701 million and current account deficit of US$228 million. In 1997 imports totalled US$2,014 million and exports US$2,504 million.
GNP – US$4,630 million (1998); US$280 per capita (1998)
GDP – US$6,946 million (1996); US$443 per capita (1996)
Total External Debt – US$4,138 million (1998)

Trade with UK	1998	1999
Imports from UK	£77,923,000	£64,815,000
Exports to UK	3,249,000	3,575,000

YUGOSLAVIA
Federativna Republika Jugoslavije – Federal Republic of Yugoslavia

AREA – 39,449 sq. miles (102,173 sq. km). Neighbours: Hungary (north), Romania and Bulgaria (east), the Former Yugoslav Republic of Macedonia and Albania (south), Bosnia-Hercegovina and Croatia (west)
POPULATION – 10,597,000 (1997 UN estimate): 66 per cent Serb and Montenegrin, 18 per cent Albanian, 8 per cent Muslim slavs, 4 per cent Hungarian, with smaller numbers of Yugoslavs (no ethnic group), Croats and Bulgarians. The majority religion is Serbian Orthodox, with significant Muslim and small Roman Catholic minorities. The main language is Serbian (Serbo-Croat) (74 per cent), with Albanian and Hungarian minorities. Serbo-Croat is a South Slav language written in the Cyrillic script
CAPITAL – Belgrade (population, 1,338,856, 1991)
MAJOR CITIES – Kragujevac (146,607); Niš (175,555); Novi Sad (178,896); Podgorica (117,875), the capital of Montenegro; Priština (108,083); Subotica (100,219), 1991
CURRENCY – New dinar of 100 paras
NATIONAL ANTHEM – Hej, Slaveni, Jošte Živi Reč Našíh Dedova (Oh! Slavs, our ancestors' words still live)
NATIONAL DAY – 27 April
NATIONAL FLAG – Three horizontal stripes of blue, white, red
LIFE EXPECTANCY (years) – male 69.88; female 74.67
POPULATION GROWTH RATE – 0.1 per cent (1997)
POPULATION DENSITY – 104 per sq. km (1997)
URBAN POPULATION – 51.4 per cent (1995)
MILITARY EXPENDITURE – 9.1 per cent of GDP (1998)
MILITARY PERSONNEL – 108,700: Army 85,000, Navy 7,000, Air Force 16,700
CONSCRIPTION DURATION – 12–15 months
ILLITERACY RATE – 6.7 per cent
ENROLMENT (percentage of age group) – primary 69 per cent (1990); secondary 62 per cent (1990); tertiary 22.5 per cent (1996)

The climate is continental. Montenegro and southern Serbia are extremely mountainous, while the north is dominated by the low-lying plains of the Danube. The major rivers are: the Danube, which flows through the north of Serbia from Romania and Bulgaria; the Sava, which flows eastwards from Bosnia to join the Danube at Belgrade; the Drina, which flows along most of the Serbian–Bosnian border to join the Sava; and the Morava, which flows from the extreme south to join the Danube in the north.

HISTORY AND POLITICS

Serbia emerged from the rule of the Byzantine Empire in the 13th century to form a large and prosperous state in the Balkans. Defeat by the Turks in 1389 led to almost 500 years of Turkish rule. After gaining autonomy within the Ottoman Empire in 1815, Serbia became fully independent in 1878 and a kingdom in 1881. Montenegro was part of the Serbian state before it was conquered by the Turks in 1355; it became independent in 1851. At the end of the First World War Serbia and Montenegro joined with the former Austro-Hungarian provinces of Slovenia, Croatia and Bosnia-Hercegovina to form the 'Kingdom of Serbs, Croats and Slovenes' which was renamed Yugoslavia in 1929. Yugoslavia was occupied by Axis forces in 1941 and reformed as a Communist federal republic under the presidency of partisan leader Josip Tito in 1945.

Tito died in 1980 and the delicate political balance of a rotating federal presidency was unable to contain the growing nationalist movements after his death. Efforts by the six republican presidents to negotiate a new federal or confederal structure for the country failed in 1991. On 25 June 1991 Slovenia and Croatia declared their independence from Yugoslavia

In Croatia the ethnic Serb minority refused to accept Croatia's independence and fighting began in July 1991 between Croat Defence Forces and Serbian guerrillas backed by the Yugoslav National Army (JNA). By September 1991 this had escalated into war between Croatia and Serbia. The war in Croatia continued until January 1992 when the EU and the UN were able to bring about a cease-fire (see Croatia).

Macedonia declared its independence on 18 September 1991.

Bosnia-Hercegovina declared its independence on 1 March 1992. Independence was supported by the Bosniacs (Muslims) and Croats but rejected by the ethnic Serbs and fighting between Bosniacs and Serbs broke out in March 1992. The JNA intervened against the Bosniacs but in May 1992 withdrew to Serbia and Montenegro (see Bosnia-Hercegovina).

On 27 April 1992 the two remaining republics of the former Socialist Federal Republic of Yugoslavia, Serbia and Montenegro, announced the formation of a new Yugoslav federation, which they invited Serbs in Croatia and Bosnia-Hercegovina to join.

Federal legislative elections were held in November 1996. The Serbian Socialist Party emerged as the largest party in the federal legislature and formed a coalition government with Yugoslav United Left and New Democracy. Legislative elections were held in Montenegro in May 1998 and were won by reformists led by President Djukanović. Kosovo has been under UN administration since June 1999. Presidential and Federal Assembly elections were scheduled for 24 September 2000.

On 2 November 1999, Montenegro made the German mark legal tender alongside the Yugoslav dinar, a move which was ruled illegal by the Yugoslav Constitutional Court in January 2000.

INSURGENCY

The province of Kosovo in the south of Serbia is more than 90 per cent ethnically Albanian. Kosovo was an autonomous region within Serbia until 1989, when Slobodan Milošević, then leader of the League of Communists of Serbia, revoked Kosovo's autonomous status, resulting in the progressive exclusion of the Albanian majority from public life. In defiance of the Serbian authorities, presidential and parliamentary elections were held in Kosovo in May 1992, and were won by the Democratic League of Kosovo and its leader Ibrahim Rugova. Following clashes between ethnic Albanians and Serbian police in February and March 1998, the Serbian military attacked civilians in the province on the pretext of eliminating support for the Kosovo Liberation Army (KLA), an ethnic Albanian organisation fighting for independence for the province. The international community condemned the brutality of the Serbian forces and a UN arms embargo was imposed on Yugoslavia, but the situation deteriorated with clashes between the KLA and security forces becoming commonplace. The civil unrest

deteriorated into a state of open war. Following early gains by the KLA, Serbian forces fought back, sending tanks and artillery to engage in the systematic destruction of entire villages in the region in order to drive out KLA troops. International organisations detailed widespread human rights abuses by the security forces; NATO and Russia ordered both sides to attend a peace conference in Paris on 6 February 1999, which was unsuccessful. Talks resumed on 15 March and the Kosovar Albanian delegation signed the internationally mediated agreement that offered Kosovo autonomy within Serbia and provided for the deployment of a NATO peacekeeping force. The Yugoslav authorities refused to sign and peace talks were abandoned. Tens of thousands of Kosovar Albanians fled when Yugoslav forces began to attack Kosovar villages. Following warnings to the Yugoslav authorities, NATO commenced air strikes against military targets in Yugoslavia 24 March 1999. Over eight hundred thousand of people fled or were forced to leave their homes and sought refuge in Albania, Macedonia or Montenegro, which, although part of the Yugoslav Federation, had refused to become involved in the fighting; more than five hundred thousand people were displaced within Kosovo. NATO intensified its bombing campaign, now targeting industrial, communications and power links.

On 27 May 1999, the UN War Crimes Tribunal indicted President Milošević of Yugoslavia, President Milutinović of Serbia, and other senior Yugoslav officials for crimes against humanity.

On 3 June President Milošević accepted a peace plan agreed by NATO and Russia and on 10 June Yugoslav forces began to withdraw; NATO air operations were immediately suspended and NATO and Russian forces entered Kosovo the following day. By 20 June all Yugoslav forces had been withdrawn from Kosovo and the Kosovar refugees had begun to return. Since the Yugoslav withdrawal, Kosovo has been under the administration of the UN's Interim Administration Mission in Kosovo (UNMIK), who have established the Kosovo Transitional Council composed of four UN and four Kosovar representatives. The NATO-led Kosovo Force (KFOR) has established five command sectors, administered by UK, US, French, German and Italian troops respectively. In addition, parts of the French, German and US sectors are patrolled by Russian troops. KFOR has facilitated the disarming of the KLA and the return of over 850,000 Kosovar Albanian refugees, but at least 200,000 Kosovar Serbs have fled, fearing reprisal attacks, which have frequently occurred.

POLITICAL SYSTEM

The Federal Republic has a bicameral parliament with a directly elected 138-seat (108 Serbian, 30 Montenegrin) lower house, the Chamber of Citizens, and an indirectly elected 40-seat (20 Serbian, 20 Montenegrin) upper house, the Chamber of Republics. Both houses serve four-year terms. Executive power is vested in a federal president and government.

Following constitutional amendments approved by the legislature on 24 July 2000, the Chamber of Republics will be directly elected and the president will be able to seek re-election.

HEAD OF STATE

Federal President, Slobodan Milošević, *elected by parliament* 15 July 1997

FEDERAL GOVERNMENT *as at September 2000*

Prime Minister, Momir Bulatović (SNP)
Deputy PMs, Danilo Vuksanović (SNP); Nikola Sainović (SPS); Vladan Kutlesić (SPS); Maja Gojković (SRS); Tomislav Nikolić (SRS)
Agriculture, Nedeljko Sipovac (SPS)
Co-operation with International Financial Organisations,

Borka Vucić (SPS)
Defence, Gen. Dragoljub Ojdanić (SNP)
Development, Science and Environment, Nada Sljapić (JUL)
Economy, Milan Beko (SPS)
External Trade, Borislav Vuković (SPS)
Finance, Dragisa Pesić (SNP)
Foreign Affairs, Zivadin Jovanović (SPS)
Information, Goran Matić (JUL)
Internal Affairs, Zoran Sokolović (SPS)
Internal Trade, Milovan Erić (SRS)
International Cultural Co-operation, Cedomir Mirković
Justice, Petar Jojić (SRS)
Labour, Miodrag Kovac (SNP)
Refugees and Displaced People, Bratislava Morina (JUL)
Sports, Velizar Djerić (SPS)
Telecommunications, Ivan Marković (JUL)
Transport, Dejan Drobnjaković (SNP)
Without Portfolio, Goran Cvetanović; Matija Dabović;
   Zelidrag Nikcević (SNS); Nebojsa Velicković (SRS);
   Zoran Vujović (SPS)

JUL Yugoslav United Left; SNP Montenegrin Socialist
   National Party; SPS Socialist Party of Serbia; SRS
   Serbian Radical Party

MONTENEGRO
AREA – 5,331 sq. miles (13,812 sq. km)
POPULATION – 615,000: 62 per cent Montenegrin,
   14.5 per cent Bosniac, 6.5 per cent Albanian and
   3 per cent Serb
CAPITAL – Podgorica (population, 117,875, 1991)

The Montenegrin Social Democrat Party (former Communists) won multiparty elections in November 1996 for the 85-seat republican assembly and formed a government. The most recent presidential election was won by Milo Djukanović, a reformist candidate favouring greater independence for the province.

President, Milo Djukanović, *elected* 19 October 1997
Prime Minister, Filip Vujanović

BRITISH COUNCIL, British Information Centre,
   Njegoseva 22, 81000 Podgorica;
   e-mail: varjam.bic@cg.yu

SERBIA
AREA – 34,175 sq. miles (88,538 sq. km)
POPULATION – 9,300,000, of whom 66 per cent are Serbs
CAPITAL – Belgrade (population, 1,338,856, 1991)

Serbia includes the provinces of Kosovo (population 1.6 million), of great historic importance to Serbs, and Vojvodina (population 2 million); the autonomy of both was ended in September 1990. Vojvodina, with its capital at Novi Sad, has a large Hungarian minority (21 per cent). Kosovo, with its capital at Priština, is predominantly Albanian (90 per cent). Following the conflict in Kosovo, more than 200,000 people have been left homeless and entire villages have been destroyed.

The Socialist Party of Serbia (SPS) (formerly the Communists) emerged as the largest party in multiparty elections for the 250-seat National Assembly, held in November 1996, although the results of the election were disputed.

President, Milan Milutinović
Prime Minister, Mirko Marjanović

ECONOMY

Since 1991 the economy has been devastated by the wars in Croatia and Bosnia-Hercegovina, by the UN economic sanctions and trade embargo, and because of the lack of free-market reforms. Only the country's agricultural self-sufficiency has kept it afloat. In 1997, agriculture accounted for 21.3 per cent of GDP and employed 22.6

per cent of the workforce.

The UN voted to lift economic sanctions on 22 November 1995 following the conclusion of the Dayton Peace Accord, but re-imposed sanctions in 1998 as the situation in Kosovo deteriorated. Industrial production remains extremely low and there is high unemployment, estimated to be around 40 per cent in 1997. Following the conflict in Kosovo, the USA and EU froze all Yugoslav assets within their jurisdiction and banned all investment in the country.

GDP – US$10,475 million (1996); US$1,018 per capita
   (1996)
ANNUAL AVERAGE GROWTH OF GDP – 4.3 per cent (1996)
INFLATION RATE – 117.4 per cent (1991)
TOTAL EXTERNAL DEBT – US$13,742 million (1998)

Trade with UK	1998	1999
Imports from UK	£42,596,000	£27,038,000
Exports to UK	30,876,000	315,573,000

ZAMBIA
Republic of Zambia

AREA – 290,587 sq. miles (752,618 sq. km). Neighbours:
   Democratic Republic of Congo and Tanzania (north),
   Malawi (east), Mozambique, Zimbabwe and Namibia
   (south), Angola (west)
POPULATION – 8,478,000 (1997 UN estimate). English is
   the official language; other languages spoken include
   Bemba, Kaonda, Lozi, Lunda, Luvale, Nyanja and
   Tonga
CAPITAL – Lusaka (population, 982,362, 1990)
MAJOR CITIES – Chingola (186,769); Kabwe (166,519);
   Kitwe (348,571); Luanshya (147,747); Mufulira
   (175,025); Ndola (376,311)
CURRENCY – Kwacha (K) of 100 ngwee
NATIONAL ANTHEM – Stand and Sing of Zambia, Proud
   and Free
NATIONAL DAY – 24 October (Independence Day)
NATIONAL FLAG – Green with three small vertical stripes,
   red, black and orange (next fly); eagle device on green
   above stripes
LIFE EXPECTANCY (years) – male 50.70; female 53.00
POPULATION GROWTH RATE – 0.7 per cent (1997)
POPULATION DENSITY – 11 per sq. km (1997)
URBAN POPULATION – 39.4 per cent (1990)
MILITARY EXPENDITURE – 1.9 per cent of GDP (1998)
MILITARY PERSONNEL – 21,600: Army 20,000,
   Air Force 1,600; Paramilitaries 1,400
ILLITERACY RATE – 22.0 per cent
ENROLMENT (percentage of age group) – primary 75 per
   cent (1995); secondary 16 per cent (1994); tertiary 2.5
   per cent (1994)

Zambia lies on the plateau of Central Africa. With the exception of the valleys of the Zambezi, the Luapula, the Kafue and the Luangwa rivers, and the Luano valley, elevations vary from 3,000 to 5,000 feet above sea level, but in the north-east the plateau rises to occasional altitudes of over 6,000 feet. Although Zambia lies within the tropics, and fairly centrally in the African land mass, its elevation relieves it from extremely high temperatures and humidity.

HISTORY AND POLITICS

Northern Rhodesia came under British rule in 1889. It achieved internal self-government when the Federation of Rhodesia and Nyasaland was dissolved in 1963 and became an independent republic within the Commonwealth on 24 October 1964 under the name of Zambia. Zambia was a one-party state (the United National

Independence Party) from 1973 until 1990, when pressure from opposition groups led to a new constitution (August 1991) and multiparty legislative and presidential elections in October 1991. The Movement for Multiparty Democracy (MMD) won 125 of the 150 seats in parliament, and the MMD candidate Frederick Chiluba defeated Kenneth Kaunda, who had ruled since independence, in the presidential election; Kaunda was later stripped of his Zambian citizenship.

Following an abortive coup attempt in October 1997, the president declared a state of emergency. 90 people were subsequently arrested in connection with the coup, including former President Kaunda, of whom 59 were sentenced to death in September 1999. The state of emergency was lifted in March 1998.

HEAD OF STATE

President, Frederick J. Chiluba, *elected* October 1991, *re-elected* 18 November 1996
Vice-President, Lt.-Gen. (retd) Christon Tembo

CABINET *as at September 2000*

Agriculture, Food and Fisheries, Suresh Desai
Commerce, Trade and Industry, William Harrington
Communications and Transport, Nkandu Luo
Community Development and Social Services, Dawson Lupunga
Defence, Chitalu Sampa
Education, Brig.-Gen. Godfrey Miyanda
Energy and Water Development, David Saviye
Environment and Natural Resources, vacant
Finance and Economic Development, Katele Kalumba
Foreign Affairs, Keli Walubita
Health, David Mapamba
Home Affairs, Peter Machungwa
Information and Broadcasting Services, Newstead Zimba
Labour and Social Security, Edith Nawakwi
Lands, Samuel Miyanda
Legal Affairs, Vincent Malambo
Local Government and Housing, Ackson Sejani
Mines and Mineral Development, Syamujaye Syamukayumbu
Presidential Affairs, Eric Silwamba
Science, Technology and Vocational Training, Abel Chambeshi
Tourism, vacant
Without Portfolio, Michael Sata
Works and Supply, Godden Mandandi
Youth, Sport and Child Development, Syacheye Madyenkuku

HIGH COMMISSION FOR THE REPUBLIC OF ZAMBIA

2 Palace Gate, London W8 5NG
Tel: 020-7589 6655
High Commissioner, vacant
Deputy High Commissioner, Geoffrey P. Alikipo
Defence Adviser, Brig.-Gen. M. G. Lisita

BRITISH HIGH COMMISSION

Independence Avenue, PO Box 50050, 15101, Lusaka
Tel: (00 260) (1) 251133
e-mail: brithc@zamnet.zm
High Commissioner, HE Thomas Young, apptd 1997
Deputy High Commissioner, P. W. D. Nessling
First Secretary (Development and Economic), A. J. Wardhaugh

BRITISH COUNCIL DIRECTOR, M. Fryars, Heroes Place, Cairo Road (PO Box 34571), Lusaka; e-mail: bclusaka@zamnet.zm

ECONOMY

In 1991, the MMD government began the transition from a state-controlled economy to a free market system. Privatisation has been encouraged, foreign exchange controls have been removed and the Kwacha has been floated. Price subsidies and tariffs have been lowered or abolished, but increased imports have affected manufacturing. In 1997, 71.1 per cent of the workforce were engaged in agriculture, which accounted for 19 per cent of GDP in 1996. Principal agricultural products are maize, sugar, groundnuts, cotton, livestock, vegetables and tobacco. The principal exports are copper and cobalt. The principal imports are industrial goods, machinery and transport equipment, fuel and foodstuffs.

In 1997 imports totalled US$819 million and exports US$915 million.

GNP – US$3,234 million (1998); US$330 per capita (1998)
GDP – US$1,690 million (1996); US$204 per capita (1996)
ANNUAL AVERAGE GROWTH OF GDP – 6.5 per cent (1996)
INFLATION RATE – 24.8 per cent (1997)
TOTAL EXTERNAL DEBT – US$6,865 million (1998)

Trade with UK	1998	1999
Imports from UK	£35,387,000	£24,024,000
Exports to UK	24,582,000	15,184,000

ZIMBABWE
Republic of Zimbabwe

AREA – 150,872 sq. miles (390,757 sq. km). Neighbours: Zambia (north), Mozambique (east), South Africa (south), Botswana and Namibia (west)
POPULATION – 12,294,000 (1997 UN estimate); 10,400,000 (1992 census): 77 per cent Shona, 17 per cent Ndebele, 1.4 per cent Europeans. The official language is English, with Shona the largest indigenous language group
CAPITAL – Harare (population, 1,189,103, 1992)
MAJOR CITIES – Bulawayo (621,742), the largest town in Matabeleland; Chitungwiza (274,912)
CURRENCY – Zimbabwe dollar (Z$) of 100 cents
NATIONAL ANTHEM – Ngaikomberarwe Nyika Ye Zimbabwe (Blessed be the country of Zimbabwe)
NATIONAL DAY – 18 April (Independence Day)
NATIONAL FLAG – Seven horizontal stripes of green, yellow, red, black, red, yellow, green; a white, black-bordered, triangle based on the hoist containing the national emblem
LIFE EXPECTANCY (years) – male 58.00; female 62.00
POPULATION GROWTH RATE – 3.9 per cent (1997)
POPULATION DENSITY – 31 per sq. km (1997)
MILITARY EXPENDITURE – 5.0 per cent of GDP (1998)
MILITARY PERSONNEL – 39,000: Army 35,000, Air Force 4,000; Paramilitaries 21,800

HISTORY AND POLITICS

European colonisation of Zimbabwe began in 1890 when settlers forcibly acquired Shona lands, followed by the seizure of Ndebele lands in 1893. It became a self-governing colony under the name of Southern Rhodesia in 1923. A unilateral declaration of independence on 11 November 1965, which resulted in UN sanctions against the country, was finally terminated on 12 December 1979. Following elections in February 1980 the country became independent on 18 April 1980 as the Republic of Zimbabwe, a member of the British Commonwealth.

The independence constitution was amended in 1987, making the presidency an executive post. The president is popularly elected for a six-year term, appoints the Cabinet and can veto parliamentary bills. The unicameral legislature, the House of Assembly, has 150 members: 120 elected, ten traditional chiefs and 20 others appointed by the president. Amendments to the constitution, which would have strengthened the role of the president and allowed the state to seize land without compensation, were rejected by the electorate in February 2000

President Mugabe was re-elected for a six-year term in March 1996, following the withdrawal of the other two contenders. The most recent general election was held on 24–25 June 2000. The Zimbabwe African National Union - Patriotic Front (ZANU-PF) won 62 of the 120 elective seats, and the Movement for Democratic Change, a new opposition grouping formed by various civic groups and the Zimbabwe Congress of Trade Unions, won 57 seats. There was widespread intimidation and violence against the opposition during the election campaign.

The occupation of white-owned farms by protestors, led by former veterans of the war against the white minority regime, began in February 2000. On 6 April, the House of Assembly approved the Land Acquisition Act, which amended the constitution to enable the government to take over white-owned farms without compensation and redistribute them to landless blacks.

The country is divided into eight provinces: Manicaland, Masvingo, Matabeleland North, Matabeleland South, Midlands, Mashonaland West, Mashonaland Central and Mashonaland East.

HEAD OF STATE

Executive President, C.-in-C. of the Defence Forces, Robert Gabriel Mugabe, *elected* 30 December 1987, *re-elected* March 1990, March 1996
Vice-Presidents, Joseph Msika; Simon Muzenda

CABINET *as at September 2000*

The President
Defence, Moven Mahachi
Education, Sports and Culture, Simbarashe Mumbengegwi
Environment and Tourism, Francis Nhema
Finance and Economic Development, Simba Makoni
Foreign Affairs, Dr Stanislaus Mudenge
Health and Child Welfare, Dr Timothy Stamps
Higher Education and Technology, Herbert Murerwa
Home Affairs, John Nkomo
Industry and International Trade, Nkosana Moyo
Information and Publicity, Jonathan Moyo
Justice, Legal and Parliamentary Affairs, Patrick Chinamas
Lands, Agriculture and Rural Development, Joseph Made
Local Government, Public Works and National Housing, Ignatius Chombo
Mines and Energy, Sidney Tigere Sekeramayi
National Security, Nicholas Goche
Public Service, Labour and Social Welfare, July Moyo
Rural Resources and Water Development, Joyce Mujuru
Transport, Swithen Mombeshora
Youth Development and Employment Creation, Border Gezi

HIGH COMMISSION OF THE REPUBLIC OF ZIMBABWE

Zimbabwe House, 429 Strand, London WC2R 0QE
Tel: 020-7836 7755
High Commissioner, HE Simbarashe Simbanenduku Mumbengegwi, apptd 1999
Deputy High Commissioner, Pavelyn Tendai Musaka
Minister-Counsellor, T. Jamu
Defence Adviser, Col. J. J. Murozvi
Senior Commercial Attaché, J. Foroma

BRITISH HIGH COMMISSION

Corner House, Samora Machel Avenue (PO Box 4490), Harare
Tel: (00 263) (4) 772990/774700
High Commissioner, HE Peter Longworth, apptd 1998
Deputy High Commissioner, T. Hay-Campbell, LVO
Defence Adviser, Col. J. S. Field, CBE
First Secretaries, D. Seddon (*Commercial*); J. Liddell (*Consular*)

BRITISH COUNCIL DIRECTOR, Dr J. Taylor, 23 Jason Moyo Avenue, PO Box 664, Harare;

e-mail: general.enquiries@bc-harare.sprint.com.
There is a regional office in Bulawayo

ECONOMY

Ten years of socialism and central planning in 1980–90 brought the economy to crisis point before free-market economic reforms were introduced in 1990. The programme has been partially implemented but the economy remains highly regulated and weak. Inflation and unemployment remains high and rises in the prices of basic commodities and fuel resulted in widespread strike action and protests. Zimbabwe's involvement in the civil war in the Democratic Republic of Congo has required substantially higher military expenditure. The value of the Zimbabwe dollar has fallen sharply, but fuel prices have not been increased accordingly, which led to shortages in January 2000 after the National Oil Company of Zimbabwe defaulted on debts. There is a grave shortage of foreign exchange, which has led to Zimbabwe defaulting on loan repayments.

Agriculture accounted for 28 per cent of GDP in 1998. The agricultural sector is well-developed and employs 66 per cent of the workforce. Tobacco remains the most important crop in terms of export (Zimbabwe is the largest exporter in the world), and maize the most important for domestic consumption. Other crops include wheat, cotton, sugar, horticultural products, fruit and vegetables. Beef is exported to the EU.

The manufacturing sector is very dependent on the agricultural sector for raw materials. Industry is also dependent on imports e.g. fuel oil, steel products and chemicals, as well as heavy machinery and items of transport. The mining sector, although contributing a relatively small portion to GDP, is important to the economy as a foreign exchange earner. Almost all mineral production is exported. Gold is the most important product; others are asbestos, diamonds, silver, nickel, copper, platinum, chrome ore, tin, iron ore and cobalt. There is a successful ferro-chrome industry and a substantial steel works which has been heavily subsidised by government.

Tourism is of growing importance, with 1.7 million visitors in 1997.

The principal exports are agricultural products (especially tobacco), manufactured goods and unprocessed minerals. The principal imports are machinery and transport equipment, manufactures, chemical products, oil and oil products, and foodstuffs. The main trading partners are South Africa and the UK.

In 1994 Zimbabwe had a trade surplus of US$158 million and a current account deficit of US$425 million. In 1995 imports totalled US$2,660 million and exports US$2,119 million.

GNP – US$7,214 million (1998); US$620 per capita (1998)
GDP – US$8,876 million (1996); US$776 per capita (1996)
ANNUAL AVERAGE GROWTH OF GDP – 6.0 per cent (1996)
INFLATION RATE – 31.8 per cent (1998)
TOTAL EXTERNAL DEBT – US$4,716 million (1998)

Trade with UK	1998	1999
Imports from UK	£77,603,000	£73,689,000
Exports to UK	122,784,000	122,696,000

EDUCATION

Education is compulsory, and the language of instruction is English. Over 80 per cent of schools are government-aided. There are four universities; the University of Zimbabwe was founded in 1955.

ILLITERACY RATE – 7.3 per cent
ENROLMENT (percentage of age group) – tertiary 6.5 per cent (1996)

Currencies of the World

AND EXCHANGE RATES AGAINST £ STERLING

Country/Territory	Monetary Unit	Average Rate to £ 31 August 1999	Average Rate to £ 1 4 September 2000
Afghanistan	Afghani (Af) of 100 puls	Af 7429.49	Af 6936.19
Albania	Lek (Lk) of 100 qindraka	Lk 211.892	Lk 215.387
Algeria	Algerian dinar (DA) of 100 centimes	DA 105.034	DA 112.936
American Samoa	Currency is that of the USA	US$ 1.5878	US$ 1.4603
Andorra	French and Spanish curriencies in use	—	Francs - 10.6435
			Peseta - 269.976
Angola	Readjusted kwanza (Krzl) of 100 lwei	Krzl 4081484.3	Krzl 10.7745
Anguilla	East Caribbean dollar (EC$) of 100 cents	EC$ 4.2871	EC$ 3.9427
Antigua and Barbuda	East Caribbean dollar (EC$) of 100 cents	EC$ 4.2871	EC$ 3.9427
Argentina	Peso of 10,000 australes	Pesos 1.5872	Pesos 1.4593
Armenia	Dram of 100 louma	Dram 851.474	Dram 775.539
Aruba	Aruban florin	Florins 2.84104	Florins 2.6139
Ascension Island	Currency that of St Helena	at parity with £ sterling	
Australia	Australian dollar ($A) of 100 cents	$A 2.5102	$A 2.5365
Norfolk Island	Currency that of Australia	$A 2.5102	$A 2.5365
Austria	Schilling of 100 Groschen	Schilling 20.8988	Schilling 22.3274
Azerbaijan	Manat of 100 gopik	Manat 6529.11	Manat 6391.52
The Bahamas	Bahamian dollar (B$) of 100 cents	B$ 1.5878	B$ 1.4603
Bahrain	Bahraini dinar (BD) of 1,000 fils	BD 0.5986	BD 0.5505
Bangladesh	Taka (Tk) of 100 poisha	Tk 78.5962	Tk 78.9266
Barbados	Barbados dollar (BD$) of 100 cents	BD$ 3.1756	BD$ 2.9205
Belarus	Rouble of 100 kopeks	Roubles 500157.2	Roubles 1486.54
			(market rate)
Belgium	Belgian franc (or frank) of 100 centimes (centiemen)	Francs 61.2671	Francs 65.4551
Belize	Belize dollar (BZ$) of 100 cents	BZ$ 3.1756	BZ$ 2.9205
Benin	Franc FCA	Francs 996.250	Francs 1064.35
Bermuda	Bermuda dollar of 100 cents	$ 1.5878	$ 1.4603
Bhutan	Ngultrum of 100 chetrum (Indian currency is also legal tender)	Ngultrum 69.0693	Ngultrum 66.8065
Bolivia	Boliviano ($b) of 100 centavos	$b 9.3204	$b 9.0244
Bosnia-Hercegovina	Convertible marka	Marka 2.9385	Marka 3.1735
Botswana	Pula (P) of 100 thebe	P 7.3374	P 7.5290
Brazil	Real of 100 centavos	Real 3.0653	Real 2.6628
			(floating rate)
Brunei	Brunei dollar (B$) of 100 sen (fully interchangeable with Singapore currency)	B$ 2.6802	B$ 2.5123
Bulgaria	Lev of 100 stotinki	Leva 2.9555	Leva 3.1583
Burkina Faso	Franc CFA	Francs 996.250	Francs 1064.35
Burundi	Burundi franc of 100 centimes	Francs 969.612	Francs 1133.37
Cambodia	Riel of 100 sen	Riel 6020.84	Riel 5621.96
Cameroon	Franc CFA	Francs 996.250	Francs 1064.35
Canada	Canadian dollar (C$) of 100 cents	C$ 2.3721	C$ 2.1517
Cape Verde	Escudo Caboverdiano of 100 centavos	Esc 150.381	Esc 181.384
Cayman Islands	Cayman Islands dollar (CI$) of 100 cents	CI$ 1.3231	CI$ 1.2168
Central African Republic	Franc CFA	Francs 996.250	Francs 1064.35
Chad	Franc CFA	Francs 996.250	Francs 1064.35
Chile	Chilean peso of 100 centavos	Pesos 817.479	Pesos 822.632
China	Renminbi Yuan of 10 Jiao or 100 fen	Yuan 13.1427	Yuan 12.0890
Hong Kong	Hong Kong (HK$) of 100 cents	HK$ 12.3284	HK$ 11.3886
Colombia	Colombian peso of 100 centavos	Pesos 3055.72	Pesos 3234.45
The Comoros	Comorian franc (KMF) of 100 centimes	Francs 781.147	Francs 796.139
Congo, Dem. Rep. of	Congolese franc	CFr 7.1451	CFr 6.5711
Congo, Rep. of	Franc CFA	Francs 996.250	Francs 1064.35
Costa Rica	Costa Rican colón (₡) of 100 céntimos	₡ 461.066	₡ 447.275
Côte d'Ivorie	Franc CFA	Francs 996.250	Francs 1064.35
Croatia	Kuna of 100 lipa	Kuna 11.5632	Kuna 12.2506
Cuba	Cuban peso of 100 centavos	Pesos 33.3438	Pesos 30.6653
Cyprus	Cypurs pound (C£) of 100 cents	C£ 0.8781	C£ 0.9289

Country	Currency	Rate 1	Rate 2
Czech Republic	Koruna (Kcs) of 100 halécru	Kcs 55.6659	Kcs 57.3711
Denmark	Danish krone of 100 Øre	Kroner 11.2892	Kroner 12.1033
Fare Islands	Currency is that of Denmark	Kroner 11.2892	Kroner 12.1033
Dijbouti	Dijbouti franc of 100 centimes	Francs 282.184	Francs 253.646
Dominica	East Caribbean dollar (EC$) of 100 cents	EC$ 4.2871	EC$ 3.9427
Dominican Republic	Dominican Republic peso (RD$) of 100 centavos	RD$ 25.1190	RD$ 26.6350
Ecuador	Sucre of 100 centavos	Sucres 17735.7	Sucres 36506.3 (official rate)
Egypt	Egyptian pound (£E) of 100 piastres of 1,000 millièmes	£E 5.4462	£E 5.1365
El Salvador	El Salvador colón (₡) of 100 centavos	₡ 13.8155	₡ 12.7334
Equatorial Guinea	Franc CFA	Francs 996.250	Francs 1064.35
Eritrea	Nakfa	–	–
Estonia	Kroon of 100 sents	Kroons 23.7512	Kroons 25.3740
Ethiopia	Ethiopian birr (EB) of 100 cents	EB 11.9355	EB 11.8894
Falkland Islands	Falkland pound of 100 pence	at parity with £ sterling	
Fiji	Fiji dollar (F$) of 100 cents	F$ 3.1631	F$ 3.1608
Finland	Markka (Mk) of 100 penniä	Mk 9.0302	Mk 9.6475
France	Franc of 100 centimes	Francs 9.9625	Francs 10.6435
French Guiana	Currency if that of France	Francs 9.9625	Francs 10.6435
French Polynesia	Franc CFP	Francs 181.171	Francs 195.498
Gabon	Franc CFA	Francs 996.250	Francs 1064.35
The Gambia	Dalasi (D) of 100 butut	D 18.6885	D 19.1294
Georgia	Laria of 100 tetri	–	Laria 2.8986
Germany	Deutsche Mark (DM) of 100 Pfennig	DM 2.9705	DM 3.1735
Ghana	Cedi of 100 pesewas	Cedi 4125.12	Cedi 10294.8
Gibraltar	Gibraltar pound of 100 pence	at parity with £ sterling	
Greece	Drachma of 100 leptae	Drachmae 495.902	Drachmae 547.754
Greenland	Currency is that of Denmark	Kroner 11.2892	Kroner 12.1033
Grenada	East Caribbean dollar (EC$) of 100 cents	EC$ 4.2871	EC$ 3.9427
Guadeloupe	Currency is that of France	Francs 9.9625	Francs 10.6435
Guam	Currency is that of the USA US$ 1.4603	US$ 1.5878	
Guatemala	Quetzal (Q) of 100 centavos	Q 12.4287	Q 11.4170
Guinea	Guinea franc of 100 centimes	Francs 2166.96	Francs 2381.67
Guinea-Bissau	Franc CFA	Francs 996.250	Francs 1064.35
Guyana	Guyana dollar (G$) of 100 cents	G$ 274.690	G$ 266.204
Haiti	Gourde of 100 centimes	Gourdes 26.2257	Gourdes 32.1255
Honduras	Lempira of 100 centavos	Lempiras 22.8485	Lempiras 21.7870
Hungary	Forint of 100 fillér	Forints 384.184	Forints 424.071
Iceland	Icelandic króna (Kr) of 100 aurar	Kr 116.751	Kr 117.930
India	Indian rupee (Rs) of 100 paisa	Rs 69.0693	Rs 66.8065
Indonesia	Rupiah (Rp) of 100 sen	Rp 12067.3	Rp 12083.6
Iran	Rial	Rials 4763.40	Rials 2551.79 (official rate)
Iraq	Iraqi dinar (ID) of 1,000 fils	ID 0.4933	ID 0.4540
Ireland Republic of	Punt (IR£) of 100 pence	IR£ 1.1962	IR£ 1.2779
Israel	Shekel of 100 agora	Shekels 6.7438	Shekels 5.8629
Italy	Lira of 100 centesimi	Lire 2940.75	Lire 3141.77
Jamaica	Jamaican dollar (J$) of 100 cents	J$ 62.7975	J$ 61.3305
Japan	Yen	Yen 177.357	Yen 154.422
Jordan	Jordanian dinar (JD) of 1,000 fils	JD 1.1297	JD 1.0382
Kazakhstan	Tenge	Tenge 209.669	Tenge 208.356
Kenya	Kenya shilling (Ksh) of 100 cents	Ksh 119.284	Ksh 112.804
Kiribati	Australian dollar ($A) of 100 cents	$A 2.5102	$A 2.5365
Korea, Dem. People's Rep. of	Won of 100 chon	Won 3.4932	Won 3.2126
Korea, Republic of	Won	Won 1877.57	Won 1614.53
Kuwait	Kuwaiti dinar (KD) of 1,000 fils	KD 0.4845	KD 0.4493
Kyrgyzstan	Som	–	Som 70.1436
Laos	Kip (K) of 100 at	K 12146.7	K 11046.8
Latvia	Lats of 100 santims	Lats 0.9423	Lats 0.8872
Lebanon	Lebanese pound (L£) of of 100 piastres	L£ 2394.41	L£ 2210.82
Lesotho	Loti (M) of 100 lisente	M 9.6697	M 10.1670
Liberia	Liberian dollar (L$) of 100 cents	L$ 1.5878	L$ 1.4603
Libya	Libyan dinar (LD) of 1,000 dirhams	LD 0.7145	LD 0.737
Liechtenstein	Swiss franc of 100 rappen (or centimes)	Francs 2.4322	Francs 2.5143
Lithuania	Litas	Litas 6.3536	Litas 5.8425

Luxembourg	Luxembourg franc (LF) of 100 centimes (Belgian currency is also legal tender)	LF 61.2671	LF 65.4551
Macao	Pataca of 100 avos	Pataca 12.7353	Pataca 11.7346
Macedonia	Dinar of 100 para	Dinars 93.1193	Dinars 95.4931
Madagascar	Franc malgache(FMG) of 100 centimes	FMG 10420.7	FMG 9588.00
Malawi	Kwacha (K) of 100 tambala	K 69.1568	K 89.1265
Malaysia	Malaysian dollar (ringgit) (M$) of 100 sen	M$ 6.7005	M$ 5.5490 (official rate)
Maldives	Rufiyaa of 100 laaris	Rufiyaa 17.9263	Rufiyaa 17.1872
Mali	Franc CFA	Francs 966.250	Francs 1064.35
Malta	Maltese lira (LM) of 100 cents of 1,000 mils	LM 0.6442	LM 0.6534
Marshall Islands	Currency is that of the USA	US$ 1.5878	US$ 1.4603
Martinique	Currency is that of France	Francs 9.9625	Francs 10.6435
Mauritania	Ouguiya (UM) of 5 khoums	UM 334.781	UM 352.490
Mauritius	Mauritius rupee of 100 cents	Rs 40.0682	Rs 38.1856
Mayotte	Currency is that of France	Francs 9.9625	Francs 10.6435
Mexico	Peso of 100 centavos	Pesos 14.8952	Pesos 13.4343
Micronesia, Federated States of	Currency is that of the USA	US$ 1.5878	US$ 1.4603
Moldova	Leu	Leu 17.5174	Leu 18.0706
Monaco	French franc of 100 centimes	Francs 9.9625	Francs 10.6435
Mongolia	Tugrik of 100 möngö	Tugriks 1653.28	Tugriks 1565.87
Montserrat	East Caribbean dollar (EC$) of 100 cents	EC$ 4.2871	EC$ 3.9427
Morocco	Dirham (DH) of 100 centimes	DH 15.7153	DH 15.7328
Mozambique	Metical (MT) of 100 centavos	MT 20166.7	MT 23510.1
Myanmar	Kyat (K) of 100 pyas	K 9.9265	K 9.1290
Namibia	Namibian dollar of 100 cents	at parity with SA Rand	
Nauru	Australian dollar ($A) of 100 cents	$A 2.5102	$A 2.5365
Nepal	Napalese rupee of 100 paisa	Rs 109.130	Rs 106.774
The Netherlands	Gulden (guilder) of florin of 100 cents	Guilders 3.3470	Guilders 3.5757
Netherlands Antilles	Netherlands Antilles guilder of 100 cents	Guilders 2.8104	Guilders 2.5847
New Caledonia	Franc CFP	Francs 181.171	Francs 195.498
New Zealand	New Zealand dollar (NZ$) of 100 cents	NZ$ 3.0924	NZ$ 3.4130
Cook Islands	Currency is that of New Zealand	NZ$ 3.0924	NZ$ 3.4130
Niue	Currency is that of New Zealand	NZ$ 3.0924	NZ$ 3.4130
Tokelau	Currency is that of New Zealand	NZ$ 3.0924	NZ$ 3.4130
Nicaragua	Córdoba (C$) of 100 centavos	C$ 19.0700	C$ 17.0192
Niger	Franc CFA	Francs 966.250	Francs 1064.35
Nigeria	Naira (N) of 100 kobo	N 156.414	N 151.355
Northern Mariana Islands	Currency is that of the USA	US$ 1.5878	US$ 1.4603
Norway	Krone of 100 Øre	Kroner 12.6111	Kroner 13.1471
Oman	Rial Omani (OR) of 1,000 baisas	OR 0.6113	OR 0.5622
Pakistan	Pakistan rupee of 100 paisa	Rs 82.2878	Rs 79.9560
Palau	Currency is that of the USA	US$ 1.5878	US$ 1.4603
Panama	Balboa of 100 centésimos (US notes are also in circulation)	Balboa 1.5878	Balboa 1.4603
Papua New Guinea	Kina (K) of 100 toea	K 4.6362	K 3.8916
Paraguay	Guarani (Gs) of 100 céntimos	Gs 5255.62	Gs 5117.45
Peru	New Sol of 100 cénts	New Sol 5.3509	New Sol 5.0693
The Philippines	Philippine peso (P) of 100 centavos	P 63.1151	P 65.9303
Pitcairn Islands	Currency is that of New Zealand	NZ$ 3.0924	NZ$ 3.4130
Poland	Zloty of 100 groszy	Zloty 6.3266	Zloty 6.3915
Portugal	Escudo (Esc) of 100 centavos	Esc 304.487	Esc 325.300
Puerto Rico	Currency is that of the USA	US$ 1.5878	US$ 1.4603
Qatar	Qatar riyal of 100 dirhams	Riyals 5.7804	Riyals 5.3157
Réunion	Currency is that of France	Francs 9.9625	Francs 10.6435
Romania	Leu (Lei) of 100 bani	Lei 25714.4	Lei 33666.1
Russia	New rouble of 100 kopeks	Roubles 39.3933	Roubles 40.5468
Rwanda	Rwanda franc of 100 centimes	Francs 537.931	Francs 524.271
St Christopher and Nevis	East Caribbean dollar (EC$) of 100 cents	EC$ 4.2781	EC$ 3.9427
St Helena	St Helena pound (£) of 100 pence	at parity with £ sterling	
St Lucia	East Caribbean dollar (EC$) of 100 cents	EC$ 4.2781	EC$ 3.9427
St Pierre and Miquelon	Currency is that of France	Francs 9.9625	Francs 10.6435
St Vincent and the Grenadines	East Caribbean dollar (EC$) of 100 cents	EC$ 4.2871	EC$ 3.9427
Samoa	Tala (S$) of 100 sene	S$ 4.8931	S$ 45.112
San Marino	San Marino and Italian currencies are in circulation	Lire 2940.75	Lire 3141.77

Country	Currency	Rate 1	Rate 2
Sao Tomé and Príncipe	Dobra of 100 centavos	Dobra 3794.84	Dobra 3490.00
Saudi Arabia	Saudi riyal (SR) of 20 qursh or 100 halala	SR 5.9551	SR 5.4769
Senegal	Franc CFA	Francs 996.250	Francs 1064.35
Seychelles	Seychelles rupee of 100 cents	Rs 8.4749	Rs 8.3660
Sierra Leone	Leone (Le) of 100 cents	Le 2817.08	Le 2976.21
Singapore	Singapore dollar (S$) of 100 cents	S$ 2.6802	S$ 2.5123
Slovakia	Koruna (Sk) of 100 halierov	Kcs 67.1847	Kcs 69.3437
Slovenia	Tolar (SIT) of 100 stotin'	Tolars 298.428	Tolars 339.107
Solomon Islands	Solomon Islands dollar (SI$) of 100 cents	SI$ 7.8226	SI$ 7.3836
Somalia	Somali shilling of 100 cents	Shillings 4160.04	Shillings 3825.86
South Africa	Rand (R) of 100 cents	R 9.6697	R 10.1670
Spain	Peseta of 100 céntimos	Pesetas 252.702	Pesetas 269.976
Sri Lanka	Sri Lankan rupee of 100 cents	Rs 114.115	Rs 114.119
Sudan	Sudanese dinar (SD) of 10 pounds	SD 403.301	SD 377.913
Suriname	Surinamese guilder of 100 cents	Guilders 1098.01	Guilders 1182.07
Swaziland	Lilangeni (E) of 100 cents (South African currency is also in circulation)	E 9.6697	E 10.1670
Sweden	Swedish krona of 100 öre	Kronor 13.2296	Kronor 13.6183
Switzerland	Swiss franc of 100 rappen (or centimes)	Francs 2.4322	Francs 2.5143
Syria	Syrian pound (S£) of 100 piastres	S£ 71.4510	S£ 76.6632
Taiwan	New Taiwan dollar (NT$) of 100 cents	NT$ 50.5794	NT$ 45.3846
Tajikistan	Tajik rouble (TJR) of 100 tanga	–	–
Tanzania	Tanzanian shilling of 100 cents	Shillings 1261.51	Shillings 1166.74
Thailand	Baht of 100 satang	Baht 60.8049	Baht 59.6878
Togo	Franc CFA	Francs 996.250	Francs 1064.35
Tonga	Pa'anga (T$) of 100 seniti	T$ 2.5102	T$ 2.5365
Trinidad and Tobago	Trinidad and Tobago dollar (TT$) of 100 cents	TT$ 9.7162	TT$ 9.0828
Tristan da Cunha	Currency is that of the UK		
Tunisia	Tunsian dinar of 1,000 millmes	Dinars 1,9094	Dinars 2.0456
Turkey	Turkish lira (TL) of 100 kurus	TL 710651.8	TL 952995.7
Turkmenistan	Manat of 100 tenesi	–	–
Turks and Caicos Islands	US dollar (US$)	US$ 1.5878	US$ 1.4603
Tuvalu	Australian dollar ($A) of 100 cents	$A 2.5102	$A 2.5365
Uganda	Uganda shilling of 100 cents	Shilling 2322.16	Shilling 2507.98
Ukraine	Kryvna of 100 kopiykas	Kryvnas 7.0261	Kryvnas 7.9620
United Arab Emirates	UAE dirham (Dh) of 100 fils	Dirham 5.8316	Dirham 5.3635
United Kingdom	Pound sterling (£) of 100 pence		
United States of America	US dollar (US$) of 100 cents	US$ 1.5878	US$ 1.4603
Uruguay	Uruguayan peso of 100 centésimos	Pesos 18.5201	Pesos 18.0487
Uzbekistan	Sum of 100 tiyin	Sum 992.375	Sum 1131.69
Vanatu	Vatu of 100 centimes	Vatu 207.288	Vatu 204.654
Vatican City State	Italian currency is legal tender	Lire 2940.75	Lire 3141.77
Venezuela	Bolívar (Bs) of 100 céntimos	Bs 982.531	Bs 1005.46
Vietnam	Dŏng of 10 hào or 100 xu	Dŏng 22168.1	Dŏng 20618.7
Virgin Islands, British	US dollar (US$) (£ sterling of EC$ also circulate)	US$ 1.5878	US$ 1.4603
Virgin Islands, US	Currency is that of the USA	US$ 1.5878	US$ 1.4603
Wallis and Futuna Islands	Franc CFP	Francs 176.887	Francs 195.498
Yemen	Riyal of 100 fils	Riyals 235.233	Riyals 237.145
Yugoslavia	New dinar of 100 paras	NewDinars 17.8645	New Dinars 17.7813
Zambia	Kwacha (K) of 100 ngwee	K 3842.49	K 4840.74
Zimbabwe	Zimbabwe dollar (Z$) of 100 cents	Z$ 41,4120	Z$ 60.8129

The Commonwealth Games

The Games were originally called the British Empire Games. From 1954 to 1966 the Games were known as the British Empire and Commonwealth Games, and from 1970 to 1974 as the British Commonwealth Games. Since 1978 the Games have been called the Commonwealth Games.

BRITISH EMPIRE GAMES

I	Hamilton, Canada	1930
II	London, England	1934
III	Sydney, Australia	1938
IV	Auckland, New Zealand	1950

BRITISH EMPIRE AND COMMONWEALTH GAMES

V	Vancouver, Canada	1954
VI	Cardiff, Wales	1958
VII	Perth, Australia	1962
VIII	Kingston, Jamaica	1966

BRITISH COMMONWEALTH GAMES

IX	Edinburgh, Scotland	1970
X	Christchurch, New Zealand	1974

COMMONWEALTH GAMES

XI	Edmonton, Canada	1978
XII	Brisbane, Australia	1982
XIII	Edinburgh, Scotland	1986
XIV	Auckland, New Zealand	1990
XV	Victoria, Canada	1994
XVI	Kuala Lumpur, Malaysia	1998
XVII	Manchester, England	2002

UK Overseas Territories

AREA – 37 sq. miles (96 sq. km)
POPULATION – 12,394 (1998 estimate)
CAPITAL – The Valley (population, 2,400, 1994)
CURRENCY – East Caribbean dollar (EC$) of 100 cents
FLAG – British blue ensign with the coat of arms and three dolphins in the fly
POPULATION GROWTH RATE – 8.6 per cent (1998)
POPULATION DENSITY – 83 per sq. km (1996)
GDP – US$88 million (1997); US$7,383 per capita (1997)
ILLITERACY RATE – 4.6 per cent

Anguilla is a flat coralline island in the Caribbean, about 16 miles in length, three and a half miles in breadth at its widest point and its area is about 37 sq. miles (96 sq. km).

HISTORY AND POLITICS

Anguilla has been a British colony since 1650. For much of its history it was linked administratively with St Christopher, but three months after the Associated State of Saint Christopher (St Kitts)-Nevis-Anguilla came into being in 1967, the Anguillans repudiated government from St Kitts. A Commissioner was installed in 1969 and in 1976 Anguilla was given a new status and separate constitution. Final separation from St Kitts and Nevis was effected on 19 December 1980 and Anguilla reverted to a British dependency. A new constitution was introduced in 1982, providing for a Governor, an Executive Council comprising four elected Ministers and two ex-officio members (the Attorney-General and Deputy Governor), and a 12-member legislative House of Assembly, consisting of seven elected members, two nominated members, two ex-officio members (the Attorney-General and Deputy Governor) and presided over by a Speaker. The most recent general election was held in March 2000.

The 1982 Constitution (Amendment) Order 1990 came into operation on 30 May 1990. Among the new constitutional provisions are a Deputy Governor, a Parliamentary Secretary, Leader of Opposition and Deputy Speaker.

Governor, HE Peter Johnson, *apptd* 2000
Deputy Governor, Roger Cousins, OBE, *apptd* 1997

EXECUTIVE COUNCIL *as at June 2000*

Chairman, The Governor
Chief Minister, Osbourne Fleming
Attorney-General, Ronald Scipio
Communications, Public Utilities and Works, Kenneth Harrigan
Finance, Victor Banks
Social Services, Eric Reid
Member, The Deputy Governor

ECONOMY

Low rainfall limits agricultural output and export earnings are mainly from sales of fish and lobsters. Tourism has developed rapidly in recent years and accounts for most of the island's economic activity. In 1998 there were 43,874 tourists and a further 69,922 day visitors.

TRADE WITH UK	1998	1999
Imports from UK	£5,697,000	£2,058,000
Exports to UK	24,000	27,000

ASCENSION
— *see* St Helena

AREA – 20 sq. miles (53 sq. km)
POPULATION – 64,000 (1994 UN estimate)
CAPITAL – ΨHamilton (population, 2,277, 1994)
CURRENCY – Bermuda dollar of 100 cents
FLAG – British red ensign with the shield of arms in the fly
LIFE EXPECTANCY (years) – male 70.23; female 78.01
POPULATION GROWTH RATE – 0.9 per cent (1996)
POPULATION DENSITY – 1,208 per sq. km (1996)
GDP – US$2,047 million (1995); US$32,495 per capita (1995)

The Bermudas, or Somers Islands, are a cluster of about 100 small islands (about 20 of which are inhabited) situated in the west of the Atlantic Ocean, the nearest point of the mainland being Cape Hatteras in North Carolina, about 570 miles distant.

HISTORY AND POLITICS

The colony derives its name from Juan Bermudez, a Spaniard, who sighted it before 1515. No settlement was made until 1609 when Sir George Somers, who was shipwrecked there on his way to Virginia, colonised the islands.

Internal self-government was introduced in 1968. There is a Senate of 11 members and an elected House of Assembly of 40 members. Independence from the UK was rejected in a referendum in August 1995.

The last general election was held on 9 November 1998. The Progressive Labour Party won 26 of the 40 seats.

Governor and Commander-in-Chief, HE Thorold Masefield, CMG, *apptd* 1997
Deputy Governor, Tim Gurney

CABINET *as at June 2000*

Premier, Jennifer Smith
Deputy Premier, Minister of Finance, C. Eugene Cox
Attorney General, Dame Lois Brown-Evans
Development, Opportunity and Government Services, Terry E. Lister
Education, L. Milton Scott
Environment, Arthur D. O. Hodgson
Health and Family Services, Nelson Bascombe, Jr
Labour, Home Affairs and Public Safety, Paula A. Cox
Telecommunications and E-Commerce, M. D. Renee Webb
Tourism, David H. Allen
Transport, Ewart Brown
Works and Engineering, W. Alex Scott
Youth, Sport, Parks and Recreation, P. Lister

ECONOMY

The islands' economic structure is based on tourism, the major industry, and international company business, attracted by the low level of taxation and sophisticated telecommunications system. In 1996 a total of 576,628 visitors arrived by air and cruise ship.

In November 1995, the US, UK and Canadian governments handed over 1,500 acres of land (roughly 10 per cent of the colony), to the government. The land, which had been used for military bases, included an airport on St David's Island.

TRADE WITH UK	1998	1999
Imports from UK	£40,214,000	£183,655,000
Exports to UK	3,701,000	29,092,000

COMMUNICATIONS

One daily and two weekly newspapers are published in Bermuda. Three commercial companies operate radio and television services, including a cable-television system. The Bermuda Telephone Company and Cable and Wireless provide telecommunications links to more than 140 countries.

THE BRITISH ANTARCTIC TERRITORY

AREA – 660,000 sq. miles (1,709,340 sq. km.)
POPULATION – No permanent population
FLAG – British white ensign, without the cross of St George, with the coat of arms of the Territory in the fly

The British Antarctic Territory was designated in 1962 and consists of the areas south of 60°S. latitude and bounded by longitudes 20°W. and 80°W. The territory includes the South Orkney Islands, the South Shetland Islands, the mountainous Antarctic Peninsula (highest point Mount Jackson, 10,443 ft above sea level) and all adjacent islands, and the land mass extending to the South Pole. The territory has no indigenous inhabitants and British population consists of the scientists and technicians at the British Antarctic Survey stations. These numbered 42 during the 1998–9 winter, but this number increases considerably in the southern hemisphere's summer months with the arrival of field scientists. Argentina, Brazil, Bulgaria, Chile, China, Korea (South), Poland, Russia, Spain, Ukraine, Uruguay and the USA also have scientific stations in the territory.

The first two British Antarctic Survey stations were established in the South Shetland Islands in 1944, and by 1956 the number of stations had risen to 12. Due to the completion of field work in some areas and increased mobility, this number has now been reduced to four: Rothera (Adelaide Island), Halley (Brunt Ice Shelf, Caird Coast) and, in summer only, Fossil Bluff (Alexander Island) and Signy Island (South Orkney Islands). Four other stations are at present unoccupied.

Commissioner (non-resident), Charles John Branford White, *apptd* 1997

THE BRITISH INDIAN OCEAN TERRITORY

AREA – 23 sq. miles (59 sq. km.)
POPULATION – No permanent population
FLAG – Divided horizontally into blue and white wavy stripes, with the Union Flag in the canton and a crowned palm-tree over all in the fly

The British Indian Ocean Territory was established by an Order in Council in 1965 and included islands formerly administered from Mauritius and the Seychelles. The

islands of Farquhar, Desroches and Aldabra became part of the Seychelles when it became independent in 1976; since then the Territory has consisted of the Chagos Archipelago only.

The Chagos Archipelago consists of six main groups of islands situated on the Great Chagos Bank and covering some 21,000 sq. miles (54,389 sq. km). The largest and most southerly of the Chagos Islands is Diego Garcia, a sand cay with a land area of about 17 sq. miles approximately 1,100 miles east of Mahé, used as a joint naval support facility by Britain and the USA.

The other main island groups of the archipelago, Peros Banhos (29 islands with a total land area of 4 sq. miles) and Salamon (11 islands with a total land area of 2 sq. miles) are uninhabited.

Commissioner, John White, *apptd* 1998
Administrator, Louise Savill, *apptd* 1996

TRADE WITH UK	1998	1997
Imports from UK	£2,561,000	£1,406,000
Exports to UK	14,000	863,000

BRITISH VIRGIN ISLANDS

AREA – 58 sq. miles (151 sq. km)
POPULATION – 19,000 (1997 estimate; by island: Tortola 15,687; Virgin Gorda 2,885; Anegada 191; Jost Van Dyke 170; other islands 172)
CAPITAL – ΨRoad Town (population, 3,983, 1994)
CURRENCY – US dollar (US$) (£ sterling and EC$ also circulate)
FLAG – British blue ensign with the shield of arms in the fly
POPULATION GROWTH RATE – 2.9 per cent (1996)
POPULATION DENSITY – 126 per sq. km (1996)
GDP – US$268 million (1995); US$14,122 per capita (1995)

The Virgin Islands, divided between the UK and the USA, are situated at the eastern extremity of the Greater Antilles. Those of the group which are British number 46, of which 11 are inhabited, and have a total area of about 58 sq. miles (151 sq. km). The principal islands are Tortola, the largest (area, 21 sq. miles), Virgin Gorda (8 sq. miles), Anegada (15 sq. miles) and Jost Van Dyke (3 sq. miles).

HISTORY AND POLITICS

Under the 1977 constitution the Governor, appointed by the Crown, remains responsible for defence and internal security, external affairs and the civil service but in other matters acts in accordance with the advice of the Executive Council. The Executive Council consists of the Governor as Chairman, one ex-officio member (the Attorney-General), the Chief Minister and three other ministers. The Legislative Council consists of a Speaker chosen from outside the Council, one ex-officio member (the Attorney-General), and 13 elected members returned from ten electoral districts.

Governor, HE Frank Savage, CMG, OBE, LVO, *apptd* 1998
Deputy Governor, Elton Georges, OBE

EXECUTIVE COUNCIL *as at June 2000*
Chairman, The Governor
Chief Minister and Minister of Finance, Ralph O'Neal, OBE
Attorney-General, Dancia Penn
Communications and Works, Alvin Christopher
Health, Education and Welfare, Eileene L. Parsons
Natural Resources and Labour, Julian Frazer

ECONOMY

Tourism is the main industry but the financial centre is growing steadily in importance. Other industries include a rum distillery, three stone-crushing plants and factories manufacturing concrete blocks and paint. The major export items are fresh fish, gravel, sand, fruit and vegetables.

TRADE WITH UK	1998	1999
Imports from UK	£10,477,000	£5,371,000
Exports to UK	3,654,000	2,499,000

COMMUNICATIONS

The principal airport is on Beef Island, linked by bridge to Tortola, and an extended runway of 3,600 ft enables larger aircraft to call.

CAYMAN ISLANDS

AREA – 102 sq. miles (264 sq. km)
POPULATION – 38,000 (1998 estimate)
CAPITAL – ΨGeorge Town (population, 20,000, 1994)
CURRENCY – Cayman Islands dollar (CI$) of 100 cents
FLAG – British blue ensign with the arms on a white disc in the fly
POPULATION GROWTH RATE – 4.4 per cent (1998)
POPULATION DENSITY – 144 per sq. km (1998)
GDP – US$1,095 million (1998); US$30,476 per capita (1998)

The Cayman Islands consist of three islands, Grand Cayman, Cayman Brac, and Little Cayman. About 150 miles south of Cuba, the islands are divided from Jamaica, 180 miles to the south-east, by the Cayman Trench, the deepest part of the Caribbean. The nearest point on the US mainland is Miami in Florida, 450 miles to the north.

HISTORY AND POLITICS

The colony derives its name from the Carib word for the crocodile, 'caymanas', which appeared in the log of the first English visitor to the islands, Sir Francis Drake. Although tradition has it that the first settlers arrived in 1658, the first recorded settlers arrived in 1666–71. The first recorded permanent settlers followed the first land grant by Britain in 1734. The islands were placed under direct control of Jamaica in 1863. When Jamaica became independent in 1962, the islands opted to remain under the British Crown.

The constitution provides for a Governor, a Legislative Assembly and an Executive Council, and effectively allows a large measure of self-government. Unless there are exceptional reasons, the Governor accepts the advice of the Executive Council, which comprises three official members and five ministers elected from the 15 elected members of the Assembly. The official members also sit in the Assembly. The Governor has responsibility for the police, civil service, defence and external affairs. The Governor handed over the presidency of the Legislative Assembly to the Speaker in 1991. The normal life of the Assembly is four years, with a general election next due in November 2000.

Governor, HE Peter Smith, CBE, *apptd* 1999

EXECUTIVE COUNCIL *as at June 2000*

President, The Governor
Chief Secretary, James Ryan, MBE

Agriculture, Environment, Communications and Natural Resources, John McLean, OBE
Attorney-General, David Ballantyne
Community Development, Sports, Women's Affairs, Youth and Culture, Juliana O'Connor-Connolly
Education, Aviation and Planning, Truman Bodden, OBE
Financial Secretary, George McCarthy, OBE
Health, Social Welfare, Drug Abuse Prevention and Rehabilitation, Anthony Eden, OBE
Tourism, Commerce, Transport and Works, Thomas Jefferson, OBE

Speaker of Legislative Assembly, Capt. Mabry Kirkconnell, MBE

CAYMAN ISLANDS GOVERNMENT OFFICE, 6 Arlington Street, London SW1A 1RE. Tel: 020-7491 7772.
Government Representative, Jennifer Dilbert

ECONOMY

With a complete absence of direct taxation, the Cayman Islands has become successful over the past 30 years as an offshore financial centre. With representation from 62 countries, there were, at the end of 1999, 571 banks and trust companies, of which local offices were maintained by 101. In addition, there were 527 licensed insurance companies and 54,566 registered companies. The Cayman Islands stock exchange opened in January 1997. Tourism, with an emphasis on scuba diving, has also been developed successfully. There were 394,534 visitors by air and 1,035,522 cruise ship callers in 1999.

TRADE WITH UK	1998	1999
Imports from UK	£9,762,000	£10,561,000
Exports to UK	324,000	1,023,000

FALKLAND ISLANDS

AREA – 4,700 sq. miles (12,173 sq. km)
POPULATION – 2,221 (1996)
CAPITAL – ΨStanley (population, 1,636, 1994)
CURRENCY – Falkland pound of 100 pence
FLAG – British blue ensign with the arms on a white disc in the fly
POPULATION GROWTH RATE – 0.0 per cent (1996)
URBAN POPULATION – 76.0 per cent (1991)

The Falkland Islands, the only considerable group in the South Atlantic, lie about 300 miles east of the Straits of Magellan. They consist of East Falkland (area 2,610 sq. miles; 6,759 sq. km), West Falkland (2,090 sq. miles; 5,413 sq. km) and over 700 small islands. Mount Usborne (E. Falkland), the loftiest peak, rises 2,312 feet above sea level.

HISTORY AND POLITICS

The Falklands were sighted first by Davis in 1592, and then by Hawkins in 1594; the first known landing was by Strong in 1690. A settlement was made by France in 1764; this was subsequently sold to Spain, but the latter country recognised Great Britain's title to a part at least of the group in 1771. The first British settlement was established in 1765. After Argentina declared independence from Spain, the Argentine government in 1820 proclaimed its sovereignty over the Falklands and a settlement was founded in 1826. The settlement was destroyed by the Americans in 1831. In 1833 occupation was resumed by the British for the protection of the seal-fisheries, and the islands were permanently colonised. Argentina continued to claim sovereignty over the islands (known to them as *las Islas Malvinas*), and in pursuance of this claim invaded the islands on 2 April 1982 and also occupied South Georgia. A naval and military force dispatched from Great Britain recaptured South Georgia on 25 April and after landing at San Carlos on 21 May, recaptured the islands from the Argentines, who surrendered on 14 June 1982. A British naval and military garrison of 1,700 personnel remains in the area. A military zone of 55 miles (previously 80) remains around the islands within which Argentinian naval and air forces may not intrude. A commercial airlink to Argentina resumed in August 1999.

Under the 1985 constitution, the Governor is advised by an Executive Council consisting of three elected members of the Legislative Council and two ex-officio members, the Chief Executive and the Financial Secretary. The Legislative Council consists of eight elected members and the same two ex-officio members.

Governor and Chairman of the Executive Council, HE Donald Lamont, *apptd* 1999
Chief Executive, Dr Michael D. Blanch
Attorney-General, David G. Lang, CBE, QC
Commander, British Forces, Falkland Islands,
    Brig. Geoffrey P. Sheldon
Financial Secretary, Derek F. Howatt
FALKLAND ISLANDS GOVERNMENT OFFICE, Falkland House, 14 Broadway, London SW1H0BH. Tel: 020-7222 2542. *Government Representative*, Miss S. Cameron

ECONOMY

The economy was formerly based solely on agriculture, principally sheep farming with a little dairy farming for domestic requirements and crops for winter fodder. Since the establishment of an interim conservation and management fishing zone around the islands in 1987 and the consequent introduction of a licensing regime for vessels fishing within the 200-mile zone, the economy has diversified. Income from the associated fishing activities, mainly for illex squid, is now the largest source of revenue. The increase in government revenue from fishing licences has led to the establishment of a substantial health, education and welfare system. The islands are now self-financing except for defence. Chief imports are provisions, alcoholic beverages, timber, clothing and hardware. Tourism is a small but expanding industry. At 30 June 1999 the government had a budget deficit of £1.16 million.

TRADE WITH UK	1998	1999
Imports from UK	£42,237,000	£16,228,000
Exports to UK	12,635,000	24,946,000

GIBRALTAR

AREA – 2.5 sq. miles (6.5 sq. km)
POPULATION – 27,192 (1997 estimate)
CAPITAL – ΨGibraltar
CURRENCY – Gibraltar pound of 100 pence
FLAG – White with a red stripe along the lower edge; over all a red castle with a key hanging from its gateway
POPULATION GROWTH RATE – 1.6 per cent (1996)
POPULATION DENSITY – 4,667 per sq. km (1996)

Gibraltar is a rocky promontory which juts southwards from the south-east coast of Spain, with which it is connected by a low isthmus. It is about 20 miles (32 km) from the opposite coast of Africa. The town stands at the foot of the promontory on the west side.

HISTORY AND POLITICS

Gibraltar was captured in 1704, during the War of the Spanish Succession, by a combined Dutch and English force, and was ceded to Great Britain by the Treaty of Utrecht (1713). Several attempts have been made to retake it, the most celebrated being the great siege of 1779 to 1783, when General Eliott held it for three years and seven months against a combined French and Spanish force. The Treaty of Utrecht stipulates that if Britain ever relinquishes its colonial rights over Gibraltar the colony would return to Spain. In a 1967 referendum on the colony's status, 12,138 people voted to remain a British Dependent Territory and 44 voted to join Spain. Spain closed the border with Gibraltar from 1969 to 1985 and refused to engage in any trade.

The 1969 constitution makes provision for certain domestic matters to devolve on a local government of ministers appointed from among elected members of the House of Assembly. The House of Assembly consists of an independent Speaker, 15 elected members, the Attorney-General and the Financial and Development Secretary.

The Governor retains responsibility for external affairs, defence, internal security and financial security, while the local government is responsible for other domestic matters. The Gibraltar government has recently been pressing for more local autonomy especially in its relations with the EU, and this has led to tension with the UK and Spanish governments. Gibraltar is part of the EU (with the UK government responsible for enforcing EU directives affecting Gibraltar) but is not a fully-fledged member. The Gibraltar Social Democrats won the last election in February 2000.

Governor and Commander-in-Chief, HE the Rt. Hon. David Durie, CMG
Commander British Forces, HM Naval Base, Gibraltar,
    Cdre A. N. Willmett
Deputy Governor, P. A. Speller
Attorney-General, R. Rhoda
Chief Justice, Derek Schofield
Chief Minister, Peter Caruana
Deputy Chief Minister, Trade, Industry and Telecommunication, Keith Azopardi
Education, Training, Culture and Health,
    Dr Bernard Linares
Employment and Consumer Affairs, Hubert Corby
Housing, Jaime Netto
Public Services, Environment, Sport and Leisure,
    Ernest Britto
Social Affairs, Yvette Del Agua
Speaker, John Alcantara , CBE
Tourism and Transport, Joe Holliday

ECONOMY

Gibraltar has an extensive shipping trade and is a popular shopping centre and tourist resort. The chief sources of revenue are the port dues, the rent of the Crown estate in the town, and duties on consumer items.

A total of 5,926 merchant ships (129.4 million gross registered tons aggregate) entered the port during 1999. There are 53 km of roads.

TRADE WITH UK	1998	1999
Imports from UK	£81,077,000	£93,355,000
Exports to UK	10,075,000	12,791,000

EDUCATION

Education is compulsory and free for children between the ages of five and 15 whose parents are ordinarily resident in Gibraltar.

MONTSERRAT

AREA – 39 sq. miles (102 sq. km)
POPULATION – 4,500 (1998 estimate)
CAPITAL – ΨPlymouth (destroyed by volcanic activity)
CURRENCY – East Caribbean dollar (EC$) of 100 cents
FLAG – British blue ensign with the shield of arms in the fly
POPULATION GROWTH RATE – 0.0 per cent (1996)
POPULATION DENSITY – 108 per sq. km (1996)
GDP – US$25 million (1999); US$5,600 per capita (1999)

Montserrat is about 11 miles long and seven miles wide. It is volcanic with several hot springs. About two-thirds of the island is mountainous, the rest capable of cultivation but volcanic activity has caused the evacuation of two-thirds of the island.

HISTORY AND POLITICS

Discovered by Columbus in 1493, Montserrat became a British colony in 1632. The first settlers were predominantly Irish indentured servants from St Christopher. Montserrat was captured by the French in 1664, 1667 and 1782 but the island reverted to Britain within a few years on each occasion and was finally assigned to Great Britain in 1783.

A ministerial system was introduced in Montserrat in 1960. The Executive Council is presided over by the Governor and is composed of four elected members (the Chief and three other Ministers) and two ex-officio members (the Attorney-General and the Financial Secretary). The four Ministers are appointed from the members of the political party or coalition holding the majority in the Legislative Council. The Legislative Council consists of the Speaker, two ex-officio members (the Attorney-General and the Financial Secretary), two nominated members and seven elected members. Following elections in November 1996 the elected element of the legislature comprised the following parties: Movement for National Reconstruction (MNR) 2; People's Progressive Alliance (PPA) 2; National Progressive Party 1; Independents 2.

Governor, HE Anthony Abbott, OBE, *apptd* 1997

EXECUTIVE COUNCIL *as at June 2000*

President, The Governor
Chief Minister and Minister of Finance and Economic Development, David Brandt
Agriculture, Lands, Housing and the Environment, Brunel Meade
Attorney-General, Brian Cottle
Communications and Works, Rupert Weekes
Education, Health, Community Services and Labour, Adelina Tuitt
Financial Secretary, Charles. T. John, OBE

Speaker of the Legislative Council, Dr Howard. A. Fergus, CBE

ECONOMY

The economy, which consists of tourism, related construction activities, offshore business services and agriculture, has been seriously affected by relocation to the north of the island due to volcanic activity.

TRADE WITH UK	1998	1999
Imports from UK	£2,000,000	£1,414,000
Exports to UK	56,000	71,000

PITCAIRN ISLANDS

AREA – 2 sq. miles (5 sq. km)
POPULATION – 54 (1999). Since 1887 the islanders have generally been adherents of the Seventh-day Adventist Church
CURRENCY – Currency is that of New Zealand
FLAG – British blue ensign with the arms in the fly.

Pitcairn is the chief of a group of islands situated about midway between New Zealand and Panama in the South Pacific Ocean. The island rises in cliffs to a height of 1,100 feet and access from the sea is possible only at Bounty Bay, a small rocky cove, and then only by surf boats. The other three islands of the group (Henderson, lying 105 miles east-north-east of Pitcairn, Oeno, lying 75 miles north-west, and Ducie, lying 293 miles east) are all uninhabited.

HISTORY AND POLITICS

First settled in 1790 by the Bounty mutineers and their Tahitian companions, Pitcairn was left uninhabited in 1856 when the entire population was resettled on Norfolk Island. The present community are descendants of two parties who, not wishing to remain on Norfolk, returned to Pitcairn in 1859 and 1864 respectively.

Pitcairn became a British settlement under the British Settlement Act 1887, and was administered by the Governor of Fiji from 1952 until 1970, when the administration was transferred to the British High Commission in New Zealand and the British High Commissioner was appointed Governor. The local Government Ordinance of 1964 provides for a Council of ten members of whom six are elected.

Governor of Pitcairn, Henderson, Ducie and Oeno Islands, HE Martin J. Williams, CVO, MBE (*British High Commissioner to New Zealand*)
Island Mayor, Steve Christian

ECONOMY

The islanders live by subsistence gardening and fishing. Wood carvings and other handicrafts are sold to passing ships and to a few overseas customers. Other than small fees charged for gun and driving licences there are no taxes and government revenue is derived almost solely from the sale of postage stamps and income from investments. Communication with the outside world is maintained by cargo vessels travelling between New Zealand and Panama which call at irregular intervals, and by means of a satellite service providing telephone, telex and fax facilities.

TRADE WITH UK	1998	1999
Imports from UK	£1,459,000	£333,000
Exports to UK	—	12,000

EDUCATION

Education is compulsory between the ages of five and 15.

ST HELENA

AREA – 47 sq. miles (122 sq. km)
POPULATION – 5,157 (1994 UN estimate)
CAPITAL – ΨJamestown (population, 884, 1998)
CURRENCY – St Helena pound (£) of 100 pence
FLAG – British blue ensign with the shield of arms in the fly
POPULATION GROWTH RATE – 0.8 per cent (1996)

POPULATION DENSITY – 40 per sq. km (1996)
URBAN POPULATION – 39.2 per cent (1998)
ILLITERACY RATE – 3.6 per cent (1998)

St Helena is situated in the South Atlantic Ocean, 955 miles south of the Equator, 702 miles south-east of Ascension, 1,140 miles from the nearest point of the African continent, 1,800 miles from the coast of South America and 1,694 miles from Cape Town. It is 10.5 miles long and 6.5 broad.

HISTORY AND POLITICS

St Helena was probably discovered by the Portuguese navigator, João da Nova in 1502. It was used as a port of call for vessels of all nations trading to the East until it was annexed by the Dutch in 1633. It was never occupied by them, however, and the English East India Company seized it in 1659. From 1815 to 1821 the island was lent to the British government as a place of exile for the Emperor Napoleon Bonaparte who died in St Helena on 5 May 1821, and in 1834 it was annexed to the British Crown.

The government of St Helena is administered by a Governor, with the aid of a Legislative Council, consisting of a Speaker, three ex-officio members (Chief Secretary, Financial Secretary and Attorney-General) and 12 elected members.

Governor, HE David Hollamby, *apptd* 1999
Attorney-General, Kurt de Freitas, OBE
Chief Administrative Health Officer, Robert Essex
Chief Agriculture and Natural Resources Officer, Roderick J. Steele
Chief Auditor, Rupert Bladon
Chief Development Officer, Mrs Corinda S. S. Essex
Chief Education Officer, John Price
Chief Employment and Social Services Officer, John MacDonald
Chief Engineer, vacant
Chief Finance Officer, Desmond H. Wade
Chief Justice, Geoffrey W. Martin, OBE
Chief Personnel Officer, Mrs Sylvia I. Ellick
Chief Secretary, Michael J. Clancy
Chief of Police, G. G. Yon
Deputy Secretary, Ms Ethel C. Yon
Financial Secretary, Matthew J. Young
Postmistress, Mrs Iva I. Henry

ECONOMY

St Helena receives an annual grant from the UK which amounted to £3.184 million in 1999. The only significant export is canned and frozen fish. The other exports are a small amount of high quality coffee and cottage industry products (including lace, decorative woodwork and beadwork). James's Bay, on the north-west of the island, possesses a good anchorage.

TRADE WITH UK	1998	1999
Imports from UK	£6,993,000	£8,781,000
Exports to UK	654,000	1,111,000

ASCENSION ISLAND

AREA – 34 sq. miles (88 sq. km)
POPULATION – 1,049 (1999 census)
CAPITAL – ΨGeorgetown
CURRENCY – Currency is that of St Helena or the UK

The small island of Ascension lies in the South Atlantic some 750 miles north-west of the island of St Helena. It is a rocky peak of purely volcanic origin. The highest point (Green Mountain), some 2,817 ft, is covered with lush vegetation and has a farm of some ten acres, producing vegetables and livestock. The island is a breeding area for green turtles and for the sooty tern, or wideawake. Other wildlife includes feral donkeys and cats, nine varieties of sea birds and five of land birds.

Ascension Island's residents consist of the employees and families of the British organisations, of the contractors of the US Air Force and RAF and of the St Helena government.

HISTORY AND POLITICS

Ascension is said to have been discovered by João da Nova in 1501 and two years later was visited on Ascension Day by Alphonse d'Albuquerque, who gave the island its present name. It was uninhabited until the arrival of Napoleon in St Helena in 1815 when a small British naval garrison was stationed on the island. As HMS *Ascension* it remained under the supervision of the Board of Admiralty until 1922, when it was made a dependency of St Helena.

The British Foreign Secretary appoints the Administrator who is responsible to the Governor resident in St Helena.

Administrator, Geoffrey Fairhurst, *apptd* 1999

COMMUNICATIONS

Cable and Wireless PLC operates the international telephone and cable services and maintains an internal telephone service. The BBC opened its Atlantic relay station broadcasting to Africa and South America in 1967.

TRISTAN DA CUNHA

AREA – 38 sq. miles (98 sq. km)
POPULATION – 288 (1994 UN estimate)
CAPITAL – ΨEdinburgh of the Seven Seas
CURRENCY – Currency is that of the UK

Tristan da Cunha is the chief island of a group of islands in the South Atlantic which lies some 1,260 nautical miles (2,333km) south-south-west of St Helena. Inaccessible Island lies 20 nautical miles south-west and has an area of 4 sq. miles (10 sq. km), and the three Nightingale Islands lie 20 nautical miles south of Tristan da Cunha and have an area of three-quarters of a sq. mile (2 sq. km). Gough Island lies some 230 nautical miles south-south-east of Tristan da Cunha and has an area of 35 sq. miles (91 sq. km).

All the islands are volcanic and steep-sided with cliffs or narrow beaches. Tristan itself has a single volcanic cone rising to 6,760 feet (2,060 m) and a narrow north-western coastal plain on which the settlement of Edinburgh is situated.

Inaccessible Island is a lofty mass of rock with sides two miles in length; the island is the resort of penguins and seabirds. Cultivation was started in 1937 but has been abandoned.

The Nightingale Islands are three in number, of which the largest is one mile long and three-quarters of a mile wide, and rises in two peaks, 960 and 1,105 feet above sea level respectively. The smaller islands, Stoltenhoff and Middle Isle, are little more than huge rocks. Seals, penguins, and sea-birds visit these islands.

Population is centred in the settlement of Edinburgh on Tristan da Cunha. In addition, there is a meteorological station maintained on Gough Island by the South African government. Inaccessible Island and the Nightingale Islands are uninhabited.

HISTORY AND POLITICS

Tristan da Cunha was discovered in 1506 by a Portuguese

admiral (Tristão da Cunha) after whom it was named. In 1760 a British naval officer visited the islands and gave his name to Nightingale Island. In 1816 the group was annexed to the British Crown and a garrison was placed on Tristan da Cunha, but this force was withdrawn in 1817. Corporal William Glass remained at his own request with his wife and two children. This party, with two others, formed a settlement. In 1827 five women from St Helena, and afterwards others from Cape Colony, joined the party.

In October 1961 a volcano, believed to have been extinct for thousands of years, erupted and the danger of further volcanic activity led to the evacuation of inhabitants to the UK. An advance party returned to Tristan da Cunha in 1963 and subsequently the main body of the islanders returned to the island.

GOVERNMENT

In 1938 Tristan da Cunha and the neighbouring islands of Inaccessible, Nightingale and Gough were made dependencies of St Helena. They are administered by the Governor of St Helena through a resident Administrator, with headquarters at Edinburgh. Under a constitution introduced in 1985, the Administrator is advised by an Island Council of eight elected members, of whom one must be a woman, and three appointed members. There is universal suffrage at 18. Elections are held every three years.

Administrator, Brian Baldwin, *apptd* 1998

ECONOMY

The island is almost financially self-sufficient; UK government aid finances training scholarships and a resident medical officer at the hospital. The main industries are crayfish fishing, fish-processing and agriculture, with the shore-based fishing industry having been developed with the construction of the boat harbour in 1967 and the re-establishment of the lobster factory in 1966. There are no taxes, income being derived from the royalties from the rock lobster fishery around the islands, interest from the reserve fund, and the sales of stamps and handicrafts, as well as vegetables, to passing ships.

COMMUNICATIONS

Scheduled visits to the island are restricted to about six calls a year by fishing vessels from Cape Town and annual calls of the RMS *St Helena* and the *SA Agulhas*, also from Cape Town. A wireless station on the island is in daily contact with Cape Town and a radio-telephone service was established in 1969, the same year that electricity was introduced to all the islanders' homes. A marine satellite system providing direct dialling telephone, telex and fax facilities was installed in 1992.

SOUTH GEORGIA AND THE SOUTH SANDWICH ISLANDS

AREA – 1,580 sq. miles (4,092 sq. km)
POPULATION – No permanent population

South Georgia is an island 800 miles east-south-east of the Falkland group. The population comprises a small military garrison (which is due to be withdrawn in 2001 and replaced by a scientific research station operated by the British Antarctic Survey) and the curator of the museum at King Edward Point, and staff of the British Antarctic Survey at Bird Island, to the north-west of South Georgia.

The South Sandwich Islands lie some 470 miles southeast of South Georgia. The group is a chain of uninhabited, actively volcanic islands about 150 miles long, with a wholly Antarctic climate.

The present constitution came into effect in 1985.

In 1993 the UK government decreed an extension of Crown sovereignty and jurisdiction from 12 miles around South Georgia and the South Sandwich Islands to 200 miles around each in order to preserve marine stocks.

Commissioner for South Georgia and the South Sandwich Islands, Donald Lamont, *apptd* 1999

TURKS AND CAICOS ISLANDS

AREA – 166 sq. miles (430 sq. km)
POPULATION – 23,000 (1999 estimate)
CAPITAL – ΨGrand Turk (population, 3,691, 1994)
CURRENCY – US dollar (US$)
FLAG – British blue ensign with the shield of arms in the fly
POPULATION GROWTH RATE – 3.7 per cent (1996)
POPULATION DENSITY – 35 per sq. km (1996)

The Turks and Caicos Islands are about 50 miles southeast of the Bahamas of which they are geographically an extension. There are over 30 islands, of which eight are inhabited, covering an estimated area of 166 sq. miles (430 sq. km). The principal island and seat of government is Grand Turk.

HISTORY AND POLITICS

A constitution was introduced in 1988, and amended in 1993, which provides for an Executive Council and a Legislative Council. The Executive Council is presided over by the Governor and comprises the Chief Minister and five elected Ministers, together with the ex-officio Chief Secretary and Attorney-General.

At the general election of 4 March 1999, the People's Democratic Movement won nine seats and the Progressive National Party four seats in the Legislative Council.

Governor, HE Mervyn T. Jones *apptd* 2000

EXECUTIVE COUNCIL *as at June 2000*

President, The Governor
Attorney-General, David Jeremiah
Chief Minister, Derek H. Taylor
Chief Secretary, Cynthia Astwood, MBE
Ministers, Hilly Ewing (*Deputy Chief Minister*); Larry Coalbrooke; Noel Skippings; Oswald Skippings; Clarence Selver

ECONOMY

The most important industries are fishing, tourism and offshore finance. The islands were visited by 111,855

TRADE WITH UK	1998	1999
Imports from UK	£1,529,000,000	£1,284,000
Exports to UK	30,000	67,000

tourists in 1998.

COMMUNICATIONS

The principal airports are on the islands of Grand Turk and Providenciales. Air services link Providenciales and Grand Turk with Miami, the Bahamas, Haiti and the Dominican Republic.

Events of the Year

1 September 1999 to 31 August 2000

SEPTEMBER 1999

3. In Paris, a judicial inquiry concluded that the 1997 car crash in which Diana, Princess of Wales, Dodi Fayed and their driver, Henri Paul, died was caused solely by Paul being under the influence of alcohol and prescribed medication. **10.** *The Times* newspaper revealed that an 87-year-old British woman, Melita Norwood, had spied for the Soviet Union for 40 years. On 20 December the Solicitor-General (Ross Cranston) announced she would not be prosecuted. On 11 September a former detective, John Symonds, was also revealed to have been a spy. On 13 September the Home Secretary (Jack Straw) ordered an investigation of the Security Service's handling of the situation. Two British academics were subsequently revealed as former East German spies. **13.** The TUC conference opened in Brighton. On 15 September the conference passed a motion supporting British membership of the euro. A Home Office report criticised levels of racism, sexism and homophobia in the Fire Service. **19.** The Liberal Democrat conference opened in Harrogate. **20.** The Agriculture Minister (Nick Brown) announced an extra £150m package to aid farmers. **23.** Labour won the by-elections in Hamilton South and Wigan. **24.** The government signed an agreement for handling compensation claims for up to 100,000 miners with diseases. **27.** The Labour Party conference opened in Bournemouth. On 28 September 16,000 people demonstrated outside the conference against the proposed ban on foxhunting. **29.** Eurotunnel announced plans to construct road tunnels between Britain and France.

OCTOBER 1999

10. The Secretary of State for Health (Frank Dobson) announced he would resign in order to seek the Labour Party's nomination as candidate for Mayor of London. **11.** Tony Blair reshuffled his Cabinet; Jack Cunningham and Frank Dobson left office, Geoff Hoon and Andrew Smith entered the Cabinet for the first time, Mo Mowlam was moved and Peter Mandelson returned to the Cabinet. **14.** A cross-party pro-EU group, Britain in Europe, was launched in London. **16.** The 440-foot London Eye Millennium Wheel was raised on the River Thames in London. **19.** The Chinese President Jiang Zemin began a state visit to the UK. **21.** The Labour MP Kali Mountford (Colne Valley) was suspended from the House of Commons for five days and her colleague Don Touhig (Islwyn) for three days for leaking a draft report. **24.** Over 10,000 people demonstrated in Norwich against the proposed banning of fox-hunting. The Agriculture Minister (Nick Brown) insisted that French meat was safe to eat and would not be banned in the UK, following revelations that French animals had been fed on sewage. On 27 October the Leader of the Opposition (William Hague) called for imports of French meat to be banned. On 2 November Mr Brown agreed with his French counterpart that British beef should be subject to further tests before being exported to France.

NOVEMBER 1999

1. The Queen awarded a Royal Charter to the Prince's Trust charity. **2.** The Lord Mayor of London hosted a lunch for 300 people, including The Queen, who were deemed to have made important contributions to British life in the 20th century. **3.** At the second reading of the Welfare Reform and Pensions Bill in the House of Commons, 54 Labour MPs voted against the government. On 8 November the House of Lords rejected those parts of the Bill concerning changes to incapacity benefit and war widows' pensions. On 9 November the Commons overruled this and the Lords accepted the Bill. **5.** The names of the 75 hereditary peers elected to remain in the House of Lords were announced. **7.** The Queen and the Duke of Edinburgh began a state visit to Ghana. On 8 November they arrived in South Africa for the Commonwealth Heads of Government meeting. On 15 November they arrived in Mozambique for a state visit. **9.** The Chancellor of the Exchequer (Gordon Brown) presented his Pre-Budget Report to the House of Commons; measures included extension of the 'New Deal' programme, an end to annually escalating petrol taxes and free television licences for everyone aged over 75. **18.** It was announced that the Prime Minister's wife, Cherie Blair, was expecting a baby in May 2000. **25.** The Conservative candidate, Michael Portillo, won the Kensington and Chelsea by-election. **30.** The government announced that it would lift the ban on beef on the bone.

DECEMBER 1999

9. The Charity Commission denied charitable status to the Church of Scientology, saying it could not be regarded as a religion. The Scottish First Minister (Donald Dewar) dismissed his chief of staff for falsely alleging to newspapers that death threats had been made against the health minister. **12.** The Deputy Prime Minister (John Prescott) announced an £80,000 million 'ten-year plan' to improve Britain's transport infrastructure. **17.** The ban on selling beef on the bone was lifted. Cuts of almost 40 per cent in fishing quotas across the EU in 2000 were agreed by ministers. **18.** Shaun Woodward, the Conservative MP for Witney, announced he was joining the Labour Party. **21.** The Government announced it would cancel the debts owed by 41 of the world's poorest countries. Andrew Cubie's inquiry recommended to the Scottish Executive that university tuition fees be deferred and maintenance grants be restored to some students in Scotland.

JANUARY 2000

1. The Queen led celebrations of the arrival of the year 2000 at the Millennium Dome in London; huge open-air parties took place throughout the UK. **4.** Mike and Fiona Thornewill became the first married couple to walk to the South Pole; their companions Catharine Hartley and Mrs Thornewill are the first British women to walk there. Diana Hoff, 55, from Glasgow, became the oldest person to row the Atlantic. **7.** Former cabinet minister Jonathan Aitken was released from prison. **12.** The Committee on Standards in Public Life (the Neill Committee) recommended new methods of dealing with alleged misconduct or corruption among MPs. **17.** The Government announced pay increases of between 3.3 per cent and 7.8 per cent for NHS workers. **20.** The Royal Commission on reforming the House of Lords published its proposals. **21.** Thirty-one of the Free Church of Scotland's 110 ministers resigned from the church in a dispute over ecclesiastical law. **25.** A Church of England report proposed changes in church law regarding marriage of divorcees. **27.** The Welsh Health Secretary (Jane Huitt) announced an independent inquiry into an incident at Prince Philip Hospital, Llanelli where a patient had the wrong kidney removed; he died on 1 March. **30.** The Under-Secretary of State for Defence (Peter Kilfoyle) resigned.

FEBRUARY 2000

1. William Hague reshuffled his shadow cabinet. **4.** Plaid Cymru won the by-election at Ceredigion. Lord Archer of Weston-super-Mare was expelled from the Conservative Party for five years for having falsified an alibi at a libel trial in 1987. **5.** Jennie Page, chief executive of the New Millennium Experience Company, resigned and was replaced by Pierre-Yves Gerbeau. **7.** An Ariana Boeing 727, with 165 people aboard, which had been hijacked on an internal flight in Afghanistan, arrived at Stansted airport in Essex. Some hostages were soon freed, and four crew members escaped. The hijacking ended peacefully on 10 February. Thirteen people were charged with the hijacking. **9.** The First Secretary of the National Assembly for Wales, Alun Michael, resigned before facing a confidence vote; on 15 February he was replaced by Rhodri Morgan. **15.** An inquiry into child abuse at children's homes in Clwyd and Gwynedd revealed years of abuse in the 1970s and 1980s. **18.** The Health and Safety Executive published a report revealing a number of safety problems at the Sellafield nuclear reprocessing plant. The chief executive of British Nuclear Fuels Limited resigned on 28 February and nine senior managers left in April. **28.** The first pets to receive 'passports' entered Britain without having to go into quarantine.

MARCH 2000

6. Ken Livingstone, MP for Brent East, announced that he was to stand as an independent candidate for Mayor of London; he was immediately suspended from the Labour Party. On 15 March he was rebuked by the House of Commons Standards and Privileges Committee for failing to declare all his business interests. **10.** In the first ballot of its kind, parents in Ripon, N. Yorks, voted against converting the town's grammar school to a comprehensive. John Major announced he would retire from his Huntingdon constituency at the next general election. **16.** The Conservatives won the Scottish Parliament by-election at Ayr. **17.** The Queen began a visit to Australia. **21.** Gordon Brown presented the Budget to the House of Commons. **22.** Cormac Murphy-O'Connor, hitherto Bishop of Arundel and Brighton, was installed as Archbishop of Westminster and leader of the Roman Catholic Church in England and Wales. **30.** A new list of life peers was announced, including the Conservative Party Treasurer Michael Ashcroft, whose peerage was conditional on his taking up residence in Britain.

APRIL 2000

1. Tony Blair confirmed that he would offer the Liberal Democrats seats in his Cabinet if Labour fails to win a second landslide victory at the next election. **3.** An investigation began into allegations that Ken Livingstone was breaking company law by taking approximately £40,000 in loans from the firms he set up, in order to finance his political activities. **6.** Two Leeds supporters were stabbed to death during football riots in Istanbul. **27.** Michael Heseltine announced that he would retire as an MP at the next election.

MAY 2000

4. The Liberal Democrats won the Romsey by-election, the Conservatives made gains in the English local elections and Ken Livingstone was elected Mayor of London. The 'ILOVEYOU' computer virus disrupted computer systems worldwide. **12.** The Greater London Assembly met for the first time. **15.** The Dunkirk Veterans Association celebrated its 60th anniversary at the Imperial War Museum, London. **17.** Rioting between Arsenal and Galatasaray football supporters before the UEFA cup final in Copenhagen left at least five people seriously injured. **20.** Tony Blair's wife, Cherie, gave birth to a baby boy whom they named Leo. **29.** David Hempleman-Adams became the first person to fly solo across the Arctic Ocean in a balloon.

JUNE 2000

2. A flotilla of boats crossed the English Channel from Dover to Dunkirk to commemorate the 60th anniversary of the evacuation of allied soldiers. **3.** The leader of Plaid Cymru, Dafydd Wigley, announced his resignation. **7.** Tony Blair was heckled and slow-hand-clapped while making a speech to the Women's Institute. **9.** The Prince of Wales's Press Secretary, Sandy Henney, resigned. **12.** The Burns report into hunting with dogs was published. **16.** Around 200 English football fans attending the Euro 2000 tournament were arrested in the centre of Brussels after serious violent clashes with police. **17.** English and German fans were involved in serious fighting before their Euro 2000 football match in Charleroi, Belgium. A total of 824 Britons were arrested. **18.** The England Football team was threatened with expulsion from the Euro 2000 tournament by UEFA if further violence occurred. **19.** The Revd Peter Stone announced his intention to become the first Church of England priest to undergo a sex change operation. **22.** Following the death of Bernie Grant, MP, the by-election for the constituency of Tottenham took place and was won by David Lammy. **28.** It was agreed by the Royal Household and the Chancellor of the Exchequer, that the money the Queen receives from the Government through the Civil List would be frozen at £7.9 million until 2011. **29.** Defence Secretary, (Geoff Hoon), announced that further supplies of weaponry would be sent to Sierra Leone. **30.** Lieutenant Corporal Jodi Breen of the Australian Federation Guard became the first woman to undertake royal guard duty in the history of the household division.

JULY 2000

3. Tony Blair was told by senior police officers that a government proposal for on-the-spot cash fines for antisocial behaviour was unworkable. **5.** The Prisons Minister (Paul Boateng) announced that he would invite private security firms to run Brixton Prison, after a report from the Chief Inspector of Prisons (Sir David Ramsbotham) revealed problems. **6.** Tony Blair's 16-year-old son, Euan, was arrested in Leicester Square, London for being drunk and incapable. The Foreign Secretary (Robin Cook) commented that Britain's membership of the single European currency was 'inevitable'. Sufiah Yusof, a 15-year-old student of Oxford University who had been missing for a fortnight, was found safe in a London hotel. **7.** Tony Blair announced plans to speed up the process of adoption by introducing a national adoption register. **12.** Betty Boothroyd announced she would resign from her post as The Speaker of the House of Commons and as MP for West Bromwich West. **16.** A memo written by Tony Blair which stated that he felt 'out of touch with gut British instincts' was leaked to the press. **17.** The government published new crime statistics which showed increases in the rates of violent crime, robbery and muggings. The leader of the Scottish National Party (Alex Salmond) announced his intention to stand down in the autumn. Prince Charles lodged a complaint with the Press Complaints Commission when an article in *The Sunday Times* claimed that he had approached the Church of Scotland on the matter of re-marrying. **18.** The Government announced its plan for an increase in spending on public services of £43 billion over the next three years. **20.** The official car of the Home Secretary (Jack Straw) was stopped by police speeding at 103mph on the M5 motorway. The Deputy Prime Minister (John Prescott) announced a ten-year spending plan of £180 billion to improve roads, motorways, local transport schemes and train services. **21.** Tony Blair attended the G8 summit in Okinawa, Japan, to discuss the scrapping of Third World debt with other world leaders. **24.** The House of Lords voted to retain Section 28 legislation, which prevents the promotion of homosexuality by local councils. It was announced that the Ministry of Agriculture would be streamlined with a loss of about 1,400 jobs. **27.** The Government announced a ten-year investment plan designed to radically improve the National Health Service.

August 2000

2. Prison Officers walked out of over 50 prisons around the country in protest over Government proposals that the running of some prisons should be privatised. **3.** Gordon Brown married his long term girlfriend Sarah Macaulay in his constituency of North Queensferry, Scotland. **4.** The Queen Mother celebrated her 100th birthday with a parade through central London from Clarence House to Buckingham Palace. **5.** The Prisons Minister (Paul Boateng) stated that the government would not make details of paedophiles available to the public. **9.** Baroness Young of Old Scone announced that she would stand down as vice-chairman of the BBC and chairman of English Nature to become the new Chief Executive of the Environment Agency. **26.** Eleven troops from the Royal Irish Regiment were taken hostage in Sierra Leone by a group of renegade soldiers. Five of the 11 soldiers were released on the 30 August. **30.** Blockades of ports by French fisherman, in protest at rising marine fuel prices, prevented thousands of British people from travelling between Britain and France. The Home Secretary announced that the number of people joining the police force in England and Wales fell by 16 per cent last year.

NORTHERN IRELAND AFFAIRS

September 1999

6. Former US Senator George Mitchell, who chaired negotiations leading to the 1998 Good Friday Agreement, held separate talks with political parties in Belfast in an attempt to renew progress. **9.** Chris Patten's commission on policing in Northern Ireland published its proposals, including re-naming the RUC the Northern Ireland Police Service and increasing the number of Roman Catholic officers. On 19 January 2000 the Northern

Ireland Secretary (Peter Mandelson) announced that the RUC would be renamed the Police Service of Northern Ireland. **14.** Johnny Adair, a leading loyalist terrorist was released from the Maze prison after serving four years of a 16-year sentence for organising terrorism. **20** Michelle Williamson, whose parents were murdered by a terrorist, was given leave to appeal against the Northern Ireland Secretary's decision that the IRA's cease-fire was intact.

October 1999

12. George Mitchell and the main Northern Ireland political parties began talks in London. The talks ended without a breakthrough on 14 October and later resumed in Belfast.

November 1999

11. An apparent breakthrough in the talks at Stormont collapsed after the Ulster Unionist Party leader (David Trimble) failed to secure sufficient backing from his party to proceed. **12.** The ten-week-long review of the Good Friday Agreement was adjourned in Belfast. **15.** The Independent International Commission on Decommissioning called for those paramilitaries who had still to disarm to appoint go-betweens so that the process could get underway. **16.** David Trimble said that if the IRA appointed such an 'interlocutor' he would be willing to enter devolved government with Sinn Féin from December. Sinn Féin said that it was committed to decommissioning and making devolved government a success. **17.** The IRA Army Council said it would not appoint a go-between until a devolved government including Sinn Féin had been established. On 3 December the IRA said it had nominated its go-between, but did not announce the name. On 5 December the IRA said its go-between had met with the decommissioning body. The loyalist Ulster Freedom Fighters announced on 8 December that they had appointed go-betweens. **23.** The RUC was awarded the George Cross; the Queen presented the award on 12 April 2000. **27.** The UUP's Council approved the plan for devolution by 58 to 42 per cent after David Trimble said the UUP would resign from the Executive if IRA decommissioning did not begin by February 2000. **29.** The Northern Ireland Assembly met and nominated ministers to the Executive. Power was officially devolved from Westminster on 1 December and the new Executive met for the first time on 2 December.

December 1999

8. The Sinn Féin President (Gerry Adams) accused British intelligence of being responsible for bugging devices found in a car used by Sinn Féin. **13.** The North-South Ministerial Council, comprising the Northern Ireland Executive and the Irish cabinet, held its first meeting in Armagh. **17.** The British-Irish Council (the Council of the Isles) held its first meeting.

January 2000

10. Richard Jameson, believed to be a commander of the Ulster Volunteer Force was shot dead in Portadown. **27.** Gerry Adams said that the IRA would not begin disarming by 1 February, the deadline set by David Trimble.

February 2000

1. Two loyalist terrorists were jailed for life for murdering two friends, one Roman Catholic and one Protestant. **3.** Peter Mandelson announced that the government would introduce legislation to revert from devolved government to direct rule unless decommissioning began within a few days; Tony Blair and the Irish Taoiseach (Bertie Ahern) held emergency talks about the situation. **6.** A bomb exploded outside a hotel in Irvinestown, Co. Fermanagh. No-one was injured; republicans opposed to the peace process were thought to be responsible. **11.** After emergency legislation cleared Parliament and received the Royal Assent, the Northern Ireland Assembly was suspended and direct rule re-imposed. An IRA offer on decommissioning was rejected by the government as too equivocal. **15.** The IRA announced it was ending links with General de Chastelain's decommissioning body.

MARCH 2000

25. David Trimble was re-elected UUP leader after a challenge from the Revd Martin Smith, MP for Belfast South. The party also voted against participation in the Northern Ireland Executive unless proposals to change the name of the Royal Ulster Constabulary were dropped. **27.** An official inquiry began into the 'Bloody Sunday' shootings in 1972.

APRIL 2000

2. Peter Mandelson commented that there was a risk of Northern Ireland 'slipping back into the conflict of the past' unless the power sharing government was reconvened. **4.** Peter Mandelson held separate talks with Portadown Orangemen and the Garvaghy Road Residents' Coalition in an attempt to avoid conflict when the Orange Order Drumcree parade takes place in July. **6.** The Ulster Unionist Party conducted a half-day Commons debate to discuss the future of the Royal Ulster Constabulary. The motion to postpone the reforms was defeated. **8.** Sinn Féin member Martin McGuinness denied having fired any shots on Blood Sunday. **18.** Tony Blair returned to Northern Ireland in an attempt to revive the peace talks.

MAY 2000

2. The main political leaders involved in the peace process held talks with Tony Blair and Bertie Ahern at Downing Street. **5.** After further talks at Hillsborough, Tony Blair and Bertie Ahern set a deadline of 22 May for the resumption of the devolved institutions. **6.** The IRA announced they would put their arms 'beyond use' and allow inspection of their arms dumps. **11.** The UUP threatened to pull out of any power sharing deal unless given assurances about the future of the RUC. **16.** The Police (Northern Ireland) Bill was published giving the Northern Ireland Secretary the power to decide the future name of the Royal Ulster Constabulary. **27.** The UUP voted to return to the power-sharing executive with Sinn Féin. **29.** Devolved government was restored to Northern Ireland from midnight on this day.

JUNE 2000

20. The loyalist terrorist group the Ulster Freedom Fighters (UFF) threatened to abandon their cease-fire in order to 'defend the protestant community'. **26.** The Parades Commission barred a forthcoming march by Orangemen down the Garvaghy Road, Co. Armagh. The Government disclosed that the IRA had opened one of its weapons dumps to be examined by inspectors.

JULY 2000

2. Leading Orangemen urged loyalists to take to the streets in protest against the Parades Commission decision to ban a march down the Garvaghy Road. **5.** Armed soldiers were called into Belfast for the first time in two years, when loyalists protesting against the banning of the Orange March in Drumcree attacked police. **7.** The official legislative title of the new police service in Northern Ireland was stated in the Police (Northern Ireland) Bill as 'the Police Force of Northern Ireland (incorporating the

Royal Ulster Constabulary)'. **19.** A bomb found on the London Underground line at Acton, which was believed to have been planted by the 'Real IRA', was exploded by police. A number of coded warnings were received by news organisations in Dublin, in a campaign believed to have been mounted to disrupt the celebrations of the Queen Mother's 100th Birthday in London. **23.** It was announced that 87 terrorist prisoners would be released from the Maze prison under the terms of the Good Friday agreement. **24.** Michael Stone, who was convicted of killing three men at an IRA funeral in 1989, was released.

AUGUST 2000

11. Police discovered a bomb in the back of a van believed to be part of a plot by the Real IRA to blow up a loyalist Apprentice Boys parade in Londonderry. The Ulster Freedom Fighters fired at police, claiming it needed to rearm itself in order to protect Protestants from Republican attacks. **19.** Several people were injured and several houses attacked during fighting between loyalist groups in the Shankill area of Belfast. **21.** Peter Mandelson authorised the admittance of British troops back into Northern Ireland, after two people were shot dead in North Belfast following further infighting between loyalist groups. **22.** The leader of the Ulster Freedom Fighters, Johnny Adair, was rearrested after it was ruled that he had breached the terms of his early release. **23.** A 21-year-old man, with connections to the Ulster Volunteer Force, was shot dead at his home. **26.** Peter Mandelson sent hundreds of military reinforcements to the Shankill area of Belfast in an attempt to prevent further bloodshed. **30.** The Ulster Volunteer Force and the Ulster Defence Association carried out 30 attacks on houses in three loyalist estates in Carrickfergus, East Antrim.

ACCIDENTS AND DISASTERS

SEPTEMBER 1999

3. Eight of the 11 people aboard a Cessna 404 flying from Glasgow to Aberdeen were killed when it crashed into a field outside Linwood, Paisley, shortly after take-off. **5.** All 15 people aboard a Necon Airlines Avro aircraft on an internal flight in Nepal were killed when it crashed into a cellular telephone tower. **7.** At least 32 people were killed when an earthquake measuring 5.9 on the Richter scale struck Athens, Greece. **8.** Four steelworkers died when a gantry on the Avonmouth Bridge on the M5 near Bristol gave way. **13** At least seven people were killed when an aftershock hit north-eastern Turkey, a month after a major earthquake. **14.** Hurricane Floyd caused extensive damage in the Bahamas before moving north to the eastern United States, where over three million people fled their homes. **18.** Three men were killed when their Grumman AA5 light aircraft crashed into a parked cargo plane at Luton airport. **19.** Two boys, aged 13 and 14, died and six other children were injured when the car they were illegally driving collided with a lorry in Lincolnshire. **20.** At least 2,000 people were killed when an earthquake measuring 7.6 on the Richter scale struck Taiwan. Powerful aftershocks caused more damage in subsequent days. **22.** Two women were killed by lightning in Hyde Park, London. **26.** At least 26 people were killed in a series of explosions originating in an illegal fireworks dump in Celaya, Mexico. **27.** Twenty-six British tourists were killed when their coach crashed near Lydenberg, South Africa. **30.** A nuclear accident at a uranium processing plant in Tokaimura, Japan resulted in 14 workers receiving dangerous doses of radiation; around 300,000 residents were advised to remain indoors for some hours to avoid contamination.

OCTOBER 1999

5. Thirty people were killed and 259 injured when two trains collided and caught fire near Paddington station, London; one of the trains had passed a red signal. The government announced a public inquiry headed by Lord Cullen and a separate inquiry into train safety systems led by Sir David Davies. On 8 October safety inspectors ordered Railtrack to make immediate improvements to 22 signals that had repeatedly been passed at red. On 3 November a woman seriously injured in the crash died. **14.** The two crewmen of an RAF Tornado were killed when it crashed at Kearsley Fell, Northumberland. **25.** The golfer Payne Stewart and four others were killed when their aircraft crashed in South Dakota, USA. **30.** Fifty-four people died in a fire at a karaoke bar in Inchon, South Korea. **31.** All 217 people aboard an Egypt Air Boeing 767 aircraft flying from New York to Cairo died when it crashed into the Atlantic off Massachusetts.

NOVEMBER 1999

12. An earthquake measuring 7.2 on the Richter scale struck western Turkey, killing at least 120 people. Three British aid workers were among 24 people killed when a United Nations ATR 42-500 aircraft crashed in Kosovo.

DECEMBER 1999

2. Up to 40 people were killed when a gas explosion destroyed an apartment block in Wilhelmsburg, Austria. **5.** Five people died and four were seriously injured in a crowd stampede outside the Olympic stadium in Innsbruck, Austria. **19.** Around 30,000 people were reported dead and thousands more were left homeless after flash floods and mudslides in Venezuela. **22.** The four crewmen of a Korean Airlines Boeing 747 cargo aircraft were killed when it crashed into a field shortly after take-off from Stansted airport, Essex. **24–28.** At least 138 people were killed by storms in northern Europe, over 68 of them in France.

JANUARY 2000

4. At least seven people were killed when two trains collided at Astå, Norway. **11.** All seven crewmen on a fishing boat, the *Solway Harvester*, drowned when it sank in the Irish Sea. The boat was raised from the sea on 3 February. **13.** Seventeen people died, at least five of them British, when a Swiss aircraft crashed in Libya. **30.** A Kenya Airways airbus crashed into the sea off Abidjan, Côte d'Ivoire, killing 169 out of the 179 people aboard.

FEBRUARY 2000

21. Six skiers died in avalanches in the Alps. **24.** The Conservative MP for Romsey, Michael Colvin, and his wife Nichola died in a fire at their home.

MARCH 2000

1. As flooding worsened in Mozambique, the President, Joachim Chissano, called for more international help; at least 5,000 people had died and up to a million were homeless. **10.** Two trains collided at Waterloo station, London, injuring 30 people. **25.** Three teenage boys died in a fire in a garden shed in Birmingham. **28.** Eleven skiers died in an avalanche near Kaprun, Austria.

APRIL 2000

11. At least 143 people drowned when a ferry sank in the Philippines. **18.** An Air Philippines Boeing 737 crashed in Mindanao, killing all 131 people aboard. **25.** A British woman tourist was killed by an elephant in Thailand.

MAY 2000

6. A Swansea City football supporter was crushed to death by a police horse before a match in Rotherham. **13.** The fireworks warehouse in Enschede, the Netherlands caught fire and exploded, killing 20 people. **21.** A BA-31 Gulfstream aircraft crashed in Pennsylvania, USA, killing all 21 people aboard. Three workmen died when their crane collapsed at Canary Wharf, London. **28.** Safety investigations were launched when two people died on fairground rides in two separate incidents.

JUNE 2000

1. Jockeys Frankie Dettori and Ray Cochrane were injured and their pilot killed when their Piper Seneca aircraft crashed at Newmarket, Suffolk. **5.** Over 100 people died in an earthquake on the Indonesian island of Sumatra. **14.** All five people aboard the Isle of Man air ambulance, died when it crashed into the river Mersey near Liverpool. **19.** The bodies of 58 illegal immigrants were found dead in the back of a freight lorry at Dover. **22.** Ten British tourists died when a backpacker's hostel in the town of Childers in Queensland, Australia, caught fire. **24.** John Dawson-Damer, the brother of the Earl of Portarlington, was killed and two marshals seriously injured, when the vintage Lotus 63 car he was racing veered off the track at the Goodwood Festival of Speed, West Sussex. **27.** Five people survived when the driver of the car they were in accidentally reversed off a cliff near Beachy Head, East Sussex.

JULY 2000

1. Thirty three people were killed and more than 200 injured in an explosion at a firework factory in Jiangmen, China. Eight fans were trampled to death at the Danish Roskilde Music Festival as the audience pushed forward to get nearer to the stage. **6.** Twenty-eight people, including 21 school children, were killed when a school bus collided with a lorry in Soria, Spain. A heat-wave across southeastern Europe caused the deaths of 24 people when temperatures reached 45°C (113°F). **9.** Twelve people were trampled to death during a World Cup qualifying match in Harare, Zimbabwe, when police caused panic by firing tear gas into the crowd. **10.** Forty-six people died in the Phillipine capital, Manila, when heavy rainfall caused a mountain of rubbish to collapse onto the shanty homes in which they lived. **12.** Over 100 people died in Bombay after heavy rainfall caused flooding and landslides. **17.** An Alliance Air aircraft crashed on approach to Patna airport in the Indian state of Bihar, killing 51 people on board and four on the ground. **21.** The theme park, Thorpe Park, was evacuated when fire broke out on one of its rides. **25.** An Air France Concorde, flying from Paris to New York, crashed in the Paris suburb of Gonesse killing all 109 people on board and four on the ground.

AUGUST 2000

3. The worst wildfires for 50 years burned out of control across the American west destroying an estimated 3.76 million acres of land. **7.** Fifteen-year-old Craig Norsworthy was killed and eleven other children were injured, when a coach transporting British children to a holiday camp crashed near Vierzon, France. Heavy monsoon rain across the Indian subcontinent and the subsequent flooding around the Brahmaputra river and its tributaries, caused the deaths of 300 people and left more than two million homeless. **9.** Two small aircraft collided in mid-air, killing eleven people in New Jersey, USA. **14.** 120 Russian sailors were trapped in the nuclear submarine, the

Kursk, after an explosion caused it to sink to the bottom of the Barents Sea. Repeated attempts by the Russian Navy to rescue them using a diving bell, failed. The hatch was released on the 21 August and it was discovered that the whole vessel was flooded and that all the sailors on board had lost their lives. **17.** The body of a child found in the sea off Brancaster Beach, Norfolk, was identified to be that of Jake Parker, who had gone missing on the 13 August. **18.** A fighter pilot was killed when his plane crashed into the sea during a display of aerobatics in Eastbourne, East Sussex. **22.** This day was marked as a national day of mourning in Russia for the 120 sailors who died aboard the *Kursk*. **23.** More than 130 people were killed when an Airbus A320 crashed while trying to land at Bahrain International Airport. **24.** Two schoolgirls, Hayleigh Hinton and Lousie Wood, drowned after falling into a pond while playing on a rope swing. **27.** Four people died in a fire in the 1,780 ft main television tower in Moscow. **30.** Twenty-four people were injured when a underground train of the Paris Metro was derailed at Notre-Dame-de-Lorette station. **31.** Twenty-three people were injured when two carriages on the world's tallest roller-coaster collided at Blackpool's Pleasure Beach.

ARTS, SCIENCE AND MEDIA

SEPTEMBER 1999

3. A woman from Suffolk, Jane Ingram, gave birth to triplets, one of whom had developed ectopically, the first time that such babies and their mother have survived. **16.** A flag and compass used by Captain Robert Scott and Sir Ernest Shackleton in their polar expeditions were bought by the National Maritime Museum. **17.** The Secretary of State for Culture, Media and Sport, Chris Smith, announced that analogue television services would be discontinued once 95 per cent of viewers had digital television sets. **22.** Doctors in New York announced they had replaced ovarian tissue in a woman whose ovaries had been removed, in the first operation of its kind. **29.** The actor Dudley Moore announced that he was suffering from progressive supranuclear palsy.

OCTOBER 1999

8. The Secretary of State for Health announced that Glaxo Wellcome's new anti-influenza drug, Relenza, would not be prescribed by the NHS, partly because of the expense. **14.** The BBC Symphony Orchestra announced that Leonard Slatkin would replace Sir Andrew Davis as conductor in autumn 2000. **25.** J. M. Coetzee won the 1999 Booker Prize for his novel *Disgrace*, becoming the first person to win the prize twice. **24.** Two visitors to the Tate Gallery were arrested for having a pillow fight on an unmade bed which was one of the shortlisted exhibits for the Turner Prize. **27.** Glaxo Wellcome withdrew its antibiotic Raxar, which had been linked to the deaths of seven people worldwide.

NOVEMBER 1999

5. A memorial concert dedicated to Yehudi Menuhin took place at the Albert Hall, London. **14.** Astronomers in the USA announced that they had observed a planet orbiting a star 153 light years away in the Pegasus constellation, the first time a planet has been seen outside the solar system. **15.** Digital One, the UK's first commercial digital radio station went on air. **30.** The Turner Prize for 1999 was won by Steve McQueen.

DECEMBER 1999

1. The Royal Opera House, Covent Garden, reopened after a three-year refurbishment. **7.** NHS Direct Online, a new NHS internet information and diagnosis service, began operation. **9.** Sculptor Phillip King was elected to replace Sir Philip Dowson as President of the Royal Academy of Arts. **14.** The Radio Authority fined two radio stations a record £50,000 each for obscenity. **17.** Virgin Radio gave a prize of £1 million to a quiz winner, the first such award in Britain. **20.** Results of experiments suggested that a higher proportion of the population may be at risk of the BSE variant Creutzfeldt-Jakob disease than was previously thought.

JANUARY 2000

1. The Prince of Wales broadcast 'Thought for the Day' on BBC Radio 4's *Today* programme. **7.** A report published in *The Lancet* suggested that screening women for breast cancer was unnecessary; the government said it remained committed to screening. **10.** The Health Secretary (Alan Milburn) said that the NHS was under 'real pressure' trying to cope with the influenza outbreak across the UK. **15.** Surgeons in Lyons, France carried out the world's first double arm transplant. **25.** The Human Fertilisation and Embryology Authority announced that women who had frozen their eggs would be permitted to use them in an attempt to conceive.

FEBRUARY 2000

9. The European première of *The Beach*, starring Leonardo di Caprio, was held at the Empire cinema, London. Physicists at the CERN laboratory, Geneva, announced that they had recreated a state of matter that had last existed ten microseconds after the beginning of the universe. **21.** The government announced that the BBC's digital television services would be paid for by increases in the licence fee. **22.** The chairman and chief executive of Sotheby's resigned over price-fixing allegations. **29.** The government confirmed that 58 baroque paintings owned by the art collector Sir Denis Mahon would be left to public galleries in Britain after his death.

MARCH 2000

23. The Tate Gallery at Millbank, London was re-launched as Tate Britain, showing only British art. **26.** The Academy Awards (Oscars) ceremony took place in Los Angeles.

APRIL 2000

3. Greg Dyke, the new Director-General of the BBC, said he would make some managers redundant in order to spend more on programme-making. **25.** The Independent Television Commission told ITV that the number of people watching its news programmes had fallen to an unacceptable level since the end of *News at Ten*. **30.** Novelist Maeve Binchy announced she was retiring from writing.

MAY 2000

4. The Queen opened the new Ondaatje Wing of the National Portrait Gallery. **9.** The Queen opened the new Millennium Bridge over the River Thames in London; on 12 June it was closed to the public as it had begun to sway. **10.** Piers Morgan, the Editor of *The Mirror* newspaper was censured by the Press Complaints Commission over a share tipping scandal. FilmFour, a subsidiary company of Channel 4 announced a joint venture with Warner Brothers to make seven films over the next three years. **11.** The Queen opened the new Tate Modern Gallery at

Bankside, London. **16.** Virgin Radio was fined a record £75,000 by the Radio Authority after DJ Chris Evans endorsed London mayoral candidate Ken Livingstone on-air. **22.** The Queen's collection of rare stamps went on display at the Royal Mail Stamp Show 2000 in London. **29.** Two genes that contribute to the development of schizophrenia were identified by the Medical Research Council of Human Genetics.

JUNE 2000

5. The National Art Collections Fund received a bequest of £5 million from the estate of an elderly widow. **6.** The Government advised 5,000 women who had breast implants made from soya bean oil to have them removed because of a cancer risk. **14.** The BBC lost the right to televise Premier League football highlights when ITV made a higher bid. **14.** The Iceland supermarket chain announced that it would buy around 40 per cent of the world's organic vegetables to sell in its stores. **19.** A re-enactment of the journey of bluestone from Pembroke-shire to Stonehenge failed when boats carrying the stone drifted apart and it fell into the sea. **21.** Greg Dyke, announced plans to revamp BBC1 and BBC2 after criticism from BBC governors of the quality of pro-grammes. Stonehenge was opened to the public for the summer solstice for the first time since 1985. **22.** The Independent Television Commission ordered ITV to re-schedule its 11pm nightly news bulletin to an earlier time, due to the loss of two million viewers. **23.** The two rival bidders to run the National Lottery, Camelot and Sir Richard Branson's 'Peoples Lottery', were turned down by the Lottery Commission and told to improve their bids. **24.** A fashion student from the University of East London designed an aero-dynamic running suit which could be worn by any athlete sponsored by Nike, in the Sydney Olympics. **26.** The first drafts of the entire human genetic code were unveiled simultaneously by British and Amer-ican scientists. **27.** The Tate Modern celebrated the attendance of its millionth visitor since its opening in May, greatly exceeding the attendance figures that it had predicted. **27.** A famous sculpture by Degas, *'Petite Danseuse de Quatorze Ans'* was sold at Sotheby's auction house in London for £7.7 million.

JULY 2000

3. An operation to restore sight by implanting artificial retinas made from silicone chips, was attempted for the first time. **6.** The BBC and the Tussaud's Group discussed an offer with the Deputy Prime Minister (John Prescott) to take over the running of the Millennium Dome. *'The portrait of Giacomo Doria'* by Titian was purchase by the Oxford Ashmolean Museum for over £2.4 million. **11.** The book *'Harry Potter and the Goblet of Fire'* by J. K. Rowling broke all previous records by selling a third of a million copies on its first day of release. **16.** A scientist from Edinburgh University's Centre for Reproductive Biology claimed that the male contraceptive pill could be available in five years time. **18.** A survey of GPs revealed that the number of people suffering from attacks of asthma was decreasing in the UK. **20.** The ITV viewing figures for the coverage of the Queen Mother's Birthday Pageant peaked at 7.3 million. **23.** The tabloid newspaper the *News of the World* published the faces of 49 known paedophiles as a reaction to the murder of eight-year-old Sarah Payne. Its action was later criticised by the Home Secretary (Jack Straw), the police and the NSPCC. **28.** The Lottery funded Pop Music Museum in Sheffield announced that it would close after falling into financial trouble.

AUGUST 2000

1. Prof. Sir Richard Doll, who first discovered the link between smoking and lung cancer, announced new evidence that stopping smoking before the age of 35 could cut the risk of developing the disease by 90 per cent. **3.** The *SS Great Britain*, an iron hulled propeller-driven ship designed by Isambard Kingdom Brunel, was awarded a £7 million grant from the Heritage Lottery Fund for restoration costs. **5.** Scientists discovered the near-complete fossil of an Ichthyosaur near Whitby, North Yorkshire. **6.** Astronomers have discovered a planet orbiting the star Epsilon Erdidani, ten light years from Earth. The BBC confirmed its intention to launch two new television channels, BBC Three and BBC Four, to replace its digital channels, BBC Choice and BBC Knowledge. **10.** The British Library announced that it had changed its policy of holding every book published in Britain since 1662 and had disposed of 80,000 books over the last two years. **25.** Greg Dyke announced plans to spend up to an extra £500 million a year on programmes after admitting that the main BBC channels were not good enough. **26.** A man from Birmingham became the first heart disease victim in the world to be saved by a unique miniature electric heart pump.

CRIMES AND LEGAL AFFAIRS

SEPTEMBER 1999

2. A British man, James Mawdsley, was sentenced to 17 years' imprisonment in Myanmar for distributing anti-government material. On 16 September a British woman, Rachel Goldwyn, was sentenced to seven years' hard labour for protesting against the government in Myanmar. She was released six weeks later. **4.** The body of nine-year old Laura Kane, who disappeared ten days earlier, was found at a house in Murton, Co. Durham. On 14 June Colin Bainbridge was convicted of her murder. **8.** Sandor Bata, aged 73, was sentenced to life imprisonment in Birmingham for killing a neighbour, Mick Wilson, in a dispute about an allotment. **16.** Seven people, including four children, were killed when a man opened fire inside a church in Fort Worth, USA; the gunman also killed himself. In Bloemfontein, South Africa, an army officer killed seven colleagues before being shot dead. **22.** The American singer Diana Ross was arrested and cautioned by police at Heathrow Airport after an alleged assault. **23.** The Earl of Hardwicke was convicted of cocaine dealing and received a two-year suspended sentence. **24.** The body of Vicky Hall, a 17-year-old who had been missing for five days, was found in Creeting St Peter, Suffolk. The High Court in London gave former boxer Michael Watson the right to sue the British Boxing Board of Control for brain damage he suffered in a fight in 1991. Former Italian Prime Minister Giulio Andreotti was acquitted of con-spiracy to murder in Perugia, Italy. **24.** An employment tribunal in Inverness ruled that a sub-postmistress was entitled to be paid the minimum wage. **27.** The European Court of Human Rights ruled that the British armed forces ban on homosexuals was unlawful. On 14 October the Defence Secretary (Geoff Hoon) announced that the policy would be changed as soon as possible. The ban was formally lifted on 12 January 2000. An extradition case brought by the Spanish government against General Augusto Pinochet, the former Chilean President, opened in London. On 8 October the court ruled that Pinochet could be extradited to face charges of torture. On 11 January 2000 the Home Secretary said that he may release Pinochet on health grounds; he was released on 2 March.

OCTOBER 1999

1. A British childminder, Manjit Basuta, was sentenced to 25 years imprisonment for causing the death of a 13-month old boy in her care in San Diego, USA. **4.** A man was believed to have stabbed his wife and three children to death before hanging himself, after all five bodies were discovered at a house in Birmingham. **4.** The commandant of a World War II concentration camp, Dinko Savić, was sentenced to 20 years' imprisonment in Zagreb, Croatia. **14.** The Radio 2 DJ Johnnie Walker was convicted of possessing cocaine and fined £2,000 in London. **15.** The Metropolitan Police paid £50,000 compensation to Winston Silcott, whose conviction for murdering a police officer during a riot in 1985 was quashed. The President of the High Court Family Division (Dame Elizabeth Butler-Sloss) recommended that more homosexual couples be allowed to foster or adopt children. Christopher Thomas was sentenced to life imprisonment for the murder of a man who had sexually abused him as a child. **22.** Police in Limoges, France said that the British student Isabel Peake, whose body was found by a railway line, had been murdered. This was later linked to two other murders in France. On 11 January 2000 a suspect was arrested in Portugal. **27.** A court in Los Angeles, USA, granted a British male couple the right to be named as parents on the birth certificates of surrogate twin babies. **28.** David Hampson was sentenced to six years' imprisonment for killing his wife in 1996; he was convicted of manslaughter on grounds of diminished responsibility because of his wife's alleged nagging. **29.** A student who falsely claimed she had been raped was jailed for two months in Exeter. **30.** In Colombia, Luís Alfredo Garavito admitted murdering 140 children, making him one of the worst serial killers in history.

NOVEMBER 1999

1. A 16-year-old shot dead two people and injured seven before killing himself in Bad Reichenhall, Germany. **4.** Two 14-year-old boys, Sergio Pantano and Terence Lambert, who killed a man 'for fun' were ordered to be detained at Her Majesty's pleasure by a court in Luton. **6.** The body of a woman, Elizabeth Stacey, was found in an office at the University of Westminster. **8.** A jury in London returned an open verdict in the case of Ricky Reel, who was found dead in the River Thames in October 1997; there were suspicions he had been the victim of a racial attack. **9.** A solicitor, Sally Clark, was convicted of murdering her two baby sons in Chester. On 26 October she received two life sentences. A deaf man lost his appeal against disqualification from jury service on the grounds that it would be illegal for his sign language interpreter to be in the jury room. **10.** A woman teacher was cleared of indecently assaulting a 15-year-old male pupil after she claimed that her pupils had conspired against her. **12.** The pop singer Gary Glitter was jailed for four months for possession of child pornography; earlier in the day a court in Bristol had acquitted him of sexually abusing a teenage girl. He was released on 11 January 2000. **24.** John Taft was sentenced to life imprisonment in Liverpool for the 1983 murder of Cynthia Bolshaw, the 'beauty in the bath'. **28.** Eleven people were injured by a man with a samurai sword during a church service in Thornton Heath, London. He was acquitted of attempted murder on 2 June 2000 on the grounds of insanity and sent to a secure hospital indefinitely. **29.** The former England rugby union player Jeremy Guscott was acquitted of assault at Bristol Crown

Court. **30.** Violence broke out at Euston station in London during an anti-capitalism demonstration.

DECEMBER 1999

8. The European Commission fined British Steel £8 million for alleged participation in price-fixing. **14.** The Lord Chancellor (Lord Irvine of Lairg) announced that Lord Auld would lead a review of the English and Welsh criminal courts system. Goran Jelisić, a former Bosnian Serb concentration camp guard, was jailed for 40 years for crimes against humanity by the UN International War Crimes Tribunal. **16.** The European Court of Human Rights ruled that the two boys convicted of murdering toddler James Bulger in 1993 did not receive a fair trial. On 13 March Jack Straw referred the case to the Lord Chief Justice, Lord Bingham of Cornhill, for a decision on how long they should spend in prison. The European Court of Justice ruled that the Government must pay winter fuel payments to men aged between 60 and 65 as well as women. The Prime Minister rejected a unanimous resolution from the Scottish Parliament to repeal the Act of Settlement. **21.** The former Conservative MP Neil Hamilton lost his libel action against Harrods owner Mohammed Al Fayed over corruption allegations. One man was convicted of murder and another of manslaughter in the case of Michael Menson, who was set on fire in a racially motivated attack in 1997; another man was convicted in Northern Cyprus of his manslaughter. **23.** Albert Wilson, a British man sentenced to death in the Philippines for raping his stepdaughter, was released after his conviction was quashed. **29.** Police began investigating the case of Konrad Kalejs, an alleged war criminal from Latvia, found living in Leicestershire. On 3 January 2000 the Home Secretary ordered his deportation to Australia, but Kalejs left the country on 5 January. **30.** George Harrison was stabbed in the lung by an intruder at his home in Oxfordshire. A man was charged with attempted murder.

JANUARY 2000

3. Angelo Fusco, a convicted IRA murderer who escaped in 1980, was arrested in Co. Kerry, Ireland. The Irish High Court halted his extradition to Northern Ireland on 4 January. **14.** Five Bosnian Croats convicted of massacring Bosnian Muslims in 1993 were sentenced to between six and 25 years' imprisonment by the International Criminal Tribunal for the former Yugoslavia. **13.** The Home Secretary decided to allow US boxer Mike Tyson to enter the UK despite being convicted of rape. **18.** Government figures showed that recorded crime had risen for the first time in six years. **26.** The High Court approved a woman's application for her severely mentally handicapped 28-year-old daughter's womb to be removed without her consent. **28.** Nigel Jones, the Liberal Democrat MP for Cheltenham, was injured and an assistant killed when they were attacked by a man with a sword during a constituency surgery. **31.** Dr Harold Shipman, a GP from Manchester, was sentenced to life imprisonment at Preston Crown Court for murdering 15 of his patients, making him Britain's worst serial killer. Police believe he may have murdered over 150 patients. On 1 February the government announced an independent inquiry into the case, chaired by Lord Laming of Tewin.

FEBRUARY 2000

18. A convicted paedophile was shot dead outside his home in east London in what was believed to be a contract killing. **20.** Lawrence Collins, QC, became the first solicitor to be appointed a High Court judge. **24.** A man was jailed for life for murdering his next-door neighbour after she had a sexual relationship with his underage son. **29.** A six-year-old boy shot dead a girl in his class at a primary school in Michigan, USA.

MARCH 2000

7. John Allan, a chemist, was jailed for life at Liverpool Crown Court for the murder of his girlfriend with cyanide while on holiday in Egypt. **10.** A judge at Liverpool High Court rejected the Moors murderer Ian Brady's request to be allowed to starve himself to death. **18.** The bodies of around 470 members of a cult were found after a fire in a church in Kanungo, Uganda. Several more mass graves of murdered cult members were later found, the total death toll was thought to be around 900. **20.** A couple were jailed for a total of four and a half years at Lewes Crown Court for cruelty to five of their children; they had previously been cleared of murdering three children. **28.** A report by the Police Foundation called for lighter sentences for some drugs offenders. **30.** Kenneth Noye was convicted at the Old Bailey of the murder of a man in a 'road rage' attack on the M25 in 1996; his plea of self-defence was rejected and he was jailed for life.

APRIL 2000

6. Nawaz Sharif, the former Prime Minister of Pakistan, was jailed for life and had all his property confiscated after being convicted of hijacking and terrorism. **7.** The Court of Appeal quashed the conviction of a man who had spent 14 years in jail for rape. **11.** David Irving, a historian, lost his libel action against an author who had accused him of denying the Holocaust. **12.** Six people were convicted of murdering a student in London whom they had beaten unconscious and thrown into the River Thames. **19.** A farmer, Tony Martin, who shot dead a teenager who had broken into his house was convicted of murder and sentenced to life imprisonment at Norwich Crown Court. **21.** Two hundred and eighty former members of the armed services announced they were suing the Ministry of Defence because they had developed psychological problems.

MAY 2000

1. Anti-capitalism demonstrators defaced the Cenotaph and the statue of Winston Churchill in Whitehall, London. On 9 May a man was convicted of criminal damage to the statue and jailed for 30 days. **3.** A specially-constituted Scottish court in the Netherlands began trying two Libyans for the 1988 Lockerbie Pan-Am aircraft bombing. **9.** Robert Jebson was sentenced to life imprisonment for the 'Babes in the Wood' murder of two children in 1970. **11.** The inquiry into the disappearance of estate agent Suzy Lamplugh 14 years ago was relaunched. **28.** British Formula 1 racing driver Jensen Button was ordered to pay a fine of 5,000 francs for speeding at 141 mph on a motorway in France. Barry George, also known as Barry Bulsara, was charged with the murder of television presenter Jill Dando.

JUNE 2000

2. Police shot and seriously injured an armed man who had been holding 25 children and three teachers hostage in Luxembourg. **8.** Brigadier Stephen Saunders, the British defence attaché in Greece, was shot dead by terrorists in Athens. **13.** Mehmet Ali Agca, who shot the Pope in 1981, was pardoned by the Italian President and returned to Turkey, where he was imprisoned for earlier offences. **15.** Former South African cricket captain Hansie Cronje gave details to an inquiry in Cape Town of how he had accepted money from bookmakers, but denied having deliberately lost matches. **21.** A police custody officer,

Sgt Paul Banfield, was sentenced to 18 years imprisonment for the rape and indecent assault of a number of women prisoners. **22.** A paediatric community nurse was suspended from work when Essex police began an inquiry into the deaths of 18 terminally ill children in her care. **23.** A Birmingham man was given a one year prison sentence by a Belgian Court, for inciting violence and assaulting police in Brussels before England's Euro 2000 match against Germany. **28.** The killer of British student, Isabel Peake, who had been studying in France, committed suicide in his cell in Lisbon, Portugal, whilst awaiting completion of extradition proceedings. **30.** David Copeland was sentenced to six life sentences for the planting of bombs in Soho, Brick Lane and Brixton in London, which injured 139 people and caused the deaths of three.

JULY 2000

1. Eight-year-old Sarah Payne went missing in West Kingston, W. Sussex. A body later confirmed to be hers was found next to the A29 near Pulborough, around 15 miles from the point where she disappeared. A suspect who had already been questioned by police was re-arrested on the 31 July and released on bail the following day. **3.** A British psychiatric nurse was sentenced to death by hanging for drug trafficking in Malaysia. **10.** Olatunde Adetoro, who kidnapped a woman driving in Manchester whilst trying to evade police and shot at passers-by, was found guilty of 21 counts of attempted murder, kidnap, hijacking of two cars and grievous bodily harm. **11.** A man who posed as a film director in order to convince women to attend bogus auditions was found guilty of rape and later sentenced to nine years in jail. **16.** The families of five civilians killed in the NATO bombing of Radio Television Serbia last year, are taking their case against Britain and 16 other NATO countries, to the European Court of Human Rights. **17.** The parents of Louise Woodward appeared in court on charges of fraud. They were later acquitted. The bodies of a woman and her two children were found murdered in their home in Northampton. **20.** A gynaecologist, who was allowed to practice in Britain after being struck off the Canadian Medical Register in 1985, was found guilty of maiming patients by the General Medical Council and was later struck off their register. **24.** The bodies of a man, his wife and their four children were found at their home in Barry, South Wales. Police concluded the man had killed his family before hanging himself. **26.** Three 16-year-old boys were sentenced to be detained at Her Majesty's pleasure for murdering a 15-year-old boy. Legal proceedings against David Duckenfield, the police officer in charge at the Hillsborough football ground in Sheffield when 96 people were crushed to death in 1989, were halted after a jury failed to reach verdicts on manslaughter charges. **28.** A school teacher was given a three month suspended sentence for slapping a pupil.

AUGUST 2000

4. Five Scotland Yard detectives were jailed for a corruption scandal involving the selling of drugs which had been seized during police raids. **7.** Two British policemen being held by the Yugoslav army were charged with committing terrorist acts. **10.** A British backpacker, Kirsty Sara Jones was found murdered in a hotel room in Chiang Mai, Thailand. A high court judge ruled that a 19-year-old man with advanced motor neurone disease, whose only means of communication was blinking, could indicate his choice to doctors that he wished his life support system to be turned off, in order to die naturally. **11.** The Marquess of Blandford was found not guilty of stealing goods to the value of £237 from the store Harvey

Nichols in Knightsbridge, London. **14.** A new Home Office study examining the link between crime and drug taking found that 70 per cent of offenders arrested by police test positive for drugs. **21.** The former M15 employee David Shayler returned to Britain to face charges of breaking the Official Secrets Act. His lawyers planned to contest the allegations claiming that the act conflicts with the right of freedom of expression. **23.** An inquest ruled that Christopher Alder, a black ex-paratrooper, who was found dead in police cell in 1998, had been unlawfully killed by the police officers at the scene. **25.** A High Court judge ordered the surgical separation of Siamese twins against the parents' wishes even though the operation would mean that the weakest baby would die. A Tottenham Hotspur fan photographed punching a woman during a Wembley cup final was cleared of assault after a jury accepted that he acted in self-defence. **26.** Jack Straw announced that the 1960's east end criminal, Reggie Kray, who had advanced terminal cancer, should be released from jail and allowed to die at home. **27.** Police began to hunt the murderer of 17-year-old Heather Tell whose body was discovered in bushes near her home at Stonydelph, Tamworth. **28.** A man was stabbed to death whilst attending the Notting Hill Carnival, adding to an overall increase in levels of violence which totalled 129 arrests. **31.** Tony Blair announced an extra £109 million would be available to police to finance a national DNA register.

ECONOMIC AND BUSINESS AFFAIRS

SEPTEMBER 1999

1. The employment agency Select Appointments accepted a £1,140 million take-over by Dutch services group Vedior, creating Europe's third-largest employment agency. **3.** British Airways announced 1,000 job losses. **8.** The Bank of England raised bank base rates by 0.25 per cent to 5.25 per cent. **14.** Barclays Bank announced it was closing all its business in Russia. **15.** Government statistics showed that 1,211,000 people were unemployed in the UK in August 1999, the lowest level since April 1980. The Japanese yen reached its highest levels for three years against the dollar and pound. **16.** Hambros Bank was fined £270,000 and ordered to pay £80,000 costs by the Securities and Futures Authority for its use of confidential information during an attempted take-over of the Co-operative Wholesale Society in 1997. The Automobile Association's members voted 96 per cent in favour of the AA being sold to Centrica for £1,100 million. **20.** Rolls-Royce announced an agreed £576 million take-over of the Vickers engineering company. **23.** Hewlett-Packard said it had given its new chief executive, Carly Fiorina, a stock and options package that could be worth £57 million over three to five years. **24.** Bank of Scotland announced a £21,000 million hostile take-over bid for NatWest. On 29 November the Royal Bank of Scotland launched a rival £25,500 million take-over bid for NatWest. NatWest agreed to the latter offer on 9 February. **26.** Fifteen European central banks announced a moratorium on gold sales; the Bank of England would join the moratorium after its planned sale of 415 tonnes. **30.** The low-cost airline Debonair suspended flights and went into receivership, leaving hundreds of passengers stranded.

OCTOBER 1999

7. Unilever announced that it was suing Mercury Asset Management for £100 million over alleged negligence with its pension fund. **8.** Direct Line insurance bought Green Flag motor breakdown service. **14.** A merger was announced between Daimler Chrysler's defence arm and Aérospatiale-Matra, which will create the world's third-largest aerospace company. **15.** The Dow Jones Industrial Average index fell 266 points and ended the week at 10,019.71, 630 points below its opening value. **21.** The German telecommunications company Mannesmann announced an agreed take-over of the mobile telephone company Orange. **27.** NatWest Bank announced 12,000 job losses by 2002.

NOVEMBER 1999

2. Prudential announced 1,400 job losses. Marks and Spencer announced a 58 per cent drop in profits to £114 million in the first half of 1999. **4.** The Bank of England raised bank base rates by 0.25 per cent to 5.5 per cent. Railtrack announced a five per cent increase in half-year profits and said track access charges may have to be increased to meet investment requirements. **5.** Anglo American announced a £1,200 million take-over of Tarmac. **15.** The price of oil reached $25 per barrel in London, its highest level for three years. The Gucci fashion house announced a £625 million take-over of Sanofi Beauté, which owns Yves Saint Laurent. **16.** Vodafone AirTouch announced a hostile take-over bid for German telecommunications company Mannesmann; the take-over was eventually approved on 3 February 2000, the largest such deal ever (£225 billion). **17.** Government statistics showed that 27.5 million people were in employment, the highest number ever.

DECEMBER 1999

1. eCompanies bought the right to use the address 'business.com' for £4.6 million, the largest internet name sale deal ever. **2.** The euro's value briefly fell below that of the dollar. **6.** The price of gold fell by over $4 per ounce to $276 after the Dutch central bank announced sales of 300 tonnes over five years. **14.** A US consortium including Nabisco announced a £1.2 billion take-over bid for United Biscuits. **23.** The FTSE 100 index at the London Stock Exchange, the Dow Jones in New York and Nasdaq all reached record high levels.

JANUARY 2000

4. The stock market suffered its worst one-day fall ever, closing down 264.3 points at 6,665.9. **10.** The internet company America Online and Time Warner media group announced a merger worth £220 billion. On 24 January Time Warner and EMI announced merger plans, which would create the largest music recording company in the world. **14.** Ginger Media Group, the television and radio company, was sold to Scottish Media Group for £225 million. **13.** The Bank of England raised bank base rates by 0.25 per cent to 5.75 per cent. **17.** Glaxo Wellcome and SmithKline Beecham announced a £107 billion merger, creating the world's largest pharmaceutical company, Glaxo SmithKline. **26.** The Government announced plans to extend the Financial Services Authority's regulatory powers to part of the mortgage market. Coca-Cola announced 6,000 job losses worldwide, 20 per cent of its workforce. **27.** The euro fell to record lows of 98.69 cents against the dollar and 60.33p against the pound. **28.** Britain's oldest colliery, at Annesley Bentinck, Notts., was closed.

FEBRUARY 2000

2. The US Federal Reserve raised interest rates by 0.25 per cent. BT announced 3,000 job losses. **10.** The Bank of England raised bank base rates by 0.25 per cent to 6 per cent. **21.** Norwich Union and CGU insurance companies announced a £20 billion merger, which will lead to 4,000 job losses in the UK.

MARCH 2000

7. FTSE International announced that ten new companies would be added to its 100 index, while a number of well-known older companies would be dropped. The Dow Jones Industrial Average index fell 374.47 points, its fourth-largest ever decline in one day. **13.** The government announced it would invest £530 million in the new Airbus A3XX airliner. **14.** The internet company lastminute.com was floated on the London Stock Exchange and was valued at £733 million by the close of trading; however the share price later fell. **20.** A government review of banking services in the UK concluded that neither individuals nor businesses were receiving proper treatment from banks. **29.** The government postponed its plans for partial privatisation of BNFL following safety concerns. **31.** Pearson announced it was acquiring the publishers Dorling Kindersley. On 7 April Pearson and Bertelsmann announced a merger of their television interests.

APRIL 2000

3. A court in Washington DC, USA ruled that Microsoft had illegally abused its dominant market position and should be broken up. **4.** Share prices of internet companies fell heavily on the New York and Nasdaq stock exchanges. **5.** The London Stock Exchange lost almost a day's trading due to computer failures. **13.** BT announced it was splitting into four companies. **14.** The New York and Nasdaq stock exchanges suffered their largest-ever one-day declines, although prices later rose. **28.** The auction of licences to provide third-generation mobile communications services ended; the government had raised a total of £22 billion. **28.** BMW threatened the complete closure of the Rover plant at Longbridge, after talks on selling the plant failed. The euro fell to a record low of 58p.

MAY 2000

3. A merger between the London and Frankfurt Stock Exchanges, to be called iX, was announced. **9.** The Rover car manufacturer was sold to Phoenix Group by BMW for £10. **10.** Sports Internet group was sold to BSkyB for £301 million. **11.** The Pound fell below $1.50 for the first time in four years. **15.** Thomson Travel agreed to a £1.8 billion take-over by Germany's biggest tour operator, Preussag. **16.** The Stewart-Liberty family agreed to sell the Liberty store in London to Marylebone Warwick Balfour for £72 million. **17.** boo.com, the internet retailer, went into receivership. **30.** The mobile phone company Orange was sold by Vodafone to France Telecom.

JUNE 2000

15. Retailer C&A announced it would close all of its stores in the UK, with the loss of 5,000 jobs. In his Mansion House speech, Gordon Brown said that the government would stick to its policy of remaining outside the euro until certain economic conditions were met. **16.** Richard Branson announced that the profits of Virgin Atlantic are expected to have halved due to increased jet fuel prices. **19.** The Post Office announced a loss for the last year of over £250 million, its first in 25 years. Swedish furniture retailer Ikea announced a £60 million expansion plan to build eight new stores, creating 4,500 jobs. **22.** The Halifax acquired Bank One's UK credit card operations for £200 million, adding 200,000 new customers to its existing 1.2 million. **26.** The Granada Media Group announced a proposed merger with United News and

Media and Carlton Communications, following a de-merger from Granada Group. This deal later fell through due to intervention from the Competition Commission. A number of car manufacturers, including General Motors, Fiat, Ford and DaimlerChrysler began bidding for the South Korean company, Daewoo Motors, after the financial collapse of the Daewoo Group last year. **27.** Members of the Standard Life insurance company voted in favour of retaining its mutual status.

JULY 2000

3. The Government was warned by the British Ambassador to Japan, Sir Stephen Gomersall, that Japanese companies were considering closing their factories in Britain due to the strength of the pound. **9.** The confectionery manufacturer Nestlé said that the future of its factory in York was under threat due to the strength of the pound. De Beers formally ended its role as the official cartel of the diamond industry. **11.** Barclays Bank agreed that it would introduce the policy of calculating interest on all its mortgage accounts daily instead of annually. **14.** Bradford and Bingley customers voted in favour of converting the building society to a bank. **20.** The mutual insurance company Equitable Life was forced to put itself up for sale when the House of Lords ruled it was breaking its contract with customers by cutting bonus rates on pensions. **21.** United News and Media was put for sale when its proposed merger with Carlton Communications collapsed. On 27 July, Granada Media agreed to buy United News and Media's television networks for almost £2 billion. **24.** The oil company BP AMOCO was criticised for introducing a new company logo at a cost of £136 million, during a period of increasing controversy about the high price of petrol.

AUGUST 2000

7. The global Chief Executive of Arthur Andersen resigned after it was announced by an international arbitrator that its sister company, Andersen Consulting, could separate without incurring termination repayments. It was ruled that in order to split Anderson Consulting would have to change its name and pay Arthur Anderson £555 million. **11.** Barclays Bank announced the £5.3 billion purchase of Woolwich. **18.** The Treasury had a cumulative surplus for the current tax year of £19.38 billion compared with a deficit of £63 million at the same stage last year. **29.** OM Group, the owners of the Stockholm Stock Exchange unveiled a hostile £820 million take-over bid for the London Stock Exchange. London Stock Exchange had been expected to merge with Deutsche Börse. The pound fell to its lowest level against the dollar since February 1994.

ENVIRONMENT

SEPTEMBER 1999

8. At a meeting of eight EU countries in Kilkee, Republic of Ireland, the British government said it would expand its list of candidate sites for Special Area of Conservation status. **15.** A United Nations report, *Global Environment Outlook 2000*, predicted serious environmental disasters in the 21st century as a result of global warming. **17.** Environment minister (Michael Meacher) admitted that the government's granting permission for tests of genetically-modified oilseed rape had been 'technically unlawful.' **29.** The Secretary of State for the Environment, Transport and the Regions (John Prescott) proposed the creation of new National Parks in the New Forest and the South Downs.

OCTOBER 1999

6. A form of malaria killed all 26 rare penguins at Marwell Zoo in Hampshire and several deaths occurred at Edinburgh Zoo. **7.** A British architect, Charlie Paton, won an architectural award at the Design Museum for his pioneering new building which uses sunlight to turn salt water into fresh water for growing vegetables and for drinking water. **12.** A survey by the United Nations Food and Agriculture Organisation has found that of the 5,500 breeds of farm animals worldwide, 30 per cent are at risk of extinction. **15.** An international conference of ornithologists and scientists in Kaula Lumpar reported that one in eight of the world's birds are facing extinction in the next millennium. **23.** Following years of warnings from conservationists that tigers would become extinct in the next millennium, new evidence shows that tiger populations have stabilised and are now growing strongly in some parts of Asia. **24.** South West Water is to plant a 196,000 acre forest at Roadford Lake in Devon with cash aid from the Forestry Commission.

NOVEMBER 1999

3. The Indonesian Wildlife Forum said that the Sumatran tiger faced extinction within two years. **11.** The World Wide Fund for Nature said that plans to protect the Iberian Lynx were inadequate and that numbers had fallen to around 600.

DECEMBER 1999

8. The first Europe-wide study of butterflies found that one-eighth of species was in danger of extinction. **21.** A Maltese oil tanker, the *Erika*, broke up off the coast of Brittany, causing a widespread oil slick which killed over 100,000 seabirds.

JANUARY 2000

1. A scarlet toadstool called Cytidia saclicina, believed to have been extinct in Britain for ten years, was rediscovered in Keilder Forest in Northumberland. **4.** Some of the worst storms to hit France in history destroyed 270 million trees, ranging from 18th century oaks in Paris gardens to entire plantations in the Vosges mountains.

FEBRUARY 2000

2. It was announced that an offshore wind farm, the first in the UK, is to be built off Blyth, Northumberland. **11.** The National Gamekeepers Organisation announced their intentions to hold the largest shoot in history in an attempt to protect winter crops.

MARCH 2000

1. The carcass of an adult woolly mammoth which died over 20,000 years ago was found preserved in a block of frozen mud in Khatanga, 500 miles north of the Arctic Circle. **5.** Conservationists warned that around half of Britain's hedgerows, which are home to birds, butterflies and wild flowers, are being destroyed by farmers worried about the anti-fraud ruling aimed at ensuring that farmers only claim subsidy payments for land under cultivation. **7.** John Prescott announced the building of 860,000 new homes in the south-east of England over the next ten years. **31.** The Japanese volcano, Mount Usu, dormant for over 20 years, erupted.

APRIL 2000

17. A worldwide ban on ivory sales was reimposed by the Convention on International Trade in Endangered Species (CITIES).

MAY 2000

2. The first red kite chick to be hatched in captivity in the United Kingdom was hatched from an incubator at the National Birds of Prey Centre in Newent, Gloucestershire. **17.** The government admitted that over 30,000 acres of genetically-modified oilseed rape had been planted in Britain accidentally, despite a ban on commercial growing of such crops. **25.** The Government announced its aim to introduce doorstep collections of recyclable materials to most households in Britain within the next three years.

JUNE 2000

30. A report into European fisheries policy by the Oslo Paris Commission concluded that two thirds of commercial fish in the region, such as North Sea Cod were being fished 'beyond safe limits.'

JULY 2000

5. The Italian government announced at it will solve the problem of a plague of 'super mosquitoes' by releasing the Gambusia fish into lakes where the larvae breed. **11.** The Royal Society for the Protection of Birds paid £1 million for wildlife reserves at Aveley, Wennington and Rainham Marshes on the Thames Estuary. East Blean Wood near Canterbury, Kent, was designated a National Nature Reserve because it supports Britain's largest population of the rare heath fritillary butterfly. **13.** The twaite shad, one of the most endangered fish in British waters has been successfully bred in captivity for the first time by the Environment Agency. **14.** The Italian Marine Research Institute discovered 85 species of tropical fish in Mediterranean waters which were previously unknown on a significant scale. **16.** A fire at the Australian Reptile Park near Sydney caused the deaths of over 1,000 crocodiles, snakes and turtles. **20.** The walled flower and fruit garden of Osborne House, Isle of Wight, which was originally planted by Queen Victoria's husband Prince Albert, was replanted by English Heritage and reopened to the public. **21.** NASA reported that global warming was causing the Greenland ice sheet to melt at a rate of 12 cubic miles per year, causing a seven per cent rise in sea levels. **24.** A British conservationist secured the release of 500 endangered Asiatic Black Bears from captivity in an agreement with the Chinese government. **28.** The European Commission reported that the bathing water at 47 of Britain's beaches was unsafe due to high levels of pollution.

AUGUST 2000

14. The European Commission banned the export of live pigs from Britain following an outbreak of swine fever in East Anglia. **15.** The RSPB reported that two red kites which had been released into the Yorkshire Dales in the hope they would breed, were deliberately killed with bait laced with a pesticide. **25.** An 11-year-old boy was attacked by a young panther-like animal while playing near his home in Trellech, Monmouthshire. A search was mounted to track the animal following a number of sightings. **30.** Scientists from the British Geomorphological Research Group announced that significant reductions in levels of acid rain meant that the stone of some of London's historical buildings was being eroded at half the rate of ten years ago.

AFRICA

SEPTEMBER 1999

6. President Mubarak of Egypt suffered a light wound to the arm when a man armed with a knife lunged at him.

16. In Algeria, a referendum proposing an amnesty for opponents of the government who had not been involved in acts of violence was endorsed by more than 98 per cent of those who voted. President Bouteflika had urged the population to vote in favour. 15. The South African government approved arms purchases worth 21,300 million rand (£2,200 million). 17. In Zambia, 59 soldiers were sentenced to death for taking part in a coup attempt against the democratically elected government in October 1997. 21. The editor of *The Times of Swaziland* was forced to resign after publishing a photograph of a topless woman chosen to be the seventh wife of King Mswati III. 25. President Mubarak of Egypt won a further six years in power after collecting 93.79 per cent of the vote in a referendum.

OCTOBER 1999

7. De Beers banned the purchase of diamonds from non-government sources in Angola, the main source of funding for the UNITÀ movement. 10. In Brandfort, South Africa, President Mbeki and the Duke of Kent laid wreaths at the graves of British soldiers, Boer civilians and black concentration camp victims; the ceremony inaugurated a three-year commemoration of the 1899-1902 Boer war. 18. President Mugabe promised compensation to the families of those killed by the army following unrest in Matabeleland in 1983. 22. The UN Security Council voted unanimously to send a 6,000-strong peacekeeping force to help to maintain the peace settlement in Sierra Leone.

NOVEMBER 1999

7. In the Democratic Republic of Congo, rebel forces declared the cease-fire to be null and void, claiming that the government was violating the pact. 10. The Queen addressed a state banquet in Pretoria, South Africa, saying that the 100th anniversary of the outbreak of the Boer War was a time for reconciliation. 11. President Museveni ordered the closure of all but six of Uganda's overseas diplomatic missions on economic grounds; the High Commission in London would remain. 16. Angolan government forces claimed to have surrounded the last UNITÀ outpost. 21. President Mugabe threatened to let squatters invade farms owned by whites if Britain refused to fund Zimbabwe's programme of land redistribution. 25–26. Two days of ethnic clashes between Christian Yorubas and Muslim Hausas in Lagos, Nigeria, resulted in the deaths of more than 40 people; President Obasanjo ordered police to shoot rioters and criminals on sight. 28. In Algeria, Muslim rebels killed at least 28 people in two separate massacres. 30. The first units of a 6,000-strong UN force arrived in Sierra Leone to help restore order after the civil war. President Mugabe of Zimbabwe issued a decree trebling the pay of MPs and ministers.

DECEMBER 1999

4. In Algeria, Islamic fundamentalists killed 11 people 180 miles south of Algiers. 5. In Namibia, Sam Nujoma won a third consecutive term as President, receiving 77 per cent of the vote; the ruling South West African People's Organisation (SWAPO) also received 77 per cent of the vote in concurrent legislative elections. 13. Namibia's Chief of Staff, Maj.-Gen. Martin Shalli announced that the country would allow Angolan troops to use the country's territory to attack the Angolan rebel movement UNITÀ. 14. The Swiss government announced that Swiss banks had frozen 120 bank accounts containing £360 million belonging to the former Nigerian President Gen. Sani Abacha. 22. Joaquim Chissano was re-elected President of Mozambique, winning 52 per cent of the vote;

his Frelimo party captured 133 seats in the 250-member assembly. 23. In Côte d'Ivoire, a military coup deposed President Henri Konan Bédié, who fled into exile, ending four decades of rule by the Côte d'Ivoire Democratic Party (PDCI). Ahmed Benbitour was named as Algeria's new Prime Minister. 26. In Angola, Bishop Eugenio del Corso said that government troops had burnt to death 47 villagers at Muambunda, 600 miles east of Luanda.

JANUARY 2000

3. Sixteen people died after three days of violence between Muslims and Christians in villages in southern Egypt. 11. In Algeria, the Islamic Salvation Army, the armed wing of the Islamic Salvation Front, agreed to disband following a government amnesty for Islamist guerrillas. On 22 January, government troops began an operation, code-named 'Sword of the Holy War', to eliminate groups which refused to disarm. 26. The South African parliament passed the Equality Bill, establishing equality courts to enforce provisions against discrimination on the grounds of race, gender, sex, pregnancy, marital status, ethnic or social origin, colour, sexual orientation, age, disability, religion, conscience, belief, culture, language and birth. 27. Zamfara state, Nigeria, formally adopted *Shari'ah* (Islamic law), but the state governor indicated that it would only apply to Muslims in the state. 29. Petrol rationing was introduced in Zimbabwe as its financial crisis deepened. 31. The Zimbabwe Broadcasting Corporation defied a High Court order by refusing to broadcast television and radio programmes made by the National Constitutional Assembly, an alliance of civic groups campaigning against the proposed new constitution in the referendum due on 12–13 February.

FEBRUARY 2000

13. Kenya issued an emergency appeal for food aid as drought threatened to bring famine to the country. 14. In Zimbabwe, President Mugabe accepted defeat in the referendum on a new constitution held on 12–13 February; the proposal had been defeated by 54.7 per cent to 45.3 per cent. 18. King Letsie III of Lesotho married Karabo Motsoeneng in Maseru. 21. Foday Sanko, the Vice-President of Sierra Leone and former rebel leader, was expelled from South Africa after violating a United Nations travel ban. 21–22. At least 200 people were killed in Kaduna, Nigeria, during clashes between Muslims and Christians over the introduction of *Shari'ah* law. 22. President Mugabe of Zimbabwe announced that he would not contest Presidential elections after the expiry of his term of office in 2002. 25. The Pope appealed for an end to employment discrimination against Christians in Egypt during a Mass in Cairo.

MARCH 2000

1. The Libyan General People's Congress abolished much of Libya's central government; only foreign policy, national security, information and the national Oil Company would continue to be determined at national level. Nigeria's northern states announced that they would withdraw the legislation implementing *Shari'ah* following an emergency meeting presided over by President Olusegun Obasanjo. 2. In Zimbabwe, the government appealed to the squatters who had occupied white-owned farms since the defeat of the constitutional referendum in February to leave. 9. The UK High Commissioner in Harare was recalled after Zimbabwean customs officials breached diplomatic convention by opening crates containing goods intended for the British High Commission. 11. President Mugabe of Zimbabwe gave official approval to the occupation of land by

squatters in an interview for *The Herald* newspaper. Encouraged by his remarks, thousands of squatters launched a new wave of farm invasions the following day. **14.** Zimbabwe's Commercial Farmers' Union appealed to the High Court in Harare to declare the invasion of white-owned farms illegal. **15.** In Swaziland, Mgabhi Dlamini, the parliamentary speaker, resigned after receiving death threats; he had been accused of stealing a piece of cow dung from the king's cattle enclosure to use in a traditional ritual to strengthen his standing with the king. **19.** Abdoulayé Wade won the Presidential election in Senegal, ending 40 years of uninterrupted rule by the Socialist Party. **21.** Zimbabwean Agriculture Minister Kumbirai Kangai appeared in court charged with corruption; he denied two counts of fraud totalling £3.5 million in connection with contracts to rebuild the country's grain reserves. **23.** President Pasteur Bizimungu of Rwanda resigned. **26.** President Mugabe postponed the general election that was to have been held in April. **28.** In Zimbabwe, it was revealed that more than one million acres of land compulsorily purchased from white farmers has been distributed to a group of around 400 people, many of them political allies of President Mugabe. **29.** It was announced in Egypt another pyramid had been discovered at Saqqara near Cairo.

APRIL 2000

1. In Zimbabwe, supporters of the President attacked a peaceful demonstration organised by the National Constitutional Assembly (NCA), singling out white protestors. **3.** The Secretary of the Zanu-PF Central Committee, Didymus Mutasa, warned that the Zimbabwean government would not tolerate the opposition MDC and branded it a puppet of the British government. **6.** The Zimbabwean parliament voted by 100 votes to nil to amend the constitution, giving the government the right to seize white-owned farms without compensation and stating that the UK, as the former colonial power, should compensate the farmers. **7.** Col. Muammar Gaddafi announced that seven years of sanctions had cost Libya more than £21,500 million. **9.** In Zimbabwe, Morgan Tsvangirai, the MDC leader, called President Mugabe 'a deranged despot' in a full-page advertisement in a Zimbabwe newspaper. **11.** At least nine people were killed during a student protest in Banjul, Gambia. **17.** In Rwanda, Paul Kagame, who led the rebel army that ended the 1994 genocide and ousted the former Hutu government, was elected President, the first Tutsi to hold the position. **18.** Speaking on the 20th anniversary of independence from the UK, President Mugabe accused white farmers of seeking to reverse independence. **21.** Southern African leaders publicly endorsed President Mugabe's land policy and demanded that the UK pay for land redistribution. **27.** Talks between Foreign Secretary Robin Cook and a Zimbabwean ministerial delegation in London failed to produce a pledge to end the violent occupation of properties. **28.** The UN warned that Zimbabwe could face starvation if the illegal seizure of white-owned farms continued during harvesting and planting seasons.

MAY 2000

1. In Kenya, more than 70 people were killed in a clash between Somali and Borana tribesmen near Isiolo in the Eastern province. **2.** On the day that the Nigerian-led West African force, Ecomog, officially withdrew from Sierra Leone, rebels killed seven Kenyan UN peacekeepers and 48 peacekeepers were being held hostage. The Commonwealth Ministerial Action Group ordered its Secretary-General, Don McKinnon, to deliver a rebuke to President Mugabe for the violence, loss of life, illegal occupations of property, failure to uphold the rule of law and political intimidation; it also resolved to send observers to monitor the elections. **3.** President Mugabe accused the Commonwealth of acting as a mouthpiece of British propaganda. Nineteen people were killed and 26 wounded when Islamic rebels attacked a bus that drove through a roadblock in Hamdania, Algeria. **5.** President Thabo Mbeki of South Africa publicly told President Mugabe to end the land invasions and seek a consensus rather than confrontation with white farmers. **6.** In Sierra Leone, it was reported that the RUF had kidnapped around 318 UN personnel; another 200 Zambian peacekeepers were reported missing. The UK despatched an emergency task force of 1,500 Royal Marines and paratroopers to Sierra Leone. Nelson Mandela, condemned leaders who used power to enrich themselves while their people went hungry and said that 'the public must bring these tyrants down by picking up rifles' in a clear reference to the situation in Zimbabwe. **8.** In Sierra Leone, 20 people were shot dead and more than 54 were wounded by rebels when around 10,000 protestors marched on the house of Foday Sankoh, the RUF leader. **9.** British paratroopers began the evacuation of British, EU and Commonwealth passport holders from Sierra Leone; the UN began evacuating all non-essential staff and Oxfam announced that it had withdrawn aid workers. The UN admitted that the RUF had captured the town of Masiaka only 40 miles from Freetown after three platoons of UN troops withdrew after they ran out of ammunition. In Kenya, squatters invaded the farm of Basil Criticos, a junior government minister and the country's only white MP; he was sacked on 12 May after he complained about the occupation. **10.** In Zimbabwe, MDC leader Morgan Tsvangirai called on the international community to consider drastic action, including economic sanctions. **12.** Fighting resumed on several fronts along the disputed border between Ethiopia and Eritrea. In South Africa, the Supreme Court of Appeal halved the six-year sentence previously imposed on Allan Boesak, the former anti-apartheid leader, for misusing charity funds. In Zimbabwe, the government and the Commercial Farmers' Union agreed to establish a land commission with a mandate to redistribute white-owned farms, in return for a public statement from the President calling on squatters to refrain from violence. **14.** The Zimbabwean government announced that British passport holders with dual nationality were to be stripped of their Zimbabwean citizenship. The farm of Ian Smith, Rhodesia's last white Prime Minister, was occupied by squatters. **15.** President Mugabe announced that a parliamentary election would be held on 24–25 June. In Ethiopia, more than 100,000 protestors demonstrated to support the renewed war against Eritrea. **16.** It was announced in Namibia that white-owned farmland would be expropriated by the government, which would pay 'just compensation' for redistribution among landless blacks. President Mugabe met Commonwealth Secretary-General Don McKinnon and agreed to accept 40 election observers from the Commonwealth. In Zambia, ex-President Kenneth Kaunda resigned as leader of the opposition United National Independence Party. **18.** In Sierra Leone, Foday Sankoh, the RUF leader, was seized by armed militiamen in Freetown. **19.** Ethiopian troops captured the Eritrean town of Barentu; the UN Security Council imposed a year-long arms embargo on both countries. In Zimbabwe, Dr Chenjerai Hunzvi, the leader of the War Veterans' Association, was convicted on contempt charges for defying orders to end the occupation of white-owned land; he escaped a jail term only after the Commercial

Farmers' Union, who had initiated the case, asked the judge to impose a non-custodial sentence, fearing that imprisoning him would be inflammatory. **22.** In Sierra Leone, an attempt by RUF rebels to seize President Kabbah and use him to barter for the release of Fodeh Sankoh was foiled. **23.** In Nigeria, violence between Christians and Muslims left at least 300 people dead in Kaduna. **24.** The Zimbabwean government issued an edict allowing President Mugabe to seize white-owned farms, declaring that it would pay compensation only for improvements to the land and that compensation for the land would have to come from the UK government. Ethiopia captured the Eritrean border town of Zalambessa. **28.** In South Africa, ANC General Secretary Kgalena Motlanthe, called on the UK to honour its colonial obligations and hand over the £36 million promised to Zimbabwe for land reform. **29.** Peace talks sponsored by the Organisation of African Unity, aimed at finding a solution to the war between Eritrea and Ethiopia, resumed in Algiers. In Zimbabwe, former President Canaan Banana lost an appeal against his conviction on sodomy and sexual assault charges and was ordered to serve a year in jail. **30.** In Sierra Leone, the RUF recaptured the town of Lunsar after the Sierra Leonean army ran out of bullets. **31.** Ethiopian Prime Minister Meles Zenawi declared that all Ethiopian territory occupied by Eritrea had been liberated, implying that the war was over.

JUNE 2000
2. President Mugabe released a list of 804 white-owned farms that were to be seized, comprising about 5.2 million acres; owners were to be compensated for buildings and roads, but not the land. Egypt marked the 2,000th anniversary of the flight of Mary, Joseph and Jesus to Egypt with celebrations that were attended by the Sheikh of Al-Azhar, Egypt's highest Islamic authority, and the Coptic Pope Shenouda III. **9.** The UN Zimbabwe election monitoring team was recalled after President Mugabe told them they could act only as observers. **13.** The USA, Japan, Canada, Switzerland, Australia and New Zealand protested against the election campaign in Zimbabwe. **14.** President Mugabe warned that the confiscation of white-owned farms would be followed by the seizure of British and foreign-owned mines. The Royal Marines withdrew from Sierra Leone; two hundred British soldiers remained in the country to train 1,000 recruits in the Sierra Leone army. **18.** Ethiopia and Eritrea signed an OAU-brokered cease-fire accord to end their two-year war. **21.** In Nigeria, Kano state announced that *Shari'ah* would be introduced in December 2000. **22.** In Sudan, President Omar Bashir offered unconditional amnesty to all his opponents, which was rejected by the main rebel group, the Sudan People's Liberation Army. **25.** In South Africa, the New National Party, the remnant of the old party of apartheid, announced that it was to merge with the Democratic Party to form the Democratic Alliance. **27.** President Mugabe called for political reconciliation and 'unity across race, tribe and ethnicity' after his party narrowly won the election. The opposition Movement for Democratic Change said it would lodge appeals against the results in a test group of ten constituencies, which it claims it lost because of systematic political intimidation by Zanu-PF.

JULY 2000
1. In Zimbabwe, the head of the EU election monitors, Pierre Schori, criticised an interim statement by Commonwealth observers that failed to blame Zanu-PF

for widespread violence and intimidation. Observer groups from the OAU and the South African Development Community had concluded that the election was free and fair. **2.** In Uganda, 90.7 per cent of voters rejected the reintroduction of multi-party politics in favour of the existing 'no-party' system in a referendum organised by President Museveni in 1986. **5.** In South Africa, the Director-General of the land affairs ministry warned that white farmers could have their land expropriated if they did not make more land available for the resettlement of landless blacks. Dozens of white farmers later abandoned their properties in KwaZulu after a surge of invasions by landless squatters. **7.** Following the imposition of *Shari'ah* in some northern states, the Nigerian medical council decreed than any doctor who amputated a healthy limb on the orders of an Islamic Court would be stuck off the medical register for unethical conduct. **9.** The President of Botswana, Festus Mogae, warned that his country faced catastrophe because of the spread of Aids; more than one-third of adults in Botswana are infected with the virus. **13.** In Nigeria, about £43 million of fraudulently obtained funds deposited by the late dictator Sani Abacha in Switzerland was returned. **18.** In Zimbabwe, around 40 white farmers in the Glendale district shut down their operations and demanded that the police restore order. On 24 July, 180 other white farmers stopped work following the murder of a white farmer in Karoi. **21.** In Sierra Leone, UN troops attacked a rebel base, freeing 233 UN peacekeepers who had been besieged for two months. **22.** In Zimbabwe, the opposition MDF announced that it would go to the High Court to challenge more than 20 results in the parliamentary election held in June. **25.** In Zimbabwe, Morgan Tsvangirai, the leader of the MDC leader, expressed his support for the striking white farmers and warned President Mugabe that urban workers might strike in solidarity with farm workers. **28.** The Zimbabwe Congress of Trade Unions approved a general strike over the breakdown of law and order. **30.** President Taylor of Liberia was warned by the USA to stop arming the rebels in Sierra Leone or face international sanctions. **31.** The Zimbabwean government threatened to add a further 2,237 farms to the 804 it has already listed for compulsory acquisition.

AUGUST 2000
2. It was estimated that 90 per cent of the workforce joined a general strike called by the Zimbabwe Congress of Trade Unions. **7.** In Swaziland, King Mswati III married Liphovela Senteni Masango, who became his seventh wife. **8.** Leaders of the Southern African Development Community urged President Mbeki to press the UK government to pay compensation for farms seized by the Zimbabwean government. In Nigeria, Yobe state became the seventh to announce its intention to introduce *Shari'ah*, to take effect from 1 October 2000. **11.** President Mugabe vowed to press on with land seizures and accused the UK of leading a crusade to destroy Zimbabwe at the annual Heroes Day ceremony in Harare, which was attended by fewer than 2,000 people. **18.** In Zimbabwe, another 229 white-owned farms were listed for compulsory acquisition. **21.** In Sierra Leone, the RUF announced that it had replaced Foday Sankoh with a new leader, Issa Sesay. **22.** In Zimbabwe, police removed more than 700 squatters and arrested 13 ringleaders from white-owned farms in the first such operation since land invasions began. **24.** In Kenya, Fr John Kaiser, an American priest who had been an outspoken critic of the government, was shot dead. On 30 August, hundreds of demonstrators marched through Nairobi in protest at his killing. **26.** In Liberia, a Channel

Four television crew was freed after being detained on charges of espionage on 21 August; they were freed after apologising to President Taylor. **27.** Abdiqassim Salad Hassan was sworn in as Somalia's first President for nine years at a meeting of representatives of the country's clans, which was held in Djibouti. In Sierra Leone, a gang known as the West Side Boys took 11 British soldiers hostage. Five were released unharmed on 30 August; they were freed by British forces on 10 September. **29.** In Libya, a welcoming ceremony was held in Tripoli for six western hostages who had been freed by Abu Sayyaf rebels in the Philippines after Libyan intervention. **30.** In Zimbabwe, Finance Minister Simba Makoni told parliament that the total cost of sending 11,000 soldiers to the Democratic Republic of Congo had amounted to more than £175 million.

THE AMERICAS

SEPTEMBER 1999

2. The Francophone Community held its biennial summit in the Canadian town of Moncton, New Brunswick. US marshals raided the headquarters of the FBI for evidence about the 1993 Waco siege in which 86 cult members were killed. **10.** Paraguay withdrew its ambassador to Argentina and its foreign minister resigned, after the Argentine government refused to extradite Gen. Lino Oviedo, who had been charged with ordering the murder of the Paraguayan Vice-President Luis María Argaña in March 1999. **12.** In Chile, two died, eight were wounded and 23 arrested in clashes between supporters of Augusto Pinochet and Salvador Allende on the anniversary of the 1973 military coup. **17.** The USA announced a relaxation of economic sanctions against North Korea following North Korea's conditional freeze on long-range ballistic missile testing. The President of the Microsoft Corporation, Bill Gates, set up a US$1 billion scholarship programme to enable students from ethnic minorities to attend university. **21.** President Andres Pastrana of Colombia asked the USA for £2,250 million in aid to end his country's worst recession in 70 years and a surge in illegal drug production. **22.** In Brazil, Hildebrando Pascoal, a congressman from the western Amazon state of Acre, was accused of multiple murders and drug trafficking; the Congress voted to remove his parliamentary immunity. President Clinton offered clemency to 16 Puerto Rican separatists, members of the Armed Forces of National Liberation (FALN) despite a warning from the head of the FBI that they remained hardened terrorists dedicated to using violence. **23.** President Clinton blocked a Republican bill that aimed to reduce taxes by US$792 thousand million over ten years. **30.** President Clinton moved to write off all Third World debt owed to the USA, provided that the countries could prove that the money freed would be spent on reducing poverty.

OCTOBER 1999

7. Adrienne Clarkson was sworn in as Canada's 26th Governor-General. **9.** President Castro agreed a deal to allow thousands of Cuban Jews to emigrate to Israel. **13.** The comprehensive nuclear test ban treaty, which had been signed by President Clinton in 1996, was rejected by Congress; the treaty had been signed by 150 countries, but cannot enter into force unless approved by the 44 nuclear-capable countries. **13.** The United States army announced the creation of two highly mobile brigades with the capability to deploy anywhere in the world within 96 hours. **15.** Chilean President Eduardo Frei appealed to Tony Blair for the release of Gen. Pinochet on

humanitarian grounds. **21.** Basil O'Brien was appointed High Commissioner for the Commonwealth of the Bahamas. **24.** In Argentina, Fernando de la Rue, the Alliance Party candidate, won the Presidential elections with 54 per cent of the vote. **25.** Over two million Colombians protested in Bogotà against the 35-year civil war as the latest round of peace talks between the government and the largest rebel group began; mass demonstrations were also held in other Colombian cities.

NOVEMBER 1999

12. Venezuela declared it was to honour Simón Bolívar by renaming itself the Bolívarian Republic of Venezuela. **12.** The ship carrying Christmas supplies to St Helena broke down in the Bay of Biscay, causing panic buying on the island. Shipping authorities despatched a freighter from South Africa on 30 November to provide replacement supplies. **15.** A two-day summit of Latin American countries plus Spain and Portugal opened in Havana; it was attended by the King and Queen of Spain, the first time a Spanish monarch had visited Cuba. **28.** Jorge Batlle, the Colorado Party candidate, won the Uruguayan Presidential election with 51.5 per cent of the vote. **30.** In the USA, protestors succeeded in delaying the formal opening of the World Trade Organisation talks in Seattle, Washington. President Clinton called for action after a report issued by the government-sponsored Institute of Medicine found that up to 98,000 people died each year because of medical mistakes.

DECEMBER 1999

6. The USA denounced Cuban demands for the return of Elian González, a boy rescued after a refugee boat sank off Florida, drowning his mother and stepfather. **13.** Communist rebels launched an attack on a Colombian naval base on the border with Panama, killing 45 marines. **14.** The ceremonial hand-over of the Panama Canal took place, with ex-President Carter representing the USA, President Moscoso of Panama, King Juan Carlos of Spain and the Presidents of six Latin American countries present; the canal reverted to Panamanian control on 31 December 1999. **15.** The USA agreed to pay China US$28 million in compensation for the NATO bombing of the Chinese Embassy in Belgrade. **27.** Alfonso Portillo of the Guatemalan Republican Front won the first peacetime Presidential election in nearly 40 years. President Chávez of Venezuela was heavily criticised for his handling of the flood disaster earlier in the month that killed an estimated 10,000 people. **30.** The US International Trade Commission said it would conduct a detail study on a plan to include the UK in NAFTA; the UK would be required to leave the EU before being given membership.

JANUARY 2000

3. In Peru, opponents of President Fujimori mounted protests in Lima against his attempt to run for the presidency a third time, in defiance of the constitution. **8.** Elian González was subpoenaed to appear before Congress after the US Immigration and Naturalisation Service had decided to return the six-year-old boy to Cuba. **11.** The Central Bank of Ecuador approved a government plan to scrap the sucre, and adopt the US dollar as Ecuador's legal currency; the sucre had lost 70 per cent of its value in 1999. **16.** In Chile, Ricardo Lagos, the candidate for the Concertación Centre-Left Coalition, was elected President after defeating Joaquín Lavin in the second round of the Presidential elections. **21.** In Ecuador, a three-man junta which had deposed President Jamil Mahuad just earlier was dissolved by the military chief Gen. Carlos Mendoza after American officials warned that Ecuador could lose its foreign aid and investment if it did not restore power to the elected government. President Mahuad was replaced by Vice-President Noboa.

FEBRUARY 2000

2. In the New Hampshire primary elections, the first in the 2000 election campaign, Senator John McCain won the Republican primary and Vice President Al Gore won the Democratic primary.

MARCH 2000

4. Gen. Pinochet, who had been allowed to return to Chile from the UK after being deemed unfit to face trial, was welcomed by supporters in Santiago; meanwhile around 4,000 people demonstrated for him to face trial in Chile for the killings and torture committed during his 17-year rule. **11.** In Arizona, the first legally binding online election took place for the Democratic primary; conventional voting was also permitted. **14.** In El Salvador, former left-wing guerrillas, the Farabundo Marti National Liberation Front, took more than 35 per cent of the vote and won mayoral elections in most main cities. **15.** Al Gore won the Democratic nomination and George W. Bush won the Republican nomination after winning the six southern states of Florida, Louisiana, Mississippi, Oklahoma, Tennessee and Texas.

APRIL 2000

3. In the USA, the Microsoft Corporation was found guilty of using its monopoly to stifle competition; on 7 June, Microsoft was ordered to submit plans to divide the company into two companies within four months. Penalties were expected to be announced in October 2000. **9.** In the USA, the CIA sacked the officer it claimed was responsible for the wrongful bombing of the Chinese embassy in Belgrade during NATO's air campaign against Serbia in May 1999; six other employees were reprimanded. **16.** Riot police dispersed hundreds of protesters who broke through barricades as the IMF and World Bank began their annual meeting in Washington. **20.** In Brazil, thousands of Amerindians converged on the north-eastern state of Bahia to protest against celebrations to mark the 500th anniversary of the country's discovery by Pedro Alvares Cabral.

MAY 2000

2. One man was killed and scores injured in a wave of protests across Brazil by Movimento Sem Terra, the Landless Rural Workers' Movement, who invaded farms and government buildings in protest at the slow pace of land reform. **7.** The Federal Bureau of Investigations announced that violent crime had fallen in the USA for the eighth year running. **11.** In the USA, the Nation of Islam leader Louis Farrakhan admitted that his comment that rival black leader Malcolm X was a traitor who was worthy of death might have been partly responsible for his assassination in 1965. **14.** In the Dominican Republic, Hipólito Mejía, a Social Democrat, claimed victory in the Presidential election after obtaining 49.8 per cent of the vote, just less than the 50 per cent required. **16.** In Colombia, a woman extortion victim was decapitated by an explosive 'necklace' placed around her neck by guerrillas after she refused to pay £5,000 to the Revolutionary Armed Forces of Columbia (FARC). A bomb technician who was helping to remove the bomb was also killed. **19.** The Mayor of New York, Rudolph Giuliani, announced his withdrawal from the senatorial election scheduled for 7 November 2000; he had planned to contest the same seat as Hilary Clinton. **23.** In Chile, the court of

appeal withdrew Gen. Augusto Pinochet's immunity from prosecution for alleged human rights abuses during his 17-year rule from 1973 to 1990. **28.** In the Peruvian Presidential election, Alberto Fujimori won the second round with a landslide majority after his rival, Alejandro Toledo, had withdrawn from the contest on 22 May, accusing the incumbent President of electoral fraud. International observers said conditions for a free election had not been met. **31.** President Clinton announced that he was prepared to share US missile defence system technology with other civilised nations.

JUNE 2000

2. President Clinton became the first US President to be awarded the Charlemagne prize for his work on promoting European unity. **5.** In Chile, the Court of Appeals declared that it had stripped Gen. Augusto Pinochet's immunity from prosecution. **13.** President Fernando de la Rua of Argentina apologised for the protection given to Nazi war criminals by his country after the Second World War. A pair of computer hard disks belonging to the US Nuclear Emergency Search Team containing information on all US thermonuclear weapons was reported missing. **19.** Madeleine Albright, the Secretary of State, announced that the USA no longer considered Iraq, Iran, Libya and North Korea as 'rogue states'; following some improvements, they were now classified as 'states of concern'. **23.** A Pentagon report leaked to the *Washington Times* claimed that China was building up its military forces in preparation for a possible war with the USA over Taiwan. **27.** The US Congress voted to lift the food and medicine embargo against Cuba.

JULY 2000

2. In Mexico, the Presidential election was won by Vicente Fox of the National Action Party (PAN) with 42.8 per cent of the vote, to 35.7 per cent for Francisco Labastida, the candidate of the Institutional Revolutionary Party (PRI), that had ruled the country for 71 years. **11-25.** President Clinton hosted a summit between Israeli President Ehud Barak and Palestinian National Authority leader Yasser Arafat at Camp David; the delegations failed to reach an agreement. **19.** An Argentine lawsuit against the UK over the sinking of the cruiser *General Belgrano* brought before the European Court of Human Rights was ruled inadmissible because there had been no attempt to exhaust all legal remedies in the UK first. **26.** In Cuba, President Fidel Castro led a march of more than a million people to protest against the continuing US economic embargo against Cuba. In the USA, George W. Bush, the Republican Presidential candidate, announced that he had chosen Dick Cheney to be his vice-Presidential running mate. **28.** In Peru, President Alberto Fujimori was inaugurated for a third five-year term; protesters demanding a return to democracy fought riot police and set three government buildings alight. **30.** In the Venezuelan Presidential election, President Chávez secured a further term in office, with 59 per cent of the vote.

AUGUST 2000

8. Chile's Supreme Court stripped former President Gen. Augusto Pinochet of his immunity from prosecution. **14.** Mexico's President Vicente Fox appealed to the USA to open its borders and urged closer economic union. **16.** In Colombia, government forces accidentally shot dead six schoolchildren, who were caught in crossfire between troops and left-wing guerrillas. Six other children were seriously injured. **22.** In Paraguay, Julio Cesar Franco was elected Vice-President.

ASIA

SEPTEMBER 1999

1. Thousands of people fled into the UN compound for safety as militiamen fired at pro-independence campaigners in Dili, East Timor. The UN rejected a call by New Zealand for a security operation in East Timor. **2.** The Chief of Staff of anti-separatist forces in East Timor, Herminio da Silva da Costa, threatened civil war if the referendum favoured independence. Australia announced that it would favour deployment of a peacekeeping force. Indonesia indicated that it would almost certainly allow a UN force to go to East Timor. The birth control pill went on sale for the first time in Japan. **4.** In East Timor, independence from Indonesia was chosen by nearly 80 per cent of the 451,792 who voted. **5.** A general strike began in Pakistan after opposition parties protested against huge tax rises. **6.** Indonesia imposed martial law in East Timor. **7.** The UN drew up plans to send a 7,000-strong force to restore law and order in East Timor, under Australian command. José Alexandre Gusmão, the pro-independence campaigner, was released in Jakarta and immediately accepted sanctuary in the British Embassy. **8.** The UN Security Council met in emergency session to consider demands for an international force in East Timor. **12.** Indonesia agreed to allow a UN peacekeeping force into East Timor after an appeal by the UN Secretary General, Kofi Annan. The Sri Lankan military launched a major air and ground offensive against Tamil Tiger Rebels in the north-western district of Mannar. **14.** The UN compound in Dili was set on fire following the airlifting of about 1,500 East Timorese refugees and more than 50 UN personnel to Australia. **18.** Tamil Tiger rebels killed more than 50 villagers in eastern Sri Lanka. Former Gurkha soldiers and their families protested in Nepal for pensions and benefits equal to their counterparts in the British Army. **19.** The first peacekeeping troops arrived in East Timor, headed by Maj.-Gen. Peter Cosgrove. At least 38 people died in a series of landmine blasts in Bihar, India, which were blamed on two banned guerrilla organisations that had urged a boycott of the general election. In Malaysia, riot police fired water cannon and teargas at protestors demanding an investigation into allegations that the jailed former Deputy Prime Minister, Anwar Ibrahim, had been poisoned; he had been admitted to hospital suffering from arsenic poisoning. **20.** The vanguard of the 8,000-strong international force arrived in Dili and secured the airport and port. India's Election Commission ordered fresh ballots in areas of four states after violence marred polling. **23.** Indonesian troops began pulling out of Dili after destroying their bases and setting fire to buildings. Indonesia lifted martial law in East Timor. Thousands of students fought with police in Jakarta over a bill that would give the military emergency powers. **27.** The commander of the Indonesian forces in East Timor, Gen. Kiki Syahnakri, departed. **28.** Indonesia's Finance Minister Boediono expressed 'deep regret' over the loss of life in East Timor at the annual meetings of the IMF and World Bank.

OCTOBER 1999

1. Hundreds of thousands of troops and civilians paraded past Tiananmen Square to mark the 50th anniversary of the People's Republic of China. A group of Myanmar dissidents stormed the Myanmar Embassy in Bangkok, taking 89 hostages; the siege ended peacefully after the intervention of the Thai Deputy Foreign Minister;

Myanmar closed its border with Thailand on 3 October in protest at the release of the dissidents. **3.** India's general election was won by the BJP-led National Democratic Alliance with a slender majority. **4.** Pakistani police fought to stop hundreds of members of the Jammu and Kashmir Liberation Front from marching across a cease-fire line into the Indian part of Kashmir. **8.** The Taliban leader, Mullah Omar, announced that Afghanistan was ready to co-operate with the international community by closing terrorist camps and returning to Pakistan Islamic militants wanted for killing Shia Muslims. **12.** In Pakistan, the government was overthrown by the army after the Prime Minister, Nawaz Sharif, had tried to sack Gen. Pervez Musharraf; the President, Prime Minister and all ministers were placed under house arrest. **13.** Gen. Musharraf declared himself Chief Executive and dissolved the legislature; martial law was imposed the following day. **16.** The Pakistani army ordered the freezing of assets of ministers, MPs and members of regional assemblies. **19.** Indonesian President Habibie withdrew from the Presidential election after losing a vote of confidence in parliament by 355 votes to 322. **20.** Indonesia's Consultative Assembly voted to approve the independence of East Timor; they also chose Abdurrahman Wahid as President and Megawati Sukarnoputri as Vice-President. **21.** In Pakistan, the 19-party Grand Democratic Alliance and Islamic fundamentalist parties endorsed the army coup. **22.** Xanana Gusmão, the East Timorese independence leader, returned to East Timor from Australia. **25.** In Pakistan, Gen. Musharraf named a military-backed government, the National Security Council, which would have seven members, the three service chiefs and four civilians. **30.** The last Indonesian troops left East Timor. **31.** Abdollah Nouri, a key aide of President Khatami, went on trial on charges including opposing the teachings of Ayatollah Khomeini and advocating relations with the USA and Israel.

NOVEMBER 1999

1. It was announced that to the world's next Disney theme park was to be built in Hong Kong. **4.** China denied that the Panchen Lama had died while in police custody. **5.** The Pope arrived in Delhi, where he was to meet the bishops of the Asian synod. **8.** About 500,000 protestors gathered in Banda Aceh, the capital of Aceh province, demanding independence from Indonesia. **10.** The deposed Premier of Pakistan, Nawaz Sharif, and eight other senior officials were accused of treason and kidnapping. **14.** UN sanctions imposed on Afghanistan after the Taliban militia, which controlled most of the country, refused to hand over Osama bin Laden to face trial on charges that he masterminded the bombings of US embassies in East Africa in 1998. **21.** Indonesia's human rights commission accused Gen. Wiranto, the former armed forces Commander-in-Chief, of being directly responsible for the destruction of East Timor; other senior officers were also named. China launched its first unmanned spacecraft, the *Schenzhou*, which was in space for 21 hours and orbited the Earth 14 times. **23.** In Afghanistan, the Taliban said it was ready for unconditional talks with the USA about the extradition of Osama bin Laden. **28.** In Iran, Abdullah Nouri, a cleric and ally of President Khatami, was jailed for five years for religious and political dissent. **29.** In Malaysia, the ruling National Front Coalition won 148 of the 193 seats in the general election; the opposition alliance gained 42 seats. **30.** President Wahid welcomed Xanana Gusmão to Jakarta and pledged to establish close ties with the soon-to-be-independent East Timor.

DECEMBER 1999

10. In a joint statement in Beijing, the Presidents of Russia and China declared that human rights considerations should never overrule national sovereignty **18.** President Chandrika Kumaratunga of Sri Lanka was wounded in a suicide bombing attack during an election campaign rally in Colombo. The state radio later claimed that police had found evidence of a conspiracy to establish a military regime had the assassination attempt succeeded.**19.** Macao reverted to Chinese sovereignty after 442 years of Portuguese rule; like Hong Kong, it is to be a Special Administrative Region for a period of 50 years. **22.** Chandrika Kumaratunga was re-elected as President of Sri Lanka. **24.** An Indian Airlines aircraft was hijacked on a flight from Kathmandu to Delhi; it landed in Kandahar, Afghanistan on 25 December. More than 160 passengers were held hostage; the hijackers demanded the release of Maulana Masood Azhar, a leading ideologue of Harakat-ul-Mujahidin, a Muslim militant group fighting in Kashmir in return for their release. **26.** Four Falun Gong leaders were sentenced to between seven and 18 years in jail; the Chinese government alleged that Falun Gong was responsible for the deaths of 1,400 members who had followed advice against seeking medical help when sick. **29.** In Indonesia, the military took control of security in Maluku province to quell sectarian violence between Muslims and Christians.

JANUARY 2000

3. In Hong Kong, opposition parties appealed for free elections, demanding full democracy by 2008. **6.** The 17th Karmapa of the Kagyupa sect of Tibetan Buddhism, Ugyen Trinley Dorje, escaped from Tibet to India. China announced that it was to ban its vast bureaucracy from using Microsoft's Windows 2000 software in favour of a Chinese operating system known as 'Red Flag'. **16.** Afghanistan's Taliban regime recognised the independence of Chechnya. **17.** China announced that it had ordained a two-year-old Tibetan lama as the 7th Reting Rinpoche, a senior lamaship; the exiled Tibetan government in India denounced the move. **18.** Four days of fighting between Muslims and Christians left 250 people dead in Ambon, capital of Maluku province, Indonesia. **19.** In Pakistan, deposed Prime Minister Nawaz Sharif and six associates were charged with attempted murder, kidnapping, hijacking and terrorism. **25.** Thai commandos killed nine armed Myanmarese guerrillas and freed the remainder of up to 700 hostages who were being held in Ratchaburi hospital, Thailand; the gunmen were from God's Army, a Karen guerrilla breakaway faction of the Christian Karen National Union, and had already freed more than 70 hostages. Myanmarese government forces raided the Kamaplaw base of the faction the following day. **26.** In Pakistan, the Chief Justice and five of his colleagues in the Supreme Court were dismissed and replaced after they refused to swear an oath of allegiance to the military regime. **31.** President Abdurrahman Wahid of Indonesia sacked Gen. Wiranto, the Security Minister and former head of the army.

FEBRUARY 2000

3. In East Timor, the National Council for East Timorese Resistance announced it would replace Bahasa Indonesia with Portuguese as the national language. **11.** China ordered Tibetan women to be sterilised after their second child, in breach of earlier promises that they would be exempt from strict family planning rules. **12.** Twenty-six people were killed in the Indian state of Bihar as polling began in local elections. **17.** United Nations Secretary-General, Kofi Annan visited East Timor. **18.** In the

general election in Iran, liberals supporting President Muhammad Khatami won 141 seats, hard-liners 44 seats and independents 10, with a turnout of over 80 per cent; the remaining 65 seats were to be decided by a second round of elections. **20.** In India, at least 22 policemen were killed when a landmine planted by suspected left-wing extremists exploded in Bustar, Madhya Pradesh. **21.** China threatened a military invasion if Taiwan delayed negotiations aimed at reuniting it with China. **26.** The Hong Kong authorities announced that the remaining 1,400 Vietnamese boat people were to be given residency status. **29.** Indonesian President Abdurrahman Wahid visited East Timor and apologised for brutalities that occurred during Indonesia's 24-year occupation. The Japanese Defence Ministry said that the Aum Shinrikyo cult, accused of a gas attack in which 12 people died, may have been involved in the installation of its computer system; the launch of the system was postponed indefinitely.

MARCH 2000

5. It was revealed that an internal document distributed by the Central Military Commission of the Chinese Communist Party to regional military commanders advised them to prepare to fight the USA; on 7 March, China announced a 12.7 per cent rise in defence spending. **10.** In Karachi, Pakistan, gunmen shot dead Iqbal Raad, the lawyer who had been defending the former Prime Minster Nawaz Sharif. **15.** The Chinese Prime Minister, Zhu Rongji, warned Taiwan ahead of its general election that China was ready 'to shed blood' to prevent Taiwan declaring itself independent. **16.** In the Philippines, Muslim separatists mounted attacks on six army bases in Mindanao, leaving 17 people dead. **18.** In the Presidential election in Taiwan, Chen Shui-bian, a pro-independence politician, was elected to the presidency with 39 per cent of the vote, ending more than half a century of Nationalist Party rule by election; the President-elect promised that he would not declare independence unless mainland China made plans to invade. Five Muslim rebels holding 300 hostages were shot dead by troops in the southern Philippines. **20.** In India, 35 Sikhs were massacred in Chadisinghpoora, a predominantly Sikh village in Kashmir. The Muslim terrorist group Lashkar-e-Tayyeba (Army of the Pure) believed to be behind the attack denied responsibility. In Pakistan, the prosecution in the trial of the former Prime Minster Nawaz Sharif and six others charged with hijacking, terrorism and attempted murder, requested the death penalty. **28.** In Japan, old age pensions for new retirees were cut by five per cent and it was announced that the retirement age was to be raised.

APRIL 2000

2. The Japanese Prime Minister, Keizo Obuchi, suffered a stroke and remained in hospital until his death on 14 May 2000. Mikio Aoki immediately took over as Acting Prime Minister. **5.** Yoshiro Mori was selected as the new Prime Minister of Japan. In Pakistan, the Foreign Minister, Abdul Sattar, announced that action would be taken against the Islamic militants who had launched incursions into Indian Kashmir. **6.** In Pakistan, the former Prime Minister Nawaz Sharif was sentenced to life imprisonment for hijacking and terrorism. The judge also ordered that all his property should be confiscated; charges of kidnapping and attempted murder were dismissed, as were all charges against the six other accused. **10.** In Taiwan, President-elect Chen Shui-bian appointed Gen. Tang Fei, the former Defence Minister, as Prime Minister. In a joint statement, the governments of North and South Korea announced that the leaders of the two states would meet in June. **13.** In the South Korea, the opposition Grand National Party won the largest number of seats in elections to the national assembly. **21.** In Pakistan, Gen. Pervaiz Musharraf announced that honour killings of women by relatives would be treated as murder. **23.** In Sri Lanka, Tamil Tiger rebels overran a strategic base that controlled access to the city of Jaffna, the guerrilla's former stronghold. **24.** In the Philippines, Abu Sayyaf, an Islamic separatist group, claimed responsibility for seizing 21 hostages from Sipadan, a Malaysian holiday island off the eastern coast of Borneo; they were taken to the Philippines on 2 May. Thousands of people rioted in western Gujarat in an attempt to obtain water following a drought in Rajasthan and Gujarat. **26.** Five thousand students demonstrated at Ahvaz University in support of President Mohammad Khatami. On the following day, there were disturbances in Tehran after two reformist newspapers were banned.

MAY 2000

1. In an espionage trial of 13 Iranian Jews, one confessed on television to being an agent for Mossad, the Israeli secret service. On 3 May, two more of the defendants admitted links with Mossad. On 1 July, ten of them were sentenced to between four and 13 years in prison for spying for Israel. **3.** In the Philippines, four Filipino hostages were killed when the armed forces rescued ten of 27 hostages being held by Abu Sayyaf rebels. **6.** In Iran, reformist candidates consolidated gains made in the first round of elections in February 2000. **8.** The Sri Lankan government rejected an offer from the Tamil Tigers of a temporary cease-fire to allow it to withdraw its 28,000 troops from the Jaffna peninsula. In the Philippines, three people were arrested in Manila in connection with the 'Love Bug' computer virus, which appeared on 4 May and affected at least 10 million computer users around the world. **9.** In Sri Lanka, the Tamil Tigers launched two attacks on a military base near Jaffna. **11.** Hundreds of demonstrators from the banned Falun Gong sect were detained in Tiananmen Square in Beijing. **12.** The Pakistani Supreme Court ruled that the military coup in October 1999 was legal because the government it had overthrown was corrupt and ruled that the military government had three years and three months from the date of the coup to return the country to democracy. **14.** In Sri Lanka, the Tamil Tigers warned residents of Jaffna to flee to safer areas of the peninsular. Heavy bombing by Sri Lankan airforce fighter-bombers on the following day halted the Tamil Tiger advance. **15.** In India, the Kashmiri State Minister for Power, Ghulam Hasan Bhatt, and four other people were killed in a bomb attack by Muslim militants in Kashmir. **16.** India formally requested the return of the Koh-i-Noor diamond, part of the Crown Jewels in the Tower of London. **17.** In Indonesia's first human rights trial, 24 soldiers and a civilian were convicted of murdering 26 villagers during a massacre in Aceh province in June 1999. In Sri Lanka, at least 23 people were killed and 75 injured when a bomb exploded in Batticaloa at a temple where Buddhists were celebrating the *Wesak* religious holiday. **20.** The Chinese Communist leadership launched a drive to install party cells in the nation's private businesses in order to reassert its grip on the economy. **29.** In Indonesia, former President Suharto was placed under house arrest; prosecutors expected that he would be charged with embezzlement. **30.** In Indonesia's Maluku province, a group of 1,000 Muslim extremists killed about 50 people in an attack on two Christian villages on Halmahera Island. **31.** It was revealed that Kim Jong-il, the North Korean leader, had just returned from a secret visit to Beijing, his first overseas trip since 1983. In Japan, a law was passed to compensate thousands of Koreans and Taiwanese who had been forced to join the Japanese Imperial Army in the Second World War, but subsequently refused pensions.

JUNE 2000

9. Eight policemen and two terrorists were killed when hundreds of Maoist guerrillas attacked a police post in northern Nepal. **12.** In India, two feudal landlords were massacred when the village of Asarfi in Bihar state was attacked by landless peasants, in apparent revenge for the murder of five poor farm workers. On 18 June, 11 people were arrested after the killing of 34 villagers in Miapur, Bihar, which was believed to have been committed by the banned Ranvir Sena, a private militia of upper caste landlords, in revenge for the killing of the landlords. **13.** North Korean President Kim Jong-il greeted South Korean President Kim Dae-jung at Pyongyang airport. **15.** Following a three-day summit, the South Korean President agreed to help rebuild the economy of North Korea in exchange for an end to the threat of war, family reunions and the reconnection of international railway lines severed in 1945. **20.** In Pakistan, mullahs and merchants joined forces to protest against proposed new sales taxes. **25.** In the Japanese general election, the coalition led by the Liberal Democratic Party retained power, winning 271 of the 480 seats. **27.** Indonesia declared a state of civil emergency in Maluku province following religious conflict between Muslims and Christians.

JULY 2000

1. In Hong Kong, thousands of protestors demonstrated to demand democracy and the resignation of Chief Executive Tung Chee-hwa. **2.** In Afghanistan, the Taliban militia launched a major offensive against the opposition Northern Alliance despite threats of fresh UN sanctions. **3.** In the Mongolian general election, the Mongolian People's Revolutionary Party, the former communist party, was returned to power with a landslide victory, winning 72 of 76 seats in the Great Hural. **8.** In Indonesia, Muslim militants killed 22 Christians and injured another 57 in an attack on a village on Ambon. **11.** In Japan, the Fujikoshi Corporation, a bearing manufacturer became the first Japanese company to agree to compensate foreign workers for slave labour during the war. **13.** Vietnam and the USA signed an agreement that removed many restrictions on trade between the countries. **17.** In the Philippines, the Moro Islamic Liberation Front massacred 21 Christians in the village of Sumagod, a week after their leaders declared a holy war. In Japan, two members of the Aum Shinrikyo cult were sentenced to death for their part in a nerve gas attack on the Tokyo underground in 1995, in which 12 people were killed. **18.** In Beijing, China, President Jiang Zemin and Russian President Vladimir Putin signed a joint statement which denounced the US plan to construct a ballistic missile defence system. **19.** President Putin of Russia and President Kim Jong-il of North Korea met in Pyongyang; North Korea offered to abandon its missile programme in exchange for help with peaceful space research. **22.** In Pakistan, ex-Prime Minister Nawaz Sharif was sentenced to 14 years' hard labour for corruption, disqualified from public office for 21 years and fined £251,000. **24.** In East Timor, a New Zealand soldier was killed by suspected pro-Indonesian militiamen near the border with Indonesian-controlled West Timor, the first combat casualty since UN peacekeepers arrived in September 1999. **26.** In Indonesia, it was announced that ex-President Suharto was to be charged with corruption; President Wahid announced that Suharto would be pardoned if convicted. **28.** In Afghanistan, Mullah Mohammad Omar, supreme leader of the Taliban militia, which was in control of most of the country, declared a ban on the cultivation of opium poppies. **30.** North and South Korea agreed to re-open liaison offices in the truce village of Panmunjom and to hold regular high-level peace talks. **31.** In Assam state, India, a bomb killed 12 people on a passenger train; the explosion was blamed on separatists.

AUGUST 2000

1. In India, Islamic militants killed 101 people in Jammu and Kashmir in nine separate incidents; a curfew was imposed in several Indian cities to prevent sectarian clashes after Hindu crowds shouted anti-Muslim slogans. In Indonesia, a bomb attack outside the Philippines Embassy in Jakarta killed two people and injured the ambassador. **3.** Peace talks began between India and Muslim guerrilla group Hizbul Mujahidin, but ended unsuccessfully on 6 August. The Hong Kong SAR government announced that all Mainland Chinese who had overstayed their visas would be deported immediately. In Indonesia, former President Suharto was formally charged with corruption; the trial, which was due to commence on 31 August, was postponed due to Suharto's ill health. **6.** In Iran, Leader of the Islamic Republic Ayatollah Ali Khamenei issued a decree banning the Iranian parliament from reversing press censorship laws that had resulted in the forced closure of most pro-reform newspapers. **7.** In Indonesia, President Wahid apologised to the People's Consultative Assembly for his handling of Indonesia's problems and vowed to learn from his mistakes. He also promised to grant special autonomy to Aceh and Irian Jaya before the end of the year. **8.** In India, Hizbul Mujahidin called off its 15-day cease-fire, saying that India had frozen Pakistan out of the talks. In Malaysia, former Deputy Prime Minister Anwar Ibrahim was convicted of sodomy and sentenced to nine years in jail. **9.** Indonesia's President Wahid stated that he would hand over the day-to-day running of the country to Vice-President Megawati Sukarnoputri after a court called him to testify in a £2.6 million embezzlement case. **10.** In Sri Lanka, Prime Minister Sirmavo Bandaranaike stepped down; she had been the world's first woman Prime Minister when she was originally appointed in1960. **14.** In Pakistan, Chief Executive Gen. Pervez Musharraf announced that local and district elections would be held between December 2000 and July 2001 as a first step towards restoring democracy. **15.** In Korea, following improved relations between the North and the South, the first family reunions took place in the two capitals, Seoul and Pyongyang. **16.** In Afghanistan, the ruling Taliban ordered the closure of UN-funded women's bakeries which feed around 50,000 widows, as part of a ban on the employment of Afghan women by aid organisations. **21.** The Singaporean government announced a package of financial measures designed to encourage larger families. **24.** In Myanmar, opposition leader Aung San Suu Kyi and about a dozen supporters were surrounded by police and ordered to return after they tried to leave the capital, Yangon. **27.** In the Philippines, five hostages were released by Abu Sayyaf guerrillas and a sixth was freed the following day. **29.** In the Philippines, Abu Sayyaf gunmen kidnapped an American tourist, demanding the release of Ramzi Youssef, an Islamic terrorist imprisoned in the USA for bombing the World Trade Centre seven years ago. **30.** In East Timor, the National Council of Timorese Resistance voted to ask foreign troops to remain in the territory after the withdrawal of the UN force, which was scheduled to follow legislative elections in 2001. In Jiangzi province, China, paramilitary units managed to restore order after five days of clashes

involving more than 20,000 farmers protesting about taxes; at least three people were believed to have died.

AUSTRALASIA AND THE PACIFIC

OCTOBER 1999

13. Leaders from Australia's 400,000-strong Aboriginal population met the Queen at Buckingham Palace to ask for formal recognition as the country's indigenous people. **27.** John Howard, the Prime Minister of Australia, urged voters to reject a republic and declared his support for the constitutional monarchy.

NOVEMBER 1999

6. In Australia, 54.2 per cent of those voting rejected proposals to make the country a republic. **28.** In New Zealand, the Labour Party won 52 of the 120 seats and its coalition partners the Alliance won 11.

FEBRUARY 2000

23. In Tuvalu, Prime Minister Ionatana said that citizens were being canvassed to see if they wished to become a republic.

MARCH 2000

20. The Queen arrived in Sydney at the start of a two-week visit to Australia.

APRIL 2000

7. Tuvalu sold the rights to '.tv', its world wide web country code, to Idealab!, a US internet company for US$50 million, a sum equivalent to three times its annual gross domestic product. **10.** In New Zealand, Prime Minister Helen Clark announced that the titles of knight and dame were to be abolished, taking effect from the next Queen's Birthday Honours list; those with existing titles could retain them. **12.** In a review of its system of justice, the New Zealand Attorney General, Margaret Wilson moved to sever the 160-year old link with the Privy Council in the UK. **14.** In Samoa, two former Cabinet Ministers, Leafa Vitale and Toi Aukuso Cain, were sentenced to death for murdering Luagalau Levaula Kamu, the Works Minister, at a political function last July; the sentences were commuted to life imprisonment on 12 May.

MAY 2000

19. In Fiji, Prime Minister Mahendra Chaudhry and most of the Fijian Cabinet were taken hostage after a gang of seven gunmen led by George Speight, a local businessman, attacked the parliament building; they declared a civil coup on behalf of the indigenous people of Fiji and appointed an interim administration. Rioting broke out in the capital, Suva. The army and police declared their loyalty to the elected government and said they would take orders only from President Ratu Sir Kamisese Mara, who declared a state of emergency, imposed a curfew and appealed for calm. **23.** The leaders of the coup in Fiji rejected a plea from the Great Council of Chiefs for the release of the Prime Minister and other hostages. **25.** The Great Council of Chiefs capitulated to the demands of the gunmen and unanimously approved the replacement of the democratically elected government and a pardon for the coup plotters. **26.** President Ratu Sir Kamisese Mare sought to end the coup by dismissing the democratically elected government and Prime Minister. **27–28.** Corroboree 2000, a weekend of ceremonies of reconciliation between Aboriginals and white Australians, was attended by PM John Howard and Aboriginal leaders in Sydney. An estimated quarter of a million people took part in a reconciliation march across the Sydney Harbour Bridge. **28.** In Fiji, a television station building was devastated by a 300-strong mob after an interview was broadcast in which a political commentator condemned the leader of the coup. **29.** Cdre Frank Bainimarama imposed martial law in Fiji following the resignation of the President. **30.** Cdre Bainimarama promised to abolish the multi-racial 1997 constitution and nominated Epeli Nailatikau as the new Prime Minister. The following day, he yielded to objections from George Speight and withdrew the nomination.

JUNE 2000

4. In the Solomon Islands, the Malaitan Eagles, a rebel group representing immigrants from Malaita Island, put Prime Minister Bartholomew Ulufa'alu under house arrest, took over key installations and set up road blocks in Honiara, the capital. The coup had been triggered by a land dispute between local residents on Guadalcanal, the main island, and Malaitan settlers. **5.** In Fiji, Cdre Bainimarama announced that the coup leaders would not form part of a planned interim government, citing the threat of EU sanctions; the EU buys most of Fiji's sugar, its main income source, at above market prices. **6.** The Solomon Islands' Prime Minister Ulufa'alu offered to resign in order to avert civil war; he was freed the next day. **25.** In Fiji, five female hostages were released. Twenty-seven male hostages remained in captivity.

JULY 2000

3. In Fiji, the military rulers named an interim government to rule until elections could be held. **4.** In the Solomon Islands, the Malaita Eagles Force threatened to increase attacks on a rival militia, the Isatabu Freedom Movement, after a cease-fire collapsed. **13.** In Fiji, the remaining 18 hostages were freed by the rebels from the parliamentary compound where they had been held since 19 May, after the Great Council of Chiefs refused to appoint a new President or Prime Minister until the hostages were released. Nine hostages had been released on 11 July. **18.** The UK, Australia and New Zealand recalled their High Commissioners from Fiji. **27.** The Fijian army arrested more than 350 rebels, including George Speight.

AUGUST 2000

1. In Fiji, rebel leader Speight was charged with minor crimes, including unlawful assembly; he appeared in court under his Fijian name, Ilikini Naitini. **11.** Speight was charged with treason for overthrowing the elected Government of Fiji. **24.** In New Zealand, Dame Silvia Cartwright was named as the next Governor-General and will assume the position in March 2001.

EUROPE

SEPTEMBER 1999

1. Presidents Rau of Germany and Kwaśniewski of Poland commemorated the 50th anniversary of the start of the Second World War by joining hands at the Westerplatte peninsula, Gdańsk (Danzig), where the first shots had been fired in 1939. **5.** In Russia, Islamic rebels from Chechnya launched a second invasion of Dagestan and took control of several villages. **7.** The Pope cancelled his planned visit to Greece, part of his Millennium tour of biblical sites, following attacks on him by the Orthodox

Church. **15.** The Dagestan Liberation Army, a previously unknown group, claimed responsibility for a series of bomb attacks on apartment blocks and a shopping centre in which over 100 people died and many more were injured. **16.** In Belarus, Viktor Gonchar, the Deputy Speaker of the disbanded parliament, disappeared in strange circumstances, one of several opponents of President Lukashenko to have vanished in recent months. **20.** The Kosovo Liberation Army (KLA) and the NATO Kosovo force (KFOR) signed an agreement turning the KLA into a purely civilian body. **21.** Ehud Barak, the Israeli Prime Minister, became the first official guest of the German government to be welcomed to the new capital, Berlin. **23.** Russian troops mounted a massive operation to seal off Chechnya by constructing a 400-mile *cordon sanitaire* of trenches, ramparts and minefields. Bulgaria, Romania and Ukraine appealed to the EU for aid to clear the Danube river of debris left by NATO air strikes on Yugoslavia. **28.** Germany expelled three Americans on suspicion of spying for the CIA. **29.** A meeting between the leaders of Chechnya and Dagestan had to be called off after Dagestani villagers blocked roads in protest against recent raids by Chechen guerrillas. **30.** Serbian police clashed with protesters in Belgrade when 60,000 people tried to march on President Milošević's home. Russia asked for increased assistance from the USA to safeguard stocks of plutonium and uranium removed from redundant intercontinental ballistic missiles.

OCTOBER 1999

3. The Social Democrats became the largest party following the Austrian general election, gaining 65 seats in the 183-seat parliament; the Freedom Party and the People's Party each gained 52 seats. **6.** President Maskhadov of Chechnya imposed martial law and called on Chechnya's Muslim clergy to declare a holy war on Russia. **7.** Russian ministers refused an offer by the EU to mediate in the conflict. More than 40 refugees from the fighting in Chechnya died after their bus was apparently fired on by a Russian tank. **8.** The Swiss parliament voted in favour of closer ties with the EU, adopting measures aimed at fostering the free movement of people and goods as well as removing technical barriers to trade and agriculture; the decision was to be put to a referendum in May 2000. President Maskhadov of Chechnya appealed to NATO to intervene in the conflict. **10.** The Socialist Party was re-elected in the Portuguese general election; the Social Democrats remained the largest opposition group. **17.** In Belarus, around 20,000 demonstrators, protesting against President Lukashenko and a proposed union between Belarus and Russia clashed with police in Minsk. **20.** Thousands of civil servants marched through the centre of Berlin to demonstrate against Chancellor Schröder's programme of spending cuts. **21.** Russia relinquished control of a radar base in Skrunda, Latvia, its last military outpost in the Baltic states. **22.** A Russian missile attack on central Grozny left at least 137 people dead. **24.** In a general election in Switzerland, the far-Right Swiss People's Party (SVP), which is opposed to immigration and the EU, became the second largest party in the ruling four-party coalition. Valery Lebedev, the Russian Nuclear Energy minister, announced that security had been tightened at nuclear plants following fears of sabotage by Chechen fighters. **26.** Albania's Prime Minister, Pandeli Majko, resigned after losing the leadership of the Socialist Party to Fatos Nano. President Mejdani appointed Ilir Meta as Prime Minister on 27 October. Talks between the leading political parties of Serbia and Montenegro aimed at preventing the disintegration of Yugoslavia commenced in Belgrade.

27. The Armenian Prime Minister Vazgen Sarkissian, the Energy Minister, Leonard Petrosian and six other deputies were shot dead and some 50 deputies were taken hostage when gunmen took over the Armenian parliament; the gunmen laid down their arms and freed the hostages the following day after President Robert Kocharian promised to spare their lives and ensure a fair trial. **28.** Russian Prime Minister Vladimir Putin vowed to rebuild Russia's military strength and said that military spending would be increased by 57 per cent in 2000 to 146 billion roubles (£3.5 billion). **31.** The Red Cross accused Russian forces of opening fire on a group of their vehicles in Chechnya; two local Red Cross workers were killed and a third was seriously injured.

NOVEMBER 1999

2. French Finance Minister Dominique Strauss-Kahn resigned over corruption allegations. In Spain, Baltasar Garzon, the judge seeking the extradition of Gen. Augusto Pinochet, ordered international warrants to be issued for the arrest of 98 former Argentine military and police officers, including Gen. Galtieri, who had led the military junta at the time of the Falklands War, to face charges of genocide, terrorism and torture allegedly committed during the military dictatorship between 1976 and 1983. **3.** In Armenia, President Kocharian appointed Aram Sarkissian, the younger brother of the former Prime Minister as the country's new Prime Minister. **4.** In Montenegro, the deutsche mark became legal tender alongside the Yugoslav dinar. **7.** In Georgia, Eduard Shevardnadze's Citizens' Union party won 42 per cent of the vote and an absolute majority of seats in the general election. **8.** The Pope visited Tbilisi, Georgia, his first trip to the Transcaucasus; the following day he said Mass before 10,000 people, including President Shevardnadze. **8.** In Germany, Egon Krenz, the last President of the German Democratic Republic, was jailed for six and a half years after losing his appeal against an earlier conviction for his part in the killing of refugees who tried to cross the east-west German frontier. **9.** Celebrations were held in Germany to mark the tenth anniversary of the fall of the Berlin Wall. **12.** Russian forces claimed to have captured Gudermes, the second largest city in Chechnya. **14.** President Kuchma of Ukraine won a second term in office, gaining nearly 60 per cent of the vote. In Macedonia, Boris Trajkovski, the Deputy Foreign Minister, won Presidential elections with 53 per cent of votes cast. **19.** Riots broke out in central Athens in protest at the visit of President Clinton; his planned three-day visit to Greece had been shortened to 22 hours because of opposition by the media and left-wing groups. At the summit of the Organisation for Security and Co-operation in Europe (OSCE), Russia accepted the principle that a political solution was essential in Chechnya and agreed to allow the OSCE chairman, Kurt Vollebæk, to visit to the region. **23.** President Clinton received a rapturous reception from ethnic Albanians on his first visit to Kosovo since the end of NATO's campaign against Yugoslavia and appealed for an end to retribution and violence. The Vatican accused Israel of fomenting religious differences in Bethlehem following Israel's approval of a new mosque next to the Basilica of the Annunciation; the following day, the Israeli Foreign Minister said that Vatican's allegation was a lie. **24.** In Croatia, a law was passed allowing President Franjo Tudjman, who was gravely ill, to be replaced temporarily by Vlatko Pavletić, the Speaker of the Parliament. The wall built around a Romany housing estate in Usti nad Labem in the Czech Republic was demolished following pressure from the government and the EU. **25.** France and the UK agreed to share military

supplies in operations where both governments agree on all aspects of a military mission at an Anglo-French summit. An appeals court upheld the death sentence for treason on Abdullah Öcalan, the Kurdish rebel leader; the European Court of Human Rights asked Turkey to suspend the death sentence on 30 November. **27.** The Basque guerrilla group ETA announced it was to end its 14-month cease-fire. **30.** Sweden's four main newspapers published a joint story naming members of Nazi groups or criminal biker gangs, saying that they endangered democracy by threatening law enforcement officers, journalists and politicians; they also published photos of 62 people listed as either Nazis or members of criminal biker gangs.

DECEMBER 1999

1. Ireland became a member of the NATO Partnership for Peace programme. **2.** The Irish Prime Minister Bertie Ahern signed the document amending the Irish constitution to remove references to the Republic's territorial claim to Northern Ireland, which had been a part of the Irish constitution since 1937; a referendum in 1998 had approved the change. **8.** The signing ceremony of the Russian-Belarusian union pact took place. Russian forces issued an ultimatum to the residents of Grozny, the capital of the breakaway Republic of Chechnya, to leave by 11 December or be killed; Chechen leaders appealed for foreign observers to monitor the exodus of civilians from Grozny. Russian forces took control of the town of Urus Martan. **10.** President Franjo Tudjman of Croatia died. **11.** Turkey formally accepted an invitation to become a candidate for membership of the EU. **13.** The Russian Duma refused to ratify the Start II treaty signed by Russia and the USA in 1993. The inaugural session of the North-South Ministerial Council took place in Armagh. **14.** In Romania, President Emil Constantinescu dismissed Prime Minister Radu Vasile after he lost the support of his Cabinet. Russian troops entered Grozny; Chechen rebels repulsed the assault the following day. **17.** President Johannes Rau of Germany publicly asked for forgiveness from the surviving Second World War forced labourers; compensation payments of £3,300 million (11,000 million DM) are to be paid. **19.** In the Russian general election, the Communist Party remained the largest single party, but four centrist parties gained over 50 per cent of the vote and the newly formed pro-Kremlin Unity Party scored 24 per cent. **20.** Prime Minister Massimo d'Alema stood down as head of Italy's 56th post-war government; President Ciampi asked him to form a new government on the following day. **22.** Grand Duke Jean of Luxembourg announced that he would abdicate in September 2000, allowing his eldest son, Prince Henri to succeed him. **23.** Montenegrin Foreign Minister Branko Perović resigned over alleged involvement in smuggling and criminal association with the Italian Mafia. **24.** The Pope officially ushered in Holy Year by opening the Holy Door of St Peter's. **26.** Greek police confiscated the car of Albania's Public Order minister, Spartak Poci, who was on an official visit to discuss crime, after finding it registered as stolen. **28.** Russia claimed to be in control of most of Grozny's suburbs. **31.** Russian President, Boris Yeltsin announced his resignation.

JANUARY 2000

1. The Swedish Lutheran church was disestablished, ending nearly five centuries as the state church. **3.** In Croatia, the centre-left alliance of Social Democrats and Social Liberals won an overwhelming victory in the general elections **11.** German women won the right to serve as soldiers after the European Court in Luxembourg overturned the law forbidding them from bearing arms. **12.** Turkey suspended the death sentence on Abdullah Öcalan pending a ruling on an appeal by his lawyers to the European Court of Human Rights. Germany's highest court ruled that Egon Krenz, the last leader of the German Democratic Republic, would have to serve six and a half years in jail for the killing by border guards of people trying to escape the GDR. **14.** A new military doctrine published in Moscow lowered the threshold at which nuclear weapons would be used in the event of an attack on Russia. **15.** Zeljko Raznatović, known as 'Arkan', who had been indicted by the International Criminal Tribunal in The Hague in 1997 for ordering the killing of thousands of Muslims during the war in Bosnia, was shot dead in Belgrade, Serbia. **20.** The first official visit by a Greek Foreign Minister to Turkey began. **21.** An army officer was killed and three passers-by injured when two car bombs planted by ETA, the Basque terrorist group, exploded in Madrid. In Austria, coalition discussions following the inconclusive October 1999 general elections between the Socialist Party and the People's Party collapsed. **22.** Shamil Basayev, a leading Chechen commander, was shot and wounded by Magomed Khambiyev, Chechnya's Defence Minister and a rival warlord, according to Chechen sources. A report by the German Federal Intelligence Service claimed that Liechtenstein was the world's biggest money laundering centre. **23.** More than a million people marched through Madrid to protest against renewed violence by ETA. The Belgian government threatened to take legal action against the UK unless Gen. Pinochet was forced to undergo new medical tests to determine his ability to stand trial. **24.** Two thousand Kosovar Albanians demonstrated in Priština, Kosovo, demanding the release of hundreds of people still being held in prison by the Serbs since the end of the war. **25.** The Czech government agreed to return property seized from Jews during the Nazi occupation. **27.** In Russia, Vladimir Putin, the Acting President, pledged a 50 per cent increase in spending on military equipment. **30.** The heads of government of the other 14 EU member states sent a communiqué warning that Austria would face a suspension of all bilateral official contacts, a refusal to receive Austrian ambassadors in EU capitals and the withdrawal of all support for Austrian candidates for international positions if the People's Party formed a coalition with the far-right Freedom Party; agreement was reached between the two parties and a coalition government was sworn in on 4 February. **31.** Belgium appealed against a High Court judge's decision to refuse a judicial review of the Home Secretary's decision to free Gen. Pinochet.

FEBRUARY 2000

1. The Chechen capital Grozny fell to Russian forces. **4.** In Kosovo, at least seven people died in a demonstration in the divided city of Mitrovica, in which Kosovar Albanian protestors attacked French peacekeepers with stones and bottles, accusing them of failing to protect them from Serb attacks. **6.** Tarja Halonen was elected President of Finland, gaining 51.6 per cent of the vote. Stipe Mesić, the Centre-Left Alliance candidate, won the Presidential election in Croatia. **7.** In Yugoslavia, Defence Minister Pavle Bulatović was shot dead in a restaurant in Belgrade. **7–8.** In El Elide in south-eastern Spain, 52 people were injured in two days of violence against immigrants, after an immigrant murdered a local woman on 6 February. **11.** US$31,800 million of loans borrowed by Soviet and Russian governments from western banks were rescheduled following a meeting with the London Club of Creditors. **17.** In Serbia, Slobodan Milošević was re-elected President of the Socialist Party. **18.** In Liechtenstein, Prince Hans-Adam II announced that he would hold a referendum on constitutional reform; he threatened to abdicate and go into exile if his proposals were not accepted. **20.** In Kosovo, NATO peacekeepers sealed off and searched Mitrovica in an attempt to end weeks of ethnic violence which left more than 12 people dead. In Austria, nearly 250,000 protestors demonstrated against the Freedom Party in Vienna, the largest demonstration in the city since the Second World War. **21.** NATO gave a formal warning to Yugoslavia that it would not tolerate harassment of ethnic Albanians in the Bujanovac-Presevo-Medveda area of southern Serbia. In Latvia, Justice Minister Valdis Birkavs began a hunger strike to protest against accusations of his involvement in a 600-strong paedophile ring that allegedly included Prime Minister Adris Skele. **22.** Russian forces began an offensive to destroy the last main pocket of Chechen rebel resistance in the Argun gorge. In Spain, Fernando Buesa, a provincial Secretary-General of the Socialist party, and his bodyguard were killed in a car bomb attack blamed on ETA; demonstrations were held throughout Spain on the following day. **28.** In Austria, Jörg Haider announced his intention to resign as leader of the Freedom Party; he stepped down and was succeeded by Vice-Chancellor Susanne Riess-Passer on 1 May. **29.** Shatoi, the last remaining Chechen town under rebel control, fell to Russian forces.

MARCH 2000

3. The Russian government announced that 1,420 Russian soldiers were killed and 3,869 injured during the Chechnya campaign. Allegations were published in the Paris newspaper, *Le Point*, that the late President Mitterrand personally benefited from commissions paid by the Elf oil company. **6.** Serbia imposed a full economic blockade on Montenegro. President Havel urged Madeleine Albright, the Czech-born US Secretary of State, to run for the Czech presidency when his term expires in three years. A 'baby bank' was introduced in Hamburg, Germany, where mothers could deposit unwanted new-borns who might otherwise be dumped in cardboard boxes or rubbish skips. **7.** Sixteen French peacekeepers were wounded in Mitrovica, Kosovo, after an argument between Kosovar Albanians and Serbs degenerated into a gunfight; 20 Serbs and five Albanians were also wounded. **9.** In Norway, Prime Minister Kjell Magne Bondevik resigned after his coalition government was defeated in the Norwegian parliament over plans to build new gas power stations; he was succeeded on 17 March by Jens Stoltenberg, the Labour Party leader. **9.** Irish Foreign Minister Brian Cowen said that the UK should scale down its military presence in Northern Ireland in order to break the deadlock in the peace process. **10.** In Sweden, delegates at a congress of the ruling Social Democrat party voted in favour of adopting the euro subject to a referendum endorsing membership. **12.** In the Spanish general election, the Popular party won 183 seats in the 350-seat Cortes. In Russia, Mikhail Gorbachev was elected head of the Social Democratic Party, which he had founded in October 1999. **17.** In Germany, the Bundesrat voted to lift the ban on the importation of British beef on condition that its origin was clearly indicated. **21.** The Lord Mayor of Dublin, Mary Freehill, authorised the first Orange Order march in the city since 1937, which was due to take place on 28 May. The Orange Order cancelled the march on 1 May following threats of violence. **26.** In the Russian Presidential election, acting President Vladimir Putin was elected with over 52 per cent of the vote.

30. British troops crossed into Serbia for the first time since their deployment in Kosovo following reports that Yugoslav army armoured vehicles had violated the three-mile-wide demilitarised zone on the Serbian side of the border with Kosovo. Russian commandos freed 15 men from slavery in Ratlub, a village in Dagestan.

APRIL 2000

2. Mary Robinson, the UN High Commissioner for Human Rights, visited Chechnya to investigate allegations of persistent human rights violations. **3.** In Bosnia, a French-led team of commandos seized Momcilo Krajisnik, the deputy of the Bosnian Serb civil war leader Radovan Karadzić; he was transferred to The Hague to face trial on charges of genocide. **7.** In Germany, the men's fashion company Hugo Boss agreed to pay £500,000 into a compensation fund for slave labourers. **9.** In the Greek general election, Pasok, the socialist party, emerged as the largest party with 43.8 per cent of the vote. The opposition New Democracy party got 42.7 per cent. In Georgia, President Shevardnadze won a further term in office; accusations of ballot rigging were made after the electoral commission declared him to have won a significantly higher majority than that predicted by exit polls. **13.** The Austrian government announced that the long-term unemployed would be compelled to work for benefits from 1 June; those who refused would have their benefits stopped. **14.** In Russia, the Duma voted overwhelmingly to ratify the Start II treaty, which obliges Russia and the USA to reduce their stocks of strategic weapons to 3,500 nuclear warheads each, down from 6,000–7,000 each at present. **15.** It was announced that the state-owned Belarusian military hardware company Beltechexport had agreed to upgrade Iraq's air defence systems, re-equip the Iraqi air force and provide air defence training for Iraqi troops in defiance of the UN arms embargo. **16.** In Ukraine, a referendum endorsed proposals to give the President increased powers over parliament to tackle corruption and quicken the pace of political and economic reform. **17.** President Vladimir Putin, insisted that Russia would not reduce its arsenal of nuclear warheads if the USA were allowed to base part of a proposed new missile shield in the UK. **19.** In Italy, Prime Minister Massimo D'Alema resigned. Giuliano Amato was nominated by the Centre-Left Coalition to replace him the following day, was sworn in on 26 April and won a confidence vote in parliament on 28 April. Spain agreed to recognise Gibraltarian identity cards and financial institutions following talks with the UK. **20.** In Slovakia, former Prime Minister Vladimir Meciar was arrested after police commandos used explosives to break into his home and end a three-week siege. He was charged with abuse of power by a public official and fraud, offences that carry terms of three to ten years' imprisonment. **24.** In Yugoslavia, seven members of a group calling itself the Serb Liberation Army went on trial on charges of plotting an armed take-over and the assassination of President Miloević. **26.** José Maria Aznar was re-elected Prime Minister by the Congress of Deputies following the victory of his Popular Party in elections in March; he was sworn in on 27 April. Spain's most decorated police officer, Gen. Enrique Rodríguez Galindo of the Civil Guard, was sentenced to 71 years in prison for the kidnapping and murder of two members of ETA. **27.** Eurocorps, comprising troops from France, Germany, Spain, Belgium and Luxembourg, took over military command from NATO of the international peacekeeping force in Kosovo.

MAY 2000

5. In Turkey, Ahmed Necdet Sezer was elected President by parliament; he called for democratic reforms and said he would protect secularism. **6.** Russian troops killed 41 Chechen guerrillas in bombing raids on Vedeno gorge in southern Chechnya. **8.** Vladimir Putin was inaugurated as President of Russia. **11.** Chechen guerrillas ambushed a Russian convoy in Ingushetia resulting in 18 deaths. **12.** German Foreign Minister Joschka Fischer called for a European government with far-reaching executive powers and a directly-elected President and written constitution. **13.** Following the visit of Pope John Paul II to the Portuguese village of Fatima, the Vatican revealed the 'Third Secret of Fatima', a prophesy given to three children but secret until now; it was announced that it had predicted the failed attempt on the life of the Pope in 1981. **14.** In Germany, the Social Democratic Party won the provincial election in North Rhine Westphalia with 42.8 per cent of the vote. In Yugoslavia, Bosko Perosević, the head of the Vojvodina provincial government, was murdered; the ruling Socialist Party accused opposition parties of involvement. **15.** In Russia, President Putin announced that seven regions were to be created, each with an envoy who would have wide-ranging powers. **17.** In Yugoslavia, about 30,000 people rallied in Belgrade to protest against a crackdown on opposition parties in which dozens of people were arrested and newspapers and television stations closed. **18.** President Putin announced plans to strip the 89 regional governors of their seats in the upper house of parliament and to set up a mechanism to dismiss them and local assemblies if they violate national laws. The Russian army admitted that it had lost 2,004 troops in its eight-month campaign in Chechnya. Thousands of Roman Catholic clerics gathered in Rome to celebrate the 80th birthday of Pope John Paul II. **19.** The Russian *Kommersant* newspaper cited a three-year study, which found that two thirds of Russian men died drunk, with more than half of those in extreme stages of alcoholic intoxication. **21.** In Italy, a referendum aimed at ending the proportional representation voting system was unsuccessful as less than 36 per cent of the electorate voted; Italian law requires more than 50 per cent for a referendum to be valid. **24.** Russia threatened airstrikes against Afghanistan, which was backing radical opposition movements in Central Asia and Chechnya. **25.** Germany's senior general, Gen. Hans-Peter von Kirchbach, was sacked in a dispute over cuts in the size and budget of the armed forces, a day after Defence Minister Rudolf Scharping announced that the number of military staff would be reduced by 100,000. **20.** In Switzerland, a referendum on strengthening links with the EU was approved by over 67 per cent of voters.

JUNE 2000

4. Kosovo Serb leaders said that they would boycott the province's main institutions in protest at the murder of about 20 ethnic Serbs, blamed on Albanians, in two months. **5.** In Ukraine, Presidents Clinton and Kuchma announced that Chernobyl power station would close on 15 December 2000. **6.** In Gracanica, Kosovo, British troops opened fire, wounding three Serbs after 300 Serbs rioted following a grenade attack on a street market. **7.** Presidents Putin and Clinton met in Moscow at their first summit. They agreed to create a permanent joint US-Russian early warning system to detect nuclear missile strikes and to reduce their plutonium stocks. **8.** President Putin of Russia took personal control over Chechnya in a move that was denounced as unconstitutional. The British military attaché, Brig. Stephen Saunders, was shot dead in Athens by two gunmen believed to be from the November 17 terror group, a Marxist group thought to have previously killed 22 people. On 10 June, a meeting of the Greek Cabinet decided to establish dedicated terrorist courts. 9. Germany and France announced that they were to build a joint satellite reconnaissance system; other EU nations were to be invited to participate. 12. Montenegrins voted in two local polls in Podgorica, where there was a pro-government majority, and Herceg Novi, where the pro-Serbia 'Yugoslavia' coalition won. 14. In Germany, Federal Chancellor Gerhard Schröder announced that Germany would close its 19 nuclear power stations over a 20-year period. An estimated 1,500 left wing and anarchist protestors rioted outside an OECD summit in Bologna, Italy. 15. Vuk Drasković, head of the Serbian Renewal Movement, the main Serbian opposition party, was shot and slightly injured when gunmen opened fire on his holiday home in Budva, Montenegro. 16. In Poland, the Freedom Union withdrew from the coalition government. The Solidarity Electoral Alliance remained in power, but without a majority in the National Assembly. 22. The French government ordered an inquiry into allegations that the Principality of Monaco had promoted money laundering. French MPs urged the government to withdraw the administrative and financial support that France gives to Monaco. 26. The Vatican published the full text of the third secret of Fatima. The President of Slovakia, Rudolf Schuster, was critically ill with pneumonia after complications from intestinal surgery. 27. In Spain, three members of the Basque terrorist group ETA were jailed for 47 years for organising a series of attacks against public figures. 28. In Germany, it was announced that a special investigation had found that Helmut Kohl's government had destroyed millions of key documents immediately after the 1998 general election. 30. The bridge and tunnel link across the Öresund linking Copenhagen and Malmö was opened on 1 July by King Karl Gustav XVI of Sweden and Queen Margrethe II of Denmark.

JULY 2000

3. In Russia, a series of suicide bombings by Chechen rebels resulted in 54 deaths. 3. Cyprus and Greece reacted angrily after Turkey moved troops 300 yards towards the Greek Cypriot village of Strovilia, a move that was condemned by the UN. 4. The Austrian government announced it would hold a referendum in October or November 2000 to seek a popular mandate to allow it to block expansion of the EU if sanctions against it had not been lifted by that time. 8. Montenegro's parliament declared illegal changes to the federal Yugoslav constitution, which were to change the voting system, enabling President Milošević to stand for a further term of office. 10. President Djukanović of Montenegro said that Montenegro would not take part in the Yugoslav federal legislative elections due to be held in the autumn and that by ignoring Yugoslav constitutional changes, Montenegro had effectively left the Yugoslav system. The French government produced a devolution plan for Corsica. In Russia, figures published by Goskomstat, the central statistical agency, indicated that the birth rate has more than halved since the final years of the USSR; only one in ten pregnancies resulted in a normal birth and less than a third of recorded pregnancies produced a live birth. 12. In Madrid, eight people were injured, four of them seriously, when a car bomb exploded. 14. In Germany, the Bundestag passed a tax reduction bill, which was to reduce corporation tax from 40 per cent to 25 per cent and the top rate of income tax from 51 per cent to 43 per cent from 2001. 22. The German Evangelical Church admitted that

it had used slave labourers to dig graves, maintain forests and perform other tasks in the Second World War. 23. In Switzerland, a magistrate investigating corruption and money laundering claimed that up to £3,200 million or a 1998 IMF loan to Russia might have been diverted to a secret Swiss bank account. 24. In France, Xavière Tiberi, the wife of the mayor of Paris, appeared in court on vote-rigging charges; she was suspected of adding 7,228 names to the electoral roll of her husband's parliamentary constituency. At their 37th congress near Copenhagen, 120 Father Christmases and elves from 15 countries met to discuss if they had any role in the third millennium. 27. In Yugoslavia, President Slobodan Milošević called a Presidential election for 24 September, after approving a constitutional amendment to which will introduce direct election of the President.

AUGUST 2000

3. In Montenegro, two British policemen and two Canadians, who had been returning to Kosovo from a coastal holiday resort, were arrested on suspicion of terrorism by the Yugoslav government. UN Secretary General Kofi Annan called for their release the following day. 4. In Chechnya, the severed heads of two Russian army officers abducted by Chechen guerrillas were thrown into a Russian military base; they had been abducted the previous week. 6. Zinedine Zidane, the footballer who helped France to victory in the 1998 World Cup and Euro 2000, was voted the most popular person in France. 7. In France, Jean-Michel Rossi, a founder member of the Corsican National Liberation Front was killed in a machine gun attack in a bar in L'Île Rousse, Corsica; it was believed that the attack had been committed by extremists opposed to his acceptance of the peace process. 8. In Russia, at least eight people were killed and more than 50 injured in Moscow when a bomb exploded in a busy pedestrian subway during the rush hour. 11. In Poland, Lech Wałęsa, the founder of the Solidarity movement, was cleared of allegations that he had been a secret police agent in the Communist era. 13. In Spain, the authorities in the Basque region appealed for police reinforcements to help combat the wave of terrorist violence, a day after around 5,000 separatist supporters demonstrated to pay tribute to four terrorists who died on 7 August when a bomb they were carrying exploded. 14. In Russia, Tsar Nicholas II and his family were canonised by the Russian Orthodox Church. British troops clashed with hundreds of Kosovar Serbs in Mitrovica, Kosovo, after UNMIK forces forced a Serb-owned lead smelter to close after the plant's management had refused to co-operate with the international administration in putting pollution reducing filters into place. 25. In Russia, following severe criticism of the government's handling of the failed attempts to rescue the crew of the stricken submarine Kursk, the Fund for Mothers' Justice, a group representing military mothers, announced that it would take legal action against the President, the government and the Ministry of Defence on behalf of the bereaved families. 26. In Yugoslavia, former Serbian President Ivan Stambolić, who had brought Slobodan Milošević into government, but latterly criticised him, disappeared while on a morning run. 29. French Interior Minister Jean-Pierre Chevènement resigned in protest over peace plans for Corsica. 30. In France, fishermen blockaded the Channel ports for 27 hours in protest at high taxes on diesel. 31. In Yugoslavia, a military court refused to release two Britons and two Canadians arrested on suspicion of terrorism; Vojislav Mihailović, the grandson of the wartime Serb Cetnik leader Draza Mihailović, was selected as the Presidential candidate of the Serbian Renewal Party, the largest

opposition party. In Liechtenstein, an Austrian special prosecutor brought in to investigate claims of money laundering made by the German Federal Intelligence Service, found that most of the assets involved had already been 'pre-washed' in other countries, including the UK, the USA, Switzerland and Luxembourg.

THE MIDDLE EAST

SEPTEMBER 1999

4. Israel and the PLO signed an agreement in which Israel agreed to withdraw from a further 11 per cent of the West Bank and release 350 prisoners; the *Knesset* approved the agreement on 8 September. American intelligence warned that Iraq was rebuilding missile factories destroyed in allied bombing raids. The UK and the USA continued pressing for a resumption of weapons inspections. **6.** Israel's Supreme Court banned the *Shin Bet* security service from using torture on detainees. **12.** In the first meeting of Arab foreign ministers in Iraq since the invasion of Kuwait in 1990, Yasser Arafat urged reconciliation. **13.** The Final Status talks began between Israel and the PLO to decide the boundaries of a Palestinian state and who controls Jerusalem. **21.** American and British warplanes struck military radar sites in southern Iraq. **22.** The political leader of Hamas, Khaled Meshaal, and two other senior officials were detained as they flew into 'Ammān, Jordan. **24.** Ali Abdullah Saleh, President for the last 12 years, won Yemen's first direct election for a head of state. **25.** A Yemeni court upheld jail sentences against ten Muslim militants, including eight Britons, convicted of terrorism charges.

OCTOBER 1999

11. Rafa al-Tikriti, the Iraqi intelligence chief and second cousin to Saddam Hussein, was executed in Baghdad for leaking information about arms deals with Russia. **13.** Israel agreed to allow the construction of a mosque close to the Basilica of the Annunciation in Nazareth, despite protests by Christian groups. **15.** Israel freed 151 Arab prisoners. **17.** In Yemen, Abul Hassan was executed after being found guilty of the kidnapping of 16 westerners in 1998; he had been condemned to death in May 1999. **22.** Operation Bright Star 99, a vast military exercise involving 73,000 troops from 11 countries, began in Egypt, the biggest gathering of troops in the Middle East region since the 1991 Gulf war. Amr Mussa, the Egyptian Foreign Minister, later denied that the exercises were aimed at Iraq. **25.** A safe passage was opened across Israel linking the Gaza strip and the West Bank town of Tarqumiya; travellers were required to pass an Israeli security test before being issued with transit permits; those considered security risks could travel in buses under armed guard. **31.** Troops fired bullets and tear gas to end two days of rioting by Egyptian workers in Kuwait.

NOVEMBER 1999

8. Israel and the Palestinians began talks in Ramallah, in the West Bank, aimed at achieving a framework agreement within less than three months and a final peace treaty by September 2000. **10.** More than 1,000 Israeli soldiers and police demolished Havat Maon, an illegal Jewish settlement on the West Bank. **12.** In the Palestinian territories, Yasser Arafat appointed Abdel-Latif Abdel-Fattah, a convicted torturer, as his new general prosecutor. **23.** A decree by the Emir of Kuwait to give women full political rights was overturned in parliament. Opposition came from a coalition of Sunni Muslim Islamists and liberals,

who defeated the decree by 41 votes to 21; the liberals reintroduced the measure in an amended form on 30 November, but it was again defeated by 32-30, with two members abstaining.

DECEMBER 1999

4. Hackers discovered that the PLO had a fortune of over £5,000 million in accounts in Zürich, Geneva and New York. **6.** Yasser Arafat, the leader of the Palestinian National Authority, ordered his negotiators to break off final-status talks with Israel until it stopped expanding Jewish settlements on occupied land. **13.** Two members of the militant Islamic group Hamas were killed and three were captured in a shootout with Israeli troops in Beit Awa on the West Bank. **19.** The Deputy Prime Minister of Iraq, Tariq Aziz, rejected a British-drafted UN resolution on sanctions and arms inspections; the official Iraqi news agency claimed that a total of 10,295 people had died in November because of sanctions imposed by the UN. **28.** Israeli warplanes struck suspected guerrilla targets in south Lebanon after an attack on an Israeli base at Beaufort Castle. **29.** Jewish settlers in Hebron clashed with Israeli police and soldiers, who were trying to dismantle a shrine that the settlers had built to Baruch Goldstein, who had killed 29 Muslims before being beaten to death by survivors in 1994.

JANUARY 2000

4. Israel and Syria began a new round of peace talks in Shepherdstown, West Virginia, USA; talks were postponed on 17 January after Syria insisted formally that Israel accept a full withdrawal from the Golan Heights behind the pre-1967 border. At least 11 Sunni Muslim rebels and three of their hostages were killed when the Lebanese Army seized the rebel-held village of Kfar Habou in northern Lebanon. **7.** Israel's leading orthodox rabbis, the Council of Torah Sages, issued a ruling banning the Internet from Jewish homes. **12.** Iraq agreed to allow the International Atomic Energy Authority to resume inspections that had been suspended by the Iraqi government in 1998. **27.** The Israeli attorney general ordered the One Israel party to pay fines of £2 million for circumventing laws restricting foreign donations to Israeli political parties. **30.** In Jordan, demonstrators carried 3.5 million pencils to the Iraqi border in protest against the UN-imposed trade sanctions against Iraq; pencils were subject to sanctions because the graphite they contain can be used for military purposes.

FEBRUARY 2000

8. Israel bombed three electricity sub-stations in Lebanon in revenge for Hezbollah attacks in which five Israeli soldiers had died; a state of emergency was declared in the north of Israel and about 250,000 Israelis sought safety in underground bunkers or fled the area in anticipation of Hezbollah revenge attacks. The senior UN humanitarian co-ordinator in Iraq, Hans von Sponeck, called for an end to UN sanctions against Iraq. **10.** An official report covering 1988–92 into torture by the Israeli security services revealed that torture sessions were concealed and accused the security services of lying about them to the courts and their superiors. **16.** In the first speech delivered by a German politician in the Knesset, President Rau asked for forgiveness for the Holocaust and pledged to fight anti-Semitism. **22.** Saudi Arabia agreed to allow a British diplomatic mission to Mecca, the first time a predominantly Christian state had been granted permission. **26.** Palestinian students pelted the visiting French Prime Minister Lionel Jospin with stones at the Birzeit

University near Ramallah, after he described guerrillas fighting Israel's occupation of south Lebanon as terrorists. **29.** The Israeli authorities released the prison diary of the Nazi war criminal Adolf Eichman; he had been convicted of war crimes and hanged in Israel in 1962.

MARCH 2000

1. In Israel, the Knesset passed a proposal requiring that any peace deal with Syria be put to a referendum in which a majority of all registered voters would be needed, rather than just a majority of those voting. **5.** The Israeli Cabinet decided to withdraw all troops from Lebanon by July, ending the 18-year occupation of a border security zone. **7.** Following the resignation of the Syrian government, President Assad appointed Mustafa Muhammad Miro as the new Prime Minister. **20.** The Pope began his visit to the Holy Land in the Jordanian capital 'Ammān with a plea to the peoples of the Middle East to spare no effort to solve the 'grave issues of justice' that beset the region. **21.** Israel transferred a further 6.1 per cent of the occupied West Bank to Palestinian control. **23.** The Pope expressed the deep regret of the Roman Catholic Church for its past persecution of the Jews at Yad Vashem, the Holocaust museum in Jerusalem. **26.** On the final day of his visit to the Holy Land, the Pope prayed at the Wailing Wall and left a piece of paper bearing a prayer asking for forgiveness for the sins of Christians towards Jews. **28.** An Israeli police report recommended that former Prime Minister Binyamin Netanyahu should face criminal charges including fraud and theft of public property.

APRIL 2000

5. The Syrian Foreign Minister, Farouq al-Sharaa, said that Israel's planned unilateral withdrawal from Lebanon would not end the conflict unless there were a peace treaty with Syria. **6.** Israeli police announced that they had failed to find sufficient evidence to prosecute President Weizman for corruption; he could still be forced to resign after their report accused him of breach of trust and fraud. **12.** President Jiang Zemin arrived in Israel, the first visit by a Chinese leader. **19.** In Iraq, journalists awarded Uday Hussein, the eldest son of Saddam Hussein, the title of 'Journalist of the Century'. **23.** King Abdullah of Jordan paid his first visit to Israel as head of state and held talks with Prime Minister Ehud Barak in Eilat. **24.** Following a drastic reduction in the numbers of wild animals, the Israeli government ordered a three-year ban on hunting. **25.** King Abdullah met with PLO leader Yasser Arafat in Ramallah. **26.** The Lebanese government announced that it would allow international peacekeepers into the south of the country after the planned Israeli withdrawal in July 2000. **28.** George Habash resigned as leader of the Popular Front for the Liberation of Palestine, a grouping that had hijacked several planes in the 1960s and 1970s.

MAY 2000

3. In Kuwait, the criminal court upheld the death sentence for treason on Alaa Hussein, who headed Iraq's occupation government after its invasion of Kuwait in 1990. **4.** Lebanese Hezbollah guerrillas unleashed two rocket attacks on Kiryat Shemona, northern Israel, killing an Israeli soldier and wounding 30 people; in response, Israel launched air raids on electricity sub-stations and a guerrilla base in Lebanon and President Weizman declared that any future attacks would be even more severely punished. **10.** Israeli Arabs boycotted Israel's Independence Day celebrations, because they claimed that the Prime Minister had done nothing to lessen the economic gap between Jews and Arabs. **12.** Israel formally proposed that the Palestinians establish their own state on up to 80 per cent of the West Bank, the first official indication of how much land Israel was prepared to offer in a final peace settlement. **13.** In Iraq, a dissident Shia Muslim group claimed responsibility for eight rockets fired into a residential neighbourhood of Baghdad, killing one person and wounding four. **14.** Thousands of Palestinians clashed with Israeli troops in protests than left one person dead and at least 30 injured in the Gaza Strip and the West Bank. **15.** Fighting broke out between Israeli soldiers and Palestinian police after an Arab day of protest marking 'Al-Nakba' (The Catastrophe), the anniversary of the founding of the state of Israel in 1948. At least three Palestinians were killed and 268 wounded and nine Israeli soldiers were injured. The Israeli cabinet approved the handover of three Jerusalem suburbs to full Palestinian control. The National Religious Party withdrew from the coalition government in protest and the government narrowly won a vote of confidence in the Knesset. **16.** Palestinian police restored order after riots in the West Bank and Gaza Strip. **21.** Israel suspended peace talks with the Palestinians after a firebomb attack on an Israeli car near Jericho in which a two-year-old girl was badly burnt. **22.** Hundreds of Lebanese civilians marched to their homes in the Israeli-occupied security zone, accompanied by Hezbollah guerrillas. South Lebanese Army troops fled or surrendered. **23.** Israeli troops began to withdraw from southern Lebanon. **24.** Israel completed its withdrawal from Lebanon and its airforce bombed its abandoned positions to prevent them falling into the hands of Hezbollah. Israel warned Syria and Lebanon that any future attacks would be regarded as an act of war and dealt with appropriately.

JUNE 2000

11. In Syria, President Hafez al-Assad died. He had ruled since 1971. The ruling Ba'ath party unanimously nominated his son, Bashar al-Assad, to succeed him. Vice-President Khaddam announced a constitutional change to lower the minimum age for the presidency from 40 to 34. **13.** In Israel, the Shas party suspended its membership of the coalition government, removing the government's parliamentary majority. On June 20, the Shas party formally resigned from the ruling coalition, but rejoined on 22 June, when the Prime Minister gave in to their demands. **15.** In Israel, the Meretz party resigned from the coalition government. **17.** Israeli defence sources claimed that Israel had secretly carried out its first test launches of cruise missiles from submarines capable of carrying nuclear warheads. **27.** In Syria, Bashar Assad's nomination for the presidency was unanimously approved by the Syrian parliament. Israel announced that it was to buy 1.8 billion cubic feet of fresh water a year from Turkey, following a prolonged drought. **28.** A gunman attacked a UN FAO building in Baghdad, killing two staff members and injuring seven after taking all the employees hostage and threatening to blow up the building. The gunman later surrendered to police.

JULY 2000

3. In Israel, the Knesset voted for a bill that would give ultra-Orthodox Jewish men a formal exemption from military service, a move strongly opposed by the nation's secular majority. **4.** Israel and the Palestinians exchanged threats of military confrontation after the PLO announced that it would unilaterally set up a Palestinian state on or before 13 September. **4.** Kuwait's highest court rejected a case by four women who said that the ban on votes for women violated the constitution, which guaranteed equal rights to both sexes. **5.** In the Jordanian capital Amman,

15 passengers were injured when security forces foiled an attempt by three Syrian hijackers to take over an aircraft bound for Damascus. **10.** In Israel, President Ezer Weizman resigned following allegations of financial impropriety and the government narrowly survived a parliamentary vote of no confidence. In Syria, a referendum was held to confirm Bashar al-Assad as President; he was approved after winning 97.29 per cent of the vote. **11-25.** The Camp David Summit between the Israeli Prime Minister Ehud Barak, the Palestinian leader Yasser Arafat and President Clinton took place. It ended without agreement. **28.** UN troops began to deploy along the Lebanese-Israeli frontier. **31.** In Israel, Moshe Katsav was voted President in a parliamentary vote, gaining 63 votes to 57 for Shimon Peres, who had been the favourite. The Israeli government of Ehud Barak narrowly survived another confidence vote.

SEPTEMBER 2000

2. Israeli Deputy Prime Minister and Foreign Affairs Minister David Levy resigned in protest at government readiness to concede areas of Jerusalem to the Palestinians as part of a peace deal. **13.** Iraq condemned Saudi Arabia and Kuwait for providing air bases for western aircraft patrolling the no-fly zones imposed after the 1991 Gulf war after two civilians were killed on 11 August when US and UK jets bombed Samawa. **27.** In the West Bank, Mahmoud Abu Hanoud, a militant suspected of masterminding suicide bombings was captured by Palestinian security forces custody after escaping from Nablus, where three Israeli soldiers had died in a gun battle.

EUROPEAN UNION

SEPTEMBER 1999

10. The EU needs to become a single legal area with its own public prosecutor to succeed in combating fraud, according to *Corpus Juris*, a report published by the team who had prompted the mass resignation of the Commission in March 1999. **11.** Allegations were made that the European Investment Bank had lost more than £180m in speculation on financial markets. **14.** European Commission President Romano Prodi set out his vision of an EU of as many as 30 states and asked for a radical reform of the EU institutions in the December Intergovernmental Conference. **15.** Prodi was officially confirmed as the new President of the Commission after the European Parliament voted to accept him by 414 votes to 142. On 24 September he promised sweeping administrative reform of the Commission, including a cut in the number of departments and the adoption of a new code of conduct; he had earlier promised that he would take seriously any demand from the European Parliament to replace any commissioner who performed badly. **29.** Vice-President Neil Kinnock announced that appointments would henceforth be made on the basis of merit, not nationality; some key positions had hitherto been reserved for certain nationals. **29.** The new Commissioners renounced their right to claim exemption from VAT and excise duty on wine, spirits, cigarettes, petrol and a range of other goods. **30.** The Commission announced it was to give €2.5 million to farm unions in central and eastern European countries to help them adjust to EU agriculture laws.

OCTOBER 1999

1. The European Commission threatened France with legal action over its refusal to lift the ban on British beef. **4.** Paul van Buitenen, an auditor employed by the

European Commission who had disclosed fraud and mismanagement, received a formal reprimand. **6.** Javier Solana left NATO vowing to use his new job as the EU's first High Representative for Foreign Affairs to help build a common defence policy for Europe. **8.** Ministers approved the Eurocac scheme, under which asylum seekers wanting refuge in any EU state would automatically be fingerprinted and their details held on a central European database. **13.** The Commission proposed an ambitious programme that aimed to reform the EU budget and institutions by the end of 2002 and expand the EU to as many as 27 states. Turkey was to be given candidate status, although negotiations could not be opened yet. EU scientists asked the UK to provide updated statistics on the current incidence of BSE after studying a French report that raised fresh doubts about the safety of British beef. **15.** France, Germany and the UK proposed that Javier Solana, the EU High Representative, should also be the Secretary-General of the Western European Union. **15 –16.** The EU summit in Tampere, Finland was held, the first exclusively devoted to justice and home affairs. **25.** The Commission announced the start of legal proceedings against the UK over the quality of waters at its bathing beaches, saying that the UK was still failing to meet standards 15 years after the deadline expired for complying with cleanliness rules

NOVEMBER 1999

3. The European Commission set a ten-day deadline for France to lift its ban on British beef or be taken to the European Court of Justice. It launched legal proceedings against France on 16 November, giving it only two weeks' notice instead of the customary two months to explain its continued ban. **10.** European Commission President Prodi called for changes in the EU treaty that could end a government's right of veto on taxation. **16.** The European Parliament overwhelmingly voted to reduce the working week for junior doctors to 48 hours within four years; the European Commission had proposed a time scale of seven years, but pressure from the UK and Ireland in the Council of Ministers had increased it to 13 years.

DECEMBER 1999

9. The Helsinki European summit began; the UK refused to sign a deal on the withholding tax, a measure aimed at reducing the outflow of capital to countries which had low taxes on investments; the UK had demanded the complete exemption of Britain's Eurobond market. **10.** The EU summit condemned Russia's bombardment of Chechnya and the treatment of refugees; the summit also approved Anglo-French plans to create a Euroforce with up to 60,000 troops ready for peacekeeping and humanitarian missions by 2003. **11.** The heads of government of the EU member states signed a 'millennium declaration' to the people of the EU that spoke of the benefits of economic and monetary union. **14.** The European Commission gave France five working days to abide by the EU ruling to permit the sale of British beef. European Commission Vice-President Neil Kinnock introduced positive discrimination for senior jobs in the Commission; women are to be given precedence over equally qualified men to redress the imbalance of only 21 of the Commission's 247 most senior posts being held by women. **17.** Reductions in fishing quotas were agreed by fisheries ministers in an attempt to save stocks in the North Sea and Irish Sea from collapse.

JANUARY 2000

5. Romano Prodi invited the Libyan leader Col. Gaddafi to visit the Commission; he cancelled the invitation on

23 January after intense pressure from member states. **12.** A European Commission White Paper proposed the creation of an EU-wide European Food Authority to cover all aspects of food production. **24.** Foreign ministers agreed to impose £90 million of punitive damages against Russia, following criticism of Russia's handling of the Chechnya crisis, but stopped short of imposing trade sanctions or suspending the EU's partnership agreement. **26.** The European Commission produced proposals covering most areas of economic activity, which would replace the national veto with qualified majority voting for all forms of taxation that impinge on the functioning of the internal market.

FEBRUARY 2000

6. The European Commission published a critical report on the failure of the French authorities to control a growing epidemic of BSE. **9.** Romano Prodi launched a five-year strategic plan for the political integration of the EU, to be discussed at the intergovernmental conference (IGC) in Nice in December 2000. **15.** The European Commission commenced legal proceedings against Germany for failing to lift its ban on British beef. **24.** The European Parliament called for the creation of a European public prosecutor and an extension of the EU's sphere of control to cover policing and criminal justice.

MARCH 2000

2. The constitutional affairs committee of the European Parliament voted overwhelmingly for a legally binding Charter of Fundamental Rights to be incorporated into treaty law. **11.** The environment commissioner stated that she would withhold regional aid grants until member states fully implemented the Habitats Directive and the Wild Birds Directive. **24.** EU leaders agreed to a ten-year programme to embrace information technology; they claimed the plan would generate an average annual economic growth rate of three per cent and raise the employment rate from 61 to 70 per cent by 2010. **27.** Prodi ordered an investigation into allegations that three former commissioners, Jacques Santer, Martin Bangemann and Padraig Flynn, had offered to sell access for money or rewards.

APRIL 2000

4. The *Frankfurter Allgemeine Zeitung* published allegations that European commissioners were planning to topple Romano Prodi. The European Commission moved rapidly to deny the allegations. **5.** The EU agreed at the Africa-Europe summit in Cairo that money embezzled by corrupt African regimes should be returned to the country of origin. **13.** The European Parliament refused to discharge the 1998 budget until the Commission handed over sensitive documents and tackled a series of corruption cases; it approved a report on curtailing the national veto and giving the EU a legally binding constitution. **28.** The euro fell to a record low after it emerged that Jean-Claude Trichet, the Governor of the Bank of France, who was due to be the next President of the European Central Bank, was under investigation for his role in financial irregularities at Crédit Lyonnais.

MAY 2000

3. Romano Prodi announced a reshuffle of senior staff in his office, replacing his press officer, chief of staff and secretary general. The value of the euro fell to below 90 cents, deepening the crisis of confidence in the single currency. On 5 May, Wim Duisenberg, the President of the European Central Bank, said that the bank would monitor the euro exchange rate closely, as further devaluation could fuel inflation and damage confidence in monetary union. **10.** The European Commission proposed a budget for 2001 of €96,926 million, up three per cent on 2000. The proposed budget would represent 1.07 per cent of the EU's total national spending, as compared to 1.11 per cent of that of 2000. **29.** EU ministers approved the Convention on Mutual Legal Assistance, which would allow EU member states to request records of suspected criminals in other countries.

JUNE 2000

7. It was announced that Greece would participate in the meetings of the Euro-11, the 11 countries that are part of the euro currency area, from July; it was to become a full member from 1 January 2001. A report issued by the Health and Consumer Protection Scientific Steering Committee stated that Germany, Italy and Spain, were probably infected with BSE, although they claimed to be free of it, and said that infection was unlikely, but could not be excluded, in six other EU countries. **20.** EU heads of state agreed to the ultimate goal of establishing a mandatory EU-wide information exchange scheme within nine years to avoid tax avoidance by non-resident investors, but said it could only come into effect if the EU could secure the participation of other international financial centres.

JULY 2000

5. The European Court of Justice rejected the challenge by France against the Court's decision to lift the world-wide export ban on British beef. **12.** The European Court of Human Rights appointed a panel of three 'wise men' to assess human rights in Austria and monitor the performance of the Freedom Party.

AUGUST 2000

7. A report by a senior committee of MEP's accused the European Commission of financial mismanagement after discovering that £12,000 million of aid remained unspent; it was found that countries promised aid by the EU had to wait an average of four and a half years before it was delivered.

INTERNATIONAL RELATIONS

SEPTEMBER 1999

1. Russia resumed its representation at NATO headquarters, five months after its withdrawal in protest at airstrikes on Yugoslavia. **28.** The IMF withheld a US$640 million loan to Russia after the Russian Central Bank ceased its co-operation with the US Justice Department who were investigating allegations of money-laundering.

OCTOBER 1999

6. Javier Solana ended his term as NATO Secretary-General. On 14 October he was replaced by Lord Robertson of Port Ellen. **16.** The UN Security Council issued an ultimatum to Afghanistan to hand over Osama bin Laden for trial for the two US Embassy bombings in Africa within one month or face sanctions. **18.** The Commonwealth Ministerial Action Group condemned the coup in Pakistan and suspended its membership of the Commonwealth. **25.** The UN Security Council voted to adopt a resolution drafted by the UK to send nearly 11,000 UN troops to East Timor to oversee its transition to independence.

NOVEMBER 1999

7. A report by the Commonwealth's Foreign Policy Centre called for Zimbabwe, Kenya, Zambia and Sri Lanka to be expelled from the Commonwealth if they did not improve their human rights record. **12.** Koichiro Matsuura was elected Director-General of UNESCO, winning 146 of 166 of votes cast by UNESCO's general conference. The Queen opened the Commonwealth's 50th anniversary gathering in Durban, South Africa. **24.** At the summit of the Organisation for Security and Co-operation in Europe (OSCE), 54 countries, including almost every European country, plus Russia and the USA, signed the Conventional Forces in Europe (CFE) treaty cutting conventional weapon levels in Europe, but most of them insisted that it would not be ratified until Russia reduced its forces in the Caucasus. A Charter for European Security was also signed. **29.** OSCE Chairman Knut Vollebæk met the Russian Foreign Minister, Igor Ivanov, to arrange a fact-finding visit to Chechnya.

DECEMBER 1999

9. The WHO announced that for the first time ever, there had not been a single case of polio in Europe in the past year. **10.** The UN Security Council voted unanimously to approve a six-month extension to the 'oil-for-food' programme in Iraq; Iraq would be allowed to sell US$5.26 thousand million worth of oil to buy food, medicine and other supplies. **17.** The UN voted to send weapons monitors back to Iraq, a year after their withdrawal. In return for full co-operation with the monitors, to be observed over four months, economic sanctions would be lifted.

JANUARY 2000

6. The WHO launched a campaign to eradicate polio by the end of 2000. **22.** Finance ministers of the G7 group urged Japan to proceed with structural reform to enable the world economy to achieve more balanced growth. **26.** Hans Blix was appointed as head of the UN Monitoring, Verification and Inspection Committee for Iraq. **28.** NATO Secretary-General Lord Robertson announced that NATO would give assistance to Ukraine to modernise its armed forces. **29.** The World Economic Forum took place in Davos, Switzerland; electronic commerce and free trade were discussed. **30.** A Biosafety Protocol to the UN Convention on Biodiversity was agreed in Montréal, Canada, which aimed to prevent contamination by genetically altered species; it will only come into force after it has been ratified by 50 nations.

FEBRUARY 2000

16. NATO and Russia agreed to resume contacts suspended during the Balkan conflict in 1999. **24.** The UN Security Council voted to send an observer force into the Democratic Republic of Congo to monitor the cease-fire and prepare for a possible UN peacekeeping operation.

MARCH 2000

9. The UN started distributing condoms to peacekeepers to prevent them spreading Aids; troops were to receive one per day, with surplus condoms to be distributed to the local population. **12.** A UN investigation of sanction evasion by Angola's UNITÀ rebels criticised Belgium for its lax controls over the diamond market in Antwerp, which handles 85 per cent of the world's rough stones. **23.** NATO Secretary-General Lord Robertson accused European governments of failing to keep their promises to augment their defence capabilities. **29.** The Managing Director of the IMF, Horst Köhler, outlined his plans for

reform of the institution, accepting the need for the fund to concentrate on short-term lending rather than longer-term development projects.

APRIL 2000

6. The Council of Europe voted to commence suspension proceedings against Russia because of its conduct in Chechnya. The Russian delegation walked out after a separate vote to suspend its voting rights. **15.** The UN Security Council admitted responsibility for failing to stop the 1994 genocide in Rwanda, in which at least 500,000 people, mainly Tutsis, were killed. **17.** Agreement was reached at a summit on the Convention on International Trade in Endangered Species in Nairobi to postpone any ivory sales until 2002 summit at the earliest; Botswana, Namibia, South Africa and Zimbabwe had wanted to sell their stockpiled ivory.

MAY 2000

3. An agreement to abolish restrictions on 99 per cent of imports from the 48 poorest countries was endorsed by the EU, the USA, Japan and Canada at a meeting of the World Trade Organisation's governing council. Gen. Joe Ralston replaced Gen. Wesley Clark as NATO's Supreme Allied Commander, Europe (SACEUR). **4.** UN Secretary-General Kofi Annan asked the members of the UN Security Council members to send troops to reinforce the peacekeepers in Sierra Leone. **10.** Lt.-Gen. Carlo Cabigiosu, of the Italian army, was appointed to serve as the commander of the NATO mission in Kosovo from October 2000, when the term of Eurocorps commander Lt.-Gen. Juan Ortuño ended. **18.** The UN Security Council voted unanimously to impose an immediate arms embargo on Ethiopia and Eritrea in an attempt to limit the border dispute. **20.** The five nuclear powers on the UN Security Council agreed to work towards eliminating their nuclear arsenals. A total of 187 countries signed the Nuclear Non-Proliferation Treaty after four weeks of discussions.

JUNE 2000

6. The Commonwealth Ministerial Action Group suspended Fiji from the councils of the Commonwealth, and told the Solomon Islands that it faced similar disciplinary action unless it restored democratic rule. **18.** The UN Security Council agreed to accept a report from the Secretary-General, Kofi Annan, that the Israeli army had finally withdrawn from Lebanese territory. **26.** The OECD said 35 tax havens, some of which with close links with the UK and the USA, were harming world trade and investment by giving a shelter to tax dodgers. Monaco, the Channel Islands, Gibraltar and the Isle of Man were among those named.

JULY 2000

23. At the G-7 summit, government leaders promised to help poor countries reduce their indebtedness, fight disease and gain the benefits of the power of new technologies.

AUGUST 2000

14. The UN Security Council voted unanimously to create a special court to prosecute Sierra Leone rebel leaders for war crimes including killing and maiming of tens of thousands of civilians.

Obituaries

Adam Smith, Janet, OBE, author and journalist, aged 93 – d. 11 September 1999, b. 9 December 1905

Adamson, Sir Campbell, Director-General of the CBI 1969–76; Chairman of Abbey National 1978–91, aged 78 – d. 21 August 2000, b. 26 June 1922

Aga Khan III, Begum, aged 94 – d. 1 July 2000, b. 15 February 1906

Albert, Carl, Speaker of US House of Representatives 1971–6, aged 91 – d. 4 February 2000, b. 10 May 1908

Anderson, Marjorie, broadcaster, aged 86 – d. 14 December 1999, b. 7 November 1913

Annan, Baron, OBE, Provost, King's College Cambridge 1956–66, University College London 1966–78; Vice-Chancellor University of London 1978–81, aged 83 – d. 21 February 2000, b. 25 December 1916

Arkan (Zelko Raznjatovic), Serbian paramilitary leader and indicted war criminal, aged 47 – d. (assassinated) 15 January 2000

Aspinall, John, zoo owner, aged 74 – d. 29 June 2000, b. 11 June 1926

Assad, Hafez al-, President of Syria 1970–2000, aged 69 – d. 10 June 2000, b. 6 October 1930

Austin, Bunny, tennis player, aged 94 – d. 26 August 2000, b. 26 August 1906

Bainton, Alan, Controller of Operations for the Prison Service 1967–72, aged 87 – d. 8 June 2000, b. 10 May 1913

Bannen, Ian, actor, aged 71 – d. (in a car accident), 3 November 1999, b. 29 June 1928

Barks, Carl, cartoonist, aged 99 – d. 25 August 2000, b. 27 March 1901

Barnes, Dame Josephine, DBE, FRCP, FRCS, FRCOG, obstetrician and gynaecologist, aged 87 – d. 28 December 1999, b. 18 August 1912

Beesley, Prof. Michael, CBE, economist, aged 75 – d. 24 September 1999, b. 3 July 1924

Belsky, Franta, sculptor, aged 79 – d. 5 July 2000, b. 6 April 1921

Black, Sir Robert, GCMG, OBE, Governor and Commander-in-Chief, Singapore 1955–7, Hong Kong 1958–64, aged 93 – d. 29 October 1999, b. 3 June 1906

Bouchier, Chili, actress, aged 89 – d. 9 September 1999, b. 12 September 1909

Bourguiba, Habib, President of Tunisia 1957–87, aged 96 – d. 6 April 2000, b. 3 August 1903

Bowie, Lester, bandleader and jazz trumpeter, aged 58 – d. 8 November 1999, b. 11 October 1941

Bowles, Rt Revd Cyril, Bishop of Derby 1969–87, aged 83 – d. 14 September 1999, b. 9 May 1916

Braine of Wheatley, Baron, PC, Conservative MP for Billericay 1950–5, South East Essex 1955–83, Castle Point 1983–92, Father of the House 1987–92, aged 85 – d. 4 January 2000, b. 24 June 1914

Bresson, Robert, French film director, aged 98 – d. 18 December 1999, b. 25 September 1901

Brewer, Rt Revd John, Roman Catholic Bishop of Lancaster 1985–2000, aged 70 – d. 10 June 2000, b. 24 November 1929

Broackes, Sir Nigel, chairman, Trafalgar House 1969–92, aged 65 – d. 28 September 1999, b. 21 July 1934

Brockman, Vice-Adm. Sir Ronald Vernon, KCB, CSI, CIE, CVO, CBE, naval officer, aged 90 – d. 3 September 1999, b. 8 March 1909

Brown, Rt Revd Leslie, CBE, Archbishop of Uganda, Rwanda and Burundi 1961–5; Bishop of St Edmundsbury and Ipswich 1966–78, aged 87 – d. 27 December 1999, b. 10 June 1912

Brück, Hermann, CBE, Astronomer-Royal for Scotland 1957–75, aged 94 – d. 4 March 2000, b. 15 August 1905

Bullwinkel, Vivian, MBE, nurse, aged 84 – d. 3 July 2000, b. 18 December 1915

Burg, Josef, Israeli politician, aged 90 – d. 15 October 1999, b. 31 January 1909

Caldecote, 2nd Viscount, KBE, DSC, aged 81 – d. 20 September 1999, b. 8 October 1917

Cartland, Dame Barbara, DBE, novelist, aged 98 – d. 21 May 2000, b. 9 July 1901

Champernowne, Professor David, FBA, Professor of Economics and Statistics at Cambridge University 1970–78, aged 88 – d. 19 August 2000, b. 9 July 1912

Charteris of Amisfield, Baron, PC, GCB, GCVO, OBE, Private Secretary to The Queen 1972–7, aged 86 – d. 23 December 1999, b. 7 September 1913

Chelmsford, 3rd Viscount, aged 68 – d. 15 December 1999, b. 7 March 1931

Clark, Alan Kenneth McKenzie, MP, Conservative MP for Plymouth, Sutton 1974–92, for Kensington and Chelsea 1997–9, minister for employment 1983–6, for trade 1986–9 and for defence 1989–92, aged 71 – d. 5 September 1999, b. 13 April 1928

Clough, Prunella, artist, aged 80 – d. 26 December 1999, b. 14 November 1919

Coggan, Rt Revd Lord (Donald), Archbishop of Canterbury 1974–80, aged 90 – d. 17 May 2000, b. 9 October 1909

Comfort, Alex, Ph.D., D.Sc., doctor and writer, aged 80 – d. 26 March 2000, b. 10 February 1920

Coote, Rt Revd Roderick, Bishop for Guinea, Gambia, Senegal, and the Cape Verde Islands (1951–57), Bishop of Fulham, Bishop of Colchester, aged 86 – b. 13 April 1915

Couve de Murville, Maurice, French Foreign Minister 1958–68; Prime Minister 1968–9, aged 92 – d. 24 December 1999, b. 24 January 1907

Craigie, Jill, film director, aged 85 – d. 13 December 1999, b. 7 March 1914

Crichton, Charles, film director, aged 89 – d. 14 September 1999, b. 6 August 1910

Crisp, Quentin, author, aged 90 – d. 21 November 1999, b. 25 December 1908

Cullberg, Birgit, choreographer, aged 91 – d. 8 September 1999, b. 3 August 1908

Cunningham, Sir Josias, President of the Ulster Unionist Party, aged 66 – d. (in a car accident) 9 August 2000, b. 20 January 1934

Danco, Suzanne, Belgian soprano, aged 89 – d. 10 August 2000, b. 22 January 1911

Day, Sir Robin, Kt, broadcaster, aged 76 – d. 6 August 2000, b. 24 October 1923

de Botton, Gilbert, founding chairman of Global Asset Management and parton of the arts, aged 65 – d. 27 August 2000, b. 16 February 1935

Dell, Edmund, Rt. Hon., Labour MP for Birkenhead 1964–79, Secretary of State for Trade 1976–8, Chairman Channel Four 1980–7 – d. 1 November 1999, b. 15 August 1921

Denman, Prof. Donald, Ph.D., FRICS, land economy pioneer, aged 88 – d. 2 September 1999, b. 7 April 1911

Deutsch, André, CBE, publisher, aged 82 – d. 11 April 2000, b. 15 November 1917

Donnelly, Martin, New Zealand cricketer and England rugby player, aged 82 – d. 22 October 1999, b. 17 October 1917

Dougall, Robert, MBE, BBC newsreader, aged 86 – d. 18 December 1999, b. 27 November 1913

Duff, Sir Anthony, GCMG, DSO, DSC, PC, wartime submarine commander, Ambassador to Nepal 1964–65, and Deputy Governor to Southern Rhodesia 1979–80, aged 80 – *d.* 13 August 2000, *b.* 25 February 1920

Dunlop, William Joseph (Joey), MBE, OBE, Motorcycle World Champion 1982–86, Isle of Man TT winner 26 times, aged 48 – *d.* 2 July 2000, *b.* 25 February 1952

Dunrossil, 2nd Viscount, CMG, aged 73 – *d.* 22 March 2000, *b.* 22 May 1926

Durack, Elizabeth, CMG, OBE, Australian artist, aged 84 – *d.* 25 May 2000, *b.* 6 July 1915

Dury, Ian, singer, aged 57 – *d.* 27 March 2000, *b.* 12 May 1942

Fairbanks, Douglas Jnr., American actor, aged 90 – *d.* 7 May 2000, *b.* 9 December 1909

Fanfani, Amintore, Prime Minister of Italy 1954, 1958–9, 1960–5, 1987, aged 91 – *d.* 20 November 1999, *b.* 6 February 1908

Farndale, Gen. Sir Martin, KCB, Commander-in-Chief British Army of the Rhine 1985–7, aged 71 – *d.* 10 May 2000, *b.* 6 January 1929

Faulds, Andrew, actor, Labour MP for Smethwick 1966–74, for Warley East 1974–97, aged 77 – *d.* 31 May 2000, *b.* 1 March 1923

Fitzgerald, Penelope, author, aged 83 – *d.* 28 April 2000, *b.* 17 December 1916

Foley, Rt Revd Brian, Bishop of Lancaster 1962–85, aged 89 – *d.* 23 December 1999, *b.* 25 May 1910

Foot, Baron, aged 90 – *d.* 17 October 1999, *b.* 17 February 1909

Fox, Sir (Henry) Murray, GBE, Lord Mayor of London 1974–5, aged 87 – *d.* 9 November 1999, *b.* 7 June 1912

Fuchs, Sir Vivian, FRS, Director, British Antarctic Survey 1958–73, first person to cross Antarctica, aged 91 – *d.* 11 November 1999, *b.* 11 February 1908

Fussey, David, Ph.D., Vice-Chancellor, University of Greenwich 1993–2000, aged 56 – *d.* 16 March 2000, *b.* 5 September 1943

Gielgud, Sir John, OM, CH, actor, aged 96 – *d.* 21 May 2000, *b.* 14 April 1904

Glock, Sir William, CBE, Controller of Music at the BBC 1959–72, aged 92 – *d.* 28 June 2000, *b.* 3 May 1908

Glover, Gen. Sir William, KCB, MBE, DL, Commander-in-chief, UK Land Forces 1985–7, aged 71 – *d.* 4 June 2000, *b.* 25 March 1929

Gorbachev, Raisa, wife of the former President of the Soviet Union, Mikhail Gorbachev, aged 67 – *d.* 20 September 1999, *b.* 5 January 1932

Graaff, Sir De Villiers, MBE, 2nd Baronet, aged 85 – *d.* 4 October 1999, *b.* 8 December 1913

Grant, Bernie, Labour MP for Tottenham 1987–2000, aged 56 – *d.* 8 April 2000, *b.* 17 February 1944

Grey of Naunton, Baron, GCMG, GCVO, OBE, Governor of British Guiana 1959–64, of The Bahamas 1964–8, of Northern Ireland 1968–73, aged 89 – *d.* October 1999, *b.* 15 April 1910

Guinness, Sir Alec, CH, CBE, actor, aged 86 – *d.* 5 August 2000, *b.* 2 April 1914

Halsbury, 3rd Earl of, FRS, FRENG., aged 91 – *d.* 14 January 2000, *b.* 4 June 1908

Hamilton, Willie, Labour MP for Fife West 1950–74, Fife Central 1974–87, aged 82 – *d.* 23 January 2000, *b.* 26 June 1917

Harrison, Ginette, mountaineer, aged 41 – *d.* (killed by an avalanche) 24 October 1999, *b.* 28 February 1958

Harsanyi, Professor John, economist, philosopher and 1994 Nobel Prize winner, aged 80 – *d.* 9 August 2000, *b.* 29 May 1920

Hart-Davis, Sir Rupert, publisher, aged 92 – *d.* 8 December 1999, *b.* 28 August 1907

Hartling, Poul, Prime Minister of Denmark 1973–5. UN High Commissioner for Refugees 1978–85, aged 85 – *d.* 30 April 2000, *b.* 14 August 1914

Heller, Joseph, author, aged 76 – *d.* 12 December 1999, *b.* 1 May 1923

Henderson of Brompton, Baron, KCB, Clerk of the Parliaments 1974–83, aged 77 – *d.* 13 January 2000, *b.* 16 September 1922

Hetherington, Alastair, Editor, The Guardian 1956–75, aged 79 – *d.* 3 October 1999, *b.* 31 October 1919

Holland, Rt Revd Thomas, DSC, DD, Bishop of Salford 1964–83, aged 91 – *d.* 30 September 1999, *b.* 11 June 1908

Hollaway, Anthony, stained glass designer, aged 72 – *d.* 9 August 2000, *b.* 8 March 1928

Hood, 7th Viscount, aged 85 – *d.* 2 October 1999, *b.* 11 March 1914

Houghton, Rt Revd Michael, Bishop Suffragan of Ebbsfleet 1998–9, aged 50 – *d.* 18 December 1999, *b.* 14 June 1949

Hughes, Baron, CBE, PC, Lord Provost of Dundee 1954–60; minister in the Scottish Office 1964–70, 1974–5, aged 88 – *d.* 31 December 1999, *b.* 22 January 1911

Hunte, Sir Conrad, Barbadian cricketer, aged 67 – *d.* 3 December 1999, *b.* 9 May 1932

Jakobovits, Baron, Chief Rabbi of the United Hebrew Congregations of the Commonwealth 1967–91, aged 78 – *d.* 31 October 1999, *b.* 8 February 1921

Jenkins, Clive, general secretary, Association of Scientific, Technical and Managerial Staffs 1970–88, aged 73 – *d.* 22 September 1999, *b.* 2 May 1926

Jones, Sir Emrys, Principal of the Royal Agricultural College 1973–78, aged 84 – *d.* 29 June 2000, *b.* 6 July 1915

Kirschlager, Rudolf, President of Austria 1974–86, aged 85 – *d.* 30 March 2000, *b.* 20 March 1915

Kraus, Alfredo, opera singer, aged 71 – *d.* 10 September 1999, *b.* 24 November 1927

Lama, Ganju, VC, MM, aged 77 – *d.* 30 June 2000, *b.* 7 July 1922

Lamb, Sir Larry, Editor of The Sun 1969–72, 1975–81, Daily Express 1983–6, aged 70 – *d.* 19 May 2000, *b.* 15 July 1929

Layfield, Sir Frank, QC, barrister, aged 78 – *d.* 2 February 2000, *b.* 9 August 1921

Leverhulme, Viscount, KG, TD, former Lord Lieutenant of Cheshire, aged 85 – *d.* 4 July 2000, *b.* 1 July 1915

Likhachev, Dmitri, Russian intellectual, aged 92 – *d.* 30 September 1999, *b.* 28 November 1906

Llewellyn, Desmond, actor, aged 85 – *d.* 19 December 1999, *b.* 12 September 1914

Mackenzie-Stuart, Baron, President European Court of Justice 1984–8, aged 75 – *d.* 1 April 2000, *b.* 18 November 1924

MacLehose of Beoch, Baron (Murray MacLehose), KT, GBE, KCMG, KCVO, Governor of Hong Kong 1971–82, aged 82 – *d.* 27 May 2000, *b.* 16 October 1917

Macleod of Borve, Baroness, aged 84 – *d.* 17 November 1999, *b.* 19 February 1915

Manwaring, Thomas, GC, miner, awarded Edward Medal (later George Cross) in 1949 for rescuing colleagues from a flooded pit, aged 83 – *d.* 7 March 2000, *b.* 11 December 1916

Marsh, Joan, actress, aged 87 – *d.* 10 August 2000, *b.* 10 July 1913

Marshall, Malcolm, West Indies cricketer, aged 41 – *d.* 4 November 1999, *b.* 18 April 1958

Martin, Prof. Sir Leslie, RA, architect, aged 91 – *d.* 28 July 2000, *b.* 17 August 1908

Matthau, Walter, actor, aged 79 – *d.* 1 July 2000, *b.* 1 October 1920

Matthew, Colin, D. Phil., FBA, Historian, Editor of the New Dictionary of National Biography, aged 58 – *d.* 29 October 1999, *b.* 15 January 1941

Matthews, Sir Stanley, CBE, footballer, aged 85 – *d.* 23 February 2000, *b.* 1 February 1915

McCue, Bill, opera singer, actor and entertainer, aged 65 – *d.* 10 September 1999, *b.* 17 August 1934

Miralles, Enric, Catalan architect, aged 45 – *d.* 3 July 2000, *b.* 12 February 2000

Mitchell, Dame Roma, AC, DBE, CVO, Australian lawyer and judge; Governor of South Australia 1991–6, aged 86 – d. 5 March 2000, b. 2 October 1913

Montague of Oxford, Baron, CBE, Chairman, Yale and Valor plc 1965–91, Montague Multinational Ltd 1991–99, aged 67 – d. 5 November 1999, b. 10 March 1932

Moondog (Louis T. Hardin), American street entertainer, poet, and composer, aged 83 – d. 8 September 1999, b. 26 May 1916

Morgan, John, author, aged 41 – d. 10 July 2000, b. 28 May 1959

Morita, Akio, Chief Executive, Sony Corporation 1976–94, aged 78 – d. 3 October 1999, b. 26 January 1921

Mortimer, Penelope, author, aged 81 – d. 19 October 1999, b. 19 September 1918

Mostyn, 5th Lord, MC, aged 80 – d. 5 June 2000, b. 17 April 1920

Mueller, Dame Anne, DCB, Second Permanent Secretary, Cabinet Office and Treasury 1984–90, aged 69 – d. 8 July 2000, b. 15 October 1930

Nagako, Empress, The Dowager Empress of Japan, aged 97 – d. 18 June 2000, b. 6 March 1903

Nebiolo, Primo, President, International Amateur Athletic Federation 1981–99, aged 76 – d. 7 November 1999, b. 14 July 1923

Nyerere, Julius, President of Tanzania 1964–85, aged 77 – d. 14 October 1999, b. 13 April 1922

O'Brian, Patrick, CBE, author, aged 85 – d. 2 January 2000, b. 12 December 1914

Obuchi, Keizo, Prime Minister of Japan 1998–2000, aged 62 – d. 14 May 2000, b. 25 June 1937

O'Halloran, Michael, MP for Islington North 1969–83 (Labour 1969–81, SDP 1981–2, Independent Labour 1983), aged 66 – d. 29 November 1999, b. 20 August 1933

Oliphant, Sir Mark, KBE, FRS, physicist, aged 98 – d. 14 July 2000, b. 8 October 1901

Oppenheimer, Harry, Chairman, Anglo-American Corporation 1957–82; De Beers Consolidated Mines 1957–84, aged 91 – d. 19 August 2000, b. 28 October 1908

Oram, Baron, Labour and Co-operative MP for East Ham South 1955–74, Parliamentary Secretary, Ministry of Overseas Development 1964–9, Lord in Waiting 1976–8, aged 86 – d. 4 September 1999, b. 13 August 1913

Patterson, Sidney, world track cycling champion 1949, 1950, 1952, 1953, aged 72 – d. 29 November 1999, b. 14 August 1927

Pearson, Daphne, GC, WAAF Officer, aged 89 – d. 25 July 2000, b. 25 May 1911

Pham Van Dong, Prime Minister of North Vietnam 1955–76, of Vietnam 1976–86, aged 49 – d. 29 April 2000, b. 1 March 1906

Pindling, Sir Lynden, PC, KCMG, first Prime Minister of the Commonwealth of the Bahamas, aged 70 – d. 26 August 2000, b. 22 March 1930

Platt, Sir Peter, BT., AM, musicologist, aged 76 – d. 3 August 2000, b. 6 July 1924

Powell, Anthony, CH, CBE, author, aged 94 – d. 28 March 2000, b. 21 December 1905

Reilly, Patrick, GCMG, OBE, British Ambassador, Moscow 1957–60, Paris 1965–8, aged 90 – d. 6 October 1999, b. 17 March 1909

Riabouchinska, Tatiana, ballerina, aged 84 – d. 25 August 2000, b. 25 May 1916

Richard, Maurice 'Rocket', Canadian ice hockey player, aged 78 – d. 27 May 2000, b. 4 August 1921

Roman, Ruth, actress, aged 75 – d. 9 September 1999, b. 23 December 1923

Runcie, The Rt. Revd Lord Robert, Archbishop of Canterbury 1980–91, aged 78 – d. 11 July 2000, b. 2 October 1921

Salam, Saeb, Prime Minister of Lebanon 1943–56, 1960–1, 1970–3, aged 95 – d. 20 January 2000, b. 17 January 1905

Sarkisyan, Vazgen, Prime Minister of Armenia June–October 1999, aged 40 – d. (assassinated) 27 October 1999, b. 1959

Scarsdale, Viscount, landowner, aged 76 – d. 2 August 2000, b. 28 July 1924

Schulz, Charles M., cartoonist, aged 77 – d. 12 February 2000, b. 26 November 1922

Schumacher, Emil, German abstract expressionist artist, aged 87 – d. 4 October 1999, b. 29 August 1912

Scott, George C., American actor, aged 71 – d. 22 September 1999, b. 18 October 1927

Segal, George, American sculptor, aged 75 – d. 11 June 2000, b. 26 November 1924

Sharma, Shankar Dayal, Ph.D., President of India 1992–7, aged 81 – d. 26 December 1999, b. 19 August 1918

Shaw, Sir Giles, Conservative MP for Pudsey 1974–97, aged 68 – d. 12 April 2000, b. 16 November 1931

Simon, William, US Treasury Secretary 1974–7, banker, aged 72 – d. 3 June 2000, b. 27 November 1927

Snagge, Dame Nancy, DBE, Director of the WRAF 1950–6, aged 93 – d. 9 October 1999, b. 2 May 1906

Snow, Hank, American singer, aged 85 – d. 20 December 1999, b. 9 May 1914

Southern, Sir Robert, CBE, General Secretary, Co-operative Union 1948–72, aged 92 – d. September 1999, b. 17 March 1907

Southgate, Very Revd John, Dean of York 1984–94, aged 73 – d. 18 December 1999, b. 2 September 1926

Stafford-Clark, David, MD, FRCP, FRCpsych., psychiatrist, aged 83 – d. 9 September 1999, b. 17 March 1916

Statham, Brian, CBE, cricketer, aged 69 – d. 11 June 2000, b. 17 June 1930

Stephens, Dame Anne, DBE, Director of the Royal Women's Air Force 1960–63, aged 87 – d. 26 July 2000, b. 4 November 1912

Stewart, Payne, American golfer, aged 42 – d. (in an aeroplane crash), 25 October 1999, b. 30 January 1957

Stronach, George, GC, merchant navy World War II hero, aged 87 – d. 12 December 1999, b. 14 April 1912

Stuart, Francis, Irish writer, aged 97 – d. 2 February 2000, b. 29 April 1902

Stuart of Findhorn, Viscount, aged 75 – d. 24 November 1999, b. 20 June 1924

Stubblefield, Sir James, D.SC., FRS, Director, Geological Survey of Great Britain and Museum of Practical Geology 1960–6, aged 98 – d. 23 October 1999, b. 6 September 1901

Swanton, E. W., CBE, cricket writer, aged 91 – d. 22 January 2000, b. 11 February 1907

Takeshita, Noboru, Prime Minister of Japan 1987–89, aged 76 – d. 19 June 2000, b. 26 February 1924

Taylor, Frank, CBE, QPM, Chief Constable of Durham 1988–97, aged 66 – d. 3 October 1999, b. 27 March 1933

Tinn, James, Labour MP for Cleveland 1964–74, Redcar 1974–87, aged 77 – d. 18 November 1999, b. 23 August 1922

Tomislav of Yugoslavia, Prince, aged 72 – d. 12 July 2000, b. 19 January 1928

Tomlinson, David, actor, aged 83 – d. 24 June 2000, b. 7 May 1917

Tranter, Nigel, OBE, author, aged 90 – d. 9 January 2000, b. 23 November 1909

Trimble, Joan, pianist and composer, aged 85 – d. 6 August 2000, b. 18 June 2000

Tudjman, Franjo, President of Croatia 1990–9, aged 77 – d. 10 December 1999, b. 14 May 1922

Vadim, Roger, French film director, aged 72 – d. 11 February 2000, b. 26 January 1928

Valiani, Leo, Italian politician and author, aged 90 – d. 18 September 1999, b. 9 February 1909

van Straubenzee, William, MBE, Conservative MP for Wokingham 1959–87, aged 75 – d. 2 November 1999, b. 27 January 1924

Vaughan, Frankie, singer and entertainer, aged 71 – d. 17 September 1999, b. 3 February 1928

Waddilove, Lewis, CBE, Director of the Joseph Rowntree
Memorial Trust 1946–79, aged 85 – *d.* 21 August 2000,
b. 5 September 1914

Walker, Colin John Shedlock, OBE, Chairman of the
National Blood Authority 1993–8, aged 64 – *d.*
1 September 1999, *b.* 7 October 1934

Walker, Jack, businessman and owner of Blackburn Rovers
football club, aged 71 – *d.* 18 August 2000, *b.* 18 May 1929

West, Morris, AO, author, aged 83 – *d.* 9 October 1999,
b. 26 April 1916

Westwood, Rt Revd William, Bishop of Peterborough
1984–95, aged 73 – *d.* 15 September 1999, *b.* 28 December
1925

Wharton, Baroness (Myrtle), Vice-president of the RSPCA,
aged 66 – *d.* 15 May 2000, *b.* 20 February 1934

White, Baroness, Labour MP for East Flint 1950–70; Colonial
Office Minister 1964–6; Foreign Office Minister 1966–7;
Welsh Office Minister 1967–70; Deputy Speaker, House of
Lords 1979–89, aged 90 – *d.* 23 December 1999, *b.* 7
November 1909

Wilton, 7th Earl of, aged 78 – *d.* 1 October 1999, *b.* 29 May
1921

Wintour, Charles, CBE, Editor of London Evening
Standard 1959–76 and 1978–80, aged 82 – *d.* 4
November 1999, *b.* 18 May 1917

Young, Loretta, actress, aged 87 – *d.* 11 August 2000,
b. 6 January 1913

Zavaroni, Lena, singer, aged 35 – *d.* 2 February 2000,
b. 9 August 1965

Zoubi, Mahmoud al-, former Prime Minister of Syria,
aged 62 – *d.* (committed suicide) 21 May 2000, *b.* 1938

Archaeology

SEAHENGE

One of the more remarkable discoveries, or rather rediscoveries, was described by Mark Brennand and Maisie Taylor in *Current Archaeology* (March 2000); it was a circular wooden structure of posts surrounding what was shown to be an inverted tree stump of considerable antiquity suggested by the discovery of a bronze axe immediately adjacent. The site lying in an inter-tidal area on the sands at Holme-next-the-Sea in Norfolk inevitably became known as Seahenge. With a protective layer of peat rapidly eroding, the site was deteriorating and, regularly covered by the tide, was difficult to excavate, which was the preferred method of treatment after other options had been rejected. A summary of the site is given as follows: In the spring of 2050 BC a mature oak tree was blown over, perhaps during a great storm.

At some point during the following year the upper part of the tree was chopped away from the bole with a bronze axe, and tow holes were expertly cut in the lower part of the trunk. In the same season of the following year, 2049 BC, the great bole was harnessed with rope manufactured from interwoven strands of honeysuckle and a family or small community dragged it across the landscape to a flat and wet marsh. It was accompanied by 55 whole or split large oak branches and trunks, which perhaps acted as skids or rollers to aid the dragging of the bole. A pit was excavated and the bole was inverted into the hole, with the roots pointing towards the sky. A trench was excavated around the bole and the large timber posts were placed within the trench to form a solid palisade. Except for the occasional crack between the timbers, there was no way to see into the centre. The only point where access was possible was through a forked post, which had been blocked, perhaps as a final gesture when the original ceremonies were finished. The use of honeysuckle as a rope is, so far as is known, the first time this plant had been used as rope in prehistory. No doubt post-excavation will reveal much more important information possibly even the purpose of the structure which probably stood in a freshwater backswamp naturally protected from the then high tide limit.

If the archaeological challenges were severe, they were matched by environmental and indeed philosophical considerations. The site is one of Special Scientific Interest supporting a large population of a bird known as a knott and a number of interest groups accused English Heritage and the archaeologists in general of arrogance in excavating a site which had a mystical significance for Druids and others of related persuasions. Even the felling of mature timber by Channel 4's *Time Team* programme to construct a replica caused controversy. It is reported that a Forum has been established by Norfolk Museum Service to decide upon the future of the excavated timbers, but the fact that a range of special interest groups need to be consulted demonstrates the extent today to which alternative religious concepts claim parity of esteem with scientific archaeology.

A NEOLITHIC LONGHOUSE

A new, and highly important, source of archaeological evidence is being revealed by excavations along the line of the Channel Tunnel Rail Link which runs for some 50 miles through the County of Kent. Many of the more significant discoveries to date are summarised in *Current Archaeology* (May 2000) and it is noted that the biggest surprise was perhaps the best example of a Neolithic longhouse yet found in this country, discovered at White Horse Stone: are these the Neolithic settlers? In the report on the work undertaken by the Oxford Archaeological Unit it is observed that for many years, archaeologists have been looking for traces of Neolithic longhouses in Southern England, similar to those so well-known in Northern and Central Europe. Now in Kent a longhouse of impressive continental type has been discovered at White Horse Stone, at the foot of the chalk escarpment of the North Downs, near Maidstone, close to the Pilgrim's Way.

The area is an important one for Neolithic studies because it lies on the edge of the eastern group of Medway megaliths. These Medway megaliths are two small groups of megalithic tombs on either side of the River Medway, which are virtually the only visible Neolithic monuments in Kent and indeed in south east England. The best known is Kits Coty House, and the new site lies only a kilometre away, at the foot of the hill slope. The site discovered under a substantial covering of hillwash revealed a continental type of longhouse of post-hole construction and very large size. There was probably an entrance with a porch leading into the centre of the house and there were also a number of pits and hearths. Three post holes produced small sherds of plain bowls of early Neolithic type. Using continental parallels, it is likely that these longhouses should be mainly dated to the sixth and fifth Millennia BC thereafter on the Continent, as in Britain, such longhouses are extremely rare. A few rectangular longhouses are known in England: a similar one was discovered at Lismore Fields in Derbyshire, and a very close parallel has recently been excavated at Yarnton in Oxfordshire.

THE ZENECA COIN HOARD

A hoard of 58 Iron Age gold coins discovered on land belonging to Zeneca Agrochemicals was declared to be Treasure under the Treasure Act and acquired by Reading Museum Service. The coins are described in some detail by Jill Greenaway in *Minerva* (March–April 2000) and it is noted that the hoard contains only two types of Iron Age coins – the Gallo-Belgic E class four and the British Q. Both were current in the middle of the first century BC and would have been in use at the time of Julius Caesar's two invasions of Britain in 55 BC and 54 BC. The hoard must have been deposited about the middle of the first century BC. It is the first hoard of this date discovered in Berkshire, although individual coins have been found before and a number of this type were present in the Waltham St. Lawrence hoard. The hoard could be the symbolic wealth of an important individual. However, in view of the political situation at the time of its accumulation, it could have a greater significance. In 54 BC Julius Caesar invaded Britain for the second time. He was opposed by a temporary confederacy of British tribes led by Cassivellaunus. As part of the terms of the peace at the end of this campaign, hostages were given by the tribes and an annual levy of tribute money imposed. It is tempting to regard the Zeneca hoard as an accumulation of gold intended to form part of a tribute payment. The question as to why the hoard was buried is more difficult and the author asks in her discussion: "Could this hoard have been left as an offering to please or appease a deity at a sacred place?"

A MINERVA FIGURINE

New evidence relating to the religious faiths which were followed in Roman London are described by Jenny Hall and Bruce Watson in *Minerva* (March–April 2000). As a consequence of excavations for foundations of the new Merrill Lynch Regional Headquarters in King Edward Street, the Museum of London Archaeology Service investigated the basal portion of a Roman well, which had been lined with a wine barrel made of silver fir tree wood. The contents of the well included a headless, pipe-clay figurine of the goddess Minerva. This is the first such figurine to be found in the City. Such pipeclay figurines of the deities were mould-made and mass produced in France and the Rhineland, especially in the Allier region, and imported into London in quite large numbers during the late first and early second centuries AD. The most common type of clay figurine found is Venus – the goddess of love, for which over 53 examples have been found. It is suggested that the figure could have been bought for use in a temple during the annual Minerva Festival or for domestic worship, although many such figures were used as charms and cult objects.

The context of the discovery of the figure from the back-fill of the well included a bronze saucepan or bowl as well as a vast amount of pottery, mostly flagons (AD 70–120), produced in the Verulamium region (St Albans, Hertfordshire). Because of the quantity of flagons it is suggested that the well was abandoned and infilled by the mass disposal of the contents of a workshop or tavern during the early second century. The fact that the figurine is headless is of considerable interest although the reason remains a matter of conjecture with the authors reflecting that, "The removal of the figurine's head may have been a ritualistic act, carried out when the well was no longer needed. The act of breaking the figurine could have been done to both liberate the spirit of the figurine and to disperse any residue of evil that the water deities of the well may have invoked when it was abandoned. Almost all the Roman clay figurines found in London are already broken, often headless, and therefore their breaking and discarding may be interpreted as a deliberate act."

WANBOROUGH TEMPLE

Wanborough near Guildford in Surrey is already well known as the site of a Romano-Celtic temple of double square plan and also as the location of an Iron Age coin hoard of some 10,000–20,000 coins which was looted

and dispersed in a quite reprehensible manner. As David Williams explains in *Current Archaeology* (March 2000) another temple has been excavated by the Surrey Archaeological Society; this was also shown to be Roman in date but circular in form. It is noted that circular temples of this date are rare in Britain; the more substantial temple on Hayling Island near Portsmouth is the best known but the undated polygonal temple in Chanctonbury Ring may be a better parallel; both had entrance porticos on the east. This latest excavation has enabled suggestions to be made as to the sequence of occupation on what was clearly a complex religious site. The newly discovered circular temple which appears to have had a relatively short life, there was no demolition debris and it can be suggested that the collapsing building was carefully dismantled and the material used in the building of the adjacent square temple, its successor in about 150–60. If this is correct, then the circular temple had a short life of perhaps 60 years. In an earlier excavation of the square temple archaeologists had revealed a foundation deposit under the temple, where the head-dresses and regalia of the temple priests had been buried: five chain head-dresses were recovered, three of which were of unique form with circular wheel-like finials suggesting that the god may have been a Celtic form of Jupiter, the wheel god. Also 20 bronze tubes, which were interpreted as handles for sceptres.

THE SHAPWICK HOARD

A hoard of over 9,000 Roman silver coins has been conserved and processed at the British Museum and is described by Richard Abdy in *Minerva* (May–June 2000): "by far the biggest silver hoard of the earlier empire to be found in Britain" was located on a farm at Shapwick in Somerset by a metal detectorist at his first attempt. Although archaeologists were not present at the recovery, it is reported that the Somerset archaeologists were able to establish that the coins had come from a round-bottomed pit and therefore had presumably been contained within some sort of bag, no trace of which now remained. What was especially exciting was that the place where the coins were discovered is clearly in the corner of a small room. The act of hoarding wealth is of necessity a secret affair, buried we must assume at some deliberately hidden location away from prying eyes. In this case, however, the owner must have had some connection with this building. A geophysical survey was carried out by English Heritage, and the results were simply astonishing. They revealed the small room to be deep within a complex of buildings forming a giant courtyard villa whose robbed walls had lurked unseen beneath the soil since remote antiquity. As to the coins themselves, Abdy reports that "The latest coins of the Shapwick-hoard date to AD 224, early in the reign of Severus Alexander (AD 222–235), the last member of the Severan dynasty, and it is clear from analysis that it shows all the characteristics of a sample of the coin population circulating around that date. In other words, Shapwick is a prime example of a late Severan denarius hoard of which a number of examples are known, such as the 'East of England' hoard (otherwise known as the Colchester hoard) which with *c.* 3000 coins had been the largest of its type known from Britain since its discovery during the 1890s." Abdy asks: "What of the original owner of all this wealth? That a major treasure such as this should be found in the context of an important villa site is unparalleled in Romano-British archaeology. At *c.* 9,200 denarii the Shapwick treasure must surely have belonged to either the one-time owner or to a very senior manager of the estate, for it represents more than ten years' pay for an ordinary legionary soldier of the time."

ROMANS IN GREENWICH

Channel 4's *Time Team* programme continues to promote archaeology to a wide audience. One of the programmes related to a joint project by the Museum of London, University of London's Birkbeck College and Channel 4's *Time Team* involving the excavation of the Roman remains in Greenwich Park in south-east London, a site which had been investigated in 1902 and 1978. Hedley Swain and Harvey Sheldon in *Minerva* (May–June 2000) write that this "appears to have been an important Romano-British site occupied between the first and fourth centuries AD which investigation has shown has the potential to answer major research questions about Roman Greenwich, Roman London and, indeed, Roman Britain". The excavation uncovered remains of what we can now almost certainly call a small Roman temple and, significantly, evidence for a complex of out-buildings. Roman Watling Street from Canterbury to London is aligned on the temple site but deviates close to it on its approach to the Thames Valley; indeed, the temple marks the last piece of high ground before the road enters the valley. We now know that the temple sat on a small mound which has been much disturbed in recent centuries, including probably re-modelling as part of the early landscaping of the park. Amongst the finds from the excavations were two of the utmost significance: a small fragment of a stone inscription and a piece of roof tile stamped PPBRL (Provincial Procurator of Britain, London) was found in a post-hole. This is the stamp of the Imperial Procurator, e.g. the emperor's personal financial representative in Britain. This is very significant. It is the first of these stamps found outside the Roman city in a stratified Roman context and suggests that the Greenwich temple was built by Imperial order.

CUXTON CEMETERY

Excavations by the Museum of London Archaeology Service prompted by the need to investigate the line of the Channel Tunnel Rail Link in Kent revealed an Anglo-Saxon Cemetery overlooking the River Medway across from Rochester. In *Current Archaeology* (May 2000) it is reported that "Thirty-six inhumations were excavated from what may have formed the core of a small family cemetery. This was a late cemetery of the sixth and seventh centuries, possibly the last generation before the advent of Christianity. Eleven of the graves had been under small mounds marked by penannular ditches; most of them had a central post-hole in the entrance, presumably originally a grave marker, perhaps with the name or sign of the person buried. Some of the grave cuts had internal ledges, perhaps to hold a lid to the burial, while one appeared to have had a canopy above it, for there were a number of post holes in the side of the grave cut. The finds show that it was a middle ranking cemetery; there were no swords but there were spearmen with their shield bosses, while the richest women had keys, rings and the objects known as chatelaines. There were also jewellery and glass bead neck-

laces, the more mundane knives, buckles and shears, as well as coins, pots and two purses." There were two pottery vessels buried within graves and there is some indication that Cuxton may be a transitional cemetery with both pagan and Early Christian elements: the graves are mostly east-west and several graves contained pottery flagons which are sometimes held to be used in the transitional phase just before Christianity.

PRINCELY BURIALS

Excavations by the Canterbury Archaeological Trust and Wessex Archaeology on the line of the Channel Tunnel Rail Link at Saltwood in south-eastern Kent revealed the re-use of three Bronze Age barrows in the Anglo-Saxon period. It is reported in *Current Archaeology* (May 2000) that "The richest cemetery was that surrounding the barrow at the western end, which attracted nearly 100 Anglo-Saxon burials in all, two of which contained Coptic bowls of the type well-known in eastern Kent as marking the grave of princes. These two princely graves were probably the earliest graves on the site." Amongst other grave goods described were a sword and two shields. Next a second even more magnificent burial was made just outside the barrow to the south. Here a new barrow was constructed, surrounded by a penannular ditch. At the centre was a chamber, two metres by four metres, with a coffin inside it. In one corner of the chamber was a large wooden bucket, twice the size of the average Saxon bucket, bound with iron hoops. A shield lay up against it. In the centre of the chamber was the coffin with the body inside it with a sword and covered by a second shield. There was also a very large throwing spear of a type known as an angon – nearly a metre long, with barbs near the tip. It is continental in form – traditionally called Merovingian. This lay just outside the coffin together with the Coptic bowl. The third burial between the other two had a spectacular wooden coffin in a hollowed out tree trunk which contained a sword as well as a shield.

Nearly 100 other graves surrounded these three very rich examples and the former produced some four swords, eight shields, and 18 spears, although there was only one brooch. There were some women in this cemetery, as indicated not least by a group of keys because in Anglo-Saxon society it was the women who kept the keys. Nevertheless the overall impression is that of a society of warriors, ostentatiously buried with their swords and their shields. There was yet another cemetery with at least ten burials provisionally dated to the sixth century AD. Two at least of the graves can be counted as princely: one grave produced a sword and an iron shield boss, while an adjacent grave contained a bronze buckle with gilt buckle plates, amber and glass beads, and three elaborate brooches, two of them being a pair of white metal square-headed brooches, while the third was a silver disc brooch with red garnet inlays. A fine tapering glass drinking vessel was retrieved from the subsidiary group of graves. There was a further cemetery consisting of some 18 graves. It is noted that all these graves were late, dating from the sixth through into the seventh centuries, the latest date for Anglo-Saxon pagan cemeteries.

WIGMORE CASTLE

The expenditure of £1m at Wigmore Castle over a three-year project is explained by Mark Palmer in *Heritage Today*

(December 1999) to mark the re-opening of this important 13th-century castle to the public. It is explained that "The original Wigmore Castle was built by William FitzOsbern, Earl of Hereford, one of William the Conqueror's captains at the Battle of Hastings. It was one of a series of castles designed by the Normans to keep out the Welsh. Nothing is known about the first Wigmore Castle and it wasn't long before it passed into the hands of the Mortimer family. It was when it came under the ownership of Roger Mortimer in 1304 that the castle was built very much in the form that we see today". Mortimer became one of the most powerful men in England with Queen Isabella, wife of the homosexual King Edward II, as his mistress and it was Mortimer who had the King murdered by the application of a red-hot poker at Berkeley Castle. King Edward III had him executed and Queen Isabella sent to a convent. After this colourful period, the castle declined in significance and was sold by Elizabeth I in 1601, suffered considerable damage in the Civil War and decayed naturally thereafter. Given centuries of dereliction when English Heritage acquired the site in 1995 the problem was how to treat Wigmore Castle and of the various options, a novel solution was adopted. Instead of partially or fully excavating the site and laying out the result amongst neat lawns and gravel, Wigmore Castle has been consolidated as found. At the end of the project and the expenditure of a substantial sum of money, it is not clear that any work has been undertaken at all, or rather it may be clear now, but as repairs to the stonework whether and as vegetation grows back it will be less obvious in time. The intention was to make the existing structure safe for visitors, while at the same time finishing with a site that was clearly a ruin possessing a wild and unkempt look. The intense isolation of the site, some ten miles north-west of Leominster near the border with Wales, was an important factor and the desirability of preserving, and by judicious management enhancing, the flora and fauna was taken into account during the consolidation project. If the treatment of this important ancient monument was unusual then so is the way in which the matter of visitor facilities has been treated in that there will be no permanent staff, the site is open without an admission charge, and there are no parking or toilet facilities. As Palmer reports: "Access to the castle is via the tiny village of Wigmore. There is no parking at the castle itself, which means that visitors have to walk across the same field that noblemen and peasants alike used right up until just before the Civil War. It's a pretty walk up a narrow street past the church, that becomes cobbled as it approaches a grassy bank leading to the field outside the castle's perimeter. Fewer than 400 people live in the village of Wigmore and the local shop and pubs have struggled to survive, but it is hoped that the 2,500–4,500 who are expected to visit the castle each year will spark a revival."

BRITISH MUSEUM EXCAVATIONS

The relocation of the British Library away from Bloomsbury has enabled a massive redevelopment project to be undertaken at the British Museum which should be completed at the end of 2000. While there is rightly much public interest in this major scheme which has attracted substantial financial support from the Heritage Lottery Fund, what is much less well known is that archaeological excavations have been undertaken as the work progresses and these have been described by Tony Spence of the

British Museum in *Minerva* (September–October 1999 and January–February 2000). While much of the archaeological investigation has related to the relationship of the first Museum building, Montagu House, purchased in 1754 and demolished in the 1840s, to the present British Museum building and while the disturbance to the site has destroyed much of the stratigraphy, nevertheless significant discoveries have been made especially at the very lowest levels. Spence reports that: "As excavation for the new Great Court facilities continued attention turned to the substantial gravel deposits lying across the site. These approach four metres deep in places and belong to the Lynch Hill/Corbets Tey terrace sequence dating to c. 300,000 years ago. They represent material brought down by an earlier, unconfined River Thames, and consist largely of rounded flints with a varying sand component. Fortunately slight evidence of early human activity has been found in the form of a hand axe, a roughout and half a dozen flint flakes from the manufacture of other hand axes. These had been carried to their recovered location by the river, and were not associated with any fauna."

ANTI-AIRCRAFT GUNSITES

Contrary to a commonly held view archaeology is not confined to any particular period in the distant past; indeed it is relevant to all periods for which material evidence survives and all that happens is that the limits are moved. For example, there has been much interest in the archaeology of the two World Wars in the 20th-century, both at home and overseas. This is important because it is easier for many people to accept the fighting during the Civil War than it is for a younger generation to accept that major population centres of Britain were bombed in World War Two. It is very much to the credit of English Heritage that its Monuments Protection Programme (MPP) has since 1994 been reviewing 20th-century defences from airfields to air raid shelters, from Cold War structures to anti-aircraft gunsites. This project has multiple aims: to develop an understanding of the subject, to present the results to a wide audience, and to ensure that some sites are preserved for the benefit of future generations. A summary of the work done to date was given by Mike Anderton and John Schofield in the *English Heritage Conservation Bulletin* (December 1999). This has included searching the archives, especially at the Public Record Office, commissioning an Aerial Survey with the aim of checking "for selected monument classes whether sites identified in the archives have survived, and to what extent, with a view to determining appropriate management action. This latter study has produced some interesting and useful results which will now lead to the first scheduling recommendations to arise from this systematic review." The authors describe the methodology adopted and this is important because "The results provide a rare insight into what the recently published Monuments at Risk Survey describes as 'wholesale monument loss', measured, almost uniquely, against knowledge of the original population of a monument class. We now have accurate records for what was actually built – the original whole population – and what now survives; we know the land-use history, and for a sample of sites we will soon have information on when sites were removed. Together this will enable us to measure decay to an unprecedented level of detail. As such, this study may have significance in helping us towards understanding change among monuments of earlier periods for which we never have evidence for the original population, and where measuring loss is more subjective". The authors give significant statistics for four categories of gunsite, namely Heavy Anti-Aircraft (HAA), Light Anti-Aircraft (LAA) and Operation *Diver* (these were constructed to resist attacks from German flying bombs and are limited to the south and east coasts of England) sites similarly divided. Having established the original distribution of these gunsites and their typology, and having subsequently established what survives and in what condition, we can now begin to plan their future management. There is some urgency about this, given their vulnerability to development schemes and their removal in the name of landscape enhancement.

Architecture

TATE MODERN
Bankside, London
Architect: Herzog and de Meuron

Few cultural events in recent years have had such an impact on the public consciousness as the high profile opening of the Tate Modern, whose blaze of publicity extended to a televised all-night party and celebrity interviews, and queues of eager visitors stretching back along of London's south bank.

Sir Giles Gilbert Scott's monumental and cavernous Bankside Power Station has been transformed into what is destined to be one of the world's top ranking galleries devoted to 20th century and contemporary art. The Tate Gallery's decision to select the largely disused building located in a hitherto neglected area of Southwark was a courageous step, but the superb setting on the riverside opposite St Paul's Cathedral provided raw material of unusual power and potential. Herzog and de Meuron were the winners of an international architectural competition in 1995, with an entry that was the least interventionist of the shortlisted schemes. Offering a conceptually simple conversion of the power station's massive spaces, it respected the character and integrity of the subtly detailed brick cladding, with its monumental central chimney anchoring the building to its site and responding to the dome of St Paul's high above the opposing riverbank, as well as exploiting the industrial nature and scale of the internal spaces and massive steel structure.

The new gallery has been formed from the combined turbine hall and boiler house spaces of the original power station. Future plans include the conversion of the switch house wing into additional gallery spaces, and new uses for the remarkable sequence of interlocking circular spaces hidden below ground that were once the oil storage tanks.

The most obvious intervention has been the addition of a two-storey penthouse structure at roof level over the wing of galleries created within the former boiler house. Outwardly this takes the form of a clean crisp 'light-box' running the whole length of the building, its tall, slender translucent panels acting as a cool and ordered foil to the massive brickwork facades and its horizontality as a counterpoint to the vertical thrust of the chimney. The lower of the two levels contains a Members' Room as well as mechanical plant rooms, while the upper level contains a café/restaurant and a room for meetings. The long, glazed corridor linking the two spaces along the north side has stunning views over the river towards St Paul's and the City, to which the gallery is linked by the new Millennium Bridge.

The Tate Modern's gallery spaces are constructed on five levels, with a completely new steel structure inserted into the boiler house volume. This space was almost entirely filled with a chaotic jumble of pipework and machinery and had to be completely gutted, back to the basic structure, before the new gallery wing could be started. The long line of massive steel columns between the boiler house and turbine hall have been retained and form the ordering discipline for what is effectively the only new elevation of the gallery, the internal façade facing the central circulation space of the turbine hall.

This new façade is essentially a blank wall at the upper gallery levels, punctuated only by further renditions of the 'light box' concept, which provide luminous projecting balcony enclosures opening up views into the awesome volume of the turbine hall from the public landings around the central bank of escalators, and providing extra illumination to the architecture of the central hall.

The colour scheme of the central hall is essentially grey and black, relieved by the tall strip windows at either end, the long glazed rooflight overhead and the luminous white faces of the projecting light-box balconies. The one exception to this palette is the fascia to the platform bridge which spans the turbine hall at its midway point and is a bright yellow. The central platform is the one remaining section of the original turbine hall floor, and is a dramatic viewing point.

The removal of the remaining parts of the turbine hall floor constitutes the other major architectural intervention, and is linked to the introduction of the long entry ramp which starts its descent a substantial distance away from the west façade and brings visitors down to basement level in the centre of the turbine hall, where the entrance to the galleries and the banks of escalators are located. This placing of the ramp links the central hall to the surrounding landscape.

The turbine hall remains an indisputably industrial space, the huge steel columns and gantry beams (the existing gantry cranes have been retained to assist with transporting heavy pieces of sculpture) and the exposed steel trusses supporting the roof, generate strong images of its past function.

The galleries themselves, by contrast, are substantially proportioned, often tall, austere rooms with simply detailed white walls and ceilings, and floors finished either in polished concrete or untreated sawn white oak boards providing a strong yet neutral background for the artworks. The suites of rooms are a generous 5 metres in height and in selected locations rise through two storeys. Where they touch the perimeter they too benefit from controlled natural lighting through the tall slot-like windows that characterise Giles Gilbert Scott's elevations. At level 5 situated above the top level of the external windows, the tall central galleries are provided with a band of clerestory glazing forming the bottom section of the 'light beam' structure around voids in the level 6 plan, while the outer galleries, set behind blank brick walls, are illuminated from above by glazed rooflight panels.

This strategy not only imbues the galleries with all the variable lighting conditions that daylight can bestow, backed up by artificial lighting organised into luminous flat panels set into the ceiling, but constantly relates the potentially clinical and introspective gallery environment to the outside world. The rooms are arranged in traditional suites, one to each side of the central concourses and banks of escalators, and are interlinked in a way that enables visitors to create their own routes through each of the suites.

Additional facilities include a bookshop and education centre at basement level, and at ground level a café, with an outdoor terrace created by cutting away sections of the external brick walls, the Starr Auditorium and a further smaller film/seminar room.

The total project cost for the building has reached £134 million, of which the construction works have accounted for £81 million. For this the Tate Gallery has acquired 34,000 m² of floor space, including 3,300 m² in the turbine hall, 3,000 m² of special exhibition space and 6,000 m² for works from the Tate's Permanent Collection, arranged in four suites. Substantial funding from the Millennium Commission contributed some £50 million and a further £6.2 million was raised from the Art's Council's Lottery Fund. Formally opened by the Queen on 11 May 2000 and to the public a day later, the Tate Modern will be recognised as one of the great art museums of the world, a tribute to the confidence of the clients and a triumph for the Swiss architects who have at once conserved, reworked and transformed a redundant but noble piece of architecture into a masterful and thoroughly contemporary vehicle for the popularisation of modern art.

ART GALLERY
Walsall
Architect: Caruso St. John Architects

With the completion of this competition-winning design Walsall, lying to the north-west of Birmingham, has now acquired an outstanding and finely crafted art gallery that promises to elevate the area into the international artistic limelight, and amply repay the enlightened public patronage that has ensured its realisation.

Caruso St. John were selected as the winners of an open international competition in 1996. The building was required to provide a gallery setting in which to display the Garman Ryan Collection, as well as provide a new cultural and artistic focus for the townspeople. The Garman Ryan Collection had been assembled by Lady Kathleen Garman, widow of the sculptor Jacob Epstein and a local resident, in conjunction with the artist Sally Ryan, and had been generously presented by her to the town in 1973. It includes drawings, paintings and sculpture, featuring the works of many recognised masters of European art and represented a gift of exceptional importance and value.

The collection is housed within a two-storey suite of display spaces, entered at first floor level and arranged around a double height hall with its own internal circulation routes and stairs, almost a gallery within a gallery, and in many ways reflecting the type of spatial arrangements that such a collection would have enjoyed within the domestic scale of an English stately home. The rooms are of an appropriate scale and, unlike many contemporary gallery spaces, are planned with a series of windows connecting the galleries to the surrounding urban context.

In addition to the Garman Ryan suite there is a variety of additional gallery spaces, a bookshop and café, library, education facilities, and at roof level, a conference room with a substantial external terrace. The majority of these spaces are set out within a solid four square tower form, with circulation organised so as to generate a complex series of separate spatial experiences within the overall simplicity of the external form. At ground level the planning breaks free of the overriding discipline of the tower above, as sections are cut away and others projected beyond the square plan form. At the upper levels the restaurant and conference areas are set back, creating the generous terrace that provides a second 'ground level' and affords excellent views out over the town, while one corner of the tower extends upwards by a further two storeys to accommodate mechanical plant.

The external form is reinforced by the selection of cladding materials, primarily grey terracotta tiles (laid overlapping like shingles), and mill-finished stainless steel sheet. The stainless steel is organised into tall panels to form a plinth base at street level and is used also to clad the inner faces of the set back elevations of the terrace and plant tower. The remaining external faces of the building receive the rain screen cladding of large terracotta tiles,

that are set out with progressively diminishing course heights as they rise up the building. Its general aesthetic tone borrows heavily from industrial sources, yet is executed with finesse and great attention to detail.

A corresponding hardness of tone is evident internally, particularly in the ground floor entrance hall, where exposed concrete finishes predominate, relieved only by the restrained application of areas of vertical Douglas Fir boarding and stainless steel panels. The ceiling is heavily beamed, with closely ranged pre-cast concrete joists and trimming beams reproducing the visual character of a mediaeval oak-beamed floor, while exposed concrete walls bear the board marks of their shuttering forms, the narrow strips picked up by the applied timber boarding. The structural frame of the building is constructed from 300 mm thick in-situ concrete walls, and this contributes to a substantial wall thickness which emphasises the contradiction between the apparent solidity of the interiors and the relatively lightweight expression of the exterior.

Within the simple, almost cubic form, the architects have devised a meandering pattern of circulation, with changes in direction, and contrasts between short dog-leg stairs at lower levels and long single direction multi-flight stairs towards the top, linking the constituent parts in a carefully composed sequence of gallery spaces, that utilise both natural and artificial lighting sources. The punched windows to the Garman Ryan suite on the first and second floors contrast with the long slot of glazing provided for the temporary exhibition galleries on the third floor, which wraps around the corners of the tower form, visually separating the upper parts from the base, and apparently contradicting the heavy and massive forms of construction evident in the interior.

Completed in late 1999 at a cost of £18 million, a sum met by funding contributions from, among various sources, the Arts Council, the European Regional Development Fund and Walsall City Challenge, the gallery opened its doors to the public early in the New Year. The meticulously constructed elevations exert a calming and dignified presence at the termination of a branch of the local canal, where a new basin has been created surrounded by an artistically inspired groundscape of striped tarmac, designed by Richard Wentworth. Its restrained architectural language and austere palette of materials enable the building to fit in with the surrounding semi-industrial hinterland without resorting to pastiche or gratuitous gestures, and demonstrate the application of a considerable intellectual rigour in the creation of a finely crafted building designed to last for many generations.

LIBRARY AND MEDIA CENTRE
Peckham, London
Architect: Alsop and Störmer

This new public library and media centre forms a key element in the ongoing regeneration of the central area of Peckham in south-east London, establishing an important new urban square just a few yards from Peckham High Street. Its highly unconventional form is visually arresting and yet based on a logical approach to the placing of the building's constituent functional parts.

The brief put together by the client, the London Borough of Southwark, required a building of architectural merit, flexible and adaptable to changing future requirements, that would bring prestige to the borough and provide a 'welcome psychological boost'. Importance was attached to the need to relate to local needs and enable the local community to feel pride in and be comfortable with the architecture.

In response to the brief, the architect has designed a building that is in section in the form of an inverted L. The horizontal part of the L, a double height space containing the main lending library, is propped up some 12 metres above the ground, one side supported by a thin, five-storey block of entrance, circulation and office spaces, the other side by a series of variously angled columns. Beneath the extensive overhang of the library is created a new public outdoor space which can be used for open air events during the summer, and which offers a focal point for connections to a network of local pedestrian routes.

Entry to the library is made from this sheltered approach into the double height ground floor of the vertical wing. A lobby and foyer give access to a 'one-stop shop' for community advice and information and the main staircase and a pair of glazed lifts rise up against the glazed curtain walling of the exposed north elevation. Two floors of back-up offices and meeting rooms occupy the intermediate levels below the principal floor of the lending library, which is the only floor level to occupy the full extent of the site area. On entering the library from the circulation core, one is presented with a large double height naturally-lit space and the presence of three dominating gourd-like volumes propped off the main floor level on tripod legs. Clad in a patchwork of stapled plywood panels, these curvaceous organic forms accommodate specific ancillary functions and are accessed either by a bridge from the mezzanine level of the vertical block or by spiral staircase from the main library level. They house, in turn, a children's activity area, an Afro-Caribbean literature centre and a meeting room. Set in line along the length of the library, the two outer pods push through the volume and penetrate the roof plane, so their tops can be seen from some distance away. The central pod is open to the library volume as it is effectively sliced off half way up. Directly over the central pod is a large circular glazed clerestorey light surmounted by an orange-red rain-screen clad roof.

The two projecting pods have their own double-glazed skylights with automatic opening lights for ventilation as well as internal motorised shutters to control the level of daylighting to the inside. Artificial lighting is provided by means of specially commissioned fittings, made by artist Joanna Turner, from stainless steel woven braiding which combines the functions of light diffusion and acoustic absorption. The projecting external parts of the pods are clad in silver powder coated rain-screen cladding panels.

The elevational treatment features a range of materials and treatments. The east and west elevations, expressing the L-shape with simple clarity, and the linking south face of the library space, are clad in turquoise pre-patinated copper panels. The panels are punctuated by windows set flush into the plane of the façade, some rectangular, others forming trapezoidal shapes defined by the geometry of the angled joint lines.

The north elevation, rising to the full five-storey height, is an all-glazed façade featuring the extensive use of brightly coloured glass as well as clear. Areas of red, green and yellow glass are disposed in simple geometric patterns to generate a striking and artful design, punctuated by the sequences of top-hung opening windows at each storey. The sheltered glazed south elevation of the vertical block, as well as the extensive soffit under the projecting library volume, is over-clad with an external mesh woven from stainless steel rods and cables. This is supported on a stainless steel support framework to form a faceted surface which reflects sunlight and at night picks up the coloured flood-lighting suspended from the soffit.

A combination of concrete and steel forms of construction was utilised for the main structural elements.

The vertical block employs an in-situ reinforced concrete frame, which is exposed to view and finished with a light sandblasted texture and a light grey paint. Similarly, the exposed diagonal cross-bracing members are of circular section in-situ concrete. The projecting section of the library utilises deep steel trusses at 3 metre centres, spanning from the concrete frame of the vertical block on one side and supported at the leading edge on the seven circular angled columns. These are 323 mm diameter tubular steel columns filled with concrete, and their angled disposition provides additional bracing and stability to the overall structure. The construction of the pods in the topmost storey made use of prefabricated techniques and employs curved timber ribs clad with a double skin of triple-ply oriented strand board.

Construction of this building took approximately 20 months, with completion in October 1999, for a total cost of £4.5 million, and after a period for fitting out, was opened in March 2000. A radical departure from the traditional notions of public architecture, and the occasionally pompous and stuffy surroundings associated with traditional public libraries, this exciting addition to the Peckham neighbourhood demonstrates a keen awareness of the real needs and aspirations of its young, multicultural and forward-looking clientele.

LONDON UNDERGROUND
Jubilee Line extension – Westminster to Stratford
Various Architects

The long awaited extension to London Underground's Jubilee Line, connecting the West End with the East End via Southwark, Docklands, Canary Wharf and the Greenwich Peninsular, is the most important addition to the Underground Network since the completion of the Victoria Line in the 1960s. The £3.5 billion project has involved the construction of eleven new stations, some independent, others linked to existing underground and mainline stations, each one designed by a different architect under the overall co-ordinating influence of London Transport's Jubilee Line extension design co-ordinator, Roland Paoletti. Whereas during the great expansion of the network in the 1930s, Frank Pick and Charles Holden had imprinted a stamp of commonality over all the station buildings, producing a recognisable house style of lasting quality, here Paoletti's intention has been to realise a similar level of architectural distinction but with a greater potential for stylistic variety in the interpretation of a brief based on a set of common principles.

High amongst these principles was a desire to create a passenger-friendly environment, spacious, easily understandable, with high standards of public safety, and based firmly on the use of the latest technology, that would extend from the street level concourse right down to platform level. The complexity of the works involved with each individual station was such as to justify the spreading of the design workload amongst a selected group of architects, and it is all the more remarkable therefore that such a consistently high standard of design has been achieved throughout the new stations. The publicity surrounding the (relatively) last-minute opening of the line to serve the Millennium celebrations at the Dome on Greenwich Peninsular on New Year's Eve precluded much critical appraisal of the architecture itself, but the system has now been up and running for over six months and has been steadily closing the psychological gap that previously existed in people's minds between the rival centres of Canary Wharf and the City/West End.

Westminster, the first stop on the continuation of the line from Green Park, is one of the most impressive in spatial and dramatic terms. Designed by Mickael Hopkins and Partners, architects for the new parliamentary building, Portcullis House, whose basement footprint the new station occupies, this station links the Jubilee with the District and Circle Lines, which cut diagonally across the site and which were actually lowered marginally during the construction operations. The new station is designed integrally with the building above, which is quadrangular, around a large courtyard, and all the loads from the inner walls of the courtyard are channelled into six massive columns which rise through the multi-storey escalator hall below the ticket and entrance halls. Loads around the perimeter are taken by a very rigid concrete box designed to restrain the earth forces around the station and with careful attention paid to the adjacent and rather sensitive structure of Big Ben. It is this structure which defines the overwhelming impression of a vast, almost Piranesian, underground chamber, criss-crossed by banks of escalators partially enclosed in exaggeratedly panelled, ribbed and facetted grey casings and the carefully articulated struts and braces linking the freestanding columns. The side walls are themselves panelled with a grid of deep concrete beams and columns projecting beyond the rough concrete faces of the diaphragm walls, that give one the impression of entering some unearthly catacomb. Grey predominates in the colours of the concrete and the cladding, with flashes of stainless steel, and is carried into the perforated steel cladding and frame sections of the platforms, where for the first time the tracks are separated by a glazed screen incorporating sliding doors to coincide with those of the trains.

Waterloo and London Bridge stations were both handled by the JLE in-house architects department, assisted at London Bridge by Weston Williamson. At Waterloo the new station had to be threaded into one of the most complex interchanges on the network and features the use of travelators linking to other lines. Work at both stations was heavily influenced by the massive undercrofts of the Victorian railway terminus structures. At London Bridge the brick vaults have been exposed and cleaned up, with lighting, telecommunications and safety systems co-ordinated into an overhead linear services gantry suspended from the vaults on angled steel rods. The aim at both stations has been to simplify the architecture and make the routing and way-finding largely self-evident. At London Bridge the separation of the services components from the spatial envelope assists in controlling visual clutter, enabling both the brick vaults and the new purpose designed cast-iron tunnel cladding system to read clearly as directional controllers of space.

MacCormac Jamieson and Pritchard, the designers of Southwark Station, were presented with the difficult task of creating clarity and simplicity out of a complicated set of circumstances. Located underneath the tracks of the main-line railway passing through Waterloo East, the platforms are connected to entrances directly from the mainline station as well as from the junction where The Cut meets Blackfriars Road. At the street level entrance the architects have created a direct reference to the distinctive forms of Charles Holden, with a double height circular ticket hall reached down flights of steps from the pavement. Four columns support a ring beam enclosing a shallow plaster dome punctuated at the centre by a glazed drum, the roof of which is supported by a fifth column rising into the void. A second and larger glazed drum illuminates the head of the escalator bank leading down to the lower concourse levels. The entrance from Waterloo East takes its design theme from the station's Victorian cast-iron work and encloses the ticket hall in a curvaceous outward leaning glass and metal framed superstructure.

The masterstroke has been to gather the east and west approaches into an intermediate concourse controlling access to the lower level concourse between the platforms. This is a subterranean space flooded with daylight from above. The three shafts rising from the lower concourse emerge through arches cut into a massive ashlar-like wall, made of polished grey concrete blocks laid in varying course heights, into a semi-circular space defined by a sloping curved 'cone wall' lined with triangular blue en-amelled glass panes held on stainless steel multiple patch fixings, designed by glass artist Alexandra Beleschenko.

Bermondsey, by Ian Ritchie Architects, is less showy in spatial terms, but has achieved a clear and honest synthesis of architecture and heavy engineering. The station sits within a concrete box whose diaphragm walls are braced by enormous horizontal open concrete trusses that allow light to filter down to the lower levels from the largely glazed station concourse above, approached from Jamaica Road. The glazed roof is supported on steel beams lined with perforated stainless steel casings that glint and sparkle, reflecting light into the depths below.

Canada Water, by JLE architects and Herron Associates, was the first to be designed and is marked by a large glazed drum which floods the ticket hall with daylight and allows light also to reach the lower levels. The station is intimately linked with a new surface level bus station, whose wing-like canopies are cut away on the diagonal to nestle up to but not quite touch the glazed drum. The station's spaces are unpretentious and robust but the routing through a complex layout has been cleverly organised and is immediately apparent from the glass sided bridge that leads into the main ticket hall.

Canary Wharf, by Foster & Partners, is perhaps the key station on the line, having the greatest passenger capacity and by far the most impressive structure. At 313 metres long, constructed within the drained West India Dock, it is as long as Canary Wharf tower is high, and has an epic scale to it. It sits beneath a landscaped park, within which are placed the entrances to the station, marked with curved steel and frameless glass canopies bulging out of the landscape like lenses. They offer weather protection to the entrances while admitting light deep into the lower levels of the station. From the platform level concourse 27 metres below ground, it is possible to read the whole station as one majestic cathedral-like volume, with seven soaring elliptical columns supporting an elegant wing-profiled roof vault articulated by sinuous curving ribs. The bases of the columns are clad in stainless steel and elliptical bearings absorbing differential movement between roof and columns act visually as capitals. Twenty banks of escalators carry passengers up and down from the entrances to the trains and ticketing facilities are ranged along the concourse sides to maximise the space for passenger movement.

North Greenwich, by Alsop & Lyall, serves the Millennium Dome, and is accessed from beneath the enormous wing-shaped roof, 160 metres wide, of the bus station. The 405 metre long concourse is an independent U-shaped structure suspended from the station's roof, and the platform areas are much enlivened by the lines of paired canted columns, clad in blue mosaic. It is the largest of the JLE stations and designed to accommodate 7,000 passengers per hour.

Canning Town, by John McAslan & Partners, connected five different transport networks. Here the Jubilee Line reaches ground level and is closely linked with the Docklands Light Railway which is elevated and runs along the same axis. This enables both railways to be accessed from a common concourse and ticket hall below ground level. These spaces are daylit by two rooflights, whose glass sheets are suspended from a spine beam with cast stainless steel outriggers and provide dramatic views up into the high level DLR structure, which is supported on two rows of Y-shaped precast concrete columns.

Van Heyningen and Haward's design for West Ham unusually features brickwork as a facing material, in response to the residential buildings nearby. Much use is also made of glass block to provide translucent walls, its modular character sitting well within the tight 6 m × 6 m structural and servicing grid, and it adds to the impact of the new buildings at night.

The line ends at Stratford, now East London's major transport interchange. Here Wilkinson Eyre's new surface level station functions as interchange and terminus for the Jubilee Line. A dramatic sweeping roof, curving up from the ground at one side and propped on a canted glazed façade at the other, with the structural members extended to form a projecting frieze, encloses the ticket hall and concourse functions. Extensive use of glazing in the end and side walls ensures excellent visibility.

The completion of these stations has demonstrated the value of inspired and determined client leadership in maintaining high architectural quality in the face of huge cost and programme difficulties, through one of the most extensive programmes of architectural patronage of recent years. Roland Paoletti has masterminded a refreshingly inventive and stimulating series of stations that will set a new standard for the quality of London's transport infrastructure for decades to come.

THE LOWRY ARTS CENTRE
Salford Quays, Manchester
Architect: Michael Wilford & Partners

L.S. Lowry, that renowned creator of an intensely personal, stylised and still potent vision of the industrialised urban landscape could be said to be the least likely of all artists to be so intimately associated with this shining, brash, chaotic and extrovert new building. However, while the Lowry Arts Centre has indeed taken the name of one of Salford's favourite sons, this complex and dramatic project is much more than just a gallery for showing off a collection of his works.

It is situated on a site of extreme prominence at the tip of the promontory known as Pier 8, where the longest of the Salford Quays joins the Manchester Ship Canal. The building's roughly triangular plan form, responding to the tapering site profile, contains two major performance spaces, the 1,730 seat Lyric Theatre and the smaller adaptable 466 seat Quays Theatre, with all the attendant back-of-stage facilities; two art galleries, one for touring exhibitions, the other providing a new home for the collection of some 340 of Lowry's works which has been transferred from the Salford City Art Gallery, conference facilities, bars and cafés, all linked by ample promenade areas and foyers.

The design displays an interesting mix of the formal and the chaotic in its development in plan, section and modelling. Viewed as a plan at almost every level it has a strongly axial layout, the central spine formed by the two performing arts auditoria, arranged with stage areas innermost, utilising a common central scenery and stage set store, and with the corresponding curved banks of seating reflected in the circular and faceted forms of the outer walls. The two series of gallery spaces, with cafés and restaurants, and the theatre dressing rooms interspersed at different levels are ranged out along the sides of the spine in a series of stepped or angled plans that create an overall arrowhead form, displaying a strong sense of symmetry. This is underlined by the two vertical tower forms framing

the main entrance and foyer at the base of the arrow-form, one circular, containing a shop, a small gallery space and at the top, a picture store/archive; the other hexagonal, containing another shop, a gallery entrance, a hospitality suite and a plant room.

The circular tower is drawn up to a much greater height and acts as a marker beacon for the whole composition. The shiny striated pattern of the steel panels entwining the cylindrical form is cut away at the top to reveal the underlying diamond pattern framework of the structure. Also framing the main entrance is a gigantic canopy structure, its huge curved soffit and segmented form suggesting a kind of elongated radio telescope, perched on stumpy splayed legs that turn out on close inspection to be less monumental, rather more transparent, being constructed of a perforated stainless steel mesh on tubular steel framing.

This wild exterior is clad almost entirely in stainless steel or glass. The stainless steel is broken down into rectangular panels, laid with overlapping and interlocking edges, sometimes arranged conventionally, elsewhere laid at sharp angles to the vertical to add extra impetus and energy to the bold geometric forms. In some sections the panels have been cut away in strips to reveal the metal-framed glass window wall passing behind, and to admit daylight into the interior. The combination of glass and stainless steel gives the building a sleek and reflective quality, which works well, reflecting the sunlight off the waters of the canal as well as providing the perfect foil for dramatic floodlighting at night. The absence, and use, of colour provides the other dramatic contrast between inside and outside, though in earlier stages of development of the design this had not always been the case.

One step inside the front door and the eyes are assaulted by a palette of the most vivid hues, as orange staircases hurtle in and out of sloping purple walls, and red ceilings compete with yellow walls and blue terrazzo floors. Both the theatre spaces are also vividly coloured, while the gallery spaces, understandably, revert largely to colourless mode.

The Lyric Theatre, the larger of the two, is a superb auditorium which attempts to recapture the glamour and sweeping excitement of traditional halls in a totally contemporary style. Designed to permit the staging of opera, dance, musicals, recitals and theatre, it is a comfortable and, for its size, surprisingly intimate space, finished in shades of purple, lilac and blue, its seating set out in three broadly curved tiers. A 25 metre high structural concrete wall surrounds the theatre space. Around the rear of the hall, fronting the entrance foyers, it leans outwards towards the top, expressing the rake of the seating, and where the volume breaks through the general roof line generates the dynamic sloping faceted façade visible across the water at the heart of the composition.

The Quays Theatre is designed to be highly adaptable and enables a much closer rapport between performers and audience. The space is horseshoe shaped, with the seating in three tiers, the upper two of which are suspended from the roof structure in order to ensure a column-free space. A number of different seating and staging arrangements can be set up to meet changing performance requirements.

Directly above the Quays Theatre, anchoring the apex of the triangular plan, is a circular rehearsal studio and function room. This takes the form of a glazed drum, surrounded by a roof terrace and surmounted by a shallow saucer-shaped roof, the classic device for marking a focal point in the building's mass and for turning the elevations round the sharp corner at the tip of the promontory.

The Lowry is clearly intended to be a generating force for new commercial, leisure and residential development in what is for the most part an inhospitable area, and its attempt to cater for a wide range of popular cultural activities has enabled the commissioning body, the Lowry Trust, to benefit from very substantial funding contributions of Lottery money from the Heritage, Arts and Millennium budgets. Over £60 million came from these sources. The building contract was completed in March 2000 and the centre was formally opened by the Minister for Culture, Chris Smith, the following month. The almost manic exuberance of this building is no doubt intended to leave an indelible impression in the minds of its visitors while the layout of the various parts of the centre, and their inter-visibility from the embracing promenade areas is aimed at fostering the chance discovery of other art forms of potential interest. While first signs are not encouraging, it is to be hoped that future development in the area will be of a quality that enables the somewhat hyperactive vigour of the Lowry to transcend its locational disadvantages and develop a reputation for quality and integrity with lasting appeal for the public.

Bequests to Charity

The following list represents some of the principal charitable bequests from wills publicly probated since the last edition. The exact values of residuary legacies cannot be assessed accurately, since prior bequests in the will and inheritance tax on personal bequests and lifetime gifts both have to be deducted from the net estate shown. All charitable gifts under wills continue to be free from any inheritance tax.

The largest estate of the year and also the one containing the largest charitable gift was that of Christina Batty, better known as Christina Foyle, head of the famous book shop, who, after a few small bequests, including £5,000 to the Book Sellers Provident Association, left the residue of her £59,029,581 estate for such charities or charitable purposes as her Trustees thought fit. Londoner Gwyneth Forrester also left the residue of her £21,664,629 estate in exactly the same manner, as did Alice Hodge, of Parkstone, Dorset, who left £785,048. Edna Linnell, of West Peckham, Kent, left the residue of her £1,940,229 estate to the Maharishi Foundation or other charitable objects as her Trustees thought fit, and Joyce Maylett, of Ickenham, Middx, left the residue of her £2,943,191 estate to the Charities Aid Foundation to be distributed among charities according to her known wishes. Ruth Smart, of Clavering, Essex, left the residue of her £4,887,384 estate for charitable purposes for the relief of the suffering of animals of any species, the maintenance of refuges, rescue homes, hospitals, sanctuaries and other facilities for unwanted animals and the treatment of sick or ill treated animals, all at the discretion of her Trustees.

Several estates in the list featured substantial gifts to charity through family trusts, the largest being the residue of the £15,028,978 estate of Roger Turner, of Upper Arley, Worcs, which he left to the R. D. Turner Charitable Trust. His will also included bequests of £250,000 to the National Trust, a further £200,000 to the National Trust for Scotland, and £50,000 to Kings College Chapel, Cambridge. Alison Hillman, of Birmingham, left the residue of her £3,159,125 estate to the Alison Hillman Charitable Trust. Mary Day, of Coddenham, Suffolk, left the residue of her £2,316,432 estate to the Day Foundation, which she and others had established in 1987. Sir Ronald Stewart, of Maulden, Beds, left the residue of his £977,253 estate to the Sir Malcolm Stewart Bart General Charitable Trust. Dorothy Klein, of Winchester, left the residue of her £986,280 estate equally between the RNID and the Carl Klein Trust. Finally, Lady Ellen Leech, of Morpeth, Northumberland, left the residue of her £646,484 estate to the William Leech Charity, desiring that substantial gifts be made to the Save the Children Fund and Christian Aid.

There were four other unusually large charitable estates all left by women, with Norfolk resident Sagle Bernstein leading the way with her £11,991,393 estate, which listed a large number of charitable bequests, including £500,000 to the RNLI, for the benefit of the Cromer Lifeboat and Lifeboat Station, and £250,000 to Addenbrookes Hospital, Cambridge, for the benefit of its patients, with the residue going to Cromer Hospital, for the improvement of its general facilities. Somerset resident Enid Jackson-Barstow left the residue of her £10,972,894 estate equally between Barnardo's, the League of Friends of Weston-super-Mare Hospitals and Weston Hospiscare. Diana Wray-Bliss, of Corsham, Wilts, left half the residue of her £9,405,483 estate to the National Trust and the other half equally between the Landmark Trust, Emmaus UK, Imperial Cancer Research Fund and the Carr Gomm Society while Brenda Knapp, of Esher, Surrey, left the residue of her £5,492,816 estate to the National Art Collections Fund. Among her prior bequests was £5,000 to Age Concern, "as a token of my appreciation for the Meals on Wheels service which they provided for me".

Among the less usual bequests in the list was the residue of the £3,000,329 estate of Joseph Vigoureux, of East Molesey, Surrey, which he left to the Society of St Pius X, and Sybil Edwards, of Guisborough, Cleveland, left £100,000 to the National Trust, and the residue of her £2,690,519 estate to the Christian Science Trust. Dr Robert Strain, of Badgeworth, near Cheltenham, left £100,000 to the Royal Ulster Constabulary Benevolent Fund, and £50,000 to the Ulster Unionist Party, and shared the residue of his £2,311,914 estate between 12 charities in Northern Ireland and the UK. Dr Josephine Lomax-Simpson left the residue of her £3,248,479 estate to her local Guild of Social Welfare in Wimbledon. Josephine Boraston, who lived on Anglesey, left the residue of her £2,276,448 estate to the RSPB, with the somewhat unusual request that they set up an animal hospital "for dogs, sheep and any other small animals". Londoner John Donovan, left the residue of his £1,631,853 estate to the National Investment and Loans Office, for the reduction of the National Debt.

Cambridge's Kings College further benefitted from the £2,065,885 estate of Eva Carlton, of Poole, who left the residue for the upkeep of the Chapel. Dame Bertha Jeffreys, of Cambridge, left most of her £1,546,638 estate between Girton and St John's Colleges, Cambridge, and Newcastle University. Audrey Macbeth, of Church Hanborough, in Oxfordshire, left the residue of her £978,164 estate to St Anne's College, Oxford, while Peter Delme-Radcliffe, who lived in nearby Deddington, left £250,000 to "the Cathedral Church of Christ in Oxford of the Foundation of King Henry VIII", better known as Christ Church College. He also left the residue of his £2,719,958 estate equally between the Imperial Cancer Research Fund, RNIB, Multiple Sclerosis Society and Stroke Association.

Dr Frederick Porges, of Hale Barns, Cheshire, left £200,000 to Manchester University, for Alzheimers Disease research, and the residue of his £3,755,495 estate between ten national charities, While another Cheshire man Harvey Garlick, of Prestbury, left most of his £2,411,686 estate between the Royal Society of Chemistry Benevolent Fund, Nathan House at Manchester's Christie Hospital, the National Trust, Kings College, London, and Kings College Hospital, London, the last two respectively endowing scholarships and beds in his memory. Finally on the education front, and not listed below, is the will of Edward Wignall, of Crawley, West Sussex, who left £1,000 to St Catharine's College, Cambridge, for its Development Fund, and a further £500 to the College's Junior Combination Room, for the replenishment of alcoholic and non-alcoholic drinks on the second day of each term, but stipulating "that no Don shall benefit from this legacy in view of their predecessors in 1949–50 having consumed my banana allowance without so much as a please or thank you"!

Anfield, Phyllis Mary, of Curzon Park, Chester, £1,575,527 (£100,000 to the Royal Masonic Benevolent Institution, for the Llandudno Home or any Home in or near Chester, £10,000 each to Barnardo's and Salvation Army, £5,000 each to Grosvenor Nuffield Hospital, Chester, and RNLI, and the residue to the Cancer Research Campaign)

Bacs, George, of Chelsea Manor Street, London SW3, £544,244 (the residue to CAFOD)

Barrone, Brian, of Wingate, Co. Durham, £711,044 (all his estate equally between the Cleveland Branches of the RSPCA and PDSA)

Batty, Christine Agnes Lilian, of Maldon, Essex, £59,029,581 (£5,000 each to the Book Sellers Provident Association, Cinnamon Trust, Penzance, Battersea Dogs Home and the Royal Society of Arts, and the residue to such charity or charities or for such charitable purpose or purposes as her Trustees think fit)

Bertstein, Sagle Norah, of Cromer, Norfolk, £11,991,393 (£500,000 to the RNLI, for the Cromer Lifeboat and Lifeboat Station, £250,000 to Addenbrookes Hospital, Cambridge, for equipment for the patients, £100,000 to the Norwich Blind Institute, £60,000 to the East Anglian Ambulance NHS Trust, for an ambulance for Cromer, £50,000 each to the RSPCA, for use in Norfolk, the Salvation Army, RAF Association, the Shaare Zedek Hospital, Jerusalem, the Bnai Brith Stepney Jewish Club and Settlement, and the Ramot Shapira, Harrow, £20,000 to the Boys Town, Jerusalem, £10,000 each to the Burma Star Association and Sheringham Rotary Club Charities, £5,000 to the Cancer Relief Macmillan Fund, for Macmillan Nursing in the locality of Cromer, £2,000 to Cromer District Nurses Fund, and the residue to Cromer Hospital, for improvement of facilities)

Bolton, Hilda Mary, of Sidcup, Kent, £1,150,354 (£50,000 to the National Trust, and the residue equally between the Salvation Army, and the Hospital for Sick Children, Great Ormond Street, London)

Boraston, Josephine Lavinia, of Llanfairpwll, Anglesey, £2,276,448 (the residue to the RSPB, to set up an animal hospital known as Tyddyn Nathanial Hospital, "for dogs, sheep and any other small animals")

Bowdler, Nora, of Market Drayton, Salop, £740,935 (all her estate to the Guide Dogs for the Blind Association)

Bowers, Arnold, of Ossett, West Yorks, £620,982 (the residue to Wakefield Hospice)

Broadhead, Florence Barbara Ann, of Bessacarr, South Yorks, £1,574,006 (the residue to the RNLI, for a lifeboat in memory of her late husband Donald and herself)

Brown, Constance Rosemary, of Blackburn, Lancs, £2,253,333 (£10,000 to the Convent of the Sisters of Nazareth House, Blackburn, and the residue equally between Pleasington Priory, Blackburn, the Guide Dogs for the Blind Association, PDSA, RSPCA and the Bristol Alzheimers Research Centre, all for use in the Blackburn area, SSAFA, Motor Neurone Disease Association, and the Marie Curie Memorial Foundation, for the care and treatment of terminal cancer cases being nursed at home in Lancashire)

Brown, Robert, of Blewbury, Didcot, Oxon, £1,461,164 (£50,0000 to Parkinson's Disease Society, and the residue to the Royal Society, London)

Burdett, Phyllis Emily, of Edgware, Middlesex, £804,613 (four-fifths of the residue to the National Trust, and one-fifth to the Gardeners Royal Benevolent Society)

Burr, Norah, of Lightcliffe, Halifax, £3,180,631 (half the residue to the RNLI, for a lifeboat in memory of her son William Gordon Burr, and one-sixth of the residue each to the RNIB, Cancer Research Campaign, and the Calderdale Society for Continuing Care)

Cant, Constance Joyce, of Dorking, Surrey, £2,270,376 (the residue equally between DGAA Homelife and the National Canine Defence League)

Carlton, Eva, of Poole, Dorset, £2,065,885 (the residue to Kings College, Cambridge, for the upkeep of the Chapel)

Clarke, Florence Emily, of East Carlton, Nottingham, £1,086,900 (the residue to the National Society for Cancer Relief)

Crossley, Roland, of Old Colwyn, Conwy, £1,900,867 (the residue equally between the British Red Cross Society, Alzheimers Disease Society and Multiple Sclerosis Society)

Cuddon, Denis Bernard, of Sidmouth, Devon, £1,857,819 (all his estate to the British Red Cross Society)

Dawson, Ann Christal, of Cleadon Village, Tyne and Wear, £2,259,926 (£50,000 to the Sailors Children's Society, Hull, £15,000 to the University of Sunderland, to establish a Model Pharmacy, and two-thirds of the residue to the National Trust, for the purchase of property in the Scottish Borders, Northumberland and the old North and East Ridings of Yorkshire, and one-third of the residue to the RSPB, for reserves north of the Humber)

Day, Mary Elizabeth, of Coddenham, Suffolk, £2,316,432 (the residue to the Day Foundation, a charity established by her and others in 1987)

Delme-Radcliffe, Peter, of Deddington, Oxon, £2,719,958 (£250,000 to "the Cathedral Church of Christ in Oxford of the Foundation of King Henry VIII", and the residue equally between the Imperial Cancer Research Fund, RNIB, Multiple Sclerosis Society and the Stroke Association)

Dugdale, Ivy, of Deane, Bolton, Lancs, £1,342,343 (£100,000 to the RNLI, for a lifeboat to be named "James Dugdale", and the residue to the Christie Hospital, Manchester)

Durden, Frederick William, of East Leake, Loughborough, Leics, £502,123 (the residue to the Royal British Legion)

Edwards, Sybil Katherine, of Guisborough, Cleveland, £2,690,519 (£100,000 to the National Trust and £10,000 to its Cleveland Association, £100,000 each to the Claremont Fan Court School, Esher, Surrey, and the Endowment Fund of Principia Elsah, Illinois, USA, £20,000 to the First Church of Christ Scientist, Guisborough, £10,000 each to Cleveland Youth Association, Cleveland Wildlife Trust, the Northern Horticultural Society, British Trust for Conservation Volunteers, Worldwide Fund for Nature, Send a Cow, Barnardo's, RSPCC, Save the Children Fund, and the Aid for Christian Scientists in Need of Nursing Care Fund, and the residue to the Christian Science Trust)

Evans, Olive Margaret, of Greet, Birmingham, £601,327 (the residue to the RNLI)

Franklyn, Finch, June Hildegard, of Petworth, West Sussex, £2,347,941 (£10,000 each to Shelter, the Brooke Hospital for Animals, London, the RSPCA, and Newnham College, Cambridge, and the residue to the Royal College of Surgeons of England)

Forrester, Gwyneth May, of Portland Place, London W1, £21,664,629 (the residue for such charitable purposes as her Trustees think fit)

Fothergill, Hilda, of Eaglescliffe, Stockton on Tees, Cleveland, £2,577,588 (the residue equally between the Society for the Protection of Animals Abroad, RSPCA, Jerry Green Foundation Trust, Blue Cross, National Canine Defence League and PDSA)

Garland, Susan Michelle, of Fairfax Road, London NW6, £675,895 (all her estate to the Cancer Research Campaign)

Garlick, Harvey Satchell, of Prestbury, Cheshire, £2,411,686 (£5,000 and one-fifth of the residue to the Royal Society of Chemistry Benevolent Fund, £2,500 and one-fifth of the residue to Nathan House at the Christie Hospital, Manchester, and one-fifth of the residue each to the National Trust, Kings College, London, for scholarships in his memory, and Kings College Hospital, for the endowment of beds in his memory)

Garwood, Mary Catherine Clee, of Paignton, Devon, £902,070 (£10,000 to the Royal United Hospital, Bath, and the residue to the Rowcroft Hospice, Torquay)

Gibson, John, of Hedon, East Yorks, £1,491,889 (the residue to the RNLI, for a new lifeboat at Spurn to be called "The Daniel L. Gibson" after his late son)

Gordon, Sir Alexander John, of Llanblethian, Cowbridge, Glamorgan, £703,830 (£50,000 each to the South Wales Cancer Research Council and the Cancer Research Campaign, and the residue to the Architects Benevolent Society)

Grier, John Burton, of Caernarfon, Gwynedd, £1,367,199 (£10,000 to the Jat British Officers Education Trust India, and the residue to the Salvation Army)

Harney, William, of Keswick, Cumbria, £1,816,426 (£16,000 to the Friends of Keswick Hospital, £4,000 each to the British Red Cross Society, and Crosthwaite Church, Keswick, and the residue equally between the Phyllis Harney Trust, and the Calvert Trust, Keswick)

Hartog, Geoffrey Barthold Numa, of Pall Mall, London SW1, £959,241 (the residue equally between Jewish Care and the Western Marble Arch Synagogue)

Hayes, Lilian Florence, of Leamington Spa, Warwickshire, £1,439,156 (the residue equally between the Myton Hamlet Hospice, Warwick, the RNLI, British Red Cross Society and the D'Oyly Carte Opera Company)

Heath, Anne Eiddig, of Eastbourne, East Sussex, £1,274,300 (the residue to St Wilfrid's Hospice, Eastbourne)

Heather, Marjorie Ethel, of Merstham, Redhill, Surrey, £3,103,914 (the residue equally between the Institute of Cancer Research, RNIB and Arthritis and Rheumatism Council)

Hillman, Alison Patricia, of Harborne, Birmingham, £3,159,125 (the residue to the Alison Hillman Charitable Trust)

Hodge, Alice Mary, of Parkstone, Dorset, £785,048 (the residue for such charity or charities as her Trustees determine)

Hogg, Elizabeth Frances, of West Clandon, Surrey, £1,062,962 (£20,000 to the National Trust, £10,000 to St Mark's Church, Surbiton, and the residue to the Sue Ryder Home, Leckhampton, Glos)

Holt, Elvira Gwendoline, of West Hill, London SW15, £528,675 (all her estate to the Royal Hospital and Home, Putney)

Irwin, Cyril Grafton, of Hanham, Glos, £4,587,108 (two-sevenheenths of the residue each to Frenchay Hospital, Bristol, and the Royal National Hospital for Rheumatic Diseases, Bath, and one-seventeenth each to the National Eye Research Centre, Bristol, St Peter's Hospice, Bristol, Macmillan Cancer Relief, Imperial Cancer Research Fund, Marie Curie Cancer Care, NSPCC, RSPCA, Oxfam, British Red Cross Society, St Dunstan's, British Heart Foundation, Alzheimers Disease Society, and Brunel Care, Bristol)

Isherwood, Helen Margaret, of Bickley, Kent, £1,532,226 (£50,000 each to the Cancer Research Campaign, Age Concern and RSPB, £40,000 each to the NSPCC, Poor Clergy Relief Corporation and Salvation Army, £30,000 each to the Guide Dogs for the Blind Association and RSPCA, £20,000 each to Mission Care, Bromley, and Multiple Sclerosis Society, £15,000 to Alzheimers Disease Society, £10,000 each to the Church of St Peter and St Paul, Bromley, Girl Guides Association, and St Christopher's Hospice, Sydenham, £5,000 each to St Augustine's Church, Bickley, South Bromley Hospiscare, Mencap, Scout Association and Cheltenham Ladies College Benefactors Fund, and the residue for such charitable institutions or objects in England as her Trustees select)

Jackson-Barstow, Enid Sybil, of Christon, Axbridge, Somerset, £10,972,894 (£5,000 to St Mary's Church, Christon, and the residue equally between Barnardo's, Weston Hospiscare and the League of Friends of Weston-super-Mare Hospitals)

Jeavons, Edith Mary, of Penn, Wolverhampton, £2,880,635 (£20,000 each to Staffordshire Lawn Tennis Association, for coaching underprivileged children, the local Red Cross Ambulance Service, Salvation Army and Barnardo's, £10,000 each to Wordsley Hospital, Stourbridge, All Saints Church, Sedgley, and St Leonard's Church, Bilston, and the residue equally between New Cross Hospital, Wolverhampton, the Compton Hall Hospice, Wolverhampton, the Wolverhampton and District Institute for the Blind, RNLI, and the County Air Ambulance Service, Dudley)

Jeffreys, Dame Bertha, of Cambridge, £1,546,638 (her home, some effects and one-third of the residue to Girton College, Cambridge, her late husband's scientific manuscripts and other effects and one-third of the residue to St John's College, Cambridge, and one-third of the residue to Newcastle University)

Joyce, Anne Christine, of Tenby, Pembrokeshire, £1,432,535 (£10,000 and two signed pictures by Fred Uhlman and Augustus John to Tenby Museum and Picture Gallery, and the residue to Battersea Dogs Home)

Kennedy, Constance, of Scarborough, North Yorks, £826,468 (£10,000 to Scarborough Hospital Renal Unit Fund, £5,000 to the Scarborough Flower Fund Homes, and the residue to St Catherine's Hospice, Scarborough)

King, Beryl Gladys, of Canterbury, Kent, £548,266 (all her estate to the RNLI)

Kings, Brian Ernest Sydney, of Lickey End, Bromsgrove, Worcs, £1,014,593 (£10,000 to Lickey End First School, and the residue to the RSPB, to purchase nature reserves)

Kitcher, Michael Frederick, of Fawley, Hants, £548,555 (£20,000 each to St Mary's Church, South Baddesley, and the Guide Dogs for the Blind Association, New Forest Branch, and the residue to the League of Friends of Oakhaven Hospice, Lymington)

Klein, Dorothy Eileen, of Winchester, Hants, £986,280 (the residue equally between the RNID and the Carl Klein Trust)

Knapp, Brenda Ulrica Washington, of Esher, Surrey, £5,492,816 (the residue to the National Art Collections Fund)

Knopf, Ilse, of Holland Park Avenue, London w11, £1,773,138 (£10,000 to the Association of Jewish Refugees, £5,000 each to the National Star Centre for Disabled,Youth,,Cheltenham, and the Royal Ballet Benevolent Fund, and the residue to the Central British Fund for World Jewish Relief)

Laufer, Malvine, of Gerrards Cross, Bucks, £1,092,315 (the residue to the Weizmann Institute Foundation, London)

Leech, Lady Ellen, of Morpeth, Northumberland, £646,484 (£10,000 to Mitford Church, Morpeth, and the residue to the William Leech Charity, desiring that substantial gifts be made to the Save the Children Fund and Christian Aid)

Linnell, Edna Rosemarie, of West Peckham, Kent, £1,940,229 (the residue to the Maharishi Foundation, or other charitable objects as her Trustees think fit)

Lomax-Simpson, Josephine Mary, of Malcolm Road, London sw19, £3,248,479 (the residue to the Wimbledon Guild of Social Service)

Lucas, Kenneth John, of Poole, Dorset, £1,714,850 (£10,000 to Lilliput Surgery, Parkstone, Poole, for equipment, and the residue equally between the RNLI, Guide Dogs for the Blind Association and RSPCA)

Macbeth, Audrey Ethelwyn O'Brien, of Church Hanborough, Oxon, £978,164 (the residue to St Anne's College, Oxford)

Mainzer, Kathleen Edith, of Stanmore, Middlesex, £2,012,706 (the residue equally between the Association of Jewish Refugees, Help the Aged, RNIB, and Cryo Research at Harefield Hospital, Middlesex)

Maylett, Joyce Rita, of Ickenham, Middlesex, £2,943,191 (the residue to the Charities Aid Foundation, to be distributed in accordance with her known wishes)

Nanney, Phyllis, of Hereford, £1,248,508 (£20,000 to the Methodist Homes for the Aged, Derby, in memory of her parents Jessie and Morris Nanney, and the residue equally between RUKBA and Imperial Cancer Research Fund)

Nicot, Marie Louise, of Coulsdon, Surrey, £682,840 (the residue to the Roman Catholic Diocese of Southwark, for the education of candidates for the priesthood and for the care of the sick, the elderly and the dying in the Diocese)

Noake, Margaret Valentine, of Worcester, £1,028,806 (the residue to the Abbeyfield Worcester Society)

Page, Elizabeth Alice, of Sidmouth, Devon, £1,113,828 (the residue equally between Sidmouth Victoria Cottage Hospital,Comforts Fund and Sidmouth Voluntary Services)

Parker, Herbert Frederick Charles Elliot, of Ducklington, Oxon, £1,870,160 (25 per cent of the residue each to the Leukaemia Research Fund and the Oxford Kidney Unit Trust, 20 per cent of the residue each to the Royal Agricultural Benevolent Institution and Royal Agricultural Society of England and Wales, and 10 per cent of the residue to the Harper Adams Foundation)

Pashley, Barbara Frances, of Richmond, Surrey, £3,267,419 (the residue to Macmillan Cancer Relief, for the Macmillan Nurses)

Perrin, Moyra Robins, of Holland Villas Road, London W14, £5,586,112 (£7,000 each to Age Concern, Action for the Blind, Alzheimers Disease Society, Macmillan Nurses Fund for Cancer Relief, PDSA, Blue Cross, and St Luke's Hospice, Hartford, Cheshire, and the residue equally between the British Red Cross Society and National Trust)

Philip, Flora, of Newmarket, Suffolk, £1,058,007 (the residue equally between the National Trust for Scotland and Cancer Research)

Porges, Frederick Benjamin, of Hale Barns, Cheshire, £3,755,495 (£200,000 to the University of Manchester, for Alzheimers Disease research, and the residue equally between the Children and Youth Aliyah, Imperial Cancer Research Fund, Muscular Dystrophy Group, Parkinsons Disease Society, RNLI, Arthritis and Rheumatism Council, British Heart Foundation, RNIB, Multiple Sclerosis Research Fund and the Save the Children Fund)

Preston, Raymond, of Cheltenham, Glos, £842,814 (all his estate to the Children's Society)

Rhodes, Gwendoline Mary, of Newton Solney, Staffs, £1,085,002 (the residue equally between the British Heart Foundation, and St Giles Hospice, Whittington, Lichfield)

Ripley, Violet Maud, of Bridlington, East Yorks, £1,427,896 (£5,000 each to the Yorkshire Cancer Research Campaign and the Hull and East Riding Institute for the Blind, and the residue to the RNLI, Bridlington Branch)

Roberts, Edna, of Hale, Altrincham, Cheshire, £2,144,003 (one-third of the residue to the PDSA, and one-sixth of the residue each to the RSPCA, Donkey Sanctuary, Sidmouth, Age Concern and Imperial Cancer Research Fund)

Rogers, William Montague, of Gillingham, Kent, £811,153 (the residue to the RNLI)

Russell, Laurence Hugh, of Ramsden Heath, Essex, £2,113,878 (£20,000 to the Samaritans, £10,000 each to the RSPCA, PDSA, Invalid Children's Aid Association, Age Concern Greater London, Imperial Cancer Research Fund and Salvation Army, £4,000 each to the Donkey Sanctuary, Sidmouth, Redwings Horse Sanctuary, Norwich, the Blue Cross, British Heart Foundation, Horder Centre for Arthritics and Help the Aged, and the residue to St Joseph's Hospice, Hackney)

Sell, Mima Elizabeth, of Bath, £1,095,352 (the residue to the RNLI, towards a new lifeboat to be named "Beth Sell")

Sheridan, Margaret Frances Patricia, of Penylan, Cowbridge, Glamorgan, £1,638,323 (£20,000 each to the Mousehole Wild Bird Hospital and Sanctuary, Cornwall, and the Cinnamon Trust, Penzance, £10,000 to the Irish Council Against Blood Sports, and 50 per cent of the residue to the National Canine Defence League, for the Bridgend Branch, and 25 per cent of the residue each to the Compassion in World Farming Trust and Compassion in World Farming Supporters)

Shooman, Barbara Ruth, of Scarcroft, Leeds, £1,168,150 (a sum up to £25,000 to Etz Chaim Synagogue, Leeds, to dedicate and equip a library room with reference books on Judaism, and £50,000 for the purchase of an ambulance and half the residue to the Friends of Magen David Adom, and half the residue to the JNF Charitable Trust)

Simes, Robert Henry, of Horsham, West Sussex, £737,617 (the residue to the RNIB)

Simister, Hilda, of Barton on Sea, Hants, £4,893,677 (the residue equally between the Birmingham Association of Youth Clubs, the Royal Masonic Institution for Boys and the Birmingham Institute for the Deaf)

Smart, Ruth Elizabeth, of Clavering, Essex, £4,887,384 (the residue for such charitable purposes for the relief of the suffering of animals of any species, the maintenance of refuges, homes, animal hospitals, sanctuaries and other facilities for unwanted animals, and the treatment of sick or ill treated animals as her Trustees think fit)

Steel, Yvonne, of Rugby, Warwickshire, £5,325,077 (a quarter of the residue each to the Incorporated Benevolent Fund of Electrical Engineers, the Musicians Benevolent Fund and the RSPB, and one-eighth of the residue each to the Police Dependants Trust and the Police Convalescence and Rehabilitation Trust)

Stewart, Sir Ronald Compton, of Maulden, Beds, £977,253 (£10,000 to St Mary's Parish Church, Maulden, £5,000 to Stewartby United Church, and the residue to the Sir Malcolm Stewart Bart General Charitable Trust)

Strain, Robert William Magill, of Badgeworth, Glos, £2,311,914 (£100,000 to the Royal Ulster Constabulary Benevolent Fund, £50,000 to the Ulster Unionist Party, and the residue equally between Bryson House, Belfast, the Royal Belfast Academical Institution, the Presbyterian Church in Ireland, RNLI, National Canine Defence League, Battersea Dogs Home, Sight Savers International, Royal British Legion, Salvation Army, Royal Medical Benevolent Fund, RSPB, and Queens University Masonic Lodge, Belfast)

Tait, Edward Andrew, of Southport, Merseyside, £1,192,116 (half the residue to the RNLI, to be used in Scotland)

Tait, Elizabeth Ogilvie, of Gosforth, Newcastle upon Tyne, £869,163 (£10,000 to the Salvation Army, Newcastle upon Tyne, £5,000 each to the Cancer Relief Macmillan Nurses and Marie Curie Nurses, both for use in the Newcastle area, the Royal Star and Garter Home, Richmond, and the Association for International Cancer Research, and the residue for the Mountain Rescue Committee of Scotland, St John Ambulance and for heart equipment for hospitals in Newcastle and Northumberland, as her Trustees select)

Tombs, Richard, of Shaw, Newbury, Berks, £1,547,747 (two-thirds of the residue to the Newbury Hospital Helpers League and one-third of the residue to the Blue Cross)

Trill, Joan Madeline Dampier, of Newnton, Tetbury, Glos, £859,540 (the residue, including any car she may own at her death, to the National Canine Defence League)

Turner, John Robert, of St Martins Avenue, London E6, £1,119,516 (£10,000 to the United Reformed Church, Ilford, and the residue to the London Chest Clinic)

Turner, Roger Douglas, of Upper Arley, Bewdley, Worcs, £15,028,978 (£250,000 to the National Trust for Scotland, £200,000 to the National Trust, £50,000 to Kings College Chapel Foundation, Cambridge, £25,000 each to St Peter's Church, Upper Arley, and Dunblane Cathedral, £20,000 to

Kidderminster Disabled Club, £10,000 to the Order of St John, Kidderminster Division, and the residue to the R. D. Turner Charitable Trust)

Vigoureux, Joseph Evenor Paul Louis, of East Molesey, Surrey, £3,000,329 (the residue to the Society of St Pius X)

Watts, John Harry, of Alfreton, Derbyshire, £597,724 (the residue to the Derby Diocesan Board of Finance, for such charitable purposes as it decides)

Wolstencroft, Edna, of Seaton, Devon, £3,870,356 (£10,000 to St Gregory's Parish Church, Seaton, and the residue equally between the RAF Association, for their Homes in the south west, the Cancer Research Campaign, Salvation Army, RNLI, National Trust, RNIB, Royal Star and Garter Home, Richmond, Musicians Benevolent Fund, and the Leonard Cheshire Foundation, for their Home at Littleborough, Lancs)

Wray-Bliss, Diana Rosemary, of Corsham, Wilts, £9,405,483 (£50,000 each to St Bartholomew's Church, Corsham, Julian House, c/o Bath Churches Housing Association, the Wiltshire Wildlife Trust, the Dulwich Picture Gallery, the Corrymeela Community, Belfast, the Watermill Theatre, Newbury, the Berkeley Reafforestation Trust, Tree Aid, Water Aid, Council for the Protection of Rural England, NCH Action for Children, Voluntary Service Overseas, Winged Fellowship Trust, Intermediate Technology Development Group, The Weston Spirit, Cats Protection League, Sue Ryder Foundation, SOS Sahel, London, the Fellowship of Meditation, Dorchester, and the Reg Gilbert International Youth Friendship Trust, Frome, and half the residue to the National Trust, and one-eighth of the residue each to the Landmark Trust, Emmaus UK, Imperial Cancer Research Fund and the Carr-Gomm Society)

Young, Olive Mary, of Claydon, Ipswich, Suffolk, £2,110,231 (£50,000 each to St Elizabeth's Hospice, Ipswich, the Suffolk Wildlife Trust, RNLI, RSPB, PDSA, Samaritans, National Trust, Guide Dogs for the Blind Association, and the East Anglia Children's Hospice, Milton, Cambridge, and the residue equally between the British Heart Foundation, Imperial Cancer Research Fund and National Asthma Campaign)

Broadcasting

TELEVISION

In many ways the year 1999–2000 was one that the main channels (ITV and BBC1), would prefer to forget. For much of the period ITV was embroiled in a long-running row over its main evening news bulletin as politicians and commentators called for *News at Ten* to be reinstated. Matters came to a head when the regulator, the Independent Television Commission, demanded that the 11 pm *Nightly News* be moved to earlier in the evening. ITV's troubles were exacerbated as it struggled to achieve audience targets promised to advertisers. Similarly BBC1 found itself in trouble when for the third year running the board of governors criticised the channel for a lack of 'quality shows'.

Commentators agreed that BBC1 needed to improve, particularly in the crucial areas of drama series and entertainment. It was hoped that the BBC's new director general, Greg Dyke, who took over in January, will have better luck with BBC1 than his predecessor, John Birt. The central plank of the BBC's millennium celebrations, a 28-hour continuous live broadcast involving more than 60 broadcasters world-wide, also struck a sour note with critics.

Meanwhile amidst much controversy regarding declining standards, Channel 5 steadily gained ground against the established networks, principally by offering audiences a programming menu strong on sex and titillation. If only the new generation of digital stations, most of them doomed to subsist on miniscule budgets and even smaller audiences, could generate as much publicity for themselves. Digital television, with 100s of viewing options, was here to stay, helped, no doubt, by free receiving equipment, but the traditional terrestrial channels still dominated viewing patterns accounting for around 85 per cent of the time spent in front of the set in British homes.

For most viewers, perhaps the biggest change in programme trends was the decline of the docu-soap and the emergence of an even more voyeuristic form of small screen entertainment known as 'reality shows'. In January BBC1 introduced a group of strangers to one another for the first instalment of *Castaway 2000*. Hailed as a 'real life social experiment', the cameras captured life in the raw as 36 volunteers attempted to build a new community on the remote Scottish island of Taransay. In certain respects the more colourful of the participants became minor celebrities in their own right. A more extreme version of this phenomenon, described as 'peek-a-boo' television by the American trade paper, *Variety*, was *Big Brother*, shown during the summer by Channel 4 in a haze of publicity. Generally the station had much to be proud of during the year, but some commentators insisted that this show brought nothing but shame on the station. In fact, *Big Brother* was half documentary and half game show. A group of young people were effectively imprisoned in a specially converted house in London's east end. An army of cameras recorded the minutia of their daily lives. At the end of each week the occupants had to vote to see who should be thrown out of the house. The eventual winner would be the one remaining inside the house (and by inference the most popular) at the end of the series. Some critics felt that the show smacked of desperation as

Channel 4 sought to come up with new ways of entertaining its audience.

CHANNEL 4 HITS A COMIC NERVE

Also aimed at the under-25s, but wining a wider audience for Channel 4 was Ali G, British television's most original new comic star of the year. Originally a character in the station's late night sketch series, *The Eleven O'Clock Show*, Ali G was given his own vehicle, *Da Ali G Show*, to showcase the wit of his creator, Sacha Baron Cohen, and his usually hapless guests. At its best the programme contained multiple layers of irony and social observation satirising young white men who mimic black culture. Some, unfairly, claimed the programme suggested racist tendencies, perhaps forgetting that the inspiration for Ali G came from people like the white Radio 1 rap DJ Tim Westwood. A more justified criticism came from those who said Channel 4 risked losing the opportunity to nurture and develop a truly original talent because of its keenness to over promote Ali G's success.

Channel 4's archrival BBC2 struggled to match the likes of Ali G and much of the station's other, successful entertainment series. The majority of its new comedy formats lacked the spark of previous recent hits like *The Royle Family* (a huge success for BBC1 in 1999–2000) although, if anything, the second series of *The League Of Gentlemen* was even more bizarre than the first.

In situation comedy BBC2 failed to deliver with the latest offering from Father Ted writers Arthur Matthews and Graham Linehan, *Hippies*, set in the swinging sixties. Also disappointing was *Coupling*, a smutty comedy about a group of twenty-somethings and their relationships. Neither were a match for Channel 4's surreal, Friday night sitcom, *Spaced*, or its continued championing of American humour in the guise of *Frasier* and *South Park*. One Friday night show showing signs of tiredness was Chris Evans' *TFI Friday*, finally axed in the spring.

The station's tackiest new entertainment show of the year was *Something For The Weekend*, in which contestants were asked to reveal details of their family's sex lives. But this was almost staid compared with some of the shows shown on Channel 5, which, most critics agreed, was plumbing new depths in bad taste television. *Ex-Rated*, a so-called adult game show, was perhaps as bad as it got.

It should be added that the station's programme director Dawn Airey claimed that material of this nature comprised only a small part of the network's schedule and the Independent Television Commission (ITC), in its annual performance review, praised Channel 5 for 'establishing areas of undoubted strength in documentaries, news, religious programmes and feature films'. However, Channel 5's entertainment programmes, said the regulator, remained weak, and aside from its nightly soap opera, *Family Affairs*, the station made little impact with the few original dramas it aired.

Overall BBC1 struggled to break new ground in comedy and entertainment although the second and final series of *dinnerladies* continued to delight audiences and critics alike. A new format for Saturday night's lottery show, *Red Alert*, hosted by pop veteran Lulu, flopped badly. For the second year running, BBC1 was unable to come up with anything to match the sheer popularity of ITV's *Who Wants To Be A Millionaire?* The big, £1 million prize still eluded contestants and there were signs of viewer fatigue, as ITV became over reliant on the series to lift ratings and revenue.

COSTUME DRAMA PUTS ON A SHOW

Throughout the year drama remained the backbone of ITV's schedule. In fact, generally there was plenty to praise across the main terrestrial stations as they continued to invest considerable sums in small screen fiction. The boom in period drama continued despite indications that the BBC's Greg Dyke would like to see a renewed commitment to contemporary drama. Commentators complained that audiences were being short-changed when both ITV and BBC1 decided to screen their big literary autumn classic adaptations, *Oliver Twist* and *Wives and Daughters*, at the same time on Sunday evenings. Yet despite this unfortunate scheduling, both programmes achieved audiences of more than seven million.

Alan Bleasdale's version of *Oliver Twist*, featuring an all-star cast including Robert Lindsay and Julie Walters, was the least favourably received of the two. But then the BBC did rely on the ubiquitous Andrew Davies for the script. *Wives and Daughters*, starring Michael Gambon, Justine Waddell and Francesca Annis, received rave reviews. An ITV film based on E. Nesbit's children's classic, *The Railway Children*, starring Jenny Agutter, proved viewers still have a big appetite for family drama.

Another literary success for the BBC's television drama department was a two-part serialisation of *David Copperfield* shown over Christmas. The programme featured some unusual casting, most notably Nicholas Lyndhust as *Uriah Heep*. The year's most ambitious TV adaptation of a literary classic was BBC2's version of Mervyn Peake's surreal Gothic fantasy, *Gormenghast*. Despite a £6 million budget and a line-up of premium British acting talent, including Ian Richardson and Christopher Lee, *Gormenghast* failed to live up to its hype 'as the drama of the millennium'. Ratings plummeted 40 per cent in the first two weeks – this caused the *Evening Standard* to dub the serial '*Gormenghastly*' – but several critics said the BBC's ambition should be admired. More successful was a provocative retelling of Flaubert's *Madame Bovary* starring Greg Wise and Frances O'Connor.

MICHAEL GAMBON IS TIMELESS IN LONGITUDE

Channel 4 also delved into the past for two high-profile costume dramas, *Longitude* and Tolstoy's *Anna Karenina*. *Longitude*, based on Dava Sobel's short novel, was a surprising success considering the challenges imposed by a story set in two different centuries. Michael Gambon, was brilliant as the tenacious clockmaker John Harrison. *Anna Karenina* received more mixed notices. The press outcry over the sex scenes was predictable. The station also scored with Jimmy McGovern's *Dockers*, a throwback to the social realism of television drama of the 60s and 70s.

On the mainstream channels, both ITV and BBC1 attempted to ring the changes by offering audiences a more varied diet than the customary mix of cops, docs and vets. Thus ITV's Christmas line-up contained a fresh episode of *A Touch Of Frost* and the first new Poirot for five years, *The Murder of Roger Ackroyd*. Less conventional was ITV's critically acclaimed drama based on the Stephen Lawrence case, *The Murder of Stephen Lawrence*, and a new television family with a difference in the shape of *At Home With The Braithwaites*. Another ITV highlight was the second series of Granada's comedy drama, *Cold Feet*, but, surprisingly, the latest ITV John Thaw vehicle, *Monsignor Renard*, the story of a French Catholic priest who returns home to France in 1940 as the Germans invade, failed to achieve a huge audience. Ex-*EastEnders* star Ross Kemp, signed to ITV at great expense, played a security guard in *Hero Of The Hour*. The verdict, though, was that the script was hackneyed and Kemp's performance was run of the mill.

On BBC1, the most critically acclaimed drama of the year was Peter Kosminsky's *Warriors*, a harrowing and brilliantly realised documentary-style account of British peace keeping forces in the Balkans. Also impressive was *All The King's Men*, starring David Jason and Maggie Smith, recounting how an entire British First World War battalion had gone 'missing' during the Gallipoli campaign.

In series drama, BBC1 still failed to come up with a programme that could match the success of ITV's Sunday night ratings juggernaut, *Heartbeat*, but several new shows showed promise. *Monarch of the Glen*, starring Richard Briers, Susan Hampshire and Alastair Mackenzie, may in turn prove a worthy successor to *Ballykissangel*. Meanwhile *Clocking Off*, scripted by Paul Abbott, brought a new dimension to Sunday night mainstream drama by being set in a factory instead of a hospital or a police station. A remake of *Randall and Hopkirk (Deceased)* starring Vic Reeves and Bob Mortimer helped refresh BBC1's often dismal Saturday night line-up.

The new series of Tony Garnett's naturalistic police saga, *Cops*, over on BBC2, was anything but cliché-ridden and proved as riveting as its debut a year earlier. In a similar vein was *Nice Girl*, a BBC2 film described as a *Cathy Come Home* for our times. Played out against the background of post-industrial south Wales, the central character was a school girl mother who appeared doomed to repeat the same mistakes as her own mother.

WALKING WITH DINOSAURS OUTPACES HOLLYWOOD

While the soaps, *Coronation Street* and *EastEnders* (celebrating its 15th anniversary in February), continued to dominate the ratings, the year showed that factual programmes do not have to be voyeuristic to attract wide appeal and critical attention. *Walking With Dinosaurs* hailed by the BBC as its most popular science programme ever, achieved audiences in excess of 13 million. Most people agreed that the series' computer generated dinosaurs were easily a match for anything produced by Hollywood but several commentators criticised the BBC for claiming that *Walking With Dinosaurs* was scientifically sound. The script, read by Kenneth Branagh, was less than challenging. Science of a very different kind was in evidence for what many critics agreed was the most original documentary series of the summer, *Brain Story*, presented by the charismatic neuroscientist Professor Susan Greenfield.

Another high point was *The Mayfair Set*, a searing criticism of city and political misdeeds during the Wilson and Heath years. Joan Bakewell, who quit as the presenter of *Heart Of the Matter* complaining that the BBC had marginalised religious programmes, re-emerged to host BBC2's *My Generation*, an entertaining slice of social history featuring such luminaries as Jonathan Miller, Beryl Bainbridge and John Peel. Cookery shows remained much in evidence, particularly on BBC2, where *The Naked Chef*, a.k.a. Jamie Oliver, emerged as a real star, writing best sellers and giving Delia Smith a run for her money with his streetwise charm and 'anyone can cook' charisma.

However, it was not only the BBC that provided audiences with some memorable documentaries. ITV's original take on a familiar subject, *The Second World War In Colour*, narrated by John Thaw, was one of the autumn's surprise hits. Made by Carlton, the series unearthed rare colour footage of some of war's key events, both on the battlefield and from the home front. Later in the year

ITV scored with a personal post mortem on Nato's action to prevent Serbian dominance of Kosovo, *A Kosovo Journey*, presented by Jonathan Dimbleby. Unfortunately this disturbing film was shown at 10.45pm on a Sunday evening. Equally compelling was another ITV documentary, albeit one examining a more conventional subject, *The Hunt for the Yorkshire Ripper*.

For innovation in the factual arena Channel 4 left the other networks gasping to catch up. *The 1900 House*, in which a family agreed to live their daily lives as their Victorian counterparts did a 100 years earlier, was an original, if somewhat inconsistent series. There was wholehearted praise for a forward-thinking programme, *The Day The World Took Off*, re-examining the industrial revolution from a novel perspective. Steve Humphries' oral history series, *Green and Pleasant Land*, depicting 20th century rural life in Britain in bleakly honest fashion, was another series that challenged convention. While David Starkey's televisual portrait of *Elizabeth*, the first Queen Elizabeth, made a big impact.

Overall current affairs continued to wane, a decline symbolised by the death in August of television's greatest political inquisitor, Sir Robin Day. *Newsnight* chalked up its 20th anniversary but few expected it still to be around in 20 years' time. One welcome exception from the 'dumbing down' was Peter Taylor's three-part BBC2 series, *The Brits*, this exemplary journalist's latest small screen examination of Northern Ireland. The new, more sensational approach to the genre was typified by the success of BBC1's *MacIntyre Uncovered*, which carried out exposés of football hooliganism and abuse in care homes. Fears that serious television was being undermined lay behind the decision by the ITC to force ITV to axe the *Nightly News* and re-introduce a high-profile news bulletin earlier in the evening. The watchdog claimed that since *News At Ten* was dumped in March 1999, audiences for news programmes on ITV had slumped by 13 per cent. The fact that digital viewers now had a new 24 hour news service from ITN was besides the point, argued the ITC, which had earlier approved the changes. A lengthy court battle was on the cards as ITV refused to obey the ITC's demands.

GREG DYKE'S BAPTISM OF FIRE

As politicians and regulators pondered the future of broadcasting prior to the publication of a new communications white paper, attention turned to Greg Dyke's new leadership at the BBC. His first weeks in charge led to a bruising row over some Granada shares that the *Sunday Times* claimed he had neglected to sell. In May there was an even bigger row involving Dyke. This time controversy raged over the BBC's decision not to cover the Queen Mother's centenary pageant. Dyke stood firm in the face of the *Daily Mail*-inspired campaign leaving the way open for ITV to broadcast the event in a programme hosted by Sir Trevor McDonald. As the new regime got into its stride, insisting that more money would be spent on programmes and less on the BBC's famed civil service-style bureaucracy, it was announced that around 1,100 jobs would go and that the wilder excesses of John Birt's internal market be curbed. Dyke was feeling the benefit of a licence fee increase although some commentators wondered if the government's new insistence on agreeing major editorial changes at the BBC in advance with the department of culture was not too heavy a price to pay.

The increased funds for programmes was not enough to prevent the BBC losing out to a joint bid by BSkyB and ITV worth £1.11 billion and £183 million for rights to screen Premier League football. This meant that the BBC, suffering from a huge loss of top sport during the latter years of the Birt era, would no longer be able to screen *Match Of The Day*, for so long a fixture of BBC1's Saturday night line-up. In May the *Guardian* reported that an edition of Grandstand had to be cancelled because of a lack of sport. Nevertheless, the BBC's coverage of the *Euro 2000* football tournament drew bigger audiences than ITV's, proof that people still turned to the national broadcaster for key sports events. A further embarrassment for the BBC was a much-publicised initiative aimed at discovering new talent for the corporation's services. Veteran broadcaster Terry Wogan dismissed the scheme as a 'public relations stunt' adding: 'When you're useful to the BBC, they'll employ you. When they've used you up, out you go'.

There was further alarm when the director of television, Mark Thompson, speaking at the Banff television festival in June, suggested that BBC1 and 2 should abandon their traditional public service remit to offer a wide range of programmes and instead concentrate on providing a more specialised viewing menu in future. BBC1 would evolve into an entertainment-led channel enabling BBC2 to concentrate on more serious fare. It was feared that more difficult programmes like *Panorama*, throughout the year suffering from poor ratings and a lack of profile, and *Omnibus*, would be shunted from BBC1 to 2, where they would be watched by even smaller audiences. John Tusa, the former head of the World Service, denounced the idea as 'miserable small-mindedness'. The idea was that BBC1 and 2, together with the digital channels, BBC Choice and Knowledge, should be re-launched as BBC1, 2, 3 and 4 along the lines of Radios 1, 2, 3 and 4 with each network more closely targeted at a particular audience. 'The medium', argued Thompson, 'was changing and changing profoundly' as viewers with digital channels increasingly turned way from conventional mixed stations to watch more specialist services.

RADIO

As Greg Dyke's proposed reforms of BBC Television reverberated around the broadcasting world, his impact on radio looked certain to be less radical, and, in the short term, minimal. Compared with the upheavals affecting television, and the perceived threat from digital services, radio per se experienced few major convulsions during the year. What upheavals there were tended to be in the commercial sector, which found itself in the peculiar position of having to come to terms with the fact that both the BBC's network and local stations were gaining listeners. Figures published in August gave BBC Radio an overall audience share of 51.1 per cent against the commercial sector's 47.2 per cent.

DIGITAL FAILS TO CONQUER

Digital TV had been kick started by the arrival of Sky Digital and On Digital in the autumn of 1998. Digital radio, on the other hand, had so far remained stillborn, hampered by the high cost of a set (around £600), enormous start-up costs and a lack of new stations. In June the BBC's chairman, Sir Christopher Bland, took the unusual step of admitting that the corporation had been wrong to invest so heavily in developing digital radio in the recent past. He also knew that while BBC1 struggled to come to terms with the 21st century, broadly speaking BBC Radio was in good shape.

Conservative politicians and commercial radio chiefs might occasionally suggest that Radio 1 and 2 be privatised but there was no denying that John Birt's legacy had, with one or two exceptions, been helpful to radio giving each of the five national networks a clear identity that could only be envied by BBC1 and 2. When it emerged that Radio 4's once reviled controller James Boyle was to retire, the ex-head of BBC Radio Liz Forgan, who had left the organisation after clashing with Birt, expressed admiration for Boyle's achievements. Forgan, writing in the *Evening Standard*, said that Boyle had left behind 'an altogether tougher, less stodgy and more competitive station than the one he had inherited'. She went on: 'He has applied rigorous intellectual coherence, faced up to some old problems, fought brave battles and won most of them'. And in a swipe at what many regarded as the 'dumbed down' world of television, Forgan said features programmes on Radio 4 was not somewhere 'where everything is interactive, short-lived, instant and brand-reliant'. Audience figures appeared to support Forgan's thesis; in February it emerged that Radio 4 was now more popular in London than the pop station, Capital FM.

Despite advertising revenue worth around £500 million, many commentators felt that there was far too little to distinguish one commercial station from another. This monotonous style was characterised by computerised playlists and similar presentation styles. But while Chris Evans struggled to increase the audience for his breakfast show on Virgin Radio, Classic FM continued to add listeners. The service was voted station of the year at the Sony Awards in May; Culture Secretary Chris Smith praised its 'clear on-air identity' and 'natural sound'. While Classic FM went from strength to strength, 1999–2000 turned out to be a challenging period for Talk Radio and its outspoken boss, ex-*Sun* editor Kelvin MacKenzie. During the year Talk Radio was relaunched as TalkSport after sacking most of its presenters including Anna Raeburn, but to date it is yet to establish itself as a serious threat to the sports dominated Radio 5 Live, which took a record 4.4 per cent share of listening. While BBC television failed to retain or win major sports contracts, Radio 5 Live struck deals to cover football, rugby and tennis. 'I wish I had gone down the sports route faster...' admitted MacKenzie, 'but nothing is going to stop us now'. In March it was reported that Talk Sport lost out to the BBC in the battle for a five-year Test Match cricket deal even though the station apparently outbid the Corporation.

It was also a fruitful year for the BBC's least listened to network, Radio 3. Under new controller Roger Wright there were indications that the service was gradually repositioning itself as an arts and culture network, instead of strictly adhering to its traditional base as a pure classical music service. Explained Wright: 'If you're describing what it's about in terms of numbers, then you'll see that it's driven by classical music. But if you're looking for a big umbrella to define it, then culture or arts would probably be it'.

LATE JUNCTION WINS CRITICAL APPROVAL

From a critical perspective one of the most talked about radio programmes of the year was Radio 3's *Late Junction*, broadcast five nights a week at 10.15. Showcasing an extraordinarily eclectic mix of music, ranging from jazz to Buddhist chants, and hosted by Fiona Talkington and Verity Sharp, *Late Junction* won the Broadcasting Press Guild radio award. The *Evening Standard's* television critic, Victor Lewis-Smith, summed up its appeal. It was, he said, 'a consistently intelligent and absorbing programme that tries to attract listeners, rather than repel them'. Other Radio 3 highlights included *Shakespeare For*

The Millennium, although some critics were disappointed, and a new daily series, *Work in Progress*, in which artists mused on their current work.

Not that it was all plain sailing for BBC Radio during the year. Radio 1, criticised in some quarters for not offering enough of a genuine alternative to its commercial rivals, scored an own goal when in May one its most loyally listened to presenters, Andy Kershaw, was sacked. Writing in *The Times* David Sinclair argued that Kershaw had been 'a victim of the ruthlessly ageist streamlining policy that has seen Radio 1 go in recent years from being an alert, broadly inclusive popular music station into an ideologically-driven, pop/dance/yoof ghetto actively designed to repel anyone over the age of 24'. Kershaw, however, was promptly signed up by Radio 3 to present a World Music show. GWR boss Steve Orchard echoed this view when he told *Broadcast* magazine: 'I listen to Radio 1 and try to work out what the hell it is spending £40 million on. It's a waste of money and waste of frequency'. The departure of Zoe Ball from the breakfast show was mourned in some quarters. Ms Ball's successor was ex-Channel 4 presenter Sara Cox, who got off to a promising if hardly sensational start.

The commercial sector also looked with envy upon Radio 2, which continued to build on its appeal to the sixties 'baby boomers' generation without alienating too many older fans. With more than ten million listeners a week Radio 2 convincingly bridged the gap between middle-of-the-road broadcasters like Terry Wogan, still presenting his breakfast show, *Wake Up Wogan*, the timeless *Sing Something Simple*, and shows aimed at younger audiences hosted by the likes of Mark Lamarr and Jonathan Ross.

The latter's Saturday morning show helped the station build its popularity with the under-50s. Also of note was a series of well-informed documentaries on soul music presented by veteran broadcaster and writer Charlie Gillett. When Radio 2 DJ Johnnie Walker was suspended from work following allegations of cocaine abuse, published in the *News of the World*, the station's reputation for being hip reached new levels. Walker was subsequently reinstated.

FOUR FORGES AHEAD

At Radio 4 James Boyle was succeeded by Helen Boaden, who joined the meagre ranks of BBC senior female editorial figures. Unlike Boyle, she has kept a low profile preferring to build on her predecessor's successors instead of following his example and embarking on a fundamental overhaul of the programme menu. Launching her first schedule in August she said her approach would be one of 'consolidation and calm'. An innovation involved a plan to reintroduce a regular children's programme, beginning in 2001. The move followed a prolonged campaign to reinstate broadcasts for younger listeners on BBC Radio.

To mark the millennium Radio 4 celebrated *A Thousand Years Of Spoken English*, while Melvyn Bragg's *The Routes of English* travelled the United Kingdom to explore the English language in all its variations. Drama included Alan Bennett reading his own, *Father! Father! Burning Bright*, a short story about a family at the bedside of a dying father. Less successful was a new comedy from *After Henry* creator Simon Brett, *Smelling of Roses*. Prunella Scales played a single mother caught between a headstrong daughter and her granddaughter.

The Archers, the network's second most popular show after *Today*, was back in the headlines. When the serial broadcast a passionate encounter in the shower, commentators wondered if the rural community of Ambridge was intent on doing anything to increase ratings. Not so, said editor Vanessa Whitburn. She said: 'The sex scene hoo-ha was the result of spin by the media'.

Listeners enjoyed the story. But when an episode in which one of the characters discussed Tony Blair's speech to the National Farmers' Union incited accusations of political bias, Greg Dyke, an Archers fan, agreed. The series profile rose higher still when Whitburn introduced a storyline involving Ruth and a diagnosis of breast cancer.

In news and current affairs *Today* and *The World At One* increased their share of listening. *The Long View*, presented by Jonathan Freedland, was hailed as an innovative history series. Meanwhile *The Food Programme* clocked up its 20th anniversary.

Conservation and Heritage

COUNTRYSIDE AND RIGHTS OF WAY

The most important legislation since 1981 affecting wildlife and access to the countryside was passing through Parliament during summer and autumn 2000. The Countryside and Rights of Way Bill will strengthen the protection of Sites of Special Scientific Interest (SSSI) and gives the public rights of access to some 1.6 million hectares of moorland, downland and registered common land. This right of access may be extended to coastal land in England and Wales, after an environmental appraisal. It does not extend to enclosed farmland or private woodlands, but an incentive scheme will allow landowners to dedicate land for public access. They will have the right to close off areas vulnerable to disturbance at certain times of year, for example on nesting bird colonies. Landowners will also be able to close land to the public for up to 28 days per year, except on weekends and bank holidays.

On SSSIs, the Bill gives the wildlife agencies powers to refuse consent for any damaging proposal and to restore damaged or mismanaged land. For deliberate damage, a successful prosecution could lead to fines of up to £20,000 in the Magistrates Court, or unlimited fines in the Crown Court. A loophole allowing third parties to escape prosecution is to be closed. However, it seems that none of these sanctions will apply to SSSIs owned by public bodies. This part of the Bill won cross-party support, and went through virtually unchanged.

GM CROP TESTING

Controversy over the testing of genetically modified crops (GMOs) in Britain was *the* environmental story of the year 2000. Greenpeace contrived to keep the subject newsworthy by its well-publicised raids on GM crops, resulting in the arrest and trial of protestors led by Lord Melchett. Prince Charles commented on GM crops in his contribution to the BBC Reith Lectures, urging biotech companies to 'work with the grain of nature' and to 'rediscover a reverence for the natural world'.

The potential effect on natural biodiversity of growing GM crops is hard to predict. In the patchwork landscape of lowland Britain, pollen from GM crops will escape more easily into the wild than in the North American mid-west, where GM crops are grown routinely. The Government introduced a three-year moratorium on their commercial use while possible ecological affects are tested. Responding to public disquiet, many retailers refused to sell food products made from GM crops.

International trade in GMOs is controlled by a Biosafety Protocol, signed by Britain in January, giving governments the right to decide whether to import GM food. However the ultimate power lies with the World Trade Organisation, which has been accused of promoting trade above environmental issues and bullying Third World nations into adopting unsustainable practices against their long-term interests. In December 1999 protests by environmentalists forced the closure of the World Trade Organisation's talks in Seattle, Washington.

EU CONSERVATION LEGISLATION

Under European legislation, all member states are required to designate sites of international interest for birds (Special Protection Areas, known as SPAs), and for other species and their natural habitats (as Special Areas for Conservation or SACs). The two categories are expected to form a Europe-wide network of conservation sites called Natura 2000. Member states, including the UK, were criticised by the EU Environment Commissioner for dragging their feet over the 'candidate' list of SACs, and for significant omissions when they finally did produce it. After hearing evidence from the World Wide Fund for Nature and other conservation bodies, the Commission deemed the UK list inadequate for certain habitats, such as bogs, Atlantic oakwoods and salmon rivers. In the meantime, Greenpeace won a legal ruling that the UK should have included marine SACs within its full 'Exclusive Economic Zone' of 200 miles, and not merely within its 12-mile territorial waters, in order to protect whales and dolphins. At present the wildlife agencies are undergoing the lengthy process of consultation with landowners and other users of proposed SACs, and reviewing extant planning permissions and land management against the requirements of the Habitats Regulations.

The European Union has been less helpful in protecting what remains of Britain's hedgerows. To prevent farmers from claiming more money for their arable crops than they are entitled to, the European Court of Auditors instructed member countries to ensure that field boundaries must be no more than two metres wide, or four metres wide in the case of adjacent fields. The EC Agriculture Commissioner agreed to delay implementing this proposal until some exemption can be made to protect our broader hedges, some of which are protected under another Regulation! In August, the Minister of Agriculture, Nick Brown, announced that he had negotiated a 'derogation' enabling farmers to obtain arable payments without ploughing up their field margins.

BURNS INQUIRY ON HUNTING

Lord Burns's report into hunting covered the probable consequences of a hunting ban on the rural economy and on the control of quarry species. Broadly it accepted the view that the issue is a moral and cultural one, rather than one with significant implications for predator control or nature conservation. Hunting makes only a minor contribution to keeping fox numbers down, although in upland areas and forestry plantations alternative means of control are limited. The inquiry found no scientific evidence that foxes suffered unduly compared with alternative methods of pest control like snaring or shooting, although 'we are satisfied that the activity of digging out and shooting a fox involves a serious compromise of its welfare'. It concluded that a hunting ban would be unlikely to result in the loss of hedgerows and copses, since these are also used for pheasant-rearing and shooting.

The inquiry found no pest control reason to hunt the Brown Hare, since this is already a declining species. However, since hare numbers tend to be higher in places where they are 'coursed' with dogs, a ban on hunting might have the paradoxical effect of reducing their numbers still further.

ARTIFICIAL WILDERNESSES

The Wetland Centre which opened in May aims to achieve Peter Scott's dream of a wildfowl reserve in the heart of London. The 42 hectare site, in a loop of the River Thames at Barn Elms, is the result of eight years of planning and engineering to convert redundant Victorian reservoirs into natural-seeming wetland, including reed-bed, marshland and woodland as well as open water. The process of moving some 500,000 cc of soil, and planting around 30,000 trees and shrubs, followed the granting of detailed planning permission in 1995. The Wildlife and Wetlands Trust and Thames Water financed the project partly from the sale of nearby surplus land for housing.

The Centre includes educational facilities and bird hides overlooking the lakes, including a novel three-storey hide with a lift for the disabled. A large variety of wild duck use the area, especially in winter, and declining species like Redshank, Lapwing and Snipe have started to nest here. Some 18 species of dragonfly have also been recorded. After the initial planting, the area is being left to develop naturally, with the water levels controlled by sluices.

A second ambitious exercise in wilderness creation is underway at Needingworth in the Cambridgeshire Fens. By agreement with the RSPB, Hanson Aggregates are set to transform some 1,000 hectares of sand and gravel pits into a large area of wetland. Half this area will be turned into reedbeds, in the hope of halting the decline of birds such as Bearded Tit and Bittern, whose current population is thought to be only 20 pairs. The hydrological work is scheduled to begin in 2002, and will be gradually handed over to the RSPB, over a 30-year period, to manage as a nature reserve.

Heathland Restored

Preserving lowland heath, one of the most diminished natural habitats in Britain, is the object of an umbrella programme called Tomorrow's Heathland Heritage, run by English Nature. Some 19 projects, substantially funded by the Heritage Lottery Fund, are currently underway, most of which aim to restore heathland and improve its biodiversity by re-introducing livestock grazing. The past year saw the launch of the Surrey's Last Wilderness project, headed by Surrey County Council, which hopes to restore some 2,500 hectares of heathland in Surrey and Berkshire by tackling invasive scrub, bracken and coarse grass. It will also try to create larger blocks of wild habitat by linking isolated heaths. A key partner in the project is the Ministry of Defence, which owns over 60 per cent of Surrey's surviving heaths. Another goal of the project is to encourage public participation, through dialogue with local communities, an interactive website and public events.

Bird Winners and Losers

In an assessment of the prospects of our 204 regularly breeding birds, the ornithologist Chris Mead reckoned that 39 are doing very well, 79 quite well, 56 quite badly and 30 very badly. The Red Kite was dubbed 'the bird of the century'. Down to a single breeding female at the lowest point of its fortunes in the 1930s, there are now 300 pairs, thanks mainly to reintroductions since 1990, but also due to an increase in the resident population in Wales.

The Mediterranean Gull enjoyed its most successful season ever in by raising 38 young in its main colony at Langstone Harbour, Hampshire. Another successful colonist is the Little Egret which is now breeding in several counties in southern England and Ireland. There are now 'several dozen' pairs breeding in trees alongside Herons. This bird has benefitted from the recent run of mild winters. Another possible colonist is the Spoonbill, a pair of which bred in 2000, in Dumfries and Galloway, for the first time since the 17th-century.

Among the losers are birds on farmland, a key indicator of sustainability in a recent Government report. Many familiar species, such as Skylark, Linnet, Tree Sparrow and Corn Bunting, have suffered serious declines, which are probably linked to early ploughing, thus depriving them of waste seeds in stubble fields, and also to the loss of natural pasture. Another bird in serious trouble is the Black Grouse, whose numbers have fallen by 95 per cent during the course of the 20th-century. One reason is that the birds tend to crash into deer fences, another that their favourite food, bilberry, is declining through over-grazing by sheep or deer. The inoffensive Turtle Dove may also be on the way out. Large numbers are shot as they migrate through Europe, but the main reason is probably agricultural herbicides, which have wiped out most of the crop weeds on which these birds depend in the breeding season.

Insect Colonists and Extinctions

British dragonflies are among the best-known insects, and so two new species found breeding in southern England are almost certainly recent colonists. The Lesser Emperor (*Anax parthenope*) has become a frequent visitor to the south-west, and it bred successfully for the first time in Cornwall. The Small Red-eyed Damselfly (*Erythromma viridulum*) was discovered breeding at three ponds in Essex, and seems to be well-established there. This species has spread through northern Europe, and probably arrived in East Anglia from the Netherlands. Two more dragonflies, the Red-veined Darter and Yellow-veined Darter, hitherto regarded as scarce migrants, are now breeding more regularly.

Another apparent newcomer is the Suffolk Ant-lion (*Euroleon nostras*), which has colonised coastal sand-hills and heaths in East Anglia. The larva of this nocturnal, dragonfly-sized insect digs pits in the sand to trap unwary ants and other invertebrates. The characteristic conical depressions were first found on the RSPB's nature reserve at Minsmere in 1994, and have since been found elsewhere on the Suffolk 'Sandlings'. In the same area, the Queen of Spain Fritillary butterfly, hitherto thought of as a very rare migrant, has been seen in most years since the mid-1990s, and has probably formed a small breeding colony.

Among the moths, two attractive species have probably colonised Britain from the continent in the past few years. One, the Small Ranunculus, is already well-established on wasteland and in gardens near the Thames Estuary, where it lays on Wild Lettace plants. The Oak Rustic moth was discovered on the Isle of Wight in 1999, possibly having spread from Jersey where it is a resident species. Its larva feeds on Holm Oak, which is common in parts of the island.

Added to other recent observations, like the successful overwintering of butterflies, like the Red Admiral and Painted Lady, or the expansion northwards of others like the Comma, these discoveries may well be signs of climate change.

Unfortunately more insects are dying out than are colonising Britain. According to English Nature, one insect in 14 has become extinct over the past century. Locally the rate is even higher. A survey of Warwickshire's insects, conducted by Oxford University, suggests that one in five kinds of insects have vanished there since 1960.

Beavers for Scotland

In August, a breeding group of three European beavers were released in a secure wetland site in Scotland as the start of a project to re-establish the beaver in Britain after an absence of at least 400 years. The animals, from the Popielno nature reserve in Poland, were quarantined at an animal sanctuary before their release. It is planned that more beavers will be released over the next seven years, and their progress carefully monitored. Following their extinction from fur-trapping, beavers have been successfully reintroduced into several European countries, including France and Germany, and an analysis of potential habitat suggests that Scotland could support 'several hundred' animals. Conservationists back the project not only for the beaver's sake but because the animals' dam-building habits create pools and other small-scale habitats where other wildlife can flourish.

ERIKA OIL-SPILL

In December 1999, the tanker MV Erika foundered and broke up off the Brittany coast. Some 25,000 tonnes of heavy fuel oil leaked from the vessel and polluted over 400 km of Atlantic shoreline between south-west Brittany and La Rochelle. By the following spring, more than 60,000 oiled seabirds had been recovered, most of them Guillemots and Razorbills. Most of those with leg-rings were from Britain or Ireland. This spill was especially damaging because much of it was blown into bays and inlets where birds shelter during winter storms. Even so, the incident should not harm the long-term prospects of Guillemots, which are increasing by some 10 per cent per annum in Scotland and northern England. Despite the occasional, much-publicised oil-spill, fewer sea-birds are oiled today and the clean-up techniques have become much less environmentally harmful. However, following the Erika wreck, the French authorities have decided to impose the obligatory use of double-hulled tankers within its national waters.

CARDIFF BAY

Cardiff Bay is a rare example of the effective destruction of an officially protected wildlife site by a government-sponsored development. The controversial barrage across the bay was completed in November 1999, enabling the conversion of tidal mudflats to a marina. The SSSI-designated mudflats were used by up to 5,000 redshank and dunlin which now have to find alternative feeding grounds. The planners' purpose is to make the Cardiff seafront look more attractive, and attract businesses into the area. However, the European Union considered that Cardiff Bay should have been included in the Severn Estuary 'Special Protection Area' (SPA). This means that the UK Government must provide a compensation site nearby. However bird experts claim that the compensatory 375 ha nature reserve on the Gwent Levels is insufficient to feed the large numbers of migratory birds that wintered in Cardiff Bay. It was hoped that, in the interests of the birds, the barrage would be left open, and the tide allowed to take its natural course, until spring 2000. However Cardiff Bay Development Corporation, in charge of the project, thought otherwise. The sluice gates were promptly shut late in 1999, only to be re-opened shortly afterwards because of fears that waterfront homes could be flooded. The gates are designed to open automatically when the water level in the bay exceeds 4.9 metres.

Other environmental concerns include the high levels of toxic metals in the mud, which may require to be dredged, and the low oxygen levels in summer.

UK SEED BANK OF NATIVE PLANTS

The Seed Bank of the Royal Botanic Gardens, situated at Wakehurst Place in Surrey, now stores seed samples from 93 per cent of the UK's native wild flowers and trees – some 1,370 species. The seeds have been collected mainly by volunteers over the past three years. The remaining seven per cent are plants which either produce seed rarely, if at all, or produce seed which cannot survive long. The Bank now includes seeds from 147 species considered endangered or vulnerable, thus holding genetic material for reintroduction attempts in case any of these plants become extinct in the wild.

The project included research into techniques that have refined the methods used to store seed. For example, the dust, like seeds of wild orchids and parasitic broomrapes can now be stored in nutrient-containing 'beads'. Another tricky group, the willows, may soon become storable, now that research has shown that they can be dried successfully. The Seed Bank, which is funded by the Millennium Commission and the Wellcome Trust, a medical research charity, has become a major contributor to the conservation of plant biodiversity, both in the UK and overseas.

THE BUILT ENVIRONMENT

HERITAGE REVIEW

Much of the year 2000 was absorbed in what was trumpeted as the most far-reaching Heritage Review since the War. Initiated following a recommendation of the Culture, Media and Sport Committee of the House of Commons and entrusted by the Secretary of State to English Heritage the Review was designed to be the most democratic ever conducted. EH provided the secretariat only, the ideas and suggestions coming from Working Parties, on which EH representatives were always in a minority, and from two broad consultation campaigns among the general public. The principal consultation paper was despatched to 3,500 addresses. At the time of writing, the collation process was underway with the anticipation of a Government response by the end of the year.

The year 2000 marked the launch of the Register of Architects Accredited in Conservation which allowed the public for the first time to identify architects who can be trusted in the repair of historic buildings.

THE HERITAGE LOTTERY FUND

The principal source of money remained the Heritage Lottery Fund financed from the National Lottery. The Department for Culture, Media and Sport estimated in the course of the year that the HLF would have at its disposal £305 million in 1999–2000, £315 million in 2000–1, and £325 million in 2001–2. Against that background and following a consultation exercise the HLF trustees declared that the percentage allocations to the various sectors for which it was responsible over those three years would be: Museums and Galleries (including acquisitions) 24 per cent, Historic Buildings 28 per cent, Land and Countryside 22 per cent, Libraries and Archives eight per cent, Industrial, Maritime and Transport Schemes nine per cent and Revenue (as opposed to Capital) Schemes nine per cent. Fifty percent of the budget would go to grants below £1 million in order to facilitate the trickle down effect which Ministers and Trustees sought.

As at 4 August 2000 the total value of capital and revenue grants announced by the HLF was £1,523,284,909. Of this £30,412,500 has gone on the Townscape Heritage Initiative and £31,431,408 under the Joint Places of Worship Scheme, the English Heritage contribution to this being on top. Of the 5,627 capital and revenue grants by that date, 1,199 had been completed. The average UK success rate for applications was a really quite respectable, 56 per cent.

A selection of the grants offered can provide only a taster of the catholicity with which the HLF interprets the word 'Heritage'. The name of the beneficiary is followed by the amount of grant offered in parenthesis – St Frances Xavier Church, Liverpool (£514,600), to allow joint church and university use of a building previously threatened by an application to demolish, Temple Newsam House, Leeds, West Yorkshire (£1,300,000) to repair and enhance one of Yorkshire's greatest country houses, St Nicholas's Church, Burnage, Manchester (£1,108,000) to repair and lend new life to one of the greatest inter-war churches built in 1938, Robert Owen's School at New Lanark (£2,435,000) to continue the ambitious programme of conservation at perhaps the best known idealistic settlement of the 19th-century, St Ethelburgha's Bishopsgate, in the City of London (£243,000) to finish the reconstruction of the church blown up by the IRA in 1993, Albert Park, Middlesbrough, Cleveland (£3,369,000) a representative example of one of the many HLF grants to the country's Urban Parks, Blackwell, Windermere, in the Lake District (£2,225,000) to permit the purchase by the Abbott Hall Museum at Kendal of this memorable house of 1898 designed by the Arts and Crafts architect, Baillie Scott, the Williton Workhouse, West Somerset (£674,000) to permit the repair of this long-derelict workhouse designed in 1838 by Sir George Gilbert Scott, Staffordshire Archive Service (£89,900) to permit the cataloguing of the papers of the Dukes of Sutherland and the Marquises of Anglesey, Saltwell Park, Gateshead, Tyne and Wear (£6,949,000) to conserve the 12 listed buildings within the park opened in 1876, Ripon Market Place, North Yorkshire (£1,233,000) to conserve and improve the buildings and floorscape, including the abolition of 40 per cent of the existing car parking spaces, the establishment of new museums at Hackney (£396,500), Padstow in Cornwall (£199,000) this one to be sited in the towns former railway station and Llanidloes in, Powys (£190,000) to consolidate and expand the collection housed in the listed town hall, Saltburn Pier, Cleveland (£995,000) the last remaining pier on the North East coast, Thurnham Castle, Kent (£67,500) to allow the County Council to acquire and repair this motte and bailey castle, the Chatterley Whitfield Colliery, Stoke-on-Trent (£463,500) to employ a project co-ordinator to take forward the conservation of the largest and best surviving example of a mining complex in the UK first mined in 1884, Llanerchaeron, Dyfed (£2 million), a further grant to the National Trust to allow it to complete the repair of what remains the most complete example of John Nash's work in the Principality, the Community Lifeline Canal Project, Sandwell in West Midlands (£1,287,000) to conserve 17.5 km of canal as a Heritage Route linking the Convention Centre in Birmingham and the Black Country Museum in Dudley, the Victoria County Histories (£179,500) to support the work of the single greatest agency engaged in the compilation of local history, the British Hindu Oral History Project (£86,200) to create an oral history archive recording all aspects of the history and culture of the Hindu community of Britain, Sheffield General Cemetery (£87,900) to improve access to, and understanding of, this poetic, romantic, picturesque landscape, rich with monuments and buildings of the 19th-century, the Handel House Museum, 25 Brook Street, in Mayfair (£500,000) to create a museum to the great Baroque composer in what was his house from 1723 until 1759, the Lawrence Olivier Archive (£500,000) to allow the papers of Britain's greatest 20th-century actor to be lodged, conserved and catalogued at the British Library, the Nenthead Mines Heritage Centre at Alston in Cumbria (£599,500) to conserve one of the most important surviving examples of

a mining landscape centred on lead and zinc working and smelting works from the 18th-century, and the Centre for Buckinghamshire Studies, Aylesbury (£463,500) to bring for the first time under one roof, records and books on the history of this county.

The year also saw the opening of many major schemes grant aided by the Lottery, whether through the HLF, the Arts Council or the Millennium Commission. These included many in London the revamped National Portrait Gallery, extension by Rick Mather to Dulwich Picture Gallery, Tate Modern on the south bank of the Thames, the Gilbert Collection at Somerset House in the Strand, the Wallace Collection at Hertford Square in central London, the £48 million Wellcome Wing at the Science Museum and the new covered courtyard at the British Museum. Outside London the World of Glass Museum at St Helens in Lancashire opened in March, the Lowry Centre in Salford followed in April with other newcomers at Stoneleigh Abbey in Warwickshire where the state rooms opened to the public for the first time after a dangerous period of near dereliction, the National Centre for Early Music based at the former church of St Margaret's, at Walmgate in York and the new educational centre adjacent to Canterbury Cathedral, designed by Sir William Whitfield where the HLF provided half the total cost of £5.5 million.

ENGLAND

The HLF is financed by those buying lottery tickets, English Heritage gains its income, aside from membership subscriptions, gate receipts and publication sales, from the tax payer. In the summer of 2000 it acquired a new Chairman, Sir Neil Cossons, a distinguished industrial archaeologist, who came to the post following retirement as Director at the Science Museum. His predecessor, Sir Jocelyn Stevens, remained in charge of EH's thorniest project, the recreation of the setting and the provision of new visitor facilities at Stonehenge. The last available Annual Report published in November 1999 showed that the agency attracted non-Governmental income in 1998–9 of £28.3 million, an increase of ten per cent over the previous years, and offered some £35.5 million in grants to England's historic buildings, monuments and landscapes. Its new Centre for Archaeology was up and running at Fort Cumberland in Portsmouth, whilst its membership totals now exceeded 400,000. Shortly before it had announced a re-focusing of its grant regimes with four new priority categories – urgent repairs to buildings and monuments at risk included with its own Register of Buildings at Risk (which included 1,600 items in the list for 2000), grants for historic parks and gardens where there was a significant risk of important historic landscape features being lost, grants to private owners covering both 'Great Treasure Houses' and smaller houses which have been in the same family ownership for at least 30 years where the project involved work urgently necessary to keep the building structurally stable and watertight and grants for repair projects with significant social or economic regeneration benefits. It also expanded its already comprehensive publication programmes with new books on Heritage-led regeneration, London suburbs, the architecture of England's prisons, the architectural and archaeological evidence of the gunpowder industry, the Directory of Building Sands and Aggregates and a new 'Heritage Dictionary' containing over 10,000 official standards of terminology, to be made available on the Internet. It also published guidance, to stand alongside that issued by the Joint Committee of

National Amenity Societies, on the vexed problem of 'Enabling Development', that is the construction of new houses or other development in the grounds of a derelict listed building in order to generate money to go towards its rescue.

WALES

In Wales the nearest equivalent to EH is Cadw, advised by the Historic Buildings Council, although the former remains internal to the Welsh Office rather than functioning as a quasi-autonomous Governmental body or quango. The last available Annual Report for Cadw printed on 29 October 1999 reported the total of listed buildings in Wales as at 31 March 1999 as 22,308, with the agency on target to complete the National Resurvey of Listed Buildings by 2005. Reports of the Historic Buildings Council describe the Cadw grants at greater length, beneficiaries including Penrhyn Castle (£119,400), the monastery off the Pembrokeshire coast on Caldey Island (£75,000), the 17th-century plaster ceilings at 5 Lion Street, Brecon (£9,400), the only Welsh work by the distinguished Arts and Crafts architect, Voysey, in Cardiff (£70,000) and the Round House at the The Kymin (£16,000) which was built in 1794 as a banqueting pavilion by a gentleman's club at a cost of 80 guineas. The Register of Historic Parks and Gardens in Wales took two large steps towards completion with the publication in 1999 of two new volumes covering Conwy, Gwynedd and the Isle of Anglesey in one, and Powys in the other.

SCOTLAND

North of the border, Historic Scotland, ranks alongside English Heritage as a quango. It too has its own distinguished technical publishing programme, the most recent subjects tackled including lime harling, Scottish Aggregates, the treatment of graffiti on historic surfaces, the conservation of parchment, water repellents for sandstone and Scottish turf construction. The series is unsurpassed in its excellence and there is at present no published equivalent in Wales or England to the 'Churches to Visit in Scotland', a guide to over 600 churches of all denominations open to the public throughout 2000 (compiled by Scotland's Church Scheme).

LISTED BUILDINGS

Britain has more listed buildings than any other country in the world (depending on how you assess the total in Italy). Recent additions to the lists include a private theatre in Bournemouth built for the son of the poet Shelley, Telegraph Farm in Kent built in the early 19th-century to take a shutter telegraph on the roof to provide early warning of a possible Napoleonic invasion, a grotto in Leicestershire designed by William Wordsworth, a mid-19th century onion-drying floor in Bedfordshire, a corn-drying house in Snowdonia of 1729, the Essex Country cricket pavilion of 1886, at Leyton, the library to St Hilda's College Oxford designed in 1934 by Sir Edwin Cooper, the Stanton Guildhouse in Gloucestershire built in the Arts and Crafts idiom as late as 1963–73 under the inspiration of Mary Osborn, a number of surviving buildings on the Hafod estate in Dyfed, one of the greatest Picturesque estates of the 18th-century, an architectural fragment in an Italian garden in Hertfordshire said to have been from the Palace of Westminster, an old sail-loft occupied by sail-makers near Cardigan, in Dyfed, a petrol pump of 1934 at Oxton in Nottinghamshire, the synagogue at Carmel College at Crowmarsh in Oxfordshire of 1963 and the planned 18th-century farmstead, part of the Holkham

estate in Norfolk at South Creake. Other buildings have been upgraded in light of new evidence including another synagogue of 1831–3 at Ramsgate, the clock tower in the docks at Middlesbrough in Cleveland, the work of Philip Webb, Highpoint One at North Hill in London Borough of Haringey already Grade II* but now raised to Grade I as one of the iconic buildings of the Modern Movement (1933–5 by Lubetkin). The year also saw the completion of a special study of cinemas as a building type with recommendations to add 30 more to the statutory lists alongside the existing total of 123.

As at the end of 1999 the number of listed buildings in England had risen to 453,111. In terms of the counties Devon had the most at over 20,000 followed by Kent with nearly 18,000. At the equivalent point of reckoning there were 8,819 conservation areas in England, 17,759 scheduled ancient monuments, newcomers including two cockpits near Warrington, alum works at Loftus in Cleveland, a castle at Christchurch and a mediaeval enclosure near Berwick-upon-Tweed. The total entries within the Register of Historic Parks and Gardens stood at 1,335, by May 1999, the 40 additions in the year prior to that including the post war landscape at the Commonwealth Institute in Kensington. The parallel Register of Battle-fields by that time had 43 entries.

The equivalent of listing on the international scale is designation as a World Heritage Site. The decisions are taken by UNESCO on the recommendations of national governments and on the 29 November 1999 the former agreed to inscribe 42 new sites located in 33 countries. They included Robbin Island off South Africa the scene of the recent imprisonment of Nelson Mandela but with continuos history of use from the 17th-century, another island with kinder memories the so-called Museum Island at Berlin housing five museums built between 1824 and 1930, the city of Graz in Austria, the belfries of Flanders and Wallonia in Belgium, Hadrian's Villa at Tivoli in Italy, Campeche in Mexico, the wooden churches of Maramures in Romania, the Brimstone Hill Fortress on St Kitt's in the West Indies, two sites in Vietnam, Hoi, a trading port of the 15th to the 19th centuries and My Son Sanctuary a series of tower temples the first one dating from the fourth century.

NEW ATTRACTIONS

Identifying, protecting and grant-aiding historic buildings can be the initial steps before increasing access to them. Historic properties opening for the first time in 1999 or for their first complete season included Rodmarton Manor in Gloucestershire one of the great Arts and Crafts houses of the end of the century, the British Schools of 1837–1905 at Hitchin in Hertfordshire, Longner Hall at Uffington in Shropshire by John Nash of 1803, Cothay Manor at Wellington in Somerset of the medieval period and Lowfield Heath Windmill at Charlwood in Surrey, the Great Hall at Winchester of 1220, reopened to the public in May after the completion of an extensive repair campaign whilst that most evocative representation of 18th-century life at 18 Folgate Street in Spitalfields in east London built in the early 18th-century passed into the care of the Spitalfields Trust following the death in December 1999 of Dennis Severs who had saved the buildings and opened it to an enraptured public. In the millennial year of 2000 many of London's hitherto closed historic buildings opened for a single year under the 'String of Pearls' project – a year long equivalent to the Heritage Open Days weekends in September, now established as a regular event. In 2000 plans were also announced for a National Centre for the Culinary Arts to be established in the redundant but listed hospital at

Stafford whilst a trust was formed to take into care the outstanding but roofless mediaeval barn at Pilton in Somerset, built in the 14th-century for Glastonbury Abbey.

The year also saw new acquisitions by The Landmark Trust which buys idiosyncratic properties under threat for conversion to holiday lets. They acquired Pugin's house 'The Grange' at Ramsgate, Beckford's Tower in Bath and opened their latest 'landmark' at Wilmington Priory in Sussex. The similar but smaller body, the Vivat Trust, opened a new property – the tower at Halbar at Braidwood near Glasgow. The Churches Conservation Trust which owns more than 300 disused Anglican churches in England took into care the fine mediaeval church of St Augustine's in Norwich and included among its vestings in 1998–9 St Peter's Northampton with considerable Norman remains and Christchurch Waterloo in Merseyside of 1891 which had been proposed for demolition. The non-Anglican equivalent to the CCT, the Historic Chapels Trust, also continues to expand its holdings, with three new vestings in 2000 – Penrose Methodist Chapel in Cornwall, Umberslade Baptist Church in Warwickshire of 1877 and the Votive Chapel of Our Lady of Lourdes at Blackpool dating from only 1957 and one of the last works of the leading Catholic architect FX Velarde. In November 1999 the Friends of Friendless Churches accepted the first, four, vestings of redundant churches in Wales as part of the arrangement under which Church and State offered 100 per cent contributions towards the cost of its serving as the equivalent within the Principality of the Churches Conservation Trust.

THREATS

In 1999 applications were lodged to demolish 210 listed buildings in England and Wales. The principal threats were to Dennis Hall at Amblecote in the West Midlands of circa 1770, the four listed buildings in Brecon threatened by an inner relief road, St Cuthbert's Church Gateshead, Tyne and Wear designed by John Dobson, St Mary's Church Halifax, the former Bethesda Baptist Chapel in Prince of Wales Road, Swansea and the body of St Augustine's Roman Catholic Church at Preston in Lancashire. Other cases falling short of demolition which stoked controversy involved extensions to the art gallery within Pallant House in Chichester, the proposed supermarket at Hadleigh in Suffolk, the redevelopment of the currently vacant site adjacent to Clifford's Tower in central York and the closure and sale of the 17th-century almshouses known as the Lucas Hospital in Wokingham, Berkshire and the great Victorian convent at Clewer in suburban Windsor.

Dance

The Royal Opera House reopened in December 1999 with a spectacular gala – spectacular at least on the part of the Royal Ballet – but spent the rest of the season fielding criticism that its planned programme had been too ambitious and that technical problems had yet to be ironed out. Several productions were cancelled and there were renewed complaints about ticket prices. But the new house offers a magnificently restored main auditorium as well as two new studio theatres, a proper rehearsal base for the Royal Ballet, and spacious and exciting public spaces, including the rebuilt Floral Hall and a terrace overlooking Covent Garden. By the summer of 2000, the House had wiped out its deficit, announced lower ticket prices for the following season, and was hosting a highly successful visit by the Kirov Ballet and Opera companies. Michael Kaiser, the chief executive of the Royal Opera House, who was appointed in 1998 and has been largely responsible for holding the organisation together and getting its finances in order, announced at the end of the season that he would leave in 2001. The search for his replacement, for probably the most demanding job in the arts world, has already begun.

Technical problems were not the only drawbacks to the Royal Ballet's opening programme in the new House. Obviously determined not to be accused of timidity, the company presented an evening of 'International Choreography' that also included new works by the British choreographers Siobhan Davies and Ashley Page. The latter produced a disappointing work, *Hidden Variables*, to music by Colin Matthews; the piece looked and sounded like a repetition of earlier, more exciting, Page works. Asking Siobhan Davies, a highly respected choreographer from the world of contemporary dance, to make a work on the classically-trained dancers of the Royal Ballet seemed to indicate a lack of confidence in classical dance itself. Her work, *A Stranger's Taste*, was fluent and professional but failed to exploit the particular qualities of the dancers. The other items on the programme ranged from Nacho Duato's highly enjoyable *Remanso*, danced with grace and humour by three of the company's leading men, to *Tagore*, an uninspired *pas de deux* by Glen Tetley danced by Greta Hodgkinson and Rex Harrington from the National Ballet of Canada.

The rest of the Royal Ballet's season was much more successful, and included evenings in homage to Diaghilev, MacMillan, Ashton and de Valois. Works presented included an interesting reconstruction of Nijinsky's 1913 work *Jeux*, a welcome revival of Jerome Robbins's wickedly funny *The Concert* and a revival of MacMillan's curious 1975 work *Rituals*, based on Japanese ceremonial and theatrical arts. The company also revived de Valois' 1954 production of *Coppélia*, a work inexplicably absent from the repertoire for 30 years. Perhaps the greatest interest of the season was excited by the revival of Ashton's *Marguerite and Armand*, only ever danced before by its creators, Fonteyn and Nureyev. Ashton never allowed any other dancers to take on the roles, and one can only wonder what he would have made of Sylvie Guillem and Nicolas le Riche. Audiences, unsurprisingly, were thrilled with the result. The only world première of the later part of the season was, however, a disaster. William Tuckett's *The Crucible*, based on Arthur Miller's play, was a wildly ambitious work set to a score by Charles Ives and with clever but unsuitable designs by the cartoonist Ralph Steadman.

The real problem lay with the concept and the choreography, where Tuckett, a normally capable dance-maker, showed a total lack of understanding of how to present characters on stage.

In March 2000 it was announced that Ross Stretton, currently director of the Australian Ballet, would take over from Sir Anthony Dowell as director of the Royal Ballet on Sir Anthony's retirement in 2001. The appointment was a surprise and met with a mixed reaction. Stretton's career to date has been largely in the USA and in Australia, his country of origin, and he is known to be unfamiliar with the repertoire and dancers of the Royal Ballet. However, he trained in Melbourne under Peggy van Praagh and Robert Helpmann, both crucial figures in the Royal Ballet's history, and he has had considerable success at the Australian Ballet and before that as assistant director of American Ballet Theatre. Stretton will work closely with his fellow Australian, Gailene Stock, who is now director of the Royal Ballet School. The company will also be seeking a new music director following the appointment of the current director, Andrea Quinn, to New York City Ballet from 2001. At the end of the season, one of the Royal Ballet's most popular principal dancers, Bruce Sansom, retired at the age of 36 after a distinguished career with the company.

Derek Deane, the director of English National Ballet (ENB) and a former Royal Ballet principal, had been tipped as one of the frontrunners to take over from Dowell. He led his company through another largely successful season, and was awarded an OBE in the Queen's Birthday Honours in June 2000. In October he brought MacMillan's powerful 1962 work *The Rite of Spring* into ENB's repertoire for the first time. Also new to the company was Glen Tetley's beautiful 1973 ballet *Voluntaries*, set to Poulenc's Concerto in G minor for Organ, Strings and Timpani and made in memory of the British choreographer John Cranko who had died in an air crash in June 1973. Less moving but more spectacular was Deane's third in-the-round production at the Royal Albert Hall, London. *The Sleeping Beauty* premièred in June 2000 and seemed to excite nearly as much comment about the personal life of the glamorous Russian guest ballerina who took the role of Carabosse (Anastasia Volochkova) as for its artistic qualities (which were slight). Also in June 2000, ENB announced the appointment of Angela Rippon, the former BBC newsreader, as its chairman on the retirement after ten years of Pamela, Lady Harlech. The company celebrated its 50th birthday at the end of the season; it dates its existence from 14 August 1950 when a group of dancers gave a programme of one-act works at the King's Theatre, Southsea. A special series of films was shown at the National Film Theatre in August 2000 to mark the anniversary.

Birmingham Royal Ballet's big new production of the season was, like ENB's *The Sleeping Beauty*, an attempt to tell a story of good conquering evil with the help of magic forces. Unfortunately, David Bintley's *Arthur*, too, had more visual impact than choreographic worth. A retelling of the Arthurian legend set to a score by John McCabe, it was handsomely designed by Peter J. Davison and costumed by Jasper Conran; but it failed to tell its story clearly and was choreographically uninspired. More successful was a new production of *Giselle* by Bintley and Galina Samsova, which provoked a certain amount of ridicule for introducing live animals (a large white horse and a couple of beagles) into the action, but was nevertheless an authentic and effective production. The most important revival of the season was Ashton's *Dante Sonata*. This work, created in wartime Britain in 1940, had not been seen in its entirety since 1951 and was recreated by one of its original cast, Jean Bedells, with the assistance of other former dancers. It depicts a battle between the Children of Light and the Children of Darkness, and is set to Liszt's sonata *After Reading Dante*; the famously simple designs are by Sophie Fedorovitch. This was a chance to view a seminal work that proved to be as powerful and dramatic as contemporary accounts had reported. It was placed at the centre of a triple bill with two of Ashton's other masterworks, *Enigma Variations* and *Scènes de Ballet*, the latter newly acquired by the company. Another successful triple bill included a jazzy new work by Bintley, *The Shakespeare Suite*, set to Duke Ellington, which proved a great hit with audiences.

Rambert Dance Company also presented a major new work with elaborate designs and a complicated scenario this season. Christopher Bruce's first full-length work as a solo choreographer, *God's Plenty*, was described as a 'theatrical pageant' and was inspired by a variety of medieval sources, including Chaucer's *The Canterbury Tales*. It is set to a score by Dominic Muldowney, with set and costume design by Es Devlin. A blend of speech, song and dance, the work proved to be confusing, choreographically dull and lacking in dramatic focus. Far more successful was a revival of Glen Tetley's fascinating and influential *Pierrot Lunaire*, with Conor O'Brien excelling as the Pierrot. Tetley's *Embrace Tiger and Return to Mountain*, created in 1968 and inspired by the ancient Chinese discipline of t'ai chi, also made a welcome return to the repertoire, and Bruce's dramatic *Ghost Dances*, a tribute to the victims of political oppression in South America, proved as popular as ever. Merce Cunningham's *Beach Birds*, set to music by John Cage and performed by the company for the first time in June 2000, provided a serenely beautiful contrast to some of the company's more dramatic works. Rambert continued its successful collaboration with London Musici in the year under review.

Yet another ambitious narrative work was created during the year. Northern Ballet's new artistic director, Stefano Giannetti, mounted a production of *Great Expectations* to selected pieces of music by Elgar and with designs by Benita Roth. Although Giannetti attempted to simplify Dickens's plot, and turned away from the more literal productions staged by his predecessor, Christopher Gable, he was not entirely successful in transforming the densely written novel into a comprehensible dance narrative. Unusually in the company's recent history, it also mounted a triple bill of shorter works, including a revival of Gillian Lynne's popular 1987 ballet *A Simple Man*, based on the life of the artist L. S. Lowry. In April 2000 Giannetti suddenly resigned as director of the company, leaving its future identity once more uncertain.

Scottish Ballet has, at least in theory, just emerged from a long period of uncertainty precipitated by the resignation of its artistic director, Galina Samsova, in 1997. For the next two years it was led by an acting artistic director, Kenn Burke, while boardroom disputes raged above the dancers. In September 1999 the established choreographer Robert North, a former director of London Contemporary Dance Theatre and Ballet Rambert, took over as director, and in November 1999 Duncan McGhie was appointed chairman of Scottish Ballet/Scottish Opera, the new joint company for the merged technical and administrative departments of the two organisations. Scottish Ballet held its 30th anniversary season in autumn

1999. The company grew out of Western Theatre Ballet, founded in Bristol in 1957, which transferred to Glasgow in 1969 to become the Scottish Theatre Ballet. Its artistic director until 1987 was Peter Darrell, whose works still appear regularly in the repertoire. This season Scottish Ballet presented his production of *Giselle* dating from 1971, and his popular *Tales of Hoffmann* (1972), starring the former Royal Ballet dancer Adam Cooper, who is now an Associate Artist at Scottish Ballet and took the lead role in the British première of North's own production of *Romeo and Juliet* in June 2000. North is obviously intending to mount many of his own works on the company, and in his first season has put the emphasis on bright, popular, accessible works. The world première of Robert Cohan's *Aladdin* is planned for autumn 2000.

Contemporary dance does not in general aim at being either popular or accessible. A major exception to this is the American choreographer Mark Morris, whose company gave two London seasons in the year under review. The first was as part of the Dance Umbrella festival, when his company performed three works, including the sublime *Gloria*, set to Poulenc, at Sadler's Wells Theatre in October 1999. The second visit, also with assistance from Dance Umbrella, brought three major works to the London Coliseum in a collaboration with English National Opera in summer 2000. Morris created the choreography for a new production of Virgil Thomson's 1934 *Four Saints in Three Acts*, with its quirky Gertrude Stein libretto, and himself took the leading roles of Dido and the Sorceress in Purcell's *Dido and Aeneas*, with his own choreography created in 1989. The summer season ended with Handel's *L'Allegro, il Penseroso ed il Moderato*, created by Morris during his residence in Brussels in 1988 and last given in London in 1997. Once more, audiences could revel in the constant flow of beautiful, imaginative, inventive and musical dance, created and performed with an apparently effortless brilliance. At the end, ecstasy does indeed triumph over order and moderation.

The rest of the Dance Umbrella season presented the London première of Siobhan Davies's first full-evening work, *Wild Air*, and included works by Mark Baldwin, Compagnie Maguy Marin, Aletta Collins Dance Company, Russell Maliphant, Nigel Charnock, Bill T. Jones and others. Richard Alston Dance Company presented two new works by Alston in the year under review. *A Sudden Exit*, set to late Brahms piano works (from Opus 118 and 119), was premièred in Cambridge in October 1999 and *The Signal of a Shake*, set to a selection of movements from Handel's Concerti for Organ and Strings, was first performed in Canterbury in February 2000. Both showed that Alston is still making interesting, high-quality work. Mark Murphy's *V-Tol* dance company presented Murphy's new work, *Without Trace*, in October 1999; as usual with Murphy, dance is only one element in a mixed-media staging, with film playing an essential role in telling the story of a woman who goes out shopping never to return. In March 2000, Wayne McGregor presented another mixed-media work, Aeon, for his Random Dance Company; intermittently intriguing, it built to an exhilarating climax.

Lloyd Newson's DV8 Physical Theatre presented his latest work, *The Happiest Day of My Life*, in autumn 1999. The work examines the wedding of Kate and Rob (the real names of the performers), and its sad results. Newson's work is, as usual, inventive, funny and constantly watchable. Matthew Bourne's new production for Adventures in Motion Pictures, *The Car Man*, is also highly enjoyable. It premièred in June 2000 and is an entertaining reinvention of Bizet's *Carmen* subtitled 'An Auto-Erotic Thriller'. The company also toured its now famous *Swan Lake* in autumn

1999 following a successful Broadway season, and presented what were described as the 'last ever' London performances of the production in March 2000.

In April 2000, the choreographer Jeremy James died suddenly at the age of 38. Royal Ballet-trained, he had performed with many of Britain's contemporary dance companies before deciding to concentrate on choreography, for which he had won critical acclaim. Another loss during the year was June Brae, the former principal dancer of the Vic-Wells (now Royal) Ballet, who died in January 2000 at the age of 82.

A wide range of companies visited Britain in the year under review. The Lowry Centre in Salford presented the first British season by Paris Opera Ballet for 16 years, with a production of *La Bayadère*. San Francisco Ballet visited London for the first time and presented a highly successful season at Sadler's Wells Theatre. The Norwegian National Ballet brought Michael Corder's *Romeo and Juliet* to the same theatre, and the Atlanta Ballet presented *Peter Pan* at the Royal Festival Hall. Peter Schaufuss Ballet brought *The King*, inspired by Elvis Presley, to Sadler's Wells and New York City Ballet were due to appear at the 2000 Edinburgh Festival.

Three new building projects are planned for leading dance organisations. Work has already begun on a major redevelopment programme at The Place, London, which will provide better facilities for performers, for the audience, and for students at the London Contemporary Dance School. The Laban Centre, an important institution for dance training and education based in south London, is building a new home in Deptford including a 300-seat theatre, 13 dance studios and a library; it is scheduled to open in 2002. Finally, the Royal Ballet School is planning to follow the Royal Ballet Company from Barons Court in west London to new premises in Covent Garden, so that the dancers of the future can continue to be enthused and inspired by the dancers of the present.

PRODUCTIONS

ROYAL BALLET
Founded 1931 as the Vic-Wells Ballet
Royal Opera House, Covent Garden, London WC2E 9DD
World premières:
A Stranger's Taste (Siobhan Davies), 8 December 1999. A one-act ballet. Music, Tobias Hume, Marais Marais, Carl Friedrich Abel, Antoine Forqueray and John Cage; design, David Buckland. Cast led by Bruce Sansom, Peter Abegglen, Deborah Bull, Nicola Roberts and Jenny Tattersall
Lento (John Neumeier), 8 December 1999. A *pas de deux*. Music, Dmitry Shostakovich; costumes, John Neumeier. Dancers, Darcey Bussell and Otto Bubeníček
Hidden Variables (Ashley Page), 8 December 1999. A one-act ballet. Music, Colin Matthews; design, Antony McDonald. Cast led by Mara Galeazzi, Carlos Acosta and Laura Morera
The Crucible (William Tuckett), 12 April 2000. A one-act ballet. Music, Charles Ives; design, Ralph Steadman. Cast led by Irek Mukhamedov, Zenaida Yanowsky and Sarah Wildor

Company premières:
Tagore (Glen Tetley), 8 December 1999. A *pas de deux*. Music, Alexander Zemlinsky; design, John Macfarlane. Dancers, Greta Hodgkinson and Rex Harrington
Remanso (Nacho Duato), 8 December 1999. A one-act

ballet. Music, Enrique Granados; design, Nacho Duato. Dancers, Carlos Acosta, Jonathan Cope, Inaki Urlezaga
Barber Violin Concerto (second movement) (Peter Martins), 8 December 1999. A *pas de deux*. Music, Samuel Barber; costumes, William Ivey Long. Dancers, Darci Kistler and Jack Soto
The Four Seasons ('Summer' *pas de deux*) (James Kudelka), 8 December 1999. Music, Antonio Vivaldi; costumes, Carmen Alie and Denis Lavoie. Dancers, Greta Hodgkinson and Rex Harrington
The Vertiginous Thrill of Exactitude (William Forsythe), 20 January 2000. A one-act ballet. Music, Schubert. Cast led by Johann Kobborg
Known by Heart ('Junk Man' *pas de deux*) (Twyla Tharp), 20 January 2000. Music, Donald Knaack. Dancers, Susan Jaffe and Ethan Stiefel
L'Après-Midi d'un Faune (Nijinsky, revived by Ann Hutchinson Guest and Claudia Jeschke), 6 May 2000. A one-act ballet. Music, Debussy; design, Bakst. Cast led by Carlos Acosta (matinée); Irek Mukhamedov (evening)
Jeux (after Nijinsky; reconstruction and staging, Millicent Hodson), 6 May 2000. A one-act ballet. Music, Debussy; design, after Bakst. Dancers, Sarah Wildor, Jane Burn and Inaki Urlezaga (matinée); Deborah Bull, Gillian Revie and Bruce Sansom (evening)
Full-length ballets from the repertoire: *The Nutcracker* (Ivanov, prod. Wright 1984 with revisions 1999), *Coppelia* (de Valois after Ivanov and Cecchetti, 1954), *Manon* (MacMillan, 1974), *Giselle* (Coralli/Perrot, prod. Wright 1985).
One-act ballets and *pas de deux* from the repertoire: *Concerto* (MacMillan, 1966), *Rituals* (MacMillan, 1975), *Gloria* (MacMillan, 1980), *Les Rendezvous* (Ashton, 1933), *Symphonic Variations* (Ashton, 1946), *Marguerite and Armand* (Ashton, 1963), *Thaïs pas de deux* (Ashton, 1971), *Serenade* (Balanchine, 1934), *The Concert* (Robbins, 1956), *Les Biches* (Nijinska, 1924), *The Firebird* (Fokine, 1910).
The company took part in a gala to celebrate the reopening of the Royal Opera House, London, on 1 December 1999; the programme was repeated on 4 December. Extracts were performed from the following works: *The Sleeping Beauty* (Petipa), *Symphonic Variations* (Ashton), *Cinderella* (Ashton), *Ballet Imperial* (Balanchine), *Birthday Offering* (Ashton), *La fille mal gardée* (Ashton), *Napoli* (Bournonville), *Le Corsaire* (after Petipa), *The Good Humoured Ladies* (Massine), *La Bayadère* (Nureyev), *Les Biches* (Nijinska), *Romeo and Juliet* (MacMillan), *Raymonda* (Petipa), *Manon* (MacMillan), *Elite Syncopations* (MacMillan), *The Concert* (Robbins), *A Month in the Country* (Ashton), *Gloria* (MacMillan), 'Still Life' at the *Penguin Café* (Bintley), *La Bayadère* (Makarova), *The Prince of the Pagodas* (MacMillan), *Fearful Symmetries* (Page), *Steptext* (Forsythe), *Mr Worldly Wise* (Tharp) and *The Firebird* (Fokine, final tableau).
In June 2000 the company presented a two-week season of new and recent works at the Linbury Studio Theatre at the Royal Opera House. The choreographers involved included Michael Corder, Poppy Ben David, Vanessa Fenton, Jacopo Godani, Matthew Hart, Wayne McGregor, Ashley Page, William Tuckett and Christopher Wheeldon.
The company toured to Belfast in June 2000, performing works by Michael Corder, Nacho Duato, Matthew Hart, Wayne McGregor, William Tuckett and Christopher Wheeldon. Dancers from the company also participated in a gala in homage to Nijinsky in Hamburg, Germany, in July 2000, and in the Royal Ballet School performance at the Royal Opera House on 19 July 2000.

BIRMINGHAM ROYAL BALLET
Founded 1946 as the Sadler's Wells Opera Ballet
Birmingham Hippodrome, Thorp Street, Birmingham
B5 4AU

World premières:
Giselle (Petipa after Coralli and Perrot, prod. David
Bintley and Galina Samsova), 30 September 1999. Music,
Adam; design, Hayden Griffin. Cast led by Leticia Müller,
Andrew Murphy and Catherine Batcheller
The Shakespeare Suite (David Bintley), 6 October 1999. A
one-act ballet. Music, Duke Ellington; set, Steve Scott;
costumes, Jasper Conran. Cast led by Robert Parker
Arthur (David Bintley), 25 January 2000. A full-length
ballet, the first part of a two-part work. Music, John
McCabe; set, Peter J. Davison; costumes, Jasper Conran.
Cast led by Robert Parker, Joseph Cipolla, Andrew
Murphy, Monica Zamora, Sabrina Lenzi and Leticia
Müller

Company premières:
Slaughter on Tenth Avenue (Balanchine), 6 October 1999. A
one-act ballet. Music, Richard Rogers; design, Kate Ford.
Cast led by Monica Zamora and Joseph Cipolla
Five Brahms Waltzes in the Manner of Isadora Duncan
(Ashton, 1975), 5 April 2000. A solo. Music, Brahms.
Dancer, Molly Smolen
Walk to the Paradise Garden (Ashton, 1972), 5 April 2000. A
one-act ballet. Music, Delius; design, William Chappell.
Cast led by Joseph Cipolla and Sabrina Lenzi
Tweedledum and Tweedledee (Ashton, 1977), 5 April 2000. A
one-act ballet. Music, Percy Grainger. Dancers, Michael
O'Hare, David Justin and Rachel Peppin
Voices of Spring (Ashton, 1977), 5 April 2000. A *pas de deux*.
Music, Strauss; design, Julia Trevelyan Oman. Dancers,
Ambra Vallo and Robert Parker
Scènes de Ballet (Ashton, 1948), 14 April 2000. A one-act
ballet. Music, Stravinsky; design, André Beaurepaire. Cast
led by Nao Sakuma and Sergiu Pobereznic
Dante Sonata (Ashton, 1940), 14 April 2000. A one-act
ballet. Music, Liszt; design, Sophie Fedorovitch. Cast
included Monica Zamora, Andrea Tredinnick, Wolfgang
Stollwitzer and Dominic Antonucci
Full length ballets from the repertoire: *The Nutcracker*
(Ivanov, prod. Wright, additional choreography by Red-
mon, 1990) (including a special one-off performance, *The
Cracked Nut*, on 15 December 1999), *The Two Pigeons*
(Ashton, 1961).
One-act ballets from the repertoire: *The Nutcracker
Sweeties* (Bintley, 1996), *Enigma Variations* (Ashton, 1968).
In addition to three seasons at the Birmingham Hippo-
drome and one at the Birmingham Repertory Theatre, the
company toured to Plymouth, Sunderland and Bradford
(two seasons each), London (the Royal Opera House) and
Manchester. It also performed *Edward II* (Bintley, 1995) at
the Hong Kong Arts Festival in March 2000.

ENGLISH NATIONAL BALLET
Founded 1950 as London Festival Ballet
Markova House, 39 Jay Mews, London SW7 2ES

World première:
The Sleeping Beauty (Deane), 8 June 2000. A production in
the round at the Royal Albert Hall, London. Music,
Tchaikovsky; design, Roberta Guidi di Bagno. Cast led by
Erina Takahashi, Dmitri Gruzdyev, Anastasia Volochkova
and Cecilia Kerche

Company premières:
The Rite of Spring (MacMillan, 1962), 12 October 1999.
Music, Stravinsky; design, Yolanda Sonnabend. Cast led
by Tamara Rojo

Voluntaries (Tetley, 1973), 29 February 2000. Music,
Poulenc; design, Rouben Ter-Arutunian. Cast led by
Daria Klimentova
Full-length ballets from the repertoire: *The Nutcracker*
(Deane, 1997), *Coppelia* (Petipa and Cecchetti, prod. Hynd
1985), *Alice in Wonderland* (Deane, 1995).
One-act ballets from the repertoire: *La Bayadère* Act III
(Petipa, prod. Makarova, 1980), *Sphinx* (Tetley, 1977), *Les
Sylphides* (Fokine, 1909), *Etudes* (Lander, 1948).
The full company toured to Stoke-on-Trent, South-
ampton, Bristol (two seasons), Oxford (two seasons),
Liverpool (two seasons), Manchester (two seasons) and
London (the Coliseum and the Royal Albert Hall).
In April 2000 the company split into two groups and went
on two small-scale tours (called *Tour de Force*). One group
toured *Les Sylphides*, *Three Preludes* (Stevenson, 1969),
Swan Lake Act II pas de deux, *Le Corsaire pas de deux* and
Who Cares? (Balanchine, 1970) to Cheltenham, Poole,
Blackpool, Swindon and Truro. The other group toured
Apollo (Balanchine, 1928), *Impromptu* (Deane, 1982), *Alice
in Wonderland pas de deux*, *Tchaikovsky Pas de Deux* and
the *Grand Pas Classique* from *Raymonda* to Barnstaple,
Tunbridge Wells, Scunthorpe, Barrow-in-Furness,
Cambridge and Bexhill-on-Sea.
The company also performed at the Granada Festival,
Spain, in July 2000, with a repertoire of *Apollo*, *Don Quixote
pas de deux*, *Three Preludes*, *Tchaikovsky Pas de Deux*, *Etudes*,
Les Sylphides, *Impromptu*, *Le Corsaire pas de deux*, *Swan Lake
Act III pas de deux*, and the *Grand Pas Classique* from
Raymonda.

RAMBERT DANCE COMPANY
Founded 1926 as the Marie Rambert Dancers
94 Chiswick High Road, London W4 1SH

World première:
God's Plenty (Christopher Bruce), 15 September 1999.
A full-length work. Music, Dominic Muldowney; design,
Es Devlin

Company première:
Beach Birds (Merce Cunningham), 6 June 2000. Music,
John Cage; design, Marsha Skinner
Works from the repertoire: *Ghost Dances* (Bruce, 1981),
Gaps, Lapse and Relapse (James, 1998), *Four Scenes* (Bruce,
1998), *The Golden Section* (Tharp, 1981), *Embarque*
(Davies, 1988), *Swansong* (Bruce, 1987), *Greymatter*
(Veldman, 1997), *August Pace* (Cunningham, 1989),
Rooster (Bruce, 1991), *Pierrot Lunaire* (Tetley, 1962),
Embrace Tiger and Return to Mountain (Tetley, 1968),
Meeting Point (Bruce, 1996).
The company performed in Manchester, High Wycombe,
Edinburgh, Sheffield, London (two seasons at Sadler's
Wells Theatre), Plymouth, Canterbury, Woking,
Norwich, Leeds, Milton Keynes and Oxford.
It also toured to Cyprus in September 1999, performing
Embarque, *Ghost Dances* and *Rooster*, and to Germany
(Cologne and Neuss) in November 1999, performing
Gaps, Lapse and Relapse, *Ghost Dances*, *The Golden Section*,
August Pace and *Embarque*. It returned to Germany
(Munich) in February 2000, with a repertoire of
Embarque, *Ghost Dances* and *The Golden Section*.
A workshop season of new works created and performed
by members of the company was given at the Lilian Baylis
Theatre, London, in February–March 2000.

RICHARD ALSTON DANCE COMPANY
Founded 1994
Cecil Sharp House, 2 Regent's Park Road, London
NW1 7AY

All works danced by the company are choreographed by Richard Alston.

World premières:
A Sudden Exit, 8 October 1999. Music, Brahms
The Signal of a Shake, 15 February 2000. Music, Handel; costumes, Jeanne Spazani

Company première:
Roughcut, 8 October 1999. Music, Steve Reich
Works from the repertoire: *Red Run* (1998), *Slow Airs (Almost All)* (1999), *Light Flooding into Darkened Rooms* (1997).

The company performed in Cambridge (two seasons), Bromley, Edinburgh, Manchester, Malvern, High Wycombe, Brighton, Stevenage, Nottingham, Canterbury, Norwich, Northampton, London (Queen Elizabeth Hall) and Blackpool.

It also appeared at the first European Festival of Contemporary Dance in Moscow in October 1999.

SCOTTISH BALLET
Founded 1956 as the Western Theatre Ballet
261 West Princes Street, Glasgow G4 9EE

World première:
Frederick (Mehmet Balkan), 25 April 2000. Music, Chopin; design, Mehmet Balkan

Company premières:
Prince Rama and the Demons (Robert North), 27 January 2000. Score, Christopher Benstead; design, Robert North with Tim Palmer; costumes, Monia Tochia; masks, Panaro. Cast led by Yi-Lei Cai, Ivan Dinev, Ari Takahashi, Ersin Aycan and Simon Stewart
Miniatures (Robert North), 29 January 2000. Music, Stravinsky; design, Andrew Storer
Offenbach in the Underworld (Robert North), 29 January 2000. Music, Offenbach and Stravinsky; design, Andrew Storer. Cast led by Preston Clare and Nicci Theis
Romeo and Juliet (Robert North), 1 June 2000. Music, Prokofiev; design, Andrew Storer. Cast led by Adam Cooper and Mia Johannson
Full-length ballets from the repertoire: *Giselle* (Darrell, 1971), *Tales of Hoffmann* (Darrell, 1972).
One-act ballet from the repertoire: *Light Fandango* (North, 1999).
The company performed in Glasgow (three seasons), Inverness (two seasons), Aberdeen (two seasons), Woking and Edinburgh.
In April–May 2000 it divided into two groups to tour to local venues in fifteen towns and villages in Scotland with a programme including *Light Fandango, Miniatures* and *Frederick*.

Film

The buzz word in film circles at the turn of the millennium has to be *convergence*. It seems to sum up the way the industry is coming together, and the way new technologies are influencing movie-makers and audiences alike.

The biggest financial story of the year was undoubtedly the proposed merger of Time Warner and America Online (AOL), the largest deal in history, worth an estimated $337 billion. Announced on the tenth anniversary of the merger of Warner Communications with Time Inc., 10 January 2000, the deal had symbolic value as well. On paper it would seem lop-sided, given that Time Warner includes among its assets a movie studio, Time magazine, CNN, HBO, People magazine, Entertainment Weekly, Sports Illustrated, Fortune, Warner Music Group, Looney Tunes and the Cartoon Network, as well as a pedigree stretching back nearly 100 years, while AOL is just 15-years old, and can only bring Compuserve, Netscape, and 26 million subscribers to the table. The assumption is that the explosive and unprecedented growth in internet activity will be sustained and indeed vastly enhanced with the arrival of faster, better broadband and internet distribution within the next five years; that the net will become the primary source of news and home entertainment – and probably much else besides, including commercial traffic and work communications – and that distributors like AOL will be able to charge a toll or subscription fee for access to content; like Warner movies and music, CNN, Time and so on. A similar prognostication underlies the recent acquisition of Seagram (including Universal Studios) by the French water utilities firm Vivendi, which includes the European film and television giant Canal Plus and has its own internet portal vizzavi.com. If things go according to plan, software commodities like videotapes, compact discs and dvds will soon become redundant: why own a movie if you can order it up at will on the world's most comprehensive video jukebox?

If the Time Warner/AOL mergers goes through – and rivals like Disney complain that it would substantially restrict market freedom – it would create the world's largest multi-media company and could profoundly alter the nature of the internet. What the implications may be for cinema remain to be seen, but the signs are that they may be both subtle and far-reaching: from the way movies are promoted to the way they are distributed and exhibited. In turn this will effect who makes films, how they do it and why.

It's still very early days, but this year threw up some fascinating portents. First, and most unexpectedly, the astonishing success of a low-budget horror movie, *The Blair Witch Project*. Made by a couple of film students, Daniel Myrick and Eduardo Sanchez, with a principle cast of three unknowns (who also doubled up as the crew), *Blair Witch* was picked up at the Sundance Festival in January 1999 by a relatively new distribution company, Artisan.

The film was shot in a documentary style, handheld, switching between film and video imagery, and presented as found footage, the last remaining traces of three students who disappeared in the Black Hills forest in Maryland in 1994 while investigating a local legend armed with a 16mm film camera and a camcorder.

Artisan and the film-makers orchestrated an ingenious and very elaborate campaign by way of the internet (which attracted 190 million hits in six months), which had everyone across America wondering whether the movie was fiction or reality. By the time it opened on just 27 screens, interest had reached fever pitch, and by the end of the summer 1999 it had made $140 million in the US alone, making it the most profitable movie against cost ever made.

While it proved impossible to recreate the mystery on a comparable scale in other territories, where the news was spread predominantly through traditional broadcast media rather than the internet, the film was already such a phenomenon it was accorded honorary blockbuster status–indeed the only movie which generated more newsprint in the UK in 1999 was *Star Wars Episode One: The Phantom Menace* (released earlier in the summer). Inevitably there was some backlash, but the film did exert a creeping dread. Interestingly, it did so by going against everything the horror move has become over the last 30 years. Myrick and Sanchez rejected gross-out gore and special effects; the only special effects in their movie are simple man-like talismans fashioned out of twigs. Instead they relied on the power of suggestion. This was back-to-basics horror; deep in the dark woods of our tenebrous imagination.

It is hard to know how the model of *The Blair Witch Project* might be replicated (though the inevitable sequel is fast upon us), but not since *Easy Rider* has a movie come out of nowhere and assumed such cultural and commercial significance. Assuredly it convinced Hollywood that the net was the most direct route to the key youth audience. Doubtless it also encouraged would-be film-makers everywhere that not only might they make their movies using the latest cheap digital recording equipment – but they could also be rewarded with a substantial and appreciative audience.

At Sundance 2000 Artisan picked up just such a venture: *Chuck and Buck* is a quirky comedy which happens to feature a homosexual stalker who appears to be mentally deficient, and who (we're invited to speculate) may harbour paedophilic tendencies. It's impossible to imagine a Hollywood studio optioning this perverse mixture of *Forest Gump*, *Philadelphia* and *Fatal Attraction* – but by filming on digital video cameras, director Miguel Artega could shoot it for a fraction of the budget he'd have need for 35mm film. *Chuck and Buck* looks terrific. It has not emulated *Blair Witch* at the box-office, but it didn't take long to make a profit, and garnered some of the best reviews of the year for its provocative and original slant on repression and desire.

Mike Figgis's *Time Code* was another boldly experimental work which could only have been made on digital video. Figgis borrowed a trick from Andy Warhol by splitting the screen into four, but took it a stage further by insisting that each quadrant play out a single unbroken shot in real-time. To make it even more complicated, he choreographed a series of interactions between the characters from each corner of the screen. A virtuoso technical feat, and often very witty, *Time Code* was something of a stunt; likely the way it was exhibited will prove more revolutionary than the way it was shot. While Sony distributed a conventional 35mm transfer of the original, the director also toured with a video disc of the film, along with a portable video projector and a mixing desk. He was then able to in effect DJ the movie, switching between dialogue tracks at will, bringing in different music (he composed the score himself) as the tempo of the event demanded. He happily reported that he was an instant convert to video projection. What's more, it took no more than an hour to set up the projector. And because there is no projector noise, all you need is the equipment, a room and some chairs to make yourself a viable cinema. Theoretically, Figgis concluded, you could showcase your own independent movie in the same way you open a play – and if a studio then wanted to come in and distribute it, you would have already test-screened it for them.

In February incidentally, *Toy Story 2* became the first movie to be digitally projected to UK audiences when the Odeon Leicester Square availed themselves to the new technology. While the technology is still in its infancy this remains an expensive alternative to celluloid; however within five or ten years it is expected that most cinemas will have converted, which will mean a significant savings for distributors in terms of striking and transporting prints.

After the creative doldrums of recent times, Hollywood had a strong year, with at least a dozen intelligent, sharply executed movies. The big winners at the Academy Awards was *American Beauty* from producer Steven Spielberg's Dreamworks studio. This was the first feature directed by 34-year-old British theatre wunderkind Sam Mendes; when he picked up the Oscar for best film as well as best director it was rather opportunistically adopted as a local triumph by the British press.

It is an impressive piece of work, a sardonic male angst comedy starring Kevin Spacey (the year's best actor) as a middle-aged man who realises his life is an empty sell-out when he unexpectedly loses his job. The film's belated rehabilitation of counter-culture values is a bit simplistic, and Annette Bening's caricatured careerist wife borders on sexist, but screenwriter Alan Ball's subversive wit, a handful of fine performances and Mendes' sympathetic, nuanced mise-en-scene allows *American Beauty* to transcend its limitations.

The losers on Oscar night included Paul Thomas Anderson's extraordinary *Magnolia*, an ambitious and even more cutting dissection of family dysfunction than *American Beauty*; *The Talented Mr Ripley*, a very polished piece of craftsmanship from Anthony Minghella with a standout performance from Jude Law; the clever psychological chiller *The Sixth Sense*, directed by the hotly-touted and evocatively-named M. Night Shyamalyn; and David Lynch's sentimental octogenarian road movie *The Straight Story*, with twinkle-eyed ex-stunt man Richard Farnsworth getting the role of his lifetime.

The Oscar for best actress went to Hilary Swank in *Boys Don't Cry* for her stunning interpretation of a mid-western girl – Teena Brandon – who was murdered after successfully masquerading as a guy, Brandon Teena. Based on a notorious true story a few years ago, Kimberly Peirce's film was a true independent, made for under $5 million but subsequently picked up for distribution by Fox Searchlight. The film raised difficult, challenging questions about sexual identity, social conditioning and male rage, never felt the need to soft pedal Teena's flaws, and presented a desperately bleak picture of life in the middle-American heartlands. The Oscar recognition was deserved but in some ways surprising.

Boys Don't Cry was one of a number of films which ran into controversy for dealing with real-life stories. In the case of Peirce's film, Teena's girlfriend Lana – sympathetically played in the movie by Chloe Sevigny – complained the film romanticised their relationship. Michael Mann's *The Insider* hit tougher slack, which probably cost it Oscar recognition. Certainly you could make a strong case that Russell Crowe pulled off a more difficult role than Spacey, playing nearly 20-years older than he really is, as a scientist who blows the whistle on the tobacco industry – exposing the cynical way it exploits nicotine's addictive qualities – at grievous cost to himself and his family. A study in integrity, pride and corporate ethics, *The Insider* worked both as a penetrating character study and as a conspiracy thriller. It also names real corporate names – including CBS and *60 Minutes*. While impressive in itself, such candour invited close scrutiny, and rightly or wrongly *The Insider* was criticised for taking too much creative licence. Steven Soderbergh's *Erin Brockovich* – with a knockout performance from Julia Roberts – was attacked by Brockovich's former boyfriend; while serial killer David Berkowitz accused Spike Lee of cynicism from his prison cell for making the underrated *Summer of Sam*.

More serious charges were levelled against a fictional film, *The Patriot*. Directed by Roland Emmerich and written by Robert Rodat the movie was a historical epic in a similar heroic vein to star Mel Gibson's *Braveheart*, this time about a renegade soldier in the American War of Independence. The film only claimed to be loosely inspired by historical characters, but critics on both sides of the Atlantic took offence to the way it stereotyped the British as stock Hollywood villains, and especially the film's appropriation of Nazi atrocities from World War II in a sequence in which an English colonel rounds up an entire village in the local church, bolts the doors and sets it alight. There is something arrogant about the filmmakers' carelessness with history here, though in their defence, you could make a case that *The Patriot* is an attempt to explore the more recent horrors we have witnessed in the Balkans: genocide and ethnic cleansing. That said, on those terms the film must be counted an abject failure.

Much better was *The Perfect Storm*, a crudely scripted but nevertheless powerful account of the last voyage of the swordboat Andrea Gail in the tempestuous Atlantic ocean – with digital effects not only whipping up a storm to remember, but also supplying extraordinarily life like fish. Wolfgang Petersen's film was a rare blockbuster which eschewed genre and celebrated the real-life heroics of working-class people.

It was a great year for *Perfect Storm* star George Clooney, who worked with the Coen brothers in their screwball double-homage to Preston Sturges and Homer, *O Brother Where Art Thou?*, and scored another critical and commercial hit with a very edgy Gulf War black comedy, *Three Kings*.

Clooney's *Three Kings* co-star Spike Jonze made the strangest American movie of the year, the surreal comedy *Being John Malkovich*, in which a depressed puppeteer (John Cusack) happens across a portal into the brain of John Malkovich (played with delicious disdain by John Malkovich). In true American fashion, the puppeteer exploits his discovery for fame and fortune, but brings only psychic chaos down upon himself. Finally, the least appreciated Hollywood movie of this bumper year must have been David Fincher's breathtaking *Fight Club*, a millennial howl of confused masculinity brilliantly adapted from Chuck Palahniuk's cult novel. Admittedly the movie loses its footing in the final third, but it still managed to throw up more scabrously funny and radically subversive ideas than any other American film this year. *Fight Club* had the misfortune to follow the political onslaught which sought to lay the blame for the Columbine High School massacre in Denver, Colorado on Hollywood and was branded fascist art by conservative critics. In fact it's a mess of conflicting emotions – but at least it's an honest mess, and very funny with it. The happy ending sees the terror-bombing of American corporate banking … a thought which chimed with events in Seattle, Washington.

In Britain the press routinely castigated a surfeit of bad British movies. The boom was lottery-sponsored to a degree, but also inspired by the confidence engendered by a long string of British successes, including *Four Weddings and a Funeral*, *Trainspotting*, *Bean*, and *Lock, Stock and Two Smoking Barrels*. The latter was especially influential, ushering in a seemingly endless cycle of gangster flicks, good (very occasionally), bad (most of the time) and ugly (always). The line-up includes *Circus*, *Essex Boys*, *Lover, Honour and Obey*, and the spectacularly misbegotten All-Saints' vehicle *Hones*. Marginally more fun was Guy Ritchie's own *Snatch*, with Brad Pitt imported to play an Irish bare-knuckle fights; and the only film of any distinction, *Gangster Number One*, a nasty piece of work which at least showed some flair and imagination.

Mercifully, these films weren't the whole story, even if the doom and gloom of the press tended to overshadow some genuine bright spots. Among them, Shane Meadows' *A Room for Romeo Brass*, an eccentric and unpredictable film which smuggled a disturbing portrait of male violence into what seems to be a nostalgic and parochial coming-of-age story; David Yates' Ealing-esque 19th-century tale of fortune hunting *The Tichborne Claimant*; Christopher Nolan's stylish and elusive *Following*; Neil Jordan's accomplished Catholic guilt-trip *The End of the Affair*; and Mike Leigh's acclaimed Gilbert and Sullivan backstage drama *Topsy Turvy* were all reasons to keep the faith.

On the other hand, three years into the government-sponsored lottery franchise scheme it seems to be shaping into a political embarrassment. Although there has been the odd critical and commercial success (*Ratcatcher*; *The Ideal Husband*) the perception is that too many films have been rushed into production with under-developed scripts and insufficient thought. While it would be fairer to judge the results on the original six-year time-span, the government's plane for the new Film Council suggest that the scheme will be wound down. John Woodward, formerly head of the BFI, now director of the Film Council, announced the first tier of proposals in the late spring of 2000. These included £5 million per annum for a new Film Development fund to strengthen the quality of screenplays; £10 million per annum for the Premier Production Fund, money earmarked for brokering higher budget, populist British Film; and £5 million per annum for the New Cinema Fund, with a remit to back new talent, radical and experimental film. In addition, there would be money for children to make films, a film training fund, and a new office to explore better co-ordination with European partners. Again, it will take some years before the Film Council may be held to account. In the meantime, it will also have to square up to even more difficult questions about the distribution of British film in a market place that has been dominated by Hollywood for so long.

In all this excitement about the future, one film in particular reminded us of the value of the past. Directed by the prolific Chilean avant-gardeist Raoul Ruiz, and starring a dazzling pantheon of French stars (Catherine Deneuve, Emmanuelle Béart, Vincent Perez, Edith Scob – and a French speaking John Malkovich), *Time Regained* had the supreme audacity to transform the last volume of Proust's *Remembrance of Things Past* into pure cinema. Ruiz employs an ingenious array of camera tricks to bend space, time and motion to his own greater design... the effect is sometimes surreal or even downright bewildering, but ultimately meditative and very poignant. Like only the greatest art can, it catches a man's life even as it slips away from him. The film opened in London on the first weekend of the new millennium, astonished everyone by becoming the talk of the town, and even catapulted Proust into the best-sellers lists. As for the impish Ruiz, who claims to have made more than 80 films in some shape or form, he explained he was experimenting with digital video cameras next.

FILM AWARD WINNERS

ACADEMY AWARDS 1999

Best picture – *American Beauty*
Best director – Sam Mendes, *American Beauty*
Best actor – Kevin Spacey, *American Beauty*
Best actress – Hilary Swank, *Boys Don't Cry*
Best supporting actor – Michael Caine, *The Cider House Rules*
Best supporting actress – Angelina Jolie, *Girl, Interrupted*
Best original screenplay – Alan Ball, *American Beauty*
Best adapted screenplay – John Irving, *The Cider House Rules*
Best foreign language film – *All About My Mother*
Best original musical or comedy score – *Shakespeare in Love*
Best original score – *The Red Violin*
Best original song – *You'll Be in my Heart*
Best cinematography – *American Beauty*
Best art direction – *Sleepy Hollow*
Best film editing – *Saving Private Ryan*
Best costume design – *Topsy-Turvy*
Best sound – *Saving Private Ryan*
Best sound effects editing – *The Matrix*
Best visual effects – *The Matrix*
Best make-up – *Topsy-Turvy*
Best animated short – *The Old Man and the Sea*
Best documentary feature – *One Day in September*
Best short documentary – *King Gimp*
Best short film – *My Mother Dreams the Satan's Disciples in New York*

BAFTA AWARDS 1999

Best film – *American Beauty*
David Lean award (best achievement in direction) –
    Pedro Almodovar, *All About My Mother*
Best actor – Kevin Spacey, *American Beauty*
Best actress – Annette Bening, *American Beauty*
Best supporting actor – Jude Law, *The Talented Mr Ripley*
Best supporting actress – Maggie Smith, *Tea with Mussolini*
Alexander Korda award (British film of the year) – *East is East*
Best foreign language film – *All About My Mother*
Best original screenplay – Charlie Kaufman, *Being John Malkovich*
Best adapted screenplay – Neil Jordan, *The End of the Affair*
Academy Fellowships – Michael Caine, Stanley Kubrick
Michael Balcon Award for contribution to British cinema:
    Joyce Herlihy

GOLDEN GLOBE AWARDS 2000

Best picture – *American Beauty*
Best actress – Janet McTeer, *Tumbleweeds*
Best actress in drama – Hilary Swank, *Boys Don't Cry*
Best actor in drama – Denzel Washington, *The Hurricane*
Best actor in musical or comedy – Jim Carrey, *Man on the Moon*
Best supporting actor – Tom Cruise, *Magnolia*
Best director – Sam Mendes, *American Beauty*
Best screenplay – Alan Ball, *American Beauty*
Best original song Phil Collins, *You'll be in My Heart*

Literature

It was another phenomenal year for J. K. Rowling and her *Harry Potter* books (published by Bloomsbury). The first three books of the series continued to dominate the bestseller lists, selling to adults and children alike, and the first print run for the fourth, *Harry Potter and the Goblet of Fire*, which was 600 pages long, was a record one million copies, solely for the UK market. The title of the fourth volume was kept secret until a matter of days before publication. There were two muggings and a break-in at the printer connected to the wish to find out the title in advance. *The Times* got the wrong end of the stick from an American website and wrongly predicted that the book would be called Harry Potter and the Doomspell Tournament. For the launch of the book at King's Cross, a steam train was painted red to look like the Hogwarts Express, and left on a nationwide author tour from a specially labelled Platform 9¾. On 8 July, the first day of publication, 256,246 were copies sold through bookshops and shops alone (that is, not through online booksellers) which was more than double the previous record, held by Delia Smith's *How to Cook Book Two*, which sold 110,425 copies in its first three days. Including sales over the Internet, the total number of copies sold was 372,775 on the first day, and over half a million copies had been sold in shops by the end of the first week. Harry Potter books accounted for 19 per cent of the books sold through retail that week. The only book that nudged into the top five of the bestseller list for any length of time after publication of *Harry Potter and The Goblet of Fire* was Helen Fielding's second volume of *Bridget Jones Diaries: The Edge of Reason*.

HARRY POTTER POPULARITY CONTINUES

The fourth Harry Potter book was arguably the darkest yet of the series. Four characters meet their deaths in it, not all of them peripheral to the story. One is a schoolchild. *The Goblet of Fire* also deals with the experience of having celebrity you did not ask for thrust upon you, discovering that even your best friend can be envious, and finding that the media presumes to intrude and says what it likes. It is hard not to interpret Harry's experience as related to that of the author, whose unprecedented success with these books was more than she could ever have sought to begin with, while some of the newspaper coverage (despite general acclaim) has manifested a certain envious backlash.

Volume three, *Harry Potter and the Prisoner of Azkaban*, caused a stir at the Whitbread awards in January. After considerable pressure on the Whitbread organisers from inside and outside the book trade to allow the Children's Book of the Year to be a contender for the overall Whitbread Book of the Year award, as an acknowledgement of the quality of books that are published for children, the rules were changed. The Whitbread Book of the Year award used to have five categories: first novel, novel, poetry, biography and children's book, and the children's book was given its own separate £10,000 prize in 1996 with the intention of making more of the genre. Many felt that it had the opposite effect, by suggesting that children's books could never measure up to books for adults, because it could not compete against the winners of the other categories for the overall prize. So for the 1999 Award, presented in January 2000, the final jury read the four shortlisted children's books (an arrangement designed to allow them to see children's books in context),

as well as the winners of the four other categories. They chose *Harry Potter and the Prisoner of Azkaban* as the Children's Book of the Year, after some debate, over competition from Jacqueline Wilson's story of sisters dealing with a manic depressive mother, *The Illustrated Mum* (Doubleday), Michael Morpurgo's tale of a Japanese soldier living out his life on a desert island, *Kensuke's Kingdom* (Heinemann), and Carol Ann Duffy's funny and touching collection of poetry, *Meeting Midnight* (Faber). It was then a close run vote for Book of the Year. Television pundits outside the judging chamber, including Ian Hislop, were rooting for Harry, and among the judges Robert Harris, Nigel Williams, and chair Eric Anderson, rector of Lincoln College, Oxford, were strongly in favour. But there was vehement opposition from Anthony Holden, who believed that choosing a children's book would 'send the wrong message' to the world. With the support of model Jerry Hall, MP Anne Widdecombe and actress Imogen Stubbs, the Whitbread Book of the Year went to the poetry book, Seamus Heaney's 'page-turner' *Beowulf*, a translation of the Anglo-Saxon epic. This was Heaney's second Whitbread win, and a double triumph for Faber, which had won (with Heaney and Ted Hughes) four years in a row.

... AND CONTINUES

Harry Potter and the Prisoner of Azkaban was again in contention against Jacqueline Wilson's *The Illustrated Mum* on the shortlist for the prestigious Library Association Carnegie Medal. But on the day before publication of the Goblet of Fire, the winner was announced at Imperial College London: it was neither of these books, but Aidan Chambers' challenging novel for teenagers, *Postcards from No Man's Land* (The Bodley Head), whose dual narrative concerned modern-day Amsterdam and wartime Arnhem, and did not shrink from such issues as euthanasia and homosexuality. The simultaneous winner of the Kate Greenaway Medal for outstanding illustration was Helen Oxenbury's exuberant new version of *Alice's Adventure's in Wonderland* (Walker). The prize crowned victories for both the illustrator and the publisher: Oxenbury's Alice had also won the Kurt Maschler Award for illustration, and she was also the winner of the Best Book for Babies Award, sponsored for the last time by Sainsbury's, with *Tickle*. Walker meanwhile was the proud publisher of seven of the nine books on the Greenaway shortlist, in the year that it celebrated its twentieth anniversary.

There were a few other Harry Potter-related dramas during the year. An attempt by a US publisher to produce an unofficial companion to the Harry Potter series was thwarted, with the author's agent, Christopher Little, promising to 'vigorously oppose any so-called companion books', because Rowling plans to write her own companion books for the series. And there were claims of plagiarism in the US from an author who says her own books originated some elements of Rowling's, including the term 'muggle'.

Casting of the Warner film was announced, with and a long hunt for the face of Harry was ended with the choosing of Daniel Radcliffe. (Other casting includes Alan Rickman as Professor Snape, Robbie Coltrane as Hagrid and Maggie Smith as Professor McGonagall). Release of the film is scheduled for autumn 2001 – which may be before volume five is published. There were rumours that the author, who had been expected to produce the books annually, would need more time for the next one, which may not appear until summer 2002.

BOOKER PRIZE CONTROVERSY

The Booker Prize controversy for 1999 was, as so often, over the books that were missed out of the shortlist. Three surprise omissions were Salman Rushdie's homage to rock 'n' roll *The Ground Beneath Her Feet* (Cape), Vikram Seth's multi-layered emotional cliff-hanger about obsessive love *An Equal Music* (Phoenix House) and Roddy Doyle's historical novel of the life story of a legendary Irish republican, *A Star Called Henry* (Cape). The bookshop chain Books Etc responded by setting up its 'Booker Etc' alternative shortlist as a promotional gimmick. The favourite among the shortlisted titles was Michael Frayn's *Headlong* (Faber) – also shortlisted for the Whitbread novel prize, about a man who faces a moral dilemma when he discovers a lost painting by Breughel, but the winner in the end was J. M. Coetzee's *Disgrace*. This was Coetzee's second Booker win (after *The Life and Times of Michael K*) and it told the story of an academic brought down by charges of sexually harassing a student, and it moved on to a wider canvas of politics and violence in rural South Africa. The chair of the judges, Gerald Kaufman MP, used the Booker ceremony to attack the submission system, which he said resulted in an unmanageable workload for the judges, and should be discontinued. In fact a subsequent change in the rules means that the next judges had to read yet more books – over 130 – since publishers continued to be allowed to submit only two titles for the prize, while also being able to include any books by authors who had either won the Booker or been shortlisted in the past 10 years. The previous rule was that only one title in each of these categories was eligible.

WOMEN ONLY

The £30,000 Orange Prize, open only to women, also made news, with the appointment of opposition leader William Hague's wife, Ffion, to the judging panel. The favourites on the shortlist were Rebecca Wells's huge seller *Divine Secrets of the Ya-Ya Sisterhood* (Macmillan), and Zadie Smith's acclaimed first novel of three generations of one family in multi-cultural Britain, *White Teeth* (which was signed up with a second book by her publisher, Hamish Hamilton for a rumoured £250,000). The book was a bestseller, but the author was burnt by the experience of an interview with the *Mail on Sunday* in which she seemed to be critical of the prize. She was quoted as saying 'I'm not going to be at the Orange Prize. It's just another award. I'm not ungrateful. I'd just rather not win.' But Smith said later that the article was a 'complete travesty' and 'a misrepresentation': 'The Orange is a wonderful prize and I'm glad and proud to be nominated for it'. She did attend the ceremony, but did not win: the prize went to Linda Grant for *When I Lived in Modern Times* (Granta), the story of a 20-year-old East London hairdresser who goes to Palestine in 1946, which explores themes of nationalism and personal identity. At the time of the announcement of the Prize shortlist, Orange also revealed the results of research into national reading tastes which claimed that 'any mention of love or a book cover in a pastel shade will stop men reading a book'.

MORE PRIZES

The Pulitzer Prize for fiction was awarded to Jhumpa Lahiri's stories of the yearnings of exiles (particularly of Indians in Boston), *The Interpreter of Maladies*, first published in the UK by Flamingo in 1999. The book had already won the PEN/Hemingway Award for the year's best short fiction. Nicola Barker's character-rich tale set on the Isle of Sheppey, with weighty themes but a light touch, *Wide Open* (Faber) won the biggest international literary award, the £75,000 Impac award.

The surprise on the shortlist for the £30,000 Samuel Johnson Prize for non-fiction was Tony Hawks' comic diary *Playing the Moldovans at Tennis* (Ebury), which struck a lighter than usual note among the contenders. David Cairns' Whitbread-category-winning biography of Berlioz took the prize. Also on the shortlist was Francis Wheen's widely admired biography of Karl Marx (Fourth Estate). But the non-fiction book that all the literati had an opinion on was Martin Amis's autobiography *Experience* (Cape), which intertwined episodes from his own and his father Kingsley's lives.

BOUQUETS AND BRICKBATS

Among noteworthy literary novels of the year were Jane Smiley's *Horse Heaven* (Faber), a complex satirical novel about horse racing, which was 'written with Hemingway' gutsiness and Jane Austen's precision'; Kazuo Ishiguro's *When We Were Orphans* (Faber), an elegant study, like many of Ishiguro's books, of self-deception, in which a reticent 1930s detective returns to his native Shanghai to solve the mystery of his parents' disappearance, and Rose Tremain's sensuous and atmospheric *Music and Silence* (Vintage), which won the Whitbread novel category.

The conspicuous dud of the year was Amy Jenkins' *Honeymoon* (Flame), for which the publishers paid £600,000 on the basis of the author's track record of involvement with the successful sitcom *This Life*. The book got lots of publicity and disastrous reviews.

Among the important book-related news stories of the year was the libel case revisionist historian David Irving brought against Penguin, which he accused of being 'reckless and foolhardy', for publishing Deborah Lipstadt's *Denying the Holocaust*, in which he claimed he was libelled. Irving lost the case resoundingly, although it cost Penguin £2m to defend their author, and, by extension, the Jews who were under threat from Irving's biased misinformation, since the central issue was what standards of historical research should be applied to examining the Holocaust. The judge, Mr Justice Charles Gray, concluded that Irving was 'an active Holocaust denier; that he is anti-Semitic and racist', and that 'no fair-minded historian would have serious cause to doubt that there were gas chambers at Auschwitz and that they were operated on a substantial scale to kill hundreds of thousands of Jews.' Irving's credibility as a historian was shattered, and truth triumphed. Penguin, which took a valiant stand over *Lady Chatterley's Lover* in 1960 and over Salman Rushdie's *The Satanic Verses*, which it continued to publish despite death threats not only to its author but to its employees, distinguished itself for a third time as a champion of integrity. Meanwhile the publisher sought permission to publish the judge's full verdict in the trial, and considered reissuing Lipstadt's book, with a new chapter by the author, concerning the trial. Demand had increased for the book because of the case, though the figures were small: book trade sources tracked sales of nearly 400 copies in the first four months of 2000, against 79 copies in 1999.

The Mithrokin Archive (Allen Lane) by Cambridge historian Christopher Andrew was serialised in *The Sunday Times* in September 1999 and revealed that 87-year-old grandmother Melita Norwood was a spy. The book used transcriptions made by the man who had been in charge of the KGB's foreign intelligence archives, and prompted the government to have to consider whether to prosecute. The content of the book was kept secret by the publishers at Penguin Press for two and a half years, and was referred to in-house only as Project G. 150,000 copies of the book were sold into the bookshops without revealing its contents.

BRITISH LIBRARY BLUNDER

The British Library was caught up in a furore after it was revealed that it had taken the decision to dispose of 80,000 books from its collections. The British Library defended itself by arguing that the books were foreign titles. But publishers were angered by a move that they saw as flying in the face of the British Library's tradition of collecting every volume published in the UK. Some argued that they should no longer be obliged to donate their books free to the Library.

HITTING THE HEADLINES

Publishers of unauthorised biographies of living people could benefit from the decision by celebrity footballer David Beckham and his pop star wife Victoria to withdraw from a £250,000 legal action against Michael O'Mara, publisher of a book about them by Andrew Morton. The publisher called it 'a victory for free speech'.

Other headline-hitting books included *First Person: An Astonishingly Frank Portrait of Russia's President Vladimir Putin* which was published to coincide with Mr Putin's presidential inauguration on 7 May by Random House imprint Hutchinson only three weeks after acquiring the title. And Little, Brown published *The Bodyguard's Story*, by Trevor Rees-Jones, who survived Princess Diana's fatal car crash.

E-HORROR

The age of the e-book came a step closer when in March horror writer Stephen King published his short story/novella *Riding the Bullet* exclusively on the website of US publisher Simon & Schuster, which claimed that it sold 400,000 copies within the first 30 hours of becoming available, earning the author about £300,000. King went on to make his latest work, *The Plant*, available only on his own Website, http://www.stephenking.com, at a cost of $1 (about 60 pence) per episode. It was to be published in monthly instalments provided not less than 75 per cent of those who downloaded each chapter paid. This was a less successful than his previous venture, prompting just over 150,000 downloads for the first episode. But King was still confident of substantial profits, especially if the downloaders continued to pay for each instalment, although whether he had terrified publishers, as he expected to (calling the project 'big publishing's worst nightmare') was a matter for debate. He did, though, inspire at least one fellow writer to follow suit. Douglas Adams, author of *The Hitchhiker's Guide to the Galaxy*, declared his intention to publish his next book on the Internet in e-book format in autumn 2000.

Print-on-demand technology was the basis of a new 'ground-breaking' publishing house, Stratus Publishing, which could thereby keep all an author's books 'in print'. It also committed itself to sharing 10 per cent of annual profits with authors, and then snatched up the rights to such names as Joyce Cary, Neville Shute and Brian Aldiss, as well as Anthony Buckeridge's Jennings and Derbyshire school stories, which had, as had been pointed out in dismay be the press, been allowed to go out of print.

Microsoft, Barnesandnoble.com, Random House and Simon & Schuster also joined forces in May to offer free e-book versions of bestselling titles. The titles were to be available exclusively through Barnesandnoble.com to users of Microsoft Reader using pocket PCs.

WORLD BOOK DAY AND THE WORD

World Book Day moved permanently to the first Thursday in March instead of Shakespeare's birthday in April (in order to involve schools) and generated more than £500,000 worth of extra book sales through UK shops, making it the most successful WBD in its three-year history. Among the thousands of events that took place, members of the public were offered £5 rewards for apprehending famous authors including Jane Austen, Robert Burns, Charles Dickens, William Shakespeare and Oscar Wilde whose lookalikes roamed Birmingham, Bristol, Cardiff, Glasgow and Manchester. On the day the results of a poll of adults and children to find the Nation's Favourite Author crowned Roald Dahl, out of a shortlist of 20 authors announced in February.

The Word, the London literature festival, moved in its second year from March to September, with a 'whole-sale revamp of its organisation and promotion', after problems created by 'over-ambitiousness' in the first year. J. G. Ballard was booked to open the Festival at Shakespeare's Globe Theatre on Bankside.

BEST OF BRITISH

Finally, among the year's top sellers were, in non-fiction, Delia Smith's *How to Cook* (which in late 1999 outsold Harry Potter 3's record of 68,000 books in one day by selling 110,000 in as long), Alex Ferguson's autobiography *Managing My Life* (Hodder), former Spice Girl Geri Halliwell's autobiography *If Only*, and *Walking With Dinosaurs*, the tie-in to the BBC television series in autumn 1999. Television chef Jamie Oliver's *The Return of The Naked Chef* (Michael Joseph) was also a bestseller, with Nigella Lawson's *How to Eat*, boosted by her TV series *Nigella Bites*, beginning to invade his kitchen space. Fiction bestsellers included Frank McCourt's sequel to *Angela's Ashes*, *'Tis* (Flamingo) and Terry Pratchett's *The Big Elephant* (Doubleday). Maeve Binchy's *Tara Road* rode high in the bestseller lists, as did her next novel, *Scarlet Feather*, which she announced would be her last, as she wished to retire from the pressures of publicity. Rosamunde Pilcher made a similar declaration. And Colin Dexter fans were dismayed that the author also retired from his hero: Inspector Morse died in *The Remorseful Day*.

BOOKER PRIZE WINNERS

1999 – *Disgrace*, J. M. Coetzee
1998 – *Amsterdam*, Ian McEwan
1997 – *The God of Small Things*, Arundhati Roy
1996 – *Last Orders*, Graham Swift
1995 – *The Ghost Road*, Pat Barker
1994 – *How Late It Was, How Late*, James Kelman
1993 – *Paddy Clarke Ha Ha Ha*, Roddy Doyle
1992 – *The English Patient*, Michael Ondaatje
1991 – *The Famished Road*, Ben Okri
1990 – *Possession*, A. S. Byatt
1989 – *The Remains of the Day*, Kazuo Ishiguro
1988 – *Oscar and Lucinda*, Peter Carey
1987 – *Moon Tiger*, Penelope Lively
1986 – *The Old Devils*, Kingsley Amis
1985 – *The Bone People*, Keri Hulme
1984 – *Hotel du Lac*, Anita Brookner
1983 – *Life and Times of Michael K*, J. M. Coetzee
1982 – *Schindler's Ark*, Thomas Keneally
1981 – *Midnight's Children*, Salman Rushdie
1980 – *Rites of Passage*, William Golding
1979 – *Offshore*, Penelope Fitzgerald
1978 – *The Sea, The Sea*, Iris Murdoch
1977 – *Staying On*, Paul Scott
1976 – *Saville*, David Storey
1975 – *Heat and Dust*, Ruth Prawer Jhabvala
1974 – *The Conservationist*, Nadine Gordimer and
          Holiday, Stanley Middleton
1973 – *The Siege of Krishnapur*, J. G. Farrell
1972 – *G*, John Berger
1971 – *In a Free State*, V. S. Naipaul
1970 – *The Elected Member*, Bernice Rubens
1969 – *Something to Answer For*, P. H. Newby

Opera

COVENT GARDEN OPERA HOUSE

After months of speculation the Royal Opera House, Covent Garden re-opened its doors, on time and on budget. After a Celebratory Gala, the first half opera, the second half ballet, on 4 December 1999, the theatre opened officially on 6 December with a new production of Verdi's *Falstaff*. Welsh baritone Bryn Terfel sang the title role and the music director, Bernard Haitink, conducted. The dark red and gold of the auditorium were hardly changed, but everything back-stage was new. The front-of-house amenities were greatly enhanced by the vast Vilar Floral Hall, with bars, a restaurant and an escalator up to a terrace overlooking the Piazza. The Amphitheatre was no longer segregated from the rest of the auditorium.

A certain amount of valuable rehearsal time had been lost, owing mainly to strikes by the electricians, and the stage staff were denied the time and opportunity of getting to know the new, computer-based machinery. As a result, the operatic production, *Le Grand Macabre* by György Ligeti, had to be cancelled, while the opening nights of several other productions were postponed. By the end of April everyone had become accustomed to the new machinery, and the British premiere of the original version of *The Greek Passion* by Bohuslav Martinu, was an elaborate production on a huge set.

Elaine Padmore arrived at the beginning of January to take up her position as director of opera. She had been artistic director of The Royal Danish Opera in Copenhagen since 1993 and spent 13 years as artistic director of the Wexford Festival. Unfortunately Michael Kaiser, whose short stint as executive director had achieved the new financial stability and artistic excellence of the house, announced he would depart in January 2001. A new executive director is being sought.

During this opening season the new Linbury Studio Theatre, capable of seating around 450 people, played host to various organisations, including the British Youth Opera, The Classical Opera Company, The BOC Covent Garden Festival of Opera and the Guildhall School of Music and Drama. At the end of the season the main stage was invaded by the Kirov Opera and Ballet. The most interesting of the six Russian operas performed were Tchaikovsky's *Mazeppa* and two works by Sergei Prokofiev, *War and Peace* and *Semeon Kotko*. Tantalising echoes of *The Fiery Angel* and pre-echoes of *War and Peace* were found insufficient to carry this story of the Russian Revolution.

ENGLISH NATIONAL OPERA

English National Opera (ENO) enjoyed a very successful season. The major event was the world premiere of *The Silver Tassie*, an opera by Mark-Anthony Turnage with text by Amanda Holden based on Sean O'Casey's anti-war play, which benefited enormously from a series of pre-rehearsals with orchestra, chorus and singers at the ENO Studio. The production was directed by Bill Bryden and designed by William Hudson, both working at ENO for the first time. Both the opera and performance received tremendous applause, the warmest going to Canadian baritone Gerald Finley, who sang Harry Heegan, the Dublin football hero wounded in the first world war and destined to spend his life in a wheel chair.

Later in the season ENO gave the London stage premiere of John Adams' *Nixon in China*, with baritone James Maddelena as Nixon and the production team was headed by director Peter Sellars. Paul Daniel, ENO's music director, who received a CBE in the New Year Honours, conducted *Nixon in China* and Debussy's *Pelléas et Mélisande*, a new production staged by Richard Jones. Francis Poulenc's *Dialogues of the Carmelites*, directed by Phyllida Lloyd, a joint production by ENO and Welsh National Opera (WNO) won the 1999 Royal Philharmonic Society's award for best Opera production.

WNO received high praise for a new production of Britten's chamber opera, *The Turn of the Screw*. This production was conducted by Carlo Rizzi, WNO's music director, who announced that he will be leaving in July 2001 after nine years with the company. During that time his very wide repertory has included operas by Verdi, Puccini, Rossini, Strauss, Mussorgsky and Wagner. He will be greatly missed in Cardiff. Meanwhile conductor emeritus Sir Charles Mackerras celebrated a 50-year association with the company by conducting *Carmen*. WNO received an Olivier Award for best new Opera production for *Hansel and Gretel*, directed by Richard Jones.

OPERA NORTH

Opera North made its first week-long visit to London for 15 years, presenting three new productions at Sadler's Wells Theatre in the autumn of 1999 including *Kátya Kabanová*, by Leoš Janáček, Verdi's *La traviata* and Mozart's *Don Giovanni*. Opera North also appeared at the Edinburgh International Festival 2000 in August, taking Schumann's infrequently performed opera *Genoveva*, conducted by Steven Sloane and staged by David Pountney, who had provided a new English translation. *Genoveva* was also given a new production by Garsington Opera earlier in the summer, marking the 150th anniversary of the opera's premiere at Leipzig in 1850.

SCOTTISH OPERA

Scottish Opera also appeared at the Edinburgh International Festival, with *Das Rheingold*. A new production of Wagner's *Der Ring das Nibelungen*, was conducted by Richard Armstrong and directed by Tim Albery and is to be built up over the next four years. Earlier in the season, Luc Bondy's much praised staging of Verdi's *Macbeth*, scored a tremendous success and was invited to the Vienna Festival in May. The premiere of a new opera by Scottish composer David Horne, *Friend of the People*, marking the bi-centenary of the death of the political reformer, Thomas Muir of Huntershill, was not as well received.

GLYNDEBOURNE

The 2000 season at Glyndebourne marked the end of an era, when Sir Andrew Davis, the music director, and Graham Vick, director of productions, made their departures. Both will be greatly missed. Vick did not leave before completing his trilogy of Mozart/Da Ponte operas, with new and sometimes controversial productions of *Le nozze di Figaro* and *Don Giovanni* (the final scene) to join that of *Così fan tutte*. Revivals of Nikolaus Lehnhoff's powerful production of *Jenůfa* and of John Cox's staging of *The Rake's Progress*, designed by David Hockney were greatly appreciated.

Earlier in the year, *Zoe*, a new opera for young people, with music by John Lunn and words by Stephen Plaice (the team responsible for *Misper* in 1997), scored a huge popular hit. With a large cast of Sussex school children, superbly directed by Stephen Langridge, and the Brighton Youth Orchestra conducted by James Morgan, together with a handful of professional singers, *Zoe* gave enormous pleasure to its participants and audiences alike. Glyndebourne Touring Opera also featured a new opera, the British premiere of *The Last Supper*, dramatic tableaux by Harrison Birtwistle, with text by Robin Blaser and premiered in Berlin in April was received with respect, rather than genuine warmth.

Michael Berkeley's new chamber opera, *Jane Eyre*, had its premiere at the Cheltenham Festival on 30 June, scoring both critical and popular success. David Malouf, the librettist, has whittled down the large cast in Charlotte Bronte's novel to five characters. Inevitably, perhaps, comparisons were drawn with Britten's *The Turn of the Screw*, which also features a young governess arriving at a large country house. An excellent performance by Music Theatre Wales, who later took the work on tour, at the Buxton Festival and other venues. Almeida Opera gave the world premiere of *Ion* at Aldeburgh in June with music by Faram Vir and text by David Lan. This was the third Almeida-Aldeburgh collaboration. The Aldeburgh Festival also included a concert performance at Snape Maltings of *Peter Grimes*, surprisingly the first time that Britten's best known opera had been given there.

ROYAL ALBERT HALL

Operas performed at the Royal Albert Hall Promenade Concerts included the Glyndebourne *Figaro*, Wagner's *Parsifal* with the Rotterdam Philharmonic conducted by Sir Simon Rattle, and *Aufsteig und Fall der Stadt Mahagonny* by Kurt Weill, the centenary of whose birth and 50-year anniversary of his death, both fell in 2000. The death of baritone Roy Henderson, eight months after he had celebrated his 100th birthday, was received with particular sadness at Glyndebourne, where he sang in the six pre-war seasons as Count Almaviva in *Figaro*, Guglielmo in *Cosi van tutte*, Masetto in *Don Giovanni* and Papageno in *Die Zauberflöte*. Henderson had also appeared at Covent Garden. Polish bass Marian Nowakowski, who sang many roles, including Boris Godunov, at the Royal Opera House in the immediate post-war years, died at the age of 87, while Dutch soprano Gre Brouwenstein died aged 84. She had given several notable performances during the 1950s, including three Verdi roles, *Aida*, Desdemona in *Otello*, and Elisabeth in *Don Carlos*, presented in 1958 to mark the centenary of the opening of the Covent Garden Theatre.

Other singers who died during the period under review included British tenor Alexander Young, aged 79. He sang with Sadler's Wells Opera (now English National Opera) for many years. His wide repertory covered operas by Gluck, Mozart, Richard and Johann Strauss, as well as Janáček and Britten. His two most memorable roles were Rossini's Count Ory and Stravinsky's Tom Rakewell. Spanish tenor Alfredo Kraus, greatly admired for his performances in Italian and French operas at Covent Garden, died at the age of 71. An unrivalled stylist, Kraus excelled in roles such as Edgardo in *Lucia di Lammermoor*, the Duke in *Rigoletto* and Massenet's Werther, by general consent his finest assumption.

Scottish composer Iain Hamilton, who died aged 78, had three full-length operas performed by British companies: *The Royal Hunt of the Sun* (1968), based on Peter Shaffer's play, *Anna Karenina* (1978), based on Tolstoy's novel, both commissioned and produced by English National Opera and *The Catiline Conspiracy* (1874), based on Ben Jonson's tragedy, were performed by Scottish Opera. Baritone Thomas Hemsley, now a successful singing teacher, who sang Caesar in *The Catiline Conspiracy*, was appointed CBE in the New Year Honours, when the same honour was awarded to Welsh tenor Dennis O'Neill and New Zealand tenor Keith Lewis. Dramatic soprano Anne Evans, renowned for her performances of Wagner roles, in particular that of Brunnhilde in *Der Ring des Nibelungen*, was appointed DBE in the Queen's Birthday Honours.

PRODUCTIONS

In the summaries of company activities shown below, the dates in brackets indicate the year that the current productions entered the company's repertory.

ROYAL OPERA

Founded 1946
Royal Opera House, Covent Garden, London WC2E 9DD
Productions from the repertory: *Gawain* (1991), *Roméo et Juliette* (1994), *La bohème* (1974), *Der Rosenkavalier* (1984), *Der fliegende Holländer* (1992), *Die Meistersinger von Nürnberg* (1993).

New Productions:
Falstaff (Verdi), 6 December 1999. Conductor, Bernard Haitink; director, Graham Vick; designer, Paul Brown. Bryn Terfel (Falstaff), Barbara Frittoli (Alice), Bernadette Manca di Nissa (Mistress Quickly), Diana Montague (Meg), Desiree Rancatore (Nannetta), Roberto Frontali (Ford), Kenneth Tarver (Fenton)

La clemenza di Tito (Mozart), 22 January. Conductor, Nicholas McGeegan; director and designer, Karl Ernst and Ursel Hermann. Vinson Cole (Tito), Patricia Schuman (Vitellia), Vesselina Kasarova (Sesto), Christiane Oelze (Servilia), Ruxandra Donose (Annio), Lorenzo Regazzo (Publio)

Otello (Rossini), 31 January. Conductor, Gianluigi Gelmetti; director and designer, Pier Luigi Pizzi. Bruce Ford (Otello), Mariella Davia (Desdemona), Juan Diego Florez (Rodrigo), Octavio Arevalo (Iago), Alastair Miles (Elmiro), Leah-Marian Jones (Emilia)

The Greek Passion (Martinů), 25 April. Conductor, Charles MacKerras; director, David Pountney; designers, Stefanos Lazaridis (set), Marie-Jeanne Lecca (costumes). Jorma Silvasti (Manolios), Marie McLaughlin (Katerina), Jeremy White (Archon), Timothy Robinson (Yannakos), Esa Ruuttunen (Grigoris), Fotis (Gwynne Howell), Peter Auty (Michelis), Robin Leggate (Panait)

Norma (Bellini), 24 May. Concert performance Conductor, Paul Wynne Griffith. Nelly Miriciou (Norma), Susanne Mentzer (Adalgisa), Franco Farina (Pollione). Eric Owens (Oroveso), Julie Unwin (Clotilde)

La battaglia di Legnano (Verdi) 30 June. Concert performance at Royal Festival Hall. Conductor; Mark Elder. Veronica Villarroel (Lida), Placido Domingo (Arrigo), Anthony Michaels-Moore (Rolando), Orlin Anastassov (Barbarossa)

ENGLISH NATIONAL OPERA

Founded 1931
London Coliseum, St Martin's Lane, London WC2N 4BS
Productions from the repertory: *Der Rosenkavalier* (1994), *Orfeo* (1981), *Figaro's Wedding* (1991). *King Priam* (1995), *La bohème*, (1993), *Peter Grimes* (1991), *The Magic Flute* (1988), *The Pearl Fishers* (1987), *Madam Butterfly* (1984), *Eugène Onegin* (1994), *L'Allegro, il Penseroso ed il Moderato* (1997).

New Productions:
Der Freischütz (Weber), 10 September 1999. Conductor, Mark Elder; director, David Pountney; designers, Ian MacNeil (set), Marie-Jeanne Lecca (costumes). Alwyn Mellor (Agathe), Lisa Milne (Aennchen), John Daszak (Max), Gidon Saks (Caspar), Mark Richardson (Kuno), Andrew Greenan (Hermit)

The Diary of One Who Vanished (Janáček), 14 October at Royal National Theatre. Pianist, Julius Drake; director, Deborah Warner; designers, Jean Kalman, Tom Pye, John Bright. Ian Bostridge (Young Man), Ruby Philogene (Gypsy)

Alcina (Handel), 29 November. Conductor, Charles MacKerras; director, David McVicar; designers, Michael Vale (set), Sue Blane (costumes). Joan Rodgers (Alcina), Sarah Connolly (Ruggiero), Lisa Milne (Morgana), Christine Rice (Bradamante), Toby Spence (Oronte), Mark Richardson (Melisso)

The Silver Tassie (Turnage), world premiere, 16 February 2000. Conductor, Paul Daniel; director, Bill Bryden; designer, William Dudley; Gerald Finley (Harry Heegan), Sarah Connolly (Susie), David Kempster (Teddy), Anne Howells (Mrs Heegan), Vivian Tierney (Mrs Foran), Mary Hegarty (Jessie), Gwynne Howell (the Croucher). John Graham-Hall (Sylvester), Leslie John Flanagan (Barney), Mark le Brocq (Dr Maxwell)

Pelléas and Mélisande, 23 March. Conductor, Paul Daniel; director, Richard Jones; designers, Antony McDonald (set), Nicky Gillibrand (costumes). Joan Rodgers (Mélisande), Garry Magee (Pelléas), Robert Hayward (Golaud), Rebecca de Pont Davies (Geneviève), Clive Bayley (Arkel), David Wigram (Yniold)

St John Passion (Bach), 5 April. Conductor, Stephen Layton; director, Deborah Warner; designers, Jean Kalman, Tom Pye. Mark Padmore (Evangelist), Paul Whelan (Jesus), David Kempster (Pilate), Natalie Christie (soprano), Catherine Wyn-Rogers (alto), Barry Banks (tenor), Michael George (bass)

Ernani (Verdi), 6 May. Conductor, David Parry; director, Mike Ashman after Elijah Moshinsky; designer, Irene Bohan after Maria Björnson. Julian Gavin (Ernani), Sandra Ford (Elvira), Alan Opie (Don Carlo), Peter Rose (Silva)

Nixon in China (Adams), 7 June (London stage premiere). Conductor, Paul Daniel; director, Peter Sellars; designers, Adrianne Lobbel (set), Dunya Ramicova (costumes). James Maddalena (Richard Nixon), Janice Kelly (Pat Nixon), Robert Brubaker (Mao Tse-tung), David Kempster (Chou En-lai), Judith Howarth (Chiang Ching), Stephen Owen (Henry Kissinger)

Four Saints in Three Acts (Thomson), 28 June. Conductor, Andrea Quinn; director, Mark Morris; designers, Maira Kalman (set), Elizabeth Kurtzman (costumes). Mary Plazas (St Teresa I), Ethna Robinson (St Teresa II), Riccardo Simonetti (St Ignatius), Richard Roberts (St Chavez), Mark Richardson (Compere), Rebecca de Pont Davies (Commere)

Dido and Aeneas (Purcell), 28 June. Conductor, Anthony Legge. Production, as above. Sarah Connolly (Dido/Sorceress), Riccardo Simonetti (Aeneas)

OPERA NORTH

Founded 1978
Grand Theatre, 46 New Briggate, Leeds LS1 6NU
Productions from the repertory: *Madama Butterfly* (1996), *Falstaff* (1997), *La Gioconda* (1993), *Orpheus in the Underworld*

New productions:
La traviata (Verdi), 16 September 1999. Conductor, Richard Farnes; director, Annabel Arden; designer, Nicky Gillibrand. Janice Kelly (Violetta), Thomas Randle (Alfredo), Keith Latham (Germont), Sarah Pring (Flora), Christopher Saunders (Gastone), Iain Dickson (Baron Douphol), Christine Bryan (Annina)

Katya Kabanova (Janáček), 27 September. Conductor, Steven Sloane; director, Tim Albery; designer, Hildegard Bechtler. Vivian Tierney (Katya), Ann Taylor (Varvara), Gillian Knight (Kabanova), Alan Oke (Boris), Andrew Forbes-Lane (Tikhon), Jamie MacDougall (Kudryash), Jeremy White (Dikoy)

Don Giovanni (Mozart), 7 October. Conductor, Dominic Wheeler; director, David McVicar; designer, Kevin Knight. Majella Cullagh (Donna Anna), Claron McFadden (Donna Elvira), Lucy Schaufer (Zerlina), Paul Nilon (Don Ottavio), Garry Magee (Don Giovanni), Jonathan Best (Leporello), Roderick Williams (Masetto), Clive Bayley (Commendatore)

A Midsummer Night's Dream, 16 December. Conductor Steven Sloane; directors, Moshe Leiser & Patrice Caurier; designers, Christine Fenouillat (set), Agostino Cavalca (costumes). Christopher Josey (Oberon), Claron McFadden (Tytania), Helen Williams (Helena), Ann Taylor (Hermia), Nicholas Sears (Lysander), Mark Stone (Demetrius), James Rutherford (Theseus), Ruth Peel (Hippolyta), Jonathan Best (Nick Bottom), Andrew Slater (Quince), Christopher Saunders (Flute), Jan Knightley (Puck)

Radamisto (Handel), 13 May 2000. Conductor, Harry Bicket; director, Tim Hopkins; designer, Charles Edwards. David Walker (Radamisto), Helen Williams (Polissena), Emma Bell (Tigrane), Alice Coote (Zenobia), Elizabeth McCormack (Fraarte), Michael John Pearson (Tiridate)

Genoveva (Schumann), 31 August at Edinburgh International Festival. Conductor, Steven Sloane; director, David Pountney; designers, Ralph Koltai (set), Sue Wilmington (costumes). Patricia Schuman (Genoveva), Christopher Purves (Siegfried), Paul Nilon (Golo), Sally Burgess (Margaretha), Keith Latham (Hidulfus), Drago (Clive Bayley)

Performances were given at the Grand Theatre, Leeds, and on tour to Sadler's Wells, London; Newcastle, Manchester, Nottingham and The Lowry, Salford.

SCOTTISH OPERA

Founded 1962
39 Elmbank Crescent, Glasgow G2 4PG
Productions from the repertory: *Kátya Kabanová* (1993), *The Marriage of Figaro* (1995), *Tosca* (1980), *Macbeth* (1999), *Salome* (1990).

New productions:
Carmen (Bizet), 22 October 1999. Conductor, Nicholas Braithwaite; directors, Patrice Caurier & Moshe Leiser; designers, Christian Fenouillat (set), Agostino Cavalca (costumes); Patricia Bardon (Carmen), John Hudson (Don José), Mary Callan Clarke (Micaela), Simon Thorpe (Escamillo), Jonathan May (Zuniga)

Friend of the People (David Horne), world premiere, 6 November. Conductor, Richard Farnes; director Christopher Alden; designers, Allen Moyer (set), Joanna Parker (costumes); Peter Savidge (Thomas Muir), Philip Salmon (Lapslie/James Grant/Don Pedro), Clarissa Meek (Annie Fisher), Ann Archibald (Anna Barbauld/'Ceres'), Michael Druiett (Dalrymple/Captain Dorr)

Parsifal (Wagner), 4 March 2000. Conductor, Richard Armstrong; director/ designer, Silviu Purcarete; assistant designer, Doina Florian. John Horton Murray (Parsifal), Anne-Marie Owens (Kundry), Matthew Best (Amfortas), David Pittman-Jennings (Klingsor), Manfred Hemm (Gurnemanz)

Das Rheingold (Wagner), 21 August, as part of the Edinburgh International Festival 2000. Conductor, Richard Armstrong; director Tim Albery; designers, Hildegard Bechler (set), Ana Jebens (costumes). Matthew Best (Wotan), Loge (Peter Bronder), Anne Mason (Fricka), Rachel Hynes (Freia), Helena Ranada (Erda), Carsten Stabel (Fasolt), Markus Hollop (Fafner), Peter Sidhom (Alberich), Alasdair Elliott (Mime)

Performances were given at the Theatre Royal, Glasgow, and on tour at Edinburgh, Aberdeen, Sunderland.

WELSH NATIONAL OPERA

Founded 1946
John Street, Cardiff CF10 4SP
Productions from the repertory: *Don Giovanni* (1996), *Rigoletto* (1990), *Turandot* (1994), *The Barber of Seville* (1986), *Carmen* (1997), *Der Rosenkavalier* (1990).

New productions:
The Carmelites (Poulenc), 2 October 1999. Conductor, Gareth Jones; director, Phyllida Lloyd; designer, Anthony Ward. Catrin Wyn Davies (Blanche), Elizabeth Vaughan (Mme de Croissy), Suzanne Murphy (Mme Lidoine), Sally Burgess (Mother Marie), Natalie Christie (Sister Constance), David Barrell (Marquis de la Force), Nicholas Serars (Chevalier de la Force), Neil Jenkins (Father Confessor)

Cosi fan tutte (Mozart), 11 February 2000. Conductor, Robert Spano; director, Calixto Bieito; designers, Alfons Flores (set), Merce Paloma (costumes). Cara O Sullivan (Fiordiligi), Imelda Drumm (Dorabella), Linda Kitchen (Despina), Gregory Turay (Ferrando), Neal Davies (Guglielmo), Donald Maxwell (Don Alfonso)

The Turn of the Screw (Britten), 15 May. Conductor, Carlo Rizzi; director, John Crowley; designer, Rob Howell. Jamice Watson (Governess), Yvette Bonner (Flora), Mary Lloyd-Davies (Mrs Grose), Geraldine McCreevy (Miss Jessel), Paul Nilon (Peter Quint/ Prologue), Gregory Monk (Miles)

Performances were given at the New Theatre, Cardiff, and at Southampton, Bristol, Belfast, Birmingham, Liverpool, Oxford, Plymouth, Swansea, Llandudno.

GLYNDEBOURNE FESTIVAL OPERA

Founded 1934
Glyndebourne, Lewes, East Sussex BN8 5UU
The Festival ran from 20 May to 27 August 2000. *Jenůfa* (1989), *Cosi fan tutte* (1998), *Peter Grimes* (1992), *The Rake's Progress* (1975) were revived.

New productions:
Le nozze di Figaro (Mozart), 20 May. Conductor, Andrew Davis; director, Graham Vick; designer, Richard Hudson. Peter Mattei (Figaro), Christiane Oelze (Susanna), Mariusz Kwiecien (Count Almaviva), Maria Costanza Nocentini (Countess Almaviva), Marina Comparato (Cherubino), Diana Montague (Marcellina), Andrew Shore (Bartolo), Ryland Davies (Don Basilio)

Don Giovanni (Mozart), 15 July. Conductor, Andrew Davis; director, Graham Vick; designer, Richard Hudson. Natale de Carolis (Don Giovanni), Barbara Frittoli (Donna Anna), Sandra Zeltzer (Donna Elvira), Patricia Biccire (Zerlina), Bruce Ford (Don Ottavio), Alessandro Corbelli (Leporello), Gwynne Howell (Commendatore), Nathan Berg (Masetto)

GLYNDEBOURNE TOURING OPERA

La bohème (Puccini), 10 October 2000. Conductor, Louis Langree; director, David McVicar; designers, Michael Vane (set), Mikki Engelsbel (costumes). Alfred Boe (Rodolpho), Luca Grassi (Marcello), Nicolas Teste (Colline), Riccardo Novaro (Schaunard), Simona Todaro (Mimi), Claron McFadden (Musetta)

The Last Supper (Birtwistle), UK premiere, 21 October. Conductor, Elgar Howarth; director, Martin Duncan; designer, Alison Chitty. William Dazeley (Jesus), Susan Bickley (Ghost), Thomas Randle (Judas). Geoffrey Moses (Simon/Peter), Colin Judson (Andrew), Andrew Rupp (John), Paul Reeves (Matthew)

La bohème, *The Last Supper* and *Don Giovanni* were performed at Glyndebourne, Woking, Norwich, Milton

Keynes, Plymouth, Oxford and Stoke-on-Trent, from
10 October to 9 December 1999.

GARSINGTON OPERA

Founded 1989
Garsington Manor, Garsington, Oxford OX44 9DH
The season ran from 11 June to 9 July 2000. *Il mondo della
luna* (1991) was revived.

New productions:
Le nozze di Figaro (Mozart), 14 June. Conductor,
Stephen Barlow; director, Stephen Unwin; designers;
Neil Warmington (set), Mark Bouman (costumes). Mark
Stone (Figaro), Hulda Bjork Gardarsdottir (Susanna),
Peter Savidge (Count), Franzita Whelan (Countess),
Louise Innes (Cherubino), Jennifer Rhys-Davies
(Marcellina)
    Genoveva (Schumann), 25 June. Conductor, Elgar
Howarth; director, Aidan Lang; designer, Ashley Martin-
Davis. Susannah Glanville (Genoveva), Nigel Robson
(Golo), Johannes Mannov (Siegfried), Kathryn Turpin
(Margaretha)

ENGLISH TOURING OPERA

Founded 1980 as Opera 80
Carmen (Bizet) and *Macbeth* (Verdi) were toured to
Richmond, Buxton, Canterbury, High Wycombe, Bath,
Wolverhampton and Weston-Super-Mare between 13
October and 27 November 1999.
    The Rake's Progress (Stravinsky) and *Carmen* (Bizet)
were toured to Cambridge, Crewe, Ipswich, Darlington,
Reading, Brighton, Truro, Poole, Exeter, Yeovil, Lincoln,
Cheltenham, Crawley, Ulverston, Preston and Carlisle
between 28 February and 20 May 2000.

Parliament

In the spill over period from the 1998–99 session of Parliament, the Government pushed through the last of their Constitutional Reform Bills of the session and completed the programme outlined in the Queen's Speech the previous November. In what might have been taken as a final show of defiance before their reform was completed, the House of Lords inflicted several high profile defeats on the Government in a number of the core Bills of their legislative programme.

On the first day of the Report Stage of Greater London Authority Bill on 12 October an amendment moved by Conservative peer Baroness Miller of Hendon to Clause 2, requiring the Mayor to nominate his Deputy before the election, was passed by 213 votes to 117, a majority against the Government of 96. This, along with the earlier defeats inflicted on the Government by the Lords before the Summer Recess were overturned under a guillotine motion in the Commons on 8 November. The Bill received Royal Assent on 11 November.

On the first day of the Report Stage of the Welfare Reform and Pensions Bill, 11 October, the Government were defeated when a Conservative amendment moved by Lord Higgins to allow people taking out stakeholder pensions to delay retirement beyond the present age limit of 75 was passed by 145 votes to 137, a majority against the Government of eight. On the second day of the Report Stage, 13 October, the Government suffered five defeats to their plans to cut disability benefits. Labour peer Lord Ashley sponsored three of the amendments expressing the view that "this Government have an outstanding record of helping disabled people but this is one of the few blots on their record . . . the Minister failed to deny the fact that this Clause will cause immense suffering" – firstly over plans to restrict entitlement to incapacity benefit when Peers voted by 251 votes to 95, a majority of 156, against Ministers' proposals to deny benefit to disabled people who had not worked for two years before claiming; then an amendment removing the means-testing of incapacity benefit to take into account pension payments (198 votes to 90, a majority of 108) and finally an amendment overturning the proposed abolition of the severe disability allowance. Earlier the Government had been defeated when peers had voted by 193 votes to 114, a majority of 79 for a Conservative amendment (Lord Astor) extending the payment of the new bereavement allowance for widows and widowers from six months to two years, and finally by 185 votes to 163, a majority of 18 for a Conservative amendment (Baroness Crawley) overturning Government plans to close a tax loophole used by individuals setting up one-man personal service companies (IR 35). At Third Reading on 27 October a Conservative amendment (Baroness Strange) extending war pensions for widows was accepted by 166 votes to 107, a majority against the Government of 59. All the eight defeats that the Government had received in the Lords were overturned in the Commons under a guillotine motion on 3 November, although on Clause 58 (Incapacity Benefit) some 54 Labour Backbench MPs voted against the Government. On 8 November, the Upper House stuck to its guns on the extension of war pensions to widows (by 153 votes to 140, a majority of 13) and on the denial of incapacity benefit to those who had not claimed it for two years (by 260 votes to 127, a majority against the Government of 133). An amendment to make it easier

for disabled people with occupational pensions to qualify for incapacity benefit was approved without division. All three of these defeats were overturned in the Commons on 9 November and the Bill received Royal Assent on 11 November.

On the second day of the Report Stage on Immigration and Asylum Bill, 20 October, a New Clause moved by the Bishop of Southwark to halt the introduction of the voucher system for asylum seekers, was passed by 161 votes to 116, a majority against the Government of 45. This too was overturned in a guillotine motion in the Commons on 9 November and the Bill received Royal Assent on 11 November.

On the Bill to reform the Lords themselves, the House of Lords Bill, Peers did not vote down the Government, with the measure gaining its Third Reading in the House on 26 October by 221 votes to 80, a Government majority of 140. This occasion was marked, however, by the expulsion from the House of the Earl of Burford, son of an hereditary peer the Duke of St Albans, with the right, therefore, to listen to proceedings from the steps of the Throne, for staging a protest. At Prorogation on 11 November many of the Hereditary Peers who would not be returning took the opportunity to bid farewell to the House of Lords.

In the Queen's Speech opening the 1999–2000 Session on 17 November the Government outlined a larger than usual legislative programme with over 28 Bills being foreshadowed and indeed some 39 eventually being brought forward by the Summer Recess. This number of Bills itself, caused problems with a backlog building up by the summer recess, but the Leader of the House, Margaret Beckett, was quick to point out that "as one looks back over the years of Conservative Governments – especially in the 1980s – the programmes of legislation that they put through were substantially heavier than that currently being undertaken."

If the Government had expected an easier time from the reformed House of Lords (without the Hereditary Peers the composition was 232 Conservative, 186 Labour, 166 Cross Benchers, 56 Liberal Democrats and 32 others, with four having Leave of Absence) and in turn they had expected the Government to curtail their use of the guillotine to reduce Parliamentary debate, both sides would be disappointed in the 1999–2000 Session. The Government faced some 40 defeats in the Lords (not all of which were overturned) and the Government guillotined discussion on Government legislation in the Commons a record 36th time under Mr Blair's premiership. The repeated theme of the session was that the Government was bypassing Parliament, making announcements outside the Chamber and only at best, tolerating scrutiny by MPs. It was generally accepted that this was by far the worst year for the Government since it came to power. Indeed on 13 July the Conservatives forced the Prime Minister Tony Blair to defend his record and position in an Opposition debate on Parliament and the Executive. His lack of practice at speaking in the Chamber except at Question Time was exposed when he kept referring to the Deputy Speaker, Sir Alan Haselhurst as "Madam Speaker", who sits on the Throne during Question Time but not always during debates. When the Speaker of the Common, Betty Boothroyd, announced her resignation on 12 July many speculated that this was one of the reasons for her departure and in her valedictory speech on 26 July she made some less than veiled references to the issue, "Let us make a start by remembering that the function of Parliament is to hold the Executive to account . . . it is in Parliament in the first instance that Ministers must explain and justify their policies." She was also critical of the attitude of some new Members to the Chamber who were keen to modernise the House and change working practices, "the House must be prepared to put in the hours necessary to carry out effective examination of the Government's legislation . . . if that means long days or re-arrangement of the Parliamentary year, so be it." She was saddened that "the high reputation of Westminster abroad is not entirely reflected at home." The election of a New Speaker will be the first and only business of the Commons when it returns from the summer recess on 23 October. Arguments about modernisation also overshadowed Parliamentary proceedings. The Opposition claimed there was a reluctance for later night sittings (past 10.00 p.m.) which meant that the opportunity for proper scrutiny of the Government's plans was curtailed. Leader of the Opposition, William Hague, felt that the Modernisation Committee had "tragically failed its own remit . . . it proposes changes to the programming of legislation and the timing of votes that would shift the terms of trade in the opposite direction by generally reducing the opportunities for the Opposition and the Government's own Back-benchers to scrutinise legislation and hold the Executive to account." First time Labour Backbench MPs Tess Kingham and Jenny Jones announced that they would not be standing again for Parliament as the working conditions were not conducive to family life. There was continued criticism of the Government, with its majority of 177, for the way in which it was handling legislation under guillotine motions, timetabling or restricting discussion. The underlying accusation of spin over substance was one that would not disappear and certainly harmed the image of the Government.

The Government's problems over legislation with the House of Lords began with the Criminal Justice (Mode of Trial) Bill (Lords), a measure designed to remove the ability of defendants to elect Crown Court trial in either-way cases as recommended by the Royal Commission on Criminal Justice, which had its Second Reading in the Lords on 2 December. It is a convention that the House of Lords do not vote against the Second Reading of a Government Bill and although many Lords, including Law Lords spoke against the Bill it did receive an unopposed Second Reading. When, however, it came to Committee consideration on 20 January, an all-party alliance of Peers led by Conservative Home Affairs spokesman Lord Cope of Berkeley who claimed that "the removing of the long-standing right . . . will damage confidence in the criminal justice system" then passed an amendment to the Bill which preserved the right to jury trial by 222 votes to 126 a majority against the Government of 96. This was the first defeat for the government in the Lords since the majority of hereditary peers were removed and also, coincidentally, came on the same day as plans were published for long-term reform of the Upper Chamber. As a result the Government withdrew the Bill but Jack Straw promised that another Bill containing the proposals would be introduced in the House of Commons later in the Parliamentary session. The Criminal Justice (Mode of Trial) (No 2) Bill was given its Second Reading by 315 votes to 188 on 7 March, when Mr Straw argued that "in no sense does the Bill undermine the availability of trial by jury for appropriate offences" but a reasoned amendment declining a Second Reading was only defeated by 315 votes to 214, a majority for the Government of 111

when 20 Labour MPs voted with the main Opposition Parties. The Bill completed its Third Reading, under a guillotine, on 25 July by 282 votes to 199 (including 25 Labour MPs) and will be sent to the Lords for consideration in the over-spill period. Even here there was controversy as Mr Straw claimed that the measure "enjoys the active endorsement of the Lord Chief Justice, Lord Bingham" a statement that subsequent correspondence released by the Opposition seemed to contradict.

The Home Office also ran into difficulty with the Lords over the Local Government Bill to give local authorities the chance to innovate and provide better services for the public, ensuring value for money and to establish powers to promote the well-being of communities and develop comprehensive community strategies by including provision to repeal Section 2A of Local Government Act 1986 (Section 28 of 1988 Act) preventing local authorities from intentionally promoting homosexuality. The Government announced it would follow through on its election promise to repeal the law in England and Wales hard on the heels of a similar move in Scotland. The Bill was introduced in the House of Lords receiving an unopposed Second Reading on 6 December when Junior Department of the Environment, Transport and the Regions Minister Lord Whitty stressed that the reasoning behind this part of the Bill was "to tackle the reasons that certain groups of people are marginalised or excluded from society . . . we want a society in which everyone is valued and in which everybody has the opportunity to participate, regardless of their race, their sex and also regardless of their sexual orientation. We need local authorities to help build such a society." Even at this stage Conservative Peer Baroness Young objected to this part of the Bill. As predicted the House of Lords overturned the plans to lift the Section 28 ban on the promotion of homosexuality by local authorities at Committee stage on 7 February when after a six hour debate Peers voted by 210 votes (including 15 Labour peers defying their Party whip) to 165, a majority against the Government of 45 for Baroness Young's amendment to keep Section 28. When the Bill came to the Commons for Second Reading on 11 April the Minister for Local Government and the Regions (Hilary Armstrong) said that "the Government are committed to its repeal and will table the amendments to achieve that. Contrary to popular belief the section does not apply to schools and therefore has no effect on what is taught in the classroom . . . it does, however, inhibit local authorities from addressing the legitimate needs of a particular section of their communities." Their amendment was duly passed in Standing Committee A on 20 June.

When the Bill returned to the Lords for consideration of Commons amendments on 24 July they again voted it down – defeating the measure for the second time after a two-hour debate by 270 votes to 228, a majority of 42, with more peers voting in favour of the status quo. This was closer than the previous occasion as some 30 Labour and Liberal Democrat Peers had been created since the original vote. Baroness Young said "the House of Lords has once again shown that, on this issue they are more representative of the British people than the House of Commons." Eighteen Labour rebels, four Bishops and a former Archbishop of York, Lord Habgood, were among the 270 peers who supported Lady Young's amendment. The Government remained committed to scrapping Section 28, but was not prepared to continue its fight with the Lords and risk losing the Local Government Bill altogether and so did not insist on reinstating the Clause on 25 July. Ministers were considering their options. It is possible they may introduce a one line bill to repeal the clause in the Queen's speech in the autumn, but it is more likely that the government will rule out a change before the next election. The Bill, without this section, received Royal Assent on 28 July.

Similar arguments also dogged the progress through the Lords of the Learning and Skills Bill (Lords). The Bill was intended to set up a framework for planning, funding and delivery of post-16 education and training but the Government were defeated twice on issues not strictly addressed by the Bill. On the same day the Government also suffered two further defeats on matters central to the Bill – on an amendment moved by Lord Pilkington of Oxenford (Con) concerning "disproportionate expenditure" by the new Learning and Skills Councils approved by 173 votes to 127, a majority against the Government of 46 and on an amendment moved by Baroness Sharp of Guildford (LibDem) on the provision of Careers services approved by 157 votes to 142, a majority against the Government of 15. These defeats were overturned at Committee Stage in the Commons and an attempt by Conservative Backbench MP Gerald Howarth to reinstate an amendment calling for pupils to be taught that "marriage provides for a strong foundation for stable relationships and the most reliable framework for raising children" at Third Reading on 27 June was rejected without a vote. When the Lords considered the Commons amendments to the Bill on 18 July peers voted by 234 votes to 220 to reject an attempt by Baroness Young to give a greater emphasis to marriage in the guidelines. The Bill received Royal Assent on 28 July.

The flagship Transport Bill to establish a Strategic Railway Authority, to deliver the proper regulation of buses at the local level, to give powers to Local Authorities to introduce road user charges and workplace parking charges and to allow for setting up of a Public Private Partnership to deliver air traffic services in the UK ran into trouble in the Commons at the Second Reading on 20 December when former Labour Transport Secretary, Gavin Strang, tabled a reasoned amendment considering that the Transport Bill was not an acceptable measure because it contains provisions the purpose of which is to pave the way for the partial privatisation of National Air Traffic Services (NATS). He was supported by the Labour Chair of the House of Commons Transport Sub-Committee, Gwyneth Dunwoody who, although welcoming much of the measure felt that on NATS "it is not in the general interest and will not really offer improvements . . . nor do I think that the suggestions for the protection of public interest are sufficient to result in the level of care that we need." Deputy Prime Minister, John Prescott, stressed the Government view that "a Private Public Partnership will ensure that NATS is able to finance its future within a stable regulatory framework . . . I am happy to assure the House that safety will continue to be the overriding priority . . . and the Government will have power to issue directions to NATS in the interests of national security." Although Mr Strang wished to withdraw his amendment, the Liberal Democrats forced a vote on it an it was defeated by 321 votes to 33 (all LibDem or other minority Parties). At Report Stage on 9 May, however, this dissent manifested itself when the Government suffered its third largest backbench revolt in the Commons, when 46 Labour MPs rebelled against plans to partially sell off NATS and a sizeable number of MPs abstained. During two votes, the rebel MPs called for NATS to be transferred to a publicly-owned company or a non-profit making trust – the Government defeated both moves, but its majority slumped to 60 during the second vote. MPs voted by 307 to 99 against an amendment moved by Mrs Dunwoody to set up NATS as a publicly-owned corporation along the lines of the Post Office.

A second rebel Labour amendment moved by Dr Strang, seeking to allow transfer of existing property, rights or liabilities only to a non-profit making company, was defeated by 308 to 248. A further Labour rebel amendment moved by veteran Backbench MP Tam Dalyell, which required a vote by both Houses of Parliament on any transfer scheme made by the Civil Aviation Authority or the Transport Secretary, was defeated by 310 to 244. The Bill received its Third Reading by 304 votes to 159, a Government majority of 145 on 10 May and passed to the Lords, where, ironically, it had an easier passage on NATS as the Conservative Opposition were in favour of wholesale privatisation. It still has to complete its stages in the Lords in the spill-over period.

The Utilities Bill, designed to set a modern, transparent and accountable framework for utility regulation by giving regulators a new primary duty to protect the consumer interest and establish independent consumer councils for each utility sector and align the regulatory systems for gas and electricity under a single regulatory authority (OFGEM) had its Second Reading in the Commons on 31 January. The Bill had nearly completed its Commons Committee stage when Trade and Industry Secretary, Stephen Byers, answered an oral question in the Commons on April 2 to announce that the Government had dropped telecoms and water industries from the provisions of the Bill, following complaints from telecom operators who alleged the bill would hinder the growth of e-commerce. Telecoms firms would now be covered in a Communications Bill, plans for which would be published later in the year and the Department of Transport would issue a draft bill to cover water companies "in the coming months." The Utilities Bill would cover just the gas and electricity industries. Conservative Trade & Industry spokesman Angela Browning was outraged at the affront to the important business sectors involved and felt the Trade Secretary's "reputation and that of his Department is that they are unbusinesslike and do not know what they are doing." Liberal Democrat Trade & Industry spokesperson Norman Baker called it a case of "joined up chaos rather than joined up government . . . the Utilities Bill is a shambles and he will have to answer the question of whether its remaining threads hang together at all." Despite this the reduced Bill completed all its stages and received Royal Assent on 28 July.

At the very final stage of consideration – Third Reading in the Commons on 28 June – of the Limited Liability Partnerships Bill (Lords), a measure to create an additional form of business entity with limited liability in the UK, the Government had to accept an amendment from Labour Backbench MP Stuart Bell to ensure that "the British branch of an oversea limited liability partnership will be able to continue to use the name that concludes with the word 'limited liability partnership', 'LLP' or their Welsh language equivalents. As drafted, the Bill would make it an offence for people to describe themselves as a limited liability partnership or LLP unless they were incorporated in this country."

The long awaited Freedom of Information Bill, hailed by Jack Straw on Second Reading on 7 December as "a good Bill, which will transform the culture in which Governments operate . . . everyone will benefit from the Bill, which will deliver a more responsive, better informed and more accountable public service," although opposed by the Conservatives was given a Second Reading by 377 votes to 138, a Government majority of 239. At Report Stage on 4 and 5 April the Government suffered a series of rebellions over the Bill, with five backbench revolts involving up to 36 Labour MPs. The rebels included many formerly loyal MPs, including Commons Public

Administration Select Committee Chair, Dr Tony Wright, who voted against his own party for the first time, and the former Labour Cabinet Minister, Dr David Clark who drew up Labour's original freedom of information legislation as well as more likely rebels such as the veteran backbench MP Tony Benn. The core of the rebellion centred on the Home Secretary's decision to keep secret elements of factual information used to advise ministers on policy and the rebels were also angered by Mr Straw refusing to back down on proposals to give Cabinet Ministers the power to override the proposed Information Commissioner. On an amendment to Clause 13 on Discretionary Disclosures, Dr Wright's amendment on the issue of policy advice, was defeated by 311 votes to 202, a Government majority of 109, but 36 Labour MPs, including four Select Committee Chairs voted with the Conservative and Liberal Democrat Opposition. On a Liberal Democrat amendment to Clause 28 (Investigations & Proceedings Conducted by Public Authorities), moved by Liberal Democrat spokesperson Simon Hughes, allowing investigating bodies to withhold information if disclosure would be likely to prejudice investigations they were conducting some 25 Labour MPs voted with the Liberal Democrats and some 26 Labour MPs voted with both main Opposition Parties for another Simon Hughes amendment to Clause 33 designed to deny Ministers powers to withhold information used to develop Government policy. Eighteen Labour MPs registered their protest against Ministers' determination to allow information to be withheld on the "reasonable opinion" of themselves or officials if it was likely to harm the working of government, councils and other public bodies, by voting with the Liberal Democrats for their amendment to Clause 34. Finally, some 24 Labour MPs voted against new Clause 6 allowing Cabinet Ministers the right to override the Information Commissioner. The Bill completed its passage through the Commons with an unopposed Third Reading on 5 April and had its Second Reading in the Lords on 20 April. It is awaiting its Committee Stage consideration in the spill-over.

Similarly the Political Parties, Elections and Referendum Bill to put into effect the recommendations of the 5th report of the Neill Committee on Standards in Public Life and limit expenditure on campaigns having passed all its Commons stages also disappeared after its first day in Committee in the Lords on 11 May.

The Sexual Offences (Amendment) Bill, designed to equalise the age of consent and strengthen the protection of people from the abuse of trust, which had been lost in the Lords in the last session of Parliament, was re-introduced and passed all its Commons stages but it has been awaiting Committee stage discussion in the Lord since its Second Reading on 11 April when Conservative Peer Baroness Young, who led the campaign to save Section 28 on homosexuality, has said she will table amendments to the Bill.

The Regulation of Investigatory Powers Bill had a Second Reading in the Commons on 6 March. Jack Straw saw it as "a significant step forward for the protection of human rights in this country ... for the first time law enforcement activities will be properly regulated by law and externally supervised" gaining its Third Reading on 8 May by 330 votes to 139. By the time, however, it reached Committee Stage in the House of Lords on 12 June some 229 amendments had been tabled from a range of groups concerned that the Bill actually harmed privacy and imposed a costly burden on business. Conservative spokesman Lord Cope of Berkeley quoted a report from the British Chambers of Commerce that suggested "the Bill as it stands is entirely inadequate as a

mechanism to achieve efficient and reasonable interception and surveillance and that its effect is likely to be loss of confidence in e-commerce, unacceptable costs to business and to the UK economy, confusion and uncertainty at numerous levels of business activity and an onerous imposition on the rights of individuals." For the Liberal Democrats Lord McNally suggested that "would it not be better to take away the Bill and perhaps hold some public hearings and obtain some more expert advice on it ... I believe that the Government are heading for the rocks if they do not realise that the warnings that have been given from some responsible quarters are valid." Although the Government were not defeated in Committee they bowed to the pressures and tabled several of their own amendments to the Bill including one that meant the Home Secretary had to sign a warrant before an individual's e-mail could be monitored, one to inform company directors if their staff were asked to hand over the passwords or encryption keys used to protect e-mail and ones to reassure Internet Service Providers (ISPs) that they would not incur excessive costs. Despite this, the Government were defeated at Report Stage on 12 and 13 July when amendments moved by Lord Cope to set up a Technical Advisory Board was passed by 155 votes to 130, a majority against the Government of 25, and by Viscount Astor (Con) to ensure that the Home Secretary could make compensatory payments to ISPs were passed by 131 to 119, a majority against the Government of 12. Lord Cope's proposal that only the Home Secretary should authorise e-mail surveillance – as with telephone tapping – was defeated by 120 votes to 119, just one vote. As a result the Government announced further concessions to ensure that Chief Constables must notify the independent Surveillance Commissioner after they have used their power to tap e-mails and at Third Reading on 19 July tabled further amendments to put in place a new safeguard allowing business to sue the security services if their confidentiality was breached as a result of the interception of e-mails and creating tighter regulation of the measures contained in the Bill so that police would be required to inform a judge within seven days of serving an order on a company. Other changes included accepting a Technical Advisory Board to oversee the installation of intercept capabilities at ISPs. The Bill returned to the Commons for endorsement of the Lords amendments on 25 July and received Royal Assent on 28 July.

The Countryside and Rights of Way Bill that sets down tougher laws to give the public right of way over open countryside as well as protect wild species and habitats had its Second Reading in the Commons on 20 March by 334 votes to 138. Environment Minister Michael Meacher denied that the bill favoured the urban population over rural people and said the changes should not burden farmers and other landowners with any significant extra costs. The arguments widened to include fox-hunting after Labour Backbench MP Gordon Prentice, with the support of some 100 MPs proposed amending the Bill at Report Stage to ban the sport unless the government gave a "cast iron statement" promising to introduce legislation before the next election. Jack Straw unveiled plans on 13 July for a bill containing a number of options ranging from a complete ban to leaving the sport unchanged, which would have a free vote for MPs, following the publication of the Burns report into the impact of a hunting ban, and this was enough for Mr Prentice to withdraw his motion.

Opening the Commons Second Reading debate on the Terrorism Bill, replacing counter-terrorist legislation with permanent UK-wide laws, on 14 December, Jack Straw said the legislation would not remove the right to peaceful demonstration, "it is not designed to be used in situations where demonstrations unaccountably turn ugly" but Human Rights groups and backbench MPs voiced concerns that the new definition of terrorism in the bill would see groups like Greenpeace targeted. Labour backbench MP Jeremy Corbyn warned the bill could threaten the right of people in exile to campaign for political change in their home countries and his Labour colleague Alan Simpson MP said a number of the party's MPs were concerned about the wider definition of terrorism in the bill, that when the Commons considered the Remaining Stages of the Bill on 15 March the House sat until 2.40 am with Government backbenchers expressing their alarm at the implications of the Bill for civil liberties. The Bill gained a Third Reading by 210 votes to one, a Government majority of 209. After consideration in the Lords it received Royal Assent on 20 July.

Northern Ireland Secretary Peter Mandelson admitted during the Second Reading of the Police (Northern Ireland) Bill in the Commons on 6 June that with a Bill "paving the way for the most complex changes in policing practices and culture ever attempted ... it is hardly surprising that such a complex task should spark controversy" but Conservative Northern Ireland spokesman Andrew McKay moved an amendment declining a Second Reading as the Bill "failed to preserve the proud title and insignia of the Royal Ulster Constabulary and enables the political representatives of paramilitary organisations to sit on the Policing Board and District Policing Partnerships without a start to the decommissioning of illegally held arms and explosives." This was rejected by 342 votes to 142, a Government majority of 200. In Committee on 6 July Ulster Unionist MP, Ken Maginnis, hoped he had saved the name RUC when an amendment retaining the title was accepted but the Government insisted that the force would be known as the Police Service of Northern Ireland for 'operational purposes.' When the Remaining Stages on the Bill were discussed on 11 July it was under a guillotine that. Only three MPs were able to speak on Third Reading that day with the result that the First Minister of Northern Ireland, David Trimble MP was unable to speak in the debate. Third Reading was passed by 307 votes to 16 but left such an ill feeling with Opposition Parties that they forced divisions on five pieces of delegated legislation that would normally have been nodded through, which kept MPs in the Chamber until 12.56 am. The Bill will complete its Lords stages in the spill-over period.

The Opposition had criticised the Government for failing to introduce legislation to deal with football hooligans prior to the rioting involving English fans at the Euro 2000 competition with Shadow Home Secretary Ann Widdecombe accusing the Government of "a complacent attitude and woeful inaction" during an oral statement on the situation on 19 June. When the Football (Disorder) Bill was introduced the Government hoped to rush it through its Parliamentary scrutiny to ensure it gained Royal Assent before the Summer recess and would thus be law before the next series of England football internationals. It was given a Second Reading in the Commons on 14 July by 206 votes to 6 (five Conservative and one Labour), but several MPs from all Parties expressed concerns at the civil liberties aspects of a bill that stopped people from travelling even in the absence of previous convictions and called for changes to be made in Committee. The Bill completed all its Commons stages on 17 July with Third Reading passed by 171 votes to 42 (mostly Liberal Democrat) and went immediately to the Lords for Second Reading on 20 July. The Bill was taken in Committee on 24 July when the Lords sat until 5.12 p.m.

and Backbench Conservative Peer Lord Marlesford's motion demanding a extra day's debate was passed by 143 votes to 124. Report Stage was taken on 25 July and an amendment moved by Lord Cope of Berkeley to review the Bill after two years (rather than the four envisaged) was passed by 174 votes to 136, a majority of 38. This was reluctantly accepted by the Government, approved by the Commons on 27 July and the Bill duly gained Royal Assent on 28 July.

The Prime Minister's seemingly poor year was perhaps typified by the weekly Prime Minister's Question Time every Wednesday when most observers agreed that the Leader of the Opposition William Hague got the better of Mr Blair more often than not. This was not helped by a series of highly embarrassing leaks of Government Memos to the Press suggesting that the Government were out of touch and on 5 July when he was sufficiently distracted by Mr Hague's accusation of "actually I was asking the Prime Minister a question to which he does not give the answer" that he referred to a war memorial for American service men and women rather than Australian, in front of five Australian Prime Ministers who were in the Gallery watching the exchanges. It was also revealed (in a leak to the Press) that he had asked his advisers to come up with "killer points" with which he could counteract the Leader of the Opposition. William Hague accused Mr Blair of expecting the media to behave as the "unquestioning mouthpiece" of the Government and "behave like Pravda."

The Chancellor of the Exchequer, Gordon Brown, was also criticised. Following what was seen as a well received Budget on 22 March, he was criticised again for failing to mention in his speech certain crucial fiscal changes such as the change to Double Taxation Relief. William Hague accused the Chancellor of increasing business taxes by £30 million, putting "taxes up by 8 pence in the pound for businesses, pensioners, drivers, savers, home owners and millions of families" and the Government of "promising that there would be no tax increases and having cynically and totally broken their promises." In the Committee of the Whole House debate on the Finance Bill on 3 May Conservative Treasury spokesman Oliver Letwin returned to the issue of Double Taxation of Mixer Companies "when I say that the Government misestimated, I do not mean they got it wrong by 5 per cent or 10 per cent ... they got it wrong roughly speaking, tenfold. If the Chancellor of the Exchequer got things wrong to that extent in general, he would bankrupt us and use up our gross domestic product about five times over." Paymaster General Dawn Primarolo announcing further consultation with industry on this measure, did not accept the figures that the Inland Revenue were wrong – "the figures we have are for companies claiming relief do not match those figures: a simple, straightforward attack is being made on the Inland Revenue and the Treasury." The Finance Bill completed its Commons stages on 28 June. After consideration in the Lords the Finance Bill received Royal Assent on 28 July.

The Chancellor was also criticised by the Opposition for double counting when announcing the Government's spending plans in the Comprehensive Spending Review on 19 July although the plans for an extra £43 billion of public expenditure were generally well received.

Nor was the Deputy Prime Minster John Prescott spared the accusations of double counting and use of spin when he unveiled the Ten Year Transport plan "based on long-term investment by Government and industry to modernise the country's transport system" on 20 July. Conservative Transport spokesman Bernard Jenkin called it "not real money but a ten year plan from a one term

Government who cannot see further than the headlines in tomorrow's newspapers."

Conservative backbench MPs Eric Forth (Bromley & Chislehurst) and David Maclean (Penrith & the Border) continued to ensure that no Bills went through the House without proper scrutiny or that the Private Member's route was not being used for legislation that was more properly the responsibility of central Government. They even caused the Remaining Stages of the Royal Parks (Trading) Bill, a Government bill to outlaw illegal trading in the royal parks to protect the public from unprincipled traders by providing powers of enforcement similar to those exercised by the City of Westminster, which had failed as a Private Member's Bill in the previous session, to have to be carried over for a second day on 22 May. This Bill received Royal Assent on 20 July. Their actions also led to the Government taking the most unusual step of allocating Government time for the Commons stages of the Census (Amendment) Bill (Lords), a Private Member's Bill introduced by Lord Weatherill (Cross Bencher) to effect a change to the Census Act 1920 in order to enable a question on religious affiliation to be included in the next census, which had failed to make it onto the Statute Book in the previous session. This received Royal Assent on 28 July.

Not everything went wrong for the Prime Minister. High profile Conservative MP Shaun Woodward made a very public defection to Labour in late December citing intolerance in the Conservatives towards homosexuals.

As Parliament rose for the Summer Recess on 28 July there was a palpable feeling of relief on the Government benches but several hurdles remained to be faced. The Government is under pressure to get the remaining legislation of this parliamentary session through the House of Lords in the short period after the end of the summer recess and the next Queen's Speech. It is thought a major bill might have to be sacrificed to achieve this. It is felt that they could be preparing to drop the Countryside and Rights of Way Bill because of a backlog of legislation awaiting passage through the House of Lords with more than 300 amendments having been tabled to the bill, raising the prospect of it running out of parliamentary time. Even though the House of Lords returns from recess in late September, nearly a whole month earlier than the Commons, Government business managers will be stretched to get the five remaining major bills as well as several other more minor bills through the Upper Chamber before the State Opening of Parliament.

SECRETARIES OF STATE FOR FOREIGN AFFAIRS since 1900

In 1782 the Northern Department was converted into the Foreign Office, and Charles James Fox was appointed first Secretary of State for Foreign Affairs. With the merger of the Foreign Office and the Commonwealth Office on 1 October 1968 the post was redesignated as Secretary of State for Foreign and Commonwealth Affairs.

Year appointed	Name	Year appointed	Name
1895	Marquess of Salisbury	1955 *Dec.*	Selwyn Lloyd
1900	Marquess of Lansdowne	1960	Earl of Home
1905	Sir Edward Grey	1963	R. A. Butler
1916	Arthur Balfour	1964	Patrick Gordon Walker
1919	Earl Curzon	1965	Michael Stewart
1924 *Jan.*	Ramsay MacDonald	1966	George Brown
1924 *Nov.*	Sir Austen Chamberlain	1968	Michael Stewart
1929	Arthur Henderson	1970	Sir Alec Douglas-Home
1931 *Aug.*	Marquess of Reading	1974	James Callaghan
1931 *Nov.*	Sir John Simon	1976	Anthony Crosland
1935 *June*	Sir Samuel Hoare	1977	David Owen
1935 *Dec.*	Anthony Eden	1979	Lord Carrington
1938	Viscount Halifax	1982	Francis Pym
1940	Anthony Eden	1983	Sir Geoffrey Howe
1945	Ernest Bevin	1989 *July*	John Major
1951 *March*	Herbert Morrison	1989 *Nov.*	Douglas Hurd
1951 *Oct.*	Anthony Eden	1995	Malcolm Rifkind
1955 *April*	Harold Macmillan	1997	Robin Cook

SECRETARIES OF STATE FOR THE HOME DEPARTMENT since 1900

In 1782 the Southern Department was converted into the Home Office. The conduct of war was removed from the Home Secretary's hands in 1794 to a separate Secretary for War. Colonies were similarly transferred in 1801 to the Secretary for War and Colonies.

Year appointed	Name	Year appointed	Name
1895	Sir Matthew White-Ridley	1945 *Aug.*	Chuter Ede
1900	Charles Ritchie	1951	Sir David Maxwell-Fyfe
1902	Aretas Akers-Douglas	1954	Gwilym Lloyd-George
1905	Herbert Gladstone	1957	R. A. Butler
1910	Winston Churchill	1962	Henry Brooke
1911	Reginald McKenna	1964	Sir Frank Soskice
1915	Sir John Simon	1965	Roy Jenkins
1916 *Jan.*	Herbert Samuel	1967	James Callaghan
1916 *Dec.*	Sir George Cave	1970	Reginald Maudling
1919	Edward Shortt	1972	Robert Carr
1922	William Bridgeman	1974	Roy Jenkins
1924 *Jan.*	Arthur Henderson	1976	Merlyn Rees
1924 *Nov.*	Sir William Joynson-Hicks	1979	William Whitelaw
1929	John Clynes	1983	Leon Brittan
1931	Sir Herbert Samuel	1985	Douglas Hurd
1932	Sir John Gilmour	1989	David Waddington
1935	Sir John Simon	1990	Kenneth Baker
1937	Sir Samuel Hoare	1992	Kenneth Clarke
1939	Sir John Anderson	1993	Michael Howard
1940	Herbert Morrison	1997	Jack Straw
1945 *May*	Sir Donald Somervell		

This list of Public Acts commences with twelve Public Acts which received the Royal Assent before September 1, 1999. Those Public Acts which follow received the Royal Assent after August 31 1999. The date stated after each Act is the date on which it came into effect..

Finance Act 1999, c. 16 July 27 1999
grants certain duties, alters others and amends the law relating to the National Debt and Public Revenue. Inter alia it provides for exemption as a benefit in kind mobile phones provided to employees for 1999–00; and restricts the married couples allowance to those reaching 65 before 2000–01.

Disability Rights Commission Act 1999, c. 17 various dates, some to be appointed
establishes a Disability Rights Commission and makes provision as to its functions; and for connected purposes.

Adoption (Intercountry Aspects) Act 1999, c. 18 various dates, some to be appointed
makes provision for giving effect to the Convention on Protection of Children and Co-operation in respect of Intercountry Adoption concluded at the Hague on May 29, 1993; makes further provision in relation to adoptions with an international element; and for connected purposes. Inter alia it makes, with certain exceptions, a person habitually resident in the British Islands who at any time brings into the UK for the purposes of adoption a child who is habitually resident outside the Islands guilty of an offence.

Company and Business Names (Chamber of Commerce, Etc.) Act 1999, c. 19 day to be appointed
makes provision concerning the approval of company or business names containing the expression "chamber of commerce" or " siambr fasnach" or any related expression; and for connected purposes.

Commonwealth Development Corporation Act 1999, c. 20 July 27, 1999
makes provision about the Commonwealth Development Corporation.

Football (Offences and Disorder) Act 1999, c. 21 September 27, 1999
makes further provision in relation to football-related offences; for the purposes of preventing violence or disorder at or in connection with football matches; and for connected purposes.

Access to Justice Act 1999, c. 22 various dates, some to be appointed
establishes the Legal Services Commission, the Community Legal Service and the Criminal Defence Service; amends legal aid law in Scotland; makes further provision relating to legal services, appeals, courts, judges and court proceedings, magistrates and magistrates courts and other matters connected with the courts and judicial functions.

Youth Justice and Criminal Evidence Act 1999, c. 23 various dates, some to be appointed
provides for the referral of offenders under 18 to youth offender panels; makes provision in connection with giving of evidence or information for the purposes of criminal proceedings; and for connected purposes. Inter alia it brings special provisions for child witnesses and for screening a witness in appropriate cases, prohibits the cross-examination of the complainant witness by the accused in person where charged with a sexual offence.

Pollution Prevention and Control Act 1999, c. 24 various dates, some to be appointed
makes provision for implementing Council Directive 96/61/EC for preventing and controlling pollution; about certain expired or expiring disposal or waste management licences; and for connected purposes.

Criminal Cases Review (Insanity) Act 1999, c. 25 July 27 1999
makes provision in England, Wales and Northern Ireland to enable verdicts of guilty but insane to be referred to and reviewed by the Court of Appeal.

Employment Relations Act 1999, c. 26 various dates, some to be appointed
amends the law relating to employment, to trade unions and to employment agencies and businesses, inter alia it amends the law dealing with leave for family and domestic reasons; disciplinary and grievance hearings; and the law relating to unfair dismissal of workers taking part in official industrial action.

Local Government Act 1999, c. 27 various dates, some to be appointed
makes provision imposing on local and certain other authorities requirements relating to economy, efficiency and effectiveness; and makes provision for the regulation of council tax and precepts.

Food Standards Act 1999, c. 28 various dates, some to be appointed
establishes the Food Standards Agency and provides for its functions, powers and main organisational and account-ability arrangements; amends the law relating to food safety and relevant consumer interests and enables provision to be made relating to the notification of tests for food-borne disease and animal feeding stuffs.

Greater London Authority Act 1999, c. 29 various dates, some to be appointed
establishes and makes provision for the Greater London Authority, the Mayor of London and the London Assembly; makes provision in relation to the London borough councils and the Common Council of the City of London; makes provision about policing in Greater London and adjusts the metropolitan police district; and for related and connected purposes.

Welfare Reform and Pensions Act 1999, c. 30 various dates, some to be appointed
makes provision about pensions and social security, e.g. provides for the establishment and registration of stake-holder pension schemes; introduces measures to reduce the under-occupation of dwellings by housing benefit claimants; makes provision for pension sharing orders on divorce, sharing of rights under pension arrangements and as to the supply of information for child support purposes; and for changes to certain social security benefits.

Contracts (Rights of Third Parties) Act 1999, c. 31 November 11, 1999 but, with exceptions,
does not apply to a contract entered into before May 11, 2000
reforms the law of privity of contract [the basic rule of which is that only a party to a contract may enforce it] by providing for the enforcement of contractual terms by third parties where the contract expressly provides this or purports to confer a benefit.

Mental Health (Amendment) (Scotland) Act 1999, c. 32 January 11, 2000
authorises hospital managers to continue to hold, expend and dispose of the property of persons to whom the 1984 Act s. 94(1) no longer applies.

Immigration and Asylum Act 1999, c. 33 various dates, some to be appointed
makes provision about immigration and asylum including the giving, refusing or varying leave to enter the UK, exemptions from immigration control, removal of over-stayers and persons unlawfully in the UK; support for asylum seekers; about procedures in connection with marriage on superintendent registrar's certificate; appeals to the Immigration Appeal Tribunal; and for connected purposes.

House of Lords Act 1999, c. 34 various dates
reforms the membership of the House of Lords by restricting membership of hereditary peers and makes provision about disqualifications for voting at elections to and membership of the House of Commons; and for connected purposes.

Consolidated Fund (No. 2) Act 1999, c. 35 December 20, 1999
applies certain sums out of the Consolidated Fund to the service of the years ending March 31, 2000 and 2001

Northern Ireland Act 2000, c. 1 part on February 10, 2000, the remainder on February 12, 2000
provides for the suspension of devolved government in Northern Ireland and for the exercise of certain functions conferred by or under Part V of the 1998 Act; and for connected purposes.

Representation of the People Act 2000, c. 2 various dates, some to be appointed
makes new provision with respect to the registration of voters for the purposes of parliamentary and local government elections and makes provision in relating to voting at such elections; and for connected purposes.

Consolidated Fund Act 2000, c. 3 March 21, 2000
applies certain sums out of the Consolidated Fund to the service of the years ending March 1999, 2000 and 2001.

Armed Forces Discipline Act 2000, c. 4 various dates, some to be appointed
amends the Army Act 1955, the Air Force Act 1955 and the Naval Discipline Act 1957 in relation to custody, the right to elect court martial trial and appeals against findings made or punishments awarded on summary dealing or summary trial; and for connected purposes.

Nuclear Safeguards Act 2000, c. 5 various dates, some to be appointed
enables effect to be given to the protocol signed at Vienna on September 22, 1998 (Cm 4282) additional to the agreement for the application of safeguards in the UK in connection with the Treaty on the Non-Proliferation of Nuclear Weapons; allows effect to be given to that agreement in certain territories outside the UK; and for connected purposes.

Powers of Criminal Courts (Sentencing) Act 2000, c. 6 various dates, some to be appointed
consolidates, with amendments, certain enactments relating to the powers of courts to deal with offenders and defaulters and to the treatment of such persons to give effect to recommendations of the Law Commission and the Scottish Law Commission.

Electronic Communications Act 2000, c. 7 various dates, some to be appointed
makes provision to facilitate the use of electronic communications and electronic data storage, and provides for the modification of licences granted under the Telecommunications Act 1984, s. 7; and for connected purposes.

Financial Services and Markets Act 2000, c. 8, various dates, some to be appointed
makes provision about the regulation of financial services and markets; provides for the transfer of certain statutory functions relating to building societies, friendly societies, industrial and provident societies and certain other mutual societies; and for connected purposes.

Appropriation Act 2000, c. 9 July 20, 2000
applies a sum out of the Consolidated Fund to the service of the year ending March 31 2000; appropriates the supplies granted in this Session of Parliament; and repeals certain Consolidated Fund and Appropriation Acts.

Crown Prosecution Service Inspectorate Act 2000, c. 10 day to be appointed
makes provision for inspection of the CPS.

Terrorism Act 2000, c. 11 various dates, some to be appointed
makes provision about terrorism; temporary provision for Northern Ireland about the prosecution and punishment of certain offences, preservation of peace and maintenance of order. For example, there is provision for an independent assessor of military complaints procedures in Northern Ireland.

Limited Liability Partnerships Act 2000, c. 12 various dates, some to be appointed
makes provision for limited liability partnerships.

Royal Parks (Trading) Act 2000, c. 13 July 20, 2000
makes provision about certain offences under Parks Regulation (Amendment) Act 1926, s. 2. for example increases the standard scale for park trading offences to level 3 .

Care Standards Act 2000, c. 14 various dates, some to be appointed
establishes a National Care Standards Commission; makes provision for the registration and regulation of (amongst others) children's homes, independent hospitals, and voluntary adoption agencies; makes provision for the regulation and inspection of local authority fostering and adoption services; establishes a General Social Care Council, a Care Council for Wales and a Children's Commissioner for Wales; and for purposes connected therewith and with, inter alia, child minding, social care workers, protection of children and vulnerable adults.

Television Licences (Disclosure of Information) Act 2000, c. 15 July 20, 2000
makes provision about the disclosure of certain information [to the BBC] for purposes connected with television licences – the objective is to assist with licences for which no or a reduced fee is payable.

Carers and Disabled Children Act 2000, c. 16 various dates, some to be appointed
makes provision about the assessment of carers' needs; provides for services to help carers; provides for payments in lieu of services to carers and disabled children over 16; and for connected purposes.

Finance Act 2000
Sea Fishing Grants (Charges) Act 2000
Child Support, Pensions and Social Security Act 2000
Government Resources and Accounts Act 2000
Learning and Skills Act 2000
Local Government Act 2000
Regulation of Investigatory Powers Act 2000
Census (Amendment) Act 2000
Football (Disorder) Act 2000
Postal Services Act 2000
Utilities Act 2000

WHITE PAPERS, REPORTS ETC

Building Trust in Statistics was presented to Parliament by Economic Secretary to The Treasury (Melanie Johnson) on 18 October 1999. It included the following main proposals:
- The new framework for National Statistics needs to: strengthen statistic priority setting; ensure professional freedom in statistical outputs; ensure high standards; ensure greater accountability.
- Results of consultation arising from the Green paper *'Statistics – A matter of trust'* showed 70 per cent supported the establishment of the independent Statistics Commission. The Government decided this should be a non-executive body to advise ministers on statistical integrity issues relating to National Statistics. The commission will comprise of seven members with a Chairman and will be supported by a small permanent staff.
- The Government will appoint a National Statistician who will take over the role of the Director of the Office for National Statistics to become the UK Government's chief professional adviser on statistical matters. The National Statistician will set up a code of practice.
- The intention was stipulated to produce statistics free from political interference.
- The Statistics Commission are advise Government on the scope of National Statistics.
- The Government has noted the need for co-ordination and co-operation between Scotland, Wales and Northern Ireland to ensure that devolution does not damage the consistency of National Statistics. The National Statistician will retain the responsibility for UK statistical obligations.
- The National Statistician, overseen by the Statistics Commission will ensure that high standards to professionalism are maintained in the production of National Statistics.

Defence White Paper 1999 was presented to Parliament by the Secretary of State for Defence (Geoffrey Hoon) on 20 December 1999. It discussed the progress that had been made since the *Strategic Defence Review* White Paper of July 1999 and outlined some new issues to be addressed.
- Britain requires armed forces which can operate in support of diplomacy, alongside economic trade and developmental levers, to strengthen security, avert conflict and conduct effective military operations throughout the crisis spectrum. The highest priority is to have robust forces available to contribute to the maintenance of international peace and stability and participate in current and future operations where necessary.
- Concern was raised in the proliferation of weapons of mass destruction and their delivery systems. Although it is agreed that there is no threat to the UK for some years, consultation with the US is taking place to improve our defences.
- Advances in our technology have taken place rapidly in recent years.
- The analytical process of a new annual defence strategic planning cycle providing a regular process of re-evaluation is being formalised.
- It is noted that NATO remains crucial for Britain's security interests.
- Joint co-operation and integration amongst service personnel and civilian staff is the objective both during operations and in peacetime. This includes the formulation of the Joint Rapid Reaction Forces (JRRF),

Joint Helicopter Command, Joint Force 2000 (RN Harrier Aircraft), Joint Doctrine and Concepts Centre, Joint Nuclear and Biological Chemical Defence Regiment and Joint Ground Based Defence.
- Measures have been introduced to ensure that people working in defence are of good quality, well trained and highly motivated.
- Britain continues to adopt the approach to international situations of 'Peace Support Operations'.
- There is a focus on Defence Diplomacy which relates to the non-operational activities such as verification of arms control agreements.

IGC: Reform for Enlargement. The British Approach to the European union Intergovernmental Conference was presented to Parliament by the Secretary of State for Foreign and Commonwealth Affairs (Robin Cook) on the 15 February 2000. The Intergovernmental Conference began in February 2000 and is expected to conclude in December when it is decided how the European Union is to enlarge and the institutional changes required before the next enlargement. The White paper included the following main proposals and discussion points:
- The Government will be playing an active and constructive role during the IGC negotiations.
- The IGC will focus on changing voting arrangements in the Council of Ministers so the country voting weight more accurately reflects its size; extending qualified majority voting in the council, so that decisions can be taken effectively in an enlarged Union; Commission reform to prevent it becoming top heavy as enlargement increases the number of Commissioners.
- The IGC may also discuss: the reform of the European Court of Justice and the European Court of Auditors, the possibility of increasing the co-decision line, the ways in which commissioners are disciplined and dismissed, the number of seats that each member state will have in the European Parliament.
- The UK Government's position on the main issues to be discussed by the IGC are: to have one Commissioner per state with a possible cap on the total number of Commissioners should the Commission continue to expand; voting in the Council to be re-weighted; endorsement of proposed Qualified Majority Voting.

Time for Reform: Proposals for the Modernisation of our Licensing Laws was presented to parliament by the Home Secretary (Jack Straw) on the 10 April 2000. It included the following main proposals:
- A single integrated scheme for licensing premises which sell alcohol, provide public entertainment and provide refreshment at night.
- personal licences which allow holders to sell or serve alcohol on or off any premises.
- new measures to uphold restrictions on under-aged drinking.
- Personal licences to be issued for ten years following a test of licensing laws and social responsibilities.
- Licences to include operating conditions.
- Flexible opening hours.
- Tougher new powers for police.
- Children to be allowed access.
- Personal and premises licences to be issued by local authorities.
- Appeal for parties through the Crown Court.
- New safety requirements for the sale of alcohol on boats.
- New arrangements for non-profit making register clubs.

Report of Committee of Inquiry into Hunting with Dogs in England and Wales was presented to parliament by the Home Secretary (Jack Straw) on 12 June 2000. It included the following main conclusions:

- The remit of the inquiry was to explore the practical aspects of the different types of hunting with dogs and its impact of the rural economy, agriculture and pest control, the social and cultural aspects, the management and conservation of wildlife, animal welfare and the consequences of banning hunting with dogs. The committee was not required to explore ethical or moral issues.
- It concluded that hunting with dogs is a diverse activity.
- There are about 200 registered packs of hounds in England and Wales.
- The registered packs are estimated to kill 21,000–25,000 foxes a year.
- There are three registered staghound packs in Devon and Somerset. They kill around 160 red deer a year, around 15 per cent of the numbers which need to be culled to maintain a stable population.
- There are 24 registered hare coursing clubs which kill about 250 hares a year. There is a good deal of illegal hunting/coursing.
- The 20 minkhound packs kill between 400 and 1,400 mink a season.
- Hunting should be viewed in the wider social context of the countryside where the population is increasing and agriculture is in decline.
- Complex relationships exist between hunting and a range of economic activities.
- It is estimated that between 6,000 and 8,000 full time jobs presently depend on hunting although the number of people involved may be higher.
- It is not possible to give a precise figure of the number of jobs which would be lost if hunting were banned. In the long term (seven–ten years) most if not all of the effects would be offset as resources were diverted to new activities.
- Those with specialised skills, which are not easily transferable, would find it hard to find alternative employment.
- Farmers would suffer the economic loss of a free means of 'pest control'.
- The part played by hunting in the social and cultural life of rural communities varies greatly. The impact of a ban would be felt more greatly in isolated rural areas. Areas of greater populated density would feel a lesser impact.
- In most areas of England and Wales farmers and landowners consider it necessary to manage fox populations. It is generally accepted that deer numbers in Devon and Somerset need to be controlled. There is little or no need to control overall hare numbers. Mink can cause localised damage to wildlife.
- Suffering and compromises to welfare were established in the 'traditional' methods of hunting of red deer, foxes, hares and mink. Welfare implications were also mentioned for horses and hounds.
- Hunting causes many cases of trespass, disruption and disturbance.
- Recommendations are given on the processes involved in the implementation of a ban.

Raising Standards and Upholding Integrity: The Prevention of Corruption – The Government's Proposals for the reform of the Criminal Law of Corruption in England and Wales was presented to parliament by the Home Secretary (Jack Straw) on 20 June 2000. It included the following main proposals:

- The acceptance of the Law Commission's recommendation that there should be a single offence of corruption to cover both public and private sectors.

- Abolition of the current assumption of corruption for public servants in the prevention of Corruption act 1916.
- A statutory definition of what is meant by acting corruptly and a definition of the concept of an 'agent' is to be formulated.
- The Inclusion in the offence of corruption of 'trading in influence' where the decision making of public officials by intermediaries is targeted.
- The corruption of, or by a public official is not confined to the public of the United Kingdom.
- Extending jurisdiction over offences of corruption to cover both offences committed in the whole or in part within the jurisdiction and those committed by UK nationals abroad.
- Evidence relating to an offence committed or alleged to have been committed by a member of either House of Parliament to be admissible notwithstanding Article 9 of the Bill of Rights.
- The Law Commission's recommendations that the new offence of corruption should continue to be triable either in the Magistrate's Court or in the Crown Court, and the Government view that the current maximum penalty of seven years imprisonment should be unchanged.
- Retention of the requirement for the consent of the Law Officers for prosecution.

Spending Review 2000 – New Public Spending Plans 2001–4 was presented to parliament by the Chancellor of the Exchequer (Gordon Brown) on 18 July 2000. It included the following main proposals:

- The Department of Social Security to receive a Welfare Modernisation Fund of £404 million for 2001–2; £786 million for 2002–3 and £680 million for 2003–4.
- To be allocated between the Lord Chancellor's Department, the Northern Ireland Court Service, the Public Records Office and HM Land Registry is £2,635 million 2000–1; £2,719 million 2001–2; £2,772 million 2002–3; £2,782 million 2003–4.
- To be allocated between the Crown Prosecution Service, the Serious Fraud Office and the Treasury Solicitors Department is £352 million 2000–1; £422 million 2001–2; £432 million 2002–3; £444 million 2003–4.
- Housing, the regions and the environment is to have an 11 per cent per year increase in spending over the next three years. £8.7 billion will be spent from 2003–4. An increase of £4.2 billion will be spent on transport.
- Foreign and Commonwealth Office spending will rise to £1,143 million in 2001–2; to £1,198 million in 2002–3 and to £1,238 million in 2003–4.
- Annual increases outlined for the Chancellor's Departments of the Inland Revenue, Customs and Excise, HM Treasury, the Office for National Statistics and National Savings.
- Public services in Scotland will receive increased funding, £3.4 billion higher in 2003–4 than in 2000–1.
- Modernisation of Local Government via a 3.1 per cent per annum increase.
- Increased resources to be provided for the National Assembly for Wales to improve public services. The increases over 2000–1 provision are 0.7 billion in 2001–2; £1.4 billion in 2002–3 and 2 billion in 2003–4.
- The Department of Culture Media and Sport is to receive an additional £105 million in 2001–2; £155 million in 2002–3 and £225 million in 2003–4 above the current year.
- The Department for International Development is to receive a 6.2 per cent increase in funding per annum

over the next three years. The total budgets will be 2000–1, £2,760 million; 2001–2, £3,115 million; 2002–3, 3,348 million; 2003–4, 3,560 million.
- Department of Health is to receive an increase in funding for the NHS of 6.1 per cent per annum until 2004.
- The Northern Ireland Executive and the Northern Ireland Office are to receive increases on the 2000–1 baseline of £361 million in 2001–2; £667 million in 2002–3 and £988 million in 2003–4.
- Department for Education and Employment is to have spending increased from £45.8 billion in 2000–1 to £57.7 billion in 2003–4, an increase of 5.4 per cent per year.
- Ministry of Defence budget to increase from £22,975 million in 2000–1 to £24,978 million by 2003–4.
- Department of Trade and Industry is to receive annual average increases in total spending of 6.6 per cent over the next three years.
- Other areas of cross departmental increased spending are tackling disadvantage in deprived areas; resources for conflict prevention; tackle child poverty and social exclusion.
- Home Office spending on police is planned to rise by 3.8 per cent a year over the next three years. This includes an extra £1.4 billion in 2002–2 rising to an extra £2.7 billion by 2003–4.
- Ministry of Agriculture, Fisheries and Food spending plans have been projected as £983 million for 2000–1; £1185 million for 2001–2; £1250 million for 2002–3 and £1270 million for 2003–4.

Excellence and Opportunity: a science and innovation policy for the 21st Century was presented to Parliament by the Secretary of State for Trade and Industry (Stephen Buyers) on 26 July 2000. It included the following main proposals:
- To ensure our science base is strong and excellent and that we can transform the results of scientific innovation quickly into products and services to improve quality of life.
- To ensure Britain has a first class process for pursuing scientific advance. To have the ability to generate, harness and exploit the creative power of modern science.
- Recognition of the importance of funding university research projects and to create the right climate and incentives to encourage companies to use science and technology to build competitiveness.
- Creating a market for innovative products. Encouraging public confidence and support in the notion of science by ensuring that it is regulated and accountable.
- The strategies outlined in the White paper are for the whole of the UK.
- Educational policy will play a key role in producing creative and knowledgeable scientist.
- The Government has stated its intention to: invest £1 billion in partnership with the Wellcome Trust to renew the infrastructure for science; give a £250 million boost to research; to increase support of postgraduate research to £9,000 a year; to recruit up to 50 top researchers; make 2001–2 Science Year; establish a Higher Education Innovation Fund of £140 million; launch a new Foresight Fund; create new Regional Innovation Funds of £50 million; support 20 Business fellows to forge links with businesses; introduce the Small Business Research Initiative to finance Research and Development.
- All Government departments have to play a role in encouraging innovation.
- The importance of Intellectual Property of publicly-funded science should increase. Research bodies will own the Intellectual Property Rights.

THE BUDGET

Budget 2000: *Prudent for a Purpose: Working for a Stronger and Fairer Britain*

The Chancellor of the Exchequer (Gordon Brown) presented his budget to the House of Commons on 21 March 2000. It included the following main points:
- an immediate £2 billion in funding to the NHS for the coming year with spending set to rise by 6.1 per cent over the next four years
- an extra £1 billion for education, £285 million for fighting crime and £280 million for transport
- a new £40 million programme of Action Teams to match unemployed people to job vacancies
- a new job grant of £100, Income Support for Mortgage Interest and Housing Benefit Extended Payments Scheme to ease transition from welfare to work
- £4.35 a week increase to the under-16 child credit in the Working Families Tax Credit
- 50p per week increase in the Children's Tax Credit
- 0.3 per cent point reduction in employer's NIC's from April 2001 and a further 0.1 per cent reduction from April 2002
- a new employment tax credit to be introduced from April 2003
- a £100 increase to the Sure Start Maternity Grant
- a new integrated system of child credit to be introduced in 2003
- a new network of local children's funds
- £50 increase in the winter fuel payment to £150 every year for every 60-plus household
- capital limit attached to the minimum income guarantee increased to £6,000 of savings for pensioners. Upper limit increased to £12,000
- road fuel and most alcohol duties are increased in line with inflation and tobacco duties are raised by five per cent
- VAT on women's sanitary protection to be cut to five per cent from January 2001
- New rates of Stamp Duty on property transactions. Over £250,000 rising to three per cent, over £500,000 rising to four per cent
- duty on flights within the European Economic Area to be reduced to £5. Flights from the Scottish Highlands and Islands will be free from duty
- reform of capital gains tax and permanent 40 per cent capital allowance for small-medium sized firms
- the business assets taper to be shortened from ten to four years
- increase to 15 employees in small companies to be eligible for new Enterprise Management Incentives
- 100 per cent first-year capital allowances for small enterprises investing in information and communications technology equipment
- £55 reduction in the rate of Vehicle Excise Duty for cars with up to 1,200cc engines
- new graduated Vehicle Excise Duty system from March 2001
- A company car taxation to be introduced in April 2002
- 1p per litre cut in duty on ultra low sulphur petrol and a freeze on duty rate for road fuel gases
- new aggregates levy to be introduced from April 2002 to encourage use of recycled materials
- reduced rate of VAT for the installation of energy saving materials to all homes
- relief of stamp duty for new developments on brownfield land
- relief of stamp duty for some Registered Social Landlords
- £1 per tonne rise in the standard rate of landfill tax

CHANCELLORS OF THE EXCHEQUER since 1900

Year appointed	*Name*
1895	Sir Michael Hicks-Beach
1902	Charles Ritchie
1903	Austen Chamberlain
1905	Herbert Asquith
1908	David Lloyd George
1915	Reginald McKenna
1916	Andrew Bonar Law
1919	Austen Chamberlain
1921	Sir Robert Horne
1922	Stanley Baldwin
1923	Neville Chamberlain
1924 *Jan.*	Philip Snowden
1924 *Nov.*	Winston Churchill
1929	Philip Snowden
1931	Neville Chamberlain
1937	Sir John Simon
1940	Sir Kingsley Wood
1943	Sir John Anderson
1945	Hugh Dalton
1947	Sir Stafford Cripps
1950	Hugh Gaitskell
1951	R. A. Butler
1955	Harold Macmillan
1957	Peter Thorneycroft
1958	Derick Heathcoat Amory
1960	Selwyn Lloyd
1962	Reginald Maudling
1964	James Callaghan
1967	Roy Jenkins
1970 *June*	Iain Macleod
1970 *July*	Anthony Barber
1974	Denis Healey
1979	Sir Geoffrey Howe
1983	Nigel Lawson
1989	John Major
1990	Norman Lamont
1993	Kenneth Clarke
1997	Gordon Brown

The Queen's Awards for Enterprise

The Queen's Award for Export Achievement and The Queen's Award for Technological Achievement were instituted by royal warrant in 1975. The two separate awards took the place of The Queen's Award to Industry, which had been instituted in 1965. In 1992 the scheme was extended with the launch of a third award, The Queen's Award for Environmental Achievement. In December 1998 it was announced that a review committee, chaired by the Prince of Wales, would examine all aspects of the awards and recommend any changes it felt necessary. The three awards are now: The Queen's Award for International Trade, The Queen's Award for Innovation and The Queen's Award for Environmental Achievement.

The awards differ from a personal royal honour in that they are given to a unit as a whole, management and employees working as a team. They may be applied for by any organisation within the United Kingdom, the Channel Islands or the Isle of Man which meet the criteria for the awards.

Awards are held for five years and holders are entitled to fly the appropriate award flag and to display the emblem on the packaging of goods produced in this country, on the goods themselves, on the unit's stationery, in advertising and on certain articles used by employees. Units may also display the emblem of any previous current awards during the five years.

Awards are announced on 21 April (the birthday of The Queen) and published formally in a special supplement to the London Gazette.

AWARDS OFFICE

All enquiries about the scheme and requests for application forms should be made to: The Secretary, The Queen's Awards Office, 151 Buckingham Palace Road, London SW1W 9SS. Tel: 020-7222 2277. Alternatively, a variety of information about the awards can be found at http://www.queensawards.org.uk.

INTERNATIONAL TRADE

The criteria for an award for international trade are "outstanding achievement in international trade, resulting in substantial growth in overseas earnings and in commercial success, sustained over not less than three years, to levels which are outstanding for the goods and services concerned and for the size of the applicant's operations" or "continuous achievement in international trade, resulting in substantial overseas earnings with growth and commercial success, sustained over not less than six years, to levels which are outstanding for the goods or services concerned and for the size of the applicant's operations".

In 2000, The Queen's Award for International Trade was conferred on the following concerns:

AES Engineering Ltd, Rotherham – *mechanical seals*
Abercrombie & Kent Europe Ltd, Burford, Oxfordshire – *tour operator*
Air Bearings Ltd, Poole, Dorset – *air bearing drilling spindles*
Aircraft Leasing & Management Ltd, Gatwick, W. Sussex – *airline consultancy and advisory services*
Alcatel Submarine Networks Ltd, London SE10 – *undersea telecommunications systems*
Andergauge Ltd, Aberdeen, Scotland – *specialist drilling tools and services for the global drilling industry*
Andor Technology Ltd, Belfast, Northern Ireland – *scientific cameras for spectroscopy and imaging applications*
Applied Satellite Technology Ltd, Great Yarmouth, Norfolk – *satellite telephone and communication systems, autotracking marine satellite television antenna systems and support services*
Artemi Ltd, London N18 – *spacemaker hooks*
Baillie Gifford Overseas Ltd, Edinburgh, Scotland – *investment management*
Bridge of Weir Leather Company Ltd, Renfrewshire, Scotland – *leather*
CIL International Ltd, London N4 – *shopfittings and merchandising equipment*
Baby Products, Division of Cannon AVENT Group plc, Glemsford, Suffolk – *baby feeding equipment and accessories*
Case United Kingdom Ltd – Doncaster Tractor Assembly Plant, Doncaster – *agricultural tractors*
Cash Bases Ltd, Newhaven, E. Sussex – *cash drawers*
Clear Channel International Ltd, London W1 – *street furniture funded by outdoor advertising*
ColorMatrix Europe Ltd, London W1 – *liquid colorants for plastics*
Geo J. Cox Ltd, Wellingborough, Northamptonshire – *fashion footwear*
DANDO Drilling International Ltd, Littlehampton, W. Sussex – *drilling rigs and equipment*
De La Rue Security Print, Dunstable, Bedfordshire – *security printed documents*
Epichem Ltd, Wirral – *chemicals for the electronics industry*
Fibrin Ltd, Beverley, East Yorkshire – *synthetic fibres for concrete*
Firmdale Hotels plc, London, SW7 – *hotel services*
Flomerics Ltd, East Molesey, Surrey – *computer aided engineering analysis software*
GB Airways Ltd, Gatwick, W. Sussex – *international scheduled air services*
Garrad Hassan and Partners Ltd, Long Ashton, Bristol – *wind energy consultancy*
Geotek Ltd, Daventry, Northamptonshire – *geological and oceanographic equipment*
Graseby Dynamics Ltd, Watford, Hertfordshire – *chemical warfare agent detection systems*
John Guest Ltd, West Drayton, Middx – *plastic push-in tube fittings*
HP:ICM (ICM International Ltd), London, W1 – *exhibition, 3D, graphic and interactive design; event management; conference, film, video and digital media*
Hotels and More Ltd, Harrow, Middx – *tour operator*
Hydrosearch Associates Ltd, Woking, Surrey – *technical and management consultancy services*
IMC Geophysics Ltd, Sutton-in-Ashfield, Nottinghamshire – *geophysical contracting and consultancy*

IOP Publishing Ltd, Bristol – *journals, books, reference works and websites, all in physics and related subjects*

Image Processing & Vision Company Ltd, Coventry – *systems and software for scientific imaging*

Imagination Technologies Ltd, Power VR Technology Division, Kings Langley, Hertfordshire – *design and licensing of multimedia technology*

International Television Enterprises London, London WC2 – *television programme distributor*

JCB Heavy Products Ltd, Uttoxeter, Staffordshire – *tracked and wheeled excavators*

Jaguar Cars Ltd, Coventry – *luxury cars*

Kings College London, Chester-le-Street, County Durham – *hydraulic excavators*

Leagas Delaney Group Ltd, London, WC2 – *advertising, web consultancy and site design*

Linx Printing Technologies plc, St Ives, Cambridgeshire – *continuous ink jet printers*

The Macallan Distillers Ltd, Banffshire, Scotland – *highland malt Scotch whisky*

Mannesmann Rexroth Ltd, Glenrothes, Scotland – *hydraulic motors*

Manor Farm Ducklings, Thetford, Norfolk – *fresh and frozen duck and geese*

Mathmos Ltd, London, EC1 – *a range of comestic kinetic lighting including the original "lava lamp"*

Matra BAe Dynamics (UK) Ltd, Stevenage, Hertfordshire – *guided weapon systems*

Messier – Dowty Ltd, Gloucester, Gloucestershire – *landing gear systems for commercial and military aircraft*

Micromass UK Ltd, Wythenshawe, Manchester – *mass spectrometers*

Motorola Ltd, GSM Systems Division, Swindon – *computer based cellular radio telephone equipment*

Netcom Consultants (UK) Ltd, Reading – *specialist telecommunication consulting services*

Nycomed Amersham plc, Imaging Division, Little Chalfont, Buckinghamshire – *in vivo diagnostic imaging agents and radiopharmaceuticals for the treatment of prostate cancer*

Ove Arup Partnership Ltd, London W1 – *consultants for the built environment*

Oxford Magnet Technology Ltd, Witney, Oxfordshire – *magnet systems for use in medical imaging equipment*

P&M Products Ltd, Merstham, Surrey – *creative colouring products*

Pascall Electronics Ltd, Ryde, Isle of Wight – *electronic systems and components*

Pfizer Ltd, Sandwich, Kent – *research, development, manufacture and sale of pharmaceutical and animal health products*

Polycarb Ltd, Doncaster – *polycarbonate and acrylic sheets*

Psion Dacom plc, Milton Keynes – *mobile communications and connectivity products*

John Ross Jr (Aberdeen) Ltd, Aberdeen, Scotland – *smoked salmon and fresh fish*

Semefab (Scotland) Ltd, Glenrothes, Scotland – *integrated circuits and other semi-conductor related products*

Silberline Ltd, Leven, Scotland – *aluminium pigments in paste and granule form*

Singletons Dairy Ltd, Preston, Lancashire – *cheese*

Smith & Ouzman, Eastbourne, E. Sussex – *security printed documents*

Software 2000 Ltd, Oxford, Oxfordshire – *computer software*

Special Contingency Risks Ltd, London, EC3 – *insurance broking and risk management consultancy services*

Spectrum Technologies plc, Bridgend, Wales – *laser wire marking and processing systems*

Spheric Engineering Ltd, Crawley, W. Sussex – *high precision balls and modified balls*

Stephenson Group Ltd, Bradford – *speciality chemicals*

Sunseeker International (Boats) Ltd, Poole, Dorset – *powerboats*

Targus Europe Ltd, Hounslow, Middx – *carry cases and accessories for portable computers*

Technology Publishing Ltd, London SW1 – *advertising, marketing services and subscriptions*

Tesla Engineering Ltd, Storrington, W. Sussex – *electro-magnets*

Traditional Weatherwear Ltd, Glasgow, Scotland – *genuine mackintoshes and quality outerwear*

Tripos Receptor Research Ltd, Bude, Cornwall – *novel chemical compounds and research for the pharmaceutical industry*

University of Westminster, London, W1 – *higher educational services*

INNOVATION

The criteria for an award for innovation are "outstanding innovation, resulting in substantial improvement in business performance and commercial success, sustained over not less than two years, to levels which are outstanding for the goods or services concerned and for the size of the applicant's operations" or "continuous innovation and development, resulting in substantial improvement in business performance and commercial success, sustained over not less than five years, to levels which are outstanding for the goods or services concerned and for the size of the applicant's operations". Achievement may be assessed in any of the following fields: invention, design, production, performance, marketing, distribution, after sales support.

In 2000, The Queen's Award for Innovation was conferred on the following concerns:

AVS Graphics Ltd, Loughborough, Leicestershire – *omnibus TV station automation system*

Alcatel Submarine Networks Ltd, London, SE10 – *design of optical WDM transmission equipment for undersea telecommunications networks*

Aspects Software Ltd, Edinburgh, Scotland – *PC-based tools to test, develop, monitor and simulate Smart Care information and application*

BG Technology Ltd, Loughborough, Leicestershire – *field service and diagnostic systems*

Beamech Group Ltd, Trafford Park, Trafford – *flexible foam slab stock equipment*

British Gas Services Ltd, Staines, Middx – *field service and diagnostic systems*

Baby Products, Division of Cannon AVENT Group plc, Glemsford, Suffolk – *AVENT ISIS breast pump*

Celsis International plc, Cambridge, Cambridgeshire – *Celsis Advance System for personal care product testing*

Codemasters Group Ltd, Southam, Warwickshire – *developer and publisher of video games*

Crocodile Clips Ltd, Edinburgh, Scotland – *software simulator for teaching physics*

Davis Schottlander & Davis Ltd, Letchworth Garden City, Hertfordshire – *low allergy dental gloves*

Fox Brothers & Company Ltd, Wellington, Somerset – *lightweight wool and cashmere cloth*

Genevac Ltd, Ipswich, Suffolk – *solvent evaporation system*

Gripple Ltd, Sheffield – *device for joining and tensioning strands of wire and wire rope*

Hydra-Tight Ltd (Power Generation Group), Darlaston, Walsall – *high temperature hydraulic nut*

Imagination Technologies Ltd. Power VR Technology Division, Kings Langley, Hertfordshire – *design of silicon chips for 3D graphics*

LH Group Services Ltd, Burton on Trent, Staffordshire – *remanufacture of engines and transmissions for the rail industry*

Lightbody Celebration Cakes Ltd, Hamilton, Scotland – *manufacture of celebration cakes*

Eli Lilly and Company Ltd, Basingstoke, Hampshire – *Zyprexa*^{TM} (*generic name olanzapine*) *for the treatment of schizophrenia*

Marconi Applied Technologies Ltd, Safety and Security Group, Chelmsford, Essex – *fire fighters thermal imaging camera*

Marks and Spencer Womenswear Group, Lingerie, London, W1 – *"secret support" supportive liner inside vests etc*

J. McIntyre Machinery Ltd, Nottingham, Nottinghamshire – *TARDIS – aluminium dross cooling system*

Heatric, A Division of Meggitt (UK) Ltd, Poole, Dorset – *printed circuit heat exchangers (PCHEs)*

Micromass UK Ltd, Wythenshawe, Manchester – *Q-TOF tandem mass spectrometers*

Nortel Networks (Northern Ireland) Ltd – Newtownabbey, Northern Ireland – *Saturn Multiplexers*

Optare Group Ltd, Crossgates, Leeds – *Optare "Solo" floor accessible midibus*

Sondex Ltd, Hook, Hampshire – *MIT multi-finger imaging tool*

Strix Ltd, Ronaldsway, Isle of Man – *control/heating systems for domestic and other water boiler appliances*

Styles and Wood Ltd, Salford – *retail interior fit-out services*

TNT UK Ltd, Atherstone, Warwickshire – *TNT express business delivery services*

Ultra Electronics Card Systems, Weymouth, Dorset – *MAGICARD range of dye sublimation ID card printers*

Zychem Ltd, Wilmslow, Cheshire – *3D tactile image reproduction to enable visually impaired people to read*

ENVIRONMENTAL ACHIEVEMENT

The criteria for an award for Environmental Achievement include "an outstanding advance in environmental performance resulting in a substantial improvement in business performance and commercial success".

In 2000, The Queen's Award for Environmental Achievement was conferred on the following concerns:

Crossfield Ltd, Warrington – *MACROSORB systems for treating and recycling textile waste waters*

Paxton Division of McKechnie Components Ltd, Walsall – *Maxi-Nest reusable transport packaging system*

The Renewable Energy Company, Stroud, Gloucestershire – *"Ecotricity"*

Strattons Hotel, Swaffham, Norfolk – *hotel/restaurant*

TSL Group plc, Wallsend, North Tyneside – *pollution-free synthetic silica*

D. W. Windsor Ltd, Hoddesdon, Hertfordshire – *Diamond Optic*^{TM} *light control system*

Science and Discovery

THE EARTH'S MAGNETIC FIELD

The Earth's magnetic field can be likened to a simple bar magnet situated in the interior of the Earth but it has been known for a long time that this idea is untenable for many reasons. The centre of the Earth consists of a solid inner core surrounded by a fluid outer core consisting of molten iron and nickel. But this is much too hot to produce a magnetic field like that of a bar magnet. To overcome this difficulty, the dynamo theory was proposed in which the magnetic field was produced by the movement of this liquid core flowing under certain critical conditions but it has, until recently, not been possible to verify this theory.

Scientists at Riga, Latvia and at Dresden, Germany, have recently carried out experiments which confirm this theory. According to the dynamo theory, a moving conductive fluid can generate and sustain its own magnetic field, but before it can get going it has to be jump-started by a disturbance such as a small electric field. This field is stretched and distorted by the moving fluid, resulting in new currents and magnetic fields. These eventually lead to a large stable magnetic field. In the experiments carried out in the laboratory, liquid sodium was passed down a pipe with a propeller producing a rotary motion. The liquid metal was then forced back to the top in a small channel along side the main pipe. When a small field was applied to the fast flowing metal it produced a magnetic field which remained after the seed field was removed. Although the experiment appeared to be fairly straight forward, there were numerous problems that had to be overcome and more work will have to be carried out before the results are confirmed.

HOW GECKOS WALK ON CEILINGS

The ability of geckos to walk on ceilings has long puzzled scientists but work carried out by a team led by Kellar Autumn from Lewis and Clark College, Portland, Oregon, has finally solved the mystery. They have discovered that the gecko's feet are covered by a billion hair-like fringes, called setae, which produce a force that can attach them to even the smoothest surfaces.

Detailed examination of a gecko's feet shows that each foot has 500,000 setae, each one having a diameter of about one tenth of that of a human hair and each seta splays into hundreds of finer, spatula-shaped microfilaments about 0.3 microns long, roughly only a thousand times larger than the hydrogen atom. At such small distances Van de Waals forces operating on small objects are extremely strong. As an indication of the strength of such forces under these conditions, if a gecko stuck all the setae attached to one foot on to a smooth surface, the force would be equivalent to ten times the atmospheric pressure. The orientation of the setae on the foot is towards the heel so that as the animal walks the setae and spatulae are pressed to the surface of the ceiling and pulled backwards parallel to it. In this way the microfilaments make the most efficient contact with the ceiling. To move forward the gecko lifts its foot off the ceiling in a manner like peeling off adhesive tape.

FORMATION OF THE SAHARA DESERT

It has been known for some time that the region now known as the Sahara desert was at one time fertile and inhabited. Why this region changed to a barren desert along with similar areas in the Middle East has remained a mystery although several theories have been put forward, none of which have been very satisfactory. Recently a team of scientists at Potsdam Institute for Climate Change, headed by Martin Claussen, have used a computer to develop a model which could explain the reason for the change.

Over a period of about 3,000 years starting roughly 9,000 years ago, the tilt of the Earth's spin axis underwent one of its periodic changes, from 24.14 degrees to 23.45 degrees, a value which is close to the current one of 23.40 degrees. In addition, because the Earth orbits the Sun in an ellipse the perihelion e.g. its nearest point to the Sun, moves slowly with time. Nine thousand years ago this occurred in July and it has gradually come earlier in the year and is currently in January. The reason for the changes in the tilt of the Earth's spin axis is not understood but it is thought to be due to movements of material deep in the Earth's molten core.

The net effect of the two changes mentioned above is to alter the weather systems. Before the change the northern hemisphere would have been much hotter during the summer, resulting in monsoons etc. with the production of abundant vegetation. After the change the African monsoons decreased and plants began to wither. As they stopped retaining water, this was released back into the atmosphere. The net effect was for less rain to fall and the rivers gradually dried up.

The computer studies have shown a very close relationship between vegetation, atmosphere and ocean currents, with small changes producing drastic effects. In the case of the Sahara, the change from a fertile land to a desert shrubland took place in just a few hundred years. Because the changes in the tilt of the Earth's spin axis and the timing of the perihelion are continuing to occur, one can only speculate their effects for the future.

EARLIEST FISH IN THE FOSSIL RECORD

The discovery of fossil fish in Cambrian deposits in the Chengjiang region of Yunnan Province in southern China has made it necessary to revise our current ideas on the evolution of animals with backbones.

A team of Chinese scientists led by Professor Degan Shu of the Northwest University in Xi'an and Professor Simon Conway Morris of Cambridge University discovered two specimens, each just under three centimetres long in rock sediments about 530 years old. These sediments have previously provided many fossils with ages ranging between 500 and 540 million years, when life on the Earth went through an explosive growth in evolution.

Both the fish had fins, mouths and possibly eyes, typical of more advanced vertebrates. One of them, given the name Haikouichthys, had gills supported by gill bars whilst in the second specimen, Myllokunmingia, had more primitive gills with a series of pouch-like structures. Both fish had the typical zig-zag muscle formation.

Professor Conway Morris said that finding animals so old and at the same time so easily recognisable as fish was a sensational event. It was previously thought that fish did not evolve from their more primitive ancestors until roughly 50 million years later than the age of these fossils. Biologists believed that during the Cambrian period conditions were such that there was a burst in the evolutionary pattern leading to the formation of animal groups such as the vertebrates. This new discovery seems to indicate that this process was much faster than was thought.

STONEHENGE – A KILLING SITE?

The recent examination of a skeleton found in a shallow grave at Stonehenge in 1923 has created quite a stir in archaeological circles. The bones were originally sent to the Royal College of Surgeons where they were put into storage with the remains of a second skeleton found at the site. On the outbreak of World War Two the College's most precious specimens were dispersed to various sites for safe keeping and it was thought that the Stonehenge fossils were destroyed when the College was destroyed during the blitz. Fortunately the skeleton was found recently in a cardboard box at the Natural History Museum although the second specimen has yet to be found.

Originally it was thought the man had died from natural causes but an examination of the skeleton has shown that the person was decapitated by a heavy metal sword. The fourth neck vertebra had been chopped and the angle of the break was in line with a nick on the chin showing that the blow had come from the back. Because the cut was clean, it is thought that it was inflicted by a narrow blade slicing through the bone, a clear sign that it was a ritual killing. The use of a metal sword suggests a date between 100 BC and AD 1000. This surprised archaeologists because it was thought that Stonehenge was not used after 1500 BC.

The body was then buried in a shallow grave southeast of the main circle but well inside the Aubrey Holes. At the moment, it not possible to give a reasonably accurate date for the killing but it must have been before the 12th century, otherwise there would have been a record of the event. Mike Pitts, an independent archaeologist, hopes to have the results of a carbon dating soon. Paul Budd of the University of Bradford has analysed the ratio of lead, strontium and oxygen isotopes in the skeleton's tooth enamel and deduced that the victim was from the south of England. He was about 35 years old, about 1.65 metres tall, in good health with strong teeth.

SPREAD OF EARLY HUMANS

Archaeologists have been puzzled for some time to explain why the earliest evidence for modern humans in Europe is 40,000 years old whereas there is evidence to show their presence in Australia some 60,000 years ago. This problem has been partly solved by the discovery on the Eritrean coast which suggests that early humans were beachcombers and migrated along coastlines in search of food.

A team of scientists led by Robert Walter of the Centro de Investigacion Cientifica de Educacion Superior in Ensenada, Mexico, found stone tools about 125,000 years old at a site on the Red Sea coast, which was rich in edible shell fish. These stone tools included tear-shaped pieces of sharpened stone and what appeared to be deliberately shaped pieces of volcanic glass capable of cutting flesh. The tools match those found at other sites in Africa where modern humans were known to have lived. In addition to the tools, the team found the remains of several edible marine animals such as oysters, mussels and crabs.

Professor Chris Stringer, head of Human Origins at the Natural History Museum in London said that the finds support the theory that the first humans migrated out of Africa along the eastern coastline. As the population grew and the depletion of food in a particular area, there would have been a natural movement along the coast. Professor Stringer said that moving along the coast at one mile per year it would have only taken 10,000 years to reach Australia. It would have enabled the migrants to get as far as Java without using boats. After that it would have been

necessary to use boats reach the Australian mainland, a relatively easy task in those days.

EATING HABITS OF TYRANNOSAURUS REX

Much has been learned of the size and structure of the largest of the carnivorous dinosaurs, Tyrannosaurus Rex, from the many fossils studied over the years but little positive information was known about the way it fed. The discovery of fossilised dung from the dinosaur in 1995 in the Canadian province of Saskatchewan has enabled a detailed study to be carried out.

Timothy Tokaryk of the Royal Saskatchewan Museum in Regina carried out an analysis on a fragment the size of a loaf of bread. The tremendous size of the faecal mass implied that it could only have come from the world's largest predator. The fossil faeces, known as a coprolite, is the first to be discovered from a meat eating species.

The study shows that the dinosaur first crushed the bones of the victim into very small pieces before swallowing. The lack of grinding molars showed that the food could not be chewed, so it relied on the immense force of its bite from the many peg-like teeth. Analysis of the bones showed that the victim was probably a young herbivore about the size of a cow. Much of the crushed bone in the coprolite escaped damage, showing that the digestive juices were very weak and entirely different from those of a crocodile which dissolve the bones eaten.

It is thought by Peter Andrews of the Natural History Museum in London that because the bone is in such pristine condition it may be possible to study its DNA. This would provide much data on the life style of the dinosaur. The overall study of the faeces has for the first time provided accurate data on the internal workings of the creature which dominated the Earth over 65 million years ago.

NEW ATOMIC WASTE PRODUCT DANGER

Plans for the long term storage of plutonium from nuclear power stations and military weapons may have to be rewritten in the light of the discovery that plutonium dioxide is not as inert as was once thought. Spent fuel from conventional reactors is reprocessed to form the oxide, a yellow crystalline solid. It is also a key component of the mixed oxide fuel (MOX) used in Japanese and some European power stations. It has always been thought that it was insoluble and easy to contain.

Work carried out by John Haschke and colleagues at the Los Alamos National Laboratory in New Mexico has shown that plutonium dioxide reacts slowly with water and oxygen to form a new oxide, a green crystalline compound which is richer in oxygen, although the exact composition has not yet been determined. The problem is that this new oxide is soluble in water. Another hazard is that during the chemical reactions which produce this new oxide, hydrogen is also produced. Long time storage could therefore generate sufficient hydrogen to produce a highly dangerous mixture.

The production of this new oxide could explain why contamination from nuclear tests sites in Nevada has spread so rapidly in the groundwater. Another team from Los Alamos and the Lawrence Livermore National Laboratory, reported in 1999 that plutonium from one blast had migrated 1.3 kilometres in 30 years.

These new findings have caused a stir in some quarters. Charles Madic, Research Director at the fuel cycle division of the French Atomic Energy Commission has already started a re-evaluation of the storage of plutonium. He has commented that the storage in water tight compartments will have major consequences for the price of this spent fuel.

SUSPECTED SUB-ATOMIC PARTICLE IDENTIFIED

For several decades the existence of a particular type of neutrino has been postulated. It was first suspected in 1978 when Nobel Prize winner Martin Perl of Stanford University put forward the theory of the existence of a tau neutrino but until recently its existence has never been verified. Now a team of scientists from the National Accelerator Laboratory near Chicago, Illinois have found that the first direct evidence of this elusive particle.

There are 12 sub-atomic particles recognised in the current standard model, three of which are neutrinos. The electron neutrino was identified in 1956 and the muon neutrino in 1962. The third, the tau neutrino, was confidently known to exist but proved to be very elusive. Neutrinos are sub-atomic particles with no electric charge and a mass which is exceedingly small tending towards zero. Hence they have very little interaction with other matter. Although they exist in large quantities, they are very difficult to track down.

The particle was identified using the world's most powerful particle accelerator, Fermilab's Tevtron. Neutrinos were squeezed into a narrow beam and fired through a multi-layered sandwich of sheets of metal covered in a manner similar to that of a photographic emulsion. Four cases were recorded of a track with a distinctive kink in it, identifying the existence of the tau neutrino.

There is still much to be discovered in the field of sub-atomic particles. Fermilab and the European particle physics laboratory Cern near Geneva, Switzerland are currently trying to track down the elusive Higgs Boson and possibly a fourth type of neutrino known as the sterile neutrino.

RARE METEORITE HITS YUKON

In the early hours of the morning of 18 January 2000, a large piece of interplanetary material exploded in the sky over north-western Canada, leaving a lingering smoky trail. The explosion scattered fragments of dark coloured meteorites over the snow covered terrain near Whitehorse, Yukon. Normally these fragments would have remained undisturbed due mainly to the fact that they fell in a sparsely populated area in winter, but a local resident found some of the black stones just a few days after the fall and placed them in clean plastic bags, and then sent them still frozen to geologists at the University of Calgary and the Geological Survey of Canada. It was then that the full significance of the fall was fully appreciated. Canadian scientists visited the area and collected some 500 fragments and put them into deep-freeze storage. The fall is now known as the Tagish Lake meteorite. This fall is possibly the largest one witnessed from space. Two U.S. Department of Defence satellites the fireball's passage through the atmosphere using on board infrared and optical sensors.

It was quickly found that the meteoritic fragments, weighing about a total of about one kg, were of a rare type, called carbonaceous chondrites. Only about two per cent of known meteorites are of this particular type. Apart from their unusual composition, their rarity is attributed to the facts that the rock is very crumbly and is easily destroyed during its passage through the atmosphere and if it survived this it quickly eroded when on the Earth's surface.

It is thought that these stones were formed some 4.6 billion years ago and are thought to be the earliest material to condense from the solar nebula. They are rich in carbon and a large variety of volatile organic compounds.

There have been two well documented falls of carbonaceous chondrites in the past, the Allende fall in Mexico and the Murchison in Australia and the results of the research on these revolutionised our ideas of the early days in the formation of the Solar System. The full analysis of the Yukon fall in Canada could produce similar findings.

MARTIAN METEORITE

Analysis of the meteorites found on the surface of the Earth has shown small percentage originated from the planet Mars. Currently the number of such meteorites is 14, the latest coming to light after the rock had spent the last 20 years stored in a box and completely forgotten about. Rock collector Robert S. Verish went out to the Mojave Desert in southern California some 20 years ago looking for interesting specimens and amongst other material found a couple of dark coloured basaltic rocks and put them into a box. Recently whilst cleaning out old boxes he found the specimens and thought that they looked like meteorites. He took them to Alan Rubin, a geochemist at the University of California at Los Angeles. Rubin and a colleague Paul Warren who specialises in igneous meteorites came quickly to the opinion that it looked very similar to previously discovered meteorites which were thought to have come from Mars. The results of their analysis showed this without doubt. The reasons for a Martian origin is based on two facts. Firstly the composition of the gases trapped in the rock matches that of the Martian atmosphere and the other the ratio of deuterium to ordinary hydrogen is unlike that of other rocks, whether terrestrial or meteoritic. Another famous martian meteorite, ALH 84001, hit the headlines in 1996 with claims that it contained fossilised signs of life. This claim has now been rejected by a large portion of the scientific community.

ASTEROID EROS SEEN IN DETAIL

After a four year journey, the spacecraft Near Earth Asteroid Rendezvous (NEAR) successfully went into orbit around the minor planet 433 Eros, on 14 February 2000, taking photographs of its surface in detail. The polar orbit achieved placed the spacecraft ranging between 323 and 370 km above its surface. This was the first time a spacecraft had successfully achieved an orbit around a minor planet. The photographs and spectra taken during approach phase and after orbiting the asteroid has given a much better understanding of these rather small members of the Solar System.

Eros is an odd shaped body measuring 33 by 13 km and is covered with so many craters that its surface must very be old. Because of the density of the craters, it is thought that the idea that the body was ejected into a near Earth vicinity by a relatively recent collision within the asteroid belt must be rejected, because such an impact would have erased most the surface detail. Because there are numerous giant boulders lying on the surface, it is thought that they were blasted from its interior by impacts.

Eros is classed as an S-type asteroid, implying that either it could consist of primitive rocky material, substantially unchanged since its formation in the early days of the formation of the Solar System or that it melted at some stage to produce distinct layers of rock and metal. Early examination shows tantalising hints of widespread layering.

Orbital analysis has shown it has an overall density of about 2.4 grams per cubic centimetre, typical of that of the Earth's crustal rocks, suggesting that the asteroid is fairly solid.

The spacecraft was being gradually lowered towards the surface of Eros to end up with a height of about 50 km. It will then be possible to use its magnetometer, X-ray and gamma-ray spectrometers for studying the composition of the rocks, and a pulsed-laser altimeter to measure variations in the contours of the asteroid. Results of these are eagerly awaited.

INTERGALACTIC PLANETARY NEBULAE

It was not too long ago when it was thought that the space between galaxies was more or less empty but over the years this idea has gradually been found to be untenable. Now it is thought that the space between these galaxies if full of material. One particular aspect involves the space between dense galaxy clusters. In these clusters, one galaxy will often pass another at close range and in doing so will strip stars from each other and cause them to populate the intergalactic space. Evidence obtained several years ago from photographs taken with the Hubble Space Telescope allowed astronomers to identify such stars in the Virgo Cluster of galaxies. Some time later the identification of intergalactic planetary nebulae within the Virgo Cluster gave support to the earlier work.

There was however the danger that the hydrogen emissions from highly redshifted galaxies may be confused with the sought-for-oxygen emissions from planetary nebulae. A team lead by Kenneth C. Freeman of Mount Stromlo and Siding Spring Observatories used the 3.9 metre Anglo-Australian telescope to obtain spectra of the 31 suspected objects previously discovered in the Virgo Cluster. It was shown that two-thirds of these suspected objects were in fact planetary nebulae.

These results imply that between a fifth and half of the stars in the Virgo Cluster lie between the galaxies and not confined to the limits of the galaxies. These results have important significance to cosmologists and it is obvious that much more research will be carried out in this field of study in the near future.

PRODUCTION OF HEAVY ELEMENTS

The synthesis of elements up to iron is reasonably well understood and is known to occur during the lifetime of stars similar in mass to that of the Sun. But for those elements heavier than iron, some alternative process is required. Nuclear physicists are generally of the opinion that all the elements in the periodic table beyond iron are formed inside stars of greater mass than that of the Sun during critical times in their evolution. There are two processes which are capable of doing this. The first process involves stars which are in the red giant stage and is referred to as the slow-neutron-capture or s-process. The rapid-capture or r-process occurs where conditions are far more extreme and can produce all of the nuclei heavier than bismuth-209 and many of the isotopes of the lighter elements where the nuclei are rich in neutrons.

It was at one time thought that the r-process occurred in certain Type-II supernovae but this theory has been shown to be unsatisfactory in many respects. Until recently no better explanation has been widely accepted. Christian Freiberghaus, Stephen Rosswog and Friedrich-Karl Thielemann, physicists at the University of Basel, Switzerland have now come up with an explanation which seems to remove most of the objections raised previously. They used a computer model to see what happens when two neutron stars spiral together and merge. They estimate that such events occur once every 100,000 years per galaxy. They found that about one per cent of the neutron stars material is flung away, where it expands and turns into ordinary matter and at the same time creates an environment which will allow the r-process to create the observed array of heavy isotopes. Only time will tell whether or not this explanation clears up all the difficulties.

JUPITER'S SATELLITE GANYMEDE

Much has been learned about Jupiter's satellites in the last five years mainly from the highly successful Galileo spaceprobe. Ganymede, the largest satellite in the Solar System, surprised astronomers by the fact that it had its own magnetic field. This was one of the first discoveries made but there are strange features about this field. As it is only 5,268 km in diameter, it is thought that its core should have frozen a long time ago, but a magnetic field implies a liquid metal core. Nevertheless the field strength is such that it is strong enough to shield the equatorial region from Jupiter's magnetosphere. In this region the field lines form closed loops but from midlatitudes to the polar regions the field lines extend outwards and merge with the Jovian field. Over this range of latitudes the surface of Ganymede is covered with snow and ice. Although there seems to be a close link between the magnetic field and the ice covering, studies in detail show that there is not a perfect match, suggesting that the magnetic field is more complicated than first thought.

To complicate matters it has been found that Ganymede has a tenuous atmosphere of oxygen and ozone and a larger corona of atomic hydrogen. Researchers have also found that the satellite has a double glow, an ultraviolet emission at the poles which produces an aurora and a red glow round the equatorial regions. This red glow is caused by oxygen atoms being exited by a torus of trapped low energy electrons derived from atmospheric gases in a region protected by the moon's magnetic field from direct bombardment from the Jovian magnetosphere. The polar aurora is caused by electrons from Jupiter's magnetosphere flowing along the satellite's magnetic lines into the lower atmosphere where they break up the oxygen molecules and in doing so emit the ultraviolet light.

SUNGRAZING COMETS

The SOHO spacecraft, designed to monitor activity on the Sun, is situated some 1.5 million kilometres sunward from the Earth and is admirably situated to detect sungrazing comets. On 4 February 2000 it registered its 100th new comet in four years. Generally these objects are fairly small being about 50 metres in diameter and would not have been noticed but for the fact that they glowed in the intense heat as they passed very close or hit the Sun. They were picked up as tiny specks of light in the surveillance photographs of the solar corona taken by SOHO's Large Angle and Spectrometric Coronograph. Very few of the comets survive the close encounter with the Sun. Of the 100 seen only eight emerged successfully.

It has been found that almost all of the comets had similar orbits prior to the solar encounter. They were members of the Kreutz group, a group identified by the German astronomer Heinrich Kreutz a century ago. Notable members of this group include the Great Comet of 1882 and Ikeya-Seki seen in 1965. Kreutz believed that they are fragments of a single precursor that broke up in the distant past. These sungrazers have orbital periods of about 800 years. Brian Marsden of the Harvard-Smithsonian Center for Astrophysics suspects that the 'mother comet' may have been observed by the Greek astronomer Ephorus in 357 BC. He reported that the comet went too close to the Sun and split into two. Subsequent fragmentation, Marsden thinks, would have created the current sungrazing population.

Since February SOHO has picked up more of these sungrazers. The rate of discovery is currently about two per month and so a very careful watch is being made in case something special turns up.

MILKY WAY GALAXY IS A BARRED SPIRAL

Until recently all books on astronomy have said that our Milky Way Galaxy, e.g. the galaxy containing our Sun and all the naked-eye stars visible on a clear night, is a typical spiral galaxy, with photographs of nearby spiral galaxies showing what our galaxy would look like if we could position ourselves outside our galaxy. But studies carried out over the last few years have shown that this picture is wrong and that we actually live in a barred spiral in which the spherical central hub is replaced by a barred structure. Unfortunately this bar structure cannot be seen by us because it is totally obscured by interstellar dust.

Radio and infrared studies can penetrate this dust and maps of the Milky Way taken in infrared radiation give evidence to support the barred structure. The strongest evidence however comes from a study of the motions of stars in the neighbourhood of the Sun.

Most of these stars, including the Sun, share the same general motion through space, in roughly circular paths around the centre of the galaxy. However, from data collected from the Hipparcos satellite, there is a population of older and middle aged stars which tend to travel in a distinctly different direction and with a different speed. Work carried out by Walter Dehnen of the Max Planck Institute for Astronomy in Germany has shown that the presence of a bar would produce the observed motions. He has calculated that the barred structure rotated round the centre of the galaxy in about 120 million years, a much shorter time than the 240 million years taken by the Sun to travel round the galaxy.

MARS – THE PLANET WITH EXTREMES

Data collected from NASA's Mars Global Surveyor has enabled scientists to compile a topographical map of the planet with elevations to an accuracy of 13 metres. The map has revealed two sensational features which have placed them amongst the leading positions for structures in the Solar System.

Data sent back from the early Mariner spacecraft showed the Hellas Basin to be a deep circular feature but the estimates of the depth of the basin were not very precise. The new map of the Hellas Basin shows that the crater is 4,000 km across with a depth of nine km. The once thought rim of Hellas with a diameter of 2,300 km actually lies on the inner slope some two km lower than the Martian equivalent of sea level. This makes the Hellas Basin the largest impact structure in the Solar System.

On the other side of the planet more sensational data presented itself. Water cannot exist on the surface of the planet at the present time but it has been accepted for some time now that at some time in the past, several billion years ago, catastrophic floods occurred on the planet, gouging out huge features such as the Valles Marineris and Ares Vallis. Research carried out by James M. Dohm of the University of Arizona and Robert C. Anderson of the Jet Propulsion Laboratory have identified evidence for what might be the biggest floods in the history of the Solar System. The region in question lies just west of the group of huge volcanoes in the Tharsis region and consists of what look like floodplains, as seen elsewhere on the planet but these are much larger. They are partly obscured by lava flows, but there is sufficient evidence to suggest that at the time the peak discharge may have equalled all the other outflows combined, perhaps equivalent to 50,000 times the current outflow of the River Amazon.

COMMON SALT FOUND IN METEORITES

On 22 March 1998, two meteorites fell at Monahans, Texas one of which narrowly missed some children playing basketball. The stones which looked like normal stony chondrites were sent to NASA's Johnson Space Center where detailed analysis revealed that the meteorite contained microscopic droplets of liquid water trapped in purplish crystals of nearly pure halite, common salt. Michael E. Zolensky of Johnson Space Center commented that it takes a large body of water to make large halite crystals and so the 4.6 billion year old meteorite must have quite a story to tell.

An examination of a 175 kg chondrite which fell at Zag in Morocco in August 1998 by a team led by James Whitby of the University of Manchester also showed the presence of halite. Within the halite crystals were traces of xenon-129, an isotope which is formed by the radioactive decay of iodine-129 and argon-40, which is a decay product of potassium-40. Analysis has shown that the halite was just over 4.5 billion years old, only a few million years of the oldest known mineral of the Solar System. The salt in the sample indicates that it must have existed in the water even earlier and that the salt was left when the water evaporated. Whitby thinks that the extreme age of the halite implies that a planetesimal about ten km in diameter would have been required to provide the necessary amount of water for the formation of the halite.

ASTRONOMICAL DISTANCES

Astronomical textbooks and articles often quote distances to nearby galaxies etc. but few give an estimate of the accuracy of the distances quoted. The techniques used in estimating distances are commonly based on a statistical treatment of some physical property which provides values which are not in conflict with current knowledge. For galactic and cosmic distances, the accuracy depends on the accuracy of the distance of the Large Magellanic Cloud (LMC). This distance is the yardstick for all such measurements. The trouble is that the knowledge of this distance remains stubbornly inexact. The distance of the LMC has over the last few years been quoted within the range of 135,000 to 180,000 light years, with astronomers tending to fall into two categories, either the lower value or the higher one.

It is possible that this controversy may soon end because the most modern data and techniques are being used to refine a well established distance measuring method based on eclipsing binary stars.

The method is simple. An accurate light curve gives the sizes of the stars compared to their orbits round each other. A measurement of the line of sight velocity (using a Doppler technique) gives the actual size of these orbits. Temperature measurement gives the surface brightness and knowing the surface area gives the total luminosity. If this value is compared with the star brightness as seen from the earth, the distance of the star can be computed. The weak link in the chain is the surface brightness.

A group of workers at Villanova University claim to have removed this difficulty by using the Hubble Space Telescope to obtain stellar spectra to a very high precision and then fitting these spectra to computer models of stellar atmospheres. The techniques also allow the effects of interstellar absorption to be removed. The overall result allows a determination of the star's effective temperature to a very high precision.

Based on two binaries so far, the distance of the LMC has been calculated to be 149,000 light years with an uncertainty of about three to four per cent. The group are currently working on three other binary systems and feel that the initial results will be confirmed. A more precise value for the distance to the LMC will produce better confidence in distances using Cepheid variables and to techniques for the more distant objects.

NEW TYPE OF VARIABLE STAR

The identification of a variable star into what is already a quite complicated system of classification has recently been made more so by the discovery of a new class of variables. The variability in brightness of this new class is not readily obvious but careful monitoring has revealed that the star involved behaves in an unusual manner.

The prototype of this new class, 4th-magnitude Gamma Doradus has been known to vary since the 1960s, although the variation in brightness amounts to only a small fraction of a magnitude. Most of its variations occur in two distinct 18 hour cycles. More recently a second star was discovered in the constellation of Auriga which behaved in a similar manner but the time scales of the variations ranged between 31 and 70 hours.

Work carried out in the mid-90s showed that variation in light from Gamma Doradus was due to non-radial pulsations in which some parts of the outer layers of the star expanded outwards whereas other parts of the star shrunk in size. In the other well known class of variables, the Cepheid variables, the star's surface expands and shrinks as a unit. It is thought that the complex atmospheric motions of Gamma Doradus are due to gravitational effects.

The Gamma Doradus variables are main sequence stars more massive than that of the Sun and are slightly hotter. They are however cooler than the Delta Scuti variables which lie in the so-called instability strip on the Hertzsprung-Russell diagram. The new class lies outside this region but nevertheless they still vary.

EARLIEST MAN-MADE STRUCTURE

Until recently the earliest known building made by man was from the remains of a structure at Terra Amata in France, thought to be 200,000 to 400,000 years old. However a recent discovery by Japanese archaeologists of an artificial structure on a hillside at Chichbu, north of Tokyo, has pushed this date back to 500,000 years.

The site was discovered during the construction of a park on a flat area with a commanding view over a river. At the bottom of two metres of river deposits lay a volcanic layer into which post holes appear to have been dug. These holes were filled with loose material not associated with the volcanic layer. The holes, which had well-defined edges, formed two pentagons 1.3 and 1.7 metres across and apart from the ones on the south side were roughly equally spaced. It is thought that the ones to the south were possibly the entrances. Thirty stone tools made of chert and shale were found in the area, some of which were found inside the pentagons.

The age of the site is based on the facts that the volcanic layer is between 500,000 and 600,000 years old whilst the alluvial layer lying above it is more than 400,000 years old. This suggests that the site is roughly half a million years old.

The remains must throw light on the way that Homo erectus lived.

DINOSAUR'S HEART DISCOVERED

Much argument has been expressed for a long time over the metabolism of the dinosaurs. Until recently most palaeontologists were of the opinion that dinosaurs were cold-blooded creatures like the present day reptiles and crocodiles but over the last few years many have come to the conclusion that dinosaurs generated their own heat allowing them to live a more active life. This latter view has been strengthened by the discovery of a fossilised heart in the chest cavity of a herbivore dinosaur which died some 66 million years ago.

The fossil, from a 300 kg plant-eating dinosaur, was found in a dry river bed in north-western South Dakota. Its ribcage was unusually well preserved because sand had filled the cavity. An Oregon fossil collector suspected that a hard iron-rich lump inside the ribcage might be a heart so it was sent for further examination. A CT scan revealed two ventricular-like cavities and a cardiac structure of the correct volume for an animal of that size. Mike Stoskopf of North Carolina State University said that the single aorta which originates and arches back from the left ventricle suggests that the dinosaur had an active birdlike metabolism, but John Ruben of Oregon State University in Corvallis suggests that a second aorta may not have been preserved. His suspicions were aroused because the pulmonary arch was also missing.

ORIGIN OF GAMMA RAY BURSTS?

Although gamma ray bursts are the most powerful explosions known in the universe, their cause has not been fully understood. In less than a second they emit roughly the same energy as that of a supernova. Many theories have been proposed for explaining these outbursts but none have been really satisfactory. It has been generally agreed that the fading of gamma ray bursts fits the theory put forward by Martin Rees of Cambridge University and Peter Meszaros of Pennsylvania State University, in which matter heated to billions of degrees explodes at a speed close to the speed of light, the shocks generated causing the gamma rays. Until now no satisfactory explanation has been put forward to explain the cause of this explosion.

Amongst the ideas proposed have been the merging of two neutron starts and the swallowing up of a neutron star by a black hole, but more recently the possibility of stars collapsing catastrophically into black holes has been seriously considered. The problem is that a black hole is surrounded by a horizon from which nothing, not even light, can escape. Because superhot matter was not capable of escaping, this idea has been rejected. Suggestions put forward by Roy Maartens of the University of Portsmouth, Pankaj Joshi of the Tata Institute of Fundamental Research in Bombay and Naresh Dadhich of the Inter-University Centre for Astronomy and Astrophysics in Poona involve the moments before the black hole takes over. They have suggested that the horizon may not form immediately after the collapse and that for a few milliseconds the window could remain open but it could be long enough to energise a relativistic fireball. The gamma ray bursts could therefore be the last evidence before the black hole takes command. Not all astronomers are in agreement with these ideas but there is much support. Obviously much more work has to be done before the problem is completely solved.

NEW SPECIES OF ELEPHANT RECOGNISED

It has been known for a very long time that the African elephant was a completely different species from that found in India, because the differences in appearance are so apparent. Now it has been found that the African elephant is not unique and that there are two species, the savannah elephant and the forest elephant, the latter being relatively rare.

The recognition that the forest elephant was different has come about by recent research carried out at the Natural History Museum in Paris, although this had been suspected for some time. Genetic studies on Coco the elephant at Vincennes Zoo in Paris have now put this beyond doubt. African forest elephants tend to be stockier than the savannah animals and they have straighter tusks and more rounded ears.

The biologists first tested DNA from his mitochondria, the maternally inherited energy-providing structures found in cells and discovered that they differed as much from those of the savannah elephant as they did from the Indian species. They have also found that similar differences exist between the animals' nuclear DNA. Although these differences exist between Coco and the other species, it is thought, especially by Nick Ellerton of Knowsley Safari Park, Liverpool, who is a recognised expert on elephants, that more work must be carried out on further animals of the forest species.

THE CAUSE OF AURORAE ETC.

Although it has been known for a long time that polar aurorae, magnetic storms etc., have been caused by the effect of solar activity on the Earth's magnetic field, the exact mechanism has not been fully understood. A chance observation has now cleared up the basic difficulty of how the solar wind can penetrate the magnetic shield which forms a cocoon round the Earth.

In 1996 an American spacecraft named Polar designed specially to investigate the mechanism of the way in which the charged particles pouring out from the Sun in the form of the solar wind penetrated the Earth's magnetic field, happened to passed through what appeared to be a tear in this magnetic cocoon. Until now it has been thought that these tears, known as magnetic disconnections, were too small to be seen directly. Since that date Polar has passed through about 40 of these tears.

Normally the Earth's magnetosphere is powerful enough to repel the magnetic fieldlines generated by the solar wind but occasionally, the solar wind is strong enough to stretch the magnetosphere breaking its field lines. The Earth's field lines then connect with the solar field lines, creating two new lines each attached to the Sun at one side and the Earth at the other. By measuring the thickness of the tears, it has been found that a tear will occur when the field lines are as narrow as one kilometre. If the tear occurs on the side of the Earth facing the Sun, the solar wind stretches these new lines round the Earth like rubber bands forming a trailing tail on the night side. Eventually the two ends rejoin reforming a line which is linked to the Earth at both ends plus a second anchored to the Sun. At this point the release in the tension causes a ball of charged particles to be fired towards the Earth. This causes the aurora and disrupts satellite communication links.

SURFACE AREA OF SOAP BUBBLES

Simple phenomenas are quite often the most difficult to explain from a theoretical point of view. One such case is the proving that complex bubbles have a minimum surface area for the amount of air trapped in the bubble. Mathematicians have now proved that the shape taken up by a double soap bubble could not be otherwise.

Interest in the shapes of soap bubbles was taken up seriously by the physicist Joseph Plateau in the 1830s, when he started dipping wire frames into soap solutions. Despite years of research, his observations have not yet been fully explained theoretically. The simplest case for a complex bubble is the double bubble, which contains two bubbles joined together. The two bubbles are parts of spheres and the area where they are joined is also part of a sphere bending a little into the bigger sphere .The angle at which the spheres join is 120 degrees. A mathematical proof to show that this configuration is the only possible one has been difficult to achieve.

In 1995, it was proved that this was true for two equal bubbles. Joel Hass at the University of California and Roger Schafly of the computer firm Real Software in Santa Cruz showed that the criterion for a minimum volume ruled out all bizarre shapes. This relatively simple problem required powerful computers to work out over 200,000 different integrals.

Now four mathematicians led by Frank Morgan of Williams College in Williamstown, Massachusetts have proved the general case for every other possible combination of bubbles, the proof involving far more possibilities than any computer could ever hope to calculate, yet the technology requires no more advanced than pencil and paper. Work is now going on by undergraduates under Morgan's direction extending the field to bubbles that exist in four-dimensional space and beyond.

FIRST SIGHTING OF A STELLAR PLANET

The identification of the existence of planetary objects orbiting stars has now become common place. During the last few years, over 30 extrasolar planets have been detected by very accurate studies of the motion of the star, deviations detected by precise spectroscopic measurements of the Doppler shifts recorded by the star as the plant travels round it. Theoretically these observations only provide indirect evidence of the existence of the planets and even if this idea is accepted it provides no information on the orientation of the planet's orbit, and consequently it limits the data that can be deduced about the planet's mass.

If the orbital plane of a planet's edge was on the line of sight from the Earth, this theoretically would mean that the planet would at times pass in front of the star and hence diminish some of the stars light in a periodic way. Such a case has been found.

David Charbonneau of the Harvard-Smithsonian Centre for Astrophysics, Timothy M. Brown of the National Centre for Atmospheric Research and colleagues examined several cases of suspected planets and computed that if their orbits were edge-on or nearly so, then the times of transit could be calculated. The idea turned out to be successful. HD209458, a star similar to the Sun lying at a distance of 174 light years in the constellation of Pegasus was recorded as falling in brightness by 0.017 magnitude for 2.25 hours every three and a half days. The planet responsible is about 30 per cent larger than Jupiter with a mass of some 37 per cent less and orbits the star at a distance of 0.05 astronomical units. The deduced density of 0.38 grams per cubic centimetre makes it even more rarified than that of our own Saturn.

Evidence has also come to light that a second team of workers have independently recorded data for transits of this planet.

SEA DINOSAUR

Australian fishermen have recently discovered the fossil remains of what is thought to be a plesiosaur, a sea dinosaur which once roamed the world's inland seas. It was found in sedimentary rocks on the banks of a slow running river in northern Queensland and is thought to be 112 million years old.

The skeleton was virtually intact, one of the most complete ever found in the country and it is considered that the specimen will provide much information about sea dinosaurs and their environment. The skeleton was found in a five-ton slab of rock and taken to Brisbane. It is estimated that it will take about 18 months of careful chiselling to extract the fossil completely.

It is thought that it weighed about 700 kg and to have swum in an inland sea in the area in which it was found. It had four very large flippers and a long tail on which was a fairly large fin. The body was flat and it had a snake-like neck. It is thought that because it was found belly up and as there was no evidence of damage to its bones, it died from natural causes. The plesiosaur was a carnivore and fed on ammonites, worms and shellfish.

Due to the advent of the wet season, it was not possible to extract the head of the fossil from the rock but as soon as is practical geologists will return to the site and complete the operation. The actual site is being kept secret to prevent damage and theft.

PLANET FOUND NEAR ONE OF THE NEAREST STARS

During the last few years, improved observing techniques has provided astronomers with the power to identify exceptionally small oscillations in the motion of stars which are the telltale signs that the star is being orbited by a planet. A new discovery of a planet orbiting a relatively near star has brought the total to 42.

The star in question is a fourth magnitude object, Epsilon Eridani, lying 10.5 light years away from the Sun. It is a sun-like star and the size of the oscillations in its path through the star background indicates that a planet about the size of Jupiter orbits the star at a distance of about 3.2 astronomical units. (One astronomical unit is the distance of our Earth from the Sun.) This corresponds roughly to the distance of our Minor Planet belt.

Because of its nearness to the Earth and the fact that the planet is large, it may be possible for the Hubble Space Telescope to record it directly. If this is possible it will be the first occasion for a sighting of an extrasolar planet. Another interesting possibility is that, because the star is similar to the Sun and because the planet is only marginally nearer to the star than Jupiter is to the Sun, there may be further planets in orbit round Epsilon Eridani.

COMET HYAKUTAKE'S TAIL

The first of the 1990's spectacular comets, C/1996 B2 Hyakutake, which appeared as a spectacular naked-eye object in the spring of 1996, had a long beautiful ion tail stretching right across the sky. Observers situated at dark-sky sites reported a tail with a length of over 100 degrees from the comet's head. If as generally accepted the ion tail is straight, as has been the case for other lesser comets, this is far longer than it should have been even if the tail extended in a straight line to infinity. Much doubt has therefore been expressed on these excessively long tails. Recent work has now come to light showing that the original observations were in fact correct.

It happened by chance that old data from the Ulysses spacecraft was being analysed by Geraint Jones and Andre Balogh of Imperial College and Tim Horbury of Queen Mary and Westfield College, London and they found strong evidence that, by a sheer fluke, Hyakutake's tail swept right across Ulysses on 1 May 1996, when the spacecraft was 3.8 astronomical units from the comet's head. For the spacecraft to have encountered the comet's tail, the tail must have been strongly curved.

At the time of the encounter the solar wind would have to have taken eight days to have carried the gases in the tail that distances whilst the comet's head journeyed in its curved path in its orbit round the Sun. The assumption of a straight tail had been based on the much shorter ion tails seen on most comets. The calculated curvature was in line with the observed straight tail as seen from the Earth.

The chances of a spacecraft passing through an ion tail of a future comet are quite small, but scientists have now been alerted to the usefulness of such intersections and possibly plan for such events.

Nobel Prizes

For prize winners for the years 1901–96, *see* earlier editions of *Whitaker's Almanack*.

The Nobel Prizes are awarded each year from the income of a trust fund established by the Swedish scientist Alfred Nobel, the inventor of dynamite, who died on 10 December 1896 leaving a fortune of £1,750,000. The prizes are awarded to those who have contributed most to the common good in the domain of:

Physics – awarded by the Royal Swedish Academy of Sciences
Chemistry – awarded by the Royal Swedish Academy of Sciences
Physiology or Medicine – awarded by the Karolinska Institute
Literature – awarded by the Swedish Academy of Arts
Peace – awarded by a five-person committee elected by the Norwegian Storting
Economic Sciences (instituted 1969) – awarded by the Royal Swedish Academy of Sciences

The prizes are awarded every year on 10 December, the anniversary of Nobel's death. The first awards were made on 10 December 1901.

The Trust is administered by the board of directors of the Nobel Foundation, Stockholm, consisting of five members and three deputy members. The Swedish Government appoints a chairman and a deputy chairman, the remaining members being appointed by the awarding authorities.

The awards have been distributed as follows:

PHYSICS

American 68, British 20, German 19 (1948–90, West German 8), French 12, Soviet 7, Dutch 8, Swedish 4, Austrian 3, Danish 3, Italian 3, Japanese 3, Canadian 2, Chinese 2, Swiss 2, Indian 1, Irish 1, Pakistani 1

CHEMISTRY

American 44, German 27 (1948–90, West German 10), British 26, French 7, Swiss 5, Swedish 4, Canadian 3, Dutch 3, Argentinian 1, Austrian 1, Belgian 1, Czech 1, Finnish 1, Hungarian 1, Italian 1, Japanese 1, Mexican 1, Norwegian 1, Soviet 1; Egyptian 1

PHYSIOLOGY OR MEDICINE

American 79, British 23, German 15 (1948–90, West German 4), French 7, Swedish 7, Swiss 6, Danish 5, Austrian 4, Belgian 4, Australian 3, Italian 3, Canadian 2, Dutch 2, Hungarian 2, Russian 2, Argentinian 1, Japanese 1, Portuguese 1, South African 1, Spanish 1

LITERATURE

French 12, American 10, British 8, Swedish 7, German 7 (1948–90, West German 1), Italian 6, Spanish 5, Danish 3, Irish 3, Norwegian 3, Polish 3, Soviet 3, Chilean 2, Greek 2, Japanese 2, Swiss 2, Australian 1, Belgian 1, Colombian 1, Czech 1, Egyptian 1, Finnish 1, Guatemalan 1, Icelandic 1, Indian 1, Israeli 1, Mexican 1, Nigerian 1, Portuguese 1, South African 1, Trinidadian 1, Yugoslav 1, Stateless 1

PEACE

American 18, Institutions 18, British 11, French 9, Swedish 5, German 4 (1948–90, West German 1), South African 4, Belgian 3, Israeli 3, Swiss 3, Argentinian 2, Austrian 2, East Timorese 2, Irish 2, Norwegian 2, Soviet 2, Burmese 1, Canadian 1, Costa Rican 1, Danish 1, Dutch 1, Egyptian 1, Guatemalan 1, Italian 1, Japanese 1, Mexican 1, Palestinian 1, Polish 1, Tibetan 1, Vietnamese 1, Yugoslav 1

ECONOMICS

American 26, British 7, Norwegian 2, Swedish 2, Canadian 1, Dutch 1, French 1, German 1, Indian 1, Soviet 1; Canadian 1

The Swedish Embassy can provide a full list of winners.

Prize	1997	1998	1999
Physics	Prof. S. Chu (American) Prof. C. Cohen-Tannoudji (French) Dr W. Phillips (American)	Prof. R. Laughlin (American) H. Störmer (American) Prof. D. Tsui (American)	Prof. Gerardus t'Hooft (Dutch); Prof. Martinus J. G. Veltman (Dutch)
Chemistry	Dr J. Walker (British)	Prof. W. Kohn (American) Prof. J. Pople (British)	Prof. Ahmed H. Zewail (Egyptian/American)
Physiology or Medicine	Prof. S. Prusiner (American)	Prof. R. Furchgott (American) Prof. L. Ignarro (American) Prof. F. Murad (American)	Prof. Günter Blobel (American)
Literature	Dario Fo (Italian)	José Saramago (Portuguese)	Günter Grass (German)
Peace	The International Campaign to Ban Land-mines and the campaign co-ordinator, Jody Williams (American)	John Hume (Irish) David Trimble (British)	Médecins sans Frontières (International non-governmental organisation)
Economics	Prof. M. Scholes (American) Prof. R. Merton (American)	Prof. A. Sen (Indian)	Prof. Robert Mundell (Canadian)

Theatre

MRS ROBINSON

To judge from the newspapers, the most important event of the year was Kathleen Turner's agreement to drop her towel as Mrs Robinson in Terry Johnson's adaptation of *The Graduate*. Naked people can be seen on the television and in the cinema every night of the year, but nudity in the theatre is strangely still cause for comment. Turner stood right at the back of the stage in the dimmest of lights and revealed all for no more than a few seconds, but that didn't stop the great volume of publicity. There was an equal flurry when Jerry Hall agreed to take over in the role after Turner's contract came to an end. Hall is, of course, better known as a model and for her now-dissolved marriage to Mick Jagger than for her acting. Turner was ideal casting as the frustrated, middle-aged housewife who seduces the young and flustered Benjamin. Hall looked glamorous but inevitably lacked the experience to sustain such a major role. For most people, however, the desire to see her in the flesh overcame any scruples about the quality of the production. There is, apparently, no end to the Hollywood stars who want to take their clothes off on London's stages. As the year ends, it was announced that Daryl Hannah is planning to come to London to appear in *The Seven Year Itch* and is likely to bare all too. *The Graduate* may have attracted the most publicity but there were other more important events to considered. Most notably, it was the year in which a number of Lottery projects came to fruition. Unlike the Dome, some of these fulfilled their promise. The Royal Court had been one of the first organisations to put in an application when the Lottery was first launched. For years, the structure of the theatre in Sloane Square had been deteriorating and was rapidly falling foul of health and safety regulations. The then Artistic Director Stephen Daldry seized the opportunity that the launch of the Lottery offered to invite the architects Steve Tompkins and Graham Haworth to come up with a radical design to include a rehearsal room, the installation of a lift, and a restaurant stretching under Sloane Square. There were difficulties in raising sufficient money to make up the difference between the grant from the Lottery of £18.8 million and the final cost of about £26 million. The Jerwood organisation finally and controversially came to the rescue and both the theatres upstairs and downstairs now carry the Jerwood name.

The Royal Court is physically in a difficult position, caught between an underground river on one side and the tube station on the other, and the opening of the building was much delayed. The production of Conor McPherson's *Dublin Carol* with Brian Cox had to play first at the Old Vic before Christmas and finally moving to its rightful home in January. Nevertheless, Topkims and Haworth were widely praised for their work and their ability to combine a respect for the old with a modern sensibility. Silky concrete sits next to remnants of war damage. The foyer is dominated by a new drum-shaped vermilion red painting by Antoni Malinowski while the floor is covered by an old mosaic revealed when the previous carpet was removed. In the much-loved theatre, the relationship between audience and actors has been left untouched.

SOTTO THEATRE

Publicity for the opening of the £10.6 million Soho Theatre in Dean Street was somewhat swamped by the delayed opening of the Royal Court. Created out of an old synagogue by Paxton Locher, the architects have made great use of the site to include a restaurant on the ground floor and basement and flats at the top (the sale of which contributed to the cost of the theatre). As well as an informal studio space seating 200, the West End's first purpose-built theatre for new plays, there are extensive facilities for conducting writer's workshops as well as three small rooms fitted with computers for the use by playwrights trying to escape the distractions of working at home. Seat prices are deliberately kept low, and the theatre, dedicated to the work of playwrights at the beginning of their careers, has been consistently full since it opened, most praise heaped on *Jump Mr Malinoff*, *Jump* about a Russian emigré family living in dead-end Southend.

LOTTERY FUNDING

There were protests generally about the amount of Lottery money being spent on major projects in London. One exception was the opening of the Lowry Centre in the Salford Quays, a huge complex of galleries, theatres, shops, restaurants and bars on regenerated land where the dockers once held sway. The Centre contains two theatres, one a large lyric theatre capable of accommodating ballet, and opera as well as major theatrical productions, and the other a 400-seat flexible studio. Michael Wilford Associates were praised for a design which used steel and glass to pay tribute to the area's industrial past.

Sir John Gielgud died in May at the age of 96. His long career in the theatre had been distinguished by a lyrical ability to speak verse, a fine sensibility as a director, a notable generosity towards his fellow professionals, as well as a seemingly endless capability for dropping bricks. He played Hamlet on numerous occasions, famously swapped the roles of Mercutio and Romeo with Laurence Olivier, and, in later years, shifted with the times to appear in plays by Harold Pinter and David Storey. His very last piece of work was recorded just shortly before his death; a film of Samuel Beckett's *Catastrophe* directed by David Mamet with Pinter in the cast which has yet to be seen.

THE END OF AN ERA

Later this year, the death of Sir Alec Guinness was also announced. Born in 1914, he was the last representative of a generation of brilliant actors that included, as well as Gielgud and Guinness, Laurence Olivier, Ralph Richardson, Peggy Ashcroft, Michael Redgrave, Edith Evans and Sybil Thorndyke. Unusually for that group, Guinness was equally at home in the theatre, television and film and in the later years he became extremely choosy about what he appeared in on stage (as much as he came to regret appearing in the *Star Wars* films, they made him a rich man). Nevertheless, even his *Macbeth* at the Royal Court, a production that was reviled at the time, in retrospect came to be seen as a landmark. He was also noted for his playing of Richard II, the transvestite criminal in Simon Gray's *Wise Child*, T. E. Lawrence in Terence Rattigan's *Ross*, and Harcourt Reilly in T. S. Eliot's *The Cocktail Party*. He was always known as a master of disguise, forever exemplified in the classic film comedy *Kind Hearts and Coronets*.

WEST END TRANSFORMS

The West End in which both these actors made their name is changing fast. Last year, the energetic, warm Australian, Janet Holmes Court, put all her ten theatres on the market including the two flagships, the Theatre Royal Drury Lane and the London Palladium. There were fears that they would be bought by someone who would run them solely for profit and be disinclined to play a positive role in encouraging a vibrant West End. The prospect of the West End turning into Broadway where the rents are extremely high, a straight play is rare, and many theatres remain dark for many months of the year, was a gloomy one. The battle in the end was between an American oil magnate Max Weitzenhoffer, and Andrew Lloyd Webber, already the owner of two West End theatres, in collaboration with NatWest Equity Partners. There was considerable relief when Lloyd Webber's offer was accepted in spite of it being at £87.5 million, lower than the £100 million asked for. Lloyd Webber is now by some way the most powerful person in British theatre. By coincidence, the nine ACT theatres also went up for sale in the summer of 1999 – including the Albery, Comedy, Donmar Warehouse, Phoenix, Piccadilly, Whitehall and Wyndhams. Their fate was happily resolved when they were bought by the Ambassadors Theatre Group adding to their property portfolio of the New Ambassadors and the Duke of York's. The future of the Old Vic, too, looked more secure with the announcement that it was to become the home of Adventures in Motion Pictures, and also that a new company called Old Vic Productions was to be set up, helped on its way by a six figure donation from Kevin Spacey who performed in the theatre when *The Iceman Cometh* transferred from the Almedia. Individual investors were invited to take a stake in the theatre's productions for as little as £2,000.

THE LION KING

On stage in the West End, *The Lion King* arrived with a great roar. Remarkable, Julie Taylor, a director form the more avant garde branch of American theatre, managed to transform an animated film into a live theatrical event that had something to offer in its own right. Taymor's great skill was to allow the audience to use its imagination. Drawing on Far Eastern traditions of representation, she introduced plenty of spectacle but made no attempt to hide how it was done. The opening number *Circle of Life* thrillingly saw all the animals coming down the aisles to congregate at the waterhole on stage. Elton John's music and Tim Rice's lyrics were enhanced by contributions from Lebo M. Backed by Disney, *The Lion King* confirmed that the pendulum for creating commercially popular musicals has once more swung back to the United States.

MUSICALS

Cameron Mackintosh, who so successfully caught the taste of the times in the 1980s and 1990s, produced his first large-scale musical since *Martin Guerre*, turning to John Dempsey and Dana P. Rowe, two Americans whose careers he had championed since producing *The Fix* at the Donmar Warehouse. The pair chose to adapt *The Witches of Eastwick*, originally a novel by John Updike and then adapted into a film with Jack Nicholson as the demonic Darryl van Horne. After such serious musicals as *Les Misérables, Phantom of the Opera and Miss Saigon, Witches of Eastwick* proved a sexy musical comedy of a more old-fashioned variety with Maria Friedman, Lucie Arnaz and Joanna Riding as the three central frustrated women all in great form, and Ian McShane as the louche seducer.

Traditionally, it is the American tourists who have packed out London's musicals. A new trend emerged, however, with the opening of *Notre-Dame de Paris*, Charles Aznavour's *Lautrec*, and the Spanish *La Cava*. These three musicals, as well as the long-running *Mamma Mia*, have attracted thousands of European tourists, no doubt helped by all the existence of Eurostar. *Notre Dame* in particular was mauled by the critics as a piece of stadium rock rather than theatre, but its European fans are flocking to London and sustaining the show in the West End.

A surprise hit of a non-musical variety in the West End was *Stones in His Pockets* which arrived at the New Ambassadors via the Tricycle Theatre and the Lyric Belfast. The play b Marie Jones describes the disruptive effect of a Hollywood film unit in County Kerry seen through the eyes of two local boys who are take on as extras in a film, the story of which grossly romanticises the history of rural poverty in Ireland. What makes this play so remarkable is that all the parts are played by just two actors – Sean Campion and Conleth Hill – ranging from the old codger in the bar, through the film star struggling with her Irish accent, to the over enthusiastic personal assistant to the director. Campion and Hill managed to go in and out of character several times in the length of time it took them to cross the stage. Their skill has attracted fans of a very high order including Tom Hanks, Tom Cruise, Kevin Spacey, Mel Brooks and Donald Sutherland.

Sutherland was in London to appear in a French play *Enigmatic Variations* translated by his own son. His performance as the reclusive genius, visited seemingly by a doting fan and journalist, was far too subdued, and the play, full of improbable twists, skirted issues of gender and lover without really exploring them. Sutherland was greatly hurt by the critical reception and hit back ferociously. More happily, Maggie Smith returned to the West End in Alan Bennett's *Lady in the Van*, ad adaptation of his diary description of a female tramp who parked her camper van in his drive and stayed there until her death. To illustrate Bennett's own divided feelings about this woman – torn between horror at the smell of that wafted out of her rundown vehicle, and concern for her homelessness – he himself was played by two actors; Kevin McNally and Nicholas Farrell. In another comedy, Alan Ayckbourn's *Comic Potential* provided a horrific vision of a future in which television actors would be dispensed with in favour of robots emotionally programmed from the control room in a virtually reality world. As a robot who discovers a sense of humour and falls in love, Janie Dee won several awards.

ARTS COUNCIL FUNDING

Subsidised theatre, and in particular regional repertory theatres, took heart from the news that the Arts Council's campaign to raise its annual overall grant from the government by £100 million a year had been successful. It is the biggest increase in funding in the Arts Council's 44-year history. The only flaw is that the money £25 million of which should go towards drama – is not due to arrive until 2003 and there is the very real possibility that some theatres might go to the wall before then. In 2003, £40 million will pay for a new Creative Partnership initiative to bring art, theatre and film to schools and deprived communities. The challenge to all theatres, not just David Lan the new Artistic Director of the Young Vic, is to attract young people into the theatre for the very first time. The extra money means that there will no longer be any excuse for repertory companies to put on *Educating Rita*, not because someone has a burning desire to direct it, but because it only has a cast of two and is cheap to do.

THE NATIONAL THEATRE

The National Theatre under Trevor Nunn was at the receiving end of both brickbats and praise. The ensemble continued to reveal its considerable strengths. Especially impressive was Nunn's production of *Summerfolk* which opened last autumn in the Olivier. Gorky's play, premiered shortly after Chekhov's *The Cherry Orchard*, reveals itself to be acutely aware of the seismic shifts about to engulf Russia in its description of the middle classes in the country. In so far as there is a central character, it is the miserable and critical Varvara (Jennifer Ehle) but this is, above all, a company play and Patricia Hodge's feminist Maria, Roger Allam's oafish Bassov, Henry Goodman's sauve Shalimov and Simon Russell Beale's defeated Dudakov all made an important contribution to the production. Russell Beale, in particular, showed just what an exceptional actor can do with a small part.

While the ensemble went from strength to strength, however, and proved, if anybody didn't realise it already, the enormous advantages of actors working together over a long period, elsewhere the National's programming looked more rocky, rarely able to sport a good new play, and determinedly middle of the road. Stephen Poliakoff's *Remember This*, Nick Stafford's *Battle Royal*, David Edgar's *Albert Speer* and Tanika Gupta's *The Waiting Room* were not great triumphs. The most impressive new play of all was Joe Penhall's *Blue Orange*, an incisive investigation into how black schizophrenics are treated in hospital. Penhall, whose film *Some Voices* also came out this year, focuses on a debate raging between the young psychiatrist (Andrew Lincoln) who wants to keep Chiwetel Ejiofor's patient locked up, under supervision and on drugs, and his superior (Bill Nighy) who looks at the broader picture of how the patient became ill in the first place but also has an almost irresponsible attitude towards his future. This was one of the best new plays of the year. Musicals were another bone of contention. Nunn repeatedly reiterates that he sees no reason why they should be treated as any less of an art form that plays. *Honk!*, *Singing in the Rain* and *The Villains Opera* have already been produced this year and there are plans to present *My Fair Lady* next.

ROYAL SHAKESPEARE COMPANY

In contrast, the Royal Shakespeare Company much improved its reputation as it embarked on an ambitious trawl through Shakespeare's history plays to celebrate the Millennium. Usually, each play has a different director so there is no consistency of style, nor of period in which each production is set. Steven Pimlott's production of *Richard II* in The Other Place in Stratford-upon-Avon was a cool, modernist examination of politics with Sam West in the lead. Michael Attenborough's rumbustious production of the two parts of *Henry IV* in the Swan, however, was more traditional with Desmond Barrit make a mountainous, memorable Falstaff. The company scored a rare success too with *Macbeth*, not for nothing known as the most unlucky of plays. Gregory Doran's production in the Other Place, and later at the Young Vic, created a real momentum and – played without an interval – was the most exciting and compelling for years. Antony Sher's Macbeth was a burly, military man betrayed by his own imagination, fighting a ware that more closely resembled Rwanda or Bosnia today than Scotland in the middle ages, and Harriet Walter, his aristocratic, gracious wife, was driven with the desire for power, unable to anticipate the consequences for herself as well as for others.

The Almeida in Islington and the Donmar in Covent Garden continued to show their flair for programming. In its most ambitious project year, the Almeida opened a season at the old Gainsborough Studios in Shoreditch – where Hitchcock first learnt his trade – of Shakespeare's *Richard II* and *Coriolanus*. In both cases these title roles were played by Ralph Fiennes. The studios, now largely derelict and about to be turned into flats, were radically restructured for the productions. Most strikingly, designer Paul Brown created a massive fissure in the back wall of the stage to represent a divided England. Real grass covered the vast stage for *Richard II*. But the actors often looked lost as they wandered around the huge space in their mediaeval costumes. Fiennes made a giggly king uneasily aware of his own weakness and easily intimidated by Linus Roache's strong-minded Bolingbroke in an old-fashion production by Jonathan Kent. Fiennes and Roache crossed swords again in *Coriolanus* in which Barbara Jefford made a forceful Volumnia. The public appeared to have no difficulty in finding its way to the unusual venue. Meanwhile, back at its home base *Celebration*, a new play by Harold Pinter was staged in a double bill with his first. *Celebration* is an unusually comic play by the master of menace, set in a well-known restaurant depicting the loutish, aggressive rich at play. Forty years ago, Pinter, then a struggling actor, was unfamiliar with flash restaurants. A rundown bed-sit room is the setting for *The Room* where Rose (an unusually dowdy Lindsay Duncan) feels here grip on her territory sliding away as it is invaded by a succession of visitors. It made for a fascinating pairing.

Unbelievably, at the same time, the theatre managed to launch Nicholas Wright's *Cressida* in the West End with Michael Gambon as a guardian and teacher of the young boys employed to play the female roles in Jacobean theatre. It was most remarkable for the scene in which Gambon's character teaches a new boy everything he knows about acting. Like the film *Shakespeare in Love*, there is a sense that in fundamental ways the theatre always remains the same. Other Almeida successes included *Bash* by the American writer and film director Neil LaBute, and Richard Eyre's heavily adapted translation of Jean-Paul Sartre's *The Novice*.

Over at the Donmar, the year was largely dominated by the Oscar that the Artistic Director Sam Mendes won for *American Beauty*. Suddenly, the world's press were attracted to the small theatre in Covent Garden. An American revival of David Mamet's *American Buffalo* brought the film buff's favourite William H. Macy to the London stage for the very first time in a rather underpowered production. Other revivals included *Juno and the Paycock*, Peter Nichols' *Passion Play* which later transferred to the West End, and Nicholas Hytner's production of *Orpheus Descending* with Helen Mirren.

Two productions of the mystery plays welcomed the arrival of the new millennium and Peter Whelan created his own version of *The Nativity* in Birmingham. In London, Bryden revived his legendary production in the Cottesloe, adapted from various cycles by Tony Harrison, beginning with the creation and culminating in the Last Judgement. Bryden went out of his way to emphasise the close working communities that created the cycles in the middle ages. God appeared on a forklift truck wearing a miner's lamp, the entrance to Hell was the jaws of a garbage truck, and all the props were made from familiar, everyday objects. All seats were removed from the floor of the Cottesloe, the actors pushing their way through the standing members of the audience in order to create a space in which to perform. The music was inspired by folk culture rather than religion. In June, the York Minster played host for the first time to the York cycle of mystery plays written in 1376. Gregory Doran directed a cast that included 200 local people as well as Ray Stevenson as

Christ. And the Creative Briton of the Year? Barrie Rutter
who won the Prudential award of £200,000, the richest
arts prize in Britain. Rutter and his company Northern
Broadsides produced Shakespeare in bus depots, cattle
markets and prisons. Next year there are plans to mount
the world premiere of Ted Hughes' translation of
Euripides' *Alcestis*.

PRODUCTIONS
September 1999 to August 2000

LONDON PRODUCTIONS

ADELPHI, WC2. *Chicago*, since November 1997

ALBERY, WC2 (8 September 1999) *Quartet* (Ronald Harwood) with Stephanie Cole, Alec McCowen, Donald Sinden, Angela Thorne; director, Christopher Morahan. (4 April) *Cressida* (Nicholas Wright) with Michael Gambon, Daniel Broklebank, Anthony Calf, Lee Ingleby; director, Nicholas Hytner. (21 June) *Baby Doll* (Tennessee Williams adapted by Lucy Bailey) with Jonathan Cake, Charlotte Emmerson, Paul Brennen, George Anderson; director Lucy Bailey.

ALDWYCH, WC2. *Whistle Down the Wind*, since July 1998

ALMEIDA, N1 (September 1999) *The Jew of Malta* (Marlowe) with Ian McDiarmid, Adam Levy, David Yelland; director, Michael Grandage.

APOLLO, W1 (16 September) *A Saint She Ain't* (Dick Vosburgh, Denis King) with Barry Cryer, Pauline Daniels; director, Ned Sherrin. (28 February) *Side Man* (Warren Leight) with Jason Priestley, Jeff Binder, Angelica Torn, Edie Falco; director, Michael Mayer. (15 June) *Personals* (David Crane, Marta Kauffman and Seth Friedman) with Cameron Blakely, Marcus Allen Cooper, Carmen Cusack, Christina Fry; director: Dion McHugh. (7 September) *They Shoot Horses Don't They?* (Ray Herman, novel by Horace McCoy) director: Edward Wilson.

APOLLO LABATTS, W6 (27 July 1999) *Oh! What a Night* (Kim Gavin, Christopher Barr, Stuart Littlewood) with John Altman, Kid Creole, Will Mellor, Lucy Moorby; director, Kim Gavin.

APOLLO VICTORIA, SW1. *Starlight Express*, since 1984

BARBICAN, EC2 (15 September 1999) *Endgame* (Beckett) with Alan Stanford, Barry McGovern; director, Antoni Libera. (24 September) *Life is a Dream* (Calderon, trans. John Clifford), a Royal Lyceum production; director, Calixto Bietio. (28 October) *King Lear* (Shakespeare) with Nigel Hawthorne, Robin Weaver, Anna Chancellor, William Armstrong, John Carlisle; director, Yukio Ninagawa. (November) *The Taming of the Shrew* Stuart McQuarrie, Monica Dolan; director, Lindsay Posner. (4 December) *A Midsummer Night's Dream* (Shakespeare) Nicholas Jones, Josette Simon; director Michael Boyd. (18 December) *Oroonoko* (Aphra Behn) with Nicholas Monu, Ewart James; director Gregory Doran. (24 February 2000) *Timon of Athens*, transferred from the Royal Shakespeare Theatre, Stratford. (6 January) *Othello* (William Shakespeare) with Richard Cordery, Henry Ian Cusick, Ray Feardon, Aidan McArdle; director Michael Attenborough. (19 January) *Antony and Cleopatra* (William Shakespeare) with Alan Bates, Henry Ian Cusick, Guy Henry, Francis de la Tour; director, Steven Pimlott. (1 March) *Timon of Athens* (William Shakespeare) with Sam Dastor, Geoff Francis, Graham Ingle, Peter Kelly; director, Gregory Doran. (18 April) *The Seagull* (Anton Chekhov, Peter Gill) with Mark Hadfield, Richard Johnson, John Light, Richard Pasco; director, Adrian Noble.

THE PIT (21 September 1999) *Scenes from an Execution* (Howard Barker) with Kathryn Hunter, Ian Pepperrell; director, Howard Barker. (27 October) *The Taming of the Shrew* (Shakespeare) with Stuart McQuarrie, Monica Dolan; director, Lindsay Posner. (2 December) *Volpone*,

transferred from the Swan, Stratford. (15 December) *Oroonoko*, transferred from the Royal Shakespeare Theatre, Stratford. (20 December) *Oroonoko* (aphra Behn, adapt. Biyi Bandele) with Rod Arthur, David Collins, Michael Fenner, Geff Francis; director Gregory Doran. (18 January) *Don Carlos* (Friedrich Schiller, trans. Robert David MacDonald) with Ray Feardon, Rupert Penry-Jones, Claire Price, John Rogan; director, Gale Edwards. (29 February) *The Family Reunion* (T. S. Eliot) with Richard Cordery, Lynn Farleigh, Christopher Good, Greg Hicks; director, Adrian Noble. (23 August) *Clear Water* (Christopher Rodiquez) with Arnold Goindhan, Melanie Hudson, Nicholai La Barrie, Mark Nottingham; director, Femi Elufowoju Jnr and Wendell Manwarren.

BUSH, W12 (8 September) *Mainstream*, a Suspect Culture production; director, Graham Eatough. (15 October) *Drink, Dance, Laugh and Lie* (Samuel Adamson). (15 October) *One Life and Counting* (Mette M. Bølstad). *Mrs Steinberg and the Byker Boy* (Michael Wilcox) with Miriam Karlin, Paul Nicholls; director, Natasha Betteridge.

CAMBRIDGE, WC2. (6 October 1999) *Great Balls of Fire* with Bill Geraghty; director, Simon Usher. (19 September) *The Beautiful Game* (Andrew Lloyd Webber, Ben Elton) with Jamie Golding, Michael Shaeffer, Alex Sharpe, Hannah Waddingham; director, Robert Carsen.

COMEDY, WC2 (7 October 1999) *2 Pianos 4 Hands* (Ted Dykstra, Richard Greenblatt) with Ted Dykstra, Richard Greenblatt; director, Jeremy Sams. (1 February) *Peggy for You* (Alan Plater) with Maureen Lipman, Tom Espiner, Crispin Redman, Selina Griffiths; director Robin Lefevre. (21 June) *Passion Play* (Peter Nichols) with Cherie Lunghi, Nicola Walker, Cheryl Campbell, Martin Jarvis; director, Michael Grandage. (6 September) *The Mystery of Charles Dickens* (Peter Ackroyd) with Simon Callow; director, Patrick Garland.

CRITERION, W1. *The Complete Works of William Shakespeare (Abridged)* and *The Complete History of America (Abridged)*, since 1996

DOMINION, W1. *Beauty and the Beast*, since May 1997. (23 May) *Note-Dame de Paris* (Victor Hugo, Luc Plamondon, Richard Cocciante, Will Jennings) with Tina Arena, Daniel Lavoie, Garou, Steve Balsamo; director: Gilles Maheu.

DONMAR WAREHOUSE, WC2 (9 September) *Juno and the Paycock* (O'Casey) with Dearbhla Molloy, Colm Meaney, Ron Cook; dierctor, John Crowley. (8 March) *Helpless* (Dusty Hughes) with Ron Cook, Craig Kelly, Art Malik, Charlotte Cornwell; director, Robin Lefevre. (18 April) *Passion Play* (Peter Nichols) with Cherie Lunghi, Nicola Walker, Cheryl Campbell, Martin Jarvis; director Michael Grandage. (27 June) *Orpheus Descending* (Tennessee Williams) with Helen Mirren, Stuart Townsend, Saskia Reeves; director, Nicholas Hytner. (14 September) *To the Green Fields Beyond* (Nick Whitby) director, Sam Mendes.

DRURY LANE THEATRE ROYAL, WC2. (26 May 2000) *The Witches of Eastwick* (John Dempsey, Dana Rowe, John Updike) with Ian McShane, Maria Friedman, Lucie Arnaz, Peter Joback; director, Eric Schaeffer.

DUCHESS, WC2 (5 February 1999) *Copenhagen*, transferred from the Royal National. DUKE OF YORK'S, WC2 (12 October 1998) *The Weir* (Conor McPherson) with Miles Anderson, Daniel Flynn, Ruth Gemmel, Karl Johnson; director, Ian Rickson. (29 June) *Speed-the-Plow* (David Mamet) with Neil Morrissey, Nathaniel Parker, Gina Bellman; director, Peter Gill.

(21 August) *Stones in his Pockets*, transferred from New Ambassadors.

FORTUNE, WC2. *The Woman in Black*, since 1986. Also the 'Lost Musicals' series: (5 September) *Finian's Rainbow* (Burton Lane, E. Y. Harburg, Fred Saidy) with Sam Kelly, Jessica Martin, Gary Raymond; director Ian Marshall Fisher.

GARRICK, WC2. *An Inspector Calls*, the 1992 National Theatre production, since 1995

GATE, W11 (24 September 1999) *Powder Keg* (Dejan Dukovski) with Alan White, Daniel Cerqueira; director, Philippe le Moine.

GIELGUD, W1 (20 October 1999) *Song at Twilight* (Coward) with Vanessa Redgrave, Kika Markham, Corin Redgrave; director, Sheridan Morley. (5 April) *The Graduate* (Terry Johnson, adapt. from Charles Webb, Calder Willingham, Buck Henry movie screenplay) with Jerry Hall, Josh Cohen, Lucy Punch; director, Terry Johnson.

GLOBE, SE1 (7 August 1999) *Augustine's Oak* (Peter Oswald) with Terry McGinity, Yolanda Vazquez, Martin Turner; director, Tim Carroll. (26 May) *The Tempest* (William Shakespeare) with Venessa Redgrave, Kanunu Kirimi, Will Keen; director, Lenka Udovicki. (9 June) *Hamlet* (William Shakespeare) with Mark Rylance; director, Giles Block. (4 August) *Two Noble Kinsmen* (William Shakespeare, John Fletcher) director, Tim Carroll. (18 August) *The Antipodes or The World Upside Down* (Richard Brome) director, Gerald Freedman.

HAMPSTEAD, NW3 (6 September 1999) *You be Ted and I'll be Sylvia* (Simon Smith) with Nichola McAuliffe, Mary Wimbush; director, Jonathan Church. (October) *Moonshine* (Snoo Wilson) with Ian Gelder, Robin Soans; director, Simon Stokes.

HAYMARKET THEATRE ROYAL, SW1 (November 1999) *Collected Stories* (Donald Margulies) with Helen Mirren, Anne-Marie Duff; director, Howard Davies. (6 November) *The Importance of Being Earnest* (??) with Patricia Routledge, Alan Cox, Adam Godley; (29 February) *Miss Julie* (August Strinberg, Frank McGuinness) with Christopher Eccleston, Aisling O'Sullivan, Maxine Peake; director, Michael Boyd. (6 June) *Hard Times: The Musical* (Christopher Tookey and Hugh Thomas) with Brian Blessed, Roy Hudd, Patsy Rowlands, Susan Jane Turner; director: Christopher Tookey.

HER MAJESTY'S, SW1. *Phantom of the Opera*, since October 1986

LONDON PALLADIUM, W1. *Saturday Night Fever*, since May 1998. (3 May) *The King and I* (Richard Rodgers, Oscar Hammerstein II, Margaret Landon) with Elaine Paige, Jason Scott Lee; director Christopher Renshaw.

LYCEUM, WC2 (October 1999) *The Lion King* (Elton John, Tim Rice, Lebo M) ; director, Julie Taymor.

LYRIC, W1 (13 October 1999) *Comic Potential* (Alan Ayckbourn) with Janie Dee, Matthew Cottle, David Soul; director, Alan Ayckbourn. (19 June) *A Busy Day* (Fanny Burney) with Stephanie Beacham, Sara Crowe, John McCallum, Ben Moor; director, Jonathan Church.

LYRIC, W6 (20 September 1999) *Gumboots* (13 October) *Comic Potential* (Ayckbourn) with Janie Dee, Matthew Cottle, David Soul (December) *Hansel and Gretel* (Brothers Grimm) with Tom Fisher, Grant Masters, Joyce Henderson; director, Polly Irvin. (20 July) *20/20* (Julia Pascal, music by Billy Cowie) with Barb Jungar;

director, Wolfgang Stange. (7 September) *The White Devil* (John Webster) with Jane Bertish, Shaun Dooley, Sebastian Harcombe, David Rintoul; director; Philip Franks.

LYRIC STUDIO (September 1999) *2:18 Underground*, a National Youth Theatre production. (September) *Riddance* (Linda McLean), a Paines Plough production; director, Vicky Featherstone.

NEW AMBASSADORS, WC2 (September 1999) *Drummers*, an Out of Joint production; director Max Stafford-Clark. (October) *Some Explicit Polaroids* (Mark Ravenhill) an Out of Joint production; director Max Stafford-Clark. (16 March) *Speed-the-Plow* (David Mamet) with Mark Strong, Patrick Marber, Kimberly Williams; director Peter Gill. (26 April) *Mother Courage and her Children* (Bertolt Brecht, Lee Hall) with Kathryn Hunter, Nicholas R. Bailey, Haley Carmichael, David Fielder; director Nancy Meckler. (24 May) *Stones in his Pockets* (Marie Jones) with Sean Campion, Conleth Hill; director Ian McElhinney. (30 August) *In Flame* (Charlotte Jones) with Kerry Fox, Marcia Warren, Jason Hughes, Rosie Cavaliero; director, Anna Mackmin.

NEW LONDON, WC2. *Cats*, since 1981

OLD VIC, SE1 (1 October 1999) *Antigone* (Sophocles, adapt. Declan Donnellan) with Tara Fitzgerald, Jonathan Hyde, Anna Calder-Marshall, Zubin Varla; director, Declan Donnellan. (31 March) *Troilus and Cressida* (William Shakespeare) with Matt Lucas, Jordan Murphy, Eileen Walsh, Paul Ritter; director, Dominic Dromgoole. (4 May) *Dolly West's Kitchen* (Frank McGuiness) with Donna Dent, Pauline Flanagan, Catherine Byren, Simon O'Gorman; director, Patrick Mason. (13 September) *The Car Man* (Terry Davies, Rodion Shchedrin adapted from Georges Bizet) with Alan Vincent, Ewan Wardrop, Will Kemp, Ben Hartley; director, Matthew Bourne.

OPEN AIR, REGENT'S PARK (12 June) *Midsummer Nights Dream* (William Shakespeare) with Paul Bradley, Harry Burton, Nicola Redmond, Michael Medwin; director, Rachel Kavenaugh. (16 June) *Much Ado About Nothing* (William Shakespeare) with Tom Mannion, Michael Medwin, Nicola Redmon, Ian Talbot; director, Alan Strachan. (28 July) *Pirates of Penzance* (Arthur Sullivan, W. S. Gilbert) with Paul Bradley, Jimmy Johnston, Gay Soper; director, Ian Talbot. (1 August) *Alice An Adventure in Wonderland* (Charles Way, adapt. from Lewis Carroll) with Rosalind Paul, Lynette Clark, Ben Fox, James Lailey; director, Emily Gray.

PALACE, WC2. *Les Miserables*, since 1985

PHOENIX, WC1. *Blood Brothers*, since 1991

PICCADILLY, W1 (5 October 1999) *Spend, Spend, Spend* (Steve Brown, Justin Greene) with Barbara Dickson, Rachel Leskovac; director, Jeremy Sams. (21 August) *La Cava*, transferred from Victoria Palace Theatre.

PLAYHOUSE, WC2 *Much Ado About Nothing*, since June 1998. (19 September) *Hedwig and the Angry Inch* (John Cameron Mitchell, Stephen Trask) with Michael Cerveris; director, Peter Askin.

PRINCE EDWARD, W1 (6 April 1999) *Mamma Mia!* (Catherine Johnson, Benny Andersson, Bjorn Ulvaeus) with Siobhan McCarthy, Lisa Stokke; director, Phyllida Lloyd.

PRINCE OF WALES, W1 *West Side Story*, since January 1999. (8 February) *Fosse* (Richard Maltby Jr, Ann Reinking, Chet Walker) with Nicola Hughes, Darren Carnall, Cavin Cornwall Daniel Crossley; directors, Richard Maltby, Anne Reinking.

QUEENS, W1 (7 December 1999) *The Lady in the Van* (Alan Bennett) with Maggie Smith, Kevin McNally, Nicholas Farrell; director, Nicholas Hytner.

ROYAL COURT DOWNSTAIRS, SW1 (6 April) *Hard Fruit* (Jim Cartwright) with Nicholas Woodeson, Alan Gear, Richard Hope, Gary Grant; director, James Macdonald. (16 May) *The Country* (Martin Crimp) with Juliet Stevenson, Owen Teale, Indra Varma; director, Katie Mitchell. (3 July) *On Raftery's Hill* (Marina Carr) with Kieran Ahern, Tom Hickey, Cara Kelly, Valerie Lilley; director, Garry Hynes. (7 September) *My Zinc Bed* (David Hare) with Steven Macintosh, Julia Ormond, Tom Wilkinson; director, David Hare.

THEATRE UPSTAIRS, SW1 (10 April) *Force of Change* (Gary Mitchell) director, Robert Delamere. (31 May) *Fireface* (Marius von Mayenburg, translated by Maja Zade) director, Dominic Cooke. (24 June) *4.48 Psychosis* (Sarah Kane) with Daniel Evans, Jo McInnes, Madeiaine Potter; director, James Macdonald. (14 September) *Under the Blue Sky* (David Eldridge) with Jonathan Cullen, Samantha Edmonds, Sheila Hancock, Lisa Palfrey; director, Rufus Norris.

ROYAL NATIONAL THEATRE, SE1, COTTESLOE (24 September) *The Oresteia 1: The Home Guard* (Aeschylus, adapt. Ted Hughes); director, Katie Mitchell. (6 October) *The Merchant of Venice* (Shakespeare) with Henry Goodman, Derbhle Crotty, David Bamber; director, Trevor Nunn. (9 November) *The Darker Face of the Earth* (Rita Dove) (December) *The Orestela* with Ted Hughes; director, Katie Mitchell. (1 December) *The Oresteia–Part 1: The Home Guard* (Aeschylus, Ted Hughes) with Anastasia Hille, Lilo Baur, Robert Bowman, Michael Gould; director, Katie Mitchell. (1 December) *The Oresteia–Part 2: The Daughters of Darkness* (Aeschylus, Ted Hughes) with Anastasia Hille, Lilo Baur, Robert Bowman Michael Gould; director, Katie Mitchell. (18 December) *Mysteries: The Nativity/The Passion/Doomsday* (Tony Harrison) with Peter Armitage, Stephen Bent, David Bradley, Cathryn Bradshaw; director Bill Bryden. (30 May) *Blue/Orange* (Joe Penhall) with Chiwetel Ejiofor, Bill Nighy; director, Roger Mitchell. (30 May) *The Waiting Room* (Tanika Gupta) with Shabana Azmi, Paul Bazely, Lolita Chakrabarti, Kulvider Ghir; director Indhu Rubasingham. (6 July) *All My Sons* (Arthur Miller) with Ben Daniels, James Hazeldine, Catherine McCormack, Julie Walters; director, Howard Davies.

LYTTELTON (22 September 1999) *Quartermaine's Terms* (Simon Gray) (15 October) *Remember This* (Stephen Poliakoff) with Stanley Townsend, Geraldine Somerville; director, Ron Daniels. (November) *The Oresteia* (Aeschylus) with Anastasia Hille, Michael Gould; director, Katie Mitchell. (December) *Battle Royal* (Nick Stafford) with Zoe Wanamaker, Simon Russell Beale, Gemma Jones; director Howard Davies. (7 March) *Baby Doll* (Tennessee Williams, Lucy Bailey) with Georgine Anderson, Jonathan Cake, George Calil, Charlotte Emmerson; director, Lucy Bailey. (14 April) *The Island* (Athol Fugard, John Kani, Winston Ntshona) with John Kani, Winston Ntshona; director, Athol Fugard. (25 May) *Albert Speer* (David Edgar, Gitta Sereny) with Alex Jennings; director, Trevor Nunn. (13 June) *The Heiress* (Ruth and Augustus Goetz, Henry James) with Ann Bell, Eve Best, Caroline faber, Alan Howard; director Philip Franks. (9 August) *House and Garden* (Alan Ayckbourn) with Jane Asher, David Haig, Suzy Aitchison, James Bradshaw; director, Alan Ayckbourn. (5 September) *Hamlet* (William Shakespeare) with Simon Russell Beale,

Cathryn Bradshaw, Sara Kestelman, Peter McEnery; director, John Caird.

OLIVIER (28 August) *Summerfolk* (Gorky), a New York Ensemble production; director, Trevor Nunn. (29 November) *The Merchant of Venice* (William Shakespeare) with Henry Goodman, David Bamber, Oliver Cotton, Raymond Coulthard; director Trevor Nunn. (10 February) *Summerfolk* (Gorky, Nick Dear) with Juliet Aubrey, Cathryn Bradshaw, Patricia Hodge, Roger Allam; director, Trevor Nunn with Fiona Buffini. (11 April) *The Villains Opera* (Nick Dear, Stephen Warbeck) with Alex Hanson, Clive Rowe; director, Tim Supple. (22 June) *Singin' in the Rain* (Betty Comden, Adolph Freed) with Mark Shannon, Zoe Hart, Paul Robinson, Rebecca Thornhill; director, Jude Kelly. (9 August) *Garden (House and Garden)* (Alan Ayckbourn) with Jane Asher, David Haig, Suzy Aitchison, James Bradshaw; director, Alan Ackbourn.

ST MARTINS, WC2. *The Mousetrap*, since 1974

SAVOY, WC2 (14 June) *Hay Fever* (Coward) with Geraldine McEwan, Peter Blythe, Stephen Mangan; director, Declan Donnellan. (10 November) *Tess of the D'Urbervilles* (Hardy, adapt. Stephen Edwards) with Alasdair Hervey, Poppy Tierney, Jonathan Monks; director, Karen Louise Hebden. (24 February) *HMS Pinafore* (Arthur Sullivan, W. S. Gilbert) with Joseph Shovelton, Sam Kelly, Tom McVeigh, Yvonne Barclay (31 May) *Enigmatic Variations* (Eric-Emmanuel Schmitt, trans. by Roeg Sutherland) with Donald Sutherland, John Rubinstein; director, Anthony Page. (15 September) *The Mikado* (Gilbert and Sullivan) with The D'Oyly Carte Opera Company; director, Ian Judge.

SHAFTESBURY THEATRE, WC2. *Rent*, since 1998. (4 December 1999) *Casper the Musical* (David H. Bell) with Robert Austin (6 April) *Lautrec* (Charles Aznavour, book by Shaun McKenna) with Sevan Stephan, Hannah Waddingham; director, Rob Bettinson. (30 September) *Napoleon* (Andrew Sabiston, Timothy Williams) director, Francesca Zambello.

STRAND, WC2. *Buddy*, since 1995

TRICYCLE, NW6 (22 September) *Emma* (Jane Austen, adapt. Martin Millar, Doon Mackichan) with Isabel Brook, Jaye Griffiths; director, Guy Retallack. (November) *Four Nights in Knaresborough* (Paul Corcoran) with Jonny Lee Miller, Christopher Fulford, Martin Marquez; director, Richard Wilson

VAUDEVILLE, WC2 (15 September 1999) *East* (Steven Berkoff); director, Steven Berkoff. (3 April) *Wit* (Margaret Edson) with Kathleen Chalfant, Jaye Griffiths, Ed Stoppard, Irene Sutcliffe; director Leigh Silverman. (5 June) *Mindgame* (Anthony Horowitz) with Simon Ward, Christopher Blake, Helen Hobson; director, Richard Baron. (1 August) *Pageant* (Bill Russell, Frank Kelly, music by Albert Evans) with Lionel Blair, Miles Western, Dale Mercer, Leon Maurice-Jones; director, Bill Russell.

VICTORIA PALACE, SW1 (September 1999) *The Pajama Game* (George Abbott, Richard Bissell, Richard Adler, Jerry Ross) with Leslie Ash, Graham Bickley, John Hegley, Anita Dobson; director, Simon Callow. (1 June) *La Cava the Musical* (Dana Broccoli, Laurence O'Keefe, John Calflin, Stephen Keeling, Shaun McKenna) with Oliver Tobias, Julie-Alanah Brighten, Paul Keating; director, Steven Dexter.

WHITEHALL, SW1 (7 September 1999) *50 Revolutions* (Murray Gold) an Oxford Stage Company production;

director, Dominic Dromgoole. (28 September) *A Penny for A Song* (John Whiting) with Julian Glover, Jeremy Clyde, Charles Kay; director, Paul Miller. (22 November) *Anna Weiss* (Mike Cullen) with Catherine McCormack; director, Michael Attenborough. (14 March) *Cooking with Elvis* (Lee Hall) with Frank Skinner, Joe Caffrey, Charlie Hardwick, Sharon Icy; director, Max Roberts.

WYNDHAM'S, WC2. *Art*, since 1996

YOUNG VIC, SE1 (1 October 1999) *'Tis Pity She's A Whore* (Ford) with Jude Law, Eve Best; director, David Lan. (December) *The Nativity)* (David Farr) director, David Farr. (10 February) *The Servant of Two Masters* (Carlo Goldoni, adapt. Lee Hall) with Ariyon Bakare, Geoffrey Beevers, Paul bentall, Nikki Amuka-Bird; director, Tim Supple. (20 April) *Macbeth* (William Shakespeare) with Anthony Sher, Ken Bones, Nigel Cooke, John Dougall; director, Gregory Doran. (28 June) *Tales from Ovid* (Ted Hughes, Tim Supple, Simon Reade) with Mark Bonnar, Anthony Byrne, Sam Dastor, Andrew Denniss; director Tim Supple. (5 July) *The Prayer* (Grant Buchanan Marshall) with Jean Breeze, Gordon Case, Anthony Lennon, Dominic Letts; director Michael Buffong.

OUTSIDE LONDON

BIRMINGHAM: REPERTORY (October 1999) *Silence* (Moira Buffini) ; director, Anthony Clark. (26 October) *Baby Doll* (Tennessee Williams) with Tom Mannion, Charlotte Emmerson, Jonathan Cake; director, Lucy Bailey. (December) *A Time of Fire* (Charles Mulekwa) with Ali Sichilongo, Nicholas R Bailey, Christopher Tajah; director, Indhu Rubasingham.

BRISTOL: OLD VIC (22 September 1999) *One for the Road* (Willy Russell) with Gary Wilmot; director, Andy Hay. (28 October) *Hamlet* (William Shakespeare) with Colin Tierney; director, Gemma Bodinetz. (2 December) *Jack and the Beanstalk* (Chris Denys, Chris Harris) with Chris Harris; director, Elwyn Johnson. (16 December) *Bitter with a Twist* (Simon Treves) with Ian Lindsay, Roy Heather; director, Gareth Machin. (3 February) *Blues Brother Soul Sisters* (Kwame Kwei-Armah) with Kwame Kwei-Armah, Ruby Turner, Paulette Ivory, Dawn Michael; director, Andy Hay. (3 February) *Anatomy of a Mad Man*(Patrick Miller) with Patrick Miller; director, Gareth Machin. (7 April) *A Busy Day*(Fanny Burney) with Sara Crowe, Googie Wither, John McCallum; director, Jonathan Church. (12 May) *Denial* (Arnold Wesker) director, Andy Hay. (24 May) *A Tender Prayer* (Lucy Catherine); director, Gareth Machin.

CHICHESTER: FESTIVAL

MINERVA (September 1999) *The School of Night* (Peter Whelan) with Colin Wells, Peter Aubry; director, Jack Shepherd. (6 October) *The Retreat from Moscow* (William Nicholson) with Janet Suzman, Edward Hardwicke.

EDINBURGH: ROYAL LYCEUM (September 1999) *Feuergesicht* (Marius von Mayenburg), a Deutsches Schauspielhaus production; director, Thomas Ostermeier. (17 September) *Lovers* (Brian Friel). (November) *Macbeth* (Shakespeare) with Tom McGovern, Jennifer Black

GLASGOW: CITIZENS (17 September 1999) *Pygmalion* (Shaw) with simon Dutton, Lise Stevenson; director, Philip Prowse. (September) *Filth* (Irvine Welsh) with Tam Dean Burn; director, Harry Gibson.

LEEDS: WEST YORKSHIRE PLAYHOUSE (September 1999) *Carnival Messiah* (October) *Macbeth* (Shakespeare) with Patrick O'Kane, Mairead McKinley; director, Jude Kelly. (December) *Singin' in the Rain* with Paul Robinson, Don Lockwood, Zoë Hart and Rebecca Thornhill; director, Jude Kelly. (17 February) *Visiting Mr Green* (Jeff Baron) with Warren Mitchell, Reece Dinsdale; director Natasha Betteridge. (7 March) *Much Ado About Nothing* (William Shakespeare) with Conrad Nelson, Deborah McAndrew; director, Barrie Rutter. (21 March) *The Free State* (Janet Suzman) with Janet Suzman; director Janet Suzman. (4 April) *Mother Courage & Her Children* (Bertolt Brecht, trans. Lee Hall) with Kathryn Hunter; director Nancy Meckler.

COURTYARD.

LEICESTER: HAYMARKET (September 1999) *The Playboy of the Western World* (J. M. Synge) (September) *A Play of the Asian World* (Vayu Naidu). (October) *Sunday in the Park with George* (Sondheim) with Dave Willetts, Josefina Gabrielle; director, Paul Kerryson.

MANCHESTER: ROYAL EXCHANGE (September 1999) *King Lear* (Shakespeare) with Tom Courtenay, Gillian Kearney, Helen Schlesinger, Ashley Jensen, Ian Bartholomew, David Tennant director, Gregory Hersov. (??Oct/Nov) *Prize Night* (Jim Cartwright) with Jim Cartwright, Anthony Booth; director, Gregory Hersov.

LIBRARY THEATRE

MOLD: CLWYD THEATRE CYMRU, EMLYN WILLIAMS (23 November 1999) *Song of the Earth* (Alexander Cordell, adapted by Manon Eames) with Alun ap Brinley, Ifan Huw Dafydd, Richard Elfyn, Sara Harris-Davies; director, Terry Hands. (10 December) *Dick Whittington and the Coolest Cat in Town* (Peter Rowe, Alan Ellis) with Wendy Parkin, Johnson Willis, Gary Turner, James Neal; director, Peter Rowe. (23 December) *Under Milk Wood* (Dylan Thomas) with Alun ap Brinley, Ifan Huw Dafydd, Richard Elfyn, Sara Harris-Davies; director, Terry Hands. (3 February) *The Alexander Cordell Trilogy, Rape of the Fair Country, Hosts of Rebecca, song of the Earth* (Alexander Cordell, adapted by Manon Eames) with Alun ap Brinley, Ifan Huw Dafydd, Richard Elfyn, Sara Harris-Davies; director, Terry Hands. (7 April) *The Threepenny* (book and lyrics by bertoit Brecht, music by Kurt Weill) with Stepehn Aintree, Peter Eldridge, Jeremy Harrison, Kim Harwood; director, Terry Hands.

ANTHONY HOPKINS.

NOTTINGHAM: PLAYHOUSE (7 October 1999) *Kiss of the Spider Woman* (Manuel Puig, trans. Allan Baker) director, Philip Franks. (16 February) *The Amen Corner* (James Baldwin) with Kennie Andrews, Earlene Bentley, Corrine Skinner Carter; director Anton Phillips. (28 April) *The Deep Blue Sea* (Terence Rattigan) director, Dana Fainaru. (2 June) *Wonderful Tennessee* (Brian Friel) director, Giles Croft. (29 June) *The Secret Garden* (Frances Hodgson Burnett, dramatised Neil Duffield) director, Jacob Murray.

PLYMOUTH: THEATRE ROYAL

SCARBOROUGH: STEPHEN JOSEPH (September 1999) *Body Language* (Ayckbourn), a Stephen Joseph Theatre Company production with Peter Laird, Alexandra Mathie, Terence Booth, Robert Blythe; director, Alan Ayckbourn. (1 October) *Hobson's Choice* (Harold Brighouse) with Sarah Hadland, Carolyn Backhouse, Charlie Hayes, John Hoggarth; director, Alan Strachan. (5 November) *Larkin with Women* (Ben Brown) with Oliver Ford Davies, Carolyn Blackhouse, Susie Blake, Suzy Aitchison; director, Alan Strachan. (4 December) *Callisto #7* (Alan Ayckbourn) with Sherry Baines, Lindsey Fawcett, Charlie Hayes, Mark Stratton; director, Alan Ayckbourn. (June) *Private Lives* (Noël Coward) with Dale Rapley, Daisy Beaumont, Andrew Havill, Celia Nelson; director, Sam Walters. (2 June) *Private Lives* (Noel Coward) with Celia Nelson, Dale Rapley, Daisy Beaumont, Andrew Havill; director, Sam Walters. (8 August) *The Mikado* (Gilbert and Sullivan) with Shobna Gulati, Nicky Adams, Chris Garner, Howard Gay; director, Chris Monks. (24 August) *Candida* (Bernard Shaw) director, Matthew Francis.

SHEFFIELD: CRUCIBLE

SOUTHAMPTON: NUFFIELD (23 September 1999) *Twelfth Night* (Shakespeare); director, Patrick Sandford.

STRATFORD: ROYAL SHAKESPEARE THEATRE (24 November 1999) *The Lion, the Witch and the Wardrobe* (C. S. Lewis, adapt. Adrian Mitchell) with Emily Pithon, Patrice Naiambana, Estelle Kohler; director, Adrian Noble. (* December) *King Lear*, transferred from the Pit, London. (23 March 2000) *As You Like It* (William Shakespeare) with Alexandra Gilbreath, Nancy Carroll, Adrian Schiller; director, Gregory Doran. (20 April) *The Comedy of Errors* (William Shakespeare) with David Tennant; director, Lynne Parker. (5 July) *Romeo and Juliet* (William Shakespeare) with David Tennant, Alexandra Gilbreath, Adrian Schiller; director Michael Boyd.

(31 August) *Henry V* (William Shakespeare); director, Edward Hall.

SWAN (16 November 1999) *Macbeth* (William Shakespeare) with Anthony Sher, Harriet Walter, John Dougal, Ken Bones; director, Gregory Doran. (7 December) *The Taming of the Shrew*, transferred from the Swan, Stratford. (1 February 2000) *The Seagull* (Chekhov, adapt. Peter Gill). (23 March) *The Rivals* (Richard Brinsley Sheridan) with Benjamin Whitrow, David Tennant, Jacqueline Defferary; director, Lindsay Posner. (30 March) *The Rivals* with Benjamin Whitrow; director, Lindsay Posner (19 April) *Henry IV: Part I* (William Shakespeare) with Desmond Barrit, Nancy Carroll, Clifford Rose, David Troughton; director, Michael Attenborough. (29 June) *Henry IV: Part 2* (William Shakespeare) with Desmond Barrit, Nancy Carroll, Clifford Rose, David Troughton; director, Michael Attenborough.

THE OTHER PLACE (15 December 1999) *The Servant of Two Masters* (Carlo Goldoni, adapt. Lee Hall) with Jason Watkins, Nikki Amuka-Bird, Claire Cox, Orlando Seale; director, Tim Supple. (29 March 2000) *Richard II* (William Shakespeare) with David Killick, David Troughton, Samuel West; director, Steven Pimlott. (4 July) *La Lupa* (Giovanni Verga, new version by David Lan); director, Simona Gonella. (30 August) *Back to Methuselah* (George Bernard Shaw) director, David Fielding.

Weather

JULY 1999

Rainfall totals were generally above normal and it was the driest July since 1911, the mean value for the month being 1.3°C (2.34°F) above the 1961–1990 normal. Manchester had its driest July since records began in 1942. The 1st produced some heavy showers in southern areas but was otherwise mainly dry. The 2nd was thundery in the south again with heavy showers. The thunder spread to most of England and Wales on the 3rd but the heaviest rain was in Scotland. The 4th produced only scattered showers but the 5th saw thunderstorms return to most areas and 33.4 mm (1.32 ins) of rain fell at Middle Wallop (Hampshire). 83.0 mm (3.27 ins) of rain fell at Caring (Kent) late on the 5th. There were many reports of funnel clouds and mini tornadoes particularly in the Midlands. Flooding was reported at Cannock (Staffordshire). Fog was the main feature of the 6th while the 7th had rain in Scotland but was otherwise dry. The 8th to the 12th were all fine days generally but light rain fell almost everywhere on the 13th. The 14th produced only very light showers mostly over the south and the Midlands but the 15th had some heavier showers over Scotland. The 16th and 17th were also showery over Scotland. The 19th brought more general rain to all areas with Thunder in Southern Wales. This rain persisted into the 20th with the heaviest over Scotland. The rain turned to showers on the 21st and 22nd. The 23rd was a generally dry day everywhere but 54.9 mm (2.48 ins) of rain fell in an isolated storm at Dalmally (Strathclyde). On the 30th early morning fog formed over most areas but did not persist. Thunderstorms affected southern England on the 31st with some heavy showers. Monthly mean temperatures were generally higher than normal. The highest temperature recorded was 31.6°C (88.7°F) at Brabourne (Worcester) on the 31st and the lowest was 2.2°C (35.96°F) at Dalmally (Strathclyde) on the 26th. Sunshine totals were higher than normal, the highest daily total being 15.8 hours at Dyce (Grampian) on the 26th.

AUGUST 1999

Rainfall totals were generally well above normal making it the wettest and dullest August since 1992. Cardiff and Birmingham had their wettest Augusts on record with 176 mm (6.9 ins) and 154 mm (6.1 ins) respectively. The 1st was foggy at first in the north followed by widespread thunderstorms and heavy rain in places. Thunderstorms were widespread over England and Wales on the 2nd. The 3rd brought rain to most areas with thunder in Norfolk. Heavy rain fell in southern areas on the 4th when 45.4 mm (1.79 ins) of rain fell at Aberporth (Dyfed). The 5th produced thunderstorms mainly in northern England, the Midlands and East Anglia whilst the 6th brought heavy rain to southern areas and 60 mm (2.36 ins) fell at Aberdaron (Gwynedd). The 7th was another wet day but dry over Scotland. Thunderstorms were widespread over southern areas on the 8th when 47.8 mm (1.88 ins) of rain fell at High Wycombe (Buckinghamshire) and 57 mm (2.2 ins) fell at Coleshill (Birmingham) in 12 hours. There were some very heavy thunderstorms over East Anglia on the 9th and 57 mm (2.2 ins) of rain fell at Basingstoke (Hampshire) and 71.1 mm (2.84 ins) fell at Hemsby (Norfolk). This rain tended to peter out on the 10th but there were some very heavy local downpours. Farnborough reported a fall of 23.2 mm (0.91 ins) in just

under one hour. Mainly light rain fell over England and Wales on the 11th and 12th becoming widespread everywhere on the 13th. Thunderstorms were again widespread in the south on the 14th and a gust of 52 kts (60 mph) occurred at Honnington (Suffolk) during a storm. Rain was mostly confined to Scotland on the 15th but became more general with thunderstorms in the southern half of the Kingdom on the 16th. Funnel clouds and mini tornadoes were reported from Monmouthshire on the 16th. On the 17th rain was widespread with thunder in many places and 34.6 mm (1.36 ins) of rain fell at Newcastle (Tyne & Wear). The 18th was a similar day and 38.2 mm (1.50 ins) of rain fell at Newcastle (Tyne & Wear). The 24th produced heavy rain over southern England when 43.2 mm (1.70 ins) fell at Cardinham (Cornwall). Rain and thunderstorms were widespread over England and Wales on the 25th when 41 mm (1.61 ins) of rain fell at Bulmer (Northumberland), 35.2 mm (1.39 ins) of rain fell at Rosehearty (Aberdeen) on the 26th but the 27th was another dry day generally as were the remaining days of the month. Monthly mean temperatures were above normal generally. The highest temperature recorded was 32.7°C (90.86°F) at Heathrow (Greater London) on the 1st and the lowest was -0.9°C (30.38°F) at Aboyne (Aberdeen) on the 24th. Sunshine totals were generally below normal. The highest daily total was 15.3 hours at Fair Isle (Shetland) on the 4th.

SEPTEMBER 1999

Rainfall totals were generally above normal. It was the wettest September since 1995. The 1st was a generally fine day with fog in southern areas. The 2nd was very similar but 25.8 mm (1.02 ins) of rain at Aultbea (Ross & Cromarty). Morning fog was widespread on the 3rd. The 4th was a dry day but the 5th produced thunderstorms in southern England. 32 mm (1.3 ins) of rain fell at Kilmony (Highland). Purley (Surrey) recorded very heavy hail which broke windows. The 6th had extensive fog at first followed by some heavy rain in northern areas and 34.0 mm (1.34 ins) fell at Capel Curig (Gwynedd). The 7th produced more extensive rain which was again confined to the north on the 8th when 35.2 mm (1.4 ins) fell at Tulloch Bridge (Inverery). The 9th and 10th were dry days generally but 36.8 mm (1.45 ins) of rain fell at Carmoney (Londonderry) on the 10th. Rain was scattered widely on the 11th and 47.6 mm (1.88 ins) fell at Kilmony (Highland). Only light scattered rain fell on the 12th and 13th but the 14th brought heavy rain to south east England when 49.6 mm (1.95 ins) fell at Wattisham (Suffolk). Rain or showers were widely scattered on the 16th. The 17th brought thunderstorms to central southern England and a funnel cloud was observed off Jersey in the evening. Between the 11th and 18th the frequent heavy downpours caused flooding in East Anglia, south east and central England, the west Midlands and parts of northern Wales. Rain was widespread on the 18th when 62 mm (2.44 ins) fell at Dunkeswell (Devon) giving rise to flooding in east Devon. Wilmington (Devon) received 51 mm (2.0 ins) of rain in 3 hours. Heavy rain was widespread on the 19th when 56.4 mm (2.36 ins) fell at Ballypatrick (Antrim). The 20th was very wet with scattered thunder and 57.8 mm (2.54 ins) of rain fell at Kepley (Greater London) and 41.0 mm (1.6 ins) at Aboyne (Aberdeen). From the 18th to 20th Brabourne (Worcester) recorded

90 mm (3.54 ins) of rain. The 22nd brought frequent thunderstorms to many areas and 34.8 mm (1.37 ins) of rain fell at Bracknell (Berkshire). The 23rd had more widely scattered thunder and 33.8 mm (1.33 ins) of rain fell at Capel Curig (Gwynedd). Showers were mainly confined to southern areas on the 25th and 37.6 mm (1.48 ins) of rain fell at Coltishall (Norfolk). The 26th was wet in the south and 36.2 mm (1.43 ins) of rain fell at Pembrey Sands (Dyfed). The last week brought much flooding to north Wales and at Tryweryn (nr.Bala) 85 mm (3.35 ins) of rain fell in 36 hours (65 in 24). A tornado occurred in Wallasay and a waterspout was seen near Llanddulas (Powys). The 28th had widely scattered rain and widely scattered showers on the 29th produced a fall of 37.0 mm (1.5 ins) at Capel Curig (Gwynedd). Light showers were widespread on the 30th. Monthly mean temperatures were generally well above normal. The highest temperature recorded was 30.4°C (86.7°F) at Gravesend (Kent) on the 11th (the highest September since 1973) and the lowest was 0.0°C (32°F) at Aboyne (Aberdeen) and at Aviemore (Highland) on the 15th. Sunshine totals were well above normal and the highest daily total was 12.6 hours at Kirkwall (Orkney) on the 4th.

OCTOBER 1999

Rainfall totals were generally below normal but some heavy rain fell late in the month. The 1st was a generally wet day and 44.8 mm (1.76 ins) fell at Capel Curig (Gwynedd). The 2nd was a showery day as was the 3rd with scattered thunderstorms. The 4th was essentially dry and winds touched gale force along northern and eastern coasts. The 5th and 6th were generally dry days but the 7th brought rain to most areas. From the 8th to the 20th it was generally dry with only light widely scattered rain or showers. The 17th was so dry that the maximum fall in 24 hours was 0.6 mm (0.02 ins) at Scilly (Isles of Scilly). The 21st produced some heavy rain in many places. The heavy rain was confined mainly to southern areas on the 22nd and 23rd. Some very heavy rain fell in southern areas on the 24th when 61.8 mm (2.71 ins) of rain fell at Rhyl (Clwyd). A gust of 61 kts (70 mph) was recorded at Portland (Dorset) on the 24th. On the 25th Scotland had light rain or drizzle. The 26th and 27th were generally dry but 36.3 mm (1.43 ins) of rain fell at Waterstein (Highland) on the 27th. The 28th was a generally dry day with some fog in the south becoming more widespread on the 29th. Only light widely scattered rain fell on the 30th and 31st but an isolated shower gave 44.8 mm (1.76 ins) of rain at Tulloch Bridge (Highland). Monthly mean temperatures were mostly near normal. The highest temperature recorded during the month was 20.7°C (69.3°F) at Herne Bay (Kent) on the 10th and the lowest was -3.5°C (25.7°F) at Redesdale (Northumberland) on the 6th. Sunshine totals were generally well above normal and the highest daily total was 10.6 hours at St Mawgan (Cornwall) on the 4th.

NOVEMBER 1999

Rainfall totals were generally below normal making this the driest November since 1989. The 1st was a generally wet day with gales along the English Channel for a time. The 2nd was a drier day except in Scotland. The 3rd was generally dry but 49 mm (1.93 ins) of rain fell at Aultbea (Ross & Cromarty). Rain fell mainly over Scotland on the 4th when 51.6 mm (2.03 ins) fell at Knockareven (Fermanagh). The 5th was a generally wet day and 46.4 mm (1.83 ins) of rain fell at Capel Curig (Gwynedd). Ennerdale and Summergrove (Cumbria) had between 90 and 100 mm (3.54 and 3.94 ins) of rain. The 6th was mainly dry with only light scattered showers. Heavy rain

was confined to Scotland on the 7th and the 8th was mainly dry. The 9th to the 14th were mostly dry with only light scattered showers. The rain became heavier on the 15th and 16th but still widely scattered. Some heavy rain fell in southern England on the 17th and 18th becoming scattered showers again on the 19th and 20th. The 21st was generally dry but the 22nd brought rain back to southern areas and the Midlands. The 23rd was mainly dry but the 24th brought scattered heavy rain to England and Wales when 38.6 mm (1.52 ins) fell at Capel Curig (Gwynedd). The 25th was similar but the 26th brought some heavy rain to Scotland. The 26th was also a windy day and gusts of 72 kts (82.9 mph) at Stornoway, 67 kts (77.2 mph) at Valley and 73 kts (83.1 mph) at Lerwick were recorded. The 27th was mainly dry but 43.2 mm (1.70 ins) of rain fell at Tulloch Bridge (Highland).

This was also a very windy day and a gust of 74 kts (85.2 mph) was recorded at Muckle Holm (Orkney). Heavy rain fell in many areas on the 28th when 70 mm (2.76 ins) fell at Keswick (Cumbria) and a gust of 70 kts (80.6 mph) was recorded at Capel Curig (Gwynedd). Heavy rain fell over southern England on the 29th but 43.6 mm (1.72 ins) fell at Loch Glascarnoch (Ross & Cromarty). The 30th was similar and yet again it was Loch Glascarnoch that received most rain, 41.8 mm (1.65 ins). This was a windy day and gusts of 72 kts (83 mph) at Kirkwall (Orkney) and 63 kts 72.5 mph at Leeds (Yorkshire) were recorded. Monthly mean temperatures were generally above normal and the highest temperature recorded during the month was 17.8°C (64.0°F) at Gravesend (Kent) on the 1st and the lowest was -6.0°C (21.2°F) at Redesdale (Northumberland) on the 21st. The highest daily sunshine total was 8.6 hours at St Mawgan (Cornwall) on the 10th.

DECEMBER 1999

Rainfall totals were well above normal making this a very wet month with 148 per cent of normal rainfall. Local flooding was extensive. The 1st was mostly showery as was the 2nd when 49.4 mm (1.95 ins) of rain fell at Knockareven (Fermanagh). The 3rd produced widespread rain with snow over Scotland Shap (Cumbria). It was a windy day with gales in the north. Gusts of 83 kts (95.6 mph) at Capel Curig (Gwynedd), 80 kts (92.1 mph) at Aberdaron (Gwynedd), 78 kts (89.8 mph) at Crosby (Sefton) and 76 kts (87.5 mph) at Leeds (Yorkshire) were recorded. Showers were prevalent in Scotland on the 4th and heavy rain fell over southern Scotland and northern England on the 5th with 72.1 mm (2.83 ins) of rain falling at Dalmally (Strathclyde). The 6th was generally wet and 36.2 mm (1.43 ins) of rain fell at Capel Curig (Gwynedd). Thunderstorms affected many areas on the 7th. The 8th brought rain to most areas and 33 mm (1.30 ins) fell at Angelo (Fermanagh). A gust of 67 kts (77 mph) was recorded at Aberdaron (Gwynedd). The 9th was generally showery but the 10th brought heavy rain to most areas of England. 58.6 mm (2.30 ins) of rain fell at Cardinham (Cornwall). The 11th was a generally wet day and 53.4 mm (2.11 ins) of rain fell at Capel Curig (Gwynedd). Rain stayed mainly in the south on the 12th and 13th with snow over East Anglia. Snow spread to southern England on the 14th. Thunder was reported in northern England on the 15th with rain and snow over Scotland. Some heavy rain fell in northern districts on the 16th when 49.2 mm (1.94 ins) fell at Glascarnoch (Ross & Cromarty). Rain fell almost everywhere on the 17th when 47.2 mm (1.86 ins) fell at Cardinham (Cornwall). The 18th brought snow to southern England and 150–200 mm (6–8 ins) lay on Salisbury Plain, the Cotswolds and southern Wales by the evening. 98.4 mm (3.88 ins) of rain fell at Cardinham

(Cornwall). The 19th and 20th were generally dry but the 21st was generally wet and 50 mm (1.97 ins) of rain fell at Lochranza (N. Arran). The 22nd was another generally wet day and 37.2 mm (1.47 ins) of rain fell at Dalmally (Strathclyde). Heavy rain fell in southern England and Scotland on the 23rd when 52.8 mm (2.1 ins) fell at Tulloch Bridge (Highland). Rain was generally lighter on the 24th but 38.8 mm (1.53 ins) fell at Dalmally (Strathclyde). It was a windy day and gusts of 74 kts (85.2 mph) were recorded at Aberdaron (Gwynedd). The 25th was also very windy and gales along Channel coasts of 86 kts (99 mph) were recorded at Plymouth. Some heavy snow fell in Scotland. Winds were still strong on the 26th but it was generally dry. The 27th was also generally dry. Jersey recorded gusts up to 60 kts (69.1 mph). Monthly mean temperatures were near or slightly above normal. The highest temperature recorded was 14.9°C (58.8°F) at Thorney Island on the 1st and the lowest was -14.0°C (6.8°F) at Senney Bridge on the 20th. Sunshine totals were well above average. The highest daily total was 7.5 hours at Camborne (Cornwall) on the 19th.

YEAR 1999

Rainfall totals were near or slightly above normal. The outstanding feature of the year 1999 is that it was the warmest year on record since 1659, the second warmest being 1990. A temperature of 16.3°C (59.54°F) was recorded on the 6th January at Gravesend (Kent). The record for London was broken with a temperature of 15.7°C (60.26°F). On the 14th April Bristol had 8 cms (3.1 ins) of level snow. July was the driest since 1911 despite flash floods and 83 mm (3.27 ins) recorded in a thunderstorm at Charing (Kent) on the 5th. Cardiff with 176 mm (6.93 ins) of rain had its wettest August on record as did Birmingham with 154 mm (6.07 ins). Gravesend (Kent) had its warmest September since 1949 with a temperature of 30.4°C (86.72°F), this being the highest United Kingdom temperature for September since 1973. A mini-tornado at Pagham (W. Sussex) caused over one million pounds worth of damage. It was the sunniest October since 1959 and the sunniest December since 1962. For central London it was the sunniest since records were started in 1929 and also beat the previous record for Kew (72.0 hours) in 1886. Lerwick observatory recorded its highest rainfall total for any month since records started in 1921. It was the sunniest year since 1995.

JANUARY 2000

Rainfall totals were generally below normal but the highest daily rainfall total was 103.6 mm (5.36 ins), this being the centrepiece of a total fall of 180 mm (7.09 ins) in 60 hours. Scattered rain fell in many areas on the 1st and 44.0 mm (1.73 ins) fell at Aultbea (Ross & Cromarty). The 2nd was drier with gales in the far north where Lerwick (Shetland) recorded a gust of 55 kts (63.3 mph). The 3rd was very similar except the gales extended much further south and gusts of 92 kts (106 mph) at Stornoway and 92 kts (106 mph) at Lerwick were recorded. The 4th had only very scattered light rain as did the 5th except for an isolated fall of 57.2 mm (2.25 ins) at Glascarnoch (Ross & Cromarty). There were gales in the west and gusts of 68 kts (78.3 mph) at Capel Curig (Gwynedd) and 99 kts (114 mph) at Aonach Mor (Highland). The 6th was a dry day but gusts of 70 kts (80.6 mph) were recorded at Stornoway. The 7th had only light scattered rain and the 8th had light scattered showers in the north. Widespread frost developed after the passage of a cold front on the 8th. The 9th was a dry day but the 10th brought some heavy scattered rain when 47.8 mm (1.88 ins) fell at Capel Curig (Gwynedd), this being the start of 180 mm

(7.09 ins) in a 60 hour period at Capel Curig (Gwynedd). The 11th was similar and 103.6 mm (5.36 ins) of rain fell at Capel Curig (Gwynedd). The 12th had scattered heavy rain and 38.0 mm (1.53 ins) of rain fell at Moel-y-Crio (Clwyd). The 13th had light rain in the south and south east. The 14th, 15th and 16th had only widely scattered rain or showers. From the 17th to the 27th very light rain, showers or drizzle fell in very scattered patches but on the 28th 47.8 mm (1.88 ins) of rain fell at Dalmally (Strathclyde). The 29th brought gales to the north and very strong winds generally. A gust of 97 kts (111.7 mph) was recorded at Kirkwall (Orkney), this being the second highest on record. The 30th was also a windy day with gusts of 66 kts (76 mph) at Leeds (Yorkshire) and 70 kts (80.6 mph) at Kirkwall being recorded. 40.9 mm (1.60 ins) fell at Dalmally (Strathclyde). Gusts of 60 kts (69.1 mph) or more were recorded initially on the 31st but the winds died down. However, 75.5 mm (2.97 ins) of rain fell at Dalmally (Strathclyde). Monthly mean temperatures were near or slightly above normal and the highest temperature recorded was 16.0°C (60.8°F) and the lowest was -9.4°C (15.08°F) at Redhill (Surrey) on the 27th. Sunshine totals were well above normal and the highest recorded during the month was 9.9 hours at the Isle of Portland (Dorset) on the 25th.

FEBRUARY 2000

Rainfall totals were generally higher than normal making this a wet month. The 1st brought heavy rain to south east England but on the 2nd only light showers affected Scotland. The 3rd was almost dry but 30.8 mm (1.21 ins) of rain fell at Capel Curig (Gwynedd). The 4th and 5th were generally dry . The 6th was also dry but thunder was reported from Stornoway and severe gales affected northern Scotland when Stornoway recorded gusts of 66 kts (76 mph). The 7th was also windy and Kirkwall (Orkney) recorded gusts of 68 kts (78.3 mph). The 8th was generally showery while the 9th was mainly dry but 38 mm (1.50 ins) of rain fell at Glencarnoch (Ross & Cromarty). Some heavy rain fell in south east England on the 10th and in isolated parts of Scotland on the 11th. The 12th brought hail showers to western areas but the 13th was mainly dry. Widespread rain fell on the 14th and 15th. On the 16th, 20 cm (7.87 ins) of snow lay around Eskdalemuir (Dumfries & Galloway) and light snow showers fell. The 17th was drizzly generally but the 18th had only light showers. The 19th and 20th were dry days but the 21st produced some heavy rain in central areas. The 22nd was mainly dry but the 23rd produced rain or drizzle generally. Heavy rain fell in southern areas on the 24th. The 26th was a generally dry day but 41 mm (1.61 ins) of rain fell at Tulloch Bridge (Inverness). On the 27th, 62.6 mm (2.46 ins) of rain fell at Capel Curig (Gwynedd) as heavy rain spread across southern areas, the 28th was mainly showery while the 29th brought heavy rain to southern areas once again. For the winter as a whole it was very sunny, wet and mild. It was the sunniest winter on record since 1900, the wettest winter on record since 1706 and the mildest on record since 1659. Monthly mean temperatures were generally above normal making this the eighth consecutive month with temperature above normal. Since January 1999 only June has had a negative temperature anomaly.

MARCH 2000

Rainfall totals were very low. Light widespread showers were prevalent on the 1st turning to widespread heavy rain on the 2nd when 67.4 mm (2.66 in) fell at Capel Curig (Gwynedd). The 3rd saw scattered showers again and the 4th was almost dry. It was dry on the 5th but the 6th produced some heavy rain and 39.9 mm (1.57 ins) fell at

Dalmally (Strathclyde). Heavy rain fell in widely scattered areas on the 8th and 53.7 mm (2.11 ins) fell at Dalmally (Strathclyde). Rain petered out on the 9th to give dry days on the 10th, 11th and 12th. The 13th was also dry but winds reached gale force in the north when Muckle Holm (Shetland) recorded a gust of 64 kts (73.7 mph). The 14th was another fine day. 36.2 mm (1.43 ins) of rain fell at South Uist (Western Isles) on the 15th.The 16th to 19th produced a fine dry spell broken by fog on the 20th and 21st. The fog was more widespread and persistent on the 22nd but the 23rd brought heavy rain to most areas and 30.0 mm (1.88 ins) fell at Lochranza (Bute). The 24th brought very isolated rumbles of thunder to the west and midlands. On the 25th thunder occurred in East Anglia and on the 26th it occurred over Wales. Rainfall was slight on both days. The 27th produced an abundance of showers generally but rainfall amounts were very low. The 30th was a dry day and the 31st was almost dry except for very widely scattered (mainly coastal) showers. Monthly mean temperatures were 7°C (44.6°F) which is 2.34°F above the 1961–1990 normal of 5.7°C (42.26°F). The highest temperature recorded was 17.9°C (64.22°F) at Hawarden Bridge (Clwyd) on the 8th and the lowest was -5.8°C (21.56°F) at Aviemore (Inverness) on the 23rd. Sunshine totals were well above normal to give a sunny month. It was the 9th month in succession that was warmer than normal and the 7th consecutive month with above normal sunshine. The highest daily total was 11.4 hours at Tiree (Strathclyde) on the 27th.

APRIL 2000
Rainfall totals were more than twice the normal making this a very wet month with record breaking rainfall. The 1st was a generally wet day but the max fall in 24 hrs was 31.6 mm (1.24 ins) at Cattleyerd (Tyrone). The 2nd was similar with a max fall of 32.4 mm (1.27 ins) at Moel-y-Crio (Clwyd). On the 3rd the rainfall was generally heavier and 33.0 mm (1.30 ins) fell at Beaufort Park (Bracknell). Between 4 and 8 cm (1.6–3.0 ins) of snow lay on high ground away from East Anglia and the south east on the 4th and London had its coldest day for 34 years with a maximum temperature of 4.2°C (39.56°F). Rain eased off on the 4th, 5th and 6th only to return on the 7th. 14.7 mm (0.57 ins) max fall and then fell again on the 8th and 9th (max rainfall 1.4 mm (0.056 ins) at Sunderland, Tyne and Wear. The 10th produced some rain over Scotland and the 11th was another generally wet day with 28.6 mm (1.12 ins) of rain at Brize Norton (Oxfordshire). The 12th was very similar with 29 mm (1.14 ins) of rain at Glenlivet (Banff). A gust of 55 kts (63.3 mph) was recorded at Stornaway (Hebrides). On the 13th rain, sleet or drizzle covered the whole country with outbreaks of heavy rain with thunder and hail on the 12th and 13th. Precipitation was less persistent on the 14th but picked up again on the 15th, 16th and 17th over southern areas. Rainfall was very persistent over southern areas of the country on the 18th and 19th. The 20th brought much lighter falls to most areas with some isolated thunderstorms in Wales. The showers became less frequent and were pushed further north on the 21st and 22nd. Thunderstorms affected south west England, Wales, northern England and much of Scotland. On the 23rd thunderstorms were reported from many places and two funnel clouds were seen over Suffolk. On the 24th thunderstorms were more general. On the 25th thunderstorms were very widespread across southern England. 34.8 mm (1.37 ins) of rain fell at Inverbervie (Kincardineshire). On the 26th early morning fog developed into showers often thundery over the whole of England and Wales. From the 27th to the 30th apart from a wet day on

the 28th most parts had long sunny spells with very warm temperatures. Monthly mean temperatures were exactly 7.9°C (46.2°F) which is exactly the 1961 to 1990 normal. The highest temperature recorded was 28°C (82.4°F) at London and the lowest was -8.4°C (16.88°F) in Glenllivet (Banff) on the 4th. Sunshine totals were around normal and the highest daily total was 14.3hrs at Leuchars (Fife) on the 30th.

MAY 2000
Rainfall totals were well above normal making this another wet month and it was the wettest May since 1983. The month started dry and fine but by the evening of the 2nd drizzle moved into East Anglia and covered the whole of south east England and Wales on the 3rd. The 4th became dry again but on the 5th thunder was reported in southern England. The 7th brought severe thunderstorms to southern counties and Bracknell (Berkshire) recorded 65.8 mm (2.59 ins). Thunderstorms continued into the 8th causing flooding along parts of the Darenth and Medway basins. The 9th to the 16th brought more thundery rain to Essex, Hertfordshire and Bedfordshire but the main feature of these days was scattered persistent fog. After a foggy start the 10th became fine. The 11th and 12th were mainly dry but on the 13th 20.4 mm (0.81 ins) of rain fell in 1 hour at Redhill (Surrey). The 14th was mainly dry but the 15th produced some widespread thunderstorms over Kent, Essex, East Anglia, Lincolnshire and the Pennines. The 16th became mainly dry but the 17th produced heavy rain in many areas. 32.8 mm (1.29 ins) of rain fell at Capel Curig (Gwynedd). The 19th produced some heavy showers over the whole country. Hail was recorded at London and Wittering. Rain affected all areas on the 20th and 21st but had almost petered out by the 22nd. The 23rd was again a wet day in most areas but the 24th was wet only over south east areas. The 25th developed widespread showers, many of which were heavy, blustery with hail and thunder at times. There was heavy rain, mainly in southern areas, on the 26th. 28.1 mm (1.1 ins) of rain fell at Guernsey. The 27th brought blustery showers to southern England and 31.0 mm (1.22 ins) of rain fell at Lossiemouth (Grampian). Prolonged heavy rain and thunderstorms caused severe local flooding in parts of the south-east on the 28th as some rivers burst their banks. Clacton (Essex) had over 100 mm (nearly 4 inches) of rain in three days the 27th–29th. Taken as a whole, this has been the wettest Spring (March, April, May) since 1983. The 28th and 29th brought thunder to many areas of England and southern Scotland. On the 30th the thunder spread to further areas but the rainfall was not noteworthy. On the 31st heavy rain fell in southern districts and 25.2 mm (.99 ins) of rain fell at Pembrey Sands (Dyfed). Monthly mean temperatures were very near or slightly above normal. The highest daily value recorded was 26.9°C (80.4°F) at Northolt (Greater London) on the 15th and the lowest was -1.5°C (29.3°F) at Glenlivet (Banff) on the 4th. Sunshine totals were slightly above normal for the month and the highest daily totals was 15.8 hours at Lerwick (Shetland) on the 12th.

JUNE 2000
Rainfall totals were well below normal generally and it was the driest June since 1996. The 1st had generally light scattered rain but 30.4 mm (1.19 ins) fell at Capel Curig (Gwynedd). The light rain moved northwards during the 2nd and 3rd but 46.6 mm (1.23 ins) of rain fell at Sunderland (Tyne and Wear) on the 3rd. The 4th was a generally dry day as was the 5th but there were thunderstorms, prolonged heavy rain and local flooding in northern England. Parts of the Yorkshire dales had over

3 inches of rain 76.2 mm in 48 hours. The 6th produced
some thundery showers in northern England, Norfolk
and Essex. The 7th was a mainly dry day and the 8th, 9th
and 10th became even finer. Some light rain fell in
northern Scotland on the 11th, 12th and 13th. Persistent
drizzle affected south west England and the Channel
Islands on the 14th. The 15th–19th were virtually dry
everywhere and became hot or very hot over most of
England and Wales. London reached a maximum temperature of 32.4°C (90.32°F) on the 19th, its hottest day
for 10 years and its hottest June day since 1976. Coltishall
(Norfolk) had 32.8°C (91.04°F), the highest temperature
recorded so far this year but some light rain affected
southern areas on the 20th and 21st when 38.0 mm
(1.5 ins) of rain fell at Capel Curig (Gwynedd). On the
22nd thunder was reported near Aberdeen but the 23rd
was mainly dry again. From the 24th–30th only very
light scattered rain, showers or drizzle, affected the
whole country to give an almost dry period of weather.
Monthly mean temperatures were above normal to give
the warmest June since 1993. The highest temperature
recorded was 32.8°C (91.04°F) at Coltishall (Norfolk) on
the 19th and the lowest was -1.4°C (29.48°F) on the 3rd
at Glenlivet (Banff). Sunshine totals were close to or a little
above normal. The highest total was 15.8 hours at Valley
(Gwynedd) on the 27th.

AVERAGE AND GENERAL VALUES 1998–2000 (June)

	Rainfall (mm) Average 1961–90	1998	1999	2000	Temperature (°C) Average 1961–90	1998	1999	2000	Bright Sunshine (hrs per day) Average 1961–90	1998	1999	2000
ENGLAND AND WALES												
January	77	119	120	195	3.8	5.3	7.7	4.7	1.6	1.7	2.1	3.3
February	55	23	47	190	3.8	7.4	5.1	6.0	2.4	3.3	3.0	3.9+
March	63	98	64	112	5.6	8.0	7.2	7.2	3.5	2.5	3.8	4.8
April	53	125	72	101	7.7	7.9	9.2	7.6	4.9	4.3	5.6	6.4
May	56	34	53	61+	10.9	12.9	12.6	11.7+	6.2	6.8	5.7	5.9+
June	58	124	78	75+	13.9	14.2	13.6	14.5+	6.4	5.0	7.0	—
July	56	54	88	—	15.7	15.3	17.1	—	6.0	5.4	7.6	—
August	68	47	66	—	15.6	15.8	16.0	—	6.0	7.3	5.1	—
September	70	88	173	—	13.6	14.6	15.3	—	4.5	4.4	5.3	—
October	77	144	110	—	10.7	10.6	10.6	—	3.2	3.4	4.0	—
November	81	82	184	—	6.6	6.1	7.6	—	2.2	2.7	2.5	
December	82	83	261	—	4.7	5.7	4.7	—	1.5	1.4	2.0	—
YEAR	796	1321	1316	—	9.4	10.3	10.5	—	4.0	4.0	4.5	—
SCOTLAND												
January	117	165	138	185+	3.1	4.3	3.7	4.1+	1.3	1.2	1.4	1.5+
February	78	200	88	190+	3.1	7.4	3.4	4.0+	2.4	1.3	2.9	2.3+
March	94	122	79	112+	4.6	6.0	5.3	5.8+	3.2	2.3	3.8	2.7+
April	60	122	74	101+	6.1	6.1	7.4	5.6+	4.8	4.9	4.9	4.6+
May	67	57	81	61+	4.3	10.5	9.8	9.5+	5.6	5.4	5.9	7.9+
June	67	144	87	75+	12.1	11.3	11.1	11.1+	5.6	5.7	5.1	5.4+
July	74	109	88	—	13.6	12.6	14.0	—	4.9	3.9	5.4	—
August	92	89	66	—	13.5	13.0	13.2	—	4.9	4.2	5.1	—
September	111	66	173	—	11.5	12.2	12.8	—	3.5	3.8	3.5	—
October	120	165	110	—	9.1	7.6	9.1	—	2.6	3.5	2.2	—
November	118	141	184	—	5.3	4.9	6.2	—	1.7	2.1	1.5	—
December	115	110	261	—	3.9	4.7	2.4	—	1.0	1.1	1.2	—
YEAR	1113	1495	1429	—	7.9	8.8	8.2	—	3.5	3.3	3.6	—

+ Provisional figures subject to alteration by the Met Office
Source: Data provided by the Met Office

WEATHER RECORDS

WORLD RECORDS

Maximum air temperature	57.8°C/136°F
San Louis, Mexico, 11 August 1933	
Minimum air temperature	-89.2°C/-128.56°F
Vostok, Antarctica, 21 July 1983	
Greatest rainfall in one day	1870 mm/73.62 in
Cilaos, Ile de Réunion, 16 March 1952	
Greatest rainfall in one calendar month	9300 mm/366.14 in
Cherrapunji, Assam, July 1861	
Fastest gust of wind	201 knots/231 mph
Mt Washington Observatory, USA, 12 April 1934	

UNITED KINGDOM RECORDS

Maximum air temperature — 37.1°C/98.8°F
  Cheltenham, Glos, 3 August 1990
Minimum air temperature — -27.2°C/-17°F
  Braemar, Grampian, 11 February 1985 and 10 January 1982
Greatest rainfall in one day — 280 mm/11 in
  Martinstown, Dorset, 18 July 1955
Greatest annual rainfall total — 6528 mm/257 in
  Sprinkling Tarn, Cumbria, 1954
Fastest gust of wind — 150 knots/173 mph
  Cairngorm, Highland, 20 March 1986
Fastest low-level gust* — 123 knots/141.7 mph
  Fraserburgh, Grampian, 13 February 1989
Highest mean hourly speed — 92 knots/106 mph
  Great Dun Fell, Cumbria, December 1974
Highest low-level mean hourly speed* — 72 knots/83 mph
  Shoreham-by-Sea, Sussex, 16 October 1987

*below 200 m/656 ft

WIND FORCE MEASURES

The Beaufort Scale of wind force has been accepted internationally and is used in communicating weather conditions. Devised originally by Admiral Sir Francis Beaufort in 1805, it now consists of the numbers 0–17 each representing a certain strength or velocity of wind at 10 m (33 ft) above ground in the open.

Scale no.	Wind Force	mph	knots
0	Calm	1	1
1	Light air	1–3	1–3
2	Slight breeze	4–7	4–6
3	Gentle breeze	8–12	7–10
4	Moderate breeze	13–18	11–16
5	Fresh breeze	19–24	17–21
6	Strong breeze	25–31	22–27
7	High wind	32–38	28–33
8	Gale	39–46	34–40
9	Strong gale	47–54	41–47
10	Whole gale	55–63	48–55
11	Storm	64–72	56–63
12	Hurricane	73–82	64–71
13	—	83–92	72–80
14	—	93–103	81–89
15	—	104–114	90–99
16	—	115–125	100–108
17	—	126–136	109–118

TEMPERATURE, RAINFALL AND SUNSHINE
At selected climatalogical reporting stations, July 1999–June 2000 and calendar year 1999

Ht   hcight (in metres) of station above mean sea level
°C   mean air temperature
Rain   total monthly rainfall
Sun   monthly total (hours)
Source data supplied by the Met Office

		July 1999			*August 1999*			*September 1999*			*October 1999*		
	Ht	°C	Rain	Sun	°C	Rain	Sun	°C	Rain	Sun	°C	Rain	Sun
	m		mm	hrs		mm	hrs		mm	hrs		mm	hrs
Lerwick	82	11.5	53.0	124.7	12.1	74.2	154.7	12.2	143.8	89.2	8.8	156.2	59.8
Stornoway	15	13.5	70.5	176.3	13.6	54.5	194.0	12.9	118.7	114.2	9.9	132.3	84.7
Dyce	65	15.1	48.4	161.2	13.6	35.0	156.0	13.8	83.6	129.8	10.0	68.4	68.8
Eskdalemuir	242	14.5	69.5	159.1	13.2	72.7	131.8	12.8	145.7	110.1	8.0	106.0	68.6
Aldergrove	68	16.2	39.4	192.2	15.0	73.0	132.2	14.2	162.4	113.5	10.7	43.4	97.8
Leeds	64	18.4	20.5	229.9	16.7	45.4	152.8	16.4	77.7	180.9	11.0	67.5	111.5
Valley	10	16.6	16.8	242.9	15.8	86.1	159.6	15.2	148.2	144.5	11.7	59.0	128.9
Coleshill	—	17.7	11.8	—	16.2	162.5	—	15.73	46.8	—	10.6	72.9	—
Skegness	6	17.5	40.3	228.6	16.4	94.4	162.5	16.5	57.6	167.0	11.4	85.4	127.3
Bristol	42	19.1	7.8	257.6	17.9	104.0	168.6	16.8	107.3	173.5	12.1	75.0	148.8
St. Mawgan	103	17.1	6.0	260.2	16.7	96.2	202.5	15.5	113.0	179.2	11.9	39.6	153.0
Hastings	45	18.4	18.6	296.8	17.8	99.3	215.0	17.3	124.0	160.3	12.3	69.1	122.9

	November 1999			*December 1999*			*The Year 1999*			*January 2000*			*February 2000*		
	°C	Rain	Sun	°C	Rain	Sun	°C	Rain	Sun	°C	Rain	Sun	°C	Rain	Sun
		mm	hrs		mm	hrs		mm	hrs		mm	hrs		Mm	hrs
Lerwick	6.8	151.3	38.1	3.0	274.2	12.6	7.5	129	42.3	4.4	156.7	29.8	3.7	160.7	68.4
Stornoway	7.1	151.8	38.1	3.8	214.0	31.1	8.7	129	55.4	5.5	195.1	32.8	4.9	202.3	56.6
Dyce	6.9	52.4	65.0	2.8	91.0	67.6	8.9	58	57.9	4.8	29.2	65.9	4.7	21.6	113.7
Eskdalemuir	5.6	215.2	57.7	1.7	282.3	39.2	7.8	154	48.9	2.8	183.7	65.9	3.5	244.4	48.6
Aldergrove	7.1	73.8	66.3	4.2	150.4	44.1	9.8	76	57.5	4.8	35.0	44.8	5.7	68.2	76.2
Leeds	8.2	25.4	72.6	4.7	90.5	66.6	11.1	55	70.1	5.8	28.7	82.8	6.5	33.0	95.0
Valley	9.1	67.2	65.8	6.8	97.6	39.1	9.7	75	67.5	6.4	84.2	61.5	7.1	98.2	97.3
Coleshill	7.3	52.7	—	4.6	79.6	—	10.2	73	39.1	4.8	24.0	—	6.0	56.3	—
Skegness	8.3	43.0	73.6	4.4	58.3	87.5	10.7	60	68.8	5.2	19.2	86.3	5.9	58.3	109.0
Bristol	9.1	62.8	80.4	6.6	170.3	74.5	12.0	87	77.4	6.0	31.8	62.9	7.6	101.4	94.6
St.Mawgan	9.3	64.8	108.4	7.6	214.6	49.0	11.4	84	81.7	6.2	46.8	88.2	7.8	121.6	82.8
Hastings	8.5	37.9	—	5.8	141.9	—	11.6	66	47.5	5.4	33.9	—	7.0	58.6	101.3

	March 2000			*April 2000*			*May 2000*			*June 2000*		
	°C	Rain	Sun	°C	Rain	Sun	°C	Rain	Sun	°C	Rain	Sun
		mm	hrs		mm	hrs		mm	hrs		mm	hrs
Lerwick	4.5	158.3	85.6	5.1	83.5	118.7	8.7	42.6	223.2	9.2	77.7	152.3
Stornoway	6.6	120.7	84.6	6.1	81.5	150.0	9.5	53.5	239.6	10.6	80.6	181.5
Dyce	6.5	39.6	119.9	6.2	130.0	124.3	9.6	85.2	241.4	11.5	28.6	186.9
Eskdalemuir	5.7	108.4	80.9	5.7	93.1	123.9	9.8	72.4	235.9	11.3	95.2	106.1
Aldergrove	7.3	34.6	83.3	7.2	65.8	166.4	11.5	62.6	278.7	13.6	56.8	162.0
Leeds	7.9	21.9	131.4	8.2	136.5	133.8	12.4	35.6	217.8	15.3	65.7	167.1
Valley	7.7	35.0	134.2	8.0	67.6	179.7	12.3	46.0	285.9	14.1	24.4	189.9
Coleshill	7.6	26.6	—	7.8	105.8	—	11.8	59.6	—	15.2	28.0	—
Skegness	7.3	20.5	113.2	8.5	108.3	157.0	11.5	88.3	190.8	15.2	22.3	168.1
Bristol	8.8	30.2	128.1	8.9	153.1	149.9	13.2	80.0	189.4	16.6	26.6	189.7
St.Mawgan	7.8	27.4	153.1	8.3	119.4	175.9	12.3	75.0	188.1	14.4	25.2	183.2
Hastings	8.1	36.7	121.4	8.8	138.5	168.1	13.1	91.1	—	15.6	2.3	—

METEOROLOGICAL OBSERVATIONS London (Heathrow)

Temperature maxima and minima cover the 24-hour period 9–9 h; mean wind speed is 10 m above the ground; rainfall is for the 24 hours starting on 9 h on the day of entry; sunshine is for the 24 hours

Source: Data provided by the Met Office

JULY 1999

Day		Temperature Max °C	Min °C	Wind knots	Rain mm	Sun hrs
Day	1	21.5	13.3	8.8	0.2	2.2
	2	26.0	14.0	6.5	5.4	10.8
	3	23.9	18.2	9.3	0.0	5.0
	4	21.0	14.3	5.9	0.2	1.6
	5	23.2	14.2	3.4	0.2	7.9
	6	25.5	13.8	3.7	0.0	8.7
	7	24.7	15.7	4.5	0.0	7.5
	8	27.6	16.1	3.8	0.0	11.8
	9	25.2	18.0	7.3	0.0	5.5
	10	26.6	13.2	6.8	0.0	14.0
	11	27.2	14.6	8.7	0.0	14.4
	12	24.4	14.6	7.6	0.0	12.3
	13	26.1	12.4	5.5	0.0	8.5
	14	19.9	13.0	7.2	0.0	6.9
	15	21.6	11.0	6.5	0.0	7.6
	16	22.1	11.9	6.6	0.0	3.7
	17	25.9	16.1	5.9	0.0	8.6
	18	28.0	13.5	2.7	0.0	14.9
	19	26.0	16.7	7.0	2.6	7.4
	20	24.7	16.4	11.8	0.0	7.6
	21	20.8	13.6	11.8	0.0	5.9
	22	16.8	11.2	6.3	0.0	0.5
	23	25.5	9.2	2.7	0.0	13.4
	24	29.8	14.5	3.9	0.0	14.1
	25	27.8	16.7	5.8	0.0	7.4
	26	23.0	14.6	10.7	0.0	8.7
	27	21.7	12.6	10.8	0.0	14.6
	28	25.3	14.4	9.4	0.0	9.6
	29	28.6	13.9	8.3	0.0	10.6
	30	29.4	14.6	4.0	0.0	12.5
	31	31.3	17.1	3.3	0.0	11.7

AUGUST 1999

Day		Temperature Max °C	Min °C	Wind knots	Rain mm	Sun hrs
Day	1	32.7	16.5	0.0	13.1	5.4
	2	31.9	18.8	1.0	9.3	6.8
	3	23.9	18.6	1.2	2.3	3.0
	4	27.6	15.3	14.4	6.0	5.6
	5	26.2	17.5	0.0	10.5	5.4
	6	26.9	15.1	6.0	5.3	7.5
	7	24.4	16.7	3.0	6.0	2.8
	8	22.7	16.9	27.4	2.5	5.0
	9	21.3	15.9	38.4	3.7	2.8
	10	17.2	14.4	0.0	0.1	5.2
	11	20.5	12.2	0.0	6.7	3.4
	12	21.7	14.2	0.4	2.0	2.8
	13	22.4	13.9	0.6	1.4	5.6
	14	22.4	15.2	2.8	8.8	6.9
	15	21.4	11.5	0.2	7.3	5.7
	16	19.1	10.4	4.2	5.3	2.3
	17	17.0	9.5	4.6	0.2	5.9
	18	19.9	13.1	19.0	6.2	6.0
	19	19.9	12.5	0.0	9.2	7.0
	20	21.2	9.7	0.0	11.5	3.9
	21	19.1	9.7	0.0	13.5	3.8
	22	19.3	10.4	0.0	5.7	6.7
	23	21.2	13.5	0.0	9.2	7.4
	24	20.4	14.0	Trace	0.0	7.0
	25	25.0	14.8	1.6	2.2	2.5
	26	24.0	17.5	0.0	6.9	6.8
	27	22.3	12.7	0.0	9.3	3.8
	28	24.8	12.0	0.0	9.3	3.8
	29	24.0	13.3	0.0	8.0	3.9
	30	23.0	14.7	0.0	10.0	2.1
	31	23.0	13.7	0.0	6.1	1.5

SEPTEMBER 1999

Day		Max °C	Min °C	Wind	Rain	Sun
Day	1	24.5	13.0	1.6	0.0	8.3
	2	26.3	14.2	3.2	0.0	12.0
	3	26.7	16.0	4.7	0.0	11.4
	4	27.0	13.5	4.5	0.0	9.8
	5	27.4	15.2	2.5	3.6	9.0
	6	26.7	14.1	2.7	0.0	10.3
	7	23.9	15.7	5.6	Trace	6.4
	8	24.3	10.9	5.3	0.8	3.0
	9	21.6	13.0	2.8	0.0	8.3
	10	24.8	11.5	3.2	0.0	9.5
	11	28.5	16.5	4.7	0.0	6.5
	12	21.7	16.7	3.5	0.0	4.4
	13	19.7	10.2	1.7	1.2	5.2
	14	13.7	11.9	2.0	4.2	0.0
	15	17.2	12.3	2.7	1.8	0.0
	16	18.9	10.4	4.1	6.1	2.4
	17	20.1	9.6	5.3	0.0	8.8
	18	19.0	11.3	9.3	0.8	3.5
	19	18.8	14.9	7.3	14.8	0.0
	20	16.7	14.6	3.5	8.6	0.1
	21	20.5	12.3	2.9	0.6	7.6
	22	21.0	13.4	4.3	17.8	2.4
	23	20.0	13.9	7.5	7.6	5.4
	24	20.0	15.0	7.6	5.0	4.0
	25	19.9	13.8	5.3	1.6	4.9
	26	17.9	11.6	4.6	2.6	4.8
	27	18.8	13.0	7.5	0.4	2.8
	28	18.0	11.3	6.5	0.6	5.5
	29	18.5	13.8	7.4	8.6	4.4
	30	18.1	12.7	5.6	Trace	4.3

OCTOBER 1999

Day		Max °C	Min °C	Wind	Rain	Sun
Day	1	17.0	9.9	7.2	0.8	10.7
	2	15.8	8.3	Trace	8.3	9.5
	3	16.1	7.3	0.8	6.0	6.0
	4	13.7	6.6	0.0	8.4	4.8
	5	14.1	3.5	0.0	10.0	1.3
	6	14.7	3.2	0.0	9.9	0.9
	7	15.3	6.2	0.8	0.1	4.3
	8	17.0	10.2	0.0	0.8	5.8
	9	17.8	12.1	0.0	1.7	4.8
	10	19.1	14.2	0.0	1.8	4.5
	11	15.1	11.6	0.0	8.3	2.2
	12	15.9	3.6	0.0	9.0	0.9
	13	16.2	4.3	0.0	9.6	1.3
	14	16.5	401	0.0	9.4	3.6
	15	15.9	10.0	0.0	5.3	6.0
	16	16.8	7.8	0.0	7.7	3.4
	17	14.8	7.5	0.0	9.4	7.4
	18	13.5	6.9	0.0	9.1	9.0
	19	12.6	6.4	0.0	8.8	10.0
	20	10.7	6.8	6.4	0.0	8.8
	21	14.5	8.5	5.2	0.0	7.5
	22	16.6	8.6	5.0	0.3	5.4
	23	16.0	10.2	17.8	0.6	5.8
	24	12.8	10.0	4.6	0.2	8.7
	25	15.7	8.5	0.2	5.5	3.1
	26	16.4	5.8	0.0	4.8	1.9
	27	16.1	6.2	0.0	7.6	4.0
	28	16.9	9.3	0.2	7.0	2.1
	29	15.8	7.5	0.2	0.7	2.5
	30	17.6	8.7	0.4	1.4	8.5
	31	16.2	10.2	0.4	8.0	9.0

NOVEMBER 1999

Day	Temperature Max °C	Min °C	Wind knots	Rain mm	Sun hrs
1	17.3	12.2	10.2	1.0	0.0
2	13.8	9.9	5.5	0.0	7.0
3	14.6	5.4	2.8	Trace	2.7
4	14.2	8.7	3.9	0.0	2.7
5	13.3	8.3	10.4	6.6	0.1
6	11.6	6.9	8.2	0.0	6.8
7	11.3	2.2	3.4	0.0	3.4
8	12.9	5.3	2.0	0.2	0.0
9	12.8	9.0	4.5	0.0	4.0
10	11.6	7.4	6.9	0.0	1.1
11	11.0	6.9	5.5	0.4	0.1
12	9.4	6.1	4.6	0.0	3.6
13	11.1	4.0	4.6	Trace	5.2
14	10.9	6.1	4.8	0.0	0.3
15	10.2	5.5	2.0	1.6	3.0
16	9.5	5.0	4.2	2.2	5.4
17	6.8	2.3	5.2	2.6	7.9
18	6.3	1.1	6.0	0.4	6.5
19	7.4	2.9	9.2	0.4	4.1
20	6.8	3.6	7.0	Trace	1.7
21	8.0	3.0	2.6	0.8	0.8
22	8.4	2.9	3.0	0.2	0.0
23	12.1	2.7	2.1	Trace	0.1
24	13.5	6.1	8.9	0.6	0.2
25	13.4	11.2	7.3	0.0	5.4
26	11.0	9.7	11.2	4.4	0.1
27	13.0	5.3	4.6	0.0	4.7
28	13.5	6.4	13.0	3.4	2.0
29	9.6	8.7	2.5	6.2	0.0
30	12.5	0.7	8.4	0.2	0.1

DECEMBER 1999

Day	Temperature Max °C	Min °C	Wind knots	Rain mm	Sun hrs
1	12.7	4.9	7.8	0.2	2.2
2	11.5	3.5	8.1	0.0	4.8
3	13.2	5.4	14.7	1.6	0.9
4	7.4	3.1	8.7	0.2	6.6
5	10.3	0.1	4.8	0.0	5.3
6	12.2	1.3	12.8	0.2	0.0
7	11.4	9.1	9.1	1.4	2.5
8	11.4	5.2	11.3	3.6	0.0
9	9.1	5.9	13.6	0.0	6.7
10	11.9	3.3	6.9	2.8	3.0
11	12.9	4.7	11.2	2.1	0.0
12	8.0	7.0	9.0	5.8	0.1
13	8.3	2.6	7.2	2.8	0.9
14	4.3	-0.4	3.5	0.2	4.4
15	4.0	0.3	9.0	Trace	5.3
16	9.8	-1.0	4.5	0.2	5.2
17	11.3	2.9	10.7	1.8	0.0
18	4.3	2.4	3.5	3.9	0.0
19	1.8	-1.3	3.6	0.0	7.4
20	4.1	-5.5	2.1	1.6	4.1
21	6.3	-4.0	8.2	0.2	0.0
22	12.0	2.2	12.8	7.4	0.0
23	11.2	4.9	12.1	10.6	5.4
24	12.9	6.5	17.0	11.2	0.0
25	6.8	4.3	14.9	6.4	1.5
26	8.2	2.6	8.6	2.8	3.7
27	5.2	1.3	3.7	0.0	0.4
28	4.4	2.4	4.7	0.0	0.0
29	6.1	-2.2	4.5	1.4	4.9
30	7.8	-0.9	4.4	7.8	0.0
31	8.8	3.2	3.7	1.0	0.0

JANUARY 2000

Day	Temperature Max °C	Min °C	Wind knots	Rain mm	Sun hrs
1	9.1	4.9	1.5	Trace	0.4
2	10.8	5.0	4.2	0.2	0.7
3	11.5	7.2	9.0	6.0	0.0
4	9.5	4.4	3.8	0.2	2.9
5	11.0	1.9	9.6	0.8	1.3
6	10.8	7.0	8.0	0.0	0.6
7	11.0	3.4	9.8	2.0	2.2
8	9.2	5.7	6.1	0.0	6.4
9	7.2	-0.7	1.3	0.2	7.1
10	7.8	-3.3	3.0	0.0	3.7
11	10.2	0.6	8.1	Trace	0.1
12	8.2	7.8	11.7	2.8	0.0
13	5.0	2.7	5.3	0.2	0.0
14	6.3	-0.5	4.9	0.3	4.2
15	6.7	2.6	4.9	0.0	0.9
16	7.2	2.2	2.9	0.0	3.9
17	8.6	0.3	3.6	0.0	3.8
18	8.4	1.2	4.8	0.2	0.0
19	7.3	3.6	3.6	0.0	0.6
20	5.3	-2.2	1.5	0.0	0.0
21	9.2	0.7	3.6	0.2	6.2
22	7.8	2.6	9.2	1.2	2.1
23	7.3	0.8	5.4	0.0	5.4
24	5.8	0.4	1.8	0.0	6.0
25	3.7	-2.7	1.0	0.0	0.8
26	6.1	0.2	1.8	0.0	7.2
27	5.2	-3.5	1.8	0.0	8.1
28	10.8	-1.8	10.8	2.2	0.1
29	13.5	3.4	17.1	Trace	3.3
30	12.9	10.4	14.7	0.0	0.3
31	12.7	10.3	12.3	Trace	0.3

FEBRUARY 2000

Day	Temperature Max °C	Min °C	Wind knots	Rain mm	Sun hrs
1	10.7	9.1	9.8	0.0	8.8
2	10.6	5.8	0.0	6.9	5.2
3	9.3	2.7	Trace	0.5	3.4
4	11.0	4.7	0.0	0.0	7.3
5	11.6	7.3	0.0	1.8	6.0
6	12.1	7.2	1.8	0.1	7.7
7	11.0	5.0	3.8	0.0	10.2
8	13.8	7.0	2.2	3.6	11.5
9	10.6	2.9	0.6	2.6	8.0
10	10.1	5.9	3.0	2.0	11.7
11	10.4	-0.1	3.8	6.2	5.7
12	9.6	3.2	0.8	3.4	9.8
13	9.9	4.8	0.0	8.5	3.5
14	10.2	-1.1	1.8	1.2	3.0
15	8.6	2.3	1.2	2.2	6.4
16	8.0	1.4	Trace	7.8	10.6
17	9.6	2.3	2.2	7.2	6.1
18	11.0	3.1	0.2	3.5	9.0
19	9.1	6.1	0.2	5.2	6.2
20	8.7	-1.0	0.6	8.2	1.8
21	10.0	1.5	0.0	5.9	4.0
22	9.5	-0.3	0.0	3.7	2.7
23	11.7	3.9	Trace	0.1	6.0
24	11.2	7.6	16.8	1.5	6.3
25	10.0	2.2	0.0	9.3	4.3
26	10.6	-0.3	Trace	6.4	5.2
27	13.0	4.2	5.2	0.0	15.7
28	10.4	6.8	2.6	4.6	10.6
29	10.1	5.5	5.6	0.1	10.5

MARCH 2000

		Temperature Max °C	Min °C	Wind knots	Rain mm	Sun hrs
Day	1	9.3	1.6	0.2	6.9	8.3
	2	11.2	0.3	7.2	0.1	11.5
	3	10.8	5.2	0.2	5.9	11.3
	4	7.8	0.8	0.0	9.1	5.4
	5	10.4	-0.3	0.0	6.0	5.4
	6	11.5	4.9	Trace	0.0	8.7
	7	13.9	8.2	Trace	2.0	10.5
	8	14.6	10.3	Trace	0.0	12.3
	9	16.6	11.2	0.0	3.1	9.8
	10	14.2	10.8	0.0	2.7	6.8
	11	13.6	7.4	0.0	5.7	6.0
	12	14.5	2.9	0.0	8.9	2.3
	13	15.0	4.9	Trace	1.0	2.8
	14	13.0	8.5	0.0	2.2	10.1
	15	12.7	2.6	0.0	9.9	5.9
	16	12.2	3.9	0.0	0.1	4.0
	17	10.6	8.3	0.0	0.0	4.5
	18	10.8	7.5	0.0	6.8	6.5
	19	12.5	2.5	0.0	8.8	3.5
	20	13.9	1.7	0.0	2.3	4.0
	21	14.3	3.7	0.0	7.5	4.8
	22	15.5	3.5	0.0	4.4	0.8
	23	14.8	5.3	1.6	0.0	6.9
	24	14.1	7.7	0.2	5.0	7.1
	25	12.3	5.9	2.6	6.7	6.8
	26	11.2	1.6	0.8	6.5	3.2
	27	10.2	4.0	2.0	6.1	9.0
	28	8.2	4.3	1.2	0.3	10.7
	29	7.1	3.7	Trace	0.0	10.0
	30	8.2	5.0	0.0	0.0	6.8
	31	10.0	5.0	0.0	2.4	2.4

APRIL 2000

		Temperature Max °C	Min °C	Wind knots	Rain mm	Sun hrs
Day	1	11.8	1.7	5.1	0.6	2.8
	2	13.7	7.1	6.8	16.0	0.6
	3	9.1	8.2	8.9	17.2	0.0
	4	6.0	1.9	11.0	1.2	0.0
	5	10.1	2.7	7.6	0.0	5.9
	6	10.9	0.7	6.0	0.0	12.0
	7	14.9	2.3	4.1	0.0	10.9
	8	17.3	2.0	2.0	3.6	11.2
	9	14.7	6.4	9.3	0.0	9.6
	10	12.4	3.6	6.5	0.6	10.6
	11	7.1	3.4	3.8	6.0	0.0
	12	6.6	1.8	5.3	6.4	0.0
	13	9.2	3.6	5.3	1.8	2.2
	14	10.2	4.0	5.2	11.8	1.0
	15	8.4	3.2	7.5	1.8	0.0
	16	12.8	0.3	6.6	2.6	7.7
	17	11.9	6.3	11.1	5.6	4.9
	18	12.2	5.8	7.8	5.2	0.6
	19	16.1	6.7	7.0	2.4	9.2
	20	14.0	10.2	9.3	2.0	0.3
	21	15.5	8.2	10.5	0.8	5.1
	22	15.8	7.2	5.5	0.0	6.9
	23	14.3	6.1	2.7	0.2	1.6
	24	15.3	5.8	7.3	5.0	5.9
	25	16.1	10.0	9.5	3.8	1.1
	26	15.2	9.4	6.6	0.2	4.8
	27	16.0	6.8	5.2	Trace	3.3
	28	13.3	10.0	3.5	4.8	0.0
	29	18.7	9.1	5.2	0.0	13.3
	30	16.6	6.5	3.6	0.0	4.3

MAY 2000

		Temperature Max °C	Min °C	Wind knots	Rain mm	Sun hrs
Day	1	16.6	7.5	6.3	0.0	5.0
	2	14.6	8.6	7.5	0.3	4.0
	3	11.2	8.2	7.4	Trace	0.0
	4	12.6	8.2	8.1	0.0	0.1
	5	20.5	7.4	7.7	0.0	10.0
	6	24.1	8.6	6.4	0.0	11.1
	7	23.3	12.7	4.5	0.0	7.6
	8	19.4	10.5	3.3	0.2	3.9
	9	23.4	12.3	3.9	0.0	7.3
	10	17.9	13.0	6.7	4.6	0.8
	11	17.8	10.9	10.4	2.6	3.7
	12	19.5	8.5	4.5	0.0	4.1
	13	24.9	13.0	2.0	0.0	9.3
	14	25.3	12.5	3.3	2.4	13.4
	15	26.6	15.4	4.8	0.0	12.6
	16	22.5	15.2	8.8	0.0	11.5
	17	15.9	11.1	12.4	4.2	4.0
	18	15.5	7.2	7.4	4.4	8.2
	19	14.3	9.2	7.2	2.0	7.1
	20	15.8	55.1	3.4	11.6	6.4
	21	16.0	8.3	4.4	1.8	4.8
	22	18.6	7.8	6.5	0.0	12.1
	23	14.3	11.6	10.6	2.2	0.0
	24	16.2	9.6	3.9	8.6	3.8
	25	16.8	9.2	8.6	0.2	12.2
	26	12.8	10.4	7.3	18.8	0.0
	27	14.8	7.0	11.5	19.0	10.2
	28	15.6	5.9	8.5	3.0	6.4
	29	17.4	6.2	5.3	Trace	12.5
	30	15.7	9.3	1.7	0.0	2.3
	31	19.0	6.3	4.9	1.4	8.5

JUNE 2000

		Temperature Max °C	Min °C	Wind knots	Rain mm	Sun hrs
Day	1	16.8	12.3	11.5	Trace	3.3
	2	18.8	12.9	6.9	0.0	0.4
	3	22.9	12.1	1.8	0.0	8.9
	4	18.1	11.3	4.3	0.0	7.4
	5	16.1	10.6	3.0	0.0	0.1
	6	18.9	9.8	6.5	0.0	7.4
	7	20.6	8.7	5.0	0.0	11.4
	8	22.4	12.5	9.5	0.2	11.0
	9	17.8	14.4	5.3	4.2	4.1
	10	20.3	8.6	6.5	0.0	13.0
	11	19.3	11.3	7.7	0.0	8.9
	12	25.1	12.1	8.5	0.0	12.1
	13	22.6	14.4	8.0	0.0	5.8
	14	22.5	15.2	8.6	0.0	1.3
	15	20.1	15.0	4.2	0.0	0.8
	16	22.3	14.3	5.3	0.0	1.0
	17	25.9	13.1	8.2	0.0	13.2
	18	30.8	15.6	8.2	0.0	15.1
	19	31.4	19.4	7.0	0.0	12.8
	20	21.6	15.4	5.1	3.8	0.2
	21	19.5	15.5	13.4	Trace	5.2
	22	19.0	13.4	13.0	2.4	4.4
	23	19.7	12.7	7.7	Trace	3.2
	24	16.1	8.5	5.5	0.0	0.1
	25	18.0	10.1	2.8	Trace	3.2
	26	19.9	12.5	3.1	0.0	3.9
	27	21.9	11.2	2.8	0.0	8.7
	28	20.9	13.2	3.4	Trace	1.4
	29	20.3	14.5	3.9	8.2	0.1
	30	20.8	13.6	6.4	0.4	1.1

Sports Results

ALPINE SKIING

WORLD CUP 1999–2000

MEN
Combined: Kjetil-André Aamodt (Norway), 200 points
Downhill: Hermann Maier (Austria), 800 points
Slalom: Kjetil-André Aamodt (Norway), 544 points
Giant Slalom: Hermann Maier (Austria), 520 points
Super Giant Slalom: Hermann Maier (Austria), 540 points
Overall: Hermann Maier (Austria), 2,000 points

WOMEN
Combined: Rentate Götschl (Austria) 100 points
Downhill: Regina Häusl (Germany), 529 points
Slalom: Spela Pretnar (Slovenia), 645 points
Giant Slalom: Michaela Dorfmeister (Austria), 684 points
Super Giant Slalom: Renate Götschl (Austria), 554 points
Overall: Renate Götschl (Austria), 1,631 points

AMERICAN FOOTBALL

AFC Championship 2000: Tennessee Titans beat Jacksonville Jaguars 33–14
NFC Championship 2000: St Louis Rams beat Tampa Bay Buccaneers 11–6
XXXIV Superbowl 2000 (Atlanta, 30 January): St Louis Rams beat Tennessee Titans 23–16
World Bowl 2000: Rhein Fire beat Scottish Claymores 13–10

ANGLING

NATIONAL COARSE CHAMPIONSHIPS 2000
Division: 1
Venue: Leeds and Liverpool Canal; *no. of teams*: 79
Individual winner: T. Flannery
Team winners: Daiwa Gordon League

Division: 2
Venue: River Nene; *no. of teams*: 58
Individual winner: D. Flaymaker
Team winners: Colins Green

Division: 3
Venue: Upper River Nene; *no. of teams*: 87
Individual winner: A. Robertson
Team winners: Popletts M. G.

Division: 4
Venue: Cam and Ely Ouse; *no. of teams*: 58
Individual winner: A. Campbell
Team winners: Preston Innovation Delcac

Division: 5
Venue: Oxford Canal; *no. of teams*: 20
Individual winner: S. Parsley
Team winners: Fosters Tipton VDE

Ladies' Championship
Venue: River Soar
Winner: Jane Burrows

ASSOCIATION FOOTBALL

LEAGUE COMPETITIONS 1999–2000

ENGLAND AND WALES
Premiership
1. Manchester United, 91 points
2. Arsenal, 73 points
Relegated: Wimbledon, 33 points; Sheffield Wednesday, 31 points; Watford, 24 points

Division 1
1. Charlton Athletic, 91 points
2. Manchester City, 89 points
Third promotion place: Ipswich
Relegated: Walsall, 46 points; Port Vale, 36 points; Swindon, 36 points

Division 2
1. Preston, 95 points
2. Burnley, 88 points
Third promotion place: Gillingham
Relegated: Cardiff, 44 points; Blackpool, 41 points; Scunthorpe, 39 points; Chesterfield, 36 points

Division 3
1. Swansea, 85 points
2. Rotherham, 84 points
3. Northampton, 82 points
Fourth promotion place: Peterborough
Relegated: Chester, 39 points

Football Conference
Champions: Kidderminster, 85 points
Relegated: Welling, 47 points; Altrinhcam, 46 points; Sutton United, 34 points

League of Wales: Barry Town, 76 points
Women's Premier League: Croydon

SCOTLAND
Premier Division
1. Rangers, 90 points
2. Celtic, 69 points

Division 1
1. St Mirren, 76 points
2. Dunfermline, 71 points
Relegated: Clydebank, 10 points

Division 2
1. Clyde, 65 points
2. Alloa, 64 points
Relegated: Hamilton, 29 points (deducted 15 points for failing to fulfil a fixture)

Division 3
1. Queen's Park, 69 points
2. Berwick, 66 points
Bottom: Albion, 22 points

NORTHERN IRELAND
Irish League Championship: Linfield, 79 points

FRANCE
French League Champions: Monaco 65 points

GERMANY

German League Champions: Bayern Munich 73 points

ITALY

Italian League Champions: Lazio 72 points

SPAIN

Spanish League Champions: Deportivo Coruna 69 points

CUP COMPETITIONS

ENGLAND

FA Cup final 2000 (Wembley, 20 May): Aston Villa beat Chelsea 2–0
Worthington (League) Cup final 2000: Leicester beat Tranmere 1–0
Auto Windscreens Shield final 2000: Stoke City beat Bristol City 2–1
FA Vase final 2000: Deal Town beat Chippenham Town 1–0
FA Trophy final 2000: Kingstonian beat Kettering Town 3–2
Charity Shield 2000: Chelsea beat Manchester United 2–0
Women's FA Cup final 2000: Croydon beat Doncaster Bells 2–1
Women's League Cup final 2000: Arsenal beat Croydon 4–1

WALES

Welsh Cup final 2000: Bangor City beat Cwmbran Town 1–0
League of Wales Cup final 2000: Barry Town beat Bangor City 6–0

SCOTLAND

Scottish Cup final 2000 (Hampden Park, 27 May): Rangers beat Aberdeen 4–0
League Cup final 1999 (Hampden Park, 19 March) : Celtic beat Aberdeen 2–0

NORTHERN IRELAND

Irish Cup final 2000: Glentoran beat Portadown 1–0

EUROPE

European Champions' Cup final 2000 (Paris): Real Madrid beat Valencia 3–0
European Cup-Winners' Cup final 1999 (Villa Park): Lazio beat Real Mallorca 2–1
UEFA Cup final 2000: Galatasaray beat Arsenal 4–1 on penalties
European Super Cup final 2000: Galatasary SK beat Real Madrid 2–1
InterToto Cup final 1999: West Ham beat Metz 3–2 on aggregate

INTERNATIONALS

AFRICAN NATIONS CUP 2000

Cameroon beat Nigeria 4–3 on penalties

EURO 2000

ROUND ONE

10 June	Brussels	Belgium 2, Sweden 1
11 June	Arnhem	Italy 2, Turkey 1
	Bruges	France 3, Denmark 0
	Amsterdam	Netherlands 1, Czech Republic 0
12 June	Liège	Germany 1, Romania 1
	Eindhoven	Portugal 3, England 2
13 June	Rotterdam	Norway 1, Spain 0
	Charleroi	Yugoslavia 3, Slovenia 3
14 June	Brussels	Italy 2, Belgium 0
15 June	Eindhoven	Sweden 0, Turkey 0
16 June	Bruges	France 2, Czech Republic 1
	Rotterdam	Netherlands 3, Denmark 0
17 June	Arnhem	Portugal 1, Romania 0
	Charleroi	England 1, Germany 0
18 June	Amsterdam	Spain 2, Slovenia 1
	Liège	Yugoslavia 1, Norway 0
19 June	Brussels	Turkey 2, Belgium 0
	Eindhoven	Italy 2, Sweden 1
20 June	Charleroi	Romania 3, England 2
	Rotterdam	Portugal 3, Germany 0
21 June	Bruges	Spain 4, Yugoslavia 3
	Arnhem	Slovenia 0, Norway 0
	Liège	Czech Republic 2, Denmark 0
	Amsterdam	Netherlands 3, France 2

QUARTER-FINALS

24 June	Amsterdam	Portugal 2, Turkey 0
	Brussels	Italy 2, Romania 0
25 June	Rotterdam	Netherlands 6, Yugoslavia 1
	Bruges	France 2, Spain 1

SEMI-FINALS

28 June	Brussels	France 2, Portugal 1
29 June	Amsterdam	Italy 0, Netherlands 0 Italy won on penalties 3–1

FINAL

2 July	Rotterdam	France 2, Italy 1

FOOTBALLER OF THE YEAR

1999	Rivaldo (Brazil)
1998	Zinedine Zidane (France)
1997	Ronaldo (Brazil)
1996	Ronaldo (Brazil)
1995	George Weah (Liberia)
1994	Romario (Brazil)
1993	Roberto Baggio (Italy)
1992	Marco van Basten (Netherlands)
1991	Lothar Matthäus (Germany)

ATHLETICS

WORLD HALF MARATHON CHAMPIONSHIPS
Palermo, Italy, 3 October 1999

MEN

Individual: Paul Tergat (Kenya), 61min. 50sec.
Team result: South Africa, 3 hr. 06 min. 01 sec.

WOMEN

Individual: Tegla Loroupe (Kenya), 1 hr. 08min. 48sec.
Team result: Kenya, 3 hr. 27 min. 40 sec.

EUROPEAN CROSS-COUNTRY CHAMPIONSHIPS
Velenje, Slovenia, 12–13 December 1999

MEN (9.25 km)

Individual: Paulo Guerra (Portugal), 32min. 45sec.
Team: Great Britain, 35 points

WOMEN (4.95 km)

Individual: Anita Weyermann (Switzerland), 18min. 53sec.
Team: France, 34 points

AAA INDOOR CHAMPIONSHIPS
Birmingham, 29–30 January 2000

MEN

	min.	sec.
60 *metres*: Jason Gardener (Wessex and Bath)		6.53
200 *metres*: Christian Malcolm (Cardiff)		20.74
400 *metres*: Daniel Caines (Birchfield)		46.89
800 *metres*: Luke Kipkoech (Kenya)	1	51.72
	min.	sec.
1,500 *metres*: Gareth Turnbull (Ireland)	3	44.06
3,000 *metres*: Rob Whalley (Stoke)	8	02.40
60 *metres hurdles*: Tony Jarrett (Haringey and Enfield)		7.65
3,000 *metres walk*: Robert Hefferan (Ireland)	11	38.20
		metres
High jump: Stuart Ohrland (Newham EB)		2.19
Pole vault: Ben Flint (Belgrave)		5.35
Long jump: Chris Tomlinson (Mandale)		7.57
Triple jump: Julian Golley (TVH)		16.56
Shot: Stephan Hayward (Sale)		17.67
Heptathlon: Paul Jones (Colwyn Bay)		5,277 points

WOMEN

	min.	sec.
60 *metres*: Marcia Richardson (Windsor, Slough and Eton)		7.25
200 *metres*: Christine Bloomfield (Woodford Green/Essex Ladies)		23.31
400 *metres*: Michelle Thomas (Birchfield)		55.26
800 *metres*: Emma Davies (Andover)	2	07.34
1,500 *metres*: Shirley Griffiths (Wakefield)	4	25.69
*3,000 *metres*: Zara Hyde-Peters (Havant)	9	16.89
60 *metres hurdles*: Diane Allahgreen (Liverpool)		8.24
3,000 *metres walk*: Gillian O'Sullivan (Ireland)	12	33.11
		metres
High jump: Wanita May (Canada)		1.84
Pole vault: Janine Whitlock (Trafford)		4.20
Long jump: Jade Johnson (Herne Hill)		6.46
Triple jump: Deborah Rowe (Birchfield)		12.47
Shot: Judy Oakes (Croydon)		18.30
Pentathlon: Julia Bennett (Epsom and Ewell)		4,216 points

*Held at Birmingham, 23 January 2000

EUROPEAN INDOOR CHAMPIONSHIPS
Glen, Belgium, 25–27 February 2000

MEN

	min.	sec.
60 *metres*: Jason Gardener (GB)		6.49
200 *metres*: Christien Malcolm (GB)		20.54
400 *metres*: Ilya Dzhivondov (Bulgaria)		46.63
800 *metres*: Yuri Borzakovski (Russia)	1	47.92
1,500 *metres*: Jose Redolat (Spain)	3	40.51
3,000 *metres*: Mark Carroll (Ireland)	7	49.24
60 *metres hurdles*: Stanislavs Olijars (Latvia)		7.50
4 × 400 *metres relay*: Czech Republic	3	06.10
		metres
High jump: Vyacheslav Voronin (Russia)		2.34
Pole vault: Alex Averbukh (Israel)		5.75
Long jump: Petar Dachev (Bulgaria)		8.26
Triple jump: Charles Friedek (Germany)		17.28
Shot: Alexander Bagach (Ukraine)		21.18
Heptathlon: Tomas Dvorak (Czech Republic)		6,424 points

WOMEN

	min.	sec.
60 *metres*: Ekaterini Thanou (Greece)		7.05
200 *metres*: Muriel Hurtis (France)		23.06
400 *metres*: Svetlana Pospelova (Russia)		51.68
800 *metres*: Stephanie Graf (Austria)	1	59.70
1,500 *metres*: Violeta Szekely (Romania)	4	12.82
3,000 *metres*: Gabriele Szabo (Romania)	8	42.06
60 *metres hurdles*: Lidia Ferga (France)		7.88
4 × 400 *metres relay*: Russia	3	32.53
		metres
High jump: Kajsa Bergquist (Sweden)		2.00
Pole vault: Paula Hamackova (Czech Republic)		4.40
Long jump: Erica Johansson (Sweden)		6.89
Triple jump: Tatyana Lebedeva (Russia)		14.68
Shot: Larisa Peleshenko (Russia)		20.15
Pentathlon: Karin Ertl (Germany)		4,671 points

NATIONAL CROSS-COUNTRY CHAMPIONSHIPS
Stowe, 26 February 2000

MEN
Individual: Glynn Tromans (Coventry Godiva), 40min. 19sec.
Team: Tipton Harriers, 141 points

WOMEN
Individual: Tara Krzywicki (Charnwood), 27min. 21sec.
Team: Shaftesbury Barnet, 56 points

WORLD CROSS-COUNTRY CHAMPIONSHIPS
Vilamoura, Portugal, 18–19 March 2000

MEN (12.3 km)
Individual: Mohammed Mourhit (Belgium), 35min. 00sec.
Team: Kenya, 18 points

MEN (4,180 METRES)
Individual: John Kibowen (Kenya), 11 min. 11sec.
Team: Kenya, 10 points

WOMEN (8,080 METRES)
Individual: Derartu Tulu (Ethiopia), 25min. 42sec.
Team: Ethiopia, 20 points

WOMEN (4,180 METRES)
Individual: Kutre Dulecha (Ethiopia), 13min. 00sec.
Team: Portugal, 46 points

LONDON MARATHON
16 April 2000

Men: Antonio Pinto (Portugal), 2 hr. 06 min. 36 sec.
Women: Tegla Loroupe (Kenya), 2 hr. 24 min. 33 sec.

EUROPEAN CUP SUPER LEAGUE
Gateshead, 15–16 July 2000

MEN

	min.	sec.
100 *metres*: Darren Campbell (GB)		10.09
200 *metres*: Christian Malcolm (GB)		20.45
400 *metres*: Jamie Baulch (GB)		46.64
800 *metres*: Mehdi Baala (France)	1	47.90
1,500 *metres*: Mehdi Baala (France)	3	41.75
3,000 *metres*: Driss Maazouzi (France)	7	58.70
5,000 *metres*: Mustapha Essaid (France)	13	47.44
3,000 *metres steeplechase*: Bouabdallah Tahri (France)	8	27.28
110 *metres hurdles*: Falk Balzer (Germany)		13.52
400 *metres hurdles*: Chris Rawlinson (GB)		48.84
4 × 100 *metres relay*: Great Britain		38.41
4 × 400 *metres relay*: France	3	04.50

	metres
High jump: Stefan Holm (Sweden)	2.28
Pole vault: Yevgeni Smiryagin (Russia)	5.85
Long jump: Vitali Shkurlatov (Russia)	8.22
Triple jump: Larry Achike (GB)	17.31
Shot: Paolo Dal Soglio (Italy)	19.99
Discus: Lars Riedel (Germany)	63.30
Hammer: Christophe Epalle (France)	78.51
Javelin: Sergei Makarov (Russia)	89.92

Team points: Great Britain 101.5; Germany 101; France 97; Italy 96.5; Russia 88.5; Greece 88.5; Sweden 75; Hungary 62

WOMEN

	min.	sec.
100 *metres*: Ekaterini Thanou (Greece)		10.84
200 *metres*: Muriel Hurtis (France)		22.70
400 *metres*: Svetlana Pospelova (Russia)		50.63
800 *metres*: Irina Mistyukevich (Russia)	2	02.52
1,500 *metres*: Helen Pattinson (GB)	4	12.05
3,000 *metres*: Gabriela Szabo (Romania)	8	43.33
5,000 *metres*: Tatyana Tomashova (Russia)	14	53.00
100 *metres hurdles*: Linda Ferga (France)		12.93
400 *metres hurdles*: Tatyana Tereshchuk (Ukraine)		54.68
4 × 100 *metres relay*: France		42.97
4 × 400 *metres relay*: Russia	3	25.50

	metres
High jump: Monica Dinescu (Romania)	1.93
Pole vault: Svetlana Feofanova (Russia)	4.35
Long jump: Olga Rublyova (Russia)	6.87
Triple jump: Tatyana Lebedyeva (Russia)	14.98
Shot: Astrid Kumbernuss (Germany)	18.94
Discus: Nicoleta Grasu (Romania)	63.35
Hammer: Mihaela Melinte (Romania)	70.20
Javelin: Ana Termure (Romania)	63.23

Team points: Russia 123, Germany, 110; France 86; Romania 80; Italy 78; Great Britain 77; Ukraine 70; Greece 55

AAA CHAMPIONSHIPS
Birmingham, 11–13 August 2000

MEN

	min.	sec.
100 *metres*: Dwain Chambers (Belgrave)		10.11
200 *metres*: Darren Campbell (Belgrave)		20.49
400 *metres*: Mark Richardson (Windsor, Slough and Eton)		45.55
800 *metres*: James McIlroy (Ballymena)	1	50.08
1,500 *metres*: John Mayock (Barnsley)	3	45.29

5,000 *metres*: Andres Jones (Cardiff)	13	45.86
*10,000 *metres*: Kamiel Maase (Netherlands)	27	56.94
3,000 *metres steeplechase*: Christian Stephenson (Cardiff)	8	28.21
110 *metres hurdles*: Colin Jackson (Brecon)		13.54
400 *metres hurdles*: Chris Rawlinson (Belgrave)		48.95
10,000 *metres walk*: Matthew Hales (Steyning)	43	12.85

	metres
High jump: Ben Challenger (Belgrave)	2.22
Pole vault: Kevin Hughes (Enfield)	5.50
Long jump: George Audu (Puma TVH)	7.89
Triple jump: Phillips Idowu (Belgrave)	16.87
Shot: Stephan Hayward (Sale)	18.24
Discus: Bob Weir (Birchfield)	62.13
Hammer: Mick Jones (Belgrave)	71.51
Javelin: Steve Backley (Cambridge Harriers)	86.70

WOMEN

	min.	sec.
100 *metres*: Marcia Richardson (Windsor, Slough and Eton)		11.41
200 *metres*: Sarah Wilhemy (Southend)		23.39
400 *metres*: Donna Fraser (Croydon)		50.94
800 *metres*: Kelly Holmes (Ealing)	2	02.08
1,500 *metres*: Hayley Tullett (Swansea)	4	06.44
5,000 *metres*: Paula Radcliffe (Bedford)	15	05.48
*10,000 *metres*: Elana Meyer (South Africa)	31	41.10
100 *metres hurdles*: Diane Allahgreen (Liverpool)		13.24
400 *metres hurdles*: Keri Maddox (Sale)		55.22
10,000 *metres walk*: Lisa Kehler (Wolverhampton)	45	09.57

	metres
High jump: Jo Jennings-Steele (Rugby)	1.89
Pole vault: Janine Whitlock (Trafford)	4.10
Long jump: Joanne Wise (Coventry Godiva)	6.44
Triple jump: Michelle Griffith (Windsor, Slough and Eton)	13.67
Shot: Judy Oakes (Croydon)	17.91
Discus: Shelley Drew (Sutton)	59.03
Hammer: Lorraine Shaw (Sale)	66.85
Javelin: Kelly Morgan (Windsor, Slough and Eton)	58.45

*Held at Watford, 22 July 2000

BRITISH GRAND PRIX
Crystal Palace, London, 5–6 August 2000

MEN

	hr.	min.	sec.
100 *metres*: Bruny Surin (Canada)			10.16
200 *metres*: Barnard Williams (USA)			20.45
400 *metres*: Greg Haughton (Jamaica)			44.91
800 *metres*: Tony Whiteman (GB)		1	45.81
1 *mile*: Hicham El Guerrouj (Morocco)		3	45.96
5,000 *metres*: Haile Gebrselassie (Ethiopia)		13	06.23
110 *metres hurdles*: Allen Johnson (USA)			13.35
400 *metres hurdles*: Angelo Taylor (USA)			48.66

	metres
High jump: Vyacheslav Voronin (Russia)	2.40
Pole vault: Nick Hyong (USA)	5.80
Triple jump: Jonathan Edwards (GB)	17.34
Javelin: Aki Parviainen (Finland)	87.81

WOMEN

	hr.	min.	sec.
100 *metres*: Marion Jones (USA)			10.78
400 *metres*: Ana Guevara (Mexico)			50.12
1,500 *metres*: Violeta Szekely (Romania)		4	05.01
5,000 *metres*: Ayelech Worku (Ethiopia)		14	41.23
400 *metres hurdles*: Sandra Glover (USA)			53.92

	metres
Long jump: Inessa Kravets (Ukraine)	6.92

GB v. USA
Scotstoun, Glasgow, 2 July 2000

MEN

	min.	sec.
100 *metres*: Jason Gardener (GB)		10.40
200 *metres*: Christian Malcolm (GB)		20.65
400 *metres*: Danny McCray (USA)		45.59
800 *metres*: Derrick Peterson (USA)	1	46.95
1 *mile*: John Mayock (GB)	4	00.65
110 *metres hurdles*: Colin Jackson (GB)		13.65
400 *metres hurdles*: Chris Rawlinson (GB)		49.12
4 × 100 *metres relay*: United States		38.90

	metres
Discus: Tony Washington (USA)	61.19
High jump: Charles Austin (USA)	2.28
Javelin: Steve Backley (GB)	82.19

WOMEN

	min.	sec.
100 *metres*: Inger Miller (USA)		11.55
400 *metres*: Katharine Merry (GB)		50.99
1,500 *metres*: Helen Pattinson (GB)	4	12.05
100 *metres hurdles*: Anjanette Kirkland (USA)		12.96
40 × 100 *metres relay*: United States		44.56

	metres
Shot: Connie Price-Smith	18.02
High jump: Jo Jennings-Steele (GB)	1.88

Team Points: United States 129, Great Britain 120

BADMINTON

ENGLISH NATIONAL CHAMPIONSHIPS 2000
Burgess Hill, Bournemouth, February

Men's Singles: Colin Haughton beat Mark Constable 15–5, 15–9
Ladies Singles: Julia Mann beat Jill Pittard 11–2, 11–1
Men's Doubles: Simon Archer and Nathan Robertson beat Anthony Clark and Ian Sullivan 15–8, 15–10
Ladies Doubles: Ella Miles and Sara Sankey beat Emma Chaffin and Donna Kellogg 15–6, 15–6
Mixed Doubles: Ian Sullivan and Gail Emms beat James Anderson and Sara Sankey 15–4, 15–4

SCOTTISH NATIONAL CHAMPIONSHIPS 2000
Edinburgh, February

Men's Singles: Bruce Flockhart beat Alun Biggart 15–7, 15–0
Ladies' Singles: Fiona Sneddon beat Susan Hughes 11–4, 11–8
Men's Doubles: Alastair Gatt and Craig Robertson beat Russell Hogg and Kenny Middlemiss 10–15; 15–7, 15–4
Ladies' Doubles: Kirsteen McEwan and Sandra Watt beat Alexis Blanchflower and Carol Tedman 15–8, 15–5
Mixed Doubles: Kirsteen McEwan and Kenny Middlemiss beat Alexis Blanchflower and Russell Hogg 15–10, 15–11

WELSH NATIONAL CHAMPIONSHIPS 2000
Llanelli, February

Men's Singles: Richard Vaughan
Ladies' Singles: Kelly Morgan
Men's Doubles: Christopher Rees and Neil Cottrill
Ladies' Doubles: Jo Muggeridge and Felicity Callum
Mixed Doubles: Kelly Morgan and Richard Vaughan

ALL-ENGLAND CHAMPIONSHIPS 2000
Birmingham, March

Men's Singles: Xia Xuanze (China) beat Taufik Hidayat (Indonesia) 15–6, 15–13
Ladies' Singles: Gong Zhichao (China) beat Dai Yun (China) 11–5, 8–11, 11–5
Men's Doubles: Ha Tae-kwon and Kim Dong-moon (Korea) beat Lee Dong-soo and Yoo Yong-sung (Korea) 15–4, 13–15, 17–15
Ladies' Doubles: Ge Fei and Gu Jun (China) beat Chung Jae-hee and Ra Kyung-min (Korea) 15–5, 15–3
Mixed Doubles: Kim Dong-moon and Ra Kyung-min (Korea) beat Liu Yong and Ge Fei (China) 15–10, 15–2

BASEBALL

American League Championship Series winners 1999: New York Yankees
National League Championship Series winners 1999: Atlanta Braves
World Series 1999: New York Yankees beat Atlanta Braves 4–0

BASKETBALL

MEN
League Trophy final 2000: London Towers beat Manchester Giants 74–73
National Cup final 2000: Sheffield Sharks beat Manchester Giants 89–80
Premier League Championship 2000: Manchester Giants

WOMEN
Championship play-off final 2000: Sheffield Hatters beat Spelthorne Acers 64–52
National Cup final 2000: Rhondda Rebels beat Spelthorne Acers 65–38
National League Championship 2000: Sheffield Hatters

NORTH AMERICA
National Basketball League (NBA): Los Angeles Lakers beat Indiana Pacers 4–2 (best of 7 series)

BOBSLEIGH

COREL WORLD CUP STANDINGS
2-man bob: 1. Christian Reich (Switzerland); 2. Reto Götschi (Switzerland); 3. Marcel Rohner (Switzerland)
4-man bob: 1. Marcel Rohner (Switzerland); 2. Sandis Prousis (Latvia); 3. Pierre Lueders (Canada)
2-man nation: 1. Switzerland I; 2. Germany I; 3. Switzerland II
4-man nation: 1. Switzerland I; 2. Germany I; 3. Latvia I
Combined: 1. Marcel Rohner (Switzerland); 2. Christian Reich (Switzerland); 3. Pierre Lueders (Canada)

BOWLS – OUTDOOR

MEN
NATIONAL CHAMPIONSHIPS 2000
Worthing, August

Singles: John Ottaway (Wymondham Dell, Norfolk) beat Andy Wise (Marlow, Bucks) 21–9
Pairs: Wigton, Cumbria beat Felixstowe and Suffolk, Suffolk 24–13
Triples: Northern Electric, Northumberland beat Civil

Service Portsmouth, Hampshire 15–12
Fours: Acton Bridge, Lancashire beat Courtfield, Cumbria 24–14

BRITISH ISLES CHAMPIONSHIPS 2000
Llandridrod Wells, Wales, July

Singles: Nicky Brett (England) beat Mark Williams (Wales) 21–3
Pairs: Wales beat England 20–16
Triples: Wales beat Ireland 19–16
Fours: Wales beat Ireland 21–10

Home International Championship 2000: Scotland
Middleton Cup (Inter-County Championship) final 2000: Durham beat Norfolk 123–117

WOMEN

WORLD CHAMPIONSHIP 2000
Australia, March

Singles: Margaret Johnson (Ireland)
Pairs: Margaret Letham and Joyce Lindores (Scotland)
Triples: New Zealand
Fours: Australia
Team: England

NATIONAL CHAMPIONSHIPS 2000
Royal Leamington Spa, August
Singles (four woods): Anne Amderson (Co. Durham)
Singles (two woods): Maureen Tims (Warkwickshire)
Pairs: Pauline Morgan and Sue Langdon (Somerset)
Triples: Margaret Lawrence, Shân Maylin, Caroline Duarte (Surrey)
Fours: Ann Hayward, Rose Castle, Gill Carver, Shirley Page (Hertfordshire)

BRITISH ISLES CHAMPIONSHIPS 2000
Royal Leamington Spa, June

Singles: Hazel Wilson (Wales)
Pairs: Jean Morris and Jill Edson (England)
Triples: Marie Tormey, Patsy McCann and Pauline Day (Ireland)
Fours: Ina Culligan, Mary Elliott, Deidre McCulloch and Maeve Hoey (Ireland)

Home International Championship 2000: Wales
Johns Trophy (Inter-County Championship) final 2000: Surrey
Double Rink (Inter-county): Lincolnshire

BOXING

PROFESSIONAL BOXING
as at 1 September 2000

WORLD BOXING COUNCIL (WBC) CHAMPIONS
Heavy: Lennox Lewis (GB)
Cruiser: Juan Carlos Gomez (Cuba)
Light-heavy: Roy Jones (USA)
Super-middle: Glenn Catley (GB)
Middle: Keith Holmes (USA)
Light-middle: Javier Castillejo (Spain
Welter: Shane Moseley (USA)
Light-welter: Kostya Tszyu (Russia)
Light: Jose Luis Castillo (Mexico)
Super-bantam: Erik Morales (Mexico)
Bantam: Veeraphol Sahaprom (Thailand)
Super-fly: Cho In-joo (S. Korea)
Fly: Malcolm Tunacao (Philippines)
Light-fly: Yosam Choj (S. Korea)
Straw: Jose Antonio Aguirre (Mexico)

WORLD BOXING ASSOCIATION (WBA) CHAMPIONS
Heavy: vacant
Cruiser: Fabrice Tiozzo (France)
Light-heavy: Roy Jones (USA)
Super-middle: Bruno Girard (France)
Middle: William Joppy (USA)
Light-middle: Felix Trinidad (Puerto Rico)
Welter: James Page (USA)
Super-light: Sharmba Mitchell (USA)
Light: Takanori Hatakeyama (Japan)
Super-feather: Joel Casamayor (Cuba)
Feather: Freddy Norwood (USA)
Super-bantam: Clarence Adams (USA)
Bantam: Paulie Ayala (USA)
Super-fly: Hideki Tokada (Japan)
Fly: Sornpichai Kratchingdaeng (Thailand)
Light-fly: Phichit Chor Siriwat (Thailand)
Straw: Noel Arambulet (Venezuela)

WORLD BOXING ORGANISATION (WBO) CHAMPIONS
Heavy: Chris Byrd (USA)
Cruiser: Johnny Nelson (GB)
Light-heavy: Daruisz Michalczewski (Germany)
Super-middle: Joe Calzaghe (GB)
Middle: Armand Kranjnc (Sweden)
Welter: Ahmed Kotiev (Russia)
Light-welter: Randall Bailey (USA)
Light: Artur Grigorian (Uzbekistan)
Super-feather: Acelino Frietas (Brazil)
Feather: Naseem Hamed (GB)
Super-bantam: Marco Antonio Barerra (Mexico)
Bantam: Johnny Tapia (USA)
Super-fly: Adonis Rivas (Nicaragua)
Fly: Isidro Garcia (Mexico)
Light-fly: Peter Culshaw (GB)
Straw: Kermin Guardia (Columbia)

INTERNATIONAL BOXING FEDERATION (IBF) CHAMPIONS
Heavy: Lennox Lewis (GB)
Cruiser: Vassily Jirov (Kazakhstan)
Light-heavy: Roy Jones (USA)
Super-middle: Sven Ottke (Germany)
Middle: Bernard Hopkins (USA)
Light-middle: Fernando Vargas (USA)
Welter: vacant
Light-welter: Zab Judah (USA)
Light: Paul Spadafora (USA)
Super-feather: Diego Corrales (USA)
Feather: Paul Ingle (GB)
Super-bantam: Lehlo Ledwaba (S. Africa)
Bantam: Tim Austin (USA)
Super-fly: vacant
Fly: Irene Pacheco (Colombia)
Light-fly: Ricardo Lopez (Mexico)
Straw: Zolani Petelo (S. Africa)

BRITISH CHAMPIONS
Heavy: Julius Francis
Cruiser: vacant
Light-heavy: Clinton Woods
Super-middle: David Starie
Middle: Howard Eastman
Light-middle: Ensley Bingham
Welter: Derek Roche
Light-welter: Jason Rowland
Light: Bobby Vanzie
Super-feather: vacant
Feather: Jon Jo Irwin
Super-bantam: Drew Docherty

Bantam: Paul Lloyd
Fly: Keith Knox

EUROPEAN CHAMPIONS

Heavy: Vladimir Klitschko (Ukraine)
Cruiser: Alexei Iliin (Russia)
Light-heavy: Clinton Woods (GB)
Super-middle: Bruno Girard (France)
Middle: Erland Betare (France)
Light-middle: Roman Karmazin (Russia)
Welter: Alessandro Duran (Italy)
Light-welter: Thomas Damgaard (Denmark)
Light: Billy Schwer (GB)
Junior-light: Dennis Holbek (Denmark)
Feather: Steve Robinson (GB)
Super-bantam: Michael Brodie (GB)
Bantam: Johnny Bredahl (Denmark)
Fly: vacant

COMMONWEALTH CHAMPIONS

Heavy: Julius Francis (GB)
Cruiser: Bruce Scott (GB)
Light-heavy: Clinton Woods (GB)
Super-middle: David Starie (GB)
Middle: vacant
Light-middle: Tony Bedea (Canada)
Welter: Kofi Jantuah (Ghana)
Light-welter: Eamonn Magee (NI)
Light: Bobby Vanzie (GB)
Super-feather: vacant
Feather: Paul Ingle (GB)
Super-bantam: Michael Brodie (GB)
Bantam: Paul Lloyd (GB)
Fly: Keith Knox (GB)

AMATEUR BOXING

AMATEUR BOXING ASSOCIATION (ABA) CHAMPIONSHIP
WINNERS 2000

Super-heavy (91+ kg): John McDermott
Heavy (91 kg): David Dolan
Cruiser (86 kg): James Dolan
Light-heavy (81 kg): Peter Haymer
Middle (75 kg): Stephen Swales
Light-middle (71 kg): Chris Bessey
Welter (67 kg): Francis Doherty
Light-welter (63.5 kg): Nigel Wright
Light (60 kg): Andrew McLean
Feather (57 kg): Henry Castle
Bantam (54 kg): Steve Foster
Fly (51 kg): Dale Robinson
Light-fly (48 kg): James Mulhearn

CHESS

PCA World Champion: Garry Kasparov (Russia)
FIDE World Champion 2000: Alexander Khalifman (Russia)
British Champion 2000: Julian Hodgson
FIDE Women's World Champion 2000: event being held in October 2000
British Women's Champion 2000: Humpy Koneru (India)

CRICKET

TEST SERIES

ENGLAND V. SOUTH AFRICA

Johannesburg (25–28 November 1999): S. Africa beat England by an innings and 21 runs. England 122 and 260; S. Africa 403–9 dec.
Port Elizabeth (9–13 December): Match drawn. S. Africa 450 and 224–4; England 373 and 153–6
Durban (26–30 December): Match drawn. England 366–9 dec.; S. Africa 156 and 572–7
Cape Town (2–6 January 2000): S. Africa beat England by an innings and 37 runs. England 258 and 126; S. Africa 421
Centurion (14–18 January): England beat S. Africa by 2 wickets. S. Africa 248–8; England 251–8 (England forfeited 1st innings, S. Africa forfeited 2nd innings)

ENGLAND V. ZIMBABWE

Lord's (18–21 May): England beat Zimbabwe by an innings and 209 runs. Zimbabwe 83 and 123; England 415
Nottingham (1–5 June): Match drawn. England 374 and 147; Zimbabwe 285–4 dec. and 25–1

ENGLAND V. WEST INDIES – WISDEN TROPHY 2000

Birmingham (15–17 June): West Indies beat England by an innings and 93 runs. West Indies 397. England 179 and 125
Lord's (29 June–1 July): England beat West Indies by 2 wickets. West Indies 267 and 54; England 134 and 191
Manchester (3–7 August): Match drawn. West Indies 157 and 438–7 dec. England 303 and 80–1
Headingley (17–18 August): England beat West Indies by an innings and 39 runs. England 272; West Indies 172 and 61
The Foster's Oval (31 August–4 September)

ONE-DAY INTERNATIONALS

ENGLAND TOUR OF SOUTH AFRICA AND ZIMBABWE

Centurion (9 February): game abandoned
Bulawayo (16 February): England beat Zimbabwe by 5 wickets. England 199–5; Zimbabwe 194–7
Bulawayo (18 February): England beat Zimbabwe by 1 wicket. England 134–9; Zimbabwe 131
Harare (20 February): England beat Zimbabwe by 85 runs. England 248–7; Zimbabwe 163

TRIANGULAR TOURNAMENT 2000

Johannesburg (21 January): South Africa beat Zimbabwe by 6 wickets. South Africa 229–4; Zimbabwe 226
Bloemfontein (23 January): England beat South Africa by 9 wickets. England 185–1; South Africa 184
Cape Town (26 January): South Africa beat England by 1 run. South Africa 204–7; England 203–9
Cape Town (28 January): Zimbabwe beat England by 104 runs. Zimbabwe 211–7; England 107
Kimberley (30 January): England beat Zimbabwe by 8 wickets. England 162–2; Zimbabwe 161–9
Durban (2 February): Zimbabwe beat South Africa by 2 wickets. Zimbabwe 223–8; South Africa 222–7
East London (4 February): South Africa beat England by 2 wickets. South Africa 233–8; England 231–6
Port Elizabeth (6 February): South Africa beat Zimbabwe by 53 runs. South Africa 204–7; Zimbabwe 151
Final Johannesburg (13 February): South Africa beat England by 38 runs. South Africa 149; England 111

NATWEST SERIES 2000

Bristol (6 July): Zimbabwe beat West Indies by 6 wickets. Zimbabwe 233–4; West Indies 232–7
London (8 July): Zimbabwe beat England by 5 wickets. Zimbabwe 210–5; England 207
London (9 July): No result. England 1, West Indies 1
Canterbury (11 July): Zimbabwe beat West Indies by 70 runs. Zimbabwe 256–4; West Indies 1868
Manchester (13 July): England beat Zimbabwe by 8

wickets. England 115–2; Zimbabwe 114
Chester-le-Street (15 July): England beat West Indies by 10
wickets. England 171; West Indies 169–8
Chester-le-Street (16 July): Zimbabwe beat West Indies by
6 wickets. Zimbabwe 290–4; West Indies 287–5
Birmingham (18 July): England beat Zimbabwe by 52 runs.
England 262–8; Zimbabwe 210–9
Nottingham (20 July): West Indies beat England by 3 runs.
West Indies 195–9; England 192
London (22 July): England beat Zimbabwe by 6 wickets.
England 170–4; Zimbabwe 169–7

OTHER INTERNATIONAL CUPS

Asia Cup 2000: Pakistan beat Sri Lanka by 39 runs.
Pakistan 277–4; Sri Lanka 238
Coca Cola Cup 2000: Pakistan beat South Africa by 16 runs.
Pakistan 263–6; South Africa 247

OTHER INTERNATIONAL DOMESTIC
CHAMPIONSHIPS

Australia: ACB Cup 1999–2000: Victoria Second XI beat
South Australia Second XI by 3 wickets. Victoria Second
XI 182–7; South Australia Second XI 178; Pura Milk
Cup 1999–2000: Match drawn. Queensland beat
Victoria; Mercantile Mutual Cup 1999–2000: Western
Australia beat Queensland by 45 runs. Western
Australia 301–6; Queensland 256
Bangladesh: Chittagong beat Barisal by 189 runs.
Chittagong 200 and 198–4; Barisal 135 and 74–9
India: Challenger Series 1999–2000: India beat India 'A'
by 84 runs. India 320–9; India 'A' 236–9; Duleep
Trophy: Match drawn. North Zone beat West Zone;
Irani Trophy 1999–2000: Rest of India beat Karnataka
by an innings and 60 runs. Rest of India 321.
Karnataka170 and 91; Ranji Trophy 1999–2000:
Mumbai beat Hyderabad by 297 runs. Mumbai 376 and
409. Hyderabad 195 and 293; *Wills Trophy 1998–9*:
Madhya Pradesh beat Bengal by 32 runs. Madhya
Pradesh 225; Bengal 193
New Zealand: Hawke Cup 1999–2000: Dunedin
Metropolitan beat Bay of Plenty by 10 runs. Dunedin
199 and 129. Bay of Plenty 177 and 141; National Club
Championship 1999–2000: Match abandoned between
Green Island and Wanderers; Shell Cup 1999–2000: 1st
Final Canterbury beat Auckland by 2 runs. Canterbury
185–8. Auckland 183–9; 2nd Final Canterbury beat
Auckland by 7 wickets. Canterbury 225–3. Auckland
224–6; Shell Trophy 1999–2000: Northern Districts
beat Auckland by 267 runs. Northern Districts 292 and
367. Auckland 208 and 184
Pakistan: NBP Cup 1999–2000: Habib Bank Limited beat
Khan Research Labs by 19 runs. Habib Bank 182. Khan
Research Labs 163; Quaid-e-Azam Trophy 1999–2000:
Pakistan International Airlines beat Habib Bank
Limited by 8 wickets. Pakistan International Airlines
112 and 106. Habib Bank 171 and 166–2; Tissot Cup
1999–2000: Pakistan International Airlines beat Redco
Pakistan Ltd by 38 runs. Pakistan International Airlines
310–4. Redco Pakistan 272–9
South Africa: Standard Bank Cup 1999–2000: Boland beat
Eastern Province by 36 runs. Boland 209–6. Eastern
Provice 173–8; SuperSport Series 1999–2000: Gauteng
beat Border by 3 wickets. Gauteng 387 and 182–7.
Border 346 and 222; UCB Bowl (one day) 1999–2000:
Free State 'B' beat Zimbabwe Board XI by 5 runs. Free
State 'B' 195–9. Zimbabwe Board XI 190
West Indies: Busta Cup 1999–2000: Jamaica beat Leeward
Islands in 1st innings. Jamaica 333. Leeward Islands 142;
Red Stripe Bowl 1999–2000: Jamaica beat Leeward
Islands by 10 runs. Jamaica 177–6. Leeward Islands
228–7

Zimbabwe: Logan Cup 1999-2000: Mashonaland beat
Manicaland by 257 runs. Mashonaland 345 and 275–5
dec. Manicaland 123 and 240; Vigne Cup 1999–2000:
Old Hararians beat Harare Sports Club by 5 wickets.
Old Hararians 95–4. Harare Sports Club 92

OTHER RESULTS 2000

Benson and Hedges Cup final: Gloucestershire beat
Glamorgan by 7 wickets. Gloucestershire 226–3;
Glamorgan 225
NatWest Trophy final: Gloucestershire beat Warwickshire
by 22 runs (Duckworth/Lewis Method).
Gloucestershire 122–3; Warwickshire 205–7
National League Champions: Division 1, Lancashire;
Division 2, Sussex
ECB County Cup final: Herefordshire beat Cheshire by
42 runs. Herefordshire 291–6; Cheshire 249–9
Varsity Match (one-day): Cambridge beat Oxford by 2
wickets. Cambridge 234–8; Oxford 233–9
Varsity Match (three-day): Cambridge drew with Oxford.
Cambridge 382–4 dec; Oxford 71

CYCLING

Tour of Burgos: Leonardo Piepoli (Italy)
Tour of Italy 2000: Stefano Garzelli (Italy)
Tour de France 2000: Lance Armstrong (USA)
Tour of Spain 2000: Roberto Heras Friere (Spain)
Tour of Switzerland 2000: Roberto Heras Friere (Spain)
World Cup series overall winner 2000: Johan Museeuw
(Belgium)
World Cyclo-Cross Championship 2000: Richard
Groenendaal (Netherlands)
World Cyclo-Cross series overall winner 2000: Sven Nus
(Belgium)
British Cyclo-Cross Championship 2000: Roger Hammond
(Collstrop)
British Road Race Championship 2000: John Tanner
(Pro Vision-plant X)

Women's World Road Race Championship 1999:
E. Pucinskaite (Lithuania)
Women's National Road Race Championship 2000
Ceris Gilfillan (Alsager)

DARTS

Embassy World Championship 2000: Ted Hankey (England)
beat Ronnie Baxter (England) 6–0

EQUESTRIANISM

SHOW JUMPING

World Cup final 2000: Rodrigo Pessoa (Brazil) on Gandini
Baloubet du Rouet
British Jumping Derby 2000 (Hickstead): John Whitaker
(GB) on Virtual Village Welham

THREE-DAY EVENTING

European Championships 1999:
Individual: Pippa Funnell (GB) on Supreme Rock
Team: Great Britain

Badminton Horse Trials 2000: Mary King (GB) on
Star Appeal
British Open Horse Trials 2000 (Gatcombe Park): William
Fox-Pitt (GB) on Moon Man
Burghley Horse Trials 2000: Andrew Nicholson (New
Zeland) on Mr Smissy

ETON FIVES

Amateur Championship (Kinnaird Cup) 2000: James Toop and Matthew Wiseman beat Ed Taylor and Ian Hutchinson 3–0
Alan Barber Cup final 2000: Old Olavians beat Old Salopians 3–0
County Championship final 2000: Kent beat Berkshire 3–0
League Championship (Douglas Keeble Cup) 2000: Old Olavians
Holmwoods Schools' Championship 2000: Harrow I beat Shrewsbury I 3–0
Holmwoods Preparatory Schools' Tournament 2000: Highgate beat Ludgrove 2–1

FENCING

MEN

WORLD CHAMPIONS 1999
Seoul, Korea, November

Foil: Sergei Goloubitski (Ukraine)
Epée: Arnd Schmitt (Germany)
Sabre: Damien Touya (France)
Team Foil: France
Team Epée: France
Team Sabre: France

EUROPEAN CHAMPIONS 2000
Madeira, Portugal, April
Foil: Max Kristian Hellström (Sweden)
Epée: Robert Andrzejuk (Poland)
Sabre: Fernando Casares (Spain)
BRITISH CHAMPIONS 2000
RAF Cosford, Albrighton, July
Foil: James Beevers (Sussex House)
Epée: Simon Austin (London Thames)
Sabre: James Williams (Salle Jakeb)
Team Foil: Sussex House

Corble Cup 2000 (international sabre world cup series): Stanislav Pozdniakov (Russia)
Glasgow Cup 2000 (international epée world cup series): Kaido Kaaberma (Estonia)

WOMEN

WORLD CHAMPIONS 1999
Seoul, Korea, November
Foil: Valentina Vezzali (Italy)
Epée: Laura Flessel-Colovic (France)
Sabre: Yelena Jemaeva (Azerbaijan)
Team Foil: Germany
Team Epée: Hungary
Team Sabre: Italy

EUROPEAN CHAMPIONS 2000
Madeira, Portugal, April
Foil: Bianca Becker (Germany)
Epée: Mojca Matko (Slovenia)
Sabre: Cecile Argiolas (France)
Team Foil: Germany
Team Espée: Hungary
Team Sabre: Italy
BRITISH CHAMPIONS 1999
RAF Cosford, Albrighton, July
Foil: Linda Strachan (Salle Boston)
Epée: Georgina Usher (Haverstock)
Sabre: Beth Davidson (Salle Stretton)

Team Foil: Salle Boston
Ipswich Cup 2000 (international epée world cup series): Tatiana Logounova (Russia)

GOLF (MEN)

THE MAJOR CHAMPIONSHIPS 2000
US Masters (Augusta, Georgia, 6–9 April): Vijay Singh (Fiji), 278
US Open (Pebble Beach, California, 15–18 June): Tiger Woods (USA), 272
The Open (St Andrews, 20–23 July): Tiger Woods (USA), 269
US PGA Championship (Valhalla Golf Club, Louisville, 17–20 August): Tiger Woods (USA), 270

WORLD RANKINGS (AS AT 11 SEPTEMBER 2000)
1. Tiger Woods (USA); 2. Ernie Els (S. Africa); 3. David Duval (USA); 4. Colin Montgomerie (GB); 5. Phil Michelson (USA); 6. Hal Sutton (USA): 7. Lee Westwood (GB); 8. David Love III (USA); 9. Vijay Singh (Fiji); 10. Jesper Parnevik (Sweden)

PGA EUROPEAN TOUR 1999
Belgacom Open (Knokke-Le-Zoute): Robert Karlsson (Sweden) 272
WGC-Anderen Consulting Matchplay (Carlsbad, California) Jeff Maggert (USA) beat Andrew Hagee (USA) at 2nd extra hole
Volvo PGA Championship (Surrey): Colin Montgomerie (Scotland), 270
European Tour Order of Merit 1999: 1. Colin Montgomerie (GB); 2. Lee westwood (GB); 3. Sergio Garcia (Spain)

PGA EUROPEAN TOUR 2000
Alfred Dunhill (Johannesburg): Anthony Wall (GB), 204
Mercedes-Benz South African Open Championship (Johannesburg): Mathias Gronberg (Sweden), 274
Heineken Classic (Perth, Australia): Michael Campbell (New Zealand), 268
Greg Norman Holden International (Sydney, Australia): Lucas Parsons (Australia), 273
Benson and Hedges Malaysian Open (Kuala Lumpur): Yeh Wei-Tze (Taiwan), 278
Algarve Portuguese Open (Penina): Gary Orr (GB), 275
WGC-Andersen Consulting Match Play (Carlsbad, California): Darren Clarke (N. Ireland)
Dubai Desert Classic: Jose Coceres (Argentina), 274
Qatar Masters (Doha): Rolf Muntz (Netherlands), 280
Madeira Island Open: Niclas Fasth (Sweden), 279
Brazil Rio de Janeiro 500 Years Open (Rio de Janeiro): Roger Chapman (GB), 270
Brazil Sao Paulo 500 Years Open (Sao Paulo): Padraig Harrington (Ireland), 270
Moroccan Open (Marrakech): Jamie Spence (GB) 266
Peugeot Open de Espana (Girona, Spain): Brian Davis (GB), 274
Novotel Perrier Open de France (Paris, France): Colin Montogmerie (GB), 272
Benson and Hedges International Open (The Belfry): Jose Maria Olazabal (Spain), 275
Deutsche Bank – SAP Open TPC of Europe (Hamburg Germany): Lee Westwood (GB), 273
Volvo PGA Championship (Wentworth): Colin Montgomerie (GB), 271
The Compass Group English Open (Warwicks): Darren Clarke (N. Ireland), 275

The Celtic Manor Resort Wales Open (Newport): Steen Tinnring (Denmark), 273
Compaq European Grand Prix (Slaley Hall): Lee Westwood (GB), 276
Murphy's Irish Open (Co. Kerry): Patrick Sjöland (Sweden), 270
Smurfit European Open (Dublin): Lee Westwood (GB), 276
Standard Life Loch Lomond: Ernie Els (S. Africa), 273
TNT Dutch Open (Hilversum): Stephen Leaney (Australia), 269
Volvo Scandinavian Masters (Malmö): Lee Westwood (GB), 270
Victor Chandler British Masters (Milton Keynes): Gary Orr (GB), 267
Buzzgolf.com North West of Ireland Open (Co. Cavan): Massimo Scarpa (Italy), 275
Scottish PGA Championship (Glenagles): Pierre Fulke (Sweden), 271
BMW International Open (Munich): Thomas Björn (Denmark), 268
Canon European Masters (Crans-sur-Sierre): Eduardo Romero (Argentina), 261
Lancôme Trophy (St-Nom-la-Bretêche): Retief Goosen (S. Africa), 271

World Matchplay Championship Final 1999 (Wentworth): Colin Montgomerie (GB) beat Mark O Meara (USA) 3 and 2

MAJOR TEAM EVENTS

Alfred Dunhill Cup final 1999 (St Andrews, 7–10 October): Spain beat Australia 2–1
Walker Cup 1999 (Nairn, 11–12 September): Great Britain and Ireland beat USA 15–9

AMATEUR CHAMPIONSHIPS

British Amateur Championship 2000 (Royal Liverpool and Wallasay): Mikko Iionen (Finland)
English Amateur Championship 2000 (Royal Lytham and St Anne's): Paul Casey (Burhill)
Welsh Amateur Championship 2000 (Royal St David's): J. G. Jermine (Sunningdale)
Scottish Amateur Championship 2000 (Royal Dornoch): Steven O'Hara (Colville Park)
Brabazon Trophy (English Open Strokeplay) 2000 (Woodhall Spa): Jochen Lupprian (Germany), 284
Welsh Open Strokeplay 2000 (Ashburnham): J. R. Donaldson (Macclesfield)
Scottish Open Strokeplay 2000 (Letham Grange): Simon Mackenzie (West Linton)
Lytham Trophy 2000 (Royal Lytham and St Anne's): David Dixon (GB), 286
Berkshire Trophy 2000 (The Berkshire): Colin Edwards (Bath) and Kevin Freeman (Gerrards Cross), 281
Eisenhower Trophy: (Berlin): USA 841
Home International Championship 2000 (Carnoustie): Scotland
* After a play-off

GOLF (WOMEN)

US Women's Open 2000 (Merit Club, Libertyville, Illinois): Karrie Web (Australia), 282
Women's World Championship 1999 (Rush Creek Golf Club, Maple Grove, Minnesota): Se Ri Pak (Korea), 280

EUROPEAN LPGA TOUR 1999

Air France Open (Le Phare Biarritz): Sofia Gronberg Whitmore (Sweden), 200

Marrakesh Open: Trish Johnson (GB), 204
European Cup (Praia d'El Rey, Portugal): Men's Senior Tour 10, European LPGA Tour 10. Men's Senior Tour retained cup
European Tour Order of Merit 1999: 1. Laura Davies (GB); 2. Catrin Nilsmark (Sweden); 3. Alison Nicholas (GB)

EUROPEAN LPGA TOUR 2000

Royal Marie-Claire Open (Evian): Silvia Cavalleri (Italy), 215
Evian Masters (Evian-les-Bains, France): Annika Sörenstam (Sweden), 276
British Masters (Prestbury): Trish Johnson (GB), 207
Chrysler Open (Halmstad, Sweden): Carin Koch (Sweden), 277
French Open (Arras): Patricia Meunier Lebouc (France), 271
Austrian Open (Frohnleiten): Patricia Meunier Lebouc (France), 206
German Open (Treudelberg): Joanne Morley (GB), 274
Championship of Europe (Gleneagles): Laura Davies (GB), 280*
British Open (Walton Heath): Sophie Gustafson (Sweden), 282
Compaq Open (Malmo, Sweden): Juli Inkster (USA), 282
Laura Davies Invitational (Brocket Hall, Herts): Sofia Gronberg Whitmore (Sweden), 275*
Irish Open (Faithlegg): Marine Monnet (France), 209
Expo 2000 Open (Hanover): Alison Munt (Australia), 212
Italian Open (Florence): Sophie Gustafson (Sweden), 284

AMATEUR CHAMPIONSHIPS

British Open Championship 2000 (Walton Heath): Rebecca Hudson (GB)
English Amateur Championship 2000 (Hunstanton): Emma Duggleby (Malton and Norton)
Welsh Amateur Championship 2000 (Pyle and Kenfig): Kathryn Evans (Conwy)
Scottish Amateur Championship 2000 (Machrihanish): Lynn Kenny (Dunblane)
British Strokeplay 2000 (Royal County Down): Rebecca Hudson (Wheatley)
English Strokeplay 2000 (Silloth-on-Solway): Rebecca Hudson (Wheatley)
Welsh Strokeplay 2000 (Ashburnham): Rebecca Prout (Betchworth Park)
Scottish Strokeplay 2000 Portland and Royal Troon/ Rebecca Hudson (Wheatley)
Home International Championship 2000 (Royal St David's): England
European Amateur Championship 2000 (Amber Baltic, Poland): Emma Duggleby (GB) 283*
European Amateur Team Championship 2000 (Castelconturbia, Italy): Italy
*After a play-off

GREYHOUND RACING

1999
Cesarewitch (Catford): Bubbly Prince
Gold Collar (Catford): Rio Scorpio
Laurels (Belle Vue): Derbay Flyer
The Derby (Milton Keynes): Black Head
Oaks (Wimbledon): Spring Time
St Leger (Wimbledon): Tessas Dilemma
Summer Cup (Milton Keynes): Farloe Bonus
Television Trophy (Wimbledon): Hollinwood Poppy 2000

2000
Grand National (Wimbledon): Tuttles Minister
Grand Prix (Walthamstow): Palace Issue
Derby (Wimbledon): Rapid Ranger
The Greyhound Derby (Peterborough): Reactabond Rebel
Ladbroke Golden Jacket (Crayford): Knappogue Oak
The Masters (Reading): Jicky
The Regency (Brighton): Knappogue Oak
Scurry Gold Cup (Catford): El Boss

GYMNASTICS

BRITISH MEN'S CHAMPIONSHIPS 2000
Wigan, July

British Champion: Kanukai Jackson (Harrow)
Individual Apparatus Champions:
Floor: Dominic Brindle (Leeds)
Pommel Horse: Ross Brewer (Woking)
Rings: John Smethurst (Manchester)
Vault: David Colvin (Fromeside)
Parallel Bars: Barry Collie (Hinckley)
High Bar: Barry Collie (Hinkley)
British Men's Team Champions 2000: Hinckley

BRITISH WOMEN'S CHAMPIONSHIPS 2000
Guildford, July

British Champion: Emma Williams (Liverpool)
Individual Apparatus Champions:
Floor: Annika Reeder (S. Essex)
Beam: Emma Williams (Liverpool)
Vault: Emma Williams (Liverpool)
Assymetric Bars: Caroline Gilbert (S. Essex)
British Women's Team Champions 2000: S. Essex

WORLD CUP SERIES, GRAND PRIX
Glasgow, November 1999

MEN

Floor: Jordan Jovtchev (Bulgaria) 9.825
Pommel Horse: Marius Urzica (Romania) 9.900
Rings: Szilvester Sollany (Spain) 9.850
Vault: Gervasio Deferr (Spain) 9.750
Parallel Bars: Jesus Carballo (Spain) 9.800
High Bar: Jesus Carballo (Spain) 9.775

WOMEN

Floor: Elana Produnova (Russia) 9.775
Beam: Andrea Raducan (Romaina) 9.800
Vault: E. Zamolodchikova (Russia) 9.725
Assymetric Bars: Svetlana Khorkina (Russia) 9.825

HOCKEY

MEN
English Hockey League Premier Division 2000: Canterbury
English Hockey League Premiership final 2000: Cannock beat
   Canterbury 3–2
National Indoor Club Championship final 2000: Old
   Loughtonians beat St Albans 10–7
County Championship final 2000: Surrey beat
   Gloucestershire 2–1
Champions Trophy final 1999: Netherlands beat Germany
   3–1
European Club Championship final 2000: Der Alster
   Hamburg (Germany) 1, Bloemendaal (Netherlands)
   1. Germany won 5–3 on penalties
European Nations Cup final 2000: Spain

European Indoor Club Champion final 2000: Dürkheimer
   (Germany)
European Cup Winners' Cup final 2000: Athletic Terrassa
   (Spain) beat Reading (GB) 4–3
Varsity Match 2000: Oxford beat Cambridge 2–1
WOMEN

English Hockey League Premier Division 2000: Hightown
English Hockey League Premiership final 1999: Hightown
   beat Ipswich 3–1
English Hockey Indoor League Premier Division 2000:
   Chelmsford
Champions Trophy final 2000: Netherlands beat Germany
   3–2
European Nations Cup final 2000: The Netherlands
European Club Championship final 2000: Den Bosch
   (Netherlands) beat Berliner (Germany) 7–0
European Indoor Club Championship final 2000:
   Rüsselsheim (Germany)
European Cup Winners' Cup final 2000: Rot Weiss Cologne
   (Germany) beat Amsterdam (Netherlands) 4–3
Varsity Match 2000: Cambridge 1, Oxford 1

HORSE-RACING

RESULTS
CAMBRIDGESHIRE HANDICAP
(1839) Newmarket, 1 mile

1996	Clifton Fox (4y), (8st 2lb), N. Day
1997	Pasternak (4y), (9st 1lb), G. Duffield
1998	Lear Spear (3y), (8st 4lb), N. Pollard
1999	She's Our Mare (6y), (7st 12lb), F. Norton

PRIX DE L'ARC DE TRIOMPHE
(1920) Longchamp, 1½ miles

1996	Helissio (3y), (8st 11lb), O. Peslier
1997	Peintre Célèbre (3y), (8st 11lb), O. Peslier
1998	Sagamix (3y), (8st 11lb), O. Peslier
1999	Montjeu (3y), (8st 11lb), M. Kinane

CESAREWITCH
(1839) Newmarket, 2 miles and about 2 f

1996	Inchcailloch (7y), (7st 10lb), R. Ffrench
1997	Turnpole (6y), (7st 10lb), L. Charnock
1998	Spirit of Love (3y), (8st 8lb), O. Peslier
1999	Top Cees (9y), (8st 10lb), K. Fallon

CHAMPION STAKES
(1877) Newmarket, 1 mile, 2 f

1996	Bosra Sham (3y), (8st 8lb), P. Eddery
1997	Pilsudski (5y), (9st 2lb), M. Kinane
1998	Alborada (3y), (8st 8lb), G. Duffield
1999	Alborada (4y), (8st 13lb), G. Duffield

*HENNESSY GOLD CUP
(1957) Newbury, 3 miles and about 2½ f

1997	Suny Bay (8y), (11st 8lb), G. Bradley
1998	Teeton Mill (9y), (10st 5lb), N. Williamson
1999	Ever Bless (6y), (10st), T. J. Murphy

*KING GEORGE VI CHASE
(1937) Kempton, about 3 miles

1996	One Man (8y), (11st 10lb), R. Dunwoody
1997	See More Business (7y), (11st 10lb), A. Thornton
1998	Teeton Mill (9y), (11st 10lb), N. Williamson
1999	See More Business (9y), (11st 10lb),
	M. A. Fitzgerald

*DUBAI WORLD CUP
(1957) Dubai, 1 mile and 2 f

| 2000 | Dubai Millennium (4y), (10st 8lb), L. Dettori |

THE CLASSICS
ONE THOUSAND GUINEAS
(1814) Rowley Mile, Newmarket, for three-year-old fillies

Year	Winner	Betting	Owner	Jockey	Trainer	No. of Runners
1997	Sleepytime	5–1	C. Wacker III	K. Fallon	H. Cecil	15
1998	Cape Verdi	100–30	Godolphin	F. Dettori	Saeed bin Suroor	16
1999	Wince	4–1	Prince K. Abdulla	K. Fallon	H. Cecil	22
2000	Lahan	14–1	Hamdan Al Maktoum	R. Hills	J. Gosden	18

Record time: 1 minute 36.71 seconds by Las Meninas in 1994

TWO THOUSAND GUINEAS
(1809) Rowley Mile, Newmarket, for three-year-olds

Year	Winner	Betting	Owner	Jockey	Trainer	No. of Runners
1997	Entrepreneur	11–2	M. Tabor	M. Kinane	M. Stoute	16
1998	King of Kings	7–2	Mrs J. Magnier/M. Tabor	M. Kinane	A. O'Brien	18
1999	Island Sands	10–1	Godolphin	F. Dettori	Saeed bin Suroor	16
2000	King's Best	13–2	Saeed Suhail	K. Fallon	Sir Michael Stoute	27

Record time: 1 minute 35.08 seconds by Mister Baileys in 1994

THE DERBY
(1780) Epsom, 1 mile and about 4 f, for three-year-olds

The first winner was Sir Charles Bunbury's Diomed in 1780. The owners with the record number of winners are Lord Egremont, who won in 1782, 1804, 1805, 1807, 1826 (also won five Oaks); and the late Aga Khan, who won in 1930, 1935, 1936, 1948, 1952. Other winning owners are: Duke of Grafton (1802, 1809, 1810, 1815); Mr J. Bowes (1835, 1843, 1852, 1853); Sir J. Hawley (1851, 1858, 1859, 1868); the 1st Duke of Westminster (1880, 1882, 1886, 1899); and Sir Victor Sassoon (1953, 1957, 1958, 1960).

Record times are: 2min. 32.31sec. by Lammtarra in 1995; 2min. 33.80sec. by Mahmoud in 1936; 2min. 33.84sec. by Kahyasi in 1988; 2 min. 33.88 by High-Rise in 1998; 2min. 33.9sec. by Reference Point in 1987.

The Derby was run at Newmarket in 1915–18 and 1940–5.

Year	Winner	Betting	Owner	Jockey	Trainer	No. of Runners
1997	Benny The Dip	11–1	L. Knight	W. Ryan	J. Gosden	13
1998	High Rise	20–1	Sheikh Mohammed Obaidh Al Maktoum	O. Peslier	L. Cumani	15
1999	Oath	13–2	Prince Ahmed Salman	K. Fallon	H. Cecil	16
2000	Sinndar	7–1	Aga Khan	J. Murtagh	J. Oxx	8

THE OAKS
(1779) Epsom, 1 mile and about 4 f, for three-year-old fillies

Year	Winner	Betting	Owner	Jockey	Trainer	No. of Runners
1997	Reams of Verse	5–6	Prince K. Abdulla	K. Fallon	H. Cecil	12
1998	Shahtoush	12–1	Mrs D. Nagle/Mrs J. Magnier	M. Kinane	A. O'Brien	8
1999	Ramruma	3–1	Prince Fahd Salman	K. Fallon	H. Cecil	10
2000	Love Divine	9–4	Lordship Stud	T. Quinn	H. Cecil	18

Record time: 2 minutes 34.19 seconds by Intrepidity in 1993

ST LEGER
(1776) Doncaster, 1mile and about 6 f, for three-year-olds

Year	Winner	Betting	Owner	Jockey	Trainer	No. of Runners
1996	Shantou	8–1	Sheikh Mohammed	F. Dettori	J. Gosden	11
1997	Silver Patriarch	5–4	P. Winfield	P. Eddery	J. Dunlop	10
1998	Nedawi	5–2	Godolphin	J. Reid	Saeed bin Suroor	9
1999	Mutafaweq	11–2	Godolphin	R. Hills	Saeed bin Suroor	9

Record time: 3 minutes 1.60 seconds by Coronach in 1926 and Windsor Lad in 1934

*CHAMPION HURDLE
(1927) Cheltenham, 2 miles and about $\frac{1}{2}$ f

1997	Make A Stand (6y), (12st), A. McCoy
1998	Istabraq (6y), (12st), C. Swan
1999	Istabraq (7y), (12st), C. Swan
2000	Istabraq (8y), (12st), C. Swan

*QUEEN MOTHER CHAMPION CHASE
(1959) Cheltenham, about 2 miles

1997   Martha's Son (10y), (12st), R. Farrant
1998   One Man (10y), (12st), B. Harding
1999   Call Equiname (9y), (12st), M. Fitzgerald
2000   Edredon Bleu (8y), (12st), A. P. McCoy

*CHELTENHAM GOLD CUP
(1924) 3 miles and about $2\frac{1}{2}$ f

1997   Mr Mulligan (9y), (12st), A. McCoy
1998   Cool Dawn (10y), (12st), A. Thornton
1999   See More Business (9y), (12st), M. Fitzgerald
2000   Looks Like Trouble (8y), (12st), R. Johnson

LINCOLN HANDICAP
(1965) Doncaster, 1 mile

1997   Kuala Lipis (4y), (8st 6lb), T. Quinn
1998   Hunters Of Brora (8y), (9st), J. Weaver
1999   Right Wing (5y), (9st 5lb), T. Quinn
2000   John Ferneley (5y), (8st, 10lb), F. Fortune

*GRAND NATIONAL
(1837) Liverpool, 4 miles and about 4 f

1997   Lord Gyllene (9y), (10st), A. Dobbin
1998   Earth Summit (10y), (10st 5lb), C. Llewellyn
1999   Bobbyjo (9y), (10st), P. Carberry
2000   Papillon (9y), (10st 12lb), R. Walsh

Record times: 8 minutes 47.8 seconds by Mr Frisk in 1990;
9 minutes 1.9 seconds by Red Rum in 1973

*WHITBREAD GOLD CUP
(1957) Sandown, 3 miles and about 5 f

1997   Harwell Lad (8y), (10st), Mr R. Nuttall
1998   Call It A Day (8y), (10st 10lb), A. Maguire
1999   Eulogy (9y), (10st), B. Fenton
2000   Beau (7yr), (10st 9lb), C. Llewellyn

JOCKEY CLUB CUP
(1894) Newmarket, 2 miles, 24 yds

1997   Time Allowed (4y), (8st 6lb), J. Reid
1998   Romanov (4y), (8st 9lb), J. Reid
1999   Rainbow High (4y), (9st), M. Hills

KENTUCKY DERBY
(1875) Louisville, Kentucky, $1\frac{1}{2}$ miles

1997   Silver Charm, G. Stevens
1998   Real Quiet, K. Desormeaux
1999   Charismatic, C. Antley
2000   Fusaichi Pegasus, K. Desormeaux

PRIX DU JOCKEY CLUB
(1836) Chantilly, $1\frac{1}{2}$ miles

1997   Peintre Célèbre (9st 2lb), O. Peslier
1998   Dream Well (9st 2lb), C. Asmussen
1999   Montjeu (9st 2lb), C. Asmussen
2000   Volvoreta (9st), T. Thulliez

ASCOT GOLD CUP
(1807) Ascot, 2 miles and about 4 f

1997   Celeric (5y), (9st 2lb), P. Eddery
1998   Kayf Tara (4y), (9st), L. Dettori
1999   Enzeili (4y), (9st), J. Murtagh
2000   Kayf Tara (6y), (9st 2lb), J. Kinane

IRISH SWEEPS DERBY
(1866) Curragh, $1\frac{1}{2}$ miles, for three-year-olds

1997   Desert King (9st), C. Roche
1998   Dream Well (9st), C. Asmussen
1999   Montjeu (9st), C. Asmussen
2000   Sinndar (9st), J. P. Murrtagh

ECLIPSE STAKES
(1886) Sandown, 1 mile and about 2 f

1997   Pilsudski (5y), (9st 7lb), M. Kinane
1998   Daylami (4y), (9st 7lb), F. Dettori
1999   Compton Admiral (3y), (8st 10lb), D. Holland
2000   Giant's Causeway (3y), (8st 10lb), G. Duffield

KING GEORGE VI AND QUEEN ELIZABETH DIAMOND
STAKES
(1952) Ascot, 1 mile and about 4 f

1997   Swain (5y), (9st 7lb), J. Reid
1998   Swain (6y), (9st 7lb), L. Dettori
1999   Daylami (5y), (9st 7lb), L. Dettori
2000   Montjeu (4yr), (9st 7lb), M. J. Kinane

GOODWOOD CUP
(1812) Goodwood, about 2 miles

1997   Double Trigger (6y), (9st), M. Roberts
1998   Double Trigger (7y), (9st 5lb), D. Holland
1999   Kayf Tara (5y), (9st 7lb), L. Dettori
2000   Royal Rebel (4y), (9st 2lb), M. J. Kinane

*National Hunt
†Run on 6 January 1996 because of bad weather

STATISTICS

WINNING FLAT OWNERS 1999

Godolphin	£2,643,688
Hamdan Al-Maktoum	1,341,897
The Thoroughbred Corporation	988,581
K. Abdulla	892,763
Maktoum Al Maktoum	745,145
H. H. Aga Khan	677,812
HRH Prince Fahd Salman	567,972
Sheikh Mohammed	518,526
M. Tabor and Mrs J. Magnier	450,325
Shiekh Ahmed Al Maktoum	406,366

WINNING FLAT TRAINERS 1999

Saeed bin Suroor	£2,643,688
H. R. A. Cecil	2,381,217
R. Hannon	1,496,459
B. W. Hills	1,490,116
J. L. Dunlop	1,430,143
Sir Michael Stoute	1,340,881
J. H. M. Gosden	1,056,706
M. Johnston	954,275
I. A. Balding	755,630
L. M. Cumani	728,467

WINNING FLAT SIRES 1999

	Races won	Stakes
Fairy King by Northern Dancer	22	£1,182,894
Sadler's Wells by Northern Dancer	22	740,476
Diesis by Sharpen Up	26	685,458
Warning by Known Fact	61	681,051
Indian Bridge by Ahonoora	64	663,509
Alzao by Lyphard	35	561,950
Doyoun by Mill Reef	15	558,311
Silver Hawk by Roberto	23	544,711
Royal Academy by Nijinsky	44	517,772
Green Desert by Danzig	52	504,885

WINNING FLAT JOCKEYS 1999

	1st	2nd	3rd	Unpl.	Total	mts
K. Fallon	202	155	124	507		988
T. Quinn	151	117	126	523		917
L. Dettori	132	94	89	312		627
K. Darley	119	100	95	540		854
T. Sprake	111	94	8386	609		900
P. Eddery	104	85	86	464		739
R. Hughes	95	90	75	443		703
J. Fortune	94	88	81	446		709
M. Hills	94	83	70	367		614
S. Sanders	90	54	75	538		757

WINNING NATIONAL HUNT TRAINERS 1999–2000

M. C. Pipe	£1,616,791
P. F. Nicholls	890,005
N. J. Henderson	838,478
P. J. Hobbs	817,072
N. A. Twiston-Davies	799,490
Miss V. Williams	665,892
Mrs M. Reveley	544,286
Miss H. C. Knight	492,424
A. King	381,211
M. Pitman	375,414

WINNING NATIONAL HUNT JOCKEYS 1999–2000

	1st	2nd	3rd	Unpl.	Total	mts
A. P. McCoy	245	135	92	331		803
R. Johnson	143	153	130	432		858
N. Williamson	123	71	67	277		538
M. A. Fitzgerald	107	99	78	267		551
A. Dobbin	71	39	42	254		406
C. Llewellyn	68	55	62	286		471
A. Thornton	66	66	57	319		508
T. J. Murphy	64	48	43	295		450
J. Tizzard	63	59	57	220		399
A. Maguire	63	57	68	273		461

The above statistics have been provided by *Timeform*, publishers of the *Racehorses* and *Chasers and Hurdlers* annuals

ICE HOCKEY

World Championship 2000: Czech Republic beat Slovakia 5–3
Stanley Cup final 2000: New Jersey Deveils beat Dallas Stars 4–2
Super League Champions 2000: London Knights
Super League Champion 2000: Bracknell Bees
Benson and Hedges Cup 2000: Manchester Storm

ICE SKATING

BRITISH CHAMPIONSHIPS 1999
Dundonald, Northern Ireland, November

Men: Neil Wilson (Northern Ireland)
Women: Tasmin Sear (Oxford)
Pairs: Sarah Kemp and Daniel Thomas (Chelmsford)
Ice Dance: Julie Keeble (Wales) and Lukas Zalewski (England)
EUROPEAN CHAMPIONSHIPS 2000
Vienna, Austria, February

Men: Evgeni Plushenko (Russia)
Women: Irina Slutskaya (Russia)
Pairs: Maria Petrova and Alexei Tikhonov (Russia)
Ice Dance: Marina Anissina and Gwendal Piezerat (France)

WORLD CHAMPIONSHIPS 2000
Nice, France, March

Men: Alexei Yagudin (Russia)
Women: Michelle Kwan (USA)
Pairs: Maria Petrova and Alexei Tikhonov (Russia)
Ice Dance: Marina Anissina and Gwendal Piezerat (France)

JUDO

BRITISH NATIONAL CHAMPIONSHIPS 1999
Sheffield, December

MEN

Heavyweight (over 100 kg): Danny Sargent
Light-heavyweight (100 kg): Keith Davis
Middleweight (90 kg): Peter Cousins
Welter (81 kg): Luke Preston
Lightweight (73 kg): Eric Bonti
Junior lightweight (66 kg): James Warren
Bantamweight (60 kg): David Johnson

WOMEN

Heavyweight (over 78 kg): Michelle Rogers
Light-heavyweight (78 kg): Chloe Cowan
Middleweight (70 kg): Amanda Sneddon
Welter (63 kg): Gemma Hutchins
Lightweight (57 kg): Nicola Fairbrother
Junior lightweight (52 kg): Elise Summers
Bantamweight (48 kg): Donna Robertson

MOTOR CYCLING

500 CC GRAND PRIX 1999

Brazilian (Rio): Norick Abe (Japan), Yahama
Japanese (Motegi): Kenny Roberts (USA), Suzuki
Australian (Phillip Island): Tadayuki Okada (Japan), Honda
Riders' Championship 1999: 1. Alex Criville (Spain), Honda, 246 points; 2. Tadayuki Okada (Japan), Honda, 202 points; 3. Kenny Roberts (USA), Suzuki, 179 points

500 CC GRAND PRIX 2000

South Africa (Welkom): Garry McCoy (Australia), Yamaha
Malaysia (Sepang): Kenny Roberts (USA), Suzuki
Japan (Suzuka): Norick Abe (Japan), Yamaha
Spanish (Jerez): Kenny Roberts (USA), Suzuki
French (Le Mans): Alex Criville (Spain), Honda
Italian (Mugello): Loris Capirossi (Italy), Honda
Catalunya (Barcelona): Kenny Roberts (USA), Suzuki
Dutch (Assen): Alex Barros (Brazil), Honda
British (Donington Park): Valentino Rossi (Italy), Honda
German (Sachsenring): Alex Barros (Brazil), Honda
Czech (Brno): Max Biaggi (Italy), Yamaha
Portugal (Estoril): Garry McCoy (Australia), Yamaha
Valencia: Garry McCoy (Australia), Yamaha

WORLD SUPERBIKES 2000

World Superbike Champion 1999: Carl Fogarty (GB, Ducati)
South Africa (Kyalami): Race 1 – Colin Edwards (USA), Honda; Race 2 – Colin Edwards (USA), Honda
Australia (Philip Island): Race 1 – Antony Gobert, Bimota; Race 2 – Troy Corser (Australia), Aprilla
Japan (Sugo): Race 1 – Hitoyasu Izutzu (Japan), Kawasaki; Race 2 – Hitoyasu Izutzu (Japan), Kawasaki
United Kingdom (Donington Park): Race 1 – Colin Edwards (USA), Honda; Race 2 – Neil Hodgson (GB), Ducati

Italy (Monza): Race 1 – Pierfrancesco Chili (Italy), Suzuki; Race 2 – Colin Edwards (USA), Honda
Germany (Hockenheim): Race 1 – Simon Bayliss (Australia), Ducati; Race 2 – Noryuki Haga (Japan), Yamaha
San Marino (Misano): Race 1 – Troy Corser (Australia), Aprilla; Race 2 – Troy Corser (Australia), Aprilla
Spain (Valencia): Race 1 – Troy Corser (Australia), Aprillia; Race 2 – Noryuki Haga (Japan), Yamaha
United States (Laguna Seca): Race 1 – Noryuki Haga (Japan), Yamaha; Race 2 – Troy Corser (Australia); Aprilla
Great Britain (Brands Hatch): Race 1 – Simon Bayliss (Australia), Ducati; Race 2 – Neil Hodgson (GB), Ducati
Netherlands (Assen): Race 1 – Colin Edwards (USA), Honda; Race 2 – Noryuki Haga (Japan), Yamaha
Germany (Oschersleben): Race 1 – Colin Edwards (USA), Honda; Race 2 – Colin Edwards (USA), Honda
Senior TT 2000, Isle of Man: David Jefferies (Yamaha)
Junior TT 2000, Isle of Man: David Jefferies (Yamaha)
500cc World Motocross Champion 2000: Frédéric Bolley (France), Honda

MOTOR RACING

FORMULA ONE GRAND PRIX 1999

Malaysian (Kuala Lumpur): Mika Hakkinen (Finland), McLaren-Mercedes
Japanese (Suzuka): Michael Schumacher (Germany), Ferrari
Drivers' World Championship 1999: 1. Mika Hakkinen (Finland), McLaren-Mercedes, 76 points; 2. Eddie Irvine (GB), Ferrari, 74 points; 3. Heniz-Harold Frentzen (Germany), 54 points
Constructors' World Championship 1999: 1. Ferrari, 128 points; 2. McLaren-Mercedes, 124 points; 3. Jordan, 61 points

FORMULA ONE GRAND PRIX 2000

Australian (Melbourne): (12 March) Michael Schumacher (Germany), Ferrari
Brazilian (São Paulo): (26 March) Michael Schumacher (Germany), Ferrari
San Marino (Imola): (9 April) Michael Schumacher (Germany), Ferrari
British (Silverstone): (23 April) David Coulthard (GB), McLaren-Mercedes
Spanish (Barcelona): (7 May) Mika Hakkinen (Finland), McLaren-Mercedes
European (Nurburgring): (21 May) Michael Schumacher (Germany), Ferrari
Monaco (Monte Carlo): (4 June) David Coulthard (GB), McLaren-Mercedes
Canadian (Montreal): (18 June) Michael Schumacher (Germany), Ferrari
French (Magny-Cours): (2 July) David Coulthard (GB), McLaren-Mercedes
Austrian (Spielberg): (16 July) Mika Hakkinen (Finland), McLaren-Mercedes
German (Hockenheim): (30 July) Rubens Barrichello (Brazil), Ferrari
Hungarian (Budapest): (13 August) Mika Hakkinen (Finland), McLaren-Mercedes
Belgian (Spa-Francorchamps): (27 August) Mika Hakkinen (Finland), McLaren-Mercedes
Italian (Monza): (10 September) Michael Schumacher (Germany), Ferrari
USA (Indianapolis): (24 September)

Indianapolis 500 2000: Juan Pablo Montoya (Columbia), G Force Oldsmobile
Le Mans 24-hour Race 2000: Frank Biela (Germany), Tom Kristensen (Denmark) and Emmanuele Pirro (Italy), Audi
Paris-Dakar-Cairo Rally: Cars – Jean-Louis Schlesser (France), Schelesser-Renault; Bikes – Richard Sainct (France), BMW Motorrad; Trucks – Vladimir Tchaguine (Russia); Kamaz

MOTOR RALLYING

1999

San Remo Rally: Tommi Makinen (Finland), Mitsubishi Lancer
Rally Australia: Tommi Makinen (Finland), Mitsubishi Lancer
Network Q Rally of Great Britain: Richard Burns (GB), Mitsubishi Lancer
Drivers' World Championship 1999: Tommi Makinen (Finland), Mitsubishi Lancer, 62 points
Manufacturers' World Championship 1999: Toyota, 109 points

2000

Monte Carlo Rally: Tommi Makinen (Finland), Mitsubishi Lancer
Swedish Rally: Marcus Groholm (Finland), Peugeot
Safari Rally: Richard Burns (GB), Subaru
Rally of Portugal: Richard Burns (GB), Subaru
Rally de Espana: Colin McRae (GB), Ford Focus
Argentine Rally: Richard Burns (GB), Subaru
Acropolis Rally: Colin McRae (GB), Ford Focus
New Zealand Rally: Marcus Groholm (Finland), Peugeot
Rally Finland: Marcus Groholm (Finland), Peugeot
Cyprus Rally: Carlos Sainz (Spain), Ford Focus

Rally of Wales 2000: Mark Higgins (GB), Vauxhall Astra
Scottish Rally 2000: Tipio Laukkanen (Finland), Volkswagen Golf
Pirelli Rally 2000: Marko Ipatti (Finland), Mitsubishi Lancher
Jim Clark Rally 2000: Mark Higgins (GB), Vauxhall Astra
MSA Rally 2000: Neil Wearden (GB), Vauxhall Astra

NETBALL

Inter-County Championship final 2000: Derbyshire
National Clubs Championship 2000: Star and Sheffield Open
English Counties League Championship 2000: Essex Met
National Clubs League Championship 2000: Linden

NORDIC EVENTS

BIATHLON WORLD CHAMPIONSHIPS 2000
MEN

10km Sprint: Frode Andersen (Norway) 23 minutes 51.2 seconds
15km Pursuit: Frank Luck (Germany) 33 minutes 21.9 seconds
20km Individual: Wolfgang Rottman (Austria) 53 minutes 36.2 seconds

WOMEN
7.5km Sprint: Liv Grete Skjelbried (Norway) 20 minutes

51.9 seconds
10km Pursuit: Magdalena Forsberg (Sweden) 31 minutes
53.8 seconds
15km Individual: Corinne Niogret (France) 45 minutes
30.9 seconds

BIATHLON OVERALL CHAMPIONS
MEN

1. Raphael Poiree (France) 470 points
2. Ole Einar Björndalen (Norway) 448 points
3. Sven Fischer (Germany) 434 points

WOMEN

1. Magdalena Forsberg (Sweden) 510 points
2. Olena Zubrilova (Ukraine) 424 points
3. Corinne Niogret (France) 411 points

CROSS-COUNTRY OVERALL CHAMPIONS
MEN

1. Johann Muehlegg (Spain) 948 points
2. Jari Isomatsae (Finland) 708 points
3. Odd-Björn Hjelmeset (Norway) 586 points

WOMEN

1. Bente Martinsen (Norway) 1,176 points
2. Kristina Smigun (Estonia) 1,165 points
3. Larissa Lazutina (Russia) 1,008 points

NORDIC-COMBINED

1. Samppa Lajunen (Finland) 1,720 points
2. Bjarte Engen Vik (Norway) 1,500 points
3. Ladislav Rygl (Czech Republic) 1,062 points

WORLD CUP SKI-FLYING
INDIVIDUAL

1. Sven Hannawald (Germany) 410.7 points
2. Janne Ahonen (Finland) 402.3 points
3. Andreas Goldberger* (Austria) 401.1 points

*Goldberger set a new world record of 225 metres at
Planica, Slovenia on 18 March

TEAM

1. Germany 772.8 points
2. Finland 745.6 points
3. Japan 691.6 points

WORLD CUP SKI-JUMPING
OVERALL

1. Martin Schmitt (Germany) 1,833 points
2. Andreas Widhölzl (Austria) 1,452 points
3. Janne Ahonen (Finland) 1,437 points

POLO

Prince of Wales's Trophy final 2000: Royal Pahang beat
  Woodchester 13–11
Queen's Cup final 2000: Geebung beat Les Lions 12–9
Warwickshire Cup final 2000: Woodchester beat Black
  Bears 8–7
Gold Cup (British Open) final 2000: Geebung beat Black
  Bears 13–8
Coronation Cup 2000: Argentina beat England 10–9
Prince Philip Trophy 2000: Black Bears beat England 'A'
  12–10
Arena Gold Cup 2000: F. C. T. beat Argosy 19–18
Arena Nations 000: England beat Argentina 16–11
Varsity Match 2000: Oxford beat Cambridge 6–0

RACKETS

Professional Singles Championship final 2000: Toby Sawrey-
  Cookson beat Mark Hubbard 3–0
British Open Singles Championship final 2000: James Male
  beat Peter Brake 5–1
British Open Doubles Championship final 2000: James
  Male and Mark Hue Williams beat G. Barker and
  A. Robinson 4–2
Amateur Singles Championship final 2000: James Male
  beat A. Robinson 3–1
Amateur Doubles Championship final 2000: James Mail
  and Mark Hue Williams beat G. Barker and
  A. Robinson 4–2
National League 2000: Old Haileyburians beat Old
  Etonians 3–0
Noel Bruce Cup final 1999 (public schools' old boys'
  doubles championship): Harrow beat Cheltenham 4–0
Varsity Match 2000: Oxford beat Cambridge 3–0

REAL TENNIS

Professional Singles Championship final 2000: N. Wood beat
  M. Gooding 3–1
Professional Doubles Championship final 2000: F. Filippelli
  and J. Male beat N. Wood and A. Phillips 3–1
British Open Singles Championship final 1999: J. Male beat
  M. Gooding 3–1
British Open Doubles Championship final 1999: R. Gunn and
  S. Virgona beat J. Snow and J. Male 3–1
Amateur Singles Championship final 2000: J. Snow beat
  J. Willcocks 3–0
Amateur Doubles Championship final 2000: J. Snow and
  A. Gray beat J. Willcocks and A. Hombrecher 3–0
Henry Leaf Cup final 2000 (public schools' old boys'
  doubles championship): Winchester beat Cranleish 2–1
Women's British Open Singles Championship final 2000:
  P. Lumley beat C. Cornwallis 2–0

ROAD WALKING

RWA MEN'S NATIONAL 20 KM WALK
Nottingham, 12 March 2000
Individual: Darrell Stone (Steyning), 1 hr. 27 min. 08 sec.
Team: Steyning, 13 points

RWA WOMEN'S NATIONAL 20 KM WALK
Nottingham, 12 March 2000
Individual: Lisa Kehler (Wolverhampton and Bilston),
  1 hr. 39 min. 28 sec.
Team: Dudley and Stourbridge, 23 points

RWA MEN'S NATIONAL 35 KM WALK
Dartford, 7 May 2000
Individual: Chris Cheeseman (Surrey WC), 2 hr. 51 min.
  20 sec.
Team: Steyning, 19 points

RWA WOMEN'S NATIONAL 10 KM WALK
Dartford, 7 May 2000
Individual: Sharon Tonks (Bromsgrove and Redditch),
  52 min. 00 sec.
Team: Steyning, 27 points

RWA MEN'S NATIONAL 50 KM WALK
Victoria Park, 9 September 2000
Individual: Darrell Stone (Steyning), 4 hr. 21 min. 23 sec.

Team: Steyning, 6 points

RWA WOMEN'S NATIONAL 5 KM WALK
Victoria Park, 9 September 2000
Individual: Niobe Menendez (Steyning), 24 min. 19 sec.
Team: City of Sheffield, 16 points

ROWING

NATIONAL CHAMPIONSHIPS 2000
Nottingham, July

MEN
Coxed pairs: London
Coxless pairs: London/Tideway Scullers School
Coxed fours: London
Coxless fours: Molesey
Single sculls: P. Gardner (Leander C)
Double sculls: Leander A
Quad sculls: Tideway Scullers School
Eights: Leander/Nottinghamshire County Rowing
   Association/Tideway Scullers School/Worcester

WOMEN
Coxless pairs: Kingston/Newcastle University
Coxed fours: Nautilus
Coxless fours: University of London/Tyrlan
Single sculls: D. Flood (Tideway Scullers School B)
Double sculls: Nottinghamsire County Rowing
   Association/Star
Quad sculls: Molesey
Eights: Upper Thames/Kingston/Thames

THE 146th UNIVERSITY BOAT RACE
Putney–Mortlake, 4 miles 1 f, 180 yd, 25 March 2000

Oxford beat Cambridge by 3 lengths; 18 min. 4 sec.
Cambridge have won 76 times, Oxford 69 and there has
been one dead heat. The record time is 16 min. 19 sec.,
rowed by Cambridge in 1998

Women's Boat Race 2000 (Henley): Cambridge beat
   Oxford by 1 length; 6 min. 01 sec. (a record time)

HENLEY ROYAL REGATTA 2000

Grand Challenge Cup: Australian Institute of Sport
   (Australia) beat Leander and Queen's Tower by $1\frac{1}{4}$
   lengths
Ladies' Challenge Plate: Brown University (USA) beat
   Rostock and Heidelberg (Germany) by a canvas
Thames Challenge Cup: Molesey A beat Crabtree by $\frac{1}{2}$ length
Temple Challenge Cup: Yale University (USA) beat Oxford
   Brookes University A by 2/3 length
Princess Elizabeth Challenge Cup: St Joseph's Preparatory
   School (USA) beat Groton School (USA) by $1\frac{3}{4}$ lengths
Stewards' Challenge Cup: Leander Club beat University of
   Technology, Sydney Haberfield (Australia) by 2/3
   length
Prince Philip Challenge Cup: Leander and Oxford Brookes
   University beat Notts County by 5 length
Queen Mother Challenge Cup: Nereus and Laga
   (Netherlands) beat Australian Institute of Sport (Aus-
   tralia) by $3\frac{1}{4}$ lengths
Visitors' Challenge Cup: Oxford Brookes University A beat
   University of London by 1 length
Wyfold Challenge Cup: Worcester beat Queen's Tower by
   $1\frac{3}{4}$ lengths
Britannia Challenge Cup: Cambridge University beat
   Imperial College, London by 1/2 length

Fawley Challenge Cup: Leander Club and Llandaff beat
   Tiffin School by $3\frac{1}{2}$ lengths
Silver Goblets and Nickalls' Challenge Cup: G. M. P. Searle
   and E. R. Coode (GB) beat R. Di Clementé and D. Cech
   (South Africa) by $1\frac{3}{4}$ lengths
Double Sculls Challenge Cup: B. Kaliszan and B. Samuelson
   (Denmark) beat M. K. Langridge and P. J. Wells (GB)
   easily
Diamond Challenge Sculls: A. H. Abdullah (USA) beat S. D.
   Goodbrand (GB) by 2/3 length
Princess Royal Challenge Cup: D. K. Flood (GB) beat
   M. H. Brandin (GB) by 1 length
Women's Eights: University of Washington (USA) beat
   University of Victoria (Canada) by $\frac{1}{2}$ length

OTHER ROWING EVENTS
Oxford Torpids 20000: Cancelled due to flooding
Oxford Summer Eights 2000: *Men*, Oriel; *Women*,
   Pembroke
Head of the River 2000: *Men*, Queen's Tower I; *Women*,
   Marlow A
Scullers Head of the River 2000: Ross Hunter
   (Leander Club)
Doggett's Coat and Badge 2000: Billie Rickner
   (Globe Rowing Club)
Wingfield Sculls 2000: Peter Haining (Auriol Kensington
   RC)
London Cup 2000: Tom Gale (Tideway Scullers' School)
Thames World Sculling Challenge 1999: *Men*, Vaclav
   Chalupa (Czech Republic); *Women*, Ekaterina Karsten
   (Belarus)

RUGBY FIVES

National Singles Championship final 1999: Hamish
   Buchanan beat Ian Fuller 15–8, 15–9
National Doubles Championship final 2000: John Beswick
   and Neil Roberts beat Ian Fuller and Dave Hebden
   15–10, 15–6
National Club Championship final 2000: Manchester YMCA
   beat Alleyn Old Boys 86–85
National Schools' Singles Championship final 2000: Paul
   Mann (St Paul's) beat James Bristow (Winchester) 11–9,
   11–0
National Schools' Doubles Championship final 2000: St Paul's
   I beat Winchester 11–1, 11–2
Varsity Match 2000: Oxford beat Cambridge 244–226

RUGBY LEAGUE

COMPETITIONS
Super League Grand Final 1999 (Old Trafford, 9 October):
   St Helens beat Bradford Bulls 8–6
Challenge Cup final 2000 (Murrayfield, 29 April): Bradford
   Bulls beat Leeds Rhinos 24–18
Northern Ford Premiership Grand Final 2000 (Bury, 29
   July): Dewsbury Rams beat Leigh Centurions 13–12

Varsity Match 2000: Oxford beat Cambridge 35–17
AMATEUR RUGBY LEAGUE 1999–2000
County Championship: Cumbria
National Conference League First Division Champions:
   Oullon Raiders
National Conference League Second Division: Eastmoor
   Dragons

RUGBY UNION

WORLD CUP 1999

1 Oct	Cardiff	Wales 23, Argentina 18
	Beziers	Fiji 67, Namibia 18
2 Oct	Twickenham	England 67, Italy 7
	Dublin	Ireland 53, USA 8
	Galashiels	Uruguay 27, Spain 15
	Beziers	France 33, Canada 20
3 Oct	Belfast	Australia 57, Romania 9
	Murrayfield	South Africa 46, Scotland 29
	Bristol	New Zealand 45, Tonga 9
	Wrexham	Samoa 43, Japan 9
8 Oct	Bordeaux	France 47, Namibia 13
	Murrayfield	Scotland 43, Uruguay 12
9 Oct	Dublin	Romania 27, USA 25
	Twickenham	New Zealand 30, England 16
	Cardiff	Wales 64, Japan 15
	Bordeaux	Fiji 38, Canada 22
10 Oct	Leicester	Tonga 28, Italy 25
	Murrayfield	South Africa 47, Spain 3
	Dublin	Australia 23, Ireland 3
	Llanelli	Argentina 32, Samoa 16
14 Oct	Toulouse	Canada 72, Namibia 11
	Limerick	Australia 55, USA 19
	Cardiff	Samoa 38, Wales 31
	Huddersfield	New Zealand 101, Italy 3
15 Oct	Dublin	Ireland 44, Romania 14
	Glasgow	South Africa 39, Uruguay 3
	Twickenham	England 101, Tonga 10
16 Oct	Cardiff	Argentina 33, Japan 12
	Murrayfield	Scotland 48, Spain 0
	Toulouse	France 28, Fiji 19
20 Oct	Lens	Argentina 28, Ireland 24
	Murrayfield	Scotland 35, Samoa 20
	Twickenham	England 45, Fiji 24
23 Oct	Cardiff	Australia 24, Wales 9
24 Oct	Murrayfield	New Zealand 30, Scotland 18
	Dublin	France 47, Argentina 26
	Paris	South Africa 44, England 21
30 Oct	Twickenham	Australia 27, South Africa 21
31 Oct	Twickenham	France 43, New Zealand 31
4 Nov	Cardiff	South Africa 22, New Zealand 18
6 Nov	Cardiff	Australia 35, France 12

SIX NATIONS' CHAMPIONSHIP 2000

5 Feb	Rome	Italy 34, Scotland 20
	Twickenham	England 50, Ireland 18
	Cardiff	France 36, Wales 3
19 Feb	Cardiff	Wales 47, Italy 16
	Dublin	Ireland 44, Scotland 22
	Paris	England 15, France 9
4 March	Twickenham	England 46, Wales 12
	Dublin	Ireland 60, Italy 13
	Murrayfield	France 28, Scotland 16
18 March	Cardiff	Wales 26, Scotland 18
	Rome	England 59, Italy 12
19 March	Paris	Ireland 27, France 25
1 April	Dublin	Wales 23, Ireland 19
	Paris	France 42, Italy 31
2 April	Murrayfield	Scotland 19, England 13

	P	W	D	L	Points		Total
					F	A	
England	5	4	0	1	183	70	8
France	5	3	0	2	140	92	6
Ireland	5	3	0	2	168	133	6
Wales	5	3	0	2	111	135	6
Scotland	5	1	0	4	95	145	2
Italy	5	1	0	4	106	228	2

European Cup final 2000 (Twickenham, 27 May): Northampton beat Munster 9–8
European Shield final 2000 (Toulouse, 25 May): Pau (France) beat Castres (France) 34–21
Super 12 final 2000 (27 May): Canterbury Crusaders (New Zealand) beat ACT Brumbies (Australia) 20–19
Women's (Inaugural) Five Nations' Championship 1999: England

DOMESTIC COMPETITIONS

Premiership: Division 1, Leicester, 51 points; Division 2, Rotherham, 48 points
National League: Division 1, Otley, 45 points; Division 2 (north), Kendal, 48 points; Division 2 (south), Esher, 46 points
County Championship final 2000: Yorkshire beat Devon 16–9
Tetley's Bitter Cup final 2000: Wasps beat Northampton Falcons 31–23
Scottish Premiership: Division 1, Heriot's F. P., 74 points; Division 2, Boroughmuir, 77 points; Division 3, Edinburgh Academicals, 68 points
Scottish Cup final 2000: Boroughmuir beat Glasgow Hawks 35–10
Irish League: Division 1, St Mary's College; Division 2, Blackrock College; Division 3, Ballynahinch; Division 4, Dublin University
Varsity Match 1999: Oxford beat Cambridge 16–13
Middlesex Sevens final 2000: Penguins beat Saracens 47–19

SHOOTING

131th NATIONAL RIFLE ASSOCIATION IMPERIAL MEETING
Bisley, July 2000

Queen's Prize: Jo F. Hossacks, 294.27 v-bulls
Grand Aggregate: Peter D. Bramley, 696.78 v-bulls
Prince of Wales Prize: Zainal Abidin M. Zain, 75.13 v-bulls
St George's Vase: Dr Parag Patel, 150.24 v-bulls
Allcomers Aggregate: Roger E. Ellis, 373.47 v-bulls
National Trophy: England, 2,060.246 v-bulls
Kolapore Cup: Great Britain, 1,182.146 v-bulls
Chancellor's Trophy: Cambridge University, 1,157.123 v-bulls
Musketeers Cup: Edinburgh University, 590.68 v-bulls
Vizianagram Trophy: House of Commons, 390.29 v-bulls
County Long-Range Championship: Sussex, 587.64 v-bulls
Mackinnon Challenge Cup: England, 1,162.124 v-bulls
The Ashburton: Stamford, 550.46 points
The Elcho: England, 1,710.176 v-bulls
The Albert: Paul S. Gray, 206.16 v-bulls
Hopton Challenge Cup: Mike Baillie-Hamilton, 875.84 v-bulls
Millennium World T. R. Championships: Jon C. Underwood, 793.98 v-bulls

CLAY PIGEON SHOOTING 2000
World Sporting Championship: Richard Faulds (England)
British Open Sporting Championship: George Digweed (England)
International Down-the-Line Cup: England
British Open Down-the-Line Championship: Jim Doherty (Ireland)
British Open Skeet Championship: Mike Bradley (England)

SNOOKER

1999–2000

Champions Cup: (Croydon) Stephen Hendry (Scotland) beat Mark J. Williams 7–5

British Open: (Plymouth) Stephen Hendry (Scotland) beat Peter Ebdon (England) 9–5

Regal Scottish Masters: (Motherwell) Matthew Stevens (Wales) beat John Higgins (Scotland) 9–7

Preston Grand Prix: (Preston) John Higgins (Scotland) beat Mark J. Williams (Wales) 9–8

Benson Hedges Championship: (Malvern) Ali Carter (England) beat Simon Bedford (England) 9–4

Liverpool Victoria UK Championship: (Bournemouth) Mark J. Williams (Wales) beat Matthew Stevens (Wales) 10–8

China International: (Shanghai) Ronnie O'Sullivan (England) beat Stephen Lee (England) 9–2

Nations Cup: (Reading) England beat Wales 6–4

Regal Welsh Open: (Cardiff) John Higgins (Scotland) beat Stephen Lee (England) 9–8

Benson Hedges Masters: (Wembley) Matthew Stevens (Wales) beat Ken Doherty (Rep. of Ireland) 10–8

Rothmans Grand Prix: (Malta) Ken Doherty (Rep. of Ireland) beat Mark J. Williams (Wales) 9–3

Thailand Masters: (Bangkok) Mark J. Williams (Wales) beat Stephen Hendry (Scotland) 9–5

Benson Hedges Irish Masters: (Kildare) John Higgins (Scotland) beat Stephen Hendry (Scotland) 9–4

Regal Scottish Masters: (Aberdeen) Ronnie O Sullivan (England) beat Mark J. Williams (Wales) 9–1

Embassy World Championship: (Sheffield) Mark J. Williams (Wales) beat Matthew Stevens (Wales) 18–16

Women's British Open 1999: Kelly Fisher (England) beat June Banks (Wales) 4–2

Women's Grand Prix 1999: Lynette Horsburgh (Blackpool) beat Emma Bonney (Portsmouth) 4–2

Women's UK Championship 1999: Kelly Fisher (England) beat Emma Bonney (England) 4–0

Connie Gough National Championship 2000: Kelly Fisher (Stourbridge) beat Kim Shaw (Kingston) 4–1

Women's Regal Scottish Masters 2000: Kelly Fisher (Stourbridge) beat Lynette Horsburgh (Blackpool) 4–0

Women's Welsh Open 2000: Lynette Horsburgh (Blackpool) beat Kelly Fisher (Stourbridge) 3–1

Women's World Championship 2000: Kelly Fisher (England) beat Lisa Ingall (England) 4–1

SQUASH RACKETS

MEN

World Open Championship final 1999: Peter Nicol (GB) beat Ahmed Barada (Egypt) 3–0

European Team Championship final 2000: England beat France 4–0

European Club Championship 1999: Colets (GB)

National Championship final 2000: Peter Marshall (Notts) beat David Evans (Wales) 3–0

World Team Championship final 1999: Egypt beat Wales 3–0

World Junior Men's Championship Final 2000: England beat Egypt 2–1

WOMEN

World Open Championship final 1999: Cassie Campion (England) beat Michelle Martin (Australia) 3–0

World Team Championship final 1999: Australia beat England 3–0

European Team Championship final 2000: England beat Germany 3–0

National Championship final 2000: Cassie Campion (Norfolk) beat Sue Wright (Kent) 3 2

SWIMMING

WORLD CHAMPIONSHIPS 2000–Short Course
Athens, March

MEN

50 metres freestyle: Mark Foster (GB) 21.58
100 metres freestyle: lars Frolander (Sweden) 46.80
200 metres freestyle: Bela Szabados (Hungary) 1:45.27
400 metres freestyle: Chad Carvin (USA) 3:41.13
1,500 metres freestyle: Jorg Hoffmann (Germany) 14:47.57
50 metres backstroke: Neil Walker (USA) 23.99
100 metres backstroke: Neil Walker (USA) 50.75
200 metres backstroke: Gordan Kozulj (Croatia) 1:53.31
50 metres breaststroke: Mark Warnecke (Germany) 27.22
100 metres breaststroke: Roman Sloudnov (Russia) 58.57
200 metres breaststroke: Roman Sloudnov (Russia) 2:07.59
50 metres butterfly: Mark Foster (GB) 23.30
100 metres butterfly: Lars Frolander (Sweden) 50.44
200 metres butterfly: James Hickman (GB) 1:53.57
100 metres medley: Neil Walker (USA) 52.79
200 metres medley: Jani Sievinen (Finland) 1:56.27
400 metres medley: Jani Sievinen (Finalnd) 4:09.54
4 × 100 metres freestyle relay: Sweden 3:09.57
4 × 200 metres freestyle relay: USA 7:01.33
4 × 100 metres medley relay: USA 3:30.03

WOMEN

50 metres freestyle: Therese Alshammar (Sweden) 23.59
100 metres freestyle: Therese Alshammar (Sweden) 52.17
200 metres freestyle: Yu Yang (China) 1:56.06
400 metres freestyle: Lindsay Benko (USA) 4:02.44
800 metres freestyle: Hua Chen (China) 8:17.03
50 metres backstroke: Antje Buschschulte (Germany) 27.90
100 metres backstroke: Sandra Voelker (Germany) 58.66
200 metres backstroke: Antje Buschschulte (Germany) 2:07.29
50 metres breaststroke: Sarah Poewe (S. Africa) 30.66
100 metres breaststroke: Sarah Poewe (S. Africa) 1:06.21
200 metres breaststroke: Rebecca Brown (Australia) 2:23.41
50 metres butterfly: Jenny Thompson (USA) 26.13
100 metres butterfly: Jenny Thompson (USA) 57.67
200 metres butterfly: Mette Jacobsen (Denmark) 2:08.10
100 metres medley: Martina Moravcova (Slovakia) 59.71
200 metres medley: Yana Klochkova (Ukraine) 2:08.97
400 metres medley: Yana Klochkova (Ukraine) 4:32.45
4 × 100 metres freestyle relay: Sweden 3:35.54
4 × 200 metres freestyle relay: Great Britain 7:49.11
4 × 100 metres medley relay: Sweden 3:59.53

EUROPEAN CHAMPIONSHIPS 2000
Helsinki, Finland – July

MEN

50 metres backstroke: Stev Theloke (Germany) 25.60
100 metres backstroke: David Ortega (Spain) 55.50
200 metres backstroke: Gordan Kozulj (Croatia) 1:58.62
50 metres breaststroke: Mark Warnecke (Germany) 27.75
100 metres breaststroke: Domenico Fioravanti (Italy) 1:02.02
200 metres breaststroke: Dmitri Komornikov (Russia) 2:13.09
50 metres butterfly: Jere Hard (Finland) 23.88

100 metres butterfly: Lars Frolander (Sweden) 52.23
200 metres butterfly: Anatoli Poliakov (Russia) 1:56.73
50 metres freestyle: Alexander Popov (Russia) 21.95
100 metres freestyle: Alexander Popov (Russia) 48.61
200 metres freestyle: M. Rosolino (Italy) 1:47.31
400 metres freestyle: Emiliano Brembilla (Italy) 3:48.56
1500 metres freestyle: Igor Chervynskiy (Ukraine) 15:05.31
200 metres medley: M. Rosolino (Italy) 2:00.62
400 metres medley: Istvan Bathazi (Hungary) 4:18.51
4 × 100 metres freestyle: Russia 3:18.75
4 × 100 metres medley: Russia 3:39.29
4 × 200 metres freestyle: Italy 7:16.52

WOMEN

50 metres backstroke: Nina Zhivanevskaya (Spain) 28.76
100 metres backstroke: Nina Zhivanevskaya (Spain) 1:01.02
200 metres backstroke: Nina Zhivanevskaya (Spain) 2:09.53
50 metres breaststroke: Agnes Kovacs (Hungary) 31.68
100 metres breaststroke: Agmes Kovacs (Hungary) 1:08.38
200 metres breaststroke: Beatrice Caslaru (Romania) 2:26.76
50 metres butterfly: A-K Kammerling (Sweden) 26.40
100 metres butterfly: Martina Moravcova (Slovakia) 58.72
200 metres butterfly: Otylia Jedrzejczak (Poland) 2:08.63
50 metres freestyle: Therese Alshammar (Sweden) 24.44
100 metres freestyle: Therese Alshammar (Sweden) 54.41
200 metres freestyle: N. Baranouskaya (Bulgaria) 1:59.51
400 metres freestyle: Yana Klochkova (Ukraine) 4:09.41
800 metres freestyle: Flavia Rigamonti (Switzerland) 8:29.16
200 metres medley: Beatrice Caslaru (Romania) 2:12.57
400 metres medley Yana Klochkova (Ukraine) 4:39.78
4 × 100 metres freestyle: Sweden 3:42.38
4 × 100 metres medley: Sweden 4:06.00
4 × 200 metres relay: Romania 8:03.17

DIVING

MEN

1 metre: Alexander Mesch (Germany)
3 metres: Dmitry Sautin (Russia)
3 metres synchronised: Tobias Schellenberg and Andreas Wels (Germany)
Platform: Dmitry Sautin (Russia)
Platform synchronised: Dmitry Sautin and Igor Loukashin (Russia)

WOMEN

1 metre: Vera Ilyina (Russia)
3 metres: Youlia Pakhalina (Russia)
3 metres synchronised: Youlia Pakhalina and Vera Ilyina (Russia)
Platform: Svetlana Timoshinina (Russia)
Platform synchronised: Anke Piper and Ute Wetzig (Germany)

NATIONAL CHAMPIONSHIPS 2000
Sheffield, July

MEN

50 metres freestyle: Mark Foster (University of Bath) 22.42
100 metres freestyle: Mark Stevens (City of Cardiff) 50.44
200 metres freestyle: Paul Palmer (University of Bath) 1:48.42
400 metres freestyle: Paul Palmer (University of Bath) 3:49.61
1,500 metres freestyle: Paul Palmer (University of Bath) 15:17.53
50 metres backstroke: Brett Lummis (Ipswich) 26.61
100 metres backstroke: Adam Ruckwood (Stockport Metro) 55.81
200 metres backstroke: Adam Ruckwood (Stockport Metro)

2:00.51
50 metres breaststroke: Darren Mew (University of Bath) 28.39
100 metres breaststroke: Darren Mew (University of Bath) 1:01.78
200 metres breaststroke: Adam Whitehead (City of Coventry) 2:14.14
50 metres butterfly: Greg Phillips (Portsmouth Northsea) 25.04
100 metres butterfly: James Hickman (City of Leeds) 52.87
200 metres butterfly: Stephen Parry (Stockport Metro) 1:57.13
200 metres medley: James Hickman (City of Leeds) 2:03.85
400 metres medley: Simon Militis (Portsmouth Northsea) 4:20.07
4 × 100 metres freestyle relay: University of Bath 3:83.46
4 × 200 metres freestyle relay: City of Coventry 7:54.65
4 × 100 metres medley relay: Loughborough University 3:50.18

WOMEN

50 metres freestyle: Alison Sheppard (Milngavie and Bearsden) 25.20
100 metres freestyle: Karen Pickering (Ipswich) 55.58
200 metres freestyle: Karen Legg (Ferndown) 2:00.45
400 metres freestyle: Victoria Horner (Stockport Metro) 4:15.91
800 metres freestyle: Rebecca Cooke (Reading) 8:39.18
50 metres backstroke: Zoë Cray (Ispwich) 29.82
100 metres backstroke: Katy Sexton (Portsmouth Northsea) 1:01.80
200 metres backstroke: Helen Don-Duncan (Ashton Central) 2:11.25
50 metres breaststroke: Zoë Baker (City of Sheffield) 32.24
100 metres breaststroke: Heidi Earp (Nova Centurion) 1:10.16
200 metres breaststroke: Jaime King (University of Bath) 2:29.95
50 metres butterfly: Caroline Forst (Kingston upon Hull) 27.73
100 metres butterfly: Margaretha Pedder (Portsmouth Northsea) 1:00.74
200 metres butterfly: Georgina Lee (Camphill) 2:11.36
200 metres medley: Susan Rolph (City of Newcastle) 2:14.90
400 metres medley: Rachael Corner (Wigan Wasps) 4:49.15
4 × 100 metres freestyle relay: TS London West 3:58.98
4 × 200 metres freestyle relay: Leatherhead 8:46.92
4 × 100 metres medley relay: Nova Centurion 4:18.02

TABLE TENNIS

EUROPEAN CHAMPIONSHIPS 2000
Bremen, Germany, April–May

Men's Singles: Peter Karlsson (Sweden) beat Zoran Primorac (Croatia) 3–0
Women's Singles: Quinhong Gotsch (Germany) beat Mihaela Steff (Romania) 3–2
Men's Doubles: Patrick Chila and Jean-Philippe Gatien (France) beat Kalinikos Kreanga (Greece) and Ilija Lupelesku (Yugoslavia) 2–0
Women's Doubles: Csilla Batorfi and Krisztina Toth (Hungary) beat Ni Xia Lian and Peggy Regenwetter (Luxembourg) 2–1
Mixed Doubles: Aleksander Karakasic (Yugoslavia) and Ruta Budiene-Garkauskaite (Lithuania) beat Ilija Lupulesku (Yugoslavia) and Marie Svensson (Sweden) 2–0

Men's Team: Sweden beat Germany 4–1
Women's Team: Hungary beat Germany 4–2
World Cup final 1999: Vladimir Samsonov (Belarus) beat
   Werner Schlager (Austria) 30
World Team final 2000: Sweden beat China 3–2

ENGLISH NATIONAL CHAMPIONSHIPS 2000
Sheffield, May

Men's Singles: Matthew Syed (Surrey) beat Alan Cooke
   (Derbys) 2–0
Women's Singles: Nicola Deaton (Derbys) beat Helen
   Lower (Staffs) 2–1
Men's Doubles: Alex Perry (Devon) and Gareth Herbert
   (Bucks) beat Terry Young (Berks) and Andrew Baggaley
   (Bucks) 2–1
Women's Doubles: Nicola Deaton (Derbys) and Helen
   Lower (Staffs) beat Linda Radford (Essex) and Kubrat
   Owolabi (Middx) 2–0
Mixed Doubles: Helen Lower (Staffs) and Alex Perry
   (Devon) beat Nicola Deaton and Alan Cooke (Derbys)
   2–1
Under 21 Men's Singles: Andrew Baggaley (Bucks) beat
   Dale Barham (Cambs) 21
Under 21 Women's Singles: Georgina Walker (Notts) beat
   Natalie Bawden (Essex) 2–1

TENNIS

MAJOR CHAMPIONSHIPS 2000

AUSTRALIAN OPEN CHAMPIONSHIPS
Melbourne, 17–30 January

Men's Singles: Andre Agassi beat Yevgeny Kafelnikov
   (Russia) 3–6, 6–3, 6–2, 6–4
Women's Singles: Lindsay Davenport (USA) beat Martina
   Hingis (Switzerland) 6–1, 7–5
Men's Doubles: Ellis Ferreira (South Africa) and Rick Leach
   (USA) beat Wayne Black (Zimbabwe) and Andrew
   Kratzmann (Australia) 6–4, 3–6, 6–3, 3–6, 18–16
Women's Doubles: Lisa Raymond (USA) and Rennae
   Stubbs (Australia) beat Martina Hingis (Switzerland)
   and Mary Pierce (France) 6–4, 5–7, 6–4
Mixed Doubles: Jared Palmer (USA) and Rennae Stubbs
   (Australia) beat Todd Woodbridge (Australia) and
   Arantxa Sanchez Vicario (Spain) 7–5, 7–6

FRENCH OPEN CHAMPIONSHIPS
Paris, 29 May–11 June

Men's Singles: Gustavo Kuerten (Brazil) beat Magnus
   Norman (Sweden) 6–2, 6–3, 2–6, 7–6
Women's Singles: Mary Pierce (France) beat Conchita
   Martinez (Spain) 6–2, 7–5
Men's Doubles: Todd Woodbridge and Mark Woodforde
   (Australia) beat Paul Haarhuis (Netherlands) and
   Sandon Stolle (Australia) 7–6, 6–4
Women's Doubles: Martina Hingis (Switzerland) and Mary
   Pierce (France) beat Virginia Ruano-Pascaul (Spain)
   and Paola Suarez (Argentina) 6–4, 6–2
Mixed Doubles: Mariaan de Swardt and David Adams
   (South Africa) beat Rennae Stubbs and Todd
   Woodbridge (Australia) 6–2,6–4

ALL-ENGLAND CHAMPIONSHIPS
Wimbledon, 21 June–4 July

Men's Singles: Pete Sampras (USA) beat Pat Rafter
   (Australia) 6–7, 7–6, 6–4, 6–2
Women's Singles: Venus Williams (USA) beat Lindsay
   Davenport (USA) 6–3, 7–6
Men's Doubles: Mark Woodforde and Todd Woodbridge

(Australia) beat Paul Haarhuis (Netherlands) and
   Sandon Stolle (Australia) 6–3, 6–4, 6–1
Women's Doubles: Venus Williams and Serena Williams
   (USA) beat Julie Halard-Decugis (France) and Ai
   Sugiyama (Japan) 6–3, 6–2
Mixed Doubles: Don Johnson (USA) and Kimberly Po
   (USA) beat Lleyton Hewitt (Australia) and Kim Clijsters
   (Belgium) 6–4, 7–6

US OPEN CHAMPIONSHIPS
New York, 30 August–12 September

Men's Singles: Marat Safin (Russia) beat Pete Sampras
   (USA) 6–4, 6–3, 6–3
Women's Singles: Venus Williams (USA) beat Lindsay
   Davenport (USA) 6–4, 7–5
Men's Doubles: Lleyton Hewitt (Australia) and Max Mirnyi
   (Belarus) beat Ellis Ferreira (S. Africa) and Rick Leach
   (USA) 6–4, 5–7, 7–6
Women's Doubles: Ai Sugiyama (Japan) and Julie
   Halard-Decugis (France) beat Cara Black (Zimbabwe)
   and Elena Likhovtseva (Russia) 6–0, 1–6, 6–1
Mixed Doubles: Jared Palmer (USA) and Arantxa
   Sanchez-Vicario (Spain) beat Max Mirnyi (Belarus)
   and Anna Kournikova (Russia) 6–4, 6–3

TEAM CHAMPIONSHIPS
Davis Cup final 1999: Australia beat France 3–2

VOLLEYBALL

MEN
World Cup 1999: Russia 22 points
World League 1999: Italy
National League Championship 2000: London Malory
National Cup final 2000: London Malory beat Wessex 3–0

WOMEN
World Cup 1999: Cuba 22 points
Grand Prix final 2000: Cuba beat Russia 3–1
National League Championship 2000: Ashcombe Dorking
National Cup final 2000: Ashcombe Dorking beat
   London 3–2

BEACH VOLLEYBALL

MEN
British Grand Prix: Grant Pursey and Tim Hollis
British Open: Grand Pursey and Tim Hollis

WOMEN
British Grand Prix: Cathy Norman and Melissa Coutts
British Open: Cathy Norman and Melissa Coutts

YACHTING

America's Cup 2000: (February) New Zealand beat Prada
   Challenge (Italy) 5–0

Sports Records

All the world records given below have been accepted by the International Amateur Athletic Federation except those marked with an asterisk* which are awaiting homologation. Fully automatic timing to 1/100th second is mandatory up to and including 400 metres. For distances up to and including 10,000 metres, records will be accepted to 1/100th second if timed automatically, and to 1/10th if hand timing is used.

MEN'S EVENTS

TRACK EVENTS	hr.	min.	sec.
100 metres			9.79
Maurice Greene, USA, 1999			
200 metres			19.32
Michael Johnson, USA, 1996			
400 metres			43.18
Michael Johnson, USA, 1999			
800 metres		1	41.11
Wilson Kipketer, Denmark, 1997			
1,000 metres		2	11.96
Noah Ngeny, Kenya, 1999			
1,500 metres		3	26.00
Hicham El Guerrouj, Morocco, 1998			
1 mile		3	43.13
Hicham El Guerrouj, Morocco, 1999			
2,000 metres		4	44.79
Hicham El Guerrouj, Morocco, 1999			
3,000 metres		7	20.67
Daniel Komen, Kenya, 1996			
5,000 metres		12	39.36
Haile Gebrselassie, Ethiopia, 1998			
10,000 metres		26	22.75
Haile Gebrselassie, Ethiopia, 1998			
20,000 metres		56	55.6
Arturo Barrios, Mexico, 1991			
21,101 metres	1	00	00.0
(13 miles 196 yards 1 foot)			
Arturo Barrios, Mexico, 1991			
25,000 metres	1	13	55.8
Toshihiko Seko, Japan, 1981			
30,000 metres	1	29	18.8
Toshihiko Seko, Japan, 1981			
Marathon	2	05	42
Khalid Khannouchi, Morocco, 1999			
110 metres hurdles (3 ft 6 in)			12.91
Colin Jackson, GB, 1993			
400 metres hurdles (3 ft 0 in)			46.78
Kevin Young, USA, 1992			
3,000 metres steeplechase		7	55.72
Bernard Barmasai, Kenya, 1997			

RELAYS		min.	sec.
4 × 100 metres			37.40
USA, 1992, 1993			
4 × 200 metres		1	19.11
Santa Monica TC, 1992			
4 × 400 metres		2	54.20
USA, 1998			
4 × 800 metres		7	03.89
GB, 1982			
4 × 1,500 metres		14	38.8
Federal Republic of Germany, 1977			

FIELD EVENTS	metres	ft	in
High jump	2.45	8	0½
Javier Sotomayor, Cuba, 1993			
Pole vault	6.14	20	1¾
Sergei Bubka, Ukraine, 1994			
Long jump	8.95	29	4½
Mike Powell, USA, 1991			
Triple jump	18.29	60	0¼
Jonathan Edwards, GB, 1995			
Shot	23.12	75	10¼
Randy Barnes, USA, 1990			
Discus	74.08	243	0
Jürgen Schult, GDR, 1986			
Hammer	86.74	284	7
Yuriy Sedykh, USSR, 1986			
Javelin	98.48	323	1
Jan Zelezny, Czech Rep., 1996			
Decathlon†	8,994 points		
Tomas Dvorak, Czech Rep., 1999			

†Ten events comprising 100 m, long jump, shot, high jump, 400 m, 110 m hurdles, discus, pole vault, javelin, 1500 m

WALKING (TRACK)	hr.	min.	sec.
20,000 metres	1	17	25.6
Bernard Segura, Mexico, 1994			
29,572 metres (18 miles 660 yards)	2	00	00.0
Maurizio Damilano, Italy, 1992			
30,000 metres	2	01	44.1
Maurizio Damilano, Italy, 1992			
50,000 metres	3	40	57.9
Thierry Toutain, France, 1996			

WOMEN'S EVENTS

TRACK EVENTS		min.	sec.
100 metres			10.49
Florence Griffith-Joyner, USA, 1988			
200 metres			21.34
Florence Griffith-Joyner, USA, 1988			
400 metres			47.60
Marita Koch, GDR, 1985			
800 metres		1	53.28
Jarmila Kratochvilova,			
Czechoslovakia, 1983			
1,500 metres		3	50.46
Qu Yunxia, China, 1993			
1 mile		4	12.56
Svetlana Masterkova, Russia, 1996			
3,000 metres		8	06.11
Wang Junxia, China, 1993			
5,000 metres		14	28.09
Jiang Bo, China, 1997			
10,000 metres		29	31.78
Wang Junxia, China, 1993			
Marathon	2	20	43
Tegla Loroupe, Kenya, 1999			

100 metres hurdles (2 ft 9 in)		12.21
Yordanka Donkova, Bulgaria, 1988		
400 metres hurdles (2 ft 6 in)		52.61
Kim Batten, USA, 1995		

RELAYS	min.	sec.
4 × 100 metres		41.37
GDR, 1985		
4 × 200 metres	1	27.46*
USA, 2000		
4 × 400 metres	3	15.17
USSR, 1988		
4 × 800 metres	7	50.17
USSR, 1984		

FIELD EVENTS	metres	ft	in
High jump	2.09	6	10¼
Stefka Kostadinova, Bulgaria, 1987			
Pole vault	4.63*	15	2¼
Stacy Dragila, USA, 2000			
Long jump	7.52	24	8¼
Galina Chistiakova, USSR, 1988			
Triple jump	15.50	50	10¼
Inessa Kravets, Ukraine, 1995			
Shot	22.63	74	3
Natalya Lisovskaya, USSR, 1987			
Discus	76.80	252	0
Gabriele Reinsch, GDR, 1988			
Hammer	75.97	249	2
Mihaela Melinte, Romania, 1999			
Javelin (new implement in 1999)	69.48*	227	11
Trine Hattestad, Norway, 2000			
Heptathlon†		7,291 points	
Jackie Joyner-Kersee, USA, 1988			

†Seven events comprising 100 m hurdles, shot, high jump, 200 m, long jump, javelin, 800 m

ATHLETICS NATIONAL (UK) RECORDS
AS AT 9 SEPTEMBER 2000

Records set anywhere by athletes eligible to represent Great Britain and Northern Ireland

MEN

TRACK EVENTS	hr.	min.	sec.
100 metres			09.87
Linford Christie, 1993			
200 metres			19.87
John Regis, 1994			
400 metres			44.36
Iwan Thomas, 1997			
800 metres		1	41.73
Sebastian Coe, 1981			
1,000 metres		2	12.18
Sebastian Coe, 1981			
1,500 metres		3	29.67
Sebastian Coe, 1985			
1 mile		3	46.32
Steve Cram, 1985			
2,000 metres		4	51.39
Steve Cram, 1985			
3,000 metres		7	32.79
David Moorcroft, 1982			
5,000 metres		13	00.41
David Moorcroft, 1982			
10,000 metres		27	18.14
Jon Brown, 1998			
20,000 metres		57	28.7
Carl Thackery, 1990			
20,855 metres	1	00	00.0
Carl Thackery, 1990			
25,000 metres	1	15	22.6
Ron Hill, 1965			
30,000 metres	1	31	30.4
Jim Alder, 1970			
3,000 metres steeplechase		8	07.96
Mark Rowland, 1988			
110 metres hurdles			12.91
Colin Jackson, 1993			
400 metres hurdles			47.82
Kriss Akabusi, 1992			

RELAYS	min.	sec.
4 × 100 metres		37.73
GB team, 1999		
4 × 200 metres	1	21.29
GB team, 1989		
4 × 400 metres	2	56.60
GB team, 1996		
4 × 800 metres	7	03.89
GB team, 1982		

FIELD EVENTS	metres	ft	in
High jump	2.37	7	9¼
Steve Smith, 1992, 1993			
Pole vault	5.80	19	0¼
Nick Buckfield, 1998			
Long jump	8.23	27	0
Lynn Davies, 1968			
Triple jump	18.29	60	0¼
Jonathan Edwards, 1995			
Shot	21.68	71	1½
Geoff Capes, 1980			
Discus	66.64	218	8
Perris Wilkins, 1998			
Hammer	77.54	254	5
Martin Girvan, 1984			
Javelin	91.46	300	1
Steve Backley, 1992			
Decathlon		8,847 points	
Daley Thompson, 1984			

WALKING (TRACK)	hr.	min.	sec.
20,000 metres	1	23	26.5
Ian McCombie, 1990			
30,000 metres	2	19	18
Christopher Maddocks, 1984			
50,000 metres	4	05	44.6
Paul Blagg, 1990			
26,037 metres (16 miles 315 yards)	2	00	00.0
Ron Wallwork, 1971			

WOMEN

TRACK EVENTS	min.	sec.
100 metres		11.10
Kathy Cook, 1981		
200 metres		22.10
Kathy Cook, 1984		
400 metres		49.43
Kathy Cook, 1984		
800 metres	1	56.21
Kelly Holmes, 1995		
1,500 metres	3	58.07
Kelly Holmes, 1997		

1 mile		4	17.57
Zola Budd, 1985			
3,000 metres		8	27.40*
Paula Radcliffe, 1999			
5,000 metres		14	43.54*
Paula Radcliffe, 1999			
10,000 metres		30	27.13*
Paula Radcliffe, 1999			
100 metres hurdles			12.80
Angela Thorp, 1996			
400 metres hurdles			52.74
Sally Gunnell, 1993			

RELAYS	min.	sec.
4 × 100 metres		42.43
GB team, 1980		
4 × 200 metres	1	31.57
GB team, 1977		
4 × 400 metres	3	22.01
GB team, 1991		
4 × 800 metres	8	23.8
GB team, 1971		

FIELD EVENTS	metres	ft	in
High jump	1.95	6	4¾
Diana Elliott, 1982			
Pole vault	4.35*	14	3¼
Janine Whitlock, 2000			
Long jump	6.90	22	7¾
Beverley Kinch, 1983			
Triple jump	15.15	49	8½
Ashia Hansen, 1997			
Shot	19.36	63	6¼
Judy Oakes, 1988			
Discus	67.48	221	5
Margaret Ritchie, 1981			
Hammer	67.44*	221	3
Lorraine Shaw, 2000			
Javelin	77.44	254	1
Fatima Whitbread, 1986			
Heptathlon		6,831* points	
Denise Lewis, 2000			

*Awaiting ratification

SWIMMING WORLD RECORDS
AS AT 9 SEPTEMBER 2000

MEN	min.	sec.
50 metres freestyle		21.64
Alexander Popov, Russia		
100 metres freestyle		47.84
Pieter van den Hoogenband (Netherlands)		
200 metres freestyle	1	45.35
Pieter van den Hoogenband (Netherlands)		
400 metres freestyle	3	40.59
Ian Thorpe, Australia		
800 metres freestyle	7	46.00
Kieren Perkins, Australia		
1,500 metres freestyle	14	41.66
Kieren Perkins, Australia		
100 metres breaststroke	1	00.37
Roman Sloudov, Russia		
200 metres breaststroke	2	10.16
Mike Barrowman, USA		
100 metres butterfly		51.81
Michael Klim, Australia		

	min.	sec.
200 metres butterfly	1	55.22
Denis Pankratov, Russia		
100 metres backstroke		53.60
Lenny Krayzelburg, USA		
200 metres backstroke	1	55.87
Lenny Krayzelburg, USA		
200 metres medley	1	58.16
Jani Sievinen, Finland		
400 metres medley	4	12.30
Tom Dolan, USA		
4 × 100 metres freestyle relay	3	13.67
Australia		
4 × 200 metres freestyle relay	7	07.05
Australia		
4 × 100 metres medley relay	3	33.73
USA		

WOMEN	min.	sec.
50 metres freestyle		24.13
Inge de Bruijn, Netherlands		
100 metres freestyle		53.80
Inge de Bruijn, Netherlands		
200 metres freestyle	1	56.77
Franziska van Almsick, Germany		
400 metres freestyle	4	03.85
Janet Evans, USA		
800 metres freestyle	8	16.22
Janet Evans, USA		
1,500 metres freestyle	15	52.10
Janet Evans, USA		
100 metres breaststroke	1	06.52
Penny Heyns, South Africa		
200 metres breaststroke	2	23.64
Rebecca Brown, Australia		
100 metres butterfly		56.61
Inge de Bruijn, Netherlands		
200 metres butterfly	2	05.81
Susan O Neill, Australia		
100 metres backstroke	1	00.16
Cihong He, China		
200 metres backstroke	2	06.62
Krisztina Egerszegi, Hungary		
200 metres medley	2	09.72
Wu Yanyan, China		
400 metres medley	4	33.59
Jana Klochkova (Ukraine)		
4 × 100 metres freestyle relay	3	36.61
USA		
4 × 200 metres freestyle relay	7	55.47
GDR		
4 × 100 metres medley relay	3	58.30
USA		

The Olympic Games

Venues of the modern Olympic Games

I	Athens, Greece	1896
II	Paris, France	1900
III	St Louis, USA	1904
*	Athens	1906
IV	London, Britain	1908
V	Stockholm, Sweden	1912
VI	Berlin, Germany	1916
VII	Antwerp, Belgium	1920
VIII	Paris, France	1924
IX	Amsterdam, Netherlands	1928
X	Los Angeles, USA	1932
XI	Berlin, Germany	1936
†XII	Tokyo, Japan, then Helsinki, Finland	1940
†XIII	London, Britain	1944
XIV	London, Britain	1948
XV	Helsinki, Finland	1952
XVI	Melbourne, Australia	1956
XVII	Rome, Italy	1960
XVIII	Tokyo, Japan	1964
XIX	Mexico City, Mexico	1968
XX	Munich, West Germany	1972
XXI	Montreal, Canada	1976
XXII	Moscow, USSR	1980
XXIII	Los Angeles, USA	1984
XXIV	Seoul, South Korea	1988
XXV	Barcelona, Spain	1992
XXVI	Atlanta, USA	1996
XXVII	Sydney, Australia	2000
XXVIII	Athens, Greece	2004

WINTER OLYMPIC GAMES

I	Chamonix, France	1924
II	St Moritz, Switzerland	1928
III	Lake Placid, USA	1932
IV	Garmisch-Partenkirchen, Germany	1936
V	St Moritz, Switzerland	1948
VI	Oslo, Norway	1952
VII	Cortina d'Ampezzo, Italy	1956
VIII	Squaw Valley, USA	1960
IX	Innsbruck, Austria	1964
X	Grenoble, France	1968
XI	Sapporo, Japan	1972
XII	Innsbruck, Austria	1976
XIII	Lake Placid, USA	1980
XIV	Sarajevo, Yugoslavia	1984
XV	Calgary, Canada	1988
XVI	Albertville, France	1992
XVII	Lillehammer, Norway	1994
XVIII	Nagano, Japan	1998
XIX	Salt Lake City, USA	2002
XX	Turin, Italy	2006

*The 'Intercalated' Games
†These Games were scheduled but did not take place owing to World Wars
Equestrian events were held in Stockholm, Sweden

Weights and Measures

SI UNITS

The Système International d'Unités (SI) is an international and coherent system of units devised to meet all known needs for measurement in science and technology. The system was adopted by the eleventh Conférence Générale des Poids et Mesures (CGPM) in 1960. A comprehensive description of the system is given in *SI The International System of Units* (HMSO). The British Standards describing the essential features of the International System of Units are *Specifications for SI units and recommendations for the use of their multiples and certain other units* (BS 5555:1993) and *Conversion Factors and Tables* (BS 350, Part 1:1974).

The system consists of seven base units and the derived units formed as products or quotients of various powers of the base units. Together the base units and the derived units make up the coherent system of units. In the UK the SI base units, and almost all important derived units, are realised at the National Physical Laboratory and disseminated through the National Measurement System.

Base Units

metre (m) = unit of length
kilogram (kg) = unit of mass
second (s) = unit of time
ampere (A) = unit of electric current
kelvin (K) = unit of thermodynamic temperature
mole (mol) = unit of amount of substance
candela (cd) = unit of luminous intensity

Derived Units

For some of the derived SI units, special names and symbols exist; those approved by the CGPM are as follows:

hertz (Hz) = unit of frequency
newton (N) = unit of force
pascal (Pa) = unit of pressure, stress
joule (J) = unit of energy, work, quantity of heat
watt (W) = unit of power, radiant flux
coulomb (C) = unit of electric charge, quantity of electricity
volt (V) = unit of electric potential, potential difference, electromotive force
farad (F) = unit of electric capacitance
ohm (Ω) = unit of electric resistance
siemens (S) = unit of electric conductance
weber (Wb) = unit of magnetic flux
tesla (T) = unit of magnetic flux density
henry (H) = unit of inductance
degree Celsius (°C) = unit of Celsius temperature
lumen (lm) = unit of luminous flux
lux (lx) = unit of illuminance
becquerel (Bq) = unit of activity (of a radionuclide)
gray (Gy) = unit of absorbed dose, specific energy imparted, kerma, absorbed dose index
sievert (Sv) = unit of dose equivalent, dose equivalent index
radian (rad) = unit of plane angle
steradian (sr) = unit of solid angle
Other derived units are expressed in terms of base units. Some of the more commonly used derived units are the following:

Unit of area = square metre (m^2)
Unit of volume = cubic metre (m^3)
Unit of velocity = metre per second ($m\,s^{-1}$)
Unit of acceleration = metre per second squared ($m\,s^{-2}$)
Unit of density = kilogram per cubic metre ($kg\,m^{-3}$)
Unit of momentum = kilogram metre per second ($kg\,m\,s^{-1}$)
Unit of magnetic field strength = ampere per metre ($A\,m^{-1}$)
Unit of surface tension = newton per metre ($N\,m^{-1}$)
Unit of dynamic viscosity = pascal second (Pa s)
Unit of heat capacity = joule per kelvin ($J\,K^{-1}$)
Unit of specific heat capacity = joule per kilogram kelvin ($J\,kg^{-1}\,K^{-1}$)
Unit of heat flux density, irradiance = watt per square metre ($W\,m^{-2}$)
Unit of thermal conductivity = watt per metre kelvin ($W\,m^{-1}K^{-1}$)
Unit of electric field strength = volt per metre ($V\,m^{-1}$)
Unit of luminance = candela per square metre ($cd\,m^{-2}$)

SI Prefixes

Decimal multiples and submultiples of the SI units are indicated by SI prefixes. These are as follows:

multiples		*submultiples*	
yotta (Y)	$\times 10^{24}$	deci (d)	$\times 10^{-1}$
zetta (Z)	$\times 10^{21}$	centi (c)	$\times 10^{-2}$
exa (E)	$\times 10^{18}$	milli (m)	$\times 10^{-3}$
peta (P)	$\times 10^{15}$	micro (μ)	$\times 10^{-6}$
tera (T)	$\times 10^{12}$	nano (n)	$\times 10^{-9}$
giga (G)	$\times 10^{9}$	pico (p)	$\times 10^{-12}$
mega (M)	$\times 10^{6}$	femto (f)	$\times 10^{-15}$
kilo (k)	$\times 10^{3}$	atto (a)	$\times 10^{-18}$
hecto (h)	$\times 10^{2}$	zepto (z)	$\times 10^{-21}$
deca (da)	$\times 10$	yocto (y)	$\times 10^{-24}$

METRIC UNITS

The metric primary standards are the metre as the unit of measurement of length, and the kilogram as the unit of measurement of mass. Other units of measurement are defined by reference to the primary standards.

Measurement of Length

Kilometre (km) = 1000 metres
Metre (m) is the length of the path travelled by light in vacuum during a time interval of 1/299 792 458 of a second
Decimetre (dm) = 1/10 metre
Centimetre (cm) = 1/100 metre
Millimetre (mm) = 1/1000 metre

Measurement of Area

Hectare (ha) = 100 ares
Decare = 10 ares
Are (a) = 100 square metres
Square metre = a superficial area equal to that of a square each side of which measures one metre
Square decimetre = 1/100 square metre
Square centimetre = 1/100 square decimetre
Square millimetre = 1/100 square centimetre

MEASUREMENT OF VOLUME

Cubic metre (m^3) = a volume equal to that of a cube each
   edge of which measures one metre
Cubic decimetre = 1/1000 cubic metre
Cubic centimetre (cc) = 1/1000 cubic decimetre
Hectolitre = 100 litres
Litre = a cubic decimetre
Decilitre = 1/10 litre
Centilitre = 1/100 litre
Millilitre = 1/1000 litre

MEASUREMENT OF CAPACITY

Hectolitre (hl) = 100 litres
Litre (l or L) = a cubic decimetre
Decilitre (dl) = 1/10 litre
Centilitre (cl) = 1/100 litre
Millilitre (ml) = 1/1000 litre

MEASUREMENT OF MASS OR WEIGHT

Tonne (t) = 1000 kilograms
Kilogram (kg) is equal to the mass of the international
   prototype of the kilogram
Hectogram (hg) = 1/10 kilogram
Gram (g) = 1/1000 kilogram
*Carat (metric) = 1/5 gram
Milligram (mg) = 1/1000 gram

*Used only for transactions in precious stones or pearls

METRICATION IN THE UK

The European Council Directive 80/181/EEC, as
amended by Council Directive 89/617/EEC, relates to
the use of units of measurement for economic, public
health, public safety or administrative purposes in the
member states of the European Union. The provisions of
the directives were incorporated into British law by the
Weights and Measures Act 1985 (Metrication) (Amendment) Order 1994 and the Units of Measurement Regulations 1994; these instruments amended the Weights and
Measures Act 1985. Parallel statutory rules amending
Northern Ireland weights and measures legislation were
made in May 1995.

   The general effect of the 1994 and 1995 legislation is to
end the use of imperial units of measurement for trade,
replacing them with metric units – *see* below for timetable
for UK metrication. Imperial units can, however, be used
in addition to metric units, as supplementary indications.

IMPERIAL UNITS

The imperial primary standards are the yard as the unit
of measurement of length and the pound as the unit of
measurement of mass. Other units of measurement are
defined by reference to the primary standards. Most of
these units are no longer authorised for use in trade in the
UK – *see* below.

MEASUREMENT OF LENGTH

Mile = 1760 yards
Furlong = 220 yards
Chain = 22 yards
Yard (yd) = 0.9144 metre
Foot (ft) = 1/3 yard
Inch (in) = 1/36 yard

MEASUREMENT OF AREA

Square mile = 640 acres
Acre = 4840 square yards
Rood = 1210 square yards
Square yard (sq. yd) = a superficial area equal to that of a
   square each side of which measures one yard

Square foot (sq. ft) = 1/9 square yard
Square inch (sq. in) = 1/144 square foot

MEASUREMENT OF VOLUME

Cubic yard = a volume equal to that of a cube each edge of
   which measures one yard
Cubic foot = 1/27 cubic yard
Cubic inch = 1/1728 cubic foot

MEASUREMENT OF CAPACITY

Bushel = 8 gallons
Peck = 2 gallons
Gallon (gal) = 4.54609 cubic decimetres
Quart (qt) = 1/4 gallon
*Pint (pt) = 1/2 quart
Gill = 1/4 pint
*Fluid ounce (fl oz) = 1/20 pint
Fluid drachm = 1/8 fluid ounce
Minim (min) = 1/60 fluid drachm

MEASUREMENT OF MASS OR WEIGHT

Ton = 2240 pounds
Hundredweight (cwt) = 112 pounds
Cental = 100 pounds
Quarter = 28 pounds
Stone = 14 pounds
*Pound (lb) = 0.453 592 37 kilogram
*Ounce (oz) = 1/16 pound
*†Ounce troy (oz tr) = 12/175 pound
Dram (dr) = 1/16 ounce
Grain (gr) = 1/7000 pound
Pennyweight (dwt) = 24 grains
Ounce apothecaries = 480 grains
Drachm (ʒ 1) = 1/8 ounce apothecaries
Scruple (϶1) = 1/3 drachm

*Units of measurement still authorised for use for trade in
the UK
†Used only for transactions in gold, silver or other precious
metals, and articles made therefrom

PHASING-OUT OF IMPERIAL UNITS IN THE UK

The Weights and Measures Act 1985 enacted the legal
units for the United Kingdom. It was amended to
implement the provisions of European Council Directive
80/181/EEC, as amended by Directive 89/617/EEC, by
the Weights and Measures Act 1985 (Metrication)
(Amendment) Order 1994 and the Units of Measurement
Regulations 1994, and by parallel statutory rules in
Northern Ireland in May 1995.

   The effect of the amended legislation is to phase out the
use of imperial units for trade, replacing them with metric
units. With effect from 30 September 1995 imperial units
ceased to be authorised for use in the UK for economic,
public health, public safety and administrative purposes,
with the following exceptions:

Units of measurement authorised for use in specialized
fields between 1 October 1995 and 31 December 1999

Unit	Field of application
fathom	Marine navigation
fluid ounce ⎫	Beer, cider, water, lemonade, fruit juice in
pint ⎬	returnable containers
ounce ⎫	
pound ⎬	Goods for sale loose from bulk
therm	Gas supply

Units of measurement authorised for use in specialised fields from 1 October 1995, without time limit

Unit	Field of application
inch	
foot	Road traffic signs, distance and speed
yard	measurement
mile	
pint	Dispense of draught beer or cider
	Milk in returnable containers
acre	Land registration
troy ounce	Transactions in precious metals

MEASUREMENT OF ELECTRICITY

Units of measurement of electricity are defined by the Weights and Measures Act 1985 as follows:

ampere (A) = that constant current which, if maintained in two straight parallel conductors of infinite length, of negligible circular cross-section and placed 1 metre apart in vacuum, would produce between these conductors a force equal to 2×10^{-7} newton per metre of length

ohm (Ω) = the electric resistance between two points of a conductor when a constant potential difference of 1 volt, applied between the two points, produces in the conductor a current of 1 ampere, the conductor not being the seat of any electromotive force

volt (V) = the difference of electric potential between two points of a conducting wire carrying a constant current of 1 ampere when the power dissipated between these points is equal to 1 watt

watt (W) = the power which in one second gives rise to energy of 1 joule

kilowatt (kW) = 1000 watts

megawatt (MW) = one million watts

WATER AND LIQUOR MEASURES

1 cubic foot = 62.32 lb
1 gallon = 10 lb
1 cubic cm = 1 gram
1000 cubic cm = 1 litre; 1 kilogram
1 cubic metre = 1000 litres; 1000 kg; 1 tonne
An inch of rain on the surface of an acre (43560 sq. ft) = 3630 cubic ft = 100.992 tons
Cisterns: A cistern 4 × 2½ feet and 3 feet deep will hold brimful 186.963 gallons, weighing 1869.63 lb in addition to its own weight

WATER FOR SHIPS

Kilderkin = 18 gallons
Barrel = 36 gallons
Puncheon = 72 gallons
Butt = 110 gallons
Tun = 210 gallons

BOTTLES OF WINE

Traditional equivalents in standard champagne bottles:
Magnum = 2 bottles
Jeroboam = 4 bottles
Rehoboam = 6 bottles
Methuselah = 8 bottles
Salmanazar = 12 bottles
Balthazar = 16 bottles
Nebuchadnezzar = 20 bottles

A quarter of a bottle is known as a *nip*
An eighth of a bottle is known as a *baby*

ANGULAR AND CIRCULAR MEASURES

60 seconds (″) = 1 minute (′)
60 minutes = 1 degree (°)
90 degrees = 1 right angle or quadrant
Diameter of circle × 3.1416 = circumference
Diameter squared × 0.7854 = area of circle
Diameter squared × 3.1416 = surface of sphere
Diameter cubed × 0.523 = solidity of sphere
One degree of circumference × 57.3 = radius*
Diameter of cylinder × 3.141 6; product by length or height, gives the surface
Diameter squared × 0.7854; product by length or height, gives solid content

*Or, one radian (the angle subtended at the centre of a circle by an arc of the circumference equal in length to the radius) = 57.3 degrees

MILLION, BILLION, ETC.

Value in the UK

Million	thousand × thousand	10^6
*Billion	million × million	10^{12}
Trillion	million × billion	10^{18}
Quadrillion	million × trillion	10^{24}

Value in USA

Million	thousand × thousand	10^6
*Billion	thousand × million	10^9
Trillion	million × million	10^{12}
Quadrillion	million × billion US	10^{15}

*The American usage of billion (i.e. 10^9) is increasingly common, and is now universally used by statisticians

NAUTICAL MEASURES

DISTANCE

Distance at sea is measured in nautical miles. The British standard nautical mile was 6080 feet but this measure has been obsolete since 1970 when the international nautical mile of 1852 metres was adopted by the Hydrographic Department of the Ministry of Defence. The cable (600 feet or 100 fathoms) was a measure approximately one-tenth of a nautical mile. Such distances are now expressed in decimal parts of a sea mile or in metres.

Soundings at sea were recorded in fathoms (6 feet). Depths are now expressed in metres on Admiralty charts.

SPEED

Speed is measured in nautical miles per hour, called knots. A ship moving at the rate of 30 nautical miles per hour is said to be doing 30 knots.

knots	m.p.h.	knots	m.p.h.
1	1.1515	9	10.3636
2	2.3030	10	11.5151
3	3.4545	15	17.2727
4	4.6060	20	23.0303
5	5.7575	25	28.7878
6	6.9090	30	34.5454
7	8.0606	35	40.3030
8	9.2121	40	46.0606

TONNAGE

Under the Merchant Shipping Act 1854, the tonnage of UK-registered vessels was measured in tons of 100 cubic feet. The need for a universal method of measurement led to the adoption of the International Convention on Tonnage Measurements of Ships 1969, which measures, in cubic metres, all the internal spaces of a vessel for the gross tonnage and those of the cargo compartments for the net tonnage. The convention has applied since July 1982 to new ships, ships which needed to be remeasured because of substantial alterations, and ships whose owners requested remeasurement. On 18 July 1994 the convention became mandatory and all vessels should have been remeasured by that date; however, there is a backlog and some vessels have not yet been remeasured.

DISTANCE OF THE HORIZON

The limit of distance to which one can see varies with the height of the spectator. The greatest distance at which an object on the surface of the sea, or of a level plain, can be seen by a person whose eyes are at a height of five feet from the same level is nearly three miles. At a height of 20 feet the range is increased to nearly six miles, and an approximate rule for finding the range of vision for small heights is to increase the square root of the number of feet that the eye is above the level surface by a third of itself. The result is the distance of the horizon in miles, but is slightly in excess of that in the table below, which is computed by a more precise formula. The table may be used conversely to show the distance of an object of given height that is just visible from a point on the surface of the earth or sea. Refraction is taken into account both in the approximate rule and in the table.

Height in feet	range in miles
5	2.9
20	5.9
50	9.3
100	13.2
500	29.5
1,000	41.6
2,000	58.9
3,000	72.1
4,000	83.3
5,000	93.1
20,000	186.2

TEMPERATURE SCALES

The SI (International System) unit of temperature is the kelvin, which is defined as the fraction 1/273.16 of the temperature of the triple point of water (i.e. where ice, water and water vapour are in equilibrium). The zero of the Kelvin scale is the absolute zero of temperature. The freezing point of water is 273.15 K and the boiling point (as adopted in the International Temperature Scale of 1990) is 373.124 K.

The Celsius scale (formerly centigrade) is defined by subtracting 273.15 from the Kelvin temperature. The Fahrenheit scale is related to the Celsius scale by the relationships:

temperature $°F$ = (temperature $°C \times 1.8$) + 32
temperature $°C$ = (temperature $°F - 32$) ÷ 1.8

It follows from these definitions that the freezing point of water is 0°C and 32°F. The boiling point is 99.974°C and 211.953°F.

The temperature of the human body varies from person to person and in the same person can be affected by a variety of factors. In most people body temperature varies between 36.5°C and 37.2°C (97.7–98.9°F).

Conversion between scales

°C	°F	°C	°F	°C	°F
100	212	60	140	20	68
99	210.2	59	138.2	19	66.2
98	208.4	58	136.4	18	64.4
97	206.6	57	134.6	17	62.6
96	204.8	56	132.8	16	60.8
95	203	55	131	15	59
94	201.2	54	129.2	14	57.2
93	199.4	53	127.4	13	55.4
92	197.6	52	125.6	12	53.6
91	195.8	51	123.8	11	51.8
90	194	50	122	10	50
89	192.2	49	120.2	9	48.2
88	190.4	48	118.4	8	46.4
87	188.6	47	116.6	7	44.6
86	186.8	46	114.8	6	42.8
85	185	45	113	5	41
84	183.2	44	111.2	4	39.2
83	181.4	43	109.4	3	37.4
82	179.6	42	107.6	2	35.6
81	177.8	41	105.8	1	33.8
80	176	40	104	zero	32
79	174.2	39	102.2	− 1	30.2
78	172.4	38	100.4	− 2	28.4
77	170.6	37	98.6	− 3	26.6
76	168.8	36	96.8	− 4	24.8
75	167	35	95	− 5	23
74	165.2	34	93.2	− 6	21.2
73	163.4	33	91.4	− 7	19.4
72	161.6	32	89.6	− 8	17.6
71	159.8	31	87.8	− 9	15.8
70	158	30	86	−10	14
69	156.2	29	84.2	−11	12.2
68	154.4	28	82.4	−12	10.4
67	152.6	27	80.6	−13	8.6
66	150.8	26	78.8	−14	6.8
65	149	25	77	−15	5
64	147.2	24	75.2	−16	3.2
63	145.4	23	73.4	−17	1.4
62	143.6	22	71.6	−18	0.4
61	141.8	21	69.8	−19	−2.2

PAPER MEASURES

Printing Paper
516 sheets = 1 ream
2 reams = 1 bundle
5 bundles = 1 bale

Writing Paper
480 sheets = 1 ream
20 quires = 1 ream
24 sheets = 1 quire

BROWN PAPERS

	inches		inches
Casing	46 × 36	Imperial Cap	29 × 22
Double Imperial	45 × 29	Haven Cap	26 × 21
Elephant	34 × 24	Bag Cap	24 × 19$\frac{1}{2}$
Double Four Pound	31 × 21	Kent Cap	21 × 18

PRINTING PAPERS

	inches		inches
Foolscap	17 × 13$\frac{1}{2}$	Double Large	
Double Foolscap	27 × 17	Post	33 × 21
Quad Foolscap	34 × 27	Demy	22$\frac{1}{2}$ × 17$\frac{1}{2}$
Crown	20 × 15	Double Demy	35 × 22$\frac{1}{2}$
Double Crown	30 × 20	Quad Demy	45 × 35
Quad Crown	40 × 30	Music Demy	20 × 15$\frac{1}{2}$

Double Quad		Medium	23 × 18
Crown	60 × 40	Royal	25 × 20
Post	$19\frac{1}{4} \times 15\frac{1}{2}$	Super Royal	$27\frac{1}{2} \times 20\frac{1}{2}$
Double Post	$31\frac{1}{2} \times 19\frac{1}{2}$	Elephant	28 × 23
		Imperial	30 × 22

Writing and Drawing Papers

	inches		*inches*
Emperor	72 × 48	Copy or Draft	20 × 16
Antiquarian	53 × 31	Demy	$20 \times 15\frac{1}{2}$
Double Elephant	40 × 27	Post	$19 \times 15\frac{1}{4}$
Grand Eagle	$42 \times 28\frac{3}{4}$	Pinched Post	$18\frac{1}{2} \times 14\frac{3}{4}$
Atlas	34 × 26	Foolscap	$17 \times 13\frac{1}{2}$
Colombier	$34\frac{1}{2} \times 23\frac{1}{2}$	Double Foolscap	$26\frac{1}{2} \times 16\frac{1}{2}$
Imperial	30 × 22	Double Post	$30\frac{1}{2} \times 19$
Elephant	28 × 23	Double Large Post	33 × 21
Cartridge	26 × 21	Double Demy	31 × 20
Super Royal	27 × 19	Brief	$16\frac{1}{2} \times 13\frac{1}{4}$
Royal	24 × 19	Pott	$15 \times 12\frac{1}{2}$
Medium	$22 \times 17\frac{1}{2}$		
Large Post	$21 \times 16\frac{1}{2}$		

INTERNATIONAL PAPER SIZES

The basis of the international series of paper sizes is a rectangle having an area of one square metre, the sides of which are in the proportion of $1{:}\sqrt{2}$. The proportions $1{:}\sqrt{2}$ have a geometrical relationship, the side and diagonal of any square being in this proportion. The effect of this arrangement is that if the area of the sheet of paper is doubled or halved, the shorter side and the longer side of the new sheet are still in the same proportion $1{:}\sqrt{2}$. This feature is useful where photographic enlargement or reduction is used, as the proportions remain the same.

Description of the A series is by capital A followed by a figure. The basic size has the description A0 and the higher the figure following the letter, the greater is the number of sub-divisions and therefore the smaller the sheet. Half A0 is A1 and half A1 is A2. Where larger dimensions are required the A is preceded by a figure. Thus 2A means twice the size A0; 4A is four times the size of A0.

Subsidiary Series

B sizes are sizes intermediate between any two adjacent sizes of the A series. There is a series of C sizes which is used much less. A is for magazines and books, B for posters, wall charts and other large items, C for envelopes particularly where it is necessary for an envelope (in C series) to fit into another envelope. The size recommended for business correspondence is A4.

Long sizes (DL) are obtainable by dividing any appropriate sizes from the two series above into three, four or eight equal parts parallel with the shorter side in such a manner that the proportion of $1{:}\sqrt{2}$ is not maintained, the ratio between the longer and the shorter sides being greater than $\sqrt{2}{:}1$. In practice long sizes should be produced from the A series only.

It is an essential feature of these series that the dimensions are of the trimmed or finished size.

A Series

	mm		*mm*
A0	841 × 1189	A6	105 × 148
A1	594 × 841	A7	74 × 105
A2	420 × 594	A8	52 × 74
A3	297 × 420	A9	37 × 52
A4	210 × 297	A10	26 × 37
A5	148 × 210		

B Series

	mm		*mm*
B0	1000 × 1414	B6	125 × 176
B1	707 × 1000	B7	88 × 125
B2	500 × 707	B8	62 × 88
B3	353 × 500	B9	44 × 62
B4	250 × 353	B10	31 × 44
B5	176 × 250		

C Series / DL

C Series	*mm*	DL	*mm*
C4	324 × 229	DL	110 × 220
C5	229 × 162		
C6	114 × 162		

BOUND BOOKS

The book sizes most commonly used are listed below. Approximate centimetre equivalents are also shown. International sizes are converted to their nearest imperial size, e.g. A4 = D4; A5 = D8.

		inches	*cm*
Crown 32mo	C32	$2\frac{1}{2} \times 3\frac{3}{4}$	6 × 9
Crown 16mo	C16	$3\frac{3}{4} \times 5$	9 × 13
Foolscap 8vo	F8	$4\frac{1}{4} \times 6\frac{3}{4}$	11 × 17
Demy 16mo	D16	$4\frac{3}{8} \times 5\frac{5}{8}$	11 × 14
Crown 8vo	C8	$5 \times 7\frac{1}{2}$	13 × 19
Demy 8vo	D8	$5\frac{5}{8} \times 8\frac{3}{4}$	14 × 22
Medium 8vo	M8	$5\frac{3}{4} \times 9$	15 × 23
Royal 8vo	R8	$6\frac{1}{4} \times 10$	16 × 25
Super Royal 8vo	suR8	$6\frac{3}{4} \times 10$	17 × 25
Foolscap 4to	F4	$6\frac{3}{4} \times 8\frac{1}{2}$	17 × 22
Crown 4to	C4	$7\frac{1}{2} \times 10$	19 × 25
Imperial 8vo	Imp8	$7\frac{1}{2} \times 11$	19 × 28
Demy 4to	D4	$8\frac{3}{4} \times 11\frac{1}{4}$	22 × 29
Royal 4to	R4	$10 \times 12\frac{1}{2}$	25 × 31
Super Royal 4to	suR4	$10 \times 13\frac{1}{2}$	25 × 34
Crown Folio	Cfol	10 × 15	25 × 38
Imperial Folio	Impfol	11 × 15	28 × 38

Folio = a sheet folded in half
Quarto (4to) = a sheet folded into four
Octavo (8vo) = a sheet folded into eight
Books are usually bound up in sheets of 16, 32 or 64 pages. Octavo books are generally printed 64 pages at a time, 32 pages on each side of a sheet of quad.

CONVERSION TABLES FOR WEIGHTS AND MEASURES

Bold figures equal units of either of the columns beside them; thus: 1 cm = 0.394 inches and 1 inch = 2.540 cm

LENGTH			AREA			VOLUME			WEIGHT (MASS)		
Centimetres		*Inches*	*Square cm*		*Square in*	*Cubic cm*		*Cubic in*	*Kilograms*		*Pounds*
2.540	**1**	0.394	6.452	**1**	0.155	16.387	**1**	0.061	0.454	**1**	2.205
5.080	**2**	0.787	12.903	**2**	0.310	32.774	**2**	0.122	0.907	**2**	4.409
7.620	**3**	1.181	19.355	**3**	0.465	49.161	**3**	0.183	1.361	**3**	6.614
10.160	**4**	1.575	25.806	**4**	0.620	65.548	**4**	0.244	1.814	**4**	8.819
12.700	**5**	1.969	32.258	**5**	0.775	81.936	**5**	0.305	2.268	**5**	11.023
15.240	**6**	2.362	38.710	**6**	0.930	98.323	**6**	0.366	2.722	**6**	13.228
17.780	**7**	2.756	45.161	**7**	1.085	114.710	**7**	0.427	3.175	**7**	15.432
20.320	**8**	3.150	51.613	**8**	1.240	131.097	**8**	0.488	3.629	**8**	17.637
22.860	**9**	3.543	58.064	**9**	1.395	147.484	**9**	0.549	4.082	**9**	19.842
25.400	**10**	3.937	64.516	**10**	1.550	163.871	**10**	0.610	4.536	**10**	22.046
50.800	**20**	7.874	129.032	**20**	3.100	327.742	**20**	1.220	9.072	**20**	44.092
76.200	**30**	11.811	193.548	**30**	4.650	491.613	**30**	1.831	13.608	**30**	66.139
101.600	**40**	15.748	258.064	**40**	6.200	655.484	**40**	2.441	18.144	**40**	88.185
127.000	**50**	19.685	322.580	**50**	7.750	819.355	**50**	3.051	22.680	**50**	110.231
152.400	**60**	23.622	387.096	**60**	9.300	983.226	**60**	3.661	27.216	**60**	132.277
177.800	**70**	27.559	451.612	**70**	10.850	1147.097	**70**	4.272	31.752	**70**	154.324
203.200	**80**	31.496	516.128	**80**	12.400	1310.968	**80**	4.882	36.287	**80**	176.370
228.600	**90**	35.433	580.644	**90**	13.950	1474.839	**90**	5.492	40.823	**90**	198.416
254.000	**100**	39.370	645.160	**100**	15.500	1638.710	**100**	6.102	45.359	**100**	220.464

Metres		*Yards*	*Square m*		*Square yd*	*Cubic m*		*Cubic yd*	*Metric tonnes*		*Tons (UK)*
0.914	**1**	1.094	0.836	**1**	1.196	0.765	**1**	1.308	1.016	**1**	0.984
1.829	**2**	2.187	1.672	**2**	2.392	1.529	**2**	2.616	2.032	**2**	1.968
2.743	**3**	3.281	2.508	**3**	3.588	2.294	**3**	3.924	3.048	**3**	2.953
3.658	**4**	4.374	3.345	**4**	4.784	3.058	**4**	5.232	4.064	**4**	3.937
4.572	**5**	5.468	4.181	**5**	5.980	3.823	**5**	6.540	5.080	**5**	4.921
5.486	**6**	6.562	5.017	**6**	7.176	4.587	**6**	7.848	6.096	**6**	5.905
6.401	**7**	7.655	5.853	**7**	8.372	5.352	**7**	9.156	7.112	**7**	6.889
7.315	**8**	8.749	6.689	**8**	9.568	6.116	**8**	10.464	8.128	**8**	7.874
8.230	**9**	9.843	7.525	**9**	10.764	6.881	**9**	11.772	9.144	**9**	8.858
9.144	**10**	10.936	8.361	**10**	11.960	7.646	**10**	13.080	10.161	**10**	9.842
18.288	**20**	21.872	16.723	**20**	23.920	15.291	**20**	26.159	20.321	**20**	19.684
27.432	**30**	32.808	25.084	**30**	35.880	22.937	**30**	39.239	30.481	**30**	29.526
36.576	**40**	43.745	33.445	**40**	47.840	30.582	**40**	52.318	40.642	**40**	39.368
45.720	**50**	54.681	41.806	**50**	59.799	38.228	**50**	65.398	50.802	**50**	49.210
54.864	**60**	65.617	50.168	**60**	71.759	45.873	**60**	78.477	60.963	**60**	59.052
64.008	**70**	76.553	58.529	**70**	83.719	53.519	**70**	91.557	71.123	**70**	68.894
73.152	**80**	87.489	66.890	**80**	95.679	61.164	**80**	104.636	81.284	**80**	78.737
82.296	**90**	98.425	75.251	**90**	107.639	68.810	**90**	117.716	91.444	**90**	88.579
91.440	**100**	109.361	83.613	**100**	119.599	76.455	**100**	130.795	101.605	**100**	98.421

Kilometres		*Miles*	*Hectares*		*Acres*	*Litres*		*Gallons*	*Metric tonnes*		*Tons (US)*
1.609	**1**	0.621	0.405	**1**	2.471	4.546	**1**	0.220	0.907	**1**	1.102
3.219	**2**	1.243	0.809	**2**	4.942	9.092	**2**	0.440	1.814	**2**	2.205
4.828	**3**	1.864	1.214	**3**	7.413	13.638	**3**	0.660	2.722	**3**	3.305
6.437	**4**	2.485	1.619	**4**	9.844	18.184	**4**	0.880	3.629	**4**	4.409
8.047	**5**	3.107	2.023	**5**	12.355	22.730	**5**	1.100	4.536	**5**	5.521
9.656	**6**	3.728	2.428	**6**	14.826	27.276	**6**	1.320	5.443	**6**	6.614
11.265	**7**	4.350	2.833	**7**	17.297	31.822	**7**	1.540	6.350	**7**	7.716
12.875	**8**	4.971	3.327	**8**	19.769	36.368	**8**	1.760	7.257	**8**	8.818
14.484	**9**	5.592	3.642	**9**	22.240	40.914	**9**	1.980	8.165	**9**	9.921
16.093	**10**	6.214	4.047	**10**	24.711	45.460	**10**	2.200	9.072	**10**	11.023
32.187	**20**	12.427	8.094	**20**	49.421	90.919	**20**	4.400	18.144	**20**	22.046
48.280	**30**	18.641	12.140	**30**	74.132	136.379	**30**	6.599	27.216	**30**	33.069
64.374	**40**	24.855	16.187	**40**	98.842	181.839	**40**	8.799	36.287	**40**	44.092
80.467	**50**	31.069	20.234	**50**	123.555	227.298	**50**	10.999	45.359	**50**	55.116
96.561	**60**	37.282	24.281	**60**	148.263	272.758	**60**	13.199	54.431	**60**	66.139
112.654	**70**	43.496	28.328	**70**	172.974	318.217	**70**	15.398	63.503	**70**	77.162
128.748	**80**	49.710	32.375	**80**	197.684	363.677	**80**	17.598	72.575	**80**	88.185
144.841	**90**	55.923	36.422	**90**	222.395	409.137	**90**	19.798	81.647	**90**	99.208
160.934	**100**	62.137	40.469	**100**	247.105	454.596	**100**	21.998	90.719	**100**	110.231

Abbreviations

A	Associate of
AA	Alcoholics Anonymous
	Automobile Association
AAA	Amateur Athletic Association
AB	Able-bodied seaman
ABA	Amateur Boxing Association
abbr(ev)	abbreviation
ABM	Anti-ballistic missile
abr	abridged
ac	alternating current
a/c	account
AC	Aircraftman
	(*Ante Christum*) Before Christ
	Companion, Order of Australia
ACAS	Advisory, Conciliation and Arbitration Service
ACT	Australian Capital Territory
AD	(*Anno Domini*) In the year of our Lord
ADC	Aide-de-Camp
ADC (P)	Personal ADC to The Queen
adj	adjective
Adj	Adjutant
ad lib	(*ad libitum*) at pleasure
Adm	Admiral
	Admission
adv	adverb
AE	Air Efficiency Award
AEEU	Amalgamated Engineering and Electrical Union
AEM	Air Efficiency Medal
AFC	Air Force Cross
AFM	Air Force Medal
AG	Adjutant-General
	Attorney-General
AGM	air-to-ground missile
	annual general meeting
AH	(*Anno Hegirae*) In the year of the Hegira
AI	Artificial intelligence
AIDS	Acquired immune deficiency syndrome
AIM	Alternative Investment Market
alt	altitude
am	(*ante meridiem*) before noon
AM	(*Anno mundi*) In the year of the world
	amplitude modulation
	Member of the Welsh Assembly
amp	ampere
	amplifier
ANC	African National Congress
anon	anonymous
ANZAC	Australian and New Zealand Army Corps
AO	Air Officer
	Officer, Order of Australia
AOC	Air Officer Commanding
AONB	Area of Outstanding Natural Beauty
AS	Anglo-Saxon
ASA	Advertising Standards Authority
	Amateur Swimming Association
asap	as soon as possible
ASB	Alternative Service Book
ASEAN	Association of South East Asian Nations
ASH	Action on Smoking and Health
ASLEF	Associated Society of Locomotive Engineers and Firemen
ASLIB	Association for Information Management
ATC	Air Training Corps
AUC	(*ab urbe condita*) In the year from the foundation of Rome
	(*anno urbis conditae*) In the year of the founding of the city
AUT	Association of University Teachers
AV	Audio-visual
	Authorised Version (*of Bible*)
AVR	Army Volunteer Reserve
AWOL	Absent without leave
b	born bowled
BA	Bachelor of Arts
BAA	British Airports Authority
	British Astronomical Association
BAF	British Athletics Federation
BAFTA	British Academy of Film and Television Arts
Bart	Baronet
BAS	Bachelor in Agricultural Science
	British Antarctic Survey
BBC	British Broadcasting Corporation
BBSRC	Biotechnology and Biological Sciences Research Council
BC	Before Christ
	British Columbia
B Ch (D)	Bachelor of (Dental) Surgery
BCL	Bachelor of Civil Law
B Com	Bachelor of Commerce
BD	Bachelor of Divinity
BDA	British Dental Association
BDS	Bachelor of Dental Surgery
B Ed	Bachelor of Education
BEM	British Empire Medal
B Eng	Bachelor of Engineering
BFI	British Film Institute
BFPO	British Forces Post Office
BL	British Library
B Litt	Bachelor of Letters *or* of Literature
BM	Bachelor of Medicine
	British Museum
BMA	British Medical Association
B Mus	Bachelor of Music
BOTB	British Overseas Trade Board
Bp	Bishop
B Pharm	Bachelor of Pharmacy
B Phil	Bachelor of Philosophy
Br(it)	Britain
	British
BR	British Rail
Brig	Brigadier
BSc	Bachelor of Science
BSE	Bovine spongiform encephalopathy
BSI	British Standards Institution
BST	British Summer Time
Bt	Baronet
BTEC	Business and Technology Education Council
B Th	Bachelor of Theology
Btu	British thermal unit
BVM	(*Beata Virgo Maria*) Blessed Virgin Mary
BVMS	Bachelor of Veterinary Medicine and Surgery
c	(*circa*) about
C	Celsius
	Centigrade
	Conservative
CA	Chartered Accountant (*Scotland*)
CAA	Civil Aviation Authority
CAB	Citizens' Advice Bureau
Cantab	(of) Cambridge
Cantuar:	of Canterbury (*Archbishop*)
CAP	Common Agricultural Policy
Capt	Captain
Caricom	Caribbean Community and Common Market
Carliol:	of Carlisle (*Bishop*)
CB	Companion, Order of the Bath
CBE	Commander, Order of the British Empire
CBI	Confederation of British Industry
CC	Chamber of Commerce
	Companion, Order of Canada
	City Council
	County Council
	County Court
CCC	County Cricket Club
CCF	Combined Cadet Force
C Chem	Chartered Chemist
CD	Civil Defence
	compact disc
	Corps Diplomatique
Cdr	Commander
Cdre	Commodore
CDS	Chief of the Defence Staff
CE	Christian Era
	Civil Engineer
C Eng	Chartered Engineer
Cestr:	of Chester (*Bishop*)
CET	Central European Time
	Common External Tariff
cf	(*confer*) compare
CF	Chaplain to the Forces
CFC	Chlorofluorocarbon
CFS	Chronic Fatigue Syndrome
CGC	Conspicuous Gallantry Cross
Cgeol	Chartered Geologist
CGM	Conspicuous Gallantry Medal
CGS	Centimetre-gramme-second (*system*)
	Chief of General Staff
CH	Companion of Honour
ChB/M	Bachelor/Master of Surgery
CI	Channel Islands
	The Imperial Order of the Crown of India
CIA	Central Intelligence Agency
Cicestr:	of Chichester (*Bishop*)
CID	Criminal Investigation Department
CIE	Companion, Order of the Indian Empire
cif	cost, insurance and freight
C-in-C	Commander-in-Chief
CIPFA	Chartered Institute of Public Finance and Accountancy
CIS	Commonwealth of Independent States
CJD	Creutzfeld-Jakob disease
C Lit	Companion of Literature

CLJ	Commander, Order of St Lazarus of Jerusalem	DNA	deoxyribonucleic acid	FAO	Food and Agriculture Organisation (*UN*)
CM	(*Chirurgiae Magister*) Master of Surgery	DNB	*Dictionary of National Biography*	FBA	Fellow, British Academy
CMG	Companion, Order of St Michael and St George	do	(*ditto*) the same	FBAA	Fellow, British Association of Accountants and Auditors
CND	Campaign for Nuclear Disarmament	DoE	Department of the Environment	FBI	Federal Bureau of Investigation
c/o	care of	DOS	Disk operating system (*computer*)	FBIM	Fellow, British Institute of Management
CO	Commanding Officer conscientious objector	DP	Data processing	FBS	Fellow, Botanical Society
COD	Cash on delivery	D Ph *or* D Phil	Doctor of Philosophy	FC	Football Club
C of E	Church of England	DPP	Director of Public Prosecutions	FCA	Fellow, Institute of Chartered Accountants in England and Wales
COI	Central Office of Information	Dr	Doctor		
Col	Colonel	D Sc	Doctor of Science	FCCA	Fellow, Chartered Association of Certified Accountants
Con	Conservative	DSC	Distinguished Service Cross		
cons	consecrated	DSM	Distinguished Service Medal	FCGI	Fellow, City and Guilds of London Institute
Cpl	Corporal	DSO	Companion, Distinguished Service Order		
CPM	Colonial Police Medal			FCIA	Fellow, Corporation of Insurance Agents
CPRE	Council for the Protection of Rural England	DSS	Department of Social Security		
		DTI	Department of Trade and Industry	FCIArb	Fellow, Chartered Institute of Arbitrators
CPS	Crown Prosecution Service				
CPVE	Certificate of Pre-Vocational Education	DTP	Desk-top publishing	FCIB	Fellow, Chartered Institute of Bankers
		Dunelm:	of Durham (*Bishop*)		
CRE	Commission for Racial Equality	DV	(*Deo volente*) God willing		Fellow, Corporation of Insurance Brokers
CSA	Child Support Agency	E	East		
CSE	Certificate of Secondary Education	Ebor:	of York (*Archbishop*)	FCIBSE	Fellow, Chartered Institution of Building Services Engineers
		EBRD	European Bank for Reconstruction and Development		
CSI	Companion, Order of the Star of India			FCII	Fellow, Chartered Insurance Institute
		EC	European Community		
CVO	Commander, Royal Victorian Order	ECG	Electrocardiogram	FCIPS	Fellow, Chartered Institute of Purchasing and Supply
		ECGD	Export Credits Guarantee Department		
				FCIS	Fellow, Institute of Chartered Secretaries and Administrators
d	(*denarius*) penny	ECSC	European Coal and Steel Community		
DA	District Attorney (*USA*)			FCIT	Fellow, Chartered Institute of Transport
DBE	Dame Commander, Order of the British Empire	ECU	European Currency Unit		
		ED	Efficiency Decoration	FCMA	Fellow, Chartered Institute of Management Accountants
dc	direct current	EEC	European Economic Community		
DC	District Council District of Columbia	EEG	Electroencephalogram	FCO	Foreign and Commonwealth Office
		EFA	European Fighter Aircraft		
DCB	Dame Commander, Order of the Bath	EFTA	European Free Trade Association	FCP	Fellow, College of Preceptors
		eg	(*exempli gratia*) for the sake of example	FD	(*Fidei Defensor*) Defender of the Faith
D Ch	(*Doctor Chirurgiae*) Doctor of Surgery				
		EIB	European Investment Bank	FE	Further Education
DCL	Doctor of Civil Law	EMS	European Monetary System	fec	(*fecit*) made this
DCM	Distinguished Conduct Medal	EMU	European Monetary Union	ff	(*fecerunt*) made this (*pl*) folios following
DCMG	Dame Commander, Order of St Michael and St George	EOC	Equal Opportunities Commission		
				ff	(*fortissimo*) very loud
		EPSRC	Engineering and Physical Sciences Research Council	FFA	Fellow, Faculty of Actuaries (*Scotland*)
DCMS	Department for Culture, Media and Sport				
		ER	(*Elizabetha Regina*) Queen Elizabeth		Fellow, Institute of Financial Accountants
DCVO	Dame Commander, Royal Victorian Order				
		ERD	Emergency Reserve Decoration	FFAS	Fellow, Faculty of Architects and Surveyors
DD	Doctor of Divinity	ERM	Exchange Rate Mechanism		
DDS	Doctor of Dental Surgery	ERNIE	Electronic random number indicator equipment	FFCM	Fellow, Faculty of Community Medicine
DDT	dichlorodiphenyltrichloroethane				
del	(*delineavit*) he/she drew it	ESA	European Space Agency	FFPHM	Fellow, Faculty of Public Health Medicine
DETR	Department of the Environment, Transport and the Regions	ESP	Extra-sensory perception		
		ESRC	Economic and Social Research Council	FGS	Fellow, Geological Society
DFC	Distinguished Flying Cross			FHS	Fellow, Heraldry Society
DfEE	Department for Education and Employment	ETA	*Euzkadi ta Askatasuna* (Basque separatist organisation)	FHSM	Fellow, Institute of Health Service Management
		et al	(*et alibi*) and elsewhere		
DFID	Department for International Development		(*et alii*) and others	FIA	Fellow, Institute of Actuaries
		etc	(*et cetera*) and the other things/ and so forth	FIBiol	Fellow, Institute of Biology
DFM	Distinguished Flying Medal			FICE	Fellow, Institution of Civil Engineers
DG	(*Dei gratia*) By the grace of God Director-General	et seq	(*et sequentia*) and the following		
		EU	European Union	FICS	Fellow, Institution of Chartered Shipbrokers
DH	Department of Health	Euratom	European Atomic Energy Commission		
DHA	District Health Authority			FIEE	Fellow, Institution of Electrical Engineers
Dip Ed	Diploma in Education	Exon:	of Exeter (*Bishop*)		
Dip HE	Diploma in Higher Education			FIERE	Fellow, Institution of Electronic and Radio Engineers
Dip Tech	Diploma in Technology	*f*	(*forte*) loud		
DJ	Disc jockey	F	Fahrenheit	FIFA	International Association Football Federation
DL	Deputy Lieutenant		Fellow of		
D Litt	Doctor of Letters *or* of Literature	FA	Football Association	FIM	Fellow, Institute of Metals
DM	Deutsche Mark	FANY	First Aid Nursing Yeomanry	FIMM	Fellow, Institution of Mining and Metallurgy
D Mus	Doctor of Music				

FInstF	Fellow, Institute of Fuel	FRPharmS	Fellow, Royal Pharmaceutical	HH	Her/His Highness
FInstP	Fellow, Institute of Physics		Society		Her/His Honour
FIQS	Fellow, Institute of Quantity	FRPS	Fellow, Royal Photographic		His Holiness
	Surveyors		Society	HIM	Her/His Imperial Majesty
FIS	Fellow, Institute of Statisticians	FRS	Fellow, Royal Society	HIV	Human immunodeficiency virus
FJI	Fellow, Institute of Journalists	FRSA	Fellow, Royal Society of Arts	HJS	(*hic jacet sepultus*) here lies buried
fl	(*floruit*) flourished	FRSC	Fellow, Royal Society of	HM	Her/His Majesty('s)
FLA	Fellow, Library Association		Chemistry	HMAS	Her/His Majesty's Australian
FLS	Fellow, Linnaean Society	FRSE	Fellow, Royal Society of		Ship
FM	Field Marshal		Edinburgh	HMC	Headmasters' Conference
	frequency modulation	FRSH	Fellow, Royal Society of Health	HMI	Her/His Majesty's Inspector
fo	folio	FRSL	Fellow, Royal Society of	HML	Her/His Majesty's Lieutenant
FO	Flying Officer		Literature	HMS	Her/His Majesty's Ship
fob	free on board	FRTPI	Fellow, Royal Town Planning	HMSO	Her/His Majesty's Stationery
FPhS	Fellow, Philosophical Society		Institute		Office
FRAD	Fellow, Royal Academy of	FSA	Fellow, Society of Antiquaries	HNC	Higher National Certificate
	Dancing	FSS	Fellow, Royal Statistical	HND	Higher National Diploma
FRAeS	Fellow, Royal Aeronautical		Society	HOLMES	Home Office Large Major
	Society	FSVA	Fellow, Incorporated Society of		Enquiry System
FRAI	Fellow, Royal Anthropological		Valuers and Auctioneers	Hon	Honorary
	Institute	FT	*Financial Times*		Honourable
FRAM	Fellow, Royal Academy of Music	FTI	Fellow, Textile Institute	hp	horse power
FRAS	Fellow, Royal Asiatic Society	FTII	Fellow, Chartered Institute of	HP	Hire purchase
	Fellow, Royal		Taxation	HQ	Headquarters
	Astronomical Society	FZS	Fellow, Zoological Society	HR	Human resources
FRBS	Fellow, Royal Botanic Society			HRH	Her/His Royal Highness
	Fellow, Royal	G7	Group of Seven (Canada,	HSE	Health and Safety Executive
	Society of British Sculptors		France, Germany, Italy,		(*hic sepultus est*) here lies buried
FRCA	Fellow, Royal College of		Japan, UK, USA)	HSH	Her/His Serene Highness
	Anaesthetists	GATT	General Agreement on	HWM	High water mark
FRCGP	Fellow, Royal College of		Tariffs and Trade		
	General Practitioners	GBE	Dame/Knight Grand Cross,	I	Island
FRCM	Fellow, Royal College of Music		Order of the British Empire	IAAS	Incorporated Association of
FRCO	Fellow, Royal College of	GC	George Cross		Architects and Surveyors
	Organists	GCB	Dame/Knight Grand Cross,	IAEA	International Atomic
FRCOG	Fellow, Royal College of Obste-		Order of the Bath		Energy Agency
	tricians and Gynaecologists	GCE	General Certificate of	IATA	International Air Transport
FRCP	Fellow, Royal College of		Education		Association
	Physicians, London	GCHQ	Government Communications	ibid	(*ibidem*) in the same place
FRCPath	Fellow, Royal College of		Headquarters	IBRD	International Bank for Recon-
	Pathologists	GCIE	Knight Grand Commander,		struction and Development
FRCPE *or*	Fellow, Royal College of		Order of the Indian Empire	ICAO	International Civil Aviation
FRCPEd	Physicians, Edinburgh	GCLJ	Knight Grand Cross, Order of		Organisation
FRCPI	Fellow, Royal College of		St Lazarus of Jerusalem	ICBM	Inter-continental ballistic missile
	Physicians, Ireland	GCMG	Dame/Knight Grand Cross,	ICFTU	International Confederation of
FRCPsych	Fellow, Royal College of		Order of St Michael and		Free Trade Unions
	Psychiatrists		St George	ICJ	International Court of Justice
FRCR	Fellow, Royal College of	GCSE	General Certificate of	ICRC	International Committee of
	Radiologists		Secondary Education		the Red Cross
FRCS	Fellow, Royal College of	GCSI	Knight Grand Commander,	id	(*idem*) the same
	Surgeons of England		Order of the Star of India	IDA	International Development
FRCSE *or*	Fellow, Royal College of	GCVO	Dame/Knight Grand Cross,		Association
FRCSEd	Surgeons of Edinburgh		Royal Victorian Order	IDD	International direct dialling
FRCSGlas	Fellow, Royal College of Physi-	GDP	Gross domestic product	ie	(*id est*) that is
	cians and Surgeons of Glasgow	Gen	General	IEA	International Energy Agency
FRCSI	Fellow, Royal College of	GHQ	General Headquarters	IFAD	International Fund for
	Surgeons in Ireland	GM	George Medal		Agricultural Development
FRCVS	Fellow, Royal College of	GMB	General, Municipal,	IFC	International Finance
	Veterinary Surgeons		Boilermakers and Allied		Corporation
FREconS	Fellow, Royal Economic Society		Trades Union	IHS	(*Iesus Hominum Salvator*)
FREng	Fellow, Royal Academy of	GMT	Greenwich Mean Time		Jesus the Saviour of Mankind
	Engineering	GNP	Gross national product	ILO	International Labour
FRGS	Fellow, Royal Geographical	GNVQ	General National Vocational		Office/Organisation
	Society		Qualification	ILR	Independent local radio
FRHistS	Fellow, Royal Historical Society	GOC	General Officer Commanding	IMF	International Monetary Fund
FRHS	Fellow, Royal Horticultural	GP	General Practitioner	IMO	International Maritime
	Society	Gp Capt	Group Captain		Organisation
FRIBA	Fellow, Royal Institute of British	GSA	Girls' Schools Association	Inc	Incorporated
	Architects	HAC	Honourable Artillery Company	incog	(*incognito*) unknown,
FRICS	Fellow, Royal Institution of	HB	His Beatitude		unrecognised
	Chartered Surveyors	HBM	Her/His Britannic Majesty('s)	INLA	Irish National Liberation Army
FRMetS	Fellow, Royal Meteorological	HCF	Highest common factor	in loc	(*in loco*) in its place
	Society		Honorary Chaplain to the Forces	Inmarsat	International Maritime
FRMS	Fellow, Royal Microscopical	HE	Her/His Excellency		Satellite Organisation
	Society		Higher Education	INRI	(*Iesus Nazarenus Rex Iudaeorum*)
FRNS	Fellow, Royal Numismatic		His Eminence		Jesus of Nazareth, King of
	Society	HGV	Heavy Goods Vehicle		the Jews

inst	(*instant*) current month
Intelsat	International Telecommunications Satellite Organisation
Interpol	International Criminal Police Commission
IOC	International Olympic Committee
IOM	Isle of Man
IOU	I owe you
IOW	Isle of Wight
IQ	Intelligence quotient
IRA	Irish Republican Army
IRC	International Red Cross
Is	Islands
ISBN	International Standard Book Number
ISO	Imperial Service Order International Standards Organisation
ISSN	International Standard Serial Number
ITC	Independent Television Commission
ITN	Independent Television News
ITU	International Telecommunication Union
ITV	Independent Television
JP	Justice of the Peace
K	Köchel numeration (*of Mozart's works*)
KBE	Knight Commander, Order of the British Empire
KCB	Knight Commander, Order of the Bath
KCIE	Knight Commander, Order of the Indian Empire
KCLJ	Knight Commander, Order of St Lazarus of Jerusalem
KCMG	Knight Commander, Order of St Michael and St George
KCSI	Knight Commander, Order of the Star of India
KCVO	Knight Commander, Royal Victorian Order
KG	Knight of the Garter
KGB	(*Komitet Gosudarstvennoi Besopasnosti*) Committee of State Security (*USSR*)
kHz	kiloHertz
KKK	Ku Klux Klan
KLJ	Knight, Order of St Lazarus of Jerusalem
ko	knock out (*boxing*)
KP	Knight, Order of St Patrick
KStJ	Knight, Order of St John of Jerusalem
Kt	Knight
KT	Knight of the Thistle
kV	Kilovolt
kW	Kilowatt
kWh	Kilowatt hour
L	Liberal
Lab	Labour
Lat	Latitude
lbw	leg before wicket
lc	lower case (*printing*)
LCJ	Lord Chief Justice
LCM	Least/lowest common multiple
LD	Liberal Democrat
LDS	Licentiate in Dental Surgery
LEA	Local Education Authority

LHD	(*Literarum Humaniorum Doctor*) Doctor of Humane Letters/Literature
Lib	Liberal
Lic	(*Licenciado*) lawyer (*Spanish*)
Lic Med	Licentiate in Medicine
Lit	Literary
Lit Hum	(*Literae Humaniores*) Faculty of classics and philosophy, Oxford
Litt D	Doctor of Letters
LJ	Lord Justice
LLB	Bachelor of Laws
LLD	Doctor of Laws
LLM	Master of Laws
LM	Licentiate in Midwifery
LMS	Local management in schools
LMSSA	Licentiate in Medicine and Surgery, Society of Apothecaries
loc cit	(*loco citato*) in the place cited
log	logarithm
Londin:	of London (*Bishop*)
Long	Longitude
LS	(*loco sigilli*) place of the seal
LSA	Licentiate of Society of Apothecaries
Lsd	(*Librae, solidi, denarii*) £, shillings and pence
LSE	London School of Economics and Political Science
Lt	Lieutenant
LTA	Lawn Tennis Association
Ltd	Limited (liability)
LTh *or* LTheol	Licentiate in Theology
LVO	Lieutenant, Royal Victorian Order
LW	long wave
LWM	Low water mark
M	Member of Monsieur
MA	Master of Arts
MAFF	Ministry of Agriculture, Fisheries and Food
Maj	Major
max	maximum
MB	Bachelor of Medicine
MBA	Master of Business Administration
MBE	Member, Order of the British Empire
MC	Master of Ceremonies Military Cross
MCC	Marylebone Cricket Club
MCh(D)	Master of (Dental) Surgery
MD	Managing Director Doctor of Medicine
MDS	Master of Dental Surgery
ME	Middle English Myalgic Encephalomyelitis
MEC	Member of Executive Council
MEd	Master of Education
mega	one million times
MEP	Member of the European Parliament
MFH	Master of Foxhounds
Mgr	Monsignor
MI	Military Intelligence
micro	one-millionth part
milli	one-thousandth part
min	minimum
MIRAS	Mortgage Interest Relief at Source
MLA	Member of Legislative Assembly
MLC	Member of Legislative Council
MLitt	Master of Letters
Mlle	Mademoiselle

MLR	Minimum lending rate
MM	Military Medal
Mme	Madame
MN	Merchant Navy
MO	Medical Officer/Orderly
MoD	Ministry of Defence
MoT	Ministry of Transport
MP	Member of Parliament Military Police
mph	miles per hour
M Phil	Master of Philosophy
MR	Master of the Rolls
MRC	Medical Research Council
MS	Master of Surgery Manuscript (*pl* MSS) Multiple Sclerosis
MSc	Master of Science
MSF	Manufacturing, Science and Finance Union
MSP	Member of Scottish Parliament
MTh	Master of Theology
Mus B/D	Bachelor/Doctor of Music
MV	Merchant Vessel Motor Vessel
MVO	Member, Royal Victorian Order
MW	medium wave
MWA	Member of the Welsh Assembly
N	North
n/a	not applicable not available
NAAFI	Navy, Army and Air Force Institutes
NASA	National Aeronautics and Space Administration
NAS/UWT	National Association of Schoolmasters/Union of Women Teachers
NATO	North Atlantic Treaty Organisation
NB	New Brunswick (*nota bene*) note well
NCIS	National Criminal Intelligence Service
NCO	Non-commissioned officer
NDPB	Non-departmental public body
NEB	New English Bible
nem con	(*nemine contradicente*) no one contradicting
NERC	Natural Environment Research Council
nes	not elsewhere specified
NFT	National Film Theatre
NFU	National Farmers' Union
NHS	National Health Service
NI	National Insurance Northern Ireland
NIV	New International Version (*of Bible*)
No	(*numero*) number
non seq	(*non sequitur*) it does not follow
Norvic:	of Norwich (*Bishop*)
NP	Notary Public
NRA	National Rifle Association
NS	New Style (*calendar*) Nova Scotia
NSPCC	National Society for the Prevention of Cruelty to Children
NSW	New South Wales
NT	National Theatre National Trust New Testament
NUJ	National Union of Journalists

NUM National Union of Mineworkers
NUS National Union of Students
NUT National Union of Teachers
NVQ National Vocational Qualification
NWT Northwest Territory
NY New York
NZ New Zealand

OAPEC Organisation of Arab Petroleum Exporting Countries
OAS Organisation of American States
OAU Organisation of African Unity
Ob *or* obit died
OBE Officer, Order of the British Empire
OC Officer Commanding
ODA Overseas Development Administration
OE Old English
omissions excepted
OECD Organisation for Economic Co-operation and Development
OED *Oxford English Dictionary*
Offer Office of Electricity Regulation
Ofgas Office of Gas Supply
OFM Order of Friars Minor (*Franciscans*)
Ofsted Office for Standards in Education
OFT Office of Fair Trading
Oftel Office of Telecommunications
Ofwat Office of Water Services
OHMS On Her/His Majesty's Service
OND Ordinary National Diploma
OM Order of Merit
ONO or near offer
ONS Office for National Statistics
op (*opus*) work
OP Opposite prompt side (*of theatre*)
Order of Preachers (*Dominicans*)
out of print (*books*)
op cit (*opere citato*) in the work cited
OPCS Office of Population Censuses and Surveys
OPEC Organisation of Petroleum Exporting Countries
OPRAF Office of Passenger Rail Franchising
OPS Office of Public Service
ORR Office of the Rail Regulator
OS Old Style (*calendar*)
Ordnance Survey
OSA Order of St Augustine
OSB Order of St Benedict
OSCE Organisation for Security and Co-operation in Europe
O St J Officer, Order of St John of Jerusalem
OT Old Testament
OTC Officers' Training Corps
Oxon (of) Oxford
Oxfordshire
p page
p (*piano*) softly
PA Personal Assistant
Press Association
PAYE Pay as You Earn
pc (*per centum*) in the hundred
PC personal computer
Police Constable
politically correct
Privy Counsellor
PCC Press Complaints Commission

PDSA People's Dispensary for Sick Animals
PE Physical Education
PEP Personal equity plan
Petriburg: of Peterborough (*Bishop*)
PFI Private Finance Initiative
PGA Professional Golfers Association
PGCE Postgraduate Certificate of Education
PhD Doctor of Philosophy
pinx(it) he/she painted it
pl plural
PLA Port of London Authority
PLC Public Limited Company
PLO Palestine Liberation Organisation
pm (*post meridiem*) after noon
PM Prime Minister
PMRAFNS Princess Mary's Royal Air Force Nursing Service
PO Petty Officer
Pilot Officer
Post Office
postal order
POW Prisoner of War
pp pages
(*per procurationem*) by proxy
PPARC Particle Physics and Astronomy Research Council
PPS Parliamentary Private Secretary
PR Proportional representation
Public relations
PRA President of the Royal Academy
Pro tem (*pro tempore*) for the time being
Prox (*proximo*) next month
PRS President of the Royal Society
PRSE President of the Royal Society of Edinburgh
Ps Psalm
PS (*postscriptum*) postscript
PSBR Public sector borrowing requirement
psc passed Staff College
PSV Public Service Vehicle
PTA Parent-Teacher Association
Pte Private
PTO Please turn over
PVC Polyvinyl chloride

QARANC Queen Alexandra's Royal Army Nursing Corps
QARNNS Queen Alexandra's Royal Naval Nursing Service
QB(D) Queen's Bench (Division)
QC Queen's Counsel
QED (*quod erat demonstrandum*) which was to be proved
QGM Queen's Gallantry Medal
QHC Queen's Honorary Chaplain
QHDS Queen's Honorary Dental Surgeon
QHNS Queen's Honorary Nursing Sister
QHP Queen's Honorary Physician
QHS Queen's Honorary Surgeon
QMG Quartermaster General
QPM Queen's Police Medal
QS Quarter Sessions
QSO Quasi-stellar object (quasar)
Queen's Service Order
quango quasi-autonomous non-governmental organisation
qv (*quod vide*) which see

R (*Regina*) Queen
(*Rex*) King
RA Royal Academy/Academician
Royal Artillery
RAC Royal Armoured Corps
Royal Automobile Club
RADA Royal Academy of Dramatic Art
RADC Royal Army Dental Corps
RAE Royal Aerospace Establishment
RAEC Royal Army Educational Corps
RAeS Royal Aeronautical Society
RAF Royal Air Force
RAM Random-access memory (*computer*)
Royal Academy of Music
RAMC Royal Army Medical Corps
RAN Royal Australian Navy
RAOC Royal Army Ordnance Corps
RAPC Royal Army Pay Corps
RAVC Royal Army Veterinary Corps
RBG Royal Botanic Garden
RBS Royal Society of British Sculptors
RC Red Cross
Roman Catholic
RCM Royal College of Music
RCN Royal Canadian Navy
RCT Royal Corps of Transport
RD Refer to drawer (*banking*)
Royal Naval and Royal Marine Forces Reserve Decoration
Rural Dean
RDI Royal Designer for Industry
RE Religious Education
Royal Engineers
REME Royal Electrical and Mechanical Engineers
Rep Representative
Republican
Rev(d) Reverend
RFU Rugby Football Union
RGN Registered General Nurse
RGS Royal Geographical Society
RHA Regional Health Authority
RHS Royal Horticultural Society
Royal Humane Society
RI Rhode Island
Royal Institute of Painters in Watercolours
Royal Institution
RIBA Royal Institute of British Architects
RIP (*Requiescat in pace*) May he/she rest in peace
RIR Royal Irish Regiment
RL Rugby League
RM Registered Midwife
Royal Marines
RMA Royal Military Academy
RMN Registered Mental Nurse
RMT National Union of Rail, Maritime and Transport Workers
RN Royal Navy
RNIB Royal National Institute for the Blind
RNID Royal National Institute for the Deaf
RNLI Royal National Lifeboat Institution
RNMH Registered Nurse for the Mentally Handicapped
RNR Royal Naval Reserve
RNVR Royal Naval Volunteer Reserve
RNXS Royal Naval Auxiliary Service
RNZN Royal New Zealand Navy

Ro	(*Recto*) on the right-hand page
ROC	Royal Observer Corps
Roffen:	of Rochester (*Bishop*)
ROI	Royal Institute of Oil Painters
ROM	Read-only memory (*computer*)
RoSPA	Royal Society for the Prevention of Accidents
RP	Royal Society of Portrait Painters
rpm	revolutions per minute
RRC	Lady of Royal Red Cross
RSA	Republic of South Africa
	Royal Scottish Academician
	Royal Society of Arts
RSC	Royal Shakespeare Company
RSCN	Registered Sick Children's Nurse
RSE	Royal Society of Edinburgh
RSM	Regimental Sergeant Major
RSPB	Royal Society for the Protection of Birds
RSPCA	Royal Society for the Prevention of Cruelty to Animals
RSV	Revised Standard Version (*of Bible*)
RSVP	(Répondez, s'il vous plaît) Please reply
RSW	Royal Scottish Society of Painters in Watercolours
RTPI	Royal Town Planning Institute
RU	Rugby Union
RUC	Royal Ulster Constabulary
RV	Revised Version (*of Bible*)
RVM	Royal Victorian Medal
RWS	Royal Water Colour Society
RYS	Royal Yacht Squadron
s	second
	(*solidus*) shilling
S	South
SA	Salvation Army
	South Africa
	South America
	South Australia
SAE	stamped addressed envelope
Salop	Shropshire
Sarum:	of Salisbury (*Bishop*)
SAS	Special Air Service Regiment
SBN	Standard Book Number
SBS	Special Boat Squadron
ScD	Doctor of Science
SCM	State Certified Midwife
SDLP	Social Democratic and Labour Party
SEAQ	Stock Exchange Automated Quotations system
SEN	State Enrolled Nurse
SERPS	State Earnings Related Pension Scheme
SFO	Serious Fraud Office
SHMIS	Society of Headmasters and Headmistresses of Independent Schools
SI	(*Système International d'Unités*) International System of Units
	Statutory Instrument
sic	so written
Sig	Signature
	Signor
SJ	Society of Jesus (*Jesuits*)
SLD	Social and Liberal Democrats
SMP	Statutory Maternity Pay
SNP	Scottish National Party
SOE	Special Operations Executive
SOS	Save Our Souls (*distress signal*)
sp	(*sine prole*) without issue
spgr	specific gravity

SPQR	(*Senatus Populusque Romanus*) The Senate and People of Rome
SRN	State Registered Nurse
SRO	Self Regulating Organisations
SS	Saints
	Schutzstaffel (Nazi paramilitary organisation)
	Steamship
SSC	Solicitor before Supreme Court (*Scotland*)
SSF	Society of St Francis
SSN	Standard Serial Number
SSP	Statutory Sick Pay
SSSI	Site of special scientific interest
STD	(*Sacrae Theologiae Doctor*) Doctor of Sacred Theology
	Subscriber trunk dialling
stet	let it stand (*printing*)
stp	Standard temperature and pressure
STP	(*Sacrae Theologiae Professor*) Professor of Sacred Theology
Sub Lt	Sub-Lieutenant
SVQ	Scottish Vocational Qualification
TA	Territorial Army
TB	Tuberculosis
TCCB	Test and County Cricket Board
TD	Territorial Efficiency Decoration
TEC	Training and Enterprise Council
TEFL	Teaching English as a foreign language
temp	temperature
	temporary employee
TES	Times Educational Supplement
TGWU	Transport and General Workers' Union
THES	Times Higher Education Supplement
TLS	Times Literary Supplement
TNT	trinitrotoluene (*explosive*)
trans	translated
trs	transpose (*printing*)
TRH	Their Royal Highnesses
TT	Teetotal
	Tourist Trophy (*motorcycle races*)
	Tuberculin tested
TUC	Trades Union Congress
TVEI	Technical and Vocational Education Initiative
U	Unionist
UAE	United Arab Emirates
uc	upper case (*printing*)
UCAS	Universities and Colleges Admissions Service
UCATT	Union of Construction, Allied Trades and Technicians
UCL	University College London
UDA	Ulster Defence Association
UDI	Unilateral Declaration of Independence
UDM	Union of Democratic Mineworkers
UDR	Ulster Defence Regiment
UEFA	Union of European Football Associations
UFF	Ulster Freedom Fighters
UFO	Unidentified flying object
UHF	ultra-high frequency
UK	United Kingdom
UKAEA	UK Atomic Energy Authority
UN	United Nations

UNESCO	United Nations Educational, Scientific and Cultural Organisation
UNHCR	United Nations High Commissioner for Refugees
UNICEF	United Nations Children's Fund
UNIDO	United Nations Industrial Development Organisation
Unita	National Union for the Total Independence of Angola
UPU	Universal Postal Union
URC	United Reformed Church
US(A)	United States (of America)
USDAW	Union of Shop, Distributive and Allied Workers
USM	Unlisted Securities Market
USSR	Union of Soviet Socialist Republics
UTC	Co-ordinated Universal Time system
UVF	Ulster Volunteer Force
v	(*versus*) against
VA	Vicar Apostolic
	Victoria and Albert Order
VAD	Voluntary Aid Detachment
V and A	Victoria and Albert Museum
VAT	Value added tax
VC	Victoria Cross
VCR	video cassette recorder
VD	Venereal disease
	Volunteer Officers' Decoration
VDU	Visual display unit
Ven	Venerable
VHF	very high frequency
VIP	Very important person
Vo	(*Verso*) on the left-hand page
VRD	Royal Naval Volunteer Reserve Officers' Decoration
VSO	Voluntary Service Overseas
VTOL	Vertical take-off and landing (*aircraft*)
W	West
WCC	World Council of Churches
WEA	Workers' Educational Association
WEU	Western European Union
WFTU	World Federation of Trade Unions
WHO	World Health Organisation
WI	West Indies
	Women's Institute
Winton:	of Winchester (*Bishop*)
WIPO	World Intellectual Property Organisation
WMO	World Meteorological Organisation
WO	Warrant Officer
WRAC	Women's Royal Army Corps
WRAF	Women's Royal Air Force
WRNS	Women's Royal Naval Service
WRVS	Women's Royal Voluntary Service
WS	Writer to the Signet
WTO	World Trade Organisation
YMCA	Young Men's Christian Association
YWCA	Young Women's Christian Association
Ψ = seaport	

Index

Stop-Press

CHANGES SINCE PAGES WENT TO PRESS

PEERAGE

Died: Lord Hamar-Nicholls; Lord Errol of Hale; Baroness Brooke of Ystradfellte; Duke of Sutherland

BARONETAGE AND KNIGHTAGE

Died: *Vice-Adm.* Sir Peter Compston; Sir James Starritt; Sir John Beith; Sir Julian Critchley; Sir John Astor; Sir Philip Woodfield; Sir Toby Coghill; Sir Antony Read; Sir Antony Pilkington

PARLIAMENT

Died: Audrey Wise, *Lab.* Preston
at the time of going to press, Betty Boothroyd's successor had not been announced

GOVERNMENT DEPARTMENTS AND PUBLIC OFFICES

Additions to the Competition Commission Appeal Panel – Professor Andrew Bain, OBE; Michael Blair, QC; Peter Clayton; Michael Davey; Professor Peter Grinyer; The Hon. Anthony Lewis; Graham Mather; Prof. John Pickering; Patricia Quigley; Mrs Vindelyn Smith-Hillman; Prof. John Stoneman; Prof. Graham Zellick.
Paul Geroski to replace Graham Corbett, CBE as Deputy Chairman of the Competition Commission.
Regional Co-ordination Unit – Rob Smith has been appointed as the first Director General of the Regional Co-ordination Unit. He will be responsible for the work of the Government Office for the Regions and for the newly established Unit.
Pupil Support and Inclusion Group – Rob Smith is no longer the Director of the Pupil Support and Inclusion Group.
Highways Agency – Tim Matthews appointed Chief Executive.
Paul Regan has become head of the Hunting Bill Unit at the Constitutional and Community Policy Directorate at the Home Office.
Prof. Macpherson and Prof. Sir Netar Mallick are no longer members of the Unrelated Live Transplant Regulatory Authority (ULTRA). Prof. J. Bradley, K. Rigg and R. Gokal are newly appointed members.
Police Ombudsman for Northern Ireland: New Cathedral Buildings, St, Anne's Square, 11 Church Street, Belfast BT1 1PG. *Ombudsman*: Nuala O'Loan

LAW COURTS AND OFFICES

Circuit Judges – John Hargreaves Reddihough and Robin William Onions (Midland and Oxford)

DEFENCE

Admiral Sir Michael Boyce to be Chief of the Defence Staff from February 2001.

EDUCATION

Changes to Cambridge University Masterships:
Prof. H. Ahmed, ScD, FEng – Master of Corpus Christi College; Prof. D. S. Ingram – St Catherine's; Prof. R. J. Bowring – Selwyn; Prof. P. F. Clarke – Trinity Hall
Mastership of Jesus – *vacant*

HEALTH

SCOTLAND

NET COSTS OF THE NATIONAL HEALTH SERVICE 1999

REVENUE AND CAPITAL EXPENDITURE

£ thousand

Health Board Administration	78,415
Hospital and Community Health Services	
Revenue	3,177,270
Capital	78,113
Family Practitioner Services	1,106,964
Central Health Services	
Revenue	120,482
Capital	5,271
State Hospital	
Revenue	17,904
Capital	607
Training	3,464
Research	10,374
Disabled Service	2,620
Welfare Foods	12,211
Miscellaneous Health Services[1]	18,776
Total NHS Cost	4,632,471
NHS Contributions	568,855
Net Cost to Exchequer	4,063,616
Central Government Administration[2]	12,378
Total Cost	4,644,849

[1] This includes Port Health which is charged to Local Authority in National Accounts
[2] Includes cost of collection of NHS contributions

LOCAL GOVERNMENT

The election of the Lord Mayor of London 2000–1 took place on 1 October 2000. Please contact the Corporation of London on 020-7606 3030 for details of this election.

THE PRESS

Address of *Athletics Weekly:*
13 Cavell Court, Lincoln Road, Peterborough PE1 2RJ
Tel: 01733-898440; Fax: 01733-898441

Financial Times:
Circulation – 461,498

TRADE UNIONS

The President of the Transport and General Workers Union (TGWL) 2000–1 is Bill Morris

INTERNATIONAL ORGANISATIONS

Amendments to the World Intellectual Property Organisation profile:
WIPO administers 21 treaties and had 175 members as at July 2000
The WIPO budget for 2000–1 is SFr 410 million
Director General: Dr Kamil Idris (Sudan)
The International Union for the Protection of New Varieties of Plants had 45 members as at July 2000

COUNTRIES OF THE WORLD

Lebanon Prime Minister Salim al-Hoss conceded defeat after the legislative election on 3 September

OBITUARIES

20 August 1999

Vice. Adm Sir Peter Compston KCB, Deputy Supreme Allied Commander Atlantic 1968–79, aged 84.

EVENTS – SEPTEMBER 1999

WORLD

2. In Myanmar, Aung San Suu Kyi and other activists from the National League for Democracy, who had been detained by security forces at the roadside when they attempted to leave Yangon on 24 August, were forcibly returned to the capital; she was subsequently put under house arrest until 14 September. **3.** In Israel, Aryeh Deri, the founder of the Shas party, began a three-year jail sentence for corruption; he had been found guilty of taking bribes worth £97,000. **5.** More than 150 presidents, prime ministers and rulers gathered in New York for the opening of the three-day UN millennium summit in what was the largest gathering of world leaders in history. **6.** In Indonesia, three UN workers were murdered by militiamen after their offices were attacked in Atambua, West Timor; the following day, all aid agencies withdrew from the region. **8.** The final report of the panel of three 'wise men' appointed by the EU to investigate Austria's human rights record urged the EU to end its diplomatic sanctions, finding no evidence that the Austrian government had breached human rights; the sanctions, which had been imposed in February 2000, were lifted on 12 September. **10.** A British paratrooper was killed and twelve others wounded when airborne forces freed six British soldiers who had been taken hostage in Sierra Leone in August by the West Side Boys, a rebel militia. Twenty-five rebels were killed in the attack. The Palestinian Central Council, which had threatened to declare statehood on 13 September, decided to delay the declaration of statehood for at least two months. **11.** In Melbourne, Australia, at least eight people, including five policemen, were injured when about 2,000 anti-globalisation protesters blockaded the opening of the World Economic Forum. **14.** In South Africa, the health committee of the ANC urged President Mbeki to acknowledge that HIV was the cause of AIDS. **15.** In Zimbabwe, armed police stormed the main offices of the opposition Movement for Democratic Change and seized all its documentation. **17.** In Peru, following criticism of the presidential election in April and May 2000, President Alberto Fujimori announced that a new presidential election would be held and that he would not seek re-election.

BRITISH

4. Cabinet Office Minister Mo Mowlam announced that she would be standing down as an MP at the next general election. **5.** The Millennium Dome received a further emergency payment from the government of £47 million to avoid bankruptcy. **7.** The government came under increasing pressure to reduce the VAT on fuel as petrol prices were expected to reach almost four pounds a gallon, due to the rising price of crude oil. It was reported that on the 31 August, an Asteroid one third of a mile wide passed within 2.4 million miles of Earth, which is classed as a 'near miss'. **8.** Protesters in France set up road blocks at refineries and fuel depots to highlight the high cost of fuel. **9.** The fuel shortages continued as people began panic buying fuel after Shell warned that the majority of their pumps would be dry by the end of the week. **10.** The oil crisis worsened as demonstrations outside refineries and fuel depots spread throughout the country. **11.** Following reports showing that over a quarter of all British petrol stations were dry, Tony Blair declared that he would never give in to the protestors. **12.** A limited number of tankers were released from blockades around the country in order to meet the needs of the emergency services and other essential industries. Ninety per cent of petrol stations remained closed. The Japanese bid for the Millennium Dome, worth £105 million was withdrawn, once again putting the future of the Dome in doubt. The British owner of the Thai guesthouse where the Welsh backpacker Kirsty Jones was murdered, was arrested in connection with her death. **13.** Troops were put on standby to intervene in the fuel crisis as the health service went on emergency alert, schools and businesses closed and supermarkets introduced rationing. **14.** Protesters lifted the blockades at oil refineries around the country but threatened that the blockades would return if tax on fuel was not cut within 60 days. **15.** The Environment agency issued flood warnings to five English counties as an average month's rainfall took place in one day. The popular Channel Four game show *Big Brother* was won by bricklayer Craig Phillips from Liverpool, following the largest ever television vote of 7.5 million people. The Chief Executive of the London Stock Exchange, Gavin Casey announced his resignation after its shareholders called on him to stand down. Ford announced that it would not pursue its £5 billion bid to take-over the South Korean car manufacturer Daewoo. **18.** The government backed down on its plan to introduce emergency powers to protect fuel supplies.

SPORT

The Olympic Games took place in Sydney, Australia between 15 September–1 October. Due to production and scheduling constraints it was not possible to incorporate the medal winners and results of the Olympic events into this edition of *Whitaker's Almanack*. However, readers wanting to obtain complimentary information on events and medallists should contact the editorial team on 020-7873 8442.

Motor Racing: Formula 1, USA–Michael Schumacher (Germany), Ferrari

Motor Cycling: 500cc, Valencia–Garry McCoy (Australia), Yamaha

Swimming: New World Records–100m freestyle and 200m freestyle, Pieter van den Hoogenband (Netherlands) (47.84) and (1:45.35); 400m freestyle, Ian Thorpe (Australia) (3:40.59); 4 × 100m freestyle (Australia) (3:13.67); 4 × 200m freestyle (Australia) (7:07.05); 4 × 100m medley (USA) (3:33.73)

BY-ELECTION

ANTRIM SOUTH

(21 September 2000)

E. 69, 414 *T* 43.02%

W. McCrea, *DUP*	*11,601*
D. Burnsidde, *UUP*	*10,779*
D. McClelland, *SDLP*	*3,496*
M. Meehan, *SF*	*2,611*
D. Ford, *All.*	*2,031*
D. Collins, *NLP*	*49*
DUP Majority	882

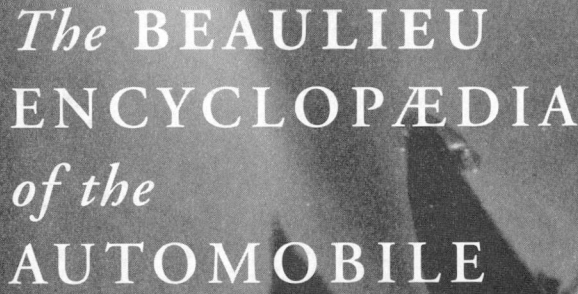